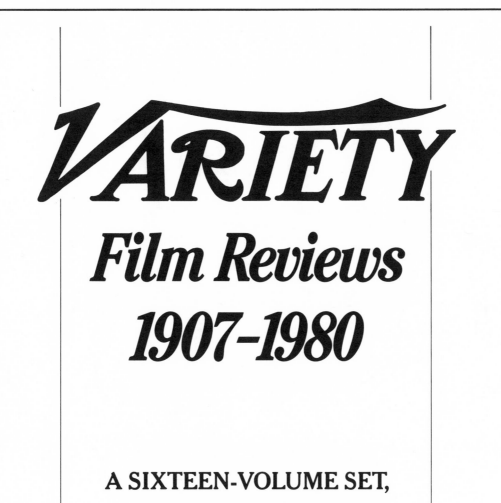

VARIETY
Film Reviews
1907-1980

A SIXTEEN-VOLUME SET,

Including an Index to Titles

Garland Publishing, Inc.
New York and London
1983

Contents

OF THE SIXTEEN-VOLUME SET

1. *1907–1920*

2. *1921–1925*

3. *1926–1929*

4. *1930–1933*

5. *1934–1937*

6. *1938–1942*

7. *1943–1948*

8. *1949–1953*

9. *1954–1958*

10. *1959–1963*

11. *1964–1967*

12. *1968–1970*

13. *1971–1974*

14. *1975–1977*

15. *1978–1980*

16. *Index to Titles*

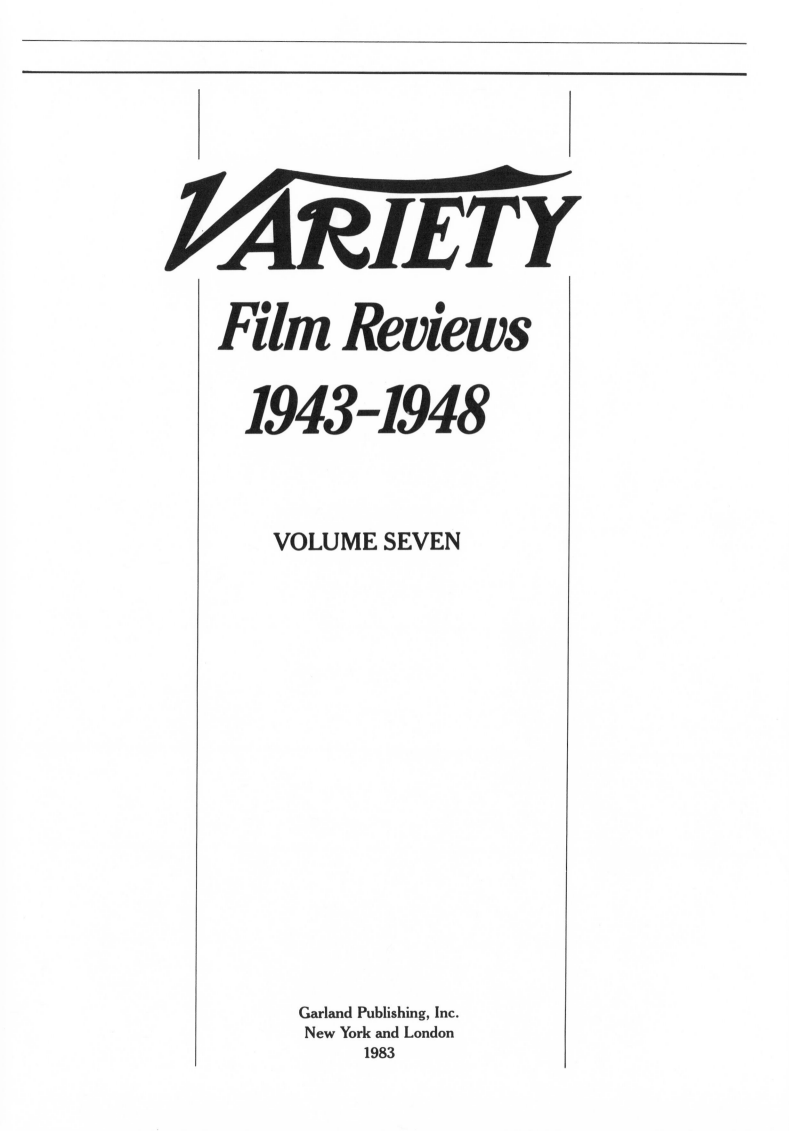

VARIETY
Film Reviews
1943-1948

VOLUME SEVEN

Garland Publishing, Inc.
New York and London
1983

Library of Congress Cataloging in Publication Data
Main entry under title:

Variety film reviews.
  Includes index.

  1. Moving-pictures—Reviews.   I. Daily variety.
PN1995.V34   1982   791.43′75   82-15691
ISBN 0-8240-5200-5 (v. 1)
ISBN 0-8240-5206-4 (v. 7)

Manufactured in the United States of America

Printed on acid-free,
250-year-life paper

User's Guide

The reviews in this collection are published in chronological order, by the date on which the review appeared. The date of each issue appears at the top of the column where the reviews for that issue begin. The reviews continue through that column and all following columns until a new date appears at the top of the page. Where blank spaces occur at the end of a column, this indicates the end of that particular week's reviews. An index to film titles, giving date of review, is published as the last volume in this set.

1943

Miniature Reviews

'Three Hearts for Julia' (Music) (M-G). Ann Sothern and Melvyn Douglas must carry this through kep spots .

'A Night to Remember' (Col). Brian Aherne, Loretta Young in mild mystery comedy.

'Miss V From Moscow' (PRC). So-so spy melodrama featuring Lola Lane. Dual supporter for regular runs.

'Undercover Man' (UA). Good Hopalong Cassidy below-the-border yarn with William Boyd and Antonio Moreno.

'Eyes of the Underworld' (U). Adequate meller item for the duals.

3 HEARTS FOR JULIA

(WITH MUSIC)

Hollywood, Jan. 5.

Metro release of John W. Considine, Jr., production. Stars Ann Sothern, Melvyn Douglas; features Lee Bowman, Richard Ainley, Marta Linden, Reginald Owen, Felix Bressart. Directed by Richard Thorpe. Original screenplay by Lionel Houser; camera, George Folsey; editor, Irvine Warburton. Tradeshown in L. A. Jan. 5, '42. Running time, **89 MINS.**

Julia Seabrook....................Ann Sothern
Jeff Seabrook....................Melvyn Douglas
David Torrance....................Lee Bowman
Philip Barrows....................Richard Ainley
Anton Ottoway....................Felix Bressart
May Elton....................Marta Linden
John Girard....................Reginald Owen
Mattie ....Marietta Canty

This effort to inject spontaneity and verve into marital separation problems falls short of the objective, and winds up as a standard programmer of mild entertainment rating. Co-starring duo of Ann Sothern and Melvyn Douglas will have to carry it through any key bookings for nominal grosses even in these days of hot boxoffices.

Story has few new twists to the familiar tale of a wandering husband whose work takes him away from the family fireside while the wife's love cools and she finds new interests. Douglas returns from war correspondent post abroad to discover wife, Miss Sothern, immersed in a musical career, bent on divorce, and pursued by Lee Bowman and Richard Ainley. In stuttering and static fashion, yarn goes through the usual familiar passages for the husband to discount each of his competitors, and finally wind up in the happy reunion.

Premise has been utilized numerous times before for screen presentation with more or less success. This one emerges in minor key on the entertainment side, but has sufficient light moments — although obviously strained to achieve their objectives—to get it by for supporting fare.

Lionel Houser, credited with original screenplay, fails to provide proper spontaneous foundation for the proceedings, and Richard Thorpe had little chance to liven things up on the directing end under the circumstances. Miss Sothern is handicapped with the material provided, and same applies to Douglas. Bowman and Ainley are standard as the two suitors, while Felix Bressart is best in support as the European conductor who makes the most of his confusion over the strange surroundings in the new country.

Best angle of the picture is inclusion of several symphonic interludes by a woman's orchestra, with Miss Sothern spotted as concert master. One performance at Ft. McHenry under USO campshow auspices is displayed, while symphonic tempo of standard and familiar American tunes is best attention-catcher on the musical side. *Walt.*

NIGHT TO REMEMBER

Columbia release of Samuel Bischoff production. Stars Loretta Young, Brian Aherne; features Sidney Toler, Jeff Donnell, Lee Patrick, Blanche Yurka. Directed by Richard Wallace. Screenplay by Richard Flournoy, Jack Henley from story by Kelley Roos; camera, Joseph Walker; editor, Charles Nelson. At State, N. Y., week Dec. 31, '42. Running time, **92 MINS.**

Nancy Troy....................Loretta Young
Jeff Troy....................Brian Aherne
Anne Carstaire....................Jeff Donnell
Scott Carstairs....................William Wright
Inspector Hankins....................Sidney Toler
Mrs. DeVee....................Gale Sondergaard
Bolling....................Donald MacBride
Polly Franklin....................Lee Patrick
Eddie Turner....................Don Costello
Mrs. Salter....................Blanche Yurka
Lingle....................Richard Gaines
Pat Murphy....................James Burke

Possible the producers of 'My Sister Eileen' reasoned if that story, concerning writers and folks in Greenwich Village, would click, why not try another with similar setting? The idea of poking fun at murder mystery and sleuthing can be made click screen fare, as it has been done many previous times, but this film often is neither mysterious nor funny. For the dual setups.

Flippant Brian Aherne and his pert wife, Loretta Young, are planted in a N. Y. Greenwich Village basement apartment. She's taken him there so he can write a love story instead of his successful string of murder mystery novels. As soon as they move in at No. 13 Gay street, both are aware of mysterious goings-on. But it's not until a near-nude dead man is discovered in their small backyard that anything tangibly mysterious develops. This brings in the gendarmes, and the plot is off on one of those 'young author solves great mystery' chases. Only here it is done so methodically, with trite excursions into trivia, one seldom cares when or if the blackmailing-killer is captured. Far too much reaching for laugh lines creates many voids.

Aherne makes a first-rate scribbler of murder mysteries, who abjectly seems to wonder what all the shooting is about. Miss Young, looking better than she has for some time, manages to create wholesome interest and scream frantically at stated intervals. Jeff Donnell seen as the young married woman living upstairs in the Village apartment house again shows possibilities. Sidney Toler, away from his Charlie Chan character, manages to make the police inspector a realistic character. Blanche Yurka is buried in a meaningless character role while Lee Patrick has too little to do. Capable support is provided by Gale Sondergaard, Don Costello and Richard Gaines.

Neither the screenplay nor so-called original indicate too much care in formulating. Chief blame rests on the script. Richard Wallace's direction is not bad, considering. Charles Nelson edited probably with the idea of letting the picture run at least an hour and a half. It would have been much better in 60 minutes. *Wear.*

Miss V From Moscow

Producers Releasing Corp. release of an M & H production. Features Lola Lane, Noel Madison, Howard Banks, Paul Weigel, John Vosper. Directed by Albert Herman. Original story and screenplay, Arthur St. Clair and Sherman Lowe; camera, Marcel LePicard; editor, W. L. Brown. At New York, N. Y., dual, Dec. 30, '42. Running time, **68 MINS.**

Vera Marova....................Lola Lane
Capt. Anton Kleis....................Noel Madison
Steve Worth....................Howard Banks
Henri Devallier....................Paul Weigel
Col. Wolfgang Heinrich....................John Wosper
Mme. Finchon....................Anna Demetrio
Capt. Richter....................William Vaughn
Pierre....................Juan De La Cruz
Minna....................Kathryn Sheldon
Gerald Naughton....................Victor Kendell
Dr. Suchevsky....................Richard Kipling

Only the title carries any marquee voltage in this new PRC release. Once inside, the customers will find themselves confronted with a typical cinematic spy melodrama. Aside from its opening shot of Moscow's Red Square and a fadeout message from a Soviet commissar, pointing up the need for a continued United Nations all-out war effort, it's a so-so tale of espionage in occupied France with Lola Lane as Stalin's favorite agent.

Its pace and suspense leave much to be desired, with resort to library clips required to hypo audience reaction. Thus midway through the picture, with action lagging, Hitler is put through the paces haranguing a multitude of swastika-studded troops for—even at this date—one of film's big punches, and toward the end a convoy of Russian-bound ships is shown engaged in enemy action, with equal results. That the two sequences carry dramatic effect is a tipoff on the shortcomings of the yarn itself.

Because of her close resemblance to a Nazi femme spy, Miss Lane, as the Russ agent, is sent to Paris to uncover data on operation of German subs interfering with U. S. lend-lease and food supplies. Action is built around a secret French coin that proves her real identity to underground workers. How she fools the Gestapo and the head of the German ministry of information and eventually makes her escape after the coin betrays her, could have made for good, actionful melodrama, but its stirring moments are few and far between. Love interest is spasmodic and virtually neglected, built around escape of an American in British service who gets stranded on French coast after raid, accidentally meets up with Russ agent and helps her flight to Moscow.

Film provides big, and much-needed, laugh when the Nazi info minister, falling for the Moscow gal's line, confides in her that the 'Russians have been annihilated.'

Director Albert Herman has turned in a good job at character development but allows too many pauses. Miss Lane is always effective, with Noel Madison as the Paris Gestapo chief and John Wosper as the Nazi bigwig who takes the rap for betraying Hitler's secrets to the gal, also convincing. Paul Weigel and Anna Demetrio are also okay in lesser roles. *Rose.*

Un Nuevo Amanecer

('A New Beginning')
(ARGENTINE-MADE)

Buenos Aires, Dec. 15.

Sono Film production and release. Stars Silvia Legrand and Carlos Cores; features Elena Lucena, Semillita, Froilan Varela, Enrique Chaico, Eduardo Cuitino, Alberto de Mendoza, Pedro Fiorito and Salvador Sinai. Directed by Borcosque. Story, Carlos A. Petit; adapted by Carlos Borcosque and Jack Hall; photography, Antonio Merayo. Reviewed at Monumental, Buenos Aires. Running time, **76 MINS.**

'Un Nuevo Amanecer' is interesting principally because it introduces Carlos Cores, a good-looking juve of whom much is expected, in his first starring role. Cores looks somewhat like Tyrone Power and has, in addition, a Latin style and spirit that already has femme audiences here swooning in the aisles. According to reports, Hollywood is cabling. He'll need plenty of handling before coming up to the Yankee standards, but possibilities are definitely there.

Story is one of those hackneyed yarns that serves mainly as a vehicle for the principal players. Cores is cast as a youngster just out of a reformatory who returns to the neighborhood of his youth and learns of the death of his mother. His old pals get him a job in a factory, where his childhood sweetheart works. Meantime, she's been promised to the son of the owner, and another gal who wants him tries to make trouble. He gets involved when the factory is burned but, of course, it turns out o.k. in the end when the true firebug tells all.

Film is overly melodramatic throughout and dialog unconvincing. There are some strong episodes well carried out, but film doesn't have Carlos Borcosque's usual forcefulness, with comparatively little action and too much dialog. Semillita, a local kid comic, supplies the touches of humor, but Silvia Legrand, one of the Legrand twins, hasn't much to do and doesn't do too much with what she has. Photography fair. *Ray.*

Eyes of the Underworld

Hollywood, Jan. 1.

Universal release of Ben Pivar production. Stars Richard Dix; features Wendy Barrie, Lon Chaney, Don Porter, Billy Lee, Lloyd Corrigan. Directed by Roy William Neill. Screenplay by Michael L. Simmons, Arthur Strawn; original, Maxwell Shane. Previewed in L. A., Dec. 29, '42. Running time, **61 MINS.**

Richard Bryan....................Richard Dix
Betty Standing....................Wendy Barrie
Benny....................Lon Chaney
J. C. Thomas....................Lloyd Corrigan
Edward Jason....................Don Porter
Mickey Bryan....................Billy Lee
Gordon Finch....................Marc Lawrence
Lance Merlin....................Edward Pawley
Kirby....................Joseph Crehan
Sergt. Clancy....................Wade Boteler
Hub Gelsey....................Gaylord Pendleton
District Attorney....................Mike Raffetto

This one follows familiar melodramatic line of racketeers mixed up with corrupt politicians and police for standard program support in the general runs. Picture carries moderate budget outlay with no attempt to follow other than straight-line presentation of regulation underworld formula. Despite dated story, starring label of Richard Dix with Lon Chaney featured, gives picture more than passable strength for dual datings.

Dix is the aggressive police chief cleaning up town after a three-year tenure. Sudden outburst of auto and tire thefts and car strippings brings in state investigator Don Porter to shadow Dix. When auto thief Marc Lawrence is caught red-handed he confronts Dix with latter's early prison record and the chief, rather than be blackmailed by racketeers, resigns. After setting up this background, picture then swings into lusty action with usual gunfighting for climax.

Script tries hard but not too successfully to inject romance between Dix and Wendy Barrie. Dix provides usual good performance as chief with Chaney okay as his chauffeur-bodyguard. Porter is personable as scientific investigator with Miss Barrie handicapped by obvious lines of script. Adequate support by Lloyd Corrigan, Billy Lee, Marc Lawrence, Ed Pawley, Joe Crehan and Wade Boteler. Direction by R. William Neill grooves to gangster standard, although slow getting under way for pace expected of a picture of this type. *Walt.*

Fortress On the Volga

(RUSSIAN-MADE)

Artkino release of Lenfilm Studios production. Scenario and direction by Sergei and Georgi Vassiliev; music, Nikolai Kriukov; camera, Yefim Dudko, Mikhail Ivanov, Alexei Sigayev; English titles, Charles Clement. At Stanley, N. Y., Dec. 24, '42. Renning time, **77 MINS.**

Stalin....................Mikhail Gelovani
Voroshilov....................Nikolai Bogoliubov
Percrikhim....................Mikhail Zharov
Katya Davidova....................Barbara Miasnikova
Parkhomenko....................Sergei Nikashin
Rudniev....................Piotr Kadochnikov
Nosovich....................Alexander Gremin
Rindin....................Vyacheslav Safronov
Moldavsky....................Boris Babochkin
Mamontov....................Dmitri Dmokhovsky
Yesaul....................Kyrll Chepurnov
Timofeyich....................Ivan Sladkopyevatov

In 1918, during the Russian revolution that resulted in the USSR, the city of Tsaritsin, now known as Stalingrad, was besieged by the Germans and White Russians. Then, as now, the military men saw no hope and wanted to retreat. But the city was important to the revolution for through it came the food that helped feed Russia.

To the city came Stalin, then a commisar, to vitalize the defense, to hold the city until a volunteer army led by Voroshilov could break through the enemy lines and relieve the city. And the people stood fast, ignoring the rumors of the defeatists and fifth columnists, and the city was held until Voroshilov came.

With this story to tell and the news headlines to capitalize upon the Russians have, for once, muffed a grand opportunity. 'Fortress on the Volga' is strictly a minor effort, one that rambles without rhyme, and defeats its own purpose. For if the analogy of Tsaritsin to Stalingrad is true then it was German stupidity that lost and not Russian virility that held and won.

The best of this one is either on the cutting room floor here in New York or the fact that it was allegedly made last summer, while the Nazis were driving on Stalingrad, hastened its completion without the usual attention to detail. The transitions from one sequence to another are abrupt and crude; the jumps from the Voroshilov army to Tsaritsin and Stalin are not bridged. Consequently, the audience has to do a lot of imagining to project the plot.

The outdoor shots were filmed around Stalingrad and show much of the territory that is now in the news. A couple of the scenes carry through the basic theme of the picture, i.e., the analogy of Tsaritsin in 1918 to Stalingrad 1942. But that's about all. And the final battle scene, with the Germans marching in close order with a military band leading the way, will annoy the most amateurish military mind for its disregard of the fundamentals of warfare. The night club sequence is strictly an obvious try at loading-up the production. Might conceivably be effective in Russia but it's puny production by American standards.

Mikhail Gelovani, as Stalin, and Nikolai Bogoliubov, as Voroshilov, give startlingly true-to-life performances. Aside from them only Mikhail Sharov, as a Cossack, and Barbara Miasnikova, as a civilian organizer, are worthy of comment.
Fran.

UNDERCOVER MAN

United Artists release of Harry Sherman production. Features William Boyd, Andy Clyde, Jay Kirby, Antonio Moreno, Nora Lane and Esther Estrella. Directed by Lesley Selander; screenplay, J. Benton Cheney; camera, Russell Harlan. At New York, N. Y., dual, Dec. 30, '42. Running time, **68 MINS.**

Hopalong Cassidy	William Boyd
California	Andy Clyde
Breezy	Jay Kirby
Thomas Gonzales	Antonio Moreno
Donna Louise	Nora Lane
Miguel	Chris Pin Martin
Dolores Gonzales	Esther Estrella
Ed Carson	John Vosper
Rosita	Eva Puig
Bob Saunders	Alan Baldwin
Captain Hawkins	Jack Rockwell

Another in the Hopalong Cassidy series of hoss operas, 'Undercover Man' sticks close to the Hollywood formula, except that it takes time out at intervals to inject topical interest by orations on the need for strengthening Mex-Americana solidarity. It's a good dual supporter that wastes little footage in unfolding yarn, with a better than average bid for comedy, plus good direction.

Scripter J. Benton Cheney has hit on the idea that a gang of outlaws operating on both sides of the border, pillaging villages, robbing the hard-toiling Mexicans of countless pesos in gold unearthed from the El Dorado mines and stealing cattle and horses, was disrupting unity between the two nations. The No. 1 citizen south of the Rio Grande brings in Cassidy to clean up the mob and run down the top culprit. There's a leak somewhere,

emanating from the immediate vicinity of the respectable Mex citizen's ranch, and in order to ferret out the bad man the leak must be plugged up. Cassidy gets his man, exposes the leak (it's a gal kin of the law-and-order Mex and her son, both of whom have been blackmailed and forced into the banditry), but not before Cassidy and a lot of other innocent border folk are suspected. With plenty of gun totin', the film will have lots of appeal for the juniors.

William Boyd is his usual good self as Cassidy while Antonio Moreno, the vet of the silent era; Jay Kirby, Nora Lane, Andy Clyde and Chris Pin Martin handle supporting roles in satisfactory manner. Clyde and Martin are particularly effective in several comedy sequences.

This is one of the Paramount pix taken over by UA for release.
Rose.

SHADOW OF A DOUBT

Hollywood, Jan. 8.
Universal release of Jack Skirball production. Stars Teresa Wright, Joseph Cotten. Directed by Alfred Hitchcock. Screenplay by Thornton Wilder, Sally Benson and Alma Reville; original by Gordon McDonell; camera, Joseph Valentine; editor, Milton Carruth; asst. director, William Tummel; score, Dimitri Tiomkin. Previewed in studio projection room, Jan. 7, '43. Running time. **106 MINS.**

Young Charlie	Teresa Wright
Uncle Charlie	Joseph Cotten
Jack Graham	MacDonald Carey
Joseph Newton	Henry Travers
Emma Newton	Patricia Collinge
Herbie Hawkins	Hume Cronyn
Fred Saunders	Wallace Ford
Ann Newton	Edna May Wonacott
Roger Newton	Charles Bates
Station Master	Irving Bacon
Pullman Porter	Clarence Muse
Louise	Janet Shaw
Catherine	Estelle Jewell

The suspenseful tenor of dramatics associated with director Alfred Hitchcock in previous pictures is again utilized here to good advantage in unfolding a story of a small town and the arrival of what might prove to be a murderer. Brimful of typically deft Hitchcock weaving, to hold suspense at a high pitch, picture will play a profitable tune at the boxoffices.

Hitchcock poses a study in contrasts when the world-wise adventurer, Joseph Cotton, eludes police in Philadelphia to journey to his sister's home and family in the small California town of Santa Rosa. His deb-age niece, Theresa Wright, is not only named young Charlie after her uncle, but knows there's a mental contact somewhere along the line. Amid the typical small-town family life, she intuitively feels that Cotten has a guilty conscience, and finally ties the ends together to cast suspicion on him as a murderer and fugitive. This shadow is intensified with the arrival of detectives MacDonald Carey and Wallace Ford, and Cotten's refusal to see them or be photographed. When the girl is certain that Cotten is a fleeing criminal, he provides a convincing argument to trust him. But his later attempts to murder Miss Wright, though presumably by accident on two occasions, settles all doubt, and the finale comes fast and conclusive. Miss Wright finds romance with Carey for the finish.

Miniature Reviews

'Shadow of a Doubt' (U). Suspenseful drama in typical Alfred Hitchcock style. Good entertainment of type. Will click.

'Chetniks' (20th). Good dramatic reenactment of adventures of Jugoslav guerrillas battling Nazi invaders. Okay biz.

'Margin for Error' (20th). Dull comedy adapted from stage play of same name. For duals.

'The Meanest Man in the World' (20th). Jack Benny and Rochester's radio followers will have to support this one chiefly.

'Immortal Sergeant' (20th). Topical adventure drama of warfare in the Lybian desert good entertainment and b.o.

'Silver Queen' (UA). Strictly B featuring Priscilla Lane, George Brent and Bruce Cabot.

'Sundown Kid' (Rep). Entertaining western with fresh slants, starring Don 'Red' Barry.

'Boss of Big Town' (PRC). Racketeering item that will serve satisfactorily on the lesser time.

'La Novia De Primavera' (Argentine). Fair Argentine made, based on radio drama.

Hitchcock deftly etches his small-town characters and homey surroundings. Miss Wright provides a sincere and persuasive portrayal as the girl, while Cotten is excellent as the motivating factor in the proceedings. Strong support is provided by Henry Travers and Patricia Collinge as heads of the family, in addition to children Edna May Wonacott and Charles Bates. Hume Cronyn gets attention as the small-town amateur sleuth whose deductions on crime stories fly about in contrast to the real drama unfolding around him. Carey is good as the detective, although restricted in footage with his sidekick Wallace Ford.

Picture carries fullest small town atmosphere, having been produced—insofar as exteriors are concerned—right on the ground at Santa Rosa when the unit spent several weeks in that town. Camera work by Joseph Valentine is consistently good throughout.
Walt.

CHETNIKS
('The Fighting Guerrillas')

Hollywood, Jan. 9.
20th Century-Fox release of Sol M. Wurtzel production. Features Phillip Dorn, Anna Sten, John Sheppard, Virginia Gilmore, Martin Kosleck. Directed by Louis King. Screenplay by Jack Andrews, E. E. Paramore; original by Andrews; camera, Glen MacWilliams; editor, Alfred Day; dialog director, Paul Le Pere. Tradeshown in L. A., Jan. 8. '43. Running time. **73 MINS.**

Gen. Draja Mihailovitch	Philip Dorn
Lubitca Mihailovitch	Anna Sten
Alexis	John Sheppard
Natalia	Virginia Gilmore
Colonel Brockner	Martin Kosleck
General Von Bauer	Felix Basch
Major Danilov	Frank Lackteen
Nada	Patricia Prest
Mirko	Merrill Rodin
Captain Savo	Leroy Mason

'Chetniks' is a straightforward drama detailing an episode in the current battle of the courageous Jugoslav army of fighters led by General Draja Mihailovitch against the Nazi occupants of their country. Contrasting activities of the fighting guerrillas with the attempts of Nazi military and Gestapo leaders to swing the populace into line, picture carries solid dramatic content, and will provide good entertainment generally. Lacking sufficient cast marquee dressing, picture needs exploitation to carry it through keys as solo or billtopper in the regular bookings.

Film biography of the Chetnik leader was lined up with cooperation of the Jugoslav embassy in this country, with dramatic situations incorporated in the screen display based on fact and newspaper reports from the country. The heroics and daring of Mihalovitch and his guerrilla band are capably presented on the screen, and his outsmarting of the Nazis at every turn makes for good theatre.

Tale opens with the guerrillas capturing an Italian supply column and runs through fast-paced melodramatic happenings that includes visit of Mihalovitch and his aides to German headquarters in the village under flag of truce to demand that the natives be provided with food to prevent starvation plans of the Nazis. Leader's wife and two children remain in the town under assumed names, but are finally uncovered by Gestapo chief Martin Kosleck. Latter and military leader Felix Basch use the prisoners as bait to force disbanding of the guerrilla army, but Mihailovitch engages in deft strategy to catch the Germans off guard, destroy their occupational forces, and capture the town.

Cast is well selected, with Philip Dorn excellently handling portrayal of the patriotic and battling leader. Anna Sten is his wife, John Shepperd and Frank Lacteen his aides, and Kosleck and Basch the Nazi Gestapo and military commanders of the town. Script by Jack Andrews and Ed Paramore develops in a straight line and maintains consistent pace throughout. Direction by Louis King amply displays the dramatic factors of the picture. *Walt.*

MARGIN FOR ERROR

Hollywood, Jan. 8.
20th Century-Fox release of Ralph Dietrich production. Features Joan Bennett, Milton Berle and Otto Preminger. Directed by Preminger. Screenplay, Lillie Hayward; from play by Clare Boothe; camera, Edward Cronjager; editor, Louis Loeffler. Tradeshown in Los Angeles Jan. 8, '43. Running time, **74 MINS.**
Sophie Baumer ....Joan Bennett
Moe Finkelstein ....Milton Berle
Karl Baumer ....Otto Preminger
Baron Von Alvenstor ....Carl Esmond
Otto Horst ....Howard Freeman
Frieda ....Poldy Dur
Dr. Jennings ....Clyde Fillmore
Mrs. Finkelstein ....Ferike Boros
Solomon ....Joe Kirk
Fritz ....Hans Von Twardowski
Saboteurs............{ Ted North
{ Elmer Jack Semple
{ J. Norton Dunn
Kurk Moeller ....Hans Schumm
Captain Mulrooney ....Ed McNamara
Coroner ....Selmar Jackson

This film adaptation of Clare Boothe's Broadway comedy of three years ago falls short of present audience requirements in screen fare.

Story picks up the original idea of New York's Mayor LaGuardia in delegating Jewish policemen to guard the German consulate. Otto Preminger, who handled the stage role of the Nazi consul, repeats here in addition to directing. There are strange manipulations and sneaky happenings within the consulate walls, including Joan Bennett as the loveless wife who's forced to stick with the Nazi to protect her father in Czechoslovakia; Carl Esmond as the consulate secretary who is being maneuvered to take the rap for unaccounted funds dissipated by Preminger; bundleader Howard Freeman, a milquetoast and flustery type being given the brushoff by the dominating Nazi consul.

It all sums up to death of Preminger during a Hitler broadcast, with indications pointing to knife murder by Freeman and shooting by Miss Bennett. It's all quite hazy, but scientific analysis discloses that the no-good consul died of poison which he had intended for Esmond. Picture has brief prolog and epilog, with copper Milton Berle bound on troopship overseas along with Esmond, and former tells the doughboys of his experiences in the consulate.

Angle of having the Jewish cops guard the Nazi headquarters predicated chances for some snappy and explosive comedy and dialog quips, but they soon faded out entirely, and Berle found himself smothered by a cumbersome script. Preminger directed with a heavy hand and retains more of stagey dialog rather than giving comedy aspects to the piece as was done in the second half of the original play.

Cast is handicapped by material. Berle is only able to generate a few snickers that are spaced too far apart. Preminger's part is too unimportant for such high rating. Miss Bennett is mainly decorative; Esmond is okay and so is Freeman. Others in support include Poldy Dur, Clyde Fillmore and Ed McNamara. Picture is virtually a one-setter, further restricting tempo required of picture versions of plays. *Walt.*

The Meanest Man in the World

Hollywood, Jan. 8.
20th Century-Fox release of William Perlberg production. Stars Jack Benny. Priscilla Lane; features Rochester (Eddie Anderson). Directed by Sidney Lanfield. Screenplay by George Seaton and Allan House, based on play by George M. Cohan; camera, Peverell Marley; editor, Robert

Bischoff. Tradeshown in L. A., Jan. 7, '43. Running time, **57 MINS.'**
Richard Clark....................Jack Benny
Janie......................Priscilla Lane
Shufro ....Rochester
Frederick P. Leggitt......Edmund Gwenn
Mr. Brown..................Matt Briggs
Kitty Crockett................Anne Revere
Mrs. Leggitt..............Margaret Seddon
Wife........................Helene Reynolds
Husband......................Don Douglas
Mr. Chambers..............Harry Hayden
Mr. Billings....................Arthur Loft
Judge......................Andrew Tombes
Farmer........................Paul Burns

It will take all of the radio-acquired marquee voltage of Jack Benny and Rochester to put this one through the regular runs for more than passing attention. It's a loosely-bundled and not-too-explosive comedy more closely related to the Benny radio technique than picture lines.

Entire comedy side is dependent on by-play, crossfire, and banter between Benny and his handyman Rochester. The late George M. Cohan would never recognize much semblance to his play. Picture shows that the by-play between Benny and Rochester can linger too long when spotlighted on the screen, and director Sidney Lanfield seemed to have had the ball intercepted in the first reel, and he never recovered it for the rest of the footage.

What fragile story there is concerns Benny as a young small-town lawyer who's romantically inclined towards Priscilla Lane. He's too soft-hearted, and when moving to New York to make fame and fortune, clients are missing, until he simulates meanness. Candid camera shot of him taking candy stick from a child, published in local daily, brings him raft of clients and tab of 'meanest man in the world.' There's arrival of Miss Lane and father in the big town when he's broke and takes over a swank apartment, and again at the finish for a most synthetic clinch.

Picture is a lot of froth without foundation underneath. Comedy situations are of synthetic nature, wherein Benny or Rochester chiefly toss quips into the microphone. As such, it's mildly diverting entertainment, but hardly solid enough to hold up beyond nominal rating for the regular bookings when soloed or toplined. It's had re-take trouble and the cutting has pruned it down to less than an hour.

Benny and Rochester display their radio personalities throughout, especially in delivery of respective lines. Miss Lane is okay as the girl, and does what she can with the slight and inadequate material. Edmund Gwenn, Matt Briggs, Anne Revere and Margaret Seddon provide bulk of support. *Walt.*

IMMORTAL SERGEANT

Hollywood, Jan. 11.
20th Century-Fox release of Lamar Trotti production; screenplay by Trotti. Stars Henry Fonda, Maureen O'Hara; features Thomas Mitchell. Directed by John Stahl. From novel by John Brophy; camera, Arthur Miller; editor, James B. Clark. Tradeshown in L. A. Jan. 8, '43. Running time, **90 MINS.**
Corporal Colin Spence.........Henry Fonda
Valentine..................Maureen O'Hara
Sergeant Kelly............Thomas Mitchell
Cassidy....................Allyn Joslyn
Benedict.................Reginald Gardiner
Pilcher....................Melville Cooper
Symes....................Bramwell Fletcher
Cottrell......................Morton Lowry
Specialty Dancers........{ Bob Mascagno
{ Italia De Nubila
Nurse........................Jean Prescott

With the North African campaign currently getting headline attention and slated to remain on the front pages for the next several months, 'Immortal Sergeant' is a timely war melodrama that will roll through the regular runs for profitable biz. Exploitation-minded exhibs can generate added coin through concentration on picture's North African desert battle background.

Story is a compact drama, interestingly told, of a lost sunrise patrol on the Libyan desert. It's an intimate

study of characters and hardships encountered in the desert, until four survivors of the original 14 finally get back to their base. There's the sergeant, Thomas Mitchell, resourceful tactician of the last war and a most inspiring leader for the unit. It's his influence, after fatal wounding, that drives corporal Fonda on with the remnants of the outfit and transforms Fonda from a self-effacing individual into a determined, confident personality. Desert warfare is vividly displayed, with the little group facing the rigors of forced marches across the sands with limited supplies; and mixing in several engagements against enemy units encountered along the way, including the climactic blasting of a German camp set up in an oasis. Neatly dovetailed via cutbacks is romance between Fonda and Maureen O'Hara.

Producer-writer Lamar Trotti provides director John Stahl with a neatly-woven script, and Stahl directs in deft style, highlighting and accentuating the characters of the piece.

Fonda gives an impressionable performance as the reticent individual who is regenerated via army experience and influence of the sarge, while Mitchell clicks solidly as the veteran soldier. Allyn Joslyn, Melville Cooper and Morton Lowry are prominent as the three privates led through the sand wastes by Fonda, while Reginald Gardiner is an aggressive war correspondent supplying third angle to the romantic triangle.

Two spectacular sequences provide vivid war encounters. First is the enemy plane attack on the trucks and light tanks of the patrol; and the final demolishment of the German oasis encampment by the quartet in a desert wind and sandstorm which provide a most suitable climax for the expedition.

Production layout naturally concentrates most of the footage on desert locations, and latter have been excellently selected. Photography by Arthur Miller is excellent throughout. *Walt.*

SILVER QUEEN

United Artists release of Harry Sherman production. Features George Brent, Priscilla Lane, Bruce Cabot, Lynne Overman and Eugene Pallette. Directed by Lloyd Bacon. Screenplay by Bernard Schubert and Cecile Kramer from an original story by Forrest Halsey and William Allen Johnston; photography, Russell Harlan. At Globe theatre, N. Y., Jan. 9, '43. Running tme, **81 MINS.**
James Kincaid................George Brent
Coralie Adams..............Priscilla Lane
Gerald Forsythe.............Bruce Cabot
Hector Bailey............Lynne Overman
Steve Adams..............Eugene Pallette
Mrs. Forsythe...............Janet Beecher
Blackie.........Guinn 'Big Boy' Williams

One of the more ambitious productions attempted by Harry Sherman and one of his few non-saddle sagas, 'Silver Queen' emerges strictly a 'B' which should do o.k. as a dual supporter. That it doesn't realize its full potentialities as a b.o. attraction on its own is due to the hackneyed gambling yarn it unfolds. Otherwise, Sherman has taken advantage of all the basic entertainment elements it affords.

Budgeted far beyond the average 'B' product, it leans heavily on atmospheric settings, boasts an excellent cast of b.o. reliables who get down to the business of unfolding the trite narrative without distractions, and carries a fair measure of suspense in Lloyd Bacon's competent directing. For good measure, Sherman has tossed in a climactic fistic fray between the two male principals, George Brent and Bruce Cabot, that packs a terrific wallop for several minutes. Be it nostalgia or just a way of reminding audiences that at heart he's still a top western producer, Sherman has given the

bare knuckle sequence everything he's got. So do the participants. Film is one of the Par pix taken over by UA for release.

Yarn is localed in New York and later in Frisco, in the '70's, and is spun around an aristocratic dame (Priscilla Lane) who is left holding a bagful of creditors when her papa (Eugene Pallette) kicks in after gambling away the family fortune, including deed to a once prosperous Nevada mine. Latter was acquired via the poker route by a professional gambler (Brent), who falls for the Lane gal but bows out when he learns she's going to marry a guy (Cabot) who can give her lots of security and social prestige. As a token of his own love, Brent turns the deed over to Cabot as a gift for the gal, but the fiance keeps the paper for himself. Cursed with papa's gambling instincts, Miss Lane changes her mind about marrying and heads for Frisco where, bent on discharging the family debts, she opens a fabulous joint called the 'Silver Queen' and cleans up. She sends the money back to Cabot with instructions to pay off, but latter uses coin in quest of new vein of ore in mine. Brent shows up in time for inevitable exposure and final clinch.

Miss Lane and Brent do the best they can with their roles, with Cabot at all times convincing as the cheat. In lesser parts, Pallette, Lynne Overman, Janet Beecher and Guinn Williams, latter as Brent's stooge, are likewise o.k. Russell Harlan's camera work stands out, with ample footage on N. Y. upper crust life and the later Frisco and Nevada background sequences providing opportunity for a colorful pattern. *Rose.*

SUNDOWN KID

Republic release of Eddy White production. Stars Don 'Red' Barry; features Ian Keith, Helen MacKellar, Linda Johnson, Emmett Lynn. Directed by Elmer Clifton. Story and adaptation, Norman S. Hall; editor, William Thompson; camera, Ernest Miller. At New York, N. Y., dual, week Jan. 5, '43. Running time, **55 MINS.**
Red Tracy }
Red Brannon } ....Don 'Red' Barry
J. Richard Spencer................Ian Keith
Lucy Randall.............Helen MacKellar
Lynn Parsons..............Linda Johnson
Pop Tanner....................Emmett Lynn
Vince Ganley................Wade Crosby
Jim Dawson....................Ted Adams
Mrs. Peabody....................Fern Emmett
Nick Parker......................Bud Geary
Luke Reed......................Bob Kortman
Tex Bronner..................Ken Duncan

Don 'Red' Barry may not be the average conception of a western star, nor is he the accepted romantic type but when it comes to performance, notably in using his fists, the young saddle-leather star has considerable on the ball. In 'Sundown Kid' he has a vehicle that will force him ahead, meantime giving followers of western adequate entertainment value.

With producers of westerns trying to get away from rustlers and water poachers, Eddy White gives 'Sundown Kid' a counterfeiting background. The role handed Barry is that of a Pinkerton detective, again a switch from marshals or sheriffs. With film opening in a prison, Barry is spotted there as a Pink with a view to getting a line on a counterfeiting ring from a fellow prisoner.

Action shifts to the wide open spaces where the counterfeiting mob is in operation. Joining up with them though the phoney-money manufacturers are suipicious of him, Barry learns a rich recluse is being mulcted of her property through the use of the bad coin. Plot also finally reveals Barry as the long-lost son of the old lady, while the girl is a reporter from Chicago rather than the customary daughter or niece of a rancher. She's Linda Johnson, who does a nice job.

Ian Keith plays a smalltown attorney, the higher-up in the counterfeiting ring, while Ted Adams is one of his principal henchmen. Both acquit themselves creditably. Helen MacKellar does the recluse appropriately. *Char.*

BOSS OF BIG TOWN

Producers Releasing Corp. release of Jack Schwarz production. Features John Litel, Florence Rice. H. B. Warner, Jean Brooks, John Miljan. Directed by Arthur Dreifuss. Story and adaptation, Edward Dein; editor, Charles Henkel; camera, Marcel le Picard. At New York, dual, week Jan. 5, '43. Running time, 65 MINS.
Michael Lynn...................John Litel
Linda Gregory................Florence Rice
Jeffrey Moore.................H. B. Warner
Iris Moore.....................Jean Brooks
Craige..........................John Miljan
Dr. Gil Page...................David Bacon
Mrs. Lane.....................Mary Gordon
Bram Hart..................Frank Ferguson
Foster.......................John Maxwell
Graham..........................Paul Dubov
Inspector Torrence..........Lloyd Ingram
Francis Hart.................Patricia Prest

Dated as to the racketeering angle, but possessing some timeliness due to the fact food, now scarce, is involved, 'Boss of Big Town' is sufficiently well put together to serve suitably in lesser runs and particularly as the associate feature on double bills.

The story concerns the operations of a gang of racketeers who control the wholesaling of food, notably milk, and gets theirs through pushing up prices. Seeking to swing the superintendent of a big city market to their side, their racket is smashed only after John Litel finally goes over to their camp under the guise of playing ball, but actually with a view to uncovering the higherups. Brains of the mob is H. B. Warner, a prominent attorney who is looked upon as a public-spirited citizen.

Litel, as the city market official, turns in a smooth and convincing performance, while Florence Rice, opposite him, does acceptably. Warner's job is in the familiar groove but okay. Jean Brooks plays Warner's daughter and John Miljan a racketeer, latter imparting to the role his usual suavity.

Jack Schwarz' production is ample and the direction by Arthur Dreifuss commands approval. *Char.*

La Novia De Primavera
('Spring Bride')
(ARGENTINE-MADE)

Buenos Aires, Jan. 2.

Lumiton production and release. Stars Maria Duval; features Roberto Airaldi, Federico Mansilla, Aurelia Ferrer, Norma Castillo, Jose Capilla, Pola Alonso, Rene Fischer Bauer, Roberto Soria, Lony Pagano, Elisa Landi, Amelia Pena, Elina Colomer, and Martha Quinteros. Directed by Carlos Hugo Christensen. Story, Julio Porter; adapted by Francisco Oyarzabal; camera, Pablo Tabernero. Reviewed at the Broadway, Buenos Aires. Running time, 68 MINS.

Based on a radio dramatization, 'La Novia de Primavera' ('Spring Bride') retains too much of its microphone background to make it a really acceptable piece, but listening audience should make it a solid grosser, particularly in nabe houses. Notable chiefly for improvement it shows in the work of Maria Duval, a youthful star who carries the weight of the plot and indicates strong possibilities for Hollywood.

Plot deals with a young girl who pretends to her friends that she is the fiancee of a famed author. When he arrives at her home, as a gag he keeps up the deception. Gal takes the 'engagement' seriously and believes her love reciprocated, only to suffer disillusionment when she discovers that it is her big sister the writer has fallen for. Yarn ends in the manner of some of the earlier Durbins, with a youthful sweetie on hand to ease the pain.

Roberto Airaldi, in the male lead, is fair, and Norma Castillo, w.k. on radio, is o.k. but hardly photogenic. Comedienne Teresita is outstanding in the supporting cast, as is Elina Colomer.

While sound and photography only so-so, simplicity of the story and particularly charm of the cast should help at the b.o. *Ray.*

Miniature Reviews

The Crystal Ball' (UA). Romantic comedy with unique plot that should do very well.

'Forever and a Day' (RKO). Topnotch cast in romantic drama geared for healthy b.o.

'Cinderella Swings It' (RKO). Guy Kibbe, Gloria Warren in typical 'Scattergood Baines' yarn; strong dualer.

'Mug Town' (U). Dead End Kid combo in routine tough guy melo O.K. filler.

'Silver Skates' (Musical), (Mono). Ice revue cinch profit maker for all bookings.

'Youth On Parade' (Rep). Frothy musical, good for strong spot on dualers.

'Lost Canyon' (UA) (One Song). Second Hopalong Cassidy western for UA typical actioner of series.

'Truck Busters' (WB). Action meller suitable as No. 2 feature on duals.

'Tarzan Triumphs' (Lesser-RKO). Adequate entry of its type for juvenile trade as program supporter in subsequents.

'The Old Chisholm Trail' (Songs) (U). Johnny Mack Brown and Tex Ritter in standard western that should please.

'Lady From Chungking' (PRC), Anna May Wong in a 'B' about Chinese guerrillas. Strictly for lesser duals.

'Amor Ultimo Modelo' (Argentine). Weak Argentine-made.

THE CRYSTAL BALL

United Artists release of Richard Blumenthal production. Stars Ray Milland, Paulette Godard; features Gladys George, Virginia Field, William Bendix, Mary Field, Frank Conlon, Ernest Truex, Iris Adrian, Mabel Paige, Don Douglas. Directed by Elliott Nugent. Story, Steven Vas; adaptation, Virginia Van Upp; editor, Doane Harrison; camera, Leo Tover. Reviewed in projection room, N. Y., Jan. 15, '43. Running time, 80 MINS.
Toni Gerard.............Paulette Goddard
Brad Cavanaugh............Ray Milland
Jo Ainsley...................Virginia Field
Madame Zenobia..........Gladys George
Biff Carter...............William Bendix
Pop Tibbets................Cecil Kellaway
Foster.........................Mary Field
Dusty........................Frank Conlan
Mr. Martin..................Ernest Truex
Mrs. Martin...................Iris Adrian
'Lady With a Pekingese'.....Mabel Paige
Mrs. Harlan Smythe.......Regina Wallace
Leonard......................Peter Jamieson
Cavanaugh's Sec...............Faye Helm
Govt. Investigator...........Don Douglas
Stukov.......................Nestor Paiva
Waiter..........................Sig Arno

A story with a unique plot, a cast of seasoned performers, very capable direction and good comedy relief combine to make this one thoroughly acceptable entertainment. It should do from better-than-average to very good everywhere played.

Picture is among those which United Artists bought from Paramount early last fall when it purchased three regular program features as well as several westerns made by Harry Sherman.

Though the title may not suggest it, 'The Crystal Ball' carries a strong romantic flavor with Ray Milland and Paulette Goddard paired, while Virginia Field is the frustrated fiancee in the triangular setup. Miss Field plays a rich widow, Miss Goddard a stranded gal who goes to work as a shill for a shooting gallery, a job procured for her by a friendly fortune-teller of shady rep.

When the fake medium takes sick, Miss Goddard doubles on the fortune-telling racket and nearly gets Milland into trouble by advising that he take an option on some property that the Government is after. Ultimately, through efforts

by Miss Goddard, now deeply in love with Milland, the latter, an attorney, is cleared. Not until the end, however, does Milland discover that the little lady is the seeress he and others have patronized.

The comic relief is light and refreshing but more could have been done with Ernest Truex and Iris Adrian, a scrapping married couple. Additional humor is supplied by William Bendix, playing a chauffeur and Sig Arno, a waiter.

Richard Blumenthal's production is meritorious. Direction is by Elliott Nugent, who has provided nice pace and kept the action rolling. *Char.*

FOREVER AND A DAY

RKO release of Anglo-American production. Directors: Rene Clair, Edmund Goulding, Cedric Hardwicke, Frank Lloyd, Victor Saville, Robert Stevenson, Herbert Wilcox. Writers: Charles Bennett, C. S. Forrester, Lawrence Hazard, Michael Hogan, W. P. Lipscomb, Alice Duer Miller, John Van Druten, Alan Campbell, Peter Godfrey, S. M. Herzig, Christopher Isherwood, Gene Lockhart, R. C. Sherriff, Claudine West, Norman Corwin, Jack Hartfield, James Hilton, Emmet Lavery, Frederick Lonsdale, Donald Ogden Stewart, Keith Winter. Camera: Robert de Grasse, Lee Garmes, Russell Metty, Nicholas Musuraca; editors: Elmo J. Williams, George Crone. Tradeshown in New York, Jan. 19, '43. Running time, 104 MINS.
Cast: Brian Aherne, Ida Lupino, Merle Oberon, Robert Cummings, Roland Young, Gladys Cooper, Cedric Hardwicke, Dame May Whitty, Charles Laughton, Jessie Matthews, Anna Neagle, Herbert Marshall, C. Aubrey Smith, Ray Milland, Claude Rains, Ian Hunter, Buster Keaton, Nigel Bruce, Reginald Gardner, Arthur Treacher, Edmund Gwenn, Halliwell Hobbes, Montague Love, Patric Knowles, Elsa Lanchester, Richard Haydn, Clyde Cook, Kent Smith, Victor McLaglen, Ruth Warrick, Gene Lockhart, Reginald Owen, Edward Everett Horton, Donald Crisp, George Kirby, Connie Leon, Ernest Grooney, Billy Bevan, Aubrey Mather, Barbara Everest, Ben Webster, Alan Edmiston, Alec Craig, Daphne Moore, Cecil Kellaway, Wendy Barrie, Eric Blore, Walter Kingsford, Una O'Connor, Ivan Simpson, Marta Gale, Doreen Monroe, Joy Harrington, Ethel Griffies, Stuart Robertson, Charles Irwin, Doris Lloyd, Isobel Elsom, Wendell Hulett, Dennis Hoey, Robert Coote, Arthur Mulliner, May Beatty, Harry Allen, June Lockhart, Gerald Oliver Smith, Lumsden Hare, Claud Allister, Helena Pickard, Clifford Severn, Anna Lee, June Duprez, Odette Myrtil, Emily Fitzroy, Anita Bolster, Pax Walker, Jean Prescott.

'Forever and a Day' is slated to garner from good to excellent grosses. It's a sentimental romantic-adventure yarn, encompassing in cavalcade manner Britain's epochal struggles to retain the integrity of an empire and the freedom of its people in face of periodical threats of would-be world conquerors. Interwoven is the quaint history of a picturesque London mansion—its illustrious builder and his descendants—built during the Napoleonic period, that withstands the ravages of time and world-shattering conflict until the days of the Nazi blitz.

In a star-studded cast, including some 45 name players, a number of topnotchers are necessarily limited. However, a large proportion of the subordinate sequences have been handled with telling effect.

Picture, which has been in the making for about a year, rolled up a negative cost of around $500,000 at RKO, which financed the production. This is exclusive of the players, who undertook the assignment on a gratis basis, some 21 niteries and the seven accredited directors who also contributed their services. Proceeds, over and above the actual cost of production and distribution, go to Anglo-American war charities.

In outstanding bit parts are Sir Cedric Hardwicke, as the Dickensonian bath-tub inventor; Charles Laughton, as the butler; Elsa Lanchester as waitress-maid; Jessie Matthews, Ian Hunter, Herbert Marshall, Buster Keaton and Dame May Whitty.

Perhaps the most effective of the important interludes is the touching, deftly-handled romantic sequence with Merle Oberon and Robert

Cummings. Latter, as an American doughboy in London during World War I, falls for the receptionist in the historic old house, long since converted into a residential hotel. Here, also, Gladys Cooper and Roland Young come through with a corking interpretation as the parents of the 21-year-old flying ace, killed in action, in whose honor all the inmates of the hostelry are meantime staging a reception. Theirs are easily the most moving, skillfully presented performances in the production.

Ida Lupino and Brian Aherne are runners-up for top honors, former as the household maid, and the latter as the coalman-mechanic, who emigrate to America.

Yarn revolves about the fusing of two families after a feud dating back to the early part of the 19th century when C. Aubrey Smith, as the robust, swashbuckling British admiral first built the house. Claude Rains, as the vindictive guardian of Anna Neagle, who runs away to marry one of the Smith tribe, does not impress as the menace.

Story is told via the flashback technique with the two youngest survivors of the feuding families meeting during the London blitz in the bomb shelter over which the old house stands. Kent Smith, as the U.S. newspaperman, is barely adequate as the romantic lead, unimpressive and somewhat awkward in enunciation. Ruth Warrick, as the last of the other clan, photographs like a winner. Opening sequences and intro by narrator are unnecessarily long. *Mori.*

Cinderella Swings It

(WITH SONGS)

RKO release of Jerrold T. Brandt production. Stars Guy Kibbee; features Gloria Warren, Helen Parrish, Dick Hogan, Leonid Kinskey, Dink Trout. Directed by Christy Cabanne. Screenplay by Michael L. Simmons, adapted from 'Scattergood Baines' stories by Clarence Budington Kelland; songs by George Jessel-Ben Oaklanl. Ted Grouya-Jerri Kruger; camera, Arthur Martinelli; editor, Richard Cahoon. Trade-shown in N. Y., Jan. 18, '43. Running time, **70 MINS.**

Scattergood Baines	Guy Kibbee
Betty Palmer	Gloria Warren
Salily Burton	Helen Parrish
Tommy Stewart	Dick Hogan
Vladimir Smitkin	Leonid Kinskey
Butch & Buddy	Billy Lenhart and Kenneth Brown
Pliny Pickett	Dink Trout
Hipp	Willy Best
Brock Harris	Pierre Watkin
Ed Potts	Lee 'Lasses' White
Clara Potts	Fern Emmett
Lem	Ed Waller
Madame Dolores	Kay Linaker
Secretary	Christine McIntyre
Tap Dancer	Grace Costello

'Cinderella Swings It' is palatable 'B' feature entertainment. Never attempts to be more than that. Hence, it will fit in well as support on double-features.

Another in the 'Scattergood Baines' series, any title reference is removed, but the film spells a certain ready-made audience. Story concerns young femme singer who makes good when she adopts the swing style. It focuses more attention on the warbler, her tutor and the tough struggle to make the grade than on Baines, but back of it all, of course, is the sound reasoning of Guy Kibbee ('Scattergood') who urges singing in the modern-day style.

Production advances the career of Gloria Warren, who played a similar role in Warners' 'Always in My Heart,' nearly a year ago. Still no great actress, her tiptop voice enables dodging the thespic pitfalls. Leonid Kinskey is the music tutor, and members of the 'Scattergood' stock company include Helen Parrish, Lee White, Fern Emmett and Willy Best.

Aside from operatic arias and classics that Miss Warren warbles, she also sings 'Flag's Still There, Mr. Key,' by George Jessel and Ben Oakland, and 'I Heard You Cried Last Night,' by Ted Grouya and Jerri Kruger. Former is climax song of film, and a tuneful standout. Film is well directed by Christy Cabanne despite a rather trite screenplay. *Wear.*

MUG TOWN

Hollywood, Jan. 15.

Universal release of Ken Goldsmith production. Features Dead End Kids and Little Tough Guys. Directed by Ray Taylor. Screenplay by Brenda Weisberg, Lewis Amster, Harold Tarshis, Henry Sucher; original, Charles Grayson; camera, Jack MacKenzie; editor, Edward Curtiss. Previewed in studio projection room, Jan. 14, '43. Running time, **58 MINS.**

Tommy	Billy Halop
Pig	Huntz Hall
Norene Steward	Grace McDonald
Ape	Bernard Punsly
String	Gabriel Dell
Clinker	Edward Norris
Mrs. Bell	Virginia Brissac
Steve	Tommy Kelly
Don Bell	Dick Hogan
Mack Steward	Jed Prouty
Shorty	Murray Alper
Marco	Paul Fix

This is another in the Universal group of dramas built around remnants of the Dead End Kids. Without too much stress on either originality or credulity, picture still retains sufficient dramatics of type to pass as supporting dualer in the secondary houses where previous issues have been accepted.

Story is forced in attempting to display further antics of the recalcitrant tough guys. After taking runaway Tommy Kelly under their wing, kid is killed in freight-hopping episode, and the four continue to his home in a small town to break the news to his mother. But they keep the secret while steered onto the road of rehabilitation and work. Leader Billy Halop gets job in service station, a stopover for long-haul trucks, and is made victim of pilfering gang. But he gets the thieves in a chase to vindicate himself and pals. Then the quartet enlists in the Army.

Halop, Huntz Hall, Bernard Punsly and Gabriel Dell comprise the youthful knights of the road, performing in regular style with usual overlay of mugging. Attempts to inject comedy through silly routines handed Hall are decidedly sophomoric. Grace McDonald is the girl for limited footage, while Virginia Brissac makes a homey mother. Direction by Ray Taylor is standard for a modest budgeter of this calibre. *Walt.*

SILVER SKATES

(MUSICAL)

Hollywood, Jan. 13.

Monogram release of Lindsley Parsons production. Features Kenny Baker, Patricia Morison and Belita. Directed by Leslie Goodwins. Screenplay, Jerry Cady. Musical director, Edward Kay. Songs and musical score, David Oppenheim and Roy Ingraham; camera, Mack Stengler; editor, Richard Currier. Previewed at Paramount, Hollywood, Jan. 11, '43. Running time, **73 MINS.**

Danny	Kenny Baker
Claire	Patricia Morison
Belita	Belita
Frick & Frack	By Themselves
Katrina	Irene Dare
Billie	Danny Shaw
Eugene Turner	By Himself
Lucille	Joyce Compton
Eddie	Frank Faylen
Hayes	Paul McVey
Mrs. Martin	Ruth Lee
Blake	John Maxwell
Tom	Henry Wadsworth
George Stewart	By Himself
Jo Ann Dean	By Herself

Ted Fio Rito Orchestra

'Silver Skates' is by far Monogram's most expensive and pretentious production, but results justify the outlay. Picture is a neat combo of ice specialties by several expert blade-steppers an adequate but not too intrusive a story thread and excellent musical background provided by Ted Fio Rito's orch, in addition to songs delivered by Kenny Baker. Picture is a cinch for profits, particularly at theatres where the ice spectacles do not show.

Major portion of the 73 minutes' running time is devoted to specialties on the ice. Production backgrounds are modest generally, but this condition serves to focus attention on the blade performers rather than on elaborate settings.

Story is rather routine. Patricia Morison is burdened with debt in operating the skating revue, but inclusion of Belita hops the grosses so promoter has chance for even break until skater gives notice to get married. Kenny Baker, vocalist with the show, is engaged to Miss Morison, who makes a play for Belita to keep her with the show. After jockeying around, financial difficulties are overcome and the romantic tangles are straightened out.

Belita displays her skating versatility with several solos and tandemed with Eugene Turner, champ blade-stepper. Little Irene Dare, who appeared in two skating pictures for Sol Lesser several years ago, comes on for three appearances, while the comedy duo of Frick and Frack clicks solidly with a comedy routine on ice. Danny Shaw, teenager, has a brief cowboy turn solo, and then teams with Miss Dare for a juvenile twosome.

Baker provides sideline vocals for 'Lovely Lady,' 'Love Is a Beautiful Song' and finale, 'Sing a Song of the Sea.' In addition, he delivers 'A Girl Like You—a Boy Like Me' for romantic tune aimed at Miss Morison. Balance of eight numbers, written by David Oppenheim and Roy Ingraham, serve for choral renditions and background music by Ted Fio Rito's orch.

Miss Morison and Baker carry major load of the story in good style, with Belita displaying ease in delivery of her role off the skates. Frank Faylen provides brief comedy interludes, teaming at several points with Joyce Compton. Balance of support is neatly set up.

William Shapiro displayed the ice sequences in intimate and showmanly style, with Leslie Goodwins keeping the framework story moving at a good clip. Camera of Mack Stengler is exceptional, especially follow shots on the ice performers. *Walt.*

YOUTH ON PARADE

(MUSICAL)

Republic release of Albert J. Cohen production. Features John Hubbard, Ruth Terry, Martha O'Driscoll, Tom Brown, Charles Smith. Directed by Al Rogell. Screenplay, George Carleton Brown; added dialogue, Frank Gill, Jr.; camera, Ernest Miller; editor, Howard O'Neill; songs by Jule Styne, Sammy Cahn; dances staged by Dave Gould. At Strand, Brooklyn, week Jan. 15, '43, dualed. Running time, **72 MINS.**

Patty Flynn)	
Prof. Gerald Payne	John Hubbard
Betty Reilly (	Ruth Terry
Sally Carlyle	Martha O'Driscoll
Bingo Brown	Tom Brown
The Dean	Ivan F. Simpson
Willie Webster	Charles Smith
Emmy Lou Piper	Lynn Merrick
Frosty	Nana Bryant
Bruce	Bruce Langley
Eddie Reilly	Chick Chandler
Marlyn	Marlyn Schild

Frothy little musical is sure to furnish strong support on dualers.

Idea of young college kids trying to pull the wool over the eyes of a youngish psychology professor is not especially new. Nor is ringing in of the inevitable school musical show. But it's given numerous clever twists and swift pace for neat returns. There's considerable aftermath stress about students staying in college to finish their courses instead of joining the colors. But it's Director Al Rogell's swift pacing of outlandish goings-on that makes the film.

John Hubbard makes a likely psychology professor, while Martha O'Driscoll, photographing like a million, is superb as the student lure he falls for. Ruth Terry, as the madcap phoney student; Tom Brown, as the effervescent collegiate leader; and Charles Smith, from the Henry Aldrich film series, as the hep student, all are well cast.

'You Gotta Study, Buddy,' 'You're So Good to Me' and 'I've Heard That Song Before,' by Jule Styne and Sammy Cahn, are outstanding among six songs. *Wear.*

LOST CANYON

(ONE SONG)

Hollywood, Jan. 14.

United Artists release of Harry Sherman production; associate prolucer, Lewis Rachmil. Stars William Boyd; features Jay Kirby, Andy Clyde, Lola Lane. Directed by Lesley Selander. Original screenplay by Harry O. Hoyt; camera, Russell Harlan; editor, Sherman A. Rose. Previewed in studio projection room, Jan. 13, '43. Running time, **61 MINS.**

Hopalong Cassidy	William Boyd
Breezy Travers	Jay Kirby
California Carlson	Andy Clyde
Laura	Lola Lane
Jeff Burton	Douglas Fowley
Clark	Herbert Rawlinson
Rogers	Guy Usher
Haskell	Carl Hackett

'Lost Canyon,' second of the Hopalong Cassidy series distributed through United Artists, is cut from familiar western pattern to develop into standard entry for the action-minded audiences.

Basic, oft-told drama of the west has plenty of fast riding and gun-popping, with inclusion of several bits of elemental comedy for the juvenile trade displayed by Andy Clyde. Young Jay Kirby is accused of a bank holdup and flees, which brings Hopalong Bill Boyd into the picture to prove his innocence and uncover the guilty bandits. There's the pitch for the rancher's holdings to round out a secret irrigation project, and cattle rustling to force the sale. Climax hits with an old-fashioned pitched gun battle between the outlaws and the sheriff's posse.

Cast is standard for the series, with Boyd, Kirby and Clyde teaming for the three western pals. Lola Lane is the girl, while Douglas Fowley is ringleader of the heavies, and Herbert Rawlinson the ranchowner. Direction by Lesley Selander steps along at a good pace. Producer Harry Sherman inserted the Sportsmen Quartet for rendition of 'Jingle, Jangle, Jingle.' *Walt.*

TRUCK BUSTERS

Hollywood, Jan. 19.

Warner Bros. production and release. Features Richard Travis, Virginia Christine, Charles Lang, Ruth Ford. Directed by B. Reeves Eason. Original screenplay, Robert E. Kent and Raymond L. Schrock; camera, Harry Neumann; editor, Clarence Kolster. Traleshown Jan. 18, '43. Running time, **58 MINS.**

Casey Dorgan	Richard Travis
Eadie Watkins	Virginia Christine
Jimmy Dorgan	Charles Lang
Pearl	Ruth Ford
Limey	Richard Fraser
Dave Todd	Michael Ames
Police Captain Gear	Frank Wilcox
Bonetti	Don Costello
Al Wilson	Rex Williams
Joe Moore	Bill Crago
Scrappy O'Brien	Monte Blue
Tim Shaughnessy	Bill Kennedy
Stephen S. Gray	William B. Davidson
Andy Panopolos	George Humbert
Babe	Peggy Diggins
Maxie	John Harmon
District Attorney Danton	John Maxwell
Mack	Glenn Cavender
George Havelock	Frank Ferguson
Landis	Robert Middlemass
Elliott	Edward Keane
Waitress	Jean Ames

'Truck Busters' is deliberately set up as an action meller for dual support, and hits that mark without detours. It's a secondary booking for the subsequent houses, dished up on extremely moderate budget.

Story involves a trucking battle between big operators and the independents, most of latter with one truck. Anticipated war boom and profits has the big boys combining to shunt indies out of business via hiring racketeer Don Costello and his mob. In addition to putting trucks and customer produce-merchants out of commission, Costello takes over auto finance outfit to repossess independents trucks through overdue payments.

Heroic Richard Travis operates lone truck and heads indie truckers, successfully blocking Costello plans, resulting in death of Travis' brother Charles Lang. In usual climactic finish with pitched gun battle, Costello and gang are rounded up, and the independents roll again. Picture has plenty of lusty and familiar action in its unreeling, with players getting little chance to tarry for acting displays. Script by Robert Kent and Ray Schrock, although unfolding obvious tale of type, is closely-knit, while direction by Reeves Eason hits lively clip. *Walt.*

TARZAN TRIUMPHS

Hollywood, Jan. 19.

RKO release of Sol Lesser production. Features Johnny Weissmuller and Johnny Sheffield. Directed by William Thiele. Screenplay, Roy Chansler and Carroll Young; from story by Young; based on characters created by Edgar Rice Burroughs; camera, Harry Wild; editor, Hal Kern; assistant director, Clem Beauchamp. Tradeshown in L. A., Jan. 19, '43. Running time, 76 MINS.

Tarzan...............Johnny Weissmuller
Boy....................Johnny Sheffield
Zandra..................Frances Gifford
Col. Von Reichart.........Stanley Ridges
Sergeant...................Sig Ruman
Patriarch.............Pedro de Cordoba
Bausch.................Philip Van Zandt
Archmet..................Stanley Brown
Schmidt...................Rex Williams
Cheta ....Herself

This is the first of at least two Tarzan features that Sol Lesser will turn out for RKO release, after Metro wound up its interest in the jungleman's adventures last fall. 'Tarzan Triumphs' will catch strong attention from the juvenile trade, otherwise it's a dual supporter generally.

Virtually all jungle stuff, 'Tarzan' has good portion of stock animal shots and includes a hidden city for convenient takeover by a squad of Nazi paratroops and subsequent battle in which Tarzan, with the aid of the subjugated natives, knocks off the invaders and restores peace in the jungle territory.

U s u a l tree-swinging, dashes through the jungle undergrowth, and other familiar Tarzanian ingredients are again on display. Also boy (little Johnny Sheffield), the chimp Cheta and the small elephant. Inability to obtain Maureen O'Sullivan for this picture switches script for her to be visiting in England, with Frances Gifford filling in as the girl from the hidden city.

Weissmuller and Johnny Sheffield run around as usual without necessity of displaying much acting ability. Miss Gifford is okay as the native girl, while Stanley Ridges, Sig Ruman, Philip Van Zandt and Rex Williams are sufficiently acceptable as the Nazi invaders. Direction by William Thiele hits usual standard for the Tarzan features. *Walt.*

OLD CHISHOLM TRAIL
(SONGS)

Universal release of Oliver Drake production. Stars Johnny Mack Brown, Tex Ritter; features Fuzzy Knight, Jennifer Holt, Jimmy Wakely Trio. Directed by Elmer Clifton. Screenplay by Clifton from original by Harry Fraser; camera, William Sickner; musical director, H. J. Salter. At New York, N. Y., dual, Jan. 13, '43. Running time, 59 MINS.

Dusty Gardner........Johnny Mack Brown
Montana Smith................Tex Ritter
Polario..................Fuzzy Knight
Mary Lee.................Jennifer Holt
Belle Turner................Mady Correll
Chief Hopping Crow........Earle Hodgins
Ed......................Roy Barcroft
Joe Rankin................Edmund Cobb
Hank......................Budd Buster
          Jimmy Wakely Trio

This western figures to be just as popular with the cowpoke addicts as were the production line gas buggies that come out of Detroit. It's a standard job, completely equipped with the usual line of action, romance and adventure.

This time the story is about a fight for free water on 'The Old Chisholm Trail' along which cattlemen actually did travel their herds to market. Johnny Mack Brown is the spokesman for a group of cattlemen whom Mady Correll, a shrewd cookie, tries to hijack by fencing off the only available supply of water.

The songs are incidental to the action, and sung by Tex Ritter and the Wakely Trio. *Fran.*

Lady From Chungking

Producers Releasing Corp. release of Alfred Stern and Arthur Alexander production. Stars Anna May Wong; features Harold Huber, Mae Clarke. Directed by William Nigh. Screenplay, Sam Robins; from original by Milton Raison and Sam Robins; camera, Marcel LePicard; editor, Charles Henkel, Jr. Reviewed at New York, N. Y., dual, Jan. 13, '43. Running time, 71 MINS.

Kwan Mei................Anna May Wong
General Kaimura..........Harold Huber
Lavara....................Mae Clarke
Rodney Carr..............Rick Vallin
Pat O'Roulke...............Paul Bryar
Leutenant Shimoto..........Ted Hecht
Hans Gruber...............Louis Donath
Chen....................James Leong
Mochow....................Archie Got
Lu-Chi................Walter Soo Hoo

'Lady From Chungking' has a noteworthy objective, the fight of the Chinese guerrillas against the Japs. And just as PRC fluffed its 'Commando' picture, released some months ago, this one comes a cropper for the same reason: 'big' pictures are rarely made on short budgets. This is just grist for the grinds.

Anna May Wong is a guerrilla leader who secretly organizes farmers. Harold Huber is a Jap general. Mae Clarke is a singer at the local hostelry. Huber likes the gals, so Miss Wong sheds her fieldhand garb for silks and satins, cons the general into tipping his plans and feeds him a knockout drop. Then her guerrillas go into action. All the leading players are killed but not before the two Flying Tigers make their escape. *Fran.*

Amor Ultimo Modelo
('Love, Latest Model')
(ARGENTINE-MADE)
(With Songs)

Buenos Aires, Jan. 1.

EFA production and release. Stars Alberto Vila, Anna Maria Lynch; features Rufino Cordoba, Sussy del Carril, Adrian Cuneo, Berta Moss, Emilio Robertie, Hilda Sour. Special roles by Luis Sandrini, Hugo del Carril, Amanda Ledesma, Cesar Ratti and Emma Martinez. Directed by Roberto Ratti. Reviewed at Monumental, Buenos Aires. Running time, 73 MINS.

'Amor Ultimo Modelo' is Roberto Ratti's first megging job after considerable experience as a local film writer. He fails to make the grade. Pic is lethargic, over talky and, in spots, downright silly, with audience at preem frequently guffawing at the wrong places, particularly at the poorly set up fashion-show-production number which is supposed to be one of the features.

It's the first by Alberto Vila since his return from a stint in Hollywood, and, judged by this effort, he appears to have gone backward.

He's cast as a dress designer working for a loose-minded boss. Boss wants to get a hefty order from a certain famed countess who's arriving in town, and Vila, who knew her when, gets the assignment. Complications follow when he borrows the boss' car, picks up the old man's daughter, and goes through a series of pretentions until it is all worked out. Frequent spots where the film is reminiscent of 'Roberta,' but the frou-frou atmosphere seems way off base, and the music and model shows interjected don't help.

Comedian Luis Sandrini, singer Hugo del Carril, Amanda Ledesma, Cesar Ratti and Emma Martinez have taken the assignments in special characterizations, with Ratti's drunk scene best of the lot. *Ray.*

Miniature Reviews

'**It Comes Up Love**' (Musical) (U). Donald O'Connor, Gloria Jean in comedy, suited as strong twin-bill support.

'**Squadron Leader X**' (RKO). British-made, anti-Nazi pic, okay for U. S. after certain cuts.

'**Border Patrol**' (UA). Satisfactory Hopalong western.

'**Secrets of a Co-Ed**' (PRC). Weak programmer featuring Otto Kruger and Tina Thayer.

'**Yolanda**' (Promesa) (Mexican-made). Better-than-average Spanish lingualer drama with ballet background.

IT COMES UP LOVE
(MUSICAL)

Universal release of Ken Goldsmith production. Stars Gloria Jean, Donald O'Connor, Ian Hunter; features Louise Allbritton, Frieda Inescort, Charles Coleman. Directed by Charles Lamont. Screenplay by Dorothy Bennett, Charles Kenyon, suggested by story of Aleen Leslie, Jay Dratler; camera, George Robinson; editor, Paul Landres; music by Leo Edwards, J. L. Malloy, Ernest Lecuono, Rubin Guevara. At Palace, N. Y., dual, week Jan. 21, '43. Running time, 64 MINS.

Victoria Peabody.............Gloria Jean
Tom Peabody.................Ian Hunter
Ricky.................Donald O'Connor
Portia Winthrop.........Frieda Inescort
Edo Ives.............Louise Allbritton
Constance Peabody..Mary Lou Harrington
Carlton Winthrop...........Raymond Roe
Tilton..................Charles Coleman
Orchestra Leader.............Leon Belasco
Bernice.................Beatrice Roberts

Latest in Universal's string of pop-titled youthful musicals such as 'What's Cookin',' 'Get Hep to Love' and 'Bit of Heaven,' this carries Gloria Jean and Donald O'Connor close to top as starring material. The two youngsters have come far in little more than a year's time at this studio, with this their best all-around effort to date. 'It Comes up Love,' receiving generous production for a 'B' production, is strong fare as support on twin bills.

Crisp dialog and standout performances by all juveniles in the cast generate sturdy entertainment, with spontaneous laughs so closely spotted they drown out succeeding lines. Young O'Connor, progressively better in similar vehicles for Universal, looms as a find judging from his work here. While reminiscent of Mickey Rooney of earlier days, the youngster stands largely on his own as a bright actor. Miss Jean, who's been in six previous films, shapes up better than in earlier vehicles.

The Dorothy Bennett-Charles Kenyon screenplay cashes in solidly on the best angles in the Aleen Leslie-Jay Dratler original. The fable of the business man with a femme secretary who's in love with him and his efforts to bring two motherless daughters home to live with him is smartly developed for popular consumption. All plot possibilities that bring the two 'teen-age girls in contact with N. Y. youngsters and a typical modern youth of their age are nicely projected. The older daughter sings—but only old-fashioned tunes. Said modern youth fixes that up by introducing her to swingeroo songs and dancing. It follows the familiar pattern, but solid as done in this film.

Besides the standout performances by O'Connor and Miss Jean, Dorothy Allbritton, as the efficient, comely secretary, again measures up to promise indicated in earlier Universal features. Ian Hunter is as suave as ever as the architect and her boss, who manages to fall in love with the sec despite his two daughters and a conspiring widow. Frieda Inescort contributes her customary strong thespian effort as the widow but Raymond Roe is a bit stilted and actorish as her son. Charles Lamont's keen handling of the youngsters in cast stems from his years spent directing juveniles. *Wear.*

Squadron Leader X

London, Jan. 5.

RKO production and release. Stars Ann Dvorak, Eric Portman. Directed by Lance Comfort. Screenplay and adaptation, Wolfgang Wilhelm; story, Emeric Pressburger; camera, Mutz Greenbaum. At London Pavilion. Running time, **94 MINS.**

Erich Kohler.................Eric Portman
Barbara.......................Ann Dvorak
Inspector Milne..........Walter Fitzgerald
Mr. Krohn..................Martin Miller
Mrs. Krohn................Beatrice Varley
Dr. Schultz...................Henry Oscar
Bruce Fenwick................Barry Jones
Marks......................Charles Victor
Miss Thorndike..............Mary Merrall
Colonel ir Luftwaffe...........Carl Jaffe
Mrs. Agnew.............Margery Rhodes
Inspector Siegel.........Frederick Richter

Reversing the usual formula of having a British airman attempting to get back from the Continent, this one presents the opposite situation. It is, on the whole, more than usually consistent in the matter of avoiding detection, etc., being quite within the range of likelihood that a German squadron leader, who lived most of his life in England, could evade capture for a considerable period. A very workmanlike job on which time and money must have been lavishly expended, intelligently cast, directed and photographed, but, before going into general release, should in many scenes be cut to render them more comprehensive to the average cinemagoer. When this is done the picture should be a good feature for the general run of American theatres.

The bestial character of the Nazi air ace, wearing a British uniform, is admirably portrayed by Eric Portman. The outstanding characterization is that of a Swiss cook who is blackmailed into assisting the Nazi espionage in England. Temperamentally his technique is more that of an Italian, but he, nevertheless, gives an especially moving performance. His name, Martin Miller, is unknown, but report has it he is an Austrian refugee. He gives promise as a character actor. Second only to Miller is Beatrice Varley as his wife. The remainder of the cast comprises players of more than average competence. *Jolo.*

BORDER PATROL

Hollywood, Jan. 25.

United Artists release of Harry Sherman production. Stars William Boyd; features Andy Clyde. Directed by Lesley Selander. Story, Clarence E. Mulford; camera, Russell Harlan. Previewed in Hollywood, Jan. 25, '43. Running time, **65 MINS.**

Cast: Jay Kirby, Duncan Renaldo, Claudia Drake, George Reeves, Russell Simpson, Cliff Parkinson.

Third of Hopalong Cassidy series for United Artists, 'Border Patrol' is satisfactory western with usual heroics, riding and shooting to make it acceptable booking for the action houses.

In line with present good-neighbor policies toward Mexico, melodramatics are laid along the Mexican border of Texas, with William Boyd, Andy Clyde and Jay Kirby as Texas Ranger trio who discover importation of Mexicans to work an isolated mine this side of border as enforced peonage of the workers by ruthless operator. Trio blasts through the closed district, are given kangaroo court trial and rigged for hanging, but break through to release the Mexican captives at the mine and dispose of the band led by Russell Simpson. Despite its familiar vein, picture rolls along at a good pace and provides exciting moments for western-minded audiences. Boyd continues to carry major prominence as Hopalong, with Clyde dishing out elemental comedy for kid appeal. Kirby is the romanticist of the trio. Simpson is best in support, with George Reeves and Duncan Renaldo good as Mexican military officers. Production layout is standard for series and direction paceful. *Walt.*

SECRETS OF A CO-ED

Producers Releasing Corp. release of Leon Fromkess production. Features Otto Kruger and Tina Thayer. Directed by Joseph H. Lewis; story and screenplay by George W. Sayre; camera, Robert Cline. At New York, N. Y., dual, Jan. 20, '43 Running time, **67 MINS.**

Reynolds ....Otto Kruger
Brenta ....Tina Thayer
Nick ....Rick Vallin
Bill ....Russell Hoyt
Laura ....Marcia Mae Jones
Tessie ....Geraldine Spreckels
Maria ....Diana Del Rio
Soapy ....Herburt Vigran
Flo ....Patricia Knox
Miss Wilson ....Claire Rochelle
District Attorney........Addison Richards
Dean Sophie ....Isabell La Mal

This one'll just about get by as a supporting dualer, thanks chiefly to performances by Otto Kruger, Tina Thayer and Rick Vallin. With only Kruger's name carrying any semblance of marquee strength, performances by girl and Vallin, latter cast in sinister role, will come as surprise. Talents of trio probably the only thing worth remembering about this new PRC release, which, so far as story material goes, is a sorry affair. Nor does directorial job by Joseph H. Lewis contribute to poor sum total.

This is a rehash of the noted criminal lawyer who's the secret boss of a mob of gamblers. His collegiate daughter likes to break the rules, which in turn breaks dad's heart, and rather than see her fall for his handsome strong-arm front man, the boss has him wiped out. It all leads up to the inevitable climax of the gal being accused of the murder, with papa winning her an acquittal via the self-exposure route. Gal goes back to collegiate boy friend, whom papa favored all the time.

Kruger is his usual smooth self as the lawyer-gambler boss, providing the film with one of its few stirring scenes in the climactic courtroom defense of his errant daughter. In latter role, Miss Thayer is excellent and obviously bears watching. Vallin, as the menace-lover, acts with conviction. Adequate support is furnished by Russell Hoyt, as the collegiate; Marcia Mae Jones, Geraldine Spreckles and Diana Del Rio. *Rose.*

YOLANDA

(MEXICAN-MADE)

Promesa Films (Manuel Reachi) production. Stars Irina Baronova, David Silva; features Miguel Arenas, Leon Greanin and Ballet Theatre. Co-directed by Dudley Murphy and Roberto Gavaldon. Screenplay by Anne Anthony, with dialog by Justine Fernandez, Elena Amor, Inigo de Martino; camera, Alexis Phillips. Previewed at Museum of Modern Art, N. Y., Jan. 26, '43. Running time, **105 MINS.**

Yolanda Petrova............Irina Baronova
Julio Castro.....................David Silva
Carlos Villagren............Miguel Arenas
Niko, ballet impresario......Leon Greanin
Father Paul...................Alberto Galan
Anita, Julio's fiancee.........Lucy Delgado
Fanny, housekeeper..........Fanny Anitua
Secretary of War.............Jose Morcillo
Prison Warden.................Hernan Vera
Cadets.......................Crox Alvarado, Ricardo Adalid
The Ballet Theatre

(In Spanish; No Subtitles)

Seeking a release in Latin America through the channels there of one of the major U. S. distributing companies, Manuel Reachi had as his guests Monday (26), at the initial screening in this country of 'Yolanda,' foreign managers and the U. S. and Latin American press. Preview was held at the Museum of Modern Art, N. Y., through the cooperation, although not under the sponsorship, of the Coordinator of Inter-American Affairs. Effort to aid the producer was a gesture of Pan-American good will by the Coordinator's office, which is giving encouragement to picture-making in the other nations of this hemisphere.

'Yolanda' is a better-than-average Latin-made production, although it suffers from the standard fault of such pictures—overlength and dragginess. That's less a defect in Latin America, however, than it would be for a film to be distributed in this country, as the Latinos are willing to accept everything on a slower pace. Story bears no freshness and direction is less than crisp, but rather good acting by prima ballerina Irina Baronova (in her first picture appearance) and by other members of the cast compensates considerably.

From a technical standpoint, 'Yolanda' is a Hollywood primitive. Yet it is considerably better than most Latin American productions. More skilled editing would have counted for much, as would have such details as better lighting and makeup. A primary fault, however, of a film which makes much of a number of lengthy ballet sequences is the fact that the theatre used (it appears to be the mccoy, rather than a set) has much too small a stage to let the terpers really extend themselves.

Baronova is pictured as a Russian ballerina invited to Mexico in a troupe headed by Leon Greanin. Political bigwig Miguel Arenas (who looks like a Latin Monty Woolley) falls for her at about the same time she goes for a young Army officer, David Silva. With Baronova's father about to be shot in Russia (this is 1909), Arenas pressures her into marrying him by promising he'll help her family. A year later she again sees Silva and the old flame blazes anew. Arenas finds out and the picture turns into heavy 'drahma' with the lover shot and Baronova and Arenas taking poison in a fade-out scene that fails to click.

The ballet background gives opportunity for three major numbers by the Ballet Theatre troupe of New York. Dances are of a popular type and should have wide appeal. Baronova is a sparkling prima, and the entire group displays attractive charm and grace. They dance against a fine, full orchestral background.

Pic is claimed by Reachi to have cost more than $75,000 in U. S. coin, although such opulence is scarcely evident in sets, cast or other aspects of the production.

Miniature Reviews

'Air Force' (WB). Sock entertainment. Will mop up.

'Flight for Freedom' (RKO). Rosalind Russell and Fred MacMurray co-starred, geared for profitable biz.

'How's About It' (Songs) (U). Andrews Sisters in another cinematic song display. Entertaining dualer.

'Two Weeks to Live' (RKO). Lum and Abner's radio vogue must get it over with the customers.

AIR FORCE

Warner Bros. release of Hal B. Wallis-Howard Hawks production, directed by Hawks. Features John Garfield, Gig Young, Harry Carey, George Tobias, Arthur Kennedy, James Brown, John Ridgeley. Original screenplay, Dudley Nichols; camera, James Wonge Howe; air photography, Elmer Dyer, Chas. Marshall; special effects, Roy Davidson, Rex Wimpy, H. F. Koenekamp; editor, George Amy; chief pilot, Paul Mantz; music, Franz Waxman; Leo F. Forbstein, Jack Sullivan. Tradeshown in N. Y., Feb. 2, '43. Running time, **124 MINS.**

Pilot..........................John Ridgely
Co-Pilot..........................Gig Young
Bombardier,.................Arthur Kennedy
Navigator...................Charles Drake
Crew Chief.....................Harry Carey
Asst. Crew Chief...........George Tobias
Radio Operator................Ward Wood
Asst. Radio Operator.....Ray Montgomery
Aerial Gunner...............John Garfield
Pursuit Pilot................James Brown
Major Mallory.............Stanley Ridges
Colonel...................Willard Robertson
Commanding Officer..........Moroni Olsen
Sgt. J. J. Callahan.....Edward S. Brophy
Major W. G. Roberts........Richard Lane
Lieut P. T. Moran.............Bill Crago
Susan McMartin............Faye Emerson
Major Daniels............Addison Richards
Major A. M. Bagley.........James Flavin
Mary Quincannon...............Ann Doran
Mrs. Chester.............Dorothy Peterson

'Air Force' is one of the sock war pictures of this or any other war. It will mop up.

It's comparable to 'In Which We Serve' as the saga of a Flying Fortress (the 'Mary Ann,' a Boeing B-17), akin to Noel Coward's saga of a British battleship.

It is gripping, informative, entertaining, thrilling. It is a patriotic heart-throb in celluloid without preaching; it is inspirational without being phoney in its emotions.

The affection of the members of the crew of the 'Mary Ann' is genuine, manly and sentimental. It points up a type of team-work which may well be construed as a pattern for all Americans in the manner in which our team-work, on the home-front and at the battle-fronts, will achieve the ultimate victory.

The manner in which the nine original members of the Boeing B-17 are shown coordinating their jobs is something that will doubtlessly gladden Washington officialdom from Lowell Mellett to Air Force Chief General Arnold. It certainly will enlighten the average fan or casual student of aeronautics who may have focused complete attention on the pilot or co-pilot, thought it's patent how the bombardier, the navigator, the crew chief, the asst. crew chief, the radio operator and his assistant, and the aerial gunner are essential to the over-all, smooth operating of a Flying Fortress.

For dramatic values, James Brown engagingly personates a pursuit pilot who becomes an emergency passenger, en route from Hawaii to Manila, where he is urgently needed. Brown eventually concedes to the prowess of the Boeings, although traditionally partial to his own piloting of pursuit planes.

Unfolded in a gripping two hours is a visualization of what we have experienced from the treachery of

Pearl Harbor through the fall of Wake Island, the Philippines, etc. The great battle of the Coral Sea, the 'Shangri-La' blitzing of Tokyo and all the rest are dovetailed into a sock filmization which bespeaks of our growing power and prowess in the air.

True, for a spell, our planes are so successfully strafeing the Nipponese task force that it makes one wonder that, despite this decisive naval battle, how come we still found ourselves pushed into the South Pacific, but the general overtone is that we were caught off base; that it's still an uphill battle, and that with time we will emerge victorious.

Despite the historic overtones, and even emphasizing the Lincolnian prolog and the Rooseveltian epilog, 'Air Force' basically is solid film entertainment, not inhibited or hamstrung by 1942 chronology.

Its showmanship will do everybody proud, from production and direction to casting. Perhaps the best known cast component is John Garfield and it's the more effective that the principals are not as well known. John Ridgley is Capt. Quincannon and Gig Young his co-pilot, both capital. Arthur Kennedy plays the bombardier; Charles Drake gives new and usually not suspected importance to the navigator's role in a Flying Fortress. Harry Carey gives a corking performance as the veteran crew chief, a career Sgt. from way back, who is proud of his son, because he won his wings and his lieutenancy (only to learn he was blitzed by the treacherous Japs, even before he could take off at Wake Island).

George Tobias's comedy registers as Corp. Weinberg, asst. crew chief from Brooklyn, who rides Ward Wood, the radio operator from Minneapolis. Ray Montgomery is the asst. radio operator, and the surly Sgt. Winocki, aerial gunner, is excellently played by John Garfield. Having flunked out as a flying officer, Garfield looks forward to three weeks hence, when his enlistment is over, but of course the Pearl Harbor debacle regenerates him into a vindictive American who stays on indef.

While the romance values are at a minimum, there is plenty of heart throb which stems from the officers' wives; the enthusiastic kid (Montgomery) who is riddled by the Nips while parachuting out, etc.

As a war picture, 'Air Force' is more than a cinematic interlude; it's a graphic symbol of an awakened America. It's rousing, rah-rah and Yankee Doodle.   *Abel.*

Flight for Freedom

Hollywood, Feb. 2.
RKO release of David Hempstead production. Stars Rosalind Russell, Fred MacMurray; features Herbert Marshall, Eduardo Ciannelli, Walter Kingsford. Directed by Lothar Mendes. Screenplay. Oliver H. P. Garrett and S. K. Lauren; adaptation, Jane Murfin; original, Horace McCoy; camera, Lee Garmes; special effects. Vernon L. Walker; editor, Roland Gross; asst. directors, J. D. Starkey, Ruby Rosenberg. Tradeshown in L. A., Feb. 1, '43. Running time, 101 MINS.

Tonie Carter	Rosalind Russell
Randy Britton	Fred MacMurray
Paul Turner	Herbert Marshall
Johnny Salvini	Eduardo Ciannelli
Admiral Graves	Walter Kingsford
Pete	Damian O'Flynn
Hill	Jack Carr
Mac	Matt McHugh
Mr. Yokohata	Richard Loo
Flyer	Charles Lung

Picture, with strong blend of romance and aviation neatly interwoven despite its extended running time of 101 minutes, is geared for healthy biz in the regular runs as solo or billtopper, with marquee voltage of the starring team of Rosalind Russell and Fred MacMurray accentuating the wicket-spinning.

'Flight for Freedom' in a fictional rendition of the flying experiences of an American aviatrix, from the time of her first solo flight back in

1932 until she deliberately nosed her plane into the waters of the Pacific a out six years later in order that the American Navy could survey the Jap fortifications on mandated islands. Although RKO apparently veers away from any resemblance of the tale to the life story of the late Amelia Earhart, strange disappearance of the latter while on a trans-Pacific flight several years ago is bound to have numerous onlookers tying up the fictional and factual parallels.

After a brief prolog of current war bombings of Jap bases in the Pacific, and commentary which predicated these newsreel clips on the earlier daring and patriotism of a noted American aviatrix, story opens with Miss Russell bumping into noted flyer MacMurray on her initial solo flight, a torrid albeit brief romance developing before he shoves off on assignment to South America. She becomes the ace flyer of her sex, participates in the Bendix cross-country race, and smashes the Los Angeles-New York record. Then she tries a round-the-world flight, but the Navy enlists her services in a daring episode to uncover possible Jap fortifications in the far Pacific mandate islands. Flying east around MacMurray at Lae, New Guinea, and the romance revives despite her engagement to Herbert Marshall. Apprised that Jap agents are wise to plan for her to be lost on a coral isle, so the fleet can scout the Nip fortified islands, she goes on her way and eventually dips the plane in the sea for a heroic death.

Despite its basic foundation of flying, picture keeps on the ground for major portion of the unreeling, and eliminates what might be boring and over-extended air footage. It's an adventurous tale, with strong romantic content for the women customers, despite the fact that MacMurray is absent for most of the middle portion. Even when he's off the screen, it's apparent that his influence is paramount in the mind of the girl aviatrix, and that's sufficient for the femmes to keep them keyed up.

Miss Russell provides a competent and sincere performance as the girl flyer, with MacMurray providing his usual portrayal as the object of the femme's affections. Marshall is fine as the flying school operator and designer who's brought along to success through backing of his confidence in the aviatrix. Good support is provided by Eduardo Ciannelli and Walter Kingsford.

Story is rather episodic, but neatly dovetails into a coherent entity through workmanlike script by Oliver H. P. Garrett and S. K. Lauren, and paceful direction by Lothar Mendes. Lee Garmes adds topnotch photography to the layout, with Vernon Walker's special effects of high standard throughout.   *Walt.*

HOW'S ABOUT IT
(SONGS)

Hollywood, Jan. 29.
Universal release of Ken Goldsmith production. Stars Andrews Sisters; features Robert Paige, Grace McDonald, Shemp Howard, Walter Catlett. Directed by Erle C. Kenton. Screenplay by Mel Ronson; adaptation, John Grey; original, Jack Goodman and Albert Rice; camera, Woody Bredell; editor, Charles Maynard; dances, Louis DaPron; music director and arranger, Vic Schoen. Previewed at studio Jan. 28, '43. Running time, 60 MINS.
Andrews Sisters—Patty Andrews, Maxene Andrews, LaVerne Andrews.

George Selby	Robert Paige
Marion Bliss	Grace McDonald
Alf	Shemp Howard
Whipple	Walter Catlett
Orchestra Leader	Buddy Rich
Oliver	David Bruce
'Mike' Tracy	Mary Wickes
Bobby	Bobby Scheerer
Waitress	Dorothy Babb

'How's About It' is a lightweight programmer that will have to carry through the dual supporting spots mainly on the strength of the Andrews Sisters. Aside from the five

songs capably delivered by the trio, picture is lightweight.

Story is a fragile affair with many loose ends tangled together, and which never completely tie up into component whole. Locale is a music building which houses radio and song-publishing enterprises, with the Andrews trio as elevator operators with a yen for a break in the music field. Robert Paige is a songwriter and publisher accused of plagiarism of lyrics by Grace McDonald. He gets her to take a job on his staff and call off damage suit, and the pair conveniently fall in love for the eventual conclusion. The singers, of course, also get their chance to click a. the finish.

Picture carries two tunes that have a chance for pop attention; Sid Robbins' 'East of the Rockies,' and 'Going Up,' by Irving Gordon and Allen Roth. Each displays excellent rhythm, with delivery by the Andrews expertly putting the pair across. Patriotic lyrics by Lt. Commander C. P. Oakes for the melody of 'Beer Barrel Polka' provide plenty of zest for 'Here Comes the Navy,' which is effectively utilized for the finale, with Buddy Rich and his orchestra providing musical background and setting. Other songs of moderate rating are 'Don't Mind the Rain' by Ned Miller and Chester Cohn, and 'Take It and Git' by William and Mel Chapman, James T. Marshall and John Green.

Picture spotlights attention on young Bobby Scheerer, a tap dancer in his teens who clicks with two fast stepping routines along the line. Paige and Miss McDonald are teamed for the romantic side of the tale, while elemental comedy, with much mugging, is provided by Shemp Howard, Mary Wickes and Walter Catlett. A few laughs drop here and there.   *Walt.*

TWO WEEKS TO LIVE

Hollywood, Feb. 2.
RKO release of Jack William Votion (Ben Hersh) production. Stars Lum & Abner (Chester Lauck and Norris Goff). Directed by Malcolm St. Clair. Original screenplay by Michael L. Simmons and Roswell Rogers; camera. Jack MacKenzie; editor, Duncan Mansfield; asst. director. Charles Kerr. Tradeshown in L. A. Feb. 2, '43. Running time, 75 MINS.

Lum	Chester Lauck
Abner	Norris Goff
Mr. Pinkney	Franklin Pangborn
Mrs. Carmen	Kay Linaker
Gimpel	Irving Bacon
Stark, Sr.	Herbert Rawlinson
Professor Frisby	Ivan Simpson
Nurse	Rosemary LaPlanche
Postman	Danny Duncan
Secretary	Evelyn Knapp
Kelton	Charles Middleton
Van Dyke	Luis Alberni
Hotel Clerk	Jack Rice
Higgens	Tim Ryan
Squire Skimp	Oscar O'Shea
Doctor	Edward Earle

Lum & Abner swing through their usual rural antics here, and whatever radio voltage the homespun pair enjoys with hinterland audiences will be required to give this more than passing attention. Otherwise it's filler for the duals in the family houses.

Picture is decidedly episodic and overlength, with commonplace story putting the team through experiences in Chicago, in which they are continually out-slickered by the big-towners, until the finale in which they emerge victorious. Excuse for projecting the crossroad characters to the city is provided by notice that Abner has been willed a railroad, with Lum accompanying him east to claim the estate. Natives are sold shares in the railroad before estate was settled, requiring pair to generate sufficient coin to pay back. Title comes from medical examination mixup with Abner given two weeks to live, and he goes through various daredevil stunts to raise the coin.

Lum & Abner's familiar rural characterizations are supported chiefly by Irving Bacon, Franklin Pangborn and Kay Linaker.

Original script by Michael J. Simmons and Roswell Rogers stretches the footage considerably with sideline episodes that look like obvious padding to get the picture out in sufficient running time. Yarn is not too imaginative, while direction by Malcolm St. Clair does as well as possible with the material provided by the writers.   *Walt.*

Miniature Reviews

'The Outlaw' (Hughes). Roadshown in Frisco to fair results. Can stand and needs exploitation.

'Cabin in the Sky' (M-G). Sincere, painstaking film version of the Negro stage musical fantasy; moderate grosser.

'Amazing Mrs. Holliday' (U) (Songs). Deanna Durbin in timely drama with human interest angles. Bright boxoffice.

'Young and Willing' (UA). Weak comedy adaptation from stage play; mild boxoffice.

'Something to Shout About' (Col) (Musical). Formula backstage filmusical. Moderate biz.

'Hi 'Ya Chum' (U) (Songs). Typical Ritz Bros. burlesque. OK programmer.

'A Stranger in Town' (M-G). Frank Morgan topping cast in 'B' that should do okay on dualers.

'Siege of Leningrad' (Artkino). Sock Russian documentary of the 18-month siege of the Soviet city.

'Secrets of the Underground' (Rep). Above-average murder mystery with novel slant on Axis agents.

'Fighting Frontier' (RKO). Actionful western with Tim Holt, albeit routine story.

'Two Fisted Justice' (Mono). Below-par Ranger Busters dualer geared for juve trade.

CABIN IN THE SKY

(MUSICAL)

Metro release of Arthur Freed production (associate producer, Albert Lewis). Stars Ethel Waters, Eddie Anderson, Lena Horne; features Louis Armstrong, Rex Ingram, Hall Johnson choir. Directed by Vincente Minelli. Screenplay, Joseph Schrank, based upon musical play of same title; book, Lynn Root; lyrics, John Latouche; music, Vernon Duke; additional songs by Harold Arlen, E. Y. Harburg; musical adaptation, Roger Edens; musical direction, Georgie Stoll; orchestration, George Bassman; choral arrangements, Hall Johnson; camera, Sidney Wagner; editor, Harold F. Kress. Reviewed in projection room, New York, Feb. 3, '43. Running time, **98 MINS.**

Petunia Jackson............Ethel Waters
Little Joe......Eddie 'Rochester' Anderson
Georgia Brown..................Lena Horne
The Trumpeter............Louis Armstrong
Lucius / Lucifer, Jr. ....Rex Ingram
Rev. Green / The General ....Kenneth Spencer
Domino........'Bubbles' (John W. Sublett)
The Deacon / Fleetfoot ....Oscar Polk
First Idea Man..........Mantan Moreland
Second Idea Man..............Willie Best
Third Idea Man....Moke (Fletcher Rivers)
Fourth Idea Man.......Poke (Leon James)
Bill...........................Bill Bailey
Messenger Boy.'Buck' (Ford L. Washington)
Lily.....................Butterfly McQueen
Mrs. Kelso................Ruby Dandridge
Dude ....Nicodemus
Jim Henry...............Ernest Whitman
Duke Ellington and Orchestra
Hall Johnson Choir

Although it was only a moderate Broadway boxoffice success, 'Cabin in the Sky' was one of the artistic and critical hits of a couple of seasons ago, winning a limited, but intensely loyal following, many of whom went back to see the show one or more times. The fate of this film version of the musical may be somewhat parallel. It has been made with obvious sincerity and good will, but its appeal is likely to be somewhat restricted, with the Ethel Waters and Eddie Anderson names as help.

Some of the boxoffice limitations of 'Cabin' are inherent in the original work. In the first place, it's fantasy, which is inclined to be tough to sell. Secondly, it's an all-Negro show, making it doubtful material for the south and likely to decrease its audience in other parts of the country. Only all-Negro picture ever to click commercially was the great 'Green Pastures,' which had a tremendous advance rep as a legit show. Finally, the picturization of 'Cabin' lacks the imagination and skill that such a subject should have. So, though it's a tender, affectionate film, it is a disappointment.

The picture version is little changed from the original stage show. It still tells of Little Joe Jackson's weakness for dice, likker and the seductive Georgia Brown, of his mortal wound in a barroom brawl, and of his six-month period of grace obtained by his eternally-devoted wife, Petunia. It still shows the contest between Lucifer, Jr., and the General for Little Joe's soul, with Little Joe's final tumble from grace and his orgy at Jim Henry's cabaret, and his and Petunia's ultimate salvation on a 'technicality.' Unlike the stage original, howev r, the picture presents all this fantasy as a dream flashback, and brings Joe back to life for the fadeout.

In the legit version, 'Cabin' seemed constantly to be constricted by the limitations of the stage. But difficult has not been solved in the present film adaptation. The yarn still appears weighed down by unimaginative conception, the few changes in the screen medium merely filling out the story, without expanding or developing its fantasy. In only one of two moments, such as the stairway to heaven finale, is there any apparent effort to utilize the facilities of the camera. There are far too many closeups, particularly in the vocal numbers.

Ethel Waters remains the one transcendant asset of the film 'Cabin,' just as she was in the original. Her sincerity, compassion, personal warmth and dramatic skill, plus her unique talent as a singer make her performance as Petunia an overpowering accomplishment. Eddie Anderson, best known as 'Rochester' on the Jack Benny radio program, is effective in the comedy moments of the Little Joe part, but his mugging mars the emotional scenes and his singing is strictly for laughs. Lena Horne is a definite click, both vocally and dramatically, as the fatal Georgia Brown, while Louis Armstrong has merely a few moments on the trumpet and a couple of lines as one of the Lucifer, Jr., 'idea men.' Rex Ingram scores in his original role of Lucifer, Jr., while Kenneth Spencer, John (Bubbles) Sublett, Oscar Polk and Ford (Buck) Washington are acceptable in supporting parts.

Besides the original songs, including 'Taking a Chance on Love' and 'Cabin in the Sky,' there are three new tunes, 'Happiness Is a Thing Called Joe,' 'Life's Full of Consequences' and 'Li'l Black Sheep.' The Hall Johnson choir provides notable help, Duke Ellington's orchestra plays a hot number and there are several good dance sequences.

Regardless of the boxoffice reception of 'Cabin,' the sincerity evident in its production may provide an answer to the liberal and Negro groups that criticized Metro for its production of 'Tennessee Johnson.' And whatever its boxoffice fate, 'Cabin' is a worthwhile picture for Metro to have made, if only as a step toward Hollywood recognition of the place of the colored man in American life.

Hobe.

Amazing Mrs. Holliday

(SONGS)

Hollywood, Feb. 5.

Universal release of Bruce Manning (Frank Shaw) production, directed by Manning. Stars Deanna Durbin; features Edmond O'Brien, Barry Fitzgerald, Arthur Treacher. Screenplay by Frank Ryan and John Jacoby; adaptation by Boris Ingster and Leo Townsend; original, Sonya Levien; camera, Woody Bredell; editor, Ted Kent; musical director, Charles Previn; score, Frank Skinner and H. J. Salter. Previewed at Filmarte, Feb. 4, '43. Running time, **97 MINS.**

Ruth.......................Deanna Durbin
Tom......................Edmond O'Brien
Timothy..................Barry Fitzgerald
Henderson................Arthur Treacher
Commodore...............Harry Davenport
Edgar.......................Grant Mitchell
Karen......................Frieda Inescort
Louise..................Elisabeth Risdon
Ferguson..................Jonathan Hale
Lucy...........................Esther Dale
Jeff...........................Gus Schilling
Dr. Kirke...............J. Frank Hamilton
The Children—Christopher Severn, Yvonne Severn, Vido Rich, Mila Rich, Teddy Infuhr, Linda Bieber, Diane Dubois, Bill Ward, and the Chinese Baby.

Her first release in more than a year, 'The Amazing Mrs. Holliday' displays Deanna Durbin as a young miss permanently removed from the ingenue class but still retaining that screen personality and charm that has made her substantial star value at the wickets. Picture is a timely drama with human interest pull, carrying sufficient—though minor—romantic interest. Biz prospects at the theatre boxoffices are bright.

Story is rather Cinderella-ish adventure, dished up with human sugarcoating through Miss Durbin's determination to get a group of Occidental orphan children out of south China and to safety in America. In order to retain possession and care of the youngsters, boat-steward Barry Fitzgerald poses her as the wife of his former boss, skipper of a torpedoed ship, head of a steamship line, and thought lost. Despite skepticism of the aged magnate's family, Miss Durbin establishes the kids in the huge family mansion, but confesses her fraud to the skipper's grandson, Edmond O'Brien, who naturally protects her for the romantic interludes. Everything turns shipshape when the magnate turns up and tosses off his crustiness to take the kids under his wing and let the romance hit the uual conclusion.

Miss Durbin again capably displays her acting abilities, providing a sincere and fine portrayal as the protector of the war orphans. Fitzgerald makes the most of a particularly fat role by clicking continually with his sly manipulations while O'Brien does well as the boy. Arthur Treacher familiarly portrays the butler in the manse, while good support is supplied by Grant Mitchell, Frieda Inescort, Elisabeth Risdon and Jonathan Hale. Group of youngsters add interest in the proceedings throughout.

Unusual presentation of two songs by Miss Durbin in Chinese gets a good reception, particularly that of 'Rock-a-Bye Baby.' Star also sings three other numbers along the route: Puccini's 'Visi D'Arte,' 'The Old Refrain,' by Fritz Kreisler and Alice Mattullath, and the standard 'Mighty Lak' a Rose.'

Bruce Manning, who stepped in as producer of the Durbin starrers at Universal a year ago, also took over the direction. With intimate knowledge of her abilities through scripting on several previous pictures, Manning welds together a good piece of general entertainment, and accentuates every possible incident deftly for favorable audience reaction. Script by Boris Ingster and Leo Townsend is compactly packaged, and production has been provided with usual topgrade mounting accorded Durbin features.

Walt.

THE OUTLAW

San Francisco, Feb. 5.

Howard Hughes production (roadshow); directed by Howard Hughes. Stars Jane Russell, Jack Buetel; with Thomas Mitchell, Walter Huston, Mimi Aguglia, Joe Sawyer, Gene Rizzi. Supervising film director, Otho Lovering. Screenplay by Jules Furthman; photography, Gregg Toland; music direction, Victor Young; effects, Roy Davidson; asst. director, Sam Nelson; editor, Wallace Grissell. At Geary, San Francisco, Feb. 5, '43. Running time, **121 MINS.**

Billy ....Jack Beutel
Rio ....Jane Russell
Pat ....Thomas Mitchell
Doc ....Walter Huston
Guadalupe ....Mimi Aguglia
Charley ....Joe Sawyer
Stranger ....Gene Rizzi

Commercial possibilities of Howard Hughes' 'The Outlaw' rely immeasurably on manner and extent of exploitation ballyhoo given its roadshow engagements. Picture has had benefit of tremendous s. a. campaign to pep run at the Geary and, on strength of curiosity aroused by 'bosom art' splashes of Jane Russell in newspapers and posters, prospects for initial week look promising. Beyond sex attraction of Miss Russell's frankly displayed charms, picture, according to accepted screen entertainment standards, falls short. Continued hypoing of exploitable factors will measure extent of business it can expect in other bookings.

Plot is based on legend Billy the Kid wasn't killed by the law but continued to live on after his supposed death. Pace is series of slow-moving incidents making up continuous chase as directed by Hughes and isn't quickened by the two hours running time, but slowness is not so much a matter of length as a lack of tempo in individual scenes. This variation of the checkered film career of Billy the Kid has the outlaw joining forces with legendary Doc Halliday, played by Walter Huston, to escape the pursuing Sheriff Pat Garrett (Thomas Mitchell). Mixing strangely into the kid's life is Rio, Latin charmer, as portrayed by Miss Russell.

Sex seldom rears its beautiful head in simonpure prairie dramas, but since this is an unorthodox, almost burlesque, version of tried and true desert themes, anything can and often does happen. Needless to recount, the Kid makes good his final escape from the Sheriff and subdues the fiery Rio for the finale. Feature of film is the outdoor scenery as caught by Gregg Toland's camera and the interior photography. Camera takes advantage of scenic possibilities in the chases, particularly when the Kid, Doc and the Sheriff join in common cause to escape a band of Indians, forgetting their personal feud for the time.

Of the two screen newcomers, Jack Buetel seems to show most promise, although Miss Russell may benefit from her publicity name. Veterans Walter Huston and Thomas Mitchell appear to enjoy free rein given them by direction and indulge in characterizations not touched by restraint that usually features their work.

If Hughes adds the western burlesque angle to the exploitation of 'The Outlaw,' public paying roadshow prices will not be disappointed.

Brog.

YOUNG AND WILLING

United Artists release of Cinema Guild (Edward H. Griffith) production, directed by Griffith. Stars William Holden, Eddie Bracken, Susan Hayward, Robert Benchley; features Martha O'Driscoll, Barbara Britton. Screenplay, Virginia Van Upp; adapted from play by Francis Swann; camera, Leo Tover; editor, Eda Warren. Previewed in projection room, N. Y., Feb. 8, '43. Running time, **83 MINS.**

Norman Reese...............William Holden
George Bodell..................Eddie Bracken
Arthur Kenny...............Robert Benchley
Kate Benson..................Susan Hayward
Dottie Coburn..............Martha O'Driscoll
Marge Benson................Barbara Britton
Tony Dennison...................James Brown
Muriel Foster..........Florence MacMichael
Mrs. Garnet......................Mabel Paige
Mr. Coburn.......................Jay Fassett
First Cop...........................Paul Hurst
Second Cop......................Olin Howlin
Phillips............................Billy Bevan

The bromide that two can live as cheaply as one has been enlarged in its scope for the purposes of this United Artists release, a weak comedy that achieved mild success two seasons ago on Broadway as 'Out of the Frying Pan.' The film version only emphasizes what was all too apparent in the play—it's bound to get lost among the heftier competition. Strictly for the duals, with its young names possibly enhancing its boxoffice values where the adolescent draw is concerned.

'Young and Willing' is of the old pattern that engendered 'Room Service' and other such comedies. Take a group of starving people, put them into a limited space—and watch the fur fly, firstly, in their vain attempts to get out from under and then, secondly, after a series of escapades, their ultimate success in paying the landlord.

This time the pattern has been cut to suit the purposes of a group of young hopefuls, all of whom, three girls and three boys, have pooled their meager resources within the confines of a two-room New York apartment pending their 'big chance.' The 'big chance' happens to be a Broadway producer with a penchant for cookery (obviously a take-off on Crosby Gaige), who happens to live in the apartment directly below theirs. The difficulties that arise in their efforts to interest the gourmet-producer afford only mild diversion in a comedy that's too intent on action and too little concerned with dialog and original situations.

The four stars, William Holden, Eddie Bracken, Robert Benchley and Susan Hayward, along with the two featured performers, Martha O'Driscoll and Barbara Britton, do as well as can be expected with the lame script. Florence MacMichael, with a squeaky voice that achieves a few laughs, rounds out the better performances.

Direction by Edward Griffith, who also produced, is up to par, while the production indicates a limited budget. 'Young and Willing' is another in the group UA took over from Paramount some time ago.

Kahn.

Something to Shout About

(MUSICAL)

Hollywood, Feb. 5.

Columbia release of Gregory Ratoff production, directed by Ratoff. Stars Don Ameche, Janet Blair, Jack Oakie; features William Gaxton, Cobina Wright, Jr., Hazel Scott. Screenplay by Lou Breslow, Edward Eliscu; adaptation, George Owen; based on original by Fred Schiller; songs, Cole Porter; camera, Franz Planer; editor, Otto Meyer; dialog director, Serge Bertensson; asst. director, Milton Carter; dances, David Lichine; musical direction, M. W. Stoloff. Previewed at Pantages, Feb. 4, '43. Running time, **88 MINS.**

Ken Douglas....................Don Ameche
Jeanie Maxwell....................Janet Blair
Larry Martin....................Jack Oakie
Willard Samson..............William Gaxton
Donna Davis..............Cobina Wright, Jr.
Flo.......................Veda Ann Borg
Hazel Scott....................Hazel Scott
Dan Howard....................Jaye Martin
Lily.......................Lily Norwood
Chuckles..............James 'Chuckles' Walker
The Bricklayers
Teddy Wilson and His Band

Gregory Ratoff apparently decided to let the customers outside of metropolitan key cities know that vaudeville is back—so he transmits his message via a picture running 88 minutes with hot and cold results. It's a typical backstage filmusical yarn with little variation, displaying some excellent talent and acts along the way, while tossing in some that could be left in the cutting room. Despite its handicaps in part, picture carries sufficient diversion to get by in the regular runs for nominal biz, with the topline trio of Don Ameche, Janet Blair and Jack Oakie required to carry it through for voltage in the billtopping positions.

Two acts are show stoppers—Hazel Scott in two spots to tickle the ivories in her inimitable and capable manner, and the Bricklayers, dog act near the close that rings the bell with slick presentation and comedy angles. Also included are several production numbers, best being a South American setting for presentation of Miss Blair singing 'Hasta Luego.' Latter is a likely tune of its type that will catch popular fancy with radio plugging.

Story is a fragile framework on which to display the various talent and acts assembled. It is launched when former chorine Cobina Wright, Jr., tabs walloping alimony settlement, and decides to toss some of it in backing a musical. She bankrolls producer William Gaxton, who draws Ameche is as press agent. Latter has met Miss Blair, Cinderella girl composer from the sticks, and maneuvers her score into the setup. Then there's the theatrical boarding house where Jack Oakie holds forth as landlord, and when Miss Wright's tryout appearance flops in the musical, Ameche and Oakie team up to present a vaude revival at the Broadway house where rent is paid in advance. Conclusion is obvious, vaude comes back, and Ameche and Miss Blair blend okay.

Ameche and Oakie provide their usual standard performances, but the picture is not too brilliant a followup for Miss Blair after her recent 'Sister Eileen.' She does the best she can under wraps of script and direction provided, and surprises by capably presenting several songs—both informally and on the stage for the two show ventures. Gaxton is submerged in role of the play producer, getting too few laughs based on his capabilities. Miss Wright has a thankless role, being forced—for some reason or other—to shout her lines and look vapid most of the footage. Others in support as credited have minor flashes.

Cole Porter's score totals nine numbers, with Miss Blair singing most of them, but in a couple of instances having duos with Jaye Martin, and one with Ameche. Aside from 'Hasta Luego,' the best include the title song, 'And There You Were,' and the sentimental number, 'So Nice to Come Home To,' which is already a radio familiar.

Ratoff's direction fails in both timing and pace, and is decidedly bumpy throughout on the story end. Yarn is obvious, with scripters providing little ingenuity in the setup. Production layout is okay, with spread for a couple of elaborate settings.

Walt.

HI'YA CHUM

(SONGS)

Hollywood, Feb. 6.

Universal release of Howard Benedict production. Stars Ritz Bros.; features Jane Frazee, Robert Paige, June Clyde, Paul Hurst, Andrew Tombes. Directed by Harold Young. Original screenplay by Edmund L. Hartman; camera, Charles Van Enger; editor, Maurice Wright; Asst. director, Mack Wright; songs, Don Raye, Gene de Paul; special material, Edward Cherkose, Jacques Press. Previewed in studio projection room, Feb. 6, '43. Running time, **60 MINS.**

Merry Madcaps.................. { Al Ritz, Jimmy Ritz, Harry Ritz }
Sunny.........................Jane Frazee
Tommy Craig....................Robert Paige
Madge.........................June Clyde
Archie Billings..................Paul Hurst
Terry Barton..........Edmund MacDonald
Eddie Gibbs.....................Lou Lubin
Cook.......................Andrew Tombes
Jackson.......................Ray Walker

This is another in the Universal series of moderate budget program filmusicals, with the Ritz Bros. providing their usual zany antics, with a few song numbers tossed in to extend the proceedings to an hour's running time. The comic trio dish out with broadest burlesque and slapstick in style acceptable to audiences familiar with their proceedings, and picture will slip in as a dual supporter in the secondary houses.

Nothing new or original in the Ritz routines, virtual carbon copies of past screen appearances. Trio deliver three comedy songs with knockabout deliveries while more subdued tunes are handled by Jane Frazee, Robert Paige and June Clyde. Best of the straight songs are 'Two on a Bike,' which carries good rhythm, and 'He's My Guy,' which was a pop tune, but now on the downgrade.

Story is decidedly fragile and hangs together with plenty of reef-knots. Ritz Bros. are comics in a floppo tab which folds in the middle west, and the boys head for Hollywood in a stuttering model T, taking along Miss Frazee and June Clyde. They wind up in a former California ghost town, which has become a mining boomtown, and the girls take over the local eatery. Paige is a chemical engineer who falls for Miss Frazee, while gambler Edmund MacDonald moves in to the district to pitch his layout of phoney apparatus. But the girls backfire with importation of glamour girls to take the play away from the joint, and it's a success all around.

Ritz Bros. sow plenty of corn along the route, and harvest a moderate amount of laughs with their standard hokum. Miss Frazee does well in the girl lead, knocking off a couple of duos with Miss Clyde to pleasing reaction. Paige is confined to a walk-through, and has little to do in the proceedings. Paul Hurst is the victim of ome ineffectual Ritzian barbs.

Harold Young directs in standard fashion for this moderate budgeter, while script by Edmund L. Hartman is sophomoric.

Walt.

A STRANGER IN TOWN

Metro release of Robert Sisk production. Features Frank Morgan, Richard Carlson, Jean Rogers, Porter Hall. Directed by Roy Rowland. Screenplay, Isobel Lennart, William Kozlenko; camera, Sidney Wagner; music, Daniele Amfitheatrof and Nathaniel Shilkret; editor, Elmo Veron. Previewed in projection room, N. Y., Feb. 4, '43. Running time, **67 MINS.**

John Josephus Grant........Frank Morgan
Bill Adams...................Richard Carlson
Lucy Gilbert....................Jean Rogers
Austin Harkley..................Porter Hall
Mayor Connison..............Robert Barrat
Vinnie Z. Blaxton........Donald MacBride
Tom Cooney...................Walter Baldwin
Roscoe Swade...............Andrew Tombes
Homer Todds....................Olin Howlin
Charles Craig......................Chill Wills
Orrin Todds....................Irving Bacon
Henry...........................Eddie Dunn
Birdie..........................Gladys Blake
Hart Ridges....................John Hodiak

There's a certain familiar ring about 'Stranger in Town,' but it's insufficient to impair its boxoffice value as a 'B' dualer. It's an entertaining feature that will bear inevitable comparison to Columbia's early-season 'Talk of the Town,' but it has enough novelty on its own to suit the production's purposes.

Both 'Stranger' and 'Talk' are alike in their basic themes—a Supreme Court justice, while on vacation, comes up against a situation that demands he exercise his judicial offices. In 'Stranger' Frank Morgan plays one of his few serious roles, that of the justice who, as plain Joe Grant, goes on a little duck-hunting vacation. The small town that he chooses for his rest is rife with the crooked politics of the city hall machine in power. The subordinate theme concerns the mayoralty campaign that finds the incumbent crooked mayor opposed by a young, honest lawyer whose hands are tied by the net of circumstances that the machine has woven around him. But when Joe Grant becomes Justice John Josephus Grant, all that's changed.

Morgan plays the name title part excellently, while Richard Carlson, as the young lawyer who ultimately wins the election; Jean Rogers, as Morgan's secretary and the romantic interest opposite Carlson; Robert Barrat, the mayor; Porter Hall, the judge, and Donald MacBride, a muscleman, also do well.

Robert Sisk's production was achieved with a limited budget, which bespeaks particular merit for the film, whose scripting was ably handled by William Kozlenko and Isobel Lennart. Roy Rowland's direction is above par.

Kahn.

Siege of Leningrad

(RUSSIAN-MADE)

Artkino release of Lenfilm Newsreel Studios production. A documentary filmed by 23 Soviet cameramen. Edited by Paul Capon. English commentary written by John Gordon, narrated by Edward R. Murrow. Previewed in N. Y., Feb. 8, '43. Opens at Stanley, N. Y., Feb. 10. Running time, **56 MINS.**

(English Commentary)

'Siege of Leningrad' is without a doubt one of the documentary epics of the war. It's a standout not only photographically, but because never before has a city lived through such drama for so long a time. And never before has a camera recorded—even in previous Soviet documentaries—such fortitude, such stoicism by so many people in face of such great danger. No one in the United States—especially the 'patriots' who complain of only three pairs of shoes a year, lack of gas, one pat of butter and the myriad other 'hardships' currently being suffered—should miss seeing this. It gives an entirely new aspect to war.

Stalin felt so strongly about the picture he presented a print to Wendell Willkie, who brought it back from Russia with him. The version about to preem in New York, however, has previously been shown in London. It was there that the English commentary was written by John Gordon, of the London Express, and narrated by Edward R. Murrow, European chief of the Columbia Broadcasting System.

Even at Stalingrad it is unlikely that Soviet cameramen have been able to capture such scenes of hardships suffered by a civilian population. It is in this picturing of the calmness, courage and hardihood of the people, rather than in showing the siege as a military campaign, that the film excels. It is a completely human document, so much so that it would seem occasionally desirable to show by animated maps or otherwise the movement of the fighting lines. That would make still clearer the peril in which the 3,000,000 inhabitants lived through the 18 months of Nazi encirclement.

The most terrifying pictures of the bombing of London are the only ones that come near comparison with these of the devastation and havoc wrought by a combination of aerial bombs, heavy artillery shells and the almost complete cutting off of the city from the rest of Russia. For months on end, with heavy snow on the ground, Leningrad had no form of transportation, no electric or other power, no fuel but burnable rubble, no water—and plenty of low temperatures.

Through it all the people of Leningrad lived on. Not only lived on, but fought on. And through it all their great factories kept operating. Gloved and overcoated workmen (no heat) hardly had the treads on tanks before the giant armored vehicles were in the battle. Production line and firing line were virtually one.

Unforgettable are the scenes of the people of Leningrad gathering around a hole in the ice with dippers. That was their source of water. In the background a woman with a tub wrings out clothes. With buses and streetcars mired in snow, the people do the next best thing, they trundle their burdens on sleds. And among those burdens—on sleds such as kids here might play with—were their dead.

But not even a ration of 4½ ounces of bread a day seemed to turn the stoic and determined people of Leningrad from as normal a life as possible under such circumstances. Not even the arts were forgotten. An unidentified composer, who well might be Shostakovitch, is pictured in boots, overcoat and muffler, seated at a piano in an otherwise empty room, writing music. And even as workmen clear the street of wreckage, a painter is seen at his easel recording the sad vista.

Cutting a road through the snow on Lake Ladoga provided the icy lifeline by which Leningrad kept up its sole contact with the rest of Russia. As spring came and the ice melted, truck convoys continued over the road until they were hub-deep in water. Then came the lifting of the siege. A camera has seldom caught more sincere happiness than in the faces of the people as the first streetcar ran again. It's in recording bits like that that the 23 Lenfilm cameramen who made this documentary show that real propaganda films are not the things of brawn and might and bombast that the Nazis would make them.

Just as 'Moscow Strikes Back' found its way, via Republic, into wider U.S. distribution than Artkino could give it, so should 'Siege of Leningrad' be exhibited to American audiences who will find in it much to admire, much to be thankful for, and an extremely interesting 56 minutes.

Secrets of Underground

Republic production and release. Features John Hubbard, Virginia Grey and Lloyd Corrigan. Directed by William Morgan; screenplay, Robert Tasker and Geoffrey Homes, from original story by Homes; editor, Arthur Roberts; camera, Ernest Miller. At New York theatre, N. Y., dual, Feb. 3, 1943. Running time, **70 MINS.**

P. Cadwallader Jones	John Hubbard
Terry	Virginia Grey
Maurice	Lloyd Corrigan
Marianne	Robin Raymond
Paul Panois	Miles Mander
Oscar	Olin Howlin
Joe	Ben Weldon
Mrs. Perkins	Maria Shelton
Kermit	Neil Hamilton
Cleary	Ken Christy
Maxie	Dick Rich

Lack of names shouldn't prove much of a deterrent for Republic's 'Secrets of the Underground.' Thanks to a workmanlike scripting job, capable direction and bangup acting by the principals, 'Secrets' emerges as an above-average dualer that should please juveniles and adults alike. Romance angle involving a d.a. and a sob-sister is dovetailed neatly, providing the film with its nicely-grooved lighter touches. Otherwise it gets down to job of unravelling murder mystery with a maximum of interest.

Scripters have based it all on the home-front menace. Brains of a mob of Axis agents who peddle counterfeit War Stamps is the proprietor of a fashionable gown shop. Murder is only a sideline, and it's distributed freely, with bodies popping out of wardrobe trunks and elevators. Victims are even used for decorative war-slanted window displays. Chief idea, however, is to create widespread panic among Uncle Sam's patriotic customers when they learn they've been falling for the bogus securities. Snoopy gal reporter, next in line for erasure, and the d.a. track the boss agent down to his upstate farm for a climactic episode that rings in a contingent of helpful WAACs for further topical interest.

John Hubbard and Virginia Grey turn in smart performances as the sleuthing romantics, with Lloyd Corrigan also outstanding as the Axis ringmaster. Good support is provided by Robin Raymond, Neil Hamilton and B. Olin Howlin. Arthur Roberts' photography is an asset.

Rose.

FIGHTING FRONTIER

RKO release of Bert Gilroy production. Stars Tim Holt; features Cliff Edwards, Ann Summers. Directed by Lambert Hillyer. Story by Bernard McConville; camera, Jack Greenhalgh; editor, Les Millbrook. Tradeshown in N. Y., Feb. 8, '43. Running time, **57 MINS.**

Kit	Tim Holt
Ike	Cliff Edwards
Jeannie	Ann Summers
Walton	Eddie Dew
Slocum	William Gould
Judge Halverson	Davison Clarke
Sheriff Logan	Slim Whitaker
Snap	Tom London
Pete	Monte Montague
Ira	Jack Rockwell

Familiar formula of the daring cowboy who poses as member of highway gang to trap the bandits is given splendid pacing in 'Fighting Frontier.' Result is a topflight oats opera that will satisfy Tim Holt's western following.

Plot follows the posing-with-outlaws routine even to the extent of having the hero jailed and about to become a victim of a necktie party. Lambert Hillyer's superb direction represents nice balance between action, suspense and comedy. Latter is handled by the effervescent Cliff Edwards, who incidentally is back with his uke strumming and warbling.

Tim Holt makes a likely cowboy daredevil as the Kit Russel who works as undercover agent with the banditti. Ann Summers, in chiefly for decorative purposes provides the slight femme interest. She is no great shakes as an actress and suffers in closeups. Davison Clarke, William Gould, Eddie Dew and Slim Whitaker are standard western characters who fill in nicely.

Wear.

TWO FISTED JUSTICE

Monogram release of George W. Weeks production. Features John King, David Sharpe and Max Terhune. Directed by Robert Tansey; screenplay by William Nolte; editor, Roy Claire; camera, Robert Cline. At New York theatre, N. Y., dual Feb. 3, 1943. Running time, **59 MINS.**

Dusty	John King
David	David Sharpe
Alibi	Max Terhune
Joan	Gwen Gaze
Sunny	Joel Davis
Hodgins	John Elliot
Trigger	Charles King
Decker	George Chesbro
Harve	Frank Ellis
Miss Adams	Cecil Weston
Sam	Hal Price

'Two Fisted Justice,' latest in the Monogram series of 'Range Busters' frontier sagas, suffers from most of the ills usually attendant upon poorer grade 'B' westerns. It's handicapped by a 'lazy' script that resorts to the tried and found-wanting formula of ridding the prairie town (this time it's Dry Gulch) of its wave of lawlessness without the injection of a single refreshing quality; its acting is mediocre throughout; the pace set by Robert Tansey's direction leaves much to be desired while the comedy, too, is below standard. Film has the usual quota of gunplay and fisticuffs, but it's geared strictly for the juves.

This time the trio of Range Busters is out to mop up the villains, who have things pretty much their way whooping it up in Dry Gulch and making stagecoach driving a hazardous venture. The town's good citizens recruit John King as their sheriff, and latter, with assistance of David Sharpe and Max Terhune as deputies, restore law and order via the routine buckaroo channels.

King's cowboy stint is below par, with Sharpe's and Terhune's attempts at comedy more on the sorry side, the latter with his ventriloquial dummy interludes. Gwen Gaze furnishes the ornamental background. The menace is Charles King, the ex-musicomedy star.

Rose.

HI, BUDDY

(MUSICAL)

Hollywood, Feb. 12.

Universal release of Paul Malvern production. Directed by Harold Young. Original screenplay, Warren Wilson; camera, John W. Boyle; editor, Charles Maynard; asst. director, Joseph A. McDonough; musical director, Charles Previn. Previewed Feb. 11, '43. Running time, **66 MINS.**

Dave O'Connor	Dick Foran
Gloria Bradley	Harriet Hilliard
Johnny Blake	Robert Paige
Mary Parker	Marjorie Lord
Tim Martin	Bobs Watson
Spud Winslow	Tommy Cook
Miss Russell	Jennifer Holt
Downbeat Collins	Gus Schilling
Michael O'Shane	Wade Poteler
Pat	Drew Roddy

and

The Kings Men, The Step Brothers, Lorraine Krueger, Marilyn Kay, Dick Humphries, Norman Ollstead, The Four Sweethearts, Geraldine Chantlind, Dolores Diane

'Hi, Buddy' is another in Universal's series of program filmusicals, designed to provide light entertainment in the general runs and family houses as dual fodder. Displaying 18 tunes that run through list of standard pop favorites, in addition to several song and dance specialties, picture emerges as a good entry of its type.

Story is lightly scaffolded to framework the musical numbers. An East Side boys' club finds itself in financial straits and due to fold unless steady stream of money can be tapped. Robert Paige is discovered for a radio singing spot, and he arranges to give the extra coin to the club. But while on army camp tour, a designing manager diverts the funds to his own use, and it's up to soldier Dick Foran to come forward to stage a serviceman's benefit show. Paige gets back in time to get the witheld coin so the club can continue.

Song solos by Paige and Harriett Hilliard are augmented by quartet and choral groups. Brief singing appearance of youngster, Dolores Diane, displays girl with good personality and delivery who's entitled to another and more extended turn to better display talent that seems to be there. The Kings Men heads the four male quartets used for the military revue, while the Four Sweethearts provide background harmony for Paige's mike appearances. Brief songs of old time memory run through a pair of Stephen Foster numbers and standard pops of the 'teens and early 20s. New tunes are all military tempo numbers, with exception of title song by Milton Rosen and Everett Carter, which Paige presents.

Most prominent in the cast are Paige, Miss Hilliard, Foran, Marjorie Lord, Bobs Watson and Gus Schilling. Specialties interwoven pass through mostly in kaleidoscopic fashion, with little pause for adequate presentation and buildup. Direction by Harold Young is standard.

Walt.

IDAHO

(SONGS)

Republic production and release. Stars Roy Rogers; features Smiley Burnette. Directed by Joseph Kane. Story, Roy Chanslor and Olive Cooper; camera, Reggie Lanning; editor, Arthur Roberts; muscal director, Morton Scott. Previewed in N. Y., Feb. 12, '43. Running time, **70 MINS.**

Roy	Roy Rogers
Frog Millhouse	Smiley Burnette
Themselves	Bob Nolan and The Sons of the Pioneers
Terry	Virginia Grey
Judge Grey	Harry J. Shannon
Belle Bonner	Ona Munson
Duke Springer	Dick Purcell
Chief Ranger	Onslow Stevens
Spike Madagan	Arthur Hohl
Bud	Hal Taliaferro

And The Robert Mitchell Boy Choir

There's more to 'Idaho' than the eye catches from the billing. While it follows the tried and true formula and should have the kids cheering, it's a dandy Roy Rogers subject.

Manner in which the old pattern has been put together makes it one of the best of the series.

Story has Harry J. Shannon as a crusading judge who sets up a prairie 'Boys' Town,' seeking to rid the county of a saloon and gambling joint presided over by a notorious operator played by Ona Munson. It turns out that the judge is an ex-convict bank robber. Two bandits who knew him when reveal his identity to the woman. She tries to blackmail him to lay off the crusade but he refuses, whereupon the two bandits rob the local bank and frame the judge.

Rogers is a state ranger. When the chief ranger seeks to arrest the judge, Rogers turns in his badge, and with the aid of the judge's daughter and the ranch kids captures the bandits as they are about to stick up a pay truck.

There's the usual hard-riding chase scenes. Notable credit for some of the picture's appeal, however, goes to the Robert Mitchell Boy Choir, and Bob Nolan and Sons of the Pioneers, a cowboy singing unit.

Smiley Burnette provides the comedy material with good results. Virginia Grey, as the love interest opposite Rogers, turns in a neat performance. Rogers plays in his usual style. Onslow Stevens, as the chief ranger, and Arthur Hohl and Hal Taliaferro, as the bandits, are in familiar roles.

Of the seven song numbers, 'Idaho,' 'Holy, Holy, Holy,' and 'Lone Buckaroo' stand out.

Laugh Your Blues Away

(SONGS)

Columbia release of Jack Fier production. Stars Bert Gordon, Jinx Falkenburg. Directed by Charles Barton. Story and screenplay by Harry Sauber; added dialog, Ned Dandy; camera, Philip Tannura; editor, Richard Fantl. At Fox, Brooklyn, dual, week Feb. 12, '43. Running time, **65 MINS.**

Pam Crawford	Jinx Falkenburg
Boris Rascalnikoff	Bert Gordon
Jimmy Westerly	Douglass Drake
Mrs. Westerly	Isobel Elsom
Blake Henley	Roger Clark
Mr. Westerly	George Lessey
Mrs. Conklin	Vivien Oakland
Mr. Conklin	Dick Elliott
Priscilla Conklin	Phyllis Kennedy
Wilfred	Robert Greig

Nora Lou and the Pals of the Golden West

The producers haven't done well by Bert Gordon (the Mad Russian of radio) in this. Consequently, 'Laugh Your Blues Away' is not likely to measure up to that billing. Whenever given half a break or tolerable lines, Gordon gives every hint of being as comical on the screen as he is on the airwaves. But this hashed-up hokum doesn't help him. Only for minor duals.

Harry Sauber's script and Charles Barton's direction lack originality. It's the extremely familiar formula of the ex-rich dowager trying to marry off her son to the daughter of a rich Texas cattleman. Plot adopts the artifice of having jobless actors serve as guests at a party held to impress the western visitors. Most important of these are Boris (Bert Gordon) and sister, Olga (Jinx Falkenburg). Pair attempt to emulate a Russian count and countess.

This develops the expected—she falls for the formerly wealthy woman's son, and Gordon nearly captures the homely daughter of the Texan. To make such climax even worse, story drags in a dumb cowboy who suddenly decides to marry the Texan's offspring, leaving the mad Russian merely as a dialectic Cupid.

Gordon usually is funny despite the lines and situations. His radio patter registers best, but too few and far between. Informal drinking sequence with the butler is standout. Nora Lou, who is about as tall as Miss Falkenburg, and sings well, warbles enough like Miss Falkenburg to have doubled for the tall player in several song sessions the latter does. These, incidentally, are the dullest portions of the film. In contrast, Gordon's one unbilled song registers.

Douglas Drake as Jimmy must have been picked for height chiefly. Miss Falkenburg plays opposite him in fairly capable fashion. Remainder of cast is routine excepting Phyllis Kennedy, who shows some animation as the Texan's daughter.

Wear.

Miniature Reviews

'Frankenstein Meets the Wolf Man' (U). Good chiller-thriller entertainment for the horro-minded customers.

'Power of Press' (Col). Lee Tracy, Guy Kibbee in another mild newspaper meller; for lower dualers.

'The Mysterious Doctor' (WB). Inferior chiller, needs strong dual support.

'Kid Dynamite' (Mono.) Okay dualer about the East Side Kids.

Frankenstein Meets the Wolf Man

Hollywood, Feb. 19.

Universal release of George Waggner production. Stars Lon Chaney, Ilona Massey, Patric Knowles, Lionel Atwill. Directed by Roy William Neill. Original screenplay by Curtis Sidmak; camera, George Robinson; editor, Edward Curtiss; asst. director, Melville Schyer; special effects, John P. Fulton. Previewed Feb. 18, '43. Running time, 72 MINS.

The Wolf Man	Lon Chaney
Baroness Elsa Frankenstein	Ilona Massey
Dr. Mannering	Patric Knowles
Mayor	Lionel Atwill
Monster	Bela Lugosi
Maleva	Maria Ouspenskaya
Inspector Owen	Dennis Hoey
Franzec	Don Barclay
Vazec	Rex Evans
Rudi	Dwight Frye
Gune	Harry Stubbs

Universal tosses its Wolf Man of previous issues in with the legendary Frankenstein monster to give this one a double-barreled horror aspect. Expertly contrived, and carrying suspenseful chiller tenor throughout, picture will prove a profitable booking in all spots where the customers plunk down the coin for horror films.

In order to put the Wolf Man and the Monster through further film adventures, scripter Curtis Siodmak has to resurrect the former from a tomb, and the Frankenstein creation from the ruins of the castle where he was purportedly killed in his last cinematic adventure. But he delivers a good job of fantastic writing to weave the necessary thriller ingredients into the piece, and finally brings the two legendary characters together for a battle climax that will give the next writer something to unravel—which is a cinch to eventuate.

Eerie atmosphere generates right at the start, when Lon Chaney, previously killed off with the werewolf stain on him, is disinterred and returns to life. After one transformation, he winds up in a hospital to gain the sympathetic attention of medico Patric Knowles, then seeks out gypsy Maria Ouspenskaya for relief, and she takes him to the continent and the village where Frankenstein held forth. This allows Chaney to discover and revive the monster, role handled by Bela Lugosi, and from there on its a creepy affair in grand style until the two stage a battle and are swept away by the floodwaters of a bursting dam.

Miss Massey is the daughter of the deceased scientist Frankenstein, and is teamed with Knowles for mild romantics. Cast is neatly slotted for routine performances, with little opportunity to give out in picture of this type. Director Roy William Neill deftly paces the film with both movement and suspense to keep audience interest on sustained plane, while low key lighting in photography by George Robinson is effective.

Walt.

POWER OF PRESS

Columbia release of Leon Barsha production. Features Guy Kibbee, Gloria Dickson, Lee Tracy, Otto Kruger, Victor Jory. Directed by Lew Landers. Story by Sam Fuller; screenplay, Robert D. Andrews; camera, John Stumar; editor, Mel Thorsen. At Strand, Brooklyn, week Feb. 19. '43.

Running time, 64 MINS.

Ulysses Bradford	Guy Kibbee
Edwina Stephens	Gloria Dickson
Griff Thompson	Lee Tracy
Howard Rankin	Otto Kruger
Oscar Trent	Victor Jory
Jerry Purvis	Larry Parks
Chris Barker	Rex Williams
Mack Gibson	Frank Sully
Pringle	Don Beddoe
Whiffle	Douglas Leavitt
John Carter	Minor Watson

'Power of the Press' is another in the long line of screen mellers concerning newspapers, crooks, politics and honest editors, only here an attempt is made to link up the war effort. Both as a melodrama and patriotic story it fails to jell, being loaded with implausibilities, bad scripting and mild direction. It's a minor dualer.

Picture points up the feeble results achieved when a producer attempts to make a moral out of newspapers not abusing the freedom of the press in wartime. Main difficulty with the plot is that, from the premise that editors should not step out of bounds in periods of national emergency, the story links up a notorious publisher with gunmen and gangsters, depicting them as his paid henchmen.

Yarn further loads on impossible angles by having this outlaw publisher (vaguely represented as a disappointed politico) heighten his power by killing off everybody in his path. In the city represented here, apparently no organized police force operated. There also is a feeble attempt to bring in the hoarding situation, only it turns out that the Washington dollar-per-year man actually was stocking a warehouse as part of a war shipment overseas. Mighty difficult to stomach. Then the overly worked device of using a fake front-page to wring a confession from the 'dastardly' publisher finally winds up the story.

Production crew apparently had only a hazy idea of how a N. Y. newspaper operates. And the type of country editor they make Guy Kibbee surely will not make real country eds happy. Lee Tracy, of original 'Front Page' fame, again assumes his venerable screen role of a resourceful managing editor. It's a reasonable facsimile though one wonders why a m.e. should do the work of a rewrite man. Gloria Dickson is the honest editor's loyal secretary, but the attempt to develop a romantic angle between her and Tracy is wasted. Gal stands out on straight thespian effort. Otto Kruger makes a vivid villainous publisher who has his partner slain. Victor Jory is head gunman. Minor Watson and Larry Parks head the support.

Lew Landers direction varies from tedious, involved passages to jerky fast-action. Columbia made another 'Power of Press', a silent film, back in 1928. It was authored by Fred C. Thompson and directed by Frank Capra, being rated by 'Variety' as one of Columbia's best. About the only resemblance to this picture apparently is that both concern newspapers.

Wear.

The Mysterious Doctor

Warner Bros. production and release. Features John Loder, Eleanor Parker and Bruce Lester. Directed by Ben Stoloff. Screenplay, Richard Weil; camera, Henry Sharp; editor, Clarence Kolster. Previewed n projection room, New York, Feb. 18, '43. Running time, 57 MINS.

Sir Henry Leland	John Loder
Letty Carstairs	Eleanor Parker
Lt. Christopher Hilton	Bruce Lester
Dr. Frederick Holmes	Lester Matthews
Hugh Penhryn	Forrester Harvey
Bart Raymond	Matt Willis
Saul Bevans	Art Foster
Herbert	Clyde Cooke
Luke	Creighton Hale
Ruby	Phyllis Barry
Tom Andrews	David Clyde
The Peddler	Harold de Becker
Simon Tewksbury	Frank Mayo
Roger	Hank Mann
Orderly	LeWolf Hopper
Watson	Jack Mower
The Commandant	Crawford Kent

This is strictly a witches brew concocted to scare the pants off little Johnny if he is unfortunate enough to catch it at a special Saturday matinee. Hobgoblins, headless ghosts and village idiots galore flit aimlessly through the mist-blanketed English landscape. This Warner 'action' flicker will have to be part of a dual billing, and the other feature better be good.

'The Mysterious Doctor' has very little to do with doctors. But it's concerned considerably with a tin mine and headless corpses. A lonely British village has ceased operating its tin mine because a headless, knife-wielding ghost is said to inhabit the pit. No appeal to patriotism, no grave warnings as to England's need for tin to beat the Axis can pursuade the frightened villagers to go near the mine. Nor film-goers to flock to the b.o.

John Loder, Eleanor Parker, Bruce Lester, featured trio, and the rest of the cast are hampered by the script. They do what little is required of them. Matt Willis plays a convincing idiot at times, though he seems too bright for the part at other intervals, for he solves the mystery in a very sane manner.

Direction by Ben Stoloff was likewise circumscribed by the story.

KID DYNAMITE

Monogram release of Sam Katzman and Jack Dietz. Associate producer, Barney Sarecky. Directed by Wallace Fox. Screenplay, Gerald Schnitzer, from story by Paul Ernst; additional dialog, Morey Amsterdam; camera, Mack Stengler; editor, Carl Pierson. At New York theatre, N. Y., dual, week Feb. 17. Running time, 73 MINS.

Mugs	Leo Gorcey
Glimpy	Huntz Hall
Danny	Bobby Jordan
Wycoff	Gabriel Dell
Ivy	Pamela Blake
Scruno	Sammy Morrison
Beanie	Benny Bartlett
Skinny	Dave Durand
Stoney	Bobby Stone
Mrs. McGinnis	Daphne Pollard
Glendick	Vince Barnett
Klinkhammer	Henry Hall

Tempo of the times saves this East Side Kids picture from being below mediocre. With the four leading characters going into the army, navy, marine corps and WAAC's, the film sizes up passably for duals, particularly for those who have followed the antics of the toughies.

Story, which appeared in the Saturday Evening Post, was written by Paul Ernst and apparently looked like a natural for the ex-Dead Enders. It's about a champion eastside kid boxer (Leo Gorcey) who is to box the westside champ. The eastsider is kidnapped by thugs who place a bet on his opponent, but another member of the kid gang, played by Bobby Jordan, steps in and wins the match.

Rest concerns the leads joining the various armed services, Gorcey in the navy, Huntz Hall, marines; Jordan, army, and Pamela Blake, WAACs. The latter part gives the film a popular appeal in keeping with present-day ideas.

In addition to Gorcey, Hall and Jordan, Gabriel Dell turns in a stereotyped performance. Miss Blake is well cast for the love interest opposite Jordan. Daphne Pollard and Vince Barnett also give good performances. Direction of Wallace Fox does much to keep action brisk.

Miniature Reviews

'The Human Comedy' (M-G). Brilliantly written, directed and acted. Sock b.o. for extended datings.

'The Youngest Profession' (M-G). Light comedy-drama of adolescent adventures provides good dual support.

'Slightly Dangerous' (M-G). Will have to depend on Lana Turner and Robert Young for the draw.

'Keep 'Em Slugging' (U). Typical Dead End Kids meller display of familiar pattern. Dual supporter for family houses.

'Tenting Tonight on the Old Camp Ground' (U). A Johnny Mack Brown, Tex Ritter run-of-the-mill oater.

THE HUMAN COMEDY

Hollywood, Feb. 24.

Metro release of Clarence Brown production, directed by Brown. Stars Mickey Rooney; features Frank Morgan. Original by William Saroyan. Screenplay by Howard Estabrook. Camera, Harry Stradling; editor, Conrad A. Nervig; score, Herbert Stothart. Tradeshown in L. A. Feb. 23, '43. Running time, 119 MINS.

Homer Macauley .... Mickey Rooney
Willie Grogan .... Frank Morgan
Tom Spangler .... James Craig
Diana Steed .... Marsha Hunt
Mrs. Macauley .... Fay Bainter
Mr. Macauley .... Ray Collins
Marcus Macauley .... Van Johnson
Bess Macauley .... Donna Reed
Ulysses Macauley .... Jack Jenkins
Mary Arena .... Dorothy Morris
Tobey George .... John Craven
Mrs. Sandoval .... Ann Ayars
Miss Hicks .... Mary Nash
Charles Steed .... Henry O'Neill
Mrs. Steed .... Katharine Alexander
Brad Stickman .... Alan Baxter
Lionel .... Darryl Hickman
Fat .... Barry Nelson
Helen Elliot .... Rita Quigley
Henderson .... Clem Bevans
Librarian .... Adeline De Walt Reynolds

William Saroyan's initial original screenplay is a brilliant sketch of the basic fundamentals of the American way of life, transferred to the screen with exceptional fidelity by director Clarence Brown and cast headed by Mickey Rooney. Overall represents picture of upper-bracket boxoffice potentialities that is destined for both strong audience reaction and critical attention. It's a holdover candidate in every booking.

Saroyan, after being promoted by Metro to write an original screenplay, reportedly wrote his script in 18 days. Studio heads acclaimed it a 'masterpiece,' until advised that yarn would consume nearly four hours of running time, and then chilled on the tale. Saroyan collected $60,000 for the original screenplay, in addition to $18,000 on the Metro writing payroll. He departed from the lot when a purported agreement for him to produce and direct his own yarn was jettisoned. Figuring the picture would never be produced by Metro, Saroyan returned to northern California and batted out a novel of the yarn, which is being published concurrently. But Clarence Brown, assured he could obtain Mickey Rooney to handle the lead, as originally intended by the writer, decided to get front office approval to make a film version of the Saroyan tale. Result is a picture of outstanding merit on the boxoffice side.

Author's tale is a human and intimate story, with punchy accentuation of typical American family life—its humor and tragedy displaying the intimacies of small-town life with its patriotic and religious fervor that makes up the backbone of the United States. Script is episodic, but this is easily overlooked in the entity of the production. Saroyan's original script was lengthy for current picture requirements, and even when it was in rough-cut form for initial sneak review, ran about 170 minutes. Editing required that whole chunks and episodes be lifted out, and this is accomplished without detracting from the entertainment factors remaining.

Rooney is the major breadwinner of his little family following departure of his older brother, Van Johnson, into army service. Hickey, going to high school, gets a night job as a telegraph messenger to keep things going. At home there are the understanding and sympathetic mother, Fay Bainter; deb-age sister, Donna Reed, and toddling brother, Jack Jenkins—typical of any family in the hinterlands. At the office, Frank Morgan is the veteran telegraph operator, a tippler of long standing; and personable manager James Craig, wooed by socialite Marsha Hunt in a cross-the-tracks romance. There are brief interludes of army intimacies, with brother Van Johnson and John Craven as buddies striking up palship in service that carries impact. Climactic final reel hits to the tragic side, with Morgan keeling over from heart attack, and word that Johnson has given his life in battle.

Picture is studded with brilliant expositions of the family, patriotic and religious undertones of American life. Only an inveterate student of Americana could have woven these three basic factors into a picture, but Saroyan achieved that purpose in what apparently was easy dramatic magic. Author's understanding of the thoughts of youngsters, exemplified by the opening scene of the curious and questioning Jack Jenkins watching a gopher digging his hole, and the continual cutbacks to the toddler naively questioning with actions or verbal surprises on explanations of life, are most convincingly transferred to the screen. The army palship between Johnson and Craven—also woven intermittently through the footage—provides a strong dramatic tug, especially in these times. Numerous other episodes flash indelibly by, with Rooney's classroom dissertation on noses, and his youthful ambition to enter the school track meet, a standout.

Rooney, displaying the strongest performance of his career under the Metro banner, shines brilliantly as the boy of Saroyan's tale. But tiny Jack Jenkins, son of Doris Dudley and grandson of columnist Bide Dudley, is right up there with Rooney in one of the most natural and outstanding kid performances ever transferred to the screen. (Youngster, discovered by Clarence Brown's secretary, is naturally retained by Metro under a term ticket.) Of the others, Frank Morgan clicks solidly as the vet telegrapher, while casting of the smaller parts displays rare judgment. Spotlight acting honors also go to Miss Bainter, Craig, Miss Hunt, Johnson, Craven, Darryl Hickman, and Mary Nash.

Clarence Brown directs with humaneness and understanding, to provide maximum audience attention. Production mounting is excellent, with photography by Harry Stradling noteworthy. *Walt.*

Youngest Profession

Hollywood, Feb. 27.

'Metro release of B.E. Zeldman production. Features Virginia Weidler, Edward Arnold, John Carroll, Ann Ayars. Directed by Edward Buzzell. Screenplay by George Oppenheimer, Charles Lederer, Leonard Spigelglass; based on book by Lillian Day; camera, Charles Lawton; editor, Ralph Winters. At Westwood Village Feb. 26, '43. Running time, 81 MINS.

Joan Lyons .... Virginia Weidler
Barton V. Lyons .... Edward Arnold
Dr. Hercules .... John Carroll
Susan Thayer .... Ann Ayars
Edith Lyons .... Marta Linden
Douglas Sutton .... Dick Simmons
Miss Feathertone .... Agnes Moorehead
Patricia Drew .... Jean Porter
Schuyler .... Raymond Roe
Secretary .... Dorothy Merrie
Junior Lyons .... Scotty Beckett
Vera Bailey .... Marela Mae Jones
Sister Lassie .... Sara Haden
Thyra Winter .... Beverly Jean Saul
Mrs. Drew .... Marjorie Gateson
Mr. Drew .... Thurston Hall
Lilybud .... Jessie Grayson
Guest Stars.... Lana Turner, Greer Garson, Walter Pidgeon, Robert Taylor, William Powell.

Antics of adolescent autograph hounds form basic story for this lightly woven number that qualifies as good support in the family houses, where the younger generation will tab plenty of laughs by their prototypes parading on the screen.

Autograph seekers of high-school age are targets for good-natured barbs by the scripters, but it's all displayed with farcical treatment that gets across in acceptable fashion. Virginia Weidler heads the film autograph club of a New York girls' high school, and tracks down Greer Garson at latter's hotel for sympathetic reception. She meets Walter Pidgeon, and has Robert Taylor virtually dropped at her front door. After toying with the celeb-seeking angle, yarn switches to family problems when governess Agnes Moorehead busybodies romantic affair between the father, Edward Arnold, and his secretary. Miss Weidler, in stepping in to protect the family situation, gums it up for rounds of broadly sketched episodes, until explanations eventually clear up the affair.

Cast is adequate throughout, with Jean Porter catching attention as the youngster who trails Miss Weidler throughout the proceedings. Edward Arnold and Marta Linden team as the parents; John Carroll is a professional Hercules hired by the daughter to assist in fixing things; and others in cast include Ann Ayars, Agnes Moorehead, Dick Simmons, Dorothy Morris and Scotty Beckett.

Lana Turner, Greer Garson, Pidgeon, Taylor and William Powell make brief guest appearances in brief clips to add authenticity to the autograph-hunter angles to the tale. Edward Buzzell swings the unreeling along at a fairly good pace, with several breezy episodes materially assisting in holding things together. *Walt.*

Slightly Dangerous

Metro release of Ramiro S. Berman production. Stars lana Turner and Robert Young; features Walter Brennan, Dame May Whitty. Directed by Wesley Ruggles. Screenplay, Charles Lederer and George Oppenheimer; story, Ian McLellan Hunter and Aileen Hamilton; camera, Harold Resson; editor, Frank E. Hull. Previewed in projection room, N.Y., Feb. 25, '43. Running time, 94 MINS.

Peggy Evans .... Lana Turner
Bob Stuart .... Robert Young
Cornelius Burden .... Walter Brennan
Baba .... Dame May Whitty
Durstein .... Eugene Ballette
English Gentleman .... Alan Mowbray
Mrs. Roanoke-Brooke .... Florence Bates
Mr. Quill .... Howard Freeman
Baldwin .... Millard Mitchell
Jimmy .... Ward Rand
Mitzi .... Pamela Blake
Snodgras .... Ray Collins
Stanhope .... Paul Stanton

'Slightly Dangerous' is a diffusion of ideas and production credits. A casual inspection of the cast and the production names involved would immediately stack the cards in the film's favor. But the unspooling is still the thing. That's where this hypothetical flimsy shows itself up.

Since the beginning of film storytelling (or, for that matter, any kind of narration) there has been, of one sort or another, the yarn to be told of the poor little shopgirl who would transform her whole circumspect life to one of glamour and riches. 'Slightly Dangerous' tries to do this with discouraging results.

Lana Turner is the girl, Robert Young the boy. She's the small-town soda jerk in a department store, and he's the new manager who soon becomes an ex-new manager through a series of nebulous circumstances involving Miss Turner, who, the town believes, has been driven to suicide by Young. Actually, however, she's gone to New York where, with her meager savings, she glamourizes herself into headline prominence as a long-lost heiress who'd been kidnapped as a child. The rest deals with her carry-out of the fraud and the attempt by Young to seek the disappearing soda-jerk in order to vindicate himself in the eyes of the small-towners.

Miss Turner, as usual, is a lassie with a chassis, and the photography makes capital of it. Her performance is as good as the limited story will permit, while Young is likewise retarded by the scope of the film. Walter Brennan, Dame May Whitty, Eugene Pallette and Alan Mowbray do as well as possible under the circumstances in lesser roles.

Wesley Ruggles directed with an eye to pace, but the story's entanglements and dialog were insurmountable. *Kahn.*

KEEP 'EM SLUGGING

Hollywood, Feb. 26.

Universal release of Ben Pivar production. Directed by Christy Cabanne. Screenplay by Brenda Weisberg; original, Edward Handler, Robert Gordon; camera, William Sickner; editor, Ray Snyder. Previewed Feb. 25, '43. Runnnig time, 60 MINS.

Pig .... Huntz Hall
Tommy .... Bobby Jordan
String .... Gabriel Dell
Ape .... Norman Abbott
Sheila .... Evelyn Ankers
Suzanne .... Elyse Knox
Frank .... Frank Albertson
Jerry .... Don Porter
Binky .... Shemp Howard
Curruthers .... Samuel S. Hinds
Mrs. Banning .... Mary Gordon
Duke Redman .... Milburn Stone
Lela .... Joan Marsh

Again parading the antics and dramatics of Universal's Dead End Kids and Little Tough Guys, 'Keep 'Em Slugging' follows familiar formula for previous issues in the series. Cranked out on low budget, it's a supporter for the duals that have found customers receptive to this type of product.

There's little originality in either the story, comedic horseplay of the tough youths or the dramatics unreeled. To get in wartime step, the four boys—Huntz Hall, Bobby Jordan, Gabriel Dell, and Norman Abbott—seek jobs for summer vacations. Even with the labor shortage they get only rebuffs, until Jordan lands in shipping department of a department store. But he's framed on jewelry theft charge, and enlists aid of his pals to track down a hi-jacking ring to clear himself for the fadeout.

Abbott is a new addition to the troupe, nephew of comedian Bud Abbott. There's a slight amount of romance generated between Evelyn Ankers and Don Porter; but cast members drop into general groove designed by the unimaginative script. Christy Cabanne keeps things moving at consistent pace, although under handicap of obvious yarn. *Walt.*

Tenting Tonight on the Old Camp Ground

(SONGS)

Universal release of Oliver Drake production. Features Johnny Mack Brown, Tex Ritter, Fuzzy Knight, Jennifer Holt. Directed by Lewis D. Collins. Screen play by Elizabeth Beecher from an original story by Harry Fraser; camera, William Sickner; editor, Charles Maynard. At New York theatre, N. Y., dual, week Feb. 24. Running time, 59 MINS.

Wade Benson .... Johnny Mack Brown
Bob Courtney .... Tex Ritter
Si Dugan .... Fuzzy Knight
Kay Randolph .... Jennifer Holt
Talbot .... John Elliott
Judge Higgins .... Earle Hodgins
Zeke Larkin .... Rex Lease
Duke Merrick .... Lane Chandler
Matt Warner .... Allen Bridge
Ed Randolph .... Dennis Moore
Pete .... Tom London
Jimmy Wakely Trio

The title 'Tenting Tonight on the Old Camp Ground' suggests a sentimental prairie musical, which is scarcely the case. Except for several numbers by the Jimmy Wakely trio, which includes 'Tenting,' this film is a run-of-the-mill shooting, ridin', way-out-west opus with delusions of historical grandeur. However, it's a passable dualer that should pick up b.o. in action situations.

The story is one of rivalry over the building of a stage coach road, and the pot of gold is a juicy Govt. mail contract. While Johnny Mack Brown tries to drive his men with patter about the destiny of the west depending upon the completion of the road, the other side uses a dive complete with hostess Jennifer Holt to lure Brown's workers from the job. They employ murder, too, but free likker and attractive Miss Holt are much more potent. All is finally saved, including the mail contract.

Featured players Brown, Tex Ritter, Fuzzy Knight and Miss Holt turn in competent performances as do the others in the cast. So long as the pintos keep running and the guns shooting, as they do for most of the film, Director Collins has done his duty.

At the Front in No. Africa
(DOCUMENTARY)
(COLOR)

Warner Bros. release for WAC of U.S. Army Signal Corps production. Photographed by U. S. Army and Navy cameramen. Previewed in Projection Room, N.Y., Feb. 24, '43. Running time, 41 MINS.

Compilation of interesting views along the North African front making up this film represent the best effort to date in covering the battlefront via military cameramen. Gives an insight on the difficulties ahead in North Africa, but fails to measure up to documentaries produced by other Allied nations, such as Canada. While known in the trade as Col. Darryl Zanuck's African pictures, there is no reference in credits to him. Exhibitors may find fault with the running time, since it is too long to rate as a short and too brief to fill the normal feature category.

Color in 'At the Front in North Africa' is standout, some shots such as the sunset and night scenes being photographic gems. The tank battle, really superb, is the highlight of the production, but too brief. On the debit side is the uneven cutting job, some photography out of focus, ordinary musical background-ing and dispirited spoken narration. Latter plus listless script looms as the principal flaw. Despite these technical flaws, enormous present-day interest in American fighting forces, particularly the North African front, make it a subject bound to attract widespread attention. It is merely too bad the finished job could not have been better.

Opening footage, all too prolonged, shows landing of tanks and supplies at Bone. First real action is the fight between Allied planes and Axis bombers, though a bit confused. Hospital train plainly marked by Red Cross identification and a lone, isolated church, both badly damaged by Nazi bombers, are given as illustrations of what's going on in Africa.

Tanks and supplies moving up a winding mountain road are seen preliminary to the tank battle of Teborba in Tunisia. Cameramen did yeoman work in giving a closeup view of conflict, the fast retreat from the scene by enemy tanks and anti-tank guns being plainly seen. There are camp scenes that include chasing turkeys and preparing them for Thanksgiving, besides shots of Zanuck and Commander John Ford, latter astride a burro. No explanation is made why Ford, producer-

director of 'How Green Was My Valley,' is there.

The average audience may find fault with the background music and effects. However, choice of 'Over There' and 'Onward Christian Soldiers' music near the film's end is the most effective part of the scoring. Audiences also may find fault with scenes depicting U. S.-British troops again on the receiving end of enemy attacks when the opposite was true, at least at the time the pictures were taken. Obviously this resulted because no cameramen were able to capture views of our forces attacking the Nazis from the air.

Wear.

Miniature Reviews

'Moon Is Down' (20th). John Steinbeck's novel makes powerful tale of Nazi-oppressed people. Sure-fire boxoffice.

'Hello, Frisco, Hello' (20th). Alice Faye, John Payne, Jack Oakie in pretentious musical; solid moneymaker.

'Assignment in Brittany' (M-G). Potent adventure thriller based on the best-selling novel should do sock business.

'Hit Parade of 1943' (Musical) (Rep). A hit.

'Harrigan's Kid' (M-G). Better-than-average 'B', with racetrack background.

'Dixie Dugan' (20th). Misses fire; a dualer.

'Rhythm of the Islands' (U) (musical). Light program filmusical in tropical isle setting, okay support for the duals.

'He Hired the Boss' (20th Dualer about mild-mannered clerk who makes good.

'Ridin' Down the Canyon'. (Rep). Fair western.

'Night for Crime' (PRC). Tedious murder meller.

MOON IS DOWN

20th-Fox release of Nunnally Johnson production. Stars Sir Cedric Hardwicke, Lorris Bowden, Margaret Wycherly, Henry Travers; features Peter Van Eyck, E. J. Ballantine, Henry Rowland, Lee Cobb, Hans Schumm. Directed by Irving Pichel. Screenplay by Nunnally Johnson from novel by John Steinbeck; camera, Arthur Miller; editor, Louis Loeffler; special camera effects, Fred Sersen. Tradeshown March 5, '43. Running time, 90 MINS.
Col. Lanser..........Sir Cedric Hardwicke
Mayor Orden...............Henry Travers
Dr. Winter..................Lee J. Cobb
Molly Morden.............Dorris Bowden
Madame Orden.........Margaret Wycherly
Lieut. Tonder.............Peter Van Eyck
Alex Morden............William Post. Jr.
Capt. Loft...............Henry Rowland
George Corell.............E. J. Ballantine
Inn Keeper..................Irving Pichel
Peder's Wife.............Violette Wilson
Capt. Bentick............Hans Schumm
Major Hunter.............Ernest Dorian
Lieut. Prackle............John Banner
Annie......................Helene Thimig
Joseph.......................Ian Wolfe
Orderly....................Kurt Kreuger
Albert.......................Jeff Corey
Schumann....................Louis Arco
Moeller.....................Ernst Hausman
Ole........................Charles McGraw
Foreman...................Trevor Bardette
Staff Officer...............John Mylong
Sergeants ....{ Otto Reichow
                       { Sven Hugo Borg
Mother..................Dorothy Peterson

John Steinbeck's 'The Moon Is Down,' despite propaganda aspects and lack of big marquee names, looks as surefire boxoffice for extended runs everywhere. Its ready-made audience from the widely-read novel and successful legit road tours make it likely to justify the strong advance praise. If properly exploited, 'Moon' promises to blaze as an outstanding picture of this year.

Instead of centering interest entirely on the rape of Norway, story concerns all invaded nations and their will to continue resistance despite Hitler's terroristic methods. There are many instances where the Norwegian undercover operations well apply to similar measures against the invading hordes in Belgium, Netherlands, Russia and France. Such treatment makes the film something more than just a story of Norway's struggle against Nazi oppression.

The story is the thing here and the way it's treated on casting, direction, sound and production justifies 20th-Fox investment of $300,000 for the basic film rights. Though lacking names that mean much to film-goers, casting for every role is socko from Sir Cedric Hardwicke down to the bit appearance by Dorothy Peterson.

The propaganda content is the perfect type because it's the sort that is believed. Propagandistic angle always is intelligently treated. The film gains strength by showing the Nazi officers as doubting Hitler's invincibility, some even longing to return home. Further it gains weight by focusing interest in three characters—the widow Molly Morden, Col. Lanser and Mayor Orden.

Story of Norway's invasion and resulting undercover uprising is familiar. Here it becomes the fight of inhabitants to survive in all conquered lands. There's the punishing of obdurate citizens, the executions to halt sabotage and dropping of dynamite by 'chute to help this program with blasting of rail lines, bridges, radio, etc., finally bringing the mass hanging of top village officials. Hanging, which is Quisling Corell's idea, brings skeptical retort from Col. Lanser who says that each execution produces 10 vengeful enemies that must be dealt with later. More disbelief is expressed by the home-loving Lieut. Tonder when he laughingly tells fellow officers how he dreamed Hitler was crazy.

Irving Pichel's superb direction never loses its vitality or pace. Nicety for detail is evident where the German bandleader halts directing his outfit to write in word 'still' on the Nazi theme song, 'We're Sailing Against England.' It is evident, too, when the town mayor slips on way to gallows and he thanks the Nazi guard who helps him up. Another is when the young Molly admits Lieut. Tonder into her bedroom and the audience indirectly knows he has been knifed to death.

Hardwicke, doing a tough assignment as Lanser, the Nazi colonel in the village, is admirable. A stickler for military detail, as portrayed, film shows him as a disbeliever in all Nazi methods—a man who knows from World War I experience that terroristic methods accomplish little. Dorris Bowden, young mother from 'Grapes of Wrath,' plays the chief femme role though widowed early by Nazi firing squad. Her scene with the Lieut. Tonder, when she admits loneliness, is super-fine. Henry Travers makes his role of town mayor an actuality, while Margaret Wycherly is excellent as his wife, a lesser role.

Exact opposite of the Nazi colonel is Henry Rowland's brutal German captain. Peter Van Eyck, as Lieut. Tonder, is another deft casting job. E. J. Ballantine, from original Broadway stage play, makes the quisling Corell as despicable as in the legiter. Lee J. Cobb is the likeable doctor. Director Pichel also plays an innkeeper bit in the dramatic snub scene when all village celebrants leave soon after the arrival of the Nazi lieutenant, and proves he's still a polished screen performer.

Nunnally Johnson's adaptation and all-round production is tops. Louis Loeffler's editing and Arthur Miller's photography measure up to the high-class vehicle. Novel use of sound on the introductory titles is the best way this medium has been employed in years. Production crew has cashed in on all means to make sound, standout all through film, accentuate plot. For each execution, there is typical Nazi drum-beating, while for each festive occasion is the playing of 'We're Sailing.'

Wear.

Hello, Frisco, Hello
(Technicolor)
(MUSICAL)

20th-Fox release of Milton Sperling production. Stars Alice Faye, John Payne, Jack Oakie, June Havoc; features Lynn Bari, Laird Cregar. Directed by Bruce Humberstone. Screenplay by Robert Ellis, Helen Logan, Richard Macauley; camera, Charles Clarke, Allen Davey; editor, Barbara McLean; dances, Hermes Pan, Val Raset; technicolor director, Natalie Kalmus; special effects, Fred Sersen. Tradeshown in N. Y. March 8, '43. Running time, 98 MINS.

Trudy Evans....................Alice Faye
Johnny Cornell....................John Payne
Dan Daley....................Jack Oakie
Bernice Croft....................Lynn Bari
Sam Weaver....................Laird Cregar
Beulah Clancy....................June Havoc
Sharkey....................Ward Bond
Charles Cochran....................Aubrey Mather
Ned Clark....................John Archer
Lou....................Frank Orth
Proprietor....................George Lloyd
Missionary....................Frank Darien
Burkham....................Harry Hayden
Foreman....................Eddie Dunn
O'Riley....................Charles Cane
Auctioneer....................Frank Thomas
Specialty Singer....................Kirby Grant
Cockney Maid....................Mary Field

20th-Fox has come up with another moneymaking musical. 'Hello, Frisco, Hello' looks stout enough to repeat the successes scored by such tunepix as 'Tin Pan Alley' and 'Springtime in the Rockies.' It follows the general formula, and deftly, of 'Tin Pan' and 'Alexander's Ragtime Band.' Having Alice Faye, Jack Oakie and John Payne, who also had leads in the former, it possesses plenty of marquee lustre. Nostalgic nature of much of music also should prove an added asset. Picture shapes as a big grosser, in larger keys as well as smaller houses, and good for extended dates.

Per usual the typical musical comedy plot is no great shakes, but nicely studded with laughs, pathos and innumerable musical interludes. Laid in San Francisco at the turn of the century when, as the story has it, men were still prospecting for gold nearby, story spots John Payne as the leader of a foursome that includes Alice Faye, Jack Oakie and June Havoc. It's a typical tavern combo that leans on their warbling to keep a regular job in the metropolis' leading saloon.

Rise of quartet, with Payne as business man and showman, is phenomenal until all four are rolling in coin. The yen of Payne to make the grade in Nob Hill society brings the usual complications, he finally marrying a socialite when she becomes broke and he enormously wealthy. His former sweetheart, Alice Faye, makes a success as singer in London musical comedy. And, of course, stakes him to another whirl in the Frisco cabaret business, unknown to him, with the customary payoff.

Into this rather incongruous fable are injected many hit songs of older days, such as 'Hello, Frisco, Hello,' 'Strike Up the Band, Here Comes a Sailor,' 'I Got a Gal in Every Port,' 'They Always Pick On Me,' 'Tulip Time in Holland,' 'Bedelia,' 'Sweet Cider Time,' 'The Grizzly Bear,' 'Has Anybody Here Seen Kelly,' 'Gee, It's Great to Meet a Friend,' and 'By the Light of the Silvery Moon.' Last named, the tune Miss Faye uses in the London stage debut, is given unusually handsome backgrounding and sold as an outstanding song.

'Tulip Time' is given a big lift via a roller-skating ballet and vocal chorus. 'You'll Never Know,' a Mack Gordon-Harry Warren new composition that is lilting enough to catch on, is the key song employed by Miss Faye in her romantic scenes. It runs through the whole film, even topping 'Frisco,' title number, in prominence.

Like other 20th-Fox's recent musicals, the color in this one is superb. The sound also is significant through its entirety and vital to such type production. Bruce Humberstone has handled the variegated scenes with keen directional sense, inserting plenty of comedy to balance the more dramatic episodes. Milton Sperling, now in the U. S. Marines, has done a forthright job on production, down to all authentic detail. One wonders, however, how the street mission band in Frisco of that era turned up as an augmented orchestra just for Payne's asking.

Alice Faye, who has the task of selling the vast majority of tunes, is a revelation in this film. She's far ahead of recent screen efforts and very capable in the romantic scenes opposite Payne. Payne makes a sufficiently zestful business manager for the quartet, though one wonders why he falls so hopelessly for Lynn Bari, the Nob Hill socialite. Jack Oakie, as the happy-go-lucky hoofer, and his partner, June Havoc, make sufficient contrast as the other half of the foursome. Oakie also cashes in on some tricky tap dances and his usual mugging. All four fit nicely in their song-dance routines.

Lynn Bari is the haughty gal who falls for Payne only when she loses her father's millions. A happy casting. Laird Cregar, disguised in a heavy beard, has little more than a bit as the heavy-drinking prospector who's always trying to get a new stake from Payne. Support is high-grade and chorus numbers are smartly staged. *Wear.*

Assignment in Brittany

Metro release of J. Walter Ruben production. Features Pierre Aumont, Susan Peters. Directed by Jack Conway. Screenplay, Anthony Veiller, William H. Wright, Howard Emmett Rogers, from Helen MacInnes novel of same title; camera, Charles Rosher; special effects, Arnold Gillespie; score, Lennie Hayton; editor, Frank Sullivan. Reviewed in projection room, N. Y., March 4, '43. Running time, **94 MINS.**

Capt. Metard / Bertrand Conlay....................Pierre Aumont
Anne Pinot....................Susan Peters
Kerenor....................Richard Whorf
Mme. Corlay....................Margaret Wycherly
Elise....................Signe Hasso
Col. Trane....................Reginald Owen
Capt. Deichgraper....................John Emery
Capt. Holz....................George Coulouris
Albertine....................Sarah Padden
Col. Fournier....................Miles Mander
Henri....................George Brest
Etienne....................Darryl Hickman

A tipoff on Metro's 'Assignment in Brittany,' adapted from the Helen MacInnes best-seller of the same name, is that it should help establish several of its actors at the boxoffice. Pierre Aumont, the French import, gets an advantageous intro to U. S. audiences, while Susan Peters, Richard Whorf, Margaret Wycherly and George Coulouris have juicy parts and give performances that will enhance their standing. And as usually is the case when there are a number of showy acting roles, the picture is a solid click.

Several time-tested story devices are effectively combined in 'Assignment.' There's the angle of having the hero impersonate someone else, even to the extent of making love to the original's sweetheart. There's strong use of the chase technique and, as modern touches, there are illustrations of Nazi terrorism and the underground movement in the occupied countries. Finally, there is a blazing cliff-hanger finish worthy of western hoss-operas, with the hero and heroine together as the sound track roars 'the Marseillaise.'

As readers of the MacInnes novel will recall, the hero, played by Aumont, is sent to Brittany to pose as a wounded, captured Frenchman, whom he remarkably resembles and whom the English suspect as a Quisling. The early scenes, as the situation and characters are established, are quiet, with touches of sinister mystery and a gradually developing suspense. But once the action gets under way, the yarn becomes taut with interest and the excitement increases to a terrific pitch at the climax. This final scene, in which a Commando raid wrecks a secret U-boat base on the Brittany coast, is magnificency produced with process stuff and mob action.

In the dual part of the hero and collaborationist, Pierre Aumont is a distinct hit. He's good looking enough to suit the femmes, somewhat resembling Paul Henried and the late Phillips Holmes, and he underplays agreeably. Susan Peters, who drew attention as the ingenue in 'Random Harvest,' has a bigger part in 'Assignment' and turns in a fuller, more effective performance. Her resemblance to Judy Garland probably won't help her pictures and she still hasn't had a testing part, but she continues to show definite promise.

Richard Whorf, as a crippled French patriot; Margaret Whycherly, as the traitor's mother; Signe Hasso, as a pretty, two-timing Fifth Columnist; Reginald Owen, as a British intelligence officer, and John Emery, as a soft-spoken Nazi, are generally effective in varyingly colorful roles, while George Coulouris deftly skims the edge of overacting at a diabolical Gestapo officer. The production, direction, photography and editing are expertly done, and the special effects are notable.

With so many memorable assets, 'Assignment in Brittany' can hardly fail to capitalize on its book rep for a boxoffice cleanup. *Hobe.*

HIT PARADE OF 1943
(MUSICAL)

Republic release of Albert J. Cohen production. Stars John Carroll, Susan Hayward; features Gail Patrick, Eve Arden, Melville Cooper, Walter Catlett, Mary Treen, Freddy Martin, Count Basie and Ray McKinley bands. Directed by Albert S. Rogell. Original, Frank Gill, Jr.; additional dialog, Frances Hyland; camera, Jack Marta; editor, Thomas Richards; songs, Jule Styne and Harold Adamson, J. C. Johnson and Andy Razaf; orchestrations Marlin Skiles; dances, Nick Castle; music director, Walter Scharf. Previewed March 5, '43. Running time, **90 MINS.**

Rick Farrell....................John Carroll
Jill Wright....................Susan Hayward
Toni Jarrett....................Gail Patrick
Belinda Wright....................Eve Arden
Bradley Cole....................Melville Cooper
J. MacClellan Davis....................Walter Catlett
Janie....................Mary Treen
Westinghouse....................Tom Kennedy
Joyce....................Astrid Allwyn
Brownie....................Tim Ryan
Jack Williams, the Harlem Sandman
Dorothy Dandridge
Pops & Louie
Music Maids
3 Cheers
Chinita
Golden Gate Quartet
Freddy Martin and Orchestra
Count Basie and Orchestra
Ray McKinley and Orchestra

Republic has itself a hit picture in 'Hit Parade of 1943.' Filmusical will do very hefty business and will further Rep's rep as the major league independent. The strides made by this company with its 'Flying Tigers,' a sock grosser last fall, are further progressed by 'Hit Parade.'

Film blends some pretty good picture names—John Carroll, Susan Hayward, Gail Patrick and Eve Arden—with three w.k. bands, maestroed by Freddy Martin, Count Basie and Ray McKinley, plus an assortment of socko Harlem talent. The sum total is a pleasing 90-minute package for anybody's theatre.

Republic, with its current 'Hit Parade,' incidentally, takes its place with another surprise industry grosser, 'Hitler's Children' (Eddie Golden-RKO) in proving that it requires no super-duper investment to boff the boxoffice with the same impact and for the same gross revenue—and more—if there is judicious and astute showmanship in what is being sold.

Here's a little musical which is 'little' only compared to some of the majors' past gargantuan efforts, but which actually blends a fetching set of songs, a wealth of variety talent, mostly colored, to a fair story, and it comes up very lovely for the b.o.

The cast names aren't breath-taking as some of the others stabled in the major league studios, but from Al Cohen's production and Al Rogell's direction to the dance-staging and songsmithing it's a very satisfying confection indeed.

The plot is also-ran so far as filmusical librettos are concerned, but it's no worse, and in some respects better, than many another musical comedy book.

You may get captious with the idea of making a thieving songwriter your hero, which is what John Carroll personates, but thus is Susan Hayward, talented young tunesmith, thrown together with him. In fact, the characterization of Rick Farrell, who even continues to let Miss Hayward ghost his songs, is never wholly palatable, but Carroll's personal charm glorifies the double-crossing, two-timing lothario of Lindy's into a model swain in time for the fadeout.

Gail Patrick is the light heavy whom Carroll double-crosses, she in turn giving Melville Cooper the business. Cooper is the Ziegfeld of the bistros, a somewhat unbelievable sap for Miss Patrick, and unbelievable also in that his niteries seemingly put on floorshows which outdo Lew Walters and Clifford C. Fischer in their pretentiousness. In fact, they're Ringling-type shows, not cafe revues.

But that's now accepted as a minor detail, in the interests of the basic entertainment. Thus, his cafes showcase the new tunes 'written' by Carroll, who also sings them. The 'Tahm-Boom-Bah' number touches off the expose by Miss Hayward, who had submitted it under another title to the plagiaristic hero.

The songs, seven of 'em, are all solid and all will register. Jule Styne and Harold Adamson wrote six, 'Do These Old Eyes Deceive Me?' 'Who Took Me Home Last Night?' 'A Change of Heart,' 'Harlem Sandman,' 'That's How to Write a Song,' and 'Tahm-Boom-Bah'; Andy Razaf and J. C. Johnson fashioned 'Yankee Doodle Tan,' which the Golden Gate quartet does as a patriotic specialty.

Nick Castle's dance-staging is clicky. For 'Tah-Boom' he does a drum sequence that's excellent, wherein Chinita does her terp specialty, with Ray McKinley at the traps of his band. Count Basie, with the personable Dorothy Dandridge, from the Harlem niteries, is in the 'Harlem Sandman' routine, headed by Jack Williams, the Harlem Sandman, and with Pops & Louie boffing over with their legmania.

Freddy Martin's band dominates in the rest, building up to 'Change of Heart.' In between the Music Maids, the 3 Cheers and Golden Gaters do their stuff.

Carroll does a fine job as the juve lead, foiled by Walter Catlett as his music publishing partner. Miss Hayward registers as the not so naive ingenue, who knows how to handle herself in the clinches. (A 'wolfing' sequence in his apartment, with cutouts uttering the inner voices of **both Miss Hayward and Carroll, makes for some good fun, as director Rogell has handled it). Eve Arden dominates with her brilliant handling of some good and brittle lines accorded her, and Miss Patrick is effective as the sophisticate.**

Abel.

HARRIGAN'S KID

Metro release of Irving Starr production. Features William Gargan, Frank Craven, Bobby Readick. Directed by Charles F. Riesner. Screenplay, Alan Friedman and Martin Berkeley; adaptation, Henry Blankfolt, based on story by Borden Chase; camera, Walter Lundin; music, Daniele Amfitheatrof; editor, Ferris Webster. Previewed in projection room, N. Y., March 5, '43. Running time, **80 MINS.**

Benny McNeil....................Bobby Readick
Mr. Garnet....................Frank Craven
Tom Harrigan....................William Gargan
Jed Jerrett....................J. Carrol Naish
McNamara....................Jay Ward
'Skip'....................Douglas Croft
Joe....................Bill Cartledge
Dink....................Irving Lee
Mr. Ranley....................Selmer Jackson
Etley....................Allen Wood
Sam....................Jim Toney
Jockey....................Mickey Martin
Col. Lowry....................Russell Hicks

A modestly budgeted 'B,' 'Harrigans Kid' should do considerably better than break even. It's a turf yarn, and because there are so few of that type being produced these days it should click for that reason and also because of its general excellence by 'B' standards. It's strictly for the duals, of course, and its lone unfavorable factor lies in the dearth of names for the marquee.

If anything, Metro has come up

with what may well become a find in Bobby Readick, a youngster who's given to overacting a bit right now, but who should, with proper handling, emerge as a performer at least approaching stellar standards. Young Readick here plays a young jockey geared for crooked riding by his mentor, a former outstanding saddler who had been ruled off the tracks. The story isn't much, being mainly concerned with the ultimate switch by the latter in encouraging his young charge, just before the big race, to play it straight.

Gargan, albeit looking much too heavy for even the most remote conception of his former jockeyship, gives his usually dependable performance, while Frank Craven, as the trainer who gives Readick a chance, is also top-drawer in performance. *Kahn.*

DIXIE DUGAN

Hollywood, March 8.

20th-Fox release of Walter Morosco production. Features James Ellison, Charlotte Greenwood, Charlie Ruggles, Lois Andrews. Directed by Otto Brower. Screenplay by Lee Loeb and Harold Buchman; based on Joseph P. McEvoy character; camera, Peverell Marley; editor, J. Watson Webb. Tradeshown March 8, '43. Running time, **63 MINS.**

Roger Hudson..................James Ellison
Mrs. Dugan..........Charlotte Greenwood
Pa Dugan....................Charlie Ruggles
Dixie Dugan..................Lois Andrews
Jean Patterson............Helene Reynolds
J. J. Lawson...........Raymond Walburn
Imogene Dugan...................Ann Todd
Matt Hogan..................Eddie Foy, Jr.
Mr. Kelly........................Irving Bacon
Mrs. Kelly....................Sarah Edwards
Mr. Sloan.....................George Melford
Mrs. Sloan.........................Mae Marsh
Editor..........................Morris Ankrum
Phillips..........................Dick French
Senator Patterson..........George Lessey
Sign Painter......................Paul Burns
Sergeant's Wife..............Ruth Warren
Policeman.......................Eddie Dunn
Pressmen ....Milt Kibbee / Bily Wayne
Postman...............Clarence Hennecke
F.B.I. Man.........................Sam Wren
Burns............................Ray Walker
Artist...............................Jack Chefe
Copy Boy..........................Dick Baron
Secretary......................Byron Foulger
Announcer.........................John Wald
Salesman.....................Emmett Vogan
Night Porter..................Sam McDaniel

Lois Andrews, former wife of George Jessel, is 'introduced' by studio in this one but the introduction is far from impressive. Same goes for the basic story—with result that picture is a rather bumpy and dull affair that will have to garner datings as dual filler.

Story attempts to satirize present living conditions and operation of Government agencies in Washington, but is generally more ridiculous than humorous. Miss Andrews gets a secretary job with James Ellson, a Government bureau head, and in order to get rid of her he puts her to making a public survey. Latter turns out to be sensational, after girl forces Ellison to get it out of pigeonhole and digest it.

Intermixed is a romance between Miss Andrews and Eddie Foy, Jr., and one of Ellison and Helene Reynolds; in addition to plenty of footage on screwball family of Miss Andrews, with Charlotte Greenwood and Charlie Ruggles cast as the parents. Cast members find inadequate script and static direction too great a handicap to overcome for more than walking through lines and display of broad characterizations. *Walt.*

Rhythm of the Islands

(MUSICAL)

Hollywood, March 5.

Universal release of Bernard Burton production. Stars Allan Jones, Jane Frazee, Andy Devine. Directed by Roy William Neill. Screenplay by Oscar Brodney and M. M. Musselman; original by Brodney; camera, George Robinson; editor, Paul Landres; asst. director, Melville Shyer; musical director, Charles Previn; songs, Dave Franklin, Louis Herscher-Andy Iona, Inez James-Buddy Pepper-Frank Skinner. Previewed at studio March 4, '43. Running time, **60 MINS.**

Tommy..........................Allan Jones
Joan Holton.....................Jane Frazee
Eddie Dolan....................Andy Devine
Mr. Holton....................Ernest Truex
Mrs. Holton...............Marjorie Gateson
Susie Dugan....................Mary Wickes
Luani ....Acquanetta
Chief Nataro....................Nestor Paiva
Martin...........................John Maxwell
Abercrombie...............Maceo Anderson
The Step-Brothers
The Horton Dancers

Another in Universal's series of program filmusicals, 'Rhythm of the Islands' acceptably fulfills its purpose of providing an hour's diverting footage for dual support in the general runs.

There's no attempt to be serious, and yarn unfolds with tongue-in-cheek attitude towards previous South Sea Island romantic numbers. It's a slight framework for story background, but sufficient on which to hang the several songs and periodic laugh lines.

Specific island is synthetic setup for tourists, with Allan Jones posing as native chief, and Andy Devine as a beachcomber. In regulation coconut and palm-tree setting, pair try to unload purchase contract of the isle, and wind up peddling it to millionaire Ernest Truex, while latter's daughter, Jane Frazee, falls in love with synthetic chieftain Jones. Yarn is spun deliberately on diverting tempo, and carries unpretentious mounting.

Jones and Miss Frazee team up for the romantic interludes, while Andy Devine dashes off moderate potions of comedy with elongated Mary Wickes. Adequate support is provided by Truex, Marjorie Gateson, Acquanetta and John Maxwell, while the Step Bros., dance trio, and Horton Dancers are on briefly for specialty numbers.

Total of five songs and unreeled, with Jones handling them with good delivery. Best seems to be 'I've Set My Mind On You,' a romantic tune with good rhythm. Direction is okay. *Walt.*

HE HIRED THE BOSS

Hollywood, March 8.

20th-Fox release of Sol M. Wurtzel production. Features Stuart Erwin, Evelyn Venable. Directed by Thomas Z. Loring. Screenplay by Ben Markson and Irving Cummings, Jr.; based on a story by Peter B. Kyne; camera, Glen MacWilliams; editor, Louis Loeffler. Tradeshown March 8, '43. Running time, **72 MINS.**

Hubert Wilkins...............Stuart Erwin
Emily Conway..............Evelyn Venable
Mr. Bates.....................Thurston Hall
Sally Conway..................Vivian Blaine
Don Bates....................William T. Orr
Jimmy.........................Bennie Bartlett
Clark...............................James Bush
Fuller.........................Chick Chandler
Jordan........................Hugh Beaumont
Stokes...............................Ken Christy
Mason..............Robert Emmett Keane
Hank........................Harold Goodwin
Driver...............................Eddie Acuff
Butler........................Charles Coleman
Mailman...............................Syd Saylor
Perry..........................Emmett Vogan
Carter...............................Ralph Dunn

This remake of '$10 Raise,' originally turned out seven years ago, is a decidedly synthetic tale of a timid milquetoaster who finally turns into an aggressive individual in the final half reel. Low marquee voltage and other factors drop this to dual support spot.

Peter B. Kyne's original tale has been modernized, bringing it up to current date with indirect war motivation sprinkled along the way. Stuart Erwin is a methodical bookkeeper for importer Thurston Hall, waiting for a $10 raise to marry stenographer Evelyn Venable. Latter takes initiative in romance but Erwin gets army induction notice, fails final physical and returns for old job, getting a lower post from blustering Hall. Latter finds difficulty in paying a bank loan, while Erwin assumes the lots from a breezy salesman who defaulted in personal debt. Property turns out to be coin bonanza, with Erwin taking over firm by paying debts with proceeds—and he hires his boss to run the layout.

Script drags in a gang of silk thieves hijacking stocks from firm's warehouse, giving Erwin chance for actionful climax. Picture has several mild laugh moments, but on the whole hits moderate gait that holds it to regulation dual programmer category.

Director Thomas Z. Loring did the best he could with the material at hand and same applies to cast. Erwin, in portraying timid plodder, does okay, and Miss Venable marks her screen return in satisfactory fashion.

Ridin' Down the Canyon

(SONGS)

Republic release of Harry Gray production. Stars Roy Rogers and George 'Gabby' Hayes; features Bob Nolan and Sons of Pioneers, Dee 'Buzzy' Henry, Linda Hayes, Addison Richards and Lorna Gray. Directed by Joseph Kane. Story, Robert Williams and Norman Houston; adaptation, Albert DeMond; songs, Tim Spencer and Bob Nolan; editor, Edward Mann; camera, Jack Marta. At New York, N. Y., half dual bill, week March 2, '43. Running time, **55 MINS.**

Roy...............................Roy Rogers
'Gabby'..............George 'Gabby' Hayes
Themselves........Bob Nolan and the Sons of the Pioneers
Bobbie Blake...........Dee (Buzzy) Henry
Alice Blake.....................Linda Hayes
Jordan.....................Addison Richards
Barbara Joyce....................Lorna Gray
Jailer................................Olin Howlin
Burt Wooster......................James Seay
Pete...........................Hal Taliaferro
Jim Fellowes................Forrest Taylor
Lafe Collins.....................Roy Barcroft

With rustlers hard to avoid in westerns, 'Ridin' Down the Canyon,' another in the Roy Rogers series, gives it a bit of a twist by using horses instead of cattle as prey of the badmen. The result is only fair since the story lacks strength, but an offset is a lot of excellent dialog, principally for comedy purposes. This and the performances save the picture from being considerably below average.

Plot concerns a well-organized gang of rustlers posing as respectable citizens, who plunder ranchers of the wild horses they have rounded up for sale to the Government for wartime uses. Leader is the operator of a dude ranch, which serves as setting for one of the songs done by Rogers, Bob Nolan and the Sons of the Pioneers choral group. It is 'Blue Prairie,' by Tim Spencer and Nolan, a good tune. Others, both by Spencer, are 'Sagebrush Symphony' and 'Curley Joe,' last-mentioned a novelty number of merit.

Love interest, tied to Rogers and Linda Hayes, is on the light side. A fine kid actor, Dee 'Buzzy' Henry, who speaks and screens well, figures rather prominently.

George 'Gabby' Hayes shoulders most of the comedy, doing very well, especially in view of the snappy laugh lines handed him. Others in the cast include Addison Richards, Lorna Gray, Olin Howlin and James Seay, all of whom acquit themselves creditably. *Char.*

NIGHT FOR CRIME

Producers Releasing Corp. release of Lester Cutler production. Stars Glenda Farrell, Lyle Talbot; features Lina Basquette, Donald Kirke, Ralph Sanford, Forrest Taylor, Lynn Starr, Marjorie Manners. Directed by Alexis Thurn-Taxis. Story, Jimmy Starr; adaptation, Arthur St. Claire and Sherman Lowe; editor, Fred Bain; camera, Marcel Le Picard. At New York, N. Y., half dual bill week March 2, '43. Running time, **75 MINS.**

Susan..........................Glenda Farrell
Joe...................................Lyle Talbot
Mona.........................Lina Basquette
Hart............................Donald Kirke
Hoffman......................Ralph Sanford
Williams.....................Forrest Taylor
Carol..................................Lynn Starr
Arthur..............................Ricki Vallin
Telephone Operator...........Edna Harris
Ellen Smith..............Marjorie Manners

Tedious murder melodrama localed in Hollywood, this one could have been edited to about 60 minutes, but it still would probably have been slow. Boxoffice potentialities appear slender.

Story, an original by Jimmy Starr, Hollywood columnist, is a detailed and complicated one involving the murder of a film extra and the disappearance of a star in the middle of a picture's production. Others concerned include the production head of a studio, who recovers love letters that are endangering him; his publicity director, a Hollywood newspaper gal and local police.

Glenda Farrell and Lyle Talbot are paired above the title but vainly struggle with the action and the dialog. This is also true of others except that Ralph Sanford, as a dumb cop, gets along nicely and manages to produce some laughs.

Lina Basquette, of the old silent days, plays the film siren who disappears and is ultimately found dead, while Donald Kirke wrestles with the assignment of studio boss. Lessers include Forrest Taylor, police official; Lynn Starr, film player, and Marjorie Manners, extra who is strangled in the first reel. Routine performances are given by all.

Starr and three other Hollywood columnists appear in a brief inquest sequence, others being Erskine Johnson, Edwin Schallert and Harry Crocker.

Production of Lester Cutler is generally shoddy and the direction of Alexis Thurn-Taxis uninspired. *Char.*

Miniature Reviews

'This Land Is Mine' (RKO). Sincere, absorbing and generally moving war drama; should draw profitable business.

'It Ain't Hay' (U). (Songs.) Typical Abbott and Costello comedy built for laugh purposes and aimed for usual socko biz.

'The Heart of a Nation' (Graetz) (in French; English subtitles). French-made pic with names nifty for arty houses.

'The Desperadoes' (Col). (Color.) Regulation western meller in Technicolor okay for regular runs.

'Ladies Day' (RKO). Baseball comedy helped by Lupe Velez and bright direction; nice dual support.

'The Ape Man' (Mono). Weak Bela Lugosi chiller.

'Dead Man's Gulch' (Republic). Good Don Barry western.

'He's My Guy' (U) (songs). Lightweight romance concerning vaudevillians.

'The Falcon Strikes Back' (RKO). Lively whodunit. Will be neat dual support.

'Hoppy Serves a Writ' (UA). Fast western entry in the Hopalong Cassidy series.

'Tomorrow We Live' (Lion). Nazi occupation of France looms as strong British entry, aided by all-English cast.

'Buckskin Frontier' (UA). Better - than - average western with Richard Dix and Jane Wyatt.

'I Walked With a Zombie' (RKO). Voodooism plot suited for lower half of dualers.

'The Kid Rides Again' (PRC). Western along familiar lines.

THIS LAND IS MINE

RKO release of Jean Renoir-Dudley Nichols production. Stars Charles Laughton, Maureen O'Hara; features George Sanders, Walter Slezak, Kent Smith, Una O'Connor, Philip Merrivale, Thurston Hall, George Coulouris, Nancy Gates, Ivan Simpson, John Donat. Directed by Jean Renoir. Screenplay, Dudley Nichols; music, Lothar Perl; musical director, C. Bakaleinikoff; dialog director, Leo Bulgakov; camera, Frank Redman; editor, Frederic Knudtson. Reviewed in projection room, N. Y., March 12, '43. Running time, **103 MINS.**

Albert Lory....................Charles Laughton
Louise Martin....................Maureen O'Hara
George Lambert....................George Sanders
Major Von Keller....................Walter Slezak
Paul Martin....................Kent Smith
Mrs. Emma Lory....................Una O'Connor
Prof. Sorel....................Philip Merivale
Mayor....................Thurston Hall
Prosecutor....................George Coulouris
Julie Grant....................Nancy Gates
Judge....................Ivan Simpson
Edmund Lorraine....................John Donat
Lt. Schwartz....................Frank Alten
Little Man....................Leo Bulgakov
Mr. Lorraine....................Wheaton Chambers
Mrs. Lorraine....................Cecil Weston

There are bound to be a number of questions arising out of pictures such as 'This Land Is Mine.' However, it seems likely that this film, at least, should do profitable business.

A propaganda drama about civil resistance and sabotage in occupied France, 'This Land' bears certain inevitable resemblances to various other films of similar subject matter, such as the forthcoming 'The Moon Is Down' (20th), 'Assignment in Brittany' (M-G), 'The Hangman' (M-G), and 'The Hangman Also Died' (UA). Whether the story likenesses will result in diminishing boxoffice returns remains to be seen. And if so, whether the propaganda value of such pictures is sufficient to justify their possibly decreasing draw is also a moot point. It is probably a fact that in wartime, even more than normally, the public likes escapist entertainment (if that term itself isn't redundant), particularly romantic comedies and musicals.

Turned out by the ace director-writer combination of Jean Renoir and Dudley Nichols, 'This Land' is a steadily engrossing film based on the inner drama of character rather than the exciting physical action of some of the recent war films. Its theme is the invincibility of ideas over brute force, and its story is of how circumstances and the realization of responsibility turn a craven weakling into a heroic champion of freedom. That is epic subject matter and it is given sincere, dignified and eloquent treatment.

Not that the picture is by any means perfect. Some of its incidents tax belief, and the presentation at times is ultra-obvious, possibly to clarify the meaning for the broadest possible audience. Similarly, although such scenes as Charles Laughton's courtroom espousal of the cause of patriotism, civil disobedience and even of sabotage, or his defiant schoolroom reading of 'The Rights of Man,' are suspiciously theatrical, the speeches themselves are magnificent.

One plausible aspect of the story is that the Nazis and the French collaborationists are understandably, if not sympathetically, motivated. Thus, the German officer in command of the town, like the much-disputed Colonel character in 'The Moon Is Down,' is a philosophical and highly literate man who realizes that the terroristic methods he is forced to use are doomed to defeat themselves by aggravating the violence they're supposed to quell. Similarly, the collaborationist mayor is shown as trying to save his townsmen, if incidentally himself. And the traitorous railroad executive, who betrays the saboteur, kills himself when faced with his own shame.

As usual when a picture has such compulsion and distinction, the individual roles are rewarding and the performances impressive. As the blubbering coward who rises to heroism in a crisis, Charles Laughton gives a shrewdly conceived and developed portrayal, although he occasionally mugs a bit. Maureen O'Hara is believably intense as the lovely, tragic patriot school teacher.

George Sanders properly projects the mental turmoil of the traitorous informer, while Walter Slezak turns in an acting gem in the rich role of the Nazi major. Kent Smith, as the saboteur; Una O'Connor, as a fatally-doting mother; Philip Merivale, as a martyr schoolmaster; Thurston Hall, as the mayor, and George Coulouris, as the prosecutor, also score in principal supporting parts, while Nancy Gates, Ivan Simpson and John Donat register in character bits.

A notable aspect of the film is that there is no attempt to suggest the French or German language. Most of the players speak in their normal accents, and such things as the outlaw newspapers, street signs, etc., are printed in English. That is justifiable and sane theatrical license. However, some of the physical production is manifestly artificial, possibly due to Government limitations on set construction. *Hobe.*

IT AIN'T HAY

(SONGS)

Hollywood, March 12.

Universal release of Alex Gottlieb production. Stars Bud Abbott and Lou Costello. Directed by Erle C. Kenton; screenplay by Allen Boretz and John Grant; based on story, 'Princess O'Hara,' by Damon Runyon; words and music by Harry Revel and Paul Francis Webster; camera, Charles Van Enger; film editor, Frank Gross. Previewed at Pantages, March 11, '43. Running time, **79 MINS.**

Grover....................Bud Abbott
Wilbur Hoolihan....................Lou Costello
Kitty McCloin....................Grace McDonald
King O'Hara....................Cecil Kellaway
Gregory Warner....................Eugene Pallette
Peggy, Princess O'Hara...Patsy O'Connor
Private Joe Collins....................Leighton Noble
Umbrella Sam....................Shemp Howard
Colonel Brainard....................Samuel S. Hinds
Harry the Horse....................Eddie Quillan
Slicker....................Richard Lane
Chauncey the Eye....................David Hacker
Big Hearted Charlie....................Andrew Tombes
Major Harper....................Pierre Watkin
Banker....................William Forrest
Reilly....................Wade Boteler
Grant....................Selmer Jackson

and
The Vagabonds
The Hollywood Blondes
Step Brothers

Bud Abbott and Lou Costello again parade their broadly-burlesqued and zany antics in this very slight adaptation of Damon Runyon's story, 'Princess O'Hara.' Comics, displaying their regular and familiar cinematic activities, dominate the proceedings throughout—with exception of a few songs. But the team of A. & C. will make ticket vending machines jingle merrily for smacking biz in all bookings.

Costello, driving a dilapidated taxi, endeavors to get a horse for hack of Cecil Kellaway. Tipped off there's a nag ready for carting away at Empire racetrack, comics grab one—but it's a champ race. Kellaway drives a fare to Saratoga, with chase to the spa and eventual big race in which Costello jockeys around the track. After plenty of absurd and screwball happenings, horse is returned to its owner and everybody's happy.

Script is studded with laugh routines by A. & C. Grace McDonald and Leighton Noble carry the slight romantic thread, while little Patsy O'Connor is prominently spotted in the early reels, and then shunted to the background. Eugene Pallette, an efficiency expert continually crossing the path of the comedians; Runyonesque trio of Shemp Howard, Eddie Quillan and David Hacker, and Kellaway, are most prominent in support.

Four songs by Harry Revel and Paul Webster are neatly spotted, with 'Sunbeam Serenade' and 'Hang Your Troubles on a Rainbow' best of the quartette. Patsy O'Connor sings two of the tunes, with Grace McDonald and Noble teaming up for a third number, and the other is used for finale production ensemble. Specialties by The Vagabonds, The Hollywood Blondes, and Step Brothers are briefly displayed along the route.

Direction by Erle Kenton unfolds at a lively pace, spotlighting the Abbott and Costello routines for maximum audience reaction. Script lacks smoothness of pace, but suitable for talents of the comedians. *Walt.*

HEART OF A NATION

(FRENCH MADE)

Produced and released by Paul Graetz. Stars Michele Morgan and Raimu; features Louis Jouvet, Suzy Prim and Lucien Nat. Commentator, Charles Boyer. Directed by Julien Duvivier. English titles by Ted Strauss. Previewed in New York March 16, '43. Running time, **111 MINS.**

Pierre Froment }
Felix } ....Louis Jouvet
Jules Froment....................Raimu
Estelle....................Suzy Prim
Bernard....................Lucien Nat
Gabrielle....................Renee Devillers
Alain....................Jean Mercanton
Marie....................Michele Morgan
Robert Leonard....................Harry Krimer
Christian....................Pierre Jordan

(In French; English Subtitles)

'The Heart of a Nation' would be a solid grosser for the arty houses even if it did not offer unusual publicity-exploitation possibilities. But with the unique story it has behind it, this biography of a Paris family from the Franco-Prussian War (1871) to the World War II, may well find a niche with 'Grand Illusion,' 'Carnival in Flanders' and other such French product which has earned immortality in America's 250-seater 'cinemas.'

The film was completed in France just a few months before the Germans marched into Paris and was never released. The Nazis took one look at it and decreed it never should be. Negative and prints were at once destroyed. One fine grain lavender, however, remained and a refugee film man fleeing from Paris is reputed to have buried it along the road. Almost two years later he was able to get his secret into Nazi-dominated France and the lavender was delivered to him in bits and pieces in the unoccupied zone. From there it was another smuggling match with customs guards and, again in one and two-reel units, 'The Heart of a Nation' arrived in the U. S. The producer, Paul Graetz, had arrived in New York himself in the meantime.

Film is not only a sometimes delightful, sometimes touching, sometimes poignant yarn, but the first new picture to come from France in almost three years. And add to that a flock of names which have become rather well known here—Michele Morgan (now an RKO star), Raimu, Louis Jouvet, Suzy Prim and Julien Duvivier, the director. Graetz gave it still another hypo by having Charles Boyer appear in a prelude and do an intermittent English commentary. Ted Strauss, second-string film critic for the N. Y. Times, contributed the mediocre English titling job.

Boyer's overlong introduction, backed with well-worn Nazi newsreel footage of German troops, sets the theme of the film. It starts in 1871 with a Montmartre family suffering hunger and privation after Paris had been under a state of siege by the Germans for four months. The film skips 20 years to find the child of the Montmartre family, Bernard, on his wedding day. Bicycles have just become the rage and all concerned in the marriage ceremony participate while astride two-wheelers. More years pass and a rich and jolly uncle from Marseille (Raimu) appears to take Bernard and his wife to see the new and popular Can-Can at the Moulin Rouge. Then it's 1906 and Bernard's son, Alain, assists in an early airplane flight; 1914—War; 1918—and the husband of Alain's sister, Marie (Michele Morgan), returns minus an arm. Many scenes fill in until 1939 and the third call to arms for France, more suffering, and a final prayer after defeat (contrived by editing in this country) for ultimate victory.

The film is of necessity episodic and occasionally overlong. Likewise it is sometimes difficult to follow the intricate family relationships. But that is all minor compared to the greatness of the unbilled writers and of Duvivier's direction in getting at 'the heart of France.' By clever choice of scene and incident in the 70-year period, they have uniquely succeeded in capturing and in making understandable and likeable the character of the French people. What writers and commentators have been vainly trying to explain since 1940 suddenly comes clearly into focus on the screen—why the French preferred the Can-Can and weddings on bicycles to the goose-step and the Panzer division; why each war finds them just as unprepared as the last.

THE DESPERADOES

(IN COLOR)

Hollywood, March 11.

Columbia release of Harry Joe Brown production. Stars Randolph Scott, Glenn Ford, Claire Trevor, Evelyn Keyes, Edgar Buchanan; features Guinn Williams and Raymond Walburn. Directed by Charles Vidor; screenplay by Robert Carson; original story by Max Brand; camera, George Meehan; technicolor photography, Allen M. Davey; film editor, Gene Havlick. Previewed at Pantages, March 10, '43. Running time, **85 MINS.**

Steve Upton....................Randolph Scott
Cheyenne Rogers....................Glenn Ford
Countess Maletta....................Claire Trevor
Allison MacLeod....................Evelyn Keyes
Willie MacLeod....................Edgar Buchanan
Judge Cameron....................Raymond Walburn
Nitro Rankin....................Guinn Williams
Stanley Clanton....................Porter Hall
Sundown....................Joan Woodbury
Jack Lester....................Bernard Nedell

Dan Walters..................Irving Bacon
Lem........................Glenn Strange
Cass........................Ethan Laidlaw
Tolliver..................Charles Whittaker
Blackie.....................Edward Pawley
Rollo......................Chester Clute

In Technicolor mounting, and displaying some excellent exterior photography of the Utah district, 'The Desperadoes' dispenses the usual lusty and vigorous melodramatics of the early west. Despite the usual tenor of the tale, picture is good boxoffice of its type and will hit profitable biz in the regular runs as solo or billtopper.

This is the first color photography venture for Columbia, and the tinting lifts the picture from the ordinary program western class to status of topliner for the regular runs. Nothing new is injected into the story, which has been retold many times before in cinematic form. Randolph Scott is the sheriff of the Utah county in the 60's, when a bank robbery is staged, and shortly after Glenn Ford wanders into town. He's a former pal of Scott—also boyhood sweetheart of Claire Trevor, who's operating the town's hotel and gambling layout—and is a fugitive with heavy coin riding on his head. But romantic influence of Evelyn Keyes persuades him to go straight—he's convicted of the bank holdup; escapes with Scott's aid and then rides back to town to release the sheriff and get the real culprits to confess. He's on the straight path when Miss Keyes falls in his arms.

Characters are all hewn to regulation western type. Ford does well as the youth who's a prototype of Wild Bill Hickok. Scott ably portrays the two-gun and two-fisted sheriff; Miss Trevor is an eyeful glamour girl; and Guinn Williams a rather dumb outlaw pal of Ford. Miss Keyes handles romantic interest in good style, while Edgar Buchanan provides a spotlight characterization as the droll postmaster and background manipulator of the robberies and town underworld. Porter Hall, as the conniving banker; Bernard Nedell, as the bank robber, and Raymond Walburn, as the judge, are most prominent in support.

In addition to its regulation western dramatic elements, picture displays a good barroom fight, a spectacular wild horse stampede that is the visual highlight of the picture, and a roaring gunfight to add to the proceedings. Start of the wild horse stampede on the desert is particularly effective theatrics.

Director Charles Vidor keeps action moving sufficiently, with script by Robert Carson an okay presentation. Scenically, exterior photography is topnotch, but interiors strived for unusual lighting effects that were not accomplished. Scenic backgrounds in the Utah desert country add much to the eye appeal of the picture. *Walt.*

LADIES' DAY

RKO release of Bert Gilroy production. Features Lupe Velez, Eddie Albert, Patsy Kelly, Max Baer, Jerome Cowan. Directed by Leslie Goodwins. Screenplay by Charles E. Roberts and Dane Lussier, from play by Robert Considine, Edward C. Lilley, Bertrand Robinson; camera, Jack Mackenzie; editor, Harry Marker. Tradeshown in N. Y., March 11, '43. Running time, **62 MINS.**

Pepita.........................Lupe Velez
Wacky.........................Eddie Albert
Hazel...........................Patsy Kelly
Hippo............................Max Baer
Updyke.....................Jerome Cowan
Kitty............................Iris Adrian
Joan..........................Joan Barclay
Dan.............................Cliff Clark
Marianna..................Carmen Morales
Doc......................George Cleveland
Marty...........................Jack Briggs
Smokey..........................Russ Clark
Tony........................Nedrick Young
Spike..........................Eddie Dew
House Detective............Tom Kennedy
Umpire......................Ralph Sanford

The 'Mexican Spitfire' series continues on with Lupe Velez, but in this one there is no reference to the old 'Spitfire' tag. 'Ladies Day' represents considerable improvement over the old formula. It has more capable people, more action and more comedy. Film is a 'B Special' and should do well when coupled with a strong entry on twinners.

Picture obviously is geared for the baseball months, since it concerns the efforts of a temperamental ball club to win a pennant and cop the world series. One of the heaviest hitters is worried about his wife having a baby. Another has a yen for blondes when his spouse is not on hand. A third loses all control as star pitcher every time he starts a new romance.

This stellar hurler, Wacky, is the real problem child. Hence, the plot revolves about attempts of the baseballers' wives to keep him away from his newlywed. Pepita (Lupe Velez), until after the world's championship is won. Wives kidnap and hold her in a hotel room until the series is nearly cinched.

Lupe Velez looks and acts vastly better than in her recent 'Spitfire' films. She manages to keep things rolling along. Eddie Albert makes a satisfying Wacky, star moundsman, while Patsy Kelly also is standout as wife of the dumb-flirtatious catcher. Max Baer. Reminiscent of Maxie Rosenbloom in mannerisms and talk, he has possibilities for further screen development. Jerome Cowan, as the rep of the bank owning the ball club; Iris Adrian, Tom Kennedy and Joan Barclay are nice in support.

Despite obvious twists in the story and absurd moments on the ball field, Leslie Goodwins has maintained pace in direction. Screenplay is as unoriginal as the play from which adapted. Photography by Jack Mackenzie is okay, though the switches from the N. Y. baseball parks with world series crowds and the studio locations are n.g. *Wear.*

THE APEMAN

Monogram release of Sam Katzman and Jack Dietz production. Features Bela Lugosi, Wallace Ford, Louise Currie. Directed by William Beaudine; screenplay, Barney Sarecky; camera, Mark Stengler; editor, Carl Pierson. At New York, N. Y., dual, week March 15, '43. Running time, **64 MINS.**

Dr. Brewster....................Bela Lugosi
Jeff Carter....................Wallace Ford
Billie Mason...................Louise Currie
Agatha Brewster............Minerva Urecal
Dr. Randall.....................Henry Hall
Zippe.......................Ralph Littlefield
Captain................J. Farrell MacDonald
Butler.........................George Kirby
Brady......................Wheeler Oakman
The Ape....................Emil Van Horn

Monogram has borrowed liberally from 'Dr. Jekyll and Mr. Hyde,' 'Dracula' and other time-worn horror film ideas and is now serving them up as a potpourri called 'The Ape Man.' It's good for laughs which aren't in the script, and Bela Lugosi, rigged out in a shaggy beard and formal morning attire, ambling like an ape and sharing a cage with a gorilla, scares nobody. It's strictly for dual support.

All happens because of a little experiment Lugosi performs in the Dr. Jekyll tradition. To resume his normal form, all he needs is fresh human spinal fluid, which he proceeds to get by having his gorilla strangle several people. Then his best friend crosses him up by refusing to inject the priceless ingredient and Lugosi promptly strangles him. Wallace Ford and Louise Currie enter the scene as a couple of story-starved newshawks, and are almost mauled by Lugosi and his gorilla pal, but are saved by the timely intervention of the police.

Lugosi seems somewhat bewildered and bemused by his role and acts accordingly. As for Wallace Ford and Billie Mason, they offer outmoded impersonations of the fourth estate. Emil Van Horn makes a very sympathetic gorilla.

Direction n.g.

DEAD MAN'S GULCH

Republic release of Eddy White production. Features Don 'Red' Barry with Lynn Merrick, Clancy Cooper and Emmett 'Pappy' Lynn. Directed by John English. Screenplay by Norman S. Hall and Robert Williams; camera, Ernest Miller; editor, Arthur Roberts. At New York, N. Y., dual, week March 15, '43. Running time, **55 MINS.**

Tennessee Colby..........Don 'Red' Barry
Mary Logan.................Lynn Merrick
Walt Bledsoe...............Clancy Cooper
Fiddlefoot..........Emmett 'Pappy' Lynn
Tommy Logan..Malcolm 'Bud' McTaggart
Bat Matson....................Jack Rockwell
Hobart Patterson.............John. Vosper
Curley Welch..................Pierce Lyden
Fred Beecher...................Lee Shumway
Steve Barker......................Rex Lease
Buck Lathrop.....................Al Taylor

Despite a conventional title, 'Dead Man's Gulch' is a convincing above-average western that moves along at a brisk pace and gives the feeling that more than cursory attention was paid to scripting and producing.

It's a exciting and believable tale of transportation competition, wardheel tactics and out-and-out gangsterism in the wild west. Forces of law and order, personified by 'Red' Barry, smash an organization of ruthless freight line operators, who use 20th century strong-arm methods to retain their monopoly and launch a reign of terror to prevent a Congressional investigation of the territory which is ripe for statehood. They are aided by Barry's best pal, 'Bud' McTaggart, who will do anything for money. This makes Barry's job harder, but even friendship falls before the claims of justice.

Barry is convincing as a deputy marshal, Lynn Merrick is innocuous as McTaggart's sister, while 'Pappy' Lynn peddles an inferior brand of comedy. McTaggart makes an appealing yet relentless killer. The other members of the cast perform adequately. Director John English allows for no letups in this quick-trigger oater.

HE'S MY GUY
(SONGS)

Universal release of Will Cowan production. Stars Joan Davis; features Dick Foran, Irene Hervey, Fuzzy Knight, Gertrude Niesen, Diamond Bros., and Mills Bros. Directed by Edward F. Cline. Story, Kenneth Higgins; adaptation, M. Coates Webster and Grant Garrett; film editor, Fred Feitshans; songs, Milton Rosen, Everett Carter, Don Raye, Gene de Paul, Bud Green, Ray Henderson, Saul Chaplin, Sammy Cahn, Dorothy Parker and Jack King; camera, John Boyle. At Palace, N. Y., dual, week of March 11, '43. Running time, **65 MINS.**

Van Moore.........................Dick Foran
Terry Allen.....................Irene Hervey
Madge Donovan....................Joan Davis
Sparks..........................Fuzzy Knight
Kirk..............................Don Douglas
Johnson......................Samuel S. Hinds
Elwood..........................Bill Halligan
and
Gertrude Niesen, Diamond Brothers, Mills Brothers, Louis Da Pron, Lorraine Krueger, Dorene Sisters

This is a lightweight romantic item with songs and dances that will provide only the most meagre support on double bills as the associate feature. Thin as to story structure, it is also disappointing musically.

Joan Davis, comedienne starred above the title, is one of the brighter elements of the film, while the Diamond Bros., standard in vaudeville, and the Mills Bros., long established, are also entertaining. The Diamonds figure in comedy and dancing, as well as song stints. Mills quartet do two numbers, while the same chore is assigned to Gertrude Niesen, also from the varieties, who gets over satisfactorily. Team of Irene Hervey and Dick Foran, paired romantically in the picture, vocal two songs, including 'He's My Guy.' Another that impresses is 'Heads Up.'

The story has to do with a group of former vaudevillians who stage morale-building shows in defense plants. Fuzzy Knight, who has long been in westerns as comedy relief, is among them, but the material provided him is quite lame. Knight plays a vaude theatre electrician rather than an actor, however.

Foran, also known in the westerns field, and Miss Hervey make an impressive team, though they, as well as Miss Davis and others, are handicapped by the material assigned them. Don Douglas plays the part of personnel manager of a defense plant effectively.

Though the picture runs only 65 minutes, its pace is slow. It's a good fit, however, for double bills where the top feature is long on running time. *Char.*

The Falcon Strikes Back

Hollywood, March 12.

RKO release of Maurice Geraghty production. Features Tom Conway. Directed by Edward Dmytryk; screenplay by Edward Dein and Gerald Geraghty; story by Stuart Palmer; based on character created by Michael Arlen; camera, Jack MacKenzie; film editor, George Crone; tradeshown in L. A. March 12, '43. Running time, **65 MINS.**

Falcon...........................Tom Conway
Gwynne Gregory..........Harriet Hilliard
Marcia Brooks..............Jane Randolph
Smiley Dugan..............Edgar Kennedy
Goldy..........................Cliff Edwards
Mia Bruger.......................Rita Corday
Rickey Davis...................Edford Gage
Mrs. Lipton.................Wynne Gibson
Jerry..............................Richard Loo
Bruno Steffen................Andre Charlot
Inspector Donovan............Cliff Clark
Bates............................Ed Gargan

This is a bright programmer detailing further adventures of the wily and wise amateur detective, the Falcon. Following familiar basic lines of previous story in the series, picture gets added lift via deft direction by Edward Dmytryk to make it a solid dual supporter in the regular runs.

Falcon is strangely maneuvered into a spot which throws suspicion of a huge war-bond robbery in his direction. Clues send him to a vacation lodge in the mountains, where number of suspects are individually lined up for audience attention when a murder takes place. Solution of the crime is gradually unwound by the Falcon, until the real perpetrator is brought forth with valid reasons for knocking off members of the gang.

Tom Conway takes over the Falcon spot on his own this time, after switching real and screen brother assignments in the previous picture with George Sanders. Conway ably handles the assignment, assisted in his sleuthing by Cliff Edwards and reporter-sweetheart Jane Randolph. Wynne Gibson is the ringleader of the bond theft ring, with Rita Corday, Erford Gage and Harriett Hilliard as accomplices. Cliff Clark continues as the inspector, with Ed Gargan as his dumb assistant.

Despite its familiar formula for Falcon adventures, picture hits a lively pace throughout, with some good comedy and surprise moments injected to liven things up. Production layout is okay throughout. *Walt.*

Hoppy Serves a Writ

Hollywood, March 13.

United Artists release of Harry Sherman production. Stars William Boyd. Directed by George Archainbaud. Associate producer, Lewis Rachmil; screenplay by Gerald Geraghty; camera, Russell Harlan; film editor, Sherman A. Rose; assistant director, Glenn Cook. Previewed in studio projection room, March 12, '43. Running time, **66 MINS.**

Hopalong Cassidy..........William Boyd
California Carlson.............Andy Clyde

Johnny Travers	Jay Kirby
Tom Jordan	Victor Jory
Steve Jordan	George Reeves
Jean Hollister	Jan Christy
Greg Jordan	Hal Taliaferro
Ben Hollister	Forbes Murray
Rigney	Bob Mitchum
Danvers	Byron Foulger
Jim Belnap	Earle Hodgins
Colby	Roy Barcroft

Plenty of fast riding, shooting and other western theatrics in this entry in the Hopalong Cassidy series, which swings along at a fast clip to rate with the better Hoppys. It's solid western entertainment for the action fans.

Locale is the northern border of Texas, across the line from Oklahoma territory where the law is absent. After a stage holdup and serious cattle rustling, sheriff William Boyd takes an undercover trip into Oklahoma to locate the desperados. He's joined by sidekicks Andy Clyde and Jay Kirby, and the trio eventually round up the gang, decoying them across the Texas line for local arrests.

Several wild chases, a lusty barroom fight, and pitched gun battles are included to satisfy action-minded audiences. Boyd ably handles the main hero spot, with Clyde continuing to supply elemental comedy. Kirby is juvenile member of the trio, while support includes Victor Jory, George Reeves, Jan Christy and Hal Taliaferro. Direction by George Archainbaud is speedy, while exterior photography by Russell Harlan is excellent. *Walt.*

TOMORROW WE LIVE

(BRITISH MADE)

London, Feb. 20.

British Lion-Sam Smith production and release. Stars John Clements, Godfrey Tearle, Hugh Sinclair. Directed by George King. Screenplay by Anatole de Grunwald. Camera, Otto Heller, Guy Drisse. At Regal, London. Running time, **85 MINS.**

Jean Baptiste	John Clements
The Mayor	Godfrey Tearle
Major Von Kleist	Hugh Sinclair
Marie Duchesne	Greta Gynt
Germaine	Judy Kelly
Madame Labouche	Yvonne Arnaud
Seitz	Karel Stepanek
Mathieu	Bransby Williams
Pogo	Allan Jeayes
Station Master	Anthony Holles
Dupont	Gibb McLaughlin

A number of things, outside of the film's merits, will contribute to boxoffice success here of 'Tomorrow We Live.' Among these are the official cooperation of General de Gaulle and the French National Committee and that the premiere here was an important social event. This gave it additional billing privilege by the Government which has drastically cut the amount of ad paper. Strong cast, nearly all-star for an English film, helps.

Film is a good propaganda story of the underground movement in France with its sabotage activities. Possibilities in England are bright and film may prove very interesting to American audiences.

Basic idea of a French village occupied by German troops and ruthless persecution of the natives is not new to films. But depicted by a strong British cast, and progressively unfolded, it makes interesting entertainment.

John Clements portrays a young Frenchman trying to escape to England with information about the German submarine base at St. Nazaire. He joins a group of patriots who constantly annoy the boches. Theatrical, yet a good heroic performance. Godfrey Tearle unconventionally handles the conventional role of town mayor with dignity. Greta Gynt, as his daughter, enacts the lead with verve. Judy Kelly, as a German spy, also is splendid, hinting Hollywood possibilities. Yvonne Arnaud is the emotional little housewife, whose husband was killed in the last war, and whose son is fighting in the present one. In opening sequences her makeup was not flattering, but she acquits herself creditably. Karel Stepanek, as a gestapo official, is more than competent. Splendid bits are by Bransby Williams and Allan Jeayes.

Photography and direction just so-so, but on the whole a workmanlike production. *Jolo.*

Buckskin Frontier

United Artists release of Harry Sherman production. Stars Richard Dix and Jane Wyatt; features Albert Dekker, Lee J. Cobb, Victor Jory, Lola Lane, Max Baer, Joe Sawyer. Directed by Lesley Selander; screenplay by Norman Houston with additional dialog by Bernard Schubert, based on story by Harry Sinclair Drago. Tradeshown in N. Y., March 10, '43. Running time, 75 MINS.

Stephen Bent	Richard Dix
Vinnie Marr	Jane Wyatt
Gideon Skene	Albert Dekker
Jeptha Marr	Lee J. Cobb
Champ Clanton	Victor Jory
Rita Molyneux	Lola Lane
Tiny	Max Baer
Brannigan	Joe Sawyer
McWhinny	Harry Allen
Duval	Francis McDonald
Jeff Collins	George Reeves
Whiskers	Bill Nestell

Harry Sherman's prairie saga anent the opening up of the west to the railroads, and the desperate attempts made to prevent the Iron Horse visionaries from encroaching on the wagon-wheeled freight business, is developed at a consistently fast pace. It should fit neatly as supporting fare in the regular program houses.

Despite trite scripting, 'Buckskin Prairie' is a smoothly assembled job with an above-average cast for buckaroo fare and a bangup direction job by Lesley Selander. Tempo in the well-spaced gun and fistic battles and the other ingredients that go into a biff-bang western is perhaps the film's outstanding virtue.

Plot deals with the attempt to run the Missouri Central through the Santa Fe cutoff land to clip 120 miles off the mountainous route, opening up new trade vistas for the hide dealers. Owner of the land, of course, is agin' it, as it would doom his own primitive freight monopoly, and the methods he adopts in an effort to halt the Iron Horse's advance make for some dramatic sequences. Love interest is tied in via the landowner's daughter succumbing to r.r. visionary's ambitions and helping to break down papa's resistance.

Richard Dix and Jane Wyatt turn in satisfactory performances and are surrounded by an unusually strong cast of supporters, including Albert Dekker, Victor Jory, Lee J. Cobb, whose spurs-and-saddle assignment is a far cry from his roles as one of the mainstays of the N. Y. Group Theatre; Max Baer and Lola Lane.

This is one of the Sherman productions taken over from Par by UA. *Rose.*

I Walked With A Zombie

RKO release of Val Lewton production. **Features** James Ellison, Frances Dee, Tom Conway. Directed by Jacques Tourneur. Screenplay by Curt Siodmak and Ardel Wray, based on original by Inez Wallace; camera, J. Roy Hunt; editor, Mark Robson. Tradeshown in N. Y., March 15, '43. Running time, **69 MINS.**

Rand	James Ellison
Betsy	Frances Dee
Holland	Tom Conway
Mrs. Rand	Edith Barrett
Dr. Maxwell	James Bell
Jessica	Christine Gordon
Alma	Teresa Harris
Calypso Singer	Sir Lancelot
Carre Four	Darby Jones
Dancer	Jeni LeGon

Another in the horror cycle, 'I Walked With A Zombie' fails to measure up to the horrific title. Film contains some terrifying passages, but is overcrowded with trite dialog and ponderous acting. It's suited for lower half duals and absence of b.o. names doesn't help.

Scripters Curt Siodmak and Ardel Wray haven't particularly improved the Inez Wallace original, which hinges on the premise that West Indies' Voodoo priests actually can produce a 'Zombie,' a live person unable to speak, hear or feel. Weird yarn has two half-brothers competing for the love of a girl, married to one of the pair, and their mother employing Voodooism to turn the girl into a robot-like existence. Climax, where one of the brothers walks into the ocean with the girl and both are drowned, is an overdone bit.

With few exceptions, cast walks through the picture almost as dazed as the zombies. James Ellison makes a loud but totally ineffective 'bad' brother; his love affair with his brother's wife starts the whole cycle of strange mishaps. Frances Dee, as a comely nurse, tries to make sense in the inanimate proceedings. Tom Conway is terrifically British as the righteous brother, but inexcusably dull most of the time. Edith Barrett is halfway acceptable as mother of the two brothers, while Teresa Harris is impressive as a personable servant. Others so-so. *Wear.*

The Kid Rides Again

Producers Releasing Corp. release of Bert Sternbach production. Features Buster Crabbe, Al (Fuzzy) St. John, Iris Meredith. Directed by Sherman Scott. Screenplay, Fred Myton; camera, Jack Greenhalgh; editor, Holbrook N. Todd. At New York, N. Y., dual, week March 9, '43. Running time, 55 MINS.

Billy the Kid	Buster Crabbe
Fuzzy Jones	Al (Fuzzy) St. John
Joan	Iris Meredith
Tom	Glenn Strange
Vic	Charles King
Mort	I. Stanford Jolley
Ainsley	Ed. Peil, Sr.
Sheriff	Ted Adams
Texas Sheriff	Slim Whitaker

This is a true-to-formula addition to the 'Billy the Kid' series with Buster Crabbe. Action addicts will find all the ingredients present; rustling, gun fights and chases.

'The Kid Rides Again' is the thrice-told tale of the unjustly jailed Billy. Rather than stand trial for a train robbery he didn't commit, Buster Crabbe breaks jail to find the real holdup man and clear his own fair name. In the process he uncovers rustlers, fronting as respectable ranchers. He not only puts a crimp in their rustling, but recovers loot of the bank robbery which they committed and tried to pin on him.

Romantic interest is provided by Iris Meredith; a deft comedy touch is injected by Al (Fuzzy) St. John, who is the only standout in the cast. Buster Crabbe makes a handsome but colorless title character.

Fighting Sea Monsters

(NATURE FEATURE)

Astor Pictures release of Capt. John D. Craig production. Narrated by Ted Webbe; associate producer, Herbert T. Edwards; continuity, Ira Knaster; music, Edward Craig. At New York, N. Y., dual, week March 9, '43. Running time, **56 MINS.**

'Fighting Sea Monsters' is a unique and thrilling camera record of a West Indian fishing trip made by several Hollywood fishermen and deep-sea divers. Marlin, shark and manta ray are the monsters in question. Slightly foggy, but skillful photography records their depredations and death struggles, as well as the more peaceful pursuits of their finny neighbors in a place called Silver Shoals.

Fish that look like flowers, fish that blow themselves into balls, fish that are nightmarish in form parade before the undersea cameras used by the expedition. The feature is well paced by Ted Webbe's humorous and dramatic narration.

Miniature Reviews

'Edge of Darkness' (WB). Powerful b.o. in story of Norway vs. Nazis starring Errol Flynn and Ann Sheridan.

'China' (Par). Fast-paced Sino-Jap war meller; good b.o.

'Hangmen Also Die' (UA)—Czech hostage story told in dramatic terms; profitable b.o. entry.

'Diary of a Nazi' (Artkino). Hard-hitting picturization by Russians of German-occupied Europe.

'The Purple V' (Rep). Stereo Nazi-themed meller; okay for the duals.

'The Silver Fleet' (GFD). British version dealing with Nazi occupation of Holland; likely b.o. entry.

'High Explosive' (Par). Okay action meller for strong support in the program houses.

'Aerial Gunner' (Par). Top-notch action meller displaying training of Uncle Sam's flying gunners.

EDGE OF DARKNESS

Warner Bros. release of Henry Blanke production. Stars Errol Flynn and Ann Sheridan; features Walter Huston, Nancy Coleman, Judith Anderson and Ruth Gordon. Directed by Lewis Milestone; screenplay, Robert Rossen, based on novel by William Woods; camera, Sid Hickox; editor, David Weisbart. Tradeshown in N. Y. March 19, '43. Running time, **120 MINS.**

Gunnar Brogge	Errol Flynn
Karen Stensgard	Ann Sheridan
Dr. Martin Stensgard	Walter Huston
Katja	Nancy Coleman
Hammer	Tom Fadden
Gerd Bjarnesen	Judith Anderson
Capt. Koenig	Helmut Dantine
Mrs. Anna Stensgard	Ruth Gordon
Kaspar Torgersen	Charles Dingle
Johann Stensgard	John Beal
Lars Malken	Roman Bohnen
Frida	Helene Thimig
Petersen	Monte Blue
Solveig Brategaard	Dorothy Tree
Pastor Aalesen	Richard Fraser
Sixtus Andresen	Morris Carnovsky
Knut Osterholm	Art Smith
Major Ruck	Henry Brandon
Paul	Tonio Selwart
Clerk	Torben Meyer

A 'hate-the-Nazis' exposition, 'Edge of Darkness' looks like another big boxoffice winner in Warners' cycle of war stories. It's a dramatic, tense, emotion-stirring story of the ravaging of Norway, superbly acted by a fine cast and firmly directed by Lewis Milestone.

There's only one loose end in the entire picture, and that is strictly the fault of the cutting room. The trimming of some redundancy and the elimination of a couple of extraneous bits would have sharpened the story to an appreciable extent; also necessary, naturally, is cutting the 120-minute running time to give exhibitors more room for turnover.

Norway has received attention in a couple of films, but chiefly as a focal point for commando raids. In 'Darkness,' as in 'Moon Is Down,' the story treats with internal conditions and unrest, and, more important, the ruthlessness of the Nazis. The populace of Trollness seethes under the yoke of the Germans and finally erupts into a bloody revolt. It's propaganda, true, but news stories filtering out of Norway point up that this is fictional-fact as well.

Best feature of this film is its cast. Errol Flynn and Ann Sheridan, as the stars, provide the proper romantic note, plus the necessary dash as the leaders of the Trollness underground. Both turn in some of their best film acting to date, yet some of the cast's lesser-knowns eclipse them in dramatic power. Notable in this respect are Morris Carnovsky, Ruth Gordon, Judith Anderson, Charles Dingle and Nancy Coleman.

Carnovsky, as an aged schoolmaster, is outstanding in a throat-catching scene when he pits his culture and kindliness against the brutish thinking of the Nazi commander, played by Helmut Dantine, who is guilty of most of the film's over-acting. This bit, which within a few moments lays bare many of the facets of modern Germany's terroristic philosophy, is a major piece of Hollywood theatrics. It also contains the finest writing in the script.

There's one other particularly outstanding scene—the meeting of the underground in the church under the guise of a religious service. Original in concept, it's emotion-gripping in executon. A refugee from another Norwegian town remains seated among the congregation and recites the terror visited upon his neighbors until they revolted with secretly-delivered British arms. He tells the people of Trollness that they, too, would be sent arms by the British, and then the congregation takes a vote on whether they will use them in open force against the Nazis. The pro and con debate furnishes a striking lesson that lives are cheap payment for freedom. The pastor, well played by Richard Fraser, takes the side against positive action, but at the film's climax he wields a machine gun very effectively against a Nazi firing squad.

How the armed revolt is finally forced when a Nazi sergeant rapes Miss Sheridan, resulting in her father-doctor, Walter Huston, running amok and murdering a German soldier, is merely one segment in a multi-sectioned drama. There are many other tense scenes and also some exceptionally warm acting, as, for instance, Ruth Gordon's portrayal as the mother of Miss Sheridan and wife of Huston. She plays a mousey little woman who, seemingly, doesn't fully grasp the meaning of the Nazi occupation, nor the treachery of her Quisling son, played by John Beal, and the machinations of her Quisling brother, Charles Dingle. Latter plays ball with the Nazis and goes insane after the revolt. He is the only one left in the town when a German rescue force arrives to find the entire Nazi garrison wiped out. Unable to question Dingle, a German officer orders him shot.

There isn't a single weak performance in the picture, and even Dantine's over-acting can be accepted as intentional for propaganda effect. He certainly makes the Nazi officer a loathesome specimen. Miss Anderson is strong as the hotel keeper and one of the leaders of the underground. Miss Coleman, as a Polish girl pressed into harlotry by Dantine; Tonio Selwart, as a German soldier in love with Miss Anderson, and all the others, from the stars to the bit players, rate bows.

Sid Hickox's photography, plus the production accoutrements provided by producer Henry Blanke, are other strong tssets. *Scho.*

CHINA

Hollywood, March 20.

Paramount release of Richard Blumenthal production. Stars Loretta Young and Alan Ladd; features William Bendix. Directed by John Farrow. Screenplay by Frank Butler, based on play by Archibald Forbes; camera, Leo Tover; film editor, Eda Warren. Process photography, Farciot Edouart; special photographic effects, Gordon Jennings. Tradeshown in L. A. March 19, '43. Running time, **78 MINS.**

Carolyn Grant..........Loretta Young
Mr. Jones..........Alan Ladd
Johnny Sparrow..........William Bendix
First Brother—Lin Cho..........Philip Ahn
Kwan Su..........Iris Wong
Third Brother—Lin Wei..........Sen Yung
Tan Ying..........Marianne Quon
Student..........Jessie Tai Sing

Story of this one closely parallels that of 20th-Fox's 'China Girl.' Despite the similarity of basic locale and dramatic theme, 'China' carries good dramatic conviction in its unfolding to provide okay biz in the regular runs as solo or billtopper attraction. Title and setting provides exploitation opportunities for showmen to generate extra customers.

Tale opens in an interior China town, with Jap planes attacking the spot and populace. Among quick evacuees is Alan Ladd, who's been trucking gasoline to the Jap armies out of Shanghai. William Bendix is his sidekick. Along the road, truck is stopped and Ladd is forced to take aboard group of Chinese femme university students in charge of American instructress Loretta Young. Ladd is arrogant and unconcerned over the Jap atrocities against the Chinese, but wakes up when a Jap plane strafes his truck. From then on, he's with the Chinese in the battle and bent on killing Nips. He kills three Japs who have ravaged a Chinese girl, and then falls in love with Miss Young. Changing his route to get the girls to safety in the interior, he stops along the way long enough to join group of Chinese guerrillas in rousing raid on Jap unit constructing a bridge, and later directs dynamiting of mountain pass to destroy a Nip column—deliberately going to his death in the execution of the plans.

Frank Butler generates authenticity in the dramatic evolvement of his screenplay, while director John Farrow neatly blends the human and melodramatic elements of the yarn. Interest is hypoed in the early reels with pickup of a Chinese baby by Bendix at the bombed town, and gradual breakdown of Ladd's attitude towards the youngster until the point where the latter is murdered by the Jap soldiers and Ladd is transformed into a battler for the Chinese cause.

Ladd capably handles the lead, with Miss Young sympathetic as the American mentor of the Chinese girls. Bendix provides his usual strong performance as the burly and soft-hearted Yankee. Good support of Chinese players has Iris Wong, Sen Yung and Philip Ahn most prominent.

Production mounting provides excellent replicas of the Chinese countryside, with Leo Tover's photography top-grade throughout. Noteworthy is special photographic effects by Gordon Jennings, and process work by Farciot Edouart. *Walt.*

HANGMEN ALSO DIE

United Artists release of Arnold Pressburger production. Stars Brian Donlevy, Walter Brennan and Anna Lee; features Gene Lockhart, Dennis O'Keefe and Alexander Granach. Directed by Fritz Lang. Screenplay by John Wexley, with adaptation and original story by Bert Brecht and Lang; camera, James Wong Howe; editor, Gene Fowler, Jr. Previewed in N. Y., March 17, '43. Running time: **131 MINS.**

Dr. Svoboda..........Brian Donlevy
Prof. Novotny..........Walter Brennan
Mascha Novotny..........Anna Lee
Czaka..........Gene Lockhart
Jan Horek..........Dennis O'Keefe
Alois Gruber..........Alexander Granach
Aunt Ludmilla..........Margaret Wycherly
Mrs. Novotny..........Nana Bryant
Beda Novotny..........Billy Roy
Heydrich..........Hans V. Twardowski
Haas..........Tonio Selwart
Dedic..........Jonathan Hale
Gabby..........Lionel Stander
Bartos..........Byron Foulger
Landlady..........Virginia Farmer
Schirmer..........Louis Donath
Mrs. Dvorak..........Sarah Padden
Dr. Pilar..........Edmund MacDonald
Necval..........George Irving
Worker..........James Bush
Camp Officer..........Arno Frey
Hostage..........Lester Sharpe
Votruba..........Arthur Loft
Viktorin..........William Farnum
Ritter..........Reinhold Schuenzel

With 'Hangmen Also Die,' United Artists get the jump on other studios rushing into production films based on the Czech blood-bath that followed the assassination of Reinhardt Heydrich, the Nazi executioner. This is a fiercely dramatic story aimed for good business.

From a directorial standpoint, the new UA entry is a triumph for Fritz Lang, who has succeeded with singular success in capturing the spirit of the Czech people in the face of the Nazi reign of terror. **So forceful a document is it that it will incite the filmgoer to an intense hatred of the Nazi barbarian, and as such is probably one of the most effective pieces of propaganda to emerge from Hollywood.**

From a b.o. standpoint, 'Hangmen' might suffer somewhat by becoming unbearable in the awfulness of what it pictures. It's an unrelenting piling up of horror upon horror, Nazi cold-blooded ruthlessness and bestiality. Throughout its two hours and 11 minutes of unfolding, it provides no relief to pent-up emotions, leaving the audience literally wrung dry. Film could easily have retained its impact and benefited by judicious cutting.

UA sunk plenty of coin into the picture. Technically and artistically, it adds immeasurably to the prestige of those associated in its production. Cameraman James Wong Howe, in particular, has turned in a magnificent job.

While lacking high-voltaged marquee strength, the cast, topped by Brian Donlevy and Walter Brennan, is uniformly splendid, with the performances of Gene Lockhart, as a cowering Quisling Czech, and Alexander Granach, as a shrewd, calculating and ruthless inspector of the Gestapo, being particularly outstanding. Story continuity is fine and absorbing throughout, but essentially it's the incisive terms of the message propounded that sets 'Hangmen' apart and conclusively points up the fact that propaganda can be art.

Saga of the courageous spirit of the Czechs starts with the assassination of Heydrich, the hangman, by an appointed member of the underground (Donlevy), but the plans for his escape go awry and, due to the stringent curfew laws, he is forced to spend the night at the home of a professor and his daughter. In order to save her father, who is held as hostage along with several hundred others until the assassin will be given up, she goes to the Gestapo to reveal his identity, but realizes that the spirit of the Czech people has made of him a symbol of freedom and that the underground will protect him at all costs. Her fiance, brooding over the stranger's overnight stay at her home, inadvertently leads the Gestapo inspector to suspect the assassin's identity, but once more the Czech spirit rises and the underground frames a Quisling, piling up such overwhelming evidence that the Nazis, although realizing they've been outwitted, are forced to accept the 'people's choice.'

Both Donlevy and Brennan, as the professor, are excellent, the latter emerging in the film a figure of heroic proportions. Tonio Selwart and Reinhold Schuenzel, as Gestapo bigwigs, and Anna Lee, in the role of Brennan's daughter, are likewise standout in the fine cast. *Rose.*

DIARY OF A NAZI

(SOVIET MADE)

Artkino release of Mikhail Romm production. Features Y. Anazhevskaya, M. Bernes, S. Ditlovich, N. Komissarov, L. Kmit, V. Bubnov, V. Mironova and B. Runghe. Directed by Igor Savchenko, V. Braun and M. Donskoy. English titles by Charles Clement; camera, Y. Ekelchik, D. Demutsky and A. Mishurin. Previewed in N. Y., March 22, '43. Running time, **67 MINS.**

(In Russian; English Titles)

'Diary of a Nazi,' actually three-films-in-one, is a powerful picture of Nazi-occupied Europe. Each of the sub-films derives its title from a specific district or event mentioned in a diary taken by the Russians from the body of a slain Nazi S. S. officer. The sub-divisions have individual directors, cameramen and featured players. Herein lies the uniqueness and weakness of the overall production.

The first film-within-a-film is titled 'District No. 14,' a section in Warsaw visited by the S.S. man. It makes an obvious play for Polish collaboration and understanding by depicting the fundamental brotherhood of Poles and Russians in their common fight against the 'Brown Plague,' Nazism. **It is a gripping episode, revealing the Nazi technic of terror in a most impersonal and inhuman manner.**

The second sub-film, 'The Blue Cliff,' derives its title from an incident described by a Czech woman rescued by the Russians from the Germans. It is a straight-forward tale of Czech resistence and self-sacrifice.

Episode three, 'The Signal,' bears virtually no relation to either the first or second sub-divisions. The only link is resistence to the enemy by civilians, the underlying theme of the overall production.

The acting in all sections is in the typical Russian tradition. Real people, not puppets are portrayed on the screen, and the uncanny ability to characterize Nazis, which stems from the years of practice portraying White Guardist officers, is convincingly demonstrated.

Photography is also effective despite technical imperfections, but this serves to lend a documentary, front-line atmosphere. Direction is generally excellent, lapsing occasionally to permit propagandist speeches and political dissertations.

THE PURPLE V

Republic release of George Sherman production. Directed by George Sherman. Features John Archer, Mary McLeod, Fritz Kortner. Screenplay, Bertram Millhauser and Curt Siodmak; adaptation by Bertram Millhauser, from story by Robert R. Mill; camera, Ernest Miller; editor, Charles Craft. Tradeshown in New York March 19, '43. Running time, **58 MINS.**

Joe Thorne..........John Archer
Katti Forster..........Mary McLeod
Thomas Forster..........Fritz Kortner
Paul Forster..........Rex Williams
Johann Keller..........Kurt Katch
Otto Horner..........Walter Sande
Oberst Von Ritter..........William Vaughn
Roger..........Peter Lawford
Walter Heyse..........Kurt Kreuger
Marta..........Eva Hyde
Mrs. Vogel..........Irene Seidner

Conventional cops and robbers formula under a Nazi, war-themed background, will serve in the smaller situations and provide okay support for key duallers.

Production values are good. Director George Sherman has developed suspense deftly and, for the most part, kept action moving at a fast clip.

Apart from Mary McLeod, femme lead, who photographs poorly and otherwise fails to impress, cast is capable. Outstanding, of course, is Fritz Kortner, as the pre-Hitler German liberal schoolmaster who helps the lost American flyer back to Allied lines with secret information on the North African campaign. Though a little stagey, Kortner is convincing as the friend, philosopher and sage who eventually dies in the fight against the new German order.

Opening sequences are draggy, with some awkwardness evidenced in laying groundwork for the ostensibly obvious meller pattern. *Mori.*

THE SILVER FLEET

(BRITISH-MADE)

London, March 5.

General Film Distributors' release of Archer producton. Stars Ralph Richardson. Directed by Vernon Campbell Sewell, Gordon Wellesley. Script by Wellesley; camera, Edwin Hillier, Cecil Cooney. At Leicester Square, London. Running time,

88 MINS.

Jaap van Leyden	Ralph Richardson
Helene van Leyden	Googie Withers
Von Schiffer	Esmond Knight
Krampf	Beresford Egan
Captain Muller	Frederick Burtwell
Willem van Leyden	Willem Akkerman
Janni Peters	Dorothy Gordon
Bastiaan Peters	Charles Victor
Jost Meertens	John Longden
Markgraf	Valentine Dyall
Chief of Police	Philip Leaver
Admiral	Ivor Barnard

This psychological study of a patriot who endures the shame of treason falters because the authors fail to show completely the infamy attaching to a Quisling in conquered lands. 'Occupied country' films are no longer top draws here, but the merits of this picture as to story, production, direction, casting, etc., makes it loom as an exception.

Story has little novelty in plot, but is so ably treated that only occasionally does the suspense wear thin. It deals with sabotage in Holland of Nazi-controlled Dutch submarines. The leading character is a Dutch shipyard engineer, who agrees to stay on and supervise building up ships for the Germans. Because of this he is considered a Quisling even by his own wife. But he succeeds in getting all important Gestapo officials in his community to accompany him on a submarine's trial. He equips this with dynamite so it will blow up, destroying all on board.

Direction largely is competent although generally the tempo is a bit slow. Obviously the directors stressed the artistic value of underacting, resulting in a monotone of self-repression by all the characters, detracting from the star's performance.

The central character moves placidly through the long footage. As a modern Piet Hein (a legendary Dutch hero of three centuries ago), Richardson turns in his usual flawless, authoritative performance, dominating the picture throughout. If the few love scenes with his wife are the least convincing moments of the action, the blame is not his. The outstanding supporting performance of a generally adequate cast is by Esmond Knight, the young actor who was blinded in the sinking of the Bismarck. The deadly menace underlying his Gestapo chief is ever present. Googie Withers, as the unhappy wife, hitherto associated with comic roles, has been badly treated by script and direction.

Although due credit is given the Royal Netherlands and the British Navy, nearly all action is confined to land locations, the surface and under-water sequences are few and unconvincing. Judged by the success of the better British war films in America, this one ought to get over nicely there. **Jolo.**

AERIAL GUNNER

Hollywood, March 23.

Paramount release of Pine-Thomas production. Stars Chester Morris, Richard Arlen and Jimmy Lydon; features Lita Ward and Dick Purcell. Directed by William H. Pine; screenplay by Maxwell Shane. Camera, Fred Jackman, Jr.; film editor, William Ziegler. Tradeshown in L. A. March 22, '43. Running time, 78 MINS.

Foxy Pattis	Chester Morris
Ben Davis	Richard Arlen
Peggy Lunt	Lita Ward
Sandy Lunt	Jimmy Lydon
Gadget Blaine	Dick Purcell
Sergt. Jones	Keith Richards
Private Laswell	Billy Benedict
Barclay	Ralph Sanford

Despite the fact it kept within a moderate negative cost, 'Aerial Gunner' is one of the best melodramas of pre-combat training to be wheeled out by any studio. Packed with lusty and punchy action, besides providing inside information on rigid instruction courses for American fliers, picture will display good box-office strength in the regular runs, and can surprise in those spots where exhibs give it exploitation push.

Army cooperated to fullest extent in providing the Harlingen aerial gunnery school base for setting and backgrounds. Story is a straightforward drama of two men—enemies in civilian life—who find themselves tossed together in service at the gunnery training camp and wind up as buddies on Uncle Sam's fighting team. Richard Arlen shows up at Harlingen to find ex-antagonist Chester Morris a sergeant and squad instructor. There's the regular conflict of personalities and attitude, with both vying for the attention of Lita Ward, sister of Jimmy Lydon. Latter, developing fear complex on plane gunnery trial, makes a second attempt and crashes. But the graduated gunners, along with Morris, pull out for combat duty in the south Pacific area. Climax comes on Jap bombing mission, in which bomber squadron is attacked by flock of Zeros and there's a forced landing on an outlying island occupied by the Japs. Morris sacrifices his life so that the plane and Arlen can take off for return to American territory. Story is unfolded via cutbacks of conversation by Arlen in base hospital after return from the mission.

Training routine conducted at Harlingen is displayed at every step, including target range, moving target car, and towed targets in the air. Combat scenes of the Jap bombing and running fight with the Zeros are effectively staged.

Picture marks first directorial effort of William Pine, senior member of the producing partnership of Pine and Thomas. He points constantly at the adventurous angles of the compact script, and takes full advantage of the facilities and equipment provided by the Army base.

Arlen and Morris are neatly cast as the two principals, both turning in slick two-fisted portrayals. Lita Ward is okay as the romantic interest, and Jimmy Lydon is prominent as the kid carried along by Arlen. Dick Purcell has a strong supporting role, while others in foreground include Keith Richards, Billy Benedict and Ralph Stanford. **Walt.**

HIGH EXPLOSIVE

Hollywood, March 23.

Paramount release of Pine-Thomas production. Stars Chester Morris, Jean Parker and Barry Sullivan. Directed by Frank McDonald. Screenplay by Maxwell Shane and Howard J. Green; original story by Joseph Hoffman; camera, Fred Jackman, Jr.; film editor, William Ziegler. Tradeshown in L. A. March 23, '43. Running time, 60 MINS.

Buzz Mitchell	Chester Morris
Connie Baker	Jean Parker
Mike Douglas	Barry Sullivan
Jimmy Baker	Rand Brooks
Doris Lynch	Barbara Lynn
Squichy Andrews	Ralph Sanford
Dave	Dick Purcell
Man	Vince Barnett
Joe	Addison Randall

This is a good action melodrama of regular program calibre that will garner full share of support datings in the general runs, and an okay entry in the Pine-Thomas series for Paramount.

Story is woven around adventures of drivers of nitro-glycerine trucks, and informative in displaying care required to handle the cans of high explosive.

Chester Morris returns west to take up his expert driving of the dangerous vehicles for trucker Barry Sullivan. In getting romantic with secretary Jean Parker, he takes her young brother under his wing to teach him all the ramifications of the trade. But the kid is blown up in a runaway truck. Climax points up a burning oil tank on hill above a munitions plant, with no nitro handy. So Morris flies a planeload in and, when the fog closes in to prevent landing, he dives the plane at the fire for resultant snuff-out

explosion to save the war plant.

Picture unfolds at a speedy pace, and contains sufficient excitement and meller ingredients to satisfy the action-minded customers. Frank McDonald neatly paces direction from compact script by Maxwell Shane and Howard J. Green.

Morris gives his usual characterization in the lead, with both Miss Parker and Sullivan providing strong support. **Walt.**

Miniature Reviews

'**Desert Victory**' (20th). 60-minute documentary of British Eighth Army's defeat of Rommel's Afrika Korps terrific and best battle film thus far.

'**Tonight We Raid Calais**' (20th). Annabella headlining occupied-France meller; mainly for secondary spots on duals.

'**Sherlock Holmes in Washington**' (U). Good entry in sleuth series.

'**The Alibi**' (Rep). British-made thriller. Okay for dualers.

'**Tahiti Honey**' (Rep) (Songs). Neat program comedy; okay for dual support.

'**Man of Courage**' (PRC). Barton MacLane, Lyle Talbot, Dorothy Burgess in humdrum meller.

'**Rangers Take Over**' (PRC). (Songs.) Dave O'Brien in mild musical western.

'**Don Winslow of Coast Guard**' (Serial) (U). Actionful chapter-play is strong for this type of fare.

DESERT VICTORY

(NEWSREEL DOCUMENTARY)

20th Century-Fox release of British Army Film Unit production. Previewed in the Projection Room, N. Y., March 30, '43. Running time, 60 MINS.

The greatest battle film of the war —one that few Americans should miss—is the only description fitting 'Desert Victory.' The source of its greatness is easy to determine—it puts the audience right in the middle of one of the war's most terrible battles. It puts a rifle, a tommy gun, a hand grenade in the fist of even the most timid soul, and sends him charging with General Montgomery's Eighth Army across the sands of Egypt and Libya after Marshal Rommel's Afrika Korps.

'Desert Victory' was made by a score or more of British army cameramen up in the front lines as General Montgomery's men started almost at the gates of Alexandria and chased the Nazi fighters right through Tripoli. A number of the lensers are said to have been killed in the shooting of the footage. And that's easily believable, as the camera dives into a shellhole and finds Nazi riflemen there, or advances cautiously over open ground with only a burning German tank for cover. The story is that the photogs were given a rifle and a camera and told: 'When you get close enough to use your rifle, lay it aside and use your camera.'

The captious certainly will find room for criticism of a film sold as 100% McCoy battle footage, for some of it, to anyone familiar with picture-making, is obviously not that. Likewise, 'Desert Victory' may be regarded as much if not more of a triumph for the film editors as for the lensmen. It's the overall effect, however, that counts, and 'Desert Victory' gives a vividly realistic idea of the terror and immensity of modern warfare.

What if shots of the strained faces of men awaiting the zero hour were reconstructed in the studio? There's no doubt how Montgomery's soldiers looked, even if no lens, no matter how fast, could actually pick them up in a pitch-dark desert. What if an editor's tricky use of a black screen is made to add drama? It certainly is no more dramatic than the actuality of earth-shaking combat artillery fire.

Some of the film has been seen briefly in the newsreels, but the British withheld hundreds of feet of the most hair-raising sequences for 'Desert Victory,' the result being a surprising quantity of brand new footage to American audiences. In addition, the fine editing and the smoothly written and narrated commentary, done in the typically understated British manner, lift the film completely out of the newsreel class and make it comparable only to an occasional recent Russian release.

High point of 'Desert Victory' is the zero hour for the start of the push back against Rommel from Egypt. Every man gets the plan of attack. Then there's the nerve-straining wait until darkness falls, the hands of the synchronized watches crawling toward the zero hour. WHAM!! And the screen literally rocks with the flash and thunder of shells as one of the world's greatest bombardments begins. For half-an-hour it lasts and then the engineers go forth on the dangerous mission of locating and digging out mines and laying white tape to mark the cleared path. Actually within five feet of the camera a sapper falls over as a sniper's bullet gets him. A few more minutes and the infantry attack begins. With bayonet drawn, the camera—and with it, of course, the audience—leaps into the fray, kills Nazis, sets tanks aflame, takes prisoners. The most experienced of soldiers was never nearer war than this. And captured German footage is spliced in to give an idea of what was happening on the other side of the lines.

Inasmuch as the U. S. Signal Corps film, 'At the Front,' supervised by Col. Darryl F. Zanuck, is being released to theatres at the same time and also is laid in Africa, comparison is inevitable. The comparison really is unfair, however, because the U. S. forces were engaged in a piddling little campaign at the time, as against the tremendous warfare which the British cameramen had as their subject. Nevertheless, it shows the English many times ahead of the Americans in knowing how to make full use of the footage they have. It's unfortunate that the two pictures should be distributed at the same time, but will be valuable in showing the U. S. War Department the folly of its lengthy delay in releasing 'At the Front' and in demonstrating to the Washington brass-hats what valuable purpose battle pictures can serve.

Incidentally, the black-and-white of the British film appears much more effective than the Technicolor of the American crews. Ordinary film gives a starkness and realism to war that the colored stock seems to impart with a candy-stick gloss.

The British cameramen and editors and, above all, the enlightened High Command that allowed 'Desert Victory' to be made deserve a loud cheer. Americans who see this film will be waiting anxiously for the next—and a U. S. equivalent.

Tonight We Raid Calais

20th-Fox release of Andre Daven production. Features Annabella, John Sutton, Lee J. Cobb, Beulah Bondi, Blanche Yurka. Directed by John Brahm; screenplay by Waldo Salt from story by L. Willinger and Rohama Lee; camera, Lucien Ballard; editor, Allen McNeil. Tradeshown in N. Y., March 25, '43. Running time, **70 MINS.**

Odette	Annabella
Geoffrey Carter	John Sutton
M. Bonnard	Lee J. Cobb
Mme. Bonnard	Beulah Bondi
Widow Grelieu	Blanche Yurka
Sergeant Block	Howard Da Silva
Jacques Grandet	Marcel Dalio
Mme. Grandet	Ann Codee
Danton	Nigel de Brulier
Maurice Bonnard	Robert Lewis
Captain	Richard Derr
Captain Baird	Leslie Denison
Bell Ringer	Billy Edmunds
Major West	Lester Matthews
Commander	Reginald Sheffield
Kurz	John Banner
English Pilot	Leslie Vincent
Lieutenants	Robert O. Davis, George Lynn

'Tonight We Raid Calais' is a lesser effort in the long string of recent screen vehicles depicting the workings of the underground in Nazi-conquered lands. Picture will have to lean on what boxoffice lustre Annabella possesses. It appears best suited for dual support.

'Calais' falls rather flat. Feebleness in direction, scripting and part of the acting is most to blame. Numerous implausible passages don't help.

Story, whipped up by L. Willinger and Rohama Lee and transferred to screen by Waldo Salt, basically starts out as a one-man expedition from England to blast a munitions factory near Calais. The one-man commando, John Sutton, is ordered to get behind Nazi lines, disguised as a Frenchman, and light up the munitions plant so the R.A.F. can blast it. He enlists the aid of a farmer and his wife, over the protests of their comely daughter (peeved at the British because her brother was killed at Oran when the English sank many French warships).

None of the major points is driven home, and there is no over-all feeling that the French underground is working smoothly. That is mainly due to over-reaching for melodramatics, such as captures, releases and executions by the Nazis. Casting flaws are evident, with Howard Da Silva, as the Nazi sergeant on the 'make' for the farmer's daughter, especially ineffectual.

Annabella, in contrast, gives a good performance as the French girl who feels the British are not friends of France until she sees the Nazis execute her parents. Beulah Bondi is excellent as the farmer's wife, while Lee J. Cobb contributes a first-rate job as her mate. Blanche Yurka, as the widow who leads the French peasants in their field-burning feat to aid the British, is superb in a lesser role. John Sutton's work is better than usual.

Camera work of Lucien Ballard is satisfactory, but John Brahm's direction is routine. *Wear.*

Sherlock Holmes in Wash.

Universal release and production. Stars Basil Rathbone and Nigel Bruce; features Marjorie Lord, John Archer, George Zucco, Henry Daniell. Directed by Roy William Neill. Screenplay by Bertram Milhauser and Lynn Riggs from original story by Milhauser; camera, Lester White; editor, Otto Ludwig. Previewed in N. Y., March 25, '43. Running time, **71 MINS.**

Sherlock Holmes	Basil Rathbone
Dr. Watson	Nigel Bruce
Nancy Partridge	Marjorie Lord
William Easter	Henry Daniell
Stanley	George Zucco
Lt. Pete Merriam	John Archer
Bart Lang	Gavin Muir
Detective Lt. Grogan	Edmund MacDonald
Howe	Don Terrry
Cady	Bradley Page
Mr. Ahrens	Holmes Herbert
Santor Babcock	Thurston Hall

Universal widens the scope for the operations of Sherlock Holmes by transferring the modernized sleuth and his aide to Washington amid war intrigue. It's one of the best to date in the Holmes series, despite the fact that Bertram Milhauser and Lynn Riggs have concocted a script that seldom ventures beyond the established formula. Director Roy William Neill has turned in a very workman-like job, while Basil Rathbone and Nigel Bruce, with the aid of a fine supporting cast, are, as usual, the film's chief assets. As sleuth sagas go, it has received a generous production and should be strong support on twin bills.

The fact that the Holmes fables are apt to strain one's credulity (some of the magnifying glass conclusions are pulled out of a hat) are no longer a detriment to the sleuth sagas. They're expected now as part and parcel of the series.

'Holmes in Washington' resorts to the tried and true formula of building story around a packet of matches, within the covers of which has been concealed a microfilmed document. Secret service operative, Washington-bound with valuable info from England, knows he's been marked by enemy agents and slips packet into unsuspecting gal's handbag. From that point on it's the story of the adventures of the tiny match folder as it passes in and out of enemy agents' hands, with only Holmes aware of its important contents. Fact that the packet seems to hold an inexhaustible supply of matches doesn't detract from the film's suspenseful moments.

Rathbone is up to his usual standards, while Bruce, as Watson, extracts from the comedy sequences their full value. Marjorie Lord, Edmund MacDonald, George Zucco and Henry Daniell are particularly effective in supporting roles. *Rose.*

THE ALIBI

(BRITISH-MADE)

Republic release of Josef Somlo production. Stars Margaret Lockwood and Hugh Sinclair; features James Mason and Raymond Lovell. Directed by Brian Desmond Hurst; screenplay by R. Carter, Juttke, Companeez; adapted from story by Marcel Achard; camera, W. McLeod; film editor, Alan Jaggs. Previewed in N. Y., March 26, '43. Running time, **66 MINS.**

Helene	Margaret Lockwood
Calas	Hugh Sinclair
Andre Laurent	James Mason
Professor Winkler	Raymond Lovell
Dany	Enid Stamp-Taylor
Gordon	Hartley Power
Delia	Jane Carr
Winkler's Assistants	Rodney Ackland and Edana Romney
Singer	Elisabeth Welch
Mlle. Loureau	Olga Lindo
Madame Bretonnet	Muriel George
Bourdille	George Merritt
Josette	Judy Gray
Dodo	Philip Leaver
Gerard	Derek Blomfield

Claire Wear's Embassy Orchestra

This one's not to be confused with the 1931 English-made film of the same title based on the play in which Charles Laughton appeared. Current Republic release, an adaptation of the story 'L' Alibi,' was done in French with Erich von Stroheim and released by Columbia here in 1939. Not a particularly good film in its French version, Josef Somlo's English production has little more to recommend it. It's not difficult to understand the temptation to refilm Marcel Achard's suspenseful story, for, basically, the material is there. But director Brian Desmond Hurst has failed to realize its full potentialities and there is an uneven quality about the production as a whole. It's strictly for the dualers.

Abruptness with which the sequences follow one another indicates that the film was not helped any in the cutting process. Picture also suffers from poor photography and bad lighting. Its chief assets are strong performances by Margaret Lockwood, Hugh Sinclair and Raymond Lovell.

Production starts off on pretentious scale with lavish setting in Paris cafe, where the menace, a psychic, has top billing. Latter bumps off one of the patrons whom he recognizes as the guy who exposed him and so terminated his lucrative career as a mystic in New York. He creates an alibi by offering one of the hostesses a large bribe to admit he spent the night with her, the gal accepting unaware of the murder rap. How the inspector of police finally runs down the alibi might have made for more edge-of-the-seat tenseness. It's here, chiefly, that the film falls short. Love interest is tied in via one of the inspector's staffers, who pulls the romance gag to extract info only to be caught in his own trap by the real thing.

While Miss Lockwood, as the framed hostess, and Sinclair, as the inspector, give skillful portrayals throughout, both are handicapped by script limitations. Lovell, as the mystic-murderer, except for moments when he tries to mimic Laughton, is an able menace, while James Mason does adequately in the dual role of detective-lover. *Rose.*

TAHITI HONEY

(SONGS)

Hollywood, March 29.

Republic release of John H. Auer production. Stars Simone Simon and Dennis O'Keefe; features Michael Whalen, Lionel Stander, Wally Vernon and Tommye Adams. Directed by John Auer. Screenplay by Lawrence Kimble, Frederick Kohner and W. Hanemann; based on original story by Frederick Kohner; camera, Jack Marta; editor, Richard Van Enger. At the Orpheum, L. A. Running time, **66 MINS.**

This is a neat little program number of comedy and song that will fit nicely into supporting spots in the regular runs and family houses. 'Tahiti Honey' is a lightly textured romantic affair, but is strong enough to carry the various song and band numbers interspersed along the route.

O'Keefe is a band leader and pianist stranded in 'Tahiti,' and, when business is bad, he picks off singer Simone Simon from the opposition cafe. Band members are cool to the inclusion of the girl, but O'Keefe takes her along to San Francisco and a succession of floppo engagements. The girl pursuades the band to change over to sweet music, and the aggregation finally clicks.

O'Keefe and Simone are lovebirds on the sly, setting up a phantom naval officer who is supposed to be engaged to her. One officer does pop up in Miami and provides competition for O'Keefe, but officer steps aside and it all ends okay with O'Keefe and the entire band in navy togs for the finish.

O'Keefe carries the role of romantic bandleader in good style, and Simone Simon is very cute as the girl. Good support is provided by Michael Whalen, Lionel Stander and Wally Vernon. The direction is paced at good speed, catching the utmost in laugh content of a good script. Simone Simon delivers several songs, the best being the title number, which is far from a hit. *Walt.*

MAN OF COURAGE

(SONG

Producing Releasing Corp. release of Lester Cutler production. Features Barton MacLane, Charlotte Wynters, Lyle Talbot, Dorothy Burgess. Directed by Alexis Thurn-Taxis. Screenplay by Arthur St. Clair, Barton MacLane and John Vlahos, from story by MacLane, Herman Ruby, Lew Pollack; camera, Marcel LePicard; editor, Fred Bain. At New York, N. Y., dual week March 23, '43. Running time, **66 MINS.**

John Wallace	Barton MacLane
Joyce Griffith	Charlotte Wynters
George Dickson	Lyle Talbot
Sally Dickson	Dorothy Burgess
Mary Ann	Patsy Nash
Mary Crandall	Forrest Taylor
Tom Haines	John Ince
Mrs. Black	Jane Novak
Erskine Johnson	Erskine Johnson
Alice	Claire Grey
Judge Roberts	Steve Clark
Mike Wilson	Billy Gray
Pete	Frank Yaconelli

This is neither fish nor fowl, being a cross between a gangster meller, a politico crook drama and a courtroom opus. Barton MacLane, top featured player, plus four others, dabbled in the original story and screenplay. Comes close to achieving a new low in corny dialog, situations and overacting. An extremely minor entry suited for some dualers, and then only as secondary entry.

Chief fault of the picture is its inability to decide on plot development. Scripters begin with a typical crooked political yarn. Then the plot swings into dramatic courtroom fare. Then there is a touch of prison life and mother-love theme. Suddenly the kidnapping of a youngster is injected, a gang killing and ultimately the capture of the slayer who started the whole fireworks.

Such a hodge-podge is not helped by Alexis Thurn-Taxis' haphazard directing. Even such capable players as Barton MacLane, as the honest d. a.; Lyle Talbot and Dorothy Burgess show up badly, fault being largely the poor dialog and sad direction.

Charlotte Wynters, as the night club singer, warbles 'Now and Then,' written by Lew Pollack, but this is marred by faulty sound. *Wear.*

RANGERS TAKE OVER

(SONGS)

Producers Releasing Corp. release of Alfred Stern and Arthur Alexander production. Stars Dave 'Tex' O'Brien, Jim Newill; features Iris Meredith, Guy Wilkerson, Cal Shrum and Rhythm Rangers. Directed by Albert Herman; screenplay by Elmer Clifton; camera, Robert Cline; editor, Charles Henkel, Jr. At New York, N. Y., dual, week March 23, '43. Running time, **59 MINS.**

Tex Wyatt	Dave (Tex) O'Brien
Jim Steele	Jim Newill
Panhandle Perkins	Guy Wilkerson
Jean Lorin	Iris Meredith
Capt. Wyatt	Forrest Taylor
Rance Blair	Stan Jolley
Kip Lane	Charles King
Weir Slocum	Carl Matthews
Bill Summers	Harry Harvey
Block Nelson	Lynton Brent
Pete Dawson	Bud Osborne

Cal Shrum and his "Rhythm Rangers"

Typical wasters, lacking outdoor opera names, depends on its musical moments for chief appeal. Mild entry for lesser twin bills.

'Rangers Take Over' follows cactus meller pattern having to do with cattle rustlers and the work of Texas Rangers in stamping out a powerful cattle-rustling gang. Father-son angle is worked in by having the son (Dave O'Brien) join the Ranger outfit commanded by his dad. This brings the expected development of having the son discharged from the ranks and take up with the cattle rustlers. He tips the Rangers on the outlaws' hideout and joins the Texas law enforcers during the showdown gun battle.

O'Brien looks and acts like a Ranger, while Jim Newill, top kick with the outfit, also does well. Burden of most of songs rests with the latter and Cal Shrum's Rhythm Rangers. Original music is by Tex Coe, Robert Hoag and Jack Williams, latter two doing 'Roll Out, Cowboy,' one of better tunes. Iris Meredith is more attractive than most cowboy film femmes. *Wear.*

When We Are Married

(BRITISH-MADE)

London, March 16.

Anglo-American Film Corp. release of British National production. Stars Sidney Howard. Directed by Lance Comfort. Screenplay by Austin Melford, Barbara K. Emary from play by J. B. Priestley. Camera, James Wilson, Arthur Grant. At Cambridge theatre, London. Running time, **90 MINS.**

Henry Ormonroyd	Sidney Howard
Joe Helliwell	Lloyd Pearson
Albert Parker	Raymond Huntley
Gerald Forbes	Barry Morse
Nancy Holmes	Lesley Brookes
Maria Helliwell	Olga Lindo
Clara Soppitt	Ethel Coleridge
Ruby Birtle	Patricia Hayes
Mrs. Northrup	Marjorie Rhodes
Landlord	George Carney
Fred Dyson	Cyril Smith
Lottie Grady	Lydia Sherwood
Mr. Northrup	Charles Victor
Annie Parker	Marian Spencer

Filmization of J. B. Priestley's play looks a boxoffice winner in provincial England, and satisfactory elsewhere in England. Main handicap for it in U. S. will be its Yorkshire dialect though this has been made understandable. It is a little story of rural domesticity that frequently borders on farce. Laid in Yorkshire of 40 years ago, yarn is well told in pungent language, as in the play produced here about five years ago.

It concerns three middle-aged couples, married on the same day, who are about to celebrate their 25th anniversary. At the last moment it is discovered the minister who married them had not been officially ordained, making the marriages illegal. Their reaction to the situation, which points up that these respectable 'chapel' folk had been 'living in sin' for a quarter of a century, provides most of the humor. The types are admirably drawn.

The solid cast has many opportunities and takes full advantage of them with the exception of George Carney, who has only one scene that stands out. *Jolo.*

Tu M'Ami-To T'Amo

('Her First Love')
(ITALIAN-MADE)

Hoffberg release of Cinecita production. Features Alida Valli, Amedeo Nazzari. Directed by Max Neufeld; camera, Vaclav Vich. At 55th St. Playhouse, N. Y., starting Feb. 27, '43. Running time, **95 MINS.**

(In Italian; no English Titles)

Rather lengthy farce comedy is suited for Italian-speaking patrons only. It is meaningless for arty theatres as film now stands because lacking English titles.

Picture, also known as 'You Love Me, I Love You,' which is literal translation of Italian tag, is loaded with verbiage. Film is noteworthy, however, in showing Alida Valli as a likely femme screen personality and Amedeo Nazzari as an ingratiating male player. He looks like Errol Flynn.

Picture apparently was brought into this country via South America, but looks old enough to have reached the U. S. before Italy entered the war. Theatre uses foreword to explain that it is shown for Italian residents in the U. S. who are no more in sympathy with the present Mussolini regime than many people living in Italy.

Story is the familiar one about the young student who falls in love with a man older than she. In this case, it is a doctor who helps her feign illness in order to cover her dismissal from high school. Many farcical passages, though, develop from the girl's yen to step out after she finds wedded life with the medico monotonous.

Max Neufeld's direction is slow. Vaclav Vich, at one time an outstanding Czech cameraman, turned in a strong photography job. Sound is poor. *Wear.*

LASSE-MAJA

(SWEDISH-MADE)

Scandia release of Europa production. Stars Sture Lagerwall; features Liane Linden, Emil Fjellstrom and John Ekman. Directed by Gunnar Olsson. Screenplay by Torsten Floden; camera, Harold Berglund. At 48th Street theatre, N. Y., starting March 20, '43. Running time, **110 MINS.**

Lars Molin (Lasse-Maja)	Sture Lagerwall
'Silver'-John	Emil Fjellstrom
Sheriff Halling	John Ekman
Anders of Lilltorpet	Arthur Natorp
His Daughter Lena	Liane Linden
Baron Krusenhjelm	Rune Carlsten
Madame Agathe	Hjordis Pettrsson
Karl XIV	Karl Magnus Thulstrep

(In Swedish; English Titles)

Latest Scandia film import is overdrawn account of the adventures of a Swedish version Robin Hood. As a cook's tour of the Swedish countryside and as a 19th century costume piece the picture has merit, but there are too much loose dramatic ends, too much inconsistent characterization and sloppy direction.

Story concerns supposedly stupid cook, who is actually a swashbuckling hero, stealing from the rich to help the poor. Sture Lagerwall does most of his second-story work in female disguise, changing with confusing frequency. Confusion also characterizes most of the story. It is a chase film, with the police pursuing Lagerwall and Lagerwall pursuing Liane Linden, whose house he had saved with a timely tax payment. The police eventually catch up with the hero, and Lagerwall eventually catches up with Miss Linden.

Lagerwall acts with gusto, but too many quick changes of character and costume cramp his style. Liane Linden belies the popular conception that all Swedish actresses are blonde facsimiles of Garbo or Bergman. Miss Linden is a raven-haired young lady on the Hedy Lamarr lines, and struggles valiantly with a poor script to give a convincing performance. Rest of cast has a tendency to overplay roles. Subtitles frequently fade or are lost against screen background. However, when legible, they prove adequate.

Don Winslow of The Coast Guard

(SERIAL)

Universal release of Henry MacRae production. Features Don Terry, Walter Sande, Elyse Knox, June Duprez, Philip Ann, Lionel Royce, Nestor Paiva. Directed by Ray Taylor, Lewis D. Colins. Screenplay by Paul Huston, George H. Plympton, Griffin Jay; based on newspaper feature, 'Don Winslow of the Navy'; camera, William Sickner; editor, Saul A. Goodkind. Previewed in Projection Room, N. Y., March 26, '43. In 13 chapters, each about **20 MINS.**

Commdr. Don Winslow	Don Terry
Lt. 'Red' Pennington	Walter Sande
Mercedes Colby	Elyse Knox
Hirota	Philip Ahn
Tasmia	June Dupres
C.P.O. Ben Cobb	Edgar Dearing
Reichter	Lionel Royce
Mussanti	Charles Wagenheim
The Scorpion	Nestor Paiva

Interest in Coast Guard activity in keeping the sea lanes open has inspired Universal into a followup of the Don Winslow 'In the Navy' adventures, with the heroic naval commander duplicating his feats with the Coast Guard. New serial should find good adult as well as juve response. Defense of the Pacific coast against the Nipponese figures in bulk of episodes.

'The Scorpion' is back in this new serial, being the conspirator who is working hand-in-glove with the Japs in their efforts to cut the U. S. supply lines to the South Pacific. There are giant Jap subs capable of launching small planes, super submarines and secret sub-supply bases worked into the plot.

Opening chapter concerns the transfer of Winslow from the Navy to Coast Guard intelligence, and his quick-thinking deeds in averting disaster for himself and an oil tanker. Vivid newsreel clips have been deftly inserted into the staged sequences for maximum of action.

Nicely picked cast is headed by Don Terry in the title role. June Duprez, Walter Sande and Nestor Paiva. Direction by Ray Taylor and Lewis D. Collins manages to maintain an even tempo. *Wear.*

Miniature Reviews

'Pilot No. 5' (M-G). Moderately entertaining programmer.

'My Friend Flicka' (20th) (Color). Fine sentimental outdoor drama about a horse; moderate to good b.o.

'The More the Merrier' (Col). Jean Arthur, Joel McCrea and Charles Coburn in socko farce-comedy.

'Cowboy in Manhattan' (U) (Songs.) Backstage drama good entertainment for supporting slots in duals and family houses.

'The Fighting Buckaroo' (Col). Satisfactory hoss opera with Charles Starrett.

'The Leather Burners' (UA). This Hopalong Cassidy falls short in series but may ride through on rep of predecessors.

'King of the Cowboys' (Rep). Best of the Roy Rogers entries to date.

'Dead Men Walk' (PRC). Preposterous yarn of black magic geared strictly for dualers.

PILOT NO. 5

Metro-Goldwyn-Mayer release of B. P. Fineman production. Stars Franchot Tone, Marsha Hunt and Gene Kelly; features Van Johnson, Alan Baxter, Dick Simmons, Steve Geray and Howard Freeman. Directed by George Sidney. Story and adaptation, David Hertz; film editor, George White; camera, Paul Vogel. Previewed in N. Y., April 1, '43. Running time, **70 MINS.**

George Braynor Collins	Franchot Tone
Freddie	Marsha Hunt
Vito S. Alessandro	Gene Kelly
Everett Arnold	Van Johnson
Winston Davis	Alan Baxter
Henry Willoughby Claven	Dick Simmons
Major Eichel	Steve Geray
Hank Durban	Howard Freeman
Nikola	Frank Puglia
American Soldier	William Tannen

The turbulent events in the life of an Army aviator, prior to the suicide flight he makes wiping out a Jap carrier, is told in flashback fashion in a moderately entertaining programmer known by the odd title of 'Pilot No. 5.' Not strong enough to command major booking, it will suit as an associate feature on the general run of double bills.

Except for a brief stretch of footage toward the end, when Franchot Tone dives his plane into the enemy carrier, as the only way out, there is no war action, but this sequence ending Tone's career provides several exciting moments. Scene of the bombed carrier, explosions and resultant fire has been exceedingly well done.

Despite the title, the story mainly concerns the unfortunate connections made by Tone as a young lawyer and the romance affected by the disgrace befalling him. Tone becomes involved with a crooked gubernatorial machine and, after redeeming himself in the eyes of the citizens by helping to elect another governor, he joins the air force.

As the story opens at a lone Allied outpost, with Tone are four other pilots, including Gene Kelly, also a former attorney who had become entangled with the corrupt governor of an unnamed state, played very well by Howard Freeman. With only one plane left to be taken on a mission seeking to destroy a Jap carrier, Tone is chosen to do the job by a Dutch major who's in command. After he has gone, the other four fliers tell what they know about Tone, but it's mainly Kelly, his former legal associate, who does most of the talking. What he relates is carried out by the flashback method, with the romantic side of the story a fairly dominating factor.

Marsha Hunt, who finally marries Tone after he has gotten his wings, turns in a nice job. Tone himself is excellent, though at times he doesn't photograph to the best advantage. Kelly impresses as an Italian who used to think Il Duce was the tops, while lesser assignments are handled capably by Van Johnson, Alan Baxter, Dick Simons and Steve Geray.

Production and direction are both adequate. *Char.*

MY FRIEND FLICKA

(COLOR)

20th-Fox release of Ralph Dietrich production. Features Roddy McDowall, Preston Foster, Rita Johnson. Directed by Harold Schuster; screenplay, Lillie Hayward; adaptation by Francis Edwards Faragoh, based on novel by Mary O'Hara; camera, Dewey Wrigley; editor, Robert Fritch. Previewed in New York March 31, '43. Running time, **89 MINS.**

Ken McLaughlin..........Roddy McDowall
Rob McLaughlin..........Preston Foster
Nell..........Rita Johnson
Gus..........James Bell
Tim Murphy..........Jeff Corey
Hildy..........Diana Hale
Charley Sargent..........Arthur Loft

Excellent direction and fine scripting in the screen version of this best-selling novel will largely account for moderate to good grosses in all situations. Fine color photography, capable performances by Roddy McDowall, Preston Foster, Rita Johnson and, of course, the magnificent horses, are assets.

Basic theme, necessarily limited in appeal since it's the story of the influence of a wild pony (Flicka), on the lives and philosophy of a small family group, required all the top-notch production values which the producer has provided in order to ensure commercial returns.

Essentially it's the story of a day-dreaming youngster's longing for a colt of his own, the boy's complete transformation once his rancher-father fulfills his desire, and the trials and tribulations in taming and nursing the filly back to health.

Skillfully interwoven is the theme of inherited insanity in animals, with the rancher (Foster) cautioning the boy not to break his heart over a horse whose dam was 'loco.' The boy banks on the sire's substantial blood strain to win out in the filly.

It's a tug-of-wills between father and son, with the boy's judgment finally vindicated when the filly proves that she has become a friend and companion. It's a stirring, sentimental drama. *Mori.*

The More the Merrier

Hollywood, April 1.

Columbia release of George Stevens production, directed by Stevens; associate producer, Fred Guiol. Stars Jean Arthur, Joel McCrea, Charles Coburn; screenplay by Robert Russell, Frank Ross, Richard Flournoy, Lewis R. Foster; story by Russell and Ross; camera, Ted Tetzlaff; editor, Otto Meyer; asst. director, Norman Deming. Previewed at Pantages, March 31, '43. Running time, **101 MINS.**

Connie Milligan..........Jean Arthur
Joe Carter..........Joel McCrea
Benjamin Dingle..........Charles Coburn
Charles J. Pendergast..........Richard Gaines
Evans..........Bruce Bennett
Pike..........Frank Sully
Senator Noonan..........Clyde Fillmore
Morton Rodakiewicz..........Stanley Clements
Harding..........Don Douglas

As producer-director, George Stevens delivers a sparkling and effervescing piece of entertainment in 'The More the Merrier,' which will make customers happy and smack the boxoffices for upper-bracket grosses. Picture is one of the most spontaneous farce-comedies to be released in this wartime era, and will rate both holdovers in the keys and socko biz in the subsequent datings.

Although Jean Arthur and Joel McCrea carry the romantic interest, Charles Coburn takes fullest advantage of a particularly meaty character role to walk off with the honors. Part is the best film assignment for the 'Old Bill' of 'Better 'Ole' stage fame of World War I era; and he smacks over every opportunity to score as the provocative intruder who brings the boy and girl together for an ultimate romantic conclusion.

Story is premised on the housing conditions existing in wartime Washington. Coburn arrives in town and sublets half interest in Miss Arthur's minute apartment, and when he finds the girl without a boy friend, conveniently picks up McCrea—Air Force sergeant in town to get orders for secret mission—to become partner in his share of the housing layout. Naturally complications ensue in hilarious fashion until Coburn backs out to watch the culmination of the romance he very effectively cooks up.

Under most skillful direction by Stevens, picture is studded with brilliant laugh lines and situations. Although Coburn is spotlighted with his oldster characterization of the mischievous cupid, Miss Arthur and McCrea team for several standout episodes that hit the highest mark of screen farce. Love scene between the pair is one of the most effective and hilarious episodes ever staged—expertly directed by Stevens, and played to the hilt by Miss Arthur and McCrea.

Yarn unfolds with concentration on the laugh lines and situations, which continually tumble on top of each other in rapid-fire and spontaneous fashion. Despite the somewhat lengthy running time of 101 minutes, there's no letdown in the fast pace generated by Stevens at the outset.

Although overcrowded conditions existing in present-day Washington prominently background the basic premise, story is an intimate affair which is mostly confined to the two-by-four apartment. But Stevens is not shackled by the restricted quarters—in fact, the reverse is true, and he misses no opportunities to utilize situations available to the utmost.

Coburn, who has been around Hollywood for several years, finally cracks through with a role tailored to his specialized farcical talents, and he scores most effectively. Miss Arthur makes the most of what is undoubtedly the best screen role of her long Hollywood career, and pushes Coburn strong all the way for the top honors. McCrea is effective as the young man who moves into the overcrowded quarters and is the pawn of Coburn's romantic designing. Richard Gaines and young Stanley Clements are most prominent in support, although each is confined to brief footage.

Stevens hits the peak in development of sparkling laugh entertainment for widest audience reaction. Script, as developed by the two writing teams of Robert Russell and Frank Ross, and Richard Flournoy with Lewis R. Foster, is one of the most compact farce-comedies developed in some time. *Walt.*

Cowboy in Manhattan

(SONGS)

Hollywood, Apr. 2.

Universal release of Paul Malvern production. Features Robert Paige, Frances Langford, Leon Erroll, Walter Catlett, Joe Sawyer. Directed by Frank Woodruff. Screenplay by Warren Wilson, original by William Thomas, Maxwell Shane and Wilson; camera, Woody Bredell; editor, Fred R. Feitshans, Jr.; songs, Everett Carter and Milton Rosen; musical director, H. J. Salter; dances, Aida Broadbent. Previewed April 1, '43. Running time, **58 MINS.**

Bob..........Robert Paige
Babs..........Frances Langford
Hank..........Leon Errol
Ace..........Walter Catlett
Louie..........Joe Sawyer
Mitzi..........Jennifer Holt
Wild Bill..........George Cleveland
Higgins..........Will Wright
Tommy..........Dorothy Granger
Potter..........Lorin Raker
Count Kardos..........Marek Windheim
Cab Driver..........Matt McHugh
Headwaiter..........Jack Mulhall
Mac..........Tommy Mack
Bill..........Billy Nelson

This is a program filmusical with backstage setting which, despite its familiar background, has sufficient brightness in lines, situations and numbers to carry it through as an above-par dual supporter in the subsequent and family bookings. Its brevity also will catch good share of support datings in the key spots.

Story carries more substance than ordinarily for this type of picture, with Robert Paige and Frances Langford neatly teamed for the leads, and with particularly strong comedy support from Leon Errol and Walter Catlett. Texas hotel group is promoted by Catlett to back a Broadway musical as exploitation for the state as tourist attraction. Miss Langford is signed for the singing lead and, after rehearsals start, Paige puts in appearance to try and get a couple of his range songs into the show. Catlett and Errol use him for publicity stunt in buying out the house for a week, during which time he sells his tunes for the production and falls in love with Miss Langford. Novel idea makes show a success with the public, and after sufficient complications everything works out for usual happy ending.

Paige adequately teams with Miss Langford for the singing and romantic interludes, with Errol and Catlett taking fullest advantage of the comedy opportunities. Good support is provided by Joe Sawyer, Dorothy Granger, George Cleveland, Jennifer Holt and Will Wright. Script is compact package of entertainment for regular audiences, with Frank Woodruff's direction keeping things moving at a fast pace.

Miss Langford sings three of the five songs provided by Everett Carter and Milton Rosen, with Paige delivering the other two. Numbers are spotted either at rehearsals of the show or at the finale opening, with several having mixed song-and-dance ensemble backgrounds. *Walt.*

The Fighting Buckaroo

Columbia release of Jack Fier production. Stars Charles Starrett; features Kay Harris, Arthur Hunnicutt, Stanley Brown, Ernest Tubb, Wheeler Oakman and Johnny Luther's Ranch Boys. Directed by William Berke; screenplay by Luci Ward; camera, Benjamin Kline; editor, William Claxton. At New York, N. Y., dual, week March 30, '43. Running time, **58 MINS.**

Steve Harrison..........Charles Starrett
Carol Comstock..........Kay Harris
Arkansas..........Arthur Hunnicutt
Dan McBride..........Stanley Brown
Ernie..........Ernest Tubb
Sam Thacher..........Wheeler Oakman
Mark Comstock..........Forrest Taylor
Fletch Thacher..........Robert Stevens
Buckshot..........Norma Jean Wooters
Sheriff..........Roy Butler

This hoss opera follows the familiar formula of the cowboy stranger who steps into town to exonerate a boyhood chum, unjustly accused of tieing in with a cattle rustlin' outfit. As such will satisfy the hoss opera addicts, particularly the juves.

From a production standpoint, its merits are few and the usual emphasis on the comedy is lacking. But what counts are the rootin', tootin', two-fisted aspects. And Charles Starrett's in there punching sufficiently not to impair its b.o. values.

Luci Ward's script rehashes the idea of the prez of a local cattlemen's association brainchilding the rustlin' activities, but manages to put the finger on a bankrupt neighbor, the latter's previous prison stretch on a trumped-up larceny charge lending conviction to the frameup. However, Starrett, with the aid of the prez's daughter, who likes the framed neighbor, brings in the real culprit via the usual channels of engineering a coup to trap the banditti.

Starrett makes a likeable cowboy throughout, while Kay Harris furnishes the ornamental femme background in satisfactory manner. Stanley Brown, as the once rowdy but now honest rancher who almost takes the rap, and Forrest Taylor and Wheeler Oakman, as the chief menaces, are also good in supporting roles. *Rose.*

LEATHER BURNERS

Hollywood, April 3.

United Artists release of Harry Sherman production; associate producer, Lewis J. Rachmil. Stars William Boyd. Directed by Joseph Henabery. Screenplay by Jo Pagano. Based on story by Bliss Lomax and characters created by Clarence E. Mulford; camera, Russell Harlan; editor, Carroll Lewis; director, Glenn Cook. Previewed in studio April 3, '43. Running time, **66 MINS.**

Hopalong Cassidy..........William Boyd
California Carlson..........Andy Clyde
Johnny..........Jay Kirby
Dan Slack..........Victor Jory
Sam Bucktoe..........George Givot
Sharon Longstreet..........Shelley Spencer
Bobby Longstreet..........Bobby Larson
Harrison Brooke..........George Reeves
Lafe..........Hal Taliaferro
Bart..........Forbes Murray

Hopalong Cassidy and his sidekicks ride along in his standard western of formularized dramatics that will slip through regular bookings for the action series on reputation of Hoppy and previous releases of the group.

Both story and script provide a moderate amount of action required for attention of the kids and action-minded customers, but the writers failed to gear up more than regulation melodramatics that have been done innumerable times. Only the usual excellent exterior photography lifts the picture above lower-budget and run-of-the-mill westerns.

Story delivers Hoppy and Andy Clyde to the cattle town, where rustlers' activities have continued despite rancher attempts to uncover the ring. Pair go to work for Victor Jory; soon discover he's involved in the outlaw activities and are accused of both rustling and murder by Jory henchmen. Unimaginative script brings in an abandoned mine, which turns out to be used as runway for the stolen cattle. There's a pitched gun-battle in the mine, a cattle stampede through the tunnels, and eventual roundup of the outlaws.

William Boyd provides his usual characterization of the western hero, with Clyde along for comedy aimed to please to youngsters. Third member of trio, Jay Kirby, has little to do, and same goes for the girl, Shelley Spencer. Little Bobby Larson does well as the young western kid who steps in to help Hoppy in several pinches. Joseph Henabery, veteran director of silents 20 odd years ago, does well in his assignment, but is unfortunately handicapped with the poor story material provided. *Walt.*

King of the Cowboys

(SONGS)

Republic production and release. Stars Roy Rogers; features Smiley Burnette, Bob Nolan, Sons of Pioneers, Peggy Moran, Lloyd Corrigan. Directed by Joseph Kane. Screenplay by Olive Cooper and J. Benton Cheney, from original by Hal Long; camera, Reggie Lanning; editor, Harry Keller. Tradeshown April 2, '43. Running time, **67 MINS.**

Roy..........Roy Rogers
Frog..........Smiley Burnette
Themselves..........Bob Nolan and Pioneers
Judy..........Peggy Moran
Maurice..........Gerald Mohr
Ruby Smith..........Dorothea Kent
Kraly..........Lloyd Corrigan
Dave..........James Bush
Governor..........Russell Hicks
Alf Cluckus..........Irving Bacon
Buxton..........Norman Willis

Latest Roy Rogers entry, his best by far to date, emerges as a neat job into which has been blended in correct proportions the elements of a western, a tent show and a saboteur ring. Film has been nicely paced, the action hits a lively clip and provides okay entertainment that will fit neatly as supporting fare. Republic has budgeted it beyond the usual buckeroo fare.

Rogers shows up here as a rodeo

star chosen by the governor as a special investigator to run down a sabotage ring. Mysterious series of explosions which level warehouses are linked with the perigrinations of a tent show. Rogers tied in with the outfit and finds the leak via a code word coming from the audience during the mystic's act. Governor's aide is the brains behind the ring but before he's exposed there's the usual bundle of trigger-point climaxes in regulation scenario style.

Rogers handles his work in good style throughout, as does Smiley Burnette, who provides the comedy interludes with fine results. Peggy Moran, as the girl, Gerald Mohr and Lloyd Corrigan as the menaces and Russell Hicks as the governor are all okay.

Framework of story permits for a tent show production number, unusual for an oats opera, and the introduction of a half dozen tunes by Rogers and Bob Nolan and the Sons of the Pioneers. *Rose.*

DEAD MEN WALK

Producers Releasing Corp. release of Sigmund Neufeld production. Features George Zucco and Mary Carlisle. Directed by Sam Newfield; screenplay by Fred Myton; camera, Jack Greenhalgh; editor, Holbrook N. Todd. At New York, N. Y., dual, week March 30, '43. Running time, 63 MINS.

Dr. Lloyd Clayton }	George Zucco
Dr. Elwyn Clayton }	
Gayle	Mary Carlisle
Dr. Bentley	Nedrick Young
Zolarr	Dwight Frye
Kate	Fern Emmett
Harper	Robert Strange
Sheriff	Hal Price
Minister	Sam Flint

PRC's excursion into black magic, via the spirit of a corpse which emerges from its tomb nightly to stalk the village streets bringing death to innocent townsfolk, fails to ring the bell as a horror story. It's suspenseful moments are few and far between; the direction mediocre and the acting ditto. Strictly for the lesser dual situations.

Mysterious murders break out in countryside after death of a reputable doctor's twin brother, latter's delving into occult powers and bizarre mysteries having been kept a secret from the respectable burghers. Dead man, with aid of his servant, a sinister hunchback, who nightly removes him from his tomb, practices his nocturnal vampirism on the doctor's ward. The medico alone suspects the supernatural implications, but the villagers, seeing the vampire's silhouetted form, blame the doctor for the midnight crimes and arrange a noose party, with inevitable nick-of-time climactic sequences.

Script offered several possibilities, which, however, were not realized, due chiefly to director Sam Newfield's inability to inject proper punch and excitement in development of yarn.

Performance by George Zucco, in dual role of the doctor and his vampire-brother, alone stands out, although it, too, lacks conviction at times. In so-so support are Mary Carlisle, as the ward upon whom the vamp tries in vain to exercise his black magic, and Nedrick Young, the girl's fiance.

Photography is n.s.g. *Rose.*

La Hija Del Ministro

('Daughter of Minister')
(ARGENTINE-MADE)
Buenos Aires, March 23.

Lumiton production and release. Stars Enrique Serrano, features Juan Carlos Thorry, Silvana Roth, Osvaldo Miranda. Directed by Francisco Mugica. Story by Sixto Pondal Rios, Carlos Olivari; screenplay by Francisco Oyarzabal. At Monumental. Running time, 78 MINS.

First question asked about 'La Hija del Ministro' ('Daughter of the Minister') is how it compares with 'Los Martes Orquideas,' also by Sixto Pondal Rios and Carlos Olivari. It

doesn't compare. 'Hija' is an above-average Argentine-made with a sufficient laugh, a topical political background, and a new romantic team to carry interest when comic Enrique Serrano isn't on screen. Nevertheless it drags in spots.

Marquee values and smooth direction by Francisco Mugica, however, should make it a good grosser in the Latin-Americas. It's a story of a business man (Enrique Serrano) who takes over the Ministry of Social Legislation of an unnamed Latin-American country following a scandal. He has no particular desire for the job, but his daughter (Silvana Roth) wants him to tote the portfolio because it will add to her social prestige. Serrano moves in but no sooner is he set than a young Deputy (Juan Carlos Thorry) sets to work on him, hauling him unmercifully over the coals in his first session before Congress. Daughter is mad over this and disguises herself as a working gal in her dad's old factory, meets the Dep and starts leading him to the slaughter. The work of Enrique Salvador is fine, Serrano is solid, Thorry shows considerable improvement, and Senorita Roth makes an attractive femme lead. Best sequences are those in the Chamber of Deputies, but in view of Argentina's state of seige, which puts a hush-hush on political gags, Mugica has been careful to make sure there's no ribbing of recognizable characters. Photography is only so-so. Music and sound is okay. *Ray.*

Miniature Reviews

'White Savage' (U) (Color).— Maria Montez, Jon Hall and Sabu in a good mass entertainment film for profitable regular runs.

'Cheyenne Roundup' (U). Formula western with Johnny Mack Brown in a dual role; fair b.o.

'Chatterbox' (Songs) (Rep). Joe Brown and Judy Canova unable to keep ancient comedy situations. Filler dualer.

'The Payoff' (PRC). Above average for this outfit, thanks to Lee Tracy; okay b.o.

'Candida, La Mujer Del Ano' (Argentine). Weakie all the way, including boxoffice prospects.

WHITE SAVAGE

Hollywood, April 12.
Universal release of George Waggner production. Stars Jon Hall, Maria Montez, Sabu; features Don Terry, Turhan Bey, Sidney Toler. Directed by Arthur Lubin. Original, Peter Milne; screenplay by Richard Brooks; camera (Technicolor), William Snyder, (black and white) Lester White; editor, Russel Schoengarth; music, Frank S. Kinney. Previewed April 12, '43. Running time, 75 MINS.

Kaloe	Jon Hall
Princess Tahia	Maria Montez
Orano	Sabu
Chris	Don Terry
Tamara	Turhan Bey
Miller	Thomas Gomez
Wong	Sidney Toler
Erik	Paul Guilfoyle
Blossom	Constance Purdy

Universal again teams Maria Montez, Jon Hall and Sabu in Technicolored display of escapist romance and vigorous adventure, unfolded on a South Sea Island. Although following familiar pattern for pictures of its type, 'White Savage' is diverting entertainment for current audience reception and will follow profit lines in regular key and subsequent bookings as solo or billtopper.

Recent releases of 'Arabian Nights' with starring trio will provide lift to marquee values. Color photography greatly enhances pictorial backgrounds and settings, story unwinds at consistent pace, with neat admixture of action, melodramatics, and idyllic romance.

Arthur Lubin capably handles directing chores. Miss Montez is the native princess ruling over a small island in the Coral Seas just across the channel from a larger isle which serves as the commercial center for district. Shark fisherman Jon Hall arrives to obtain fishing privileges of island, while trader Thomas Gomez is bent on getting possession of native pool which is lined with gold and jewels. Sabu is the native urchin who acts as self-appointed Cupid for romantic display between the princess and fisherman.

Fabled tale pits Hall against machinations of Gomez, with usual obvious melodramatics along the line until Gomez and his henchmen invade island for theft of gold and jewels. Natives' guardian god on the mountaintop provides the necessary earthquake to send them to their deaths.

Miss Montez deftly underplays her characterization of the princess, delivering her best performance to date. Hall is a vigorous hero, per usual, while Sabu provides lightness with his nimble and mischievous antics. Sidney Toler displays an interesting character as a jack-of-all-trades Chinaman who befriends Hall and is the key to smashing Gomez's ambitions. Latter is typically the heavy, with good assistance from Paul Guilfoyle. Turhan Bey and Don Terr are also prominent in support.

Picture has been given 'A' production mounting throughout, with Technicolor photography by Lester White and William Snyder particu-

larly effective in presenting colorful settings and investitures. *Walt.*

CHEYENNE ROUNDUP
(SONGS)

Universal release of Oliver Drake production. Stars Johnny Mack Brown and Tex Ritter; features Fuzzy Knight, Jennifer Holt and the Jimmy Wakely Trio. Directed by Ray Taylor. Screenplay, Elmer Clifton and Bernard McConville; camera, William Sickner; editor, Otto Ludwig. At New York, N. Y., dual, week April 6, '43. Running time, 56 MINS.

Gila Brandon	Johnny Mack Brown
Buck Brandon	Johnny Mack Brown
Steve Rawlins	Tex Ritter
Cal Cawkins	Fuzzy Knight
Ellen Randall	Jennifer Holt
Blackie Dawson	Harry Woods
Slim Layton	Roy Barcroft
Judge Hickenbottom	Robert Barron
Bonanza	Budd Buster
Perkins	Gil Patric
The Jim Wakely Trio	

This western sticks pretty much to formula. Johnny Mack Brown gets plenty of chance to emote as twins, one an ornery cuss, the other a strong right arm of law and order. Add Tex Ritter's tight-lipped straight-from-the-shoulder sheriff portrayal and this pinto drama is fair fodder for the action fans.

Brown, as the bad brother, takes over a mining ghost town after having been run out of one county by Ritter. When Brown and his gang get out of hand, Fuzzy Knight writes to his friend, Rititer, to move in and clean up the town. Ritter does, but not until he and his posse kill the nefarious twin, who dies in the arms of his long-lost, law-abiding brother. Ritter and the twin then make a deal to wipe out the gang, the twin masquerading as his dead brother.

Acting is par for westerns, with Brown, Ritter, Knight and Jennifer Holt delivering as per script. The Jimmy Wakely Trio does a musical once-over-lightly, and the rest of the cast goes through the proper motions. Film lagged in spots, but was generally well-paced.

CHATTERBOX
(SONGS)

Hollywood, April 7.
Republic release of Albert J. Cohen production. Stars Joe E. Brown, Judy Canova. Directed by Joseph Santley. Original screenplay by George Carleton Brown and Frank Gill, Jr.; camera, Ernest Miller; editor, Ernest Nims; special effects, Howard Lydecker; songs, Harry Akst and Sol Meyer; musical director, Walter Scharf. Previewed April 6, '43. Running time, 75 MINS.

Rex Vane	Joe E. Brown
Judy Boggs	Judy Canova
Carol Forrest	Rosemary Lane
Sebastian Smart	John Hubbard
Gillie	Gus Schilling
Wilfred Peckinpaugh	Chester Clute
Vivian Gale	Anne Jeffreys
Roger Grant	Emmett Vogan
Joe	George Byron
Black Jake	Billy Bletcher
Milla Brothers	
Spade Cooley and His Boys	

This one strings together a series of moth-eaten comedy episodes for unfunny conclusion. Even the familiar antics of Joe Brown and Judy Canova fail to lift the shoddy material provided in the script.

Brown, radio cowboy broadcaster, is signed for a film and arrives in western town on location. When tumbling off a horse, he's saved by Miss Canova, but publicity provides adverse public reaction, and girl is signed to appear with him for face-saving. After winding through various film-making and synthetic romantic episodes, pair are conveniently placed on mountain-top which is to be dynamited for new state road. Finale utilizes the toppling and balancing mountain cabin with the couple inside, but it's crudely timed and executed, hence falls flat.

Brown and Miss Canova are directed to mug broadly and generally over-act, which does not help the proceedings. Supporting cast stumbles through the impossible situations provided. Miss Canova sings three songs in typical hillbilly style, while the Mills Bros. are in briefly and lost in delivering one tune. *Walt.*

THE PAYOFF

Producers Releasing Corp. release of Jack Schwarz production. Features Lee Tracy, Tom Brown, Tina Thayer and Evelyn Brent. Directed by Arthur Dreifuss. Screenplay, Edward Dein; camera, Ira Morgan; editor, Charles Henkel, Jr. At New York, N. Y., dual, week April 6, '43. Running time, **74 MINS.**

Brad McKay....................Lee Tracy
Guy Morris....................Tom Brown
Phyllis Walker................Tina Thayer
Alma Dorene...................Evelyn Brent
John Angus....................Jack La Rue
Inspector.....................Ian Keith
Moroni........................John Maxwell
Sergeant Brenen...............John Sheehan
Dr. Steele....................Harry Bradley
Hugh Walker...................Forrest Taylor
Reporter......................Pat Costello

With Lee Tracy as the cynical, solve-all reporter, 'The Payoff' rates several notches above usual PRC standards. It will draw stubholders who like a mixture of murder and newshounds and cling to the illusion that fourth-estaters cover stories with one arm around a burnet, a gin bottle in the free hand, and tell the police how to run their business. Tracy does all this.

A special prosecutor, about to prepare evidence against the city's biggest racketeer, is killed in a suspenseful opening scene. After that the film is all Tracy's. He's a star reporter who has been working on the racket probe. Sleuthing on his own, he discovers the killer, aided by Tom Brown, a cub reporter and son of the paper's owner; Tina Thayer, daughter of a man who knows the answers, and Evelyn Brent, who portrays a shady lady with her heart in the right place. Half-way through the film the man behind the murder is easy to spot, but the actual climax is excitingly done.

Tracy has enough of the old sparkle to take top acting honors. Miss Brent lends particularly good support, but needs better costuming. Tina Thayer and Tom Brown hit it off in the puppy-love scenes. Direction, like script, is above average for PRC.

Candida, La Mujer Del Ano

('Candida, Woman of the Year')
(ARGENTINE-MADE)

Buenos Aires, April 1.

Sono Film production and release. Stars Nini Marshall and features Augusto Codeca, Carlos Morganti, Julio Renato, Alfredo Jordan, Edna Norrell, Blanca Vidal, Lalo Malcolm and Carlos Bellucci. Directed by Enrique Santos Discepolo. Story and adaptation by Meanos, Menasche and Discepolo. Reviewed at the Ocean. Running time, **73 MINS.**

(In Spanish)

A few more like this one and comedienne Nini Marshall, one of Latin-America's top film stars, is going to slip a few rungs. Story is weak, direction indifferent and cast mediocre. About the worst of the 'Candida' series which Sono Film has put out in a long time, and while Marshall name will bring some biz to the boxoffice, it will hardly be a strong grosser.

Senorita Marshall once again handles the Candida characterization based on a servant girl whose ability to get into complicated situations provides most of the laughs. *Ray.*

Miniature Reviews

'Crash Dive' (Technicolor) (20th). Exciting submarine saga starring Tyrone Power geared for top grosses.

'They Came to Blow Up America' (20th). George Sanders, Anna Sten in saboteur meller; strong dual supporter.

'Good Morning, Judge' (Songs) (U). Program comedy-drama with good pace to carry through as standard dual supporter.

'Taxi, Mister' (UA). Hal Roach streamliner will satisfy in usual slot as supporting programmer.

'I Escaped From the Gestapo' (Mono). Spy meller okay for supporting datings in the secondary duals.

'Keep 'Em Slugging' (U). Dead End Kids and Little Tough Guys in a program meller.

'Shantytown' (songs) (Rep). Non-war tale of a tomboy. Okay for duals.

CRASH DIVE

(TECHNICOLOR)

20th-Fox release of Milton Sperling production. Stars Tyrone Power, Anne Baxter, Dana Andrews; features James Gleason, Dame May Whitty, Henry Morgan, Ben Carter. Directed by Archie Mayo. Screenplay, Jo Swerling, based on original by W. R. Burnett; camera, Leon Shamroy; special effects, Fred Sersen; editor, Walter Thompson. Tradeshown April 17, '43. Running time, **105 MINS.**

Lieut. Ward Stewart........Tyrone Power
Jean Hewlitt...............Anne Baxter
Lieut. Commdr. Connors....Dana Andrews
McDonnell..................James Gleason
Grandmother...........Dame May Whitty
Brownie....................Henry Morgan
Oliver Cromwell Jones..........Ben Carter
Hammond...................Charles Tannen
Captain Bryson.............Frank Conroy
Doris......................Florence Lake
Curly......................John Archer
Crew Member...............George Holmes
Butler.....................Minor Watson
Miss Bromley...........Kathleen Howard
Lieutenant..................David Bacon
Captain...................Stanley Andrews
Clerk........................Paul Burns
Sailor.......................Gene Rizzi

'Crash Dive' is 20th-Fox's salute to the submarine crews of the U. S. Navy. It packs terrific wallop and is geared to exceptional b.o. grosses in all situations.

Endowed with a fine cast, headed by Tyrone Power for marquee strength, it has been directed with consummate skill and artistry by Archie Mayo, unfolds a tense, dramatic series of undersea warfare episodes and, visually, through its excellent Technicolor treatment, is at all times highly distinctive.

True, the script concocted by Jo Swerling from an original by W. R. Burnett can hardly lay claim to originality, with the film having a tendency to slip during its maudlin boy-chases-gal sequences in the early chapters, but once the preliminaries have been disposed of and the U.S.S. Corsair starts hitting the high seas, it's a tense, arresting saga of sub warfare that's as educational as it is entertaining. When the picture deals with the adventures of the sub's crew in maneuvering the ship through narrow channels to elude sub nets and a profusion of mines, with only a matter of inches the difference between life and death, it creates an overwhelming suspense. The fact that many of the film's top moments are derived from an examination of the intricacies involved in the complex operation of the submersible is a tribute to director Mayo for his ability to dramatize the technical aspects of the sub's mechanisms with such vividness and clarity, and endow it with a maximum of entertainment. Throughout the latter part, the film is charged with surefire episodes, such as the sub's crash diving to the floor of the ocean as depth charges from an enemy Q-boat explode about her, with the resultant sinking of the enemy vessel via a ruse whereby the sub fires dummies to the surface and ejects oil to convey to the Germans that she has been sunk. 'Crash' was made in cooperation with the U. S. naval sub base at New London, Conn., where many of its sequences were filmed.

Tale opens on a weak note with Lt. Tyrone Power transferred from a PT mosquito boat to submarine service. En route to Washington for instructions he meets up with Anne Baxter, a New London teacher taking a group of junior misses on an educational tour of the capital. The officer gets off on the wrong foot through a lower berth mixup and later they wind up at the same hotel where, through another sleeping arrangement maneuver, he puts on a wolf act to gain her affections. It's trite, but solid stuff for the Power fans. Back in New London, where the gal has returned to her teaching post, he continues his play for her, finally winning her over only to learn she's the fiancee of his superior officer, Dana Andrews. Thus is laid the background for the conflict between the two officers which is only submerged by their allegiance to the Corsair and their respect for each other's abilities.

It's when the triangle situation is properly relegated to a background that the film's interest hypoes, with the sea episodes building up to a sock climactic sequence when the sub is ordered back into the North Atlantic waters to find and destroy a Nazi minelaying base in the vicinity of its first encounter with the Q-boat. The manner in which the sub's crew blasts the shore installations and torpedoes subs and other enemy craft, while required to work with split-second accuracy, offers moments of terrific excitement and permits for maximum production presentation, enhanced considerably by the Technicolor.

Power is expertly cast both in the romantic role and as the sub officer. Andrews also turns in a top performance, as does Miss Baxter. In supporting roles, James Gleason, Dame May Whitty, Henry Morgan and Ben Carter, latter as the sub's colored mess attendant, likewise rate kudos. *Rose.*

They Came to Blow Up America

20th-Fox release of Lee Marcus production. Stars George Sanders, Anna Sten; features Ward Bond, Ludwig Stossel. Directed by Edward Ludwig. Screenplay by Aubrey Wisberg from original by Michel Jacoby; editor, Nick De Maggio; camera, Lucien Andriot; special effects, Fred Sersen. Tradeshown in N. Y. April 19, '43. Running time, **73 MINS.**

Carl Steelman..............George Sanders
Frau Reiker....................Anna Sten
Craig..........................Ward Bond
Colonel Taeger...............Dennis Hoey
Dr. Herman Baumer...........Sig Ruman
Julius Steelman.............Ludwig Stossel
Captain Kranz...............Robert Barrat
Helga Lorenz...................Poldy Dur
Heinrich Burkhardt...........Ralph Byrd
Mrs. Henrietta Steelman.....Elsa Janssen
Eichner.....................Rex Williams
Zellerbach................Charles McGraw
Commander Houser.......Sven Hugo Borg
Schonzeit.....................Kurt Katch
Fritz.......................Otto Reichow
Zugholtz....................Andre Charlot
Kranz' Aide....................Arno Frey
Jones..........................Sam Wren
Theresa....................Etta McDaniel
Gertzer.....................Peter Michael
Coast Guardsman..............Dick Hogan
Saleslady......................Lisa Golm
Schlegel..................Wolfgang Zilzer

Lacking big marquee names and handicapped by its elongated title, 'They Came to Blow Up America' nevertheless is a deftly concocted melodrama of Nazi sabotage efforts in U. S.

Yarn concerns the German saboteurs who were landed off Long Island, N. Y., opening with the sentencing of the eight Nazi espionage agents. Flashback method is used to detail what supposedly backgrounded their capture. However, main thread of fable follows the efforts of an F.B.I. operative to ferret out Nazi sabotage ahead of actual event.

Despite the fact that the story follows the accepted pattern in showing how the Gestapo and espionage boys are trained in Germany, Edward Ludwig's well-paced direction makes an exciting tale out of obviously melodramatic, and sometimes implausible, material. Loyal F.B.I. agent substitutes for a dead Bund operative in U. S. and ingratiates himself with the Nazi Naval Intelligence in Germany, George Sanders being the agent who goes on the exciting trip inside enemy headquarters. He's just landed on Long Island from a German sub when word is flashed that he should be executed forthwith because a spy.

Somebody in Sanders' own family had talked to one of his best friends (the family doctor), and word was flashed back to Germany nearly in time to cause his death. However, Sanders lands successfully and goes through with the trial with his true identity not revealed by the F.B.I. until later.

Sanders turns in a solid performance as a convincing American-German type in the F.B.I. employ. Anna Sten, as the Austrian beauty tied up with the underground movement in Germany, is excellent though in a secondary role. Her affair with Sanders is all too brief. In contrast, Poldy Dur, as the wife of the dead Bundist who nearly traps Sanders, is given a meaty part. Ludwig Stossel is remarkably fine as Sanders' German dad, who is sickened by the prospect that his son is falling for the Bundist movement. Ward Bond, as the F.B.I. chief, makes something of his role. Support is headed by Ralph Byrd, Dennis Hoey, Sig Ruman, Robert Barrat and Elsa Janssen.

Besides the exciting direction, trim camera work by Lucien Andriot and outstanding special photo effects by Fred Sersen help the all-round strong production afforded by Lee Marcus. *Wear.*

Good Morning, Judge

(SONGS)

Hollywood, April 16.

Universal release of Paul Malvern production. Stars Dennis O'Keefe, Louise Allbritton; features Mary Beth Hughes, J. Carroll Naish. Directed by Jean Yarbrough. Screenplay by Maurice Geraghty and Warren Wilson; original, Geraghty and Winston Miller; camera, John W. Boyle; editor, Edward Curtiss; songs by Milton Rosen, Everett Carter. Previewed April 15, '43. Running time, **66 MINS.**

David Barton..............Dennis O'Keefe
Elizabeth Christine Smith.Louise Allbritton
Mira Bryon.............Mary Beth Hughes
Andre....................J. Carrol Naish
Cleo......................Louise Beavers
J. P. Gordon.............Samuel S. Hinds
Ben Pollard.................Frank Faylen
Harry Pollard...............Ralph Peters
Magistrate.................Oscar O'Shea
Nicky Clark..................Marie Blake
Biscuit Face................Don Barclay

This is a compact little package of comedy-drama, with accent on familiar but brightened comedic situations, that will carry it through the program houses as a good supporter for more serious fare.

Dennis O'Keefe is a music publisher with both a song hit and a warbling blonde, Mary Beth Hughes, on his hands. He's sued for plagiarism, with portia Louise Allbritton handling plaintiff's case and insistant on trial rather than settlement. Publisher and femme attorney meet without knowing each other's identity and dine together. But when O'Keefe realizes girl is to appear in court against him the next day, he tosses her a mickey finn. Yarn unravels in merry and not too serious fashion, with O'Keefe in and out of court between running gag of further mickeys liberally dispensed. There's a brief but aggressive battle between Miss Hughes and portia for another court rendevous, and finally clinch between O'Keefe and the girl attorney.

Yarn is lightly set up and not in too serious a vein, with both good script and paceful direction by Jean Yarbrough combining to keep up interest in the proceedings. O'Keefe competently handles his assignment of the music publisher, with Miss Allbritton catching attention in her first light role as the femme attorney. Miss Hughes and J. Carroll Naish provide solid support, with others in cast turning in good performances including Frank Faylen, Ralph Peters, Samuel S. Hinds, Louise Beavers, Oscar O'Shea, Marie Blake and Don Barclay.

Miss Hughes, displayed as musical revue star chasing O'Keefe, sings two numbers by Milton Rosen and Everett Carter—'Spellbound' and 'Sort of a Kinda.' Former gets two deliveries along the line, and is a good tune, but not strong enough for more than passing attention. *Walt.*

TAXI, MISTER

United Artists release of Hal Roach (Fred Guiol) production. Features William Bendix, Grace Bradley. Directed by Kurt Neumann. Screenplay, Earle Snell, Clarence Marks; camera, Robert Pittack; editor, Richard Currier. At Palace, N. Y., dual, April 15, '43. Running time, 45 MINS.

Tim McGuerin	William Bendix
Sadie McGuerin	Grace Bradley
Eddie Corbett	Joe Sawyer
Glorio	Sheldon Leonard
Stretch	Joe Devlin
Van Nostrum	Jack Norton
Silk	Frank Faylen
Joe	Mike Mazurki
Henry	Sig Arno
Hogan	Clyde Fillmore
Objector	Jimmy Conlon
Lew Kelly	Lew Kelly
Waitress	Iris Adrian
Chorus Girl	Lona Andre

This is the third in the series about the Brooklyn McGuerins and, like the streamliners preceding, fills the bill nicely as a supporting programmer for family trade picture houses.

It's a light but pleasant comedy, not geared for belly-laughs, but satisfying in conjunction with heavier dramatic material.

Yarn, handled via the flashback technique, tells how Tim McGuerin (Bendix) and his partner (Joe Sawyer) build up a taxi company from scratch to 1,000 cabs. McGuerin owes it all to a curve he developed as a pitcher on a backyard baseball team. He gets a $10,000 award for capturing a notorious racketeer whom he downs by throwing a fancy curve with a monkey wrench.

Bendix and Sawyer, as the partners, register as an amiable team of funsters while Grace Bradley does well as the burlesque queen with a yen for a marriage ring and a cottage. Girl displays shapely gams in the burlesque sequences. *Mori.*

I Escaped From the Gestapo

Hollywood, April 11.

Monogram release of King Brothers production. Stars Dean Jagger, John Carradine and Mary Brian. Directed by Harold Young. Screenplay, Henry Blankfort and Wallace Sullivan; original, Blankfort; camera, Ira H. Morgan; editor, S. K. Winston; asst. directors, Arthur Gardner and Herman King. Previewed at Ambassador, April 10, '43. Running time, 74 MINS.

Lane	Dean Jagger
Martin	John Carradine
Helen	Mary Brian
Gordan	Bill Henry
Bergen	Sidney Blackmer
Gerard	Ian Keith
Lokin	Anthony Ward
Lunt	Billy Marshall
Rodt	Norman Willis
Haft	Charles Waggenheim
Domack	Ed Keane
Hilda	Greta Grandstadt
Billy	Spanky McFarland

'I Escaped From the Gestapo' is a satisfactory spy melodrama grooved for dual support in the secondary houses. Despite the low budget restrictions that are apparent on the production side, picture carries good cast toppers in trio of Dean Jagger, John Carradine and Mary Brian to lift it above par for a Monogram release.

Despite title implications, it's not a European background but domestic locale that displays operations of the Gestapo ring. Jagger is an expert counterfeiter who's aided in jailbreak by the Nazis so they can kidnap and use him for engraving forged plates of various securities of both the United States and neutral countries. Although he wises up to the Gestapo aims, Jagger presumably agrees until he can get word outside for the eventual roundup. Story weaves through the usual melodramatics until it reaches that conclusion.

Jagger is pitted against Carradine, head of the Gestapo group, in development of the tale, with Miss Brian briefly seen as the girl for very minor romantic interest. Good support is provided by Bill Henry, Sidney Blackmer and Ian Keith. Direction is adequate in concentrating on the suspense provided by the script. *Walt.*

KEEP 'EM SLUGGING

Universal release of Ben Pivar production. Features Huntz Hall, Bobby Jordan, Gabriel Dell, Norman Abbott, Evelyn Ankers, Don Porter, Elyse Knox, Frank Albertson. Directed by Christy Sabanne. Screenplay by Brenda Weisberg from original story by Edward Handler and Robert Gordon; camera, William Sickner; editor, Ray Snyder. At New York theatre, N. Y., dual, week April 14. Running time, 60 MINS.

Pig	Huntz Hall
Tommy	Bobby Jordan
String	Gabriel Dell
Ape	Norman Abbott
Sheila	Evelyn Ankers
Suzanne	Elyse Knox
Frank	Frank Albertson
Jerry	Don Porter
Binky	Shep Howard
Curruthers	Samuel S. Hinds
Mrs. Banning	Mary Gordon
Duke Redman	Milburn Stone
Lela	Joan Marsh

Hampered by poor story material this latest of the Dead End Kids-Little Tough Guys series has little to offer except to the clientele of the cast. Yarn is weak from the time it gets under way. Only one sequence stands out—the capture of truck robbers by the gang with the aid of a fire hose.

Kids turn in their usual typed performances as toughies who get jobs in a department store, where Frank Albertson, as head of the delivery department, is implicated with thieves. Albertson has an interest in Evelyn Ankers, employed in the jewelry department. When Albertson frames Bobby Jordan with some stolen jewelry, the Kids are jailed. On getting released Jordan tails Albertson and, with the gang, captures the thieves.

Huntz Hall, Gabriel Dell and Norman Abbott get what they can from their parts, which isn't much. Miss Ankers and Don Porter as the love interest turn in good performances. Direction is ordinary.

SHANTYTOWN

(SONGS)

Republic release of Harry Grey production. Directed by Joseph Santley. Features Mary Lee, John Archer, Marjorie Lord. Screenplay, Olive Cooper; adaptation, Henry Moritz; camera, Ernest Miller; editor, Thomas Richards. Previewed in N. Y. April 16, '43. Running time, 63 MINS.

Liz Gorty	Mary Lee
Bill Allen	John Archer
Virginia Allen	Marjorie Lord
Doc Herndon	Harry Davenport
Papa Ferrelli	Billy Gilbert
Mrs. Gorty	Anne Revere
Mr. Gorty	J. Frank Hamilton
Whitey	Frank Jenks
Shortcake	Cliff Nazarro
Bindy	Carl 'Afalfa' Switzer
Dugan	Robert Homans
Ace Landers	Noel Madison

Matty Malneck and His Orchestra

One of the few of the recent low-budget pictures without a war theme, 'Shantytown' will prove okay in the lesser dual situations. Film has good direction, four songs, as many orchestra numbers and a conglomeration of entertainment values to suit almost every taste.

Mary Lee, as the girl from the other side of the railroad tracks whose parents operate a ramshackle boarding house, is given an opportunity to display all her talents, from a hoydenish sand-lot baseball player to a singer, with dramatic acting interspersed throughout.

Story concerns the kid tomboy falling for John Archer, an innocent mechanic, who had been intrigued by a band of auto thieves. Archer gets a job in the girl's home town and she brings him to her home to live. The lad is married, wife being played by Marjorie Lord. About the time the wife arrives at the boarding house, the racketeers stop at the garage where Archer is employed and force him to drive a getaway car for a bank holdup. Archer tries to signal a cop by flashing on the lights. But the holdup is committed, one of the robbers killed and Archer escapes. His wife expects a child and Mary Lee endeavoring to urge him to return goes on an amateur-hour program and gets her message over.

Anne Revere, Harry Davenport, Billy Gilbert, Frank Jenks, Cliff Nazarro and Carl 'Alfalfa' Switzer turn in good performances, while Marjorie Lord's screen personality is photographed to advantage.

Miniature Reviews

'Presenting Lily Mars' (M-G) (Songs). Judy Garland and Van Heflin in escapist entertainment, will hit profitable grosses.

'Above Suspicion' (M-G). Joan Crawford-Fred MacMurray spy meller. Okay for nominal biz.

'Captive Wild Woman' (U). Sprightly horror thriller; strong dual support.

'Hoppy Serves a Writ' (UA). Slick Hopalong Cassidy western with William Boyd in title role.

'Follow the Band' (U) (Songs). Wrap-up of musical specialties in moderate budget programmer

'Reveille With Beverly' (Col). Thin musical with numbers by Frank Sinatra and four name bands. For swing fan audiences only.

'Junior Army' (Col). Very poor programmer.

'My Son, The Hero' (PRC). Mild comedy. Fair b.o.

Presenting Lily Mars

(SONGS)

Hollywood, April 27.

Metro release of Joseph Pasternak production. Stars Judy Garland, Van Heflin; features Fay Bainter, Richard Carlson, Spring Byington, Marta Eggerth, Connie Gilchrist, Leonid Kinskey, Tommy Dorsey orchestra, Bob Crosby orchestra. Directed by Norman Taurog. Screenplay by Richard Connell, Gladys Lehman, based on novel by Booth Tarkington; camera, Joseph Ruttenberg; special effects, Warren Newcombe; editor, Albert Akst; songs, Walter Jurmann, Paul Francis Webster, E. Y. Harburg, Burton Lane, Roger Edens; musical adaptation by Edens; musical direction, Georgie Stoll; dances, Ernst Matray. Tradeshown in L. A. April 27, '43. Running time, 106 MINS.

Lily Mars	Judy Garland
John Thornway	Van Heflin
Mrs. Thornway	Fay Bainter
Owen Vail	Richard Carlson
Mrs. Mars	Spring Byington
Isobel Rekay	Marta Eggerth
Frankie	Connie Gilchrist
Leo	Leonid Kinskey
Poppy	Patricia Barker
Violet	Janet Chapman
Rosie	Annabelle Logan
Davey	Douglas Croft
Charlie Potter	Ray McDonald

Tommy Dorsey and His Orchestra
Bob Crosby and His Orchestra

'Presenting Lily Mars' spotlights Judy Garland and Van Heflin in a stage Cinderella yarn that supplies minor switches to regulation formula, but mainly depends on performances, direction and musical mounting, to carry it through as a profitable grosser.

Songs are about equally divided between Judy Garland and Marta Eggerth, with both putting over respective numbers in scintillating fashion. Connie Gilchrist catches attention in a brief episode in delivery of the oldie, 'Every Little Movement,' with Miss Garland joining in for duo rendition. Although Bob Crosby and his orchestra and Tommy Dorsey and his band are provided with featured billing, each aggregation is on for minor footage and fails to be spotlighted.

Story is a typical Cinderella tale, with Miss Garland an aspiring and stagestruck youngster who attempts to catch attention of producer Van Heflin in a small Indiana town. She makes a pest of herself for 40 minutes of the running time until she follows him into New York, gets a job in his new show, and eventually falls in love with the producer. Romance results in walkout of star, Miss Eggerth, induction of the youngster into the lead for rehearsals, and eventual return of Miss Eggerth for the opening performance. But the neophyte Miss Garland eventually clicks on Broadway as predicted by Heflin.

Picture is decidedly overlength, and deep cutting of the running time of 106 minutes could help materially in tightening process. After all, it's a backstage tale, but the 40 minutes of preliminaries should have been clipped for tighter footage. In this early sector, there's plenty of diverting by-play only cemented by deft direction and slick performances.

Heflin adequately handles the assignment of the young producer who eventually falls in love with Miss Garland. Latter delivers in her usual effective style as the aspiring actress, putting across her numbers in top fashion. Marta Eggerth provides solid support on both acting and singing ends, while others prominent in support include Fay Bainter, Richard Carlson, Spring Byington, Patricia Barker and Leonid Kinskey.

Best tune of several incorporated into the production looks like 'When I Look at You.' Miss Eggerth delivers it in good style for introduction, with Miss Garland taking it up later for typical delivery and then a pantomime delivery for comedy reaction. Second in importance is Miss Eggerth's rendition of 'Is It Really Love,' while 'Tom, Tom, the Piper's Son' is a novelty tune presented by Miss Garland.

Bob Crosby band is on for one tune in a nightspot where Miss Garland heads for the mike to sing a song, while Tommy Dorsey and his ork appears for the finale accompaniment to song and dance by Miss Garland.

Norman Taurog directs in a straight line, and turns in good account of himself despite the overlength script. There's a moderate amount of comedy and diverting entertainment along the line. *Walt.*

ABOVE SUSPICION

Hollywood, April 27.

Metro release of Victor Saville production; associate producer, Leon Gordon. Stars Joan Crawford, Fred MacMurray; features Conrad Veidt, Basil Rathbone, Reginald Owen. Directed by Richard Thorpe. Screenplay by Keith Winter, Melville Baker, Patricia Coleman, based on novel by Helen MacInnes; camera, Robert Plank; editor, George Hively. Tradeshown in L. A. April 26, '43. Running time, **90 MINS.**

Frances Myles	Joan Crawford
Richard Myles	Fred MacMurray
Hassert Seidel	Conrad Veidt
Sig von Aschenhausen	Basil Rathbone
Dr. Mespelbrunn	Reginald Owen
Peter Galt	Richard Ainley
Countess	Cecil Cunningham
Aunt Ellen	Ann Shoemaker
Aunt Hattie	Sara Haden
Mr. A. Werner	Felix Bressart
Thornley	Bruce Lester
Frau Kleist	Johanna Hofer
Ottilie	Lotta Palfi

This is another in the familiar current cycle of European spy dramas, developed along familiar lines and not too clearcut in its exposition. Picture will require all of the marquee voltage generated by starring team of Fred MacMurray and Joan Crawford to carry it through the regular runs as billtopper, and even then will need strong support for more than passable biz.

After establishing MacMurray and Miss Crawford as newlywed Americans in England, planning honeymoon in south of Germany just prior to outbreak of the war, yarn has British secret service drafting them for mission to secure vital confidential plans for the secret weapon—a magnetic mine. Pair pick up the trail in Paris and then hop to Salzburg, where it becomes a mysterious chase with various and sundry characters peering out of shadows and suddenly turning up in the most approved spy fashion. When suspicion of the Gestapo is cast in their direction, they assume disguises in attempt to get over the border. Girl is captured but rescued from outlying castle headquarters of the Gestapo in regulation heroics, and they make the final dash for safety.

Picture is filled with various incidents that crop up and then vanish, with no reason for their inclusion except to confuse the audience and by-pass straight-line exposition of the tale. Deeper cutting could materially speed up tempo of the piece to make it more acceptable for audience consumption.

Both MacMurray and Miss Crawford competently handle their roles, despite drawbacks of script material. The late Conrad Veidt clicks solidly in major supporting spot, along with brief appearances of Basil Rathbone as a Gestapo leader. Others listed in support are mainly on for minor footage and in episodes off the main trend. Richard Thorpe's direction is standard, but he's obviously handicapped by story material provided. *Walt.*

Captive Wild Woman

Universal release of Ben Pivar production. Features Acquanetta, Evelyn Ankers, John Carradine, Milburn Stone; directed by Edward Dmytryk; screenplay by Henry Sucher and Griffin Jay from original by Ted Fithian and Maurice Pivar; camera, George Robinson; editor, Milton Carruth. Previewed in N. Y., April 26, '43. Running time, **61 MINS.**

Beth Colman	Evelyn Ankers
Paula Dupree	Acquanetta
Dr. Sigmund Walters	John Carradine
Dorothy Colman	Martha MacVicar
Fred Mason	Milburn Stone
John Whipple	Lloyd Corrigan
Curley Barret	Vince Barnett
Miss Strand	Fay Helm

Another horror thriller, packed with the usual implausibilities, 'Captive Wild Woman' is an exploitable picture that should rack up some coin for Universal. While much of the plot is strictly off the cob, this film has enough excitement and strange elements to appease the thrill patrons. Should be a strong secondary attraction on twin bills.

Story of a crazed medico who transfuses blood from a human into the veins of an animal is reminiscent of other horror vehicles such as 'Frankenstein,' etc. In this instance, a wild animal hunter furnishes a feminine ape involuntarily and the animal turns up as part human and part ape. Plot has the strange creature in love with the animal hunter-trainer and helping him to pacify a cage of ferocious beasts.

Hair-raising climax has the trainer working in a cage with cats despite a terrific storm and being rescued by the ape at the last minute.

Acquanetta makes an effective 'wild woman' (the ape who is transformed into a partly human being), though given a minimum of lines to speak. Milburn Stone as the hunter-trainer is life-like enough to be Clyde Beatty, who is credited with technical help on the production. Evelyn Ankers makes something of the role of his sweetheart, whose efforts to cure her sister of a glandular disorder starts the strange parade of events. John Carradine is the slightly demented surgeon who concocts the strange beast. Nice support is headed by Vince Barnett and Fay Helm.

Edward Dmytryk's intelligent direction points up the numerous suspenseful episodes. Henry Sucher and Griffin Jay have done a tight script. Lion, tiger and cage footage, which appears to have come from some previous animal thriller, is deftly dovetailed into picture via process photography. Since Beatty is credited with assisting on production, it seems likely that this older footage may have come from some Beatty wild animal opus. *Wear.*

Hoppy Serves A Writ

United Artists release of Harry Sherman production. Stars William Boyd; features Andy Clyde, Jay Kirby, Victor Jory. Directed by George Archainbaud. Screenplay, Gerald Geraghty; based on character created by Clarence E. Mulford; camera, Russell Harlan; editor, Sherman A. Rose. At New York, N. Y., dual, week of April 20, '43. Running time, **67 MINS.**

'Hopalong' Cassidy	William Boyd
California Carlson	Andy Clyde
Johnny Nelson	Jay Kirby
Tom Jordan	Victor Jory
Steve Jordan	George Reeves
Jean Hollister	Jan Christy
Ben Hollister	Forbes Murray

Fiftieth in the Hopalong Cassidy series with William Boyd has all the familiar action ingredients plus top-notch direction. It should do well boxofficially.

Story is built around ticklish legal situation that confronts Boyd. He knows the identity of a gang of rustlers and highwaymen, but since he can only act in Texas and they hide out in Oklahoma, he has to find a way of luring them back into Texas before he can make the pinch. How he accomplishes this is the basis of an exciting plot. Nor is there a lack of hard ridin', fast shootin', barroom brawls and suave sleuthin'.

Boyd makes a very convincing sheriff. He is ably supported by Andy Clyde, Jay Kirby and Victor Jory.

FOLLOW THE BAND

(SONGS)

Hollywood, April 23.

Universal release of Paul Malvern production. Directed by Jean Yarbrough. Screenplay by Warren Wilson, Dorothy Bennett, from Collier's story by Richard English; camera, Woody Bredell; editor, Milton Carruth; asst. director, Mack Wright; musical director, Charles Previn. Previewed at Fairfax, April 22, '43. Running time, **60 MINS.**

Marvin Howe	Eddie Quillan
Dolly O'Brien	Mary Beth Hughes
Big Mike O'Brien	Leon Errol
Juanita Turnbull	Anne Rooney
'Pop' Turnbull	Samuel S. Hinds
Tate Winters	Bob Mitchum
Jeremiah K. Barton	Russell Hicks
Cootie	Bennie Bartlett
Bert	Frank Coghlan, Jr.
Lucille Rose	Jean Ames

Skinnay Ennis and the Groove Boys

'Follow the Band' is another in the group of Universal program filmusical series designed to provide support in the dual houses. Despite its fragile story, there's sufficient musical talent on display to carry it through the family and hinterland bookings in okay style.

Lightly frameworked yarn which sends farm-worker Eddie Quillan to New York to get membership in National Dairy Association, projects him into a nightspot band as trombone player and several complications until the usual happy windup. Along the line, there's a number of specialty acts, including guest appearances by Frances Langford for delivery of 'My Melancholy Baby,' and Leo Carillo for a monolog.

Specialty numbers are provided by The King's Men, Hilo Hattie, Ray Eberle, Alvino Rey and the King Sisters, and the Bombardiers. There's a sprinkling of old and new tunes on display, with Skinnay Ennis and his band providing the accompaniment. Mary Beth Hughes, cast as the night club singer making pitch for the hayseed, sings two songs, 'Swingin' the Blues' and 'Ain't Misbehaving.' Anne Rooney displays spark of showmanship delivery with the oldie, 'So What Do You Want to Make Those Eyes at Me For.' With exception of latter number, all songs are part of the night club show in the one set.

Quillan lightly handles the lead assignment in okay fashion, with Miss Rooney the country girl in contrast to blonde charmer Miss Hughes.

Standard support is provided by Leon Errol, Samuel S. Hinds, Bob Mitchum and Jean Ames. Direction by Jean Yarbrough paces the brief yarn through the various musical interludes satisfactorily. *Walt.*

Reveille With Beverly

(MUSICAL)

Columbia release of Sam White production. Features Ann Miller, William Wright, Dick Purcell. Directed by Charles Barton. Original screenplay, Howard J. Green, Jack Henley, Albert Duffy; camera, Philip Tannura; musical director, M. W. Stoloff; editor, James Sweeney. At Abbey, N. Y., April 23, '43. Running time, **78 MINS.**

Beverly Ross	Ann Miller
Barry Lang	William Wright
Andy Adams	Dick Purcell
Vernon Lewis	Franklin Pangborn
Mr. Kennedy	Tim Ryan
Eddie Ross	Larry Parks
Mrs. Ross	Barbara Brown
Mr. Ross	Douglas Leavitt
Evelyn Ross	Adele Mara
Canvassback	Walter Sande
Stomp McCoy	Wally Vernon
Mr. Smith	Andrew Tombes

Also Bob Crosby orch, Freddie Slack orch with Ella Mae Morse, Duke Ellington orch, Count Basie orch, Frank Sinatra, Mills Bros., Radio Rogues.

Based on the idea of a local recorded radio program in the Rocky Mountain district, 'Reveille With Beverly' is a mild little programmer aimed for the hepcat phonograph record fans. It'll draw them in droves, but is a missout for general appeal.

Story is an embarrassingly synthetic one about a gal who runs a waker-upper record jockey program intended primarily for the soldiers at a nearby camp. With that as the excuse, the picture cuts periodically to single numbers by the Bob Crosby, Freddie Slack, Duke Ellington and Count Basie bands, all playing steaming jive.

And although Frank Sinatra, on the strength of his present popularity, gets top marquee billing on this New York showing, he also has only one number, lugubrious, clumsily directed and photographed vocal of 'Night and Day,' likewise introduced via phonograph recording. The specialty acts of the Mills Bros. and Radio Rogues are introduced as parts of a camp show.

It's all painfully inept in the writing, production and, with few exceptions, in performance. The single excuse, the hot swing by the various bands and the Sinatra vocal, will be good for boxoffice, but won't satisfy even the jitterbug customers, since every one of the names offers only a single number. Ann Miller has one ordinary dance routine and the rest of the time has to make a stab at acting a fatuous part. The others are no better or worse than their material. *Hobe.*

JUNIOR ARMY

Columbia release of Colbert Clark production. Features Freddie Bartholomew, Billy Halop, Huntz Hall, Bobby Jordan. Directed by Lew Landers. Story, Albert Bein; adaptation, Paul Gangelin; editor, Mel Thorsen; camera, Charles Schoenbaum. At Fox, Brooklyn, dual, week April 22, '43. Running time, **70 MINS.**

Freddie Hewlett	Freddie Bartholomew
Jimmie Fletcher	Billy Halop
Cowboy	Bobby Jordan
Bushy Thomas	Huntz Hall
Major Carter	Boyd Davis
Cadet Capt. Rogers	William Blees
Cadet Sergt. Sable	Richard Noyes
Mr. Ferguson	Joseph Crehan
Saginaw Jake	Don Beddoe
Cadet Pell	Charles Lind
Cadet Baker	Billy Lechner
Cadet Wilbur	Peter Lawford
Horner	Robert O. Davis

Freddie Bartholomew, who tops the cast, has gone into the Army since this picture was produced by Colbert Clark. He plays an English refugee who is living on his uncle's ranch in this country. After Bartholomew saves the life of a former Dead Ender, Billy Halop, who's hoboing, his uncle, recognizing the possibilities of regenerating Halop, sends the lad to a class military academy with Bartholomew. While latter gets along nicely as a cadet, Halop incurs the enmity of his classmates and only at the last redeems himself when aiding in the capture of a group of saboteurs who are trying to flee in a plane. A minor dualer.

The story is thin and uneventful, while the dialog fails to rise above the mediocre. Production and direction, latter by Lew Landers, follow the lines of least resistance.

Bartholomew and Halop, who fail to give impressive performances, are supported by Huntz Hall and Bobby Jordan, who like Halop come from the Dead End school, and numerous lessers. *Char.*

MY SON, THE HERO

Producers Release Corp. release of Peter R. Van Duinen production. Features Patsy Kelly, Roscoe Karns, Joan Blair, Carol Hughes, Maxie Rosenbloom, Luis Alberni. Directed by Edgar G. Ulmer. Screenplay, Doris Malloy and Edgar G. Ulmer; camera, Robert Cline and Jack Greenhalgh; editor, Charles Henkel, Jr. At New York, N. Y., dual, week of April 20, '43. Running time, **66 MINS.**

Gerty	Patsy Kelly
Big Time	Roscoe Karns
Cynthia	Joan Blair
Linda	Carol Hughes
Kid Slug	Maxie Rosenbloom
Tony	Luis Alberni
Michael	Joseph Allen, Jr.
Nancy	Lois Collier
Lambie	Jennie Le Gon
Nicodemus	Nick Stewart
Manager	Hal Price
Night Clerk	Al St. John
Rositta	Elvira Curcy
Mrs. Olmstead	Isabel La Mel
Girl Reporter	Maxine Leslie

Mildly amusing comedy has to stretch for laughs. Strictly for the duals, film has fair b.o. possibilities.

The hard-on-the imagination story concerns a small-time fight promoter, Roscoe Karns, who puts on the dog for his hero war correspondent son, Joseph Allen, Jr. Allen is the product of a former marriage to Joan Blair, and the audience is led to believe that he is ignorant of his sire's perpetually broke status. When the son wires he's coming to bunk with Karns, Karns gets panicky, since he can't make good his bluff. But with the help of his fighter's (Maxie Rosenbloom) ex-wife, Patsy Kelly, plus a one-man war bond drive, among other things, everything turns out okay.

It's the brassy clowning of Patsy Kelly, and the mugging of Rosenbloom and Luis Alberni that net the picture laughs. Karns, stymied by poor material, is unable to turn in one of his usually top performances. Carol Hughes lends a very winsome touch to the rough-and-tumble comedy, while the rest of the players do a thankless but workmanlike job. Direction is so-so.

Miniature Reviews

'Mission to Moscow' (WB). Strong grosser based on exciting report by former Ambassador Joseph E. Davies.

'Five Graves to Cairo' (Par). Melodrama of Rommel's North African campaign a strong b.o. potential.

'Du Barry Was a Lady' (Color; Songs). (M-G). Beautiful production, but stage musical too sapolioed for pix; will do biz.

'Lady of Burlesque' (Songs). (UA). Hunt Strumberg's backstage whodunit meller for profitable biz as solo or billtopper.

'Dr. Gillespie's Criminal Case' (M-G). Not up to standard of the series.

'Mr. Lucky' (RKO). Cary Grant in refreshing drama of the gambler and the rich girl. Solid biz, with key holdovers.

'Swing Shift Maisie' (M-G). Ann Sothern in a weak comedy concerning Maisie's adventures in a war plant; dualer.

'Gildersleeve's Bad Day' (RKO). Harold Peary in the title role; dualer.

'The Leopard Man' (RKO). Standard chill melodrama of whodunit texture for dual filler datings.

'Swing Your Partner' (Songs) (Rep). Corny comedy drama with music. Aimed entirely at rural audiences.

'Clancy Street Boys' (Mono). Programmer with Dead End Kids and others fairly entertaining.

'West of Texas' (PRC). Pretty good western.

MISSION TO MOSCOW

Washington, April 28.

Warner Bros. release of Robert Buckner production. Directed by Michael Curtiz. Stars Walter Huston and Ann Harding; features Oscar Homolka, George Tobias, Gene Lockhart, Helmut Dantine. Screenplay, Howard Koch; based on book by Joseph E. Davies; camera, Bert Glennon; montages, Don Siegel, James Leicester; editor, Owen Marks; asst. director, Frank Heath; dances, Leroy Prinz. Previewed at the Earle, Washington, D. C., April 28, '43. Running time, **123 MINS.**

Joseph E. Davies	Walter Huston
Mrs. Davies	Ann Harding
Litvinov	Oscar Homolka
Freddie	George Tobias
Molotov	Gene Lockhart
Madame Molotov	Frieda Inescort
Emlen Davies	Eleanor Parker
Paul	Richard Travis
Major Kamenev	Helmut Dantine
Byshinsky	Victor Francen
Minister von Ribbentrop	Henry Daniell
Mrs. Litvinov	Barbara Everest
Churchill	Dudley Field Malone
Krestinsky	Roman Bohnen
Tanya Litvinov	Maria Palmer
Colonel Faymonville	Moroni Olsen
Loy Henderson	Minor Watson
Kalinin	Vladimir Sokoloff
Dr. Botkin	Maurice Schwartz
Spendler	Jerome Cowan
Bukharin	Konstantin Shane
Stalin	Mannart Kippen
Lady Chilston	Kathleen Lockhart
Timoshenko	Kurt Katch
Dr. Hjalmar Schact	Felix Basch
Judge Ulrich	Frank Puglia
Grinko	John Abbott
Secretary Cordell Hull	Charles Trowbridge
Haile Selassie	Leigh Whipper
Paul Van Zeeland	George Renevant
Anthony Eden	Clive Morgan
Pierre Laval	Alex Chirva
Mrs. Churchill	Doris Lloyd

Also Olaf Hytten, Art Gilmore, Don Clayton, George Sorel, Duncan Renaldo, Mino Bellini, Ferd Schuman-Heinck, Rolf Lindau, Peter Michael, George Davis, Jean Del Val, Emory Parnell, Pat O'Malley, Mark Strong, Albert D'Arno, Rudolph Steinbeck, Gino Corrado, Glen Strange, Oliver Cross, Ray Walker, Captain Jack Young, Ernst Hauserman, Frank Faylen, Joseph Crehan, Ross Ford, Warren Douglas, Barbara Brown, Isabel Withers, George Lossey, Wallis Clark, Hans Schumm, Dr. Ernest Golm, Lisa Golm, Henry Victor, Louis Arco, Alfred Ziesler, Richard Ryen, Erwin Kaiser, Pierre Watkin, Edward Van Sloan, Esther Zeitlin, Nina Blagoi, Tanya Somova, Nikolai Celikhovsky, Michael Visaroff, Nick Kobliansky, Gabriel Lenoff, Alex Akimoff, Sam Savitsky, George Glebeff, Mike Tulligan, Adia Kutnetzoff, Dimitris Alexis, Henry Guttman, Robert Baikoff, Mischa Westfall, Elizabeth Archer (Scherbachova), Rosa Margot, Valya Terry, Sandor Szabo, Virginia Christine, Ivan Tresault, Daniel Ocko, David Hoffman, Lumsden Hare, Peter Goo Chong, Robert C. Fischer, Charles La Torre, Alex Caze (Rene Plaissetty), Frank Reicher, Leonid Snegoff, Edgar Licho, Marie Melesch, Michael Mark, Martin Noble, Lee Tung Foo, Victor Wong, Luke Chan, Allen Jung, John Dilson, Jean de Briac, George Sorel, Ted E. Jacques, Billie Louie, Loulette Sablon, Marian Lessing, Joan Winfield, Tina Menard, Peggy Watts, Irene Pedrini, Louis Jean Heydt, John Hamilton, Frank Ferguson, Bill Kennedy, William Forrest, Alex Melesch, Marek Windheim, Ivan Lebedeff, Gregory Golubeff, Jack Gardner, Sam Goldenberg, Egon Brecher, Zina Torchina, Vera Richkova, Jean Wong, Irina Semochenko, Christine Gordon, Alexander Granach, Mischa Westfall, Joseph Kamaryt, Baroness Yvonne Hendricks, Tamara Shayne, Olga Uljanovskaja, Patricia Fung, Igorde Navrotsky, Doris Lloyd, James Flavin, William B. Davidson, Herbert Hayes, George Carlton, Charles Trowbridge, Francis Pierlot, Forbes Murray, Edward Keane, William Gould, Harry Cording, Zoia Karabanova, Betty Roadman, Hooper Atchley, Eugene Eberly, Arthur Loft, Alec Campbell, Mike Mazurki, Nicco Romoff, Noel Cravat, Tom Tully, Lionel Royce, Emile Rameau, Eugene Borden, Feodor Chaliapin, John Maxwell, Jacqueline Dalva, Herbert Ashley, Oliver Prickett, Monte Blue, Frank Penny, Ernie Adams, Eddie Kane, Eddie Cobb, Howard Mitchell, Frank Wayne, Jack Kenny, Ben Erway, Mauritz Hugo, Gene Gary, Frank Jacquet, Fred Essler, John Wenglaf, Robert Shayne, Michel Panaieff, Lily Norwood, Sid Charisse.

'Mission to Moscow' is a powerful historical document. It is also a strong b.o. entry for the first-runs. It's a picture tied to the headlines, which will guarantee continued interest in it as Nazi and Russian troops thunder at each other this summer.

What will assure heavy trade in the earlier runs is the exceedingly controversial nature of the subject matter. Former Ambassador to Russia Joseph E. Davies, author of the best-seller which the picture faithfully follows, presents a strong case for the Soviet and fires heavy guns at U. S. isolationists. Resultant talk and controversy are bound to bring lucre to the till.

Film, however, is of a highly intellectual nature, requiring constant attention and thought if it is to be fully appreciated. It is pretty much in the nature of a lengthy monolog, with little action. Resultantly, femme and kid trade as the film moves into subsequents and hinterland towns cannot be expected to hold up.

The picture represents such a daringly different approach to the screen medium—an adventure for which Warner Bros. deserves the utmost commendation—that it can't possibly be reviewed as an ordinary film. It is truly a documentary; Hollywood's initial effort at living history. Every character is the counterpart of an actual person. Real names are used throughout—Roosevelt, Churchill, Stalin, Davies, Litvinov, et al.—and the casting is aimed for physical likeness to the person portrayed. The jolting realism of the likenesses is far from the least of the picture's interesting aspects.

Actors in the film are entirely secondary to the parts they play and must so be judged. Rather than purely histrionic ability, determining factors in the success of their portrayals are frequently physical characteristics and makeup. Outstanding in the tremendous cast are Walter Huston as Davies, Ann Harding as Mrs. Davies, Oscar Homolka at Litvinov, Gene Lockhart as Molotov, Barbara Everest as Mrs. Litvinov, Vladimir Sokoloff as Kalinin, Dudley Field Malone as the British Prime Minister, Frieda Inescort as Mrs. Molotov, George Tobias as the Davies chauffeur, Helmut Dantine as a young Soviet officer (in striking contrast to his usual Nazi parts), Victor Francen as the Russian state prosecutor during the purge trials, Maurice Schwartz as Dr. Botkin, Roman Bohnen and Kurt Katch as Timoshenko.

Approach in the picture is very similar to that used by Davies in his book, which was made up of a diary and journal which he himself kept, plus portions of numerous official reports he sent to the Department of State. Film follows pretty much in chronological order from the time of Roosevelt's appointment of the progressively-minded, capitalist-corporation lawyer to the Moscow post. It is Davies' big business background that primarily makes 'Mission to Moscow' so convincing a pro-Soviet document. In addition, of course, is the fact that this is the first film to really humanize the Russian rulers, who seem to Americans always to have lived in a world apart.

The Executive Mansion and a rear view of President Roosevelt's film counterpart—but in good simulation of F.D.R.'s voice—telling Davies what he wants is followed by the new Ambassador's departure with his wife and daughter for Germany and then Moscow. In Russia he presents his credentials and meets the top officialdom. That's followed by numerous tours of the country, its war plants, an exhibition of its armed strength, a sequence featuring Mrs. Davies to show what Russian women are doing in business and industry, and a scene of Davies' daughter at play with her Russian friends, which does much to humanize the people.

There are many other sequences to bring out particular points, but by far the most interesting—and controversial—is a lengthy reaction of the famed purge trials of 1937. By using what Davies claims to be an actual transcript of the trial, exact words of the confessions of guilt made by the leaders later executed are given by the actors playing the parts. These confessions reveal that with the aid of Trotzky, the men on trial conspired with Germany and Japan to sabotage Russia's preparations for defense and otherwise weaken the country so that the conspirators could oust the regime and take over. It's espoused that the purge of the traitors in 1937 is giving the United Nations such a strong ally on the eastern front in 1943. Treatment of the purge trial is one of the picture's most controversial scenes.

Davies' last act before departure from Russia is a talk with Premier Stalin, which provides a much-needed and highly-important explanation of how Chamberlain and the other British Tory leaders were stalling him, driving him into an alliance with Germany so that he might have time to build up his arms.

On his way back to Washington, Davies stops to see Churchill, warning him of the catastrophe to come. His arrival back in the United States is marked by an impassioned speaking tour, in which he predicts inevitable U. S. embroilment in the war and fights isolationism. This is one of the most significant portions of the film, for in making clear the fallacious thinking of the isolationists, it is bound to have a strong effect on the post-war thinking of the people of this country.

Manner of presentation of the film is the use of Huston's voice off-screen, employing the first person, to describe his tours and many of the events. Then, where the action permits, the film lapses into regular direct dialog among the characters on the screen. Top credit must be given Howard Koch, who wrote the screenplay, and Michael Curtiz, who directed, for making something so exciting out of a script that must necessarily be talky.

As might be expected in any picture so unusual, it has some minor defects. A notable point in the film that may annoy the more hep audiences is the terrific buildup it gives Davies. It makes of him a veritable oracle who foresaw everything and knew just what to do about it. His talk with Churchill is a prime example.

Naturally enough, too, in a film of this type, it is episodic. The quick flashes are not really objectionable, however, seeming to lend realism and give pace to the unfolding.

But rather than hunt for defects, the overall effect of the film must be considered. It is a story vitally needed at this time, when the homespun patriots are sniping at our great ally and isolationists are again rearing their heads.

Those who object to the broad internationalism of Davies' views must also object to President Roosevelt and Vice-President Wallace. The cry has already gone up of 'fourth term propaganda.' That it is, just as must be any document which goes beyond narrow, nationalistic, anti-anything-New Deal lines.

To the exhibitor it must be obvious from the foregoing that 'Mission to Moscow' offers a challenge. It has every element a film needs for exploitation, with page one headlines providing new selling points every edition. The amount of business the picture does will depend almost entirely on the imagination, ingenuity and effort put in the sales campaign. Every exhib will be doing both himself and his country a favor by devising and executing the greatest exploitation campaign he has ever staged. Warners' own exploiteers already have laid a magnificent groundwork. Its National Press Club premiere in Washington should snowball into a wealth of controversial pros and cons, all for benefit of b.o.

5 GRAVES TO CAIRO

Paramount release of Charles Brackett production. Stars Franchot Tone, Anne Baxter, Akim Tamiroff, Erich von Stroheim, Peter Van Eyck, Fortunio Bonanova. Directed by Billy Wilder. Screenplay by Charles Brackett and Billy Wilder based on play by Lajos Biro; camera, John Seitz; editor, Doane Harrison. Tradeshown in N. Y., May 3, '43. Running time, 96 MINS.

John J. Bramble............Franchot Tone
Mouche........................Anne Baxter
Farid..........................Akim Tamiroff
Field Marshal Rommel..Erich von Stroheim
Lieut. Schwegler..........Peter Van Eyck
General Sebastiano......Fortunio Bonanova
Major Von Buelow......Konstantin Shayne
Major Lamprecht..............Fred Nurney
British Colonel..............Miles Mander
British Captain.............Leslie Denison
British Captain.................Ian Keith

As timely as today's headlines from North Africa, 'Five Graves to Cairo,' with fairly sturdy b.o. names to bally, shapes up as a strong grosser. Fictionized version of what enabled the British to halt Rommel before Cairo backgrounds, it's an espionage thriller of the North African campaign. Film has story, cast, direction and swift movement, each done respectively with polish and deftness.

Franchot Tone, Erich von Stroheim, Anne Baxter, Akim Tamiroff and Peter Van Eyck give the exhibitor plenty to work on, coupled with current interest in the Allies' victorious drive against Rommel and his cohorts. Besides abundance of exploitation possibilities, it is the sort of picture that will build on word-of-mouth.

Idea of making Field Marshal Rommel's campaign into an exciting fable is by Lajos Biro, Hungarian writer, who did so many successful Ernst Lubitsch screen hits. It affords a vivid picture of Rommel, Stroheim doing a capital job. The characterization is tailor-made for him.

Surprisingly for such a dynamic, moving vehicle, there is a minimum of actual battle stuff. Director Billy Wilder has handled the varied story elements, countless suspenseful moments and vivid portrayals in excellent fashion. In some instances the absence of spoken word or muffled sentences have been pointed up through skillful pantomime and action.

Basically 'Five Graves' is the story of a British corporal, Franchot Tone, who impersonates a Nazi spy to gain military information from the Germans as they sweep towards Cairo. Sole survivor of a tank crew, he stumbles into a deserted village hotel only a few moments before the Germans arrive. Akim Tamiroff, hotel proprietor, hides him. He and the hostelry's maid (Anne Baxter) agree to keep his identity secret though she believes the British gave the French short shrift at Dunkirk (she's originally from France). While he's working to wangle information from Rommel, she intrigues first with Rommel, unsuccessfully and then with a German staff officer (Peter Van Eyck) in trying to spring her brother from prison. Rommel's brushoff to her when she substitutes for the spy, working as waiter at the hotel, to serve coffee to him in bed, is a masterpiece of sarcasm. His reprimand is that he does not like women in the morning.

Crackling dialog and fine scripting by director Wilder and Charles Brackett enhance the Biro original. Camera work of John Seitz is outstanding, as is the film editing by Doane Harrison. Use of sound effects, indicating superb recording, especially during the running gun fight, also is topflight.

All the key actors turn in trim performances. Anne Baxter's French maid bespeaks a bright future for this comely miss. Franchot Tone does one of his most polished jobs as the corporal who impersonates the Nazi spy-advance agent. Peter Van Eyck is the stern but youthful aspiring staff officer who falls for Mouche. Akim Tamiroff is the nervous, worried African hotelkeeper, also a standout portrayal. Bonanova, as the singing Italian general being pushed about by Rommel, has several of the barbed, humorous passages besides several impromptu bathroom ballads. One crack to the effect, 'How can a nation that belches understand a nation that sings?' obviously refers to Germany as contrasted to his native Italy. *Wear.*

Du Barry Was a Lady

(Musical)

(COLOR)

Metro release of Arthur Freed production. Features Red Skelton, Lucille Ball, Gene Kelly, Virginia O'Brien. Directed by Roy Del Ruth. Screenplay, Irving Brecher; adaptation, Nancy Hamilton; additional dialog, Wilkie Mahoney; based on the play by Herbert Fields and B. G. DeSylva; songs, Cole Porter; additional songs, Lew Brown, Ralph Freed, Burton Lane, Roger Edens, E. Y. Harburg; camera, Karl Freund; editor, Blanche Sewell. Previewed at Loew's Lexington, N. Y., April 27, '43. Running time, 96 MINS.

Louis Blore / King Louis..................Red Skelton
May Daly / Mme. Du Barry..............Lucille Ball
Alec Howe / Black Arrow.................Gene Kelly
Ginny......................Virginia O'Brien
Charlie / Dauphin.................'Rags' Ragland
Rami, the Swami / Taliostra............Zero Mostel
Mr. Jones / Duc De Choiseul............Donald Meek
Willie / Duc De Rigor........Douglass Dumbrille
Cheezy / Count De Roquefort.........George Givot
Niagara...................Louise Beavers
Tommy Dorsey and His Orchestra

'There's nothing for Hollywood in 'Du Barry,' except possibly an idea; any film adaptation would require practically a complete rewrite for a Hays office nod.' That was the opinion expressed by 'Variety's' reviewer the night the B. G. DeSylva musical opened in New Haven, Nov. 9, 1939. And there's very little in Metro's current screen version to cause a revision of that opinion. While the capital production, the title, some of the names for the marquee and the fact that all musicals are doing well, means at least fair business is assured, no smash can be expected. 'Du Barry's' too much of a lady now.

DeSylva-Herbert Fields-Cole Porter musical ran for almost a year on Broadway to consistently strong grosses. But at least a good part of its appeal was in the utter ribaldry of its men's room-attendant plot and the latrine-verse quality of the Porter lyrics. Hollywood obviously had to duck that. Partially accountable for the musical's success, too, was the gagging afforded by putting a bunch of lowdown 52d streeters in the court of Louis XV, and mixing up the Broadway talk with ruffled collars and pantaloons. Irving Brecher's screenplay takes so long getting Red Skelton from 52d street to France that much of the possibility for fun around this point is lost.

As if to compensate for the story and lack of powerful tunes, Metro has given the picture topnotch production and a Technicolor setting. Sets and costumes are as lavish as a state dinner, and there's enough cheesecake for all the calendars in the world for the next 20 years. From that angle, 'Du Barry' must attract exhib attention.

Not to be overlooked, either, is the current b.o. strength of Skelton. Opposite him is Lucille Ball. They fill the spots held by Bert Lahr and Ethel Merman in the original. Gene Kelly and Virginia O'Brien are the pic replacements for Ronald Graham and Betty Grable. To add b.o. strength for the 'teen-trade, Metro has tossed in Tommy Dorsey's orch and a specialty by the Oxford Boys trio. Comic Zero Mostel also debuts in the film.

In sapolioing the script for celluloid, the studio has taken Skelton out of the men's room and put him in the coat room. Otherwise it follows the general outlines of the original: the club caddy falls for the top warbler at the spot (Miss Ball). She pays no attention to him, being enamored of a broke songsmith, Gene Kelly, while she plays Douglas Dumbrille for his chips. Then Skelton wins a Derby pot and some attention from Miss Ball, only to get a Mickey intended for Kelly mixed up with his own drink, which sends him into a dream sequence. He finds himself Louis XV and Miss Ball his Du Barry.

With the weak plot and weaker dialog, Skelton has a tough time living up to his rep as a funnyman. Miss Ball does a bit better, while Gene Kelly, whose forte is terping, suffers from the histrionic and singing demands of his role and lack of opportunity to make with the feet. Miss O'Brien is disappointing, too, except for the one tune she's given, 'Salome Was the Grandma of Them All,' in which she literally sparkles.

Zero Mostel fails to get the same results in Technicolor that he does in the flesh. As the swami in a night club, he gets a chance to do some variations of the numbers which socked him over at Cafe Society, N. Y., but they don't seem to take with the same strength. He requires an intimacy that the screen does not afford. 'Rags' Ragland, out of burley, is diverting as the check-room understudy who becomes the Dauphin. George Givot and Donald Meek strain to make funny the roles of waiter and tax-collector.

Except for the title tune and 'Friendship,' most of the original Cole Porter lyrics and melodies are missing. In their place is nothing particularly memorable. Among the numbers are 'If You Don't Love an Esquire Girl,' 'Madame, I Came Here for Love,' and 'Fight for the Freedom of France.' Last-named seems to be rather ill-timed, incidentally, so far as this plot's concerned.

LADY OF BURLESQUE

(SONGS)

Hollywood, April 29.

United Artists release of Hunt Stromberg production. Stars Barbara Stanwyck; features Michael O'Shea. Directed by William Wellman. Screenplay by James Gunn, from novel, 'The G-String Murders,' by Gypsy Rose Lee; camera, Robert de Grasse; editor, James Newcom; production manager, Joseph C. Gilpin; asst. director, Sam Nelson; songs, Harry Akst, Sammy Cahn; dances, Danny Dare; score, Arthur Lange. Previewed at Filmarte, April 28, '43. Running time, 89 MINS.

Dixie Daisy...............Barbara Stanwyck
Biff Brannigan..............Michael O'Shea
S. B. Foss............J. Edward Bromberg
Gee Gee Graham....................Iris Adrian
Dolly Baxter.................Gloria Dickson
Lolita La Verne.............Victoria Faust
Princess Nirvena.......Stephanie Bachelor
Inspector Harrigan.........Charles Dingle
Alice Angel...................Marion Martin
Russell Rogers...............Frank Fenton
Stacchi........................Frank Conroy
Jake.......................George Chandler
Mandy............................Pinky Lee
Officer Pat Kelly............Eddie Gordon
Louie Grindero...............Gerald Mohr
The Hermit........................Lew Kelly
Sandra.......................Claire Carleton
Janine..........................Janis Carter
Sammy...........................Bert Hanlon
Joey...............................Sid Marion
Moey...............................Lou Lubin
Lee..................................Lee Trent
Don..................................Don Lynn
Wong...............................Beal Wong
Policewoman.................Florence Auer
Cossack......................David Kashner

This is Hunt Stromberg's initial independent production for UA release after nearly two decades with Metro as producer of numerous top money pictures. Despite its grooving into regulation backstage whodunit melodramatics, Stromberg invests it with his usual showmanship flare of color and movement to make film a profitable attraction for toplining in the keys and regular datings.

Although 'Lady of Burlesque' is based on Gypsy Rose Lee's novel, 'G-String Murders,' story plows an obvious straight line in generating the whodunit angles, and two gal burlesque performers are knocked off in succession before the culprit is disclosed. But gallant trouping by Barbara Stanwyck, colorful background provided by Stromberg, and speedy direction by William Wellman, carry picture through for good entertainment for general audiences.

Story centers around a burlesque stock company established in an old opera house. Miss Stanwyck is the strip-tease star in process of buildup by manager J. Edward Bromberg, with Michael O'Shea the lowdown comedian who's continually making romantic pitches to the girl. Various backstage characters are introduced, with usual number of jealousies, until sufficient number of suspects are around to launch the first murder. While this is unsolved, a second killing takes place, and it remains for the stripper and comic to set a trap for the killer.

O'Shea, film newcomer plucked by producer from the stage play, 'Eve of St. Mark,' displays plenty of screen personality and ability to keep him around Hollywood for a long time. Miss Stanwyck turns in a solid performance in the title spot, and does much to maintain interest in the proceedings.

Bromberg clicks as the burlesque producer, with usual group of girls in various cast categories for glamour-dressing and to serve as victims and suspects. Coterie has been neatly cast for respective assignments, and includes Iris Adrian, Gloria Dickson, Marion Martin, Victoria Faust and Stephanie Bachelor. Miss Faust catches attention in her film debut, as does Miss Bachelor in initial screen appearance, although both are called on for unsympathetic characterizations. Frank Fenton, Charles Dingle, Frank Conroy, Pinky Lee, Eddie Gordon and Bert Hanlon also are okay in supporting spots.

Picture gets off to zestful start, with stage show background in which Miss Stanwyck socks over 'Take Off the E String, Play It on the G String,' and Fenton deliberately off-keys 'So This Is You.' There's a sudden raid and wagon backup; release on bail and then slowdown to generate various motives for the coming murders. After swinging into the strange use of a G-string for strangulation of the victims, it's just a matter of time before the windup.

Stromberg spent close to a million on his first independent venture, and production investiture is naturally topgrade throughout. Camera work by Robert de Grasse is of high standard. *Walt.*

Dr. Gillespie's Criminal Case

Metro production and release. Stars Lionel Barrymore, features Van Johnson, Donna Reed, Key Luke, John Craven, Nat Pendleton, Alma Kruger, William Lundigan, Walter Kingsford and Marilyn Maxwell. Directed by Willis Goldbeck. Based on characters created by Max Brand; adaptation, Martin Berkeley, Harry Ruskin and Lawrence P. Bachmann; editor, Laurie Vejar; camera, Norbert Brodine. Previewed in projection room, N. Y., April 20, '43. Running time, 89 MINS.

Dr. Leonard Gillespie....Lionel Barrymore
Dr. Randall Adams..........Van Johnson
Marcia Bradburn..............Donna Reed
Dr. Lee Wong How.............Keye Luke
Roy Todwell....................John Craven
Joe Weyman...................Nat Pendleton
Molly Byrd.....................Alma Kruger
Alvin F. Peterson.......William Lundigan
Margaret...................Margaret O'Brien
Dr. Walter Carew.......Walter Kingsford
Ruth Edly..................Marilyn Maxwell
Sergeant Patrick J. Orisin..Michael Duane
Warden Kenneson...........Henry O'Neill
Sally..............................Marie Blake
Irene...........................Frances Rafferty

The strain of keeping Dr. Gillespie alive as a screen character in a series that has extended over the years is beginning to tell. This latest starring Lionel Barrymore in a wheelchair called for the combined efforts of three script writers and a very capable cast, yet all hands concerned have failed to provide anything but mediocre screen entertainment.

Poorly edited and running much too long—89 minutes—it is tedious from the start.

Three writers — Martin Berkeley, Harry Ruskin and Lawrence P. Bachmann—did not concoct much of a plot to begin with, but also stand guilty of penning trite dialog. Comedy relief is in a minor key.

The character of Roy Todwell in the last Gillespie release went to jail for murder. In this one, with Todwell played by another actor, John Craven, the efforts of Dr. Gillespie to have him transferred to a proper institution on the ground the confessed murderer is insane come to naught as result of a prison break and the killing of Todwell by cops.

In addition to testing two young internes to determine who shall be Gillespie's assistant, not settled, the story concerns an erysipelas epidemic among children and trouble doctors have in trying to get a former flier to try to walk on wooden legs which he doesn't want.

Barrymore, Van Johnson, Donna Reed, Keye Luke, Nat Pendleton, Walter Kingsford, Alma Kruger and Marie Blake are carryovers in the Gillespie series. A newcomer for the glamour ranks, whose prospects are exceedingly bright, is Marilyn Maxwell, who is paired for romantic interest with Johnson. Latter, while a good performer, is hardly a doctor type. William Lundigan, who ably plays the legless soldier, is appearing in the series for the first time. *Char.*

MR. LUCKY

Hollywood, May 4.

RKO release of David Hempstead production. Stars Cary Grant; features Laraine Day, Charles Bickford, Gladys Cooper, Alan Carney. Directed by H. C. Potter. Screenplay by Milton Holmes and Adrian Scott; original, Holmes; camera, George Barnes; special effects, Vernon Walker; editor, Theron Warth; asst. director, Harry Scott; production designed by William Cameron Menzies. Tradeshown in L. A. May 3, '43. Running time, 98 MINS.

Joe...............................Cary Grant
Dorothy.........................Laraine Day
Hard Swede...............Charles Bickford
Capt. Steadman............Gladys Cooper
The Crunk.....................Alan Carney
Mr. Bryant............Henry Stephenson
Zepp...........................Paul Stewart
Mrs. Ostrander...............Kay Johnson
The Gaffer......................Erford Gage
Convoy Commissioner....Walter Kingsford
McDougal.....................J. M. Kerrigan
Foster.......................Edward Fielding
Greek Priest...........Vladimir Sokoloff

'Mr. Lucky' is as fresh as this week's ration coupon. Expertly devised to provide top entertainment as a romantic drama of unusual and breezy tenor, it's a solid attraction for the key spots and general runs as a solo or billtopper aiming for hefty grosses. Marquee voltage of Cary Grant in starring spot will keep the wickets spinning and generate holdovers.

Story is one of the freshest angles that has come out of Hollywood in many months. Despite its underlying dramatic foundation, it's studded with light and breezy episodes that catch strong audience reaction, and concentrates interest in the proceedings throughout without a letdown.

Grant is a resourceful and opportunist gambling operator, figuring on outfitting his outlawed gaming ship for trip to Havana. But coin and draft registration balk his departure. Assuming name and draft card of a dying 4-F, he launches drive to raise the moola and runs into society heiress Laraine Day. Pursuing her for romantic pitches, he lands as member of the war relief agency and proceeds to ply his con to help the outfit with supplies and boat charters. Proposing handling the gambling concession on a relief ball, Grant whips it through, and the take is healthy until former partner Paul Stewart moves in to grab the haul for himself. Girl, figuring Grant has given both herself and the organization the double-cross on the coin, gets it all back, and then discovers his former gambling boat has been chartered to the war relief group for transportation of the supplies overseas. Then there's the natural happy ending.

Picture carries an authentic ring to operations of bigtime gamblers, and it faithfully follows the professional premise of 'never give the sucker a break, but never cheat a friend.' Writer Milton Holmes, in selling his first screen original, hews closely to the lines of actual incidents rather than depending on synthetic dramatics to drop it into the groove of obvious cinematic dramatics.

Grant does a slick job in portraying the gambling operator, and makes the most of the smart material, lines and situations provided by the script, although at times the direction rather overstresses his delivery of dialog. Miss Day catches attention as the girl, and picture should do a lot for her in raising her boxoffice status. Alan Carney clearly etches the character of Grant's sidekick and aide; his prototype will be found in any class gaming establishment. Charles Bickford gives his usual good performance as the ship's skipper; Henry Stephenson delivers as the girl's irascible grandfather, while Paul Stewart, Gladys Cooper and Kay Johnson are most prominent in remaining support.

David Hempstead ably handles production reins, while H. C. Potter's direction swings the tale along at a consistent and interesting clip. Photography by George Barnes is topnotch in line with grade-A mounting provided for the production. *Walt.*

SWING SHIFT MAISIE

Metro release of George Haight production. Stars Ann Sothern; features James Craig, Jean Rogers, Fred Brady, Wiere Bros. Directed by Norman Z. McLeod. Screenplay by Mary C. McCall, Jr., and Robert Halff based on characters created by Wilson Collison; camera, Harry Stradling; editor, Elmo Veron. Previewed in N. Y., April 30, '43. Running time, 87 MINS.

Maisie Ravier.....................Ann Sothern
'Breezy' McLaughlin..........James Craig
Iris Reed...........................Jean Rogers
Maw Lustvogel...........Connie Gilchrist
Horatio Curley...................John Qualen
Ann..............................Kay Medford
The Schmitt Brothers......Wiere Brothers
Grace.....................Jacqueline White
Ruth.............................Betty Jaynes
Judd Evans......................Fred Brady
Emmy Lou Grogan..........Marta Linden
Helen Johnson.................Celia Travers

There appears to have been a lull in the 'Maisie' series, and this shows it. Maybe the producers have lost their enthusiasm. Ann Sothern, who has been away from the series, struggles hard to save this from sagging but it's too much.

'Swing Shift Maisie' takes Masie Ravier (Ann Sothern) from a dog act into an airplane plant on the Coast. She went with the dog troupe cross-country just so she could get a war-work job. She falls in love with a test pilot at the factory, befriends a supposedly forlorn beauty aspiring to screen fame and is rewarded by having the movie-struck dame snatch her man. All familiar angles are included with many developments telegraphed way in advance of actual occurrence. Thus the fact that the two-timing girl friend is going to frame Ann at the plant is tipped bluntly a couple of reels in advance.

Miss Sothern is her customary zestful self, working overtime to breathe some reality into the overworked situations. James Craig, as the test pilot, is handsome but otherwise undistinguished. Jean Rogers, cast as the screen hopeful, manages a distasteful part with some distinction. Connie Gilchrist, as Mrs. Lustvogel, the boarding house operator where the plant workers live, makes a neat characterization of this minor role. The Wiere Bros., playing the Schmitt Brothers, acrobat threesome, friends of Ann, are virtually wasted in a brief sequence.

The script by Mary C. McCall, Jr., and Robert Halff is loosely written, and not improved by Norman McLeod's lacklustre direction. *Wear.*

Gildersleeve's Bad Day

RKO release of Herman Schlom production. Features Harold Peary, Jane Darwell, Nancy Gates. Directed by Gordon Douglas. Screenplay, Jack Townley; editor, Les Milbrook; music, C. Bakaleinikoff; camera, Jack Mackenzie. Previewed in N. Y., April 30, '43. Running time, 62 MINS.

Gildersleeve.......................Harry Peary
Aunt Emma.......................Jane Darwell
Margie.............................Nancy Gates
Judge Hooker....................Charles Arnt
Leroy............................Freddie Mercer
Jimmy:............................Russell Wade
Birdie..........................Lillian Randolph
Al......................................Frank Jenks
Louie.........................Douglas Fowley
Toad...............................Alan Carney
Henry Potter..................Grant Withers
Peavey.......................Richard LeGrand
Otis.................................Dink Trout
George Peabody..............Harold Landon
Police Chief....................Charles Cane
Bailiff...............................Ken Christy

One of the lesser RKO dualers, 'Gildersleeve's Bad Day,' featuring Harold Peary in the title role he created for radio, is strictly for the family audiences at whom it's aimed.

The laughs are negligible, mostly because of the trite script, but Peary has built himself a radio following and for them his strictly corny comedy will probably find an appreciative outlet.

Peary, still using the equine laugh that has become his trademark, is this time concerned in the trial of a yegg. As the foreman of the jury, Peary is insistent—the only member of the jury who is—on the innocence of the thug. Circumstances then point at Peary as the unwitting victim of bribe-taking from the defendant's friends, and the rest concerns complications that arise from his attempt to establish his innocence.

Peary gives a standard performance, while Jane Darwell and Nancy Gates, in lesser parts, do as well as could be expected. Production is okay, in keeping with the modest budget. *Kahn.*

THE LEOPARD MAN

Hollywood, May 4.

RKO release of Val Lewton production. Features Dennis O'Keefe, Margo. Directed by Jacques Tourneur. Screenplay by Ardel Wray; added dialog, Edward Dein; from novel, 'Black Alibi,' by Cornell Woolrich; camera, Robert de Grasse; editor, Mark Robson; asst. director, William Dorfman. Tradeshown in L. A. May 3, '43. Running time, 65 MINS.

Jerry Manning...............Dennis O'Keefe
Clo-Clo ....Margo
Kiki Walker......................Jean Brooks
Maria...........................Isabel Jewell
Dr. Galbraith......................James Bell
Teresa Delgado...........Margaret Landry
Charlie How-Come........Abner Biberman
Raoul Belmonte.............Richard Martin
Consuelo Contreras.............Tula Parma
Chief Robles...........................Ben Bard
Eloire...............................Ariel Heath
Rosita...........................Fely Franquelli

With RKO figuring that group of program mystery-thrillers would prove profitable for both the producer and theatres following 'Cat People,' studio has embarked on such a series. 'Leopard Man' is the second issue of the group, carrying regulation formula for generating audience suspense, and succeeding partially in attaining that premise.

Story and script both lack the clear-cut and direct line treatment accorded 'Cat People' and follows too many confusing paths to make it more than passable fare for the general audiences. After brief introduction, it's a series of chases and murders, with a tame leopard blamed for the latter until strange happenings are pinned on one of the players. It's all confusion, in fact too much for an audience to follow.

Dennis O'Keefe is press agent for a New Mexican nitery and rents a tame black leopard for a publicity stunt which backfires when the cat escapes and a girl is presumably killed by the fugitive. Yarn then spins through regulation eerie channels with two other strange murders enacted—one being in the timeworn setting of a cemetery and windstorm combined. O'Keefe and Margo stick around long enough to trip the real culprit by time for the fadeout to come along.

Both script and direction noticeably strain to achieve effects of 'Cat People,' but fall far short of latter standard. O'Keefe and Margo acceptably handle the two leads, with satisfactory support from Jean Brooks, Isabel Jewell, James Bell, Abner Biberman, Ben Bard, Tula Parma and Margaret Landry. *Walt.*

Swing Your Partner

(SONGS)

Hollywood, April 28.

Republic release of Armand Schaefer production. Features Lulubelle & Scotty, Vera Vague, Dale Evans, Ransom Sherman, Harry 'Pappy' Cheshire, Richard Lane, George 'Shug' Fisher, Tennessee Ramblers. Directed by Frank McDonald. Original screenplay by Dorrell and Stuart McGowen; camera, Bud Thackery; editor, Richard Van Enger; dances, Josephine Earl; music, Morton Scott. Previewed April 27, '43. Running time, 70 MINS.

Johnny Murphy...................Roger Clark
Caroline Bird.....................Esther Dale
Judy.................................Judy Clark
Digby...........................Charles Judels
Secretary...............Rosemary LaPlanche
Teal..................................Sam Flint

Morningside.......................Forbes Murray
Duffy.......................Elmer Jerome

Lulubelle & Scotty
Vera Vague
Dale Evans
Ransom Sherman
Harry 'Pappy' Cheshire
Richard Lane
George 'Shug' Fisher
The Tennessee Ramblers
Peppy & Peanuts

There's plenty of corn planted in this cinematic aggregation of backwoods radio favorites culled from various sections of the country. Not much of a harvest for the city folk, but the hix in the sticks will find it good entertainment along lines they understand from constant association with the backwoods comics. Unreeling mainly to highlight specialties of the radioites, picture will have to depend on audiences of the latter to carry it through for passable coin in the hinterlands.

Yarn revolves around workers in outlands dairy plant of big company presided over by crusty Esther Dale. She hops to the place incognito, and sticks around long enough to humanize the operations, with the radio performers handling their several specialties in song and musical displays and characterizations.

Homespun corn in both comedy and dramatic kernels is planted on rather barren ground, but the crossroads audiences will react favorably to the proceedings. Dale Evans clicks with delivery of two songs, 'Cheesecake' and 'In the Cool of the Evening,' and demonstrates that Republic has a good prospect under contract for both acting and singing roles. Lulubelle & Scotty handle three numbers in good style, while Tennessee Ramblers are on several times with musical interludes.

Story was obviously written around talents of the air performers rounded up, with direction handicapped accordingly. *Walt.*

CLANCY STREET BOYS

Monogram release of Sam Katzman-Jack Dietz production. Features Leo Gorcey, Huntz Hall, Bobby Jordan, Bennie Bartlett, Noah Beery, Lita Ward, Ric Vallin and Martha Wentworth. Directed by William Beaudine. Story and adaptation, Harvey Gates; editor, Carl Pierson; camera, Mack Stengler. At New York, N. Y., half dual bill, week April 27, '43. Running time, **66 MINS.**

Muggs.......................Leo Gorcey
Glimpy.......................Huntz Hall
Danny.......................Bobby Jordan
Bennie.......................Bennie Bartlett
Pete.......................Noah Beery Sr.
Judy.......................Lita Ward
George.......................Ric Vallin
Mrs. McGinnis.......................Martha Wentworth
Flanagan.......................J. Farrel MacDonald
Stash.......................Dick Chandlee
Scruno.......................Sammy Morrison
Dave.......................Eddie Mills

Comedy element in 'Clancy Street Boys' makes it a fairly entertaining programmer aside from a plot that is somewhat unique for remnants of the Dead End kids and other slum ruffians who are dubbed the East Side Kids in the picture. Should provide good support on double bills.

In addition to the one gang headed by the wisecracking, smart-alecky Leo Gorcey, the story has made room for a rival bunch of tough young hoodlums who aid in providing action through free-for-all fights and the like.

Harvey Gates' story is based on amusing situations that involve Gorcey and a rich uncle from Texas. Gorcey's mother has permitted the uncle to believe that she is the mother of seven children, whereas Gorcey is the only one she has. Result is that Gorcey gets his mob to pose as his mother's brood, including one of them as a girl. Though the uncle gets wise later, he forgives all after they rescue him and his daughter from kidnapers.

In addition to Gorcey, the East Side Kids include Huntz Hall, Bobby Jordan, Dick Chandlee, Sammy Morrison and Bennie Bartlett. The uncle is played effectively in an exaggerated Texas manner by Noah Beery, while his daughter, also laying on that southwestern accent, is Lita Ward, a looker. Others doing satisfactorily are Ric Vallin, Martha Wentworth and J. Farrel MacDonald.

William Beaudine, veteran director, has piloted the picture capably. *Char.*

WEST OF TEXAS

(SONGS)

Producers Releasing Corp. release of Alfred Stern-Arthur Alexander production. Stars Dave (Tex) O'Brien and Jim Newill, features Guy Wilkerson, Frances Gladwin, Marilyn Hare, Robert Barron and Henry Hall. Directed by Oliver Drake. Story and adaptation, Oliver Drake; songs, Dave (Tex) O'Brien and Jim Newill; editor, Charles Henkel; camera, Ira Morgan. At New York, N. Y., half dual bill, week April 27, '43. Running time, **59 MINS.**

Tex Wyatt.......................Dave (Tex) O'Brien
Jim Steele.......................Jim Newill
Panhandle Perkins.......................Guy Wilkerson
Marie Moenette.......................Frances Gladwin
Ellen Yaeger.......................Marilyn Hare
Bert Calloway.......................Robert Barron
Steve London.......................Tom London
Bart Yaeger.......................Henry Hall
Gabe Jones.......................Jack Rockwell
Sheriff.......................Roy Butler
Blackie.......................Jack Ingraham
Clem.......................Art Fowler

Rather good western, action in which moves at a gingerly pace. Where horse operas are played, this one should have no trouble pleasing audiences.

Dave (Tex) O'Brien and Jim Newill, who wrote the three songs in the picture, are excellent prairieland types whose chances to graduate into regular features are sanguine. The team plays Texas Rangers who go to New Mexico with a view to setting up a Ranger outfit in that state as a means of protecting ranchers whose land is being grabbed by dishonest railroad surveyors. They succeed in rounding up those responsible for the pillaging but at times the plot becomes a little involved and implausible.

There are two girls, Marilyn Hare, who figures in a romantic way, and Frances Gladwin, a saloon dancer who serves as a spy for the villain group. She has a brief dance specialty at one point. Miss Hare a likely comer. Among others in the supporting cast are Guy Wilkerson, comedy type, and Robert Barron, excellent heavy.

O'Brien and Newill's three songs, which they sing, are 'Whistle a Song,' 'El Lobo' and 'Tired of Rambling.' They listen well. *Char.*

Miniature Reviews

'Stage Door Canteen' (musical) (Lesser-UA). A mopup; all-star cast reads like a dream benefit show.

'Ox-Bow Incident' (20th). Henry Fonda in top-rate western based on Walter Clark's best-selling novel; medium grosser.

'Bombardier' (RKO). Good grosser, with thriller finish.

'The Bells Go Down' (UA). British-made, featuring Tommy Trinder and James Mason, that should do okay.

'Prelude to War' (Capra-U. S. Gov't.). Dramatic documentary of aggressor nations preparing for war.

'Pardon My Gun' (Col). Charles Starrett topflight western; packed with action.

'Johnny Doughboy' (Rep). Gives Jane Withers a glamor buildup. Should appeal to juves; a dualer.

'Mantrap' (Rep). Murder mystery of minor importance.

'Ghost and the Guest' (PRC). James Dunn, Florence Rice in harum-scarum gangster comedy; strong dual supporter.

'Capitan Veneno' (Argentine-made). Comic Luis Sandrini in dramatic role fails to come off. Poor b.o. likely.

'Cuando Florezca El Naranjo' (Argentine-Made). Romantic comedy aimed for good grosses throughout Latin America.

'Passion Island' (Maya). Mexican-made melodrama, geared for nice b.o. at foreign-language houses.

Stage Door Canteen

(MUSICAL)

United Artists release of Sol Lesser production (Barnett Briskin associate producer). Directed by Frank Borzage. Original by Delmer Daves; camera, Harry Wild; asst. directors, Lew Borzage, Virgil Hart; editor, Hal Kern; music, Freddie Rich; director, C. Bakaleinikoff; songs, Al Dubin-Jimmy Monaco, Rodgers & Hart, Joe Moody, Harry Miller-Bob Reed, Al Hoffman-Mann Curtis-Cy Corbin-Jerry Livingston, Albert Hay Mallotte, Castro Valencia-Joe Pafumy. Running time, **132 MINS.**

STARS AT CANTEEN

Judith Anderson	Aline MacMahon
Kenny Baker	Elsa Maxwell
Tallulah Bankhead	Harpo Marx
Ralph Bellamy	Helen Menken
Edgar Bergen and Charlie McCarthy	Yehudi Menuhin
	Ethel Merman
Ray Bolger	Ralph Morgan
Ina Claire	Alan Mowbray
Katharine Cornell	Paul Muni
Jane Cowl	Merle Oberon
Virginia Field	George Raft
Gracie Fields	Lanny Ross
Lynn Fontanne	Selena Royle
Vinton Freedley	Martha Scott
Virginia Grey	Cornelia Otis Skinner
Helen Hayes	Ned Sparks
Katharine Hepburn	Bill Stern
Hugh Herbert	William Terry
Jean Hersholt	Cheryl Walker
Sam Jaffe	Ethel Waters
Allen Jenkins	Johnny Weismuller
George Jessel	Arleen Whelan
Otto Kruger	Dame May Whitty
Gypsy Rose Lee	Ed Wynn
Alfred Lunt	Elliott Nugent

BANDS

Count Basie	Kay Kyser
Xavier Cugat	Guy Lombardo
Benny Goodman	Freddie Martin

CAST

Eileen.......................Cheryl Walker
'Dakota' Ed Smith.......................William Terry
Jean.......................Marjorie Riordan
'California'.......................Lon McCallister
Ella Sue.......................Margaret Early
'Texas'.......................Michael Harrison
Mamie.......................Dorothea Kent
'Jersey'.......................Fred Brady
Lillian.......................Marion Shockley
The Australian.......................Patrick O'Moore

What stood a good chance of emerging a 'big short' under less skillful hands than Sol Lesser proves a sock filmusical of great stature. It has a cast that reads like an out-of-this-world benefit, and a romance as simple as Elsie Dinsmore—and the blend is plenty boffo. It will mop up.

Film constitutes a terrific institutional ballyhoo for all of show business and what we are doing in this war effort. By design or otherwise, and perhaps its casualness is the more purposeful, this impact of Americanism and unselfish service by the greats of the theatre is a shining recording of what all forces in stage, screen and radio have been doing for the lonesome servicemen of all the United Nations.

'Stage Door Canteen' is a skillful admixture by two casts, in itself a departure. One cast projects the simple love story—Eileen and her 'Dakota'; Jean and her 'California'; Ella Sue and her 'Texas'; Mamie and her 'Jersey.' Another cast comprises the Stars of the Stage Door Canteen, and but few of them do walk-through parts.

Plausibly and smoothly, these stars are introduced into their natural habitat, the Stage Door Canteen on West 44th Street, just off Broadway, where Lunt and Fontanne and Vera Gordon, Sam Jaffe, George Raft and Allen Jenkins, Ned Sparks, Ralph Morgan and Hugh Herbert—these, among others, are shown doing their menial back-in-the-kitchen chores.

Then, up front, performing for the visiting men in uniform, gobs, doughboys, marines—no officers—is paraded a galaxy of talent that's a super-duper, all-star array which reads like a casting agent's dream of paradise.

Thus are paraded six bands—Basie, Cugat, Goodman, Kyser, Lombardo and Martin, in sock specialties all.

Thus is introduced Yehudi Menuhin in a longhair rendition of 'Ave Maria' and another excerpt that would tame even a Paramount theatre jitterbug.

Thus, interspersed throughout the lengthy footage—a 132 minutes which, incidentally, doesn't seem as long as it may sound—come a galaxy of name personalities for bows, introductions, and, above all, socko specialties. Kenny Baker, Edgar Bergen, Ray Bolger, Gracie Fields, George Jessel, Gypsy Rose Lee, Elsa Maxwell, Harpo Marx (with his madcap automobile horn business), Ethel Merman, Lanny Ross, Ethel Waters and Ed Wynn—alphabetized billing, you'll note, throughout—do their stuff.

And, to project the mechanics of the Canteen, showing the officer-of-the-day, the senior hostesses, the dancing junior hostesses, or as parts of the plot motivation (as with Katharine Cornell's skillful bit of 'Romeo and Juliet,' and Paul Muni's part as rehearsing his own play), there are introduced another array of stars and legit personalities: Helen Hayes, Ina Claire, Tallulah Bankhead, Vinton Freedley, Merle Oberon, Brock Pemberton, Katharine Hepburn and the others are intertwined into the lonely-soldier-boy-meets-romantic-stage-girl plot.

The quartet of buddies, hailing from Dakota, California, Texas and New Jersey, hence their nicknames, are cast opposite Cheryl Walker (a looker and fine young actress, as Eileen), and Marjorie Riordan, Margaret Early and Dorothea Kent as ambitious girls of the stage, who are doing their patriotic bit at the Canteen. The boys, Bill Terry, Lou McCallister, Michael Harrison and Fred Brady, are capital. And it was good showmanship, for purposes of realism, to utilize these unknowns. They won't remain unknown for long, however.

Scripter Delmer Daves did a deft writing job, and Frank Borzage's direction smoothly splices the sum total into a very palatable cohesive entity.

The 24-hour-leave medium motivates the plot. The kids migrate to the Canteen for their New York fun, before embarking for overseas. Comes another 24-hour respite, and still a third night, all cementing the romantic interest struck up on the first night, a genuine spark, although it is established that the cheek-to-cheek ends within the confines of the Canteen; no after-hour dating, etc., under penalty of dismissal. However, the casual meetings blossom into genuine romance, and while a marriage date before the convoy's sailing is set, an Australian (Patrick O'Moore) brings the news that the boys will meet them again after they return. Katharine Hepburn, officer-of-the-day on that day, gives them solace and urges them to continue their Canteen chores until such reunion.

There are a flock of songs, in keeping with the prolific musical talent, most of them original. Lanny Ross' ballad, 'We Mustn't Say Goodbye' is good; Cugat's specialty is 'Bombshell from Brooklyn'; Ethel Merman is on early with 'Marching Through Berlin'; Gracie Fields does the 'Machine Gun Song' and the 'Lord's Prayer,' the latter highly effective; Kenny Baker reprises the thematic, 'Good Night Sweetheart'; Benny Goodman's 'Why Don't You Do Right'; Ray Bolger's 'The Girl I Love to Leave Behind' (okay ditty by Rodgers & Hart); the Lombardos' 'Sleep, Baby, Sleep in Your Jeep'; Ethel Waters' 'Quicksands'; also 'A Rookie and His Rhythm' and 'Don't Worry Island' all will get a radio play, more or less.

Sol Lesser's showmanship has incorporated fitting salutes to the Aussies, the bravery of the Chinese, and the courage of the Russians, with Sam Jaffe hosting a quintet of non-jiving caviar kiddies, including a femme sea mariner.

The stars, playing themselves, are shown dancing with the boys, most of whom recognize them and in genuine simulation are flabbergasted to be rubbing shoulders with their stage and screen idols.

Of the specialists, their pacing is consistently effective and all of it good. Perhaps Bolger is boffier than the others, or Bergen is a shade overboard, but it's all ultra. Jessel's telephone bit is another good showmanship touch as he tells momma what is coming on next, but at no time is any one set formula adhered to, so that it risks palling. The bands are punchy, each in his own idiom, although there's no gainsaying the showmanly impact of Kay Kyser and his crew. Goodman for jive (including an unidentified, but neat looking, blonde warbler with him), Cugat for rhumba, Basie for bounce (and as backup for Ethel Waters), Lombardo and Martin for smooth dansapation make for another neat blend.

All in all, it's a winner. *Abel.*

OX-BOW INCIDENT

20th-Fox release of Lamar Trotti production. Stars Henry Fonda; features Dana Andrews, Jane Darwell, Paul Hurst. Directed by William A. Wellman. Screenplay, Lamar Trotti, from novel by Walter Van Tilburg Clark; camera, Arthur Miller; editor, Allen McNeil. Previewed in projection room, N. Y., May 8, '43. Running time, **75 MINS.**

Gil Carter....................Henry Fonda
Martin....................Dana Andrews
Rose Mapen....................Mary Beth Hughes
Mexican....................Anthony Quinn
Gerald....................William Eythe
Art Croft....................Henry Morgan
Ma Grier....................Jane Darwell
Judge Daniel Tyler....................Matt Briggs
Arthur Davies....................Harry Davenport
Major Tetley....................Frank Conroy
Farnley....................Marc Lawrence
Monty Smith....................Paul Hurst
Darby....................Victor Kilian
Pancho....................Chris-Pin Martin
Kinkaid....................Frank Orth
Joyce....................Ted North
Mr. Swanson....................George Meeker
Miss Swanson....................Almira Sessions
Mrs. Larch.................Margaret Hamilton
Mapes....................Dick Rich
Old Man....................Francis Ford
Bartlett....................Stanley Andrews
Greene....................Billy Benedict
Gabe Hart....................Rondo Hatton
Winder....................Paul Burns
Sparks....................Leigh Whipper
Jimmy Carnes....................George Chandler
Moore....................George Lloyd

A powerful preachment against mob lynching, 'The Ox-Bow Incident' will have to lean heavily on the popularity of Walter Clark's vivid novel to get this into more important boxoffice brackets. Picture may get some nice coin in certain deluxers, but bulk of it likely will come from twin setups where it should get top billing. In either case, it represents a heavy selling job for both exhibitor and distributor.

Screen version of the best-selling book depends too much on the hanging theme, developing this into a brutal closeup of a Nevada necktie party. Hardly a gruesome detail is omitted. Where the pleading by the three innocent victims doubtlessly was exciting on the printed page, it becomes too raw-blooded for the screen. Chief fault is that the picture over-emphasizes the single hanging incident of the novel, and there's not enough other action.

Western opus follows the escapades of two cowboys, played by Henry Fonda and Henry Morgan, in town after a winter on the range. They are tossed into the turmoil of the usually quiet western community which is aroused by the report of a cattleman's slaying by rustlers. A buddy of the supposedly slain rancher stirs the pot-boiling, and a posse is formed to get the culprits and handle them 'western style.' Remainder of story concerns efforts of the few law-abiding gentry to halt the lynching, and triumph of the mob element.

Director William Wellman has skillfully guided the characters and driven home the point that hanging is unwarranted.

Fonda measures up to star rating, as one of the few level-headed cowhands. His brief scene with Mary Beth Hughes, the flashy belle of the village, following her sudden marriage, is topflight. He helps hold together the loose ends of the rather patent plot. Andrews offers a powerful characterization as the stranger who is unjustly accused of the 'killing' and hung. Frank Conroy makes a believable ex-Confederate major, while William Eythe is superb as his mild-mannered son. Paul Hurst, as the town's drunken bully, gives a fine portrayal.

Anthony Quinn, the Mexican member of the triple hanging; Harry Davenport, the peacemaker; Francis Ford, one of the victims; Henry Morgan, Jane Darwell, Marc Lawrence, Leigh Whipper and Chris-Pin Martin head the strong support.

Camera work by Arthur Miller helps, particularly in the few outdoor scenes. His skill helps cover several obviously phoney sets.

Wear.

BOMBARDIER

RKO release of Robert Fellows production. Stars Pat O'Brien, Randolph Scott; features Anne Shirley, Eddie Albert, Walter Reed, Robert Ryan, Barton MacLane. Directed by Richard Wallace. Screenplay, John Twist; from story by Twist and Martin Rackin; music, Roy Webb; musical director, C. Bakaleinikoff; camera, Nicholas Musuraca; editor, Robert Wise. Tradeshown in N. Y., May 10, '43. Running time, **97 MINS.**

Major Chick Davis....................Pat O'Brien
Captain Buck Oliver....................Randolph Scott
Burt Hughes....................Anne Shirley
Tom Hughes....................Eddie Albert
Jim Carter....................Walter Reed
Joe Connors....................Robert Ryan
Sergeant Dixon....................Barton MacLane
Jap Officer....................Leonard Strong
Chito Rafferty....................Richard Martin
Paul Harris....................Russell Wade
Captain Rand....................James Newill
Chaplain Craig....................John Miljan
Instructor....................Charles Russell

The theory of modern high-level precision bombing, as practiced by the U. S. Army Air Forces, is explained and fairly well dramatized in this somewhat obvious romantic thriller. While 'Bombardier' has its drawbacks, it's reasonably good as war propaganda. It will get its share of biz.

Picture suffers from the lack of powerful names and excessive length. Sequences seem to have been added after the regular yarn was completed. From appearances, this extra footage was aimed to give the picture timely punch. Under the circumstances, it fits the basic story surprisingly well, although stretching the running time too much.

The technical phases of the story, dealing with the theory of high-level bombing and the instruction of bombardier cadets, are interesting and illuminating, although manifestly presented in popularized terms. These sequences contain some excellent aerial stuff, including several genuinely exciting scenes.

But from the news of Pearl Harbor and the departure of the bomber unit to action in the Pacific, the yarn takes a definitely topical turn. With unmistakable parallel, it shows a bomber raid on Japan, with the torture and execution of one captured Flying Fortress crew, and with a thoroughly hoked-up and implausible finish.

From a propaganda standpoint, 'Bombardier' offers at least a rudimentary lesson in U. S. Army bombing. But more important, it shows the Japs as merciless, inhuman murderers and torturers, although it does present them as not too efficient fighters and foemen. Still, the scene of murder and torture of prisoners, coming so soon after the execution of Doolittle's men, should have some value. There is nothing to indicate the basic issues of the war, however.

Of the performances, Pat O'Brien and Randolph Scott, as the stars, have by far the best parts as the fanatical exponent of high-level bombing and the daredevil pilot, respectively, so they're more effective than the others. O'Brien is still troubled by his old habit of reading almost every line as if he were trying to be heard above the roar of a bomber engine, but otherwise his playing is properly direct and convincing. Scott gives one of his usual quiet performances. Of the others, Anne Shirley is too much the stock ingenue to seem at home amid the bomber school surroundings, but Eddie Albert, Walter Reed, Robert Ryan and Barton MacLane are acceptable in stereotype cadet roles.

Hobe.

THE BELLS GO DOWN

(BRITISH-MADE)

London, April 17.

United Artists' release of Ealing Studios-Michael Balcon production. Features Tommy Trinder, James Mason. Directed by Basil Dearden. Screenplay, Roger MacDougall, adapted from book of same name by Stephen Black; camera, Ernest Palmer, G. Gibbs. At London Pavilion. Running time, **86 MINS.**

Tommy Turk....................Tommy Trinder
Ted Robbins....................James Mason
Bob....................Philip Friend
Sam....................Mervyn Johns
Brookes....................Billy Hartnell
Susie....................Meriel Forbes
Ma Turk....................Beatrice Varley
Nan....................Philippa Hiatt
Officer MacFarlane....................Finley Currie
Pa Robbins....................Norman Pierce
Ma Robbins....................Muriel George
Lou Freeman....................Julian Vedey
P. C. O'Brien....................Richard George

Current film must compete with 'Fires Were Started,' a government documentary with a similar basic idea which was released only a few weeks ago. Both depict the activities of life in the London Auxiliary Fire Service. But the first one out was more legitimate in that it was portrayed by actual members of the service. However, it'll do okay at the b.o.

Viewed as mere low comedy, 'The Bells Go Down' ambles along amiably. There is a running commentary patterned on the lines of those made familiar by Quentin Reynolds, and the fire scenes alternate with the wisecracking of Tommy Trinder, which are often without provocation. Thrillingly effective conflagration scenes deserve a large share of the honors

Trinder's numerous fans will accept him unreservedly without for a moment analyzing the whys and wherefores. He enacts a lovable East Side young man whose mother runs a fish and chip shop, and who owns a racing greyhound that never wins until his comrades have gone broke backing the pooch.

The supporting cast was very well chosen, with Mervyn Johns offering another one of the numerous portrayals in which he has been so frequently scintillating. James Mason, as a fireman, scores, as usual; Beatrice Varley, as Trinder's mother, and fully a score of others can be set down as efficient support. Direction, production and photography are praiseworthy. *Jolo.*

PRELUDE TO WAR

War Activities Committee release of U. S. War Dept. production. Prepared by Lt. Col. Frank Capra and staff of U. S. Army Signal Corps writers and technicians; previewed in N. Y. May 6, '43. Running time, **53 MINS.**

First in the series of seven 'Why We Fight' films produced for the U. S. War Dept. by Lt. Col. Frank Capra, of the Special Service Division, Army Service Forces, 'Prelude to War,' which was originally intended for exclusive use in the Army's orientation courses, is scheduled for theatrical release May 27, and public reaction to the documentary will decide whether the remaining films will be distributed generally. The public's attitude, however, is a foregone conclusion. For in piecing together the collection of clips—many of them released for the first time—giving the causes and events leading up to the present conflict, Capra has turned out a forceful, dramatic and ofttimes spectacular presentation.

'Prelude' lacks the terrific impact of the second and third in the series, 'The Nazis Strike' and 'Divide and Conquer' (reviewed in last week's 'Variety'), but not having these succeeding films for comparative standards, it will stand out in front of other home-made factual pictures backgrounding our entry into the war. It's a triumph for Capra and those associated with him in the production of the film and is singularly outstanding for the War Dept's courage in placing great stress on this country's fatal error—of being lulled into a false sense of security by two oceans when the aggressor nations, as far back as 1931, were on the march.

Capra makes every inch of footage count; there isn't a dull second in the 53 minutes of running time, nor one that doesn't conclusively prove the main point of the film—how America was caught asleep as Germany, Japan and Italy built up its well-trained war machine for world conquest. The commentary and animated maps are equally as effective. Throughout Capra uses the technique of comparing the men and ideals of a free world and those of the slave world. As the U. S. was sinking its ships in a futile attempt to cement peace after the last war, the aggressor nations, with their inbred love of regimentation and discipline, were preparing to strike anew with newer and more powerful war machines and campaign of lies.

Particularly stirring is a marching sequence showing how, almost from infancy, the youth of Germany, Italy and Japan were being trained, drilled and regimented. As the drums keep beating their ominous rhythm, the complete training of the child to manhood is vividly portrayed with appropriate flashbacks to the counterpart of American training of its future manhood. The steadily mounting tension produced by these reels is greatly intensified by the repetitious and increasing tempo of the drums. Sequence as used is damning in its contrast, conclusively pointing up America's lack of planning and preparation.

Latter portion of film deals with Japan's invasion of Manchuria and China and finally Mussolini's march into Ethiopia, with the commentary throughout reiterating 'why should we go to war for a few mud huts?' to emphasize again U. S. isolationism and lack of vision. Film ends as Hitler, fully prepared, is also ready to march. *Rose.*

PARDON MY GUN

Columbia release of Jack Fier production. Stars Charles Starrett. Directed by William Berke. Story and screenplay, Wyndham Gittens; camera, George Meehan; editor, Mel Thorsen. At New York, N. Y., dual, week May 4, '43. Running time, **56 MINS.**

Steve Randall............Charles Starrett
Dodie Cameron............Alma Carroll
Arkansas.................Arthur Hunnicutt
Tex......................Texas Jim Lewis
Judge....................Noah Beery, Sr.
Clint....................Dick Curtis
Ace......................Ted Mapes
Whitey...................Lloyd Bridges
Corks....................Dave Harper
Sheriff..................Roger Gray
Texas Jim Lewis and His Lone Star Cowboys

Rather facetious title fails to convey the action and fairly original twists in this sturdy western. 'Pardon My Gun' measures up to best in this group starring Charles Starrett, and will do well where previous outdoor epics did business. Length makes it suited for twinners, where it belongs.

Film differs from many of its ilk in that there's a murder in the first few minutes, and the many plot ramifications develop from this killing. Rancher is slain for $100,000 in money he is taking to town, but the daughter of a sheepman cops the coin when the money-satchel is tossed into the bushes. She's immediately placed on the spot by the rustlers and crooked judge, leader of the cutthroats, because she knows too much about the killing and location of the $100,000. Engineer (Starrett) who's surveying land for a dam comes to her rescue, with a real romance developing. There's the usual mistaken identity angle, with the engineer jailed for a second shooting. The customary finish is embellished with a clinch between the femme and the engineer.

Charles Starrett is the rangy, good-looking cowboy-engineer who knows more about riding and handling a gun than surveying. Alma Carroll makes a comely daughter of the sheep-owner who's in love with him. Remainder of cast is standard for a cowboy opus, with Dick Curtis again the heavy, Noah Beery, Sr., as the crooked judge; Arthur Hunnicutt and Texas Jim Lewis and His Lone Star Cowboys. Last-named is a string musical combo that lifts this into the musical western category. *Wear.*

JOHNNY DOUGHBOY

(SONGS)

Republic release of John H. Auer production. Stars Jane Withers; features Henry Wilcoxon and Patrick Brook. Directed by Auer. Screenplay, Lawrence Kimble, based on original story by Frederick Kohner; camera, John Alton; editor, Wallace Grissell. Reviewed at RKO Palace, N.Y., May 5, '43. Running time, **64 MINS.**

Ann Winters } Penelope Ryan }............Jane Withers
Olive Lawrence...........Henry Wilcoxon
Johnny Kelly.............Patrick Brook
Harry Fabian.............William Demarest
'Biggy' Bigsworth........Ruth Donnelly
Mammy....................Etta McDaniel
Jennifer.................Joline Westbrook
Members of the 20 Minus Club: Bobby Breen, Baby Sandy, 'Alfalfa' Switzer, 'Spanky' McFarland, Butch & Buddy, Cora Sue Collins, Robert Coogan, Grace Costello, the Falkner Orchestra, Karl Kiffe.

Glamorization of Jane Withers is theme of the script and purpose of the studio in 'Johnny Doughboy,' which should appeal to juves. But it's strictly a dualer.

Story gives Miss Withers ample opportunity to strut in a bathing suit, model latest 'junior miss' creations and go in for heavy emoting as a 16-year-old film star who is tired of playing kid roles. She runs away to seek romance and finds a middle-aged playwright, Henry Wilcoxon, who builds her up to a big letdown. She drowns her sorrows by joining a juve edition of the 'Hollywood Caravan,' called 'Junior Victory Caravan.' It plays the camps with a troupe of teen-age actors and hoofers (members of a 20-Minus Club), and Miss Withers has opportunity to exhibit newly acquired tap routine.

Despite efforts of makeup and wardrobe departments, Miss Withers is no glamour girl, but she does well at her acting. Wilcoxon is okay as the tweedy, pipe-smoking playwright, while Patrick Brook clicks in his song-and-dance routines. Incidentally, Bobby Breen, child star of some years ago, is seen and heard in a bit role, but he does no singing, as his voice has changed drastically.

MANTRAP

Republic release of George Sherman production, directed by Sherman. Features Henry Stephenson, Lloyd Corrigan, Joseph Allen, Jr., Dorothy Lovett, Edmund MacDonald, Alice Fleming. Story and adaptation, Curt Siodmak; editor, Arthur Roberts; camera, William Bradford. At Strand, Brooklyn, dual, week May 6, '43. Running time, **57 MINS.**

Sir Humphrey Quilp.....Henry Stephenson
Anatol Duprez..........Lloyd Corrigan
Eddie Regan............Joseph Allen, Jr.
Jane Mason.............Dorothy Lovett
Asst. D. A. Knox.......Edmund MacDonald
Miss Mason.............Alice Fleming
Robert Berwick.........Tom Stevenson
Patrick } Thomas } Berwick.........Frederic Worlock
Miss Woolcott..........Jane Weeks

That venerable character actor, Henry Stephenson, here plays a retired detective in the manner of a Sherlock Holmes, whose exploits have often been picturized, but his efforts and those of the assorted cast of minor importance fail to lift 'Mantrap' above the ordinary. It's a minor dualer.

Even though the picture runs but 57 minutes, it tires as result of a lot of routine detail involved in piecing together clues and arriving at deductions in the solving of a murder which should not have stumped police as much as it obviously does. Stephenson, a former Scotland Yard man and now at the age of 70 devoting himself to writing books on criminology, is called in by the D.A.'s office to aid them in pinning a murder charge on a suspect. While the d.a. and a police lieutenant are certain they have solved the crime, they ask Stephenson's aid as a tribute to him on his birthday. He upsets their modern calculations and comes up with a surprise solution.

Teamed with Stephenson is his doctor friend, Lloyd Corrigan, an amusing character, while romantic interest is supplied by Joseph Allen, Jr., playing a dick, and Dorothy Lovett, daughter of Stephenson's housekeeper. For all concerned in the cast it's a struggle to hold attention, partly because of the slowness of the action and also in the face of lifeless dialog. *Char.*

Ghost and the Guest

Producers Releasing Corp. release of Arthur Alexander-Alfred Stern production. Stars James Dunn, Florence Rice. Directed by William Nigh. Screenplay by Morey Amsterdam from Milt Gross' original story; camera, Robert Cline; editor, Charles Henkel, Jr. At New York, N. Y., dual, week April 4, '43. Running time, **59 MINS.**

Webster Frye.............James Dunn
Jackie Frye..............Florence Rice
Mabel....................Mabel Todd
Harmony Jones............Sam McDaniel
Ben Bowron...............Robert Dudley
Herbie...................Eddy Chandler
Police Chief.............Jim Toney
Smoothie Lewis...........Robert Bice
Josie....................Renee Carson
Killer Blake.............Tony Ward
Ted......................Anthony Caruso
Harold...................Eddie Foster

With James Dunn and Florence Rice in principal roles, producers here have turned out a neat little farce comedy, suited for the dual combos. Milt Gross' original has been scripted into lively fare by Morey Amsterdam.

Yarn about a honeymooning couple that bumps into gangsters after the hidden diamonds, an empty coffin, an eerie country house with its trap doors, sliding panels and other trick gadgets is played with tongue-in-cheek attitude for real guffaws. Director William Nigh keeps the many plot ramifications on an even and plausible keel, with most events turned into solid laugh material. Meaningless title is a handicap; otherwise, it's forthright comedy fare.

James Dunn, once a major company potential, shapes up like his old self as the groom who finally decides the quiet country house (picked for a honeymoon) is an exact replica of Grand Central station. Florence Rice, capable young femme lead, tries her hand in a comedienne role as his wife with nice results. Mabel Todd, cast as the man-crazy, jittery gangster's moll, also contributes some funny moments. Sam McDaniel, too, is good as the frightened colored chauffeur. Robert Dudley, comparative newcomer, heads the support as the wry county hangman. Robert Cline's cameraing is excellent, while Charles Henkel, Jr., turns in a trim editing job. *Wear.*

CAPITAN VENENO

('Captain Poison')
(ARGENTINE MADE)

Buenos Aires, April 16.

EFA production and release. Stars Luis Sandrini; features Rosa Rosen, Aline Marney, Joaquin Garcia Leon, Bertha Moss, Hector Quintanilla, Maria Ramos, Gregorio Verdi, Alberto Ballerini, Lalo Bosch, Jose Krause, Vicente Alvarez. Screenplay by Enrique Amorim and Roman Gomez Masia, original by Pedro A. de Alarcon. Reviewed at the Broadway, Buenos Aires. Running time, **90 MINS.**

(In Spanish)

This is the first dramatic role attempted by Latin comic Luis Sandrini, and it doesn't come off too well. Like other Latin players (and a good many outside Latin America), Sandrini wanted to do something more than the kind of parts that brought him fame and cash. 'Capitan Veneno' is adapted from the work of a w.k. Spanish author, Pedro A. de Alarcon, and screen version turns out to be disconnected, full of weak situations, and only isolated effective scenes. Fact that it is Henri Martinent's maiden effort at handling the meg doesn't help.

Story tells with slight changes history of irascible soldier Jore de Cordoba, who was given the nickname Captain Poison because of his violent temper. Locale has been shifted to Argentina at end of last century. Wounded captain is taken to the home of a widow with two daughters whose attentive care soon finds its mark. One of the gals falls for him and little by little he comes around. Casting of Sandrini, in the opinion of most critics, was an error, but he does fairly well, turns in a generally intelligent performance. Rosa Rosen is o.k. and Aline Marney good in role added to the story.

There are some interesting interpolations, particularly a lancer's dance under the direction of Margarita Wallmann, but certain sequences seem out of place. Music by Alberto Soifer and photography by Roque Funes are above average. Pace is a little too dull throughout and dramatic highlights missing, but with proper exploitation it should do o.k. in interior situations where the rough-riding military motif is especially sought. *Ray.*

Cuando Florezca El Naranjo

('When the Orange Tree Flowers')
(ARGENTINE-MADE)

Buenos Aires, April 16.

Panamericana release of San Miguel production. Stars Angel Magana and Maria Duval; features Alita Roman, Felisa Mary, Juana Sujo, Rafael Frontaura, Francisco Lopez Silva, Homero Carpena, Mirtha Reid and Teresita. Directed by Alberto de Zavalia. Screenplay by Alejandro Casona. At Ambassador, Buenos Aires; running time, **75 MINS.**

(In Spanish)

Nice romantic comedy with enough of the poetic tone to appeal especially to Latin audiences, 'Cuando Florezca El Naranjo' appears a steady prospect for first-runners throughout the Americas and a solid followup which will pay dividends even though not sensational. Some of the starry-eyed connections are a little vague, but audiences south of the border like 'em and that's the best test. Albert de Zavalia, one of the best of the Latin meggers, has adroitly handled the sentimental scenes and his good taste is apparent in restraint which marks production in general.

Yarn concerns a handsome young prof who comes to a girl's boarding school. The daughter of the school's gardener, a moon-struck 'chica,' falls with a thud. She listens in as the 'maestro' tells legend of Mariquita and Martin Thompson, who were to marry 'when the orange tree blossomed.' Maria Duval, who plays the young girl's role with assurance and charm, imagines herself the reincarnation of Mariquita, but troubles develop from another score when a femme teacher pleads with the prof because she is about to have an illegitimate child. The young prof, to save her, proclaims the expected infant as his and everything looks dark until schoolmarm finally confesses and romance is allowed to proceed without a hitch.

Magana still has signs of over-affected posturing, but all in all turns in a good job. Senorita Duval's role is reminiscent of her eternal Cinderella, but good presence and smart handling help. Alita Roman, in a dramatic support, and Juanita Sujo, who handles much of the comedy relief, are outstanding among featured players. *Ray.*

PASSION ISLAND

('La Isla de la Pasion')
(MEXICAN-MADE)

Maya Films release of EMASA Studios production. Stars David Silva, Isabela Corona. Directed by Emilio Fernandez. Story and screenplay by Fernandez; English titles, Herman G. Weinberg. At World, N. Y., starting April 30, '43. Running time, **93 MINS.**

Julio....................David Silva
Lolita...................Isabela Corona
Maria....................Pituka De Foronda
'Alligator'..............Chaflan
Captain Allende..........Miguel Angel Ferriz
'Toro'...................Pedro Armendariz
The Doctor...............Antonio Bravo
Coquito..................Chela Campos

(In Spanish; English titles)

After President Roosevelt's visit to Mexico to meet President Camacho, interest in all Mexican-made pictures naturally is increased. While this may not be the top Mexican production to come from south of the Rio Grande, it certainly measures up as stout fare for foreign-language theatres in U.S. In some respects it is reminiscent of first French-made productions launched in this country some five or six years ago. Picture should make coin for its American distributors despite difficulties the film had with New York censors.

One can readily imagine how much more vivid certain passages would have been without the censorial shears. Patriotic angle has been kept to the fore despite the unrequited love theme on which the director has focused must interest. Understood that the 'soldaderas' theme was particularly objectionable to the censors although long regarded as part of the military history of Mexico—that wives and sweethearts, or just camp followers, follow their loved ones in the army wherever they go. Implication, after censorial doctoring, is that those not married have gone along just to do the clothes washing for their men.

The annexation of Clipperton Island back in 1909 forms the historical background for this picture. Story revolves about the sending of a small detachment of men to Passion Island, to hold it in the name of Mexico. When revolution breaks out under the Diaz regime, the troops have to stay on for two years instead of four months. Result is that sickness, dissatisfaction and near-starvation confront the hardy band. It all winds up in a mutiny, with usual results—the captain is killed but the hero lives to carry on the Mexican tradition after the deserters are slain.

Main theme concerns a man, disappointed in love, who joins the colors to forget his sorrow. Then there is the beautiful cafe singer, madly in love with him, who goes along to the deserted isle to attempt to win his love. Tragic ending is in the familiar Latin-American tradition.

David Silva, handsome hero of yarn, has few opportunities to act but bespeaks possibilities. The director likely is to blame for making him such a silent, unbending hero. Isabela Corona, as Lolita the cafe singer, is reminiscent of Dolores del Rio, although having the added asset of being a capable singer. Chaflan, a top cinema comedian in Mexico, is acceptable as Silva's pal. Nice performances are contributed by Pituka de Foronda, as Silva's main heart interest; Miguel Angel Ferris, as the captain; Antonio Bravo, as the doctor, and Pedro Armendariz.

Emilio Fernandez' scripting is better than his direction, which is heavy-footed at times. This indicates that Mexican producers are headed in the right direction, and with Hollywood technicians now helping may soon supplant French productions in popularity. Herman G. Weinberg has done a trim job translating the Spanish into pointed English titles. *Wear.*

Miniature Reviews

'Coney Island' (20th) (Songs) (Color). Betty Grable - George Montgomery-Cesar Romero starrer will do biz.

'Action in the North Atlantic' (WB). Murmansk-bound convoy saga for nominal biz in regular bookings.

'The Gentler Sex' (British). The British women's army glorified; should do okay b.o. in America with cutting.

'Fall In' (UA). Hal Roach comedy, running but 48 minutes, that's only mildly funny.

'Tres Hombres del Rio' (Argentine). Legendary story; unlikely for boxoffice.

'Virgin of Guadalupe' (Mex.). Excellent religious story about the Miracle of Tepeyac done by strong Mexican cast.

'Masquerade' (Soviet - made). Too melodramatic for American consumption.

'Casi Un Sueno' (Argentine). Cinderella yarn seen doing okay in domestic Argentine market.

CONEY ISLAND

(Color)

(MUSICAL)

20th Century-Fox release of William Perlberg production. Stars Betty Grable, George Montgomery, Cesar Romero; features Charles Winninger, Phil Silvers, Matt Briggs, Paul Hurst. Directed by Walter Lang. Original screenplay, George Seaton; songs, Leo Robin, Ralph Rainger; dances, Hermes Pan, musical numbers supervised by Fanchon; camera, Ernest Palmer; editor, Robert Simpson. Previewed in N. Y., May 17, '43. Running time, **95 MINS.**

Kate Farley	Betty Grable
Eddie Johnson	George Montgomery
Joe Rocco	Cesar Romero
Finnigan	Charles Winninger
Frankie	Phil Silvers
William Hammerstein	Matt Briggs
Louie	Paul Hurst
Bartender	Frank Orth
Dolly	Phyllis Kennedy
Dancer	Carmen D'Antonio
Cashier	Hal K. Dawson
Carter	Andrew Tombes
Piano Player	Harry Seymour
Organist	Byron Foulger

The true Coney Island, corny, bawdy and brash, evidently wasn't deemed sufficiently colorful for George Seaton, scripter of this film, so he just hung the title on what amounts to a 95-minute audition of Betty Grable's chassis and legs—in color. Its entertainment stemming almost wholly from the physical allure of the svelte blonde soubret, this filmusical, with exploitation, will achieve sustained boxoffice. Another saving grace is that it's escapist film fare.

Slowness marks the story all the way; also sameness. Both these negative factors were inevitable in view of the fact that Miss Grable is either dancing or singing, or both, in much of the running time. Remainder is taken up by a flash of the Coney Island midway and to sustain an oft-told story about two pals after the same girl.

In this instance the boys are portrayed as characters; one the owner of a Coney barroom-honky tonk, the other a con guy looking for a partnership in lieu of an old doublecross on a carny grift. When Cesar Romero refuses the split to George Montgomery, the latter worms his way into the joint, after a couple of asinine escapades, as producer of the floorshows. In this way he makes a lady of Miss Grable, a gaudy singing moll, and she winds up at the finish as star of a Willie Hammerstein-produced musical at the Victoria on Broadway. Fact that Willie Hammerstein didn't produce musicals, and that the Victoria was strictly a straight vaudeville theatre, evidently escaped this film's scenarist.

There's no gainsaying Miss Grable's charm for the male masses, but it's hard to conceive such wild audience acclaim as occasions every one of her fair singing stints. She's pretty with a terrific set of gams and other physical assets—period. Only in one musical number is she a boff, and that's her brownskin take-off of 'Miss Lulu from Louisville,' a pictorial review of derriere exercising. Her other Robin-Rainger songs are 'Take It from There,' 'Beautiful Coney Island' and 'There's Danger in a Dance,' latter given one of those out - of - this-world-except-in-Hollywood mammoth productions as part of Hammerstein's musical. None of the tunes is distinguished.

On the performance end, Phil Silvers and Charles Winninger steal all the honors in featured parts. Both take the play whenever they're within camera focus, Winninger as a good-natured souse-pal of Montgomery's, and Silvers as a sideshow owner. Montgomery is talking exactly like Clark Gable, but he's not as good an actor, in his unbelievable role as a con man, while the part of a frustrated wolf doesn't exactly suit Romero here.

Matt Briggs plays Willie Hammerstein, and it's hard to conceive that the late showman would have become so enraptured of a mediocre singer. Paul Hurst, per usual, does okay as a tough bouncer for Romero. Frank Orth has a nice bit as a bartender, and Carmen D'Antonio, somewhat under wraps, gains a minute's attention as a sexy torso-tosser in a Coney Island harem scene. Phyllis Kennedy, who has a promisingly funny pan, acquits herself nicely in a chorine's part. Others in the cast have only bits.

Plus the color, film also has the costuming of the early 1900 era. Also some montage of old 'Clipper' and 'Variety' front pages, with 'Variety' portrayed as giving its entire front page to the phenomenal b.o. lure of Miss Grable at Coney Island.

Production looks costly, but Walter Lang's directorial job didn't match it. However, that was most likely due to the script. Camera work, on the other hand, is all to the good. *Scho.*

Action in the North Atlantic

Hollywood, May 15.

Warner Bros. release of Jerry Wald production. Stars Humphrey Bogart; features Raymond Massey, Alan Hale, Julie Bishop, Ruth Gordon. Directed by Lloyd Bacon. Screenplay by John Howard Lawson, based on story by Guy Gilpatric; additional dialog, A. I. Bezzerides, W. R. Burnett; camera, Ted McCord; editors, Thomas Pratt, George Amy; montages, Don Siegel, James Leicester; special effects, Jack Cosgrove, Edwin B. DuPar; asst. director, Elmer Decker; dialog director, Harold Winston. Tradeshown in L. A., May 14, '43. Running time, **126 MINS.**

Joe Rossi	Humphrey Bogart
Capt. Steve Jarvis	Raymond Massey
Boats O'Hara	Alan Hale
Pearl	Julie Bishop
Sarah Jarvis	Ruth Gordon
Chips Abrams	Sam Levene
Johnnie Pulaski	Dane Clark
Whitey Lara	Peter Whitney
Rear Admiral Hartridge	Minor Watson
Caviar Jinks	J. M. Kerrigan
Cadet Robert Parker	Dick Hogan
Ensign Wright	Kane Richmond
Goldberg	Chic Chandler
Cecil	George Offerman, Jr.
Lt. Commander	Don Douglas
Pete Larson	Art Foster
Ahearn	Ray Montgomery
Sparks	Creighton Hale
Hennessy	Elliott Sullivan
McGonigle	Alec Craig
Capt. Ziemer	Ludwig Stossel
Cherub	Dick Wessel
Capt. Carpolis	Frank Puglia
Jenny O'Hara	Iris Adrian

'Action in the North Atlantic' is Warners' latest contribution to the present cycle of war-backgrounded melodramas, in this instance a cinematic salute to the members of the Merchant Marine and Navy gun crews who have battled their way through the sub packs to Murmansk. Within extended running time of 126 minutes, picture delves deeply into reactions and incidents in the lives of crew members, and the convoy passage, with sub attacks, is too lengthy to retain proper audience suspense. It's a moderate but still profitable grosser for the regular runs.

Story is launched with Humphrey Bogart first mate and Raymond Massey skipper on a tanker which is torpedoed by a Nazi sub. Pair join crew members for liferaft drift of 11 days until saved. Ashore, yarn dips deeply into lives and reactions of various crew members, and traces rather quick pitch, romance and marriage of Bogart to nitery singer Julie Bishop. Massey draws captain post on new Liberty ship, signs on Bogart, and again picks up most of his former tanker crew. Story then goes narrative in visual explanation of assemblage and formation of North Atlantic convoy groups, with this one bound for Murmansk. Off Iceland, a sub pack attacks, and the convoy scatters, with Massey's ship decoying on sub far away from the convoy, finally going through maneuvers that succeeds in sinking the sub. But Nazi dive bombers put out from Norway to rake the ship before they are downed, and the voyage ends when the listing Victory freighter limps into Murmansk.

There's plenty of action and melodramatic suspense in the brief sub and air attacks on the ship, but it's insufficient to compensate for the slow cinematic voyage up to that point. Process and special effects photography is expertly devised for realistic presentation of the ocean trip; but still these factors cannot overcome the slow and deliberate script that runs double of needed footage to unfold the tale.

Bogart provides a sterling performance as the first mate, getting maximum results from the rough-and-ready role, while Massey is neatly cast as the skipper. Alan Hale is prominent as the bo'sum mate, while Sam Levene, Dane Clark, Peter Whitney, Dick Hogan, Chic Chandler and Kane Richmond provide strong support in various assignments. Julie Bishop and Ruth Gordon are submerged in brief sequences.

There are several informative stretches and sequences on the convoy operation and setup for audience attention, but even this—combined with the spectacular phases of the sub and air attacks—is not sufficient to carry picture through for more than moderate attention. Script by John Howard Lawson is greatly overwritten, while Lloyd Bacon found direction of the lengthy document too much to generate into necessary paceful picture. *Walt.*

THE GENTLE SEX

(BRITISH-MADE)

London April 15.

General Film Distributors release of Two Cities-Concanen-Leslie Howard production. Features Joan Gates, Jean Gillie, Joan Greenwood, Joyce Howard, Rosamund John, Lilli Palmer, Barbara Waring, John Justin. Directed by Leslie Howard. Screenplay, Moie Charles; camera, Cyril Knowles, Ray Sturges. Reviewed at Odeon theatre, London. Running time, **92 MINS.**

Gwen	Joan Gates
Good Time Dot	Jean Gillie
Betty	Joan Greenwood
Anne Lawrence	Joyce Howard
Maggie Fraser	Rosamund John
Erna	Lilli Palmer
Joan	Barbara Waring
David Sheridan	John Justin
Colonel Lawrence	Frederick Leister
Mrs. Sheridan	Mary Jerrold
Mrs. Simpson	Everley Gregg
Mrs. Fraser	Elliot Mason
Sally	Rosalyn Boulter
Convoy Sergeant	Noreen Craven
Captain	Harry Welchman

Here is a British-made film that will probably have more boxoffice appeal in America than in its native precincts. The story is too close to

home for the British, who are familiar with women's war work there, whereas in U. S. it is relatively new. It should do well, however, in Britain also.

Story concerns the personalities of seven girls, drawn from various grades of society, who join the ATS (women's army) and go through the routine of breaking in before being sent to different posts. At crucial moments the girls prove themselves as brave and heroic as the male contingent, and the film ends with a toast to 'the women.' This is spoken by an unprogrammed commentator. The voice was Leslie Howard's, who also directed and co-produced.

Palpably a propaganda war picture, there is plenty of comedy, which savors a little too much of crosstalk wide-cracking. Direction and production are intelligent and artistic, but the basic plot is too one-keyish. Pic would be improved by cutting for the American market. Audience reaction, however, is invariably favorable.

Cast, even to the smallest bit parts, deserves commendation. The two outstanding characterizations are those handled by Lilli Palmer and Rosamund John. Miss Palmer enacts a Czech refugee whose family was manhandled by the Nazist, and Miss John is a Scot with a delicious and easily understood dialect. But it is Miss Palmer, in an emotional role delicately and subtly played, who has the best opportunities. *Jolo.*

FALL IN

United Artists release of Hal Roach production. Features William Tracy, Joe Sawyer, Robert Barratt, Jean Porter, Frank Faylen, Clyde Fillmore. Directed by Kurt Neumann. Story and adaptation, Eugene Conrad and Edward E. Seabrook; editor, Richard Currier; camera, Robert Pittack. At Laffmovie, N. Y., week May 14, '43. Running time, **48 MINS.**

Sergeant Doubleday.........William Tracy
Sergeant Ames.................Joe Sawyer
Colonel Elliot...............Robert Barratt
Joan..........................Jean Porter
Luke.......................Arthur Hunnicutt
Lydia........................Rebel Randall
Captain Gillis...............Frank Faylen
Benedict...................Clyde Fillmore
Carl........................Gregory Gaye
Zeb..........................Tom Fadden
Ruth....................Nancy Brinckman
Pete..........................Eddie Hall

Even though it runs only 48 minutes, 'Fall In' pads itself to about double the footage it deserves. Tiresome and detailed, it offers but minor support as the associate feature on double bills. It's on the same order as a previous Hal Roach 'streamliner.'

An army camp and two sergeants who resent each other form the background for the mild fun produced, while for slight romantic interest the cast contains Jean Porter, whose potentialities appear as bright and promising as her smile.

Story deals with a young sergeant whose memory is out of this world and another of the bully type whose lack of memory is also a precedent-setter. This, plus a group of Kentucky hillbillies who are made up into a military police platoon, are the hooks on which the gags and situation are hung, while for a slapsticky sequence Hal Roach has provided a free-for-all with a bunch of spies. Even Miss Porter and other girls take part in bopping the enemy agents.

The performances are routine but okay, William Tracy, Joe Sawyer, Robert Barratt, Frank Faylen and Clyde Fillmore the standouts. Some of the hillbilly characters are well patterned. *Char.*

Tres Hombres del Rio

('Three Men of the River')
(ARGENTINE-MADE)

Buenos Aires, May 8.

Pan-Americana release of San Miguel production. Stars Elisa Galve; featuring Jose Olarra, Luis Aldas, Agustin Irusta, Juan Jose Miguez, Leticia Scury, Homero Carpena, Roberto Ferradas, Olga Valladares, Lucy Blanco, Felipe D'Angelis and Felix Tortorelli. Directed by Mario Soffici. Story, Eliseo Montaine; adapted by Rodolfo Gonzalez Pacheco and Hugo MacDougall; photography, Francis Boeninguer. Reviewed at the Ocean, Buenos Aires. Running time, **93 MINS.**

This is one of the best to come from San Miguel in some time and has a possible interest for U. S. audiences because of its locale. Fault, however, lies in weak characterization and lack of vitality. Scenery, with swell shots of waterfalls, rivers and other assorted natural phenomena, gets in the way too often with result that pic doesn't even line up with a logical conclusion. Boxoffice prospects are just fair.

Like increasing number of Argentine-mades, 'Tres Hombres' has a legendary background. Story in this case is the tale of an Indian girl whose body is washed away after she has been violated on the sands of the river bank, on the Alta Parana. A flower springs up, which, according to the superstitious natives, must not be plucked lest it bring bad luck.

All this done in a poetic prolog that pans into modern story of three characters, smugglers and thieves. They abduct a young girl but can't go through with their kidnapping plans. In the course of their journey down the river they pick up an abandoned derelict for whom the gal falls. Jealousy angle is built up, with one of the trio going for her only to resign himself to the mysterious stranger.

Elisa Galve in the starring role is somewhat mannered and too, too, sweet, but in general turns in a good performance. Top honors, however, go to Leticia Scury, as the old Indian woman, and to Jose Olarra, one of Argentina's best character actors. Director Mario Soffici proves his already high standing as one of the best camera handlers with excellent interiors, but indoor shots are as out of place as a gaucho in the livingroom. Music by Gilardo Gilardi good. *Ray.*

Virgin of Guadalupe

('La Virgen Morena')
(MEXICAN MADE)

Soria & Santandar production and release. Stars Jose Luis Jimenez; features Amparo Morillo, Abel Salazar, Antonio Bravo. Directed by Gabriel Soria. Screenplay by Soria and Alberto Santandar, based on story by Father Carlos Heredia; camera, Augustin Solares; English titles, Herman G. Weinberg; score, Julian Carrillo. At World, N. Y., week May 15, '43. Running time, **95 MINS.**

Juan Diego.............Jose Luis Jiminez
Dona Blanca...............Amparo Morillo
Temoc, Last of the Aztec Kings.....
Abel Salazar
Juan Bernardino...........A. Soto Rangel
Xochitl, the Aztec Princess..........
Maria Luisa Zea
Delgadillo...................Antonio Bravo
Aztec Warrior.................Tito Junco

(In Spanish; English Titles)

This is the second Mexican production to play this theatre in recent weeks to indicate that Mexico's film industry is getting places. 'Virgin of Guadalupe,' explaining in dramatic form the miracle of Tepeyac hill and the role that the Virgin played in early Mexican history, has been done in excellent taste and with obvious appeal to Mexicans and Spanish-speaking people in this country. Picture, too, shapes up as a sturdy entry in foreign-language and arty theatre despite its length.

Story of church history in Mexico during the sixteenth century has been told with reverence and dignity if, at times, perhaps seemingly extra care for minute detail. Screenplay by Gabriel Soria and Alberto Santandar is a faithful translation of the story by the Rev. Carlos Heredia, historian for Shrine of Guadalupe in Mexico. The Catholic historian his interwoven historic facts surrounding the surrender of Temoc, final ruler of Aztec empire, into the legend about the miraculous vision.

Cruelty of Delgadillos' troops operating under the Conquistadores of Spain is pitted against the ruthlessness of the Aztec Indians, with the Church of Spain finally peacefully converting the Indians to Christianity. The miracle at the village of Tepeyac which brings the two factions together is nicely worked out in this vehicle. Story has the Spanish governor's daughter ultimately falling in love with the Aztec ruler, Temoc.

Jose Luis Jiminez does a remarkable job as the Indian peasant who sees the vision of Virgin of Guadalupe. Amparo Morillo, as the blonde and beautiful daughter of the Spanish governor, is a revelation as a comely actress of no mean ability. Looms as a U.S. film possibility if able to handle Americanese as well as she speaks Spanish. Abel Salazar is the stern Aztec king, but is inclined to play the role too dead-pan in his effort to make it dignified. A. Soto Rangel is excellent as Juan Bernardino, the Indian, who swings over to the Christian faith and is healed of a deadly wound. Support, headed by Antonio Bravo, Maria Luisa Zea, Jose Massot, Luis Alcoriza, Agustin Sen and Francisco Llopis, is uniformly fine.

Gabriel Soria's direction is good if not too inspired. Fine musical backgrounding is helped by the fact that it is original music by Julian Carrillo, director of the Mexican Philharmonic Society. Film includes a foreword by Monsignor Luis Martinez, Bishop of Mexico, while the intelligent English titling is well done by Herman G. Weinberg. *Wear.*

MASQUERADE

(SOVIET-MADE)

Artkino release of Lenfilm Studios production. Directed by Sergei Gerasimov. Screenplay, Gerasimov, from drama by Mikhail Lermontov; camera, V. Gardanov; music, N. Pushkov; English titles, Charles Clement. At Stanley, N. Y., week May 15, 1943. Running time, **104 MINS.**

Arbenin.................Nikolai Mordvinov
Nina....................Tamara Markarova
Prince Zvezdich...........Mikhail Sadovski
Baroness..................Sophia Magarill
Shprikh...............................E. Gall

(In Russian; with English Titles)

A Soviet-made film that reaches American shores these days is almost always notable for its war themes. 'Masquerade,' Artkino's latest release in the States, is notable for another reason. It's not a war picture.

Adapted from the sociological poetic drama of the 19th century Russian writer, Lermontov, 'Masquerade' is replete with the stark melodramatics of the period. Its suitability for American audiences is somewhat questionable in these days of escapist boxoffice values. Added to that is a conspicuously artificial manner of production similar to American film-making of the silent era.

'Masquerade' tells the story of a wealthy gambler whose extreme love for his wife brings tragedy into their home. Through circumstances he's led to believe she's been unfaithful, but her truthful protestations remain unheeded. So he poisons her. And when he learns, on the day of her funeral, that she'd actually been faithful, he goes mad.

There is some good acting, some that is misdirected, but it's mostly a story that could have been told in less than the 104 minutes consumed. Too much footage is used to set the basic situation, and there are also several extraneous scenes, mostly for color, that haven't been done so well. But, in the main, it's too starkly melodramatic, particularly at the tail end of the final reel, when madness comes upon the husband.

Nikolai Mordvinov, as the husband, and Tama Markarova, the wife, dominate the cast, though whatever performance honors there are belong to the former. However, he, too, frequently overacts. Mikhail Sadovski, as the young prince, is believable, while lesser featured performers include Sophia Magarill and E. Gall. *Kahn.*

CASI UN SUENO

('Almost a Dream')
(ARGENTINE-MADE)

Buenos Aires, May 9.

Carlos Gallart (EFA) production and release. Stars Maria Duval; features Ricardo Passano, Jr., Miguel Gomez Bao, Rafael Frontaura, Maria Santos, Tito Gomez, Paloma Cortez, Pepito Petray, Elvira Quiroga, Maria Elena Rouge and Chela Cordero. Story, Enrique Amorim and Romah Gomez Masia. Directed by Enrique Amorim and Tito Davison. Reviewed at Monumental, Buenos Aires. Running time, **74 MINS.**

'Casi Un Sueno,' latest from EFA, is another one of those Cinderella yarns that Latin pix apparently haven't yet grown tired of. Neither, seemingly, has the public south of the border, for this one did an o.k. opening biz and seems slightly better than average for second runs in the interior. Will need plenty of build-up, though. Designed apparently for the Maria Duval fans, it's been cut to fit her style, with plot occasionally wobbling but dialog making up for deficiency.

Story goes back to that time-worn device of a family adopting an orphan as a maid of all work, with the son of the patron naturally falling for her. Meantime, she has befriended a seemingly poor and lonely old gent who lives nearby, and when he dies seh gets all his coin. Riches separate the lovers, but gal is able to help land him a scholarship to study music, and film ends with a train pulling out of the station as she, with eyes tear-filled, waves a full-of-promise goodbye.

Senorita Duval is reminiscent of early Deanna Durbin, except that she doesn't warble. However, musical end has been built up with special numbers by Alejandro Gutierrez del Barrio and boys chorus. Ricardo Passano, Jr., in leading male role, doesn't quite measure up but does o.k. for a newcomer. He bears watching. Maria Santos and Miguel Gomez Bao are effective in comedy roles.

Unlike most pix here this one had a producer, Carlos Gallert, and both an artistic and a technical director. Enrique Amorim handled former role, but steady hand of Tito Davison, who gets credit for technical direction, is apparent. Davison has contributed smoothness but hasn't been able to overcome all of the somewhat faulty continuity. Photography by Jose Maria Beltran o.k. *Ray.*

Miniature Reviews

'Bataan' (M-G). Inspiring and realistic reenactment of heroism in the Bataan campaign. Geared for solid coin generally.

'Mr. Big' (Songs). (U). Donald O'Connor introduced as juvenile star in musical comedy drama that will ride nicely.

'No Place for a Lady' (Col). Murder mystery-romance of ordinary grade.

'Jitterbugs' (Songs) (20th). Laurel & Hardy in elemental comedy; dualer.

'Carson City Cyclone' (Rep). Don 'Red' Barry 'B' starrer with a neat twist; should satisfy western addicts.

'Behind Prison Walls' (PRC). Novel 'B' comedy, but it'll need hefty exploitation to click.

'Cuando Los Hijos Se Van' (Mexican). Portrays ups and downs of Mexican family. Has some appeal for Latinos.

BATAAN

Hollywood, May 25.

Metro release of Irving Starr production. Stars Robert Taylor; features George Murphy, Thomas Mitchell, Lloyd Nolan. Directed by Tay Garnett. Original screenplay by Robert D. Andrews; camera, Sidney Wagner; special effects, Arnold Gillespie, Warren Newcombe; editor, George White. Tradeshown in L. A. May 25, '43. Running time, 113 MINS.

Sergeant Bill Dane	Robert Taylor
Lieut. Steve Bentley	George Murphy
Corp. Jake Feingold	Thomas Mitchell
Corp. Barney Todd	Lloyd Nolan
Capt. Henry Lassiter	Lee Bowman
Leonard Purckett	Robert Walker
Felix Ramirez	Desi Arnaz
F. X. Matowski	Barry Nelson
Matthew Hardy	Phillip Terry
Corp. Juan Katigbak	Roque Espiritu
Wesley Eeps	Kenneth Spencer
Yankee Salazar	J. Alex Havier
Sam Malloy	Tom Dugan
Lieutenant	Donald Curtis

'Bataan' is a melodramatic re-enactment of the last ditch stand of an Americal patrol detailed to guard a road in the Philippines following the evacuation of Manila. Carrying strong patriotic appeal, and studded with a group of outstanding performances, picture is due for most profitable boxoffice reaction in the regular runs as solo or billtopper.

Picture pulls no punches in displaying the realistically grim warfare being conducted in the far Pacific. Although it's based on fighting in the Philippines, the customers can easily adjust locale to any in that battle area. 'Bataan' graphically generates public hate of the Japs, and is the first picture of that kind in the high budget class since release of 'Wake Island.'

There's a sufficient amount of jungle battle action and a couple of hand-to-hand skirmishes where bayonets are brought into play, but major portion of the extended 113 minutes running time is devoted to dramatic incidents revolving around the hastily-recruited patrol unit and their efforts to stave off the Japs' advance into the Bataan peninsula so that the main American and Philippine forces could dig in.

Story groups the patrol together near Manila, under command of Lee Bowman as captain and with Robert Taylor as veteran top sergeant, and George Murphy as a fling officer who has his disabled plane cached in the bush. Bowman is knocked off first by a Jap sniper, and Taylor takes command. Picture then wends through various hardships of the marooned band, their blowing up of a bridge to halt the Nips, gradual decimination of the unit by both malaria and snipers, and the final vivid attack by the sneaky Japs that wipes out all of the unit with the exception of Taylor. Latter is stricken with fever, sets the guns and ammunition around his own grave, and keeps shooting until he passes out heroically.

It's an all-made cast, but with terrific sock to women audiences in depicting front line adventures of their sons, husband and sweethearts. Taylor gives a strong performance as the commanding sergeant, but picture focuses attention on screen debut of Robert Walker, who smacks over an arresting portrayal as the sensitive and sympathetic young sailor who attaches himself to the outfit to get a crack at the Japs. Walker, former radio actor, who got a Hollywood brushoff in making his initial pitch for film work, is one of the top 'finds' of the year. Metro figures the same way, as he's set for starring spot in film version of 'See Here, Private Hargrove.'

Murphy makes the most of his assignment as the flyer, finally diving to a heroic death to demolish the bridge the Japs are trying to repair. Thomas Mitchell delivers his usual high-grade performance as a corporal, while Lloyd Nolan is a tough private who tangled with Taylor years previously, but does a good job of soldiering in the specific situation. Kenneth Spencer, Negro trooper in the unit, also delivers effectively, as does Desi Arnaz, Bowman, Barry Nelson, Phillip Terry, Roque Espiritu, J. Alex Havier and Tom Dugan as other members of the patrol.

Tay Garnett deftly steers the course of events, and despite the script concentration on intimate detail surrounding the conditions faced by the men, maintains an interesting pace throughout. And even though the action is restricted to the small area in which the patrol is holed up, there's plenty of graphic picturization of the actual conditions under which fighters of this country face in the foreign fields. There's no broad sweep of battle displayed, outside of the concentrated Jap attacks toward the end.. But there's strong underlying current of the bravery of American soldiers for maximum audience appeal, especially in these times when news of victories from various battlefronts are coming through regularly.

Production is carefully staged, with authentic reproduction of the Philippine jungle presented. Camera work by Sidney Wagner is of high standard throughout. *Walt.*

MR. BIG
(SONGS)

Hollywood, May 22.

Universal release of Ken Goldsmith production. Stars Donald O'Connor; features Gloria Jean, Peggy Ryan. Directed by Charles Lamont. Screenplay by Jack Pollexfen, Dorothy Bennett; original, Virginia Rooks; camera, George Robinson; editor, Frank Gross; songs, Buddy Pepper, Inez James; dances, Louis da Pron; music, Charles Previn. Previewed at Filmarte, May 21, '43. Running time, 73 MINS.

Patricia	Gloria Jean
Donald	Donald O'Connor
Peggy	Peggy Ryan
Johnny Hanley	Robert Paige
Alice Taswell	Elyse Knox
Jeremy Taswell	Samuel S. Hinds
Bobby	Bobby Scheerer
Genius	Richard Stewart
Muggsy	Mary Eleanor Donahue
Mrs. Davis	Florence Bates
Eberle	Ray Eberle

Eddie Miller's Bob Cats
Ben Carter Choir
Jivin' Jacks and Jills

Figuring that it has a potential juvenile star in the versatile Donald O'Connor, Universal spotlights attention on him in this lightly-concocted filmusical comedy-drama of program calibre. Picture is not particularly strong for starring takeoff for the youth, but will adequately satisfy as an above-par supporting attraction in the family and hinterland bookings.

Neither story nor material carries sufficient strength to justify picture as initial starrer for O'Connor, despite the fact that the latter demonstrates wealth of ability to climb into and carry starring position with proper production background. He has an infectious personality, displays veteran trouping abilities, does some crackerjack dance routines, and ably delivers comedy song numbers.

Story is lightly tied together, and along familiar lines. It concerns students in a dramatic school who are more interested in jive tempo than the classics on the curriculum. While the school head, Florence Bates, is out of town, kids concoct a musical show from book written by O'Connor. After rounds of rehearsals for insertion of various production numbers, show goes on under difficulties but proves a hit to break down resistance of the classic-minded owner.

Juvenile spontaneity and all-around ability displayed by O'Connor gets strong assistance from comedienne Peggy Ryan and Gloria Jean. Latter, as reticent youngster with a good set of pipes, does well; but it's Miss Ryan who romps through with her crazy antics and comedy song-and-dance deliveries to make a perfect teammate for O'Connor. Robert Paige and Elyse Knox pair up for mature romance in brief footage, while Samuel S. Hinds, Richard Stewart, Miss Bates and Bobby Scheerer provide good support. Ray Eberle appears for a few shots and one song delivery, 'This Must Be a Dream' in front of band.

O'Connor, Miss Ryan and Gloria Jean provide a good share of juvenile and elemental comedy to do much to keep things moving under good direction by Charles Lamont. There's too much ensemble dancing by the jitterbug background; while two appearances of the Ben Carter choir—while of high standard—are out of place in the general proceedings. A minstrel sequence in blackface could be eliminated to effectively speed up the tempo.

Vocal abilities of Gloria Jean are utilized in group of tunes more on the pop side than former semi-classical renditions by the girl. 'Moonlight and Roses' is best of the oldies, while 'We're Not Obvious' is a good romantic number that stands out as best of the seven compositions by Buddy Pepper and Inez Janes. Three of the tunes are on the comedy side for duos and trios. *Walt.*

NO PLACE FOR A LADY

Columbia release of Ralph Cohn production. Stars William Gargan, Margaret Lindsay; features Phyllis Brooks, Dick Purcell, Jerome Cowan, Edward Norris, Thomas Jackson. Directed by James Hogan. Story and adaptation, Eric Taylor; editor, Dwight Caldwell; camera, James S. Brown. At Strand, Brooklyn, dual, week May 20, '43. Running time, 66 MINS.

Jess Arno	William Gargan
June Terry	Margaret Lindsay
Dolly Adair	Phyllis Brooks
Rand Brooke	Dick Purcell
Eddie Moore	Jerome Cowan
Mario	Edward Norris
Moriarity	James Burke
Webley	Frank Thomas
Captain Baker	Thomas Jackson
Rawlins	Tom Dugan
Mrs. Harris	Doris Lloyd
Hal	Ralph Sanford
Thomas	William Hunter
Yvonne	Chester Clute

A murder mystery of mediocre quality, 'No Place for a Lady' will provide only minor support on double bills. Where singles is the policy, it is destined for the less important runs.

Picture is tinged with romance and some comedy but these factors fail to lift it out of the ordinary class. The story is hackneyed and the dialog lacks force or color, while the direction of James Hogan follows routine lines.

Cast names offer little for the marquee though all strive valiantly to overcome the handicaps of the script. William Gargan and Margaret Lindsay, over the title, are paired. Former plays a private detective who unsnarls a murder mystery and recovers a lot of tires which had been stolen from the murdered, wealthy widow. Miss Lindsay in the role of his fiancee gives a good performance.

Others, all doing well, include Phyllis Brooks, a gal who beats a murder rap; Dick Purcell, newspaper reporter; Jerome Cowan, night club singer and murderer; Edward Norris, nitery racketeer, and Thomas Jackson, police captain. *Char.*

JITTERBUGS
(SONGS)

Hollywood, May 22.

20th Century-Fox release of Sol M. Wurtzel production. Stars Laurel & Hardy; features Vivian Blaine. Directed by Mal St. Clair. Screenplay by Scott Darling; camera, Lucien Androit; editor, Norman Colbert; songs, Charles Newman, Lew Pollack; dances, Geneva Sawyer. Tradeshown in L. A., May 21, '43. Running time, 74 MINS.

Laurel & Hardy	Themselves
Susan Cowan	Vivian Blaine
Chester Wright	Bob Bailey
Bennett	Douglas Fowley
Tony Queen	Noel Madison
Dorcas	Lee Patrick
Corcoran	Robert Emmett Keane
Cass	Charles Halton

This is a generally unfunny Laurel & Hardy feature, a dualer for houses where the combo means something.

Title is also a misfit as, aside from trailer tabbing the comics as a two-man, zoot-suit band, and one brief musical display by the duo at a carnival, their musical talents disappear from all further footage. Pair team up with grifter Bob Bailey for the carny pitch, boy meets girl, and then it's a switch for the con man to recover coin from other consters who bilked the girl's mother. Comics, Bailey and girl Vivian Blaine shift to New Orleans to track down the culprits, and wend through series of episodes to pull switcheroo for recovery of the money. Laurel even goes into femme attire to masquerade as a wealthy spinster, but this fails to generate much interest in the proceedings.

Laurel & Hardy provide their usual characterizations, with usual tomfoolery much subdued and comics given little comedy to display. Vivian Blaine is passable as the girl, who steps in to sing three songs with moderate results in river boat nightclub. Script is of minor league status, with Mal St. Clair failing to inject more than old and elemental gags on the directing side. *Walt.*

Carson City Cyclone

Republic release of Eddy White production. Stars Don 'Red' Barry; features Lynn Merrick, Noah Beery, Bryant Washburn, Emmett Lynn. Directed by Howard Bretherton. Screenplay, Norman S. Hall; camera, William Bradford; editor, Edward Schroeder. At New York, N. Y., dual, week May 18, '43. Running time, 57 MINS.

Gilbert Phalen	Don 'Red' Barry
Linda Wade	Lynn Merrick
Judge Phalen	Noah Beery
Dr. Andrews	Bryant Washburn
Tombstone	Emmett Lynn
Frank Garrett	Stuart Hamblen
Joe Newman	Roy Barcroft
Sheriff Wells	Bud Osborne
Dave	Jack Kirk
Walker	Bud Geary
Tom Barton	Curley Dresden

Republic gives this western somewhat of a new twist by making Don Barry a glib lawyer bedecked like a dude. But action addicts needn't worry, for he finally emerges as a two-fisted gun-totin' true son of the cow country. It's an okay pic for the double-features.

Barry, as a shrewd criminal lawyer, is too smooth and cocky for his father, Noah Beery, who is a Carson City judge and banker. Father and son have a falling out, and Barry is unjustly accused of murdering Beery when the latter is found dead in his office. All this, a series of other killings and bank robberies, too. Lynching parties, posses, several slug fests and lots of gunplay keep things moving briskly.

Barry is more convincing in his cowboy attire and on a horse than in fancy frills addressing juries. Beery plays a judge and bank president with diginity, and Lynn Merrick, as his secretary, is highly decorative. Bryant Washburn and Emmett Iynn adequately fill out the featured cast.

Behind Prison Walls

Producers Releasing Corp. release of Andre Dumonceau production. Features Alan Baxter, Gertrude Michael, Tully Marshall. Directed by Steve Sekely. Screenplay, Van Norcross; camera, Marcel Le Picard; editor, Holbrook N. Todd. At New York, N. Y., dual, week of May 18, '43. Running time, 64 MINS.

Jonathan MacGlennon.........Alan Baxter
Elinor Cantwell..........Gertrude Michael
James J. MacGlennon......Tully Marshall
Percy Webb...............Edwin Maxwell
Mimi......................Jacqueline Dalya
Frank Lucacelli...............Matt Willis
Frederick Driscoll.........Richard Kipling
Yettie Kropatchek..............Olga Sabin
Whitey O'Neil.............Isabelle Withers
Reagan.......................Lane Chandler
Warden.......................Paul Everton
Doc...........................George Guhl
Mrs. Cantwell..............Regina Wallace

Behind the grim title is an original father-son comedy of big-business shenanigans. Limited budget and uneven direction keep this film from the 'big boxoffice' category, but with smart exploitation it should make the grade on the duals.

Steel tycoon Tully Marshall (recently deceased) is sent to prison on the testimony of his Ph.D. son, Alan Baxter, whose intense honesty and social consciousness wouldn't allow him to withhold information that his father was monkeying with the government's priorities regulations. Son also implicates himself, so he, too, is sent up.

Humorous situations develop on way to prison and in jail as Baxter tries to convert his capitalistic father to a modified socialism. When the son is pardoned, Marshall places business in his hands, hoping news of his appointment and ideas Baxter plans to carry out will depress steel stocks low enough to make a killing. Story slows down at this point.

Love angle between Baxter and Gertrude Michael is extraneous and gets laughs in the wrong spots.

Marshall is properly cantankerous as the old-fashioned individualist, and Baxter plays the theorist with the confused air expected of film-version braintrusters. Edwin Maxwell runs true to form as a pompous, blustering executive while Miss Michael has had better roles.

Cuando Los Hijos Se Van

('When Children Leave Home')
(MEXICAN-MADE)

Grovas-Oro production and release. Stars Fernando Soler and Sara Garcia; features Joaquin Pardave, Emilia Tuero, Marina Tamayo. Directed by Bustillo Oro. Screenplay, Bustillo Oro, based on story by Humberto Gomez Landero; camera, Lauron Draper. At Belmont, N. Y., week May 21, '43. Running time, 137 MINS.

Don Jose......................Fernando Soler
Dona Lupita......................Sara Garcia
Don Casimiro.............Joaquin Pardave
Raimundo........................Emilio Tuero
Jose......................Carlos Moctezuma
Erring Wife....................Gloria Marin
Amalia.......................Marina Tamayo

(In Spanish; no English Titles)

Here is a tearjerker sprinkled with comedy relief which, despite its lengthiness and lack of English titles, played to a packed and appreciative house opening night Friday (21). Audience, however, was mostly Mexican, Spanish and Latin-American. If drastically cut and furnished with English titles, it might have a wider appeal, since the theme of moral ups and downs of prominent family, redeemed by self-sacrifice of misunderstood son, has a more universal appeal.

Into the happy home dominated by Fernando Soler, the father and his devoted and soft-hearted wife, Sara Garcia, parade an unending series of domestic tragedies. The favorite son, Emilio Tuero, is unjustly accused of theft. The daughter, Maria Tamayo, elopes with a wealthy wolf old enough to be her father. Another son, Carlos Moctezuma, makes a play for Gloria Marin, wife of a man who has just given him a good job, and Tuero is also blamed for this indiscretion. What saves the film from this dreary procession of misfortune are the comic antics of Joaquin Pardave, as a steadfast friend of the family, and the suspenseful near-seduction of the curvaceous Miss Marin by Moctezuma. It is done in a very efficient, provocative manner, revealing that the young Mexican film industry is not afraid of the facts of life.

In general, the acting is reminiscent of Hollywood's silent era. There is much beating of breasts and tortuous facial expressions. Soler is strikingly righteous and repentant as head of the house. Sara Garcia cannot fail to have an audience's full sympathy as the mother. Joaquin Pardave displays boundless energy and understanding as the family friend. Tuero also has a long-suffering look which becomes his ascetic appearance. Miss Marin has little to say, but is highly effective as the flirtatious wife, and her would-be paramour. Moctezuma, smirks attractively. Marina Tamayo is intense, impassioned and convincing as the daughter who marries for pesos.

Photography is rather spotty. Direction is too slow, and scenes and narration drag, with every situation and emotion milked to the last drop.

Miniature Reviews

'Stormy Weather' (Musical) (20th). Lena Horne and Bill Robinson top very entertaining all-colored musical.

'All By Myself' (U). Evelyn Ankers, Rosemary Lane, Patric Knowles in snappy, modernistic comedy. Strong 'B' entry.

'She Has What It Takes' (Col). Jinx Falkenburg starrer carrying little weight.

'That Natzy Nuisance' (UA). Hal Roach streamliner, fair supporter on twin setups.

'Corregidor' (PRC). Weak dualer with a triangle romance localed in the Manila Bay fortress during the Jap siege.

'Murder in Times Square' (Col). Murder mystery of fair value.

'We Dive at Dawn' (British). Prototype of 'In Which We Serve,' British-made deals with a submarine; sock boxoffice.

'The Russian Story' (Artkino). Followup to other Russian pix will do biz.

'Raiders of San Joaquin' (U). Below average western in the Johnny Mack Brown series.

'Song of Texas' (Songs) (Rep). Roy Rogers musical western that will entertain.

'Spy Train' (Mono). Tiresome Nazi spy meller.

STORMY WEATHER

(MUSICAL)

20th-Fox release of Wm. LeBaron production. Features Bill Robinson, Lena Horne, Cab Calloway, Katherine Dunham Troupe, Fats Waller, Nicholas Bros., Dooley Wilson, Ada Brown. Directed by Andrew Stone Screenplay, Frederick Jackson, Ted Koehler; adaptation, H. S. Kraft; original, Jerry Horwin, Seymour B. Robinson; editor, James B. Clark; special effects, Fred Sersen; dances, Clarence Robinson; production advisor, Irving Mills; songs (pop excerpts) by Andy Razaf-Fats Waller-Harry Brooks; Dorothy Fields-Jimmy McHugh; Ted-Koehler-Harold Arlen (title song), Koehler-James P. Johnson-Irving Mills, Cab Calloway, et al. Tradeshown May 26, '43. Running time, 77 MINS.

Selina Rogers...................Lena Horne
Corky..........................Bill Robinson
Cab Calloway and Band.......Themselves
Katherine Dunham and Her Troupe... Themselves
Fats..........................Fats Waller
Nicholas Bros..................Themselves
Ada............................Ada Brown
Gabe.........................Dooley Wilson
The Tramp Band.................Themselves
The Shadracks...........Net Stanfield and Johnny Horace
Chick Bailey..................Babe Wallace
Jim Europe...............Ernest Whitman
Zuttie.....................Zuttie Singleton
Mae.......................Mae E. Johnson
Miller..................Flournoy E. Miller
Lyles.........................Johnnie Lee
Cab Calloway, Jr.............Robert Felder
Chauffeur..............Nicodemus Stewart

'Stormy Weather' will have smooth sailing at the b.o. It's chockful of the cream-of-the-crop colored talent, with a deft story skein to hold it together. Riding the crest of 'Cabin in the Sky,' the Metro all-colored musical, which has been doing business, this 20th-Fox filmusical will get its share of business also.

Bill Robinson and Lena Horne (latter the s.a. menace in 'Cabin') top the cast. It's a tribute to the affection in which Bojangles is held that the story plot is glossed over in favor of all the other components. But it's likewise a tribute to the ageless Bojangles that, despite the intra-trade concern over miscasting him as Miss Horne's romantic vis-a-vis, the illusion comes off quite well.

True, the plot is one of frustrated love, chiefly because both are cast as nomadic professionals, but for the finale, with Cab Calloway, Jr., introduced by the real-life hi-de-ho maestro, there is a solid sentimental touch, for Cab, Jr., is in the same American doughboy garb which first tees off the plot.

Story nicely spans both wars. Lt. Jim Europe's band is marching up 5th Ave. in a riotous homecoming. Dooley Wilson, Robinson and the others have come back from the wars. The big Harlem hoopla thus projects Lena Horne who takes a liking immediately to Robinson. Her partner, Babe Wallace, is the menace, a conceited professional.

Story is told via the flashback formula. A 25th Anniversary Number of 'Theatre World' ('Variety'?!?) holds the plot together. The special edition is in tribute to the great trouper, Bill Robinson. Surrounding him are the neighbors' children on his comfortable, handsome front porch. There isn't one ofay character in the plot, yet the all-colored cast is not permitted to engage in any grotesque or theatrically 'typed' concepts of Negro behaviorism. When they dance hotcha, it fits the story. Otherwise it is played straight.

Bojangles thumbs the pages. A salutory ad from Noble Sissle points up the Jim Europe homecoming. Another ad flashes back another highlight in Robinson's career. Even the heavy has a testimonial advertisement, and that, too, brings forth a memorable episode.

Thus is projected Robinson's adventures from a returned doughboy to a Memphis riverboat; a Memphis honky-tonk (where, at the Beale St. Cafe, Ada Brown and Fats Waller give out with some lowdown blues), and the rest of the plot progression. While by no means factually biographical there's a note of autobiographical conviction throughout.

Miss Horne, a star from the start, folds the Memphis joint and takes the standout acts with her, into a new revue, insisting that Robinson (who has been ekeing out a living as a waiter) also be made part of the package deal. Bojangles, frustrated by being given a tom-tom bit in a chorus number, finally breaks tradition and essays his own idea of a tom-tom dance, leaping from drumhead to drumhead (an evolution, of course, of his famed stair-dance) and thus he achieves his real opportunity. From then he becomes himself, the authentic dancing comedian and star.

As a backstage colored musical, it is in itself a novelty. There is convincing flavor to the stars and featured talent who play themselves. When Lena Horne says she is going to Paris to be a star, it rings true because she's a cinch for those Montmartre heights as soon as we again mop up that European situation, as we did in 1918, and thus paved the way for so much worthy American Negro talent to conquer Europe artistically.

Via the 'Theatre World' anniversary number, Robinson continues crossing and re-crossing paths with Miss Horne, in and out of shows, Hollywood filmusicals, etc., with Cab Calloway, Katherine Dunham and her expert troupe of ballet dancers, Fats Waller, the Nicholas Bros., the Tramp Band, The Shadracks (Ned Stanfield & Johnny Horace), Zuttie Singleton at the drums, Mae E. Johnson, Flournoy E. Miller (his partner, the late Aubrey Lyles is played here by Johnny Lee), Coleman Hawkins on sax, Taps Miller on the horn, plus others.

Ted Koehler (who collaborated on the story also) and Harold Arlen's 'Stormy Weather,' now a Tin Pan Alley classic, has been given new values under Miss Horne's interpretation, William LeBaron's production and Andrew Stone's direction. Same goes for the cavalcade of other highlight tunes, from past great colored musicals, such as the Lew Leslie 'Blackbirds' excerpts, 'Diga Diga Do' and 'I Can't Give You Anything But Love, Baby'; or Fats Waller's 'Ain't Misbehavin'' (which he wrote with Andy Razaf and Harry Brooks); or Calloway's own 'Geechy Joe' and 'Jumpin' Jive.' In the former he flashes a milk-white zoot-suit creation that is the Gargantua production of zoot-suits.

'There's No Two Ways About Love' is a sterling thematic, for intro and finale, which deftly climaxes the romantic relations between the stellar pair. Miss Horne reprises that, along with the title song, and gets more out of 'I Can't Give You Anything But Love, Baby' than did the original stage 'Blackbirds' production.

The finale is a particular zinger, with 'Ain't That Something to Shout About' combining Calloway's jive with the legmaniacal Nicholas Bros., plus the femme choristers in cute, modified zoot outfits.

The talent throughout is solid. Dooley Wilson (now so closely identified with his 'As Time Goes By' revival in 'Casablanca') here does a legit dramatic role, handling his lines with conviction and dignity; Ada Brown shouts her 'Beale St.' and 'Basin St. Blues' and later 'Lost My Sugar in Salt Lake City' effectively; and a bizarre Tramp Band, plus the Shadracks, with their own specialties, further punctuate the proceedings with highly effective variety interludes. Even a quickie of Miller & Lyles' classic crossfire is sandwiched in.

Production is lavish. Clothes are ultra, especially for Miss Horne. The theatrical specs where the action calls for a show-within-a-show are authentic and ring the bell. And Clarence Robinson's dance-staging is in high pitch, where warranted, but never out-of-line.

Another intra-trade footnote must be reference to Irving Mills, who is credited as production adviser. Mills, vet manager of colored talent, and whose Mills Music firm has published most of the notable Harlem songsmiths, unquestionably figured importantly in the assembling of this galaxy of music, talent and other values. *Abel.*

ALL BY MYSELF

(SONGS)

Universal release of Bernard W. Burton production. Features Rosemary Lane, Evelyn Ankers, Patric Knowles, Neil Hamilton. Directed by Felix Feist. Screenplay by Hugh Wedlock, Jr., Howard Snyder, from original by Dorothy Bennett, Linde Hannah; camera, Paul Ivano; editor, Charles Maynard. Previewed in Projection Room, N. Y., May 27, '43. Running time, **63 MINS.**

Val Stevenson....Rosemary Lane
Jean Wells....Evelyn Ankers
Dr. Bill Perry....Patric Knowles
Mark Turner....Neil Hamilton
J. D. Gibbons....Grant Mitchell
Willie....Louise Beavers
Tip, Tap & Toe....Loumell Morgan Trio

This is a frothy little comedy which never pretends to be anything more than an escapist 'B' feature. Yet it generates streamlined entertainment values. Title is not much help, but the dialog, which is always crisp, gives it added strength.

'All By Myself' also furthers the film career of Evelyn Ankers, this comely capable actress taking the play away from the better known Rosemary Lane and both Patric Knowles and Neil Hamilton.

The by-now familiar yarn about the advertising executive, who falls in love with a flippant nightclub singer instead of his comely, capable femme partner, is given several new twists in this original by Dorothy Bennett and Linde Hannah. The said pert partner, Evelyn Ankers, seeks solace from her family medico on learning of her boss' engagement. Result is that the doctor gradually falls in love with his patient while the ad executive, Neil Hamilton, nearly goes on the rocks with his newlywed.

Customary pattern is deftly jazzed up by having the new romance of Miss Ankers far from a smooth running affair, with a faked marriage, threatened divorces, old-fashioned drag-out drawing room battles and several musical interludes tossed in for good measure.

Aside from Miss Ankers, who is remarkably fine as the ad executives's biz partner, Rosemary Lane, as the cafe balladist, also figures importantly. Her outstanding song is 'All By Myself.' Patric Knowles chips in with a forthright interpretation of the personable medico who finally falls for Miss Ankers. Neil Hamilton makes a good ad executive who depends on his femme aide for his success and then falls for the cafe warbler.

Tip, Tap & Toe, standard vaude colored tapsters, and the Loumell Morgan Trio, colored instrumentalists, appear in the closing Reno nightclub sequence. Former scores per usual. Felix Feist has directed for maximum of laughs, keeping the farce going along in swift style. Hugh Wedlock, Jr., and Howard Snyder did a strong screenplay. Film is packed with unusually strong production values for a film of this sort, Paul Ivano's photography being standout. *Wear.*

She Has What It Takes

(SONGS)

Columbia release of Colbert Clark production. Stars Jinx Falkenburg; features Tom Neal, Constance Worth, The Vagabonds, Radio Rogues. Directed by Charles Barton. Screenplay by Paul Yawitz, from story by Yawitz and Robert Lee Johnson; camera, Phillip Tannura; editor, Al Clark; musical director, M. W. Stoloff; songs, Saul Chapman; Cindy Walker; Roy Jacobs-Gene DePaul; Don Reid; Charlie, Elliott and Henry Tobias. At Fox, Brooklyn, N. Y., week of May 28, '43. Running time, **66 MINS.**

Fay Weston....Jinx Falkenburg
Roger Rutledge....Tom Neal
June Leslie....Constance Worth
Paul Miloff....Douglas Leavitt
Lee Shuleman....Joe King
'One Round' Beasley....Mat Willis
Nick Partos....Daniel Ocko
Mike McManus....George McKay
'Shocker' Dodie....George Lloyd
Capt. Pat O'Neal....Robert Homans
George Clarke....Joseph Crehan
Chamberlain Jones....John H. Dilson
Mrs. Walters....Barbara Brown
Mr. Jason....Harry Hayden
Tony....Curly Wright
The Radio Rogues
The Vagabonds

This Jinx Falkenburg starrer hasn't much power for anything beyond the lower half of duals, in which capacity it is serving here.

Miss Falkenburg, about whom reams of publicity have been planted, shows nothing extraordinary outside of a shapely set of gams in a couple dance sequences. Direction doesn't help the tired yarn, allowing the action to become so involved, like a dime mystery, that the characters are extricated from their precarious positions in about 30 seconds flat in the final reel, and the whole thing is unexpectedly ended, to no one's satisfaction. An idea of what it's like can be gleaned from the fact that long footage is devoted to the Vagabonds, a comedy-song quartet who show up nicely, and the Radio Rogues, who contribute virtually their entire vaude act.

Miss Falkenburg is a small-time singer who masquerades as the daughter of a once well-known stage star, who had just died in poverty. She contrives to meet a screen counterpart of Walter Winchell (Tom Neal), who gets a financially flat but highly respected Broadway producer to star her in a show, as a tribute to her claimed mother who once worked for him. Other old friends of the mother provide the backing, but the bubble is exploded for the daughter when a female rival of Neal's discovers the deception.

Miss Falkenburg's handling of lines is often uncertain, almost amateurish. Neal's portrayal of the newspaper columnist, too, isn't up to snuff. Supporting characterizations by Joe King, Constance Worth and others, however, is okay. Most of the action is indoors. Of the songs, 'Let's March Together,' by Saul Chapman, stands out. *Wood.*

That Nazty Nuisance

United Artists release of Hal Roach production. Features Bobby Watson, Joe Devlin, Johnny Arthur, Jean Porter, Ian Keith, Henry Victor, Ed 'Strangler' Lewis, Abe 'King Kong' Kashey. Directed by Glenn Tryon. Screenplay by Earle Snell, Clarence Marks; camera, Robert Pittack; editor, Bert Jordan. At Laff-Movie, N. Y., week May 28, '43. Running time, **60 MINS.**

Hitler....Bobby Watson
Mussolini....Joe Devlin
Suki Yaki....Johnny Arthur
Kela....Jean Porter
Chief....Ian Keith
Von Popoff....Henry Victor
Spense....Emory Parnell
Benson....Frank Faylen
Guard....Ed (Strangler) Lewis
Second Guard....Abe (King Kong) Kashey
Goering....Rex Evans
Goebbels....Charles Rogers
Himmler....Wedgewood Nowell

This is a funnier and better-made Hal Roach streamliner than recently to come from this mill. Most of chuckles come from poking fun at Hitler, Mussolini and a Japanese dictator, 'Suki Yaki,' but even the slapstick is well done. It's a fairish supporting feature for twin bills, or, as used here, on an all-laugh program.

Mythical venture of the three Axis dictators to an Oriental land called Norom is interrupted by the landing of the small crew from a submarined American merchant vessel. One enterprising crew member substitutes for the land's most famous magico and leads to the undoing of Hitler and his two pals. Nicely hoked up with wisecracks about known traits and characteristics of the Germans, Jap and Italian rulers worked in for extra laughs.

Bobby Watson makes a clever imitation of the worried Hitler pictured in this vehicle, while Johnny Arthur is remarkably good as the Jap military ruler. Joe Devlin provides a realistic counterpart of Benito. Ian Keith in the land of Norom's ruler, who thinks more of eating and watching magical feats than signing treaties with Hitler or anybody else. Strangler Lewis and Abe 'King Kong' Kashey make two giant guards to the ruler. Jean Porter, as the magico's assistant and dancer, is okay but has little to do. Henry Victor is the principal crew member who outwits the Axis gang.

Glenn Tryon, who also is listed as associate producer, directs with imagination for such a small-budgeter. Camera work of Robert Pittack is satisfactory but the use of so many miniatures and special photo effects is not good. *Wear.*

CORREGIDOR

Producers Releasing Corp. release of Dixon R. Harwin-Edward Finney production. Stars Otto Kruger, Elissa Landi, Donald Woods; features Frank Jenks, Rick Vallin, Wanda McKay, Ian Keith. Directed by William Nigh. Original and screenplay, Doris Malloy, Edgar Ulmer; camera, Ira L. Morgan; musical director, David Chudnow; score, Leo Erdody; editor, Charles Henkel. At Globe, N. Y., May 27, '43. Running time, **74 MINS.**

Jan Stockman....Otto Kruger
Dr. Royce Lee....Elissa Landi
Michael....Donald Woods
Sergt. Mahoney....Frank Jenks
Pinky....Rick Vallin
Hey Dutch....Wanda McKay
Captain....Ian Keith
Hyacinth....Ruby Dandridge
Brooklyn....Eddie Hall
Bronx....Charles Jordan
Filipino Lieutenant....Ted Hecht
Lieutenant No. 2....Frank Hagney
Priest....Frank Jacquet
General....Jack Rutherford
Soldier No. 1....John Grant
Soldier No. 2....Stan Jolley
No. 1 Boy....Jimmy Vilan
Marine....Gordon Hayes

A transparent attempt to exploit a heroic theme, 'Corregidor' is a feeble picture that does no credit to its subject nor to the screen itself. It isn't even passable boxoffice. Only on the strength of a good upper-bill companion feature and the current filmgoing boom will it do profitable business.

Purporting to tell the story of the heroic stand of the U. S. forces who held Corregidor so long against the Japs, the picture offers a stereotype triangle plot about three doctors, one of them a femme. It's unmotivated, undeveloped, ineptly written, clumsily produced and directed and, except for an acceptable performance by Otto Kruger, is inexcusably played. The endless repetition of stock action shots is characteristic of the entire film.

Even the not-too-critical Times Square audience at the Globe, N. Y., opening night was perversely amused by the picture. *Hobe.*

Murder in Times Square

Columbia release of Colbert Clark production. Features Edmund Lowe, Marguerite Chapman, John Litel. Directed by Lew Landers. Story, Stuart Palmer; adaptation, Paul Gangelin; editor, Richard Fantl; camera, L. W. O'Connell. At Abbey, N. Y., week May 29, '43. Running time, **65 MINS.**

Cory Williams....Edmund Lowe
Melinda Matthews....Marguerite Chapman
Dr. Blaine....John Litel
Detective Lieutenant Tabor....William Wright
Supal George....Bruce Bennett
Longacre Lil....Esther Dale
Fiona Maclair....Veda Ann Borg
O'Dell Gissing....Gerald Mehr
George Nevins....Sidney Blackmer
Rob Slocumb....Leslie Denison
Henry Trigg....Douglas Leavitt
Southcote....George McKay

Who uses rattlesnake venom in committing a series of murders and why, forms the basis for a fairly interesting meller in 'Murder in Times Square,' which will serve suitably on single-policy dates of secondary importance and as an associate feature generally on duals.

Well plotted out and sustaining suspense, with suspicion of guilt in several directions carefully planted, the story deals with a doctor, who through unrequited love and jealousy, kills no less than four persons through stabbing them with a hypodermic needle containing snake poison. Trapping the M.D. responsible for the crimes does not attest to great intelligence or cunning, nor is it logical the murderer would fall for the ruse, but notwithstanding the action holds up satisfactorily.

A part of the plot concerns a Broadway panhandler and blackmailer known as Longacre Lil who plagues a vain playwright-actor who snubs her so far as a handout is concerned. She does everything to try to pin the murders on him, especially since he's in love with his leading lady, already married, who's among those snaked to death.

Edmund Lowe plays the stage egotist who ultimately falls for his press agent, Marguerite Chapman. Both give polished performances, though Miss Chapman does not have so much opportunity to show what she can do. John Litel plays the doctor-murderer in steady fashion, while Esther Dale stands out as Longacre Lil. Others include Bruce Bennett, friend of Loew's; Veda Ann Borg, murdered actress, and William Wright, detective lieutenant, latter not the cop type.

Lew Landers' direction passes muster, while Colbert Clark has provided good production and backgrounds. *Char.*

WE DIVE AT DAWN

(BRITISH-MADE)

London, May 18.

General Film Distributors release of Gainsborough-Maurice Ostrer production. Stars Eric Portman, John Mills. Directed by Anthony Asquith. Story and scenario, J. B. Williams, Val Valentine; camera, Jack Cox. At Leicester Square theatre, London. Running time, **93 MINS.**

Lieut. Taylor....John Mills
Seaman Hobson....Eric Portman
Seaman Wilson....Leslie Weston
Lieut. Brace....Louis Bradfield
Lieut. Johnson....Ronald Millar
Lieut. Gordon....Jack Watling
Chief P. O. Dabbs....Reginald Purdell
P. O. Mike Corrigan....Niall MacGinnis
Canada....Norman Williams
Spud....Lionel Grose
Chief P. O. Duncan....Caven Watson

There's enough drama and human comedy to appease the average film-goer in this film, a prototype of 'In Which We Serve,' which depicted life on a destroyer, whereas the present one is laid in a submarine. It is a tale of magnificent heroism, and gives every indication of success not only as entertainment, but valuable propaganda. Some cutting, however, is in order for the U. S. market.

The human element is well depicted, leading up to a dramatic denouement. The submarine, Sea Tiger, is sent out to sink a Nazi battleship which is due to leave Bremerhaven for the Kiel Canal, en route to the Baltic. The sub's instructions are to intercept her off the German coast before she enters the canal. Too late for this, the lieutenant in charge decides to brave the dangers of the Baltic and attack the battleship when she emerges at the other end of the canal. Sighting the enemy, she discharges her torpedoes, but owing to depth charges from accompanying destroyers, the attack results in a leakage in the sub's oil tanks and the Britisher decides to blow her up and escape to Denmark.

One of the seamen remembers there is a port on a nearby Danish island where there may be a tanker in dock. Donning the uniform of a dead German airman, he lands on the island, finds a tanker and signals to his ship to come in shore. They refuel and return home, and only then discover they have sunk the German vessel they were after.

John Mills, one of England's ace leading men, enacts the lieutenant with not only requisite dignity, but with a human touch. But it is Eric Portman, as the seaman, who has the outstanding role and scores best. Rest of the cast gives excellent performances, while direction and production were above par. *Jolo.*

THE RUSSIAN STORY

(RUSSIAN-MADE)

Artkino release of Joseph Burstyn production. Compiled from about 25 Russian-made features and shorts, with an original English commentary written by Theodore Strauss. Commentary spoken by Libby Holman, Morris Carnovsky, Martin Blaine and Strauss. Film and accompanying music edited by George Freedland. Previewed in the Projection Room, N. Y., May 27, '43. Running time, **68 MINS.**

'The Russian Story' is a unique film idea and as such will merit attention not only from those who favor the unusual in motion pictures, but from the American industry as well. Joseph Burstyn, producer of the picture subtitles it 'A Film Cavalcade of a Thousand Years of Russian Heroism.' He achieves his cavalcade effect by splicing together footage from some 25 Soviet-made fictional features and shorts, combining them to picture a half-dozen or so highlight episodes in the history of Russia from the Hun to the Nazi. Houses which have been playing Soviet pix will find an eager audience for it.

The conception of 'The Russian Story' is excellent, for, added to whatever other b.o. values it may have, is the sentimental attachment of lovers of foreign films for their fave Russian pix and actors of the past two decades. They'll find all of them in this 68-minute intermittent panorama, some of them at length, some of them in fleeting takes.

Burstyn has added a touch of showmanship by enlisting Libby Holman and Morris Carnovsky to speak the major part of the English commentary, which accompanies the action on the screen. Subtitles are resorted to only occasionally. Commentary was scripted by Theodore Strauss, second-string film crick of the N. Y. Times. He also speaks part of it.

Film's thesis is that Russia will beat back the invading Hitlerites, just as it has other would-be conquerers down through the centuries, for the fury of a Russian's love for his mother soil is unvanquishable. Going back a thousand years, it traces the onslaught of the Huns, the Swedes, the Japs and the German's of the Kaiser's day. Intertwined with battle sequences are aspects of the political, social and economic development of the nation, showing Peter the Great's efforts to westernize his people and coming down to the revolution of Lenin, Stalin and Trotzky.

Difficulties of editing the mass of assorted film into an orderly and homogenous whole proved almost insurmountable. Rather than lift scenes bodily out of other pictures, Burstyn and his editor, George Freedland, chose to select bits and pieces and attempt to weld these together into sequences. The commentary should have been designed to clarify this necessarily patchy editing. It continuously wanders off, however, into ethereal poesy and inspirational prose, while what is required is earthy fact to explain the action on the screen. There's a false assumption that the average audience knows much more Russian history than it does.

Result is that the outstanding scene is the only one which has been picked up intact from the Soviet studios. It's a corker of the battle at Smolensk in the present war. It pictures the Nazis using a shield of women and children as they advance on the Reds, with two Russian soldiers leaving their trench to rescue a baby from the arms of its dead mother in the field between the lines. A breathtaker that would stand up in any company, it was shot as a short last year and Burstyn acquired exclusive U.S. rights to it.

Raiders of San Joaquin

(SONGS)

Universal release of Oliver Drake production. Stars Johnny Mack Brown, Tex Ritter; features Fuzzy Knight, Jennifer Holt, Henry Hall, Joseph Bernard, George Eldredge. Directed by Lewis D. Collins. Story and adaptation, Patricia Harper; editor, Russel Shoengarth; camera, William Sickner. At New York, N. Y., dual, week May 25, '43. Running time, **59 MINS.**

Rocky Morgan........Johnny Mack Brown
Gil Blake........................Tex Ritter
Eustace Clairmont..........Fuzzy Knight
Jane Carter................Jennifer Holt
Bodine Carter...................Henry Hall
Jim Blake..................Joseph Bernard
Gus Sloan..................George Eldredge
Rogers.....................Henry Roquemore
Morgan.........................John Elliott
Clark.......................Michael Vallon
Detective......................Jack O'Shea
Lear..........................Jack Ingram
Johnson....................Robert Thompson
Tanner.......................Carl Sepulveda
Tripp.........................Scoop Martin
McQuarry........................Roy Brent
Deputy.........................Budd Buster
Jimmy Wakely Trio

Recently numerous westerns have turned from rustling to racketeers who muscled in on early railroad building beyond the Great Divide. 'Raiders of San Joaquin' is another in that groove, but not a particularly exciting exhibit. Below the Johnny Mack Brown average, but will get by.

Comedy relief is ordinarily strong in the Brown series with Fuzzy Knight on the assignment to dig laughs. In this case, however, the stuttering, bungling Knight isn't half as funny as he usually is, while also action is lacking to the point where frequently considerable slowness sets in.

Brown, with Knight as his roving plains pal, settle down in a community where ranchers are being mulcted of their properties by an unscrupulous gang which is grabbing land under the guise that they are obtaining right-of-way for a railroad. How Brown, related to the v.p. of the road, upsets their racket forms the basis for the major portion of the action.

Mixed in is Jennifer Holt, who has played in previous westerns and like most cactus-land heroines is where she shouldn't be at all times. Lessers include Henry Hall, Joseph Bernard and George Eldredge, all okay.

Several songs, of new and old vintage, are sprinkled through the picture. They are featured by the Jimmy Wakely trio. *Char.*

SONG OF TEXAS

(SONGS)

Hollywood, May 26.

Republic release of Harry Grey production. Stars Roy Rogers; features Bob Nolan and Sons of Pioneers. Directed by Joseph Kane. Original, Winston Miller; camera, Reggie Lanning; editor, Tony Martinelli. Previewed May 25, '43. Running time, **69 MINS.**

Roy ....Roy Rogers
Sue Bennett.....................Sheila Ryan
Jim Calvert................Barton MacLane
Sam Bennett................Harry Shannon
Hildegarde ....Arline Judge
Fred Calvert................William Haade
Miss Murray......................Eve March
Pete ....Hal Taliaferro
Alex Nahera Dancers
Bob Nolan and Sons of the Pioneers

With Roy Rogers now in top popularity spot among the Republic westerners, studio is providing him with benefit of higher budgets for his pictures. 'Song of Texas' displays unusual supporting cast for sagebrusher, good scenic backgrounds and photography, and the usual group of songs for delivery by Rogers and his musical Sons of the Pioneers (Bob Nolan). Picture will get by neatly with the Rogers and western audiences.

Rogers is a rodeo star working for crooked outfit headed by Barton MacLane, but pulls out of the show with his pals to take over operation of a stock ranch recently purchased. Along goes Harry Shannon, former big time bronc-buster, who's rehabilitated by Rogers. But when Shannon expects his daughter out from the east for vacation under impression he owns a ranch, the boys set him up as master of their outfit. But the girl's inquisitiveness results finally in sale of half the ranch to MacLane, with Rogers forced to engage in a chuck wagon race to win it back.

Rogers and Sons of the Pioneers give out with group of eight songs in familiar vein plus two standards, 'Moonlight and Roses' and 'Mexicali Rose.' Rogers turns on his pipes, heroics and personality for good audience reaction, getting major assistance from the Pioneers on the musical side.

Sheila Ryan is passable as the girl, being overshadowed by Arline Judge, her pal from the east, in second femme lead. MacLane and William Haade provide good pair of heavies, with Shannon okay in a character part. Alex Nahera Dancers are on for a brief number in a fiesta sequence

Picture carries thread of usual western dramatics, with the heavies lurking around, but major footage is utilized for songs and lightly-textured dramatic byplay, including elemental comedy touches strung out along the line. Result is dearth of shooting and wild riding generally expected by western devotees. Finale chuck wagon race, instead of usual chase is a novelty, while high Sierra setting allows for above-par photography by Reggie Lanning. Direction by Joseph Kane is standard. *Walt.*

SPY TRAIN

Monogram release of Max King production. Features Richard Travis, Catherine Craig, Chick Chandler, Thelma White, Paul McVey, Evelyn Brent, Warren Hymer and Snowflake. Directed by Harold Young. Story, Scott Littlefield; adaptation, Leslie Schwabacher, Wallace Sullivan and Bart Lytton; editor, Carl Pierson; camera, Mack Stengler. At New York, N. Y., dual, week May 25, '43. Running time, **61 MINS.**

Bruce ....Richard Travis
Jane ....Catherine Craig
Stu ....Chick Chandler
Millie ....Thelma White
Frieda ....Evelyn Brent
Italian ....Gerald Brock
Porter ....Snowflake
Detective ....Bill Hunter
Chief Nazi...................Steve Roberts
Herman ....Warren Hymer

Taking turns trying to gain possession of a traveling bag which is thought to contain important Nazi documents, but actually has a time-bomb as its contents, numerous persons, including a reporter and spies, spend most of 61 minutes causing a serious state of ennui. Although the picture has been acceptably cast and its members do as well as could be expected under the circumstances, the marketing possibilities are slender.

Virtually all of the action takes place on a streamliner where a bag, with a time-bomb in it, has been planted by mistake by Nazi agents. It moves from one compartment to another as various persons stealthily purloin it with a view to getting the important papers it's supposed to contain. As result of some detective work on the part of a newspaper reporter, spies are permitted to take it on the lam as the train stops to pick up police, the spies getting themselves blown to bits for their trouble.

Richard Travis and Catherine Craig are twinned for romantic interest. Playing a photographer and getting stabbed in the bargain is Chick Chandler, while as a wisecracky, dumb-Dora maid is Thelma White of old silent days. Lessers include Paul McVey and Evelyn Brent, latter also a star when films didn't have voice. Snowflake does well as a Pullman porter. Warren Hymer is miscast as a Nazi agent who's none too intelligent. *Char.*

Miniature Reviews

'Background to Danger' (WB). Actionful spy meller will do business.

'Hitler's Hangman' (M-G). Deals with Czechoslovakia and and extinction of Lidice; moderate entertainment.

'She Defends Her Country' (Russian). Strong entry with a war background.

'Terror House' (PRC). British chiller that should do okay.

Background to Danger

Hollywood, June 7.

Warner Bros. release of Jerry Wald production. Stars George Raft, Sydney Greenstreet; features Peter Lorre, Brenda Marshall. Directed by Raoul Walsh. Screenplay by W. R. Burnett from novel by Eric Ambler; camera, Tony Gaudio; editor, Jack Killifer; technical effects, Warren Lynch, Willard Van Enger. Tradeshown in Hollywood, June 7, '43. Running time, **80 MINS.**

Joe Barton.....................George Raft
Tamara.....................Brenda Marshall
Col. Robinson..........Sydney Greenstreet
Zaleshoff.......................Peter Lorre
Ana Remzi.....................Osa Massen
Mailler.........................Kurt Katch
Rashenko......................Daniel Ocko
Syrian Vendor...............Frank Puglia
Hassen..........................Turhan Bey
Old Turk.................Pedro de Cordoba
McNamara..............Willard Robertson

Regulation cops-and-robbers story formula is utilized in this spy melodrama laid in Turkey. Obvious in its unfolding of familiar situations, it nevertheless hits consistently fast pace to cover up story weaknesses, while topliners, George Raft, Sydney Greenstreet and Brenda Marshall for the marquee will carry it through the regular runs to average biz.

Opening describes Turkey as location for operations of spies and agents of all countries, with Germany particularly anxious to bend Turkish public opinion to the Nazi cause. Key to the yarn are forged documents being shipped into Ankara by the Nazis purporting to prove Russian intention to invade Turkey. Raft, American agent, gets possession of the package and then becomes the centre of highly theatric meldramatics indulged in by Russian and Nazi spy rings. Peter Lorre, Miss Marshall and Daniel Ocko try to get possession as Soviet agents, while Greenstreet is a German official determined to carry through the Nazi plot to conclusion. After teetering back and forth for sufficient footage, Raft finally winds up the victor over Greenstreet by turning latter over for deportation and destroying the forgeries.

Main motivation is provided by Raft, Greenstreet and Lorre as respective spy leaders, with the trio turning in okay performances for their respective assignments. Miss Marshall is buried in what is virtually a walk-on role, while most prominent support includes Osa Massen, Turhan Bey, Kurt Katch and Ocko. There's little for the cast to do other than concentrate on the display of melodramatics provided by both script and direction. Raoul Walsh, cognizant of the action requirements of the film, keeps it romping along at a fast clip, despite yarn's obviousness in getting Raft out of tough spots, reminiscent of old-time gangster pictures.

Walt.

HITLER'S HANGMAN

Metro-Goldwyn-Mayer release of Seymour Nebenzal production. Features Patricia Morison, John Carradine, Alan Curtis. Directed by Douglas Sirk. Story, Emil Ludwig and Albrecht Joseph; adaptation, Peretz Hirshbein, Melvin Levy, Doris Malloy; editor, Dan Milner; camera, Jack Greenhalgh. Previewed in Projection Room, N. Y., June 8, '43. Running time, **84 MINS.**

Jarmila.....................Patricia Morison
Heydrich.....................John Carradine
Karel..............................Alan Curtis
Himmler.....................Howard Freeman
Hanka...........................Ralph Morgan
Nepomuk......................Edgar Kennedy
Mayor Bauer.................Ludwig Stossel
Priest..............................Al Shean
Maria Bartonek.............Elizabeth Russell
Dvorak...........................Jimmy Conlin
Mrs. Hanka....................Blanche Yurka
Clara Janek.....................Jorja Rollins
Janek..............................Victor Kilian
Mrs. Bauer....................Johanna Hofer
Colonel........................Wolfgang Zilzer
Professor......................Tully Marshall

The rape of Czechoslovakia, and particularly the extermination of the little village of Lidice in sham atonement for the assassination of the late and unlamented Reich Protector Heydrich, forms the basis in 'Hitler's Hangman' for what amounts to only moderate entertainment. The title is indicative of the subject-matter, and from that angle the boxoffice may benefit to some extent. Cast names are of lesser importance.

Of the war in its more horripilating phases, the picture rather effectively emphasizes the hardness of the Nazi heel so far as the Czecks and other oppressed peoples have felt it since Hitler ran amok in Europe. The action is not as gruesome as in some productions of the past, but sufficiently so to point up the ruthlessness of the Nazis and their mania for executions.

Heydrich is pictured as a very mean man, with John Carradine giving the character all that it should have, but audiences might not like the indirect whitewash that comes when, on his deathbed, Heydrich virtually repudiates Hitler as the tin god that he is, and mentions the Allies prophetically. Himmler, with Heydrich as latter succumbs to bullet wounds, is another good Nazi character in the person of Howard Freeman. Others are of minor importance.

Resistance of Czech patriots and underground activities in subversion of the Nazi occupation lead to the ultimate killing of Heydrich and orders by Himmler to wipe out the town of Lidice. The sequence in which the townfolk are rounded up, with the men lined up to be shot, the women carted off to concentration camps, and the kids torn from parents to be sent elsewhere, offers several dramatic and tragic moments, having been well directed. At other points the action lags somewhat, causing slowness. Running time could have been cut at least 10 minutes for better results.

Film was independently produced by Seymour Nebenzal for Metro. So far as production value is concerned, nothing outstanding has been achieved, with various backgrounds failing to impress.

Patricia Morison and Alan Curtis, latter a leader in the movement to bump off Heydrich, are paired for romantic interest, but Miss Morison is killed. Ralph Morgan plays a pacifist who ultimately becomes the opposite, while Blanche Yurka is his wife. Edgar Kennedy is another Czech patriot, one who mostly roams the woods, and Ludwig Stossel does a local mayor who's on the Nazi side. Their performances are satisfactory, no more.

Picture includes portions from the Edna St. Vincent Millay poem, 'The Murder of Lidice,' which are recited by the unconquerable Czechs.

Char.

She Defends Her Country

(RUSSIAN-MADE)

Moscow, June 8.

Released in Moscow this week is a film dedicated to Soviet women entitled 'She Defends Her Country.' It was produced by the Central Amalgamated Studio of Almpata Kazakhstan, and stars the popular Moscow stage actress, Vera Maretskaya. It was directed by Feodor Ermler.

It is the story of how the residents of a captured village west of Moscow became partisans during the German drive of last year.

Technically, it is the best Rusian film produced during the war. It is excellent propaganda for the Russians and is currently packing them in. The entire audience has a good cry and emerges in a fever of hate for the Nazis.

Maretskaya portrays Praskovya Lukyanova, cornily built up as the happiest woman in the village, the best tractor driver, and an ecstatic mother of a five-year-old son. However, the film settles down when the village is evacuated under German attack. In a single day Lukyanova loses her husband while her son is cold-bloodedly shot and she ravished. She wanders through the forest where she finds distraught villagers and finds her hair turned white. She becomes 'Comrade P,' woman leader of guerrillas.

The love interest is provided by a young couple from the district who also join the guerrillas.

The film is dramatically well put together and holds interest with the same type of action as the western thrillers. The tone is tragic and American audiences might find the scenes of the shooting of children, crushing of soldiers under tank treads too strong for their stomachs.

However, totally, it is an intelligent job of interpreting the spirit of hatred which is the basis of the entire guerrilla movement—which causes peaceful farmers to join the movement which offers no quarter and whose only fate, if captured, is death.

Atrocity is brutally treated in this film and if shown in America could give reaching confirmation of what every foreign correspondent has seen. The film's sincerity overcomes its shortcomings.

Downs.

TERROR HOUSE

(BRITISH MADE)

Producers Release Corp. release of John Argyle production. Stars James Mason, Wilfrid Lawson, Mary Clare. Directed by Leslie Arliss. Screenplay, Alan Kennington; camera, Gunther Krampen. At New York, N. Y., dual, week June 1, '43. Running time, **62 MINS.**

Stephen Deremid.................James Mason
Sturrock........................Wilfrid Lawson
Mrs. Ranger........................Mary Clare
Marian Ives........................Joyce Howard
Doris..............................Tucker McGuire
Barry Randall......................John Fernald

Chiller addicts should raise their quota of goosepimples viewing this British importation, which also includes some outspoken dialog about Europe's recent history. Exhibited as a dualer, film has OK boxoffice possibilities.

Story starts conventionally enough with two schoolteachers on walking trip of storm-tossed moors. Girls get lost and wind up in the house of shellshocked musician, veteran of Spanish Civil War. Link is established between musician and friend of schoolteachers who disappeared on similar walking trip of district a year previous. Mystery further heightened by discovery of skeleton and missing girl's locket in secret room. Film works up to gruesome climax of double death in quickstand.

James Mason, as the shellshocked musician, gives an uneven performance that ranges from mediocre to excellent. Marian Ives manages to look properly prim as one of the schoolteachers, and downright luscious when she falls in love with Mason. Wilfrid Lawson, despite his star billing, contributes little to the proceedings, but Mary Clare, as Mason's nurse and double-crossing housekeeper, is convincing in her duplicity. Tucker McGuire doesn't pull any punches as a sex-starved schoolmarm, and John Fernald is highly reminiscent of Barry Fitzgerald.

Film is well-paced and maintained suspense throughout. There are, however, several hard-to-take story transitions, but since horror is the objective, picture can be said to have achieved its purpose.

SOY PURO MEXICANO

('I'm a Real Mexican')

(MEXICAN-MADE)

Oro-Film release of Paul De Anda production. Features Pedro Armendariz, Raquel Rojas, David Silva, Charles Rooner, Andres Soler, Margarita Cortes, Alfredo Valera, Jr., Pedro Vargas. Directed by Emilio Fernandez. Screenplay by Jose Bustos based on story by Emilio Fernandez; camera, Jesus Bracho and Lauron Draper. At Belmont, N. Y., week June 4, '43. Running time, **112 MINS.**

(In Spanish; no English titles)

Axis agents, Mexican bandits, corpses galore and laughs to spare (for those who understand Spanish) make up the ingredients of this anti-fascist importation from good neighbor Mexico. Judging by reaction of Spanish comprehending audience, picture should click at the boxoffice in Latin-populated regions.

Story is about bandit chief who breaks jail just a few hours before he is to be executed, which is also the day Mexico declares war on the Axis. Bodit Pedro Armendariz then hides out in a ranch, headquarters of Axis agents. Gunplay, torture, comedy and romance follow each other in quick succession as Armendariz falls for an Allied counter-espionage agent, Raquel Rojas, kills the Axis spies, and then turns Miss Rojas over to her reporter-boy friend.

It's a fast moving and at times a grim picture, with more murders and assassinations per reel than a Hollywood production would dare feature outside of a war film. The humor of the bandit chief is in the Pancho Villa vein as portrayed by Wallace Beery some years ago. The Axis agents, a German, Italian and Jap, are strikingly played and their arrogance and brutality are not exaggerated.

Technically there is much to be desired. The lighting is either insufficient or too much, rarely in-between. Part of the time the faces are shrouded in shadow and the rest of the unreeling they are over-exposed. This lack of technical perfection, however, often makes for interesting and impressionistic effects. With English titles and a more assiduous application of the scissors, 'Soy Puro Mexicano' should have been able to reach a wider audience, as it has action, comedy and song appeal. Pedro Vargas' warbling and guitaring of his own compositions is standout.

SU HERMANA MENOR

('Her Younger Sister')

(ARGENTINE MADE)

Buenos Aires, May 25.

Sono Film production and release. Stars Silvia Legrand; features Zully Moreno, Santiago Arrieta, Oscar Valicelli, Semillita and Herminia Mass. Directed by Enrique Cahen Salaberry. Story and adaptation, Carlos Aden; camera, Alberto Etchebehere; settings, Raul Soldi; music, Mario Maurano. Reviewed at the Ocean, Buenos Aires. Running time, **85 MINS.**

This is scripter Enrique Cahen Salaberry's first megging job. Proves he has possibilities which should pick up provided he pays heed to errors. Story is simple, with comparatively little originality and interest. Dialog, although clean, often gets monotonous and wordy. Continuity o.k., but action frequently slows up, and greenness of the director becomes most evident in love scenes.

Yarn opens with a young girl on the night of her engagement telling an old servant (who runs a country boarding house where she lives) about expected arrival of her older sister. Film fades into yarn she is describing. In essence tale describes how older girl, ambitious and luxury loving, returned to the sickbed of her young siter and made a solemn oath that in the future they would be together every 12th night. Later, younger sister goes to the country and there falls for poor but honest hero. When he has to go to the big town he carries along an intro to the older sister. Lad, of course. forgets his youthful love, and tangle begins to appear serious until the older girl, learning what's on the mind of her sister, turns back the boy, who rushes home to his original heart-throb.

Silvia Legrand, of the Legrand twins, gives a fair performance, but her coy, girlish tone is sometimes a little tiring. Zully Moreno, as a glamorous sister who is supposed to be a kind of local Powers girl, shows some improvement over previous performances. There's still a bit of phoniness, however, possibly due to the fact that there are no such models here as depicted in the film, and the whole idea is a borrowed impression of Hollywood. Semillita in comic role is pleasing, and Santiago Arrieta and Oscar Valicelli do well. Photography and music both above average. *Ray.*

Miniature Reviews

'Two Tickets to London' (Songs). (U). Slow melodramatic journey.

'Salute for Three' (Songs) (Par). Macdonald Carey, Betty Rhodes in lightweight musical.

'The Kansan' (UA) (Songs). Punchy action western of higher-budget calibre for datings in the regular runs.

'It's a Great Life' (Col). Standard Blondie slapstick; okay for family duals.

'Redhead from Manhattan' (Col). Lupe Velez comedy okay entertainment for program houses.

'Thumbs Up' (Songs) (Rep). May pull stubholders with hands-across-the-sea romance and songs.

'Western Cyclone' (PRC). Very good western in the Buster Crabbe 'Billy the Kid' series.

'Wild Horse Stampede' (Mono). Inferior western starring Ken Maynard and Hoot Gibson, mustang-riding vets.

'Guadalajara' (Mexican-made) (Songs). Gay musical of romantic Me-hee-co. Aided by English titles, it should do fair boxoffice.

'16 Anos' (Argentine). Argentine adaptation of English play; steady grosser.

Two Tickets to London
(SONGS)

Hollywood, June 11.

Universal release of Edwin L. Marin production, directed by Marin. Stars Michele Morgan. Screenplay, Tom Reed, based on story by Roy William Neill; camera, Milton Krasner; editor, Milton Carruth; asst. director, Howard Christie; song, Don Raye, Gene de Paul. Previewed at Fox Wilshire, June 10, '43. Running time, 78 MINS.

Jeanne	Michele Morgan
Dan Driscoll	Alan Curtis
Fairchild	C. Aubrey Smith
MacCardle	Barry Fitzgerald
Roddy	Tarquin Olivier
Mrs. Tinkle	Mary Gordon
Ormsby	Robert Warwick
Brighton	Matthew Boulton
Mr. Tinkle	Oscar O'Shea
Emmie	Doris Lloyd
Kilgallen	Holmes Herbert
Nettleton	Stanley Logan
Treathcote	Lester Matthews
Benson	Harold DeBecker
Royce	John Burton
Dame Dunne Hartley	Mary Forbes
Accordionist	Dooley Wilson

Two Tickets to London is basically a chase through most of its 78 minutes' unreeling. There's romance injected liberally, but not too deftly, and melodramatics through the efforts of the fugitive to elude the police until he can clear himself of treason charges. It's a porous tale, with many dull detours and slow spots, and hardly capable of holding up the upper bracket of the general bookings.

Yarn fails to generate the suspense and tension intended. It concerns Alan Curtis, charged by the Admiralty with treason, who escapes from his guard during a train wreck and rescues cafe entertainer Michele Morgan to use her as front for his escape. It's a slow journey to London via various conveyances, with dragnet out for the couple. Although girl is unaware of charges against him until well along, she falls in love, and tries to hide him in London. But his eventual capture, trial and resultant exoneration, provides prelude to the eventual clinch.

Miss Morgan handles her assignment okay, but role is still far below her potentialities. Curtis is okay as the American who's charged with complicity with the enemy in signaling to a Nazi sub while in convoy. Supporting cast is adequate, with Barry Fitzgerald clicking for brief appearance near the finish, and Dooley Wilson making solid impression as accordionist-singer in a pub.

Story rides at a slow pace throughout, with direction by Edwin Marin hitting the same groove. Production layout carries through numerous sequences to run up the budget. Miss Morgan sings one new number of Don Raye and 'Gene de Paul early, but Dooley Wilson clicks with his deliveries of 'You Are My Sunshine' and 'Lead, Kindly Light,' in his one brief appearance to catch audience attention. *Walt.*

SALUTE FOR THREE
(SONGS)

Paramount production and release. Stars Betty Rhodes, Macdonald Carey; features Marty May, Cliff Edwards, Jeanne Lorraine, Roy Rognan. Directed by Ralph Murphy. Screenplay by Doris Anderson, Curtis Kenyon, Hugh Wedlock, Jr., Howard Snyder from story by Art Arthur; camera, Theodor Sparkuhl; editor, Arthur Schmidt; songs, Jule Styne, Kim Gannon, Sol Meyer; dances, Jack Donohue. At Strand, Brooklyn, week June 10, '43. Running time, 74 MINS.

Judy Adams	Betty Rhodes
Buzz McAllister	Macdonald Carey
Jimmy Gates	Marty May
Foggy	Cliff Edwards
Myrt	Minna Gombell
Dona	Dona Drake
Lorraine & Rognan	

Picture starts out as a hokey farce and winds up in a blaze of patriotic flourishes. In between, the action sputters, dies and then revives, but too late. Result is that 'Salute for Three' is a minor-key farce with songs when it might have amounted to something. It will never rise above dual status despite a considerable production outlay.

Original premise of having a radio talent agent cash in on a present war hero's popularity to sell a femme client for a radio spot is a ticklish one even in most capable hands. Here it veers too close to bad taste, overcome only in part by the musical comedy technique. Had it adhered wholly to this musical treatment instead of turning suddenly dramatic the results might have been better.

There's the familiar angle of the radio femme being persuaded to play up to the returned war ace and then actually falling in love with him. In between there's the usual parting when the soldier is convinced he has been made a stooge in the plot to land her on the airwaves, followed, of course, by the customary making-up. It plays as woodenly as it sounds, with the musical specialties and songs almost wasted. Betty Rhodes makes a fetching radio singer as the love interest. Has possibilities as a singer but some of closeups are bad. Macdonald Carey understandingly has a struggle to make the hero role seem lifelike.

Cliff Edwards does stalwart work with innocuous gag lines, and again proves he is a solid seller of talky tunes with his familiar uke-strumming specialty of 'My Wife's a WAAC.' Dona Drake leads an all-girl band and dances to enhance proceedings while Marty May and Minna Gombell head the large supporting cast, necessary for the servicemen's canteen scenes. Jeanne Lorraine and the late Roy Rognan (who lost his life in the Lisbon clipper crash) score heavily with their classic comedy ballroom dancing.

Principal songs by Jule Styne and Kim Gannon are sparkling exceptions to the usual dull proceedings. Climax marching tune, 'Left-Right,' by this team, plus Sol Meyer, is appealing, but the best songs are 'I'll Do It For You' and 'What Do You Do When It Rains.' 'Don't Worry' fails to impress despite heavy build-up. Ralph Murphy's direction is unoriginal and routine but much of blame rests on the scripting. *Wear.*

THE KANSAN
(SONGS)

Hollywood, June 11.

United Artists release of Harry Sherman production. Features Richard Dix, Jane Wyatt, Albert Dekker, Victor Jory. Directed by George Archainbaud. Screenplay, Harold Shumate; from book by Frank Gruber; associate producer, Lewis Rachmil; camera, Russell Harlan; editor, Carroll Lewis; assistant director, Glenn Cook; songs, Foster Karling and Phil Ohman. Previewed in Filmarte, Hollywood, June 10, '43. Running time, 79 MINS.

John Bonniwell	Richard Dix
Eleanor Sager	Jane Wyatt
Steve Barat	Albert Dekker
Tom Waggoner	Eugene Pallette
Jeff Barat	Victor Jory
Malachy	Robert Armstrong
Soubret	Beryl Wallace
Bridge Tender	Clem Bevans
Josh Hudkins	Hobart Cavanaugh
Gil Hatton	Francis McDonald
Bones	Willie Best
Ben Nash	Douglas Fowley
Kelso	Rod Cameron
Ed Gilbert	Eddy Waller
Messenger	Raphael Bennett

'The Kansan' is the latest in the Harry Sherman series of higher-budgeted westerns that have been trademarked for combination display of action and scenic panoramas. With Richard Dix and Albert Dekker heading a strong cast for this type of entry, it's a good western attraction for the regular fans, with emphasis on datings in the family and action subsequents.

Despite the fact that the story hits familiar lines, Sherman has injected punchy and paceful episodes along the route to maintain audience interest. Dix, enroute to Oregon in pioneer days, stops off in a Kansas frontier town to scatter bank raid of the James gang and get elected town marshal. He's sponsored by Dekker, town banker who not only rules the town but wants to take over all the profitable enterprises. Usual conflict develops, with plenty of gunplay, a rousing rough-and-tumble free-for-all in the dancehall, a cattle stampede and a rather spectular bridge dynamiting. Interwoven is romance between Dix and Jane Wyatt, with Victor Jory on the triangle but graciously stepping aside to save Dix and the townsmen at the finish.

Dix provides his usually vigorous portrayal of the fearless marksman, with Dekker neatly handling the heavy assignment. Miss Wyatt displays charm and personality in prominent footage as the girl, while Jory draws a sympathetic role for a change. Strong support includes Eugene Pallette, Robert Armstrong, Clem Bevans, Hobart Cavanaugh, Willie Best, Francis McDonald, Douglas Fowley and Eddy Waller.

Camera supervision by Russell Harlan takes fullest advantage of the scenic backgrounds of the high Sierra location. George Archainbaud's direction unfolded the tale at a consistently speedy pace, accentuating the highlighted chases and battles. Beryl Wallace leads girl song-and-dance chorus in the music hall for delivery of 'When Johnny Comes Marching Home,' while King's Men briefly display new tune, 'Lullaby of the Herd.' *Walt.*

IT'S A GREAT LIFE

Columbia production and release. Features Penny Singleton, Arthur Lake, Larry Simms, Hugh Herbert. Directed by Frank Strayer. Original screenplay, Connie Lee and Karen De Wolf; camera, L. W. O'Connell; editor, Al Clark; music, M. W. Stoloff. At Fox, Brooklyn, June 11, '43; dual. Running time, 68 MINS.

Blondie	Penny Singleton
Dagwood	Arthur Lake
Alexander	Larry Simms
Timothy Brewster	Hugh Herbert
J. C. Dithers	Jonathan Hale
Alvin Fuddle	Danny Mummert
Collender Martin	Alan Dinehart
Bromley	Douglas Leavitt
Mailman	Irving Bacon
Cookie	Marjorie Ann Mutchie

The usual Blondie antics are

stirred up again in 'It's a Great Life.' The result is a typical slapstick trifle that'll please the juves at matinee showings, but is likely to be only mildly trying to adults.

The Connie Lee-Karen De Wolf screenplay offers an 'original' story, but it's standard comic strip stuff. It's loaded with broadly comic situations and sight gags, with the succession of lunacies practically falling over each other. As always, Dagwood causes the complications and his stupidity finally provides the solution. This time the plot stems from a pun, Dagwood buying a horse instead of a house. The horse, Reggie, and a pooch, Daisy, are practically the leading characters.

It's all skillfully obvious for the widest possible kid audience. The writing, direction and performance miss scarcely a trick in ridiculous contrivence. *Hobe.*

Redhead From Manhattan

Columbia release of Wallace McDonald production. Stars Lupe Velez, Michael Duane. Directed by Lew Landers. Screenplay by Rex Taylor; camera, Philip Tannura; editor, James Sweeney. At Brooklyn Paramount, week June 10, '43. Running time, 63 MINS.

Rita }
Elaine Manners } ....Lupe Velez
Jimmy Randall..............Michael Duane
Mike Glendon..............Tim Ryan
Chick Andrews..............Gerald Mohr
Polly..............Lillian Yarbo
Sig Hammersmith..............Arthur Loft
Paul..............Lewis Wilson
Joe..............Douglas Leavitt
Policeman..............Clancy Cooper
Marty Britt..............Douglass Drake

'Redhead From Manhattan' provides okay entertainment of its type and should fit neatly as supporting fare in the regular program houses. For Lupe Velez, it's her first non-'Spitfire' script in some time and thanks to Lew Landers' direction, it moves at good clip.

'Redhead' is one of those who's who mixups, with the dynamic Miss Velez in the dual role of sisters—first as a stowaway who escapes from a torpedoed ship to an isolated stretch of beach with a sax player, and later as a Broadway musicomedy star whose marital difficulties forces a switcheroo, with the twin sister, arriving in N. Y. under fortuitous circumstances, subbing in her place and the forgotten sax player, strangely enough, winding up in the orchestra pit. The inevitable complications attending mistaken identities bring into the script an assortment of characters ranging from FBI men and gangsters to a producer with a dislike for married dames in his shows.

Principals are often handcuffed by Rex Taylor's labored scripting job, but thanks to Miss Velez and Michael Duane, latter providing considerable comedy relief, proceedings are livened up. Gerald Mohr, Arthur Loft, Tim Ryan and Lewis Wilson lend satisfactory support. *Rose.*

THUMBS UP
(SONGS)

Republic release of Albert J. Cohen production. Features Brenda Joyce, Richard Fraser, Elsa Lanchester, Arthur Margetson. Directed by Joseph Santley. Screenplay by Frank Gill, Jr., based on story idea by Ray Golden and Henry Moritz; camera, Ernest Miller; editor, Thomas Richards; musical director, Walter Scharf; songs, Jule Styne, Sammy Cahn. Previewed in N. Y., June 11, '43. Running time, 67 MINS.

Louise Latimer..............Brenda Joyce
Douglas Heath..............Richard Fraser
Emmy Finch..............Elsa Lanchester
Bert Lawrence..............Arthur Margetson
Sam Keats..............J. Pat O'Malley
Janie Brooke..............Queenie Leonard
Welfare Supervisor..............Molly Lamont
Gertrude Niesen..............Herself
Foreman..............George Byron
Roy Irwin..............Charles Irwin
E. E. Cartwright..............Andre Charlot
The Hot Shots..............Themselves

The idea back of 'Thumbs Up' is good, but it's killed by a hackneyed story treatment, which wastes the first-rate acting talent of Elsa Lanchester and Arthur Margetson. However, there are boxoffice possibilities in the hands-across-the-sea romance of American Brenda Joyce and British Richard Fraser.

Yarn concerns Miss Joyce, vocalist in a cheap London nitery, who is awaiting her big break, a part in a London revue. Break fails to jell when her fiance's (Margetson) partner in a production firm decides to recruit talent from British war factories. This gives Miss Joyce an idea and she gets a job in an aircraft plant. She is 'discovered' by her fiance and his partner and wins the talent contest, but when her coworker and roommate, Elsa Lanchester, and fellow employees learn why she registered for war work they give her the cold shoulder. She also gets the brushoff from Richard Fraser, who has fallen in love with her, and she with him. However, she squares herself with Fraser, who is an RAF officer in charge of the plant, and with the workers by taking the rap for an accident caused by Fraser.

It's the familiar song and dance about an American who regards the war as a means of self-aggrandizement, but sees the light in the last reel. Other films have portrayed theme more effectively and more originally. What might have given the picture a new starting point is the idea of an American working in a British factory. Very little has been done with that, and judging from 'Thumbs Up' very little still has been done with it. But here's an angle that producers can well play around with.

This picture also has a song department, which features 'Love Is a Corny Thing,' 'Who Are the British?' and 'From Here On In' by Jule Styne and Sammy Cahn, and 'Thumbs Up' by Jaffe, O'Brien and Lee. Miss Joyce or her vocal ghost delivers nicely with 'Love,' 'From Here' and 'Thumbs.' 'Who Are the British?' which will probably embarrass the self-effacing Britishers, is socked across by Gertrude Niesen, playing herself.

WESTERN CYCLONE

Producers Releasing Corp. release of Sigmund Neufeld production. Stars Buster Crabbe; features Al St. John, Marjorie Manners, Karl Hackett, Milton Kibbee, Glenn Strange. Directed by Sam Newfield. Story and adaptation, Patricia Harper; editor, Holbrook Todd; camera, Robert Cline. At New York, N. Y., dual, week June 8, '43. Running time, 62 MINS.

Billy the Kid..............Buster Crabbe
Fuzzy Q. Jones..............Al St. John
Mary Arnold..............Marjorie Manners
Governor Arnold..............Karl Hackett
Senator Peabody..............Milton Kibbee
Dirk Randall..............Glenn Strange
Ace Harmon..............Charles King
Sheriff..............Hal Price
Hank..............Kermit Maynard

This is one of the best of the 'Billy the Kid' series starring Buster Crabbe, not only because it has plenty of action and lively dialog but also as result of the laugh value. Al St. John, going steady with Crabbe in westerns, has been provided with plenty of good comedy situations and, apparently with Crabbe's blessings, is given wide opportunity to show his stuff. That is to Crabbe's credit or the credit of director Sam Newfield, who appreciates his value.

While the story of 'Western Cyclone' follows a well-established formula, it has been well plotted out and maintains suspense to near the end, as all good westerns should. Concerns the efforts of a crooked gang to frame Crabbe and the governor of a western state who has faith in the outlaw. The girl, Marjorie Manners, is kidnapped as part of a plot to get Crabbe, already convicted of murder, into a hangman's noose.

Miss Manners is a personable type but not permitted to extend herself very far. She has a particularly entrancing figure. Crabbe, as usual, gives a fine performance, including in the fist battles he indulges. Karl Hackett makes a good governor and Milton Kibbee acquits himself creditably as a conniving senator. Not unlike dozens of other villains but okay is Glenn Strange. *Char.*

Wild Horse Stampede

Monogram release of Robert Tansey production. Stars Ken Maynard, Hoot Gibson; features Betty Miles, Ian Keith, Don Stewart, Don Baker. Directed by Alan James. Story, Francis Kavanaugh; adaptation, Elizabeth Beecher; editor, Fred Bain; camera, Marcel Le Picard. At New York, N. Y., dual, week June 8, '43. Running time, 60 MINS.

Ken..............Ken Maynard
Hoot..............Hoot Gibson
Betty..............Betty Miles
Carson..............Ian Keith
Donny..............Don Stewart
Tyler..............Bob Baker
Rawhide..............Sy Jenks
Col. Black..............John Bridges
Tip..............Glen Strange
Tex..............Reed Howes
Borman..............Kenneth Harlan

An inferior western called 'Wild Horse Stampede' serves to reintroduce Ken Maynard and Hoot Gibson to the followers of saddle-warmers. Both date back to the old silent days and may have trouble trying to compete with the more hard-hitting of sagebrush Romeos who have come up in later years.

No attempt is made in this instance to push either Maynard or Gibson into a romantic groove, that being assigned in a minor way to Bob Baker, U. S. marshal, and Betty Miles, the girl who sells a herd of horses to a pioneering railroad company only to have them rustled.

Moreover, in scenes in which fistfighting occurs, Maynard and Gibson do not hand it out like Charlie Starrett, Johnny Mack Brown and other boys of the rangeland do. The punches are so pulled in this one, as a matter of fact, as to suggest bad staging, if nothing else. Maynard particularly makes every effort to attain a miss and so do his opponents.

The story deals with the successful efforts of the Maynard-Gibson twain to wipe out a band of horse rustlers who are also inciting Indians to plunder whites who are trying to build a railroad line through the southwest. Not only is the story lightweight but in many cases the recording and photography rate below par.

Miss Miles attracts attention but hardly appears to be the type to run a horse ranch of her own. Ian Keith fills requirements as a heavy, while Bob Baker adequately carries out the assignment of the smalltown marshal. A kid part without much scope is played by Don Stewart. *Char.*

GUADALAJARA
(SONGS)
(MEXICAN-MADE)

Azteca Studio release and production. Features Pedro Armendariz, Chaflan, Esperanza Baur. Directed by Chano Urueta. Screenplay by Urueta from original by Ernesto Cortazar. Titles by J. A. Cordero. At World, N. Y., week June 11, '43. Running time, 103 MINS.

Pedro..............Pedro Armendariz
Melitan..............Chaflan
Hortensia..............Esperanza Baur
Piledonio..............Joaquin Pardave
Jorge..............Jorge Velez
Mrs. Severo..............Emma Roldan
Esther..............Rosita Lepe
Lencho..............Lorenzo Barcelata
Trio Calsveros, Trio Ascencio Del Rio

(In Spanish; English Titles)

Despite its technical shortcomings and corny plot, 'Guadalajara' has solid song and romance appeal which should prove above average boxoffice. The film is a good gesture from a good neighbor.

The billing should really be reversed, for it's the songs and instrumentalizing of Lorenzo Barcelata and the Trios Calaveros and Ascencio Del Rio that really sell the picture. Especially standout are their 'Jalisco Nunca Piere,' 'El Mariachi,' 'Guadalajara' and 'Quesera.'

You take the good with the bad in this Mexican production, which is built around an overlong story of two pairs of lovers who are almost forced into unhappy marriages by unthinking parents. A ranch hand, Pedro Armendariz, falls in love with the boss's daughter Esperanza Baur, who returns his love, but is betrothed against her wish to Jorge Velez. Nor is Velez in love with her, as he is much more interested in Rosita Lepe. An ingenious double wedding winds up what appears to be a never ending film.

Comedy played to the hilt is contributed by Joaquin Pardave and the recently deceased Chaflan. Performances of principals and supporting players are natural and to the point. Especially good is Miss Baur, whose distinctive appearance is an asset to the film.

Although far below Hollywood standards, the photography in 'Guadalajara' reveals a decided improvement over that in recent Mexican pictures.

16 ANOS
('Sixteen')
(ARGENTINE-MADE)

Buenos Aires, June 1.

Lumiton production and release. Stars Maria Duval and Jorge Rigaud; features Alicia Barrie, Amalia Sanchez Arino, Mariana Marti, Aurelia Ferrer, Francisco Lopez Silva. Directed by Carlos Hugo Christensen. Based on stage play by Aimee and Philip Stuart; adapted by Julio Porter and Francisco Oyarzabal. Reviewed at Broadway, Buenos Aires. Running time, 68 MINS.

Reversing general formula of English-mades based on Latin productions, 'Sixteen' is the initial try by Latin studios to take a successful English work and adapt it for local screens. In this case the Aimee and Philip Stuart play, which ran both in New York and London, was purchased by Lumiton with heavy drum-thumping by British Council for Cultural Relations in South America, English counterpart of Nelson Rockefeller's Office of the Coordinator of Inter-American Affairs. Inking of contract was accompanied by much ballyhoo, aided by fact that Spanish translation of legit version, done by Jose Alberto Arrieta, was fairly successful here.

Result was therefore watched with considerable interest, particularly since entire diplomatic crowd turned out for preem. in benefit of Allied charities. Spanish screen version is o.k. and should be a steady grosser, but will not set any records, particularly in second-run and interior showings.

It's an interesting psychological study of adolescent jealousy. Story is basically that of a girl who becomes enraged by the fact that her widowed mother is about to marry again. To head off the Mendelssohn march, she goes to all lengths, finally attempting suicide. Saved just before the plunge into the lake, she finally becomes reconciled.

Maria Duval, who seems to star in every other Argentine picture, is not quite up to a difficult role. Initial scenes between Alicia Barrie and Jorge Rigaud, an Argentine actor who gained considerable prominence in pre-war Parisian films, are somewhat slow.

Film does not quite succeed in conveying turmoil in the soul of a young girl, which is its principal point. Latter half of film is better than opening, with performance by Mariana Marti especially good. Presentation above average, with exteriors, shot on location in Cordoba hill region, being noteworthy. Night scenes in park are well photographed, but there are isolated defects in the sound.

Deal for purchase of play was arranged by Lawrence Smith, local rep for a number of British and American authors.

Ray.

Miniature Reviews

'**So Proudly We Hail!**' (Par). Excellent saga of the Bataan and Corregidor nurses and their heroism under fire. Has cast names; will do big biz.

'**Alaska Highway**' (Par). Alcan roadbuilding provides setting for outdoors meller with romantic triangle. Action dualer.

'**The Life and Death of Col. Blimp**' (GFD-British). Excellently made longest ever in England (163 mins). Should go well everywhere.

'**Submarine Alert**' (Par). Good actioner of type, but will have to be satisfied with dual datings.

'**Colt Comrades**' (UA). Good action entry in the Hopalong Cassidy series of westerns.

'**Get Going**' (Songs) (U). Entertaining little program number will provide amusement as dual supporter.

'**Two Senoritas From Chicago**' (Musical). (Col). Minor musical turned into fair b.o. by Joan Davis.

'**The Dark Tower**' (WB-British). Ben Lyon starred in nsg big-top mystery, made in England. Strictly for lower duals.

'**Days of Old Cheyenne**' (Rep). Don 'Red' Barry in above-average western.

'**Sarong Girl**' (Songs) (Mono). Spotty on quality but may get by as dualer if merchandised properly.

'**Rhythm Parade**' (Musical) (Mono). Musical romance should do okay.

'**A Gentle Gangster**' (Rep). Warmed - over gangster story starring Barton MacLane in routine role.

So Proudly We Hail!

Paramount release of Mark Sandrich production, directed by Sandrich. Features Claudette Colbert, Paulette Goddard, Veronica Lake, George Reeves, Sonny Tufts, Walter Abel. Original screenplay, Allan Scott; camera, Charles Lang; special effects, Gordon Jennings, Farciot Edouard; music, Miklos Rozsa; editor, Ellsworth Hoagland. Tradeshown June 22, '43. Running time, 126 MINS.

Lt. Janet Davidson	Claudette Colbert
Joan O'Doul	Paulette Goddard
Olivia D'Arcy	Veronica Lake
Lt. Summers	George Reeves
Rosemary Larson	Barbara Britton
Chaplain	Walter Abel
Kansas	Sonny Tufts
Captain 'Ma' McGregor	Mary Servoss
Dr. Jose Bardia	Ted Hecht
Flight Lt. Archie McGregor	Dick Hogan
Ling Chee	Dr. H. H. Chang
Colonel White	James Bell
Lt. Toni Bacelli	Lorna Gray
Lt. Irma Emerson	Dorothy Adams
Lt. Ethel Armstrong	Kitty Kelly
Capt. O'Rourke	Bill Goodwin
Lt. Sadie Schwartz	Mary Treen
Lt. Elsie Bollenbacker	Helen Lynd
Lt. Carol Johnson	Jean Willes
Lt. Lynne Hopkins	Jan Wiley
Lt. Fay Leonard	Lynn Walker
Lt. Margaret Stevenson	Joan Tours
Major (dock at Frisco)	William Forrest
Capt. O'Brien	James Flavin
Mr. Larson	Bryon Foulger
Georgie	Richard Crane
Mrs. Larson	Else Janssen
Young Ensign	James Millican
Second Doctor	Michael Harvey
Ensign	Fred Henry
Corporal	Victor Killan, Jr.
First Young Doctor	Damian O'Flynn
Ship Capt	Ray Godin
Nurse	Frances Morris
Nurse	Mimi Doyle
Thin Nurse	Fay Sappington
Nurse	Julia Faye
Young Officer	Keith Richards
Filipino Nurse	Isabel Cooper
Filipino Nurse	Amparo Antenorcruz

Mark Sandrich's 'So Proudly We Hail!' for Paramount will be the answer to the from-now-in trade attitude on war films. As always,

the answer is that quality product, whether it's on celluloid or from Tiffany, will command attention. In short, if the picture is good, the theme or the cycle goes by the board. This is a good one. It will do lots of business. What's more, it deserves to do so.

It's a saga of the war-front nurse and her heroism under fire. As such it's a 'new' theme, glorifying the American Red Cross and presenting the present-day, wartime nurse, in the midst of unspeakable dangers, physical and spiritual, in a new light.

An Angel of Mercy is two other fellers when she's part of a delaying action in Bataan and Corregidor. That means she's on the losing end of catastrophic battle, for the record has now made familiar how our too few troops couldn't stem the Jap hordes. Yet, despite knowledge of headline history, the saga of the eight heroine-nurses from the Philippine debacle could well have come out of official Army records—and probably did.

Director-producer Sandrich and scripter Allen Scott have limned a vivid, vital story. It's another step in the general patriotic pattern, as Hollywood is practising it, of bringing the war to the home-front, via the screen. In this case it's backgrounded against a realistic romance of how a group of brave American Nightingales came through the hellfire to Australia and thence back to blighty.

The canvas is broad and the dramatics dynamic. Perhaps some of it is too realistic. Perhaps there is no need for Capt. 'Ma' McGregor to see her son. Flight Lt. Archie McGregor, experience a crude amputation of both his legs, and then succumb under her eyes in the thick of insular warfare in the far Pacific.

Perhaps Veronica Lake's hatred of Japs who killed her fiance, and her self-annihilation with a hand-grenade, as she deliberately walks into the woman-greedy Japs' hands (presumably taking a few of them with her), is not for tender sensitivities.

Perhaps, too, the deliberate strafing by the Japs of a Red Cross hospital base, and sundry miniature Dunkirks staged as the evacuating Yanks leave the Jap-entrapped hellholes, aren't exactly 'entertainment,' per se, but it's realism that's as authentic as the rest of the gruesomeness extant in this not so civilized world.

It's certainly purposeful, even if it has to be done only by indirection, via the articulateness of Claudette Colbert, when it gets over such messages as the benefits of blood plasma and sulfa; the fact that this is 'the people's war, and once we win it we should also make sure we win a people's peace.' Or that punchy reference to the 'One World' theme which another American statesman, Wendell Willkie, has emphasized in his own manner.

The casting is excellent. It underplays everything but only heightens the general effect that way. In short order one gathers that women are fighting a man's war, yet they face bestial despoiling if they ever fall into barbaric Jap hands. But that's just an overtone to the semi-documentary treatment.

Done in flashback manner, with Claudette Colbert rapidly sinking physically, the saga of their travail pitches to the situation where, out of the past, a love letter from her officer-lover finally brings her back on the road to recovery. Paulette Goddard does a capital job as running mate, and Veronica Lake is the sullen nurse who finally sees the light, only to destroy herself.

Sonny Tufts walks off with the picture every time he's on. As 'Kansas,' the blundering ex-footballer, he's Miss Goddard's vis-a-vis. George Reeves isn't as effective as the romantic opposite to Miss Colbert.

Barbara Britton, newcomer, makes

much of her assignment; Walter Abel is expert as the chaplain; Mary Servoss troupes her 'Ma' McGregor to the hilt; Ted Hecht gets a lot out of a Filipino medico assignment; ditto Dr. H. H. Chang as a Chinese guide, and Dick Hogan as the ill-fated flight lieutenant.

Mary Treen is excellent as Lt. Sadie Schwartz; Helen Lynd as the nurse who yens fresh tomatoes after her experiences in Bataan, and Lorna Gray, Dorothy Adams, Kitty Kelly, Jean Willes, Jan Wiley, Lynn Walker and Joan Tours, as the heroic nurses, are ever prominent and thoroughly realistic.

Film's 126 minutes is overboard and there is room for judicious slicing, but as a screen document, even in its present somewhat fulsome form, it is a credit to all concerned.

Abel.

ALASKA HIGHWAY

Hollywood, June 22.

Paramount release of Pine-Thomas production. Stars Richard Arlen, Jean Parker. Directed by Frank McDonald. Original screenplay by Maxwell Shane; camera, Fred Jackman, Jr.; editor, William Zeigler. Tradeshown in L. A., June 22, '43. Running time, 66 MINS.

Woody Ormsby	Richard Arlen
Ann Coswell	Jean Parker
Frosty Gimble	Ralph Sanford
Roughhouse	Joe Sawyer
Steve Ormsby	Bill Henry
Sgt. Swithers	John Wegman
Pop Ormsby	Harry Shannon
Blair Caswell	Edward Earle
Hank Lincoln	Keith Richards
Pompadour Jones	Eddie Quillan

Construction of the Alcan road forms topical background for this action drama which displays a regulation triangle involving two brothers and a girl. Despite obvious texture of the romantic conflict, speedy pace and roadbuilding setting supply good supporting fare for the regular runs, and picture has chance to be put over in secondary key houses with smart exploitation campaigns.

Producers Bill Pine and Bill Thomas secured considerable footage of construction of the Alcan highway for insertion as stock shots and utilization for process backgrounds. This film, deftly intercut into the dramatic action, is decidedly interesting and informative in the task confronting Army engineers and roadbuilders in pushing through to the north.

Harry Shannon, father of Richard Arlen and Bill Henry, heads a construction company building roads in California when the war hits and he's commissioned a major in the Army engineers. His entire crew joins up, including the two sons, to become the pioneering unit to blaze the trail through the wilderness north from Ft. Nelson base. Jean Parker, carrying on romance with Henry, arrives in the north country, and immediately falls in love with Arlen. Then it's the usual triangle complications, narrow escapes and action melodramatics to the finish. Naturally the road is pushed through, and Henry graciously steps aside for his brother to get the girl.

Cast grooves nicely into respective roles, with Arlen and Miss Parker providing okay performances in the starring spots. Major assistance comes from Ralph Sanford, jovial pal of Arlen, who is handed fat lines and situations for comedy reaction, Joe Sawyer, Eddie Quillan, Henry, Shannon, and Edward Earle.

Speedy pace which generally characterizes the Pine-Thomas product, is again on display here; with Frank McDonald turning in okay directing job.

Walt.

Life and Death of Col. Blimp

(BRITISH-MADE)
(Color)

London, June 8.

General Film Distributors release of Archer Film Production. Stars Deborah Kerr, Roger Livesey, Anton Walbrook. Directed by Michael Powell and Emeric Pressburger who also wrote and produced picture. Music by Allan Gray; camera, Georges Perinal. Military adviser, Lieut. General Sir Douglas Brownrigg. Reviewed at Odeon, London. Running time, **163 MINS.**

Clive Candy	Roger Livesey
Edith Hunter / Barbara Wynne / Johnny Cannon	Deborah Kerr
Theo. Kretschmar-Schuldorf	Anton Walbrook
Spud Wilson	James McKechnie
Period Blimp	Spencer Trevor
Colonel Betteridge	Roland Culver
Frau von Kalteneck	Ursula Jeans
Pebble	Phyllis Morris
Murdoch	John Laurie
von Schonborn	Valentine Dyall
Embassy Counsellor	Arthur Wontner
Colonel Berg	Count Zichy
Major Davis	Harry Welchman
von Reumann	Carl Jaffe
von Ritter	Albert Lieven
Colonel Goodhead	Eric Maturin

Here is an excellent film whose basic story could have been told within normal feature limits, but which, instead, is extended close to three hours. Longer or shorter, this panorama of British army life is depicted with a technical skill and artistry that marks it as one of the really fine pix to come out of a British studio.

This is the longest picture ever made in England. It was carefully and intelligently written, directed and produced, and should rank as an important feature in America.

It's a clear, continuous unreeling of events in the life of an English military man, from the Boer War, through the last war and including the present one, up to the completion of the training and equipment of England's Home Guard. Story revolves around an officer (Clive Candy) who has spent all his life in the army and still feels it is the right thing to play fair with the Germans even after we have won the present war. He insists on believing the German people as a whole are decent human beings, and that they're only the tools of their war lords.

The role of Candy is spasmodically well enacted by Roger Livesey, who looks a little too mature in the scenes of his younger days and a bit too virile at the finish. More generous praise should go to Anton Walbrook as an Uhlan officer. This is an excellent characterization depicted with delicacy and sensitiveness. Deborah Kerr contributes attractively as the feminine lead in three separate characters through the generations, and a score of other artists leave little to criticize from the histrionic side.

Title is based on the symbolic figure of the old-time English officers who have been axed, not only due to age but because of their constant reiteration, in their clubs, of their contempt for present methods of warfare as compared with 'the good old days,' when cavalry anteceded mechanized combat. Cartoonist Low, in the Evening Standard, christened them 'Colonel Blimps,' but the title would mean nothing outside England, and it's suggested that a more felicitous one should be utilized for the export trade. *Jolo.*

SUBMARINE ALERT

Hollywood, June 22.

Paramount release of Pine-Thomas production. Stars Richard Arlen, Wendy Barrie; features Nils Asther, Roger Pryor, Abner Biberman. Directed by Frank McDonald. Original screenplay by Maxwell Shane; camera, Fred Jackman, Jr.; editor, William Zeigler. Tradeshown June 21, '43. Running time, **66 MINS.**

Lee Deerhold	Richard Arlen
Ann Patterson	Wendy Barrie
Dr. Arthur Huneker	Nils Asther
G. B. Fleming	Roger Pryor
Com. Toyo	Abner Biberman
Vincent Belga	Marc Lawrence
Mr. Bambridge / Capt. Hargas	John Miljan
Tina	Patsy Nash
Freddie Grayson	Ralph Sanford
Henry Haldine	Dwight Frye
Dr. Barclay	Edward Earle
Engineer	William Bakewell
Clerk	Stanley Smith

'Submarine Alert' is a good example of how a picture can get out of date via extended period between production windup and eventual release. Typical spy meller with usual melodramatic contents has been held on the shelf for a year and, in these fast-moving times, emerges as a rather dated piece in general setup. Filler for the duals.

Picture carries the usual fast action which has characterized the Pine-Thomas product. Secret radio shortwave portable transmitter results in wholesale sinkings of American tankers off the Pacific coast by a Jap submarine. FBI, in attempt to track the spies, has group of radio engineers fired—among them Richard Arlen. Latter is eventually selected by the gang to repair the set, and when he gets wise to the sabotaging efforts it's the usual meller mixup until the mob is rounded up. There's slight tinge of romance injected between Arlen and Wendy Barrie, herself an FBI operative.

Years ago, audiences would have accepted this as a good program actioner, but it's now on the far end of a cycle of spy tales. Direction is fast, and cast provides good performances generally. *Walt.*

COLT COMRADES

Hollywood, June 17.

United Artists release of Harry Sherman (Lewis J. Rachmil) production. Stars William Boyd. Directed by Lesley Selander. Screenplay by Michael Wilson; camera, Russell Harlan; editor, Sherman A. Rose; asst. director, Glenn Cook; production manager, Dick Johnston. Previewed in studio projection room, June 16, '43. Running time, **67 MINS.**

Hopalong Cassidy	William Boyd
California Carlson	Andy Clyde
Johnny Nelson	Jay Kirby
Lin Whitlock	George Reeves
Lucy Whitlock	Gayle Lord
Wildcat Willy	Earl Hodgins
Jebb Hardin	Victor Jory
Joe Brass	Douglas Fowley
Varney	Herb Rawlinson

'Colt Comrades' is another of the Hopalong Cassidy series of westerns which have held a top rank in the action field for several years. It's a good entry in the series, excellently photographed against scenic panoramas that have become a trademark for the Hoppys, containing sufficient action, riding and gunplay to get favorable reaction from western-minded audiences.

Story has Hoppy and his two sidekicks, Andy Clyde and Jay Kirby, breeze into the western town as U. S. marshals, rounding up a robber with a $5,000 price on his head. Trio decides to settle down for a spell, and buy half interest in cattle ranch of George Reeves. But conflict develops with Victor Jory, who charges excessive price for water to the valley ranchers and has a gang of gun-toters to back up his racket. Clyde gets hooked with an old con game, but makes the promoter drill—to bring in water. Jory then tries to frame Hoppy as a rustler, but winds up on the short end of the deal in a rousing gun battle.

William Boyd continues his strong characterization of Hopalong, with Andy Clyde providing the usual comedy sidelight, and Jay Kirby completing the trio as the juvenile member. Jory and Douglas Fowley are typed as the heavies, with Earl Hodgins the oil promoting artist.

Although story hits some familiar trails, it's mounded for a speedy trip to accentuate the action angles with Lesley Selander expertly handling the direction. Photography still maintains the high standard of Sherman outdoor production, with backgrounds materially assisting the scenic reproductions. *Walt.*

GET GOING

(SONGS)

Hollywood, June 18.

Universal release of Will Cowan production. Features Robert Paige, Grace McDonald, Vera Vague, Walter Catlett, Milburn Stone. Directed by Jean Yarbrough. Original by Warren Wilson; camera, George Robinson; editor, Ray Snyder; songs, Milton Rosen, Everett Carter. Previewed in studio projection room, June 17, 43. Running time, **57 MINS.**

Bob Carlton	Robert Paige
Judy King	Grace McDonald
Matilda Jones	Vera Vague
Horace Doblem	Walter Catlett
Doris	Lois Collier
Bonnie	Maureen Cannon
Mr. Tuttle	Milburn Stone
Vilma Walters	Jennifer Holt
Mrs. Daugherty	Nana Bryant
Hank	Frank Faylen

'Get Going' is an unpretentious comedy-drama with sufficient verve and sparkle to provide good support in the regular runs. It's a tongue-in-cheek tale about housing and male shortages in Washington, and makes little effort to be serious.

Grace McDonald arrives in Washington from New England, and shares room and clothes with Vera Vague, Maureen Cannon and Lois Collier. Getting typing job in a bureau, girl attracts attention of Robert Paige by dropping hints she might be employed by enemy spies. While tracking her down, the pair fall in love to provide humorous complications until windup when Miss McDonald really uncovers headquarters of a spy ring.

Paige and Miss McDonald team in good style to carry the major assignments; with broad comedy supplied by Vera Vague, Walter Catlett and Frank Faylen. Lillian Cornell smacks over personality with delivery of 'Siboney' in a night club sequence, while Maureen Cannon sings two Milton Rosen-Everett Carter tunes, 'Got Love' and 'Hold That Line.' Milburn Stone, Lois Collier and Nana Bryant are okay in support. Direction by Jean Yarbrough swings along at a zestful pace, with gag lines and situations neatly timed for audience reaction. *Walt.*

2 Senoritas From Chicago

(SONGS)

Columbia release of Wallace MacDonald production. Features Joan Davis, Jinx Falkenburg. Directed by Frank Woodruff. Screenplay, Stanley Rubin and Maurice Tombragel, based on original by Steven Vas; camera, L. W. O'Connell; editor, Jerome Thoms. At Strand, Brooklyn, N. Y., dual, June 18, '43. Running time, **63 MINS.**

Daisy Baker	Joan Davis
Gloria	Jinx Falkenburg
Maria	Ann Savage
Lena	Leslie Brooks
Louise	Ramsey Ames
Jeff Kenyon	Bob Haymes
Rupert Shannon	Emory Parnell
Sam Grohman	Douglas Leavitt
Gilberto Garcia	Muni Seroff
Armando Silva	Max Willenz
Mike	Stanley Brown
Bruiser	Frank Sully
Chester T. Allgood	Charles C. Wilson
Miffins	Romaine Callender

Joan Davis' solid comedy characterization helps sell an otherwise third-rate film about show biz. Bob Haymes' vocalizing and the voices of Jinx Falkenburg and Ann Savage account for the rest of the picture's limited b.o.

Play agents may be offended, but Joan Davis, a refuse-sorter in a Chicago hotel, peddles plays on the side. She manages to sell a discarded Portguese script to a New York producer without the consent or knowledge of its authors. Jinx Falkenburg and Ann Savage, sporting phoney Porto accents, pass themselves off as the authors' sisters and talk their way into leading roles. Production is set, rehearsals underway when the real authors sell the original copy of the play to another producer. Two rival hoofers, Leslie Brooks and Ramsey Ames, spill the beans and this leads to unauthorized jail sentences for Misses Davis, Falkenburg and Savage and their producer Emory Parnell. Broadway careers for all are insured, however, when Bob Haymes, Parnell's assistant, is pursuaded to produce a musical he has had up his sleeve.

The entire plot is a plot to get Miss Falkenburg to sing and display her well-tanned limbs in several rhumba numbers. But in the last analysis she and the other cast members merely play straight man for Miss Davis, whose burlesque is broad and whose antics get the laughs.

THE DARK TOWER

(BRITISH-MADE)

London, June 8.

Warner Bros. production and release. Features Ben Lyon, Anne Crawford, David Farrar. Directed by Joyn Harlow. Screen adaptation by Brock Williams from play by George S. Kaufman and Alexander Woollcott. Reviewed at Warner theatre, London, June 7 '43. Running time, **90 MINS.**

Phil Danton	Ben Lyon
Mary	Anne Crawford
Tom Danton	David Farrar
Torg	Herbert Lom
Willie	Frederick Burtwell
Towers	Bill Hartnell
Madame Shogun	Josephine Wilson
Eve	Elsie Wagstaffe
Dr. Wilson	J. H. Roberts

A rambling melodrama with little boxoffice appeal, 'The Dark Tower' unfolds 90 minutes of trite entertainment. Devoid of originality, carrying no punch in its overlong footage, it's destined to play a minor role on double features.

As a buildup for two potential stars, it's a sorry tryout, too; Anne Crawford and David Farrar, starred with the veteran Ben Lyon, prove stilted and amateurish, although the inane dialog is a factor, too. Herbert Lom, however, gives a hint of promise, although he should play down his marked acting resemblance to Peter Lorre.

Story is a muddled affair of mesmerism with a circus background. One Torg, gifted with hypnotic powers, is given a job in a big top whose owner's brother is a trapeze artist in love with the partner in his act. The owner upsets their act and romance, climaxing his melodramatics by hypnotizing the girl into trying to kill her partner.

Uncertain in its treatment, the situation loses dramatic value, and the tame finale—with the death of the villain at the hands of another member of this strange circus—leaves the spectator wondering what it is all about—and why it was ever made.

The overlong footage could be considerably cut, for two or three circus acts are extraneously brought into the proceedings.

Incidentally, Miss Crawford, too, bears a resemblance to another Hollywood star—Jeannette Macdonald. Ben Lyon wanders aimlessly through the vapid goings-on.

Days of Old Cheyenne

Republic release of Eddy White production. Stars Don 'Red' Barry; features Lynn Merrick, William Haade, Herbert Rawlinson, Emmett 'Pappy' Lynn. Directed by Elmer Clifton. Screenplay, Norman S. Hall; camera, Reggie Lanning; editor, Harry Keller. At New York, N. Y., dualed week June 15, '43. Running time, **56 MINS.**

Clint Ross	Don 'Red' Barry
Nancy Carlyle	Lynn Merrick
Big Bill Harmon	William Haade
Tombstone Boggs	Emmett 'Pappy' Lynn
Gov. Shelby	Herbert Rawlinson
John Carlyle	Charles Miller
Steve Brackett	William Ruhl
Bobby	Harry McKim
Slim Boyd	Robert Kortman
Higgins	Nolan Leary
Pete	Ken Duncan

With Don Barry in the lead, this shapes up as a strong dual entry for prairie-meller patrons.

Barry plays a cowpuncher whose handy dukes win him the job of town marshal shortly after he arrives in Cheyenne, down to his last dollar. He wins the favor of William Haade, political boss of the Wyoming territory, and is ultimately kicked upstairs to governor. Showdown comes when Barry fails to cotton to Haade's crooked schemes. Climax, when Barry single-handedly nabs Haade for the murder of a youngster, winds up into a nifty gun duel.

Barry maintains his rep for riding, shooting and general action, while Haade does okay on the villainy. Emmett 'Pappy' Lynn is excellent as Barry's sidekick. Herbert Rawlinson has a minor role as the retiring governor while Lynn Merrick again registers as the femme. Harry Mc-Kim and Charles Miller head the support.

Direction by Elmer Clifton, camera by Reggie Lanning and story by Norman S. Hall are satisfactory.

Wear.

SARONG GIRL
(MUSICAL)

Monogram release of Philip N. Krasne production. Stars Ann Corio; features Tim Ryan, Irene Ryan, Mantan Moreland, Bill Henry, Damian O'Flynn, Johnny 'Scat' Davis, Mary Gordon. Directed by Arthur Dreifuss. Story and adaptation, Charles R. Marion and Arthur Hoerl; additional dialog, Tim Ryan; editor, Carl Pierson; songs, Lou Hercher and Andy Liona; camera, Mack Stengler. At Palace, N. Y., dual, week June 17, '43. Running time, 60 MINS.

Dixie Barlow......................Ann Corio
Tim Raynor........................Tim Ryan
Irene Raynor......................Irene Ryan
Maxwell.....................Mantan Moreland
Jeff Baxter.......................Bill Henry
Gil Gailord.................Damian O'Flynn
Scat Davis...............Johnny 'Scat' Davis
Mattie..........................Mary Gordon
Mr. Jefferson Baxter........Henry Kolker
Barbara.........................Gwen Kenyon
Sergeant O'Brien............Charles Jordan
Miss Ellsworth................Betty Blythe
Mr. Chase................Charles Williams

'Sarong Girl,' third picture for the former strip-teaser, Ann Corio, fails to increase her stock as a film personality, though in spots it has entertainment quality and, on the musical side, is fairly good. Strictly a dualer.

The Johnny 'Scot' Davis band, which plays several hot numbers, and the comedy contributions by the former radio team of Tim and Irene Ryan, as well as the song, 'I'm Nobody's Child,' which Miss Ryan does well, help to offset the weaknesses of the story and the listlessness of Arthur Dreifuss' direction. Nor does Philip N. Krasne's production offer much.

Miss Corio, who sings and dances, plays a burlesque queen who is arrested at the instigation of a bluenose and placed on probation for 160 days after her attorney has put up a heartwringing plea in behalf of Miss Corio's mother, who doesn't exist. In order to carry out the court decision placing the burlesque gal in the custody of her mother, the counselor digs up an inmate of an old ladies' home to play the part. After Miss Corio sets her cap for the son of the reformer who caused her arrest, in order to get even with him, the phony mother turns on her and squeals but ultimately agrees to adoption, squaring things.

Miss Corio is paired with Damian O'Flynn, who plays her attorney and does a nice job of it. Figuring temporarily on the romantic side is Bill Henry, whose performance is not as impressive as that of O'Flynn's. Tim Ryan is a bookie, while Irene Ryan appears as his heckling wife. Mantan Moreland, vet colored comic as Ryan's man Friday, does well and looks to be going places.

The Davis band is spotted in a night club setting. 'Tawai,' an Hawaiian number, is sung by Miss Corio, backed by a chorus line, and 'Woofie Hula,' in the nature of Ha-

waiian jive, is done by the star and Davis, together with the chorines. Davis, who plays a hot trumpet, also gives out vocally with the old favorite, 'Darling Nellie Gray.' *Char.*

RHYTHM PARADE
(MUSICAL)

Monogram release of Sydney Williams production. Features N.T.G. (Nils T. Granlund), Gale Storm, Robert Lowery, Margaret Dumont, Chick Chandler, Cliff Nazarro, Ted Fio Rito's orchestra, Mills Bros., Candy Candido and Florentine Gardens Revue. Directed by Howard Bretherton and Dave Gould. Story and adaptation, Carl Foreman and Charles R. Marion; editor, Carl Pierson; camera, Mack Stengler; songs, Dave Oppenheim, Roy Ingraham and Charles Cherokee. At Abbey, N. Y., week of June 18, '43. Running time, 68 MINS.

Granny.............N.T.G. (Nils T. Granlund)
Sally............................Gale Storm
Jimmy........................Robert Lowery
Ophelia....................Margaret Dumont
Speed.......................Chick Chandler
Rocks........................Cliff Nazarro
Connie...........................Jan Wiley
Candy.......................Candy Candido
Sparkie.........................Julie Milton
Patsy...........................Sugar Geise
Dancer....................Jean Foreman
Florentine Gardens Revue, Mills Bros.,
Ted Fio Rito's Orchestra.

The N.T.G. (Nils T. Granlund) floor show from his Florentine Gardens in Hollywood, including the Ted Fio Rito band, a line of 36 girls and others, form the background in 'Rhythm Parade,' a musical romance that should do satisfactorily in face of the present demands for more escapist entertainment. Film includes three new numbers, 'Mimi From Tahiti,' 'Tootin' My Own Horn' and 'Petticoat Army,' as well as several old ones such as 'Tiger Rag,' 'In a Victory Garden,' 'Sweet Sue,' 'Dark Eyes' and 'Wait Till the Sun Shines Nellie.' Mills Bros. do exceptionally well with a special arrangement of 'Darling Nellie Gray.' Other songs are handled by Gale Storm, the Fio Rito band, Robert Lowery, Jan Wiley and others.

A nitery forms the setting for the picture, while the story concerns the efforts of a singer (Miss Wiley) to spoil the professional chances of Miss Storm after learning that the latter is taking care of an eight-month's old baby, the nephew of her sister. The baby (Julie Milton) is planted in Miss Storm's dressing room but for a happy finish the kid's real mother returns from Honolulu to clear up the parentage problem. Lowery, leading man of Rock's legit show, is paired with Miss Storm on the romantic end, while the double-talking Cliff Nazarro is gambler and backer of a new show. Chick Chandler does an impressive job as Miss Storm's press agent. In addition to mixing into the story, N.T.G. acts as master of ceremonies for his Florentine Gardens revue. Featured with the Fio Rito band is Candy Candido, comedy bass viol player, while others include Jean Foreman and Sugar Geise, dancers.

Film has been ably directed by Howard Bretherton and Dave Gould, moves at a snappy pace and has been given good production by Sydney Williams. *Char.*

A GENTLE GANGSTER

Republic release of W. W. Hackel production. Stars Barton MacLane; features Molly Lamont, Dick Wessel, Joyce Compton, Jack LaRue. Directed by Phil Rosen. Screenplay, Jefferson Parker, Al Martin; camera, Harry Neumann; editor, Martin G. Cohn. At Strand, Brooklyn, N. Y., June 18, '43. Running time, 57 MINS.

Mike Hallit...............Barton MacLane
Ann Hallit...................Molly Lamont
Steve Parker..................Dick Wessel
Kitty Parker................Joyce Compton
Hugo............................Jack LaRue
Al Malone........................Cy Kendall
Helen Barton................Rosella Towne
Joe Barton........................Ray Teal
Rev. Hamilton.............Crane Whitley
Lefty.......................Elliott Sullivan
Charles...................Anthony Warde

A warmed-over story about a racketeer who goes straight, 'A Gentle Gangster' gives Barton MacLane

ample opportunity to strut his stuff as a two-fisted fighter both against and for law-and-order. For those weaned on gangster films, however, this is a mild offering.

MacLane, Dick Wessel and Ray Teal ran a speak and hustled beer back in 1923 but gave it up for legit careers when their girl friends, Molly Lamont, Joyce Compton and Rosella Towne, threatened to leave them. The conversion isn't very convincing, as everybody appeared to have been thriving on the rackets. However, 20 years later finds the trio and their wives respectable citizens of a respectable community. There is no clue as to how they got that way. The old days seem slated for a comeback with the appearance of Jack LaRue, his roadhouse and strongarm men. When LaRue tries to muscle in on the peaceful community, MacLane and his former guerrillas beat him at his own game and drive him out of town, preserving its purity and innocence.

Strictly a dualer, 'A Gentle Gangster' also has little to recommend it in the way of acting. MacLane, the principals and the supporting players do a routine job of routine roles. Fortunately, direction permits for no lagging and the film is over before it can overstay its welcome.

Miniature Reviews

'Best Foot Forward' (Filmusical) (Technicolor) (M-G). Smart and spontaneous youthful filmusical with Harry James and ork. Solid biz in all runs.

'Dixie' (Musical) (Color) (Par). OK for the summer b.o. Light Technicolored filmusical, with Crosby and Lamour.

'The Constant Nymph' (WB). Drama of frustrated love should have moderate appeal for women to hit profitable biz.

'Hit the Ice' (Songs) (U). Smash Abbott and Costello laugh hit; one of their best. Top biz and holdovers indicated.

'Henry Aldrich Swings It' (Par). Okay entry in the Aldrich series will provide support for the family bookings.

'The Black Raven' (PRC). Murder mystery for lower half of duals.

'Yanks Ahoy' (UA). Lesser Hal Roach comedy; dualer.

'Wings Over the Pacific' (Mono). Robert Armstrong and Inez Cooper in lightweight meller; for twinners.

'Santa Fe Scouts' (Rep). Only moderately okay western.

BEST FOOT FORWARD
(Color)
(MUSICAL)

Hollywood, June 29.

Metro release of Arthur Freed production. Stars Lucille Ball; features William Gaxton, Virginia Weidler, Tommy Dix, Nancy Walker, June Allyson, Kenny Bowers, Gloria De Haven, Jack Jordan, Harry James and his Music Makers. Directed by Edward Buzzell. Screenplay by Irving Brecher and Fred F. Finklehoffe; book by John Cecil Holm; songs, Hugh Martin and Ralph Blane, as produced on the stage by George Abbott; camera, Leonard Smith; editor, Blanche Sewell; musical direction, Lennie Hayton; dances, Charles Walters. Tradeshown in L. A., June 29, '43. Running time, 93 MINS.

Lucille Ball.....................By Herself
Jack O'Riley...............William Gaxton
Helen Schlessenger.......Virginia Weidler
Bud
Elwood C. Hooper }........Tommy Dix
Blind Date (Nancy)........Nancy Walker
Minerva.......................June Allyson
Dutch........................Kenny Bowers
Ethel.....................Gloria De Haven
Hunk...........................Jack Jordan
Miss Delaware Water Gap...Beverly Tyler
Chester Short....................Chill Wills
Major Reeber................Henry O'Neill
Miss Talbert.....................Sara Haden
Captain Bradd..........Donald MacBride
Greenie....................Bobby Stebbins
Killer.......................Darwood Kaye
Colonel Harkrider........Morris Ankrum
Mrs. Dalyrimple..............Nana Bryant
Harry James and His Music Makers

This Technicolored filmusical version of George Abbott's stage production retains all of the youthful enthusiasm and spontaneity of the original, with addition of Harry James and his orchestra for generous supply of his trumpeteering and jump music. Result is slick entertainment for solid biz in all datings—and that Harry James flash for the marquees will catch heavy trade from the juves and collegians all around the country.

Although picture is aimed directly at the younger generation, there's sufficient diversion and lightness to provide strong appeal for the adults. Following the lines established by Abbott with the stage presentation, Metro displays a number of new faces and teen-age talent including five—Tommy Dix, Nancy Walker, June Allyson, Kenny Bowers and Jack Jordan—from the original stage cast.

Scholastic zest and pep, and the musical interludes, successfully carry the extremely fragile story premise. Annual prom and commencement ceremonies of the military prep school provides excuse for Hollywood film star to make an appearance to further her publicity efforts, and to accept wildly-made promise of stude to make her queen of the dance. Complications resulting from the youth and his pals trying to renege and keep the glamour gal under cover during the evening, gives wide latitude for many rounds of humorous situations.

Prep school dance allows for generous appearances of Harry James and his orch, with the maestro giving out plentifully with jump and jive tunes that will have the kids stomping and romping in the aisles. James is showmanly displayed several times performing on the trumpet for camera closeups, with his followers also being treated to shots of various sections of his aggregation. He also steps onto the dance floor for comedy routine with comedienne Nancy Walker which is a laugh highlight.

Only three of the original songs in the show are retained in the picture—'Buckle Down Winsocki,' 'Ev'ry Time,' and 'The Three B's.' But five new ones are delivered by Ralph Lane and Hugh Martin, who wrote the show score and were brought to the studio to supply the added tunes. Best of the additions is a fast jump number, 'Alive and Kicking,' effectively delivered by Nancy Walker with the James band providing strong spotlight accompaniment. Second in probable importance of the new tunes is 'Wish I May,' a novelty number used for production display and choral and band rendition.

Metro effectively combines the three stage juves with young talent from around Hollywood. Tommy Dix is most prominently displayed among the boys as the bewildered kid who invites Miss Ball to the affair, and is focal point of the resultant complications. Miss Walker is a comedienne of wide talents; stumbling, mugging, singing and dancing with veteran timing and delivery in each endeavor. She can stick around pictures for a long time. June Allyson, also from stage version, is both a looker and good vocalist. Bowers and Jordan are prominent as Dix's pals. Virginia Weidler neatly handles role of the girl shelved to supply prom admittance for Miss Ball, while Goria De Haven (daughter of Carter De Haven) grooves nicely in a supporting spot.

Oldsters, in comparison to the scholastic-age performers, include the glamorous Miss Ball, who's an eyeful with Technicolor, accentuating the dazzle of her brilliant red hair-do; William Gaxton as the go-getting press agent; hick photog Chill Wills; school head Henry O'Neill, and Donald McBride.

Studio gives the picture elaborate production mounting in the few sets required and in dance ensembles of boys and girls for background to spotlight the various routines. Production number for 'My First Prom' is outstanding color display, with the girls in white gowns carrying bouquets of deep red roses a most contrasting effect. Director Eddie Buzzell turns in a most showmanly job, neatly tempoing the humorous adventures of the prep school proceedings. Dance direction by Charles Walters effectively presents the various ensembles, while photography by Leonard Smith adds much to the richness of the general production. *Walt.*

DIXIE

(Color)
(MUSICAL)

Paramount release of Paul Jones production. Stars Bing Crosby, Dorothy Lamour; features Marjorie Reynolds, Billy de Wolfe, Lynne Overman, Raymond Walburn, Eddie Foy, Jr. Directed by A. Edward Sutherland. Screenplay, Karl Tunberg, Darrell Ware; adaptation, Claude Binyon; story, Wm. Rankin; songs, Johnny Burke, James Van Heusen (besides Dan Emmett's originals); music direction, Robt. Emmett Dolan; dances, Seymour Felix; vocal arrangements, Joseph J. Lilley; music asst., Arthur Franklin; settings and costumes, Raoul Pene duBois; camera, William C. Mellor, Morgan Padelford, Gordon Jennings; editor, Wm. Flannery. At Paramount, N. Y., week June 23, '43. Running time, 89 MINS.

Dan Emmett....................Bing Crosby
Millie Cook....................Dorothy Lamour
Mr. Bones....................Billy de Wolfe
Jean Mason....................Marjorie Reynolds
Mr. Whitlock....................Lynne Overman
Mr. Cook....................Raymond Walburn
Mr. Pelham....................Eddie Foy, Jr.
Mr. Mason....................Grant Mitchell
Mrs Mason....................Clara Blandick
Homer....................Tom Herbert
Mr. Devereau....................Olin Howard
Mr. La Plant....................Robert Warwick
Headwaiter....................Fortunio Bonanova
Man in Restaurant....................Brandon Hurst
Woman in Restaurant...Josephine Whittell
Headwaiter in Restaurant.....Paul McVay
Captain of Waiters.......Charles La Tone
News Vendor....................Charles R. Moore
Bar Keeper....................Tom Kennedy

'Dixie' is a Technicolorful moneygetter, ideal for the summer b.o. It has charm, lightness, good new songs by Johnny Burke and Jimmy Van Heusen, the classic oldies by Dan Emmett ('Dixie'), and some spirituals, such as 'Swing Low Sweet Chariot.' And it has Bing Crosby and Dorothy Lamour for the marquee.

'Dixie' is the saga of pre-Civil War minstrel man and songwriter, Daniel Decatur Emmett (Crosby), who had a song in his soul, and an innate showmanship which inspired what later became the standard blackface minstrel makeup. Born of duress and privation, the vagabond troupers in a New Orleans music hall set a standard which, as the story develops, wound up in the rousing and spirited 'I Wish I Were in Dixie,' as result of a catastrophic backstage fire.

The story itself is literally a three-fire affair. It seems as if Crosby's careless corncob pipe is always getting him into red-hot trouble. It runs the gamut of burning down his fiancee's father's house (opening), and the backstage finale, which, however, caused Crosby to heroically keep singing 'Dixie,' accelerating it into the spirited tempo with which we now identify the classic American folk song.

As a story it's lightweight. It's also doubtlessly a very free fictionization of Dan Emmett's career, but it's sufficient unto the purpose thereof. Thus are introduced Dorothy Lamour as the landlord's daughter of fickle heart; Marjorie Reynolds as Crosby's paralyzed bride; and Billy de Wolfe, making his film debut as Mr. Bones, from whence supposedly stemmed the now time-honored Bones and Tambo end-men nomenclatures of minstrelsy. Self-styled world champion bones-player, there is more emphasis on de Wolfe's card-cheating and easy virtue, ranging from gypping the New Orleans French restaurateurs out of epicurean productions to cheating a theatre-owner into an unwilling partnership. This was de Wolfe's first and last Par picture before going into the service and he's a cinch for a comeback. The former nitery-vaude mimic reads his lines with conviction and deports himself with much poise and ease.

Lynne Overman's last performance as the luckless trouper is in his usual vein of superfine characterization. Ever a facile farceur, the veteran actor's post-mortem screen performance is a fitting tribute to his histrionic prowess, long recognized and long familiar.

For the rest, Eddie Foy, Jr., is likewise an excellent minstrel; Raymond Walburn is the kindly landlord, himself formerly of the theatre, hence his weakness for indigent actors (with result his fretful daughter, Miss Lamour, is forever hounding them for back-rent). Grant Mitchell is Miss Reynolds' impatient father, and the rest are bits.

The new songs are clicko. 'Sunday, Monday and Always' and 'She's from Missouri' are Hit Parade material, and the Negro spiritual on the riverboat was effectively introduced by Crosby.

Productionally there is plenty of good stuff for both the nostalgic hepcats and for the uninitiate who may take their mistrelsy yak-yak-yak laughs straight. The Crosby and de Wolfe frightwigs are something to behold, the boys evidencing they personally enjoyed the old hokum bucketfuls they were called on to dispense. The challenge song-and-dance of the end-men, the impromptu manner of variety entertainment, the evolution of the interlocutor (only whiteface member of the cast), the gay and colorful habiliments of minstrelsy (Raoul Pene duBois did a dandy costume-designing job here) and all the rest of it are in the best 1943 tradition.

Per usual, Crosby is in high with his vocalizing. Whether it's 'Dixie' or the new Tin Pan Alley interpolations, the crooner is never from Dixie when it comes to lyric interpretations. The weaker the film vehicles, the greater is the impact of the Crosby technique. And while this isn't exactly a weak-sister, the book is one of those things. But between the Eddie Sutherland direction, plus Paul Jones' very okay production, and Crosby's singing and trouping, it more than offsets the libretto. Crosby now is as standard among the male singing toppers as the Four Freedoms, and today he shapes up more and more as the Will Rogers-type of solid American actor-citizen. He enjoys a stature, especially because of his radio programs, enjoyed by no other singing star in show business. And, so, if Paramount calls on him to forego the sirenish Lamour for the chair-ridden Marjorie Reynolds, that's OK too. Yet despite all the above, it's significant too that newcomer de Wolfe almost steals the picture when it comes to the airy persiflage, a field wherein Crosby is no slouch either, excepting that in this instance de Wolfe has the saucier lines. *Abel.*

The Constant Nymph

Hollywood, June 26.

Warner Bros. release of Henry Blanke production. Stars Charles Boyer, Joan Fontaine, Alexis Smith; features Charles Coburn, Brenda Marshall, Dame May Whitty, Peter Lorre. Directed by Edmund Goulding. Screenplay, Kathryn Scola, from novel and play by Margaret Kennedy, Basil Dean; camera, Tony Gaudio; editor, David Weisbert; asst. director, Jack Sullivan; music, Erich Wolfgang Korngold; arrangements, Hugo Friedhofer; music director, Leo F. Forbstein. Tradeshown at studio, June 25, '43. Running time, 106 MINS.

Lewis Dodd....................Charles Boyer
Tessa Sanger....................Joan Fontaine
Florence Creighton....................Alexis Smith
Charles Creighton....................Charles Coburn
Toni Sanger....................Brenda Marshall
Lady Longborough......Dame May Whitty
Fritz Bercovy....................Peter Lorre
Paula Sanger....................Joyce Reynolds
Kate Sanger....................Jean Muir
Albert Sanger....................Montagu Love
Roberto....................Edward Ciannelli
Marie....................Jeanine Crispin
Miss Hamilton....................Doris Lloyd
Lina....................Joan Blair
Dr. Renee....................Andre Charlot
Kiril Trigorin....................Richard Ryan
Thorpe....................Crauford Kent
Georges....................Marcel Dalio
Concert Soloist....................Clemence Groves

This is the film version of the novel and play of several years ago under same title. Despite its over-length, there's moderate women's appeal presented in the frustrated love dramatics to provide profitable biz in the regular runs. Marquee voltage of starring trio of Charles Boyer, Joan Fontaine and Alexis Smith will add to its general pull.

Picture has been finished for about a year, but held back on release due to subsequent topical features that could not be shelved with any degree of safety. Devoting plenty of footage to character delineations and incidental episodes, it results in a bumpy screen tale with interlay of both draggy and interesting sequences. Major portion of excess footage is on the front end, where 40 minutes is consumed in setting up detailed background for the final event, which is a love triangle, with Boyer the focal point for conflict between teen-ager played by Miss Fontaine and the older Miss Smith. That 40-minute stretch hits yawning periods.

This early portion serves to detail movement of Boyer, composer of promise but lacking the necessary fire to write his outstanding composition, from Brussels to home of his friend and mentor (Montagu Love) in Switzerland. Of the four daughters in the house, Miss Fontaine is next to the youngest, with adolescent adoration for Boyer. When Love dies and girls' uncle (Charles Coburn) arrives from England with his own daughter (Miss Smith), Boyer and latter embark on romance culminating in marriage. Miss Fontaine and younger sister (Joyce Reynolds) are taken back to England for schooling, while the socialite wife endeavors to parade her husband's musical talents in her circle. Boyer finally rebels, and when Miss Fontaine returns from school and provides inspiration for his writing, the wife senses the girl's influence as love, and proceeds to combat her by making things miserable. Boyer, placed in the center of the dramatics, endeavors without success to smooth things over, until finally he discovers he's also in love with the young girl. During presentation of his new symphonic poem, latter dies of a heart attack due to elation over his initial success.

Miss Fontaine brilliantly handles her role, with Boyer also neatly cast. Miss Smith is excellent, while Coburn provides his usual strong performance as the crusty Englishman. Miss Reynolds demonstrates ability and personality, while balance of support has been carefully chosen.

Script covers plenty of ground and detail, but general tightening would have helped materially. There's a tang of the stage in the unfolding, which director Edmund Goulding found impossible to overcome with his careful and even-tempoed direction. Photography by Tony Gaudio is topgrade, and picture carries 'A' production background in all departments. *Walt.*

HIT THE ICE

(SONGS)

Hollywood, June 25.

Universal release of Alex Gottlieb production. Stars Bud Abbott, Lou Costello; features Ginny Simms. Directed by Charles Lamont. Screenplay, Robert Lees, Frederic Rinaldo, John Grant from original by True Boardman; camera, Charles Van Enger; editor, Frank Gross; assistant director, Howard Christie; songs, Harry Revel, Paul Francis Webster; musical numbers staged by Sammy Lee; music director, Charles Previn; skating number staged by Harry Losee. Previewed at Pantages, June 24, '43. Running time, 81 MINS.

Flash Fulton....................Bud Abbott
Weejie McCoy....................Lou Costello
Marcia Manning....................Ginny Simms
Dr. Bill Elliot....................Patric Knowles
Peggy Osborne....................Elyse Knox
Buster....................Joseph Sawyer
Phil....................Marc Lawrence
'Silky' Fellowsby.........Sheldon Leonard
Johnny Long Orch
with
Helen Young, Gene Williams, The Four Teens

Packed with solid laugh entertainment, 'Hit the Ice' should roll up top grosses in all bookings. Utilizing the comedic abilities of Bud Abbott and Lou Costello in a compact script, in contrast to previous Abbott and Costello features, this one carries more than passing semblance of story credulity. This is their last before Lou Costello because incapacitated.

Not to be overlooked, in addition to the script by Robert Lees, Frederic Rinaldo and John Grant, is the expert direction by Charles Lamont. Latter, with extensive experience in the two-reel field of silent comedy, rounds out every comedy sequence with tailored precision.

Abbott and Costello, street candid cameramen, become mistaken for Detroit gunmen by bank robber Sheldon Leonard, are bystanders at the bank holdup and finally head west to Sun Valley to evade arrest on suspicion. Also going west is Leonard and his two thugs, medico Patric Knowles, nurse Elyse Knox, songstress Ginny Simms and Johnny Long with his orchestra, with Miss Simms and band to launch engagement at the winter resort. With the two comics performing as waiters, and laying plans to recover the stolen bank coin, picture proceeds to unfold several laugh episodes in the snow and ice district until Abbott and Costello capture the bandit trio and recoup the money.

Comedians launch a fast pace at the start, with the bank robbery, visit to the hospital and wild race to a fire providing plenty of opportunity for physical and dialog zaniness. Even train trip west gives the boys something to do, while Costello's adventures as end man on a snap-the-whip routine on the ice rink is a smackeroo laugh highlight. Climactic routine slides the two boys down the mountainside is a standout chase which also includes Leonard and his confederates.

Abbott and Costello romp in their usual top style, with strong support from Miss Simms, Knowles, Miss Knox, Long and orch. and gang trio of Leonard, Marc Lawrence and Joseph Sawyer.

Miss Simms sings four songs by Harry Revel and Paul Francis Webster, 'I'm Like a Fish Out of Water,' 'Happiness Bound,' 'I'd Like to Set You to Music' and 'Slap Polka,' with the first three having best chance for public consideration. In addition to clicking in presenting the tunes, Miss Simms has advantage of excellent photography throughout. Long and his band, the Four Teens, Helen Young and Gene Williams add to the musical end of the proceedings, although brief appearances of Long in front of the camera for lines display his self-consciousness.

Production layout is of 'A' rating throughout, with photography by far the best provided for the comedy team at Universal. There's class to the settings and general technical contributions. *Walt.*

Henry Aldrich Swings It

(ONE SONG)

Hollywood, June 23.

Paramount release of Walter MacEwen (Michel Kraike) production. Features Jimmy Lydon. Directed by Hugh Bennett. Screenplay by Muriel Roy Bolton; camera, Daniel Fapp; editor, Archie Marshek; song, Jule Styne, Kim Gannon. Tradeshown in L. A. June 22, '43. Running time, 64 MINS.

Henry Aldrich	Jimmy Lydon
Dizzy Stevens	Charlie Smith
Mr. Aldrich	John Litel
Mrs. Aldrich	Olive Blakeney
Mimi Gray	Mimi Chandler
Mr. Bradley	Vaughan Glaser
Louise Elliott	Marion Hall
Margie	Beverly Hudson
Josef Altman	Fritz Feld
Boyle	Charles Arnt

Henry Aldrich stumbles his way in and out of trouble in this standard entry in the series which will get adequate reaction in the family houses as a dual supporter. Despite the obvious concoction of misadventure for the juvenile to become focal point of involvement, picture has sufficient basic lightness to carry through as a second feature in the subsequent houses.

Henry, again portrayed by Jimmy Lydon, becomes involved in puppy-love affair with the new high school music teacher, Marion Hall. This projects him into the band as a violinist; his dad gets a slight crush for the teacher; visiting concert violinist loses his valuable Strad through unintentional switch by Henry; and then it becomes the usual merry-go-round until the Strad is returned, and fiddle thieves are thwarted.

Lydon continues to groove neatly as the scholastic muddler who always gets into trouble, with Charlie Smith typed as his dizzy sidekick. Mimi Chandler, daughter of Kentucky senator Happy Chandler, steps in as Lydon's doting 'steady,' with Miss Hall turning in okay performance as the music teacher. John Litel and Olive Blakeney again appear as the parents, with Vaughan Glaser the grouchy principal. Fritz Feld is the temperamental violinist, with Charles Arnt a fast-talking insurance investigator.

Along the line of Henry's musical career, group of the school orch forms a swing band which gets into trouble by playing at a nightspot which is raided by the cops. Beverly Hudson, with brief role of a youthful comedienne, steps in to be vocalist with the band, and handles warbling for one tune by Jule Styne and Kim Gannon, 'Ding Dong, Sing a Song.' Direction by Hugh Bennett maintains good pace to the proceedings. *Walt.*

THE BLACK RAVEN

Producers Releasing Corp. release of Sigmund Neufeld production. Features George Zucco, Wanda McKay, Noel Madison, Bob Randall, Byron Foulger, Charlie Middleton, Robert Middlemass. Directed by Sam Newfield. Story and adaptation, Fred Myton; editor, Holbrook N. Todd; camera, Robert Cline. At New York, N. Y., half dual bill, week June 22, '43. Running time, 62 MINS.

Bradford	George Zucco
Lee Winfield	Wanda McKay
Mike Bardoni	Noel Madison
Allen Bentley	Bob Randall
Horace Weatherby	Byron Foulger
Sheriff	Charlie Middleton
Tim Winfield	Robert Middlemass
Sandy	Glenn Strange
Whitey Cole	I. Stanford Jolley

Only virtue of 'The Black Raven' is its sometime suspense. It requires a generally faster pace, more inspired direction and peppier dialog. Rates considerably below average for low-budgeters.

Action takes place on a rainy night in a country inn known as the Black Raven, whose owner has a shady past. An assortment of droppers-in, caught in the storm, include an escaped convict who wants to even an old score with the proprietor of the inn, a bank cashier who has absconded $50,000, a boy and gal who are trying to get to Canada to get hitched, the father of the girl who's trying to intercept their elopement, and a man wanted by police who's after the 50 grand. A local sheriff trying to unravel two murders also figures.

The cast lacks impressiveness. Includes George Zucco, Wanda McKay, Noel Madison (vet villian), Bob Randall, Byron Foulger, Charlie Middleton and Robert Middlemass. Only comedy relief, and slight at that, is furnished by Middleton, playing the country sheriff. *Char.*

YANKS AHOY

United Artists release of Hal Roach-Fred Guiol production. Stars William Tracy, Joe Sawyer; features Marjorie Woodworth, Minor Watson, William Bakewell, Romaine Callender, Walter Woolf King, Robert Kent. Directed by Kurt Neumann. Screenplay, Eugene Conrad, Edward E. Seabrook; camera, Robert Pittack; editor, Richard Currier; special effects, Roy Seawright. Previewed in Projection Room, N. Y., June 24, '43. Running time, 60 MINS.

Sgt. Doubleday	William Tracy
Sgt. Ames	Joe Sawyer
Phyllis	Marjorie Woodworth
Capt. Scott	Minor Watson
Capt. Gillis	Walter Woolf King
Lt. Reeves	Robert Kent
Col. Elliott	Romaine Callender
Ensign Crosby	William Bakewell
Jenkins	Frank Faylen
Miss Potter	Marga Ann Deighton
Helmsman	Tom Seidel
Lt. Ransome	Lt. John Canady
Dr. Hadley	Irwin Stanley
Jap	Richard Loo
German	Frank Reicker
Second German	Rudolph Lindau
Corp. Quinn	Bud McTaggert
Sailor	Dan Lloyd
Cook Flynn	James Finlayson

This slaphappy comedy achieves what may well be a new low for clowning about the armed services in the current war. The old Sergeant Quirk-Capt. Flagg enmity angle is carried out by Sgts. Doubleday and Ames, played by William Tracy and Joe Sawyer, respectively, apparently being a continuation of their adventures in the army. Dull direction, ordinary scripting of a so-called original and the facial-gyration type of acting are further burdens. It's a minor entry for twinners.

Tracy finally wins overseas service as a sergeant despite his puny size. His ability to memorize anything he glims wins him the boat ride and keeps him in there punching despite the disparaging efforts of Sawyer. Once aboard the transport, it becomes a series of oldie slapstick gags, climaxing with the capture of a two-man Jap submarine with a fishing line. Others date back to the silent-comedy era.

Tracy is somewhat funny when given a chance. Sawyer, as his husky rival, mugs it but manages fairly well to portray the tough, blundering non-com. Marjorie Woodworth is the blonde nurse the two men flirt with, but she's in there primarily for decorative purposes. Minor Watson heads the support. Special effects by Roy Seawright most of time look like the minatures they are. *Wear.*

Wings Over the Pacific

Monogram release of Lindsley Parsons production. Features Inez Cooper, Edward Norris, Montagu Love, Robert Armstrong. Directed by Phil Rosen. Screenplay, George Sayre; camera, Mack Stengler; editor, Carl Pierson. At New York, N. Y., dualed week June 15, '43. Running time, 59 MINS.

Nona	Inez Cooper
Allan	Edward Norris
Butler	Montagu Love
Pieter	Robert Armstrong
Kurt	Henry Guttman
Harry	Ernie Adams
Chief	Santini Pauiloa
Taro	John Roth
Native	James Lono
2d Native	George Kamel
3d Native	Hawksha Paia
Jap Officer	Alex Havier

This is a badly done melodrama with unoriginal plot and inane dialog. Even the presence of Robert Armstrong, Montagu Love and Henry Guttman fail to lift it out of the category of extreme hokum. Extremely lesser picture for lower part of dualers.

Story about the veteran of World War No. 1 who seeks peace on a quiet Pacific isle, only to be disturbed by a German fighter pilot and U. S. Navy aviator, has been given considerable production. The American naval officer and Nazi advance scout for the Japs, both forced to land on the island after a dogfight, are interned by the peace-loving American and the native ruler. Of course, the Yank falls for the island beaut, daughter of the American. The real fireworks begin when the Nazi discovers oil on the isle and signals the Japs to land troops.

Montagu Love (recently deceased) lends some realism to his role of Jim Butler, the Yank gone native. Not as much can be said for Inez Cooper, as his daughter. She's rather attractive but neither acts or sings well. Ernie Adams, as Butler's pal and man-of-all work, provides a few invigorating comedy moments. Guttman makes a thoroughly despicable Nazi aviator while Edward Norris is passable as the Yank Navy man.

Robert Armstrong, as Dutch trader turned espionage agent for the Nazis, is not at home in this villain role, with his accent one of those things that he turns on and off. Support is headed by Satini Paulia, as the island chief. *Wear.*

SANTA FE SCOUTS

Republic release of Louis Gray production. Stars Tom Tyler, Jimmie Dodd, Bob Steele; features Lois Collier, John James, Elizabeth Valentine, Tom Chatterton. Directed by Howard Bretherton. Based on characters created by William Colt MacDonald; story and adaptation, Morton Grant and Betty Burbridge; editor, Charles Craft; camera, Reggie Lanning. At New York, N. Y., dual, week June 22, '43. Running time, 55 MINS.

Tucson Smith	Bob Steele
Stony Brooke	Tom Tyler
Lullaby Joslin	Jimmie Dodd
Claire Robbins	Lois Collier
Tim Clay	John James
Minerva Clay	Elizabeth Valentine
Neil Morgan	Tom Chatterton
Billy Dawson	Tom London
Wid Neighton	Budd Buster
Frank Howard	Jack Ingram
Ben Henderson	Kermit Maynard

Tom Tyler, Jimmie Dodd and Bob Steele, known as the Three Mesquiteers, have only what amounts to moderate horse-opera entertainment in 'Santa Fe Scouts.' It has less action than the average and is built around a story that fails to pack much interest.

The Mesquiteers, in this instance, come to the rescue of a prospective groom who is about to fall heir to ranch property owned by his mother. He is framed on a murder charge by outlaws who are occupying the ranch and hope to gain possession through a squatters' rights bill that has been passed. Meantime, the squatters are extorting money from ranchers who use the property to water their stock while driving it to market, something they are not supposed to do.

After finally getting evidence against a crooked lawyer who represents the owners of the ranch and learning the murder allegedly committed was not committed at all, they succeed in running the poachers off the property they're after.

Tyler, Dodd and Steele, a good trio combination, have able support in the two romantic leaders, John James and Lois Collier, while others include Elizabeth Valentine, mother of James, and Tom Chatterton, the conniving lawyer. Miss Valentine is an odd but effective westerns type who appears she could outcuss the best. *Char.*

Miniature Reviews

'Victory Through Air Power' (UA-Disney). Excellent transmutation of the Major de Seversky best-seller.

'Gals, Inc.' (Songs) (U). Program filmusical with 12 numbers to dominate footage. Okay dualer.

'Crime Doctor' (Col). Good meller entertainment.

'Laws of the Northwest' (Col). Average Chas. Starrett western.

'False Faces' (Rep). Trivial whodunit, strictly in the filler category.

'Ghosts on the Loose' (Mono). Another East Side Kids comedy thriller; lower half of duals.

'Fire in the Straw' (French-made). Jean Benoit-Levy production; a topflight French film.

'Under Secret Orders' (Guar). A dull remake about a German Mata Hari.

'Maravilla Del Toreo' (Mexican-made). Weak on script, but strong on bullfight shots. English titles.

Victory Thru Air Power

(COLOR)

United Artists release of Walt Disney production. By and with Major Alexander P. de Seversky. Seversky scenes directed by H. C. Porter; animation supervision, David Hand; story direction, Perc Pearce; story adaptation, T. Hee, Erdman Penner, Wm. Cottrell, Jim Bodrero, Geo. Stallings, Jose Rodriquez; music, Edward Plumb, Paul J. Smith, Oliver Wallace; sequence directors, Clyde Geronimi, Jack Kinney, James Algar; narration, Art Baker; director of photography, Ray Hennehan; editor, Jack Keefe; corps of artists, backgrounders and animators. Tradeshown in N. Y., July 2, '43. Running time, **65 MINS.**

'Victory Through Air Power' is as timely as the Allied's invasion plans. In fact it's almost out of tomorrow's headlines, excepting that Major Alexander P. de Seversky has been pounding the issue long since. Under Walt Disney's aegis, in 65 snappy minutes, a combination of super-animation, all in color, plus Technicolored photography with the Major himself participating, this is a highly skilled narration of the aerial scheme of things.

It's graphic enough for a 10-year-old to savvy, and it's interesting all the way. It's a skillful blend of cartoonics, documentation and prophesy which should combine well for the boxoffice. Apart from its entertainment values it should be made a must for anybody and everybody who is interested in the welfare of the Allied's war cause.

Historically, albeit kaleidoscopically, Disney and Major de Seversky trace the progress of aviation. It flashes back from the prophetic Gen. Billy Mitchell—to whom the film is dedicated—to 1903 when the Wright Bros. first succeeded in lifting a heavier-than-air craft off the ground. As it is unfolded, it indeed staggers the imagination, even in these fast-moving times, how much progress has been made in aviation.

In cartoon and narration is traced the Luftwaffe's exploits, plus the concluding arguments by de Seversky of how to beat Hitler in his Fortress Europa and finally how to overcome the Japs' present air-based advantages. The strategy of the use of air power, both across the Atlantic lifeline versus Hitler, and in the Pacific against Tojo, brings the war close to the auditor in a highly informative and graphic manner.

Disney and his battalion of artists, animators and backgrounders have not permitted the seriousness of the theme to completely dwarf their humor. There are the usual imaginative complement of Disneyisms in his cartoonics, and an excellent musical score to point it up.

Abel.

GALS, INCORPORATED

(SONG)

Hollywood, July 2.

Universal release of Will Cowan production. Features Leon Errol, Harriet Hilliard, Pied Pipers, Casa Loma orch. Directed by Leslie Goodwins. Screenplay by Edward Dein, suggested by story by Dave Guold and Charles Marion; camera, Jerome Ash; editor, Arthur Hilton; dances, Josephine Earl; musical director, Charles Previn; songs, Milton Rosen, Everett Carter. Previewed at studio July 1, '43. Running time, **60 MINS.**

Cornelius	Leon Errol
Gwen	Harriet Hilliard
Molly	Grace McDonald
Bill	David Bacon
Bets Moran	Betty Kean
Bubbles	Maureen Cannon
Vicki	Lillian Cornell
Jennifer	Minna Phillips
Virginia	Marion Daniels

Pied Pipers
Glen Gray and Casa Loma Orchestra

Musical numbers—to total of 12—predominate in this program number that will suffice as supporter in the subsequent duals. It's another in the moderate budgeter group of musicals on the Universal program.

Idea of group of girls operating a nightspot, backed by a senile playboy, provides necessary, but decidedly fragile, framework for plentiful display of songs, dance specialties and musical numbers by Glen Gray and the Casa Loma ork. Playboy, Leon Errol, masquerades Grace McDonald as his wife when his sister arrives from the west to cut off his income unless he's settled down. Usual farcical episodes ensue, including arrival of Errol's son to grab the girl from the pater.

Gray and his band provide musical accompaniment throughout, and also step in for three spotlighted band numbers. Grace McDonald, Harriet Hilliard and Lillian Cornell split up the solos, while Pied Pipers (quartet of three men and a girl) deliver two songs. Betty Kean catches attention with two comedy dance routines, while Margery Daye does an acrobatic dance at floorshow. Three new songs by Milton Rosen and Everett Carter are handled by Misses McDonald and Hilliard. Former sings 'All the Time It's You' and 'Here's Your Kiss,' with latter having fair chance for plug attention. Miss Hilliard steps in front of the band to solo 'Hep, Hep, Hooray.'

Errol broadly sketches the elderly playboy, with okay assistance from the girl contingent headed by the Misses McDonald, Hilliard and Kean. Leslie Goodwins keeps things moving at fairly consistent pace, but the gags in dialog and situations on the story side are all familiar.

Walt.

CRIME DOCTOR

Columbia release of Ralph Cohn production. Stars Warner Baxter; features Margaret Lindsay, John Litel. Directed by Michael Gordon. Based on radio program, 'Crime Doctor,' by Max Marcin; story, Graham Baker and Louis Lantz; adaptation, Jerome Odlum; editor, Dwight Callwell; camera, James S. Brown. At Globe, N. Y., week July 3, '43. Running time, **66 MINS.**

Robert Ordway	Warner Baxter
Grace Fielding	Margaret Lindsay
Three Fingers	John Litel
Dr. Carey	Ray Collins
Joe	Harold Huber
Nick	Don Costello
Captain Wheeler	Leon Ames
Betty	Constance Worth
Pearl	Dorothy Tree
Myrtle	Vi Athens

'Crime Doctor,' starring Warner Baxter, long with 20th-Fox and the old Fox company but now under contract to Columbia, is a much-better-than-average melodrama which, in spite of a denouement that is slightly fantastic, holds interest all the way. The market potentialities are good.

This is the first of what is likely to become a series with Col, which obtained the rights to the 'Crime Doctor' air programs written by Max Marcin and on the CBS network for the Philip Morris cig people. The screenplay, by Graham Baker and Louis Lantz, and the adaptation by Jerome Odlum, expertly done, make 'Crime Doctor' entertainment of the better grade in the meller class largely through the careful plotting of the yarn and the suspense maintained.

Baxter plays the former brains of a burglary gang who loses his memory as result of being batted on the head by his suspicious comrades in crime and then, starting out from scratch, becomes a famous spychiatrist. All along the line he is trying to find out who he formerly was but not until he has become head of a state parole board and getting hit on the head again, in getting mixed up with old cronies, does he learn of his criminal past. The suspended sentence he receives is a bit contrary to expectations, also the fact that fingerprints fail to identify him, but palpably there was no other way out for the happy ending achieved.

Margaret Lindsay, as a parole worker, plays opposite Baxter, giving an impressive performance. A trio of gangsters are well portrayed by John Litel, Harold Huber and Don Costello. Lessers include Ray Collins, a doctor who helps to push Baxter after treating him for amnesia; Leon Ames, a convict Baxter reforms; Constance Worth, a nurse, and Dorothy Tree and Vi Athens, gals who got in dutch with the law. Miss Tree is not on long in a parole board hearing sequence but makes the minutes count and appears to be in line for better things.

Ralph Cohn's production is adequate and the direction of Michael Gordon skilled.

Char.

Law of the Northwest

Columbia release of Jack Fier production. Stars Charles Starrett; features Shirley Patterson, Arthur 'Arkansas' Hunnicutt. Directed by William Berke; story and screenplay by Luci Ward; camera, Benjamin Kline; editor, Jerome Thoms. At New York, N. Y., dual, week June 29, '43. Running time, **57 MINS.**

Steve King	Charles Starrett
Michel Darcy	Shirley Patterson
Arkansas	Arthur Hunnicutt
Neal Clayton	Stanley Brown
George Bradley	Douglas Leavitt
Frank Mason	Donald Curtis
Paul Darcy	Douglass Drake
Tom Clayton	Davison Clark
Jean Darcy	Reginald Barlow

Charles Starrett is playing the smart mountie again in this western, which is in the usual outdoor opus groove and up to standard of this series.

This one is about the race to get a road constructed in time to transport valuable war minerals for Allied forces. Angle is so vaguely developed that it looks as though added at the last minute. Main theme is the struggle between law-and-order boys (represented by the Northwest Mounted Police) and a crooked contractor. There's plenty of gunplay as mountie Starrett personally sees that the road is rushed to completion in time.

Per usual with recent westerns, dramatic moments are tipped by the exciting music. Picture has more than usual quota of night scenes, all well photographed by Benjamin Kline.

Starrett is not overly burdened with bright lines, but chips in with his familiar suave hero role. Shirley Patterson shapes up well as the femme of the production, while Arthur Hunnicutt provides a neat comedy portrayal. Stanley Brown, Douglas Leavitt and Douglass Drake head the support.

Wear.

FALSE FACES

Republic release of George Sherman production, directed by Sherman. Features Stanley Ridges, Bill Henry, Rex Williams, Veda Ann Borg. Screenplay, Curt Siodmak; camera, William Bradford; editor, Arthur Roberts. At Strand, Brooklyn, July 1, '43. Running time, **58 MINS.**

Stanley Harding	Stanley Ridges
Don Westcott	Bill Henry
Craig Harding	Rex Williams
Joyce Ford	Veda Ann Borg
Diana	Janet Shaw
Capt. O'Brien	Joseph Crehan
Manager	Chester Clute
Stewart	John Maxwell
Mallory	Dick Wessel
Jimmy	Billy Nelson
Magnolia	Etta McDaniel
Mac	Nicodemus

An ill-contrived whodunit, lacking suspense and weakly motivated, 'False Faces' falls into filler category for the subsequents.

It opens with a shot of a man (Rex Williams) in a nitery bar looking into a glass. He registers sadness. Maybe because the girl (Veda Ann Borg) is singing. Possibly because the glass is empty.

Later there's a brawl with a mysterious, unidentified stranger. The girl is eventually killed. The district attorney's son, Williams again, is implicated. So's his pal Bill Henry. It finally turns out to be the fat little hotel manager whodunit.

Williams registers photogenically as long as he keeps his hat on. Otherwise his hair is combed high up, like a Zulu warrior. Bill Henry, as the band leader, fills a colorless role nicely while Stanley Ridges as the conventional, hard-boiled district attorney, handles his assignment capably.

Mori.

Ghosts on the Loose

Monogram release of Sam Katzman-Jack Dietz production. Stars Leo Gorcey, Huntz Hall, Bobby Jordan, Bela Lugosi; features Ava Gardner. Directed by William Beaudine. Screenplay by Kenneth Higgins; camera, Mack Stengler; editor, Carl Pierson. At New York, N. Y., dual, week June 29, '43. Running time, **64 MINS.**

Mugs	Leo Gorcey
Glimpy	Huntz Hall
Danny	Bobby Jordan
Emil	Bela Lugosi
Betty	Ava Gardner
Jack	Ric Vallin
Hilda	Minerva Urecal
Tony	Wheeler Oakman
Stash	Stanley Clements
Benny	Billy Benedict
Scruno	Sammy Morrison
Dave	Bobby Stone

Loosely constructed comedy thriller contains plenty of laughs despite the long procession of venerable gags. 'Ghosts on the Loose' differs little from other East Side Kids epics, which means the muggs hog most of footage. Okay for supporting feature on twinners.

While main theme of yarn centers about a mystery house, found later to be headquarters for Nazi undercover agents in N. Y., many initial sequences concern a wedding and the clowning of the East Siders in aiding Huntz Hall's (a gang member) brother to get married. This is detailed too much, with the youngsters' choir practice stretched threadbare. Newlyweds are supposed to spend their honeymoon in a haunted house, but don't. Instead, the East Side Kids visit the dwelling, expecting to get it into shipshape after they learn that the married couple is going on a trip out of town. Usual sliding panels, disappearing pictures, hidden passageways and trick gadgets provide the bulk of the hoke. Of course, the kids ultimately uncover the hiding place of Nazi underground operatives.

Leo Gorcey, the 'little toughie' leader of the kids, is tops, in the troupe, though mugging far too much. Huntz Hall, his No. 1 stooge, is okay. Bobby Jordan and Billy Benedict also do well as other young mobsters. Bela Lugosi, as the principal menace, is the Nazi chief, but has little to do.

Picture is almost a screentest for Ava Gardner as the newlywed, and fairly good. Ric Vallin is the groom. William Beaudine's direction is far better than the plot. *Wear.*

FIRE IN THE STRAW

('Le Feu de Paille')
(FRENCH-MADE)

Carl Laemmle release of Jean Benoit-Levy production, directed by him. Features Orane Demazis, Jean Fuller, Lucien Baroux. Screenplay by Jean Benoit-Levy and Henri Troyat; adapted from Henri Troyat's novel, 'Grandeur Nature'; camera, Marcel Lucien; editor, Darlowe. At World, N. Y., week July 1, '43. Running time, **89 MINS.**

Antoine Vautier..............Lucien Baroux
Jeanne Vautier..............Orane Demazis
Christian Vautier..............Jean Fuller
Monica..........................Jeanne Helbling
Gueretrain ....Aimos

(In French; English titles)

Story of a French musical comedy actor who can't resist the smell of grease-paint though the parade has passed him by has been made into a potentially strong French production by Jean Benoit-Levy. While not up to his 'Ballerina' and 'La Maternelle,' it is easily the best French picture seen in the U.S. in months. 'Fire in the Straw' should prove worthwhile boxoffice at foreign language and arty theatres.

Benoit-Levy has taken a Goncourt prize novel, 'Grandeur Nature,' by Henri Troyat, and made something of a yarn that obviously was not too weighty as a screen vehicle. It traces the rise of a school child to fame in motion pictures, only to find that the public has become tired of him after his initial successes—and that the acting profession is a tough one, just as his father had discovered. The director pictures the disappointment of the little boy's father, not only over the lad's sudden rise but high-salaried fame while he is struggling to get bits in radio or pictures.

While inclined to be a bit wordy, the skillful portrayal of the lad's father and mother in their happiness and disappointment over the precocious youngster's rise and fall makes a forthright vehicle. Produced well ahead of Nazi occupation of Paris, the whole picture represents considerable outlay in production values. Scenes in the picture studio are excellently done.

Jean Fuller, 12-year-old French actor, contributes much to the realism of the story. Shift from the typical schoolboy to the important screen star is never overdone. Lucien Baroux makes a typical actor-father, who is babied by his pretty wife, and spurred to have faith in himself despite his cruel disappointments on the stage. Orane Demazis, French actress who has been in numerous French pictures lately, is highly effective as his faithful wife.

Jeanne Helbling, cast as the impetuous blonde dancer who's always on the make for Baroux, is outstanding in the supporting cast. Even in the disrobing scene (which the censors have cut to less than a flash), she is convincing in an unsympathetic role. Jean Benoit-Levy's direction is intelligent, aside from the old tendency to draw out sequences. English-titling is topflight. *Wear.*

Under Secret Orders

(BRITISH-MADE)

Guaranteed Pictures release. Directed by Edmond Greville. Features Erich Stroheim, Dita Parlo, John Loder, Claire Luce. Story by George Neveux and I. Cube; scenario, Ernest Betts; adaptation, R. Bernaur; camera, Otto Heller; editor, Ray Pitt. At Strand, Brooklyn, July 1, '43. Running time, **66 MINS.**

Col. Mathesius }
Simonis }..............Erich Stroheim
Lieut. Peter Carr..............John Loder
Anne-Marie Lesser..............Dita Parlo
Gaby..........................Claire Luce
Lieut. Hans Hoffman.........Gyles Isham
Coudoyan....................Clifford Evans
Armand..........................John Abbott
Mario.......................Anthony Holles
Carr's Orderly..............Edward Lexy
French General.............Robert Nainby
Col. Burgoyne...................Brian Powley
Prop. of Blue Peacock..................
Molly Hamley Clifford
Col. von Steinberg.........Raymond Lovell
Col. Marchand............Frederick Lloyd
Capt. Fitzmaurice............Claud Horton

This British pic is a silly piece about espionage during World War I. It's a trite, insipid tale and if a remake or a reissue it's certainly ill-timed. There's no tie-in with the current war, not that it would help any if the yarn were more topical. Moreover, there's an almost pro-German slant in the treatment accorded Dito Parlo, as the German Mata Hari.

Trying to act the glamor girl, Miss Parlo flops miserably. She's too mature aside from being photogenically inadequate.

There's a 'It Happened One Night' bedroom scene wherein John Loder and Miss Parlo photograph so unattractively and are so stagily handled that it's not even suggestive.

Erich von Stroheim is the German secret service mastermind. In Salonika he does a Sherlock Holmes in wig and mustache which fools nobody except the cast. Miss Parlo purloins the plans about British troop movements from the unbelievably stupid British captain. British secret service finally catches up with the German agents and Miss Parlo and Stroheim are shot—66 minutes too late. *Mori.*

Maravilla Del Toreo

('Marvels of the Bull Ring')
(MEXICAN-MADE)
(Songs)

Clasa Studios production and release. Stars Conchita Cintron: features Pepe Ortiz. Directed by Raphael J. Sevilla. Screenplay, Pepe Ortiz; camera, Ross Fischer, R. Martinez-Solares; music, Carlos M. Baena. At Belmont, N. Y., week July 2, '43. Running time, **105 MINS.**

Rosita.....................Conchita Cintron
Jose Morera..........................Pepe Ortiz
Fernanda..............Pituka de Foronda
Curro....................Florencio Castello
Rerre..........................Rafael Icardo
Don Pedro....................Manuel Arvide
Ricardo...............................Tony Diaz
'Chiclanero'..............Rafael Banquells

(In Spanish; No English Titles)

Despite a hackneyed overlong story weighted down further by the lack of English titles, 'Maravilla Del Toreo' should draw bullfight fans and readers of Hemingway. The bull-ring sequences built around the activities of two bona fide practitioners of the art, Conchita Cintron and Pepe Ortiz, are intensely interesting because they avoid phoney dramatics.

Miss Cintron is known as the world's top femme bull fighter and Ortiz is Mexico's No. 1 matador. Unfortunately their skill in the bull ring does not carry over to the sound stage, so they emerge as a couple of top athletes 'gone Hollywood' to cash in on their reps.

The story itself revolves around Ortiz's 'discovery' of Miss Cintron on a Peruvian ranch. As the daughter of a ranch owner she has acquired considerable riding skill and amateur bull fighter status. Ortiz, a great Mexican matador, takes her under his wing. Their ultimate triumphs in the arenas of Mexico and Spain are overshadowed by their love for each other despite Ortiz's marriage, and his growing blindness. His wife conveniently runs off with his manager and they're killed making the getaway. Ortiz and Miss Cintron have a clear field, but he nixes the idea after he has gone blind.

The top players are too wooden in their roles, and only come to life when they are shown in the bull ring. But the other members of the cast perform with adequate professional poise. The camera work, in general, is poor. The scenes have either too much or too little lighting, and the bull-ring episodes are muffed. The camera roves around promiscuously, passing by some excellent action opportunities.

On the other hand, the film is musically standout, especially a flamenco song and dance number. Mexican guitar and chorus routines also help give the picture a much-needed lift.

JUVENILIA

(ARGENTINE-MADE)

Buenos Aires, June 18.

San Miguel production released by Panamericana. Stars Elisa Galve; featuring Jose Olarra, Ernesto Vilches, Ricardo Passano, Jr., Eloy Alvarez, Hugo Pimentel, Mario Medrano, Rafael Frontaura, Gregorio Verdi, Domingo Marquez, Francisco Lopez Silva, Jorge Villoido, Salvador Lotito, Nelly Daren, Gogo Andreu, Iris Portillo, Marcos Zucker, Alfredo Almanza, Chela Cordero, Mary Dormal, Enrique Chaico, Pepito Petray, Morena Chiolo, Fausto Fornoni and A. Bernia. Directed by Augusto Cesar Vatteone. Story by Miguel Cane; screenplay by Dr. Pedro E. Pico, A. de la Guardia and Manuel Agromayor; camera, Francis Boeninger and Hugo Chiesa. Reviewed at Ambassador, Buenos Aires. Running time, 105 MINS.

Based on book that has already become a standard text in Argentina and other Latin American schools, 'Juvenilia,' first important production by Manuel Pena Rodriguez for Estudios San Miguel, is a definite step forward for the national industry. It is an interesting possibility for elsewhere in the Americas and U. S. Rodriguez, former film critic for 'La Nacion,' daily here, becomes the first independent Argentine producer with this. Previously there were no producers, directors being responsible to studio heads. It's likely that the Hollywood pattern will be followed more in the future.

Job of transferring the Miguel Cane story to screen was difficult because of its episodic character. A sort of Latin 'Good-bye Mr. Chips,' it needed cinema punch, which often is lacking.

Parade of sketches resulting has led to gaps in development and to a slow start due to over emphasis on detail. However, it picks up considerably and the scenes of student life go over well. Story is laid in Buenos Aires of 1860 when the city was starting to grow up. As directed by Augusto Cesar Vatteone, story humanizes the characters, their furtive loves, their midnight feasts, their books and songs, and their rivalries.

While given feature billing, Elisa Galve is not outstanding, but vivacious. Veteran Jose Olarra, as the wise and audacious professor Jacques, cops lead acting honors, and Ernesto Vilches, as the understanding Padre Aguero, is also sure-fire. Interest centers, however, on Ricardo Passano, Jr., young juve, who carries the principal student role.

Film's emphasis on national theme and its pro-democratic overtones are also rare for here, most nationals to date having been purely escapist fare. Photography by Francis Boeninger and Hugo Chiesa is somewhat uneven. Music by Alejandro Gutierrez del Barrio and R. Garcia Morillo is adequate. *Ray.*

Miniature Reviews

'Hers to Hold' (U). One of Deanna Durbin's strongest b.o. films.

'Behind the Rising Sun' (RKO). An exploitation special that will hit hefty grosses and holdovers in regular runs.

'Bomber's Moon' (20th). Exciting, suspenseful entertainment; good b.o.

'The Falcon in Danger' (RKO). Another in the series; well-knit tale, will groove as supporter in regular runs.

'Prairie Chickens' (UA). Hal Roach streamlined comedy; poor entertainment.

'Petticoat Larceny' (RKO). Joan Carroll in juvenile adventure slated to provide filler support in the family houses.

'Leather Burners' (UA). Very good western in the Hopalong Cassidy series.

'Cowboy Commandos' (Mono). Fairly worthy western dealing with cow-country saboteurs.

'World of Plenty' (BMI). British-made documentary on food, with special emphasis on wartime distribution, splendid.

'Marines Come Through' (Astor). Grant Withers, Wallace Ford, Toby Wing in dud patriotic film gone haywire.

'Silent Village' (BMI). British-made documentary on Lidice is slow, and suffers from overabundance of predecessors.

'Luisito' (Argentine). Paulina Singerman starrer; okay for Latin trade.

Hers to Hold

(SONGS)

Hollywood, July 13.

Universay release of Felix Jackson production. Stars Deanna Durbin. Joseph Cotten: features Charles Winninger. Evelyn Ankers, Gus Schilling, Nella Walker, Ludwig Stussel. Directed by Frank Ryan. Story, John D. Klorer; adaption, Lewis R. Foster; songs, Cole Porter, Amy Woodforde-Finden, Laurence Hope, Jimmy McHugh, Herb Magidson, Georges Bizet and F.W. Rosier: editor, Ted Kent; camera, Elwood Bredell. Previewed at Filmarte, N.Y., July 12, '43. Running time, 93 MINS.

Penelope Craig..............................Deanna Durbin
Bill Morley......................................Joseph Cotten
Judson Craig..............................Charles Winninger
Flo..Evelyn Ankers
Rosey Blake......................................Gus Schilling
Dorothy Craig....................................Nella Walker
Rinns..Ludwig Stossel
Dr. Crane......................................Samuel S. Hinds
Hannah Gordon......................................Fay Helm
Arlene..Iris Adrian
Foreman..Murray Alper
Mr. Cartwright...................................Douglas Wood
Mrs. Cartwright................................Minna Phillips
Nurse Willing..................................Nydia Westman
Dr. Bacon..Irving Bacon

In 'Hers to Hold' Deanna Durbin successfully and permanently completes transition from cinematic sub-deb to young ladyhood. Picture is straight romantic drama constructed with eye on lightness and tongue-in-cheek love affair. One of the strongest boxoffice entries for Miss Durbin in several pictures.

Fluffy and escapist theme, in tune with present audience requirements, will carry it through as potential holdover in all bookings. Felix Jackson, formerly associated as writer on numerous early Durbin starrers, makes his bow as the star's producer here, and clicks solidly. He gets able assistance from freshness and pace in both script by Lewis Foster and direction by Frank Ryan, together with strong performances by supporting cast, and an excellently mounted production overall.

Story, although lightly contrived, generates audience attention through the deft business generously inserted in the script and carried through via direction. Rich deb Durbin is object of amorous flirtation by Joseph Cotten, trifling love-and-leave-'em adventurer, and what starts out as boy chases girl winds up as girl chases boy. When she coyly falls for his pitches after a fast campaign, he tries to get from under when he sees that look in her eye, but his brush-off is unsuccessful and she follows him to an aircraft plant to get job to seek him out. It's a merry-go-round of entertainment until Cotten is called for active service in air corps and he finally resolves himself to being hooked permanently for the final clinch.

Miss Durbin again demonstrates capabilities in carrying acting responsibilities of lead, with her four song numbers neatly spotted along the way. Two are on display at noon-time lunch entertainments for aircraft workers. 'Begin the Beguine' and 'Say a Prayer for the Boys Over There.' Latter is a new tune by Herb Magidson and Jimmy McHugh, of topical nature that might catch on moderately. Star also delivers 'Seguidilla' from 'Carmen' and the 'Kashmiri Song.' There's lightness and charm in Miss Durbin's portrayal, while her vocal renditions are of usual high caliber.

Cotten is excellent opposite Durbin to provide sterling performance of flirtatious wanderer. Charles Winninger clicks as the absent-minded father of girl, with Nella Walker again in role of her mother. Gus Schilling and Ludwig Stossel milk maximum reactions from two character comedy parts, while Murray Alper catches brief attention as aircraft foreman.

Audience is taken inside Vega aircraft plant for several sequences that provides pictorial idea of magnitude and workings of Coast plane factories. Clips from previous Durbin starrer, especially her four earliest pictures, are expertly dovetailed into screening as a 16 mm. family reel compiled by proud father Winninger. Brief unreeling is deftly set up into most interesting episode through creation of business and dialog during showing.

Picture has advantage of top production mounting, as is the usual case with Durbin starrers. Sound quality of musical numbers is excellent, with Woody Breedell contributing topflight photography.

Walt.

Behind the Rising Sun

Hollywood, July 13.

RKO production and release. Features Margo, Tom Neal, J. Carroll Naish, Robert Ryan. Directed by Edward Dmytryk. Original screenplay by Emmett Lavery, based on book by James R. Young; camera, Russell Metty; special effects, Vernon L. Walker; editor, Joseph Noriega; asst. director, Ruby Rosenberg. Tradeshown in L. A. July 13, '43. Running time, 88 MINS.

Tama .... Margo
Taro .... Tom Neal
Publisher .... J. Carroll Naish
Lefty .... Robert Ryan
Sara .... Gloria Holden
O'Hara .... Don Douglas
Boris .... George Givot
Grandmother.... Adeline DeWalt Reynolds
Tama's Father .... Leonard Strong
Woman Secretary .... Iris Wong
Max .... Wolfgang Zilzer
Servant .... Shirley Lew
Jap Officer .... Benson Fong
Dinner Guest .... Lee Tung Foo
Jap Wrestler .... Mike Mazurki

This is an exploitation special of timely interest that will roll up hefty grosses and holdovers in the regular runs as solo or billtopper. Screenplay, spun by Emmett Lavery who handled similar assignment on same company's 'Hitler's Children,' is from factual information contained in book by James R. Young, International News Service correspondent in Tokio for several years prior to the war's outbreak at Pearl Harbor.

Although foreword points out that the characters are imaginary, facts woven into the dramatics are real. Result is a good drama of inside info on the Jap indoctrination and thinking that will give American audiences plenty to hiss about. Added to the general American attitude against the Nips, forecasting a major offensive against the latter is likely to break out in number of spots, makes this as timely as the morning newspaper.

Story is an intimate affair of a Jap family of the upper class; and the impress of the Nip conquests in Asia and war against the United States on both father and son. Father is influential newspaper publisher (J. Carroll Naish), while son is Cornell-educated Tom Neal. When latter arrives from America after completing college education and figures to embark on career as an engineer with Don Douglas, there are family objections for a time. But when Neal further falls in love with lower-caste Jap girl, Margo, marriage is impossible. Naish, with close inner government connections, is all for Jap empirical expansion and eventual domination of the world, while the son holds opposite views with pro-American attitude. But outbreak of the war in China, with induction of Neal into the Nip army for duty as an engineer in northern China, finally makes the son a killer and advocate of the Jap military plan of world conquest. Some months later, when Neal returns from China, his father is minister of propaganda and concerned with possible eventual downfall of Japan, but the boy is indoctrinated with the new Jap credo of 'all for the emperor.' This new doctrine also results in his turning on American friends shortly after the Pearl Harbor incident—and also against Margo, his betrothed. Transferred to the air force, Neal is shot down when the American bombers raid Tokio, and Naish—with defeatism attitude for Japan's chances—commits hari-kari.

Despite its intimate dramatics of a Jap father and son, picture carries sufficient display of Nip atrocities against the Chinese and Americans to focus hate attention from domestic audiences. There are few battle scenes—and these are brief clips of Jap forays against the Chinese armies. But where the dramatic strength lies is in the atrocities committed against Chinese women and children in occupied areas—in addition to the tortures inflicted on Americans caught in Tokio at the time of the sneak attack on Pearl Harbor. These sequences are melodramatic in themselves, but given added weight due to current and past newspaper headlines.

Naish is most prominent as the Jap publisher, although efforts are made to focus attention on Neal. Former does an excellent job with his role, while Neal—handicapped by obvious makeup—is passable as the Jap recently returned from America. Margo grooves neatly as the girl; while strong support is provided by Douglas, Robert Ryan, Gloria Holden, George Givot and Adeline DeWalt Reynolds.

During its unfolding, picture gives insight into the intimate and fundamental attitude of the Japs towards the army and emperor, which provides background for necessity of all-out battles in the Pacific area before the Japs are routed. Fight between Jap wrestler Mike Muzurki and American boxer Ryan is a rouser, and gives detailed comparison of the overall battle between this country and the sneaky Japs.

Lavery's script is deftly contrived from material furnished by Young, while Dmytryk's direction hits a general suspenseful pace. Photography and special effects by Russell Metty and Vernon Walker, respectively, are excellent throughout.

Walt.

BOMBER'S MOON

20th Century-Fox release of Sol M. Wurtzel production. Stars George Montgomery, Annabella; features Kent Taylor, Walter Kingsford, Martin Kosleck, Dennis Hoey, Robert Barrat. Directed by Charles Fuhr. Story, Leonard Lee; adaptation, Kenneth Gamet and Aubrey Wisberg; editor, Robert Fritch; camera, Lucien Ballard. Previewed in N. Y., July 8, '43. Running time 70 MINS.

Captain Jeff Dakin.... George Montgomery
Alec .... Annabella
Captain Paul Husnik .... Kent Taylor
Friederich Mueller .... Walter Kingsford
Major Von Streicher .... Martin Kosleck
Major Von Grunow .... Dennis Hoey
Ernst .... Robert Barrat
Karl .... Kenneth Brown
Henrik Vanseeler .... Victor Kilian
Priest .... Robert Lewis
Kurt .... Mike Mazurki
Johann .... Christian Rub
Hans .... Otto Reichow
Dr. Hartman .... Frank Reicher
Elsa .... Grete Dupont

The title may not be the best that could have been tacked to this picture but here's thoroughly exciting and suspenseful entertainment based on the circuitous route taken by two Nazi-caught prisoners in making their escape to England. It possesses warm romantic strength, has been very ably produced and directed to establish authenticity, includes some excellent air scenes and is extremely well acted. The boxoffice potentialities are good but advisable that the account sell the picture as a romance rather than as a war item, especially since the title would suggest this is strictly a so-called 'shooting' picture. It isn't that except for a couple brief sequences dealing with bomber combat.

George Montgomery, who made a good type as a westerns star and in this instance works exceedingly well opposite Annabella, plays an American flying captain who is forced into a crash dive on enemy territory. He is thrown into a German prison, which includes as one of its inmates a woman lieutenant in the Soviet medical corps. Together they effect an escape with Kent Taylor and hazardously make their way to the home of a friend of Annabella's, only to learn that Taylor actually is a German spy who has trapped them.

Annabella, who does not quite look a Russian medico, and Montgomery then make their way to Holland where arrangements have been negotiated to get them back to England on a fishing boat. Annabella goes but Montgomery, who learns there's a flying field nearby, disguises himself as a Nazi soldier and wiggles himself out of captor's hands again, taking off for England in an enemy bomber.

On the way he intercepts the German flier who cold-bloodedly killed his brother when latter bailed out of the plane Montgomery was forced to crash. What heightens the suspense is difficulty of Montgomery in getting British army officials to believe he's coming back in a Nazi plane but Annabella finally convinces the commanding officer in time.

The picture ends rather abruptly. When Annabella and Montgomery parted, they had made a date to meet in a pub back in England, where it is expected the big embrace on home soil would take place. That never occurs.

Annabella screens effectively in her army uniform but it's a little unreasonable that Montgomery does not recognize her at the outset when they made their escape from prison. Taylor gives a steady, even performance, while lessers, all good, include Walter Kingsford, Martin Kosleck, Dennis Hoey and Robert Barrat.

Char.

FALCON IN DANGER

Hollywood, July 13.

RKO release of Maurice Geraghty production. Features Tom Conway. Directed by William Clemens. Screenplay by Fred Niblo, Jr., Craig Rice, based on character created by Michael Arlen; camera, Frank Redman; editor, George Crone; asst. director, Fred Fleck. Tradeshown July 13, '43. Running time, 69 MINS.

Falcon .... Tom Conway
Iris .... Jean Brooks
Nancy .... Elaine Shepard
Bonnie .... Amelita Ward
Donovan .... Cliff Clark
Bates .... Ed Gargan
Palmer .... Clarence Kolb
Morley .... Felix Basch
Ken .... Richard Davies
Georgie .... Richard Martin
Evan .... Erford Gage
Grimes .... Eddie Dunn

For the addicts of the Falcon's cinematic adventures as a master sleuth, and to general run of customers who can sit back and relax while the suave deductioner unravels clues and situations to a crime or baffling situation, this entry will amply fill requirements. It's one of the most compact and interesting of the series, and rates as a strong supporter of its type in the regular bookings.

Tom Conway, as the Falcon, continues his winning ways as both a lady-killer and solver of mysterious crimes. This time, he's brought in to unravel the strange disappearance of two industrialists from a commercial plane in midair. Daughter of one and niece of the other both seek out Conway to assist them in finding the missing men. The trail leads through strange maze of circumstances until everything's finally cleared up.

Script by Fred Niblo, Jr., and Craig Rice combines with paceful direction by William Clemens to maintain suspense throughout for neat conception of cinematic sleuthing. Conway ably handles the lead assignment, keeps his eye on all pretty girls who cross his path, and the particular problem at hand. He's provided with three femmes in this instance—fiancee Texan and baby-talker Amelita Ward, Jean Brooks, and Elaine Shephard—with trio turning in good performances. Cliff Clark and Ed Gargan are back again as the inspector and dumb assistant. Production mounting is adequate for intent of moderate budgeter. *Walt.*

PRAIRIE CHICKENS

United Artists release of Hal Roach production. Features Jimmy Rogers, Noah Beery, Jr. Directed by Hal Roach, Jr. Story, Donald Hough; adaptation, Arnold Belgard and Earle Snell; editor, Bert Jordan; camera, Robert Pittack. Running time, 46 MINS.

Jimmy .... Jimmy Rogers
Pidge .... Noah Beery, Jr.
Albertson .... Joe Sawyer
Lucy .... Marjorie Woodworth
Yola .... Rosemary La Planche
Henry Lewis-Clark .... Jack Norton
Jeff .... Raymond Hatton
Miss Billows .... Marga Ann Deighton
Bus Driver .... Ed Gargan
Clem .... Frank Faylen
Farnsworth .... Dudley Dickerson

Running only 46 minutes, this slapstick comedy will probably come in handy on double bills, especially where turnover is desired. Otherwise it's a very poor comedy.

Deals with a couple of zanies who are trying to get somewhere with a broken-down Ford, one of whom is mistaken for the rich owner of a ranch who is expected. Last-mentioned arrives at the western town that is decked out for him but is pushed to one side for purposes of comedy and, together with a bevy of gals on a sightseeing tour of the cow-country, are shunted to the ranch-house, which is supposed to be haunted. The results rate low.

Jimmy Rogers and Noah Beery, Jr., play the roaming pals who get themselves involved with the owner of the ranch, a drunk-nutsy type done by Jack Norton. *Char.*

PETTICOAT LARCENY

Hollywood, July 13.

RKO release of Bert Gilroy production.

Directed by Ben Holmes. Screenplay by Jack Townley, Stuart Palmer; camera, Frank Redman; editor, John C. Grubb; asst. director, William Dorfman. Tradeshown July 12, '43. Running time, 61 MINS.

Pat Mitchell..................Ruth Warrick
Joan Mitchell..................Joan Carroll
Bill Morgan..................Walter Reed
Sam Colfax..................Wally Brown
Pinky..................Tom Kennedy
Jitters..................Jimmy Conlin
Stogie..................Vince Barnett
Joe Foster..................Paul Guilfoyle
Detective Hogan..................Grant Withers
Mr. Crandall..................Earl Dewey
Higgins..................Charles Coleman
Lt. Hackett..................Cliff Clark

This is a lightweight number, built on very moderate budget, that will suffice as a dual filler for the family and juvenile trade.

Little Joan Carroll displays ability as the child star of a radio program who decides to get first-hand knowledge of how underworld characters talk and act after balking at the vacuous scripts provided for her air shows. She runs into thieving trio of Tom Kennedy, Jimmy Conlin and Vince Barnett, who unconsciously hide her out when the papers headline her kidnapping. Kid reforms the trio, but not before her fabricated father arrives to abduct her to a gambling ship for rousing fight at the finish.

Kennedy, Conlin and Barnett team for broad and easily delivered comedy as the three lugs; but Wally Brown's attempt to portray a keyhole columnist gets nowhere through lack of footage. Ruth Warrick is okay as the youngster's aunt, while Walter Reed is romantic interest for her as the kid's press agent. Director Ben Holmes unfolds the yarn at a good tempo, and catches laughs through antics of the comedy trio.

Walt.

The Leather Burners

United Artists release of Harry Sherman production. Features William Boyd, Andy Clyde, Jay Kirby, Victor Jory, George Givot, Shelley Spencer, Bobby Larson. Directed by Joseph E. Henabery. Story, Bliss Lomax; adaptation, Jo Pagano; editor, Carroll Lewis; camera, Russell Harlan. At New York, N. Y., dual, week July 6, '43. Running time, 66 MINS.

Hopalong Cassidy..................William Boyd
California Carlson..................Andy Clyde
Johnny..................Jay Kirby
Dan Slack..................Victor Jory
Sam Bucktoe..................George Givot
Sharon Longstreet..................Shelley Spencer
Bobby Longstreet..................Bobby Larson
Harrison Brooke..................George Reeves
Lafe..................Hal Taliaferro
Bart..................Forbes Murray

To steal from the title, this is another leather-burner in the popular Hopalong Cassidy series which appear to maintain a steady high standard in westerns entertainment. William Boyd, who came from regular features some years ago to become a Hollywood cowboy, gives his usual good performance, including with the mitts. His two pearl-handled revolvers and the white horse must be the envy of every kid who knows his Hopy.

With Andy Clyde still at his side for laughs, Boyd this time cleans out a gang of rustlers who have been using an old mine shaft as a hiding place for themselves and the purloined cattle. Included in the cast of of characters is an old man, now insane, who was deprived of his mine and is imprisoned in it. He finally goes on a killing tear toward the end, with this and a stampede of mine-trapped cattle adding to the excitement of the climax. A good kid actor, Bobby Larson, who figures rather importantly in the story, is clutched from the path of the stampeding bovines by Boyd just in time.

He's the brother of the heroine, Shelley Spencer, who looks nice but offers nothing particularly histrionic. Jay Kirby, playing the romantic lead; Victor Jory, leader of the rustlers, and George Givot, as the lunatic, are the more important of the others. Givot, Greek dialectician, for years in vaudeville, does a swell job as the old man who was robbed of his mine.

Char.

Cowboy Commandos

(SONG)

Monogram release of George W. Weeks production. Features Ray Corrigan, Dennis Moore, Max Terhune, Evelyn Finley. Directed by S. Roy Luby. Story, Clark Paylow; adaptation, Elizabeth Beecher; editor, Ray Claire; camera, Edward Kull. At New York, N. Y., dual, week July 6, '43. Running time, 53 MINS.

Crash..................Ray Corrigan
Denny..................Dennis Moore
Alibi..................Max Terhune
Joan..................Evelyn Finley
Slim..................Johnny Bond
Werner..................Bud Buster
Fraser..................John Merton
Katie..................Edna Bennett
Bartlett..................Steve Clark
Hans..................Bud Osborne

The possibility that Nazis may be everywhere, even in the cow country, forms the premise for a fairly exciting western which has as one of its virtues a short running time of 53 minutes. Thus it will create no problem on double-bill turnover.

George W. Weeks produced from a story by Clark Paylow, which was adapted by Elizabeth Beecher. While the dialog fails to have much brilliance, the plot carries considerable suspense and the various roles are played capably. Weeks' trio working together in westerns, Ray (Crash) Corrigan, Max (Alibi) Terhune and Dennis Moore, are featured, while the girl, Evelyn Finley, is a comely type.

The yarn concerns the efforts of Corrigan, appointed sheriff, and his two pals in tracking down a group of Nazi agents who are sabotaging mine shipments of magnesite and are planning to ultimately blow up the mine itself. Several excellently staged fist fights figure, together with a sufficient amount of gunplay. There is one song in the picture, 'I'll Get the Fuehrer Sure as Shootin,' written in the western manner and sung by Johnny Bond, a cowpuncher who's in mostly for laughs.

Corrigan, Moore and Terhune all turn in good performances, while well cast as Nazi saboteurs are Bud Buster, John Merton, Edna Bennett and Bud Osborne. Steve Clark, character actor, plays the owner of the mine.

Picture has very effective opening which at the same time delivers a message to buy bonds. Miss Finley is rehearsing a stunt riding routine and, on finishing, faces the camera to make a plea for the purchase of bonds. It's not directed at the audience, being a rehearsal for a bond-selling tour, but appears that way and thus has trailer value. *Char.*

WORLD OF PLENTY

(British-Made Documentary)

British Ministry of Information release of Paul Rotha production, directed by Rotha. Written by Eric Knight; additional dialog by Miles Malleson; commentary spoken by Knight, Robert St. John, E. V. H. Emmett; music, William Alwyn. Previewed at Museum of Modern Art, N. Y., July 1, '43. Running time, 45 MINS.

Britain's wartime filmmakers, who have already earned themselves ranking as the world's foremost documentary technicians, affirm and strengthen that reputation with 'World of Plenty.' While 'Desert Victory' established the British as tops among makers of battle pictures, 'Plenty' will similarly rate them in the much more difficult field of documentaries on complicated economic subjects. Despite the complexity of the material dealt with and its dry, statistical character, producer Paul Rotha and author Eric Knight (recently killed) have succeeded in making it not only absorbing to the layman, but downright entertaining. Any theatre audience will be grateful for seeing it. It is the epitome of educational picturemaking.

No small part of its interest, of course, lies in its subject matter—food, its production, distribution and consumption. That's a vital topic to everyone at the moment and it is extremely interesting to see how Britain, with much greater experience than we in rationing and other wartime measures, has handled the problems with which the United States is now struggling. The picture goes much beyond that, however, for it speaks of proper feeding in both war and peace and not only in England, but as an international problem.

A sense of humor, with which so many of the better British documentaries are blessed, is the crowning grace of 'Plenty.' Without it, it would be as nothing. With it, even the graphs and statistics become things of life, something to be amused as well as instructed by. There's action in everything and the speedy editing allows nothing to linger. An impressive group of experts on all aspects of food are called to the screen to give evidence and advice on various problems raised, but there are no lectures, no lengthy speeches. A sentence or two and gone are such men as Lord Woolton, British Minister of Food; Claude R. Wickard, U. S. Secretary of Agriculture; Wellington Koo, Chinese Ambassador to Great Britain, and Sir John Orr, nutrition expert. In addition, there are significant passages from speeches by President Roosevelt, while part of Vice-President Wallace's famed words on 'The Century of the Common Man' provides a stirring epilog.

The film is in three parts, opening with the pre-war anomaly of overproduction and glutted markets while three-fourths of the world starved. The second part shows the control being exercised over production, distribution and price during the present war—with particular interest aroused by the success with which the much more stringent controls of Britain are meeting, while we flounder. The film ends with a picture of what might be done, when peace comes again, by world-wide control of food production, according to world needs, and the planning of distribution on a large enough scale to do away with surplus and scarcity. It makes a plea for establishment of such control.

Amusing to contemplate is the reaction this film would receive both in and out of Congress had it been made by the OWI or some other U.S. Government agency, instead of by the British government. Its pointing out of errors of the past and call for more control in the future most certainly would have had the makers' heads as 'Communists' and 'visionary world-planners.' Produced by our British allies, however, it no doubt will be accepted for what it is—a common-sense view of the world's greatest problem and an effort at a solution.

Marines Come Through

Astor Pictures release of George A. Hirliman production. Features Grant Withers, Toby Wing, Wallace Ford. Directed by Louis Gasnier. Original by Lawrence Meade; screenplay, D. S. Leslie; camera, J. Burgi Contner. At Strand, Brooklyn, dual, week July 8, '43. Running time, 60 MINS.

Singapore..................Wallace Ford
Linda Dale..................Toby Wing
Jack..................Grant Withers
Maisie..................Sheila Lynch
Lt. Landers..................Michael Doyle
Dick Weber..................Don Lanning
Beckstrom..................Frank Rasmussen
Charles..................Roy Elkins
Top Sergeant..................James Neary
Col. Dale..................Thomas McKeon

Packed with artificiality, this one is so weak it is difficult to single out the one thing that makes the picture so bad. Principal blame should be shouldered by the writers and director because Grant Withers, Wallace Ford and Toby Wing are good enough screen troupers when given direction and story breaks. They have neither here. 'Marines Come Through,' so thin it looks amateurish, will have a tough time making the grade in the lower slot of any dual combo.

Marines themselves really take the rap because of the way they're pictured here, and not likely to make them happy about future films made in Florida where screen credits this one to have been produced. Yarn is a far-fetched something about Nazi efforts to grab plans for a newly-invented bomb sight. But hundreds of feet of shallow events are paraded on screen before anything happens. Silly action, obvious padding in a phoney nightclub sequence and other inane events, clutter up the aimless story.

While Louis Gasnier's direction, which undoubtedly hits a new low for him, is sad enough, it gets close competition from the trite, badly conceived dialog and stupid story. Many outdoor sequences, supposed to be night shots, merely are foggy. Sound is equally poor.

Thespian efforts of Withers, Miss Wing and Ford certainly add nothing to their screen reps. Ford and Withers are teamed as a couple of quarreling marine aviation mechanics. Even that is overdone. Remainder of cast is much worse. They laughed at the wrong time or hooted this one in Brooklyn—and it's no wonder. *Wear.*

The Silent Village

(British-Made Documentary)

British Ministry of Information release of Crown Film Unit (British Government) production. Produced and directed by Humphrey Jennings. Camera, H. E. Fowle; editor, Stewart McAllister. Previewed at Museum of Modern Art, N. Y., July 1, '43. Running time, 35 MINS.

Another effort at celluloid immortalization of the slaughter of Lidice, 'The Silent Village' suffers from the numerous other films which have preceded it on the same subject. In addition, the idea of using a town in Wales similar to Lidice to dramatize the Nazi scourge of Czechoslovakia is one of those things which looks great on paper, less great on film. 'The Silent Village' will find little place on American screens.

For his picture, producer-director Humphrey Jennings selected the town and people of Cwmgiedd. As was Lidice, this is a mining village. It is in about the same economic plane—or was, before Hitler's barbaric stooges razed Lidice to the ground, murdered its men and sent into concentration camps its women and children.

'Village' first describes the peacetime life of Cwmgiedd, its enjoyment of freedom, its old tradition and native culture. Then it shows the effect of the conquest of Czechoslovakia by the Nazis. The notorious slaughter scene is followed by a description of the resurrection of Lidice in the minds of men to whom freedom is dear and the dedication of the people of Cwmgiedd to the liberation of the people of the world.

Welsh talk is interesting, the traditional choral singing entertaining and the photography is frequently unusual. The film is slow, however, and it presents insufficient compensations for the fact the story has been heard and seen so frequently before.

LUISITO

(ARGENTINE-MADE)

Buenos Aires, June 17.

Sono Film production and release. Stars Paulina Singerman; features Santiago Arrieta, Adrian Cuneo, Julio Renato, Sarita Olmos, Enrique Chaico, Liana Moabro and

Arturo Bamio. Story, Gabriel Pena, based on idea of Florencio Parravicini; adapted and directed by Luis Cesar Amadori; photography, Alberto Etchebehere; music, Mario Maurano. Reviewed at Monumental, Buenos Aires. Running time, **88 MINS.**

Fast-moving, entertaining farce, well-megged by Luis Cesar Amadori, 'Luisito' will be a strong grosser not only on first runs in Argentina but throughout Latin America. Should be especially solid in Cuba and the Canal Zone, where the blonde Senorita Singerman, Argentine-born of Russian parentage, is especially popular. As usual with Amadori comedies, plot isn't overly original, but Senorita Singerman playing a dual role helps to fill out the weak spots.

Yarn deals with a pert cafe waitress-entertainer who meets by chance a one-time playboy now on his uppers. Cupid steps in, but since he is out of cash, plans go ahead for him to marry the daughter of a big shot. Senorita Singerman happens along at the bachelor dinner his pals are tossing and decides to dress up as a boy and get a job as a secretary to break up the pending aisle march. Not only succeeds in the end but discovers the boyfriend's prospective father-in-law is a no-good and was about to pull a fast deal himself and get away with valuable property the hero didn't know was his.

Santiago Arrieta in leading male role is far better than in anything he has done, and La Singerman doesn't hog the lens as much as in some previous efforts. Dialog at times is somewhat wordy and theatrical but, generally speaking, it sparks. Adrian Cuneo and Sarita Olmos also good in supporting roles. Story by Gabriel is based on an idea of the late famed Argentine actor, Florencio Parravicini. Photography neat, especially effects in early scenes, and music adequate, with one sock waltz, 'Luisito,' sung with good effect. *Ray.*

'EL ESPEJO'
('The Mirror')
(ARGENTINE-MADE)

Buenos Aires, July 1.
Lumiton production and release. Stars Mirtha Legrand; features Alicia Barrie, Roberto Airaldi, Ana Arneodo, Tito Gomez, Rafael Frontaura, Maria Santos, Tilda Thamar, Jorge Salcedo, Quico Moyano, Martin Zabalua and Emilia Noda. Directed by Francisco Mugica. Reviewed at Broadway, Buenos Aires.

This looks like one of the best all-round efforts of the local industry this season. Excellently constructed, well balanced, artistically conceived, it's by Carlos Olivari and Sixton Pondal Rios, the same team who did 'Los Martes Orquideas.' Both Mirtha Legrand, the star, and Francisco Mugica, the director, surpass previous work. Although in the final scenes some quality is lost, the film gains in dramatic effect what it loses in purity.

Story, told in retrospect, employs dramatic theme of a mirror which evokes the past of an old mansion and its people. Opens with an elderly woman, seeking a traveling blanket for her nephew, who finds among her ancient moth-ball possessions an old glass. Gazing into it she relives episodes of her life. There are scenes of old affairs, babies, intrigue and melancholia.

Mirtha Legrand works the sentiment to excellent advantage and Alicia Barrie gives out an excellent performance. Roberto Airaldi appears a little washed out, Tito Gomez is amusing and entertaining in a comedy supporting role while Maria Santos fills the bill in another character study. Starlet Tilda Thamar-is neat in supporting role.

Story has been carried out with a firm hand with fine shades of expression. Photography is unusually good. *Ray.*

Report from the Aleutians
(Documentary)
(COLOR)

U. S. Signal Corps production. Photographed under supervision of Capt. John Huston; commentary written and narrated by Capt. Huston, with additional narration by Walter Huston. Previewed at the Museum of Modern Art, N. Y., June 18, '43. Running time, 45 MINS.

The U. S. Army, which has consistently trailed its British allies in the making of war documentaries, moves up a peg with 'Report from the Aleutians.' The 45-minute film, beautifully photographed in color, has scope, depth and—above all—feeling. It leaves a real impression —bound to make every American puff with pride, trite as that sounds —at the splendid quality of the young men who make up our Army and Air Force and the great way they are conquering not only the Japs, but the elements, on this toughest of all battlefronts.

Outstanding is the mature, professional standard of 'Aleutians.' Which is not surprising, since it was supervised, edited, written and partially narrated by Capt. John Huston, who scripted such Warner Bros. b.o. toppers as 'Sergeant York' and 'Maltese Falcon,' and directed 'Falcon,' 'In This Our Life' and 'Across the Pacific.' Walter Huston, the captain's father, contributed part of the narration.

All war documentaries must perforce, forevermore, be compared with the greatest of them all, 'Desert Victory.' From this standpoint of exciting battle action, 'Aleutians' falls far short for the simple reason that no such ground-fighting took place here. Huston, who spent five months on the islands, left before the recent battle of Attu. This is a different kind of picture, however, and in its way—aside from terrific sequences of a bomber raid on Kiska —is almost as exciting as 'Desert Victory.' It is a successful attempt to bring to the American people a picture of the tough conditions under which their boys are fighting and the minor human angles which don't make newspaper headlines, but are the background to every battlefront.

That bomber raid on Kiska, incidentally, with which the picture ends, is one of the best-photographed of such actions yet seen. It's a breath-taker, which is at the same time remarkable for its unity, clarity and completeness. Huston obviously made many flights with the bomber crews and carefully edited his material to provide a well-rounded and in every way exciting picturization of the takeoff, the long trip to the target, the quick and dangerous bombing run and the voyage home.

Majority of the film was shot on the isle of Adak, locale of a U. S. bomber base. It shows the landing, the conquest in double time of the bleak Arctic weather to build the airfield, the way the boys live, what they do, how they act. The footage in the film was offered by the Army to the newsreels and bits of it have already been seen, notably shots of planes sending up torrential geysers as they land on a field covered with several feet of water.

Distribution of the film has been temporarily withheld, pending settlement of a dispute between the Army and the film industry over the length in which it shall be released. The Army wanted it to go into theatres in its present 4½ reels, while the War Activities Committee of the industry objects to that as an awkward length and wanted it in two reels or less to better fit theatre programs. It has been finally set for 1½ reels. Truth is that fine as it now is, trimming probably will improve it. Definitely, however, it will suffer from the severe shaving being demanded by the WAC. It hardly can be ex-

pected in that length to retain the fine, friendly, human quality which, contrasted against the bleak background, is its strength.

Miniature Reviews

'For Whom the Bell Tolls' (Color) (Par). Super-boxoffice.

'Heaven Can Wait' (20th). ─Lubitsch comedy-drama geared for big grosses and holdovers.

'Appointment in Berlin' (Col). Spy meller should do okay, especially as a dualer.

'Mexican Spitfire's Blessed Event' (RKO). Usual confusion and elemental comedy display for finale of series. Moderate entry as dual supporter.

'Bar 20' (UA). Hopalong Cassidy and his pals in actionful western with plenty of riding.

'Lucky Mr. Yates' (Col). Good idea bogged down by mock heroics and oversentimentalization: mediocre b.o.

'Silver Spurs' (Rep). Roy Rogers starrer that should click provincially.

'Spotlight Scandals' (Songs). (Mono). Billy Gilbert and Frank Fay in moderate-budget backstage comedy-drama.

'Wild Horse Rustlers' (PRC). Nazi-filled western, limited b.o.

For Whom the Bell Tolls
(COLOR)

Paramount release of Sam Wood production, directed by Wood. Executive producer, B. G. DeSylva. Stars Gary Cooper. Ingrid Bergman; features Akim Tamiroff. Arturo de Cordova, Joseph Calleia, Katina Paxinou. From novel by Ernest Hemingway; screenplay, Dudley Nichols; camera, Ray Rennahan; special effects, Gordon Jennings and Farciot Edouart; Technicolor, Natalie Kalmus, Morgan Padelford; production designed by Wm. Cameron Menzies; art, Hans Dreier, Haldane Douglas; music, Victor Young; editors, Sherman Todd, John Link. Opened July 14, 1943. Rivoli, N. Y., twice daily, $2.20 top. Running time, 166 MINS.

Robert Jordan	Gary Cooper
Maria	Ingrid Bergman
Pablo	Akim Tamiroff
Agustin	Arturo de Cordova
Anselmo	Vladimir Sokoloff
Rafael	Mikhail Rasumny
Fernando	Fortunio Bonanova
Andres	Eric Feldary
Primitivo	Victor Varconi
Pilar	Katina Paxinou
El Sordo	Joseph Calleia
Joaquin	Lilo Yarson
Paco	Alexander Granach
Gustavo	Adia Kuznetzoff
Ignacio	Leonid Snegoff
General Golz	Leo Bulgakov
Lieut. Berrendo	Duncan Renaldo
Andre Massart	George Coulouris
Captain Gomez	Frank Puglia
Colonel Miranda	Pedro de Cordoba
Staff Officer	Michael Visaroff
Karkov	Konstantin Shayne
Captain Mora	Martin Carralaga
Sniper	Jean del Val
Colonel Duval	Jack Mylong
Kashkin	Feodor Chaliapin
Frederico Gonzales	Pedro de Cordoba
Ricardo	Mayo Newhall
Benito Garcia, Mayor	Michael Dalmatoff
Guillermo	Antonio Vidal
Faustino Rivero	Robert Tafur
Julian	Armand Roland
Spanish Singer	Trini Varela
Sergeant—Elias Man	Dick Botiller
Elias Man	Franco Corsaro
Elias Man	Frank Lackteen
Bored Sentry	George Sorel
Peasant—Flails Gonzales	John Bleifer
Man—Flails the Mayor	Harry Cording
First Soldier	William Edmunds
Second Soller	Albert Morin
Third Soldier	Pedro Regas
Guillermo's Wife	Soledad Jiminez
Drunkard	Luis Rojas
Officer of the Civil Guards	Manuel Paris
One of the Civil Guards	Ernesto Morelli
One of the Civil Guards	Manuel Lopez
One of the Civil Guards	Jose Tortosa
Young Cavalry Man	Yakima Canutt
First Sentry	Tito Renaldo

Girls in Cafe—Maxine Ardell, Marjorie Deanne, Yvonne de Carlo, Alice Kirby, Marcella Phillips, Lynda Grey, Christopher King, Louise La Planche.

'For Whom the Bell Tolls' is one of the important pictures of all time. It will do plenty of business. Paramount took no chances when it pre-advertised that 'it will not be shown at popular prices before 1945.' Despite some of the captious criticism by the dailies, some of it justified, particularly as regards the length. 'Bell' is a boxoffice bellringer. The problem of fulsome footage is obviously open to easy solution and, as is detailed in this issue in a news story, producer-director Sam Wood recognizes this and will return to New York shortly to cut out plenty of footage; at least 20 minutes.

None can dispute that almost three hours of running time can overdo a good thing. If for no other reason, these tense wartimes are not attuned to marathon entertainment. Running sans intermission, the saga of Roberto and Maria (Gary Cooper and Ingrid Bergman) asks for too much concentrated attention on what is basically one dramatic episode, that of blasting a crucial bridge, in order to foil the Nationalists.

On a beautiful Technicolor canvas is projected an equally beautiful romance which, perhaps, lays a little too much emphasis on the amorous phase. It's one thing to punch up boy-meets-girl sequencing, but the nature of Hemingway's best-seller, of course, was predicated on a political aura resulting in the Spanish civil war. Whether or not with an eye to Franco's sensitivities in Madrid, there is little provocative in the film save for one speech by Cooper to explain to the Spanish gypsies why he, an instructor of Spanish in America, became partial to and part of the Loyalist cause.

Masterful have been the combined talents of producer-director Wood, scripter Dudley Nichols, executive producer Buddy DeSylva, and artisans such as William Cameron Menzies, who designed the production, along with the skillful cinematographers in all departments. In transmuting Hemingway to the screen they have captured the spirit of the strife that took Axis planes and tanks to bring the Republicans to their knees.

In flashback style are shown the cruelties of the Loyalists themselves, as they make Nationalist mayor and sympathizers run the gauntlet to their doom over a precipice. This is one of the film's few failings in direction and action, since the Fascist cruelties are chiefly spoken of, never depicted, save for one mountain-top foray by a group of strafing planes; whereas more graphically is shown what Loyalist mob rule did to one group of Francoites.

Maria (Miss Bergman) always speaks of how she, a mayor's daughter, was closely-cropped of tresses, and how she was physically abused in the former City Hall headquarters of her murdered father, the Mayor. (Reference to the bestial mass rape is delicately skimmed over, and is never as frank as in the book). Her first, clinging love is beautifully pointed up in the sequences with Cooper (Robert Jordan) where she tells him she has never really been kissed; and the passages where she wants to know 'what happens with the noses when people kiss,' are among the more definite audience values. Likewise, the intimacies in the sleeping bag, on the mountain-crags, are skillfully handled with little likelihood of censorial sensitivities.

Histrionically, 'Bell Tolls' is a triumph for the four sub-featured players. Katina Paxinou, onetime foremost in her native Greek theatre, dominates everything by a shade. A masculine woman who, however, has known of love and beauty, despite her realistic self-abnegation that she is ugly, is standout in everything she does. A vibrant actress, her American debut in Hollywood impresses her as one who will be reckoned with henceforth. The passages of the philosophy of exterior feminine ugliness and the hidden beauty within are almost epic in their writing and interpretation.

Akim Tamiroff, now an habitual scene-stealer, gives the best performance of his career as the sotted Pablo, the onetime brave warrior, now remorseful and wine-beclouded in remorse over his cruelties of the past, as he made the Nationalists run the flaylings. In a succession of character studies, the vagaries of his befuddled mind emerge into a spark of his former self, as he assists the sabotaging plans of Cooper. Arturo de Cordova and Joseph Calleia are capital as Augustin and El Sordo, fierce Loyalists despite their gypsy vagaries, and Vladimir Sokoloff likewise clicks in his philosophic assignment as aide to the anti-Francoites.

Cinematurgically, the sequencing of the action is open to more judicious editing for purposes of dramatic compactness. The fol-de-rol attendant to the main chore of blowing up the bridge, in some spots, creates for dangerous restlessness. The action tees off well. There is a train-wreck; Cooper has to shoot his aide as part of the pact that none should ever fall prisoner, alive, to the Francoites; there is an exciting blitz of a cafe; but soon thereafter it bogs down.

Scenically and cinematographically, the beauteous Sierra Nevadas have created an eye-filling Spanish background which approaches portraiture in many respects. William Cameron Menzies' designs, and the combined lensing of Ray Rennahan and his crew, plus the Technicolorations by Mrs. Kalmus and Morgan Padelford, are superlative.

For the record, 'Bell' cost around $150,000 for the screen rights (Hemingway's book sales determined the overage on top of the basic $100,000 price) and the production cost is officially a few thousands under $3,000,000.

For the record, also, 'Gone With Wind' (with which 'Bell' is being compared, in merchandizing, etc.) ran 217 minutes. *Abel.*

HEAVEN CAN WAIT

(COLOR)

20th-Fox release of Ernst Lubitsch production, directed by Lubitsch. Stars Gene Tierney, Don Ameche, Charles Coburn. Screenplay, Samson Raphaelson, based on play by Lazlo Bus-Fekete; editor, Dorothy Spencer; camera, Edward Cronjager. Tradeshown at RKO 23d St., N. Y., July 19, '43. Running time, 112 MINS.

Martha	Gene Tierney
Henry Van Cleve	Don Ameche
Hugo Van Cleve	Charles Coburn
Mrs. Strabel	Marjorie Main
His Excellency	Laird Cregar
Bertha Van Cleve	Spring Byington
Albert Van Cleve	Allyn Joslyn
E. F. Strabel	Eugene Pallette
Mademoiselle	Signe Hasso
Randolph Van Cleve	Louis Calhern
Peggy Nash	Helene Reynolds
James	Aubrey Mather
Jack Van Cleve	Michael Ames
Flogdell	Leonard Carey
Jasper	Clarence Muse
Henry Van Cleve (age 15)	Dickie Moore
Albert Van Cleve (age 15)	Dickie Jones
Jane	Trudy Marshall
Mrs. Craig	Florence Bates
Grandmother	Clara Blandick
Mrs. Cooper	Anita Bolster
Jack (as a boy)	Nino Pipitone, Jr.
Miss Ralston	Claire Du Brey
Nurse	Maureen Rodin-Ryan

'Heaven Can Wait' is a charming, sentimental comedy-drama which will roll up top grosses. It's a cinch for profitable holdovers in the key situations and will click easily in the subsequents as well.

Built in episodic fashion, via the flashback style, and containing a number of familiar situations, nimble writing and sparkling dialog have, however, imparted a freshness which assures strongly favorable word-of-mouth.

Provided with generous slices of comedy, skillfully handled by producer-director Ernst Lubitsch, it is for most of the 112 minutes a smooth, appealing and highly commercial production. Lubitsch has endowed it with light, amusing sophistication and heart-warming nostalgia. He has handled Don Ameche and Gene Tierney, in (for them) difficult characterizations, dexterously.

The Lazlo Bus-Fekete piece covers the complete span of a man's life, from precocious infancy to, in this case, to the sprightly senility of a 70-year-old playboy. It opens with the deceased (Ameche) asking Satan for a passport to hell, which is not being issued unless the applicant can justify his right to it.

This is followed by a recital of real and fancied misdeeds from the time the sinner discovers that, in order to get girls, a boy must have plenty of beetles, through the smartly fashioned hilarious drunk scene with a French maid at the age of 15, to the thefting of his cousin's fiancee, whom he marries.

Encompassing the picturesque handle-bar mustache era of the '80s and '90s in New York, there is what is tantamount to a series of engaging animated family tintype scenes.

Charles Coburn as the fond grandfather who takes a hand in his favorite grandson's romantic and domestic problems, walks away with the early sequences in a terrific comedy performance. Standouts in subordinate roles are Marjorie Main and Eugene Pallette as the Kansas beef tycoons, with a statue to a cow named Mabel on their front lawn, whose daughter (Gene Tierney) marries Ameche. Allyn Joslyn, as the staid, colorless cousin who loses the girl; Laird Cregar, as a very bland, very human, very understanding Satan; Dickie Moore and Dickie Jones in the juve roles; Louis Calhern as the father who learns the facts of life at 43; and Spring Byington, provide excellent support.

Technicolor and other uniformly high production values bespeak the hefty negative cost. *Mori.*

Appointment in Berlin

Columbia release of Samuel Bischoff production. Features George Sanders, Marguerite Chapman, Onslow Stevens, Gale Sondergaard. Directed by Alfred E. Green. Story, B. F. Fineman; adaptation, Horace McCoy and Michael Hogan; editors, Al Clark and Reg Browne; camera, Franz F. Planer. At Rialto, N. Y., week July 16, '43. Running time, 77 MINS.

Keith Wilson	George Sanders
Ilse Preissing	Marguerite Chapman
Rudolph Preissing	Onslow Stevens
Gretta Van Leyden	Gale Sondergaard
Colonel Patterson	Alan Napier
Sir Douglas Wilson	H. P. Sanders
Bill Banning	Don Douglas
Babe Forrester	Jack Lee
Smitty	Alec Craig
MacPhail	Leonard Mudie
Von Ritter	Frederic Worlock
Henri Bader	Steve Geray
Cripple	Wolfgang A. Zilzer

Dealing with counter-espionage under somewhat unique circumstances, 'Appointment in Berlin' is acceptable albeit not sockful entertainment. Despite its 77 minutes which causes dragginess toward the end, picture holds sufficient interest to indicate that it will do satisfactorily, particularly as a dualer.

Central figure is George Sanders, playing a wing-commander in the R.A.F. whose resentment over the Munich pact cashiers him out of service. However, a British intelligence official, who has faith in Sanders, inducts him into the secret service but carefully conceals his identity. Even after consorting with a group of Nazi spies and getting arrested, the British intelligence service declines to avert Sanders' imprisonment for 18 months.

After that, the action switches to Berlin where Sanders ingratiates himself into the confidence of the Nazis and becomes a sort of Lord Haw-Haw, doing shortwave broadcasts as the 'Voice of Truth.' While the broadcasts appear to be viciously anti-British, they are so done, through a code, as to supply vital information to London.

Finally the Nazis get wise to Sanders and he is forced to flee. With him is the sister of a Nazi spy who has turned but, for her trouble, she gets shot, thus removing the female lead of the story. Sanders, fleeing in a stolen Nazi plane, also meets death, a finish for him that isn't expected. He is posthumously decorated for the work he had done. Both Sanders and Marguerite Chapman, playing opposite him, give sturdy performances.

Gale Sondergaard, working in Berlin as a British intelligence agent, is another who bites the dust at the hands of the Nazis. She plays her role convincingly and effectively. Doing the brother of Miss Chapman is Onslow Stevens, a good type as a Nazi spy. Lessers include Alan Napier, H. P. Sanders and Don Douglas.

Samuel Bischoff has provided adequate production and the direction by Alfred E. Green is capable. *Char.*

Mexican Spitfire's Baby

Hollywood, July 15.

RKO release of Bert Gilroy production. Stars Lupe Velez, Leon Errol. Directed by Leslie Goodwins. Screenplay by Charles E. Roberts, Dane Lussier; original by Roberts; camera, Jack MacKenzie; editor, Harry Marker; asst. director, James Casey. Tradeshown in L. A. July 14, '43. Running time, 62 MINS.

Carmelita	Lupe Velez
Lord Epping / Uncle Matt	Leon Errol
Dennis	Walter Reed
Aunt Della	Elisabeth Risdon
Lady Epping	Lydia Bilbrook
Mr. Sharpe	Hugh Beaumont
Mrs. Pettibone	Aileen Carlyle
Bartender	Alan Carney
Verbena	Marietta Canty
Mrs. Walters	Ruth Lee
Desk Clerk	Wally Brown

This is the last of the 'Spitfires' which have tarried around for several years. Finale of series displays the usual complications on light framework for display of broadest farce and horseplay. It's a standard supporting entry for the program houses where levity is required to contrast dramatic top attraction.

Lupe Velez's acquisition of a baby cub starts the routine misunderstandings of an expectant heir, which allows corralling of the series characters at an Arizona inn. Leon Errol again handles dual role of Uncle Matt and Lord Epping for the usual hit-and-miss episodes of confused identities, while Lupe's explosions are frequent as usual. Bound up in the proceedings is a vague plot of Navy officer Walter Reed and Hugh Beaumont to secure signature of Epping to a contract of some kind.

Yarn sets up convenient situations to display laugh material that will get reaction from the family and juve customers and those not hard to please. Errol broadly plays the two characters, but injects expert timing to delivery to take major attention throughout. Direction by Leslie Goodwins is standard for the entries. *Walt.*

BAR 20

Hollywood, July 17.

United Artists release of Harry Sherman production; associate producer, Lewis J. Rachmil. Stars William Boyd; features Andy Clyde and George Reeves. Directed by Lesley Selander. Screenplay by Morton Grant, Norman Houston, Michael Wilson; camera, Russell Harlan; editor, Carroll Lewis; asst. drector, Glenn Cook. Previewed in studio projection room, July 16, '43. Running time, 54 MINS.

Hopalong Cassidy	William Boyd
California	Andy Clyde
Lin Bradley	George Reeves
Marie Stevens	Dustine Farnum
Mark Jackson	Victor Jory
Slash	Douglas Fowley
Mrs. Stevens	Betty Blythe
Richard Adams	Bob Mitchum
One Eye	Francis McDonald
Tom	Earle Hodgins

Good action western, with Hopalong Cassidy and his two sidekicks running through most of the footage in fast rides or shooting it out with the frontier bad men. Will tab plenty of bookings where Hoppy series and westerns have a following among the customers.

Trek of Hoppy, Andy Clyde and George Reeves from Bar 20 ranch to a distant point to buy herd of pedigreed cattle, sets the stage for unfolding of regulation situation where gang of outlaws are preying on the valley. Naturally, Hoppy becomes the frontier sleuth to make necessary deductions and bring the leader to time. Gang, in this case, get away with haul of jewels in stagecoach robbery, and follow this up with snatch of Hopalong's money earmarked for cattle purchase. Balance of tale is devoted to lusty riding and plenty of funfighting; with broad comedy of Clyde aimed for juve reaction and getting over with more footage than is generally the case.

Although script is set up in regulation western formula, speedy direction by Lesley Selander fulfills audience requirements. Boyd, Clyde and Reeves again continue their standard characterizations which have combined to become the most popular western threesome on the screen. Victor Jory is the gang leader, with Douglas Fowley and Francis McDonald his henchmen. In addition to oldtimers McDonald and Betty Blythe, producer Harry Sherman introduces Dustine Farnum as the girl. Latter is daughter of the late Dustin Farnum, early western film star.

Photography by Russell Harlan maintains the high standard which he has set for previous issues of the series. *Walt.*

Good Luck, Mr. Yates

Columbia release of David Chakin production. Features Claire Trevor. Edgar Buchanan, Jess Barker, Tom Neal, Albert Basserman. Directed by Ray Enright. Screenplay, Lou Breslow and Adele Comandini from story by Hal Smith and Sam Rudd; camera, Philip Tannura; editor, Richard Fantle. At Strand. Brooklyn, N. Y., dual, week July 15, '43. Running time, 69 MINS.

Ruth Jones	Claire Trevor
Jonesey Jones	Edgar Buchanan
Oliver Yates	Jess Barker
Charlie Edmonds	Tom Neal
Dr. Carl Hesser	Albert Basserman
Johnny Zaloris	Tommy Cook
Jimmy Dixon	Scotty Beckett
Joe Briggs	Frank Sully
Monty King	Douglas Leavitt
Mike Zaloris	Henry Armetta
Katy Zaloris	Rosina Galli
Plunkett	Billy Roy
Bob Coles	Conrad Binyon
Ross	Bobby Larson
Wilson	Rudy Wissler
The Bob Mitchell Boy Choir	
The Sheriff's Boys Band	

Columbia starts out with a swell idea; the psychological plight of a 4-F schoolteacher in a community where a young man out of uniform just doesn't rate; and then gums the works with an overdrawn piece of mock heroics, that will have a tough time pleasing either the juves or their elders.

The conflict starts early. Jess Barker, a teacher in a military academy, loses the students' respect because he's not in uniform. He finally induces the draft board to release him from his essential classification, and enlists, only to discover that the army won't take him due to a punctured eardrum. Rather than return to school where he's now regained stature, Barker takes a shipyard job. The plot then takes a vacation.

Barker leads the kids to believe he's in the army by answering letters addressed to him in camp, which are forwarded by a soldier pal. This leads to suspicion that he's a deserter. A Nazi spy charge is also thrown in when he has his ear treated by Albert Basserman, of the heavy accent. Complications are topped by a romance with Claire Trevor, a fellow welder, and a fire at the shipyard in which Barker emerges as a hero.

The military school angle is oversentimentalized, and using the army as a mail forwarding organization, without the officers catching wise is hard to take. Performances also run an uneven course, with juve, Scotty Beckett, copping honors. He portrays a juvenile delinquent cadet going straight, and he does it without the benefit of Dead End Kid diction.

Claire Trevor is okay in modern wedding garb, minus her shady lady routine. Edgar Buchanan, who usually clicks as a comedian, plays straight and as a consequence lacks that surefire Buchanan appeal. Barker, reminiscent of the late Phillips Holmes, seems capable of handling solid dramatics.

Film in general is paced too slowly, which doesn't help the weak script.

SILVER SPURS
(SONGS)

Republic release of Harry Grey production. Stars Roy Rogers; features Smiley Burnette, John Carradine, Phyllis Brooks, Jerome Cowan, Joyce Compton, Bob Nolan, Sons of Pioneers. Directed by Joseph Kane. Screenplay, John K. Butler and J. Benton Cheney; camera, Reggie Lanning; editor, Tony Martinelli; musical director, Morton Scott. Reviewed July 16, '43. New York, N. Y. Running time, 68 MINS.

Roy	Roy Rogers
Smartest Horse in the Movies	Trigger
Frog Millhouse	Smiley Burnette
Lucky Miller	John Carradine
Mary Hardigan	Phyllis Brooks
Jerry Johnson	Jerome Cowan
Mildred "Millie" Love	Joyce Compton
Buck Walters	Dick Wessel
Steve Corlan	Hal Taliaferro
Judge Pebble	Forrest Taylor
Mr Hawkins	Charles Wilson
Justice of Peace	Byron Foulger
Bob Nolan and	
The Sons of the Pioneers	

Republic doesn't help its Roy Rogers buildup campaign any with this farfetched combination western and newspaper story. The hoss opera stuff is in the groove, but the fourth estate angle is just so much unnecessary and unbelievable business. It's still strong b.o. for action fans and out-of-town houses, but won't make much of a dent with the city crowd.

Story concerns ranch foreman Roy Rogers' attempt to get his boss, Jerome Cowan's, signature okaying a railroad right-of-way across the ranch to complete a local oil well project. Resort operator, John Carradine, wants the ranch and piece of oil well for himself, so he gets Cowan drunk, takes him for plenty in a card game, and induces him to hitch up with a mail order bride. All this is supposed to delay the signing of the right-of-way and place Cowan in Carradine's power. 'Bride' is supplied by the Lonely Hearts club of a big city newspaper, and Phyllis Brooks, sheet's star reporter, is assigned to pose as bride-to-be.

Action then centers on Miss Brooks' unscheduled marriage to Cowan, Cowan's murder by Carradine's gunman, two unjustified murder raps charged against Rogers and the ultimate righting of wrongs. When the story sticks to the western format, it's fast moving, exciting material. But the mail order bride routine with Phyllis Brooks and her editor, who cooked up the scheme, is too phoney, even for an actioner. Rogers, however, manages to play a two-fisted, smooth-singing cowboy very convincingly throughout all the shenanigans. He is ably aided by his horse, Trigger, and right hand man, Smiley Burnette. Carradine, Cowan, and the Misses Brooks and Compton, who represent the film's urban set, go through their parts without too much distinction. Both Cowan and Carradine, who are actually topnotch performers, don't attempt to rise above the script. The distaff side is content to look pretty, cute, coy and indignant as the occasion demands.

Joseph Kane's direction is good, keeping the film moving at a gallop. Camera work is also above average, with some neat landscape and action shots.

Spotlight Scandals
(SONGS)
Hollywood, July 16.

Monogram release of Sam Katzman-Jack Dietz production; associate producer, Bar-

ney Sarecky. Features Billy Gilbert, Frank Fay, Bonnie Baker. Directed by William Beaudine. Screenplay, Wm. X. Crawley, also Biryl Sachs; camera, Jack Stengler; editor, Carl Pierson; asst. director, Arthur Hammond; musical director, Edward Kay; dances, Jack Boyle. Previewed at Hollywood Paramount, July 15, '43. Running time, 78 MINS.

Billy Gilbert	By Himself
Frank Fay	By Himself
Bonnie Baker	By Herself
Butch	Billy Lenhradt
Buddy	Chas. K. Brown
Oscar	Harry Langdon
Bernice	Iris Adrian
Radio Rogues	Jimmy Hollywood
	Eddie Bartell
	Syd Chalton
Jerry	James Bush
Betty	Claudia Dell
Eddie Parks	By Himself
Mrs. Baker	Betty Blythe
Henry King	By Himself
Herb Miller	By Himself
Suzy	Lottie Harrison
Blondel	Jim Hope
Dance Director	Jack Boyle

Monogram teams Billy Gilbert and Frank Fay for surprising results in this moderately-budgeted program filmusical which will garner good share of datings in supporting spots of the program and family houses.

Despite fact picture needs major editing job to eliminate extraneous footage and unnecessary sequences, work of Gilbert and Fay carries it along fairly successfully. Both work straight, and let their gags slip in with some degree of credulity. Despite the good crop of corn planted along the way, it's diverting for the customers.

Fay, vaude actor stranded in the midwest, picks up barber Gilbert as partner—mainly to get transportation back to New York. But under Fay's tutelage, the hick amateur becomes a valuable stooge to catapult the pair to stardom. Gilbert steps aside to allow Fay to go single in radio. However, the pair reunite when Fay gets in trouble and Gilbert comes to his aid.

Backstage setting allows for several production numbers, brief musical interludes by the Henry King and Herb Miller bands, specialties by the Three Radio Rogues, and songs by Bonnie Baker.

Editing can smooth out the poor job of spotting the various talent on display. The two band aggregations are not used for maximum attention, while in comparison, four songs by Bonnie Baker could be sliced to half that number. Her tunes include: 'The Restless Age,' 'Goodnight Now,' 'Oh. Johnny,' and 'The Lilac Tree.' Claudia Dell has too weak a voice to lead frontier dancehall number with 'Tempo of the Trail.' Radio Rogues click with their impersonations for best specialty of the picture.

Supporting cast includes Butch & Buddy, Harry Langdon. Iris Adrian, James Bush. Jim Hope and Betty Blythe. Despite the overload of numbers, William Beaudine gets plenty out of the Gilbert-Fay episodes for the credit side of the ledger. Production mounting indicates the economy budget. *Walt.*

Wild Horse Rustlers

Producers Release Corp., release of Sigmund Neufeld production. Features Bob Livingston, Al St. John, Linda Johnson. Directed by Sam Newfield; screenplay, Steve Braxton; camera, Robert Cline; editor, Holbrook N. Todd. Reviewed at New York, N. Y., dual, week of July 13, '43. Running time, 56 MINS.

Tom Cameron	Bob Livingston
Fuzzy	Al St. John
Ellen	Linda Johnson
Smoky	Lane Chandler
Collins	Stanley Price
Jake	Frank Ellis
Sheriff	Karl Hackett

PRC gives this western a topical twist by introducing Nazi horse rustlers, but it's the mugging of Al St. John that gives the film an even chance as entertainment. There's also the identical twin angle; one, a 100% patriotic American ranch foreman, the other, a nazi agent trying

to sabotage the Army's horse procurement program.

The identical twin business is hard on the imagination. The foreman is acceptable, but the audience is supposed to swallow a western drawl sported by the long-lost brother, who's lived in Germany since he was knee-high to a gopher. There is another shortcoming. Despite the Government's and private agencies' advice to treat the Nazi agents here as serious menaces, 'Wild Horse Rustlers' portrays the Axis heavies as jerks with an I.Q. of minus 50.

Film is otherwise a run-of-the-mill actioner with the normal quota of hard riding and shooting which rarely seems to hurt anybody, the actual punishment being inflicted via slugfests.

Bob Livingston and Linda Johnson, who share top billing with St. John, play poor seconds to the be-whiskered comedian as far as audience reaction is concerned. Livingston, however, is featured in most of the action and wears his cowboy regalia with the proper amount of dash. Lane Chandler, who plays the twins, is okay as the ranch foreman, but n.s.g. as the phoney Nazi agent.

Miniature Reviews

'Watch On The Rhine' (WB). Magnificent picturization of stinging, anti-fascist stage play. Should pull powerful grosses.

'Salute to the Marines' (M-G). should do good biz; stars Wallace Beery.

'I Dood It' (M-G) (Musical). Red Skelton-Eleanor Powell musical okay boxoffice via marquee names.

Murder on the Waterfront (WB). Weak in entertainment and b.o. values. Short length poses booking problem.

'Headin' For God's Country' (Rep). With smart exploitation of Jap angle, film can register as dualer.

'What's Buzzin', Cousin?' (Col). Dull musical with a strong marquee cast.

'Honeymoon Lodge' (Songs) (U). Fairly diverting comedy-drama with music and specialties for dual supporting spot.

'The Stranger From Pecos' (Mono). Excellent Johnny Mack Brown western.

Watch on the Rhine

Warner Bros. release of Hal B. Wallis production. Stars Bette Davis, Paul Lukas: features Geraldine Fitzgerald, Lucile Watson. Beulah Bondi. George Coulouris. Directed by Herman Shumlin. Screenplay by Danniell Hammett, from stage play by Lillian Hellman: music, Max Steiner: camera, Merritt Gerstad and Hal Mohr; editor, Rudi Fehr: orchestral arrangements, Hugfo Friedhofer: musical director, Leo F. Forbstein. Previewed in projection room. N.Y. July 23, '43. Running time. 109 MINS.

Sara Muller....Bette Davis
Kurt Muller....Paul Lukas
Marthe de Brancovis....Geraldine Fitzgerald
Fanny Farrelly....Lucile Watson
Anise....Geulah Bondi
Teck de Brancovis....George Coulouris
David Farrelly....Donald Woods
Phil von Ramme....Henry Daniell
Joshua....Donald Buka
Bode....Eric Roberts
Babette....Janis Wilsonb
Mrs. Mellie Sewell....Mary Young
Herr Blecher....Kurt Katch
Dr. Klauber....Edwin Kalser
Oberdorff....Robert O. Davis
Sam Chandler....Clyde Fillmore
Joseph....Frank Wilson
Horace....Clarence Muse

'Watch on the Rhine' is a distinguished picture. It is even better than its powerful original stage version. It expresses the same urgent theme, but with broader sweep and in more affecting terms of personal emotion. It is enthralling entertainment and at the same time irresistibly stirring drama. It should be a tremendous boxoffice success and, more important, it carries a message of incalculable topical importance.

The film more than retains the vital theme of the original play. It actually carries the theme further and deeper, and it does so with passionate conviction and enormous skill. There is no compromise on controversial matters. Fascists are identified as such and, although the point is not brought home as it might have been, the industrial-financial support that makes fascism possible is also mentioned. But it is the basic idea of the play, the universal threat of fascism, even into peaceful, everyday American homes before Pearl Harbor, and the humble, noble courage of those who fight it, that is transcendantly expressed in this screen edition. That message is now more timely than ever.

Besides expanding and giving greater dimension to the Lillian Hellman original, the film clarifies the story and makes some of the characters and situations more coherent. That is achieved not so much by utilizing the greater scope of the screen to carry the action outside the walls of the suburban Washington living room, but by rearranging scenes and dialog to give slightly different continuity and greater plausibility to the story.

Thus, the picture opens with the refugee Muller family entering the U. S. from Mexico and crossing the desert in a grubby day coach, in contrast to the luxurious home they are about to enter. Similarly, the quarrels between Teck and Marthe de Brancovis, which were so awkward in the play, are spread into several different scenes and placed in more logical locales on the screen. Also, the villainous Count's visits to the German embassy, merely a reference in the legit version, are actually shown in the film in all their sinister aspects.

Nearly all the original dialog remains, but with a few minor changes and numerous lines that retain the sense and flavor of the play. Some of the lines have been switched from one character to another. Most such instances involve building up the Bette Davis part of the anti-fascist's wife. But though most of her added lines have been taken from Paul Lukas' part, the effect is not harmful. A scene at the very end, obviously added to enlarge Miss Davis' role, is anti-climactic and disappointing, but even that does not vitally lessen the picture's dramatic impact.

Just as he was in the play, Paul Lukas is the outstanding star of the film. Anything his part may have lost in the transfer of key lines to Miss Davis is offset by the projective value of the camera for closeups. So, although his performance in the same part was voted by the New York drama critics as the best of the 1940-41 season, he surpasses it on the screen. His portrayal of the heroic German has the same quiet strength and the slowly gathering force that it had on the stage, but it now seems even better defined and carefully detailed, and it has much more vitality. It is the best part Lukas has ever had on the screen (just as it was on the stage) and he responds with by far the finest performance of his career.

In the lesser starring part of the wife (created on the stage by Mady Christians), Miss Davis gives a performance of genuine distinction. Only in a single scene, a dress-making bit which adds significant detail to the tender relationship between Muller and his wife, is there any compromise with the appropriately dowdy appearance of the character. But more important, Miss Davis' playing suggests a blend of humility and magnetism, of reticence and articulateness, and of quiet patience and iron willpower. Some of her scenes with Lukas are overpoweringly touching.

Lucile Watson, whose incisive playing of the shrewd matriarch was a gem in the original play, is even more striking in the expanded part on the screen. Her performance of the old gal's capriciousness still sets the tone for the early scenes, but some added passages later have given her greater scope, which she capitalizes brilliantly. And although one or two of her lines have been given to Miss Davis, notably the quotation of a saying by old Judge Farrelly, an added line about how she wishes she had been the kind of woman her daughter has turned out to be, gives the part more stature and the entire picture more point.

Geraldine Fitzgerald is believable and attractive as the unhappily-married Countess, which is a tribute to her acting, but also to the greatly clarified part (which Helen Trenholme artfully made acceptable in the stage original). George Coulouris is more subdued and thus more believably menacing than he was in the legit edition. Donald Woods makes young David Farrelly much more pliable and thus more logical and attractive than the character seemed on the stage. Eric Roberts, as the youngest child, and Frank Wilson, as the butler, repeat their original characterizations convincingly. Beulah Bondi is excellent in the slightly diminished part of the French governess-companion, while Donald Buka and Janis Wilson are credible as the older Muller children. Kurt Katch contributes a juicy bit as a Nazi agent, and Mary Young offers a graphic miniature of a gossipy Washington matron.

Although credit for such a magnificent picture as 'Watch on the Rhine' must rightfully be shared by everyone associated with it, Herman Shumlin rates particular praise for his remarkably expressive direction. Even more than with the original play, he seems to have seen and understood the depth of the characters and the story, to have been able to project them in graphic terms and to evoke eloquent performances from his cast. He has used the camera skillfully, achieved deft pace, created atmosphere and a steadily mounting suspense and, with few exceptions, has compressed the story continuity into a smooth flow. There are flaws in some of the film's technical details, such as faulty tone in the sound track for outdoor scenes, and certain strident passages in the musical score. But they are relatively inconsequential. *Hobe.*

Salute to the Marines

(COLOR)

Metro release of John W. Considine, Jr., production. Stars Wallace Beery; features Fay Bainter, Reginald Owen, Keye Luke, Ray Collins, Marilyn Maxwell, William Lundigan, Donald Curtis. Directed by S. Sylvan Simon. Story, Robert D. Andrews; screenplay, George Bruce; adaptation, Wells Root; editor, Fredrick Y. Smith; camera, Charles Schoenbaum and W. Howard Green. Previewed in projection room, N. Y., July 21, '43. Running time, 101 MINS.

Sgt. Major William Bailey....Wallace Beery
Jennie Bailey....Fay Bainter
Mr. Caspar....Reginald Owen
'Flashy' Logaz....Keye Luke
Colonel Mason....Ray Collins
Helen Bailey....Marilyn Maxwell
Rufus Cleveland....William Lundigan
Randall James....Donald Curtis
Adjutant....Noah Berry, Sr.
Corporal Mosley....Dick Curtis
Private Hanks....Russell Gleason
Mrs. Carson....Rose Hobart

'Salute to the Marines' is exactly what its title implies. The fine production given the picture by John Considine, Jr., the able direction of S. Sylvan Simon and the superlative acting, plus excellent color, entitle it to good to strong boxoffice results.

Wallace Beery, starring, is cast as a marine who's been in the service 30 years. Beery has proved himself himself has never seen action, a fact that burns him because he's after battle stripes.

When Beery is refused permission to embark with a battalion for action in China, he suffers a spell of despondency and, after hitting the bottle, gets into a fight with a flock of merchant seamen. This lands him in the brig, and since his wife has gone anti-war, wanting him to give up army life, he decides to retire. Some of the best moments of the picture are those in which Beery, out of uniform and no one to yell at, tries vainly to relax in the atmosphere of home life, where chewing tobacco, among other things, is verboten. He's almost a pitiful figure, while the wife becomes an increasingly unsympathetic character, especially when she tries to take Beery's dress uniform away from him, a proud possession mirrowing 30 years of faithful military service.

When the Japs suddenly invade the Philippines, Beery goes into action by directing the evacuation of his town and the defenses necessary in an attempt to beat off the 'mustard-colored monkeys,' as he calls 'em. It's the first battle he's seen and he goes to it like a horse to water, his strategy ultimately aiding in an enemy retreat.

Film ends back at San Diego, where Marilyn Maxwell, now in uniform herself, receives a decoration on behalf of her father who, with Fay Bainter, as the mother, perished in the Philippines' defense. Miss Maxwell photographs niftily in color and gives a fine performance. This is also true of Miss Bainter, who ultimately makes up with Beery when both face actual war in the P.I. Reginald Owen is a surprise as the store owner who turns out to be a Nazi, despite his decided English accent. Keye Luke plays a Filipino, a former fighter in the U. S. who is hopeful of regaining the ring crown. He does well, while Ray Collins makes a good marine colonel. William Lundigan is paired with Miss Maxwell for romantic interest. He acquits himself creditably, as does Donald Curtis, a brother flier in the marines. *Char.*

I DOOD IT

(MUSICAL)

Metro release of Jack Cummings production. Stars Red Skelton and Eleanor Powell; features Richard Ainley, Patricia Dahe, Sam Levene, Thurston Hall, Lena Horne, Hazel Scott and Jimmy Dorsey's orch with Bob Eberly and Helen O'Connell. Directed by Vincente Minnelli. Screenplay, Sig Herzig and Fred Saldy; songs, Don Raye, Gene De Paul, Lew Brown, Ralph Freed, Sammy Fain, Count Basie, Cole Porter, Vernon Duke, John La Touche, Ted Fetter, Leo Robin, Richard Myers; arrangement of 'Jericho,' Kay Thompson; music direction, George Stoll; dance direction, Bob Connolly; camera, Ray June; editor, Robert J. Kern. Previewed in projection room, N. Y., July 22, '43. Running time, 102 MINS.

Joseph Rivington Renolds....Red Skelton
Constance Shaw....Eleanor Powell
Larry West....Richard Ainley
Suretta Brenton....Patricia Dane
Ed Jackson....Sam Levene
Kenneth Lawlor....Thurston Hall
Lena Horne....By Herself
Hazel Scott....By Herself
Roy Hartwood....John Hodiak
Annette....Butterfly McQueen
Mrs. Spelvin....Marjorie Gateson
Mr. Spelvin....Andrew Tombes
Jimmy Dorsey and Orchestra
with Helen O'Connell and Bob Eberly

Metro has wrapped Red Skelton and Eleanor Powell, among other names, around a popular Skelton radio phrase that's being used for the film's title, and the net result is moderate entertainment. With the two stars pacing a featured lineup that includes Jimmy Dorsey's orchestra (with Bob Eberly and Helen O'Connell), Lena Horne, Hazel Scott, Richard Ainley, Patricia Dane, Sam Levene and Thurston Hall, the pic's b.o. seems assured.

'I Dood It' is, by Metro's usual standards, not one of its best musicals, but that's due mostly to the screenplay. While the plot of a musical can generally be accepted only as a cue for the song-and-dance, the failing is particularly apparent in 'Dood It.' The yarn is too unbelievable, though the absurdities fashioned for Skelton have their compensations in the actual performance.

'Dood It' is enhanced by its specialties, notably by the Dorsey personnel, the dancing of Miss Powell, the pianistic swingology of Miss Scott and the sultry warbling of Miss Horne, the latter two in an all-Negro production number. This sequence, incidentally, emphasizes the film's lack of continuity by the obviously contrived manner in which it is introduced.

Story is a retake of an old situation, dealing with the love of a valet aide for a dancing star. That would be Skelton and Miss Powell. Skelton courts Miss Powell from a distance, a fashion plate through borrowal of his customers' clothes. Then follows a series of situations that find him mixed up in a 'spite' marriage with Miss Powell, followed by his discovery and rout of a spy plot. It's all very hectic and uncertain, but pretends to be nothing more than a vehicle for the comic's fol-de-rol.

Skelton remains a topnotch comedian with his standard dumb-cluck type of business, though the material is somewhat spotty, while Miss Powell is seen at her best advantage during the production numbers, in which she hoofs with her usual sock results.

Dorsey's outfit, a boxoffice factor in itself, is in and out a[redacted]rnment to the presentation routines, and always acquits itself niftily, ably backed by its two singers, Bob Eberly and Helen O'Connell. There's plenty production backgrounding for the Misses Scott and Horne in a number with lots of s.a. as evidenced by the two colored principals. Richard Ainley, Patricia Dane, Sam Levene and Thurston Hall have lesser parts and they handle them capably.

There are a flock of tunes from some of the top songsmiths in the biz, some of them now standard, and all help towards the film's plus marks. Vincente Minnelli has directed for speed, but there are enough draggy spots to warrant at least a 10-minute cut. The dances are colorful and the over-all production investiture bespeaks hefty expenditure. *Kahn.*

Murder on the Waterfront

Warner Bros. production and release. Features Warren Douglas, Joan Winfield, John Loder, Ruth Ford. Directed by B. Reaves Eason. Screenplay, Robert E. Kent, from play by Ralph Spencer Zink; camera, Harry Neumann; editor, James Gibbon. Previewed in projection room, N. Y., July 23, '43. Running time, **49 MINS.**

Joe Davis....................Warren Douglas
Gloria....................Joan Winfield
Lt. Com. Holbrook....................John Loder
Lana Shane....................Ruth Ford
Lt. Dawson....................Bill Crago
1st Officer Barnes....................Bill Kennedy
Capt. David Towne..William B. Davidson
Gordon Shane....................Don Costello
Com. George Kalin....................James Flavin
Guard....................Bill Edwards
2d Sentry....................Ross Ford
1st Sentry....................DeWolf Hopper
Daniel Lewis....................John Maxwell
Connors....................Phil Van Zandt
Petty Officer Thomas........Frank Mayo
Capt. Beal....................Fred Kelsey

Any picture as feeble as 'Murder on the Waterfront' immediately evokes the question, 'How come?' Not only is it negative entertainment, but it's dubious propaganda and is even awkward length (49 minutes) for booking, either for dual bills or as a short.

Ostensibly, the film is a whodunit, but with a couple of tepid specialty acts. Localed at a Pacific coast port, the yarn deals with the attempts of a Nazi agent to steal a secret thermostat used by the U. S. Navy. There's one murder, plus several attempts and, in a shoot-the-works finish, a wholesale shooting match. Since all the visible clues fakes and the real culprit is shown hardly at all until the denouement, it all makes scant sense.

In addition, the picture presents Naval officers and men as not only nitwits addicted to loose gab of military info (there are any number of instances of characters telling where and when they're sailing, with no indication such behavior is foolish or dangerous), but as acting senselessly and inefficiently in a crisis. What's more, there's the ludicrous supposition that a troupe of entertainers would give a show for the sailors on the very eve of their sailing, the implication that a Navy and Merchant Marine includes spies and murderers, that a Navy court marshall has been guilty of injustice, that camp-show performers may include revenge-killers, and even the spectacle of a naval intelligence officer making a veiled suggestion of incitement to lynching.

All this is scattered through a puerile script, embarrassing production and direction, and stilted performance. *Hobe.*

Headin' for God's Country

Republic release of Armand Schaefer production. Features William Lundigan, Virginia Dale, Harry Davenport, Harry Shannon, Addison Richards. Directed by William Morgan. Screenplay, Elizabeth Meehan and Houston Branch, based on original by Houston Branch; camera, Bud Thackery; editor, Arthur Roberts. Reviewed at Brooklyn Strand, Brooklyn; dual, week of July 22, '43. Running time, **78 MINS.**

Michael Banyan........William Lundigan
Laurie Lane....................Virginia Dale
Clem Adams....................Harry Davenport
Albert Ness....................Harry Shannon
District Commissioner....Addison Richards
Hilary Higgins........J. Frank Hamilton
Hugo Higgins....................Eddie Acuff
Jim Talbot....................Wade Crosby
Jeff....................Skelton Knaggs
Nickolai....................John Bleifer
Hank....................Eddy Waller
Willie Sohn....................Charlie Lung
Chuck....................Ernie Adams
Gim Lung....................Eddie Lee
Japanese Officer..........James B. Leong
Mrs. Nilsson..........Anna Q. Nilsson

In trying to cash in on U. S.-Jap fighting in the Aleutians, Republic has dished up a far-fetched production which, nevertheless, can create a mild b.o. stir as a dualer with proper exploitation.

Angle is the annihilation of a Jap raiding party. Story, which is full of inconsistencies, has William Lundigan as a 'mysterious stranger' in an isolated Alaskan village. The entire populace, except two, are suspicious and hostile. These two are Virginia Dale, a weather station operator, and Harry Davenport, who doubles as newspaper publisher and barber.

To get back at the town bluenoses who have him jailed for vagrancy, Lundigan cooks up a fantastic story that the U. S. is at war with an unknown power. He plants it in one copy of Davenport's sheet while the latter is drunk. Everybody falls for the war yarn, which can't be checked because all news from the outside has been cut off when the weather station's receiver is kiboshed. And when Pearl Harbor does roll around, nobody but the local fifth columnist, Harry Shannon, knows about it. Shannon is the one who swipes the tube and maintains contact with the Japs, whom he later leads to the village. The Jap attack and their defeat is the film's highlight and exciting climax.

Lundigan has lots to do but little to say, and makes a fast-moving hero. Miss Dale is out of place in this outdoor opus; Davenport, on the other hand, can, seemingly fit into any setting as a character actor, but performance honors go to J. Frank Hamilton, who portrays a heel, and Charlie Lung, who makes a very convincing not-so-bright Eskimo.

Direction is good, for in spite of an erratic script, the film has few slow spots.

What's Buzzin' Cousin?

(MUSICAL)

Columbia release of Jack Fier production. Stars Ann Miller, Edward (Rochester) Anderson, Freddy Martin Orch, John Hubbard. Directed by Charles Barton. Screenplay, Harry Sauber; based on story by Aben Kandel; camera, Joseph Walker; editor, James Sweeney; reviewed at Loew's State, N. Y., July 22, '43. Running time: **75 MINS.**

Ann Crawford....................Ann Miller
Rochester....................Edward Anderson
Jimmie Ross....................John Hubbard
Freddy Martin....................Freddy Martin
Josie....................Leslie Brooks
Billie....................Jeff Donnell
May....................Carol Hughes
Blossom....................Theresa Harris
Jim Langford....................Roy Gordon
Pete Hartley....................Bradley Page
Dick Bennett....................Warren Ashe
Jed....................Dub Taylor
Saree....................Betsy Gay
Hill-Billy....................Louis Mason

'What's Buzzin', Cousin?' is a listless filmusical, burdened with an unusually dull book and indifferent tunes (for the most part), yet peopled with a strong and talented name cast. Ann Miller, Freddy Martin's orchestra and Rochester on the marquees will help considerably in selling the picture for nominal to moderately good grosses.

Scripting is an insurmountable handicap. Texture of the yarn is uneven, motivation is weak and neither dialog nor situations hold much smart comedy. Miss Miller shines with her corking terp numbers, especially in the finale, a nicely routined bond-selling number entitled 'Eighteen Seventy-Five.' Miss Miller photographs attractively in abbreviated dancing costumes.

Rochester clicks on occasions where he manages to lift mediocre lines while the Freddy Martin orch, appealing all the way, comes through with a topper in a sock interpretation of Liszt's second Hungarian rhapsody. Another outstanding number is 'Nevada,' when a singing guitarist impresses strongly with his vocals.

John Hubbard fills a niche as an attorney turned singer with the Martin band who revives a droopy hotel in a forsaken town for the sake of the girl who, with her friends, invested money in the place.

Romantic interludes are underplayed and never convincing. *Morg.*

HONEYMOON LODGE

(SONGS)

Hollywood, July 23.

Universal release of Warren Wilson production. Directed by Edward Lilley. Screenplay, Clyde Bruckman; original story, Warren Wilson; camera, Paul Ivano; editor, Russell Schoengarth. Previewed at Fairfax, July 22, '43. Running time, 63 MINS.

Bob Sterling....................David Bruce
Lorraine Logan..........Harriet Hilliard
Carol Sterling....................June Vincent
Big Boy....................Rod Cameron
Cathcart..........Franklin Pangborn
Judge Wilkins..........Andrew Tombes
George Thomas....................Martin Ashe
Ozzie Nelson and Orchestra
Veloz and Yolanda
Tip, Tap & Toe
Booby Brooks, Hattie Noel, Ray Eberle

Despite its story fragility, and obvious padding through insertion of several song and dance specialties, 'Honeymoon Lodge' has sufficient diverting moments to carry it through secondary houses in supporting slots.

Story opens with David Bruce and June Vincent halting their divorce proceedings to try for a new start with re-enactment of their first meeting and courtship in a mountain resort. But plans go awry when Harriet Hilliard teams with Bruce, and Rod Cameron pursues Miss Vincent, to develop dual jealousies. Resultant confusion, until eventual reunion, is built with obvious material.

Leads are handled by two newcomers, with both Bruce and Miss Vincent displaying good screen personalities for future development. Miss Hilliard, Cameron and Franklin Pangborn are okay as main support.

Ozzie Nelson's orchestra provides musical background, with Miss Hilliard (Mrs. Nelson) neatly delivering two standard pop tunes, one a comedy number with Nelson. Ray Eberle delivers one, while high-tenor Bobby Brooks handles 'Do I Worry.' Tip, Tap & Toe do a fast dance routine, while Veloz and Yolanda are on for a ballroom turn.

Script by Clyde Bruckman provides some amusing episodes despite the shallow yarn, while direction by Edward Lilley is okay. *Walt.*

The Stranger From Pecos

Monogram release of Scott R. Dunlap production. Stars Johnny Mack Brown; features Raymond Hatton, Kirby Grant, Christine McIntyre, Steve Clark, Sam Flint, Roy Barcroft, Robert Frazer. Directed by Lambert Hillyer. Story and adaptation, Jess Bowens; editor, Carl Pierson; camera, Harry Newmann. At New York, N.Y., half dual bill, week July 20, '43. Running time, 58 MINS.

Nevada....................Johnny Mack Brown
Sandy....................Raymond Hatton
Tom....................Kirby Grant
Ruth....................Christine McIntyre
Clem....................Steve Clark
Ward....................Sam Flint
Sheriff....................Roy Barcroft
Burstow....................Robert Frazer
Burt....................Edmond Cobb
Harmond....................Charles King
Gus....................Bud Osborne
Ed....................Artie Ortega

A well-plotted story in which the suspense is expertly maintained makes this new entry in the Johnny Mack Brown series a sure-shot for accounts playing saddle-warmers. In addition to the good yarn and the compactness of action, the casting adds value.

Brown, of the quick draw and the punching fists, plays a U. S. marshal who's been detailed to a western outpost where a local biggie, grabbing property when mortgages can't be met, has lined up with a crooked sheriff in a game that also includes murder and plunder. Considerable shooting, hard riding and fighting with the mitts figure though there's less of the last-mentioned than in most Brown westerns.

An excellent western character is Raymond Hatton, as Brown's sidekick. Hatton shines particularly in a poker game sequence in which he intentionally loses to a rancher whose $3,000, due him on the sale of a shipment of cattle, has been stolen.

Romantic lead opposite Kirby Grant is Christine McIntyre, who plays a waitress. She makes a nice impression though getting minor footage. Grant also is more or less in the background as a murder suspect. Lessers include the girl's father, Steve Clark; Sam Flint, as a local gangster, and Roy Barcroft, sheriff. *Char.*

Miniature Reviews

'This Is the Army' (Musical; Color) (WB). Rah-rah-rousing boxoffice.

'Girl Crazy' (Musical) (M-G). Rooney, Judy Garland as stars, plus Gershwin score, point to excellent b.o.

'We've Never Been Licked' (U). Should receive warm b.o. reception.

'The Man From Down Under' (Song). (M-G). Refreshing tale laid in Australian background will click for good biz.

'Tartu' (M-G). Robert Donat-Valerie Hobson in above-average English-made spy meller; should do satisfactorily.

'Young Ideas' (M-G). Amusing farce with dramatic trimmings will provide solid suport in regular runs.

'Hi Diddle Diddle' (Songs) (UA). Lively and wacky farce will click for summer datings.

'Calaboose' (UA). A 45-minute Hal Roach 'streamlined' comedy that employs dated technique.

'Someone to Remember' (Rep). Best customer reaction in the family houses as dual supporter.

'Here Comes Kelly' (Mono.). Good laugh producer, but strictly a light dualer.

'Saint Meets the Tiger' (Rep). Another British-made link in 'Saint' chain. For duals.

'Scream in the Night' (Indie). Mild meller about gem thieves in the Orient, with Lon Chaney, Jr., in dual role.

'La Suerte Llama Tree Veces' (Argentine). Poor story, weak direction don't give this Argentine-made much chance.

'Los Hijos Artificiales' (Argentine). Minor Argentine-made will do okay in Latin-America.

'Border Buckeroos' (songs) (PRC). Has good vocalizing and enough action to get by as lower dualer.

'Eclipse De Sol' (Argentine). Libertad Lamarque starred in Argentine musical; okay for Latin audiences.

'Cafe Concordia' (Mexican). Old hat stuff partially redeemed by Raquel's sock dance routines.

THIS IS THE ARMY

(Color)
(MUSICAL)

Warner Bros. production of Irving Berlin's soldier show in Technicolor. Starring Men of the Armed Forces and George Murphy, Joan Leslie, Lt. Ronald Reagan, Geo. Tobias, Alan Hale, Chas. Butterworth, Kate Smith. Produced by Jack L. Warner and Hal B. Wallis. Directed by Michael Curtiz. Screenplay, Casey Robinson and Capt. Claude Binyon; songs, Irving Berlin; camera, Bert Glennon, Sol Polito; special effects, Jack Cosgrove; montages, Don Siegel, Jas. Leicester; editor, Geo. Amy; Technicolor directors, Natalie Kalmus, Richard Mueller; sound, C. A. Riggs; dialog director, Sgt. Edward Blatt; dances, LeRoy Prinze and M/Sgt. Robt. Sidney; costumes, Pvt. Orry Kelly; arrangements, Ray Heindorf; musical directors, Leo F. Forbstein, Frank Heath. World premiered at $55 top for Army Emergency Relief (which gets 100% of the film's profits) at Hollywood, N. Y., July 28, '43; grind thereafter. Running time, **120 MINS.**

Jerry Jones................George Murphy
Eileen Dibble....................Joan Leslie
Maxie Twardofsky...........George Tobias
Sgt. McGhee.........................Alan Hale
Eddie Dibble..........Charles Butterworth
Mrs. Davidson.............Dolores Costello
Rose Dibble.........................Una Merkel
Major Davidson..............Stanley Ridges
Ethel.....................Rosemary De Camp
Mrs. O'Brien...................Ruth Donnelly
Mrs. Nelson...............Dorothy Paterson
Cafe Singer..................Frances Langford
Singer.........................Gertrude Niesen
Herself..................................Kate Smith
Mrs. Twardofsky...............Ilka Gruning
Johnny Jones.............Lt. Ronald Reagan
Joe Louis.........................Sgt. Joe Louis
Tommy...................T/Sgt. Tom D'Andrea
Ollie Twardofsky..........Sgt. Julie Oshins
Ted Nelson..................Sgt. Robt. Shanley
Danny Davidson....Cpl. Herbert Anderson

As Soldiers

1st. Sgt. Allan Anderson	Sgt. Earl Oxford
	Sgt. Philip Truex
M/Sgt. Ezra Stone	Cpl. James MacColl
S/Sgt. James Burrell	Cpl. Ralph Magelssen
Sgt. Ross Elliott	Cpl. Tileston Perry
Sgt. Alan Manson	Pfc. Joe Cook, Jr.
Sgt. John Prince Mendes	Pfc. Larry Weeks
	The Allon Trio

'This Is the Army' is a boxoffice tornado.

That $10,000,000 gross for the Army Emergency Relief Fund, which benefits 100% from the profits of this filmization of the Irving Berlin soldier show, looks a cinch. Everything about it is b.o. boff. It's a picture which can share its kudos with everybody; there is so much about it that is creditable that there is plenty to spread around. That the major chunk should go to Berlin goes without saying.

After the history of World War II is written, the Warner Bros. filmization will stand out like the Empire State Bldg. amidst the many other highlights in the motion picture industry's contributions to the home front and war front. It's that kind of an all-embracing job.

Firstly, it's socko entertainment. Two, it's a dynamic linking of World War I and II, with its respective soldier shows—'Yip Yip Yaphank' and 'This Is the Army,' both by Irving Berlin. Third, it's a fulsome contribution from the entertainment industry for benefit of an altruistic arm of our national defense—the Army Emergency Relief Fund.

Thus, all this is morale in capital letters. It's democracy in action to the hilt. It's showmanship and patriotism combined to a super-duper Yankee Doodle degree.

Skillfully linked are both generations, with George Murphy capital as the yesteryear musicomedy star who suffers a leg injury, which doesn't curb his skill as a theatrical impresario post-1918, and Lt. Ronald Reagan, as Johnny Jones, his son, who carries the romance interest in World War II. George Tobias and Sgt. Julie Oshins are father-and-son to span both periods, and Joan Leslie is the 1943 femme offspring of Charles Butterworth, another of the 'Yip Yip Yaphankers.' She is the romantic vis-a-vis to Reagan.

The blend of the two generations is a skillful job all told, considering the basic difficulty of linking up the two. Alan Hale, as the tough Sgt. McGhee, is capital as the career soldier of both wars, and, throughout, this coupling of two major catastrophes of our times is done with sentimental overtones.

But putting the story aside, the socko Berlin songs—17 of them—tie the whole package together. Starting from Gertrude Niesen's recruiting rally in 1917 of 'Your Country and My Country,' the chronology of numbers practically tells the story. Murphy is shown a hit in the Follies doing a song-and-dance to 'My Sweetie,' when he receives his draft call from Uncle Sam. Tobias' specialty is 'Poor Little Me, I'm on K.P.' Murphy, Tobias and Alan Hale do 'We're On Our Way to France,' with the soldiers getting their marching orders in the midst of this stage number, and thus they parade to their transports through the audience. It's a highlight of this film as it was when Berlin used the same thought in his 'Alexander's Ragtime Band' filmusical for 20th-Fox in 1938.

Kate Smith's 'God Bless America' is a socko specialty next. She looks great and sings her now classic trademark ballad in voice to match. Frances Langford is introduced in a cafe scene with a modern lullaby, 'What Does He Look Like,' the lone new song written by Berlin. (Reprised from 'Yaphank' are the 'KP,' 'France' and 'Oh How I Hate to Get Up in the Morning' songs. Added are 'God Bless America,' 'My Sweetie,' 'Your Country' and 'What Does He Look Like?' The rest are from the basic 'Army' score, as the show was toured last season.)

Starting with 'This Is the Army, Mr. Jones,' sung by Cpl. Sidney Robin, Cpl. Wm. Roerich and Pfc. Henry Jones, the rest of the sequence is a cinematic transmutation of Berlin's World War II soldier show. It's made part of a show-within-a-show, against which is backgrounded the Ronald Reagan-Joan Leslie romance. This portion of the script is a lovelorn chase, as 'Army' is shown playing from coast-to-coast, winding up in Washington before President Roosevelt (instead of Frisco, as was actually the case), and with Miss Leslie chasing Reagan.

'I'm Getting Tired So I Can Sleep,' sung by S/Sgt. James Burrell is a click. S/Sgt. Dick Bernie, as interlocutor, with Sgt. Alan Manson and Cpl. John Draper, do their 'Hunting Story,' which is somewhat verbose; and 'Mandy' is the punch, per heretofore, of the minstrel sequence. Cpl. Ralph Magelssen leads it; Sgt. Richard Irving does a terrific 'dame' as 'Mandy,' and Sgt. Fred Kelly is 'her' vis-a-vis. In the Military Vaude Show, Pfc. Joe Cook, Jr. is the unicyclist; Cpl. Larry Weeks the juggler; Pfc. Hank Henry the mess sgt., and Sgt. John Prince Mendes a click with his magico routine. Sgt. Ross Elliott plays the captain; and the amazing Allon Trio (Sgt. Geno Erbisti, Cpl. Angelo Buono and Cpl. Louis Bednarcik) are aided by the acrobatic Sgt. Gene Berg, S/Sgt. Arthur Steiner, Sgt. Belmonte Cristiani and Cpl. Pinkie Mitchell. Alan Hale impresses here in 'Ladies of the Chorus.'

'Well-Dressed Man in Harlem,' next, is perhaps the highlight of the entire picture, with the sepia entertainers whamming over a terrific score. The champ, now Sgt. Joe Louis, does a bagpunching specialty, with number led by Pvt. James Cross and danced by Cross, Pvt. William Wyckoff and a hotcha Harlem group.

'How About a Cheer for the Navy' segues into 'Stage Door Canteen' with Cpl. Tileston Perry, Sgt. Alan Manson and Pvt. James McColl terrific as Lynn Fontanne, Jane Cowl and Alfred Lunt. It's here that Sgt. Earl Oxford (a good picture bet for the future, incidentally, as are several of the others) re-creates 'I Left My Heart at the Stage Door Canteen' with Sgt. Philip Truex as 'Eileen.' (Ernest Truex is shown in an audience flash admiring his real-life son in reel-life). Sgt. Robert Shanley, another good bet for the future, clicks with 'With My Head in the Clouds' and 'American Eagles,' given an impressive aeronautical 'production'; and the Oldtimers reprise 'Oh, How I Hate to Get Up in the Morning,' showing Irving Berlin, in his old Sgt. suit of World War I, vocalizing the song. It's a notable interlude, showmanly incorporated for the best visual highlighting of the songwriter-showman who inspired both 'Yip' and 'Army.' 'This Time Is the Last Time' makes for the rousing finale.

The hark-backers may wonder about Julie Oshins and Ezra Stone, of the songwriter-showman who were so memorable in the stage original, and why photogenic restrictions caused so much to wind up on the cutting room floor. The intra-trade stuff on how one of the vocal highlights of the film was dubbed by another boy, who did the stage original, is also a detail that's not pertinent to the sum total as unreeled. What Warners has produced leaves little room for captiousness.

Under the Jack Warner-Hal Wallis production supervision and with Mike Curtiz's expert direction—all of whom donated their services, along with the rest of it—'This Is the Army' looks like a $3,000,000 Technicolor production instead of the $1,400,000 it cost to bring it in.

Abel.

GIRL CRAZY

(MUSICAL)

Metro release of Arthur Freed production. Stars Judy Garland, Mickey Rooney; features Gil Stratton, 'Rags' Ragland, Nancy Walker, Robert E. Strickland, June Allyson, Guy Kibbee, Tommy Dorsey Orchestra. Directed by Norman Taurog. Screenplay by Fred Finklehoffe, based on musical comedy by Guy Bolton and Jack McGowan; songs, George and Ira Gershwin; vocal arrangements by Hugh Martin and Jack Blane; 'I Got Rhythm' number directed by Busby Berkeley; dances, Charles Walters; camera, William Daniels and Robert Planck; editor, Albert Akst. Tradeshown in N. Y., July 30, '43. Running time, **97 MINS.**

Danny Churchill, Jr.........Mickey Rooney
Ginger Gray.......................Judy Garland
Bud Livermore......................Gil Stratton
Henry Lathrop........Robert E. Strickland
'Rags'.............................'Rags' Ragland
Specialty............................June Allyson
Polly Williams..................Nancy Walker
Dean Phineas Armour..........Guy Kibbee
Marjorie Tait...............Frances Rafferty
Mr. Churchill, Sr...............Henry O'Neill
Governor Tait...............Howard Freeman
Tommy Dorsey and His Orchestra

Fred Finklehoffe took some liberties with the original Guy Bolton-Jack McGowan book of this 1930-31 stage click, cleaned it up considerably, and it emerges on the screen as a nifty escapist musical. The Gershwin score and the Judy Garland-Mickey Rooney dressing for the marquee should total plenty at the boxoffice, with the picture easily holding the customers once inside.

This is the second film treatment of 'Girl Crazy,' the first being an RKO 'B' starring Wheeler and Woolsey, with all of the crack tunes tossed out at that time except 'I Got Rhythm.' Not so this time, but, coincidentally, 'Rhythm' is again over-dressed in production.

Judy Garland is in the role originally played by Ginger Rogers on the stage, while Nancy Walker, new to the screen in 'Best Foot Forward,' is in a semblance of Ethel Merman's part. But all the double entendre is tossed out, with the locale switched from a dude ranch to a western university. It's to the latter that a N. Y. newspaper publisher sends his playboy son, Rooney. That was Billy Kent's part in the stage version, only he transformed a dude ranch into a roadhouse-speakeasy, while all Rooney does is put the university on its financial feet and make it co-educational. The girls he attracts, and there are plenty, are plenty pretty.

The story thread is light, but enough to string together the George and Ira Gershwin songs, i.e., 'Embraceable You,' 'Treat Me Rough,' 'Bidin' My Time,' 'Could You Use Me' and 'Not for Me.' There's an added Gershwin starter in 'Fascinating Rhythm,' which gives the Dorsey band a major inning with expert collaboration from Rooney at the piano. Latter doesn't look like a dubbing, with Rooney known to be an okay ivory-tickler.

Miss Garland is a nifty saleswoman of the numbers, right down to the over-produced 'Rhythm' finale which was Busby Berkeley's special chore. Her 'Embraceable You' delivery is standout; ditto 'Bidin' My Time' and 'Not for Me.' She's also got two nice dancing sessions, first with dance director Charles Walters and later in 'Rhythm' with Rooney. Latter is in a typical Rooney characterization and plenty forte as Miss Garland's vis-a-vis.

Miss Walker, the tough kid with a great comedy pan and pace, repeats her click in 'Best Foot Forward' in this screen treatment. June Allyson, likewise in 'Foot,' has a singing bit at the opening, doing 'Treat Me Rough,' and then isn't seen again. Gil Stratton and Bob Strickland acquit themselves well in juve roles, while 'Rags' Ragland, in the transition from Gaiety burlesque to Hollywood, is in a cowboy part, but minus the Indian-Hebe dialectics of Willie Howard in the stage musical. Guy Kibbee, as the kindly university dean; Henry O'Neill, as Rooney's father, and Howard Freeman, as a governor, are okay in more adult roles.

Lack of body in the screenplay stymies the pace somewhat, but director Norman Taurog managed to inject zing where possible. Arthur Freed can take a bow for excellent production investiture, with the camera work likewise an asset.

Scho.

We've Never Been Licked

(SONGS)

Universal release of Walter Wanger production. Features Richard Quine, Noah Beery, Jr., Anne Gwynne, Martha O'Driscoll. Directed by John Rawlins. Story, Norman Reilly Raine; adaptation, Raine and Nick Grinde; editor, Phil Cahn; song, 'Me for You, Forever,' Harry Revel, Paul Francis Webster; camera, Milton Krasner. Previewed in N. Y., July 29, '43. Running time, 101 MINS.
Brad Craig.................Richard Quine
Cyanide Jenkins........Noah Beery, Jr.
Nina.......................Anna Gwynne
Deedee..................Martha O'Driscoll
Nishikawa...............Edgar Barrier
Fat Man..................William Frawley
'Pop' Lambert............Harry Davenport

Using Texas Agricultural & Mechanical College for background, with most of the action shot at the famous southwestern institution of learning, Walter Wanger has built a long but interesting picture around the character of a student there who finally made the supreme sacrifice in the war against Japan. While too long, running 101 minutes, there is sufficient body to the story, plus action and atmosphere, to warrant a warm reception at the boxoffice despite the lack of name talent.

Film is not a college story per se nor is it strictly of the war, though combining the two effectively. Majority of the action takes place at Texas A. & M. at College Station, Texas, whose entire enrollment of over 7,000 men appear in the footage. It is at this college, rich in tradition, where students are put through a rigorous military training, and discipline all its own is maintained. The story of Texas A. & M. in itself makes good entertainment.

Richard Quine, newcomer to the screen, plays the son of an officer, former grad of the college, who's now seeing active service. He immediately becomes unpopular, including because he seems to side with the cause of Japan, where he had spent several years before coming to Texas A. & M. He is ultimately dismissed from the college after turning over the formula for a gas antidote to a Jap ring operating at the school and goes to Tokio, where he becomes a yellow-peril Lord Haw-Haw. While the implication is strong that he has turned pro-Axis, actually Quine has disgraced himself in the eyes of his fellow students and others in order to use his Jap connections in tipping off a planned sea battle. Permitted to accompany a bomber squadron, he kills the pilot, and dives the plane into a Jap aircraft carrier to which finishing touches of destroyal are lent by an Allied bombardment from the air. The battle scenes, in which Wanger had the cooperation of the Navy, are extremely exciting and well photographed.

Quine and Noah Beery, Jr., are paired as Texas A. & M. roommates. Beery gives a more impressive performance than Quine but latter fits the role laid out for him very well. The girl, daughter of a professor at the college who's fond of Quine and knew his father before him, is played by Anne Gwynne, who has an excellent screen personality. Her father is played effectively by Harry Davenport. Lessers include Martha O'Driscoll, Edgar Barrier and William Frawley, last-mentioned an American who is directing pro-Japanese activities in this country.

In addition to Texas A. & M. college songs, the picture contains a ballad, 'Me For You, Forever,' written specially by Harry Revel and Paul Francis Webster. It is inserted in a ball sequence. The college numbers are 'Spirit of Aggieland,' 'Aggie War Hymn' and 'I'd Rather Be a Texas Aggie.' *Char.*

The Man From Down Under

(ONE SONG)

Hollywood, Aug. 3.

Metro release of Robert Z. Leonard-Orville O. Dull production, directed by Leonard. Stars Charles Laughton; features Binnie Barnes, Richard Carlson, Donna Reed. Screenplay by Wells Root and Thomas Seller, based on story by Bogart Rogers and Mark Kelly; camera, Sidney Wagner; special effects, Arnold Gillespie; editor, George White; song by Earl Brent. Tradeshown in L. A., Aug. 3, '43. Running time, 102 MINS.
Jocko Wilson..............Charles Laughton
Aggie Dawlins...............Binnie Barnes
'Nipper' Wilson............Richard Carlson
Mary Wilson..................Donna Reed
'Nipper' as a child.....Christopher Severn
Ginger Gaffney................Clyde Cook
'Dusty' Rhodes...........Horace McNally
Father Polycarp...........Arthur Shields
Mary, as a child.............Evelyn Falke
'Boots'...............Hobart Cavanaugh
Father Antoine............Andre Charlot

Charting a refreshing screen tale which detours formulaized lines, 'Man From Down Under' will hit profitable grosses in all runs as a billtopper and provide adequate entertainment for all classes of audiences.

Producer-director Robert Z. Leonard has injected nice pace to the unfolding, from a compact script which imparts a verve and unusual dramatic angles to the general runs of screen tales. Despite opening and closing war backgrounds it's sufficient 'escapist' in general texture to conform to present audience requirements.

Australian sergeant Charles Laughton picks up two Belgian orphans, boy and girl, when embarking for home in 1919, but he leaves entertainer Binnie Barnes standing on the dock. Laughton, former boxer, brings the boy up to point where he becomes lightweight champ of Australia, sustaining torn shoulder ligaments that prevents future fighting. Girl, meanwhile, has been educated in private school. Laughton buys a northern Queensland estate for hotel with fight winnings, but customers are scarce until Miss Barnes shows up as a rich widow. She takes the place from Laughton via cards and dice, as revenge for Laughton's perfidy many years before. Despite the supposed relation of sister-brother between boxer Richard Carlson and Miss Reed, there's a strong attraction while American reporter Horace McNally is romancing the girl; and situation is sensed by the discerning Miss Barnes. When the war hits, group is brought back to the country hotel by devious means to go through a Jap bombing attack and eventually disclose boy and girl are not blood relations, while Laughton and Miss Barnes finally clinch.

There's plenty of interesting sidelights to the tale during its unfolding, accentuated by skillful direction by Leonard, deft writing, and excellent performances. Laughton's character is vividly etched, as is also that of Miss Barnes as a blonde who's been around. Both Carlson and Miss Reed deliver topnotch performances as the boy-girl duo, while excellent support is provided by Clyde Cook, McNally, Arthur Shields and Christopher Severn.

Story setting in Australia provides opportunity for generous display of Aussie dialect and slang. Latter is not laid on too thick, but sufficient to provide audiences with refreshing background. Picture is well-mounted productionally.

Walt.

TARTU

(BRITISH-MADE)

Metro release of Gainsborough production. Stars Robert Donat, Valerie Hobson; features Walter Rilla, Glynis Johns, Phyllis Morris. Directed by Harold S. Bucquet. Screenplay, John Lee Mahin and Howard Emmett Rogers, from story by John C. Higgins; editor, D. Myers; camera, John J. Cox. Previewed in projection room, N. Y., July 28, '43. Running time, 103 MINS.
Terrence Stevenson..........Robert Donat
Maruschka Brunn..........Valerie Hobson
Paula Palacek..................Glynis Johns
Inspector Heidrich............Walter Rilla
Anna Palacek..................Phyllis Morris
Colonel Perry...........Lawrence O'Madden
General Weymouth.......Frederick Leister
Mrs. Stevenson..........Mabel Terry-Lewis
Nurse......................Josephine Wilson
Boy Patient..............Maurice Rhodes

Title of this Gainsborough-made British production suggests a South Sea Island escapist film (the studio purportedly was anxious to erase any marquee stigma of war overtones), but actually 'Tartu' is an above-average spy meller with a Czechoslovakian background that should have no trouble selling itself on its merits in both England and America. From both the standpoint of action and story-telling it's effective, enhanced by capital performances by its stars, Robert Donat, in the title role, and Valerie Hobson.

Despite some closing sequences that strain one's credulity, 'Tartu' has been provided with a proper tenseness and briskness by director Harold Bucquet. The fact, however, that it's essentially still another sabotage yarn may limit its b.o. potentialities in light of the current public emphasis on non-war sagas.

Commendable scripting by John Lee Mahin and Howard Emmett Rogers is focused chiefly around the underground Czech movement and the Nazi operation of the Skoda armament factory. Donat, as a chemical engineer and delayed-bomb expert, is detailed by the British War Office to maneuver the blowing up of a Nazi poison gas factory in Prague. Thus the film gets its dubious title from a liquidated Roumanian Iron Guardist, with Donat masquerading in his stead in getting safe conduct to Czechoslovakia. From then on it's high action only now and then given to over melodramatics.

Miss Hobson plays the haughty toast of the Nazis who, in reality, is one of the Czech underground, and aids Donat in his successful flight back to England. Glynis Johns, as a Skoda worker shot for committing sabotage, and Walter Rilla, as a sadistic Nazi S.S. man, are always convincing.

Photography by John J. Cox is excellent and the other technical credits are first rate. *Rose.*

YOUNG IDEAS

Hollywood, July 30.

Metro release of Robert Sisk production. Stars Susan Peters, Herbert Marshall, Mary Astor; features Elliott Reid, Richard Carlson, Allyn Joslyn. Directed by Jules Dassin. Original, Ian McLellan Hunter and Bill Noble; camera, Charles Lawton; editor, Ralph E. Winters. Tradeshown in L. A., July 29, '43. Running time, 75 MINS.
Susan Evans..................Susan Peters
Michael Kingsley.........Herbert Marshall
Jo Evans......................Mary Astor
Jeff Evans....................Elliott Reid
Tom Farrell..............Richard Carlson
Adam.......................Allyn Joslyn
Co-Ed......................Dorothy Morris
Co-Ed.....................Frances Rafferty
Pepe.......................George Dolenz
Judge Kelly.................Emory Parnell

When a pair of college kids attempt to disrupt the marriage of their writer-lecturer mother to a supposedly staid and serious college professor stationed in a midwest town, result must be a farcical drama enriched by human touches that will get general reaction. This is the situation in 'Young Ideas,' an amusing offering that will get by as a solid supporter in all bookings.

Script has many bright moments,

especially the conflict between the prof and the two children who are bent on getting their mother out of the small town and back to New York. But the boy fails to reckon on his sister falling in love with a young dramatics professor, but even this fails to prevent splitup and divorce action of the elders until the kids hit a rock and everything pans out okay. Scholastic connivings of the offspring confuse the new stepfather throughout, until the blowoff, when he finally realizes he's the butt of their machinations.

Picture is a lightly concocted and amusing affair, and as such is in tune with present audience requirements for diverting entertainment. Mary Astor and Herbert Marshall team effectively as the elder newlyweds, while Susan Peters and Elliott Reid catch attention as the disrupting youngsters. Richard Carlson steps up another notch as the dramatic prof, while Allyn Joslyn ably handles role of the literary agent.

Walt.

CALABOOSE

United Artists release of Glenn Tryon production. Stars Jimmy Rogers, Noah Beery, Jr.; features Mary Brian, Bill Henry, Paul Hurst, Marc Lawrence, William Davidson. Directed by Hal Roach, Jr. Story, Donald Hough; adaptation, Harvey Thew and Arnold Belgard; editor, Bert Jordan; camera, Robert Pittack. At Palace, N. Y., dual, week July 29, '43. Running time, 45 MINS.
Jim.......................Jimmy Rogers
Pidge..................Noah Beery, Jr.
Doris Lane..................Mary Brian
Tom Prendergast..............Bill Henry
Ed Hopkins..................Paul Hurst
Sluggsy Baker...........Marc Lawrence
Sheriff.............William Davidson
Major Barbara..............Jean Porter
Ma.......................Iris Adrian
Colonel..................Sarah Edwards

One of the Hal Roach 'streamliners,' running only 45 minutes, 'Calaboose' is a slapsticky comedy of the old school which in former years, as now, merits no more than two-reeler production. The situations and gags are strictly elementary.

The title refers to the jail of a small western town where the niece of the sheriff has taken up the curing of criminals as a hobby. For this reason both Jimmy Rogers and Noah Beery, Jr., try to get themselves arrested, young Beery succeeding in that direction. Because of the ridiculous luxuries afforded him in the calaboose, his roving partner, Rogers, frames the arrest of a hardened gangster who has just been released from a bigtown hoosegow. As result, Mary Brian, the jail reformer, goes to work on the real hoodlum who ultimately is sprung by pals. A gun battle ensues in a barroom between the big city gang and the plains-country townsmen under a coating of slapstick that reminds of the pie-throwing days.

Supporting Rogers, Beery and Miss Brian are Bill Henry, in for slight romantic consideration; Paul Hurst, a bartender; Marc Lawrence, gangster, and William Davidson, the sheriff. All are okay in spite of the bad material. *Char.*

Someone to Remember

Hollywood, July 28.

Republic release of Robert North production. Features Mabel Paige, John Craven, Dorothy Morris. Directed by Robert Siodmak. Screenplay by Frances Hyland; original by Ben Ames Williams; camera, Jack Marta; editor, Ernest Nims. Previewed at studio, July 27, '43. Running time, 79 MINS.
Mrs. Freeman..................Mabel Paige
Dan Freeman..................John Craven
Lucy Stanton..............Dorothy Morris
Jim Parsons................Charles Dingle
Tom Gibbons...............Harry Shannon
Bill Hedge..................Tom Seidel
Ike Dale....................David Bacon
Paul Parker................Richard Crane
Mr. Roseby.................Chester Clute
Mr. Stanton.................Russell Hicks
Mrs. Mayberry..............Leona Maricle
Mrs. Stanton................Madeline Grey

This is an intimate drama that depends on incidental episodes for its unfolding. Devoid of names for advertising, picture must depend on expert showmanship for putting it over on the basic theme of the age-old subject of mother-love for more than support in the nabe duals. In latter spots, picture is a cinch for favorable customer reaction.

Picture is far and away out of the line usually hewn by Republic, and as such might be considered rather arty. It's a femme reverse on RKO's 'Man to Remember,' which was turned out several years ago.

Mabel Paige is a white-haired and kindly old lady whose contract with owners of an old hotel allows her to remain on when the university takes over the building for a men's dormitory. The boys think she's great, and she awaits return of her son, who flunked out of school and vanished a quarter century ago. So when John Craven turns up as a freshman with same name as her son, the old lady takes it for granted Craven is her grandson. She keeps the boy on the right track, and even injects herself successfully into his romance with Dorothy Morris for eventual marriage. But eventual appearance of Craven's father proves too much for the old lady, who dies smilingly prior to reunion with her expected son; but events prove otherwise, for her own boy had been killed many years before without her knowledge.

Picture, because of its texture, plods a slow but consistent pace, with both script and direction combining to provide sympathetic dramatic appeal for the mothers of the world, and the whitehaired Mabel Paige in particular. Latter angle is a strong one for the family trade, where picture will catch best audience reaction.

Cast is neatly set up, with Miss Paige neatly grooved as the main character. Craven and Miss Morris do well as the romantic pair, while good support is provided by Charles Dingle, Harry Shannon and Tom Seidel. *Walt.*

HERE COMES KELLY

(SONG)

Monogram release of William Lackey production. Features Eddie Quillan, Joan Woodbury, Maxie Rosenbloom, Armida and Sidney Miller. Directed by William Beaudine. Screenplay, Charles R. Marian from original by Jeb Aschery; camera, Arthur Martinelli; editor, Carl Pierson. At New York, N. Y., dual, week July 27, '43. Running time, **65 MINS.**

Jimmy Kelly....................Eddie Quillan
Margie....................Joan Woodbury
Trixie Bell....................Maxie Rosenbloom
Carmencita....................Armida
Sammy Cohn....................Sidney Miller
Mrs. Kelly....................Mary Gordon
L. Herbert Oakley....................Ian Keith

There are lots of laughs in 'Here Comes Kelly,' laughs for those who go in for unsophisticated 'gas house district' comedy. It's a notch above a 'dead-end-kid' picture, but it will take the same kind of exploitation and get by as a light dual offering.

Eddie Quillan struts about like a 'B'-version Jimmy Cagney. He portrays a cocky Irishman who can't keep a job because he can't keep his mitts to himself. This brings him into conflict with the law, his fiancee, Joan Woodbury, and his mother. He finally goes straight by becoming a process server with his pal Sidney Miller.

However, he almost loses his gal when he serves a summons on temperamental Armida (who gets in a Latin song and dance routine). And becomes a minor hero when he slaps the papers on 'Slapsie' Maxie Rosenbloom. But in the end the draft board cuts short his respectable career and further postpones his marriage.

Cast manages to squeeze the last ounce of humor out of each situation, and honors are equally shared by all. Direction is snappy, catching spirit of the script.

Saint Meets the Tiger

(BRITISH-MADE)

Republic release of William Sistrom production. Features Hugh Sinclair, Jean Gillie, Gordon McLeod, Clifford Evans, Wylie Watson. Screenplay, Leslie Arliss, Wolfgang Wilhelm, from novel, 'Meet the Tiger,' by Leslie Charteris; camera, Bob Krasker; editor, Ralph Kemplen. Previewed in projection room, July 30, '43. Running time, **70 MINS.**

Simon Templar....................Hugh Sinclair
Pat Holmes....................Jean Gillie
Inspector Teal....................Gordon McLeod
Tidmarsh....................Clifford Evans
Horace....................Wylie Watson
Bentley....................Dennis Arundell
Bittle....................Charles Victor
Aunt Agatha....................Louise Hampton
Merridow....................John Salew
Police Constable....................Arthur Hambling
Mrs. Jones....................Amy Veness
Mr. Jones....................Claude Bailey
Burton....................Noel Dainton
Frankie....................Eric Clavering
Joe....................Ben Williams
Eddie....................John Slater
Paddy....................Tony Quinn
Tailor....................Alf Goddard

This British-made adaptation of a Leslie Charteris novel is strictly for the lower half of dualers. With Hugh Sinclair enacting the name role, which he's done in other films of the same crime series, 'The Saint Meets the Tiger' has too many loopholes to escape better billing.

The Sinclair series, incidentally, is the British-made counterpart to the RKO 'Saint' pix done until recently in America with George Sanders in the lead part. Tom Conway, Sanders' brother, has since taken over as the Saint in the Hollywood versions. Produced by William Sistrom for RKO as a British quota production, 'Tiger' has been bought by Republic for American releasing, but the film's British origin is unbilled.

Film opens with a murder, committed on Sinclair's doorstep. Three words by the expiring visitor send the 'Saint' off on a chase of gold thieves who have bunked the loot in an abandoned gold mine with the ultimate intention of 'discovering' a vein and moving the stuff out legally. The Saint, of course, fixes all that.

Sinclair's performance is good throughout; ditto that of Jean Gillie, the romantic vis-a-vis. Gordon McLeod as a Scotland Yard man is a bit stuffy, while Clifford Evans gives a strong performance as 'The Tiger.' Wylie Watson provides good comedy relief as Sinclair's valet. Camera and settings are good throughout. *Wood.*

Scream in the Night

Astor Pictures release of Ray Kirkwood production. Stars Lon Chaney, Jr. Directed by Fred Newmeyer. Story, Norman Springer; camera, Bert Longnecker; editor, Fred Bain. At Strand, Brooklyn, week July 29, '43. Running time, **58 MINS.**

Jack Wilson } Butch Curtain }....................Lon Chaney, Jr.
Moora....................Zara Tazil
Edith....................Sheila Terry
Johnny Fly....................Manuel Lopez
Yuting....................Philip Ahn
And Dick Cramer, John Ince, Merrill McCormick, John Lester Johnson.

Looking as though it were made several years ago, judging by general production technique, this indie is extremely mild even as secondary feature.

Yarn of a notorious gem thief operating in the Orient devotes too much footage to closeups of Lon Chaney, Jr., in a dual role, that of a murderous aide to Manuel Lopez and also as the detective who disguises himself as Curtain.

Chaney helps lift what little plot there is. Zara Tazil is fairly good in an unsympathetic role, while Lopez makes a typical villain. Sheila Terry has little to do. Supporting cast is mainly humdrum. *Wear.*

CREO EN DIOS

('Believe in God')
(MEXICAN-MADE)

Fernando de Fuentes, S. de R. L. Production, distributed by Clasa Mohme, Inc. Stars Fernando Soler. Script and direction by Fernando de Fuentes; camera, Gabriel Figueroa. At Belmont, N. Y., week July 16, '43. Running time, **103 MINS.**

El Padre Bernal....................Fernando Soler
Carmen....................Isabela Corona
Don Jose....................Miguel Angel Ferriz
Luisa....................Matilde Palou
Antonio....................Miguel Inclan
Gertrudis....................Lolita Camarillo

(In Spanish; no English Titles)

This tedious treatise will neither do its stuff as a cementer of cordial relations nor pulmotor trade in either Mex or Spanish cinemas north of the border. Sans English titles doesn't enhance it. It's all done in Spanish and without mirrors. If there's another cut in raw film stock down Mexico way, this would have done it, through consuming more than twice the film footage necessary for thin, melodramatic story reeled.

It's the saga of a Catholic priest, who because of indoctrination oath is headed for the gallows after conviction for a murder he did not commit. The murderer's wife has told all in confession but true to his doctrine, the loveable padre cannot reveal a confessional confidence, even to save his life.

It seems the real murderer 'borrowed' the padre's robes as disguise and then goes out and polishes off a pawnbroker. This 'fingers' the padre. He is convicted on circumstantial evidence and condemned to die. Before the ox-bow incident catches up with him, real culprit signs confession and suicides. Latter's wife does a photo finish race to save the padre.

All this is unraveled tediously, devoid of action through long-winded dialog. Star and support do the best they can with material at hand and neither are exciting.

Even theme is not new here. The late Hal Reid wrote and appeared in 'The Confession' some 40 years ago, which at the time was the crux of much controversy but yielded handsome returns to the boxoffice. Only b.o. this one has is the wrong kind.

La Suerte Llama Tres Veces

'Jack Called 3 Times'
(ARGENTINE-MADE)

Buenos Aires, July 13.

EFA production and release. Stars Luis Sandrini; features Ana Maria Lynch, Fanny Navarro, Nelly Hering, Berte Liana, Maria Ester Buschiazzo, Eduardo Sandrini and Francisco Donadio. Directed by Luis Bayon Herrera. Reviewed at Monumental, Buenos Aires.

Another instance of poor story and weak direction for Luis Sandrini, one of the top local stage and screen comics. Its story of a poor boy who triumphs in the end has already been done to death locally.

Film is adequate only for local dualers where it won't have to drag its own weight. *Ray.*

Los Hijos Artificiales

('Artificial Sons')
(Songs)
(ARGENTINE-MADE)

Buenos Aires, July 10.

Pan-American release of San Miguel production. Features Francisco Alvarez, Felisa Mary, Malisa Zini, Pedrito Quartucci, Maria Santos, Raimundo Pastore, Sarita Olmos, Adrian Cuneo, Mecha Lopez, Alberto Terrones, Iris Portillo, Agustin Barrios, Olimpio Bobbio, Marcos Zucker. Directed by Antonio Momplet. Story, Reparaz and Abati; adapted by Homero Manzi; photography, Jose Maria Beltran; music, Mario Maurano.

A minor effort designed for popular consumption, 'Los Hijos Artificiales' should nevertheless do fairly well in Argentina and serve principally for duals in Latin American cities. Slow at first but gradually picking up, film succeeds in purpose despite theatrical tone and overhefty dialog. It's principally a vehicle for Francisco Alvarez, comic star, who turns in a good performance.

Yarn deals with the judge from a small town who, to cover up his frequent jaunts from the hinterland to Buenos Aires, says he has to see 'his son,' offspring of a long-dead affair. The lad falls in love with the judge's daughter without knowing his supposed pop and comes to the burg to seek her hand. Matters become complicated and hizzoner is soon involved in a net of lies in an attempt to retain reputation. He embroils a friend in his troubles, claiming buddy is the real dad, and then works in a few chorus-girl friends of his gayer days. Of course, it all ends with everything cleared, and even the last-minute duel is avoided.

Antonio Momplet has tried to step up interest with some of the snappiest sex appeal seen in local films, and interpolated Latin version of the strip tease drew frowns from some critics. Malisa Zini is expressive and natural in leading femme role, and Felisa Mary, Pedrito Quartucci and Sarita Olmos do o.k. in supporting parts. *Ray.*

BORDER BUCKEROO

(SONGS)

Producers Releasing Corp. release of Alfred Stern-Arthur Alexander production. Features Dave (Tex) O'Brien, Jim Newill, Guy Wilkerson. Directed by Oliver Drake. Screenplay and original, Oliver Drake; camera, Ira Morgan; editor, Charles Henken, Jr. At New York, N. Y., dual, week of July 27, '43. Running time, **60 MINS.**

Tex Wyatt....................Dave (Tex) O'Brien
Jim Steele....................Jim Newill
Panhandle Perkins....................Guy Wilkerson
Betty Clark....................Christine McIntyre
Marge Leonard....................Eleanor Counts
Cole Melford....................Jack Ingraham
Hank Dugan....................Ethan Laidlow
Rance Daggett....................Charles King
Seth Higgins....................Michael Vallon
Tom Bancroft....................Ken Duncan

With the principal characters masquerading as two other guys, 'Border Buckaroos' is a standard western with enough action to get by as a minor dualer.

Dave O'Brien and Jim Newill swap their Texas Ranger characters for those of a gunman and ranch heir, respectively. This is done to keep a valuable ranch and mine from falling into the hands of the former owner's murderers. Naturally these proceedings entail considerable gunplay, slugfests, and fast riding. As an added attraction Newill, O'Brien and Guy Wilkerson go in for some smooth vocalizing, and instrumental effects.

Acting, like the script, is of the usual low-budget western caliber.

ECLIPSE DE SOL

('Eclipse of the Sun')
(ARGENTINE-MADE)

San Miguel production, released by Panamericana. Stars Libertad Lamarque; features George Rigaud, Angelina Pagano, Alita Roman, Juanita Sujo, Pedro Quartucci, Raimundo Pastore, Celia Geraldy, Alberto Terrones, Oscar Villa, Benita Puertolas, Berta Moss, Ines Murray and Iris Martorell. Directed by Luis Saslavsky. Story, Enrique Garcia Velloso; adapted by Homero Manzi; camera, Jose Maria Beltran; music, Paul Misraki. Reviewed at Broadway, Buenos Aires. Running time, **84 MINS.**

With many scenes and situations frankly borrowed from Hollywood production, 'Eclipse de Sol' is nevertheless fast-paced, expensively done comedy that, because of its top star, Libertad Lamarque, and generally o.k. direction by Luis Saslavsky, should do well. Based on a theatre work by Enrique Garcia Velloso, adapted by Homero Manzi, it is dressed up with musical numbers.

For the femme trade Senorita Lamarque's conversion from raven-hued tresses to blonde locks is another outstanding feature and reception proves Latin audiences sometimes aren't as keen on the dark-haired gals as they are on blondes.

Saslavsky has obviously tossed in a good many pesos and finished product shows it, even though continuity is frequently rather jumpy.

Jorge Rigaud is excellent as the husband and Pedro Quartucci as the original sweetie is also good, and Angelina Pagano as the grandma wins honors. Juanita Sujo, Raimundo Pastore and Alita Roman are fair. Song numbers by French composer-arranger Paul Misraki deserve better play, but Argentine items are given adequate handling. Decorations by Ralph Pappier and photography by Jose Maria Beltran are strong. *Ray.*

HI DIDDLE DIDDLE

(SONGS)

Hollywood, July 29.

United Artists release of Andrew Stone (Edward F. Finney) production; directed by Stone. Stars Adolphe Menjou, Martha Scott; features Pola Negri, Dennis O'Keefe, Billie Burke, June Havoc. Screenplay, Frederick Jackson; camera, Charles Schoenbaum; editor, Harvey Manger; songs, Foster Carling and Phil Boutelje; cartoon sequence, Leon Schlesinger. Previewed at studio, July 28, 43. Running time, **72 MINS.**

Col. Hector Phyffe.........Adolphe Menjou
Janie Prescott.........Martha Scott
Genya Smetana.........Pola Negri
Sonny Phyffe.........Dennis O'Keefe
Mrs. Prescott.........Billie Burke
Leslie Quayle.........June Havoc
Senator Simpson.........Walter Kingsford
Peter Warrington, III.........Barton Hepburn
Spinelli.........Georges Metaxa
Pianist.........Marek Windheim
Croupier.........Eddie Marr
Impresario.........Paul Porcasi
A Friend.........Lorraine Miller
Boughton.........Richard Hageman
Fat Man.........Bert Roach
Chauffeur.........Chick Chandler
Maid.........Ellen Lowe
Cashier.........Barry McCollum
Bartender.........Joe Devlin
Minister.........Hal K. Dawson
Doorman.........Andrew Tombes
Watson.........Byron Foulger
Sandra.........Ann Hunter

This is one of the fastest and wackiest screen farces of the season. It's geared to current audience requirements for laugh entertainment, and is a natural release for the summer season. Picture will give a profitable account of itself in all bookings, and can surprise with hefty grosses in many situations.

Every line and situation is displayed in the broadest farcical vein, with smart lines for the sophisticates neatly blended with easily understood basic comedy, slackstick and accentuated mugging. It's rollicking and spontaneous throughout, with Andrew Stone deftly utilizing the talents of his cast to the limit.

Story is a light framework on which to project the various laugh episodes, but smartly dovetailed together. Martha Scott is to marry gob Dennis O'Keefe, whose ship is delayed in docking to provide hysterical pause in the ceremony. After latter finally takes place, and pair are off on 48-hour honeymoon, there are continual interruptions to distract the lovers until only a few hours of the sailor's leave remain. Frustrated newlyweds are surrounded by wild characters parading continual wacky episodes to delay their romantic inclinations. There's Billie Burke in her usual flustery characterization as the girls' mother; Adolphe Menjou, impecunious con man and father of the boy; Pola Negri, opera star and jealous wife of Menjou; and glamorous night club singer, June Havoc. Supporting cast wanders in singly and in groups to further confuse proceedings for the couple. This 'comeback' pic for Negri, who has been off the screen for many years, is a good reentry.

Picture is filled with bright and sparkling lines. One of best for the picture-wise is running gag handed Menjou, who recognizes a girl at various spots, and finally turns to Miss Burke and declares 'I've seen that girl somewhere before.' Quick retort is: 'She's a particular friend of the director, who uses her in all of his pictures.' Another slick episode is display of June Havoc in slottie-movie singing 'Man in the Big Sombrero,' while she stands beside machine delivering duet wtih herself on the film.

Miss Negri sings 'Evening Star,' while Miss Havoc displays plenty of showmanship in delivery of 'Big Sombrero' and a good torcher tune, 'Loved Too Little Too Late.' She also gets into the swing of things with a broadly farcical characterization of the temperamental singer. Despite the major league competition of the other leads, Miss Havoc catches the spotlight with a fine performance, punching over her lines with excellent timing and personality.

O'Keefe and Miss Scott capably handle the lead spots, with Menjou scoring as the fast-talking and quick-thinking roue and suave con man. Miss Burke is also prominent with her absent-minded dialog. Walter Kingsford and Barton Hepburn are okay in major supporting spots. *Walt.*

CAFE CONCORDIA

(MEXICAN-MADE)

Clasa release and production. Features Raquel David Silva, Jr., Tomas Perrin, Jr., and Julio Villareal. Directed by Alberto Goat. Screenplay, Pedro Zaplain; camera, Alex Phillips; music, Hugo Riesenfeld and Jorge Perez. At Belmont, N. Y., week July 30, '43. Running time, **79 MINS.**

Dancer.........Raquel
Julian.........David Silva, Jr.
Ernesto.........Tomas Perrin, Jr.
Don Antonio.........Julio Villareal

With Mimi Derba, Matilde Corel, Agustin Isunza Raoul Guerrero, Nina de Eijo, Josefina Escobedo.

(In Spanish; No English Titles)

This piece was taken out of the mothballs and presented without the benefit of a dusting off or streamlining for 1943 audiences. Redeeming feature is Raquel's dancing, and even that is somewhat marred by poor lighting and camera work.

With so many vital activities going on in Mexico and Latin America, it's hard to understand why Mexico's most recent entertainment media persists in palming off ancient plots such as 'Cafe Concordia,' which may have appealed to the grandparents of the modern film-going generation. In art, music and in radio Mexico has not only kept in step with the modern tempo, but in some instances has set the pace. However, for reasons known only to Mexican scripters and producers, their films are remote and meaningless in terms of the modern spirit.

'Cafe Concordia' reaches back into the 19th century, and for 79 minutes struggles along with the now insignificant problems of a society youth's love for a famous dancer. Raquel, whom he can't marry because of then existing social barriers. There are also triangular complications. A bearded wolf wants the dancer for his mistress, and tangles with his honorably-intentioned rival. This leads to a duel, and an-according-to-hoyle finale, with the dancer stepping into the path of the bullets, dying in her true love's arms.

If Mexican films hope to achieve a small part of the rep earned here by pre-World War II French, German and Russian pictures, they should take a cue from the modern revolutionary tradition built up and enjoyed by other Mexican art and entertainment forms.

Miniature Reviews

'Let's Face It' (Songs) (Par). Plenty laughs, plenty boxoffice in this Bob Hope-Betty Hutton starrer.

'Hostages' (Par). Disappointing Nazi melodrama geared for moderate grosses.

'True to Life' (Songs) (Par). Pleasant albeit lightweight escapist romance.

'Tornado' (Songs) (Par). Chester Morris and Nancy Kelly in fast action melodrama. Strong supporter for regular duals.

'The Good Fellows' (Par). Ridiculous farce of boresome calibre; filler dualer.

'Frontier Badmen' (U). Actionful western provides good entertainment of its type. Strong supporter for regular duals.

'The Law Rides Again' (Mono). Ken Maynard, Hoot Gibson ride again; standard western.

LET'S FACE IT

(SONGS)

Paramount release of Fred Kohlmar production. Stars Bob Hope, Betty Hutton; features ZaSu Pitts, Phyllis Povah, Dave Willock, Eve Arden, Cully Richards, Marjorie Weaver, Dona Drake. Directed by Sidney Lanfield. Screenplay by Harry Tugend; based on musical play by Dorothy and Herbert Fields and Cole Porter, suggested by play by Norma Mitchell and Russell G. Medcraft; songs by Cole Porter, Sammy Cahn & Jule Styne; camera, Lionel Lindon. At Paramount, N. Y., week Aug 4, '43 Running time, **76 MINS.**

Jerry Walker.........Bob Hope
Winnie Potter.........Betty Hutton
Cornelia Pigeon.........ZaSu Pitts
Nancy Collister.........Phyllis Povah
Barney Hilliard.........Dave Willock
Maggie Watson.........Eve Arden
Frankie Burns.........Cully Richards
Jean.........Marjorie Weaver
Muriel.........Dona Drake
Julian Watson.........Raymond Walburn
Judge H. Clay Pigeon.........Andrew Tombes
George Collister.........Arthur Loft
Sergeant Wiggins.........Joe Sawyer
Mrs. Wigglesworth.........Grace Hayle
Mrs. Taylor.........Evllyn Dockson
Milk Maid.........Andria Moreland
Canteen Hostess.........Kay Linaker
Milk Maid.........Brooks Evans
Dance Team.........Nicco & Tanya

Laughs are boxoffice and 'Let's Face It' is loaded. It's another big winner for Bob Hope, this time co-starring with madcap Betty Hutton and supported by an excellent cast.

Harry Tugend's screenplay closely follows the Herbert and Dorothy Fields-Cole Porter musical, which, in turn, had basic similarities to the play, 'Cradle Snatchers,' with the writers of that, Norma Mitchell and Russell G. Medcraft, included in the screen credit. The yarn is about a wacky soldier, who, with two pals, gets involved with three a.k. dames figuring to get revenge on their philandering husbands by hiring soldiers as consorts. There's the dual denouement of the soldiers' girl friends and the dames' husbands, latter with their respective cuties in tow, surprising the soldiers in their reluctant love-making. Only deviation from the stage plot is the screwball finale, in which Bob Hope, Cully Richards and Dave Willock capture a German sub in Long Island Sound.

Tugend, however, has managed to inject many more laughs than was in the Broadway musical click, which was highlighted by Danny Kaye's delivery of 'Melody in 4-F,' replaced here with a Sammy Cahn-Jule Styne number, 'Who Did? I Did, Yes I Did.' The laughs, in fact, come so often and so fast as to be stepping on one another, with the audience estimated as missing 25% of the gags.

Cole Porter's score has been sacrificed for the comedy content, with 'Let's Not talk About Love,' which Betty Hutton bounces in a cafe scene, and 'Let's Face It' the only tunes retained—the latter strictly incidental. There are no production numbers.

Bob Hope, a master at fast vaudeville timing of comedy material, and Betty Hutton, glamorized to an unprecedented degree for a hoydenish singer, are an okay romantic team. They are given better than average support by Cully Richards and Dave Willock, as Hope's pals; and Eve Arden, who was in the Broadway cast, ZaSu Pitts and Phyllis Povah playing the three matrons in search of romance. Dona Drake, Marjorie Weaver, Raymond Walburn, Andrew Tombes and Arthur Loft, latter as the husbands, are in capable assist, and a standout job is delivered by Joe Sawyer, as a tough sergeant.

One of the highlights of the film is a comedy dance routine by Nicco and Tanya, working in a cafe setting and utilizing some original business in their knockabout ballroom routine. Necco, teamed with his wife, Grace, who was ill when this film was made, is appearing this week at Loew's State, on Broadway, in the same dance routine.

Director Sidney Lanfield kept the pace fast and the over-all result is an A-1 light comedy. Camera work is likewise good. *Scho.*

HOSTAGES

Paramount release of Sol C. Siegel production. Stars Luise Rainer, Paul Lukas, Arturo de Cordova and William Bendix; features Oscar Homolka, Katina Paxinou. Directed by Frank Tuttle. Screenplay, Lester Cole and Frank Butler; adapted from novel by Stefan Heym; camera, Victor Milner; music, Victor Young; editor, Archie Marshek. Previewed in projection room, N. Y., Aug. 5, '43. Running time, **88 MINS.**

Paul Breda.........Arturo de Cordova
Milada Preissinger.........Luise Rainer
Janoshik.........William Bendix
Jan Pavel.........Roland Varno
Lev Preissinger.........Oscar Homolka
Maria.........Katina Paxinou
Rheinhardt.........Paul Lukas
Capt. Patzer.........Fred Giermann
Dr. Wallerstein.........Felix Basch
Solvik.........Michael Visaroff
Peter Lobkowitz.........Eric Feldary
Proskosch.........John Mylong
Joseph.........Mikhail Rasumny
Lieut. Eisner.........Phillip van Zandt
Lieut. Marschmann.........Rex Williams
Lieut. Glasenapp.........Hans Conried
Young Nazi Soldier.........Louis Adlon
Elderly Nazi Soldier.........Richard Ryen
Sergeant.........Kurt Neumann

Stefan Heym's novel of the past season is the basis for this Paramount melodrama about the Czech underground movement, an always intensely interesting picture because of the subject matter. **But as a film with its miscasting, leisurely pace and indecisive story development, it's unlikely to achieve more than moderate boxoffice success. It will have to depend mostly on the novel's reputation and the cast headed by Luise Rainer, Paul Lukas, William Bendix and Arturo de Cordova for its b.o. draw.**

'Hostages' actually is just a commonplace story. The Nazis are the villains—and there you are. That point is hammered home to a point of exhaustion, as if this was the first film about Nazis.

Basically, it's the story of 26 Czechs held as hostages after a Nazi army officer dies by drowning. Even after the coroner has called it a suicide, their freedom is denied. A couple of Nazi schemers have decided to weave the circumstantial net to make it appear like murder so that one of the prisoners, the influential Preissinger (Oscar Homolka), can be relieved of his wealth through confiscation, despite his collaboration with the Nazis.

Among the hostages also is Janoshik (William Bendix), the underground leader whose identity is unknown to his captors until he makes his escape and leads the sabotage of the Nazi munitions dumps. Around Janoshik stems the film's major action, with the Gestapo chief (Paul Lukas), the collaborationist's daughter (Miss Rainer) and another underground leader (de Cordova) comprising the other major links in the drama.

Two of the stars, Bendix and

Lukas, are badly miscast, particularly the former. Having achieved considerable prominence of late through his 'dese-dose-dem' film roles, Bendix is straining credence in a part that's antithetical to that for which he's become known. As a Czech patriot, he occasionally lapses into Brooklynese. Lukas is too intelligent an actor to make his miscasting distinct, but it's a little far-fetched to fathom him so stupid as the part of the Gestapo chief would have him.

Miss Rainer's part is poorly defined, though she does well in a role that's comparatively minor despite the star billing. In the book the characterization of the collaborationist's daughter was more clearly etched. Homolka gives what is probably the film's outstanding performance. De Cordova is creditable, too, as an undergrounder who's unsuspected by the Nazis, though in constant contact with them.

Rest of the cast, headed by Katina Paxinou, are outstanding for types, while the direction notably lacks incisiveness and development of the characters. Lester Cole and Frank Butler adapted, and they followed the book pretty closely in a wordy script. *Kahn.*

TRUE TO LIFE

Paramount release of Paul Jones production. Stars Mary Martin, Franchot Tone, Dick Powell; features Victor Moore. Directed by George Marshall. Screenplay, Don Hartman, Harry Tugend; original, Ben and Sol Barzman, Bess Tafel; songs, Hoagy Carmichael, Johnny Mercer; score, Victor Young; camera, Charles Lang, Jr.; asst. director, Arthur Black. Tradeshown Aug. 9, '43. Running time, **94 MINS.**

Bonnie Porter	Mary Martin
Fletcher Marvin	Franchot Tone
Link Ferris	Dick Powell
Pop Porter	Victor Moore
Mom Porter	Mabel Paige
Twips	Beverly Hudson
Clem	Raymond Roe
Jake	Bill Demarest
Oscar Elkins	Ernest Truex
Mr. Huggins	Clarence Kolb
Mr. Mason	Harry Shannon
Gabe, the Butler	Charles Moore
Mr. Mammal	Tim Ryan
Mrs. Barkow	Betty Farington
Expressman	Charles Cane
Bit Man	J. Farrell MacDonald
Bit Cop	Fred A. Kilsey
Bit Woman	Grace Hayle
Foreman of Bakery	Stanley Andrews
Announcer	Ken Carpenter
Program Director	Harry Tyler
Radio Pop	Harry Hayden
Radio Kitty	Ann Doran
Radio Mom	Madora Keene
Radio Sister	Shirley Mills
Radio Heavy	Billy Bletcher
Radio Jake	Bud Jamison
Radio Sonny	Robert Winkler
Radio Man	Jack Gardner
Stage Doorkeeper	Paul Newlan
Girl	Christopher King
Girl	Maxine Ardell
Girl	Yvonne De Carlo
Girl	Alice Kirby
Girl	Marcella Phillips
Man on Bus	Jack Baxley
Guide on Bus	Don Kerr
Beggar	Marjorie Deanne
Taxicab Driver	Matt McHugh
Man in Subway	Walter Soderling
Woman in Subway	Constance Purdy
Bit Girl	Dorothy Granger
Subway Guard	Edward S. Chandler
Bit Man on Bus	Frank Coleman
Bit Woman on Bus	Edna Bennett
Bit Woman	Ethel Clayton
Bit Woman	Gloria Williams

Taking the premise, in an audible intro title that 'life should mirror the movies, instead of the movies reflecting life,' the escapist theme of 'True to Life' is quickly set. What unfolds is not weighty, nor even sturdy, but sufficient unto the light entertainment purpose thereof. And with Mary Martin, Franchot Tone, Dick Powell, Victor Moore, plus some good direction and scripting, this one emerges as satisfactory film fare.

It treats radio family serials with tongue-in-cheek but utilizes the radio soap opera appeal for the plot bulwark of a frothy film. Tone and Powell are the all-written-out radio scripters on the verge of losing their $1,000-a-week jobs because their 'Kitty Farmer' serial has become too phoney. Powell, in search for down-to-the-peasants material, runs into hash-house waitress Mary Martin whose real-life family and their zany behaviorisms provide the authors with almost literal librettc.

Her family in Sunnyside (N. Y. suburb) is one of those 'You Can't Take It With You' families. Pa Victor Moore is a slap-happy inventor and overly ardent air-raid warden. Suffering ma has a shiftless brother, Bill Demarest, to whom Moore doesn't speak, although sharing the same roof and board. The kid sister and brother are characters all their own, and even Ma (well trouped by Mabel Paige) isn't exactly always on the beam.

Powell takes down their daily household sayings literally; the radio script suddenly becomes a top Crossley; Tone, a frank wolf, meantime wants to cut in on Miss Martin; and in between all of this Dick Powell tries to keep the Sunnyside Porter family from ever hearing the radio 'Farmer Family,' for fear of their ire, especially the romance interest.

Action shuttles between the bourgeois Sunnyside family menage and the lush apartment and slick Radio City environment of the Powell-Tone team. Three songs, all good, are skillfully interwoven and the finale is a madcap radio pickup of how things right themselves. Miss Martin handles 'Mr. Bluebird' as an incidental in the intro of her lunch-wagon scene; and Powell punches out 'Old Music Master' and 'There She Was.'

Well-paced direction by George Marshall and some excellent scripting from Don Hartman and Harry Tugend do much to hold the madcap proceedings together. What might have evolved a clambake comes out all right, aided and abetted by seasoned bit players who troupe everything they do to the hilt. Thus, Charles Moore as the colored butler; Clarence Kolb as the apoplectic radio sponsor; Ernest Truex and Harry Shannon as his aides; Beverly Hudson and Raymond Roe as the Porter kids, and so on down the line come up with a satisfying collective job. *Abel.*

TORNADO
(SONGS)

Hollywood, Aug. 10.

Paramount release of Pine-Thomas production. Stars Chester Morris, Nancy Kelly. Directed by William Berke. Screenplay by Maxwell Shane, adapted from story by John Guedel; camera, Fred Jackman, Jr.; editor, William Zeigler; songs, Ralph Freed, Frederick Hollander, Frank Loesser. Tradeshown in L. A. Aug. 9, '43. Running time, **80 MINS.**

Pete Ramsey	Chester Morris
Victory Kane	Nancy Kelly
Bob Ramsey	Bill Henry
Charlie Boswell	Joe Sawyer
Sally Vlochek	Gwen Kenyon
Diana Linden	Marie McDonald
Gary Linden	Morgan Conway
Old Man Linden	Frank Reicher
Big Joe Vlochek	Nestor Paiva

Latest in the Pine-Thomas series of action features for Paramount provides stronger dramatic tale than has usually been the case with previous issues of the PT product. 'Tornado' is a well-told and neatly-paced melodrama that will catch plenty of datings as a strong dual supporter.

Coal mining district of Illinois forms background for the plot which—although hitting usual dramatic strides—has some new twists injected to hold audience interest in good style. Chester Morris is a young miner, who falls in love with wandering showgirl, Nancy Kelly, who breezes into town to get singing spot in miners' cafe hangout. Girl is particularly ambitious for wealth and position, and pushes Morris until he becomes a shaft superintendent. Finding coal outcropping on farm willed to Miss Kelly—who's secretly married to Morris—latter forms new company and gets capital for operation. While struggling to make things go, the wife gets involved in affair with Morgan Conway, socialite mine operator who connives to prevent Morris' shaft from producing. After weaving through series of lusty dramatics, climax comes when tornado twister disposes of the wife and Conway, while Morris gets his finances in shape for successful operation.

Maxwell Shane has devised an interesting script, which is unfolded at a fast and consistent pace by director William Berke. Morris capably handles the lead spot, with Miss Kelly okay as the scheming and opportunist wife. Good support is provided by Bill Henry, Joe Sawyer, Gwen Kenyon, Conway, Frank Reicher and Nestor Paiva. Miss Kelly sings two songs—'I'm Afraid of You' and 'There Goes My Dream'—but delivery is rather weak.

Adequate production mounting is provided, with several sequences unfolding around the mine shafts and tunnels. Camera work by Fred Jackman, Jr., is okay. *Walt.*

THE GOOD FELLOWS

Hollywood, Aug. 10.

Paramount release of Walter MacEwen production. Features Cecil Kellaway, Mabel Paige, Helen Walker, James Brown, Diana Hale. Directed by Jo Graham. Screenplay by Hugh Wedlock, Jr., and Howard Snyder, based on play by George S. Kaufman and Herman Mankiewicz; camera, Theodor Sparkuhl; editor, Arthur Schmidt. Tradeshown in L. A., Aug. 9, '43. Running time, **69 MINS.**

Jim Hilton	Cecil Kellaway
Miss Kent	Mabel Paige
Ethel Hilton	Helen Walker
Tom Drayton	James Brown
Spratt	Diana Hale
Mary Hilton	Kathleen Lockhart
John Drayton	Douglas Wood
Mrs. Drayton	Norma Varden
Reynolds	Olin Howlin
Harvey	Tom Fadden
Blake	William B. Davidson

This one fumbles and stumbles through 69 minutes of running time in ineffectual attempt to put over a light farce that fails to jell anywhere along the route. It's a bore-some and unfunny tale which will get support playdates when nothing else is available for fill-in bookings. Story attempts to broadly sketch the humor of fraternal order enthusiasts, but misses completely in both script and direction. Cecil Kellaway is the head of a small-town lodge, and is in continual financial difficulties at home through his contributions to the fraternal order. It's synthetic all the way, with lodge meetings on display at several points bending to the silly side. After winding through series of episodes that project Kellaway further into debt, situations finally develop for him to hit the jackpot and gain financial stability.

Play on which film is based, which was known as 'The Good Fellow,' was produced in 1926 by Crosby Gaige but flivved.

Cast is forced to overplay the various assignments, and direction is far below par. Best thing about the picture is the title. *Walt.*

FRONTIER BADMEN

Hollywood, Aug. 5.

Universal release of Ford Beebe production, directed by Beebe. Features Robert Paige, Anne Gwynne, Noah Beery, Jr., Diana Barrymore, Leo Carrillo, Andy Devine, Thomas Gomez, William Farnum, Lon Chaney. Original screenplay by Gerald Geraghty and Morgan B. Cox; camera, William Sickner; editor, Fred Feitshans, Jr. Previewed at Hillstreet, L. A., Aug. 5, '43. Running time, **74 MINS.**

Steve	Robert Paige
Chris	Anne Gwynne
Jim	Noah Beery, Jr.
Claire	Diana Barrymore
Chinito	Leo Carrillo
Slim	Andy Devine
Ballard	Thomas Gomez
Cherokee	Frank Lackteen
Courtwright	William Farnum
Chango	Lon Chaney

'Frontier Badmen' is actionful and exciting entry in the higher-budget western field and will shape up as strong programmer of its type for good support in all datings. Current audience interest in 'escapist' action drama insures profitable biz.

Picture carries usual quota of western heroics, including fist and gun fights, to make it hit usual groove. Universal combined large group of its contract featured talent—several in first western appearances—in the cast. Robert Paige, Anne Gwynne, Diana Barrymore and Lon Chaney join up with western vets Noah Beery, Jr., Andy Devine, Leo Carrillo and William Farnum to provide good cast mounting.

Yarn concerns efforts of Texas ranchers to break up cattle-buying monopoly at the Abilene (Kan.) railhead, with Paige leading the battle to prevent rooking of the ranchers through controlled low prices for cattle. Noah Beery, Jr., as Paige's sidekick, generates a restrained romance with Texas girl, Miss Gwynne, while Paige initially outwits card dealer Diana Barrymore, but flirts around long enough to fall in love with the latter. Devine and Carrillo provide their usual comedy and dialect routines for generous audience reaction. Thomas Gomez heads the cattle ring, while Chaney is his willing henchman axious for gunplay at all times.

Ford Beebe, handling combo of producer-director chores, keeps the tale moving at a fast gait, and injects two cattle stampedes through the town to heighten excitement for the customers. Cast is well set up. Paige fits nicely as the heroic and happy-go-lucky Texan, with Beery, Jr., delivering able performance as the conservative member of the duo. Miss Gwynne clicks as the Texas charmer, while Miss Barrymore catches attention as the dealer, despite her minor footage. Devine and Carrillo are in for usual standard comedy relief, with aid from Frank Lackteen, a stoic Indian knife-tossing expert. Chaney grooves okay as aide to heavy Gomez. *Walt.*

The Law Rides Again

Monogram release of Robert Tansey production. Stars Ken Maynard, Hoot Gibson; features Jack LaRue, Betty Miles. Directed by Alan James. Screenplay, Frances Kavanaugh; camera, Marcel Le Picard; editor, Fred Bain. At New York, N. Y., week Aug. 3, '43, dual. Running time, **56 MINS.**

Ken	Ken Maynard
Hoot	Hoot Gibson
Betty	Betty Miles
Dillon	Jack LaRue
Eagle Eye	Emmett Lynn
Hampton	Kenneth Harlan
Indian	Chief Thunder Cloud
Commissioner Lee	Bryant Washburn
Jess	John Bridges
Hank	Fred Hoose
Marshal	Chas. Murray, Jr.
Sheriff	Hank Bell
Barking Fox	Chief Many Treaties

Hoot Gibson and Ken Maynard, known as 'Trail Blazers' in this series, go through routine western gymnastics in this oats opera.

A convicted bandit is employed to trap a band of badmen stirring up injun trouble in Arizona. Gibson and Maynard use LaRue as a means of uncovering a supposedly honest Indian agent. It requires about six reels to bring the phoney agent and his gang to justice.

Maynard and Gibson, both now appearing slightly overweight, make a good pair of western heroes. Both can ride, fight and shoot. Betty Miles, boasting a southern accent, is okay as the heart-interest. Kenneth Harlan, vet of silent films, does okay as the crooked Indian agent while LaRue goes over, as usual. Bryant Washburn, another lead of bygone screendays, has a minor bit as commissioner. *Wear.*

Miniature Reviews

'Thank Your Lucky Stars' (musical) (WB). Star-studded musical can't miss as top grosser.

'Claudia' (20th). Effectively sentimental adaptation of the stage hit. Should draw potent grosses, particularly femmes.

'Lassie Come Home' (color) (M-G). Sentimental dog story will serve well in duals.

'Phantom of the Opera' (color; songs) (U). Completely new version, with music and in Technicolor, headed for okay b.o.

'The Fallen Sparrow' (RKO) (Song). John Garfield and Maureen O'Hara in spy melodrama; OK for regular runs.

'A Lady Takes a Chance' (RKO). Top romantic comedy starring Jean Arthur and John Wayne.

'Destroyer' (Col). Navy service meller of moderate rating for the regular program houses.

'Passport to Suez' (Col). Warren William is standard lone wolf sleuth thriller.

'Adventures of a Rookie' (RKO). New team of Wally Brown and Alan Carney in service comedy; duals.

'So This Is Washington' (RKO). Lum 'n' Abner in entertaining entry for their radio following and rural districts.

'Melody Parade' (Mono). Mildly entertaining musical for duals.

'The Seventh Victim' (RKO). 'B' meller that hasn't a chance.

'Undercover' (UA - British). British-made saga of guerrilla warfare against Nazis. Name players alone may mean b.o.

'Calle Corrientes' (Argentine). Just fair yarn for interior native theatres.

'Robin Hood of the Range' (Col). Fast western dualer, with Charles Starrett providing plenty of action.

'Escape to Danger' (RKO-British). Ann Dvorak-Eric Portman starred in exciting spy drama; okay for biz.

'Black Sea Fighters' (Artkino). Rates with the best of the Russian war documentaries.

'West Side Kid' (Rep). Donald Barry turns gangster in amusing comedy-meller; okay for duals.

'The Man in Gray' (British). British-made historical yarn okay for Britons; doubtful for the States.

'Adventure in Blackmail' (English). Ordinary British-made.

'Asi Se Quiere en Jalisco' (Songs; Color) (Mex). With Jorge Negrete starred; okay for Spanish fans; limited otherwise.

Thank Your Lucky Stars

(MUSICAL)

Warner Bros. release of Mark Hellinger production. Stars Eddie Cantor, Dinah Shore, Bette Davis, Humphrey Bogart, Olivia de Havilland, Errol Flynn, John Garfield, Joan Leslie, Ida Lupino, Dennis Morgan, Ann Sheridan, Alexis Smith; features George Tobias, Jack Carson, Alan Hale, E. E. Horton, Ruth Donnelly, Don Wilson, Willie Best, Henry Armetta, Joyce Reynolds, S. Z. Sakall, Hattie McDaniel, Spike Jones & City Slickers. Directed by David Butler. Screenplay by Norman Panama, Melvin Frank and James V. Kern based on original story by Everett Freeman and Arthur Schwartz; songs, Schwartz, Frank Loesser; vocal arrangements, Dudley Chambers; musical director, Leo F. Forbstein; dances, Leroy Prinz; asst. director, Phil Quinn; camera, Arthur Edeson; editor, Irene Morra. Previewed in projection room, N. Y., Aug. 13, '43. Running time, 127 MINS.

With virtually all the stars and featured performers on the Warner lot written into the script for bit sequences, the new Eddie Cantor-Dinah Shore WB musical, 'Thank Your Lucky Stars,' is a b.o. natural that'll garner top grosses everywhere. On the basis on its marquee strength alone it'll sell. But it's far from the smash filmusical it might have been, considering the super-duper aspect of the production as a whole.

As a Cantor vehicle it's been topped by some of his previous efforts but it's chiefly due to the banjo-eyed comedian that the thing is pulled together during its sagging moments. As such it's a triumph for Cantor. Film's two hours and seven minutes has long stretches that are under par; the musical and star participation interludes are dovetailed together by a story that often gets lost in the shuffle and is something less than inspiring; a few of the star bits have dubious entertainment value. But even the most captious will admit to its many moments of diversion.

In novelty, 'Stars' packs a wallop. The idea of a dual Cantor role, on the one hand a film star portrayed strictly as a heel, with a crush on any Cantor gag, and the other a film colony bus guide whose affliction is that he can't land a picture job because he looks 'too much like that Cantor guy' has solid merit in itself. But that idea goes astray too. For novelty there's also Bette Davis being tossed around in a swank nitery by a frenzied jitterbug, lamenting her fate of resorting to a.k.'s and adolescent pups in a vocalization of Arthur Schwartz's sock tune, 'They're Either Too Young or Too Old.' Or Errol Flynn as a cockney sailor singing a sea chanty, with Gilbertian overtones, only to emerge in the finale reprise by kidding the dubbed vocal.

List among its assets, too, John Garfield's vocal satirization of his own WB 'Blues in the Night'; an old-time vaude routine by Jack Carson and Alan Hale; a hot za-zu-zass number by Olivia de Haviland, George Tobias and Ida Lupino; a briefie by Humphrey Bogart who takes a verbal dressing down and slinks away wondering aloud what the Bogart fans'll think.

There's also an all-round slick performance by Joan Leslie; Dinah Shore looking fetching and at her singing best with a trio of tunes; a sock production finale that reprises the film's top moments and a pleasant score by Schwartz which gets a fine assist in Frank Loesser's lyrics. These, plus Cantor's performance, are what redeem 'Stars' and will help send the customers out forgetful of its duller interludes.

That Warners has sunk considerable coin in the production is apparent throughout, aside from the star calvacade aspect. Mark Hellinger has given it a painstaking production and David Butler does a commendable directing job. That the pace is often slow is not the fault of Butler's. Both he and Hellinger, incidentally, are in for a brief scene in which they sympathize with a guy (the bus guide) who even remotely resembles Cantor.

Story pattern uses as film's mainstays Cantor, the Misses Leslie and Shore, Dennis Morgan, Edward Everett Horton and S. Z. Sakall, with the various stars introed chiefly via a 'Calvacade' benefit that Sakall and Horton are promoting. Latter show up at a Cantor-Shore broadcast (Garfield's worked into the scene as a program guester) bent on lining up the songstress for their all-star shindig, but the gimmick is that Cantor wants to run the show, or else no Dinah. Promoters regard Cantor as a ham but they yield. Comedian's idea of a production number is to dress the chorus up as boiled potatoes and let them dive into a mammoth bowl of sour cream, which gives an idea of what the promoters got themselves into. From then on it's a case of kidnapping the real Cantor, with the bus guide tossed in as the Cantor poseur to wham over a routine as the benefit's highlight. It's through the latter maneuver, too, that Morgan and Miss Leslie, as two film aspirants who can't get a tumble from the real Cantor, finally click for the fadeout.

'Stars' marks Miss Shore's film debut and she's a standout in the three production numbers in which she's featured, particularly in her rendition of Schwartz's top tune, 'How Sweet You Are.' She photographs well, can wear clothes that are keyed strictly to eye-appeal, and though the picture offers her little opportunity to act, she demonstrates she can hold her own in the latter department. From here on, the songstress is a natural for films.

Spike Jones and His City Slickers are worked in for their usual corn session with a Schwartz-Loesser tune, 'I'm Riding for a Fall,' with Ann Sheridan also spotted for a vocalization of one of the better numbers, 'Love Isn't Born, It's Made.' Hattie McDaniel and Willie Best, with a troupe of colored singers and dancers, lend distinction to an effective 'Ice Cold Katie' production number, while Dennis Morgan's warbling of 'Good Night, Good Neighbor' and an Alexis Smith terps routine are okay.

Photography is excellent. *Rose.*

CLAUDIA

20th-Fox release of William Perlberg production. Features Dorothy McGuire, Robert Young, Ina Claire, Reginald Gardiner, Olga Baclanova. Directed by Edmund Goulding. Adapted by Morrie Ryskind, from stage play by Rose Franken; music, Alfred Neuman; camera, Leon Shamroy; editor, Robert Simpson. Reviewed in projection room, N. Y., Aug. 12, '43. Running time, 91 MINS.

Claudia	Dorothy McGuire
David Naughton	Robert Young
Mrs. Brown	Ina Claire
Jerry Seymour	Reginald Gardiner
Mme. Daruschka	Olga Baclanova
Julia	Jean Howard
Fritz	Frank Tweedell
Bertha	Elsa Janssen
Carl	John Royce
Hartley	Frank Fenton
Mr. Feiffer	Ferdinand Munier
Mrs. Feiffer	Winifred Harris
Maid	Jessie Grayson

As it was on the stage, 'Claudia' is a happily sentimental tearjerker that should draw hefty business and satisfy audiences—especially femmes. Despite a number of disappointing aspects, the picture has enough appeal to indicate it may be the forerunner of several sequels. The basis is there for a juicy series.

Since the story is altered or expanded only slightly from the legit version, chief interest in this film adaptation is in the performance of Dorothy McGuire, who makes her screen debut in the title part she created on the stage. She has a captivating personality and her playing is believable and expressive, particularly in the emotional scenes later in the picture, but she is handicapped by unbecoming makeup, costuming and murky lighting.

Robert Young gives an admirably direct and plausible performance as David, the husband, while Ina Claire skillfully suggests the gallantry of the doomed mother without allowing the part to lapse into pathos. Reginald Gardiner overplays the role of the British playwright, completely missing the wry quality John Williams gave it in the original stage production. Olga Baclanova repeats the opera diva caricature she gave in the play, while Frank Tweedell clicks again in the butler part he created on the stage.

The film edition has little more scope than the play. Even the few times the action moves outdoors the effect is innocuous, and the reference to the butler's criminal background, which was a trifle obscure in the stage version, is badly muddled in the picture. In addition, the outdoor settings look palpably faked and even the interior scenes suggest a labyrinth rather than a quaint Connecticut farmhouse. Edmund Goulding's direction is deftly paced, but the picture appears to have been ineptly edited.

Despite these faults, 'Claudia' is generally appealing. Even a slightly arch quality fails to mar the frivolous opening scenes seriously. And when the yarn moves into its intense passages it is undeniably affecting. At those moments it won't leave a dry eye in the house.

Just as the play did, the picture edition of 'Claudia' closes on the sort of inconclusive note that would readily permit sequelization. If that were desired there is ample material available in the Red Book mag stories from which Miss Franken dramatized her play. In that case the studio would presumably have to buy the rights from the authoress, but wouldn't have to pay John Golden, who produced the legit edition. Incidentally, General Foods sponsored a radio version of the same material, under the title of 'Claudia and David' two summers ago. *Hobe.*

LASSIE COME HOME

(COLOR)

Metro release of Samuel Marx production. Features Roddy McDowall, Donald Crisp, Dame May Whitty, Edmund Gwenn, Nigel Bruce, Elsa Lanchester and Lassie. Directed by Fred M. Wilcox. Screenplay, Hugo Butler, based on novel by Eric Knight; camera, Leonard Smith; editor, Ben Lewis. Tradeshown in N. Y., Aug. 13, '43. Running time, **90 MINS.**

Joe Carraclough	Roddy McDowall
Sam Carraclough	Donald Crisp
Dally	Dame May Whitty
Rowlie	Edmund Gwenn
Duke of Rudling	Nigel Bruce
Mrs. Carraclough	Elsa Lanchester
Priscilla	Elizabeth Taylor
Dan'l Fadden	Ben Webster
Hynes	J. Patrick O'Malley
Jock	Alan Napier
Andrew	Arthur Shields
Snickers	John Rogers
Buckles	Alec Craig

And Lassie

A sentimental story of a dog's devotion, 'Lassie Come Home' will be moderate b.o.

From the pen of the late Major Eric Knight, and with Fred M. Wilcox directing his first feature picture, 'Lassie' emerges as nice entertainment enhanced by color photography and good scenic shots.

One of the film's major assets is its cast, good from top to bottom. Lassie, a beautiful collie, is given a great deal of camera attention and is docile, if not extraordinarily trained. The dog is the focal point for a great deal of pathos throughout the film's 90 minutes.

Her Yorkshire owner, Donald Crisp, sells her to the lord of the manor, thus depriving his son, Roddy McDowall, of his bosom companion. The dog escapes a couple of times to rejoin McDowall, then finally makes a trek of hundreds of miles from Scotland to England to get back to the kid. The windup is happy, however, when the wealthy dog-lover gives Crisp a job as his kennelman, thus reuniting child and dog.

The sentimental angles are something akin to McDowall's recent 'My Friend Flicka' film for 20th-Fox.

That the kid is a solid trouper has been proven in the past, and he doesn't let down in this. Crisp, as his father, is excellent; ditto Elsa Lanchester, playing McDowall's mother. Good portrayals are likewise contributed by Edmund Gwenn, as an itinerant peddler who befriends the dog; Dame May Whitty and Ben Webster, who likewise shelter the animal during a stopover by the collie on the long hike back to England; Nigel Bruce, as the wealthy dog fancier, and J. Patrick O'Malley, playing a cruel dog-handler. Elizabeth Taylor, a pretty moppet, shows up to good advantage as Bruce's granddaughter.

Considering this is Wilcox's first effort with a feature film, his work is promising. His characters are believable and that's especially important in a film of this type. Leonard Smith's photography in some spots is outstanding. *Scho.*

Phantom of the Opera

(Color)

(SONGS)

Universal release of George Waggner production. Directed by Arthur Lubin. Stars Nelson Eddy, Susanne Foster, Claude Rains. Screenplay, Eric Taylor, Samuel Hoffenstein; adaptation, John Jacoby; based on composition, 'Phantom of the Opera,' by Gaston Leroux; stage director, opera sequences, William Wymetal; musical director, Edward War; camera, Hal Mohr; technicolor camera, Duke Green; operatic score and libretto by Edward Ward and George Waggner; 'Lullaby of the Bells' music by Edward Ward, lyrics by Waggner. Tradeshown in N. Y. Aug. 12, '43. Running time, **92 MINS.**

Anatole Carron..................Nelson Eddy
Christine Dubois...........Susanna Foster
Enrique Claudin.............Claude Rains
Raoul de Chagny............Edgar Barrier
Biancarolli.........................Jane Farrar
The Aunt....................Barbara Everest
Vercheres.......................Steve Geray
Villeneuve......................Frank Puglia
Marcel..........................Hans Herbert
Lacours..............................Fritz Feld
Amolt................J. Edward Bromberg
Gerard.........................Hume Cronyn
Jennie............................Gladys Blake
Maid................................Elvira Curci
Maid...............................Rosina Galli
Franz Liszt........................Fritz Leiber

Resurrection of the 'Phantom' as a talker, after nearly 20 years (it was first filmed as a silent in 1924), has resulted in a vivid, elaborate and, within its original story limitations, an effective production geared for substantial grosses. Claude Rains now portrays the role of the 'Phantom' originated by Lon Chaney in the silent.

Topnotch production values, fortified with colorful and melodious operatic interludes of a type aimed for mass appeal, will largely overcome the paucity of suspense.

It's far more of a musical than a chiller, though this element is not to be altogether discounted, and holds novelty appeal which provides a broad base for exhibitor exploitation.

Tuneful operatic numbers and the splendor of the scenic settings in these sequences, combined with excellent group and solo vocalists, count heavily. Nelson Eddy, Susanna Foster and Jane Farrar (niece of operatic star Geraldine Farrar) score individually in singing roles and provide marquee dressing. Third act from 'Martha' and two original opera sketches based on themes from Chopin and Tschaikowsky have been skillfully interwoven.

For the rest it is, of course, a struggle against a familiar story structure. Bereft of elements of surprise and action, the theme has obviously taxed the ingenuity of both director and writers. Musical and production effects have been skillfully employed to counterbalance.

Outstanding performance is turned in by Claude Rains as the musician who, from a fixation seeking to establish the heroine as a leading opera star, grows into a homicidal maniac. Eddy, Miss Foster, and Edgar Barrier, as the Parisian detective, are awkward in movement and speech, though much like opera performers restricted by their medium. Miss Foster, of course, impresses as a strong bet for future filmusical assignments.

Since its original release 'Phantom' was reissued in 1929 with sound. Story is about the mad musician who haunts the opera house and kills off all those who are in his protege's way towards becoming the headliner.
Mori.

The Fallen Sparrow

(WITH SONG)

Hollywood, Aug. 17.

RKO release of Robert Fellows production. Stars John Garfield, Maureen O'Hara. Directed by Richard Wallace. Screenplay by Warren Duff, based on novel by Dorothy B. Hughes; camera, Nicholas Musuraca; special effects, Vernon L. Walker; editor, Robert Wise; asst. director, Sam Ruman. Tradeshown in L. A. Aug. 17, '43. Running time, **91 MINS.**

Kit...............................John Garfield
Toni Donne..............Maureen O'Hara
Dr. Skaas...................Walter Slezak
Barby Taviton.............Patricia Morison
Whitney Hamilton.......Martha O'Driscoll
Ab Parker.....................Bruce Edwards
Anton...........................John Banner
Inspector Tobin................John Miljan
Prince Francois...........Sam Goldenberg
Otto Skaas...............Hugh Beaumont

This is a spy melodrama with sufficient content of suspense to carry through the regular runs as billtopper for nominally profitable biz. Starring combo of John Garfield and Maureen O'Hara provides marquee strength.

During its progress, story details that Garfield is a veteran of the Spanish civil war; escaped from a Franco prison camp after mental and physical tortures that resulted in enforced recuperation at an Arizona ranch. He returns to New York when hearing his childhood pal had been bumped off, and links the murder with his secret possession of a Nazi battle flag captured from a German battalion on the Spanish battlefield. Garfield traces through a maze of melodramatics, personal danger and usual mystery, until he finally uncovers the Nazi ringleader to bump him off at finish. In his sleuthing, Garfield tabs three girls—Maureen O'Hara, socialite Patricia Morison and nitery singer Martha O'Driscoll—as leads in his investigations; but finally settles on Miss O'Hara for romantic interludes, but she turns out to be a strong Nazi operator who's exposed at the end.

Garfield handles the lead in particularly strong fashion, dominating the proceedings throughout. Miss O'Hara is excellent as the girl agent, with Miss O'Driscoll singing a Scandinavian folksong as one number while capably handling her acting assignment. Support includes Walter Slezak, Bruce Edwards, John Banner, John Miljan and Hugh Beaumont.

Despite script attempt to keep the audience confused and bewildered during most of the proceedings, director Richard Wallace keeps the yarn moving at a good and suspenseful pace. Production and technical contributions are of a fine calibre throughout.
Walt.

A Lady Takes a Chance

RKO release of Frank Ross production. Stars Jean Arthur and John Wayne, features Charles Winninger, Phil Silvers, Mary Field, Don Costello, John Philliber, Grady Sutton, Grant Withers and Hans Conreid. Directed by William Seiter. Story, Jo Swerling; adaptation, Robert Ardrey; editor, Theron Warth; camera, Frank Redman. Previewed in N. Y. projection room, Aug. 11, '43. Running time, **85 MINS.**

Mollie Truesdale................Jean Arthur
Duke Hudkins...................John Wayne
Waco ....Charles Winninger
Smiley Lambert..................Phil Silvers
Florrie Bendix......................Mary Field
Drunk ....Don Costello
Storekeeper ....John Philliber
Malcolm ....Grady Sutton
Bob ....Grant Withers
Gregg ....Hans Conreid
Jitterbug ....Peggy Carroll
Flossie ....Ariel Heath
Linda Belle........................Sugar Geise
Lilly ....Joan Blair
Mullen ....Tom Fadden

'A Lady Takes a Chance' is strictly 'escapist,' going back to 1938, when seemingly everyone had a car, fed the dog steak and didn't have to carry ration books. It's an highly entertaining romantic comedy that should be powerful boxoffice.

'Lady' gives Jean Arthur one of her best roles. Opposite her is an equally appealing character played by John Wayne, as a rodeo performer who loves his horse better than anything else until Miss Arthur finally wins his favor.

Miss Arthur, as a working girl from N. Y., signs up for a back-breaking vacation tour of the west by bus and, at one stop, in the land of the prairie playboys, becomes smitten with Wayne and gets stranded. Her trials and tribulations during the period she must wait to pick up the bus on its way back make for rich comedy, the sequence spent on the desert with Wayne and his rodeo partner, Charles Winninger, being one of the amusing highlights of the picture.

Dialog of Robert Ardrey, who adapted the Jo Swerling story on which picture is based, has crispness as well as a pattern that makes it appear he wrote with Miss Arthur in mind. For sheer delight of dialog one of the best scenes is the one in which Miss Arthur and Wayne lie on a wagon filled with hay, talking about the respective merits of the horses they love. It's a quiet and slow scene but one that has much charm.

Production of Frank Ross has high merit and the direction by William Seiter excellent. Even the free-for-all brawl in the beerhall-gambling joint is done with finesse that distinguishes it from scores of similarly-staged sequences in westerns. Rodeo performances on two different occasions also fit in conveniently, though there could have been a little cutting there.

Winninger is most important among the support, most of whom are of a minor nature, including Don Costello, in for a drunk bit; John Philliber, a storekeeper; and three eastern boy friends who see Miss Arthur off on her vacation trip, Gray Sutton, Grant Withers and Hans Conreid. Also not getting much footage, though tops in what he does, is Phil Silvers, as a bus guide.
Char.

DESTROYER

Hollywood, Aug. 11.

Columbia release of Louis F. Edelman production. Stars Edward G. Robinson; features Glenn Ford, Marguerite Chapman. Directed by William A. Seiter. Screenplay by Frank Wead, Louis Meltzer and Borden Chase; original by Wead; camera, Franz E. Planer; editor, Gene Havlick; asst. director, Milton Carter; technical adviser, Lt. Comm. H. D. Smith, U.S.N.. Previewed at Pantages, Aug. 10, '43. Running time, **97 MINS.**

Steve Boleslavski......Edward G. Robinson
Mickey Donohue........................Glenn Ford
Mary Boleslavski.....Marguerite Chapman
Kansas Jackson............Edgar Buchanan
Sarecky............................Leo Gorcey
Lt. Comm. Clark..................Regis Toomey
Casey..................................Ed Brophy
Lt. Morton.....................Warren Ashe
Bigbee...........................Craig Woods
Yasha................................Curt Bois

'Destroyer' is a regulation service drama of standard rating, that will catch nominal attention in the regular runs. It hits regulation formula in unfolding melodramatics afloat and ashore, with light touches on the directing side by William Seiter holding it together for passable attention.

Edward G. Robinson, veteran of World War I Navy, who shipped on the destroyer John Paul Jones, is shipyard worker on new vessel of same name. Enlisting to sail on the new Jones, he wangles post of chief bo'sun mate from skipper Regis Toomey, gaining enmity of sailor Glenn Ford in process. Everything goes wrong on the shakedown cruise, with crew antagonistic to the oldline mate, and Robinson replaced as chief by Ford. Speed trial also discloses construction deficiencies, and ship is transferred to a mail dispatch boat for the northwest Pacific area. En route to Dutch Harbor, destroyer is attacked by Jap planes, gets hole below water line, but Robinson crawls in to repair while ship is being stalked by Nip sub. At dawn, destroyer sights the sub and rams latter; and back at the base, Robinson is the hero of the enterprise. In between, there's romantic development between Ford and Marguerite Chapman, Robinson's daughter.

Familiar cruise is charted by the story plot, which is stereotyped for a Navy meller. Basic story premise, which displays an American ship turned out in U. S. yards as being shoddily constructed, so that it could not stand up in battle line, will not be pleasing to the customers. This factor is likely to generate much adverse comment.

Robinson delivers his standard characterization as the loyal Navyite who's bent on getting back into service. Ford does well as the young seaman, and Marguerite Chapman is decorative as the girl. Edgar Buchanan abandons his whiskers for a tar role, while Leo Gorcey provides a few snatches of smart-aleck comedy. Toomey clicks as the ship captain.

Despite the formularized yarn, Seiter injects good pace into the proceedings, while process and miniature work, which consumes large amount of footage, is excellently contrived by Dave Allen.
Walt.

PASSPORT TO SUEZ

Columbia release of Wallace MacDonald production. Stars Warren William; features Eric Blore, Ann Savage. Directed by Andre de Toth. Screenplay, John Stone; camera, L. W. O'Connell; editor, Mel Thorsen. At Strand, Brooklyn, week Aug. 12, '43, dualed. Running time, **72 MINS.**

Michael Lanyard ....Warren William
Valerie King ....Ann Savage
Jameson ....Eric Blore
Donald Jameson............Robert Stanford
Johnny Booth..............Sheldon Leonard
Fritz ....Lloyd Bridges
Karl ....Gavin Muir
Rembrandt ....Lou Merrill
Sir Roger Wembley.......Frederic Worlock
Cezanne ....Jay Novello
Whistler ....Sig Arno

This is the eighth Lone Wolf (Michael Lanyard) production for Warren William. And while generally up to standard in group of private sleuth mystery mellers, 'Passport to Suez' becomes cluttered with n.s.g., mystifying developments near its close. Letdown is all the more apparent because earlier passages shape up slickly.

Customary artifice of having the Lone Wolf suspected unjustly is used. This time, he's eyed by the British admiralty at Alexandria, Egypt, as conniving with a German spy ring to get secret plans of the Suez canal. Actually he's attempting, of course, to outwit the Nazi agents—and does ultimately. Story builds to a smash climax, with the Lone Wolf about to seize the thefted plans almost from under the noses of the Nazi espionage agents. Then the film goes haywire with a double-cross of the Alexandria spy coterie plus an exciting autoplane chase.

A new spy bobs up every several hundred feet, but both scripter John Stone and director Andre de Toth keep interest centered well enough on the Lone Wolf and his faithful butler until the absurd anti-climax. Usual hidden codes, trick doors and gunplay in other Lone Wolf ventures enliven the plot.

William again clicks as Michael

Lanyard, the Lone Wolf. Eric Blore, as the butler, proves as droll as ever. Story has the butler with a hitherto unknown son—in the British navy. That helps complicate the plot since he's in love with an alleged femme war correspondent (Ann Savage). She's plenty effective in this role despite the later development showing her to be a German agent. Sheldon Leonard, as Lanyard's pal of N. Y. speakeasy days, chips in with a vivid ex-bootlegger characterization. Support, which is excellent, is topped by Lou Merrill, Frederic Worlock, Jay Novello and Sig Arno. *Wear.*

Adventures of a Rookie

Hollywood, Aug. 17.

RKO release of Bert Gilroy production. Stars Wally Brown and Alan Carney. Directed by Leslie Goodwins. Screenplay, Edward James; original and adaptation by William Bowers, M. Coates Webster; camera, Jack MacKenzie; editor, Harry Marker; asst. director, James Casey. Tradeshown in L.A. Aug. 17, '43. Running time, 64 MINS.

Jerry Miles....................Wally Brown
Mike Strager....................Alan Carney
Bob Prescott....................Richard Martin
Sgt. Burke....................Erford Gage
Peggy Linden....................Margaret Landry
Patsy....................Patti Brill
Ruth....................Rita Coprday
Sgt. Wilson....................Robert Anderson
Colonel....................John Hamilton
Mrs. Linden....................Ruth Lee
Eve....................Lorraine Krueger
Margaret....................Ercelle Woods
Betty....................Toddy Peterson
Mr. Linden....................Byron Foulger

Wally Brown and Alan Carney are launched as a new comedy team by RKO in 'Adventures of a Rookie,' with studio figuring to turn out series of Rookie Army comedies starring the pair during the coming season. Parading silly—and at times ridiculous—episodes at training camp, picture is sufficiently corny to get through the subsequent duals as a supporter where the customers are not too particular.

Brown is a glib, fast-talker in contrast to the stoutish, dumbish and slow-thinking Carney. Basically, RKO has potential comedy starring timber in the duo, but they need stronger material than provided here. Picture is just a jumble of sequences tied together on a very slender thread, with much of the comedy yanked out from deep down in the bag.

Picture opens with quick flashes to establish drafting of Brown from a nightclub floor; Carney from a shipping room, and Bob Prescott from a mansion. Trio land in induction center, and then to training camp. Brown and Carney go through series of misadventures, with Prescott generally along to become the victim of the duo's antics. At the finish, boys are conveniently released from jam that sends them aboard a transport with their unit for overseas duty.

Two comics hold the center of all footage to show flashes of ability despite the nostalgic material provided. Erford Gage is a broadly-sketched tough top sergeant, while Prescott does okay as butt of Brown-Carney Army jams. Balance of cast comes in for minor footage. Direction by Leslie Goodwins lacks timing that could lift the aged material beyond present level. *Walt.*

So This Is Washington

Hollywood, Aug. 17.

RKO release of Ben Hersh production. Stars Lum 'n' Abner (Chester Lauck and Norris Goff). Directed by Raymond McCarey. Screenplay by Leonard Praskins and Roswell Rogers, from original by Rogers and Edward James; camera, Harry Wild; editor, Duncan Mansfield; asst. director, Ruby Rosenberg. Tradeshown in L. A. Aug. 16, '43. Running time, 64 MINS.

Lum....................Chester Lauck
Abner....................Norris Goff
Mr. Marshall....................Alan Mowbray
Robert Blevins....................Roger Clark
Jane Nestor....................Mildred Coles
Aunt Charity....................Sarah Padden
Mrs. Pomeroy....................Minerva Urecal
Grandpappy....................Dan Duncan
Stranger....................Matt McHugh
Taxi Driver....................Barbara Pepper

Radio team of Lum 'n' Abner continue their cinematic series in this lightly-concocted comedy-drama aimed for attention in the rural and crossroads houses. Basic story is unimportant, but picture is held together mainly through good pace on direction side by Ray McCarey. It's a filler for the duals where the customers are familiar with the colloquial characterizations of the radio duo.

Story opens with Lum and Abner operating their general store, and Abner taking up radio plea to invent something for the war effort. He hits on concoction that Lum tabs as synthetic rubber, and pair are off to Washington to turn it over to the proper Government agency. Before finally reaching that objective, duo go through series of adventures in the capital with amusing results for the rural customers.

Chester Lauck and Norris Goff provide their familiar characterizations of the two hicks; Alan Mowbray broadly plays the Government official; and Roger Clark teams with Mildred Coles for minor romantic interludes.

Raymond McCarey adequately handles the directorial assignment, holding together the lightly-frameworked and synthetic yarn through well-timed delivery. *Walt.*

MELODY PARADE

(SONGS)

Monogram release of Lindsley Parsons production. Features Mary Beth Hughes, Eddie Quillan, Tim and Irene Ryan. Directed by Arthur Dreifuss. Screenplay, Tim Ryan and Charles Marion; dance director, Jack Boyle; music, Eddie Cherkose, Ed Kay; editor, Dick Currier. At Paramount, Brooklyn, week of Aug. 13. Running time, 73 MINS.

Anne O'Rourke ....Mary Beth Hughes
Jimmy Tracy....................Eddie Quillan
Happy Harrington....................Tim Ryan
Gloria Brewster....................Irene Ryan
Skidmore ....Mantan Moreland
Carroll White ....Andre Charlot
Jedson ....Kenneth Harlan
Adams ....Cy Ring

Specialties: Armida, Jerry Cooper, Anson Weeks and His Orchestra, Ted Fio Rito and His Orchestra, Loumell Morgan Trio, Ramon Ros, Ruloff, Follette and Lunard.

This non-name musical is mildly entertaining and should hold up on most dual situations. Eddie Quillan and Mary Beth Hughes have the leads.

Chockful of dancing, music and singing, 'Musical Parade,' though its dialog and direction are frequently faulty, draws many laughs, mainly from the screwball part played by Irene Ryan and the performer-aspirations of Mantan Moreland, cast as a porter. It's the type of comedy, however, that will find most favor in the sticks. It's a limited budgeter.

Monogram brought in several variety acts to fortify this effort. One, Ruloff, Follette and Lunard, proves one of the highlights. Spotted as part of a nitery floor show, the burlesque ballroom trio click solidly with their knockabout. Another standout bit is contributed by the Loumell Morgan Trio, Negro instrumentalists. Jerry Cooper is used as a crooner in his initial appearance, but he's better in the finale. Anson Weeks' and Ted Fiorito's bands also are used.

There isn't much to the story. Quillan is a busboy in a nitery and he has producer aspirations. He's continually auditioning people. Meanwhile, the spot is due to fold unless new money is forthcoming, and when Miss Norton shows up she is taken for an heiress, the club gets new life, only to wilt again when she's discovered for what she is. This on-again, off-again business prevails to a rather mixed up finale, in which Mary Beth Hughes, playing a hat-check girl, finally gets her chance to sing, which Quillan is promising all along.

Miss Hughes gives a satisfactory performance. Quillan is okay, but with the exception of the aforementioned laugh getters, the remainder of the lineup is unimpressive. There are several songs in the film, none of which seems to have outstanding value. *Wood.*

THE SEVENTH VICTIM

RKO release of Val Lewton production. Features Tom Conway, Isabel Jewell, Kim Hunter. Directed by Mark Robson. Screenplay, Charles O'Neal and De Witt Bodeen; camera, Nicholas Mesuraca; music, Roy Webb; music director, C. Bakaleinikoff; editor, John Lockert. Previewed in projection room, N. Y., Aug. 13, '43. Running time, 71 MINS.

Dr. Louis Judd....................Tom Conway
Mary Gibson....................Kim Hunter
Jacqueline....................Jean Brooks
Gregory Stone....................Hugh Beaumont
Jason Hoag....................Erford Gage
Frances....................Isabel Jewell
Mr. Romari....................Chef Milani
Mrs. Romani....................Marguerita Sylva
Natalie Cortez....................Evelyn Brent
Mrs. Redi....................Mary Newton
Durk....................Wally Brown
Mr. Brun....................Ben Bard
Leo....................Feodor Chaliapin

A particularly poor script is the basis for the ills besetting this mystery melodrama. Even the occasional good performance can't offset this minor dualer.

Tom Conway has the lead, and while he's generally a satisfactory performer, he, too, can't extricate himself from the maze of circumstances that abound in this totally unbelievable hocus-pocus about a strange Greenwich Village coterie.

There isn't a name in the list, which will make it more difficult to sell. *Kahn.*

UNDERCOVER

(BRITISH-MADE)

London, July 27.

United Artists release of Ealing Studios Production. Features John Clements, Godfrey Tearle, Tom Walls, Mary Morris, Michael Wilding. Directed by Sergei Nolbandov. Screenplay, John Dighton, M. Danischewsky from original by George Slocombe; camera, W. Cooper. At London Pavilion, July 27, '43. Running time, 90 MINS.

Milosh Petrovitch....................John Clements
Kossan Petrovitch....................Tom Walls
Anna Petrovitch....................Mary Morris
General Von Staengel....................Godfrey Tearle
Constantine ....Michael Wilding
Dr. Jordan ....Niall MacGinnis
Colonel Von Brock....................Robert Harris
Maria Petrovitch....................Rachel Thomas
Dr. Stevan Petrovitch....................Stephen Murray
Sergeant ....Charles Victor
Dragutin ....Ben Williams
Yugoslav General....................George Merritt

This film of Yukoslav guerrillas, originally titled 'Chetnik,' is being released as 'Undercover.' Story is entirely about peasant resistance to the Nazis and it's a fast-moving drama whose value is somewhat dissipated for America due to the U. S.-made 'Chetniks' last year, which deals with the same theme.

Despite admirable direction and players, 'Undercover' is made up of unoriginal situations and has insufficient plot to sustain interest for 90 minutes. John Clements has the leading role, that of a peasant who organizes the Yugoslav resistance. Tom Walls, as the latter's father, is just plain Tom Walls, waiting for his laughs just as he did when playing farce. Godfrey Tearle looks too decent to play a German general issuing ruthless orders as the military governor of the occupied town. More than a dozen other players effectively portray their roles. *Jolo.*

CALLE CORRIENTES

(ARGENTINE-MADE)

Buenos Aires, July 25.

Lumiton production and release. Features Tito Lusiardo, Severo Fernandez, Alberto Anchart, Elena Lucena, Carmen Del Moral, Emilio De Grey, Leonor Rinaldi, Paquita Vehil, Juan Porta, Vincente Forastieri, Gerardo Rodriguez, Alfredo Capuano, Hector Calcagno, Fernando Campos. Direction, story and adaptation by Manuel Romero. Photography, by Fulvio Testi. Reviewed at Monumental, Buenos Aires. Running time, 91 MINS.

Calle Corrientes is B. A.'s Broadway. This is first time it's been made subject of a film. Result, while interesting, is not so hot because the script, adaptation and direction of Manuel Romero haven't much to work with. It's strictly for interior theatres.

Story deals with a young attorney who develops a yen to be a tango singer, and in spite of opposition of father and fiancee he abandons the bar and tries to crash 'Corrientes.' Gets that way about a femme warbler and papa cooks up all kinds of obstacles to discourage him, but he finally makes the grade. Singer, who has a more spotless record than the original fiancee, tries to get him to go back to his first love and law books by telling him she's to marry another, but love and tango win in the end.

Tito Lusiardo and Elena Lucena do well considering the material. Alberto Anchart, one of the top comedians of the Maipo theatre revues, is teamed with Severo Fernandez, but they don't come off quite as well as they do behind the footlights. Carmen Del Moral and Emilio De Grey sing well, but latter is weak in acting. Comparatively little use made of street scene which provides motif. *Ray.*

Robin Hood of Range

(SONGS)

Columbia release of Jack Fier production. Features Charles Starrett, Arthur Hunnicutt, Kay Harris, Kenneth MacDonald. Directed by William Berke. Screenplay, Betty Burbridge; camera, Benjamin Kline; editor, Jerome Thoms. At New York, N.Y., dual, week of Aug. 10, '43. Running time, 54 MINS.

Steve Marlowe....................Charles Starrett
Arkansas....................Arthur Hunnicutt
Julie Marlowe....................Kay Harris
Henry Marlowe....................Kenneth MacDonald
Ned Harding....................Douglass Drake
Sheriff....................Hal Price
Grady....................Ed. Peil, Sr.
Carter....................Frank LaRue
Thompson....................Bud Osborne
Santana....................Stanley Brown
The Jimmy Wakely Trio

Charles Starrett delivers plenty of action as a western Robin Hood aiding homesteaders in their fight against a land-hungry railroad company. The story has often been worked over, but in 'Robin Hood of the Range' it has the added twist of making the hero a foster son of the railroad manager.

Starrett takes up the work of the 'Vulcan,' the region's original hooded Robin Hood, a former homesteader evicted for non-payment of rent by the railroad in a phoney land-grab deal. As the 'law-abiding' railroad manager's foster son, and as the new 'Vulcan,' Starrett is kept busy changing costumes, chasing himself and keeping the homesteaders from losing their property.

In between chase scenes the Jimmy Wakely Trio gives out with several nicely delivered prairie ballads. Love interest, however, is non-existent. Kay Harris, the femme lead, portrays Starrett's sister.

Photography is above average for a limited-budget western. Direction is also good keeping the 54 minutes brisk.

ESCAPE TO DANGER

(BRITISH-MADE)

London, July 22.

RKO production and release. Stars Ann Dvorak, Eric Portman. Directed by Victor Hanbury, Lance Comfort, Mutz Greenbaum. Story, Patrick Kirwan. At Cambridge theatre, London. Running time, 92 MINS.

Anthony Lawrence....................Eric Portman

Joan Grahame.................Ann Dvorak
Franz Von Brinkmann.....Karel Stepanek
Rupert Chessman.............Ronald Ward
George Merrick............Ronald Adam
Sir Alfred Horton...........Felix Aylmer
Lieut. Surgeon Leighton.......David Peel
Hoelder.....................Hay Petrie
Rear Admiral Leighton....A. E. Matthews
P. O. Flanagan............Charles Victor
Works Manager............George Merritt
Mrs. Pickles.............Marjorie Rhodes
Lisbon Attache.............Anthony Shaw

This RKO British-made production, another in the Nazi spy cycle, is excellent entertainment. Building to a gripping climax, it's geared for good grosses both in home and foreign markets.

Ann Dvorak plays a school teacher from Denmark whose espionage finally brings out the German fleet on an unsuccessful mission to trap elusive invasion barges. Following a false wireless beam, they're caught by combined operations, but the schoolmarm does not live to enjoy the fruits of the rather exaggerated tour de force. Eric Portman is excellent as a drunken Englishman whose 'lack' of patriotism unfortunately will not fool the average audience. Rest of the cast okay.

BLACK SEA FIGHTERS
(DOCUMENTARY)

Artkino presents Central Newsreel production. Directed by Vasili Belyaev; assistant director, A. Yevsikov; commentary, Clifford Odets; narrator, Fredric March; photography, A. Krichevsky, G. Donetz, A. Smolka, V. Mikosha, D. Rimarev, F. Korotkevich. Presented at Stanley, N. Y., July 27, '43. Running time, 64 MINS.

'Black Sea Fighters,' the new Moscow Central Newsreel production which Artkino is distributing in the U. S., packs a terrific wallop via its graphic newsreel shots. It further boasts a simple though always forceful commentary written by Clifford Odets and narrated eloquently by Fredric March.

The inspiring defense of their city by the people of Sevastopol during the eight-month attack by the Nazis has aroused the admiration and feeling of all civilized peoples but it remains for this newest documentary to reveal the marvelous synchronization and superb courage of the fighting soldiers of the Soviet Union and her less-acclaimed sailors and marines. The heroism of the people has been shown before in all its horrible detail, but the epic of the seaport city, surrounded on three sides by Nazi-held shores and garrisoned as a sea fortress with no protection against land forces, has never been portrayed so vividly as in 'Black Sea Fighters.' Film is punctuated with closeups of men and women, young and old, taking up arms to take their toll of 300,000 German dead and wounded until only 11 buildings are left standing in the entire city. Equally as tense and exciting are the sea battles by Russia's trained forces, including a number of clips not previously released in this country.

The cameramen who took these actual battle shots are not the least of Russia's heroes. Although the film still has the flickering, clouded appearance of the preceding Russian documentaries, taking the hazardous shots, which seem to project the cameraman into the heart of the battle, pushes this technically into the background.   *Rose.*

WEST SIDE KID

Republic release of George Sherman production. Stars Donald Barry; features Henry Hull, Dale Evans. Directed by George Sherman. Screenplay, Albert Beich and Anthony Coldewey; camera, Jack Marta; editor, Ernest Nims. At Strand, Brooklyn, week Aug. 12, '43, dualed. Running time, 57 MINS.

Johnny April ....Donald Barry
Sam Winston...............Henry Hull
Gloria Winston.............Dale Evans
Shoelace ....Chick Chandler
The Worrier.......Matt McHugh
Mrs. Winston.............Nana Bryant
Ramsey Fehsel..........Walter Catlett

Donovan ....Edward Gargan
Gwylim.............Chester Clute
Jerry Winston..........Peter Lawford
Dr. Kenton.............George Metaxa

Donald Barry quits his chaps and spurs to become a gangster in this melodrama. He's cast as one Johnny April, a role reminiscent of the recent Johnny Eager characterization by Robert Taylor in the Metro picture of that name. Okay for duals.

Barry plays a guy who, just out of prison, turns slightly soft in reforming the family of rich publisher. Plot is a bit implausible at times but does establish Barry as suited for mobster roles.

Henry Hull plays a newspaper publisher who's so fed up on the eccentricities of spoiled members of his family that he hires a gangster to have himself killed. Barry is employed at $25,000 to bump him off. Instead, latter becomes convinced that the head of the family has had a raw deal and manages to straighten out the whole tribe while falling for the daughter. Plot starts out with rare possibilities but continuity goes awry.

Barry makes a typical gangster, with even his most ardent western followers likely to be surprised at the ease with which' he fits into his new characterization. Dale Evans, as the spoiled daughter, shapes up as a comer.

Hull does first-rate as the publisher. Good support includes Chick Chandler, Walter Catlett, Chester Clute and George Metaxa. George Sherman's direction shows good pace.   *Wear.*

THE MAN IN GRAY
(BRITISH-MADE)
London, Aug. 6.

General Film Distributors release of Gaumont-British-Gainsborough production. Features Phyllis Calvert, Margaret Lockwood, James Mason. Directed by Leslie Arliss. Screenplay, Margaret Kennedy, Leslie Arliss; based on novel by Lady Eleanor Smith; camera, Arthur Crabtree. At Gaumont, Haymarket. Running time, 115 MINS.

Clarissa ....Phyllis Calvert
Hesther Shaw ....Margaret Lockwood
Lord Rohan ....James Mason
Swinton Rokeby ....Stewart Granger
Prince Regent ....Raymond Lovell
Miss Patch ....Martita Hunt

Lady Eleanor Smith has written some colorful novels, usually period and with a circus background, some of which have been transferred to the screen. In this latest one, with Regency London as the background, a dramatic and interesting story is unfolded. It is Leslie Arliss' first direction job, and in all ways a credit to him. It should do well in England, though doubtful for America because of the yarn's background.

Story opens with auction sale of effects at a peer's mansion in Grosvenor Square. A chance meeting between a flying officer and a girl naval officer fades into the story of their ancestors' part in the house's history.

Phyllis Calvert is a lovely heroine, exuding the charm and kindly disposition essential to the character. Margaret Lockwood neatly carries off the wanton go-getter role and James Mason's usually sombre personality suits the title role. A newcomer, Stewart Granger, makes a promising start as the hero. Scenes of Bath, Vauxhall Gardens and kindred topical sets are effectively photographed.   *Clem.*

Adventure in Blackmail
(BRITISH-MADE)

English Films, Inc., release of Mercury production. Stars Clive Brook and Judy Campbell; features C. V. France, Marguerite Allan, Percy Walsh and Dennis Arundell. Directed by Harold Huth. Story, Emeric Pressburger; adaptation, Roland Pertwee; editor, Sidney Cole; camera, Jack Cox. At Strand, Brooklyn, dual, week

Aug. 5, '43. Running time, 70 MINS.
Peter Conroy.................Clive Brook
Pamela Lawrence.........Judy Campbell
Morgan.................C. V. France
Pamela Rose........Marguerite Allan
Saxon Rose..................Percy Walsh
Philip...................Dennis Arundell
The Professor.............George Merritt
Sir Hamar...............David Horne
Sir William...............Charles Victor
Judge...............Aubrey Mallalieu
Rex........................Tony Bazell

A production that rates under average, and suffering also from substandard recording and photography as well as a British slant that will make it difficult to make a go of it in America, 'Adventure in Blackmail' is strictly a secondary feature.

Clive Brook, who stars opposite Judy Campbell, will be recalled as the former Paramount star in America, dating back to silent days. He still makes a fine appearance and, unlike others in the cast, records acceptably for American ears. His Hollywood experience doubtlessly helps. One of the general difficulties, if it's not the recording, is that most members of the cast speak too fast.

Brook essays the role of a playwright who becomes involved in a breach-of-promise suit but agrees to marry the girl during the trial rather than await a verdict. However, he and the lass ultimately fall in love after a series of scenes highlighting the resentment they feel for each other. The girl is Miss Campbell, who fails to impress much, while the notable support includes C. V. France, Marguerite Allan, Percy Walsh, Dennis Arundell, George Merritt, Aubrey Mallalieu and Tony Bazell.   *Char.*

Asi Se Quiere en Jalisco
('Love in Jalisco')
(MEXICAN-MADE)
(Songs, Color)

Grovas-Mohme release of Fernando de Fuentes production; direction and screenplay by de Fuente. Stars Jorge Negrete. Story by Guz Aguila based on idea by Don Carlos Arniche; camera, John W. Boyle; music, Manuel Esperon. At Belmont, N. Y., week Aug. 6, '43. Running time, 140 MINS.

Lupe.................Maria Elena Marques
Don Pancho..............Antonio Frausto
Dona Pepa.................Lupe Inclan
Juan Ramon...........Jorge Negrete
Don Luis...............Carlos Moctezuma

(In Spanish; English titles)

'Love in Jalisco' is one of the outstanding features to come from Mexico City film studios. As the initial all-color feature production from Mexico and with Jorge Negrete, Mex. fave, it represents topflight b.o. for Spanish-speaking audience in arty U. S. cinemas. Though a typically wordy Spanish screen vehicle it should attract recent students of Espanol. Present length of film and dearth of action makes it highly questionable for most American houses.

Musical background plus a couple of typical (and swingy) Mexican songs partly overcome the obviously verbose character of the story. Plot is the familiar one about the wealthy man who tries to pressure a girl into marriage by taking care of the mortgage on her parent's ranch. After loaning the money, the rich man, a ranch owner, agrees to employ the femme as his housekeeper. Usual developments result, with the gal's real sweetheart ultimately winning out.

Jorge Negrete as the sweetheart is as effective as usual. Besides being a capable screen actor, he possesses a nice voice and sings the two best songs of film. First he's a ranch overseer, doubling as an orchestra leader (this gives him a chance to warble), and finally as a wandering minstrel. Maria Elena Marques is excellent as femme interest, im-

pressing with her looks and acting, while Carlos Moctezuma, as the ranch owner, is effective as the third in the triangle. Support is standard.

Fernando de Fuentes, who scripted from Guz Aguila's story, also directs and produced. This possibly explains the film's length. While it's a workmanlike job of direction, many story angles need pruning. *Wear.*

Miniature Reviews

'Holy Matrimony' (20th). Monty Woolley and Gracie Fields in comedy-drama slated for big boxoffice.

'Shrine of Victory' (20th). Documentary on Greece's courageous fight to overcome Nazi yoke.

'Follies Girl' (PRC). Name bands and capable cast fail to make this musical jell; strictly for lower half of dualers.

'The Flemish Farm' (British). Skillfully produced war drama okay for duals.

'Hoosier Holiday' (Songs) (Rep.). Corny, but likeable back-to-soil saga; should do well on dualers.

'Al Son de La Marimba' (Mexican). Musical farce with Fernando Soler; strong for Spanish-language houses.

'Stukas' (German-Made). German-language, Spanish-subtitled film, glorifying Nazi flying squadron. Purely propaganda.

'Los Hombres Las Prefieren Viudas' (Argentine). Okay comedy for Latin-American audiences.

HOLY MATRIMONY

20th-Fox release of Nunnally Johnson production. Stars Monty Woolley, Gracie Fields; features Laird Cregar, Eric Blore, Alan Mowbray, Melville Cooper, Franklin Pangborn, Fritz Feld, Una O'Connor, George Zucco. Directed by John Stahl. Screenplay, Nunnally Johnson from Arnold Bennett's novel, 'Buried Alive'; camera, Lucien Ballard; editor, James B. Clark; music, Emil Newman. Tradeshown in N. Y. Aug 19, '43. Running time, **87 MINS.**

Priam Farll	Monty Woolley
Alice Challice	Gracie Fields
Clive Oxford	Laird Cregar
Mrs. Leek	Una O'Connor
Mr. Pennington	Alan Mowbray
Dr. Caswell	Melville Cooper
Duncan Farll	Franklin Pangborn
Lady Vale	Ethel Griffies
Henry Leek	Eric Blore
Mr. Crepitude	George Zucco
Critics	Fritz Feld, William Austin
Judge	Montagu Love
John Leek	Richard Fraser
King Edward VII	Edwin Maxwell
Solicitor	Leyland Hodgson
Harry Leek	Whitner Bissell
Matthew Leek	Geoffrey Steele
Lady Vale's Footman	Lumsden Hare
Court Clerk	Thomas Louden
Stawley	Ian Wolfe
Clerk	Milton Parsons
Aylmer	Alec Craig

Arnold Bennett's early 20th century novel, 'Buried Alive,' has been resurrected by Nunnally Johnson as a Monty Woolley-Gracie Fields starrer that can't miss. The production and casting credits are all on the plus side in this comedy-drama themed in England at the turn of the century. It can play single dates in all situations.

Produced and written for the screen by Johnson, 'Holy Matrimony' is sparked mainly by the novel story, excellent dialog, pacey direction by John Stahl and, above all, fine performances by the co-stars.

To the non-initiates who might discern similarity between 'Matrimony' and other, more modern yarns it must be emphasized that Arnold Bennett's stories are almost as notable today for the predilection of modern writers to copy his style. Bennett wrote 'Buried Alive' in 1908.

'Matrimony' is a study of characters, and Johnson's script has defined, and Stahl's direction developed, them excellently. Woolley is dominant throughout as Priam Farll, a painter whose fame for 25 years had mounted in England while he worked in solitude in the South Seas, accompanied only by a valet. When a command appearance is ordered by King Edward so he can be knighted, the trip back to England marks a turn of events that form the crux for the story.

The valet contracts pneumonia and dies on the return to England, and the doctor mistakenly inserts the name of the painter on the death certificate. And so all England, even King Edward, goes into mourning for the man whom no one actually knew. Seeing a chance to retain his cherished physical anonymity, Farll adopts the name of Henry Leek, the valet. Thereafter the film rapidly increases in interest, going through the various situations in which Farll finds himself as Leek, including his acquisition of a wife through a matrimonial agency, and up to the climactic court scenes that finally determine Farll's real identity.

There are a number of excellent touches given the picture through the combined Johnson-Stahl auspices. The funeral rites at Westminster Abbey, where the real Priam Farll is chased as a crasher—and at his own funeral, too—is ironical comedy that's pointed up dramatically but always with an austere sense of proportion that could have been lost in less skillful hands. The King's acknowlegement, too, that Priam Farll was to be buried in London's famed cloisters also has its irony in Farll's realization—and even regret—at actually not being able to achieve his—and the lifelong desire of every Englishman—to be laid to rest in the Abbey's hallowed halls.

The film's development abounds with a story line that at no times strains credibility. Miss Fields, as the widow in search of a husband, gives the film a highly human touch instead of the ludicrousness that the situation might normally suggest. The British comedienne, who's achieved note by her droll Lancashire humor, is essaying a straight dramatic part, and, if anything, she underplays. She's a perfect mate for Woolley's cantankerous characterization, and the two might very well be teamed in other pictures where suitable stories can be lined up for them.

Rest of the cast, all of them types, is excellent. The more notable featured players are Laird Cregar, Una O'Connor, Alan Mowbray, Melville Cooper, Franklin Pangborn, Eric Blore (the valet) and George Zucco. There are a number of bits, all done well. *Kahn.*

The Shrine of Victory

(BRITISH-MADE)

Twentieth-Fox release of Casanave-Artlee production. Features Vrassidas Capernaros, officers and men of Greek Navy. Directed by Charles Hasse. Based on Greek Testament by M. Danischewsky. Michael Balcon and Cavalcanti in charge of production; commentary by Frank Owen and Angus MacPhail; editor, Sidney Cole; original music, Ernest Irving. Previewed in Projection Room, N. Y., Aug. 16, '43. Running time, **45 MINS.**

(Partly in Greek; English Titles)

Story of the Nazi conquest of Greece, and manner in which the Greek race subsequently has fought back, is intelligently done in this British-made documentary. Earlier passages, containing a maximum of newsreel clips, lean entirely on spoken commentary and occasional English titles to carry the thin plot thread. Once the leading figure in the yarn (Petty Officer Leonides) escapes to England the pace quickens and the regulation sound track carries along the action. It is a timely feature, calculated to interest Greek-speaking Americans and others interested in the Greek cause.

Picture lacks the action associated with more recently completed British productions and consequently it possesses limited appeal for average U. S. film audiences. (Feature will be given its American preem Thursday (19) night at the World, N. Y., with the Greek War Relief Assn. as beneficiary.)

Vrassidas Capernaros, only player listed in film credits, portrays Petty Officer Leonides—a typical, courageous Greek, who survives the German onslaught, to live and fight in the reconstructed Greek navy off the British Isles. He is depicted as a wine grower who decides to do something when his native land is invaded. At first his task is concentrated in aiding the escape of luckless Greeks from their homeland. When the Nazis are about to pounce on him he, too, successfully quits Greece and ships to England. There he becomes an officer on a new Greek battlewagon; training of men, launching of boat and its work in protecting convoys providing bulk of incidents.

There is nothing particularly new in the newsreel footage, though it has been nicely interwoven with the staged sequences. The famine that followed the oppressive Nazi measures in Greece is vividly pictured as well as incidents of the underground movement. Episode where the petty officer escapes, with the singing of a native high on a shoreline cliff to tip off that the Germans are not wise, is particularly well done.

Commentary by Frank Owen and Angus MacPhail is crisply read but the script at times goes overboard in praising the British help to the Greeks without mentioning the U. S., Canada or other Allies. This is understandable because it was made in England and with the Greek navy construction going on there. Charles Hasse's direction is not inspired but fairly even. Vrassidas Capernaros proves a smart choice for the single outstanding character, typifying the rugged Greek personality. *Wear.*

FOLLIES GIRL

(MUSICAL)

PRC release of William Rowland production, directed by Rowland. Features Wendy Barrie, Doris Nolan, Gordon Oliver, J. C. Nugent, Arthur Pierson, Cora Witherspoon, Fritzi Scheff, and Johnny Long, Bobby Byrne, Ray Hetherton, Ernie Holst bands. Screenplay by Marcy Klauber and Charles Robinson from original by Klauber and Art Jarrett; added dialog, Pat C. Flick, Lew Hearn; camera, George Webber; Editor, Samuel Datlowe; dances, Larry Ceballos; musical director, Ernie Holst; songs, Nick Kenny, Charles Kenny, Sunny Burke, John Murphy, Kim Gannon, Ken Lane, Robert Warren, Fred Wise, Buddy Kaye, Sid Lippman, Mary Schaeffer. At Strand, Brooklyn, dual, week Aug. 19, '43. Running time, **71 MINS.**

Anne Merriday	Wendy Barrie
Francine La Rue	Doris Nolan
Pvt. Jerry Hamlin	Gordon Oliver
Bunny	Anne Barrett
Sgt. Bill Perkins	Arthur Pierson
J. B. Hamlin	J. C. Nugent
Mrs. J. B. Hamlin	Cora Witherspoon
Jimmy Dobson	William Harrigan
Andre Duval	Jay Brennan
Lew	Lew Hearn
Cliff	Cliff Hall
Trixie	Marion McGuire
Patsy	Pat C. Flick
Somers	Anthony Blair
Jerri	Jerri Blanchard
Scarini	Serjei Radamsky
Doorman	G. Swayne Gordon

'Follies Girl' has name bands, some capable players and specialty combos, several tuneful numbers and an idea, yet it never quite jells. Main trouble is the lack of tight script and sock gags, plus the wealth of material that slows proceedings. Idea of using a servicemen's canteen and a nearby hoity-toity burlesque show as background for usual boy-girl romance undoubtedly was new when this picture was produced about a year ago, but by release time, several features had incorporated the canteen background, outstanding being 'Stage Door Canteen,' while 'Lady of Burlesque' also was released. This one is strictly for secondary dualers.

Scripters Marcy Klauber and Charles Robinson employ a servicemen's canteen for locale on a yarn about a burlesque warbler, a dress designer and the Army private who falls in love with the attractive designer while trying to save his dad from a supposed affair with her. The father, who owns the dress design outfit, is sold on the idea that streamlined, richly costumed burlesque can be put over at Broadway musical show prices. The 'Follies' of the title refers to the burley queen (who never strips) but wins her way with her warbling.

Venerable gag lines and the continued obtrusion of musical numbers hinder the pace. Ray Heatherton's band plays at the canteen and for the film while Johnny Long, Bobby Byrne (long since in the Air Corps), Heatherton and Ernie Holst figure in an informal ensemble near the end. Claire & Arena, ballroom team; Charles Weidman dance group, Song Spinners, Heat Waves and Lazara & Castellanos are outstanding among specialists but badly presented.

Of numerous songs, 'No Man in the House,' by Nick and Charles Kenny, Sunny Burke; 'Someone to Love,' by Robert Warren, and 'I Told a Lie,' by Nick Kenny, Kim Gannon and Ken Lane, are the more tuneful. George Webber's photography takes the rap for the faulty lighting evident in several scenes. William Rowland directs capably enough considering the story.

Wendy Barrie, as the dress designer, comes closest to giving a pat performance. Doris Noland, the burley prima donna, clicks with her vocals. J. C. Nugent, who plays the wealthy dressshop owner; Cora Witherspoon, as his wife, and Gordon Oliver, as the son, most of the time are uninteresting, their lines being largely to blame. Lew Hearn, Cliff Hall, Pat C. Flick and Anne Barrett are lost in lesser roles.

Fritzi Scheff, who is introed near the finale, screens fairly well and does her best to put over 'Keep the Flag A-flying, America,' a rather uninspired tune. *Wear.*

THE FLEMISH FARM

(BRITISH-MADE)

London, Aug. 4.

General Film Distributors release of Two Cities Film. Stars Clive Brook, Jane Baxter, Clifford Evans. Directed by Jeffrey Dell. Screenplay, Jill and Jeffrey Dell; camera, Eric Cross; music, Ralph Vaughan Williams. At Leicester Square theatre, London. Running time, **82 MINS.**

Major Lessart	Clive Brook
Duclos	Clifford Evans
Trescha	Jane Baxter
Matagne	Philip Friend
Belgian Minister	Brefni O'Rorke
Flemish Farmer	Wylie Watson
Van der Velde	Martin Walker
Madame Duclos	Mary Jerrold
Flemish Farmwife	Lilli Kahn
Squadron Leader Hardwick	Ronald Squire
Captain Scheldheimer	Richard George

A skillfully produced film with a carefully selected cast and exceptional camerawork, but the basic story seems insufficient to hold attention. The author staked too much on a single incident. It's okay for duals, however.

Story is allegedly based on an actuality, dealing with an incident on the Belgian invasion of the present war.

Clifford Evans, Clive Brook and Jane Baxter head the cast. The male stars acquit themselves well, while Miss Baxter appears to be too much a comedic type for the tragic part she plays. The supporting cast is excellent. *Jolo.*

HOOSIER HOLIDAY

(SONGS)

Republic release of Armand Schaefer production. Starring Hoosier Hot Shots, The Music Maids, George D. Hay, Isabel Randolph, George 'Shug' Fisher and Lillian Randolph. Featuring Dale Evans, George Byron, Emma Dunn, Thurston Hall, Ferris Taylor, Georgia Davis, 'Sleepy' Williams and His Three Shades of Color. Directed by Frank McDonald. Original and screenplay by Dorrell & Stuart McGowan, based on idea by Edward James; camera, Reggie Lanning; songs, Johnny Marvin and Charles Henderson; dances, Josephine Earl.

Previewed in N. Y. Aug. 20, '43. Running time, **72 MINS.**

Old Judge....................George D. Hay
Dale Fairchild....................Dale Evans
Abigail Fairchild..........Idabel Randolph
Jim Baker....................George Byron
Molly Baker....................Emma Dunn
Henry P. Fairchild..........Thurston Hall
Aloysius Lincoln...............'Nicodemus'
Gov. Manning.................Ferris Taylor
Grace Manning...............Georgia Davis
'Sleepy' Williams and 3 Shades of Rhythm
Hoosier Hot Shots
Music Maids
George 'Shug' Fisher
Lillian Randolph

Corn pops aplenty in this one, but it's all likeable stuff that should particularly ring the bell with the hinterland folk.

'Hoosier Holiday' has ostensibly been set up and woven around the Hoosier Hot Shots, novelty band with a hillbilly tinge. In that and other respects it achieves its object. Story is old hat, yet there's plenty of fun sprinkled throughout by the band boys and others.

It's a back-to-the-soil saga, pointing up the premise that the land army of food-growers are every whit as important as the army on the global warfronts. There's also the inevitable feud which takes entire unravelling of the film to iron out.

Hoosier tooters essay the Baker boys, sons of the soil, mothered by Ma Baker (Emma Dunn), who double between vegetating the land and broadcasting on local station's Good Earth program, handled by the Solemn Old Judge (George D. Hay). Boys are popular with everybody but Henry and Abigal Fairchild. To them they're good-for-nothing hoodlums. Reason is pivot upon which ensuing plot rotates.

Beneath the denim garb of the Baker lads is a yen to quit the farm for active service in the air corps, but Fairchild, head of the draft board, nixes out of spite. Fairchild's five gals return from finishing school and chase around with the Bakers. Boys conspire to rush the gals so that Fairchild may relent and okay them for service, if for no other reason than break up attachments. It nearly works until Fairchild has a change of heart and seems willing to unload his quintet of hoydens on the Bakers. He's also patched things up with Molly, and Abigail is again purring at the judge before it's over.

Band boys are augmented by George Byron, as Jim Baker, vis-a-vis to Dale Evans in romantic interest. Miss Evans, too, is augmenting Musical Maids, harmony foursome, who double as Fairchild girls and handle vocals in the film. Emma Dunn capably handles assignment as the Baker boys' Ma, and Thurston Hall is convincing as the blustering Fairchild. Other cast members are adequate in respective roles.

Interspersing action is several numbers by band and harmony vocals by Miss Evans and Music Maids, comprising 'Hoosier Holiday' and 'Grandaddy of Boogie Woogie,' effectively sold and well spotted.

Frank McDonald, who directed, keeps it moving at lively pace. Photography by Reggie Lanning is also okay.

Al Son de la Marimba

('Song of the Marimba')
(MEXICAN-MADE)
(Musical)

Clasa-Mohme release of Grovas Films production. Stars Fernando Soler. Directed by Bustillo Oro. Screenplay by H. Gomez Landero. At Belmont, N. Y., starting Aug. 20, '43. Running time, **131 MINS.**

The Ambitious Father.....Fernando Soler
The Equally Ambitious Mother.Sara Garcia
Their Daughter............Marina Tamayo
The 'Rich Catch'.............Emilio Tuero
His Wise Counsel........Joaquin Pardave

(In Spanish; no English titles)

This newest import from Mexico is a hybrid farce-musical comedy, with most stress on the latter. With Fernando Soler, rated Mexico's leading character actor, starred, some above-average tunes and the Latin-American miramba orchestra, 'Song of the Miramba' is plenty forte for Spanish language houses and a few arty spots. Fact that it has no English titles confines its business possibilities to this field.

Film is packed with crisp dialog, superbly handled by ths cast. Result is that Spanish-speaking auditors virtually tumble in the aisles. But to those not savvying Espanol, the quips mean nothing.

This is the oldie about the venerable family of good name but thin financial status knocking themselves out to marry off their comely daughter to a rich rancher. Lavish spending of the new son-in-law's money (the scheming parents always succeed) brings out the old artifice of testing the loyalty of the sponging parents and other relatives. Payoff runs to form with the elderly couple disclaiming that the lad's coin is their sole interest.

Requires far too long to tell but okay for Spanish-speaking patrons because loaded with humorous incidents. Like so many foreign-language producers launching extensive feature film-making, the tendency of Mexican producers is towards going overboard on dialog. Understandable with Mexican producers, because native audiences are accustomed to verbose legit drama and seemingly like their screen fare the same way.

H. Gomez Landero's screenplay is overly long considering limited action but director Bustillo Oro does nicely in milking every possible guffaw from material available. Fernando Soler is brilliant as the scheming father, while Sara Garcia is adequate as the mother. Marina Tamayo, as the eligible daughter, who weds the wealthy rancher, is comely and fetching. Emilio Tuero, playing the young rancher 'rich catch,' and Joaquin Pardave, his pal, are above average. *Wear.*

STUKAS

(GERMAN-MADE)

Buenos Aires, Aug. 7.

Ufa production and release. Stars Karl Raddatz, Hannes Stelzer, Herbert Wilk and Albert Hehn; features Ernst von Klipstein, Otto E. Hasse, Else Knott. Adapted. Directed by Karl Ritter. Opened at the Astoria, Buenos Aires. Running time, **90 MINS.**

(In German; with Spanish Sub-titles)

In the 14 months since the Nazis first tried to smuggle this pic into Buenos Aires on the Portuguese vessel Serpa Pinto, only to have it nabbed by customs authorities, every Latin-American country except Argentina has severed relations Axis-yard and, coincidentally, banned showings of German pictures. Releasing of 'Stukas' after much string-pulling and fine-paying was one of the last acts of the ousted Castillo administration. New government is apparently following same practice regarding Axis films as the previous administration, and therefore Argentina is about the only country in this hemisphere where propaganda picts such as this can still be shown. Resultingly, although there's little chance the pic will ever be openly screened outside this country, it's interesting as an example of the Berlin war film technique as contrasted to Hollywood.

'Stukas' is supposed to be a kind of Nazi counterpart to Warners' 'Air Force.' But comparison, even leaving out admitted prejudice of this Yanqui observer, is such that neutral critics here can't even give the Goebbels-inspired effort any credit. Done in German with Spanish sub-titles, it's a glorification of a Stuka squadron operating just about the time of the fall of France against Liege, against French tank formations, and opposite Dunkirk and French positions on the Marne.

Adapted and directed by Karl Ritter, it's apparently intended more for home consumption than export. Every attempt is made to develop idea that the squadron has an 'esprit de corps' that can't be beaten. There's a constant effort to depict high morale and good spirits of the force. There's no love interest. Everyone in the cast hollers from end to end. Some of the language, incidentally, for any one who understands Unter den Linden slang, is enough to make one blush. Local censors, and the Minister of Interior, who had to personally o.k. film, base blue-pencilling, however, on translated titles only, and since these are mild it is said that comparatively few cuts have been made. *Ray.*

Los Hombres Las Prefieren Viudas

(Songs)
(ARGENTINE-MADE)

Buenos Aires, Aug.

Pan-Americana release of San Miguel production. Features Catalina Barcena, Santiago Gomez Cou, Rosa Cata, Alita Roman, Oscar Villa, Marcial Manet, Rosa Rosen, Iris Portillo, Francisco Lopez Silva, Perlita Mux, Max Citelli, Mario Faig and Alberto D'Salvio. Directed by Gregorio Martinez Sierra. Story, Gregorio Martinez Sierra, adapted by Pedro E. Pico and C. Cordoba Iturburo; photography, Fulvio Testi; music, Julian Bautista. Reviewed at Broadway, Buenos Aires. Running time, **62 MINS.**

Gregorio Martinez Sierra, prominent local writer who not long ago turned to film megging, has taken one of his own playscripts, had it adapted by Pedro E. Pico and C. Cardoba Iturburo and turned out a satisfactory comedy with music that should do o. k. comercially in Latin-America, although hardly likely to set any records. Result is a film in good taste, suitable for all kinds of audiences, despite the story.

Story deals with an old maid who's particularly conscious of getting older. Anxious to marry, she decides to risk all on the theory that men prefer widows. Taking advice of a friend who has tried it herself, she passes herself off as the widow of an aviator reportedly lost in flight. Sure enough, she becomes the center of attraction and has a grand time until who should turn up but the pseudo-dead airman curious to see his 'widow.' He becomes one of her train of admirers, then pretends to expect to exercise his marital rights and brings about a series of complications which end, of course, with him and the alleged widow falling in love.

Catalina Barcena, w.k. Spanish actress, has leading role and, while a trifle miscast, turns in a finished performance. Original play from which the film was adapted shows through, and since adaptation was done by writers more accustomed to the footlights than the screen they haven't been able to avoid pitfalls. Santiago Gomez Cou is overshadowed in top supporting role, but the rest of the cast is o.k.

Songs by Julian Bautista good. Specialties by dance team of Muguet and Albaicin add considerably.

Ray.

Miniature Reviews

'Johnny Come Lately' (UA) James Cagney starrer should gross big at the b.o.

'Black Market Rustlers' (Mono). Routine yarn, strictly for lower dualers.

'Girls In Chains' (PRC). Good fare for low budgeter.

'Revenge of the Zombies' (Mono.) Incredible yarn, strictly for the duals.

'Seeds of Freedom' (Indie). Modernized version of 'Potemkin,' plus English dialog, limited to arty audiences.

Johnny Come Lately

United Artists release of William Cagney production. Directed by William K. Howard. Stars James Cagney. Screenplay, John Van Druten, based on 'McLeod's Folly,' by Louis Bromfield; camera, Theodore Sparkuhl; editor, George Arthur. Previewed in N. Y. Aug. 23. Running time, **97 MINS.**

Tom Richards................James Cagney
Vinnie McLeod..............Grace George
Gashouse Mary.............Marjorie Main
Jane.........................Marjorie Lord
Aida.......................Hattie McDaniel
W. M. Dougherty...........Ed McNamara
Pete Dougherty..................Bill Henry
Bill Swain..................Robert Barrat
Willie Ferguson..........George Cleveland
Myrtle Ferguson.......Margaret Hamilton
Dudley Hirsh................Norman Willis
Blaker....................Lucien Littlefield
Winterbottom...............Edwin Stanley
Chief of Police..................Irving Bacon
First Cop.........................Tom Dugan
Second Cop..................Charles Irwin
Third Cop....................John Sheehan
Butler.......................Clarence Muse
First Tramp......................John Miller
Second Tramp...........Arthur Hunnicutt
Tramp in Box Car............Victor Kilian
Bouncer....................Wee Willie Davis

James Cagney's first independent production via brother Bill Cagney's unit, coming at a time when the star's b.o. power is at its zenith, is likely to hit from good to hefty business. Cagney comes through with a topnotch performance in the story of the crack tramp newspaperman, afflicted with a wanderlust complex, who temporarily halts in his tracks to help an old lady continue publication of her newspaper and battle the crooked politico-financial forces in her town.

Whatever elements of suspense, action and motivation the Louis Bromfield book, 'McLeod's Folly,' may have held to attract the Cagney production staff, the screen treatment which has emerged is, for the most part, familiar melodrama.

Cagney's performance, however, combined with William Howard's direction, offset scripting flaws.

Production is studded with excellent comedy 'character' bits which, combined with Cagney, give the yarn a terrific lift. Marjorie Main, though overplaying slightly as the turbulent dancehall operator who prides herself on running 'a straight place,' furnishes sturdy support. Hattie McDaniel turns in a corking performance as the family cook, friend and guide. Marjorie Lord and Bill Henry fill the bill nicely as the youthful romantic leads, while Grace George registers as the frail but determined old lady set to carry on the heritage of intrepid journalism bequeathed by her husband. George Cleveland, in a bit as drunken reporter, and Margaret Hamilton, as a sourpuss bookkeeper, also stand out.

Action revolves mainly about Cagney's journalistic attacks on the village tycoon (Ed McNamara) after the lady publisher (Miss George) saves him from a stretch in the hoosegow on vagrancy charges.

Mori.

Black Market Rustlers

Monogram release of George W. Weeks production. Features Ray Corrigan, Dennis Moore and Max Terhune. Directed by S. Roy Luby. Screenplay, Patricia Harper; camera, Edward Kull; editor, Roy Claire. At New York, N. Y., week of Aug. 26, '43, dual. Running time, 54 MINS.

Crash	Ray Corrigan
Dennis	Dennis Moore
Alibi	Max Terhune
Linda	Evelyn Finley
Prescott	Steve Clark
Parry	John Merton
Corbin	Glen Strange
Sheriff	Carl Sepulveda
Blade	George Chesebro
Slim	Hank Warden
Kyser	Frank Ellis
Ed	Frosty Royce

A dull affair, 'Black Market Rustlers' struggles to tie in with black markets. It's strictly for lower half of rural double bills.

Routine yarn deals with rustlers selling cattle to black marketers, only to be apprehended by Ray Corrigan, Dennis Moore and Max Terhune, employed by the Cattlemen's Assn. There's the usual hard riding and fist thumping, but not much else of interest. Pic is another in George Weeks' 'Range Busters' series.

GIRLS IN CHAINS

Producers Releasing Corp. release of Peter Van Duinen (Leon Fromkess) production. Features Arline Judge and Roger Clark. Directed by Edgar R. Ulmer. Screenplay, Albert Beich; camera, Ira Morgan; editor, Charles Henkel, Jr. At New York, N. Y., week of Aug. 26, '43, dual. Running time, 72 MINS.

Helen	Arline Judge
Frank Donovan	Roger Clark
Rita	Robin Raymond
Ruth	Barbara Pepper
Mrs. Peters	Dorothy Burgess
Marcus	Clancy Cooper
Johnny Moon	Allan Byron
Jean	Patricia Knox
Pinkhead	Sidney Melton
Delvers	Russell Gaige
Lionel Cleeter	Emmett Lynn
Tom Haverfield	Richard Clarke
Mrs. Grey	Betty Blythe
Jerry	Peggy Stewart
George	Beverly Boyd
Dr. Orchard	Bob Hill
Judge Coolidge	Henry Hall
Mrs. McCarthy	Mrs. Gardener Crane
Rev. Greene	Crane Whitley
Jury Foreman	Francis Ford

Good dual fare for a low budgeter. Starting with a slight twist on the ordinary detective yarn, film opens with the murderer revealed and then builds to a fast finish with much suspense. Although subject matter is trite, being a rehash on rehabilitation of wayward gals confined to an institution, tight scripting compensates considerably.

Roger Clark plays the dick who helps Arline Judge, sister-in-law of a crook, get the culprit. Gal, fired from teaching school by the board because her sister is married to the gangster, lands a teaching job in the girls' reformatory and there gets the goods on the nemesis through his illegal tieup with the superintendent of the institution.

Direction has things moving swiftly and doesn't neglect the lesser roles, notably that of Allan Byron as the gangster. A handful of toughlooking gals put on the leer effectively. Emmet Lynn provides necessary comedy relief.

Revenge of the Zombies

Monogram release of Lindsley Parsons production. Stars John Carradine; features Gale Storm, Robert Lowery, Mantan Moreland, Bob Steele. Directed by Steve Sekely. Screenplay, Edmund Kelso and Van Norcross; editor, Richard Burrier; camera, Mack Stengler. At Strand, Brooklyn, dual, week Aug. 26, '43. Running time, 61 MINS.

Von Altermann	John Carradine
Larry	Robert Lowery
Jen	Gale Storm
Lila	Veda Ann Borg
Jeff	Mantan Moreland
Scott	Mauritz Hugo
Keating	Barry Macollum
Agent	Bob Steele

Lazarus	James Baskett
Beulah	Mme. Sul-Te-Wan
Rosella	Sybil Lewis
Pete	Robert Cherry

Monogram's newest 'Zombie' release is one of the incredibly fantastic yarns that borders on the ludicrous and fails singularly in creating anything near the suggestion of tenseness or suspense that characterized its predecessor, 'I Walked With a Zombie.' It's strictly for the lower half of the dualers and as such will probably get by in the smaller situations.

Picture tries to tie in a war-tempoed motif with the zombie creator this time portrayed as a mad medico operating in the U. S. bayou country who also turns out to be a Nazi agent and tries to convert his army of 'between life and death' creatures to Hitler's use. His ally in the conspiracy is a local sheriff who eventually turns out to be an FBI man. How the latter and the medico's murdered wife and master of the 'zombie' clan turn on saturnine villain and drag him into the swamp bayou might have made for more horror sequences, but director Steve Sekely's slow pace reacts to the detriment of the film.

John Carradine as the cracked German scientist is properly villainous as he tries to make the most of an impossible role. In supporting roles, Veda Ann Borg, as the wife with superhuman qualities, plus Robert Lowery and Gale Storm lend adequate assistance. *Rose.*

SEEDS OF FREEDOM
(RUSSIAN-MADE)

Potemkin production and release. Features Henry Hull and Aline MacMahon plus original stars of Sergei Eisenstein's 'Potemkin.' Contemporary scenes directed by Hans Burger, with revised production supervised by William Sekely; original script, N. Agedzunov, S. Eisenstein; dialog, contemporary story, Albert Maltz; camera, E. Tisse, William Kelly; editor, Marc Sorkin. At Stanley, N. Y., week Aug. 24, '43. Running time, 67 MINS.
Original cast: A. Antonov, G. Alexandrov, V. Barsky, sailors of Red Navy, citizens of Odessa.
Added American players: Henry Hull, Martin Wolfson, Wendell Phillips, Grover Burgess, John Berry, Peter Frye, Aline MacMahon, Lucy Heim, Louis Sorin, Russell Collins, Stanley Phillips and James Elliott.
Speakers: Julius Matthews, Charles Henderson, Martin Wolfson, John Boyd, Harry Kadison, Hester Sondergaard, Lou Polen, Jack Lambert, Jay Meredith and William Beach.

The brave stand of Odessa against the Nazi hordes is reportedly the inspiration for this 'modernization' of 'Potemkin,' an outstanding Russian film production of many years ago with the courage of Odessa citizens highlighting the picture. Actually, 'Seeds of Freedom' ties up the present fight of brave Russian guerrilla bands against German forces (via several U.S produced interior shots) with the original 'Potemkin' film, with footage from latter picture representing most of story. Film's best appeal is in houses drawing Russian sympathizers. Technically, because of dated scenes and dated acting technique from the original 'Potemkin,' the film likely will have limited appeal even in dual setups, except in arty or foreign language spots.

William Sekely, production chief on current version, and editor Marc Sorkin deserve credit for an inordinately clever job of combining old with newly photographed footage, plus dubbing of American voices onto the Russian original. But despite their astuteness, they are unable to overcome the disadvantage of having to work with those original scenes, where fashions and thespian efforts forcibly expose their antiquity.

Even despite this handicap, introduction of a new plot showing a typical Russo guerrilla group planning to halt a Nazi advance and liberate relatives and captured troops ties up smartly with the production's theme. This simply is that the spirit of Odessa of 1905, when its citizens helped the first revolt against the Czar, still lives and is being perpetuated by Russian fighters on today's battlefronts. Leader of the guerrillas, Henry Hull, recounts his experiences as a 'Potemkin' sailor, with story fading into original Russian screen version. The Russian actors, of course, now speak English in this version.

Hull makes a suitable guerrilla leader (he's 52 in story) to tell the new recruits of 20 years how Russia first started its fight for freedom back in 1905. Aline MacMahon plays the role of a leading citizen of Odessa, figuring most importantly in a prophetic speech about the fight for freedom during mourning ceremonies for a slain member of the Potemkin crew. Others figuring in new sequences are Wendell Philips, Peter Frye, Lucy Heim and James Elliott.

Both William Kelly, who photographed the new footage, and Hans Burger, who directed the added modern scenes, do well considering. *Wear*

The City That Stopped

Paramount release of Artkino production. Compiled by Central Newsreel Studios in the U.S.S.R. from pictures taken by Soviet cameramen on the Don and Stalingrad fronts; editor, Leonid Varlomov; musical arrangement, V. Smirnov; 'Song of Stalingrad,' V. Lebedev-Kumach and V. Mokrousov; narration, John Wexley, spoken by Brian Donlevy. Tradeshown in New York, Aug. 27, '43. Running time, 58 MINS.

The horrors of a besieged, shattered Stalingrad, which for more than five months in 1942 withstood the Nazi blitz at its mightiest, are told in graphic pictorial terms in a newsreel compilation that Paramount has taken over for distribution in the United States. No more horrific documentary of the present war—unless it be the 'Desert Victory' film of the African campaign—can tell in such mute, and yet so eloquent, terms the tale of the Soviet defense of the great industrial city. It is a newsreel compilation for which not only the valiant Soviet fighters must have been rewarded. The cameramen were no less the heroes. Eight of them were killed in line of duty.

The film's 58 minutes will make it difficult for single spotting, but for the double bills it's a natural, though certainly not for sensitive stomachs.

Titled 'The City that Stopped Hitler—Heroic Stalingrad,' this picture pointedly reveals how the city whose fall once seemed a matter of hours, dug itself in for the defense that must go down in history as the turning point of the European theatre of war. Not a building was left standing; it was at Stalingrad that the Nazi machine which had thundered through Europe undefeated was speared by the spirit of a people who wouldn't be beaten—all this, and more, the cameramen have caught in as spine-tingling a document as has ever been filmed.

'Heroic Stalingrad' also points up Russian military tactics by graphs and actual maneuvers. Their now famed 'Katusha,' or flaming rocket, is seen in pictorial action for the first time. Its operating principle, of course, remains secretive.

It's a pic that doesn't skimp on the horrors—the dead lying in uncovered graves, the gangrenous wounded, the civilians forced to flee, the falling defenders—they're all here in a picture whose year-old datedness won't make it any the less newsworthy. Some of the film, too, is of German origin, being among the booty taken when the last vestige of Nazidom had been cleared from the city.

John Wexley has written the commentary, and its excellence is emphasized by Brian Donlevy's reading. There's no denying its propaganda purposes, but its informative value and tribute to the Soviet people by far exceeds the basic element of propaganda. There can be no coloring of a courage that has turned back superior numbers.

With constant rumors of a possible separate Soviet peace with Hitler, the pic may help clarify the multiple confusions that prevail in the world capitals. For there arises an all-important question:

Is the Stalingrad defense to be forgotten for a negotiated peace that would be an admission of Soviet weakness?

Washington and London should feel heartened that in this film there is too much to remind the Soviet that there can be no just peace through negotiation; that her just place is at the peace table with the Allies. *Kahn.*

Miniature Reviews

'The Sky's the Limit' (songs) (RKO). Fred Astaire-Joan Leslie musical o.k. for b.o.

'Larceny with Music' (Songs) (U). Satisfactory filmusical for dualers.

'Sherlock Holmes Faces Death' (U). Standard in the Holmes-Dr. Watson mysteries.

'First Comes Courage' (Col). War picture localed in Norway; will do average biz.

'Fugitive From Sonora' (Rep). Above average low-cost western starring Don 'Red' Barry.

'Lone Star Trail' (U). Action-filled cowboy yarn with Johnny Mack Brown. Okay dualer.

'Submarine Base' (PRC). Lightweight saga of gangster who aids Nazi agents, repents and is killed. Okay for duals.

'Los Ojos Mas Lindos del Mundo' (Argentine). Argentine-made melodrama; mediocre.

'Alejandra' (Mexican). Drawn out tear-jerker, starring Arturo de Cordova, strictly for Latin trade.

THE SKY'S THE LIMIT
(SONGS)

RKO release of David Hempstead (Sherman Todd, associate) production. Stars Fred Astaire, Joan Leslie; features Robt. Benchley, Robt. Ryan, Elizabeth Patterson, Marjorie Gateson, Eric Blore, Freddie Slack orch. Directed by Edward H. Griffith. Original, Frank Fenton, Lynn Root; songs, Johnny Mercer, Harold Arlen; dances, Astaire; music director, Leigh Harline; camera, Russell Metty, Vernon L. Walker; asst. director, Ruby Rosenberg; editor, Roland Gross. At RKO Palace, N. Y., week Sept. 3, '43. Running time, **90 MINS.**

The above starred and featured cast is a handful of players indeed to carry Fred Astaire's newest, but carry it they do, and into more than averagely pleasing results. On the Astaire rep and performance, coupled with Joan Leslie's ever-mounting impact for the marquee, plus her surprising agility on the hoof, 'The Sky's the Limit' will do business.

Story is thin and the three Mercer-Arlen songs are by no means socko, but it's all in the modern idiom of escapology, which is sufficient to get it by. Plot doesn't weigh one down —in truth, there isn't enough of it there to bother—but the general aura is modern and contemporaneous enough to sound like something out of the newsreels.

Astaire is a returning hero from the Flying Tigers campaign and, bored with one of those War Heroes Tours, he changes into mufti—somewhat bizarre dude ranch clothes—which, while a military violation, is overlooked for plot purposes. Miss Leslie is one of those Life-like photogs who bawls her publisher, Robert Benchley, why can't she go to Russia or some other war-front if Margaret Bourke-White, et al. have done it.

From then on it becomes a chase and on-the-make routine by Astaire with Miss Leslie, segueing into a nitery and Canteen sequence where, as part of an 'impromptu' show, they do very smooth specialties, song, dance and otherwise.

The 10-day leave is the excuse for Astaire's whirlwind persistence and in between, they crowd in 'My Shining Hour,' 'I've Got a Lot in Common With You' and 'One for My Baby and One for the Road.' The latter in a stew scene, which is kinda corny for Astaire, is a torcher, but it permits him to utilize the lavish bistro bar for a terp setting, including a highly destructive piece of business with shattering of the bar glasses, etc. 'Hour' is the thematic, first chirped by the stage-struck lenser, Miss Leslie. 'Lot in Common With You' may prove the sturdiest survivor of all three Mercer-Arlen tunes.

Choreographically, Astaire has done wonders with Miss Leslie, who will be a general surprise on the time-step stuff, although trade insiders know of her former song-and-dance sister acts in vaude and the niteries, prior to pix. She's not quite in the Ginger Rogers league—that seems to be a bane of all Astaire partners; they must inevitably suffer comparison with Miss Rogers, and especially from the customers' viewpoint—but she is by no means 'carried' by Astaire. He gets special credit for the dance routines and it's a tribute to his tutoring that Miss Leslie is as OK for hoof as she is for sight and sound.

For the rest, Freddie Slack's band is merely the background although the Capitol Recording artist suggests film possibilities, via his music and nice personality. Robert Benchley's hokum with a toastmaster routine, at a dinner to an aviation tycoon, is merely a perversion of his former 'Treasurer's Report' nonsense, here overdone.

As Astaire filmusicals go, this is as ultra in its general aura, yet the cost is probably more moderate than some of his RKO predecessors. There's no palpable cheating, but the compactness of the plot automatically limited the production nut.

Abel.

LARCENY WITH MUSIC
(SONGS)

Universal release of Howard Benedict production. Stars Allan Jones, Kitty Carlisle, Leo Carrillo; features King Sisters, Alvino Rey Orchestra. Directed by Edward Lilley. Original screenplay, Robert Harari; editor, Paul Landres; camera, Paul Ivano; musical director, Charles Previn. Reviewed in projection room, N. Y., Sept. 7, '43. Running time; **64 MINS.**

Ken Daniels....Allan Jones
Pamela Mason....Kitty Carlisle
Gus Borelli....Leo Carrillo
Mike Simms....William Frawley
Austin J. Caldwell....Gus Schilling
Agatha Parkinson....Lee Patrick
Brewster....Samuel S. Hinds
Zybisco....Sig Arno
King Sisters....King Sisters
Alvino Rey Orchestra

Current upswing in demand for escapist entertainment should enhance chances for Universal's new musical romance, 'Larceny With Music,' although its weak story and direction gear the film strictly into the 'B' class. As a dualer, it should do satisfactory business, although it will need exploitation.

Although picture is in the nature of a comeback for Kitty Carlisle, who's been missing from the screen for several years, it's the King Sisters, spotted solo and with the Alvino Rey orchestra, who get the choice break in 'Larceny.' With a quartet of tunes, the foursome, particularly in their 'When You Wore a Tulip' number, are standouts and give every evidence of being a natural for films. Miss Carlisle, on the other hand, is handcuffed by the poor scripting job, though she can still sell an operetta aria with sock results.

Scripter Robert Harari apparently hadn't wasted much time and effort concocting his yarn of the hoax perpetrated on the owner of the swank Blue Room nitery (Leo Carrillo) whose phobia for chamber music quintets has put his spot on the skids, with a resultant eviction coming on. The manager for Allan Jones, who is vocalist with the Alvino Rey band, playing for peanuts in the Eight Ball Club, sells Carrillo the cooked-up story that Jones has fallen heir to a fortune. Carrillo, envisioning a 50% slice, books Jones, the orchestra and the King Sisters. The quintet with its soloist, Miss Carlisle, are tossed out. Latter turns from chamber music to chambermaid to hang around the nitery-hotel to ferret out the scheme, with the inevitable complications when she exposes Jones to the boite proprietor. By that time, however, the buildup for Jones has been terrific, so he stays in, as does Miss Carlisle.

Jones does a creditable acting and singing job, but the Alvino Rey outfit is unfortunately relegated to the background. William Frawley as the scheming manager turns in an impressive chore.

Film's pace is too leisurely, while Howard Benedict's production is 'B'-grooved throughout. *Rose.*

Sherlock Holmes Faces Death

Universal release of Roy William Neill production. Stars Basil Rathbone and Nigel Bruce. Directed by Neill. Screen play, Bertram Millhauser, based on story by Sir Arthur Conan Doyle; camera, Charles Van Enger; editor, Fred Feitchans; music director, H. J. Salter. Previewed in projection room, N. Y., Sept. 2, '43. Running time, **68 MINS.**

Sherlock Holmes....Basil Rathbone
Dr. Watson....Nigel Bruce
Sally Musgrave....Hillary Brooke
Capt. Vickery....Milburn Stone
Dr. Sexton....Arthur Margetson
Brunton....Halliwell Hobbes
Lestrade....Dennis Hoey
Philip Musgrave....Gavin Muir
Geoffrey Musgrave....Frederic Worlock
Capt. MacIntosh....Olaf Hytten
Major Langford....Gerald Hamer
Lieut. Clavering....Vernon Downing
Mrs. Howells....Minna Phillips
Mrs. Hudson....Mary Gordon

The Sherlock Holmes series remains obviously grooved 'B' detective melodrama as emphasized by this particular Universal release, 'Sherlock Holmes Faces Death.' As long as there is the fingernail-bitting clan buying tickets at the boxoffice, there will always be such pictures as these. And thus the Holmes-Dr. Watson pictures remain saleable.

Holmes, of course, is this time called in by Dr. Watson to unravel the mystery of the Musgrave estate, where several usual murders occur under the usually complicated circumstances. It's all obvious stuff that might draw snickers from the sophisticates, but they're not the ones at whom this pic is aimed.

Basil Rathbone and Nigel Bruce, as Holmes and Watson, respectively, contribute their standard performances, while lessers who acquit themselves well are Hillary Brooke, a blonde looker; Arthur Margetson, Halliwell Hobbes and Gavin Muir.

Kahn.

First Comes Courage

Columbia release of Harry Joe Brown production. Stars Merle Oberon, Brian Aherne; features Carl Esmond, Fritz Leiber, Erville Alderson, Erik Rolf, Reinhold Schunzel, Isobel Elsom. Directed by Dorothy Arzner. Story, Elliott Arnold; adaptation, George Sklar; editor, Violet Lawrence; camera, Joseph Walker. At State, N. Y., week Sept. 2, '43. Running time, **86 MINS.**

Nicole Larsen....Merle Oberon
Captain Allan Lowell....Brian Aherne
Major Paul Dichter....Carl Esmond
Dr. Aanrud....Fritz Leiber
Soren....Erville Alderson
Ole....Erik Rolf
Col. Kurt Von Elser....Reinhold Schunzel
Rose Linstrom....Isobel Elsom

Another war picture of familiar cut dealing with underground activities in Naiz-occupied countries and, for added color, with English Commandos. Norway is the setting for this one, but while the romantic interest develops to an appreciably acceptable point with the ending somewhat of a surprise, on the whole 'First Comes Courage' is not strong enough to command better than average business.

The story, written by Elliott Arnold and adapted by George Sklar, is routine, while the dialog fails to have much punch. Plot concerns a girl in a Norwegian coastal town who's friendly with a Nazi major, on the surface because she loves him, but, unknown to townsmen, actually as a means of gathering military information that is relayed to England through a doctor friend.

A British Commando captain, who had met the girl prior to the war, is despatched to Norway on a secret mission and is again thrown across her path following capture by the Germans. However, he's aware of the work the femme Norwegian patriot is doing and, finally, following various plot situations, they are rescued by a group of Commandos who have landed in Norway to blow up oil dumps. Brian Ahern, playing the Commando in love with Merle Oberon, the Norwegian underground worker, pleads with her to return to England with him, but at the last minute she declines in order to continue in intelligence duty on home shores. This decision on her part is a bit unexpected.

Also unusual is the fact that the Nazi major goes through with his marriage to Miss Oberon earlier in the action although he has learned she is using him as a means of obtaining valuable information for the enemy. Only he knows, however, with result that when he's bumped off by Aherne, Miss Oberon feels that her position henceforth in intelligence work will be greatly strengthened since no one would suspect the widow of a slain German officer.

Ahern gives a smooth albeit not impressive performance, while Miss Oberon is generally stiff. Carl Esmond is good as the Nazi major, and Reinhold Schunzel is an acceptable Nazi colonel. Lessers include Fritz Leiber, doctor relaying info to Britain; Erville Alderson, a butler; Erik Rolf, Norwegian patriot, and Isobel Elsom, a nurse *Char.*

Fugitive From Sonora

Republic release of Eddy White production. Stars Don 'Red' Barry; features Wally Vernon, Lynn Merrick. Directed by Howard Bretherton. Screenplay, Norman S. Hall; camera, William Bradford; editor, Richard van Enger. At New York, N. Y., dual, Sept. 1, '43. Running time, **57 MINS.**

Keeno Phillips....Don 'Red' Barry
Dave Winters....Don 'Red' Barry
Jackpot Murphy....Wally Vernon
Dixie Martin....Lynn Merrick
Iron Joe Martin....Harry Cording
Hack Roberts....Ethan Laidlaw
Slade....Pierce Lyden
Tom Lawrence....Gary Bruce
Cole....Ken Duncan
Ed....Tommy Coats
Harris....Frank McCarroll

This pic is above average for low-cost western, and it should satisfy on duals. Combo of gun-totin' in dual role played by Don 'Red' Barry, and comedy antics of Wally Vernon, lifts film all the way. Acting is above par, too, with Barry, Vernon, and Gary Bruce standouts.

Story revolves around twin brothers, one as a parolee killer, other as a fighting, traveling parson trying to bring religion to lawless towns. Barry ably plays both parts, with most of the action centering on the preacher role. With the help of Lynn Merrick, who plays niece of head of gang that force parolees to either join the gang or go back to the pen, he helps clean up the town. Of course, parson's brother does an about-face at the last minute, dying to save his brother.

LONE STAR TRAIL
(SONGS)

Universal release of Oliver Drake production. Stars Johnny Mack Brown, Tex Ritter; features Fuzzy Knight, Jennifer Holt, Jimmy Wakely Trio. Directed by Ray Taylor. Screenplay, Oliver Drake from original by Victor Halperin; camera, William Sickner; editor, Ray Snyder. At New York, N. Y., dual, Sept. 1, '43. Running time, **56 MINS.**

Blaze Barker..........Johnny Mack Brown
Fargo Steele....................Tex Ritter
Angus MacAngus............Fuzzy Knight
Joan Winters................Jennifer Holt
Doug Ransom............George Eldredge
Jonathan Bently...........Michael Vallon
Sheriff Waddell............Harry Strang
Cyrus Jenkins..............Earle Hodgins
Dan Jason....................Jack Ingram
and the Jimmy Wakely Trio

Another in the low-budgeted Oliver Drake series, featuring Johnny Mack Brown, Tex Ritter and Fuzzy Knight, 'Lone Star Trail' packs plenty of b.o. punch for the double bills. Although yarn includes traditional western treatment, film is sound cowboy fare for any nabe house going for the actioners.

Yarn deals with Johnny Mack Brown clearing himself of a $75,000 train robbery after being framed and serving two years for the crime. Paroled, he returns to nab the quartet of cattle rustlers who pinned the robbery on him. Tex Ritter and Fuzzy Knight ably back Brown.

Jimmy Wakely Trio, standard in the series, harmonize cowboy tunes. Film's musical background is a standout.

SUBMARINE BASE

PRC release of Jack Schwartz production. Stars John Litel, Alan Baxter; features Fifi D'Orsay, Eric Blore. Directed by Albert Kelley. Screenplay, Arthur St. Clair and George Merrick; camera, Marcel Le Picard; editor, Holbrook N. Todd. At Strand, Brooklyn, week Sept. 2, '43, dual. Running time, 65 MINS.
Jim Taggart....................John Litel
Joe Morgan..................Alan Baxter
Maria......................Fifi D'Orsay
Spike........................Eric Blore
Dorothy......................Iris Adrian
Judy....................Jacqueline Dalaya
Kroll.....................Georges Metaxa
Styx.....................Luis Alberni
Felipo..................Rafael Storm
Cavanaugh................George Lee
Angela..................Anna Demetrio
Mueller................Lucien Prival

'Submarine Base' is acceptable fare for a low budgeter.

Set on a small, remote island, it has sufficient atmosphere and intrigue to hold the auditor, but lacks wallop above the lower-B rating. It's the saga of a former gangster who has found sanctuary from police on a forgotten island. He ties in with a Nazi agent and assists in re-fueling of Nazi subs. He rescues a survivor of a torpedoed vessel, whom he recognizes as a N. Y. copper gone merchant marine for the duration. Latter recognizes the mobster and the conflict begins. Tag has the gangster giving the Nazis a bum steer and being shot by the Nazi agent. He dies in the arms of the copper.

Story packs some thrills but is practically nil on the romantic side, save for a brief interlude of torchy stuff between Alan Baxter and Jacqueline Dalaya. Latter is one of a trio of entertainers stranded on the island and entertaining at the Half Way House. Entertainment, however, never shows up in the film. When Delaya finds out how Morgan is getting his coin she will have none of him. The inn keeper's daughter (Fifi D'Orsay) has a yen for Baxter but he can't see her, and that's all for romance.

Baxter is smooth and convincing, as is John Litel. Miss D'Orsay has little to do, Eric Blore spears hard for comedy that isn't there as the cockney pal, and the others are just adequate in subordinate roles. Albert Kelley keeps direction at an even pace and does remarkably well with the commonplace screenplay.

Los Ojos Mas Lindosdel Mundo

(ARGENTINE-MADE)

Buenos Aires, Aug. 25.
Argentina Sono Film production and release. Stars Amelia Bence and Pedro Lopez Lagar; features Roberto Airaldi, Ernesto Vilches, Amelia Sanchez Arino, Maria Santos, Cesar Flaschi, Judith Sulian and Benita Puertolas. Directed by Luis Saslavsky. Reviewed at the Ambassador, Buenos Aires. Running time, 89 MINS.

This is an unusual pict, especially to come from Sono Film, which generally is among the most commercial of local producers. Director Luis Saslavsky has taken a story by a French writer, Jean Sarment, and given somewhat complicated plot good handling, although falling into the usual Latin over-melodramatics.

Deals with two old maids of a wealthy family raising a nephew. To give the lad a companion they adopt a washwoman's son. Pair are like brothers, nephew weak, poor lad strong. When they're about 18—story, incidentally, is laid at the turn of the century—they fall in love with the daughter of a friend of the family. Adopted lad, talented and with a gift of gab, appears to be winning the girl. Nephew tries suicide, and the old maids appeal to the gratitude of the adopted boy, who backs out, leaving field to the nephew. Rest is rather melodramatic and ends on a tragic note which is perhaps more in keeping with its general sentimental tone than if a happier version had been adopted.

Amelia Bence, as the girl, has not improved much in her acting, and her coquettish mannerisms don't add anything to the honesty of the telling. Pedro Lopez Lagar is noble throughout but shades performance better than in previous roles. Roberto Airaldi is rather hammy, especially in suicide scene. Judith Sulian good in brief role as a dancer.

Dialog generally excellent, although at times a bit declamatory, theatrical and over-burdensome. Some of the photography excellent but elsewhere extremely mediocre with plenty of evidence it was done in a hurry. *Ray.*

ALEJANDRA

(Songs)
(MEXICAN-MADE)

Filmex release and production. Stars Arturo de Cordova. Directed by Jose Benavides. Screenplay, Catalina D'Erzell; camera, Augustin Martinez. At Belmont, N. Y., week Sept. 3, '43. Running time, 106 MINS.
Ricardo Ibanez..........Arturo de Cordova
Irene......................Anita Blanche
Dona Elena................Sara Garcia
Manuel..................Julio Villareal
Alejandra..............Susanna Guizar

(In Spanish, no English Titles)

For nearly two hours, 'Alejandra,' the latest Mexican import, wallows in tear-jerking emotions which should appeal to Spanish-savvying filmgoers whose tastes run to 'Way Down East' screen fare. Nor does the presence of Arturo de Cordova, prominent in 'For Whom the Bell Tolls,' make this picture less tiresome.

It is a bewhiskered story laboriously detailing the complicated love affairs of wealthy novelist de Cordova. First he has an affair with Anita Blanche, and when his passion cools she vindictively drops a basketful of baby on his doorstep, a note stating that the child is theirs. However his mother gets the note before he does and conceals the child's identity. Therefore when de Cordova returns from Paris after a 15-year absence, he finds a beautiful young lady (Alejandra), falls in love with her and proposes. But his mother reveals the girl's identity. He turns to drink, the girl almost dies of a broken heart and all seems headed for a double tragedy when his ex-sweetheart confesses that the child isn't theirs.

Not only does the story drag, but the acting is over-dramatic and over-tragic. Both the star and principals milk every situation for twice what it's worth. Anita Blanche and Susanna Guizar play the elder and younger sweetheart roles with a maximum of bosom-heaving. With more restraint they might make the U. S. grade, for they have looks and so a plus. Technically, 'Alejandra' is above average for Mexican films. The camera work and lighting begin to compare with some of the lesser Hollywood product. *Wawa.*

THOUSANDS CHEER

(Technicolor)
(MUSICAL)

Metro release of Joseph Pasternak production. Features Mickey Rooney, Judy Garland, Red Skelton, Eleanor Powell, Ann Sothern, Lucille Ball, Virginia O'Brien, Frank Morgan, Lena Horne, Marsha Hunt, Marilyn Maxwell, Donna Reed, Margaret O'Brien, June Allyson, Gloria DeHaven, John Conte, Sara Haden, Don Loper & Maxine Barratt; the Kay Kyser, Bob Crosby and Benny Carter bands; also Jose Iturbi's screen debut; along with the below regular cast. Directed by George Sidney. Original screenplay, Paul Jarrico, Richard Collins; camera, Geo. Folsey; editor, George Boemler; songs, Ferde Grofe, Harold Adamson; Lew Brown, Ralph Freed, Burton Lane; Walter Jurmann, Paul Francis Webster; Earl Brent, E. Y. Harburg; Dmitri Shostakovitch, Harold J. Rome, E. Y. Harburg; music direction, Herbert Stothart. Tradeshown Sept. 13, '43. Running time, 126 MINS.
Kathryn Jones..........Kathryn Grayson
Eddy Marsh..................Gene Kelly
Hyllary Jones................Mary Astor
Colonel William Jones..........John Boles
Chuck Polansky................Ben Blue
Marie Corbino............Frances Rafferty
Helen....................Mary Elliott
Sergeant Kozlack............Frank Jenks
Alan........................Frank Sully
Captain Fred Avery.........Dick Simmons
Pvt. Monks....................Ben Lessy

'Thousands Cheer' is a musical mopup. Metro has a smash in this all-star, technicolorful filmusical.

On marquee values alone 'Thousands Cheer' is a boxoffice boff. The studio threw everything into the picture, fortifying the basically showmanly story with virtually its entire studio roster. There aren't many missing nor are they missed. In fact, while Spencer Tracy and Hedy Lamarr and the servicemen stars like Gable and Taylor are among the few from Leo the Lion's stable not in the cast, it has more than enough as is.

Comparison of 'Thousands Cheer' to 'Stage Door Canteen' is inevitable and natural. Both have the same format. Kathryn Grayson is the colonel's (John Boles) daughter who puts on a super-duper camp show which not only re-introduces Jose Iturbi as part of the entertainment—the eminent pianist-maestro is already made part of the regular plot—but it brings forth Mickey Rooney, Judy Garland, Red Skelton, Eleanor Powell, Loper & Barrat, three name bands and others (see cast above).

Paramount keynote of this expert filmusical is the tiptop manner in which young George Sidney has marshalled his multiple talents so that none trips over the other. And whether the seasoned guidance of producer Joe Pasternak figures, it's a triumph for Sidney on his first major league effort.

Paul Jarrico and Richard Collins supplied a smooth story to carry the mammoth marquee values. Casting Kathryn Grayson as herself, a click diva, making her longhair farewell at an Iturbi concert, is as plausible as it is appealing. Her idea to move with papa Boles to his camp, in an endeavor to reconcile him and Mary Astor (the mother), is well interlarded with romance and basic Americanism. It's as timely as the headlines, replete with the democratic keynote which is the leitmotif of what we are fighting for.

Gene Kelly capably projects that in his gripe against a supposed prejudice that Joe Soldier and the Colonel's daughter can't get clubby and romantic. This is fast dissipated as the action progresses.

Miss Grayson's personal charm and her superlative sopranoing further her along the road to becoming Metro's No. 1 diva as she handles the sundry vocal assignments. These run the gamut from the Ferde Grofe 'Daybreak' to the Dmitri Shostakovitch finale, 'United Nations On the March' (Harold J. Rome and E. Y. Harburg collaborators). 'I Dug a Ditch' (Lew Brown-Ralph Freed-Burton Lane) gets a songplugger's dream production and reprise; the Walter Jurmann-Paul Francis Webster ballad, 'Three Letters in the Mail Box,' and the thematic 'Let There Be Music' (by Earl Brent and Harburg) are the other numbers.

There is considerable showmanship to the idea of Miss Grayson singing 'Daybreak' as her father's favorite. This follows an opening patriotic medley, which leads into an operatic aria as part of the legitimate longhair concert. It eases the idea, for the diehards, of showing maestro Iturbi pianologing a Tin Pan Alley excerpt like 'Daybreak.' The pianist looks well, handles his lines authoritatively and in this, his cinematic debut, he is auspiciously introduced.

At one of the post theatre's lesser shows the 'Mail Box' song by Miss Grayson helps set the romantic clash with Gene Kelly, while Ben Lessy (ex-Oshins & Lessy) gets a good bite into the 'Wichita' pop. Sgt. Julie Oshins, now of 'This Is the Army' (stage and screen), has nothing on the opportunity Metro accorded his ex-saloon partner. The diminutive Lessy has a good comedy pan for pix.

The circus stuff with the Flying Corbinis (Kelly was the former star of that circus troupe); the business on how to control a 21-year-old daughter, where Boles asks his fellow-officers (one of them Bryant Washburn, Sr., and why isn't there more of him?); and that sequence where Iturbi plays a piano solo by phone are all good touches throughout.

Kelly has a good tap solo opportunity while on KP duty. And a sequence wherein he and the colonel reverse positions, and he ad libs what would be a just punishment for his own misbehaviorism in a deft piece of writing.

The boff of the picture, of course, is the big camp show, and Metro's opulence makes possible a revue such as no camp will ever see. Rooney emcees, introducing the sundry specialists. Thus, Eleanor Powell does her standard tapstering; Virginia O'Brien deadpans 'In a Little Spanish Town,' with Bob Crosby's band for assist, and June Allyson and Gloria deHaven stand out in vocal bits.

Frank Morgan with John Conte have a medico skit on the WAVES, wherein Ann Sothern, Lucille Ball and Marsha Hunt strut the s.a.

Kay Kyser's consummate showmanship asserts itself anew with 'Wichita,' wherein Harry Babbitt, his ace singer, again impresses as likely to step out on his own as one of those croon-swooners, with proper tutelage and grooming. It's in this session that Georgia Carroll, former No. 1 mag model from N. Y., gets a 'presentation' that should give every Conover and Powers gal something to dream about. She's a terrific blonde looker and her photogenic impact is properly staged as part of the Kyser specialty.

Don Loper and Maxine Barrat are justly given a big samba ballet build-up in an opulent flash presentation. Rooney's own specialty is a Gable-Barrymore (Lionel) takeoff. Lena Horne's 'Honeysuckle Rose' is a self-thematic, the lyric lending audible interpretation to her looks, as Benny Carter's band gives her support. The mirrored presentation accorded her is a nice flash.

Red Skelton's drugstore scene is a triple-threat blackout in a number of bits, among them flashing the personable Bunny Waters, another erstwhile showgirl beaut from Broadway who proves she can handle lines with authority—and the 'lines' are dialog, not visual. Little Marilyn Maxwell is a highlight here.

Judy Garland's 'Joint Is Jumpin' Down at Carnegie Hall' (unbilled specialty) is the cue for Iturbi to boogie-woogie; and his Steinwaying straight or barrelhouse, is something for the cats. Shostakovitch's 'United Nations On the March' is a rousing finale, handsomely produced.

Withal, from production to direction, 'Thousands Cheer' will send 'em out cheering. Not the least of the whyfores will be those Metro beauts who dress the atmosphere.

Story is well tied together albeit sketchy. The underlying theme of teamwork, whether in the Flying Corbinis' hazardous aerial daredeviltry, or in the Army, is well projected. Miss Grayson is highly sympathetic and, above all, competently articulate as the Little Miss Fixit between her estranged parents, Boles and Miss Astor. Frank Jenks as a soldier-maestro; Dick Simmons as a captain; and Ben Blue in comedy teaming with Ben Lessy, are others prominent in the general story structure.

Abel.

WINTERTIME

(SONGS)

20th-Fox release of William Le Baron production. Stars Sonja Henie; features Jack Oakie, Cesar Romero, Carole Landis, Cornel Wilde; Woody Herman orchestra. Directed by John Brahm. Screenplay, E. Edwin Moran, Jack Jevne, Lynn Starling; story, Arthur Kober; camera, Joe MacDonald; editor, Louis Loeffler; songs, Leo Robin, Nacio Herb Brown; musical sequences supervised by Fanchon, staged by Kenny Williams. Tradeshown in New York, Sept. 8, '43. Running time, **82 MINS.**

Nora .... Sonja Henie
Skip Hutton .... Jack Oakie
Brad Barton .... Cesar Romero
Flossie Fouchere .... Carole Landis
Hjalmar Ostgaard .... S. Z. Sakall
Freddy Austin .... Cornel Wilde
Mrs. Daly .... Helene Reynolds
Russell Carter .... Matt Briggs
Jay Rogers .... Don Douglas
Jimmy .... Geary Steffen
Mr. Prentice .... Charles Trowbridge
Mrs Prentice .... Nella Walker
Bodreau .... Georges Renavent
Constable .... Jean Del Val
Advertising Man .... Arthur Loft
Moving Man .... Jean De Briac
Headwaiter .... Henri De Soto
Drunk .... Charles Irwin
Husband .... Dick Elliott
Woody Herman and His Orchestra.

Sonja Henie filmusical, backed by the corking Woody Herman orch and fortified with Fanchon's eye-filling musical sequences, shapes up as a healthy b.o. entry. In addition to the Norwegian skating star, whose blade routines continue a photogenic treat, supporting marquee values include the Woody Herman band, Jack Oakie, Cesar Romero and Carole Landis.

That ice shows have continued to draw heavily in arenas, with no sign of a drop in attendance during the past season, is an indication of public response to entertainment of this type.

Story structure while fragile, is adequate but the Leo Robin-Nacio Herb Brown tunes, on the other hand, are sturdier, with a couple, such as 'I Like It Here' and 'Dancing in the Dawn,' likely to catch on easily.

Comedy situations are built mainly around Jack Oakie, Cesar Romero and S. Z. Sakall, the latter, as a Norwegian millionaire refugee, impressing where material permits. Opposite Miss Henie in the light romantic interludes is Cornel Wilde, who, though a little awkward, photographs well and shapes up promisingly. Jack Oakie's comedy clicks in a couple of scenes.

Story revolves about a Norwegian refugee and his daughter (Miss Henie), whose destination is the Chateau Frontenac, Quebec. Oakie, who, in partnership with Wilde, operates a small, shabby hostelry called the Chateau Promenade, detours the party to his own place in order to build trade through the presence of the distinguished refugees. Frequent references to the Chateau Frontenac, incidentally, constitute a terrific plug for the Canadian Pacific Railway's ace eastern hotel; and not even the Quebec Tourist Bureau could have written stronger commercials into the film for winter sports attendance from the U. S.

Romantic interest is woven in via the familiar triangle motif, with Miss Henie chasing Wilde who temporarily devotes himself to a gal, representing a sports magazine with large circulation, in order to grab space for his hotel. Romero, as a frivolous Casanova, loses out, following a slapstick bit where he runs through the hotel in long underwear.

Miss Henie's blade sequences, solo and with a partner, enhanced by gorgeous settings, are socko as always.

Mori.

TOP MAN

(SONGS)

Hollywood, Sept. 10.

Universal release of Bernard W. Burton production. Stars Donald O'Connor, Susanna Foster, Lillian Gish, Richard Dix, and Peggy Ryan; features Anne Gwynne, Noah Beery, Jr., Count Basie orchestra, Borrah Minevitch Rascals, Bobby Brooks Quartet. Directed by Charles Lamont. Screenplay, Zachary Gold; original, Ken Goldsmith; camera, Hal Mohr; editor, Paul Landres; asst. director, Mack Wright; music, Charles Previn; dances, Louis Da Pron; special songs, Inez James and Buddy Pepper. Previewed at Pantages, Sept. 9, '43. Running time, **81 MINS.**

Don Warren .... Donald O'Connor
Connie .... Susanna Foster
Beth Warren .... Lillian Gish
Tom Warren .... Richard Dix
Jane Warren .... Peggy Ryan
Pat Warren .... Anne Gwynne
Ed Thompson .... Noah Beery, Jr.
Fairchild .... Samuel S. Hinds
Cleo .... Louise Beavers
Tommy .... Dickie Love
Erna .... Marcia Mae Jones
Archie .... David Holt
Count Basie and His Orchestra
Borrah Minevitch Rascals
Bobby Brooks Quartet

'Top Man' is a neatly-packaged comedy-drama, with liberal display of song, musical and specialty numbers to provide excellent and diverting entertainment in the regular bookings, and profitable b.o. reactions.

Picture confirms judgment of Universal studio execs in spotlighting Donald O'Connor as juvenile star for series of features. Youngster, in addition to expertly handling the lead, steps out with vivacious comedienne Peggy Ryan for two comedy song-and-dance numbers. His monolog on the sources of modern dance steps is a show-stopper.

In providing adequate story background of a typical American family, picture presents Richard Dix as the father; Lillian Gish as the mother; and sisters Peggy Ryan and Anne Gwynne for junior collegian O'Connor. Susanna Foster moves in across the street for the usual adolescent romance. When Dix is called to active duty with the Navy, O'Connor assumes responsibilities of head man in the household, and eventually winds up herding his schoolmates into the labor-shortaged war plant for four-hour shifts to break a bottleneck of production. He also teams with Miss Foster to put on the postponed school variety show at the plant for the finish.

Picture is studded with smart and sparkling lines, with the musical and dance interludes deftly spotted for a well-rounded bundle of entertainment. Miss Foster, youthful coloratura soprano, sings the standards, 'Dream Lover,' 'Jurame,' and 'Romany Life.' in excellent voice; with expert musical accompaniment and sound recording. O'Connor and Miss Ryan team for wow comedy song-and-dance delivery of 'The Road Song,' while the girl also smacks over a solo appearance for song and knockabout dance. Count Basie and his ork provides jump tunes for the warplant show, while Borrah Minevitch's harmonica ensemble click with two appearances.

Throughout the entire unreeling, O'Connor demonstrates his versatility at every turn. Miss Ryan is a perfect partner for the youth, and rates as one of the top young comediennes uncovered by films in several years. Dix and Miss Gish are effective as the understanding parents, while Miss Gwynne capably handles the older sister role. Good support is provided by Noah Beery, Jr., Samuel S. Hinds, Louise Beavers, Dickie Love, Marcia Mae Jones and David Holt.

Zachary Gold provides topnotch script, compactly set up on the story side, and brimful of effervescing lines and situations. Charles Lamont pilots at a fast pace, timing his comedy routines for maximum reaction.

Walt.

FRONTIER FURY

(SONGS)

Columbia release of Jack Fier production. Stars Charles Starrett; features Arthur Hunnicutt, Jimmie Davis and Singing Buckaroos. Directed by William Berke. Story and screenplay by Betty Burbridge; camera, Benjamin Kline; editor, Jerome Thoms. At New York, N. Y., dual, Sept. 8, '43. Running time, **55 MINS.**

Steve Langdon .... Charles Starrett
Arkansas Tuttle .... Arthur Hunnicutt
Stella Larkin .... Roma Aldrich
Dan Bentley .... Clancy Cooper
Nick Dawson .... I. Stanford Jolley
Tracy Meade .... Edmund Cobb
Clem Hawkins .... Bruce Bennett
Jim Wallace .... Ted Mapes
Chief Eagle Feather .... Bill Wilkerson
Gray Bear .... Stanley Brown
Doc Hewes .... Joel Friedkin
Jimmie Davis and His Singing Buckaroos

Another of the low cost, western horse operas, which fluctuates from fair to poor, and should get by the double bill bookings. Jimmie Davis and Buckaroos sing and play their three ballads effectively; Arthur Hunnicutt makes a good enough aid to Charles Starrett; Roma Aldrich is pretty but lacks sparkle, and Starrett does the best he can in this lightweight script job.

Starrett is an honest Indian agent who loses his job because he was robbed of the tribal income. He doesn't mind losing his job, but it means a cold and hungry winter for his Indian friends, for whom he will fight to the death. He sets out to find the robbers by searching for some rare coins which were in the stolen booty cache. He plays a lone hand in the chase, and every time he catches up with the thieves he ends up being captured or unconscious. He gallops, shoots and fights like a bear, but is always outnumbered in the end, and his friends gallop to his rescue just in the nick of time. Roma Aldrich, the love interest, finally leads our hero to the robber hideout, and although she came to marry the gang leader she sees Clancy Cooper for what he really is, and helps Starrett with the final capture. A victory over formula (and they might as well have done it) is that Starrett goes back to his job, minus the satisfying clinch; just a friendly goodbye.

DEAR OCTOPUS

(BRITISH-MADE)

London, Aug. 24.

General Film Distributors release of Gainsborough-Paul Soskin production. Features Margaret Lockwood, Michael Wilding, Helen Haye, Frederick Leister. Directed by Harold French. Screenplay, R. J. Minney, Pat Kirwin, from play by Dodie Smith, adapted by Esther McCracken; camera, Arthur Crabtree. At Gaumont, Haymarket, London, Aug. 23, '43. Running time, **86 MINS.**

Penny....................Margaret Lockwood
Nicholas....................Michael Wilding
Cynthia....................Celia Johnson
Dora Randolph....................Helen Haye
Felix Martin....................Roland Culver
Belle....................Athene Seyler
Kenneth....................Basil Radford
Charles Randolph....................Frederick Leister
Edna....................Nora Swinburne
Mrs. Vicar....................Jean Cadell
Hilda....................Antoinette Cellier
Mrs. Glossop....................Kathleen Harrison
Margery....................Madge Compton

The success of 'Dear Octopus' as a stage play was due apparently to a combination of two talents. First was that Marie Tempest, the actress, and second, Dodie Smith, the authoress, who had just passed through a list of successes. The attempt to make a film of a series of dialogs bearing little relation to each other has resulted in slight, monotonous substance. The director may well have realized this and so the pace was geared to a high speed. Unlikely b.o. for this one.

The principals (and some of the others) are given opportunities to do what in vaudeville would be a specialty. Story is of a highly respectable middle-class family, whose parents are celebrating their golden wedding anniversary. All the family come from various parts of the world for the event. As each of the family arrives there is unfolded a brief sketch of their respective lives. All of which is insufficient to sustain interest in a full-length film.

An enormous cast found it difficult to get their teeth into the task. It's distressing to see artists like Helen Haye, Roland Culver, Celia Johnson, Michael Wilding, Basil Radford and Margaret Lockwood struggling along without achieving anything. *Jolo.*

Battle of Britain

When, in the future, the story of World War II is told in its entirety, the 'Battle of Britain,' produced by Lt. Col. Frank Capra for the Special Services Division of the U. S. Army, will probably emerge as one of the vital documents depicting a people's courage when the torch of freedom flickered at its lowest.

Fourth in the series of 'Why We Fight' documentary pictures turned out by Col. Capra for the Army's orientation courses in basic training centers, the 'Battle of Britain' is a vivid 52-minute account of the indomitable spirit of the English people in the face of the 1940 blitz that first disproved Hitler's 'invincibility.' Shown privately in N. Y. before a specially invited group representing press, radio and films, on the very day the Italians capitulated to superior Allied forces, the picture's datedness (a factor that, as in the case of its two predecessors, 'The Nazis Strike' and 'Divide and Conquer,' has negated their commercial value), was all the more apparent. But, paradoxically enough, the film gains in importance with the realization that the British stand as shown in Capra's brilliant compilation was one of the factors that made possible the unconditional surrender of the Italian army. It gave the Britons time to prepare when the Luftwaffe finally got discouraged.

Composed of previously-shown clips, exclusive Army reels heretofore unreleased and captured Nazi footage, with a splendid running commentary by Walter Huston and others, all of which has been forcefully edited by Capra, 'Battle of Britain' has already been shown in London theatres through the British Ministry of Information and was received with such acclaim that U. S. correspondents in England have appealed in recent weeks for its commercial distribution in America. Regardless of its datedness, the film, unquestionably, would have tremendous morale value on the U.S. home front. Even as 'The City That Stopped Hitler—Heroic Stalingrad' packs a terrific wallop in portraying the Russian people's defense of a city, 'Battle of Britain' strikes closer home since it deals with a people whose emotional ties and kinship are linked with Americans. Of the four in the projected series of seven films outlining the background of world aggression that eventually will make up 'Why We Fight' (the fifth, 'Battle of Russia' will be available to the Army in two weeks), 'Battle of Britain' ranks with the initialer, 'Prelude to War,' and the second, 'Nazis Strike,' as great documentaries stemming from the global conflict.

The film puts less emphasis on the horror aspects of Nazi brutality such as characterized the invasion of Poland, France and the Lowlands in the previous releases, but is primarily an account of the unquenchable spirit of the Britons, and particularly the residents of London, in the six-week blitz by the Luftwaffe. The latter, it will be recalled, took a toll of 40,000 dead and 50,000 wounded at a time when the RAF was outnumbered 10 to 1 and there wasn't sufficient equipment for even one full British division.

Woven into the film's pattern are a number of animated graphs, maps and charts that are singularly effective in outlining Hitler's six-point plan of attack in annihilating England in his dream for world conquest—a dream that was shattered as the RAF and anti-aircraft batteries brought down more than 3,000 enemy planes. *Rose.*

Miniature Reviews

'Sweet Rosie O'Grady' (Musical; Color) (20th). Betty Grable is Rosie; and so will be its box-office values.

'Princess O'Rourke' (WB). Hilarious comedy-romance unfolding at fast clip. Escapist entertainment of topflight rating.

'Flash and Fantasy' (U). Heavy marquee voltage cast in unusual drama Strong b.o.

'Adventures in Iraq' (WB). Meller aiming for supporting slots in the secondary duals.

'Black Hills Express' (Rep). Don Barry in one of his better westerns.

'Man From Music Mountain' (Songs) (Rep). Roy Rogers saddler should draw on duals.

'The Unknown Guest' (Mono). Suspense-holding melodrama, featuring Victor Jory and Pamela Blake. Okay for duals.

'I Danced With Don Porfirio' (Grovas). Topflight Mexican production with Mapy Cortez in dual role.

Sweet Rosie O'Grady

(Technicolor)
(MUSICAL)

20th Century-Fox release of William Perlberg production. Stars Betty Grable, Robt. Young, Adolphe Menjou; features Reginald Gardner, Virginia Grey, Phil Regan. Directed by Irving Cummings. Screenplay, Ken Englund from stories by Wm. R. Lipman, Frederick Stephani, Edward Van Every; songs, Mack Gordon and Harry Warren, and others; dances, Hermes Pan; music supervised, Fanchon; camera, Ernest Palmer, Natalie Kalmus, Fred Sersen; editor, Robt. Simpson; music direction, Alfred Newman, Chas. Henderson. Previewed Sept. 17, 1943. Running time, **76 MINS.**

Madeleine Marlowe....................Betty Grable
Sam Magee....................Robert Young
Thomas Moran....................Adolphe Menjou
Duke of Trippingham...Reginald Gardiner
Edna....................Virginia Grey
Composer....................Phil Regan
Joe Flugelman....................Sig Ruman
Arthur Skinner....................Alan Dinehart
Clark....................Hobart Cavanaugh
Cabby....................Frank Orth
Mr. Fox....................Jonathan Hale
Danny....................Stanley Clements
Rumplemeyer....................Byron Foulger
Gracie....................Lilyan Irene
Robt. Mitchell 'Boychoir'.......Themselves
Leo Diamond Solidaires.........Themselves

With the b.o. boff of 'Coney Island' fresh in mind, exhibitors will have plenty to shout about in heralding this Betty Grable starrer, also a Technicolored musical primed for super grosses. It's in the same light, frothy, just-before-the-turn-of-the-century idiom. It's escapist film fare which won't let many loose quarters escape from the wickets.

Everything about this William Perlberg production is showmanly appealing. The casting is tiptop, with Robert Young, as the Police Gazette reporter, the romantic vis-a-vis after forcing Miss Grable to jilt Reginald Gardner, cast as an honorably enamored English duke whom she had met in London. Adolphe Menjou is the volatile Gazette ed, but the rest of the cast is also-ran save for Virginia Grey as the star's pal and Phil Regan, marking his cinematic comeback effectively in a songsmithing role.

Apart from Maude Nugent's classic title song, and sundry other excerpts such as the opener, 'Here Am I Waiting at the Church,' which is given a nice production flash, the tunes by Mack Gordon and Harry Warren are zestful and certain of popularity. They fit the action well, and in the person of pseudo-song-writing Regan, who does handsomely while tenoring the tunes he has 'just written,' they are given excellent demonstration throughout.

Ken Englund has fashioned a deft filmusicomedy plot from the combined sources of William R. Lipman, Frederick Stephani and Ed Van Every; and director Irving Cummings, a past master with musical themes of this nature, has given it everything for compactness and proper audience values.

Betty Grable, already an exhibitor's fave pinup girl on the marquees, outdoes herself in the mauve decade decolletage. A saucy title that 'if you think the Gay 90s were gay, get a load of the 1880s'—or words to that effect—sets the pace well. Even the introductory titles, sung in choral effect, are different.

Action shifts from England back to America. The Police Gazette's 'love diary' expose of the snooty star, Madeleine Marlowe, as ex-Rosie O'Grady, former burlesque queen and thrush of Flugelman's Brooklyn Beer Garden, is an 1880 version of a backstage musical, permitting for judicious interpolation of the song numbers. Thus is introduced a nostalgic oldtimers' medley—strictly out of Charles K. Harris, Edward B. Marks, et al.—along with 'My Heart Tells Me,' 'County Fair' and 'The Wishing Waltz,' the latter given a fair semblance of production flash. But considering the period it didn't call for any Hollywood furbelows (a break for the budget), although there's no production cheating.

The film moves at a fine pace, compressing a lot into its 76 minutes. The color brings out all the tint values of a colorful past—and it should also bring in the customers. *Abel.*

PRINCESS O'ROURKE

(ONE SONG)

Hollywood, Sept. 21.

Warner Bros. release of Hal B. Wallis production. Stars Olivia de Havilland, Robert Cummings; features Charles Coburn, Jack Carson, Jane Wyman. Written and directed by Norman Krasna. Camera, Ernie Haller; editor, Warren Low; asst. director, Frank Heath; song by Ira Gershwin and E. Y. Harburg. Tradeshown in L. A. Sept. 20, '43. Running time, **93 MINS.**

Princess Maria....................Olivia de Havilland
Eddie O'Rourke....................Robert Cummings
Uncle....................Charles Coburn
Dave....................Jack Carson
Jean....................Jane Wyman
Supreme Court Judge....Harry Davenport
Miss Haskell....................Gladys Cooper
Mr. Washburn....................Minor Watson
Singer....................Nan Wynn
Count Peter de Chandome.......Curt Bois
G-Man....................Ray Walker
Butler....................David Clyde
Mrs. Mulvaney....................Nana Bryant
Mrs. Bower....................Nydia Westman
Clare Stillwell. ....Ruth Ford
Stewardess....................Julie Bishop
Greek....................Frank Puglia
Greek's Wife....................Rosina Galli
Mrs. Pulaski....................Ferike Boros
Delivery Boy....................Dave Willock
Elevator Man....................John Dilson
Stranger....................Edward Gargan

'Princess O'Rourke' is one of those spritely, effervescing and laugh-explosive comedy-romances that come along too infrequently. Geared to current audience requirements for highly amusing and diverting entertainment, picture will clock upper-bracket biz in all bookings, with holdovers indicated for the metropolitan keys.

Credit for general sparkle and excellence of the picture must be tossed to Norman Krasna, who handled the writing and directing responsibilities. It's Krasna's initial directing assignment, and after completing it, he joined the Army Air Force first motion picture unit—so the industry will have to await further directing on his part until he's out of the service.

Krasna provides numerous humorous and novel twists to the tale of an American who falls in love with a girl after a whirlwind romance, and then discovers she's a refugee princess of European royalty. After approval for marriage has been given to cement relations of the two countries, the boy balks at renouncing his American citizenship, but love finally wins with quick wedding ceremony performed in the White House with Presidential blessing.

After establishing the confined luxury provided in New York for the princess, Olivia de Havilland, her caretaking uncle Charles Coburn suggests a trip west to a ranch. Plane with Robert Cummings and Jack Carson as co-pilots, makes sudden return to airfield due to zero ceiling, but the girl is punchdrunk from overdose of sleeping pills. Cummings takes her under his wing, and, unable to find her address, puts her up at his apartment. Intrigued by simplicities of the common people, girl quickly falls in love with Cummings, with latter getting her consent to marriage. An FBI agent trails the girl through various episodes, reporting to her guardian uncle at intervals. Latter, intrigued by Cummings' ancestral background of boys, sets the stage for marriage, but his plans misfire when Cummings refuses cancellation of his citizenship. That's where the girl steps in on her own to provide the happy ending, regardless of royal practices.

Picture unfolds at a spontaneously-fast pace, with Krasna studding the proceedings with toppling laughs most of the way. Final 20 minutes, when levity must be tossed aside for proper decorum within the walls of the White House, slows down considerably, but previous pace carries momentum through the romantic windup successfully.

Miss de Havilland shines brightly as the girl; with Cummings getting equal prominence for excellent portrayal of the airline pilot. Coburn clicks with his usual strong performance as the uncle, while Jack Carson and Jane Wyman catch attention as married couple who assist the romance. Brief standout bits are provided by Curt Bois, Harry Davenport and Nydia Westman.

Krasna has injected a number of sophisticated cracks, but it's all in general good taste. His dialog is bright throughout, with picture brimming with hilarious sequences broadly displayed for maximum audience reaction. Production mounting is topgrade, with photography by Ernie Haller of high standard throughout. Song, 'Honorable Moon,' by Ira Gershwin and E. Y. Harburg, is well handled by an unprogrammed singer in a nightspot sequence. *Walt.*

FLESH AND FANTASY

Hollywood, Sept. 17.

Universal release of Charles Boyer-Julien Duvivier production, directed by Duvivier. Stars Robert Benchley, Betty Field, Robert Cummings, Edward G. Robinson, Boyer, Barbara Stanwyck; features Edgar Barrier, Thomas Mitchell, C. Aubrey Smith, Anna Lee, Dame May Whitty, Charles Winninger. Screenplay by Ernest Pascal, Samuel Hoffenstein, Ellis St. Joseph, based on stories by Oscar Wilde, Laslo Vadnay and St. Joseph; camera, Paul Ivano and Stanley Cortez; editor, Arthur Hilton; dialog director, Don Brodie; asst. directors, Joseph A. McDonough and Seward Webb. Previewed at Filmarte, Sept. 16, '43. Running time, **92 MINS.**

Marshall Tyler........Edward G. Robinson
Paul Gaspar................Charles Boyer
Joan Stanley............Barbara Stanwyck
Henrietta.......................Betty Field
Michael.................Robert Cummings
Septimus Podgers.........Thomas Mitchell
King Lamarr...........Charles Winninger
Rowena...........................Anna Lee
Lady Pamela Hardwick.Dame May Whitty
Dean of Chichester......C. Aubrey Smith
Doakes...................Robert Benchley
Stranger.....................Edgar Barrier
Davis......................David Hoffman

This is a decidedly novel and unusual picture, displaying the impress on individuals of dreams, fortune-telling and other supernatural phenomena. Parading a powerhouse cast, neatly contrived and presented in three separate episodes adequately tied together 'Flesh and Fantasy' will catch excellent biz in all bookings.

Picture idea was contrived by Charles Boyer and Julien Duvivier and sold to Universal, with pair combining as producers; Duvivier also directing, and Boyer handling a major acting assignment. Current public interest, especially on part of the women, catches added boxoffice lure through showmanly presentation of the implications of dreams and palmistry, together with human abilities to break reactions to predictions or superstitions.

Clubmen Robert Benchley and David Hoffman discuss dreams, predictions and the supernatural to provide necessary interweave of the three episodes on display. Benchley is inclined to believe in a strange dream he had, with Hoffman arguing against implications, and displaying the three separate strange tales by Oscar Wilde, Samuel Hoffenstein and Ellis St. Joseph. First delves into romance of Betty Field, who's become calloused, bitter and defeated through ugly features. But on Mardi Gras night she is handed a beautiful face mask and told that beauty is within herself, and she would be loved for that rather than her facial characteristics. She romances with Robert Cummings behind the mask, and finally discovers truth in the moral: faith in yourself is the main thing. This episode runs a brief 24 minutes.

Second episode presents Thomas Mitchell as a palmist at a socialite group, and after attorney Edward G. Robinson scoffs at the predictions, latter nevertheless submits to a reading, and becomes intrigued when he's told he will commit murder. Prediction preys on him to point that it preys on his mind, and he finally embarks on plan to commit the predicted crime. After unsuccessfully targeting two victims, Robinson removes the hex by choking Mitchell for culmination of the prediction.

Boyer shares starring honors with Barbara Stanwyck in the final episode, which has the former upset by dream which predicts disaster to himself while performing as a circus high-wire artist. Dream upsets him to extent he cannot perform his thrill stunt, but on boat to America with the circus, he meets Miss Stanwyck, the girl clearly shown in the dream. He tells her they have met before, but the girl sidesteps him until pair fall in love. While he tries to toss off the 'hex,' girl conceals her real identity as member of jewel-theft mob, but her capture by police also hits him in a dream. He overcomes the psychological consciousness of his fall during the performance, but that of the girl's arrest happens as visioned. Audience is left to draw its own conclusions on the eventual happy ending.

Strange experience of Betty Field is transformation of her character from hate to love in the first episode provides excellent tempo on which to proceed with the succeeding tales. Miss Field and Cummings team for an interesting sequence. Robinson, Mitchell, Anna Lee, Dame Mae Whitty and C. Aubrey Smith are all seen to good effect in the second episode; while finale is an intimate balance of romance and the impress of dreams, with Boyer and Miss Stanwyck in fine form and aided by Charles Winninger as the circus owner.

Duvivier directs in careful style, injecting the European style of piloting with concentration on incidents that build up into prominence, and withal holding to a steady and generally suspenseful pace. Picture was carefully made, episode by episode, over greater part of a year. Production mounting and technical contributions are of A calibre, including both photography and musical background. *Walt.*

ADVENTURES IN IRAQ

Hollywood, Sept. 21.

Warner Bros. production and release. Directed by D. Ross Lederman. Screenplay by George R. Bilson and Robert E. Kent, from play ('Green Goddess') by William Archer; camera, James Van Trees; editor, Clarence Kolster; dialog director, Jack Lucas; asst. director, Wilbur McGaugh. Tradeshown in L. A. Sept. 20, '43. Running time, **64 MINS.**

George Torrence...................John Loder
Tess Torrence.......................Ruth Ford
Doug Everett..............Warren Douglas
Sheik Ahmid Bel Nor......Paul Cavanagh
Devins.........................Barry Bernard
Timah..........................Peggy Carson
Captain Bill Carson............Bill Crago
High Priest..............Martin Garralaga
Radio Operator...............Bill Edwards
Patroling Guard...............Dick Botiller
Native Officer...............Eugene Borden
Priest............................Manuel Lopez

This one has been reposing on the shelf awaiting release for a number of months. Over-dramatic meller of the Arabian desert, it looks like title was tagged on as afterthought in order to catch front page impact from the Iraq sector. Picture is strictly a supporting meller for the secondary duals.

Plot of the original stage play, 'The Green Goddess,' which was a George Arliss starrer, is now replete with over-accentuated melodramatics. Former flying tiger Warren Douglas makes a forced landing in the wild Syrian desert with passengers comprising John Loder and latter's wife, Ruth Ford. Trio treks to nearby settlement ruled by sheik (Paul Cavanaugh) and become his hostages for his three brothers who are to be executed as spies for the Nazis by the British. After required footage of heroics and familiar situations, American planes come to the rescue.

Script is illogical in its melodramatics, but maintains fast pace despite obvious tenor. Cast members are forced to overact throughout in regulation film serial fashion under direction of D. Ross Lederman. *Walt.*

BLACK HILLS EXPRESS

Republic release of Eddy White production. Stars Don 'Red' Barry; features Wally Vernon, Ariel Heath. Directed by John English. Screenplay, Norman Hall, Fred Myton from original by Fred Myton; camera, Ernest Miller; editor, Harry Keller. At New York, N. Y., week Sept. 14, '43, dualed. Running time, **55 MINS.**

Lon Walker...............Don 'Red' Barry
Deadeye.........................Wally Vernon
Gale Southern.....................Ariel Heath
Vic Fowler.....................George Lewis
Harvey Dorman..........William Halligan
Jason Phelps..............Hooper Atchley
Raymond Harper...........Charles Miller
Carl............................Pierce Lyden
The Sheriff..................Jack Rockwell
Dutch..........................Bob Kortman
Denver...............................Al Taylor

Don 'Red' Barry again portrays a hard-riding, two-gun cowboy, this time in 'Black Hills Express,' a better than average 'B' western.

Barry is a supposed outlaw sought for a string of stagecoach robberies. He's been put on the spot by the familiar crooked marshal and town banker. But Barry, of course, rounds up or outguns the real culprits.

Barry rides and shoots realistically. Wally Vernon, as the deputy sheriff, furnishes brisk comedy as the pal of Barry. Ariel Heath is the girl. Support is headed by Charles Miller and William Halligan.

John English, comparative newcomer as western director, turns in a creditable job. The Norman Hall-Fred Myton screenplay is above-average for this sort of fare. Ernest Miller does his usual slick camera job. *Wear.*

Man From Music Mountain

(SONGS)

Republic release of Harry Grey production. Stars Roy Rogers. Directed by Joseph Kane. Screenplay, Bradford Ropes and J. Benton Chaney; camera, William Bradford; editor, Russell Kimball; music director, Morton Scott. Previewed in projection room, N. Y., Sept. 17, '43. Running time, **71 MINS.**

Roy.............................Roy Rogers
Trigger (the Horse)..................Trigger
Themselves..Bob Nolan & Sons of Pioneers
Laramie Winters..................Ruth Terry
Victor Marsh.......................Paul Kelly
Penny Winters.....................Ann Gillis
Sheriff Joe Darcey.......George Cleveland
Pat..................................Pat Brady
Christina Kellog..............Renie Riano
Arthur Davis....................Paul Harvey
Dobe Joe............................Hank Bell
Barker..........................Jay Novello
Slade..........................Hal Taliaferro

This latest Roy Rogers saddler shapes up as one of the best of the series and should do okay biz on the duals.

It's full of fast action, with customary romantic interlude and plenty of opportunity for Rogers, Bob Nolan and Sons of the Pioneers to sandwich in their vocalizing without retarding action. Story is conventional, yet holds interest for the most part.

Rogers plays a former cowboy who's become the Sinatra of the prairies. He comes back to the hometown for a broadcast. His welcome is marred by a feud between cattlemen, headed by Paul Kelly, and the sheepers, represented by the winsome Ruth Terry. Rogers signs up as deputy sheriff and finally brings Kelly and his gang to justice. He's back on the air at fade-out with Miss Terry.

Rogers turns in his usually good performance as the singing cowboy who can handle his dukes and gat plenty when the occasion demands. Miss Terry lends both looks and talent. Ann Gillis is cute and convincing as Miss Terry's younger sister, while Kelly makes the heavy adequately despicable. Pat Brady and Renie Riano handle comedy well. Hank Bell, George Cleveland, Jay Novello and Hal Taliaferro are okay in support. Joseph Kane, who directed, keeps story by Bradford Ropes and J. Benton Chaney moving at lively clip, while William Bradford also rates a nod for camera work, especially several trick shots in the mountain battle scenes.

The Unknown Guest

Monogram release of Maurice King production. Features Victor Jory and Pamela Blake. Directed by Kurt Neuman. Screenplay, Philip Yordan; camera, Jackson Rose. Reviewed at Strand, Brooklyn, N. Y., Sept. 17, '43. Running time, **61 MINS.**

Chuck Williams.................Victor Jory
Julie.........................Pamela Blake
Nadroy.......................Harry Hayden
Helen.......................Veda Ann Borg
Martha Williams................Nora Cecil
Joe Williams......................Lee White
Fats.................................Paul Fix
Sheriff........................Emory Parnell
Swarthy..........................Ray Walker
Sidney...........................Edwin Mills

Neat mystery meller holds suspense; should make for acceptable dual.

Victor Jory essays title role and winsome Pamela Blake is the romantic vis-a-vis. Jory is the supposed blacksheep nephew of the Williamses (Lee White and Nora Cecil) who shows up at their inn when they're about to shutter for annual hiatus. Miserly couple gives him shabby welcome. He keeps inn going with aid of Miss Blake, waitress. Things begin to happen which directs suspicion that Jory has polished off his miserly relatives and has them buried in the cellar. The gal is sure of it but too much in love to throw him at the law. When the law is about to ambush him, the supposedly murdered couple shows up to set things aright for the final clinch of Jory and Miss Blake. Both give good performances. Others are okay.

Kurt Neuman, who directed, kept story moving with sustained suspense, and camera work of Jackson Rose is okay.

Schweik's New Adventures

(BRITISH-MADE)

London, Aug. 30.

Coronet Pictures' release of Eden Films production. Features Margaret McGrath, Lloyd Pearson. Directed by Karel Lamac; story by Karel Lamac; dialog, Con West; music, Clifton Parker. At Cambridge theatre, Aug. 27. Running time, 75 MINS.

Schweik.....................Lloyd Pearson
Madame Karova........Margaret McGrath
Gestapo Chief.............Julian Mitchell
Railway Worker.....Richard Attenborough
Gendarme..................George Carney

Schweik, pronounced to rhyme with wake, is Czechoslovakia's 'Old Bill' Bairnsfather's Cockney character of the World War. Created by Jaroslav Hasek, the Czech humorist, 'The Good Soldier Schweik' was for 25 years a best seller in Czechoslovakia. Following the occupation of the country by the Nazis, Hasek produced a new book titled 'How to Speak German.' To everybody's amazement the hand book sold like hot cakes when it was discovered the title was a clever camouflage for an underground pamphlet, 'Schweik Against the Gestapo.'

Like 'Mission to Moscow,' a living statesman, Jan Masaryk, introduces the English-made version of this Czech character. Explaining the reason for Schweik making the Nazis look more dumb than they are, Masaryk declares the main purpose of Hasek's new book is to hearten the Czech people by proving the invincibility of the Nazis is a myth. Schweik does this in the film version by resorting to low comedy, including the use of a trick dog and a box full of fleas.

Lloyd Pearson as Schweik, as well as all the other principals, plays the part as a Cockney. The brand of comedy is, however, so distinctly alien to the Britist idea that the effect of the original is lost. Julian Mitchell as chief of the Gestapo turns in a workmanlike performance, but he too is as English as a BBC news announcer.

Direction by Karel Lamac, who also wrote the script, is adequate, but with the limitations imposed by the English cast and lack of authentic Czech exterior shots, the film is never convincing as a Czech offering. In spite of this, nothing has hit the screen yet which makes such howling fun of the Hun.

As a quasi-documentary, and skilfully cut, this might have curiosity appeal in America among sophisticates. *Jolo.*

I Danced With Don Porfirio

('Yo Baile con Don Porfirio')
(MEXICAN-MADE)
(With Music)

Jesus Grovas production and release. Stars Mapy Cortes, Joaquin Pardave, Emil Tuero. Directed by Gilberto Martinez Solares. Original story, Gilberto Martinez Solares; camera, Raul Martinez Solares; music, Manuel Esperon; choreography for ballet, Eva Beltri. At Belmont, N. Y., starting Sept. 17, '43. Running time, 92 MINS.

Violeta........................Mapy Cortes
Rosa...............................Mapy Cortes
Don Severo..................Joaquin Pardave
Don Placido..................Joaquin Pardave
Alberto..............................Emil Tuero
Don Porfirio................Fernando Cortes
Don Evaristo..................Julio Villareal
Rodolfo.........................George Reyes
Dona Leonor...........Consuelo G. de Luna
Dona Ghole...................Consuelo Guiroz

(In Spanish, No English Titles)

Spotting of Mapy Cortes, clever Puerto Rican singer-dancer, and Emil Tuero in same picture lifts this Mexican-made considerably. It's a first-rate farce about mistaken identity. Miss Cortes, who appeared in RKO's 'Seven Days' Leave' last year, registers solidly in the dual role of a socialite and impetuous singer-dancer. Tuero, who might pass as a double for Harry James, clicks as a pianist and orchestra conductor. 'I Danced With Don Porfirio' shapes up as a sizable boxoffice entry from Mexico City, though without English titles it must lean almost solely on Spanish-speaking audiences in the U. S. Also has the additional asset of having been produced with the assistance of the Mexico City Ballet Theatre. Title stems from fact that the singer-dancer dances with one Don Porfirio, the Mexican president.

Plot hinges on close resemblance of the twin daughters of Don Severo (Joaquin Pardave), one being a society miss and the other a footlighter. The father keeps the singer-dancer in the background, dialog and story tipping off that she's the daughter of his mistress. Only accidentally does his wife discover the other child. An ardent suitor falls in love with the socialite daughter and then thinks he's seeing double when the other girl, his voice pupil, becomes involved. To complicate affairs, there's a second suitor who courts the singer and thinks he's being two-timed when the other daughter appears.

Director Gilberto Solares manages to squeeze every laugh possible from the pat farcical situations, even down to the comedy duel. Ballet numbers and stage sequences are deftly staged. Manuel Esperon's music is markedly tuneful.

Miss Cortes more than ever looks like a potential screen personality with improvement in her terps ability. Her forte always has been her vivacious singing and dancing, and she's in fine form in these. Tuero, as her voice tutor and pianist-band leader, figures importantly in nearly every scene. Pardave, character veteran of many Spanish pictures, is at his best. George Reyes, as the rival in the confused love affair, also clicks along with the other support. *Wear.*

Adventures of the Flying Cadets

(Serial; Chapters 1, 2, 3)

Universal release of Henry MacRae production. Directed by Ray Taylor and Lewis D. Collins. Screenplay, Morgan B. Cox, George H. Plympton and Paul Huston, from original story by Cox; editors, Alvin Todd, Paul Himm, Irving Birnbaum, Edgar Vane; music director, H. J. Salter. Previewed in proection room, N. Y., Sept. 16, '43. Running time, 21 MINS. first chapter, rest 20 MINS.

Cast: Johnny Downs, Bobby Jordan, Ward Wood, Billy Benedict, Edward Cianneili, Robert Armstrong, Charles Trowbridge, Jennifer Holt, Regis Toomey, Joseph Crehan, Addison Richards, Leland Hodgson, Ian Keith, Philip Van Zandt, Joan Blair, Selmer Jackson, Pat Flaherty, William Forrest, Louis Arco, Louis Adlon.

For those exhibs who pad their Saturday morning programs for juvenile interest, 'Adventures of the Flying Cadets' is right up their alley. There's no pretense at what 'Cadets' aims are; it's strictly for kids and, as such, sure to ignite 'em.

Yarn concerns the escapades of four cadets at a flying school, the leads being handled by Johnny Downs, Bobby Jordan, Ward Wood and Billy Benedict. There's some Nazi espionage thrown in, along with the murders of several men who apparently had the clews to some lost gold. First three of the 13 chapters were reviewed.

Performances are standard, and the direction was apparently more intent on pace than plausibility. *Kahn.*

Miniature Reviews

'Sahara' (Col). Melodramatic and suspenseful saga geared for smart grosses in all bookings and holdovers in the keys.

'Whistling in Brooklyn (M-G). Strong programmer.

'Corvette K-225' (U). Melodramatics with a convoy escort across the Atlantic. Nominally profitable biz in regular runs.

'Always a Bridesmaid' (U). Andrews Sisters top lightweight musical, strictly for the duals.

'The Avenging Rider' (RKO). Cliff 'Ukelele Ike' Edwards lifts this routine action dualer.

'El Sillon y la Gran Duquesa' (Argentina-made). Comedy starring Olinda Bozan well done with unusual plot twists.

Sahara

Hollywood, Sept. 25.

Columbia production and release. Stars Humphrey Bogart. Directed by Zoltan Korda. Screenplay by John Howard Lawson and Korda. Adaptation, James O'Hanlon; story, Philip MacDonald, based on incident in Soviet photoplay, 'The Thirteen'; camera, Rudolph Mate; editor, Charles Nelson; asst. director, Abby Berlin. Previewed at Pantages, Sept. 24, '43. Running time, 95 MINS.

Sergeant Joe Gunn......Humphrey Bogart
'Waco' Hoyt.................Bruce Bennett
Fred Clarkson................Lloyd Bridges
Tambul.............................Rex Ingram
Guiseppe.......................J. Carrol Naish
Jimmy Doyle...................Dan Duryea
Capt. Jason Halliday......Richard Nugent
Ozzie Bates................Patrick O'Moore
Jean Leroux..............Louis T. Mercier
Marty Williams.................Carl Harbord
Peter Stegman..............Guy Kingsford
Capt. Von Schletow..........Kurt Krueger
Major Von Falken............John Wengraf
Sergeant Krause..............Hans Schumm

For punchy action, realistic melodrama and sustained audience interest, 'Sahara' rates as one of the best of the current crop of war dramas. These factors, combined with Humphrey Bogart in starring spot to generate high voltage for the marquee, insures profitable biz in all datings, with indications for holdovers in the keys.

Story background displays Libyan desert fighting in 1942, when the British were huled back to the El Alemein line. It vividly focuses attention on exploits of an American tank crew headed by Bogart to escape the onrushing Nazis, and battles against desert sands and lack of water.

Picture gets off to a fast start, with Bogart heading his 28-ton tank south on the desert in drive to regain the British lines. Along the way, he picks up six Allied stragglers; Sudenese soldier Rex Ingram with latter's Italian prisoner, J. Carrol Naish; and a downed Nazi pilot, Kurt Krueger. Bogart pushes on with his assorted passengers to reach a water hole at an old desert fort which provides a trickle but enough to sustain the group. Nazi motorized battalion also heads for the water supply, with Bogart deciding to make a stand to slow up the German column while sending south for British aid. In furious battle and assault, defenders successfully hold off the Nazis until latter surrender to obtain water—with only two surviving members of the unit, Bogart and Patrick O'Moore, remaining to capture the 100 odd Germans.

Script is packed with pithy dialog, lusty action and suspense, and logically and well-devised situations avoiding ultra-theatrics throughout. It's an all-male cast, but absence of romance is not missed in the rapid-fire unfolding of vivid melodrama. Direction by Zoltan Korda deftly spotlights the intimacies and comradeship of the Allied soldiers who are through together for mutual protection in the desert battle zone.

Bogart dominates the action throughout, turning in an outstanding performance that ranks with any of his previous assignments. He's provided with excellent support through deft casting. Naish delivers a standout characterization as the Italian prisoner; Ingram clicks as the Sudenese soldier; Louis T. Mercier catches attention as the Frenchman; and Krueger ably handles the role of the Nazi flyer. Bruce Bennett and Dan Duryea score as the American tank crewmen. Richard Nugent, O'Moore, Lloyd Bridges, Carl Harbord and Guy Kingsford provide strong support.

Production mounting is topnotch throughout, with desert providing major portion of the footage. Photography by Rudolph Mate is excellent. *Walt.*

Whistling in Brooklyn

Metro release of George Haight production. Directed by S. Sylvan Simon. Stars Red Skelton; features Ann Rutherford, Jean Rogers, 'Rags' Ragland, Ray Collins, Henry O'Neill, William Frawley, Sam Levene, the Brooklyn Dodgers. Screenplay, Nat Perrin; camera, Lester White; editor, Ben Lewis. Tradeshown in New York, Sept. 28, '43. Running time, 87 MINS.

Wally Benton......................Red Skelton
Carol Lambert.............Ann Rutherford
Jean Pringle........................Jean Rogers
Chester.........................'Rags' Ragland
Grover Kendall.....................Ray Collins
Inspector Holcomb..........Henry O'Neill
Detective Ramsey.........William Frawley
Creeper..............................Sam Levene
Detective MacKenzie.........Arthur Space
Detective Finnigan.Robt. Emmet O'Connor
Whitey..............................Steve Geray
Steve Conlon....................Howard Freeman
Manager of the Beavers.......Tom Dillon
And the Brooklyn Dodgers

Sturdy programmer will fit nicely into major situations for top spotting on duals.

It's another in the series of Red Skelton comedies beginning with 'Whistling in the Dark' and revolving about a radio program crime wizard who is called upon to get out of real jams. This yarn deals with a mysterious criminal referred to as 'constant reader' who makes a practice of killing off cops among other people. The radio crime detective is suspected.

Situations and motivation are obvious. Comedy dialog and gagging are familiar but effective. Baseball sequence, with Skelton as a bearded player trying to save the police inspector, is surefire.

Skelton turns in a first-rate performance despite a sketchy theme and thin lines. Jean Rogers, as the cub girl reporter, photographs well and handles assignment easily. Ann Rutherford, the heart interest, is adequate.

Director S. Sylvan Simon rates a nod for maintaining action at a lively level. *Mori.*

Corvette K-225

Hollywood, Sept. 24.

Universal release of Howard Hawks production. Stars Randolph Scott, James Brown. Directed by Richard Rosson. Original screenplay by John Rhodes Sturdy, Lieut. R.C.N/V.R.; camera, Tony Gaudio; convoy photography, Harry Perry; editor, Edward Curtiss; asst. director, William Tummel; special effects, John Fulton. Previewed at Filmarte, Sept. 23, '43. Running time, 98 MINS.

Lieut. Com. MacClain.....Randolph Scott
Paul Cartwright..................James Brown
Joyce Cartwright..................Ella Raines
Stooky O'Meara..........Barry Fitzgerald
Walsh..................................Andy Devine
Cricket.................................Fuzzy Knight
Stone.................................Noah Beery, Jr.
Admiral..............................Richard Lane
Smithy...............................Thomas Gomez
Rawlins...............................David Bruce
Jones.................................Murray Alper
Gardner.................................James Flavin
Evans...................................Walter Sande

'Corvette K-225' details the melodramatic adventures of one of those small fighting ships that have checkmated the Nazi subs in the North Atlantic. Will be a profitable grosser for the regular runs, with reception in Canada and Great Britain certain to hit hefty figures due to display of heroics of the Dominion naval forces.

Picture, made in cooperation with the Canadian navy, has been in preparation and production for virtually a year, with director Richard Rosson making trips across the Atlantic on a corvette with a camera crew to obtain authentic sea shots. Aside from displaying work of the corvettes in accompanying convoys and battling sub packs, film's dramatic yarn reminds of Warners' 'Action in the North Atlantic.'

Randolph Scott is a lieutenant commander in the Royal Canadian Navy who's back on shore after having one corvette shot out from under him. He selects a new ship building on the ways, and indulges in tepid romance with Ella Raines before shoving off with his new K-225. The fast wave-hopper is assigned to convoy duty with group of ships being assembled for trip across the Atlantic. Passage has usual amount of melodramatics — plowing through storm at sea; attack by Nazi planes; location of the lurking subs and stiff battle between the corvette and U-boats. But convoy finally reaches port of safety in northern Ireland.

Extensive footage is devoted to intimacies of the crew of 60 aboard for the journey, with contrast in the various characters on display. Barry Fitzgerald is a salty seaman; Murray Alper and Andy Devine team for several minor comedy routines; and Fuzzy Knight catches good share of supporting footage. Scott is okay as the commanding officer, while James Brown acceptably handles the role of the cadet officer who rebels at Scott's iron rule, but finally becomes a hero of the sea battle. Miss Raines is virtually lost in the shuffle of men and events, while others in support include Thomas Gomez, David Bruce, James Flavin and Noah Beery, Jr.

Story takes too much footage for getaway, with early portion dragging considerably to offset the melodramatics and pace of the episodes when the ship puts to sea. Major audience interest will be aroused by the authentic shots displayed of the various phases of the convoy trip, with one particular highlight scene of a Nazi plane smacked by anti-aircraft fire, its trailing fire and resultant crash into the sea.

Production mounting is okay, with maritime camera work by Harry Perry, who made the corvette trips across the Atlantic, hitting the spectacular on several occasions.

Walt.

Always a Bridesmaid

(SONGS)

Universal release of Ken Goldsmith production. Features Andrews Sisters, Patric Knowles, Charles Butterworth, Grace McDonald, Billy Gilbert. Directed by Erle C. Kenton. Screenplay by Mel Ronson from original story by Oscar Brodney; camera, Louis Da Pron. In N. Y., Sept. 24, '43. Running time, **61 MINS.**

The Andrews Sisters..........Themselves
Tony Warren..............Patric Knowles
Linda Marlowe............Grace McDonald
Nick...........................Billy Gilbert
Col. Winchester.......Charles Butterworth
Mrs. Cavanaugh............Edith Barrett
Rigsy..........................O'Neill Nolan
Annie..........................Annie Rooney
Jivin' Jacks and Jills

Bunch of capable people are wasted in this trite, little musical. While obviously only intended as a secondary entry, the general mishandling seems out of place with such sincere performers as Charles Butterworth, Patric Knowles and Grace McDonald. Even the Andrews Sisters do not fare too well because forcibly injected, with their singing, into proceedings. 'Always a Bridesmaid,' a rather far-fetched title, may appeal to 'teen-age jitterbugs as a supporting feature.

Scripters have taken the Lonely Hearts club as the background for some far-fetched alleged promotional stunts being probed by the d.a. and a secret operative from the city detective bureau. A faint effort is made to carry out the angle that a phoney rubber manufacturer is using the club as headquarters for his promotional scheme. But this is lost in the desire to go on with the singing and jitterbug dancing of the Jivin' Jacks and Jills. It ultimately winds up with the assistant d.a. being wangled out of the pinch by the city operative, the comely Grace McDonald. After that the story winds up with some more song and dance.

Even the possibility of a romantic affair between the assistant district attorney and Miss McDonald is lost in the deluge of musical fare—and mugging by Billy Gilbert. Situations are further marred by silly dialog, most of it fresh from the Iowa corn fields. Gilbert is depicted as the angel (small restaurant owner) who puts the Andrews Sisters on the radio and finally opens a nightclub.

The Andrews look and sing better than usual, but every time they appear it's the signal for a lapse from even the slim plot developments. They are singing a group of tunes in this.

Butterworth, as the promoter, seldom has a chance to be funny. Knowles conducts himself creditably as the assistant d.a., but given small opportunity. Grace McDonald shapes up as a femme likely to be heard from further, indicating development as an actress with each succeeding picture. Gilbert, as the restaurant man, tries hard, but isn't too funny. Story and dialogue writers depend too much on him for humor while neglecting Butterworth.

Presence of Jivin' Jacks and Jills still remains a mystery although admittedly a capable jitterbug dancing combo. They clutter up too many sequences. Edith Barrett makes something of a rather unimportant role, that of the unattractive matron who's willing to stake the promoting Butterworth.

Wear.

The Avenging Rider

(ONE SONG)

RKO release of Bert Gilroy production. Features Tim Holt, Cliff 'Ukulele Ike' Edwards, Ann Summers. Directed by Sam Nelson. Screenplay, Harry O. Hoyt and Morton Grant; camera, J. Roy Hunt; editor, John Lockhert. Dual, New York, N. Y., week of Sept. 21, '43. Running time, **56 MINS.**

Brit.................................Tim Holt
Ike............Cliff 'Ukulele Ike' Edwards
Jean...........................Ann Summers
Grayson......................Davison Clarke
Red............................Norman Willis
Sheriff Allen.................Karl Hackett
Deputy........................Earl Hodgins
Sheriff Lewis..............Edward Cassidy
Blackie.....................Kenneth Duncan
Baxter......................Bud McTaggart
Wade...........................Bud Osborne
Harris..........................Bob Kortman

If it's possible for an actor to steal a second-rate western, then Cliff Edwards does that with 'The Avenging Rider.' His mugging, one ukulele number and all-around shenanigans give this otherwise routine actioner a lift.

Story is one of mistaken identity. Edwards and Tim Holt unwittingly fall in with the murderers of their partner, a gold mine owner, and are accused of his death and stealing $25,000 worth of gold bars. They are jailed, break out, spot the true murderers, are jailed again, make another break and finally wind up nabbing the holdup leaders.

All of this entails considerable riding and shooting. Much of it is repetitious, but there's hardly a dull moment. Holt, unlike Edwards, hasn't mastered scene-stealing tricks. Nevertheless, he makes a youngish, fast-moving 'avenging rider' who is made to perform slugging wonders despite the handicap of a bullet wound in the arm. Ann Summers, femme lead, appears in two or three sequences. Her lines are few and actions limited.

Camera work is weak from the lighting standpoint. Direction is standard.

El Sillon y la Gran Duquesa

(ARGENTINE-MADE)

Buenos Aires, Sept. 8.

EFA production and release starring Olinda Bozan; features Alberto Bello, Ernesto Vilches, Osvaldo Miranda, Billy Days, Maria Ester Buschiazzo, Francisco Donadio, Lucia Barausse; story by Alejandro Verbinsky, E. Villalba Wells, based on a Russian novel; directed by Carlos Schlieper. Reviewed at the Monumental, Buenos Aires. Running time, **62 MINS.**

An interesting comedy, 'El Sillon y la Gran Duquesa' is notable mainly for ingenious story and work of Olinda Bozan. Dialog is fast and snappy and plot twists sometimes border on farce, but it all holds together.

Yarn deals with a Russian grand duchess expatriate living in Argentina. She longs for her old-time life in czarist Russia, meets a duke, also a White Russian, the possessor of a tremendous secret. Inside dope turns out to be the location of an armchair under tapestry of which are hidden keys of a mansion in Russia where the crown jewels have lain since the revolution. He's seen the chair, recognized it in the theatre where a ballet is being given.

Duchess and friend go into theatre but complications set in. There are three chairs exactly alike on the stage, and from there on no holds are barred as the couple try to find the chair. Most likely prospect has been copped by a lady of the evening and the duke almost gets to the point of marriage in order to find the hidden fortune. Search involves various characters, some of them fairly close to stock.

Slapstick occasionally heavy, but telling has been fairly well done, with Miss Bozan as the rich gal who marries the duke particularly noteworthy. Alberto Bello is tops as the duke himself, and Osvaldo Miranda and Billy Days are o.k. in supporting roles.

Ray.

Miniature Reviews

'Paris After Dark' (20th). French underground drama, okay programmer.

'Hi 'Y Sailor' (Songs) (U). Lightweight program filmusical for dual support in secondary bookings.

'Bordertown Gun Fighters' (Rep). Wild Bill Elliott, George Hayes boosting typical western yarn into strong 'B' oats opera.

'Campus Rhythm' (Songs). (Mono). Obvious collegiate antics with songs, for dual support in subsequent houses.

Paris After Dark

(ONE SONG)

20th-Fox release of Andre Daven production. Features George Sanders, Brenda Marshall, Philip Dorn. Directed by Leonide Moguy. Screenplay, Harold Buchman, based on story by Georges Kessel; camera, Lucien Andriot; editor, Nick De Maggio; music director, Emil Newman. Tradeshown in New York, Oct. 4, '43. Running time, **85 MINS.**

Dr. Andre Marbel..........George Sanders
Jean Blanchard..................Philip Dorn
Yvonne Blanchard........Brenda Marshall
Collette...............Madeleine LeBeau
Michel...........................Marcel Dalio
Col. Pirosh...................Robert Lewis
Capt. Franck................Henry Rowland
George Bennoit...............Raymond Roe
Victor Durand.....................Gene Gary
Papa Benoit...................Jean Del Val
Max...................................Curt Bois
Mme. Benoit......................Ann Codee
Picard............................Louis Borell
Mannheim......................John Wengref
Paul.......................Michael Visaroff
Nazi Agent........................Frank Lyon

Out of today's headlines has come another in the long list of tales dealing with the underground movement against the Nazis. This time it's about the French and their efforts to keep alive the spark that has intermittently sputtered since Paris fell in 1940. There's no doubting the authenticity of the background story, since the production and cast credits reveal a number of personalities prominent in Parisian show biz before the war. But 'Paris After Dark' is essentially a dualer, which will satisfy on most bills.

It's a tale of frustration by a poilu released from a Nazi concentration camp after the fall of France and his return to his Parisian family, thoroughly convinced that the Nazis are invincible. Their cruelty to him in the camp had placed its stamp on his seared soul. Around this framework is the story of the underground and his ultimate amorphosis in becoming a factor in the movement.

Philip Dorn plays the French soldier with considerable restraint, but is nearly always convincing. Brenda Marshall is the wife to whom he returns, and she, Dorn and George Sanders form the key characters in a drama that's highlighted by generally able performances, even to the bit parts. However, the slow pace that has been characteristic of French-language films, so as to methodically set the mood for the story, is too evident in 'Paris,' a factor heightened by the knowledge that the direction was handled by Leonide Moguy, one of France's ablest meggers in better times.

Notable among the supporting players are Madeleine Le Beau, a blonde looker, who has one particularly good emotional scene; Marcel Dalio (a star in France), and Raymond Roe, teen-aged lad who shows promise.

Kahn.

Hi 'Ya, Sailor

Hollywood, Oct. 1.

Universal release of Jean Yarbrough production, directed by Yarbrough. Screenplay by Stanley Roberts, suggested by story by Fanya Lawrence; camera, Jack

Mackenzie and Jerome Ash; editor, William Austin; songs, Milton Rosen, Everett Carter; musical director, H. J. Salter. Previewed Sept. 30, '43. Running time, 61 MINS.

Bob Jackson	Donald Woods
Pat Rogers	Elyse Knox
Corky Mills	Eddie Quillan
Deadpan Weaver	Frank Jenks
Nanette	Phyllis Brooks
Lou Asher	Jerome Cowan
Bull Rogan	Matt Willis
Secretary	Florence Lake
Doorman	Charles Coleman
Sam	Mantan Moreland
Police Lieutenant	Jack Mulhall

Ray Eberle and His Orchestra
Wingy Manone and His Orchestra
Delta' Rhythm Boys
Leo Diamond Quintet
Mayris Chaney anl Her Dance Trio
George Beatty
Hacker Duo
Nilsson Sisters

Music and songs, to total of 15 oldies and new ones, are on display in this program filmusical that will adequately fill dual support datings in the family and subsequent houses.

Picture is another in the Universal group of modest-budgeted musicals, and parades six specialty acts in addition to pair of bands. New songs by Milton Rosen and Everett Carter are handled by Donald Woods, Ray Eberle and Phyllis Brooks; while Eberle sings one romantic tune in front of his own band. Then there's Wingy Manone and his fast-tempo swing orch, the harmony Delta Rhythm Boys; musical Leo Diamond Quintet; Mayris Chaney dance trio; Hacker Duo, George Beatty, the Nilsson Sisters, and other vaude personalities, with the Delta Boys and Beatty spotlighted for attention.

What story there is shapes up as a fragile affair and serves only an excuse to get into a servicemen's canteen and a night club to set the various numbers. Woods is a sailor with songwriting propensities, who gets clipped by a racket song publisher. He takes leave for trip to New York with three pals to make rounds of publishers and spots for display of the various specialties. After rounding out the hour's footage, Woods winds up with sale of his first song for an advance.

Producer-director Jean Yarbrough concentrates on staging the acts, slipping fast over the necessary story passages. Cast does okay in respective assignments, but it's strictly a modest filmusical revue for flash attention. *Walt.*

Bordertown Gun Fighters

Republic release of Eddy White production. Stars Wild Bill Elliott; features George 'Gabby' Hayes, Anne Jeffreys. Directed by Howard Bretherton. Original screenplay by Norman S. Hall; camera, Jack Marta; editor, Richard Van Enger. At New York, N. Y., week Sept. 28, '43, dual. Running time, 55 MINS.

Himself	Wild Bill Elliott
Gabby Whitaker	George 'Gabby' Hayes
Anita Shelby	Anne Jeffreys
Cameo Shelby	Ian Keith
Dave Strickland	Harry Woods
Daniel Forrester	Edward Earle
Frank Holden	Karl Hackett
Jack Gattling	Roy Barcroft
Buck Newcombe	Bud Geary
Red Dalley	Carl Sepulveda

Wild Bill Elliott, who's become increasingly important in cowboy mellers, is paired with George 'Gabby' Hayes for strong results in this typical oats opera. Elliott recently signatured a long-term pact with Republic and this is one of his initial efforts under the setup. 'Bordertown Gun Fighters' is topnotch for spots where westerns go over.

With locale along the Mexican border near El Paso, plot concerns a lottery racket operated by the typical cutthroat gambler and efforts of Elliott, operative for U. S. secret service, to bring 'em to justice. Secret service is after gang because it's swindling Mexican natives. Crooked cattle deals, stagecoach stickups and killings are sidelines.

Elliott rides and performs with typical ease. Hayes, comedy relief,

helps, too. Anne Jeffreys seems too pretty to be doing the cowgirl feats she's supposed to, but she's a trim little femme for westerns. Support is headed by Harry Woods and Ian Keith, making it better than usual. *Wear.*

Campus Rhythm
(SONGS)

Hollywood, Oct. 2.

Monogram release of Lindsley Parsons production. Features Johnny Downs, Gale Storm, Robert Lowery. Directed by Arthur Dreifuss. Screenplay by Charles R. Marion; original by Ewart Adamson, Jack White; added dialog, Al Beich, Frank Tarloff; camera, Mack Stengler; editor, Dick Currier; asst. director, Eddie Davis. Previewed at studio, Oct. 1, '43. Running time, 61 MINS.

Scoop	Johnny Downs
Joan	Gale Storm
Buzz	Robert Lowery
Harold	Candy Candido
Babs	Ge-Ge Pearson
Uncle Willie	Doug Leavitt
Hartman	Herbert Heyes
Susie	Marie Blake
Freshman	Johnny Duncan
Cynthia	Claudia Drake

This is conveniently-backgrounded at college in order to provide setting for the usual campus doings, with a half dozen songs tossed in to give it more than ordinary rating for modest budget outlay. Picture will get by in the subsequent houses as a filler booking without difficulty.

Yarn spins around decision of a youthful radio songstress to head for college and an education. She walks out on the sponsors and ad agency to turn up under assumed name at a hideaway school; goes through usual collegiate routines until finally exposed for return to broadcasting duties.

Gale Storm is the girl. She adequately sings four songs. Ge-Ge Pearson, comedienne, smacks over two comedy tunes by Edward Cherkose and Edward Kay, but gets valuable aid from Candy Candido who clicks with his quick-changing and wide range voice, in addition to broad pantomime throughout. Johnny Downs and Robert Lowery share responsibilities of the two male leads. *Walt.*

Battle for Russia
(DOCUMENTARY)

In 'The Battle for Russia,' Lt. Col. Frank Capra, of the Special Service Division, Army Service Forces, has turned out by far the most notable in the series of 'Why We Fight' Army orientation pictures. Fifth of the series of seven documentaries produced for the men of the Army to supply background information on world aggression and to explain the nature of the war they're fighting, 'Battle for Russia' is a powerful, yet simple, drama vividly depicting the greatest military achievement of all time.

As in the case of its predecessors, 'Prelude to War,' 'The Nazis Strike,' 'Divide and Conquer' and 'Battle of Brtiain,' 'Russia' is a brilliant compilation of carefully edited footage culled, in the latter instance, from official Soviet sources and from newsreel and Signal Corps film, with a good part of the Russian ma'erial made available to the War Dept. exclusively for this production. Running 80 minutes, nearly twice the length of the others in the series completed to date, 'Russia' has been flawlessly coordinated by a forceful, eloquent commentary by Capt. Anthony Veiller, who also prepared the continuity. It also stands as a tribute to Lt. Col. Anatole Litvak, who produced the film under Capra's supervision; Major William W. C. Hornbeck (formerly associated with Sir Alexander Korda) and First Lt. William A. Lyon, ex-film editor for Columbia. Latter two assembled and edited the reels. Musical score, prepared by Dimitri Tiomkin and recorded by a 65-piece Army Air Force

band at Santa Ana, Cal., does much to heighten the emotional impact by i.s utilization of excerpts from Tschaikowsky and the ominous Nazi March from the Shostakovich 7th Symphony.

Portraying the historical background of Russia from the time of Alexander Nevsky to the present, the film explains the reasons motivating the various conquests over Russia. Effective use of animated maps helps detail its enormous resources, raw materials, manpower, etc.

Keyed to Gen. Douglas MacArthur's statement that: 'The scale and grandeur of the (Russian) effort mark it as the greatest military achievement in all history,' this Capra-Litvak documentary is primarily the story of the titanic struggle up to the successful defense of Stalingrad. But 'Russia' succeeds in striking a new note previously untouched even in such Soviet releases as 'The City That Stopped Hitler' and 'Siege of Leningrad.' For its stressing of the 'human' angle that not only points up the undying spirit of the Russian people, but analyzes the reasons for their refusal to submit to the Nazi hordes. Thus 'Russia,' through its wide distribution in Army orientation courses, will unquestionably help foster a closer kinship and spiritual bond between the U. S. forces and their fighting ally. For that reason alone it emerges a document of inestimable value. Technically, it's superior to any film to date covering the phases of the Russian campaign.

'Battle for Russia' was completed two weeks ago and has just been released for use in the Army indoctrination classes. Film will also be widely distributed in war plants, though its commercial release is still in doubt. *Rose.*

Miniature Reviews

'The North Star' (RKO-Goldwyn). Good boxoffice for drama on Nazi invasion of Russia.

'The Strange Death of Adolf Hitler' (U). Moderate boxoffice possibilities.

'Dangerous Blondes' (Col). Laugh - packed, husband - wife whodunit comedy.

'A Scream in the Dark' (Rep). 'B' whodunit that's stout support on twinners despite weak scripting.

'Mystery of the 13th Guest' (Mono). Ordinary No. 2 feature for duals.

'My Learned Friend' (British-made). Comedy a natural for Will Hay fans.

'Lad From Our Town' (Soviet-made). Acting, song and battle appeal key this film for good b.o.

'Riders of the Rio Grande' (Rep). Okay western in the Three Mesquiteers series.

'Historia de un Gran Amor' (Mex-made). This Mex critics award film should do healthy b.o. in U. S. Latinas.

The North Star

RKO release of Samuel Goldwyn production; associate producer, William Cameron Menzies. Features Anne Baxter, Dana Andrews, Walter Huston, Walter Brennan, Ann Harding, Jane Withers, Farley Granger, Erich Von Stroheim. Directed by Lewis Milestone. Original story and screenplay, Lillian Hellman. Music, Aaron Copland; lyrics, Ira Gershwin; camera, James Wong Howe; editor, Daniel Mandell; choreography, David Lichine; special effects, R. O. Binger and Clarence Slifer. Previewed in N. Y. Oct. 11, '43. Running time, 105 MINS.

Marina	Anne Baxter
Kolya	Dana Andrews
Dr. Kurin	Walter Huston
Karp	Walter Brennan
Sophia	Ann Harding
Claudia	Jane Withers
Damian	Farley Granger
Dr. Von Harden	Erich Von Stroheim
Rodion	Dean Jagger
Grisha	Eric Roberts
Boris	Carl Benton Reid
Olga	Ann Carter
Anna	Esther Dale
Nadya	Ruth Nelson
Iakin	Paul Guilfoyle
Dr. Richter	Martin Kosleck
German Captain	Tonio Selwart
German Lieutenant	Peter Pohlenz
Russian Pilot	Robert Lowery
Russian Gunner	Gene O'Donnell
Petrov	Frank Wilcox
Woman on Hospital Cot	Loudie Claar
Guerrilla Girl	Lynn Winthrop
Petya	Charles Bates

Samuel Goldwyn as the producer and Lillian Hellman, the writer, have teamed for one of the most spectacular productions of the season in telling of the Nazi invasion of the Soviet. The title is 'The North Star,' and by the sheer weight of current headlines alone it is slated for big boxoffice.

As entertainment, however, there's too much running time consumed before the film actually gets into its story and, in parts, it is seemingly a too-obviously contrived narrative detailing the virtues of the Soviet regime. Setting the background for the actual climax is a long and sometimes tedious one. The early parts of the film are almost always colorful in depicting the simple life of the villagers around whom this story revolves, but it's a question of too premeditatedly setting a stage of a simple, peace-loving people who, through the bestiality of the enemy, are driven to an heroic defense that must, in time, become legendary. For this is the story of the Soviet people as seen through the eyes of a small village.

Miss Hellman's story, when she finally gets around to it, is a parallel one, dealing with a picnic group that's suddenly called on to rush arms through the German lines to their guerrilla comrades when the sudden invasion catches them unawares while on a walking trip. It is an exciting tale from here on in, and ultimately shows how, despite the travail in transit, the group is able to reach their small village just as the guerillas decided to free the families they had left behind from the Nazis who had taken over the village.

The scripters' character delineations are carefully drawn, a factor that helps maintain the film's interest when the story's backgrounds are being established. Productionally, Goldwyn has apparently spared no expense.

The cast is excellent. Anne Baxter, Dana Andrews, Walter Huston, Walter Brennan, Ann Harding, Jane Withers, Farley Granger, Erich Von Stroheim, Dean Jagger all contribute fine performances.

Lewis Milestone obviously was trying to emphasize the 'color' of the Russian people in his earlier scenes, but when once the action got under way—and it can actually be based on the start of the invasion—he's pointed it up with much emphasis. It is, generally, a noteworthy directorial contribution, as is James Wong Howe's photography. *Kahn.*

Strange Death of Adolf Hitler

Universal release of Ben Pivar production. Features Ludwig Donath, Gale Sondergaard, George Dolenz, Fritz Kortner, Ludwig Stossel, William Trenk, Joan Blair. Directed by James Hogan. Story, Fritz Kortner; adaptation, Kortner and Joe May; editor, Milton Carruth; camera, Jerome Ash. At Rialto, N. Y., week Oct. 8, '43. Running time, **72 MINS.**

Franz Huber (Hitler).......Ludwig Donath
Anna Huber............Gale Sondergaard
Herman Marbach............George Dolenz
Bauer......................Fritz Kortner
Graub.....................Ludwig Stossel
Von Zechwitz..............William Trenk
Duchess Eugenie...............Joan Blair
Hohenberg...................Ivan Triesault
Mampe......................Rudolph Anders
Godeck........................Erno Verebes
Hansl..........................Merrill Rodin
Viki...........................Charles Bates
Karl..............................Kurt Katch
Profe..........................Hans Schumm
Himmler........................Fred Gierman
Palzer..........................Richard Ryen
Halder...........................John Mylong
Youth Leader.................Kurt Kreuger
Dr. Kaltenbruch..............Lester Sharpe
Frau Reitler.................Trude Berliner
Judge................Hans von Twardowsky
Attorney.....................Wolfgang Zilzer

Somewhat unique as to plot, but far from being highly engrossing, 'The Strange Death of Adolf Hitler' is disappointing on the whole. Its title and the exploitation values entailed make for the prime b.o. equation.

As to story, it's highly synthetic as well as fantastic, with only the novelty angles involved serving as a virtue. Fritz Korner, who plays a Nazi stooge in the picture, wrote the story and, together with Joe May, did the adaptation. Ludwig Donath, also a refugee from Nazism, plays a dual role, that of Hitler and the double for the Feuhrer into which he has been transformed through plastic surgery by the Gestapo whose intent appears to be to wipe out Hitler and then let Donath pose as the boss without any power.

In seeking to accomplish this, the Gestapo grabs Donath, a minor official in Vienna, and under duress operates on him to give him the appearance of Hitler himself. Meantime, Donath's wife has been informed he has been killed for treason. Threatened with death, Donath agrees to play the game, but on a trip to Vienna he makes his identity known to a friend who plans bumping off the real Hitler, also then in Vienna. Donath's wife, however, does not know of the plot, and herself having laid plans to erase Hitler, shoots his double (her husband) instead, and, for her trouble, in turn, is liquidated.

Donath gives a steady performance and looks enough like Hitler under makeup to pass. His voice, also, resembles that of the world's No. 1 rat. Gale Sondergaard stands out as the wife, while a friend of the family, George Dolenz, playing a Swiss, does satisfactorily. Others are strictly in the Nazi groove, and okay as such, these including Kortner, Ludwig Stossel, William Trenk and Joan Blair, last-mentioned a duchess pal of Hitler's. *Char.*

Dangerous Blondes

Columbia release of Samuel Bischoff production. Features Allyn Joslyn, Evelyn Keyes, Edmund Lowe, John Hubbard, Anita Louise, Frank Craven. Directed by Leigh Jason. Screenplay, Richard Flournoy and Jack Henley; camera, Philip Tannura; editor, Jerome Thomas. At Fox, Brooklyn, dual, week of Oct. 7, '43. Running time, **81 MINS.**

Barry Craig...................Allyn Joslyn
Jane Craig...................Evelyn Keyes
Ralph McCormick..........Edmund Lowe
Kirk Fenley..................John Hubbard
Julie Taylor....................Anita Louise
Inspector Clinton...........Frank Craven
Harry Duerr...............Michael Duane
Erika McCormick.............Ann Savage
Detective Gatling.......William Demarest
Pop......................Hobart Cavanaugh
Detective Henderson..........Frank Sully
Jim Snyder.................Robert Stanford
May Ralston...................Lynn Merrick
Lee Kenyon..................Stanley Brown
Madge Lawrence............Bess Flowers
Mrs. Fleming...............Mary Forbes
Roland Smith.................John Abbott

The husband-and-wife amateur sleuthing pair, with a penchant for solving murders and getting into hot water furnish a laugh-packed session here via the antics of Allyn Joslyn and Evelyn Keyes. 'Dangerous Blondes' is a misnomer, but with smart promotion it has solid b.o. possibilities on a dual bill.

Joslyn portrays a detective story writer who goes in for real life detective work as a sideline. He is, however, constantly accompanied by his wife, Evelyn Keyes, and also constantly running into the police, personified by Frank Craven, as an inspector, who resents his interference. The murders are committed against the swank background of a class fashion studio and high society. The story achieves suspense and comedy, but falls down in the romance department when it has Anita Louise cherish a secret and unrequited love for Edmund Lowe, her boss and owner of the studio, who is unjustly accused of killing his wife. The police are made to look silly by Joslyn, first in an amusing 'detective fiction writers versus real detectives' radio quiz contest, and then during the actual murder hunt. But as a sop the cops are allowed to save Joslyn's life at the crucial moment.

The plot and the acting of 'Dangerous Blondes' immediately invite comparisons with the 'Thin Man' series. And although 'Blondes' is not in the same league, it helps fill the gap left by the absence of the husband-wife sleuth comedy. Joslyn tends to be over-cute and simpering considering that he is supposed to be a surefire detective. But his fumbling, and wolfish gleam get lots of laughs. Miss Keyes goes over neatly as the wide-eyed wife who can turn on the sex appeal or act coy with equal conviction. Anita Louise stalks through the film looking very beautiful and very frightened, while Lowe just looks lost in semi-formal clothes and a tragic role, but Frank Craven seems right at home as a down to-earth police inspector.

The film is well paced, and also registers with interesting camera effects.

A Scream in the Dark

Republic release of George Sherman production, directed by Sherman. Features Robert Lowery, Marie McDonald, Edward Brophy, Wally Vernon, Jack La Rue. Screenplay by Gerald Schnitzer, Anthony Coldewey, based on novel by Jerome Odlum; camera, Reggie Lanning; editor, Arthur Roberts. At Strand, Brooklyn, week Oct. 7, '43, dualed. Runnting time, **53 MINS.**

Mike Brooker...............Robert Lowery
Joan Allen.................Marie McDonald
Eddie Tough.............Edward S. Brophy
Clousky.......................Wally Vernon
Leo Starke.............Hobart Cavanaugh
Cross...........................Jack LaRue
Muriel.....................Elizabeth Russel
Lackey..........................Frank Fenton
Gerald Messenger..........William Haade
Stella...........................Linda Brent
Norton...........................Arthur Loft
Maisie.........................Kitty McHugh

Flimsy scripting of Jerome Odlum's novel, 'The Morgue Is Always Open,' is considerably overcome by George Sherman's forthright direction and several bright individual performances. Result is a passable 'B' whodunit which fits in snugly on twin bills.

'A Scream in the Dark' is a typical amateur sleuth mystery, with action centering about a mysterious married lady, who always turns up shortly after her deceased husbands meet sudden death. Scripters Gerald Schnitzer and Anthony Coldewey deal with most of the strange deaths in light fashion and stress the alleged humorous angle too much. Trouble is that often it is misplaced humor. There's the divorced hubby of the insurance-collecting widow, who stays around until the last and soon is suspected of being wielder of a strange umbrella that has a fancy stilleto end-piece. The mystery becomes a bit confusing near the end, partly due to poor editing, but director George Sherman usually manages to point up many suspenseful moments for good returns.

Worthy cast is topped by a quintet of players who breathe life into some of the wooden proceedings. Robert Lowery, youngish leading man, does well enough as the police reporter turned private detective, but is helped manfully over many hurdles by Edward Brophy, his humorous assistant in the sleuthing business. Marie McDonald, Lowery's sweetheart, not only is pretty, but now is shaping up as a first-rate actress. Wally Vernon, as the morgue caretaker, provides a few funny moments, while Jack La Rue is effective as a police detective. Elizabeth Russell, as the hubby-killing femme, is effective while support is headed by Hobart Cavanaugh and William Haade. *Wear.*

Mystery of the 13th Guest

Monogram release of Lindsley Parsons production. Features Dick Purcell, Helen Parrish, Tim Ryan. Directed by William Beaudine. Story, Armitage Trail; adaptation, Charles Marion, Tim Ryan; editor, Dick Currier; camera, Mack Stengler. At New York, N. Y., dual, week Oct. 5, '43. Running time, **60 MINS.**

Johnny..........................Dick Purcell
Marie.........................Helen Parrish
Burke................................Tim Ryan
Speed............................Frank Faylen
Harold..........................John Duncan
Jackson..........................Jon Dawson
Morgan............................Paul McVey
Marjory....................Jacqueline Dalya
Barksdale............................Cyril King
District Attorney.........Addison Richards

A boiler-plate murder mystery that drags in spite of being only an hour long, and will serve only in a minor way as the No. 2 feature on double bills.

The hackneyed story concerns the efforts of an uncle to knock off the beneficiary under a will, others meantime having been disposed of, but as result of good detective work and some luck the plot is exposed for the happy finish. Direction of William Beaudine is ordinary, while technically the production of Lindsley Parsons rates below par.

Dick Purcell, private detective, and Helen Parrish, the gal who's murder-menaced, are paired for romantic interest, but it never gets very hot. Lessers include Tim Ryan, Frank Faylen, John Duncan, Jon Dawson and Paul McVey. Faylen playing a dopey cop, appears to have comedy possibilities, given the right opportunity. *Char.*

My Learned Friend
(BRITISH-MADE)

London, Sept. 22.

Ealing Studios' release of Michael Balcon production. Stars Will Hay, Claude Hulbert. Directed by Basil Dearden, Will Hay; original screenplay by Angus Macphail, John Dighton; camera, W. Cooper. At Empire, London, Sept. 21. Running time, **80 MINS.**

William Fitch........................Will Hay
Claude Babbington.........Claude Hulbert
Grimshaw......................Mervyn Johns
'Safety' Wilson.............Charles Victor
Dr. Scudamore............G. H. Mulcaster
'Basher' Blake..............Eddie Phillips
Aladdin....................Maudie Edwards
Gloria...........................Derna Hazell

An amusing vehicle for Will Hay, minus his former stooges. This time his associate is Claude Hulbert as a budding lawyer sacked for failing to convict Hay on a charge of writing begging letters. It's a b.o. natural for the Hay fans.

Picture is slickly directed, never drags, and has a plausible excuse for many comic and improbable incidents. A released convict has it in for Hay, in reality a disbarred lawyer, for failing to save him from a forgery sentence, and with a maniacal look implies he intends rubbing out six people responsible for his incarceration, from the judge down to Hay himself. Thereafter ensues a desperate attempt to warn the other victims, prevent their untimely ends, and thus stave off the shyster's own doom. The two comedians are good foils to each other—the bland odiocy of the younger contrasting with the shrewd trickery of the other, supplemented by crisp, amusing dialog.

Highlight is a chase to prevent Big Ben from striking 12, when a mechanical devise set by the unhinged avenger will blow up the House of Lords, to whose final judgment he was not allowed to appeal. Clever photography showing the trio dodging around the interior workings of the famous clock and clinging by their eyebrows to the face and hands suspended over Westminster, makes for hilarious excitement.

All the characters (practically all male) are perfect types, from the East End thugs to the tawdry personnel of a cheap provincial pantomime company. Mervyn Johns scores particularly in the role of the crafty maniac-crook.

In the comedy field, excellent of its kind and no reason it shouldn't provide a novelty support in a dual program in the U. S. *Clem.*

Lad From Our Town
(Songs)
(SOVIET-MADE)

Artkino release of Central Art Film Studios production. Features Nikolai Kriuchkov, Nikolai Bogoliubov, Anna Smirnova and Nikolai Mordvinov. Directed by Alexander Stolper and Boris Ivanov; based on a play by Konstantin Simonov; English titles, Charles Clement; music, Nikolai Kriukov; camera, S. Uralov. At Stanley Theatre, N. Y., Oct. 6, '42. Running time, **65 MINS.**

Lukonin ....Nikolai Kriuchkov
Burmin ....Nikolai Bogoliubov
Varya ....Anna Smirnova
Vasnyetsov ....Nikolai Mordvinov
Sevostyanov ....V. Stepanov
Pyetka ....V. Medvedyev
Volodya ....A. Alekseyev
Safonov ....P. Liubeshkin

Despite a loosely constructed story and stiff-upper-lip theme, this latest Russian importation should prove good b.o. for houses normally exhibiting Russian films, by virtue of some vivid tank battle sequences and warm acting.

Konstantin Simonov, who authored 'The Russian People,' which had a short Broadway run last season under the aegis of the Theatre Guild, wrote the play on which 'Lad of Our Town' was based. The story itself is simple. The romance and subsequent marriage of a tank officer and an opera singer are served up against a background of peacetime military life and then war. The tank officer is one of those charming braggarts who clicks as a tactician in both love and war. The action jumps too rapidly from early courting days, to marriage, the Spanish Civil war and finally the current conflict. Some sequences fare better than others but few dovetail.

Nikolai Kriuchkov, the tank officer, impresses with his ruggedness, and clicks both as a Romeo and grim fighter. Anna Smirnova, who portrays his opera-singer wife, pleases the eye and ear with her looks, vocalizing and acting. The other members of the cast do workmanlike jobs. The music possesses the tuneful spirit so characteristic of Russian melody. In addition to story weakness, photography on camera work is fuzzy.

Riders of the Rio Grande

Republic release of Louis Gray production. Stars Bob Steele, Tom Tyler, Jimmie Dodd; features Lorraine Miller, Edward Van Sloan, Rick Vallin, Harry Worth. Directed by Howard Bretherton. Story and adaptation, Albert Demond; editor, Charles Craft; camera, Ernest Miller. At New York, N. Y.; dual, week Oct. 5, '43. Running time, **55 MINS.**

Tucson Smith....................Bob Steele
Stony Brooke....................Tom Tyler
Lullaby Joslin....................Jimmie Dodd
Janet Owens....................Lorraine Miller
Pop Owens....................Edward Van Sloan
Tom Owens....................Rick Vallin
Sam Skelly....................Harry Worth
Sarsaparilla....................Roy Barcroft
Thumber....................Charles King
Berger....................Jack Ingram

Another in the Three Mesquiteers series, 'Riders of the Rio Grande,' follows a familiar pattern, but holds the interest sufficiently to warrant booking where westerns are the diet. Not the best of its kind, picture still has enough action to get by satisfactorily.

The plot differs in at least one respect, that the town leader and banker, a benign old gentleman, decides to make the supreme sacrifice in arranging to have himself bumped off in order to make up for a wastrel son's mistakes which resulted in cleaning out the bank. Through a switch in circumstances, the banker believes the Three Mesquiteers are the gunmen he hired, whereas it's three other guys who were actually retained to do the dirty work.

While a bit unbelievable, the mix-up in identity provides situations that help keep the film rolling along, meantime developing some gunfire and other action.

Bob Steele, Tom Tyler and Jimmie Dodd, the Three Mesquiteers, ride off at the finish, as usual, with not the slightest trace of any romantic interest having intervened. The girl is a pretty, Lorraine Miller, but she's almost conspicuous by her absence. Edward Van Sloan plays the banker, while Rick Vallin appears as his ne'er-do-well son, not showing much. Harry Worth is a slick heavy.

Char.

Historia De Un Gran Amor

Films Mundiales production. Stars Jorge Negrete. Directed by Julio Bracho. From the novel, 'El Nino de la Bola,' by Pedro Antonio De Alarcon. At Belmont, N. Y., week of Oct. 8, '43. Running time, **151 MINS.**

Manuel Venegas....................Jorge Negrete
Senora Elias....................Sara Garcia
Don Elias....................Julio Villareal
Soledad....................Gloria Marin
Friar Trinidad....................Domingo Soler
Apothecary....................Andres Soler
Manuel (as a boy)....................Narciso Busquets
Antonio Arregui....................Miguel Angel Ferriz

This one is reputed as having won producers' and critics' acclaim as the super-duper Mex production of 1942. Both in running time and with cast studded with veteran boxoffice favorites down Mexico way, it should do exceptionally well to hypo b.o. takes in the Latinas of the U. S. Reaction thus far at the Belmont, N. Y., where it is showcasing, has been capacity since opening Friday (8) and if current rush continues may chalk up a new record for the house.

Story pivots on an orphaned boy's love for a girl whose father opposes match because he, although well-born, is sans moola. Hero rides off and later not only achieves his niche in the world, but becomes a millionaire and rides back to claim his senorita. Too late. She has married another, but still loves Manuel. At the fiesta he can no longer withhold his love for the girl. Culmination is death for her, presumably at the hands of her supposedly outraged husband. Negrete gives a dashing, superb performances as Mauel. Gloria Marin is charming as the girl. Others of cast are adequate in respective assignments.

Although story is somewhat run-of-the-mill tragedy, which seemingly has strong appeal with Latin audiences, this one is backgrounded by sufficient historic lore and scenics to provide an aura of documentary aside from the story which motivates it. Fiesta scenes give director Julio Bracho plenty of scope for clever manipulation of mob ensembles. Camera work, also, is especially good.

Miniature Reviews

'Northern Pursuit' (WB). Adventure melodrama, pitting Nazis against Northwest mounties. Profitable b.o. for regular runs.

'The Iron Major' (RKO). Profitable biz ahead for Pat O'Brien starrer about famed American football coach.

'Crazy House' (Filmusical). (U). Olsen & Johnson in solid 'escapist' filmusicomedy. Top b.o. and holdover loom.

'My Kingdom for a Cook' (Col). Charles Coburn starrer should do nicely at b.o.

'Find the Blackmailer' (WB). Whodunit for secondary duals.

'Mystery Broadcast' (Rep). Good short-end dualer for nabe houses.

'Nearly Eighteen' (Mono). Fluffy 'B' romance; strong for dual support.

'We Will Come Back' (Artkino). Vivid, but commercially limited, film about Russian guerilla fighting.

'Blazing Guns' (Mono). Ken Maynard, Hoot Gibson in standard cowboy meller.

'Isle of Forgotten Sins' (PRC). Exciting meller with John Carradine, Gale Sondergaard and Sidney Toler. Okay as supporter.

Northern Pursuit

Hollywood, Oct. 19.

Warner Brothers release of Jack Chertok production. Stars Errol Flynn; features Julie Bishop and Helmut Dantine. Directed by Raoul Walsh. Screenplay, Frank Gruber and Alvah Bessie; from story by Leslie T. White; camera, Sid Hickox; editor, Frank Killifer. Tradeshown in L. A., Oct. 18, '43. Running time, **93 MINS.**

Steve Wagner....................Errol Flynn
Laura McBain....................Julie Bishop
Hugo von Keller....................Helmut Dantine
Jim Austin....................John Ridgely
Ernst....................Gene Lockhart
Inspector Barnett....................Tom Tully
Dagor....................Bernard Nedell
Sergeant....................Warren Douglas
Jean....................Monte Blue
Angus McBain....................Alec Craig
Hobby....................Tom Fadden
Alice....................Rose Higgins
Heinzmann....................Richard Alden
German Aviator....................John Royce
Indian Guide....................Joe Herrera
Radio Operator....................Carl Harbaugh

This one combines the elements of Nazi spies with the lusty and vigorous adventures of a Canadian Northwest mountie. Carrying plenty of suspense, dramatic content and pace, 'Northern Pursuit' will roll through the regular runs for fairly strong biz, with marquee voltage of Errol Flynn aiding in drawing the customers.

Yarn pits Flynn as a heroic mountie against Nazi flyer Helmut Dantine, who's been dropped in the Hudson Bay region by a sub for a war mission in Canada. But Dantine is captured in the wild snow country by Flynn and John Ridgely, with Flynn devising plan to gain confidence of the flyer to smash spy ring. Nazi escapes from prison camp, while Flynn 'resigns' from the force and professes Nazi sympathies. Flyer has him contacted and deal is made for Flynn to guide Nazi party north to a secret destination, which proves eventually to be an old mine where Germans had secreted bombing plane several years before. After arrival, Flynn stands off the Nazi gang, finally bagging Dantine in a gun battle aboard the plane.

Snow-blanketed north is a fresh background for staging a Nazi spy chase; and full advantage is taken to blend the scenery with the dramatics. Particularly effective is the process photography with several spectacular shots. At opening is the surfacing of the sub in the ice-covered waters; later the snow avalanche that buries the original Nazi party except Dantine.

Flynn provides a strong and heroic mountie officer in best cinematic style. Dantine hits in strong fashion as the arrogant and despicable Nazi, who has a penchant for killing everyone who is no longer useful to him. Julie Bishop capably handles the girl role, following Flynn after his disappearance to go along for part of the journey as a hostage for the Nazis. Gene Lockhart portrays the Nazi agent in fine form, while Ridgely displays a manly mountie. Good support includes Tom Tully, Alec Craig and Joe Herrera.

Both script by Frank Gruber and Alvah Bessie, and direction by Raoul Walsh, are in keeping with the best traditions of outdoor melodramatics.

Production, with major portion of footage in the outdoors with snow-blanketed trails and mountains, is topgrade throughout. Photography by Sid Hickox is particularly praiseworthy.

Walt.

The Iron Major

Hollywood, Oct. 19.

RKO release of Robert Fellows production. Stars Pat O'Brien; features Ruth Warrick, Robert Ryan. Directed by Ray Enright. Screenplay by Aben Kandel and Warren Duff; camera, Robert de Grasse; editor, Robert Wise; music director, C. Bakeleinikoff. Previewed Oct. 18, '43. Running time, **90 MINS.**

The film biography of the late Frank Cavanaugh, dynamic and driving football coach at Dartmouth, Boston College and Fordham, despite its focus on grid activities weaves a strong story about a typical American family and its progress and happiness through the years. Grid angle is a cinch to attract the male sector, but women also will go for the family theme included for their attention.

With Pat O'Brien starred, picture is due for good and profitable business in regular runs. The story, told in retrospect, covers a stretch of 40 years and is necessarily episodic. It traces Cavanaugh from a kid of 10 through his schooldays, college and coaching years and the romance with Ruth Warrick.

While coaching at Dartmouth, Cavanaugh, who has raised a family of 10 children, enlists at the outbreak of World War I and goes overseas carrying the same driving force for victory into combat that he instilled into his football charges.

Wounded and partly blinded he returns after the war with the rank of major and resumes coaching, this time at Boston College where, despite his rapidly failing eyesight, he turns out winning teams. Advised by his doctor that he can expect only five more years of active life Cavanaugh switches to Fordham to provide security for his family after a stretch of lean years.

Film reaches climax with 1932 football season when Fordham beats Oregon State in ranking intersectional contest and the coach goes completely blind. Post-climax provides unnecessary death scene.

O'Brien delivers strong and impressive performance as Cavanaugh who lived on three precepts; love of God, country and family. Miss Warrick is excellent as the understanding and loveable mother of the household. Robert Ryan and Leon Ames are well cast as coach's pals, and Russell Wade does well with a brief shot as a doughboy at the front. Picture is liberally spotted with newsreel clips of grid games, including several shots of the B.C. team, hitting a peak with extended footage of the famous Fordham-Oregon State clash.

Through it all runs the contrast of Cavanaugh's stern drive on the gridiron with his family associations of love and sympathy. His pep talks before games are typically American in stressing our fight and drive for things we believe in. Ray Enright directed in good style under production wing of Robert Fellows. *Walt.*

Crazy House

(MUSICAL)

Hollywood, Oct. 14.

Universal release of Erle C. Kenton production. Stars Olsen & Johnson; features large cast below. Directed by Edward F. Cline. Screenplay, Robert Lees and Frederic I. Rinaldo; camera, Charles Van Enger; editor, Arthur Hilton; asst. director, Howard Christie; special effects, John P. Fulton; musical productions devised and staged by George Hale; music director, Charles Previn; music supervisor, Ted Cain. Previewed at Hillstreet, L. A., Oct. 13, '43. Running time, **78 MINS.**

Appearing with Olsen and Johnson

Sadie..........Cass Daley
Mac..........Patric Knowles
Margie..........Martha O'Driscoll
Johnny..........Leighton Noble
Wagstaff..........Thomas Gomez
Col. Merriweather..........Percy Kilbride
Roco..........Hans Conried
Hanley..........Richard Lane
Gregory..........Andrew Tombes
Stone..........Billy Gilbert
Fud..........Chester Clute
Judge..........Edgar Kennedy
Hotel Clerk..........Franklin Pangborn
Mumbo..........Shemp Howard
Jumbo..........Fred Sanborn

Also Tony & Sally DeMarco, Count Basie & Orchestra, Marion Hutton & Glenn Miller Singers, Chandra Kaly Dancers, Delta Rhythm Boys, Leighton Noble Orch.

Introducing guest stars: Allan Jones, Leo Carrillo, Andy Devine, Robert Paige, Alan Curtis.

Olsen & Johnson's screwball antics in their second picture for Universal make for solid entertainment results. It's strictly escapist, with the two comedians using broadest physical, visual and mechanical gags for laugh attention, and neatly set up song and dance support to provide top boxoffice reaction. Holdovers in the keys will be the rule rather than exception.

Film version of 'Hellzapoppin' provides best key to cinematic display of the two comics. Everything goes, and in a big way. General upset and surprise rules when they are anywhere near the camera. Under direction of Edward Cline, O. & J. romp all over the place.

Story is only a light framework on which to display the Olsen-Johnson wackiness, and the specialty numbers that are liberally sprinkled along the route. Comics arrive at Universal to make another picture, but, from the front office down, nobody wants anything to do with them. Pair decided to make picture on their own, and set up without coin on a rental lot. After it's finished and the creditors stalk in to grab the negative, they stage a preview and auction off the negative for a million. Running through is a slight romance between Patric Knowles and Martha O'Driscoll.

Picture opens at a fast clip, with the comics staging their own welcoming parade along Hollywood Boulevard, and then crashing the studio to scatter the help pellmell. Olsen & Johnson adroitly step aside for presentation of a wealth of standout talent that serves to materially lift the entertainment factors of the picture. There's a crackerjack comedienne, Cass Daley, who proves excellent foil for the pair; songs by Martha O'Driscoll, the Glenn Miller Singers, and Delta Rhythm Boys; music by Count Basie and the Leighton Noble bands, and dances by the DeMarcos and Chandra Kaly and his dancers. Allan Jones comes on as guest star to sing 'Donkey Serenade' for brief but spotlighted attention.

In addition to a few familiar tunes, picture has around 10 new songs written by various writing teams. Cass Daley handles two comedy numbers to full advantage; Miss O'Driscoll clicks with three tunes, of which 'Rainbow Song' has chance to catch on; and the Delta Rhythm Boys score solidly with tuneful arrangements. Glenn Miller Singers, with looker Marion Hutton, backed up by male foursome, are on frequently for smart delivery of several melodies.

Tony and Sally DeMarco stage some fancy terping, headlining the 'Tropicana' production number, which is expensively staged for eye and ear appeal. Other specialties include Ramsey Ames and her Tropicana Can Cans, Nick Cochrane and ork, Marjorettes Girl band, and Ward & Van. Count Basie and his band gets spotlight flood in two spots and score in usual solid style.

Olsen & Johnson again play themselves here, and everything is neatly set up to revolve around them—with accent on supporting acts and the physical and mechanical contrivances for comedy reactions. Picture has been expensively produced, with heavy outlay for talent and staging, and brings in several of Universal contract players for very brief footage. Camera and sound work is of high standard throughout. *Walt.*

My Kingdom for a Cook

Columbia release of P. J. Wolfson production. Stars Charles Coburn; features Marguerite Chapman, Bill Carter, Isobel Elsom, Edward Gargan. Directed by Richard Wallace. Screenplay, Harold Goldman and Andrew Solt, Joseph Hoffman and Jack Henley; story by Lili Hatvany and Andrew Solt; editor, Otto Meyer; camera, Franz E. Planer. At Loew's State, N. Y., week Oct. 14, '43. Running time, **81 MINS.**

Rudyard Morley..........Charles Coburn
Pamela Morley..........Marguerite Chapman
Mike Scott..........Bill Carter
Lucille Scott..........Isobel Elsom
Duke..........Edward Gargan
Agnes Willoughby..........Mary Wickes
Hattie..........Almira Sessions
Sam Thornton..........Eddy Waller
'Pretty Boy' Peterson..........Ralph Peters
Professor Harlow..........Ivan Simpson
Jerry..........Betty Brewer
Angus Sheffield..........Melville Cooper
Mrs. Carter..........Kathleen Howard
Oliver Bradbury..........Charles Halton
Abe Mason..........Andrew Tombes

'My Kingdom for a Cook' may excite no raves or boxoffice records, but its escapist comedy content indicates nice, steady business in all situations.

Plus the laughs, it has the marquee asset of Charles Coburn. Latter, however, is somewhat out of his own established character and appears to be doing a Monty Woolley—not as funny as Woolley, and, naturally, not as funny as Coburn usually is. Story contributes to this fault, though, by being stretched too thin.

Without being too pointed, yarn might be a takeoff on George Bernard Shaw, Coburn impersonating a famous English author who comes to the U. S. on a goodwill lecture tour. Being a trencherman, he's quite put out when lack of place on a plane forces his English cook to stay behind. Unable to get a cook in the U. S., Coburn swipes the faithful servant of a Massachusetts socialite, and she takes revenge by turning the whole town against him. Meanwhile, the socialite's army-flier son and Coburn's daughter mix up in a romance and this helps unmix all the Max Sennett difficulties at the finish, when Coburn apologizes to the town and asks the Americans not to judge all Englishmen by his actions.

Pretty Marguerite Chapman and Bill Carter are okay in support as the romantic duo. Ditto Isobel Elsom, as the socialite, and Edward Gargan, as the dissolute husband of the cook, Almira Sessions. Most of the others are in strictly bits, all well handled.

Richard Wallace directed with fairly good pace and Franz E. Planer's photography is average. *Scho.*

Find the Blackmailer

Hollywood, Oct. 18.

Warner Bros. production and release. Features Jerome Cowan, Faye Emerson and Gene Lockhart. Directed by D. Ross Lederman. Screenplay, Robert E. Kent, from story by G. T. Fleming-Roberts; camera, James Van Trees; editor, Harold McLernon. Tradeshown in L. A., Oct. 18, '43. Running time, **55 MINS.**

D. L. Trees..........Jerome Cowan
Mona Vance..........Faye Emerson
John M. Rhodes..........Gene Lockhart
Pandora Pines..........Marjorie Hoshelle
Harper..........Robert Kent
Detective Cramer..........Wade Boteler
Ray Hicky..........John Harmon
Farrell..........Bradley Page
Olen..........Lou Lubin
Coleman..........Ralph Peters

This is a quickie 'B' whodunit of minor program calibre which will have to struggle with filler datings in the secondary duals where the customers are not too particular. It's one of those low-budgeters turned out on the Warner lot a year ago, and dusted off after reposing in the vaults these many months.

Yarn, pivoting around adventures of a private detective, is decidedly unimaginative. Jerome Cowan is engaged by mayoralty candidate Gene Lockhart to unearth a talking crow which might incriminate him in a future murder. The victim is bumped off, and tale then wends its way through a maze of convenient situations for the eventual explanation.

Cowan slips out of his usual heavy roles to handle spot of the breezy and impecunious dick. Passable support is provided by Faye Emerson, Gene Lockhart, Marjorie Hoshelle, Robert Kent, Wade Boteler, John Harmon, Bradley Page and Lou Lubin. Direction by D. Ross Lederman hits the usual meller groove. *Walt.*

Mystery Broadcast

Republic release of George Sherman production. Features Frank Albertson and Ruth Terry. Directed by George Sherman. Screenplay, Dane Lussier; camera, William Bradford; editor, Arthur Roberts. Tradeshown in New York, Oct. 15, '43. Running time, **63 MINS.**

Michael Jerome..........Frank Albertson
Jan Cornell..........Ruth Terry
Ricky Moreno..........Nils Asther
Eve Stanley..........Wynne Gibson
A. J. Stanley..........Paul Harvey
Smitty..........Mary Treen
Bill Burton..........Addison Richards
Chief Daniels..........Joseph Crehan
Mida Kent..........Alice Fleming
Crunch..........Francis Pierlot
Announcer..........Ken Carpenter
Don Fletcher..........Emmett Vogan

George Sherman has taken a mystery script loaded with the usual mechanics and tailored an acceptable short-end dualer for nabe houses. Film moves with good pace in spite of hackneyed story, and Frank Albertson and Ruth Terry give acceptable performances as the amateur crime-solvers.

Story deals with a radio writer (Ruth Terry) of a weekly unsolved-crime program. Due to waning popularity of the stanza, the writer decides to present the solutions to unsolved crimes instead of mere dramatizations as a hypo. Result of her interest in a murder case long on the police's unsolved list is a set of further murders. All of which are finally solved by the heroine with the obvious person as the culprit.

Albertson is a rival radio mystery writer whose romanctic interest in Miss Terry involves him in the procedures. His presence, except as a romantic foil, presents what little mystery there is in the picture.

Nils Asther, on the film comeback trail, has a bit as the sleek orchestra leader-inamorata of the program sponsor's wife, played by Wynne Gibson. Rest of supporting cast does workmanlike job.

Nearly Eighteen

(WITH SONGS)

Monogram release of Lindsley Parsons production. Features Gale Storm, Bill Henry, Rick Vallin, Luis Alberni. Directed by Arthur Dreifuss. Screenplay, George Sayre, from original by Margaret Englander; camera, Mack Stengler; editor, Dick Currier. At New York, N. Y., week Oct. 12, '43, dualed. Running time, **61 MINS.**

Jane..........Gale Storm
Tony..........Rick Vallin
Leonard..........Bill Henry
Gus..........Luis Alberni
Tom..........Ralph Hodges
Dick..........Jerry Rush
Eddie..........George O'Hanlon
Harriet..........Bebe Fox

Although there are traces of several previous films in 'Nearly Eighteen,' this shapes up well as good support on dual combos though lacking names.

It's the time-worn theme of an aspiring youngster trying to make good in show business in the big city. This time it's an ambitious femme singer, with the yarn centering about the youngster's age. First she loses out on a cafe job because under 18; then, she finds she must be under 14 in order to become a pupil in a noted academy of music. Story revolves around the love affair with her tutor and efforts to keep up the deception about her age. There's the usual blowup when the sweetheart tutor learns her deception and customary reuniting the night of her swank nightclub debut. Her bookmaker friend, who's in love with every new face he encounters, forms the other end of the triangle.

Gale Storm, Texas gal who won the 'Gateway to Hollywood' contest several years ago, shows promise as a singer, potentialities as an actress, and, what's more, is a looker. In her first featured role for Monogram, she figures in several snappy dance sequences. Her best songs are 'Smiles for Sale' and 'Walkin' on Air'; no writers are credited for these tunes.

Bill Henry, the teacher, goes over nicely. Rick Vallin makes an acceptable chaser, and Luis Alberni has another typical cafe operator role that's filled with chuckles.

George Sayres' screenplay is okay, but the editing of Dick Currier leaves some gaps in the continuity. Arthur Dreifuss' direction is mainly topflight. *Wear.*

We Will Come Back

(SOVIET-MADE)

Artkino release of Art Film Studios production. Fredric Ermler, Leonid Trauberg in charge of production. Directed by Ivan Piriev. Story, Ivan Prunt; camera, V. Pavlov; English titles, Charles Clement. Reviewed at Victoria theatre, New York, Oct. 14, '43. Running time, **90 MINS.**

Stepan Kochet..........Vasili Vanin
Colonel Makenau..........Mikhail Astangov
Natasha..........Marina Ladynina
Gavrila Rusov..........Mikhail Zharov
Sasha Rusov..........Mikhail Kuznetsov
Rotman..........Boris Poslavsky
Orlov..........Victor Kulakov

In common with other Soviet-made pictures, this is a vividly realistic picturization of the mass murder of the innocents practiced by the Nazi hordes in their invasion of European countries.

It's a grim, only slightly fictionized pictorial recital of many facts which have already been prominently carried in news coverage from battle zones abroad. Some of the hanging and shooting scenes are shocking and strictly adult fare.

As a commercial proposition the film is, of course, limited. Casting is more than adequate, camerawork is okay, and direction good. Like other pictures of this type, however, it's wordy.

Yarn deals specifically with Russian guerilla warfare behind the German lines and their victory in a local engagement. 'We Will Come Back,' depicting the fighting qualities of the Russian peasantry, is a deserved tribute to the people who gave the Nazis their most important lesson in modern warfare. *Mori.*

Blazing Guns

Monogram release of Robert Tansey production. Stars Ken Maynard and Hoot Gibson. Directed by Robert Tansey. Screenplay and original story, Frances

Kavanaugh; camera, Marcel Le Picard; editor, Fred Bain. At New York, N. Y., week Oct. 12, '43, dualed. Running time, 53 MINS.

Ken....................Ken Maynard
Hoot....................Hoot Gibson
Betty....................Kay Forrester
Duke Wade....................LeRoy Mason
Jim Wade....................Roy Grent
Governor....................Lloyd Ingram

'Blazing Guns' varies little from others in this Maynard-Gibson string of westerns for Monogram. There are the usual chases, rough'n-tumble fights, customary narrow escapes and climactic mass gun battle. But nonetheless okay cowboy fare.

This time the governor sends his two marshals to clean up a particularly lawless town. Gibson and Maynard, of course, are the two marshals. Kay Forrester furnishes the brief femme lure while support is headed by LeRoy Mason, Roy Grent and Lloyd Ingram. *Wear.*

Isle of Forgotten Sins

PRC release of Peter R. Van Duinen production. Stars John Carradine, Gale Sondergaard; features Sidney Toler, Rita Quigley, Frank Fenton, Veda Ann Borg, Rick Vallin, Betty Amann. Directed by Edgar G. Ulmer. Screenplay by Raymond L. Schrock based on story by Edgar G. Ulmer; camera, Ira Morgan; editor, Charles Henkel, Jr.; special effects, Gene Stone. At Strand, Brooklyn, week Oct. 14, '43, dualed. Running time, 82 MINS.

Clancy....................John Carradine
Marge....................Gale Sondergaard
Krogan....................Sidney Toler
Burke....................Frank Fenton
Diane....................Rita Quigley
Luana....................Veda Ann Borg
Johnny Pacific....................Rick Vallin
Olga....................Betty Amann
Christine....................Tala Birell
Bobbie....................Patti McCarty
Mimi....................Marian Colby
Native Chief....................William Edmonds

'Isle of Forgotten Sins,' an ambitious PRC feature, appears to have encountered numerous Hays code pitfalls. Result is jerky continuity in several spots, and a few vapid sequences. Fact that Director Edgar G. Ulmer also cooked up the original may have caused the meandering at a couple of junctures because several capable people are often submerged by the inane developments. It's good supporting feature despite these flaws.

Picture starts out like a rip-snorting tropical meller, embellished by scantity-garbed girls. Opening shot might even indicate the interior of a South Sea brothel; that's all cleared up quickly by making 'Isle of Forgotten Sins' Inn a cabaret-gambling spot. From this opening it swings into an outright quest for $3,000,000 in gold, lost when a steamer sunk near the harbor of this tropical isle. Story would have one believe the captain and purser saved their hides and were just waiting for a pair of sea-divers to come along and rescue the fortune. They do, and the captain and his assistants then grab the gold from them. A monsoon storm sweeps all the principals into the ocean. But the so-called heroic sea-divers and their sweethearts are washed up safely—minus the gold. Apparently it had to end that way according to the code.

John Carradine makes an acceptable pugnacious sea-driver, while Frank Fenton is good as his aide and fighting companion on the diving expeditions. Sidney Toler manages to breath some realism into the role of conniving captain of the scuttled steamer while Dick Vallin walks through as the partner in crime—the purser. Gale Sondergaard, cast as the proprietor of the gambling inn, seldom has a chance. Veda Ann Borg makes something of the native girl role, while excellent support is headed by Rita Quigley and Betty Amann.

Plenty of production value is in evidence, with the climactic storm specially well done. Ulmer's direction generally is better than his original story, while Gene Stone has done an okay special effects job. *Wear.*

Miniature Reviews

'Guadalcanal Diary' (20th). Dignified, absorbing and moving adaptation of the Richard Tregaskis best-seller. Big b.o.

'You're a Lucky Fellow, Mr. Smith' (Songs) (U). Tuneful comedy-drama programmer to fit nicely in regular duals.

'Gildersleeve On Broadway' (RKO). Filler for the duals where Gildersleeve will catch dialers.

'The Dancing Masters' (20th). Standard Laurel-Hardy comedy for the duals.

'In Old Oklahoma' (Rep). Standard adventure meller for nominally profitable b.o.

'Alaska Highway' (Par). Documentary value will overshadow yarn woven around it. okay dualer.

'Here Comes Elmer' (Rep). Al Pearce and radio gang have field day. Plenty of corn, but okay dualer.

'Wagon Tracks West' (Rep). Standard western dualer featuring Bill Elliott and 'Gabby' Hayes.

Guadalcanal Diary

20th Century-Fox release of Bryan Foy (Islin Auster) production. Features Preston Foster, Lloyd Nolan, William Bendix, Richard Conte, Anthony Quinn, Richard Jaeckel. Directed by Lewis Seiler. Screenplay, Lamar Trotti; adaptation, Jerry Cady; from book by Richard Tregaskis; camera, Charles Clarke; editor, Fred Allen. Reviewed in projection room, N. Y., Oct. 25, '43. Running time, 90 MINS.

Father Donnelly....................Preston Foster
Hook Malone....................Lloyd Nolan
Taxi Potts....................William Bendix
Captain Davis....................Richard Conte
Soose....................Anthony Quinn
Private Johnny Anderson....................Richard Jaeckel
Captain Cross....................Roy Roberts
Colonel Grayson....................Minor Watson
Ned Bowman....................Ralph Byrd
Butch....................Lionel Stander
Correspondent....................Reed Hadley
Lieutenant Thurmond....................John Archer
Tex....................Eddie Acuff
Dispatch Officer....................Harry Carter
Sammy....................Robert Rose
Major....................Jack Luden
Lieutenant....................Louis Hart
Captain....................Tom Dawson
Weatherby....................Miles Mander
Colonel Thompson....................Selmer Jackson
Colonel Merton....................Warren Ashe
Colonel Roper....................Walter Fenner
Chaplain....................Larry Thompson
Marines: David Peters, Martin Black, Charles Lang, George Holmes, Bob Ford, Russell Hoyt.

As 'Wake Island' (Par) and 'Bataan' (M-G) demonstrated, grim war films with all-male casts can, if well made, mop up at the boxoffice. For that reason, and because it's a fine and compelling film on its own, 'Guadalcanal Diary' should draw potent grosses.

To anyone unfamiliar with the Richard Tragaskis book, the picture version may or may not be a faithful adaptation of the original. But it is without question a painstaking, dignified and, in general, eloquent expression of a heroic theme. It is at times a sobering film and at other times an exalting one. It is also an almost continuously entertaining one.

The diary form of the original book is utilized in the picture. Opening with a quiet scene aboard a transport on a Sunday afternoon, as the Marine Corps task force steams toward an as-yet undisclosed objective, the story is narrated by an off-screen voice, fading in and out of the action sequences. Shown thus are the rendezvous with the rest of the convoy, the tense landing on the beach, the long and bitter fighting and the final, victorious retirement as Army replacements take over.

All this is admirably free from bombast and chauvinistic boasting. Although the deeds of the men are heroic, the men themselves reveal no self-consciousness of heroism. There are no lofty speeches about patriotism, or bravery, or the glory of death in battle. There are patriotism, bravery and death in battle. But the men don't give them hifalutin names. On the contrary, they are shown as hating war and killing, as frequently being afraid, as scorning sanctimoniousness, but doing a filthy, horrible job with dogged, unpretentious courage.

All the action isn't grim, of course. There are comedy moments, generally in the form of broad gags and slapstick, as seems plausible under the circumstances. There are also passages giving at least a suggestion of how savage the fighting against the Japs has become. Such shots include the bayoneting of wounded men, the trickery and treachery of fighting tactics, and, in one throat-catching sequence, the ambushing and slaughter of a Yank force on a tide-swept beach.

Reflecting the favorable turn of the war tide since 'Wake Island' and 'Bataan' drove home the seriousness of the Japanese offensive power and the ruthlessness of the Jap soldiers, 'Guadalcanal Diary' has a generally hopeful note. Thus, the task force convoy reaches its objective safely, the initial attack is successful and the subsequent fighting is almost invariably victorious. That makes the picture more cheerful and should provide pleasanter audience reaction and better word-of-mouth comment. At the same time, some of the critical aspects of the campaign are also suggested, such as the manner in which the Marines clung to the stretch of tropical sand for nearly three months without reinforcement and with few supplies.

With minor exceptions, 'Guadalcanal Diary' is skillfully produced. A few of the incidents seem synthetic and such scenes as the sinking of the Jap submarine are rather obviously faked, but in general both the action and the manner of its presentation are genuinely believable. Lewis Seiler's direction is positive and firm, and the photography is satisfactory.

Of the cast, William Bendix stands out in a juicy comedy-straight part as a tough-soft taxi driver from Brooklyn, while Preston Foster and Lloyd Nolan give effective performances in the other principal leads. Richard Conte (known as Nicholas Conte in legit), making his screen debut, registers in a fairly good straight part, and Richard Jaeckel scores as a downy-faced juvenile. Anthony Quinn, Roy Roberts and Eddie Acuff also click. *Hobe.*

You're a Lucky Fellow, Mr. Smith

(SONGS)

Hollywood, Oct. 22.

Universal release of Edward Lilley production. Stars Allan Jones; features Evelyn Ankers, Billie Burke, David Bruce, Patsy O'Connor, Stanley Clements, Kings Men. Directed by Felix Feist. Screenplay by Lawrence Riley, Ben Barzman, Louis Lantz; original, Oscar Brodney; camera, Paul Ivano; editor, Ray Snyder. Previewed Oct. 21, '43. Running time, 63 MINS.

Tony....................Allan Jones
Lynn....................Evelyn Ankers
Aunt Harriet....................Billie Burke
Harvey....................David Bruce
Peggy....................Patsy O'Connor
Squirt....................Stanley Clements
Goreni....................Luis Alberni
Doc Webster....................Francis Pierlot
Judge....................Harry Hayden
Porter....................Mantan Moreland

'You're a Lucky Fellow, Mr. Smith' displays an oft-told tale, but is backed with sufficient topnotch vocalizing by Allan Jones, The Kings Men and Patsy O'Connor, to make it acceptable program fare for dual bill support.

Lightly-textured plot is the formula girl-must-marry idea, with Evelyn Ankers en route to Chicago for marriage to David Bruce in order to secure inheritance. Young Miss O'Connor (cousin of Donald O'Connor) is along, and when pair are tossed into carload of soldiers, mischievous miss promotes romance between sister and Jones. Couple are tricked into marriage before arrival in Chicago, and then complications ensue when wife finds her unwanted husband's signature is required on all her checks. After sufficient footage of fluffy episodes, couple get together for final clinch.

Both Jones and Miss Ankers ably handle the lead spots, with major assistance from Miss O'Connor and juvenile Stanley Clements. Billie Burke displays her usual flustery characterization, while Luis Alberni is a screwball painter. Okay support provided by Bruce, Mantan Moreland and Francis Pierlot. Felix Feist provides good pace to the unfolding.

Song section mounts a number of standard published tunes, including 'Your Eyes Have Told Me So,' 'When You're Smiling' and 'What Is This Thing Called Love.' New song by Al Sherman and Harry Tobias, 'On the Crest of a Rainbow,' is smacked over by Jones and The Kings Men and can catch on when issued. In putting over comedy number, '10 Little Men With Feathers,' Patsy O'Connor displays showmanship delivery. Kings Men handle five songs in good style. *Walt.*

Gildersleeve on B'way

Hollywood, Oct. 21.

RKO release of Herman Schlom production. Stars Harold 'Gildersleeve' Peary. Directed by Gordon Douglas. Story and screenplay by Robert E. Kent; camera, Jack MacKenzie; editor, Les Millbrook; asst. director, Harry D'Arcy. Tradeshown in L. A. Oct. 21, '43. Running time, 65 MINS.

Gildersleeve....................Harold Peary
Mrs. Chandler....................Billie Burke
Francine Gray....................Claire Carleton
Peavey....................Richard LeGrand
Leroy....................Freddie Mercer
Homer....................Robert Cavanaugh
Margie....................Margaret Landry
Window Washer....................Leonid Kinskey
Matilda....................Ann Doran
Birdie....................Lillian Randolph
Jimmy....................Michael Road

Radio followers of Harold 'Gildersleeve' Peary will have to be super-loyal to sit through this cinematic display of his penchant for dropping into trouble. Strictly filler for the duals.

Story is a shoddy affair which bounces through maze of stupid situations that are laughed at—rather than with. Gildersleeve, in getting engaged to Ann Doran, hops to New York with Richard LeGrand for a druggists' convention, gets tangled with wealthy widow Billie Burke and blonde siren Claire Carleton. After series of ludicrous and decidedly ridiculous episodes, Gildersleeve winds up his stay for happy return to the hometown.

Peary transfers his Gildersleeve characterization to the screen with minor success, but he's chiefly handicapped by the inane material provided. Claire Carleton is a looker, but cast fails to do much with the inferior tale. Most of action takes place in a hotel rather than Broadway, which keeps production costs at low level. *Walt.*

The Dancing Masters

20th-Fox release of Lee Marcus production. Stars Laurel & Hardy. Directed by Mal St. Clair. Screenplay, W. Scott Darling, suggested by story by George Bricker; camera, Norbert Brodine; editor, Normal Colbert; music, Arthur Lange; music director, Emil Newman. Previewed in projection room, N. Y., Oct. 22, '43. Running time, 63 MINS.

Laurel & Hardy....................Themselves
Mary Harlan....................Trudy Marshall
Grant Lawrence....................Robert Bailey
Wentworth Harlan....................Matt Briggs
Mrs. Harlan....................Margaret Dumont

George Worthing................Allan Lane
Silvio........................George Paiva
Jasper........................George Lloyd
Mickey........................Bob Mitchum
Clerk.........................Edward Earle
Butler........................Charles Rogers
Dentist.......................Sherry Hall
Pianist.......................Sam Ash
Truck Driver..................William Haade
Director......................Arthur Space
Mother........................Daphne Pollard

'The Dancing Masters' is in the usual vein of Laurel-Hardy comedies, the type the youngsters would enjoy most. It's strictly for the duals.

'Masters' deals with the pair as penniless operators of a dancing school and the complications that evolve when they seek to help a young inventor exploit a new type of gun. The complications are manifold and the comedy always pretty obvious, bordering frequently on the slapstick, but it has considerable laughs despite some of the obviously contrived situations.

The starred pair go through their usual slapdash stuff, Laurel as the simpleton who's continuously doing the wrong thing and Hardy as the one who invariably gets clipped by the former's fol-de-rol. A driverless bus in which they're the lone passengers, and which weaves in and out of traffic, is typical of the comedy.

Mal St. Clair has milked the situations for laughs in his direction of W. Scott Darling's screenplay. *Kahn.*

In Old Oklahoma
(WITH SONG)
Hollywood, Oct. 20.

Republic release of Robert North production. Stars John Wayne, Martha Scott; features Albert Dekker. Directed by Albert S. Rogell. Original and adaptation, Thomson Burtis; screenplay, Ethel Hill, Eleanore Griffin; camera, Jack Marta; editor, Ernest Nims; special effects, Howard Lydecker, Jr. Previewed Oct. 19, '43. Running time, 100 MINS.

Dan Somers...................John Wayne
Catherine Allen..............Martha Scott
Hunk Gardner.................Albert Dekker
Desprit Dean.................George 'Gabby' Hayes
Bessie Baxar.................Marjorie Rambeau
'Cuddles' Walker.............Dale Evans
Richardson...................Grant Withers
Teddy Roosevelt..............Sidney Blackmer
The Cherokee Kid.............Paul Fix
Mrs. Ames....................Cecil Cunningham
Ben..........................Irving Bacon
Wilkins......................Byron Foulger
Mrs. Peabody.................Anne O'Neal
Walter.......................Richard Graham

Oklahoma oil fields and wildcatting at the turn of the century provides background for this outdoor action drama which is a standard entry of its type for datings in the regular houses for nominally profitable biz. Starring team of John Wayne and Martha Scott will catch marquee attention for top billing in most situations.

Plot hits formula lines with very little deviation from the main line. Miss Scott, rural teacher, has written sexy book which drums her out of town. Aboard train, she meets oil promoter Albert Dekker and cowboy Wayne, with obvious antagonism of the pair developing immediately. In the oil boom town, Dekker tries to obtain drilling leases from the Indians, with Wayne on the other side with the townsfolk to form an opposition syndicate. Wayne gets the leases with provision that oil is delivered within a specified time, which is accomplished despite obstacles placed in his path. Naturally he ropes the girl in the process.

Despite fact picture is filled with inconsistencies, it unrolls at such a fast clip that audiences will overlook such shortcomings, with speedy and lusty direction by Albert Rogell doing a slick cover-up. When conditions arise to prevent shipment of the oil to Tulsa under the deadline, climax is generated for wild ride of large number of wagons through brush fires and other obstacles to deliver and secure the

leases. It's regulation chase stuff, but too extended in footage for a top budget picture and editing would help to accentuate the spectacular sequence.

Wayne delivers neatly as the cowboy, with Miss Scott holding important attention as the girl, Dekker ably taking over the opposition. Good support is provided by George Hayes, Marjorie Rambeau, Grant Withers, Paul Fix and Byron Foulger. Dale Evans, Republic contract songstress, warbles 'Put Your Arms Around Me Honey' in dancehall in front of line of eight dancers. *Walt.*

Alaska Highway

Paramount release of Bill Pine and Bill Thomas production. Stars Richard Arlen, Jean Parker; features Ralph Sanford, Bill Henry, Joe Sawyer, Eddie Quillan. Directed by Frank McDonald. Screenplay, Maxwell Shane, Lewis R. Foster; asst. director, Charles Kerr; editor, William Ziegler; camera, Fred Jackman, Jr., A.S.C. At Strand, Brooklyn, dual, week Oct. 21. Running time, 66 MINS.

Woody Ormsby.................Richard Arlen
Ann Caswell..................Jean Parker
Frosty Gimble................Ralph Sanford
Roughhouse...................Joe Sawyer
Steve Ormsby.................Bill Henry
Sgt. Swithens................John Wegman
Pop Ormsby...................Harry Shannon
Blair Caswell................Edward Earle
Hank Lincoln.................Keith Richards
Pompadour Jones..............Eddie Quillan

Bill Pine and Bill Thomas hopped on the timeliness of completion of Alcan Highway as background for this one. It must have been an all-around hurry job, since it looks like the writers of the screenplay were hurried, too. Hence the story structure by Maxwell Shane and Lewis R. Foster shapes up little better than a documentary narrative; so does the film.

Story is the familiar conflict, of brother against brother for top spot in the affections of a gal. It all seems trivial to their dad, a hard-boiled contractor, what with the business of completing a vital road artery is at hand.

Pop Ormsby (Harry Shannon), erstwhile private contractor, is mustered in service as a Major in charge of Army Engineer Corps, which is to construct the road which connects Alaska with Canada. Richard Arlen, the elder son, wants to chuck it all for active service until Jean Parker arrives. Between work assignments he finds time to pitch woo with the gal, only to find out that his younger brother (Bill Henry) also has romantic leanings in that direction. On showdown each wants a release from assignment to go away and forget the girl. Father is fed up, eventually brings his boys to their senses, and the road is completed in time for the final clinch between Arlen and Miss Parker. Brace of thrillers incorporated include landslide and forest fire, but neither of a sock variety.

Shannon steals the picture as the patriotic contractor. His performance throughout is superb. Arlen gives a neat portrayal also, while Miss Parker is refreshing as the girl in the case, and Henry is okay as the younger brother. Frank McDonald's direction keeps story at an even pace.

Here Comes Elmer
(SONGS)

Republic release of Armand Schaefer production. Stars Al Pearce; features Frank Albertson, Dale Evans, Gloria Stuart, Artie Auerbach (Kitzel), Arlene Harris, William Comstock, 'Pinky' Tomlin, Wendell Niles, The Sportsmen, King Cole Trio, Jan Garber Band. Directed by Joseph Santley. Screenplay, Jack Townley and Stanley Davis; editor, Richard Van Enger; camera, Bud Thackery. At Strand, Brooklyn, dual, week Oct. 21. Running time, 74 MINS.

Al Pearce }
Elmer Blurt }................Al Pearce
Jean Foster..................Dale Evans
Joe Maxwell..................Frank Albertson
Glenda Forbes................Gloria Stuart
Wally Vernon.................Wally Vernon
Nick Cochrane................Nick Cochrane
Horace Parrot................Will Wright
P. J. Ellis..................Thurston Hall

Louis Burch..................Ben Welden
Postelwaite..................Chester Clute
Dr. Ziffy....................Luis Alberni
Johnson......................Tom Kennedy

Featuring radio's popular entertainers: Artie Auerbach as 'Kitzel,' Arlene Harris, William Comstock, 'Pinky' Tomlin, Wendell Niles, The Sportsmen, The King Cole Trio, and Jan Garber and His Band.

Corn pops aplenty in this modest budgeter, which provides a field day for Al Pearce and his radio gang. Pearce essays dual character—that of himself as radio star and Elmer Blurt, low-pressure salesman of the airwaves. Pearce's radio following in the hinterlands should go for this one in a big way.

There is a slight skein of story interwoven around Pearce's antics with Frank Albertson and Dale Evans handling romantic interludes. Pearce also is involved romantically with Gloria Stuart and Arlene Harris. It all adds up for plenty of laughs.

Albertson is contracted to back the Pearce radio show in a whistle-stop station. Sponsor is hard-fisted money-lender to whom Albertson is in debt. When Pearce nixes appearance of sponsor's sister, Arlene Harris, on the program, the skinflint forecloses on the band instruments. Albertson's gal (Dale Evans) is secretary to head of N.Y. radio station. In desperation he flashes phony telegram with offer from latter, and they're off to New York. The dizzy sister finances the trip on promise of being allowed to sing with band.

With all this buildup they do land a job at swank club with aid of Jan Garber, who augments with own band and batons it. Nitery buildup lands them a sponsor, and all ends well.

Story gives scope for interpolation of Pearce's standard radio stuff, utilizing Artie Auerbach (Kitzel), Arlene Harris, Wendell Niles, William Comstock, Pinky Tomlin, The Sportsmen, King Cole Trio and Jan Garber band, all doing precisely what they have been doing on the Al Pearce radio program.

Garber's orch spots several numbers in the nightclub and broadcast sequences, with Pinky Tomlin and Dale Evans also handling a couple of vocals satisfactorily. The Sportsmen and King Cole Trio also background in the musical interludes.

Pearce promulgates corny fun throughout, especially in the Elmer Blurt sequence. Frank Albertson and Dale Evans are okay as romantic vis-a-vis. Remainder of cast do all right in respective assignments. Joseph Santley's direction keeps story in lively tempo.

Wagon Tracks West

Republic release of Lou Gray production. Features Bill Elliott and George Hayes. Directed by Howard Bretherton. Screenplay, William Lively; camera, Reggie Lanning; editor, Charles Craft. At New York, N. Y., week of Oct. 19, '43, dual. Running time, 54 MINS.

Himself......................Wild Bill Elliott
Gabby Whittaker..............George 'Gabby' Hayes
Clawtooth....................Tom Tyler
Moonbush.....................Ann Jeffreys
Fleetwing....................Rick Vallin
Robert Warren................Robert Frazer
Laird........................Roy Barcroft
Brown Bear...................Charles Miller
Lem Martin...................Tom London
Matt.........................Cliff Lyons
Sheriff Summers..............Jack Rockwell

This one should hold its own dualed in nabe houses. It holds strictly to formula.

Wild Bill Elliott and Gabby Hayes require about 53 minutes to straighten out the situation, which centers around Rick Vallin, redskin medico fresh from the white man's college. Shunned by cattlemen and Indians alike, Vallin is put on the right road by Elliott and Hayes, who subdue Tom Tyler, the crooked medicine man, and Robert Frazer, corrupt Indian agent, as well as a few other assorted heavies. Vallin saves the community from ravages of a fever traced to the cattlemen's irrigation project and polluted drinking water.

Film provides more horseraces than a charity day at Belmont, and enough shooting to satisfy the most rabid western fan.

Femme lead could have been handled by a totem pole wired for sound. Anne Jeffreys, as the Indian maid, doesn't even get a chance to smile, has very few lines, and is completely eliminated from the story by the time Elliott rescues the redskin doctor from the hangman's noose in closing footage. As usual, Elliott and Hayes ride off to new adventures as the story ends. Roy Barcroft does okay as the Indian agent's stooge.

Miniature Reviews

'Old Acquaintance' (WB). Bette Davis and Miriam Hopkins due for hefty b.o. returns.

'Never a Dull Moment' (U). Ritz Bros., Frances Langford in screwball comedy; strong 'B' support.

'The Mad Ghoul' (Songs). (U). Horror dramatics will hit good box office in regular bookings.

'Son of Dracula' (U). Well set up horror drama to catch customers addicted to thrill-chills.

'Gangway for Tomorrow' (RKO). Programmer for the duals; no names.

'False Colors' (UA). Good western in the Hopalong Cassidy series.

'Beyond Last Frontier' (Rep.). Okay mustanger for duals.

Old Acquaintance

Hollywood, Nov. 2.

Warner Bros. release of Henry Blanke production. Stars Bette Davis, Miriam Hopkins; features Gig Young, John Loder, Dolores Moran. Directed by Vincent Sherman. Screenplay by John Van Druten and Lenore Coffee from stage play by van Druten; asst. director, Art Lueker; editor, Terry Morse; music director, Leo F. Forbstein; camera, Sol Polito. Tradeshown Nov. 1, '43. Running time, **110 MINS.**

Katherine Marlowe..........Bette Davis
Millie Drake..........Miriam Hopkins
Rudd Kendall..........Gig Young
Preston Drake..........John Loder
Deirdre..........Dolores Moran
Lucian Grant..........Philip Reed
Charlie Archer..........Roscoe Karns
Belle Carter..........Anne Revere
Harriet..........Esther Dale
Mademoiselle..........Ann Codee
Editor..........Joseph Crehan
Mr. Winter..........Pierre Watkin
Margaret Kemp..........Marjorie Hoshelle
Dean..........George Lessey
Saleslady..........Ann Doran
Deirdre (child)..........Francine Rufo

Film version of John Van Druten's comedy, presented on Broadway three years ago, in addition to getting expansion on the front end of the tale, switches the piece to straight dramatics, displaying strong love triangle. Picture is a strong attraction for the women and with both Bette Davis and Miriam Hopkins turning in persuasive performances, it's due for hefty boxoffice returns and holdovers generally.

Misses Davis and Hopkins were schoolgirl chums. With former leaving home town to carve literary career, while latter settles to happy marriage to John Loder. Bette Davis returns for lecture and, as guest of former pal, finds her with child and writer of hot sexy novels which she agrees to read and submit to publishers. Eight years later, Miss Hopkins is a successful pop novelist and hits New York with Loder and daughter for opening of Miss Davis' initial play. Latter sees pending breakup of marriage, tries to prevent it, even though Loder tells of his walkout and real love for her, which she shuns on account of her best friend. She attempts unsuccessfully to effect reconciliation. Next episode unfolds another 10 years, with Loder, now an Army major, renewing acquaintance with Miss Davis, but latter is being romanced by Gig Young, 10 years her junior. Moving swiftly to involvement, dramatics tosses young daughter into arms of Young, Loder is engaged to another woman, and the two schoolgirl chums find themselves together and alone for mutual companionship.

Miss Davis, as the willing one of frustrated romances, expertly handles her assignment for a spotlight performance. Miss Hopkins is also standout as the flustery and explosive wife and novelist, while Loder delivers excellently in a particularly meaty role of the male lead. Dolores Moran makes an important contribution as the ingenue, while Young clicks in his assignment.

Van Druten and Lenore Coffee have devised fine script from the original play, deftly moulding it to particular dramatic talents of Hopkins-Davis, while Vincent Sherman provides fine directing job. Photography is topnotch, with music score by Franz Waxman adding to dramatic tempo. *Walt.*

Never a Dull Moment

(SONGS)

Universal release of Howard Benedict production. Stars Ritz Brothers, Frances Langford; features Mary Beth Hughes, Jack LaRue, Stuart Crawford, Elizabeth Risdon. Directed by Edward Lilley. Screenplay, Mel Ronson, Stanley Roberts, from original by Roberts; camera, Charles Van Enger; editor, Paul Landres. Previewed in Projection Room, N. Y., Oct. 29, '43. Running time, **60 MINS.**

Three Funny Bunnies..........{Harry Ritz / Al Ritz / Jimmy Ritz}
Julie Russell..........Frances Langford
Dick Manning..........Stuart Crawford
Mrs. Scyler Manning..........Elizabeth Risdon
Flo..........Mary Beth Hughes
Tony Rocco..........George Zucco
Joey..........Jack LaRue
Romeo..........Sammy Stein
Mrs. Vandrake..........Barbara Brown
Commodore Barclay..........Douglas Wood
Murphy..........Charles Jordan

Geared for twin bills, 'Never a Dull Moment' is first-rate light, musical entertainment, strong as supporting picture on most dualers, with Ritz Brothers and Frances Langford providing the marquee lustre. Ritzes work better and with brighter material than they've had for some time.

Familiar story is used principally as background for the Ritzes' shenanigans, variety numbers and Miss Langford's neat warbling. Ritz Bros. pose as Chicago mobsters, taking job at a N. Y. nightclub under the impression they've been hired on their vaude rep as 'the Three Funny Bunnies.' When they learn that Mary Beth Hughes is a femme pickpocket hired by the nitery operator to pass the stolen jewels to them, the whacky trio attempts to duck out. Romance concerns the nightclub singer (Miss Langford) and a socialite.

Miss Langford clicks easily as the nitery songbird and photos neatly, registering solidly with such numbers as 'Sleepy Time Gal' and 'Blue Heaven.' Ritzes do several of their better routines, all solidly sold.

The nitery sequences offer the excuse to introduce the Igor-Pogi ballroom team and Rogers Dancers, both excellent. Production values are remarkably lavish for this type of picture. Jack LaRue, one of the nightclub's strong-arm boys, goes in for some comedy, but still remains the toughie menace. Miss Hughes makes a superb feminine dip and foil for one of the Ritz freres. Stuart Crawford, Elizabeth Risdon and George Zucco also go over.

Edward Lilley directed briskly and Charles Van Enger's cameraing is topflight. *Wear.*

The Mad Ghoul

(SONGS)

Hollywood, Oct. 29.

Universal release of Ben Pivar production. Features David Bruce, Evelyn Ankers, George Zucco, Robert Armstrong, Turhan Bey, Milburn Stone. Directed by James Hogan. Screenplay by Brenda Weisberg, Paul Gangelin; original, Hans Kraly; camera, Milton Krasner; editor, Milton Carruth. Previewed Oct. 28, '43. Running time, **64 MINS.**

Ted Allison..........David Bruce
Isabel Lewis..........Evelyn Ankers
Dr. Alfred Morris..........George Zucco
Ken McClure..........Robert Armstrong
Eric Iverson..........Turhan Bey
Macklin..........Milburn Stone
Eagan..........Andrew Tombes
Della..........Rose Hobart
Gavigan..........Addison Richards
Garrity..........Charles McGraw
Caretaker..........Gus Glassmire

Title easily tabs this one for the addicts of chill-thrill horror dramas. For those audiences, it's good entry that will catch okay coin at the wickets, and might surprise with above-par biz for a regulation programmer.

Story is a typical, 'mad doctor' idea, with chemistry professor George Zucco delving into research into ancient Egyptian gases that stun its victims, and requires heart fluid of a lately-deceased person for revival. Zucco enlists aid of medical student David Bruce for the research and deliberately gives the youth a dose of the gas. Yarn then runs through series of ghoulish episodes where pair obtain heart fluid to return Bruce to normal, while they follow Evelyn Ankers around a concert circuit to put reporter Robert Armstrong on the trail. Newsman's death gives clue that corners both Bruce and Zucco—after Bruce discovers the truth and gives the doctor a dose of the chemical gas.

Bruce and Zucco handle leads as victim and Svengali, respectively. Miss Ankers is nicely spotted as the girl singer, who delivers three classical numbers along the way. Armstrong is a zippy reporter; Turhan Bey the girl's accompanist; and Milburn Stone handles role of a detective. Rose Hobart has a brief spot as a society reporter.

In directing, James Hogan accentuates the horror aspects of the tale for consistent effect—as far as such a tale can go in plausibility. *Walt.*

Son of Dracula

Hollywood, Oct. 29.

Universal release of Ford Beebe (Donald H. Brown) production. Stars Lon Chaney; features Robert Paige, Louise Allbritton, Evelyn Ankers, Frank Craven, J. Edward Bromberg. Directed by Robert Siodmak. Screenplay by Eric Taylor; original, Curtis Siodmak; camera, George Robinson; editor, Saul Goodkind; asst. director, Melville Shyer. Previewed Oct. 28, '43. Running time, **79 MINS.**

Count Dracula..........Lon Chaney
Frank Stanley..........Robert Paige
Katherine Caldwell..........Louise Allbritton
Claire Caldwell..........Evelyn Ankers
Doctor Brewster..........Frank Craven
Professor Lazlo..........J. Edward Bromberg
Judge Simmons..........Samuel S. Hinds
Madame Zimba..Adeline DeWalt Reynolds
Sheriff Dawes..........Patrick Moriarity
Sarah..........Etta McDaniel
Colonel Caldwell..........George Irving

This is another in the profitable Universal series of 'Dracula' horror features which have been periodically turned out during the past dozen years. It's a good entry of its type, and due for coinful box office reception from the thrill-inclined customers.

Plot, in detailing the legendary transformation of humans to vampire form at night through throat-bites by a previous victim, ships Dracula's son (Lon Chaney) to a small town where Louise Allbritton is an occult follower. There's the usual lonely manse with surrounding woods; and killings by the night-flying vampire to arouse the countryside. Miss Allbritton marries Chaney, whom she believes to be a Hungarian count, and comes under his influence. Her affianced, Robert Paige, figures strange things going on, and compares notes with town doctor, Frank Craven, and psychologist J. Edward Bromberg. After usual series of suspenseful episodes, Paige is able to kill vampirish forms of both Chaney and Miss Allbritton for fadeout—but it's a cinch the Dracula stain will be revived again for further cinematic adventures.

Direction by Robert Siodmak points up the scarey dramatics of the tale, while low key lighting by George Robinson assists materially in plotting the unfolding. *Walt.*

Gangway for Tomorrow

RKO release of John H. Auer production, directed by Auer. Features Margo, John Carradine, Robert Ryan, Amelita Ward, William Terry, Wally Brown, Alan Carney. Screenplay, Arch Oboler, from original story by Aladar Laszlo; camera, Nicholas Mesuraca; music director, C. Bakaleinikoff; editor, George Crone. Tradeshown in N. Y., Nov. 1, '43. Running time, **69 MINS.**

Lisette..........Margo
Wellington..........John Carradine
Joe..........Robert Ryan
Mary..........Amelita Ward
Bob Nolan..........William Terry
Fred Taylor..........Harry Davenport
Burke..........James Bell
Jim Benson..........Charles Arnt
Sam..........Wally Brown
Swallow..........Alan Carney
Dan Barton..........Erford Gage
Colonel Mueller..........Richard Ryen
Pete..........Warren Hymer
Mechanic..........Michael St. Angel
Mechanic..........Don Dillaway
Hank..........Sam McDaniels
Radio Announcer..........John Wald

The boxoffice potential of the nationalistic spirit, of course, remains as strong a bet whatever the field of entertainment, and it is this factor that qualifies 'Gangway for Tomorrow' for whatever b.o. prominence it achieves. Minus names and budgeted for the duals, 'Gangway' skirts the propaganda borderline in its retrospect narrative of five persons and the story behind their employment in an American war plant.

It's an Arch Oboler screenplay, which may explain partially the 'different' kind of story that it is, for the radio scripter has apparently used considerable imagination in weaving this yarn from an original by Aladar Laszlo. John H. Auer's direction has captured the intent of the story, and so have the performers, but the story is not for generally popular consumption.

It's a yarn that tells the motivation behind the desire of five people to go to work in a plane factory. There was the French refugee (Margo), who had been active in the French underground movement before her escape to America. She went to work in the factory because that, assuredly, was her way to do her share in achieving the ultimate victory for her people. And so on.

Margo, John Carradine, Robert Ryan, Amelita Ward, William Terry, Wally Brown and Alan Carney head the cast, and all give plausible performances, but the general treatment keeps this strictly in the dual groove, which was apparently the ultimate intention anyway. *Kahn.*

False Colors

Hollywood, Oct. 30.

United Artists release of Harry Sherman (Lewis Rachmil) production. Stars William Boyd; features Andy Clyde, Jimmy Rogers. Directed by George Archainbaud. Original screenplay by Bennett Cohen; camera, Russell Harlan; editor, Fred Berger; asst. director, Glenn Cook. Previewed Oct. 29, '43. Running time, **64 MINS.**

Hopalong Cassidy..........William Boyd
California Carlson..........Andy Clyde
Jimmy Rogers..........Jimmy Rogers
Bud }
Kit }..........Tom Seidel
Faith..........Claudia Drake
Foster..........Douglas Dumbrille
Rip..........Bob Mitchum
Sonora..........Glenn Strange
Lefty..........Pierce Lyden
Sheriff Martin..........Roy Barcroft
Judge Stevens..........Sam Flint
Lawyer Griffen..........Earle Hodgins
Stevers..........Elmer Jerome

'False Colors' is the 49th in the Hopalong Cassidy series, and contains the familiar ingredients of heroics, broad comedy, fist and gun fights, and fast riding. It's a good entry for the western audiences.

Plot gives William Boyd and his pals, Andy Clyde and Jimmy Rogers, the assignment of exposing a ring which attempts to substitute an imposter for a murdered youth who is heir to a large cattle ranch. It's done in the usual vigorous and fighting western cinematic style, providing plenty of action along the way for the paying customers.

Jimmy Rogers, son of the late Will Rogers, is introduced as Hoppy's romantically-inclined sidekick, but displays camera fright in reading of his lines. Boyd continues his familiar role as the western hero, while Clyde delivers usual quota of broad comedy. Tom Seidel adequately handles a dual role; Claudia Drake is the girl; and Douglas Dumbrille heads the manipulating mob.

Direction by George Archainbaud hits a steady clip, while trademarked scenic backgrounds of the series are again present to add eye appeal for the slick camera work by Russell Harlan. *Walt.*

Beyond the Last Frontier

Republic release of Lou Gray production. Features Eddie Dew and Smiley Burnette. Directed by Howard Bretherton. Screenplay, John K. Butler and Morton Grant; camera, Bud Thackery; editor, Charles Craft; music, Mort Glickman. At New York, N. Y., week Oct. 26, '43, dual. Running time, 55 MINS.

John Paul Revere	Eddie Dew
Frog Millhouse	Smiley Burnette
Susan Cook	Lorraine Miller
Trigger Dolan	Bob Mitchum
Big Bill Hadley	Harry Woods
'Sarge' Kincaid	Ernie Adams
Steve Kincaid	Richard Clarke
Major Cook	Charles Miller
Clyde Barton	Kermit Maynard

'Beyond the Last Frontier' starts off with something relatively fresh as the reason for all the shooting. The reason holds up fairly well until the plot based on it gets too complicated. But this hoss opry is adequate for the grade.

Pic introduces Eddie Dew as a Western hero. He is out of Coast stock and shows up as a personable young fellow who handles his not-too-difficult role easily. Smiley Burnette, co-featured, turns in an acceptable performance as Dew's heart-of-gold sidekick.

'Beyond' deals with the redoubtable Texas Rangers and a gang of outlaws trying to run contraband through Ranger territory. The prairie cops have a fingerman (Dew) planted among the badmen, and the crooks are running into plenty of trouble. Gang succeeds in planting a stool-pigeon among the Rangers. The rest of the film then revolves around these two spies chasing each other amidst much shooting and scenery.

The love interest is negligible, but counter-spy angle gets so involved the N. Y. audience snickered at one point when film was caught. Pic suffers from bad location lighting at several places. Direction and photography are standard.

Miniature Reviews

'Riding High' (Musical; Color) (Par). Fast - moving musical spells plenty of b.o. wampum.

'Cry Havoc' (M-G). Drama with all-femme cast tossed into Bataan bomb shelter. Stars will carry it.

'Happy Land' (20th). Stout boxoffice with holdovers in most spots.

'His Butler's Sister' (U). A top attraction in the Deanna Durbin series.

'No Time for Love' (Par). Claudette Colbert, Fred MacMurray starred in laugh-provoking comedy. Okay b.o.

'The Cross of Lorraine' (M-G). Well made, but heavy drama, unfolding in a German military prison camp.

'Footlight Glamour' (Col). Fourteenth in 'Blondie' series saved by plenty of slapstick. Okay as lower dualer.

'Government Girl' (RKO). Synthetic tale of overcrowded Washington will catch moderate attention in regular runs.

'Henry Aldrich Haunts a House' (Par). Satisfactory chiller for the duals.

'The Falcon and the Co-Eds' Good entry in the Falcon whodunit series.

'Yellow Canary' (Brit.). Anna Neagle and Richard Greene spy meller should do okay on both hemispheres.

'Drums of Fu Manchu' (Rep). So-so thriller adapted from serial; passable for kid audiences and nabes.

'Minesweeper' (Par). Deals with Navy's attempt to clear U.S. sea lanes of mines. OK dualer.

'Man From the Rio Grande' (Rep). Don 'Red' Barry has Twinkle Watts as support in this standard 'B' western dualer.

'Deerslayer' (Rep). Mediocre Indian drama of nickleodeon-day period. For filler dates at kid matinees.

'The Lamp Still Burns' (Brit.). Rates as one of top English films of year. Produced by late Leslie Howard.

Riding High
(Color)
(MUSICAL)

Paramount release of Fred Kohlmar production. Stars Dorothy Lamour, Victor Moore, Dick Powell; features Cass Daley, Gil Lamb, Milt Britton band. Directed by George Marshall. Screenplay by Walter DeLeon, Arthur Phillips and Art Arthur, based on play, 'Ready Money,' by James Montgomery; songs, Ralph Rainger & Leo Robin, and Johnny Mercer, Harold Arlen, Joseph J. Lilley; music, Victor Young; camera, Karl Struss, Harry Hallenberger; editor, LeRoy Stone; dances, Danny Dare; process photography, Farciot Edouart. Tradeshown N. Y., Nov. 4, '43. Running time, 89 MINS.

Ann Castle	Dorothy Lamour
Steve Baird	Dick Powell
Mortimer J. Slocum	Victor Moore
Bob 'Foggy' Day	Gil Lamb
Tess Connors	Cass Daley
Themselves	Milt Britton and Band
Chuck Stewart	Bill Goodwin
Sam Welch	Rod Cameron
Jack Holbrook	Glen Langan
Jean Holbrook	Louise La Planche
Blanche	Marie McDonald
P. D. Smith	Andrew Tombes
Brown	Douglas Fowley
Jones	Tim Ryan
Masters	Pierre Watkin
Train Conductor	Stanley Pine
Cowboy	Dwight Butcher
Cowboy	Lane Chandler
Train Conductor	James Flavin
Porter	Charles R. Moore
Cowboy	William Edwards
Pete Brown	James Burke

With Dorothy Lamour, Victor Moore and Dick Powell for the marquee, exhibs have plenty to play with in this escapist musical. The comedy is packed around a western yarn with superb Technicolor an added asset. In toto, it represents plenty of wampum at the wickets—extended runs and high grosses.

Lots of ingredients for a b.o. musical are in this one, and George Marshall makes the most of a rather flimsy framework. An ex-burlesque principal (Dorothy Lamour) lands back at her father's ill-fated silver mine out in Arizona when her show folds. She finds that mining engineer Dick Powell is also back after trying unsuccessfully to sell stock in same mine. Miss Lamour takes a job at the elaborate Dude Ranch cabaret, run by Cass Daley, in order to help her dad. Victor Moore, slick counterfeiter wanted in many states, persuades Powell to merely flash the phoney lucre. Trick works, there's a rush to grab the mining stock at any price and usual payoff, when the mine actually comes in.

Miss Lamour gets more to do and displays more talent than in previous vehicles. Also, she dances, her terps in 'Secretary to the Sultan' clicking. She's also a bit revealing in 'Injun Gal Heap Hep,' one of elaborate production bits which permits Gil Lamb to do his eccentric dancing.

Victor Moore fits snugly into the counterfeiter role, his droll witticisms being solid throughout. Opening poker game sequence, an oldie, is given a new twist, but is topped by the series of succeeding gags. Cass Daley makes the grade in her rough-'n'-ready part of Dude Ranch owner, on the make for Moore. Her mugging is held to a minimum excepting in 'Willie, the Wolf of the West,' comedy song-dance number, played with all stops out. Containing many bits from her vaude act, it's a howl. Powell is Powell again, but managing to carry the romance with Miss Lamour nicely. Lamb, as the under-sheriff seeking the counterfeiter, plays it dumb right to the hilt for top returns. He also tees off the mad act of the Milt Britton band, as an amateur musician making his debut. This builds into the familiar roughhouse band routine. All done countless times before on the stage, but deft direction and cameraing take in every angle for strong results. It's one of funniest scenes in film. There's a chuck-wagon race, with the counterfeit coin figuring, as a climax that's high slapstick, but socko.

Of the several songs, 'You're the Rainbow,' dueted by Miss Lamour and Powell, 'Whistling in the Light' and 'Secretary to the Sultan' appear most likely. 'Get Your Man,' with the femmes in 'mountie' garb, is given a nice buildup, with the chorus doing a trimly executed drill.

Picture has been given strong mounting by producer Fred Kohlmar. Karl Struss and Harry Hallenberger contribute A-1 camera work with the uniformly fine photography helped by excellent color supervision of Natalie Kalmus. *Wear.*

Cry Havoc

Hollywood, Nov. 6.

Metro release of Edwin Knopf production. Stars Margaret Sullavan, Ann Sothern, Joan Blondell; features Fay Bainter, Marsha Hunt, Ella Raines, Frances Gifford, Diana Lewis, Heather Angel, Dorothy Morris. Directed by Richard Thorpe. Screenplay by Paul Osborn, based on play by Allan R. Kenward; camera, Karl Freund; editor, Ralph E. Winters. Tradeshown in L. A. Nov. 5, '43. Running time, 96 MINS.

Lieut. Smith	Margaret Sullavan
Pat	Ann Sothern
Grace	Joan Blondell
Capt. Marsh	Fay Bainter
Flo Norris	Marsha Hunt
Connie	Ella Raines
Helen	Frances Gifford
Nydia	Diana Lewis
Andra	Heather Angel
Sue	Dorothy Morris
Sadie	Connie Gilchrist
Steve	Gloria Grafton
Luisita	Fely Franquelli

Film version of the over-theatric play which was originally presented at a Hollywood little theatre under 'Cry Havoc' and taken to New York under title of 'Proof Thro' the Night,' is a decidedly staged piece which is far removed from present film entertainment requirements. Only starring trio of Margaret Sullavan, Ann Sothern and Joan Blondell gives sufficient marquee voltage for billtopping position in key bookings.

Plot sets up all-femme cast tossed into a bomb shelter at Bataan, with nine girls rounded up from evacuation of Manila to function as volunteers at an outland field hospital. Each of the nine are from various fields of endeavor, including waitress Ann Sothern, and former burleyque performer Joan Blondell. Girls are assigned auxiliary spots around the camp, but practically all of the footage centers in the bomb shelter for lengthy dialog and mental reactions of the individuals as the going gets tougher. Miss Sullavan, as Army nurse in charge of the contingent, keeps moving despite severe suffering from malignant malaria. At the finish, with the Japs closing in, the girls bravely march out of the shelter to surrender to the Nips.

Best thing about the film is the capable cast tossed in for group of generally fine performances, despite the inadequacies of the plot in both suspense and movement. Miss Sullavan delivers strong portrayal of the Army nurse, with Misses Sothern and Blondell clicking solidly in respective roles. Others of the dozen girls do okay, although at times it is hard to distinguish individual personalities due to khaki uniforms and generally smudged faces. Richard Thorpe is restricted on direction to following too stagey a script, with no chance of generating more than nominal suspense at points where it should reach peaks. *Walt.*

Happy Land

20th-Fox release of Kenneth Macgowan production. Stars Don Ameche, Frances Dee, Harry Carey; features Ann Rutherford, Richard Crane, Larry Olsen, Henry Morgan. Directed by Irving Pichel. Screenplay by Kathryn Scola and Julien Josephson from MacKinlay Kantor's novel; camera, Joseph La Shelle; editor, Dorothy Spencer; special effects, Fred Sersen; music, Emil Newman. Tradeshown in N. Y. Nov. 9, '43. Running time, 75 MINS.

Lew Marsh	Don Ameche
Agnes	Frances Dee
Gramp	Harry Carey
Lenore Prentiss	Ann Rutherford
Gretchen Barry	Cara Williams
Rusty	Richard Crane
Tony Cavrek	Henry Morgan
Judge Colvin	Minor Watson
Peter Orcutt	Dickie Moore
Bill Beecher	William Weber
Father Case	Oscar O'Shea
Mrs. Schneider	Adeline De Walt Reynolds
Velma	Roseanne Murray
Rusty (age 12-16)	James West
Rusty (age 5)	Larry Olsen
Sam Kendall	Bernard Thomas
Arch	Terry Masengale
Bud	Edwin Mills
Everett Moore	James J. Smith
Emmy	Mary Wickes
Jake Hibbs	Walter Baldwin
Mr. MacMurray	Tom Stevenson
Mrs. Prentiss	Aileen Pringle
Mr. Prentiss	Matt Moore
Lenore Prentiss (age 12)	Darla Hood
Reverend Wood	Richard Abbott
Mattie Dyer	Lillian Bronson
Mayor	Ferris Taylor
Andy	Larry Thompson
Pop Schmidt	Paul Weigel
Jackie	Ned Dobson, Jr.
Ted	Jackie Averill
Clerk	Joe Bernard
Sam Watson	Housley Stevens
Joe	Elvin Field
Sally Pierce	Juanita Quigley
Shep Wayne	Milton Kibbee
Charles Clayton	John Dilson
Old Ben	Leigh Whipper
Teacher	Marjorie Cooley
Old Man Bowers	Robert Dudley
Dr. Hammond	Pass Le Noir

MacKinlay Kantor's novel, which appeared in serial form in the Saturday Evening Post and Reader's Digest, has been turned into a strong tear-jerker mainly through the keen production given by Kenneth Macgowan and directorial skill of Irving Pichel. Combined efforts of this pair, plus a trim writing job, sets off a string of performances topped by Don Ameche, Frances Dee, Harry Carey and Richard Crane. Story is particularly applicable to times, dealing with a father whose son is killed in action.

On sheer dramatic values and superb performances, 'Happy Land' looms as a highly profitable grosser, with holdovers likely in most spots. Picture has an extensive ready-made audience if readers of the original story can be sold.

Kathryn Scola and Julian Josephson's scripting has successfully spotlighted the situation for those who have lost sons in the present war. 'Happy Land' is the story of a typical Iowa country town and a typical family (the Marshes), their joys, disappointments and sorrows. Plot has drugstore operator Ameche bereaved over the loss of his son, killed in naval action. Return of Gramp, his father, dead for some 25 years, in the form of an apparition, is the device used to unfold the principal story up until Richard Crane is killed in service. Explanation of this visionary appearance is that Gramp has returned to set Ameche right, since the grief-stricken father claims that Crane never really lived—never had a home of his own, had not married, etc.

Flashback method then traces the life of the youngster from birth, through Boy Scout days, high school, vacations at home, work in the drugstore and finally to university—then volunteering for the Navy. It shows Ameche as he came back from the First World War, his happy marriage—and devotion to his young son. The homey, down-to-earth touches in this story of the Marsh family are the real meat of the picture. One is told that Lew Marsh imagines all this, with the vision introduced to lend realism on the screen.

Climax is when one of the boy's pals in the navy visits the Marsh family and gives them the first-hand account of how their son gave his life attempting to save others.

Don Ameche, usually in lighter roles, makes the character of Lew Marsh a vivid profile. It is a role that might easily be overdone, but isn't. Frances Dee, as his wife, is outstanding as the understanding mate. Harry Carey turns in his usual strong performance as Gramp, the Civil War veteran, who sets Marsh straight. Ann Rutherford is topnotch as Rusty's sweetheart, while Richard Crane does yeoman work as the Rusty of high school and Navy age. Larry Olsen is clever as the Rusty of five years. Henry Morgan, cast as Tony, pal of Rusty in the Navy, does well with a dramatic bit. Unusually big and well-picked supporting cast is headed by Minor Watson, Cara Williams, Dickie Moore, Oscar O'Shea, Richard Abbott and Roseanne Murray.

Besides his intelligent direction, Irving Pichel has made smart use of patriotic tunes and musical score to accentuate the yarn. Joseph La Shelle contributes a uniformly excellent camera job, while Dorothy Spencer's editing is topflight.

Wear.

His Butler's Sister
(SONGS)

Hollywood, Nov. 9.

Universal release of Felix Jackson production. Directed by Frank Borzage. Stars Deanna Durbin, Pat O'Brien and Franchot Tone; features Evelyn Ankers, Akim Tamiroff, Alan Mowbray, Frank Jenks, Walter Catlett and Elsa Jansen. Screenplay, Samuel Hoffenstein and Betty Reinhardt; editor, Ted Kent; camera, Woody Bredell. Previewed Nov. 8, '43, at Egyptian. Running time, **92 MINS.**

Ann Carter	Deanna Durbin
Martin Carter	Pat O'Brien
Charles Gerard	Franchot Tone
Liz Campbell	Evelyn Ankers
Severina	Elsa Jansen
Mortimer Kalb	Walter Catlett
Popoff	Akim Tamiroff
Buzz	Alan Mowbray
Emmet	Frank Jenks
Moreno	Sig Arno
Reeves	Franklin Pangborn
Brophy	Andrew Tombes

Universal swings strictly to the Cinderella formula for plot of Deanna Durbin's 13th starrer, 'His Butler's Sister.' Neatly contrived situations, consistently good pace, excellent cast and four songs by Miss Durbin combine to make this a top attraction of the Durbin series.

Familiar plot is embellished with fine performances and entertaining situations. Miss Durbin hits New York from her Indiana town to embark on a singing career through visit to older brother, Pat O'Brien, whom she figures wealthy but who's in reality the butler to composer Franchot Tone. She's inducted as maid in the bachelor penthouse but fired in two days on insistence of O'Brien, afraid of losing his job if she sings to catch Tone's attention. Of course the composer becomes interested in girl, they fall in love, O'Brien separates them, but the pair are finally reunited for the fadeout clinch.

Despite tale's fragility, picture is brimful of light and amusing situations to attune it perfectly to present audience requirements for escapist fare. Miss Durbin is spotlighted with fine performance as the young and ambitious singer, getting sensitive direction under Frank Borzage. Four songs, all in top voice, include the aria, 'Turnadot,' the Victor Herbert-Henry Blossom 'When You're Away,' a 'Russian Medley,' arrangement by Max Rabinowitch, and a new tune by Bernie Grossman and Walter Jurman, 'In the Spirit of the Moment,' which has a chance for pop attention.

O'Brien clicks solidly as the buttling older brother, while Tone effectively carries romantic responsibilities. Akim Tamiroff, Alan Mowbray, Frank Jenks and Sig Arno comprise a semi-comedy combo; Walter Catlett is a wacky stage producer, and Elsa Janssen stands out as the kindly cook. Borzage's direction is consistent throughout and smacks over numerous attention-arresting episodes for maximum attention. Original screenplay by Sam Hoffenstein and Betty Reinhardt displays fine craftsmanship, while producer Felix Jackson demonstrates innate knowledge of cinematic story requirements for best display of Miss Durbin's talents. Production is topgrade in all technical departments.

Walt.

No Time for Love

Paramount release of Mitchell Leisen (Fred Kohlmar) production. Directed by Leisen. Stars Claudette Colbert and Fred MacMurray; features Ilka Chase, Richard Haydn, Paul McGrath, June Havoc. Screenplay, Claude Binyon; adaptation, Warren Duff; from story by Robert Lees and Fred Rinaldo; camera, Charles Lang, Jr.; music, Victor Young; editor, Alma Macrorie. Tradeshown in N. Y., Nov. 5, '43. Running time, **83 MINS.**

Katherine Grant	Claudette Colbert
Jim Ryan	Fred MacMurray
Hoppy Grant	Ilka Chase
Roger	Richard Haydn
Henry Fulton	Paul McGrath
Darlene	June Havoc
Sophie	Marjorie Gateson
Christley	Bill Goodwin
Kent	Robert Herrick
Dunbar	Morton Lowry
Clancy	Rhys Williams
Moran	Murray Alper
Morrisey	John Kelly
Leon Brice	Jerome DeNuccio
Pete Hanagan	Grant Withers
Taylor	Rod Cameron
Company President	Willard Robertson

Escapist is the word, and 'No Time for Love' is just that, in spades. Starring Claudette Colbert and Fred MacMurray in a Claude Binyon screenplay that's heavily loaded for laughs, this Paramount pic is rather obviously contrived in some of its situations, but there's no denying a sufficiency of crack dialog—and the laughs that go with it—to make for strong boxoffice.

Mitchell Leisen has handled both the production and direction reins, giving 'No Time' both barrels on each count. There's a nifty set of characters, and some of them should be provocatively topical in their apparent copy—at least partially—from several real-life personalities of the New York and Hollywood literati set.

Story concerns a famous femme photographer for a national picture magazine (Miss Colbert), and the complications that evolve when, on an assignment to lens a tunnel construction project, she meets up with a sandhog (MacMurray).

From there on the basic story is pretty much pretense, but the laughs come fast, and the performances by Miss Colbert and MacMurray are capital. There's one riotous sequence, in particular, when MacMurray jealously eyes one of those body beauts posing for Miss Colbert and seeks to show him up. It's scathing satire aimed at the so-called 'strong' men, and Miss Colbert at times also contributes a caricature of the profession she characterizes.

Miss Colbert emphasizes her flair for comedy and doesn't spare herself either in relegating her usual sartorial elegance for the sake of serious story values, as indicated in the climactic scene when she gets spilled into a lake of spewing mud from a tunnel cave-in. The scene is played straight, and it might ordinarily have seemed dangerous for an actress of Miss Colbert's always superbly coutouriered manner to have become involved in such an undignified situation, but there should be scarcely a thought in that direction since Leisen's direction has caught the scene as intended.

Cast of supporting players is headed by Ilka Chase, Richard Haydn, Paul McGrath and June Havoc, and all give nifty performances, though their parts are limited in scope because the story is so pertinently directed at the starred pair. Miss Chase is in one of her usual sophisticated roles, that of Miss Colbert's sister. The character could have been given greater substance. Haydn is okay as the somewhat parasitic composer, McGrath is the magazine publisher and boss of Miss Colbert, with whom she's affianced until she meets Mr. Muscles, while June Havoc is the tough chorine who makes a play for MacMurray.

The story itself could have been more plausible in spots, namely the pat final scenes in which MacMurray is suddenly revealed as somewhat of an engineer—a guy with brains—instead of just another sandhog. It's a switch belied by the dese-dose-dem characterization MacMurray gives during the entire pic. But then, the 'smart' Miss Colbert couldn't very well team up with just another sandhog, could she?

Kahn.

The Cross of Lorraine

Hollywood, Nov. 10.

Metro release of Edwin Knopf production. Features Jean Pierre Aumont, Gene Kelly, Sir Cedric Hardwicke, Richard Whorf, Joseph Calleia, Peter Lorre, Hume Cronyn. Directed by Tay Garnett. Screenplay by Michael Kanin and Ring Lardner, Jr., Alexander Esway, Robert D. Andrews; based on story by Lilo Demert and Robert Aisner, and 'A Thousand Shall Fall,' by Hans Hebe; camera, Sidney Wagner; editor, Dan Milner. Tradeshown in L. A. Nov. 9, '43. Running time, **89 MINS.**

Paul	Jean Pierre Aumont
Victor	Gene Kelly
Father Sebastian	Sir Cedric Hardwicke
Francois	Richard Whorf
Rodriguez	Joseph Calleia
Sergt. Berger	Peter Lorre
Duval	Hume Cronyn
Louis	Billy Roy
Major Bruhl	Tonio Selwart
Jacques	Jack Lambert
Pierre	Wallace Ford
Marcel	Donald Curtis
Rene	Jack Edwards, Jr.
Lieut. Schmidt	Richard Ryen
Corporal Daxer	Frederick Giermann

Detailing the graphic adventures of French war prisoners who submitted to Nazi armistice promises and were carted off to German military camps, with subsequent tortures, cruelties and starvation by their captors in an attempt to bend them to the new order, 'The Cross of Lorraine' is heavy drama. Its boxoffice appeal will depend a lot on its selling.

As a cinematic reenactment of various factual information on treatment of former French soldiers in German military encampments, picture provides a vivid display of barbaric tortures by the Nazis. It's too stolid and gruesome, without any semblance of lightness.

Story unfolds slowly, with much footage given over to individual characterizations and the effect of the Nazi double-crossing of the French soldiers. The camp living conditions, the cruelties and ruthlessness of the German officers, and gradual starvation of the prisoners are vividly sketched in episodic fashion.

Opening picks up at the Franco-German armistice, with French soldiers surrendering on promises of being returned to their homes and families. One group is herded into a boxcar and dumped off at camp in occupied France. Gene Kelly is tortured without submitting to German demands to cooperate; Jean Pierre Aumont unwillingly keeps in line until time arrives to get his friends out to freedom, and across the line into unoccupied France where they can sneak off to join the Free French forces.

All-male cast is adequately set up, with entire troupe providing excellent individual characterizations under deft direction by Tay Garnett, who was not wholly able to overcome the heaviness of the script. Picture is adequately mounted in all production departments.

Walt.

Footlight Glamour

Columbia release of Frank Strayer production. Features Penny Singleton, Arthur Lake and Larry Simms. Directed by Frank Strayer. Screenplay, Karen DeWolfe and Connie Lee, based on comic strip, 'Blondie,' by Chic Young; camera, Philip Tannura; editor, Richard Fantl. At Fox, Brooklyn, dual, week of Nov. 5, '43. Running time, **68 MINS.**

Blondie	Penny Singleton
Dagwood	Arthur Lake
Alexander	Larry Simms
Vicki Wheeler	Ann Savage
J. C. Dithers	Jonathan Hale
Mr. Crum	Irving Bacon
Cookie	Marjorie Ann Mutchie
Alvin Fuddle	Danny Mummert
Randolph Wheeler	Thurston Hall
Mrs. Dithers	Grace Hayle
Jerry Grant	Rafael Storm
Daisy	Himself

This 14th in the 'Blondie' series is a routine job, but manages to net laughs in last few reels via a slapstick play-within-a-play. Thanks to this angle, it makes the b.o. grade as a dualer.

Story concerns efforts of a real estate promoter, Jonathan Hale, to induce a tool manufacturer (Thurston Hall) to set up a war plant near former's new apartment houses. Hale enlists aid of his employee, Arthur Lake. But plans are nearly gummed up when Lake's wife, Penny Singleton, helps produce a play written by Hall's daughter, Ann Savage. Hall has been opposing daughter's stage career.

Situations built around efforts to keep Hall from seeing the play, and hoked-up production of the play itself, provide the laughs. Usual slapstick devices such as wrong sound effects, trapdoors that open when they shouldn't, and fumbled lines go over big. Performances of Lake, Miss Singleton, Larry Simms and Daisy, the dog, are delivered in standard 'Bumstead' manner. Supporting players turn in workmanlike jobs.

Good pace prevents otherwise weak script from bogging down film.

Government Girl

Hollywood, Nov. 4.

RKO release of Dudley Nichols production. Stars Olivia de Havilland and Sonny Tufts; features Anne Shirley. Directed by Nichols. Screenplay, Nichols. Adapted by Budd Schulberg from story by Adela Rogers St. John; camera, Frank Redman; editor, Roland Gross. Tradeshown in L. A., Nov. 3, '43. Running time, 91 MINS.

Smokey.............Olivia de Havilland
Browne.......................Sonny Tufts
May.........................Anne Shirley
Dana..........................Jess Barker
Sergeant Joe..................James Dunn
Branch.......................Paul Stewart
Mrs. Wright..............Agnes Moorehead
Senator MacVickers.......Harry Davenport
Mrs. Harris...................Una O'Connor
His Excellency..................Sig Ruman
Miss Trask...................Jane Darwell
Count Bodinski..............George Givot

'Government Girl' satirically endeavors to picture the confusion surrounding the girls living and working in overcrowded Washington. The idea is good, but the results are not up to expectations. Picture strains to generate spontaneity, but only partially accomplishes that aim. With marquee voltage of Olivia de Havilland and newcomer Sonny Tufts, picture will roll through regular runs as a billtopper for moderately profitable biz.

Dudley Nichols debuts as a director here, but hardly measures up on that end. He overplays situations and characters, and never quite gets the tale into an effervescing groove. Miss de Havilland is forced to hit broad slapsticks and mugging in handling the title spot, and delivers a synthetic portrayal that never rings true.

Miss de Havilland plays an office worker in War Construction Board offices. Tufts is a brilliant young production engineer brought in as a dollar-a-year man to speed up the plane output. Pair's introduction is coupled with a wild and broadly Sennettized motorcycle chase around Washington, and they team up as boss and secretary in the wild confusion of the capital. Tufts breaks bottlenecks with disregard of red tape, while the girl is continually bewildered by his actions in filching priorities of other divisions in order to speed plane production. There's skullduggery, with promotion for a Senate committee investigation, with Miss de Havilland strangely appearing to make a rousing speech in Tuft's behalf to squelch the proceedings.

Running gag, which starts at opening with marriage of Anne Shirley to Army sergeant James Dunn in a crowded hotel lobby, has the couple trying to find a room for their honeymoon night, which they finally tab right at the finish. It's overdone with too frequent footage, but serves purpose for mild laughs at times.

Tufts clicks as the engineer, and again shows that he is of definite starring timber. In addition to Miss Shirley and Dunn, Jess Barker, Paul Stewart and Agnes Moorehead are most prominent in support. *Walt.*

Henry Aldrich Haunts a House

Paramount release of Michel Kraike production. Features Jimmy Lydon, Charles Smith, John Litel, Olive Blakeney, Joan Mortimer, Vaughan Glaser. Directed by Hugh Bennett. Screenplay, Val Burton, Muriel Roy Bolton; camera, Daniel L. Fapp, editor, Everett Douglas. Tradeshown in New York, Nov. 5, '43. Running time: 73 MINS.

Henry Aldrich................Jimmy Lydon
Dizzy Stevens..............Charles Smith
Mr. Aldrich......................John Litel
Mrs. Aldrich................Olive Blakeney
Elise Towers..................Joan Mortimer
Mr. Bradley...............Vaughan Glaser
Whit Bidecker..................Jackie Moran
Mr. Quid...................Lucien Littlefield
Olin Bidecker...............George Anderson
Shadow.........................Mike Mazurki
Chief of Police Reedy........Edgar Dearing
Clannahan......................Charles Cane
Clannahan's Assistant.........Kernan Cripps
Charlie..........................Jack Gardner
Kid..............................William Inman
The Mayor.......................Ferris Taylor
Mrs. Norris........................Anita Bolster
Dr. Danford...............George M. Carleton
Police Officer......................Dick Rush
Beamish............................Ray Walker
Mr. Wright...................George Sherwood
Mr. Bellows.........................Paul McVey
Sykes..............................Paul Phillips

Spook programmer, fashioned along familiar lines, will serve as an adequate dualer.

Latest in the 'Henry Aldrich' series plants the title character (Jimmy Lydon) in an old mansion filled with stuffed animals, skeletons and the usual assortment of trapdoors, creaking wall panels and miscellaneous sound effects.

Youngster swallows a new chemical, supposedly with properties designed to develop three times the normal strength. The school principal is believed murdered and the youngster at first is under the delusion that he committed the crime while under the influence of the drug.

Picture is lacking in comedy relief. Casting is okay, camera work standard and production values satisfactory. *Mori.*

Falcon and the Co-Eds
(ONE SONG)

Hollywood, Nov. 5.

RKO release of Maurice Geraghty production. Stars Tom Conway. Directed by William Clemens. Screenplay, Ardel Wray and Gerald Geraghty; original story by Ardel Wray. Based on character created by Michael Arlen; camera, Roy Hunt; editor, Theron Warth. Tradeshown in L. A., Nov. 4, '43. Running time, 67 MINS.

Falcon..........................Tom Conway
Vicky............................Jean Brooks
Marguerita......................Rita Corday
Jane.........................Amelita Ward
Mary..........................Isabel Jewell
Graelich......................George Givot
Donovan..........................Cliff Clark
Bates.............................Ed Gargan
Miss Keyes...................Barbara Brown
The Ugs.......Juanita Alvarez, Ruth Alvarez, Nancy McCollum
Beanie............................Patti Brill
Goodwillie.......................Olin Howlin
Harley..............................Ian Wolfe

The Falcon continues his cinematic super-sleuthing in this lively and neatly-concocted whodunit that will groove nicely as supporting fare in the regular dual houses.

Tom Conway is called to an exclusive girls' school to investigate the strange death of the professor-owner. Running into tangle of conflicting clues and situations, he finally tabs it as murder, and then wends through series of episodes to eventually clear things up and point to the real culprit.

Despite its obvious whodunit formula, picture gets benefit of good pace on the script and directing ends to make it a good entry in the series. Conway capably handles the title spot, getting good support from Jean Brooks, Rita Corday, Amelita Ward, Isabel Jewell, George Givot, Cliff Clark, Ed Gargan and Barbara Brown. Patti Brill sings one inconsequential song. *Walt.*

Yellow Canary
(BRITISH-MADE)

London, Oct. 19.

RKO release of Herbert Wilcox production. Stars Anna Neagle, Richard Greene. Directed by Herbert Wilcox. Screenplay by Milles Malleson, Dewitt Bodeen, from story by D. M. Bower; camera, Max Green. At Cambridge theatre, London, Oct. 19. Running time, 95 MINS.

Sally Maitland..................Anna Neagle
Jim Garrick..................Richard Greene
Betty Maitland.................Nova Pilbeam
Jan Orlock......................Albert Lieven
Madame Orlock...............Lucie Mannheim
Mrs. Towcester...........Margaret Rutherford
Sir W. Maitland................Patric Curwan
Lady Maitland..................Marjorie Fielding
German Commander.........Valentine Dyall
Admiral..........................David Horne
Major Fothergill...............Claude Bailey

Direction, cast, production and camera work are so good, it is a pity the suspensive story is not on the same plane of excellence. There is smart comedy dialog and plenty of action throughout. It has a 'mystery' start with red herring trails that lead up blind alleys, necessitating the return each time to a new start. The result is an overplus of the aforesaid 'mystery' and one or more of these trails, all of them good in themselves, might be sacrificed to quicken the progression of its ultimate ending. RKO departed from the usual practice of furnishing the story accompanying the cast on the synopsis. The idea was not to reveal the denouement. To trained reviewers, this 'secret' came as no surprise.

Anna Neagle plays Sally Maitland, daughter of an aristocratic British family. She has achieved notoriety for her pre-war association with the Nazis. Public antagonism to her is so violent that she is practically forced to leave Britain. It is a role altogether different from her previous film appearances. Her co-star is Richard Greene, and principal support comes from Nova Pilbeam, Lucie Mannheim and Albert Lieven.

Stellar reputations of Anna Neagle and Richard Greene should go a considerable way toward attracting audiences on both hemispheres. *Jolo.*

Drums of Fu Manchu

Republic release of Hiram S. Brown, Jr., production. Features Henry Brandon, William Royle, Robert Kellard and Gloria Franklin. Directed by William Witney and John English. Screenplay, Franklyn Adreon, Morgan B. Cox, Ronald Davidson, Norman S. Hall, Barney A. Sarecky, Sol Shor; based on novel by Sax Rohmer; camera, William Nobles; editors, Edward Todd and William Thompson; music, Cy Feuer. Previewed in projection room, Nov. 5, '43. Running time, 68 MINS.

Fu Manchu.................Henry Brandon
Sir Nayland Smith..........William Royle
Allan Parker.................Robert Kellard
Fah-Lo-Suee................Gloria Franklin
Dr. Petrie.......................Olaf Hytten
Professor Randolph.........Tom Chatterton
Mary Randolph...............Luana Walters
Sirdar Prahni..............Lal Chand Mehra
Professor Parker..........George Cleveland
Howard..........................John Dilson
Loki..............................John Merton
Anderson.........................Dwight Frye
Dr. Humphrey..........Wheaton Chambers
Crawford.................George Pembroke
Hang Sang........................Guy D'Ennery

Rehashed from a serial bearing the same name, 'Drums of Fu Manchu' is passable for kid audiences and as a dual in nabes.

Story revolves around efforts of Fu Manchu to obtain a fabled sceptre, possession of which would give him a hold on the emotions of wild tribesmen in India, and would facilitate his plan to conquer all Asia. Opposing him is an agent of the British Foreign Office plus sundry scientists and others. The sceptre is found, the tribesmen revolt but in the end the British agent triumphs and Fu Manchu goes to his presumable death.

With a good makeup job, Henry Brandon is properly menacing as Manchu. William Royle is sufficiently heroic as the Briton, and the others are okay for their needs. Direction is tolerable for a kid picture. The film is peculiarly distending at times, arising from the fact that it is made up of serial reels spliced together; climaxes are frequent and unresolved.

Minesweeper

Paramount release of William Pine-William Thomas production. Features Richard Arlen, Jean Parker, Russel Hayden. Directed by William Berke. Screenplay, Edward T. Lowe and Maxwell Shane; camera, Fred Jackman, Jr.; editor, William Ziegler. Tradeshown in N. Y., Nov. 5, '43. Running time, 67 MINS.

Jim Smith.....................Richard Arlen
Mary Smith.....................Jean Parker
Elliot.........................Russel Hayden
'Fixit'.........................Guinn Williams
Moms...........................Emma Dunn
Commander..................Charles D. Brown
Lt. Gilpin......................Frank Fenton
Corney Welch................Chick Chandler
Lt. Wells.......................Doug Fowley
Cox..............................Ralph Sanford
Boatswain Helms................Billy Nelson

Since these are times when Hollywood is filming practically all branches of the various services, it seemed inevitable that the Navy's minesweepers, those inveterate die-hards who clear the lanes for Uncle Sam's shipping, should find themselves the subject of celluloiding. 'Minesweeper' is the result, and it's another in the series of Pine-Thomas action films. It should do well enough on the duals.

This one is about the Annapolis graduate who has long since been broken because of his penchant for gambling. When the U. S. enters the war, patriotism grips him and he rejoins the Navy under an alias, ultimately giving his life in ferreting out a new type of Jap mine endangering American ships.

The screenplay is the notable weak spot in 'Minesweeper,' though the idea is certainly commendable. There's never any doubt as to the story's ultimate windup.

Richard Arlen is the ex-Middie, and he gives one of his standard performances, while Jean Parker hasn't much to do as the romance, with Russel Hayden as the third party in the romantic triangle. Guinn Williams contributes some mild lighter interest, while rest of the cast is mostly in for atmosphere. Direction by William Berke is as satisfactory as the script would permit. *Kahn.*

Man from Rio Grande

Republic release of Eddy White production. Stars Donald 'Red' Barry; features Wally Vernon and Twinkle Watts. Directed by Howard Bretherton. Screenplay, Norman S. Hall; camera, John MacBurnie; editor, Ralph Dixon; music, Mort Glickman. At New York, N. Y., week Nov. 3, '43, dual. Running time, 55 MINS.

Lee Grant...................Don 'Red' Barry
Jimpson Simpson..............Wally Vernon
Herself.......................Twinkle Watts
John King....................Harry Cording
Doris King.......................Nancy Gay
Tom Traynor........................Kirk Alyn
Two-Way Hanlon................Paul Scardon
Ace Holden.....................Roy Barcroft
Chick Benton...................Kenne Duncan
Curly Wells........................Jack Kirk
Art Thomas...................Kansas Moehring

Donald 'Red' Barry can still ride and handle a six-shooter, and blonde Twinkle Watts, eight-year-old Republic newcomer, is sensational on ice skates. To combine these talents in this dualled western a plot has been devised making the little girl an heiress to a million-dollar ranch which the cowboy star rescues from a scheming rancher. An adequate dualer.

There's a nifty ice-show sequence featuring little Miss Watts. Wally Vernon is an okay comic aide. Barry gives one of his standard performances. Harry Cording is a convincing heavy and Nancy Gay has looks but not much chance to emote.

There are occasional complications in the story, but for diehard western fans it'll escape much notice.

Deerslayer

Hollywood, Nov. 3.

Republic release of P. S. Harrison-E. B. Derr production. Stars Bruce Kellogg; features Jean Parker, Larry Parks, Warren Ashe and Wanda McKay. Directed by Lew Landers. Story and screenplay, Harrison and Derr; adaptation, John W. Krafft; camera, Arthur Martinelli; editor, George McGuire. Previewed in projection room, Nov. 2, '43. Running time, 67 MINS.

Deerslayer.....................Bruce Kellogg
Judith............................Jean Parker
Jingo-Good......................Larry Parks

Harry March....................Warren Ashe
Hetty..........................Wanda McKay
Wah-Tah....................Yvonne de Carlo
Mr. Hutter................Addison Richards
Bobby Hutter...............Johnny Michaels
Briarthorn..................Phil Van Zande
Chief Rivenoak.............Trevor Bardette
Chief Uncas................Robert Warwick
Chief Brave Eagle...........Many Treaties
Mr. Barlow...................Clancy Cooper
'Duenna'.................Princess Whynemah
A Huron Sub-Chief..........William Edmund

This is an amateurish, synthetic drama of early Colonial days when the Indians periodically went on the warpath. It's strictly for kid matinees where the youngsters can whoop at the wild and woolly theatrics.

Picture is the first production venture for P. S. 'Pete' Harrison, who's been reviewing films for at least a quarter century. Harrison draws a complete blank as a producer-scenarist, and the general illogical tenor of the feature is hard to understand in view of his experience in diagnosing what others have been turning out.

Plot is a disjointed display of Indian warfare that might have passed inspection in the early nickleodeon days—but hardly in these modern times. Deerslayer is a super-hero, who continuously eludes the Indians, and, when he's captured, easily escapes at the most convenient spots for script purposes. There's a peaceful tribe; also the settlers who gather inside the stockade to repel attacks; and a riverboat family that provides target for the warring braves. After sufficient footage of amateurish jumble, the battling tribe is dispersed to bring peace to the dictrict.

Jean Parker is the most important film name in the cast, which is unimpressive throughout. Direction by Lew Landers is sophomoric.

Walt.

The Lamp Still Burns
(BRITISH-MADE)

London, Oct. 20.

General Film Distributors' release of Two Cities Film. Stars Godfrey Tearle, Rosamund John, Stewart Granger. Directed by Maurice Elvey. Produced by Leslie Howard. Screenplay by Elizabeth Baron from Monica Dickens' novel, 'One Pair of Feet.' Camera, Jack Hildyard. At Leicester Square theatre, London, Oct. 19. Running time, **90 MINS.**

Hilary Clarke................Rosamund John
Sir Marshall Frayne.........Godfrey Tearle
Larry Rains................Stewart Granger
Christine Morris..............Sophie Stewart
Pamela Siddell..............Margaret Vyner
Mr. Hervey.......................John Laurie
Dr. Trevor....................Eric Mickewood
Dr. Barratt....................Joyce Grenfell
Sister Catley......................Joan Maude
Medical Student...............John Howard
Matron.......................Cathleen Nesbitt

If any English outfit followed the Hollywood custom of awarding Oscars for films, it's a cinch 'The Lamp Still Burns' would bring such posthumous honor to Leslie Howard. Here is definitely a producer's picture in the sense the trade speaks of a Lubitsch as a directors flick. From start to finish Howard's fine appreciation of the difference between sentiment and sentimentality marks every sequence, and for all the inherent grimness of the subject there are frequent touches of Howardesque humor.

Undoubtedly British audiences will view this offering through misty eyes, for it is generally known in this country what a staggering loss the native film industry suffered when the plane in which Howard was returning from Lisbon was shot down in the Bay of Biscay last June. Not as an actor, high as he stood in the esteem of film and theatregoers, but as a director-producer Howard had proved himself to be in a class by himself in this country. 'The Lamp Still Burns,' viewed unemotionally as a producer's triumph, abundantly sets the seal on his greatness.

Basically the picture is a plea for the bettering of conditions under which hospital nurses work. It is also an unequivocal damning of the system which makes British hospitals dependent on charity for their continued existence. Inasmuch as the film was made with the cooperation of the Ministry of Health, it is fair to assume there must be governmental sympathy with the argument favoring state subsidy for hospitals.

How tough life is for a hospital nurse is graphically portrayed in the experiences of a young woman architect, Hilary Clarke, who chucks up her job to dedicate her life to a nursing career. As Hilary, a relative unknown, Rosamund John walks away with the acting honors. A more intelligent, sensitive performance than this sober-visaged, self-restrained girl turns in, in a long and difficult role, has never been captured by a British camera. Up against superb competition by Godfrey Tearle, Cathleen Nesbitt and John Laurie this new star gives promise of becoming England's first lady of the screen.

Direction by Maurice Elvey is first class. Also, all too rare in Englis films, this one has been cut with Hollywood slickness. It would be difficult to find 10 superfluous feet from fade in to fade out. Production values, especially in the hospital sequences, are rich in detail and patently authentic. Topicality is introduced by an air raid during which 'walking cases' are seen to leave the wards for the shelters while the nurses and bed-ridden patients have to stick it out where they are.

Considerable advance publicity has been given to Stewart Granger, another newcomer to English stardom, as a wartime discovery of the first order. In the role of a factory owner, injured in an explosion in his works and nursed back to health by the probationer nurse, he gives an adequate performance. But it is triumphantly Miss John's picture so far as acting honors are concerned.

It is an even greater triumph for Howard, a fitting monument for a great artist.

Day After Day
(DOCUMENTARY)

Artkino release of production by Central Newsreels Studios, Moscow. Directed by Mikhail Sletzky. Scenario, Alexei Kapler; English commentary written and narrated by William S. Gailmor; additional commentary and narration, Philip Sterling and Hilda K. Simms; music, Daniel Pokrass. At Stanley, N. Y., week Nov. 5, '43. Running time, **60 MINS.**

This broadscale filming of Soviet Russia on June 13, 1942, the 356th day of the war against the Nazi aggressors, may be a little too much blood-and-guts to take at one sitting for the average filmgoer, but followers of modern military tactics and life in the Soviet should find it much to their liking. It's strictly for those houses showing Russe pix.

Source material for the 'March of Time' two-reeler released earlier this year, 'Day After Day' contains much attention to detail in 'revealing' the Soviet-Nazi war as actually fought. Casualties behind the lines are apparently filmed insensitively.

Sequences of the Soviet industrial front also are included. In short, a Soviet day on the battle and home fronts. However, the short by M. of T., prepared primarily for U. S. audiences, told the same story in less time and with just as much punch.

Miniature Reviews.

'Death Valley Manhunt' (Rep). Standard Western fare in the Wild Bill Elliott series.

'Millions Like Us' (Brit.). Finely acted study of 'common man' may find wide reception in U. S.

'El Conde de Monte Cristo' ('Count of Monte Cristo') (Mex). Dumas classic loosely spun and talky, strictly for Latinas.

'Casa de Munecas' (Argentine-Made). Adaptation of Ibsen's 'Doll's House' okay only for U. S. arty houses.

'Todo Un Hombre' (Argentine-Made).—Should do well in U. S. arties.

'Safo' (Argentine-Made).—Excellent adaptation of Daudet novel, should do strong b.o.

'Valle Negro' (Argentine-Made).—Fair dualer should appeal to femme trade.

Death Valley Manhunt

Republic release of Eddy White production. Features Wild Bill Elliott, George 'Gabby' Hayes, Anne Jeffreys. Directed by John English. Screenplay, Norman S. Hall and Anthony Coldeway; camera, Ernest Miller; editor, Harry Keller. At New York, N. Y., week of Nov. 8, '43, dual. Running time, **55 MINS.**

Wild Bill.....................Wild Bill Elliott
Gabby..................George 'Gabby' Hayes
Nicky Hobart....................Anne Jeffreys
Richard Quinn................Weldon Heyburn
Judge Jim Hobart..............Herbert Heyes
'Tex' Benson...................Davison Clark
Clayton..........................Pierce Lyden
Danny.....................Charlie Murray, Jr.
Ward................................Jack Kirk
Blaine.........................Eddie Phillips
Roberts............................Bud Geary
Lawson.............................Al Taylor

Flimsy dual fare, Universal release in the Wild Bill Elliott series should do biz in the hinterlands where action pics go, on the lure of Elliott's name. It's all standard gunplay stuff.

Yarn deals with the efforts of Elliott, as a rep of the law, to protect indie oil owners from moneyed interests moving westward. Weldon Heyburn, as a major company frontsman, attempts to play both ends against the middle. He attempts to get the indies to accept financial aid from the company, which then proceeds to take over oil property when owner can't meet the payment. Elliott, aided as usual by George 'Gabby' Hayes, has little difficulty in putting an end to the illegal activities of Heyburn.

Anne Jeffreys, blonde eyeful, is scarcely seen, but when on provides what romantic interest there is. Herbert Hayes and Davison Clark give substantial backing performances.

Millions Like Us
(BRITISH-MADE)

London, Oct. 26.

General Film Distributors' release of Gainsborough picture. Features Eric Portman, Patricia Roc, Anne Crawford, Gordon Jackson. Directed by Frank Launder, Sidney Gilliat. Screenplay by Frank Launder, Sidney Gilliat. Camera, Jack Cox, Roy Frogwell. At Gaumont, London. Running time, **103 MINS.**

Charlie Forbes................Eric Portman
Celia Crowson.................Patricia Roc
Fred Blake...................Gordon Jackson
Jennifer Knowles.............Anne Crawford
Phyllis Crowson.................Joy Shelton
Gwen Price....................Megs Jenkins
Annie Earnshaw................Terry Randal
Charters.......................Basil Radford
Caldicott....................Naunton Wayne
Jim Crowson..................Moore Marriott
Tom Crowson.....................John Boxer
Elsie Crowson...............Valentine Dunn
Dr. Gill.........................John Salew
Miss Hodge.....................Hilda Davies
Miss Wells..................Beatrice Varley
Mrs. Blythe.....................Amy Veness
Landlady........................Irene Handl

Merely the picturization of the life of the 'common people' in these parlous days. Film is designed as patriotic propaganda on the home front, minus flag waving and suchlike. Acting throughout is superior to the story, and is of such a high quality it ought to make almost any film script interesting. It would not be at all surprising if the creation of this abundance of histrionic talent was due to slickness of direction.

Film was produced by the writers of the story. This is a foundation that was well pounced upon by the scripters, and resulted in innumerable little momentary scene flashes. More frequently than is usual in most filmizations, there are homely scenes apparently so simply enacted they hurt and conjure up lumps in the throat and other emotions that 'hurt' more than actual killings would do. Not a blow is struck, not even an arm raised in an attempt to do so.

The list of players includes a pair of prominent artists who appeared in the writers' successful 'The Lady Vanishes,' when they scored smartly as a couple of silly Englishmen. An attempt was made to reproduce them in this picture, but without the same success. It really was unfair to Basil Radford and Naunton Wayne.

The main star (in point of reputation) is Eric Portman, who has a relatively small part, but gives to it a dignified and intelligent portrayal. The outstanding roles are Patricia Roc and Gordon Jackson; she a factory worker, and he a young airman. Their love-making is crudely simple, but so sincere as to lift it out of the commonplace.

The picture cannot fail to attract audiences here, and may even prove more interesting to cinemagoers across the water. In this country it is too close to the 'life' of the proletariat.

Jolo.

El Conde de Monte Cristó
('The Count of Monte Cristo')
(MEXICAN-MADE)

Filmex production directed by Chano Ureta from story of Alexander Dumas. Stars Arturo de Cordova. At Belmont, N. Y., week of Nov. 6, 43. Running time, **180 MINS.**

Edmond Dantes.........Arturo de Cordova
Haide............................Mapy Cortes
Count Morcef..................Rene Cardona
Countess of Morcef.........Consuelo Frank
Baron de Danglars....Carlos L. Moctezuma
Baroness de Danglars..........Gloria Marin
Count de Villefort...........Miguel Arenas
Countess de Villefort..........Anita Blanch
Abbot Faria.................Julio Villarreal
Morrel........................Domingo Soler
Caderousse.....................Abel Salazar
Maximilian....................Rafael Valedon
Valentina...................Esperanza Baur

(In Spanish; No English Titles)

Filmex probably speared for a Mexican 'Gone With the Wind' when deciding to transform Alexander Dumas' yarn into a three-hour spinning, but despite its massive settings and splendid cast, headed by Arturo de Cordova, 'Count of Monte Cristo' is strictly for Latina consumption on this side of the pond. Its length does not lend itself to any great turnover in Latina grinds. Roadshowed in Mexico, even the splendid acting, good direction and photography will not hypo it outside of that territory and its appeal is thus limited.

Dante's persecution and imprisonment because of his love for Mercedes, his escape as substitute corpse and his later rise to power as the Count of Monte Cristo to wreak revenge upon his persecutors is faithfully adhered to albeit slowly paced. Arturo de Cordova's delineation is at all times superb, and is another notable achievement for the star if nothing else. Producers have spared nothing in providing proper mounting, but film could easily have been held in half of currently consumed running time, but apparently that's the way they like 'em in Mexico. For U. S. Spaniards it's a draggy, almost actionless and talky affair.

Casa de Munecas
('The Doll's House')
(AGENTINE-MADE)
Buenos Aires, Oct. 15.

San Miguel production released by Distribuidora Panamericana. Stars Delia Garces and Jorge Rigaud; features Sebastian Chiola, Angelina Pagano, Orestes Caviglia, Alita Roman, Olga Casares Pearson, Mirtha Reid, Camella De Maucci, Jeannette Morel, Emilio R. Casanovas, Federico Iribarren, Maria Arriola, Augustin Barrios, Jose Maria Beltran; music, Julian Bautista. Directed by Ernesto Arancibia. Reviewed at the Ambassador, Buenos Aires. Running time, 95 MINS.

An unusual job for the Argentine industry, this screen adaptation of Ibsen's 'Doll's House' is noteworthy primarily because it represents a practically first-time attempt by the national screen to handle a classic of this size and renown. San Miguel has succeeded in fairly good measure, although it's a difficult play for filming, especially with the variations made necessary by local conditions. General comment has been that the job was somewhat too big for director Ernesto-Arancibia, although praise for the effort has been widespread.

Adaptation by Alejandro Casona has made use of the best parts of play's dialog and narrative but with setting of the story placed in Argentina. Delia Garces gives one of her best performances to date in the difficult role of Nora, the young wife. Jorge Rigaud has also come up to previous standards, although there's some criticism of his casting in the role, which was distinctly not his dish. Director Arancibia, who has originally been a designer, concentrates perhaps overmuch on scenic aspects and development of certain situations, while the soul and vigor of the characters become lost and film drags.

Story has held pretty much to the original theatrical work although done in modern dress with a prolog to hurry the story along. Film may have U. S. possibilities for art-house showings because of familiarity of its story, although it's probably not the best vehicle for introduction of either Senorita Garces or Rigaud to U. S. audiences. Ray.

Todo Un Hombre
(ARGENTINE-MADE)
Buenos Aires, Oct. 6.

Artistas Argentinos Asociados production, distributed by Distribuidora Panamericana. Stars Francisco Petrone and Amelia Bence; features Nicolas Fregues, Guillermo Battaglia, Florindo Ferrario, Ana Arneodo, Leticia Scury, Jorge Lanza, Tilda Thamar, Liana Moabro, Renee Sutil, Barlos Bellucci, Percival Murray, Juan Carrara and Rene Mugica. Story by Miguel de Unamuno. Adapted by Ulises Petit de Murat and Homero Manzi; camera, Bob Roberts. Directed by Pierre Chenal. Reviewed at the Ambassador, Buenos Aires. Running time, 94 MINS.

First locally produced film directed by French director Pierre Chenal ('Crime and Punishment'), 'Todo Un Hombre' has received a strong sendoff from local critics who consider it an important advance in Argentine production. While it lacks smoothness in some portions, total effect is high and action and movement, particularly in later portions, give it definite values for possible U. S. art-house showings.

Based on the w.k. work by Miguel de Unamuno, 'Nana Menos Que Todo Un Hombre,' it's the third production from the Artistas Argentinos Asociados group. Not overly Argentine in spirit, film is essentially the story of a strong, self-made man moved by an indomitable will and tremendous force of character. Story traces the marriage of hard-bitten Alejandro Gomez, an islander from the Argentine up-river country, scorning society, determined to impose his own will and do things as he sees it.

Tale centers on Gomez's acquisition of a wife to whom he refuses to convey his real love. Development is handled with a kind of French quality that at times almost seems alien to the local scene. Finale, which moves to a boat trip up-river which Gomez and his wife take, is done more or less in a symbolic sense. It even becomes over-melodramatic at points, but all wraps together, particularly at the close.

Francisco Petrone, in the lead, drew special attention of all critics for complete naturalness and true interpretation. Chenal also gained many verbal bouquets. Photography by Bob Roberts, only Yank photographic director here, is unusually good, camera being employed to aid movement in a way far surpassing that of previous local productions. Ray.

Safo
(ARGENTINE-MADE)
Buenos Aires, Oct. 6.

Luminton production and release. Stars Mecha Ortiz and Mirtha Legrand; features Roberto Escalada, Miguel Gomez Bao, Nicolas Fregues, Herminia Mancini, Guillermo Battaglia, Elisardo Santalla, Ilde Pirovano, Eduardo Cuitino, Ricardo Canales, Elisa Labarden. Story by Alphonse Daudet; adapted by Cesar Tiempo and Julio Porter. Directed by Carlos Hugo Christensen; camera, Alfredo Traverso. Reviewed at the Broadway, Buenos Aires. Running time, 95 MINS.

Adapted from a French novel, 'Safo' is an indication that local producers are at last learning to adapt foreign works to local Latin settings in order to produce pix which may have a broader interest than that of this country itself. Adapters Cesar Tiempo and Julio Porter, more or less respecting the epoch of Alphonse Daudet's work, have translated the action of the book to the Argentine, eliminating or changing certain episodes for the purpose of providing a better cinema sense.

Story is that of a lad from the provinces who arrives in the capital to continue his studies preliminary to a diplomatic career. He falls into the net of a prostitute, who, despite her past, sincerely loves him. In the ups and downs that follow, hero first breaks with her in order to return to his innocent love, then switches his affections once more, only to leave her again at the end. Treatment and handling are almost in the manner of the French-made films rather than those of the Argentine or of Hollywood.

Although many interesting episodes of original have been deleted, those included are sufficient to give an authentic spirit. Christensen's direction is not overly original in details and at times characters are somewhat exaggerated. All in all, however, film shows excellent handling and has done a strong opening biz at the Broadway. Ray.

Valle Negro
('Dark Valley')
(ARGENTINE-MADE)
Buenos Aires, Oct. 6.

Sono Film production and release. Stars Maria Duval and Carlos Cores; features Nelida Bilbao, Elisardo Santalla, Leticia Scury, Enrique Garcia Satur, Juan Sarcione, Ada Cornaro and Rosita Grassi. Adapted by Carlos Borcosque and Jack Hall from novel by Hugo Wast. Directed by Carlos Borcosque. Released at the Monumental. Running tie, 90 MINS.

A stark melodrama with mystery overtones, 'Valle Negro' is only a fair possibility for Argentine audiences which will probably serve as a dualer elsewhere in Latin America. Based on a novel of a famed local Latin writer, Hugo Wast, it opens with a fairly strong suspense but later drags, with everything becoming increasingly grimmer and over-much bearing down hard on the same theme. Dialog at times becomes pretty declamatory, with references to old feuds, secrets, etc., that need to be explained at length, slowing down the action and diffusing whatever attention might have been built up. All in all, it is overly theatrical, and whatever little comedy has been injected doesn't help.

Story tells of an estancia owner in Valle Negro feuding with a neighbor. Sister has an affair with the enemy, which results in an illegitimate child who remains with the father. Sister finally goes to see her child in secret, wins the offspring's love, and the complications begin. An orphan boy sheltered by the estancia owner grows up to love the girl. All sorts of murders and shootings take place to complicate the affair and it ends with the usual grim note, with the curse on Valle Negro preventing final happiness.

Maria Duval in the starring role is good, but Nelida Bilbao as the aunt steals the honors. Carlos Cores, who gets starring honors, lacks vigor, and Elisardo Santalla in a top role spoils it with over-emphasis. Rest of the cast is fair. Sob situations will appeal to feminine audiences. Ray.

Miniature Reviews

'Madame Curie' (M-G). Greer Garson and Walter Pidgeon in a great picture from every point of view. Augurs big b.o.

'Jack London' (Bronston-UA). Michael O'Shea and Susan Hayward starred in disappointing biography.

'Around the World' (songs) (RKO). Fair Kay Kyser filmusical.

'Is Everbody Happy?' (Col). Ted Lewis name on marquee will carry this mediocre pic as dual support.

'So's Your Uncle' (songs) (U). Billie Burke with Jan Garber and Jack Teagarden bands in dualer.

'Women in Bondage' (Mono). Meller of women under Hitler's regime; sturdy grosser for many spots.

'Silver City Raiders' (Col). Russell Hayden starrer with plenty of action for rabid western fans.

'Underdog' (PRC). Juve doglovers should go for this tearjerker of a farm boy and his pooch battling big-city odds.

'It Happened in Gibraltar' (Strong) (French). French spy meller for arty theatres.

Madame Curie

Metro release of Sidney Franklin production. Stars Greer Garson, Walter Pidgeon; features Henry Travers, Albert Basserman, Robert Walker, C. Aubrey Smith, Diane Way Whitty, Victor Franeen, Elsa Basserman, Reginald Owen. Directed by Mervyn LeRoy. Based on the book by Exve Currie; adaptation. Paul Osborn and Paul H. Rameau; narration, James Hilton; editor, Harold F. Kress; camera, Joseph Ruttenberg. Previewed in N.Y., Nov. 13, '43. Running time. 175 MINS.

Madame Currie	Greer Garson
Pierre Curie	Walter Pidgeon
Eugene Currie	Henry Travers
Prof. Jean Perot	Albert Basserman
David LeGros	Robert Walker
Lord Kevin	C. Aubrey Smith
Mme. Eugene Curie, Sr.	Dame May, Whitty
Pres. of University	Victor Franeen
Mme. Perot	Elsa Basserman
Dr. Becquerel	Reginald Owen
Reporter	Van Johnson
Irene	Margaret O'Brien

Every inch a great picture, 'Madame Curie' is not only a distinguished contribution to the screen in that it absorbingly tells mankind of the struggle and heartaches that ultimately resulted in the discovery of radium bu., further than that, because it is a very poignant love story, its boxoffice success is assured. Carrying a singularly strong appeal for women, at the same time it is not just a so-called woman's picture and can't miss being big everywhere.

The same hit-making combination of Sidney Franklin, producer, and Mervyn LeRoy, director, who turned out 'Mrs. Miniver' and 'Random Harves.,' have instilled into the story of Madame Curie and her scienist-husband a particularly high degree of entertainment value where in less-skilled hands the romance of radium and its discovery may have struck out. The pitfalls were there but Franklin, giving the film excellent production, and LeRoy, directing it inspiringly, have skirted them in the most intelligent and cautious manner.

While the events leading up to the discovery of radium and the fame it brought Madame Curie are of the greatest underlying importance to the picture as entertainment, it's the love story that dominates all the way. Thus, this is not just the saga of a great scientist nor just a story of test tubes and laboratories.

Film is based on the book.

'Madame Curie,' written by Eve Curie, daughter of the Polish teacher-scientist who quite by accident came upon the source of the precious radium element. It has been adapted with great skill by Paul Osborn and Paul H. Rameau, with a few stretches of narration by James Hilton. Written compellingly, with the dialog having both force and tenderness, it throws Greer Garson and Walter Pidgeon together immediately after the opening and, as the romance between them ripens, it gathers terrific momentum. The scenes in which Pidgeon, himself a struggling scientist, pleads with Miss Garson not to give up her laboratory studies (she's been using his lab as a place to experiment), and his final, rather clumsy proposal, are gems. Farther on, after Madame Curie has found radium and Pidgeon gets killed, a sequence of great pathos and touching romanticism is portrayed which will wring the doughtiest hearts and bring out the kerchiefs.

For the finish, the story skips several years, going to an impressive ceremony before solons of the University of Paris who are honoring the now graying Madame Curie on the 25th anniversary of isolation of the radium element. It marks a fitting close for a fine biography of an illustrious and fine womanan.

The picture has been directed with excellent restraint and both of its stars perform with this same admirable restraint. In all respects, it's a simple story told that way but with uncommonly strong impact.

Miss Garson and Pidgeon, latter with chin whiskers and mustache, virtually carry the picture between themselves, but in the casting of others the selections have been carefully made as to type and otherwise. These include Henry Travers and Dame May Whitty, parents of Pidgeon, and sundry scientists, professors, etc., among them Albert Basserman, Robert Walker, C. Aubrey Smith, Victor Francen, Elsa Basserman and Reginald Owen.

Though running long, the footage of 125 minutes is fully justified and the editing by Harold F. Kress leaves nothing to be desired. Franklin's production backgrounds are excellent and the photography by Joseph Ruttenberg good without being gaudy. *Char.*

Jack London

United Artists release of Samuel Bronston production. Directed by Alfred Santell. Stars Michael O'Shea, Susan Hayward; features Frank Craven, Osa Massen, Virginia Mayo, Ralph Morgan. Screenplay, Ernest Pascal, based on 'The Book of Jack London,' by Charmian London; camera, John W. Boyle; music, Fred Rich; editor, William Ziegler. Previewed in N. Y. Nov. 22, '43. Running time, **92 MINS.**

Jack London	Michael O'Shea
Charmian	Susan Hayward
Freda Maloof	Osa Massen
Pref. Hilliard	Harry Davenport
Old Tom	Frank Craven
Mamie	Virginia Mayo
George Brett	Ralph Morgan
Mammy Jenny	Louise Beavers
Kerwin Maxwell	Jonathan Hale
Capt. Tanaka	Leonard Strong
'Lucky Luke' Lannigan	Paul Hurst
Scratch Nelson	Regis Toomey
Mike	Hobart Cavanaugh
Mailman	Olin Howlin
French Frank	Albert Van-Antwerp
Whiskey Bob	Ernie Adams
Red John	John Kelly
Capt. Allen	Robert Homans
Richard Harding Davis	Morgan Conway
James Hare	Edward Earle
Fred Palmer	Arthur Loft
English Correspondent	Lumsden Hare
American Correspondent	Brooks Benedict
Geisha Dancer	Mei Lee Foo
Hiroshi	Robert Katcher
American Consul	Pierre Watkin
Japanese General	Paul Fung
Interpreter	Charlie Lung
Japanese Official	Bruce Wong
Japanese Sergeant	Eddie Lee
Spider	John Fisher
Victor	Jack Roper
Axel	Sven Hugo Borg
Pete	Sid Dalbrook
Commissioner	Davison Clark
Literary Guests	Harold Minjir, Roy Gordon, Torben Meyer
Bit Child	Charlene Newman
Bit Father	Edmund Cobb
Theodore Roosevelt	Wallis Clark
Wm. Loeb	Charles Miller
Japanese Ambassador	Richard Loo
Cannery Foreman	Dick Curtis
Cannery Woman	Sarah Padden
Indian Maid	Evelyn Finley
Charmian's Secretary	Rose Plummer

Samuel Bronston has brought to the screen one of the great men of American letters, Jack London, and if ever there was a blood-and-guts subject for Hollywood treatment, London has long seemed a natural. But the play's still the thing. 'Jack London,' an adaptation of a book written by the author's wife, Charmian, has much of the writer-adventurer's life crammed into its 92 minutes, but somewhere along the line it has missed fire. Coupled with the lack of name value for the marquee, 'London' seems slated for mild biz in the keys or where his name still spells magic as one of the great writer champions of the class struggle.

To the modern generation the name of Jack London is probably just a memory. To them he may well have been the author of one of the great bestsellers, 'The Call of the Wild,' or the lusty 'Sea Wolf.' But to another generation the name was everything his books implied, a fabulous adventurer whose character seeped into many of his novels and short stories. It was an adventuresome career so fabulous that even in its fictional transition did it excite incredulous disbelief. All this has been told in the filmization, but the story treatment is consistently wavering. It's a yarn that might well have defeated most scenarists; it seems incredible that one screen script could have attempted so full a career.

For boxoffice purposes one of the main snags to 'London' is the fact that one of the film's two most important characters—Charmian London, the author's wife—fails to appear until the film has consumed half its running time. Susan Hayward is starred in the role, as is Michael O'Shea in the title part, and for a starred performer to be absent for that length of time is dangerous scripting and directing, let alone producing.

London's career, of course, will be recalled as being divided into, possibly, two facets. One was his burning desire to cure the world's ills through his writings. That part only receives passing notice in the pic. And it was one of his great links to a world-wide public. The other was the lustiness that creeped into all his stories, and which this film treats unimaginatively.

If it has no value other than narrating the story of a great author, 'London' at least points up the Japanese menace that he apparently determined was out to rule the Pacific —this as long ago as 1904, when he covered the Russo-Jap war as a newspaper correspondent. His treatises on the subject—so the film says —were ignored as too dangerous. The United States and Japan were at that time to all intents and purposes friendly.

There is much more in the film that creates some interest, but all told at a generally languid pace. His early career as raider of oyster beds, his venture into the Yukon in '97 to join the gold rush, his seamanship on a sealing vessel, and more, are told almost perfunctorily.

O'Shea, comparative newcomer to Hollywood from the Broadway stage, is miscast in the title role. His physique, for one, is not what one might expect of a two-fisted Jack London, and a couple of the scenes in which he delivers kayo blows are too obviously staged. His performance generally is uncertain. Miss Hayward lends grace and looks to the part of London's wife, while Frank Craven is best of the large supporting cast.

This is Bronston's first production after years in the film distribution business, and there obviously was considerable coin spent on the production. But there can be considerable consolation in knowing that many another initial failure has been a rung to success. Bronston indicates sufficiently in this pic that he's got the spark and imagination to achieve that success. *Kahn.*

Around The World
(SONGS)

Hollywood, Nov. 22.

RKO release of Allan Dwan production. Stars Kay Kyser; features Mischa Auer, Joan Davis, Marcy McGuire, Wally Brown, Alan Carney, Kay Kyser's band. Directed by Allan Dwan. Original story and screenplay by Ralph Spence; special material, Carl Herzinger; camera, Russell Metty; editor, Theron Warth; musical director, C. Bakaleinikoff; songs, Jimmy McHugh, Harold Adamson; special effects, Douglas Travers; musical arrangements, George Duning; musical numbers staged by Nick Castle; art direction, Albert D'Agostino and Al Herman; set decorations, Darrell Silvers, Claude Carpenter; assistant director, Harry Scott. Previewed Nov. 22, '43. Running time, **90 MINS.**

Kay	Kay Kyser
Mischa	Mischa Auer
Joan	Joan Davis
Marcy	Marcy McGuire
Pilot-Clipper	Wally Brown
Joe Gimpus	Alan Carney
Georgia	Georgia Carroll
Harry	Harry Babbitt
Ish	Ish Kabibble
Sully	Sully Mason
Julie	Julie Conway
Diane	Diane Pendleton

Little Fred's Football Dogs and Kay Kyser's Band

Kay Kyser, his band and entertainers, with added and major assistance from Joan Davis, Mischa Auer, Marcy McGuire and bevy of eight showgirls, make an overseas camp show tour as basis for this obvious filmusical. Lightly set up, aiming for escapist fare, with accent on combination of songs and broadly sketched slapstick, picture will catch boxoffice reaction mainly on name of Kyser. Unit is picked up entertaining at an Australian canteen, and then planes to India, Chungking, Cairo and eastward across the North African desert. At each stop there are song and musical presentations by Kyser and his group in typical zippy style, intermingled with disjointed and wacky slapstick.

Scripter Ralph Spence digs deep into his memory for numerous aged dialog cracks. Story threads are started at a couple of points, but left dangling when the gang moves on, and the result is an episodic, crazy-quilt tour.

Joan Davis goes all-out with her broad comedy display for good reaction, while Auer does well in limited footage and fleeting glimpses. Young Miss McGuire, newcomer, indicates promise in both acting and singing lines, but requires better showcase than this one. Kyser competently holds spotlight for the journey, and does okay in displaying his band and entertainers in the familiar style of his radio presentations.

Jimmy McHugh and Harold Adamson have provided a good group of songs, several of which can catch popular favor. 'Roodle-ee-Doo,' introduced by Kyser's band and songsters, has good jump tempo to get wide attention; 'Candlelight and Wine' is a romantic tune with chance for popularity. Five others are standard, with 'Great News' best of group. Picture has its broad comedic moments that intrude suddenly and without reason along the route. Attempt to inject dramatics in death of Marcy McGuire's father in action towards the end pancakes into a discordant note to neutralize the finale production number. Most of production is displayed on stages, with background process shots or backdrops. Director Allan Dwan, also listed as producer, took an easy line to whip up a picture to star Kyser. *Walt.*

Is Everybody Happy?
(SONGS)

Columbia release of Irving Briskin production. Directed by Charles Barton. Features Ted Lewis orch, Nan Wynn, Michael Duane, Larry Parks, Lynn Merrick, Bob Haymes. Screenplay, Monte Brice; camera, L. S. O'Connell; editor, James Sweeney. At Fox, Brooklyn, week of Nov. 18, '43, dual. Running time, **73 MINS.**

Ted Lewis	Ted Lewis
Tom	Michael Duane
Kitty	Nan Wynn
Jerry	Larry Parks
Ann	Lynn Merrick
Artie	Bob Haymes
Joe	Dick Winslow
Bob	Harry Barris
Frank	Frank Stanford
Mrs. Broadbelt	Fern Emmett
Salbin	Eddie Kane
Lou Merwin	Ray Walker
Carl Muller	Anthony Marlowe
Missouri	George Reed

'Is Everybody Happy?' is pure corn, but for those who go for the Ted Lewis brand of music, philosophy and showmanship, the pic should be satisfying, and with the Lewis name for marquee value it should do well as a dual.

Hard to believe though it is, film purports to be some kind of biography of Lewis and, incidentally, an explanation of the advent of the jazz era. Story is a straight-away flashback proposition employing situational cliches from countless other musicals.

Lewis undertakes to convince a modern serviceman and his gal that they should wed immediately instead of waiting for the uncertainty of war to end. For this purpose he tells the couple the story of another pair of sweethearts before and after World War I. The other couple (Larry Parks and Nan Wynn) are the parents of the present-day soldier, and the best friends of Lewis. Plot details how they all met, formed a jazz band, struggled upwards, and had differences because Jerry (Larry Parks) went Broadway in a hurry.

Story, acting and direction are uninspired and hackneyed; photography is fair. Pic has no less than 18 standard tunes associated more or less with Lewis, including 'Chinatown,' 'Pretty Baby,' 'Wild About Harry,' 'Way Down Yonder in New Orleans,' 'By the Light of Silvery Moon' and 'Sunny Side of Street.' Miss Wynn delivers such standards as 'It Had to Be You' and 'Am I Blue' in okay style, but in the big 'St. Louis Blues' number she's overshadowed by an unbilled Negro contralto. There are no original tunes.

Lewis speaks lines the way he sings songs, with the same typical Lewis mannerisms, use of hands, hat, and so on, but all effective. Rest of the performances are standard.

So's Your Uncle
(SONGS)

Universal release of Jean Yarbrough production, directed by Yarbrough. Features Billie Burke, Donald Woods, Elyse Knox. Screenplay by Maurice Leo and Clyde Bruckman from original by Leonard Lee; camera, Elwood Bredell, Milton Krasner. Tradeshown in New York Nov. 23, 1943. Running time, **64 MINS.**

Minerva	Billie Burke
Steve Curtis	Donald Woods
Pat Williams	Elyse Knox
Joe Elliott	Frank Jenks
Roger Bright	Robert Lowrey
Dempster	Irving Bacon
Dinwiddie	Chester Clute
John L. Curtis	Paul Stanton

Plus Mary O'Brien, Tailor Maids, Delta Rhythm Boys, Jan Garber and Jack Teagarden orchestras.

Obviously aimed for the duals, an implausible plot is stretched to the breaking point but gets a breather via specialties in nitery sequences by Mary O'Brien, songstress; Tailor Maids, harmony trio; Delta Rhythm Boys, sepia quintet, and the Jan Garber and Jack Teagarden orchs. But even with all this pulmotoring the gossamer yarn won't raise much dust anywhere.

Donald Woods is a struggling playwright-producer chasing angel coin for his latest opus, for which he's turning actor, too. When creditors close in on him he essays his character makeup, a caricature of his wealthy uncle to escape the plasterers. He is struck by a limousine while making getaway. Elyse Knox, attractive blonde owner, insists on taking him home for medical checkup over objections of Robert Lowrey, the boy friend. Billie Burke, as the gal's Aunt Minerva, with plenty of moolah and a yen for another altar trip, goes for the pseudo middle-aged gent in a big way.

Woods grasps this opportunity to tell her about his nephew and the play and that's when complications set in that have Woods dodging in and out of the alfalfa through alternating as himself and the uncle. Everything's set to produce the play with Miss Burke's backing and they go off to a niteclub to celebrate. Here's where the Garber and Teagarden bands come in for instrumentation in brief sequences. Of course Miss Knox goes romantically overboard for Woods, sans the beard. Deception is about to be caught up with when Paul Stanton, the real uncle, arrives. For scripters' convenience he takes it from there in the romance with Miss Burke and everything points to a double wedding for the foursome at fadeout.

Woods does okay by the dual role. Miss Knox makes an attractive vis-a-vis. Miss Burke gives her usual superb delineation of the coy, chattery husband-hunter. Frank Jenks lends much to the comedy side as pal of Woods. Paul Stanton is sufficiently blustery as the tycoon uncle. Remainder of cast are adequate in the lesser roles. Mary O'Brien does okay with a vocal in nitery sequence. Ditto for Three Tailor Maids and Delta Rhythm Boys. Yarbrough's direction keeps the thin story moving at good pace, considering the material at hand.

Women in Bondage

Monogram release of Herman Millakowsky production. Directed by Steve Sekely. Stars Gertrude Michael, Gail Patrick, Nancy Kelly, H.B. Warner; features Anne Nagel, Tala Birell, Rita Quigley, Gisela Werbisek, Alan Baxter, Roland Varno. Screenplay, Houston Branch, from original story by Frank Bentick Wisbar; camera, Mack Stengler; editor, Richard Currier. Previewed in N.Y., Nov. 18, 43. Running time, 72 MINS.

Margot Bracken	Gail Patrick
Toni Hall	Nancy Kelly
Gertrude Schneider	Gertrude Michael
Deputy	Anne Nagel
Ruth Bracken	Tala Birell
Gladys Bracken	Mary Forbes
Grete Ziegler	Maris Wrixon
Herta's Grandmother	Gisela Werblack
Herta Rumann	Rita Quigley
Ritzl	Francinne Bordeaux
Blonde	Una Franks
Heinz Radtke	Bill Henry
Pastor Renz	H.B. Warner
Otto Bracken	Allen Baxter
Dr. Mensch	Felix Basch
Ernst Bracken	Roland Varne
Corp. Mueller	Ralph Lynn
Dist. Leader	Frederic Brunn

Monogram has a valuable exploitation picture in 'Women in Bondage,' and wisely is rushing it into distribution. Formerly known as 'Hitler's Women,' it has exploitable angles. Sturdy biz in many spots looms, particularly where sold to the hilt by the exhibitor.

This is a story of Nazi regimentation of its womenfolk. Plot centers around Gail Patrick, a section leader in the German youth movement, and the love affair of her servant, Nancy Kelly. Miss Patrick is pictured as the patriotic wife of a wounded German officer, the older daughter in a rich family. Her efforts to consummate a happy marriage for her servant and shield her from the harsh Nazi methods are the focal points. Brutal twist is injected via having the Nazis order Miss Patrick to become a mother, even though her husband has been paralyzed by battle wounds. Climax shows her guiding Allied planes to Berlin by disobeying blackout orders.

Miss Patrick gives depth and character to the role. Miss Kelly. Gertrude Michael, as a stern district leader of the youth movement, and H. B. Warner, as the priest who single-handed tries to battle the Nazi ruthlessness, are also standout among the 'name' players.

Roland Varno, Alan Baxter, Gisela Werbisek, Bill Henry, Anne Nagel, Tala Birell, Rita Quigley and Maris Wrixon are okay in support.

Herman Millakowsky, who turned out numerous screen productions in Germany before Hitler's rise to power, supplied relatively strong production values. Steve Sekely does as well as could be expected with the scripting though not showing much originality. The original of Frank Bentick Wisbar, who produced 'Maedchen in Uniform' in Germany, is faithfully transferred to the screen by Houston Branch. Editing of Richard Currier is okay while Mack Stengler's photography is fine.

Wear.

Silver City Raiders
(SONGS)

Columbia release of Leon Barsha production. Directed by William Berke. Stars Russell Hayden; features Bob Wills and his Texan Playboys, Dub Taylor, Alma Carroll. Screenplay, Ed Earl Repp; camera, Benjamin Kline; editor, Jerome Thoms. At New York, N. Y., dual, week of Nov. 16, '43. Running time, 55 MINS.

Lucky Harlan	Russell Hayden
Bob Wills	Bob Wills
Cannonball	Dub Taylor
Dolores Alvarez	Alma Carroll
Dawson	Paul Sutton
Steve	Luther Wills
Dirk	Jack Ingram
Ringo	Edmund Cobb
Slim	Art Mix

'Silver City Raiders' packs enough action to suit the most demanding western fan. Nor is there any stinting on melody in this limited-budget dualer.

Russell Hayden is up to his ears in red tape trying to prove that his ranch and those of his neighbors are not the property of an unscrupulous land grabber, who uses all sorts of strong-arm tactics to prevent Hayden and his pals from getting justice. Hayden straightens out the legal snarl, and then he and his neighbors muss up the land-grabber and his gang in a lusty slugfest that wrecks the local saloon.

Hayden does thorough acting job, but the standout performance is turned in by Dub Taylor, a roly-poly fellow with a thick drawl which sounds more southern than western. He has an easy comedy style. Bob Wills and his Texan Playboys deliver some okay music, alternating between vocals and instrumentalizing. Alma Carroll is an attractive brunet, who comes as a welcome change to the usual run of deadpan gals usually featured in actioners. The film is well-paced and clearly photographed.

The Underdog

Producers Releasing Corp. release of Max Alexander production. Directed by William Nigh. Features Barton MacLane, Bobby Larsons, Jan Wiley, Charlotte Wynters. Screenplay, Ben Lithman from story by Lawrence E. Taylor and Malvin Wald; camera, Robert Cline; editor, Charles Henkel, Jr. At New York, N. Y., dual, week of Nov. 16, '43. Running time, 65 MINS.

John Tate	Barton MacLane
Henry Tate	Bobby Larson
Amy Tate	Jan Wiley
Mrs. Bailey	Charlotte Wynters
Spike	Conrad Binyon
Mrs. Connors	Elizabeth Valentine
Eddie Mohr	Kenneth Harlan
Krueger	George Anderson
Officer O'Toole	Jack Kennedy
Hobo, the dog	Himself

Juve dog-lovers should go for this tear jerker, which teams a mongrel and a farmboy in their battle to win respect in the big city. Strictly for duals, lots could have been done with the film, but it misses out when it tears off in several directions.

On the one hand, the story has Bobby Larson, the boy, and his dog, Hobo, tangling with neigborhood toughs and trying to prove that by turning the other cheek and doing right by one's neighbors, virtue will be rewarded. At the same time Barton MacLane, who portrays a dispossessed farmer seeking his fortune in the city, poses another problem, and suggests another story. He and his wife, Jan Wiley, are in constant conflict. He wants to return to farming and she wants to stay in the city to keep from being lonely.

Juve delinquency also enters into the film via a gang of vandals who make life miserable for Bobby and his dog. But the scripters tie everything up by having Bobby and the dog (which had been rejected for armed service) route saboteurs and save MacLane from burning to death.

Young Larson overacts considerably, and at times his performance suggests that of a martyr, which isn't very comfortable to witness. MacLane offers very little of his usual bluster and consequently loses much of his punch and appeal. Jan Wiley and Charlotte Wynters are highly decorative and adequate, although Miss Wiley looks too attractive and well fed for a farmer's wife who's been through drought and floods.

Film lacks solid direction and continuity.

It Happened in Gibraltar
(FRENCH-MADE)

Vigor Picture Corp. release of Gibraltar Films production. Directed by Fedor Ozep. Stars Erich von Stroheim; features Biviane Romance and Roger Duchesne. Screenplay, Jean Stelli, Jacques Companeez, Ernest Neuville; camera, Ted Pahle; music, Paul Dessau; English titles, Herman G. Weinberg. At World, N. Y., starting Nov. 15, '43. Running time, 92 MINS.

Marson	Erich von Stroheim
Mercedes	Vivian Romance
Maori	George Flament
Robert Jackson	Roger Duchesne
Lloyd	Abel Jacquin
General Wilcox	Andre Roanne
Maud Wilcox	Yvette Lebon

(In French; with English titles)

Produced in 1939, before France and England entered the war, 'It Happened in Gibraltar' is a swift-moving spy meller up to usual high French pre-war standards. It should prove top boxoffice at arty theatres. Erich von Stroheim and Vivian Romance, in principal roles, are added b.o. assets for arty filmgoers.

Yarn tells of a spy ring headed by von Stroheim in trying to disrupt the military machines of England and France. Basic theme concerns efforts of the spies to obtain vital secrets of the British admiralty and blowing up Britain's troop ships after they depart from coaling at Gibraltar.

The romantic passages between Roger Duchesne, as a British naval officer, and Miss Romance are plenty hot. There is one particularly spicy boudoir episode that hardly would get the Haysian nod, and is torrid enough despite apparent clipping by N. Y. censors.

Von Stroheim stands out per usual. Miss Romance, as a Spanish dancer doing spying between cabaret appearances, makes every episode a penetrating one. She's depicted as saving her British naval sweetheart and going against the spy ring at the end. Duchesne is satisfactory, and remainder of principals are nicely picked. George Flament as the spy trigger-man being particularly effective.

Fedor Ozep, Soviet director who's now making 'Russian Girl' in Hollywood, did a crisp directorial job, being especially strong on his suspenseful scenes. Ted Pahle's camera work is mostly good though some scenes are below par on lighting. Original script by Jean Stelli, Jacques Companeez and Ernest Neuville probably would be just one of those things without such a strong cast and Ozep's direction. However, bulk of the dialog is smart.

Wear.

Miniature Reviews

'The Gang's All Here' (Musical) (20th). Alice Faye, Carmen Miranda, Phil Baker, Goodman's band insure strong b.o.

'The Heat's On' (Musical) (Col.). Musical comedy, first picture for Mae West in over three years; only average for biz.

'Where Are Your Children?' (Mono). Over average as programmer, with biz prospects promising.

'O, My Darling Clementine' (Rep) (Songs). Corn for bumpkin audiences only. Stars Roy Acuff.

'Hail to the Rangers' (Col). A Charles Starrett dualer with plenty of action.

'Tiger Fangs' (PRC). Exciting juve dual fare with Frank Buck nabbing Nazis as well as tigers.

'Carmen' (Arg.)—Bizet opera, filmed as parody, should have strong appeal south of border.

'No Mataras' (Mexican), Mexmade melodrama. No English titles. Okay for Spanish houses.

The Gang's All Here
(MUSICAL; COLOR)

20th-Fox release of William LeBaron production. Directed by Busby Berkeley. Stars Alice Faye, Carmen Miranda; features Phil Baker, Benny Goodman's orch, Charlotte Greenwood, Eugene Pallette, E. E. Horton, Sheila Ryan, James Ellison, Tony De Marco. Screenplay, Walter Bullock; based on story by Nancy Wintner, George Root, Jr., Tom Bridges; songs, Leo Robin and Harry Warren; dances, Busby Berkeley; camera, Edward Cronjager; Technicolor director, Natalie Kalmus; editor, Ray Curtiss; musical directors, Alfred Newman and Charles Henderson. Previewed in New York, Nov. 26, '43. Running time, 103 MINS.

Eadie Allen	Alice Faye
Dorita	Carmen Miranda
Phil Baker	Himself
Benny Goodman Orch	Themselves
Andrew Mason, Jr.	Eugene Pallette
Mrs. Peyton Potter	Charlotte Greenwood
Peyton Potter	Edw. Everett Horton
Tony De Marco	Himself
Sergt. Andrew Mason, Jr.	James Ellison
Vivian Potter	Sheila Ryan
Sergt. Pat Dasey	Dave Willock
Specialty Dancers	Miriam Lavelle, Charles Saggau
Benson	George Dobbs
Waiter	Leon Belasco

A marquee that includes such names as Alice Faye, Carmen Miranda, Phil Baker and Benny Goodman's orchestra, and an expensively mounted William Le Baron Technicolor musical production directed by Busby Berkeley, are surefire ingredients for most boxoffices. 'The Gang's All Here' includes all these.

A weak script is somewhat relegated by the flock of tuneful musical numbers that frequently punctuate the picture. Miss Faye has never been screened more fetchingly, and she still lilts a ballad for sock results. Miss Miranda is given her fattest screen part to date, and she's become a comedienne who can handle lines as well as put over her South American rhythm tunes. Baker makes the most of invariably drab comedy lines, while Goodman's orch is always prominently focused as a bow to the jive hounds.

There's a supporting cast, notably Eugene Pallette, Charlotte Greenwood and Edward Everett Horton, that generally backs up the principals niftily in this yarn of a romantic tangle involving Miss Faye, Sheila Ryan and James Ellison. Latter plays a wealthy doughboy who makes a pitch for Miss Faye, a nitery chorine, though engaged to wealthy Miss Ryan.

The Leo Robin-Harry Warren tunes include several potentially exploitable ones, namely 'A Journey to a Star,' which Miss Faye reprises a couple of times. A ballad, it's the best of the seven numbers used in the pic. The rhythmic 'Paducah,' done by Goodman and also by Miss Miranda, is pointed up for its novelty values.

Berkeley has used considerable imagination in the ensemble numbers, a notable absenteeism being in the chorus manpower, but he's gotten together a flock of beauts for the pretentious routines—and so the boys aren't missed appreciably. Besides, a gal's gams are always prettier.

Of the cast, Miss Miranda is outstanding, and the way she kicks around the English lingo affords much of the film's comedy. Miss Faye underplays as usual, but always clicko, while for Baker it's an effort that definitely stamps him for future comedy roles, despite his material. Charlotte Greenwood gives some indication of her once-prominent hoofing ability, but otherwise she's given too little to do. James Ellison as the love interest opposite Miss Faye is generally ineffectual in the acting department. Horton and Pallette are okay for lighter moments, while Miss Ryan is a dark-haired beaut who does well enough in a small role. Tony De Marco (minus his partner, Sally Craven) apparently wound up a victim on the cutting room floor, as did some of the others. Edward Cronjager's photography of the niftily Technicolored effects is a boff job. *Kahn.*

The Heat's On

(MUSICAL)

Columbia release of Milton Carter production. Stars Mae West, Victor Moore, William Gaxton; features Lester Allen, Mary Roche, Almira Sessions, Hazel Scott, Alan Dinehart, Lloyd Bridges, Sam Ash, Xavier Cugat orch and Lina Romay. Directed by Gregory Ratoff. Story and adaptation, Fitzroy Davis, George S. George and Fred Schiller; songs, Jay Gorney, Edward Eliscu, Henry Myers, Jule Styne and Sammy Cahn; editor, Otto Meyer; dances, David Lichine; camera, Franz E. Planer. At State, N. Y., week Nov. 25, '43. Running time, **79 MINS.**

Fay Lawrence	Mae West
Hubert Bainbridge	Victor Moore
Tony Ferris	William Gaxton
Mouse Beller	Lester Allen
Janey Bainbridge	Mary Roche
Hannah Bainbridge	Almira Sessions
Hazel Scott	Hazel Scott
Forrest Stanton	Alan Dinehart
Andy Walker	Lloyd Bridges
Frank	Sam Ash
Xavier Cugat	Xavier Cugat
Lina	Lina Romay

Appearing in 'My Little Chickadee,' released by Universal in February, 1940, this is the first picture for Mae West since then. A musical comedy, with the book and gags in the West manner, its principal pull is in several good song numbers but, taken as a whole, the audience value is not sufficient to suggest more than just average business.

The musical numbers are in generous measure, including a few production sequences of moderate stature, plus song specialties, the Xavier Cugat band and Hazel Scott at the piano. Cugat, whose orchestra has a couple sessions, figures in one scene in which he engages in the dialog, while his soloist, Lina Romay, warbles a couple tunes, 'There Goes My Heart,' in which faulty diction has a marring effect, and 'Antonio,' novelty song that scores much better. Miss Romay photographs exceptionally well.

Miss Scott, the wiz on the piano keys, does 'White Keys and Black Keys,' which scores strongly, and, following a novelty trumpet solo by one of Cugat's kiddies, does a stint playing two pianos, while immediately on top of this is 'Thinking About the Wabash,' a very listenable ballad sung by Mary Roche and Sam Ash, with a quartet backing. Subsequently, Miss Scott, with colored soldiers and girls for production background, sings 'Caissons Are Rolling Along,' another sequence that hits home satisfactorily. Victor Moore, playing the dopey brother of the head of a reformist organization, has a Victory Garden number for himself, 'They Looked So Pretty on the Envelope,' but it's not so hot.

Picture opens on 'Indiscretions,' a Broadway musical that's having trouble getting along, with Miss West singing 'I'm Just a Stronger in Town,' done in the typical Westian manner, while for the close she is surrounded by a male chorus in 'Hello, Mi Amigo,' which rates okay. 'There Goes That Guitar,' used by the Cugat band as background for a Latinesque dance double, is also a part of the structure of this musical.

Story of 'Heat's On,' with Miss West as the actress-siren, her hips a-swinging in a familiar manner and arms akimbo for added familiar effect, plus the affected hard-boiled Westian diction, concerns the efforts of a legit producer, in love with his star, to wrest her from a rival producer after latter has been hoodwinked into believing she's been blacklisted by a reform society. Moore, less funny than usual, has appropriated funds of the organization headed by his bluenose sister in order to back a Broadway show, that his niece, played cutely by Miss Roche, may have a chance for stardom. As expected, everything turns out chummily for all concerned, though the ending on the production number with Miss West is a bit abrupt.

Miss West looks well but her technique somehow seems dated. Gaxton does well as the legit producer who's soft for his glamorous star, while Alan Dinehart does okay as a rival prod. Lester Allen plays a press agent, looking ridiculous in circusy clothes most of the time. Lessers include Almira Sessions, Lloyd Bridges and Ash. *Char.*

Where Are Your Children?

(SONGS)

Monogram release of Jeffrey Bernerd production. Directed by William Nigh. Stars Jackie Cooper; features Gale Storm, Patricia Morison, John Litel, Gertrude Michael, Addison Richards, Herbert Rawlinson, Betty Blythe, Anthony Ward, Charles Williams and Evelyn Eaton. Story, Hilary Lynn; adaptation, Hilary Lynn and George W. Sayre; editor, Duncan Mansfield; camera, Mack Stengler and Ira Morgan. Previewed in N. Y. Nov. 24, '43. Running time, **73 MINS.**

Danny	Jackie Cooper
Judy	Gale Storm
Linda	Patricia Morison
Judge Evans	John Litel
Nell	Gertrude Michael
Halstead	Addison Richards
Butler	Herbert Rawlinson
Mrs. Cheston	Betty Blythe
Jim	Anthony Ward
Caesar	Charles Williams
Opal	Evelyn Eaton
Jerry	Jimmy Zaner
Matron	Sarah Edwards
Petty Officer Jones	John Laurenz
Herb	Neyle Marx

'Where Are Your Children?' may not contribute to the solution of the juvenile delinquency problem, but its intentions help rate this picture above average as a programmer. Boxoffice prospects are promising. Since the negative cost is reported at only $110,000, the chances are strong that a very substantial profit will be made.

Jeffrey Bernerd, former English producer, has assembled a film that not only delivers a strong message against juve waywardness and parental neglect but also one which carries rather strong romantic appeal. The veteran William Nigh has piloted the yarn, an original by Hilary Lynn which the latter also assisted in adapting, in such a manner as to maintain interest while at the same time trying to prove various points about causes of juvenile delinquency. As result, while the story and its unfolding veer on the preachy, it never becomes entirely a pulpit exhibit. Additionally, action is fused into the script through various scenes, notably one in which some tough girls, in custody of the law, stage a fight scene that's not just merely a hair-pulling contest. A newcomer to the screen, Evelyn Eaton, playing a toughie, goes to town in this sequence and should step ahead fast.

Story opens in a soft-drink jive joint, point of romantic contact between Jackie Cooper and Gale Storm, former a rich boy without parental attention, latter a hash-slinger. Their intentions are mistaken by the brother and sister-in-law with whom Miss Storm lives, and though latter is not a bad girl, through circumstances and the wrong associations she becomes involved in a murder from which she's ultimately cleared. Meantime, a romance has developed with Cooper, now in the Navy, who comes to her rescue and aids in absolving her.

Miss Storm, very youthful and refreshing, gives a fine performance. She's under long-term contract to Mono. Cooper does satisfactorily, while Patricia Morison excels as a juvenile court officer. Other standouts include John Litel, the judge; Herbert Rawlinson, a butler; Gertrude Michael, Addison Richards and Betty Blythe.

Two songs of considerably ancient vintage are injected, 'Glad You're Dead, You Rascal,' sung in the jive joint sequence, and 'Girl of My Dreams,' done by a sailor in a barracks setting. Both are well rendered by unidentified characters. *Char.*

O, My Darling Clementine

(SONGS)

Republic release of Armand Schaefer production. Directed by Frank McDonald. Stars Roy Acuff and Smokey Mountain Boys and Girls, Radio Rogues, Isabel Randolph, Harry 'Pappy' Cheshire, Tennessee Ramblers; features Frank Albertson, Lorna Gray, Irene Ryan. Screenplay, Sorrell and Stuart McGowan; camera, Bud Thackery; editor, Arthur Roberts; music director, Morton Scott. Tradeshown in N. Y., Nov. 26, '43. Running time, **70 MINS.**

Sheriff	Roy Acuff
Mayor	Harry 'Pappy' Cheshire
Mrs. Uppington	Isabel Randolph
Dan Franklin	Frank Albertson
Clementine	Lorna Gray
Irene (Princess Sheba)	Irene Ryan
Luke Scully	Eddie Parks
Ellie Scully	Lole Bridge
Bubbles	Patricia Knox
Bill Collector	Tom Kennedy
Hartfield	Edwin Stanley
Brown	Emmett Vogan

'O, My Clementine' should make money in districts where the 'Grand Ole Opry' program of Station WSM, Nashville, has an avid following, namely the deep south and middle-west. The presence of WSM's incredible Roy Acuff and his synthetic mountain music in the film is a big factor in the pic's b.o.

Pic deals with a group of itinerant entertainers managed by Frank Albertson who wind up in a bluenose town somewhere in Dixie. The manager's efforts to put on a show furnish the film with what might be termed its plot, and also provide openings for soggy gags and inevitable imitations of bigtime personalities. Interspersed throughout is a bunch of Acuff's songs and specialty turns by various of the hillbillies. There's romance, too, involving Frank Albertson and Lorna Gray, who does as well as can be expected under the circumstances.

Acting, photography, editing and direction are at the usual par for modest budgeters like this.

Hail to the Rangers

(SONGS)

Columbia release of Jack Fier production. Directed by William Berke. Stars Charles Starrett; features Arthur Hunnicutt and Robert Owen Atcher. Screenplay, Gerald Geraghty; camera, Benjamin Kline; editor, William Claxton. At New York, N. Y., dual, week of Nov. 23, '43. Running time, **58 MINS.**

Steve McKay	Charles Starrett
Arkansas	Arthur Hunnicutt
Bob Atcher	Robert Owen Atcher
Bonnie Montgomery	Leota Atcher
Monte Kerlin	Norman Willis
Dave Kerlin	Lloyd Bridges
Schuyler	Ted Adams
Latham	Ernie Adams
Jessup	Tom London
Major Montgomery	Davison Clark
Sheriff Ward	Jack Kirk

Charles Starrett is given plenty to do in this sagebrush dualer, which contains the usual quota of gunplay and slugfests plus some crude comedy and pleasing melody. It should register at the till with western fans.

Story offers a reverse twist to the land-grabbing plot. In 'Hail to the Rangers' phoney homesteaders try to dispossess the big ranch owner, who happens to be an ex-Ranger. But Charles Starrett and his pals team with the rancher after having lost their jobs when the Rangers are disbanded. The homesteaders are driven off, and a newspaper publisher and a gambler, who would have eventually gotten the ranch, conveniently shoot each other.

Starrett handles his part with ease and conviction. Arthur Hunnicutt is adequate as the mustached comedian sidekick, and Robert and Leota Atcher do a neat job of delivering songs, which are romantic and comic.

Film could have been tighter and better paced. Photography above-average for low-budget actioners.

Tiger Fangs

Producers Releasing Corp. release of Jack Schwarz production. Directed by Sam Newfield. Features Frank Buck, June Duprez and Duncan Renaldo. Screenplay, Arthur St. Claire; camera, Ira Morgan; editor, George M. Merrick. At New York, N. Y., dual, week of Nov. 23, '43. Running time, **57 MINS.**

Frank Buck	Frank Buck
Linda MacCardle	June Duprez
Peter Jeremy	Duncan Renaldo
Tom Clayton	Howard Banks
Geoffrey MacCardle	J. Farrell MacDonald
Ali	J. Alex Havier
Doctor Lang	Arno Frey
Henry Gratz	Dan Seymour
Takko	Pedro Regas

Juves should find this Frank Buck actioner exciting. It's a fiction piece, and not the usual jungle travelog. The fantastic 'Tiger Fang' plot is along serial lines, making it more suitable for Saturday matinee kid material rather than adult presentation.

Story has Buck tangling with Nazis who have been doping tigers, thereby making maneaters of the beasts (as if they weren't already!). With the cats on a rampage, rubber production is seriously curtailed and the United Nations' war effort jeopardized. How Buck and his United Nations associates, J. Farrell MacDonald, Duncan Renaldo and June Duprez, get into the Malay jungle to raise rubber and catch tigers is never explained. Especially in view of Japan's conquest of the region. The film does mention that a state of war exists between the Axis and the U. S. And what happened to the rubber-growing areas in the Far East following the Japs attack is very well known by now. More than one film shot looks like a leftover from Buck's early jungle safaris, although the less obviously rehashed reels are passable.

Dan Seymour, who may well be one of the fattest screen performers, tries hard to be a sinister stout fellow in the Sydney Greenstreet tradition, but he only succeeds in looking piqued and foolish. Buck has added more to his waistline than to his stature as an actor. June Duprez is as attractive a biologist as one could hope to meet up with in the middle of the jungle.

Carmen

(Argentine-Made)

(WITH SONGS)

Buenos Aires, Nov. 20.

Argentina Sono Film production and release starring Nini Marshall and featuring Juan Jose Padilla, Manuel Perales, Adrian Cuneo, Carlos Tajes, Juan Jose Pineyro, Olga Cortese, Nelly Daren and Ellen Pardi. Directed by Luis Cesar Amadori; story by

Arnaldo G. Malfatti and Tito Insausti; camera, Alberto Etchehehere; music by Bizet, arranged by Mario Maurano. Reviewed at the Ambassador, Buenos Aires. Running time, 96 MINS.

While terrific for local audiences, Sono Film's latest musical isn't quite up to the effect achieved by Mexican star Cantinflas in 'The Three Musketeers.' However, 'Carmen' has already opened to zingo biz in Buenos Aires and will have strong commercial possibilities for theatres south of the border, especially since the musical effects have been done with good style and restraint, with emphasis on their appeal to Latin filmgoers.

Story has been developed entirely for Nini Marshall, whose style might be likened to that of a Latin Gracie Fields. She's a fast-moving comedienne whose sometimes innocently phrased remarks pack plenty of comedy and who also depends on pantomime and movement to achieve effects. Her sense of gagging and timing is especially strong with Latin audiences, who like her terrific energy, her capacity for getting into scrapes and her romantic tomfoolery.

Story as scripted by Arnaldo G. Malfatti and Tito Insausti makes Nini a dressmaker who gets a blow on the head while visiting the local opera house to deliver a costume. Thereafter she dreams about getting involved in the stage production which moves beyond the footlight limits through a strongly burlesqued version of the Bizet opera.

It's the first time a parody of this kind has been done on the local screen and while not completely successful in all aspects, is generally strong, especially in the scenes where Nini dominates. Her takeoffs on the 'toreador' episodes of the Tyrone Power version of 'Blood and Sand' are especially good, as are the dance sequences featuring Juan Jose Padilla. Story has been made topical, with plenty of current references, of which the best is the smuggling scene in the mountains when rationed tires form the principal contraband. Direction by Luis Cesar Amadori is good, although following the standard Amadori pattern. Outstanding in supporting roles are Juan Jose Pineyro and Carlos Tajes. Ray.

No Mataras
('Thou Shalt Not Kill')
(MEXICAN-MADE)

Clasa-Mohme release of V. Saiso Piquer production. Directed by Chano Urueta. Features Sara Garcia, Emilio Tuero, Carmen Montejo and Rafael Baledon. Screenplay, Chano Urueta, from novel by Joaquin Margall; camera, Raoul Martinez Solares; music, Jorga Perez; editor, Jorge Bustos. At Belmont, N. Y., week of Nov. 24, '43. Running time, 107 MINS.

(In Spanish: no English titles)

'No Mataras' ('Thou Shalt Not Kill') is a strange film anomaly with limited boxoffice appeal except for those houses serving a Spanish clientele. Lack of English titles is the major handicap for other houses.

Story is relatively easy to follow, despite lack of titles, and has a number of melodramatic elements that have long since become familiar.

Pic tells tragic story of a widow with a child who is taken by a usurer and jailed for her efforts to fight him. She then makes a fresh start but along anti-social lines, finally becoming the matron of a luxurious gambling salon. To this place, a young rake brings her daughter—now grown and registered in an exclusive girl's school—where he wines, dines and seduces the gal. She becomes his mistress, but the guy marries her off to a professor from her school, meanwhile putting a blackmail bite on the mother. When the couple return from Europe with a child of their own, the blackguard threatens to expose the girl, but she jumps the gun and tells her husband herself. The husband starts out to shoot the gal, runs across the seducer—and the guy is seen falling

dead. The husband is put on trial for murder, but it turns out the mother did it to save everybody's honor.

Lighting, costuming and sound, are relatively good for a Mexican film, but all this is engulfed in a badly directed, poorly edited, cheaply-made and mounted production with a hackneyed story and poor acting in all cases except one. Only exception is Carmen Montejo, who turns in a simple, heartfelt and effective portrayal, and she's a looker, besides.

Miniature Reviews

'What a Woman!' (Col). Enough laughs to insure moderate box-office, helped by Rosalind Russel and Brian Aherne.

'She's For Me' (U). Comedy romance, with David Bruce, Grace McDonald and Lois Collier, strong dualer.

'Tarzan's Desert Mystery' (RKO). Surefire juve thriller starring Johnny Weissmuller.

'Rookies in Burma' (RKO). Second in series for comedy team of Wally Brown and Alan Carney; adequate for duals.

'The Demi - Paradise' (Brit). Laurence Olivier starrer should do strong b.o.

'Hands Across the Border' (Rep) (songs). Upped budget for Roy Rogers western; good for dual support.

'Harvest Melody' (songs) (PRC). Corny back-to-the-farm film.

'Hundred Pound Window' (WB). British - made race-track film a natural for hefty grosses.

'Fighting Valley' (PRC). Above average western dualer with plenty of action.

'Headline' (Brit.). Conventional whodunit starring David Farrar, newest femme rave.

What a Woman!

Columbia production and release. Directed by Irving Cummings. Stars Rosalind Russell, Brian Aherne; features Willard Parker, Alan Dinehart, Edward Fielding, Ann Savage, Norma Varden, Douglas Wood, Grady Sutton. Screenplay, Therese Lewis and Barry Trivers, based on original by Erik Charell; camera Joseph Walker; editor, Al Clark; music, John Leipold; music director, M. W. Stoloff. At Radio City Music Hall, N. Y., week Dec. 2, '43. Running time, 93 MINS.

Carol Ainsley	Rosalind Russell
Henry Pepper	Brian Aherne
Michael Cobb	Willard Parker
Pat O'Shea	Alan Dinehart
Senator Ainsley	Edward Fielding
June Hughes	Ann Savage
Miss Timmons	Norma Varden
Dean Shaffer	Douglas Wood
Clark	Grady Sutton
Minna	Lilyan Irene
Ben	Frank Dawson

These are times when scenarists have apparently agreed that absurdities pay off at the boxoffice, or else there wouldn't be such efforts as 'What a Woman!' This is the kind of film where plausibility is considerably secondary. The laughs are the thing. But since there can be no quarrel with a film that does have a reasonable number of chuckles—at the expense of the script, of course—'Woman!' should do well enough at the b.o. aided by such names as Rosalind Russell and Brian Aherne for the marquee.

'Woman!' has some funny situations and the earnest, brisk direction of Irving Cummings. And Rosalind Russell.

If there has heretofore been any question as to Miss Russell's flair for comedy, then it can be immediately dispelled with a gander at this pic. She is all that the title implies. It's a type of role in which she's been seen too frequently, but there's no doubt she remains one of Hollywood's stellar comediennes.

Yarn concentrates itself on the invariable triangle, all treated lightly. Miss Russell is an agent, and it's a foregone conclusion soon after the first couple of reels that Brian Aherne, as the magazine writer sent to interview her, will eventually usurp the usual fictional contrivances and get the girl. The other guy is played by Willard Parker, a newcomer from the Broadway stage.

Story concerns Miss Russell's attempt to secure a male lead for a best-selling novel she's sold to the Hollywood studios and whose author

prefers to remain anonymous. When she learns his identity and seeks to persuade him (Parker) to perform the herculean character of the book. —a character apparently modeled after his own superman physique— that's where the film's weaknesses begin to crop up. It's pretty much of a merry-go-round after that.

Cummings' direction has concentrated on Miss Russell to carry the pic, and this she does with an effect that shades a number of obvious script loopholes. Aherne is somewhat miscast, since the part seemingly called for someone a little more flip, though he does as well with the role as the situation permitted. Parker contributes a commendable performance along with Alan Dinehart and Edward Fielding. Kahn.

She's for Me
(SONGS)

Universal release of Frank Gross production. Features David Bruce, Grace McDonald, Lois Collier, George Dolenz. Directed by Reginald Le Borg. Original screenplay by Henry Blankfort; camera, Paul Ivana; editor, Paul Landrers; songs, Joan Costello, Freddy Stewart, Mitchell Parish, Harry Woods; musical director, Charles Previn. Previewed in N. Y. Dec. 2, '43. Running time, 60 MINS.

Phil Norwin	George Dolenz
Michael Reed	David Bruce
Jan Lawton	Grace McDonald
Eileen Crane	Lois Collier
Bradford Crane	Charles Dingle
Miss Carpenter	Helen Brown
The Kid	Louis Da Pron
Sam	Mantan Moreland

Modestly budgeted and lacking marquee names, 'She's For Me' turns out surprisingly entertaining for a supporting dual feature. It's not unlike several recent frothy romantic comedies Universal has turned out so well lately. Picture further accents the screen possibilities of Grace McDonald who, judged by her work in this, originally was a singer and tap dancer of considerable ability.

Yarn shows two young members of a law firm wooing the same beauty. Lois Collier, niece of the elderly man who runs the law outfit, Charles Dingle. Latter thinks she is madly in love with David Bruce, his junior partner. Bruce actually is in his modest sort of way but is confounded when his former college pal, George Dolenz (just landed with the same law firm through this friendship), starts cutting in. Dolenz proves a practiced wooer via many previous love affairs.

One of these, with a pretty singer-dancer, Grace McDonald, returns to haunt him when Bruce accidentally learns about it. Latter hires Miss McDonald to make love to Dolenz (after landing her a nightclub job) In front of Miss Collier. That produces the expected blowup; Collier girl rushes to wed Bruce but the latter decides he's in love with Miss McDonald. After the familiar comedy of errors, Miss Collier lands Dolenz and Bruce wins Miss McDonald's consent.

Director Reginald Le Borg has invested such unoriginal developments with humorous angles for a maximum of chuckles. Producer Frank Gross has provided solid production, particularly in the nightclub sequence, in which Miss McDonald clicks with two songs. In earlier tryout nitery appearance she uses 'Getting Closer and Closer to Me,' with swingy tap dance followup. In big de luxe nightclub, Miss McDonald is equally effective singing 'Living My Tomorrow Today.' Wear.

Tarzan's Desert Mystery

RKO release of Sol Lesser production. Directed by William Thiele. Stars Johnny Weissmuller, Nancy Kelly, Johnny Sheffield; features Otto Kruger, Joe Sawyer. Screenplay, Edward T. Lowe from story by Carroll Young, based on Edgar Rice Burroughs characters; camera, Harry Wild and Russ Harlan; editor, Ray Lockert. Previewed in New York Dec. 6, '43. Running time, 70 MINS.

Tarzan..............Johnny Weissmuller

Boy..........................Johnny Sheffield
Connie Bryce....................Nancy Kelly
Hendrix.........................Otto Kruger
Karl.............................Joe Sawyer
Prince Selim...................Robert Lowery

'Tarzan's Desert Mystery' doesn't miss a thing with its quota of Nazi agents and gruesome animals plus the usual Tarzan jungle scenes, the film should lure the juves in droves to the dual setup for which this pic is headed.

Picture opens with Johnny Weissmuller, Johnny Sheffield and the chimp Cheta setting out across a desert to find a cure-all herb ordered by Mrs. Tarzan in London. On the way they run into Nancy Kelly, an American vaude performer who is on her way to warn a local sheik that Otto Kruger and Joe Sawyer are a couple of Nazi agents trying to stir up trouble. Things look tough for Tarzan and his crew when he is accused of stealing a stallion intended for the Sheik and Miss Kelly is framed on a murder charge and sentenced to be hanged. But it all winds up with the usual rescue.

Miss Kelly, who has replaced Maureen O'Sullivan as the femme lead in this Tarzan picture, turns in a workmanlike performance as an American magician. Weismuller, young Sheffield and Cheta are per usual. Kruger just doesn't belong as the Nazi. Film is nicely paced and photography highly effective.

Rookies in Burma

Hollywood, Dec. 7.

RKO release of Bert Gilroy production. Features Wally Brown, Alan Carney, Erford Gage. Directed by Leslie Goodwins. Original story and scenario, Edward James; camera, Harry Wild; editor, Harry Marker. Tradeshown Dec. 6, '43. Running time, **61 MINS.**

Jerry Miles.....................Wally Brown
Mike Strager.....................Alan Carney
Sgt. Burke.......................Erford Gage
Janie..........................Claire Carleton
Connie...........................Joan Barclay
Capt. Tomura........................Ted Hecht

This is second in group of features designed to spotlight RKO's new comedy team of Wally Brown and Alan Carney. It's corny tomfoolery in broadly burlesqued strokes, but carries sufficient elemental laughs to slip through the program houses as lower half of the duals.

Picture is a continual chase, with several crossfire displays of dialog banter between the comedians. Brown delivers his usual jumbled talk while Carney is the dumbbell of duo. Pair are captured in Burma along with Sergeant Erford Gage, but trio manages quick escape from Jap military camp. They pick up two American showgirls stranded in Burmese nightclub to make fivesome. Nips keep chasing until group reaches battlefront, with last hop made in captured Jap tank.

Brown and Carney show potentialities as cinematic comedy team, but need much stronger material than displayed here to get them into key houses even as support. Gags and situations have whiskers, with best audience reaction obtained from the physical action on display. Gage is overplayed as typical movie version of tough sergeant, while the two girls are okay to lend femme angle to the chase. Ted Hecht adequately handles heavy role of pursuing Jap officer. Most of the action in exteriors, with few interior sets. Most sustained laughs come at finish when fivesome rolls between the Jap and American lines in crazy fashion for sufficient footage until rescued. *Walt.*

The Demi-Paradise

(BRITISH-MADE)

London, Nov. 16.

General Film Distributors' release of Two Cities Film. Stars Laurence Olivier; features Penelope Ward, Leslie Henson. Directed by Anthony Asquith; written and produced by Anatole de Grunwald. Music by Nicholas Brodszky; camera, Bernard Knowles. At Odeon theatre, London, Nov. 16, '43. Running time, **115 MINS.**

Ivan Dimitrievitch Kouznetsoff, ...Laurence Olivier
Ann Tisdall....................Penelope Ward
Mrs. Tisdall.................Marjorie Fielding
Rowena Ventnor......Margaret Rutherford
Leslie Henson..................Leslie Henson
Herbert Tisdall...............George Thorpe
Richard Christie.............Guy Middleton
Mr. Walford.................Michael Shepley
Mr. Runalow......................Felix Aylmer
Mrs. Pawson...................Joyce Grenfell
Mrs. Flannel....................Everley Gregg
Winifred Tisdall..................Edie Martin
Mrs. Tisdall-Stanton...........Muriel Aked

'The Demi-Paradise' runs five minutes less than two hours and its entertainment value would be improved by the deletion of half an hour or more. Most of it is narration, and from that angle is one of the finest scripts ever put out anywhere, its splendid satirical dialog poking amusingly and bitingly at the English themselves. British people laugh at themselves as no other nation.

'Demi-Paradise' script consists of a wealth of character drawings with a thin web of a story about a young Russian engineer, the inventor of a new-type propellor for use on icebreakers. He arrives in England some months before the war, with humorous misconception of the average native of Britain. He is bewildered by its conventions, smugness and capacity for muddling through. It takes him some time to know these people for what they really are, with their foibles, humors and idiosyncrasies. A good many things happen before a mutual respect and understanding comes about. There is a slight love story between the young Russian and an English girl.

Outstanding is a performance by Laurence Olivier. It is an accumulation of matured acting greatly exceeding the normal development that comes to an artist with increased experience. Replete with Russian accent, he gives a dignified and serious performance full of sincerity and repose that puts him in the top rank of British actors. For years an ace artist, he reaches a height in this film that will court comparison with the greatest of his contemporaries. Ablest support comes from Felix Aylmer, veteran stage actor, as a wealthy shipbuilder with a series of eccentricities that would excite risibility in a mummy. Penelope Ward is the leading lady and offers a much more acceptable performance than anything with which she has hitherto been identified.

There is a cast of over 30 that could hardly be improved upon, being selected for their known talents as character performers. This includes a star of the magnitude of Leslie Henson, who makes a brief appearance as himself in a cafe, doing a bit as a pianist with his inimitable Rachmaninoff piano solo.

Photography is excellent, production borders on the massive, and director Anthony Asquith has caught the spirit of the idea. *Jolo.*

Hands Across the Border

(SONGS)

Republic release of Harry Grey production. Stars Roy Rogers and 'Trigger'; features Ruth Terry, Guinn Williams, Onslow Stevens, Mary Treen, Bob Noland, The Sons of the Pioneers. Directed by Joseph Kane. Screenplay by Bradford Ropes and J. Benton Cheney; camera, Reggie Lanning; editor, Tony Martinelli; dances directed by Dave Gould. Tradeshown, New York, N. Y., Dec. 3, '43. Running time, **72 MINS.**

Roy..............................Roy Rogers
Trigger (His Horse)...................Trigger
Themselves..............Bob Nolan and the Sons of the Pioneers
Kim Adams........................Ruth Terry
Teddy Bear......Guinn 'Big Boy' Williams
Brock Danvers...............Onslow Stevens
Sophie Lawrence..................Mary Treen
Jeff Adams....................Joseph Crehan
Juan Morales................Duncan Renaldo
Col. Ames...................Frederick Burton
Mac Marclay.......................Leroy Mason
Col. Carter.........................Larry Steers
Senor Morales..................Julian Rivero
Rosita Morales....................Janet Martin
The Wiere Bros...................Themselves

Ostensibly a horse-opera, 'Hands Across the Border' is in reality closer to being a musical than a Western. It has been produced on a higher budget and scale than is customary for shootin' mellers, and the result shows it. Pic supplies a very satisfying 70 minutes of fine scenery, beautiful horseflesh, good songs well sung, production numbers and, above all, 'Trigger,' the gifted equine who is a show in himself. Film is good dual support.

Story is very thin, but there's so much else that this doesn't matter. It deals with the performer-daughter (Ruth Terry) of a rancher, who takes over the job of turning out good horses for the Army when her father is killed through the machinations of a rival breeder, who is also the gal's suitor. Roy Rogers helps her, makes a success of the horse venture, and everything ends happily.

Pic is loaded with good tunes by Hoagy Carmichael, Ned Washington and Phil Ohman, and these are delivered well by Rogers. Miss Terry and the rest of the cast. Miss Terry turns out to be possessed of a nifty selling style. For competition she has a relatively-unknown runnerup in Janet Martin. Latter has good voice and distinctive style in performing a Spanish number, and looks good, too. Mention should go to two young dancers, Betty Marion and Chiquita, who deliver a couple of swell routines combined out of ballet, tap and flamenco.

There are two production numbers styled by Dave Gould. One, a Spanish fiesta number, is graceful and highly entertaining. The second, a 'Hands Across the Border' number, seems too long, but is packed with good stuff. Both are done without the pretentiousness reserved for such items in big pix, and they prove that much can be accomplished with taste and intelligence instead of heavy budgets.

Harvest Melody

(SONGS)

PRC release of Walter Colmes production; features Rosemary Lane, Johnny Downs, The Vigilantes, Radio Rogues, Eddie Le Baron orch. Directed by Sam Newfield. Screenplay by Allan Gale, from original by Martin Mooney and Ande Lamb; camera, James Brown; editor, Holbrook N. Todd. At Strand, Brooklyn, dual, week of Dec. 2, '43. Running time, **70 MINS.**

Gilda Parker...............Rosemary Lane
Tommy.........................Johnny Downs
Chuck.......................Sheldon Leonard
Nancy.....................Charlotte Wynters
Cafe Manager......................Luis Alberni
Daisy.........................Claire Rochelle
Spot................................Syd Saylor
Jane........................Marjorie Manners
Sunny Fox.........................Sunny Fox
Pa Nelson..........................Henry Hall
Canvas...........................Billy Nelson
Cigarette Girl..............Frances Gladwin

This indie film plugs the farmer's contribution to the war effort in phoney fashion. But farmers will probably flock from miles around to get a horse laugh from PRC's idea of how they are solving the man and woman power shortage.

Pipe dream of a story, which is superimposed on a solid set of songs and specialty numbers, has Rosemary Lane, an ex-film star, pitching hay on a farm as a publicity stunt. Idea was dreamed up by her press agent, Sheldon Leonard, who induces his other clients to join her. He also has her pitch woo with the farmer's son, Johnny Downs, and later inveigle lad into an engagement. She gets her publicity, sets up national farm labor clubs, but then goes righteous by turning down a fat film contract, sticking to her farm work, and releasing the farm boy.

There's very little rhyme or reason to 'Harvest Melody' except that it gives Rosemary Lane a chance to warble several numbers with Johnny Downs, and Eddie Le Baron's orch an opportunity to play rumbas on a haystack. The Radio Rogues toss off impersonations of Jack Benny, Don Wilson and several others which are above par.

Performances of top featured players and supporting cast are on par with the corny story, so the actors can't be blamed too much.

The Hundred Pound Window

(BRITISH-MADE)

London, Nov. 17.

Warner Bros. production and release. Features Anne Crawford, Mary Clare, David Farrar, Frederick Leister. Directed by Brian Desmond Hurst. Adaptation by Brock Williams from screenplay by Abem Finkel, based on original story by Mark Hellinger; additional dialog by Rodney Ackland; music by Hans May; lyrics, Alan Stranks. At Studio One, London, Nov. 16, '43. Time, **90 MINS.**

Joan Draper...................Anne Crawford
George Graham..................David Farrar
Ernest Draper...........Frederick Leister
Millie Draper.......................Mary Clare
Tommy Draper......Richard Attenborough
Chick Slater..................Niall McGinnis
Steve Halligan............David Hutcheson
Captain..........................Francis Lister
Hon. Freddie..................Claude Allister
Van Rayden...............Peter Gawthorne
John Humphries..............Claude Bailey
O'Neil................................John Slater
Baldwin.............................David Horne
Evans..............................Tony Hawtrey

This English adaptation of Mark Hellinger's original American racing story has all the earmarks of a natural for war-film-weary audiences on both sides of the Atlantic. Slickness of plot development suggests a faithful following of the original American script by Abem Finkel, but in every detail incident and atmosphere is as English as the Derby.

What the American title may have been is a secret in the WB London office, but it certainly could not have been more mystifying than 'The Hundred Pound Window,' pounds thus used in England meaning only weight. Even the correct £100 would not help much, inasmuch as it would convey an idea of the worth of some window. Actually it refers to a super totalizator booth where the minimum bet is the sterling equivalent of $500.

With due consideration to wartime difficulties, the casting of this one is little short of a triumph for the Warners' Teddington studio, even the smallest of the bits being filled perfectly. Acting honors are shared by Anne Crawford and Mary Clare, with Frederick Leister turning in a convincing portrait of an auditor with years of faithful service suddenly catapulted into the maelstrom of the race track where he presides at the tote window of the title.

Of the others, a brand-new beauty with a really good singing voice and an A-1 figure, Hazel Bray, has to be seen and heard to be believed. If she doesn't find herself in possession of a one-way ticket to Hollywood when the Wardour street talent scouts of the big American companies spot her they will all have to be afflicted with deafness and blindness.

Second only to flawless performances by the 18 principal characters, the production value of this one is exceptional.

Direction by Brian Desmond-Hurst, coupled with more than usually effective editing, keeps the story moving with a smooth swiftness all too rare in English movies.

Unfortunately for his growing number of British fans, David Farrar, in the relatively unimportant role of a Scotland Yard detective on the track of black market crooks, has little to do.

For all its escapism, here is one as topical as it is gripping entertainment.

Fighting Valley

Producers Releasing Corp. release of Alfred Stern and Arthur Alexander production. Directed by Oliver Drake. Features Dave (Tex) O'Brien, Jim Newill, Guy Wilkerson. Screenplay, Oliver Drake; camera, Ira Morgan; editor, Charles Hinkle, Jr. At New York theatre, N. Y., dual. Running time, **60 MINS.**

Tex Wyatt	Dave (Tex) O'Brien
Jim Steele	Jim Newill
'Panhandle' Perkins	Guy Wilkerson
Joan Manning	Patti McCarty
Dan Wakely	John Merton
Paul Jackson	Robert Bice
Tuscon Jones	Stanley Price
Ma Donovan	Mary McLaren
Frank Burke	John Elliot
Slim	Charles King

This hour-long dual western makes for above-average interest for films of this type. It's another in the Oliver Drake series, featuring Dave (Tex) O'Brien, and furnishes plenty of fist-slinging, hoss riding and gunplay.

Yarn deals with the efforts of O'Brien, Jim Newill and Guy Wilkerson, as Texas Rangers, to break up the conspiracy of a large ore smelting company trying to put the squeeze on indie operators. Patti McCarty, femme interest, is one of the indie owners and unwittingly plays into the hands of the larger firm through her fiance, Robert Bice, who is trying to play both ends.

O'Brien is standout, with Wilkerson providing laughs. Miss McCarty is satisfactory also, while Bice and John Merton make for suitable wrong-guys.

Headline
(BRITISH-MADE)

London, Nov. 17.

Ealing Distribution release of John Corfield production. Stars John Stuart. Directed by John Harlow. Screenplay by Maisie Sharman, from adaptation by Ralph Bettinson of Ken Attiwill's novel, 'The Reporter.' Camera, Geoffrey Faithful. At Studio One, London, Nov. 16, '43. Running time, **75 MINS.**

Broogie	David Farrar
Anne	Anne Crawford
L. B. Ellington	John Stuart
Mrs. Ellington	Antoinette Cellier
Dell	Billy Hartnell
Grayson	Anthony Hawtrey
Jones	Richard Goolden
Betty	Lorna Tarbat

David Farrar, newest rave of British femmes, has it all his own way in this newspaper melodrama. In the role of a crime reporter, Farrar does things which in any real newspaper office, English or American, would put him in the breadline for life. So film audiences, ignorant of the way newspapers are run, will undoubtedly find his performance tops.

The picture itself is badly balanced. After an intriguing opening, with more than a touch of Noel Coward smartness in the dialog, the story degenerates into conventional whodunit.

A John Corfield production, made at Riverside Studios and handled by Ealing Distribution, Ltd., 'Headline' has had too many better predecessors in the way of newspaper picts to make much headway in the American market.

Antoinette Cellier does her best with a hopelessly melodramatic part. But, as seems frequently to be the case in present-day English pictures, the minor roles offer the biggest opportunities, and are the best played. Of these an amateur, 'psychological' detective, as portrayed by Richard Goolden, of BBC fame in the 'Mr. Penny' series, steals the film from the principals.

Direction by John Harlow is at all times adequate, but greater directorial genius than his could not make plausible the incongruities of this script.

Miniature Reviews

'Desert Song' (Musical; Color) (WB). Modernized operetta in color looks good for hefty grosses.

'Higher and Higher' (RKO). Starring Michele Morgan, Jack Haley and Frank Sinatra; and rates, high for b.o.

'The Woman of the Town' (UA) (songs). High-budgeted wesern. Stars, Albert Dekker and Claire Trevor; good for duals.

'Calling Dr. Death' (U). First of cinematic Inner Sanctum whodunits strong programmer for regular bookings.

'Crime Doctor's Strangest Case' (Col). Murder mystery that should do fairly well on double bills.

'Pistol Packin' Mama' (Songs) (Rep). Diverting filmusical comedy woven around pop song title. Strong program supporter.

'Doughboys in Ireland' (songs) (Col). Kenny Baker and the Jesters in lightweight comedy; mild supporter for dual bills.

'Mr. Muggs Steps Out.' (Mono). 'East Side Kid' comedy, with Park avenue setting. Nets lots of laughs, for lower duals.

'La Piel De Zapa' (Argentine). Adaptation from Balzac novel; strictly for Spanish-speaking audiences.

'Canyon City' (Rep). Don 'Red' Barry starrer, which delivers its money's worth in action.

The Desert Song
(Color)
(OPERETTA)

Hollywood, Dec. 13.

Warner Bros. production and release. Stars Dennis Morgan, Irene Manning; features Bruce Cabot, Lynne Overman, Gene Lockhart. Directed by Robert Florey. Based on play by Lawrence Schwab, Otto Harbach, Oscar Hammerstein 2d, Sigmund Romberg and Frank Mandel; camera, Bert Glennon; editor, Frank Magee; art director, Charles Novi; dances, Leroy Prinz; set, Jack McConaghy; asst. director, Art Lueker. Previewed Dec. 13, 1943. Running time, **90 MINS.**

Paul Hudson	Dennis Morgan
Margot	Irene Manning
Colonel Fontaine	Bruce Cabot
Caid Yousseff	Victor Francen
Johnny Walsh	Lynne Overman
Benoit	Gene Lockhart
Hajy	Faye Emerson
Tarbouch	Marcel Dalio
Heinzelman	Felix Basch
Haasan	Gerald Mohr
Abdel Rahman	Noble Johnson
Francois	Curt Bois
Muhammad	Albert Morin
Lieutenant Bertin	Jack LaRue
Suliman	William Edmunds
Pajot	Wallis Clark

Warners' modernized film version of the popular 'Desert Song' operetta is mounted in eyeful Technicolor. It's a combo of tuneful escapist entertainment that will catch strong boxoffice reaction in all runs—with key holdovers indicated.

In modernizing story, German agents and plans to construct new railroad in North Africa for terminus at Dakar, provides motivation for Riff uprising and leadership by Dennis Morgan, an American piano player in Morocco nightspot, who's been fighting Franco in Spain prior to moving across the Mediterranean to Africa. Irene Manning is the new singer at the cafe, with mutual romance developing. Riffs are rounded up by French officers to work on the railroad, with native Victor Francen, a tool of the Nazis, impressing the natives to work. But Morgan, as El Khobar, leader of the Riffs, circumvents the plans by periodic appearances on the desert and in Morocco to lead the natives in revolt against the forced labor regulations. From there on it's series of chases across the desert sands, pitched battles, and wild adventure until Morgan convinces the French colonel, Bruce Cabot, of Francen's duplicity, to eventually obtain freedom and rights for the Riffs through edict of France.

Despite modernization to provide film technique and movement to the operetta, basic entertainment qualities of 'Desert Song' are retained to provide most diverting audience reaction at this time. Uncredited script from the Schwab-Harbach-Hammerstein II-Romberg-Mandel play is expertly directed by Robert Florey, aided by excellent production mounting and exterior color photography notable for its sharpness and depth.

Morgan is neatly cast as the Red Rider, delivering both dramatic and vocal assignments in top style. Irene Manning capably handles the girl spot as singer and actress; with strong support provided by Lynne Overman, Gene Lockhart, Faye Emerson, Curt Bois and Marcel Dalio. Sylvia Opert displays a provocative nautch dance that was obviously trimmed for footage.

In addition to the standard and well known 'Riff Song,' 'One Alone' and 'Desert Song,' delivered in solo and duo by Morgan and Miss Manning, new film version inserts four additional tunes—two by Romberg—but none of the quartet has strength for current popularity.

Warners backgrounded the picture, made about 18 months ago, with expensive background of Morocco and the desert country for top production values and eye entertainment.

Walt.

Higher and Higher
(MUSICAL)

RKO release of Tim Whelan production. Stars Michele Morgan, Jack Haley and Frank Sinatra; features Leon Errol, Marcy McGuire, Paul and Grace Hartman, Barbara Hale, Dooley Wilson, Victor Borge, Mary Wickes, Elisabeth Risdon, Mel Torme and Ivy Scott. Directed by Tim Whelan. Based on legit musical production of same name, with book by Gladys Hurlbut and Joshual Logan; score by Rodgers and Hart; adaptation, Jay Dratler and Ralph Spence, with additional dialog by William Bowers and Howard Harris; special songs, Jimmy McHugh and Harold Adamson; musical numbers staged by Ernst Matra; film editor, Gene Milford; camera, Robert De Grasse. Previewed in N. Y. Dec. 1, '43. Running time, **90 MINS.**

Millie	Michele Morgan
Mike	Jack Haley
Frank	Frank Sinatra
Drake	Leon Errol
Mickey	Marcy McGuire
Sir Bictor Fitzroy Victor	Victor Borge
Sandy	Mary Wickes
Mrs. Keating	Elisabeth Risdon
Katherine	Barbara Hale
Marty	Mel Torme
Byngham	Paul Hartman
Hilda	Grace Hartman
Oscar	Dooley Wilson
Mrs. Whiffin	Ivy Scott
Mr. Green	Rex Evans
Hotel Manager	Stanley Logan
Maid	Ola Lorraine
Mr. Duval	King Kennedy
Announcer	Robert Anderson

With a good cast, among whom is Frank Sinatra, the 1940 legit musical, 'Higher and Higher,' with added script material and new songs, emerges on the screen under excellent production treatment by Tim Whelan as first-rate entertainment.

Light in vein but rich in comedy and song values, plus having very fine pace, the picture is destined to rank high at the boxoffice. Among other things, it's as escapist as they come. The lads and lassies in the service are bound to take to it warmly.

There may be some folks who can't figure out the reasons for Sinatra's meteoric rise, or might be wondering whether he's here to stay or not, but in his first starring role on the screen he at least gets in no one's way. Though a bit stiff on occasion and not as photogenic as may be desired, he generally handles himself ably in song as well as a few brief dialog scenes. Several good song numbers, turned out specially for the film by Jimmy McHugh and Harold Adamson, are a strong asset to Sinatra, while the book assigns the crooner to carefully plotted romantic and other situations.

The song-studded story is laid principally in the mansion of Leon Errol, who learns, as it opens, that he has gone bankrupt and will have to vacate unless getting up a hunk of coin in a hurry. His valet gets the bright idea of picking one of the servants, having her pose as Errol's daughter, and getting her married off. Since none of the long list of servants in Errol's employ has been paid in many months, a corporation is formed in order to include them in the deal.

The scullery maid, who has a waving acquaintance with Sinatra, living across the way from her, is chosen to carry out the marriage end of the plot, which, as a starter, is designed to bring the gal out as the new season's No. 1 deb. Michele Morgan plays this part, and reluctantly agrees to go through with it, with most of the amusing comedy situations being built around her continued efforts to back out, plus the boners she makes in trying to pose as a deb. Her scenes at the butler's ball are extremely funny.

Maneuvering the scullery maid's marriage to Victor Borge, who everyone thinks is a titled gentleman but actually is a crook in disguise, the ceremony is about to be performed when Jack Haley, the valet, breaks it up. He has discovered a secret door leading to a huge wine-cellar filled with priceless vintages and containing an historic old harpsichord that's worth a fortune, all of which saves the day for Errol and his crew. The cellar is turned into a night club and forms the scene for a production sequence built around 'Minuet in Boogie,' very good number in which all hands take part. It also includes reprising of two hit tunes, 'I Couldn't Sleep a Wink Last Night,' earlier soloed by Sinatra, and 'I Saw You First,' previously doubled by Sinatra and Marcy McGuire, cute little songstress with loads of personality and a long, open road ahead of her.

Two other songs that stack up strongly are Sinatra's 'The Music Stopped,' directed to Miss Morgan and Barbara Hale at the butler's ball, and 'This Is a Lovely Way to Spend an Evening,' done by the crooner and Miss Morgan. Still another number, handled in a group manner, that listens well is 'When It Comes to Love You're on Your Own.'

Mixing into the latter vocally as well as for light, gay comedy are Errol, Haley, Miss McGuire, Mary Wickes, Paul and Grace Hartman, Dooley Wilson and Mel Torme, plus Sinatra. All the musical numbers have been expertly staged by Ernst Matra, with fast pace and novelty a commanding characteristic of Matra's work. This is also particularly true of Whelan's direction, while his production backgrounds are all that may be desired.

Miss Morgan, she of the charming naivette, and Haley, with whom she's secretly in love, both turn in fine jobs. This is also true of Errol, whose opening drunk bit tees the picture off very entertainingly. Miss Hale, a legit deb, pairs romantically with Sinatra for the finish.

Except for Borge, who has a brief novelty piano session at one point, and a few lessers, the cast is playing servants' roles, all good. They include the Hartmans, with Paul playing a butler and Grace an upstairs maid in Errol's household. Both do very well in their comedy and singing parts, their dancing being virtually conspicuous by its absence all along the line. Mary Wickes, comedienne type reminding a little of Joan Davis, scores strongly as Errol's secretary, as do Wilson, his colored chauffeur; Torme, pantry boy, and Ivy Scott, buxom cook.

While this is Sinatra's first starring role, he was in a picture last season, 'Reveille With Beverly,' made by Columbia, in which the lean-looking crooner did one song number.
Char.

The Woman of the Town
(SONGS)

United Artists release of Harry Sherman production. Directed by George Archainbaud. Stars Albert Dekker and Claire Trevor; features Barry Sullivan, Henry Hull, Marion Martin, Porter Hall, Percy Kilbride, Beryl Wallace, Arthur Hohl and Clem Bevans. Screenplay, Aeneas MacKenzie, from story by Norman Houston; camera, Russell Harlan; editor, Carrol Lewis. Previewed in New York, Dec. 10, '43. Running time, **87 MINS.**

Dora Hand..........Claire Trevor
'Bat' Masterson..........Albert Dekker
King Kennedy..........Barry Sullivan
Inky Wilkinson..........Henry Hull
Daisy Davenport..........Marion Martin
Dog Kelly..........Porter Hall
Rev. Samuel Small..........Percy Kilbride
Louella Parsons..........Beryl Wallace
Robert Wright..........Arthur Hohl
Buffalo Burns..........Clem Bevans
Fanny Garretson..........Teddi Sherman
Judge Blackburn..........George Cleveland
The Publisher..........Russell Hicks
Doc Sears..........Herb Rawlinson
Annie Logan..........Marlene Mains
Belle..........Dorothy Grainger
Waddy Kerns..........Dewey Robinson
Crockett..........Wade Crosby
Wagner..........Hal Taliaferro
Walker..........Glenn Strange
Eddie Foy, Sr..........Charley Foy
Mrs. Wright..........Claire Whitney
Sime..........Russell Simpson
Mrs. Brown..........Eula Guy
Mrs. Logan..........Frances Morris

'Woman of the Town' is a comparatively high-budgeted western starring Albert Dekker and Claire Trevor in a biographical film highlighting the romance of 'Bat' Masterson and Dora Hand. Masterson, it will be recalled, was famous in U. S. folk history as the tough, straight-shooting marshal of Dodge City who later became a crack newspaperman. Dora Hand was a high-minded honky tonk singer, who launched him on newspaper career. It's a fast moving feature, providing first-rate entertainment, and appealing to femmes and action fans. It should do healthy biz.

Film opens with shot of Masterson (Albert Dekker) at his desk as editor of the old New York Morning Telegraph in 1919. Then there's a flashback to Dodge City of 1871. The picture deals with that period of Masterson's life when he became marshal (despite the fact that he wanted a newspaper job), and remained in that post until he drove several gangs of outlaws from the frontier cattle center. It was during this period that he fell for Dora Hand (Claire Trevor), who doubled as a saloon singer and social worker. She wanted Masterson to give up marshaling and go east to do newspaper work. He, in turn, wanted her to give up professional singing. A third party, King Kennedy (Barry Sullivan), complicated matters. He was a rich Texas cattledealer, playboy and gunman, and until Masterson took over as marshal nobody tried to curb his lawlessness. Masterson, however, made him and his gang toe the mark. But Kennedy and his gunmen finally cut loose when he tries to kidnap Dora Hand. She was accidently killed by Kennedy during the fighting that takes place. Before she died she made Masterson promise to throw away his guns. He carried out the promise, but also succeeded in bringing Kennedy to justice.

The screenplay takes its title from an editorial Masterson wrote in the Dodge City paper while he was marshal, in which he praised the social work and church efforts of Dora Hand and denounced the stuffed-shirts who tried to exclude her from the church. It is a well-scripted screenplay which combines plenty of action with convincing dialog.

Dekker and Miss Trevor handle their roles neatly and receive strong support from Sullivan, Percy Kilbride, who portrays the town preacher; Clem Bevans and Henry Hull. Direction is firm and fast-paced, and photography is clear. Considering, however, that 'Woman of the Town' is essentially a western, there are no panoramic scenic shots, which are expected of higher-priced actioners.

Calling Dr. Death

Universal release of Ben Pivar production. Stars Lon Chaney; features Patricia Morison, J. Carrol Naish, David Bruce, Ramsay Ames, Fay Helm. Directed by Reginald LeBorg. Original screenplay by Edward Dein; camera, Virgil Miller; editor, Norman A. Cerf; special photography, John P. Fulton. Previewed Dec. 9, '43. Running time, **62 MINS.**

Doctor Steele..........Lon Chaney
Stella..........Patricia Morison
Inspector Gregg..........J. Carrol Naish
Robert Duval..........David Bruce
Maria Steele..........Ramsay Ames
Mrs. Duval..........Fay Helm
Butler..........Holmes Herbert
Watchman..........Alec Craig
Father..........Fred Giermann
Mother..........Lisa Golm
Coroner..........Charles Wagenheim
Marion..........Mary Hale
District Attorney..........George Eldredge
Priest..........John Elliott

Universal, which specializes in supernatural thrillers, is launching a new series of 'Inner Sanctum Mysteries' with this whodunit about 'self-hypnosis.' The 'Inner Sanctum' tag is by arrangement with the Simon & Schuster publishing house, which has a modest rep for its mystery novels. This initial feature, 'Calling Dr. Death,' is a reasonably compact and compelling yarn told in semi-radio style, with a smattering of pseudo-scientific mumbo-jumbo. It's an okay programmer for whodunit fans.

The story deals with a neurologist who hates his beautiful, faithless wife and who, when her mutilated body is found, doesn't know if he murdered her in a state of self-hypnotic jealousy. The other principal characters are the doc's seemingly loyal nurse-assistant and the relentless detective who apparently suspects him of the crime. The piece is patently concocted, but is fairly taut and moves with reasonable pace to a suspenseful denouement. However, the stream-of-consciousness soundtrack spiel by the doctor (precisely the kind of thing used too much in radio) is artificial and distracting.

Reginald LeBorg's direction has satisfactory tempo and emphasis, which the cutting has apparently helped. Lon Chaney is direct and believable as the doctor, but from a marquee standpoint isn't ideally cast. Patricia Morison is acceptable as the nurse and J. Carrol Naish registers as the uncannily shrewd sleuth. Technically, the picture is all right.
Hobe.

Crime Doctor's Strangest Case

Columbia release of Rudolph C. Flothow production. Stars Warner Baxter; features Lynn Merrick, Reginald Denny, Barton MacLane, Jerome Cowan, Rose Hobart, Gloria Dickson. Directed by Eugene J. Forde. Based on radio program, 'Crime Doctor,' by Max Marcin; story and adaptation, Eric Taylor; editor, Dwight Caldwell; camera, James S. Brown. At Fox, Brooklyn, week Dec. 9, '43. Running time, **68 MINS.**

Robert Ordway..........Warner Baxter
Ellen..........Lynn Merrick
Paul Ashley..........Reginald Denny
Rief..........Barton MacLane
Mallory Cartwright..........Jerome Cowan
Diana Burns..........Rose Hobart
Mrs. Keppler..........Gloria Dickson
Patricia Cornwall..........Virginia Brissac
Jimmy Trotter..........Lloyd Bridges
Betty Watson..........Constance Worth
Yarnell..........Thomas E. Jackson
Addison Burns..........Sam Flint

Though plotted well, sustaining suspense, 'Crime Doctor's Strangest Case' has a tendency to drag due to detail involved in running down clues and questioning of suspects in the murder that has been committed. Should do fairly well, however, and will provide suitable support on double bills.

Latest in the 'Crime Doctor' series, all starring Warner Baxter, concerns the mysterious poisoning of a retired realty operator who at one time was partnered in a cafe venture with a man who supposedly vanished with $50,000 but actually had been killed and his body left in the cafe for 30 years. After pointing the finger of guilt in many directions, it develops that a nephew of the slain man did the poisoning with a view to getting at the latter's money.

Baxter, who in the first of the 'Crime Doctor' series retired from the parole board, now practices psychiatry and, in spare moments, indulges in amateur detective work. No romantic interest revolves around him, this being mainly shouldered by Lynn Merrick and Lloyd Bridges, who perform neatly.

Reginald Denny plays the murderer well, while Rose Hobart is suitable as the widow suspect. Others include Jerome Cowan, who with Barton MacLane and Thomas E. Jackson, provide some comedy relief. It isn't much, however. Gloria Dickson does the wife of Cowan in an okay manner. She's also one of the suspects, as is Virginia Brissac. A minor part is played by Constance Worth.
Char.

Pistol Packin' Mama
(SONGS)

Hollywood, Dec. 8.

Republic release of Eddy White production. Directed by Frank Woodruff. Screenplay by Edward Dein and Fred Schiller. Original by Arthur Caesar and Dein; camera, Reggie Lanning; editor, Tony Martinelli; music director, Morton Scott. Previewed in projection room, Dec. 7, 1943. Running time, **63 MINS.**

Vicki Norris / Sally Benson..........Ruth Terry
Nick Winner..........Robert Livingston
The Joker..........Wally Vernon
Johnny Rossi..........Jack LaRue
J. Leslie Burton III..........Kirk Alyn
Mike..........Eddie Parker
Joe McGurn..........Joe Kirk
Young Wife..........Helen Talbot
Mrs. Burton..........Lydia Bilbrook
Mr. Burton..........George Lessey
Themselves..........The King Cole Trio

This cinematic filmusical is a neatly concocted affair based on the song title, and will provide strong support for the regular bookings, including key dualers, where title will attract added patronage.

In view of necessity of whipping up a yarn and getting film through production fast to catch current popularity of the song hit, picture is above par in entertainment of its type. Arthur Caesar and Edward Dein teamed to brew a light and fluffy tale in typical musical vein, satisfactorily hitting the mark of diverting and not-to-be-taken-seriously entertainment. Director Frank Woodruff paces the unreeling at a consistent gait, and songs are showmanly spotted and presented.

Ruth Terry, as the gat-packer, is introduced as the warbling owner of a gambling tavern in Nevada. Robert Livingston, a slick opportunist and con man muscled out of New York by gangleader Jack LaRue, steps up to switch dice and break the house. He returns east to open a swank gambling nightspot; with girl following when she discovers his crooked coup. She takes singing job in the casino and tricks him into high-card cut to get possession in retaliation for original deal. LaRue and mob try to move in, but girl shoots gang up and finds at finish it's time for clinch with Livingston.

Miss Terry capably delivers 'Pistol Pack' several times along the way, wildly waving her shooting irons to accentuate presentation. She also sings 'I've Heard That Song Before' and 'Love Is a Corny Thing.' King Cole trio is spotlighted with one tune, 'I'm an Errand Boy for Rhythm.' Wally Vernon functions as Livingston's wacky pal for various comedy interludes, and does one turn on the nightclub floor for okay reaction. LaRue is typed for the gangleader, while Kirk Alyn is spotted as a socialite suitor of the girl.

Picture carries adequate production mounting for above-par filmusical programmer.
Walt.

Doughboys in Ireland
(SONGS)

Columbia release of Jack Fier production. Stars Kenny Baker; features Jeff Donnell, Lynn Merrick, The Jesters. Directed by Lew Landers. Original screenplay by Howard J. Green; added dialog, Monte Brice; camera, L. W. O'Connell; editor, Mel Thorsen. At Strand, Brooklyn, week Dec. 9, '43, dualed. Running time, **61 MINS.**

Danny O'Keefe..........Kenny Baker
Molly Callahan..........Jeff Donnell
Gloria Gold..........Lynn Merrick
Chuck Mayers..........Guy Bonham
Corny Smith..........Red Latham
Tiny Johnson..........Wamp Carlson
Ernie Jones..........Bob Mitchum
Jimmy Martin..........Buddy Yarus
Michael Callahan..........Harry Shannon
Mrs. Callahan..........Dorothy Vaughan
Captain..........Larry Thompson
Sergeant..........Syd Saylor
Larry Hunt..........Herbert Rawlinson

Even Kenny Baker's superb ballading fails to save 'Doughboys in Ireland' from being a lightweight supporting feature. Plot leans too much on Baker and his voice to carry it over the bumps. Numerous scripting errors, such as switching from farce comedy to heavy dramatics, could not be overcome even by Lew Landers' usual fine direction. Why Baker's valuable singing voice should be wasted on this trite vehicle is difficult to comprehend. He's given faulty lighting, uneven photography and haphazard makeup—none of which is calculated to enhance his future screen possibilities.

Baker is an orchestra leader at a pop N. Y. nightclub; also chief vocalist. Other entertainers include The Jesters, the four of them leaving after a farewell laudatory appearance to enter the Army. There's also Lynn Merrick, a passably good singer at the club, who's ambitious to get into a Broadway musical. There's the typical 'wolf' Broadway producer, too, and he's out making a play for Miss Merrick in competition with Baker. Latter is hornswoggled into believing she is madly in love with him.

With the foursome off to Ireland, Baker moons over his failure to get any news from his 'sweetheart,' Miss Merrick, though everybody in his barracks is hep to how she's gone for the Broadway producer when he lands her a show. Baker falls for the Irish colleen, Jeff Donnell, but does an about-face when, quaintly enough, Miss Merrick lands in the camp as special entertainer. When he gets the brushoff, Baker returns to the arms of Miss Donnell. There is a heavily miniaturized Ranger attack on some invasion coast and Baker is badly wounded. The next scene he's out of the hospital and singing again to Miss Donnell. It's that simple.

Kenny Baker sings admirably, if perhaps a bit too often, with many songs dragged in by the forelock. Most of them are Irish ballads. 'I Have Faith' is his best in the pop category. The Jesters are okay on several brief appearances, doing their own instrumental playing per usual with their comedy numbers. Jeff Donnell makes an effective shy Irish miss who falls for Baker, but Lynn Merrick is overly stilted as the nightclub singer (Baker's first love). Jesters turn actors here, figuring importantly in story. Support is headed by Dorothy Vaughan, Harry Shannon and the Jesters, Guy Bonham, Red Latham and Wamp Carlson. Picture moans for a couple of outstanding thespians.
Wear.

Mr. Muggs Steps Out

Monogram release of Sam Katzman and Jack Dietz production. Features Leo Gorcey, Huntz Hall, Gabriel Dell, Billy Benedict and Joan Marsh. Directed by William Beaudine. Screenplay and story, William X. Crowley and Beryl Sachs; camera, Marcel le Picard; editor, Carl Pierson. At New York, N. Y., dual, week of Dec. 7, '43. Running time, 63 MINS.

Muggs	Leo Gorcey
Glimpy	Huntz Hall
Nolan	Gabriel Dell
Pinkie	Billy Benedict
Judge	Noah Beery, Sr.
Brenda	Joan Marsh
Margaret	Betty Bl the
Diamonds	Nick Stuart
Maisie	Patsy Moran
Virgil	Stanley Brown
Charney	Halliwell Hobbes

The survivors of the original 'Dead End Kids' company, re-christened the 'East Side Kids' by Monogram, are served up in a corny comedy that should register with 'Kids' fans on double bills.

Leo Gorcey, titlerolist, is saved from a reform school term by Park avenue matron Betty Blythe, whose hobby is to hire jailbirds as servants, thereby satisfying her social conscience and solving the servant problem. Gorcey gets a job as chauffeur to the matron and her daughter, Joan Marsh, despite the objections of former's husband. Hiring Gorcey and his gang, who act as waiters for an engagement party, turns out to be a smart move, when the gang nabs thieves who had crashed the party and lifted a diamond necklace.

Repartee between Gorcey and Miss Marsh is amusing, and manner in which Gorcey has gang do his dirty work nets laughs. Story itself is old stuff, but dialog and 'Kids' antics liven the proceedings.

The original dead-enders—Gorcey, Huntz Hall and Gabriel Dell—are picking up too much weight and maturing much too rapidly to continue playing 'juve' delinquents. They look ripe for full-fledged gangster roles. Miss Marsh is easy to look at, although she frequently overacts.

Direction is good, photography is blurred and scenes poorly lighted.

La Piel De Zapa

(Argentina-Made)

(SONGS)

Buenos Aires, Nov. 20.

EFA production and release. Stars Hugo del Carril; features Alda Luz, Florence Marly, Santiago Gomez Cou, Francisco Lopez Silva, Alberto Contreras, Maria Esther Buschiazzo, Ricardo Canales, Alberto Terrones, Francisco Donadio, Berta Aliana, Mario Faig, Ambrosio Radrizzani, Jucky Namba, Nora Gilbert, Celia Geraldy, Rodolfo Rocha, Vicente Lubino, Lina Estevez, Pedro Gonzales and Iris Gorosito. Directed by Luis Bayon Herrera. Story, Honore de Balzac; adapted by Leopoldo Torres Rios and Raimundo Roxal; camera, Roque Funes; music, Alejandro Gutierrez del Barrio. Reviewed at the Broadway, Buenos Aires. Running time, 82 MINS.

This newest from EFA is in line with the increasing local trend for screen adaptations of famed classics. Based on Balzac's 'Ass' Skin,' screen version, done in Spanish by Leopoldo Torres Rios and Raimundo Roxal, closely follows the original. It's strictly for local b.o.s.

Atmosphere of the novel has been retained by director Luis Bayon Herrera and interest holds throughout, despite certain passages which drag. Production better than average, sets being rich in detail and street and ball scenes particularly strong. Attempt to film the French novel in itself required a bit of courage here. Film also introduces Florence Marly, French actress-wife of Parisian director Pierre Chenal, who is now working in Argentine studios. Hugo del Carril takes the starring role, his biggest to date, and while he doesn't do too badly, part requires more dramatic power than he possesses.

As in the original, story dwells on the case of a man about to commit suicide who finds a bewitched ass' skin at an antique shop. The skin

will grant him any wish, but it shrinks with each favor granted, shortening the life of the owner. Central motive is interwoven with a passionate love story, and the dialog and etching of the characters give the production considerable quality.

Carril sings several numbers in French, but is hardly the romantic sideburned Parisian—his forte is the tango. Photography is not so hot, and music is fair. *Ray.*

Canyon City

Republic release of Eddy White production. Stars Don 'Red' Barry; features Wally Vernon, Helen Talbot and Twinkle Watts. Directed by Spencer Bennett; screenplay, Robert Yost; camera, John MacBurnie; editor, Harry Keller. At New York, N. Y., dual, week of Dec. 7, '43. Running time, 56 MINS.

Terry Reynolds ⎰	
The Nevada Kid ⎱	Don 'Red' Barry
Beauty Bradshaw	Wally Vernon
Edith Gleason	Helen Talbot
Twinkle Hardy	Twinkle Watts
Craig Morgan	Morgan Conway
Emerson Wheeler	Emmett Ovgan
Alfred Johnson	Stanley Andrews
Jeff Parker	Roy Barcroft
Webb Hepburn	Leroy Mason

An action-packed western with Don 'Red' Barry accounting for the lion's share of the shenanigans. A sure draw for the outdoor fans.

Story concerns efforts of Barry to catch a city promoter who is trying to pull a fast deal on a utility company and ranchers. Barry poses as an escaped killer, is accused of an additional murder committed by the promoter, is tossed into jail, but makes his getaway in time to trap the latter.

Barry plays a tough, hard-riding, fast-shooting westerner as if he really means it. He is ably aided by comedian Wally Vernon, who portrays a cowboy from Brooklyn; Helen Talbot, one of the better looking and more talkative western femme leads, and Twinkle Watts, a cute kid whether she's performing on iceskates or on a pony.

Film is well-paced and neatly photographed.

Stella

(ARGENTINE-MADE)

Buenos Aires, Nov. 20.

Pampa Film production and release starring Zully Moreno and featuring Florinda Ferrario, Stella Rio, Rafael Fronteura, Guillermo Battaglia, Marla Santos, Mary Pareta, Chela Cordero, Hugo Pimentel, Lidia Denis, Fernando Lamas, Carlos Lagrotto, Elina Colomar, Lydia Quintana, Cesar Blasco, Liana Moabro, Maria Ines Guerra, F. Lacroze, Perla Nelson, Delia Diasne. Quico Moyana, Martha Glusman, Juan Carlos Morales. Directed by Benito Perojo. Story by Cesar Duayan. Adapted by Benito Perojo. Music by Paul Misrakl. Reviewed at the Monumental, Buenos Aires. Running time, 92 MINS.

As the first production directed here by Benito Perojo, film megger —formerly in Spain, 'Stella' is of unusual interest. Perojo, who has been under fire from pro-democratic forces in the local industry, has apparently been aware of this, however, for pic contains no elements which might be construed as propaganda, thus avoiding criticism on that ground. Film is essentially a melodrama and holds closely to the well-known novel of Cesar Duayan. Production is fairly well done, at times excessively romantic and oversweet, presentation is above average.

Story deals with the orphan daughter of a Swedish explorer who returns to her late mother's home in Buenos Aires with her little paralyzed sister. Daughter becomes the secretary of her uncle and discovers that his sons have been systematically robbing him. Her situation becomes increasingly difficult, for the cousins humiliate her and cause her misery which she must accept for the sake of the invalid sister.

Tale develops sentimental touches

which give it a special femme appeal, but dramatic action slows up in latter half when heroine returns to Sweden only to later come back to Argentina to discover that her former sweetheart has devoted his life to building a home for orphan children.

Some scenes, particularly those of the costume ball which highlights opening are good, but local critics have pointed out inaccuracies in handling of details of gaucho life. Zully Moreno is better than usual and Florinda Ferrario as the uncle turns in a good performance. Stella Rio excellent in role of the invalid younger sister. *Ray.*

Miniature Reviews

'Song of Bernadette' (20th). Franz Werfel's novel made into absorbing drama for top returns.

'Destination Tokyo' (WB). Cary Grant and John Garfield in smash boxoffice war drama.

'Gung Ho' (U). Randolph Scott starred in thriller about Makin Island raid; geared for strong boxoffice.

'Gangway for Tomorrow' (RKO). Margo topping routine cast in uninspired meller; dualer.

'Swingtime Johnny' (Songs) (U). Andrews Sisters starrer, strictly dual fare.

'The Chance of a Lifetime' (Col). Chester Morris in a fast-moving 'Boston Blackie' cops-and-robbers. Good dualer.

'Moonlight in Vermont' (U) Songs). Minor league comedy-drama with songs for the nabe duals.

'Overland Mail Robbery' (Rep). Standard newcomer in Wild Bill Elliott western series; suitable for duals.

'Up With the Lark' (British) (songs). Minor comedy slated for British consumption.

The Song of Bernadette

Hollywood, Dec. 21.

20th-Fox release of William Perlberg production. Features Jennifer Jones, Charles Bickford, Gladys Cooper, Charles Dingle, Vincent Price, Lee J. Cobb, Roman Bohnen, Anne Revere, Blanche Yurka. Wm. Goetz in charge of production. Directed by Henry King. Screenplay by George Seaton based on novel by Franz Werfel; camera, Arthur Miller; editor, Barbara McLean; music, Alfred Newman; special effects, Fred Sersen. Previewed Dec. 20, '43. Running time, 158 MINS.

Bernadette Soubirous	Jennifer Jones
Peyramale	Charles Bickford
Sister Marie Therese	Gladys Cooper
Jacomet	Charles Dingle
Dutour	Vincent Price
Dr. Dozous	Lee J. Cobb
Francois Soubirous	Roman Bohnen
Louise Soubirous	Anne Revere
Aunt Bernarde	Blanche Yurka
Jeanne Abadie	Mary Anderson
Antoine Nicolau	William Eythe
Croisine Bouhouhorts	Edith Barrett
Charles Bouhouhorts	Manart Kippen
Lacade, Mayor of Lourdes	Aubrey Mather
Bouriette	Sig Rumann
Empress Eugenie	Mona Maris
Louis Napoleon III	Fortunio Bonanova
Madame Bruat	Tala Birell
Callet, the Policeman	Marcel Dalio
Madame Nicolau	Eula Morgan
Bishop of Tarbes	Charles Waldron
Marie Soubirous	Ermadean Walters
Mother Superior	Nana Bryant
Estrade	Jean del Valle
Father Pomian	John Maxwell Hayes
Bishop of Nevers	Andre Charlot
Chaplain	Moroni Olsen

'Song of Bernadette' is an absorbing, emotional and dramatic picturization of Franz Werfel's novel. It's big in every respect; will rate fine critical attention; great in prestige for the industry; and due for top boxoffice reaction.

Film version is a warming and intimate narrative of godly visitation on the young girl of Lourdes which eventuated in establishment of the Shrine at Lourdes, a grotto for the divine healing of the lame and halt. It's a strong and inspirational religious theme, particularly strengthening in these troublous times when people are turning to God.

Sensitively scripted and directed in best taste throughout, 'Bernadette' unfolds in leisurely fashion with attention held through deft characterizations and incidents, rather than resort to synthetic dramatics. Many times during the extended running time of 158 minutes there are sideline episodes inserted, but even these fail to lessen intense attention to the major theme. Rightly, 20th-Fox and producer William Perlberg provide finest production mounting —it always remains intimate and never veers towards spectacular effects to detract from the tempo and tenor.

Cast, extensively running through 39 credits, is one of the most expertly-selected in several years, and even the one-shot bits click solidly in fleeting footage. Jennifer Jones, in title role, delivers an inspirationally sensitive and arresting performance that sets her solid as a screen personality. Wistful, naive, and at times angelic, Miss Jones takes command early to hold control as the motivating factor through the lengthy unfolding. Support is studded with numerous brilliant portrayals, including Charles Bickford, William Eythe, Vincent Price, Lee J. Cobb, Gladys Cooper, Anne Revere, Roman Bohnen, Aubrey Mather, Charles Dingle, Blanche Yurka, Edith Barrett, John Maxwell Hayes and many others.

Story introduces Bernadette as the asthmatic daughter of a jobless father living meagerly in the town jail with his large brood. While wood-gathering near the Grotto, girl is visited by vision of the Holy Mother. Scoffed at and berated by parents, town officials and church authorities, she continues her visits to dig at the spring, as directed, for waters to carry miracle healing powers. Finally convincing Jean Bickford of her sincerity and God-delivered inspiration, he guides her to a convent for novitiate and finally sisterhood. Years slip by, she's stricken with dread disease, and passes, on to God's kingdom and sainthood on earth, as exemplified by the Shrine at Lourdes.

Technical contributions are excellent in every department, with outstanding photography by Arthur Miller hitting high mark of quality. Music by Alfred Newman is meritorious, especially orchestral and choral passages on periodic revelations of the Vision at the Grotto. Despite the deeply religious tone of the dramatic narrative, theme has been handled with utmost taste and reverence. Foreword and the short commentary by Bickford sums it up completely: 'To those who believe in God, no explanation is necessary. To those who do not believe, no explanation is possible.'

But to every person who sees 'Bernadette,' there is warmth, inspiration and pause for reflection regardless of creed or non-belief. *Walt.*

Destination Tokyo

Warner Bros. release of Jerry Wald production. Directed by Delmer Daves. Stars Cary Grant and John Garfield; features Dane Clark, Robert Hutton, Warner Anderson, John Ridgely, Alan Hale, William Prince. Screenplay, Delmer Daves and Albert Maltz, from original story by Steve Fisher; camera, Bert Glennon; editor, Chris Nyby; montages, James Leicester; special effects, Lawrence Butler and Willard Van Enger; music, Franz Waxman; music director, Leo Forbstein. Previewed in N. Y. Dec. 17, '43. Running time, **135 MINS.**

Captain Cassidy	Cary Grant
Wolf	John Garfield
Cockie	Alan Hale
Reserve Officer	John Ridgely
Tin Can	Dane Clark
Executive Officer	Warner Anderson
Pills	William Prince
Tommy	Robert Hutton
Dakota	Peter Whitney
Mike	Tom Tully
Mrs. Cassidy	Faye Emerson
Diving Officer	Warren Douglas
Sparks	John Forsythe
Sound Man	John Alvin
Gunnery Officer	Bill Kennedy
Quartermaster	William Challee
Yoyo	Whit Bissell
Admiral's Aide	Stephen Richards
Communications Officer	John Whitney
Chief of Boat	George Lloyd
Toscanini	Maurice Murphy

In a season replete with many war dramas, 'Destination Tokyo' is a standout addition. For sheer intensity of melodrama it certainly must take its place with any film to come out of this war. Its excellence as a document paying tribute to a valiant unit of the American Navy—the submarine—is something that must go unquestioned. Nor can there be any doubt as to its smash boxoffice prospects.

What Warners has done for America's air heroes, in 'Air Force,' it has achieved for America's undersea fighters. For this is an exciting and absorbing story of how a single submarine paved the way for the Flying Fortress attack on Japan more than a year ago.

How much of it is fact, and how much fiction, is not to be determined casually. That some of it is based on fact there can be no doubt. Its credulity can be best measured in terms of the past year's headlines.

'Destination Tokyo' runs two hours and 15 minutes, and that's a lot of film. But none of it is wasted. In its unspooling is crammed enough excitement for possibly a couple of pictures. It is tightly compact, and exhibitors can merchandize a film of such magnitude and cost to the fullest.

Here is a film whose hero is the Stars and Stripes; the performers are merely symbols of that heroism. Here is a film whose marquee may convey the stellar billing of Cary Grant and John Garfield, but the two are no less the stars than the comparatively insignificant character one may find at the very bottom of the casting credits. Here is a film fully representative of a wartime Lady Liberty. Here is a film of superbly pooled talents.

As in 'Air Force,' which detailed a single mission of a Flying Fort, 'Destination Tokyo' tells of a single mission undertaken by a sub. Its destination is Tokyo.

Under sealed orders opened 24 hours after it has sped from San Francisco Harbor, the sub first has a rendezvous with a Navy plane near Kiska. There it takes aboard a meteorologist whom the sub is to deposit in Japan to survey conditions as a guide to the attack of the Fortress armada taking off from the aircraft carrier Hornet.

Fantastic may well describe this story, and fantastic though it may be there is enough to indicate that it has been no concoction of the sheerest fancy. Only the war's end could possibly clarify its variable factors.

It is a film of action, but not continuously so. Where it does lapse in movement there is always retained the thought of impending action. This is no film where an audience can afford to sit back.

Considerable of the situational drama is little short of terrific. There is an exciting two or three minutes when a crew member unfastens the detonator cap on what is presumably a dud dropped by a Jap plane into the hold of the sub—all this in hushed expectancy lest a slight jar set it off. There is the emergency appendicitis operation performed on one of the sub's crew by a pharmacist's mate without previous surgical experience—an operation performed from instructions in a surgical manual. There is the expectancy of the seemingly inevitable as the sub flees the Jap fleet whose every depth charge sends the sub closer to its doom.

The credits are lavish, and each one in his turn has turned in a spectacular job. Jerry Wald handled the production, and he must have spent plenty. Delmer Daves' direction achieved the superlative in dovetailing script with performance. Daves doubled into the scripting with Albert Maltz. The special montage effects lend the illusion of realism, particularly in the Tokyo bombing scene. The musical score is a fine one.

Cary Grant has never been better as the sub's skipper, underplaying the role and so setting the performance pace for the entire pic. John Garfield gives one of his fine portrayals as the sailor with a perpetual femme yen, and the roster of featured performers gives capital characterizations all the way down the line. Among the more notable performances are those of Alan Hale, Warner Anderson, William Prince, Robert Hutton, Dane Clark and John Ridgely.

A film without feminine allure is an anomaly in these days of filmmaking, but 'Destination Tokyo' is such a picture. It has only two brief shots of femmes, but they have no link with the story. This story doesn't miss them.

The film academicians can maintain their stand of more 'escapist' pix to help forget the war, but 'Destination Tokyo' need make no apologies on that score. There can be no escape from reality. *Kahn.*

Gung Ho

Universal release of Walter Wanger production. Stars Randolph Scott; features Noah Beery, Jr., Alan Curtis, Grace McDonald, J. Carroll Naish, Sam Levene, David Bruce. Directed by Ray Enright. Screenplay, Lucien Hubbard, based on factual story, 'Gung Ho,' by Lieut. W. S. Le Francois, USMC; additional dialog, Joseph Hoffman; camera, Milton Krasner; music, Frank Skinner; music director, H. J. Salter; editor, Milton Carruth. Previewed in projection room, N. Y., Dec. 17, '43. Running time, **88 MINS.**

Col. Thorwald	Randolph Scott
Kathleen Corrigan	Grace McDonald
John Harbison	Alan Curtis
Kurt Richter	Noah Beery, Jr.
Lt. Cristoforos	J. Carroll Naish
Larry O'Ryan	David Bruce
Kozzarowski	Peter Coe
Pigiron	Bob Mitchum
Capt. Dynphy	Richard Lane
Rube Tedrow	Rod Cameron
Transport	Sam Levene
Commander Blade	Milburn Stone
Frankie Montana	Harold Landon
Buddy Andrews	John James
Lt. Roland Browning	Louis Jean Heydt

It was just a few weeks ago that the telegraphic flash, 'Makin Taken,' spun around the world, and now Universal can capitalize on the headlines with a film telling of the initial push by the Marines' Col. Carlson and his raiders on the tiny island in the Pacific. It will be recalled as the first offensive step taken by the Americans to recapture territory taken from them early in the war with the Japs. 'Gung Ho' gives an exciting account of the American attack and should do well at the b.o.

Randolph Scott has the lead in this story, adapted from what is said to be a factual account written by Lieut. W. S. Le Francois, USMC. There's considerable authenticity given the yarn by the counsel to the producer by Carlson himself.

'Gung Ho' is apparently a modest-budgeter that should stack up well as a subject for exploitation. It certainly has its promotional angles. But its title is not a saleable one, being of obscure Japanese origin and meaning 'work together.'

Pertinently, it's the story of how, out of thousands of trainees, a picked group of Marines is slated for a special mission—the first raid on Makin Island. It's an at-times loosely written script. The 'boot training' preliminaries to the raid are just so much of a wait, but the actual attack has its compensating and exciting moments.

Scott gives one of his usually fine heroic performances, while J. Carroll Naish is a tough lieutenant who, somehow, doesn't look the part. Noah Beery, Jr., and David Bruce play half-brothers in a heat over the same blonde (Grace McDonald). Sam Levene, in a small role as a sergeant, is best of the support.

The direction has geared the pic for pace but some of that dialog is strictly for the younger element. The story has been needlessly glamourized, and it's here that it bogs down. It has a love yarn where one need not necessarily exist, and that's with all due respect to the producer's obvious attempt to woo feminine interest at the b.o. But the romance attempt makes for amateurish scripting. It obviously was part of the additional treatment given the original story by the studio. But dead Japs and live blondes don't mix.

Kahn.

Gangway for Tomorrow

RKO release of John H. Auer production, directed by Auer. Features Margo, John Carradine, Robert Ryan, Amelita Ward, William Terry, Wally Brown, Alan Carney. Screenplay by Arch Oboler from original story by Aladar Lazzlo and Oboler; camera, Nicholas Musuraca; editor, George Crone. At RKO Albee, Brooklyn, week Dec. 16, '43, dualed. Running time, **69 MINS.**

Lisette	Margo
Wellington	John Carradine
Joe	Robert Ryan
Mary	Amelita Ward
Bob Nolan	William Terry
Fred Taylor	Harry Davenport
Burke	James Bell
Jim Benson	Charles Arnt
Sam	Wally Brown
Swallow	Alan Carney
Dan Barton	Erford Gage
Col. Mueller	Richard Ryen
Pete	Warren Hymer

Idea back of 'Gangway for Tomorrow' is to retrace highlights in lives of five central figures, all now employed in a U. S. war plant where now overlooking their miseries by laboring for a better world in which to live. But the telling is belabored and hardly rates laurels for Arch Oboler's screenplay and original which he is co-credited with Aladar Lazzlo. Result is a routine dualer.

Use of flashbacks is timeworn and has been done much more effectively in recent films. Probably the best passage, concerning Margo's heroism for Free France, looks like a page ripped from any number of previous yarns about the French underground. There's also Robert Ryan, the racetrack driver who's been hurt while speeding at Indianapolis and kept out of the U. S. air force. There's also Amelita Ward, the gal who's been disillusioned as 'Miss America.' Episodes further include John Carradine who abandoned a life of loafing to aid the war effort and the grim yarn about the prison warden who's forced to sub as electrocutioneer and turn the juice to kill his own brother. There seems little excuse for the last-named. Such horrific material may be okay for radio chillers but suffers in telling on the screen.

Per usual with an Arch Oboler yarn, there's over-emphasis on clanking chains, slamming doors, muffled talking, marching feet, etc. Had the bulk of the story been centered on the tale about the French underground and Margo's heroic singing to stir the Free French this would have been considerably stronger. But as is, it is merely one of several episodes; a strong one and considerably detailed, but lost in the welter of other developments.

Margo is tops, both in her thespian efforts and several vocal tries. Best of other cast members is Amelita Ward, a comparative newcomer but excellent in the yarn about a 'Miss America' who is suddenly awakened. There's also a nice bit by Harry Davenport. Others featured are William Terry, Robert Ryan and John Carradine.

John H. Auer's direction is not particularly inspired, and often is stodgy. Cameraing by Nicholas Musuraca is uniformly trim even if going in for a plethora of closeups.

Wear.

Swingtime Johnny
(SONGS)

Universal release of Warren Wilson production. Stars Andrews Sisters; features Harriet Hilliard, Peter Cookson, Matt Willis, Bill Phillips, Tim Ryan, Mitch Ayres orchestra. Directed by Edward F. Cline. Original, Warren Wilson; screenplay, Clyde Bruckman; music, Vic Schoen; numbers, Charles O'Curran; editor, Edward Curtiss; camera, Jerome Ashe. At Loew's State, N. Y., week of Dec. 16. Running time, **60 MINS.**

Themselves	Patty Andrews Maxene Andrews LaVerne Andrews
Linda	Harriet Hilliard
Jonathan	Peter Cookson

Sparks..........Tim Ryan
Monk..........Matt Willis
Steve..........William (Bill) Phillips
Gruff Character..........Tom Dugan
Mike..........Ray Walker
Blonde..........Marion Martin
Caldwell..........John Hamilton
Raffle Wheel Barker..........John Sheehan
Sea Food Barker..........Syd Saylor
Bill..........Jack Rice
Chairman of Board..........Emmett Vogan
Pop..........Herbert Heywood
Pierre..........Alphonse Martell
Mitch Ayres and His Orchestra

Andrews Sisters' latest for Universal is a weak story that depends almost entirely on numerous pop and standard melody interpretations to move it along. Premiering in the N. Y. area at Loew's State the production is in over its head; its groove is the duals where it will do OK.

Despite the weakness of the yarn, which depicts the Andrews trio, Harriet Hilliard and members of Mitch Ayres' orchestra as alternate nightclub entertainers and workers in a pipe-organ factory converted to war production, the item becomes likable enough because of its music. Spotted throughout are such tunes as 'When You and I Were Young, Maggie,' 'Ta-ra-ra-boom-der-e,' 'Poor Nell,' 'You Better Give Me Lots of Lovin' and 'Auld Lang Syne.' Added to these are several modern things, 'Sweet and Low,' 'Boogie Woogie Choo-Choo,' 'Boogie Woogie Bugle Boy,' et al.

Use of so many tunes, of course, indicates that the Andrews group are always in evidence. They are. Every 100 feet of film seems to bring up an excuse for them to exercise and the resulting prominence, plus the acting parts they are assigned, can do nothing but help their cause regardless of the lack of a story. In the latter the girls and Miss Hilliard switch from night club floor to the Chadwick factory, for no obvious reason. The procedure hooks Miss Hilliard up with Peter Cookson who, as descendant of the founder, is endeavoring to make the place pay in the face of sabotage from a trusted employee, in the employ of another combine. It all works out, of course, with Miss Hilliard winding up in Cookson's affections.

One of the best comedy scenes comes up in the factory, with the girls scooting around looking for the 'key to the situation' (machine). Another is a sequence built around 'Poor Nell,' in which the girls do a good job of hokum.

Performances are generally good. Cookson stands out; Miss Hilliard is okay, but the remaining small parts are all stiffly handled. Mitch Ayres' band is used in virtually all of the scenes behind songs, but never is projected alone.

Photography is fair and the various sets inexpensively turned out.

Wood.

The Chance of a Lifetime

Columbia release of Wallace MacDonald production. Features Chester Morris, Erik Rolf, Jeanne Bates, Richard Lane, George E. Stone. Directed by William Castle. Screenplay, Paul Yawitz; camera, Ernie Miller; editor, Jerome Thoms. At Strand, Brooklyn, N. Y., dual, week of Dec. 16, '43. Running time, **66 MINS.**

Boston Blackie..........Chester Morris
Dooley Watson..........Erik Rolf
Mary Watson..........Jeanne Bates
Inspector Farraday..........Richard Lane
The Runt..........George E. Stone
Arthur Manleder..........Lloyd Corrigan
Matthews..........Walter Sande
Nails Blanton..........Douglas Fowley
Jumbo Madigan..........Cy Kendall
Johnny Watson..........Larry Joe Olson
Richie Adair..........Sally Cairns
Manny Vogel..........Trevor Bardette
Egyp. Hines..........Harry Semels
Tex..........Arthur Hunnicutt

Further adventures of Boston Blackie, as played by Chester Morris in this 66-minute package of action, should fare well at dual policy b.o.'s. 'Chance of Lifetime' moves swiftly in the groove already established by earlier releases in the series and seems well able to satisfy those who like gunplay heroics plus a smattering of nobleness tossed into their underworld film diet.

Easy-to-follow plot finds Morris sponsoring parole of a handful of cons so they may accept employment at Lloyd Corrigan's tool shop working on war contracts. Among those sprung is Erik Rolf, doing time for a $60,000 stickup in which two confederates escaped capture. Before reporting for work at the war plant Rolf is allowed to visit his wife and young son and, while there, a scuffle ensues in which one of the hoodlums is killed by a shot from his own gun. He was struggling with Rolf at the time so the other gunman plans to accuse Rolf of murder unless he hands over the holdup money.

Rolf's wife, Jeanne Bates, persuades him to turn the money over to police and place his trust in Morris. Fast moving tale pits latter against Richard Lane, a not-too-bright detective, and Douglas Fowley, holdup artist who tries to frame Rolf, and sees Morris arrested for the 'Murder' on his own confession. He escapes, not once but several times, and makes things tough all around for the dimwit cops. Final scenes, naturally, wind everything up in wonderful style and set the stage for next adventure of the reformed crook.

Morris does a good job and carries the action throughout. George E. Stone works in some comedy as Morris' right hand man and laughs also come through in work of Lane as the inspector. Other police characters bring in humorous touches and Lloyd Corrigan, as the harassed plant manager, delivers well in a natural comedy role. Distaff side is most inconspicuous but Jeanne Bates makes a convincing loyal wife and performed as well as part would allow.

Rolf, as the unjustly accused excor, rounds out a well-balanced and capable cast.

Donn.

Moonlight in Vermont

(SONGS)

Hollywood, Dec. 17.

Universal release of Bernard Burton production. Stars Gloria Jean; features Ray Malone, George Dolenz, Fay Helm, Betty McCabe, Sidney Miller, Vivian Austin. Directed by Edward Lilley. Original screenplay by Eugene Conrad; camera, Jerome Ash; editor, Charles Maynard; dancers, Louis Da Pron; songs, Inez James and Sidney Miller. Previewed Dec. 16, '43. Running time, **60 MINS.**

Gwen Harding..........Gloria Jean
Richard Ellis (Slick)..........Ray Malone
Lionel Devereau..........George Dolenz
Lucy Meadows..........Fay Helm
Joan..........Betty McCabe
Cyril..........Sidney Miller
Brenda Allenby..........Vivian Austin
Alice..........Patsy O'Connor
Elvira..........Mira McKinney
Abel..........Billy Benedict
Aunt Bess..........Virginia Brissac
Uncle Rufus..........Russell Simpson

This is a stereotyped tale of a rural girl singer who hits for New York and a dramatic school, and winds up back home when the coin gives out. Unimaginative throughout and tugging continually against the synthetically-brewed yarn, picture is celluloid moonshine, a filler for the family and backwoods duals where supporting 60 minutes are needed.

Along the line there are several songs by Gloria Jean and a few song-and-dance routines by newcomer Ray Malone (plucked from New York nightclub floors for Universal contract). These specialties are okay, but fail to lift the sophomoric material and direction provided.

Miss Jean is the gal from a Vermont farm who arrives at the N. Y. drama school; is target for catty attitude of Vivian Austin, and puppy-love attentions of Malone. When the farm needs hands she returns home, to be followed by the students to help with the harvesting. It's natural that the kids turn in also to stage a show for the ruralites as excuse for presenting a few production turns.

Malone, juvenile performer who displays possibilities of sticking around pictures for some time with good personality and footwork, needs better takeoff than this one. Miss Jean is also under wraps in both the acting and singing lines; and other cast members are handicapped by forced theatrics of the script and direction. Best of group of songs contributed by Inez James and Sidney Miller is 'Be a Good, Good Girl,' but it's too weak for pop attention.

Walt.

Up With the Lark

(BRITISH-MADE)

(Songs)

London, Dec. 1.

New Realm Pictures production and release. Directed by Phil Brandon. Stars Ethel Revnell, Gracie West. Screenplay, James Seymour from original story by Val Valentine. At Rialto, London, Nov. 25, '43. Running time, **83 MINS.**

Ethel..........Ethel Revnell
Gracie..........Gracie West
Martel..........Anthony Holles
Mr. Blitt..........Anthony Hulme
Mr. Tanner..........Johnny Schofield
Mabel..........Lesley Osmond
Fred Tomkins..........Alan Kane
Rev. Swallow..........Ian Fleming

If you can picture Martha Raye teamed with Gracie Allen (of Burns and Allen) you'll get the rough idea of this one. Ethel Revnell and Gracie West have been wowing 'em in BBC broadcasts years now in an act they call 'The Long and Short of It,' and New Realm Pictures has starred them in 'Up With the Lark' to cash in on a ready-made British market. The flick may do as well in this country as a similar attempt by RKO to put Amos 'n' Andy across on the American screen, but its chances in American houses rate less than that one.

Against a background of Black Market operations Miss Revnell (tall and 'goofy') and Miss West (smaller and 'dumb') do their stuff as detectives disguised as Land Army girls. The mess they make includes every slapstick gag ever invented.

Production is adequate, and Phil Brandon's direction is as good as the story deserves.

Of seven songs, 'A Place in the Sun for Everyone' and 'You're a Sweetheart in a Million' are good.

Overland Mail Robbery

Republic release of Louis Gray production. Directed by John English. Features Wild Bill Elliott, George 'Gabby' Hayes, Anne Jeffreys. Story and screenplay, Robert Yost; camera, John MacBurnie; editor, Charles Craft; music, Mort Glickman. At New York, N. Y., week Dec. 14, '43, dual. Running time, **56 MINS.**

Wild Bill..........Wild Bill Elliott
Gabby..........George 'Gabby' Hayes
Judy Goodrich..........Anne Jeffreys
Mrs. Patterson..........Alice Fleming
John Patterson..........Weldon Heyburn
Tom Hartley..........Kirk Alyn
David Patterson..........Roy Barcroft
Lola Patterson..........Nancy Gay
Jimmy Hartley..........Peter Michael
Slade..........Bud Geary
Sheriff..........Tom London

This is a standard addition to the Wild Bill Elliott western series. Hackneyed plot and static direction make this just a filler on the duals.

Story deals with an effete easterner who goes west to take over the family stagecoach line coveted by a gang headed by an innocent-appearing but hard-as-a-nut mother of a crooked brood. With the aid of Elliott, friend of the easterner's murdered brother, Peter Michael, as the easterner, manages to defeat the gang and win the girl, Anne Jeffreys.

Difficulties of the plot might have been overcome with more paceful direction and less standard action shots.

Miniature Reviews

'A Guy Named Joe' (M-G). Fantasy starring Spencer Tracy and Irene Dunne should do satisfactorily at boxoffice.

'The Heavenly Body' (M-G). William Powell and Hedy Lamarr will carry this comedy.

'Tender Comrade' (RKO). Ginger Rogers in emotional yarn geared for smash b.o.

'Song of Russia' (One Song) (M-G). Headed by Robert Taylor and Susan Peters for OK b.o.

'Sing a Jingle' (Songs) (U). Okay program filmusical for supporting slots in regular duals.

'The Ghost Ship' (RKO). Disappointing dualler starring Richard Dix.

'Suspected Person' (British) (PRC). Minor dualer for average returns.

'Cattle Stampede' (PRC). Dual western in 'Billy the Kid' series; fair b.o.

'Smart Guy' (Mono). Slow-moving pic for lower dualers.

A Guy Named Joe

Metro release of Everett Riskin production. Stars Spencer Tracy and Irene Dunne; features Lionel Barrymore, Van Johnson, James Gleason, Ward Bond, Barry Nelson. Directed by Victor Fleming. Screenplay, Dalton Trumbo, adaptation by Frederick Hazlitt Brennan from original story by Major Chandler Sprague and David Boehm; editor, Frederick Brennan; camera, George Folsey and Karl Freund. Reviewed at Capitol theatre, New York, Dec. 23, '43. Running time, **120 MINS.**

Pete Sandidge..........Spencer Tracy
Dorinda Durston..........Irene Dunne
Ted Randall..........Van Johnson
Al Yackey..........Ward Bond
Nails Kilpatrick..........James Gleason
The General..........Lionel Barrymore
Dick Rumney..........Barry Nelson
Ellen Bright..........Esther Williams
Colonel Sykes..........Henry O'Neill
James J. Rourke..........Don DeFore
Sanderson..........Charles Smith

In taking a fling at the spirit world, Metro hasn't quite succeeded in reaching the nebulous but has managed to turn out an entertaining and excellently performed picture. With Spencer Tracy and Irene Dunne contributing the marquee strength and giving two of their top performances, coupled with the title lure and love story, 'A Guy Named Joe' should add up to satisfactory boxoffice.

Had the fantasy been interpreted wholly in terms of the sharp wit and dry humor which Tracy, as a ghostly visitor, only occasionally injects, instead of investing it with spiritual counselling, the film might have attained smash proportions. As it is, there hovers over too many scenes in the cloudy strata a fogginess that isn't made any more acceptable by the final solution. The latter only changes the mood of the film from one of light cockiness to the realm of metaphysics. It's all the more regrettable that the picture couldn't have emerged as a piece of clever whimsy, for in all other respects Metro has given it an overall fine production, only going overboard on its two-hour running time. As it stands, a good half-hour could be cut advantageously.

Tracy is cast as a squadron commander at an English base who's in a constant jam because of his foolhardy heroics. He steps out of bounds once too often and gets transferred to a remote reconnaisance spot in Scotland. Through all this his gal, Irene Dunne, a ferry pilot, sticks by him in the casual, undemonstrative love-making manner characteristic of the Tracy pix. Fulfilling a premonition felt by Miss Dunne, he crashes on his last heroic stunt, proceeding to the land where all dead pilots go. There he meets up with The Boss, and is assigned to guide and instruct the new pilots in the earthly world who are making a bid for their wings. It's at this point that the serious overtones of the picture intrude themselves, with the offering of the matter-of-fact solution that 'life must go on for the living' too abruptly thrust into the story's continuity. Had that philosophical concept been developed logically it might have been more acceptable. As it is, Tracy's blithe spirit, as it nonchalantly weaves in and out when it takes up with his old associates, provides the film with its more entertaining moments while it at no time tries to convert the audience to a belief in those spiritual preachments.

Through a freak of circumstance (or was it scripting?), Tracy's initial assignment is a young student officer whom he ferries right into the life of Pilot Dunne, his ex-sweetheart. As they become emotionally involved Tracy develops some unspiritual jealousy but is brought back into line by The Boss, and by his ghostly guidance releases Miss Dunne for 'life with the living.'

Tracy gives a fine performance throughout, making a very likeable ghost, while Miss Dunne is nifty to look at and turns in a sufficiently restrained but emotionally convincing portrayal. Ward Bond, as his buddy in Tracy's earthly existence, likewise contributes a top performance, while James Gleason, Lionel Barrymore and Don DeFore are good in supporting roles. On the other hand, Van Johnson has difficulty in being convincing as Tracy's successor for Miss Dunne's affections because of his extreme youth.

Victor Fleming's direction is fine, limited only by the script's deficiences. *Rose.*

The Heavenly Body

Metro release of Arthur Hornblow, Jr., proluction. Stars Hedy Lamarr and William Powell: features James Craig, Fay Bainter, Spring Byington. Directed by Alexander Hall. Screenplay, Michael Arlen and Walter Reisch; adapted by Harry Kurnitz from original by Jacques Thery; camera, Robert Planck; score, Bronislau Kaper; era, Robert Planck; score, Bronislau Kaper; editor, Blanche Sewell. Tradeshown in N. Y. Dec. 28, '43. Running time, **95 MINS.**

William S. Whitley.........William Powell
Vicky Whitley...............Hedy Lamarr
Lloyd X. Hunter.............James Craig
Margaret Sibyll...............Fay Bainter
Prefessor Stowe............Henry O'Neill
Nancy Potter..............Spring Byington
Strand........................Robert Sully
Dr. Green..................Morris Ankrum
Sebastian Melas...........Franco Corsaro
Beulah Murphy...........Connie Gilchrist

Metro is dabbling in things astronomical in 'The Heavenly Body,' one of those husband-wife comedies that should do well at the boxoffice on the basis of the Hedy Lamarr-William Powell names.

The script is inclined to be one of those far-fetched things, and there's a frequent stretch for laughs, but where there's a sufficient reelage of Miss Lamarr no picture can be very far off the b.o. beam. The guys witnessing this pic will be entranced by Miss Lamarr's beaut looks; the dolls will be impressed. The camera has been particularly good to her in this one, and her clothes are also plenty eye-appealing.

Yarn attempts to tell what happens when the usual triangle evolves from a situation involving Miss Lamarr and Powell as the husband-wife, James Craig as an air-raid warden, and the astronomical pursuits of Powell. The crux of the story is woven around the fact that Powell works at night, as an astronomer, leaving his wife prey for prowling air-raid wardens. It may sound funny on paper, but it doesn't quite come off as expected. There are some extraneous slapstick situations that fail to achieve the laughs intended.

Direction points up the laugh situations as well as could be expected. Powell gives one of his standard performances, but occasionally overacts, while Craig, as the air-raid warden, looks and acts enough like Gable to get by.

But the question remains—what exactly did Metro mean by that title? Miss Lamarr can be very fetchingly decollete. *Kahn.*

Tender Comrade

RKO release of David Hempstead production. Stars Ginger Rogers; features Robert Ryan, Ruth Hussey, Patricia Collinge, Mady Christians, Kim Hunter, Jane Darwell, Richard Martin. Directed by Edward Dmytryk. Story and screenplay, Dalton Trumbo; camera, Russell Metty; music, Leigh Harline; music director, C. Bakaleinikoff; editor, Roland Gross. Tradeshown in N. Y. Dec. 28, '43. Running time, **102 MINS.**

Jo...........................Ginger Rogers
Chris.........................Robert Ryan
Barbara......................Ruth Hussey
Helen Stacey..............Patricia Collinge
Manya.....................Mady Christians
Doris..........................Kim Hunter
Mrs. Henderson.............Jane Darwell
Jo's Mother....................Mary Forbes
Mike.......................Richard Martin

In this or any war one of the most poignant elements of human drama remains the wives our servicemen must leave behind. In 'Tender Comrade,' in which RKO has starred Ginger Rogers, it is an element propelled home with the dramatic impetus that can mean only one thing for exhibitors. The word is boxoffice —and plenty of it.

This is a woman's picture. Not that it hasn't a basic value of understanding for the stronger sex. It's just that here is a picture about women and one that's more pertinently for women. It is a drama in which its characters will take their places in the homes of Mr. and Mrs. America. It is one which, because of the effect it has had on every home in America, should have a terrific emotional surge for most audiences.

Centered around five women, all of whom have their men in the services and all of whom are contributing to the war effort in one way or another, 'Tender Comrade' is a preachment for all that democracy stands for.

All the basic ingredients for entertaining drama are here, from David Hempstead's production down to, and notably including, Edward Dmytryk's direction and an excellent performance by Miss Rogers that paces the entire cast. It is, in fact, one of Miss Rogers' finest characterizations.

It is a picture of considerable charm despite its terrific emotional effects. And if the emotional impact is sometimes achieved with what may seem to be overdone dramatics, then it's to be marked off to what one can assume to be an enactment of what is actually real-life drama. Each of the women has her own private little drama, of course, and around them are concentrated much of the picture's sensitive values.

These little dramas require a somewhat episodic treatment of the film, but all this has been achieved well. There's the story of Jo, who married Chris, and when Jo wanted a baby, Chris said no because he felt he would soon be in the army; then Barbara, whose husband was in the Navy, and the other girls were always cautioning her about her infidelities to a man who was serving his country; Helen had a husband and son in the service; Doris was anxiously anticipating a real furlough from her soldier-husband so they could consummate a marriage whose vows were taken when he had had just a few moments' leave. All worked in a defense plant, and lived together with Manya, their refugee housekeeper, whose husband, too, was in the Army.

Miss Rogers gives an unrestrained performance throughout, and where several scenes are almost dawdling, she perks it up with neat bits of business. Ruth Hussey as Barbara, Kim Hunter as Doris and Patricia Collinge as Helen also give excellent portrayals. Mady Christians plays the housekeeper satisfactorily, while Jane Darwell, though featured, is only in for a brief flash.

Dalton Trumbo has contributed a story and screenplay compact and replete with plenty of excellent dialog. A notably big factor in the film's pace is Dmytryk's direction of the sometimes slow, but never tedious story. *Kahn.*

Song of Russia
(ONE SONG)

Metro release of Joseph Pasternak production. Stars Robert Taylor and Susan Peters; features Robert Benchley. Directed by Gregory Ratoff. Screenplay, Paul Jarrico and Richard Collins, based on story by Leo Mittler, Bictor Trivas and Guy Endore; music, Peter Ilyich Tschaikowsky and modern Russian composers adapted for screen by Herbert Stothart; conducted by Albert Coates; song, 'And Russia Is Her Name,' by E. Y. Harburg and Jerome Kern; dance direction, David Lichine; camera, Harry Stradling; editor, George Hively. Tradeshown in N. Y., Dec. 28, '43. Running time, **107 MINS.**

John Meredith................Robert Taylor
Nadya Stepanova.............Susan Peters
Boris..........................John Hodiak
Hank Higgins.............Robert Benchley
Petrov......................Felix Bressart
Stepanov..................Michael Chekhov
Peter......................Darryl Hickman
Anna....................Jacqueline White
Peter Meremblum's California Jr. Symphony Orchestra

The glory of Russian courage against Nazi infamy has been paid tribute once again in 'Song of Russia,' which Joseph Pasternak has produced for Metro with a sweep that suggests epochal intentions. That these intentions go awry can be attributed considerably to a script that too frequently sacrifices realism for what is seemingly more a love story than an epic of a gallant people's fight against enslavement. 'Song of Russia's' boxoffice returns will be dependent to a considerable degree on Robert Taylor's name.

Another b.o. factor is that it's been too long since one has read of Soviet defensives; the shoe has long since been on the other foot. But for the marquee there's something else to be considered. Russian heroism, whatever the degree, still remains a popular b.o. commodity.

'Russia' has the benefit of a fine production, faithful to detail. No Pasternak production could be otherwise. And Gregory Ratoff, the director, certainly is keenly aware of his Russian backgrounds. But when the boy-meets-girl situation projects itself, the picture becomes involved with its rather belabored romantic interludes amid scenes of, firstly, a peaceful, then a war-torn Russia.

But if it achieves nothing else, 'Song of Russia' at least establishes the stellar value of a comparative newcomer; this is Susan Peters' most important role to date. It reveals her as one of the finest young dramatic actresses to emerge from Hollywood in some time. The word-of-mouth on her performance, beauty and expressive underplaying should make her a 'must' in any future Metro plans.

This is a yarn whose characters, mainly those who background, are more real than the story itself. It is a story of a famous American symphonic conductor who is caught in the midst of the Nazi invasion of Russia after he has become intrigued by, and married, a young Russian pianist (Miss Peters). The pair's digress loyalties—he for his music, she for her little village threatened by the invaders—bring what is intended to be a temporary parting until such time when he can join her.

Notable in the film is the music. Tschaikowsky's cleffings are particularly prominent, and additional music has been supplied by 'modern Russian composers,' none of whom is billed. The Jerome Kern-E. Y. Harburg combination has contributed the tuneful 'And Russia Is Her Name,' which is bound to achieve wider appeal than it has already gained.

Outside of Miss Peters' performance, there is none among the lead players who shows distinctively. Robert Benchley is wasted as Taylor's manager. And it's a question of whether Taylor could be popularly accepted as a noted symphonic conductor. One who batons Tschaikowsky, no less. *Kahn.*

Sing a Jingle
(SONGS)

Hollywood, Dec. 24.

Universal release of Edward Lilley production, directed by Lilley. Stars Allan Jones; features June Vincent, Betty Kean, Gus Schilling, Kings Men, 4 Society Girls. Screenplay, John Grey, Eugene Conrad, Lee Sands, Fred Rath; camera, Jerome Ash; special photography, John Fulton; editor, Charles Maynard; songs, Buddy Pepper, Inez James, Sidney Miller. Previewed Dec. 23, '43. Running time, **61 MINS.**

Ray King.......................Allan Jones
Muriel Crane.................June Vincent
J. P. Crane..............Samuel S. Hinds
Bucky.......................Gus Schilling
Myrtle..........................Betty Kean
Andrews....................Jerome Cowan
Abbott.....................Edward Norlis
Vera Grant......................Joan Castle
Wilbur Crane................Richard Love
Ann........................Vivian Austin
Wiggins......................Billy Newell
Benny........................Dean Collins
Kings Men
Four Society Girls

Another in the Universal group of program filmusicals designed for dual supporting datings. Despite formula story structure, it holds together sufficiently to achieve aim intended.

Allan Jones delivers six songs in good voice, with comedienne Betty Kean clicking with two comedy tunes and some well-timed comedic dances. Best of the new songs by Inez James and Sidney Miller is 'Sing a Jingle,' a lilting tempo that could catch on for pop attention. Other Jones contributions are 'The Night We Called It a Day,' 'Love, You Are My Music,' and 'Beautiful Love'—all previously published.

Story hits familiar strides, with Jones—as radio baritone star—slipping off to a hinterlands war plant after getting Army physical turndown. After initial conflict with the boss' daughter, pair fall in love, and he steps in under radio name to put over benefit show for a war bond campaign.

Jones does well in the lead, with June Vincent okay as the girl. In addition to pair of song and dance numbers, Miss Kean teams up with Gus Schilling for slapstick comedy romance to inject levity into the proceedings. Young Richard Love is on for two tap numbers in addition to being overplayed as the juve genius. Samuel Hinds, Jerome Cowan, Edward Norris and Joan Castle comprise support.

Script is unimpressive though adequate, and direction by producer-director Edward Lilley maintains adequate tempo to hold interest for the abbreviated running time. *Walt.*

The Ghost Ship

RKO release of Van Lewton production. Stars Richard Dix; features Russell Wade, Edith Barrett, Ben Bard, Edmund Glover. Directed by Mark Robson. Screenplay, Donald Henderson Clarke; camera, Nicholas Musuracca; editor, John Lockert. At Rialto, N. Y., week of Dec. 24, '43. Running time, **69 MINS.**

Captain........................Richard Dix
Tom.........................Russell Wade
Ellen.........................Edith Barrett
Bowns..........................Ben Bard
Sparks....................Edmund Glover
Finn.......................Skelton Knaggs
Benson........................Tom Burton
Ausman.....................Steve Winston
Raphael......................Robert Rice
Louie...................Lawrence Tierney
Boats....................Dewey Robinson
Mm..........................Charles Lung
John...................George de Normand
Peter..........................Paul Marion
Billy.........................Sir Lancelot
Roberts........................Boyd Davis

Story of a psychological struggle

between Richard Dix, ship captain, and Russell Wade. his new. youthful third officer, never gets started so couldn't jell. A dualer.

Star is called upon to do a deadpan lunatic for most of the footage but breaks into a face-twitching routine near the close which finds him murdered by Skelton Knaggs, a crew member. Latter, incidentally, is cast as a Finnish mute who, through the miracles of modern screen technique, is wired for sound. Strange and philosophical maxims are wafted from the 'dummy' in a ghostly. off-screen voice every once in a while. This helps not at all in making the vague yarn any clearer.

Wade. as the mystified third mate acts mystified enough, but probably will have to be content with an also-ran position when compared with 'Ghost Ship' audiences. Rest of the cast seems even more mystified than Wade.

Script, which evidently aimed for a Joseph Conrad groove. fails to put over temperamental conflict idea in understandable fashion, and direction does not overcome this handicap. Dix as a heavy should have been built as such in earlier scenes to offer fuller appreciation by dual audiences used to seeing him in nobler moods.   *Donn.*

Suspected Person
(BRITISH-MADE)

PRC release of Associated British production. Features Clifford Evans. Patricia Roc, David Farrar and Anne Firth. Directed by Lawrence Huntington. Screenplay. Huntington; camera. Ronald Anscombe; editor, Flora Newton. At New York, N. Y.. week of Dec. 20, dual. Running time, 78 MINS.
Jim Raynor..................Clifford Evans
Joan Raynor..................Patricia Roc
Thompson.....................David Farrar
Carol............................Anne Firth
Franklin.....................Robert Beatty
Dolan.......................Eric Clavering
Tony Garrett................Leslie Perrins
David.....................Eliot Makeham
Jones..........................John Salew
Saunders....................Billy Hartnell

An Associated British film. which PRC is distributing in the U. S., is a suspenseful mystery-drama which exhibs should find adequate in filling out a program.

Story takes place in London where

Clifford Evans is in possession of money from a bank holdup in America, obtained when he fled country after two of his accomplices were arrested. These two win acquittals and track down Evans, all the while under scrutiny of Scotland Yard, which bides time in nabbing trio until the hiding place of the dough is revealed.

Patricia Roc, as Evans' sister, and David Farrar, as the inspector, turn in good performances as do Evans and his cinematic sweetheart, Anne Firth. Direction by Lawrence Huntington has even pacing with Ronald Anscombe's photography at par.

Cattle Stampede

PRC release of Sigmund Neufeld production. Features Buster Crabbe and Al St. John. Directed by Sam Newfield. Original and screenplay. Joe O'Donnell; camera, Robert Cline; editor, Holbrook Todd. At New York, N. Y., week of Dec. 20; dual. Running time, 58 MINS.
Billy the Kid...............Buster Crabbe
Fuzzy Jones..................Al St. John
Mary.. ....Frances Gladwin
Coulter......................Charles King
Sam Dawson....................Ed Cassidy
Ed Dawson..................Hansel Werner
Stone.......................Ray Bennett
Elkins........................Frank Ellis
Turner.......................Steve Clark
Slater........................Roy Brent
Doctor.......................John Elliott
Jensen........................Bud Buster

This Sigmund Neufeld production in the 'Billy the Kid' series for PRC is a routine dual western. Buster Crabbe and Al St. John are featured, with the latter's comedy providing the highlight.

Crabbe and St. John lead a group of Oklahoma ranchers in their fight to break the rustling combine headed by Charles King, whose practice is stampeding herds and buying whatever is left at his own price. Some good hand-to-hand brawls and fast gunplay spice up the proceedings.

Frances Gladwin has the only female role, a minor one. Sam Newfield's direction brings out average performances.

Smart Guy

Monogram release of John T. Coyle production. Directed by Lambert Hillyer. Stars Rick Vallin; features Veda Ann Borg. Bobby Larson. Screenplay. Charles R. Marior and John W. Krafft, based on original by Harrison Jacobs; camera. Mack Stengler; editor, Carl Pierson; music, Edward Kay. At New York, N. Y.. week Dec. 14, '42. dual. Running time, 63 MINS.
Johnny.......................Rick Vallin
Bobby......................Bobby Larson
Lee.......................Veda Ann Borg
Jean.........................Wanda McKay
Taylor.......................Jack La Rue
Maggie.......................Mary Gordon
Kilbourne....................Paul McVey
District Attorney........Addison Richards
Kearns.......................Roy Darmour
Evans.........................Jon Dawson

Lambert Hillyer directed this one strictly according to formula. A minor dualer.

Slow-moving picture concerns itself with the rehabilitation of a tough gambler. Rick Vallin is the gambler who 'adopts' a newsboy to get favorable publicity in order to beat a manslaughter rap. Amusing angle is that he's actually innocent, but the d.a. is out to get him. The gambler jumps bail and takes refuge in the country, accompanied by the kid. He finally gives up after the moral lessons taught him by the newsboy and the country girl, Veda Ann Borg, proprietress of the inn where he hides.

1944

Miniature Reviews

'The Lodger' (20th). Merle Oberon, Laird Cregar, George Sanders in top boxoffice film; due for extended runs.

'Miracle of Morgan's Creek' (Par). Rather amusing romantic comedy that will do better than average to good.

'Three Russian Girls' (UA). Documentary display of Soviet nurses working behind front lines; dualer.

'Standing Room Only' (Par). Fred MacMurray and Paulette Goddard in romantic comedy headed for healthy b.o.

'The Uninvited' (Par). Fanciful melodrama starring Ray Milland and Ruth Hussey.

'Henry Aldrich, Boy Scout' (Par.). Rather dull Aldrich subject dealing with Boy Scout activities.

'Timber Queen' (Par). Conventional timberlands meller; okay for twin bills.

'Courageous Mr. Penn' (British). Saga of William Penn's life. Limited for arty houses.

The Lodger

20th-Fox release of Robert Bassler production. Stars Merle Oberon, George Sanders, Laird Cregar; features Sir Cedric Hardwicke, Sara Allgood. Directed by John Brahm. Screenplay by Barre Lyndon from novel by Mrs. Marie Belloc Lowndes; camera, Lucien Ballard; editor, J. Watson Webb, Jr.; special camera effects, Fred Sersen. Tradeshown in N. Y., Jan. 3, '43. Running time, **84 MINS.**

Kitty	Merle Oberon
John Warwick	George Sanders
The Lodger	Laird Cregar
Robert Burton	Sir Cedric Hardwicke
Ellen	Sara Allgood
Supt. Sutherland	Aubrey Mather
Daisy	Queenie Leonard
Jennie	Doris Lloyd
Sergeant Bates	David Clyde
Anne Rowley	Helena Pickard
Dr. Sheridan	Lumsden Hare
Sir Edward	Frederick Worlock
Harris	Olaf Hytten
Harold	Colin Campbell
Charlie	Harold De Becker
Wiggy	Anita Bolster
Publican	Billy Bevan
Cobbler	Forrester Harvey
Comedian	Charles Hall
Costermonger	Skelton Knaggs
Manager	Edmund Breon
Conductor	Harry Allen

With a pat cast, keen direction and tight scripting, 20th-Fox has an absorbing, and, at times, spine-tingling drama concocted from Mrs. Marie Belloc Lowndes' widely read novel, 'The Lodger.' It looks like a sturdy boxoffice entry, calculated to win extended runs in many spots.

Where it fails to register top coin, only lukewarm exploitation will be to blame, because 'The Lodger' is the sort of film that will benefit from word-o'-mouth. It's a super chiller-diller in its picturization of a Scotland Yard manhunt for London's Jack the Ripper.

Picture's title may prove a handicap in attracting those unversed as to the Lowndes' novel, but that much stronger for those familiar with her book. This is far from being an outright man's vehicle, although the romance is slight. With Laird Cregar as the principal menace, Merle Oberon's popularity and all-round appeal of George Sanders the film has balanced marquee lustre.

Director John Brahm and scripter Barre Lyndon have made it as much a psychological study of the half-crazed 'Lodger' (Laird Cregar), as it is a deftly paced horrific who-dunit. In trying to outline some explanation for the repeated throat-slashings of London stage women, neither has even slightly deviated from the swift weaving of events. Result is a tempo sure to grip the most blase. Aside from preliminary steps, sequence of events mounts in rapid succession with suspense injected time after time with telling effect.

Plot spots the 'lodger' early as a possible suspect as he calmly conducts his medical 'experiments' in the attic rooms of a modest London home occupied by a middle-aged couple. He wanders in and out via the rear entrance, doing work in a hospital sometimes during the day. The Scotland Yard inspector, George Sanders, has his suspicions almost as soon as he meets him, but not until almost too late to save his sweetheart, Miss Oberon, does he feel certain he is 'The Ripper.' Yarn depicts 'The Ripper's' killings as prompted by revenge for his brother's early death, blamed on an unfaithful actress.

It is Laird Cregar's picture. As 'The Ripper' he gives an impressive performance. It is a relentless, at times pathetic character as he pursues his self-appointed task of avenging his brother. His precise diction and almost studied poise makes his characterization all the more impressive. Merle Oberon is highly effective as Kitty, the dancer, of respectable family whose stardom is nearly abruptly ended. Stage sequences show her a graceful dancer in abbreviated skirt and provide the bright contrast to somber and melodramatic passages. Kept more or less in the background initially, her scene in the dressing room, when she pleads for her life, is the high dramatic spot of the production. George Sanders, again cast as a sleuth, is strong. He has several romantic interludes with Miss Oberon.

Sir Cedric Hardwicke, as Robert Burton, the middleclass Londoner who takes in a lodger, provides a sturdy supporting role. Sara Allgood is tremendously effective as his wife. Helena Pickard makes something of a bit, an unsuccessful music hall entertainer, who is one of the first victims of 'The Ripper.' Support is headed by Queenie Leonard, Doris Lloyd, Lumsden Hare and Aubrey Mather.

Robert Bassler has provided plenty of production values in carrying out with authenticity the London of the gaslight era. Lucien Ballard has turned in a superb job of photography, his use of light and shade being fine throughout. John Brahm's direction, making a maximum reliance on suspense, is possibly the strongest feature of the picture. Barre Lyndon's scripting from the novel also is standout. There was a tendency, however, to overplay the sound effects. *Wear.*

Miracle of Morgan's Creek

Paramount production and release. Stars Eddie Bracken, Betty Hutton; features Diana Lynn, William Demarest, Porter Hall, Emory Parnell, Alan Bridge, Julius Tannen, Victor Potel. Written and directed by Preston Sturges. Editor, Stuart Gilmore; camera, John Seitz. Previewed in N. Y. Dec. 29, '43. Running time, **101 MINS.**

Norval Jones	Eddie Bracken
Trudy Kockenlocker	Betty Hutton
Emmy Knockenlocker	Diana Lynn
Officer Kockenlocker	William Demarest
Justice of the Peace	Porter Hall
Mr. Tuerck	Emory Parnell
Mr. Johnson	Alan Bridge
Mr. Rafferty	Julius Tannen
Newspaper Editor	Victor Potel
Wife of J. P	Almira Sessions
Sally	Esther Howard
Sheriff	J. Farrell MacDonald
First M. P	Frank Moran
Cecilia	Connie Tompkins
Mrs. Johnson	Georgia Caine
Doctor	Torben Meyer
U. S. Marshal	George Melford

'Miracle of Morgan's Creek' is a diverting picture that will do from better than average to good business in all situations.

Aside from that longish title, there is nothing at the outset to suggest that this is a comedy. Morgan's Creek is the name of the town where the action takes place and the miracle, as Sturges terms it, is the birth to Eddie Bracken and Betty Hutton of a set of sextuplets.

Done in the satirical Sturges vein, and directed with that same touch, the story makes much of characterization and somewhat wacky comedy, plus some slapstick, with excellent photography figuring throughout. The Sturges manner of handling crowds and various miscellaneous characters who are almost nothing more than flashes in the picture, such as the smalltown attorney and the justice of the peace, contribute enormously to the enjoyment derived.

However, some of the comedy situations lack punch, and the picture is slow to get rolling, but ultimately picks up smart pace and winds up quite strongly on the birth of the sextuplets with the retiring Bracken and Miss Hutton as national heroes. The publicity, newspaper headlines and the worry that it even causes Hitler, provide a fast strip of action that is typically Sturges and clever.

Bracken is a smalltown bank clerk who yearns to get into uniform and is madly in love with Miss Hutton. Getting out on an all-night party with soldiers, the latter wakes up to remember that she married a serviceman, but can't remember the name, what the spouse looked like, or anything except that they didn't give their right names. Finally Bracken and Miss Hutton evolve a scheme under which he'll dress up in a uniform (of World War I vintage) and they'll get married under the name which the girl vaguely remembers was that of the soldier on her big night out. They both get in a jam over this but, for the happy finish, their marriage is declared the only legal one Miss Hutton had. In between are numerous amusing scenes, notably the one in which Bracken proposes to Miss Hutton and the one in which he is escaping from jail.

Bracken does a nice job. He's a comedian who is coming along rapidly and should attain major stature ere long. Miss Hutton and he make a desirable team. In this instance, the fiery little song bombshell who came to pictures from niteries, plays a straight light comedy role and does it exceptionally well. She's real star material.

Among the supporting cast, largest assignment is that given William Demarest, smalltown cop father of Miss Hutton, who has his troubles with his daughters, the other being attractive Diana Lynn. There are many lessers in the cast, but all are in parts of a minor character. A standout among them is Alan Bridge, an attorney, while another who impresses in a short amount of footage is Porter Hall.

The editing, by Stuart Gilmore, represents a consummate job in most respects, but the running time could have been chopped somewhat to tighten the picture, particularly in the first two reels. *Char.*

Three Russian Girls
(SONGS)

Hollywood, Dec. 23.

United Artists release of Gregor Rabinovitch production; associate producer, Eugene Frenke; assistant to producer, Carley Harriman. Stars Anna Sten, Kent Smith; features Mimi Forsaythe, Alexander Granach, Kathy Frye, Paul Guilfoyle, Kane Richmond. Directed by Fedor Ozep and Henry Kesler. Adapted from 'Girl From Leningrad,' by Maurice Clark and Victor Trivas; screenplay, Aben Kandel, Dan James; camera, John Mescall; special effects, Frank Hills; editors, S. K. Winston and Gregg Tallas; ass't director, Joseph Depew. Previewed at Egyptian Dec. 22, '43. Running time, **80 MINS.**

Natasha	Anna Sten
John Hill	Kent Smith
Tamara	Mimi Forsaythe
Major Braginski	Alexander Granach
Chijik	Kathy Frye
Trishin	Paul Guilfoyle
Sergei	Kane Richmond
Doctor	Manart Kippen
Misha	Jack Gardner
Shoora	Marcia Lenack
Zina	Mary Herriot
Olga	Anna Marie Stewart
Manya	Dorothy Gray
Terkin	Feodor Chaliapin

This American remake of the Russian feature, 'Girl From Stalingrad,' is factual narrative rather than film entertainment as required by current audience requirements. Detailing a stolid and plodding tale of the fortitude and patriotism of Soviet volunteer nurses working behind the lines, picture even fails to take advantage of oppportunities to inject a fairly strong romance into the proceedings by tossing it off in matter-of-fact manner. A dualer.

Story starts off in June of 1941, when volunteer Red Cross unit headed by Anna Sten is called for duty at the front. Field hospital in an old mansion gives them opportunity to minister to the wounded—which is expounded in extended footage. Then Kent Smith, an American technical engineer, seriously injured in a plane crash, is brought in. Vivid clinical operation is displayed, and while Kent is hovering between life and death, mild romance develops between the American and Miss Sten. Patients and staff of hospital are moved when Russian army retreats to Leningrad; and then the Soviet's winter counter-attack with white-clad ski troops, tanks and heavy equipment participating provides a vivid and spectacular battle episode which, nevertheless, comes too late to do more than catch momentary interest. Back at the base hospital, the boy and girl nonchalantly say goodbye to end a very mild flirtation for the finish.

Russ winter attack carries a wallop in divulging the methods and operations under the sub-zero climates. Apparently the footage was acquired from the original Soviet production but regardless of source, it's highly dramatic.

Anna Sten's lead spot is a tough assignment, an unlightened and burdensome characterization that fails to catch attention. Mimi Forsaythe and Kathy Frye, as members of the volunteer corps, shine in various sequences, but both are handicapped by the stolid proceedings. Alexander Granach and Paul Guilfoyle are in support, with Kent Smith unable to take advantage of the situation at any time. *Walt.*

Standing Room Only

Paramount release of Paul Jones production. Stars Fred MacMurray, Paulette Goddard; features Edward Arnold, Roland Young, Hillary Brooke, Porter Hall. Directed by Sidney Lanfield. Screenplay, Darrel Ware and Karl Tunberg, based on a story by Al Martin; score, Robert Emmett Dolan; editor, William Shea; camera, Charles Lang. Previewed in N. Y. Dec. 29, '43. Running time, **83 MINS.**

Lee Stevens	Fred MacMurray
Jane Rogers	Paulette Goddard
T. J. Todd	Edward Arnold
Alice Todd	Hillary Brooke
Ira Cromwell	Roland Young
Major Cromwell	Anne Revere
Glen Ritchie	Clarence Kolb
Mrs. Ritchie	Isobel Randolph
Hugo Farenhall	Porter Hall
Opal	Marie McDonald
Miss Becker	Josephine Whittell
Peggy Fuller	Veda Ann Borg

War crowded Washington again is the nucleus for a timely comedy based on the trouble people have in securing living accommodations and the red tape involved in getting in to see officials on business in the nation's capital. Fred MacMurray and Paulette Goddard, plus an excellent supporting cast, should help 'Standing Room Only' to good boxoffice.

This is a picture for all the family. All problems are dealt with in the light vein used by most predecessors based on similar themes. With the acting ability of MacMurray and Miss Goddard, ably abetted by Edward Arnold, Roland Young and Porter Hall, and the snappily paced direction of Sidney Lanfield, the film is escapist entertainment with many amusing sequences.

Script by Darrel Ware and Karl Tunberg gives the two stars plenty opportunities to prove their capabilities. MacMurray, as the butler, is especially funny in a scene where he drops a cherry from the fruit salad which he is serving into the lap of one of the women and endeavors to snare the elusive condiment with a knife and spoon, while she continues her conversa ion with one of the guests. Miss Goddard gives a pleasing performance throughout. Porter Hall, as owner of an opposition factory who tries to secure a government contract; Clarence Kolb, as the blustering official, and Hillary Brooke, as Arnold's daughter, give proper portrayal to their roles. Roland Young plays his usual dwadling self in extremely capable fashion.

Paul Jones, associate producer, has given the production depth and understanding, avoiding pitfalls which were apparent from the outset, but which failed to materialize.

The Uninvited

Paramount release of Charles Brackett production. Stars Ray Milland, Ruth Hussey; features Donald Crisp, Cornelia Otis Skinner, Gail Russell, Dorothy Stickney. Directed by Lewis Allen. Screenplay by Dodie Smith and Frank Partos, based on novel by Dorothy Macardle; score, Victor Young; editor, Doane Harrison; camera, Challes Lang. Previewed in N. Y., Dec. 30, '48. Running time, **98 MINS.**

Roderick Fitzgerald	Ray Milland
Pamela Fitzgerald	Ruth Hussey
Commander Beech	Donald Crisp
Miss Holloway	Cornelia Otis Skinner
Miss Bird	Dorothy Stickney
Lizzie Flynn	Barbara Everest
Dr. Scott	Alan Napier
Stella Meredith	Gail Russell
Miss Ellis	Jessica Newcombe
Foreword Narrator	John Kieran
Maid	Rita Page

The supernatural is dealt with seriously in this dynamic, suspenseful melodrama, chock full of fine acting, that will hold audiences glued to their seats for its entire 93 minutes. Once in, they'll like it, but because of the unusual and controversial subject, its b.o. may be moderate.

Audiences are asked to accept the fact that living characters portrayed on the screen are harassed by two ghosts. And the ghosts remain just that throughout the picture. One is heard but never seen. The other materializes completely out of mist for one short, terrific scene at the end.

Ray Milland and Ruth Hussey give excellent performances as brother and sister, who tire of living in a London flat, find a house overlooking the ocean on the coast of England, buy it and settle down to enjoy suburban life, only to find that the past permeates throughout the building. But the real treat in 'The Uninvited' is a starlet Paramount has been keeping under wraps in 'B' pictures, who is given a part with plenty of meat in this one, and comes through like a veteran. Her name is Gail Russell, and she definitely belongs.

Miss Russell plays the 20-year-old daughter of the woman who is believed to be haunting Windward House. Kept from entering the edifice since she was three by her grandfather (Donald Crisp), she becomes friendly with Milland and Miss Hussey. On visiting the mansion she is faced by the ghost of her mother, faints, becomes a victim of shock when she awakens. When she returns to her grandfather's home, he has her whisked away to a mental rest home owned by Cornelia Otis Skinner. How she is rescued, with the truth coming out concerning her late mother, lends itself to a strong climax.

Dodie Smith and Frank Partos have written a tight screenplay from Dorothy Macardle's best-selling ghost novel. Camera work by Charles Lang is especially commendable, with deft direction by Lewis Allen keeping the picture moving at a rapid pace throughout.

Performances of Milland and Miss Hussey are unrestrained and convincing in a picture that could have been very unconvincing. Donald Crisp, as Commander Beech, retired grandfather of Miss Russell; Dorothy Stickney, from the Broadway stage, who is on screen in one short scene as a patient at the mental institution, and Alan Napier, as Dr. Scott, who endeavors to help Miss Russell during her alleged illness, all lend dignity and authority to the film.

This is Cornelia Otis Skinner's first picture in which she is a featured player. A capable actress on the stage, she also proves her worth on the screen, and will definitely be heard from as far as films are concerned in the future. Although Miss Skinner does not appear until more than half the film has unwound, she is impressive in her role.

Henry Aldrich, Boy Scout

Paromount release of Michel Kraike production. Features Jimmy Lydon. Directed by Hugh Bennett. Screenplay, Muriel Roy Bolton; story, Agnes Christine Johnston; camera, Daniel Fapp; editor, Everett Douglas. Tradeshown in N. Y., Dec. 30, '43. Running time, **66 MINS.**

Henry Aldrich	Jimmy Lydon
Dizzy Stevens	Charley Smith
Sam Aldrich	John Litel
Mrs. Aldrich	Olive Blakeney
Elise	Joan Mortimer
Ramsey Kent	Minor Watson
Peter	Darryl Hickman
Irwin Barrett	David Holt
Beaney	Richard Haydel

This is a dull, overlong piece suitable chiefly for the lower half of duals. It's lacking in suspense and action, with tiresome scripting largely responsible for the unsatisfactory result. Paramount has given this small budgeter relatively good production values, Hugh Bennett's direction is better than the trite motivation allows for, and Daniel Fapp's camera work is okay.

Yarn is about the tribulations of a senior patrol scout leader in a small town, with Jimmy Lydon, as Henry Aldrich, in the lead.

Lydon portrays a long-suffering scout leader, taking the blame for the misdeeds of a mischievous youngster (Darryl Hickman), the son of a friend of Aldrich, Sr. Henry (Lydon) finally winds up with the coveted appointment of junior assistant scoutmaster, following a series of misadventures in the woods during a scout contest. Darryl Hickman shows promise as a kid actor and looks like a good bet for more important assignments. *Mori.*

Timber Queen

Paramount release of William Pine and William Thomas production. Features Richard Arlen, Mary Beth Hughes. Directed by Frank McDonald. Screenplay, Maxwell Shane, Edward T. Lowe; camera, Fred Jackman; editor, Howard Smith. Tradeshown in N. Y., Dec. 30, '43. Running time, **66 MINS.**

Russ	Richard Arlon
Elaine	Mary Beth Hughes
Lil	June Havoc
Smacksie	Sheldon Leonard
Squirrel	George E. Stone
Milt	Dick Purcell
Talbot	Tony Hughes
Birdsdell	Edmund MacDonald
Rawson	Bill Haade
Barney	Clancy Cooper
Wenzel	Dewey Robinson
Rodney	Horace McMahon
Strudel	Jimmy Ames

Though 'Timber Queen' follows the familiar and obvious pattern indicated by the title, it will serve nicely for double-feature setup. Director Frank McDonald has managed to maintain action at a satisfactory pace, casting is adequate, and the yarn holds attention most of the way despite a few corny sequences.

Story has Arlen as a returned Army flyer, honorably discharged for physical disability, coming back to civilian life in time to save the widow of his friend (killed in action) from a ruinous finanacial tangle. In order to retain the timber lands left to the widow (Mary Beth Hughes), Arlen has to lift a mortgage by getting a certain amount of timber cut and delivered. Situation is complicated by Arlen's partner, who is trying to prevent the timber from reaching him on time so he can foreclose the property.

Couple of fist fights, some aviation sequences, and a gang of racketeers who are finally enlisted in the service of the widow to salvage their own investment in the project, are developments employed to heighten suspense. Romantic interludes with Arlen and Miss Hughes are interwoven. *Mori.*

Riders of the Deadline

United Artists release of henry Sherman production. Directed by Lesley Selander. Stars Willaim Boyd; features Andy Clyde, Jimmy Rogers, Frances Woodward and Bob Mitchum. Screenplay, Bennett Cohen from characters created by Clarence E. Mulford; camera, Russell Harlan. At New York theatre, Week Dec. 28, dualled. Running time, 70 MINS.

Hopalong Cassidy	William Boyd
California Carson	Andy Clyde
Jimmy	Jimmy Rogers
Tim	Richard Crane
Crandell	William Halligran
Sue	Frances Woodward
Madigan	Tony Ward
Drago	Bob Mitchum
Tex	Jim Bannon
Martin	Hugh Prosser
Captain	Herb Rawlinson

This is an above-average western for the duals, wi h story and direction both credible.

Story deals with the efforts of William Boyd, in his usual role of Hopalong Cassidy, and his two sidekicks, Andy Clyde and Jimmy Rogers, to track down a band of firearms smugglers operating close to the Mexican border.

Gal is Frances Woodward, and she does an adequate job. There's no time for romance or sentimentality of any sort, as the action is tight throughout. Tony Ward and William Halligan do a good job as leaders of the outlaws.

Courageous Mr. Penn
(BRITISH-MADE)

J. H. Hoffberg release of Richard Vernon production. Stars Clifford Evans, Deborah Kerr. Directed by Lance Comfort. Original story and screenplay by Anatole de Grunwald; music, London Symphony orchestra. At 55th Street Playhouse, N. Y., starting Dec. 22, '43. Running time, 78 MINS.

William Penn	Clifford Evans
Gulielma	Deborah Kerr
Charles II	Dennis Arundell
King's Chaplain	Aubrey Mallalieu
Lord Arlington	D. J. Williams
Lord Lecil	O. B. Clarence
Fox	James Harcourt
Admiral Penn	Charles Carson
Pepys	Henry Oscar
Elton	Max Adrian
Bindle	John Stuart
Cook	Marie O'Neill
Bushell	Edward Rigby
Lord Mayor of London	Joss Ambler
Ford	J. H. Roberts
Ship's Captain	Edmund Willard
Ship's Mate	Gus McNaughton
Holme	Percy Marmont
Indian Chief	Gibb McLaughlin
Cockle	Herbert Lomas

Some vivid passages have been managed from a rather methodical script and an obviously weighty subject. Lacking any player halfway familiar to average American audiences, and further burdened by slowly-paced direction, 'Courageous Mr. Penn' looks suited only for a few arty theatres.

Starting with his youth in the London of 1667, when he spearheaded the Quaker movement, story is extremely wordy and lacks sufficient action. It's all done with integrity in production detail, and helped by a uniformly excellent and large cast.

This British has depicted Penn as an almost dashing figure, spotlighting his attempt to gain free speech and equality. Unfortunately, the plot focuses too much attention on Penn alone and overlooks several important surrounding characters. For instance, even though not shown in too favorable light, King Charles II gives every indication of being an outstanding character (and he was); yet, it's relegated in the long procession of events. Yarn ultimately shows Penn leading his ardent freedom lovers to U. S.

Clifford Evans makes a remarkably interesting, if a bit wordy, Penn, not only as a zealous Quaker but as an ardent lover and husband. Deborah Kerr is nicely cast as his sweetheart and wife. Dennis Arundell plays Charles II plausibly. Of the support, John Stuart, Max Adrian, D. J. Williams and O. B. Clarence shape up best.

Anatole de Grunwald's scripting has apparently taken liberties with history. Dialog shows up well. *Wear.*

The Girl from Monterey
(SONGS)

PRC release of Jack Schwarz (Harry B. Edwards) production. Features Armida, Elgar Kennedy, Veda Ann Bord, Jack La Rue. Directed by Wallace Fox. Screenplay, Arthur Hoerl, from original story by George Green and Robert Gordon. Camera, Marcel Le Picard; editor, Robert Grandall. At New York, N. Y., week of Dec. 18, dual. Running time, 60 MINS.

Lita	Armida
Doc Hogan	Edgar Kennedy
Flossie	Veda Ann Borg
Johnson	Jack La Rue
Jerry O'Leary	Terry Frost
Baby	Anthony Caruso
Harry	Charles Williams
Commissioner	Bryant Washburn
Perrone	Guy Zanett
Announcer	Wheeler Oakman

'Girl From-Monterey' is a minor dualer. Pic offers little diversion outside of a few exciting boxing shots.

Deals with the efforts of Armida, who manages her prizefighting brother, played by Anthony Caruso, to keep him from fighting Terry Frost, also a fighter, and one with whom gal is in love. Climax, of course, comes when Boxing Commission sets fight, with Fros.'s manager apparently fixing the fight through siren Veda Ann Borg, who is to keep Caruso out of condition. Gal spills beans and everything ends right side up.

Pic makes poor usage of good song material, when Armida, who has a Spanish accent, sings 'Jive, Brother, Jive,' a song built for a swing singer, not a coloratura soprano. Edgar Kennedy gets the laughs, and Jack La Rue is capable as the 'fixit' manager.

Title refers to the Mex origin of Miss Armida, but action is otherwise localed in New York.

Oro En La Mano
('Gold in the Hand')
(ARGENTINE-MADE)

Buenos Aires, Dec. 15.

Pampa Film production and release. Stars Pepita Serrador, Sebastian Chiola, Jose Olarra, Domingo Sapelli, Froilan Barela, Nestor Deval, Jose Ruzo. Directed by Adelqui Millar. Story, Manuel Villegas Lopez; adapted by Manuel Villegas Lopez; photography, Gumer Barreirro; music, Lucio Demare. At Monumental, Buenos Aires. Running time, **100 MINS.**

This one is not quite up to Pampa's past standards although an interesting example of local production, particularly since it reverses usual trend of local films and moves story outdoors to a region not unlike the American west. Yarn deals with a medico who, because of an error, is ruined and abandoned by his friends. He heads for the mountain regions, becomes a miner and falls in love with the wife of one of his companions. To get the funds to escape with her, he steals from his pal and a series of incidents ending in a tragic climax follows.

Mining scenes have been fairly well done and the superstitions and brutality that still mark the distant regions of Argentina are well painted. But film lacks punch and has been acted without brilliance, with the result that it fails to really take advantage of its possibilities. Should be of interest for provincial Latinos, however, because of the background and of the frequently well-realized action sequences. *Ray.*

Miniature Reviews

'Lifeboat' (20th). Alfred Hitchcock thriller, based on John Steinbeck's powerful original, a b.o. winner.

'Sherlock Holmes and the Spider Woman' (U). Mystery should prove strong dual supporter.

'Ali Baba and 40 Thieves' (Color) (Song) (U). Adventurous and colorful escapist fare. Should get strong biz.

'Charlie Chan in the Secret Service' (Mono.). Sidney Toler in so-so mystery.

'There's Something About a Soldier' (Col). Interesting combination of documentary and romantic plot; good for duals.

'La Guerra La Gano Yo' (Argentine). Spanish languager, one of best-made native pix of Argentine season.

'The Sultan's Daughter' (Musical) (Mono.). Fairly neat, production; strong dual support.

'Death Rides the Plains' (PRC). Western dualer with Bob Livingston, Al St. John; average b.o.

Lifeboat

20th-Fox release of Kenneth Macgowan production. Stars Tallulah Bankhead; features William Bendix, Walter Slezak, Mary Anderson, John Hodiak, Henry Hull, Hume Cronyn, Canada Lee. Directed by Alfred Hitchcock. Story, John Steinbeck; screenplay, Jo Swerling; camera, Glen MacWilliams; editor, Dorothy Spencer. At Astor, N. Y., for run starting Jan. 11, '44. Running time, 96 MINS.

Connie Porter..........Tallulah Bankhead
Gus....................William Bendix
The German.............Walter Slezak
Alice Mackenzie........Mary Anderson
Kovac..................John Hodiak
Ritterhouse............Henry Hull
Mrs. Higgins...........Heather Angel
Stanley Garrett........Hume Cronyn
Joe....................Canada Lee

'Lifeboat' looks like a big grosser. John Steinbeck's devastating indictment of the nature of Nazi bestiality, at times an almost clinical, dissecting room analysis, though it is always carried along for strong audience values under the impetus of exciting narrative, emerges as powerful adult motion picture fare.

This is one of the first films to deal with the problem of the people of Germany. It is not a problem picture, however, and its sociological implications are neatly and expertly fictionized. Neither is there any effort to solve any problem. Yet a provocative issue is raised, one of a kind calculated to stir theatregoers throughout the country. The question Steinbeck poses is, 'What can you do with people like that?'—meaning the Germans.

The picture is based on an original idea of director Alfred Hitchcock's. Hitchcock, from accounts, first asked Steinbeck to write the piece for book publication, figuring that if it turned out a big seller the exploitation value for film purposes would be greatly enhanced. The author, however, would not undertake the more ambitious assignment and wrote the story for screen purposes only, with Jo Swerling handling the adaptation.

Patterned along one of the simplest, most elementary forms of dramatic narration, the action opens and closes on a lifeboat. It's a lusty, robust story about a group of survivors from a ship sunk by a U-boat. One by one the survivors find precarious refuge on the lifeboat. Finally they pick up a survivor from the German U-boat. Despite the fierce hatred of the suspicious Kovac (John Hodiak), an American of Czech descent, the majority vote against killing the Nazi. He is first

tolerated and then welcomed into their midst. They share their food and water with the Nazi. And in the end he repays their trust and confidence with murderous treachery.

The Nazi, who turns out to be the captain of the submarine which sunk the ship originally, hoards vitamin-food and water while the others go hungry and thirsty. He steers the lifeboat off its course, heading it straight for German waters. He torments the suffering group with extravagant boasts of Nazi 'master race' superiority. And when he is finally disposed of there is a momentary sense of loss among the survivors, as if 'the motor is gone.' Yet, when the group of Americans and Britishers is confronted later with another Nazi whom they rescue from the sea, they appear likely to repeat their first mistake. Have they so soon forgotten Willie, the first Nazi? Maybe not, but as humans they cannot murder another defenseless human in cold blood.

Walter Slezak, as the fat, greasy, conceited German, comes through with a terrific delineation. Henry Hull as the millionaire, William Bendix as the mariner with a jitterbug complex who loses a leg, John Hodiak as the tough, bitter, Nazi-hater, and Canada Lee as the colored steward, deliver excellent characterizations.

Tallulah Bankhead, as Mrs. Porter, a cynical newspaper writer, is not photogenically acceptable in the brief, fiercely romantic interludes with Hodiak. The camera treats her unkindly throughout, except in one or two instances.

While the film has no top picture names, it is a production that holds first-rate exploitation possibilities.

Hitchcock has piloted the piece skillfully, ingenuously developing suspense and action. Despite that it's a slow starter, the picture, from the beginning, leaves a strong impact and, before too long, develops into the type of suspenseful product with which Hitchcock has always been identified. *Mori.*

Sherlock Holmes and the Spider Woman

Universal release of Roy William Neill production, directed by Neill; assistant director, Melville Shyer. Features Basil Rathbone, Nigel Bruce, Gale Sondergaard, Dennis Hoey, Vernon Downing. Screenplay, Bertram Millhauser, based on story by Sir Arthur Conan Doyle; camera, Charles Van Enger; editor, James Gibbon. Previewed in N. Y., Jan. 5, '43. Running time, 62 MINS.

Sherlock Holmes..........Basil Rathbone
Dr. Watson...............Nigel Bruce
Adrea Spedding...........Gale Sondergaard
Lestrade.................Dennis Hoey
Norman Locke.............Vernon Downing
Radlik...................Alec Craig
Mrs. Hudson..............Mary Gordon
Gilflower................Arthur Hohl
Larry....................Teddy Infuhr

A mysterious succession of 'pyjama' suicides throws London into a turmoil. Sherlock Holmes, convinced the dead were all murder victims, rounds up the gang of killers. It's all interesting enough, and the picture will serve as strong support on duals.

Strangely, all the victims are found in locked rooms with death resulting from wounds inflicted by bullets from guns found in their hands. However, Holmes believes that a woman is behind the alleged suicides. On a fishing trip with Dr. Watson he disappears, with his death announced in London papers. Of course, he comes back to life soon enough, solves the reason for the murders, escapes death twice at the hands of the gang, and they wind up in the hands of the police.

Basil Rathbone, as Sherlock Holmes, and Nigel Bruce, as Dr. Watson, give their usual substantial performances in this film, one of a series of mysteries based on novels by Sir Arthur Conan Doyle. Gale Sondergaard, as Adrea Spedding,

does a bewitching job as the diabolic head of a group of killers-for-life insurance benefits. Rest of the players, including Dennis Hoey, as Lestrade of Scotland Yard; Vernon Downing, brother of Adrea; Alec Craig and Mary Gordon portray their small roles in capable fashion.

Direction by Roy William Neill, who also produced, is in keeping with past films in this series. Screenplay by Bertram Millhauser is not too wordy, with action moving right along. One gets the impression that the Sherlock Holmes series must be a good money-maker for Universal, since the pictures are so obviously produced on limited budgets. *Sten.*

Ali Baba and the 40 Thieves

(TECHNICOLOR; ONE SONG)

Hollywood, Jan. 7.

Universal release of Paul Malvern production. Stars Maria Montez, Jon Hall, Turhan Bey; features Andy Devine, Fortunio Bonanova, Frank Puglia, Ramsay Ames, Moroni Olsen, Kurt Katch. Directed by Arthur Lubin. Original screenplay by Edmund L. Hartmann; camera, George Robinson and W. Howard Greene; special photography, John P. Fulton; editor, Russell Schoengarth; dialog director, Stacy Keach; asst. director, Charles Gould; score and direction, Edward Ward; song, Ward and J. K. Brennan. Previewed at Pantages, Jan. 6, '44. Running time 85 MINS.

Amara....................Maria Montez
Ali Baba.................Jon Hall
Jamiel...................Turhan Bey
Abdullah.................Andy Devine
Hulagu Khan..............Kurt Katch
Cassim...................Frank Puglia
Baba.....................Fortunio Bonanova
Caliph...................Moroni Olsen
Nalu.....................Ramsay Ames
Fat Thief................Chris-Pin Martin
Ali (as child)...........Scotty Beckett
Amara (as child).........Yvette Duguay
Mongol Captain...........Noel Cravat
Little Thief.............Jimmy Conlin
Mahmoud..................Harry Cording

'Ali Baba and the 40 Thieves' is a colorful and exciting melodrama that will play a happy tune at the theatre wickets and catch holdovers generally in key bookings. Picture is strictly escapist entertainment, but deftly contrived and presented for maximum audience reaction.

Following success of 'Arabian Nights,' Universal decided to turn out series of dramatic fantasies, with 'Ali Baba' second in group. No question of picture's ability to duplicate or surpass b.o. reaction of 'Nights.' In utilizing the Ali Baba idea, producer Paul Malvern expertly dishes up an adventurous screen tale that is noteworthy for fast pace and eye-appeal through costumes and sets photographed in some of the best Technicolor to date.

Tale centers around Bagdad at the time of the Mongol invasion which enslaved the populace and killed the caliph. But latter's young son escapes to the hills and stumbles on secret cave of the 40 thieves to become adopted member of the band. Ten years later he is the heroic leader, pitting his group against the ruling Mongol khan of Bagdad until the people can be freed. There's the inevitable romance with Maria Montez, daughter of the traitorous Frank Puglia, her forced betrothment to the khan, and eventual victory for Ali Baba.

Picture moves at express speed and pauses but briefly for characterizations. Maria Montez, as the princess, catches attention with a good performance and many excellently-photographed shots that accentuate eye-reaction, particularly two bathing episodes. Jon Hall, as Ali Baba, is a fast riding and robust hero in typical cinematic vein; while Turhan Bey clicks as a slave boy with ease of handling his particular assignment. Andy Devine is in for his usual comedy antics that catch favorable reaction; Kurt Katch delivers a solid portrayal of the khan, and Puglia is prominent as the traitor. Ramsay Ames is a formful slave girl, and Fortunio Bonanova does well in brief appearances as the original Baba.

Mounting is excellent. There's color in the sets and costumes, and gorgeous exteriors that react to fullest values through the expert photography of George Robinson and Howard Greene. Action predominates, with cameras catching wide scope of battle climax in the khan's palace grounds when the populace rush in to join the 40 thieves in overthrow of the invaders.

Edward Ward did a slick job in preparing the musical score and directing the background music, joining with J. K. Brennan in writing a riding song, '40 Thieves and One for All,' which is sung by male chorus when thieves are riding to battle. *Walt.*

Charlie Chan in the Secret Service

Monogram release of Philip N. Krasne-James S. Burkett production. Stars Sidney Toler; features Gwen Kenyon, Mantan Moreland and Lelah Tyler. Directed by Phil Rosen. Story, George Callahan; camera, Ira Morgan; editor, Marty Cohen; assistant director, George Moskov. At Brooklyn Strand, N. Y., Jan. 6. '43, dual. Running time, 65 MINS. .
Chan...........................Sidney Toler
Inez...........................Gwen Kenyon
Birmingham..............Mantan Moreland
Iris.......................Marianne Quon
Jones........................Arthur Loft
Mrs. Winters.................Lelah Tyler
Tommy.......................Benson Fong
Vega.....................Gene Stutenroth
Lewis.....................Eddie Chandler
Slade.....................George Lessey
Paul.......................George Lewis
Peter......................Muni Seroff

Charlie Chan has moved over to the Monogram lot from 20th-Fox, and the script supplied the veteran detective for his first venture under the new banner is not one of the series' best. Actionless mystery is strictly a program filler.

Signey Toler, who shifted to Monogram along with the Chan stories, tries hard to create interest in Chan's new adventure but is hampered by halting direction and wordy material.

Chan, as a government agent, is assigned to solve mystery surrounding death of an inventor and also to find secret plans stolen from latter. In doing so, he is aided by Gwen Kenyon, Mantan Moreland, Delah Tyler and others in average performance. Majority of sequences take place in home of murdered inventor, thus confining the action and adding to the stodginess of the film.

There's Something About a Soldier

Columbia release of Samuel Bischoff production. Directed by Alfred E. Green. Features Tom Neal, Evelyn Keyes, Bruce Bennett, John Hubbard, Jeff Donnell. Screenplay, Horace McCoy and Barry Trivers; camera, Philip Tannura and George Meehan; editor, Richard Fantl; music director, M. W. Stoloff. At Fox, Brooklyn, week Dec. 31, '43, dual. Running time, 81 MINS. .
Wally Williams....................Tom Neal
Carol Harkness.............Evelyn Keyes
Frank Mallov................Bruce Bennett
Michael Crocker..............John Hubbard
Jean Burton....................Jeff Donnell
Alex Grybinski...............Frank Sully
Bolivar Jefferson...........Lewis Wilson
George Edwards.........Robert Stanford
General Sommerton........Jonathan Hale
Lieut. Martin............Hugh Beaumont
Sgt. Cummings...........Kane Richmond
Burroughs.................Douglass Drake
Jonesy........................Craig Woods

An informal film, with the thread of a plot, this pic adds up to well-paced entertainment which should do well as a dualer.

Story concerns itself with the fates of five boys who go to the Officer Candidate School of the Anti-Aircraft Artillery Command at Camp Davis, N. C. In this way, a picture of the rigid training and discipline that goes to make an officer in this branch of the Army is well delineated. Plot deals with the wise guy (Tom Neal) who, through a girl

(Evelyn Keyes) and a veteran of the North African campaign (Bruce Bennett), sees the light and ultimately sacrifices his own ambitions.

Interest is mostly developed by shots of the training given the future officers. Alfred Green neatly dovetailed the film's information values with story by his direction.

La Cuerra La Gano Yo
('I Win the War')
(ARGENTINE-MADE)

Buenos Aires, Jan. 1.
Lamilton production and release. Stars Pepe Arias, features Ricardo Passano, Alberto Contreras, Virginia Luque, Gogo Andreu, Chela Cordero, Perla Alvarado, Esperanza Palomero, Jorge Salcedo, Carlos Montalvan, Malena Podesta, Bernardo Perrone, Percival Murray, Mercedes Gisper, Warly Cerinni, Sofia Merli. Directed by Francisco Mugica. Story, Sixto Pondal Rios and Carlos Olivari; music, Bert Rose. Photography, Alberto Traverso. At Ambassador, Buenos Aires. Running time, 71 MINS.

This is one of the best local-mades released here this season—a comedy with smash possibilities, especially in the Argentine, not only because of its comedy but because it smacks at Argentine neutrality and particularly at those who've speculated and profited on the basis of Argentine fence-sitting. Even with the cuts made by the Ramirez military administration, picture has plenty of strength and its onceover on certain Argentine traits is such that if it had been done in Hollywood or Mexico, touchy local patrons would have torn down the house.

Pepe Arias, who rates close to Mexico's comic, Cantinflas, in overall b.o. popularity, has done the best work of his career in this pic. Direction of Francisco Mugica is steady throughout. Story by Sixto Pondal Rios and Carlos Olivari is one of the first topical pix done here in some time, for Argentine films have been principally of the escapist variety, especially since ex-President Castillo imposed the ban on freedom of speech by imposition of a state of siege in December, 1941.

Story casts Arias as the co-partner in a neighborhood almacen, or grocery, a local institution which combines all the traditions of the U. S. village store and the A. & P. Arias and his Spanish partner, Alberto Contreras, are well characterized and the buildup of the early scenes, family tie-ins and picturization of middle-class Argentine life are packed with laugh potentialities and sharp characterization. Story shifts when Arias, discovering that he is snubbed by the socialite mama of a boy interested in his daughter, decides to, go in for speculation on the rubber tire market. Success is immediate and he expands into other fields, outfitting himself in a luxurious office, riding around town with a liveried chauffeur, and sending his son (Ricardo Passano, Jr.) off to a swang naval school. Handling of these sequences is truer to life than any film done here since the outbreak of war, and the cracks at Argentine price-raising, selling to both the Allies and the Nazis, etc., are powerful, more so by their humorous touches.

Payoff comes when Arias, after turning down an English offer for his manganese supplies, because it's not up to what the Germans would pay, gloats over the sinking of the ship on which the material is being carried because he can now double his price. He awakens with a heart-sickening thud when he finds that his son, who has left home because his fellow naval students have pointed out his father's wartime speculation, is on the torpedoed vessel. There's a happy ending tagged on but, essentially, the effectiveness of the story is there. It's not so much the indictment of Argentine neutrality as it is the finger pointing at the many Argentine war-profit speculators that gives the picture point and

purpose. Arias dominates but Contreras is excellent in a supporting role, as are Passano, Jorge Salcedo and Chela Cordero. *Ray.*

The Sultan's Daughter
(MUSICAL)

Monogram release of Philip S. Krasne-James S. Burkett production. Stars Ann Corio; features Charles Butterworth, Tim and Irene Ryan, Eddie Norris, Fortunio Bonanova and Jack Large. Directed by Arthur Dreifuss. Screenplay, M. M. Raison and Tim Ryan; music, Karl Hajos; camera, Johnny Alton; editor, Dick Currier. At Brooklyn Strand. Jan. 6, '43, dual. Running time, 64 MINS.
Patra............................Ann Corio
Sultan.................Charles Butterworth
Tim..............................Tim Ryan
Irene...........................Irene Ryan
Jimmy.........................Eddie Norris
Kuda....................Fortunio Bonanova
Rata...........................Jack Large
Ludwig...................Gene Stutenroth
Merchant.................Cris-Pin Martin
Benson.................Joseph J. Greene
Freddy Fisher & His Orchestra

Monogram officials announced several months ago that during the 1943-44 season they planned to spend more money on several of the company's higher-budget productions than ever before. Apparently, this picture falls in that category, and it is a step in the right direction. However, 'The Sultan's Daughter' falls short of the mark in a number of respects. Result is a light musical that will fit into a dual program.

Ann Corio portrays the sultan's offspring in a stodgy, rigid manner, giving stuffiness to a role that called for effervescence. Her good points are outlined expertly by the costumes she wears. Tim and Irene Ryan do their best to liven up the festivities throughout with their expert nonsense and showmanship. Tim Ryan, incidentally, collaborated on the screenplay with M. M. Raison, and they turned out a workmanlike script, all things considered.

Film has two production numbers featuring a line of dancing girls dressed as members of the sultan's harem. 'Clickety-Clack Jack,' sung by Tim Ryan, and 'I'd Love to Make Love to You,' rendered by Eddie Norris, have possibilities for popularity with proper exploitation.

Charles Butterworth, as the sultan who refuses to have his daughter sell her oil properties to German agents; Norris, as a young American vaudevillian stranded in the desert country with Tim Ryan, and Fortunio Bonanova, as the righthand man to the Sultan and who schemes with the German agents to get the oil lands but fails, do their best to put the production over. Freddy Fisher's band swings out with the corn in a couple of spots.

All in all, co-producers Philip N. Krasne and James S. Burkett have done a fairly good job, with direction by Arthur Dreifuss substantial. Musical director Karl Hajos displays his wares capably.

Death Rides the Plains

PRC release of Sigmund Neufeld production. Stars Bob Livingston and Al St. John. Directed by Sam Newfield. Screenplay, Joe O'Donnell from story by Patricia Harper; camera, Robert Cline; editor, Holbrook Todd. At New York, N. Y., week Jan. 11, '44, dualed. Running time, 53 MINS.
Rocky Cameron.............Bob Livingston
Fuzzy Jones..........Al (Fuzzy) St. John
Virginia........................Nica Doret
Ben Gowdey.....................Ray Bennett
Rogan.....................J. Stanford Jolley
Trent...................George Chesebro
Marshal.......................John Elliott
Jed.......................Kermit Maynard
Sheriff.....................Slim Whitaker
Simms..........................Karl Hackett

Usual brand of western fare featuring Bob Livingston and Al St. John is offered in PRC's dualer, 'Death Rides the Plains.' It should do average b.o.

Story is better than most in this series. It concerns crooked dealing of Ray Bennett, who lures prospec-

tive buyers to his ranch through newspaper ads, then winds up murdering the victims and swiping the dough. But Livingston and St. John track him down.

Nica Doret is only fair in minor femme role, while others, with exception of St. John, turn in dull performances, despite good script by Joe O'Donnell.

Miniature Reviews

'Broadway Rhythm' (Songs) (Color) (M-G). Elaborate filmusical, packed with name specialty talent, due for good b.o.

'The Fighting Seabees' (Rep). Romantic tale of Navy's base-builders. Strong billtopper on duals.

'Riders of the Deadline' (UA). Formula western for Hopalong Cassidy entry, with sufficient gunplay for western addicts.

'Uncensored' (20th) (British. Mild boxoffice likely in States because of lesser-known (in U.S.) all-British cast.

'Jive Junction' (Musical) (PRC). Dickie Moore and Tina Thayer heading youthful cast in musical dualler for juve trade.

'The Texas Kid' (Mono). Adequate dual western with Johnny Mack Brown and Raymond Hatton. Should do okay.

'San Demetrio—London' (Balcon-British). Thriller about British Merchant Marine; boff biz in England, okay for U.S.

'The Shipbuilders' (British). Clive Brook starred in mediocre drama about Britain's shipbuilding.

'La Gallina Clueca' (Mexican). Suitable for Spanish houses. Domestic story sans English titles.

Broadway Rhythm

(Technicolor)
(FILMUSICAL)

Hollywood, Jan. 18.

Metro-Goldwyn-Mayer release of Jack Cummings production. Stars George Murphy, Ginny Simms; features Charles Winninger, Gloria De Haven, Nancy Walker, Ben Blue, Lena Horne, Eddie 'Rochester' Anderson, Tommy Dorsey orchestra, Hazel Scott, Kenny Bowers, Ross Sisters, Dean Murphy. Directed by Roy del Ruth. Screenplay by Dorothy Kingsley and Harry Clork; story by Jack McGowan and based on musical, 'Very Warm for May,' by Jerome Kern and Oscar Hammerstein 2d; camera, Leonard Smith; editor, Albert Akst. Tradeshown at L. A. Jan. 17, '44. Running time, **115 MINS.**

Jonnie Demming	George Murphy
Helen Hoyt	Ginny Simms
Sam Demming	Charles Winninger
Patsy Demming	Gloria DeHaven
Trixie Simpson	Nancy Walker
Felix Gross	Ben Blue
Fernway de la Fer	Lena Horne
Eddie	Eddie 'Rochester' Anderson
Hazel Scott	Herself
Ray Kent	Kenny Bowers
Maggie, Aggie, Elmira	Ross Sisters
Hired Man	Dean Murphy
Farmer	Louis Mason
Bunnie	Bunny Waters
Doug Kelly	Walter B. Long

Tommy Dorsey and His Orchestra

'Broadway Rhythm' is a typical backstage filmusical wheeled out in the usual Metro elaborate and colorful style. Displaying group of top-rank specialties and names among the entertainers, the fragile and hodge-podge yarn stops periodically while the guest stars appear. For diverting filmusical entertainment, picture will do good biz in the regular bookings as billtopper. Raft of marquee names won't hurt either.

Overload of specialties and dragging story unwinds the footage for extensive running time of 115 minutes. Picture would be much sharper with at least 25 minutes clipped, even though such editing should lose some of the name turns.

Story follows run-of-mill formula for a backstager. George Murphy is a top musical comedy producer readying his next show for Broadway. Ginny Simms, Hollywood film star, hits town for a whirl at the stage after being stymied on new contract in films. Charles Winninger, veteran song-and-dance man, is Murphy's dad, while Gloria DeHaven is the young sister with stage ambitions. Producer flirts with film star, winding up by signing her for his show, but she turns it down as a floppo. Winninger digs out old playscript, which is used for strawhat tryout in the hinterland and convincer for Murphy to stage for success on Broadway.

Tommy Dorsey and his orchestra provide the musical backgrounds, and are spotlighted for opening number to get picture away to a good start and one other number later. Lena Horne socks over two songs—the Gershwins' 'Somebody Loves Me,' and 'Brazilian Boogie,' by Hugh Martin and Ralph Blane—and both are smartly presented for maximum effect.

Miss Simms capably handles rendition of 'Amor,' by Gabriel Ruiz and Ricardo Lopez Mendez, assisted by background of male dancers for eyeful production number, and 'All the Things You Are,' from the original 'Very Warm for May' score. In the first sequence, Murphy teams with Jane Hale for a smart dance turn, but latter obviously was trimmed deeply for final runoff. Hazel Scott also makes a solo appearance for one piano number, in which she displays usual showmanship style.

Gloria DeHaven gets prominence teamed with Kenny Bowers for delivery of the old-time fave, 'Pretty Baby' and Martin & Blane's good tune, 'What Do You Think I Am.' Helen Walker and Ben Blue also team for a comedy song presentation. Ross Sisters deliver showstopping acrobatic turn, Dean Murphy scores with impersonations of prominent personages. Walter Long is on for a fast tap dance—and there's the usual super-elaborate finale which is rich in gorgeousness and color.

George Murphy and Miss Simms do much to hold the yarn together with their performances in the lead spots. Winninger, Miss DeHaven, Ben Blue and Eddie 'Rochester' Anderson are most prominent in the support.

Production is elaborately mounted, with full advantage taken in set construction and staging for the Technicolor photography utilized. *Walt.*

The Fighting Seabees

(ONE SONG)

Republic release of Albert J. Cohen production. Stars John Wayne and Susan Hayward; features Dennis O'Keefe, William Frawley, Leonid Kinskey, J. M. Kerrigan and Grant Withers. Directed by Edward Ludwig. Story, Borden Chase; adaptation, Borden Chase and Aeneas MacKenzie; song, Peter de Rose and Sam M. Lewis; musical score, Walter Scharf; editor, Richard Van Enger; camera, William Bradford. Previewed in N. Y., Jan. 17, '44. Running time, **100 MINS.**

Wedge Donovan	John Wayne
Constance Chesley	Susan Hayward
Lt. Comdr. Robert Yarrow	Dennis O'Keefe
Eddie Powers	William Frawley
Johnny Novasky	Leonid Kinskey
Sawyer Collins	J. M. Kerrigan
Whanger Spreckles	Grant Withers
Ding Jacobs	Paul Fix
Yump Lumkin	Ben Welden
Lt. Kerrick	William Forrest
Captain Joyce	Addison Richards
Joe Brick	Jay Norris
Juan	Duncan Renaldo

Republic has come through with a film on the U. S. Navy's construction battalions that will hold its own as a billtopper on duals. Exploitation possibilities are abundant, and exhibitors have plenty of material to help them put this one over for good grosses.

John Wayne and Susan Hayward, with Dennis O'Keefe completing the inevitable triangle, as stars of 'The Fighting Seabees' do a workmanlike job. Their performances are above average, as are the rest of the actors comprising the supporting cast. Story upon which the production is based is another matter; in some sequences plausibility is given the go-by.

Producer Albert J. Cohen has delved into the archives of the Seabees, from the unit's formation, to round out this picture. He has had the technical advice of Lt. Cmdr. Hubert Hunter and Lt. Cmdr. William A. McManus. Fact that liberties have been taken by writer Borden Chase and his co-adapter, Aeneas MacKenzie, to add a romantic angle adds selling points, that will work to advantage at the boxoffice.

Wayne, as head of a construction company, is vexed at the Navy for not arming his men to fight off Japs, causing losses among his personnel. However, he aids O'Keefe, a Naval officer, in convincing Washington brasshats that the Navy should have battalions of men, trained in warfare, to construct bases. Wayne is given a commission, helps in a recruiting drive, and goes through with his mission in true Naval tradition, being killed by Japs on a Pacific Island in the process. Miss Hayward portrays a wire-service correspondent assigned to Australia, and forms the prime romantic interest with O'Keefe.

Scene near the close of the picture, in which the Americans are outnumbered by Jap attackers but save the supply depot which they have been building, is one of the best war sequences of recent vintage.

'Song of the Seabees,' by Peter De Rose and Sam M. Lewis, is a rousing tune with a catchy refrain. *Sten.*

Riders of the Deadline

Hollywood, Jan. 14.

United Artists release of Harry Sherman production. Stars William Boyd; features Andy Clyde and Jimmy Rogers. Directed by Les Selander. Original screenplay, Bennett Cohen, from characters created by Clarence Mulford; camera, Russell Harlan; editor, Walter Hannemann. Previewed in projection room, Jan. 13, '44. Running time, **68 MINS.**

Hopalong Cassidy	William Boyd
California Carlson	Andy Clyde
Jimmy	Jimmy Rogers
Tim	Richard Crane
Sue	Frances Woodward
Crandall	William Halligan
Madigan	Tony Ward
Drago	Bob Mitchum
Tex	Jim Bannon
Martin	Hugh Prosser
Capt. Jennings	Herb Rawlinson
Calhoun	Montie Montana
Sourdough	Earle Hodgins
Kilroy	Bill Beckford
Sanders	Pierce Lyden

With this release the Hopalong Cassidy series hits the 50 mark, which gives the Hoppys some sort of distinction. But the yarn is strictly formula and oft-told, with only the familiar characters of the series and the background exteriors holding the feature up for more than passing attention in the western houses.

Hoppy (William Boyd), in attempting to get his young friend, Richard Crane, out of a jam with gamblers and smugglers, gets phoney dismissal from the rangers to join the outlaws and finally tab the top man. Along the line there's some fast riding and liberal gunplay.

Boyd is in his familiar spot as Hoppy, with Andy Clyde supplying elemental comedy, and Jimmy Rogers as the juve member of the trio. William Halligan nicely handles role of the town banker. Tony Ward is the typical outlaw leader, and Bob Mitchum is a tough customer who continually tangles with Boyd. Girl is Frances Woodward. *Walt.*

Uncensored

(BRITISH-MADE)

20th-Fox release of Edward Black production. Features Eric Portman, Phyllis Calvert, Griffith Jones. Directed by Anthony Asquith. Screenplay, Rodney Ackland and Terrence Rattigan, from story by Wolfgang Wilhelm, based on book by Oscar E. Millard; camera, Arthur Crabtree. Tradeshown in N. Y. Jan. 18, '44. Running time, **83 MINS.**

Andre Delage	Eric Portman
Julie Lanvin	Phyllis Calvert
Father de Gruyte	Griffith Jones
Charles Neels	Peter Glenville
Victor Lanvin	Frederick Culley
Von Koerner	Raymond Lovell
Frau Von Koerner	Irene Handl
Kohlmeier	Carl Jaffe
Press Officer	Stuart Lindsell
Col. von Hohenstein	Felix Aylmer
Abbe de Moor	Eliot Makeham
Father Corot	J. H. Roberts
Van Heemskerk	Walter Hudd
Louis Backer	Aubrey Mallalieu
Arthur Backer	Ben Williams
Gaston	Arthur Goullet
Theophile	John Slater
Lou	Philip Godfrey
Cabaret Manager	Lloyd Pearson

Efforts of the Belgian underground to thwart the Nazi grip form the basis for this thrilling melodrama, which often reaches the melodramatic heights of '39 Steps.' Publication of La Libre Belgique, put out by the underground in World War No. 1, is revived in 'Uncensored.' Picture contains about an hour of suspenseful action. **Despite infinite care on production details, well-picked cast and obvious appeal as a meller, this film, released in the U. S. by 20th-Fox, must lean on a terrific selling job if it amounts to more than average returns at the U. S. boxoffice. The reason is that all-British cast,** headed by Eric Portman, is not familiar to American audiences.

Director Anthony Asquith has done much to develop this yarn. Whole action centers about the efforts of Belgium's patriots to maintain regular publication of an underground paper as a constant thorn to the Nazi occupational troops. Scripters Rodney Ackland and Terrence Rattigan have taken Wolfgang Wilhelm's story and framed it around the apparently unpatriotic Portman, who quietly continues his underground operations while entertaining nightly at a cabaret for Nazi toppers. Walter Hudd is the editor of paper while at the same time turning out material for the Nazi publication, at a fee. After Peter Glenville, Portman's cabaret partner, jealously tries to turn in the underground paper's staff, a series of incidents and the ardent patriotism of the Belgian underground operatives enable them to continue publication. Story ends on the note that despite all Nazi persecution, the Belgian spirit will carry on.

Portman, slightly reminiscent of Cary Grant, contributes a standout performance. Phyllis Calvert, as the wistful, but faithful Belgian worker, provides several romantic interludes with Portman. Griffith Jones supplies a nifty characterization as the priest who manages to maintain his religious attitude while aiding the underground movement.

Well-chosen supporting cast is topped by Peter Glenville, Frederick Culley, Walter Hudd, Raymond Lovell, Felix Aylmer and John Slater. Camera work of Arthur Crabtree is uniformly good. *Wear.*

Jive Junction

(MUSICAL)

PRC production and release. Stars Tina Thayer, Dickie Moore; features Gerra Young, Johnny Michaels, Jack Wagner, Jan Wiley, Bill Halligan. Directed by Edgar G. Ulmer. Screenplay, Irving Wallace, Walter Doniger, Malvin Wald; camera, Ira Morgan; music, Leo Erdody; dances, Don Gallaher; editor, Robert Crandall. At New York, N. Y., week Jan. 11, '44, dual. Running time, **62 MINS.**

Peter	Dickie Moore
Claire	Tina Thayer
Gerra	Gerra Young
Jimmy	Johnny Michaels
Grant	Jack Wagner
Miss Forbes	Jan Wiley
Cubby	Beverly Boyd
Maglodian	Bill Halligan
Frank	Johnny Duncan
Chick	Johnny Clark
Feher	Frederick Feher
Mary	Carol Ashley
Girl	Odessa Laurin
Sheriff	Bob McKenzie

Former child star Dickie Moore carries most of the load in this musical which, as title indicates, is aimed at teen-agers who probably will accord it fair support on the two-for-ones.

Revolving around problems of a music conservatory product transplanted to a modern high school where student body leans more to

Tin Pan Alley tunes, tale brings young Moore into the jive fold as leader of his school's orch and glee club. The unit carries off top honors in nationwide competition in closing footage.

Inconsequential tale gives minor focus to adolescent romance between Moore and Tina Thayer and struggle by former to win popularity among fellow studes. After death of his aviator dad overseas, Moore switches into popular music field to provide entertainment for servicemen stationed nearby as means of forgetting grief.

Gerra Young, a newcomer, has the important singing assignments and impresses with finished rendition of the Bell Song from 'Lakme,' 'We're Just in Between.' Latter gets production treatment in finale.

Musical numbers help to offset story's seriousness, but a little more sweetness and light would help.
Donn.

The Texas Kid

Monogram release of Scott R. Dunlap production. Stars Johnny Mack Brown; features Raymond Hatton. Directed by Lambert Hillyer; original story, Lynton W. Brent; screenplay, Jess Bowers; camera, Harry Neumann; editor, Carl Pierson. At New York, N. Y., week of Jan. 11, '44, dual. Running time, 56 MINS.
Nevada................Johnny Mack Brown
Sandy...................Raymond Hatton
Kid...................Marshall Reed
Nancy..................Shirley Patterson
Naylor...................Robert Fiske
Scully...................Edmund Cobb
Ed...................Stanley Price
Jess...................Lynton Brent
Steve...................Bud Osborne
Alex...................Kermit Maynard
Roy...................John Judd
Atwood...................Cyrus Ring

This Johnny Mack Brown western should fill the bill at dual houses without much trouble as regular formula of gunplay, wild riding and a smattering of romance is followed.

Film is light on comedy, however, with Raymond Hatton given few chances for laughs and not doing much with those offered. He and Brown are U. S. marshals detailed to wipe out band of highwaymen staging series of stagecoach holdups which prevents ranchowners from meeting payrolls and carrying on their operations.

Marshall Reed as the Texas Kid is sufficiently strong and silent as the onetime member of the gang who gets shot after going straight, trying to outwit his former criminal sidekicks and bring the stagecoach with its load of gold through. Brown and Hatton, however, round up the gang and gallop off to new exploits while the ranchers prepare for business as usual.

Direction holds to good level and there are some better-than-average outdoor shots. *Donn.*

San Demetrio—London
(BRITISH-MADE)
London, Dec. 8.

Ealing Studios release of Michael Balcon production. Features Walter Fitzgerald, Mervyn Johns, Ralph Michael, Robert Beatty, Gordon Jackson, Frederick Piper. Directed by Charles Frend. Screenplay, Robert Hamer and Charles Frend, from official records by F. Tennyson Jesse. At Cambridge theatre, London, Dec. 7, '43. Running time, 93 MINS.

If for only one reason—and there are a number of others—here is one of the best factual thrillers to come from a British studio since the war began. The cast is that terrific.

If American filmgoers are in the market for not only a story of unparalleled, true-life heroism, but one that's the very reverse of the Hollywood star system, here is one to line them up at the boxoffice. Except for a short sequence in a Galveston department store, where members of the tanker's crew buy silk stockings for their womenfolk from a fly femme clerk, there is not a woman in the cast.

Whether wittingly or accidentally, the presentation of this epic tale of the British Merchant Marine omits the customary cast of characters in the screen credits. Thus does it emphasize the genuineness of the personalities concerned in the unfolding of a gripping drama. So one prefers to believe the man who plays the skipper of the San Demetrio is Captain Waite in person, just as the tough, nameless Texan who joins the tanker in Galveston is a tough Texan imbued with the idea of Britain's needing help to win the war. If the chief engineer—who performs miracles in the half-flooded, fire-swept engine room by not only restarting the engines, but by cooking a pailful of potatoes in live steam from a leaking valve—is not a c.e. in real life, it really doesn't make any difference. And this goes for all of them, from the bosun to the kid apprentice whose first voyage it is. To audiences they're real-life characters.

Much credit must go to Michael Balcon, the producer, and Charles Frend, who directed. How much F. Tennyson Jesse's official account on salvaging of the San Demetrio, after she had been abandoned for two days and nights 900 miles from her port, helped Robert Hamer and the director in their writing of the script can only be surmised, but the dialog is unvaryingly authentic.

What 'Desert Victory' did for Montgomery's 8th Army, what 'Target for Tonight' did for the R.A.F., and what 'In Which We Serve' did for the Royal Navy (and Noel Coward), 'San Demetrio—London' does certainly as much for the British Merchant Marine.

The Shipbuilders
(BRITISH-MADE)
London, Dec. 14.

Anglo-American Film Corp. release of British National-John Baxter production. Stars Clive Brook. Directed by John Baxter. Screenplay, Gordon Wellesley; music, Kennedy Russell; camera, James Wilson, Arthur Grant. At Cambridge, London. Running time, 88 MINS.

Granted it has a wealth of detail that's authentic and as effectively presented as a 'March of Time' opus, 'Shipbuilders' lacks entertainment value.

In one respect the flick seemingly establishes a record. Not only is there no love interest, but for the first time since the days of the Fort Lee one-reelers, the hero, married and the father of a boy, lives through the 13 years covered by the story without once mentioning, much less being shown with his wife. As for the boy, about whom there is a prodigious amount of talk, he figures in one fleeting sequence with his father in an ornate nursery set, the sole shot to establish that the millionaire shipbuilder has a home.

Admirers of Clive Brook, who plays the fifth of a line of Clydeside shipbuilders, will have no grounds for complaint, so far as his dominating the story is concerned. The occasions when he is absent from the screen are few, and even when he is not facing the camera his unmistakable voice frequently carries the history of British shipbuilding in the approved 'March of Time' manner. The idea behind this one is obviously a plea to keep British shipbuilding from going to the dogs after the war.

Besides Brook, Morland Graham, as a riveter, has the best acting opportunities, and turns in a workmanlike performance as a fanatically loyal employe, unwavering in his faith in the ability of the boss to bring prosperity back to the Clyde. In the friendship between the magnate and the riveter a somewhat labored attempt is made to strike a human note that's intensified when news comes of the death at sea of their sons.

La Gallina Clueca
('Cackling Hen')
(MEXICAN-MADE)

Clasa-Mohme release of Augustin J. Fink production. Stars Sara Garcia; features Domingo Soler, Emma Roldan, David Silva, Gloria Marin. Directed by Fernando de Fuentes. Camera, Jorge Fernandez; music, Raul Lavista and Mario Ruiz Saltrez. At New York, N. Y., Dec. 24, '43. Running time, 120 MINS.
Teresa...................Sara Garcia
Angel Chapa...................Domingo Soler
Rosario...................Emma Roldan
Jose...................David Silva
Laura...................Gloria Marin
Gono...................Lalito Montemayor
Tita...................Carmen Molina

Here is a light-hearted domestic story of a mother's trials in rearing her four children. Since it carries no English titles, the film is suitable only to those audiences understanding Spanish.

Sara Garcia plays a mother who's stranded with her youngsters in a broken-down jalopy. Domingo Soler comes along in his truck and plays the benefactor. The two middle-aged folk go into business and make a success. They finally marry upon official notification of the death of Miss Garcia's husband.

The Augustin Fink production is competent with good direction by Fernando de Fuentes. Photography by Jorge Fernandez is okay, and supporting roles were capably handled by Soler, Emma Roldan and David Silva, though Miss Garcia is the standout.

Miniature Reviews

"Rationing" (M-G). Wallace Beery and Marjorie Main comedy geared for mild returns.

"Phantom Lady" (U) (Song). Mystery meller with sustaining suspense, aiming for profitable—and likely—b.o.

"Texas Masquerade" (UA-Sherman). Better-than-average Hopalong Cassidy western starring William Boyd.

"Swing Out the Blues" (songs) (Col). Bob Haymes-Lynn Merrick in whacky comedy; strong dual supporter.

"Cowboy in the Clouds" (Col). Western fans will like this one. It should register well at dual houses.

"Casanova in Burlesque" (Rep) (musical). Joe E. Brown in mild comedy for duals.

"Lady, Let's Dance" (Mono) (musical). Despite weak, overlong story, picture should do well in regular runs.

"What a Man!" (Mono). Better-than-average comedy that will fit snugly into any dual bill.

Rationing

Metro release of Orville O. Dull production. Stars Wallace Beery, Marjorie Main; features Donald Meek, Dorothy Morris, Tommy Batten, Gloria Dickson, Carol Ann Beery. Directed by Willis Goldbeck. Screenplay, William R. Lipman, Grant Garrett, Harry Ruskin; camera, Sidney Wagner; editor, Ferris Webster. Tradeshown in N. Y., Jan. 21, '44. Running time, 93 MINS.
Ben Barton...................Wallace Beery
Iris Tuttle...................Marjorie Main
Wilfred Ball...................Donald Meek
Dorothy Tuttle...................Dorothy Morris
Cash Riddle...................Howard Freeman
Mrs. Porter...................Connie Gilchrist
Lance Barton...................Tommy Batten
Miss McCue...................Gloria Dickson
Senator Edward A. White...Henry O'Neill
Teddy...................Richard Hall
Ezra Weeks...................Charles Halton
Mr. Morgan...................Morris Ankrum
Carol Ann Beery...................By Herself
Dixie Samson...................Douglas Fowley
Roberts...................Chester Clute

Hampered by a non-selling title, weighted with slapsticky situations and lacking originality, Wallace Beery and Marjorie Main have a slipshod comedy in "Rationing." Team lends what little entertainment value this "B" picture possesses and all their help will be needed for mild returns.

Original script by William R. Lipman, Grant Garrett and Harry Ruskin has not enhanced comedy's palatability. Beery plays a storekeeper and local meatpacker, as usual squabbling with Miss Main, postmistress and in charge of doling out ration stamps. Beery's adopted son joins the colors and there's a slight romance between him and the postmistress' daughter. But he goes off to training, and then plot switches into familiar slapstick. In the final reels, the yarn gets down to its main premise, the black market in meat.

Beery is as good as could be expected with the inferior role. His real-life daughter, Carol Ann, appears for a fleeting glimpse in a bit role as one of the store customers. Miss Main renews her by-now standard cinema feud with Beery, and is okay as usual. Dorothy Morris does nicely as the postmistress' daughter and manages to make something of the all too-brief love scenes with Tommy Batten. Latter shows real possibilities as Beery's adopted son. Donald Meek has virtually a bit, while Gloria Dickson, appearing a bit plump, is okay as the lady barber and town catch.

Support is topped by Howard Freeman, as Beery's partner; Henry O'Neill and Chester Clute. Willis

Goldbeck's direction was fairly well paced but routine. Sidney Wagner has supplied excellent camera work.
Wear.

Phantom Lady
(ONE SONG)

Hollywood, Jan. 21.

Universal release of Joan Harrison production. Stars Franchot Tone, Ella Raines, Alan Curtis; features Thomas Gomez, Aurora, Elisha Cook, Jr., Fay Helm, Andrew Tombes. Directed by Robert Siodmak. Screenplay, Bernard C. Schoenfeld, based on novel by William Irish; camera, Woody Bredell; editor, Arthur Hilton; music director, H. J. Salter. Previewed at Pantages, Hollywood, Jan. 20, '44. Running time, **85 MINS.**

Jack Marlow............Franchot Tone
Carol Richman............Ella Raines
Scott Henderson............Alan Curtis
Estela Monteiro............Aurora
Inspector Burgess............Thomas Gomez
Ann Terry............Fay Helm
Cliff............Elisha Cook, Jr.
Bartender............Andrew Tombes
Detective............Regis Toomey
Detective............Joseph Crehan
Kettisha............Doris Lloyd
Dr. Chase............Virginia Brissac
District Attorney............Milburn Stone

"Phantom Lady" is an expertly contrived, suspenseful mystery meller developing along unusual cinematic lines. Catching and holding attention at the opening sequence, it rolls through a maze of episodes to allow a femme amateur detective to unravel a strange murder. Picture, as intriguing and suspenseful film dramatics of its type, is headed for profitable boxoffice reaction, and can easily surprise as a sleeper attraction with expert exploitation.

Plot has Alan Curtis picking up a strange woman in a bar, and he takes her to a show. During the evening his wife is murdered, and he eventually is convicted on circumstantial evidence when he cannot find or identify his woman companion of the night, whose main distinguishing feature is an odd hat creation. While Curtis is facing execution, secretary Ella Raines embarks on sleuthing tour to find the woman with the hat. Blocked at every turn, she finally locates the owner, and then discovers that Curtis' best friend, Franchot Tone, is a paranoiac and the real murderer during a fit of insanity. The audience is let in on the secret of Tone's duplicity at about the halfway mark, to accentuate the suspense and dramatics of the latter portion when Tone poses as the girl's friend in unwinding the mystery. Naturally, Curtis is saved to realize the love of Miss Raines.

Picture is the first producer chore for Joan Harrison, who was associated with producer-director Alfred Hitchcock for eight years as secretary, reader and scripter, "Phantom Lady" demonstrates that the pupil absorbed much of Hitchcock's technique in displaying screen suspense in her first production responsibility.

In addition to a fine script prepared by Bernard C. Schoenfeld, director Robert Siodmak maintains an arresting pace, utilizing camera angles and intimations to greatest effect.

Miss Raines capably handles the lead assignment. Tone is excellent, while Curtis clicks, too. Aurora (Miranda), sister of Carmen, appears briefly as star of the musical show to sing a Brazilian tune, "Chick-Ee-Chick," composed by Jacques Press and Eddie Cherkose. Thomas Gomez delivers in prominent spot as the police inspector, Elisha Cook, Jr., provides the portrait of the drummer, and Andrew Tombes fits neatly as a bartender. Fay Helm has one brief but important sequence as the mentally-deranged womanwearer of the important hat.

Sound effects and silent track without dialog are used to maximum effect to heighten the suspense of the picture. Photography by Woody Bredell is excellent in minor key lighting throughout.
Walt.

Texas Masquerade

United Artists release of Harry Sherman production. Stars William Boyd; features Andy Clyde, Jimmy Rogers. Directed by George Archainbaud. Screenplay, Norman Houston and Jack Lait, Jr., from characterizations created by Clarence Mulford; editor, Walter Hanneman; camera, Russell Harlan. Tradeshown in N. Y. Jan. 24, '44. Running time, **59 MINS.**

Hopalong Cassidy............William Boyd
California Carlson............Andy Clyde
Jimmy Rogers............Jimmy Rogers
Virginia Curtis............Mady Correll
Ace Maxson............Don Costello
J. K. Trimble............Russell Simpson
James Corwin............Nelson Leigh
Sam Nolan............Francis McDonald
John Martindale......J. Farrell McDonald
Mrs. Martindale............June Pickerell
Jeff............John Merton
Al............Pierce Lyden
Rowbottom............Robert McKenzie
Sykes............Bill Hunter

Another in the Hopalong Cassidy group of westerns produced by Harry Sherman, "Texas Masquerade" is better than par for the series and should do commensurately well at the boxoffice.

It hasn't anything basically new in the scripting, but it's fast enough, directed well and, what's more, has a musical score that deserves more than its lack of billing.

William Boyd, as Hoppy, is again teamed with Andy Clyde and Jimmy Rogers as his sidekicks. This time they're out to break up the combine seeking to secure a flock of ranches through the usually crooked machinations. This phase of the yarn has been done innumerable times, of course, but there's enough shooting, riding and fisticuffs to warrant more than passing attention from the hoss opry fans.

Boyd gives a good performance, as do most of the others, but some of that dialog could have been edited more closely. Photography, mostly exteriors, is also topgrade.
Kahn.

Swing Out the Blues
(SONGS)

Columbia release of Sam White production. Features Bob Haymes, Lynn Merrick, Vagabonds, Janis Carter, Tim Ryan, Joyce Compton. Directed by Mal St. Clair. Screenplay by Dorcas Cochran from story by Doris Malloy; camera, Arthur Martinelli; editor, Jerome Thoms. At Paramount, Brooklyn, week Jan. 20, '44, dual. Running time, **73 MINS.**

Rich Cleveland............Bob Haymes
Penelope Carstairs............Lynn Merrick
The Vagabonds............Pete Peterson, Till Risso, Al Torrieri, Don Germano
Dena Marshall............Janis Carter
Dudley Gordon............Tim Ryan
Kitty Grogan............Joyce Compton
Larry Stringfellow............Arthur Q. Bryan
Aunt Amanda............Kathleen Howard
Gregg Talbot............John Eldredge
Malcolm P. Carstairs............Dick Elliott
The Duchess............Lotte Stein
Weight Lifter............Tor Johnson

Whacky comedy about swing musicians makes no pretense at being anything but a 'B' comedy with songs. It has turned out as first-rate entertainment, and never dull.

"Swing Out the Blues" serves to spotlight Bob Haymes both as a new juvenile and screen crooner. Not to be confused with Dick Haymes, this Haymes croons admirably like the other. Plot is framed around him and his crooning ability, one line in script referring to him as "the poor man's Sinatra."

Actually, the farce belongs to The Vagabonds, singing-instrumental foursome whose zany tricks often remind of the Ritz Bros., though leaning on vocalizing and perfect timing for laurels. Swingster combo produces the funniest, most lively moments in the film. Story concerns their efforts to keep the wolf away and prevent their solid meal ticket, Haymes, from tossing them overboard when he weds a young socialite, Lynn Merrick. Fable pictures this femme as a loyal spouse while depicting Haymes' agent, Janis Carter, as a conniving vamp.

From a "goodwill court" radio program opening that spots The Vagabonds telling their problem to the "judge," picture develops into a recital to the "radio jedge" of their experiences in night spots. Main problem winds up as a battle to keep the crooner, Haymes, and his wife happy despite the machinations of Miss Carter. Plenty of ludicrous moments emerge in showing the harum-scarum existence of the foursome in a theatrical flat. Film also is dotted with other humorous incidents such as the rugcutting Vagabonds trying to play society chamber music at the home of the socialite's aunt.

Best songs by Haymes are "It Can't Be Wrong" and "Prelude to Love," first looking like a screen test for the warbler. Vagabonds register strongest with "Tahitian Lullaby," "Dark Eyes" and the comedy numbers, "We Should Be Ever So Quiet," "Beethoven's Minuet" and "Tahitian War Chant," last being a hula lulu. Quartet also clicks nicely with "Rockabye Baby," with unbilled baby stealing closing sequences of film.

Haymes is a personable chap with excellent pipes, and a likely singing find. Lynn Merrick really blossoms out as a first-rate femme star as the socialite who snubs her rich aunt to wed Haymes. The Vagabonds figure as vital ingredients to the whole production. Janis Carter is okay as the agent, Joyce Compton excellent in a lesser role as one of the Vagabonds' wives, while Tim Ryan does all right as the radio judge. Support is headed by Kathleen Howard and Dick Elliott.

Mal St. Clair's direction has much to do with the overall strength of the comedy. Jerome Thoms' editing is topnotch.
Wear.

Cowboy in the Clouds
(SONGS)

Columbia release of Jack Fier production. Stars Charles Starrett; features Dub Taylor, Julie Duncan, Jimmy Wakely and Jesters. Directed by Benjamin Kline. Story and screenplay, Elizabeth Beecher; editor, Aaron Stell; camera, George Meehan; asst. director, William O'Connor. At New York, N. Y., Jan. 10, '43. Running time, **55 MINS.**

Steve Kendall............Charles Starrett
Cannonball............Dub Taylor
Dorrie Bishop............Julie Duncan
Glen Avery............Jimmy Wakely
Amos Fowler............Davison Clark
Hadley............Hal Taliaferro
Roy Madison............Dick Curtis
Sheriff Page............Edward Cassidy
Dean............Paul Zaremba
Thripp............Charles King, Jr.
Mack Judd............John Tyrrell
The Jesters

Here's a western with a novel twist that has more thrills than the run-of-the-mill hoss opera. It should register well at dual houses.

Charles Starrett portrays the role of a ranch boss who goes to the aid of the Civil Air Patrol under fire from the richest man in the state. Story carries Starrett and his cohorts through dangers of thundering hoofs, gunfire, airplane exploits and the menace of a forest fire, battling their way to final victory and justification of the air patrol.

Julie Duncan and Dub Taylor are prominent in the action. The Jesters lend their brand of comedy and song to music supplied by Jimmie Wakely and his saddle pals. Outdoor shots are good and direction by Benjamin Kline keeps the picture moving.
Sten.

Casanova in Burlesque
(SONGS)

Republic release of Albert J. Cohen production. Directed by Leslie Goodwins. Stars Joe E. Brown; features June Havoc, Dale Evans. Screenplay, Frank Gill, Jr., based on story idea by John Wales; camera, Reggie Lanning; musical director, Walter Scharf; musical supervisor, Albert Newman; songs, Kim Gannon, Walter Kent; editor, Ernest Nims; dance director, Dave Gould. Previewed in N. Y. Jan. 21, '44. Running time, **74 MINS.**

Joseph M. Kelly, Jr............Joe E. Brown
Lillian Colman............June Havoc
Barbara Compton............Dale Evans
Lucille Compton............Marjorie Gateson
John Alden Compton............Lucien Littlefield
J. Boggs-Robinson............Ian Keith
Joseph M. Kelly, Sr............Roger Imhof
Bucky Farrell............Harry Tyler
Peewee Dixon............Patricia Knox
Fannie............Sugar Geise
Al Gordon............Jerome Franks, Jr.
Guest............Marga Dean

Compound of Joe E. Brown and Shakespeare lends itself to exploitation angles, but film should appeal mainly to Brown devotees. Okay for bottom rung on duals.

Basic idea of a burlesque company playing Shakespeare in jive genre is geared for laughs, but this interlude doesn't crop up until the tail end of yarn, by which time there isn't much left to salvage.

Story gyrates around efforts of Brown to lead a split life, making his summer stand as a comic on the girly wheel and taking French leave every winter to act as Shakespearean professor in a tank-water college.

Situation becomes involved when Brown's secret is discovered by June Havoc, a burley peeler, who demands the leading role in the school's summer festival of Shakespearean repertoire. Also expecting the lead is a wealthy dowager, backer of the festival, who gets in a pitch, too, for her niece, Dale Evans, a jive hound.

Story reaches its crux when the cast walks out because of Miss Evans' hamming, and Brown, well in his cups, calls his original burley cast to take over for burlesque "Taming of the Shrew," as the only way out of a bad deal. Crossfire jive talk and musical interludes are amusing and cleverly done.

Early sequences permit Brown to gag through several purported burley skits. Comic is stymied throughout by weak lines and situations.

Miss Havoc turns in a middling chore as the stripper and Dale Evans and Marjorie Gates, respectively, are acceptable as the dowager and her niece. Latter furnishes the romance angle and, together with Miss Havoc, goes through a mild repertoire of songs and dances. Ian Keith gets by nicely as a Shakespearean thespian of the old school.

Lady, Let's Dance
(MUSICAL)

Hollywood, Jan. 19.

Monogram release of Scott R. Dunlap production. Stars Belita; features James Ellison. Directed by Frank Woodruff. Screenplay, Peter Milne and Paul Gerard Smith; adapted from story by Bradbury Foote and Scott R. Dunlap; camera, Mack Stengler; editor, Richard Currier; music director, Edward Kay; production numbers staged by Dave Gould; ballet directed by Michael Panaieff; songs, David Oppenheim and Ted Grouya; Lew Pollock and Charles Newman. Previewed at Paramount, Hollywood, Jan. 18, '44. Running time, **86 MINS.**

Belita............Belita
Jerry............James Ellison
Frick............Frick
Frack............Frack
Timber............Walter Catlett
Snodgrass............Lucien Littlefield
Manuelo............Maurice St. Clair
Eugene............Eugene Mikeler
Henry Busse............Henry Busse
Fraser............Harry Harvey
Given............Jack Rice
Stack............Emmett Vogan
Dolores............Barbara Woodell
The Orchestras of Henry Busse, Eddie LeBaron, Mitch Ayres, Lou Bring

"Lady, Let's Dance," is Monogram's most ambitious production thus far, and company obviously tossed plenty of coin into this second showcase for skating star Belita. Latter, in addition to displaying expert skill as a skater, clicks solidly as a dancer, performing both ballroom and ballet numbers to make her one of the most versatile artists in Hollywood. Despite the story's overlength, picture packs plenty of dance and skating entertainment for profitable boxoffice reaction in regular runs.

Story is a thin line on which to hang the dance-skating specialties and ensembles. Picture sags in spots, and would be more compact with elimination of about 10 minutes in the story. James Ellison plays an entertainment director for a California resort who's forced to get a replacement for girl member of dance team. A refugee from Holland, Belita is drafted and clicks, Ellison sending her along with Henry Busse and band for Chicago engagement. There she's picked up by agents who spot her with an ice show for eventual stardom. Ellison loses his job at the resort and bounces around in many spots until he finally winds up in the Army for overseas duty. Invalided home, Belita grabs him for the final clinch.

Busse's orchestra handles major portion of the musical end, with Busse also taking a role, as himself, for moderate results. Eddie LeBaron's rhumba orch appears in one sequence for musical background of dance by Belita and Maurice St. Clair, with band soloist singing the standard "Esperanza." Mitch Ayres' band supplies background for ice number of "Silver Shadows and Golden Dreams," capably performed by Belita and partner with male chorus background.

Finale is billed as "Spirit of Victory" number, with Belita soloing in climactic ice routine that is a showstopper. It has Statue of Liberty backdrop, with skater garbed in white costume to accentuate her whirls, twirls, swans and jumps with triple turns. Two ballroom dances by Belita and St. Clair are expertly contrived and delivered, with one a particular boff. Skating comedy team of Frick and Frack is on for two ice numbers and scores.

Belita ably carries the lead, with Ellison adequate as the aggressive and thunder-voiced end of the romance. Walter Catlett is neatly spotted as an eccentric westerner who brings the pair together. Good support is provided by Lucien Littlefield, Barbara Woodell, Jack Rice, Harry Harvey and Emmett Vogan. Camera work of Mack Stengler is excellent throughout, especially on the dance and skating sequences.   *Walt.*

What a Man!

Monogram release of Barney A. Sarecky production. Stars Johnny Downs, Wanda McKay; features Robert Kent, Etta McDaniels, Harry Holman. Directed by William Beaudine. Original screenplay, William X. Crowley and Beryl Sachs; editor, Carl Himm; camera, Marcel LePicard; asst. directors, Dick L'Estrange and Lew Brandt. At New York theatre, Jan. 10, '43. Running time, 67 MINS.
```
Henry Burrows..............Johnny Downs
Jean Rankin................Wanda McKay
Steve Jackson..............Robert Kent
Buelah.....................Etta McDaniels
Prewitt....................Harry Holman
Constance..................Lillian Bronson
Detective..................Wheeler Oakman
Doctor.....................John Ince
Parsons....................I. Stanford Jolley
Boyle......................Jack Gardner
```

Direction, scripting and some swell make-believing by Johnny Downs and newcomer Wanda McKay combine to make 'What a Man!' an amusing picture. It's a better-than-average escapist film that will fit snuggly into any dual bill.

Surprise twists in a story based on "the worm turns," often-used formula, will give this picture good word-of-mouth. Downs, a milquetoast white collarite, becomes involved in a murder when he finds that an attractive blonde (Miss McKay) has moved into his bachelor apartment. To make sure she will not be evicted, the young lady, who allegedly is on the lam, feigns illness. At the office, Downs becomes involved in a financial scandal. His transformation from a meek clerk to office manager, and the resultant winning of the girl, who proves to be the boss' daughter, add up to a neat 67 minutes of film fare.

Etta McDaniels (no relation to Hattie McDaniel), in the role of colored maid for bachelor Downs, gives a good account of herself. Robert

Kent portrays a brash salesman whose "wolfish" tactics fail to score with Miss McKay. Harry Holman, as Prewitt the office manager, is also a capable support.

Direction by William Beaudine cuts corners and molds the script by William X. Crowley and Beryl Sachs into a tight package in keeping with the modest budget obviously allowed for this picture.   *Sten.*

Miniature Reviews

"Jane Eyre" (20th). Joan Fontaine and Orson Welles in well-produced dramatization of Charlotte Bronte novel; big b.o.

"In Our Time" (WB). Drama of pre-war Poland geared for profitable biz in regular runs as top attraction.

"Swing Fever" (M-G) (musical). Kay Kyser in slow comedy.

"The Bridge of San Luis Rey" (UA) Top-drawer drama headed for holdovers in first-runs and strong grosses generally.

"Weekend Pass" (U) (Songs). Light program comedy-drama to satisfy as dual support.

"Return of the Vampire" (Col). Bela Lugosi and Frieda Inescort in first-rate horror thriller.

"Passport to Adventure" (RKO). Fantastic, unpretentious drama okay as dual supporter, satisfying general audiences because of originality.

"Death Valley Rangers" (Mono). Okay sagebrush dualer backed by name appeal of Hoot Gibson, Ken Maynard.

"Secreto Eterno" (Grovas). Mexican-made Spanish drama with no English subtitles, headed for limited grosses.

Jane Eyre

20th-Fox release of William Goetz production. Stars Joan Fontaine and Orson Welles; features Margaret O'Brien, John Sutton, Sara Allgood, Henry Daniell, Agnes Moorehead. Directed by Robert Stevenson. Screenplay, Aldous Huxley, Robert Stevenson and John Houseman, from novel by Charlotte Bronte; camera, George Barnes; music, Bernard Herrmann; editor, Walter Thompson. Tradeshown in N. Y. Jan. 31, '44. Running time, 97 MINS.
```
Edward Rochester..........Orson Welles
Jane Eyre.................Joan Fontaine
Adele Varens.............Margaret O'Brien
Jane (as a child)........Peggy Ann Garner
Dr. Rivers................John Sutton
Bessie....................Sara Allgood
Brocklehurst..............Henry Daniell
Mrs. Reed................Agnes Moorehead
Colonel Dent..............Aubrey Mather
Mrs. Fairfax.............Edith Barrett
Lady Ingram..............Barbara Everest
Blanche Ingram...........Hillary Brooke
Grace Poole..............Ethel Griffies
Leah......................Mae Marsh
Miss Scatcherd...........Elly Malyon
Mrs. Eshton..............Mary Forbes
Sir George Lynn..........Thomas Loudon
Mason....................John Abbott
John.....................Ronald Harris
Auctioneer...............Charles Irwin
```

Charlotte Bronte's Victorian novel, "Jane Eyre," which has been on the library lists for nearly a century, has again reached the screen in a drama that is as intense on celluloid as it is on the printed page. Joan Fontaine and Orson Welles are the stars, and 20th-Fox has produced a picture geared for hefty grosses.

For the exacting who have read and recall the original story there will be much in the film to win their favor. This picture has taken liberties with the novel that may be chalked off to cinematic expediency, but there is, nonetheless, a certain script articulation that closer heed to the book could possibly not have achieved.

The story's basic framework remains present in the film. There have been excluded certain elemental features, however, that tended to give the original story some of its colorful passages. It's a picture, however, that has achieved more than the original deserved. For "Jane Eyre," in case one forgets, has long been fanciful, tragic prose in the schoolboy-schoolgirl idiom.

"Jane Eyre" will be remembered as the story of a girl who, after a childhood during which she was buffeted about in an orphanage, secures a position as governess to the ward

of one Edward Rochester, sire of an English manor house called Thornfield. Jane Eyre eventually falls in love with him, and he with her. When their wedding is interrupted by a man who accuses Rochester of already being married, there is divulged the secret that Rochester has kept for many years, that he has a wife who is a raving maniac and whom he keeps locked up in a tower at Thornfield. Jane's flight from Thornfield, the privations she endured and her ultimate heeding of a "telepathic" call from Rochester culminate in her return to him. She then learns of the death of his wife in a fire that destroys Thornfield and in which Rochester has become blinded and maimed in attempting to rescue Mrs. Rochester after she had set fire to the house.

The original story was as pat as all that. Full of improbabilities and with a remarkable naivete for an author whose fame has been as great as Charlotte Bronte's.

In the novel there are some fine love passages in those final scenes that have not been transferred to the screen. The film's end, in fact, comes too abruptly and too patly.

But, withal, this is a film that should be seen. Miss Fontaine and Welles are excellent, though the latter is frequently inaudible in the slur of his lines. It is a large cast and one that acquits itself well. Notable in the support are Henry Daniell, as Brocklehurst, the cruel overseer of the orphanage; Margaret O'Brien, as ward of Rochester; John Sutton, as Dr. Rivers (the original novel had no such character, if memory serves correctly, though there was a St. John Rivers, the cleric who wished to marry Jane Eyre); Sara Allgood; Agnes Moorehead, as the cruel aunt of Jane Eyre, and Edith Barrett as Mrs. Fairfax, the Rochester housekeeper.

There is some excellent photography by George Barnes, practically all in light and shadow to emphasize the eeriness of the story, and the direction by Robert Stevenson has heightened the illusion of action where, frequently, none existed. And William Goetz has endowed the production with all the niceties of expensive film-making. But, basically, "Jane Eyre," the novel, remains something for the highschool classroom, a study in the literature of another day. The picture is something else again. It is intriguing adult entertainment.   *Kahn.*

In Our Time

Hollywood, Feb. 1.

Warner Bros. release of Jerry Wald production. Stars Ida Lupino and Paul Henreid. Directed by Vincent Sherman. Screenplay, Ellis St. Joseph and Howard Koch; camera, Carl Guthrie; editor, Rudi Fehr; montages, James Leicester. Tradeshown in L. A. Jan. 31, '44. Running time, 109 MINS.
```
Jennifer Whittredge.......Ida Lupino
Count Stephen Orvid.......Paul Henreid
Janina Orvid..............Nancy Coleman
Mrs. Bromley.............Mary Boland
Count Pavel Orvid........Victor Francen
Zofya Orvid..............Nazimova
Uncle Leopold............Michael Chekhov
Antique Dealer...........Marek Windheim
Bujanski.................Ivan Triesault
Wladek...................John Bleifer
Wanda....................Lotte Palfe
Father Josef.............Wolfgang Zilzer
Richard Ordynski.........Pyotr
```

Life, class distinctions and political moves of Poland just prior to the German invasion are on display in this dramatic exposition of a romance in Warsaw. Carefully produced and excellently acted, picture, however, dwells too much on incidental material for extended overlength to make it more than a nominally profitable billtopper on regular bookings.

Stripped of its sideline characterizations and incidents, story is decidedly Cinderellaian, with English girl, Ida Lupino, going to Warsaw as companion to antique collector Mary Boland. She meets and falls in love with Paul Henreid, count and member of an aristocratic family steeped in traditions of class distinctions. Despite his family's objections, pair marry and the girl assists Henreid in mechanizing the farming estate with resultant success and disproving stand of family objectors. Peasant farmers are cut in for profits of the harvest, but invasion and the siege of Moscow blanket the happiness, with the estate getting scorched-earth policy from Henreid and the farmers to prevent anything falling into the hands of the Nazis. But the Poles walk forth with determination that the country will survive regardless of current adversity, with the couple in the van.

Looks like story concocters Ellis St. Joseph and Howard Koch try to give an insight into the general breaking down of class divisions and century-old traditions in Poland and other European countries just prior to the war's outbreak. Much footage and incident are utilized in stressing that point throughout. Result is an uneven and overlong picture which would be better and more compact with a half-hour edited out.

Miss Lupino provides a strong performance as does Henreid. Michael Chekhov scores with neat rendition as the philosopher-poet who befriends the girl in the otherwise antagonistic setting. Miss Boland is okay and Nancy Coleman capably displays the cold, resentful sister of Henreid; Nazimova is excellent as the stately countess, and Victor Francen strongly characterizes the head of the family and a Polish appeaser of Nazi pressure.

Direction by Vincent Sherman accentuates the characters and incidents in fine style, but he cannot overcome the too-long script. Production is of "A" calibre throughout, with photography by Carl Guthrie adequate. *Walt.*

Swing Fever
(MUSICAL)

Metro release of Irving Starr production. Stars Kay Kyser. Features Marilyn Maxwell, William Gargan, Nat Pendleton, Lena Horne. Directed by Tim Whelan. Screenplay, Nat Perrin, Warren Wilson from original by Matt Brooks, Joseph Hoffman; songs, Herb Brown, Lew Brown, Ralph Freed, Sammy Fain, Walter Donaldson, Sonny Skyler; camera, Charles Rosher; editor, Ferris Webster. Reviewed at Loew's State, New York, Jan. 28, '44. Running time, **80 MINS.**
Lowell Blackford...............Kay Kyser
Ginger Gray...................Marilyn Maxwell
"Waltzy" Malone...........William Gargan
Lena Horne........................By Herself
"Killer" Kennedy............Nat Pendleton
Nick Sirocco......................Curt Bois
Dan Conlon..................Morris Ankrum
Dr. Clyde L. Star..........Andrew Tombes
"Rags"....................Maxie Rosenbloom
Mr. Nagen.................Clyde Fillmore
Lois..........................Pamela Blake
Kid Mandell......................Lou Nova
"Sledgehammer"...............Jack Roper
The Merriel Abbott Dancers
Kay Kyser and His Orchestra

Kay Kyser filmusical is for the duals, where it should fare moderately well as a supporting feature. Production misses fire because of flimsy scripting and absence of effective gag situations necessary in productions of this type.

On the credit side, of course, are Kay Kyser and his orch, a few listenable tunes and Marilyn Maxwell. Miss Maxwell flashes an exceptionally attractive profile, though not quite as fetching when facing the camera. Her vocals are adequate.

Lena Horne has one number, "You're So Indifferent," a corking bit but hardly presented in a manner calculated for maximum results. Other tunes in the picture include "I Planted a Rose" (by Herb Brown, Lew Brown and Ralph Freed); "Mississippi Dreamboat" (Lew Brown, Sammy Fain, Ralph Freed), "Thinking Of You" (Walter Donaldson), "Don't Make a Sound" (Sonny Skylar).

Uninteresting yarn deals with a round-heeled prizefighter, a flighty fight manager and his girl, and a backwoods composer with a hypnotic eye. The gal tricks the country boy (Kyser) into using his hypnotic powers in behalf of the fight manager so as to win a championship bout and a wad of coin. When the boy discovers that he's been tricked he refuses to go through with the plan but changes his mind at the last minute in order to save the girl because of fears that she would be rubbed out. *Mori.*

Bridge of San Luis Rey
(SONGS)

United Artists release of Benedict Bogeaus production. Stars Lynn Bari, Akim Tamiroff, Francis Lederer; features Alla Nazimova, Louis Calhern, Blanche Yurka, Donald Woods. Directed by Rowland V. Lee. Screenplay, Howard Estabrook; adaptation, Estabrook and Herman Weissman, from novel by Thornton Wilder; musical director, Dimitri Tiomkin; editor, Harvey Manger; camera, John Boyle. Previewed in N. Y., Jan. 31, '44. Running time, 107 MINS.
Michaela.........................Lynn Bari
Uncle Pio...................Akim Tamiroff
Manuel.)
Esteban)..............Francis Lederer
The Marquesa...................Nazimova
The Viceroy.................Louis Calhern
The Abbess.................Blanche Yurka
Brother Juniper.............Donald Woods
Dona Mercedes...............Emma Dunn
Don Rubio.................Barton Hepburn
Pepita.........................Joan Lorring
Maita....................Abner Biberman
Servant to Uncle Pio.........Minerva Urecal
Antonio Triana and His Dancers.

Benedict Bogeaus hasn't spared the budget in this remake of Thornton Wilder's Pulitzer prizewinning novel. Result is out of the top drawer. "Bridge of San Luis Rey" is headed for extended runs in key houses and strong returns in the subsequents.

Bogeaus surrounded himself with some high-calibre technical talent for what is his first venture as an independent producer. He chose as his initial endeavor a novel from which Metro, back in 1929, made one of its biggest successes, a film which featured Lili Damita, Ernest Torrence, Raquel Torres and Don Alvarado. As a remake for present-day audiences, up to their ears in war news, this picture will be a welcome divertissement.

Lynn Bari, Akim Tamiroff and Francis Lederer, supported by Louis Calhern, Alla Nazimova and Blanche Yurka from the Broadway stage, give telling performances in a story that attempts to clarify, spiritually, why the Almighty chose five persons to die in the collapse of an ancient bridge. It is a search for truth as seen through the eyes of a young priest (Donald Woods).

In a series of flashbacks the priest learns of the spectacular rise of the street dancer, Miss Bari, to a position as consort of the Viceroy (Calhern). He learns of the love and hate, violence and hypocrisy which took place in Peru during the days when Spaniards ruled that country. But in the end he learns that mere man can never understand the ways of the Almighty or His purposes.

Tamiroff turns in one of his best characterizations as Uncle Pio, dramatic tutor, who takes the dancer of the streets under his wing and makes her the "toast" of Peru. He paces the film's performances. Francis Lederer portrays twins—one a seafaring, happy-go-lucky man who wins the affections of the dancer; the other, a scribe for the wealthy who loves his brother so much that he is driven to a suicide attempt when he is convinced that the girl is ruining the sailor's life.

Lynn Bari has her first starring role in a top-budget "A" picture in "Bridge of San Luis Rey." At times she portrays her role with depth and understanding. However, her performance is uneven in several sequences, and it is apparent that director Rowland V. Lee had to use all the acumen at his disposal to draw from her the sturdy acting which is required of her role.

Settings and montage are in good taste, and costuming by Reynaldo Luza, who was brought from his native Peru to work on this film, should come in for special commendation. Dimitri Tiomkin, musical director, also wrote, in collaboration with Herbert Stollberg, the three songs used—"Mi Chicos," "What Is Love" and "The Marquesa"—none of which is catchy. *Sten.*

Weekend Pass
(SONGS)
Hollywood, Jan. 28.

Universal release of Warren Wilson production. Stars Martha O'Driscoll and Noah Beery, Jr.; features Delta Rhythm Boys, George Barbier, Andrew Tombes, Leo Diamond and His Harmonaires, Mayris Chaney Dancers and The Sportsmen. Directed by Jean Yarbrough. Screenplay, Clyde Bruckman, from original by Warren Wilson; camera, William Sickner; special photography, John P. Fulton; editor, Edward Curtiss. Previewed at Four Star, Hollywood, Jan. 27, '44. Running time, 61 MINS.
Barbara..................Martha O'Driscoll
Johnny.....................Noah Beery, Jr.
Bradley.....................George Barbier
Constable..................Andrew Tombes
Sheriff........................Irving Bacon
Ray.........................Dennis Moore
Motor Cop.................Edgar Dearing
Kendall.....................Pierre Watkin
Hilda.........................Lottie Stein
Waikowsky....................Eddie Acuff
Jenkins.........................Jack Rice
Murphy.....................Perc Launders

This is a program comedy-drama, with inclusion of several song and dance specialties, that will moderately satisfy in the general bookings as a supporting attraction where brief running time is required.

Despite the synthetic and fragile story, it holds together fairly well for nominal entertainment. Noah Beery, Jr., is a shipyard worker who gets bonus and weekend leave after 18 months' perfect record. He hies for a rural hotel where he can loll in a bathtub and relax in a big bed. But he bumps into Martha O'Driscoll, runaway socialite who wants to join the Wacs against objections of her grandfather. Yarn weaves through series of at-times humorous episodes until the girl is returned home and Beery goes back to work.

Picture displays several specialties, including the Delta Rhythm Boys for one appearance harmonizing "All Or Nothing At All"; Mayris Chaney and partner in a ballroom dance; Leo Diamond and harmonica trio for two tunes; the Sportsmen for vocal ensembles; and various songs warbled by Miss O'Driscoll. Best is "I Like to Be Loved," by Milton Rosen and Everett Carter.

Miss O'Driscoll and young Beery are okay in the leads, with George Barbier heading list of adequate support—most of which are brief bits. Jean Yarbrough's direction is passable. *Walt.*

Return of the Vampire

Columbia release of Sam White production. Features Bela Lugosi, Frieda Inescort, Nina Foch, Miles Mander. Directed by Lew Landers. Screenplay, Griffin Jay, based on idea by Kurt Neumann; camera, John Stumar and L. W. O'Connell; editor, Paul Borofsky. At Rialto, N. Y., week starting Jan. 28, '44. Running time, 69 MINS.
Armand Tesla..................Bela Lugosi
Lady Jane Ainsley.........Frieda Inescort
Nicki Saunders................Nina Foch
John Ainsley................Roland Varno
Sir Frederick Fleet........Miles Mander
Andreas Obry.................Matt Willis
Elsa........................Ottola Nesmith
Professor Saunders.........Gilbert Emery
Lynch......................Leslie Denison
Gannett.............William C. P. Austin

Bela Lugosi is back in another horror thriller, this time spotted as the vampire who's restored from his grave via cinematic miracle. It's the usual supernatural stuff, "Return of Vampire" being suited for nice dual biz.

Story shows Lugosi spending his days in his coffin and nights seeking out girls. And there's a wolf man as an assistant. Developments are telegraphed in advance, with dialog being unduly trite, but Lew Landers managed nicely on his direction, even overcoming some of the more implausible episodes. He's also tossed in plenty of suspense.

Lugosi's villainy remains standard for him and Frieda Inescort, as one who saves the life of a vampire victim and helps trap Lugosi, contributes the outstanding portrayal. Miles Mander makes a realistic Scotland Yard operative. Nina Foch shows promise as the gal saved from the vamp. Matt Willis is excellent as the servant turned wolfman. John Stumar and L. W. O'Connell have done topflight photography. *Wear.*

Passport to Adventure
Hollywood, Jan. 28.

RKO release of Herman Schlom production. Directed by Ray McCarey. Screenplay, Val Burton and Muriel Roy Bolton; camera, Jack Mackenzie; special effects by Vernon L. Walker; editor, Robert Swink; dialog director, Hal Yates. Tradeshown in L. A. Jan. 27, '44. Running time, 65 MINS.
Ella........................Elsa Lanchester
Franz......................Gordon Oliver
Grete.......................Lenore Aubert
Dietrich.....................Lionel Royce
Hausmeister....................Fritz Feld
Lieutenant Bosch..........Joseph Vitale
Lord Haw Haw................Gavin Muir
Professor Walthers........Lloyd Corrigan
Agnes......................Anita Bolster
Millie....................Lydia Bilbrook
Captain.....................Lumsden Hare
Prison Warden..............Hans Schumm

"Passport to Adventure" is a rather arty and usual yarn which, because of its novelty, will garner plenty of playdates as dual support in the general runs. Lacking any marquee names in the cast, it nevertheless is deftly developed from an intriguing premise to hold attention for the customers after they're inside.

Story is unpretentious and tending towards the fantastic side of drama, with goodly share of light moments. Elsa Lanchester is a London charwoman, widow of a sergeant-major, who decides to head for Berlin to bump off Hitler. She's sped on her journey by a magic eye which kept her late husband out of trouble in foreign climes. She stows away on a boat going to France, travels with her pail and scrub-brush right into Berlin, and, posing as a deaf mute, gets a charwoman's job in the Reich chancellory. She fails to meet the Feuhrer, but upsets things generally until escape with Nazi-opposed officer, Gordon Oliver, and latter's sweetheart, Lenore Aubert.

Miss Lanchester ably carries the piece in the main role, taking full advantage of slick script provided by Val Burton and Muriel Roy Bolton, and excellent direction by Ray McCarey. Various characters are neatly etched in the unfolding, with Oliver, Lionel Royce, Fritz Feld, Gavin Muir, Joseph Vitale, Lloyd Corrigan and Miss Aubert providing fine support. *Walt.*

Death Valley Rangers

Monogram release of Robert Tansey production. Stars Ken Maynard, Hoot Gibson and Bob Steele. Directed by Robert Tansey. Screenplay, Elizabeth Beecher, from original by Robert Emmett and Frances Kavanaugh; camera, Edward Kull; editor, Carl Pierson. At New York, week Jan. 26, '44, dual. Running time, 59 MINS.
Ken..........................Ken Maynard
Hoot.........................Hoot Gibson
Bob...........................Bob Steele
Lorna.......................Linda Brent
Kirk.....................Kenneth Harlan
Blackie......................Charlie King
Red.......................George Chesboro
Cal.........................John Bridges
Ross.......................Al Ferguson
Ranger.......................Robert Allen

Standard hoss opera totes plenty of b.o. for sagebrush followers, with starring trio of Ken Maynard, Hoot Gibson and Bob Steele for extra marquee values. Should fill in nicely as dualer.

Story has Maynard, Gibson and Steele, the Trail Blazers, on lookout for hijackers sacking gold shipments carted by Death Valley stagecoach. Blazers catch up with marauders when Steele furnishes opening via clever ruse of joining gang.

There's plenty of gunplay and fist-exchanging when rival groups meet head-on in finale scene, with starred trio, following conventional pattern, emerging unscathed.

Film opens and shuts with slight romantic pitch between Steele and Linda Brent, but amour buildup is negligible and never intrudes upon two-fisted saga. Supporting cast and direction okay.

Secreto Eterno
("The Eternal Secret")
(MEXICAN-MADE)

Jesus Grovas release of V. Saiso Piquer production. Stars Marina Tamayo and Carlos Orellana; features David Silva, Matilde Palou, Miguel Ferriz and Virginia Manzano. Directed by Carlos Orellana. At Belmont theatre, N. Y., Jan. 23, '44. Running time, **97 MINS.**

Dolores	Marina Tamayo
Don Justo	Carlos Orellana
Luis	David Silva
Emilia	Matilde Palou
Eduaro	Miguel A. Ferriz
Borja	Alejandro Cobo
Teresa	Virginia Manzano
Pablo	Armando Davila

(In Spanish; no English Titles)

Without any English subtitles, this Mexican-made, despite its technical qualifications, is headed for limited grosses in the United States. Strictly for Spanish-speaking audiences.

Acting, direction and yarn are above the usual level of releases from south of the Rio Grande. Story unwinds in rapid pace, telling of a woman (Marina Tamayo) who is married to a widower (Carlos Orellana) with two grown daughters who hate their stepmother. Gals get her charged with a murder of which she is innocent. Convicted through circumstantial evidence, she's released from prison several years later when the real murderer confesses. Meanwhile, her young daughter from the marriage to the widower, who was adopted by a wealthy family after his death, learns of her plight and takes her in.

Producer V. Saiso Piquer and director Orellana have blended their talents for few lapses of interest. The two stars acquit themselves well; supporting roles by David Silva, Matilde Palou, Miguel Ferriz and Virginia Manzano are handled capably, without the stiltedness so usual in these Spanish-language films. *Sten.*

Miniature Reviews

"Up In Arms" (RKO) (Musical; Color). Danny Kaye, new film comedy star, introduced in top escapist b. o. entertainment.

"The Sullivans" (20th-Fox). A fine picture; good boxoffice.

"The Impostor" (U). Adventures of Free French units in Africa provide mildly entertaining drama. Good dualer.

"Devil Riders" (PRC). Buster Crabbe in average buckskin meller, okay as dual supporter.

Up in Arms
(MUSICAL; COLOR)

Los Angeles, Feb. 5.

RKO release of Samuel Goldwyn production. Stars Danny Kaye; features Dinah Shore, Dana Andrews and Constance Dowling. Directed by Elliott Nugent. Screenplay, Don Hartman, Allen Boretz and Robert Pirosh, suggested by character from "The Nervous Wreck," by Owen Davis; camera, Ray Rennahan; editors, Daniel Mandell and James Newcom; special photographic effects, Clarence Slifer and R. O. Binger; songs, Harold Arlen and Ted Koehler, Sylvia Fine and Max Liebman; dances staged and directed by Danny Dare; musical director, Louis Forbes; musical numbers arranged and conducted by Ray Heindorf. Tradeshows in L. A., Feb. 4, '44. Running time, **106 MINS.**

Danny Weems	Danny Kaye
Virginia	Dinah Shore
Joe	Dana Andrews
Mary Morgan	Constance Dowling
Colonel Ashley	Louis Calhern
Blackie	George Mathews
Butterball	Benny Baker
Info Jones	Elish Cook, Jr.
Sgt. Gelsey	Lyle Talbot
Major Brock	Walter Catlett
Ashley's Aide	George Meeker
Ashley's Aide	Richard Powers
Mrs. Willoughby	Margaret Dumont
Singer at Dock	Donald Dickson
Mr. Higginbotham	Charles Arnt
Dr. Freyheisen	Charles Halton
Pitchman	Tom Dugan
Waiter	Sig Arno
Dr. Weavermacher	Harry Hayden
Mr. Campbell	Charles D. Brown
Dr. Jones	Maurice Cass
Head Waiter	Fred Essler
Band Leader	Rudolf Friml, Jr.

And the Goldwyn Girls

Expertly showcasing the comedic talents of Danny Kaye in his first film starrer, "Up in Arms" is a filmusical that's expensively mounted in Technicolor and in the best Samuel Goldwyn tradition of elaborateness. Picture is fine escapist fare and will hit healthy biz and holdovers as solo or billtopper in all situations.

Kaye, whose solid hit in "Let's Face It" on Broadway provided rush of film producers to sign him for pictures, is definitely star material. Another newcomer, Constance Dowling, is both an eyeful and talented in a straight acting part. She also should go far in pictures.

Character portrayed by Kaye is a broadly-sketched version of Owen Davis' "Nervous Wreck"—a wacky hypochrondiac who's inducted by the Army for a series of wild misadventures. At start, before Kaye is drafted, yarn introduces him as reticent suitor for Miss Dowling, while Dinah Shore has designs on snagging Kaye and Dana Andrews is in love with Miss Dowling. While Kaye and Andrews go into service together, the girls enlist as Army nurses. On transport going to the South Pacific, quartet are thrown together for further episodes to hold thread of yarn together, with main routine on shipboard being a wild chase evolving from Kaye's efforts to hide stowaway, Miss Dowling. Arriving at a tropic isle, Kaye disappears, is captured by the Japs, but turns tables on the Nips to bring them into the camp for hero's reception. It's a rather abrupt ending.

Kaye has great sense of timing in putting over his comedy for maximum effect. He also smartly delivers three song specialties especially written by Sylvia Fine (Mrs. Kaye) and Max Liebman; an extended number in a theatre lobby, a jive duet with Miss Shore, and his "Melody in 4-F," which he smacked over in "Let's Face It."

Miss Shore, in addition to handling an important role, clicks with two songs, "Now I Know" and "Tess' Torch Song," both by Harold Arlen and Ted Koehler. Former is best candidate for pop attention. Songwriting team also composed "All Out for Freedom," a lilting march tune delivered by male soldier chorus.

Every set is elaborately displayed to take advantage of the Technicolor photography, and the "Goldwyn Girls" are on display via a new crop of dazzling lookers, but are only briefly glimpsed.

Picture has fine acting support, with Louis Calhern, George Mathews and Benny Baker most prominent.

Top production number is a Kaye dream sequence with an unusually staged background of "the Goldwyn Girls" perched in trees, with ground-fog to accensuate the effect. Comedian and Miss Shore duet the jive number here, and it's a well-staged, colorful and deftly executed setting.

Elliott Nugent capably handled the directing, getting good script from Don Hartman (also associate producer), Allen Boretz and Robert Pirosh, which continually points up the abilities of Kaye. Goldwyn spent plenty of coin on the production, but it should all roll back along with plenty of profit. *Walt.*

The Sullivans

20th Century-Fox release of Sam Jaffe production. Features Anne Baxter, Thomas Mitchell, Selena Royle. Directed by Lloyd Bacon. Story, Edward Doherty and Jules Schermer; adaptation, Mary C. McCall, Jr.; editor, Louis Loeffler; camera, Lucien Andriot. Previewed in N. Y. Jan. 26, '44. Running time, **111 MINS.**

Katherine Mary	Anne Baxter
Mr. Sullivan	Thomas Mitchell
Mrs. Sullivan	Selena Royle
Al	Edward Ryan
Genevieve	Trudy Marshall
Frank	John Campbell
George	James Cardwell
Matt	John Alvin
Joe	George Offerman, Jr.
Father Francis	Roy Roberts
Lieutenant	Ward Bond
Gladys	Mary McCarty
Al (child)	Bobby Driscoll
Genevieve (child)	Nancy June Robinson
Frank (child)	Marvin Davis
George (child)	Buddy Swan
Matt (child)	Billy Cummings
Joe (child)	Johnny Calkins
Admiral	Jorn Nesbitt
Damage Control Officer	Selmer Jackson
C.P.O.	Harry Shannon
Nurse	Barbara Brown
Yeoman	Larry Thompson
Naval Captain	Addison Richards

A glorious tribute to the modest Waterloo (Ia.) family which sacrificed five sons to the cause of World War II, and a fine picture in many respects, the saga of "The Sullivans" is a fine film record. Despite too much detail to some sequences which tends to a certain amount of slowness, the exploitation potentialities are great. There's much downright good entertainment, and it all adds up to strong grosses.

The story is that of the five Sullivan boys who enlisted in the U. S. Navy immediately after Pearl Harbor and went down with their ship, later to be honored by the christening of a battle-wagon named after them. That is fact, this being the true story of the Sullivans of Waterloo. It has been done with assumed fidelity and no doubt will be richly cherished as a documentary account of heroism by the Sullivan family of the small midwestern town, whether or not it achieves exceptional support from the general public as entertainment.

The warmth of its humor, its homespun qualities, and the excellent performances by a large cast, in addition to the general strength of the dialog, combine to make "The Sullivans" very intriguing amusement in many spots. There are innumerable scenes which stand out in particularly sharp contrast to those where there is too much detail and added wordage, such as the radio broadcast on the Pearl Harbor attack, rehashing that all over again, the lengthy "goodbye" to the Sullivan boys, etc.

The first half deals with the five Sullivan lads as little boys, with much homey humor derived from their pranks and the worries they cause their folks. One of the peak scenes is the one in which Papa Sullivan has caught the kids smoking cornsilk in the shed behind their house. Instead of spanking them, he imposes what is supposedly an all-time cure by telling them that since they want to smoke, they should be men and use tobacco, so passes out cigars to all. Their efforts to stomach such a strong smoke makes for big laughs. Another sequence that plays havoc with the risibilities is the one in which the kids decide to build a woodbox for their mother which would extend through the kitchen wall, saving them the trouble of having to lug the wood through a door.

Skipping several years, the second half deals with the boys as adolescents, four of the Sullivans now working on various jobs, while the youngest, Al, is still in high school. It is here that the romance between Al and Katherine Mary (Anne Baxter) develops, reaching full flower quickly and with a baby born to them. Since the boys had always stuck together through thick and thin, including all the fights they won as little boys, Al goes along with the other four when latter decide to enlist in the Navy. He is urged to do this by his wife who realizes he is fighting the desire to do so in the face of his marital responsibilities.

A brief sequence covering a naval battle off the Solomons in which the Sullivans perished when their ship exploded, precedes the sad anti-climax when word of their loss arrives at home and the pride which enlivens the scene in connection with the launching.

Outstanding on performance is that of Bobby Driscoll, playing Al when he was a boy of perhaps five or six years old, although Thomas Mitchell, as the father, and others are transcendentally fine in their work. Little Driscoll, however, captures top prize and in that first half is responsible for most of the warm, fireplace-like humor which the film contains. He is so natural before the camera it's amazing. The other boys, his brothers, are Marvin Davis, Buddy Swan, Billy Cummings and Johnny Calkins, who also rate encomiums.

That these boys are missed when older ones take their place is to be expected but their successors do nicely, including Edward Ryan (Al), John Campbell, James Cardwell, John Alvin and George Offerman, Jr. The casting reflects the typical, average smalltown such as Waterloo, this including Mitchell as the father, a freight-train conductor, and his wife Selena Royle. Miss Baxter likewise is the refreshing, attractive little-town belle who fits in admirably with the surroundings and the faithful production backgrounds furnished by Sam Jaffe. Lloyd Bacon's direction fails only in that he was in no hurry to get the picture to a finish. He and his film editor, Louis Loeffler, could have cut out plenty, notably in the second half. Photographic crew under Lucien Andriot has done a superior job. *Char.*

The Impostor

Hollywood, Feb. 4.

Universal release of Julien Duvivier production. Stars Jean Gabin. Directed by Duviver. Screenplay, Duvivier; dialog adapted from the french by Stephen Longstreet; added dialog, Marc Connelly and Lynn Starling; cameram Paul Ivano; editor, Paul Landres; special photography, John P. Fulton; music score and direction by Dimitri Tiomkin. Previewed atv Pantages, Hollywood, Feb. 3, '44. Running time. 93 MINS.

Clement	Jean Gabin
Lieutenant Varenne	Richard Whorf
Bouteau	Allyn Joslyn

Yvonne ... Ellen Drew
Hafner ... Peter Van Eyck
Colonel De Bolvin ... Ralph Morgan
Corhery ... Eddie Quillen
Monge ... John Qualen
LaFargo ... Dennie Moore
Clauzel ... Milburne Stone
Mortourart ... John Philliber
Menessler ... Charles Mcgraw
Matown ... Otho Gaines
Free French Corporal ... John Forrest
Priest ... Fritz Leiber
Sergeant Clerk ... Jim Wolfe
Adjutant ... William Davidson
Prosecutor ... Frank Wilcox
Officer ... Warren Ashe
Soldier ... Peter Cookson
Toba ... Leigh Whipper
Ekopa ... Ernest Whitman
Captain ... Grandon Rhodes
Prosecuter ... George Irving

Fall of France in 1940. and subsequent formation of Free French units in Africa. forms basis for this adventure drama. which unfolds tale of regeneration of a confirmed criminal through the comradeship in arms. Written, produced and directed by Julien Duvivier, and with Jean Gabin starred, audience interest is mainly held by fresh background and informative display relevant to the re-gathering of French soldiers to continue the battle against the Nazis. In stressing these points, Duvivier fails to generate pace fast enough to carry picture along for more than moderate attention, and it will have to groove in the duals, except in spots where exploitation can attract pro-French customers.

Story tells of how Gabin is saved from the guillotine, for murder, at Tours by Nazi air bombing, heads south and assumes the identity, papers and uniform of a dead French soldier along the road. Joining group of refugee soldiers who enlist in the Free French forces, Gabin's army association gradually transforms the criminal; he leads a small unit overland for attack on Italian desert base and is decorated for gallantry, under the name of the dead man whose identity he assumed. Conscience-stricken, he confesses masquerade and is broken to the ranks, but distinguishes himself for climax with death raid on machinegun nest to protect his battalion.

Duvivier dwells much on characterizations, neatly etching the various characters assembled in the Free French forces. Gabin turns in a good performance while support, including Richard Whorf, Allyn Joslyn, John Qualen, Peter Van Eyck and Eddie Quillen, is uniformly good. Ellen Drew is only femme in cast, appearing in limited footage. *Walt.*

Devil Riders

PRC release of Sigmund Neufeld production. Stars Buster Crabbe; features Al St. John. Directed by Sam Newfield. Story and screenplay, Joe O'Donnell; camera, Robert Cline; editor, Robert Crandall. At New York, week Jan. 26, '44, dual. Running time, **56 MINS.**

Billy Carson ... Buster Crabbe
Fuzzy Jones ... Al "Fuzzy" St. John
Sally Farrell ... Patti McCarthy
Del Stone ... Charles King
Jim Higgins ... John Merton
Red ... Kermit Maynard
Tom Farrell ... Frank LaRue
Turner ... Jack Ingram
Curley ... George Chesebro
Doc ... Ed Cassidy

Conventional stagecoach saga, furnishing two-fisted background for Buster Crabbe, is an okay amalgam of action and comedy and should level off well as supporting dualer.

Open-and-shut story poses Crabbe as a pony express rider who sides in with new stagecoach company being bucked by a crooked lawyer and his henchmen. Bad hombres are after a parcel of rich land the government is about to grant to the stage operator. After horse rustling, a labor sitdown, and plenty of fist exchanging, Crabbe manages to expose the heavies and makes possible the successful run of the stagecoach line. In the process of mopping up, Crabbe manages also to corral the heroine, daughter of the stagecoach operator.

Story is considerably lightened by Al St. John's comedy. He lends some vestige of credibility to an otherwise loosely-woven yarn.

Photography is better than in the usual buckskin meller.

El Fin De La Noche
("End of the Night")
(ARGENTINE-MADE)
(SONGS)

Buenos Aires, Jan. 25.

San Miguel production distributed by Distribuidora Panamericana. Stars Libertad Lamarque; features Alberto Bello, Juan Jose Miguez, Florence Marly, Ernesto Raquen, Maria E. Buschiazzo, Elisardo Santalla, Cesar Fiaschi. Directed by Alberto de Zavalia. Story by Hugo MacDougall; camera, Jose Maria Beltran. Music by Paul Misraki. At the Ambassador, Buenos Aires. Running time, **95 MINS.**

An anti-Nazi war film coming out of Argentina now is news. Based on subsequent events—Argentina quitting Axis—producers may have had foresight as to the future. Voluntarily censored by the producers, then reluctantly okayed by the official censors (held up for another look reportedly because of protest by the German Embassy), it's a pity that the picture isn't better.

May be that the restraint which Director Alberto de Zavalia had to use prevented development of a more suspenseful story. Where story misses is its similarity with many U. S. pix dealing with occupied Europe. Libertad Lamarque, Argentina's top singing star, is shown as a South American singer eager to leave a European country, clearly occupied France. An anti-Vichy Frenchman, wounded in a street battle with the invaders, hides in her home. She covers up his tracks when the Germans (never tagged with Swastikas but obvious by their accents and uniforms) come searching. Subsequently, the local Nazi Gestapo boss, seeing her warbling in the little theatre where she works, persuades her to carry out a job in return for the exit visa she needs to leave the country with her child.

As a foreigner and an artist, she's to work her way in with the anti-Vichy crowd. From this point on the story becomes sadly complicated since the Free Frenchman she is to trip up is the same handsome guy who hid in her cellar.

Honors go to Zavalia for his direction, still among the best in the Latin industry. Senorita Lamarque, while she has her moments, apparently can't help piling on the emotion like singing a tear-jerking tango. Close-ups do not flatter her, especially scenes with Juan Jose Miguez, male lead. Alberto Bello turns in a good job as the Gestapo boss. Photography by Jose Maria Beltran is above average, and the music by French composer Paul Misraki, now living here, is also noteworthy. *Ray.*

Miniature Reviews

"Lady in the Dark" (Color) (Par.). Lavishly produced and very entertaining, this one will range from big to terrif b.o.

"Passage to Marseille" (WB). Humphrey Bogart and an all-star cast in a thrilling melodrama headed for top grosses.

"Action in Arabia" (RKO). Entertaining spy meller unfolding in the Near East. Okay biz.

"Chip Off the Old Block" (U) (Musical). Effervescing juvenile comedy-drama for wide audience appeal. Should do okay.

"Raiders of the Border" (Mono). Slow-moving western which should fill the lower half of a dual bill.

Lady in the Dark
(SONGS)
(COLOR)

Paramount release of Mitchell Leisen production, directed by Leisen. Stars Ginger Rogers, Ray Milland, Jon Hall, Warner Baxter; features Barry Sullivan, Mischa Auer. Based on play by Moss Hart; adaptation, Frances Goodrich and Albert Hackett; songs, Kurt Weill, Ira Gershwin, Johnny Burke and James Van Heusen; editor, Alma Macrorie; photography, Ray Rennahan, Gordon Jennings, Paul Lerpae and Farciot Edouart; dances, Billy Daniels. Previewed in N. Y. Feb. 3, '44. Running time, **100 MINS.**

Liza Elliott ... Ginger Rogers
Charley Johnson ... Ray Milland
Randy Curtis ... Jon Hall
Kendall Nesbitt ... Warner Baxter
Dr. Brooks ... Barry Sullivan
Russell Paxton ... Mischa Auer
Maggie Grant ... Mary Phillips
Allison DuBois ... Phyllis Brooks
Dr. Carlton ... Edward Fielding
Adams ... Don Loper
Miss Parker ... Mary Parker
Miss Foster ... Catherine Craig
Martha ... Marietta Canty
Miss Edwards ... Virginia Farmer
Miss Bowers ... Fay Helm
Barbara—17 years ... Gail Russell
Miss Stevens ... Marian Hall
Liza's Mother ... Kay Linaker
Liza's Father ... Harvey Stephens
Office Boy ... Billy Daniels
Miss Sullivan ... Georgia Backus
Ben ... Rand Brooks
Clown ... Pepito Perez

Produced on a lavish scale in Technicolor, and in very fine taste against backgrounds of a glittering character, with costuming that fills the eye, "Lady in the Dark" is at the outset a technically superior piece of craftsmanship. But more than that, in all directions, an extremely entertaining film. It can't miss being boffo at the boxoffice.

Crammed with diversion of rich consistency for all, though some of its more sophisticated aspects may be less enjoyed by children than others, the picture carries singularly strong appeal for the women. The beautiful costuming alone contributes importantly to that. Paramount spent $185,000, and total negative nick is reported at $2,800,000. It looks it.

Mitchell Leisen produced and also directed from a surefire script based on the Broadway stage hit by Moss Hart, with music by Kurt Weill and lyrics by Ira Gershwin. An additional song, "Suddenly It's Spring," was written by Johnny Burke and James Van Heusen. The able adaptation was in the hands of Frances Goodrich and Albert Hackett, an obviously superb writing team. In all other departments, too, including the dance staging, the lighting, photography and orchestral score, nothing is to be desired. Photography in particular is the last word, notably the process shots. Ray Rennahan served as director of photography, with Natalie Kalmus as color director. Special photographic effects are credited to Gordon Jennings and Paul Lerpae, while the process work was under the direction of Farciot Edouart. Among other things, a plethora of many combinations of brilliant colors stamps the production as perhaps the finest ever turned out in tints, with the modern settings, dream backgrounds and costuming especially lending themselves to color treatment.

Picture has considerable scope as against the limitations of the stage when "Lady" was done in legit. A few of the musical numbers of the stage version were omitted in the interest of emphasizing the story, but studio facilities have permitted a display of fantastic effects in the dream sequences which were not possible on the stage. The three dream portions have been very elaborately and cleverly staged. In addition to choral backgrounding in the "Blue Dream," "Wedding Dream" and "Circus Dream" production numbers, there are some dance portions in which Miss Rogers, Don Loper, Mary Parker and Billy Daniels figure. In addition to "Suddenly It's Spring," there are two Weill-Gershwin numbers from the stage original, "My Ship" and "Jenny." Last-mentioned, used extensively and cleverly in the Circus Dream sequence, led by Miss Rogers and with all members of the cast taking part, is the best of the trio.

Miss Rogers plays the editor of a fashion magazine who, realizing she's on the edge of a nervous breakdown, finally places herself in the hands of a psycho-analyst. She resists his ministrations but ultimately goes through with it all and finally finds herself, the wall she had built around herself and her emotions since childhood ultimately being broken down. The dream sessions are reflections of her disturbed mind. Very ingeniously pieced in are some scenes of Miss Rogers in her childhood, which had been unhappy.

Playing the ad manager for the society mag and the only man in her life who has sought to set himself up as Miss Rogers' superior, irritating her all along the line, Ray Milland gives an excellent performance. At first dropping Warner Baxter on romantic grounds after he has divorced his wife, Miss Rogers then turns to a glamor picture star in the person of Jon Hall [Victor Mature was the original "beautiful hunk of man"], but sours on him, too.

Tearing down the barriers that have stood between them, Milland and Miss Rogers go into a clinch for a very unique finish. This comes when Mischa Auer, embattled photographer for the magazine who sticks his head in the door and in utter amazement sees the clinch, exclaims, "This is the end, the absolute end." And it is.

Auer, Mary Phillips, Phyllis Brooks and lessers contribute much to the smart and sophisticated light comedy relief, which together with the crispy dialog go a long way toward making "Lady" an exceedingly diverting picture. The cast includes numerous persons of a minor nature in addition to the many who figure in the production numbers. *Char.*

Passage to Marseille

Warner Bros. release of Hal B. Wallis production. Stars Humphrey Bogart; features Michele Morgan, Claude Rains, Sydney Greenstreet, Philip Dorn, Helmut Dantine, Peter Lorre, George Tobias, Victor Francen, John Loder. Directed by Michael Curtiz. Screenplay, Casey Robinson and Jack Moffitt, from novel by Charles Nordhoff and James Norman Hall; music, Max Steiner; camera, James Wong Howe; special effects, Jack Cosgrove and Edwin DuPar; editor, Owen Marks. Previewed, N. Y., Feb. 4, '44. Running time, **110 MINS.**

Matrac ... Humphrey Bogart
Paula ... Michele Morgan
Capt. Freycinet ... Claude Rains
Renault ... Philip Dorn
Major Duval ... Sydney Greenstreet
Marius ... Peter Lorre
Manning ... John Loder
Petit ... George Tobias
Grandpere ... Vladimir Sokoloff
Chief Engineer ... Edward Ciannelli
First Mate ... Konstantin Shayne
Capt. Malo ... Victor Francen
Garou ... Helmut Dantine
2nd Engineer ... Louis Mercier
2nd Mate ... Monte Blue
Lt. Hastings ... Stephen Richards
Jourdain ... Hans Conreid
Bijou ... Frederick Brunn

Mess Boy........................Billy Roy
Lt. Lenoir....................Chas. La Torre

There is nothing wrong with this picture although a little tightening, with some 15 minutes less footage, which can be edited easily without hurting continuity, would help. Nonetheless, Warner Bros. has a thrilling melodrama which will do big business right down the line.

As presented now, several sequences, in which speeches are made concerning France, its enemies, allies and inhabitants, are just a mite lengthy.

Exhibitors will be impressed with the exploitation possibilities that will zoom this film into the top-grossing class. They are many, and will not have to be concocted, because they are so obvious. It is a natural for showmanship.

The film pulls no punches. No kid gloves are used to soothe the feelings of either the isolationists or the pacifiists who have been using the news columns of late in an effort to impress people with the advisability of securing a negotiated peace with our enemies. The message of this picture is forthright and rings true.

To bring all this about, producer Hal B. Wallis has gathered a cast that is boxoffice in itself. Practically every actor, from Humphrey Bogart to Helmut Dantine, portrays roles with sincerity and understanding, giving added meaning to the screenplay by Casey Robinson and Jack Moffitt from the novel by Charles Nordhoff and James Norman Hall.

Yarn, dedicated to the Fighting French, unwinds in a series of flashbacks, as related by a French liaison officer (Claude Rains) to an American newspaperman (John Loder), who seeks background for a story dealing with activities of these Frenchmen who are fighting, and flying, on the side of the Allies. Rains goes back many months in the telling, when a ship he was on picked up a group of men in a lifeboat in the Atlantic. The survivors admit, when pressed, that they are escaped prisoners from Devil's Island, who wish to return to France to fight for their country. This act of mercy fails to meet with the approval of Major Duval (Sydney Greenstreet), a professional army man, who hated the Republic and admired the fascism of Marshal Petain.

After the rescue, the freighter settles down to its normal routine, continuing back to Marseille, its destination, only to be disturbed again when the wireless crackles with the news of French surrender to the Nazis. The captain of the ship (Victor Francen) secretly orders its course changed toward England, but Major Duval heads a mutiny which takes over the boat for a short time. In the end, the mutiny is subdued, but not before the fascist wireless operator radios the ship's position to a German patrol bomber, which attacks, does great damage, kills several men, but is finally brought down by a deck gun. Conclusion of the narrative by Rains describes what each of the Frenchmen who escaped from Devil's Island are doing at the moment to aid the cause.

Humphrey Bogart, as Matrac, a journalist whose opposition to the appeasers at the time of Munich resulted in his conviction on a trumped up charge of murder and treason and his banishment to Devil's Island, gives a forthright performance as one of the escaped convicts rescued by the freighter. Others in this motley crew include Philip Dorn, Peter Lorre, Helmut Dantine and George Tobias. Michele Morgan, as the wife of Matrac, left in France, and Victor Francen, as skipper of the freighter, go through their paces impressively—Francen, especially, in a scene where he stands on the bridge of his ship and reads, with tears, the message announcing France's downfall, calling it "The blackest day in French history." Charles La Torre, as the aide to Greenstreet who yesses the major at every turn, does extremely well in the few scenes in which he is shown.

But the best job of all is done by Rains. Not only does he have the biggest part in the picture, but he captures practically all the acting honors in a film filled with good acting.

Direction by Michael Curtiz keeps the action moving during majority of the 110 minutes, but he could have easily cut several of the over-long speeches without much trouble. Special effects by Jack Cosgrove and Edwin DuPar are realistic, with the camera work of James Wong Howe, using all the tricks at his disposal, responsible for several entertaining highlights. *Sten.*

Action in Arabia

Hollywood, Feb. 15.

RKO release of Maurice Geraghty production. Features George Sanders, Virginia Bruce, Leonore Aubert, Gene Lockhart. Directed by Leonide Moguy. Screenplay, Philip MacDonald and Herbert Biberman; camera, Roy Hunt; special photographic effects, Vernon L. Walker; editor, Robert Swink. Tradeshown in L. A. Feb. 15, '44. Running time, **75 MINS.**

Gordon....................George Sanders
Yvonne....................Virginia Bruce
Mounirah....................Lenore Aubert
Danesco....................Gene Lockhart
Reed....................Robert Armstrong
Rashid....................H. B. Warner
Latimer....................Alan Napier
Leroux....................Andre Chariot
Chakka....................Marcel Dalio
Chalmers....................Robert Anderson
Kareem....................Jamiel Hasson
Hamilton....................John Hamilton
Hotel Clerk....................Rafael Storm
Hamid....................Mike Ansara

Agents and spies of the Nazis, Vichy French, and Free French predominate in this well-assembled melodrama backgrounded in Damascus and nearby desert. Although sticking close to formula in setting up mysterious situations and characters for eventual clarification, picture develops on a straight line and at good pace. Low on marquee name voltage, picture can stand for billtopping in secondary first runs with good support. Otherwise, it's a strong dualer for any situation.

Number of years ago, Meriam Cooper and E. B. Schoedsack made a trip to the Arabian desert and shot much footage for a proposed picture for RKO. On their return to the studio, however, production was abandoned and the exposed film tossed on the shelf. Quite a lot of the footage is utilized here, with shots of large camel and bedouin assemblages in the desert being neatly dovetailed into the story for hefty production effect.

George Sanders plays an American newspaper correspondent stationed in the Near East for some time, arriving in Damascus in 1941. It's the headquarters for espionage and plotting, with the French and Germans attempting to win favor of the Arab tribes in the war. Sensing a story, Sanders sticks around to run into many strange and mysterious characters, and finally gets on track of Nazi aim to stir up the tribes. Virginia Bruce, ostensibly working for the Nazis but in reality agent for the Free French, and Sanders form romantic portion of the yarn. After uncovering identity of the Nazi plotters, Sanders follows them to desert castle to prevent coup with traitorous Arab leaders, and the enemies are neatly disposed of at the finish.

Sanders gives a good performance, as does Miss Bruce; Alan Napier and Andre Charlot are Vichy French operators; Gene Lockhart is prominent as a flustering gossip-peddler; Lenore Aubert is an Arab girl; and Robert Armstrong is attache of the American consulate.

Philip MacDonald and Herbert Biberman provided a compact and fast-paced original script, with Leonide Moguy aiding with direction that maintains interest in both the characters and the proceedings. Production mounting generates colorful background, while the desert camel caravans are decidedly unusual. *Walt.*

Chip Off the Old Block

(MUSICAL)

Hollywood, Feb. 11.

Universal release of Bernard W. Burton production. Stars Donald O'Connor, Peggy Ryan, Ann Blyth. Directed by Charles W. Lamont. Screenplay, Eugene Conrad and Leo Townsend; original story by Robert Arthur; camera, Charles Van Enger; editor, Charles Maynard; dance director, Louis Da Pron; musical director, Charles Previn; songs, Inez James and Sidney Miller; Grace Shannon and William Crago. Previewed at Pantages, Feb. 10, '44. Running time, **76 MINS.**

Donald Corrigan....................Donald O'Connor
Peggy....................Peggy Ryan
Glory Marlow, 3rd....................Ann Blyth
Glory Marlow, Jr....................Helen Vinson
Glory Marlow, Sr....................Helen Broderick
Quentin....................Arthur Treacher
Judd Corrigan....................Patric Knowles
Blaney Wright....................J. Edward Bromberg
Henry McHugh....................Ernest Truex
Milly....................Minna Gombell
Dean Manning....................Samuel S. Hinds
Prof. Frost....................Irving Bacon
Quiz Kid....................Joel Kupperman

Donald O'Connor continues his merry pace as a fast-rising juvenile film personality in this, his third starrer for Universal. Comedienne Peggy Ryan and newcomer Ann Blyth share starring position and contribute materially to the overall zestful, spontaneous entertainment. It's entirely escapist fare, studded with laugh lines and situations, songs, and comedy dances by the O'Connor-Ryan team. Best of his three starrers, picture will get profitable reception as billtopper in all bookings, and can hit surprise biz in the nabes and hinterlands.

Although young O'Connor is spotlighted with Miss Ryan for youthful exhuberance and comedy, 16-year-old Ann Blyth catches attention in her initial film appearance. Girl, signed by U from stage cast of "Watch on the Rhine," has been held for several months awaiting proper spot for introduction. Delay was no mistake. Girl displays fine personality and ease in front of the cameras, in addition to a fine lyric soprano and ability to put over a song for maximum reaction.

Director Charles Lamont took full advantage of a fine script by Eugene Conrad and Leo Townsend to smack over the lines with telling effect.

O'Connor, son of a seafaring family, is given leave from prep naval academy pending return of his father from sea duty with the fleet. Enroute to New York, he picks up acquaintanceship with Miss Blyth; gets along fine with juve flirtation, until Miss Ryan meets him at the station to spoil everything. From there on it's case of boy pursuing Miss Blyth, while comedienne chases him. Miss Blyth plays third generation of stage stars, Helen Vinson and Helen Broderick, both of whom had been wooed—but not won—by boy's father and grandfather, respectively, in bygone years. Complications unfold at a happy clip; O'Connor persuades the girl to take star role in a stage musical; he gets Miss Ryan into the show; and returns to school to prepare for a naval career.

Quiz Kid Joel Kupperman is introduced for two brief but amusing sequences to lisp his answers to questions. Brevity of footage accentuates his appearance for shrewd production guidance.

O'Connor duets one romantic number with Miss Blyth and then teams, as usual, with Miss Ryan for three comedy tunes that wind up with pair going into dance turns. Miss Blyth sings the Lew Brown-Ray Henderson standard, "My Song," and "Love Is Like Music," by Milton Schwarzwald, Inez James and Sidney Miller. Both display her lyric soprano to best advantage.

In the well-rounded production, supporting cast adds much to the overall results. The Misses Vinson and Broderick are fine as the two veteran stage stars; Arthur Treacher is excellent in his familiar butling role; Ernest Truex and J. Edward Bromberg are play producers; Minna Gombell, Patric Knowles, Samuel Hinds and Irving Bacon also deliver creditably.

Coincidental with trade preview of "Chip Off the Old Block," young O'Connor was inducted into the Army this week. However, Universal has completed three other O'Connor features that will be spaced out on the releasing schedule during the coming year. *Walt.*

Raiders of the Border

Monogram release of Scott R. Dunlap production. Stars Johnny Mack Brown, Raymond Hatton. Directed by John P. McCarthy. Screenplay by Jess Bowers based on story by Johnston McCulley; camera, Harry Neumann; editor, Carl Pierson; musical director, Edward Kay. At New York, week Feb. 8, '44. Running time, **53 MINS.**

Nevada....................Johnny Mack Brown
Sandy....................Raymond Hatton
Joe....................Craig Woods
Bonita....................Ellen Hall
Harsh....................Raphael Bennett
McGee....................Edmund Cobb
Whiskey....................Ernie Adams
Steve....................Dick Alexander
Davis....................Lynton Brent
Blackie....................Stanley Price

Slow-moving carbon of western prototype provides Johnny Mack Brown ample opportunity to display his fistic abilities. Short length poses problem in booking but should manage in lower dual slot.

Brown and Hatton are U. S. marshals huntin' down them cattle rustlers. Hatton hides behind an ear trumpet while Brown is the front man and fighter of the pair. The rustlers who are exchanging their stolen beef for equally illicit Mexican jewels, are finally rounded up after a series of chases. Musical background for the chases is a somewhat garbled and thoroughly incongruous extract from the Red Army song, "Meadowland."

In between their bouts with the rustlers, the pair of marshals manage to play Cupid for Craig Woods and Ellen Hall. Naturally, the rustlers are finally rounded up and jugged.

Kings of the Ring

Irwin A. Lesser and Martin J. Lewis production and release. Edited by M. J. Lewis; photography director, Jack Rieger; narration written and delivered by Nat Fleischer. At World, N. Y. Running time, **95 MINS.**

Reissued fight film runs for about 90 minutes and supplies first-class screen entertainment for male audiences. Film stands by itself with no support from shorts, newsreels or comedies, depending on its appeal solely as a sequence of notable fights edited for latter-day consumption. Nat Fleischer, editor of Ring magazine, handles most of the commentary.

Appealing directly to hosts of uniformed males magneted to the Broadway area, "Kings of the Ring" bases most of its b.o. appeal on recent ring appearances of Joe Louis. Billy Conn and Lou Nova fights, Louis' last ring appearances, are conspicuously absent, the first for unexplained reasons and the second probably because the fight was so disappointing that skedded showings of the pictures ringsided by Pathe were cancelled by Garden execs less than an hour after the bout.

Documentary films, including the Jack Johnson-Stanley Ketchell, Tommy Burns and Bill Squires, Dempsey Carpentier, Benny Leonard-Lew Tendler, Dempsey-Firpo and both Dempsey-Tunney title fights, are included as well as a revealing round-by-round celluloid version of the Madison Square Garden, N. Y., contest between Primo Carnera and

Ernie Schaaf from which the latter never regained consciousness. Interesting angle in this clip is that, although cry of "fake" was raised after kayo registered by weak-hitting Italian, obvious distress of Schaaf is plainly revealed by the camera and it would seem that everyone at Garden ringside must have known that he was badly hurt.

For contrast Tony Galento and Max Baer toss in some comic antics both in and out of ring.

"Kings" looks set for prolonged run on Broadway with good likelihood, industry circles believe, that servicemen's camp show tieup here and abroad is in offing. *Donn.*

Miniature Reviews

"The Purple Heart" (20th). Stirring drama dealing with fate of captured U. S. airmen who bombed Tokyo. Strong b.o.

"See Here Private Hargrove" (M-G). Sentimental romantic comedy with Army background. Surefire boxoffice.

"Curse of the Cat People" (RKO). Simone Simon, Kent Smith in alleged horrific film that never jells; for lesser duals.

"Klondike Kate" (Songs) (Col). A weak "B."

"Pride of the Plains" (Rep.) Good western for duals support.

"Million Dollar Kid" (Mono). "East Side Kids" turn righteous in this one; dualer.

"Nabonga" (PRC). Jungle film offers exploitation possibilities for the duals.

"Que Hombre Tan Simpatico" (Mundiales). Entertaining Spanish musical, limited to Latin audiences.

The Purple Heart

20th-Fox release of Darryl F. Zanuck production. Directed by Lewis Milestone. Features Dana Andrews, Richard Conte, Farley Granger, Kevin O'Shea, Donald Barry, Sam Levene, Charles Russell, John Craven. Screenplay, Jerome Cady; story, Melville Crossman; camera, Arthur Miller; editor, Douglas Biggs. Tradeshown in New York, Feb. 21, '44. Running time, 99 MINS.

Capt. Harvey Ross	Dana Andrews
Lieut. Angelo Canelli	Richard Conte
Sergt. Howard Clinton	Farley Granger
Sergt. Jan Skvoznik	Kevin O'Shea
Lieut. Peter Vincent	Donald Barry
Mrs. Ross	Trudy Marshall
Lieut. Wayne Greenbaum	Sam Levene
Lieut. Kenneth Bayforth	Charles Russell
Sergt. Martin Stoner	John Craven
Johana Hartwig	Tala Birell
General Ito Mitsubi	Richard Loo
Mitsuru Toyama	Peter Chong
Peter Vorosbevski	Gregory Gaye
Karl Keppel	Torben Meyer
Ludwig Kruger	Kurt Katch
Manuel Siva	Martin Garralaga
Karl Schleswig	Erwin Kalser
Boris Evenik	Igor Dolgaruki
Francisco De Los Santos	Nestor Paiva
Paul Ludovegu	Alex Papana
Yuen Chiu Ling	H. T. Tsiang
Moy Ling	Benson Fong
Admiral Kentaro Yamagichi	Key Chang
Itsubi Sakai	Allen Jung
Police Captain	Wing Foo
Court Clerk	Paul Fung
Procurator	Joseph Kim
Court Stenographer	Luke Chan
Toma Nagota	Beal Wong
Hank Morrison	Marshall Thompson

One of the most dramatic episodes in the history of this or any other war has been wrought into this screenplay. From the boxoffice viewpoint "The Purple Heart" is a hefty grosser.

More than that, however, the celluloid version of the tragic events which followed the capture of eight of the American flyers who bombed Tokyo will likely penetrate the public consciousness more forcefully than the stories of Jap atrocities which have appeared in cold type, hair-raising as these reports have been. In a fashion, the headlines have served as a trailer for this type of production and from the looks of things will continue to ensure the timeliness of such films for a long spell to come.

Despite or because of the restraint which has been exercised in story detail, performance and direction the horrendous nature of the enemy becomes all the more pronounced. The Jap military caste, their matter-of-fact innate, senseless cruelty, their insanely nationalistic fanaticism, have been drawn in cold, stark, deliberate, devastating strokes. It is, so far, the strongest indictment of the savagery and sadism of the Japs to be projected.

Withal, it's an intensely moving piece, spellbinding though gory at times, gripping and suspenseful for the most part. Scenes depicting, by inference, the tortures which the

American boys were subjected to, strike home with terrific impact. About a dozen individual performances are outstanding, with acting honors being shared fairly evenly among all the principals in the drama.

It's an excellent casting job, even minor roles having been handled with good judgment. Medieval costuming, somewhat bizarre and barbaric, though apparently authentic, of the Japanese court officials, in sharp contrast to the modern courtroom, emphasizes the fantastic nature of the proceedings.

Under Darryl Zanuck's production guidance and Lewis Milestone's deft direction, Jerome Cady's yarn emerged as taut, swift-paced fare. Topnotch continuity was authored by Zanuck under nom-de-plume of Melville Crossman.

The story is about eight captured American flyers on trial before a Jap civil court on a murder rap, charged with purposely bombing and machine-gunning Jap civilians. Protests by Lieut. Wayne Greenbaum (Sam Levene) that civil courts have no jurisdiction over military prisoners and that the proceedings constitute a violation of the Geneva Convention are ignored. Action takes place mainly in the Jap courtroom, with war correspondents from Axis nations only admitted.

The lying testimony of a traitorous Chinese official, working with the Japs, is the flimsy basis upon which the Jap prosecution hangs the charge that the flyers gloried in bombing hospitals and schools. A phoney film, made during an air raid practise drill in a Jap city, is another bit of evidence used in the attempt to prove the men guilty.

On the whole, however, the crux of the situation lies in the bitter hatred and intense jealousy between the Jap army and navy leaders, each trying to place the blame for the bombing on the other. General Ito Mitsubi (Richard Loo) tries to prove that the bombers took off from an aircraft carrier, and thus must have penetrated the supposedly impregnable Jap navy defenses. Admiral Yamgichi (Key Chang) contends that the bombers, because of their size, could not possibly have taken off from even the largest aircraft carrier in existence. Sitting in judgment is Mitsuru Toyama, sinister, powerful political figure, head of the Black Dragon Society, who ranks both military leaders.

The Americans are given the choice of telling where they came from and being sent to a regular prisoners' camp or facing torture and eventual death. One by one the men are beaten and maimed. But no confession is forthcoming and the men are marched to their doom. Earlier, during the proceedings, word is received in the courtroom that Gory regidor has fallen. The scene where the puppet-like Jap soldier mannikins and the austere judges suddenly go into a fierce, aboriginal dance to the accompaniment of loud shrieks of "banzai" is but another gruesome and effective reminder of the subhuman quality of the enemy.

Outstanding among the Oriental performers are Peter Chang, in a sock interpretation of the harsh-voiced Black Dragon society head; Richard Loo, as the oily, dangerous head of the Jap military staff and Army Intelligence; Key Chang, as the suave, supercilious chief of naval intelligence.

Dana Andrews turns in an excellent performance as the leader of the American group, with other topnotch characterizations by Charles Russell, Richard Conte, John Craven, Donald Barry, Kevin O'Shea, Sam Levene and Farley Granger. *Mori.*

See Here, Private Hargrove
(ONE SONG)

Metro release of George Haight production. Directed by Wesley Ruggles. Features Robert Walker, Donna Reed. Screenplay, Harry Kurnitz; based on book by Marion Hargrove; camera, Charles Lawton; editor, Frank E. Hull. Tradeshown in New York, Feb. 16, '44. Running time, 101 MINS.

Private Hargrove	Robert Walker
Carol Holliday	Donna Reed
Private Mulvehill	Keenan Wynn
Mr. Holliday	Robert Benchley
Brodie S. Griffith	Ray Collins
First Sergeant Cramp	Chill Wills
Bob	Bob Crosby
Mrs. Holliday	Marta Linden
Uncle George	Grant Mitchell
Private Esty	George Offerman, Jr.
General Dillon	Edward Fielding
Sergeant Heldon	Donald Curtis
Private Burk	Wm. "Bill" Phillips
Captain Manville	Douglas Fowley

"See Here, Private Hargrove," despite the military connotation, is a pleasant, exhilarating, sentimental comedy which will ring up healthy grosses in the keys and all the way up and down the line.

Based on Marion Hargrove's book of the same title, this autobiog combines such surefire ingredients as sprightly dialog, corking comedy situations, a smartly handled romantic motif, with pointed though inoffensive joshing about army life (in the early phases following induction) as the underlying base.

Director Wesley Ruggles, working from Harry Kurnitz's finely-textured continuity, set and maintained a fast pace throughout. The book, of course, was a find and the cost of the film rights reasonable because the purchase was made long before the Hargrove piece hit the bookstalls and the best-seller class.

Robert Walker chalks up another impressive score as a romantic lead in this picture but Donna Reed, photographing like the proverbial million, is the topper. Under unusually clever camera treatment Miss Reed registers stunningly both for appearance and delivery. She's missed when not in action. As a team the couple appear in a few all too brief romantic interludes which are the highlights of the picture. The scenes are skilfully played for laughs as well as love interest. And this relatively subordinate phase of the yarn is conveyed with a poignancy which will leave audiences hankering for more.

"Hargrove" is the story of an awkward cub reporter, alternately the joy and bane of his editor's existence, who carries his ineptitude into the Army. His witless blunders lead him to K.P. regularly, usually scrubbing metal ashcans. He sells a share in his literary career to Keenan Wynn and two other Army buddies for the loan of enough money to go to New York to see his girl on his furlough.

Wynn, as a petty chiseler who conducts a private loan business among his acquaintances, clicks easily in a nifty comedy characterization. Only serious thought introduced is when Wynn persuades Walker to apply for a transfer from combat duty to an office chore in the Army and they incur the displeasure of the other two members of the friendly quartet. They effect a last-minute transfer back into the combat unit. Robert Benchley is in for a small but effective bit as the girl's father.

While this is a picture with a wartime background, it is not a combat story and comes strictly under the heading of escapist entertainment.

Production standards are first rate all the way, with an extra nod rated by the camera for its handling of Miss Reed. There's one song, the pop "In My Arms," by Frank Loesser and Ted Grouya. *Mori.*

Curse of the Cat People

RKO release of Val Lewton production. Features Simone Simon, Kent Smith, Jane Randolph. Directed by Gunther V. Fritsch and Robert Wise. Screenplay by DeWitt Bodeen; camera, Nicholas Musuraca; editor, J. R. Whittredge. Previewed in N.Y., Feb. 10, '44. Running time, **70 MINS.**

Irena	Simone Simon
Oliver Reed	Kent Smith
Alice Reed	Jane Randolph
Amy	Ann Carter
Barbara	Elizabeth Russell
Miss Callahan	Eve March
Julia Farren	Julia Dean
Capt. State Troopers	Erford Gage
Edward	Sir Lancelot
Donald	Joel Davis
Lois	Juanita Alvarez

Made as sequel to the profitable "Cat People," this is highly disappointing because it fails to measure up as a horrific opus. Even though having the same principals as in the original "Cat" chiller, this is such an impossible lightweight that it will have trouble even on the lower half of twin bills. Chief trouble seems to be the over-supply of palaver and concern about a cute, but annoying, child.

Two directors worked on "Curse of the Cat People," suggesting production headaches. Pair has turned out a strange cinema stew that is apt to make audiences laugh at the wrong scenes. Many episodes are unbelievably bad, with hardly anything happening in the first three reels.

Plot has the offspring of the first wife of a naval architect, Kent Smith, apparently suffering from the same supernatural beliefs that brought the death of the child's mother. Yarn tries to show the child living in a dream world and imagining she is playing with her mother, Simone Simon. Youngster's visit to a supposedly haunted house where a half-crazed character actress, Julia Dean, lives with her daughter, Elizabeth Russell, builds into the slight horrific angle of film, resulting in the best episodes in the production.

Miss Simon, appearing as the spirit of the dead mother, does almost a bit, a silly characterization. Smith walks through the father portrayal. Jane Randolph, as his wife, is so-so. Miss Dean does as much as possible, under the circumstances, in the half-crazed role, while Elizabeth Russell is standout as her disowned daughter though given small opportunity. Ann Carter does alright as the dream world kid, but probably wondered what all the fuss was about. Eve March heads the support.

Direction of Gunther V. Fritsch and Robert Wise is uneven, but suffered from a lukewarm script.

Wear.

Klondike Kate
(SONGS)

Columbia release of Irving Briskin production. Stars Ann Savage, Tom Neal, Glenda Farrell; features Constance Worth, Lester Allen, Sheldon Leonard. Directed by William Castle. Screenplay, M. Coates Webster, from story by Webster and Houston Branch. Musical director, M. W. Stoloff; songs, Harry Revel and Paul F. Webster; editor, Mel Thorsen; camera, John Stumar. At Brooklyn Fox, Feb. 18, '44. Running time, **64 MINS.**

Kathleen O'Day	Ann Savage
Jefferson Braddock	Tom Neal
Molly	Glenda Farrell
Lita	Constance Worth
Sometime Smith	Sheldon Leonard
Duster Dan	Lester Allen
Judge Crossit	George Cleveland
Bartender	George McKay
Piano Player	Dan Seymour

"Klondike Kate" is an unentertaining porridge of idea patterns that never jell. A weak "B."

The contemplated lynching by a mob of a man under suspicion of murder is just forgotten; the Great Northern Hotel burns down conveniently so that neither the man who bought the place from a conniving manager, the gambler who wins it at the turn of a card, nor the girl who comes to the Klondike to claim it as her inheritance, win out. Screenplay by M. Coates Webster, from a story by Webster and Houston Branch, is neither logical nor worthwhile.

Acting, direction, and the production itself, are done tongue-in-cheek with an apparent attitude, of, "We'll be glad when we get this one in the can." Several songs are sung and dances staged which also are not outstanding or worth recalling. Ann Savage, Glenda Farrell and Tom Neal, as well as the supporting actors, are stumped by the illogical script throughout.

Sten.

Pride of the Plains

Republic release of Louis Gray production. Stars Bob Livingston and Smiley Burnette. Directed by Wallace Fox. Screenplay, John K. Butler and Bob Williams, from story by Oliver Drake; camera, John MacBurnie; editor, Charles Craft. At New York, N. Y., week Feb. 16, '44, dualed. Running time, **55 MINS.**

Johnny Revere	Bob Livingston
Fred Milhouse	Smiley Burnette
Joan Bradford	Nancy Gay
Kenny Revere	Stephen Barclay
Hurley	Kenneth MacDonald
Grant Bradforl	Charles Miller
Snyder	Kenne Duncan
Steve Craig	Jack Kirk
Gerard	Bud Geary
Bowman	Yakima Canutt

Differing in some respects from the garden variety of buckskin fare, "Pride of the Plains" will reap biz on the duals commensurate with popularity of its stars. Bob Livingston and Smiley Burnette. Latter's comic rep as erstwhile screen sidekick of Gene Autry continues to stand him in good stead on the marquee front.

Yarn concerns efforts of the heavy to repeal protectorate law governing wild horse site, idea being to then step in and slaughter horses for illegal gain through the usual devious scheming. But Livingston and Burnette expose the setup.

Cast is uniformly good, with Nancy Gay, in particular, lending credence to an unconvincing role. Camera work better than average.

Million Dollar Kid

Monogram release of Sam Katzman-Jack Dietz production. Stars Leo Gorcey, Huntz Hall; features Gabriel Dell, Billy Benedict, Louise Currie, Noah Beery, Sr., Iris Adrian. Directed by Wallace Fox. Story and screenplay, Frank Young; editor, Carl Pierson; camera, Marcel Le Picard. At Brooklyn Strand, week Feb. 18, '44. Running time, **66 MINS.**

Muggs	Leo Gorcey
Glimpy	Huntz Hall
Lefty	Gabriel Dell
Skinny	Billy Benedict
Louise	Louise Currie
Captain	Noah Beery, Sr.
Maisie	Iris Adrian
Cortland	Herbert Heyes
Spevin	Robert Greig
Roy	Johnny Duncan
Andre Dupree	Stanley Brown
Mrs. Glimpy	Patsy Moran
Mrs. McGinnis	Mary Gordon
Herbie	Al Stone
Danny	Dave Durand
Pinkie	Bud Gorman
Stinkie	Jimmy Strand
Spike	Pat Costello

Monogram's "East Side Kids" turn to the side of righteousness in their latest opus, giving an otherwise run-of-the-mill picture a fairly diverting twist. But despite good direction by Wallace Fox, "Million Dollar Kid" will wind up on the lower rung in dual houses.

Leo Gorcey, Huntz Hall and their cohorts rescue a wealthy man from a group of ruffians. He invites them to his home, where he explains that his son has become wayward. The boys decide to rid the neighborhood of the ruffians, and find that the wealthy gent's son is one of the latter. Word arrives that the twin, brother of the wealthy youth has been killed in action, causing the father to become ill. The "East Side Kids" find the young man, bring him to his senses and impart the news of his brother's death. They clean out the gang, and the rich lad is absolved from any crimes the gang may have committed.

Gorcey, Hall, Billy Benedict and Gabriel Dell, who have been playing these rough-and-tough roles for years, will please those who go for this type of film fare. Rest of the cast, including Noah Beery, Sr., Louis Currie and Iris Adrian run through their roles in convincing fashion.

Sten.

Nabonga

PRC release of Sigmund Neufeld production. Stars Buster Crabbe; features Barton MacLane, Fifi D'Orsay and Julie London. Directed by Sam Neufield. Original story and screenplay, Fred Myton; camera, Robert Cline; editor, Holbrook N. Todd. At New York, N. Y., week Feb. 16, '44, dualed. Running time, **72 MINS.**

Ray Gorman	Buster Crabbe
Marie	Fifi D'Orsay
Carl Hurst	Barton MacLane
Doreen Stockwell	Julie London
Hunter	Bryant Washburn
Stockwell	Herbert Rawlinson
Tobo	Prince Modupe
Doreen (child)	Jackie Newfield
Gorilla	Nabonga

PRC incorporates all the familiar Edgar Rice Burroughs elements in "Nabonga," title purportedly being a native translation of "gorilla." Okay for dual support. Film's exploitation possibilities should help.

Gossamer story deals with an embezzler who planes out of New York with his daughter and a cargo of securities and jewels. Plane crashes in the Belgian Congo, where embezzler and pilot are wiped out, child surviving after befriending a wounded ape (Nabonga), who assumes protectorate over her as she grows into womanhood.

Picture jumps ahead several years and shows Buster Crabbe searching the Congo for the stolen booty, and tangling with Barton MacLane.

Acting throughout is wooden and never rises above story. Julie London, in her first film, hasn't much to do except slink around in a modified sarong and mouth an occasional phrase in pidgin English. Photography and direction get by.

Que Hombre Tan Simpatico!
("What a Charming Fellow")
(SONGS)

Film Mundiales release of Diane S. de Fontanals production. Stars Fernando Soler; features Gloria Marin, Blanca De Castejon, Rafael Banquells, Manuel Medel, Directed by Fernando Soler. Music, Manuel Esperon. At Belmont, N. Y., opening Feb. 18, '44. Running time, **100 MINS.**

Amable Corcuera	Fernando Soler
Fanny Jiminez	Gloria Marin
Dona Blanca	Blanca De Castejon
Paquito	Rafael Banquells
Feito	Manuel Medel

(In Spanish; no English titles)

Acting and directing of Fernando Soler helps make this an entertaining, if verbose, musical of Mexican genre. All-Spanish dialog will limit audiences to followers of the espanol school, but b.o. should make for better than even break in those situations.

Musical is built around incident in the life of roue bachelor (Soler) who sponges on medical student for livelihood in return for getting him out of series of jams. Stude, who is supported by rich uncle, makes a play for more dough by telling the old man that he has just married, and thus complicated situation follows.

Film could do with wholesale snipping, but never approaches the tiresome stage. All parts are well done, with Soler standing out in a well-rounded characterization. Music is catchy and camera work is generally above par.

The Negro Soldier

A two-fisted plea for tolerance, told simply, honestly and conscientiously, is the 42-minute documentary, "The Negro Soldier," made by the War Department under the supervision of Col. Frank Capra. It presents a message that should reach every theatregoer, especially in those areas where inter-racial outbreaks have been common.

Plans are now underway to exhibit the picture at theatres throughout the nation, backed by the film industry's War Activities Committee. Production was handled by a crew of 14 U. S. Army technicians and Carlton Moss, Negro author, who scripted and plays the leading role of the pastor. Group visited more than 30 camps and reportedly took two years to complete the picture.

"The Negro Soldier" reveals two phases of the title subject, firstly showing what the race has done to earn its place in the American way of life, and, secondly, deals with the Negro soldier and WAC. The documentary should receive more than cursory attention from regular film audiences.

Facts are presented about the Negro that are not generally known to the average person. Pertinently, the role of the Negro soldier, from Crispus Attucks, mulatto hero of the Boston Massacre in 1770, to Robert Brooks, first American soldier to die in World War II. The Negro Minute Men at Lexington and Concord during the Revolutionary War—Peter Salem, who fought at Bunker Hill; Prince Whipple, who was with Washington when he crossed the Delaware, and the hundreds of other Negroes who shared the hardships of Valley Forge—are screened vividly.

In dramatic sequence the film tells of the Negro sailors who were with Perry at Lake Erie; soldiers who fought with Stonewall Jackson at New Orleans, and it also dwells on the Mass. 54th Regiment of volunteers in the Civil War. It follows Negro fighters through the Spanish-American conflict and World War I.

But the main part of "The Negro Soldier" deals with his activities in the present conflict. An enlisted man is picked up and followed through basic training, additional fundamentals, and through actual combat. These scenes, and those showing Negro WACs in training, will drive home the picture's message harder than anything else caught by the Army cameras.

Sten.

Miniature Reviews

"Knickerbocker Holiday" (UA). Nelson Eddy, Charles Coburn in smash adaptation of Broadway musical, top grosser.

"You Can't Ration Love" (Par) (Musical). Moderately entertaining college story; moderate b.o.

"The Navy Way" (Par). Good service melodrama about Great Lakes Naval Station; profitable for regular runs.

"Voice in the Wind" (U). Francis Lederer and Sigrid Gurie starred in morbid, romantic drama; doubtful b.o.

"Beautiful, But Broke" (Songs) (Col). Joan Davis in slap-happy jive musical, okay for lesser duals.

"Sweethearts of the U.S.A." (Mono) (Songs). Flimsy fantasy about femme war worker; dualer.

"No Greater Love" (Artkino). Russian-made, dubbed into English, should do good biz.

Knickerbocker Holiday
(MUSICAL)

United Artists release of Harry Joe Brown (PCA) production. Stars Nelson Eddy, Charles Coburn, Constance Dowling; features Ernest Cossart, Shelley Winter, Johnnie "Scat" Davis and Fritz Feld. Directed by Harry Joe Brown. Adaptation, Thomas Lennon; screenplay, David Boehm and Rowland Leigh, from stage play by Maxwell Anderson and Kurt Weill. Additional music, Forman Brown, Werner R. Heymann, Franz Steininger, Jule Styne and Sammy Cahn; music direction, Jacques Samossoud; editor, John F. Link; camera, Phil Tannura. Previewed in N. Y., Feb. 28, '44. Running time, **85 MINS.**

Brom Broeck	Nelson Eddy
Peter Stuyvesant	Charles Coburn
Tina Tienhoven	Constance Dowling
Tienhoven	Ernest Cossart
Ulda Tienhoven	Shelley Winter
Tenpin	Johnny "Scat" Davis
Jailer	Percy Kilbride
Roosevelt	Otto Kruger
Tammany	Richard Hale
Poffenburgh	Fritz Feld
Town Crier	Chester Conklin

Carmen Amaya and Her Company

"Knickerbocker Holiday" may not have been much for the b.o. as a Broadway stageplay with music some five years ago, but as filmed by Producers Corp. of America it is a rousing escapist musical geared for top grosses in all situations.

Sig Schlager, Producers Corp. of America prexy, has not spared the budget in readying this adaptation from the original by Maxwell Anderson and Kurt Weill. Harry Joe Brown, who produced and directed for the screen, has done much to emphasize the film's humor, gaiety and songs in a fast-moving pic that will find a ready audience of all ages

The marquee has not been neglected, either. Nelson Eddy, Charles Coburn and Constance Dowling, plus a supporting cast of sturdy character actors, will aid plenty in bringing the customers into the theatre.

A comedy set to music, film is laid in old New Amsterdam of Peter Stuyvesant's day. It deals with a gay, singing but fighting newspaper publisher who fights for freedom in the colony and relief from the oppressed from conniving politicians. He crosses the path of the crafty, humorous Governor Stuyvesant in his political and newspaper crusading, and also in his desire to wed the daughter of a politician.

Eddy is given seven vocal opportunities. As the crusading, happy-go-lucky publisher, he gives a neat performance. Charles Coburn, in the role of the governor played on the stage by Walter Huston, portrays a roue, impishly and in topflight fashion. Miss Dowling, the sought-after young lady, follows her initial film smash, in Danny Kaye's "Up in Arms," with another forthright portrayal. Ernest Cossart, Shelley Winter, Johnnie "Scat" Davis, Otto Kruger, Percy Kilbride, Fritz Feld and others turn in workmanlike characterizations.

Film has nine songs, five more than the Broadway show. The music ties the production together neatly. Four songs—lyrics by Anderson, music by Weill—are carried over from the original. They are "Nowhere to Go But Up," "It Never Was Anywhere You," "Indispensable Man" and "September Song," first two sung by Eddy, last two by Coburn. Eddy also breaks into song with "Love Has Made This Such a Lovely Day," by Jules Styne and Sammy Cahn, in a duet with Miss Dowling. Several other substantial numbers have been written by Werner Heymann, Forman Brown, Franz Steininger and two by Eddy himself, "Oh, Woe!" and "Holiday," latter sung by Johnnie "Scat" Davis.

Two of the outstanding scenes in "Knickerbocker Holiday" are the gypsy dances of Carmen Amaya and her troupe. She stamps and terps through her dynamic routine to the accompaniment of guitarist Sabicas.

Sten.

You Can't Ration Love
(SONGS)

Paramount release of Michel Kraike production. Features Betty Rhodes, Johnnie Johnston, Bill Edwards, Marjorie Weaver, Marie Wilson, Johnnie "Scat" Davis, Mabel Paige, Jean Wallace, Roland Rupree, Christine Forsythe, and D'Artega's All-Girl Orchestra. Directed by Lester Fuller. Story, Muriel Roy Bolton; adaptation, Val Burton and Hal Fimberg; editor, Tom Neff; songs, Lester Lee and Jerry Seelen; camera, Stuart Thomson. Previewed in N. Y., Feb. 24, '44. Running time, **78 MINS.**

Betty	Betty Rhodes
John	Johnnie Johnston
Pete	Bill Edwards
Marian	Marjorie Weaver
Bubbles	Marie Wilson
Kewpie	Johnnie "Scat" Davis
Miss Hawks	Mabel Paige
Madge	Jean Wallace
Pickles	Roland Dupree
Christine	Christine Forsythe
Band	D'Artega All-Girl Orch

This one bubbles over with youth and escapism, aided by several light, airy songs, but on the whole it adds up only moderately well and cannot be expected to do much more than that at the boxoffice unless cleverly exploited.

This is another of those stories based upon college life. Cast, while suiting the requirements of the story and the songs, offers nothing for marquee lettering.

Mythical Adams college provides the background, while the somewhat unique wartime idea behind the story is the rationing of dates with boyfriends. It's a co-ed institution and the point value of the remaining males in school ranges downward from 30 points for the more desirable guys to "Two-Point" Simpson, a chemistry student who's anything but a lady's man. However, out of jealousy, one of the girls decides to make a big play for Simpson, glamourizing him and finally developing him into a swoon-crooner who takes the school by storm. While the original intent was a prank, the girl, Betty Rhodes, falls for "Two-Point" (Johnnie Johnston) after he has become a quarry for every girl in the college, even to one scene where they gang up on him a la Sinatra. This sequence provides one of the few laughs in the picture, comedy values being generally lacking.

A varsity show and rehearsals for it, in addition to other backgrounding, pave the way for the several songs, best-sounding being "Love Is This," a ballad which is reprised for the finish, and "Ooh-Ah-Oh." These, plus others, were written by Lester Lee and Jerry Seelen, while also thrown in is "Louise," by Leo Robin and Richard A. Whiting, which originally was written for "Innocents of Paris," first American vehicle for Maurice Chevalier and released in 1929 by Paramount. Number is done by Miss Rhodes and Johnston as a double. Together they also do "Look What You Did to Me."

Miss Rhodes solos "Nothing Can Replace a Man" early in the proceedings, topped by a dancing chorus which also vocalizes. Possessing a good crooning type of voice, Johnston scores nicely on "Ooh-Ah-Oh," playing the guitar, while several gals mix into the number with him for bits. His "Love Is This" sells very nicely. He does this solo, number being reprised at the end with Miss Rhodes. "How Did It Happen?" is nicely done as a double by Marie Wilson and Johnnie "Scat" Davis, with a novelty acrobatic dance team (Roland Dupree and Christine Forsythe) topping. The D'Artega all-girl orchestra, backgrounding on the music, has the spotlight to itself for a medley of three numbers, "I Don't Want to Walk Without You," "Oodles of Noodles" and "One O'Clock Jump."

In addition to Miss Rhodes and Johnston, good performances are given by Bill Edwards. Marjorie Weaver, Miss Wilson, Davis, Mabel Paige and Jean Wallace. *Char.*

The Navy Way

Hollywood, Feb. 25.

Paramount release of Pine-Thomas production. Directed by William Berke. Screenplay, Maxwell Shane; camera, Fred Jackman, Jr.; editor, Howard Smith; music, Willy Stahl. Tradeshown in L. A. Feb. 24, '44. Running time, **74 MINS.**

Johnny Jersey	Robert Lowery
Ellen Sayre	Jean Parker
Mal Randall	Bill Henry
Frankie Gimble	Roscoe Karns
Trudy	Sharon Douglas
C. P. O. Harper	Robert Armstrong
Steve Appleby	Richard Powers
Billy Jamison	Larry Nunn
Agnes	Mary Treen

Another in the series of service action dramas contributed by the Pine-Thomas organization for Paramount release, and backgrounded at the Great Lakes Naval Training Station, "The Navy Way" hits fast pace and is cinch for smart exploitation. Picture can be easily sold for bill-topping position in the regular runs for profitable returns.

Group of recruits from all walks of life are thrown together for training at Great Lakes. Robert Lowery, fighter who has had to battle his way through childhood and youth, resents induction when ready to hit heavy coin in fight with the champ. He's a recalcitrant inductee, but gradually transformed into a fine graduate, guided along the way by romance with Wave Jean Parker. But, at the finish, latter decides she's in love with Bill Henry and Lowery becomes reconciled and ships out with his unit for duty aboard a new ship.

Lowery, under termer to Pine-Thomas for buildup, neatly handles the lead assignment and demonstrates ease of performance and good screen personality. Miss Parker fills in nicely as the girl, and support consisting of Henry, Roscoe Karns, Richard Powers, Larry Nunn, Robert Armstrong, Sharon Douglas and Mary Treen provides well-rounded cast.

William Berke directed at a good clip, ably dovetailing the characterizations with the highlights of Great Lakes training. Virtually all exterior footage was shot at Great Lakes, with Navy extending fullest cooperation. *Walt.*

Voice in the Wind

United Artists release of Rudolph Monter-Arthur Ripley production. Stars Francis Lederer and Sigrid Gurie; features J. Edward Bromberg, J. Carroll Naish and Alexander Granach. Directed by Arthur Ripley. Screenplay, Frederick Torberg, from original story by Ripley; music, Michel Michelet; editor, Holbrook N. Todd; camera, Dick Fryer. Premiered at Lyric, Camden, N. J., Feb. 28, '44. Running time, **85 MINS.**

Jan Volny / El Hombre	Francis Lederer
Marya	Sigrid Gurie
Dr. Hoffman	J. Edward Bromberg
Luigi	J. Carroll Naish
Angelo	Alexander Granach
Marco	David Cota
Anna Hoffman	Olga Fabian
Captain Von Neubach	Howard Johnson
Piesecke	Hans Schumm
Bartender	Luis Alberni
Detective	George Sorel
Policeman	Martin Garralaga
Portuguese Girl	Jacqueline Dalya
Novak	Rudolph Myzet
Vasek	Fred Nurney
Guard No. 1	Bob Stevenson
Guard No. 2	Otto Reichow
Refugee	Martin Berliner

Because of a morbid theme, bleak lighting that adds to the moroseness of the entire picture, and direction that slows the action throughout, "Voice in the Wind" will be a tough one to sell.

Francis Lederer and Sigrid Gurie, who are starred, are over-dramatic at times in this pointless, romantic, tragic drama. Camera work and lighting, in endeavoring to put over the sadness of theme, actually shroud some of the action, and during flashbacks, when full lighting is used, makeup and background react to detriment of both stars. Angles at which Miss Gurie is caught by photog Dick Fryer fail to do her justice in the majority of sequences. She's much more of a looker than pictured.

Notable are the excellent musical score and musicianship of whoever played the piano for Lederer, who portrays a Czech concert pianist banished to a concentration camp for playing Smetana's "Moldau" during one of his engagements despite specific instructions from Nazi agents barring playing of the song.

Film opens with a shot of the ocean at night, dark and bleak, and a voice, that of Arthur Ripley, who directed, pointedly informing audience the picture concerns those who have not been fortunate enough to get out of Europe from under the Nazi heels. Told by flashback, story deals with a musician, obviously a victim of mental depression, a resident of Guadalupe—which might be any haven beyond the reach of the Nazis—who is attracted to a piano in a saloon because of his love for music. Film then segues back to Czechoslovakia shortly after German occupation.

Despite being ordered not to play "Moldau," the concert artist does and is arrested, but not before making arrangements for his wife (Sigrid Gurie) to escape. On the train to the Nazi concentration camp, the musician becomes incensed at his guards for taunting him, battles with them, escapes to a coastal town, stows away on a boat which runs the blockade and reaches the island haven. There he works for Angelo (Alexander Granach) at times, one of a sinister brotherhood who traffics in smuggling and murdering refugees. In a lucid moment, the musician opens the sea-cock of their ship, which is tied to a dock, and it sinks. He is shot by Luigi, brother of Angelo (J. Carroll Naish). Both brothers quarrel over this act, Angelo killing Luigi but not before he, too, is fatally wounded.

Physical violence of the tussle snaps the musician's mind back to normal. He makes his way to the bedside of his wife, who has just died from an unknown malady, in a house across the street from the saloon. He joins her in death.

"Voice in the Wind," initial independent production from Rudolph Monter and Arthur Ripley, originally was to be distributed by Producers Releasing Corp. but will now be released by United Artists. It was made in 12 days on a comparatively small budget.

Even three veteran character actors, J. Edward Bromberg, who plays the role of a doctor in whose apartment Miss Gurie is bedded during the illness which results in her death; Alexander Granach and J. Carroll Naish, appear stumped by the whole thing. *Sten.*

Beautiful But Broke
(SONGS)

Columbia release of Irving Briskin production. Stars Joan Davis; features Jane Frazee, Judy Clark. Directed by Charles Barton. Adapted by Manny Seff, based on story by Arthur Housman; camera, L. W. O'Connell; editor, Richard Fantl. At Strand, Brooklyn, week Feb. 24, '44. Running time, 74 MINS.

Dottie.............................Joan Davis
Bill Drake.....................John Hubbard
Sally Richards................Jane Frazee
Sue Ford..........................Judy Clark
Jack Foster..................Bob Haymes
Rollo..........................Danny Mummert
Maxwell McKay...........Byron Foulger
Station Master...............George McKay
Mayor..........................Ferris Taylor
Mrs. Grayson............Isabel Withers
Waldo Main.................John Eldredge
Birdie Benson.................Grace Hayle
Putnam.........................John Dilson
Willie, West and McGinty

"Beautiful But Broke" proves again that it takes more than a radio comedienne to make a solid screen vehicle. Also that even Joan Davis, crackerjack airwaves comic, and Willie West & McGinty, hilarious vaude combo, can't prevent this from being other than a commonplace "B" entry.

Miss Davis does a workmanlike job with her funny antics and facial gyrations but she can't overcome the familiar fable of the stranded theatrical act. This time, it's the theatrical agent who specializes in name bands that figures in this formula. Miss Davis takes over agency when her boss is called to the colors, but she soon finds out that there aren't many male bands around. Getting together a femme orchestra, she lands a Cleveland nitery date. Then her screwball mentality leaves her two pals, femme singers, and the girl band stranded in a Nevada warplant community. Payoff is that the outfit never reaches the remunerative playdate, various gals going romantic and even Miss Davis falling for a prankster. It's all pretty haphazard.

Joan Davis is standout as the agent who has her troubles with the all-femme band. Jane Frazee and Judy Clark are her two crooning assistants, both doing well with stuff like "Shoo Shoo Baby" and "Pistol Packin' Papa." Willie, West & McGinty, aided by Miss Davis, who's an added entry to their standard bricklayer routine used for years in vaude, hit the laugh peak. Act is even more ludicrous on the screen than on stage. John Hubbard heads the obviously subordinated male portion of the cast. Unbilled girl band does okay, and has several lookers.

Charles Barton is happiest when he is directing familiar slapstick scenes but gets small help from the Manny Seff adaptation of Arthur Housman's story. Richard Fantl has done a neat cutting job, but L. W. O'Connell's cameraing is only fair.
Wear.

Sweethearts of U. S. A.
(SONGS)

Monogram release of Lester Cutler production. Stars Una Merkel; features Parkyakarkus, Donald Novis, Lillian Cornell and Jan Garber, Henry King, Phil Ohman orchestras. Directed by Lew Collins. Screenplay, Arthur St. Claire, Sherman Lowe, Mary Sheldon, based on original by Mary Sheldon; editor, George M. Merrick; camera, Ira Morgan; music director, David Chudnow; songs, Lew Pollack, Charles Newman, Joe Goodwins. At New York, N. Y., week Feb. 22, '44, dual. Running time, 63 MINS.

Patsy...........................Una Merkel
Parky........................Parkyakarkus
Don Clark.....................Donald Novis
Helen Grant................Lillian Cornell
Loretta.........................Judith Gibson
Bill Craige.......................Joel Friend
Mrs. Carver...........Cobina Wright, Sr.
Josephine....................Marion Martin
Clipper........................Vince Barnett
Gilhooley.....................Ralph Sanford
Napoleon......................Joseph Kirk
Also Georgann Smith, Joe Devlin, Edmund Cobb, Dorothy Bradshaw and Charles Williams.
Jan Garber orchestra.
Henry King orchestra.
Phil Ohman orchestra.

Flimsy fantasy, in the serio-comic vein only makes a stab at continuity.

It's a dualer that's lacking in good comedy and fails to get over its serious premise—the job being done by women defense workers. The songs are somewhat redeeming.

Plot deals with the dream of a woman defense worker (Una Merkel) after she knocks herself out while demonstrating to her foreman what's wrong with the contraption she's working on. Dream mechanism permits the entry of the nonsense purveyed by Parkyakarkus, as an addlepated detective on the hunt for some bank robbers and a lover of bands on the side. Interplay of the cops-robbers and patriotic themes leads to confusion and makes the proceedings generally ridiculous.

Jan Garber, Henry King and Phil Ohman orchs provide what little amusement there is in the 63 minutes. *Turo.*

No Greater Love
(RUSSIAN-MADE)

Artkino release of Central Artfilm Studios-Frederick Ermler production, directed by Ermler. Story and adaptation, M. Bleiman and I. Bondin; English version, I. R. Lopert and W. A. Pozner; English dialog, William C. Write, Alexander Bakshy and I. Elman; dialog director, Peter Frye; editor, Geraldine Lutten; camera, V. Rappaport and A. Zavialov. At Victoria, N. Y., week Feb. 24, '44. Running time, 76 MINS.

Pasha......................Vera Meretskaya
Fenya......................Anna Smirnova
Senya......................Peter Aleinikov
Nikolai...............Alexander Violinov
Lukyanov..............Nikolai Bogoliubov
Orlova......................Irina Fedorova
Stepan Orlov.................I. Peltzer

A starkly realistic account of guerrilla warfare against the Nazis in Russia shortly after that country was invaded and Moscow was threatened. With the picture dubbed into English, first time this has been done with a Russe import, it has much more than the average appeal for the American market and should do well.

The title, "No Greater Love," brings to mind the quotation of John the Baptist, "Greater love hath no man than this, that a man lay down his life for his friends," except that in this case it also strongly means country as well as friends or relatives. In 1932 Columbia made a picture also called "No Greater Love," while away back in 1915 Selig produced one called "Greater Love Hath No Man." This Russian-made could also have been titled "No Greater Hate" since it deals with a group of partisans who are grim in their determination for vengeance against the Nazis in the face of the atrocities visited upon their land.

The band is organized and led by Pasha who is implacably resolved to wreak vengeance on the invaders for the brutality of which they stand accused, including the wanton murder of her husband and child, latter being run over by a tank. Ultimately, Pasha catches up with the driver of that tank, crushing him against a mountainside with it. These and several other scenes are not only stark but also quite gruesome, including one shot in which Pasha sinks an axe into a German she catches up with. There is one spot where a censorial cut was imposed. It's where Pasha is left alone with a captured Nazi general. Shot that was knocked for exhibition on this side is one in which she goes to work on the German in an unladylike manner. A brief subtitle is thrown on the screen after the cut to the effect that "he talked."

Picture goes over considerable ground and includes some excellent war action shorts in which a tank column figures. Gaining wide prominence throughout the land as a crusader, the Nazis finally take Pasha into custody and are about to hang her when partisan followers effect her rescue, living to see the tide turned against the Nazis and recapture of invaded territory.

The English-dubbing job, exceptionally well done, adds much to the worthiness of the import but some of the photography is below par. Performances are generally good, although Vera Maretskaya, playing Pasha, is often quite theatrical. Love interest is carried by Anna Smirnova and Peter Aleinikov, whose jobs are over average. Others include Alexander Violinov, Nikolai Bogoliubov, Irina Fedorova and I. Peltzer, members of the partisan group led by Pasha. *Char.*

Miniature Reviews

"Going My Way" (Par) (Songs). Bing Crosby starrer due for hefty profit and holdovers in regular runs.

"Cover Girl" (Musical; Color) (Col). Rita Hayworth and Gene Kelly in socko filmusical.

"The Hour Before the Dawn" (Par). Familiar tale of Nazi spies in nEgland.

"The Falcon Out West" (RKO). Standard whodunit in Falcon series; strong support for program houses.

"Hat Check Honey" (U) (Musical). Lightweight but okay for dual support.

"Career Girl" (PRC). Frances Langford in weak story with theatrical pretensions; for the lower duals.

"Voodoo Man" (Mono). Programmer in approved thriller style, starring Bela Lugosi.

"Trail of Terror" (PRC). Headed for good response among western devotees.

Going My Way
(SONGS)

Los Angeles, Feb. 26.
Paramount release of Leo McCarey production. Stars Bing Crosby; features Rise Stevens. Directed by McCarey. Screenplay, Frank Butler and Frank Cavett; camera, Lionel Lindon; editor, Leroy Stone; songs, Johnny Burke and James Van Heusen. Tradeshown in L. A. Feb. 25, '44. Running time, 126 MINS.

Father Chuck O'Malley........Bing Crosby
Jenny Linden ....Rise Stevens
Father Fitzgibbon........Barry Fitzgerald
Ted Haines, Jr............James Brown
Ted Haines, Sr.............Gene Lockhart
Carol James...................Jean Heather
Father O'Dowd.............Frank McHugh
Mrs. Carmody...............Eily Malyon
Tony Scaponi..............Stanley Clemens
Tomaso Bozzani..........Fortunio Bonanova
Mrs. Quimp.................Anita Bolster
Herman ....Carl Switzer
Mr. Belknap...................Porter Hall

Bing Crosby gets a tailor-made role in "Going My Way," and with major assistance from Barry Fitzgerald and Rise Stevens, clicks solidly to provide topnotch entertainment for wide audience appeal. Picture will hit hefty biz on all bookings.

The overlong 126 minutes contain many episodes which could be deleted for more compactness. Despite this drawback, however, picture is a warm, human drama studded liberally with bright episodes and excellent characterizations accentuated by fine direction of Leo McCarey. Intimate scenes between Crosby and Fitzgerald dominate throughout, with both providing slick characterizations.

Crosby plays a young priest interested in athletics and music who's assigned as assistant to crusty Fitzgerald in an eastside church saddled with burdensome mortgage that might be foreclosed by grasping Gene Lockhart. Progressive youth and staid oldster clash continually, but Crosby gradually bends Fitzgerald to his way. Crosby gets the tough kids of the neighborhood to organize a choir through smattering of athletics, ballgames and shows, does the usual round of kindly deeds in blithesome manner and eventually sells a song to pay the church mortgage.

Major thread of gaiety runs through the proceedings, and McCarey has liberally sprinkled sparkling individual episodes along the way for cinch audience reaction. Rise Stevens comes on for the second half, introduced as a Metropolitan Opera star and old friend of Crosby when both were interested in music. She sticks around to sing aria from "Carmen" and title song of "Going My Way," and to assist in providing funds to save the church from foreclosure. In addition to scoring with her song presentations, Miss Stevens does well in her acting assignment.

Crosby's song numbers include three new tunes by Johnny Burke and James Van Heusen—"Going My Way," "Would You Like to Swing On a Star" and "Day After Forever." Trio are topgrade and due for wide pop appeal due to cinch recording and airings by the Bing. He also delivers "Ave Maria," "Adeste Fidelis" and "Silent Night" in addition to a lively Irish folksong, "Toora-loora-loora" with boys' choir accompaniment.

Supporting cast is neatly set up for generally fine performances. *Walt.*

Cover Girl

(MUSICAL; COLOR)

Hollywood, March 2.

Columbia release of Arthur Schwartz production; stars Rita Hayworth, Gene Kelly; features Lee Bowman, Phil Silvers, Jinx Falkenburg, Leslie Brooks, Eve Arden, Otto Kruger, Jess Barker, Anita Colby, Curt Bois and Cover Girls. Directed by Charles Vidor. Assistant to the producer, Norman Deming. Screenplay by Virginia Van Upp; adaptation, Marion Parsonnet and Paul Gangelin; story, Erwin Gelsey; songs by Jerome Kern and Ira Gershwin. Camera, Rudolph Mate and Allen M. Davey; editor, Viola Lawrence; asst. director, Oscar Boetticher, Jr.; art, Lionel Banks and Cary Odell; dances, Val Raset, Seymour Felix; musical director, M. W. Stoloff. Previewed at Pantages, March 1, '44. Running time, **105 MINS.**

Rusty Parker	Rita Hayworth
Danny McGuire	Gene Kelly
Noel Wheaton	Lee Bowman
Genius	Phil Silvers
Jinx	Jinx Falkenburg
Maurine Martin	Leslie Brooks
Cornelia Jackson	Eve Arden
John Coudair	Otto Kruger
John Coudair (young man)	Jess Barker
Anita	Anita Colby
Chem	Curt Bois
Joe	Ed Brophy
Tony Pastor	Thurston Hall

Columbia steps out with one of the best packages of gaysome filmusical entertainment in "Cover Girl." Overflowing with all elements for widest pop audience reaction, picture is a standout entry for heavy grosses and holdovers in all runs.

There is strong and effervescent audience appeal in every sector. Rita Hayworth's standout performance is matched by that of Gene Kelly, with his acting, singing and dancing display. The songs by Jerome Kern and Ira Gershwin are fine; ditto the compact story of comedy, drama and romance, dazzling gowns to catch the feminine fans, and solo and duo dances by Miss Hayworth and Kelly that are showstoppers.

Arthur Schwartz, in his initial film producer spot after years of experience with stage musicals, deftly injects surefire showmanship into the picture, neatly blending the talents of the players with an inspired script by Virginia Van Upp, fine and consistently-paced direction by Charles Vidor, and taking fullest advantage of the technical contributions.

Plot is neatly concocted to get over idea of sudden rise to theatrical fame of Miss Hayworth as result of winning a Cover Girl contest. Kelly, operating the modest Brooklyn nightspot where he stages the floorshows, is in love with Miss Hayworth, a dancer. Latter wins the contest to give the room immediate fame with the upper-crust customers from Manhattan. Otto Kruger, responsible for her prominence, had youthful romance with her grandmother when latter was an entertainer 40 years previously at Tony Pastor's, and figures she should be lifted out of the lowly nightspot to a Broadway show. Result is break between the girl and Kelly when latter stubbornly blows off steam. Miss Hayworth joins Broadway revue produced by Lee Bowman, latter eventually proposing marriage. But he's deserted at the altar as she returns to Kelly and helps him resume operation of the night club, which had been closed when she left the show.

Dance sequences spotlighting the terping abilities of both Miss Hayworth and Kelly are expertly staged. Kelly devised his own routines for the picture, and one—a synchronized dance with his inner conscience in a dead-end street—is one of the top performances of its type ever to be screened.

Score by Jerome Kern and Ira Gershwin, comprising seven tunes, is of high calibre. "Make Way for Tomorrow" has a good chance for pop attention.

Charles Vidor hits major league status for his paceful direction of a standout and entertainment-filled filmusical. Virginia Van Upp rates attention for the compact and neatly-blended screenplay. Marion Parsonnet and Paul Gangelin did a good job on the adaptation of Erwin Gelsey's original, and uncredited executive producer Sidney Buchman deserves kudos for assemblage of the talent and general setup. *Walt.*

Hour Before the Dawn

Los Angeles, Feb. 25.

Paramount release of William Dozier production. Stars Franchot Tone and Veronica Lake; features John Sutton and Binnie Barnes. Directed by Frank Tuttle. Screenplay, Michael Hogan; adaptation, Lesser Samuels, from novel by W. Somerset Maugham; camera, John Seitz; editor, Stuart Gilmore. Tradeshown in L. A. Feb. 24, '44. Running time, **74 MINS.**

Jim Hetherton	Franchot Tone
Dora Bruchmann	Veronica Lake
May Hetherton	Binnie Barnes
Roger Hetherton	John Sutton
General Hetherton	Henry Stephenson
Sir Leslie Buchanan	Philip Merivale
Capt. Atterley	Leslie Dennison
Kurt Bruchmann	Nils Asther
Tommy Hetherton	David Leland
Freddy Merritt	Edmond Brlon
Farmer Searle	Donald Stuart
Maid	Viola Moore
Mrs. Parkins	Aminta Dyne
Sam	Harry Cording

Somerset Maugham's tale of Nazi spying and intrigue in England early in the war is tedious and generally uneventful. "The Hour Before the Dawn" is a weak b.o. entry for the duals.

Story develops according to formula. Franchot Tone in his youth acquires aversion to killing, so when the war breaks out, he's a conscientious objector and deferred for farm work. Veronica Lake is governess in his family mansion, and she as Nazi spy marries him at war's outbreak for protection. Yarn spends much footage explaining the grooving of his family into the war effort, it weaves wearisome episodes of Miss Lake working for the enemy, attempts to get Tone to front for the agents in peace campaign and finally sees unmasking of the wife after a German air blitz of the countryside in attempt to knock out a secret airfield. Tone then proceeds to kill his wife and joins the air force for fadeout.

Direction by Frank Tuttle adds nothing. Tone and Miss Lake are lustreless. Henry Stephenson rises slightly above the poor material as best of the supporting cast. *Walt.*

The Falcon Out West

Hollywood, March 3.

RKO release of Maurice Geraghty production. Stars Tom Conway. Directed by William Clemens. Original screenplay by Billy Jones and Morton Grant, based on character created by Michael Arlen; camera, Harry Wild; editor, Gene Milford; dialog director, Donald Dillaway; asst. director, James Casey. Tradeshown in L. A., March 2, '44. Running time, **64 MINS.**

Falcon	Tom Conway
Vanessa	Carole Gallagher
Marion	Barbara Hale
Mrs. Irwin	Joan Barclay
Donovan	Cliff Clark
Bates	Ed Gargan
Colby	Minor Watson
Hayden	Don Douglas
Tex	Lyle Talbot
Dusty	Lee Trent
Red	Perc Launders
Sheriff	Wheaton Chambers
Eagle Feather	Chief Thunderbird

The Falcon continues his avocation of amateur sleuthing in this latest entry of the whodunit series which seems to be a successful entry on the RKO program. Picture will provide good support in the program houses for customers who go for the formula murder mysteries and spotting of the culprit out of a maze of suspects.

Story wastes little time in bumping off the first victim for the Falcon (Tom Conway) to step in and figure out a solution. Murder is committed via rattlesnake venom on a playboy westerner, which calls for quick shift to the open spaces to pick up the clues and other suspects. Conway weaves through the problem in regulation fashion as a gentleman sleuth, coming up with solution at the finish.

There's little extraneous footage in the picture, with consistently-paced direction by William Clemens getting the most from compact script by Billy Jones and Morton Grant. Conway capably handles the sleuthing assignment, with adequate cast comprising Carole Gallagher, Barbara Hale, Joan Barclay, Cliff Clark, Ed Gargan and Minor Watson. *Walt.*

Hat Check Honey

(MUSICAL)

Hollywood, Mach 3.

Universal release of Will Cowan production. Directed by Edward F. Cline. Screenplay, Maurice Leo and Stanley Davis; story, Al Martin; camera, Milton Krasner; editor, Saul Goodkind; dialog director, Phil Brown; special process photography, John P. Fulton; songs, Milton Rosen and Everett Carter. Previewed in studio projection room, March 2, '44. Running time, **66 MINS.**

Susan Brent	Grace McDonald
Dan Briggs, Jr.	Richard Davis
Happy Dan Briggs	Leon Errol
Tim Martel	Walter Catlett
Mona Mallory	Ramsay Ames
David Courtland	Milburn Stone
Alan Dane	Lee Bennett
Mr. Worthington	Russell Hicks
Uniformed Officer	Chester Clute
Jennie	Mary Gordon
Lynn	Emmett Vogan
C. B	Jack Rice

Freddie Slack and His Orchestra
Harry Owens and His Royal Hawaiians
Ted Weems and His Orchestra
Jimmy Cash

"Hat Check Honey" is another in the Universal series of program filmusical dramas and follows the familiar story formula and presentation. With brief running time and despite story fragility, it has sufficient musical interludes and broad comedy strokes to get by as dualer.

Picture programs three bands, but only Freddie Slack's group gets prominence for several tunes. Harry Owens' Royal Hawaiians are shown in a few flashes and some soundtrack footage, while Ted Weems' orch is confined to one number coming out of a coin film machine. Ray Eberle steps into soundtrack as double for Richard Davis in three Milton Rosen-Everett Carter songs along the line.

Leon Errol plays a carny comic teamed with son, Davis. Former tosses the boy out for shot at the bigger time, and youth lands as singer with Slack's band through efforts of newly-acquired sweetheart, hatchecker Grace McDonald. Davis clicks and is picked up with band for picture engagement in Hollywood by film star, Ramsay Ames. Then there's the usual complications when Davis clicks, Miss McDonald and Errol arrive at the studio, and general mixup until boy gets girl, with assistance of dad.

Lightweight story is held together through broad direction by Edward Cline, who takes advantage of the comedics of Errol and Walter Catlett at every turn. Miss McDonald is okay as the girl, while Davis needs experience to handle lead spots. Support includes Miss Ames, Milburn Stone, Russell Hicks, Mary Gordon and Jack Rice. Songs and musical numbers are liberally spotted along the way, but none of the tunes shapes up for attention. *Walt.*

Career Girl

(SONGS)

PRC release of Jack Schwarz production; associate producer, Harry D. Edwards. Stars Frances Langford; features Edward Norris, Iris Adrian, Craig Woods. Directed by Wallace W. Fox. Screenplay, Sam Neuman from original by Dave Silverstein and Stanley Rauh; songs, Morey Amsterdam, Tony Romano, Sam Neuman, Michael Breen; editor, Robert Crandall; camera, Gustave Peterson. At Brooklyn Strand, dual, week March 2, '44. Running time, **67 MINS.**

Joan	Frances Langford
Steve	Edward Norris
Glenda	Iris Adrian
James	Craig Woods
Thelma	Linda Brent
Pop	Alec Craig
Sue	Ariel Heath
Ann	Lorraine Krueger
Polly	Renee White
Janie	Gladys Blake
Felix Black	Charles Judels
Louis Horton	Charles Williams

A weak and obvious distillation of George S. Kaufman's and Edna Ferber's "Stage Door," "Career Girl" must lean heavily on Frances Langford's radio rep for b.o. action. It's a mild dualer.

Story deals with a Kansas City hopeful (Miss Langford) who winds up in New York and the inevitable theatrical boarding house. After meeting with the usual Broadway reverses, she manages to wind up as singing star of a new revue that, presumably, is going to be a wow. Audience never knows because film comes to an abrupt end while show is still in rehearsal.

Picture is replete with anachronisms and trite phrases ("there's a broken heart for every light on Broadway"), and camera work emerges as heavy-handed as the shooting script. Miss Langford, who's out-numbered all the way, never rises story's obstacles, which include four songs of no particular distinction. Supporting cast is poor. *Jona.*

Voodoo Man

Monogram release of Sam Katzman-Jack Dietz production. Stars Bela Lugosi, John Carradine and George Zucco; features Michael Ames, Wanda McKay and Ellen Hall. Directed by William Beaudine. Screenplay, Robert Charles; editor, Carl Pierson; camera, Marcel Le Picard. At New York theatre, N. Y., week of March 1, '44, dual. Running time, **62 MINS.**

Dr. Marlowe	Bela Lugosi
Job	John Carradine
Nicrolas	George Zucco
Ralph	Michael Ames
Betty	Wanda McKay
Mrs. Marlowe	Ellen Hall
Sally	Louise Currie
Sheriff	Henry Hall
Deputy	Dan White
Grego	Pat McKee
Girl	Terry Walker
Zombies	Ethelreda Leopold, Claire James, Dorothy Bailer

"Voodoo Man" is negligible as a chiller.

Story finds Bela Lugosi, with John Carradine and George Zucco as his assistants, kidnaping young girls and reducing them to zombie state in an effort to restore his spellbound wife to normalcy. But they are caught when they kidnap one girl too many.

Lugosi, as the mad physician; Zucco, dressed up in robe and feathers, and Carradine, stalking around idiotically, bending at his master's will, try their best with the material at hand. Rest of the cast gives so-so performances.

Direction by William Beaudine is in the approved thriller-chiller vein. *Sten.*

Heaven Is Round Corner

(BRITISH-MADE)

(With Songs)

London, Feb. 16.

Anglo-American Film Corp. release of British National production. Stars Will Fyffe, Leni Lynn. Directed by Maclean Rogers. Screenplay by Austin Melford from story by A. Hillarius, P. Knepler; music by Kennedy Russell; lyrics by Desmond O'Connor; camera, James Wilson, Arthur Grant.

At Cambridge theatre, London, Feb. 15. Running time, **105 MINS.**

Joan Sedley....................Leni Lynn
Dougal....................Will Fyffe
Robert Sedley....................Leslie Perrins
Musette....................Magda Kun
Donald McKay....................Peter Glenville
Dorothy Trevor....................Barbara Waring
Mrs. Trevor....................Barbara Couper
John Cardew....................Austin Trevor
Mrs. Harcourt....................Toni Edgar Bruce

Will Fyffe admirers won't believe their eyes if and when they see this opus. Fyffe is on the screen most of the picture, yet his role, that of a colorless farmhand, could have been safely left to a bit player. Pic for lower half of duals, and for British audiences only.

Co-starred with Fyffe is Leni Lynn, a chubby-faced youngster who vaguely calls to mind Clara Bow in one of her rare sedate moments. Story is built around her singing. There are the usual operatic arias for her benefit, and for the most part she gets away with them well enough to make reasonable her singing teacher's raves. Hit number is "Heaven Is Round the Corner," which she sings to welcome the dawn on a Paris roof top when her sweetheart, for no reason at all, asks her to warble to him.

Production is at least worthy of the trite script. Especially well handled and mounted are sequences of the British Embassy in Paris, climaxing with an effective ballroom scene on the eve of Britain's declaration of war.

The featured players, including Austin Trevor, Magda Kun, Peter Glenville, Barbara Waring, Leslie Perrins and Barbara Couper are consistently good. All have greater opportunities to score than Fyffe.

Trail of Terror

(SONGS)

Producers Releasing Corp. release of Alfred Stern-Arthur Alexander production. Stars Dave (Tex) O'Brien and Jim Newill; features Guy Wilkerson, Patricia Knox and Jack Ingram. Directed by Oliver Drake. Screenplay by Drake. Songs, Tex O'Brien and Jim Newill; music director, Lee Zahler; editor, Charles Henkel, Jr.; camera, Ira Morgan. At New York theatre, N. Y., week of March 1, '44. Running time, **63 MINS.**

Tex Wyatt / Curly Wyatt ....Dave (Tex) O'Brien
Jim Steele....................Jim Newill
Panhandle Perkins....................Guy Wilkerson
Belle Blaine....................Patricia Knox
Nevada Simmons....................Jack Ingram
Hank....................I. Stanford Jolley
Monte....................Bud Buster
Sam....................Ken Duncan
Joe....................Frank Ellis
Capt. Curtis....................Robert Hill

This western, in a slightly higher plane than the average cut-and-dried hoss opera, should receive a better-than-average reception from audiences who go for this type of dual film.

Curly Wyatt's early death gives his Texas Ranger twin brother, Tex, an opportunity to join the gang of which the errant Curly was a member. Tex is doing alright with the outlaws, even with Curly's girl friend, until his pals, Jim and Panhandle, arouse the gang's suspicions that something is wrong. Follows the showdown, with the Rangers nabbing the outlaws and getting back the money which the latter had been stealing from stagecoaches.

Dave (Tex) O'Brien, singing Jim Newill and Guy Wilkerson, as the Texas Rangers, give forthright characterizations. Patricia Knox, Jack Ingram, I. Stanford Jolley and Bud Buster are among the notable supporting players.

Three songs written by Newill and O'Brien are fairly good. Oliver Drake, who wrote and directed, kept the action moving, cutting corners neatly. *Sten.*

Tunisian Victory

The joint British-American military operation that emerged as the Allied North African victory has resulted, finally, in the impending release of the campaign's actual battle pictures under joint auspices of the British and United States governments. "Tunisian Victory" is really a must-see.

Somewhat anti-climatic, perhaps, when one considers the headlines that have long since been made on the war fronts, "Tunisian Victory," nevertheless, is a compelling documentary whose sweep and scope should find it an advantageous booking for most exhibitors. It'll be a question, perhaps, of first getting the customers into the theatres, in view of the film's datedness; but, once inside, the patrons will be amply intrigued by the pictures themselves.

Specifically, this is a film produced by the British Army Film Unit and the U. S. Army Signal Corps, and edited in Hollywood by Lt. Col. Hugh Stewart, of the British Army, and Lt. Col. Frank Capra, of the United States Army. It is a pooling of footage shot independently by both British and American Army cameramen. Dubbed-in voices of Bernard Miles (of "In This We Serve") and Lt. Burgess Meredith, both of whom represent, respectively, a British tommy and an American doughboy, give the pic a considerable earthiness. And with Capt. Anthony Veiller, former Hollywood scripter, handling the writing of the Yank commentary, and J. L. Hodson, British author and war correspondent, doing likewise with the British narration, the finished product is something of intense interest through practically all of its 75 minutes.

Most of the pic contains battle scenes whose proximity to the camera certainly bears out the information that four cameramen were killed and several others wounded during the lensing. Approximately 50 photographers, all of whom were armed equally with both photographic and firearm equipment, participated in getting the original 300,000 feet of film.

"Tunisian Victory" tells the photographic story of the entire North African campaign, from the initial landings at Casablanca, Oran and Algiers by the British and Americans, to Tunis and Bizerte capitulation. It is replete with maps and sotto voce explanations of the British-American plan of operation—a plan described simply by its coded title of "acrobat." It's military strategics reduced to terms of layman acceptance.

There are close-to-the-front scenes of figures prominently identified with the campaign . . . Eisenhower, Montgomery, Clark, Spaatz and Tedder, among others, along with Rommel and Kesselring, the latter being among the captured German films.

Some of the footage closely resembles pix long since shown in the newsreels, but these are few and fail to dissipate the value of the remainder.

Official government groups releasing "Tunisian Victory" are the British Ministry of Information, for the Empire, and the Office of War Information, for the U. S. Metro, specifically, is handling the American distribution. *Kahn.*

Miniature Reviews

"The White Cliffs of Dover" (M-G). A top grosser with a fine cast headed by Irene Dunne and Alan Marshal.

"Four Jills in a Jeep" (Musical) (20th). Moderately pleasing.

"Shine On Harvest Moon" (Musical) (WB). Cinematic biog of Nora Bayes; nominal biz for regular runs.

"Buffalo Bill" (20th). Joel McCrea, Maureen O'Hara, in super western on Bill Cody's career; stalwart b.o. in most spots.

"Hi Good-Looking" (U) (Songs). Okay comedy-drama for duals.

"Sailor's Holiday" (Col). Arthur Lake in an at-times funny dualer.

"California Joe" (Rep). Well-paced dual westerner with historical background.

White Cliffs of Dover

Metro-Goldwyn-Mayer release of Sidney Franklin production. Stars Irene Dunne and Alan Marshall; features Frank Morgan, Roddy McDowall, Van Johnson, C. Albrey Smith, Dame May Whitty, Gladys Cooper, Peter Lawford. Directed by Clarence Brown. Based on poem, "The White Cliffs," by Alice Duer Miller, with additional poetry by Robert Nathan; adaptation, Claudine West, Jan Lustig and George Froeschel. Previewed in N. Y., March 8, '44. Running time, **126 MINS.**

Susan Ashwood....................Irene Dunne
Sir John Ashwood....................Alan Marshall
Hiram Porter Dunn....................Frank Morgan
John Ashwood II (boy)....................Roddy McDowall
Sam Bennett....................Van Johnson
Colonel....................C. Aubrey Smith
Nanny....................Dame May Whitty
Lady Jean Ashwood....................Gladys Cooper
John (young man)....................Peter Lawford
Reggie....................John Warburton
Rosamund....................Jill Esmond
Gwennie....................Brenda Forbes
Mrs. Bland....................Norma Varden

A poignant love story commingled with the tragedies that come from war. "The White Cliffs of Dover" is the saga of an American girl who went to England for a vacation in 1914, fell in love with a title, learned to love Britain and remained there to go through World War I and see the coming of the second. Boxoffice potentialities being great, this one will command top rentals and extended dating. It's superlative entertainment and in England, incidentally, should be an outstanding grosser as it will be on this side.

Based on the Alice Duer Miller poem, "The White Cliffs," the picture is, among other things, a powerful but intelligent approach to a better understanding between the English and the Yanks.

Strongly a woman's picture but not singularly for them only, picture is much more a distillate of romantic elements than it is of war. Actual war scenes are held to a minimum.

As the story opens, Irene Dunne, a Red Cross supervisor in an English Army hospital, is awaiting the arrival of casualties from what ostensibly was the Dieppe raid. At her desk, prepared for a heavy load of injured soldiers, she begins to muse about the white cliffs and the first time she saw them as a young girl on her arrival in England back in '14.

From this, the action cuts back to that time and carries Miss Dunne through her marriage to Sir John Ashwood (Alan Marshall), her grief over his loss in the first World War, and finally to the second which claims their son.

At the end, it is Miss Dunne's son who's among the casualties brought to the hospital, while outside American and English soldiers are on the march, with bands playing, same as occurred in World War I when Miss Dunne, her baby boy in arms, joyfully cheered the arrival of Yanks in Dieppe when the strains of "Over There" added to the thrill that she was an American.

Miss Dunne gives an excellent performance, as does Alan Marshall, playing her husband, while Roddy McDowall stands out sharply as their son. Peter Lawford plays the boy when it comes time to enter the service. For pungent comedy relief there are Frank Morgan, C. Aubrey Smith and to a lesser extent Dame May Whitty. Van Johnson, young American in love with Miss Dunne, does not get much footage but performs ably, as do Gladys Cooper, John Warburton and others.

Sidney Franklin's production background and impressive settings give the picture a stable framework, while Clarence Brown's direction is of the most competent order. *Char.*

Four Jills in a Jeep

(MUSICAL)

Twentieth Century-Fox release of Irving Starr production. Features Kay Francis, Carole Landis, Martha Raye, Mitzi Mayfair, Jimmy Dorsey orchestra, John Harvey, Phil Silvers, Dick Haymes, Alice Faye, Betty Grable, Carmen Miranda, George Jessel, Lester Matthews, Glen Langan and Paul Harvey. Directed by William A. Seiter. Story, Froma Sand and Fred Niblo, Jr.; adaptation, Robert Ellis, Helen Logan and Snag Werris; songs, Jimmy McHugh and Harold Adamson; editor, Ray Curtiss; camera, Peverell Marley and Fred Sersen. Previewed in N. Y., March 9, '44. Running time, **89 MINS.**

Kay Francis....................Herself
Carole Landis....................Herself
Martha Raye....................Herself
Mitzi Mayfair....................Herself
Jimmy Dorsey Orchestra....................Themselves
Ted Warren....................John Harvey
Eddie....................Phil Silvers
Lieut. Dick Ryan....................Dick Haymes
Alice Faye....................Herself
Betty Grable....................Herself
Carmen Miranda....................Herself
George Jessel....................Himself
Captain Lloyd....................Lester Matthews
Captain Stewart....................Glen Langan
General....................Paul Harvey
Colonel Hartley....................Miles Mander
Lady Carlton-Smith....................Winifred Harris
Nurse Captain....................Mary Servoss
Soldier....................B. S. Pully

The USO tour made by Kay Francis, Carole Landis, Martha Raye and Mitzi Mayfair, which took them first to England and thence into North Africa, provided the inspiration for this one. While pleasing and diverting, plus having good pace, picture is far from socko and may not be relied upon to do outstanding business. However, the exploitation boys have plenty to work with, since the "Four Jills" of the title afford opportunities. Also, there are plenty of names as an aid.

"Four Jills in a Jeep" records some of the girls' experiences away from fire, and under it, too, but mainly dwells upon the laughter and entertainment the Hollywood quartet brought to the fighting fronts. In addition to the top foursome around whom the film is built, there are Alice Faye, Betty Grable, Carmen Miranda, Dick Haymes, Phil Silvers and George Jessel for selling assistance, plus the Jimmy Dorsey band, which does a swing number effectively and backgrounds in other spots for specialties.

There isn't much story to "Four Jills" except for charting the movements of the Francis-Landis-Raye-Mayfair troupe and the love interest tacked on principally so far as Miss Landis and Miss Mayfair are concerned. Former is paired with Dick Haymes, while Miss Mayfair ultimately lands John Harvey. Miss Raye and Silvers strike a similar chord. Speaking of the story, Carole Landis authored a "Four Jills" series in the Satevepost (which is additionally good exploitation, incidentally), but the screen play is not of her doing.

Numerous songs intersperse the action, including old and new. Crooner Haymes, who is making his first film appearance—and screening acceptably, too—sings three new Jimmy McHugh - Harold Adamson numbers, "How Blue the Night," "You Send Me" and "How Many

Times Do I Have to Tell You." Last-mentioned is the best of the three, while the other two listen agreeably. Another new one, "Crazy Me," sold well by Miss Landis, lands well on the ears.

Old songs include "Cuddle Up a Little Closer," rendered by Miss Grable: "You'll Never Know," sung by Miss Faye; Carmen Miranda's "Ay, Ay, Ay," with a Latin string group backing, and Miss Raye's old favorite, "Mr. Paganini," with the clowning thrown in. The Grable-Faye-Miranda numbers are cut into the picture through broadcasts, with Jessel acting as m.c. for one that emanates from Hollywood and is tuned in at an army base in England. Miss Mayfair does two tap routines that click as well as some jitterbugging with soldiers. Entertainment halls at Army camps and a home in London where a Red Cross benefit is held form the background for the numbers done on the other side.

Light comedy is supplied mainly by Silvers and Miss Raye. Former, as a sergeant driving a jeep and assigned to transport the four USO entertainers, does an exceedingly good job and wrings as many laughs from his part as possible. Miss Francis acts as chaperone for the other three girls, all turning in nice jobs. John Harvey acquits himself acceptably, as do lessers like Lester Matthews, Glen Langan and Paul Harvey.

Char.

Shine On Harvest Moon
(SONGS; PART COLOR)

Los Angeles, March 10.

Warner Bros. release of William Jacobs production. Stars Ann Sheridan, Dennis Morgan, Jack Carson, Irene Manning; features S. Z. Sakall, Marie Wilson, Robert Shayne. Directed by David Butler. Screenplay, Sam Hellman, Richard Weil, Francis Swann and James Kern; original by Weil; camera, Arthur Edeson; editor, Irene Morra; songs, M. K. Jerome and Kim Gannon; Cliff Friend and Charlie Tobias; music director, Leo F. Forbstein. Tradeshown in L. A. March 9, '44. Running time, 111 MINS.

Nora Bayes	Ann Sheridan
Jack Norworth	Dennis Morgan
The Great Georgetti	Jack Carson
Blanche Mallory	Irene Manning
Poppa Karl	S. Z. Sakall
Margie	Marie Wilson
Dan Costello	Robert Shayne
Police Sergeant	Bob Murphy
Dance Team	The Four Step Bros.
Dance Team	The Ashburns
Tim Donovan	William Davidson
A Drunk	Will Stanton
William Fowler	James Bush
Harry Miller	Joseph Crehan
Soubrette	Betty Bryson
Dancer	Don Kramer
Dancer	George Rogers
Juggler	Harry Chas. Johnson
Acrobat	Walter Pietilla

Warners started out to make this a cinematic life story of Nora Bayes; what's on the screen is something else again. To those vets of show biz with memories, the presentation does not jibe with historical facts, but the customers will accept "Shine On Harvest Moon" as just another backstage drama, with songs, for moderate attention. Picture needs full heft of Ann Sheridan and Dennis Morgan.

Footage, hitting 111 minutes, is overboard. Result is inclusion of too many incidental episodes which, if eliminated, would have speeded tempo considerably. However, there are a number of individually interesting sequences.

Aside from recalling memories of backstage and pop songs of the 1910 period—including a number of tunes popularized by the Nora Bayes-Jack Norworth team—film drops into regulation backstage formula. In addition to display of old pop tunes—several written and introduced by Bayes and Norworth—("Apple Blossom Time in Normandy," "Every Little Movement," "What's the Matter With Father?" "Pretty Baby," and "Harvest Moon"), picture presents two new numbers by M. K. Jerome and Kim Gannon, "I Go for You" and "So Dumb But So Beautiful," and "Time Waits for No One," by Cliff Friend and Charlie Tobias. Latter is best candidate for radio plugs, with "I Go for You" a good tune for novelty band arrangements.

Miss Sheridan displays a good soundtrack singing "voice" for solos and harmonies with Morgan. Latter smacks over his vocal assignments in fine style, as does Miss Manning with four tunes. Jack Carson and Marie Wilson team for presentation of the comedy number, "So Dumb But So Beautiful."

Morgan and Miss Sheridan excellently team to maintain interest in their characterizations, and pair gets major support from Miss Manning, Carson, and Miss Wilson. S. Z. Sakall, Robert Shayne, William Davidson, and Bob Murphy (formerly of vaude) are briefly seen in support.

After black and white photography till final 10 minutes, picture swings into Technicolor for "Follies" production number with dancing ensemble and chorus girls, and the Four Step Brothers are on for a few minutes to perform a scarecrow dance. Setting gives opportunity for extended and visual presentation by Morgan and Miss Sheridan of "Harvest Moon." Direction by David Butler is standard, although he gets plenty out of the cast members despite script deficiencies.

Walt.

Buffalo Bill
(COLOR)

20th-Fox release of Harry A. Sherman production. Stars Joel McCrea, Maureen O'Hara, Linda Darnell; features Thomas Mitchell, Edgar Buchanan, Anthony Quinn. Directed by William A. Wellman. Screenplay, Aeneas MacKenzie, Clements Ripley, Cecile Kramer; based on story by Frank Winch; camera, Leon Shamroy; Technicolor director, Natalie Kalmus; editor, James B. Clark. Tradeshown in N. Y., March 10, '44. Running time, 90 MINS.

Buffalo Bill	Joel McCrea
Louisa Cody	Maureen O'Hara
Dawn Starlight	Linda Darnell
Ned Buntline	Thomas Mitchell
Sergeant Chips	Edgar Buchanan
Yellow Hand	Anthony Quinn
Senator Frederici	Moroni Olsen
Murdo Carvell	Frank Fenton
General Blazier	Matt Briggs
Mr. Vandervere	George Lessey
Sherman	Frank Orth
Trooper Clancy	George Chandler
Tall Bull	Chief Many Treaties
Medicine Man	Nick Thompson
Crazy Horse	Chief Tundercloud
Theodore Roosevelt	Sidney Blackmer
Doctor	Edwin Stanley
President Hayes	John Dilson
Queen Victoria	Evelyn Beresford
Barber	William Haade
Bellboy	Merrill Rodin
Old Indian Woman	Talzumbie Dupea

Primarily escapist fare, "Buffalo Bill" is a super-western and often a tear-jerker. Filming it in color against colorful outdoor panorama, Harry A. Sherman has made it a magnificent production, one calculated to ring up strong grosses in most keys. Film has innumerable angles for bally. Marquee lure is plenty evident with Joel McCrea, Maureen O'Hara, Linda Darnell and Thomas Mitchell.

Those familiar with the story of William F. Cody may wonder why this cinema version did not lay more stress on his career as a showman and less on his romance and wedded life. But few residents of Cody, Wyo., Council Bluffs or the Platte river country will find fault with the sweep of the redskin-white man struggle done so skillfully by Director William A. Wellman.

Head-on battle between U. S. cavalry and Cheyenne tribe at War Bonnet Gorge is the story's focal point, with Buffalo Bill, famed scout and friend of the Indian, becoming the yarn's hero in man-to-man combat with his former redskin pal, thereby enabling the remainder of cavalry troop to arrive in time to defeat the Indians. For this, Buffalo Bill is awarded the Congressional Medal of Honor, after which he goes east, to be greeted first as a fabled hero and then discredited because he antagonizes a railroad magnate. He finally lands a job as a sharpshooter in a N. Y. museum and ultimately becomes world-famous with his wild-west show.

Outstanding and particularly unusual in such an outdoor opus is the sound recording. Wellman has directed evenly for dramatic values. However, the humorous angle need not have been so neglected. Leon Shamroy's cameraing is topflight, while Natalie Kalmus deserves bends for her tinting.

Joel McCrea makes a realistic Buffalo Bill. Maureen O'Hara, as the daughter of a senator who goes west to push through a railroad line, and later weds McCrea, is satisfying. Linda Darnell, the Indian schoolteacher who loves Cody, has too little to do but does that little with charm. Thomas Mitchell is the eastern newspaperman who authors books about Buffalo Bill's fame in the west and acts as his promoter when he visits the east. Per usual, a shipshape characterization.

Sergeant Chips is played by Edgar Buchanan. Few funny lines are tossed his way as the sole humorous character in the piece. Anthony Quinn, as the young Indian chief, plays the role to the hilt. Okay support is headed by Moroni Olsen, George Lessey and Matt Briggs. Merrill Rodin, a youngster, has a small bit that registers solidly.

Wear.

Hi Good-Lookin'
(SONGS)

Hollywood, March 10.

Universal release of Frank Gross production. Directed by Edward Lilley. Screenplay, Paul Gerard Smith, Bradford Ropes and Eugene Conrad. Story, Smith Camera, Jerome Ash; editor, Edgar Zane. Previewed in projection room, March 9, '44. Running time, 60 MINS.

Kelly Clark	Harriet Hilliard
Dynamo Carson	Eddie Quillan
King Castle	Kirby Grant
Peggy	Betty Kean
Archie	Roscoe Karns
Phyllis	Vivian Austin
Mrs. Hardacre	Marjorie Gateson
Joe Smedley	Fuzzy Knight
Bill Eaton	Milburn Stone
Gib Dickson	Frank Fenton
Homer Hardacre	Robert Emmett Keane

Ozzie Nelson and His Orchestra
Jack Teagarden and His Orchestra
Delta Rhythm Boys
Tip, Tap and Toe

"Hi Good-Lookin'" is a diverting programmer that will adequately fill in as supporter on duals. In addition to passable plot there's a dozen song and orch numbers.

Kirby Grant, newcomer from radio, shows screen possibilities in first camera appearance. He has pleasant personality, displays ease in front of the camera and sings several songs in good style. Harriet Hilliard is okay lead, teamed with Grant for harmonizing of four songs; while Eddie Quillan, Betty Kean and Fuzzy Knight handle the comedy. Ozzie Nelson's orchestra is in for fast-tempoed renditions, and Jack Teagarden's group makes one brief appearance. Delta Rhythm Boys click with fine arrangement of "Paper Doll," and Tip, Tap and Toe deliver one dance turn.

Story unfolds around radio biz in Hollywood. Miss Hilliard arrives from the midwest for singing pitch, falls for radio vocalist Grant and uses latter in click tryout on small station. On account of bigtime commitment, he's anonymous, but team-up proves success when pair are grabbed as "replacement" for Grant when latter's option is not lifted by sponsor.

Picture rolls along at a consistently fast pace to provide diverting amusement for the customers, with direction by Edward Lilley responsible for the zestful tempo.

Walt.

Sailor's Holiday

Columbia release of Wallace MacDonald production. Stars Arthur Lake; features Jane Lawrence, Bob Haymes, Shelley Winters and Lewis Wilson. Directed by William Berke. Screenplay, Manny Seff; music director, M. W. Stoloff; editor, Paul Borofsky; camera, Burnett Guffey. At Brooklyn Strand, week of March 9, '44. Running time, 60 MINS.

Marble Head Tomkins	Arthur Lake
Clementine Brown	Jane Lawrence
Bill Hayes	Bob Haymes
Gloria Flynn	Shelley Winter
Iron Man Collins	Lewis Wilson
Ferd Baxter	Edmund MacDonald
Studio Guide	Pat O'Malley
Director	Herbert Rawlinson
Assistant Director	Buddy Yarus
Maid	Vi Athens
Ronald Blair	George Ford

"Sailor's Holiday" is a sometimes humorous dualler.

Thread of a plot deals with two engagements that are broken because each party has fallen in love with someone else. But not before a tour of a film studio, Columbia, is made showing several stars in person and pictures being produced, followed by a fire, a fight and a love affair.

Arthur Lake, Bob Haymes and Lewis Wilson, as merchant mariners on the loose in Los Angeles; Jane Lawrence, who went to the Coast from the Broadway cast of "Oklahoma," and Shelley Winters, from the Broadway "Rosalinda," breeze through in accepted slapstick style.

Sten.

California Joe

Republic release of Eddy White production. Stars Don "Red" Barry; features Wally Vernon, Helen Talbot, Twinkle Watts, Brian O'Hara, Terry Frost. Directed by Spencer Bennet. Screenplay, Norman S. Hall; editor, Harry Keller; camera, Ernest Miller. At New York theatre, N. Y., week of March 7, '44. Running time, 55 MINS.

Lt. Joe Weldon	Don "Red" Barry
Tumbleweed Smith	Wally Vernon
Judith Cartaret	Helen Talbot
Twinkle	Twinkle Watts
Delancey Cartaret	Brian O'Hara
Melbourne Tommy Atkinson	Terry Frost
Col. Burgess	Edward Earle
Breck Colton	Leroy Mason
Ashley	Charles King
Harper	Pierce Lyden
Dave	Edmund Cobb
Ned Potter	Karl Hackett
Bradshaw	Robert Kortman
Gov. Glynn	Edward Keane

Well-paced hoss opera with a Civil War background, "California Joe" won't let the westerner clientele down and adequately fills the bill as a supporting dualer.

Story deals with a Union cavalry lieutenant whose mission is to thwart a group of rebel sympathizers. Switch in the plot is that the Southerners are themselves being double-crossed by their leader, who wants to set up a personal empire. Don Barry, as the Union officer in mufti, is rough, tough and equal to all occasions, while Helen Talbot, as a southern gal who turns against the seekers of personal glory, provides the other half of the romantic interest. Wally Vernon is the comic relief, while the appearance of Twinkle Watts, child iceskating star, on a pony instead of gliders seems somewhat incongruous and a waste of talent.

Turo.

Miniature Reviews

"**It Happened Tomorrow**" (UA). Escapist comedy-drama; good audience reaction.

"**Up In Mabel's Room**" (UA). Should fare well in duals.

"**Ladies Courageous**" (U). Cinema dramatics of femme ferry pilots needs exploitation hypo to catch nominal biz.

"**The Lady and the Monster**" (Rep). More clinical research than horror in so-so meller. Needs plenty of exploitation.

"**The Memphis Belle**" (WAC-Par). Fine documentary.

"**Westward Bound**" (Mono). Okay dual stagecoacher featuring Ken Maynard, Hoot Gibson and Bob Steele.

"**Heroes Are Made**" (Artkino). Dramatic, Soviet-made portrayal of a youthful revolutionary's development; moderate b.o.

It Happened Tomorrow

Hollywood, March 14.

United Artists release of Arnold Pressburger production. Stars Dick Powell, Linda Darnell and Jack Oakie. Directed by Rene Clair. Screenplay and adaptation, Dudley Nichols and Rene Clair; based on originals by Lord Dunseny, Hugh Wedlock and Howard Snyder, and ideas of Lewis R. Foster; added dialog, Mclene Fraenkel; camera, Archie Stout; editor, Fred Pressburger. Previewed at Egyptian, March 17, '44. Running time, 84 MINS.

Larry Stevens	Dick Powell
Sylvia	Linda Darnell
Cigolini	Jack Oakie
Inspector Mulrooney	Edgar Kennedy
Pop Benson	John Philliber
Jakw Schomberg	Edward Brophy
Mr. Gordon	George Cleveland
Mr. Bernstein	Sig Rurnon
Shep	Paul Guilfoyle
Bob	George Chandler
Jim	Eddie Acuff
Nurse	Marion Martin
Reporter	Jack Gardner
Sweeney	Eddie Cole
Mulcahey	Robert Hormans
Mrs. Keever	Emma Dunn

"It Happened Tomorrow" poses a novel premise on which to spin a comedy-drama—what happens when a cub reporter gets a copy of tomorrow's newspaper. Screen results provide diverting escapist entertainment for all audiences, with many sparkling moments and episodes along the line. Picture will catch nominal billtopping dates in the first runs, but best spot is bill-sharing with film of similar rating.

Although there are numerous broadly sketched sequences aimed for laugh reaction, picture carries undercurrent of Continental directing technique of Rene Clair. The welding is more than passably successful, but main credit for picture's status can be handed to script by Clair and Dudley Nichols; it picks up every chance for a chuckle or laugh in both dialog and situation.

Powell, cub on the sheet, is befriended by the rag's veteran librarian who, after death, hands the youth copies of the next day's paper for three successive days. First day, he's on hand to witness a holdup he's anticipated, on second he expects capture at a bank; he figures quick cleanup at races for third day by getting advance gander at race results, but the third sheet also headlines his death in a hotel lobby.

Interweaved is his meeting and quick romance with Linda Darnell, medium and niece of mindreader Jack Oakie. Complications result in Oakie insisting on shotgun marriage route; trio head for the race track to parlay five straight winners, but are robbed en route home. Powell tries to duck the inevitable prediction of the newspaper yarn, but inadvertently winds up in the hotel lobby. But the victim of shooting is the holdup gent, who lifted his wallet, this breaking the hex.

Powell lightly handles the reporter spot to good effect; Miss Darnell is okay as the girl, while Oakie gives out with broad comedy with blustering characterizations. Edgar Kennedy is a bewildered police inspector. Others in brief supporting spots are well cast.

Three-minute prolog displays 50th wedding anniversary of Powell and Darnell for flashback unfolding of the strange tale, and gives audience inkling of final outcome for better reaction. Photography by Archie Stout is excellent throughout. *Walt.*

Up in Mabel's Room

United Artists release of Edward Small production. Features Marjorie Reynolds, Dennis O'Keefe, Gail Patrick, Mischa Auer, Charlotte Greenwood. Directed by Allan Dwan. Screen adaptation, Tom Reed; based on stage play by Otto Harbach and Wilson Collison; camera, Charles Lawton; editor, Grant Whytock. Previewed at Loew's Sheridan theatre, New York, March 20, '44. Running time, 76 MINS.

Geraldine Ainsworth	Marjorie Reynolds
Gary Ainsworth	Dennis O'Keefe
Mabel Essington	Gail Patrick
Boris	Mischa Auer
Martha	Charlotte Greenwood
Arthur Weldon	Lee Bowman
Jimmy Larchmont	John Hubbard
Alicia Larchmont	Binnie Barnes
Priscilla	Janet Lambert
Johnny	Fred Kohler, Jr.
Justice of the Peace	Harry Hayden

"Up in Mabel's Room," conventional bedroom farce of a pattern which was much in vogue in the 1920s and earlier, should hold up pretty well in the neighborhoods as the top feature and fill in satisfactorily on dual bills in first-run situations, exclusive of de luxers.

Some 17 years have elapsed since the Otto Harbach-Wilson Collison play was produced and, of course, much of the dialog, as well as situations and other comedy business are rather dated and familiar. Despite the obvious formula, where punches are telegraphed way ahead of developments and minimize elements of surprise and suspense, it appears likely to fare moderately well.

Some of the timeworn gagging and other tepid material still retains potency and will ring up a substantial laugh score. In addition it's a commercial title, and while the cast holds no outstanding names, there are several who are exploitable.

Yarn is about a bespectacled, newly-wedded Caspar Milquetoast, played by Dennis O'Keefe, who in a pre-marital moment of weakness bestowed an autographed slip upon a girl (Gail Patrick) to whom his business partner (Lee Bowman) is to be married.

O'Keefe's young wife (Marjorie Reynolds) suspects him of more serious indiscretions and one of those mixups which defeat all attempts at a solution until the last moment, further adds to the confusion during a weekend party.

Much of the comedy revolves about the double entendre relating to the object which O'Keefe is supposed to have slipped the "other woman" in Mexico. Series of compromising situations, in which two gals are involved, serves as basis for climaxers.

O'Keefe registers favorably in his comedy interpretation, Miss Reynolds photographs interestingly as the petulant wife, and Mischa Auer plays the waiter, whose mission it is to recover the incriminating lingerie, for laughs. Charlotte Greenwood is okay in a subordinate role. *Mori.*

Ladies Courageous

Hollywood, March 16.

Universal release of Walter Wanger production. Stars Loretta Young and Geraldine Fitzgerald. Directed by John Rawlins. Story and screenplay by Norman Reilly Raine and Doris Gilbert; suggested by book, "Looking for Trouble," by Virginia Spencer Cowles; camera, Hal Mohr; editor, Phillip

Cahn; dialog director, Harold Tarshin; asst. director, William Tummel; special photog., John P. Fulton. Previewed at Pantages March 15, '44. Running time, 95 MINS.

Roberta Harper	Loretta Young
Vinnie Alford	Geraldine Fitzgerald
Nadine	Diana Barrymore
Gerry Vail	Anne Gwynne
Wilhelmina	Evelyn Anhern
Tommy Harper	Phillip Terry
Frank Garrison	David Bruce
Jill	Lois Collier
Mary Frances	June Vincent
Brig. General Wade	Samuel S. Hinds
Colonel Brenman	Richard Fraser
Snapper	Frank Jenks
Bee Jay	Janet Shaw
Alex Anderson	Kane Richardson

Exploits of the WAFS (Women's Auxiliary Ferrying Squadron) provides basis for this over-theatricalized drama of the early femme ferry pilots who argued and pouted to be taken into regular Army service. Wandering, and at times confusing, continuity fails to generate much punch for audience attention, and picture will have to depend on heavy exploitation to carry through regular runs for more than nominal biz.

Intermingled among the serious air queens are a few who allow personal emotions and jealousies to interfere with their work—and to dull the cinema accomplishments of the entire group. Over-dialoged script hops aimlessly between girls' quarters at the airfield, takeoffs and landings, and several flashbacks to give onlookers an idea of previous events that projected several of the girls into the service. In continually slipping off the direct beam, picture unrolls at an uneven and yawning pace.

Loretta Young is the serious executive officer of the original two dozen WAFS, determined that the girls who ferry ships overseas should get recognition from Army brasshats. Her main job is to keep her charges in line and their minds on responsibilities at hand. Geraldine Fitzgerald is her publicity-seeking sister who nearly washes out the entire group after cracking up a plane. Aside from this pair, the other girls wander in and out of the proceedings for brief and extended sequences of minor importance. Frank Jenks provides snatches of broad comedy, while Richard Fraser is commanding officer of the flying field. Phillip Terry, David Bruce and Kane Richmond are each in a few shots for inconsequential romantic tieups.

Picture has been given adequate production mounting around the ferrying airfield. Direction by John Rawlins is handicapped by the loosely knit and over-dialoged script. *Walt.*

The Lady and Monster

Hollywood, March 15.

Republic release of George Sherman production. Stars Vera Hruba Ralston. Features Richard Arlen and Erich von Stroheim. Directed by Sherman. Screenplay, Dane Lussier and Frederick Kohner; from story, "Donovan's Brain," by Curt Siodmak; camera, John Alton; editor, Arthur Roberts. Previewed in RCA projection room, March 14, '44. Running time, 86 MINS.

Janice Farrell	Vera Hruba Ralston
Prof. Franz Mueller	Erich Von Stroheim
Patrick Cory	Richard Arlen
Mrs. Fame	Mary Nash
Eugene Fuller	Sidney Blackmer
Chloe Donovan	Helen Vinson
Collins	William Henry
Grimes	Charles Kane
Mary Lou	Juanita Quigley
Dr. Martin	Harry Hayden
The Husky Man	Jack Kirk
Antonio Triana and Lola Montes	

Although title directly implies that this is a thrill-chill melodrama, and tag will catch plenty of customers in spots where such fare is accepted, picture is more of a clinical adventure. Picture's b.o. success will be in direct proportion to exploitation of the title in each individual situation, but at best it's a dual supporter for the regular runs.

Erich von Stroheim plays a scientist conducting research on keeping the brain alive after death. Vera Hruba Ralston and Richard Arlen

are his two assistants in an Arizona desert castle.

Miss Hruba, former iceskating star, makes bid for dramatic buildup here, but is handicapped by role. Arlen is okay while Von Stroheim is most prominent.

Story unfolds at a stolid pace, with too few suspenseful episodes. Production shows substantial expenditure. *Walt.*

Memphis Belle

(DOCUMENTARY)

"Memphis Belle" is a timely dedication to the U. S. Army Eighth Air Force, 41 minutes of thrilling film that will bring home to the nation's audiences exactly what our flyers are up against on European bombing missions.

Details of these missions, namely their planning by army strategists and the actual flights over Germany itself, are all vividly, excitingly documented in color, and it has an impact that is equally compelling. Footage was taken by a camera crew of three Air Force officers headed by Lt. Col. William Wyler and including Major William C. Clothier and the late Lt. Harold Tannenbaum. Latter, a veteran of the last war, joined up in this one at the age of 47 and lost his life while on a flight taking films incorporated in this picture.

Titled after a Flying Fortress which returned from 25 missions over Europe. "Memphis Belle" has two climaxes: one, an explanation by narrator Ed Kern, of the OWI, with the use of a map, of how six different flights are sent out from English bases to divide up Nazi defenses and lessen the risk of the mission; the other, films of the planes and their crews after they return from one of the raids, with many crewmen hurt and many of the planes shot up so badly it is surprising they returned at all.

Paramount will distribute the picture, starting in April, to the nation's film houses through the War Activities Committee. *Sten.*

Westward Bound

Monogram release of Robert Tansey production. Stars Ken Maynard, Hoot Gibson and Bob Steele. Directed by Robert Tansey. Story and screenplay, Frances Kavanaugh; camera, Marcel Le Picard; editor, John C. Fuller. At New York theatre, N. Y., week of March 14, '44, dual. Running time, 54 MINS.

Ken	Ken Maynard
Hoot	Hoot Gibson
Bob	Bob Steele
Enid Barrett	Betty Miles
Ira Phillips	John Bridges
Roger Caldwell	Harry Woods
Henry Wagner	Karl Hackett
Albert Lane	Weldon Heyburn
Jasper Tuttle	Hal Price
Will	Roy Brent
Judd	Frank Ellis
Monte	Curly Dresden

Featuring Ken Maynard, Hoot Gibson and Bob Steele, "Westward Bound" is a fast mustanger for duals. Yarn concerns the efforts of the Trail Blazers (Steele, Gibson, Maynard) to cope with desperadoes trying to victimize ranchers of their property. But, as usual, Maynard, Gibson and Steele beat them to the draw.

Script, direction and camera work are par for this type of fare.

On Approval

(BRITISH-MADE)

Gaumont-British production and release. Stars Clive Brook, Beatrice Lillie. Directed by Clive Brook. Adapted from Frederick Lonsdale's play by Clive Brook. Camera, C. Frieste-Greene. At Leicester Square theatre, London. Running time, 30 MINS.

George, Duke of Bristol	Clive Brook
Maria Wislack	Beatrice Lillie
Helen Hale	Googie Withers
Richard Halton	Roland Culver
Dr. Graham	O.B. Clarence
Parkes	Lawrence Hanray
Mrs. McCosh	Elliot Mason

Landlord .... Hay Petrie
Cook .... Marjories
Jeanne .... Molly Munks

Cleverest thing about this film is a trick opening sequence and an equally unconventional finish. Otherwise, the Frederick Lonsdale play not only does not lend itself to the screen, but it has too much chatter between the four principals. When Clive Brook as Duke of Bristol is not playing the silly ass with Roland Culver, his bachelor pal, Beatrice Lillie is engaging in Victorian misbehavior with Googie Withers, her rich American girl friend. Presence of Clive Brook and Beatrice Lillie may help put this over in U. S., but even then only for very mild returns.

"On Approval" was not only produced and directed by Brook, but he made the screen adaptation. So he gets any kudos attached to the smart opening. There's also novel treatment of the story, but it is doubtful if any director could make this outdated tale convincing to 1944 audiences. By the same token not one of the principals is able to bring reality to their roles. Admittedly "daring" for end of last century, it is patently dull today. And it is not even funny.

After the drawn-out plot development, the final pungent wise cracks only serve to emphasize the dullness of what has gone before.

Heroes Are Made

(SOVIET MADE)

Artkine release of Mark Donakoy production. Stars V. Periat-Petrenko, D. Sagal, I. Pedotova; features V. Bubnov, V. Krusnovlisky, A. Dunaysky, A. Khvillis, R. Runghe, V. Bulashov. Directed by Mark Donshoy. Screenplay, Mark Donshoy. based on novel by Nikolai Omtrosky; music, L. Schwartz; camera, R. Monsatirsky; English titles, Charles Clement. At Stanley theatre, N.Y., March 10, '44. Running time, 76 MINS.

Pavel Korchagin .... V. Periat-Petrenko
Sailor .... D. Sagal
Tonia .... J. Pedotova
Artem Korchagin .... V. Bubnov
German Officer .... V. Krasnovitsky
Ukranian Interpreter .... A. Dunsysky
Dolinnik .... A. Khvilla
Seryozha .... B. Runghe
Victor Leachinsky .... V. Balashov

Filming of a 14-year-old's revolutionary development provides intense drama hampered by technical deficiencies. Film's appeal will be restricted to those who avidly follow the Soviet releases.

Yarn deals with a young kitchen boy in a railroad buffet who, through the example of a partisan sailor leader, turns to active opposition of German occupation, 1918 vintage. Boy organizes a youthful underground but is forced to leave his friends when he helps the sailor to escape the police. He joins the Red Army and takes part in the rescue of these same friends who are caught in the interim and sentenced to be hanged. Adolescent love affair which develops into the real thing with growing maturity, provides the romantic relief. *Turo.*

Candlelight in Algeria

(BRITISH MADE)

London, March 1.

British Lion production and release. Stars James mason, Carla Lehmann, Walter Rilla. Directed by Geroge King. Screenplay by Brock Williams, Katherine Strueby from story by Dorothy Hope: camera, Otto Heller, Gus Drisse, Patrick Gay. At Regal, London, starting Feb. 18. Running time, 85 MINS.

Alan Thurston .... James Mason
Susan Ann Foster .... Carla Lehmann
Von Alven .... Raymond Lovell
Marlian .... Enid Stamp-Taylor
Doktor Muller .... Walter Rilla
Yvette .... Pamela Sirling
Henri de Lange .... Leslie Bradley
Police Commissioner .... Michael Morel
General Mark Clark .... Bart Norman

Events move so quickly in wartime that so-called big events become quickly outdated. That's what has happened with this film. The hush-hush activities and spy intrigues leading up to General Mark Clark's secret disembarkation from a British submarine to a meeting of allied chiefs on the deserted North African coast prior to the Anglo-American invasion there form the basic plot.

A year ago that would have made a timely theme, but not today. Despite the theme, its chances in U. S. appear slim even on duals, the all-British cast being an obvious handicap. This is more melodrama than a war story about an outstanding event in the North African invasion.

Carla Lehmann is efficient as the unwilling accomplice of the British-er (James Mason). Nice role is played by Pamela Stirling as French grisette, who gives her life more for love of the hero than love of France. Walter Rilla also scores, while Mason is okay, if a bit dour as the British officer. Backgrounds are adequate, but not outstanding. *Clem.*

Miniature Reviews

"Follow the Boys" (Musical) (U). Name-loaded show biz saga, a cinch for big b.o.

"Tampico" (20th). Disappointing war drama; will need dual support.

"Two-Man Submarine" (Col). Lower dualer about espionage in the South Pacific.

"Nine Girls" (Col).—Likeable whodunit, with cast of glamor gals, that should hold its own on the duals.

"Jamboree" (Musical) (Rep). Entertaining dualer.

"Partners of the Trail" (Mono). Routine western, okay dualer.

Follow the Boys

(MUSICAL)

Universal release of Charles K. Feldman production; associate producer, Albert L. Rockett. Stars George Raft, Vera Zorina. Guest stars: Sophie Tucker, Ted Lewis, Jeanette MacDonald, Orson Welles, Marlene Dietrich, Dinah Shore, Donald O'Connor, Peggy Ryan, W. C. Fields, Andrews Sisters, Artur Rubinstein, Carmen Amaya, Delta Rhythm Boys, Leonard Gautier's Bricklayers, Freddie Slack orchestra, Charlie Spivak, orch., Louis Jordan orch. Directed by Eddie Sutherland. Original screenplay, Lou Breslow and Gertrude Purcell; camera, David Abel; editor, Fred R. Feitshans, Jr.; Asst. director, Howard Christie; special effects, John Fulton; music, Leigh Harline; dances, George Hale. Tradeshown in N. Y. March 23, 1944. Running time, 122 MINS.

Tony West .... George Raft
Gloria Vance .... Vera Zorina
Nick West .... Charlie Grapewin
Kitty West .... Grace McDonald
Louie Fairweather ...... Charles Butterworth
Walter Bruce .... George Macready
Annie .... Elizabeth Patterson
William Barrett .... Theodore Von Eltz
Dr. Henderson .... Regis Toomey
Laura .... Ramsay Ames
Martha O'Driscoll .... Martha O'Driscoll
Maxie Rosenbloom ...... Maxie Rosenbloom
Junior .... Spooks

Victory Committee Sequence

Louise Allbritton, Evelyn Ankers, Noah Beery, Jr., Turhan Bey, Louise Beavers, Nigel Bruce, Lon Chaney, Lois Collier, Peter Coe, Alan Curtis, Andy Devine, Susanna Foster, Thomas Gomez, Samuel S. Hinds, Gloria Jean, Maria Montez, Clarence Muse, Robert Paige, Gale Sondergaard.

Guest Stars in Order of Appearance

Jeanette MacDonald, Orson Welles' Mercury Wonder Show, Marlene Dietrich, Dinah Shore, Donald O'Connor, Peggy Ryan, W. C. Fields, the Andrews Sisters, Artur Rubinstein, Carmen Amaya and her company, Sophie Tucker, Delta Rhythm Boys, Leonard Gautier's Bricklayers. Ted Lewis, Freddie Slack, Charlie Spivak and Louis Jordan bands.

Prime trouble with "Follow the Boys" is its over-generosity. The two hours and two minutes running time show that a good thing can be overdone. However, by and large, this salute to show business, with its galaxy of names, even though many are walk-throughs, makes "Boys" a cinch for biz boxoffice.

Charles K. Feldman, Hollywood agent and "package" producer, who has been prominent in Hollywood Victory Committee and allied USO-Camp Shows activities, conceived the idea of glorifying the professional undertaking with which he has long been associated and familiar. The sum total is a highly entertaining film package.

For show business, it's a timely tribute. For the fans, it smacks of authentic inside stuff. Big names are bandied about in casual conversation; and equally big names are shown playing themselves as guest stars at the sundry service camp entertainments.

Just as the danger arises that it's approaching the appearance of becoming a big short, the plot snaps back, but none the less there is so much room for paring it's surprising this hasn't been done.

Plot after a spell wears thin. George Raft and Vera Zorina, as the married stars, part because of what seems a rather thin reason. But from this is motivated Raft's preoccupation with organizing the Hollywood Victory Committee, and thus are paraded Jeanette MacDonald, Orson Welles, Dietrich, Dinah Shore, W. C. Fields, Andrews Sisters, Artur Rubinstein (another longhair, like Iturbi, to go cinematic), Carmen Amaya, Sophie Tucker, Delta Rhythm Boys, et al. There are also the Ted Lewis, Freddie Slack, Charlie Spivak and Louis Jordan bands. In the HVC sequence there is discovered another galaxy of names.

The transition from the final night of the famed Palace on Broadway to Hollywood is extended but more authentic than the multiplicity of specialties which follow. A number each by the Misses MacDonald and Shore could be dropped for instance; ditto the Andrews and Miss Tucker. Not that all aren't expert, but it soon surfeits. Of the specialists, really socko are Donald O'Connor and Peggy Ryan, right off the Universal lot.

Everybody does something, the songs running the gamut of the Hit Parade of three decades. Raft even gets in his "Sweet Georgia Brown," and W. C. Fields revives an almost forgotten pooltable scene he did in an earlier "Ziegfeld Follies." A real tug is Miss MacDonald's "I'll See You in My Dreams" with a blinded young soldier in a hospital bed as the vis-a-vis. Sock song is the Deltaites' treatment of "The House I Live In." Finale is a radio reading of an excerpt from Joe Schoenfeld's "Soldiers in Greasepaint," but with the original "Variety" source not credited. It's part of a worldwide Command Performance, and herein is tied in the Special Services branch of the army.

Considering the attempt to embrace all the show biz groups—UTWAC, USO, HVC, SS, Bond Caravans, etc.—it was indeed a weighty all-inclusive task but director Eddie Sutherland managed it all rather well. None the less, the kaleidoscope could have been trimmed closer for greater compactness. *Abel.*

Tampico

20th-Fox release of Robert Bassler production. Stars Edward G. Robinson, Lynn Bari, Victor McLaglen. Directed by Lothar Mendes. Screenplay, Kenneth Gamet, Fred Niblo, Jr., Richard Macaulay; original story and adaptation, Ladislas Fodor; camera, Charles Clarke; special effects, Fred Sersen; dances, Geneva Sawyer; editor, Robert Fritch; music, David Raksin; music director, Emil Newman. Tradeshown in N. Y., March 23, '44. Running time, 75 MINS.

Capt. Bart Manson .... Edward G. Robinson
Kathie Hall .... Lynn Bari
Fred Adamson .... Victor McLaglen
Watson .... Robert Bailey
Valdez .... Marc Lawrence
Silhouette Man .... E. J. Ballantine
Dolores .... Mona Maris
Kruger .... Tonie Selwart
Mueller .... Carl Ekberg
Crawford .... Roy Roberts
Stranger .... George Sorel
Naval Officer .... Charles Lang
Quartermaster .... Ralph Byrd
Crew Members .... { Louis Hart, Paul Kruger, Martin Cinchy, Constantin Romanoff, Oscar Hendrian }
Justice of Peace .... Antonio Moreno
Naval Commander .... Nestor Paiva
Rodriguez .... Muni Seroff
Photographer .... Juan Varro
Dr. Brown .... Ben Erway
Mrs. Kelly .... Helen Brown
Serra .... Martin Garralaga
Proprietor .... Margaret Martin
Messenger Boy .... David Cota
Navigator .... Arno Frey
Waiters .... { Chris-Pin Martin, Trevor Bardett }
Captain .... Peter Helmers
Second Lieutenant .... Otto Heichow
Commander .... Ludwig Donath
Radio Operator .... Rudolph Lindau
Port Pilot .... Jean Del Val
Second Officer .... Hans Von Morhart

"Tampico" suggests it started out to be one of those "big" 20th-Fox war thrillers, but somewhere along the line it missed fire. It emerged, instead, as a 75-minute sea drama for the dualers.

Picture is disappointing mainly because of a poorly developed script and characters. Names of Edward G. Robinson, Victor McLaglen and Lynn Bari, for the marquee, aren't likely to dissipate the film's minus values.

Robinson plays the captain of an oil tanker, and McLaglen is his first mate. Miss Bari comes into the picture when she's picked up, along with other survivors, in the Gulf of Mexico after her ship has been torpedoed. Thereafter it's a conflicting story of romance, between Robinson and Miss Bari, and the intrigues of wartime espionage in the gulf city of Tampico.

The script hasn't done right by Robinson, which is unusual for him since he generally can make the best of bad situations. McLaglen hasn't much to do, while Miss Bari lends a decorative touch. *Kahn.*

Two-Man Submarine

Columbia release of Jack Fier production. Features Tom Neal, Ann Savage and J. Carrol Naish. Directed by Lew Landers. Screenplay, Griffin Jay and Leslie T. White; camera, Lew Landers; editor, Jerome Thoms. At Fox, Brooklyn, dual. Running time, 62 MINS.

Jerry Evans	Tom 'Neal
P..t Benson	Ann Savage
Dr. Augustus Hadley	J. Carrol Naish
Walt Hedges	Robert Williams
Gabe Fabian	Abner Biberman
Normann Fosmer	George Lynn
Fuzzytop	J. Alex Havier

A hollow attempt to capitalize on espionage efforts to decipher the secret of penicillin, "Two-Man Sub" is a standard dual meller employing all the familiar hoke ingredients.

Story tells of efforts by Japs and Nazis to wrest from American research workers on a South Pacific island the secret of the drug. Attempts are properly frustrated, but not until half the American group is killed off and the miscreants share a similar fate aboard a submarine.

Direction and acting fail to break through the unbelievable script.

Nine Girls

Columbia release of Burt Kelly production. Features Ann Harding, Evelyn Keyes, Jinx Falkenburg, Anita Louise, Leslie Brooks. Directed by Leigh Jason. Screenplay, Karen De Witt, Connie Lee; adapted by Al Martin from the play by Wilfrid H. Pettit; score, John Leipold; camera, James Van Trees. At Paramount, Brooklyn, dual, March 24. Running time, 78 MINS.

Grace Thornton	Ann Harding
Mary O'Ryan	Evelyn Keyes
Jane Peters	Jinx Falkenburg
Paula Canfield	Anita Louise
Roberta Holloway	Leslie Brooks
Eva Sharon	Lynn Merrick
"Butch" Hendricks	Jeff Donnell
Alice Blake	Nina Foch
"Tennessee" Collingwood	Shirley Mills
Shirley Berke	Marcia Mae Jones
Capt. Brooks	Willard Robertson
Walter Cummings	William Demarest
Horace Canfield	Lester Matthews

Fairly diverting whodunit that enlists topflight glamour gals in cast, plus Ann Harding, Sans rapid paced action, which usually obtains in this type of flicker, it's likeable enough fare for dualers. With plenty of material among the gals for cheesecake and other exploitation angles should do moderately well on twin bills.

Yarn is woven around a sorority group and their teacher. Brief vacation has been declared for a hiatus in a log cabin attendant to the initiation of two of the girls into the sorority. Upon arrival they learn that one of their group, Anita Louise, has been murdered on the way. Finger of suspicion points at Nina Foch and Evelyn Keyes.

Early spinning is somewhat slow and tedious, but when yarn hits its stride in the later reels, it keeps rolling at a lively pace. The denouement is a nifty surprise.

Ann Harding gives a superb portrayal of the frustrated teacher. Her eloquent shading bespeaks well her years of experience in stage and film work. Evelyn Keyes turns in a neat job, while Willard Robertson gets the most out of the gentleman copper role. Bill Demarest is okay for laughs as Robertson's dumb assistant. Lester Matthews has the brief role of the slain girl's father. Jinx Falkenburg and the rest of the glamour group give good account in the lesser roles.

Direction by Leigh Jason is adequate for material at hand, and camera work by James Van Trees is remarkably good.

Jamboree
(SONGS)

Republic release of Armand Schaefer production. Stars Ruth Terry; features George Byron; Paul Harvey, Edwin Stanley, Freddie Fisher band, Music Maids. Directed by Joseph Santley. Screenplay, Jack Townley from original by Townley and Taylor Caven; musical director, Morton Scott; editor, Richard Van Enger; camera, William Bradford. Previewed in N. Y., March 24, '44. Running time, 71 MINS.

Ruth Cartwright	Ruth Terry
Joe Mason	George Byron
P. J. Jarvis	Paul Harvey
Sam Smith	Edwin Stanley

Freddie Fisher and His Schnickelfritz Band
The Music Maids
Ernest Tubb and His Texas Troubadors
Don Wilson
Isabel Randolph as Mrs. Uppington
Rufe Davis
Shirley Mitchell as Alice Darling
George "Shug" Fisher

Republic has come up with a rustic musical that should prove an entertaining dualer.

Ruth Terry is supported by a group of radio entertainers who dispense with the "corn" during the majority of the 71 minutes of "Jamboree." Seven songs, with several encores of some tunes, are played or sung by Freddie Fisher and his Schnickelfritz band, Ernest Tubb and his Texas Troubadors, and the Music Maids, who are joined by Miss Terry. Most notable of the tunes are "Jamboree," composed by Fisher, and "Maggie Went to Aggie," by Charles Henderson.

Plot deals with the tough luck Fisher's band meets in getting a job. Their manager (George Byron) walks out on them when he finds that their type music is not saleable. Byron learns that a prospective radio sponsor is interested in Tubb and his group, hies himself out to a farm, where they are supposedly employed, but finds they have left. He phones the Schnickelfritzers to come out to the farm and take the part of Tubb's outfit in auditioning for the sponsor. They get the job, but cannot get "availability certificates" to leave their essential farm jobs from Miss Terry, who is their employer. Tubb's outfit, in the city, takes over as Fisher's band, the climax coming with the mixup in identities being ironed out to everyone's satisfaction.

Other radio entertainers in the cast besides Fisher and his band are: The Music Maids, quartet from the Bing Crosby program; Don Wilson, in the film the sponsor's right-hand man, who is with Jack Benny's air troupe; Isabel Randolph, the Mrs. Uppington on "The Great Gildersleeve" radio stanza, and Rufe Davis, a standard vaude and radio turn. *Sten.*

Partners of the Trail

Monogram release of Scott R. Dunlap production. Stars Johnny Mack Brown. Directed by Lambert Hillyer. Screenplay and story, Frank H. Young; camera, Harry Neumann; editor, Carl Helm. At New York theatre, N. Y., week of March 31, '44, dual. Running time, 55 MINS.

Nevada	Johnny Mack Brown
Sandy	Raymond Hatton
Kate	Christine McIntyre
Joel	Craig Woods
Edwards	Robert Frazer
Dobbey	Harry F. Price
Trigger	Jack Ingram
Lem	Lynton Brent
Baker	Marshall Reed
Duke	Ben Corbett
Cobly	Steve Clark
Applegate	Lloyd Ingraham

Conventional westerner provides plenty of action and also incorporates a minor mystery pattern to lend sustaining interest. Okay as dualer.

Plot deals with efforts of Johnny Mack Brown and Raymond Hatton, roving U. S. marshals, to clear up mystery surrounding the wanton killing of ranchers for no apparent reason. Denouement is reached after the usual slugging spree and free gunplay.

Hatton lends good support in quasi-humorous role. Direction and lenswork standard.

Miniature Reviews

"**Uncertain Glory**" (WB). Errol Flynn and Paul Lukas melodrama will get business.

"**Meet the People**" (Musical) (M-G). Lightweight entertainment will have to depend on names for nominal biz.

"**Andy Hardy's Blonde Trouble**" (M-G). Fourteenth in the series; OK entertainment.

"**Her Primitive Man**" (U). Louise Allbritton, Robert Paige, Robert Benchley in lively farce; strong dual supporter.

"**Lumberjack**" (UA). Another Hopalong Cassidy to please William Boyd fans.

"**Weird Woman**" (U). Meller okay dualer in program houses.

"**Arizona Whirlwind**" (Mono). Conventional western.

"**Rosie the Riveter**" (Rep). Lively dualer with warplant background.

"**Lady in the Death House**" (PRC). Minor meller, can pass as sub-dualer.

"**Cowboy and the Senorita**" (Rep). Roy Rogers western gets fine support from Mary Lee. Okay dualer.

Uncertain Glory

Warner Bros. release of Robert Buckner production. Stars Errol Flynn and Paul Lukas; features Jean Sullivan and Lucile Watson. Directed by Raoul Walsh. Screenplay, Lazlo Vadnay and Max Brand, from story by Joe May and Laszlo Vadnay; camera, Sid Hickox; editor, George Amy; music, Adolph Deutsch; music director, Leo F. Forbstein. Previewed in N. Y., April 3, '44. Running time, 102 MINS.

Jean Picard	Errol Flynn
Marcel Bonet	Paul Lukas
Marianne	Jean Sullivan
Mme. Maret	Lucile Watson
Louise	Faye Emerson
Captain Mobile Guard	James Flavin
Police Commissioner	Douglas Dumbrille
Father Le Clerc	Dennis Hoey
Henri Duval	Sheldon Leonard
Mme. Bonet	Odette Myrtil
Prison Priest	Francis Pierlot
Razeau	Wallis Clark
Latour	Victor Kilian
Saboteur	Ivan Triesault
Vitrac	Van Antwerp
Warden	Art Smith
Innkeeper	Carl Harbaugh
Drover's Wife	Mary Servoss
Restaurant Keeper	Charles La Torre
Executioner	Pedro de Cordoba
Pierre Bonet	Bobby Walberg
Drover	Erskine Sanford
German Officer	Felix Basch
Veterinary	Joel Friedkin

France under the Nazis is again being portrayed, this time in Warners' "Uncertain Glory," a psychological, melodramatic study that is lengthy and frequently tedious. However, with Errol Flynn and Paul Lukas for the marquee it will do OK.

"Glory" is more a yarn of two people than any group of people; it is scattered in its development of both narrative and characters; it is slow-paced and possessive of little action. Lack of action, perhaps, might be excusable in melodrama—providing that there is the omniscient thought of impending action. Warners brought home that thought very forceably in its recent "Destination Tokyo." Story is involved, dealing with a surete inspector and the object of his longtime chase (Flynn).

The film's opening finds Flynn being led to the guillotine for murder. A British flying squadron bombs the prison, upsetting the execution and leading to Flynn's escape. Then follows once again the chase by Lukas, the capture and the subsequent plan by Flynn, at first for escape reasons, to give himself up as a saboteur so that 100 French hostages could go free. The idea is that thus he would be doing the only redeeming thing in his life.

Lukas' performance is as commendable as the story permits while Flynn is the victim of an unlikely, poorly developed characterization. Jean Sullivan, newcomer, is an interesting face as the romance opposite Flynn, though she still needs schooling in the straight dramatics. Lucile Watson has little to do as the town matriarch.

Film seems to be difficult to cut, though that's what it needs badly.

Kahn.

Meet the People

(MUSICAL)

Hollywood, April 4.

Metro release of E. Y. Harburg production. Stars Lucille Ball, Dick Powell; features Virginia O'Brien, Bert Lahr, Rags Ragland, June Allyson, Vaughn Monroe orchestra, Spike Jones City Slickers. Directed by Charles Reisner. Screenplay by S. M. Herzig and Fred Saidy, suggested by story by Sol and Ben Barzman and Louis Lantz; camera, Robert Surtees; editor, Alexander Troffey. Tradeshown in L. A. April 3, '44. Running time 99 MINS.

Julie Hampton....................Lucille Ball
Wm. "Swanee" Swanson......Dick Powell
"Woodpecker" Peg.........Virginia O'Brien
The Commander.....................Bert Lahr
Mr. Smith.................."Rags" Ragland
Annie..........................June Allyson
Uncle Felix......................Steve Geray
"Buck".............................Paul Regan
Mr. Peetwick..............Howard Freeman
Steffi.............................Betty Jaynes
John Swanson.....................John Craven
Monte Rowland...............Morris Ankrum
Miriam........................Miriam LaVelle
Ziggie............................Ziggie Talent
Oriental Dancers.............Mata and Hari

When "Meet the People" was staged as a musical revue in Hollywood, mainly with new talent, back about five years, Metro bought the film rights. Resemblance between the two ends with the title. Story is both innocuous and unimportant, dragging in many spots, and only serves to mount number of production numbers and specialties. Laugh moments are spaced too far apart, and picture will do only fair biz in the regular runs without much chance of holdovers in the keys.

There's a flock of talent on display. Some is spotlighted to fine advantage, while other personalities are lost in the shuffle. Spike Jones and his City Slickers, novelty and clowning musical group, catch attention with production number built around song, "Schicklegruber," by Sammy Fain and E. Y. Harburg, which is one of the best caricatures of Hitler and Mussolini filmed to date. Oriental dance team of Mata and Hari cleverly and showmanly stop the show.

Vaughn Monroe and his orchestra open with a fast musical routine, with Ziggie Talent clicking with gesticulating presentation of the vocal, to get picture off to good start. Monroe and band are on later for Monroe to sing "In Times Like These" and to assist with song, "I Like to Recognize the Tune," which June Allyson delivers in solid style with Monroe, Talent, Virginia O'Brien and harmony girls aiding.

Bert Lahr's particular brand of comedy is restricted, with comedian getting one specialty, a dropped-in number for him to deliver "Heave Ho" with male chorus, Rags Ragland also gets one rather unfunny blackout, but Virginia O'Brien breaks through with a nifty comedy tune, "Say That We're Sweethearts Again," which is delivered in her inimitable style. Other production numbers, including the finale, fail to measure up to standard, and are not too well spotted.

Story is routine. Lucille Ball is stage glamour girl who makes personal appearance at Maryland shipyard, and finds herself romantically attracted to welder Powell. Latter sells her play, which is in turn sold to producer Morris Ankrum. But Powell is dissatisfied with rehearsals and stops the proceedings. Actress gets job in the shipyard to regain rights to the play, but—after usual romantic complications and misunderstandings—is frozen to her job and sticks around long enough to put show on at ship launching with yard talent.

Powell ably carries the lead spot, despite handicaps of the script, and sings two numbers, "In Times Like These" and "Meet the People." Miss Ball is decorative; while Lahr garners a few laughs in his infrequent appearances. Direction by Charles Reisner is bumpy.

Walt.

Andy Hardy's Blonde Trouble

(ONE SONG)

Metro-Goldwyn-Mayer production and release. Features Mickey Rooney, Lewis Stone, Fay Holden, Sara Haden, Herbert Marshall, Bonita Granville, Keye Luke, Lee Wilde and Lyn Wilde. Directed by George B. Seitz. Based upon characters created by Aurania Rouveral; story and adaptation, Harry Ruskin, William Ludwig and Agnes Christine Johnston; editor, George White; camera, Lester White. Previewed in N. Y., March 30, '44. Running time, 107 MINS.

Judge Hardy......................Lewis Stone
Andy Hardy...................Mickey Rooney
Mrs. Hardy........................Fay Holden
Aunt Milly.......................Sara Haden
Dr. M. J. Standish......Herbert Marshall
Kay Wilson................Bonita Granville
Katy Anderson...................Jean Porter
Dr. Lee.............................Keye Luke
Lee Walker.........................Lee Wilde
Lyn Walker.........................Lyn Wilde
Mrs. Townsend................Marta Linden

This series goes on like Tennyson's brook, which is almost true of "Andy Hardy's Blonde Trouble." It's way overboard at 107 minutes. The 14th in the Hardy series, all of which have featured Lewis Stone and Mickey Rooney, it will probably do all right, though it's under par. Editor George White could have found many spots where the scissors could have done valuable service.

This time Rooney goes to college, the same one from which Stone, playing his father, had graduated. It's now co-ed, however, and Rooney, doing a likeable but partly impish role, gets himself into plenty of hot water, especially with twins and another girl. His difficulties ultimately reach the point where he's going to leave college but through a chance visit of his father, as he's about to push off, things are cleared up to the satisfaction of the dean. Herbert Marshall plays the latter in a very polished and ingratiating manner.

Both Rooney and Stone perform smoothly although handicapped by the slowness of the script as well as some inconsequential scenes. Outstanding and very cute are the young Wilde twins (Lee and Lyn), while Bonita Granville acquits herself creditably. Lee Wilde sings a brief portion of a song, "You'd Be So Easy to Love," topped by a short dance bit with the other Wilde girl. Cast members not in much footage include Fay Holden, Sara Haden, Keye Luke, Jean Porter and Marta Linden. All do satisfactorily.

Char.

Her Primitive Man

Universal release of Michael Fessier-Ernest Pagano production. Stars Louise Allbritton, Robert Paige; features Robert Benchley, E. E. Horton, Helen Broderick, Walter Catlett, Ernest Truex. Directed by Charles Lamont. Screenplay by Michael Fessier, Ernest Pagano from story by Dick Irving Hyland; camera, Charles Van Enger; editor, Ray Snyder. At State, N. Y., week March 30, '44. Running time, 80 MINS.

Sheila Winthrop.............Louise Allbritton
Pete Matthews...................Robert Paige
Martin Osborne..............Robert Benchley
Orrin Tracy.........Edward Everett Horton
Mrs. Winthrop...............Helen Broderick
Marcia Stafford..........Stephanie Bachelor
Uncle Hubert.....................Ernest Truex
Hotel Clerk.....................Walter Catlett
Gerald Van Horn.........Louis Jean Heydt
Aunt Penelope..............Nydia Westman
Jonathan........................Oscar O'Shea
Aunt Martha.....................Sylvia Field
Caleb................................Ian Wolfe
Mr. Smith........................Irving Bacon

Co-starring combo of Louise Allbritton and Robert Paige again clicks nicely in this second feature in which they're starred. Making no pretense of being more than a whacky farce-comedy, "Her Primitive Man" is a solid dualer.

Fable is a screwball one about book-publisher Robert Benchley who loses plenty when anthropolgy society prexy, Louise Allbritton, brands his work on head-hunters a fraud. Robert Paige, who's been authoring this book from a Havana casino, aided and abetted by Edward Everett Horton, bartender, who frames the yarn from his old jungle experiences, is stranded financially and decides to get revenge on very social Miss Allbritton. Frames her to go on an expedition after a savage and manages to disguise himself as a head-hunter. Per usual in such a screwy yarn, he's brought back to N. Y. by Miss Allbritton so she can study his reactions to civilization, and incorporate them in a novel.

At the same time, Paige cuts himself in for $10,000 by promising an expose of her socialite, uppish mansion while masquerading as a savage. With such a setup, further complications develop because Paige is pursued by a man-crazy heiress to whom he's indebted for $10,000. Farcical possibilities are aided by crisp dialog.

Louise Allbritton, who made this before her overseas trek, is superb as anthropology society prexy who tests the primitive man's reactions. Robert Paige makes an adroit partner as he shifts from savage garb to that of author to maintain the deception. Robert Benchley has a typical role, though secondary, as are Horton and Helen Broderick, as a stuffy socialite. Oscar O'Shea, though not featured, steals many scenes as the father who wants his daughter (Miss Allbritton) happily married, and not to a stuffed shirt. Walter Catlett and Ernest Truex have virtual bits. Stephanie Bachelor is brilliant as the "other woman," the rich young gal pursuing Paige. Support is topped by Sylvia Field, Ian Wolfe and Nydia Westman.

Scripting by Michael Fessier and Ernest Pagano (credited also as producers) makes this jell. Camera work of Charles Van Enger is bright.

Wear.

Lumberjack

United Artists release of Harry A. Sherman production. Stars William Boyd; features Andy Clyde, Jimmy Rogers, Herbert Rawlinson and Ellen Hall. Directed by Lesley Selander. Screenplay, Norman Houston, from characters created by Clarncee E. Mulford; camera, Russell Harlan. Reviewed in projection room, N. Y., March 31, '44. Running time, 65 MINS.

Hopalong Cassidy...............William Boyd
California Carlson.................Andy Clyde
Jimmy Rogers...................Jimmy Rogers
Buck.......................Herbert Rawlinson
Julie...................................Ellen Hall
Abbey................................Ethel Wales
Keeper.....................Douglas Dumbrille
Fenwick....................Francis McDonald
Jordan..............................John Whitney
Taggart..............................Hal Taliaferro
Slade...................................Henry Wills
Big Joe............................Charles Morton
Mrs. Williams..................Frances Morris
Sheriff..............................Jack Rockwell
Justice..................................Bob Burns

Like its 52 predecessors in the Hopalong Cassidy series, this film is geared for profitable business in the subsequents on the lower rung of dual bills.

Action-filled with some fancy horse-riding by William Boyd, as Hoppy, and his cohorts, and with some fairly realistic knock-down-drag-out fisticuffs, picture was filmed in the woodlands of the High Sierras and has caught the beauty of that locale.

Yarn finds Ellen Hall, whose husband has been killed by an unknown assailant, inclined to make a deal with two conniving land agents for her virgin-timber property, despite the advice of Boyd not to sign the papers. Because of the loafing by the lumberjacks who are in cahoots with the businessmen, Miss Hall is unable to meet delivery date on the lumber, but, fortunately, Boyd convinces the homesteaders, who formerly worked the land but had been evicted, to come back to work. He also succeeds in tracking down the killer.

Interspersed is the comedic character acted by Andy Clyde, who, as usual, does neatly.

Sten.

Weird Woman

Hollywood, March 31.

Universal release of Oliver Drake production. Stars Lon Chaney, Anne Gwynne, Evelyn Ankers. Directed by Reginald Le Borg. Screenplay by Brenda Weisberg; adapted by W. Scott Darling, based on Inner Sanctum Mystery by Fritz Leiber, Jr.; camera, Virgil Miller; editor, Milton Carruth. Previewed March 30, 1944. Running time, 62 MINS.

Norman Reed....................Lon Chaney
Paula Reed.....................Anne Gwynne
Ilona Carr.....................Evelyn Ankers
Prof. Millard Sawtelle........Ralph Morgan
Grace Gunnison...........Elisabeth Risdon
Margaret...........................Lois Collier
Evelyn Sawtelle..........Elizabeth Russell
Prof. Septimus Carr.........Harry Hayden
David Jennings.................Phil Brown
Student............................Kay Harding

This is second of Inner Sanctum mysteries which are based on the mental, rather than physical, stress which results in murders and usual mysterious imagination and superstition. It's a standard dual supporter and okay for the secondary and nabe houses.

Picture hits slow pace in early reels to establish characters and foundation for the series of mysterious events, after which it gains momentum and fairly fast clip through directorial efforts of Reginald Le Borg.

Reared by natives of a South Sea island, Anne Gwynne marries professor Lon Chaney who brings her to the college town, along with charms and rituals to dispell evil spirits. Evelyn Ankers jealously starts whispering campaign against Chaney and his bride, resulting in a suicide and murder, in addition to intense mental confusion of the couple, before prof figures solution through trapping of Miss Ankers to admit her machinations.

Chaney, Miss Gwynne and Miss Ankers combine adequately for the three leads. Support is okay.

Walt.

Arizona Whirlwind

Monogram release of Robert Tansey production. Stars Ken Maynard, Hoot Gibson and Bob Steele. Directed by Robert Tansey. Screenplay, Frances Kavanaugh; camera, Edward Kull; editor, John C. Fuller. At New York theatre, N. Y., week of March 28, '44, dual. Running time, 59 MINS.

Ken Maynard.................Ken Maynard
Hoot Gibson....................Hoot Gibson
Bob Steele.........................Bob Steele
Polini..................................Ian Keith
Ruth Hampton....................Myrna Dell
Donny Davis....................Don Stewart
Duke Rollins....................Charles King
Steve Lynch.....................Karl Hackett
Ace..............................Geo. Chesebro
Jim Lockwood....................Dan White
Ted Hodges..............Chas. Murray, Jr.
Lefty...................................Frank Ellis

Third in stagecoach series built around Ken Maynard, Hoot Gibson and Bob Steele, "Arizona Whirlwind" is standard western fare with broad doses of comedy. Prime for the duals, with plenty of name values for hoss opera coterie.

Yarn has protagonists meeting band of diamond-looters intent on disposing of gems via ruse. Heavies are thwarted, but not until Jimmy Valentine situation is introduced and boys are forced to shoot it out on several fronts.

Starring trio gives good account of itself despite story deficiencies. Camera and direction hold up.

Rosie the Riveter

(SONGS)

Republic release of Armand Schaefer production. Stars Jane Frazee and Frank Albertson; features Vera Vague, Frank Jenks and Lloyd Corrigan. Directed by Joseph Santley. Screenplay, Jack Townley and Aleen Leslie, from story by Dorothy Curnow Handley; music director, Morton Scott; camera, Reggie Lanning; editor, Ralph Dixon. Reviewed in projection room, N. Y., March 30, '44. Running time, 75 MINS.

Rosie Warren.....................Jane Frazee
Charlie Doran..............Frank Albertson
Vera Watson......................Vera Vague
Kelly Kennedy..................Frank Jenks
Clem Prouty.................Lloyd Corrigan
Wayne Calhoun................Frank Fenton
Grandma Quill...............Maude Eburne
Buzz...................Carl "Alfalfa" Switzer
Mabel.........................Louise Erickson

Stella Prouty	Ellen Lowe
Sgt. Mulvaney	Arthur Loft
Piano Mover	Tom Kennedy

This is a light, fairly amusing film that should find little trouble garnering bookings on the duals.

Based on the Satevepost story, "Room for Two," by Dorothy Curnow Handley, "Rosie the Riveter" is a modernized, lower-budgeted version of "You Can't Take It With You," with that boardinghouse aura plus a warplant background. Jane Frazee and Frank Albertson, in the leading roles, supported by an able cast headed by Vera Vague and Frank Jenks, give added value to the pic.

Yarn deals with four warplant workers who are forced to live in one room because of a housing shortage, the men using the room at certain hours and the two women lodging there the remainder of the time. With something always going on in the boarding house due to the exuberance of the landlady's large family, and the constant tiffing of the four who share the one room, several amusing sequences are registered. Conclusion finds Miss Frazee and Albertson paired off, and Miss Vague and Jenks a cooing duo.

Miss Frazee sings two songs, unbilled and not too memorable, in neat fashion. A production number winding up the 75 minutes presents a line of dancing girls, a chorus of singers and Miss Frazee giving out with the title tune. *Sten.*

Lady in the Death House

PRC release of Jack Schwarz production. Stars Jean Parker and Lionel Atwill; features Douglas Fowley. Marcia Mae Jones and Robert Middleman. Directed by Steve Sekley. Screenplay. Harry O. Hoyt, from original by Frederick C. Davis; camera, Gus Peterson; editor, Robert O. Crandall. At New York theatre, N.Y., week of March 29, '44, dual. Running time, 56 MINS.

Mary	Jean Parker
Finch	Lionel Atwill
Brad	Douglas Fowley
Suzy	Marcia Mae Jones
State's Attorney	Robert Middleman
Detective	Cy Kendall
Snell	John Maxwell
Gregory	George Irving
Warden	Forrest Taylor

"Lady in the Death House" is an overcharged meller that's short on credibility and dated in its dramatic motif. Can fill as dualer.

Hoary theme deals with an innocent gal (Jean Parker) who is saved from the hot seat through the last-minute efforts of Lionel Atwill and Douglas Fowley. Atwill plays criminologist who rounds up the real culprit, and Fowley furnishes heart interest opposite Miss Parker.

Acting and production fairish, both being hamstrung by stilted yarn.

Cowboy and the Senorita
(SONGS)

Republic production and release. Stars Roy Rogers; features Mary Lee and Dale Evans. Directed by Joseph Kane; screenplay, Gordon Kahn from story by Bradford Ropes; music director, Walter Scharf; camera, Reggie Lanning; editor, Tony Martinelli; songs, Ned Washington, Phil Ohman; dance direction, Larry Ceballos. Reviewed in projection room, March 24, '44. Running time, 77 MINS.

Roy	Roy Rogers
Chip Williams	Mary Lee
Ysobel Martinez	Dale Evans
Craig Allen	John Hubbard
Teddy Wear	Guinn "Big Boy" Williams
Fuzzy	Fuzzy Knight
Lulubelle	Dorothy Christy
Judge Loomis	Lucien Littlefield
Ferguson	Hal Taliaferro
Sheriff	Jack Kirk

Specialty Dancers: Cappella and Patricia, Jane Beebe and Ben Rochelle, Tito and Corinne Valdez.
Themselves: Bob Nolan and the Sons of the Pioneers.

There's enough routine cowboy stuff in this combo musical-western to satisfy the average cinema thrill-seeker, but chief appeal rests in the musical and dance sequences.

Weak story revolves around treasure buried in goldmine bequeathed to Mary Lee and efforts of John Hubbard to take possession. Roy

Rogers performs as usual with guitar, and with pipes putting over title tune in good form. Singing honors, however, rest with personable Miss Lee, for whom role as the 16-year-old sparkplug was made to order.

Dale Evans, Bob Nolan with Sons of the Pioneers, and the dance teams, Cappella and Patricia, Jane Beebe and Ben Rochelle, Tito and Corinne Valdez, are well spotted. Guinn Williams, Fuzzy Knight, Dorothy Christy and Lucien Littlefield do okay by comedy. *Donn.*

Miniature Reviews

"**Lost Angel**" (M-G). Margaret O'Brien comedy-drama geared for substantial biz.

"**None Shall Escape**" (Col). Searing indictment of Nazism makes for sturdy programmer.

"**My Best Gal**" (Songs) (Rep). Jane Withers starrer for the duals.

"**Moon Over Las Vegas**" (Songs) (U). Lightweight filmusical handicapped by weak story. Okay for dual filler datings.

"**Hey, Rookie**" (Songs) (Rep). Entertaining film, suitable for duals.

Lost Angel

Metro release of Robert Sisk production. Stars Margaret O'Brien; features James Craig, Marsha Hunt, Philip Merivale, Henry O'Neill, Donald Meek, Keenan Wynn, Sara Haden. Directed by Roy Rowland. Screenplay, Isobel Lennart, based on an idea by Angna Enters; camera, Robert Surtees; editor, Frank Hull. At Criterion, N.Y., opening April 8, '44. Running time, 91 MINS.

Alpha	Margaret O'Brien
Mike Regan	James Craig
Katie Mallory	Marsha Hunt
Professor Peter Vincent	Philip Merivale
Professor Pringle	Henry O'Neill
Professor Catty	Donald Meek
Packy	Keenan Wynn
Mr. Woodring	Alan Napier
Rhoda Kitterick	Sara Haden
Mrs. Catty	Kathleen Lockhart
Professor Endicott	Walter Fenner
Professor Richards	Howard Freeman
Mrs. Pringle	Elizabeth Risdon
Jerry	Bobby Blake

If there was any doubt about Margaret O'Brien as a child star, "Lost Angel" dispels it. She takes a "B" and makes it a "sleeper" that will probably be among Metro's high grossers of its comparatively inexpensive productions this season.

"Lost Angel" reveals the O'Brien girl as a foundling picked by a group of scientists as the subject for experiment in human behavior. A genius at the age of six, the human element, however, has been overlooked. But then a police reporter (James Craig) is assigned to check on the prodigy, and the rest chiefly concerns a rehabilitation to her innate child consciousness with Craig as her tutor. There's a gangster angle brought in but only incidentally.

Roy Rowland has intelligently directed the moppet, and his ability to keep the more implausible moments down to a minimum is worthy of note. Isobel Lennart's scripting also fits nicely into the child characterization.

Craig is satisfying as the reporter. Marsha Hunt helps supply the slight love interest (with Craig) in nice fashion. Keenan Wynn, as a mobster, chips in with a neat characterization. Philip Merivale is satisfactory as the professor heading the group of child investigators, while Sara Haden contributes nicely as a teacher. Support also includes, notably, Henry O'Neill, Alan Napier and Donald Meek. *Wear.*

None Shall Escape

Columbia release of Samuel Bischoff production. Features Marsha Hunt and Alexander Knox. Directed by Andre De Toth. Story, Alfred Neuman and Joseph Than; editor, Charles Nelson, camera, Lee Garmes. At Loew's State, N.Y., April 6, '44. Running time, 85 MINS.

Marja Pacierkowski	Marsha Hunt
Wilhelm Grimm	Alexander Knox
Father Warecki	Henry Travers
Karl Grimm	Erik Rolf
Willie Grimm (as a man)	Richard Crane
Janina	Dorothy Morris
Rabbi Levin	Richard Hale
Alice Grimm	Ruth Nelson
Lt. Gersdorf	Kurt Kreuger
Anna Oremska	Shirley Mills
Jan Stys (as a boy)	Elvin Field
Jan Stys (as a man)	Trevor Bardette
Dr. Matek	Frank Jaquet
Oremski	Ray Teal
Stys	Art Smith
Presiding Judge	George Lessey

"None Shall Escape" hews to the premise that the first World War incubated the present conflict and that extension of Germanic hatred can be halted only by a judicious peace. In expanding this premise, film offers an interesting and entertaining episodic recital of Nazi bestiality but offers no solution. While lacking in names, it's a sturdy programmer.

Told in flashback fashion, theme deals with an embittered and crippled German soldier who returns after the first World War to resume his teaching position in a small German-Polish border village. His vengeful ideology causes his fiancee to turn from him and eventually leads to his being forced to leave the village after he has violated one of his girl students. His rise in the Nazi party and the wave of terrorism that follows his return to the village as a commandant set the keynote for picture's searing climax.

Alexander Knox and Marsha Hunt are forceful and convincingly cast as the Nazi commander and his one-time fiancee. Henry Travers is okay as the village priest, and Richard Hale is outstanding as the rabbi who dies for his convictions rather than suffer the Nazi depredations. Remainder of the cast is similarly adept and Andre De Toth's direction has merit.

My Best Gal
(SONGS)

Republic release of Harry Grey production. Stars Jane Withers features Frank Craven, Jimmy Lydon, Fortunio Bonanova. Directed by Anthony Mann. Screenplay, Olive Cooper and Earl Fenton from original by Richard Brooks; songs, Kim Gannon and Walter Kent; editor, Ralph Dixon; camera, Jack Marta. At Brooklyn Fox, week of April 7, '44. Running time, 67 MINS.

Kitty O'Hara	Jane Withers
Johnny McCloud	Jimmy Lydon
Danny O'Hara	Frank Craven
Charlie	Fortunio Bonanova
Ralph Hodges	George Cleveland
Mr. Porter	Franklin Pangborn
Miss Simpson	Mary Newton
Freddy	Jack Boyle

Jane Withers' talents are wasted in this one. A dualer.

Story deals with a father's efforts to get his daughter interested in the trouper traditions of the family, and revolves around the gal's endeavors to get a backer interested in a musical written by youthful Johnny McCloud (Jimmy Lydon).

Miss Withers, Lydon, Frank Craven and Fortunio Bonanova are given few opportunities because of the maze of story incongruity and poor direction. Music and dances are uninspiring, and the production has the earmarks of haste. Whatever plus value the film has is supplied by the affable singing and dancing chores of Miss Withers. *Sten.*

Moon Over Las Vegas
(SONGS)

Hollywood, April 7.

Universal release of Jean Yarbrough production, directed by Yarbrough. Features Anne Gwynne, David Bruce, Vera Vague. Screenplay by George Jeske and Clyde Bruckman; original by Jeske; camera, Jerome Ash; editor, Milton Caruth. Previewed Apr. 6, '44. Running time, 65 MINS.

Marian Corbett	Anne Gwynne
Richard Corbett	David Bruce
Auntie	Vera Vague
Grace Towers	Vivian Austin
Hal Blake	Alan Dinehart
Mrs. Blake	Lee Patrick
Joe	Jow Sawyer
Jim Bradley	Millburn Stone
Judge	Addison Richards
Porter	Mantan Moreland
Conductor	Eddie Dunn
Herman	Tom Dugan
Taxi Driver	Pat West
Walter	Muni Scroft

Gene Austin & Sherrell Sisters, Connie, Haines, Cappella & Patricia, Lillian Fornell, Ann Triola, Jimmy Dodd, the Sportsmen.

This is a lightweight entry in the Universal series of moderate-budgeted program filmusicals, handicapped by a weak story thread, but still displaying sufficient song specialties to carry it through the family houses as a dual supporter.

On the music side, there's Gene Austin delivering two songs, "You Marvelous You" and "My Blue Heaven" in his usual intimate style. Connie Haines is floorshow entertainer presenting "Touch of Texas" and "A Dream Ago"; Lillian Cornell handles the title song; Jimmy Dodd and the Sportsmen, harmony group, are also on the talent list. Ann Triola makes brief appearance with an accordion, while Spanish dance team of Cappella & Patricia catch attention with a fast number.

Story concerns Anne Gwynne and David Bruce, who get court approval for separation, although pair are still in love. They journey to Las Vegas on same train, where husband gets innocently entangled with Vivian Austin. After rising complications and general marital mixup and confusions, couple are reunited in happy fashion.

Script lacks smoothness, and direction does little to overcome this situation. Result is episodic melange, with many quick breaks in cutting. Cast struggles along with the static dialog at hand, with Vera Vague sup- [illegible] what few laughs are dropped along the way. *Walt.*

Hey, Rookie

(SONGS)

Columbia release of Irving Briskin production. Stars Joe Besser, Ann Miller, Larry Parks; features Joe Sawyer, Jimmy Little Selmer Jackson. Directed by Charles Barton. Screenplay, Henry Myers, Edward Ellsen. Jay Gorney, from play by K.B. and Doris Culvan; camera, L.W. O'Connell; editor, James Sweeney. At Brooklyn Strand, week of April 6, '44. Running time. 71 MINS.

Pudge Pfeiffer .... Joe Beamer
Winnie Clark .... Ann Miller
Jim Lighter .... Larry Parks
Sergeant .... Joe Sawyer
Bert - Pfeiffer .... Jimmy Little
Colonel Robbins .... Selmer Jackson
Captain Jessup .... Larry Thompson
Mrs. Clark .... Barbara Brown
Gen. Willis .... Charles Trowbridge
Sam Jonas .... Charles Wilson
Corporal Trupp .... Syd Saylor
Maxon .... Doodles Weaver

Hi, Lo, Jack and a Dame, Condos Brothers, The Vagabonds, Johnson Brothers, Jack Gilford, Judy Clark and the Solid Senders, Bob Evans with Jerry O'Leary, Hal McIntyre Orchestra.

"Hey, Rookie" is fair entertainment, a pleasant vaudeville-type film that will fit snugly into the lower rung of dual bills.

Produced inexpensively by Irving Briskin, the film is livened considerably by a steady parade of stage and radio personalities, including zany Joe Besser, from Broadway's "Son's o' Fun." Seven songs are spaced evenly throughout the proceedings, written by Sgt. J. C. Lewis, Jr., Henry Myers, Edward Eliscu and Jay Gorney. The latter three also wrote the screenplay. Ann Miller cavorts, sings and terps alone, and with Larry Parks, who plays the male romantic lead. Miss Miller is an experienced dancer who registers well.

Film is based on an army musical play which held the stage of L. A.'s Belasco theatre for 36 weeks. It deals with a musical comedy producer, in the army, who is assigned to put on a show to entertain his fellow-soldiers in camp. His trials in staging the show, hindered by the antics of Besser and Jimmy Little, form the nucleus of the plot. Hi, Lo, Jack and a Dame, Condos Bros., Jack Gilford, Bob Evans and his dummy, and Hal McIntyre and his orch are included in the activities. All in all, [illegible]ne is brief, to the point, and will do. *Sten.*

Miniature Reviews

"Show Business" (Musical) (RKO). Eddie Cantor in top form. Will hit profitable b.o. in all runs.

"Pin Up Girl" (musical; color) (20th). Betty Grable starrer okay escapology.

"Bermuda Mystery" (20th). Routine whodunit, budgeted for duals.

"Address Unknown" (Col). Disappointing film that will lean heavily on Paul Lukas' name for boxoffice draw.

"Slightly Terrific" (Songs) (U). Program filmusical for dual support.

"Coastal Command" (RKO). Absorbing documentary; fine dual supporter.

"Hot Rhythm" (Songs) (Mono). Mildly amusing comedy suitable for duals.

"Blazing Frontier" (PRC). Routine western with some high comedy spots.

"Ukraine in Flames" (Soviet). Fine documentary for houses showing Russian pix.

Show Business

(MUSICAL)

Hollywood, April 18.

RKO release of Eddie Cantor production. Stars Cantor, George Murphy, Joan Davis, Nancy Kelly, Constance Moore, Don Douglas. Directed by Edwin L. Marin. Screenplay by Joseph Quillan and Dorothy Bennett; story, Bert Granet; added dialog, Irving Elinson; camera, Robert de Grasse; special effects, Vernon L. Walker; editor, Theron Warth; asst. director, Clem Beauchamp; song, George Jessel, Ben Oakland. Musical numbers created and staged by Nick Castle. Tradeshown April 18, '44. Running time, 90 MINS.

Eddie Martin .... Eddie Cantor
George Doane .... George Murphy
Joan Mason .... Joan Davis
Nancy Gaye .... Nancy Kelly
Constance Ford .... Constance Moore
Charles Lucas .... Don Douglas

"Show Business" is Eddie Cantor's first film as a producer. It's an auspicious start, with Cantor wisely splitting top importance with George Murphy, Joan Davis and Constance Moore; and giving latter trio plenty of opportunity to catch attention in their particular fields. Picture is a speedy and well-assembled piece of diverting entertainment geared for profitable biz in all runs.

Title immediately tabs backstage setting. But that's not a drawback in view of present trend to spot every filmusical that way. In addition to Cantor, Murphy and Joan Davis there are plenty of laugh lines and situations, with the horseplay ideally set up between Cantor and Miss Davis. It's all for laughs, and several oldies are brushed up a bit to still catch attention from the customers due to spontaneous delivery and smart timing.

Story thread carries through period of years in the 'teens, when Murphy is straight man at Miner's Bowery in era of belles, bloomers and beers. Cantor shows up for amateur night, cops first prize when he speeds up song and prances around stage to duck produce tossed at him, and teams with Murphy as comic. Murphy is a chaser, pursued by soubrette Nancy Kelly, but falls for Constance Moore who has Miss Davis in sister act. Four eventually team up for vaude act; Murphy and Miss Moore marry; there's the formula separation; he goes overseas as soldier in last World War; Cantor follows as an entertainer; Cantor and Miss Davis sign with Ziegfeld for a "Follies" and uncover Murphy at a down-and-out Frisco speakeasy for reunion of quartette in "Follies" and a double marriage.

Cantor revives several of his old and standout tunes including "Alabamy Bound," "Dinah," "I Don't Want to Get Well," and "Making Whoopee"—latter a standout towards the finish, with Eddie effectively smacking over delivery without benefit of costly production setting. Other pop tunes of 20 or more years ago are utilized by Murphy, Miss Moore and Nancy Kelly; with the Cantor-Murphy-Davis-Moore quartet clicking with comedy presentation of "Sextette from Lucia," and a straight rendition of "Dinah," both as vaude turns.

Cantor is Cantor throughout, working with enthusiasm at every turn. Murphy provides his usual strong performance as the song-and-dance man; teaming with Miss Moore for the straight romantic story thread. Miss Davis is spotlighted as comedienne working opposite Cantor, and pair provide solid laughs with antics on numerous occasions. Miss Kelly is okay as third member of romantic triangle, while Don Douglas carries role of vaude agent also in love with Miss Moore.

Direction by Edwin L. Marin is topnotch, providing picture with fast tempo and getting utmost out of every comedy line and situation. Stage acts and songs are smartly inserted for smooth unfolding. Production mounting and technical contributions are high grade, especially photography by Robert de Grasse and special effects by Vernon Walker. *Walt.*

Pin Up Girl

(COLOR; MUSICAL)

20th-Fox release of William LeBaron production. Stars Betty Grable; features Martha Raye, Joe E. Brown, Joh Harvey, Charlie Spivak Band. Directed by Bruce Humberstone. Screenplay, Robt. Ellis, Helen Logan, Earl Baldwin; original, Libbie Block. Songs, Mack Gordon-James Monaco; dances, Hermes Pan, Alice Sullivan, Gae Foster, Fanchon; camera, Ernest Palmer; special effects, Fred Sersen; music direction, Emil Newman, Chas. Henderson. Tradeshown April 14, 1944, N.Y. Running time. 85 MINS.

Lorry Jones .... Betty Grable
Tommy Dooley .... John Harvey
Marian .... Martha Raye
Eddie .... Joe E. Brown
Barney Briggs .... Eugene Pallette
Skating Vanities .... Themselves
Kay .... Dorothea Kent
Dud Miller .... Dave Willock
Specialty Dancers .... Condos Brothers
Charlie Spivak and Orchestra .... Themselves
Stage Doorman .... Robert Homans
Headwaiter .... Marcel Dalio
George .... Roger Clark
Captain of Waiters .... Leon Belasco
Window Cleaner .... Irving Bacon
Messenger Boy .... Walter Tetley
Scrubwoman .... Ruth Warren
Walter .... Max Willenz
Manton Moreland
Red Cape .... Charles Moore

Betty Grable in "Pin Up Girl"—a natural. The title and the star are right and even if the story isn't they make it right for the b.o.

This is one of those escapist filmusicals which you accept, or else. It makes no pretenses at ultra realism, and if you get into the mood fast that it's something to occupy your attention for an hour and a half, it's all very pleasing and pleasant.

Producer William LeBaron, director Bruce Humberstone and the cast, scripters, et al. have treated "Pin Up Girl" in uniform spirit. The Missouri gal who crashes the party of a welcome - to - a - Guadalcanal - hero (John Harvey) in one of New York's top niteries brooks no plot examination. From there the action shifts to Washington, again a nitery. All of it makes for song-and-dance specialty numbers set in bistros which contract into intime boites or expand into guargantuan proportions, with stages bigger than the Roxy and space larger than Madison Square Garden. Thus are sandwiched in the Skating Vanities, doing their stuff on rollers, and that precision military finale that looks like the West Point parade grounds.

Right from the start, when Betty Grable is almost trapped in her gate-crashing, she poses as a musicomedy actress, mounts the rostrum pronto and Charlie Spivak picks up the music cue and it all comes out all right. Just like that!

Mack Gordon and James Monaco have provided some good tunes, including "Time Alone Will Tell," "Yankee Doodle Hayride," "Don't Carry Tales Out of School," "Red Robins, Bob White and Blue Birds."

Joe E. Brown as the cafe prop and Martha Raye as his jealous star carry the low comedy against which are backgrounded expert hoofology by the Condos Bros., Spivak's stuff, the rollerskating routines (which Gae Foster first did at the N. Y. Roxy) and the military finale.

In Technicolor Miss Grable is a looker in pastel shades and spades. The costumes of the spec numbers have likewise been contrived for ultra sartorial resplendence. All combined it makes for merry movie moments. *Abel.*

Bermuda Mystery

20th-Fox release of William Girard production. Stars Preston Foster, Ann Rutherford. Directed by Benjamin Stoloff. Screenplay, W. Scott Darling, from story by John Larkin; camera, Joseph La Shelle; editor, Norman Colbert. Tradeshown April 17, '44. Running time, 65 MINS.

Steve Carromond .... Preston Foster
Constance Martin .... Ann Rutherford
Dr. Tilford .... Charles Butterworth
Angela .... Gelene Reynolds
Mrs Tilford .... Jean Howard
Det. Sergeant Donovan .... Richard Lane
Mr. Best .... Roland Drew
Mr. Brooks .... John Eldredge
Mr. Cooper .... Theodore Von Eltz
Mr. Bond .... Pierre Watkin
Dunham .... Jason Robards
Mr. Martin .... Kane Richmond
Judge .... Holmes Herbert

In "Bermuda Mystery" 20th-Fox has dished up a routine whodunit with stock situations and obvious development. Too many characters are rung in as possible villains to make the yarn at all plausible and some weak comedy doesn't help it along. A "B" film obviously aimed for the duals, this is apparently mounted on a modest budget.

Six buddies, World War I vets, have pooled some money together for investment, the kitty and whatever profits to be shared after 10 years by all or whoever survives. Comes the week the money is to be divvied, and the partners start to keel over. Police say heart attacks, but the niece of one (Ann Rutherford) suspects foul play.

Rest of the film is spent in her naive methods to track the murderer down. Preston Foster, as an unwilling private detective rung in on the case, never seems to be putting too much heart in his work. Between amateur sleuthing and open love-making to Foster (who is about to be married), Miss Rutherford never seems convincing. Charles Butterworth and Roland Drew have most to do in the brief parts given the six buddies, and Gelene Reynolds is good as the "other woman."

Address Unknown

Columbia release of William Cameron Menzies production, directed by Menzies. Stars Paul Lukas, K. T. Stevens; features Carl Esmond, Peter Van Eyck, Mady Christians, Morris Carnovsky. Screenplay, Herbert Dalmas; from story by Kressmann Taylor; camera, Rudolph Mate; editor, Al Clark; music, Ernst Toch; music director, M. W. Stoloff. At Globe, N. Y., week April 15, '44. Running time, 80 MINS.

Martin Schulz .... Paul Lukas
Baron von Friesche .... Carl Esmond
Heinrich Schulz .... Peter Van Eyck
Elsa .... Mady Christians
Max Eisenstein .... Morris Carnovsky
Griselle .... K. T. Stevens
Postman .... Emory Parnell
Mrs. Delancey .... Mary Young
Jimmie Blake .... Frank Faylen
Pip-Squeak .... Charles Halton
Stage Director .... Erwin Kaiser
Professor Schmidt .... Frank Reicher
Carl .... Dale Cornell
Wilhelm .... Peter Newmeyer
Youngest .... Larry Joe Olsen
Hugo .... Gary Gray

The corruption and degeneration of a repatriated German-American who returns to his homeland is the basis of this film weighed down by artificial dramatics. However, with Paul Lukas' name value, it should fare well at the boxoffice.

Based on Kressmann Taylor's story, told in a series of letters exchanged between two German partners in an American art firm, the picture has been translated into a slow-moving, ponderous tale that lacks the intensity of the book, and never comes up to expectations, due to the fact that the story, while pertinent 10 years ago, has become dated by time and events.

Discarding the letter device, camera moves back and forth between Germany and America, recounting the story of one partner who has taken his family, and the actress-daughter of his Jewish associate, back to Germany in the early days of the Hitler regime, leaving his eldest son, engaged to the actress, behind to help run the business.

His inculcation of Nazi doctrines leads to the point where he refuses to protect his daughter-in-law-to-be from the Gestapo, after she flouted Nazi intolerance from the stage.

Her flight from her pursuers, and the process whereby he falls prey to the cause he espoused, makes for the only real action in the picture.

Lukas strives mightily to instil importance and interest to the role of the former American turned Nazi, but the inadequacies of the script are too great to be overcome. K. T. Stevens, in her first starring performance, does well in the little she is called upon to do. Carl Esmond, Peter Van Eyck, Mady Christians and Morris Carnovsky provide fine support, though they seldom have the opportunity to display their abilities.

The story never measures up to the excellent photography and handsome production given it.

Slightly Terrific
(SONGS)

Hollywood, April 14.

Universal release of Alexis Thurn-Taxis production. Directed by Edward F. Cline. Screenplay by Edward Dein and Stanley Davis; original, Edith Watkins, Florence McEnany; camera, Paul Ivano; special photography, John P. Fulton; editor, Norman A. Cerf; songs, Milton Rosen, Everett Carter. Previewed April 13, '44. Running time, **61 MINS.**

Tuttle	Leon Errol
Julie Bryant	Anne Rooney
Charlie	Eddie Quillan
Mike Hamilton	Richard Lane
Marie Mason	Betty Kean
Joe Bryant	Ray Malone

Also: Lillian Cornell, The Stardusters, Maritza Dancers, The 8 Rhythmeers, Donald Novis, Loraine Krueger, Jayne Forrest.

This lightweight program filmusical has a few diverting moments scattered through an inane and sophomoric plot. Strictly a dual supporter in the secondary houses.

Plot is a rather silly hodge-podge detailing efforts of a young theatrical group to get attention. Eccentric Leon Errol shows up with promise to put show on at distant town where his twin brother is prominent manufacturer. Mixup of the two look-alikes around hotel, which conveniently has dance floor and band for presentation of several numbers, creates confusion to carry through for sufficient footage.

Eddie Quillan is head of the juve troupe, with Anne Rooney, comedienne Betty Kean and Ray Malone as principals. Lillian Cornell, Jayne Forrest, Starduster harmony quartet, Miss Rooney and Miss Kean handle total of nine songs, seven new ones supplied by Milton Rosen and Everett Carter. Director Eddie Cline supplies broadest comedy technique in attempt to hold script together throughout. *Walt.*

Coastal Command
(Documentary)
(BRITISH-MADE)

RKO release of Crown Film Unit produced in England for the British Government with cooperation of Royal Air Force and Royal Navy. Supervised by Ian Dalrymple; direction, J. B. Holmes; photography, Jonah Jones; music, R. Vaughan Williams. Reviewed in N. Y. April 19, '44. Running time, **60 MINS.**

A British counterpart of our own "Memphis Belle," this absorbing, full-length factual film on the work of the R. A. F. division which protects Britain's coasts and life-giving convoys, is one of the most thrilling and graphic pictures the war has brought forth.

Hero of the film is a Sunderland flying boat, "T for Tommie," that goes out day after day to protect incoming convoys. Presenting a week in the life of the Sunderland, with Nazi fighters attacking the ship, the film has as its climax the detection and subsequent destruction of a German raider, in a battle comparable to the sinking of the Bismarck off Iceland by British.

With the actual secret Operational Room of the Coastal Command being shown, and with superb photography, the picture is an engrossing and moving account of men's heroism and quiet courage in performing a vital job in a commonplace and unspectacular manner.

Hot Rhythm
(SONGS)

Monogram release of Lindsley Parsons production. Directed by William Beaudine. Features Dona Drake, Robert Lowery, Tim and Irene Ryan, Sidney Miller. Story and screenplay, Tim Ryan, Charles Marion; camera, Ira Morgan; editor, Richard Currier. At Brooklyn Strand, week of April 13, '44. Running time, **79 MINS.**

Mary	Dona Drake
Jimmy	Robert Lowery
O'Hara	Tim Ryan
Polly	Irene Ryan
Sammy	Sidney Miller
Taylor	Jerry Cooper
Strobach	Robert Kent
Whiffle	Harry Langdon
Brown	Lloyd Ingraham
Jackson	Cyril Ring
Receptionist	Joan Curtis
Cafe Owner	Paul Porcasi

"Hot Rhythm" is mildly amusing with a good idea and some okay gags, but with the comedy for the most part corny and obvious. The idea—that of kidding spot radio commercials—isn't developed too thoroughly or brightly, and film drags. The few good gags and the half-dozen songs should carry the film in the neighborhoods as a dualer.

Story centers around a couple of jingle writers and the love of one for a singer. Attempts to get the singer lined up with a name band cause mild complications and account for the comedy. Songs are spaced through the film and, though pleasant, are undistinguished. Robert Lowery is personable as the hero and Sidney Miller is comic as his long-suffering sidekick. Dona Drake is an attractive ingenue, with a nice singing personality, notably in warbling "Where Were You" and "Talk Me Into It."

Irene Ryan, as a wacky secretary, is sometimes funny and is good with a talking-character song, "Happiest Girl in Town." But for most part her comedy is standard slapstick, as is Tim Ryan's and Harry Langdon's. Latter, former silents comic, has only a bit role.

Blazing Frontier

PRC release of Sigmund Neufeld production. Stars Buster Crabbe, Al "Fuzzy" St. John. Directed by Sam Newfield. Original story and screenplay, Patricia Harper; camera, Robert Cline; editor, Holbrook N. Todd. At N. Y. theatre, N. Y., week of April 4, '44, dual. Running time, **59 MINS.**

Billy the Kid	Buster Crabbe
Fuzzy Jones	Al (Fuzzy) St. John
Helen	Marjorie Manners
Barstow	Milt Kibbee
Sharp	I. Stanford Jolley
Pete	Kermit Maynard
Tragg	Frank Hagney
Slade	George Chesebro
Biff	Frank Ellis

More exploits of Billy the Kid, portrayed this time by Buster Crabbe, with good comedy support provided by Al "Fuzzy" St. John, giving stock yarn much-needed lift. Minus any love interest, film has plenty of hard riding to satisfy the hoss-opera brigade. Should fill in nicely as dualer.

Plot has heroes joining band of railroad detectives set on robbing settlers of their land, and working from within to thwart their efforts. Blackguards receive just deserts in a series of gunplay and fisticuffs.

Starring duo gives satisfactory account of itself, despite evident shortcomings of story. Direction and production fair.

Ukraine in Flames

Artkino release of Alexander Dovzhenko production. Commentary and editing, Alexander Dovzhenko; English commentary, Alexander Werth; narrated by Bill Downs. At Stanley theatre, N. Y. Running time, **56 MINS.**

Moving documentary of Red Army's battle for the Ukraine. "Ukraine in Flames" is also notable for fine photography by cameramen who advanced with shock troops during battle that broke the Nazi grip on Russia.

Starts with pre-war shots of productive farms and industrial advances made under five-year plans, hops to German devastation of land and introduces survivors of Nazi cruelties. Incorporating a number of clips from captured German newsreels, film offers evidence of Nazi atrocities, showing mass graves of murdered civilians and soldiers on the outskirts of Kharkov. Also has some thrilling scenes of Russian partisans in action plus touching shots of Russian soldiers being greeted by inhabitants of recaptured cities.

Narration by Bill Downs, European correspondent for the Columbia Broadcasting System, is adequate.

Miniature Reviews

"The Story of Dr. Wassell" (Color) (Par). Spectacular war picture, with romance and comedy, should be a big grosser.

"Two Girls and a Sailor" (Musical) (M-G). Lack of story and length of footage makes this musical pot-pourri disappointing entertainment.

"Double Indemnity" (Par). Fred MacMurray, Barbara Stanwyck, Edward G. Robinson in big b.o. murder meller.

"And the Angels Sing" (Songs) (Par). MacMurray-Lamour musical light escapist fare for mild b.o.

"The Hitler Gang" (Par). Documentary-melo of Nazi party growth.

"Once Upon a Time" (Col). Cary Grant-Janet Blair in novel, controversial film due for b.o.

"Gambler's Choice" (Par). Fast-action meller; good dualer.

"Cobra Woman" (Color) (U). Jungle romance should prove good b.o. fare.

"Seven Days Ashore" (Musical) (RKO). Thoroughly enjoyable minor musical which will please on dual bills.

"Henry Aldrich Plays Cupid" (Par). Entertaining and good dual supporter.

"Man From Frisco" (Rep). Modern shipbuilding story should do okay with right exploitation.

"Trocadero" (Rep.) Lightweight musical for dual support.

The Story of Dr. Wassell
(TECHNICOLOR)

Paramount release of Cecil B. DeMille production, directed by DeMille. Stars Gary Cooper; features Laraine Day, Signe Hasso, Dennis O'Keefe. Based upon story as related by Commander Corydon M. Wassell and upon story by James Hilton; adaptation, Alan LeMay and Charles Bennett; editor, Anne Bauchens; camera, Victor Milner, William Snyder, Gordon Jennings, Farciot Edouart, Wallace Kelley. Previewed at Constitution Hall, Washington, D. C., April 1, '44. Running time, **136 MINS.**

Dr. Corydon M. Wassell	Gary Cooper
Madeline	Laraine Day
Bettina	Signe Hasso
Hopkins (Hoppy)	Dennis O'Keefe
Three Martini	Carol Thurston
Lieut. Dirk van Daal	Carl Esmond
Murdock	Paul Kelly
Anderson (Andy)	Elliott Reid
Commander Bill Goggins	Stanley Ridges
Johnny	Renny McEvoy
Alabam	Oliver Thorndike
Ping	Philip Ahn
Ruth	Barbara Britton

Because this is the factual story of Dr. Wassell's heroic evacuation of 12 men, plus himself, from Java in earlier stages of the war, it packs more interest than otherwise might have been the case. The exploits of the by-now famed Naval Commander have been brought to the screen on a lavish scale by Cecil B. DeMille, with an exceptionally fine cast and good comedy relief. The entertainment value, even had the scenario been fictional, is very strong. Production excellence and good color photography are added assets. Gross possibilities are exceptionally favorable despite any trend away from so-called war pictures.

While the running time of 136 minutes is much longer than the average and there are portions where cuts could have been made, the story and DeMille's spectacular production possess so much body and covers so much ground, with many incidents of a romantic or non-war character included, that there is justification for the extent of the footage.

There can be no quarrel with the

cast. While Gary Cooper bears no particular resemblance to Commander Wassell himself, who's 60 and a weather-beaten type, the star imparts to the role much vigor, color and sympathetic interest. It's one of Cooper's best performances. The story, based upon facts as related by Commander Wassell, through various cutbacks, takes Cooper from his early horse-and-buggy country doctor days in Arkansas through medical research in China before the war and, finally, to Australia after he has successfully transported wounded men to that point. Instead of being court-martialed there for having disobeyed orders to leave stretcher cases behind in Java, Dr. Wassell, as most of the public should know, was awarded the Navy Cross and his heroic deed made the subject of a broadcast by President Roosevelt.

Battle scenes as well as others are very effectively staged and photographed. It's a wonder DeMille himself doesn't have plenty of casualties in view of the realistic manner in which he directs bombing and other sequences.

Comedy touches and romance go a long way toward lightening any likely strain from the war ingredients. Renny McEvoy, who is strong for the native girls and through that predilection is left behind with Dr. Wassell and his stretcher cases, together with others furnish the laughs. McEvoy is a terrific character in all respects. Laraine Day, who first cast her eyes upon Dr. Wassell in China before the war, shoulders the love interest opposite the famed naval doctor, while Signe Hasso figures in a romantic light with Carl Esmond and Elliott Reid. The combination of O'Keefe and Carol Thurston, the native Javanese nurse with whom he gets marooned in the jungles at the mercy of approaching Japs, strike an exceptionally strong note. This is Miss Thurston's first film appearance but it won't be her last. She's a very ingratiating type. Paul Kelly is excellent as a morose wounded man, while Stanley Ridges gives an impressive performance as a naval doctor who's also among the wounded. *Char.*

Two Girls and a Sailor
(MUSICAL)

Metro release of Joe Pasternak production. Features Van Johnson, June Allyson, Gloria DeHaven, Jose Iturbi, Jimmy Durante, Gracie Allen, Lena Horne, Tom Drake, Henry Stephenson, Henry O'Neill, Ben Blue, Carlos Ramirez, Frank Sully, Albert Coates, Donald Meek, Amparo Novarro, Virginia O'Brien, the Wilde Twins, Dick Deyo, Harry James and Xavier Cugat orchestras. Directed by Richard Thorpe. Story and adaptation, Richard Connell and Gladys Lehman; editor, George Boemler; camera, Robert Surtees; vocal arrangements, Kay Thompson; dances, Sammy Lee. Previewed at Ziegfeld, N. Y., April 24, '44. Running time, 124 MINS.

John Dyckman Brown III.....Van Johnson
Patsy Deyo.....June Allyson
Jean Deyo.....Gloria DeHaven
Jose Iturbi.....By Himself
Billy Kipp.....Jimmy Durante
Concerto Number.....Gracie Allen
Specialty.....Lena Horne
Frank Miller.....Tom Drake
John Dyckman Brown I..Henry Stephenson
John Dyckman Brown II.....Henry O'Neill
Ben.....Ben Blue
Carlos.....Carlos Ramirez
Private Adams.....Frank Sully
Albert Coates.....By Himself
Mr. Nizby.....Donald Meek
Amparo Novarro.....By Herself
Virginia O'Brien.....By Herself
The Wilde Twins.....By Themselves
Dick Deyo.....Frank Jenks
Harry James' Orc with Helen Forrest
Xavier Cugat Orchestra with Lina Romay

Weakness of story, a very thin one in this instance, reduces "Two Girls and a Sailor" to little more than a salmagundi of band numbers by Harry James and Xavier Cugat, with their soloists, plus Jimmy Durante, of whom there isn't enough, and various other specialties ranging from Lena Horne to the concert pianist Jose Iturbi. Running 124 minutes, it is too long and generally slow. The boxoffice prospects hinge chiefly on the marquee.

The tenuous book, by Richard Connell and Gladys Lehman, which mainly records a romance between a girl singer and a sailor with a prominent family background, unknown to her until near the end, is not only a disappointing foundation upon which to build a musical but, also, the dialog lacks brilliance and comedy relief is more lacking than in evidence.

The Schnoz, who was on this lot some years ago as a featured player and since has staged a big comeback, plays a character role as well as doing a couple numbers. He's an old-time actor who assists two girls in running a canteen for servicemen. But more than the early number at the piano and, toward the finish, "Inky, Dinky Do," could be stood from such a seasoned and forceful singing entertainer.

June Allyson and Gloria DeHaven play a sister act, featured in a few short numbers. Headliners at a nightclub with the James and Cugat orchestras, they turn their home into a place where servicemen may be entertained after they're through with their nitery chores. This leads, through strange circumstances, to a storage warehouse, apparently willed to them, which is converted into a canteen. It's all been arranged by the sailor of rich parents, unbeknownst to the sister team. He falls for one, Gloria DeHaven, then switches to the other, June Allyson.

In addition to the band numbers, with Helen Forrest as soloist with the James outfit and Lina Romay with Cugat, specialties include a spanish baritone solo by Carlos Ramirez; a rather clever comical one-finger piano concerto by Gracie Allen; clever comedy interpretation of "Take It Easy" by Virginia O'Brien; short dance number in which Ben Blue works with a girl partner; Jose Iturbi playing a ritual fire dance on the piano, assisted by his sister, unbilled but announced on the screen, and Lena Horne singing "Paper Doll."

Miss Allyson, who should not be far from stardom, turns in a very fine performance despite the poorness of the script, which also is true of Van Johnson, opposite her as the sailor boy. Miss DeHaven and Tom Drake, latter doing a soldier, fare suitably though not impressively, while lessers of a well-established character school who come through as usual are Henry Stephenson, Henry O'Neill and Donald Meek.

Joe Pasternak's production backgrounds are to some extent impressive but on the tinsel and theatrical side, though his dream sequence is very effective. Photography suffers in spots. *Char.*

Double Indemnity

Paramount release of Joseph Sistrom production. Stars Fred MacMurray, Barbara Stanwyck, Edward G. Robinson. Directed by Billy Wilder. Screenplay, Wilder and Raymond Chandler, from novel by James M. Cain; editor, Doane Harrison; music, Miklos Rozsa; camera, John Seitz. Tradeshown in N. Y. April 21, '44. Running time, 103 MINS.

Walter Neff.....Fred MacMurray
Phyllis Dietrichson.....Barbara Stanwyck
Barton Keyes.....Edward G. Robinson
Mr. Jackson.....Porter Hall
Lola Dietrichson.....Jean Heather
Mr. Dietrichson.....Tom Powers
Nino Zachette.....Byron Barr
Mr. Norton.....Richard Gaines
Sam Gorlopis.....Fortunio Bonanova
Joe Pete.....John Philliber

James M. Cain's Liberty story, "Double Indemnity," apparently based on a sensational murder of the '20s, has become an absorbing melodrama in its Paramount adaptation. It is certain boxoffice insurance. And double indemnity with such marquee names as Fred MacMurray, Barbara Stanwyck and Edward G. Robinson.

There are unmistakeable similarities between the Paramount pic and the famous Snyder-Gray murder wherein Albert Snyder was sashweighted to death 17 years ago in his Queens Village, N. Y., home by his wife, Ruth, and her lover, Judd Gray. Both the fictional and the real murders were for the slain men's insurance. Both were committed by the murdered men's wives and their amours.

"Indemnity" is rapidly moving and consistently well developed. It is a story replete with suspense, for which credit must go in a large measure to Billy Wilder's direction. He was also co-author of the screenplay.

The story's development revolves mainly around the characterizations of MacMurray, Miss Stanwyck and Robinson, the first two as the lovers and Robinson as an insurance claims agent who balks the pair's "perfect crime" from becoming just what they had intended it to appear—an accidental death from a moving train, for which there would have been a double indemnity.

Miss Stanwyck plays the wife of an oilman, and when MacMurray, an insurance salesman, becomes her paramour, they sell to the husband, fraudulently, an accidental-death policy. They then kill him and place his body on the railway tracks. Their plans go awry, however, when MacMurray learns that Miss Stanwyck has been using him as a dupe, and he shoots her to death. It is a story told in flashback, film opening with MacMurray confessing voluntarily the entire setup into a dictaphone for use by the claims agent, from which the narrative then unfolds.

MacMurray has seldom given a better performance. It is somewhat different from his usually light roles, but is always plausible and played with considerable restraint. Miss Stanwyck is not as attractive as normally with what is seemingly a blonde wig, but it's probably part of a makeup to emphasize the brassiness of the character. Her performance, however, is consistent though the character in the final reel would have been stronger had not the scripters sought to reflect some sense of human understanding for her. Robinson, as the infallible insurance executive quick to determine phoney claims, gives a strong performance, too. It is a typically brash Robinson role. Lessers who do well are Porter Hall, Jean Heather, Tom Powers (the murdered man) and Richard Gaines.

Joseph Sistrom has contributed a grade A production, and there's an enterprising score by Miklos Rozsa. *Kahn.*

And The Angels Sing
(SONGS)

Paramount release of E. D. Leshin production. Stars Dorothy Lamour, Fred MacMurray; features Betty Hutton, Diana Lynn, Mimi Chandler, Raymond Walburn, Eddie Foy, Jr. Directed by George Marshall. Screenplay by Melvin Frank, Norman Panama; original, Claude Binyon; camera, Karl Struss; editor, Eda Warren; songs, Johnny Burke, James Van Heusen; music direction, Victor Young; arrangements, Joseph J. Lilley, Arthur Franklin, Lester Lee and Jerry Seelen; musical numbers by Danny Dare. Tradeshown in N. Y. April 20, '44. Running time, 95 MINS.

Nancy Angel.....Dorothy Lamour
Happy Morgan.....Fred MacMurray
Bobby Angel.....Betty Hutton
Josie Angel.....Diana Lynn
Patti Angel.....Mimi Chandler
Pop Angel.....Raymond Walburn
Fuzzy Johnson.....Eddie Foy, Jr.
Oliver.....Frank Albertson
Schultz.....Mikhail Rasumny
Holman.....Frank Faylen
House Man.....George McKay
Saxy.....Harry Barris
Mickey.....Donald Keer
Miller.....Pere Launders
Potatoes.....Tom Kennedy

"And the Angels Sing" is a pretty tired filmusical with a band and a madcap femme quartet as the focal romantic action. It will need all the marquee support of Fred MacMurray (as the maestro) and Dorothy Lamour and Betty Hutton, half of the sister act (the 4 Angel Sisters) to bolster the flimsy plot. In its b.o. favor is the plot's complete escapology, predicated on a wacky family.

The climactic situation where MacMurray is the harried swain, literally running between the Misses Lamour (whom he loves) and Hutton (whose love is unrequited), reminds one of those old Al Woods bedroom farces with the principals running in and out of doors, strangely just missing each other amidst ludicrous albeit not humorous complications.

The action even beggars maestro MacMurray and Eddie Foy, Jr., his colleague in the band biz, into doing one of those Tyrolean shoe-platter, song-and-dance routines in a Polish cabaret, for throw money, all because they've got to raise $190 for the gals. Action shifts from a small town to N. Y., where MacMurray (incidentally back at the sax, which is how he started) has gone.

There are topical musical moments such as "Hello Mary, How Does Your Garden Grow?", with a Victory Garden motif; and Miss Hutton is her usual energetic self with a scat routine, while Miss Lamour ballads "It Could Happen to You." The film's title is borrowed from a yesteryear pop-song hit, but the pic does not reprise that song. *Abel.*

The Hitler Gang

Hollywood, April 21.

Paramount release of B. G. De Sylva production. Features Robert Watson, Roman Bohnen, Martin Kosleck, Victor Varconi, Luis Van Rooten, Alexander Pope, Ivan Triesault. Directed by John Farrow. Screenplay, Francis Goodrich, Albert Hackett; camera, Ernest Laszlo; editor, Eda Warren; music, David Buttolph. Tradeshown in L. A. April 20, '44. Running time, 101 MINS.

Adolf Hitler.....Robert Watson
Captain Ernst Roehm.....Roman Bohnen
Joseph Goebbels.....Martin Kosleck
Rudolph Hess.....Victor Varconi
Heinrich Himmler.....Luis Van Rooten
Hermann Goering.....Alexander Pope
Pastor Niemoeller.....Ivan Triesault
"Geli" Raubal.....Poldy Dur
Angela Raubal.....Helene Thimig
General Ludendorff.....Reinhold Schunzel
Geh. Von Hindenburg.....Sig Ruman
Julius Streicher.....Alexander Granach
Gregor Strasser.....Fritz Kortner
Alfred Rosenberg.....Tonio Selwart
Adolf Wagner.....Richard Ryen
Cardinal von Faulhaber.....Ray Collins
Gustav von Kahr.....Ludwig Donath
Anton Drexler.....Erno Verebes
Franz von Papen.....Walter Kingsford
General von Epp.....Fred Nurney
Col. von Reichenau.....Arthur Loft
Fritz Thyssen.....Lionel Royce

"The Hitler Gang" is a melodrama exposition of the start and progress of the Nazi party and Hitler through formative years and up to start of present world war. As a documentary and re-creation of key events in Germany between the two wars, picture holds certain interest, but it's not entertainment for current audience requirements. Biz will be spotty, with best chance in key centers where customers will delight in hissing the Nazis.

Paramount produced the picture mainly as a contribution to the war effort, according to studio spokesmen during production, and had full cooperation of the Government in the endeavor. Factual line has been taken throughout rather than resort to accentuated theatrics. Finish is non-climactic, resorting to montages of marching soldiers and United Nations flag-waving to get to the end title.

Hitler is picked up in a German military hospital in 1918 suffering from emotional shock, and tabbed a paranoiac case. Shortly after he's used by the high command as a political spellbinder to form the National Socialist Party and attract Roehm, Hess, Goebbels, Himmler, Goering and others. As the organization progresses, Hitler lies and rants for continual double-crossing of those groups he enlists for aid.

The Munich beer hall meetings and eventual putsch is re-enacted, with

Hitler getting light jail sentence where he compiles "Mein Kampf" from various other books and pamphlets. It's there that astrology influences his moves, and on release Hitler retires to the country to let the party proceed. Called back, new campaign for power is launched, with wild promises, appointment as Reichschancellor, and total power through decree. Then follows reign of terror against all opposition, drives against churches and religion; indoctrination of children; and the purge of 1934.

Robert Watson handles role of Hitler in good style with other Nazi leaders effectively depicted by Roman Bohnen, Martin Kosleck, Victor Varconi, Luis Van Rooten, Alexander Pope and Tonio Selwart. Extended cast is in and out for the various sequences. Picture has plenty of authentic sets to carry outlay to heavy negative costs. Technical contributions are okay thorughout. *Walt.*

Once Upon a Time

Columbia release of Alexander Hall production, directed by Hall. Stars Cary Grant, Janet Blair; features James Gleason, Ted Donaldson, William Demarest. Screenplay, Lewis Meltzer and Oscar Saul; adapted by Irving Fineman, from original story by Norman Corwin and Lucille Fletcher Herrmann; editor, Gene Havlick; music, Frederick Hollander; music director, M. W. Stoloff; camera; Franz F. Planer. Previewed in N. Y., April 24, '44. Running time, **88 MINS.**

Jerry Flynn	Cary Grant
Jeanne Thompson	Janet Blair
The Moke	James Gleason
Pinky Thompson	Ted Donaldson
McKenzie	Howard Freeman
Brant	William Demarest
Gabriel Heatter	Art Baker
Dunhill	Paul Stanton
Fatso	Mickey McGuire

One of the more novel scripts of the year, "Once Upon a Time" is certainly bizarre—and yet charming. It's unfathomable—and yet intriguing. It is certainly absurd—and yet boxoffice.

"Once Upon a Time" will certainly excite a national wave of conflicting theories on its merits. It certainly must have required considerable courage for Columbia to have undertaken a production that manifests so few popular ingredients that make for big b.o. Because of its central character, such as it is. "Once Upon a time" is, actually, the story of—a caterpillar! A dancing caterpillar! One that dances only to "Yes Sir, That's My Baby!"

"Once Upon a Time" was originally a radio play called "My Friend Curly," by Norman Corwin (from an idea by Lucille Fletcher Herrmann). It excited considerable comment in radio circles when it was produced on CBS, but its film version, because of a more extensive production starring Cary Grant and Janet Blair, bids fair to create an even greater word-of-mouth.

The film's leading "character," of course, is one that's unbilled—that would be Curly, the caterpillar. Curly is the pal, of nine-year-old Pinky, and it dances when Pinky plays "That's My Baby" on his mouth-organ. When a flop Broadway producer learns of this phenomenon, he sees a chance to gain its possession and exploit it sufficiently so that he can salvage his theatre from the bankers. Gabriel Heatter hears about the dancing caterpillar and gives it nationwide prominence in discussing it on his radio program. Then follows a deluge of offers to exploit the insect—and there's even a scene of Walt Disney, over long-distance phone from Hollywood, offering $100,000 for it.

The basic story may have difficulty in "reaching" an audience at first, but if one can accept the sheer fantasy for what it's worth, it can very well be excellent entertainment. There's considerable charm in the youngster's attachment for the insect though the close link that existed in the original radio play between the theatrical agent and the boy (in the film the agent is the theatrical producer) is somewhat lost. And that final reel—when the youngster has been overcome with grief over the loss of his caterpillar, only to learn that it wasn't lost at all but had since become a butterfly—is an exercise in screen fantasy.

Both Grant and Miss Blair may be starred in this film, but they must bow in performance to others not equally billed. Namely, Ted Donaldson, the youngster, who, in his first film appearance, is what publicity departments would call a find. James Gleason, William Demarest and Howard Freeman are among the major supporting players who do okay.

That title really tells it. There's a foreword that suggests to the audience, in effect, to pull up a chair and relax. It's the kind of suggestion that had best be taken literally. *Kahn.*

Gambler's Choice

Hollywood, April 21.

Paramount release of Pine-Thomas production. Features Chester Morris, Nancy Kelly, Russell Hayden, Sheldon Leonard, Lee Patrick. Directed by Frank McDonald. Screenplay, Maxwell Shane, Irving Reis; original, Howard Emmett Rogers, James Edward Grant; camera, Fred Jackman; editor, Howard Smith. Tradeshown in L. A. April 20, '44. Running time, **66 MINS.**

Ross Hadley	Chester Morris
Vi Parker	Nancy Kelly
Mike McGlennon	Russell Hayden
Chappie Wilson	Sheldon Leonard
Fay Lawrence	Lee Patrick
Ulysses S. Rogers	Lloyd Corrigan
Benny	Tommy Dugan
Yellow Gloves Weldon	Lyle Talbot
McGrady	Charles Arnt
Bonnie D'Arcy	Maxine Lewis
Danny May	Billy Nelson

"Gambler's Choice" follows the usual line of fast-action melodrama which characterizes the Pine-Thomas product and shapes up as a strong program supporter for the regular runs.

Colorful era of 1910 provides setting for adventures of Chester Morris in launching swank gambling room in the N. Y. tenderloin district, opposition from competitors and final closure by reform wave.

Russell Hayden, childhood pal of Morris, is the police lieutenant of the district who raids the gambling layouts following death of a cop and is subsequently shipped to the wilds of the Bronx. Nancy Kelly is nightclub singer who is romantically pursued by gambler and cop. Latter wins when Morris saves him from frameup by gambling interests and Morris conveniently dies from gunfight to clear way for clinch of Miss Kelly and Hayden.

Original story by Howard Emmett Rogers and James Edward Grant weaves an actionful tale while script by Maxwell Shane and Irving Reis is decidedly compact. Morris, Miss Kelly and Hayden provide good trip in top spots. Miss Kelly sings two old tunes, "Hold Me Just a Little Closer" and "Sidewalks of New York," as entertainer in night club. Sheldon Leonard, Lee Patrick and Lloyd Corrigan provide interesting supporting characterizations. *Walt.*

Cobra Woman
(TECHNICOLOR)

Hollywood, April 21.

Universal release of George Waggner production. Stars Maria Montez, Jon Hall, Sabu; features Edgar Barrier, Lon Chaney, Lois Collier, Mary Nash, Moroni Olsen, Samuel S. Hinds. Directed by Robert Siodmak. Screenplay by Gene Lewis, Richard Brooks, based on original by W. Scott Darling; camera, George Robinson, W. Howard Greene; color, Natalie Kalmus; editor, Charles Maynard; dances, Paul Oscard; music, Edward Ward; special effects, John Fulton. Tradeshown in Hollywood, April 21, '44. Running time, **70 MINS.**

Tollea / Naja	Maria Montez
Ramu	Jon Hall
Kado	Sabu
Martok	Edgar Barrier
Queen	Mary Nash
Veeda	Lois Collier
Father Paul	Samuel S. Hinds
MacDonald	Moroni Olsen
Hava	Lon Chaney

"Cobra Woman" is a super-fantastic melodrama backgrounded on a mythical island that might exist somewhere in the Indian Ocean. Elaborately and colorfully mounted for Technicolor photography and constant eye-appeal, and continuing the starring trio of Maria Montez, Jon Hall and Sabu. Picture unfolds at fast pace to concentrate on action features of the tale. It's profitable b.o. fare for the regular runs as solo or billtopper.

Plot combines jungle-island romance with melodramatic complications, temple rituals, chases and fights. Miss Montez is kidnapped on eve of wedding to Jon Hall and carried back to an island where her twin sister rules ruthlessly as high priestess and preys on religious superstitions of the natives to keep latter under control. Hall follows his betrothed to the forbidden island, accompanied by native boy, Sabu, to rescue Miss Montez; discovers she's brought back to take rightful place as high priestess instead of twin sister; and sticks around for fast-moving series of melodramatic episodes, including periodic eruptions of nearby volcano, until things are satisfactorily settled for eventual sail-away of the lovers.

Miss Montez is decidedly shapely and eyeful as sarong-draped native girl and dazzlingly gowned as the high priestess. She handled the dual assignment very well. Hall and Sabu are typed in regular characterizations. Lon Chaney is the powerful guard of queen Mary Nash. Edgar Barrier makes adequate heavy, with Lois Collier, Samuel S. Hinds and Moroni Olsen in supporting slots.

Robert Siodmak's direction keeps events moving at a fast pace, taking full advantage of the actionful script. Background music by Edward Ward also is a major asset. Photography by George Robinson, with W Howard Greene as Technicolor associate, is of high standard. In addition to the tropical exteriors, picture has huge temple sets for extravagant mounting for better display via color photography. *Walt.*

Seven Days Ashore
(MUSICAL)

RKO release of John H. Auer production, directed by Auer. Stars Wally Brown, Alan Carney; features Marcy McGuire, Gordon Oliver, Virginia Mayo, Amelita Ward, Elaine Shepard, Dooley Wilson, Freddie Slack orchestra, Freddie Fisher band. Screenplay, Edward Verdier, Irving Phillips, Lawrence Kimble; from story by Jacques Deval; camera, Russell Metty; editor, Harry Marker; songs, Mort Greene, Lou Pollock; dances, Charles O'Curran; musical director, C. Bakaleinikoff; special effects, Vernon Walker. At Palace, N. Y., week April 25, '44. Running time, **72 MINS.**

Monty	Wally Brown
Orval	Alan Carney
Dot	Marcy McGuire
Dan Arland	Gordon Oliver
Carol	Virginia Mayo
Lucy	Amelita Ward
Annabelle	Elaine Shepard
Jason	Dooley Wilson
Mrs. Arland	Marjorie Gateson
Mr. Arland	Alan Dinehart
Hazel	Miriam LaVelle
Mrs. Croxton-Lynch	Margaret Dumont
Captain Harvey	Emory Parnell
Process Server	Ian Wolfe

Freddie Slack Orchestra
Freddie Fisher Band

Making no pretense of being more than a relatively inexpensive production without any big marquee names, this musical is a lot more frolicksome and tuneful than many of its more expensive and elaborate counterparts, and should fit very well as a good dual supporter.

Shenanigans involve efforts of a wealthy playboy in the Merchant Marine to extricate himself from the clutches of two girl violinists, while engaged to a society deb. He turns the musical duo over to his shipmates, Carney and Brown, after the girls slap breach-of-promise suits against him. Boys naturally fall for gals and get married, while playboy gets gal he wants, all to the tune of comedy cavortings.

Team of Carney and Brown score heavily, and with right material should soon be among the top-rung comedians. Gordon Oliver makes a convincing playboy, while the three girls in plot are all lookers and do well. Marcy McGuire puts over three songs in sock fashion, and Dooley Wilson does fine in his two numbers. Freddie Slack has the hepcats jumping, and Freddie Fisher and his corny band are quite funny in the one number they do.

The entire thing comes out as thoroughly enjoyable fare under the neat handling of John Auer.

Henry Aldrich Plays Cupid

Paramount production and release. Stars Jimmy Lydon and Charles Smith; features John Litel, Diana Lynn and Vera Vague. Directed by Hugh Bennett. Screenplay, Muriel Roy Bolton and Val Burton, from story by Aleen Leslie; camera, Daniel Fapp; editor, Everett Douglas. Previewed in N. Y., April 20, '44. Running time, **65 MINS.**

Henry Aldrich	Jimmy Lydon
Dizzy Stevens	Charles Smith
Mr. Aldrich	John Litel
Mrs. Aldrich	Olive Blakeney
Phyllis Michael	Diana Lynn
Mr. Bradley	Vaughn Glaser
Blue Eyes	Vera Vague
Senator Caldicott	Paul Harvey
Male Teacher	Harry Bradley
Female Teacher	Betty Farrington
Male Teacher	Gladden James
Western Union Girl	Shirley Coates

Another in the "Aldrich" series, this one is pleasantly amusing and shouldn't have any difficulty snaring bookings on the duals.

In this one, Henry Aldrich has been bequeathed $5,000 by a deceased uncle for an education at Princeton providing he graduates high school with honors. He does well in all his subjects with the exception of biology, where he incurs the displeasure of his instructor, a dour bachelor who is also the school principal. As a result, he is given so many demerits, he is in danger of not graduating. Believing that a wife would serve as an antidote to the instructor's unpleasant disposition, Henry starts a matrimonial bureau to get him married off. His efforts, as usual, go awry, with droll consequences which involve his parents, a state senator who is a political enemy of his father, and assorted individuals with whom he comes in contact. But, as usual, everything is finally reconciled to the satisfaction of all.

Jimmy Lydon, Charles Smith, John Litel and Olive Blakeney, the usual members of the cast, perform smoothly, with some outstanding assists by Diana Lynn and Vera Vague.

Man From Frisco

Republic production and release. Stars Michael O'Shea and Anne Shirley; features Gene Lockhart, Dan Duryea, Stephanie Bachelor, Ray Walker, Tommy Bond. Directed by Robert Florey. Screenplay, Ethel Hill and Arnold Manoff; original story, George W. Yates and George C. Brown; camera, Jack Marta; music, Marlin Skiles; editor, Ernest Mims. Previewed April 25, '44. Running time, **91 MINS.**

Matt Braddock	Michael O'Shea
Diana Kennedy	Anne Shirley
Joel Kennedy	Gene Lockhart
Jim Benson	Dan Duryea
Ruth Warnecke	Stephanie Bachelor
Johnny Rogers	Ray Walker
Russ Kennedy	Tommy Bond
Bruce McRae	Robert Warwick
Eben Wheelock	Olin Howlin
Martha Kennedy	Ann Shoemaker
Dr. Hershey	Russell Simpson
Chief Campbell	Stanley Andrews
Maritime Commissioner	Forbes Murray
Judge McLain	Erville Alderson
Baby Warnecke, Jr.	Michael Barnitz

"Man from Frisco" started with a good idea—that of a dynamic construction engineer who revolutionizes shipbuilding — but foundered along the way and got stuck in the mud of a stereotyped plot. Title itself is none too descriptive, and would seem to apply more to the Barbary Coast in the 1880's than to a saga of modern shipbuilding. However, with the proper exploitation and the appeal of its stars, picture should do all right for itself on either end of dual bills in nabe houses.

Picture loses effectiveness when it becomes just another romance between the two principals and moves slowly. It is only in the shipyard scenes that the film catches some of the power and drama which goes into the making of the sinews of war. O'Shea never rings true as the Henry Kaiser-like production genius. Anne Shirley is satisfactory as the girl who is first repelled and then attracted to him. Lockhart does fine work in a supporting role, as does Stephanie Bachelor, who contributes one of the few good dramatic sequences in the role of a war worker whose husband is in the Navy.

Production is good, while the direction should have been more demanding as far as realism is concerned.

Trocadero

(SONGS)

Republic release of Walter Colmes production. Stars Rosemary Lane, Johnny Downs; features Ralph Morgan, Dick Purcell, Sheldon Leonard. Directed by William Nigh. Screenplay, Allen Gale, from story by Charles F. Chaplin and Garret Holmes; music, Jay Chernis; camera, Jackson Rose; editor, Robert Crandall. At Brooklyn Strand, week of April 20, '44. Running time, 74 MINS.

Judy.........................Rosemary Lane
Johnny......................Johnny Downs
Sam..........................Ralph Morgan
Spike.........................Dick Purcell
Mickey.....................Sheldon Leonard
Cliff Nazarro...................By Himself
Marge........................Marjorie Manners
Erskine Johnson................By Himself
Dave Fleischer.................By Himself
Carson........................Emmett Bogan
Tony..........................Charles Calvert
Bullfrog.....................Dewey Robinson
Cigarette Girl...................Ruth Hilliard
Master of Ceremonies.......Eddie Bartell
Specialties: Bob Chester band, Eddie Le Baron band, Matty Malneck band, Gus Arnheim band, Wingy Mannone, Ida James, Stardusters, Radio Rogues.

A story of a Hollywood nitery, "Trocadero" is a mildly entertaining musical with a potpourri of talent that should make it right for the duals.

Story has two adopted children, played by Johnny Downs and Rosemary Lane, being left a night club at the end of Prohibition by their foster-father. Pickings are lean until they hire a swing band that skyrockets the club to fame. Separate romances of both children make for the love interest.

Eight new songs are introduced in addition to two revivals, none of them outstanding. Following the vogue of having "name" bands, picture has Eddie LeBaron (actual owner of the Troc), Bob Chester, Matty Malneck and Gus Arnheim. Wingy Mannone is in for one bit doing a musical and vocal rendition of "The Music Goes Round and Round," Ida James warbles "Shoo Shoo Baby," and the Stardusters do one number. Club background is also used to drag in the Radio Rogues with their imitations, Cliff Nazarro singing and making with the double-talk, and cartoonist Dave Fleischer doing some drawing.

Rosemary Lane, looking very well, is convincing in the emotional scenes, and does several songs in good style, while Johnny Downs does a hoofing routine and acts with assurance. Rest of the cast do satisfactorily.

Miniature Reviews

"Adventures of Mark Twain" (WB). Fredric March-Alexis Smith starred in topflight screen biog.

"Song of the Open Road" (Songs) (UA). Moderately entertaining tale of scholastic crop-pickers. Okay b.o.

"This Is the Life" (Songs) (U). Donald O'Connor, Susanna Foster and Peggy Ryan starred in lively juvenile adventures.

"The Whistler" (Col). Richard Dix in stout supporting gangster meller for dualers.

"Days of Glory" (RKO). Without names, limited b.o.; for the duals.

"Arizona Trail" (U). Above average western.

"Three Men in White" (M-G). Another Dr. Gillespie adventure, modestly budgeted for the duals.

"Raiders of Red Gap" (PRC). Standard western fare for duals.

"Allergic to Love" (Songs) (U). Okay farce for dual support.

"Pardon My Rhythm" (Songs) (U). Lightweight program filmusical for the juve trade and nabe houses.

"Jam Session" (Musical) (Col). Must depend on its band names; a dualer.

Adventures of Mark Twain

Warner Bros. release of Jesse L. Lasky production. Stars Fredric March, Alexis Smith; features Donald Crisp, Alan Hale, C. Aubrey Smith, John Carradine, Bill Henry, Robert Barrat, Walter Hampden, Joyce Reynolds. Directed by Irving Rapper. Screenplay, Alan LeMay; adaptation, LeMay, Harold M. Sherman; additional dialog, Harry Chandlee (based on works controlled by Mark Twain Co. and the play by Sherman); score, Max Steiner; camera, Sol Polito, Laurence Butler, Edwin Linden, Don Siegel, Jas. Leicester; editor, Ralph Dawson; dialog director, Herschel Daugherty; arrangements, Bernard Kaun; music director, Leo F. Forbstein. Previewed in N. Y. April 27, '44. Running time, 130 MINS.

Samuel Clemens............Fredric March
Olivia Langdon...............Alexis Smith
J. B. Pond....................Donald Crisp
Steve Gillis....................Alan Hale
Oxford Chancellor........C. Aubrey Smith
Bret Harte...................John Carradine
Charles Langdon............William Henry
Horace E. Bixby...........Robert Barrat
Jervis Langdon............Walter Hampden
Clara Clemens...............Joyce Reynolds
Joe Goodwin................Whitford Kane
Billings.......................Percy Kilbride
Mrs. Langdon................Nana Bryant
Sam Clemens (15 years)......Dickie Jones
Jane Clemens................Kay Johnson
Sam Clemens (12 years)......Jackie Brown
Huck Finn...................Eugene Holland
Tom Sawyer.................Michael Miller
Promoter...................Joseph Crehan
Prospector.....................Cliff Saum
Assistant Editor............Harry Tyler
Editor........................Roland Drew
William Dean Howells......Douglas Wood
George........................Willie Best
Oliver W. Holmes............Burr Caruth
John G. Whittier..........Harry Hilliard
Ralph W. Emerson........Brandon Hurst
Henry W. Longfellow.......Davison Clark
Captain......................Monte Blue
Boss Deck Hand..............Paul Newlan
Stoker.....................Ernest Whitman
Repeater....................Emmett Smith
Captain's Mate..............Pat O'Malley
Judge.......................Chester Conklin
Henry H. Rogers...........George Lessey
Kate Leary................Dorothy Vaughan
Susie (child)........Gloria Ann Crawford
Susie..........................Lynne Baggett
Clara (child)............Carol Joyce Coombs
Jean (child)..............Charlene Salerno
Jean..........................Joyce Tucker
Dr. Quintard..............Charles Waldron
Rudyard Kipling............Paul Scardon

One of the great American sagas is the life of Samuel Langhorne Clemens, and Jesse L. Lasky, who interpreted so well the cinematic biography of a more contemporaneous American, Sgt. Alvin York (the George Gershwin film biog is as yet unreleased), has done a capital job with "The Adventures of Mark Twain." It's as American as apple pie, and deserves the b.o. patronage

it will get. Despite its length, it grips all the way.

So rich and full was the life of Mark Twain, born Sam Clemens, that it requires the two hours-plus to tell the full tale. It is a film that has its measure of symbolism; linking the humorist's lifetime of 75 years to appearances of Halley's Comet. The astronomical display was visible when Sam Clemens was born in Hannibal, Mo., on the banks of the Mississippi, and 75 years later, when the Chancellor of Oxford extols the great American writer, at a time when the famed university is also paying honor to Rudyard Kipling with an honorary doctorate of literature, it again makes its astral appearance.

In between Clemens has adventured as a river boatman, journeyman reporter, and western goldrusher, only to find sudden fame with his saga of the jumping frogs. Soon follow renown and fortune as Tom Sawyer, Huck Finn and the rest of his "funny books" capture the hearts and the minds of all America, only to be dissipated in abortive attempts with an automatic printing press, extravagant publishing ventures and the like.

Against this panorama is projected a beautiful love story, with Fredric March capital as Twain and Alexis Smith clicking as his beloved Livvy. Donald Crisp as his publisher, Alan Hale as his fellow-adventurer into the California gold rush, John Carradine as Bret Harte are prominent in the early and late adventures of the midwestern writer who finds himself compelled to keep writing "those funny books" in order to pay off for an ideal. And when all else fails he goes on a globe-girdling lecture tour to pay off for that ideal, namely, publishing General Grant's memoirs with all the profits to the soldier-President but bankruptcy for Mark Twain's Pub. Co.

Warners and producer Jesse L. Lasky bring to the screen an educational yet highly entertaining biography of the immortal American. In a business which has done so handsomely by and for the glorification of, say, British historical events and other foreign personalities, vis., Pasteur, Rothschild, Zola, Disraeli, Queen Victoria, et al., the discriminating film audience will recognize in "The Adventures of Mark Twain" something that is more than a little sentimentally close to their hearts.

The stars, notably, perform their assignments with extraordinary compassion and understanding, particularly March in the title role. Alexis Smith assumes new histrionic stature as his spouse. Director Irving Rapper has accomplished an intelligent job in the general direction; the stage technique serves in good stead here. The scripting is likewise topdrawer. Alan LeMay having fashioned an expert screenplay from an original by himself and Harold M. Sherman. They err only in over-generosity, and there is opportunity enough for judicious editing to get under that 130 minutes. Not the least of the affirmative attributes is a stirring, dramatic score composed by Max Steiner. Withal, a credit all around.　　　　　　　　　　*Abel.*

Song of the Open Road

(SONGS)

Hollywood, April 28.

United Artists release of Charles R. Rogers production. Features Edgar Bergen and Charlie McCarthy, Bonita Granville, W. C. Fields, Sammy Kaye orchestra, Jane Powell. Directed by S. Sylvan Simon. Screenplay by Albert Mannheimer, based on story by Irving Phillips and Edward Verdier; camera, John W. Boyle; editor, Truman K. Wood; production manager, Val Paul; assistant to producer, William J. Fender; songs, Walter Kent, Kim Gannon. Previewed at Egyptian, April 27, '44. Running time, 93 MINS.

Charlie McCarthy........Charlie McCarthy
Edgar Bergen..............Edgar Bergen
Jane Powell................Jane Powell
W. C. Fields..............W. C. Fields
Bonnie...................Bonita Granville
Peggy....................Peggy O'Neill

Jack..........................Jackie Moran
Bill..........................Bill Christy
Director Curtis...........Reginald Denny
Conners..................Regis Toomey
Mrs. Powell................Rose Hobart
Spolo.........................Sig Arno
Miss Casper.................Irene Tedrow
Pat Starling.................Pat Starling
　　　Sammy Kaye Orchestra

"Song of the Open Road" is woven around activities of high school groups in assisting in harvesting of crops, introducing a newcomer, 14-year-old Jane Powell in typical poor-little-rich-girl tale. Name and unknown talent on display will provide sufficient marquee voltage to pilot picture through regular runs for okay biz.

Miss Powell has a fine voice for the recording channels, and good camera presence in her screen debut. Producer Charles Rogers surrounds her with combination of veteran performers and some youthful newcomers that emerge as major league talent. Hollywood Canteen Kids is a slick group of young musicians who catch attention with two numbers, while Lipham Four, composed of four young acrobats (one is a girl of around five years) executes several unusual stunts for strong audience reaction.

Walter Kent and Kim Gannon supply four new songs, with "Too Much in Love" due for strong radio and disc plugging. In addition to handling three of the new tunes to good advantage, Miss Powell sings the classical "Carmena"—all, with good display of her high soprano voice.

Girl is a film star, tired of constant supervision at the studio and home, who walks out in disguise to join the crop-pickers and a fling at freedom. Her enthusiasm generates antagonism from the boys and girls in the unit, until she discloses her true identity. Then Jack Moran, head of the group, discovers the orange crop on his brother's ranch is in jeopardy due to help shortage, and Jane returns to Hollywood to enlist services of Bergen, Fields and the Sammy Kaye band for attraction of onlookers for the orange picking chores. Jane is then satisfied to return to her film work.

Looks like producer Rogers has a strong potential in Miss Powell, but future material needs to be carefully selected. Bergen appears twice for specialties with Charlie McCarthy; Sammy Kaye and band handle two numbers, and Fields does a monolog at the orange grove. Condos Bros.' dances are displayed to good advantage with routine on the studio set. Cast of scholastic youngsters display plenty of spontaneity to decidedly lift the unimaginative script. Jackie Moran and Bonita Granville team for romantic interest, while Peggy O'Neill and Bill Christy contrast with comedy affair. Rose Hobart, Regis Toomey and Reginald Denny are prominent in support.

Picture gets good production mounting, opening on studio stage and quickly moving to the outdoors. Harvesting by the youths in traveling groups will give metropolitan audiences an idea of farm problems. Finale, with crowds pitching in for orange harvest, is straight filmusical comedy presentation. Camera work by John Boyle is uniform, while director S. Sylvan Simon provides general lightness to the picture.

　　　　　　　　　　Walt.

This Is the Life

(SONGS)

Hollywood, Apr. 26.

Universal release of Bernard W. Burton production. Stars Donald O'Connor, Susanna Foster, Peggy Ryan; features Louise Allbritton, Ray Eberle and orchestra. Directed by Felix Feist. Screenplay by Wanda Tuchock, based on stage play by Sinclair Lewis and Fay Wray; camera, Hal Mohr; editor, Ray Snyder; asst. director, Charlie Gould; special photography, John Fulton. Previewed at Fox Wilshire, April 25, '44. Running time, 85 MINS.

Jimmy.....................Donald O'Connor
Angela....................Susanna Foster
Sally McGuire.............Peggy Ryan

Harriet......Louise Allbritton
Hilary Jarret......Patric Knowles
Aunt Betsy......Dorothy Peterson
Doctor Plum......Jonathan Hale
Gus......Eddie Quillan
Eddie......Frank Jenks
Music Teacher......Frank Puglia
Leon......Maurice Marsac
Mrs. Tiggett......Virginia Brissac
Ray Eberle and His Orchestra
Bobby Brooks Quartet

Adventures of romantic youth form basis for this diverting comedy-drama embellished with the musical talents of Susanna Foster, the all-around abilities of young Donald O'Connor, and the slaphappy antics of Peggy Ryan. Various elements blend with sufficient story content and consistent pace to provide good general entertainment in all bookings, with youthful starring trio providing marquee strength.

Story is based on stage play, "Angela Is 22," and describes the adolescent infatuation of 18-year-old Miss Foster for fortyish Patric Knowles recuperating from campaign in the South Pacific. O'Connor is in love with the girl, and disturbed by her sudden growing-up antics, especially when she follows him to New York, from the small town, with excuse she is to take voice lessons. Knowles is disturbed by her puppy-love but finally consents to engagement with idea girl will cool in short order. O'Connor makes trip to the big town, sizes up the situation and bumps into Louise Allbritton, former wife of Knowles, who is still in love with him and her photographic career. From there on it's obvious conclusion that O'Connor will maneuver the couple together so he can regain the affections of Susanna.

Script develops at a lively pace, tossing out a good supply of laugh lines along the route. Episode of O'Connor in nightspot, trying to snag cherry from lemonade glass, is one of the best laugh routines devised in some time—and O'Connor milks it to the hilt. Miss Foster capably handles several songs, including "Ciribiribin," "L'Amour, Tourjours, L'Amour," "With a Song in My Heart," and "Open Thy Heart." Peggy socks over pair of comedy song-and-dance numbers with O'Connor, and effectively handles novelty "Gremlin Walk" alone. Ray Eberle vocalizes one tune with his orch. accompaniment, while Bobby Brooks quartet is also on for one number.

O'Connor continues to demonstrate his versatility as a screen entertainer, in the singing, dancing and acting lines. Miss Foster does well as the lovesick ingenue, while Peggy Ryan clicks as the young comedienne. Knowles and Miss Allbritton do well in prominent supporting spots. Direction by Felix Feist is topgrade. *Walt.*

The Whistler

Columbia release of Rudolph Flothow production. Stars Richard Dix; features J. Carrol Naish, Floria Stuart, Alan Dinehart, Joan Woodbury. Directed by William Castle. Screenplay, Eric Taylor, from story by J. Donald Wilson, suggested by CBS radio program, "The Whistler"; camera, James S. Brown; editor, Jerome Thoms. At Rialto, N. Y., week April 28, '44. Running time, 59 MINS.

Earl Conrad......Richard Dix
The Killer......J. Carrol Naish
Alice Walker......Gloria Stuart
Gorman......Alan Dinehart
Lefty Vigran......Don Costello
Toni Vigran......Joan Woodbury
Bartender......Cy Kendall
The Thief......Trevor Bardette
Charles McNear......Robert E. Keane
Briggs......Clancy Cooper
Bill Tomley......George Lloyd
Flophouse Clerk......Byron Foulger
Jennings......Charles Coleman
Dock Watchman......Robt. Homans

"The Whistler" is a new type of gangster-killer melodrama. Patterned after the CBS radio show of the same name, it could have been made into a powerful thriller. As is, this production never makes any pretense of being anything but a "B" supporting meller. As such it will provide strong support.

Biggest difficulty encountered by scripters and the director on this picture was in concentrating on the main thesis—an attempt to kill a man by fear. There are too many offshoots of this central theme, with interest suffering as a result. Yarn has Richard Dix suffering mental torture over the drowning of his wife and paying $5,000 to have himself bumped off. When he receives word that his wife is alive, Dix tries to have the "killer" order recalled but finds that his go-between with the professional gunman himself has been killed.

From then on it becomes an exciting bout of wits to see whether Dix will crack under the strain of being shadowed by this pro-killer or be able to bring the man to terms. Before this obviously strongest part of the story is reached, there is considerable deviation with a wild auto race, a silly adventure in a flop house, etc. Film gets its title from a mysterious character, The Whistler, whose odd whistle saves Dix from death several times. He acts more or less as a background voice, with the whistle not tied in with this shadowy character until the last.

Richard Dix does well enough as the wealthy merchant who employs a gangster to have himself bumped off. J. Carrol Naish, again a tough mobster, makes a realistic killer. Alan Dinehart is submerged in a virtual bit role, as the wealthy gangster, but great. Gloria Stuart is superb as the loyal secretary to Dix, while support is headed by Joan Woodbury and Otto Forrest, "The Whistler."

William Castle's direction is a bit uneven, though okay in the final suspenseful episodes. Jerome Thoms has done a slick editing job. James S. Brown's cameraing is satisfactory. *Wear.*

Days of Glory

RKO release of Casey Robinson production. Stars Tamara Toumanova, Gregory Peck; features Alan Reed, Maria Palmer, Lowell Gilmore. Directed by Jacques Tourneur. Screenplay, Robinson, from original by Melchior Lengyel; editor, Joseph Noriega; music, Daniele Anfitheatrof; music director, C. Bakaleinikoff; camera, Tony Gaudio. Previewed in N. Y., April 28, '44. Running time, 86 MINS.

Nina......Tamara Toumanova
Vladimir......Gregory Peck
Sasha......Alan Reed
Yelena......Maria Palmer
Semyon......Lowell Gilmore
Fedor......Hugo Haas
Olga......Dena Penn
Mitya......Glenn Vernon
Dmitri......Igor Dolgoruki
Petrov......Edward L. Durst
Johann Staub......Lou Crosby
Ducrenko......William Challee
Seminov......Joseph Vitale
Col. Prilenko......Erford Gage
German Lieutenant......Ivan Triesault
Vera......Maria Bibikov
Anton......Edgar Licho
Mariya......Greti Dupont
Von Rundhol......Peter Helmers

"Days of Glory" is a rather expensive way for RKO to showcase its new screen talent, but it has its compensations. Namely in a pair of newcomers whom the company has starred in this story of Russian guerrilla warfare against the Nazi invaders. But overall, it's for the duals.

The aforementioned newcomers are Tamara Toumanova and Gregory Peck. They head a cast of whom all are new to films. The former is the ballerina star, and she possesses a dark, arresting type of beauty that screens well. Her thespic abilities, however, will require considerably more schooling, although she has possibilities. After all, this is her first picture. Peck shows his seasoning, being from the Broadway stage, while the rest of the cast contribute okay characterizations in what is essentially a slow, talky drama with too little action. *Kahn.*

Arizona Trail

Universal production and release. Stars Tex Ritter, Fuzzy Knight; features Janet Shaw, Dennis Moore, Johnny Bond's Valley Boys. Directed by Vernon Keays. Screenplay, William Lively; camera, William Sickner; editor, Alvin Todd. At New York theatre, week of April 26, '44. Running time, 57 MINS.

Johnnie......Tex Ritter
Kansas......Fuzzy Knight
Wayne Trent......Dennis Moore
Martha Brooks......Janet Shaw
Ace Vincent......Jack Ingram
Dan Trent......Erville Alderson
Doc Wallace......Joseph Greene
Matt Baker......Glenn Strange
Sheriff......Dan White
Curley......Art Fowler
Johnny Bond and His Red River Valley Boys

This is better-than-average western fare, both in the action and production departments. With plenty of quick trigger work and hell-for-leather riding, film is prime for duals.

Story concerns estranged son of a wealthy landowner who returns home to his ailing father to help combat the greedy machinations of a land grabber, attempting to wrest the coveted property.

Cast is competent, especially Dennis Moore, who seems a likely prospect to develop as a leading non-singing cowboy star. Red River Valley Boys sing several songs, to satisfy the "music-in-westerns" crowd.

Three Men in White

Metro production and release. Features Lionel Barrymore, Van Johnson, Keye Luke, Marilyn Maxwell and Ava Gardner. Directed by Willis Goldbeck. Original screenplay by Martin Berkeley and Harry Ruskin, based on characters created by Max Brand; camera, Ray June; editor, George Hively. Tradeshown in N. Y. April 28, '44. Running time, 85 MINS.

Dr. Leonard Gillespie......Lionel Barrymore
Dr. Randall Adams......Van Johnson
Ruth Edley......Marilyn Maxwell
Dr. Lee Wong How......Keye Luke
Jean Brown......Ava Gardner
Molly Byrd......Alma Kruger
Hobart Genet......"Rags" Ragland
Nurse Parker......Nell Craig
Dr. Walter Carew......Walter Kingsford
Conover......George H. Reed

This is another in the Dr. Gillespie series, with Lionel Barrymore continuing as the chair-ridden surgeon who solves all problems, medical or love. A weaker story than its predecessors, film should carry on the strength of the series' buildup for a modest success as a dualer.

The film has the usual mysterious medical cases and inevitable romance. But the medical problems and solutions are rather naive, suggesting that a doctor ought to be called in as consultant when scripts are prepared. Love interest, too, is a little silly. In this day and age it's difficult to believe that a good-looking boy will dodge a better-looking gal for eight reels, hesitant even over a first kiss.

In this film, Barrymore finally decides on the momentous question of who, between Van Johnson and Keye Luke, is to be his assistant. Both boys are given cases to solve, Luke curing a child of a sugar allergy, Johnson easing a woman out of an "incurable" arthritis. Both men are convincing as medicos, Johnson less plausible as a lover. Barrymore, of course, is his usual crotchety, mugging self as the great diagnostician.

Marilyn Maxwell, pursuing Johnson boldly throughout the film, makes a toothsome blonde menace, and Ava Gardner is attractive as a girl with a problem. Alma Kruger and Walter Kingsford are back in familiar roles as head nurse and hospital head, but "Rags" Ragland has replaced Nat Pendleton as the thick-skulled ambulance assistant.

Raiders of Red Gap

PRC release of Sigmund Neufeld production. Stars Bob Livingston and Al "Fuzzy" St. John. Directed by Sam Newfield. Story and screenplay, Joe O'Donnell; camera, Robert Cline; editor, Holbrook N. Todd. At New York theatre, N. Y., week of April 18, '44, dual. Running time, 57 MINS.

Rocky Cameron......Bob Livingston
Fuzzy Jones......Al (Fuzzy) St. John
Jane......Myrna Dell
Roberts......Ed Cassidy
Bennett......Charles King
Bradley......Kermit Maynard
Butch......Roy Brent
Jed......Frank Ellis
Sheriff......George Chesebro

Another in the Lone Rider series, "Raiders of Red Gap" is conventional western fare that should fit nicely on the lower rung of dual bills in the subsequent-runs.

With plenty of hard riding to satisfy the sagebrush crowd, yarn concerns efforts of a cattle company to gain control of all grazing lands in Arizona in order to break the eastern meatpackers. Assigned by state officials to aid the harassed ranchers, Bob Livingston and Al St. John are mistaken for gunmen whom the cattle firm has imported. Distrusted by the ranchers and discovered as imposters by the cattle outfit, they are opposed by both factions, but finally corral the gang after the usual complications.

Bob Livingston and rest of cast do adequately, while comedy character portrayed by Al "Fuzzy" St. John is a definite asset. Camera and direction hold up.

Allergic to Love
(SONGS)

Hollywood, April 29.

Universal release of Warren Wilson production. Stars Martha O'Driscoll and Noah Beery, Jr. Features David Bruce, Franklin Pangborn, Fuzzy Knight and Maxie Rosenbloom. Directed by Edward Lilley. Screenplay, Warren Wilson; original by Wilson, Jack Townley and John Larkin; camera, George Robinson; editor, Philip Cahn. Previewed in Hollywood, April 28, '44. Running time, 64 MINS.

Pat......Martha O'Driscoll
Kip......Noah Beery, Jr.
Roger......David Bruce
Ives......Franklin Pangborn
Charlie......Fuzzy Knight
Max......Maxie Rosenbloom
Louie......Henry Armetta
Dr. Kardos......Marek Windheim
Mr. Bradley......Paul Stanton
Mrs. Bradley......Olive Blakeney
Cuthbert......Grady Sutton
Mr. Henderson......William Davidson
Dr. McLaughlin......John Hamilton
Joe......George Chandler
Sam Walker......Olin Howlin
Mrs. Beamish......Lotte Stein
Miss Peabody......Edna Holland
Whitey......Dudley Dickerson
Antonio Triana and Montes, Chinita
Guadalajara Trio

This is a mildly amusing farce of program status that will provide standard support in dual houses. It's a fairly new twist to the separated-newlyweds formula, this time when bride breaks out with hayfever when hubby is around.

Script embarks couple on a South America-bound ship for honeymoon, with young doctor friend along to attempt diagnosis of the ailment. Medic gives decision that separation and divorce is necessary, but the girl takes things into her own hands to force a solution of the trouble to make everything okay.

Miss O'Driscoll and Noah Beery, Jr., are okay in the leads, with David Bruce as the doctor and Franklin Pangborn as a jittery stock broker. Chinita sings two songs in nightclub sequence; Antonio Triana and Montes offer a Spanish dance, and the Guadalajara Trio strums one tune. Direction by Edward Lilley has good tempo. *Walt.*

Pardon My Rhythm
(SONGS)

Hollywood April 27.

Universal release of Bernard W. Burton production. Stars Gloria Jean; features Evelyn Ankers, Patric Knowles, Walter Catlett, Marjorie Weaver, Bob Crosby orchestra. Directed by Felix Feist. Screenplay by Val Burton, Eugene Conrad; based on story by Hurd Barrett; camera, Paul Ivano; editor, Edward Curtiss. Previewed April 26, '44. Running time, 61 MINS.

Jinx Page......Gloria Jean
Tony Page......Patric Knowles
Julia Munson......Evelyn Ankers
Dixie Moore......Marjorie Weaver
Michael O'Bannon......Walter Catlett
Ricky O'Bannon......Mel Torme

Doodles Weaver	....	Patsy O'Connor
Mrs. Doan	....	Ethel Griffies
Announcer	....	Jack Slattery

Bob Crosby and His Orchestra

"Pardon My Rhythm" is a lightweight issue in the Universal group of modest-budget filmusicals detailing adventures of talented youth. Musical end lifts static story to get picture through as average dual supporter in the program datings.

Gloria Jean has adolescent romance with Mel Torme, who's a hot drummer and organizer of a kid orchestra which participates in a national radio contest. Bob Crosby hears the youngster, and has Marjorie Weaver turn on glamour to get him under contract. Jealous Gloria Jean swings into action by tossing her playwright father at Miss Weaver, generating confusion via series of episodes conveniently set up by the scripters. Torme snaps out of it to rejoin the band to win the contest.

Gloria Jean and Miss Weaver capably handle two songs each, with Bob Crosby crooning the standard, "I'll See You in My Dreams," and providing the musical background with his orchestra. Young Torme gives out with some hot rhythm displays on the drums that will catch attention of the juve trade.

Cast is restricted by haphazard script, which director Felix Feist cannot aid. Gloria Jean is okay in top spot; with Torme showing surprising camera presence for a newcomer. Crosby is good as himself, and support is adequate. *Walt.*

Arturo Toscanini

Produced by Overseas Motion Picture Bureau of Office of War Information, distributed by United Films. Features Arturo Toscanini, Jan Peerce, Westminster Choir and NBC Symphony Orchestra. Directed by Irving Lerner and Alex Hackenschmidt. Philip Dunne in charge of production; Archie Houghton, producing. Writer, May Sarton; camera, Peter Glushonock; sound, Robert Johnson, NBC; Clarence Wall, RCA; Harry Jones, OWI. Editor, Irving Lerner. Narrator, Burgess Meredith. Previewed in N. Y. April 27, '44. Running time, 33 MINS.

This musical documentary, first of its kind, is a stirring film—Arturo Toscanini's musical tribute to democracy, and a musical summation of his long fight against fascist tyranny. A film study of an NBC Symphony orchestra performance of Verdi's "La Forza del Destino" Overture and Verdi's "Hymn of the Nations" at Studio 8H in N. Y., interspersed with shots of Toscanini at his Riverdale, N. Y., home, this gives a narrator the chance to describe briefly the maestro's long struggle against oppression. Camera travels around as orchestra plays, giving long shots, getting closeups of the maestro and solo players.

Verdi "Hymn" is in Toscy's adaptation, ending with national anthems of France, England, Russia and U. S. ("Internationale" is used for Russia, this still being the Soviet anthem at time the maestro did his rescoring). Tenor Jan Peerce and the Westminster Choir of Princeton, N. J., assist in the "Hymn," Peerce singing brilliantly, with a thrilling overall effect of the "Hymn" and concluding anthems. Sound track is clear, with chorus and orchestra in fine blend.

All artists contributed services free. Film was produced by OWI for use overseas, but it may be released in the U. S. later. the Treasury trying to get it in time for the 5th War Loan drive. English and Italian versions now in use, with 20 other languages planned later.

Jam Session
(MUSICAL)

Columbia release of Irving Briskin production. Stars Ann Miller; features Jess Barker, Nan Wynn, Charlie Barnet, Louis Armstrong, Alvino Rey, Jan Garber, Glen Gray, Teddy Powell bands and Pied Pipers. Directed by Charles Barton. Screenplay, Manny Seff, from story by Harlan Ware and Patterson McNutt; camera, L. W. O'Connell; editor, Richard Fantl; musical director, M. W. Stoloff. At Palace, N. Y., week May 2, '44. Running time, 78 MINS.

Terry Baxter	....	Ann Miller
George Carter Haven	....	Jess Barker
Raymond Stuart	....	Charles D. Brown
Lloyd Marley	....	Eddie Kane
Berkley Bell	....	George Eldredge
Miss Tobin	....	Renie Riano
Henry	....	Clarence Muse
Evelyn	....	Pauline Drake
Coletti	....	Charles La Torre
Neva Cavendish	....	Anne Loos
Fred Wylie	....	Ray Walker

With Charlie Barnet and His Orchestra; Louis Armstrong and His Orchestra; Alvino Rey and His Orchestra; Jan Garber and His Orchestra; Glen Gray and His Casa Loma Orchestra; Teddy Powell and His Orchestra; Pied Pipers; Nan Wynn.

"Jam Session" merely furnishes band music to please the hepcats and, on the strength of its six bands, should fit into the nabe dualers. Dull story deals with small-town girl who wins trip to Hollywood in local dance contest. There she meets a film writer, gets involved in many mishaps, but finally lands both a job and the writer.

The six bands which are dragged in, perform oldies in rhythmic fashion. Pied Pipers sing one ditty and Nan Wynn warbles "Brazil" in an appealing manner.

Ann Miller does well in the finale dance routine, and attempts to inject interest in the trivial plot, while Jess Barker is likeable and pleasing as the brash writer. Rest of the cast adequate.

Miniature Reviews

"Gaslight" (M-G). Charles Boyer - Ingrid Bergman - Joseph Cotten starred in b.o. meller adaptation of "Angel Street."

"Between Two Worlds" (WB). "Outward Bound" remake should be money-getter, though difficult to sell in smaller towns.

"For Those in Peril" (Ealing). British documentary; worthy successor to "Desert Victory," others.

"Outlaw Trail" (Mono). So-so western; dualer.

"Internado Para Senoritas" ("Girls' Boarding School") (Mexican). Pleasing musical.

"Sol Over Klara" (Songs) (Swedish). Amusing film grooved for Svenska audiences.

"Que Lindo es Michoacan" (Songs) (Mexican). Tito Guizar starred in farce, with English titles, due for fair returns.

"One Inch From Victory" (Indie). Feature length documentary with interesting clips of Nazi side of Battle of Russia.

"Hotel de Verano" (Musical) (Astro). Mexico's first try at super-musicals; okay.

"El Penon de las Animas" (Mexican). Latin version of Romeo and Juliet with several outstanding performers.

Gaslight

Metro release Arthur Hornblow, Jr., production. Stars Charles Boyer, Ingrid Bergman, Joseph Cotten; features Barbara Everest, Dame May Whitty. Directed by George Cukor. Screenplay, John van Druten, Walter Reisch, John L. Balderston, based on play by Patrick Hamilton; camera, Joseph Ruttenberg; music, Bronislau Kaper; editor, Ralph E. Winters. At Capitol, N. Y., May 5, 44. Running time, 114 MINS.

Gregory Anton	....	Charles Boyer
Paula Alquist	....	Ingrid Bergman
Brian Cameron	....	Joseph Cotten
Miss Thwaites	....	Dame May Whitty
Nancy	....	Angela Lansbury
Elizabeth	....	Barbara Everest
Maestro Guardi	....	Emil Rameau
General Huddleston	....	Edmund Breon
Mr. Mufflin	....	Halliwell Hobbes
Williams	....	Tom Stevenson
Lady Dalroy	....	Heather Thatcher
Lord Dalroy	....	Lawrence Grossmith
Pianist	....	Jakob Gimpel

Patrick Hamilton's London stage melodrama, which is in its third year on Broadway as "Angel Street," has been given an exciting screen treatment by Arthur Hornblow, Jr.'s excellent production starring Charles Boyer, Ingrid Bergman and Joseph Cotten. It can't miss at the boxoffice.

The screen version has retained the play's original title, "Gaslight," and it is a faithful adaptation, conspicuously notable for fine performances of the stars and the screenplay by John van Druten, Walter Reisch and John L. Balderston. There are times when the screen treatment verges on a type of drama that must be linked to the period upon which the title is based, but this factor only serves to hypo the film's dramatic suspense where normally it might be construed as corny theatrics. Its sober screenplay and the performances, particularly that of Miss Bergman, however, do much to dissipate whatever lack of values that element might have sustained.

"Gaslight" will be recalled as being the story of a murderer who has escaped detection for many years. He had killed a famous opera singer for her jewels but was never able to uncover the baubles. Years later he marries the singer's niece so that he can continue his search for the gems in the late singer's home, which has been inherited by her niece and in which the newlyweds make their home. How a young Scotland Yard detective uncovers the real identity of the husband and killer, after the latter has plotted to have his young wife committed to an asylum so that he can have a freer rein in his search of the house, forms an exciting climax.

Director George Cukor has kept the film at an even pace and has been responsible for the film lacking the ten-twent-thirt element that has been a factor in the stage play. It is an apparently expensive production in the usual Metro tradition, and Boyer, as the homicidal husband, Miss Bergman, as the wife, and Cotten, the detective, have given carefully studied, restrained performances that have captured the full intent of the script. They are playing the respective roles originally created on Broadway by Vincent Price, Judith Evelyn and Leo G. Carroll. *Kahn.*

Between Two Worlds

Warner Bros. release of Mark Hellinger production. Stars John Garfield, Paul Henreid, Sydney Greenstreet and Eleanor Parker; features Edmund Gwenn, George Tobias, George Coulouris, Faye Emerson, Sara Allgood, Dennis King, Isobel Elsom and Gilbert Emery. Directed by Edward A. Blatt. Based upon play, "Outward Bound," by Sutton Vane; adaptation, Daniel Fuchs; editor, Rudi Fehr; camera, Carl Guthrie. Previewed in N. Y., May 4, '44. Running time, 112 MINS.

Tom Prior	....	John Garfield
Henry	....	Paul Henreid
Thompson	....	Sydney Greenstreet
Ann	....	Eleanor Parker
Scrubby	....	Edmund Gwenn
Pete Musick	....	George Tobias
Lingley	....	George Coulouris
Maxine	....	Faye Emerson
Mrs. Midget	....	Sara Allgood
Rev. William Duke	....	Dennis King
Mrs. Cliveden-Banks	....	Isobel Elsom
Cliveden-Banks	....	Gilbert Emery
Dispatcher	....	Lester Matthews
Clerk	....	Pat O'Moore

An artistic transcription of "Outward Bound," the Broadway stage hit of 1925, this film was once before brought to the screen by Warner Bros. under that title and released in 1930. Picture will be a good money-maker in spite of its somewhat morbid theme. The merchandising will count heavily, especially if mass attention is to be captured.

The new version, beautifully produced by Mark Hellinger and skillfully acted by a fine cast, has been given the very fitting title of "Between Two Worlds." It's class entertainment on the allegorical side.

A modern 1944 opening has been provided, the locale being an unidentified port in England from which a small assorted group of persons is preparing to sail for America. Unable to leave because his papers aren't in order is Paul Henreid, former pianist, who recently had fought with the Free French. As result he and his wife, played with much feeling by Eleanor Parker, take to the gaspipe, both wanting to die together. Meantime, in an air raid the bus carrying others to the evacuation ship are killed.

From here the action shifts to a mystery ship which, it finally becomes evident, is bound for the Great Beyond, with Henreid, Miss Parker and the group which had been killed in the bomb raid. Brilliant dialog and excellent performances, as well as thoughtful, imaginative direction by Edward A. Blatt, neatly sustain the interest aboard ship on the long voyage. There is no place in the story for comedy relief.

On reaching High Olympus and judgment day, Sydney Greenstreet enters the scene as the examiner, taking his new arrivals one by one. His performance is exceptionally outstanding, and the sequence, though quite lengthy, represents a productional, directional and acting triumph. For the finish, the action returns to England, where Henreid and Miss Parker have experienced their weird dream under the influence of gas, from which they are saved by a fortuitous bombing which shattered the windows of their apartment.

In the first production of "Outward Bound" the late Leslie Howard played the role here assigned to the capable Henreid. As the profligate, disillusioned reporter, John Garfield stands out sharply, while as his girl friend, an actress, Faye Emerson does very well. George Tobias lends color to the role of a merchant seaman who's going "home" to his wife and baby, George Coulouris makes his part of a scheming industrialist an important one, and Dennis King rates highly as a minister. Others include Sara Allgood, whose performance is arresting; and Edmund Gwenn, Isobel Elsom and Gilbert Emery, all good.

In a technical way, notably the photography, "Between Two Worlds" represents a superior achievement.

Char.

For Those in Peril

(BRITISH-MADE)

London, March 30.

Ealing Studios release of Michael Balcon production. Features David Farrar, Ralph Michael, Robert Wyndham, John Slater, John Batten. Directed by Charles Crichton. Screenplay by Harry Watt, J. O. C. Orton, T. E. B. Clarke from story by Richard Hillary. At Studio One, London, March 29. Running time, **67 MINS.**

Another worthy companion piece to the growing list of "factuals" which began with "Desert Victory" is this contribution from Ealing Studios. Except for being too short to rate top billing, "For Those in Peril" is as gripping and authentic as a presentation of the Air Sea Rescue work as "San Demetrio" was an actual story of wartime oil tankers.

Both producer Michael Balcon and director Charles Crichton have had the advantage of an intelligent script. With the exception of a momentary glimpse of a pretty barmaid, there's not a femme in the big cast, and no love interest. Balcon has chosen to follow the Hollywood boxoffice formula at the cost of destroying the reality of this he-men saga. Two outstanding performances are turned in by David Farrar and Ralph Michael among many in picture.

Story presents the Air Sea Rescue service as a dumping ground for would-be fliers who fail to come up to R.A.F. physical requirements. The disgruntled, disappointed lads, who find themselves at sea in speed boats instead of in planes, learn that their job of saving lives of pilots from the "drink" is just as important and thrilling as the air service.

Although there is not a single American accent in this film, it is a matter of official record this Air Sea Rescue outfit has saved scores of Yank fliers from watery graves.

Camera work, especially montage superimposed on actual English Channel seascapes, measures up to the generally high standard of production and direction. "For Those in Peril" is tops among English documentaries.

Outlaw Trail

Monogram release of Robert Tansey production. Stars Hoot Gibson, Bob Steele and Chief Thundercloud; features Jennifer Holt, Cy Kendall and Rocky Camron. Directed by Tansey. Screenplay, Frances Kavanaugh, from original by Alvin Neitz; camera, Edward Kull; editor, John C. Fuller. At N. Y. theatre, N. Y., week May 3, '44. Running time, **53 MINS.**

Hoot	Hoot Gibson
Bob	Bob Steele
Thundercloud	Chief Thundercloud
Alice Thornton	Jennifer Holt
"Honest John" Travers	Cy Kendall
Sheriff Rocky Camron	Rocky Camron
Carl Beldon	George Eldridge
Chuck Walters	Charles King
H. A. Fraser	Hal Price
Ed Knowles	John Bridges
Blackie	Bud Osborne
Spike	Jim Thorpe

Ken Maynard drops out of the Trail Blazers series of westerns in this one, but Hoot Gibson and Bob Steele are joined by Chief Thundercloud in tracking down the doers of evil, resulting in a fair hoss opera geared for the duals.

It all revolves about Cy Kendall's portrayal of the supposed civic leader, Honest John, who owns the town lock, stock and barrel, collecting tribute from all, and issuing money of his own, printed by his henchmen, for the oppressed ranchers. Come the Trail Blazers and the shenanigans are brought to an end.

Some run-of-the-mill dialog and a few unbelievable situations will probably be overlooked by devotees of this type film. Add up the credits and the debits—credits including more than the usual amount of gunplay and hard riding—and "Outlaw Trail" is good enough all around.

Sten.

Internado Para Senoritas

("Girls' Boarding School")

(MUSICAL)

(MEXICAN-MADE)

Clasa Studios release of Mauricio de la Serna production. Directed by Gilberto Martinez Solares. Stars Mapy Cortes, Emilio Tuero; features Prudencia Grifell, Fernando Cortes, Maria Luisa Zea, Della Magana. Songs, Alberto Dominguez. At Belmont, N. Y., May 5, '44. Running time, **94 MINS**

(In Spanish; no English titles)

A light, frothy musical about a girls' boarding school in Mexico, which scores as pleasant entertainment even without English titles. Film should please regular Spanish filmgoers.

Plot has schoolgirl secretly in love with literature professor, unaware of her affection. Crush is unearthed and girl is about to be expelled by the usually stern director when preoccupied pedagogue declares his devotion for his youthful admirer.

Mapy Cortes makes a pretty, vivacious schoolgirl and sings and dances with equal facility. Emilio Tuero is perfect as the shocked and dismayed professor, while Fernando Cortes contributes some uproarious scenes as another professor.

Dance sequences are well staged and costumes are eye-filling.

Sol Over Klara

("Sun Over Klara")

(SWEDISH-MADE)

(Songs)

Scandia release of Europa production. Stars Edvard Persson; features Babro Flodqvist, Bjorn Berglund and Stina Stahle. Directed by Emil A. Lingheim. Music, Alvar Kraft and Sven Runo; camera, Harold Berglond. At 48th St. theatre, N. Y., week of April 29, '44. Running time, **100 MINS.**

Ararat	Edvard Persson
Sylvia	Barbro Flodqvist
The Water-colorist	Bjorn Berglund
Mrs. Soderheim	Stina Stahle
Reuben	Bror Bugler
Tirolius	Frithjof Hedwall
The Portrait Painter	Nils Ekstam
The Grey-haired One	Martin Sterner
Manne	Tord Bernheim
The Magician	Arne Lindblad

Geared for okay boxoffice in U. S. houses that play Swedish product, this film, about the Bohemian artists' quarters of Stockholm during wartime, has a sparse use of English subtitles, which would leave non-Swedish speaking audiences in a quandary as to what much of the humor is all about.

Edvard Persson portrays the principal role, a painter. He performs in a leisurely manner and with considerable personality. The several songs he does, with possibly two exceptions, are sung effectively, and the title tune is a catchy, lilting gavotte.

Yarn finds Persson as peacemaker between two impecunious artist friends, both rivals for the love of a pretty model. He, too, is pursued by a wealthy widow, and, in the course of making up his mind, situations arise, among them an art contest, a wedding feast and other extraneous sequences that seemingly lend themselves to much humor but nurse the footage along to an unwarranted 100 minutes.

Sten.

One Inch From Victory

(DOCUMENTARY)

Scoop Productions release of Robert Velaise production. Commentary written and narrated by Quentin Reynolds. Noel Meadow in charge of production; supervised by Maurice Lev. Reviewed in projection room, N. Y., April 24, '44. Running time, **68 MINS.**

This is a documentary assembled from captured German films shown in Nazi newsreels in Berlin, occupied France and South America for propaganda purposes, at a time when the German Wehrmacht was running roughshod over its enemies. It's strictly for houses showing Soviet pix.

The clips are notable in that they present the Battle of Russia from the Nazi side. Intertwined in the 68 minutes of film are shots of the memorable occasion in 1933 when President Roosevelt announced the reopening of trade with Russia; scenes of Heydrich's funeral in Prague and the last rites for the Hangman in Berlin attended by Hitler; scenes of U.S. Secretary of State Hull's flying trip to Moscow to clear the way for the Teheran conference, and finally scenes of that historic event with F.D.R., Prime Minister Churchill and Premier Stalin and their entourages present.

Narration, written and spoken by Quentin Reynolds, serves as an antidote when the supposedly pro-Nazi footage is flashing across the screen. It describes how the Nazi hordes, continuing a march through Poland, Czechoslovakia, Norway, Belgium and France, planned to take Russia in a six-week, three-pronged assault, converging on Leningrad in the north, Moscow in the center of Russia and Stalingrad to the south.

The Red Army withstood these assaults in the towns of Kharkov, Sevastopol and Voronezh, losing them eventually but not before these cities were completely devastated and of no use to the enemy.

Noel Meadow, who operates the Stanley theatre, N. Y., and Maurice Lev did an excellent job of editing the footage. Reynolds' deft narration aids in holding the picture together.

Sten.

Hotel de Verano

("SUMMER HOTEL")

(In Spanish)

(MUSICAL)

Mexico City, May 9.

Astro Films production and distribution. Features Ramon Armengod. Stars Janice Logan, Enrique Herrera; Consuelo Guererod de Luna, Blanquita Amaro, Jorge Reyes, Carlos Villarias, Rafael Icardo, Salvator Quiroz, Jose Nava, and Ramon & Renita. Directed by Rena Cardona; Ramon Reachi, dance director. At Cine Palacio, Mexico City. Running time, **95 MINS.**

This is Mexico's first super musical and measures up fairly well. Astro Films is reputed to have sunk $500,000 (Mex.) in picture, high for Mexico. Rene Cardona, film star, turns megger for this, and is okay. Production has a special interest for Americans as it marks the debut in Mexican films of Janice Logan, late of Hollywood, who has joined Sally Blane and June Marlowe as American-Mexican screen players.

Story is good. Enrique Herrera, rich widower, is set to marry Miss Logan, daughter of an American he befriended in his last illness, pact being that when the time comes his daughter is to marry him, to settle this debt. There is a radio singer, and usual triangle started and customary rows before the happy solution is reached.

Ramon Reachi contributes much to the vehicle with the dance numbers. He also does a ballroom number with Renita (Mrs. Reachi) that goes over well. Much of production was made at Acapulco, Pacific port-resort.

El Penon de las Animas

("The Rock of Souls")

(MEXICAN-MADE)

Clasa Studios production and release. Stars Jorge Negrete, Maria Felix; features Rene Cardona, Carlos Mocteuma, Miguel A. Ferriz, Virginia Manzano. Direction and story by Miguel Zacarias; camera, V. Herrera; music, Manuel Esperon; songs, Ernesto Cortazar. At Belmont, N. Y., April 28, '44. Running time, **110 MINS.**

(In Spanish; with English Titles)

This heavy dramatic piece reveals the great strides which Mexican production has made within the past few years, making its film industry a leading contender for the Latin-American market. Picture should do very well in Spanish language houses.

A Latin version of Romeo and Juliet, containing all the pathos and tragedy of the work from which it was adapted, the film emerges as a sensitive, poignant tale of love, vengeance and death, unfolded to the accompaniment of fine musical background.

Maria Felix, a new star, who combines beauty and talent, gives an exceptionally good performance, and should become a favorite with South American audiences.

The characterizations of Jorge Negrete and Rene Cardona as opposing swains, are equally as effective, while the rest of the cast contributes capably.

Que Lindo es Michoacan

("Beautiful Michoacan")

(SONGS)

(MEXICAN-MADE)

Clasa Studios release of Ismael Rodriguez production. Directed by Ismael Rodriguez. Stars Tito Guizar; features Gloria Marin, Angel Garasa, Victor Manuel Mendoz, Evita Munoz, Dolores Camarillo and Emma Duval. Story, Ernesto Cortazar; music, Francisco Dominguez; camera, Jose Ortiz Ramos. Reviewed at Belmont, N. Y., April 21, '44. Running time, **105 MINS.**

(In Spanish with English titles)

A pretentious production by the largest film studio in Mexico City, made in the tropical province of Michoacan, this picture should garner fair grosses in art houses and other situations where Tito Guizar has a following.

Primarily this is the singer-guitarist's project from beginning to end. And he more than holds his own, singing, playing and acting his way through a rather lengthy but nevertheless interesting farce in which he portrays a boorish roue who causes a rich, beautiful heroine to fall—but hard.

Gloria Marin plays a difficult role excellently, with strong support from rest of the cast, but poor direction, camera and other technical aspects of the picture will hurt its value.

Sten.

Miniature Reviews

"The Eve of St. Mark" (20th). Adaptation of Maxwell Anderson stage hit due for OK biz.

"The Hairy Ape" (UA). Eugene O'Neill's play makes a very good picture, which should show up strongly at b. o.

"Make Your Own Bed" (WB). Wacky farce for good audience reaction and profitable biz.

"The Yellow Rose of Texas" (songs) (Rep). Roy Rogers musical hits boxoffice register.

"Beneath Western Skies" (Rep). Complicated, incredible rope-twirler, for dual programs.

"The Monster Maker" (PRC). Fine acting of J. Carrol Naish fails to put this horror film over.

The Eve of St. Mark

20th-Fox release of William Perlberg production. Features Anne Baxter, William Eythe, Michael O'Shea. Directed by John M. Stahl. Screenplay, George Seaton; adapted from stage play by Maxwell Anderson; editor, Louis Sackin; camera, Joseph La Shelle; music, Cyril J. Mockridge; music direction, Emil Newman. Previewed in N. Y., May 15, '44. Running time, **96 MINS.**

Janet Feller....................Anne Baxter
Private Quizz West..........William Eythe
Private Thomas Mulveray..Michael O'Shea
Private Francis Marion.......Vincent Price
Nell West......................Ruth Nelson
Deckman West..................Ray Collins
Private Glinka.............Stanley Prager
Private Shevlin..............Henry Morgan
Corporal Tate...............Robert Bailey
Lill Bird......................Joann Dolan
Sal Bird........................Toni Favor
Sergeant Ruby............George Mathews
Private Carter.................John Archer
Sergeant Kriven..............Murray Alper
Zip West.....................Dickie Moore
Pepita........................Joven E. Rola
Chaplain.....................Harry Shannon
Guide..........................David Essex
Sheep Wagon Driver..........Arthur Hohl
The Captain....................Roger Clark
Neil West......................Jimmy Clark

In these days of "invasion" headlines, when Wake and Guam and Corregidor are seemingly of a too-remote past, "The Eve of St. Mark" will require considerable salesmanship and exploitation. It is a well-produced war story, and no small factor in its favor is the dialog retained from the Maxwell Anderson stageplay from which the film was adapted. Its appeal for the femmes, mothers especially, is vital.

Anderson's stage hit of the 1942-43 season will be remembered as a subtle flag-waver whose basic purposes were shrouded by the always terse, down-to-earth dialog of American doughboys, pre-and post-Pearl Harbor. Much of this quality the film has retained, though for the screen there was an inevitable elimination of some of the play's salty lines and sex implications. In short, "St. Mark" has become a homey comedy-drama of a farmboy inductee, his family, sweetheart and barracks comrades. It remains almost a Johnny Doughboy documentary.

It would seem to be almost a distortion in the film of the play's original, ideological ending, in which an effective realism was gained with the death on a Philippines island of the small group of soldiers who defended it. The film concludes on a note of hope that the group escaped after accomplishing its desired delaying action.

Corregidor may be dated in the newsprints, but there can be no mere dismissal of its catastrophic effects. It is unlikely that this group of hemmed-in doughboys could have escaped under the circumstances, and Anderson certainly never intended for them to escape. It's a disturbance of realism, however, that has its compensations. If 20th-Fox's purpose was to give hope to friends and relatives of Philippine defenders "missing in action"—and there's little question that such was its intent—then it's a commendable token of how Hollywood has done much in this war to promote the morale of the American civilian.

It is a picture of superlative performances. William Eythe, as the farmboy inductee, has his biggest part to date, and does much with it. He and Anne Baxter share the romance, and she, too, gives a fine characterization, as does, notably, Michael O'Shea, in the same role he created in the Broadway stage version, when he was known as Eddie O'Shea. Eythe and Miss Baxter have the parts created on the stage by William Prince and Mary Rolfe. Vincent Price, as the poetical southerner played originally by James Monks; Ruth Nelson as the mother (Aline MacMahon was the original); Ray Collins, the father; Stanley Prager and George Mathews are others who stand out in a cast of standouts.

William Perlberg has manifested an eye for production values, and John M. Stahl has done surprisingly well in his direction of a talky script. George Seaton's screenplay has followed the original as far as could be permitted by screen license. *Kahn.*

The Hairy Ape

United Artists release of Jules Levey production. Features William Bendix, Susan Hayward, John Loder, Dorothy Comingore, Roman Bohnen, Tom Fadden, Alan Napier, Charles Cane. Directed by Alfred Santell. Based on play by Eugene ONeill; adaptation, Robert D. Andrews and Decla Dunning; editor, William Ziegler; camera, Lucien Andriot. Perviewed in N. Y., May 12, '44. Running time, **90 MINS.**

Hank.......................William Bendix
Mildred....................Susan Hayward
Lazar............................John Loder
Helen.................Dorothy Comingore
Paddy......................Roman Bohnen
Long..........................Tom Fadden
MacDougald...................Alan Napier
Gantry.......................Charles Cane
Aldo........................Raphael Storm
Portuguese Proprietor.....Charles La Torre
Concertina Player..............Don Zolaya
Waitress......................Mary Zavian
Police Captain...............George Sorrel
Doctor..........................Paul Weigel
Musician.....................Egon Brecher
Refugee Wife..............Gesela Werbsek
Young Girl..................Carmen Rachel
Water Tender...............Jonathan Lee
Third Engineer...............Dick Baldwin
Head Guard.....................Ralph Dunn
Lieutenant................William Halligan
Doorman....................Tommy Hughes
Bartender........................Bob Perry

Going back more than 20 years for material but daring to tackle the subject of Eugene O'Neill's trenchantly written "The Hairy Ape," Jules Levey has come up with a very good picture, although innumerable liberties have been taken with the O'Neill play. Skillfully skirting the danger portions of O'Neill's drama, switching it around, including a different ending, and inserting scenes of his own, Levey may be accused of taking the liberties he has, but the results are gripping entertainment. The boxoffice potentialities are very strong.

The O'Neill play, one of his earliest and one carrying plenty of gutter dialog and epithets which of necessity could not have been brought to the screen as written, dealt with the futility of brawn over brain, but also severely attacked capitalism and, at one point, concerned the old I. W. W. (International Workers of the World). Additionally, it took a poke at high society. Film transcription could not go into that, although the basic character, that of a ship's stoker who felt that his strength was all that belonged in the world, is particularly well portrayed, both so far as the part itself is concerned and in the interpretation by William Bendix. He imparts to it all the ape-like qualities that could exist in a man in line with the O'Neill play. Part was done on the stage by the late Louis Wolheim.

The script given Levey by Robert D. Andrews and Decla Dunning, a well-turned one containing as much of O'Neill's original dialog as possible and judicious, is of the present to furnish some wartime flavor, and opens in Lisbon, where a freighter is about to sail with a load of refugees. Love interest that ultimately peters is injected through the central woman character, Susan Hayward, who plays the snobbish, badly spoiled daughter of a steel tycoon (as called for by the O'Neill story), and John Loder, second engineer of the ship. It develops that the girl is merely enticing Loder in order to achieve her selfish aims. Also, it is she who, revolting at the sight of Bendix, labels him a hairy ape. That charge hounds him constantly, with the result his bestial prowess is finally dulled through an arrest, and in other ways. Though he goes to a circus to speak his thoughts to a caged gorilla, instead of freeing the primate and getting hugged to death, as in the play, he makes peace with the world and ships again as a stoker.

In the play the central character was called Yank, whereas in Levey's pic he's Hank. Production rates tops as to settings, background, etc. Most of the dialects, among stokehole associates of Hank's, as written by O'Neill, are missing in the film version. There is a slight attempt, however, to inject some comedy, but it's not needed. Alfred Santell's direction keeps the story moving at a good pace, with a lot of ground covered during the 90 minutes running time. Ostensibly the editing job by William Ziegler was an able one.

In addition to the outstanding performance given by Bendix and various of his lowly pals, both Miss Hayward and Dorothy Comingore acquit themselves very creditably. Loder does well as the engineer. The others, among a long list of players, are relatively lesser, but of much importance in lending the picture body as well as color. *Char.*

Make Your Own Bed

Hollywood, May 16.

Warner Bros. release of Alex Gottlieb production. Stars Jack Carson, Jane Wyman, Irene Manning; features Alan Hale. Directed by Peter Godfrey. Screenplay by Francis Swann and Edmund Joseph; adapted by Richard Weil; from play by Harvey J. O'Higgins and Harriet Ford; camera, Robert Burks; editor, Clarence Kolster; special effects, Willard Van Enger; asst. director, Les Guthrie. Tradeshown in L. A. May 15, '44. Running time, **81 MINS.**

Jerry Curtis......................Jack Carson
Susan Courtney................Jane Wyman
Walter Whirtle......................Alan Hale
Vivian Whirtle...............Irene Manning
Boris Murphy..................George Tobias
Lester Knight................Robert Shayne
Marie Gruber........................Tala Birell
Fritz Alten....................Ricardo Cortez
Elsa Wehmer...............Marjorie Hoshelle
Paul Hassen........................Kurt Katch
Mr. Brooking...................Harry Bradley
F. B. I. Man...............William Kennedy

"Make Your Own Bed" is a wacky farce sketched on broad lines, to hit present audience requirements for light and fluffy screen fare. Jack Carson and Jane Wyman take off here as a co-starring team, continuing their screwball antics first introduced by the pair in "Princess O'Rourke." Picture will click for profitable biz in all bookings.

Story is predicated on the wartime servant problem, with Alan Hale setting up phoney spy plot to get dumbbell private detective Carson to function as butler on Hale's suburban estate. Jane Wyman, who's to marry Carson when he gets enough coin, goes along to pose as the maid. Added suspects are provided for Carson by arrival of four members of Hale's radio program for weekend rehearsals. Succession of events aim for laugh situations, and at several points it's a pretty broad reach to attain the objective. Dramatic climax with comedic trimmings discloses radio actors are real German spies bent on obtaining confidential war plans from Hale. Carson fumbles through, however, to capture the agents.

Story thread is a fragile affair, with picture depending on individual sequences of physical violence and laugh lines to carry it along at a surprisingly fast pace. Peter Godfrey directs to take advantage of the comedy angles, and neatly times comedy sequence of Carson in the ladies' bathhouse and preparation of dinner by the new servants.

Carson and Miss Wyman team well for display of broad comedy and mugged as called for by type of farce on display. Hale, Irene Manning and George Tobias provide strong support. *Walt.*

Yellow Rose of Texas

(MUSICAL)

Republic production and release. Stars Roy Rogers; features Dale Evans, Grant Withers, Harry Shannon, George Cleveland, Bob Nolan and Sons of Pioneers. Directed by Joseph Kane. Screenplay, Jack Townley; camera, Jack Marta; editor, Tony Martinelli; musical director, Morton Scott; dances, Larry Ceballos. Tradeshown in N. Y. May 12, '44. Running time, **69 MINS.**

Roy ....Roy Rogers
Betty Weston....................Dale Evans
Lukas...........................Grant Withers
Sam Weston..................Harry Shannon
Capt. Joe...................George Cleveland
Buster.........................William Haade
Charlie Goss...............Weldon Heyburn
Ferguson.....................Hal Taliaferro
Sheriff Allen......................Tom London
Indian Pete........................Dick Botiller
Specialty Singer..................Janet Martin
Pinto.......................Brown Jug Reynolds
Bob Nolan and Sons of the Pioneers

Republic has hit the boxoffice register again with this handsomely produced Roy Rogers musical. Picture is a strong top-bill contender in all situations.

Rogers is a secret investigator for an insurance company trying to locate a payroll stolen five years ago. He obtains a job singing on the showboat "Yellow Rose of Texas" from Betty Weston, whose father was convicted and imprisoned for the robbery. When Weston breaks jail to clear himself of the framed charge, Rogers helps get the evidence that traps the real culprit.

The musical sequences are pleasant and well staged, enhanced by some good singing and dancing, and there is enough action to satisfy those who like excitement in their westerns.

Rogers acts and sings in his usually accomplished style, and Dale Evans makes a decorative addition to the film with her fine singing and dancing, while Bob Nolan and the Sons of the Pioneers do well with their numbers. Rest of the cast is competent.

Beneath Western Skies

Republic release of Louis Gray production. Stars Bob Livingston and Smiley Burnette; features Effie Laird, Frank Jaquet and Tom London. Directed by Spencer Bennet. Screenplay, Albert DeMond and Bob Williams, from original by DeMond; camera, Ernest Miller; editor, Charles Craft. At N. Y. theatre, N. Y., week of May 9, '44. Running time, **54 MINS**

Johnny Revere.............Bob Livingston
Frog Millhouse............Smiley Burnette
Carrie Stokes.......................Effie Laird
Samuel Webster..............Frank Jaquet
Earl Phillips......................Tom London
Lem Toller....................Charles Miller
Tadpole.....................Joe Strauch, Jr.
Bull Bricker.......................Leroy Mason
Rod Barrow....................Kenne Duncan
Spike..........................Charles Dorety
Wainwright.........................Jack Kirk
Hank..............................Bud Geary

With a plot more incredible and complicated than most films of this type, "Beneath Western Skies" is a sagebrusher that will find tough sledding. Strictly a lower-case dualer.

Bob Livingston gets conked on the head, resulting in a loss of memory. When told by the crooks that he is one of them, he believes them, but they advise him to continue being a law-enforcer. Another bop, his memory returns and he goes to work on the villains, rounding them up and regaining the faith of the township.

Comedy support of Smiley Burnette adds to his laurels, and the other members of the supporting cast, including the veteran Effie Laird, do their best with the material at hand. *Sten.*

Los Dos Rivales
("The Two Rivals")
(ARGENTINE-MADE)

Buenos Aires, May 3.

E. F. A. production and release. Stars Luis Sandrini and Hugo del Carril; features Alicia Barrie, Aida Alberti, Bertha Moss, Enrique Roldan, Golde Flam, Alberto Terrones, Billy Days, Mario Faig and Domingo Mania. Story by Arturo S. Mom; adapted by Bayon Herrera; camera, Roque Funes; music, Alberto Soifer. At Ocean, Buenos Aires. Running time, **96 MINS**

This looks like the Hollywood influence in local production with a newspaper story in the U.S. manner, adapted to local conditions. Film has had an unusual production in that while two directors worked on it, neither gets credit for actual job. Also unusual is that a number of cuts have been made by local censors.

Story tells of two newsmen, rivals in their work and romance but still buddies. They discover a gang of crooks and ransom the daughter of one of the directors. One rival is wounded but recovers and marries the girl he saved. Other weds the sister. Both wind up as directors of rival newspapers.

Action, complications, comedy, romance and gangsters are close to the U. S. mold. Luis Sandrini, a top Argentine comic, is good in title role. Hugo del Carril, an outstanding local tango singer, improves his dancing ability in a role that seems tailored to his style. Film looks good draw for Latin-American houses but not for U. S. because of similarity to American films of same pattern.

Ray.

The Monster Maker

PRC Pictures release of Sigmund Neufeld production. Stars J. Carrol Naish and Ralph Morgan; features Tala Birell, Wanda McKay and Terry Frost. Directed by Sam Newfield. Screenplay, Pierre Gendron and Martin Mooney, from original by Lawrence Williams; camera, Robert Cline; editor, Holbrook N. Todd. At N. Y. theatre, N.Y., week of May 9, '44. Running time, **64 MINS**

Markoff....................J. Carrol Naish
Lawrence....................Ralph Morgan
Maxine....................Tala Birell
Patricia....................Wanda McKay
Blake....................Terry Frost
Giant....................Glenn Strange
Butler....................Alexander Pollard
Dr. Adams....................Sam Flint
Ace....................By Himself

The ingredients are there to make this a suspenseful horror film, but somewhere along the line director Sam Newfield got sidetracked. Result is another one of those "mad scientist" things that wind up on the duals.

This one has J. Carrol Naish as a doctor interested in experimenting with human lives for the money he figures he can get out of it. Ralph Morgan, portraying a concert pianist, is the victim. Naish, in his warped mind, also figures that, by curing the old boy, he can win the latter's daughter.

Tala Birell, Wanda McKay, Terry Frost and the others in support, including Ace, the dog, find their way in and out of the plot despite everything.

Sten.

Miniature Reviews

"Roger Touhy, Gangster!" (20th). Smoothly-done gangster yarn will do good business.

"Home in Indiana" (Technicolor) (20th). A film about horse breeding and sulky racing that should do well at the b.o.

"Summer Storm" (UA). Critical attention certain, but needs selling.

"Ladies in Washington" (20th). Dull drama of girls in the capitol. For dual fillers.

"Jungle Woman" (U). Apegirl prances in good horror drama. Strong dual supporter.

"South of Dixie" (Songs) (U). Farce with songs for supporting dates in secondary duals.

"The Black Parachute" (Col). Spy melodrama for the dualers.

"The Scarlet Claw" (U). Sherlock Holmes story makes fair dualer.

"Girl in the Case" (Col). Detective tale featuring Edmund Lowe and Janis Carter, for duals.

"Detective Kitty O'Day" (Mono). Pleasantly diverting mystery-comedy, nice dual fill-in.

"The Drifter" (PRC). Below-average western starring Buster Crabbe.

"Men On Her Mind" (PRC). (Songs). Entertaiping "B."

Roger Touhy, Gangster!

20th-Fox release of Lee Marcus production. Features Preston Foster, Victor McLaglen, Lois Andrews, Kent Taylor. Directed by Robert Florey. Screenplay by Crane Wilbur and Jerry Cady, from original by Wilbur; camera, Glen MacWilliams; editor, Harry Reynolds. Tradeshown in N. Y. May 22, '44. Running time, **65 MINS.**

Roger Touhy....................Preston Foster
Owl Banghart....................Victor McLaglen
Daisy....................Lois Andrews
Captain Steve Warren....................Kent Taylor
George Carroll....................Anthony Quinn
Joe Sutton....................William Post, Jr.
Smoke Reardon....................Henry Morgan
Cameron....................Matt Briggs
Riley....................Moroni Olsen
Drake....................Reed Hadley
Gloria....................Trudy Marshall
Kerrigan....................John Archer
Troubles O'Connor....................Frank Jenks
Ice Box Hamilton....................George E. Stone
Boyden....................Charles Lang
Mason....................Kane Richmond
MacNair....................George Holmes
Clanahan....................Ralph Peters
Frank Williams....................Roy Roberts
Lefty Rowden....................John Harmon
Maxie Sharkey....................Horace MacMahon

"Roger Touhy, Gangster!" would ordinarily do satisfactorily on its merits as a fast-paced, smoothly-done gang film. Add to this that it's based on fact not too dim in the headlines, as well as the fact that Touhy, while in prison, tried to get an injunction preventing its release, and one has a film that will do good business when the obvious exploitation is used.

The film has further ring of truth in it. The state of Illinois permitted several shots to be filmed at Statesville prison in Joliet, where Touhy and his mob made their sensational break in October, 1942. There's no suggestion of the phoney about the whole business.

Where the film does suffer is in the inevitable nature of the yarn. It starts off excitingly enough in a masterful montage of shootings to end a little lamely when the gangsters are recaptured without a shot. And 20th-Fox makes the mistake of covering this up with a lecture to the audience by the prison warden on crime not paying, which only makes the tame end tamer. But on the whole the story has a taut quality, a full credibility and a cumulative effect to make it an absorbing yarn.

Starting in the gun-crazed days of the early '30s, the story carries Touhy and his mob into the kidnapping stunt that brought about their arrest and imprisonment. Shifting to Joliet prison, it shows Touhy's long patient plans for the jail-break, culminating in the mob's exciting getaway. The dragnet that state and Federal officials throw out to recapture the mob is shown in tight, direct scenes with a minimum of heroics. And the buildup for the climax, when the mob is retaken, is tense enough, if the final scene is not.

Preston Foster makes an authentic figure of Touhy without overdoing the heavy side, although one scene in which he beats up another mobster is as brutal (and effective) as anything one will ever see. Henry Morgan, Frank Jenks, George E. Stone, Horace MacMahon and Victor McLaglen give each gang-member a distinct individuality, and Kent Taylor is quietly convincing as a police captain. There are several montage views in addition to the gunplay opener that are worthy of attention. The production isn't skimpy at any time, a lavish style being laid on when needed, and Robert Florey's direction calls for commendation.

Home in Indiana
(TECHNICOLOR)

20th Century-Fox release of an Andre Daven production. Stars Walter Brennan; features Jeanne Crain, June Haver, Lon McCallister, Charlotte Greenwood, Ward Bond. Directed by Henry Hathaway. Screenplay, Winston Miller from original by George Agnew Chamberlain; music, Emil Newman; camera, Edward Cronjager; editor, Harmon Jones. Tradeshown N. Y., May 19, '44. Running time, **103 MINS**

J. F. (Thunder) Bolt....................Walter Brennan
Sparke Thornton....................Lon McCallister
Char....................Jeanne Crain
Cri-Cri....................June Haver
Penny....................Charlotte Greenwood
Jed Bruce....................Ward Bond
Godaw Boole....................Charles Dingle
Gordon Bradley....................Robert Condon
Jitterbug....................Charles Saggau
Mo....................Willie Best
Tuppy....................George Reed
Fleaflit Dryer....................Noble "Kid" Chissell
Ed....................Walter Baldwin
Sam....................George Cleveland
Blacksmith....................Arthur Aylesworth
Maid....................Libby Taylor
Old Timer....................Roger Imhof
Dave....................Matt McHugh
Bill....................Eddy Waller
Waiter....................Billy Mitchell
Soft Drink Man....................Tom Dugan
Swipes....................{Sam McDaniel / Emmett Smith}

A poignant story, framed in the beautiful setting of Indiana's horse-breeding territory, mounted in Technicolor that catches the grand scope of the blue-grass country, "Home in Indiana" is plenty on the all right side. For young and old, male and female, it will do good business in all situations, depending, of course, on word-of-mouth and proper exploitation, since marquee strength is lacking.

This picture deals with the rearing of sulky horses and the trials and tribulations of their breeders. It serves to introduce three youthful players in featured roles from whom much should be heard in the future. They are Lon McCallister, seen in "Stage Door Canteen"; June Haver, blonde eyeful who has plenty on the ball, and titian-haired Jeanne Crain, a personable miss with loads of talent.

Backed up by veterans Walter Brennan, Charlotte Greenwood, Ward Bond and a supporting cast of experienced actors, these youthful players portray their roles to the hilt. Director Henry Hathaway has dug deeply into his bag of tricks, for his work in this picture is topflight. His guidance of the younger actors, and the fine performances he has drawn from the older ones, is highly commendable.

Settings are in good taste with scenes of the crowds at the state fair especially colorful, as are those showing the young actors frolicking at the "old swimmin' hole" and again "jitterbugging" at the dance the night before the big race. Sequence at night, when the young filly is born, with the attendant ministrations and to-do, lingers in one's memory even after the film has unwound.

Story relates how McCallister comes into the life of Brennan and Miss Greenwood, following the death of his aunt back east. His love of horses results in the renewed interest of Brennan, who until then was, in semi-retirement, in life itself, and horse-breeding and sulky racing in particular. Borrowing money from Miss Crain with the help of Willie Best, Negro handyman, McCallister foals a high-bred filly, who turns into a champion trotter, winning a big-money race that again places Brennan in the respected light he once held among trotting followers. Love interest is supplied by Miss Crain and McCallister, with Miss Haver forming what proves to be an innocent triangle.

Despite the fact that 20th-Fox has taken such an obvious gamble, depending on one fair draw (Brennan) and three unknowns to entice the customers through the wickets, "Home in Indiana" should prove to be a sleeper. Except for the Technicolor budget, the film could not have been too costly to produce. In any event, there is plenty of value for filmgoers in this one.

Sten.

Summer Storm

Hollywood, May 18.

United Artists release of Seymour Nebenzal production. Stars George Sanders and Linda Darnell; features Edward Everett Horton and Anna Lee. Directed by Douglas Sirk. Adaptation by Michael O'Hara; screenplay, Rowland Leigh; added dialog, Robert Thoeren; based on Anton Chekhov's "The Shooting Party"; camera, Archie Stout; editor, Greg Tallas; original score and musical direction by Karl Hajos. Previewed at Four Star, Los Angeles, May 17, '44. Running time, **105 MINS.**

Fedor Michailovitch Petroff....................Geo. Sanders
Olga....................Linda Darnell
Nadina....................Anna Lee
Count Volsky....................Edward Everett Horton
Urbenin....................Hugo Haas
Clara....................Lori Lahner
Polycarp....................John Philliber
Kuzma....................Sig Ruman
Mr. Kalenin....................Andre Charlot
Mrs. Kalenin....................Mary Servoss
Lunin....................John Abbott
Gregory....................Robert Greig
Gypsy Singer....................Nina Koschetz
Orloff, the Gendarme....................Paul Hurst
Doctor....................Charles Trowbridge
Clerk in Newspaper Office....................Byron Foulger
Mailman....................Charles Wagenheim
Cafe Proprietor....................Frank Orth
Haughty Lady at Dinner....................Eliz. Russell
Young Lady at Dinner....................Ann Staunton
Passerby at Mailbox....................Jimmy Conlin
Woman with Umbrella....................Kate McKena
Residing Judge in Kharkov....................Fred Nurney
Beggar Woman....................Sarah Padden
Beggar Child....................Sharon McManus
Priest....................Gabriel Lionoff
Policeman....................Mike Mazurki
Young Lackey....................Woody Charles
Gypsy Girl....................Joyce Gates

"Summer Storm" is a carefully-made drama of people and passion in Russia 30 years ago, adapted from a Chekhov drama. It has dramatic strength in parts, and critics, in the majority, will probably tab it as artistic and unusual. But, lacking in strong marquee values, picture will require smart and concentrated selling campaign to catch profitable biz at key billtoppers, but it's a cinch for strong support in the regular duals.

Russian background of the Kharkov district displays intimate study in contrasts of various persons—local judge, George Sanders; young and impetuous siren, Linda Darnell, who's determined to have wealth and finery; flustery and decadent Edward Everett Horton, land-owning aristocrat; estate superintendent, Hugo Haas; and Anna Lee, engaged to Sanders. All become engulfed in tragedy when Miss Darnell marries Haas and immediately embarks on an affair with Sanders, while slyly playing Horton for the finery and jewels he can supply. After leisurely wending through lengthy footage of characters and incidents, girl is murdered by Sanders to save the others—but Haas is convicted of the crime, with Sanders assisting by his silence. Decade later, Sanders finds it impossible to live with his secret and pays for the crime with his life.

Miss Darnell is spotlighted with her particularly effective performance. Sanders is excellent, sharing supporting prominence with Horton. Lori Lahner scores as the maid who protects Sanders' secret; Anna Lee, Haas, and John Philliber are strong in support.

Script, with adaptation credited to Michael O'Hara and screenplay by Rowland Leigh, is particularly effective despite details of characters and carefully-etched situations which consume plenty of footage and tend to slow up the tempo. Direction by Douglas Sirk has the European touch, but he takes full advantage of passionate inferences in many of the sequences, although deftly skirting the taboos of the purity-sealers.

Production layout and technical contributions are topnotch throughout, especially photography by Archie Stout. *Walt.*

Ladies in Washington

Hollywood, May 17.

20th-Fox release of William Girard production. Features Trudy Marshall, Ronald Graham, Anthony Quinn, Sheila Ryan. Directed by Louis King. Screenplay, Wanda Tuchock; camera, Charles Clarke; editor, Nick De Maggio. Tradeshown in L. A. May 16, '44. Running time, **61 MINS**

Carol	Trudy Marshall
Dr. Mayberry	Ronald Graham
Michael	Anthony Quinn
Jerry	Sheila Ryan
Stephen	Robert Bailey
Helen	Beverly Whitney
Adelaide	Jackie Paley
Investigator	Carleton Young
Mother Henry	John Philliber
Vicky	Robin Raymond
Amy	Doris Merrick
Betty	Barbara Booth
Frieda	Jo-Carroll Dennison
Marjorie	Lillian Porter
Lieutenant Lake	Harry Shannon
Nellie	Ruby Dandridge
Inspector Saunders	Charles D. Brown
Dr. Crane	Pierre Watkin
Mrs. Crane	Nella Walker
Dorothy	Inna Gest
Nurse	Rosalind Keith
Susan	Edna Mae Jones

Housing problem for the abundance of girls working in Washington forms basis for this minor-league drama. It limps along with obvious theatrics and synthetic development. For filler on secondary duals.

Story is a hodge-podge and over-dialoged. Spar Trudy Marshall befriends former schoolmate Sheila Ryan but latter is upsetting influence in girls' boarding house by faking suicide and then hooking up with an enemy agent to involve several characters when the spy is killed in gun battle.

Plot struggles unsuccessfully, but neither director Louis King nor members of the cast can provide much assistance. *Walt.*

Jungle Woman

Hollywood, May 20.

Universal release of Will Cowan production. Features Acquanetta, Evelyn Ankers, J. Carrol Naish, Samuel S. Hinds, Lois Collier, Milburn Stone and Douglas Dumbrille. Directed by Reginald LeBorg. Screenplay, Bernard Schubert, Henry Sucher, Edward Dein; original by Sucher; camera, Jack MacKenzie; editor, Ray Snyder. Previewed in Hollywood, May 19, '44. Running time, **60 MINS.**

Beth	Evelyn Ankers
Dr. Fletcher	J. Carrol Naish
Coroner	Samuel S. Hinds
Joan Fletcher	Lois Collier
Fred Mason	Milburn Stone
District Attorney	Douglas Dumbrille
Bob Whitney	Richard Davis
Miss Gray	Nana Bryant
Dr. Meredith	Pierre Watkin
George	Christian Rub
Caretaker	Alec Craig
Willie	Edward M. Hyans, Jr.
Joe Fingerprint Man	Richard Powers

And Acquanetta

Another horror drama with good blend of thrills and suspense for the chiller-minded customers. Slick title and exploitation possibilities for secondary runs will provide strong support to hold up a weak billtopper.

Picture is sequel to "Captive Wild Woman," which Universal released a year ago, with Acquanetta as the ape-girl. In previous film latter had blood of a simian transfused into her veins for periodic reversion to animalistic instincts and killings. This yarn spends no time on the actual clinical work, easily bridging that phase through brief explanatory dialog to get into the story.

Ape-girl strangely appears at a sanatorium of medical research scientist, J. Carrol Naish, and immediately causes confusion. Her attraction to Richard Davis, who's engaged to Naish's daughter, Lois Collier, sets up premise for climactic disposal of the strange creature.

Dark-eyed and dark-complexioned Acquanetta is an excellent choice for the ape-girl role. Naish, Stone, Evelyn Ankers, Samuel Hinds, Miss Collier, Davis and Edward M. Hyans, Jr., are okay in support.

Direction by Reginald LeBorg is crisp throughout, accentuating the suspense and thrill sequences supplied by compact script. *Walt.*

South of Dixie
(SONGS)

Hollywood, May 20.

Universal release of Jean Yarbrough production. Features Anne Gwynne, David Bruce, Jerome Cowan and Ella Mae Morse. Directed by Yarbrough. Screenplay, Clyde Bruckman; original story, Sam Coslow; camera, Jerome Ash; editor, Paul Landres. Previewed in Hollywood, May 19, '44. Running time, **61 MINS.**

Dixie	Anne Gwynne
Danny	David Bruce
Brains	Jerome Cowan
Barbara Ann	Ella Mae Morse
Ernest	Joe Sawyer
Colonel Morgan	Samuel S. Hinds
Jay	Eddie Acuff
Annabelle	Marie Harmon
Colonel Hatcher	Oscar O'Shea
Chloe	Louise Beavers
Dean Williamson	Pierre Watkin
Announcer	Bill Bivens
Ruby	Marie Blake
Woman	Rita Gould
Mr. Platt	Edward Keane
Porter	Manton Moreland
Reporter	Ray Walker
Clerk	Eddie Bruce
Photographer	Jack Mulhall

Bobby Brooks and Quartet
Lester Cole and The Debutantes
The Charmers

"South of Dixie" is a lightweight farce with sufficient song interludes to carry it through the secondary houses as a dual supporter.

Story is decidedly flimsy. David Bruce, writer of southern pop tunes, is promoted as subject for a film biog of his life by enterprising partner, Jerome Cowan, and latter figures Bruce must go south to whip up suitable family background. Southerner Anne Gwynne goes along as tutor in proper accent, and Bruce is unwillingly projected into romance with Ella Mae Morse, daughter of a southern colonel; also subject of revival is an old family feud. After proper running time, episode is disclosed as a hoax, with Bruce and Miss Gwynne back in New York for the usual clinch.

On the tune side, Miss Morse sings her trademark, "Shoo Shoo Baby," and "Never Again." Bobby Brooks and his quartet, Lester Cole and his six Debutantes and The Charmers girl trio each make single appearances. Bruce and Miss Gwynne each deliver a solo and team for a romantic ditty. Songs and deliveries are standard. Cast and direction are adequate. *Walt.*

The Black Parachute

Columbia release of Jack Fier production. Stars John Carradine, Osa Massen; features Larry Parks, Jeanne Bates. Directed by Lew Landers. Screenplay by Clarence Upson Young; story by Paul Gangelin; camera, George Meehan; editor, Otto Meyer. At Brooklyn Fox, week of May 19, '44. Running time, **68 MINS.**

Gen. Von Bodenbach	John Carradine
Marya Orloff	Osa Massen
Michael Lindley	Larry Parks
Olga	Jeanne Bates
King Stephen	Jonathan Hale
Col. Pavlec	Ivan Triesault
Nicholas	Trevor Bardette
Joseph	Art Smith
Pilot	Robert Lowell
Kurt Vandan	Chas. Wagenheim
Erik Dundeen	Chas. Waldron
Cobbler	Ernie Adams

"The Black Parachute" is a fairly trite spy melodrama with the usual ingredients of gunplay and the wild chase. But its intriguing title, and the timeliness of its guerilla warfare theme, will lend it sufficient interest to hold up on the dual bills.

The story is set presumably in a Balkan mountain country (although its name is never mentioned) where the Nazis have taken over the king and government by treachery, and the natives are in armed revolt. It's a bloody bit of business, with the Nazis painted as stupid, ruthless murderers, and each native a quick-triggered avenger. Starting off plausibly enough with its tale of a battling underground, the story goes off into fantastic tangents, such as the American disguised as a Nazi colonel showing up at German headquarters, to destroy any credence or value to the film.

The American drops into the invaded country by means of a black parachute, the further to hide his entry in the dark night. His mission is to rescue the king, and get him out of the country, so that he may broadcast the truth to his people and keep them fighting.

Larry Parks plays the American with a certain charm and plausibility. John Carradine, although featured, has a somewhat secondary role as a brutal Heydrich-modeled Nazi general. Osa Massen makes an attractive figure as a German spy, although the motives for her individual actions are not always clear. Jonathan Hale is effective as the courageous captive king, and Jeanne Bates is convincing as a young patriot.

The Scarlet Claw

Universal release of Roy William Neill production, directed by Neill. Features Basil Rathbone, Nigel Bruce, Gerald Hamer, Paul Cavanagh, Arthur Hohl, Miles Mander. Screenplay by Edmund L. Hartmann and Neill; from story by Paul Gangelin and Brenda Weisberg; camera, George Robinson; editor, Paul Landres. At Rialto, N. Y., May 19, '44. Running time, **74 MINS.**

Sherlock Holmes	Basil Rathbone
Doctor Watson	Nigel Bruce
Potts, Tanner, Ramson	Gerald Hamer
Lord Penrose	Paul Cavanagh
Emile Journet	Arthur Hohl
Judge Brisson	Miles Mander
Marie Journet	Kay Harding
Sergeant Thompson	David Clyde
Drake	Ian Wolfe
Nora	Victoria Horne

Universal has resorted to original stories to continue the Sherlock Holmes series, but it is very apparent they don't measure up to the Conan Doyle plots, despite the presence of psychic phenomena, apparitions and premonitions, with the result that the entire thing wears thin. Picture should be fair for the duals.

This one finds the indomitable Holmes and blundering Dr. Watson in a French-Canadian village, investigating the mysterious reappearance of a legendary monster. Of course, there are the usual number of grisly murders and suspects, fog-shrouded marshes and deserted houses to lend the proper atmosphere to the proceedings, together with a very talkative murderer, and a thoroughly detached ending, in which Holmes delivers a Churchill speech eulogizing Canada.

Basil Rathbone is his customary grim and infallible Holmes, with Nigel Bruce a good foil in providing a few droll scenes, while the others are all properly suspicious looking.

Girl in the Case

Columbia release of Sam White production. Stars Edmund Lowe; features Janis Carter, Robert Williams, Richard Hale and Stanley Clements. Directed by William Berke. Screenplay, Joseph Hoffman and Dorcas Cochran, from story by Charles F. Royal; camera, L. W. O'Connell; editor, Paul Borofsky. At Brooklyn Strand, N. Y., week of May 18, '44. Running time, **68 MINS**

William Warner	Edmund Lowe
Myra Warner	Janis Carter
Malloy	Robert Williams
John Heyser	Richard Hale
Tuffy	Stanley Clements
Sylvia Manners	Carole Mathews
Tommy Rockwood	Robert Scott
Smith	Dick Elliott
Roberts	Gene Stutenroth

Columbia's effort to build Edmund Lowe and Janis Carter into an amusing detective team (a la Metro's "Thin Man" series with Myrna Loy and William Powell) falls short of the mark. Strictly a dualer.

Lowe, as a lawyer who is an expert lock-picker, is on the verge of making an anniversary present to his wife (Miss Carter) when Robert Scott walks into his office and hires him to open an old chest. Before the audience knows what the score is, Lowe is involved with a group of enemy agents while trying to untangle the mystery surrounding his client.

Film is fast-paced at times but fails to be amusing too often. Too many script loose ends are other failings. Supporting cast, including Robert Williams, as a plainclothes man; Richard Hale, as a German spy, and Stanley Clements, youngster who is assistant to Lowe, gives creditable performances. *Sten.*

Detective Kitty O'Day

Monogram release of Lindsley Parsons production. Stars Jean Parker; features Peter Cookson, Tim Ryan, Veda Ann Borg, Edward Gargan. Directed by William Beaudine. Screenplay, Tim Ryan and Victor Hammond, from original by Victor Hammond; camera, Ira Morgan; editor, Richard Currier; music director, Edward Kay. At New York theatre, N. Y., week of May 16, '44. Running time, **61 MINS**

Kitty O'Day	Jean Parker
Johnny Jones	Peter Cookson
Inspector Miles	Tim Ryan
Georgia Wentworth	Veda Ann Borg
Mike Storm	Edward Gargan
Anton Downs	Douglas Fowley
Oliver Wentworth	Edward Earle
Jeffers	Herbert Heyes
Cab Driver	Pat Gleason
Charles	Olaf Hytten

Using a succession of murders to establish its background, "Detective Kitty O'Day" emerges as a pleasantly diverting mystery comedy that should fill in nicely as a second feature in nabe houses, although, at times, it's a case of too many corpses.

There is the amateur feminine detective who leads her reluctant boyfriend into a series of situations wherein they are suspected of murdering the girl's employer. There are the usual number of murders and suspects, and the usual thickheaded police inspector, too.

Jean Parker, in the title role, is okay as the sleuth, and Peter Cookson, a screen newcomer, is fine as her swain, with the rest of the cast aiding effectively.

The Drifter

PRC release of Sigmund Neufeld production. Stars Buster Crabbe and Al "Fuzzy" St. John; features Carol Parker, Kermit Maynard, Jack Ingram. Directed by Sam Newfield. Story and screenplay, Patricia Harper; camera, Robert Cline; editor, Holbrook N. Todd. At New York theatre, N. Y., week of May 16, '44. Running time, **60 MINS**

Billy Carson / Drifter Davis	Buster Crabbe
Fuzzy Jones	Al "Fuzzy" St. John
Sally Dawson	Carol Parker
Jack	Kermit Maynard
Dirk Trent	Jack Ingram
Sam	Roy Brent
Blackie	George Chesebro
Simms	Ray Bennett
Sheriff Perkins	Jimmy Aubrey
Marshal Hodges	Slim Whitaker

PRC, in trying to build up Buster Crabbe as a western star, will have

to furnish him with better material than this. Picture is definitely a dual tailender.

Crabbe plays a dual role, a Robin Hood of the range and a bank robber who has been impersonating the R.H. in order to cover up his crimes. The mistaken identity angle has everyone confused—the audience included.

Crabbe does the best he can with the stereotyped yarn, while Al "Fuzzy" St. John provides a few humorous moments.

Men on Her Mind
(SONGS)

PRC Pictures release of Alfred Stern production. Stars Mary Beth Hughes; features Edward Norris and Ted North. Directed by Wallace Fox. Screenplay, Raymond L. Schrock; musical director, Lee Zahler; camera, Robert Cline; editor, Chas. Henkel, Jr. At Brooklyn Strand, N. Y., week of May 18, '44. Running time, 70 MINS.

Lily Durrell	Mary Beth Hughes
Jeffry Wingate	Edward Norris
Jim Lacey	Ted North
Roland Palmer	Alan Edwards
Alberti Verdi	Luis Alberni
Eloise Palmer	Kay Linaker
Mayme Munson	Claire Rochelle
"Big Joe" Monroe	Lyle Latell
Mrs. Goodwin	Claire McDowell
Gracie Tuttle	Eva Hamill
Miss Wiggins	Isabell La Mal
Frank Tuttle	Lane Chandler

A tale of an ambitious singer who refuses to let love and marriage interfere with her career. "Men on Her Mind" is a pleasant enough "B" for nabe duals.

Mary Beth Hughes displays her abilities in good fashion as the gal singer. After achieving her ambition, becoming a popular radio and nightclub vocalist, she changes her mind about one of her suitors and gives in to his offer of marriage.

Miss Hughes sings several tunes, most notable being "Heaven on Earth," written by Lee Zahler and Pat O'Dea, in a pleasant, throaty voice. Edward Norris, Ted North and Alan Edwards, as her suitors, enact their parts fairly well. Direction by Lee Zahler is in the groove. *Sten.*

Miniature Reviews

"**Bathing Beauty**" (Musical) (Technicolor) (M-G). Top budgeter with Red Skelton, Harry James, Cugat will do strong b.o.

"**Mr. Skeffington**" (WB). Bette Davis sharrer is dramatic film fodder of terrific pungency that will hit the higher b.o. brackets.

"**The Canterville Ghost**" (M-G). Neat comedy-drama geared for okay b.o.

"**Ghost Catchers**" (Songs) (U). Spooky laugh-provoker in the best Olsen & Johnson style.

"**Mystery Man**" (UA). Another Hopalong Cassidy western; a tailend dualer.

"**Secret Command**" (Col). Actionful meller of counter-espionage. Good entertainment for all customers.

"**Tawny Pipit**" (GFD). Unusual British bird yarn; may do in U. S. if given new title.

Bathing Beauty
(COLOR; MUSICAL)
(Musical)

Metro release of Jack Cummings production. Stars Red Skelton, Esther Williams; features Basil Rathbone, Bill Goodwin, Ethel Smith, Jean Porter, Carlos Ramirez. Directed by George Sidney. Screenplay, Dorothy Kingsley, Allen Boretz, Frank Waldman; adaptation, Joseph Schrank from original by Kenneth Earl, M. M. Musselman, Curtis Kenyon; music, Johnny Green; camera, Harry Stradling; editor, Blanche Sewell. Previewed at Criterion, N. Y., May 24, '44. Running time, 101 MINS.

Steve Elliott	Red Skelton
Caroline Brooks	Esther Williams
George Adams	Basil Rathbone
Willis Evans	Bill Goodwin
Organist	Ethel Smith
Jean Allenwood	Jean Porter
Carlos	Carlos Ramirez
Chester Klazenfrantz	Donald Meek

Harry James and orch. with Helen Forrest Xavier Cugat band with Lina Romay

Another one of those musicals in Technicolor which have proved to be winners at the b.o., "Bathing Beauty" has been produced in the lush, lavish manner which, by now, has become as familiar as the Metro trademark. Escapist in all respects, this picture will do from good to excellent business in all situations.

With Red Skelton, Harry James and his orch, Xavier Cugat and his band, and newcomer Esther Williams, who will gain prestige through word-of-mouth, for the marquee, this one is long on music, gals and beauty, but short on story and, except for two sequences, comedy.

Esther Williams, who formerly appeared in "Andy Hardy" films and briefly in "A Guy Named Joe," is pulled to stardom by her swim-suit straps. Dressed in either bathing togs or street finery, she is a pretty picture indeed. The former swimming champ displays her aquatic and acting abilities in the role of a collegienne who travels the rocky road of love with songwriter Red Skelton. She should prove to be an asset in future pictures, on the basis of her performance here.

Skelton is his usual effervescent self, bouncing in and out of the script, getting in and out of scrapes with his girl, and the authorities at the college she attends. His two specialty numbers are especially funny: one, where he attends a ballet dancing class with the girls of the school, dressed in a short, fluffy, pink dress with dancing slippers, endeavoring to go through the motions, and being slapped around by the instructress; the other, which he did in vaude for years prior to landing in films, is his impression of a gal getting up in the morning, prettying herself and dressing.

Unlike musicals prior to this one, Metro has invested in beautiful sequences rather than cast. Water ballet costumes by Sharaff, and the water ballet, produced under the supervision of John Murray Anderson, are memorable. One sequence with Miss Williams swimming in a pool, and water sockets gushing high, is climaxed by the appearance of torches of flame between each water spray, the water then being turned off and quenching the flames. It is unusual in every respect, probably the most ingenious water ballet sequence ever filmed.

Cugat's Latin-American specialties are given added zest by the singing of Lina Romay and the ballading of Carlos Ramirez. James' crew holds the spotlight for five tunes that should have the jitterbugs jumpin', and a tune with Helen Forrest featured. Ethel Smith, Hammond organ specialist, alumna of radio's Hit Parade, swings out with a duo of tunes as well. Altogether, 11 musical numbers run through the picture.

Producer Jack Cummings apparently was given the "go-ahead" signal on unlimited expenditures. "Bathing Beauty" is filled with expensive settings and costuming. Director George Sidney could easily have tightened up the script: his modus operandi seems to have been to allow each of the performers as much freedom as possible. *Sten.*

Mr. Skeffington

Warner Bros. release of Philip G. and Julius J. Epstein production. Stars Bette Davis; features Claude Rains, Walter Abel, Richard Waring, George Coulouris. Directed by Vincent Sherman. From novel of same name by "Elizabeth"; adaptation, the Epsteins; editor, Ralph Dawson; camera, Ernest Haller, James Leicester. Previewed in N. Y. May 19, '44. Running time, 146 MINS.

Fanny Trellis	Bette Davis
Job Skeffington	Claude Rains
George Trellis	Walter Abel
Trippy Trellis	Richard Waring
Dr. Byles	George Coulouris
Janny Junior	Marjorie Riordan
MacMahon	Robert Shayne
Jim Conderley	John Alexander
Ed Morrison	Jerome Cowan
Johnny Mitchell	Charles Drake
Manby	Dorothy Peterson
Chester Forbish	Peter Whitney
Thatcher	Bill Kennedy
Hyslop	Tom Stevenson
Soames	Halliwell Hobbes
Fanny (age 10)	Sylvia Arslan
Fanny (age 5)	Bunny Sunshine
Fanny (age 2)	Gigi Perreau
Singer	Dolores Gray
Dr. Melton	Walter Kingsford
Secretary	Molly Lamont

Fitting Bette Davis like a silk glove, the same as the gowns which she wears to intrigue the male of the species in defiance of all the laws of good womanhood, in the part of the vainglorious, selfish wife and mother, "Mr. Skeffington" is not only another triumph for this Warner star but also a picture of terrific strength. It is boxoffice in the upper brackets.

Philip G. and Julius J. Epstein, who have given the story fine production and backgrounds, also adapted the book but locale it in America rather than in England. The story moves steadily and smoothly, gathering much impact as it goes along, while also the dialog ranges from the smart to the trenchantly dramatic in limning the life of the woman who lived for her beauty but found that it wasn't of a lasting character. She also lived to regret that life, except that a pseudo-happy ending, with a strong undertone of pathos, figures in ultimately reuniting the woman with her divorced husband.

Miss Davis, playing the coquettish daughter of a once-wealthy family, progresses through the years from 1914 before the first World War to the present, going with gradual changes frfom early girlhood to around 50 years when suddenly aging badly as result of illness. Her characterization is one of the best among those which have made her one of the screen's finest actresses.

Opposite Miss Davis is the able Claude Rains, the successful Wall Street tycoon who goes blind and also prematurely ages as result of several years spent in a Nazi concentration camp following the beginning of World War II. He had succumbed to the wiles of Miss Davis when latter set her cap for him in 1914 with a view to saving her brother from disgrace over $25,000 he had mulcted from Rains' firm. Never loving him, though he does her, Miss Davis continues her merry way with men before and after divorce, alienating herself at the same time from their daughter. In spanning the years and giving impetus to the story, characterizations and situations, Vincent Sherman has provided direction of a superior grade. The montage work by James Leicester, notably in the scenes relating to hallucinations, rates tops, along with the photography of the crew under Ernest Haller.

In addition to the excellent performances by both Miss Davis and Rains, a long list of very competent portrayals include those by Walter Abel, Richard Waring, George Coulouris, Marjorie Riordan, Robert Shayne, John Alexander, Jerome Cowan, Charles Drake, Dorothy Peterson, Bill Kennedy and Peter Whitney. The Davis-Rains' daughter at the age of 10 is played effectively by Sylvia Arslan. *Char.*

The Canterville Ghost

Metro release of Arthur L. Field production. Directed by Jules Dassin. Features Charles Laughton, Robert Young, Margaret O'Brien, William Gargan, "Rags" Ragland. Screenplay, Edwin Harvey Blum; based on "The Canterville Ghost" by Oscar Wilde; camera, Robert Planck; editor, Chester W. Schaeffer. Previewed at Ziegfeld, N. Y., May 22, '44. Running time, 95 MINS.

Sir Simon de Canterville / The Ghost	Charles Laughton
Cuffy Williams	Robert Young
Lady Jessica de Canterville	Margaret O'Brien
Sergeant Benson	William Gargan
Lord Canterville	Reginald Owen
Big Harry	"Rags" Ragland
Mrs. Umney	Una O'Connor
Sir Valentine Williams	Donald Stuart
Mrs. Polverdine	Elisabeth Risdon
Lieutenant Kane	Frank Faylen
Mr. Potts	Lumsden Hare
Metropolus	Mike Mazurki
Hector	William Moss
Eddie	Bobby Readick
Bugsy McDougle	Marc Cramer
Jordan	William Tannen
Anthony de Canterville	Peter Lawford

"The Canterville Ghost" is entertaining comedy-drama, with the accent on comedy despite the mystery-chiller emphasis in the title, which should roll up from good to strong business in the keys and subsequents all the way down the line.

Tight scripting, nimble direction and excellent casting are about equally responsible for the satisfactory results.

Margaret O'Brien and Charles Laughton come through with top-notch performances, with the clever moppet, who is being groomed as one of the most important stellar properties on the Culver City lot, a solid smash and topping everything. The youngster's corking delivery will likely create strongly favorable word-of-mouth comment.

One of her outstanding bits is in a jitterbug terping number with an American soldier and her sedately demure dancing with Robert Young. Her solemn, dignified interpretation as the youthful Lady Jessica de Canterville, head of one of the great English landowning families, is terrific.

Yarn is about a 300-year-old ghost (Laughton), once walled up alive in the castle by his father because he proved a coward on the field of battle, who is looking for a kinsman to perform an act of bravery in his name so that he can be freed from his miserable existence. Robert Young, member of a platoon of

American Rangers who are billeted in the castle, turns out to be a kinsman of the ghost's. Pictured as a normal American doughboy in a crack regiment Young, when he learns of his cowardly lineage, finds himself turning coward also. Miss O'Brien instills new moral fibre in him in a climaxing scene where he saves his comrades from destruction by a delayed action bomb.

Comedy highlights are in sequences where, for a switch, the Rangers scare the ghost. *Mori.*

Ghost Catchers

(SONGS)

Universal release of Edmund L. Hartmann production; screenplay and story, Hartmann. Stars Ole Olsen & Chic Johnson; features Gloria Jean, Martha O'Driscoll, Leo Carrillo, Andy Devine, Morton Downey. Directed by Edward F. Cline. Musical director, Edward Ward; original songs, Harry Revel-Paul F. Webster, Don Raye-Gene dePaul; camera, Charles Van Enger; editor, Arthur Hilton. At Criterion, N. Y., week May 30, '44. Running time, **67 MINS.**

Ole............................Ole Olsen
Chic..........................Chic Johnson
Melinda........................Gloria Jean
Susanna..................Martha O'Driscoll
Jerry..........................Leo Carrillo
Bear...........................Andy Devine
Horsehead.....................Lon Chaney
Clay...........................Kirby Grant
Colonel......................Walter Catlett
Virginia...................Ella Mae Morse
Signatelli..................Henry Armetta
Morton Downey

In the best Olsen & Johnson tradition, "Ghost Catchers" is a tuneful, screwy concoction, brief and zippy. Grooved for the top rung on duals, it is money in the bank.

Unlike previous O&J endeavors, this film has a plot. The boys, with the aid of numerable stooges, join in aiding a southern family, which bought an old, haunted brownstone house in the city as a showcase for the two daughters who are slated to appear at Carnegie Hall, get rid of a ghost.

Before this is accomplished there is a murder or two, bodies in closets, screams, gunfire, songs by Ella Mae Morse, Morton Downey, Gloria Jean and Kirby Grant, a riot in a night club, a jitterbug number and a Gay 90's party.

Film has been edited so tightly that Downey sings but one tune, "These Foolish Things"; Miss Jean, two, "Swanee River" and, with Kirby Grant, "I'm Old Enough to Dream"; Ella Mae Morse, "Quoth the Raven," and, with the entire cast, "Three Cheers for the Customers." Downey gets a brushoff, possibly because Universal wishes to build up newcomer Grant, who has a pleasant voice, and enough on the ball to go on from here as a romantic lead.

O&J prove they are strong laugh-getters, predominating the 67 minutes, while Leo Carrillo, as owner of the nitery where they are employed, Andy Devine and Lon Chaney, as two of the men househaunters, and Martha O'Driscoll, as the blonde vis-a-vis opposite Grant, manage to have their innings, brief as they are. Veteran Walter Catlett, in the role of a southern gentleman and father of the two girls, scores best of all, giving a topflight performance.

Edmund L. Hartmann's production cuts corners at every turn, the film being showcased in not too expensive but substantial settings. Eddie Cline, an old-time comedian himself, pilots the cast in capable fashion, his direction being responsible for the fast pace. Considering everything, much credit should go to film editor Arthur Hilton, who probably kept the midnight lamps burning, separating the wheat from the chaff in this one. All in all, another "rent-payer" from Universal. *Sten.*

Mystery Man

United Artists release of Harry A. Sherman production. Stars William Boyd; features Andy Clyde, Jimmy Rogers, Don Costello and Eleanor Stewart. Directed by George Archainbaud. Camera, Russell Harlan; editor, Frederick Berger. At New York theatre, N. Y., week of May 23, '44. Running time, **58 MINS.**

Hopalong Cassidy..............William Boyd
California Carlson...............Andy Clyde
Jimmy Rogers..........................Himself
Bud Trilling......................Don Costello
Rogan.........................Francis McDonald
Sam Newhall....................Forrest Taylor
Diane Newhall................Eleanor Stewart
Ted Blane.........................Jack Rockwell

"Mystery Man" in the Hopalong Cassidy series of westerns, is a weak addition to the list, with little plot and less suspense. But enough action and gunplay serve to cover up the yarn's thinness, to make it a passable second-half of a dualer.

Film is misnamed. Story revolves around a herd of cattle owned by rancher Cassidy which the outlaw gang rustles twice, Cassidy's outfit recovering in both instances after much riding and shooting. Constant horse and gunplay pall after awhile, although background ranch and desert settings are beguiling.

Andy Clyde supplies some comedy as a braggart cowhand; Jimmy Rogers and Eleanor Stewart supply a modest love interest; William Boyd continues as Cassidy, and Don Costello is the smooth gang leader.

Secret Command

Hollywood, May 26.

Columbia release of Terneen production; produced by Phil Ryan. Stars Pat O'Brien, Carole Landis; features Chester Morris, Ruth Warrick, Barton MacLane, Tom Tully, Wallace Ford. Directed by Eddie Sutherland. Screenplay by Roy Chanslor; camera, Franz F. Planer; editor, Viola Lawrence; process photography, David Allen and Ray Cory; special effects, Robert Wright; montages, Aaron Nibley; asst. director, Rex Bailey; production manager, Jack Murphy. Previewed at Pantages, May 25, '44. Running time, **81 MINS.**

Sam Gallagher.....................Pat O'Brien
Jill McCann.....................Carole Landis
Jeff Gallagher.................Chester Morris
Lea Damaron.....................Ruth Warrick
Red Kelly.....................Barton MacLane
Brownell..............................Tom Tully
Miller..........................Wallace Ford
Max Lessing..................Howard Freeman
Ben Royall............................Erik Rolf
Curly............................Matt McHugh
Shawn...............................Frank Sully
Simms...........................Frank Fenton
James Thane.................Charles D. Brown
Joan..............................Carol Nugent

This is a lusty melodrama of counter-espionage around a large shipyard, with expert blending of action and suspense with spontaneous good humor resulting in solid entertainment for pop appeal. Picture is one of the best Pat O'Brien starrers wheeled out in some time, and will hit profitable gait in the regular runs.

Naval intelligence gets wind of Nazi sabotage plans at the large shipyard, and O'Brien is sent in to get a job as a secret agent. He starts as a pilebuck on shift bossed by brother Chester Morris, and latter is not sold on O'Brien's tale of wife (Carole Landis) and two youngsters in bungalow—with family and housing conveniently supplied by Intelligence. Yarn weaves between the dramatics of tracing the Nazi saboteurs at the shipyards, and intimacies at home with O'Brien's newly-acquired family setup. Plot steadily moves to climax when Nazis are ready to wreck the yard and a new flattop, but are rounded up by secret agents while O'Brien stages a rousing battle with the Nazi chief. O'Brien likes home life so well he proposes to Miss Landis with provision of keeping the two refugee youngsters via adoption.

O'Brien turns in a fine performance in the lead, with Miss Landis and Ruth Warrick sharing femme spots in good style. Strong support is provided by Morris, Barton MacLane, Tom Tully and Wallace Ford. Direction by Eddie Sutherland maintains a zestful pace, while Phil Ryan clicks on the producing end.

Picture carries some unusual scenes of the huge shipyards of the Coast, with process photography by David Allen and Ray Cory of exceptional merit. Photography by Franz Planer is uniform throughout. Overall spontaneity of the film might be linked to the preponderance of Irish names connected with the making, including producer Ryan, star O'Brien, director Sutherland, production manager Jack Murphy and majority of the cast. *Walt.*

A Canterbury Tale

(BRITISH-MADE)

London, May 9.

Eagle-Lion Distributors release of Archer Production. Features Eric Portman, Sheila Sim, Dennis Price, Sergeant John Sweet. Written, produced and directed by Michael Powell and Emeric Pressburger. Camera, Erwin Hillier. At Leicester Square theatre, London, May 9. Running time, **124 MINS.**

Thomas Colpeper, J.P........Eric Portman
Alison Smith.......................Sheila Sim
Bob Johnson...............Sgt. John Sweet
Peter Gibbs.......................Dennis Price
Seven Sisters Soldiers......Esmond Knight
Thomas Duckett..........Charles Hawtrey
Woodcock..........................Hay Petrie
Ned Horton.....................George Merritt
Jim Horton......................Edward Rigby
Prudence Honeywood........Freda Jackson
Fee Baker.........................Betty Jardine

Sincerity and simplicity shine through every foot of this oversized, modern version of the Chaucer epic tale. Here is rare beauty. "A Canterbury Tale" is the genuine article as far as English sincerity and dignity are concerned, but whether it will click in U. S. likely will depend on whether American audiences want to see how English people live today, as seen through a Yank doughboy's eyes.

Without belittling the highly imaginative genius inspiring the two directors, Michael Powell and Emeric Pressburger, first honors go to Erwin Hillier, whose camera work is superb. Nothing more effectively by way of a time transition shot has been conceived here than the way he carries his audience through nine centuries in a few seconds. Beginning with a close-up of a hooded falcon on the wrist of an ancient Canterbury pilgrim (400 years before Columbus discovered America), he follows the graceful bird as it soars aloft on speedy wings. When it becomes a mere speck, it turns and comes gliding back. On coming nearer, it is seen to be a Spitfire.

This Archer production meanders with leisurely charm through two-thirds of length before one gets a distant glimpse of the cathedral of Canterbury. Although near the film's end it is discovered the four principals are 20th century pilgrims, up to the denouement they are entirely ignorant and skeptical of the miracle their coming to the cathedral works.

By far the best role in a well-nigh perfect cast is filled by Sgt. John Sweet, borrowed from U. S. Army. Facing the camera for first time, he frankly does nothing more than play himself. His reactions to English customs are guaranteed to give British audiences a real bang, just as there are millions of laughs for the GI's who have been up against all the things experienced by the Yank on the screen. In civil life, Sweet is an Ohio school teacher. He has all the earmarks of a find, reminding of the late Will Rogers.

Sheila Sim, a relative newcomer to films, is the sole femme in the story. As a London shop girl, turned farmeret for the duration, she turns in a polished performance. Although giving the American GI all the best of it, there is an equally well-drawn characterization, the British tank sergeant, done so well by Dennis Price. For him the cathedral works a miracle. Trained to be a church organist he succumbs (before the war) to a $150-per-week offer as organist in a super cinema. The miracle enables him to sit at the great organ in Canterbury Cathedral and play special music for a service attended by his own regiment on the eve of its departure for the second front.

Star of the film, Eric Portman, gives a splendid, restrained performance as a small-town justice of the peace. Four miracles occur in this story, one to each of these four principal characters.

Tawny Pipit

(BRITISH-MADE)

London, April 28.

General Film Distributors' release of Two Cities Film. Features Bernard Miles, Rosamund John, Niall MacGinnis. Directed by Charles Saunders, Bernard Miles. Screenplay by Bernard Miles, Charles Saunders. Music by Noel Mewton-Wood, played by London Symphony Orchestra. Camera, Eric Cross, Ray Sturgess. At Leicester Square theatre, London, April 28. Running time, **85 MINS.**

Colonel Barton-Barrington...Bernard Miles
Hazel Broome..............Rosamund John
Jimmy Bancroft.............Niall MacGinnis
Nancy Forester.......................Jean Gillie
Russian Sniper............Lucie Mannheim
Reverend Kingsley.......Christopher Steele
Uncle Arthur................Brefni O'Rorke
Whimbrel.....................George Carney
Crasker.........................Wylie Watson
Silver.............................Lionel Watts
Shuttleworth....................Scott Harold
Pickering..........................John Salew
Mrs. Pickering............Marjorie Rhodes
Miss Penyman....................Ann Wilton
Schoolmaster.....................Ian Fleming

If the Academy had an award for the year's worst titled film, this one would cop the Oscar without a doubt. Despite this handicap, "Tawny Pipit" has everything it takes to make a boxoffice hit. The tawny pipit is a rare bird, and this film is frankly a glorification of ornithology. With such a theme, a picture could hardly be expected to have much appeal, but it actually has.

Most of action is in an English wheat field, where two such birds have made a nest, and are preparing to bring a family of quintuplets into the world. A wounded airman, on a convalescent hiking tour with his hospital nurse, spots the birds. They wire the girl's uncle, famous ornithologist, about the discovery.

From this simple start, plot unfolds with a swiftness of tempo as unexpected as the development of many gripping incidents. Under the spell there is nothing unbelievable in the rallying of the whole countryside to protect the "friendly aliens."

Sounds goofy, but if given another title it may do in the U. S.

In this country, success for the film is assured because of a cast of such established boxoffice favorites as Bernard Miles, Rosamund John, Niall MacGinnis, Jean Gillie and Lucie Mannheim. All are aided by more than usually intelligent direction of Charles Saunders and Bernard Miles.

Miniature Reviews

"Hail the Conquering Hero" (Par.). A Preston Sturges "honey," starring Eddie Bracken, is headed for top grosses.

"Christmas Holiday" (U). Deanna Durbin in heavy but effective dramatic role. Good boxoffice.

"The Mask of Dimitrios" (WB). Too-talky mystery yarn, for duals.

"The Great Moment" (Par). Entertaining biog, with Joel McCrea and Betty Field, strong grosser.

"Take It Big" (Musical) (Par). Lightweight musical with Jack Haley, Harriet Hilliard, Ozzie Nelson, okay for duals.

"The Invisible Man's Revenge" (U). Fifth of "Invisible" chiller series, starring Jon Hall, slated for good dual biz.

"A Night of Adventure" (RKO). Tom Conway is mild adventure tale; only for dualers.

"Stars On Parade" (Col) (Musical). Suitable for duals.

"Silent Partner" (Rep). Innocuous mystery drama; a programmer.

"Follow the Leader" (Mono). East Side Kids in comedy-mystery; a good dualer.

"Fanny By Gaslight" (Gen). British-made 19th-century meller will draw class trade.

"This Happy Breed" (Eagle-Lion). Noel Coward play not so good as film; cutting may aid U. S. draw.

"Taxi to Heaven" (Songs) (Artkino). Entertaining escapist fare that should do especially well in the arties.

"La Virgen Que Forjo Una Patria" (Mex). Ramon Novarro in religious-patriotic story; too tedious except for arty houses.

"Vi Hemslavinor" (Swedish). Brisk comedy dealing with the servant problem. For the smorgasbord following.

Hail the Conquering Hero

Paramount release of Preston Sturges production, directed and written by Sturges. Stars Eddie Bracken; features Ella Raines, Raymond Walburn, William Demarest. Music, Sigmund Krumgold; camera, John Seitz; editor, Stuart Gilmore. Tradeshown N. Y. June 5, '44. Running time, 101 MINS.

Woodrow Truesmith	Eddie Bracken
Libby	Ella Raines
Forrest Noble	Bill Edwards
Mayor Noble	Raymond Walburn
Sergeant	William Demarest
Corporal	Jimmie Dundee
Mrs. Truesmith	Georgia Caine
Political Boss	Alan Bridge
Jonesy	James Damore
Bugsy	Freddie Steele
Bill	Stephen Gregory
Juke	Len Hendry
Mrs. Noble	Esther Howard
Libby's Aunt	Elizabeth Patterson
Judge Dennis	Jimmy Conlin
Rev. Upperman	Arthur Hoyt
Dr. Bissell	Harry Hayden
Chairman of Committee	Franklin Pangborn
Progressive Bandleader	Victor Potel
Mr. Schultz	Torben Meyer
Regular Bandleader	Jack Norton
Sheriff	George Melford
Town Painter	Frank Moran
Western Union Man	Chester Conklin
Alfie	Merrill Rodin
Mamie	Marjean Neville
Mamie's Mother	Dot Farley
Cafe Singer	Julie Gibson
Cafe Dancer	Miriam Franklin
Cafe Manager	Paul Porcasi

This is another film on the style of "Miracle of Morgan's Creek"—only better. A comedy as funny as its predecessor, only more logical, with more human interest, "Hail the Conquering Hero" will do excellent business from the word go.

Eddie Bracken bounces back from his humorously, absent-minded performance in "Miracle" to still a stronger hold on the star ladder with his portrayal of a phoney Marine hero who is swept up in a tide of townfolk hero worship to the point where he almost becomes mayor—and then does.

The deft hand of Preston Sturges molded this film, further proof that he is one of the industry's best writer-directors. The numerous situations that lend themselves readily to comedy lines and business are taken advantage of by a cast that sparkles because of the swift pace they are put through. Neither expensive to produce nor filled with players who will draw the customers on the basis of marquee strength, word-of-mouth by filmgoers will more than do its share toward making this film a boxoffice whiz.

Yarn finds Bracken, medically discharged from the Marines after only one month of service because of hay fever, befriended by six real Guadalcanal heroes. During the course of this friendship, Bracken is clothed in his old Marine uniform, bodily taken back to his old home town, where he is welcomed as a hero. The town goes wild over him, burning the mortgage on his mother's home, planning to build a statue in Station Square honoring him and his father (a hero who was killed in World War I), and even offering him the mayoralty nomination. In the end, he confesses the phoniness of the entire buildup, but not before he has endeared himself to the populace, and it all turns out all right.

Proof that a capable director can take an actor who is willing to listen and get a better-than-good performance out of him or her is amply displayed here. Sturges has a large cast of veterans supporting Bracken, and a former boxing champion, Freddie Steele, as Bugsy, one of the six Marines. The vets all do a good job, but Steele's work is standout. The guy's well-known as a boxer, but he should get plenty of film work after his performance here.

Film runs 101 minutes, but no footage is wasted. Settings are purposeful and in good taste. *Sten.*

Christmas Holiday
(SONGS)

Universal release of Felix Jackson production; associate producer, Frank Shaw. Stars Deanna Durbin, Gene Kelly; features Richard Whorf, Dean Harens, Gladys George, Gale Sondergaard. Directed by Robert Siodmak. Screenplay, Herman J. Mankiewicz, from W. Somerset Maugham's novel; camera, Woody Bredell; editor, Ted Kent; special photog., John P. Fulton. Previewed in N. Y. June 6, '44. Running time, 93 MINS.

Jackie Lamont / Abigail Martin	Deanna Durbin
Robert Manette	Gene Kelly
Simon Fenimore	Richard Whorf
Charles Mason	Dean Harens
Valerie de Merode	Gladys George
Mrs. Manette	Gale Sondergaard
Gerald Tyler	David Bruce

Universal has taken quite a chance with its most important property, Deanna Durbin. Jumping the gal practically overnight from youthful comedy roles to one mature and dramatic, as it does in "Christmas Holiday," it heightened the danger with a heavy, brooding though effective vehicle. However, because her performance is so sincere and appealing, as well as the good supporting cast and tasteful production, the film should do well at the boxoffice to justify the risks Universal took.

Her first appearance in the film, casually slinking up to sing in a sleazy nightclub with a tired, blase manner, is as much a shock as was Greta Garbo's first talkie appearance with that hoarse voice of hers in "Anna Christie." Poor makeup accentuates Miss Durbin's strange look. The effect, patently intentional, accents the contrast when flashbacks show the adolescent Miss Durbin.

The story is Somerset Maugham's tale of a boy who grew up emotionally during a holiday in France (with the locale changed to New Orleans) and the plot switched around to pass the Hays office. A young army lieutenant, disappointed in love, finds himself stranded in the southern city, and meets up with another heartsick kid in a sad-faced singer at a cheap nightclub. From then on the story is told in flashbacks, as the singer (Miss Durbin) tells the lieutenant of her brief happy marriage to a young ne'er-do-well, her husband's arrest for murder, and his imprisonment for life.

As the nitery thrush, Miss Durbin has two incidental songs, "Spring Will Be a Little Late This Year" (Frank Loesser) and the Irving Berlin oldie, "Always." But otherwise the dramatic role is unrelieved except by a few glimpses of a happy, smiling past. In another switch from musical to heavy role is Gene Kelly, as the ne'er-do-well husband, Kelly doing an effective job. Support roles all good, Gale Sondergaard playing a proud, possessive mother; Richard Whorf a wine-bibbing reporter; Gladys George the understanding cafe proprietor, and Dean Harens the sympathetic lieutenant. *Bron.*

The Mask of Dimitrios

Warner Bros. release of Henry Blanke production. Features Sydney Greenstreet, Peter Lorre, Zachary Scott, Faye Emerson, Victor Francen. Directed by Jean Negulesco. Screenplay by Frank Gruber, from novel by Eric Ambler; camera, Arthur Edeson; editor, Frederick Richards; music, Adolph Deutsch; music director, Leo F. Forbstein. Previewed in N. Y. June 2, '44. Running time, 95 MINS.

Mr. Peters	Sydney Greenstreet
Dimitrios	Zachary Scott
Irana	Faye Emerson
Leyden	Peter Lorre
Grodek	Victor Francen
Bulic	Steven Geray
Mme. Chavez	Florence Bates
Marukakis	Edward Ciannelli
Col. Haki	Kurt Katch
Mrs. Bulic	Marjorie Hoshelle
Werner	Georges Metaxa
Pappas	John Abbott
Abdul	Monte Blue
Konrad	David Hoffman

Backgrounded with international intrigues, "The Mask of Dimitrios" has an occasional element of suspense, but those moments are comparatively few. It's a dualer.

"Dimitrios," which traces the year-long international criminal career of one Dimitrios Makropoulos (played by Zachary Scott), has the benefit of a good cast headed by Sydney Greenstreet and Peter Lorre, but it is mostly a conversational piece that too frequently suggests action in the dialog where, actually, the film itself practically has none.

Talky script slows the pace to a walk. Greenstreet and Lorre are capital as a criminal and mystery writer, respectively, while Scott gives a plausible performance as the titular character. The rest are mainly bits. *Kahn.*

The Great Moment

Paramount release of Preston Sturges production, directed by Sturges. Stars Joel McCrea and Betty Field; features Harry Carey, William Demarest, Louis Jean Heydt, Julius Tannen. Screenplay by Sturges from book by Rene Fulop-Miller; camera, Victor Milner; editor, Stuart Gilmore; music, Victor Young. Tradeshown N. Y., June 6, '44. Running time, 83 MINS.

W. T. G. Morton	Joel McCrea
Elizabeth Morton	Betty Field
Prof. Warren	Harry Carey
Eben Frost	William Demarest
Dr. Horace Wells	Louis Jean Heydt
Dr. Jackson	Julian Tannen
V. P. Medical Soc	Edwin Maxwell
President Pierce	Porter Hall
Dr. Heywood	Franklin Pangborn
Homer Quinby	Grady Sutton
Betty Morton	Donivee Lee
Judge Shipman	Harry Hayden
Dr. Dahlmeyer	Torben Meyer
Dental Patient	Vic Potel
Senator Borland	Thurston Hall
The Priest	J. Farrell MacDonald
Cashier-Charles	Robert Dudley
Mr. Abbot	Robert Frandsen
Young Mother	Sylvia Field
Young Father	Reginald Sheffield
Morton's Butler	Robert Greig
Servant Girl	Sheila Sheldon
Mr. Chamberlain	Harry Rosenthal
Porter	Frank Moran

Preston Sturges has brought to the screen the compelling biography of Dr. W. T. G. Morton, who 100 years ago discovered anaesthesia. With Joel McCrea and Betty Field supplying the marquee strength, "The Great Moment" should prove to be a good grosser in the keys and subsequents.

The film is the story of the romance, the trials and the ultimate victory of a Boston dentist, who experimented until he finally hit upon a painless means of extracting teeth, then passed on his discovery to the world of medicine. Performances of McCrea and Miss Field, as well as a solid supporting cast, are well in keeping with the dignity of the yarn.

McCrea gives an excellent portrayal in the role of the impoverished medical student, forced to forego the study of medicine in lieu of a dental career because of lack of funds. Betty Field, as the wife who sometimes gets on his nerves because of her lack of understanding of what he is endeavoring to accomplish, proves again that she is an actress with loads of talent.

Supporting roles of Harry Carey, the doctor who gives McCrea a chance to prove that anaesthesia is suitable for surgical operations as well as dental treatment, and William Demarest, as the first patient of McCrea who continues to be his human guinea pig throughout all experiments, never losing faith in the discovery, are expertly handled by them.

Despite the fact that others ridicule his aims, McCrea feels that some way must be found to end the pain which patients have while dentists work on their teeth. Finally, hitting upon a formula, he tries it out on a patient (Demarest) who goes beserk because the ether used was not highly rectified. Again experimenting with Demarest, McCrea hits upon the proper formula, calling it "Letheon," to protect it from competitors. Naturally, he becomes wealthy from its use, nullifying all barriers to pass it on to humanity, including a charge by the Massachusetts Medical Assn. that he seeks to profit by its use. In the end, he donates his discovery to the advancement of medicine. *Sten.*

Take It Big
(MUSICAL)

Paramount release of Pine-Thomas production. Stars Jack Haley, Harriet Hilliard; features Mary Beth Hughes, Richard Lane, Arline Judge, Lucile Gleason, Frank Forest. Directed by Frank McDonald. Original screenplay by Howard J. Green; added dialog, Joe Bigelow; camera, Fred Jackman; editor, Victor Lewis; songs, Lester Lee and Jerry Seelen, Johnny Burke and James Van Heusen; special lyrics by Ozzie Nelson. Previewed N. Y., June 5, '44. Running time, 76 MINS.

Jack North	Jack Haley
Jerry Clinton	Harriet Hilliard
Gaye Livingstone	Mary Beth Hughes
Eddie Hampton	Richard Lane
Pert Martin	Arline Judge
Dr. Dittenhoffer	Fritz Feld
Sophie	Lucile Gleason
Cowboy Joe	Fuzzy Knight
Harvey Phillips	Frank Forest
John Hankinson	George Meeker
NTG	Himself
Ozzie Nelson	Himself
House Detective	Ralph Peters

"Pansy the Horse" and Rochelle & Beebe

"Take It Big" is a lightweight musical—so light, in fact, that even the usual smooth comedy of Jack Haley and Harriet Hilliard's singing sometimes fail to overcome the plot.

Dude ranch setting has a band and entertainers for guests over night, band being Nelson's, and Miss Hilliard and Jack Haley, the entertainers, plus an added entry, Frank Forest, who appears a real voice find. Plot starts off with Haley, as the rear portion of "Pansy the Horse," standard act, bemoaning his fate. Story never forgets this, dialog constantly reminding the audience that Haley always rates himself as the rear portion. Horsing around with this gag for several reels Haley is finally informed he has inherited a ranch. Mistaking a dude establishment for his A-Bar-B that's been left him, Haley runs the swank joint until tossed out, and then reclaims his dilapidated A-Bar-B and rescues it from bankruptcy.

Director Frank McDonald does not help the familiar plot much. Of the several topflight tunes, outstanding is the already popular "Sunday, Monday and Always." Of the new songs, "I'm a Big Success with You" is tops.

Haley, forced to carry the full comedy burden, does well considering plot absurdities. Richard Lane, as front part of hoss act, looks strictly a heavy, with few comedy moments. Harriet Hilliard, as trainer in horse act, teams with Haley and Ozzie Nelson for several duets, and clicks solidly on her own. Arline Judge has a minor part as her pal at the nightclub, while Mary Beth Hughes is the comely hanger-on at the dude ranch who vamps Haley. Fuzzy Knight, comic in many westerns, is wasted. Support is headed by Fritz Feld, Frank Forest, Lucile Gleason and Nils T. Granlund, m.c. at nitery.

Forest, from radio and once under contract to Par, is standout when he sings, for no special reason, a complete scene from "Barber of Seville." Screens well, has a rare voice, and is passable as an actor. *Wear.*

Invisible Man's Revenge

Universal release of Ford Beebe production, directed by Beebe. Stars Jon Hall; features Leon Errol, John Carradine, Alan Curtis, Evelyn Ankers, Gale Sondergaard. Screenplay, Bertram Millhauser, suggested by "The Invisible Man," by H. G. Wells; camera, Milton Krasner; special photog., John P. Fulton; editor, Saul Goodkind. Previewed N. Y., May 31, '44. Running time, 78 MINS.

Robert Griffin	Jon Hall
Mark Foster	Alan Curtis
Julie Herrick	Evelyn Ankers
Herbert	Leon Errol
Peter Drury	John Carradine
Maud	Doris Lloyd
Feeney	Ian Wolfe
Gray Shadow	Himself
Lady Irene Herrick	Gale Sondergaard
Sir Jasper Herrick	Lester Matthews
Cleghorn	Halliwell Hobbs
Sir Frederick Travers	Leland Hodgson
Sergeant	Billy Bevan

Fifth in the "Invisible Man" series is fast-moving but preposterous yet has the saving grace of being intelligently performed and directed so that for dualers it should more than hold is own.

Cast is first-rate with Jon Hall turning in bangup job of the maniac with a persecution complex. He decides to throw in with a crackpot professor, John Carradine, to become invisible and badger titled English couple, Gale Sondergaard and Lester Matthews, into turning over their property and daughter's hand to him.

Hall shows up in England after a five-year absence to accuse the pair of having tried to murder him on safari after they had discovered a fabulous diamond mine. The invisible man's comings and goings around the English mansion provide excellent opportunities for John Fulton's camera tricks. Hall finally meets his doom in the wine cellar after unsuccessfully trying to appropriate the lifeblood of journalist Alan Curtis to prevent his invisibility from fading in.

Leon Errol reaps plenty of laughs from his cockney role and John Carradine clicks as the daffy prof.

Donn.

A Night of Adventure

RKO release of Herman Schlom production. Stars Tom Conway; features Audrey Long, Edward Brophy, Louis Borekk, Addison Richards, Jean Brooks, Nancy Gates. Directed by Gordon Douglas. Screenplay by Crane Wilbur, from play "Hat, Coat and Glove," by Wilhelm Speyer; camera, Frank Redman; editor, Les Millbrook. Tradeshown in N. Y. May 31, '44. Running time, 65 MINS.

Mark Latham	Tom Conway
Erica	Audrey Long
Steve	Edward Brophy
Tony Clark	Louis Borell
Branson	Addison Richards
Julie Arden	Jean Brooks
Connie	Nancy Gates
Benny Sarto	Russell Hopton
Ruby La Rue	Claire Carleton
Judge	Emory Parnell
Andrews	Edmund Glover

Filmed in 1934 with Ricardo Cortez, under original title of "Hat, Coat and Glove," this remake emerges a slow-moving tale, only for the duals.

Story concerns a criminal lawyer (Tom Conway), who is on the trail of an underworld gang for the FBI. As a result, he neglects his wife, who takes up with an artist. Lawyer becomes involved in a murder, when he goes to the artist's apartment to have it out with him. When the latter is unjustly accused of the crime, he undertakes his rival's defense, winning both the case and his wife.

Tom Conway, away from his "Falcon" roles, is suave as the legal light. Audrey Long, as his wife, supplies a bright spot, being not only attractive but hinting promise in future dramatic roles. Others do their stints faithfully. The trouble is that the playing merely accentuates the frailties of "A Night of Adventure."

Stars on Parade

(MUSICAL)

Columbia release of Wallace MacDonald production. Features Larry Parks, Lynn Merrick, Ray Walker, Jeff Donnell and Robert Williams. Directed by Lew Landers. Screenplay, Monte Brice; camera, L. W. O'Connell; editor, Jerome Thoms. At Strand, Brooklyn, week of June 1, '44, dual. Running time, 63 MINS.

Danny Davis	Larry Parks
Dorothy Dean	Lynn Merrick
Billy Blake	Ray Walker
Mary Brooks	Jeff Donnell
Jerry Browne	Robert Williams
J. L. Carson	Selmer Jackson
Mrs. Dean	Edythe Elliott
Nan McNair	Mary Currier

And Danny O'Neil, Frank and Jean Hubert, The Chords, King Cole Trio, The Ben Carter Choir.

"Stars On Parade," acutely misnamed because of the absence of a single star name in the cast, is a pleasant trifle about youngsters getting a start in show business. It should hold up its half of a dual program because of its variety acts, songs and a hard-working set of principals.

Built on the familiar pattern about people putting on a show, film has a routine love story enlivened by a stream of good vaude acts. The principals are two Hollywood youngsters who believe there's a lot of talent (including themselves) in L. A.'s backyard that the producers don't know about, and put on a show with this talent to convince the skeptics.

Auditions and performance give the film an opportunity to show off the Huberts in their drunk act, the Chords in musical instrument imitations, the Ben Carter Choir of young Negroes in spirituals, the King Cole Trio and tenor Danny O'Neil. Larry Parks and Lynn Merrick, as the enterprising youngsters, make an attractive team, visually and vocally. The songs, on the sentimental ballad side, are good, with "My Heart Isn't In It" and "Love, Love, Love" as standouts. Arrangement of "Ezekial Saw the Wheel" for the Carter Choir is also effective and pleasing.

Silent Partner

Republic release of George Blair production, directed by Blair. Stars William Henry, Grant Withers; features Beverly Loyd, Ray Walker, Joan Blair. Original screenplay, Gertrude Walker; editor, Ralph Dixon; camera, William Bradford. At Brooklyn Paramount, week of June 1, '44. Running time, 56 MINS.

Jeffrey Swales	William Henry
Mary Price	Beverly Loyd
Bob Ross	Grant Withers
The Drunk	Ray Walker
Lady Sylvia Marlowe	Joan Blair
Harry Keating	Roland Drew
Desk Clerk	George Meeker
Second Waiter	Wally Vernon
Blackie Barton	John Harmon
Pop	Dick Elliott
Tony, the Junk Man	Eddie Fields
Dolly Daring	Pat Knox

"Silent Partner" is an innocuous mystery drama about a newspaperman who specializes in solving crimes. A programmer.

William Henry, freelance actor who formerly appeared in Metro and Paramount films, portrays the top role of a reporter who endeavors to track down five persons listed in the address book of a murder victim. In the process of nabbing the killer, he evades several attempts upon his life.

Beverly Loyd is cast in the female lead, and gives a good account of herself in her first film chore. Joan Blair plays an adventuress, posing as a member of the English aristocracy, competently. Grant Withers, Ray Walker and the other members of the supporting cast manage not to look too bad in this, at times, unbelievable mystery.

George Blair, who directed, turned "Silent Partner" out at an obviously low budget. *Sten.*

Follow the Leader

Monogram release of Sam Katzman-Jack Dietz production. Features Leo Gorcey, Huntz Hall, Gabriel Dell, Billy Benedict, Joan Marsh, Jack LaRue. Directed by William Beaudine. Screenplay by William X. Crowley and Beryl Sachs from original story by Ande Lamb; editor, Carl Pierson; camera, Marcel Le Picard. At New York theatre, N. Y., week May 30, '44. Running time, 65 MINS.

Muggs	Leo Gorcey
Glimpy	Huntz Hall
Fingers	Gabriel Dell
Spider	Billy Benedict
Milly	Joan Marsh
Larry	Jack LaRue
Mrs. McGinnis	Mary Gordon
Cop	J. Farrell MacDonald
Danny	Dave Durand
Speed	Bobby Stone
Dave	Jimmy Strand
Skinny	Bud Gorman

Gene Austin and Sherrill Sisters

In tune with the times, the East Side Kids "get religion," and are on the side of law and order in "Follow the Leader," which molds laughs and action into a fairly entertaining film. Good supporter on twin bills.

Story shows East Side Kids Leo Gorcey and Huntz Hall, on furlough from Army, conducting a private investigation (with military and police sanction) into a series of medical warehouse robberies. One of their cronies has been unjustly accused of and jailed for these thefs. The duo experience many a close brush with the hijackers before they clear up the case.

Gorcey, Hall, Gabriel Dell and Billy Benedict make a humorous foursome. Joan Marsh does well in the leading femme role, while Jack LaRue is convincing as the nightclub operator who heads the thieves. Gene Austin and the Sherrill Sisters supply a melodious interlude during the nightclub sequences.

Fanny by Gaslight

(BRITISH-MADE)

London, May 4.

General Film Distributors' release of Gainsborough production. Stars Phyllis Calvert, James Mason, Wilfrid Lawson, Stewart Granger. Directed by Anthony Asquith. Screenplay by Doreen Montgomery from novel by Michael Sadleir. Camera, Arthur Crabtree. At Leicester Square theatre, London, May 4, '44. Running time, 108 MINS.

Fanny	Phyllis Calvert
Lord Manderstoke	James Mason
Chunks	Wilfrid Lawson
Harry Somerford	Stewart Granger
Lucy	Jean Kent
Alicia	Margaretta Scott
Mrs. Hopwood	Nora Swinburne
Kate Somerford	Cathleen Nesbett
Mrs. Somerford	Helen Haye
William Hopwood	John Laurie
Clive Seymore	Stuart Lindsell
Mrs. Heaviside	Amy Veness

In spite of its title and 19th century setting this adaptation of a current best seller, as it now stands, has merit enough to attract discriminating filmgoers in U. S. Seldom has a British picture been given such a star-studded cast. Even the lesser roles are filled by names of b.o. value in England. Resulting performances make this one well above the average British-made pix.

Unfortunately, however, Anthony Asquith's direction is hurt by the inevitable faulty film editing and irritatingly slow tempo. Although the script distorts the original story almost beyond recognition, there is still retained a lot of plot development in the house of ill-fame, which in the book is the main background. Hays organization may temper some of these sequences, if and when it reaches the American market. For all its being toned down from Michael Sadleir's frank treatment in the novel, the way the curvaceous femmes do their stuff in the underground joint hardly makes for best family trade.

As a matter of fact, the film would suffer little if all the bawdy-house sequences were removed. The main theme—the thorny path traveled by the true lovers because the man is "well born" while the girl is an illegitimate child, foster-fathered by the bawdy housekeeper—would be preserved by the mid-Victorian pillorying they both receive.

With so many good performances, it is significant that Phyllis Calvert in the lead more than holds her own. She succeeds in portraying Fanny with girlish wistfulness and appeal. Second best performance is the Lord Manderstoke of James Mason. Wilfrid Lawson's portrayal of a faithful servant. Chunks, also is splendid.

Lavish production hints that the sky was the limit on this picture.

This Happy Breed

(Technicolor)

(BRITISH-MADE)

London, April 28.

Eagle-Lion release of Noel Coward-Cineguild production. Features Robert Newton, Celia Johnston, John Mills. Directed by David Lean. Camera, Ronald Neame. At New Gallery Kinema, London, April 28. Running time, 107 MINS.

Frank Gibbons	Robert Newton
Ethel Gibbons	Celia Johnson
Billy Mitchell	John Mills
Queenie Gibbons	Kay Walsh
Bob Mitchell	Stanley Holloway
Mrs. Flint	Amy Veness
Aunt Sylvia	Alison Leggatt
Vi	Eileen Erskine
Reg	John Blythe
Sam Leadbitter	Guy Veryney

American theatregoers don't have to be sold on a Noel Coward play. "This Happy Breed" as a play hit was Coward at his best. But good theatre is not necessarily good film material, and it appears the case in this production.

Had this piece not already been praised by dramatic critics, had it not been written by Coward, and had he not lent his name to the screen production, it is doubtful if it ever would have been made. Flawless performances by all the cast, production values, effective use of Technicolor, clever lighting—all these assets don't offset the basic fact that "This Happy Breed" is not picture material.

As a foreword frankly admits, the "hero" is a suburban villa, one of a long row of dingy brick bandboxes whose gardens back onto the gardens of exactly similar, drab houses. All the traveling shots in the world, and Coward uses hundreds of feet, can't make ugliness of the smugly respectable suburbia look bright.

Aside from this fault, the film needs drastic cutting. Although the leisurely tempo can be justified on the grounds of its being consonant with the dull-witted people who come and go, no such excuse holds good for allowing the camera to roll over vapid scenes.

Robert Newton as Frank Gibbons (role created on stage by Coward) meets every requirement of his tremendous part with artistry known only to an oldtime legit actor. For the role of his wife, another grand stage artist, Celia Johnson, never puts a foot wrong in an even more difficult role. This is no less true of the others, of whom two newcomers, Kay Walsh as a manicurist who runs away with a married man to escape from her "common" environment, and Billy Mitchell as her stolid, broad-minded sailor sweetheart, turn in performances which should carry them far.

The period covered (1919-1939) permits Coward to inject all the highlights of those years in British history. Incidentally, the cheering mobs hailing Chamberlain at 10 Downing street afford Coward a chance to take a crack at his own people which, in these days, must have taken a lot of courage. Here is Coward at his best. And scattered throughout the otherwise humdrum story are numerous brilliant highspots no less Cowardesque. How much, as producer, Coward had to do with directing the film (credit is given David Lean), there is more than one directorial touch plainly bearing the cunning of this actor-stage manager which helps to disguise the static story quality.

Excellent business for this picture looms in British cinemas where Coward is emphatically boxoffice. As for American audiences on the one condition the film is adequately cut, it all depends on the strength of Coward's name as a draw. *Jolo.*

Taxi to Heaven
(Songs)
(RUSSIAN-MADE)

Artkino release of Central production. Features Ludmila Tselikovskaya, Mikhail Zharov. Directed by Herbert Rappaport. Screenplay, Eugene Petrov; music, U. Birukov; additional selections from Tschaikowsky's "Pique Dame" and Leoncavallo's "Pagliacci"; camera, A. Halpern. At Stanley, N. Y., week of May 25, '44. Running time, 71 MINS.
```
Baranov..................Mikhail Zharov
Natasha...........Ludmila Tselikovskaya
The Colonel.................Boris Blinov
Svetlovidov................Georgi Speigel
Kulikov......................B. Gribkov
Kulikova..............Tamara Govorkova
Zadunaisky....................K. Sorokin
Marusya....................L. Shabaldina
Tolya....................Boris Shishkin
Co-Pilot................Mikhail Kuznetzov
```

(In Russian; English Titles)

Artkino should hit the jackpot with this highly escapist fare that's a welcome relief from some of its predecessors. It will undoubtedly capture much moola in native houses and looks geared for good take in the arties here and in other foreign countries. After an influx of films that have accentuated Russia's war effort to extent of over-propagandizing "Taxi to Heaven" has some tinges, but subjugates for the merrier and romantic interludes.

Plot of comedy is gossamer but is kept moving at swift pace by Herbert Rappaport, whose nifty direction adds up in success of the film. It's a saga of two fellows in love with the same girl. Ludmila Tselikovskaya, blonde recruit from Moscow Art Players, who previously gave good account of herself in the Russe release of "Spring Song," projects throughout as a hoyden with much s.a. as the object of affections of Georgi Spiegel, opera singer, and Mikhail Zharov. Latter is a transport pilot, turned down for war service, but covers himself with glory when he volunteers for dangerous mission in an emergency and brings down enemy plane. Heroism triumphs over operatic warbling.

In addition to her fine portrayal Miss Tselikovskaya gives good account in the vocals, especially the operatic interludes. Acting and direction is superb throughout. Entire cast does well in respective roles. Photography is n.s.g., probably due to war limitations.

There are times when plot goes a bit Moscow Arty but not sufficiently so to stifle the lighter and gayer moments. On overall should get favorable attention and coin, too. *Edba.*

La Virgen Que Forje Una Patria
("Saint That Forged a Country")
(MEXICAN-MADE)

Clasa Studios production and release. Stars Ramon Novarro; features Gloria Marin, Domingo Soler, Julio Villareal. Directed by Julio Bracho. Story by Julio Bracho, Rene Garza. At Belmont, N. Y., week May 19, '44. Running time, 100 MINS.
```
Juan Diego..................Ramon Novarro
Brother Martin.............Domingo Soler
Aztec Slave...................Gloria Marin
Pedro de Alonso.............Paco Fuentes
Xinel.......................Felipe Montoya
Don Miguel Hidalgo.......Julio Villareal
Captain Allende.........Ernesto Alonso
Captain Juan Aldama.....Victor Urruchua
Josefa...................Fanny Schiller
```

(In Spanish; English Titles)

This is another version of Mexico's patron saint but adapted to show the social significance of the fight against tyranny. Only about 15 months ago Mexico producers turned out "Virgin of Guadalupe," which also related how a lowly peon saw the vision of the Virgin Mary and built a temple on a hill. This earlier film had the advantage of better acting and fact that it covered only one period in Mexican history while "La Virgen" covers both 1531 and 1810. This story, however, has the advantage of Ramon Novarro playing the lead. But plot is unfolded so tediously and so wordily it has slim chance in U. S. except in such arty theatres as the Belmont, where it is topflight Mexican fare.

Clasa Studios (Mexico City) have lavished plenty on production. But this is partly counterbalanced by Julio Bracho's ponderous direction. He's also credited with helping Rene Garza with the screen story.

Ramon Novarro is forthright as the peon who sees the saint, displaying some of his old screen skill. It's a difficult role, but he does it well. Domingo Soler is superb as Brother Martin, leading Father of 16th century Mexico, but Julia Villareal, in earlier sequence, makes Father Hidalgo stagey and verbose. Top femme is Gloria Marin, a looker who does splendidly in the Aztec slave role. She's a potential for American pictures, given better direction.

No question but that Mexican-made screen productions have progressed in the last three years, but they still appear miles behind the status of American or even some European film of recent vintage. *Wear.*

Vi Hemslavinor
("We Home Toilers")
(SWEDISH-MADE)

Viva production and release. Stars Dagmar Ebbesen; features Karl-Arne Holmsten, Ernst Eklund, Hjordis Petterson, Maj-Britt Hakanson, Kaj Hjelm. Directed by Schmayl Bauman. Story, Torsten Lundqvist and Bauman; camera, Hilmer Ekdahl. At 48th St., N. Y., week of May 20, '44. Running time, 88 MINS.
```
Kristiana..................Dagmar Ebbesen
Gunnar Andersson....Kari-Arne Holmsten
Johannes Larsson............Ernst Eklund
Laura, His Wife.........Hjordis Petterson
Ingrid, Their Daughter.Maj-Britt Hakanson
Pelle, Their Son...............Kaj Hjelm
Blomquist....................John Botvid
Gullan....................Dagmar Olsson
Hanna....................Julia Caesar
The Barber, Bergman.Carl-Gunnar Wingard
Anna, His Wife..........Anna-Lisa Baude
```

(In Swedish; English Titles)

A 1941 Swedish production belatedly released in this country, "Vi Hemslavinor" ("We Home Toilers") is a warm albeit overlong comedy dealing with the servant situation, a problem that apparently has universal manifestations. Film will do biz within confines of limited foreign-language audience at which it is aimed.

Story deals with a female domestic who enters the home of a wealthy Swedish family and swiftly changes

---

the pattern of their set ways. At first regarding her as an unfeeling martinet, the various family members eventually are brought to recognize her true worth, but not until after she packs her duds and leaves following the marriage of her illegitimate son to the boss' daughter. Denouement, however, finds her back in the fold again, this time as a mother-in-law rather than as a servant-problem.

Dagmar Ebbesen turns in a capital performance as the overbearing domestic and remainder of the cast are also well accounted for, especially Kaj Hjelm as the kid brother.

Essential nature of yarn would never get it past the Hays office, but director Schmayl Bauman, who also co-scripted, handles the morals situation in film with forthright candor and good taste, avoiding coy circumlocutions.

Miniature Reviews

"Henry Aldrich's Little Secret" (Par). Lukewarm entry, for duals.

"Secrets of Scotland Yard" (Rep). Spy-thriller with good cast; better-than-average dualer.

"Attack." One of the best and most thrilling OWI releases yet to reach the screen.

"Goodnight Sweetheart" (Rep). Far-fetched story; dualer.

"Song of Nevada" (Rep). Roy Rogers musical should hit the jackpot in all situations.

"Gunsmoke Mesa" (PRC). Rangers ride again in this exciting saddler, which should be okay in the duals.

"Candles at Nine" (Brit.), Jessie Matthews in meller; looks okay for U. S. market.

"Wolves of the Range" (PRC). Lively western in the Lone Rider series.

"They Met in Moscow" (Artkino). Russian-made comic opera with English titles; one of best from Moscow, but only for duals.

"Shake Hands With Murder" (PRC). Fairly diverting whodunit co-starring Iris Adrian and Frank Jenks; okay dualer.

Henry Aldrich's Little Secret

Paramount release of Walter MacEwen production. Stars Jimmy Lydon, Charles Smith; features Joan Mortimer, John Litel, Olive Blakeney, Ann Doran, John David Robb. Directed by Hugh Bennett. Screenplay, Val Burton and Aleen Leslie, from story by Miss Leslie; camera, Daniel L. Fapp; editor, Everett Douglas. Previewed in N. Y., June 7, '44. Running time, 75 MINS.
```
Henry Aldrich..............Jimmy Lydon
Dizzy Stevens.............Charles Smith
Elise Towers..............Joan Mortimer
Mr. Aldrich..................John Litel
Mrs. Aldrich...............Olive Blakeney
Helen Martin.................Ann Doran
Ricky Martin..........John David Robb
Jennifer Dale...............Tina Thayer
Mrs. Winnibegar...........Sarah Edwards
Mr. Tuttle................Harry Bradley
Mrs. O'Hara...............Lucille Ward
Aunt Maude............Almira Sessions
Mr. Luther..................Tom Fadden
Judge Hyde.............George Carleton
Bill Collector..............Byron Foulger
Miss Swithen..............Fern Emmet
Mrs. Olsen..............Dorothy Vaughn
Policeman....................Eddie Dunn
Photographer..............Hal K. Dawson
Daisy........................Noel Neill
```

In making its star an entrepreneur, lawyer, foster-parent, filibusterer and romantic lead, "Henry Aldrich's Little Secret" loads too much on the otherwise capable shoulders of its principal, with lukewarm results. For the duals.

Henry Aldrich and his pal, Dizzy, are heads of a baby-minding trust, assisted by Centerville High girls who become nursemaids to a client's baby when she leaves town to prove her jailed husband's innocence, after the local welfare board, headed by Sam Aldrich, tries to prove her an unfit parent. Farcical situation occurs when Henry pleads for his client in court, opposed by his father, representing the board. To stall for time, so as to get more proof, Henry conducts a filibuster in the best Congressional tradition, scoring a legal victory over his father.

Jimmy Lydon (as Henry) and Charles Smith (Dizzy) click neatly, while incidents involving the care and feeding of the infant are humorous and hypo an otherwise dull film. Other cast members furnish adequate support.

Secrets of Scotland Yard

Republic release of George Blair production, directed by Blair. Stars Edgar Barrier, Stephanie Bachelor; features C. Aubrey Smith, Lionel Atwill, Henry Stephenson. Screenplay, Denison Clift from novel by Clift; camera, William Bradford; editor, Fred Allen. Previewed, projection room,

N.Y., June 9, '44. Running time, **68 MINS.**
John Usher }
Robert Usher } ....Edgar Barrier
Sudan Ainger............Stephanie Bachelor
Sir Christopher Belt......C. Aubrey Smith
Waterlow.........................Lionel Atwill
Sir Reginald Meade......Henry Stephenson
Mortimer Cope.................John Abbott
Roylott Bevan............Walter Kingsford
Josef.........................Martin Kosleck
Alfred Morgan..............Forrester Harvey
Mason......................Frederic Worlock
Col. Hedley..................Matthew Boulton
David Usher....................Bobby Cooper

A strong cast lifts this spy-thriller from the doldrums it might have fallen into because of its average plot. "Secrets of Scotland Yard" should suffice for the duals.

Based on the novel, "Room 40, O.B.," by Denison Clift, the film has enough action to sustain moderate interest throughout. Edgar Barrier, who plays the roles of twin-brothers, one of whom is killed early in the picture after deciphering a secret Nazi code message, acts out his chores in commendable style. Stephanie Bachelor portrays the gal in the plot so well that, on the basis of her work here, she has been signed to a long-termer by Republic. Veterans C. Aubrey Smith and Lionel Atwill, latter enacting the heavy, also are responsible in a large measure for carrying the story through to its fairly surprising conclusion.

Yarn deals with the inner workings of an English staff who specialize in the decoding of Nazi messages. The hazards of their work bring about the death of two of their number, presumably by German agents in England. Denouement, in which the Germans are rounded up, and the capture of the staff member who is a spy, is brought about in logical sequence.

Direction by George Blair keeps things moving at a good pace, and he has cut corners to bring the film in under the budget wire without hurting the value of the picture. *Sten.*

Attack!
(The Battle for New Britain)
(DOCUMENTARY)

Office of War Information release, distributed by RKO. Produced under the auspices of the Commanding General, Southwest Pacific Area; photography, U. S. Army Signal Corps; exhibited under auspices of War Activities Committee of Motion Picture Industry. Tradeshown N. Y. June 7, '44. Running time, **56 MINS.**

Synchronized for national release simultaneous with the Fifth War Loan Drive, "Attack!" is the most detonating and grimly realistic exposition of the Second World War to be reflected by the camera lens since the carnage of Pearl Harbor.

In its overall message, its stark account of modern warfare and timeliness of subject, "Attack!" is the ultimate in puissant pursuasion, if reason need be advanced, to buy bonds until it hurts—but hard.

Produced under the auspices of the Commanding General, Southwest Pacific area, "Attack!" is the step-by-step, methodical account of the events leading up to the wresting of the island of New Britain from the Japs.

In minute detail and comprehensive scope the preparations for the Yank onslaught are brought into focus. Johnny Doughboy is shown in intimate juxtaposition with the camera. In full revelation are depicted his careful training maneuvers, his food, his weapons, his military indoctrination for the attack and his final charge—with life or death as the payoff—on the sandy beaches and steaming jungles of New Britain.

Since the Battle for New Britain was a three-pronged assault, the essential strategy of the various feints and maneuvers are explained via simple cartography. The purpose and import of each movement is revealed in advance as is also the immediate objective.

The close teamwork of the air corps, the navy and the infantry in gaining the victory is given full play, with each service entity shown as complementing the two other branches.

Camera work of the U. S. Army Signal Corps is superb in depicting the air shots and the naval cannonading. Shooting peak, however, reaches its acme in the final jungle scenes where Yank and Nippon have a go at each other. For sheer dramatic intensity and chilling impact and suspense, these internecine glimpses of modern warfare are without parallel in film annals.

"Attack!" is released through the Office of War Information, which has a cinema epic on its hands in a 56-minute film that should perforce be part of the military education of every American in civilian raiment.

Goodnight Sweetheart

Republic production and release. Stars Robert Livingston, Ruth Terry; features Henry Hull, Grant Withers, Thurston Hall, Lloyd Corrigan. Directed by Joseph Santley. Screenplay by Isabel Dawn, Jack Townley, from original by Frank Fenton, Joseph Hoffman; camera, Bud Thackery; editor, Ralph Dixon; music, Morton Scott. Previewed in N. Y. June 9, '44. Running time, **67 MINS.**
Johnny Newsome........Robert Livingston
Caryl Martin.......................Ruth Terry
Jeff Parker.........................Henry Hull
Matt Colby.....................Grant Withers
Judge James Rutherford.....Thurston Hall
Police Chief Davis..........Lloyd Corrigan
Johnny's Landlady..........Maude Eburne
Slim Taylor.......................Olin Howlin
Collins.....................Lucien Littlefield
Caryl's Landlady...................Ellen Lowe
Bottle Man...................Chester Conklin
Pete..............................Emmett Lynn
Bellboy..........................Billy Benedict

"Goodnight Sweetheart" is a far-fetched story which, as they say, "could only happen in the movies." Evident that film was made on a low budget strictly as a dual program fill-in and, as such, should fit into the niche aimed for without any great difficulty.

Plot has a brash, cocksure city reporter coming to a small town to take over his half interest in a hick paper. His use of expose tactics to build the paper's circulation by attacking the opposition sheet's mayoralty candidate backfires when the latter's niece, unknown to the scribe, double-crosses him. He in turn double-double-crosses her, but with all the two-timing, everyone is reconciled at the closeout.

Title of the picture, which was a pop ballad a few years back, is played only as background music for production credits.

Teaming up for the second time, Robert Livingston and Ruth Terry make a good combination. Livingston, ex-cowboy star who has laid aside his six guns and sombrero for the time being, is good as the smart city slicker. Comely Ruth Terry is appealing in the role of the gal who teaches him a lesson, and warbles one number competently. Henry Hull is wasted in a comparatively obscure role and the others perform passably.

Song of Nevada
(MUSICAL)

Republic production and release. Stars Roy Rogers; features Dale Evans, Mary Lee, Lloyd Corrigan, Thurston Hall, John Eldredge, Bob Nolan. Directed by Joseph Kane. Screenplay, Gordon Kahn, Olive Cooper; camera, Jack Marta; editor, Tony Martinelli; music, Morton Scott; dances, Larry Ceballos. Previewed in N. Y. June 9, '44. Running time, **75 MINS.**
Roy.................................Roy Rogers
Joan Barrabee...................Dale Evans
Kitty Hanley.......................Mary Lee
Prof. Jeremiah Hanley......Lloyd Corrigan
John Barrabee................Thurston Hall
Rollo Bingham................John Eldredge
Col. Jack Thompson.........Forrest Taylor
Calahan.........................George Meeker
Master of Ceremonies........Emmet Vogan
Ferguson.........................LeRoy Mason
Worthington.............William Davidson
Bob Nolan and the Sons of the Pioneers

Indicative of the trend to modernize westerns by placing them in present-day settings, "Song of Nevada" is a far cry from the old-time blood and thunder westerns, but is nevertheless a well-knit, fast-paced and lavishly produced film that should hit the jackpot in all situations. It should even attract a lot of people who would never have gone to see the old style "reach for your gun, pardner!" type of sagebrush thriller.

While the title pays tribute to Nevada, locale of the yarn does not distinguish the silver mining and divorce territory from any other western state, a fact that Republic could utilize for productions bearing the titles of the other 20 odd western states.

Yarn has Roy Rogers and the Sons of the Pioneers meeting a wealthy ranchowner whose plane has been forced down returning from New York, where his daughter has gone high-hat and fallen for a Park Avenue bounder. He misses his plane and decides to remain with his new friends, learning afterwards that the plane has crashed and he is considered dead. When his daughter and her boyfriend return to dispose of the ranch, the old man remains in hiding and persuades Rogers to go to the ranch to prevent the sale and wean his daughter away from the avaricious city slicker. Needless to say, he does both, to the tune of some fancy riding, pretty singing and flashing fists.

Rogers clicks throughout and Dale Evans supplies looks and a good voice to the proceedings. Mary Lee and Lloyd Corrigan are entertaining as a traveling medicine show team, while the Sons of the Pioneers contribute a polished performance vocally.

The eight songs in the film are tuneful though not outstanding, except the current pop tune, "It's Love, Love, Love," sung by Dale Evans. Musical sequences are well staged and the entire production, which bears an expensive look, has been masterfully directed by Joseph Kane.

Gunsmoke Mesa
(SONGS)

PRC release of Arthur Alexander production. Stars Jim Newill, Dave "Tex" O'Brien; features Guy Wilkerson. Directed by Harry Fraser. Screenplay, Elmer Clifton; songs, Aleth Hansen; editor, Charles Henkel, Jr.; camera, Ira Morgan. Asst. director, Clark L. Paylow. At New York, N. Y., dual, week June 7, '44. Running time, **59 MINS.**
Jim Steele..........................Jim Newill
Tex Wyatt............Dave "Tex" O'Brien
Panhandle Perkins..........Guy Wilkerson
Joan Royal.....................Patti McCarty
Henry Black.....................Jack Ingram
Sam Sneed..................Kermit Maynard
Bill Moore......................Robert Barron
Frank Lear...................Dick Alexander
Judge Plymouth............Michael Vallon
Deputy Mace Page.................Roy Brent
Sheriff Horner................Jack Rockwell

This run-of-the-mill western projects Jim Newill, Dave O'Brien and Guy Wilkerson as Texas Rangers who frustrate gang's attempt to poach on the preserves of the law-abiding folk of the Cactus plains. Oke action dualer.

In this one, the three musketeers of the saddle set out after Jack Ingram, villainous hombre who had his cousin and the latter's frau bumped off to get control of the Gold Star mine by being appointed guardian of their infant son. Before his aides can do away with the kid, the Rangers chase them off. Heroic trio turn detectives and bring the murderers, and Ingram, to justice.

During the interim there's plenty of galloping and shooting, although spaced by comedy and song interludes by the mustangers when the boys are not tracking down the killers. Newill, O'Brien and Wilkerson give their usual good performances. Ingram, Patti McCarty, Kermit Maynard, Robert Barron and Dick Alexander all turn in good performances in the lesser roles. Direction by Harry Fraser is keyed on a fast pitch. Camera work by Ira Morgan packs some dandy shots. *Edba.*

Candles at Nine
(BRITISH-MADE)

London, May 19.

Anglo-American Film Corp. release of British National Film. Stars Jessie Matthews; features Beatrix Lehmann, John Stuart. Directed by John Harlow. Screenplay by Basil Mason, John Harlow, from Anthony Gilbert's novel, "The Mouse Who Couldn't Play Ball." Camera, James Wilson, Arthur Grant. At Studio One, London, May 19, '44. Running time, **82 MINS.**
Dorothea Capper............Jessie Matthews
William Gordon....................John Stuart
Julia Carberry..............Beatrix Lehmann
Brenda Tempest...........Winifred Shotter
Charles Lacey.............Reginald Purdell
Hugh Lacey..................Hugh Dempster
Garth Hope.........................Joss Ambler
Everard Hope................Eliot Makeham
Griggs..............................John Salew
Lucille Hope.......................Vera Bogetti
Cecil Tempest........Andre Van Gyseghem

For British audiences seeking relief from the war this frankly escapist thriller has at least the merit of a striking performance by Beatrix Lehmann as a female killer as sinister as the most menacing on the screen. Generally the artificial plot and melodramatic situations are made to seem almost plausible by a cast of seasoned troupers in support of Jessie Matthews and John Stuart in the star roles. May do fairly well in U. S. as a meller. How much of a draw the Matthews name may still be with filmgoers on this side who remember when she was tops in West End musicals is dubious. But for American audiences, even though she plays a frightened young girl, Miss Matthews should help the draw.

Based on Anthony Gilbert's novel, "Mouse Who Couldn't Play Ball," the main theme revolves around the consequences of a miser's willing his half-million-dollar estate to an obscure great-niece, winner of a song-and-dance amateur competition. All six nearer relatives of the dead man, who feel they have more legitimate claims, try at first to flatter her into getting them out of financial entanglements, and then variously scheme to put her out of the way. But it remains for the housekeeper to make an actual murderous attempt on the heiress. A ubiquitous detective, John Stuart, who foils the villainess, wins the girl. Beatrix Lehmann is the sinister housekeeper.

British National Films have given the film elaborate mounting, and direction by John Harlow is adequate. Outstanding for this type film is the musical background, the featured number, "I'd Like to Share With You," is put over effectively by Miss Matthews.

Wolves of the Range

PRC release of Sigmund Neufeld production. Stars Bob Livingston, Al "Fuzzy" St. John; features Frances Gladwin, I. Stanford Jolley, Karl Hackett and Ed Cassidy. Directed by Sam Newfield. Story and screenplay, Joe O'Donnell; camera, Robert Cline; editor, Holbrook N. Todd. At New York theatre, N. Y., week of May 30, '44, dual. Running time, **60 MINS.**
Rocky Cameron.............Bob Livingston
Fuzzy Jones...........Al (Fuzzy) St. John
Ann.........................Frances Gladwin
Dorn......................I. Stanford Jolley
Corrigan..........................Karl Hackett
Brady...............................Ed Cassidy
Hammond.......................Jack Ingraham
Adams.............................Ken Duncan
Foster...............................Bud Buster
Judge Brandon.......................Bob Hill

"Wolves of the Range" is another in the Lone Rider series, with the usual quota of hard riding, fisticuffs and gunplay resulting in a lively drama of the plains that should please the westerns crowd and make a good addition to nabe dual bills.

Bob Livingston as the Lone Rider and his side-kick, Al "Fuzzy" St. John, this time come to the aid of the ranchers when the head of the cattlemen's association with his thugs starts a reign of terror to drive the ranchers from their properties so he can put through an irrigation project.

Livingston and St. John, as usual, make a smooth-working team, with the latter lending his fine comedy antics to the proceedings. Francis

Gladwin is one of the best lookers to be seen in westerns in a long time.

They Met in Moscow
(RUSSIAN-MADE)

Artkino release of Ivan Piriev production, directed by Piriev. Stars Marina Ladynina, Vladimir Zeldin. Script and lyrics by Victor Gussev; camera, Valentin Pavlov; English titles, Charles Clement; score, Tikhon Krennikov. At Victoria, N. Y., June 7, '44. Running time, 87 MINS.
Glasha Novikov..........Marina Ladynina
Musaib Gatuyev..........Vladimir Zeldin
Kuzma Petrov..........Nikolai Kriuchkov
Agrafena Vlasov......Elena Schastlivtseva
Abdusalam................Grigori Alexeyev

(In Russian; English Titles)

Adept English titles help put across this Russian comic opera. It is one of better efforts from Russe studios, with musical score and ballading standout. "They Met in Moscow" should find modest returns in some arty theatres and a few keys, but will obtain most revenue in U. S. market where deemed stout enough to fit into twin bills.

An industrious herder of swine in the cold northern area of Russia and a shepherd from the mountainous regions of the south meet, pledge undying faith, at an annual aggie fair in Moscow, and then go back to their respective means of livelihood. In between, there is some misgiving, a deliberately falsified translation of the rugged shepherd's letter by a rival stable hand, and still more misunderstanding before the two are finally brought together just before the northern femme weds the horsey rival by mistake.

Though keeping in musical comedy atmosphere most of the time, there's a vivid sequence high in the mountains where the stalwart shepherder battles three mountain wolves to save the valuable ewes. The breeding sequence, in which the feminine star figures, is strictly down to earth, and distinctly different from the usual American film brushoff for such. Camera work of Valentin Pavlov is vivid, his work in the mountains and in depicting winter scenes being standout.

Marina Ladynina, as the blonde northern gal who raises pigs, helps mightily in lending vigor and contrast to a routine yarn. Vladimir Zeldin, the cossack-looking shepherder, is excellent in what he has to do, but the real voice of the film is Grigori Alexeyev, assistant to the sheepherder. Unfortunately, he sings only once, and then too briefly. Nikolai Kriuchkov also has sturdy vocal chords, and plays a mean accordion. Supporting roles are well played even down to the moon-faced warblers in the excellent chorus. *Wear.*

Shake Hands With Murder

PRC release of American Productions. Stars Iris Adrian, Frank Jenks; features Douglas Fowley. Directed by Albert Herman. Screenplay, John T. Neville, from original by Martin Mooney; editor, George Merrick; camera, Robert Cline. At New York, N. Y., dual, week of June 7, '44. Running time, 61 MINS.
Patsy Brent....................Iris Adrian
Eddie Jones...................Frank Jenks
Steve Morgan.............Douglas Fowley
Joe Blake..................Jack Raymond
Secretary..................Claire Rochelle
John Clark............Herbert Rawlinson
Stanton.....,..........Juan De La Cruz
Haskins...................Stan Jolley
Kennedy..................Forrest Taylor
Adams....................George Kirby
Howard..................Gene Stutenroth
Waitress................Anitra Sparrow
Sergeant.r...............Buck Harrington

Fairly diverting whodunit, a setup for Iris Adrian and Frank Jenks, gives both plenty of lunges at comedic stuff to offset an otherwise commonplace murder mystery. Should do well in the dualers.

Miss Adrian and Jenks are partnered in the bail bond business. They have staked their poke in bailing out Douglas Fowley, whom they feel has been unjustly accused of larcenous

taint. Bonds have been stolen from his business partner and Howley has been tagged by the police. When Herbert Rawlinson, the partner and complainant, is found murdered, couple are more interested in recovering their moola. She goes after Howley, while Jenks goes after the cops. Of course, Howley never took the bonds, which are found in the murdered partner's manse. Real killer is also unmasked before final fadeout.

Miss Adrian, Jenks and Howley have a merry time of it throughout unravelling and turn in corking good performances. Support cast is adequate in lesser roles. Story is kept moving at fast clip by Albert Herman, who directed, and camera work by Robert Cline is on the okay side. *Edba.*

Mexico De Mis Recuerdos
("My Memories of Mexico")
(MEXICAN-MADE)

Mexico City, May 30.
Pan American Films release of Filmex production. Stars Antonio R. Frausto, Virginia Zuri and Lolita Camarilo. Written and directed by Juan Bustillo Oro. At Cine Teatro Alameda, Mexico City. Running time, 91 MINS.

This is tops for period pix of which Mexican producers are so fond and on which they have less fortunate results. Looks one of best films made in Mexico. Production in every way demonstrates a great forward step by the Mexican film industry. Scored well here.

Juan Bustillo Oro did writing and direction, and deserves the palm.

Story is of the days of Gen. Porfirio Diaz, ruler of Mexico for 30 years. Story has a Gallic simplicity: showfolk and bohemians and prudes mingling. Sofia Alvarez, radiant brunet, who has a rep as comic. is excellent in a dramatic role, as the spirited miss reared by three starchy aunts. To land her man, Luis Aldas, admirer of show girls, she goes with the troupe at the old Teatro Principal here, Mexico's ace operetta house of the times.

Joaquin Paraave, veteran comedian, is an essential ingredient as confidential aide of President Diaz and sort of protector of Miss Alvarez in the theatrical world. It is he who advises Diaz to give Soler a grand piano instead of a check as a token of appreciation for the waltz he composed and dedicated to Senor Diaz. Piano serves the bohemian composer well as a bed after his long nights of tune making. Soler is particularly good in this one. Aldas is first-rate as the cultured young-man-about-town. Antonio R. Frausto gives a good impersonation of President Diaz. *Grahame.*

Mis Hijos
("My Children")
(MEXICAN-MADE)

Mexico City, May 30.
Astro Films production and release. Stars Andres Soler, Gustavo Rojo, Ramiro Gomez Kemp, Julio Ahuet, Ruben Rojo, Rafael Icardo, Roberto Banquells, Esperanza Issa. Directed by Rene Cardona. Camera, J. Ortiz Ramos. At Cine Mazerit, Mexico City. Running time, 85 MINS.

Performances of Sara Garcia, Mexico character woman, and Andres Soler, strongly reminiscent of Lionel Barrymore in this role, are the saving graces of this one. They give vitality to an inferior story, that of a widowed mother losing track of her children for many years because of amnesia resulting from a railroad wreck. But the customers loved it here.

Production is languid Latin and too much on the weepy side. Mother gets physically as well as mentally lost. Children are taken in charge of by Soler, the family doc, who after a vain search for their mama takes them with him to Mexico City from the little old town and they all

do well, while the mother, wandering away from a state mental hospital, kills a man and is sent to prison. Released, La Garcia gets a glimmering of what it's all about. She finds the doc in Mexico City and enters his employ as a servant to be near her children. They treat her as a servant.

Big scene is when a son, Gustavo Rojo, a bullfighter, gets gored. Lots of censor trims in this one. Esperanza Lissa, the daughter, a looker, should go places in films. *Grahame.*

Miniature Reviews

"Sensations of 1945" (Musical) (UA). Okay filmusical with Eleanor Powell topping flock of variety names.

"Step Lively," (Songs) (RKO). Sinatra film should please generally; especially good for light summer film fare.

"Marine Raiders" (RKO). Exploits of the Marines in Guadalcanal dramatically re-enacted.

"Gildersleeve's Ghost" (RKO). Radioite Harold Peary in mediocre comedy attempt, for duals.

"Teen-Age" (Cont.). Routine juve problem melodrama: so-so dualer.

"The Way Ahead" (Eagle-Lion). David Niven in strong war story; likely for American market.

Sensations of 1945
(MUSICAL)

United Artists release of Andrew Stone production directed by Stone (James Nasser associate producer). Stars Eleanor Powell; features Dennis O'Keefe, W.C. Fields, Sophie Tucker, Eugene Pallete, C. Aubrey Smith, David Lichine, Dorothy Donegan, The Cristianis, Woody Herman and Cab Calloway bands. Original, Frederick Jackson; screenplay, Dorothy Bennett, Andrew Stone; camera, Peverell Marley, John Mescall; dances, David Lichine; music, Mahlon Merilek; songs, Al Sherman-Harry Tobias; acrobatic dances, Chas. O'Curran; asst. director, Henry Kesler; editor, James E. Smith. Previewed N.Y. JUne 16, '44. Running time, 85 MINS.
Ginny Walker .... Eleanor Powell
Junior Crane .... Dennis O'Keefe
Dan Lindsay .... C. Aubrey Smith
Gus Crane .... Eugene Pallette
Julia Westcolt .... Mimi Forsythe
Randall .... Lyle Talbot
The Great Gustafson .... Hubert Castle
Pendergast .... Richard Hageman
Miss Grear .... Marie Blake
Mr. Collins .... Stanley Andrews
English Girl .... Louise Currie
Girl in Penny Arcade .... Betty Wells
Photographer.................. Bert Roach
Doctor .... Grandon Rhodes
Detective .... Earl Hopkins
Mme. Angostina .... Constance Purdy
Silas Hawkins .... Joe Devlin
Martinelli .... George Humbert
Moroni .... Anthony Warde
Mrs. Gustafson .... Ruth Lee
Playing themselves: W.C. Fields, Sophie Tucker, Dorothy Donegan, The Christianis, Pallenberg's Bears, Cab Calloway and Woody Herman bands, David Lichine, Wendell Niles, Gene Rodgers, Les Paul 3, The Copelands, Mel Hall, Johnson Bros.

"Sensations of 1945" may be a misnomer but none will dispute its popular appeal. It's a boxoffice filmusical, perhaps no "sensation" literally, but Andrew Stone did contrive to blend a large variety of acts into a fairly cohesive tunefilm.

Plot is one of those things. Eleanor Powell is the ambidextrous musicomedy dancer turned p.a. whose imagination cooks up spectacular ideas calling for lavish showmanship and Miss-Fixit technique which, however, almost always involves her deeper with Dennis O'Keefe. Latter is Junior Crane, half of the father-son partnership in Crane & Co. (Eugene Pallette is the senior publicist) whose flackery is a sort of combination Myron Selznick-Brandt & Brandt-Ringling Bros.-Dick Maney outfit. That's the ridic part of the plot. P.a.s capable of handling literary memoirs, promoting a Circus-in-the-Sky nitery, a Devil's Gorge ropewalking stunt, a Times Sq. jitterbugging melee, with assorted cabaret preems and musicomedy ventures in between, makes for a story which reads like a Ziegfeldian nightmare out of Ivy Lee.

Despite the cold analysis of the curious plot motivation it all plays far more compellingly than this brief recounting would indicate. It's to producer-director Andrew Stone's credit that he has thus been able to jell the Woody Herman and Cab Calloway bands, the specialties of W. C. Fields (too brief), Sophie Tucker's two dandy numbers (with Teddy Shapiro omnipotently at the Steinway), the crack boogie-woogie-ing of Dorothy Donegan, the standout Cristiani Family, Pallenberg's Bears, David Lichine's choreography in person and back-of-the-camera, Les Paul Trio, The Copelands, the John Bros. and other vaude acts.

In between, Miss Powell, when not carrying the romance interest, demonstrates her stepping skillfully; Calloway's "Hepster's Dictionary" stampedes Times Sq. into a jitterbug panic, when the 47th street signboard (above the Pepsicola's servicemen's center) is utilized as a screen for soundpix presumably projected from the Times Bldg. in the downtown end of Times Sq.

"Starlight Night," a beautiful high-school horse, keynotes an equine conceit, with some extraordinary acrobatic dancing and "can-can" type of splits by the hardworking line under acro-choreographer Charles O'Curran's direction. Dorothy Donegan, assisted by an unidentified male boogie-woogiest, massages a revolving Steinway in the best Hazel Scott manner; Soph does one of her intimate pops.

C. Aubrey Smith is convincing as the passe but proud yesteryear impresario who is maneuvered into a comeback via a Gay 90s nitery; Mimi Forsythe bespeaks of promise as the minor ingenue (gal has a good screen face); Dennis O'Keefe is scowlingly adequate as the juve; Lyle Talbot is a mild menace; W. C. Fields does too little (in a bit with the unidentified Fritz and Jean Hubert). Both bands work hard and to good effect, and Woody Herman handles himself rather well on dialog. *Abel.*

Step Lively
(SONGS)

RKO release of Robert Fellows production. Features Frank Sinatra, Geo. Murphy, Adolphe Menjon, Gloria De Haven, Walter Slezak, Eugene Pallette. Directed by Tom Whelan, Screenplay, Warren Duff, Peter Milne; based on "Room Service," by John Murray and Allen Peretz, camera, Robt. de Grasse; music, Ernst Matray; vocals, Ken Darby; music director, C. Bakaleinikoff; arrangements, Gene Rose, Axel Stordahl; editor, Gene Milford; asst. director, Clem Beauchamp; songs, Sammy Cahn-Jule Styne. Tradeshown N.Y. June 26, '44. Running time, 86 MINS.

Glen .... Frank Sinatra
Miller .... George Murphy
Wagner .... Adolphe Menjon
Christine .... Gloria De Haven
Gribble .... Walter Slezak
Jenkins .... Eugene Pallette
Binion .... Wally Brown
Harry .... Alan Carney
Dr. Gibbs .... Grant Mitchell
Miss Abboli .... Anne Jeffreys
Mother .... Frances King
Father .... Harry Noble

The old George Abbott play, "Room Service," has been resurrected for an RKO remake, with song trimming palpably designed to fit Frank Sinatra. As a tailormade vehicle it's somewhat loosely fitted but in the main it will please. It's good summer film fare, and riding the Sinatra crest right now it's sure to do well.

The hectic machinations of theatrical shoestringers have been given a thorough going-over, especially with the last few years' wave of backstage filmusicals. But as Warren Duff and Peter Milne have revamped it, under Tim Whelan's staccato direction, it is pleasant enough celluloid divertissement.

Sinatra is first the ambitious playwright who is suddenly discovered to have a voice, and thus causes the non-bobbysox Gloria De Haven and Anne Jeffreys to swoon for him. Throwing in the sophisticated and somewhat sultry Miss Jeffreys—her sponsor's $50,000 check is the convincer to the plot's constant bankrollitis—may have been by design in order to de-bobbysox the swami of swoonerville.

It's to the credit of all the troupers that "Step Lively" maintains bounce. True, there never was a dumbbell hotel manager like Walter Slezak, nor as irascible a hotel chain supervisor as Adolphe Menjou troupes it, but the exaggerated gusto goes a lot towards offsetting the lack of plot credibility.

George Murphy is ever in command of Wally Brown and Alan Carney, as his shoestring aides, all intent on putting on that musical with a mysterious backer's 50G. Miss De Haven is the general factotum as ingenue; Eugene Pallette legal rep for the effacing San Francisco tycoon; and Sinatra practically himself, although cast as a playwright-turned-crooner.

He has a couple of good song opportunities in "As Long As There's Music" and "Where Does Love Begin." Outside of an opening audience number (bubble-bath routine) and the show-within-a-show, as part of the finale production, the production values are moderate. Director Whelan let himself go in the finale, and some of the Oriental hoke (with Murphy, et al.) is bright, as is that black-and-white terp creation. (Plot-wise, this is the show supposedly put on in five days, the idea being to beat the 50G check when it bounces back from the Frisco bank. Hectic as the plot is, nothing so lavish could be mounted in five weeks, much less five days, but the general tempo of "Step Lively" is such that audiences won't examine that phase too closely either). Incidentally, musically there is some fine choral and orchestral work evident in all the arrangements.

Sinatra, an important property now to RKO and Metro (where he is on loan), handles himself with ease but still needs some camera assists. *Abel.*

Marine Raiders
Hollywood, June 20.

RKO release of Robert Fellows production. Stars Pat O'Brien, Robert Ryan, Ruth Hussey. Directed by Harold Schuster. Screenplay by Warren Duff; original, Martin Rackin and Duff; camera, Nicholas Musuraca; special effects, Vernon L. Walker; editor, Philip Martin, Jr.; asst. director, Sam Ruman; dialog director, Melville Burke; technical director, Capt. Clay Boyd, U.S.M.C. Tradeshown in L. A. June 19, '44. Running time, 90 MINS.

Major Steve Lockhard .... Pat O'Brien
Capt. Dan Craig .... Robert Ryan
Ellen Foster .... Ruth Hussey
Sergeant Louis Leary .... Frank McHugh
Sergeant Maguire .... Barton MacLane
Jimmy .... Richard Martin
Miller .... Edmund Glover
Tony Hewitt .... Russell Wade
Lt. Harrigan .... Robert Anderson
Lt. Sherwood .... Michael St. Angel
Sally .... Martha MacVicar
Cook .... Harry Brown

"Marine Raiders" is an expertly-contrived cinematic drama saluting the U. S. Marine Corps, deftly blending battle action in Guadalcanal with a sincere and sympathetic romance, and giving the public a direct insight into the training and expansion of the Marines to a force of 500,000 toughened fighting men. Smoothly unfolding at a fast clip and contained in 90 minutes' running time, picture will be a timely attraction with the stepped-up activity in the far Pacific, and is a cinch for solidly profitable boxoffice in all datings.

Picture credits cooperation in the making to the Marine Corps, Navy, Coast Guard and the Army. There are a few official Government clips of plane attacks and salvos by the Navy against Jap-held Guadalcanal and other islands, and a fine sequence detailing the intensive training of recruit Marines with simulated battle conditions at Camp Elliott, Calif.

There's a realistic sincerity in the screen drama, especially in the warmful romance between Marine Capt. Robert Ryan and Ruth Hussey; and the close palship between Ryan and his commanding officer, Pat O'Brien. Deft and sympathetic handling of the love affair gives picture a women's appeal, which is not generally the case with service dramas.

Opening reenacts the Guadalcanal landing by the First Marine Raider battalion, and—after brief battle footage—swings to makeshift materials and supplies utilized by the men who first landed to establish the beachhead. Army forces move in to relieve the Marines, who are shunted for leave in Australia, where Ryan meets and quickly falls in love with the understanding Miss Hussey. Jap air raid hospitalizes Ryan with minor wounds, and O'Brien, fearing his officer had been taken in by a conniving gal, shanghais him, under orders, aboard boat returning the battalion to the States. After officers and men of the first train new recruits at Camp Elliott, they're off again for another major landing in the islands. Brief stopoff in Australia provides reunion and marriage of Ryan and Miss Hussey, and blessing of O'Brien. Reenactment of major operation to occupy an enemy island, with air and sea attacks to soften up and then takeoff of the paramarines under command of Ryan and regular landing forces under O'Brien, provides a stirring and dramatic climax.

O'Brien delivers solidly as the Marine major, with important support provided by Ryan and Miss Hussey in excellent performances. Frank McHugh does well as a comedy cook, with Barton MacLane his continual heckler. Support is carefully selected.

Harold Schuster does a fine job of direction under producership of Robert Fellows. Script by Warren Duff is decidedly compact and interesting throughout; while cameraman Nick Musuraca and special effects chief Vernon Walker turn in slick jobs on the photographic end. *Walt.*

Gildersleeve's Ghost
Hollywood, June 20.

RKO release of Herman Schlom production. Stars Harold Peary. Directed by Gordon Douglas. Story and screenplay by Robert E. Kent; camera, Jack Mackenzie; special effects, Vernon L. Walker; editor, Les Milbrook; asst. director, Harry Mancke. Tradeshown in L. A. June 19, '44. Running time, 63 MINS.

Gildersleeve / Randolph / Jonathan .... Harold Peary
Terry Vance .... Marion Martin
Peavey .... Richard LeGrand
Marie .... Amelita Ward
Leroy .... Freddie Mercer
Margie .... Margie Stewart
Harriet Morgan .... Marie Blake
Haley .... Emory Parnell
John Wells .... Frank Reicher
Henry Lennox .... Joseph Vitale
Birdie .... Lillian Randolph
Chauncey .... Nicodemus Stewart
Gorilla .... Charles Gemora

This is the last of the Gildersleeve series of program features from the RKO lot. It's a minor league affair, filled with elemental nonsense and broad attempts at comedy that seldom get beyond the sophomoric stage. Picture is strictly for the dualers where Harold Peary's radio characterization of Gildersleeve might have a following.

Peary is entered for office of police commissioner, with ancestral ghosts in the graveyard wandering out to set the stage to make him a hero to cop the election. Plot sends characters to a strange manor, where a research doctor is experimenting with invisibility via a girl and a gorilla. Convenient storm holds the cast in the typical eerie surroundings for usual attempts at comedy suspense, but latter does not jell sufficient for audience interest. After much horseplay and ludicrous situations. Peary emerges as the hero.

Peary does not click on the screen and is better for his radio followers in front of the mike. Marion Martin is a blonde eyeful as the girl who periodically becomes visible from a transparent state. Supporting cast is average, and direction by Gordon Douglas is handicapped by the material provided by the script. *Walt.*

Teen Age

Continental release of J. D. Kendis production; supervised by Edward E. Kaye, directed by Dick L'Estrange. Original, Elmer Clifton; camera, Eddie Kull; editor, Fred Bain. At Victoria, N. Y., week of June 17, '44. Running time, 56 MINS.

District Attorney .... Herbert Heyes
Jim Murray .... Wheeler Oakman
Dan Murray .... Johnny Duncan
Eddie Quinten .... Fred Towns
Rose Gordon .... Sylvia Stanton
Alice Gordon .... Betty Walters
Lily Miller .... Beverly Penn
Henry Cobb .... Rod Rogers
John Abbott .... Russell Horton
Mary Abbott .... Claire McDowell
Ralph Gordon .... Ted Stanhope
Mabel Lee .... Patsy Harmon

"Teen Age" is a dull and obvious bit of sermonizing on youthful delinquency, thrown together without any cohesion or taste. Little attention seems to have been paid to casting, direction or even photography. Obviously filmed as a quickie, it's routine stuff, good only for the lower rung of a dual program.

Story concerns wild young kids neglected by busy or indifferent parents, who start out on harmless joyrides and benders and end up on the wrong side of the law in petty thievery and brawls. To paint the obvious moral that petty knavery leads to stronger crime, story melodramatically brings in gambling dens, gangster battles and gunplay. There is very little originality in the film, even in the method of the flashbacks that tell the story.

Acting in the film runs from routine to painful. Herbert Heyes, as the D.A., has the embarrassing duty of occasionally directing his remarks at the theatre audience, pointing out in so many more words that crime doesn't pay. Juve members of the audience when film was caught were more bored than impressed. *Bron.*

People's Avengers
(Documentary)
(RUSSIAN-MADE)

Artkino release of Central Newsreel Studios, U.S.S.R., production. Directed by V. Belyaev. Commentary and narrative by Norman Corwin, music, D. Astradanzev; camera, I. Bykov, B. Makaseyev, M. Gileder, L. Isaacson, B. Elberg, B. Muromtaey, Y. Mestechkin, S. Skolnikov. At Stanley theatre, N.Y., June 14, '44. Running time, 55 MINS.

Complete documentation of the activities of the Russian guerillas (Partisans) harassing the Nazis behind the Eastern Front is a vivid kudo to the spirit of the common people who continued to fight fascism after the fighting front had passed them by. Film covers Partisan activities along the whole front, from the snows of the North to the swamps of the South, and from the elimination of a single sentry to the recovery of a whole town.

Camera work is necessarily hampered by stealthy nature of guerilla fighting and resultant lighting conditions, most attacks being made in semi-darkness or in wooded forests chosen for their fighting possibilities rather than their merits as film locales. The cameramen spent from two to three months behind the German lines shooting thousands of feet of film. Two of them lost their lives in shuttling between the lines.

Film is a worthy addition to the many film records of the current war and is a down-to-earth portrayal of the fighting qualities of the Russians. Norman Corwin, noted for his radio dramatizations via CBS, has written a workmanlike commentary keyed to every nuance of the film's story. *Turo.*

The Way Ahead
(BRITISH-MADE)
London, June 6.

Eagle-Lion release of Two Cities Films production. Stars David Niven. Directed by Carol Reed. Screenplay by Eric Ambler, Peter Ustinov from original story by Eric Ambler. Produced by Norman Walker, John Sutro. Camera, Guy Green. At Odean theatre, London, June 6. Running time, 115 MINS.

Jim Perry.....................David Niven
Davenport................Raymond Huntley
Sergeant Fletcher..........Billy Hartnell
Brewer.... ....Stanley Holloway
Lloyd....».................James Donald
Luke.....................John Laurie
Beck.......................Leslie Dwyer
Parsons...................Hugh Burden
Stainer....................Jimmy Hanley
Commanding Officer........Reginald Tate
Company Commander.........Lee Genn
Marjorie Gillingham.....Renee Ascherson
Mrs. Gillingham............Mary Jerrold
Col. Walmsley............A. E. Matthews
Rispoli.. ....Peter Ustinov

At last somebody has dared to blow his own horn. This is the dominating impression left by this picture. Eagle-Lion's presentation of Two Cities production. No soft-pedalling here. no understatement of British guts. but unashamed glory-ing in a nation's girding up its loins to go and conquer its enemies. David Niven. as star, and stout story may make it okay at the American box-office.

There is' no story in the accepted sense, and no love interest. There are momentary shots of femmes, chiefly wives. but no pin-up girls. This heightens the documentary value of this wartime slice of Eng-lish life. Slickness of cutting should be enough to put this among notable British films. but there is additional cleverness in keeping David Niven far less obtrusive than his star's status might seem to justify. He's a subaltern in command of a platoon. Covering the period from early 1939 to the Tunisian campaign of 1943. "The Way Ahead" shows how a totally unprepared, peace-loving people was suddenly catapulted into war; how a score of widely different individuals reacted to it. Second in command of the platoon, and rating as many close-ups as the star. Billy Hartnell as Sergeant Fletcher press-es Niven for acting honors. So to single him out from the cast of 28 is to be less than fair to the others. for the general high standard of acting applies to the smallest bit perform-ance.

Direction by Carol Reed is com-petent. and undoubtedly accounts for the underlying genuiness of the pic-ture as a semi-documentary. Reed's job was made relatively easy by the solid script turned in by Eric Ambler and Peter Ustinov.

Torpedoing of the troopship en route to North Africa. followed by a hair-raising fire-fighting sequence on the doomed vessel, provides a suc-cession of thrills as a prelude to the concluding scenes as the toughened rookies come to death grips with the Germans. Their behavior wins the grudging approval of the red-coated Chelsea Pensioners. veterans of Brit-ain's earlier wars whose earlier doubt of the stamina of modern Eng-lish youth is finally proved un-founded.

Apasionadamente
("Apasionata")
(ARGENTINA-MADE)
Buenos Aires, May 18.

Argentina Sono Film production and re-lease. Stars Pedro Lopez Lagar and Zully Moreno; features Susana Dupre, Rafael Frontaura, E. Chaico, Mauricio Castel, J. J. Pinelro. Directed by Luis Cesar Amadori. Story by Enrique Vico; camera, Antonio Merayo. At Ocean, Buenos Aires. Running time, 115 MINS.

Producers of this apparently sought to curry favor with authorities on whose goodwill they rely for raw stock. by building story around beau-ties of the Argentine lake district, considered by some better than Switzerland.

In case this avid display of scenery might pall on femme-minded Argen-tinos, Zully Moreno, a looker, adds numerous poses to backgrounds of lake and mountain. wearing a whole gamut of unsuitable costumes—in-cluding what passed for a sarong.

Tear-jerker yarn centers round taciturn painter (Lopez Lagar) whose care for paralytic daughter keeps him from arms of supposedly rich and certainly frivolous socialite (Zully Moreno). Susana Dupre's playing of paralytic moppet is high-light of picture. Theme song of story and reason for film tag is Beethoven's "Appasionata." Lopez Lagar gives customary competent performance. Story is overly melodramatic and di-rection uneven. Photography shows signs of developing technique. but sequences are badly put together. in-cluding such bad mistakes as girl en-tering a telephone booth in one cos-tume and exiting in another.

Miniature Reviews

"An American Romance" (Color) (M-G). Brian Don-levy and King Vidor have smash b.o. winner.

"Youth Runs Wild," (RKO). Feeble addition to the juve de-linquency cycle. Poor dualer.

"Hotel Reserve" (RKO) (Brit). Run-of-mill whodunit.

"Law Men" (Mono). Enter-taining hoss-opera dualer.

"We've Come a Long, Long Way." Negro documentary suit-able for colored houses.

"Johnny Doesn't Live Here Any More" (Mono). Merry comedy on overcrowded Wash-ington should ring bell in duals.

"Welcome Mr. Washington" (Anglo-Am.). British meller about Yank troops in England; thin possibilities for U. S.

"The Amazing Mr. Forrest" (PRC) (British-Made). Detec-tive fiction of an inferior quality.

"Another Dawn" (Mex). Gang-ster meller lacking sufficient action; Spanish-language houses only.

"Goyescas" (Spanish). Elabor-ate costume piece (with English titles) should please regular Spanish filmgoers.

"En Morenita Clara" (Mex). Evita Munoz makes a humdrum yarn a neat comedy; child star looks to be a find.

An American Romance
(TECHNICOLOR)

Metro release of King Vidor production. directed by Vidor. Stars Brian Donlevy; features Ann Richards, Walter Abel, John Qualen, Horace McNally. Screenplay, Her-bert Dalmas and William Ludwig, based on story by Vidor; score, Louis Gruenberg; editor, Conrad A. Nervig; camera, Harold Rosson. Tradeshown, projection room, N.Y., June 16, '44. Running time, 151 MINS.
Steve Dangos................Brian Donlevy
Anna.........................Ann Richards
Howard Clinton................Walter Abel
Anton Dubechek..............John Qualen
Teddy Dangos..............Horace McNally

Despite the fact that there is little marquee strength in the person of several proven name stars in this picture. "An American Romance" is bound to create a storm of contro-versy. based upon its plot and gen-eral treatment of labor vs. capital. So much so that this romantic drama, on the basis of that impetus, should garner topflight grosses wher-ever exhibited.

One of Metro's greatest efforts (execs state that the picture was two years in the making and cost over $3,000,000). this film will zoom Brian Donlevy into the constellations as one of Hollywood's most important actors. It's his baby from opening to closing, and his performance as the Czech immigrant who runs the gamut from poverty to become a wealthy industrialist, is one of the most understandable. warm and neatly woven portrayals to hit the screen in many a moon.

King Vidor's story, coupled with his forthright direction and the excellent acting. are assets that add up to a winning total. The one fault with "Romance" is that it is much too long in the telling. A tightening-up process, in which at least 40 minutes of the 151-minute runoff is eliminated. would aid this romantic narrative immeasurably.

Yarn takes more than an hour to get down to business. During that hour, true, Vidor lays the setting for the rest of the film, showing how Donlevy. who is held up at Ellis Island on landing in America because he did not own the equivalent of $25 in U. S. money, overcomes this pov-erty by hard work in the Mesabi iron ore pits of Minnesota, and meets the girl whom he is to marry (Ann Richards). Donlevy, eager to learn the modes and history of America, also takes advantage of the fact that she is a schoolteacher, delving into the chemistry of steel-making and the functions of industry.

With this background, Donlevy makes his way to a large city in the industrial midwest, and works his way up to foreman of a section of a steel mill. He sends for his fiancee in Minnesota, they wed, and have five children. Meanwhile, he begins the manufacture of autos. Through the aid of funds of his cousin Anton (John Qualen) and the business acumen of his partner (Walter Abel), all this soon results in the success of the business.

However, the men working in the auto plant wish to organize a union, and Donlevy's son joins with them in their demands. A confirmed individ-ualist, Donlevy refuses to give in to their demands, and so, when his board of directors votes to settle a three-month strike by acceding, he retires from the firm. In the end, though. Donlevy comes out of retire-ment to take over the outfit's new airplane building plant in California.

Photographed in beautiful Techni-color. this romantic drama is notable for the documented montage shots of the intricate mining and shipping of iron ore; the making of steel in the huge mills of the midwest; films showing the way autos are made, and the excellent details of airplane-making.

Once "Romance" starts moving, it proves to be a mighty appealing pic-ture. The support given Donlevy by Miss Richards, Walter Abel and John Qualen adds much to the enjoyment of the film, especially the job done by Abel.

Vidor hasn't had a tremendous winner in a long time. This vehicle may well be the one to again estab-lish him at the pinnacle of the pro-ducer-director ladder. With the ap-parently unlimited budget allowed him by Metro, and the fine camera work of Harold Rosson, Vidor has turned out a likable film that is going to create much discussion, all to its advantage at the b.o.   Sten.

Youth Runs Wild

RKO release of Val Lewton production. Features Bonita Granville, Kent Smith, Jean Brooks. Glenn Vernon and Tessa Brind. Directed by Mark Robson. Screen-play. John Fante; original, Fante and Her-bert Kline; camera, John J. Mescall; editor, John Lockert. Tradeshown in N. Y., June 21. '44. Running time, 67 MINS.
Teddy......................Bonita Granville
Danny.....................Kent Smith
Mary.....................Jean Brooks
Frank....................Glenn Vernon
Sarah Taylor.................Tessa Brind
Mr. Taylor..................Ben Bard
Mrs. Hauser...............Mary Servoss
Mr. Dunlop................Arthur Shields
Duncan..................Lawrence Tierney
Georgie Dunlop.............Dickie Moore
Herb Vigero..............Johnny Walsh
Rocky...................Rod Rodgers
Mrs. Taylor.............Elizabeth Russell

"Youth Runs Wild" is another film on juvenile delinquency, a feeble sermon that fails to provide much entertainment. A dualer.

Story follows a familiar, obvious pattern of kids running around in jalopies, frequenting roadhouses, slipping into crime as the means to a little spending money or excite-ment. It is, as usual, an indictment against careless or indifferent par-ents.

The producers have cast some at-tractive youngsters for the film and given it a nice production. But it's a naive approach, with stilted dialog, stodgy direction and an amateurish script. Glenn Vernon and Tessa Brind, as the teen-age leads, are wholesome and appealing. Bonita Granville gives a convincing per-formance as a wayward gal, and Jean Brooks is plausible in a big-sister role. But the other characters are undistinguished.   Bron.

Hotel Reserve
(BRITISH-MADE)

London, June 1.

RKO Radio production and release. Stars Lucie Mannheim, James Mason. Directed by Victor Hanbury, Lance Comfort, Max Greene. Screenplay by John Davenport from novel by Eric Ambler; camera, Max Greene. At Rialto, London, June 1, '44. Running time, 89 MINS.

Peter Vadassy.......James Mason
Suzanne Koche.......Lucie Mannheim
Robert Duclos.......Raymond Lovell
Monsieur Beghin.......Julien Mitchell
Mary Skelton.......Clare Hamilton
Herr Walter Vogel.......Martin Miller
Andre Roux.......Herbert Lom
Emil Schimler.......Frederick Valk
Chemist.......Ivor Barnard
Walter Skelton.......Valentine Dyall
Odette Roux.......Patricia Medina
Henri Asticot.......David Ward
Hilda Vogel.......Hella Kurty
Major Clandon Hartley.......Anthony Shaw
Police Commissaire.......Lawrence Hanray
Jacqueline.......Patricia Hayes

This pre-war thriller about French counter-espionage methods against Nazi agents is a run-of-the-mill whodunit, not rating real consideration as a first-run draw even in British communities where James Mason and Lucie Mannheim mean something. In spite of this, if and when it is seen by American talent scouts, "Hotel Reserve" may prove of interest as the picture in which Herbert Lom was "found."

In what seems a subordinate role during first of picture, this British film actor treats his more than seductive bride with all the heavy-lidded indifference which has made Charles Boyer popular. In later sequences, as he begins to merge as the central character of the spy plot, young Lom turns on the heat as a menace. If wartime conditions prevent Hollywood from grabbing him, Lom looms large as Britain's boxoffice bet. The Riviera the summer before the war provides a background against which holiday makers find themselves enmeshed in the spy hunt conducted by an unconventionally tough officer of French Naval Intelligence (played in stolid English style by Julien Mitchell). Suspicion, directed first against an Austrian medical student, gradually extends to all of the patrons of the Hotel Reserve.

As the young Austrian, James Mason is convincing as a completely bemused innocent. Lucie Mannheim as Madame Koche, charming hostess of the hotel, succeeds in making her secret love affair with Emil Schimler, one of her guests, disguised enough to keep one guessing up to the climax. Of the others, Patricia Medina, as Lom's scorned bride, is comely and has curvaceous figure, and looks a future bet.

Direction is as undistinguished as the production generally. Background music by the London Symphony orchestra lends a welcome distinction.

Law Men

Monogram production and release. Features Johnny Mack Brown, Raymond Hatton. Directed by Lambert Hillyer. Story and screenplay, Glenn Tryon; camera, Harry Neuman; editor, John Fuller; music director, Edward Kay. At New York theatre, N. Y., week of June 21, '44, dual. Running time, 55 MINS.

Nevada.......Johnny Mack Brown
Sandy.......Raymond Hatton
Phyllis.......Jan Wiley
Clyde Miller.......Kirby Grant
Bradford.......Robert Frazer
Slade.......Edmund Cobb
Gus.......Art Fowler
Hayner.......Harry F. Price
Killifer.......Marshall Reed
Auntie Mac.......Isabel Withers
Simmons.......Ben Corbett
Curley.......Ted Mapes
Wilson.......Steve Clark
Hardy.......Bud Osborne

Possessing several ingredients for an exciting western, "Law Men" emerges as a fairly entertaining double-bill pleaser for the hoss-opera coterie.

Yarn has U. S. marshals Johhny Mack Brown and Raymond Hatton arriving secretly in town to investigate various bank and stage holdups. Hatton sets himself up as a shoemaker, and Brown manages to join the gang committing the robberies. After numerous chenanigans they corral the outlaws and unmask the real leader.

Starring team works smoothly, as usual. Brown is properly convincing and Hatton is amusing. Other cast members are good, with the gal, Jan Wiley, a looker.

We've Come a Long, Long Way
(DOCUMENTARY)

Negro Marches On release of Jack Goldberg production. Narration by Elder L. S. Michaux. At World, N. Y., week of June 24, '44. Running time, 67 MINS.

A factual film tracing the rise of the American Negro during the past 75 years, "We've Come a Long, Long Way" is outright propaganda of the best variety—to bring about the realization by others that this race has as much at stake in the winning of the war by the Allies as any other.

But as a picture, its production values are negligible, its sound track at times inaudible, and its cohesion disjointed. It tries to do too much in too short a time.

Comprised chiefly of newsreel and montage shots of Negro leaders in all fields; colleges and schools which have done much for race uplift; personalities in the armed forces and the political world; and battle scenes showing colored troops and sailors in action, this picture uses too many sequences which have already been flashed on screens before to tell its story.

Notable, however, is a lively musical score featuring the world-famed "Happy Am I" choir. A full-sized symphony orch was also used to provide the musical background. Narration by Elder Lightfoot Solomon Michaux is well-written and interestingly done by the pastor of the "church on the banks of the Potomac" in the nation's capital.

Sten.

Johnny Doesn't Live Here Any More

Monogram release of Maurice and Franklin King production. Stars Simone Simon, James Ellison, William Terry; features Minna Gombel, Chick Chandler, Alan Dinehart. Directed by Joe May. Screenplay, Philip Yordan, John H. Kafka, from original by Alice Means Reeve; score, W. Franke Harling; editor, Martin G. Cohn; camera, Ira Morgan. At Fox, Brooklyn, N. Y., June 23, '44. Running time, 77 MINS.

Kathie.......Simone Simon
Mike.......James Ellison
Johnny.......William Terry
Mrs. Collins.......Minna Gombell
Jack.......Chick Chandler
Judge.......Alan Dinehart
Sally.......Gladys Blake
Jeff.......Robert Mitchum
Irene.......Dorothy Grainger
George.......Grady Sutton
Mr. Collins.......Chester Clute
Shrew.......Fern Emmett
Gremlin.......Jerry Maren
Gladys.......Janet Shaw

Overcrowded Washington comes in for another lampooning in this release which should do okay biz in the duals. Continuity romps at merry pace, sprinkling many laughs along the way either via dialog or screwy situations.

William Terry has been inducted, so he turns his former menage over to Simone Simon, forgetting he had previously given keys to a number of buddies to drop in and stay when in the Capitol City. It develops that Terry's place topped Baldpate in distribution of keys, and when the gang carrying them, mostly pals also in service, barge in, the gal is at wit's end what to do. Along comes James Ellison, a likeable gob who nearly makes her forget all about Terry. After many comic didoes there is a free-for-all for attentions of the gal and they all land before Alan Dinehart, as judge, who sets everything aright before fadeout.

Miss Simon is likeable, although a trifle lightweight as the gal, with her male supporters, principally Terry and Ellison, practically running away with the pic. Dinehart gives his usual good account as the judge, with Chick Chandler and Minna Gombel also turning in good performances. Joe May's direction is keyed in fast tempo keeping it at merry pace. Scenarists have done nifty job on screenplay, with camera work of Ira Morgan also on the okay side.

Edba.

Welcome, Mr. Washington
(BRITISH-MADE)

London, May 18.

Anglo-American Film Corp. release of British National Film. Features Barbara Mullen, Donald Stewart. Directed by Leslie Hiscott. Screenplay by Jack Whittingham from original story by Noel Streatfield. Camera, Gerald Gibbs, Gerald Moss. At Studio One, London, May 18. Running time, 95 MINS.

Jane Willoughby.......Barbara Mullen
Lieut. Johnny Grant.......Donald Stewart
Sarah Willoughby.......Peggy Cummins
Captain Abbott.......Leslie Bradley
Selby.......Roy Emerton
Miss Finch.......Martita Hunt
Murphy.......Arthur Sinclair
Albert.......Graham Moffat
Millie.......Shelagh Frazer
Martha.......Beatrice Varley
Publican.......George Carney
Katherine Willoughby.......Louise Lord
Vernon.......Paul Blake
Mrs. Curley.......Drusilla Wills

Hardships suffered by British country folk when American troops came in is the keynote of this latest in the series of hands-across-the-seas films. Main title tips what it is all about, GI's volunteering at the last moment to reap the harvest and save the community before the time limit set for demolition of farm houses to clear the way for a huge airdrome. Even before this happens it seems as if the Yanks had earned a welcome. If it gets distribution in U. S., it looks to have only limited possibilities for nabes.

As with "A Canterbury Tale," this British National offering is cinematography at its best. Bishop's Knole, a stately mansion, is the scene of a greater part of the action. Leslie Hiscott's direction, if conventional, is worthy of the "original story" by Noel Streatfield, who is daring enough to make the villain of the piece an English farmer stalking through the plot with the menace of a Boris Karloff.

Acting honors go to Peggy Cummins, who walks away with the picture in a role in which a less clever child would win scant recognition. The co-stars, Barbara Mullen and Donald Stewart, struggle valiantly as conventional as they are unconvincing. Stewart, as a U. S. Army lieutenant, is confronted with the hopeless task of being every inch the hero. As his superior officer, Leslie Bradley, not so handicapped by script, gives a more convincing portrayal.

Amazing Mr. Forrest
(BRITISH-MADE)

PRC release of Jack Buchanan production. Features E. E. Horton, Otto Kruger, Jack Buchanan, Jack LaRue. Directed by Thornton Freeland. Story and adaptation, Ralph Spence; editor, E. B. Jarvis; camera, Claude Friese-Greene. At New York, N. Y., week June 13, '44. Running time, 71 MINS.

Treadwell.......Edward Everett Horton
Mike Chadwick.......Otto Kruger
John Forrest.......Jack Buchanan
Alberni.......Jack La Rue
Alice Forrest.......Georgie Withers
Younce.......Syd Walker
Beretti.......David Burns
Prince Homouska.......Walter Rilla
Charles Cartwright.......Charles Carson
Harper.......Leslie Perrins
Spider Ferris.......Ronald Shiner

A mixture of American and British film talent figured in the production of this one, which was made in England some time ago but is now just getting release on this side. That its acceptance for sale in the American market has been delayed is not surprising since the picture is feeble entertainment. Only for the smaller runs.

"The Amazing Mr. Forrest" was produced by the English star, Jack Buchanan, who plays the title role of an insurance company investigator and runs down a ring of jewel thieves. Not only is the script trite but the attempt at comedy misses badly. It's an example of the British sense of humor at its worst.

Artists from the States in the cast include Edward Everett Horton, playing a butler and getting nowhere. Otto Kruger, racketeer nightclub owner, who's all right, and Jack LaRue, his triggerman who never showed to poorer advantage. Georgie Withers (English) is the wife of Buchanan and okay though far from outstanding. A derby-hatted detective is done suitably by Syd Walker, while Ronald Shiner is a good character as a dip. Others are lesser.

Char.

Distinto Amanecer
("Another Dawn")
(MEXICAN-MADE)

Filma Mundiales production and release. Stars Pedro Armendariz, Andrea Palma. Directed by Julio Bracho. At Belmont, N. Y., week June 9, '44. Running time, 108 MINS.

Julieta.......Andrea Palma
Octavio.......Pedro Armendariz
Ignacio.......Alberto Galan
Ruiz.......Octavio Martinez
Juanito.......Narciso Basquets
Don Santos.......Felipe Montoya

(In Spanish; No English Titles)

It had to happen ultimately—a Mexican-produced gangster meller with henchmen, crooked cafe operators, the comely femme habitue and familiar trappings a la Americano. "Another Dawn" is a fairly workmanlike effort despite the persistent Mexican film-maker habit of dragging out the dialog and forgetting the action. Aside from this, film has suspense, excellent camera work, sound direction by Julio Bracho and two deft performances by Andrea Palma and Pedro Armendariz. Okay for Spanish-language theatres or arty houses when given English titles.

Assassination of a labor leader brings two gangs into a race to obtain important official documents (never clear just what's in them). Armendariz is the dapper gunman aide to the slain laborite, and he carries on to save the valuable papers. In the meantime, he meets a former sweetheart, Miss Palma, now unhappily wed to Ignacio (Alberto Galan). The old romance between Armendariz and Palma flares again. He nearly elopes with her, but winds up using her as a stooge. Showdown scene in nightclub could have been lifted from any number of U. S. gangster films.

There's an episode where Miss Palma confronts her femme rival, latter attired only in unmentionables, that would bring Haysian eyebrow lifting even though obviously considerably trimmed for N. Y. consumption.

Andrea Palma's languid acting reminds of Dietrich, with her whole makeup apparently patterned after that actress. She shows possibilities. Pedro Armendariz, as the laborite's henchman in love with Miss Palma, is one of the more vigorous Mexican screen actors judging from this performance. Alberto Galan is capable in the role of Miss Palma's hubby. Supporting cast is as little known to American audiences, but adequate.

Wear.

Goyescas
("After Goya")
(SPANISH-MADE)

RKO release of Universal Ibero-Americana De Cinematografia production. Stars Imperio Argentina; features Rafael Rivelles, Armando Calvo, Ramon Martori, Jose Latorre. Directed by Benito Perojo. Music, Enrique Granados; camera, Michel Kelber; dances, Vincente Escudero; settings, Sig-fred Burmann. At World, N. Y., June 2, '44. Runn'-; time, 97 MINS.

Petrilla..................Imperio Argentina
Countess de Gualda.....Imperio Argentina
Capt. Fernando Pizarro.....Rafael Rivelles
Don Luis Alfonso..........Armando Calvo
Mayor of the Town.........Ramon Martori
Minister Godoy................Jose Latorre
The Queen.........................Eloisa Muro
Paquiro, the Matador........Antonio Casas
Innkeeper..................Manuel Requena
Second Innkeeper............Manuel Moran
Pepa...............................Marta Flores
Patillas, the Outlaw............Juan Calvo
El Malagueno, 2nd Outlaw..Antonio Bayon

(In Spanish; English Titles)

Made in Spain three years ago, this elaborate costume piece reveals the great shortcomings of Spanish film production which, if it were to compete with U. S. pix in the Latin-American market on technical excellence alone rather than culturally, would fall far behind Yank product. However, the film has a certain grace and charm to recommend it and should garner fair grosses in Spanish-language houses.

Based on the celebrated opera by Enrique Granados which was inspired by the paintings of Goya, which it closely follows, the picture is laid in 19th century Spain, recounting the tale of two women who resemble each other, one a bold singer, the other a capricious countess, both in love with the same man.

Vividly characterizing the Spain of that period, with its decadent aristocracy and the squalor and misery of its people, the story unfolds to the music of the famous "Intermezzo" from the opera played by the Madrid Symphony Orchestra and features the lilting dances of that period.

Imperio Argentina contributes much to the picture in her dual role, displaying a fine voice and dramatic ability, carrying the film along practically singlehandedly, with the others assisting satisfactorily, but the whole thing is marred by poor sound transmission and photography.

En Morenita Clara
("The Little Brunette")
(MEXICAN-MADE)

Clasa Studios production and release. Stars Evita Munoz; features Margarita Mora, Arturo Soto Rangel, Adelina Vehl. Directed by Joselito Rodrigues. At Belmont, N. Y., week June 2, '44. Running time, 104 MINS.

Chichita.............................Evita Munoz
Soledad........................Margarita Mora
Don Juan...............Arturo Soto Rangel
Dona Carmen......................Adelina Vehl
And Victor Urruchua, Edward Arozamena, and Manuel Noriega.

(In Spanish; No English Titles)

Diminutive Evita Munoz, star of this nicely made Mexican production, looms as the best potentiality to come thus far from Mexico City as far as concerns American films. Appearing about five years old, this tot really makes "The Little Brunette" jell. She reminds of Shirley Temple, achieving top rating through her own thespic ability. Picture, itself, looks okay for Spanish-language houses and arty theatres though in the latter it will require English titles.

Story does not represent much. Basically, it's the venerable one about the precocious child who wins over her harsh grandfather. In this case, said child is the daughter of Soledad, a gypsy, who wed the old man's son before he left for the U. S. This son is killed in an accident, which gives the excuse to bring the child and ultimately her gypsy mother into grandad Don Juan's home. Don Juan's other son, villain of yarn, attempts to break up this peaceful atmosphere in hopes of gaining his dad's fortune.

Little Evita, as the gypsy's daughter, is thoroughly captivating. Surrounding cast is standard for productions made in Mexico City, but dwarfed by this youngster's bright performance. Joselito Rodriguez directed fairly well, but has left in too many wordy scenes. *Wear.*

The Mummy's Ghost

Universal release of Ben Pivar production. Stars Lon Chaney; features John Carradine, Ramsay Ames, Barton MacLane, George Zucco, Robert Lowery. Directed by Reginald Le Borg. Screenplay, Griffin Jay, Henry Sucher, Brenda Weisberg; original, Jay and Sucher; camera, William Sickner; editor, Saul Goodkind. At Rialto, N. Y., June 30, '44. Running time, 60 MINS.

Kharis............................Lon Chaney
Yousef.........................John Carradine
Tom Hervey....................Robert Lowery
Amina...........................Ramsay Ames
Inspector Walgreen........Barton MacLane
High Priest....................George Zucco
Prof. Norman..................Frank Reicher
Sheriff.........................Harry Shannon

"The Mummy's Ghost" contains the usual stock ingredients of the horror-thriller. But careful direction keeps the suspense sustained, and a good production and plausible performances help make the film satisfactory entertainment. A good dualer.

Juxtaposition of ancient tombs of Egypt and prosaic midwest college town aid in giving the film plausibility as well as interest. Yarn concerns the remains of Princess Ananka, which were taken from Egypt to America. The Princess had been punished 3,000 years ago for loving one Kharis, a subject beneath her. Kharis' punishment has been to be kept alive in mummified form, to guard the Princess' tomb. Balance of film shows Kharis' attempts to return the Princess' incarnation, ending in a weird finish reminiscent of a famed incident in "Lost Horizon."

Lon Chaney has a weird but effective getup as Kharis, and his limping figure barging through the countryside makes good drama. John Carradine acts a modern-day Egyptian priest with plausible understatement, and George Zucco is persuasive as the high priest. Ramsay Ames is unusually attractive as the unfortunate reincarnation of the Princess, and Robert Lowery is appealing as the boy friend. *Bron.*

Law of the Saddle

PRC release of Sigmund Neufeld production. Stars Bob Livingston, features Al (Fuzzy) St. John, Betty Miles, Lane Chandler, John Elliott. Directed by Melville De Lay. Story and adaptation, Fred Myton; editor, Holbrook N. Todd; camera, Robert Cline. At New York, N. Y., dual, week June 27, '43. Running time, 60 MINS.

Rocky Cameron.............Bob Livingston
Fuzzy Jones...........Al (Fuzzy) St. John
Gayle...............................Betty Miles
Steve Kinney.................Lane Chandler
Dan Kirby........................John Elliott
Dave...............................Reed Howes
Joe..............................Curly Dresden
Bart................................Al Ferguson
Vic.................................Frank Ellis

Routine western, but one which has sufficient action to please the average follower of this type of fare. Running time is short enough at 59 minutes to make the picture a convenient fit for double bills.

Bob Livingston, starred, plays a wanderer whose specialty appears to be that of rounding up rustlers and other baddies of the plains. In this case he's called in to get the goods on a crooked sheriff, who moves from town to town with a gang of looters and highwaymen, using the expedient of getting himself elected constable as a coverup. Livingston, however, is on to the sheriff's game, and finally corners him for a kill. He has as his steady aid the wizened prairie-country character, Al (Fuzzy) St. John, who supplies comedy relief. The girl is the daughter of a rancher who gets bumped off. She's a personable young lady, Betty Miles, who might graduate from westerns ultimately.

Lane Chandler makes a good heavy as the conniving sheriff, while John Elliott does well as his first lieutenant. Lessers include Reed Howes, Curley Dresden, Al Ferguson and Frank Ellis. *Char.*

Miniature Reviews

"Take It or Leave It" (Songs) (20th). Lightweight but engaging film, with songs, okay for the summer trade.

"Forty Thieves" (UA). Another "Hopalong Cassidy" hoss opry starring William Boyd, an actionful saddler for duals.

"Mr. Winkle Goes to War" (Col.) Edward G. Robinson in strong dualer.

"Medal for the General" (British-made). British kids in this put it over; appears to have nice possibilities for America.

"El Globo de Cantolia" (Clasa) (Mex). Good comedy starring Mapy Cortes, with songs, but no English subtitles.

"His Best Pupil" (Argentine). Lucas Demare's best film and one of top ones from Argentine; may attract in U. S.

Take It Or Leave It
(SONGS)

20th-Fox release of Bryan Foy production. Stars Phil Baker; features Phil Silvers, Edward Ryan, Marjorie Massow, Stanley Prager. Directed by Benjamin Stoloff. Screenplay, Harold Buchman, Snag Werris, Mac Benoff; camera, Joseph LaShelle, Fred Sersen; editor, Harry Reynolds; music, Emil Newman; songs, divers sources. Tradeshown July 10, '44. Running time, 70 MINS.

Phil Baker..............................Himself
Phil Silvers.............................Himself
Eddie...........................Edward Ryan
Kate Collins..................Marjorie Massow
Herb Gordon..................Stanley Prager
Dr. Edward Preston.............Roy Gordon
Miss Burke......................Nana Bryant
Program Director..........Carleton Young
Secretary.......................Ann Corcoran
Mrs. Preston....................Nella Walker
Mrs. Bramble....................Renie Riano
Taxi Driver.......................Frank Jenks
Truck Driver.......................B. S. Pully

Phil Baker's "Take It or Leave It" film version is no $64 question when it comes to plot. However, it's OK summer film fare.

It's a loose affair which adequately rides the crest of Baker's radio program and, as put together, it's a curious blend of naive yet effective cinematic divertissement. The manner in which a dozen clips from past Fox and Joe Schenck film productions have been intertwined is a skillful and audience-arresting device to make the film fan participate in the quiz show.

Baker emcees the unreeling of a series of highlight scenes from 20th-Fox filmusicals—Henie, Grable-Faye, Nicholas Bros., Ink Spots, Wiere Bros., Ritz Bros., Dixie Dunbar, Jolson, Buster Keaton, et al. [The Jolson excerpt is from an old Joe Schenck (UA) production.] Thus is derived the ballyhoo of the "27 surprise stars," an excellent merchandizing stunt.

Plot is sympathetically hung on Edward Ryan, nervous young gob, who needs $1,000 for the fancy baby specialist. He and Stanley Prager have just shipped in. Marjorie Massow, as Ryan's young wife, is winsome as the mother-to-be.

When young Ryan takes her and his shipmate Prager to Baker's Take-It-or-Leave-It broadcast, and he participates, the $64 prize is rung up into several hundred as Baker recognizes that the young U. S. seaman will need more than the usual $64 jackpot to meet expenses. Ryan had picked "scenes from famous movies" as his category, which is excuse for the film-within-a-film unreeling.

Thus follow the succession of filmusical excerpts. They're well paced and spaced, with variety and novelty all the way. In fact, the audience-appeal is patent from the general attitude of "now, what is the name of that picture" approach. Incidentally, proof of how ephemeral is the average filmusical's impact is evidenced as the sundry clips unreel. Pictures of two years ago are as foggy in identification as that old Jolson and Buster Keaton clip.

Of the cast, Phil Silvers is in for a bit and B. S. Pully, lammister from the 52d street (N. Y.) niteries, does OK in a bit as the stumblebum truck driver who collects his $1 and refuses to take a chance on a deuce.

Baker, of course, could have telephoned his stuff over. He's himself, an affable conferencier, doing a celluloid version of his broadcast. But the real story line motivates around the shore-leave sailors and their concern in getting the best baby doctor for Miss Massow. She does an okay job, as does Ryan, while in Stanley Prager, 20th-Fox has an excellent comedy potential. *Abel.*

Forty Thieves

United Artists release of Harry E. Sherman production. Stars William Boyd; features Andy Clyde, Jimmy Rogers, Douglas Dumbrille, Louise Currie, Kirk Alyn. Directed by Lesley Selander. Screenplay, Michael Wilson, Bernie Kamins; based on characters created by Clarence E. Mulford. At New York theatre, N. Y., week of July 4, '44. Running time, 60 MINS.

Hopalong Cassidy................William Boyd
California Carlson...................Andy Clyde
Jimmy Rogers.....................Jimmy Rogers
Tad Hammond...............Douglas Dumbrille
Katherine Reynolds.............Louise Currie
Jerry Doyle............................Kirk Alyn
Buck Peters................Herbert Rawlinson
Judge Reynolds..................Robert Frazer
Ike Simmons.......................Glenn Stran
Sam Garms..........................Jack Rockw
Joe Garms..........................Bob Kortman

This recent "Hopalong Cassidy" western should satisfy the oater fans for okay returns on the duals.

This time, William Boyd, as Hopalong, is sheriff of Butteville, has cleaned up town, but election's coming up again and the bad 'uns ankle back hoping to install Kirk Alyn, tavern keeper and weakling, into Boyd's office by keeping honest landowners away from the polls. Boyd is defeated, and when he finds Alyn is controlled by the lawless, he takes over on his own and again cleans up the town.

Boyd gives his usually good performance Andy Clyde grabs laughs as Boyd's comedic assistant. Jimmy Rogers and Louise Currie are okay as the romantics. Alyn and Douglas Dumbrille make themselves sufficiently despicable as the menaces. Rest of cast does okay in lesser roles while Lesley Selander's direction packs plenty of action. *Edba.*

Mr. Winkle Goes to War

Hollywood, July 11.

Columbia release of Jack Moss production. Stars Edward G. Robinson; features Ruth Warrick, Ted Donaldson, Richard Lane, Robert Armstrong, Bob Haymes. Directed by Alfred E. Green. Screenplay, Waldo Salt, George Corey and Louis Solomon, from novel by Theodore Pratt; editor, Richard Fantl; camera, Joseph Walker. Previewed in Hollywood July 10, '44. Running time, 78 MINS.

Wilbert Winkle......Edward G. Robinson
Amy Winkle.......................Ruth Warrick
Barry............................Ted Donaldson
Jack Pettigrew...................Bob Haymes
Sgt. "Alphabet"..................Richard Lane
Joe Tinker...................Robert Armstrong
Ralph Westcott.................Richard Gaines
Plummer..........................Walter Baldwin
McDavid...............................Art Smith
Martha Pettigrew...........Ann Shoemaker
A. B. Simkins....................Paul Stanton
Johnson..........................Buddy Yarus
Captain.........................William Forrest
Gladys..........................Bernadine Hayes

"Mr. Winkle Goes to War" takes a case history among the over-38s drafted into Army service in early 1942 to weave a moderately interesting tale. Edward G. Robinson's marquee voltage is necessary to hold this one as a top-biller; otherwise it's a strong dualer.

Robinson is a self-conscious bank clerk tied down to a desk and figures. Actually, he's more inclined to mechanics and gadgets. His resignation at the bank to open a fix-it shop creates a conflict with his wife, but an induction notice and his entry into the Army change the entire course of his life.

He gradually loses his hypochondriac and milque-toast tendencies, shuns an Army desk job for the mechanical division of ordnance and struggles through combat training. On a Pacific island he repairs a bulldozer during a Jap raid to emerge a casualty and a hero for the return home and happy launching of his repair shop.

The dramatic narrative has several amusing situations neatly interwoven and lightly displayed, mainly through the direction of Al Green, but the script follows a standard path with little originality.

Robinson competently handles the title role, getting okay support from Ruth Warrick, Richard Lane, Robert Armstrong and Bob Haymes. Latter sings a brief chorus of "Sweet Genevieve," with Robinson, Lane and Armstrong completing the soldier quartet. Young Ted Donaldson is spotlighted as an orphan pal of Robinson interested in assisting in the shop. The lad continues to manifest talent and personality.

Picture makes use of Pacific island invasion clips for combat sequences, together with a staged battle between the Army and Japs. Photography is good. *Walt.*

Medal for the General
(BRITISH-MADE)
London, June 21.

Anglo-American Film Corporation release of British National film. Stars Godfrey Tearle, Jeanne de Casalis. Directed by Maurice Elvey. Screenplay by Elizabeth Baron. Camera, James Wilson, Arthur Grant. At Rialto, London, June 21. Running time, 100 MINS.

General Church	Godfrey Tearle
Lady Frome	Jeanne de Casalis
Bates	Morland Graham
Mrs. Bates	Mabel Constanduros
McNab	John Laurie
Dr. Sargeant	Patrick Curwen
Lord Ottershaw	Michael Lambart
Mrs. Farnsworth	Irene Handl
Snarrer	Maureen Glynne
Harry	Gerald Moore
Limpy	Brian Weske
Irma	Petula Clarke
Bobby	David Trickett
Violet	Pat Geary
Andrew	Thorley Walters
Hank	Alec Faversham
Billeting Officer	Rosalyn Boulter

English reverence of everything ancient has always operated to the hopeless disadvantage of youth on the stage and in pictures. "Medal for the General" gives six London kids a chance to show what they can do. They turn in individual performances as good as the best the "Dead End" kids ever did. These youngsters may make this film appeal to U. S. market, in almost any house.

British National doesn't star these kids in their early teens; not even featuring them. Godfrey Tearle and Jeanne de Casalis get top billing, with Morland Graham, Mabel Constanduros and John Laurie grabbing support credits.

Maurice Elvey's direction measures up to the high standard of Elizabeth Baron's excellent adaptation of the novel by James Ronald, on which "Medal for the General" is based. Picture is notable for the bright editing by Grace Garland.

Production values are outstanding, scenes in the War Office and a military club bearing the hall mark of authenticity. The General's country house, where the greater part of the story is unfolded, is as modern as a Hollywood star's beach bungalow. Incidentally, in the 1939 sequences, American housewives will find their own servant problem the more maddening as they see the staff of domestics—butler, cook, and three "upstairs" maids.

War Office red tape comes in for outspoken ribbing, while the comic pomposity of Civil Defense officials in the first days of formation is treated in the same way. Refusal of all these outfits to make use of the old general's services makes understandable his cancelling his news-

paper subscriptions and scrapping his radio, proofs of his determination to shut his mind to the war. If his turning recluse does not adequately motivate his decision to commit suicide, it at least heightens the contrast worked in him when the sextet of slum kids are billeted on him.

Of the kids, Gerald Moore, as an unregenerate guttersnipe who steals the General's medals, has a rare personality. In his scenes with Tearle this shifty-eyed Artful Dodger more than holds his own.

El Globo de Cantolla
("The Balloon of Cantella")
(MEXICAN—MADE)
(Songs)

Clasa release of Mauriele de la Serna production. Stars Mapy Cortes, Jose Cibrian; features Prudencia Grifell, Fernando Cortes, Agustin Isunza. Directed by G. Martinez Solares. At belmont, N.Y. week of July 7, '44. Running time. 100 MINS.

Luisa	Mapy Cortes
Roberto	Jose Cibrian
Angea	Josefina Martinez
Enrique	Jorge Reyes
Maria	Martha Elba
Claudio	Ramiro Gomez Kemp
Dona Eduarda	Prudencia Grifell
Don Remigio	Fernando Cortes
Fidencio	Sergio Orta
Martha	Consuelo Guerrere de Luna

(In Spanish; No English Titles)

This comedy with music is for Spanish-speaking audiences in this country. It is too bad there are no English subtitles so that the film could achieve wider distribution, because it has all the attributes of a good production.

Direction by G. Martinez Solares is especially commendable for, despite the fact that the picture unwinds in 100 minutes, there are very few dull moments. Mapy Cortes, who plays the lead, is a looker who knows how to act, giving proper treatment to her comedy lines, and playing her romantic role with understanding. Jose Cibrian, male star, and the supporting cast of some of Mexico's best actors, also do an excellent job, resulting in an all-around topflight cinema—one of the best to come from south of the Rio Grande in a long time.

Yarn deals with the trio of romances being carried on by the daughters of a Mexican family, against the wishes of their mother, who has chosen three swains for her offspring herself. The comedic ruses used by the three gents seeking their hands in marriage are surprisingly funny, and well performed. Most of the music is intertwined in the script as a suitor visualizes the type show he plans for Miss Cortes.

Musical settings are elaborate, and the film has the earmarks of being an expensive production. Seeing this one makes it understandable how Mexican-made films are beginning to give Hollywood product a strong fight for that country's playing-time. *Sten.*

Su Mejor Alumno
("His Best Pupil")
(ARGENTINE-MADE)
Buenos Aires, June 25.

AAA production and release. Stars Enrique Muino and Angel Magana; features Orestes Caviglia, Norma Castillo and Guillermo Battaglia. Directed by Lucas Demare. Story and dialog by Ulises Petit de Murat and Homero Manzi. Adapted from the book "Sarmiento" by Leopoldo Lugones, Sr.; camera, Bob Roberts. At Ambassador, Buenos Aires. Running time, 115 MINS.

This is the best Argentine film produced to date. It marks a milestone in Argentine picture production.

Lucas Demare, who was responsible for "La Guerra Gaucha," has proved that he can do it again. All associated with him in this production, based on the life of the Argentine statesman, Sarmiento, also have

done well. Should draw attention in all parts of hemisphere.

Sarmiento was perhaps Argentina's greatest statesman, educator, soldier, writer and civilizer—and a stormy character. Friend of the U. S., to which he was sent as Ambassador and from which he brought school teachers to organize Argentina's educational system, this phase of his life has not been neglected in Demare's version of his life.

Adaptation of story to screen has been most skilfully done by Manzi and Petit de Murat. Love story is faintly interwoven in remarkably good taste. Sarmiento's son lost his life at battle of Curupaity, while Sarmiento was in U. S. as Ambassador. When the statesman returned to take up Presidency of his country in succession to Bartolome Mitre, played realistically by Orestes Caviglia, the youngster was no longer there to cheer him on. Scenes are well put together and photography is good.

Muino's characterization of Sarmiento is close to unforgettable, being an uncanny reproduction of the Statesman himself. Angel Magana is superb as Sarmiento's son. *Embe.*

Miniature Reviews

"Since You Went Away" (Selznick-UA). Boffo b.o.

"Dragon Seed" (M-G). Katharine Hepburn starred in tiptop filmization of Pearl S. Buck novel. Significant film, solid b.o.

"The Seventh Cross" (M-G). Spencer Tracy starred in boxoffice drama, adapted from Anna Seghers novel.

"Wing and a Prayer" (20th). Entertainment, factual account of a carrier's mission in the war against the Japs. B.o. prospects excellent.

"Jungle Woman" (U). In the chiller groove; okay dualer.

"Minstrel Man" (Musical) (PRC). Benny Fields stands out sharply; boxoffice chances OK.

"Outlaws of Santa Fe" (Rep). Routine saddle drama aimed for the twin-billers.

"Call of the South Seas" (Rep) Routine island drama-romance; dualer.

"The Contender" (PRC). A minor dualer.

Since You Went Away

United Artists release of David O. Selznick production. Stars Claudette Colbert, Jennifer Jones, Joseph Cotten, Shirley Temple, Monty Woolley, Lionel Barrymore, Robert Walker. Directed by John Cromwell. Screenplay by Selznick from Margaret Buell Wilder's book; camera, Stanley Cortez, Lee Garmes, Jack Cosgrove, Clarence Slifer; production designed by Wm. L. Pereira; music, Max Steiner, Louis Forbes; editors, Hal C. Kern, Jas. E. Newcom, John D. Faure, Arthur Fellows, Wayland M. Hendry; prod. asst., Barbara Keon; asst. prod. mgr., Fred R. Ahern; asst. directors, Lowell J. Farrell, Edward F. Mull; dances, Marty Crail; "Together" theme, song by DeSylva, Brown & Henderson. Tradeshown July 17, '44. Running time, 152 MINS.

Cast (besides above starred): Hattie McDaniel, Jane Devlin, Lloyd Corrigan, Gordon Oliver, Agnes Moorehead, Robt. Anderson, Irving Bacon, Aileen Pringle, Chas. Williams, Wallis Clark, Nella Hart, Leomide Mostovoy, Cindy Garner, Jas. Carlisle, Cico, Chandler, John A. James, Mary Anne Durkin, Joyce Horne, Anne Gillis, Grady Sutton, Ruth Valmy, Jackie Moran, Buddy Gorman, Patricia Peters, Andrew McLaglen, Addison Richards, Geo. Lloyd, Barbara Pepper, Guy Madison, Jill Warren, Byron Foulger, Harry Hayden, Edwin Maxwell, Russell Hoyt, Loudie Claar, Don Najarian, Helen Koford, Florence Bates, Conrad Binyon, Theodore Von Eltz, Adeline de Walt Reynolds, Christopher Adams, Jimmy Dodd, Martha Outlaw, Verna Knopf, Robt. Cherry, Kirk Barron, Karl Jacobs, Cecil Ballerine, Jack Gardner, Doodles Weaver, Dorothy Adams, Jas. Westerfield, Warren Hymer, Paul Esburg, Richard C. Wood, Ralph Reed, Willard Jillson, Dorothy Mann, Peggy Maley, Robt. Johnson, Dorothy Daindridge, Shelby Bacon, Eddie Hall, Warren Burr, Lela Bliss, Eilene Janssen, Harlan Miller, Mrs. Ray Feldman, Neyle Marx, Johnny Bond, Ruth Roman, Betsy Howard, Stephen Wayne, Wm. B. Davidson, Tom Dawson, Marilyn Hare, Jonathan Hale, Walter Baldwin, Eric Sinclair, Craig Stevens, Albert Basserman, Jerry Revell, Nazimova, Jimmy Clemons, Jr., Keenan Wynn.

"Since You Went Away" is David O. Selznick's first production since "Gone With the Wind" and "Rebecca," both Academy prizewinners. This is a similar smash. It's a box-office mopup, an audience heart-tug and, in no small measure, a human document of World War II as it affects all of us. Film's dedication "to that fortress—the American Home" is inspired.

"Since You Went Away" may be viewed by some as perhaps a year late in release, but a decade hence it will still graphically mirror the emotions of USA 1943 under wartime sacrifice, love and devotion. The same captious group may also question the almost-three-hour unreeling, but retrospect will unveil much that is durable to the average film fan. It is meatier than the black-market chophouses the theme decries, and is the type of film that will get repeat trade. Being a Selznick production, and so generous in footage, it should be established pronto that "Gone With the Wind" ran almost an hour longer. And, of course, this film is not in Technicolor.

As David O. Selznick screenplayed his own production, from Mrs. Margaret Buell Wilder's book, "Since You Went Away" is a heart-warming panorama of human emotions, reflecting the usual wartime frailties of the thoughtless and the chiseler, the confusion and uncertainty of young ideals and young love, all of it projected against a panorama of utterly captivating home love and life in the wholesome American manner.

Claudette Colbert is the attractive, understanding mother of Jennifer Jones, 17, and Shirley Temple, in her earliest teens, all of whom adore their absent husband and father, Timothy, a captain off to the wars. All the emotions of "what right has an over-38 father got to leave his family and a good advertising agency post to fight a young man's war" are cannily limned. At no time is it maudlin. It is always authentic, endearing and as true-to-life as death and taxes. The father is never shown; only his photo in officer's uniform, along with closeups of other domestic memorabilia.

True, Selznick's continuity has given director John Cromwell an episodic script, but it is this narrative form which makes for so much audience-appeal. Each sequence is a closeup, a character study, a self-contained dramalet. Whether it's the cocktail lounge or the church; the hangar dance or the dining-car sequence; the convalescent ward or the steak house; the ice-cream parlor or the bowling alley; the rehabilitation ward or the shipyards; the r.r. depot or Xmas eve at the Hiltons—each and every scene is an arresting, heart-warming, ofttimes intensively soul-stirring closeup.

There is so much meat, so much contemporaneous camera portraiture it's little wonder that Selznick, Cromwell and his cutters were faced with an editing problem.

It is a film that should make the women cry with honest emotion.

It's a tough film—true—for the mothers and fathers and sisters and sweethearts, each of whom will relive their own "Since You Went Away." But it doesn't compromise with realism.

Some of these sequences may prove shockers indeed to many, but the scenes in the rehabilitation rooms, convalescent wards and psychiatrist's office bring home, realistically, how much Uncle Sam is doing to take care of his heroic nephews. The film fan who can't face this sort of cinematurgy probably ducks the newsreels for the same reason.

Productionally, the film is ultra in every respect. The stellar septet are stars all the way, and betimes hard pressed by minor bits. Joseph Cotten as the Hiltons' "best man" is capital. Monty Woolley as the captious codger turns in his usually expert performance, but Robert Walker as the shy GI shades all the males with a bellringing performance. Miss Colbert along with Jennifer Jones and Shirley Temple are dream-castings, so expert are their performances. The latter, now grown up, is a b.o. natural all over again. And Miss Jones, less monastic than in "Bernadette," is effective opposite Walker (her real-life albeit estranged husband). Not forgetting Soda, a pugnacious English bulldog who's a scene-stealer on his own. The rest of the back-of-the-camera artisans may well point to their respective credits with pride, whether it's the production design, the lensing, editing, score or whatever the technical contribution entailed. *Abel.*

Dragon Seed

Metro release of Pandro S. Berman production. Stars Katharine Hepburn, Walter Huston, Aline MacMahon, Akim Tamiroff and Turhan Bey. Directed by Jack Conway and Harold S. Bucquet. Screenplay, Marguerite Roberts and Jane Murfin, based on novel by Pearl S. Buck; camera, Sidney Wagner; special effects, Warren Newcombe; score, Herbert Stothart; editor, Harold F. Kress. Tradeshown in N. Y., July 14, '44. Running time, 145 MINS.

Jade	Katharine Hepburn
Ling Tan	Walter Huston
Ling's Wife	Aline MacMahon
Wu Lien	Akim Tamiroff
Lao Er	Turhan Bey
Lao San	Hurd Hatfield
Jap Kitchen Overseer	J. Carrol Naish
Third Cousin's Wife	Agnes Moorehead
Third Cousin	Henry Travers
Lao Ta	Robert Bice
Captain Sato	Robert Lewis
Orchid	Frances Rafferty
Wife of Wu Lien	Jacqueline De Wit
Fourth Cousin	Clarence Lung
Neighbor Shen	Paul E. Burns
Wu Sao	Anna Demetrio

In 1937 Albert Lewin completed what the late Irving Thalberg started, and so Metro had an Academy prizewinner in Pearl S. Buck's "The Good Earth." In 1944 history may be repeating itself with another Pearl Buck saga of a more contemporaneous and less idyllic China. "Dragon Seed" is a fine film in anybody's sweepstakes. It will wow 'em at the boxoffice.

China under the Jap heel; a redoubtable China tilling its soil, but later destroying its own crops rather than have them fall into Nipponese hands, looms as a beacon of hope and courage for all the civilized peoples.

As Katharine Hepburn, Walter Huston, Aline MacMahon, Akim Tamiroff, Turhan Bey, Hurd Hatfield, Frances Rafferty and all the rest of the very competent cast troupe it, they make "Dragon Seed," for all its $2\frac{1}{2}$ hours, a compelling saga. Misses Hepburn and MacMahon and Huston are especially effective histrionically, and one soon forgets Tamiroff's vodka accent in the Chinese setting.

It traces the valley of the good earth, with its peaceful inhabitants, to whom the roar of the Japs' cannons is still leagues away. But Jade (Miss Hepburn) has learned of the Nippons' evil; she learns to read, and eventually her Lao Er (Turhan Bey), her husband, is brought from petty marital jealousies into a full realization that their love must carry them beyond their village. They must help Free China remain free, and even the venerable Ling Tan (Walter Huston) and his devoted wife (Aline MacMahon) realize that turning-the-other-cheek is no way to cope with the aggressors.

As the Japs take over; as the greedy merchant (Tamiroff) collaborates and becomes the food comptroller; as the patriot brothers and cousins learn to handle arms, sabotage their occupation authorities and generally retard the militaristic might, the power of a new and greater China starts to assert itself. In Jade and Lao Er's new-born son is "Dragon Seed," the hope of the future China.

Capitally screenplayed by Marguerite Roberts and Jane Murfin, with Jack Conway and Harold S. Bucquet as directors, producer Pandro Berman has achieved an arresting film. It is almost documentary in its contemporaneous fact-presentation. But it has romance, suspense and honest emotion, for all its grim realism.

An off-screen narrator delves in and out of the screen to take up where the dramatic dialog leaves off. A soft sepia cinematography is ideal for the China wheat and rice fields. An atmospheric unobtrusive score by Herbert Stothart (who, incidentally, also did the music for "The Good Earth") is a valuable corollary here also.

"Dragon Seed' is of the same pattern which obtains in this world's present battle between the oppressors and the oppressed. The antagonists find their quislings in all races; here Akim Tamiroff imports Jap goods, because of lower costs, until finally his bazaar is burned by the young students whom he ignored or stalled too long. As his reward he becomes a Jap puppet until that fatal banquet scene when Miss Hepburn pulls a patriotic Borgia and poisons his sumptuous repast, exterminating the entire Jap command.

The pillage and the rape, the looting and the brutality that come with the conquest of every Chinese village by the hateful Nips have their counterparts in the fascist strongholds of Europe. The peace-loving Huston's plea that "all men are brothers and they should not kill each other" points its own moral. "Dragon Seed" could be transplanted from peaceful China to peaceful Norway, France, Holland, Poland or Belgium. The same factors obtain, and the appeal is universal. As Metro and its skilled artificers—thespic, directorial, production—have fashioned it, the appeal is not only universal, but good entertainment. *Abel.*

The Seventh Cross

Metro release of Pandro S. Berman production. Stars Spencer Tracy; features Signe Hasso, Hume Cronyn, Jessica Tandy, Herbert Rudley, Felix Bressart, Agnes Moorehead, Ray Collins, Kurt Katch. Directed by Fred Zinneman. Screenplay, Helen Deutsch, from novel by Anna Seghers; camera, Karl Freund; score, Roy Webb; editor, Thomas Richards. Previewed in New York, July 13, '44. Running time, 111 MINS.

George Heisler	Spencer Tracy
Toni	Signe Hasso
Paul Roeder	Hume Cronyn
Liesel Roeder	Jessica Tandy
Mme. Marelli	Agnes Moorehead
Franz Marnet	Herbert Rudley
Poldi Schlamm	Felix Bressart
Wallau	Ray Collins
Zillich	Alexander Granach
Mrs. Sauer	Katherine Locke
Bruno Sauer	George Macready
Fiedler	Paul Guilfoyle
Dr. Lowenstein	Steven Geray
Leo Hermann	Kurt Katch
Leni	Karen Verne
Fuellgrabe	Konstantin Shayne
Bellani	George Suzanne
Overkamp	John Wengraf
Fahrenburg	George Zucco
Hellwig	Steven Muller
Fraulein Bachmann	Eily Malyon

Two years ago a virtually unknown writer soared to the best-seller ranks with a fantastic tale of Nazi bestiality. It was incredible —yet utterly believable. Anna Seghers' novel, "The Seventh Cross," became a Book-of-the-Month Club selection. And now, as a Metro film starring Spencer Tracy, it has all the elements of boxoffice power.

There is much in "Cross" that Mrs. Seghers has obviously seen, as she herself is a refugee from the Third Reich now living in Mexico City. It is a tortuous drama that is, at times, slow-moving, but it never lags in suspense. It weaves a pattern around its central character that never loses interest. It is a film that has been given a fairly literal screenplay adaptation, and the production accoutrements are all there, too.

"Cross" tells the story of seven men who escape from a concentration camp, and it follows the death or capture of six of them. Upon their escape the camp's commandant has ordered seven trees stripped and crosses nailed to them. It is his plan, as each fugitive is caught, to pinion them to the crosses and let them die of exposure.

And so this becomes the story of the seventh cross—the one that was never occupied. It is the story of George Heisler, who makes good his escape amid a web of almost unbelievable circumstances. The sheer fancy, as he eludes the Gestapo at every turn, is gripping drama.

Mrs. Seghers related in her book, and Miss Deutsch has maintained that thought in her screen script, that all Germans are not necessarily Nazi. There can be no doubt that there are many Germans in the Third Reich today who are awaiting the time to overthrow the incumbent government, and it is of these people that the film treats to a considerable extent.

This is a film of fine performances. There are one or two characterizations that might possibly eclipse that of the central one, played by Tracy, who, as usual, underplays and gives one of his invariably creditable portrayals. However, there are times when he appears unusually well fed for an inmate of a concentration camp.

Of the supporting players, Hume Cronyn, of the New York stage, gives a performance at least equal to that of the star. As the rather dull-witted Paul Roeder, who aids his friend, Heisler, in his escape, Cronyn has the best of the supporting parts. Jessica Tandy, as his wife, does well in a smaller role. Others who do notably, though none of their parts is big, are Ray Collins, Signe Hasso, Agnes Moorehead, Herbert Rudley, Felix Bressart, George Macready, Paul Guilfoyle, and Kurt Katch.

"Cross" is well-directed by Fred Zinneman who maintained the element of suspense throughout. It was obviously a tough editing job that mainly achieved its purpose.

"Cross" may not be alone in its political propaganda, but it is probably the first major film story to point up—by its symbolism—the manner in which the Nazis have violated the sacraments of the Church. Mrs. Seghers has suggested in "Cross"—and humanity will agree— that Adolph Hitler has become the modern-day Pontius Pilate. *Kahn.*

Jungle Woman

Universal release of Wil Cowan production. Features Acquanetta, Evelyn Ankers, J. Carroll Naish, Samuel S. Hinds. Directed by Reginald Le Borg. Story, Henry Sucher; adaptation, Bernard Schubert, Henry Sucher and Edward Dein; editor, Ray Snyder; camera, Jack MacKenzie. At Rialto, N.Y., week July 14 '44. Running time, 60 MINS.

Paula	Aquanetta
Beth	Evelyn Ankers
Dr. Fletcher	J. Carroll Naish
Coroner	Samuel S. Hinds
Joan Fletcher	Lois Collier
Fred Mason	Milburn Stone
District Attorney	Douglas Dumbrille
Bob Whitney	Richard Davis
Miss Gray	Nana Bryant
Dr. Meredith	Pierre Watkin
George	Christian Rub
Caretacker	Alec Craig
Willie	Edward M. Hyans, Jr.
Joe, Fingerprint Man	Richard Powers

Based upon a fantastic story which converts an animal trainer's assistant into an ape and back again into human form, "Jungle Woman" is another in the chiller groove. Will serve okay in the dualers.

Acquanetta, an exotic type, plays the gal who seems to have a strange influence over wild animals. As an ape, she is shot by a policeman and taken to a sanitarium for research study. It's here that J. Carrol Naish, a doctor, becomes suspicious that the girl Acquanetta had been converted from ape form. Subduing her with a hypodermic when she is about to commit murder, the girl dies of an overdose. Picture opens on inquest where Naish is being questioned, his weird story of what happened being accepted when a reexamination of the body shows it to be that of an ape.

Naish renders his usual steady performance, while others giving a suitable account of themselves include Samuel S. Hinds, as the coroner; Milburn Stone, liontamer; Douglass Dumbrille, d.a., and Lois Collier and Richard Davis, who are paired romantically. *Char.*

Wing and a Prayer

20th Century-Fox release of William A. Batcher-Walter Morocco production. Features Don Ameche, Dana Andrews, Charles Bickford, William Kythe, Sir Cedric Hardwicke, Kevin O'Shea, Richard Jaeckel, Henry Morgan, Richard Crane. Directed by Henry Hathaway. Story and adaptation, Jerome Cady; editor, J. Watson Webb; camera, Glen MacWilliams. Previewed in N.Y. July 12, '44. Running time. 96 MINS.

Bingo Harper	Don Ameche
Moulton	Dana Andrews
Oscar Scott	William Eythe
Captain Waddell	Charles Bickford
Admiral	Sir Cedric Hardwicke
Cookie Cunningham	Kevin O'Shea
Beexy Bessemer	Richard Jaeckel
Malcolm Brainard	Henry Morgan
Ensign Gus Chisholm	Richard Crane
Executive Officer	Glenn Langas
Ensign Cliff Hale	Benny McKray
Paducah Holloway	Robert Rolley
Com. O'Donnell	Reed Hadley

This is a forcefully entertaining factual account of naval strategy shortly after Pearl Harbor when everybody was asking where our fleet was and the answer to that question which came after the memorable battle of Midway. A shooting picture of excellence, the prospects for boxoffice success are very sanguine.

There are no women in the cast, but it doesn't matter. While the stern business of waging war, in this case against the Japanese in the South Pacific, and the equally stern character carved by Don Ameche, dominate the action, dotting it is a moderate amount of pleasing comedy relief.

Called the Story of Carrier X, a footnote in the credits points out that for military reasons the name of the carrier and other ships or individuals cannot be named. The saga of a U. S. carrier which played an extremely important role in the earlier phases of the Pacific campaign, the action remains with it from the beginning to the end following the successful attack on Midway. Carrier was the one chosen by naval strategists three months after Pearl Harbor to carry out a mission designed to fool and trap the Japs by making it appear that our fleet was not only scattered but, also, that we feared engaging the bucktoothed Nips. This led to turning of the tables in the Midway encounter, official shots of which are cut into the picture to provide particularly effective combat scenes between planes and attacks not only upon an unnamed Jap carrier but also upon the one around which "Wing and Prayer" is built.

While considerable is given over to authentic naval detail aboard the carrier, in the takeoff of planes and otherwise, it is interesting rather than a detriment. The editing by J. Watson Webb, cutting the footage to 95 minutes, gives the film good pace.

Production job by William A. Bacher and Walter Morosco rates tops, while the camera crew under Glen MacWilliams has very ably lensed the film, with the before-dawn and night scenes being outstanding.

Lengthy cast is headed by Don Ameche, flight commander of the air force on the boat; Charles Bickford as captain of the carrier; Dana Andrews, a squadron commander, and numerous fliers with accent strongest on William Eythe, cast as a former film star who gets in dutch but ultimately redeems himself in the battle of Midway. Ameche gives one of the best performances of his career, looking and acting every inch the commanding taskmaster that he plays. Less important to the action but excellent is Bickford, while Eythe impresses very favorably in the picture-star role. Sir Cedric Hardwicke is in only a small amount of footage as an admiral. Kevin O'Shea and Henry Morgan stand out rather sharply among the long list of others in the cast. *Char.*

Minstrel Man
(MUSICAL)

PBC release of Harry Revel production. Stars Benny Fields, Gladys Geroge; features Alan Dinehart, Roscoe Barns, Judy Clark, Gloria Petroff, Molly Lamont, Eddie Kane. Diredted by Joseph H. Lewis. Story, Martin Mooney and Raymond I. Schank; adaptation, Irwin Franklin and Pierre Gendron; music, Harry Revel; Paul Webster; editor, Carl Pierson, camera, Marcel Le Picard. At Vietnam, N.Y., week July 13, '44. Running time, 97 MINS.

Dixie Boy Johnson	Benny Fields
Mae White	Gladys George
Lew Dunn	Alan Dinehart
Lasses White	Roscoe Barns
Caroline (Age 16)	Judy Clark
Caroline (Age 5)	Gloria Petroff
Caroline (Mother)	Molly Lamont
Bill Evans	Jerome Carson
John Raitt	John Raitt
Booking Agent	Eddie Kane

Tailored to fit Benny Fields, who works most of the time in this film under burnt cork, "Minstrel Man" is mostly entertaining because of Fields' performance although a capable cast surrounds him. It includes the youthful Judy Clark, as his singing-dancing daughter, who is likely to go places. Edited to the quick, running only 67 minutes, and hitting a generally good pace, the boxoffice possibilities appear favorable. Among other things, it's escapist diversion in a vein, that of minstrelsy, which affords some relief from the modern type of musical.

Fields not only sells his songs effectively, as he does on the stage, but also tosses plenty of personality into the cameras. In the speaking sequences he also acquits himself very creditably. He plays a minstrel who has come up from vaudeville and some years back stars in a Broadway show called "Minstrel Man." On the opening night his wife, of whom he's very fond, dies shortly after giving birth to a daughter. He walks out on the show, refuses to see the baby girl, leaves her with friends and, sorrowed by what has happened, goes off to Europe for five years. He returns to find his friends, who had reared the girl meantime, antagonistic toward him, whereupon he plays one vaude date, then runs off to a Havana nitery. It's here that he breaks down singing a song he had written years back with his wife in mind, and on the way back to the States is among those on the casualty list of a steamship, being identified in the picture as the Morro Castle. Choosing to remain unidentified, taking another name, he turns up in a San Francisco joint singing songs at a piano but is finally discovered by his former agent and lured back to New York where a modern version of his "Minstrel Man" show is about to open with his daughter, never sighted by him, as the star. This leads to the anticipated happy ending, with Fields himself also back in the show.

Harry Revel and Paul Webster wrote several numbers of minstrel flavor for the film, best of which are "Remember Me to Carolina," "I Don't Care If the World Knows About It," and "Cindy." They are reprised on several occasions, including by Fields and Miss Clark, while also thrown in is Fields' old standby, "Melancholy Baby."

Gladys George, co-starred with Fields, plays the wife of Roscoe Karns, actor, who brings up the Fields' baby, and doesn't want to give her up but finally feels that she has been unfair about it all from the beginning. Both she and Karns turn in nice performances. The Fields' daughter at the age of five, played by Gloria Petroff, is among the cuter little kids of the screen but she isn't around long. The late Alan Dinehart, character actor of wide experience, plays the part of a legit producer with usual expertness. Others in the cast are lesser. *Char.*

Outlaws of Santa Fe

Republic release of Eddy White production. Stars Don "Red" Barry; features Helen Talbot, Wally Vernon. Directed by Howard Bretherton. Screenplay, Norman S. Hall; camera, John McBurnie; editor, Charles Craft. At New York theatre, N.Y., week of July 11, '44. Running time 96 MINS.

Bob Hackett	
Bob Conray	Don "Red" Barry
Ruth Gordon	Helen Talbot
Buckebot	Wally Vernon
Winky Gordon	Twinkle Watts
Jim Hackett	Charles Morton
Henry Jackson	Herbert Reyes
Steve	Bud Geary
Triggar McGurn	Leroy Mason
Chuck	Kenne Duncan
Mayor Ward	Nolan Leary
Judge Turner	Walter Bodarilner
Marshall Billings	Edmund Ca
Bill	Frank McCarroll
Ed	Bob Kortman
Saloon Drunk	Emmett Lynn

"Outlaws of Santa Fe" is a close version of O. Henry's short story, "Alias Jimmy Valentine," this time stacked up against a Winchester-Colt background. Passable for the second-string dualers.

Don "Red" Barry, who scored as a dramatic actor in "The Purple Heart," is starred in film, thus running the pix gamut from "A" to "B." He packs plenty of authority in this buckskin series, and rates highly with the cowboy cognoscenti.

Fast-moving yarn has Barry renouncing life of crime in order to concentrate on finding his pater's murderer. He tangles with the law via a safe-opening where his bank loot is cached, but eventually proves his good intentions as a transient marshal and queers killer who did away with his father.

Wally Vernon lays on the laughs in thick gobs as Barry's pard, and Helen Talbot takes care of the distaff side, which is negligible. Camera work and direction get by.

Call of the South Seas

Republic release of Walter H. Goets production. Features Janet Martin, Allen Lane. Directed by John English. Original screenplay, Albert DeMond; camera, William Bradford; editor, Richard Van Enger; music, Thurston Knudson. At Strand, Brooklyn, N.Y., July 13, '44. Running time, 50 MINS.

Tahia	Janet martin
Kendall Gaige	Allan Lane
Russell	William Henry
Landrau	Roy Harcroft
Handsome	Wally Vernon
Aritana	Adele Maru
Charcot	Duncan Renaldo
Judge Fator	Frank Jaquat
Latona	Anna Demetrio
Bailey	Dick Alexander

"Call of the South Seas" is about what the title suggests—a routine romantic drama about lovely island paradises full of stock situations without a fresh or original variation. Sea and jungle shots are attractive, and the incidental music pleasant (even if both scenes and music are stereotyped). The plot ambles along passably enough for an hour's entertainment. A modest budgeter, this will be a fair dualer.

Pure escapist stuff, the film describes a small Pacific isle, where a pretty native rules as princess, and a gang of fugitives from U. S. justice shortchange the natives. An FBI man, disguised as a besotted beachcomber, worms his way into the gang to break it up. There's some suspense as the situation develops, and a bit of action at the close in a motorboat chase across volcanic erupting waters. A couple of romantic situations also arise between G-man and princess, and cafe dancer and police chief, for love interest.

The lighting in some of the scenes is pretty bad, with characters indistinct. Janet Martin and Allan Lane present a satisfactory pair of romantic leads and Wally Vernon tries too hard to be funny. Direction is so-so. *Bron.*

The Contender

PRC release of Bert Sternbach production. Stars Buster Crabbe, Arline Judge; features Julie Gibson, Donald Maye. Directed by Sam Newfield. Screenplay, George Sayre, Jay Dolen, Raymond Schrock from original by Sayre; camera, Robert Cline; editor, Holbrook N. Todd. At New York theatre, N.Y., week of July 11, '44. Running time 63 MINS.

Gary	Buster Crabbe
Linda	Arline Judge
Rita	Julie Gibson
Mickey	Donald Maye
Biff	Glenn Strange
Pop	Milton Kibbee
Kip	Roland Drew
Commandant	Sam Flint
Bomber	Duke York
Sparky	George Turner

"The Contender" is a homily built around the threadbare theme of a rising pug who ruins his career by shifting from arnica to amour. Film is not a main contender, but okay for duals.

It's a rehash of most pugilistic fables. Outset has Buster Crabbe shifting from truckdriver to prizefighter in order to earn enough to keep his son in an expensive military academy. He does okay inside the squared circle, egged on by Arline Judge as a femme sports writer, until he runs afoul of a gold-digging blonde. Too many bouts with night life leads to Crabbe's being washed up as heavyweight contender, but not until he has broken with his pals and the faithful Arline.

Denouement finds Buster's cronies rescuing him from the last stop on the skids and effecting a reconciliation with his son and the sports scribbler. Payoff is that the offspring doesn't want to remain in the swank military school after all, but would rather grow up and become a newspaperman. [The kid is punchy, too.]

Crabbe is okay as the vascillating pug, with Arline Judge ditto as the heart interest despite fact she's veering to the corpulent side.

Direction generally hazy, with clips from actual fights awkwardly inserted into the continuity. Newspaper shots are likewise ineptly handled.

Miniature Reviews

"Janie" (Song) (WB). Fine diverting entertainment, in tune with current audience requirements.

"Abroad with Two Yanks" (Small-UA). Service comedy-farce, with William Bendix, geared for okay biz.

"Music in Manhattan" (Songs) (RKO). Fluffy farce in tuneful mood for amusing audience reaction.

"Falcon in Mexico" (Songs) (RKO). Latest detective meller, with Mexican setting, strong supporter for all runs.

"Crime By Night" (WB). Strictly a "B" whodunit for the duals.

"Return of the Ape Man" (Mono). Average chiller, suitable for duals.

"Sundown Valley" (Col.). Pleasant western dualer.

"Una Carta de Amor" (Mex). Strong dramatic fare interspersed with plenitude of Mexican harmony.

Janie
(SONG)
Hollywood, July 25.

Warner Bros. release of Alex Gottlieb production. Features Joyce Reynolds, Robert Hutton, Edward Arnold, Ann Harding, Robert Benchley, Alan Hale. Directed by Michael Curtiz. Screenplay by Agnes Christine Johnston and Charles Hoffman from play by Josephine Bentham and Herschel V. Williams, Jr., produced by Brock Pemberton; camera, Carl Guthrie; editor, Owen Marks; dialog director, Frederick De Cordova; special effects, Lawrence Butler and Warren Lynch; asst. director, Frank Heath; song, Jule Styne, Sammy Cahn. Tradeshown in L. A. July 24, '44. Running time, **100 MINS.**

Pvt. Dick Lawrence........Robert Hutton
Charles Conway............Edward Arnold
Lucille Conway..............Ann Harding
John Van Brunt..........Robert Benchley
Reardon.........................Alan Hale
Elsbeth Conway................Clare Foley
Mrs. Thelma Lawrence.....Barbara Brown
April.....................Hattie McDaniel
Wilber "Scooper" Nolan......Dick Erdman
Mickey......................Jackie Moran
Paula Rainey....................Ann Gillis
Bernadine Dodd................Ruth Tobey
Carrie Lou Trivett.........Virginia Patton
Hortense Bennett.........Colleen Townsend
"Dead Pan" Hackett....William Frambes
Susan Wiley............Georgie Lee Settle
Photographer...............Peter Stackpole
Sgt. Carl.................Michael Harrison
Colonel Lucas...............Russell Hicks
Janie.......................Joyce Reynolds

This is a cinematic version of Brock Pemberton's play of the same name which had a successful Broadway run for two reasons. Wider latitude of presentation allowed by the camera in comparison to the stage makes it excellent diverting entertainment for profitable biz as solo or billtopper in the regular bookings.

Script of the film closely follows the play in detailing the romantic adventures of small-town adolescent Janie when an Army camp is established nearby. Her editor-father, Edward Arnold, writes editorials condemning the camp's establishment and its possible adverse effect on the highschool girls of the community. After displaying the small-towney antics of the scholastic kids, and the inability of Arnold to understand the new generation, soldier Robert Hutton turns up for a whirl of romance with Janie. Suddenly deciding she's grown up, she tries to toss over school crush, Dick Erdman, but latter stays in pitching to upset the new romance; culminating in inviting squad of soldiers to the house one night during family's absence to disrupt quiet evening of Janie and Hutton. It's a wild but orderly blowout, but Arnold blows up on return simultaneously with the cops, M. P.'s and commanding officer of the camp. Janie wiggles out of things when Alan Hale appears as priority official from Washington to give Arnold permission for new printing press. Erdman joins the Navy, and Janie bids her two flames goodbye, as the soldiers move out and the Marines move in to encamp near the town.

Picture takes fullest advantage of juvenile pranks and adventures to turn them into laugh content for the customers. Little Clare Foley, nine-year-old, is only recruit from the stage cast. As the mischievous and pestiferous kid sister who's always snooping around and finding out secrets, she provides a highlight character of the piece.

Joyce Reynolds capably handles the title spot, displaying fresh personality that will get her far on the screen. Hutton is well-cast as the young soldier, while Erdman clicks as the scholastic admirer. Arnold gives solid performance as the father, while the happy-go-lucky bachelor Robert Benchley neatly grooves for his usual excellent characterization. Ann Harding, Alan Hale, Barbara Brown, Hattie McDaniel, Ruth Tobey and Ann Gillis combine to add strong support.

Script by Agnes Christine Johnston and Charles Hoffman is compactly set up, and takes advantage of opportunities of displaying antics and talk of the younger generation. Direction by Michael Curtiz is zestful throughout. One song, "Keep Your Powder Dry," is presented by mixed chorus at the soldier party.

Walt.

Abroad With Two Yanks

United Artists release of Edward Small production. Features William Bendix, Helen Walker, Dennis O'Keefe. Directed by Allan Dwan. Scenario, Charles Rogers, Wilkie Mahoney, Ted Sills; original, Fred Guiol; adaptation, Edward E. Seabrook, Tedwell Chapman; camera, Charles Lawton; editor, Richard Heermance. Previewed at Mayfair, N. Y., July 20, '44. Running time, **80 MINS.**

Biff Koraski................William Bendix
Joyce Stuart..................Helen Walker
Jeff Reardon................Dennis O'Keefe
Cyril North.........................John Loder
Roderick Stuart..........George Cleveland
Alice...........................Janet Lambert
Sergeant Wiggins..............James Flavin
Arkie.....................Arthur Hunnicutt
Handsome....................Willard Jillson
Michael.......................Herbert Evans
Colonel Hart...............William Forrest
Salesman.........................John Abbott

"Abroad With Two Yanks" is commercial comedy-farce which should stand up strongly. Geared for hefty b.o. in the major situations it will likely do even better in the secondary and subsequent bookings.

Plainly slapstick in conception and development, "Yanks" is aimed at and will likely secure solid audience response. It contains a heavy proportion of sustained gagging sequences which chalk up an impressive laugh score. Surefire, as always, is the bit with William Bendix and Dennis O'Keefe, dressed as femmes, in a chase and fisticuff routine.

Yarn about U. S. doughboy adventures abroad, though by no means an unusual theme, is intrinsically appealing, and the production has been carried along at a swift pace by director Allan Dwan. Scripting is tight though story development is obvious. Bendix, of course, provides substantial marquee value.

Bendix and O'Keefe, who also comes through with a corking comedy interpretation, are central characters as Army buddies and competitive Casanovas usually after the same girl. O'Keefe, as the handsomer of the two, finally runs into tough opposition from Bendix in a play for an Australian girl (Helen Walker). Bendix, unable to win the girl, finally steers her away from his fair-weather Romeo pal into the arms of John Loder.

Among the stronger bits is one where Bendix sells the idea that O'Keefe, who impersonated him, is slightly berserk and can be soothed only with bagpipe music. *Mori.*

Music in Manhattan
(SONGS)
Hollywood, July 25.

RKO release of John H. Auer production, directed by Auer. Features Anne Shirley, Dennis Day, Phillip Terry. Screenplay by Lawrence Kimble; story, Maurice Tombragel, Hal Smith, Jack Scholl; camera, Russell Metty; editor, Harry Marker; asst. director, James Casey; montage, Douglas Travers; songs, Lew Pollack and Herb Magidson; score, Leigh Harline; musical director, C. Bakaleinikoff. Tradeshown in L. A. July 25, '44. Running time, **80 MINS.**

Frankie...........................Anne Shirley
Stanley..............................Dennis Day
Johnny..........................Phillip Terry
Professor................Raymond Walburn
Mrs. Pearson..................Jane Darwell
Gladys................................Patti Brill
Charlie Barnet Orchestra
Nilo Menendez Rhumba Band

"Music in Manhattan" is a light filmusical farce, with sufficient passages of laugh entertainment to carry through the general runs as a strong supporting attraction.

Plot revolves around efforts of Anne Shirley and Dennis Day to catch on as song-and-dance team in show biz. After clicking in night club circuit, pair stage show with young talent on Broadway, but the customers are scarce. In snagging plane accommodations to Washington in attempt to pry loose some coin from her father's estate, Miss Shirley is incorrectly identified as bride of war hero Phillip Terry. Girl is whisked from airport to hotel and established in Terry's suite, launching complications of bedroom farce tempo. Resultant publicity puts show over; Terry visits his pseudo-wife in her N. Y. apartment, and when his mother arrives to meet the bride, it's a round of cinch laugh reactions. Pair sneak away for secret marriage, with Terry writing annulment permission and departing for speaking tour. Miss Shirley then discovers love for the flyer, with resultant clinch in cute ending.

Miss Shirley blossoms out as a pin-up aspirant, capably handling the lead and neatly putting over several song and dance numbers. Day does well as the confused suitor who's much concerned with the marriage masquerade, and will catch attention from his radio following with three song numbers. Terry plays straight as the flyer for good effect; while Raymond Walburn, Patti Brill and Jane Darwell provide good support. Nilo Menendez and his rhumba band is on at opening as accompaniment for Day and Miss Shirley to deliver "One Night in Acapulco." Charlie Barnet and orch also appear in one production number to display fine arrangement of the snappy "I Like a Man Who Makes Music," sung by Miss Shirley with chorus aiding. The five songs provided by Lew Pollack and Herb Magidson add much to the entertainment factors of the film.

Script displays many amusing moments for cinch general audience reaction, while producer-director John Auer provides a generally-fast tempo.

Walt.

Falcon in Mexico
(SONGS)
Hollywood, July 25.

RKO release of Maurice Geraghty production. Stars Tom Conway. Directed by William Berke. Original screenplay by George Worthing Yates and Gerald Geraghty, based on character created by Michael Arlen; camera, Frank Redman; editor, Joseph Noriega; asst. director, William Dorfman; special effects, Vernon L. Walker. Tradeshown in L. A. July 25, '44. Running time, **70 MINS.**

Falcon..........................Tom Conway
Raquel...............................Mona Maris
Barbara.................Martha MacVicar
Manuel..........................Nestor Paiva
Paula Dudley.....................Mary Currier
Dolores.........................Cecilia Callejo
Winthrop Hughes............Emory Parnell
Anton..........................Joseph Vitale
Senor Ybarra..............Pedro De Cordoba
Pancho...................Fernando Alvarado
Humphrey Wade.........Bryant Washburn
Mexican Detective..........George Lewis
Mexican Doctor.............Julian Rivero
Singers..........Juanita and Ruth Alvarez

Falcon takes a trip below the border into picturesque Mexican back country to unravel a most tangled murder mystery. This is a strong entry in the Falcon series of sleuth mellers, and will provide fine support in the regular bookings.

Plot centers around the mysterious appearance of new paintings attributed to an artist supposedly dead for a decade. The Falcon gets immersed in N. Y. when assisting a Mexican girl, Cecilia Callejo, to recover painting of which she was the subject. But the art gallery owner is found murdered, and the Falcon whips into action to quickly contact the young daughter of the painter and fly to Mexico. Few hundred miles south of Mexico City there's a modern inn where suspects and clues abound. After neatly winding up the plot, the Falcon proceeds to guide the audience through series of episodes to finally pin down the culprit in workmanlike style.

Drama is crisply displayed through compact script by George Worthing Yates and Gerald Geraghty, and paceful direction by William Berke. Tom Conway continues as the amateur sleuth, and gets good support from Mona Maris, Martha MacVicar, Nestor Paiva, Mary Currier, Miss Callejo, Joseph Vitale and Fernando Alvarado. Mexican characters are displayed to fine advantage, and picture will catch plenty of attention below the border from the customers. Scenic backgrounds of a large lake and the natives adds much to production values. Two native song numbers also add color to the setting.

Walt.

Crime By Night

Warner Bros. release of William Clemens production, directed by Clemens. Stars Jane Wyman, Jerome Cowan; features Faye Emerson, Charles Lang, Eleanor Parker. Screenplay by Richard Weil and Joel Malone, from novel by Geoffrey Homes; camera, Henry Sharpe; editor, Doug Gould. Tradeshown, N. Y., July 24, '44. Running time, **72 MINS.**

Robbie Vance.....................Jane Wyman
Sam Campbell..................Jerome Cowan
Ann Marlow......................Faye Emerson
Paul Goff...........................Charles Lang
Irene Carr.....................Eleanor Parker
Larry Borden.................Stuart Crawford
Sheriff Ambers......................Cy Kendall
Dist. Attorney Hyatt.......Charles Wilson
Telephone Operator...........Juanita Stark
Grayson.......................Creighton Hale
Dick Blake.......................George Guhl
Desk Clerk..........................Hank Mann
Attendant.........................Bill Kennedy
Chauffeur..............................Dick Rich
Dad Martin..........................Fred Kelsey

This low-budget Warner film, a frankly unpretentious "B," is for the lower dualers.

Lacking marquee value, with only Jane Wyman to back up the exploitation angles, "Crime By Night" is filled with talk and tends toward boredom. Supposedly a mystery picture, anyone should be able to pick out the murderer in short order.

Dialog is so full of cliches, etc., that even the actors are hampered in their performances. Miss Wyman, in the role of secretary to private detective Jerome Cowan, goes through her paces stiltedly, while Cowan is anything but believable in his portrayal of a slick dick who is not averse to making a dollar from as many as three parties in one case. Faye Emerson, too, suffers at the hands of poor story and scripting as the phoney vaude agent who proves to be an international spy and murderess.

Direction by William Clemens fails to score in any respect. Film lacks suspense. Settings are ordinary, and even thriller fans will be disappointed with this one. *Sten.*

Return of the Ape Man

Monogram release of Sam Katzman-Jack Dietz production. Stars Bela Lugosi; features John Carradine, Frank Moran, Judith Gibson, Michael Ames. Directed by Phil Rosen. Associate producer, Barney Sarecky; associate director, Arthur Hammond. Screenplay, Robert Charles; camera, Marcel LePicard; editor, Carl Pierson. At New York theatre, N. Y., week of July 18, '44. Running time, **60 MINS.**

Prof. Dexter.........................Bela Lugosi
Prof. Gilmore.................John Carradine

Ape Monster..................Frank Moran
Anne..................Judith Gibson
Steve..................Michael Ames
Mrs. Gilmore..................Mary Currier
Sergeant..................Ed Chandler
Policeman..................Mike Donovan
Patrolman..................George Eldridge
Watchman..................Horace Carpenter
Bum..................Ernie Adams

"Return of the Ape Man" hits average in the scale of dual horror-thrillers. Film shows Bela Lugosi in another pseudo-scientific role, this time bent on bringing prehistoric apemen back to life and endowing them with enough brain and power to maneuver through a modern-day world.

Lugosi and fellow-researcher John Carradine go off to the far North, find a prehistoric man encased in a glacier and bring him back to their laboratory. Thawing the creature out, they find it bereft of any intelligence. Lugosi decides it needs a brain; after a quarrel with Carradine, he decides on the latter's brain for the experiment, and kills his fellow-scientist to make the transplanting. Balance of film deals with the escape of the monster, and the crimes it commits until it is finally destroyed.

Lugosi and Carradine give okay performances, and Frank Moran is satisfactory as the monster. Michael Ames and Judith Gibson offer stock variations of the romantic duo. Production is satisfactory and direction okay. *Bron.*

Sundown Valley

(SONGS)

Columbia release of Jack Fier production. Stars Charles Starrett; features Jeanne Bates and Dub Tailor. Directed by Benjamin Kline. Story and screenplay, Luci Ward; camera, George Meehan; editor, Aaron Stell. At New York theatre, N. Y., week of July 18, '44. Running time, 55 MINS.

Steve Denton..................Charles Starrett
Cannonball..................Dub Tailor
Sidney Hawkins..................Jeanne Bates
Mom Johnson..................Jessie Arnold
Hodge Miller..................Clancy Cooper
Bart Adams..................Jack Ingram
Cab Baxter..................Wheeler Oakman
Joe Calloway..................Joel Friedkin
Sally Jenks..................Grace Lenard
Tom Carleton..................Eddie Laughton
Gun-Sight Hawkins..................Forrest Taylor
Tennessee Ramblers
Jimmy Wakely and Saddle Pals

"Sundown Valley" presents a ranch-range loaded with patriotism. Idea of cowboys going in for defeat of the Axis is a comparatively fresh slant on westerns, and some pleasant musical interludes also help. Fist-fights and a wagon-race supply the main action for a passable double-feature thriller.

Fisticuffs instead of gunplay seem to mark this western, with Charles Starrett pitching in almost every reel or so to dispose of some villain by Marquis of Queensbury rules. Starrett has taken over the management of a gunsight plant and has to battle absenteeism, negligence and saloon and gamblinghouse keepers, in order to keep production up and the Army's needs supplied. He manages very well, aided by Jeanne Bates, the Tennessee Ramblers, and Jimmy Wakely and his Saddle Pals.

Ramblers and Pals supply hillbilly songs and music for the various shindigs Starrett rigs up to keep his factory crew happy. Acting is standard for westerns, with Dub Tailor's comedy a little on the feeble side. Satisfactory direction keeps the story moving. *Bron.*

Una Carta de Amor

("Letter of Love")
(MEXICAN-MADE)
(Songs)

Azteca release of Grovas, S. A., production. Stars Jorge Negrete. Features Gloria Marin, Andres Soler. Direction and original story by Miguel Zacarias. At Belmont, N. Y., week of July 14, '44. Running time, 115 MINS.

Alfredo..................Jorge Negrete
Martha..................Gloria Marin
Arturo, the Colonel..................Andres Soler
Martha's Mother..................Mimi Derba
Martha's Brother...Alejandro Chiangueroti
Martha's Maid..................Emma Roldan
Alfredo's Assistant......Antonio R. Fausto

Despite its protracted length (115 minutes) and overboard accent on melody, "Una Carta de Amor" emerges as sturdy fare for aficionados of the Mexican film school.

Director Miguel Zacarias, who doubled as scripter of original screenplay, has invested period story with judicious amalgam of emotionalism and comedy, tempering plot's heavy overtones. Music also plays an integral part in uniting the various sequences of film.

Chief transgression of "Una Carta de Amor" is fact that no words are minced in unravelling theme, which could well be spooled out in about half the footage expended without voiding overall effect. Result is a series of anti-climaxes making for a drawn-out finish.

Told in flashback fashion, script opens with hero in prison cell and reading letter from his dead wife while awaiting execution by his French captors who charge him with being a Mexican insurrectionist. Story then fades into account of protagonist's early romance and exigencies encountered in trying to avoid capture, ending with his wife's immolation via poison rather than betray her husband's love.

Jorge Negrete and Gloria Marin are believable and well cast as the dolorous couple, also coming in for kudos as vocalists. Additional principals hold up well, with camera work and direction likewise rating nods.

Miniature Reviews

"Wilson" (Technicolor) (20th). A smash.

"Casanova Brown" (Int'l-RKO). First of the Bill Goetz-Leo Spitz productions augurs strong b.o.; Gary Cooper starred.

"Barbary Coast Gent" (Songs) (M-G). Standard Wallace Berry starrer to roll up usual profitable biz for regular runs.

"Sweet and Lowdown" (Musical) (20th). Benny Goodman starrer good b.o. for the jive trade.

"Heavenly Days" (Song) (RKO). "Fibber McGee and Molly" (Jim and Marion Jordan) in enjoyable comedy.

"Mademoiselle Fifi" (RKO). Fair melodrama of the 1870's, starring Simone Simon; a dualer.

"Atlantic City" (Musical) (Rep). Will do all right on strength of its marquee names.

"Bride by Mistake" (RKO). Lightweight dualer starring Alan Marshal and Laraine Day.

"Shadows in the Night" (Col). Better-than-average meller in the "Crime Doctor" series.

"Three Little Sisters" (Songs) (Rep). Mildly entertaining hot-weather fare.

"Frontier Outlaws" (PRC). Very good western with swell comedy relief.

"Waterfront" (PRC). Nazi espionage item of fair entertainment value.

"Give Us the Moon" (Brit). Absurd, unlikely b.o. comedy starring Margaret Lockwood and Vic Oliver.

"Two Soldiers" (Songs) (Soviet-made). Talky rambling story limits appeal to Russian-speaking audiences.

Wilson

(TECHNICOLOR)

20th-Fox release of Darryl F. Zanuck production. Directed by Henry King. Screenplay, Lamar Trotti. Camera, Leon Shamroy; special effects, Fred Sersen; music, Alfred Newman; arrangements, Edward Powell; editor, Barbara McLean. At Roxy, N. Y., commencing Aug. 1, '44. Running time, 158 MINS.

Woodrow Wilson..................Alexander Knox
Professor Henry Holmes....Charles Coburn
Edith Wilson..................Geraldine Fitzgerald
Joseph Tumulty..................Thomas Mitchell
Ellen Wilson..................Ruth Nelson
Henry Cabot Lodge..Sir Cedric Hardwicke
William G. McAdoo..................Vincent Price
George Felton..................William Eythe
Eleanor Wilson..................Mary Anderson
Margaret Wilson..................Ruth Ford
Josephus Daniels..................Sidney Blackmer
Jessie Wilson..................Madeleine Forbes
Admiral Grayson..................Stanley Ridges
Eddie Foy..................Eddie Foy, Jr.
Colonel House..................Charles Halton
Senator E. H. Jones..................Thurston Hall
Edward Sullivan..................J. M. Kerrigan
Jim Beeker..................James Rennie
Helen Bones..................Katherine Locke
Secretary Lansing..................Stanley Logan
Clemenceau..................Marcel Dalio
William Jennings Bryan....Edwin Maxwell
Lloyd George..................Clifford Brooke
Von Bernstorff..................Tonio Selwart
Senator Watson..................John Ince
Senator Bromfield..................Charles Miller
Jennie..................Anne O'Neal
Secretary Lane..................Arthur Loft
Secretary Colby..................Russell Gaige
Secretary Payne..................Jamesson Shade
Secretary Baker..................Reginald Sheffield
Secretary Garrison......Robert Middlemass
Secretary Burleson..................Matt Moore
Secretary Houston..................George Anderson
Secretary Meredith..................Robert Barron
Judge Westcott..................Paul Everton
Francis Sayre..................Arthur Space
McCombs..................George MacCready
Ike Hoover..................Roy Roberts
Smith..................Frank Orth
Worker..................Dewey Robinson
Barney Baruch..................Francis X. Bushman

Also Cy Kendall, Emory Parnell, Ferris Taylor, Ken Christy, Guy D'Ennery, Antonio Filauri, Hilda Plowright, Joseph J. Greene, Gus Glassmire, Ralph Dunn, Davidson Clark, Tony Hughes, Isabel Randolph, Jess Lee Brooks, Gladden James, Frank Dawson, Larry McGrath, Josh Hardin, Ralph Linn, Russ Clark, Harold Schlickemeyer, Ed Mundy, Aubrey Mather, Jesse Graves, Del Henderson, John Ardell, George Mathews, John Whitney, Harry Tyler, William Forrest, Harry Carter, Jessie Grayson.

"Wilson" is a rahrah, rousing, 100% American entertainment which, post-war, can be its own Yankee good-will-getter abroad, perhaps of a value transcending statesmanship or lend-lease. For domestic consumption, it's a must. It will mop up at the boxoffice.

It's a thrilling saga of an American president whose World War I problems seem so sharply echoed in our own times. One could almost substitute Franklin Delano Roosevelt for Thomas Woodrow Wilson and make it a page out of 1944 history. Yet it has nothing to do with the New Deal or fourth term propaganda. It's American statesmanship then as now, all for the common American welfare.

Paradoxically, here is history that is entertainment. As Darryl F. Zanuck, Henry King and Lamar Trotti produced, directed and authored "Wilson" for 20th-Fox, it stresses a new avenue of biographical entertainment which may be the answer to all the prayers of the "visual education" exponents.

History that is part of our lives, that is vibrant with all the fictional emotions of conflict, romance and adventure; history that is world-influencing; and cinematurgy that is as newsy as a travelog, are captured in this production.

On a brilliant Technicolor canvas which artist-cameraman Leon Shamroy designed, right before you are brought the intimacies and wonders of the White House with all its rooms, its social functions and diplomatic splendor. Brought to you is a replica of the great hall of the palace of Versailles where Wilson's 14 points and dreams of a League of Nations were laid down but, alack, never fully respected.

Right before you is mirrored the legislative life of our nation—its political conventions, its political chicaneries and skullduggery, and its political altruism. Right to you is brought the heartsick travail which ages any man in the White House many more years than his periodic four-year terms of office as he appeases, deliberates, worries, fights, parries—all for the wellbeing of his nation.

Out of yesterday's—yes, and today's—headlines come names like William Gibbs McAdoo, Senator Henry Cabot Lodge, Clemenceau, the Tiger of France, William Jennings Bryan, the treacherous Count von Bernstorff, the sinking of the Lusitania, Newton D. Baker, Col. E. M. House, Admiral Grayson, Mrs. Edith Bolling Galt, Josephus Daniels, Wilson's three daughters, Barney Baruch, the cabinet members, and all the rest.

And then there are the human aspects of our 28th president, the ex-schoolmaster. His love of football as he cheers a losing Princeton team. His enthusiasm for vaudeville—an historic fact—especially when Eddie Foy and Lew Dockstader are the headliners (both reenacted). His penchant for parlor harmony with his wife and daughters.

And later there is his concern for the war to end war; his repeated efforts to keep us out of the 1917 bloodshed, and his constant concern over the casualty lists as they came in.

Zanuck, King, Trotti, et al. have captured all this in sweeping dramatic touches which may well be transmuted to the 1944 scene. There is the isolationistic paen of "I Didn't Raise My Boy to Be a Soldier" and the equally articulate music hall chanson that "I'm Giving My Boy to Uncle Sam."

Wilson reads an editorial which paints the President as a blackguard of the deepest dye—only it's an excerpt from a report on Lincoln when the Great Emancipator first took office. And it's an editorial which seemingly fits any White House incumbent not of your choice.

There are dynamic showmanship scenes as when Wilson talks down the arrogant von Bernstorff, indicts the Germans and "all their evil plans," which is certainly out of today's headlines.

There are newsreel excerpts of the 1917-18 days—incidentally the only black-and-white footage amidst the extraordinarily fine Technicolor—which is a memorabilia saga all its own. By itself that's a featurette of no small potency. But so cleverly is it interspliced as part of the then U. S. scene that it becomes current, rather than historic.

There are authentic Wilsonian speeches—all of them true excerpts from his talks—which will be roof-raisers. The applause is bound to be spontaneous. Just as there will be some anti feeling in the isolationistic sectors.

Through it all stalks a potent personality in Alexander Knox, a newborn star (now 50-50 owned by 20th and Columbia, where he started), supported by a flawless cast. Ruth Nelson and Geraldine Fitzgerald as the first and second Mrs. Wilson are both capital. Thomas Mitchell as Joe Tumulty; Mary Anderson as the sprightly Eleanor Wilson; Sir Cedric Hardwicke as Senator Henry Cabot Lodge; Charles Coburn as the President's professorial friend; Charles Halton as Col. House; Vincent Price as McAdoo, and down to the smallest bit—all are expertly cast. Wisely, Baruch is only a walk-through bit.

The production is said to cost over $3,000,000 and looks it. When there are crowds in the Senate, at the sundry political conventions, in the Palmer Studium, on the campus, they are there in staggering, sizable numbers.

When the period of 1912-1920 is recreated in Technicolor it is as authentic as it is splendiferous. All the detail of the White House decor of the Wilson administration; all the local color of the era and the day are faithfully brought to the canvas in a nostalgic, authentic fashion. In fact, that is the keynote of "Wilson"—authority, warmth, idealism, a search for a better world. As it is today, and will be always. *Abel.*

Casanova Brown

RKO release of International Pictures (Nunnally Johnson) production. Stars Gary Cooper, Teresa Wright; features Frank Morgan, Anita Louise, Patricia Collinge. Directed by Sam Wood. From play by Floyd Dell and Thomas Mitchell; adaptation, Nunnally Johnson; editor, Thomas Neff; camera, John Seitz. Previewed in N. Y. July 27, '44. Running time, 93 MINS.

Casanova Q. Brown..........Gary Cooper
Isabel Drury..........Teresa Wright
Mr. Ferris..........Frank Morgan
Madge Ferris..........Anita Louise
Mrs. Drury..........Patricia Collinge
Mr. Drury..........Edmond Breon
Dr. Zernerke..........Jill Esmond
Monica..........Mary Treen
Frank..........Emory Parnell
Mrs. Ferris..........Isabel Elsom
Butler..........Halliwell Hobbes

International Pictures (Bill Goetz-Leo Spitz) tees off with a straight long drive with its first for RKO, "Casanova Brown," and looks to hole out on the 18th green with a par score or close. While the romantic comedy isn't quite sensational, it is exceedingly diverting entertainment, very much on the escapist side, and will do strongly at the boxoffice. That goes for big towns as well as the small.

Nunnally Johnson, who produced, has fashioned a script that rolls along at a merry pace and carries dialog that bristles, while Sam Wood's capable direction and cast performances round out the 93 minutes of relaxation in a thoroughly agreeable manner. Production itself is all that may be desired but backgrounds are of a simple rather than an elaborate character, suggesting on that score that the budget didn't go overboard.

Gary Cooper gives a splendid performance in a part which calls upon him to play nurse to a baby—a very cute little thing at that. He's a shy young pedagogue who returns to Rossmore, Ill., and his smalltown fiancee, played by Anita Louise. Complications arise as he's about to be married when Cooper receives a letter from the head of a maternity hospital in Chicago requesting certain vital information of him. A cut-back lays the groundwork for what all this may mean, carrying Cooper back cast to a whirlwind courtship with Teresa Wright, whom he marries. There's a very funny sequence in which the girl's parents, including a mother who's bugs on astrology, look upon the marriage as a tragedy and the burning of her folks' home accidentally.

Annulment of the marriage follows but at the Chicago maternity hospital, which Cooper visits, his former wife has just given birth to a baby. Under amusing circumstances, Cooper falls for the baby girl and kidnaps her because he thinks she's to be turned over for adoption. What ensues, as he tries to nurse the kid behind closed doors in a hotel-room, makes for very amusing light comedy. Reunion of Cooper and Miss Wright winds things up with a wealth of warmth and affection.

Though the picture is Cooper's from the start, the support from Miss Wright, Frank Morgan, Anita Louise, Patricia Collinge and others is of extreme importance. Morgan stands out strongly as a smalltown man of leisure who married for money and is Miss Louise's father. The mother is Isabel Elsom but relatively unimportant. Miss Collinge, not in much footage either, is great while she's there, however. Mary Treen has a good part, well done, as a hotel servant aiding Cooper in caring for the baby and nearly marrying him. Emory Parnell contributes some comedy relief. *Char.*

Barbary Coast Gent
(ONE SONG)

Hollywood, Aug. 1.

Metro release of Orville O. Dull production. Stars Wallace Beery; features Binnie Barnes, John Carradine, Bruce Kellogg. Directed by Roy Del Ruth. Screenplay by William R. Lipman, Grant Garrett, Harry Ruskin; based on original by Lipman and Garrett; camera, Charles Salerno, Jr.; editor, Adrienne Fazan. Tradeshown L. A. Aug. 1, '44. Running time, 87 MINS.

Honest Plush Brannon..........Wallace Beery
Lil Damish..........Binnie Barnes
Duke Cleat..........John Carradine
Bradford Bellamy III..........Bruce Kellogg
Portia Adair..........Frances Rafferty
Sheriff Hightower..........Chill Wills
Pete Hanibal..........Noah Beery, Sr.
Colonel Watrous..........Henry O'Neill
Johnny Adair..........Ray Collins
Alec Veeder..........Morris Ankrum
Bradford Bellamy I..........Donald Meek
Wade Gamelin..........Addison Richards
Elias Porter..........Harry Hayden
Tim Shea..........Paul E. Burns
Jake Compton..........Paul Hurst
Curry Slake..........Victor Kilian
Jack Coda..........Cliff Clark
Bedelia..........Louise Beavers

This is a typical Wallace Beery starrer, set in 1880 background of the gold-conscious west. It's okay drama of routine texture, with Beery continually holding center of the proceedings for familiar shrugs and smirks. Biz will hit the regular profitable groove established by previous Beery starrers.

Beery is picked up as a minor league con man on San Francisco's Barbary Coast, perpetually broke but boy friend of prosperous dancehall operator, Binnie Barnes. John Carradine returns from jail stretch to engage in shooting fray with Beery, with latter skipping town to be welcomed as big financier when stepping off train at Nevada boomtown. At first prevented from taking the localities with a phoney gold mine stock deal, Beery stumbles onto a rich claim and is forced to sell shares to the natives. Carradine shows up to grab his operating bankroll, and Beery goes straight in trying to protect his investors, but outlaw in holding up stages to secure money to keep mine going till the big strike. Simultaneous with the latter, he's uncovered as the robber and finishes as first inhabitant of jail he dedicated.

Beery gives his usual performance in the title spot, getting good support from Miss Barnes, Carradine, Bruce Kellogg, Frances Rafferty, Chill Wills and Ray Collins. Miss Rafferty, teamed for minor romantic interest with Kellogg, sings one old tune as local entertainer.

Script has several bright sequences but, in contrast, there are some rather dull and overlength passages that make it a standoff. Direction by Roy Del Ruth does much to liven the pace. *Walt.*

Sweet and Lowdown
(MUSICAL)

Twentieth-Fox release of Wm. LeBaron production. Features Benny Goodman orch, Linda Darnell, Lynn Bari, Jack Oakie, James Cardwell. Directed by Archie Mayo. Screenplay, Richard English from original by English and Edward Haldeman; camera, Lucien Ballard, Fred Sersen; editor, Dorothy Spencer; songs, Mack Gordon-James Monaco; music, Emil Newman, Chas. Henderson. Tradeshown N. Y., July 27, '44. Running time, 75 MINS.

Benny Goodman and His Band..Themselves
Trudy Wilson..........Linda Darnell
Pat Sterling..........Lynn Bari
Popsy..........Jack Oakie
Johnny Birch..........James Cardwell
Lester Barnes..........Allyn Joslyn
Dixie Zang..........John Campbell
Skeets McCormick..........Roy Benson
General Carmichael..........Dickie Moore
Tony Birch..........Buddy Swan
Helen Birch..........Beverly Hudson
Mrs. Birch..........Dorothy Vaughan
Norman Wilson..........George Lessey
Coroner..........Ray Mayer
Major Ellis..........Billy Dawson
Colonel Wiseman..........Harry McKim
Tivoli Owner..........Robert Emmett Keane
Matron..........Hope Landin
Blonde..........Cara Williams
Friend..........Roger Clark
Escort..........William Colby

"Sweet and Lowdown" is for the jive trade, and the juves will give Benny Goodman good b.o. support.

Rather thin on story, nevertheless this filmusical has an authoritative and somewhat biographical ring to it. Goodman is shown making periodic reappearances at the Chi settlement house, where he was reared. James Cardwell is the tromboning aspirant whom BG gives a break and per usual the kid's head is turned by quick success and a couple of attractive dolls in the persons of Linda Darnell, socialite dilletante with a bandophile complex, and Lynn Bari, thrush with the Goodmanites.

That's the simple story, but against it is projected such cinematic nuances as a jam session; four good tunes by Mack Gordon and Jimmy Monaco, plus some oldies; and a little inside stuff on what makes a name band tick. Just because the same team continues, when it walks out on Goodman, doesn't mean it will click or do business, as the plot discloses.

Cardwell gives a good performance as the overly ambitious trombonist, and the entire plot structure is given authority by Goodman playing himself. "The maestro with the X-ray eye"—as the Local 802ers call him—handles his lines well, and is a good foil not only for Cardwell but for the Misses Darnell and Bari, plus others.

There's a cute military prep school scene where the 15-year-old "General" (well done by Dickie Moore) is alternatingly the military man, stern on Army protocol, and also the jive savant who gives out with a mess of 52nd street gutbucket chatter that only a hepcat could interpret.

"Chug, Chug, Choo-Choo, Chug" (patently a "Chattanooga Choochoo" road company) is a good tune, as are "Hey Bub! Let's Have a Ball," "10 Days With Baby" and "I'm Making Believe."

There's good inside stuff for the jazz cognoscenti such as the cracks about Sinatra, Casa Loma's co-op band, Jess Stacy and Sid Weiss, Goodman's penchant for chamber music quintets, "boogie-woogie world" stuff, etc., but the overall plot requires no very hep audience for general acceptance. *Abel.*

Heavenly Days
(ONE SONG)

RKO release of Robert Fellows production. Stars Jim and Marion Jordan ("Fibber McGee and Molly"); features Eugene Pallette, Gordon Oliver, Raymond Walburn, Barbara Hale. Directed by Howard Estabrook. Screenplay, Estabrook and Don Quinn, from original by Estabrook; camera, Roy Hunt; editor, Robert Swink. Previewed in N. Y. July 28, '44. Running time, 72 MINS.

Fibber McGee..........Jim Jordan
Molly..........Marian Jordan
Senator Bigbee..........Eugene Pallette
Dick..........Gordon Oliver
Mr. Popham..........Raymond Walburn
Angie..........Barbara Hale
Dr. Gallup..........Don Douglas
Mrs. Clark..........Frieda Inescort
Butler..........Irving Bacon
Alvin Clark..........Chas. Trowbridge
and the King's Men.

"Heavenly Days" is an unpretentious film that will please the family trade. It has many pleasant surprises. It combines lessons in good citizenship in an enjoyable manner, and could serve as an example of how a picture can be both instructive and entertaining. It well utilizes the proven talents of radio personalities.

Screenplay by Howard Estabrook and the "Fibber McGee and Molly" radio scripter, Don Quinn, has wisely followed the same formula employed by the vet husband and wife comedy team on the air, without attempting to inject a lot of other talent into the yarn that would detract from its principals. Plot has the McGees going to Washington at the request of a relative who is a bigwig in the capitol. Fibber's well-meaning attempts to show the legislators how to run the country lead to the usual amusing complications. The story is chockful of moral blandishments, done unobtrusively, that would not set well with the southern bloc. There is the character who is supposed to be Dr. Gallup, of poll fame, who is shown reading "Heaven Forbid!" Henry Wallace's "The Century of the Common Man."

Interspersed are a young league of nations that demonstrates different international groups can live harmoniously with one another; an argument for abolition of the poll-tax and full voting rights for all people; a preachment for more active participation in public affairs on the part of the average citizen and for better understanding among national groups, and a plea for pre-election registration. The whole thing comes out as firstrate picture-making that should please everyone without being didactic and forcing good citizenship down peoples' throats.

As likable though bombastic Fibber, and sweet, understanding Molly, the stars are just about what they have been for a decade or more in radio. They seem to be nearest to a Will Rogers or Irvin S. Cobb in kidding human foibles the screen has found. Rest of the cast perform capably. The King's Men, vocal quartet, are in for one number. *Kamp.*

Mademoiselle Fifi

RKO release of Val Lewton production. Stars Simone Simon; features John Emery, Kurt Kreuger and Alan Napier. Directed by Robert Wise. Screenplay, Josef Mischel and Peter Ruric, from stories by Guy de Maupassant; camera, Harry Wild; editor, J. R. Whittredge. Tradeshown in N. Y., July 26, '44. Running time, 69 MINS.

Elizabeth Rousset..........Simone Simon
Jean Cornudet..........John Emery
Lt. von Eyrick..........Kurt Kreuger
Count de Breville..........Alan Napier

His Countess	Helen Freeman
Wholesaler in Wines	Jason Robards
His Wife	Norma Varden
Manufacturer	Romaine Callendar
His Wife	Fay Helm
Young Priest	Edmund Glover
Cure of Cleresville	Charles Waldron
M. Follenvie	Mayo Newhall
Mme. Follenvie	Lillian Bronson
Coach Driver	Alan Ward
Maid	Dann Kennedy
Major	William Von Wymetal
Captain	Max Willens
Lieutenant	Marc Cramer
Fritz	John Good

Lacking marquee value, "Mademoiselle Fifi" never seems to get started. An otherwise inexpensive production, it's headed for the duals.

Simone Simon is starred in this film, which draws an analogy between the Prussian invasion of France in the 1870's and the Nazi rape of that country during the current conflict. Her performance lacks spark in a portrayal of a French laundress loyal to her nation to the very end. John Emery, as a patriot who respects her views though others kowtow to the oppressors, gives a sparkling performance, as does Kurt Kreuger, as a typical Prussian officer.

Much of the footage unwinds on a stagecoach carrying a group of aristocrats to Dieppe, and freedom in England, out of the reach of the invaders. Also in the coach are Miss Simon and Emery. They all bow to the Prussians to achieve their purpose, all except the laundress.

Direction by Robert Wise could have speeded things up by adding more action in certain sequences. Settings are in keeping with the times, costuming is fairly good.

Sten.

Atlantic City
(MUSICAL)

Republic release of Albert J. Cohen production. Stars Constance Moore, Brad Taylor; features Charley Grapewin, Jerry Colonna, Paul Whiteman and Louis Armstrong bands, Buck & Bubbles, Belle Baker, Joe Frisco. Directed by Ray McCarey. Screenplay, Doris Gilbert, Frank Gill, Jr., George Carleton Brown; original, Arthur Caesar; camera, John Alton; music, Walter Scharf, Albert Newman, Jos. Dubin; editor, Richard L. Van Enger; dances, Seymour Felix. Previewed in N. Y. July 28, '44. Running time, **86 MINS.**

Marilyn Whitaker	Constance Moore
Brad	Brad Taylor
Jake Taylor	Charley Grapewin
Professor	Jerry Colonna
Carter Graham	Robert B. Castaine
Bar Maid	Adele Mara
Senator	Pierre Watkin
Sherman	Harry Tyler
Rogers	Stanley Andrews
Oaks	Donald Kerr
Man on the Street	Charlie Williams
The Maid	Daisy Mothershed
Gallagher & Shean	Jack Kenny & Al Shean
Van & Schenck	Gus Van & Charles Marsh

Paul Whiteman and His Orchestra
Louis Armstrong and His Orchestra
Buck & Bubbles
Dorothy Dandridge
Belle Baker
Joe Frisco

Republic's "Atlantic City" will do all right at the boxoffice but chiefly on its marquee components, not the plot. Fortified with a better story, Republic could have pulled a surprise winner in the smash division. Instead, it's a stodgy tale, replete with cliche dialog.

Whether the fault of the original or the screenplay adaptors, "Atlantic City" only skims the surface although it does get across the "playground of America" and beauty pageant stuff, along with the generic evolution and development of the boardwalk resort.

Film does one thing—it brings Brad Taylor well to the fore as a leading man. Rep has a good bet in this ex-western juve. Co-starred with Constance Moore, and surrounded with important personalities who perforce, will give "AC" wider b.o. circulation, it's an excellent showcase for this player. Miss Moore handles her vocal pops well, notably "By the Sea" and "On a Sunday Afternoon," which form the basic thematics.

Plot motivation makes Taylor run the gamut of his own theatre, class nitery, amusement pier and department store, plus the civic promotional stunts of "America's Playground" and bathing beaut contest. While on the ascension he's more thoughtless than ruthless, but the venerable Charley Grapewin's advice about making friends in life finally catches up with him when the amusement pier burns down.

Interspersed are a flock of specialties, some good, most of them wasted. Paul Whiteman could have phoned his stuff over for all he does. Instead of being accorded perhaps one of those lush symphonic syncopation arrangements of the "Whispering" or "Do You Ever Think of Me?" school, he is just a bit. Louis Armstrong does better by himself with a typical Satchmo treatment of "Ain't Misbehavin'" in a "Harlem on Parade" sequence embracing Buck & Bubbles, with their standard legmania, and the personable Dorothy Dandridge with her cute song-and-dance. Belle Baker looks well in her "Nobody's Baby" specialty but, like Joe Frisco's standard yesteryear strut-and-heater dance, along with the Van & Schenck and Gallagher & Shean specialties, she's merely one-to-fill as the thin plot unspools.

Gus Van with Charles Marsh recreate "Van & Schenck" in a typical treatment of "That's How You Can Tell They're Irish," and Al Shean, with songsmith Jack Kenny in the late Ed Gallagher's role, recreate "Gallagher & Shean."

The nostaglic bits, pre-World War I, and brought up through the mid-1920s, suggest themselves as ideal escapist film fare, and on a broad scale it is, save for the plot shortcomings. Basically it's a backstage musical with a surfside chamber of commerce aura.

"By the Sea" and "Sunday Afternoon" make for an overlong intro number, but by and large Seymour Felix has gaily recaptured the yesteryear surfside atmosphere. Interspersed, as part of the boardwalk restaurant show, are such Gay '90s excerpts as "Who Put the Bird on Nellie's Hat," while "After You've Gone" is another of Miss Moore's solo opportunities which she handles rather well.

Ex-ballroomologist Bob Castaine (& Barry) makes his pic debut as the secondary juve and manages well although still a bit stiff on handling lines. The rest are bits.

Abel.

Bride By Mistake

RKO release of Bert Granet production. Stars Alan Marshal and Laraine Day; features Marsha Hunt, Allyn Joslyn, Edgar Buchanan. Directed by Richard Wallace. Screenplay, Phoebe and Henry Ephron from original story by Norman Krasna; camera, Nicholas Musuraca; editor, Les Millbrook. Tradeshow Y., July 26, '44. Running time, **81 MINS.**

Tony	Alan Marshal
Norah	Laraine Day
Sylvia	Marsha Hunt
Phil Vernon	Allyn Joslyn
Connors	Edgar Buchanan
Corey	Michael St. Angel
Ross	Marc Cramer
Donald	William Post, Jr.
Chaplain	Bruce Edwards
Janie	Nancy Gates
Samuel	Slim Summerville
Major Harvey	John Miljan
Lieut. Wilson	Robert Anderson

"Bride by Mistake" slips into the hot weather category of entertainment. Film is weak on marquee (Alan Marshal and Laraine Day starred) but shapes up okay for twin bills.

Of the several deviations of the poor-little-rich-girl theme, "Bride by Mistake" sticks to the conventional pattern of the heiress who discovers that her dough is negotiable for everything on the exchange except love.

A rich gal (Laraine Day) comes acropper when her lover gives her the heave-ho because of her retinue of hangers-on, one of whom impersonates her in public because the heroine is camera-shy. Gal then sets her sights on a convalescent flyer (Alan Marshal), who has the foresight to fall for her double, the gal he thinks totes the check book.

After the filler-in (Marsha Hunt) turns down his offer of marriage because she's already tied to Allyn Joslyn, Marshal compromises by eloping with the actual money gal. Marshal doesn't discover that he's married to the real heiress until the bridal night. Revelation that he's hooked the real heiress has him going into a high dudgeon for a brief minute, but appearance of Miss Day in a revealing negligee gives him something to think about as film closes.

Both Marshal and Miss Day acredit themselves well, within the limitations of their respective parts. Tenuous story, however, is too much to be expected to overcome. Minor roles, as well as camera work and direction, all pass muster. *Jona.*

Shadows in the Night

Columbia release of Rudolph C. Flothow production. Stars Warner Baxter; features Nina Foch, George Zucco, Jeanne Bates. Directed by Eugene J. Forde. Story and screenplay by Eric Taylor, based on Max Marcin's radio program, "Crime Doctor"; camera, James S. Brown; editor, Dwight Caldwell. At Rialto, N. Y., week of July 28, '44. Running time, **67 MINS.**

Dr. Robert Ordway	Warner Baxter
Lois Garland	Nina Foch
Frank Swift	George Zucco
Frederick Gordan	Minor Watson
Stanley Carter	Lester Matthews
Nick Kallus	Ben Welden
Jess Hilton	Edward Norris
Sheriff	Charles Wilson
Doc Stacey	Charles Halton
Adele Carter	Jeanne Bates

Another in the "Crime Doctor" series, "Shadows in the Night" is a better-than-average thriller which should satisfy the eerie atmosphere followers.

Dr. Ordway, the "Crime Doctor" who solves criminal cases through psychology, is investigating the case of an heiress who is being haunted into madness and a suicide leap over a precipitous cliff. The good doctor is confronted with the usual quota of suspects, the demented scientist who sees evil spirits, a convicted murderer, and a live ghost that stalks the stalker. But with some mighty slick sleuthing the villain is unmasked.

Warner Baxter handles the role of the doctor adeptly. Nina Foch, who plays the haunted heiress, is convincing, while the others are adequate. Direction by Eugene Forde keeps the film compact and fast moving. *Kamp.*

Three Little Sisters
(SONGS)

Republic release of Harry Grey production. Stars Mary Lee, Ruth Terry, Cheryl Walker; features William Terry, Jackie Moran, Charles Arnt, Frank Jenks. Directed by Joseph Santley. Screenplay by Olive Cooper, from original by Cooper and Maurice Clark; camera, Reggie Lanning; editor, Fred Allen; songs, Taylor & Mizzy, Kent & Gannon, E. L. Bruber. Previewed N. Y., July 27, '44. Running time, **69 MINS.**

Sue Scott	Mary Lee
Hallie Scott	Ruth Terry
Lily Scott	Cheryl Walker
Pvt. Robert Mason	William Terry
Chad Jones	Jackie Moran
Ezra Larkin	Charles Arnt
Pvt. "Rosey" Rowman	Frank Jenks
Pvt. Ferguson	William Shirley
Ambrose Pepperdine	Tom Fadden
Twitchell	Tom London
Tom Scott	Milt Kibbee
Col. Flemming	Addison Richards
Mabel	Lillian Randolph
Benjy	Sam "Deacon" McDaniel
Mayor Thatcher	Forrest Taylor

Based on the pop tune of the same title of a few seasons back, "Three Little Sisters" is mildly entertaining hot-weather fare that should make good on dual bills.

Yarn concerns correspondence between a young soldier and his dream girl, whom he has never seen. Gal's letters have described her luxurious life in the family mansion with her two sisters, who in reality wash clothes for the villagers, with the gal a wheelchair invalid herself. When the GI visits the manse with a group of soldier pals, the girls pose as socialites and switch identities, lest the soldier be disillusioned to find his dream girl a cripple.

Shenanigans involved in the deception make for several good comedy scenes which include the army, townspeople and just about everyone. The whole thing naturally comes out all right, with the soldier falling for the right gal, even with the switched identities.

Film serves to display the talents of its femme trio to advantage. Mary Lee and Ruth Terry click as the hoydenish sisters, both warbling two songs effectively. Cheryl Walker and William Terry, the "Stage Door Canteen" team, are reunited and supply the love interest in capable fashion. Rest of the cast is uniformly good and the entire production has been given impressive mounting. *Kamp.*

Frontier Outlaws

PRC release of Sigmund Neufeld production. Stars Buster Crabbe; features Al St. John, Frances Gladwin, Marin Sais, Charles King, Emmett Lynn, Jack Ingram. Directed by Sam Newfield. Story and adaptation, Joe O'Donnell; editor, Holbrook N. Todd; camera, Robert Cline. At New York, N. Y., dual, week July 25, '44. Running time, **58 MINS.**

Billy Carson	Buster Crabbe
Fuzzy Jones	Al St. John
Pat	Frances Gladwin
Ma Clark	Marin Sais
Barlow	Charles King
Taylor	Jack Ingram
Wallace	Kermit Maynard
Sheriff	Edward Cassidy
Judge	Emmett Lynn
Clerk	Bud Buster

In other respects a very good western, this one's value is enhanced markedly by its comedy, notably a courtroom scene that's of bigtime caliber for laughs. Can stand preferred time where accounts give it to westerns, as they do occasionally in various parts of the country.

The cowcountry courtroom scene is rich in burlesque and the judge, played by Emmett Lynn, is a terrific attack upon the risibilities. This comedy relief, plus that supplied by Al St. John, who's in all the Buster Crabbe westerns, is a real asset to the picture.

Story, written by Joe O'Donnell, sustains suspense nicely and moves at a fast clip. It deals with outlaws in a valley district who are indulging in everything from rustling to gold-grabbing and murder. Crabbe traps them by posing as a Mexican who's interested in buying stolen steers. The girl is Frances Gladwin, the usual westerns type. Marin Sais plays a tough ranchowner with effect, while Charles King as a gang-leader is a heavy of accepted type.

Char.

Waterfront

PRC release of Arthur Alexander production. Stars John Carradine, J. Carrol Naish; features Maris Wrixon, Edwin Maxwell, Terry Frost, John Bleifer. Directed by Steve Sekely. Story, Martin Mooney; adaptation, Irwin R. Franklyn and Mooney; editor, Charles Henkel, Jr.; camera, Robert Cline. At New York, N. Y., dual, week July 25, '44. Running time, **66 MINS.**

Victor Marlowe	John Carradine
Dr. Carl Decker	J. Carrol Naish
Freda Hauser	Maris Wrixon
Max Kramer	Edwin Maxwell
Jerry Donovan	Terry Frost
Zimmerman	John Bleifer
Mike Gorman	Marten Lamont
Mrs. Hauser	Olga Fabian
Maisie	Claire Rochelle
Butch	Billy Nelson

A cheating cheaters theme among Nazi agents and others who figure mysteriously in their Germanic activities forms the basis in "Waterfront," a wartime meller of just fair entertainment value. Running only 66 minutes, it makes a suitable fit for secondary double bills.

Action takes place on the San Francisco waterfront where a local optometrist clandestinely rules Nazi espionage work in that area. Virtually all of the story revolves around a code book which is stolen from the oculist and passes through many hands with several murders en route. While it's clear that John Carradine and J. Carrol Naish are agents of the Gestapo, the motives of others and their interest in the code book, except for one case of blackmail, are somewhat beclouded. This includes a boarding-house keeper who fears for her family in Germany and a shipping tycoon who gets killed for trying to lay hands on the code book.

Carradine plays a ruthless Nazi spy who uses his mauser on the slightest provocation and ultimately, with a view to taking control of espionage activities, wipes out Naish, the boss. He himself is grabbed at the finish in a pistol battle with police.

Both Carradine and Naish give good performances. Support includes Maris Wrixon and Terry Frost on the romantic end who do suitably; Max Kramer, businessman who gets bumped off, and John Bleifer, saloonkeeper, who also ingests a bullet.

Char.

Give Us the Moon

(BRITISH-MADE)

London, July 19.

General Film Distributors release of Gainsborough production. Stars Margaret Lockwood, Vic Oliver. Directed by Val Guest. Screenplay, Val Guest, from novel, "The Elephant Is White," by Caryl Brahams, S. J. Simon; additional dialog, Caryl Brahams, S. J. Simon, Howard Irving Young; camera, Phil Grindrod. At Leicester Square theatre, London, July 19, '44. Running time, **95 MINS.**

Nina....................Margaret Lockwood
Sascha....................Vic Oliver
Ferdinand....................Roland Culver
Peter....................Peter Graves
Pyke....................Frank Cellier
Lunka....................Eliot Makeham
Otto....................George Relph
Jacobus....................Max Bacon
Raphael....................Alan Keith
Heidi....................Jean Simmons
Tania....................Iris Lang
Marcel....................Gibb McLaughlin

"Give Us the Moon" is an absurdity which owes much to its lightness of treatment, often-witty lines, novelty, and occasional naive charm. But although the scripters evade responsibility for credulity by placing the action in postwar London (a period when anything can, and probably will, happen), the originality of theme wears thin. Cutting would help. It's due for moderate biz on this side, with American prospects unlikely.

Margaret Lockwood, with beautiful gowns and an atrocious Russian accent, plays the founder of a club for people who will not work. The odd members of this union form the background of the scenario, and among these are a constant suicide, played with a stressed leer by Vic Oliver, a coupon collector (Max Bacon), and an author who has yet to write a book.

Enticed to the club by a fake note, the son of a wealthy hotelier falls for the founder and joins the idlers. Follows the usual farrago of nonsense, which includes the standbys of the old comedy school—an early morning dual and an overlong, obvious sequence which finds Oliver in a nice line in underwear.

The pace is set by the firstrate performance of Frank Cellier. A very long, but more than competent, cast acquits itself well.

Two Soldiers

(Songs)

(RUSSIAN-MADE)

Arfkino release of I. Lukov production. Stars Mark Bernes, Borid Andreyev; features Vera Shershneva, S. Krilov, Yannina Zheime, Maxim Straukh, I. Kuznetzev, Peter Masokha. Directed by L. Lukov. Screenplay by Eugene Gabrilovich; camera, A. Ginsberg; music, N. Bogoslavsky; songs, V. Agatov, M. Golovny; titles, Charles Clement. At Stanley, N. Y., week July 26, '44. Running time, **75 MINS.**

Arkady....................Mark Benes
Sasha....................Boris Andreyev
Tasya....................Vera Shershneva
Nurse....................Yannina Zheimo
Professor....................Maxim Straukh
Galanin....................I. Kuznetzov
Major Rudoy....................S. Krilov
Okulita....................Peter Masokha

(In Russian; English Titles)

Rambling filmization about the friendship of two Red Army soldiers has a limited appeal because full effect of the niceties of dialog are lost in the translation. Dramatic background of the Leningrad scene also is dissipated through poor direction and lackadaisical scripting.

Story of a seaman from Odessa and a blacksmith from the Urals who become comrades doesn't permit the development of an interesting story line. Result is that the bulk of footage is devoted to squabbles between the two pals resulting from the Odessan's penchant for kidding his bulkier and slower-witted companion. Their last schism is bridged only in the heat of battle.

Perhaps the redeeming feature of an otherwise limp screen vehicle are the songs, "Dark Nights," "Song of Odessa," and "Song of Leningrad." Love interest is present as an extraneous injection that adds little to the proceedings. Whole adds up to a weak entry satisfactory only for Russian consumption.

Turo.

Miniature Reviews

"Greenwich Village" (Musical; Technicolor) (20th). Lightweight summer filmusical that will get by.

"Abott & Costello In Society" (U). Pop comedy combo in uproarious screen return; sock b.o.

"The Falcon in Mexico" (Songs) (RKO). One of the best in mystery series; strong dualer.

"Dangerous Journey" (20th). Adventures of Armand Denis-Leila Roosevelt expedition makes for exciting travelog.

"Gypsy Wildcat" (Technicolor; one song) (U). Maria Montez-Jon Hall starrer will please the action fans.

"It Happened One Sunday" (British). Dualer; not for American audiences.

Greenwich Village

(Musical)

(TECHNICOLOR)

20th-Fox release of Wm. LeBaron production. Features Carmen Miranda, Don Ameche, Wm. Bendix, Viviane Blaine. Directed by Walter Lang. Screenplay, Earl Baldwin, Walter Bullock; adaptation, Michael Pemier, Ernest B. Pagano, suggested by story by Fred'k Hazlitt Bresman; songs, Lee Robin-Xacie Herb Broen; dancers, Seymour Felix; camera, Leon Shamroy, Harry Jackson, Fred Sorsen; editor, Robt. Simpson; music Emil Newman, Chris Henderson. Tradeshown in N.Y., Aug. 3, '44. Running time, 83 MINS.

Princess Querida....................Carmen Miranda
Kenneth Harvey....................Don Ameche
Danny O'Mara....................Willaim Bendix
Bonnie Watson....................Vivian Blaine
Moger....................Felix Bressart
Tony and Sally De Marco....................Themselves
The Revuers....................Themselves
Brophy....................R.S. Pully
Specialty....................Four Step Brothers
Kovesky....................Emil Rameau
Cadway....................Frank Orth
Butler....................Torben Meyer
Young Man....................Herbert Evers
Cashier....................Hal K. Dawson
Dance Director....................William B. Davidson
Set Designer....................Eddie Dunn
Assistant Set Designer....................Sherry Hall
Milkman....................Paul Hurst
Bootlegger....................Tom Dugan
Ballyhoo Man....................Billy Wayne
....................Charles Arnt
Ambers....................Oliver Prickett
....................Charles Williams

Another backstage musical whose Technicolor, plus its stellar people, will have to carry the burden. By and large it will please as lightweight summer fare. No panic, but it won't chase 'em. With William Bendix among the co-featured players, that's an asset, and the ballyhoo attendant to promoting the new personality, Vivian Blaine, from the N. Y. niteries, should also have a beneficial b.o. effect.

Title places the locale. Time is in the early 1920s; i.e., the speakeasy era. Bendix is the speakeasy prop., Ameche the tyro composer from the sticks. Miranda the joint's combination fortuneteller and entertainer, and Miss Blaine the songstress toplining at Bendix's joint.

Thin story is held together by several old songs and three new good tunes by Leo Robin-Nacio Herb Brown, of which "It Goes to Your Toes" and "Give Me a Band and a Bandanna" are the best. But the mainstay is a pop interpolation, "Whispering," which is spoken of as the hero's concerto inspiration, which almost makes Carnegie Hall, but winds up as the big number of Bendix's musicomedy production. It's so patently a case of misguided enthusiasm it's surprising nobody at the studio talked the producers out of the idea. No matter how you slice it, "Whispering," an old Vincent Rose tune, is still a pretty familiar pop. What's more, why couldn't so adept a pair as Robin and Brown have fashioned some original concerto as the central musical thematic?

Miss Blaine impresses favorably on her cinematic debut, both photographically and vocally. Histrionically she needs seasoning. As for the others, Ameche is sufficiently earnest as the backwoods boy who finally makes good, and the rest do their stuff in acceptable if not altogether convincing manner.

Of the specialists, the DeMarcos are well nigh wasted, and that goes for The Revuers, who are merely bits in the Greenwich Village atmosphere stuff, sans any of their own specialties. B. S. Pully, another cafe recruit, whom 20th-Fox is trying to bring along, has yet to assert himself, being merely a stooge fill-in. Felix Bressart is the slightly slaphappy menace; the 4 Step Bros. do their hoofing specialty, and the rest are incidentals.

Abel.

Abbott and Costello in Society

(SONGS)

Universal release of Edmund L. Hartmann production. Stars Bud Abbott, Lou Costello; features Marion Hutton, Arthur Treacher, Will Osborne band. Directed by Jean Yarbrough. Screenplay by John Grant, Edmund L. Hartmann, Hal Fimberg from original story by Hugh Wedlock, Jr., Howard Snyder; camera, Jerome Ash, John P. Fulton; editor, Phillip Cahn; songs, Mann Curtis, Vic Mizzy, Bobby Worth, Stanley Cowan, Kim Gannon, Walter Kent, B. G. deSylva, Larry Spier, Con Conrad. Previewed at Orpheum, N. Y., Aug. 7, '44. Running time, **73 MINS.**

Eddie....................Bud Abbott
Albert....................Lou Costello
Elsie....................Marion Hutton
Peter....................Kirby Grant
Gloria....................Anne Gillis
Pipps....................Arthur Treacher
Drexel....................Thomas Gomez
Baron Sergei....................George Dolenz
Count Alexis....................Steven Geray
Mrs. Winthrop....................Margaret Irving
Marlow....................Murray Leonard
Mr. Van Cleve....................Thurston Hall
Mrs. Van Cleve....................Nella Walker
Parker....................William B. Davidson

In their first picture in more than a year, Abbott & Costello have just what audiences want today in "Abbott & Costello in Society." This is probably the most uproarious in the successful string of comedy vehicles the team's turned out. It's smash boxoffice, which means top coin in firstrun accounts and all down the line.

Basic idea of story spots A&C as two struggling, extra-dumb plumbers being accidentally invited to a high society weekend soiree. Their exertions and blundering efforts to adjust themselves to new surroundings furnish the pegs on which many gags are strung. But even before reaching Hollywood's idea of effete society, a bunch of new and old comedy routines are dusted off and whipped across deftly. These include the old business with flooded bathroom faucets (dates to Keystone Kop days, but wows and the familiar "Floogle Street," long a burley standby. Fox hunt, with Costello standing on back of hurricane deck of a draft horse, doing circus leaps, is one of comedy highlights. And there are others, including the knife-tossing venerable and the stern butler's efforts to get Costello to prepare for his bath. Old or new, they are expertly inserted, with song interruptions spotted logically.

Costello works in his old stride, while Abbott is more efficient, smooth-working than ever as straight in the laugh combo. Marion Hutton, a femme taxi driver, provides the slight romantic twist opposite the wealthy Kirby Grant. She's supposed to be Costello's sweetie, but that's strictly for laughs. Miss Hutton can forget being Betty Hutton's sis with this picture, because she's a potential star in her own right, with the added asset of clicking as tuneseller.

Arthur Treacher, as the dominating Butler, works well with A&C, going over per usual. Anne Gillis is the petite, young socialite, distinguishing herself mainly via the one ballad, "Rehearsin'," an okay Bobby Worth-Stanley Cowan effort. Stout supporting cast is headed by Thurston Hall and Margaret Irving.

Will Osborne's orchestra does

bangup job playing the several tunes and for backgrounds in party scenes. Three Sisters (Margie, Bea and Geri) do well enough with vocalizing of the oldie, "Memory Lane," and helping Miss Gillis with "Rehearsin'." Not bad lookers, either. However, vocal laurels go to Marion Hutton. She wows 'em with "No Bout Adout It," Curtis-Mizzy tune that's built into near-hit proportions by La Hutton. Another Curtis-Mizzy song, "My Dreams Are Getting Better All the Time," which Miss Hutton also deftly puts over. "Change in the Weather" (Gannon-Kent) is nicely done by Kirby Grant, ex-bandleader, but not as strong as other tunes. Number of sprightly tunes in this picture shows that the producer spared little to support the comedy pair.

Jean Yarbrough distinguishes himself with his swiftly paced direction. Hugh Wedlock, Jr.-Howard Snyder original has been made into a trim comedy screenplay by John Grant (he's been with team for years). Edmund L. Hartmann and Hal Fimberg. Edmund L. Hartmann's production bespeaks care for details, some of sets being lavish. Jerome Ash's cameraeing and editing of Philip Cahn measure up. *Wear.*

The Falcon in Mexico

(SONGS)

RKO release of Maurice Geraghty production. Stars Tom Conway, Mona Maris; features Martha MacVicar, Joseph Vitale, Nestor Paiva. Directed by William Berke. Screenplay, George W. Yates, Gerald Geraghty, based on character created by Michael Arlen; camera, Frank Redman; editor, Joseph Noriega. At Rialto, N. Y., week of Aug. 4, '44. Running time, 70 MINS.

Falcon	Tom Conway
Raquel	Mona Maris
Barbara	Martha MacVicar
Manuel	Nestor Paiva
Paula Dudley	Mary Currier
Dolores	Cecelia Callejo
Winthrop Hughes	Emory Parnell
Anton	Joseph Vitale
Senor Ybarra	Pedro De Cordoba
Pancho	Fernando Alvarado
Humphrey Wade	Bryant Washburn
Mexican Detective	George Lewis
Mexican Doctor	Julian Rivero
Singers	Juanita and Ruth Alvarez

Capture by the camera of the picturesque locale and customs south of the Rio Grande result in making RKO's ninth Falcon film, "The Falcon in Mexico," a strong dualer.

Most entertaining of the series, this mystery-thriller has the added ingredients of typical Mexican music and dances, as well as some good scenes of the country itself. Particularly striking are fiesta scenes in a little village, and sequences showing butterfly fishing boats at Lake Patzcuaro.

Yarn takes the Falcon south of the border to clear up the fate of a missing N. Y. artist. With three murders to solve, he finds himself in series of fairly fast-moving situations, during which he narrowly escapes an assassin's bullet.

Tom Conway again does a neat acting job as the elusive detective, while Mona Maris, in the role of a specialty dancer at a cafe, overacts a little, detracting from an otherwise interesting characterization. Rest of cast does good supporting work. Producer Maurice Geraghty and director William Berke have turned out an evenly-paced picture. Settings are quaint and costuming in keeping with the times. *Sten.*

Dangerous Journey

20th-Fox release of Armand Denis-Lella Roosevelt production, filmed by Denis-Roosevelt. Narration by Conrad Nagel; directed by Carlo de Angels. Tradeshown in New York Aug. 7, 44. Running time, 73 MINS.

A dramatic presentation of the adventures of the famous Armand Denis-Leila Roosevelt expedition into hitherto unexplored outposts, "Dangerous Journey" is an interesting, informative, oftentimes thrilling travelog that should please all the sedentary and imaginative Marco Polos.

Film marks the active reentry of George J. Schaefer, former RKO prexy, into the film business via his unbilled bankrolling of the vehicle. A major portion of the footage is from two travelreels, "Wheels Across Africa," shot in 1937, and "Wheels Across India," sponsored by the Dodge Motor Co., and available for the past two years in 16 mm. prints for non-theatrical exhibition. Under its new title, it is a refreshing breeze from the tranquil past and is far removed from the turmoil of war with its attention to the customs, strange to the civilized person, of people who are older and also numerically greater than we are.

Recording the expedition of the famed exploring couple in Africa, India, Ceylon and Burma, the film manages to capture some of the excitement of peoples and civilizations far removed from our own. The savage tribal customs of African natives, a thrilling capture of a wild elephant, and for a gripping climax, the worship of the King Cobra snake in Burma, all add up to an out-of-the-ordinary travelog.

Narration by Conrad Nagel ably recreates the spirit and feeling of the various colorful locales. *Kamp.*

It Happened One Sunday

(Songs)

(BRITISH-MADE)

London, July 28.

Pathe Pictures release of Associated British (Victor Skutezky) production. Features Barbara White, Robert Beatty. Directed by Karel Lamac. Screenplay, Victor Skutezky, Stephen Black, Frederick Gottfurt; dialog, Paul Vincent Carroll, Frank Harvey; camera, Basil Emmett. At Regal Cinema, London, July 28, '44. Running time, 97 MINS.

Tom	Robert Beatty
Moya	Barbara White
Mrs. Buckland	Marjorie Rhodes
Mr. Buckland	Ernest Butcher
Violet	Judy Kelly
Mrs. Bellamy	Irene Vanbrugh
Mrs. Purkiss	Kathleen Harrison
Porter	George Moore Marriott
Magistrate	C. V. France
Madame	Marie Ault

A well-documented script with innumerable complications and an implausible Peg O' My Heart-Cinderella story. Life in the lower strata of England sometimes proves interesting to American audiences, but the chances of this effort are small. Cut to not much more than an hour it might get by as a second feature in a dual program.

Director has taken pains to capture the atmosphere, but the story doesn't stand up. It's also handicapped by the introduction of stagey characters.

The two principals make a curious combination. Robert Beatty, shown as a ship's stoker, speaks English like a man of education; Barbara White enacts an Irish lass with the requisite brogue, but otherwise looks like a well-bred lady. In other words they fail to subordinate their personalities to their respective roles. The nearest to a genuine characterization is Marjorie Rhodes as the boisterous wife of a local grocer, albeit a trifle forensic. Judy Kelly contributes a well-restrained portrayal of a gangster's moll, never once resorting to vulgarity.

Direction efficient despite the lethargic footage. Photography is workmanlike. *Jolo.*

Gypsy Wildcat

(One Song)

(TECHNICOLOR)

Universal release of George Waggner production. Stars Maria Montez, Jon Hall, Peter Coe; features Nigel Bruce, Leo Carrillo, Gale Sondergaard, Douglass Dumbrille. Directed by Roy William Neill. Screenplay, James Hogan, Gene Lewis, James M. Cain; from original by Hogan, Ralph Stock; camera, George Robinson, W. Howard Greene; editor, Russell Schoengarth; song, Waggner, Edward Ward. Tradeshown N. Y., Aug. 2, '44. Running time, 77 MINS.

Carla	Maria Montez
Michael	Jon Hall
Tonio	Peter Coe
High Sheriff	Nigel Bruce
Anube	Leo Carrillo
Rhoda	Gale Sondergaard
Baron Tovar	Douglass Dumbrille
Valdi	Curt Bois
Captain Marver	Harry Cording

"Gypsy Wildcat" has all the stock ingredients of an old Douglas Fairbanks swashbuckler—without Fairbanks. However, film should attract fans of the Maria Montez-Jon Hall team and those who aren't too discriminating about so-called action yarns.

All the props are included. There is the medieval castle with a dungeon, surrounded by a moat; the villainous baron who, of course, meets retribution by his own hand; the fiery and flirtatious gypsy dancer who is really a countess; the stalwart, handsome soldier of fortune; the noble "other man," who is conveniently disposed of at the propitious time; an abduction, the forced marriage, knights in armor, swordplay, horse chases. The works.

Plot has a band of gypsies imprisoned in the baron's dungeon, charged with the murder of Count Orso, who has been found in the woods, an arrow piercing his heart. Of course, they are innocent, the baron's men having rubbed out the Count themselves. Jon Hall, a messenger from the king, has witnessed the whole dastardly crime and attempts to free the unjustly imprisoned gypsies. By this time, however, the not-so-good baron has his eye on the beautiful gypsy dancer, Maria Montez, whom he recognizes as the long-lost daughter of the deceased Count and heiress to the latter's lands and fortunes. He attempts to force her into marriage as the price of her people's freedom, but is foiled by the hero, to whom it makes no difference that his passion is an heiress. He loves her for herself alone, and it's mutual, as they go to live in the castle all by themselves.

Performances by Miss Montez and Hall are adequate, especially Miss Montez, whose actions speak louder than words when she wears a black silk nightgown. Peter Coe, the "other man," is a newcomer who does well in his first starring role. Leo Carrillo as the gypsy chieftain, Gale Sondergaard and Douglass Dumbrille provide effective support, while Nigel Bruce furnishes the only light moments to the entire proceedings.

Picture starts in routine fashion, with no hint as to where and when story is laid, so when mailed-uniform horsemen come into the scene, things are quite confusing until the audience accustoms itself to the medieval setup. Saving grace of the whole vehicle is the outstanding Technicolor and the colorful and lavish production utilized. Lone tune, "Gypsy Song of Freedom," sung by the chorus, is a melodic and stirring affair. *Kamp.*

Miniature Reviews

"Marriage Is a Private Affair" (M-G). Drama needs full marquee voltage of Lana Turner as star to ride through regular runs.

"Merry Monahans" (Musical) (U). Tiptop filmusical with Donald O'Connor, Peggy Ryan, Jack Oakie.

"Sing, Neighbor, Sing" (Songs) (Rep). Hillbilly radio personalities in double-bill yarn for the corn belt.

"Maisie Goes to Reno" (Song) (M-G). A lesser effort in the profitable "Maisie" series starring Ann Sothern; good dualer.

"Cry of the Werewolf" (Col). Occult mystery is a moderate b.o. dualer.

"A WAVE, a WAC and a Marine" (Songs) (Mono). Mildly amusing comedy that should prove profitable.

"Block Busters" (Mono). One of the poorer East Side Kids pictures; lower dueler.

"English Without Tears" (GFD). Elemental love story; this British production has slim chance in U. S.

"U-Boat Prisoner" (Col). Overdrawn film version of supposed autobiographical story; dualer.

"Range Law" (Songs) (Mono). Above-par dual western.

"Sombrero Des Tres Picos" (Filmex). Spicy Mexican yarn, okay for Spanish-language houses of U. S.

Marriage Is A Private Affair

Hollywood, Aug. 15.

Metro release of Robert Z. Leonard production. Stars Lana Turner; features James Craig, John Hodiak, Frances Gifford, Hugh Marlowe, Natalie Schafer, Keenan Wynn, Herbert Rudley. Directed by Leonard. Produced by Pandro S. Berman. Screenplay, David Hertz and Leonore Coffee, based on novel by Judith Kelly; camera, Ray June; editor, George White. Tradeshown in L. A. Aug. 14, 1944. Running time, 116 MINS.

Theo West	Lana Turner
Captain Miles Lancing	James Craig
Lieut. Tom West	John Hodiak
Sissy Mortimer	Frances Gifford
Joseph I. Murdock	Hugh Marlowe
Mrs. Selworth	Natalie Schafer
Maj. Bob Wilton	Keenan Wynn
Ted Mortimer	Herbert Rudley
Mr. Selworth	Paul Cavanagh
Mr. Scofield	Morris Ankrum
Martha	Jane Green
Bill Rice	Tom Drake
Mary Saunders	Shirley Patterson
Minister	Rev. Neal Dodd
Nurse	Nana Bryant
Senora Guizman	Cecilia Callejo
Mrs. Courtland West	Virginia Brissac
Ned Bolton	Byron Foulger
Col. Ryder	Addison Richards

"Marriage Is a Private Affair" dramatizes the first two years of marriage of a young couple, with the selfish and adulation-loving young wife in constant state of confusion over the restrictions of wedlock. Basically, it's a timely tale, but displayed in overlong footage that incorporates minor incidents for many dull minutes, thus failing to balance several sparkling sequences. Marquee voltage of Lana Turner will be necessary to jolt boxoffices for more than nominal biz in the regular runs.

Story is over-burdened with much extraneous material, and script is not a clear display of plot. Miss Turner, rather vacuous-brained daughter of a much-married mother, is surrounded by suitors, but marches to the altar with John Hodiak. Latter is sincere in making success of marriage, but wife feels he's neglecting her when his father dies and Hodiak is released from lieutenancy in Air Force to take over parent's post as a lens expert for the war effort.

Baby arrives in first year, there

are the usual marital bickerings and pouting of newlyweds, with the wife walking out to make certain of love of husband for brief and innocent meetings with former pursuer, James Craig. There's the inevitable separation, her plans for a Reno divorce and sudden realization of love of husband for happy reunion.

Miss Turner capably carries the lead spot, getting sterling support from Hodiak, who—despite inadequacies of the script—should increase his audience popularity. Frances Gifford makes the most of her role of a socialite who carries on secret affair with childhood sweetheart, though married. Craig, Hugh Marlowe, Natalie Schafer and Morris Ankrum are most prominent in support; with Keenan Wynn getting spotlight at the finish as a relay radio operator for reconciliation, garnering hefty laughs.

Robert Z. Leonard injected many intimacies of first-year marriage along the way, but was burdened by script to prevent telling of direct-line story. Production mounting and technical contributions are top-grade. *Walt.*

The Merry Monahans

(MUSICAL)

Universal release of Michael Fessier-Ernest Pagano release, written by same. Stars Donald O'Connor, Peggy Ryan, Jack Oakie; features Ann Blyth, Rosemary DeCamp, John Miljan. Directed by Chas. Lamont. Camera, Chas. Van Enger, John P. Fulton; dances, Louis DaPron, Carlos Romero; editor, Chas. Maynard; asst. director, Mack Wright; songs, Irving Bibo-Don George, plus interpolations; music, Hans J. Salter. Previewed Aug. 11, '44. Running time, **90 MINS.**

Jimmy Monahan.........Donald O'Connor
Patsy Monahan................Peggy Ryan
Pete Monahan.....................Jack Oakie
Sheila DeRoyce...................Ann Blyth
Lillian DeRoyce.......Rosemary De Camp
Arnold Pembroke..............John Miljan
Weldon Laydon..................Gavin Muir
Rose............................Isabel Jewell
Clerk................................Ian Wolfe
Policeman.................Robert Homans
Soubrette........................Marion Martin
Judge..........................Lloyd Ingraham

Despite the corny title, "The Merry Monahans" is a merry musical which will ring up a tuneful b.o. in anybody's theatre.

The title is strictly Gus Sun and it starts that way, a homely, appealing, nostalgic vaudeville saga of another era. With Jack Oakie in the cast, and with such artisans as Cliff Work and Nate Blumberg, production heads of the Universal studio, themselves so steeped in vaudeville, it couldn't help but ring true. There's authority and authenticity in almost every detail. The vaudeville diehards will love it and the new generation will delight in it.

Oakie as the vet vauder, sometimes given to drink, is right out of the NVA and, for that matter, so are Donald O'Connor and Peggy Ryan, as his offspring. Young O'Connor, like Mickey Rooney, is now a GI but both are in the same groove as precocious youngsters who can do about everything—and they show it in everything they do.

The action runs the gamut from 1901 into the Volstead era. There's an appealing saga of unrequited love between Oakie and Rosemary De Camp; and the youngsters, O'Connor and Miss Ryan, throw everything out of the talent directory right at the customers. They do imitations from Sophie Tucker to Jolson to Lauder. They play the corny vaude scenes with authentic tongue-in-cheek.

They reprise a yesteryear Hit Parade such as "I Hate to Lose You," "Rockabye Your Baby With a Dixie Melody," "Missouri Waltz," "In My Merry Oldsmobile," "Isle D'Amour," "What Do You Want to Make Those Eyes at Me For?", "Some of These Days," "Rose Room" and "When You Wore a Tulip and I Wore a Big Red Rose." And there are good original tunes by Irving Bibo and Don George such as "Lovely," "Beautiful to Look At" and "We're Havin' a Wonderful Time."

They do standard vaude stuff a la the Swiss bellringers and slightly corned-up song-and-danceology that's right out of the files. But it's always the McCoy, and by its very simplicity and authority it compels audience interest.

The underlying theme of the great love of the kids for their errant pop parallels his unrequited love and the amour between O'Connor and the nice singing ingenue, well done by Ann Blyth. Peggy Ryan is a match for young O'Connor as the vaudevillian scions of the veteran Oakie, and John Miljan is capital as the lammister from Swift and Armour—the hambola with an Equity card. Rosemary DeCamp, incidentally, is likewise convincing as the too—trusting mother of Miss Blyth.

The yesteryear pop song medley is an inspiration in selectivity, skillfully punctuating the entire proceedings. Even the usage of "Variety" in the script is more than the usual atmosphere prop; here it's a realistic bit whereby the kids trace their naughty pop, just out of the clink for a stew-stuff escapade.

Producers-scripters Michael Fessier and Ernest Pagano establish a convincing pattern for author-impresarios with their handling of "The Merry Monahans." They know their vaudeville, and they get over the impact of what it meant to the yesteryear vaudevillian when he played the Keith circuit.

Withal a fetching 90-min. filmusical for hot or cold weather customers. *Abel.*

Sing, Neighbor, Sing

(SONGS)

Republic release of Donald H. Brown production. Stars Brad Taylor, Ruth Terry; features Virginia Brissac, Beverly Loyd, Roy Acuff and his Smoky Mountain Boys with Rachel, Lulubelle and Scotty, Harry "Pappy" Cheshire, Milo Twins, Carolina Cotton. Directed by Frank McDonald. Screenplay, Dorrell and Stuart McGowan; camera, Reggie Lanning; editor, Ralph Dixon; songs, Fred Rose, Milo Bros., John Marvin, Krumet & Kurtis, Scott Wiseman, J. Elliott & D. Butts. Previewed in N. Y., Aug. 14, '44. Running time, **70 MINS.**

Bob Reed.........................Brad Taylor
Virginia Blake..................Ruth Terry
Cornelia Blake............Virginia Brissac
Beverly.........................Beverly Loyd
Prof. Jasper Cartwright......Charles Irwin
Joe, the Barber..............Olin Howlin
Maxine........................Maxine Doyle
Ruth.............................Mary Kenyon
Roy Acuff and his Smoky Mountain Boys with Rachel, Lulubelle and Scotty, Harry "Pappy" Cheshire, the Milo Twins, Carolina Cotton.

"Sing, Neighbor, Sing" is one of those conglomerations of hillbilly radio talent that should be popular in the corn belt, for which it's aimed. For the duals.

Yarn involves a young lothario posing as a distinguished, elderly English psychologist in a small college town. He hawks psych pamphlets that townsfolk find helpful and makes love to the varsity girl between disguises. Of course, the real psychologist turns up, but everything is ironed out when the impersonator develops a conscience, thanks to the influence of a "good woman."

Plot is so much whitewash to cover the injection of a group of w.k. hillbilly radio personalities such as Roy Acuff, of the "Grand Ole Opry," Lulubelle and Scotty, on the "National Barn Dance" show; the Milo Twins, etc. Acuff is unimpressive, with the other radio stars having more appeal on the airlanes than in this film.

None of the nine tunes in the picture is particularly meritorious, but might score on the "Corn Parade." Brad Taylor and Ruth Terry carry their share of the load with a do-or-die attitude. The others just die. *Kamp.*

Maisie Goes to Reno

(ONE SONG)

Metro release of George Haight production. Stars Ann Sothern; features John Hodiak, Tom Drake, Marta Linden, Paul Cavanagh. Directed by Harry Beaumont. Screenplay, Mary C. McCall, Jr., from original by Harry Ruby and James O'Hanlon, based upon characters by Wilson Collison; camera, Robert Planck; editor, Frank E. Hull; song, Sammy Fain, Ralph Freed. Tradeshown, N. Y., July 28, '44. Running time, **90 MINS.**

Maisie Ravier...................Ann Sothern
"Flip" Hennahan.............John Hodiak
Bill Fullerton.....................Tom Drake
Winifred Ashbourne. ....Marta Linden
Roger Pelham..............Paul Cavanagh
Gloria Fullerton..............Ava Gardner
J. E. Clave.................Bernard Nedell
Jerry..........................Roland Dupree
Tommy Cutter.............Chick Chandler
Elaine..........................Bunny Waters
Parsons.........................Donald Meek

The infectious personality of Ann Sothern has caught the fancy of the film public to such an extent that the "Maisie" series, in which she is starred by Metro, has proved to be profitable for the nation's exhibitors. This offering, while not as good as its predecessors, is enjoyable and will provide strong support in the duals.

"Maisie Goes to Reno," but not for the usual reason. Quite the contrary. On her way to the divorce spa for a rest because her nerves are shot from working overtime in a war plant, Maisie meets up with a soldier who begs her to deliver a note to his wife, in Reno for a divorce. She entertains at a nightclub, delivers the note to a woman who claims to be the soon-to-be-unspliced wife of the soldier, but who is actually one of three people working in cahoots to get the gal's dough. Maisie, meanwhile, falls hard for one of the card dealers in the hotel where she works, and before he knows what is happening, he is mixed up in her domestic-battle settling routine. It all comes out okay, however.

Miss Sothern's dumb-but-smart, lovable-but-rileable, nosy-but-pensive characterization of a fair-sex riveter, who gets in all sorts of mix-ups, is thoroughly likeable. John Hodiak, as the card dealer who is in love with Maisie despite her troublesome antics, is not a little miscast. He portrays his role as if he is angry at someone, possibly his agent for getting him the part. Performances of supporting cast are just fair.

Director George Haight could easily have cut corners to mold a more compact picture. Screenplay by Mary C. McCall, Jr., from an original by Harry Ruby and James O'Hanlon, rambles at times, but in the main is sufficiently meaty. This film, like so many being released today, is too long. It needs editing before it is distributed. *Sten.*

Cry of the Werewolf

Columbia release of Wallace MacDonald production. Features Nina Foch, Stephen Crane, Osa Massen, Blanche Yurka, Barton MacLane. Directed by Henry Levin. Screenplay by Griffin Jay and Charles O'Neal; camera, L. W. O'Connell; editor, Reg Browne. At Rialto, N. Y., week of Aug. 11, '44. Running time, **63 MINS.**

Celeste............................Nina Foch
Bob Morris..................Stephen Crane
Elsa Chauvet..................Osa Massen
Bianca.......................Blanche Yurka
Lt. Barry Lane...........Barton MacLane
Yan Spavero.................Ivan Triesault
Peter Althius..................John Abbott
Pinkie..............................Fred Graff
Mac.............................John Tyrrell
Max........................Robert Williams
Dr. Charles Morris............Fritz Leiber
Adamson.....................Milton Parsons

"Cry of the Werewolf" is an average horror-film. Hardly a distinguished addition to the series, its stodgy story and lack of originality or excitement is barely offset by a fair outlay in budget and production. A passable dualer.

The story is another occult yarn about a fair damsel changing into a werewolf and harassing the countryside. In this case she's queen of a tribe of gypsies, daughter of a mysterious figure who lived for a time as a New Orleans belle but who disappeared strangely after the death of her scientist-husband.

Daughter guards the secret of her mother's tomb, hidden away in a New Orleans museum, even to killing the museum head as well as one of her tribesmen, when the secret is about to leak out. The killings, as one can guess, come about after the gypsy queen has changed to wolf, her victims being torn to shreds.

Nina Foch makes an attractive figure as the gypsy, even to making part of her story almost credible. Stephen Crane and Osa Massen are a plausible pair of lovers, intent on clearing up a mystery that involves Crane's father. Blanche Yurka as a gypsy, John Abbott, museum guide, and Barton MacLane, police lieutenant, are effective in supporting roles. *Bron.*

A WAVE, A WAC And A Marine

(SONGS)

Monogram release of Sebastian Cristillo production; Cristillo executive producer, Edward Sherman, producer. Features Henny Youngman, Sally Eilers, Elyse Knox, Ramsay Ames, Ann Gillis, Alan Dinehart, Marjorie Woodworth, Charles "Red" Marshall, Connie Haines, Aileen Pringle, Cy Kendall, Freddie Rich and orch. Directed by Phil Karlstein. Story, Lillian Planer and Dick Hyland; adaptation, Hal Fimberg; music, Freddie Rich; lyrics, Eddie Cherkose; editor, William Austin; camera, Maury Gertsman. At Victoria, N. Y., week Aug. 12, '44. Running time, **70 MINS.**

Marian...........................Elyse Knox
Margaret Ames..............Sally Eilers
Betty........................Ramsay Ames
Judy...............................Ann Gillis
Producer R. J...............Alan Dinehart
Eileen..................Marjorie Woodworth
Henny.....................Henny Youngman
Red...............Charles "Red" Marshall
Singer..........................Connie Haines
Marty Allen.................Richard Lane
Mike..............................Cy Kendall
Newswoman..................Aileen Pringle
Freddie Rich and Orch.

"A WAVE, a WAC and a Marine" is a mildly amusing comedy with a couple songs that listen well. It introduces Henny Youngman to the feature field, while at the same time marking the producing bow of Lou (Abbott &) Costello. Costello does not take billing, however, it being Sebastian Cristillo (Costello's father) as executive producer and Edward Sherman, A. & C.'s personal manager, as producer. While only fair-to-middlin' as entertainment, picture provides the type of light fare now in demand and should be a profit-maker. It stacks as quite suitable material for double bills, especially as the No. 2 feature, in which slot it ought to offer oke support.

Youngman, who has always been fast on his chatter on the stage, speaks too rapidly with the result much of his dialog is unclear. Also, generally speaking Youngman's voice does not seem to record too well although it appears the soundmen on the picture didn't do such a good job on the whole. Youngman plays a Hollywood talent agent who's east to grab off a couple gals who are about to close in a legit show, called "A WAVE, a WAC and a Marine." By mistake he signs up the two understudies for the top roles in the show instead of the leads themselves, a rival agent getting east in time to land the latter. However, the two girls under Youngman's wing make a terrific hit on an emergency nitery assignment doing a dramatic sketch and are immediately signed for pictures. The other two actresses, already under contract to the same company to play a WAVE and a WAC, are mollified when (the late) Alan Dinehart, film company head, agrees to toss them into a different type picture.

There are three song numbers. The Music Maids, of radio, sing "Time Will Tell," nice little number in front of the Freddie Rich band in a nightclub sequence. "My G.I.

Guy," charmingly 'sold by Connie Haines, clicks very well, while at the finish "Carry On" figures as a group number. It's also a pretty good tune.

Though there are some lessers contributing to the comic side of the picture, chief laugh support is from Charles "Red" Marshall but as in the case of Youngman some of his lines are also muffled. Ann Gillis and Elyse Knox play the two Broadway understudies landing in pictures. The two girls they are at first mistaken for are Ramsay Ames and Marjorie Woodworth. All do well albeit not outstandingly. Among others are Aileen Pringle as a film colony newshound and looking the type; Sally Eilers, excellent as a studio executive; Cy Kendall, good as a nitery operator, and Richard Lane, who does nicely as an agent.
Char.

Block Busters

Monogram release of Sam Katzman-Jack Dietz production (associate producer, Barney Sarecky). Stars Leo Gorcey; features Huntz Hall, Gabriel Dell, Billy Benedict. Directed by Wallace Fox. Original story, Houston Branch; camera, Marcel Le Picard; editor, Carl Pierson. At N. Y. theatre, N. Y., week of Aug. 9, '44. Running time, 60 MINS.

Muggs	Leo Gorcey
Glimpy	Huntz Hall
Skinny	Gabriel Dell
Butch	Billy Benedict
Danny	Jimmy Strand
Tobey	Bill Chaney
Amelia	Minerva Urecal
Jinx	Roberta Smith
Judge	Noah Beery, Sr.
Higgins	Harry Langdon
Jean	Fred Pressel
Butler	Jack Gilman
Irma	Kay Marvis
Umpire	Charles Murray, Jr.

This one spreads democracy thick on a thin plot. Another in the East Side Kids series, "Block Busters" is for lower half of duals.

Film deals with antics of gang led by Leo Gorcey in taking into their midst a rich kid so he can learn the American way of life by associating with other boys. After making it almost unbearable for him, the East Side Kids realize the lad can stand up under their torments, and so he becomes one of them.

Acting, direction and production values are lacking.
Sten.

English Without Tears
(BRITISH-MADE)

London, July 29.

General Film Distributors' release of Two Cities Film. Features Lilli Palmer, Penelope Ward, Michael Wilding, Claude Dauphin. Directed by Harold French. Screenplay by Terence Rattigan, Anatole de Grunwald. Camera, Bernard Knowles, W. MacLeod. At Odeon, London, July 28. Running time, 89 MINS.

Tom Gilbey	Michael Wilding
Joan Haseltine	Penelope Ward
Brigid Knudsen	Lilli Palmer
Jean de Freycinet	Claude Dauphin
Felix Dombowski	Albert Lieven
Sir Cosmo Brandon	Roland Culver
Lady Christabel	Margaret Rutherford
Bobby Haseltine	Peggy Cummins
Schmidt	Martin Miller
Spagott	Felix Aylmer
Elise Batter-Jones	Judith Furse
Mr. Quill	Ivor Barnard

Most distinctive thing about "English Without Tears" is the continental atmosphere. This is probably because a group of foreign artists is used to augment a cast of British celebrities. Despite this, admirable direction and excellent photography, the story ambles along to no definite denouement. Therefore, it's not a strong candidate for the American market.

Smart dialog and witticisms galore are not sufficient to sustain so elemental a love story. This affair shows a young lady of an aristocratic family who falls in love with the cold and indifferent butler.

As a demonstration of British versus continental types, the picture makes interesting entertainment. A lot of preliminary care was undoubtedly spent to assemble such a large array of players. Result is a series of cameo scenes which bear little or no relation to the story.
Jolo.

U-Boat Prisoner

Columbia release of Wallace MacDonald production. Features Bruce Bennett, Erik Rolf. Directed by Lew Landers. Screenplay, Aubrey Wisberg, from story by Archie Gibbs; camera, Burnett Guffey. At Brooklyn Strand, week of Aug. 9, '44. Running time, 65 MINS.

Archie Gibbs	Bruce Bennett
Kapitan Ganz	Erik Rolf
Alfonse Lamont	John Abbott
Rudchoff	John Wengraf
Commander Bristol	Robert Williams
Clyde Hamilton	Kenneth MacDonald
Bienawicz	Erwin Kalser
Sigo Van Der Brek	Egon Brecher
First Officer Kerck	Frederick Giermann
Hagemann	Arno Frey
Durner	Sven-Hugo Borg
Lt. Hagen	Nelson Leigh
Lt. Blake	Fred Graff
Commander Prentiss	Trevor Bardette
Lt. Nolan	Paul Conrad
Braustig	Erik Feldary

"U-Boat Prisoner" is a marine meller replete with stock situations ostensibly based on the exploits of Archie Gibbs, a merchant seaman. Film, which is completely lacking in verisimilitude despite its background, is destined for the lower half of dual bills.

Unfortunate angle in "U-Boat Prisoner" is that its American protagonist is depicted as a not-too-bright jingoistic superman who outthinks and outfights an entire cordon of Nazis. Pic is a prime example of Yankee chauvinism at its worst, revealing the enemy as a setup for a left hook followed by a right cross. Impression is heightened by flag-waving cliches and a dragged-in situation involving the Star-Spangled Banner. It's patriotism delineated in its crudest form.

Fatuous story concerns a merchant seaman who changes identities with a Nazi spy after former's tanker has been torpedoed. Picked up by a Nazi sub, he's promptly accepted as a dyed-in-the-wool German but is cooped up with the other prisoners, all of them scientists en route to the Fatherland.

After blabbing his real identity, he quickly engineers a series of incidents that leads to the sub's being sunk by an American destroyer, and after knocking out half the German crew he sees to it that all concerned are saved from death on the bottom of the Atlantic.

Despite its lack of credulity, film maintains a measure of excitement part of the way. Characterizations are all synthetic with lead role, portrayed by Bruce Bennett, being especially wooden.

Photography and direction are handled in okay fashion but are hardly able to circumvent thin story.
Jona.

Range Law
(SONGS)

Monogram release of Charles J. Bigelow production. Stars Johnny Mack Brown, Raymond Hatton; features Sarah Padden, Ellen Hall, Lloyd Ingraham. Directed by Lambert Hillyer. Story and screenplay, Frank Young; camera, Harry Neumann; editor, John C. Fuller. At N. Y. theatre, N. Y., week of Aug. 9, '44. Running time, 57 MINS.

Nevada	Johnny Mack Brown
Sandy	Raymond Hatton
Boots Annie	Sarah Padden
Lucille Gray	Ellen Hall
Judge	Lloyd Ingraham
Jim Bowen	Marshall Reed
Pop McGee	Steve Clark
Phil Randall	Jack Ingram
Sheriff	Hugh Prosser
Dawson	Stanley Price
Swede Larson	Art Fowler
Zeke	Harry F. Price
Joe	Ben Corbett
Davis	Bud Osborne

A fairly diverting dual western. "Range Law" easily fills the bill for outdoor fans.

Johnny Mack Brown's riding, shooting and acting add much to the film, along with support from Raymond Hatton and the romantic duo, Ellen Hall and Marshall Reed. Director Lambert Hillyer comes in for a bow, too.

Story tells of a group that strives to swindle property because they know there's silver ore on the land. But Brown and Hatton, as U. S. marshals, clear up the trouble with plenty of fists and bullets.

Picture shows good overall supervision by Charles J. Bigelow.
Sten.

Sombrero de Tres Picos
("Three-Cornered Hat")
(SPANISH-MADE)

Filmex production and release. Features Joaquin Pardave and Sofia Alvarez. Stars Angel Garasa, Amparito Morillo, Bernardo Sancristobal, Manolo Noriega. Directed by Juan Bustillo Oro. Story by Oro. At Cine Hipodromo, Mexico City. Running time, 97 MINS.

Mexico City, Aug. 8.

Typical Spanish wit, with Mexican paprika, help this film version of Pedro Antonio de Alarcon's classic comedy of 18th Century Spain. Adaptation and direction of Juan Bustillo Oro, gold medalist in both fields, and the acting of Joaquin Pardave, veteran comic from the stage, make this solid entertainment. For U. S. it will do in Spanish-language theatres.

Story tells of mix-up of the philandering of Pardave, who allows neither his shrewish spouse nor his high office of King's deputy to hinder him when his heart dictates. He's the bee drawn to the garden of La Alvarez, the miller's wife, along with many other men, some not so young, including clerics, by her famed food and wine. High spot is his attempted kidnapping of the enchantress, neatly thwarted by Sancristobal.

Miss Alvarez does well in a glove-fitting role. Garasa is excellent as the minor cleric who is the merry bishop's shadow. Tuneful music helps this production.

Miniature Reviews

"Kismet" (songs; Technicolor) (M-G). Ideal escapist fantasy with Ronald Colman and Marlene Dietrich.

"The Doughgirls" (WB). Will get the dough for any exhibitor.

"The Impatient Years" (Col). Highly amusing comedy-drama of topical interest. Good b.o.

"Louisiana Hayride" (Songs) (Col). Comedy with music starring Judy Canova grooved for the duals.

"Sonora Stagecoach" (Mono). Above-average western with plenty of name value.

"Seven Doors to Death" (PRC). Loosely knit meller for the duals.

"Adventure in Bokhara" (Russian). Surprisingly good comedy, but strictly for class houses. Russian dialog; English titles.

Kismet
(TECHNICOLOR; SONGS)

Metro release of Everett Riskin production. Stars Ronald Colman, Marlene Dietrich; features James Craig, Edward Arnold, Hugh Herbert, Joy Ann Page. Directed by William Dieterle. Screenplay, John Meehan from Edward Knoblock's play; camera, Charles Rosher, Warren Newcombe; songs, Harold Arlen-E. Y. Harburg; editor, Ben Lewis; art, Cedric Gibbons, Daniel B. Cathcart. Opened Aug. 21, '44. Astor, N. Y. Running time, 100 MINS.

Hafiz	Ronald Colman
Jamilla	Marlene Dietrich
Caliph	James Craig
Grand Vizier	Edward Arnold
Feisal	Hugh Herbert
Marsinah	Joy Ann Page
Karsha	Florence Bates
Agha	Harry Davenport
Moolah	Hobart Cavanaugh

The sheer mystic fantasy of Bagdad and its royal pomp and splendor remain acceptable escapism. It is as entertaining in 1944 as it was in 1912, when Otis Skinner captured Gotham with his rousing production of Edward Knoblach's play at the old Knickerbocker theatre. Since then, Knaublach, like another eminent contemporaneous stage craftsman, Otto Hauerbach (Harbach), simplified the spelling to Knobloch; the Knickerbocker is no more; the Broadway of a third-of-a-century ago has undergone a sharp metamorphosis; the producer-star, Otis Skinner, is playing in some theatre of the Valhalla. But despite all this tempus fugiting, Metro and Technicolor have worked wonders with the present-day remake. And so again, it is fated, "Kismet" is a b.o. click.

The fantasy under lavish Culver City and Natalie Kalmus (Technicolor) production auspices is beautifully investitured. Ronald Colman as the beggar-sometimes-prince, Marlene Dietrich as the dancing girl with the gold-painted gams, Edward Arnold as the double-dealing Grand Vizier, James Craig as the Caliph-sometimes - turned - gardener's son, and Joy Ann Page as Colman's sheltered daughter are a convincing casting. Miss Page (Mrs. Jack Warner's daughter) is ideal as the Oriental beauty.

Colman, the king of beggars, is impressive as the phoney prince. He lends conviction to his role, so dominating the proceedings that he makes Legs Dietrich more or less of a stooge. However, she comes through in the highlight opportunity accorded her when she does her stuff for the Vizier and Colman. Miss Dietrich's terp specialty and getup is out of the dream book, but boffo. Thereafter Kismet (fate) follows the beggar-prince's hopes; his daughter really marries a prince himself disguised as the royal gardener's son). Colman, of course, is pleasantly banished with his dancing girl (Dietrich) after indulging in some Fairbanksesque heroics.

The rich Technicolor under the lavish art direction of Cedric Gibbons and Daniel B. Cathchart is an eye-filling cinematic easel throughout the entire 100 minutes. They have given the Bagdad saga size and stature. The sultry, sensuous atmosphere is as bizarre as the Haysian code permits. *Abel.*

The Doughgirls

Warner Bros. release of Mark Hellinger production. Stars Ann Sheridan, Alexia Smith, Jack Carson, Jane Wyman, Irene Manning, Charlie Ruggles, Eve Arden. Directed by James V. Kern. Screenplay, Kern and Sam Hellman: additional dialog, Wilkie Mahoney: from Max Gordon's legit production of Joseph A. Fields' comedy; camera, Ernest Haller, Jack Leicester, Wm. McCann; editor, Folmer Blangsted; dialog director, Jack Gagte; asst. director, Phil Quinn. Previewed N.Y. Aug. 21, '44. Running time, 102 MINS.

Edna....Ann Sheridan
Nan....Alexis Smith
Arthur....Jack Carson
Vivian....June Wyman
Mrs. Cadman....Irene Manning
Slade....Charlie Ruggles
Natalia....Eve Arden
Julian....JOhn Ridgely
Breckenridge Drake....Alan Mowbray
Buckley....John Alexander
Tom....Craig Stevens
Mrs. Cartwright....Barbara Brown
Lieut. Keary....Stephen Richards
Mr. Jordan....Francis Pierlot
Judge Franklin....Donald MacBride
Timothy Walsh....Regis Toomey
The Stranger....Joe DeRita

This one will get the dough—from the picture of the same name. "The Doughgirls" is a laugh marathon, topical and marquee-loaded.

There have been other pix about overcrowded Washington, but this is one film where the hectic locale is incidental to the romantic comedy context. The Joe Fields comedy could be shown 10 years after the peace and still be a wallop.

Producer Mark Hellinger, director-screenwright Jimmy Kern, and his writing confreres, Sam Hellman and Wilkie Mahoney, have done a deft job sapolioing some of the saucy situations of the original play. Now everybody wants to get married. The gals are three honeys, excepting that, for one reason or another, they are without benefit of clergy until the Russian sniper again saves the day and rings in a Russian Orthodox cleric for the triple ceremony.

Eve Arden is the Russian guerrilla heroine, in the States as the guest of the Soviet embassy. She makes it a close race with Jane Wyman for the cast standouts. Not that Ann Sheridan and Alexis Smith as Miss Wyman's femme pals don't more than sustain their assignments as the anxious brides-to-be, but it's a setup for the dumbdora Miss Wyman. Latter is expertly foiled by the choleric Jack Carson. And the vodka Dick Tracy-in-drag, as played to the hilt by the facile Miss Arden, is a vivid personality.

There are good performances right down the line from Irene Manning as the captious ex-wife, the flirtatious Charlie Ruggles, and the bombastic newscaster (Alan Mowbray), to the distrait grooms, John Ridgely and Craig Stevens, et al. The somnambulistic stranger, Joe De Rita, is another good character who bespeaks of comedy possibilities all his own. He suggests a Lou Costelloesque quality which augurs much for him.

"The Doughgirls" has another basic advantage, in that it's forthright escapism despite the hectic wartime background of the nation's capital.

And a great inside laugh is the dumbdora character's enthusiasm for the President. "Tell him how much I loved him in 'Yankee Doodle Dandy'," she screams after one of the players. Where but in America could you make FDR a straight man for Jimmy Cagney? *Abel.*

The Impatient Years

Hollywood, Aug. 19.

Columbia release of Irving Cummings production, directed by Cummings; associated producer, Virginia Van Upp. Stars Jean Arthur, Lee Bowman. Charles Coburn. Original screenplay by Miss Van Upp; camera, Joseph Walker; editor, Al Clark; asst. director, Abby Berlin. Previewed at Pantages, Aug. 18, '44. Running time, 89 MINS.

Janie Anderson....Jean Arthur
Andy Anderson....Lee Bowman
William Smith....Charles Coburn
Judge....Edgar Buchanan
Bell "Boy"....Charley Grapewin
Henry Fairchild....Phil Brown
Minister....Harry Davenport
Minister's Wife....Jane Darwell
Motel Clerk....Grant Mitchell
Top Sergeant....Frank Orth
Marriage Clerk....Charles Arnt
Attorney....Robert Emmett Keane

"The Impatient Years" hits a merry pace in intimately detailing the strain and confusion of a returning soldier and his young wife in trying to get reacquainted after his absence overseas of 18 months—especially as couple met and married originally in four days. Compactly set up, and filled with spritely dialog and episodes geared to current audience tastes, picture will hit profitable biz in all bookings. Names of Jean Arthur and Charles Coburn provide fine marquee voltage.

Problem of the young couple is one to be faced in reality by thousands of others as the war marches to a conclusion. Lee Bowman returns to his wife a virtual stranger which is entirely logical in view of the fast romance and marriage. Both are self-conscious to the breaking point, and their squabbles bring them before the judge for a divorce. Coburn, girl's understanding father, suggests that the judge decree their retracing of original meeting and honeymoon—which provides series of amusing situations for final understanding and reunion. Naturally there's a baby involved to assist in final clinch.

Original screenplay by Virginia Van Upp, who also functions as associate producer, is liberally sprinkled with sparkling episodes and dialog; with Irving Cummings directing in deft style to accent the humorous situations.

Miss Arthur is capital as the young wife who takes household duties too seriously, while Coburn gives his usual fine performance as the father. Bowman is good as the soldier-husband who re-woos his mate. Strong bits are provided by Phil Brown, Charley Grapewin, Edgar Buchanan, Frank Jenks and Frank Orth.

Picture has been given good production mounting, with camera work by Joseph Walker of standard quality. *Walt.*

Louisiana Hayride

(SONGS)

Columbia release of Charles Barton production, directed by same. Stars Judy Canova; features, Ross Hunter, Richard Lane, Lloyd Bridges. Screenplay Paul Yawitz, based on original by Yawitz, Manny Seff; camera, L. W. O'Connell; editor, Otto Meyer; songs, Kim Gannon, Walter Kent, Jerry Seelen, Saul Chaplin. At B'klyn Strand, N. Y., week of Aug. 18, '44. Running time, 67 MINS.

Judy Crocker....Judy Canova
Gordon Pearson....Ross Hunter
J. Huntington McMasters....Richard Lane
Montague Price....Lloyd Bridges
Jeb Crocker....Matt Willis
Canada Brown....George McKay
Maw Crocker....Minerva Urecal
Malcolm Cartwright....Hobart Cavanaugh
Warburton....Eddie Kane
Wiffle....Nelson Leigh
Director....Arthur Loft
Officer Conlon....Robert Homans
Forbes....Russell Hicks

A weak, low-budgeter with a couple of lively tunes, "Louisiana Hayride" is a Judy Canova comedy film headed for the lower dual bills.

Miss Canova portrays a film-struck hick from the sticks who outsmarts two con men to achieve her ambition. But not before the two crooks get part of her fortune, which is hers because of the oil potentialities on her farm. Some laughs are scored by the comedy that comes out of mixups between the star and the phoneys. But much of the humor falls flat, because the gags concocted by scripter Paul Yawitz are silly in most instances, and old in all.

Richard Lane and George McKay, as the con men, do a fairly good job, while remainder of the cast is substantial. "You Gotta Go Where the Train Goes," by Kim Gannon and Walter Kent, and "I'm a Woman of the World," by Jerry Seelen and Saul Chaplin are better-than-average songs, ably delivered by Miss Canova. Direction by Charles Barton lacks pace. *Sten.*

Sonora Stagecoach

Monogram release of Robert Tansey production, directed by Tansey. Stars Hoot Gibson, Bob Steele, Chief Thunder Cloud; features Rocky Camron, Betty Miles, Paul Kenton. Screenplay, Frances Kavanaugh; from original by Robert Emmett; editor, John C. Fuller; music, Frank Sanucci. At New York, N. Y., week of Aug. 16, '44. Running time, 51 MINS.

Hoot....Hoot Gibson
Bob....Bob Steele
Thunder Cloud....Chief Thunder Cloud
Rocky....Rocky Camron
Betty....Betty Miles
Paul Kenton....Glen Strange
Larry Payne....George Eldridge
Joe Kenton....Karl Hackett
Sheriff Hampton....Henry Hall
Blackie Reed....Charles King
Steve Martin....Bud Osborne
Weasel....Charlie Murray, Jr.
Pop Carson....John Bridges
Red....Al. Ferguson
Judge Crandall....Forrest Taylor

"Sonora Stagecoach" is a well-made, fast-moving western for the duals with plenty of name value to lasso the sage-followers.

Trio of Hoot Gibson, Bob Steele and Chief Thunder Cloud are a smooth combination who carry the action at a quick pace and provide enough gunplay, fisticuffs and hell-for-leather riding to give the film its full quota of excitement. Even gal in the yarn is superior to the average heroine in westerns, knowing what to do on a horse and being more than just a mere decorative addition to the proceedings.

Threesome are involved in clearing an innocent man from a murder charge, and as the title indicates, delivering him safely to Sonora via stagecoach for trial. Thwarting attempts to waylay the vehicle, they deliver their charge safely and choke a confession from the real killers.

Method of using an offstage voice at the start to explain their mission makes for added interest, while music, camera work and Robert Tansey's direction also rate mention. *Kamp.*

Seven Doors to Death

PRC release of Alfred Stern production. Stars Chick Chandler, June Clyde; features George Meeker, Michael Raffetto, Gregory Gay, Rebel Randall. Direction and screenplay by Elmer Clifton. Original story, Helen Kiely; camera, Robert Cline; editor, Charles Henkle. At New York, N. Y., week of Aug. 16, '44, Running time, 60 MINS.

Jimmy McMillan....Chick Chandler
Mary Rawling....June Clyde
Charles Eaton....George Meeker
Capt. Wm. Jaffe....Michael Raffetto
Henry Butler....Gregory Gay
Claude Burns....Edgar Dearing
Mable De Rose....Rebel Randall
Donald Adams....Milton Wallace
Timothy Green....Casey MacGregor

A loosely knit meller without suspense or action and thoroughly lacking credibility. "Seven Doors to Death" is slated for the bottom dual bills.

Yarn has a young architect entangled in a crime which he solves in order to lift police suspicion from himself. The "seven doors to death" are the entrances of six shops in an exclusive shopping center and one apartment house, which open onto a courtyard, the tradesmen of which are suspects together with an ape-like gardener, in a double murder and gem burglary.

The characters are all properly suspicious, both in appearance and action, and mouth conversation that is out of a story book right up to the unsurprising denouement. Chick Chandler, who has played almost every type of role, does well as the smart-cracking romantic lead, while June Clyde upholds the feminine end capably. Rest of the cast is adequate.

Picture has been given handsome mounting with the story never measuring up to the production. *Kamp.*

Adventure in Bokhara

Artkino release of Tashkent Film Studio production. Stars Lev Sverdlin; features M. Mirzaharimova. Directed by Y. Protozanov. Based on story by L. Soloviev and V. Votkovitch; music, N. Ganiev and Briunchugin; camera, D. Demutsky. At Stanley, N. Y., week of Aug. 19, '44. Running time, 85 MINS.

Nasredin....Lev Sverdlin
Guldzhan....M. Mirzakarimova
Emir....K. Mikhailov
Djafar....E. Heller

(In Russian; English Subtitles)

Despite the fact that this is a good comedy, given excellent production and entertainment values by its Russian producers, "Adventure in Bokhara" is grooved solely for class houses in this country. Action is slowed too much by transposition to English from Russ dialog.

Yarn deals with a modern Robin Hood who sets out to make the pompous ruler of Bokhara look ridiculous in the eyes of his subjects, and succeeds. He tricks the palace guard and the Emir not only into freeing the latter's newest harem acquisition, but in making him promise to free a group of alleged traitors who were supposedly hiding an adversary.

Lev Sverdlin, as Nasredin, the elusive opponent of the Emir, gives an enjoyable portrayal, adding sparkle to his role by giving the audience the impression he is having a swell time throughout. Costumes and scenes are gaudy. Age of the print of the film is noticeable—it flickers often.

However, a good musical score and some fine acting by a large cast add up to a neat 85 minutes of film fare. *Sten.*

Miniature Reviews

"Till We Meet Again" (Par). Fine romance-adventure saga of French Underground, with Ray Milland-Barbara Britton starred.

"Lost In a Harem" (Songs) (M-G). Good Abbott and Costello fare, OK for b.o.

"Reckless Age" (U). Neat 63 minutes of music and comedy starring moppet Gloria Jean; for the duals.

"The Pearl of Death" (U). Good mystery drama based on exploits of Sherlock Holmes. Standard dual support.

"San Fernando Valley" (Songs) (Rep). Roy Rogers entry will draw on the popularity of its star

"Are These Our Parents" (Mono). Juvenile delinquency yarn is a dualer; must depend on exploitation for biz.

"Enemy of Women" (Mono). Dull tale of inside Germany and life of Goebbels. Lacking b.o. and filler for the duals.

"Storm Over Lisbon" (Rep). Dull routine mystery; for the dualers.

"Valley of Vengeance" (PRC). Fairly diverting westerner.

"Call of the Jungle" (Mono). Better than former Ann Corio pix, but still far from satisfactory; dualler.

Till We Meet Again

Paramount release of Frank Borzage (David Lewis, associate) production, directed by Borzage. Stars Ray Milland, Barbara Britton. Screenplay, Lenore Coffee based on play by Alfred Maury; camera, Theodor Sparkuhl, Farciot Edouart, Gordon Jennings; editor, Elmo Veron; score, David Buttolph. At Rivoli, N. Y., starting Aug. 29, '44. Running time, 88 MINS.

John.....Ray Milland
Sister Clothilde.....Barbara Britton
Vitrey (Mayor).....Walter Slezak
Mother Superior.....Lucile Watson
Major Krupp.....Konstantin Shayne
Cabeau.....Vladimir Sokoloff
Madame Sarroux.....Marguerite D'Alvarez
Elise.....Mona Freeman
Henri Maret.....William Edmunds
Walter-Gaston.....George Davis
Examiner.....Peter Helmers
Gestapo Chief.....John Wengraf
Portress.....Mira McKinney
Mme. Bouchard.....Tala Birell

"Till We Meet Again," with its French underground theme, is more timely at this moment, because of current historical events, than when that plot form was first cinematized. In light of the French Maquis' successes, Frank Borzage's film is virtually more out of the headlines than the fiction pages. But it's equally strong as a romance. With Ray Milland and Barbara Britton starred it's surefire boxoffice.

For all its underground intrigue, Nazi brutality and Machiavellian Gestapo methods, film is a different sort of war romance. For one thing, its heroine is a novitiate nun and Milland is an almost too happily married albeit dashing American aviator, forced down in occupied France.

Sometimes Milland's love-hunger for his wife and child is a bit sticky, but it gets over a wholesome message of the American standard of love and marriage to the young French convent girl. To her it's a new-found litany of love that awakens a new perspective on the mundane world as she accompanies Milland—as his pseudo-wife—in order to aid his escape with valuable secret papers from the French Underground for London.

Miss Britton, a newcomer, is compelling as the beauteous but unworldly church disciple. Unwittingly she had betrayed her church as a haven for Allied flyers and the French underground, and so she essays to square her debt by accompanying Milland on his dangerous mission.

Against this panorama is projected Walter Slezak as the quisling provincial French mayor of their home town who, however, mercifully kills the novice when the brutal Nazi major is about to ship her to a German brothel. Konstantin Shayne is superb as the Nazi officer, shading his despicable character with a certain decorum as he constantly foils with Lucile Watson, the Mother Superior, who too is impressive in her venerable role. Vladimir Sokoloff as the gardener, Marguerite D'Alvarez and Tala Birell as French patriot women doing the dangerous job, and John Wengraf in a bit as the Gestapo chief, make their performances count.

Borzage's direction is even throughout, projecting the ethereal and romance values against the harsh martial background. Lenore Coffee's script is solid and certain lines, ascribed to the patriotic French bourgeoisie, such as "one is never through with the Germans," is a constant reminder of a too-realistic truism.

The dominant religioso aura, of course, puts "Till We Meet Again" somewhat in the cycle of "Song of Bernadette" and "Going My Way," but basically it is solid romance-adventure entertainment. *Abel.*

Lost in a Harem

(SONGS)

Metro release of George Haight production. Stars Bud Abbott and Lou Costello; features Marilyn Maxwell, John Conte, Douglass Dumbrille, Jimmy Dorsey orchestra. Directed by Charles Riesner. Screenplay, Harry Ruskin, John Grant, Harry Crane; camera, Lester White; editor, George Hively; musical supervision, Johnny Green; songs, Don Raye, Gene dePaul, Sammy Fain, Ralph Freed, Toots Camarata. Previewed at Ziegfeld, N. Y., Aug. 23, '44. Running time, 89 MINS.

Peter Johnson.....Bud Abbott
Harvey Garvey.....Lou Costello
Hazel Moon.....Marilyn Maxwell
Prince Ramo.....John Conte
Nimativ.....Douglass Dumbrille
Teema.....Lottie Harrison
Bobo.....J. Lockard Martin
The Derelict.....Murray Leonard
Chief Ghamu.....Adia Kuznetzoff
Crystal Gazer.....Milton Parsons
Mr. Ormulu.....Ralph Sanford
Jimmy Dorsey and His Orchestra

"Lost in a Harem" is good standard fare for Abbott & Costello fans. The boys are in the groove, knocking themselves out for laughs in a slapstick bit of nonsense that is plenty corny at times, but is still funny. The plot is thin and the action drags badly at times, but on the whole the boys deliver. What may be a little old-hat for a first-run Broadway house will garner laughs in the towns and nabes. Audience at the sneak review lapped up most of it. Film will do good business.

"Harem" has some fun kidding the usual desert musical-romance, even if that category includes Metro's own "Kismet." Film will also garner some unintended laughs from keen-eyed audiences who recognize some of the sets in "Harem" as having also been used in "Kismet." This isn't a terrible fault, sets fitting in nicely, and the film itself getting a lavish-enough production not to be accused of skimping on budget. There is an elaborate ballet scene, for instance, set to "Scheherazade" music, as attractive as any seen in recent films.

The film also has some neat production numbers built around appearances of Jimmy Dorsey and his orchestra. This also adds to the fun, gaudy Oriental costumes on the musicians adding to the incongruity of a modern jazz band in an exotic Bagdad kingdom. Photography in handling the Dorsey music-numbers is also fresh and original, for attractive intro of the music into the story.

Story has to do with a mystical eastern land where an American troupe has been stranded. Land is ruled by a sheik who has defrauded his nephew of the throne. Nephew (John Conte), knowing his uncle's weakness for blondes, hires Marilyn Maxwell, troupe's prima donna, and Abbott & Costello, troupe's magic act, to regain his kingdom by stealing some magic rings his uncle wears.

The quartet's efforts involves them in varied escapades, most centered about the sheik's extensive harem, until the youthful prince regains his throne. The fun centers around the blunderings of Abbott & Costello, although Murray Leonard, as a wacky derelict, grabs off a wad of laughs himself. One prison scene with Leonard and the boys, however, is much too long, spun out long after the gags are outworn. Miss Maxwell and Conte, furnishing the romantic element, make an attractive pair, and Douglass Dumbrille is suave enough as the villain. Directing pace, aside from the laugh lapses, is good. *Bron.*

Reckless Age

(SONGS)

Universal release of Felix E. Feist production. Stars Gloria Jean; features Jane Darwell, Franklin Pangborn, Henry Stephenson. Directed by Feist. Screenplay, Gertrude Purcell and Henry Blankfort, from original by Al Martin; camera, Jerome Ash; editor, Ray Curtiss; musical direction, Sam Freed, Jr. Previewed in N. Y., Aug. 28, '44. Running time, 63 MINS.

Linda Wadsworth.....Gloria Jean
J. H. Wadsworth.....Henry Stephenson
Sarah Wadsworth.....Kathleen Howard
Mr. Thurtle.....Franklin Pangborn
Mr. Cook.....Andrew Tombes
Roy Connors.....Marshall Thompson
Mrs. Connors.....Jane Darwell
Mr. Connors.....Lloyd Corrigan
Sandra Sibelius.....Judy Clark
Joey Bagle.....Jack Gilford
Jerkins.....Chester Clute
The Delta Rhythm Boys
Harold Nicholas

Supported by an excellent cast and given topflight, swiftly-paced production by Felix E. Feist, Gloria Jean in "Reckless Age" scores strongly. Picture should do well in the duals.

Neatly molded variety film includes comedy, songs and specialties, plus a fairly interesting plot. Miss Jean has been surrounded by an experienced cast, among them Jane Darwell, as a rooming-house proprietress; Franklin Pangborn, as the pixillated dime-store assistant manager, and Henry Stephenson, as her wealthy grandfather, whose well-meaning antics drive her to distraction. She sings three tunes, "Il Bacio," "Cradle Song" and "Santa Lucia," in fine voice. Notable specialties include Harold Nicholas (of pre-war Nicholas Bros.) in his standard song-and-dance routine of "Mama Eu Quero"; vocalizing by the Delta Rhythm Boys, and one by Jack Gilford, who does a very funny bit of a guy trying to keep awake while getting a pep talk from his boss (which Gilford did in the stage revue, "Meet the People"). Gilford, who has been in niteries and vaudeville, should go on from here to bigger things as a film comedian. Yarn finds Miss Jean rebelling against the home life of her grandfather, running away and obtaining a job as a clerk in one of his dime stores, unbeknownst to him.

Feist has produced and directed this picture on a fairly unpretentious budget. *Sten.*

The Pearl of Death

Hollywood, Aug. 25.

Universal release of Roy William Neill production. Stars Basil Rathbone and Nigel Bruce. Directed by Neill. Screenplay, Bertram Millhauser; based on "The Six Napoleons" by Sir Arthur Conan Doyle; camera, Virgil Miller; editor, Ray Snyder. Previewed in Hollywood, Aug. 24, 1944. Running time, 67 MINS.

Sherlock Holmes.....Basil Rathbone
Doctor Watson.....Nigel Bruce
Lestrade.....Dennis Hoey
Naomi Drake.....Evelyn Ankers
Giles Conover.....Miles Mander
Amos Hodder.....Ian Wolfe
Digby.....Charles Francis
James Goodram.....Holmes Herbert
Bates.....Richard Nugent
Mrs. Hudson.....Mary Gordon
The Creeper.....Rondo Hatton

Sherlock Holmes continues his cinematic sleuthing in this murder mystery, which should provide good entertainment on the duals for the customers partial to mystery dramas. Basil Rathbone and Nigel Bruce, previously identified as Holmes and Dr. Watson, respectively, again carry on for satisfactory results.

Plot concerns efforts of European master criminal (Miles Mander) to obtain possession of a huge pearl valued at $250,000. It's battle of wits between Mander and Holmes to track down elusive gem, with Holmes emerging the victor after formularized development of suspenseful episodes.

Rathbone and Bruce are okay in their familiar roles. Mander is good as the criminal with aid from Evelyn Ankers as accomplice. Balance of cast has brief footage individually.

Roy William Neill, as producer-director, retains the flavor of past Holmes films, while Bertram Millhauser delivers a compact and straight-line script. *Walt.*

San Fernando Valley

(SONGS)

Republic release of Eddy White production. Stars Roy Rogers, Dale Evans; features Jean Porter, Andrew Tombes. Directed by John English. Original screenplay, Dorrell and Stuart McGowan; camera, William Bradford; editor, Ralph Dixon; songs, Gordon Jenkins, Ken Carson, Tim Spencer, Charles Henderson, William Lava, Alyce Walker. Previewed in N. Y. Aug. 24, '44. Running time, 74 MINS.

Roy.....Roy Rogers
Dale Kenyon.....Dale Evans
Betty Lou.....Jean Porter
John "Cyclone" Kenyon.....Andrew Tombes
Oliver Griffith.....Charles Smith
Keno.....Edward Gargan
Hattie O'Toole.....Dot Farley
Matt.....LeRoy Mason
Bob Nolan and Sons of Pioneers
Trigger
Vernon & Draper
Morell Trio

A lavishly produced film that falls short of previous Roy Rogers entries. "San Fernando Valley" will nevertheless be profitable on the star's marquee popularity as well as the title tune.

Weakly-knit yarn, which doesn't take place in the San Fernando Valley, but merely uses the song for window dressing to display the vocal talents of the leads, concerns Rogers' efforts to woo the quick-tempered but charming mistress of a ranch, owned by her grandfather, while filling the job of cook; discouraging the ardor of the gal's kid-sister, and trying to track down some holdup men who fleeced him. He's assisted in all this by his none-too-bright pal. Inclusion of feminine cowhands to work on the ranch, replacing the Sons of the Pioneers, makes for a few good comedy sequences, with the teen-age sister, the grandpop and Rogers' sidekick carrying the none-too-heavy comedy load.

Rogers and Dale Evans continue their acting association, and are a convincing team. Duo warble title number, and each does a solo on another. Jean Porter, as the likable brat, does well and sings two numbers, one a cute double-talk affair, "I Drotled a Drit Drit." Bob Nolan and the Sons of the Pioneers are in for their usual vocal contribution, while Edward Gargan, who has done so many dumb-dick parts he seems out of his environment on a horse, pitches in with Rogers on a novelty tune, "They Went That a-Way." Rest of the cast, who don't sing, are okay. Specialties by Vernon & Draper and the Morell Trio are bits of no great consequence.

Film has been spared no expense insofar as production is involved, but direction could have been tightened. *Kamp.*

Are These Our Parents?

Monogram release of Jeffrey Bernard production. Stars Helen Vinson, Lyle Talbot; features Noel Neill, Richard Byron, Addison Richards, Ivan Lebedeff. Directed by William Nigh. Screenplay, Michel Jacoby from original by Hilary Lynn; camera, Harry Neumann; editor, Johnny Link. At Victoria, N. Y., week of Aug. 22, '44. Running time, 74 MINS.

Myra Salisbury	Helen Vinson
George Kent	Lyle Talbot
Alexis	Ivan Lebedeff
Terry Salisbury	Noel Neill
Hal Bailey	Richard Byron
Clint Davis	Addison Richards
Ma Henderson	Emma Dunn
Pa Henderson	Ian Wolfe
Mona Larson	Robin Raymond
Sam Bailey	Anthony Warde
Meg	Jean Carlin
Miss Winfield	Claire McDowell
Commissioner	Emmett Vogan
Butler	Edgar Norton

Another in the cycle of films dealing with the problem of juvenile delinquency, only this time placing the transgressions of youth on the shoulders of their elders. "Are These Our Parents?" because of its approach and treatment, would seem to fit more into the 1920s, when people were despairing of the lost younger generation and F. Scott Fitzgerald was writing of wild youth with hip flasks, than today, when totally different and far more complicated problems exist. A dualer that will have to depend on lurid exploitation for business.

Story has a young girl fed up with fashionable boarding schools and angry because of her mother's disinterest, who sneaks away to a roadhouse. She becomes involved with a boy who has discovered that his father is neglecting his defense job for a woman. Both become suspects in a murder, with the resultant investigation by a juvenile delinquency officer blaming the parents for the indiscretions of youth by their failure to exercise proper parental supervision. Chastisement has a sobering effect upon the youngster's mother and father, who welcome their children back, eager to right their wrongs.

Film attempts to lump the entire problem of youthful waywardness in the story of a wealthy kid and philandering parents. The war is brought in only incidentally, and no account is made of the greater number of doorkey children whose parents are busy working in defense plants and who have no outlets or planned recreation, while community planning for youngsters is ignored entirely. If the majority of American parents were as unconcerned and thoughtless of their children as the picture makes them out to be, we would have a whole nation of youthful criminals, and not 10 million American boys and girls in the armed forces fighting to come home to an existence which they thought pretty highly of, evidence that their parents were all right and did a good job of upbringing.

Helen Vinson and Lyle Talbot are adequate in the leads, while Noel Neill and Richard Byron are convincing as the two kids. The others are just so-so. Whole trouble with "Are These Our Parents?" is that it's 20 years too late. *Kamp.*

Enemy of Women

Hollywood, Aug. 22.

Monogram release of W. R. Frank production; associate producer, Fred W. Kane. Features Donald Woods, Claudia Drake, H. B. Warner, Paul Andor, Ralph Morgan. Directed by Alfred Zeisler. Original story and screenplay by Zeisler and Herbert O. Phillips; camera, John Alton; editor, Douglas Bagier; asst. director, Barton Adams. Previewed at Filmarte, Aug. 21, '44. Running time, 85 MINS.

Maria Brandt	Claudia Drake
Paul Joseph Goebbels	Paul Andor
Dr. Hans Traeger	Donald Woods
Colonel Brandt	H. B. Warner
Madga Quandt	Sigrid Gurie
Mr. Quandt	Ralph Morgan
Bertha	Gloria Stuart
Walburg	Robert Barrat
Jenny Hartmann	Beryl Wallace
Krause	Byron Foulger
Hanussen	Lester Dorr
Hanke	Craig Whitley
Uncle Hugo	Charles Halton
Mrs. Bendler	Marian Sais

W. R. Frank, who has been operating theatres around Minneapolis, produced and backed this film, which he originally prepared and produced under title of "The Private Life of Paul Joseph Goebbels." It's a melange of purported incidents in the life of the Nazi propagandist loosely put together and dragging along as a narrative without entertainment factors.

Title is a misnomer, apparently tagged on to give the picture some marquee value, but it's a vain attempt. Although Frank apparently spent plenty of coin on large number of sets, cast is negative for selling purposes while neither the wandering script nor uncertain direction justified the outlay.

Story picks Goebbels up in the early '20s as a struggling young playwright who makes unsuccessful advances towards Claudia Drake. He later becomes an ardent follower of Hitler, swiftly rising to power to then find Miss Drake a bit player in a Hanover stock company and use his influence to push her to stardom. He has girl's father placed on purge list, which gives her intimation of his plans. Fleeing to Austria, she meets and marries Donald Woods, but when the Nazis take over, Goebbels singles her out again for persecution. Girl is finally killed in Berlin during an air raid.

Cast is lost in the haphazard unfolding, with boresome episodes making for dull entertainment. Best thing about the picture is the number of sets and camera work by John Alton. *Walt.*

Storm Over Lisbon

Republic release of George Sherman production, directed by Sherman. Stars Vera Hruba Ralston, Erich Von Stroheim and Richard Arlen; features Otto Kruger, Eduardo Ciannelli, Robert Livingston, Mona Barrie. Original story, Elizabeth Meehan; screenplay, Doris Gilbert; camera, John Alton; editor, Arthur Roberts. Previewed N. Y., Aug. 25, '44. Running time, 86 MINS.

Maritza	Vera Hruba Ralston
John Craig	Richard Arlen
Deresco	Erich Von Stroheim
Alexis Vanderlyn	Otto Kruger
Bianco	Eduardo Ciannelli
Bill Flanagan	Robert Livingston
Evelyn	Mona Barrie
Murgatroyd	Frank Orth
Maude	Sarah Edwards
Agatha	Alice Fleming
Street Singer	Leon Belasco
Henchman	Kenne Duncan

"Storm Over Lisbon," for all its ambitious production and lineup of reliable names, is a pretty dull, routine mystery. A tale of espionage in the Portuguese capital, centering around a glamorous cafe where spies of all nations gather, the yarn is long-drawn-out, highly involved and sometimes downright confusing. A dualer.

The action is slow, the comedy by-play feeble and the dialog stilted and unnatural. The tale, when it is clear, is a stock story of familiar situations, with no particularly bright performances by its participants to lift it out of its rut. This one doesn't rate high.

Attempts to make a dramatic actress out of Vera Hruba Ralston (Czech ice-skate dancer, who first tried a straight role in Republic's "Lady and the Monster") aren't too successful, actress being too wooden. She's highly attractive, though, and a seductive dancer in a ballet sequence, for a passable lead to an undistinguished story.

Mystery-dramas can strangle themselves in too many skeins of intrigue, and this one ties itself up in knots. It concerns the manifold activities of Deresco, owner of a combination gambling den and night club, who buys and sells state secrets, and seems to be partial to Axis agents and money. He seems able to kidnap and murder, right under the noses of the Lisbon police, and in other ways act the all-highest. His attempts to intercept an American correspondent, headed for home with some vital secrets on film, form the chief thread of the yarn, into which lovely secret service agents, street singers and musicians, Axis agents and strong-arm men are all mixed.

Richard Arlen adds some verity to his role of correspondent. Erich von Stroheim, as the mysterious Deresco, is right out of the stock files, and Eduardo Ciannelli, as his killer assistant, just as stereotyped. Otto Kruger does a good job as the frightened agent whose number is up, and Mona Barrie is satisfactory in her bit. But "Storm" hardly lives up to its title, despite their efforts, simmering down to a languid breeze in entertainment. *Bron.*

Valley of Vengeance

PRC release of Sigmund Neufeld production. Stars Buster Crabbe, Al (Fuzzy) St. John; features Evely Finley, Donald May, David Polonsky. Directed by Sam Newfield. Story and screenplay, Joseph O'Donnell; camera, Jack Greenhalgh; editor, Holbrook N. Todd. At N. Y. theatre, N. Y., week of Aug. 23, '44. Running time, 56 MINS.

Billy Carson	Buster Crabbe
Fuzzy Jones	Al (Fuzzy) St. John
Helen	Evelyn Finley
Young Billy	Donald May
Young Fuzzy	David Polonsky
Marshal Baker	Glenn Strange
Burke	Charles King
Kurt	John Merton
Carr	Lynton Brent
Brett	Jack Ingram
Dad Carson	Bud Osborne
Ma Carson	Nora Bush
Happy	Steve Clark

"Valley of Vengeance" is a fairly entertaining hoss opera which should please fans of this type film fare. Grooved for the lower rung on dual bills.

Yarn has to do with the roundup of a gang, which 20 years before had wiped out the families of two friends in the wide open spaces. In the course of the hunt, the youths, now much older, meet in the town where the gang leader has full sway, and on the basis of an eyebrow-raising clue, not only nab the leader, but all his henchmen as well.

There's plenty of gunplay, lots of hard, fast riding and the usual amount of romance in this one. Buster Crabbe and Al (Fuzzy) St. John, with the aid of a good supporting cast including Evelyn Finley, as the gal, give neat performances. Settings are better than average, and cameraman Jack Greenhalgh has done a fine job of capturing the background for the action, an improvement over past films he focused. *Sten.*

Call of the Jungle

Monogram release of Philip N. Krasne-James S. Burkett production. Stars Ann Corio; features James Bush, John Davidson, Claudia Dell. Directed by Phil Rosen. Screenplay, George Callahan; editor, Martin Cohen; camera, Arthur Martinelli. At N. Y. theatre, N. Y., week of Aug. 23, '44. Running time, 60 MINS.

Tana	Ann Corio
Jim	James Bush
Harley	John Davidson
Gracie	Claudia Dell
Boggs	Edward Chandler
Louie	Muni Seroff
Carlton	I. Stanford Jolley
Malu	J. Alex Havier
Dozan	Phil Van Zandt
Kahuna	Harry Burns

This Ann Corio starrer is better than her prior efforts, but still leaves much wanting. Film has the usual South Sea setting and dress, giving the ex-burlesque queen a chance to display her figurative talents, but plot fails to sustain interest and pic falls into the lower-rung-of-duals rating.

It all has to do with the efforts of a one-man police force on an isle tracking down a couple of jewel thieves. Miss Corio takes it upon herself to aid in the search for the thieves, but she fails to inform the copper what she is doing and he becomes suspicious of her. After things are cleared up, they learn they are in love with each other.

Best feature of this picture is that it is short. Miss Corio seems to have learned little in the way of histrionics since her last film, and there is great room for improvement in that department. James Bush, as the vis-a-vis, outshines the star in his portrayal of the one-man police force, while the supporting roles are fairly capably handled. Settings show clipped-budgetitis, while direction lacks an even pace. *Sten.*

Miniature Reviews

"Arsenic and Old Lace" (WB). Comedy along chiller lines, based on Broadway longrun hit of same name, will do big b.o.

"Rainbow Island" (Musical; Color) (Par). Slow-moving Dorothy Lamour-Eddie Bracken musical augurs moderate b.o.

"Our Hearts Were Young and Gay" (Par). Bright comedy which, despite marquee shortcomings, likely to do big b.o

"Dark Mountain" (Par). Okay outdoor action drama, to provide good support for regular houses.

"The National Barn Dance" (Songs) (Par). Strong supporter in metropolitan bookings; hot boxoffice for hinterlands.

"San Diego, I Love You" (U). Jon Hall and Louise Albritton in a "sleeper"; farce-comedy looks a moneymaker for most spots.

"Port of 40 Thieves" (Rep) Tense study of femme killer; better than average "B." Duals.

"Oh, What a Night!" (Mono). Fast-moving dualer; Edmund Lowe and Jean Parker for the marquee.

Arsenic and Old Lace

Warner Bros. release of Frank Capra production, directed by Capra; Stars Cary Grant; features Raymond Massey, Jack Carson, Peter Lorre, Priscilla Lane, E. E. Horton, James Gleason, Josephine Hull, Jean Adair, John Alexander. Based on play of same name by Joseph Kesselring; adaptation, Julius J. & Philip G. Epstein; editor, Daniel Mandell; camera, Sol Polito. At Strand, N. Y., starting Sept. 1, '44. Running time, **118 MINS.**

Mortimer Brewster..........Cary Grant
Elaine Harper..........Priscilla Lane
Jonathan Brewster..........Raymond Massey
O'Hara..........Jack Carson
Mr. Witherspoon..........Edw. E. Horton
Dr. Einstein..........Peter Lorre
Lt. Rooney..........James Gleason
Abby Brewster..........Josephine Hull
Martha Brewster..........Jean Adair
Teddy "Roosevelt"..........John Alexander
Reverend Harper..........Grant Mitchell
Brophy..........Edward McNamara
Taxi Cab Driver..........Garry Owen
Saunders..........John Ridgely
Judge Cullman..........Vaughan Glaser
Dr. Gilchrist..........Chester Clute
Reporter..........Charles Lane
Gibbs..........Edward McWade

"Arsenic and Old Lace," which recently closed a run on Broadway that ran 3½ years has, in the highly capable hands of producer-director Frank Capra, become riotous screen entertainment. It faces no obstacles toward sales acceptance in any type of situation. It is definitely in the higher brackets as a money-getter.

Despite the fact that picture runs 118 minutes, Capra has expanded on the original play to a sufficient extent to maintain a steady, consistent pace. With what he has crammed into the running time film doesn't seem that long. Though the scope of the camera permits some outside and extraneous scenes, the majority of the action is confined to one set, that of the home of the two amiably nutty aunts who believe it's kind to poison people they come in contact with and their non-violently insane brother who thinks he's Teddy Roosevelt.

Cary Grant, starred, and Priscilla Lane, featured, are paired romantically. They open the picture getting married but are delayed in their honeymoon when Grant finds his two screwy aunts have been bumping off people in their house, burying them in the cellar and even holding thoughtful funeral ceremonies for them. The laughs that surround his efforts to get John Alexander, the "Teddy Roosevelt" of the picture, committed to an institution; troubles that come up when a maniacal long-lost brother shows up after a world tour of various murders with a phoney doctor, and other plot elements make for diversion of a very agreeable character. Spicing are thriller-diller ingredients. In one sudden instance, when the action is tense, there was a spontaneous audience scream at the N. Y. Strand, where picture was caught, followed by laughs, which Capra apparently hadn't figured on. With no timing to permit for this, considerable dialog goes downstream as result though doubtless of little importance.

Capra's production, not elaborate, captures the color and spirit of the play, while the able writing team of Julius J. and Philip G. Epstein has turned in a very workable, tightly-compressed script. Capra's own intelligent direction rounds out.

Grant, who ultimately learns he isn't related to the unbalanced but genial aunts and the guy who's supposed to be his wacky brother, turns in a hectic, fast-working performance. Outstanding are the two aunts, Josephine Hull and Jean Adair, from the original Broadway cast, together with Alexander, also of the show's cast. Miss Lane, somewhat lesser as to cast stature, does a creditable job as the harassed bride anxious to get going on her honeymoon. Cop role is played evenly by Jack Carson, while James Gleason, in the action toward the end, has several good moments to offer his audiences. He plays a police official who's as dumbfounded as others over what's going on. Edward Everett Horton is the sanitarium super and okay, as usual. Exceptionally good are Massey and Lorre, the former looking like Boris Karloff as result of facial operations to cloak his identity. Lorre as the doctor who performed them and likes his grog.

Warners has had this picture on spools for a long time, withholding release until now. Since it isn't the type that becomes dated, it has given precedence to other of its productions. *Char.*

Rainbow Island

(TECHNICOLOR: MUSICAL)

Paramount release of E. D. Leshin production. Stars Dorothy Lamour, Eddie Bracken. Directed by Ralph Murphy. Screenplay, Walter DeLeon, Arthur Phillips; story, Seena Owen; camera, Karl Struss; editor, Arthur Schmidt; songs, Ted Koehler, Burton Lane; dances, Danny Dare. Tradeshown in New York, Aug. 31, '44. Running time, **97 MINS.**

Lona..........Dorothy Lamour
Toby Smith..........Eddie Bracken
Pete Jenkins..........Gil Lamb
Ken Masters..........Barry Sullivan
Dr. Curtis..........Forrest Orr
Queen Okalana..........Anne Revere
High Priest Kahuna..........Reed Hadley
Alcoa..........Marc Lawrence
Executioner..........Adia Kuznetzoff
Miki..........Olga San Juan
Moana..........Elena Verdugo
Mrs. Carveth Wells.

Produced on a lavish scale (Technicolor), this musical is geared for moderate b.o. in the keys. Business will depend largely on marquee values of Dorothy Lamour and Eddie Bracken. Both the stellar and costly production assets will likely require strong selling to insure returns.

Miss Lamour, Bracken and Gil Lamb are limited by a somewhat aimless yarn and slow direction. Comedy dialog and gag sequences are not overly strong, though registering for occasionally sturdy results. Barry Sullivan, singing male lead opposite Miss Lamour, gets by. Romantic interest, however, is light throughout.

Yarn is along the familiar South Sea island lines, with the sarong motif heavily emphasized. War angle is introduced via three sailors (Bracken, Lamb and Sullivan), survivors of a ship torpedoed by the Japs, who land on a deserted island. Later, afte rcapturing a Jap plane, they make a crash landing on another island, inhabited almost exclusively by dark-skinned damsels attired in revealing costumes.

Miss Lamour, as an American girl who had been shipwrecked on the island years earlier, saves the boys from death at the hands of the hostile male natives by pointing out that Bracken looks like the island god. Bracken, falling into line with the idea, is thus obliged to refrain from eating, drinking and flirting.

Gag sequences include a female impersonation of the island queen's maid and a chase. Production numbers, along typical South Sea pattern, include routine dance numbers. Three songs—"Beloved," "What a Day" and "Boogie, Woogie, Boogie Man"—are okay. *Mori.*

Our Hearts Were Young and Gay

Paramount release of Sheridan Gibney production, screenplayed by him from book by Cornelia Otis Skinner and Emily Kimbrough. Features Gail Russell, Diana Lynn, Charlie Ruggles, Dorothy Gish. Directed by Lewis Allen. Camera, Theodor Sparkuhl, Gordon Jennings, Farciot Edouard; music, Werner Heymann; editor, Paul Weatherwax. Tradeshown N. Y. Sept. 1, '44. Running time, **75 MINS.**

Cornelia Otis Skinner..........Gail Russell
Emily Kimbrough..........Diana Lynn
Avery Moore..........James Brown
Tom Newhall..........Bill Edwards
Mrs. Otis Skinner..........Dorothy Gish
Mr. Otis Skinner..........Charles Ruggles
Miss Abigail Horn..........Beulah Bondi
Mrs. Ethel Lamberton..........Alma Kruger
Frances Smithers..........Jean Heather
Mrs. Smithers..........Helen Freeman
Nina Koshetz..........Nina Koshetz
Monsieur Darnet..........Georges Renavent
Pierre 'Cambouille..........Roland Varno
English Girl..........Joy Harrington
English Girl..........Valentine Perkins
Captain..........Holmes Herbert
Purser..........Reginald Sheffield
Guide..........Edmond Breon

"Our Hearts Were Young and Gay," from the Cornelia Otis Skinner-Emily Kimbrough autobiog. is a young and gay film. It will please plenty, at the boxoffice and as entertainment.

Not exactly skimpy in cost, it's a frankly low-cost entry, sans cast names unless you call Charlie Ruggles and Dorothy Gish, as Mr. and Mrs. Otis Skinner, such. The authoresses are expertly played by Gail Russell and Diana Lynn but their human nonsensities in this film will do more to project them to future attention than their billing would indicate in this comedy.

Right out of the F. Scott Fitzgerald era, in the mid-1920s, the summer tourism to London and Paris is an affectionate hark-back. Coming now on the threshhold of another postwar tourist season for America—many predict there will not be enough planes and boats to take Yank sightseers abroad—it's a timely and appealing saga.

As unfolded, the adventures of the Misses Skinner and Kimbrough in making their first overseas voyage; the shipboard romances; the sundry tourist characters; the little human misunderstandings and bewilderments of Americans in a strange land amidst stranger customs—all these make for a good audience film. Even the diehard opera diva who "encores" incessantly at the ship's concerts, the correct English captain, the mature femme tourists (skillfully played by Beulah Bondi and Alma Kruger), the show-the-teeth college boy, all are exceedingly well done.

But it's chiefly Miss Russell's and Miss Lynn's picture. Miss Russell looks enough like Miss Skinner to be her younger self, while the ever-breathless, slightly madcap Miss Lynn is capital in everything she does. Their two vis-à-vis juveniles likewise click. Bill Edwards is good as the young medico and James Brown ditto as the campus ladykiller. Miss Gish, marking her film comeback, is okay as Mrs. Skinner, and Ruggles does a sedate job as the famed actor-manager.

Producer-writer Sheridan Gibney and director Lewis Allen have taken every advantage of the Skinner-Kimbrough bestseller. The bit with the swinging handbags beneath their petticoats (for safekeeping passports, money, etc.), is milked, as is the innocent larceny of a femme passenger's handbag. The business with the rabbit capes, which shed (but plenty) in the swank Savoy hotel grillroom, London; their being locked in for the night atop the Notre Dame cathedral in Paris; the misunderstanding and the free-for-all in the Paris hotel lobby make for genuine and human fun.

Photography is excellent, especially the Cook's tour montage stuff which will have special appeal for the last-time-we-saw-Paris (London) trade. *Abel.*

Dark Mountain

Hollywood, Sept. 2.

Paramount release of Pine-Thomas production. Stars Robert Lowery, Ellen Drew; features Regis Toomey, Eddie Quillan, Elisha Cook, Jr. Directed by William Berke. Screenplay by Maxwell Shane, from original by Paul Franklin and Charles Royal; camera, Fred Jackman, Jr.; editor, Henry Adams. Tradeshown L. A., Sept. 1, '44. Running time, **56 MINS.**

Don Bradley..........Robert Lowery
Kay Downey..........Ellen Drew
Steve Downey..........Regis Toomey
Willie..........Eddie Quillan
Whitey..........Elisha Cook, Jr.
Sanford..........Ralph Dunn
Uncle Sam..........Walter Baldwin
Aunt Pattie..........Rose Plumber
Aletha..........Virginia Sale
Harvey Bates..........Byron Foulger
Hunk..........Johnny Fisher
Dave Lewis..........Alex Callam
Waiter..........Eddie Kane
Bookkeeper..........Angelos Desfis

"Dark Mountain" is another in the Pine-Thomas series of outdoor action dramas which have become standard program supporting attractions in the regular dualers. This one carries the outdoor flavor, with more story plot than usual for the P-T entries. It's a good dater for the supporting slots.

Robert Lowery works hard as a forest ranger to get promotion to supervisor so as to marry childhood sweetheart Ellen Drew. Finding her wedded to Regis Toomey, suave racketeer, he has Miss Drew take the car for getaway, dropping off while she continues on to Dark Mountain where Lowery sets her up in mountain cabin as hideout. Toomey shows up, keeping under cover for month while wife tries to break away, and Lowery slowly realizes outlaw is hiding on the place. Windup has wild chase over mountain roads, with Toomey killed when car crashes to allow for Lowery and Miss Drew to get together.

Direction by William Berke hits a good pace throughout, opening with brief sequence of battling a forest fire and closing with the inevitable chase. Lowery is okay in the lead, with good assists from Miss Drew, Toomey and Eddie Quillan—latter dishing out mild comedy as sidekick of Lowery. *Walt.*

National Barn Dance

(SONGS)

Hollywood, Sept. 2.

Paramount release of Walter MacEwen production. Features Jean Heather, Charles Quigley, Robert Benchley, Mabel Paige and National Barn Dance Troupe. Directed by Hugh Bennett. Original screenplay by Lee Loeb and Hal Fimberg; camera, Henry Sharp; editor, Everett Douglas; dances, Jack Crosby; music, Irvin Talbot. Tradeshown L. A., Sept. 1, '44. Running time, **76 MINS.**

Betty..........Jean Heather
Johnny..........Charles Quigley
Mr. Mitcham..........Robert Benchley
Mrs. Gates..........Mabel Paige
Mr. Gates..........Charles Dingles
Arkie..........Luther W. Ossenbrink
Pat Buttram, Joe Kelly, Lulu Belle & Scotty, Dinning Sisters, Hoosier Hot Shots.

National Barn Dance radio show, which has been going on network for many years over WLS, Chicago, provides talent for this cinema tale of how the backwoods folk were discovered and brought to the airlanes.

Well staged and assembled, carrying better than average story thread, picture provides good entertainment for the urban customers. However, will be particularly hot boxoffice in the outlands where the radioites have large followings.

Picture provides liberal offerings of the familiar members of the radio stock company. There's Lulu Belle & Scotty, the Dinning Sisters, Hoosier Hot Shots, Joe Kelly and Pat Buttram—all doing their particular specialties. Added is regulation film cast headed by Jean Heather, Charles Quigley, Robert Benchley and Mabel Paige.

Plot revolves around opportunist Quigley, who uses various devices to gain audience of advertising agency owner, Benchley, to sell latter idea for radio show. When Benchley mentions possibility of hillbilly entertainers, Quigley hies out to sign backwoods barn dance unit, bringing group back to the city. Turned down by Benchley for audition, Quigley and Barndancers pose as servants in execs home to stage impromptu show and get chance on the air.

Appearances of the radio group are deftly spotted. First sequence is at hinterland barn dance, and presents Lulu Belle & Scotty in typical song, "When Pa Was Courtin' Ma"; harmonizing of "Angels Never Leave Heaven" by the three Dinning Sisters; and a fast and corny musical turn by the Hoosier Hot Shots. Entertainers are on again for extended period with impromptu show in the kitchen, and then for two final turns when making initial airings over the air. Barndancers work with speed and enthusiasm which has made them popular radio favorites over the years.

Quigley lightly handles the lead assignment, getting okay assistance from Jean Heather for minor romantic footage. Benchley adds strength in straight role as the advertising exec. Hugh Bennett directs zestfully, and keeps up fast tempo throughout. *Walt.*

San Diego, I Love You

Universal release of Michael Fessier-Ernest Pagano production, written by them. Stars Jon Hall, Louise Allbritton; features E. E. Horton, Eric Blore, Buster Keaton. Directed by Reginald Le Borg. Original, Ruth McKenney, Richard Bransten; camera, Hal Mohr, John P. Fulton; editor, Charles Maynard. Previewed at RKO 81st, N. Y., Aug. 30, '44. Running time, **81 MINS.**

John Caldwell........................Jon Hall
Virginia McCooley.........Louise Allbritton
Philip McCooley.........Ed. Everett Horton
Nelson ....Eric Blore
Bus Driver..................Buster Keaton
Miss Jones.........................Irene Ryan
Walter McCooley..............Rudy Wissler
Joey McCooley..............Gerald Perreau
Larry McCooley..............Charles Bates
Pete McCooley.....................Don Davis
Miss Lake...................Florence Lake
Percy ....Chester Clute
Mrs. Lovelace..................Sarah Selby
Mrs. Callope..................Fern Emmett

This is a sleeper. There's little in the routine title, cast lineup or outline of the plot to tip the volatile laugh contents. "San Diego. I Love You" is patterned on the lines of "More the Merrier" and "My Sister Eileen." It's like the former because of the war-crowded San Diego (instead of D. C.), while the "Eileen" resemblance is natural since Ruth McKenney, who did that play, coauthored this. Should do sturdy biz, especially where properly sold as a whacky, laugh bellringer. It'll pay off in satisfied patrons where given that extra bally lift.

With Louise Allbritton and Jon Hall topping the capable cast, producers-authors Michael Fessier and Ernest Pagano have made a neatly gaited farce of the Ruth McKenney and Richard Bransten original. Crisp dialog, screwball situations and an overall sense of comedy are evident in nearly all sequences. Even a corny, forced sleeping car episode goes over.

Miss Allbritton is spotted as the older sister in a large family trying to mother an obstreperous batch of four youngsters (her brothers) and also peddle her dad's collapsible life raft. With this premise, director Reginald Le Borg takes this group into dizzy, crowded San Diego on the hope that the life-raft invention will be approved by a research institute. Remainder concerns her encounter with Jon Hall, third richest man in U. S., who helps the war effort with his research company searching for new inventions.

This does not account for abrupt entrances and more abrupt exits by Miss Allbritton from the scion's private office, nor detail the hilarious ventures of her four brothers, typical American youths. Nor does it cover the persistent obsequities of Eric Blore, the butler, who's fired several times daily after the family discovers that he goes with the house they buy. Nor does it adequately take in an uproarious bus ride, resulting, from Buster Keaton's decision, as pilot of the bus, to abandon the same route he's traveled for 10 years, and Hall's fight in a barber shop. He's handy with his dukes.

Bus ride blends nicely into the story, providing the first chance for Miss Allbritton and Hall to clinch, and cinches subsequent developments. These are only a few of the laugh highlights which include the mistaken roomer, the hotel lobby sleeping episode, the speedboat climax, etc.

Screen scripting of Michael Fessier and Ernest Pagano (the producers) is deft. Their production likewise bespeaks intelligent handling and adequate mounting. Director Reginald Le Borg has chipped in with the necessary tempo required for a farce of this swift pace.

Miss Allbritton, as the invention-boosting daughter, makes a fetching foil for the comedy situations, turning in her top comedienne effort to date. Hall plays the millionaire who owns most of San Diego including the research institute, and does nicely despite being made the butt of many gags. Edward Everett Horton is the high school prof with the brood of brat-like boys, these four being realistically portrayed by Rudy Wissler, Gerald Perreau, Don Davis and Charles Bates. Eric Blore is the usual eager-to-please butler. Chester Clute makes something of pretty much a bit, as the irresponsible brother of millionaire Hall. *Wear.*

Port of 40 Thieves

Republic release of Walter H. Goetz production. Features Stephanie Bachelor, Richard Powers, Lynn Roberts. Directed by John English. Screenplay, Dane Lussier; camera, Jack Marta. At New York, N. Y., week of Aug. 29, '44, dual. Running time, **58 MINS.**

Muriel (Mrs. Hartford Chaney, 3d)......
Stephanie Bachelor
Scott Barton................Richard Powers
Nancy Hubbard..................Lynn Roberts
Aunt Caroline...............Olive Blakeney
Charles Farrington.............Russell Hicks
Frederic St. Clair............George Meeker
Della..............................Mary Field
Jonesy.............................Ellen Lowe
Gladys........................Patricia Knox
Mr. Fellows.................John Hamilton
Conductor.........................Harry Depp

As a psychological chiller, "Port of 40 Thieves" is a superficial insight on the mental processes of a ruthless femme killer. Despite its shortcomings, film is off the beaten track sufficiently to classify as suspenseful entertainment, and should click in the dual spots.

Story deals with a mercenary doll who kills her wealthy husband in order to collect his estate and marry her playboy lover. Murder is kept sub rosa, general impression being that the husband, a w.k. author, has "disappeared." Daughter by husband's previous marriage suspects the truth, and when murderess engages lawyer to have her husband declared legally dead, daughter's suspicions mount. Wife tips her hand to her lover, whom she then kills in order to cover up. When she attempts two additional murders, however, plus a side order of blackmail, she overplays hand.

Yarn carries credence a good part of the way despite gossamer plot. Screenplay by Dane Lussier bridges the tenuous gaps neatly, putting heavy emphasis on character delineation of murderess to offset story.

Stephanie Bachelor is well cast as the wife. Remainder of the principals are adequate. Direction by John English is brisk most of the way and Jack Marta's camera work adds to overall effect. Film, incidentally, is virtually a one-setter, a penthouse apartment serving as centerpiece for most of the action. *Jona.*

Oh, What a Night!

Monogram release of Scott R. Dunlap production. Features Edmund Lowe, Jean Parker, Marjorie Rambeau, Alan Dinehart. Directed by William Beaudine. Screenplay, Paul Gerard Smith, from original by Marion Orth; camera, Mack Stengler; editor, Dan Milner. At Brooklyn Strand, week of Aug. 31, '44, dual. Running time, **71 MINS.**

Rand ....Edmund Lowe
Lil Vanderhoven.........Marjorie Rambeau
Valerie ....Jean Parker
Tom Gordon.....................Pierre Watkin
Detective Norris..............Alan Dinehart
Petrie ....Claire DuBrey
Boris ....Ivan Lebedeff
Sonya ....Karin Lang
Sutton ....Charles Miller
Wyndy ....Olaf Hytten
Rocco ....George Lewis
Sullivan ....Crane Whitley
Murphy ....Charles Jordan
Healy ....Dick Rush

"Oh, What a Night!" is pseudo-comedy for the lower duals.

Familiar ingredients include international jewel thieves and the unsuspecting gauche dame who harbors a fabulous diamond. Also on the scene is the pretty niece who doesn't suspect her uncle of being a crook, and the latter's partner in crime who goes pashy on the gal and turns out to be true blue.

Jean Parker plays the wide-eyed heroine in pulsating fashion and Edmund Lowe is okay as the small-time Raffles. Remainder of the cast is adequate although stymied by hackneyed yarn. Direction is brisk.

Miniature Reviews

"The Last Ride" (WB). Routine actioner for duals.

"Dead Man's Eyes" (U). Inner Sanctum mystery that proves to be no mystery lower-rung dualler.

"The Singing Sheriff" (Songs) (U). Fairish comedy with Bob Crosby. For duals.

"The Soul of a Monster" (Col). A thriller-chiller "B" for the lower rung on duals.

"Leave It to the Irish" (Mono). James Dunn returns to pix in this low-budget comedy; fair dualer.

"1812" (Artkino). One of strongest dramas to come from Russo studios; oke as secondary feature on some U. S. bills.

"Champagne Charlie" (Songs) (Ealing). British production of early-day London Music Hall; may find response in America.

"Boss of the Rawhide" (Songs) (PRC). The Texas Rangers ride again; just another western.

"They Came To a City" (Ealing). Film copy of London stage success, but U. S. possibilities look slim.

"Return of Vikings" (Ealing) (Documentary). British - made documentary on Norway's war efforts; okay for world market.

"2,000 Women" (GFD) (British-made). Good idea gone sour; mild U. S. entry even as second feature.

The Last Ride

Warner Bros. release. Features Richard Travis, Charles Long, Eleanor Parker, Jack LaRue, Cy Kendall. Directed by D. Ross Lederman. Screenplay, Raymond L. Schrock; camera, James Van Trees; editor, Harold McLernon. Previewed N. Y. Sept. 11, '44. Running time, **56 MINS.**

Pat Harrigan................Richard Travis
Mike Harrigan..................Charles Lang
Kitty Kelly..................Eleanor Parker
Joe Genna..........................Jack LaRue
Capt. Butler.......................Cy Kendall
Delaney..........................Wade Boteler
Mrs. Kelly.......................Mary Gordon
Harry Bronson..................Harry Lewis
Fritz Hummel..................Michael Ames
Hazel Dale.....................Virgina Patton
Joe Taylor..........................Ross Ford
Shannon.........................Jack Mower
Walters............................Frank Mayo
Maltby..........................Stuart Holmes
Mrs. Bronson.....................Leah Baird

Chief virtue of "The Last Ride" is its 56 minutes—which makes for easy bracketing as a dualer. Otherwise, film is familiar cops-and-robbers stuff with appeal limited strictly to the actioner devotees.

Scripter Raymond L. Schrock dug deep in the trunk to come up with "Last Ride" plot, which concerns such vintage characters of the ne'er-do-well gangster and his detective-brother, both in love with the same girl. End runs true to form, the hoodlum dying in his brother's arms after being drilled by fellow racketeer.

Contemporary note is injected between chase shots by dragging in situation involving the bootlegging of automobile tires, tying it in with a flaming youth episode that was hot stuff during the Clara Bow-jazz age era.

Film unspooled at dizzy pace with plentitude of episodes involving gunplay and chase sequences. Dialog is both terse and trite. Acting performances are about on even keel with character of film, which obviously turned out on straited budget. *Jona.*

Dead Man's Eyes

Universal release of Will Cowan production. Stars Lon Chaney; features Jean Parker, Paul Kelly, Acquanetta. Directed by Reginald Le Borg. Screenplay, Dwight V. Babcock; camera, Paul Ivano; editor, Milton Carruth. Previewed in projection room, N. Y., Sept. 12, '44. Running time, 64 MINS.

Dave Stuart....................Lon Chaney
Heather Hayden....................Jean Parker
Alan Bittaker....................Paul Kelly
Captain Drury....................Thomas Gomez
Dr. Welles....................Jonathan Hale
Stanley Hayden....................Edward Fielding
Nick Phillips....................George Meeker
Attorney....................Pierre Watkin
Policeman....................Eddie Dunn
Acquanetta

Filled with stilted dialog, lacking action and suffering from poor performances by most of the cast, "Dead Man's Eyes" is an Inner Sanctum Mystery that is strictly for the lower dual bills.

Almost from the first the audience is able to pick out the killer. Yarn deals with the blinding of an artist by his model, who switches an eye-lotion bottle with another containing a corrosive acid, because he is in love with someone else. He can be given new sight by a delicate operation requiring the use of tissues from the eye of another person, alive or dead. The inevitable triangle results in the death of an innocent man and finally in the slaying of the model, who suspects the real killer. In the end, the artist regains his sight and the murderer is caught.

Only one who gives out okay is the star, Lon Chaney, who portrays the blind artist. Jean Parker, as his intended, and Acquanetta, as the other woman, fail to impress, while remainder of the supporting cast does the best it can under the circumstances.

Direction by Reginald Le Borg lacks an even pace. It's obviously a limited budgeter. *Sten.*

The Singing Sheriff
(SONGS)

Universal release of Bernard W. Burton production. Features Bob Crosby, Fay McKenzie, Samuel S. Hinds, Joe Sawyer, Fuzzy Knight. Directed by Leslie Goodwins. Screenplay, Henry Blankfort and Eugene Conrad, from original by John Grey; camera, Charles Van Enger; editor, Edward Curtiss; music director, Sam Freed, Jr. Previewed in N.Y., Sept. 7, '44. Running time. 63 MINS.

Bob Richards....................Bob Crosby
Caroline....................Fay McKenzie
Fuzzy....................Fuzzy Knight
Lefty....................Iris Adrian
Seth....................Samuel S. Hinds
Vance....................Edward Norris
Jonas....................Andrew Tombes
Squini....................Joe Sawyer
Butch....................Walter Sande
Ivory....................Doodles Weaver
Pat Starling and Louis Da Pron
Spade Conley and His Orchestra

Universal has contrived an unorthodox western in "The Singing Sheriff" film being turned out with a tongue-in-cheek approach that joshes the standard mustangers and is patently tailored to suit the crooning stylisms of Bob Crosby. Result is a fair comedy for the duals, with Crosby's name the motivating power on the marquees.

Idea of taking the formula westerns for a ride could have been built up to a high-powered satire, but as conceived in "The Singing Sheriff" it doesn't come off all the way. Opening shots of film, in which the cowboys-and-Indians angle comes in for a ribbing, make for high expectations, but nothing comes of it after pic gets into high gear.

Crosby, who plays a tenderfoot adrift in the wild and woolly west, is afforded plenty of opportunity to indulge in his singing specialties, getting off five of film's seven songs. Numbers are listenable although none is of hit parade calibre. Singing chores are also shared by Iris Adrian, Fay McKenzie and Fuzzy Knight, adding to the overall music plentitude. Voices as well as delivery are standard.

Plot has Crosby, pinch-hitting for sick pal, winding up in a small western town after closing in a successful Broadway musical in which he'd been spotted as a cowboy crooner. Posing as the pard, he finds the sheriff incapacitated, and Crosby's expected to take over and round up the gang responsible for murder and sundry shootings. Crosby stumbles in and out of a dozen situations, including an affaire du coeur, before rounding up the mob in left-handed fashion.

Director Leslie Goodwins keeps story running at brisk pace but film suffers from stilted dialog and too many of Crosby's doubletakes. Crooner's delineation of part is entirely one-dimensional and lacking in the character shading. Yarn, which allows Crosby plenty of rope, isn't entirely at fault for its inept moments. Of the remaining characters in pic, Joe Sawyer, as the quick-on-the-draw gang leader, is outstanding, doing the part up brown. *Jona.*

The Soul of a Monster

Columbia release of Ted Richmond production. Stars Rose Hobart, George Macready; features Jim Bannon, Erik Rolf. Directed by Will Jason. Screenplay, Edward Dein; camera, Burnett Guffey; editor, Paul Borofsky. At Rialto, N. Y., week of Aug. 8, '44. Running time, 61 MINS.

Lilyan Gregg....................Rose Hobart
Dr. George Winson....................George Macready
Dr. Roger Vance....................Jim Bannon
Ann Winson....................Jeanne Bates
Fred Stevens....................Erik Rolf
Wayne....................Ernest Hilliard

Weird and supernatural doings comprise the theme of this low-budget thriller from Columbia. A "B" for the lower rung on dual bills.

Yarn relates how a dying man is saved by the supernatural powers of a fiendish woman, who keeps him under her hypnotic control to do her evil deeds. In their endeavor to save the man from her grasp, his friends manage to stay out of her hypnotic spell, and in the end he is saved.

Rose Hobart does a malevolent and menacing job as the ghoulish lass. George Macready, in the role of a doctor who is saved from death only to be cast under the spell of the woman hypnotist, gives a good portrayal to a difficult assignment. Erik Rolf, as Macready's friend, adds sympathetic treatment to an otherwise stereotyped role. Others in the cast are just fair.

Story bogs down at times, but on the whole director Will Jason keeps the action moving along at a fairly interesting level. Settings are unpretentious as are the mountings and remainder of the production. *Sten.*

Leave It to the Irish

Monogram release of Lindsley Parsons production. Stars James Dunn; features Wanda McKay, Jack La Rue, Ralph Lewis, Dick Purcell. Directed by William Beaudine. Story and screenplay, Tim Ryan and Eddie Davis; camera, Ira Morgan; editor, Dick Currier. At N. Y. theatre, N. Y., week of Sept. 5, '44, dual. Running time, 71 MINS.

Terry Moran....................James Dunn
Nora O'Brien....................Wanda McKay
Maletti....................Jack La Rue
Timothy O'Brien....................Arthur Loft
Harry....................Vince Barnett
Mrs. Hamilton....................Barbara Woodell
Gus....................Joseph DeVillard
Butler....................Olaf Hytten
Joe....................Ted Stanhope
Slim....................Eddie Allen
Biff....................Dick Scott

"Leave It to the Irish" is a low-budget comedy that will garner fair business on the duals only because of James Dunn in the cast.

This one finds murder and mystery playing second fiddle to comedy, but not too good comedy. Dunn and Wanda McKay join forces as criminal investigators, following the murder of a fur dealer. After a series of varying incidents, some tragic, some comical, the male star finds himself a murder suspect with the police at his heels.

Supporting cast, including Jack La Rue, Barbara Woodell, Dick Purcell, Vince Barnett and Arthur Loft, does its best to liven up proceedings, but screenplay by Tim Ryan and Eddie Davis hampers its efforts. *Sten.*

1812
(RUSSIAN-MADE)

Artkino release of Mosfilm Studios production. Features A. Dykki, S. Mezhinsky. Directed by Vladimir Petrov. Screenplay by V. Soloviev; camera, M. Gindin; English titles and narration by Sergei Kournakoff. At Stanley, N. Y., week Sept. 9, '44. Running time, 95 MINS.

Field Marshal Prince Kotuzov....A. Dykki
Napoleon....................S. Mezhinsky
General Barclay de Tolly....N. Okhlopkov
General Prince Bagration....S. Zakariadze
General Beningsen....................V. Gotovzev
Marshal Berthier....................E. Kalushski
Marshal Murat....................E. Brilling
Marshal Davout....................A. Palinkov
Marshal Ney....................A. Stepanov
Czar of Russia....................N. Tischenko

(In Russian; English Titles)

"1812" is one of the most spectacular war features to be turned out in Russia. Fashioned on same lines as "Charge of Light Brigade" (also concerning Napoleonic campaigns), it sketches vividly the Russian army's bitter campaign which ended in severe defeat for Napoleon Bonaparte. Because the battle scenes have been done so well and because there are so many of them, this stands the best chance of any recent Russo production to find outlet as second feature on twin bills in U. S. This despite absolute lack of any femme appeal, with hardly any feminine players appearing.

Besides the moving battlefront episodes and mob scenes, all done with great attention to detail, picture will be remembered for the magnificent characterization A. Dykki has given the role of Prince Kotuzov, field marshal commanding the Russian armies against Napoleon. S. Mezhinsky makes his Napoleon something right out of the old historical sketches. S. Zakariadze is also highly effective as Prince Bagration, who led the second Russian army, only to lose his life near Moscow. For that matter all principal supporting roles are well done by the all-Russian male cast.

Plot traces Napoleon's invasion of Russia sketchily until he nears Moscow. There a near-victory for the Russians is followed by a retreat, and decision to let the French forces occupy Moscow (after it had been partly burned and sacked by its own populace) rather than risk losing a big portion of the Russian army. Story stresses how Field Marshal Kotuzov (Dykki) skillfully plays his game of retreating and leading on the Napoleonic legions. When Nap fails to secure a peace and quits Moscow, yarn faithfully follows the text in showing how the weather, Napoleon's blunders and the harassing tactics of the Russian forces makes the retreat from Moscow a disastrous defeat for Napoleon.

Great attention has been given the mass scenes, with M. Gindin's camera work excellent. Same may be said of Vladimir Petrov's direction. *Wear.*

Champagne Charlie
(Songs)
(BRITISH-MADE)

London, Aug. 31.

Ealing Studios release of Michael Balcon production. Stars Tommy Trinder. Directed by Cavalcanti. Screenplay by Austin Melford, John Dighton, Angus MacPhail. Camera, W. Cooper. At London Pavilion, Aug. 23, '44. Running time, 105 MINS.

George Leybourne....................Tommy Trinder
The Great Vance....................Stanley Holloway
Bessie Bellwood....................Betty Warren
Dolly....................Jean Kent
The Duke....................Austin Trevor
Lord Petersfield....................Peter de Greeff
Fred Saunders....................Leslie Clarke
Tom Sayers....................Eddie Phillips
Duckworth....................Robert Wyndham
Stage Manager....................Billy Shine
Tipsy Swell....................Guy Middleton
Dresser....................Drusilla Wills
Learoyd....................Frederick Piper
Gatti....................Andrea Malandrinos
Targetto....................Paul Bonifas

Based on backstage life in the music halls of the late '60's "Champagne Charlie" should prove popular in England. It may find some favor in America because of its clear depiction of English vaudeville life of those days, being based on the life of George Leybourne, one of Britain's ace singing comics. But Music Hall sequences are too prolonged for U. S. audiences, and will need severe cutting.

Story of two coal miners who come to London to seek fame, finds one as a stage comedian and his brother as an embryo prize fighter. Latter fails as boxing expert. His brother gets an engagement at the Elephant and Castle music hall at $5 a week, plus a pork pie and two pints of beer nightly. He also fails to make good, but is given another chance by Bessie Bellwood at her Music Hall. Here he changes his name to George Leybourne and he eventually becomes one of the top stars of his day. His greatest rival is the Great Vance. Drinking songs about beer, sherry, brandy, etc., eventuating into "Champagne Charlie," figures in plot.

Star of the picture is Tommy Trinder, popular London comedian, as George Leybourne. He has a habit of smiling and smirking at his own antics in this film, but maybe it's okay as a portrayal of this Music Hall comic.

Second featured player is Stanley Holloway, as Great Vance, who uses burlesque seriousness for good returns. Betty Warren, as the then famous Bessie Bellwood, is featured also, giving an excellent performance. Austin Trevor, Billy Shine and Guy Middleton provide neat portrayals in support.

Direction and production help general effectiveness. *Jolo.*

Boss of the Rawhide
(SONGS)

PRC release of Alfred Stern production. Stars Dave O'Brien Jim Newill; features Guy Wilkerson. Directed by Elmer Clifton. Original story, Clifton; camera, Robert Cline; editor, Charles Henkel, Jr.; songs by Newill, O'Brien, Oliver Drake and Herbert Myers; music director, Lee Zahler. At N. Y. theatre, week of Sept. 5, '44, dual. Running time, 57 MINS.

Tex Wyatt....................Dave "Tex" O'Brien
Jim Steele....................Jim Newill
Panhandle Perkins....................Guy Wilkerson
Mary Colby....................Nell O'Day
Henry Colby....................Edward Cassidy
Sam Barrett....................Jack Ingram
Jed Bones....................Billy Bletcher
Frank Hade....................Charles King, Jr.
Joe Gordon....................George Chesebro
Capt. Wyatt....................Robert Hill
Minstrel....................Dan White
Mrs. Periwinkle....................Lucile Vance

Dave O'Brien, Jim Newill and Guy Wilkerson, as Texas Rangers, help make this an average westerner for the double bills.

Task encountered by the trio in "Boss of the Rawhide" is to track down the mastermind behind a gang knocking off the ranchers and then buying up their property from the widows. There is insufficient story material to require almost one hour of footage. Songs, "High in the Saddle," "Ride On Vaquero" and "I Ain't Got a Gal to Come Home To" are fairly well done by the stars, but none is tuneful enough to warrant more than passing mention.

Camera work could stand improvement. Supporting cast does not appear sufficiently enthusiastic about their roles. *Sten.*

They Came to a City
(BRITISH-MADE)

London, Aug. 17.

Ealing Studios release of Michael Balcon production. Stars John Clements, Googie Withers. Directed by Basil Dearden. Screenplay by Basil Dearden, Sydney Cole,

J. B. Priestley. Camera, Stan Pavey. At Studio One, London, Aug. 17, '44. Running time, 87 MINS.

Lady Loxfield............Mabel Terry-Lewis
Philippa......................Frances Rowe
Sir George Gedney..........A. E. Matthews
Malcolm Stritton.........Raymond Huntley
Mrs. Stritton...................Renee Gadd
Alice..........................Googie Withers
Joe Dinmore...................John Clements
Mrs. Batley.......................Ada Reeve
Cudworth....................Norman Shelley

Following faithfully the stage success, which ran nine months in London, "They Came to a City" may repeat its success with this film version.. It holds interest despite the fact that the action occurs in a symbolic atmosphere.

Aside from a prolog and epilog, which serves little purpose except to introduce Mr. Priestley to those interested, the film is an almost exact copy of the play. Even the artists repeat their roles, and without exception, give adequate characterizations. This is particularly true of Ada Reeve, a star 40 years ago, whose portrayal of the philosophical charlady is standout. U. S. boxoffice seems limited in view of what has happened to similar stories recently.

Story belongs to the "Outward Bound," "Admirable Crichton" genre, dealing with a cross section of humanity and their reactions to a new way of life; their success and failure; the awakening of conscience, and the hope and desire for a better future.

Films of this type rely first and foremost upon their dialog, with the action limited. Interest is focussed upon the speech of the players, and in this respect Priestley has delivered the goods. His idea of Utopia, admirably spoken by his adequate cast, cannot fail to evoke admiration.

Return of the Vikings
(Documentary)
(BRITISH-MADE)

London, Aug. 17.

Ealing Studios production and release of first bi-lingual film made for showing in liberated countries. Directed by Charles Frend. Produced in co-operation with Norwegian Government in London with unnamed Norwegian players. At Studio One, London, Aug. 15, '44. Running time, 54 MINS.

"The Return of the Vikings" is another milestone in film history, because it is the first film to be made bi-lingual for the purpose of distribution in a post-war Europe. To Norway and its gallant men goes the honor of this distinction, and the result is praiseworthy. The simple narrative tells of a whaling skipper caught at sea while the Nazis invade his land; of his arrival in England and his life as a member of the Free Norwegian Forces. Should fare well in the world market.

Interwoven with this tale are interesting side issues of the Norwegian Air Force raid on the Gestapo headquarters in Oslo, glimpses of Quisling and his party, and the vistas of the famed fjords.

Although its short footage may be a handicap, the film looks good as a second feature. Michael Balcon is listed as executive producer.

2,000 Women
(BRITISH-MADE)

London, Aug. 23

General Film Distributors' release of Gainsborough Picture. Stars Flora Robson, Phyllis Calvert. Directed by Frank Launder. Story by Frank Launder, Michael Pertwee. Camera, Jack Cox. At Leicester Square, London, Aug. 23, '44. Running time, 97 MINS.

Freda Thompson............Phyllis Calvert
Miss Manningford.............Flora Robson
Rosemary Brown...............Patricia Roc
Maud Wright..................Renee Houston
Alec Harvey................Reginald Purdell
Margaret Long..............Anne Crawford
Bridie Johnson....................Jean Kent
Jimmie Moore..........James McKechnie
Nellie Skinner.....................Dulcie Gray
Dave Kennedy....................Bob Arden
Sgt. Hentzner........................Carl Jaffe

An original idea has been badly botched by story treatment here which divorces this film from reality. A minor dualer.

It shows 2,00 women inmates of a concentration camp in France, caught in the German break-through of 1940. Yarn relates their constant squabblings, their loyalties, and their reactions when three English airmen are parachuted onto their prison. Given rational handling, this might have drawn attention because of its novel theme. It's done in a farcical manner here, and unbelievable. Chances in U. S. are very thin even as a second feature.

The film additionally wastes a fine artist, Flora Robson, in a secondary role, in which she obviously is unhappy.

In extremely bad taste is a supposedly comic sequence in which a corpse plays dummy at a game of bridge. A purposeless fight between two internees brings the picture to a climax in keeping with "fun" and games that have gone before.

The draw of the film's title may help, but this still remains a picture of wasted opportunities.

Miniature Reviews

"Mrs. Parkington" (Songs) (M-G). Greer Garson and Walter Pidgeon starred in excellent production for top biz.

"Frenchman's Creek" (Color) (Par). Lavish 17th century saga of piracy and romance will do okay biz.

"In the Meantime, Darling," (20th). First starrer for 20th's new femme lead, Jeanne Crain, a fair dualer.

"My Pal, Wolf" (RKO). Highly entertaining tale of a kid and a dog for wide audience attention as supporting attraction.

"Babes on Swing Street" (Songs) (U). Lightweight filmusical parading group of younger talent; standard family dualer.

"Riding West" (Col). Average mustanger, starring Charles Starrett, for the duals.

"The Big Noise" (20th). Laurel and Hardy in inept "comedy"; weak dualler.

"Machine Gun Mama" (PRC). Inept comedy for lower duals.

Mrs. Parkington
(SONGS)

Hollywood, Sept. 14.

Metro release of Leon Gordon production. Stars Greer Garson, Walter Pidgeon; features Edward Arnold, Agnes Moorehead, Cecil Kellaway. Directed by Tay Garnett. Screenplay by Robert Thoeren and Polly James, based on novel by Louis Bromfield; camera, Joseph Ruttenberg; editor, George Boemler; special effects, A. Arnold Gillespie, Warren Newcombe, Danny Hall. Tradeshown L. A. Sept. 13, '44. Running time, 123 MINS.

Susie Parkington..............Greer Garson
Major Augustus Parkington..Walter Pidgeon
Amory Stilham................Edward Arnold
Aspasia Conti..............Agnes Moorehead
Prince of Wales.............Cecil Kellaway
Duchess de Brancourt.......Gladys Cooper
Jane Stilham...............Frances Rafferty
Ned Talbot.........................Tom Drake
Lord Thornley...............Peter Lawford
Jack Stilham....................Dan Duryea
John Marbey..................Hugh Marlowe
Mattie Trounson................Selena Royle
Signor Cellini...........Fortunio Bonanova
Madeleine........................Lee Patrick
Humphrey.....................Harry Cording
Belle.............................Celia Travers
Mrs. Graham..................Mary Servoss
Al Swann.......................Rod Cameron
Helen Stilham...............Helen Freeman
Lady Norah Ebbsworth..........Tala Birell
Mr. Ernst........................Hans Conried
Taylor...................Gerald Oliver Smith
Saint Luke's Choristers

"Mrs. Parkington" is a successful picture from any angle. Film version of Louis Bromfield's novel is an absorbing and warmful presentation of the history of an American empire builder—with particular stress on the influence of his wife on his widespread success. With Greer Garson and Walter Pidgeon topping a strong cast of competent performers, there's a smooth-flowing script despite the extended running time of 123 minutes. Skillful direction and production mounting furthermore are in line with the Metro policy of the best for its big ones. Hefty b.o. and extended runs are assured.

Story covers period from 1875 to 1938, with modern portion allowing for frequent flashbacks through the years. Greer Garson is presented at opening as the grand old lady and head of the family and its huge fortune. Her brood of indolent, selfish and generally worthless grandchildren is a collection of strange characters; only sane one is great-grandchild Frances Rafferty, in love with a penniless engineer. Critical situation, calling for pledging the family fortune to save stock-manipulator Edward Arnold from jail and disgrace of the family, is resolutely handled by the wise old lady.

After establishing the family crisis, history of the founder of the fortune, Walter Pidgeon, is developed via series of numerous extended flashbacks as reminiscences of the old lady. Pidgeon is an adventurous and gambling pioneer and promoter, meeting and marrying Miss Garson in a frontier mining town when he inspected silver holdings. She's swept off to New York and luxury and, although remaining naive and unspoiled quickly adjusts herself to the new surroundings. She's sympathetic and loyal to her husband, with intuitive understanding of his egotistical and ruthless nature in business. When infrequent separations occur, she's certain of his return to her—even at one high point where she blocks him from destroying business enemies. Overall, it's a warm and absorbing drama of an American family which built a huge fortune through gambling on the future of the country; and the helpfulness of the wife in the background.

Script by Robert Thoeen and Polly James is deftly contrived to generate maximum audience interest. Dramatic highlights on the life of Parkingtons down through the years are expertly woven together, with producer Leon Gordon rating kudos for his initial big production.

Miss Garson scores solidly in the title role, catching attention with frequent natural blowing of curl on her forehead when riled. Pidgeon provides fine performance as the dashing and adventurous empire builder, while Cecil Kellaway clicks in one brief sequence as the Prince of Wales. Agnes Moorehead is great as Pidgeon's former sweetheart who sticks around to become guide and close confidante to Miss Garson; while Arnold, Gladys Cooper, Frances Rafferty, Dan Duryea and Rod Cameron are strong in excellent supporting cast. Fortunio Bonanova makes one brief appearance to sing an operatic number at the dinner reception.

Tay Garnett provides fine direction throughout, while photography by Joseph Ruttenberg is topgrade, along with all other factors of production and technical contributions.

Walt.

Frenchman's Creek
(TECHNICOLOR)

Paramount release of Mitchell Leisen production (B. G. DeSylva exec. prod., David Lewis, assoc. prod.)., directed by Leisen. Stars Joan Fontaine, Arturo de Cordova; features Basil Rathbone, Nigel Bruce, Ralph Forbes, Cecil Kellaway, Harald Ramond. Screenplay, Talbot Jennings from novel by Daphne du Maurier; camera, Geo. Barnes, Gordon Jennings, Farciot Edouard; music, Victor Young; arrangements, Leo Shuken, Geo. Parrish; editor, Alma Macrorie; costumes, Raoul Pene duBois executed by Mme. Karinska. Tradeshown Sept. 14, '44. Running time, 113 MINS.

Dona St. Columb............Joan Fontaine
The Frenchman........Arturo de Cordova
Lord Rockingham..........Basil Rathbone
Lord Godolphin.................Nigel Bruce
William.......................Cecil Kellaway
Harry St. Columb............Ralph Forbes
Edmond.....................Harald Ramond
Pierre Blanc....................Billy Daniels
Lady Godolphin..............Moyna MacGill
Henrietta.....................Patricia Barker
James...........................David James
Prue................................Mary Field
Coachman.......................David Clyde
Footman.....................Charles Coleman
Luc.................................Paul Oman
Thomas Eustick.......Arthur Gould Porter
Robert Penrose...............Evan Thomas
John Nankervis..............Leslie Denison
Philip Rashleigh.................Denis Green
Doctor Williams...............George Kirby

"Frenchman's Creek" is a 17th century romance about the lady and the pirate, beautifully Technicolored and lavishly mounted, which should fit into the present-day escapist idiom. As such, it will do business.

No smash, but the Joan Fontaine name for the marquee, the ballyhoopla attendant to building Arturo de Cordova into a male draw, the Daphne duMaurier ("Rebecca") authorship, combined with the elaborate Mitchell Leisen production, should make for b.o. attention.

Film reputedly cost over $3,000,000

to produce. Paramount's costliest investment in history. It doesn't quite look that expensive, but it's understandable that much back-of-the-scene travail and delay could fast mount the costs.

The romantic pirate from France who invades the Cornish coast of England, hiding his frigate in what thus becomes known as Frenchman's Creek, plays his role with all the musical comedy bravado the part calls for. In truth, if the public accepts the cinematurgy in that frivolous, musicomedy manner, the picture is a cinch to become a winner.

The romance is supposedly forthright and played straight. Miss Fontaine seeks refuge in the Cornish castle to get away from a stupid husband (Ralph Forbes) and a ducal menace. The scoundrelly servant at the Cornish retreat is actually the pirate chief's hireling, and the romance between the two, including a de-Haysized idyll on his piratical schooner over-night, is but one of a sequence of similar adventures.

All the trappings of the period are interlarded in this tale of hijacking an English pirate's vessel, loaded with booty from the Indies; bearding the irate English gentry in their lair; duelling against odds; the inevitable arrest and escape to the high seas, leaving Miss Fontaine and de Cordova mooning at each other through the sails and halliards. It is a romantic picture of love torn asunder by the conventions. In this case, said conventions are her two children.

The performances are sometimes unconsciously tongue-in-cheek, but withal come off well. Cecil Kellaway is particularly good as the servant. Miss Fontaine is beauteously titian and desirable as the romantically torn wife, and de Cordova gets his role off well albeit not altogether convincingly. He has yet to prove himself truly socko as a male pash. Nigel Bruce, Basil Rathbone and Forbes are otherwise satisfactory, especially Bruce. Rathbone is too leeringly the lecherous menace, and Forbes too much the dolt.

The scripting at times borders on the ludicrous, especially when almost all the sympathetic figures wax near hysteria in their scoffing at the dangers which may beset them. Productionally it is ultra. And no minor assist is that excellent Victor Young score. *Abel.*

In the Meantime, Darling

(ONE SONG)

20th Century-Fox release of Otto Preminger production, directed by Preminger. Stars Jeanne Crain; features Frank Latimore, Eugene Pallette, Mary Nash. Original and screenplay, Arthur Kober, Michael Uris; camera, Joe MacDonald; editor, Louis Loeffler; music, David Buttolph. Previewed N.Y., Sept. 15, '44. Running time, 74 MINS.

Maggie	Jeanne Crain
Lieut. Daniel Ferguson	Frank Latimer
H.B. Preston	Eugene Pallette
Mrs. Preston	Mary Nash
Lieut. Red Planatowski	Stanley Prager
Shirely	Gale Robbins
Jerry Armstrong	Jane Randolph
Mrs. MacAndrews	Doris Merrick
Mrs. Sayre	Cara Williams
Mrs. Bennett	Ann Corcoran
Major Phillips	Reed Hadley
Mrs. Nelson	Heather Angel
Mrs. Farnum	Bonnie Bannon
Lieut. Farnum	William Colby
Colonel Corkery	Cliff Clark
Mrs. Corkery	Elisabeth Risdon
Mrs. Cook	Marjorie Massow
Lieut. Sayre	Lee Bennett
Lieut. Sullivan	Roger Clark

Twentieth-Fox is giving its new femme lead, Jeanne Crain, a star buildup, but neither her first vehicle nor her performance in it, gets her off to an auspicious start. "In the Meantime, Darling" shapes up as light b.o. for the dualers.

Yarn wobbles and never settles down to one main theme, touching on several story lines, but developing none of them completely or satisfactorily. It's a sort of "First Year" tale of a newlywed Army officer, Frank Latimore, and his wife, Miss Crain. At the start, latter is unable to adjust to the regimen imposed on Army wives living in a crowded, old-fashioned hotel outside an Army camp. After her clashes with the other officers' wives, story drops the adjustment problem to go into the wife's efforts to keep her husband from being shipped overseas when the rest of his outfit is alerted. This line, in turn, is dropped for a third plot element, a misunderstanding between the young couple when the husband is inadvertently led to believe he is to become a father. Payoff is the wife's realization of her home-front responsibilities, and the young husband-officer going off to war. Film would probably have been better off had its authors stuck to the original premise, the difficulties faced by all Army wives. Subject certainly is close to many women today.

Wavering story may be partly responsible for Miss Crain's unconvincing performance, but she needs plenty more training and work before she rates the stellar billing 20th has given her. In looks she resembles Paulette Goodard and is okay. Frank Latimore, opposite her, is likewise making his film debut—he's from the legit—and makes a first-rate impression. Should do well as a juve, having an engaging personality, good appearance and an ability to handle lines.

Best work is turned in by Stanley Prager and Gale Robbins, doing comedy relief as another young Army couple. Prager is a promising comic who gave a good account of himself in "Eve of St. Mark." Miss Robbins, former vocalist with the late Ben Bernie, takes good care of her comedy assignment. Also sings one chorus of an unbilled tune okay. Gene Pallette and Mary Nash, although co-featured with Latimore, have small roles. Jane Randolph, as a widow whose serviceman husband was killed in action, is effective. Heather Angel plays a bit. *Merr.*

My Pal, Wolf

Hollywood, Sept. 19.

RKO release of Adrian Scott production. Directed by Alfred Werker. Screenplay by Lillie Hayward, Leonard Praskins, John Paxton: original, Frederick Hazlitt Brennan: camera, Jack Mackenzie: editor, Harry Marker; special effects, Vernon L. Walker; asst. director, Fred A. Fleck. Tradeshown L.A. Sept. 18, '44. Running time. 74 MINS.

Gretchen	Sharyn Moffett
Miss Munn	Jill Esmond
Mrs. Blevin	Una O'Connor
Wilson	George Cleveland
Papa Eisdaar	Charles Arnt
Ruby	Claire Carleton
Mrs. Anstey	Leona Maricle
Mr. Anstey	Bruce Edwards
Secretary of War	Edward Fielding
Mama Eisdaar	Alga Fabian
Fred	Larry Olsen
Alf	Jerry Michelson
Karl	Bobby Larson
Sergeant Blake	Marc Cramer
Wolf	Grey Shadow

This is a sleeper among the program entries, excellent and sustained entertainment for all types of audiences, and focusing attention on new child, Sharyn Moffett, whose charm, personality and ease before the cameras tabs her immediately as candidate for early starring position. Turned out on modest budget and without name values, picture will have to be content with datings as a dual supporter. But after the customers are in, the top bracket attraction will have to be hot to draw the nod over this one.

Story is slightly-new variation of the "poor-little-rich-girl" theme, with the child acquiring a lost dog for immediate audience interest in the kid-dog palship and mutual protection. Youngster is under care of a stern governess on a Virginia farm outside of Washington, with governess combatting keeping the dog and finally discovering it was really trained and owned by the Army canine corps. When jeep takes animal away, youngster follows to training camp trying to buy Wolf back with her few dimes saved from allowance. Told that the Secretary of War is the only person with authority to sell the battle-trained dog, youngster journeys to his Washington home in the middle of the night to plead for return of her pet. She's satisfied with explanation of dog's value for the war, and is finally returned home for happy reunion with parents, dismissal of the governess, and gift of a puppy from the Secretary.

Picture keeps on line of simple and natural situations is displaying the mutual affection and loyalty of the youngster and dog, and never resorts to synthetic dramatics. Result is a sympathetic and arresting piece of entertainment. In directing, Al Werker catches the maximum human interest in the child's brief adventure, and clicks in presentation of Sharyn Moffett for first screen appearance who indicates future potentialities as a marquee name.

In supporting cast, Jill Esmond is the governess, Una O'Connor provides light characterization as the kindly housekeeper, and Edward Fielding is well spotted as the War Secretary. Charles Arnt is the understanding neighbor. The Belgian shepherd, Grey Shadow, as Wolf, is well-trained. *Walt.*

Babes on Swing Street

(SONGS)

Hollywood, Sept. 15.

Universal release of Bernard W. Burton production. Features Peggy Ryan, Ann Blythe, Marion Hutton, Freddie Slack orchestra. Directed by Edward Lilley. Screenplay by Howard Dinsdale, Eugene Conrad; original, Brenda Weisberg; camera, Jerome Ash; editor, Fred R. Feitshans, Jr.; asst. director, Charles S. Gould; music, Sam Freed, Jr.: dances, Louis De Pron; songs, Sidney Miller. Inez James. Previewed at Pantages, Sept. 14, '44. Running time, 69 MINS.

Carol Curtis	Ann Blyth
Trudy Costello	Peggy Ryan
Joe Costello	Andy Devine
Malcolm Curtis	Leon Errol
Francis Carlyle	Anne Gwynne
Dick Lorimer	Kirby Grant
Fern Wallace	June Preisser
Martha Curtis	Alma Kruger
Billy Harper	Billy Dunn
Corny Panatowsky	Sidney Miller

Marion Hutton
Freddie Slack Orchestra
The Rubenettes

Universal tosses a flock of younger talent, headed by Peggy Ryan and Ann Blyth, into this moderately entertaining filmusical. Built strictly to amuse as a light offering, picture has sufficient number of specialties to provide good support in the family houses.

Versatile Peggy Ryan again clicks in fine style with her comedy, distinctive mannerisms, dancing and singing, to carry main attention. Leon Errol catches laughs as an absent-minded eccentric, hitting high gear with a high ledge balancing routine for thrill comedy. Ann Blyth handles one song, the oldie "Peg o' My Heart," and is okay in unobtrusive role. Andy Devine, Kirby Grant, Billy Dunn, Alma Kruger, June Preisser and Ann Gwynne provide support of standard calibre.

Plot is a thin excuse on which to hang the various songs and specialties. Miss Ryan is president of Settlement House group of scholastics who decide to stage night dance spot for younger folk in order to send 10 of group to music school. Ann Blyth aids to secure hall owned by her crusty aunt, Alma Kruger, but there are several stoplights before the show finally goes on with final approval of the aunt.

Freddie Slack and his orchestra are on display early in regular nightclub sequence for one number and appearance of Marion Hutton to deliver "Take It Easy." Errol gets Slack for opening of the kids' enterprise to add class to the getaway, and accompaniment for the various numbers.

Peggy Ryan has several song and dance turns of comedy vein, while June Preisser does one acrobatic dance and handles one song. Script is loosely thrown together, with several bumpy spots along the line. Edward Lilley keeps things moving at a good pace, skipping through the script inadequacies and concentrating on the comedy abilities of Errol to hold things together between the numbers. *Walt.*

Riding West

Columbia release of Jack Fier production. Stars Charles Starrett: features Shirley Patterson, Arthur Hunnicutt, Ernest Tubb and singing cowboys. Directed by William Berke. Screenplay, Luci Ward: camera, Benjamin Kline: editor, Jerome Thoms. At N.Y. theatre, N.Y., week of Sept. 14, '44. Running time. 61 MINS.

Steve Jordan	Charles Starrett
Prof. Arkansas Higgins	Arthur Hunnicutt
Alice Morton	Shirley Patterson
Ernie	Ernest Tubb
Alexander Morton	Steve Clark
Captain Amos Karnes	Wheeler Oakman
Sgt. Dobbs	J.P. "Blackie" Whiteford
Blackburn	Clancy Cooper
Red Eagle	Bill Wilkerson

A routine lariat meller with Pony Express background, "Riding West" will prove okay fare for dual runs.

Actioner centers around efforts of Charles Starrett to initiate Pony Express run in face of dirty work plotted against him by gang of crooked gamblers.

Justice trimuphs in routine fashion, with matters being settled via gunplay and fast riding. Starrett turns in good chore as buckskin protagonist who sees that the mail goes through.

Femme lead is adequately handled by Shirley Patterson, who hasn't much to do since love interest in film is virtually nonexistent. Camera work and direction average.

The Big Noise

20th-Fox release of Sol M. Wurtzel production. Stars Stan Laurel, Oliver Hardy; features Doris Merrick, Arthur Space, Veda Ann Borg. Directed by Mal St. Clair. Screenplay by W. Scott Darling: camera, Joe MacDonald; editor, Norman Colbert. Tradeshown N.Y. Sept. 14. '44. Running time, 74 MINS.

Laurel and Hardy	Themselves
Evelyn	Doris Merrick
Hartley	Arthur Space
Mayme	Veda Ann Borg
Egbert	Bobby Blake
Charlton	Frank Fenton
Hartman	James bush
Dutchy	Phil Van Zandt
Aunt Sophia	Esther Howard
Grandpa	Robert Dudley
Motor Policeman	Edgar Dearing
Manning	Selmar Jackson
Butler	Harry Hayden
Station Attendant	Francis Ford
Drunk	Jack Norton
Conductor	Charles Wilson
Speaker	Ken Christy
Jap Officer	Beal Wong
German Officer	Louis Arco

This Laurel and Hardy starrer is a concoction of silly situations that may have been comical in their time, but certainly not in this day and age. A weak dualer.

Practically every gag the fat boy and his partner use in this melange has been used on the screen before, either done by themselves or others.

Sol M. Wurtzel, who was the 20th-Fox "B" picture production topper until his resignation several months ago, is noted for giving these limited budget films good selling value. Mal St. Clair is a much better director than his job in this one would have you believe. But even they were hampered by an obviously poor screenplay. Whatever laughs there are in "The Big Noise" are merely of the hoke variety.

Yarn finds Laurel and Hardy in the roles of detectives guarding a new-type bomb, invented by a gent who fears that the missile may find its way into the hands of enemy agents. A gang, ensconced in a neighboring mansion, laying plans to rob the jewels of the sister of the inventor, changes over to the bigger game—the bomb—and in the ensuing scenes do all in their power to nab the deadly weapon.

Of the large supporting cast, most have bit parts. Doris Merrick, femme lead and a looker, does not make her appearance until almost half the footage is unwound. Direction lacks an even pace; settings are just average. *Sten.*

Machine Gun Mama

(SONGS)

PRC release of Jack Schwarz production. Features Armida, El Brendel, Wallace Ford, Jack La Rue, Luis Alberni. Directed by Harold Young. Screenplay, Sam Neuman: camera, Gus Peterson; editor, Robert O. Crandall; songs, Sam Neuman, Michael Breen; music, Mort Glickman, David Chudnow. At N.Y. theatre, N.Y., week Sept. 14, '44. Running time, 58 MINS.

Nita Cordova....Armida
Ollie Swenson....El Brendel
John O'Rielly....Wallace Ford
Jose....Jack La Rue
Ignacio....Luis Alberni
The Blonde....Ariel Heath
Alberto Cordova....Julian Rivero
First Detective....Eumenio Blance
Carlos....Anthony Warde

"Machine Gun Mama" is strung out for 58 minutes at pedestrian pace. A minor dualer.

Film, which is dragged out from opening shot to close, never gets started. Outside of flurry of action in early sequence, picture is all talk, and its dialog veers strongly to the fatuous side. Cast of good feature players, including Wallace Ford, Jack La Rue, El Brendel and Luis Alberni, is completely lost in the inept goings-on.

Loose theme deals with couple of okies, Ford and Brendel, who peddle an elephant to a traveling carnival and thereby become involved in series of events centering around the pachyderm. It's elephantine all the way, both in theme and pace.

Armida is injected in film to handle love interest and songs and does okay by both, within limitations imposed by story and music. Others in pic just about get by. Direction and camera work under par.

Miniature Reviews

"The Master Race" (RKO). As timely as current headlines. Solid biz, and can surprise with heavy grosses.

"The Climax" (Songs) (Color) (U). Good entertainment of type, will hit profitable biz in all bookings.

"Goin' to Town" (RKO). Lum & Abner in dual supporter for the nabes and hinterlands.

"Tall in the Saddle" (RKO). Top bracket western meller for ideal escapist entertainment.

"My Buddy" (Songs) (Rep). Good acting lifts this post-World War I story into above-average category; strong dualler.

"Thundering Gun Slingers" (PRC). Oat opera for lower dualers.

"Mr. Emmanuel" (Eagle-Lion). All-British cast in adaptation of novel; may do as secondary dual in U. S.

"Underground Guerrillas" (Brit.) (Col). British-made film about Yugoslav Partisans, strong dualer.

"Maria Candelaria" (Mexican-Made). Bids for attention, with Dolores Del Rio, but considerably inferior to U. S. standards.

The Master Race

Hollywood, Sept. 22.

RKO release of Edward A. Golden production; produced by Robert Golden. Direction, story and screenplay by Herbert J. Biberman. Camera, Russell Metty; dialog director, Madeleine Dmytryk; editor, Ernie Leadlay; asst. director, Sam Ruman. Tradeshown, L. A., Sept. 21, '44. Running time, 96 MINS.

Von Beck....George Coulouris
Phil Carson....Stanley Ridges
Helena....Osa Massen
Andrei....Carl Esmond
Nina....Nancy Gates
Old Man Bartoc....Morris Carnovsky
Frank....Lloyd Bridges
Altmeier....Eric Feldary
Mrs. Varin....Helen Beverly
William Forsythe....Gavin Muir
Katry....Paul Guilfoyle
Sgt. O'Farrell....Richard Nugent
Schmidt....Louis Donath
John....Herbert Rudley
Baby....Ghislaine Perreau
Jacob Weiner....Jason Robards
George Rudan....Merrill Rodin

When Eddie Golden turned out "Hitler's Children" last year to hit film grosses that looked like the Comstock lode, wiseacres predicted his first production venture was a one-shot, and Golden would have a tough time repeating. "The Master Race" is his second picture. It's timely as tomorrow's war headlines and, despite lack of cast names, picture is an exploitation special for hefty biz and key run holdovers. A natural for all bookings.

Golden originally selected the title as a likely one for a picture, and then searched for a yarn to pin it to in order to dramatically show the arrogance and synthetic character of the barbaric Germans. He selected a period when the German armies were fleeing in disorder, and the final unconditional surrender of the Nazi minions. Script follows this line with amazing forecasts, especially the occupation of a Belgian town by the advancing American and British armies and the military government set up by the American major, Stanley Ridges.

Picture opens with clips of the D-Day invasion of June 6 for brief footage, and then swings to headquarters of George Coulouris, member of the German general staff, where he tells assemblage of German officers that the war is lost and they are to proceed according to individual instructions to points designated to create dissension among the peoples of the liberated countries to further destroy Europe so that the self-styled master race can again rise to rule the continent. Coulouris enters the ruined Belgian village posing as a Belgian patriot. American troops are there to establish order and restore normal activity, self-sufficiency of the people, and rebuilding of the ruins.

There's Morris Carnovsky, elderly patriot and head of family which includes daughter Osa Massen, who has child daughter from unwilling association with a Nazi; fighting son, Lloyd Bridges, who returns when town is liberated; Helen Beverly and Nancy Gates, wife and daughter, respectively, of former collaborationist; and Paul Guilfoyle, town's underground leader who's innocent tool of Coulouris.

Neat script and direction by Herbert Biberman details the dramatic events in the town; the bewilderment of the populace, kind and sympathetic attitude of the Allied troops in contrast to the German rule, and Coulouris' conniving to upset quick return to normal. It's a direct and well-told tale, and provides solid dramatic entertainment.

Coulouris is excellent as the German militarist who goes underground for a time in the liberated area; Miss Massen scores as the Belgian girl, and Ridges ably portrays the American major. Carnovsky is splendid as the bewhiskered patriot, while Carl Esmond, Guilfoyle, Nancy Gates, Helen Beverly and Eric Feldary are fine in support. *Walt.*

The Climax

(COLOR; SONGS)

Hollywood, Sept. 21.

Universal release of George Waggner production, directed by Waggner. Stars Susanna Foster, Turhan Bey, Boris Karloff. Screenplay by Curt Siodmak, Lynn Starling, adapted by Siodmak from play by Edward Locke; camera, Hal Mohr, W. Howard Greene; dialog director, Gene Lewis; editor, Russell Schoengarth; asst. director, Charles S. Gould; score, Edward Ward; songs, Waggner and Ward. Previewed Four Star, Sept. 20, '44. Running time, 86 MINS.

Dr. Hohner....Boris Karloff
Angela....Susanna Foster
Franz....Turhan Bey
Luise....Gale Sondergaard
Count Seebruck....Thomas Gomez
Marcellina....June Vincent
Amato....George Dolenz
Carl Bauman....Ludwig Stossel
Jarmila Vadek....Jane Farrar
Brunn....Erno Verebes
Mama Hinzl....Lotte Stein
King....Scotty Beckett
Leon....William Edmunds
King's Aide....Maxwell Hayes
Miss Metzger....Dorothy Lawrence

Embellished in Technicolor, "The Climax" is an entertaining suspense drama, developing reverse twist to the Svengali-Trilby formula. With the rising romantic team of Turhan Bey and Susanna Foster starred with Boris Karloff, picture carries marquee strength for good and profitable biz in the regular runs.

In weaving story of control of Miss Foster's voice by the mentally-unbalanced physician, Karloff, plot utilizes the Royal Opera House for setting. This provides opportunity for the girl to sing several prima donna passages in deft mixture of drama and song.

Karloff, theatre physician, resents discovery of Miss Foster after he had killed his sweetheart-singer 10 years before. When girl is selected to revive deceased successful opera, Karloff gets her under hypnotic spell to prevent her singing. Bey, in love with the girl, finally contrives to get the young king to issue decree for command performance, and lays plans to trap Karloff in his nefarious plans. After building to suspenseful climax, the medic is cornered and Miss Foster delivers her performance for wide acclaim.

Karloff excellently handles the heavy spot of the maniacal physician in good style. Miss Foster does well as the young singer, and is in good voice with the several numbers handed her for delivery. Bey adds to his boxoffice strength as the young composer and lover of the girl. Support, all displayed in strength, includes Gale Sondergaard, Thomas Gomez, Ludwig Stossel, Lotte Stein, June Vincent, Jane Farrar, and George Dolenz.

In handling dual chores of producing and directing, George Waggner capably injects suspense and movement in the dramatic unfoldings. Waggner, at one time lyricist for films when he first started around Hollywood, also contributes musically, teamed with Edward Ward in four songs, of operatic tempo, all sung by Miss Foster. Ward's music is excellent. Technicolor photography by Hal Mohr and Howard Greene is of high standard. *Walt.*

Goin' to Town

Hollywood, Sept. 20.

RKO release of Jack William Votion (Frank Melford production). Stars Lum & Abner; features Barbara Hale, Florence Lake, Grady Sutton, Dick Elliott, and N. T. G. Directed by Leslie Goodwins. Original screenplay by Charles E. Roberts and Charles R. Marion; camera, Robert Pittack; editor, Hanson T. Fritch; asst. director, John E. Burch; dances, Paul Oscard. Tradeshown L. A., Sept. 19, '44. Running time, 69 MINS.

Lum....Chester Lauck
Abner....Norris Goff
Sally....Barbara Hale
Abigail....Florence Lake
Squire....Dick Elliott
Cedric....Grady Sutton
Wentworth....Herbert Rawlinson
Jimmy Benton....Dick Baldwin
Zeke....Ernie Adams
Clarke....Jack Rice
Dr. Crane....Sam Flint
Parker....Andrew Tombes
Jameson....George Chandler
Mrs. Wentworth....Ruth Lee
Grandpappy Spears....Danny Duncan
Camellia....Marietta Canty
N.T.G....Nils T. Granlund

Lum & Abner parade their usual radio characterizations in this one, latest in their series of film programers designed to catch trade through air popularity of the pair. Like past issues, it runs strictly to formula for the rural duo, and will suffice as a dual supporter in the nabes and smaller towns where L. & A. have following.

Plot is rather thin, following usual formula of the hicks outwitting the city slickers. Lum & Abner run the general store at Pine Ridge and become victims of practical joke perpetrated by visiting oil promoter. Result is formation of local capitalized company to drill for oil; resultant dry hole; prospect of the neighbors losing their property through mortgage foreclosures; and unloading of the well on the joker in Chicago for plenty of coin.

Radio characters are slotted for regulation backwoods dialog twang and situations, getting okay support from cast. Direction by Leslie Goodwins injects plenty of corn and hoke to keep things moving at a good gait. N. T. G. and his showgirls are inserted for one floorshow number, apparently to inject some production values into the proceedings. *Walt.*

Tall in the Saddle

Hollywood, Sept. 20.

RKO release of Robert Fellows production. Stars John Wayne, Ella Raines. Directed by Edwin L. Marin. Screenplay by Michael Hogan, Paul Fix; story, Gordon Ray Young; camera, Robert De Grasse; editor, Philip Martin; asst. director, Harry Scott. Tradeshown L. A. Sept. 19, '44. Running time, 86 MINS.

Rocklin....John Wayne
Arly....Ella Raines
Clara....Audrey Long
Dave....George "Gabby" Hayes
Miss Martin....Elisabeth Risdon
Garvey....Ward Bond
Harolday....Don Douglas
Clint....Russell Wade
Juan....Frank Puglia
Bob Clews....Paul Fix
George Clews....Harry Woods
Jackson....Emory Parnell
Cap....Cy Kendall
Doc Riding....Bob McKenzie
Zeke....Raymond Hatton

"Tall in the Saddle" is exciting and adventurous drama in the best western tradition. With John Wayne starred for marquee voltage, and unfolding a crisp and consistently exciting tale, picture is top-bracket entertainment of its type to click for profitable biz in all runs.

Picture, mounted with fine scenic backgrounds for the action, combines all the regulation ingredients of wild stagecoach rides, rough-and-tumble fights, gunplay and chases. Story carries unusual twists from regulation formula to provide top audience interest as strictly exciting escapist entry.

Wayne shows up at the cattle town to take job as cowhand, only to find out his employer has been murdered recently. He refuses position with Audrey Long, grandniece-heiress at the ranch, instead joining up with tempestuous Ella Raines, who operates adjoining layout. Woman-hating Wayne is caught in middle between the two girls while he antagonizes several of the town's tough guys and supposedly respectable citizens. He gradually traces clues to the murder, finds a solution to identify himself as nephew and heir to the ranch, and clinches for the fadeout with Miss Raines.

Wayne delivers a lusty and sturdy performance as "Tall," reminding of his standout "Stagecoach" several years ago. Bewhiskered Gabby Hayes scores for comedy as the waddling and cantakerous sidekick of Wayne. Miss Raines is excellently cast as the dominating and sure-shot girl of the great outdoors, while Miss Long contrasts as the demure maid from the city. Elisabeth Risdon, Ward Bond, Russell Wade, Don Douglas, Frank Puglia, and Paul Fix add strength to the overall in prominent supporting spots.

Edwin Marian neatly balances his characters for fast unfolding of the tale, and gets the utmost out of the action possibilities presented in the well-devised script by Michael Hogan and Paul Fix. Photography by Robert De Grasse takes fullest advantages of the scenic factors presented, while large amount of process photography is credited to Vernon Walker. *Walt.*

My Buddy

(SONGS)

Republic release of Eddy White production. Stars Donald Barry; features Ruth Terry, Lynne Roberts, Alexander Granach. Directed by Steve Sekely. Screenplay, Arnold Manoff from original by Prescott Chaplin; camera, Reggie Lanning; editor, Tony Martinelli. Previewed, projection room, N. Y., Sept. 22, '44. Running time, **67 MINS.**

Eddie Ballinger	Donald Barry
Lola	Ruth Terry
Lucy Manners	Lynne Roberts
Tim Oberta	Alexander Granach
Mary Ballinger	Emma Dunn
Father Jim Donnelly	John Litel
Pete	George E. Stone
Senator Henry	Jonathan Hale
Russ	Ray Walker
Nicky Piastro	Joe Devlin
Happy	Matt McHugh

This is a picture with a purpose and a message for those who will draw up the peace after this war, bringing to the fore the mistakes made concerning employment of the men who came back after the last one. As such this film is a noble endeavor, but the story-line and production values fail to measure up to what an important picture should be. Thus, "My Buddy" (that title!) is nothing more than a strong dualer.

Acting of two members of the cast, Donald Barry, the star, and Alexander Granach, Polish-born actor, stand head and shoulders above the work of anyone else in this film. Barry, as the youngster who comes back from World War I, a man, eager to go out, get a job, help his mother, and then marry the girl who waited for him, only to find "no help wanted" signs facing him wherever he turned, finally departing from the straight and narrow, bites into his meaty role with gusto. His sincerity pervades itself through the screen.

Granach is a real scene-stealer, nabbing honors whenever his visage appears, in the role of the ruthless leader of a gang of liquor-runners, who pledges to help Barry when he is imprisoned, taking the rap for the others.

Lynne Roberts as Barry's vis-a-vis; John Litel as the padre to whom he goes for advice; George E. Stone as the cellmate during his prison sojourn, and others in the cast are seen briefly, but effectively. Despite fact that film is a limited-budgeter, settings are substantial enough.

Given greater scope, more thought and better value during the course of production, "My Buddy" may well have been the sleeper of the year for Republic. Company certainly had the jump on other studios with that postwar prolog and epilog, with the important message and hope that the same thing will not follow the current conflict. Why couldn't Rep have followed through to give this film the treatment it so richly deserved?

Three tunes, "My Buddy" (the oldie), "Whodunit?" and "Waiting for the Evening Mail," both new, are delivered in capable fashion, first and last by unbilled singers, while Ruth Terry warbles second song. *Sten.*

Thundering Gun Slingers

PRC release of Sigmund Neufeld production. Stars Buster Crabbe; features Al St. John. Directed by Sam Newfield. Original and screenplay, Fred Myton; camera, Robert Cline; editor, Holbrook N. Todd. At N. Y. theatre, N. Y., week Sept. 20, '44. Running time, **58 MINS.**

Billy Carson	Buster Crabbe
Fuzzy Jones	Al (Fuzzy) St. John
Bab Halliday	Frances Gladwin
Jeff Halliday	Karl Hackett
Steve Kirby	Charles King
Vic	Jack Ingram
Ed	Kermit Maynard
Sheriff	Budd Buster
Dave	George Chesebro

"Thundering Gun Slingers" is a below-par equiner, which, judging from inferior quality of production, was given smaller budget and less shooting time than even the average western. A shoddy job, for lower half use.

Ardent hoss opera fans will find its hackneyed story dull. Plot is the oldie about the outlaw leader framing innocent ranchers on rustling charges, so's he can buy their properties for little dough. Buster Crabbe, as the nephew of one such framed cattle owner, wipes out the gang and gets himself a romance with the daughter of another rancher, similarly framed.

Performances, except for Al St. John's comedy relief and mugging behind his chin hay, are wooden. Direction and photography weak. Music sounds as though recorded on the soundtrack from poorly surfaced phonograph platters.

This one doesn't even have scenery to save it. *Merr.*

Mr. Emmanuel

(BRITISH-MADE)

London, Sept. 4.

Eagle-Lion release of Two Cities Film. Stars Felix Aylmer; features Greta Gynt, Walter Rilla. Directed by Harold French. Screenplay by Louis Golding, Gordon Wellesley from novel by Louis Golding. Camera, Otto Heller, Gus Drisse. At Gaumont, London, Sept. 3, '44. Running time, **97 MINS.**

Mr. Emmanuel	Felix Aylmer
Elsie Silver	Greta Gynt
Willi Brockenburg	Walter Rilla
Bruno	Peter Mullins
Frau Heinkes	Ursula Jeans
Herr Heinkes	Frederick Reichter
Rose Cooper	Elspeth March
Examiner	Frederick Schiller
Frau Kahn	Maria Berger
Committee Secretary	Charles Goldner
Otto	David Baxter
Klaus	Yvan Delay
Mr. Silver	Meyer Tzelnicker

Painstakingly produced and directed, "Mr. Emmanuel" moves along sturdily, but without inspiration. This may be traced in no small degree to the novel from which adapted, not being too good for a film. It sways back and forth with complete mechanical efficiency and is not likely either to prove a great success or the opposite. For the U. S., it may do as a mild secondary feature.

Slow in getting started, the measured pace is never increased. That more than competent actor, Felix Aylmer, isn't convincing in the title role. He suffers from endeavoring to perpetrate characteristic Jewish mannerisms, without resorting to dialect sufficiently. Never for a moment does one visualize him as an amiable old Jewish gentleman who spent his life in the ghetto of Manchester. There are several others in the cast who might have given Aylmer pointers.

Greta Gynt and Walter Rilla are featured second to Aylmer, and both are splendid. Half a dozen other players offer excellent portrayals. *Jolo.*

Underground Guerrillas

(BRITISH-MADE)

Columbia release of Michael Balcon production. Stars John Clements, Godfrey Tearle, Tom Walls; features Michael Wilding, Mary Morris. Directed by Sergei Nolbandov. Screenplay, John Dighton, M. Danischewsky; original, George Slocombe; camera, W. Cooper; editor, Sidney Cole. At Strand, Brooklyn, N. Y., Sept. 14, '44. Running time, **82 MINS.**

Milosh Petrovitch	John Clements
Kossan Petrovitch	Tom Walls
Maria Petrovitch	Rachel Thomas
Dr. Stevan Petrovitch	Stephen Murray
Anna Petrovitch	Mary Morris
Gen. Von Staengel	Godfrey Tearle
Col. Von Brock	Robert Harris
Constantine	Michael Wilding
Sergeant	Charles Victor
Dr. Jordan	Niall MacGinnis
Station Master	Ivor Bernard
Dragutin	Ben Williams
A Yugoslav General	George Merritt
Peter	Stanley Baker
Danilo	Tocwyn Jones
Lieut. Banse	Eynon Evans
Lieut. Franke	Norman Pierce
Lieut. Von Klotz	Eric Micklewood

"Underground Guerrillas," Columbia's British-made addition to the many films (American and Russian) about heroic resistance of various nationals to the German invaders, comes a little belatedly. The story is a familiar one by now. The film unfolds slowly, although its several climaxes are swift and exciting. Sincerity and simplicity, too, help to offset stodginess. A dualer, certainly, the film will be worth seeing, as the stronger half of any double program.

Story centers around a little Yugoslav village and its feats of sabotage against the Nazis. Principals are the Petrovitch family, the aged patriarch who still has plenty of fight in him; his surgeon son who heads a Belgrade hospital, and his other son who heads a band of guerrillas. Into a peaceful, idyllic community, whose chief activity is farming and chief pleasure is a wedding celebration, come arrogant German military. And the natives don't put up with them for a minute.

Taking to the hills, they fight back effectively. They raid the village to kill Nazi officers. They blow up bridges and tunnels, and even ammunition trains. The Nazis, of course, fight back, torturing women, shooting children in cold blood, and in other ways bringing their vaunted New Order to the conquered territory. Undying resistance, however, is a key to the future, when it is obvious the Nazis will eventually be driven out.

Some of the film's effectiveness is marred by the fact that all the English actors speak with the same clipped British accent, so that it is difficult to distinguish between German and Yugoslav, except for the uniforms. John Clements and Stephen Murray give good, restrained performances as the brothers in arms, while Godfrey Tearle and Robert Harris play Nazi officers satisfactorily. Mary Morris adds romance and a wistful quality as the guerrilla leader's wife. *Bron.*

Maria Candelaria

(MEXICAN-MADE)

Clasa release of Films Mundiales production. Stars Dolores Del Rio; features Pedro Armendariz, Margarita Cortes, Alberto Galan, Beatriz Ramos, Manuel Inclan, Rafael Icardo, Julio Ahuet, Arturo Soto Rangel. Direction, story and adaptation, Emilio Fernandez; editor, Gloria Scherman; camera, Gabriel Figueroa. At Belmont, N. Y., week Sept. 11, '44. Running time, **96 MINS.**

Maria Candelaria	Dolores Del Rio
Lorenzo Rafael	Pedro Armendaris
Lupe	Margarita Cortes
El Pintor	Alberto Galan
Reporter	Beatriz Ramos
Don Damian	Manuel Inclan
Senor Cura	Rafael Icardo
Jose Alfonso	Julio Ahuet

Judged by standards below the Rio Grande, this is probably of upper-bracket caliber and reflects a determination on the part of our neighbors to the south to turn out pictures that can compete with Hollywood. Artistic to a degree, principally because of its simplicity, and given good production as foreign-mades go, with photographic work which often impresses, "Maria Candelaria," however, is still considerably inferior to American-mades. Since it is Mexican, and Yanks will find it almost impossible to follow the story and action, local market is limited to the Spanish-speaking public. There are no English titles.

Dolores Del Rio, Mexican-born who has returned to her native land to work in pictures, no doubt is a name which, after a number of years in Hollywood, must mean something. Another picture of hers, also made in Mexico, was brought into this country last season. Miss Del Rio is exceptionally well preserved, hardly suggesting that she dates back to the silent film days in this country. In this instance she plays a tragic Indian peasant girl who, together with the man she loves, is hounded by the people of her primitive community because she is the daughter of a woman who once posed for a local artist in the nude and for that sin was stoned to death.

Miss Del Rio ultimately suffers the same fate though innocent of the same indiscretion. However, in an effort to free her boy friend from jail, whence he had gone after stealing some quinine to help cure her case of malaria, plus a nice dress for their wedding, she consents to pose for the same man of paintbrush and pallette who had brought her mother to disgrace and death. After he finishes doing her face and wants her to disrobe, Miss Del Rio flees in horror. The artist, however, has another model pose from the neck down au naturel and an angry mob embarks on another stoning spree.

Photography of Gabriel Figueroa impresses for a foreign-made, although at various times dullness of the print detracts generally.

Miss Del Rio, who turns in a fine performance, has opposite her Pedro Armendariz, who has fine acting ability but is not much of a hero-type. A standout on personality but disposed of early is Beatriz Ramos, who plays a reporter. Manuel Inclan is terrific as the villain, looking the type of Mexican heavy Hollywood likes to cast. Alberto Galan plays the artist a bit stiffly but one of his models, Margarita Cortes, attracts more than ordinary attention. In the hands of Rafael Icardo the part of a padre attains fair stature. Others in the cast are minor. *Char.*

October 4, 1944

Irish Eyes Are Smiling
(COLOR; MUSICAL)

Twentieth Century-Fox release of Damon Runyon production. Features Monty Woolley, June Haver, Dick Haymes, Anthony Quinn, Beverly Whitney, Maxie Rosenbloom, Veda Ann Borg, Clarence Kolb, Leonard Warren, Blanche Thebom, Kenny Williams. Directed by Gregory Ratoff. Story, E. A. Ellington; adaptation, Earl Baldwin and John Tucker Battle; editor, Harmon Jones; camera, Harry Jackson. Previewed in N. Y., Sept. 29, '44. Running time, **90 MINS.**

Edgar Brawley..............Monty Woolley
Mary "Irish" O'Brien........June Haver
Ernest R. Ball..............Dick Haymes
Al Jackson..................Anthony Quinn
Lucille Lacey...............Beverly Whitney
Stanley Ketchel.........Maxie Rosenbloom
Belle La Tour...............Veda Ann Borg
Betz........................Clarence Kolb
Metropolitan Opera Singers.Leonard Warren
and Blanche Thebom
Stage Manager.............Chick Chandler
Specialty Dancer..........Kenny Williams
Headwaiter...............Michael Dalmatoff
Prima Donna................Marian Martin

"Irish Eyes Are Smiling" nearly out-nostalgias all the warmly sentimental pictures for which 20th-Fox has shown a singular fondness. In color and produced on a lavish but not too gaudy a scale, this biographical musical is boxoffice manna. Its 90 minutes will provide a convenient turnover, and in that 90 minutes there's plenty for the ear and eye. Damon Runyon, the producer, and Gregory Ratoff, the director, could easily have let it run longer without complaint.

The story of Ernest R. Ball, the American composer, and the unforgettable numbers he wrote—"When Irish Eyes Are Smiling," "Mother Machree," "Let the Rest of the World Go By," "A Little Bit of Heaven," among others—form the background for this swift-moving and sentimental musical. Produced with a tender touch by Runyon and directed with superlative skill by Ratoff, the film is full of life, interest, beauty and light humor in addition to many succulent songful moments and several production numbers that have been expertly staged.

Not only does the color photography enhance the optical appreciation of the production but the musical background commands special consideration. It's one of the best musical scores ever to reach the screen. Alfred Newman and Charles Henderson are credited with the musical direction, while Mack Gordon acted as musical consultant.

Dick Haymes, who did a somewhat minor stint for 20th in "Four Jills in a Jeep" last season, plays the part of Ball, the Cleveland boy who rose to fame as a songwriter. He acquits himself creditably, not only in the singing of various ballads Ball wrote but also in enacting a straight romantic role. Opposite him is the youthful and vivacious June Haver, whose potentialities for stardom are great. She photos excellently, handles lines well, sings and dances with verve and also has a pair of gams that can't go unnoticed. Miss Haver plays the Cleveland showgirl who falls in love with Haymes.

The type of bristling dialog so suitable to Monty Woolley has been supplied him by the adaptors, Earl Baldwin and John Tucker Battle, whose scenario is likewise topdrawer. Anthony Quinn plays a mildly villainous role effectively, while Maxie Rosenbloom, as Stanley Ketchel, the fighter, provides decoration and color. Lessers include Veda Ann Borg and Clarence Kolb, both of whom give good performances.

Leonard Warren, baritone, and Blanche Thebom, soprano, of the Metropolitan Opera Co., give terrific punch to some of Ball's music. Warren solos "Little Bit of Heaven" and Miss Thebom does "Mother Machree" in addition to both reprising numbers in the finale, a niftily staged production. Miss Thebom photographs exceptionally well. Haymes does notable song jobs on "When Irish Eyes Are Smiling" and "Let the Rest of the World Go By." Miss Haver stands out on "Bessie in a Bustle," which is part of a spectacular production number. Kenny Williams, softshoe dancer, appears in another song-and-dance sequence.

In all respects "Irish Eyes" measures up to the highest standards set by the industry. *Char.*

None But the Lonely Heart

RKO release of David Hempstead (Sherman Todd) production. Stars Cary Grant; features Ethel Barrymore, Barry Fitzgerald, June Duprez, Jane Wyatt. Written and directed by Clifford Odets. From novel by Richard Llewellyn; camera, George Barnes, Vernon L. Walker; music, Hanns Eisler; editor, Roland Gross; asst. director, Ruby Rosenberg. Tradeshown N. Y. Sept. 29, '44. Running time, **110 MINS.**

Ernie Mott......................Cary Grant
Ma Mott.....................Ethel Barrymore
Twite.......................Barry Fitzgerald
Ada.............................June Duprez
Aggie Hunner....................Jane Wyatt
Jim Mordinoy..............George Coulouris
Len Tate........................Dan Duryea
Dad Prettyjohn..............Roman Bohnen
Ike Weber..............Konstantin Shayne
Ma Chalmers..........Eva Leonard Boyne
Taz.........................Morton Lowry
Sister Nurse.................Helen Thimig
Knocker....................William Chalce

Based on the Richard Llewellyn novel, author-director Clifford Odets has fashioned a purposeful film which never quite comes off. There is a combination of circumstances against "None But the Lonely Heart," including some ofttimes too-difficult-to-understand cockney dialects, and while it will get a fair share of business, the cast names will account for it chiefly. Cary Grant, Ethel Barrymore (a not too frequent film player) and Barry Fitzgerald (quite a hot article since "Going My Way") are nobody's boxoffice poison.

"Lonely Heart" had the makings of a significant picture and it is suspected something happened in midstream. One may conjecture that Clifford Odets was cued not to get too "social conscious" and hence underplayed what apparently was the basic objective—the hope for a better world for the lowly man in the street.

Instead, with the sotto voce accent on any social significance, "Heart" emerges as a medley of simple romance in London's east side, interspersed with a little melodrama. The meller phase doesn't bestir matters until almost an hour and a half from scratch when the limey hoodlums hijack Ike Weber's pawnshop and beat up the kindly loan broker.

Cary Grant starts as a shiftless cockney who lets his struggling mother (Ethel Barrymore) fend for herself with her small, second-hand shop beneath their dingy home until the pawnbroker-friend (well underplayed by Konstantin Shayne) tips him off that his mother is dying of cancer. For all of Grant's penuriousness he apparently has a way with the attractive young cellist, Jane Wyatt, and the divorced wife (June Duprez) of the London mobster (George Coulouris, who does one of his standard good jobs as the menace). Grant seemingly has his way with the not too affluent neighborhood shopkeepers from whom he cadges cookies, cigarets, etc.

When Grant sees the light and decides to cease vagabonding, he becomes an almost model son. An expert clock and furniture repairer and piano-tuner, he helps make his mother's little business thrive until he himself gets mixed up with the mob, while the mother succumbs to the temptations of dealing in stolen goods.

Barry Fitzgerald is introduced into the proceedings as the casual acquaintance who becomes a philosophical friend in need for all his eccentricity. Fitzgerald also acts as counsellor and lookout when the mob stuff figures in the plot.

The confusion of interests is what diverts fullest attention from Odets' purpose. When Miss Duprez takes the easiest way and returns to her ex-husband, the menace, and Grant succumbs to the Tschaikowsky strain, "None But the Lonely Heart," which clarions him back to the pretty cellist's affection, it makes for a purposeless conclusion.

There is some dialog about man bestirring himself to greater glory, and that one must fight to preserve these rights (with a suggestion of the RAF overhead). There is also a sequence about the Unknown Soldier in Westminster Abbey, dating from World War I. The action is pre-World War II, but seemingly not too far away.

Productionally the gaslight atmosphere of Whitechapel doesn't make for arresting cinematurgy. This, coupled with the long passages of sometimes static dialog, done up in cockney brogue, all tends to militate against fullest interest.

As offset to this, there are some deeply effective sequences, and almost always Grant, Fitzgerald and Misses Barrymore, Duprez and Wyatt and the rest make the most of them. *Abel.*

La Dama de las Camelias
(Songs)
(MEXICAN-MADE)

Azteca Films release of Jorge Velez production. Stars Emilio Tuero, Lina Montes; features Miguel Arenas, Fanny Shiller. Directed by Gabriel Soria. Screenplay, Bob Tasker, from Alexander Dumas' "La Dame aux Camelias." At Belmont, N. Y., week of Sept. 28, '44. Running time, **115 MINS.**

Armand Duval..................Emilio Tuero
Marguerite Gautier............Lina Montes
Georges Duval..............Miguel Arenas
Prudence.......................Fanny Shiller
Count de Varville...........Alejandro Cobo
Olympe........................Virginia Zuri
Gaston...............................Tony Diaz
Nannina.....................Mercedes Ferris
Suzette..................Blanca Rosa Otero
Pierre.......................Charles Rooner

(In Spanish; No English Titles)

Presented in Spanish without English titles, this is Mexico's version of "Camille." Strictly for houses catering to Spanish-speaking audiences.

Besides being a shallow production, this south-of-the-border tearjerker gives newcomer Lina Montes her first starring role. She gives a poor performance. Her portrayal of Marguerite Gautier, plagued by indebtedness, dissipation, illness, a lover's scorn and a father's ire, proves too much for her.

The supporting cast gives a good account of themselves as does Emilio Tuerco, co-star of the picture.

However, this version of "Camille" is presented with more candor than its Hollywood predecessor (Garbo-Robert Taylor). Settings and costuming are noteworthy. Picture could easily be cut about 20 minutes. *Sten.*

October 11, 1944

Miniature Reviews

"The Princess and the Pirate" (Color; Song) (RKO-Goldwyn). Bob Hope starrer a b. o. click-eroo.

"To Have and Have Not" (Songs) (WB). Humphrey Bogart starrer. OK boxoffice pic.

"Laura" (20th). Slick murder-mystery, surefire b.o.

"The Woman in the Window" (International - RKO). Punchy murder meller, starring Edward G. Robinson and Joan Bennett.

"Marked Trails" (Mono). Ordinary western dualer.

"Sundown Riders" (16mm.-color) (Major 16 Prods.). First western feature produced in color for the 16 mm. field.

"Adios Juventud" (Clasa). Fair Mexican drama, without English titles, for Spanish-speaking audiences.

"Himlaspelet" (Swedish). A humdinger; one of the best Swedish-made films of this or any other year. English titles.

The Princess and the Pirate
(One Song)
(COLOR)

RKO release of Samuel Goldwyn production (Don Hartman, assoc.). Stars Bob Hope; features Virginia Mayo, Walter Brennan, Walter Slezak, Victor McLaglen. Directed by David Butler. Screenplay, Don Hartman, Melville Shevelson, Everett Freeman; adaptation, Allen Boretz, Curtis Kenyon, suggested by story by Sy Bartlett; camera, Victor Milner, Wm. Snyder, R. O. Binger, Clarence Slifer; editor, Daniel Mandell; score, David Rose; song, Jimmy McHugh-Harold Adamson. Tradeshown N. Y., Oct. 10, '44. Running time, **92 MINS.**

Sylvester..........................Bob Hope
Margaret.....................Virginia Mayo
Featherhead................Walter Brennan
La Roche.....................Walter Slezak
The Hook..................Victor McLaglen
Pedro.......................Marc Lawrence
Cafe Proprietor..................Hugo Haas
Landlady.....................Maude Eburne
Don Jose....................Adia Kuznetzoff
Mr. Pelly....................Brandon Hurst
Alonzo.........................Tom Kennedy
Captain "Mary Ann".....Stanley Andrews
The King...................Robert Warwick

Anything called "The Princess and the Pirate," with Bob Hope starred, is a tipoff on its frank escapology. This Goldwyn production makes no pretext at anything else, and Hope plays it that way, all the way, even unto a very funny topper. In short, a boxoffice click, ideally attuned to the times.

Beautifully Technicolored, Virginia Mayo is the princess, on the lam because she loves a commoner, and Victor McLaglen is the buccaneer of another century who steers his course to capture the beautiful princess as the richest prize yet of his career. Hope is cast as the 18th century smalltimer, loaded with more Westphalian than Swift and Armour, who does a protean act—"The Great Sylvester, Man of Seven Faces"—and is admittedly a coward. He wants nought of pirates, whereas the beauteous princess, who is also brave in face of direst danger, bolsters him throughout.

Action is replete with lawlessness in the West Indies, particularly in the dissolute governor's palace, and at the Bucket of Blood, a bistro with a definite Hell's Kitchen clientele where Hope and Miss Mayo do their vaudeville specialty, with the expected comic results.

From start to finish Hope dominates the action with welltimed colloquial nifties that run the gamut from current events and the political scene to Bing Crosby. The topper is a honey where she runs into the arms of her lover, a commoner—not Hope, but Crosby who suddenly comes on the scene. This causes Hope to scream at "that bit player from Paramount" and deride his producer. "That's the last picture I'll ever make for you, Mr. Goldwyn." It's a switch on a bit Hope and Crosby did in one of the former's Paramount starrers.

While much of the farcical byplay is pretty familiar business, it's expertly treated. It runs the gamut from the snuffbox to a beer-drinking contest. Then there's the finale where Hope masquerades as The Hook while the real piratical Hook (McLaglen) also shows up on the marauding vessel. The bewildered crew is told to fetch the princess, and/or to put her in chains in the dungeon, alternatingly. There is all the rest of the familiar business, and the results make for beaucoup laughs.

Virginia Mayo's blonde beauty shows up to great advantage under the Natalie Kalmus coloration technique. Walter Brennan 'does a standout job as the harebrained pirate, as do McLaglen as the pirate and Walter Slezak as the rascally governor.

There is one song, a good one, by McHugh and Adamson, titled "Kiss Me in the Moonlight," which should assert itself, and David Ross has created an effective musical score.
Abel.

To Have and Have Not
(SONGS)

Warner Bros. release of Howard Hawks' production, directed by Hawks. Stars Humphrey Bogart; features Lauren Bacall, Walter Brennan, Dolores Moran, Hoagy Carmichael. Screenplay, Jules Furthman and William Faulkner, from novel by Ernest Hemingway; camera, Sid Hickox; editor, Christian Nyby; songs, Hoagy Carmichael-Johnny Mercer; music, Leo Forbstein. Previewed in New York Oct. 6, '44. Running time, 100 MINS.
Morgan.....................Humphrey Bogart
Eddie......................Walter Brennan
Marie......................Lauren Bacall
Helene De Bursac...........Dolores Moran
Crickett...................Hoagy Carmichael
Paul De Bursac.............Walter Molnar
Lieut. Coyo................Sheldon Leonard
Gerard.....................Marcel Dalio
Johnson....................Walter Sande
Capt. Renard...............Dan Seymour
Bodyguard..................Aldo Nadi
Beauclerc..................Paul Marion
Mrs. Beauclerc.............Patricia Shay
Bartender..................Pat West
Emil.......................Emmet Smith
Horatio....................Sir Lancelot

With an eye to the lucrative box-office of its "Casablanca," the brothers Warner have turned out another epic of similar genre in a none-too-literal adaptation of Ernest Hemingway's "To Have and Have Not." There are enough similarities in both films to warrant more than cursory attention, even to the fact that Humphrey Bogart is starred in each, but the b.o. prospects of the new pic are unlikely to approach those of "Casablanca." It should do well enough though this story of Vichy France collaborationism is not up to Warners' melodramatic story standards.

Though "Have Not" was one of Hemingway's inferior novels—whose theme of rum-running was certainly antithetical to the film's story of French collaboration—it affords considerable picture interest because of some neat characterizations. And it introduces a newcomer, Lauren Bacall, in her first picture. She's an arresting personality in whom Warners has what the scouts would call a find. She can slink, brother, and no fooling!

Yarn deals with the intrigue centering around the Caribbean island of Martinique, owned by France, and the plotting that ensued there prior to its ultimate capitulation to Allied pressure. Bogart is an American skipper there who hires out his boat to anyone who has the price. When he becomes involved in the local Free French movement, the story's pattern becomes woven around him, at times in cops-and-robbers fashion. Warners has given the pic its usually nifty productional accoutrements, and that includes casting, musical scoring and Howard Hawks'

direction, but the basic story is too unsteady.

Bogart is, of course, in his usual metier, a tough guy who, no less, has the facility of making a dame go for him, instead of he for her. That's where Miss Bacall comes in. Walter Brennan, as Bogart's drunken sidekick; Dolores Moran, as the film's second looker; and songwriter Hoagy Carmichael have lesser roles that they handle to advantage.

Carmichael as an actor is somewhat of a surprise; he's actually playing himself, a pianist-songwriter in the Martinique cafe that affords the story's background. He and Johnny Mercer have collabbed on one tune that merits more than passing attention, "How Little We Know."
Kahn.

Laura

20th Century-Fox release of Otto Preminger production, directed by Preminger. Stars Gene Tierney, Dana Andrews, Clifton Webb; features Vincent Price, Judith Anderson. Screenplay by Jay Dratler, Samuel Hoffenstein, Betty Reinhardt, from novel by Vera Caspary; editor, Louis Loeffler; camera, Joseph La Shelle. Tradeshown in N. Y. Oct. 6, '44. Running time, 88 MINS.
Laura......................Gene Tierney
Mark McPherson.............Dana Andrews
Waldo Lydecker.............Clifton Webb
Shelby Carpenter...........Vincent Price
Ann Treadwell..............Judith Anderson
Bessie Clary...............Dorothy Adams
McAvity....................James Flavin
Bullitt....................Clyde Fillmore
Fred Callahan..............Ralph Dunn
Corey......................Grant Mitchell
Louise.....................Kathleen Howard
Servant....................Lee Tung Foo
Inspector..................Cy Kendall
Detectives.....{ Harold Schlickenmayer
               { Harry Strang
               { Lane Chandler

A smart murder-mystery, expertly tailored in script, casting and direction, "Laura" is one of the neatest films of its kind to come along this season. Its fresh approach to a stock formula, the neat touches and constant new twists, and especially the intelligence that guides it throughout, tab it as aces. It's a sure thing at the boxoffice.

The film's deceptively leisurely pace at the start, and its light, careless air, only heighten the suspense without the audience being conscious of the buildup. What they are aware of as they follow the story is the skill in the telling. Situations neatly dovetail and are always credible. Developments, surprising as they come, are logical. The dialog is honest, real and adult. Producer-director Otto Preminger, screenwriters Sam Hoffenstein, Jay Dratler and Betty Reinhardt, and a good cast, have combined to keep an audience intensely absorbed in a guessing game for 88 minutes, without feeling let down at the end. That's good storytelling.

The yarn concerns an attractive femme art executive who has been brutally murdered in her New York apartment, and the attempts of a police lieutenant to solve the case. Beginning by interviewing the girl's intimates, the sleuth's trail leads him from one friend to another, all becoming suspect in the process. There is a surprising twist in mid-film which merely shifts emphasis without changing suspicions, cleverly giving the yarn fresh impetus at a point where such mystery stories are most likely to sag. Climax of the film, which may not surprise some, is still socko in its speed and unfolding.

Story is told with some flashbacks, never leaning too heavily on this trite method, however. Neat touches fill in from the start, as when the sleuth goes on his rounds of checking, taking along the suspects that he calls on en route. Tracking down clues takes the lieutenant on a round of familiar N. Y. spots, film showing glimpses of the Stork, El Morocco, Sardi's, the Algonquin and similar stopping-off spots of the Gotham sophisticate. Chief character in the film is a middle-aged radio and newspaper columnist with the omniscience

of a Winchell and the garb of a Lucius Beebe, whose interest in crime stories makes him a confederate of the sleuth, and helps to befuddle the climax.

Clifton Webb makes a debonair critic-columnist, with all the glibness to his portrayal that marks his stage appearances. Dana Andrews' intelligent, reticent performance as the lieutenant gives the lie to detectives as caricatures. Gene Tierney makes an appealing figure as the art executive and Vincent Price is convincing as a weak-willed ne'er-do-well. Judith Anderson brings force to her brief role as Price's patroness. Sets are lavish, although film's a modest-budgeter. It should clean up.
Bron.

The Woman in the Window

Hollywood, Oct. 10.
RKO release of International Pictures (Nunnally Johnson) Production. Stars Edward G. Robinson and Joan Bennett; features Raymond Massey. Directed by Brits Lang. Original Screenplay, Johnson; camera, Milton Krasner; editors, Gene Fowler, Jr., and Marjorie Johnson. Previewed in L.A. Oct ,9 '44. Running time. 90 MINS.
Richard Wanley.............Edward G. Robinson
Alice Reed.................Joan Bennett
Frank Lalor................Raymond Massey
Dr. Barkstane..............Edmond Brown
Heidt......................Dan Duryea
Inspector Jackson..........Thos. B. Jackson
Mazard.....................Arthur Loft
Mrs. Wanley................Dorothy Peterson
Steward....................Frank Dawson
Elsie......................Carol Cameron
Dickie.....................Bobbie Blake

Nunnally Johnson whips up a strong and decidedly suspenseful murder melodrama in "Woman in the Window," with the slick entertainment factors certain to be reflected for strong boxoffice returns in all bookings. It's a topliner in its particular field.

Producer, who also prepared the original screenplay, continually punches across the suspense for constant and maximum audience reaction. Added are especially fine timing in the direction by Fritz Lang and outstanding performances by Edward G. Robinson, Joan Bennett, Raymond Massey and Dan Duryea.

Opening sequence suggests that tragedies spring from little things, and anyone can become involved in a murder or criminal action. That's just what happens to Robinson; a staid and middleaged college professor whose wife and children depart for vacation in Maine. He pauses and admires a painting on exhibition in store window adjoining his club. Later he again glances at the girl's portrait and finds the model standing beside him.

Robinson visits her apartment to look over other sketches; a stranger breaks in to accuse the girl of infidelity and attacks Robinson, who stabs the visitor in self-protection. Sidetracking initial impulse to call the police, he connives with the girl to dispose of the body in the country woods. He's then projected into the role of a fugitive. Victim was a noted financial promoter; Massey, Robinson's pal at the club, is district attorney and keeps him advised of the latest clues in the case—even conducting him to point where body is found. Victim's bodyguard, Duryea, appears at the girl's house as blackmailer to grab silence coin. Robinson decides on suicide to get out of the predicament, but Duryea is shot down by police and tabbed as the real murderer as the girl phones the professor to tell him everything's okay. Finish is a surprise for smash climax.

Robinson gives everything he has to the strong role of the reserved and reticent professor, scoring solidly. Miss Bennett is most advantageous as the girl, while Massey and Duryea are outstanding in main supporting roles. Edmund Breon and Thomas Jackson are also prominent in lesser spots.

Picture gets top production mounting, with photography by Milton Krasner of high calibre.   *Walt.*

Marked Trails

Monogram release of William Strohbach production. Stars Hoot Gibson, Bob Steele, Veda Ann Borg; features Mauritz Hugo, Steve Clark. Directed by J. P. McCarthy from original by himself and Victor Hammond; camera, Harry Neumann; editor, John C. Fuller. At N. Y. theatre, N. Y., week of Oct. 4, '44. Running time, 59 MINS.
Parkford...................Hoot Gibson
Bob Stevens................Bob Steele
Blanche....................Veda Ann Borg
Slade......................Mauritz Hugo
Harry Stevens..............Steve Clark
Denver.....................Charles Stevens
Jed........................Ralph Lewis
Tex........................Lynton Brent
Sheriff....................Bud Osborne
Liveryman..................George Morrell
Mr. Bradley................Allen B. Sewall
Blackie....................Benny Corbett

Something new under the western sun is sprung by Monogram in this hoss opera—the gal is the villain. However, "Marked Trails" still is just another dualer.

Hoot Gibson and Bob Steele undertake roundup of gang putting over an oil swindle. Donning disguises, the duo meet up with Veda Ann Borg, who, with the aid of several cohorts, are in on the scheme.

Production values are ordinary outdoor scenes failing to impress. Riding and fighting are in the usual groove.   *Sten.*

Sundown Riders
(COLOR—16 MM)

Hollywood, Oct. 5.
Major 16 MM. Productions release of H. V. George production. Stars Russell Wade, Jay Kirby and Andy Clyde. Directed by Lambert Hillyer. Screenplay, Hillyer; original, Graham Walsh; camera, Alan Stensvold; editor, Ella Brouner. Previewed in Hollywood, Oct. 4, '44. Running time, 55 MINS.
Sundown Riders.....{ Russell Wade
                   { Jay Kirby
                   { Andy Clyde
Donna Fraser...............Evelyn Finley
Tug Wilson.................Jack Ingraham
Bob Casey..................Marshal Reed
Yeager.....................Hal Price
Mr. Fraser.................Steve Clark
Gilson.....................Ted Mapes
Loco.......................Bud Osborne
Curly......................Henry Wills
Jed........................Jack Shannon
Bill.......................Ted Wells
Evans......................Cliff Parkinson
Sam........................George Fuller
Indian Charlie.............Chief Many Treaties
Walker.....................Cactus Mack Peters
Pioneer....................Elmer Napier
Pioneer's Daughter.........Emily Crittenden

"Sundown Riders" is the first western produced in color for the 16 mm. market. For years, the industry has not only bypassed the rapidly-expanding 16 mm. field, but has built up resistance to making features available for that branch of the business. A few companies and producers make features available to the miniature field, but only after two or more years. Even the aged subjects have, in many instances, returned surprising grosses from the home, school, and institution circuits.

With producer H. V. George financing, and Russell Wade, Jay Kirby and cameraman Alan Stensvold taking cuts in expected profits, unit expects to make series of six over period of a year, tabbing bookings from Parent-Teacher groups for school showings in juvenile delinquency drives. Bookings on the home circuits are also figured to bring in sizable grosses, while some coin might be picked up along the way from regular theatres that have short projection throws and access to 16 mm. sound projectors.

Picture was shot on 16 mm. kodachrome, which has been widely used by amateur photographers and by commercial firms for promotional pictures. Prints struck off will be kodachrome duplicates, and, although cost is fairly high, it's still much cheaper than Technicolor in the 35 mm. size. Shot in eight days —all exteriors—picture carries negative cost of around $30,000, which is less than average black-and-white western being shot these days on 35 mm. It's all-professional cast along with crew from unions and guilds, and result is on par with regular westerns.

Plot is typical western, with plenty of riding, action and fisticuffs. Wade, Kirby and Clyde are the three western pals who clean up an outlaw gang, and then ride off to other adventures. Lambert Hillyer hit a fast pace in his direction, while the color accentuates the scenic backgrounds that add much to productional values.

Walt.

Adios Juventud
("Farewell to Youth") (MEXICAN-MADE)

Clasa release of Gregorio Wallerstein production. Stars Joaquin Pardavo; features Luis Aldas, Manolita Saval. Directed by Pardavo. Music, Manuel Esperon. At Belmont, N. Y., week of Oct. 9. Running time, **118 MINS.**

Dr. Alberto Montes..............Luis Aldas
Juanita..............Manolita Saval
Montero..............Aurora Segura
Luis..............Alfredo Varela, Jr.
Dona Maria..............Maria Luisa Serrano
Dr. Medinilla..............Joaquin Pardave

(In Spanish; No English Titles)

This overlong comedy-drama is grooved only for houses catering to Spanish-speaking audiences, since there are no English subtitles.

Yarn relates the tale of two friends who meet 20 years after their graduation from medical school. In flashback, the story reveals how the duo competed for the love of a young lady who died at the time they matriculated.

Story line and production values lack enough punch to require 118 minutes of footage. Picture contains too much dialog and not enough dances, the best part of the film (credited to a Mme. Nesley), with some excellent music by Manuel Esperon.

Sten.

Himlaspelet
("The Heavenly Play") (SWEDISH-MADE)

Wivefilm release of Alf Sjorberg production, directed by himself. Stars Rune Lindstron, Eivor Landstron; features Anders Hendrickson, Holger Lowandler. Screenplay, Rune Lindstron, Alf Sjorberg. At 48th St. Cinema, week of Oct. 8, '44. Running time, **105 MINS.**

(In Swedish; English Titles)

Produced with an artistry that **befits the ultra from Hollywood, this Swedish picture is one of the best foreign films ever to play the American market. Aided by English subtitles, its appeal is grooved for houses** that cater to foreign audiences and beyond.

Etched with a combination of caricature, whimsy and fervor, "Himlaspelet" tells of a young farm lad who sets out to seek justice of the Heavenly Father after his sweetheart has been burned as a witch. The transition of this youth from a simple farmer to a hard old man whose ill-gotten riches do him no good, when the devil allows him one last night to check his past for his friends and good deeds, omits nothing in the way of moods—comic or tragic—with eye-filling backgrounds, excellent performances and topflight photography.

Yarn is laid in the undated past, having a timeless theme. There is a Joseph and Mary; a Jerusalem where King Solomon holds court amidst revelry, and there's a Heaven, too. A notable musical score by Lille-Bror Soderlundh adds much to this picture.

Sten.

Miniature Reviews

"And Now Tomorrow" (Par). Loretta Young and Alan Ladd top familiar but pleasant quadrangle romance.

"The Conspirators" (Song) (WB). Familiar underground drama needs b.o. heft of Hedy Lamarr and Paul Henreid.

"Ministry of Fear" (Par). Ray Milland in a thrilling melodrama geared for good b.o.

"The Very Though. of You" (WB). Moderately entertaining romantic comedy-drama.

"One Body Too Many" (Par). Good mixture of comedy and suspense for solid program attraction.

"The Man In Half Moon Street" (Par). Strong "B" suspense meller, above standard for this type of tale.

"Faces in the Fog" (Rep). So-so juve delinquency yarn, for duals.

"Shadows of Suspicion" (Mono). Burlesque whodunit a fair dualer.

"Las Dos Huerfanas" (Mex.). Mexican version of "Two Orphans."

And Now Tomorrow

Paramount release of Fred Kohlmar production. Stars Alan Ladd, Loretta Young; features Susan Hayward, Barry Sullivan. Directed by Irving Pichel. Screenplay, Frank Partos and Raymond Chandler from Rachel Field's bestseller; camera, Daniel L. Fapp, Farciot Edouart; music, Victor Young; editor, Duncan Mansfield. Tradeshown N. Y., Oct. 16, '44. Running time, **86 MINS.**

Emily Blair..............Loretta Young
Dr. Merek Vance..............Alan Ladd
Janice Blair..............Susan Hayward
Jeff Stoddard..............Barry Sullivan
Aunt Em..............Beulah Bondi
Dr. Weeks..............Cecil Kellaway
Angeletta Gallo..............Helen Mack
Peter Gallo..............Anthony Caruso
Uncle Wallace..............Grant Mitchell
Dr. Sloane..............Jonathan Hale
Meeker..............George Carleton
Hester..............Connie Leon

A familiar tale but well done, with Loretta Young and Alan Ladd for the marquee, hence okay for box-office.

The Rachel Field bestseller, undoubtedly makes better reading, judging by its cinematurgical transition. It emerges as formula narration. Plot concerns sister vs. sister for the love of the man. One of the sisters is a rich, spoiled heiress (Miss Young), who is seeking to regain her hearing, lost as result of an illness. Susan Hayward is the other sister.

Ladd is the hometown boy, from the wrong side of the railroad tracks, who returns to his New England community from Pittsburgh, at request of Cecil Kellaway, playing the hometown family doctor. Of course he works the miracle, with a new ear serum, but in between times Susan Hayward, back from a European trip (this is in the mid-'30s), and Barry Sullivan, Miss Young's betrothed, become romantically attached. Thus it leaves the way clear for Miss Young and Ladd.

There is a bit of sociological exposition projected as part of the action, wherein latter visits a poor family in shantytown, to assist in an emergency mastoiditis. Helen Mack and Anthony Caruso click as the poor friends with whom Emily Blair (Miss Young) of Blairstown had gone to the local highschool. There are other good performances by Beulah Bondi and Grant Mitchell, along with the principal foursome.

Production highgrade all the way.

Abel.

The Conspirators
(ONE SONG)

Hollywood, Oct. 13.

Warner Bros. release of Jack Chertok production. Stars Hedy Lamarr, Paul Henreid; features Sydney Greenstreet, Peter Lorre. Directed by Jean Negulesco. Screenplay, Vladimir Pozner and Leo Rosten; added dialog, Jack Moffitt; from novel by Fredric Prokosch; camera, Arthur Edeson; editor, Rudi Fehr; dialog director, Herschel Daugherty; special effects, William McGann, Willard Van Enger, James Leicester; asst. director, Reggie Callow. Tradeshown L. A. Oct. 12, '44. Running time, **100 MINS.**

Irene..............Hedy Lamarr
Vincent..............Paul Henreid
Quintanilla..............Sydney Greenstreet
Bernazsky..............Peter Lorre
Von Mohr..............Victor Francen
Capt. Pereira..............Joseph Calleia
Rosa..............Carol Thurston
Miguel..............Vladimir Sokoloff
Almeida..............Edward Ciannelli
Dr. Schmitt..............Steven Geray
Lutzke..............Kurt Katch
Wynat..............Gregory Gay
Croupier..............Marcel Dalio
The Con Man..............George Macready
Mrs. Benson..............Doris Lloyd
Leiris..............Louis Mercier
Jennings..............Monte Blue
Page Boy..............Billy Roy
Antonio..............David Hoffman
The Slugger..............Otto Reichow
Waiter..............Leon Belasco
Casino Attendant..............Frank Reicher

Coming on the tail end of the extended cycle of European underground agents versus Nazi cunning, "The Conspirators" will catch only mild audience attention. It will need the boxoffice heft of Hedy Lamarr and Paul Henreid.

The oft-told drama of underground agents and cinematic outwitting of the Nazis has been told better and with more suspense many times previously.

Plot centers in Lisbon, where underground, Allied and German spies run loose in trying to outfox the others. Henreid is an escaped Hollander who fled with price on his head after committing plenty of sabotage against the Germans. He is tracked by the Nazis, but manages to reach underground ring of agents headed by Sydney Greenstreet and Peter Lorre. Also meets and falls in love with Miss Lamarr, later discovered as French girl married to Victor Francen, official of the German embassy. After jumble of murders, chases and love interludes, an underground agent is selected to go back into Holland but killed and robbed of talisman piece. Francen poses as friend of the Greenstreet group, but is finally exposed as a traitor and killed by Henreid. Latter then takes the assignment to go back to direct the Dutch underground, while Miss Lamarr promises to wait for victory.

Picture is filled with overlength footage, both in unnecessary sideline incidents and extended running of relatively unimportant sequences, bouncing all over Lisbon and environs. It never reaches the dramatic climaxes intended.

Henreid works hard in his assignment, but is under handicap of the script deficiencies. Miss Lamarr walks through her role with air of being continually afraid of the results. Greenstreet, Lorre, Francen, Joseph Calleia and Kurt Katch are most prominent in support.

Script is uninspired, and director Jean Negulesco does little with the material supplied. Production has numerous sets and locations, but it takes more than good production values to bolster a loose yarn.

Walt.

Ministry of Fear

Paramount release of Seton I. Miller production. Stars Ray Milland; features Marjorie Reynolds, Carl Esmond, Hillary Brooke. Directed by Fritz Lang. Screenplay by Seton I. Miller, based on novel by Graham Greene; camera, Henry Sharp; editor, Archie Marshek; music, Victor Young. Tradeshown N. Y., Oct. 16, '44. Running time, **84 MINS.**

Stephen Neale..............Ray Milland
Carla Hilfe..............Marjorie Reynolds
Willi Hilfe..............Carl Esmond
Mrs. Bellane No. 2..............Hillary Brooke
Prentice..............Percy Waram
Cost (Travers)..............Dan Duryea
Dr. Forrester..............Alan Napier
Mr. Rennit..............Erskine Sanford
Mr. Newland..............Thomas Louden
Mrs. Bellane No. 1..............Aminta Dyne
Blind Man..............Eustace Wyatt
Miss Penteel..............Mary Field
Mr. Newby..............Byron Foulger
Dr. Morton..............Lester Mathews

Bringing the Nazi spy thriller formula up-to-date by basing this film on the theft of plans for the invasion of the continent, Paramount, rather belatedly, endeavors to cash in on a somewhat overworked theme. However, the marquee value of Ray Milland teamed with Marjorie Reynolds should aid in garnering business for this one in all situations.

Fritz Lang, a master at getting the most out of mystery, intrigue and melodrama, in his direction apparently didn't have his way from beginning to end on "Ministry of Fear." Pic starts out to be a humdinger, and continues that way for the most part, but when the roundup of the spy gang gets underway the situation becomes drawn out and elementary, marring the footage that preceded. A more tightly written climax, without the commonplace histrionics and action, would have steered this one into the top drawer.

Milland, in the role of an ex-asylum inmate, who is released after serving two years for the "mercy" killing of his incurable wife, gives a forthright performance. He is tossed into the midst of a spy chase when, in purchasing a ticket to London upon leaving the asylum, he is drawn to the crowds at a British fair and wins a cake by guessing its weight. The cake contains a capsule which one of the spies is to have delivered to other enemy agents. It is stolen from him by a phoney blind man on the train, who is blown to bits in an air raid, and with him, the cake.

In his endeavor to find out what the whole thing is about, Milland investigates the charity organization which sponsored the country bazaar, and in that way, tracks down the entire gang. But not before Scotland Yard is drawn into the case, accusing him of the murder of a man whom he had hired as bodyguard.

Supporting cast does a worthy job. Marjorie Reynolds and Carl Esmond, who portray the role of brother and sister directors of the charity group, do justice to their roles. Percy Waram, as a police inspector, probably has the meatiest role in comparison with the others and performs credibly. Dan Duryea, a leader of the suspect crew, is true to type.

Seton I. Miller has unstintingly cased the entire production in suitable settings, with the caremawork of Henry Sharp, aided by important lighting effects, worthy of more than passing mention.

Sten.

The Very Thought of You

Hollywood, Oct. 14.

Warner Bros. release of Jerry Wald production. Stars Dennis Morgan, Eleanor Parker, Dane Clark. Directed by Delmar Daves. Screenplay by Alvah Bessie and Daves. Original by Lionel Wiggam; camera, Bert Glennon; editor, Alan Crosland, Jr.; special effects, Warren Lynch; asst. director, Art Lueker. Tradeshown L. A. Oct. 13, '44. Running time, **99 MINS.**

Dave..............Dennis Morgan
Janet..............Eleanor Parker
"Fixit"..............Dane Clark
Cora..............Faye Emerson
Mrs. Wheeler..............Beulah Bondi
Pop Wheeler..............Henry Travers
Fred..............William Prince
Molly..............Andrea King
Cal..............John Alvin
Bernice..............Marianne O'Brien
Ellie..............Georgia Lee Settle
Soda Jerk..............Dick Erdman
Minister..............Francis Pierlot

This is a light romantic comedy-drama of moderate proportions which is handicapped by extended running time of 99 minutes, where compact editing could have unfolded a faster tale with at least 20 minutes clipped from the running. Dennis Morgan will have to carry marquee voltage in the regular runs.

Story details the romantic adventures of Morgan who has put in 18 months in the Aleutians with the Army, who again meets Eleanor Parker in Pasadena when he visits his alma mater of Caltech in Pasadena. His sidekick, Dane Clark, teams up with Faye Emerson while Morgan goes to the girl's house for Thanksgiving eve dinner and gets a closeup view of various members of the family—both argumentative and kindly. Next day, pair are together for fast and mutual falling in love and a quick marriage and one night honeymoon due to his orders for report at San Diego. Few weeks later they have another brief get-together at San Diego before he again ships overseas. Girl leaves the family hearth for teamup with Miss Emerson, has a baby and everything's fine when Morgan returns wounded from action in the Mediterranean.

At numerous points picture displays possibilities of getting into the groove to generate spontaneity and verve, but then the action dips through insertion of extraneous footage of inconsequential episodes. Looks like both the script and direction tried to cover too much ground.

Morgan is fine as the soldier, while Miss Parker displays potentialities as the girl. Clark clicks solidly as the comedian, and teams nicely with Miss Emerson. Little Georgia Lee Settle, as youngest sister of Miss Parker, is spotlighted, while a good support is provided by Beulah Bondi, Henry Travers, Andrea King, John Alvin and Marianne O'Brien. William Prince catches attention in a brief bit. *Walt.*

One Body Too Many

Hollywood, Oct. 17.

Paramount release of Pine-Thomas production. Stars Jack Haley, Jean Parker, Bela Lugosi. Directed by Frank McDonald. Original screenplay by Winston Miller, Maxwell Shane; camera, Fred Jackman, Jr.; editor, Howard Smith. Tradeshown L. A. Oct. 17, '44. Running time, 74 MINS.
Albert Tuttle.................Jack Haley
Carol Dunlap.............Jean Parker
Larchmont.................Bela Lugosi
Attorney Gellman.......Bernard Nedell
Matthews................Blanche Yurka
Henry Rutherford......Douglas Fowley
Mona.................Dorothy Granger
Jim Davis................Lyle Talbot
Kenneth............Lucien Littlefield
Estelle.....................Fay Helm
Margaret...............Maxine Fife
The Professor......William Edmunds

"One Body Too Many" is a murder mystery with comedic trimmings displayed with the fast tempo and zip that characterizes the Pine-Thomas product. It's a strong program entry for general entertainment, and can carry the billtopping spot with support in the key week stands.

Despite its comedy approach, with Jack Haley as the bewildered intruder into a mansion setting for strange happenings and murders, plot carries good suspense throughout. Excellent timing in direction by Ralph Murphy is an asset to the overall results.

Plot sets up the strange will of a millionaire whose body is to remain in the house along with the group of relatives and prospective beneficiaries. Haley shows up to sell the deceased some life insurance, and sticks around to help Jean Parker. There's the regulation disappearing corpse, secret passages, and a couple of murders tossed in to heighten the dramatics for good entertainment and audience reaction. Villain in the affair is finally disclosed, with Haley clinching with Miss Parker for okay finish.

Cast is well set up. Haley romps through the proceedings in good style, with Bela Lugosi peering

around menacingly as the butler for eventual innocence. Miss Parker does well as the girl, and all others listed in cast credits are okay. *Walt.*

The Man in Half Moon Street

Hollywood, Oct. 17.

Paramount release of Walter MacEwen production. Stars Nils Asther, Helen Walker. Directed by Ralph Murphy. Screenplay by Charles Kenyon; adaptation, Garrett Fort, based on play by Barre Lyndon; camera, Henry Sharp; editor, Tom Neff; music, Miklos Rozsa. Tradeshown L. A., Oct. 16, '44. Running time, 91 MINS.
Julian Karell................Nils Asther
Eve Brandon................Helen Walker
Dr. Kurt Van Bruecken..Reinhold Schunzel
Dr. Henry Latimer.......Paul Cavanagh
Sir Humphrey Brandon....Edmond Breon
Allen Guthrie............Morton Lowry
Inspector Garth.......Matthew Boulton
Simpson, Julian's Butler..Brandon Hurst
Lady Minerva Aldergate....Aminta Dyne
Sir John Aldergate......Arthur Mulliner
Colonel Ashley.........Edward Fielding
Mr. Taper, Art Critic..Reginald Sheffield
Inspector Jawson.......Kustave Wyatt
Harris, a Cabby........Forrester Harvey
Dr. Yishanoff........Konstantin Shayne

"The Man in Half Moon Street" is a suspense drama based on clinical premise of gland transplanting to provide constant youth. It's a well-set up tale of its type, and will provide strong support in the regular bookings.

Plot has a few new twists from the formularized style of long-life mystery tales to keep interest at consistent level. Asther is a doctor and painter, who falls in love with Helen Walker after completing commission of painting her portrait. But Asther has a cloud hanging over him that necessitates research with the elderly Reinhold Schunzel. Asther is disclosed as an aged man, who requires periodic gland transplanting to keep his physical fitness. Story weaves through series of dramatic incidents to expose Asther's successive murders in getting new glands, to have him age, and collapse when new glands are not secured in time.

Script by Charles Kenyon and adaptation by Garrett Fort provide a compact and interesting cinematic tale, with direction by Ralph Murphy deftly timing the sequences for good audience reaction.

Asther does well as the subject of his own longevity theories, while Miss Walker capably handles her role opposite. Good support is provided by Schunzel, Paul Cavanagh, Edmond Breon, Matthew Boulton and Brandon Hurst. *Walt.*

Faces In the Fog
(ONE SONG)

Republic release of Herman Millakowsky production. Stars Jane Withers; features Paul Kelly, Lee Patrick, John Litel, Eric Sinclair, Dorothy Peterson, Gertrude Michael and H. B. Warner. Directed by John English. Screenplay, Jack Townley; camera, Reggie Lanning; editor, Tony Martinelli. Tradeshown N. Y. Oct. 16, '44. Running time, 71 MINS.
Mary Elliott................Jane Withers
Tom Elliott.................Paul Kelly
Cora Elliott................Lee Patrick
Dr. Mason..................John Litel
Joe Mason.................Eric Sinclair
Mrs. Mason............Dorothy Peterson
Nora Brooks.........Gertrude Michael
Defense Attorney Rankin....H. B. Warner
Mike......................Richard Byron
Sergeant O'Donnell.......Roger Clark
Gertrude...................Adele Mara
Les Elliott..............Bob Stebbins
Mr. White..........Charles Trowbridge
Alice...................Helen Talbot
Danny................Joel McGinnis
Auto Court Manager.......Tom London
Capt. Roberts............Emmett Vogan

"Faces in the Fog" is just another juve delinquency drama for the double bills. Story is pretty trite and the situations all stock and contrived. Jane Withers is appealing and believable in a straight dramatic role. Yarn points rather obviously at parents rather than their undisciplined children. That also has been said before, but better. The film goes

in for sermonizing, and feeble melodramatic situations. A likable cast gives the script some semblance of verity, but the total is negative.

Story concerns the families of two neighbors. The Elliotts, out on nightly sprees, are neglectful of their teenage son and daughter, who seem to be pretty good stock regardless. The Masons are an average, normal family, whose son Joe falls in love with Mary Elliott. When Mary is innocently involved in a hit-and-run case, Joe takes the rap, even to getting expelled from school. The two kids get married secretly, so that Mary's father, following them, shoots Joe in mistaken belief he's wronged the girl. Mary's parental loyalty is proved at the trial when she perjures herself in order to get her father off, and the situation rights itself finally when the two kids, after Joe recovers, go off on a belated honeymoon.

As the bride, Miss Withers paints a poignant portrait that keeps within the bounds of restraint while being warm and convincing. John Litel and Dorothy Peterson are believable as Joe's parents, and H. B. Warner, as a lawyer, and Gertrude Michael, as a police matron, are good in bit roles. Others in cast, such as Paul Kelly and Lee Patrick as Mary's parents, and Eric Sinclair, Joel McGinnis and Richard Byron as teen-agers, are perfunctory. *Bron.*

Shadows of Suspicion

Monogram release of A. W. Hackel production. Features Marjorie Weaver, Peter Cookson, Tim Ryan, Pierre Watkin, Clara Blandick. Directed by William Beaudine. Story by Harold Goldman; screenplay, Al Demond, Earle Snell; camera, Marcel Le Picard; editor, Martin G. Cohn. At New York, N. Y., week of Oct. 10, '44. Running time, 68 MINS.
Claire....................Marjorie Weaver
Jimmy.....................Peter Cookson
Northrup....................Tim Ryan
Randall...................Pierre Watkin
Bill.....................Anthony Warde
Red......................Frank Scannell
Paul.....................George Lewis
Steve....................Ralph Lewis
Dolan................J. Farrell MacDonald
Mrs. Randall............Clara Blandick
Hohman..................Tom Herbert
Reporter...............Lester Dorr
Express Guard..........Frank Stephens
Mr. Vanderbrook........Wilbur Mack
Mrs. Vanderbrook.....Charlotte Treadway

Hoked-up whodunit with accent on a humorous chase rather than on problem of criminals' identity should prove an adequate dualer. Audience knows from the beginning who the crooks are and interest centers around zany detective methods of the wrongdoers' pursuers.

Action deals with a private investigator (Peter Cookson), who introduces his partner (Tim Ryan of the radio team "Tim & Irene"), by casting suspicion on himself so that his partner's appearance as a member of the firm sent to check up on him as a questionable person seems plausible. Delivery of a valuable necklace and its theft by the jewelry firm manager provide the duo with ample opportunity for horseplay while tracking the criminal and his associates. Romantic interest is provided by Marjorie Weaver as the manager's secretary who's innocently involved in the case by carrying the stolen necklace in a pair of metal-plated baby-shoes as a favor for her boss.

Direction and acting is standard "B" grade with none of the cast particularly outstanding. Cookson is a new personality with a breezy style and physical appeal. He should develop with more work. Camera work is clean and opening scenes display some originality. *Turo.*

Las Dos Huerfanas
("The Two Orphans")
(MEXICAN-MADE)

Mexico City, Oct. 17.

Pan-American Films release of Filmex production. Features Julian Soler, Susana Guizar, Anita Blanch, Rafael Baledon, Virginia Zuri, Miguel Arenas, Rafael Base-

quells. Directed by Jose Benavides, Jr. Adapted by Adolfo Fernandez Bustamante. Running time, 125 MINS. Cine Orfeon, Mexico City.

Classic tale of "The Two Orphans" during the big French Revolution's Reign of Terror is done Mexican with some deftness plus a mixing of Spanish and Gallic philosophy. Tragedy, suffering and general bad luck are heavily stressed amid excellent atmosphere of the period. Guillotine sequences are done with typical Spanish love for lingering on horror. Because done by American companies and also French, this version appears headed for mild returns in U. S.

Film's length and tedious pace is enlivened by comedienne Anita Blanch, who has a big local comedy legit rep. She does okay in a rather somber role. Julian Soler and Susana Guizar rate special mention for their difficult roles.

Plot holds close to the novel and ranks high in treatment and direction. Picture is in the groove for Mexican audiences.

Miniature Reviews

"Bowery to Broadway" (musical) (U). Backstage filmusical will need b.o. strength of its stars.

"Girl Rush" (Songs) (RKO). Broad laugh entertainment for the program houses as supporter.

"One Mysterious Night" (Col). Another in the Boston Blackie series. dualer.

"Brazil" (Musical) (Rep). Tito Guizar, Virginia Bruce, in sock musical; top biz and holdovers in most spots.

"The Last Horseman" (Songs) (Col). Russell Hayden rises into hoss opera stardom in this one; a dualer.

"That's My Baby" (Songs) (Rep). Good dualer with several specialty acts helping.

"Pique Dame" (French). Interesting Gallic version of Pushkin novel.

"China Poblana" (Mex). Talky, slow story.

"Romance of Half a Century" (Chilean-made). Spanish - languager okay for south-of-border or native-language patrons.

Bowery to Broadway
(MUSICAL)

Hollywood, Oct. 20.

Universal release of John Grant production. Stars Maria Montez, Susanna Foster, Jack Oakie, Turhan Bey. Directed by Charles Lamont. Screenplay by Edmund Joseph, Bart Lytton, Arthur T. Horman; original, Joseph and Lytton; camera, Charles Van Enger; editor, Arthur Hilton; dialog director, Edward Colebrook; asst. director, Mack Wright; score and direction, Edward Ward; musical numbers staged by Carlos Romero, Louis Da Pron and John Boyle. Previewed at WB Beverly, Oct. 19, '44. Running time, **95 MINS.**

Marina....................Maria Montez
Michael O'Rourke..............Jack Oakie
Peggy Fleming.............Susanna Foster
Ted Barrie....................Turhan Bey
Bessie Jo Kirby................Ann Blyth
Dennis Dugan.................Donald Cook
Lillian Russell.........Louise Allbritton
Joe Kirby..................Frank McHugh
Bessie Kirby..........Rosemary De Camp
P. J. Fenton.................Leo Carrillo
Father Kelley................Andy Devine
Bonnie Latour..............Evelyn Ankers
Tom Harvey................Thomas Gomez
Walter Rogers...............Richard Lane
George Henshaw...........George Dolenz
Alabam ....Mantan Moreland
No-More ....Ben Carter
Madame Alda...............Maude Eburne
Cliff Brown...............Robert Warwick

In tossing group of its "name" contract personalities into the cast, Universal figured to make a big filmusical with "Bowery to Broadway." Despite the cast toppers and plenty of outlay for production cost, picture fails to achieve its objective. However, there are sufficient entertainment factors in the episodic unfolding to make it moderately acceptable as billtopper for the regular runs, with the starring quartet of Maria Montez, Susanna Foster, Jack Oakie and Turhan Bey materially aiding the b.o.

Tale covers span of 30 years, introducing Oakie and Donald Cook as competitors with Bowery nightspots. Cook is the idea man and showman, with Oakie stealing both to be expert executioner. Pair take their perpetual biz battle to 14th Street vaude theatres, and then are brought together as partners to sensationally stage filmusicals farther uptown on 42d St. Partnership splits when Cook essays dramatic shows unsuccessfully with Maria Montez. Several years later, partnership is revived via reunion for another hit presentation.

Story is episodic, and grooves into the three periods—Bowery, 14th St. and Broadway. Miss Foster is a discovery of Cook, appears briefly in the show as new star in the middle footage, and falls in love with musical director-composer Bey for virtual fadeout in later sequences. Miss Montez, as European import, checks in for first time at the hour mark, which seems quite late in the proceedings. Oakie and Cook, as the producing team which might have been lightly sketched from several real partnerships, are focal points throughout and handle majority of the footage outside of the musical and production numbers.

Louise Albritton makes the most of her brief appearance as Lillian Russell in the Bowery layout to sing the oldier, "Under the Bamboo Tree." Miss Foster delivers, in her high soprano, two neat Everett Carter-Edward Ward tunes, "The Love Waltz" and "There'll Always Be a Moon." Donald O'Connor and Peggy Ryan are cut in for one comedy song and dance number, "He Took Her for a Sleighride," but latter looks like it's a leftover from some other picture. Miss Montez is presented with one South America tempoed song, "My Song of Romance."

Picture is studded with series of elaborate production numbers, some crisp and lively, while others are too extended. Fast-patter routine by Negro pair, Ben Carter and Mantan Moreland, is presented with expert timing to rate as a high spot of the entire picture. Frank McHugh and Rosemary De Camp team nicely as a vaude pair who never quite reach Broadway.

Oakie blusters merrily throughout, in contrast to the reserved fine portrayal of Cook. Leo Carillo, Andy Devine, Thomas Gomez and Ann Blyth make brief appearances. Direction by Charles Lamont shows flashes of consistency, but he's handicapped by the disjointed and episodic script and inclusion of the extended production numbers. *Walt.*

Girl Rush
(SONGS)

Hollywood, Oct. 19.

RKO release of Sid Rogell production. Stars Wally Brown, Alan Carney, Frances Langford, Vera Vague. Directed by Gordon Douglas. Screenplay by Robert E. Kent, based on original by Laszlo Vadnay and Aladar Laszlo; camera, Nicholas Musuraca; special effects, Vernon L. Walker; editor, Duncan Mansfield; assit. director, James Casey; songs, Lew Pollack, Harry Harris. Tradeshown Alexander, Glendale, Oct. 17, '44. Running time, **65 MINS.**

Jerry Miles.....................Wally Brown
Mike Strager.....................Alan Carney
Flo Daniels...............Frances Langford
Suzie Banks.......................Vera Vague
Jimmy Smith..............Robert Mitchum
Muley ....Paul Hurst
Claire ....Patti Brill
Emma ....Sarah Padden
Barlan ....Cy Kendall
Scully ....John Merton

"Girl Rush" is broad buffoonery, sprinkled with plenty of corn and a few songs, to make it a suitable comedy supporter for the family and hinterland audiences. It's the best opportunity to date for RKO's comedy team, Wally Brown and Alan Carney, with addition of Frances Langford and Vera Vague as co-stars to lend b.o. strength.

Plot is an acceptable chassis on which to mount the broad slapstick routines of Brown and Carney, and the three songs delivered in fine style by the personable Miss Langford. Comics also deliver a comedy duet along the line on two occasions.

Brown and Carney are top comics of a tab show in Frisco music hall-saloon of century ago when gold rush kills patronage. Boys decide to hunt for gold, but wander into womanless town of Red Creek to get sacks of golddust on promise to bring girls in troupe back as entertainers and prospective brides for the miners. They intend to buy wagon train for skip to New York, but finally get untangled to route for the mining town and a wild rough-and-tumble brawl for the finish.

Comics show up well with several well-devised and timed slapstick sequences that are good for laugh reaction from the customers. Miss Langford adds strength with her songs and brief romantic spot opposite Robert Mitchum. Latter catches attention with a smooth performance and likeable personality. Vera Vague is continually on a manhunt.

Direction by Gordon Douglas neatly times the gag situations for Brown and Carney, and keeps pace at a good clip. The four songs contributed by Lew Pollack and Harry Harris are above par for a programmer. *Walt.*

One Mysterious Night

Columbia release of Red Richmond production. Features Chester Morris, Richard Lane, Janis Carter. Directed by Oscar Boetticher, Jr. Based upon character of "Boston Blackie," created by Jack Boyle; story and adaptation, Paul Yawitz; editor, Al Clark; camera, L. W. O'Connell. At Roalto, N. Y., week Oct. 20, '44. Running time, **61 MINS.**

Boston Blackie..................Chester Morris
Inspector Farraday...........Richard Lane
Dorothy Anderson.............Janis Carter
Paul Martens.................William Wright
Matt Healy................Robert Williams
The Runt....................George E. Stone
Eileen Daley..............Dorothy Maloney
George Daley...............Robert E. Scott
Matthews..........................Lyle Latell
Sergeant McNulty...........George McKay
Margaret Dean..............Early Cantrell
Jumbo Madigan...............Joseph Crehan

Another in the Boston Blackie series, one that adds up lightly as film entertainment in the detective fiction groove. Will serve adequately, however, on the lesser double bills.

Chester Morris, again as Boston Blackie, although not entirely unsuspected of having had part in a jewel robbery, is called in by police to aid in recovering a costly diamond that has been stolen at an exhibit for war relief held in a swanky hotel. With the aid of The Runt, his standby, played in the B. B. series of George E. Stone, the diamond is ultimately turned over to the police. In the meantime, Morris and Stone are tailed, as are others, by a girl reporter who gives Morris a meaningful eye at the finish after snapping his picture. A couple murders are committed en route through the rather tedious story, with police not so sure Morris isn't responsible for at least one.

Richard Lane plays a police inspector in a routine manner. Sob-sister role is carried off well by Janis Carter, a looker, while two gem thieves, doing okay, are William Wright and Robert Williams. Dorothy Maloney, switchboard operator, and Robert E. Scott, asst. manager of a hotel, are of a minor character but suitable.

On the technical side picture is a little below par, some of the photography especially being sub-standard. *Char.*

Brazil
(MUSICAL)

Republic release of Robert North production. Stars Tito Guizar, Virginia Bruce; features Edward Everett Horton, Robert Livingston, Veloz & Yolanda, Roy Rogers, Aurora Miranda. Directed by Joseph Santley. Screenplay by Frank Gill, Jr., and Laura Kerr from original by Richard English; dances, Billy Daniels; songs, Ary Barroso, Ned Washington, S. K. Russell, Hoagy Carmichael, Harolo Lobo, Milton de Olivera, Alvaro De S. Carvalho, Aloysio Oliveira; editor, Fred Allen; camera, Jack Marta. Previewed N. Y. Oct. 20, '44. Running time, **91 MINS.**

Miguel Soares.......................Tito Guizar
Nicky Henderson.............Virginia Bruce
Everett St. John Everett......E. E. Horton
Rod Walker...............Robert Livingston
Veloz and Yolanda......Veloz and Yolanda
Senhor Renato Da Silva.Fortunio Bonanova
Edward Graham...............Richard Lane
Senhor Machado...............Frank Puglia
Specialty Dancer...........Aurora Miranda
Master of Ceremonies........Alfredo de Sa
Business Man................Henry Da Silva
Airport Official...............Rico de Montez
Reporter..........................Leon Lenoir
Guest Star.........................Roy Rogers

"Brazil" is as solid as the hit tune of same name, which, incidentally, figures importantly in this film's story. Should prove a block-buster at the wickets, a musical investment for Republic that promises to outgross any previous top-bracket film from this company. With Ary Barroso, Latin-American composer who did the lilting "Brazil" song-dance number, contributing bulk of music, this is in the groove for all who like south-of-border music.

Unlike too many previous films with Latin-American locales, this has a plot that adds up. Virginia Bruce, as author of "Why Marry a Latin?" is in Rio to get material for a book on Brazil. She's hardly given a warm welcome because of that book. Otherwise, her stay in Brazil is okay because not recognized by natives. That is until she bumps into Tito Guizar. Forced to stay on, because unable to get travel priorities, her friend, Robert Livingston, member of U. S. Consulate, escorts her around swank nightclubs where she again encounters Guizar. He fakes being a tourist guide to be near her. But on learning she authored "Why Marry a Latin?" he decides to give her an object lesson, and prove that Latins aren't such lousy lovers. Of course, in trying to prove his point, Guizar falls in love with her.

Guizar personates Brazil's most famous songwriter, whose "Brazil" has copped first prize at the most recent lavish Rio carnival. He's pictured as indifferently trying to turn out a follow-up hit, this time for a U. S. music publisher. Said publisher's insistence on early delivery of tune adds complications as does Edward Everett Horton's lapse when he tells Miss Bruce that Guizar's romance is to teach her a lesson. There's the usual smoothing out of the spat with reunion at the Rio festival where Guizar's new song wins first prize.

For those who may question Tito Guizar as the romantic lead, this should build his popularity in the U. S.; and of course, he's fairly well established in the Latin-Americas. Role of Brazil's top composer is glove-fitting for him. He looks and acts better than in any previous film. Guizar carries brunt of vocal chores with nice polish, his excellent voice going over well. He warbles the picture's hit tune, "Rio de Janeiro," both in English and Portuguese, other numbers being sung in Portuguese solely. They will register with the average American.

Miss Bruce makes an excellent contrast to Guizar with her blonde beauty. She's the typically bored Yank visitor in South America. Horton provides the comedy moments, especially with his two-headed cousin gag.

Veloz & Yolanda are impressive in their brief appearance doing the Samba to the music of "Brazil." More footage than usual is devoted to their dance, but it's smart showmanship because of high-ranking musical background and unusual terps treatment. Billy Daniels, who did the outstanding dance creations, Aurora Miranda and Rita Lupino (sister of Ida) contribute another vivid dance, typically Brazilian.

Also standout, and the film's most elaborate ensemble, is the "Cafe" number. It's one of those picturesque conceits depicting how Brazil's coffee is handled.

Aside from Guizar's vocalizing, only other credited singer is Roy Rogers, doing "Hands Across the Border," tuneful effort from Hoagy Carmichael and Ned Washington. He's brought in as western film star visiting Rio during the big carnival.

Best of Ary Barroso's compositions, besides "Brazil" and "Rio de Janeiro" (latter appearing another hit of almost same stature as "Brazil") are "Vaquero Song," "Tonight You're Mine," "Moonlight Fiesta" and "Upa Upa." Ned Washington did the English lyrics for all excepting "Brazil," which were by S. K. Russell.

Stout supporting cast is headed by Fortunio Bonanova, Richard Lane and Robert Livingston. Joseph Santley's direction is topflight throughout while Robert North has given the picture elaborate production back-

grounding. Special camera crew went to Brazil for background shots, most important being the Rio carnival scenes. Jack Marta has chipped in with a crack camera job.
Wear.

The Last Horseman
(SONGS)

Columbia release of Leon Barsha production. Stars Russell Hayden; features Dub Taylor, Bob Wills, Ann Savage. Directed by William Berke. Story and screenplay, Ed Earl Rapp; camera, George Meenhan; editor, Jerome Thoms. At N. Y. theatre, N. Y., week of Oct. 18, '44, dual. Running time, **54 MINS.**

Lucky Rawlins..............Russell Hayden
Cannonball ....Dub Taylor
Bob ....Bob Wills
Judy Ware....................Ann Savage
Cash Watson.................John Maxwell
Rance Williams.............Frank La Rue
Karp ....Nick Thompson
Slade...........J. P. "Blackie" Whiteford
Cudlow ....Ted Mapes
Bert Saunders...............Forrest Taylor

Pleasant enough, but not out of the ordinary as hoss operas go, "The Last Horseman" should please western fans. Grooved for the lower rung on duals.

With Bob Wills and his Texas Playboys supplying the musical encouragement, Russell Hayden portrays the role of a ranch foreman who is robbed of $12,000 which he was delivering to his boss, proceeds from the sale of a herd of cattle. The gang turns the check over to the town banker, who plans to take over the ranch when the owner is unable to pay a note. By disguising themselves as women, Hayden and his cohorts nab the outlaws, who hold up the stage on which they are riding, save the ranch, boss, et al.

Lots of fast riding, fighting and action should please those who enjoy this type of film fare. This is Hayden's initial starring vehicle, and he turns in a fairly neat performance. Outdoor sequences are eye-filling.
Sten.

That's My Baby
(SONGS)

Republic release of Walter Comes production. Stars Richard Arlen, Ellen Drew; features Leonid Kinskey, Richard Bailey, Minor Watson. Directed by William Berke. Screenplay, Nicholas Barrows, William Tunberg, from original by Irving Wallace; camera, Robert Pittack; editor, Robert Jahns. At N. Y. theatre, N. Y., week of Oct. 18, '44, dual. Running time, **68 MINS.**

Tim Jones......................Richard Arlen
Betty Moody...................Ellen Drew
Dr. Svatzky...................Leonid Kinskey
Hilton Payne...................Richard Bailey
R. P. Moody...................Minor Watson
Miss Wilson.................Marjorie Manners
Hettie Moody.................Madeline Grey
Dr. Calloway...................Alex Callam
Barber............................P. J. Kelly
Office Boy.....................Billy Benedict
Waiter ....Jack Chefe

Richard Arlen and Ellen Drew, with a capable supporting cast, help make "That's My Baby" a better than average dualer.

Yarn finds Arlen and his fiancee, Miss Drew, faced with the problem of pulling her dad, Minor Watson, out of a psychiatric depression. Screenplay by Nick Barrows and Bill Tunberg, from Irving Wallace's original, is well written, giving the actors many opportunities. Dave Fleischer, vet of the animated cartoon field, worked on this pic, and it is his cartoon handiwork which is a key to the yarn.

Among the specialties are the Freddie Fisher and Mike Riley bands; Gene Rogers, Negro boogie-woogie pianist; Isabelita and the Guadaljara boys. All are seen briefly, with good results. *Sten.*

Pique Dame
(FRENCH-MADE)

Herbert Rosner Co. release of Michel Kagansky-Christian Stengel production. Stars Pierre Blanchar; features Marguerite Moreno and Madeleine Ozeray. Directed by Fedor Ozep. Screenplay, Bernard Zimmer, adapted from Alexander Pushkin novel; camera, Thirard and Louis Nee; English titles, Herman G. Weinberg. At 5th Ave. Playhouse, N. Y., Oct. 18, '44. Running time, **78 MINS.**

Hermann ....Pierre Blanchar
Iretzky ....Andre Luguet
La Dame de Pique.......Marguerite Moreno
Lisa ....Madeleine Ozeray
Tomski ....Abel Jaquin
The General....................Camille Bert
The Banker................................Palau
Ivan ....Roger Legris
Narumoff ....Jean Didier
Glacha ....Raymone
Nadia ....Michele Alfa
The Florist............... ....Colette Wilda

(In French; English Titles)

"Pique Dame," prewar French pic, is an interesting fable of 19th century Russian manners, which despite its many technical faults, should do well with French audiences and arty groups. French will want to see a native film again, and this one particularly because its lead, Pierre Blanchar, has distinguished himself since as radio voice of French underground during the Nazi occupation. Film is adaptation of Alexander Pushkin story.

Russian director Fedor Ozep has played around with various effects, some satisfactory, some not. Lighting is frequently bad, with attempts at mood through use of shadows not altogether successful. Acting is sometimes stilted, and film frequently drags. But story nevertheless is an interesting satire on 19th century aristocracy and its absorption in gambling, duels and fancy social affairs. Primarily it centers around a young Russian army officer and his obsession for cards. His mania leads him to making false love to a lady, risking a duel and ruining his reputation, in order to gain from an old dowager an alleged magic formula for winning at cards. Background of St. Petersburg aristocracy is intriguing, a proper setting for the satire.

Blanchar gives a generally intelligent but sometimes stylized portrait as the card-maddened officer. Marguerite Moreno, as a shrewish dowager, gives a skilled, flavorsome portrayal, and Madeleine Ozeray is a charming blonde cameo as the dowager's ward. *Bron.*

China Poblana
("The Silken Chinese Dress")
(MEXICAN-MADE)
(Color)

Clasa Mohme release of Clasa Films production. Stars Maria Felix. Directed by Fernando Palacios. Music, Manuel Esperon. At Belmont, N. Y., Oct. 19, '44. Running time, **92 MINS.**

Senora de la Barca...............Maria Felix
Don Miguel..............Miguel Angel Ferriz
El Pitarras......................Miguel Inclan
Captain de Cordoba........Augusto Novaro
Maria Tomellin................Gloria Iturbe
Calderon...........................Jose Goula
Mme. Francine....................Ana Claire
Melquiades....................Antonio Fausto

(In Spanish; No English Titles)

Transposition to the screen of the "stigma" attached to a Chinese dress of silk provides a wordy, overlong drama with only the color processing and musical background compensating for the lightweight story. In Spanish, without English titles, it certainly has little appeal for non-Latin audiences, and even Latins will find the yarn trivial.

Story concerns the wife of the first Spanish ambassador to Mexico whose determination to wear the forbidden costume leads her to investigate its history. Latter makes up the greater part of the pic and concerns an Oriental princess who is captured by pirates and bought by a noble Spaniard. Love affair develops between the princess and the noble's nephew, with latter killed in a mine mishap. The Chinese gal then dies of a broken heart. Story of the ill-fated princess only strengthens the ambassador's wife's desire to wear the costume, which she does and thus becomes the belle of the ball. Why association of the dress with the virtuous Chinese gal attaches a stigma thereto remains a mystery, with no attempt at explanation. *Turo.*

Romance De Medio Siglo
("Romance of Half a Century")
(CHILEAN-MADE)

Santiago, Chile, Oct. 10.

Band y Salas, Ltda., release of Chile Films production. Stars Ines Moreno, Florinda Ferrario, Francisco Flores; features Nieves Yanko, Orlando Castillo, America Viel, Chela Bon, Mario Gaete, Hernan Castro Oliveira. Directed by L. J. Moglia Barth. Story, C. Vattier and F. Coloane; music by Prospero Bisguertt; screenplay, L. K. Moglia Barth. At Teatro Central, Santiago. Running time, **95 MINS.**

This is the first production from these new studios, skippered by Don Andres Salas Edwards, and is good entertainment for south of the border and Spanish-language theatres in the U. S.

Story begins with a girl falling for a guy but her father balks the match because the suitor is on the "wrong side" in the Chilean Revolution of that year. The time is 1891. She marries her father's choice, and the turned-down chap goes to Paris and becomes a famous painter. Later they meet again in Valparaiso, he with his son and she with daughter. He is killed in 1906 earthquake and she brings up son with her own children. Daughter and son develop brother-sister affection, and eventually their respective grandson and grand-daughter meet, culminating in romance.

Ines Moreno is seen all through pic and plays sincerely. She ages gracefully and her performance is tenderly touching. Only other character seen all through is Orlando Castillo, as her uncle; he gives a fine character portrayal. Stars Florindo Ferrario and Francisco Flores also do well. The work of Hernan Castro Oliveira, an Arturo de Cordoba type, stands out, and the senoritas, America Viel and Chela Bon, of the studio's own dramatic school, show promise. Advantage has been taken of Chile's great store of natural scenery, and thought went into reproducing atmosphere of the various periods. Main fault, common to most Latin American productions, is slowness of movement and tendency to pose actors in positions that look artificial and affected.

Well-written musical score by Prospero Bisguertt, Chilean composer, is neatly interpreted by Chilean symphony orchestra under Armando Carvajal, leading longhair maestro of the republic.

Miniature Reviews

"Meet Me In St. Louis" (Songs; Color) (M-G). Socko all the way, from cast to story; a cinch for big grosses.

"Something For The Boys" (Musical; Color) (20th). Should prove satisfactory at the b.o.

"Dark Waters" (UA). Oberon, Tone in a melodrama which should do OK.

"Ever Since Venus" (Songs) (Col). Entertaining limited budgeter grooved for anybody's dual bill.

"Murder in the Blue Room" (Songs) (U). Lightweight whodunit; duals.

"Los Miserables" (Azteca). Mexican-made version of Victor Hugo's story is top-bracket fare; strong for foreign spots.

"The Rainbow" (Artkino). Stark filmization of Russian resistance to Nazis. Too grim for more than indifferent b.o.

Meet Me In St. Louis
(TECHNICOLOR; SONGS)

Metro release of Arthur Freed production. Stars Judy Garland; features Margaret O'Brien, Mary Astor, Lucille Bremer, Leon Ames. Directed by Vincente Minnelli. Screenplay, Irving Brecher, Fred F. Finklehoffe, from Sally Benson's book. Songs, Hugh Martin, Ralph Blane; camera, George Folsey; music, Roger Edens, Georgie Stoll, Conrad Salinger; dances, Chas. Walters; editor, Albert Akst. Tradeshown Oct. 25, N. Y., 1944. Running time, **113 MINS.**

Esther Smith.....................Judy Garland
"Tootie" Smith..........Margaret O'Brien
Mrs. Anna Smith..................Mary Astor
Rose Smith.....................Lucille Bremer
John Truett...........................Tom Drake
Katie (Maid)....................Marjorie Main
Mr. Alonzo Smith....................Leon Ames
Grandpa.....................Harry Davenport
Lucille Ballard....................June Lockhart
Lon Smith, Jr.......Henry H. Daniels, Jr.
Agnes Smith........................Joan Carroll
Colonel Darly...................Hugh Marlowe
Warren Sheffield...................Robert Sully
Mr. Neely............................Chill Wills

"Meet Me in St. Louis" is the answer to any exhibitor's prayer. Perhaps accented in these days as ideal "escapist" film fare, it would be surefire in any period. It holds everything for the film fan.

It is wholesome in story, colorful both in background and its literal Technicolor, and as American as the World's Series. Its theme is a natural for the hinterland; it's that "getting ahead and going to New York" isn't everything.

As Leon Ames plays the head of the Alonzo Smith clan it's a 1903 life-with-father. Mary Astor is the understanding and, incidentally, quite handsome mother as they worry about Judy Garland and Lucille Bremer, playing their daughters. Henry H. Daniels, Jr., is the self-sufficient brother, off to Princeton, but the romantic travail of the two older girls is the fundamental. Backgrounded are Marjorie Main, capital as the maid who almost bosses the household, and the still-gallant Harry Davenport, now 80ish, who is Grandpa.

It's the time of the St. Louis Fair, hence the title song, and everything that makes for the happy existence of a typical American family is skillfully panoramaed.

From Sally Benson's New Yorker stories (and later a book), Metro's scripters, Irving Brecher and Fred Finklehoffe, have contrived a tiptop screenplay.

Seasonal pastorals, from summer into the next spring, take the Smith clan through their appealing little problems. Judy Garland's plaint about "The Boy Next Door" (played by Tom Drake); the Paul Jones dance routine to the tune of "Skip to My Lou"; the Yuletide thematic, "Have Yourself a Merry Christmas"; and the already popular "Trolley

Song," en route to the Fairgrounds, are four socko musical highlights. They have been intelligently highlighted and well-paced by director Vincente Minnelli.

Then there is winsome Margaret O'Brien as the prevaricating and impressionable "Tootie" Smith, the youngest of the brood.

Miss Garland achieves true stature with her deeply understanding performance, while her sisterly running-mate, Lucille Bremer, a looker and a redhead out of the N. Y. nitery choruses, likewise makes excellent impact with a well-balanced performance.

Right down the line the casting is smooth. The people all seem real. Joan Carroll, another moppet, slightly older than Margaret O'Brien, is likewise a prankster. June Lockhart makes her role believable when she saves the evening at the Christmas ball by properly pairing off the love-sick couples, turning the impression that she was a N. Y. vamp. Dominant is the warm family spirit, whether it's the mild skullduggery to make papa Smith (well played by Leon Ames) dine earlier than usual, or the climactic situation when there is consternation at the thought of breaking up their St. Louis home ties to transplant themselves to New York, just because of the bigger opportunity with papa's law firm. When it suddenly dawns on him that St. Louis is where his heart also lies, it's a rousing finish to a thoroughly enjoyable unfolding of a film whose footage is replete with natural warmth and good humor. *Abel.*

Something For the Boys

(MUSICAL; COLOR)

20th Century-Fox release of Irving Starr production. Stars Carmen Miranda, Michael O'Shea, Vivian Blaine; features Phil Silvers, Sheila Ryan, Perry Como, Glenn Langan. Directed by Lewis Seiler. Based on Broadway musical, book by Herbert and Dorothy Fields, songs by Cole Porter; adaptation, Robert Ellis, Helen Logan, Frank Gabrielson; new songs, Jimmy McHugh and Harold Adamson; dances, Nick Castle; editor, Robert Simpson; camera, Ernest Palmer, Fred Sersen. Previewed N.Y. Oct. 27, '44. Running time, **87 MINS.**

Chiquita Hart..............Carmen Miranda
Sgt. Rocky Fulton..........Michael O'Shea
Blossom Hart..................Vivian Blaine
Harry Hart......................Phil Silvers
Melanie Walker.................Sheila Ryan
Sgt. Laddie Green................Perry Como
Lieut. Ashley Crothers.........Glenn Langan
Lieutenant ....Roger Clark
Secretary....................Cara Williams
Col. Jeff L. Calhoun..........Thurston Hall
Col. Grubbs.................Clarence Kolb
Supervisor ....Paul Hurst
Southern Colonel...........Andrew Tombes

While "Something for the Boys," based upon the Broadway hit of the same name, fails to reach the stature of outstanding musical entertainment, it is sufficiently diverting and tuneful to warrant more than moderate success at the boxoffice. Several of new songs which look like hits, the well-staged dance numbers and the good pace, plus elaborate productional backgrounds and superior color photography, go a considerable distance in offsetting weaknesses of other elements in the picture.

Screen adaptation of the musical play, done by Robert Ellis, Helen Logan and Frank Gabrielson, includes various amusing situations, but, taken as a whole, the story does not have partciular punch in dialog or otherwise. Also, the comedy values are somewhat spotty, though, here and there, including among the slapstick stuff, some fairly good laughs are registered. Phil Silvers works hard on the comic end and, in one clowning number, provides several minutes of surefire nature.

Though "Boys" on stage concerned a Texas ranch inherited by three distant cousins, 20th-Fox has changed the locale to a broken-down plantation at Thomasville, Ga. As result, some odd and theatrical Dixie accents, which will kill 'em in the South, have been introduced. Least authentic-sounding among cast members is the affected voice of Glenn Langan, who plays an Army lieutenant; Cara Williams (a secretary) rating as the next worst. Of course, with Silvers, who's from the North but wants to act the Southern gentleman, it's a matter of travesty.

Carmen Miranda, Vivian Blaine and Silvers are the three cousins who fall heir to the old plantation, only to learn that they are poorer by having acquired the debt-laden property. They get an idea, with cooperation of a nearby Army camp, to make it a home for Army wives, and raise money through putting on shows and otherwise to repair and maintain it. This opens the way for the various song and dance numbers.

Perry Como, singer from the radio-nitery-theatre field, makes his debut in the musical. He has two numbers, but figures in the action in only a very minor way. Making a good appearance before the camera, he does "I Wish We Didn't Have to Say Goodnight" and "In the Middle of Nowhere," both of which are quite listenable and well sold. These, among others, were written by Jimmy McHugh and Harold Adamson to supplement the small amount of Cole Porter music from the stageplay which was utilized.

"Wouldn't It Be Nice," originally a double for Michael O'Shea and Miss Blaine, reprised later on, is a probable hit. Another that stacks up very favorably is "80 Miles from Atlanta," featured by the attractive Miss Blaine as part of a production number. Two others, exceptionally well done by Miss Miranda, are "Boom Brachee" and "Samba Boogie," additional worthy contributions by McHugh and Adamson. They are also given production background. The dances are effective, staged by Nick Castle.

O'Shea, playing an Army sergeant and giving a good account of himself, is paired romantically with Miss Blaine. Miss Miranda, aside from her songs, ably assists Silvers and others in a comedy way. Others in the cast, but not in much of the footage, include Sheila Ryan, Roger Clark, Thurston Hall, Clarence Kolb, Paul Hurst and Andrew Tombes. All acquit themselves acceptably. *Char.*

Dark Waters

United Artists release of Benedict Bogeaus production. Stars Merle Oberon, Franchot Tone, Thomas Mitchell; features Fay Bainter, John Qualen, Elisha Cook, Jr. Directed by Andre de Toth. Screenplay by Joan Harrison, Marian Cockrell, from Satevepost serial by Frank and Marian Cockrell; camera, Archie Stout, John Mescall; editor, James Smith. Tradeshown, N. Y., Oct. 30, '44. Running time, **90 MINS.**

Leslie Calvin.................Merle Oberon
Dr. George Grover............Franchot Tone
Mr. Sydney...............Thomas Mitchell
Aunt Emily.....................Fay Bainter
Uncle Norbert..................John Qualen
Cleeve.....................Elisha Cook, Jr.
Pearson Jackson...............Rex Ingram
Mama Boudreaux.............Odette Myrtil
Papa Boudreaux.............Eugene Borden
Jeanette....................Eileen Coghlan
Florella................Nina May McKinney
The Doctor......................Alan Napier
The Nurse..........................Rita Beery

With Merle Oberon, Franchot Tone and Thomas Mitchell for the marquee, "Dark Waters," a melodrama that has its spine-chilling moments, should fare above average at the boxoffice in all situations.

A strong cast that handles itself superbly throughout, aided by the capable direction of Andre de Toth, is responsible for whatever entertainment value this picture might have. Obviously, the film set out to be a study in characterizations, destined to make the story itself secondary to the characters portrayed, thus giving it a lift out of the ordinary. But somewhere along the line this idea was sidetracked, and the film winds up in the usual denouement of the gal getting her man and the dastard getting his just deserts.

Merle Oberon gives one of the best portrayals of her career in the role of a young heiress beset by psychological neuroses due to the loss of her parents when a ship on which they were returning from Batavia to America is sunk, she being one of four survivors. Thomas Mitchell, as the conniver intent on driving the heiress into an asylum and gaining her riches, has some poor lines to toss away before coming through with a meaty performance. Franchot Tone's portrayal of a bayou country doctor who falls for Miss Oberon and, in the end, saves her from Mitchell's double-dealing tactics, is forthright, but never too weighty.

Producer Benedict Bogeaus hasn't stepped off the deep end in giving this one fancy values that are meaningless. On the other hand, he has gathered together a strong cast, knowing full well that they would have to do the job at hand capably, in order to give this film meaning and boxoffice. *Sten.*

Ever Since Venus

(SONGS)

Columbia release of production directed by Arthur Dreifuss, based on original screenplay by himself and McElbert Moore. Features Ina Ray Hutton, Hugh Herbert, Ann Savage, Glenda Farrell, Ross Hunter, Billy Gilbert. Camera, Benjamin Kline; editor, Otto Meyer; songs, Bernie Wayne, Ben Raleigh, Lester Lee, Harry Harris. At Fox, Brooklyn, week Oct. 27, '44. Running time, **74 MINS.**

Ina Ray Hutton.......................Herself
P. G. Grimble.................Hugh Herbert
Janet Wilson.....................Ann Savage
Tiny Lewis.......................Billy Gilbert
Babs Cartwright...........Glenda Farrell
Bradley Miller...................Ross Hunter
J. Webster Hackett........Alan Mowbray
Maud Hackett...........Marjorie Gateson
Edgar Pomeroy.............Thurston Hall
Michele..............................Fritz Feld
Clarence....................Dudley Dickerson

"Ever Since Venus" is an entertaining low-budgeter that will serve as strong support on dual bills.

Obviously the members of the cast, from featured players to extras, had a good time making this film, and that cheeriness percolates to the audience. Ina Ray Hutton, Ann Savage and Glenda Farrell divide the feminine chores, and do a good job, but the buffoonery of Hugh Herbert, in the role of an eccentric factory owner, and Billy Gilbert, as a song-writing member of a trio of lipstick manufacturers who have trouble getting started, is especially commendable. The latter duo carry the film in topflight fashion.

Yarn has to do with the trials and tribulations faced by three men who concocted a new lipstick formula, but are unable to merchandise the article. How they gain production facilities, with the aid of funds garnered by Billy Gilbert who wins a prize for writing a song, proves to be fairly interesting.

To Arthur Dreifuss, who directed and also wrote the original screenplay, teamed with McElbert Moore, goes a bow for turning out a winner on limited funds. Songs, played by Ina Ray Hutton and her band and sung by the Misses Savage, Farrell, et al., are above par. *Sten.*

Murder In The Blue Room

(SONGS)

Universal release of Frank Gross production. Features Grace McDonald, Donald Cook, Anne Gwynne, John Litel, June Preisser, Betty Kean, Regis Toomey. Directed by Leslie Goodwins. Screenplay by I. A. L. Diamond, Stanley Davis; from story by Erich Philippi; editor, Charles Maynard; camera, John P. Fulton. At Rialto, N. Y., week Oct. 27, '44. Running time, **61 MINS.**

Nan............................Anne Gwynne
Steve..........................Donald Cook
Frank Baldrich....................John Litel
Peggy.....................Grace McDonald
Betty..............................Betty Kean
Jerry..........................June Preisser
Inspector McDonald.........Regis Toomey
Linda Baldrich................Nella Walker
Dr. Carroll................Andrew Toombes
Edwards..........................Ian Wolfe
Hannagan....................Emmett Vogan
Larry.....................Bill MacWilliams
Curtin.........................Frank Marlowe

Comedy treatment of this whodunit yarn, plus songs and capable cast, with several names for the marquee, won't lift it beyond run-of-mill dualers.

Yarn has John Litel, theatre magnate, married to Nella Walker, his deceased pal's widow, reopen the house in which her former spouse was murdered. After acquiescing, there's a reception and when a whacky driver of guests to the party lets out that the place is haunted, he intrigues them to investigate. Anne Gwynne, daughter of the deceased, who had a previous fling as a nitery chirper, invites her former pals, Betty Kean, June Preisser and Grace McDonald, to come out and entertain with a view of impressing her stepdad to contract them for his theatre chain.

Usual romantic angle doesn't come off because Miss Gwynne is unwittingly involved romantically with Bill MacWilliams, son of her late father by previous marriage, known only to Andrew Toombes, the family medico. It's after this the spook hunt begins, with Betty Kean and nitery pals furnishing most of the laughs and a couple of vocals to space proceedings. MacWilliams elects to sleep in the murder room and, ofcourse, it polished off. There's a spook, supposedly the spirit of the deceased, walking about on occasion. Donald Cook, writer of mystery yarns, also elects to sleep in the murder room and tracks down the family medico as perpetrator of the double homicide. He had been blackmailing the elder victim and polished off the son when latter got too curious.

Story is thin and laughs and situations too widely spaced to amount on sock comedy score. Direction and cast do well by the thin story. Camera work is up to par. *Edba.*

Los Miserables

("Les Miserables")
(MEXICAN-MADE)

Azteca Studios release of Jose Luis Calderon production. Stars Domingo Soler; features David Silva, Manolita Saval, Andres Soler, Emma Roldan. Directed by Fernando Rivero. Screenplay by Robert Tasker, Ramon Perez, Fernando A. Rivero; from novel by Victor Hugo; camera, Ross Fisher. At Belmont, N. Y., week starting Oct. 27, '44. Running time, **103 MINS.**

Jean Valjean...............Dominugo Soler
Cosette.....................Manolita Saval
Thendler......................Andres Soler
Thendler's Wife..............Emma Roldan
Javert........................Antonio Bravo
Baron Marius...................David Silva
Eponina..................Margarita Cortes

(In Spanish; no English Titles)

This Mexican version of Victor Hugo's "Les Miserables" is surprisingly strong, possessing more than the usual amount of action and dramatics for a Spanish-language production. It stacks up as boff b.o. for foreign-tongue houses and plenty of dinero for its distributors in the world market. Film's boxoffice chances in U.S. market depend largely on whether it is given English titles before set on general distribution, since it now has no superimposed titles.

Long familiar story of Jean Valjean's struggle to evade the relentless Javert, French police inspector, is done with marked skill by a capable cast headed by Domingo Soler as Valjean. Direction of Fernando Rivero, who emerges as one of Mexico's top directors as a result of this, goes far towards making the production jell. Story of this conflict between two men and the clash of revolutionaries with the gendarmes and Paris soldiers is given adequate production and sufficient clarity by producer Jose Luis Calderon. In fact, his handling of mass scenes, new trick shots and bright closeups marks an advance for Mexico film production. While thing represents a bundle of cash.

Main complaint is inability of the studio staff to get away from the usual tedious opening sequences. But this can be overlooked in view of the spread of action in subsequent reels. Even the chase through the Paris sewers is done with utmost fidelity as to detail.

Domingo Soler is brilliant as the stalwart Jean Valjean, the man who attempted to live down his past, despite a tendency to substitute deep sighing for acting in earlier passages. Manolia Saval, as his daughter, Cosette, not only is one of the most attractive femmes from the Mexico studios, but okay as a light actress. Antonio Bravo makes his Javert deep-dyed villain, but an effective one. David Silva is the courageous Baron Marius who joins the revolutionaries and nearly loses his life. Margarita Cortes, as the other girl, is strong in a lesser role. Andres Soler is an underworld crook, and Emma Roldan his wife and partner in crime. She's okay, but he tries to make too much of a lesser character.

The screenplay by Roberto Tasker, Fernando Rivero and Ramon Perez is skillful. Camera by Ross Fisher is topflight. *Wear.*

The Rainbow

Artkino release of Kiev Studio production. Directed by Mark Donskoy; story and screenplay by Wanda Wasilewska from same author's novel; camera, Boris Monastirsky; music, Lev Schwartz; English titles, Charles Clement. At Stanley, N. Y., Oct. 21, '44. Running time, **87 MINS.**

Olena Kostiuk	Natasha Uzhvey
Pusya	Natalia Alisova
Fedosia	Elena Tiapkina
Olga	Vera Ivasheva
Okhaiko	Anton Dunaysky
Maliuchikha	Anna Lisyanskaya
Capt. Kurt Werner	G. Klering
Gaplik	Nikolai Bratersky
Maliuchikha's children	Vitya Vinogradov, Alik Letichevsky, Emma Pearlstein, Vova Ponomariov
English Voice	Anne Seymour

Produced under wartime conditions in Russia, "The Rainbow" is a grim filmization of the brutality of the Nazis and the courage of the Russian peasants in resisting them, no matter what. Its mediocre production values, however, coupled with its lack of marquee draw, spell indifferent boxoffice for the U. S.

Story centers mainly about Olena, who leaves a partisan group to return to her native village to have her child. Seized by the Germans, upon her return, she is mercilessly tortured, even on the eve of delivery, and ultimately she and the child are killed. Lesser story tangets involve a quisling mayor and the traitorous Russian mistress of the German commandant. In its transitions, according to American standards, the film is glaringly weak.

Natasha Uzhvey, people's artist of the Ukraine, gives a powerful performance as the courageous partisan, playing with restraint and simple eloquence. Part could have been hammed. Elena Tiapkina, as the mistress' maid, also does a capital job, closing the film with a stirring plea against immediate slaughter of the Germans. Her theory is that they should be made to face the future to realize the crimes they've committed and to face, ultimately, a people's court.

Although the camera and sound are weak, there are several sock scenes. Mainly they involve the torture inflicted on Olena, who is forced to walk barefoot in the snow as she approaches labor, and, shortly after, the birth itself, which takes place in a bleak and barren barn. Another superb bit is done by one of Maliuchikha's kids as he and his brothers and sisters are threatened by a German soldier. The terror which shines through the kid's eyes is so realistic it seems to be proof that he's been through a similar experience in real life.

Other performances, in the main, are good, especially in the lesser, unbilled roles portraying typical village peasants. Natalia Alisova, as the mistress; G. Klering, as the commandant, and Nokolai Bratersky, as the quisling, are all stock. Miss Alisova is a Stalin prize winner, but in this picture gives a heavy and completely unsubtle performance.

Film has some exploitation angles, primarily its production under war conditions; its prominent Russian cast and its stark realism. Full advantage will have to be taken of them to get the business in. *Merr.*

Miniature Reviews

"**Together Again**" (Col). Irene Dunne and Charles Boyer in spritely romantic farce for solid diverting entertainment.

"**I Love a Soldier**" (Par). Disappointing comedy-drama dealing with war marriages. Stars Paulette Goddard, Sonny Tufts.

"**Lights of Old Santa Fe**" (Songs) (Rep). Roy Rogers should ride to top coin in his latest sagebrusher.

"**Bowery Champs**" (One Song) (Mono). Routine dualer in which East Side Kids become newspaper reporters.

"**Delinquent Daughters**" (PRC). Dull juve problem-yarn.

"**Rustlers' Hideout**" (PRC). Buster Crabbe rides again to bring the poachers to justice.

Together Again

Hollywood, Nov 2.

Columbia release of Virginia Van Upp production. Stars Irene Dunne, Charles Raven; features Charles Coburn. Directed by Charles Vidor. Screenplay by Virginia Van Upp, F. Hugh Herbert; story, Stanley Russell, Herbert Billerman; camera, Joseph Walker; editor, Otto Meyer; asst. director, Milton Feldman. Previewed Pantages, Nov. 11, '44. Running time, 93 MINS.

Anne Crandall	Irene Dunne
George Corday	Charles Boyer
Jonathan Crandall, Sr.	Charles Coburn
Diana Crandall	Alona Freeman
Gilbert Parker	Jerome Courtland
Jessie	Elizabeth Patterson
Morton Buchanan	Charles Dingle
Witherspoon	Walter Baldwin
Lillian	Fern Emmett
Leonardo	Frank Puglia

"Together Again" is a well-devised comedy-drama, liberally sprinkled with laugh lines and situations, and spotlighting Irene Dunne and Charles Boyer, with major assistance from Charles Coburn. It's top entertainment, in tune with present audience requirements, for profitable biz in all runs andt holdover candidate for the key spots.

Story, developed in broad farcical vein, romps along at a good clip and —although at times the script reaches pretty far to generate laughs—it's so generally crazy-quilt that the overall effect is far on the credit side in entertainment values. Miss Dunne and Boyer competently team in the top spots—she as the pursued and he as the pursuer in the love match. Coburn clicks for prominent attention with his constant conniving and manipulations to develop the romance for final clinch. Mona Freeman and newcomer Jerome Courtland, scholastic-age pair carry important story responsibilities in great style. Young Courtland virtually stops the show with a sparkling puppy love romantic episode with Miss Dunne, and shows plenty of possibilities for feature buildup.

Plot is a light affair, displaying Miss Dunne as the widow of the former mayor of a small town in Vermont, who carries the elective office on her shoulders as a family obligation rather than from choice. She goes to New York to hire a sculptor to make a statue of her late husband for the town square, hires Boyer, is mistaken for a strip-tease artist in a nightclub while at dinner, and fires the sculptor. He shows up in town later to do the job, and carry his romantic pitches to the mayoress. There's the usual complications of duty vs. love for necessary footage until the eventual happy windup.

Script by Virginia Van Upp, who also handles the producing chores, is studded with amusing situations and lines. Direction by Charles Vidor is smooth and fast-paced throughout, and he neatly polishes off his gags and episodes with finesse. Production mounting and all technical contributions are high calibre. *Walt.*

I Love a Soldier

Paramount release of Mark Sandrich production, directed by Sandrich. Stars Paulette Goddard, Sonny Tufts; features Beulah Bondi, Barry Fitsgerald. Screenplay, Allan Scott; camera, Charles Lang and Farelot Edomart; music, R.E. Dolan; editor, Ellsworth Hoagland. At Paramount, N.Y., week Nov. 1, '44. Running time, 106 MINS.

Eva Morgan	Paulette Goddard
Dan Kilgore	Sonny Tufts
Cissy Grant	Mary Green
Stiff Banks	Walter Sande
Jenny	Ann Doran
Ella Lane	Beulah Bondi
Gracie	Marie McDonald
Murph	Barry Fitzgerald
Williams	James Bell
John	Hugh Beaumont
Little Soldier	Frank Albertson
Doctor	Roy Gordon

"Soldier" deals with a timely and topical problem, that of war marriages, but fails to do complete justice to its subject. It will disappoint the GI's, their girl-friends and their parents, to whom its theme has a close and personal appeal, and it will similarly disappoint at the boxoffice.

Principal reasons for the film's weaknesses are twofold. From the start the payoff is never in doubt, with little suspense induced. Secondly, its boy-meets-girl plot has a tedious overabundance of twists and turns, result being a film that runs almost two hours. Trimming wouldn't be too hard a job, since there are a number of scenes that can easily be clipped and should have been sliced in the first place. Included in this category is a wedding scene and a ship-building take that serve only to hinder proceedings. Hackneyed handling of a blind officer's homecoming could also take trimming.

Story concerns a lady welder, Paulette Goddard, who refuses to go for a war marriage and supplements her war effort chore by evening hostess work, entertaining soldiers just back from overseas or on the verge of going. She does fall, though, for Sonny Tufts, but they split twice, first when she discovers he's married although on brink of divorce, and secondly, after the reconciliation, on the self-sacrifice angle. Idea here is that if he's worried about a wife back home, he's likely to forget to concentrate on the war and get knocked off.

Supporting characters, Jenny (Ann Doran), whose husband comes home blind shortly after she's had a baby, and the spinster Etta Lane (Beulah Bondi), carry the argument for those in favor of war weddings. Miss Doran, originally advised that her man is missing in action, argues that they had each other for a short time and she has those memories to look back on. Miss Bondi says she passed up her opportunity at matrimony when her guy went off to war "40 years ago" and she's regretted it ever since.

Miss Goddard and Tufts, who teamed so well in Sandrich's "So Proudly We Hail," are the leads. She's okay in the lighter moments but not too convincing in the heavier spots. Tufts indicates that he's well on his way to b.o. potency, impressing with an ingratiating and sincere performance that's bound to help make him a femme fave. Occasionally, however, he overdoes the self-effacing approach. Mary Treen, as another welder-entertainer, but definitely on the make, and Walter Sande, as the dumb sergeant she grabs, are good in comedy support. Miss Bondi displays her talents solidly as the spinster, although the role itself is on the schmaltzy side.

Barry Fitzgerald, as a streetcar conductor, is given heavy feature billing, but has comparatively little to do. Nevertheless, he walks away with those scenes in which he does appear.

Sandrich has given the picture a sturdy production and several amusing scenes, one localed in an amusement park, one in a dancehall and one in an attic which Miss Goddard converts into an apartment. But the story didn't get enough attention before the film went into action. *Merr.*

Lights of Old Santa Fe
(SONGS)

Republic release of Harry Grey production. Stars Roy Rogers; features George "Gabby" Hayes, Dale Evans. Directed by Frank McDonald. Screenplay, Gordon Kahn, Bob Williams; music, Morton Scott; dances, Larry Ceballos; editor, Ralph Dixon; camera, Reggie Lanning. Previewed N. Y., Nov. 6, '44. Running time, 78 MINS.

Roy............Roy Rogers
Gabby............George "Gabby" Hayes
Marjorie Brooks............Dale Evans
Marty Maizely............Lloyd Corrigan
Frank Madden............Richard Powers
Rosie McGerk............Claire Du Brey
Bill Wetherbee............Arthur Loft
Ken Ferguson............Roy Barcroft
The Judge............Lucien Littlefield
The Sheriff............Sam Flint
Themselves......Bob Nolan and the Sons of the Pioneers, and Trigger

Republic should hit the jackpot with this latest Roy Rogers starrer. It has everything it takes to keep the wickets turning as top feature in the dualers and can stand on its own solo in the smaller situations. In story material, song embellishment and smooth direction it tops many of the previous Rogers screen vehicles.

Rogers, per usual, steals the show with his trick riding atop Trigger, his educated horse. This time he's cast as head of a group of cowboy troubadours, who would like to sandwich some bulldozing and bronc busting between their yodeling. When Richard Powers won't let the boys display said versatility, they walk off the lot of his streamlined rodeo to hitch their wagons to a broken down outfit run by George "Gabby" Hayes, who's taken over for his old Boss' gal, Dale Evans. Latter is ready to team up with Powers matrimonially and combine shows.

But Rogers, Bob Nolan and the Sons of the Pioneers, the cowboy pals change all this by exposing Powers' chicanery, join the gal's show to put it on the map again as the classiest rodeo touring the arenas.

Rogers gives good account, as usual, and lends a pleasant baritone to the vocals by Nolan and the Pioneers, also in a duet with Miss Evans. Latter also turns in a neat acting job and handles solo on "Amor" creditably. Hayes projects comedy as the lovable old cuss who tries to keep the gal in the dark on financial status of her rodeo. Lloyd Corrigan and Claire DuBrey also turn in good performances in support roles. Frank McDonald's direction sustains a racy pace throughout, Gordon Kahn and Bob Williams have contributed a nifty script, while camera work of Reggie Lanning is also up to par. *Edba.*

Bowery Champs
(ONE SONG)

Monogram release of Sam Katzman & Jack Dietz production (associate producer, Barney Sarecky). Stars East Side Kids (Leo Gorcey, Bobby Jordan, Huntz Hall, Gabriel Dell, Billy Benedict); features Evelyn Brent. Directed by William Beaudine. Screenplay, Earle Snell; editor, John Link; camera, Ira Morgan. At New York, N. Y., week Oct. 31, '44, dual. Running time, 61 MINS.

Muggs............Leo Gorcey
Glimpy............Huntz Hall
Skinny............Billy Benedict
Danny............Jimmy Strand
Kid............Bobby Jordan
Shorty............Bud Gorman
Jane............Anne Sterling
Jim............Gabriel Dell
Cartwright............Frank Jaquet
Scoop............Francis Ford
Gypsy............Evelyn Brent
Brother............Eddie Cherkose
Wilson............Wheeler Oakman
Duncan............Ian Keith
Diane............Thelma White
Lieutenant............Bill Rhul

The East Side Kids go reportorial in this one in tracking down a murder mystery. Although not always on even keel for a whodunit, it should do okay in the duals, especially in spots where the kids retain b.o. hypo.

Leo Gorcey is copyboy on newspaper and his pals work on delivery. A nitery owner is bumped off and Evelyn Brent, his ex-wife, is suspected. Gorcey enlists his pals, hides the suspect until it is established she's innocent and then aids materially in wrapping up Ian Keith and Thelma White as the culprits.

Gorcey has been written in for an abundance of gab and footage in this one and stands up well under the assignment. The other kids are merely fillers. Anne Sterling and Jimmy Strand are the romantics as m.c.'s sec and police reporter, respectively. The others do all right by their respective assignments. William Beaudine's direction keeps things moving. Ira Morgan's camera work is up to par. *Edba.*

Delinquent Daughters

PRC release of Donald C. McKean-Albert Herman production. Features June Carlson, Fifi D'Orsay, Teala Loring, Mary Bovard, Margia Dean. Directed by Albert Herman. Screenplay, Arthur St. Claire; editor, George Merrick; camera, Ira Morgan. At Brooklyn, N. Y., Strand, Nov. 2, '44, dual. Running time, 71 MINS.

June Thompson............June Carlson
Mimi............Fifi D'Orsay
Sally Higgins............Teala Loring
Betty............Mary Bovard
Francine Van Pelt............Margia Dean
Rocky Webster............Johnny Duncan
Hanahan............Joe Devlin
Jerry Sykes............Jimmy Zaner
Nick Gordon............Jon Dawson
Judge Craig............Frank McGlynn
Steve Cronin............Parker Gee
Roy Ford............Warren Mills

PRC adds more fuel and no light to the juve delinquency situation with its dull, long, drawnout opus, "Delinquent Daughters." Pic is trite, sermonizing and maudlin, for very mediocre entertainment. A lower-rung dualer.

Again highschool kids are shown riding around crazily in jalopies, drinking in roadhouses and engaging in petty holdups. Negligence of parents is pointed out in dull harangues before juvenile court judge. Story centers around a cafe whose proprietor eggs kids on to crime and shields them from cops. Incidents are familiar, obvious and contrived to hold little interest.

Acting in main is stereotyped, with Jon Dawson a wooden cafe proprietor, Joe Devlin, a nondescript detective, and Fifi D'Orsay a pallid hostess. Kids are also routine. Frank McGlynn, as a judge, and Johnny Duncan, as one of the kids, give some reality to their roles. *Bron.*

Rustler's Hideout

PRC release of Sigmund Neufeld production. Stars Buster Crabbe, features Al (Fuzzy) St. John. Directed by Sam Newfield. Screenplay, Joe O'Donnell; editor, Holbrook N. Todd; camera, Jack Greenhalgh. At New York, N. Y., week Oct. 31, '44, dual. Running time, 60 MINS.

Billy Carson............Buster Crabbe
Fuzzy Jones............Al (Fuzzy) St. John
Barbara............Patti McCarty
Buck Shaw............Charles King
Harry Stanton............John Merton
Jack Crockett............Terry Frost
Dave Crockett............Hal Price
Hammond............Lane Chandler
Steve............Al Ferguson
Squint............Frank McCarroll
Sheriff............Ed Cassidy

Stereotyped plot won't do much for this average mustanger.

Buster Crabbe rides again to crab the act of the cattle pilferers. His ever-faithful aide, Al (Fuzzy) St. John, rides not far behind; he's not as funny in this one as he has been in previous cactusers. During the interim Crabbe exposes the cardsharpery of Lane Chandler, who is subsequently polished off; circumvents scheme of Charles King and John Merton to divert delivery of cattle so that they can take over packing plant from Terry Frost and Hal Price. He also makes a feeble pass at Patti McCarty—but that's all for romance.

Crabbe and supporting cast do okay, with direction of Sam Newfield and camera stint of Jack Greenhalgh also acceptable. *Edba.*

Miniature Reviews

"30 Seconds Over Tokyo" (M-G). A b.o. blitz.

"Enter Arsene Lupin" (U). Detective yarn a top dualer.

"Mark of the Whistler" (Col). Second in the Whistler series, based on the CBS radio program, moderately entertaining.

"Meet Miss Bobby Socks" (Songs) (Col.). Despite two good songs, a minor dualler.

"End of the Road" (Rep). Fair meller for duals.

"Don't Take It to Heart" (GFD) (British-made). Richard Greene in smart satirical comedy; looks okay for U. S.

30 Seconds Over Tokyo

Metro release of Sam Zimbalist production. Stars Spencer Tracy, Van Johnson, Robert Walker, Phyliss Thaxter. Directed by Mervyn LeRoy. Screenplay, Dalton Trumbo from book by Capt. Ted W. Lawson and Robt. Considine; camera, Harold Rosson, Robt. Surtees. A. Arnold Gillespie, Warren Newcombe, Donald Jahraus; music, Herbert Stothart; editor, Frank Sullivan. Tradeshown N.Y. Nov. 8, 1944. Running time. 138 MINS.

Ted Lawson............Van Johnson
David Thatcher............Robert Walker
Eilen Lawson............Phyllis Thaxter
Dean Davenport............Tim Murdock
Davey Jones............Scott McKay
Bob Clever............Gordon McDonald
Charles McClure............Don DeFore
Bob Gray............Robert Mitchum
"Shorty" Manch............John R. Reilly
"Doc" White............Horace McNally
Lieut. Randall............Donald Curtiss
Lieut. Miller............Louis Jean Heydt
Don Smith............Wm. "Bill" Phillips
"Brick" Holstom............Douglas Cowan
Captain "Ski" York............Paul Langton
Lieut. Jurilis............Leon Ames
Lieut. Col. James Doolittle......Spencer Tracy

Metro's "30 Seconds Over Tokyo" is in the boxoffice groove. It's almost out of the current headlines. This is a slight contradition, in some respects in view of the chronology concerning that historic event when Col. Doolittle mapped his blitz on Japan 131 days after Pearl Harbor. History or not, as Metro has treated the Capt. Ted Lawson-Bob Considine yarn it's a boxoffice humdinger.

Not only is it a timely saga of our war in the Pacific but it's a thoroughly romantic tale which will get the femmes. For once, here's a war picture eclipsed by its romantic components. No stretching to sell the non-war factors will be necessary because of the way in which producer Sam Zimbalist and director Mervyn LeRoy have handled scripter Dalton Trumbo's tiptop treatment of the yarn.

Dominantly a sentimental story, the emphasis comes even from army officials that it would be no disgrace for any of the volunteers to bow out at any point in their arduous training, for reasons of family, wife, mother or sweetheart. The basis thus is a warm, human foundation. There is suspense as the flyers prepare themselves for their long-range training in anticipation of the secret mission.

More or less relegated but capital as the bulwark of the entire mission is Spencer Tracy's conception of Lt. Col. James H. Doolittle. Van Johnson is Ted Lawson and Phyllis Thaxter his wife. It's an inspired casting. Johnson is a hot b.o. commodity, definitely on the upbeat, and Miss Thaxter, newcomer from legit, possessed of a Margaret Sullavan wistfulness, is virtually star-made in this spotlighting. She meets all her histrionic opportunities with tenderness and consummate skill. Prominent in Johnson's crew is Tim Murdock, a standout as the co-pilot; Don DeFore as the navigator; Gordon McDonald as the bombardier; and Robert Walker, who is particularly effective as the wistful gunner-mechanic.

Their plane, the Ruptured Duck, and its pleasant little family become the focal attention henceforth. After Doolittle finally tells them of their mission to bomb Japan, the war becomes a highly personalized thing through the actions of these crew members. Skillfully and effectively, writer, director and producer have not permitted any diffusion of interest. Everything is centered around the Ruptured Duck. Forced to take off from their carrier ahead of schedule, following Doolittle who is the first to bomb Tokyo, the Duck's low-range bombing at military targets is almost underplayed, because of the ease with which they found their marks. This is one technical mistake, not because it's not historically accurate, but because it is not made sufficiently clear to the auditor that the Japs were taken by surprise at the audacious Yank flyers whom they thought were friendly planes. The Nips are even shown waving them inland.

The real drama occurs off the China coast after Lawson wrecks his plane and a leg amputation becomes necessary. The friendly Chinese succor him and his luckless mates. Later the natives bring them gifts. This is highlighted by the presentation of a pair of native slippers to the now one-legged Lawson. It's a socko touch. Incidentally, the amputation sequence is well handled, with nought of the "Moby Dick" technique, as only the preparations for the necessary severance are depicted. There is, of course, the happy ending back in the States, with Doolittle (now Brigadier-General) expediting their reunion. And the finale is touching in its human appeal as Lawson, forgetting his loss of one limb, rises from the wheelchair to greet his wife and falls flat on his face.

There is much more in "30 Seconds Over Tokyo" than meets the eye. There are excellent "X" factors which may well prove indelible morale-builders for the back-home folks. Unfolded is a cross-section of what it means to fight for America; what it means for American authority to indoctrinate our warriors; for American authority to understand our at-home problems; and how America diligently cares for our heroes. Not overdone, not piled up, much of this is exceptionally well gotten across in the more than two hours that "30 Seconds" consumes in running time. *Abel.*

Enter Arsene Lupin

Universal release of Ford Beebe production, directed by Beebe. Stars Charles Korvin, Ella Raines; features J. Carrol Naish, George Dolenz, Gale Sondergaard, Miles Mander. Original, Bertram Millhauser, based on character by Maurice LeBlanc; editor, Saul A. Goodkind; camera, Hal Mohr. Tradeshown N. Y. Nov. 14, '44. Running time, 72 MINS.

Arsène Lupin............Charles Korvin
Stacie............Ella Raines
Ganimard............J. Carrol Naish
Dubosc............George Dolenz
Bessie Seagrave............Gale Sondergaard
Charles Seagrave............Miles Mander
Constable Ryder............Leland Hodgson
Pollett............Tom Pilkington
Wheeler............Lillian Bronson
Jobson............Holmes Herbert
Inspector Cogswell............Charles LaTorre
Doc Marling............Gerald Hamer
Cartwright............Ed Cooper
Superintendent............Art Foster
Beckwith............Clyde Kenny
Conductor............Alphonse Martell

"Enter Arsene Lupin," Universal's contribution to the cops-and-robbers saga, French style, is a slick enough combination of romance, action and suspense to offset phony, far-fetched plot. Pix is a top dualer or nabe solo, where it will do good biz.

Part of appeal is new romantic team of Charles Korvin and Ella Raines in some torrid moments. Korvin, Hungarian actor who made brief Broadway stage appearance last year, isn't much of an actor, but he has the continental ease of manner and attractive face to catch the femme trade. Also a draw is the flavorsome caricature of a stupid French detective which J. Carroll Naish, in a change of pace from gangster roles, plays very amusingly, even if he does milk role. Lupin tag is also well enough known to thriller addicts to be a draw.

Yarn concerns Lupin, renowned suave French thief, who robs a lady of her fabulous emerald on the Paris-Constantinople express, but returns it to her when he falls in love. Following lady to England, Lupin discovers she's a half-English, half-Greek heiress. Discovers, too, that some cousins are planning to murder her for her fortune. Although busy at his modest vocation of lifting precious paintings and objects d'art from museums and stores, Lupin still has time to help the damsel out of her predicament. He succeeds, but only to slip into the law's clutches as a result.

Pix is produced on good scale, with some rich interiors, to help illusion. Ella Raines adds glamor and beauty to role of heiress, and Gale Sondergaard is menacing enough as one of sleek, murderous cousins. George Dolenz makes good foil for Naish as his servitor-partner in crime. Photography is good, some of love scenes having real art quality. Direction is satisfactory for the thriller. *Bron.*

Mark of the Whistler

Columbia release of Rudolph C. Flothow production. Stars Richard Dix; features Janis Carter, Porter Hall. Directed by William Castle. Suggested by CBS radio program, "The Whistler"; story, Cornell Woolrich; adaptation, George Bricker; editor, Reg Browne; camera, George Meehan. At Rialto, N. Y., week Nov. 10, '44. Running time, **60 MINS.**

Lee Nugent....................Richard Dix
Patricia Henley....................Janis Carter
Joe Sorsby....................Porter Hall
Limpy Smith....................Paul Guilfoyle
Eddie Donnelly....................John Calvert
Perry Donnelly....................Matt Willis

Second in the Columbia series built around the CBS radio meller, "The Whistler," this is moderately entertaining dualer.

Richard Dix is a down-and-out drifter who manages to lay claim to a dormant bank account. He nearly pays for it with his life since two brothers have long looked for the man who would show up to claim the money, that they might wreak vengeance on him in settling an old score which sent their father to jail. Dix escapes this fate only to learn in the end that a crippled peddler whom he has befriended, in turn benefiting by latter's friendship, is the real owner of the money.

William Castle moves the story at an even pace, with his direction in other ways capable, while Rudolph C. Flothow, with an obviously restricted budget, has given the picture adequate production value. The story and adaptation rate fair.

Dix gives a steady performance as the troubled drifter but close to a steal is registered by Porter Hall, a crafty storekeeper, who gambles on Dix by outfitting him that he may make a good appearance at the bank when claiming the dormant deposit. Janis Carter, who plays a newspaper reporter acceptably, is somewhat of a looker from whom much more should be heard. Others include Paul Guilfoyle, the cripple, and the two brothers who stalk Dix with a view to bumping him off. John Calvert and Matt Willis. They all fit well. *Char.*

Meet Miss Bobby Socks
(SONGS)

Columbia release of Ted Richmond production. Stars Bob Crosby, Lynn Merrick; features Louise Erickson, Robert White, Howard Freeman. Directed by Glenn Tryon. Original, Muriel Roy Bolton; camera, George Meehan; editor, Jerome Thoms; songs, Kim Gannon, Walter Kent, others. At Brooklyn Fox, week of Nov. 10, '44. Running time, **68 MINS.**

Don Collins....................Bob Crosby
Helen Tyler....................Lynn Merrick
Susan Tyler....................Louise Erickson
Howard Barnes....................Robert White
Mr. Tyler....................Howard Freeman
Mrs. Tyler....................Mary Currier
Gloria....................Pat Parrish
Pillow....................Sally Bliss
Swanson....................John Hamilton
Whitaker....................Douglas Wood
Quinlan....................Pierre Watkin

Bob Crosby tries his best to give this poor entry some value. Despite the fact that he sings a couple of catchy tunes during the unwinding, remainder of film is so innocuous it will even have a tough time in the duals.

Columbia apparently had a fair idea for a picture with plenty of exploitable angles, and a good title. But by the time the guy in charge of getting quickies under the wire at the least amount of dough got through with the budget on this one, there wasn't even enough coin to hire extras to fill a cabaret, during one of the scenes in this picture.

Only redeeming feature about this one is that two of the tunes which Crosby sings are better than average, "Fellow on a Furlough" and "Come With Me, My Honey." Five other tunes are either oldies, or new with little chance. The Kim Loo Sisters and Louis Jordan and his Tympany Five are seen briefly, both groups doing only one song.

Yarn has to do with the rise of a returned war vet to the realm of fan club proportions as a crooner. His fans get him a job. Lynn Merrick, as the heart interest, handles her role fairly well, but Louise Erickson and Howard Barnes fail to please in their portrayals of youthful kids intent on getting Crosby to the top. *Sten.*

End of the Road

Republic release of George Blair production, directed by himself. Stars Edward Norris, June Storey; features John Abbott. Screenplay, Denison Clift and Gertrude Walker based on a "New Yorker" mag article by Alva Johnston; camera, William Bradford; editor, Arthur Roberts. At Brooklyn Strand, week of Nov. 10, '44. Running time, **61 MINS.**

Robert Kirby....................Edward Norris
Chris Martin....................John Abbott
Kitty McDougal....................June Storey
Gregory McCune....................Jonathan Hale
District Attorney....................Pierre Watkin
Walter Gribbon....................Ted Hecht
Al Herman....................Kenne Duncan
Joe Ferrari....................Eddy Fields
Drake....................Ferris Taylor
Mannenberg....................Emmett Vogan
Jordan....................Charles Williams
Judge....................Edward Van Sloan

A melodrama in which psychology plays an important part, done fairly well for a low-budgeter, "End of the Road" is grooved for lower dualers.

Edward Norris is seen as a writer specializing in murder cases who is convinced that a man condemned as a slayer is innocent. He sets about plotting several incidents which prey upon the mind of the person whom he believes to be the actual killer, and by doing so, saves the condemned man.

June Storey, in the role of a waitress, who almost falls second victim to the sadistic, money-hungry killer, provides the heart interest, opposite Norris. John Abbott, as the neurotic suspect, does a surprisingly good job.

Story, itself, is not too well written, and loses its momentum from time to time. Production values are negligible. *Sten.*

Don't Take It to Heart
(BRITISH-MADE)

London, Oct. 11.

General Film Distributors release of Two Cities production. Stars Richard Greene. Directed by Jeffrey Dell. Written by Jeffrey Dell. Camera, Eric Cross. At Leicester Square theatre, London, Oct. 11, '44. Running time, **93 MINS.**

Peter Hayward....................Richard Greene
Sir Henry Wade, K.C....................David Horne
Lady Mary....................Patricia Medina
Mr. Pike....................Alfred Drayton
Mrs. Pike....................Joan Hickson
Arthur....................Richard Bird
Harry Bucket....................Wylie Watson
Loopy....................Claude Dampier
Butler....................Edward Rigby
Lord Chaunduyt....................Brefni O'Rourke
Mr. Smith....................Patrick Curwen
Mrs. Smith....................Marjorie Withers
Granfer....................Moore Marriott
Harriet....................Joyce Barbour
Music Lover....................Ronald Squire
Magistrate's Clerk....................Ernest Thesiger

Richard Greene, plus a score of character actors, several of them British stars in their own right, go far in making this a hit. Jeffrey Dell, who wrote and directed, also shares in the strong overall results. Treatment of some familiar material is novel. There is a nice clean story, satirically unfolded and occasionally bordering on burlesque, but in a nice manner. This should be a success in America.

Scene is laid in and about Chaunduyt Court, one of the stately homes of England. The Lord of the Manor is flat broke and manages to eke out an existence by donning the cap of a guide and showing sightseers over the mansion. He accepts no tips, but has a large bucket on a table announcing that all gratuities deposited there are for a benevolent fund. Of course, he has a charming daughter and naturally a nice young man, on one of the sight-seeing trips, falls in love with her. Not until the end does it turn out he is a baron and they eventually make a match.

A bomb destroying a portion of the building discloses valuable 400-year-old manuscripts. These papers reveal he is not the real lord but descended from the local poacher, whose descendant thus comes into the title and estates. After a series of risibility inciting incidents, the courtly old usurper is seen enjoying life to the full by poaching on the land he heretofore believed was his by right.

The strength of the film lies in the casting. Laugh scenes are never so long as to tire. Unlike some native films this does not absorb half hour or more in developing the real comedy. *Jolo.*

Miniature Reviews

"Winged Victory" (20th). Moss Hart's screen version of his own stage boff about the Army Air Force is socko boxoffice.

"The Thin Man Goes Home" (M-G). Moderately good b.o. indicated for first of new Powell-Loy whodunit series.

"3 Is a Family" (UA). Sol Lesser's screen version of John Golden's Broadway legit production solid b.o.

"Blonde Fever" (M-G). Philip Dorn, Mary Astor in lukewarm comedy.

"My Gal Loves Music" (Songs) (U). Bob Crosby, Grace McDonald in light comedy, suitable as okay supporting feature.

"Army Wives" (Mono). Lightweight dualer.

"When Strangers Marry" (Mono). Superior thriller, a top dualer.

"Love Story" (Eagle-Lion) (British-made) Dubious for American market, length being serious handicap.

"Three Hours" (French) Charming love story of a poilu.

Winged Victory

20th-Fox release of Darryl F. Zanuck production. Directed by George Cukor. Screenplay, Moss Hart, adapted from his own stage play. Music, Sgt. David Rose; camera, Glen MacWilliams; editor, Barbara McLean; special effects, Fred Sersen; choral direction, Lt. Leonard DePaur. Tradeshown N. Y., Nov. 20, '44. Running time, **130 MINS.**

Alan Ross....................Sgt. Mark Daniels
Frankie Davis....................Pvt. Lon McCallister
Danny (Pinky) Scariano....................Cpl. Don Taylor
Dorothy Ross....................Jo-Carroll Dennison
Mrs. Ross....................Geraldine Wall
Whitey....................Cpl. Red Buttons
Mr. Scariano....................George Humbert
Jane Preston....................Jane Ball
Irving Miller....................Sgt. Edmond O'Brien
Bobby Grills....................Cpl. Barry Nelson
Dave Anderson....................Sgt. Rune Hultman
Ruth Miller....................Judy Holliday
Helen....................Jeanne Crain
Jimmy Gardner....................Cpl. Richard Hogan
Col. Gibney....................Cpl. Phillip Bourneuf
Captain McIntyre....................Cpl. Garry Merrill
Colonel Ross....................Cpl. Damian O'Flynn
Major Halper....................Cpl. Alan Baxter
Lieut. Thompson....................Sgt. George Reeves
Barker....................Pfc. George Petrie
Milhauser....................Pfc. Alfred Ryder
Adams....................Cpl. Karl Malden
Gleason....................Pfc. Martin Ritt
O'Brian....................T/Sgt. Peter Lind Hayes
Cadet Peter Clark....................Cpl. Harry Lewis
Officer....................Capt. Ray Bidwell
Flight Surgeon....................Cpl. Henry Rowland
Captain Speer....................Lt. Carroll Riddle
Carmen Miranda....................S/Sgt. Sascha Brastoff
Master of Ceremonies....................Cpl. Archie Robbins
Andrews Sisters....................Cpl. Jack Slate / Cpl. Red Buttons / Pfc. Henry Slate
Doctor....................Cpl. Lee J. Cobb

It was a season or so ago that Moss Hart and the Army Air Forces brought to Broadway one of the stirring stage dramas of these or any times, and now the film version of that epic AAF story is upon us. The Broadway stage premiere of "Winged Victory" was a memorable evening in the theatre—and the picture is no less worthy. Its boxoffice prospects are seemingly limitless wherever it may play.

The coffers of the various Army charities, to which the proceeds from this picture—as from the play—are being donated, should be enriched in all boxoffice situations because this is no story of any specific segment of Americana; it is, rather, the tale of Main street and Broadway, of Texas and Brooklyn, of Christian and Jew—of American youth fighting for the preservation of American ideals. Its appeal has the punch of an Army backfield—Eisenhower, MacArthur, Patton and Arnold.

Whatever "Victory" possesses as stage artifice, as a film it has gained a breadth and scope that stage limitations could not permit. And chalk that one up for Moss Hart, who wrote both the screen and stage plays.

This is a documentation of American youth learning to fly for victory—a winged victory—and though it's fashioned in the manner of fictional entertainment, this is no less fiction than, say, Tarawa, Saipan, Aachen or Metz. Take a look at that cast. All the boys listed are bona fide members of the AAF—acting real-life roles.

The story of six boys from diverse parts of America, and how they leave behind wives and sweethearts and mothers to join the AAF, "Victory" is an honest understanding of American youth with the unsatiable urge to ride the clouds. While this is mainly the story of these six lads, it is obviously one of every American youth visioning the day when he can win his wings. It is the yarn of three close friends from a small Ohio town, a fourth from Brooklyn, another from Texas, the last from an Oregon farm. Their friendship, hopes and frustrations create a warm understanding and sentiment without becoming sticky.

The narrative follows them through basic training, the rigorous aptitude tests, and then the news on whether they had passed or were washed out. The solo flights—from which one of the sextet fails to return—and, ultimately, graduation day, followed by their assignments as either pilots, navigators or bombardiers, are all significantly told.

Of the war itself there is very little. Only in the last reel, when the scene shifts to a South Pacific island, is there the grim reminder of what these boys had studied for.

"Victory" is a film of poignant scenes. There is one that is no less touching than academic, when one of the sextet is washed out by a panel of AAF officers. There's another where one of the group is to become a father, but his wife chooses to delay telling him the news because of his wholly enveloping attention to flying. He dies in a solo flight without ever learning of his unborn child. And there's the scene where three wives, rooming together near the flying field, mark time until their men shove off for overseas. And the one in which the men see for the first time the silver-sheathed fortress for which they had worked so hard—their winged victory.

"Victory" has a flock of young players—privates and corporals and sergeants—who could grace the roster of any Broadway or Hollywood production. And have. Performers like Sgt. Edmond O'Brien, Pvt. Lon McCallister, Sgt. Mark Daniels, Cpl. Lee J. Cobb, Sgt. Peter Lind Hayes, Cpl. Alan Baxter, Cpl. Red Buttons, Cpl. Archie Robbins, Cpl. Alfred Ryder, Cpl. Jack Slate, Pfc. Henry Slate, Sgt. George Reeves, among others. And no less impressive are Jeanne Crain, Jane Ball, Judy Holliday and Jo-Carroll Dennison, of the 20th-Fox roster, who replaced the original play's distaffers. Otherwise, it's practically the same cast as that which appeared in the Broadway version.

It is a magnificent production that Darryl F. Zanuck has given "Victory," and the direction by George Cukor has kept the film moving at an even pace despite its extreme length of two hours and 10 minutes. Sgt. David Rose has written a fine score, as he did for the play, and the other productional credits are likewise notable.

For those skeptics who would point out that this film, like the play, has no names for the marquee, let him take a longer look at the billing. And then the headlines. The AAF not boxoffice? *Kahn.*

The Thin Man Goes Home

Metro release of Everett Riskin production. Stars William Powell, Myrna Loy. Directed by Richard Thorpe. Screenplay, Robert Riskin, Dwight Taylor; original story, Riskin, Harry Kurnitz, based on characters created by Dashiell Hammett; camera, Karl Freund; editor, Ralph E. Winters. Tradeshown N. Y., Nov. 21, '44. Running time, **100 MINS.**

Nick Charles..............William Powell
Nora Charles..................Myrna Loy
Mrs. Charles...............Lucile Watson
Laura Ronson.............Gloria DeHaven
Crazy Mary...................Anne Revere
Helena Draque...............Helen Vinson
Dr. Bertram Charles......Harry Davenport
Edgar Draque..................Leon Ames
Willie Crump................Donald Meek
Brogan....................Edward Brophy
Dr. Bruce Clayworth........Lloyd Corrigan
Hilda.......................Anita Bolster
Peter Berton.................Ralph Brooke
Police Chief MacGregor..Donald MacBride
And Asta

First of the new William Powell-Myrna Loy "Thin Man" productions (last one about four years ago) will likely prove a fairly substantial grosser.

Based on the characterizations originally created by Dashiell Hammett, the story by Robert Riskin, Dwight Taylor and Harry Kurnitz emerges as a neatly-fashioned whodunit. Richard Thorpe has paced the plot nicely, overcoming, before too long, the hurdles of a rather slow opening.

Production as a whole, however, lacks much of the sophistication and smartness which characterized the early "Thin Man" films. If the "Thin Man" is to remain a marquee topper instead of becoming a stock filler, need for a more vigorous approach, via brighter dialog and more intriguing situations is indicated.

As it is, the first of the revived series is pleasant enough picture house fare, with the gory aspects of homicide wisely kept at a minimum. Deficiency is mainly in the dialog and other business provided for the two leads.

Miss Loy, incidentally, while graceful and piquant for the most part, photographs unattractively in a number of sequences.

Yarn deals with an espionage ring working for a foreign power. Involves a battle of wits to secure a group of paintings which leads to a couple of killings.

Powell, as Nick Charles, back home for a visit, touches off the murders when one of the parties involved goes to the sleuth for advice. Suspense has been maintained adequately.

Casting is okay and production values generally good. *Mori.*

3 Is a Family

United Artists release of Sol Lesser production. Features Charlie Ruggles, Fay Bainter, Helen Broderick, Marjorie Reynolds. Directed by Edward Ludwig. Screenplay, Harry Chandlee, Marjorie L. Pfaelzer, based on play by Phoebe and Henry Ephron; camera, Charles Lawton; editor, Robert Crandall. Previewed N. Y., Nov. 17, '44. Running time, **81 MINS.**

Kitty Mitchell............Marjorie Reynolds
Sam Whitaker...............Charlie Ruggles
Frances Whitaker.............Fay Bainter
Irma Dalrymple..........Helen Broderick
Archie Whitaker..............Arthur Lake
Unnamed Maid...........Hattie McDaniel
Hazel Whitaker...............Jeff Donnell
Doctor Bartell...............John Philliber
Barney Meeker...............Walter Catlett
Mr. Steele..................Clarence Kolb
Adelaide......................Else Janssen
Genevieve.....................Renie Riano
Coolie.......................Warren Hymer
Mr. Spencer.................Clyde Fillmore
Bell Boy.....................Christian Rub
Susan and Patty Whitaker......Donna and Elissa Lambertson
Joe Franklin................William Terry
Marian Franklin............Cheryl Walker
Gene Mitchell.................Fred Brady
Steele's Daughter..........Margaret Early

Sol Lesser has turned out an enjoyable comedy which should click readily. By no means pretentiously mounted, "3 Is a Family" nonetheless impresses as a sturdy grosser on the strength of a solid laugh score. It's a cinch for the family trade in particular.

Basically endowed with surefire story and dialog values, the production is further insured with a first-rate cast, at least six or seven of the troupe rating nods for individual performances. With one climactic laugh sequence topping another in rapid succession, it remains for John Philliber (whose death was recently reported) to top everything with a riotous impression of an absent-minded, almost completely blind, old-fashioned medico.

Homespun rather than sophisticated, with a broad comedy motif of farcical proportions at times, yarn is fashioned for wide general appeal. Most of the action is encompassed in a single set. Charles Ruggles as the slightly henpecked husband who had made a series of unfortunate investments, has been relieved of his position as the family breadwinner and relegated to the status of a housekeeper while Fay Bainter, the femme executive, is the provider and family braintrust.

Ruggles, as usual, comes through with an expert impersonation as the Milquetoast who finally gets an opportunity to reassert himself, solve the family's housing problems, and recoup his fortunes. The Lambertson twins (Donna and Elissa) register plenty strong. Hattie McDaniel, Miss Bainter, Walter Catlett and Helen Broderick are also among the outstanders, while Arthur Lake scores handily as the jittery father experiencing the travails of fatherhood. Marjorie Reynolds clicks nicely as the young femme lead, photographing attractively throughout. Cheryl Walker, William Terry and Fred Brady are limited to subordinate bit roles. *Mori.*

Blonde Fever

Metro release of William M. Wright production. Features Mary Astor, Philip Dorn, Gloria Graham, Marshall Thompson. Directed by Richard Whorf. Screenplay, Patricia Coleman; based on play by Ferenc Molnar; camera, Lester White; editor, George Hively. Tradeshown N. Y., Nov. 16, '44. Running time, **69 MINS.**

Peter Donay...................Philip Dorn
Delilah Donay..................Mary Astor
Johnny.......................Felix Bressart
Sally Murfin...............Gloria Grahame
Freddie Bilson..........Marshall Thompson
Brillon..........................Curt Bois
Mrs. Talford..............Elisabeth Risdon
Willie.......................Arthur Walsh

"Blonde Fever" is a very placid comedy. Shapes up as a routine "B."

Ancient story of the middle-aged hubby who falls for a curvaceous blonde waitress (in his own inn-restaurant) almost under his wife's nose adheres to pattern. Film is hurt by haphazard direction, weak scripting and mediocre acting. Only Mary Astor and youngish Marshall Thompson manage to make their characters jell.

Gloria Grahame, as the blonde waitress, shows possibilities, but given a conflicting, indefinite role in this opus. First she's depicted as a dumb but innocent 19-year-old femme. Then she's painted as a worldly-wise little gold-digger, out to vamp the middle-aged gent. Particularly, is her gold-digging blatant when she learns he's won a $40,000 lottery. Yarn has the blonde about to wed the husband, as soon as he gets a divorce, although his faithful wife is the main reason his business is successful. Usual payoff when hubby discovers how mercenary the blonde flame is.

Marshall Thompson, the blonde's impetuous young suitor, manages to rise above the bad closeups and inane lines allotted him. Should do better if given anything to work with. Philip Dorn is the nearly unfaithful husband, a bit more blustering than usual. Miss Astor provides the only legitimate performance as the devoted wife who turns the tables on the blonde.

Looks as though Patricia Coleman did not improve the Ferenc Molnar play much, dialog certainly not indicating any improvement. This is one of Richard Whorf's lesser directorial efforts. *Wear.*

My Gal Loves Music
(SONGS)

Universal release of Edward Lilley production, directed by Lilley. Stars Bob Crosby, Grace McDonald; features Betty Kean, Walter Catlett, Alan Mowbray. Screenplay, Eugene Conrad, from original by Patricia Harper; camera, Hal Mohr; editor, Russell Schoengarth; songs, Milton Rosen, Everett Carter, Clarence Gaskill, Inez James, Sidney Miller. Previewed N. Y., Nov. 21, '44. Running time, **69 MINS.**

Mel Murray......................Bob Crosby
Rodney Spoonyer............Alan Mowbray
Judy Mason.................Grace McDonald
Peggy Quinn....................Betty Kean
Dr. Bilbo.....................Walter Catlett
Clarence....................Freddie Mercer
Child Pianist................Paulina Carter
Montague Underdunk.............Tom Daly
Announcer................Gayne Whitman
Chinita, Trixie

This is a harum-scarum, lightweight comedy that is light and frothy enough to stand up as secondary feature on twin bills. Presence of Bob Crosby and Grace McDonald sets it up as having enough swing tunes and songs to satisfy the younger fans. Film holds several catchy tunes, including the by-now familiar "Over and Oover."

"My Gal Loves Music" focuses on femme singer-dance team who try for a comeback after being stranded with a medicine show in the sticks. Their sponsor, Walter Catlett, who finds that vitamin pills have outmoded his snake-medicine show, dreams up the idea of having the smaller gal, Grace McDonald, pose as a 14-year-old child prodigy. In such guise she wins a trip to N. Y. and appearance on the radio for a vitamin pill company. Quack medico goes along as her uncle, and her partner in the dance act becomes her elderly aunt.

From such a hoaxed-up predicament, usual laughable developments ensue and with the customary payoff on discovering that the gal prodigy is not what she seems. There's a real attempt to swing into romantic channels with Bob Crosby falling for Miss McDonald. Although she's as hep as ever with her ballading, Miss McDonald gets no real break because she must parade in pigtails and gawky kid dresses most of picture.

Crosby makes a likeable bandleader-pianist and singer who promotes the audition for the vitamin company. Betty Kean, from vaude and Broadway musicals, is the long-limbed partner of Miss McDonald. She does surprisingly well as the aunt but is in her element with her eccentric tap terps. Catlett plays the medicine-showman with his usual droll quips while Alan Mowbray is okay as the vitamin exec. Freddie Mercer, who's the real child "voice" find in the film, displays an unusual tenor.

Top tune, "Over and Over" (Milton Rosen and Everett Carter) is done well by Miss McDonald and Crosby. Betty Kean sells "I Need Vitamin U," by Clarence Gaskill, with fine skill. "Somebody's Rockin' My Rainbow," also by Rosen-Carter, is nicely put over by Crosby.

Edward Lilley, who directed in routine fashion, gives the picture superb production. Hal Mohr's camera-ing is standout. *Wear.*

Army Wives

Monogram release of Lindsley Parsons production. Stars Elyse Knox, Marjorie Rambeau, Rick Vallin. Directed by Phil Rosen. Screenplay, B. Harrison Orkow from original idea by Joel Levy, Jr.; camera, Mack Stengler; editor, William Austin. At N. Y. theatre, N. Y., week of Nov. 20, '44. Running time, **68 MINS.**

Jerry............................Elyse Knox
Mrs. Shannahan.........Marjorie Rambeau
Barney..........................Rick Vallin
Louise.....................Dorothea Kent
Mike..........................Murray Alper
Verne.......................Hardie Albright
Pat Shannahan...............Kenneth Brown

Billy Shannahan	Billy Lenhart
Sgt. Shannahan	Eddie Dunn
Stan	Jimmy Conlin
Burke	Ralph Langford
Mrs. Lowry	Dorothy Christy
Benson	Phil Warren
Kirby	Ralph Lewis

Cheaply produced and lacking interest because of a weak story-line, "Army Wives" is a lightweight dualer.

Yarn, using all the tried truisms about needing priorities to travel, shortages of living quarters, help and other material things, at almost every opportunity, deals with the trouble gal and boy have in getting together to take the marital vows, he being in the Army and she following him from place to place.

Performances of those listed above the title, Elyse Knox, Marjorie Rambeau and Rick Vallin, are in the usaul vein of performers who find themselves in this type of production, acting in a "let's-get-it-over-quick" tempo. Remainder of cast is shown briefly. Screenplay by B. Harrison Orkow is reportedly based on an original idea by Joel Levy, Jr. Where there is any originality about this pic, in either the idea or the telling, is not readily perceived. Lindsley Parsons produced. *Sten.*

When Strangers Marry

Monogram release of Maurice and Franklin King production. Features Kim Hunter, Dean Jagger, Robert Mitchum, Neil Hamilton. Directed by William Castle. Screenplay, Philip Yordan and Dennis J. Cooper, from story by George V. Moscov; camera, Ira Morgan; editor, Martin Cohn. At Brooklyn Strand, week of Nov. 16, '44, dual. Running time, 67 MINS.

Paul	Dean Jagger
Millie	Kim Hunter
Fred	Robert Mitchum
Blake	Neil Hamilton
Houser	Lou Lubin
Charlie	Milt Kibbee
Newsstand Man	Dewey Robinson
Middle-aged Woman	Claire Whitney
Middle-aged Man	Edward Keane
Chambermaid	Virginia Sale
Prescott	Dick Elliot
Old Man	Lee ("Lasses") White

Only thing wrong with this film is its misleading title. Tag, "When Strangers Marry," suggests another of the problem plays of newlyweds when in reality pic is a taut psychological thriller about a murderer and a manhunt full of suspense and excitement. A superior sort of whodunit, film's lack of marquee names keeps it out of the solo class, but it's a top dualer for the nabes and with good exploitation should ring the boxoffice bell.

Film has smart, fresh handling throughout, in scripting, direction and especially photography. Some neat angle shots, montages and other mood-instilling camera bits are worked in for proper effect without disrupting flow of narrative. Psych mood is cleverly sustained throughout for good atmosphere.

Title fits at start only. Two strangers are married after three meetings and immediately separated. The girl goes off to find her man. Then begins another type of manhunt, the police on the trail of a killer who to all intents and purposes is the disappearing husband. Girl finds her man in hiding, and the two continue dodging the cops. All the time the finger points increasingly to the man as the criminal, the girl sticking with him despite her increasing suspicions. A smart twist at the end catches audience off guard, but in logical sequence, for a neat solution.

In addition to crisp, tight writing, film has advantage of neat little quirks throughout that give it character. Acting is on the same satisfying plane. Dean Jagger has the soft menacing air that befits the suspect. Kim Hunter, comparative newcomer, is attractive as well as immensely appealing as the distraught but loyal wife. Robert Mitchum has

a breezy quality to fit his role of boyfriend, and Neil Hamilton plays the police lieutenant quietly and with dignity. *Bron.*

Three Hours
(FRENCH-MADE)

J. H. Hoffberg release of Arnold Pressburger production. Stars Jean Pierre Aumont. Directed by Leonide Moguy. Screenplay, Marcel Achard, from story by Jacques Companez and Michel Deligne; camera, Robert Lefebvre and Andre Germann; music, Arthur Honegger and Henry Verdun; English titles, Charles Clement. At 48th St. Cinema, N. Y., Oct. 28, '44. Running time, 85 MINS.

Paul Marchand	Jean Pierre Aumont
Mrs. Marchand	Betty Bovy
Mr. Marchand	E. Delmont
Marie	Corinne Luchaire
Jean	Almos
Auguste	Roger Legris

(In French; with English Titles)

"Three Hours," French pic filmed in 1940 and now having its American premiere, is a simple love story in a war setting whose quiet charm should overcome language barriers. Story of a jealous mother and misunderstanding between two lovers has general appeal, while fidelity of locale, a French village with its typically Gallic middleclass figures, is impressive. Photography is also interesting for its many atmospheric shots.

Story begins when a troop train headed for the front is halted after a track is blown up. Train is held up for three hours near a village for rail repairs. A poilu on the train, native of the village, takes this opportunity to run home to see his parents and learn why his sweetheart hasn't written to him. He finds that his jealous mother has driven the girl, an orphan, from his home but reconciles the two.

This was Jean Pierre Aumont's last French film before he joined the French army vs. Germany, after a short stint in Hollywood. He plays the worried young poilu with the proper blend of ardor and naivete. Blonde looker Corinne Luchaire (since denounced as a collaborationist), is affecting as his sweetheart, while Betty Bovy and E. Delmont add rich characterizations as the parents. *Bron.*

Love Story
(BRITISH-MADE)

London, Oct. 9.

Eagle-Lion release of Gainsborough production. Features Margaret Lockwood, Stewart Granger. Directed by Leslie Arliss. Screenplay by Leslie Arliss, Doreen Montgomery from short story by J. W. Drawbell. Additional dialog by Rodney Ackland. Music by Hubert Bath, played by National Symphony Orchestra, conducted by Sidney Beer. Camera, Bernard Knowles. At Gaumont, London, Oct. 8, '44. Running time, 112 MINS.

Lissa	Margaret Lockwood
Kit	Stewart Granger
Judy	Patricia Roc
Tom	Tom Walls
Albert	Reginald Purdell
Carol	Moira Lister
Ray	Walter Hudd
Colonel Pitt Smith	A. E. Matthews
Mrs. Pitt Smith	Josephine Middleton
Susie	Dorothy Bramhall
Angus Rossiter	Lawrence Hanray
Miss Rossiter	Beatrice Varley

There are some things wrong with this production, but it is so well executed and dotted with such extraneous incidents that it may have some possibilities in Britain. Appears only dubious for U. S. market, length being an obvious handicap.

A young concert pianiste suffers from heart trouble and the doctor gives her only three months to live. She goes to the Cornish coast, where she meets an engineer who devotes his time to flirting. They become close friends. When she is due to die, the man learns he will go blind. Neither will tell the other, and much is made of this situation.

Plot is filled with all sorts of events from the philosophical remarks of a Yorkshire millionaire to the stuttering yokel trying to speak coherently. The coastline scenery represents fine technical photography, but there is an excess of irrelevant happenings and superfluous dialog.

There is an admirable cast, the direction artistic, but nearly two hours is too long to give an elemental plot. Margaret Lockwood is the heroine, Stewart Granger, the hero; Tom Walls, the philosopher, and Patricia Roc, a girl who always loved the engineer.

British producers are still obsessed with the idea that their first-class pictures must have surplus footage. *Jolo.*

Miniature Reviews

"Belle of the Yukon" (Songs-Color) (RKO). Backstage filmusical in a Yukon dancehall diverting and colorful.

"Main Street After Dark" (M-G). First of under-hour support features. OK meller.

"Nothing But Trouble" (M-G). Latest Laurel-Hardy a dualer.

"Strange Affair" (Col). Allyn Joslyn-Evelyn Keyes teamed in rollicking whodunit, which should do okay on duals.

"Hi Beautiful" (Songs) (U). Decidedly lightweight entry for the secondary dualers.

"Adventures of Kitty O'Day" (Mono.). Second in girl amateur detective series starring Jean Parker. Okay dualer.

"Moulin Rouge" (Musical) (French). Lucien Baroux, Rene Dary in typical French screen musical; okay for arty houses.

Belle of the Yukon
(SONGS-COLOR)

Hollywood, Nov. 25.

RKO release of International production, produced and directed by William A. Seiter. Stars Randolph Scott, Gypsy Rose Lee, Dinah Shore, Bob Burns; features Charles Winninger. Screenplay, James Edward Grant; story, Houston Branch; camera, Ray Rennahan; editor, Ernest Nims; songs, Johnny Burke and Jimmy van Heusen; score and direction, Arthur Lange. Tradeshown Nov. 24, '44. Running time, 83 MINS.

"Honest" John Calhoun	Randolph Scott
Belle Devalle	Gypsy Rose Lee
Lettie Candless	Dinah Shore
Pop Candless	Charles Winninger
Sam Slade	Bob Burns
Viola	Florence Bates
Marshall Maitland	Guinn Williams
Steve	William Marshall
George	Robert Armstrong
The Professor	Victor Kilian
C. V. Atterbury	Edward Fielding
Cherie Atterbury	Wanda McKay
The Chief	Charles Soldani

"Belle of the Yukon" is a typical backstage filmusical, utilizing a Yukon dancehall for setting. Colorful song-and-dance pic has moderate audience appeal, and is sufficiently escapist to catch present customer requirements. Picture will hit profitable biz as topliner in the regular runs.

Opening title tips off that it is not to be taken seriously, and then yarn spins with tongue-in-cheek attitude and in general light vein. Randolph Scott is a reformed confidence man who fled north from the law, and opened a successful dancehall-gambling establishment at Malamute. Gypsy Rose Lee, deserted by Scott in his flight, arrives as head of a new entertainment unit and is intrigued by his reformation to again fall in love with him. Bob Armstrong tries to muscle in on the casino play with crooked dice and wheels without success, and Scott frames him with phony weather report on the date of river freezing. Armstrong gives odds to the miners on the early date, with Scott organizing a bank to keep the wagers. But Armstrong finds out about the fake report, and there's a round of double-cross episodes among the former con men over escape with the dust, including a temporary run on the bank. Scott proves he's still on the level by thwarting all plans for filching of the coin. Threading throughout is a romance of sorts between Dinah Shore and William Marshall, in contrast to the hectic interludes of Scott and Miss Lee.

Miss Shore capably handles three songs, the oldie "I Can't Tell Why I Love You But I Do-Do-Do," "Sleigh Ride in July" and "Like Someone in Love." Latter two are new tunes by Johnny Burke and Jimmy van Heusen that will get attention. Miss Lee talks one novelty number, "Every Girl Is Different," injecting plenty of personal zing into the rendition.

Members of the cast do well in their respective assignments. Scott is good as the dancehall operator; Miss Lee clicks as the smart performer; Miss Shore fits neatly as the young singer; and Bob Burns drawls in typical characterization. Charles Winninger, Marshall, Guinn Williams, Armstrong and Florence Bates supply solid support.

William Seiter grooves the fragile tale in a light vein throughout, accentuating the characters to compensate for the slim plot. Screenplay by James Edward Grant has liberal supply of chuckling dialog. Production mounting is top grade, with Technicolor treatment greatly adding to the eye appeal. *Walt.*

Main Street After Dark

Hollywood, Nov. 28.

Metro release of Jerry Bresler (Herbert Moulton) production. Features Edward Arnold, Hume Cronyn, Selena Royle. Directed by Edward Cahn. Screenplay, Karl Kamb and John C. Higgins; original, Higgins; camera, Jackson Rose; editor, Harry Komer. Tradeshown L. A. Nov. 27, '44. Running time, **57 MINS.**

Lieut. Lorrigan..............Edward Arnold
Ma Dibson..................Selena Royle
Lefty..........................Tom Trout
Jessie Belle................Audrey Totter
Posey.........................Dan Duryea
Keller......................Hume Cronyn
Rosalie..............Dorothy Ruth Morris

"Main Street After Dark" is the first of five features Metro will release during the coming months, each designed—through under-hour running time—to provide support for the company's top A's of longer length, and enabling exhibs to team a program from the one exchange.

This one is a straight-line drama exposing operations of theft rings, especially the rolling of service men at a port of embarkation. It briefly displays the work of girls trained to lift wallets and pokes of the soldiers and sailors, and delves into the scientific apprehension of rollers through use of fluorescent powder and violet ray lights.

Selena Royle heads the petty thieves, with Audrey Totter and Dorothy Ruth Morris as her operatives. Tom Traut is released from the pen on probation and kills a cafe owner in holdup to give a certain amount of dramatic punch to the climax. Edward Arnold is the police lieutenant delegated to clean up the petty thieves.

Short cast is well-selected, and direction by Edward Cahn is okay. Picture wheels out as a moderate budgeter by Metro standards, but production standards are maintained throughout. *Walt.*

Nothing But Trouble

Metro release of B. F. Zeidman production. Stars Stan Laurel and Oliver Hardy. Directed by Sam Taylor. Screenplay, Russell Rouse, Ray Golden; added dialog, Bradford Ropes, Margaret Gruen; music, Nathaniel Shilkret; editor, Conrad A. Nervig; camera, Charles Salerno, Jr. Tradeshown in N. Y., Nov. 28, '44. Running time, **69 MINS.**

Stan...........................Stan Laurel
Oliver........................Oliver Hardy
Mrs. Hawkley..................Mary Boland
Prince Saul.................Philip Merivale
Mr. Hawkley.................Henry O'Neill
King Christopher.............David Leland
Ronetz......................John Warburton
Prince Prentiloff...........Matthew Boulton
Mrs. Flannagan............Connie Gilchrist

Latest Laurel and Hardy comedy is geared for mild returns on duals in most situations.

Story, contrasting employment void in '32 with big demand for help in '44, seems to have something, but after the introductory reels it gets lost in the shuffle. It then veers into a prop setup for the stars to revive the clowning they have done for years, with little new added.

In the depression era Laurel and Hardy, descendants of a long line of cooks and butlers, are seeking employment against great odds. When convinced there isn't a job to be had in America, they hit off on a tour of foreign lands. Same situash obtains there, and they return to America in the lush era of employment. They are grabbed by Mary Boland, social-climber, to handle chores at a dinner she and her husband, Henry O'Neill, are giving in honor of David Leland, who plays the boy regent of a mythical kingdom.

During interim, however, his scheming uncle Philip Merivale, heir apparent, tries to have the kid knocked off. Sensing machinations of the uncle, he takes refuge with L & H, who protect him right up to the moment the unc nibbles the poisoned canape by mistake. It's presumed the kid will take the pair back to the royal palace as a reward.

Laurel and Hardy project their stock tricks throughout, managing to garner laughs here and there but not as socko as in some of their previous stanzas. Young Leland turns in a neat job, ditto for Miss Boland, Merrivale and O'Neill. Sam Taylor paces pic well on direction despite yarn not lending itself to any great gait. Camera work by Charles Salerno is okay also. *Edba.*

Strange Affair

Columbia release of Burt Kelly production. Features Allyn Joslyn, Evelyn Keyes, Marguerite Chapman and Edgar Buchanan. Directed by Alfred E. Green. Screenplay, Oscar Saul, Eve Greene, Jerome Odlum, from original by Saul; music, Marlin Skiles; music director, M. W. Stoloff; editor, Richard Fantl; camera, Franz F. Palmer. At Strand, Brooklyn, N. Y., week of Nov. 23, '44, dual. Running time, **78 MINS.**

Bill Harrison..................Allyn Joslyn
Jacqueline Harrison..........Evelyn Keyes
Marie Dumont........Marguerite Chapman
Lt. Washburn..............Edgar Buchanan
Freda Brenner......................Nina Foch
Domino..........................Hugo Haas
Laundry Truck Driver......Shemp Howard
Sergeant Erwin...............Frank Jenks
Dr. Brenner....................Erwin Kalser
Leslie Carlson...............Tonio Selwart
Rudolph Kruger............John Wengraf
Johansen............................Erik Rolf
Gloria.......................Carole Mathews
Motor Cop...................Edgar Dearing
Truck Driver......................Ray Teal

Whodunit packs plenty of fun and should more than hold its own on duals. Allyn Joslyn and Evelyn Keyes, who did so niftily in "Dangerous Blondes," are teamed again.

Joslyn plays the creator of a whodunit comic strip who has a penchant for injecting his artist's theories in solving homicides. He gets into the hair of the cops and steams them up further when his seemingly cockeyed deductions crack the cases. In this instance Erwin Kalser, as head of a committee to raise funds for refugees, drops dead at banquet table. Police diagnose death due to heart attack. Joslyn establishes it as homicide via poisoning. In transit he rounds up ring that had been smuggling internees out of the country. Miss Keyes plays his mate.

Joslyn and Miss Keyes turn in neat performances while Marguerite Chapman, as mystery gal, and Edgar Buchanan, a copper, give okay support. Others do well. Burt Kelly has done well with modest budget on production and Alfred E. Green has maintained a rollicking pace of direction. Franz F. Palmer's camera work is also up to par. *Edba.*

Hi Beautiful

(SONGS)

Hollywood, Nov. 20.

Universal release of Dick Irving Hyland production. Stars Martha O'Driscoll, Noah Beery, Jr.; features Walter Catlett, Hattie McDaniel, Tim Ryan, Florence Lake. Directed by Leslie Goodwins. Screenplay by Hyland; based on story by Eleanore Griffin and William Rankin; camera, Paul Ivano; editor, Edward Curtiss; dialog director, Stacy Keach. Previewed studio projection room, Nov. 16, '44. Running time, **64 MINS.**

Patty Callahan.........Martha O'Driscoll
Jeff........................Noah Beery, Jr.
Millie.....................Hattie McDaniel
Bisbee......................Walter Catlett
Babcock..........................Tim Ryan
Mrs. Bisbee..................Florence Lake
Attendant....................Grady Sutton
Husband..........................Lou Lubin
Wife..........................Virginia Sale
Bus Driver......................Tom Dugan
Passenger.......................Dick Elliott
Soldier Specialty..............James Dodd

This is an unimportant low-cost feature on the Universal list, burdened with an innocuous script and strained dialog. A lesser dualer.

There might have been some semblance of a picture in the original story but, if so, it got lost in the sophomoric script and finished version. Picture is a loosely-knit jumble of nonsense so broadly sketched that audience will be sympathetic rather than amused.

Plot introduces Martha O'Driscoll as caretaker for a model home, with soldier Noah Beery, Jr., walking in one night for lodging when unable to find hotel accommodations. Pair suddenly fall in love for a whirlwind romance and round of difficulties and pouts to the yawning climax. Several songs only add to the slow proceedings.

Director Leslie Goodwins must have figured the inadequacies of the script, for he injects mugging and broad characterizations at every possible turn. But this just makes it more ludicrous. Cast members are handicapped by material provided. *Walt.*

Adventures of Kitty O'Day

Monogram release of Lindsley Parsons production. Stars Jean Parker, Peter Cookson; features Tim Ryan, Ralph Sanford. Directed by William Beaudine. Story, Victor Hammond; adaptation, Tim Ryan, George Callahan and Victor Hammond; editor, Richard Pike; camera, Mack Stengler. At New York, N. Y., dual, week Nov. 25, '44. Running time, ***63 MINS.**

Kitty............................Jean Parker
Johnny......................Peter Cookson
Clancy..............................Tim Ryan
Mike.........................Ralph Sanford
Tracey...............................Bill Ruhl
Jeff..........................Shelton Brooks
Sauter..........................Bill Forrest
Gloria............................Lorna Grey
Nick..........................Hugh Prosser
Bascom..........................Dick Elliott
Roberts.......................Byron Fowlger
Carla................................Jan Wiley

"Detective Kitty O'Day" carries forward on a series format and is a fairly worthy low-budgeter which, in spite of some of its obviousness, slapstick, Hollywood murder mystery cliches, etc., merits attention for the dualers.

The brassy Kitty O'Day, hotel telephone operator, this time gets further into the hair of studio-typed detectives in attempting, in her amateurish dick fashion, to solve three different murders within the walls of her hostelry, meantime getting herself and her b.f., Peter Cookson, into brushes with the police under circumstances which veer suspicion toward them. A jewel-theft plot is at the bottom of the wholesale homicides.

Production of Lindsley Parsons is adequate and the direction of William Beaudine ditto though more of the old school. That chase through hotel corridors, slides down laundry chutes, etc., for example. Story and dialog hold promise for the writers involved, and some of the comedy material clicks in a moderate way. One of the adaptors is Tim Ryan, who plays the police inspector and whose hair may be free of dandruff but never of the novice sleuth, Kitty O'Day. His partner in crime solution is Ralph Sanford, good cop type who gets a few laughs.

Jean Parker is the O'Day gal, okay in the assignment called for but hardly any more. Her viz-a-viz, Cookson, has a breeziness and youth that impresses, while among others in the cast Jan Wiley suggests particular promise. She photographs well and is distinctive looker type.

Among lessers is Shelton Brooks, the songsmith, as the colored porter, who deserves a better chance than accorded here. *Char.*

Moulin Rouge

(Musical)

(FRENCH-MADE)

Andre Hugon production and release. Stars Lucien Baroux, Rene Dary; features Genevieve Callix, Josephine Baker. Directed by Yves Mirande. Story by Mirande; songs, Jean Lenoir, Van Parys, Rene Silviano, Raoul Moretti, Lucien Pipon, Roger Beernstein; English titles, Herman G. Weinberg. At 55th St. Playhouse, N. Y., week Nov. 22, '44. Running time, **85 MINS.**

Losieau.......................Lucien Baroux
Lequerec...........................Rene Dary
Eva.......................Genevieve Callix
Director of Moulin Rouge...Pierre Larquey
Lulu...........................Annie France
Simone.....................Simone Berriau
Princess Tam-Tam........Josephine Baker

(In French; English Titles)

"Moulin Rouge" is a typical French screen musical, but of 1938-39 vintage. Made in France before the Nazis took over Paris, it's lightweight in lighting, closeups and general production technique, but even these flaws cannot eclipse the charm and spirit of the show business yarn as it's done here with happy-go-lucky Gallic flavor. Film shapes as okay for foreign language and arty theatres. It's helped by the deft English titling.

Presence of Josephine Baker in the cast in one of her typical dances may aid its U. S. boxoffice, although makeshift continuity and sharp scissoring mar her appearance. In spite of this, her jungle number is plenty torrid.

Plot concerns an ambitious crooner, Rene Dary who, when turned down, works first as an undertaker's helper and then as caretaker-guard until he makes the grade. He and his pal, Lucien Baroux, stumble into a rich-paying job as caretakers of a rich man's home. Borrowed duds enable them to crash the Moulin Rouge, where he accidentally sings and attracts the attention of the show's producer and his mistress. This permits ringing in several production numbers from the French musichall.

A rather feeble story, it still manages to click nicely in the French manner in spite of obviously dated production faults. Veteran comic of French screen, Lucien Baroux, steals the picture, even his drinking of wine being made into a highly ludicrous episode. Baroux does all the things he's done so many times before on the screen, but sold better here. Rene Dary, as the ambitious singer, ballads with the verve of a Maurice Chevalier and resembles the latter in his mannerisms, intentionally or otherwise. Standard but strong supporting cast includes Genevieve Callix, Pierre Larquey, Annie France and Simone Berriau.

Tunes by a whole string of French songsmiths are surprisingly strong, but Yves Mirande's story is better than his direction, which is inclined to be jerky. *Wear.*

Miniature Reviews

"Hollywood Canteen" (Musical) (WB). With an all-star dream cast, a b.o. socko.

"National Velvet" (Color) (M-G). An unusual film, especially good for women and kids. Stars Mickey Rooney. A b.o. winner.

"Guest in the House" (UA) Meller with an unusual psychological triangle should fare well in most situations.

"Sunday Dinner for a Soldier" (20th). Anne Baxter-John Hodiak starred in dualer geared

"Night Club Girl" (U) (Musical). Grooved for dual bills.

"La Casta Susana" (Pampa). Pretentious but dull Argentine-made operetta okay for Latin-Americas, but no dice in U. S. for modest grosses.

Hollywood Canteen
(MUSICAL)

Warner Bros. release of Alex Gottlieb production. Direction and original screenplay, Delmer Daves. Musical numbers, LeRoy Prinz; camera, Bert Glennon; editor, Christian Nyby; music, Ray Heindorf; music director, Leo F. Forbstein; asst. director, Art Lueker; songs, Cole Porter, Ted Koehler-M. K. Jerome, E. Y. Harburg-Burton Lane, Harold Adamson-Vernon Duke, Koehler-Lane, Larry Neal-Jimmy Mundy, Jean Barry-Leah Worth-Dick Charles, Obdulio Morales-Julio Blanco-Marion Sunshine, Bob Noland. Tradeshown N. Y. Dec. 1, 1944. Running time, **124 MINS.**

Andrews Sisters	Nora Martin
Jack Benny	Joan McCracken
Julie Bishop	Chef Milani
Betty Brodel	Dolores Moran
Barbara Brown	Dennis Morgan
Joe E. Brown	Janis Paige
Eddie Cantor,	Eleanor Parker
Kitty Carlisle	William Prince
Jack Carson	Joyce Reynolds
Dane Clark	John Ridgely
Joan Crawford	Roy Rogers & Trigger
Helmut Dantine	Rosario & Antonio
Bette Davis	S. Z. (Cuddles) Sakall
Faye Emerson	Zachary Scott
Victor Francen	Robert Shayne
John Garfield	Alexis Smith
Golden Gate Quartet	Sons of the Pioneers
Mary Gordon	Barbara Stanwyck
Sydney Greenstreet	Craig Stevens
Alan Hale	Joseph Szigeti
Paul Henreid	Theodore Von Eltz
Robert Hutton	Donald Woods
Andrea King	Jane Wyman
Joan Leslie	
Peter Lorre	Jimmy Dorsey & His Band
Ida Lupino	
Irene Manning	Carmen Cavallaro & Orchestra
Eddie Marr	

Author-director Delmer Daves has done it again. He scripted "Stage Door Canteen" for Sol Lesser in early '43 and he's parlayed himself into another smasheroo for Warners with "Hollywood Canteen." There isn't a marquee big enough to hold all the names in this one, so how can it miss? Besides, it's basically solid. It has story, cohesion and heart. That's not a bad parlay either.

As with the N. Y. Canteen benefiting from the earlier pic's gross, Hollywood Canteen gets a generous slice from this WB filmusical, so little wonder the cast reads like a benefit.

The names are alphabetized for tactical reasons, but it's perhaps a too cautious diplomacy since some stars might just as well have telephoned their stuff over. None the less Robert Hutton and Joan Leslie emerge as the real stars of the filmusical. They carry the story, and a human one it is, too. Hutton looks like the ideal GI Joe, back with a Purple Heart from the South Pacific, and his buddy (Dane Clark) looks the perfect Brooklynite. In short, a Dodgers addict. His Brooklyn brogue will make us demand a plebiscite for Brooklyn's return to the USA.

Story has Hutton winding up not only meeting his dream-girl, Joan Leslie, but is also the lucky winner as the millionth guest of the Hollywood Canteen. That entitles him to an Arabian Nights suite, car, gifts and his choice of actresses for his weekend date. Natch, it's Miss Leslie. What's nice is that real-life Miss Leslie plays herself with charm, poise and ease, and the plot is so glib one accepts the romance wholeheartedly.

In between are interspersed a wealth of specialties, well paced and spaced, so that it doesn't border on the "big short" idea. There are a flock of highlights and a flock of tunes. Cole Porter's "Don't Fence Me In" gets a two-ply plug, best via the Andrews Sisters. Joseph Szigeti, heralded as "the world's greatest violinist," does "The Bee," and, of course, that's a setup for Jack Benny's clowning for the topper.

Jimmy Dorsey's band plays the major background although Carmen Cavallaro mops up with his colorful "Voodoo Moon." Eddie Cantor and Nora Martin do their "We're Having a Baby (My Baby and Me)" and click, although Cantor, somehow, permitted himself a bad makeup. Sydney Greenstreet and Peter Lorre, playing themselves, make their bit count; ditto John Garfield who has been a tireless real-life worker at the Hollywood Canteen. Bette Davis is likewise herself as boss of the Canteen, and there is a good institutional trailer by WB for its Paul Henreid as the male thrill. Alexis Smith, Faye Emerson (Mrs. Elliott Roosevelt now), Joan Crawford, Victor Francen, Irene Manning, Barbara Stanwyck, Donald Woods mostly do host-hostess bits.

Little Joan McCracken, out of "Oklahoma" (so heralded) but now in "Bloomer Girl," makes her film debut, albeit brief, a real sock. It's a comedy ballet specialty (well staged by LeRoy Prinz, who also gets a flash of himself on-screen) and it counts for boff results. She lenses excellently. Kitty Carlisle does a ballad; Jack Carson and Jane Wyman do an OK song-and-dance specialty, "Rest of Your Life"; ditto Joe E. Brown, Roy Rogers, including Trigger and backed by the Sons of the Pioneers, while the Golden Gate Quartet and Rosario & Antonio with their Spanish terps, likewise register. And, of course, underlying it all is the impact of show business doing its job once again—and how!

"Don't Fence Me In" and "Sweet Dreams, Sweetheart" already are asserting themselves. A couple of the others are reprises. There's a good rhythm number in "The General Jumped at Dawn," and two patriotic nifties, "I'm Gettin' Corns for My Country" and "You Can Always Tell a Yank."

Alex Gottlieb's production doesn't skimp although nothing lavish is required, considering the focal interest in the Canteen. Withal, a dandy filmusical for anybody's theatre.

Abel.

National Velvet
(COLOR)

Metro release of Pandro S. Berman production. Stars Mickey Rooney. Directed by Clarence Brown. Screenplay, Theodore Reeves and Helen Deutsch from novel by Enid Bagnold; camera, Leonard Smith; color, Natalie Kalmus, Henri Jaffa; editor, Robert J. Kern; music, Herbert Stothart. Tradeshown N. Y., Dec. 4, '44. Running time, **125 MINS.**

Mi Taylor	Mickey Rooney
Mr. Brown	Donald Crisp
Velvet Brown	Elizabeth Taylor
Mrs. Brown	Anne Revere
Edwina Brown	Angela Lansbury
Donald Brown	Jackie Jenkins
Malvolia Brown	Juanita Quigley
Race Patron	Arthur Treacher
Farmer Ede	Reginald Owen
Miss Sims	Norma Varden
Ted	Terry Kilburn

In "National Velvet" Metro has one of the top b.o. clicks of the year. It's a horse picture with wide general appeal, a potent draw for femme and juve attendance in particular. The production also focuses attention on a new dramatic find—moppet Elizabeth Taylor, who plays "Velvet."

Film is based on a novel of the same name, written some years ago. Backgrounded in England, it tells of a former jockey (Rooney) who's become embittered through circumstances and plans to steal from a family that befriends him. But the family's 11-year old daughter, Velvet, softens him.

From this point on, early in the film, Velvet, becomes the dominant character in the story. The kid is nuts about horses. When a neighbor raffles off an unmanageable brute he's unable to handle she wins it on tickets paid for by Rooney. Over the objections of both Rooney and her father, nag is entered in the greatest race in England, the Grand National Sweepstakes. Support for this seemingly crazy move comes from the girl's mother, a philosophic, understanding woman who supports the theory that once in a lifetime a person is entitled to a move of great folly. When no jockey is available, Velvet boots the horse home, only to be disqualified when her sex is discovered. The moral victory, plus the fact that the horse has proven itself a champ, substantiating Velvet's faith, serves as ample recompense.

Story is told with warmth and understanding. There is much detail, in this direction, between husband and wife; between Velvet and her mother and between the two kids, especially when Rooney confesses to an abiding fear of horses ever since he rode in a sweepstakes which ended in another jockey's death.

Production is excellent. Clarence Brown, who directed, has used the asset of color superbly, capturing the charm of English countrysides and, above all, reproducing Aintree, the Grand National course, with fidelity.

Anne Revere, the mother, does another fine job—restrained and excellently modulated. Donald Crasp, as the kindly father who usually guesses wrong, contribs one of his usual workmanlike performances. Rooney's part is a difficult one, hampered by the lack of motivation, but he handles it well.

Merr.

Guest in the House

United Artists release of Hunt Stromberg production. Features Anne Baxter, Ralph Bellamy, Ruth Warrick, Aline MacMahon. Directed by John Brahm. Screenplay, Ketti Frings; based on stage play by Hagar Wilde and Dale Eunson; camera, Lee Garmes; editors, James Newcom, Walter Hanneman. Previewed N. Y., Dec. 1, '44. Running time, **117 MINS.**

Evelyn Heath	Anne Baxter
Douglas Proctor	Ralph Bellamy
Aunt Martha	Aline MacMahon
Ann Proctor	Ruth Warrick
Dan Proctor	Scott McKay
Mr. Hackett	Jerome Cowan
Miriam	Marie McDonald
John, the Butler	Percy Kilbride
Hilda, the Maid	Margaret Hamilton
Lee Proctor	Connie Laird

"Guest in the House" should garner from good to strong b.o. results, depending on individual situations and specialized exploitation which it requires. Chiller, with a sombre psychological motif based on a triangle motif with a different approach, will likely strike a good average.

Hunt Stromberg's film version of the Hager Wilde-Dale Eunson play is a bit on the arty side. On the other hand, another aspect is the popularity which this play has achieved among little theatre groups since the amateur production rights were released.

Transition of a legit piece of this kind, dealing with a peculiar type of neurotic, to celluloid, is obviously beset with difficulties. There are moments when the illusion is barely maintained. Yet it is a distinct credit to the direction, scripting and cast that the yarn has been made as believable as it is on the screen.

Production's most valuable asset, apart from its first-rate cast, is the suspense and action which are sustained throughout once the motivation is established. It is also bolstered with some sexy interpolations. On the debit side is the long running time. Some pruning would help considerably.

Story is about girl (Anne Baxter) with bats in the belfry and a cardiac condition besides, who is taken into the home of a happy family at the request of the young doctor (Scott McKay) who has befriended her. The girl becomes infatuated with the medico's older, married brother (Ralph Bellamy) and immediately proceeds to distill psychological poison, alienating one member of the family from another so that she can win the man of her choice.

Aline MacMahon, as the aunt who eventually finds a way to protect the young doctor from marrying the unbalanced girl, handles a difficult assignment in fine style. Miss Baxter, Ruth Warrick, as the older brother's wife, Bellamy and Marie McDonald, a blonde looker, handle the more important roles and provide substantial marquee value.

Mori.

Sunday Dinner for a Soldier

20th-Fox release of Walter Morosco production. Stars Anne Baxter, John Hodiak; features Charles Winninger. Directed by Lloyd Bacon. Screenplay, Wanda Tuchock and Melvin Levy, based on story by Martha Cheavens; editor, J. Watson Webb; music, Alfred Newman; camera, Joe MacDonald. Tradeshown Nov. 30, '44. Running time, **86 MINS.**

Tessa	Anne Baxter
Eric Moore	John Hodiak
Grandfather	Charles Winninger
Agatha	Anne Revere
Mary	Connie Marshall
Mr. York	Chill Wills
Kenneth Normand	Robert Bailey
Jeep	Bobby Driscoll
Mrs. Dobson	Jane Darwell
Michael	Billy Cummings
Samanthy	Marietta Canty
WAC Lieutenant	Barbara Sears
M.P.'s	Larry Thompson and Bernie Sell
Photographer	Chester Conklin

"Sunday Dinner for a Solider" is a modest b.o. film. It's lightweight but has a number of touching moments, particularly for the women.

"Sunday Dinner" deals with a derelict family living on a houseboat in Florida and its scrimping so it can invite a strange soldier, through the USO, to a Sunday chicken dinner. The family consists of three moppets, their adult sister, all of whom have been orphaned, and a shiftless grandfather.

Anne Baxter, as the older sister, as always, gives a plausible performance. John Hodiak is co-starred with Miss Baxter, and somewhere along the line the film has missed fire in building up the soldier character played by Hodiak. For he doesn't make his first appearance until about an hour of the 86-minute film has elapsed. Which makes it a short romance between him and Miss Baxter.

Charles Winninger is the grandfather, strutting and expostulating his way through a role that's typical for him. Connie Marshall, Billy Cummings and Bobby Driscoll are the kids, and they supply the proper atmosphere.

Lloyd Bacon's direction is even, and the production is consistent.

Kahn.

Night Club Girl

Universal release of Frank Gross production. Features Maxie Rosenbloom, Vivian Austin, Edward Norris, Judy Clark, Billy Dunn. Directed by Eddie Cline. Screenplay, Henry Blankfort, Dick I. Hyland from original by Adele Comandini; camera, Charles Van Enger; editor, Charles Maynard. Previewed N. Y., Dec. 4, '44. Running time, **61 MINS.**

Eleanor	Vivian Austin
Clark Phillips	Edward Norris
Percival	Maxie Rosenbloom
Janie	Judy Clark
Charlie	Billy Dunn
Gaston	Leon Belasco
Simmons	Andrew Tombes
Fred	Fred Sanborn
Mayor	Clem Bevans

Ma Kendall..................Virginia Brissac
Captain..........................Emmett Vogan
Carlos..............................George Davis
The Mulcays, Paula Drake, Delta Rhythm Boys

A rags-to-riches routine through the medium of thin story material, plus several specialties by three top-flight vaude and nitery acts. That sums up "Night Club Girl," a low-budget musical medley grooved for the lower dualers.

The Delta Rhythm Boys, colored quartet, are showcased doing two tunes; the Mulcays, currently in "Star Time" on Broadway, giving out with three harmonica duets; Paula Drake warbling "Wo-Ho" by Jimmy Nolan and Jim Kennedy; vocal duets and tap-dancing by Vivian Austin and Billy Dunn, and a knockabout (a la Betty Hutton) song by Judy Clark, round out the conglomeration.

Yarn has to do with the helping hand given couple of kids trying to break into the Hollywood nitery scene by the personnel of a joint run by Maxie Rosenbloom. Eddie Norris, in the role of a columnist, succeeds in getting them a tryout, but they fail dismally. Neither the dialog nor the situations originated by Adele Comadini and screenplayed by Henry Bankfort and Dick I. Hyland are out of the ordinary.

Settings, too, are run-of-the-mill, as is the direction by Eddie Cline and the photography by Charles Van Enger. *Sten.*

La Casta Susana
("Chaste Susan")
(ARGENTINE-MADE)

Buenos Aires, Nov. 7.

Pampa Film production and release. Stars Mirtha Legrand, Juan Carlos Thorry; features Alberto Bello, Hector Calcagno, Mario Santos, Homero Carpena, Thilda Thamar, Tito Climent. Directed by Benito Perojo. Adapted from Jean Gilbert's operetta by Juan Carlos Muello. Camera, Pablo Tabernero. At Gran Cine Ocean, Buenos Aires, starting Oct. 11. Running time, **95 MINS.**

Great things had been expected of this first Argentine-made screen operetta, shot at great expense at Pocitos beach in Uruguay, and with many pesos invested in lavish decorations and costuming. The result certainly does not justify the expenditure. Scenes are disjointedly put together and in some cases are entirely unrelated. Explanation has been that owing to contract difficulties with stars and shortage of raw stock, many sequences were omitted or not screened as written, with sketchy and confusing result. No go for U. S.

Gilbert's long-popular music and decidedly risque farce are worthy of more careful production and direction. Benito Perojo, Spanish director now settled in Buenos Aires, shows himself to be no Lubitsch

Mirtha Legrand, authentic ingenue, is entirely miscast as the flirtatious Susana, who is so undeservedly awarded the prize for chastity. It's disconcerting to see how entirely this youngster fails to understand the implications of the role she is playing. Juan Carlos Thorry, competent and lively as ever, does what he can to keep things going. "Can Can" ballet scenes at Moulin Rouge serve to enlighten what might otherwise be a more decided flop.

"La Casta Susana" has marquee value in Latin-Americas because of lavish production and its prestige as a highly popular operetta of the gay nineties, but cannot be classed among the best that local producers can do. *Nid.*

Miniature Reviews

"Keys of the Kingdom" (20th). Dignified transmutation of Dr. A. J. Cronin's bestseller, capitally played and produced.

"Music for Millions" (Songs) (M-G). Socko romance with music; a b.o. mopup.

"The 3 Caballeros" (Color; Musical) (Disney-RKO). Significant live action-animation feature. Strong boxoffice.

"Experiment Perilous" (RKO). Good suspense drama, with Hedy Lamarr, George Brent and Paul Lukas.

"Destiny" (U). Gangster regeneration drama will provide okay support in regular bookings.

"Carolina Blues" (Col.) (Musical). Kay Kyser, Ann Miller, Victor Moore in okay dualer.

"The Falcon In Hollywood" (RKO). Falcon invades a film studio to unravel a murder mystery. Standard entry in series.

"The Unwritten Code" (Col). Dull drama about Nazi fanaticism; a dualer.

"When the Lights Go On Again" (PRC). Tells how returning wounded vets should be treated; strong dualer.

The Keys of the Kingdom

20th-Fox release of Joseph L. Mankiewicz production. Features Gregory Peck, Thos. Mitchell, Vincent Price, Rosa Stradner, Roddy McDowall, Edmund Gwenn, Sir Cedric Hardwicke. Directed by John M. Stahl. Screenplay, Mankiewicz and Nunnally Johnson from A. J. Cronin's novel; camera, Arthur Miller, Fred Sersen; music, Alfred Newman, Edward Powell; editor, James B. Clark. Tradeshown in N. Y. Dec. 7, 1944. Running time, **137 MINS.**

Father Francis Chisholm......Gregory Peck
Dr. Willie Tulloch........Thomas Mitchell
Rev. Angus Mealy..........Vincent Price
Mother Maria-Veronica......Rosa Stradner
Francis (as a child)......Roddy McDowall
Rev. Hamish MacNabb.....Edmund Gwenn
Monsignor Sleeth.....Sir Cedric Hardwicke
Nora (as a child)........Peggy Ann Garner
Nora..............................Jane Ball
Dr. Wilbur Fiske............James Gleason
Agnes Fiske....................Anne Revere
Lisbeth Chisholm..............Ruth Nelson
Joseph............................Benson Fong
Mr. Chia......................Leonard Strong
Mr. Pao..............................Philip Ahn
Father Tarrant..............Arthur Shields
Aunt Polly.....................Edith Barrett
Sister Martha....................Sara Allgood
Lieutenant Shon................Richard Loo
Sister Clotilde......................Ruth Ford
Father Craig....................Kevin O'Shea
Hosannah Wang.................H. T. Tsiang
Philomena Wang...............Si-Lan Chen
Anna.........................Eunice Soo-Hoo
Alex Chisholm.................Dennis Hoey
Mrs. Glennie....................Ethel Griffies
Malcolm Glennie..............Terry Kilburn
Daniel Glennie...............Lumsden Hare
Ned Bannon..............J. Anthony Hughes
Bandit Captain..............Abner Biberman
Andrew.........................George Nokes

"The Keys of the Kingdom" takes its place with "Song of Bernadette" and "Going My Way" in inspired, dignified, artistic, heart-warming cinematurgy about the Church. In its 137 minutes director John M. Stahl has limned a gracious albeit sometimes too leisurely transmutation of Dr. A. J. Cronin's bestseller. The result is all on the credit side.

A cavalcade of a priest's life, played excellently by Gregory Peck, who is more and more the Gary Cooper type, what transcends all the cinemaction is the impact of tolerance, service, faith and godliness.

Where the monsignor (Sir Cedric Hardwicke) comes to out the aged, limping and poor father (Peck), he departs with humility and a new respect after he reads the good father's journal, first of unrequited love (in youth) and later in unselfish devotion, self-punishing denials and unswerving fealty to his mission as it covers more than a half century. The action starts in Scotland, shifts to China and thence back to the land of his birth.

The bishop (Vincent Price), lush and proud of his ecclesiastical achievements, and the equally regal ecclesiast (Hardwicke), his special emissary, vividly point up the contrast to the lean, gaunt priest (Peck), who gave so much and seemingly achieved so little personally.

There is a spell of prime-of-life accomplishment as he makes some headway in the far province of Chek Kow, even unto saving the life of the wealthy local mandarin's son and heir through emergency lancing of the boy's blood-poisoned arm. But comes civil war, and his mission on the beautiful Hill of the Green Jade happens to fall in direct line of fire between the authoritative army and the Chinese bandits.

More character study than vivid cinematurgy, none the less the unfolding is gripping, cogent, forceful. Rosa Stradner is the proud, unbending mother superior, finally softening when she realizes the good father's noble work. Thomas Mitchell as the medico is equally understanding, as is James Gleason, head of the American mission (Methodist). The faithful Joseph (Benson Fong), the friendly Rev. Hamish MacNabb (Edmund Gwenn), lovelorn Nora (aJne Ball) and al lthe other assorted characters of a large cast deport themselves intelligently, realistically. The boyhood ambitions, setbacks, pretenses and intensive little loves and hates are vividly portrayed under John Stahl's skillful direction. All this is unfolded as one continues flshback.

Produced by Joseph Mankiewicz, who also collaborated with Nunnally Johnson on the screenplay, they have done a capital job. True, it's slow in spots and some judicious cutting wouldn't hurt, but "The Keys of the Kingdom" is one of the films to which Hollywood can always turn with pride. *Abel.*

Music for Millions
(SONGS)

Metro release of Joe Pasternak production. Stars Jimmy Durante, Margaret O'Brien, Jose Iturbi, June Allyson. Directed by Henry Koster. Screenplay, Myles Connolly; music, Georgie Stoll, Michel Michelet, Jos. Nussbaum, Ted Duncan, Calvin Jackson; camera, Robt. Surtees; editor, Douglass Biggs. Tradeshown Dec. 8, 1944. Running time, **120 MINS.**

"Mike"........................Margaret O'Brien
Jose Iturbi............................By Himself
Andrews..........................Jimmy Durante
Barbara Ainsworth..............June Allyson
Rosalind..............................Marsha Hunt
Uncle Ferdinand.................Hugh Herbert
Doctor..........................Harry Davenport
Marie................................Marie Wilson
Larry...................................Larry Adler
Kickebush...............................Ben Lessy
Traveler's Aid Woman.....Connie Gilchrist
Elsa........................Katharine Balfour
Helen..............................Helen Gilbert
Anita..................................Mary Parker
Jane.........................Madeleine LeBeau

"Music for Millions" is one of those sleepers that comes along every couple of seasons, costs moderately, and goes out and outgrosses the $1,000,000 epics. This one will mop up.

Why? Here's why — and how. Margaret O'Brien is the waif whose faith in her elder sister, June Allyson, is greater than the latter's hope that her soldier-husband will return. Meantime she's one of the string bass players in Jose Iturbi's symphony, now almost 50% femmes because of the war's inroads. Jimmy Durante is Iturbi's general factotum, and Marsha Hunt, Marie Wilson, Madeleine LeBeau, Katharine Balfour, Mary Parker and Helen Gilbert are Miss Allyson's co-musicians, confidantes and friends.

Against this canvas is plotted a human, heart-tugging story which just about embraces the gamut of emotions. Iturbi is shown as the temperamental yet human and understanding maestro. The Great Schnozzola's honest sentiment—and that stork scene with the naively precocious Margaret O'Brien is a gem—is real trouping. The friendly cop and the Traveler's Aid worker who brings the sisters together; the errant uncle, a forger (Hugh Herbert), who almost does a good turn; the caustic theatrical boarding-house keeper; the friendly gals in the symphony—all are vividly filmed under the sterling production direction of the Pasternak-Koster team and the tiptop scripting job turned in by Myles Connolly.

In between, the cavalcade of Dvorak, Grieg, Victor Herbert, Debussy, Tschaikowsky, Liszt, Handel and Chopin is batoned by Iturbi, while the Schnoz gets off "Toscanini, Iturbi and Me" and "Umbriago," plus ad lib jam session furbelows by the otherwise legit musikers. Then there's Ben Lessy (ex-Oshins & Lessy, knockabout saloonatics) who has a schnoz to rival Durante's, and who deadpans a drummer bit for very effective results. Incidentally, even Eddie Jackson and drummer Jack Roth get in their licks—with billing yet! Not forgetting Larry Adler's socko "Clair de Lune," which he Debussys into a sentimental highlight as part of the plot motivation.

June Allyson, heretofore dominant in musicals, steps forth as a dramatic actress to be reckoned with and, show business being what it is, the crest of this click film is bound to carry a few others to the heights. One of them is Marsha Hunt, no newcomer, and the other is the relatively unknown Katharine Balfour, both in very sympathetic castings as a worried pair of gal pals. The business with the War Dept. telegram apprising of the "lost in action," and the manner in which the girls debate whether to show it, and finally decide not to do so, is a corking sequence which director Koster milks to the limit. That goes for the hospital scene, when Miss Allyson is having her baby, while little sister Margaret O'Brien refuses to leave her watchful waiting. The news "it's a boy," as it's flashed to the mixed Manhattan Symphony, and finally to maestro Iturbi, signs off the film on a high sentimentally appealing note.

Picture runs two hours flat and packs plenty into it. Thus the pace is steady, the montages well edited to embrace the camp shows and the cavalcade of classics with only a touch of Victor Herbert in the "March of the Toys" fanfare. Handel's "Messiah," with impressive mixed choir and orchestra, of course, is the topper at the double good news that the missing husband is alive and "it's a boy."

Consummate showmanship has gone into every phase of the presentation as Iturbi piano solos Debussy but segues into the gayer Chopin to cheer the heroine. The titular "Music for Millions" takes on added values as it unreels and impresses that the classics have mass appeal. But above all, holding everything together is the powerful romance story, embracing several surefire elements.

The performances are excellent all the way. While little Miss O'Brien steals it, and Miss Allyson is a warm, appealingly brave heroine, Iturbi proves himself as good histrionically as he is musicianly. Durante is not just the distrait, harassed character but handles his dramatic sequences with eclat. Marie Wilson's dumb blonde role, the s.a. Madeleine Le Beau, the sympathetic Miss Balfour, along with the Misses Parker and Gilbert, all ring the bell in their assignments. Productionally, it's ultra. *Abel.*

3 Caballeros
(COLOR; MUSICAL)

RKO release of Walt Disney production. Features Aurora Miranda, Carmen Molina, Dora Lux, with Clarence Nash, Joaquin Garay, Jose Oliveira, Frank Graham, Sterling Holloway, Fred Shield, Nestor Amaral, Almirante, Trio Calaveres, Ascencion del Rio Trio, Padua Hills Players. Camera, Ray Rennahan; art, Richard F. Irvine; dances, Billy Daniels, Aloysio Oliveira, Carmelita Maracci; Technicolor, Natalie Kalmus, Morgan Padelford, Phil Dike; process effects, Ub Iwerks, Richard Jones; editor, Don Holliday; asst. director, Harold Young; songs, Manuel Esperon, Ary Barroso, Augustin Lara, Chas. Wolcott; music direction, Chas. Wolcott, Paul J. Smith, Edward Plumb; lyrics, Ray Gilbert; animated production supervision and direction, Norman Ferguson, assisted by Larry Lansburgh; plus a corps of animators. Tradeshown N.Y., Dec. 11, '44. Running time, **71 MINS.**

Walt Disney in "The Three Caballeros" reveals a new form of cinamatic entertainment wherein he blends live action with animation into a socko feature production. Running 71 mins., it's just right for popular consumption. It's bound to please generally, and has perennial values as Latin-American relations grow closer with the succeeding years.

Unlike Disney's preceding "Saludos Amigos" (which ran only 45 mins.), this is not so closely tied in with the Coordinator of Inter-American Affairs, although the former Nelson Rockefeller committee undoubtedly helped the Disneyites no end in this one also.

It's a gay, colorful, resplendent conceit. Neatly conceived, it ties in many Pan-American highlights through the medium of irascible Donald Duck, the wiseguy Joe Carioca (first introduced in "Saludos Amigos"), and a lovable new character in Panchito, the little South American boy.

It's DD's birthday and on Friday-the-13th he gets three huge packages of gifts from his friends in Latin America. What he unwraps as his "gifts" are transplanted to this live action-animation feature. The off-screen narration is so skillfully blended with the dialog between Donald, Joe Carioca, et al., and it's all so smoothly cut and edited, one is only casually conscious of where one stops and the other begins.

Unreeled are peripatetic penguins from the South Pole, rare birds, the beauties of Baia (Brazil), a trip to Mexico on the "magic sarape" (carpet), brief stopoffs in other countries between Brazil and Mexico; highlights of the Acapulco beach resort, Vera Cruz, Mexico City, etc.

Punchily interspersed are sock songs such as the title number (by Manuel Esperon), "Baia" (by Ary Barroso), "You Belong to My Heart" (by Augustin Lara), "Mexico" (by Chas. Wolcott), and "Os Quindins de Yaya" (Barros). Each is surefire for hitdom and, as done, it's a songplugger's delight, being reprised again and again to sundry thrilling cartoon-artistry effects. The blend of the multi-hued Technicolor with the music is an eye-and-ear treat all the way. The imagination that went with it pyramids the wonderment as the footage progresses.

As the gift book is turned, to take Duck and Carioca from one locale to another; the animation blends with real-life action, chiefly song and dance. Thus are introduced Aurora Miranda (Carmen's sister), Carmen Molina, dancer, and Dora Luz, songstress. Each is a looker and especially does the beauteous Dora Luz, with her sonorous treatment of "You Belong to My Heart," boff the customers. What the Disneyites make Donald Duck do in exaggerated pash manner is about the impact this sexy looker should have on the average male customer.

The action is projected via a movie-travelog technique (the 16 mm projector is one of Duck's gifts), and as he alights from the "magic sarape" in this or that locale, commingling with the real-life players, it makes for some extraordinary comedy. Perhaps the highlight of a sequence of standout scenes is Donald's wolfing among the Mex bathing beauts on the beach of Acapulco.

Royalty-minded Disney, incidentally, has created a few more affectionate characters, from the lovable Panchito (little boy) and his Flying Burrito (a fetching flying donkey) to Pablo, the South Pole penguin, and those winsome little Mexican children in their "Las Posadas," the traditional Xmas custom. The toy market should boom plenty from these.

Of the featured trio, Aurora Miranda stands out in the Brazilian stuff, notably "Os Quindins de Yaya" (the cookie girl number) and in "Baia." Carmen Molina dances her famed "Jesusita" Chihuahua dance, against appropriate cactus backgrounds, and of course the somnolent Dora Luz, with "You Belong to My Heart," makes her impact in the other Mexican sequences. Obviously, unlike the "Saludos Amigos" accent on South America, Disney has now brought his pitch closer to home, i.e., below the Rio Grande, and the Mexican Chamber of Commerce will **probably elect him mayor for the terrific ballyhoo.**

There's no question that Disney has brought to the screen a technique of combining live action with cartoon animation which is revolutionary and significant. *Abel.*

Experiment Perilous

Hollywood, Dec. 12.

RKO release of Warren Duff production. Stars Hedy Lamarr, George Brent, Paul Lukas; features Albert Dekker, Carl Esmond, Olive Blakeney. Directed by Jacques Tourneur. Screenplay by Duff, based on novel by Margaret Carpenter; camera, Tony Gaudio; special effects, Vernon L. Walker; editor, Ralph Dawson; asst. director, Dewey Starkey. Tradeshown L. A. Dec. 5, '44. Running time, **90 MINS.**

Allida	Hedy Lamarr
Dr. Huntington Bailey	George Brent
Nick	Paul Lukas
Clag	Albert Dekker
Maitland	Carl Esmond
Cissie	Olive Blakeney
Alec	George N. Neise
Maggie	Margaret Wycherly
Elaine	Stephanie Bachelor
Miss Wilson	Mary Servoss
Deria	Julia Dean
District Attorney	William Post, Jr.
Alec (5 years old)	Billy Ward

"Experiment Perilous" is one of those strange and weird dramas that occasionally get screen presentation. This one is well done, carrying interest at good, suspenseful pitch, and has the bright marquee dressing of Hedy Lamarr, George Brent and Paul Lukas. Picture is due for profitable biz in the keys and subsequents.

Plot centers around Lukas' mansion in the 1903 era. The elderly Lukas has been married to the young and beautiful Miss Lamarr for about a decade, holding her in close confinement and restraint as he would any other possession. She, in turn, is continually dominated by fear of strange influences which can be felt but not seen. Brent, a young doctor, originally is projected into contact with the family through chance meeting with Olive Blakeney, elderly sister of Lukas, who's returning from several years in a midwest sanitarium. She comments on the unseen influences at the family home, and declares against staying there. But she dies on arrival while having tea, and Brent accepts invitation some days later to meet Miss Lamarr and inspect the place that intrigues him. Accepting Lukas' plea to help his wife, Brent gradually falls in love with her, and eventually tabs Lukas as a cunning and insane personality with Napoleonic complex who's responsible for several murders and setting up of the weird influences prevailing. Windup disposes of Lukas in a fire, for clinch of the doctor and wife.

Picture unfolds in both straightline and flashback techniques. It covers a lot of territory and sets, and depends mainly on dialog to put over its dramatic unfolding. Despite these handicaps, picture carries good pace of suspense, mainly through generally fine performances by Brent, Lukas, Miss LaMarr, Albert Dekker and Miss Blakenev. Jacques Tourneur's direction deftly keys the major premise of strange suspicions, while the motif of a wife submerged under the influence of an insane husband and her futility in trying to escape, is certain to catch attention of the women customers. Production mounting is A-calibre throughout.

Walt.

Destiny

Hollywood, Dec. 12.

Universal release of Roy William Neill production. Features Gloria Jean, Alan Curtis. Directed by Reginald Le Borg. Screenplay by Roy Chanslor and Ernest Pascal; camera, George Robinson, Paul Ivano; editor, Paul Landers; asst. director, Seward Webb. Previewed projection room, Nov. 30, '44. Running time, **65 MINS.**

Jane	Gloria Jean
Cliff	Alan Curtis
Clem	Frank Craven
Betty	Grace McDonald
Phyllis	Vivian Austin
Sam	Frank Fenton
Marie	Minna Gombell

This is a regulation drama with psychological twist and sufficient suspense to carry through the regular bookings as a supporting attraction.

Last year, Universal made "Flesh and Fantasy" through combining of several dramatic episodes. When it got to the editing stages, studio found one episode with Gloria Jean and Alan Curtis could not be included. As a result, the footage was held out and revamped and enlarged story devised to salvage the sequence. Result is "Destiny."

Original episode forced out in editing of "Fantasy" ran about 30 minutes. This is retained in toto, with a half hour tacked on the front end, and about five minutes at the finish to provide happy ending. Overall result displays an excellent job of recouping otherwise lost footage and production costs.

Added first half discloses Curtis as a convict and fugitive from the law taking a bum rap on prison sentence and an innocent victim of the holdup which had him racing to the back country to elude the law. Hateful and suspicious of everyone and everything, he lands at the farm of blind Miss Jean and her kindly father, Frank Craven. Despite the hospitality and his inability to understand the girl's intuition on things going on around her, Curtis steals money and an heirloom necklace for departure, but girl's sincerity makes him stick around for reformation treatment, including sacrifice of his liberty by taking Craven into town for medical treatment following gun accident. But Curtis is freed of charges for clinch with the girl.

Miss Jean does well in her portrayal of the blind girl in the country, with Curtis clicking as the criminal fugitive. Good support is provided by Craven, Grace McDonald, Vivian Austin and Minna Gombell. Reginald Le Borg's direction of the added footage hits a fast pace, and adequately ties to the episode originally made by Julien Duvivier.

Walt.

Carolina Blues

(MUSICAL)

Columbia release of Samuel Bischoff production. Stars Kay Kyser, Ann Miller, Victor Moore; features Jeff Donnell, Ish Kabibble (M. A. Bogue), Georgia Carroll, Harry Babbitt, Sully Mason, Diane Pendleton and Kyser's Band. Directed by Leigh Jason. Screenplay, Joseph Hoffman and Al Martin from original by M. M. Musselman and Kenneth Earl; songs, Jule Styne, Sammy Cahn, Dudley Brooks, Walter Bullock; editor, James Sweeney; camera, George Kelley. At Loew's State, N. Y., week of Dec. 7, '44. Running time, **81 MINS.**

Kay Kyser	Kay Kyser
Julie Carver	Ann Miller
Phineas J. Carver	Victor Moore
Eliott Carver	
Hiram Carver	
Horatio Carver	
Aunt Martha Carver	
Aunt Minerva Carver	
Charlotte Barton	Jeff Donnell
Tom Gordon	Howard Freeman
Georgia Carroll	Georgia Carroll
Ish Kabibble	M. A. Bogue
Harry Babbitt	Harry Babbitt
Sully Mason	Sully Mason
Diana	Diane Pendleton
Roland Frisby	Robert Williams
Skinny	Doodles Weaver
Maisie	Dorothea Kent
Cab Driver	Frank Orth
Eddie	Eddie Acuff

Harold Nicholas
The Cristianis
The Layson Brothers
The Four Step Brothers
Kay Kyser's Band

Fairly diverting musical, starring Kay Kyser, Ann Miller and Victor Moore, should be a natural as solo feature for vaudfilm houses and top rung fare for duals. For a modest budgeter it zips along, aided by plenty of sock vaude specialties.

Kyser and musicrew play returners from USO-Camp Shows tour who make bondshow appearance at war plant. Moore, poor relation of plant owner, inveigles Ann Miller, his daughter, into show as band soloist when Georgia Carroll, regular warbler, decides to quit for matrimony. Although gal clicks, Kyser burns at deception, figuring she's just a stage-struck socialite. But it all winds up okay, with Kyser and Miss Miller on the romantic end.

Kyser plays himself throughout. He and his bandsmen get in their licks and are solid, as usual. Miss Miller sings and dances neatly, while Moore gets as much comedy as part allows as the phoney tycoon. Also in trick shot essays his wealthy relatives, doing males and dames, for comic interlude. Jeff O'Donnell also contributes comedy as the band's publicist, while Miss Carroll (Mrs. Kyser in real life), Sully Mason, Harry Babbitt, Diane Pendleton and Robert Williams also do well in support.

Film is studded with four good tunes, of which "Thinkin' About the Wabash" and "There Goes That Song Again" are standouts. Another one, "Mr. Beebe," satire on the well-dressed reporter, is worked up for sock production number. Harold Nicholas and Four Step Bros. sock across nifty dance routines, and Cristianis, acrobatic troupe, give good account in bondshow sequence. Screenplay by Joseph Hoffman and Al Martin is timely and moves along under Leigh Jason's direction. Camera work by George Kelley also standout. *Edba.*

The Falcon in Hollywood

Hollywood, Dec. 12.

RKO release of Maurice Geraghty production; executive producer, Sid Rogell. Features Tom Conway. Directed by Gordon Doublas. Screenplay by Gerald Geraghty, based on character created by Michael Arlen; camera, Nicholas Musuraca; editor, Gene Milford; asst. director, James Casey. Tradeshown in L.A., Nov. 28, '44. Running time, 66 MINS.

The Falcon	Tom Conway
Peggy Callahan	Barbara Hale
Lili D'Allio	Rita Corday
Roxanna	Jean Brooks
Billie	Vida Ann Borg
Alec Hoffman	Constantin Shayne
Martin Dwyer	John Abbott
Inspector McBride	Emory Parnell
Lt. Higgins	Frank Jenks
Louie	Sheldon Leonard
Perc Saunders	Tom Burton
Ed Johnson	Walter Soderling

"Falcon in Hollywood" follows the familiar pattern in the adventures of the cinematic amateur sleuth with latter arriving in Los Angeles for his usual vacation, quickly becoming involved in a murder mystery inside a film studio. Picture carries good suspense of type, and will prove to be an okay supporter for the duals.

Conway, as the Falson, is picked up at the racetrack to introduce assorted characters, including two film actresses. Locale quickly shifts to the studio, where the sleuth stumbles on body of a leading man in corner of a dark stage. Finger of suspicion is pointed at several characters to inject the necessary audience reaction, with Conway threading his way through to finally tab the murderer.

Conway delivers his usual characterization of the amateur detective, getting adequate support from Barbara Hale, Rita Corday, Jean Brooks, Vida Ann Borg, Constantin Shayne, Sheldon Leonard, Emory Parnell and Frank Jenks.

Studio locale assisted in keeping down negative costs, but again gives film audiences a quick tour of a movie lot for added interest. Direction by Gordon Douglas maintains good pace and suspense.   *Walt.*

The Unwritten Code

Columbia release of Sam White production. Stars Ann Savage, Tom Neal; features Roland Varno, Howard Freeman. Directed by Herman Rotsten from screenplay by Leslie T. White, Charles Kenyon, based on story by Kenyon and Robert Wilmot; camera, Burnett Guffey; editor, Gene Havlick. At Brooklyn Strand, week Dec. 7, '44, dual. Running time, 61 MINS.

Mary Lee Norris..............Ann Savage
Sergeant Terry Hunter............Tom Neal
Corporal Karl Richter.......Roland Varno
Mr. Norris...............Howard Freeman
Mrs. Norris.............Mary Currier
Willie Norris................Bobby Larson
Dutchy Schultz.............Teddy Infuhr
Heinrich Krause...........Otto Reichow
Schultz....................Fred Essler
Luedtke..............Frederick Giermann
Kunze....................Tom Holland
Ulrich.................Phil Van Zandt
Schroeder.................Carl Ekberg
Sheriff...................Alan Bridge

This incredulous tale of Nazi intrigue falls flat due to poorly developed plotting and overall production. Strictly a dualer.

Yarn deals with a Nazi military officer who gets into the U.S. by taking the identity of a British officer whom he killed. Being treated as a wounded ally, he plans the escape of German prisoners. How he is foiled is hardly believable.

Ann Savage and Tom Neal, as a student nurse and Army sergeant, supply the love interest. Roland Varno does a fairly good job as the Nazi who is finally killed by armed guards at the prison camp.   *Sten.*

When the Lights Go On Again
(SONGS)

PRC release of Leon Fromkess production. Stars Jimmy Lydon, Barbara Belden; features Regis Toomey, George Cleveland, Grant Mitchell, Dorothy Peterson. Directed by William K. Howard. Screenplay by Milton Lazarus from original by Frank Craven. Songs by Eddie Seiler, Sol Marcus, Ben Benjamin and Alec Morrison; camera, Ira Morgan; editor, Don Hayes. At Brooklyn Paramount, week of Dec. 7, '44, dual. Running time, 76 MINS.

Ted Benson.................Jimmy Lydon
Arline Cary................Barbara Belden
Mr. Benson.................Grant Mitchell
Mrs. Benson...............Dorothy Peterson
Bill Regan.................Regis Toomey
Pat Benson.................George Cleveland
Tom Cary...................Harry Shannon
Joey Benson................Warren Mills
First Marine..............Williard Jielson
Second Marine.................Jac Turrell
Third Marine...................Bill Nelson
Medical Officer............Larry Thompson
Middle Aged Woman......Myrtle Ferguson
Old Panhandler..............Emmett Lynn
Peggy.......................Jill Browning
Barbara....................Roberta Carlin
Jim Bagby....................Guy Blake
First Farmer.................Al Stewart
Second Farmer.............Elmo Lincoln
Engineer..................Joseph Crehan

"When the Lights Go On Again" treats a problem that will be faced by hundreds of families during the war and afterwards in an entertaining and convincing manner. Strong dualer for all situations.

Coming from little PRC, this effort is especially noteworthy. Leon Fromkess, hasn't spared either the budget or personnel, apparently, in his endeavor to give this picture

the treatment it deserves. He has embellished a story by Frank Craven with a fine screenplay by Milton Lazarus: two good songs, a pop tune from which this film gets its title, and the newie, "Living a Dream"; a fairly good cast, including newcomer Barbara Belden, from whom much should be heard in the future, and some topflight production values that help sustain audience interest throughout.

Picture, told in flashback, unreels in categorical fashion; first, the marine suffering from shellshock is guided homeward by a reporter; then, while he is sleeping on the train, his prewar life is depicted, and finally how his family and environment help him beat his illness.

Jimmy Lydon, as the Marine, performs his role with understanding, although with a stiltedness at times. Miss Belden, as his gal and wife, enacts her part surprisingly well for an actress who hasn't been around much in pictures before. Others in the cast include Regis Toomey, as the reporter; Grant Mitchell, George Cleveland and Dorothy Peterson.

Settings, while little better than average, are more than adequate, as is the photography by cameraman Ira Morgan.   *Sten.*

Miniature Reviews

"Tomorrow the World" (UA-Cowan). Fredric March-Betty Field-Skippy Homeier filmization of Broadway hit; sock b.o.

"Here Come the Waves" (Musical) (Par). Tiptop Bing Crosby - Betty Hutton - Sonny Tufts starrer, with socko songs.

"I'll Be Seeing You" (UA). Tasteful, timely romantic drama; stars Ginger Rogers-Joseph Cotten-Shirley Temple.

"Can't Help Singing" (Songs, Color) (U). Deanna Durbin filmusical, with fine Kern score, due for top biz.

"Practically Yours" (Par). Claudette Colbert and Fred MacMurray, in Mitchell Leisen comedy, a parlay for strong b.o.

"Gentle Annie" (M-G). A western about train robbers which should do from moderate to good biz. A dualer.

"Lake Placid Serenade" (Rep). Lavish ice-romance; will do good biz as solo in certain situations.

"Between Two Worlds" (M-G). Continuation of "Dr. Kildare" series, starring Van Johnson. O.k. as top dualer.

"The Fighting Lady" (Color) 20th). One of the best documentaries of the war, gripping, exciting, and solid boxoffice.

"Double Exposure" (Par). Breezy program drama for good support in the regular duals.

"The Missing Juror" (Col). Plausible murder - mystery; good lower-rung dualer.

"House of Frankenstein" (U). Good horror meller, latest entry in the profitable series, for dials.

"The Mummy's Curse" (U). Ghoulish goings-on in the Cajun country. Strong for dual support.

"Dangerous Passage" (Par) Formula action meller geared for dual supporting spots.

Tomorrow the World

United Artists release of Lester Cowan production. Stars Fredric March, Betty Field; features Skippy Homeier, Agnes Moorehead. Directed by Leslie Fenton. Screenplay, Ring Lardner, Jr., and Leopold Atlas, from play of James Gow and Arnaud D'Usseau; editor, Ann Bauchens; camera, Henry Sharp. Previewed N. Y., Dec. 14, 44. Running time, 86 MINS.

Mike Frame................Fredric March
Leona Richards................Betty Field
Jessie...................Agnes Moorehead
Emil Bruckner............Skippy Homeier
Pat Frame..................Joan Carroll
Frieda....................Edit Angold
Stan....................Rudy Wissler
Ray.....................Boots Brown
Dennis..................Marvin Davis
Millie.............Patsy Ann Thompson
School Principal............Mary Newton
Mailman...................Tom Fadden

Reformation of Nazi youth, a problem forcefully projected in "Tomorrow the World" on Broadway a season ago, has been dealt with no less assiduously in Lester Cowan's screen presentation of the same story. "Tomorrow" as a picture is a harsh realization that such a problem exists and, as such, can scarcely be called the type film to which patrons will flock in droves for entertainment. Its grimness is too omniscient, too foreboding, but there's no denying it's a problem many will want to see unfolded. "Tomorrow" can thus hardly fail to achieve a good measure of boxoffice returns.

The play has been literally adapted, excepting, of course, for various situations whose scope could only be enlarged upon by the screen. It's a vivid story of a youngster brought to America from Germany, into the home of a college professor whose

philosophies have been governed by those of the boy's father, a well-known liberal killed by the Nazis because of his views.

The boy has been geared in the Nazi way, taught that his father had been a traitor to the Third Reich. Repudiation of the American concept and an attempt to inculcate Nazi fears into the minds of his American schoolfellows almost succeed. He would also break up the impending marriage between the professor and his Jewish fiancee, and this, too, is almost realized. But the mental distortion that prompts him almost to kill the prof's young daughter brings to a climax the boy's malfeasance. Then the sudden realization by the youngster of Nazism's fallacies.

"Tomorrow" is very objective in its treatment, and the authors believe, apparently, that all Nazi youth can be steered correctly, eventually. The authors are vague in their solution, but there's no doubt that, it's a solution that should be left untold for the present. It's somewhat different when one is dealing of fictional Nazi youth and the real thing. Time will dictate the proper course.

Fredric March and Betty Field are starred in the roles played originally by Ralph Bellamy and Shirley Booth, and both give dignity to the parts of the professor and his bride-to-be. But the main accolade must go to Skippy Homeier, as the young Nazi, in the characterization he created on Broadway for Theron Bamberger's legit production. Agnes Moorehead plays March's spinster sister, and she, too, gives a well-defined performance, as does the rest of the cast. Of the support Edit Angold, as the maid, repeats her stage role to advantage, while Joan Carroll is properly precocious as March's daughter.

Leslie Fenton establishes himself anew in Hollywood with this film, but this time as a director. The former actor, who became a British film director before joining the British Royal Navy—from which he was recently discharged—hasn't attempted to deviate from the original stageplay, and this was wise. There was very little that could have been improved upon over the original production. And "Tomorrow" as a pic should achieve a commensurate success—mainly because of one performance.   *Kahn.*

Here Come the Waves
(MUSICAL)

Paramount release of Mark Sandrich production, directed by Sandrich. Stars Bing Crosby, Betty Hutton, Sonny Tufts. Original screenplay, Allan Scott, Ken Englund. Zion Myers; songs, Johnny Mercer-Harold Arlen; music direction, Robt. E. Dolan; vocals, Jos. J. Lilley; music associate, Troy Sanders; dances, Danny Dare; camera, Chas. Lang, Gordon Jennings, Paul Lerpae; editor, Ellsworth Hoagland. Tradeshown N. Y. Dec. 15, '44. Running time, 99 MINS.

Johnny Cabot................Bing Crosby
Susie & Rosemary Allison....Betty Hutton
Windy.....................Sonny Tufts
Ruth.....................Ann Doran
Tex...................Gwen Crawford
Dorothy...................Noel Neill
Lieut. Townsend...........Catherine Craig
Isabel................Marjorie Henshaw
Band L...der.............Harry Barris
Ensign Kirk.................Mae Clarke
High Ranking Officer........Minor Watson
Double for Betty Hutton......Vera Marshe

A kinda corny title, "Here Come the Waves" manages to surmount the handle and emerges as a tiptop film. Presumably launched at a time when it was expedient to propagandize the WAVE movement, old tempus fugit and the film backlog situation have somewhat dated Mark Sandrich's production but not to the degree it's not b.o. For it is. "Here Come the Waves" has plenty to please all audiences.

Der Bingle, the effervescent Betty Hutton in a double role, and Sonny Tufts are an undeniable marquee and b.o. parlay. They play it across the board for a clean sweep.

Interspersed in Crosby's nifty

songalogy. Johnny Mercer-Harold Arlen have supplied a set of excellent songs, including a dandy novelty in "Accent-Tchu-ate the POS-itive"; two corking ballads in "Let's Take the Long Way Home" and "I Promise You," the latter as a duet with Betty Hutton playing the alter ego, and incidentally a song which seems a cinch to become as standard as Reginald de Koven's not dissimilarly titled "Oh Promise Me." Miss Hutton on her own hi-de-hos herself to a wow score with "There's a Fella in Poughkeepsie," while "Old Black Magic" is reprised in a delicious rib on Frank Sinatra.

Crosby is cast as the new pash crooner, and his mike-clutching stance, accented by the whinnying dames, leaves no secret as to whom Der Bingle refers. It's a dandy take-off on The Voice, but it's not harsh; in fact, it's a sympathetic salve for all out-of-service crooners. It's finally established that Crosby is allowed to enlist in the Navy (at first turned down for color blindness) but, because of Miss Hutton's wacky machinations, he's taken off active duty and given a specialist's rating in order to aid WAVE recruiting.

Miss Hutton plays both twins of a sister act, one her familiar zany self and the other a conservative twin sister, older by 12 minutes. The blonde is the hoyden; the darker is the more conservative and no bobbysox swooner like her madcap sister. Spurned, Crosby is intrigued by her, as against the swooning adulation of her sister. Sonny Tufts is the other guy, a pal who double-crosses and is crossed in the Quirt-Flagg tradition.

The show-within-a-show (since that's part of the WAVE recruiting technique) permits song-and-dance specialties by Crosby and Miss Hutton. The latter's yen for males introduces a scene, "If Waves Acted Like Sailors," which is a topical switch on an old legit revue scene, "If Women Played Poker Like Men." It's in this WAVEs show that Crosby and Tufts click with the rhythmic "Accent-Tchu-Ate the POSitive" along with "Promise You." "Long Way Home" is part of the romantic motivation, behind-the-scenes. Of course, being twins, the hoyden's bad deeds, in order to snafu her sister's honest romantic emotions, create the usual amount of misunderstandings through mistaken identities, but it all ends happily after a breezy 99 mins.

Producer-director Sandrich has kept the tale fluid and the pace accelerated. Scripters Allan Scott, Ken Englund and Zion Myers have supplied a basically good structure, punctuated by appropriately breezy banter, at which Crosby is a master, providing the chatter is in the groove. They do as good a job for The Groaner as does Carroll Carroll on the radio. Productionally, also, the two-ply Hutton personations are well done, a credit both to the camera and to Vera Marshe who, meritoriously, gets billing as the acting and photographic double for the star. The rest of the support is competent.

Abel.

I'll Be Seeing You

(ONE SONG)

United Artists release of Dore Schary production. Stars Ginger Rogers, Joseph Cotten, Shirley Temple; features Spring Byington, Tom Tully, Chill Wills, Dare Harris, Kenny Bowers. Directed by William Dieterle. Screenplay, Marion Parsonnet; based on radio play by Charles Martin; camera, Tony Gaudio; editor, William H. Ziegler; song, "I'll Be Seeing You," by Sammy Fain and Irving Kahal. Tradeshown in N. Y. Dec. 18, '44. Running time, **83 MINS.**

Mary Marshall ....Ginger Rogers
Zachary Morgan .... Joseph Cotten
Barbara Marshall ....Shirley Temple
Mrs. Marshall ....Spring Byington
Mr. Marshall ....Tom Tully
Swanson ....Chill Wills
Lieut. Bruce ....Dare Harris
Sailor on Train................Kenny Bowers

"I'll Be Seeing You" is a timely story about Christmas and a shell-shocked war vet. It ties up the immediate problem of the soldier psychiatric finding himself in civilian life with the perennial problem of a convict readjusting herself to society after paying her debt. A poignant, romantic drama, done with taste and honesty, and acted superbly, it is sure boxoffice.

A quietly moving, sensitive story about two misfits adapting themselves to the world and each other, the film has the right touch throughout, being never mawkish or cheap. A beautiful picture of smalltown life and an average family's problems, it tears the tear-ducts a bit but never too often. Essentially a fine femme pic, it can't miss.

The story concerns a girl on Christmas furlough from the state penitentiary, where she is serving a term for manslaughter, and an Army sergeant on furlough from the hospital where he is being treated as a neuro case. The sergeant got his shellshock after a bayonet wound in the South Pacific; the girl accidentally caused the death of her employer when she resisted his unsolicited advances.

They meet on a train, the girl going to visit relatives for the Xmas holiday, the soldier going anywhere on a 10-day leave at doctor's orders to prove that he can mingle with people again. The girl invites the soldier to her aunt's home and, in the 10-day leave both have, the soldier strives successfully to shake off his nervous ailment while falling in love with the girl. The latter, also in love with him, and trying to help the soldier in his rehabilitation, keeps her prison secret from him. When he finds out, there is a crisis, but it settles as the two renew their love again for the future when both will be free.

What distinguishes the story is its general honesty and lack of obvious histrionics, the many fine touches of family life and the performance of the cast. There are many memorable moments, as the Christmas scene when the plum pudding is served and the family sings carols; the scene in the kitchen when niece and aunt are discussing society's reactions to wrongdoers; the scene when the women buy a dress which the girl can wear only once, and finally the bedroom scene when the soldier fights off for the last time his recurring war fright.

Joseph Cotten gives a fine portrait of the slightly befuddled soldier slowly coming out of his semi-stupor under the influence of a sympathetic family, while Ginger Rogers is again a noteworthy dramatic actress as the embittered but resigned young woman struggling for a dream she once thought forever lost. Shirley Temple is a charming study of the eager awareness of a 17-year-old. And Spring Byington and Tom Tully give well-etched, human performances as understanding, sympathetic parents.

William Dieterle's direction is a little slow sometimes, but suitable to the film's mood. Dialog is simple and natural, and performances honest.

Bron.

Can't Help Singing

(MUSICAL; COLOR)

Hollywood, Dec. 14.

Universal release of Felix Jackson (Frank Shaw) production. Stars Deanna Durbin; features Robert Paige, Akim Tamiroff. Directed by Frank Ryan. Screenplay, Lewis R. Foster and Ryan; story, John Klorer and Leo Townsend, based on "Girl of the Overland Trail," by Samuel J. and Curtis B. Warshawsky; camera, Woody Bredell, W. Howard Greene; editor, Ted J. Kent; asst. director, William Holland; songs, Jerome Kern, E. Y. Harburg; score and direction, H. J. Salter; orchestrations, Frank Skinner. Previewed at Carthay Circle, Dec. 13, '44. Running time, **89 MINS.**

Caroline.........................Deanna Durbin
Lawlor...............................Robert Paige
Gregory............................Akim Tamiroff
Latham...............................David Bruce
Koppa.............................Leonid Kinskey
Senator Frost........................Ray Collins
Miss McLean......................June Vincent
Sad Sam...........................Andrew Tombes
Carstairs.........................Thomas Gomez
Aunt Cissy........................Clara Blandick
Bigelow................................Olin Howlin
Marshal.........................George Cleveland

"Can't Help Singing" is a bright, colorful and gay filmusical, notable for the collection of new tunes by Jerome Kern and the fine scenic mounting accentuated by the Technicolor photography. It's Deanna Durbin's initial color starrer, and her first filmusical comedy vehicle. Picture rates as fine "escapist" entertainment to hit hefty profits in all runs and holdovers generally.

Kern's songs, with lyrics by E. Y. Harburg, add much strength to the picture. "More and More" and "Any Moment Now" will rise high in the popular disc and radio-played tunes, while the lively "Californ-I-Ay" and "Can't Help Singing" also have a chance for their novelty tempo.

Story deliberately unfolds as a light adventure romance in musical comedy technique. It's relaxing and diverting throughout, fine framework on which to set up the musical and production numbers, and to set off the gorgeous scenery of the Utah locations displayed by the Technicolor photography.

Picture is set in the 1850 era, opening in Washington to introduce Miss Durbin as the daughter of an influential senator who's determined to marry a cavalry officer. When the senator's influence ships the latter on quick notice to a California post, the girl follows but never quite catches up. After reaching a midwest river town, she joins a wagon train, meets up with adventurous Robert Paige, and eventually falls in love with him by the time the train reaches California.

Lavish and superb production numbers frequently punctuate the proceedings for display of the Kern songs with large crowds of colorfully-costumed extras being used with apparent abandon by the production office. Frank Ryan's direction is okay, while the script inclines to loosely-assembled sequences at times, and a liberal amount of corn and slapstick is sown along the route.

Miss Durbin, most photogenic for the color cameras, excellently handles the top assignment, providing lightness to her role throughout. Paige clicks in role opposite the star, while Akim Tamiroff and Leonid Kinskey romp continually as a couple of Russian comedians with routines always on the broad slapstick side. Andrew Tombes, David Bruce, Thomas Gomez, Olin Howlin and George Cleveland provide support in brief sequences.

Walt.

Practically Yours

(ONE SONG)

Paramount release of Mitchell Leisen production. Stars Claudette Colbert, Fred MacMurray; features Gil Lamb, Robert Benchley, Cecil Kellaway. Directed by Leisen. Screenplay by Norman Krasna; camera, Charles Lang, Jr., Gordon Jennings, J. Devereaux Jennings, Farciot Edouart; music, Victor Young; song, Sam Coslow; editor, Doane Harrison. Previewed N. Y., Dec. 14, '44. Running time, **90 MINS.**

Peggy Martin....................Claudette Colbert
Lt. (S.G.) Daniel Bellamy.Fred MacMurray
Albert Beagell.............................Gil Lamb
Marvin P. Meglin...............Cecil Kellaway
Judge Simpson..................Robert Benchley
Commander Harpe.................Tom Powers
Musical Comedy Star.............Jane Frazee
Elen Macy..................Rosemary De Camp
Mrs. Meglin.....................Isabel Randolph
La Crosse......................Mikhail Rasumny

Paramount's battery of Claudette Colbert and Fred MacMurray, with Mitchell Leisen producing and directing, makes "Practically Yours" practically a boxoffice cinch.

Pic is deft combination of chuckles and heart-throbs, plus a sock patriotic theme that can't miss. Story has MacMurray brought back from the Pacific after a one-in-a-million escape when he put his Navy plane into a suicide dive to destroy a Jap carrier. Hero, in a radioed farewell to crew members of an accompanying bomber, tells of his devotion for "Peggy," in reality his pet dog. But the folks back home, who hear the farewell speech via radio transcription, jump to conclusion a former coworker (Miss Colbert) with MacMurray in a N. Y. business office, was in his thoughts when he put his ship into the "suicide" dive.

Well-meaning friends succeed in hooking the hero into marriage plans, and because they're so much in the public eye, the couple decides to keep up the pretense which, of course, soon becomes the real thing. Situash is well-handled throughout and works for a full crop of laughs. Cecil Kellaway, as the millionaire employer who "adopts" the couple; Isabel Randolph, his wife, and Gil Lamb, simp office worker, kick in neat support along with Robert Benchley, who handles his minute assignment okay.

Particularly worthy bit is that by Mikhail Rasumny, as an arty photog trying to instill some inspiration into MacMurray and Miss Colbert while he snaps a "perfect lovers" pose. Film's only song, "I Knew It Would Be This Way," is a pleasant product from Sam Coslow, handled nicely by Jane Frazee in a nitery sequence, her only appearance. Rosemary De Camp, as the wife of a flyer who didn't come back, also deserves favorable mention.

Donn.

Gentle Annie

Metro release of Robert Sisk production. Features James Craig, Donna Reed, Marjorie Main, Henry Morgan, Paul Langton, Barton MacLane, John Philliber and Morris Ankrum. Directed by Andrew Marton. Based upon novel of same name by MacKinlay Kantor; adaptation, Lawrence Hazard; editor, Chester W. Schaeffer; camera, Charles Salerno. Previewed in N. Y. Dec. 13, '44. Running time, **80 MINS.**

Lloyd Richland.....................James Craig
Mary Lingen.........................Donna Reed
Annie Goss.........................Marjorie Main
Cottonwood Goss................Henry Morgan
Violet Goss.........................Paul Langton
Sheriff Tatum..................Barton MacLane
Barrow...............................John Philliber
Gansby.............................Morris Ankrum

In the western category, "Gentle Annie" has received sufficient production values from Robert Sisk, plus good performances, to merit favorable audience reaction. Picture is not an upper-bracketer but should do from moderate to good business on the duals.

Locale is the Oklahoma territory and the time 1901. Action centers around two brothers of the school the James boys made famous and the pioneering mother with whom they live on a ramshackle ranch. Because they want to return to Missouri, from which they migrated, the trio hold up a train, but while suspicion points strongly to them, a U. S. marshal, whom they befriend by giving him shelter in their home, is loath to believe they're guilty. The circumstances leading up to evidence that the brothers and their mother committed the holdup are somewhat implausible, while also not according to Hoyle is the chance the marshal takes in letting the two boys escape after their mother has been shot. He permits them to aid in a gunfight with a local sheriff who's a crook, one of the brothers being killed in the battle. Then the marshal, instead of taking the other brother into custody, puts him on a train for a nearby point where, he tells him, a deputy will be waiting to arrest him. A waitress who quits her job and is left stranded, also being taken into the home of the train robbers, fits into the picture a bit awkwardly for romantic interest.

Title of "Gentle Annie" relates to Annie Goss, the mother, played feelingly and with warmth by Marjorie Main. She could have been dealt less dialog, however. There are some stretches where she nearly talks herself to death. James Craig gives a smooth performance as the U. S. marshal, while Donna Reed plays the romantic interest opposite him. She's okay. The two brothers are Henry Morgan and Paul Langton, good types for the roles. Barton MacLane provides suitable menace as the sheriff. John Philliber (recently deceased) as an itinerant photographer who likes his grog, is amusing in a lesser role.

Camera job by Charles Salerno is very good. *Char.*

Lake Placid Serenade
(MUSICAL)

Republic release of Harry Grey production. Stars Vera Hruba Ralston; features Eugene Pallette, Vera Vague, Robert Livingston, Stephanie Bachelor. Directed by Steve Sekely. Screenplay, Dick Irving Hylar and Doris Gilbert, from original by Frederick Kohner; camera, John Alton; editor, Arthur Roberts; song, "Winter Wonderland," by Bernard and Smith. Previewed N. Y., Dec. 18, '44. Running time, **85 MINS.**

Vera Haschek..........Vera Hruba Ralston
Carl Cermak..........Eugene Pallette
Countess..........Vera Vague
Paul Jordan..........Robert Livingston
Irene..........Stephanie Bachelor
Webb..........Walter Catlett
Haschek..........Lloyd Corrigan
Susan..........Ruth Terry
Jiggers..........William Frawley
Walter Benda..........John Litel
Mayor..........Ludwig Stossel
Club President..........Andrew Tombes

Ray Noble and Orchestra, Harry Owens' Royal Hawaiians, McGowan & Mack, Twinkle Watts, The Merry Meisters, Roy Rogers.

Republic has a nifty vehicle in "Lake Placid Serenade." Film is a lavish display of spectacle, specialty and girls with apparently the whole studio roster thrown into an essentially simple Cinderella story of a lovely immigrant skater who meets her dream prince. A routine plot and some very feeble humor are well offset by rich production numbers, some fine outdoor settings and an attractive cast. Pic, with its ice-skating background, is a timely seasonal and holiday film, and will do good biz.

Studio didn't stint on this one. There's an abundance of everything and sometimes a little too much. For what should be subordinate comic relief to a boy-and-girl romance, Republic has thrown in five comedians in Vera Vague, Walter Catlett, William Frawley, Andrew Tombes and Eugene Pallette, with only the last-named genuinely amusing and the other four (Tombes is in for only a brief sequence) practically wasted on stale gags and corny situations.

In a bewilderment of musical sequences, ice ballets and gaudy production numbers, studio has included besides the legitimate ice specialties, the music of Ray Noble and his orchestra and Harry Owens and His Royal Hawaiians. It even drags in Roy Rogers, the cowboy star, for a song sequence. Surprisingly enough, the Cinderella story stands out in spite of all the fulsome display.

This is entirely due to the appeal of the film's star, Vera Hruba Ralston, a Czech professional skating star before she became a film actress. She's in her natural element here in an ice-romance. Lovely to look at, beautifully built, and a graceful figure on skates, Miss Ralston makes an appealing heroine, especially when clad in the quaint peasant costumes of her native land. A winsome quality heightens her Cinderella role. A brilliant performance on skates polishes film off to make it essentially a star vehicle for her.

Story concerns a Czech village maid who wins the national skate championship and is sent to America to represent her country at a Lake Placid carnival. Outbreak of war prevents her return, but discovery of a rich, lost uncle (Pallette) keeps her from being stranded. When a love affair develops between skater and her uncle's junior partner, and girl discovers the man is practically engaged to her cousin, girl runs off, joining an ice-show under an assumed name to support herself. The man finally finds her, the Cinderella legend even being duplicated down to a lost shoe, to end film happily.

Plot gives ample opportunity for skate sequences and spectacles. Opening scenes in a snow-covered Czech village have a charming, story-book appeal. American scenes at Placid, and on tour with the ice-show, are gaudy and resplendent. Lavish production numbers follow each other in profusion, a Showboat number, a Hawaiian number and one with girl cadets drilling on ice, being standouts. The specialty numbers include one with a new twist, an Apache dance act on skates which McGowan & Mack carry off with great style. Miss Ralston's several skate appearances are all firstrate, with one sequence, skated to a tiny musicbox accompaniment, particularly appealing.

Robert Livingston fills the romantic role satisfactorily, Stephanie Bachelor is attractive as the "other woman," and Pallette has a bluff, human quality as sympathetic uncle. John Litel has good brief bit as a consul, and Lloyd Corrigan is genial as the Czech godfather. The Vague-Frawley-Catlett trio bounce in and out of the film as an iceshow producing combine, stumbling over each other's feeble lines. Roy Rogers appears briefly as King of Placid's New Year's celebration to sing "Winter Wonderland." Music varies through film from Czech band marches to American swing, and is both profuse and attractive. Direction is sprightly, to keep romance and spectacle at swift pace and good balance. *Bron.*

Between Two Women
(ONE SONG)

Metro release of Willis Goldbeck production, directed by Goldbeck. Stars Van Johnson; features Lionel Barrymore, Gloria De Haven. Screenplay, Harry Ruskin, based on characters created by Max Brand; camera, Harold Rosson; music, David Snell; editor, Adrienne Fazan. Tradeshown N. Y., Dec. 5, '44. Running time, **83 MINS.**

Dr. "Red" Adams..........Van Johnson
Dr. Leonard Gillespie..........Lionel Barrymore
Edna..........Gloria De Haven
Tobey..........Keenan Wynn
Ruth Edley..........Marilyn Maxwell
Molly Byrd..........Alma Kruger
Sally..........Marie Blake
Dr. Lee..........Keye Luke
Nurse Parker..........Nell Craig
Nurse Morgan..........Edna Holland
Marian..........Lorraine Miller
Dr. Walter Carew..........Walter Kingsford
Eddie Smith..........Tom Trout
Nurse Thorsen..........Shirley Patterson

Despite the currently "hot" Van Johnson in the top acting spot, with Lionel Barrymore as marquee assistance, "Between Two Women" is a weakie on its own. It will draw moderate results in the duals.

Film is an offshoot of the "Dr. Kildare" series, with some of the original "Kildare" characters, played by Barrymore, Alma Kruger and Marie Blake, participating in the story. Weakness, however, lies in the yarn, which fails to achieve impact or suspense.

The two women of the title are Gloria de Haven, as a night club singer, who becomes a patient when she faints of malnutrition, and Marilyn Maxwell, wealthy deb who aims at having Van Johnson (Dr. Adams) as her husband. Latter eschews marriage, figuring he's not ready yet. Jealousy angle enters when the deb feels the medico is on the make for the singer. But when he's unable to trace the cause of her psychiatric disturbance, itself responsible for her self-starvation, the deb uses her feminine wiles to worm it out of the singer's friends. That helps the doc cure her.

Meanwhile, another story tangent concerns Marie Blake, as the hospital operator who becomes critically ill and needs a serious operation, calling for a specialist. Because of the emergency, Johnson himself wields the scalpel and saves the girl. Entire development of the switchboard operator phase impresses as though the original plot couldn't fill the running time; actually, it has no bearing on the main theme.

Johnson isn't too much at home as the young medic, although few femmes will find fault with his bedside manner. Barrymore turns in his usual job as the hospital head. He's in a wheelchair throughout. Miss DeHaven handles one song, "I'm In the Mood for Love," an oldie, quite well and is okay generally. Miss Maxwell reveals a potent dash of s.a. and, while her part's not too forte, she does the best under the circumstances. She should become b.o. Keenan Wynn, as a nitery m.c., Walter Kingsford, as a medic, Alma Kruger as the chief nurse, and Keye Luke as an interne, are strong support. Marie Blake overdoes the ailing phone gal role.

Production levels are good, although the direction, except in the operating room scenes, isn't too zippy. *Merr.*

The Fighting Lady
(Documentary)
(COLOR)

20th-Fox release of Louis de Rochemont production. True story in Technicolor from 16-millimeter original print. Photographed in combat zones by U. S. Navy under supervision of Edward J. Stiechen and Lieut.-Commander Dwight Long; narration written by John Stuary Martin; narrator, Lieut. Robert Taylor. Tradeshown N. Y., Dec. 15, '44. Running time, **61 MINS.**

This hits a new high as a documentary, one that will stack up with many Hollywood-produced fictional stories. Running time prevents the picture from playing solo in many spots, but even in dual setups it should of a real winner and highly profitable to 20th. "The Fighting Lady" will measure up to all advance plugging given it by an exhibitor, and has a ready-made audience because of numerous Navy men spotted by the camera.

Film is compiled from a vast amount of U. S. Navy footage, with Louis de Rochemont, formerly March of Time producer, turning in a whale of a job on his first feature producer assignment. Actually the film was started by Lieut.-Commander Dwight Long, who will be recalled as the cameraman who sailed around the world in a small boat to get a cinema travel story. When he went into the Navy, his first assignment in the Bureau of Aeronautics was to follow the activities of an airplane carrier. From a small crew, the story became so large the group was expanded to 10 men. 20th-Fox was successful in obtaining the Navy story when finished, and de Rochemont was assigned to whipping it into shape for theatre use.

"The Fighting Lady" in the picture is a typical, new streamlined carrier of the U. S. Navy. Yarn traces its career from the time a full complement of planes are flown out to the huge ship until it has gone through the fierce attacks on Truk and Marianas. While the offensive against the Marianas, when 360 Jap planes and 17 Nip warships have been sunk, easily is the highlight there are so many graphic attack closeups (taken from fighter and bomber planes) that there never is a dull moment.

Producer de Rochemont has maintained skillful pace, shifting easily from the noisy and exciting battle events to episodes concerning the men aboard the carrier. The typical happenings in the lives of 3,000 men on the ship are picked up, often in closeup, with graphic results. How planes come in and take off are captured by the Navy lensmen, with actual crackups on the flattop when the fighting planes come back crippled from air offensives shown in full realism. Every one of the exciting moments comes out doubly effective in color, all material having been originally photographed in 16-mm. and then blown up to 35-mm.

This is perhaps the first documentary not using any miniature effects, only a couple of drawings and maps being employed to keep the audience on keel as to the locale where the carrier is fighting. The scenes picked up by the camera from fighting planes are uncanny, the scenes being photoed automatically no matter what happens to the ship's pilot. One remarkable shot shows a Zero plane roaring towards the carrier, reflection of the blazing enemy plane being seen before it actually plunges into the water.

Another thrilling episode comes when the carrier is attacked by a big bunch of Jap planes, and successfully wards off the onslaught. One gripping moment shows a torpedo plane coming head-on but plunging in flames on the opposite side of the ship after failing to launch its deadly charge.

Attacks on Kwajalein in the Marshall Islands, Guam, Truk and Marianas are covered, last-named being standout because this is where the U. S. found the Imperial Japanese Battle Fleet and nearly wiped it out.

Spoken narrative is deftly done by Lieut. Robert Taylor, now in the U.S. Navy. There is hardly a spoken word outside of his description of what's transpiring, yet one hardly realizes that he is not seeing a regularly produced feature. A few background noises and voices are heard, but so well put on the sound track that they sound natural. John Stuart Martin's written narration is aces. And standing out above all is the superb camera job done by the Navy photographers. *Wear.*

Double Exposure
Hollywood, Dec. 16.

Paramount release of Pine-Thomas production. Stars Chester Morris and Nancy Kelly. Directed by William Berke. Screenplay, Winston Miller and Maxwell Shane; original, Ralph Graves and Miller; camera, Fred Jackman, Jr.; editor, Henry Adams. Tradeshown L. A. Dec. 15, '44. Running time, **68 MINS.**

Larry Burke..........Chester Morris
Pat Marvin..........Nancy Kelly
Ben Scribner..........Phillip Terry
Dolores Tucker..........Jane Farrar
James B. Turlock..........Richard Gaines
Sonny Tucker..........Charles Arnt
Smitty..........Claire Rochelle
Mavis..........Roma Aldrich

"Double Exposure" is a light drama of the adventures of news photographers working for the illustrated weeklies. It's a fairly breezy affair, unfolding at the fast clip which characterizes virtually all of the Pine-Thomas product. Picture will hold up as a good program entry for the regular houses, and provide strong support in the dual situations.

Chester Morris is editor of the photo weekly, importing Nancy Kelly from the midwest on impression she's a man. While Morris starts romancing for pair to fall in love, her smalltown boy friend arrives and is introduced as her brother to develop the triangle. Girl gets some exclusive shots for the magazine and becomes a suspect in a murder mystery, going to jail despite efforts of Morris to spring her. He finally tabs the murderer through faking a picture to force a confession. The former boy friend is conveniently disposed of through marriage to another.

Morris and Miss Kelly handle the lead assignments in good style, getting okay support from Phillip Terry, Richard Gaines, Charles Arndt and Jane Farrar. Breezy direction by William Berke keeps proceedings moving at a fast tempo. *Walt.*

The Missing Juror

Columbia release of Wallace MacDonald production. Features Jim Bannon. Janis Carter, George Macready and Jean Stevens. Directed by Oscar Boetticher, Jr. Screenplay, Charles O'Neal; original, Leon Abrams and Richard Hill Wilkinson; camera, L.W. O'Connell; editor, Paul Borofsky. At Fox, Brooklyn, N.Y. Dec. 15, '44. dual. Running time, 66 MINS.

Joe Keats	Jim Bannon
Alice Hill	Janis Carter
Harry Wharton	
Jerome Bentley	George Macready
Tex	Jean Stevens
Willard Apple	Joseph Crehan
Marcy	Carole Mathews
Inspector Davis	Cliff Clark
Cahan	Edmund Cobb
Cullie	Mike Mazurki
George Sasbo	George Lloyd

While running in the conventional vein of mystery melodrama, "The Missing Juror" has sufficient suspense as well as logical story development to make it interesting. Direction is sensible and cast is satisfactory for an okay lower-case dualer.

Plot deals with a phantom killer who has murdered six members of a jury that once wrongly convicted a man of murder. Fact that the convicted man burned to death in an asylum instead of the chair doesn't seem to deter the mystery-murderer from taking vengeance on the jurors. A newspaperman interests himself in the case when the police are baffled. Suspecting that balance of jury will get theirs next, reporter trails them and eventually unravels the mystery. The convicted man hadn't died at all, but having killed the jury's foreman instead and making police believe the foreman's charred body was his, he was at liberty to wreak his mad vengeance on balance of jury. Switch isn't revealed till final scene for effective twist. Film is swift enough and dialog is good. Jim Bannon, ex-radio announcer, fills role of inquiring reporter adequately, and George Macready carries sufficient menace and mystery as the killer. Joseph Crehan is good as the city editor who doubts Bannon's hunches, while Janis Carter and Jean Stevens are attractive as girl friend and secretary.

Bron.

House of Frankenstein

Hollywood, Dec. 15.

Universal release of Paul Malvern production. Stars Boris Karloff, Lon Chaney. Directed by Erle Kenton. Screenplay by Edward T. Lowe, based on story by Curt Siodmak; camera, George Robinson; editor, Philip Cahn; special photography, John C. Fulton; asst. director, William C. Tummel. Previewed Dec. 14, '44. Running time, 70 MINS.

Doctor Niemann	Boris Karloff
Daniel	J. Carrol Naish
Larry Talbot	Lon Chaney
Dracula	John Carradine
Rita	Anne Gwynne
Carl Hussman	Peter Coe
Arnz	Lionel Atwill
Lampini	George Zucco
Ilonka	Elena Verdugo
Russman	Sig Ruman
Fejos	William Edmunds
Toberman	Charles Miller
Muller	Philip Van Zandt
Hertz	Julius Tannen
Meier	Hans Herbert
Born	Dick Dickinson
Gerlach	George Lynn
Strauss	Michael Mark
Hoffman	Olaf Hytten
Ullman	Frank Reicher
Dr. Geissler	Brandon Hurst
Monster	Glenn Strange

Frankenstein's Monster, Dracula, and the Wolf Man provide three-ply horror display in this chiller-diller meller. Aimed entirely for suspense and weird dramatics, picture is a solid entry for the attention of the horror addicts and will click for good biz generally where this type of product is popular.

Plot takes the usual twists of the suspense-chill series. Boris Karloff is the mad scientist with a penchant for delving into transplanting of brains. He escapes from prison with deformed J. Carroll Naish, takes over a traveling chamber of horror exhibit to release the skeleton of Dracula for brief forays among the populace, and then goes to the ruins of the Frankenstein castle to secure records of former transplanting research. Karloff releases the Monster and Wolf Man from icy graves, and sets up laboratories for operations. But the Wolf Man runs amuck around the countryside to arouse the citizens for a march on the castle, and destruction of the scientist and his collection of strange creatures—until the next in the series comes along.

Karloff is the usual menace in lead role of the scientist, with Naish particularly well cast as the hunchback. Lon Chaney is the Wolf Man, while John Carradine steps into the Dracula assignment. Erle Kenton generates plenty of creeps and suspense in the direction, while script has all the ingredients required of a horror show.

Walt.

The Mummy's Curse

(ONE SONG)

Universal release of Oliver Drake production. Stars Lon Chaney; features Peter Coe, Virginia Christine, Kay Harding. Directed by Leslie Goodwins; screenplay by Bernard Schubert; original story and adaptation be Leon Abrams and Dwight V. Babcock; camera, Virgil Miller; special photography by John P. Fulton; music and lyrics, Oliver Drake and Frank Orth. Previewed in New York Dec. 19, '44. Running time, 60 MINS.

Mummy	Lon Chaney
Ilzor	Peter Coe
Princess Ananka	Virginai Christine
Betty	Kay Harding
Halsey	Dennis Moore
Ragheb	Martin Kollech
Cajun Joe	Kurt Hutch
Pat Walsh	Addison Richard
Dr. Cooper	Holmes Herbert
Achilles	Charles Stevens
Sacristan	William Farnum
Goobie	Napoleon Simpson

This chiller is okay as dual support and lends itself to strong and novel exploitation. Although film deals in improbabilities and makes use of occasional cliches, suspense is maintained throughout.

Lon Chaney, in mummy wrapping, plays an Egyptian prince who long ago was buried alive as a punishment for trying to restore his gal, Virginia Christine, to life. They have been preserved in a somnolent state, and after having been transported to the Cajun country of Louisiana by archaeologists, horrify the countryside. Dennis Moore, a museum representative, finally succeeds in making the mummies safe enough to be merely museum pieces.

Cast passes muster in standard fashion.

Jose.

Dangerous Passage

Hollywood, Dec. 15.

Paramount release of Pine-Thomas production. Stars Robert Lowery and Phyllis Brooks. Directed by William Burke. Screenplay, Geoffrey Homes; camera, Fred Jackman, Jr.; editor, Henry Adams, Tradeshown L.A. Dec. 14, '44. Running time, 61 MINS.

Joe Beck	Robert Lowery
Nita Paxton	Phyllis Brooks
Daniel Bergstrom	Charles Arnt
Mike Zomano	Jack LaRue
Buck Harris	Victor Kilian
Captain Saul	Willaim Edmunds
Dawson	Alec Craig
Vaughn	John Eldredge

This is a program meller following usual dramatic formula, with fast action compensating somewhat for the usual situations. It's a supporter for the regular duals.

Plot picks up Robert Lowery at a Central American port, where he arrives from the interior to be advised by local attorney, Charles Arndt, that inheritance awaits him in Galveston. Grabbing a slow boat north, he finds the lawyer, Phyllis Brooks, and others aboard for strange and mysterious happenings and attempts on his life. Falling in love with the girl, he reneges on leaving the ship at a Mexican port, and finds the boat a victim of deliberate wrecking for insurance by the owners. He and girl stick to the shipwreck to be picked up by a scout plane for safe arrival and clinch in Galveston.

William Berke provides a fast pace to the direction. Cast is okay.

Walt.

La Guerra de Los Pasteles

("The War of the Pastries")

(MUSICAL)

(Mexican Made)

Clasa films release of Films Mundiales production. Stars Mapy Cortes; features Domingo Soler, Pedro Armendariz, Fernando Cortes. Directed by Emilio Gomez Mariel. Story, Celestino Gorosliza. At Belmont, N.Y., week of Dec. 11, '44. Running time, 83 MINS.

Suzette	Mapy Cortea
Alcalde	Domingo Soler
Antonio	Pedro Armendariz
Remoniel	Fernando Cortes
Hortensia	Delia Magana
Perico	Alfredo Varela
Mariata	Fanny Schiller

(In Spanish; no English Titles)

One of the better musicals to emanate from south of the border, this comedy, however, is headed for good business only in U. S. houses catering to Spanish-speaking audiences. There are no English subtitles.

Lines and situations that draw hearty laughs are sprinkled throughout the footage. Some neat photography, gay costumes, catchy music and better than average photography add much to the pic.

Yarn deals with two love stories and their complications: that of a baker's daughter (Mapy Cortes) with a lieutenant, who is opposed by the mayor of the town where her father has a bakery shop, and that of the baker with an old flame of the mayor's (Delia Magana), who is intent on capturing the mayor for herself.

Miss Cortes gives out with a topflight performance, and acting by remainder of the cast, including Domingo Soler, Fernando Cortes and the others, is above par. E. G. Muriel has directed this film deftly from a fairly interesting story by Celestino Gorostiza.

Sten.

Miniature Reviews

"The Suspect" (U). Charles Laughton, Ella Raines in sock melodrama.

"The Great Mike" (PRC). Stu Erwin drama about horseracing a fair dualer.

"La Pequena Madrecita" (Clasa). Fair Spanish-language drama grooved for Spanish-speaking audiences.

The Suspect

Universal release of Islin Auster production. Stars Charles Laughton, Ella Raines; features Stanley C. Ridges, Henry Daniell, Rosalind Ivan. Directed by Robert Siodmak. Screenplay by Bertram Millhauser; adapted by Arthur T. Horman from novel by James Ronald; camera, Paul Ivano; editor, Arthur Hilton. Previewed N. Y., Dec. 21, '44. Running time, 85 MINS.

Philip	Charles Laughton
Mary	Ella Raines
John	Dean Harens
Huxley	Stanley C. Ridges
Mr. Simmons	Henry Daniell
Cora	Rosalind Ivan
Mrs. Simmons	Molly Lamont
Merridew	Raymond Severn
Sybil	Eve Amber
Mrs. Packer	Maude Eburne
Mr. Packer	Clifford Brooke

"The Suspect" is a gripping screen story well told. Tale of a middle-aged storekeeper of London's gaslight era is projected with utmost fidelity and with a keen perception of dramatic values. With Charles Laughton in a somewhat different role that elevates him back to his old niche of popularity, picture looks smash boxoffice. It's one of finest productions to come from Universal in some time.

Film is a murder mystery lacking much mystery but with all the suspense of a super-whodunit. More than that, this production actually is a keen character study of a man whose married life has been a hell-on-earth and who sacrifices all to protect the one happiness in his middle-age, a sensible young stenographer who later becomes his wife. In Laughton's accomplished hands, this character becomes fascinating. Withal, he makes it a typical home-loving storeheeper accustomed to the simple things in London of that particular era.

Director Robert Siodmak constantly builds suspense, and, though one can surmise the course of events, he keeps his auditors guessing on many angles. Thus, it's fairly well established that the peaceable Laughton has become a double-murderer. An outstanding surprise, and one that brings the picture to a terrific climax, is when Laughton comes off the boat on which he's about to sail when everybody believes and secretly hopes he will make Canada safely. And, as the Scotland Yard inspector bets, voluntarily turns himself in to the law.

This is practically a new Laughton. There is less of the bluster and none of the villainy of previous vehicles. He gives an impeccable performance as the kindly, law-abiding citizen who kills only when driven to it. Matching his deft portrayal is Ella Raines as the youthful steno he weds after his wife's demise. Her English stenographer who gradually grows to love the older Laughton is undoubtedly one of her best in a string of roles. Incidentally, Laughton actually is pictured as a totally different type of lover. However, his romance with Miss Raines is overshadowed by the melodramatic events as Laughton runs head-on into Scotland Yard operatives.

Stanley C. Ridges offers the outstanding supporting role in a splendid supporting cast that's perfect even down to the smallest bit. Story development makes his interpretation of the relentless sleuth almost villainous. Rosalind Ivan makes vivid the vixen-wife of Laughton.

Henry Daniell makes considerable of the loafing, drunken husband of Laughton's pretty neighbor, the blackmail scene which ends with the latter being eliminated being an epic of word play. Mollie Lamont is superb as the neighbor's wife. Additionally s'rong in support are Eve Amber, Raymond Severn and Maude Eburne.

Those taking bows for the all-round production job are producer Islin Auster (with keen eye for detail), director Siodmak, editor Arthur Hilton and cameraman Paul Ivano. But above all, it's Laughton's picture, and he makes the most of it.
Wear.

The Great Mike

PRC release of Leon Fromkess (Martin Mooney) production. Stars Stuart Erwin; features Roberty Henry, Pierre Watkin, Gwen Kenyon, Carl Switzer. Directed by Wallace W. Fox from original by Martin Mooney and screenplay by Raymond L. Schrock; camera, Jockey A. Feindel; editor, Hugh Winn. At Brooklyn Paramount, week of Dec. 21. Running time, **72 MINS.**

Spencer	Stuart Erwin
Jimmy	Robert (Buzzy) Henry
Whitley	Pierre Watkin
Erin	Gwen Kenyon
Speck	Carl (Alfalfa) Switzer
Mrs. Dolan	Edythe Elliott
Kitty	Marian Martin
Sandy	Bob Meredith
Hildur	Lane Chandler
Pronnet	Ed Cassidy
Doc Scott	William Halligan
Junior	Leon Tyler
Doc Slagle	Charlie King
Bill Slagle	Eddie Rocco
Mike	Himself
Corky	Herself
Mickey	Himself

This neat, unpretentious drama about a horse, a dog and a boy, starring Stu Erwin, should do well in most dual situations.

Yarn deals with the faith of young "Buzzy" Henry in a horse that pulls a milkwagon, but whom the lad feels would make a great racer. He induces an eastern sportsman to allow his top runner to race the delivery animal, and sure enough the latter wins the contest. A crooked racing ring is foiled in making a "killing" involving the horse, through the actions of Henry, Stu Erwin, and the boy's dog, who gives his life in saving the runner from serious injury.

Erwin comes through with his usual droll performance, and touches of comedy, few and far between, are supplied by Carl "Alfalfa" Switzer, young "Our Gang" comedy graduate, who should appear on the screen more often. Gwen Kenyon supplies the love interest in capable style.

Settings are above par, and camera work by Jockey A. Feindel captures several exciting racing sequences.
Sten.

La Pequena Madracita

("The Little Mother")

Clasa release of Joselito Rodriguez production. Stars Evita Munoz, Narciso Busquets; features Anita Blanch, Titina, Francisco Jambrina. Directed by Rodriguez. Dialog, Rodriguez Hnos. At Belmont, N. Y., week of Dec. 20, '44. Running time, **105 MINS.**

Chachita	Evita Munoz
Pepe	Narciso Busquets
Lupe	Anita Blanch
Titina	Herself
Manuel	Francisco Jambrina
Professor	Arturo Soto Rangel
Titina's Mother	Elena D'Orgaz
Stepsister	Concha

(In Spanish; No English Titles)

This drama, starring two of Mexico's best child actors, Evita Munoz and Narciso Busquets, has touches of comedy and pathos that should please Spanish-speaking audiences in the U. S.

Yarn deals with trials and tribulations of the two children who are taken into the home of their mother's stepsister, when their mother is unable to take care of them due to her husband always being drunk. Then follows a series of incidents involv-

ing the baby of the stepsister; death of the two kids' mother and rehabilitation of their father.

Film is overlong, since most footage is taken up with dialog, and the story line, involved in spots, fails to sustain interest. Settings, though not pretentious, are substantial.

Evita Munoz is a capable little actress with a likeable personality and lots of ability. Narciso Busquets turns in a fair performance, while remainder of cast runs through its pace in workmanlike fashion.
Sten.

1945

January 3, 1945

Under Western Skies

(SONGS)

Universal release of Warren Wilson production. Stars Martha O'Driscoll; features Noah Beery, Jr., Leo Carrillo, Leon Errol. Directed by Jean Yarbrough. Screenplay by Stanley Roberts and Clyde Bruckman based on an original story by Roberts; camera, Charles Van Enger; editor, Arthur Hilton. Songs by Everett Carter and Milton Rosen. Previewed in N. Y. Dec. 28, '44. Running time, **57 MINS.**

Katie	Martha O'Driscoll
Tod	Noah Beery, Jr.
King Randall	Leo Carrillo
Willie	Leon Errol
Sheriff	Irving Bacon
Professor Moffett	Ian Keith
Charity	Jeniffer Holt
Faith	Edna May Wonacott
Mayfield	Earle Hodgins
Barton Brothers	Shaw and Lee
Maybelle	Dorothy Granger
Neil Mathews	Jack Rice

Cut and dried story, dialogue, acting and direction add up to a rather unentertaining film. Solely a dualer.

Obviously, Warren Wilson, producer, and Jean Yarbrough, director, didn't waste much time in getting this one into the can. They put the cast, headed by Martha O'Driscoll, through their paces in one-two-three fashion, with montage shots showing a stagecoach race with a bandit gang and a few outdoor scenes depicting a western town and surrounding area.

Yarn concerts the adventures of a traveling vaude show in a small Arizona community where several people want the entertainers to leave pronto. Turned down on staging the show, they talk the saloon keeper into giving them room. Meanwhile, a bandit gang is knocked off through the marksmanship of schoolteacher Noah Beery, Jr., who gets the gal, too.

Miss O'Driscoll's singing and acting talents seem especially wasted here. She delivers four of the five tunes composed by Everett Carter and Milton Rosen, none of which is especially catchy. Leo Carrillo is seen as the bandit chief, but briefly; while Leon Errol is the gal's father. Shaw and Lee, vaude vets, are also shown in one routine. *Sten.*

Western Approaches

(Color)

(BRITISH-MADE)

London.

British Lion release of Crown Film Production. Produced by Ian Dalrymple. Directed by Pat Jackson. Story by Pat Jackson. Camera, Jack Cardiff. Made with cooperation of Royal Navy, Royal Netherlands Navy, Ministry War Transport, Allied Merchant Navies. At Warner theatre, London, Dec. 6, '44. Running time, **83 MINS.**

"Western Approaches," most ambitious documentary made by Crown Film unit, and its first in Technicolor, should draw favorable comment on both sides of the Atlantic. It's a bit long to fit on duals where it will have to go in U. S. There are no professionals in the cast. The Merchant Seamen, to whom it's dedicated, are, with the exception of Pat Jackson, director, all real naval personnel. Film may do some biz in U. S.

All the convoy shots are genuine. This is reported the first time the Atlantic has been used for scenes in a color film, and there are some remarkably fine examples of same. Story set amid this technical realism tells of a lifeboat and its crew, of their sighting by the straggler from a convoy, and a climax of great intensity in which the straggler's guns fight a battle to the finish with a submarine.

Considering the great difficulties of filming at sea in the winter, the picture is not uneven, but some of dialogue will be alien to the American ear. An opportunity was missed in not making the final scenes of greater power for pop appeal. It is a painstaking effort and augurs well for future product of this sort.

January 10, 1945

Miniature Reviews

"This Man's Navy" (M-G). Wallace Beery starred in fair dualer about Navy's blimp service.

"She's a Sweetheart" (Songs) (Col). "B" comedy, okay for the duals.

"She Gets Her Man" (U). Humdrum Joan Davis comedy-mystery; dualer.

"Dixie Jamboree" (PRC). Slow-paced musical, for duals.

"I Accuse My Parents" (Songs) (PRC). Another juvenile delinquency theme; weak dualler.

This Man's Navy

Metro release of Samuel Marx production. Stars Wallace Beery; features Tom Drake, James Gleason, Selena Royle. Directed by William A. Wellman. Story and screenplay, Borden Chase, based on idea by Cmdr. Herman E. Halland, USN (ret.); camera, Sidney Wagner; editor, Irvine Warburton. Previewed in N. Y., Dec. 27, '44. Running time, **100 MINS.**

Ned Trumpet	Wallace Beery
Jess Weaver	Tom Drake
Jimmy Shannon	James Gleason
Cathey Cortland	Jan Clayton
Maude Weaver	Selena Royle
Joe Hodum	Noah Beery, Sr.
Lieut. Cmdr. Graystone	Henry O'Neill
Tim Shannon	Steve Brodie
Bert Bland	George Chandler
Operations Officer	Donald Curtis
Cadet Rayshek	Arthur Walsh
David	Will Fowler
Sparks	Richard Crockett

An ordinary programmer. Starring Wallace Beery, "This Man's Navy" should do average business.

Good direction by William A. Wellman and some excellent shots of Navy blimps in action add much to film. Story itself is ordinary, along with acting by majority of cast.

Beery, as a chief pilot, loves blimps and telling tall tales, especially about an imaginary son, although he's not married. Near the Lakehurst naval air station, however, lives a widow with an invalid youth whom Beery convinces to join the lighter-than-air service when he gets well. In that way, he outdoes James Gleason, who all along doesn't believe Beery has a boy at all, but since the widow and her son go along with the gag, Gleason is convinced. Conclusion finds the youth a hero, sinking a sub from the blimp, and Beery marries his mother.

Montage effects, actual shots of Lakehurst and the taking off and landing of the blimps, as well as the films of the hunt for subs are thrilling. Pic at 100 minutes, however, is too long. *Sten.*

She's a Sweetheart

(SONGS)

Columbia release of Ted Richmond production. Stars Jane Darwell, Jane Frazee, Larry Parks; features Nina Foch, Ross Hunter. Directed by Del Lord. Screenplay, Muriel Roy Bolton; songs by Saul Chaplin, others; camera, Benjamin Kline; editor, Al Clark. At Brooklyn Strand, week of Jan. 4, '45, dual. Running time, **69 MINS.**

Maxine LeCour	Jane Frazee
Rocky Hill	Larry Parks
Mom	Jane Darwell
Jeanne	Nina Foch
Paul	Ross Hunter
Pete Ryan	Jimmy Lloyd
Jimmy Loomis	Loren Tindall
Frances	Carole Mathews
Fred Tilly	Eddie Bruce
Matt	Pat Lane
Poker	Danny Desmond
Edith	Ruth Warren
Wes	Dave Willock

Light entertainment, this picture serves its purpose, being a low-budgeter produced as filler for nabe duals.

Yarn relates how a plumpish old lady turns her house into an overnight canteen for servicemen with short-time passes. She supplies them room, board and entertainment, and also acts as intermediary in their romantic escapades.

Jane Darwell, as the boardinghouse proprietress, overacts. Jane Frazee, who sings and dances fairly well, is an entertainer who in the end wins her man, Larry Parks, though Miss Darwell seeks to intervene in this romance. Miss Frazee and Parks, as well as the remaining members of the cast, do a forthright job.

Production values are strictly low-budget. Script is lightweight and songs are not of such quality as to be remembered. *Sten.*

She Gets Her Man

(ONE SONG)

Universal release of Warren Wilson production. Stars Joan Davis; features William Gargan, Leon Errol, Vivian Austin, Donald McBride, Paul Stanton. Directed by Erle C. Kenton. Screenplay, Warren Wilson, Clyde Bruckman; song, "For All We Know," by Sam M. Lewis and J. Fred Coots; camera, Jerry Ash; editor, Paul Landres. Tradeshown N. Y., Jan. 4, '45. Running time, **70 MINS.**

Pilky	Joan Davis
Breezy	William Gargan
Mulligan	Leon Erroll
Maybelle	Vivian Austin
Mayor	Russell Hicks
Phoebe	Virginia Sale
Brodie	Cyrus Kendall
Bleaker	Paul Stanton
Hatch	Emmet Vogan
Wright	Donald McBride

This one is strictly for Joan Davis fans. A tired double-feature comedy built around a series of fiendish murders in a small town, its humor is generally feeble, with only a few real comic moments as, for instance, the free-for-all chase at the end.

Murder can be a grim subject when handled this way, despite the comedy attempts, with persons bumped off before one's eyes being too realistic to be funny. Perpetrator is a mysterious killer who uses a gun which shoots needles into his victims. Miss Davis, daughter of a famed woman chief of police, is called in to solve the mystery. No chip off the old block, she fumbles around, goes off on false clues, while the murders keep apace. Not one moment of it makes sense, but all that's beside the point. When ready to quit Miss Davis stumbles onto a lead that solves the mystery.

Comedienne combines hillbilly and cornstalk humor plus her usual mugging for a typical characterization. Supporting cast in the main goes through its routines suggesting an awareness of the whole painful business. William Gargan tries to play a reporter in an awkward manner, while Leon Errol has some moments as a friendly police sergeant. *Bron.*

Dixie Jamboree

(SONGS)

PRC release of Jack Schwarz production. Stars Frances Langford, Guy Kibbee; features Eddie Quillan, Charles Butterworth, Fifi D'Orsay, Lyle Talbot. Directed by Christy Cabanne. Screenplay, Sam Neuman; original, Lawrence E. Taylor; camera, Jack Mackenzie; editor, Robert Crandall; songs, Michael Breen and Sam Neuman. At Fox, Brooklyn, Jan. 5, '45, dual. Running time, **69 MINS.**

Susan Jackson	Frances Langford
Captain Jackson	Guy Kibbee
Jeff Calhoun	Eddie Quillan
Professor	Charles Butterworth
Yvette	Fifi D'Orsay
Tony Sardell	Lyle Talbot
Curly	Frank Jenks
Ellabella Jackson	Almira Sessions
Sergeant	Joe Devlin
Opal	Louise Beavers
Sam	Ben Carter
Azella	Gloria Jetter
Mr. Doakes	Edward Shattuck
Mrs. Doakes	Ethel Shattuck
Double	Tony Warde
Nothing	Angel Cruz

Ben Carter Choir

This film is as slow-moving as the plodding Mississippi showboat on which all its action transpires. It has everything in it from crooning by Frances Langford, French ditties by Fifi D'Orsay, spirituals by a Negro choir and what passes for comedy by Charles Butterworth, Guy Kibbee and Frank Jenks, down to a couple of drugstore Indians—with just as much coherence as one would expect from such a setup. A lower-case dualer this, for the sticks.

The story concerns the Ellabella, last of the Mississippi showboats, droning along from port to port, putting on shows while Captain Jackson (Guy Kibbee) sells his patent medicine. On board this trip are Lyle Talbot and Frank Jenks, a pair of fugitive con men posing as health vacationers; Eddie Quillan, a tramp trumpeter, and a couple of Indians he's adopted, the trio coming on board one day when Miss Langford's dockside singing entranced them; and the showboat troupe represented by Misses Langford and D'Orsay, Kibbee and Butterworth. On this last trip, the latter had loaded two barrels of whiskey on board, mistaking them for water, and in bottling their medicinal have mixed it with this firewater. The two crooks taste the stuff, think Kibbee is a distiller, and plan highjacking boat and booze. Quillan and Miss Langford foil their plans.

All this unwinds slowly and painfully, to choppy interludes of stale jokes and pleasant songs. Miss Langford is appealing as singer and does several ballads well. Quillan plays romantic lead a little bewilderedly. Butterworth's dry humor mostly goes flat. Louise Beavers has a few moments, and a couple of scenes with the drugstore Indians are mildly amusing. *Bron.*

I Accuse My Parents

(SONGS)

PRC release of Max Alexander production. Stars Mary Beth Hughes; features Robert Lowell, John Miljan, Vivienne Osborne, George Meeker. Directed by Sam Newfield. Screenplay, Harry Fraser and Marjorie Dudley, based on original by Arthur Caesar; songs by Ray Evans and Jay Livingston; camera, Robert Cline; editor, Charles Henkel, Jr. At Brooklyn Strand, week Jan. 4, '45, dual. Running time, **68 MINS.**

Kitty Reed	Mary Beth Hughes
James Wilson	Robert Lowell
Dan Wilson	John Miljan
Mrs. Wilson	Vivienne Osborne
Charles Blake	George Meeker
Judge	Edward Earle
Al Frazier	George Lloyd
Vera Moore	Patricia Knox
Shirley Clark	Florence Johnson
Joe Holden	Richard Bartell

Another juve delinquency pic; a weak dualler.

This one tells of a highschool student accused of murdering the head of a gang of jewel thieves. He is acquitted and his parents, who gamble, drink and neglect him, are given a verbal lashing by the judge for allowing him to consort with such characters.

The whole thing takes too long to get to the point, is poorly produced and the actors probably regret ever having gotten mixed up in the proceedings. Mary Beth Hughes heads the cast. Songs, such as they are, fail to impress. Direction lacks evenness. *Sten.*

Miniature Reviews

"Hangover Square" (20th). Laird Cregar-Linda Darnell-George Sanders in Cregar's last pic; good b.o.

"The Great Flamarion" (Rep). Vivid melodrama of backstage vaude with Erich Von Stroheim; looks solid mostly in dual setups.

"Grissly's Millions" (Rep). Better-than-Average whodunit that should do well in all situations.

"Strawberry Roan" (Anglo-Am.). British-made drama of farm; extremely mild hopes for U. S. market.

"The Shanghai Drama" (French). Prewar meller of Russ-Jap intrigue. Fair draw.

"Woman Without a Soul" (Mex.-made) (Songs). Talky Mexican production, for foreign-language houses only.

"Madonna of Seven Moons" (Eagle-Lion). British-made with limited b.o. appeal.

Hangover Square

20th-Fox release of Robert Bassler production. Stars Laird Cregar, Linda Darnell, George Sanders; features Glenn Langan, Faye Marlowe, Alan Napier. Directed by John Brahm. Screenplay, Barre Lyndon, based on novel by Patrick Hamilton; editor, Harry Reynolds; music, Bernard Herrmann; camera, Joseph La Shelle. Previewed in New York, Jan. 11, '44. Running time, 77 MINS.

George Harvey Bone.......... Laird Cregar
Netta Longdon.......... Linda Darnell
Dr. Allan Middleton.......... George Sanders
Carstairs.......... Glenn Langan
Barbara Chapman.......... Faye Marlowe
Sir Henry Chapman.......... Alan Napier
Supt. Clay.......... Frederic Worlock
Detective Inspector King..... J. W. Austin
Detective Sgt. Lewis..... Leyland Hodgson
Watchman.......... Clifford Brooke
Butler.......... John Goldsworthy
Mickey.......... Michael Dyne
Yvette.......... Ann Codee
Ogilby.......... Francis Ford
Manager.......... Charles Irwin
Newsman.......... Frank Benson
Maid.......... Connie Leon
Costermonger.......... Robert Hale
English Policeman.......... Leslie Denison

There will be considerable interest attached to "Hangover Square," not so much because of its melodramatic impact, but because it was Laird Cregar's last picture—in his biggest role—before his recent demise. For boxoffice purposes the film can also stand on its own.

"Hangover Square" is eerie murder melodrama of the London gaslight era—typical of Patrick Hamilton yarns, of which this is another. And it doesn't make any pretense at mystery. The madman-murderer is known from the first reel.

It is the story of a distinguished young composer-pianist with a Jekyll-Hyde personality. When he becomes over-wrought, he's a madman—and his lustful forages are always accompanied by a loss of memory for the periods during which he is murder-bent.

Around this framework is the lesser yarn of his meeting with a double-dealing young singer and how he goes berserk when he learns of her infidelity. Her ghastly end is not for sensitive audiences.

Cregar as the madman murderer shows markedly the physical decline, through dieting, said to have been a factor in his death. Ironically, it is a picture that would have established him more strongly among Hollywood's younger stars.

Linda Darnell and George Sanders are co-stars, the former as the two-timing gal and Sanders as a Scotland Yard psychiatrist who provides the tell-tale clues responsible for the denouement. They, along with Faye Marlowe, contribute the outstanding performances.

Production is grade A, and so is the direction by John Brahm, with particular bows to the music score by Bernard Herrmann and the sharp editing (pic runs only 77 minutes).

This is a picture more notable for the omniscience of a single player than any other factor. *Kahn.*

The Great Flamarion

Republic release of William Wilder production. Stars Erich Von Stroheim, Mary Beth Hughes. Directed by Anthony Mann. Screenplay, Anne Wigton, Heinz Herald and Richard Weil, from story by Anne Wigton, based on character in "Big Shot," Collier magazine story by Vicki Baum; camera, James Spencer Brown; editor, John F. Link; musical numbers by Faith Watson, Lester Allen. At Republic, N. Y., starting Jan. 13, '45. Runing time, 78 MINS.

Flamarion.......... Erich Von Stroheim
Connie Wallace.......... Mary Beth Hughes
Al Wallace.......... Dan Duryea
Eddie.......... Stephen Barclay
Tony.......... Lester Allen
Cleo.......... Esther Howard
Night Watchman.......... Michael Mark
Detective.......... Joseph Granby
Coroner.......... John R. Hamilton
Mexican Dancers.......... Fred Velasco, Camen Lopez
Mexican Singer.......... Tony Ferrell

"The Great Flamarion" is heavy melodrama. It offers Erich Von Stroheim in one of his better screen roles. But because it leans only on him and Mary Beth Hughes for boxoffice pull, picture will have to depend mostly on dual combos for best biz.

This production might have been called "The Great Doublecross" because it's the manner in which "The Great Flamarion," crack vaudeville pistol shot, is two-timed by the femme in his act that makes the yarn. "The Great Flamarion" (Von Stroheim) lives only for his art. A love affair 15 years previously has soured him on women, and Miss Hughes, stooge in act, is regarded merely as a prop. That is until she starts to make a play for him, their affair winding up with the "accidental" death of the other assistant, her husband. But she's been playing the boys on nearly every vaude bill, and disappears with a bicycle rider on a Latin-American trek.

Von Stroheim makes his role plausible, and Miss Hughes lends plenty of sex to her part. Dan Duryea is okay as the gal's husband. Solid supporting cast is headed by Stephen Barclay, Lester Allen and Esther Howard.

Strong production values have been supplied by William Wilder while Anthony Mann's direction is imaginative and well-paced. James Spencer Brown's camera work is especially effective as is the editing of John F. Link. *Wear.*

Grissly's Millions

Republic release of Walter H. Goetz production. Features Paul Kelly and Virginia Grey. Directed by John English. Screenplay, Muriel Roy Bolton; editor, Harry Keller; camera, William Bradford. At Strand threatre, Brooklyn, N. Y., week of Jan. 10, '45, dual. Runing time, 71 MINS.

Joe Simmons.......... Paul Kelly
Katherine Palmer Bentley.... Virginia Grey
Ellison Hayes.......... Don Douglas
Leona Palmer.......... Elisabeth Risdon
Grissly Morgan Palmer.. Robert H. Barrat
Young Tom.......... Clem Bevans
Mattie.......... Elly Malyon
Marlielle.......... Adele Mara
Dr. Henny.......... Francis Pierlot
Henry Adams.......... Addison Richards
Lewis Bentley.......... Paul Fix
Fred Palmer.......... Byron Foulger
Mrs. Fred Palmer (June).......... Joan Blair
Robert Palmer, Jr.......... Grady Sutton
Robert Palmer, Sr.......... Frank Jaquet
John Frey.......... Will Wright
The Gatekeeper.......... Louis Mason
Policeman Ralph.......... Tom London

Republic comes up with a nifty whodunit that has the makings for better-than-average returns despite lack of marquee names. It projects a compact yarn with plenty of twists and suspenseful situations.

Grissly Morgan Palmer (Robert H. Barrat), retired tycoon, is surrounded by a motley crew of relatives awaiting the old gent's demise and presumed legacies. When he kicks off he leaves everything to Virginia Grey, his loyal and favorite granddaughter. This sets the rest of the gang in motion to polish off Miss Grey and get the coin. Paul Kelly, a copper who has trailed the girl's estranged husband, Paul Fix, to the household but loses him when he mysteriously vanishes within, remains to clear up that mystery and at the same time protect her from the jealous relatives. Of course, they're in on the romantic fadeout.

Miss Grey gives a neat portrayal. Kelly gives his usually slick performance. Don Douglas, Elisabeth Risdon, Joan Blair, Barrat and Fix also give good accounts of themselves. John English has paced direction of Muriel Roy Bolton's screenplay in proper tempo. William Bradford's camera work is okay, too. *Edba.*

Strawberry Roan
(BRITISH-MADE)

London, Jan. 5.

Anglo-American Film Corp. release of British National Films. Features Billy Hartness. Directed by Maurice Elvey. Screenplay by Elizabeth Baron from novel by A. G. Street. Camera, James Wilson. At Rialto, London, Jan. 5, '45. Running time, 83 MINS.

Chris.......... Billy Hartnell
Molly.......... Carol Raye
Dibben.......... John Ruddock
Mrs. Morley.......... Sophie Stewart
Mr. Morley.......... Walter Fitzgerald
Bill Gurd.......... Wylie Watson
Gladys Moon.......... Joan Maude
Mrs. Dibben.......... Joan Young
Vicar.......... Patric Curwen
Dr. Lambert.......... Norman Shelley
Kate.......... Petula Clark

This is a typical, slow-moving, back-to-the-land film, written by A. G. Street, who's done other farm yarns. It looks like blah U. S. boxoffice.

Strawberry Roan is a young heifer calf, given by a hard-working young farmer to his skittish, extravagant young bride. Heedless of the need for returning the money made from the land back into the land, the thoughtless girl, formerly a stage dancer, not only splashes money on all sorts of unnecessary luxuries, but causes her husband to neglect his work. They soon head for disaster. Following a squabble, the wife rides off on horseback, sustains a fall which proves fatal. The heartbroken and now impoverished young widower is forced to sell his farm and take work at a neighbor's estate.

Stories like this one have little to bolster them excepting peaceful shots of rural scenery. Camera work in this is strong, but it takes more than this to make a picture.

Carol Raye and Billy Hartnell get as much as possible in the leading roles. Picture has only limited appeal here.

The Shanghai Drama
(FRENCH-MADE)

David Brill release of Marc Sorkin production. Stars Louis Jouvet. Directed by G.W. Pabst. Screenplay, Leo Laniz and A. Arnoux, adapted from O.P. Gilbert novel. "Shanghai Chambard et Cio"; camera, E. Shufftan; music, Ralph Erwin; English titles, Herman G. Weinberg. At 55th St. Playhouse, N.Y., Jan 10, '44 Running time, 76 MINS.

Ivan.......... Louis Jouvet
Kay.......... Christine Mardayne
Franchon.......... Raymond Rouleau
"Big" Bill.......... Dorville
Vera.......... Suzanne Dempers
Nana.......... Elina Labourdette
Superintendent.......... Gabrielle Dorziat
Dancing Girl.......... Mila Parey
Cheng.......... Linh-Nam
"Black Dragon" agent.......... V. Inkijinoff
"Black Dragon" henchmen.......... Ky-Duyen and Hoang Dao

(In French; with English Titles)

This prewar-made Parisian film, though a little slow in pace, is an interesting melodrama of intrigue in Shanghai in 1935 before the Sino-Jap war. Setting and types seem authentic (part of pic is claimed to have been filmed in French Indo-China), background being intriguing enough to offset too melodramatic plot and occasional wooden acting of principals. Pic should be passable draw for arty foreign-film houses.

Pic presents interesting situation of White Russian refugees in Shanghai being drawn into Jap net to serve as pawns in enslaving Chinese population. Plot centers on a Russian cabaret singer serving as tool of Jap "Black Dragon" terrorist society, who tries to break away from job and ring when her daughter comes to live with her from school in Hongkong. Woman's attempts to free herself fail, but daughter manages to get away with aid of a friendly journalist when Chinese citizens revolt against Jap plotters.

Louis Jouvet, though starred, has fairly minor part as renegade Russ member of Jap ring. Christiane Mardayne is mannered, with occasional bad makeup, in lead femme role. Dorville lends character to cafe-owner's role and Raymond Rouleau is personable as helpful journalist. G. W. Pabst's direction, though leisurely, is suspenseful and always interesting. Cabaret scenes, with diversity of audience from all races—black, brown and white—are more interesting part of film, as is music, neat jazz arrangements being smartly played. English subtitles make story easy to follow. *Bron.*

La Mujer Sin Alma
("Woman Without a Soul")
(MEXICAN-MADE)
(Songs)

Cia Cinematograsca de Guadalajara release of Luis Enrique Gallinde productions. Stars Fernando Soler, Maria Felix. Directed by Fernando de Fuentes. Story by Fuents; camera, V. Herrera; songs, Oeto Ama. At Belmont, N.Y., starting Jan. 8, '45. Running time, 130 MINS.

Don Alfredo.......... Fernando Soler
Tersa.......... Maria Felix
Don Vicente.......... Andres Soler
Enrique.......... Antonio Badu
Rosita.......... Chela Campos

(In Spanish; No English Titles)

"Woman Without a Soul" is typical of the recent upbeat in Mexican pix. It has production values, an unusually capable cast, solid comedy and expert photography. But it's too long, with the dearth of action accentuating the wordy episodes. Despite this, film should be top fare in Spanish-language houses and a few arty theatres such as this, even though lacking English titles.

Maria Felix dominates every scene in which she's in. Basically, this is the story of a sewing-machine girl who weds riches but soon tires of her elderly mate. It lacks the necessary light strokes to make it palatable for the average American audience.

Besides the forthright performance by Miss Felix, Fernando Soler is fine as her godfather and confidant. A strong supporting cast is headed by Antonio Badu, Chela Campos and Andres Soler. *Wear.*

Madonna of 7 Moons
(BRITISH—MADE)

London, Dec. 18.

Eagle-Lion Distributors release of Gainsborough production. Starring Phyllis Calvert, Stewart granger, Patricia Roc. Directed by Arthur Crabtree. Screenplay by Brook Williams from novel by Margery Lawrence. Camera, Jack Cox. At Gaumont, London, Dec. 17, '44. Running time, 105 MINS.

Maddalena
Rosanna.......... Phyllis Calvert
Nino.......... Stewart Granger
Angela.......... Patricia Roc
Sandro.......... Peter Glenville
Guiseppe.......... John Stewart
Ackroyd.......... Reginald Tate
Logan.......... Peter Murray Hill
Neala.......... Dulcie Gray
Evelyn.......... Alan Haines
Mrs. Fiske.......... Hilda Bayley
Madame Baracci.......... Nancy Price

A lavishly handled production, the most interesting thing about it is the atmospheric detail. The story is far different from the usual boy-meets-girl yarn. Censor bodies in U. S. likely will do lots of cutting. American boxoffice seems mild at best.

An Italian convent-bred girl is raped · by a gypsy, resulting in a highly improbable case of dual personality. This results in the girl, married to a rich wine merchant, periodically disappearing. On these disappearing trances she is shown as the mistress of a gypsy. After these absences, she remembers nothing of her prowling escapades, resuming usual married life.

Opening announcement claims medical authority proves the authenticity of such a condition of mind.

Miniature Reviews ·

"A Tree Grows in Brooklyn" (20th). Excellent adaptation of Betty Smith's best selling novel. Sock boxoffice.

"A Song to Remember" (Color) (Col). Film biog of Chopin excellent entertainment for wide audience appeal. Hefty biz and key holdovers indicated.

"Dancing in Manhattan" (Col). (Songs). Low-budget comedy for duals.

"Jade Mask" (Mono). One of the better Charlie Chan dual whodunits.

"Thoroughbreds" (Rep). Okay horse-race dualer.

"Moscow Skies" (Artkino). Russian - made romantic war yarn has extremely mild U. S. appeal.

"Flor Sylvestre" (Clasa; Mexican). Dolores del Rio starred in interesting drama.

A Tree Grows in B'klyn

· 20th-Fox release of Louis D. Lighton production. Features Dorothy McGuire, James Dunn, Joan Blondell, Peggy Ann Garner, Ted Donaldson, Lloyd Nolan. Directed by Elia Kazan. Screenplay, Tess Slesinger and Frank Davis, adapted from the novel by Betty Smith; editor, Dorothy Spencer; music, Alfred Newman; camera, Leon Shamroy; special photographic effects, Fred Sersen. Tradeshown in N. Y. Jan. 19, '45. Running time, 132 MINS.

Katie....................Dorothy McGuire
Aunt Sissy..................Joan Blondell
Johnny Nolan.................James Dunn
McShane......................Lloyd Nolan
Francie Nolan...........Peggy Ann Garner
Neeley Nolan................Ted Donaldson
McGarrity.................James Gleason
Miss McDonough...............Ruth Nelson
Steve Edwards.............John Alexander
Christmas Tree Vendor........B. S. Pully
Grandma Rommely...........Ferike Boros
Carney...............J. Farrell MacDonald
Mrs. Waters.....Adeline De Walt Reynolds
Mr. Spencer................George Melford
{ Mae Marsh
Tynmore Sisters...........{ Edna Jackson
Henny Gaddis...............Vincent Graeff
Flossie Gaddis...............Susan Lester
Mr. Crackenbox.............Johnnie Berkes
Librarian...................Lillian Bronson
Werner......................Alec Craig
Mr. Barker................Charles Halton
Cheap Charlie..................Al Bridge
Hassler...................Joseph J. Greene
Miss Milford............Virginia Brissac
Herschel...................Harry Harvey, Jr.
Augie.....................Robert Anderson
Iceman ....Art Smith
{ Norman Field
Principals of Schools.......{ George Meader
Undertaker...............Erskine Sanford
Mother...................Martha Wentworth
Priest....................Francis Pierlot
Union Representative..............Al Eben
Barber....................Peter Cusanelli

A tree that has become one of the near-legends of these times—a tree that grew in Brooklyn—has been transplanted from the printed page to achieve distinction on celluloid. A bestseller for many months. Betty Smith's novel about the Brooklyn of a generation ago has emerged as one of the fine film dramas of the year.

The earthy quality of Brooklyn tenement squalor, about which Miss Smith wrote so eloquently in "A Tree Grows in Brooklyn," has been given a literal transition to the screen by 20th-Fox to become an experiment in audience restraint. There have been few pictures to tug at the heartstrings as this one does.

This is the story of that Brooklyn locale called Williamsburg, and of the poverty-ridden Nolan family. Katie, the young mother, had to scrub down the tenement steps to help defray the family expenses; Johnny, her husband, had more zest for fun-loving than the capacity to support his brood; Francie, their daughter, dreamed of becoming a writer; Neeley, the youngest, had a desire for food greater than the family coffers could

afford. And there was Aunt Sissy, Katie's sister, with her perpetual flair for new husbands.

Around these are woven a story that is lengthy but never tedious, a yarn whose propensity for minor details looms forever importantly, as the tale develops.

"Tree" recalls an absorbing period of a colorful tribe, of a Brooklyn neighborhood that was tough in its growing-up, where kids fought or were kicked in the slats; where on Saturday nights fathers and husbands, more often than not, loped uncertainly from the corner quenchery.

Some of this might have acquired the tinge of travesty in hands less skilled than those of Miss Smith—or director Elia Kazan—but never does the serio-comic intrude on a false note; never does this story become maudlin.

This may be fiction but there's no disguising the basis of truth for this story. The dramatic power it possesses seemingly could never have been attained from imagination alone. Miss Smith herself, through one of the characters, professes that stories are little lies that have their basis on truths.

The Nolans—and the characters forever lending strong background—make for superb studies. Katie Nolan, penny-pinching, her brow forever furrowed with worry over whether the family would have enough food—or about the new baby to come—was sometimes too circumspect in her family decisions. Katie felt she had to be. Johnny meant one day to be the best darned singing waiter in all Brooklyn—even Manhattan—but Katie—and Johnny did, too, down deep—knew that he didn't have a ghost of a chance. Everything was against them. And when Katie figured that Francie had to quit school, so she could go to work and help out because of the new baby, that incited Johnny to tramp the employment agencies so that his little girl could continue her schooling. Johnny couldn't get a job, but he got pneumonia and died trying.

To Dorothy McGuire, who has appeared in only one other film, in the title role of "Claudia," also for 20th-Fox, went the prize part of Katie Nolan. For the first reel or so it's difficult to associate the girl wife of "Claudia" with the almost-calloused character of Katie, but soon Miss McGuire develops with the part, and the part with her. It is a role that she makes distinctive by underplaying.

Johnny Nolan is a comeback part for James Dunn. The role has a greater depth than any he has ever played, and Dunn plays it excellently. Peggy Ann Garner is the teen-aged Francie, and this character must certainly have been the author's favorite. Upon Francie, Miss Smith has lavished much of the story's sympathies, and the young actress performs capitally.

Young Ted Donaldson, as Neeley, also contributes importantly. Joan Blondell as Aunt Sissy has considerable of the hoyden quality intended by Miss Smith, and Miss Blondell also gives an impressive performance. Lloyd Nolan, as a policeman, is another outstander.

The adaptation has been carefully made by Tess Slesinger and Frank Davis, with particular attention paid to the original.

Where "Tree" is frequently slow, it is offset by the story's significance and pointed up notably by the direction of Elia Kazan. This film runs two hours and 12 minutes, but Kazan's direction has paced the story admirably. The production values are evident all the way, and that includes the fine photography and musical score.

Oh, yes—the tree! Bent and twisted, it grew, somehow, amid debris and clotheslines in the backyard of the tenement where the Nolans lived. Bent and twisted—

but beautiful to Johnny and Francie Nolan. As bent and twisted—and as beautiful—as the people Betty Smith has written about.   Kahn.

A Song to Remember
(COLOR)

Hollywood, Jan. 17.

Columbia release of Sidney Buchman production. (Louis Edelman, associate producer). Stars Paul Muni, Merle Oberon; features Cornel Wilde, Nina Foch, George Coulouris. Directed by Charles Vidor. Screenplay, Sidney Buchman, from story by Ernst Marischka; camera, Tony Gaudio and Allen M. Davey; editor, Charles Nelson; music recording by William Randall; musical adaptation by Miklos Rozsa; musical supervisor, Mario Silva; music director, Lodge Cunningham. Previewed in Hollywood, Jan. 16, '45. Running time, 110 MINS.

Prof. Joseph Elsner..............Paul Muni
George Sand..................Merle Oberon
Frederic Chopin...............Cornel Wilde
Franz Liszt...............Stephen Bekassy
Constantia......................Nina Foch
Louis Pleyel............George Coulouris
Henri Dupont....................Sig Arno
Kalkbrenner................Howard Freeman
Alfred DeMusset.........George Macready
Madame Mercier............Claire DuBrey
Monsieur Jollet..............Frank Puglia
Madame Lambert............Fern Emmett
Isabelle Chopin..............Sybil Merritt

Abounding in entertainment factors, "A Song to Remember" is one of the top biographical dramas to get screen presentation to date. Based on the colorful—though brief—life of Polish composer Frederic Chopin, picture is a showmanly presentation of intimate drama and music. It's slated for most profitable biz in all runs, with holdovers indicated generally.

Plot introduces Chopin as a prodigy at 11, with Paul Muni the old music master who easily recognizes his genius. Of poor Polish parents, he becomes a patriot during his youth and member of underground band determined to throw off the Czarist rule. When 22, the student and teacher flee to Paris after Chopin refuses to perform for the Russian governor. Young Franz Liszt befriends the newcomer and arranges a concert debut, introduces him to the famous authoress, George Sand, and is directly responsible in getting him recognition. But Miss Sand falls in love with the composer, and takes him off to the island of Majorca for romantic interludes where she drives him to compose rather than return to Paris and a concert tour. But his patriotism finally emerges for him to embark on concert tour of the European capitals to raise funds for the Polish revolutionary cause, even though he is stricken with tuberculosis. He finally collapses at windup of a Paris concert to pass into the ages, with the stolid authoress ignoring his final hours.

Brilliant performances are generally turned in by the cast, with Muni provoking maximum interest with his portrayal of the proud and blustering old music teacher. Cornel Wilde is spotlighted as Chopin and establishes himself as a screen personality. Merle Oberon clicks as the cold and calculating writer. Stephen Bekassy, as Liszt, and George Coulouris, as the impresario, are most prominent in the carefully-selected supporting cast.

Jose Iturbi is not seen, but he contributes importantly in the overall with his background playing of numerous Chopin compositions, which are liberally sprinkled throughout the unreeling. Wilde does a fine job of keyboard manipulations for the various numbers, and the visual and sound components blend accurately for realistic effect.

Also important is the recording of the piano numbers—always one of the most difficult assignments for the sound engineers. Reproduction of the piano passages is the best of its kind that has so far been accomplished, and credit for the achievement must go to John Livadary and the entire Columbia sound department.

Sidney Buchman, as executive producer, has combined the wealth of talent and material into a solid piece of entertainment. Script, which was turned over to Louis Edelman to produce, is deftly and compactly set up. Direction by Charles Vidor is topgrade, and production has been given an expensive mounting in Technicolor. *Walt.*

Dancing in Manhattan
(SONGS)

Columbia release of Wallace MacDonald production. Stars Fred Brady, Jeff Donnell; features William Wright, Ann Savage, Cy Kendall. Directed by Henry Levin. Screenplay, Erna Lazarus; camera, L. W. O'Connell; editor, Richard Fantl. At Brooklyn Strand, week of Jan. 18, '45, dual. Running time, 60 MINS.

Eddie Martin	Fred Brady
Julie Connors	Jeff Donnell
Steve Crawford	William Wright
Valerie Crawford	Ann Savage
Inspector Kirby	Cy Kendall
George Hartley	Howard Freeman
Andre	Eddie Kane
Billie	Sally Bliss
Sally	Adelle Roberts
Rita	Jean Stevens
Joe	George McKay
Mrs. Bundy	Dorothy Vaughan

This "B" is notable in only one respect. It serves to introduce radio scripter-comedian Fred Brady to pic audiences. However, weak story line and comedy material make it just another dualer.

Yarn concerns a truckdriver who finds $5,000, and rather than try to find owner, he decides to blow the coin on a good time. He and his gal help capture a blackmailer. Then he is given the money by the rightful owner for aiding in the capture of the con man.

Brady has the ability to go places in pix. He has an effervescent personality, and given the right kind of breaks should make the grade. Jeff Donnell and supporting members of the cast do all right.

Songs are unworthy of mention. *Sten.*

Jade Mask

Monogram release of James S. Burkett production. Stars Sidney Toler; features Mantan Moreland, Edwin Luke, Janet Warren. Directed by Phil Rosen. Screenplay, George Callahan; camera, Harry Neumann; editor, Dick Currier. At Brooklyn Strand, week of Jan. 18, '45, dual. Running time, 69 MINS.

Charlie Chan	Sidney Toler
Birmingham	Mantan Moreland
Tommy	Edwin Luke
Jean	Janet Warren
Louise	Edith Evanson
Mack	Alan Bridge
Kimball	Ralph Lewis
Harper	Frank Reicher
Meeker	Hardie Albright
Roth	Cyril DeLevanti
Stella	Dorothy Granger
Archer	Jack Ingram
Michael	Lester Dorr
Godfrey	Henry Hall

Another in the Charlie Chan series, "Jade Mask" is above par and should do well on the duals.

They pulled out all the stops in this one. Sidney Toler, as usual, is the Chinese detective who solves the killings and clears the mystery in his usually quiet fashion.

Touches of comedy are added by Mantan Moreland, as a colored chauffeur, and Edwin Luke, as the detective's son. *Sten.*

Thoroughbreds

Republic release of Lester Sharpe production. Features Tom Neal, Adele Mara. Directed by George Blair. Screenplay, Wellyn Totman; editor, Ralph Duxon; camera, William Bradford. At Brooklyn Fox, Jan. 15, '45. Running time, 56 MINS.

Rusty Curtis	Tom Neal
Sally Crandall	Adele Mara
Harold Matthews	Roger Pryor
John Crandall	Paul Harvey
Jack Martin	Gene Garrick
Private Mulrooney	Doodles Weaver
Dapper	Eddie Hall
Pop	Tom London
Nails	Charles Sullivan

Major Lane | Alan Edwards
Pete | Sam Bernard
Roberts | Buddy Gorman

"Thoroughbreds" is a modest double-bill budgeter. Plot is simple and familiar, but story is told pleasantly.

Story concerns a steeplechase, a cavalry rider just out of the army, and a few small-fry gamblers. Turf lingo has a hep twist, but, in view of the track ban, such lines as the innocent newsstand request, "Got a form sheet?", win laughs from an audience.

Plot revolves around a cavalry sergeant released from service about the same time the Army is disposing of some horses. the sergeant's mount among them. The horse, a steeplechaser, is bought by a society gal. The sergeant gets a job as the horse's trainer, foils attempts of gamblers to keep the horse out of an important meet and rides it to victory when regular rider is disabled. And wins the dame, of course.

Tom Neal makes a plausible hero as the sarge, with Adele Mara attractive as the haughty socialite. Roger Pryor is fairly menacing as a gambler, and Paul Harvey suits as the gal's father. *Bron.*

Moscow Skies
(SOVIET-MADE)

Artkino release of Mosfilm Studios production. Stars Peter Aleinikov, Nina Masayeva. Directed by Yuri Reisman. Story by M. Bleiman, M. Bolshintzev; camera, E. Andrikanis; English titles, Charles Clement. At Stanley, N. Y., starting Jan. 20, '45. Running time, 81 MINS.

Lieut. Ilya Streltsov	Peter Aleinikov
Zoya	Nina Masayeva
Lieut.-Col. Balashev	Nikolai Bogolyubov
Capt. Goncharov	Peter Sobolyevsky
First Lieut. Cherbina	Ivan Kuznetzov

(In Russian; English Titles)

Story about the Soviet air force's daring defense of Moscow looks geared for modest returns in Russian-language theatres and a few scattered arty houses. Biggest drawback is that the picture appears to have been made two or three years ago, and the technique is even more dated.

Film's romantic element is covered by a daring Army flying lieutenant who carries on a love affair with an Army nurse. Best episodes are the newsreel clips of actual aerial combat. Even these fail to measure up to those of previous Russian films.

Story is marred by several haphazard incidents, typical being the one in which the lieutenant is delivered to his home after being apparently hurt and exhausted after his plane cracks up. Audience is led to believe he is either critically wounded or dead. Suddenly he answers the telephone and goes back to active duty.

Peter Aleinikov is effective as the hero lieutenant. Nina Masayeva, the nurse, is fairly good. Supporting cast of unknowns (to U.S. audiences) really outdoes the principals.

With bulk of scenes shot outdoors, cameraman E. Andrikanis apparently had plenty of trouble with his lighting. Result is spotty photography, some so bad it looks like a worn-out print. *Wear.*

Flor Sylvestre
("Wildflower")
(MEXICAN-MADE)
(Songs)

Clasa release of Agustin Fink-Films Mundiales production. Stars Dolores Del Rio; features Pedro Armendariz, Emilio Fernandez. Directed by Emilio Fernandez. Songs by Lucha Reyes. At Belmont, N. Y., week of Jan. 15, '45. Running time, 90 MINS.

Esperanza	Dolores Del Rio
Jose Luis Castro	Pedro Armendariz
Rogelio Torres	Emilio Fernandez
Don Francisco Castro	Miguel Angel Ferriz
Reynaldo	Chiocto
Dona Clara	Mimi Derba
Melchor	Eduardo Arozomona

(In Spanish; with English Titles)

Dolores Del Rio Mexican-made drama has plenty of impact, being suitable for class houses in this country.

Yarn is told in flashback. It relates the anguish and despair caused when a landowner's son weds a laborer's granddaughter. His father disowns him and he joins the revolutionary element in Mexico. He learns that a band of outlaws, opposed to the revolutionists, killed his father. In the end the landowner's son is executed, and his wife and son live on.

Miss Del Rio gives a capable performance as the laborer's daughter, while Pedro Armendariz, as her husband, goes through his paces rather stiltedly. Remainder of cast suffices. Story line, through strong direction, sustains interest throughout. *Sten.*

Miniature Reviews

"Objective, Burma" (WB). Errol Flynn in war film due for top grosses.

"Tonight and Every Night" (Musical; color) (Col). Excellent filmusical in Technicolor, with Rita Hayworth in starring spot. Plenty b.o.

"Thunderhead—Son of Flicka" (20th; color). Charming ranch idyll sequel in technicolor will do good biz.

"Roughly Speaking" (WB). Too-long drama of American family. Starring voltage of Rosalind Russell and Jack Carson required for nominally profitable biz.

"Here Come the Co-Eds" (U) (With Music). Latest Abbott-Costello starrer is a boxoffice wow.

"What a Blonde" (RKO). Mildly entertaining comedy, okay on duals.

"Tahiti Nights" (Musical) (Col). Low-budget "B"; dualler.

"Bluebeard" (PRC). One of better pix to come from this distrib; horror story headed for surprising business.

Objective, Burma

Warner Bros. release of Jerry Wald production. Stars Errol Flynn; features William Prince, James Brown, Dick Erdman, George Tobias, Henry Hull, Warner Anderson. Directed by Raoul Walsh. Screenplay, Ranald MacDougall and Lester Cole, from original story by Alvah Bessie; music, Franz Waxman; editor, George Amy; camera, James Wong Howe; special effects, E. B. Du Par; music director, Leo F. Forbstein. Running time, 142 MINS.

Capt. Nelson	Errol Flynn
Lieut. Jacobs	William Prince
Sgt. Treacy	James Brown
Gabby Gordon	George Tobias
Mark Williams	Henry Hull
Col. Carter	Warner Anderson
Hogan	John Alvin
Lieut. Barker	Stephen Richards
Nebraska	Dick Erdman
Miggleori	Tony Caruso
Capt. Hennessey	Hugh Beaumont
Negulesco	John Whitney
Brophy	Joel Allen
Soapy Higgins	Buddy Yarus
Capt. Li	Frank Tang
Fred Hollis	William Hudson
Sgt. Chettu	Rodric Red Wing
Ghurka	Asit Koomar
Co-Pilot	John Sheridan
Major Fitzpatrick	Lester Matthews

The brothers Warner have gone in for another task-force operation in a thriller called "Objective, Burma," a yarn about the American paratrooper invasion of Burma. It has ghastly Jap-atrocity ramifications that will dissipate considerable appeal for the femmes, but with Errol Flynn for the marquee, its general boxoffice lure will prevail.

"Air Force" and "Destination, Tokyo" have been other Warner operations in a similar genre, and comparisons are inevitable with the latest objective. "Burma" may not have the accelerated pace of the others but its overall effect is achieved despite a script that could have been cut by half an hour.

Yarn deals with a paratroop contingent dropped behind the Japanese lines in Burma to destroy a radar station. The chutists achieve their objective but while returning to a designated spot to be picked up by planes and flown back to the base they're overtaken by Japs. Then follows a series of exciting experiences by the troopers against overwhelming odds.

The film has considerable movement, particularly in the early reels, and the tactics of the paratroopers are authentic in their painstaking detail. However, while the scripters have in the main achieved their purpose of heightening the action, there are scenes in the final reels that could have been edited more closely.

There will be many who will shudder at the horror of American soldiers suffering the tortures at the hands of the Japs, as viewed late in the pic, and if "Burma" achieves nothing else, it will at least have accented that complacency should have no place in our dealing with the Nips.

Ranald MacDougall, who achieved an enormous rep with the CBS noholds-barred series, "The Man Behind the Gun," has scripted "Burma," along with Lester Cole. This adaptation of a story by Alvah Bessie likewise pulls no punches in conjuring a picture of the type of enemy we're fighting.

Flynn gives a quietly restrained performance as the contingent's leader, while supporting players who also perform capably are Henry Hull, as a war correspondent; William Prince, James Brown, George Tobias, Dick Erdman and Warner Anderson.

Raoul Walsh's direction is topflight, and so is the cameraing of James Wong Howe. The other productional accoutrements are likewise topflight. *Kahn.*

Tonight and Every Night
(MUSICAL; COLOR)
Hollywood, Jan. 24.

Columbia release of Victor Saville production. Stars Rita Hayworth; features Lee Bowman, Janet Blair, Marc Platt and Leslie Brooks. Produced and directed by Saville. Screenplay by Lesser Samuels and Abem Finkel, based on play, "Heart of the City," by Lesley Storm; camera, Rudolph Mate; editor, Viola Lawrence; special effects, Lawrence W. Butler; montages, John Hoffman; dances staged by Jack Cole and Val Raset; songs by Jule Styne and Sammy Cahn; musical director, M. W. Stoloff. Previewed in Hollywood, Jan. 23, '45. Running time, **89 MINS.**

Rosalind Bruce	Rita Hayworth
Paul Lundy	Lee Bowman
Judy Kane	Janet Blair
Tommy Lawson	Marc Platt
Angela	Leslie Brooks
The Great Waldo	Professor Lamberti
Toni	Dusty Anderson
Leslie Wiggins	Stephen Crane
Life Photographer	Jim Bannon
May Tolliver	Florence Bates
Sam Royce	Ernest Cossart
Rev. Gerald Lundy	Philip Merivale
David Long	Patrick O'Moore
Group Captain	Gavin Muir
Bubbles	Shelley Winter
Pamela	Marilyn Johnson
Frenchie	Mildred Law
Joan	Elizabeth Inglise
Mrs. Peabody	Aminta Dyne
Mrs. Good	Joy Harrington
Annette	Ann Codee

Specialty by Richard Haydn

"Tonight and Every Night" is a toprank filmusical with plenty of eye and ear entertainment, diverting for all classes of audiences. With Rita Hayworth starred, picture has strong marquee dressing for getaways in the keys, with what's on the screen a cinch to create plenty of fast and favorable word-of-mouth.

"Tonight" has plenty of pace in its backstage tale, which gets slightly away from regulation formula to carry adequately the many showmanly production numbers. Setting is a five-a-day music hall in London, which carries on with daily performances during the blitz through the courage of the performers, headed by American-born Miss Hayworth and the persistence of impresario Florence Bates. Romance is quickly developed between Miss Hayworth and RAF pilot Lee Bowman.

In addition to several excellently staged dances by Miss Hayworth, latter is presented as singing a few songs to good effect. Title tune is in patriotic march tempo, "You Excite Me" is a torch number, while "Anywhere" looks like the best bet for pop attention.

Comedy specialty handled by Miss Hayworth and Janet Blair, in twin bed setting and with both attired in woolen underwear, is neatly contrived and excellently presented by the two performers. One of the most novel and original presentations seen in years is Miss Hayworth in front of a movie screen in which she hails various characters from the projected black-and-white film to come down and join her. The monotone-hued characters walk off the side of the screen to appear down front in natural colors. Number is a standout in both design and execution, with great credit due to the technicians and engineers.

Marc Platt, plucked by Columbia from his featured role in the Broadway "Oklahoma!" makes a sensational debut early with an improvised solo dance to conform to every type of music coming over the radio, and his finale stepping to a haranguing speech by Hitler is a showstopper. Although Platt briefly appears in a few other dance numbers with Miss Heyworth, his entrance insures his sticking around films. Platt slips into a straight acting spot in the proceedings and does exceptionally well for a camera newcomer.

Miss Hayworth turns in a capable all-around performance, dancing magnificently, effectively putting over the song numbers and scoring solidly in the starring assignment. Bowman is fine as the romantically-inclined pilot, while Miss Blair catches attention as the show's ingenue with a refreshing and personable delivery. Miss Bates, Ernest Cossart and Professor Lamberti show to advantage as most prominent in support, although Lamberti's xylophone specialty should have been clipped somewhat.

Victor Saville is credited with both producer and director chores. He deftly paces the story portions. Script by Lesser Samuels and Abem Frankel is compact and interesting in both situations and dialog. Jack Cole and Val Raset expertly staged the various dance numbers.

Picture is lavishly mounted, with the outstanding Technicolor photography, by Rudolph Mate, adding much to the overall effect. *Walt.*

Thunderhead—Son of Flicka
(COLOR)

20th-Fox release of Robert Bassler production. Features Roddy McDowall, Preston Foster, Rita Johnson. Directed by Louis King. Screenplay, Dwight Cummins and Dorothy Yost, based on novel by Mary O'Hara; camera, Charles Clarke; editor, Nick De Maggio; music, Cyril J. Mockridge; musical direction, Emil Newman. Tradeshown in N. Y. Jan. 26, '45. Running time, **78 MINS.**

Ken McLaughlin	Roddy McDowall
Rob McLaughlin	Preston Foster
Nelle	Rita Johnson
Gus	James Bell
Hildy	Diana Hale
Major Harris	Carleton Young
Mr. Sargent	Ralph Sanford
Tim	Robert Filmer
Dr. Hicks	Alan Bridge

"Thunderhead — Son of Flicka," 20th-Fox's sequel to "My Friend Flicka," is a worthy successor. A simple outdoor idyll of a ranch lad and his horse, it has the same refreshing quality of its predecessor and a similar appeal. It's set for good biz throughout.

Story, like "Flicka," is filmed on open ranges of Utah and Oregon, with its rolling country, gorges and hills. In its Technicolor dress, setting is a natural, with beauty of background continually intruding into yarn.

Shots, too, of herds of horses roaming the range, always intrigue, as do brief scenes of a horse warily nosing a porcupine or violently killing a rattler. Though story is simple one of a boy rearing a colt in hopes of making him a racer, pic contains drama throughout, as in various stages of breaking in the horse or the hunt for an equine killer. And the horse race, as well as the fight between two magnificent white stallions, gives pic some peak moments of excitement. Background music also rates mention, especially towards emphasizing its drama.

Thunderhead is a wild white colt foaled by Flicka. Ken, the horse rancher's son, tries to break him and train him for racing. Ken partly succeeds, riding him towards victory in a county meet till horse pulls tendon. Thereafter Thunderhead, when he recovers, is used only as Ken's saddlehorse, until finally the horse redeems itself by saving Ken's life and rescuing the rancher's herd from a wild albino that has terrorized the county and stolen its mares. Fact that albino has sired Flicka, mother of Thunderhead, doesn't stop the two white stallions from fighting each time they meet, until the death struggle at the close.

Roddy McDowall again plays the rancher's son, as in "Flicka," with shy appeal, exhibiting, however, more of the practical rancher than the kid dreamer in this film in trying to tame Thunderhead. Preston Foster plays the rancher father with warmth. Rita Johnson is again the understanding mother and Diana Hale the amusing little busybody. James Bell reliably enacts the ranch hand again.

Directing pace is satisfactory. *Bron.*

Roughly Speaking
Hollywood, Jan. 30.

Warner release of Henry Blanke production. Stars Rosalind Russell and Jack Carson. Directed by Michael Curtiz. Screenplay by Louise Randall Pierson, from her book of same name: camera, Joseph Walker; editor, David Weisbart; montages by James Leicester; special effects by Roy Davidson, director, and Hans Koenekamp, camera; dialog director, Frederick De Cordova. Tradeshown in L. A. Jan. 30, '45. Running time, **125 MINS.**

Prolog (1902)

Mr. Randall	Ray Collins
Mrs. Randall	Kathleen Lockhart
Elinor Randall	Cora Sue Collins
Louise Randall	Ann Todd
Matt	Andy Clyde
Minister	Arthur Shields
First Maid, Olga	Helene Thimig
Second Maid, Anna	Greta Granstedt

(Beginning 1908)

Louise Randall	Rosalind Russell
Alice Abbott	Ann Doran
The Teacher	Hobart Cavanaugh
The Dean	Elly Malyon
Mr. Morton	Alan Hale
Rodney Crane	Donald Woods
Jack Leslie	Craig Stevens
Lawton Mackall	John Alvin
Rose	Mary Servoss
Doctor Lewis	Francis Pierlot
Doctor Bowditch	Manart Kippen
The Judge	George Carleton
The Professor	George Meader
Harold Pierson	Jack Carson
Tony	Frank Puglia
Svend Olsen	John Qualen
The Proprietor	Chester Clute
Customer in Music Shop	Irving Bacon
Relief Worker	Barbara Brown
George	Sig Arno

The Children: Ann Lawrence, Mona Freeman, Andrea King, Mickey Kuhn, Johnny Treul, Robert Hutton, John Calkins, Richard Wimer, John Sheridan, Jo Ann Marlowe, Patsy Lee Parsons, Jean Sullivan, Gregory Muradian, John Sheffield, Robert Arthur.

"Roughly Speaking" transference to the screen has resulted in a generally tedious tale of the life of an American girl—not particularly typical—from 12 to 50. Filled with many minor and disconnected episodes over 125 minutes, picture will hit nominally profitable gait in these days of lush b.o., mainly on the marquee voltage of Rosalind Russell and Jack Carson in the starring spots.

Brief prolog of the 1902 period introduces the character played later as an adult by Miss Russell. Louise Randall's the 12-year-old daughter of a New England merchant whose death discloses a small estate to take care of wife and two girls. Determined to make her own way in the then man's world of business, the ambitious Miss Russell takes a business course to wind up in New Haven and marry a Yale student and banker's son, Donald Woods. Latter makes slow progress in business, pair raise a brood of four youngsters, and he finally departs for another woman. She then meets and falls in love with Carson, happy-go-lucky gambler who vows to settle down. It's a happy marriage, with the trials, tribulations and haphazard fortunes of the group displayed in detail through the years until outbreak of the present, when three of the now-grown boys enter service to leave the parents with chins up for eventual family reunion.

Original biography of Louise Randall Pierson, who came to the studio to prepare the screenplay, is a rambling drama for dashes of comedy and family crisis along the route. Director Michael Curtiz deftly etches his characters, but he's burdened with too much, and a too-loose script, to deliver a compact job.

Miss Russell is spotlighted effectively as the girl who's determined to be a success but who finds vicissitudes of life too great to overcome until her fifties, when prosperity finally smiles. Carson provides a strong performance as the always-happy husband and pal of the growing kids. Woods, Andrea King, Robert Hutton, John Sheridan, Jean Sullivan and Robert Arthur are most prominent in the extended supporting cast.

Picture has been given expensive production mounting, with numerous sets required to bridge the long period covered. Photography by Joseph Walker is of high standard throughout. *Walt.*

Here Come the Co-Eds
(WITH MUSIC)

Universal release of John Grant production. Stars Bud Abbott, Lou Costello; features Peggy Ryan, Martha O'Driscoll, Lon Chaney, Donald Cook, Phil Spitalny's "Hour of Charm" all-girl orchestra. Directed by Jean Yarbrough. Screenplay by Arthur T. Horman and John Grant, based on story by Edmund L. Hartmann; camera, George Robinson; editor, Arthur Hilton; special camera work, John P. Fulton; songs by Jack Brooks, Edgar Fairchild. Previewed at RKO 58th St., N. Y., Jan. 29, '45. Running time, **88 MINS.**

Slats	Bud Abbott
Oliver	Lou Costello
Patty	Peggy Ryan
Molly	Martha O'Driscoll
Diane	June Vincent
Johnson	Lon Chaney
Benson	Donald Cook
Kirkland	Charles Dingle
Near-sighted Man	Richard Lane
Honest Dan	Joe Kirk
Bill Stern	Himself

Phil Spitalny and His Hour of Charm Orchestra

Abbott and Costello are easily up to their high laugh standards in "Here Come the Co-Eds." It's sock boxoffice. Will get holdover runs in almost all spots.

Pic is helped considerably by presence of Phil Spitalny's nifty, all-girl "Hour of Charm" orchestra and Peggy Ryan. Miss Ryan plays a typical college hepcat.

"Co-Eds" is smartly gagged, smoothly paced, and even the familiar routines are given new twists. The gags or bits cover the field from the face-slapping episodes, down through a comedy wrestling match, farcical basketball game, a mad scramble in a kitchen, to the payoff chase sequence. One of the funniest scenes is in a restaurant where Lou Costello encounters difficulty drinking his oyster stew and winds up being leered at by a pugnacious live oyster.

Yarn is one of those things, showing a moss-covered, tradition-bound femme college that's stirred out of its lethargy by Abbott and Costello. These two get jobs as caretakers at the school when Slats (Abbott) publicizes his dancing sister as wanting to earn coin to attend school. She wins the scholarship, much to the vexation of Charles Dingle, chairman of the college board. He holds a mortgage on the school and it takes a concert (by the Spitalny band), then the screwball wrestling match and, finally, the payoff basketball game, to raise the money to lift the mortgage. Script has Spitalny in for closeups as professor of music appreciation at the girls' college. He looks the part.

Of the seven tunes by Jack Brooks and Edgar Fairchild, "I Don't Care If I Never Dream Again," "Jumpin' on Saturday Night," and "Some Day, We Will Remember" loom as best. There's also a comedy number, "Let's Play House," that's catchy. It's done by Costello and Miss Ryan for top laugh returns. "Dream Again," which appears to be standout song, is the offering of the Spitalny organization, with Evelyn, Meda and Kathryn spotlighted. Given superb mounting, a real click. "Jumpin'" is entirely a triumph for Miss Ryan, youngster putting over the swingeroo tune vocally and with her clever tapstering.

John Grant, originally from musical comedy, who's done scripts from the A.-&-C. team ever since they began to go places, did well by the comedy duo on the production end. He's also responsible for the screen story, along with Arthur T. Horman. Jean Yarbrough's direction is aces. George Robinson did a particularly fine camera job.

Support, headed by Martha O'Driscoll, Lon Chaney, Donald Cook and Bill Stern (as sports announcer at basketball game), provides strong background for the comedy gyrations. *Wear.*

What a Blonde

RKO release of Ben Stoloff production. Features Leon Errol, Richard Lane, Michael St. Angel, Elaine Riley, Veda Ann Borg. Directed by Leslie Goodwins. Screenplay, Charles Roberts, from original by Oscar Brodney; editor, Edward W. Williams; camera, J. Roy Hunt. At Albee, Brooklyn, N. Y., week of Jan. 27, '45, dual. Running time, **71 MINS.**

Fowler....Leon Errol
Pomeroy....Richard Lane
Andrew....Michael St. Angel
Cynthia....Elaine Riley
Pat....Veda Ann Borg
Mrs. Fowler....Lydia Bilbrook
Mr. Dafoe....Clarence Kolb
Mrs. Dafoe....Ann Shoemaker
Guglielmi....Chef Milani
McPherson....Emory Parnell
Watson....Larry Wheat
Annie....Dorothy Vaughan
Redmond....Jason Robards

Mildly diverting comedy, which more often than not borders on farce, is geared strictly for the duals. Also, it will give Leon Errol fans a field day, since he carries most of the burden and grabs the majority of laughs throughout the gossamer interludes of a thin but more or less entertaining yarn.

Errol, in the lingerie line, is stumped for materials because of silk shortage due to war and is dependent upon Clarence Kolb, a bluenose competitor, to get materials. He's also stymied for gas and deputizes Richard Lane, his playboy butler, to hire extra riders for his car to solve this problem, so he can have a greater ration via share-the-ride. Latter sells idea to Veda Ann Borg, stranded vaude performer, who moves the other gals into the tycoon's menage. It all adds up to a galloping frolic of mistaken identities and the usual other farcical ingredients to keep Errol in hot water throughout.

Errol is at his best. Miss Borg does all right by the flashy blonde performer, the title role, with Lane doing a nifty job as playboy-butler. There is a brief romantic interest handled nicely by Michael St. Angel and Elaine Riley. Other support roles are capably handled. Leslie Goodwins has directed at required galloping pace. *Edba.*

Tahiti Nights
(MUSICAL)

Columbia release of Sam White production. Stars Jinx Falkenburg; features Dave O'Brien, Carole Mathews. Mary Treen, Florence Bates. Directed by Will Jason. Story by Lillie Hayward; camera. Benjamin Kline; editor, Jerome Thoms; songs by Harry Owens, Mitchell Parrish and Rene Touzet. At Brooklyn Strand. week of Jan. 25, '45, dual. Running time, 63 MINS.

Luana....Jinx Falkenburg
Jack....Dave O'Brien
Mata....Mary Treen
Queen Liliha....Florence Bates
Chief Enoka....Cy Kenda
Chopstick....Eddie Bruce
Tonga....Pedro de Cordoba
Temata....Hilo Hattie
Betty Lou....Carole Mathew
And the Vagabonds

A light, low-budget love story with six songs of South Seas motif, "Tahiti Nights" is a "B" for the lower rung on duals.

Story relates how an American bandleader arrives on a Tahitian isle and finds that arrangements have been made to marry him off to the princess of one of the tribes.

"Let Me Love You Tonight," by Mitchell Parrish and Rene Touzet, is the best tune in the picture and, of course, has long since been exploited for sock response. Others, composed by bandleader Harry Owens, are just fair. Jinx Falkenburg, starred, and remainder of cast go through their paces rather stiltedly. Direction is slow-paced and production values are negligible. *Sten.*

Bluebeard

PRC Pictures release of Leon Fromkess production. (Associate producer, Martin Mooney.) Features John Carradine, Jean Parker, Nils Asther, Ludwig Stossel. Directed by Edgar G. Ulmer. Screenplay by Pierre Gendron from original by Arnold Phillips and Werner H. Furst; camera, Jockey A. Feindel; editor, Carl Pierson. At Brooklyn Strand, week of Jan. 25, '45, dual. Running time, **71 MINS.**

Gaston....John Carradine
Lucille....Jean Parker
Inspector Lefevre....Nils Asther
Lamarte....Ludwig Stossel
Inspector Renard....George Pembroke
Francine....Teala Loring
Renee....Sonia Sorel
Mimi....Iris Adrian
Deschamps....Henry Kolker
Le Soldat....Emmett Lynn
Bebette....Patti McCarty
Constance....Carrie Devan
Jeanette....Anne Sterling

One of the best pictures to come out of the PRC production mill, "Bluebeard" is a horror film that should be able to bring good returns as the top film on neighborhood duals.

Locale is Paris in the 19th century. John Carradine gives an excellent portrayal of an artist with an uncontrollable desire to strangle his models after he has painted their portraits. Jean Parker, as one of the models, gives one of her better performances in bringing the killer to justice. Others who help make this chiller topflight are Nils Asther, as a member of the French Surete, and Ludwig Stossel, as an art dealer.

Production has some expensive settings and pretty costumes. *Sten.*

Miniature Reviews

"Sergeant Mike" (Col). Actionful war yarn pointing up canines' contribution to armed services; okay for duals.

"Waterloo Road" (GFD). British-made story of blitzed London has b.o. possibilities in U. S.

"El Muerto Falta a La Cita" (AAA). Strong Argentine-made romantic comedy, but absence of names makes usual extremely limited U. S. appeal.

"El Camino de los Gatos" (Clasa) (Mexican-made). Thin melodrama about Mexico in 1860's; mild for Spanish languagers.

"Rats of Tobruk" (RKO) (Australian-made). Long-anticipated Charles Chauvel film looks like b.o. dud except Down Under.

Sergeant Mike

Columbia release of Jack Fier production. Features Larry Parks, Jeanne Bates, Mike and Pearl (dogs). Directed by Harry Levin. Screenplay, Robert Lee Johnson; editor, Rey Browne; camera, L. W. O'Connell. At Strand, Brooklyn, N. Y., week of Feb. 1, '45; dual. Running time, **60 MINS.**

Allen....Larry Parks
Terry....Jeanne Bates
Simms....Loren Tindall
Patrick Henry....Jim Bannon
Sgt. Rankin....Robert Williams
Reed....Richard Powers
S. K. Arno....Larry Joe Olsen
Monohan....Eddie Acuff
Rogers....John Tyrrell
Hall....Charles Wagenheim
Mike....Himself
Pearl....Herself

This actionful war yarn, pointing up contributions of the dogs on the field of battle, will get plenty of the juve trade for which it's seemingly geared. Adults, too, will be interested, but it's the kiddies who will keep the wickets turning in most of the dual situations.

Screenplay has evidently been spun to display histrionic ability of the featured brace of canines, Mike and Pearl, which have the more meatier roles than their supporting players.

Larry Parks is none too happy over his transfer from a hard-boiled machinegun outfit to the K-9 (canine) Corps, where he is assigned to train pooches for war work. When he finds out that Mike, one of the dogs he's to train, is the gift of eight-year-old Larry Joe Olsen, whose father died in battle, he makes Mike one of the best four-footed scouts of the corps. Pearl is Mike's vis-a-vis. Both do heroic work in ferreting out machinegun nests of the Japs and carry messages through the enemy lines. Pearl is killed by Japs in one of the jungle fights but Mike carries on to bring reinforcements that whip the Nippons.

There's the inevitable romance between the soldier and Jean Bates, as the little boy's mother. Parks gives good account as the heroic GI. Miss Bates does likewise as the youthful war-widow. Remainder of cast also okay. Direction by Harry Levin is adequate. L. W. O'Connell's camera work is okay, too. *Edba.*

Waterloo Road
(BRITISH-MADE)

London, Jan. 12.

General Film Distributors' release of Gainsborough production. Features John Mills, Stewart Granger, Alastair Sim. Directed by Sydney Gilliat. Written by Sydney Gilliat from story of Val Valentine; camera, Arthur Crabtree. At Leicester Square theatre, London, Jan. 12, '45. Running time, **76 MINS.**

Jim Colter....John Mills
Ted Purvis....Stewart Granger
Dr. Montgomery....Alastair Sim
Tillie Colter....Joy Shelton
Mrs. Colter....Beatrice Varley
Ruby....Alison Leggatt
Tom Mason....George Carney
Fred....Arthur Denton
Vera....Vera Frances
Mike Duggan....Leslie Bradley
Corporal Lewis....Ben Williams

Skillful direction and admirable casting give this film satisfactory b.o. potentialities, which should be realized both here and in U.S. Played against the drab, bomb-shattered background of a London slum, story is the familiar triangle theme with use of the flashback technique not adding to its originality. But it's acted with such sincerity and is so true-to-life in its characterization that the picture grips throughout. There is a terrific climax in which the two men fight for one woman as the bombs thunder down. This brutal sequence likely will produce word-of-mouth publicity.

A soldier deserts when he learns his wife is receiving attentions from another man. Story depicts his day spent in pursuit of the pair, finally confronting them in a sports arcade.

Entire cast is adequate, but particular praise goes to Alastair Sim as the neighborhood doctor and George Carney's role of pigeon fancier.

Picture is a striking example of how sound an English production can be if it keeps to the medium it interprets best, that of the middle class character.

El Muerto Falta a La Cita
("Corpse Breaks a Date")
(ARGENTINE-MADE)

AAA release of Baires production. Directed by Pierre Chenal. Stars Angel Magana, Nelida Bilboa, Sebastian Chiola. Features Guillermo Battaglia, Maruja Quesada, Oscar Vila, Tilda Thamar, Roberto Ramos, Marcial Manena, Alberto Terrones. Screenplay by Sixto Pondal Rios and Carlos Olivari; camera, Francisco Boeniger. At Gran Rex, Buenos Aires, Dec. 7, '44. Running time, **90 MINS.**

This picture is unique in many ways. It aroused praise both from critics and public. Story is refreshingly original. And Pierre Chenal's direction is bright. The French director manages to obtain naturalness from all players. But only mild for U. S. market.

Suspenseful story concerns the trials of a bridegroom (Magana) whose bachelor friends host him too well on the wedding eve. Tearing himself away from this party, his roadster runs down a cyclist on a deserted roadway. Befuddled and horrified he drags the body into the bushes (he thinks he has killed the man) and returns to the party, and drinks himself into oblivion. Next morning the crime seems nightmarish, so he abandons his bride (Nelida Bilboa) at the altar steps.

Magana goes to the cops and the search for the supposed "corpse" proving futile, the incident is dismissed as due to his alcohol-bemused brain. Driving back, Magana gives a lift to a curious wayfarer (Sebastian Chiola) who appeared at the scene of the search. This man advises him to seek the abandoned bride's forgiveness. The lovers are reconciled, but their honeymoon is rudely interrupted by the arrival of an uninvited guest, this eccentric vagabond whose advice had reunited them. The intruder finally starts to blackmail him. Unable to raise the sums demanded, there is a showdown with the "bereaved," really the man Magana hit with his car.

Of the players, Sebastian Chiola is outstanding as the humbugging brother, proving okay in an unsympathetic part. He overshadows Angel Magana, rated among best local film material. Nelida Bilboa is appealing as the bride.

Locations have been well chosen to show something of the local countryside. Photography and cutting are about the best so far seen here. *Nid.*

El Camino de los Gatos
("Highway of Cats")
(MEXICAN-MADE)

Clasa Films production and release. Stars Emilio Tuero, Carmen Montejo. Directed by Chano Urueta. Adapted by Chano Urueta from story by Hermann Sudermann. At Belmont, N. Y., starting Jan. 26, '45. Running time, 128 MINS.

Carlos...................Emilio Tuero
Regina................Carmen Montejo
Felix.....................Tony Diaz
Pedro..................Paco Fuentes
Elena...................Esther Luquin
Don Alberto........Alfredo del Diestro
Don Arturo..............Jose Morcillo
Victor..............Victor Velazquez
Army Prosecutor........Angel T. Sala
Don Lazaro.............Lauro Benitez
Priest.................Agustin Sen
Ernesto.............Enrique Cancino
Official I...........Salvador Lozano
Official II..............Chel Lopez

(In Spanish; No English Titles)

"Highway of Cats" concerns the military campaigns of Mexico's Benito Juarez against the French from 1862 to 1867. Despite an unusual title, picture becomes tangled up with countless counter-plots, including an odd and uninteresting romantic triangle. It's lesser fare for Spanish languagers.

Whole thing centers about Emilio Tuero's efforts to make amends for his father's traitorous action in opening the "Highway of the Cats" to the invading French troops. He does this by leading the armed forces of Mexico. Main theme hardly gets past a couple of mild battle sequences before Tuero becomes involved in two romantic affairs and a fight with, first, his old pal, and then the natives he blames for killing his father. It's all a bit confusing, especially to those not understanding Spanish too well because most of plot hinges on spoken passages, and this film has no English titles.

Tuero is not seen to advantage due to direction and story. Carmen Montejo does her best to make something out of the downtrodden childhood sweetheart. Esther Luquin is the other girl in the story. *Wear.*

Rats of Tobruk
(AUSTRALIAN-MADE)
Sydney, Jan. 9.

RKO release of Charles Munro-Charles Chauvel production. Features Grant Taylor, Chips Rafferty, Peter Finch, George Wallace. Directed by Charles Chauvel. Screenplay by Mrs. Chas. Chauvel; camera, George Heath. At Mayfair, Sydney, Dec. 7, '44. Running time, 95 MINS.

Financed by RKO, Hoyts, and Charles Munro, "Rats of Tobruk" has been two years in making. Chauvel, who had the cooperation of local military authorities, has failed to give "Rats" a screen treatment worthy of so great a war epic in which Australian khaki-clads played such a magnificent part. Instead, he turns out a disjointed piece that fails to hit the target. Fact that this phase of the war is overshadowed by new campaigns also is a handicap for world market.

Listless piece of screen writing is a major drawback. Continuity is almost zero, and so-so acting, especially by the femmes, make tough sledding the prospect at the boxoffice for this one. Chances in U. S. look extremely slim.

Chauvel's direction fails to bring out any light and shade. Too much time is devoted to war sequences, with scant attention paid to story continuity. Chauvel also has rung in several newsreel clips for good measure, but not effectively.

Film opens in prewar days. It shows an English author out in Australia to secure copy for a book he's writing on local ranch life. He travels around the countryside in the company of a sheep-herder and a trapper—and recites quite a lot of poetry. Country girl gets a yen for the Englishman, even though the sheep-herder is in love with her. Arrival of the war finds all three

men in Tobruk. Shot-and-shell sequences then consume most of the running time. Englishman gets killed near the finish. Film then switches suddenly to New Guinea where the trapper is killed. This leaves only the sheep-herder to return home to the girl he loves.

Pauline Garrick as the country girl is extremely weak. Same is true of Mary Gay who is the nurse. George Wallace, from vaude-revue, does okay with a burlesque comedy role.

American audiences wouldn't understand the lingo, much less the story. Same goes for the British. Only chance for "Rats" is in Australia and New Zealand. It's a poor piece of celluloid. *Rick.*

Miniature Reviews

"The Enchanted Cottage" (RKO). Fine, sensitive drama with Dorothy McGuire, Robert Young and Herbert Marshall. Profitable biz.

"It's in the Bag" (UA). Fred Allen starrer geared for satisfactory b.o.

'Circumstantial Evidence" (20th). Mild crime meller; B-grade dualer.

"Frisco Sal" (Songs) (U). Drama and romance on Frisco's Barbary Coast in the old days. Nominally profitable biz.

"The Chicago Kid" (Rep). Fast-moving, modern gangster meller with Donald Barry; strong supporter for duals.

The Enchanted Cottage
Hollywood, Feb. 13.

RKO release of Harriet Parsons production (Jack Gross, executive producer). Stars Dorothy McGuire, Robert Young, and Herbert Marshall. Directed by John Cromwell. Screenplay by DeWitt Bodeen and Herman J. Mankiewicz, based on play by Sir Arthur Wing Pinero; camera, Ted Tetzlaff; editor, Joseph Noriega; special effects by Vernon L. Walker; music by Roy Webb; musical director, C. Bakaleinikoff. Tradeshown in L. A. Feb. 13, '45. Running time, 91 MINS.

Laura....................Dorothy McGuire
Oliver......................Robert Young
Hillgrove.................Herbert Marshall
Mrs. Minnett.............Mildred Natwick
Violet Price.............Spring Byington
Beatrice.................Hillary Brooke
Frederick...............Richard Gaines
Danny.....................Alec Englander
Mrs. Stanton..............Mary Worth
Canteen Manager.......Josephine Whittell
Marine......................Robert Clarke
Soldier....................Eden Nicholas

Modernized version of play by Sir Arthur Wing Pinero, a silent picture of 20 years ago with Richard Barthelmess and May McAvoy, is an artistic production which will catch both critical praise and plenty of audience attention. With Dorothy McGuire, Robert Young and Herbert Marshall toplining in top performances, "Enchanted Cottage" will play a merry tune at the boxoffice.

Sensitive love story of a returned war veteran with ugly facial disfigurements and the homely slavey—both self-conscious of their handicaps—is sincerely told both in the script and outstanding direction of John Cromwell. It's a timely drama which should impress on relatives and friends of the returning crippled or disfigured a necessity for tolerance of such scars to make rehabilitation of the boys easier through eliminating personal self-consciousness of their injuries.

Brief prolog establishes Young as the flyer who leases a cottage for his honeymoon, but is called to service on eve of his wedding. Two years later he returns to hide his war disfigurements from his family at the cottage, where Miss McGuire is hiding from people because of her ugliness. But the girl's tender attention to the flyer results in idyllic love, with each appearing beautiful to the other and pair sincerely believing that the cottage is enchanted and responsible for the transformations. Married, couple has shocked awakening when Young's parents shatter their dreams and they realize that the physical defects are pointedly apparent to the outside world. But the philosophies of Marshall, as the counselling blind composer and friend, prevail to have the lovers gradually lose their self-consciousness to mingle again with other people.

Miss McGuire turns in an outstanding performance, with Young also sharing the limelight. Marshall is excellent, while Mildred Natwick scores as the housekeeper. Spring Byington; Hillary Brooke, Richard Gaines and Alec Englander, provide strong support.

Cromwell's direction deftly motivates the drama in top style. Picture is first for Harriet Parsons as a producer at RKO, and—under wing of executive producer Jack Gross—she has turned in a most able job. Production mounting is fine, accentuated by the excellent photography by Ted Tetzlaff. *Walt.*

It's In the Bag

United Artists release of Jack H. Skirball production. Directed by Richard Wallace. Stars Fred Allen. Guest stars: Jack Benny, Don Ameche, Rudy Vallee, William Bendix, Victor Moore. Screen treatment, Lewis R. Foster, Fred Allen; screenplay, Jay Dratler, Alma Reville; story, Morrie Ryskind; camera, Russell Metty; editor, William M. Morgan. Previewed at Loew's Sheridan Square, N. Y., Feb. 7, '45. Running time, 87 MINS.

Fred Floogle...................Fred Allen
Himself.......................Jack Benny
Himself....................William Bendix
Eve Floogle.................Binnie Barnes
Parker....................Robert Benchley
Psychiatrist...............Jerry Colonna
Pike.......................John Carradine
Marion......................Gloria Pope
Perry.....................William Terry
Mrs. Nussbaum.............Minerva Pious
Homer.....................Dickie Tyler
Detective Sully............Sidney Toler
Hotel Manager..........George Cleveland
Arnold.....................John Miljan
Monte......................Ben Welden
Mr. Buddoo...............Emory Parnell

"It's in the Bag" should prove moderately profitable. Film packs plenty of individual sock comedy sequences, offsetting uneven, loosely-woven continuity and doubtful story values. Additionally, it's jammed with as many topnotch names as any theatre marquee can conveniently use. Exploitation potential, of firstline importance in a production of this type, is enormous.

Aside from Victor Moore, Don Ameche and Rudy Vallee, who are in for a brief but hilarious singing-waiter bit, other name players hold considerable footage. Among the outstanding sequences is one with Jack Benny and Fred Allen, in which the former's stinginess is expertly lampooned. William Bendix is also in for a lengthy bit as a namby-pamby boss racketeer who inherited the "gang" from his mother and can't stand the sound of pistol shots. Jerry Colonna scores readily in a running gag sequence as a wacky psychiatrist.

Allen handles his film assignment expertly but this vehicle does not provide the proper formula for the full and effective use of the comic's ability.

Jack Skirball has, perhaps wisely, poured everything into talent. The result is something like a series of vaudeville skits, mostly good, but inadequate as a screenplay.

Robert Benchley rates a nod as a swanky insect exterminator as does Dickie Tyler, who plays a bespectacled young genius with all the answers.

Yarn is about a flea circus operator (Allen) who suddenly finds he's inherited $12,000,000 from a granduncle and then discovers that the money has disappeared. Allen learns that some of the coin has been hidden in a chair, and most of action revolves about the hunt for the missing money. *Mori.*

Circumstantial Evidence

20th-Fox release of William Girard production. Stars Michael O'Shea, Lloyd Nolan; features Trudy Marshall, Billy Cummings, Ruth Ford, Reed Hadley, Roy Roberts, Scotty Beckett. Directed by John Larkin. Screenplay, Robert Metzler; adapted by Samuel Ornitz from story by Nat Ferber, Sam Duncan. Editor, Norman Colbert; camera, Harry Jackson. Tradeshown N. Y., Feb. 9, '45. Running time, 67 MINS.

Joe Reynolds............Michael O'Shea
Sam Lord...................Lloyd Nolan
Agnes Hannon............Trudy Marshall
Pat......................Billy Cummings
Mrs. Simms..................Ruth Ford
Prosecutor................Reed Hadley
Marty Hannon...............Roy Roberts
Freddy Hanlon.............Scotty Beckett
Bolger....................Byron Foulger

Bolger's Wife..............Dorothy Adams
Judge White..................John Eldredge
Mike...............................Eddie Marr
Warden......................Selmer Jackson
Chairman..............William B. Davidson
Governor Hanlon.............John Hamilton

A tedious, trite melodrama about a man sentenced to the chair on circumstantial evidence, this 20th-Fox film hasn't more than good intentions to recommend it. Strictly B-grade, it's a supporting dualer.

If 20th-Fox had a commendable idea in pointing out how dangerous circumstantial evidence testimony can be, the obvious way the script went about it destroys all the effect. There's no subtlety or imagination in the telling.

Story has a hotheaded parent arrested after a fight with a storekeeper results in latter's death. Three eye-witnesses saw parent lift axe to strike the other; the man claims the other fell, cracking skull on a nearby stove. Why medical testimony wasn't introduced to decide which was right isn't explained. Instead man is sentenced to chair, goes to the pen, breaks out, is persuaded to return by his son and a friend, and intricately worms his way back into the jailhouse again while the friend uncovers evidence to set him free.

The trouble and suspense in breaking back into the deathhouse are incredible. The session between judge, governor and the three original witnesses, while the man's son and his boy pals seemingly take over the cross-examination to show the witnesses they may have erred, is fantastic.

Michael O'Shea plays the parent with an engaging bluff quality. Lloyd Nolan does his best as a postman-friend. Billy Cummings is acceptably precocious as the son. But cast, on the whole, bogs down like the script. *Bron.*

Frisco Sal
(SONGS)

Hollywood, Feb. 9.

Universal release of George Waggner production. Stars Susanna Foster, Turhan Bey, Alan Curtis; features Andy Devine, Thomas Gomez, Collette Lyons, Samuel S. Hinds, Fuzzy Knight. Directed by Waggner. Screenplay, Curt Siodmak and Gerald Geraghty; camera, Charles Van Enger; editor, Edward Curtiss; musical director, Edward Ward; dances staged by Lester Horton. Previewed Feb. 8, '45. Running time, **92 MINS.**

Sally..........................Susanna Foster
Dude................................Turhan Bey
Ric..................................Alan Curtis
Bunny..............................Andy Devine
Dan...........................Thomas Gomez
Mickey........................Collette Lyons
Doc.........................Samuel S. Hinds
Hallelujah......................Fuzzy Knight
Billy................................Billy Green
McKinney.........................Ernie Adams
Judge.............................George Lloyd
Eddie.................................Bert Fiske

The San Francisco Barbary Coast at the turn of the century provides a colorful background for this drama which, despite rather formularized unfolding, emerges as good escapist b.o. entertainment for regular runs. Susanna Foster, Turhan Bey and Alan Curtis are starred.

Miss Foster arrives in the district from the east to search for her older brother, who had mysteriously disappeared in San Francisco, with only clue an old letter describing a special dish at a Barbary Coast cafe. Latter happens to be dancehall-saloon operated by Bey on fairly legitimate basis to catch the sightseers. Girl gets a job and clicks with a singing number, being headlined quickly. Curtis operates a mission as a blind for thugs and pickpockets of the area, and clashes with Bey for control of the coast operations. Bey and Miss Foster fall in love, but girl gets evidence that former was responsible for brother's disappearance. Pair get together at the finish, with Curtis disclosed as the lost brother.

Bey capably handles his role, with Miss Foster teaming nicely. She clicks with delivery of two low-register torchy songs, best of which is "Beloved," by George Waggner and Edward Ward. Collette Lyons stands out as the comedienne of the show, while Curtis, Andy Devine, Thomas Gomez, Samuel S. Hinds, and Fuzzy Knight are prominent in support.

Producer-director George Waggner provides plenty of pace to the unfolding, taking full advantage of the colorful background for lusty drama and two wild and comedic saloon brawls. Original script by Curt Siodmak and Gerald Geraghty is compact. *Walt.*

The Chicago Kid

Republic release of Eddy White production. Stars Donald Barry; features Otto Kruger, Lynne Roberts, Chick Chandler. Directed by Frank McDonald. Screenplay, Jack Townley, from story by Karl Brown; camera, William Bradford; editor, Ralph Dixon; additional dialog, Albert Beich. At Republic, N. Y., starting Feb. 10, '45. Running time, **68 MINS.**

Joe Ferrill......................Donald Barry
John Mitchell......................Otto Kruger
Mike Thurber.....................Tom Powers
Chris Mitchell..................Lynne Roberts
Bill Mitchell...................Henry Daniels
Squeak.........................Chick Chandler
Chief Rogers...................Joseph Crehan
Pinky.............................Jay Novello
Carter.............................Paul Harvey
The Warden................Addison Richards
Al..................................Kenne Duncan

This well-made, modern-day gangster meller furthers the development of Donald Barry ("Red" Barry of westerns) as a screen mobster. Transition of Barry from outdoor epics to solid gangster roles has been under way for more than a year, and the intense little actor appears to have "arrived" with "The Chicago Kid." Picture should provide strong support on duals.

Barry plays a warehouse worker trying to save enough for his father to have a country home when he's released from the big house. When latter dies before being freed, Barry sours on society in general and Otto Kruger, the auditor whose testimony sent his dad up the river, in particular. How Barry ingratiates himself with Kruger, his daughter (Lynne Roberts) and his son (Henry Daniels) lays the framework for his plans to work with mobsters.

Frank McDonald has done a good directorial job. Jack Townley's script helps maintain suspense, William Bradford's camera work is uniformly good, and Ralph Dixon's editing is deft.

Kruger, Miss Roberts, Daniels, Tom Powers and Chick Chandler also go over. *Wear.*

Toros, Amor Y Gloria
("Bulls, Love and Glory")
(SONGS)
(Mexican-Made)

Clasa release of Raul de Anda production. Directed by de Anda. Stars Lorenzo Garza; features Sara Garcia and Maria Pons. At Belmont, N. Y., week of Feb. 9, '45. Running time, **116 MINS.**

Jose Antonio...................Lorenzo Garza
"Nana" Irene......................Sara Garcia
Maria Villarreal....................Maria Pons
Andres.....................Carlos Moctezuma
Roberto Villarreal..................Jorge Reyes

(In Spanish; No English Titles)

This is an overlong, unfunny rags-to-riches comedy grooved for Spanish-speaking audiences.

Deals with a worker on a bull-breeding ranch who becomes a matador to win the hand of a wealthy gal. In the unwinding the supposedly funny antics of the matador fail to register.

Performances by the entire cast are stilted, and direction lacks pace. *Sten.*

Miniature Reviews

"God Is My Co-Pilot" (WB). Okay thriller of Flying Tigers, due for average biz.

"Bring on the Girls" (Par; Musical). Better-than-average biz for lightweight musical due to names (Bracken-Lake-Tufts).

"Keep Your Powder Dry" (M-G). Lana Turner-Laraine Day-Susan Peters in moderate boxoffice drama about the Wacs.

"Salty O'Rourke" (Par). Alan Ladd in racetrack yarn; average biz.

"Pan-Americana" (Musical) (RKO). Routine musical saluting the Latins; for duals.

"High Powered" (Par). Pine-Thomas comedy melodrama; strong B

"The Unseen" (Par). Strong murder-mystery starring Joel McCrea, Gail Russell, Herbert Marshall.

"The Body Snatcher" (RKO). Spine-tingling chiller with Boris Karloff and Bela Lugosi; strong dualer.

"Having Wonderful Crime" (RKO). Wacky and racy murder-mystery comedy. Fairly profitable for regular bookings.

"A Song for Miss Julie" (Rep). Shirley Ross lending vigor to stage-story farce, with musical backgrounding; dualer.

"Youth On Trial" (Col). Juve delinquency theme can hold its own on duals.

"Rogues Gallery" (PRC). Lightweight whodunit. Secondary billing on duals.

"The Man From Morocco" (Pathe). British-made meller good enough for second feature in Britain, but mild for U. S.

"Dona Barbara" (Clasa; Mex). Prize-winning drama in Spanish; no English titles.

God Is My Co-Pilot

Hollywood, Feb. 20.

Warner Bros. release of Robert Buckner production. Stars Dennis Morgan; features Dane Clark, Raymond Massey, Alan Hale, Andrea King, John Ridgely. Directed by Robert Florey. Screenplay, Peter Milne and Abem Finkel, from book by Col. Robert Lee Scott, Jr.; camera, Sid Hickox; aerial photography, Charles Marshall; editor Folmer BVlangsted; technical adv iser, Col. Robert Lee Scott, Jr.: special effects, Roy Davidson, Edwin DuPar, Robert Barks: musuc, Franz Waxman: musical director, Leo F. Forbstein. Previewed in Hollywood. Feb. 16, '45. Running time. 83 MINS.

Col. Robert L. Scott..........................Dennis Morgan
Johnny Petach......................................Dane Clark
Gen. Chennault..........................Raymond Massey
Big Mike..Alan Hale
Catharine..Andrea King
Tex Hill..John Ridgely
Col. Cooper.....................................Stanley Ridges
Rector...Craig Stevens
Bob Neal..Warren Douglas
Sgt. Baldridge...............................Stephen Richards
Pvt. Motley.......................................Charles Smith
Col. Haynes.......................................Minor Watson
Tokyo Joe...Richard Loo
Sgt. Aaltonen......................................Murray Alper
Lt. Sharp..Joel Allen
Chinese Captain...................................Frank Tank
Lt. Horner...Paul Brook
Lt. Wilson...Jolin Miles
John Allison..Bernie Sell
Dr. Reynolds...................................William Forrest
Frank Schiel.....................................Danny Dowling
Jap radio announcer...............................Philip Ahn

This is another of Warners' recent war films touching on the various fighting branches of our armed forces. As such it should do average business in the keys and play off okay down through the subsequents. Narrative uses flashback technique to condense life of Col. Robert Lee Scott, Jr., Army ace who's gained fame with General Chennault's Flying Tigers.

Air fight sequences bear an authentic stamp, although studio-made, and the thrills are good drama for the present-day market. Title derives from Scott's realization that a pilot doesn't face danger alone, and several of his real-life brushes with death sustain the belief.

There has been considerable condensation of Scott's story, taken from his best-selling book of same title, and undoubtedly commercial license has pointed up some incidents for better dramatic flavor. It's the story of a boy born to fly and spans his days from the time he first jumped off the barn with an umbrella, through model planes, West Point, flying the mail, instructing and his takeoff on a secret mission to China after Pearl Harbor. Mission is cancelled and Scott becomes attached to Gen. Chennault's Tigers. It is during this period he decides a pilot never flies alone.

Condensation was evidently more in the hands of the film editor than in the script by Peter Milne and Abem Finkel. Finished picture indicates there was considerable scissoring to hold footage to reasonable length. Robert Florey's direction manages authenticity and obtains excellent performances from the cast headed by Dennis Morgan. Latter is thoroughly likeable as Scott, the Macon, Ga., boy who took to the air to win honors. Andrea King, as Scott's wife, does an interesting job in the few scenes permitted her.

Raymond Massey is capable as Gen. Chennault. Dane Clark, as Johnny Petach, and John Ridgely as Tex Hill, show up best among the pilots. Alan Hale is a believeable missionary. Murray Alper, Stanley Ridges, Richard Loo, a Nip pilot, and Philip Ahn, a Jap radio announcer, rate mention among the others.

Robert Buckner's productional guidance is topflight, as are the technical functions under his wing, including Sid Hickox' camera work, the aerial photography by Charles Marshall, and special effects by Roy Davidson, Edwin DuPar and Robert Burks. *Brog.*

Bring On the Girls
(MUSICAL; COLOR)

Paramount release of Fred Kohlmar production. Stars Eddie Bracken, Veronica Lake, Sonny Tufts, Marjorie Reynolds. Directed by Sydney Lanfield. Screenplay, Karl Tunberg and Darrell Ware, from story by Pierre Wolff; songs, Jimmy McHugh and Harold Adamson; music direction, Robert Emmett Dolan; editor, William Shea; dances staged by Danny Dare; photography (in Technicolor) by Karl Struss; settings and costumes by Raoul Pene du Bois. Tradeshown in N. Y., Feb. 16, '45. Running time, **92 MINS.**

Teddy Collins.................Veronica Lake
Phil North............................Sonny Tufts
J. Newport Bates...............Eddie Bracken
Sue Thomas.................Marjorie Reynolds
Uncle Ralph.....................Grant Mitchell
Benny Lowe.......................Johnnie Coy
Swede..........................Peter Whitney
August..........................Alan Mowbray
Dr. Efrington.........................Porter Hall
Rutledge.......................Thurston Hall
Beaster........................Lloyd Corrigan
Joseph..................................Sig Arno
Gloria.........................Joan Woodbury
Dr. Spender...................Andrew Tombes
Sailor..............................Frank Faylen
Sailor...............................Huntz Hall
Sailor.............................William Moss
Aunt Martha....................Norma Varden
Spike Jones Orchestra

"Bring On the Girls" is a lightweight musical with some sprightly tunes by Jimmy McHugh and Harold Adamson, and a neat production whose marquee names such as Eddie Bracken, Veronica Lake, Sonny Tufts and Marjorie Reynolds should insure better-than-average biz in the keys.

The book is one of those things, but "Girls" is fast paced all the way and has the benefit of gorgeous Technicolor plus other productional accoutrements that stamp film as being top-budget.

It's the story of a young millionaire with a proclivity for becoming engaged to dames who are out only for his money. That would be

Bracken. So he joins the Navy, where he won't be so wellknown, but he becomes linked to a gold-digging ciggie girl (Miss Lake), who learns his identity, and thereafter the travail concerns whether or not Miss Lake will get him. Tufts plays Bracken's sidekick and Miss Reynolds is the gal with whom Bracken ultimately winds up.

Story becomes pitiful at times, and it remains for Bracken's performance to salvage much of it. Tufts and the Misses Lake and Reynolds are somewhat obscured by the story, as is true of others in the large cast, most of whom are unbilled.

McHugh and Adamson have written a quintet of sprightly tunes, with the title number seemingly having the best chance for exploitation. "How Would You Like to Take My Picture" is also of particularly sturdy quality.

There are a number of neat specialties, particularly a couple of hoofing numbers by an unbilled tapster, and there's some comedy by Spike Jones' orch that has an amusing moment or two. *Kahn.*

Keep Your Powder Dry

Metro release of George Haight production. Stars Lana Turner, Laraine Day and Susan Peters; features Agnes Moorehead, Bill Johnson. Directed by Edward Buzzell. Screenplay, Mary C. McCall, Jr., and George Bruce; camera, Ray June; musical score, David Snell; editor, Frank E. Hull. Tradeshown in N. Y., Feb. 9, '45. Running time, **93 MINS.**

Valerie Parks....................Lana Turner
Leigh Rand....................Laraine Day
Ann Darrison....................Susan Peters
Lieut. Col. Spottiswoode..Agnes Moorehead
Capt. Bill Barclay....................Bill Johnson
Harriet Corwin....................Natalie Schafer
Gladys Hopkins....................Lee Patrick
Junior Vanderheusen....................Jess Barker
Sarah Swanson....................June Lockhart
Capt. Sanders....................Marta Linden
Capt. Joseph Mannering......Tim Murdock

Metro has produced the feminine prototype of the many servicemen stories that have emerged on the screen, and "Keep Your Powder Dry" is a somewhat feeble result. It has the benefit of Lana Turner, Laraine Day and Susan Peters for the marquee, but, by and large, its story values are lacking in sustained interest. Boxoffice results should be moderate. Lack of romantic elements is another factor in the uncertain b.o.

Yarn deals with the Wacs and the conglomerate group that comprises its ranks. There's Miss Turner as a rich gal who joins to become eligible for an inheritance; Miss Day, who is of an Army family and thus reared in the traditions of the service, and Miss Peters, who supplies the film's major drama as a young wife who enlists when her newlywed husband-soldier goes overseas.

The picture's conflict elements arise between Miss Turner and Miss Day, and the story follows them and Miss Peters through basic training and their ultimate success as officer candidates.

The femme leads lend as much s.a. to the film as the uniforms will allow, and their performances are sufficient for the story's needs. Miss Peters particularly supplies a wistful, appealing characterization. Agnes Moorehead, as the Wac commander, and Bill Johnson, in first film role since being signed from the Broadway musicomedy stage, also do okay with the unimaginative story.

Edward Buzzell has directed capably, and production is in the usual topflight Metro manner. *Kahn.*

Salty O'Rourke

Paramount release of E. D. Leshin production. Stars Alan Ladd and Gail Russell; features William Demarest, Bruce Cabot, Spring Byington and Stanley Clements. Directed by Raoul Walsh. Story and screenplay, Milton Holmes; camera, Theodor Sparkuhl; editor, William Shea; music score, Robert Emmett Dolan. Previewed in N. Y. Feb. 16, '45. Running time, **100 MINS.**

Salty O'Rourke....................Alan Ladd
Barbara Brooks....................Gail Russell
Smitty....................William Demarest
Doc Baxter....................Bruce Cabot
Mrs. Brooks....................Spring Byington
Johnny Cate.....Stanley "Stash" Clements

Alan Ladd in a tough-guy role is invariably capital, and it's unfortunate "Salty O'Rourke" couldn't have been sturdier. Though it runs an hour and 40 minutes, "Salty" is actually for double-bill situations. It dawdles several times, and about 15 minutes of cutting would help considerably. It should do average biz.

"Salty" is a racetrack story, and on that basis may well have its element of boxoffice uncertainty because of the current race track ban and attendant decline in turf interest. It's an apparently modest budgeter that deals with a gambler who points his nag for a big race; a mugg jockey who would give the former the doublecross but doesn't with a climactic decision; a school teacher for whom the jockey falls, with the gal, instead, going for the gambler. Besides the romantic conflict there's one between the aforementioned gambler and another one on a payoff. It's all typical gun stuff with none of the subleties that go for better programming.

Ladd is the turfman, and he gives one of his typically tough performances, while Gail Russell, a newcomer to the screen, is darkly attractive though still wavering as a performer. Stanley Clements is the jockey, and he gives the film's best performance.

Pic is slow, but it's mainly the fault of the script rather than the directing. *Kahn*

Pan-Americana
(MUSICAL)

RKO release of John H. Auer production. Features Phillip Terry, Audrey Long, Robert Benchley, Eve Arden, Ernest Truex, Marc Cramer, Isabelita. Directed by Auer. Screenplay, Lawrence Kimble; story, Frederick Kohner and Auer; musical numbers staged by Charles O'Curran; songs by Ary Barroso, Margarita Lecuona, Gabriel Ruiz, Pepe Guizar, Carlos Castellanos, Antonio Fernandez, Bobby Collazo; English lyrics, Mort Greene; editor, Harry Marker; camera, Frand Redman. Tradeshown N. Y., Feb. 15, '45. Running time, **84 MINS.**

Dan....................Phillip Terry
Jo Anne....................Audrey Long
Charlie....................Robert Benchley
Hoppy....................Eve Arden
Uncle Rudy....................Ernest Truex
Jerry....................Marc Cramer
Lupita....................Isabelita

Also Rosario and Antonio, Miguelito Valdes, Harold and Lola, Louise Burnett, Chinita Marin, Chuy Castillon, Padilla Sisters, Chuy Reyes's Orch., Nestor Amaral's Samba Band.

"Pan-Americana" is a routine salute to our Latin-American neighbors, as inoffensive as it is unimportant. A picture-postcard tour of Central and South America is sandwiched in with a trite and sometimes dull yarn about a magazine staff. The music interludes and specialties are quite good and the film's best point, but not enough to lift it out of the dual grade despite the top budget.

Producer John H. Auer has some fresh slants in introducing his story and some novel ways of segueing from plot to musical number and back. Latin talent is authentic and of high calibre. But pic nevertheless is essentially a so-so musical with a dull book enlivened by exotic music numbers. And the succession of music numbers, though each is good, palls after a time.

Story concerns four members of the editorial staff of a New York class magazine who set out on tour of Latin-American countries to select prettiest girl of each for a musical revue the mag is sponsoring. Flitting from country to country, choosing Miss Whosis for each, gives producer opportunity for musical numbers at each stop. The mag's ace cameraman has a romance with the feature writer, and he does a little wolfing on the side, with the mag's femme managing editor trying to break the romance up. The fourth member, the foreign editor, is just along for the drinks.

Audrey Long makes an uncommonly attractive ingenue and Phillip Terry an acceptable lead. Eve Arden and Robert Benchley, as balance of quartet, struggle with some feeble lines and situations for comedy relief, and Ernest Truex, in a brief bit, isn't much more help. Marc Cramer suits as "the other man."

Film's music specialties are all rewarding. Rosario and Antonio, flamenco dance team, give two fine exhibitions of their spirited gypsy dancing. There is an unusually good snake dance by an unidentified adagio duo, as well as some good coloratura singing by attractive gal tagged as Miss Brazil. Isabelita has a cute style in song delivery to match her attractive person. Various other individuals, like Padilla Sisters, and the orch groups, are also good.

Production numbers are lavish and in good taste. Some camera angles are also outstanding. *Bron.*

High Powered

Paramount release of Pine-Thomas production. Stars Robert Lowery, Phyllis Brooks; features Mary Treen, Joe Sawyer, Roger Pryor. Directed by William Berke. Screenplay, Milton Raison and Maxwell Shane, from original by Milton Raison; camera, Fred Jackman, Jr.; editor, Henry Adams. Previewed in N. Y., Feb. 16, '45. Running time, **63 MINS.**

Tim Scott....................Robert Lowery
Marian Blair....................Phyllis Brooks
Cassio McQuade....................Mary Treen
Spike Kenny....................Joe Sawyer
Rod Farrell....................Roger Pryor
Sheriff....................Ralph Sanford
Worker....................Billy Nelson
Boss....................Ed Gargan
Worker....................Vince Barnett

"High Powered" is an highly entertaining dualer. Film more than fills the bill as a secondary feature despite dearth of name players. It's neatly acted and directed, and sharply edited.

Robert Lowery, an ace high-rigger, becomes afraid of high places after a near-fatal fall. A co-worker blames him for his brother's death in the same accident but the principal theme is Lowery's struggle to overcome his fear. Rousing climax finds him effecting a daring rescue from a swinging boom.

Phyllis Brooks and Mary Treen share honors as the femme leads. Lowery does well while Roger Pryor and Joe Sawyer, former super on the job, take top honors. Support is strong with minor bits by Vince Barnett and Ed Gargan scoring.

Direction by William Berke is one of his better jobs while the Pine-Thomas unit has given this a good production. Both the camera work of Fred Jackman, Jr., and editing of Henry Adams are worthy of a more important film. *Wear.*

The Unseen

Paramount release of John Houseman production. Stars Joel McCrea, Gail Russell, Herbert Marshall; features Phyllis Brooks, Isobel Elsom, Elisabeth Risdon, Norman Lloyd. Directed by Lewis Allen. Screenplay, Hagar Wilde, Raymond Chandler; adapted by Wilde and Ken Englund, from novel by Ethel Lina White; editor, Doane Harrison; camera, John F. Seitz. Tradeshown N. Y., Feb. 16, '45. Running time, **81 MINS.**

David Fielding....................Joel McCrea
Elizabeth Howard....................Gail Russell
Dr. Charles Evans........Herbert Marshall
Maxine....................Phyllis Brooks
Marian Tygarth....................Isobel Elsom
Jasper Goodwin....................Norman Lloyd
Chester....................Mikhail Rasumny
Mrs. Norris....................Elisabeth Risdon
Sullivan....................Tom Tully
Ellen Fielding....................Nona Griffith
Barnaby Fielding....................Richard Lyon

Murder mystery should do good biz. Plot is interesting, mood is good and suspense and interest sustained practically throughout. One or two plot flaws, a certain obviousness, and one bad miscasting keep pic out of select class.

Performances are generally good, with two youngsters showing talent without the added cloying quality so patent in some better-publicized moppets. Direction is at fluent pace and camera work is good with some novel shots.

Story deals with a young widower and his two kids who live next door to a mysterious, boarded-up house. Atmosphere in the widower's home is strained. His wife had died strangely two years before, with suspicion cast on the husband. His children are being raised indulgently by bad governesses. A new governess seems to correct the situation.

Mysterious happenings involve the boarded-up home. Prowlers are glimpsed inside at night. A maid employed by the widower is found in a nearby alley, murdered. Somehow the children know about the murder and what is going on next door. The bewildered governess slowly uncovers casual facts that, put together, suggest her employer is a murderer. Although the actual criminal can be spotted long before the finale, development and conclusion are persuasive and well set up.

Joel McCrea is good as the curt widower, with a certain harshness in his characterization explained as pic develops. Herbert Marshall also suits as family physician, with perhaps less assurance in closing reels. Gail Russell is serious flaw in film, her constant hangdog look and attitude scarcely convincing as the governess conquering the eerie, unwholesome situation.

Isobel Elsom, as owner of the next-door manse; Elisabeth Risdon, as housekeeper, and Tom Tully, as detective, act as satisfactory support. Moppets Richard Lyon and Nona Griffith are real finds, especially the latter. Young Lyon, in addition to being strikingly good-looking, has real dramatic sense. Griffith girl is pert, with no too-too-cute drawbacks. And a natural little actress. *Bron.*

The Body Snatcher

RKO release of Val Lewton production. Stars Boris Karloff; features Henry Daniell, Bela Lugosi, Edith Atwater. Directed by Robert Wise. Screenplay, Philip McDonald and Carlos Keith, based on short story by Robert Louis Stevenson; camera, Robert de Grasse; editor, J. R. Whittredge. Tradeshown in N. Y., Feb. 15, '45. Running time, **79 MINS.**

Gray....................Boris Karloff
Joseph....................Bela Lugosi
MacFarlane....................Henry Daniell
Meg....................Edith Atwater
Fettes....................Russell Wade
Mrs. Marsh....................Rita Corday
Georgina....................Sharyn Moffett
Street Singer....................Donna Lee

Containing horror in large doses, "The Body Snatcher" is a gruesome, low-budget chiller that should do strong biz in both single-feature houses catering to this type audience and on the duals.

Based on a short story by Robert Louis Stevenson, and given tightly scripted adaptation by Philip MacDonald and Carlos Keith, "Snatcher" seldom lacks interest. Yarn deals with the traffic in dead bodies by hansom cabbie Boris Karloff. Corpses are used for study purposes in a medical school mastered by Henry Daniell. Russell Wade, young assistant to Daniell, is caught in the web of the illicit dealings, with Edith Atwater playing the wife of Daniell. Bela Lugosi is seen briefly as a handyman at the med school. Denouement is really something to be remembered.

Karloff portrays his sadistic role in characteristic style, but best performance comes from Daniell. Lugosi is more or less lost, probably on the cutting floor, since he is only in for two sequences. Miss Atwater, from the Broadway stage, underacts her supporting role capably.

"Body Snatcher" is localed in Scotland over a century ago. Settings are inexpensive but sufficient for the needs. Production values, in general, however, aid materially in making this picture a winner. *Sten.*

Having Wonderful Crime

Hollywood, Feb. 15.

RKO release of Robert Fellows production. Stars Pat O'Brien, George Murphy, Carole Landis. Directed by Eddie Sutherland. Screenplay, Howard J. Green, Stewart Sterling and Parke Levy; original, Craig Rice; camera, Frank Redman; special photographic effects, Vernon L. Walker; editor, Gene Milford. Tradeshown in L. A., Feb. 14, '45. Running time, **69 MINS.**

Michael J. Malone	Pat O'Brien
Jake Justus	George Murphy
Helene	Carole Landis
Gilda	Lenore Aubert
King	George Zucco
Phyllis	Anje Berens
Lance	Richard Martin
Winslow	Charles D. Brown
Zacharias	William Davis
Elizabeth Lenhart	Blanche Ring
Myra	Josephine Whittel

"Having Wonderful Crime" is a razzle-dazzle murder mystery developed in nonsensical style. Strictly broad escapist fare, picture will do okay in regular bookings, aided by marquee voltage of Pat O'Brien, George Murphy and Carole Landis.

Loosely-knit tale never pauses long enough to establish credulity, but continually races along with accentuated slapstick. O'Brien is a criminal lawyer who's continually projected into crime-solving by his newly-married pals, Murphy and Miss Landis. Mysterious disappearance of illusionist George Zucco from a theatre stage quickly moves scene of action to a mountain resort for continual round of wild and mysterious happenings, a couple of murders and a trunk that periodically disappears with and without a corpse enclosed. But the trio solves the crimes and situations to allow the newlyweds to catch up on their honeymoon.

O'Brien, Murphy and Miss Landis romp merrily through the slapstick and zany proceedings with accentuated gestures and wisecracking dialog cracking at every turn. Zucco, Lenore Aubert, Anje Berens, Richard Martin, Charles D. Brown and William Davis provide adequate support.

Eddie Sutherland directs for broadest comedy reaction, while script has been set up in similar fashion.

A Song for Miss Julie
(SONGS)

Republic release of William Rowland-Carley Harriman production. Features Shirley Ross, Barton Hepburn, Jane Farrar, Roger Clark, Cheryl Walker and Alicia Markova and Anton Dolin. Directed by Rowland. Screenplay by Rowland Leigh from original by Michael Foster; adapted by Leighton K. Brill; camera, Mack Stengler; editor, James Smith; music and lyrics, Louis Herscher, Marla Shelton, Del Cleveland; musical director, David Chudnow; dance director, Larry Ceballos. Previewed in Projection Room, N. Y., Feb. 16, '45. Running time, **69 MINS.**

Valerie	Shirley Ross
George Kimbro	Barton Hepburn
Julie	Jane Farrar
Steve	Roger Clark
Marcelle	Cheryl Walker
Mrs. Charteris	Elisabeth Risdon
Eliza	Lillian Randolph
Pete	Peter Garey
Mrs. Calhoun	Rene Riano
John Firbank	Harry Crocker
The Robertos	The Robertos
Vivian Fay	Vivian Fay
Alicia Markova and Anton Dolin	

Despite lavish production, including a couple of songs and elaborate ensembles, "A Song for Miss Julie" never becomes more than a B. Picture will suffice as dual support.

A good idea went wrong somewhere along the production line. Film might have been better paced if the performances had been more convincing. And at times the direction was at fault. At least Shirley Ross manages to whip some vitality into the vehicle.

"Julie" is the story of two playwrights who want to use a yarn built around a southern gentleman of the 1850's, particularly some risque episodes in his life. Much of the picture is the lacklustre search for these ingredients by the two scripters for their Broadway operetta, with an elderly southern lady (oldest survivor of the family in question) battling their efforts. She's finally wangled into allowing playwrights Barton Hepburn and Roger Clark to do the musical festival in her Louisiana home town, where the pair go for story material. Later this is moulded into the Broadway show.

The operetta sequences serve to introduce to pictures Alicia Markova and Anton Dolin, of the Ballet Theatre. It also gives Miss Ross a chance to sing in her best style and for Cheryl Walker to show up effectively in slinky costumes. Miss Ross plays an ex-fan dancer who's featured in all the shows her hubby (Hepburn) writes. Hepburn's performance is faltering, while Miss Walker, as the other-side-of-tracks relative of the fine southern family, is outstanding in a subordinate role. Jane Farrar, as Julie, the daughter of the elderly southern lady (Elisabeth Risdon) acts sweet, and that's about all. Clark, playing the other playwright, completely overshadows Hepburn. Peter Garey, as a hotel bellhop, looks like a comer.

Both "Bayou Calls" and "I Love to Remember," the two principal songs, are catchy, with the latter taking top honors. The Markova-Dolin turn goes over big. William Rowland has done better on his production effort than with his direction. But then the script is mostly to blame. *Wear.*

Youth on Trial

Columbia release of Ted Richmond production. Features Cora Sue Collins, David Reed, Eric Sinclair, Georgia Bayes, Robert Williams. Directed by Oscar Boetticher, Jr. Screenplay, Michael Jacoby; editor, Gene Havlick; camera, George Meehan. At Strand theatre, Brooklyn, N. Y., week of Feb. 15, '45, dual. Running time, **59 MINS.**

Cam Chandler	Cora Sue Collins
Tom Lowry	David Reed
Denny Moore	Eric Sinclair
Meg Chandler	Georgia Bayes
Officer Ken Moore	Robert Williams
Judge Chandler	Mary Currier
Jud Lowry	John Calvert
Stacey	Boyd Bennett
Robert Reynolds	William Forrest
Mario	Muni Seroff
Maude McGregor	Florence Auer
Maryor Townsend	Boyd Davis
Commissioner Ryan	Joseph Crehan
Commissioner Collins	Edwin Stanley

This latest cinematic expose of the juve delinquency situation can hold its own in most dual situations. Its story, while not new in pattern, is well knit, sustains suspense and is neatly cast.

Mary Currier plays a judge of the adolescents' court, giving out stiff sentences to youthful malefactors. She also enlists aid of police in raiding a notorious roadhouse catering to teen-age highschool kids. Cora Sue Collins, her daughter, is there with David Reed, the highschool's bad boy, but they make a getaway. When the other kids are haled to court they snitch on the pair. The judge then realizes that while she was attempting to keep other homes in order she had neglected her own responsibilities, and at the tag she opines it's the parents rather than the kids who are to blame.

Miss Collins turns in a neat performance. Eric Sinclair and Reed also give good accounts of themselves, with Miss Currier also turning in a fine performance. Other support roles are adequately handled by Georgia Bayes, Robert Williams, John Calvert, Boyd Bennett, William Forrest, Joseph Crehan and Edwin Stanley.

Michael Jacoby has contributed compact script, nicely paced in direction by Oscar Boetticher, Jr. *Edba.*

Rogues Gallery

PRC Pictures release of Donald C. McKean-Albert Herman production. Features Frank Jenks, Robin Raymond, H. B. Warner, Ray Walker. Directed by Albert Herman. Screenplay, John T. Neville; editor, Fred Bain; camera, Ira Morgan. At Strand theatre, Brooklyn, N. Y., week of Feb. 15, '45, dual. Running time, **60 MINS.**

Eddie	Frank Jenks
Patsy	Robin Raymond
Reynolds	H. B. Warner
Jimmy	Ray Walker
Foster	Davidson Clark
O'Day	Bob Homans
Blake	Frank McGlynn
Red	Pat Gleason
Gentry	Edward Keane
Griffith	Earl Dewey
Wheeler	Milton Kibbee
Joyce	Gene Stutenroth
Duckworth	George Kirby
Seawell	Norval Mitchell
Board Member	John Valentine
Mike	Jack Raymond
Detective	Parker Gee

Lighweight whodunit of cut-and-dried pattern. Geared for lower-rung in duals.

Robin Raymond plays a gal reporter, and Frank Jenks is her news photographer pal, both assigned to interview H. B. Warner, inventor of a trick device. They stumble into a murder and a couple of near homicides before turning up Ray Walker, rival scribe, as the culprit, who's committed to steal plans of the invention.

Miss Raymond has a tendency to overplay the sobbie. Jenks manages to pack some laughs as a stupe photog. Warner, Walker and Bob Homans are okay in lesser roles. Story is weighted down by superfluous dialog. Albert Herman turns in good direction despite handicaps of yarn. *Edba.*

The Man From Morocco
(BRITISH-MADE)

London, Jan. 29.

Pathe Pictures release of Associated British production. Stars Anton Walbrook. Directed by Max Greene. Screenplay by Edward Dryhurst from story by Rudolph Cartier; adapted by Warwick Ward; additional dialog, Marguerite Steen. Music by Mischa Spoliansky. At Studio One, London, Jan. 26, '45. Running time, **110 MINS.**

Karel	Anton Walbrook
Manuela	Margaretta Scott
Sarah Duboste	Mary Morris
Ricardi	Reginald Tate
Jock	Peter Sinclair
Doctor Duboste	David Horne
Colonel Bagley	Hartley Power
Bourdille	Charles Victor
Erna	Sybilla Binder
Franz	Josef Almas
Pete	John McLaren
Galzani	Dennis Arundell
French General	Andre Randall
German General	Carl Jaffe

Here is a good second feature for key spots and better than average for top billing in the sticks. It has plenty of merit for a yarn of this sort. Lack of names will hold back its small boxoffice possibilities in the U. S.

Anton Walbrook as "The Man from Morocco" makes convincing the story's main theme—that the world is okay so long as men are willing to die for an ideal. With him is a little band of volunteers fighting Fascism in Spain, including a Jew, a Senengalese, a Yankee, a Scotsman, a Cockney and a dozen other nationalities.

It's the first film here to take a crack at Vichy Frenchmen, bringing to the screen a French officer whose cruelty and lust make Himmler almost a saint by comparison. His villainy is aided and abetted by a French woman who does not draw the line at murder as a spy in the guise of a Red Cross nurse.

Melodramatic plot involves an Italian aristocrat, leader of the Fascist spy ring in London. Essentially a tale of the sufferings by idealistic males under unspeakably brutal French officers of the Foreign Legion, "Morocco" succeeds in the purely male sequences. It is in the love interest that the story fails to convince. This is the fault of the author, rather than the actors.

Margaretta Scott as a Spanish senora of high rank is by turns queenly and weak, even to the point of marrying the lustful French officer in order to spare the lives of 2,000 French patriots. She is unable to make an impossible role credible.

Direction by Max Greene is competent, and the production generally is top notch. But chief credit goes to the exterior location man of Associated British for finding spots which appear new to the screen.

Dona Barbara
(MEXICAN-MADE)

Clasa release of Fernando de Fuentes production. Stars Maria Felix and Julian Soler; features Maria Marques, Andres Soler, Charles Rooner. Directed by de Fuentes. Screenplay by Romulo Gallegos, based on his own novel. At Belmont, N. Y., week of Feb. 16, '45. Running time, **128 MINS.**

Dona Barbara	Maria Felix
Santos Lusardo	Julian Soler
Marisela	Maria Marques
Lorenzo	Andres Soler
Guillermo	Charles Rooner
Juan	Agustin Izunsa
Meliquiades	Miguel Inclan
Melesio	Edwardo Arczamena
Antonio	Antonio R. Frausto
Coronel Pernalete	Arturo Soto Rangel
Maria Nieves	Pedro Galindo

(In Spanish; No English Titles)

Despite its length, "Dona Barbara" is a powerful drama which should do heavy business in theatres that cater to Spanish-speaking audiences. There are no English titles.

A prize-winning film in Mexico, picture has two neat performances by Maria Felix, as a wealthy landowner who achieves her position through gifts from paramours, and Julian Soler, young heir to several neighboring acres, whom the older woman learns to love, only to find that he cares for her daughter. Maria Marques, who portrays the young gal, gives forthright treatment to her role, as do the majority of the supporting cast.

Film, whose background is Venezuela, is overlong. Production values are good. *Sten.*

Miniature Reviews

"It's a Pleasure" (RKO-Int'l; Color). Sonja Henie in weak story; moderate boxoffice.

"Delightfully Dangerous" (Musical) (UA). Modest dualer sans names, best noted for Morton Gould's treatment of Strauss music.

"I Love a Mystery" (Col). Fair low-budget mystery for the duals.

"The Big Bonanza" (Rep). Richard Arlen and Jane Frazee in well-mounted western; stout support on dualers.

"Docks of New York" (Mono). East Side Kids meller; good dualer.

"There Goes Kelly" (Mono). Radio murder-mystery; lower-case dualer.

"Jubilee" (Artkino; Russ.) Amusing though thin Chekhov farce.

"Marriage" (Artkino; Russ.) Amusing short Chekhov farce.

It's a Pleasure

(One Song)

(COLOR)

RKO-Radio release of International Pictures-David Lewis production (Don Loper, associate producer). Stars Sonja Henie; features Michael O'Shea, Bill Johnson, Marie McDonald. Directed by William A. Seiter. Screenplay, Lynn Starling and Elliot Paul; editor, Ernest Nims; song, Edgar Leslie and Walter Donaldson; music, Arthur Lange. Tradeshown N. Y., Feb. 28, '45. Running time, **89 MINS.**

Chris Linden	Sonja Henie
Don Martin	Michael O'Shea
Buzz Fletcher	Bill Johnson
Mrs. Buzz Fletcher	Marie McDonald
Bill Evans	Gus Schilling
Wilma	Iris Adrian
Loni	Cheryl Walker
Cricket	Peggy O'Neill
Jack Weimar	Arthur Loft
Maid	Alyce Fleming
Hockey Referee	George Brown
Canadian Hockey Star	Jack Chefe
Dancing Partner	Don Loper
Announcer	Tom Hanlon
Photographer	Lane Watson

Third of the four pictures which International (William Goetz-Leo Spitz) has contracted for RKO release, "It's a Pleasure," starring Sonja Henie in her first for the new combine, is a weakie. Its story treatment fails to provide sufficiently sturdy background for Miss Henie's iceskating pyrotechnics. Produced lavishly in Technicolor, "Pleasure" should draw 'em moderately. It will have to be sold. Incidentally, it's the star's first film in color.

Yarn has a dual ice theme, concerning Miss Henie's marriage to a hotheaded hockey player who, for his frequent fights, is barred from the game for life. Thereafter the story deals with his comeback attempt as an ice-show performer, but here again his drinking proclivities find him on the short end, while Miss Henie eventually achieves stardom as a figure-skater. Then it's the usual clinch between the two after an enforced parting caused by their misunderstandings.

Miss Henie is the skating star, of course, and her work on the blades remains unparalleled. She's in for more story than skating in "Pleasure," which may be a weak link in the pic, but she screens niftily though some of her lines are pretty tired. Michael O'Shea is her romantic vis-a-vis, and he gives a creditable performance, as does Bill Johnson, Broadway musicomedy juve, on loanout from Metro, where he's under contract.

Marie McDonald, as the red-headed menace who makes a play for O'Shea, is a gal to watch for similar roles. She's plenty s.a., a beaut with chassis that's plenty whistle-provoking. In fact, the s.a. Miss McDonald gives the pic is probably its most dominant feature.

The production numbers are neatly staged, and there's one dance sequence, sans skates, in which Miss Henie shows a grace comparable to anything she does on the gliders. This is a routine with Don Loper. Latter, ex-nitery dancer and designer, is also credited as the film's associate producer.

William A. Seiter has done as well with the direction as the trite story would permit, although some of the hockey is too amateurishly played to suggest the professional qualities it represents. *Kahn.*

Delightfully Dangerous

(MUSICAL)

Hollywood, Feb. 27.

United Artists release of Charles R. Rogers production; associate producer, Joseph S. Tushinsky. Features Jane Powell, Ralph Bellamy, Constance Moore. Director, Arthur Lubin. Screenplay, Walter DeLeon and Arthur Phillips, based on story by Irving Phillips, Edward Verdier and Frank Tashlin; camera, Milton Krasner; music, Charles Previn; staged by Ernst Matray; songs, Morton Gould, Edward Heyman; editor, Harvey Manger. Previewed in Westwood Village, Feb. 23, '45. Running time, **92 MINS.**

Cheryl Williams	Jane Powell
Arthur Hale	Ralph Bellamy
Josephine Williams	Constance Moore
Morton Gould and his Orchestra	Themselves
Jeffers	Arthur Treacher
Hannah	Louise Beavers
Molly	Ruth Tobey
Mrs. Jones	Ruth Robinson
Professor Bremond	Andre Charlot
Nadine	Shirley Hunter Williams

This is a modest musical that will be moderately pleasing in the dual brackets. Best recommendations are the modern Morton Gould music and the old Strauss tunes as played by Gould's orchestra. It has been given production flash in several elaborate numbers but these neither impress nor overcome the episodic development and commonplace story. Theme will have some juvenile appeal as it features young Jane Powell as a youngster who plays at grownup. Running time is overlength for the material's worth and could be judiciously trimmed to speed proceedings.

"Delightfully Dangerous" is the story of a 15-year-old girl who imagines her big sister is a Broadway musical comedy star. She leaves her school to pay a surprise visit, discovers the sister is really a bump-strip artist in burlesque. Befriended by a producer, the youngster at first tries to get the sister the lead in his new show and then plays grownup to land the role herself, figuring she'll earn enough coin so the sister can give up bumps for a living. Both **girls land in the show when they prove to him that Strauss is more commercial when swung a bit.**

Jane Powell has a cuteness in playing dramatic portions of her part and her voice gets over the songs, even though enunciation isn't all that it should be. Ralph Bellamy deserves better assignments than his harassed play producer spot in this. Constance Moore does well enough by the big sister role, being properly bawdy in her burley bit while singing "I'm Only Teasin'," and handling herself okay otherwise. Arthur Treacher and Louise Beavers are in for comedy and Ruth Tobey, a plump moppet, shows up among the juvenile casting.

All the Gould-Edward Heyman tunes are melodic, with "Through Your Eyes" given best presentation in an elaborate garden number. Gould also does a small speaking part but is better in front of his orch. Strauss music is used for a waltz-jive finale number and an earlier production spot. Ernst Matray staged the musical numbers but none is particularly impressive. *Brog.*

I Love a Mystery

Columbia release of Wallace MacDonald production. Stars George Macready; features Nina Foch, Jim Banonn, Carole Mathews. Directed by Henry Levin. Screenplay, Charles O'Neal, based on radio program of same title; camera, Burnett Guffey; editor, Aaron Stell. At Brooklyn Paramount, N. Y., week of Feb. 22, '45, dual. Running time, **69 MINS.**

Jack Packard	Jim Bannon
Ellen Monk	Nina Foch
Jefferson Monk	George Macready
Doc Long	Barton Yarborough
Jean Anderson	Carole Mathews
Justin Reeves	Lester Matthews
Dr. Han	Gregory Gay
Vovaritch	Leo Mostovoy
Ralph Anderson	Frank O'Connor
Miss Osgood	Isabel Withers
Capt. Quinn	Joseph Crehan

Incongruous at times, "I Love a Mystery," nevertheless, is a fairly suspenseful low-budget chiller for the lower rung on the duals. Film gets its title from radio program of same name, which is a good exploitation point.

Yarn deals with the endeavors of an Oriental group, which offers a man-about-town $10,000 for his head, supposedly to replace the entombed dome of the founder of the organization, which is deteriorating because of age. However, it all proves to be a phoney deal, since the gent's wife financed the whole setup in order to inherit some two million bucks when he dies.

George Macready portrays in capable fashion the playboy about whom the plot revolves. Jim Bannon, as a detective, is convincing, while Nina Foch, in the role of Macready's wife, and Carole Mathews, as a mysterious gal who flits in and out of the film in unexplainable fashion, give somewhat stilted performances.

Settings are substantial, though obviously of cheap calibre. Direction and script lack smoothness. *Sten.*

The Big Bonanza

Republic release of Eddy White production. Stars Richard Arlen, Robert Livingston, Jane Frazee; features George Hayes, Lynne Roberts. Directed by George Archainbaud. Screenplay by Dorrell and Stuart McGowan, Paul Gangelin from original by Robert Presnell, Leonard Praskins; camera, Reggie Lanning; editor, Tony Martinelli. At Republic, N. Y., starting Feb. 24, '45. Running time, **62 MINS.**

Jed Kilton	Richard Arlen
Sam Ballou	Robert Livingston
Chiquita McSweeney	Jane Frazee
Hap Selby	George "Gabby" Hayes
Judy Parker	Lynne Roberts
Spud Kilton	Bobby Driscoll
Jasper Kincaid	J. M. Kerrigan
Adam Parker	Russell Simpson
Dr. Ballou	Frank Reicher
Abraham	Cordell Hickman
Jimmy	Hayward Soo Soo
Don Pendleton	Roy Barcroft
Roberts	Fred Kohler, Jr.
The Singer	Monte Hale

"The Big Bonanza" is a dressed-up western. Richard Arlen, Jane Frazee and George "Gabby" Hayes turn in smart acting jobs and that notches the picture as a strong supporting film on most twin bills. Not long enough to stand alone in most spots even where cactus epics are liked.

Story starts out with a slightly different twist, showing Arlen as an escaped U. S. Army officer of the post-Civil War days, who's unjustly courtmartialed for cowardice in battle. But from there on plot treads familiar trails, this one being about good, stalwart youth who returns home to find his boyhood pal turned crook and linked with a dancehall queen. Arlen is said stalwart while Robert Livingston is the unscrpulous lad. The familiar young brother angle is worked in, with Livingston's gang out to silence the boy because sole witness to a murder.

Per customary western pattern there's the noisy gun battle at the Big Bonanza mine, with the upright citizenry coincidentally triumphing over the gunmen. Oh yes, Jane Frazee, the dancehall queen, goes straight because of her love for the youngster.

Arlen is his usual rugged self, being in for one knock-down fistic encounter. Livingston contributes a smooth portrayal as his boyhood pal, while Miss Frazee is vivid in her role. Bobby Driscoll looks promising as the younger brother, and "Gabby" Hayes has more to do and less comedy as Arlen's sidekick. Lynne Roberts is attractive as Arlen's sweetheart.

Director George Archainbaud has made it a fast gaited vehicle while Reggie Lanning's camera work is above par for a film of this sort. *Wear.*

Docks of New York

Monogram release of Sam Katzman-Jack Dietz production. Stars Leo Gorcey, Huntz Hall, Billy Benedict, Bud Gorman; features Betty Blythe, Carlyle Blackwell, Jr., Gloria Pope, George Meeker. Directed by Wallace Fox. Screenplay, Harvey Gates; camera, Ira Morgan; editor, William Austin. At New York, N. Y., week of Feb. 24, '45, dual. Running time, **63 MINS.**

Muggs	Leo Gorcey
Glimpy	Huntz Hall
Skinny	Billy Benedict
Danny	Bud Gorman
Saundra	Gloria Pope
Marty	Carlyle Blackwell, Jr.
Naclet	George Meeker
Mrs. Darcy	Betty Blythe
Captain Jocabs	Pierre Watkin
Millie	Joy Reese
Compeau	Cy Kendall
Patriot	Maurice St. Clair

Latest in the East Side Kids series is better than average. Action is more involved and there's some amusing business. Pic is just fodder for the duals, of course, but it will do biz there.

Story has the Kids—Muggs and Glimpy particularly—tied up in some knots concerning foreign agents, jewel thieves, murder and the law. The boys find a diamond necklace in an alley near their home. They become enmeshed in intrigue, as the cops trail killers who are after the jewels. A Balkan princess even enters the picture. The boys are locked up for larceny, are released and catch the real criminals. And Glimpy's brother, of course, wins the princess.

Leo Gorcey, a little chubbier now, is still amusing and realistic as the little, tough Muggs, with Huntz Hall a good foil as his dopey stooge, Glimpy. Betty Blythe, as the princess' aunt; Carlyle Blackwell, Jr., and Gloria Pope, as the romantic pair, and Cy Kendall, as chief villain, are okay.

Film pays more attention to suspense, comedy and camera detail than most in this series. *Bron.*

There Goes Kelly

(SONGS)

Monogram release of William Strohbach production. Features Jackie Moran, Wanda McKay, Sidney Miller, Ralph Sanford. Directed by Phil Karlstein. Screenplay, Edmond Kelso; camera, William Sickner; editor, Richard Currier. At New York, N. Y., week of Feb. 24, '45, dual. Running time, **61 MINS.**

Jimmy	Jackie Moran
Anne	Wanda McKay
Sammy	Sidney Miller
Marty	Ralph Sanford
Delaney	Dewey Robinson
Rita	Jan Wiley
Farrel	Anthony Warde
Hastings	Harry Depp
Quigley	George Eldredge
Martin	Edward Emerson
Tex	John Gilbreath
Pringle	Pat Gleason
Bowers	Don Kerr
Wallis	Charlie Jordon
Stevens	Terry Frost
Norris	Ralph Linn
Stella	Gladys Blake

Not much sense to this one. A couple of wide-eyed page boys, a murderous radio executive, a blundering cop, all in a humdrum yarn, with a song or two for relief. A lower-case dualer, strictly.

A detective in charge of unraveling a crime is shown up as so puerile and ludicruous as to be fantastic.

A couple of pages at a radio station believe the receptionist whom they adore is a great singer. They plan all sorts of schemes to get her an audition at the station. Suddenly the station's star vocalist is murdered. A hillbilly singer is suspected, but flees before he can be queried. The boys, who seem to have the run of the place, barge into the case, teletype messages widespread, invade private apartments, and in general keep several steps ahead of the police unwinding the mystery. They get the gal-friend in as sub on the murdered singer's program, where she's a hit. and also find the real murderer.

Jackie Moran has the job of precocious page boy, with Sidney Miller, his pal, in for comic relief. Both try too hard, with the script no help. Ralph Sanford is the detective to end all such. Wanda McKay is attractive as the singer. Others are nondescript.

Bron.

Jubilee
(RUSSIAN-MADE)

Artkino release of Mosfilm production. Stars Victor Stanitsin, Olga Androvskaya, Vasily Toporkov, Anastasia Zuyeva. Direction and screenplay by Vladimir Petrov, from Anton Chekhov drama. Camera, Vladimir Yakovlav and N. Brusilovskaya. Music, N. Kriukov. At Stanley, N. Y., week of Feb. 21, '45. Running time, 40 MINS.

Shipuchin	Victor Stanitsin
Tatiana Alexeyevna	Olga Androvskaya
Khirin	Vasily Toporkov
Merchutkina	Anastasia Zuyeva

(In Russian; English Titles)

Short feature based on Chekhov play and made last year by Soviets to comemorate 40th anni of dramatist's death, is a somewhat labored farce with, however, some very amusing moments.

Story has slender thread which spins out even before the 40-minute length. Situation involves the plans of a stuffed-shirt bank director to celebrate the 15th anni of his establishment, and the way said plans are upset by his gabbing, tactless wife and another featherbrained female.

Slight yarn is, however, superbly acted by some fine, individual types. Anastasia Zuyeva, as the persistent wife of a provisional secretary holding up the bewildered bank president for some monies deducted from her husband's wages by a totally different bureau, contributes a priceless bit of humor. Other three principals, banker Victor Stanitsin, clerk Vasily Toporkov, banker's wife Olga Androvskaya, also fine artists. Production, too, is good. *Bron.*

Marriage
(With Music)
(RUSSIAN-MADE)

Artkino release of Tbilisi studio production. Stars Vera Maretskaya, Zoya Fyodorova, Lev Sverdlin. Screenplay and direction by Isidor Annensky. Based on Anton Chekhov play. Camera, Yuri Yekelchik; music, V. Zhelobinsky; dances, V. Burmeister. At Stanley, N. Y., week of Feb. 21, '45. Running time, 47 MINS.

The Father	Alexei Gribov
The Mother	Fanya Ranevskaya
The Groom	Ernest Garin
The Bride	Zoya Fyodorova
The Rejected Suitor	Sergei Martinson
The Flirt	Vera Maretskaya
The Guest	Omar Abdulov
The Organ Grinder	Lev Sverdlin
The General	Nikolai Konovalov

(In Russian; English Titles)

Anton Chekhov's play, filmed last year as part of commemoration of 40th anni of the great Russian dramatist's death, makes a highly diverting pic. Scene of a wedding in a lower-class family, with its attendant bickerings, jealousies and greed, is ace material for satire. And as broadly burlesqued by some excellent

Russ actors, it makes 47 minutes of high-grade fun.

Although pic contains stock actors —the rejected suitor, the bossy mother-in-law, the prying neighbors —it is acted so well to be a perfect takeoff of petty small-town folk. Scene is the banquet following the marriage of a young couple. The event wouldn't be complete without the presence of a notable, so a general is hired to attend. Snide rejected suitor makes some comment about a sparse dowry, whereupon indignant mother-in-law disrupts dinner to drag guests through house, pulling sheets out of bureaus, coats out of trunks, to demonstrate riches going with bride. Banquet ends in a free-for-all with everyone being hauled off by the cops.

Pic is peopled with fascinating types, some grotesque, some burlesqued, but all highly amusing. Faces of dancers at dinner-dance, as well as the pompous groom, the witch mother-in-law, the pathetic general, are intriguing. Pic has other good features, good production, good music, some fine song and dance interludes, to add to excellence. *Bron.*

Miniature Reviews

"Hotel Berlin" (WB). Socko meller, right out of the headlines. Exciting melodrama that will hypo anybody's b.o.

"Molly and Me" (20th). Gracie Fields - Monty Woolley - Roddy McDowall comedy-drama geared for healthy b.o.

"The Picture of Dorian Gray" (M-G). A critic's picture. Selling will determine its b.o.

"Sudan" (U) (Color). Romantic adventure costumer in rich coloring that should range from well to better than good b.o.

"The Crime Doctor's Courage" (Col). No suspense in this latest of the series; for the lower duals.

"Eadie Was a Lady" (Col) (Musical). Ann Miller and Joe Besser in light comedy with music; okay supporter for duals.

"Earl Carroll's Vanities" (Musical) (Rep). Moderate b.o. for Dennis O'Keefe-Constance Moore starrer.

Hotel Berlin

Warner Bros. release of Louis F. Edelman production. Features Faye Emerson, Helmut Dantine, Raymond Massey, Andrea King, Peter Lorre. Directed by Peter Godfrey. Screenplay, Jo Pagano and Alvah Bessie from Vicki Baum's novel; score, Franz Waxman; camera, Carl Guthrie; editor, Frank Magee; dialog director, Jack Gage; asst. dir., Claude Archer. At Strand, N. Y., week March 2, '45. Running time, 98 MINS.

Martin Richter	Helmut Dantine
Lisa Dorn	Andrea King
Arnim Von Dahnwitz	Raymond Massey
Tillie Weiler	Faye Emerson
Johannes Koenig	Peter Lorre
Hermann Plottke	Alan Hale
Joachim Helm	Geo. Coulouris
Von Stetten	Henry Daniell
Heinrichs	Peter Whitney
Frau Sarah Baruch	Helene Thimig
Kliebert	Steven Geray
Maj. Otto Kauders	Kurt Kreuger
Walter	Paul Andor
Dr. Dorf	Erwin Kalser
Bellboy No. 6	Dickie Tyler
Woman Tele. Msgr.	Elsa Heim
Fritz	Frank Reicher
Kurt	Paul Panzer
Von Buelow	John Mylong
Gretchen	Ruth Albu
Gomez	Jay Novello
Frau Plottke	Lotte Stein
Franz (Barber)	Torben Meyer

"Grand Hotel" in a 1945 Nazi setting, now known as "Hotel Berlin," is socko. It's socko as entertainment and as boxoffice, another timely break for Warners, as was "Casablanca" and "Confessions of a Nazi Spy."

A melodrama out of the headlines, this compact, punchy thriller should be an exhib's delight. The dialog reads like a footnote to Yalta, and the film plays like a trailer for the London peace conference.

There's no mincing of language and skirting of sensitivities. Unlike the guarded, double-talk of "Nazi Spy" and some of the necessary vagueness of "Casablanca," the WB version of Vicki Baum's novel (brought up to the minute, circa 1945 and not '43, when she first authored it) is one for the crystal-ball. The war's already lost—or, at least, there's that defeatist aura about Hotel Berlin—and the Nazi higherups are packing their loot for a South American getaway. already plotting World War III, with a plan "to be more skillful next time when we attempt to create unrest in North America."

For average film fan consumption that's the least of it. For average American and, for that matter, all our Allied audiences, this is arresting melodrama and an honest if. mayhaps, sometimes naive attempt to treat a world catastrophic situation in broad values.

Producer Lou Edelman has guided his charges well. Productionally the lavishness is by suggestion rather than in reality. It's still the Hotel

Berlin on one floor or another. There are the periodic Allied air blitzes which chase everybody into the shelters, but otherwise it's a Grand Hotel in the lobby or on the sundry floors. but particularly in the apartments of general (Raymond Massey), an informer (Faye Emerson), or a theatre darling (Andrea King) whose closets-full of clothes from Paris embitter the hotel harlot who hungers for one pair of shoes.

That's the action, but it's action all the way. It is kaleidoscopic but thrill-packed. Director Peter Godfrey has painted well his chiseling gauleiters and ruthless Gestapo. Alan Hale is one of these mercenary gauleiters about to be done in by the SS bunch until Miss Emerson turns on him in an air-raid shelter, after he had berated a woman from the ghetto for not wearing her Star of David. George Coulouris is the complete menace as the Gestapo leader, covetous of the dishonored general's (Massey) mistress, the darling of the Berlin theatre (Miss King). Henry Daniell is the party-chief who would give Massey an honorable way out but is ever subservient to the Gestapo.

Then there is Peter Lorre in a capital albeit somewhat vague assignment of the befuddled Prof. Koenig, whose genius was "softened up" to the Nazis' will. And back of it all is the underground, apparently in a pretty good position within Hotel Berlin to help its cause along when some crisis demanded it.

There are many suspenseful touches right along. The footage is replete with arresting meller. Whether it's Dickie Tyler as the resourceful little bellboy, or his father, a waiter, both of the underground, or the femme star who apparently first falls for Dantine (the escaped anti-Nazi) and later would turn him in, the situations are constantly intriguing. The performances match. All are excellent. Miss King as the star and Miss Emerson as the informer, hungry for a pair of new shoes, silently in love with a Jewish boy whom she thought dead, are convincing. Ditto Massey, which is merely dittoing what is generally any Massey performance. That goes for Dantine and right down the line.

Not the least of the technical assists is an excellent dramatic score by Franz Waxman. *Abel.*

Molly and Me
(SONGS)

20th-Fox release of Robert Bassler production. Stars Gracie Fields, Monty Woolley, Roddy McDowall. Directed by Lewis Seiler. Screenplay, Leonard Praskins; adaptation, Roger Burford; camera, Charles Clarke; editor, John McCafferty; from novel by Frances Marion. Tradeshown N. Y., March 2, '45. Running time, 76 MINS.

Molly	Gracie Fields
Graham	Monty Woolley
Jimmy Graham	Roddy McDowall
Peabody	Reginald Gardiner
Kitty	Natalie Schafer
Julia	Edith Barrett
Pops	Clifford Brooke
Musette	Aminta Dyne
Lily	Queenie Leonard
Mrs. Graham	Doris Lloyd
Ronnie	Patrick O'Moore
Sir Arthur Burroughs	Lewis L. Russell
Mr. Lamb	Ethel Griffies
George	Eric Wilton
Pierre	Jean Del Val
Manager	Leyland Hodgson
Perkins	Lillian Bronson
Angus	David Clyde
Messenger Boy	Jerry Shane
Lord Alexander	Boyd Irwin
Lady Alexander	Ottola Nesmith
Flower Boy	Tony Ellis
Grocery Boy	Walter Tetley
McDougall	Gordon Richards
Sergeant	Matthew Boulton
Policeman	Leslie Denison
Bar Maid	Jean Prescott

Inauspicious title cloaks a pleasant comedy-drama which should fare handsomely in the key runs and all the way down the line. Despite some incongruities in thematic development "Molly and Me" impresses favorably for its swift pace. skillful direction and compact entertainment values. It is neatly studded with belly-laugh material as well as effective bits of pathos. Above all, it holds an excellent all-round cast topped by Gracie Fields, Monty Woolley, Roddy McDowall and Reginald Gardiner.

The Fields - Woolley - McDowall combo is, of course, a nifty bundle to drop onto any marquee. The Beard clicks again in a role wherein explosive repartee is more scathing and voluminous than ever. Miss Fields, capably handling assignment as friend - philosopher - guide to the wealthy, hermit-like autocrat, is in a setting which serves as an excellent foil for the Beard's caustic dialog. Roddy McDowall appeals strongly as the lonely youngster whose father has never learned how to get along with him.

Story, with an English locale, opens with a jobless music hall entertainer (Miss Fields) taking job as a housekeeper to keep going. She revitalizes a gloomy household, discharges a parisitical group of thieving servants, makes the place seem like home to the motherless boy, and finally brings about an understanding between father and son.

Interwoven is an ancient scandal concerning the runaway wife of the one-time Parliamentarian (Woolley) who had resigned his seat in the House of Commons many years before just when he was about to be appointed to a cabinet post. Woolley has been persuaded to "stand" for parliament again when his errant wife returns with blackmail as her objective. Unbeknownst to the politician Miss Fields scares the woman out of England by framing a phoney murder in her hotel room. This, among others, is an obvious, unconvincing sequence, rather crudely handled and scarcely adequate as a solution to the "situation." It presents a troupe of ex-actors who also came to work in the politico's household after the other help had been discharged, in the staging of the scene.

On the whole, however, the slender motif has been nicely developed with corking individual performances and via deft megaphoning. Reginald Gardiner rates attention as the ex-actor turned butler, playing the part strongly for laughs at times.

Miss Fields has several fetching songs, including "Bring Back My Bonnie," "The Awfulness, the Sinfulness, the Wickedness of Men," and "Christopher Robin." *Mori.*

The Picture of Dorian Gray

(ONE SONG)

Metro-Goldwyn-Mayer release of Pandro S. Berman production. Features George Sanders, Hurd Hatfield, Donna Reed, Angela Lansbury, Peter Lawford. Directed by Albert Lewin. Based on novel by Oscar Wilde; adaptation, Albert Lewin; editor, Ferris Webster; camera, Harry Stradling. At Capitol, N. Y., week March 1, '45. Running time, **107 MINS.**

Lord Henry Wotton........George Sanders
Dorian Gray........Hurd Hatfield
Gladys Hallward........Donna Reed
Sibyl Vane........Angela Lansbury
David Stone........Peter Lawford
Basil Hallward........Lowell Gilmore
James Vane........Richard Fraser
Allen Campbell........Douglas Walton
Adrian Singleton........Morton Lowry
Sir Robert Bentley........Miles Mander
Mrs. Vane........Lydia Bilbrook
Lady Agatha........Mary Forbes
Sir Thomas........Robert Greig
Duchess........Moyna MacGill
Malvolio Jones Chairman........Billy Bevan
Young French Woman........Renie Carson
Kate........Lillian Bond

"The Picture of Dorian Gray," based upon the Oscar Wilde story, represents an interesting and daring experiment by Metro in view of the subject matter. What it may do at the boxoffice, something not as easy to foretell as with most pictures, also makes it an intriguing piece of merchandise for analysis. It's a critic's picture.

In the advertising, exploitation, publicity, etc., may lie the answer from a gross point of view. However, the ad approach is something exhibitors may have difficulty in deciding upon. The Wilde name may mean something, but the cast names do not. It would seem, especially in view of the fact that the horror and murder cycle is now enjoying popularity, that the best way to merchandise "Dorian Gray" may be to stress that angle; also, perhaps, to try to arouse the public on controversial aspects of the film.

Pandro S. Berman has invested the picture with much production value. It is reported to have cost over $2,000,000, raising the question of whether the negative cost will be returned. That again may depend a lot on the selling and how much talk about the film and its theme may count in arousing interest in seeing it. Five persons, including Dorian Gray, go dead in the picture. That might be played up, too. The first is the saloon singer who kills herself over Gray, the second his friend who did his portrait and is murdered by Gray, the third a chemist who suicides, fourth a sailor out to get Gray who's accidentally shot by a hunting party and, finally, Gray himself. It's his painting, horribly disfigured and bloodied up by Gray, which, in line with fantasy, turns on him.

The morbid theme of the Wilde story, carefully but also somewhat boldly adapted to the screen, is built around Gray; his contempt for the painting that was made of him, the fears of not retaining youth and, of course, the unregenerate depths to which Gray sinks and the evil rumors about him that have become widely circulated. His utter indifference to them, his troubled mind, the weaknesses that make him an interesting character and, on the other hand, his sadistic tendencies, all combine to make Gray a subject any psycho-analyst would like to lay his hands on. In the adaptation, Albert Lewin, who directed, has very subtly but unmistakably, pegged Gray for what he was, but it may go over the heads of a lot of people anyway. Also, much of the offscreen narration, explaining among other things what is going on in Gray's mind, plus the epigrammatic slants, might be too much for most to grasp.

Hurd Hatfield, who had a minor part in Metro's "Dragon Seed," is pretty-boy Gray. He plays it with little feeling, as apparently intended, but does it well, though he should have been aged a little toward the end. As Hatfield does the Gray part, he's singularly Narcissitic all the way. Sanders, misogynistic of mind and a cynic of the first water, turns in a very commendable performance. It's he who upsets the romance, ostensibly serious on Gray's part, which has developed with a cheap music hall vocalist. She's Angela Lansbury, who registers strongly and very sympathetically. Miss Lansbury sings "Goodbye, Little Yellow Bird," a haunting old English music hall number which is reprised several times. Another sympathetic character is Donna Reed, who also falls in love with Gray but is brushed aside. Peter Lawford plays the man she jilts, while Lowell Gilmore is the murdered painter. Richard Fraser the brother of Miss Lansbury, and Douglas Walton, the chemist suicide. All are well cast, together with numerous minor characters. *Char.*

Sudan

(COLOR; SONGS)

Universal release of Paul Malvern production. Features Maria Montez, Jon Hall, Turhan Bey, Andy Devine, George Zucco and Robert Warwick. Directed by John Rawlins. Story and adaptation, Edmund L. Hartmann; editor, Milton Carruth; songs, Everett Carter and Milton Rosen; camera, George Robinson; special photography, John P. Fulton. Previewed in N. Y. Feb. 28, '45. Running time, **76 MINS.**

Naila........Maria Montez
Merab........Jon Hall
Herua........Turhan Bey
Nebka........Andy Devine
Horadef........George Zucco
Maatet........Robert Warwick
Setna........Phil Van Zandt
Uba........Harry Cording
Bata........George Lynn
Khafra........Charles Arnt

In color and very impressive against richly-hued costuming, outdoor vistas, etc., "Sudan" is a romantic adventure of convenient length (76 mins.) which bids fair to do well at the b.o. Because of the nice tinting job, and despite the sometimes erratic photography, it has particular appeal to the eye.

Ancient Egypt, backgrounded by slave-trading, thievery and intrigue, provides the locale for the lavish production turned out by Paul Malvern and directed neatly by John Rawlins, who has efficiently handled, in particular, some of the action scenes. These include battles between rival factions, a horse race and an avalanche which is part of a scheme to wipe out an army on the way to battle a slave group.

The story, an original by Edmund L. Hartmann, has been woven together skillfully with satisfactory dialog. Production values, in addition to the glittering costuming and outdoor shots, include numerous impressive, colorful settings.

Maria Montez lends glamour to the role of an Egyptian queen who is grabbed by slave-traders but effects an escape, aided in part by Jon Hall and Andy Devine, who are a couple of roving horse-thieves and pickpockets. Captured by the slavers, the trio is about to be executed when Turhan Bey frees them in spectacular fashion.

Bey virtually steals the picture as the leader of a group of slaves whose mission is to wipe out the slave-traders. He and Miss Montez contribute the romance elements. George Zucco, as the scheming chamberlain in the Queen's royal setup, acquits himself creditably, while among others handling themselves ably is Robert Warwick, as head of a slave-trading bunch.

Two background songs for mixed choruses were specially written for the picture by Everett Carter and Milton Rosen. They are "Proud and Free," an operatic type number which impresses considerably, and "The Call to Love," led by an unseen soloist, which doesn't *Char.*

The Crime Doctor's Courage

Columbia release of Rudolph C. Flothow production. Stars Warner Baxter; features Hillary Brooke, Jerome Cowan, Robert Scott. Directed by George Sherman. Screenplay by Eric Taylor based on radio program by Max Marcin; camera, L. W. O'Connell; editor, Dwight Caldwell. At Rialto, N. Y., week of March 2, '45. Running time, **70 MINS.**

Dr. Robert Ordway........Warner Baxter
Kathleen Carson........Hillary Brooke
Jeffers Jerome........Jerome Cowan
Bob Rencoret........Robert Scott
John Massey........Lloyd Corrigan
Captain Birch........Emory Parnell
Gordon Carson........Stephen Crane
Butler........Charles Arnt
Miguel Bragga........Anthony Caruso
Dolores Bragga........Lupita Tovar
David Lee........Dennis Moore
Detective Fanning........Jack Carrington
Luga........King Kong Kashay

One of the poorer entries in the series, this "Crime Doctor" pic lacks suspense or mystery. **A lower dualer.**

Yarn finds Dr. Ordway dealing with a detective story writer, a fortune hunter, two Spanish dancers and a studious young man, in an effort to solve a murder. Everyone is suspect, but by pointing suspicion at majority of the cast and overlooking one actor, director makes the solution too obvious.

Warner Baxter gives a forthright performance as the psychiatrist turned mystery-solver. Hillary Brooke, as the gal; Robert Scott, as the eccentric youth, and Jerome Cowan, as the detective story writer, go through their paces in capable fashion. Rest of cast is seen briefly.

Script takes too much for granted, and direction lacks smoothness, jumping around without too much thought of audience reaction. Settings are substantial for this light-budgeter. *Sten.*

Eadie Was a Lady

(MUSICAL)

Columbia release of Michel Kraike production. Features Ann Miller, Joe Besser. Directed by Arthur Dreifuss. Original story and screenplay by Monte Brice; camera, Brunett Guffey; editor, James Sweeney; songs, L. Wolfe Gilbert, Ben Oakland, Saul Chaplin, Sammy Cahn, Phil Moore, Howard Gibeling, Harold Dickinson, Buddy De Sylva, Nacio Herb Brown. At Gramercy Park, N. Y., March 1-2, '45. Running time, **80 MINS.**

Eadie Allen........Ann Miller
"Professor" Dingle........Joe Besser
Tommy Foley........William Wright
Pamela Parker........Jeff Donnell
Jimmy Tuttle........Jimmy Little
Rose Allure........Marion Martin
Aunt Priscilla........Kathleen Howard
Hannegan........Tom Dugan
Dean Flint........Douglas Wood
Hal McIntyre Orchestra

That "Eadie Was a Lady" is a fairly entertaining, well produced supporting feature is largely due to Ann Miller and Joe Besser. Nicely-paced direction of Arthur Dreifus also helps pull it from the mire of implausibilities. Despite the rather weird picture it paints of burlesque, film is okay for lower rung of twin bills.

Main theme hamstrings the picture right off the bat. Scripter Monte Brice would have one believe that a co-ed (Miss Miller) from a straight-laced gals' school is living a double life by working nights as femme star at a local burley house.

Miss Miller does a slick job singing "Next Victory Day," "Eadie Was a Lady" and "I'm Going to See My Baby." "Eadie," by Buddy De Sylva and Nacio Herb Brown, is given plenty of production, and is the best tune in the film. It's not new, as are several others in film, but solid. Miss Miller cleans up with her deft tapstering as usual. Besser, as former burlesque comic turned school instructor, is funny when given a break, which is seldom. William Wright is passable as the burley manager and Miss Miller's sweetie, while Jeff Donnell clowns well as Besser's romantic viz-a-vis. Hal McIntyre's band provides trim backgrounding but is seldom spotted to best advantage. *Wear.*

Earl Carroll's Vanites

(MUSICAL)

Republic release of Albert J. Cohen production. Stars Dennis O'Keefe, Constance Moore; features Eve Arden, Otto Kruger, Alan Mowbray, Stephanie Bachelor, Pinky Lee, Parkyakarkus,, Leon Belasco, Beverly Loyd, Edward Gargan, Woody Herman's orchestra. Directed by Joseph Stanley. Screenplay, Frank Gill, Jr., based on original story by Cortland Fitzimmons; editor, Richard L. Van Enger; camera, Jack Marta; songs, Walter kent and Kim Gannon; music, Walter Scharf; dances, Sammy Lee. Previewed N.Y., Feb 2, '45. Running time, 95 MINS.

Danny Baldwin........Dennis O'Keefe
Drina........Constance Moore
Tex Donnelly........Eve Arden
Earl Carroll........Otto Kruger
Grand Duke Paul........Alan Mowbray
Claire Elliott........Stephanie Bachelor
Pinky Price........Pinky Lee
Walter........Parkyakarkus
Dashek........Leon Belasco
Cigarette Girl........Beverly Loyd
Policeman........Edward Gargan
Queen Mother........Mary Forbes
Waiter in Club........Tom Dugan
Mr. Weims........Chester Clute
The Singer........Jimmy Alexander
Doorman........Tom London
Vance, butler........Robert Greir
Mr. Thayer........Wilton Graff
Tommy........Tommy Ive
Dance Specialty........Lillane & Marie
Woody herman and His Orchestra

Earl Carroll as a showman has **long been topgrade,** and it's unfortunate that Republic Pictures could not have whipped together a better story with which to accentuate the producer's positive. "Earl Carroll's Vanities" can thus hope to achieve no more than moderate boxoffice.

This film is not one to glamorize the career of Carroll, portending to be strictly an incident in his producing lifetime. It's straight fiction, and the basic value to such a pic might well have been the beauts around whom much of his career has actually been predicated.

The picture has two elements that distinguish it, however—a song and a girl. The tune is "Endlessly," one of several by Walter Kent and Kim Gannon in this backstage musical; the gal—Constance Moore.

Of the two, it's Miss Moore who's the film's top commodity, a sock looker who needs to be "discovered" all over again for musicals. Miss Moore wears clothes as they were intended to be worn; she screens like a million and she knocks off a tune with better than passing interest. "Endlessly" is far and away the best tune in the pic.

"Vanities" specifically is about how Carroll is looking for talent for a new show and how a visiting princess from a dot on the European map winds up in the show. That would be Miss Moore, in America trying to get a loan for her country. There are complications, of course, and their development makes for more confusion than entertainment.

Dennis O'Keefe is co-starred with Miss Moore, and he makes a handsome juve, as an author who creates the show being produced by Carroll. Eve Arden is in for the caustic comedy, a type she's long done in pix and on stage, a credible job, while Otto Kruger's lines as Carroll don't do much justice to the real-life producer. Alan Mowbray is in for questionable laughs, Stephanie Bachelor is the "other woman," while other comedy typical of them is contributed by Pinky Lee and Parkyakarkus. Woody Herman's orch is in for a couple of brief musical sequences.

Production looks expensive by normal Republic standards. *Kahn.*

The Legend of a Bandit

("La Leyenda de Bandidó")

(MEXICAN-MADE)

Clasa release starring Raul de Anda and Susana Guizar; features Miguel Angel Ferriz, Tito Junco, Miguel Arenas, Agustin Isunza, El Chicote. Directed by Fernando Mendez. Music by Trio Calaveras. At Belmont, N. Y., week March 2, '45. Running time, **82 MINS.**

Benito Canales..................Raul de Anda
Isabel..........................Susana Guizar
Priest..................Miguel Angel Ferris
Capt. Rogenio.......................Tito Junco
Isabel's Father...............Miguel Arenas
"The Tall One"..............Agustin Isunza
"The Short One"....................El Chicote

(In Spanish; No English Titles)

Clasa pulled one out of its bottom drawer for this presentation. It's doubtful if the most unsophisticated Latin audience would give it much patronage.

Strictly out of the cops-and-robbers era comes the story of the honest peasant turned bandit because the captain of the local constabulary wants to wed the pretty gal and accuses the clod unjustly of murder. Hero takes to the hills and fights several companies of the state's military arm, while he has exactly three companions to his name. The three bravos die gamely, after having aided their chieftain in knocking off dozens of the pursuers. Stymied, the evil one presses the local padre into service, betrays both priest and peasant, kills latter, gets his own bullet straight into the heart. At the altar waiting for her fair one is left Isabel, having rather a hard time keeping the mascara out of her eyes.

Miguel Ferriz as the priest, who is also the narrator of the piece, turns in a workmanlike job, and Raul de Anda is not bad. Susana Guizar is good to look at, but if she can act, she doesn't show it here.

Miniature Reviews

"Murder, My Sweet" (RKO). Taut thriller with Dick Powell-Claire Trevor; a boxoffice cinch.

"Brewster's Millions" (UA), comedy should get by nicely in the duals.

"Utah" (Musical). (Rep). A good western.

"Let's Go Steady" (Songs). (Col). Mild juve-songwriter yarn, okay for duals.

"Dillinger" (Mono). Melodramatic biog of gangland killer. For duals, with no names a retarding b.o. factor.

"The Randolph Family" (English). Mild drama of family manners; dualler.

"El Rebelde" (Songs) (Mex). Jorge Negrete in a good drama with songs. English titles.

Murder, My Sweet

RKO release of Adrian Scott production (Sid Rogell, executive producer). Stars Dick Powell, Claire Trevor, Anne Shirley; features Otto Kruger, Mike Mazurki, Miles Mander, Douglas Walton, Don Douglas. Directed by Edward Dmytryk. Screenplay, John Paxton; based on novel by Raymond Chandler; camera, Harry J. Wild; editor, Joseph Noriega; special effects, Vernon L. Walker. At Palace, N. Y., opening March 8, '45. Running time, **93 MINS.**

Marlowe...........................Dick Powell
Mrs. Grayle....................Claire Trevor
Ann...............................Anne Shirley
Amthor............................Otto Kruger
Moose...........................Mike Mazurki
Mr. Grayle......................Miles Mander
Marriott......................Douglas Walton
Randall...........................Don Douglas
Dr. Sonderborg.................Ralf Harolde
Mrs. Florian..................Esther Howard

"Murder, My Sweet," a taut thriller about a private detective enmeshed with a gang of blackmailers, is as smart as it is gripping. Ace direction and fine camera-work combine with a neat story and top performances. It should pay off plenty.

Plot ramifications may not stand up under clinical study, but suspense is built up sharply and quickly. In fact, the film gets off to so jet-propulsed a start that it necessarily hits a couple of slow stretches midway as it settles into uniform groove. But interest never flags, and the mystery is never really cleared up until the punchy closing.

Director Edward Dmytryk has made few concessions to the social amenities and has kept his yarn stark and unyielding. Story begins with a private dick hired by an ex-convict to find his one-time girl friend. Copper is momentarily sidetracked by another job, to help as bodyguard to a heel who is trying to buy back a stolen jade necklace from some thieves. The job is bungled when the heel is killed and the copper himself knocked out. Then suddenly both assignments dovetail, as the dick finds himself tailing the crooks again, the dame he is seeking being tied up with the necklace, and the amorous ex-con being one of the gang.

The mystery only gets more involved, with the dame married to a wealthy socialite, playing around on the side, becoming entangled with the head of the gang, and seeking the copper's help to rid her of her encumbrances. The private dick is further enmeshed with the regular police, who step in when a couple of murders are committed, apparently suspecting him of the crimes. The tangled web neatly disengages itself at the close.

Tense quality of direction is marked throughout pic. So is the camera work, from neat angles and trick shots to clever montage effects. Neat little touches stick out constantly, and the dialog is hep and rough-hewn, as well as having its smart humorous touches.

Performances are on a par with the production. Dick Powell is a surprise as the hard-boiled copper. The portrayal is potent and convincing. Claire Trevor is as dramatic as the predatory femme, with Anne Shirley in sharp contrast as the soft kid caught in the crossfire of her father's weakness and her young stepmother's greed. Mike Mazurki, ex-pug, gives added menace as the hopheaded killer, with Otto Kruger in effective contrast as the oily gang leader. Supporting bits are no less finely-chiseled. *Bron.*

Brewster's Millions

United Artists release of Edward Small production. Stars Dennis O'Keefe, Helen Walker, June Havoc, Eddie "Rochester" Anderson; features Gail Patrick, Mischa Auer. Directed by Allan Dwan. Screenplay, Siegfried Herzig, Charles Rogers, Wilkie Mahoney; from novel by George Barr McCutcheon and stage play by Winchell Smith and Byron Ongley; camera, Charles Lawton; editor, Richard Heermance. Previewed at Mayfair, N. Y., March 8, '45. Running time, **79 MINS.**

Monty Brewster...............Dennis O'Keefe
Peggy Gray.......................Helen Walker
Jackson.......Eddie "Rochester" Anderson
Trixie Summers...................June Havoc
Barbara Drew.....................Gail Patrick
Michael Michaelovich..........Mischa Auer
Hacky Smith......................Joe Sawyer
Mrs. Gray.........................Nana Bryant
Swearengen Jones..................John Litel
Nopper Harrison..............Herbert Rudley
Colonel Drew....................Thurston Hall
Mr. Grant.........................Neil Hamilton
Attorney...........................Byron Foulger
Cab Driver.....................Barbara Pepper
Notary............................Joseph Crehan

Latest version of this hardy perennial stage farce (also a novel), filmed twice previously, once by a U. S. and later a British producer, should get by nicely in the duals. Based on apparently modest, though by no means skimpy budget, it looks like profitable biz, particularly in the subsequents.

Play, first produced some 38 years ago, remains somewhat dated despite efforts to refurbish background in this screen adaptation through introduction of wartime atmosphere. Slow, deliberate opening is a drawback. Once motivation has been established, however, yarn moves along at a fast clip with one climax topping another.

Dennis O'Keefe, Rochester, Gail Patrick and Mischa Auer are in for sturdy individual performances, with O'Keefe particularly carrying the ball neatly as the returned doughboy who inherits the millions. Helen Walker, a looker and a comer, photographs well.

Story is, of course, familiar. It's a problem play. The young, handsome soldier returns home to a swell girl waiting to marry him. He's apparently in good condition, ready to enjoy life. He finds he's inherited $8,000,000 bucks. Now here's the problem—he's got to spend $1,000,000 in two months, under the provisions of the will, or lose the entire estate. Even with the help of a flop musical show, a bankrupt banker, the stock market, the racetrack and a spending society gal he has trouble. "Millions" is a broad farce, of course, and gets over as such.

Small has provided adequate scenic backgrounds and a satisfactory cast. *Mori.*

Utah

(MUSICAL)

Republic release of Donald H. Brown production. Stars Roy Rogers; features George "Gabby" Hayes, Dale Evans, Peggy Stewart, Beverly Loyd, Grant Withers, Bob Nolan, Sons of Pioneers. Directed by John English. Screenplay, Jack Townley and John K. Butler from story by Gilbert Wright and Betty Burbridge; camera, William Bradford; music, Morton Scott; dances, Larry Ceballos; songs, Charles Henderson, Dave Franklin, Bob Palmer, Glen Spencer, Tim Spencer, Bob Nolan, Ken Carson. Tradeshown N. Y., March 7, '45. Running time, **78 MINS.**

Roy Rogers........................Roy Rogers
Gabby...............George "Gabby" Hayes
Dorothy Bryant....................Dale Evans
Jackie............................Peggy Stewart
Wanda............................Beverly Loyd
Ben Bowman....................Grant Withers
Babe...............................Jill Browning
Stella Mason....................Vivien Oakland
Steve Lacey.....................Hal Taliaferro
Sheriff...........................Jack Rutherford
District Attorney..............Emmett Vogan
Bob Nolan and Sons of Pioneers

A good western. Production is smooth, music pleasing, girls nice to look at. Roy Rogers and his intelligent horse turn in the kind of easily-flowing performance expected from them, and Gabby Hayes is as natural as springwater in his role.

Story centers about a Utah ranch heiress who's in a musical show in Chicago. Show is ready for opening when producers run out of money. Gal (Dale Evans) heads west to the ranch she owns but had never seen, to sell it and raise money for financing the show. That's where Rogers and Hayes come in, the one as the ranch foreman who wants to prevent the ranch going out of the family's hands for sound business reasons as well as because of sentiment; the other as the crotchety old neighbor who just hates women and is afraid that sheep would violate the range if the acres were sold.

Situations, too, are stock. But everything is handled with utmost smoothness. Singing is good, Bob Nolan and Sons of Pioneers turning in some fine ensemble work at times. Nolan's highlight number, "Five Little Miles," may catch on.

Let's Go Steady

(SONGS)

Columbia release of Ted Richmond production. Features Pat Parrish, Jackie Moran, June Preisser, Jimmy Lloyd, Arnold Stang, Skinnay Ennis orchestra. Directed by Del Lord. Screenplay, Erna Lazarus; story by William B. Sackheim. Songs, Mel Torme; camera, Benjamin Kline; editor, Richard Fantl. At Brooklyn Fox, week March 8, '45. Running time, **60 MINS.**

Linda..............................Pat Parrish
Roy Spencer....................Jackie Moran
Mibble Stack....................June Preisser
Henry McCoy....................Jimmy Lloyd
Chet Carson....................Arnold Stang
Larry Tyler....................Skinnay Ennis
"Streak" Edwards..................Mel Torme
Andy............................William Moss
Waldemar Oates...............Byron Foulger
Miss Schlepheimer..............Gladys Blake
Fred Williams.....................Eddie Bruce
Bertram Quill..............William Frambes

Columbia's misnamed comedy is a mild B-budgeter about a score of juve songwriters trying to crash Tin Pan Alley. Story and situations are as juvenile as the personalities involved, but just as harmless and unoffending. Pleasant songs, a few strands of simple humor and youthful enthusiasm help make the pic passable dual fare.

Story concerns group of youngsters from the hinterland who've been bilked by a New York phoney out of $50 apiece on promise to publish and exploit their songs. Kids gather in New York and decide to promote their songs themselves, getting the nets, bandleaders and recording stations to plug their tunes. When they get GI bands to play their tunes, so attracting the professionals, the kids are made. Title comes in at end, when kids pair off romantically.

Plot is excuse for Columbia to show off talents of some of its aspiring youngsters, in Jackie Moran's crooning, June Preisser's singing and dancing, Mel Torme's clowning and Jimmy Lloyd's mimicry. Arnold Stang is also in for comedy and Pat Parrish for glamour. Torme also contributes three of the tunes, "Tantza Babele," "Sioux Falls, S. D.," and "Baby Boogie." Skinnay Ennis is okay in brief speaking role, while leading his band through deft accompaniment to the singers. *Bron.*

Dillinger

Monogram release of King Bros. production. Directed by Max Nosseck. Screenplay, Phil Yordan; editor, Otto Levering; camera, Jackson Rose. Previewed at Normandie theatre, N. Y., Mahch 9, '45. Running time, **70 MINS.**

Specs..........................Edmund Lowe
Helen..........................Anne Jeffreys
Dillinger..................Lawrence Tierney
Murph.....................Eduardo Ciannelli
Doc...........................Marc Lawrence
Kirk...........................Elisha Cook, Jr.
Tony.............................Ralph Lewis
Otto...........................Ludwig Stossel
Mrs. Otto.......................Else Jannsen
Guard...........................Hugh Prosser
Guard.......................Dewey Robinson
Proprietor..........................Bob Perry
Watchman..........................Kid Chisel
Watchman........................Billy Nelson
Salesman..................Lee (Lasses) White
Walter...............................Lou Lubin

The hectic career of John Dillinger, who a dozen years ago terrorized the midwest with his spectacular bank holdups, has rather belatedly been brought to the screen by the independent producing outfit of the King Bros. With a no-name cast, "Dillinger" is doubtful boxoffice though its obvious modest budget shouldn't be difficult to recoup on the duals. [Film, incidentally, has been banned in Chicago.]

Somehow, the pic smacks of the same intensity imparted to gangland pictures of the '30s, when such films seemed the boxoffice rage. But in 1945 "Dillinger," as most such pix, seems passe.

Dillinger's career is traced from what was presumably his first holdup—which netted him $7.20—through his many bank holdups, and finally to his end, when "the lady in red" became the finger-pointer for the G-men in the now-famed episode in which he was shot down while exiting from a Chicago theatre.

Lawrence Tierney, as Dillinger, is a likely prospect with better roles, while Anne Jeffreys is another newcomer who does little more than look decorative as the gal who ultimately is responsible for gang-leader's death. Edmund Lowe has a comparatively inconspicuous part as the gang chief whom Dillinger succeeds and eventually bumps off.

The pic is slow in spots, and the script, by Phil Yordan—who, incidentally, wrote "Anna Lucasta," current Broadway stage hit—is only as good as the subject permitted. Which means that Dillinger at this late date was hardly worth the try. *Kahn.*

The Randolph Family

English Films release of Paul Soskin (Maurice Ostrer) production. Features Margaret Lockwood and Michael Wilding. Directed by Harold French. Screenplay, R. J. Minney and Pat Kerwan, from Esther McCracken adaptation of Dodie Smith's play, "Dear Octopus"; camera, Arthur Crabtree; editor, Michael Chorlton. At Little Carnegie theatre, N. Y., week of March 12, '45. Running time, **78 MINS.**

Penny Fenton..............Margaret Lockwood
Nicholas Randolph.........Michael Wilding
Cynthia.........................Celia Johnson
Felix Martin...................Roland Culver
Dora Randolph..................Helen Haye
Belle...........................Athene Seyler
Vicar's wife.....................Joan Cadell
Kenneth......................Basil Radford
Charles Randolph..........Frederick Leister
Edna........................Nora Swinburne
Hilda.....................Antoinette Collier
Marjorie....................Madge Compton
Mrs. Glossop..............Kathleen Harrison
Scrap..........................Ann Stephens
Bill...........................Derek Lansiaux
Joe..........................Alistair Stewart
Gertrude.......................Evelyn Hall
Cook.........................Muriel George
Nannie.......................Annie Esmond
Flora............................Irene Handl
Mr. Glossop.................Arthur Denton
Deidre......................Pamela Western
Burton...............................Artie Ash
Chauffeur..................Graham Moffatt
Vicar..........................Henry Morrell

A mild drama of family manners in a bygone day, this English-made pic is a dualler. Even the most hidebound English fan won't get excited over this one. American audiences will find it too chattery, and while it's patently a pre-war theme, dialog, such as tourists trips to Paris doesn't rest well in this day and age.

Story centers about a very amiable, aged couple celebrating their golden wedding anniversary in their "typical, English middle-class" country home. (There are a few million Englishmen who would dispute the typicalness of a middle-class family with at least three or four servants.) To the affair come all the children, grandchildren, and even the widow of the deceased son. Family hatreds and jealousies come to the surface, the family skeleton is exhibited starkly for all to see, and a grand bustup of the party is hinted. But one is sure it will not really happen. It doesn't.

Lovely Margaret Lockwood, excellent in her role as a sort of family companion, secretary and confidante, manages the obstreperous, successful playwright-son; a couple of daughters rise to compromise; even the wolfish daughter-in-law learns to love people, and all ends happily. The playwright declares his love for the pretty family major domo (Miss Lockwood) and all is serene.

Michael Wilding's role as the playwright simply doesn't come off, and the fault is apparently with both script and actor. Roland Culver is much better as the village bandmaster who also loves the lovely gal. And the aged couple, done by Helen Haye and Frederick Leister, are amiable enough in their parts. In fact, it's all just too amiable.

Amarga Verdad
("Bitter Truth")
(CHILEAN-MADE)

Santiago, March 1.

Features Carlos Cores, Maria Teresa Squella, Mafaldi Tinelli, Hernan Castro Oliveira, Placido Martin, Ines Yanko, Elvira Quiroga. Directed by Carlos Borcosque. Screenplay, Borcosque and Demicheli. At Teatro Real, Santiago de Chile. Running time, **88 MINS.**

This is the second production of Andres Salas Edwards, made in studios of Chile Films, and comes close to high standards set by top Mexican and Argentine pix. First showing to public drew spontaneous and enthusiastic applause. Looks big for Spanish-language houses and all Latin-America.

Story deals with the growth of two boys, born the same night, one to a rich property owner and other to one of the servants. Servant persuades his friend to change children to insure a worry-free life for her own baby. Property owner, who is epileptic, enters private nursing home on day son is born, and swapped infants are brought up together—as far as strict social barriers permit. Servant's son, who has been educated for medical profession by unknowing wife of property owner, meets and falls in love with daughter of doctor who attended birth, and who knows of epilepsy in family. His pseudo-mother's cold reception makes him realize that something is wrong, and he discovers fact of epilepsy. Scientific examination of his blood reveals to him that he is not epileptic, so he jumps to conclusion that he is illegitimate son of lady he thinks is his mother and her former sweetheart, who has remained friendly to family throughout. Real situation is eventually disclosed by servant-mother to boys, who decide to leave things as they are for sake of property owner's wife and lovers, the boy who has inherited epilepsy leaving for parts unknown.

Somewhat confusing nature of story is offset by skill of director, Carlos Borcosque (a Chilean with experience in both Hollywood and Argentina), who unfolds it cleverly, using all the technical knowledge he has acquired in his varied career. Photography and sound work are excellent, especially use of half tones to create atmosphere for the tragic theme, and comic relief is tastefully employed. Carlos Cores, star of the pic, is handsome Argentine juve with ingratiating personality, and Maria Teresa Squella, young Chilean actress who makes first film appearance in this opus, has what it takes. The work of Rodolfo Onetto, Mafaldi Tinelli, Elvira Quiroga and Hernan Castro Oliveira has fine quality. *Russ.*

El Rebelde
("The Rebel")
(SONGS)

Aguila release of Clasa production. Stars Jorge Negrete; features Frederico Pinero; Maria Elena Marques. Directed by Jaime Salvador. Story and screenplay, Juan Malaquais and Salvador; music, Manuel Esperon; camera, R. Martinez Solares. At Belmont, N. Y., week of March 10, '45. Running time, **112 MINS.**

The Rebel........................Jorge Negrete
Singing Teacher..............Frederico Pinero
Rancher's Daughter..Maria Elena Marques
Also Julio Villareal, Miguel Angel Ferriz, Felipe Montoya, Fernando Soto.

(In Spanish; English Titles)

A good drama, with four songs capably sung by star Jorge Negrete, this Mexican film should do OK in class U. S. houses since the Spanish dialog is embellished with English titles.

Yarn relates how a young man turns bandit to avenge his father's death. He captures the singing teacher of the daughter of the man who he knows is responsible, taking the latter's place, and falls in love with the daughter. But in the end he must kidnap the girl in order to get her to marry him.

Settings and camerawork are especially commendable, as is the English continuity flashed on the screen. These attributes add to the enjoyment of the drama, which holds interest because of its impact. Cast, led by Negrete, who is before the camera practically during the entire film, act out their roles as if they are enjoying themselves. Songs are in the usual Mexican vein. *Sten.*

Miniature Reviews

"Without Love" (M-G). Hepburn-Tracy insure strong boxoffice.

"A Royal Scandal" (20th). Bankhead, Coburn, Eythe in strong Lubitsch farce comedy; big boxoffice.

"House of Fear" (U). OK Sherlock Holmes series dualler.

"Tarzan and the Amazons" (RKO). An OK twinner.

"GI Honeymoon" (Mono). Lusty comedy, just short of risque, okay dualler.

"The Man Who Walked Alone" (PRC). A humorless dualer.

"Wait for Me" (Artkino) (Songs). Good for special arty houses.

"The Kid Sister" (PRC). Light comedy, nice dualer.

Without Love

Metro release of Lawrence A. Weingarten production. Stars Spencer Tracy, Katharine Hepburn; features Lucille Ball, Keenan Wynn, Carl Esmond, Patricia Morison. Directed by Harold S. Bucquet. Screenplay, Donald Ogden Stewart from Philip Barry's play (Theatre Guild); camera, Karl Freund; music, Bronislau Kaper; special effects, A. Arnold Gillespie, Danny Hall; montage, Peter Ballbusch; editor, Frank Sullivan. Tradeshown N. Y., March 16, 1945. Running time, **111 MINS.**

Pat Jamieson....................Spencer Tracy
Jamie Rowan..............Katharine Hepburn
Kitty Trimble........................Lucille Ball
Quentin Ladd...................Keenan Wynn
Paul Carrell.......................Carl Esmond
Edwina Collins...............Patricia Morison
Professor Grinza...............Felix Bressart
Anna...............................Emily Massey
Flower Girl.....................Gloria Grahame
Caretaker..........................George Davis
Elevator Boy..................George Chandler
Sergeant.........................Clancy Cooper

Competent trouping and topflight production make "Without Love" a boxoffice click despite some basic plot faults. And, of course, Hepburn-Tracy on the marquee ain't exactly b.o. poison.

But there's no gainsaying the general obviousness of it all, along with a somewhat static plot basis. True, adapter Donald Ogden Stewart has brought it up the minute in a wartime Washington locale, but the Theatre Guild production of Philip Barry's play was fundamentally uncertain.

There is a lack of conviction despite the adult trouping of the lady scientist who aids the gentleman scientist. It's a foregone conclusion that behind their mutual shells of yesteryear amours they'll clinch eventually. Hers was the idyllic love, too shortlived, but a perfect two years, until his death; and Tracy's love life is something out of a Parisian past.

A bit of that long arm of coincidence crops up when the slick menace, well done by Carl Esmond, of Madrid, New York, D. C., and points east, happens to want to rent Miss Hepburn's house. Ditto is the accidental doubling-up on a rainy night in a D. C. taxi, which throws Tracy together with the tippling Keenan Wynn, whose cousin is Miss Hepburn. Hence Tracy bivouacs in the house which he shortly takes over as a laboratory for a new aeronautical oxygen helmet.

Interspersed is an intelligent pooch who has been trained to curb Tracy's somnambulism, which is planted early for boudoir usage later. Somehow this is inconsistent with so stoic a character as Tracy, but somehow, also, it's made acceptable, as is the squabbling Wynn-Patricia Morison business, and the rest of it. All of which is wholly to the cast's credit.

Usual lush Metro appurtenances, including a very fetching Bronislau Kaper musical setting. *Abel.*

A Royal Scandal

20th-Fox release of Ernst Lubitsch production. Stars Tallulah Bankhead, Charles Coburn, Anne Baxter, William Eythe; features Vincent Price, Mischa Auer, Sig Ruman, Vladimir Sokoloff, Mikhail Rasumny. Directed by Otto Preminger. Screenplay, Edwin Justus Mayer; adapted by Bruno Frank from a play by Lajos Biro, Melchior Langyel; camera, Arthur Miller; editor, Dorothy Spencer. Tradeshown in N. Y., March 16, '45. Running time, 94 MINS.

The Czarina............Tallulah Bankhead
Chancellor................Charles Coburn
Anna......................Anne Baxter
Alexei...................William Eythe
Marquis de Fleury.........Vincent Price
Captain Sukov.............Mischa Auer
General Ronsky.............Sig Ruman
Malakoff................Vladimir Sokoloff
Drunken General........Mikhail Rasumny
Boris.......................Grady Sutton
Variatinsky................Don Douglas
Wassilikow...................Egon Brecher

"A Royal Scandal" is a highly hilarious comedy. The skill and unerring flair of Ernst Lubitsch for deftly handling sophisticated material holds solid throughout. Add to this, superb performances by Tallulah Bankhead and Charles Coburn, in particular, and the wit of the original play by Lajos Biro and Melchior Langyel, and it all adds up to fine screen entertainment. Film will click everywhere.

This version of Catherine the Great's saga turns out to be a farce of real proportions, although never eclipsing the Czarina as an extremely vigorous personality, surrounded by palace intrigue and a parade of lovers. Lubitsch and director Otto Preminger have neatly interwoven the court intrigue with her w.k. amorous proclivities. The stream of captains of the palace guards is pointed up somewhat briskly.

Yarn concentrates on impetuous William Eythe, young cavalryman, who has ridden three days and nights to warn the Czarina about two plotting generals. Because he admittedly is not tired after his strenuous ride, Catherine ignores his impetuosity and slight dumbness to have him await a nocturnal interview. That this interview is successful is borne out by subsequent events as Eythe is rapidly pyramided first to commander of the guards and ultimately to rank of general. When the Czarina actually falls in love with Eythe, she banishes Anne Baxter, to whom he is engaged and who is a lady-in-waiting to Catherine. Payoff is a plan to seize the throne which is thwarted by Eythe, so he and his sweetheart are forgiven as Catherine launches on a new romance with a romantic marquis from France.

Through the whole story the adroit maneuvering of Charles Coburn, as the Czarina's chancellor, fits in trimly. It is a meaty role and he finishes it off with his usual aplomb. Miss Bankhead, as Catherine, is excellent. First the storming, irate ruler, then the ardent femme seeking new romantic adventures, then as the forgiving queen who knows her chancellor will handle every situation, she is convincing throughout. *Wear.*

House of Fear

Universal release of Roy William Neill production, directed by Neill. Stars Basil Rathbone, Nigel Bruce; features Aubrey Mather, Dennis Hoey. Screenplay, Roy Chanslor, based on Sir Arthur Conan Doyle book; camera, Virgil Miller; editor, Saul Goodkind. At Rialto, N. Y., week of March 16, '45. Running time, 68 MINS.

Sherlock Holmes.............Basil Rathbone
Doctor Watson.................Nigel Bruce
Alastair...................Aubrey Mather
Lestrade...................Dennis Hoey
Simon Merrivale............Paul Cavanagh
Alan Cosgrave.............Holmes Herbert
John Simpson.............Harry Cording
Mrs. Monteith............Sally Shepherd
Chalmers....................Gavin Muir
Alison MacGregor........Florette Hillier
Alex MacGregor.............David Clyde

Another of the Basil Rathbone-Nigel Bruce, Sherlock Holmes-Dr. Watson mysteries in the light-budget whodunit vein for the duallers, this one is better than average.

Yarn deals with the disappearance of all members of "The Good Com-

rades Club," except one, who supposedly is to inherit the insurance policy covering the group. Holmes is called in, and with the aid of Dr. Watson, finds several clues which lead to the finding of those who faded from sight, in a secret hiding place in the cellar of a large English mansion.

Rathbone and Bruce go through their paces in the usual oh-so-British manner, aided by Dennis Hoey, as the police inspector, and Aubrey Mather, as the surviving member. Settings are substantial, dialog trite at times but interesting enough. The camera work by Virgil Miller could have been better. *Sten.*

Tarzan and Amazons

RKO release of Sol Lesser production. Stars Johnny Weissmuller, Brenda Joyce, Johnny Sheffield. Screenplay, Hans Jacoby and Marjorie L. Pfaelzer; based on characters created by Edgar Rice Burroughs; camera, Archie Stout; director, Kurt Neumann; editor, Robert O. Crandall. Tradeshown N. Y., March 16, '45. Running time. 76 MINS.

Tarzan...............Johnny Weissmuller
Jane......................Brenda Joyce
Boy.....................Johnny Sheffield
Henderson.............Henry Stephenson
Amazon Queen........Maria Ouspenskaya
Ballister..............Barton MacLane
Andres.................Don Douglas
Splivers..................J. M. Kerrigan
Athena..................Shirley O'Hara
Brenner..................Steven Geray

The usual Tarzan adventures have been screened in an African setting, with the three stars doing a good job, and the supporting cast performing competently. A good dualer.

Story concerns Tarzan's efforts to keep faith with mysterious Palmyrians whose valley hideout is peopled only by women. Queen of the Amazons trusts Tarzan, knowing he will never reveal secret.

Unwittingly, the Tarzan household chimpanzee, Cheta, reveals to group of Europeans that Palmyrians are somewhere in the neighborhood. Group, composed of scientists and a couple of greedy traders, are led to the hideout by Tarzan's son. In denouement, Europeans war against the women, all but two are killed, Tarzan traps remaining two in quicksand, rescues his erring son whom the Amazons have meanwhile sentenced to death.

Photography is good, and African wildlife is pictured smoothly. All three stars do some good swimming, and Cheta is very engaging.

GI Honeymoon

Monogram release of Lindsley Parsons production. Stars Gale Storm; features Peter Cookson. Directed by Phil Karlstein. Screenplay, Richard Weil, Jr.; adapted from play by A. J. Roblen, Robert Chapin and Marion Page Johnson; additional dialog. Tim Ryan; camera, Harry Neumann; editor, Richard Currier. At RKO Albee, Brooklyn, N. Y., week of March 15, '45. Running time, 63 MINS.

Ann.......................Gale Storm
Bob.....................Peter Cookson
Flo........................Arline Judge
Blubber.....................Frank Jenks
Ace......................Jerome Cowan
Lavinia..................Virginia Brissac
Lieut. Randall.............Ralph Lewis
Jonas.....................Earl Hodgins
Mrs. Barton................Ruth Lee
Rev. Horace............Andrew Tombes
Col. Smith...............Jonathan Hale
Mrs. Smith.................Lois Austin
Major Brown.............John Valentine
Mrs. Brown.............Claire Whitney
Capt. Stein.............Frank Stevens
Sergt. Harrigan.........Jack Overman

A fairly lusty comedy, skillfully kept from verging on the risque, this low-budgeter is acceptable fare as a minor dualler.

GI couple's efforts to consummate their marriage is being constantly frustrated through various army emergencies. When bridegroom isn't suddenly assigned to overnight duty, just as gal has donned loveliest negligee, he's too tired to care after returning from 37-mile hike.

Hilarious scene comes when gam-

bler, who has grudge against bride, manages through witless assistant to trap husband's superior officers, and at least a company of plain Joes, in newlyweds' apartment which used to be gambling joint and has been declared out of bounds. Husband goes to the clink. But bride's spinster aunt, who had been the girl-friend of young man's colonel in first world war, helps clear up the situation.

Script is lightweight stuff and dialog undistinguished. But direction is smooth and acting good throughout, an especially good job being turned in by Jerome Cowan as the gambler and Frank Jenks as his assistant.

The Man Who Walked Alone

PRC release of Leon Fromkes production. Stars David O'Brien, Kay Aldridge; features Walter Catlet and Guinn (Big Boy) Williams. Written and directed by Christy Cabanne; camera, James Brown. At New York, N. Y., week of March 17, '45. Running time, 74 MINS.

Cpt. Marion Scott...........David O'Brien
Wilhelmina Hammond........Kay Aldridge
Wiggins....................Walter Catlett
Champ.................Big Boy Williams
Mrs. Hammond..........Isabel Randolph
Alvin Baily.................Smith Ballew
Patricia Hammond...Nancy June Robinson
Aunt Harriet..............Ruth Lee
Mr. Monroe...............Chester Clute
Mrs. Monroe.............Vivian Oakland

In the hands of some people with a sense of humor, the material of which this picture is made could have been a passable film, something along the lines of "Hail the Conquering Hero." As it stands, it's a humorless piece that doesn't manage to emerge from the stockpile for a single moment. A minor dualer.

Story centers about medically discharged corporal who had decided to settle in the hometown of a dead buddy. Walking toward the town, he is given a lift by a rich girl who had taken her fiance's car for a getaway from the man she'd prefer not to marry. They get pinched twice, once for being in the automobile that had been reported stolen, again for trying to climb into the gal's country home through a window.

Hero is suspected by girl's family of being a deserter and is so reported to cops. But instead of a posse, there come the police band, plus mayor and governor, to greet the returned hero. Girl who swore she would never marry the other guy had somehow got into her wedding gown just the same, and ends up riding in the parade besides the corporal. Nothing particularly wrong with any of the cast, but there is nothing outstanding with any of them, either.

Wait for Me
(Russian-Made)
(SONGS)

Artkino release of Central Art Studios (Alma Ata, USSR) production. Features Valentina Serova, Boris Blinov, Lev Sverdlin. Screenplay, Konstantin Simonov; English dialog and lyrics throughout by Mila Eskell; music, Nikolai Kriukov; camera, S. Rubashkin. Tradeshown N. Y., March 14, '45. Running time, 87 MINS.

Lisa.......................Valentina Serova
Nikolai.....................Boris Blinov
Misha......................Lev Sverdlin
Andrei................Nikolai Nazvanov
Sonia.....................Nina Zorskala
Fedia.....................Piotr Geraga
Maria.................Elena Tiapkina
Partisan................Anton Mertenov
Pasha......................Eda Sipavina
Gunner.....................Alex Apsolon

(English dialog and songs voiced (dubbed) by Donna Keath, Alexander Scourby, Sanford Meisner, Paul Mann, Eugenie Chapel, Byron McGrath, Grace Coppin, Louis Sorin, Barbara Fuller, Will Hare, Bill Quinn.)

In "Wait for Me" the Russians have focused their cameras on the home front, producing a film that's as interesting to Americans as it is to the Kremlin folk. Theme is the faithfulness, or vice versa, of the soldier's little woman back home. Looks like

a good shot for houses specializing in Soviet fare.

Story centers about Russian airforce major (Boris Blinov) and his blonde wife (Valentina Serova). When he is officially reported missing after a crash behind the Nazi lines, she insists he's alive and will come back. Keeping the home fires burning, she throws herself into home defense work, laboring in a warplant, digging trenches for the defense of Moscow, meanwhile shunning all male attention. A year to the day later, he returns, tickled to find she had kept faith.

A thin but pleasant little song weaves its way through the story, dubbed in the American version by Donna Keath. Theme of the song, as of the entire picture, is a poem by Simonov which sold over 1,000,000 copies in the Soviet Union, and to which 18 Russian composers had set music.

On the whole, smart scripting and even production have made the picture unusually nostalgic and unmelodramatic for a Russian war film. Juxtaposing the faithful wife's staunchness is another war bride who drowns her sorrows over her "missing" husband in wild parties, until he returns to discover her infidelity. Two sequences may seem a bit hammy to more sophisticated American audiences. In one, the hero, turned Partisan, wipes out an entire Nazi outpost single-handed. In the other, Lev Sverdlin spoils an otherwise excellent performance with a remark directed too unsubtly to the audience rather than to the cast.

But these little blemishes don't mar the fact that all of the principals turn in a very good job, with Sverdlin, as a warfront photographer and pal of the flier, doing best of all.

The Kid Sister

PRC release of Sigmund Neufeld production. Stars Roger Pryor and Judy Clark; features Frank Jenks, Constance Worth. Directed by Sam Newfield. Screenplay, Fred Myton; camera, James Brown. At New York, N. Y., week of March 17, '45. Running time, 55 MINS.

J. Waldo Barnes.............Roger Pryor
Joan Hollingsworth............Judy Clark
Ethel Hollingsworth.......Constance Worth
Burglar.......................Frank Jenks
Michael, the Cop..........Tommy Dugan
Tommy.....................Richard Byron
Mrs. Wiggins...........Minerva Urecal
Mrs. Hollingsworth........Ruth Robinson
Martha.....................Peggy Wynne

This is an example of a good, light comedy done well on a very light budget. Nice supporter on a dual bill.

Younger of two daughters who's been brought up according to the psychology book decides she's grown up and goes after the man whom mama had tabbed for older sister. Judy Clark plays the youngster very well, and the rest of cast supports her capably.

At reception for the older girl's cool swain, the kid, who'd been ordered to stay in her room, crashes the gate by posing as the family maid. She gets herself embroiled with a burglar (Frank Jenks) who takes her for a moll working the same racket. She and the burglar wind up at the home of the matrimonial catch later in the night. There's no reason for this, but it's all done so smoothly, and the ensuing comedy is so engaging, that no one should mind the lack of logic. In the end, of course, the bright youngster had taken the man away from the older sister.

Women of the cast are best. Coming close to Miss Clark's good work is the job done by Minerva Urecal and Peggy Wynne. Script never takes its light material too seriously; production is in same vein; and the short running time helps make the whole thing palatable.

Miniature Reviews

"Affairs of Susan" (Wallis-Par). Joan Fontaine and George Brent in uproarious comedy; boff boxoffice and extended runs.

"The Clock" (M-G). Judy Garland and Robert Walker in a fine drama headed for big b.o.

"Power of the Whistler" (Col). Fair mystery chiller for the duals. Stars Richard Dix.

"Rough, Tough and Ready" (Col). Victor McLaglen and Chester Morris in a neat "B" comedy.

Affairs of Susan

Paramount release of Hal Wallis production. Stars Joan Fontaine, George Brent; features Dennis O'Keefe, Don DeFore, Walter Abel, Rita Johnson. Directed by William A. Seiter. Original story by Thomas Monroe and Laszlo Gorog; screenplay, Monroe Gorog, Richard Flournoy; camera, David Abel; editor, Eda Warren. Tradeshown N. Y., March 23, '45. Running time, 110 MINS.
Susan Darell....................Joan Fontaine
Roger Berton.....'............George Brent
Bill Anthony.................Dennis O'Keefe
Mike Ward.......................Don DeFore
Mona Kent........................Rita Johnson
Richard Aiken.................Walter Abel
Chick............................Byron Barr
Nancy............................Mary Field
Uncle Jemmy..............Frances Pierlot
Mr. Cusp.....................Lewis Russell
Brooklyn Girl................Vera Marshe
Brooklyn Boy................Frank Faylen
Major.........................James Millican
Lieutenant....................Robert Sully
First Captain.................John Whitney
Second Captain..............Jerry James
Colonel.....................Crane Whitney

Hal Wallis' first production for Paramount release is a whale of a comedy and boff boxoffice. With Joan Fontaine slipping into her initial screen comedy role with rare glibness, and George Brent in the other main character doing a standout job, "Affairs of Susan" looks destined for holdovers and extended runs. It's the sort of laugh vehicle that has a chance to snowball into limitless b.o. if solidly sold. Bally naturally would need to stress that Miss Fontaine is as big as a comedienne as an Academy Award dramatic winner.

In this tale about the four loves of Susan Darell (Joan Fontaine), producer Wallis has invested the picture with considerable production values, going in for nicety of detail, but, per usual, making the story and action the thing.

Miss Fontaine, as Susan, legit actress just back from a USO Camp tour, accepts Walter Abel's proposal of marriage. He soon learns that there have been three men in her life previously. In fact, he meets all three at the reception given for her new hubby-to-be.

Abel tosses a bachelor dinner party for the three, her ex-husband and stage producer, a young lumber millionaire, and the ardent author. They recite how they figured in Susan's life, with most of flashback sequences devoted to her contact with producer George Brent, her lone marriage.

Brent meets her accidentally when he seeks rest from producer worries and scheming actresses in isolated Rhode Island retreat. He falls in love with her natural acting ability, and finally with her. To him, Miss Fontaine is the child wife who bluntly tells the truth at all times. It's this failing that costs Brent a new play backer and leads to her Reno divorce.

Lumberman Don DeFore catches her on the rebound, just after getting her divorce and she is trying to become the life of the nightclubs. DeFore finds Susan a glamorous, gay person, but also a shameless liar. Miss Fontaine is studying a new stage role when she encounters novelist Dennis O'Keefe. The Susan he recalls is the brainy girl.

Recital of their experiences prompts all three to decide that Susan still is the one gal in their lives, but it winds up with the staid businessman, Abel, doing a fadeout when she decides to remarry Brent.

William A. Seiter's clever direction keeps this on an even keel, with laughs well spotted between the action and romantic scenes. It's one of his smoothest contrived pictures.

Miss Fontaine's sparkle in this first comedienne role is impressive. She swings easily from plain Jane to the seasoned actress type, then to the glamorous, and finally to the intellectual. Abel, who handles the difficult business man with aplomb, finds Miss Fontaine a composite of all these. Top male contribution is George Brent, as the producer. He's a fine combination of the hardboiled showman and admiring husband. As the lumberman, Don DeFore is plenty okay. Dennis O'Keefe comes near copping male laurels in the comparatively brief space given him as the bouncing author. Rita Johnson, as the rival actress, Mary Field, as the maid, and Francis Pierlot, as the uncle, are well picked to head the support.

Screenplay by Thomas Monroe, Laszlo Gorog and Richard Flournoy from the Monroe-Gorog original has sufficient paprika and swift movement to fit the all-round production job.   *Wear.*

The Clock

Metro release of Arthur Freed production. Stars Judy Garland, Robert Walker; features James Gleason, Keenan Wynn. Directed by Vincente Minelli. Screenplay by Robert Nathan and Joseph Schrank, based on story by Paul and Pauline Gallico; camera, George Folsey; editor, George White, special effects, G. Arnold Gillespie, Warren Newcombe. Tradeshown N. Y., March 15, '44. Running time, 90 MINS.
Alice Mayberry................Judy Garland
Corporal Joe Allen..........Robert Walker
Al Henry....................James Gleason
The Drunk.................Keenan Wynn
Bill.......................Marshall Thompson
Mrs. Al Henry..............Lucile Gleason
Helen../........................Ruth Brady

A poignant story has been made into a screenplay filled with a lot of little things that add up to something big. For this reason, plus the fact that Judy Garland and Robert Walker are strong names on anybody's marquee, "The Clock" will tingle at the boxoffice in all situations.

Producer Arthur Freed and director Vincente Minelli, the combination that scored so heavily with the Judy Garland musical, "Meet Me in St. Louis," show their versatility in this picture which is straight drama sans any music. It's her first straight dramatic role. The entire story takes place in the 48 hours that Cpl. Joe Allen (Walker) is on furlough in N. Y. City.

All the Manhattan local color is so authentic, so real and so typical of this day and age that "The Clock" will get a tremendous word-of-mouth buildup. Minelli has the knack of getting deep meaning into little footage. Running only 90 minutes, remarkable in itself these days, the director uses odd tricks to achieve his objective, and succeeds. For instance, the beanery scene where the jolly inebriate (Keenan Wynn) spouts about life and America. The entire sequence is probably four minutes long, but it is real meat. Then there's a sequence after the boy and girl get hitched in one of those quickie ceremonies at City Hall. They're sitting in a self-service restaurant, and Miss Garland is weeping because of the unattractiveness of the entire marriage ceremony. But the camera keeps concentrated on a lone diner, an unbilled character who just sits there and chews away at his food, staring at the embarrassed couple, but not uttering a word. It is memorable humor, the kind people talk about.

Processing of the N. Y. footage into the enactment is tiptop. Highly creditable performances are given by Miss Garland, Walker and James Gleason, who portrays the milk driver who gives the couple a lift.   *Sten.*

The Power of the Whistler

Columbia release of Leonard S. Picker production. Stars Richard Dix; features Janis Carter, Jeff Donnell, Loren Tindall, Tala Birell. Directed by Lew Landers. Screenplay, Aubrey Wisberg, based on radio program, "The Whistler"; camera, L. W. O'Connell; editor, Reg Browne. At Brooklyn Strand, N. Y., week of March 22, '44, dual. Running time, 66 MINS.
William Everest................Richard Dix
Jean Lang.....................Janis Carter
Francie Lang..................Jeff Donnell
Charlie Kent..................Loren Tindall
Constantina Ivaneska..........Tala Birell
Kaspar Andropolos............John Abbott
Joe Blaney....................Murray Alper
Druggist........................Cy Kendall

Another in the series based upon CBS' "The Whistler" stanzas, "Power of the Whistler" is a fair whodunit, starring Richard Dix, grooved for the dual bills.

Dix is cast as a homicidal maniac, victim of amnesia, a part that calls for strong acting and guidance from director Lew Landers. Both, however, falter in their objectives, resulting in some sequences that lack suspense. Janis Carter, as the gal who befriends Dix and almost is killed at his hands, along with Jeff Donnell, in the role of her sister and amateur detective who finally establishes his real identity, give creditable performances. Remainder of the cast is substantial.   *Sten.*

Rough, Tough and Ready

Columbia release of Alexis Thurn-Taxis production. Stars Chester Morris, Victor McLaglen; features Jean Rogers, Veda Ann Borg, Amelita Ward. Directed by Del Lord. Original screenplay, Edward T. Lowe; camera, George Meehan; editor, Walter Holscher. At Rialto, N. Y., week March 23, '44. Running time, 66 MINS.
Brad Crowder................Chester Morris
Owen McCarey.............Victor McLaglen
Jo Matheson...................Jean Rogers
Lorine Gray................Veda Ann Borg
Kitty Duval...............Amelita Ward
Paul......................Robert Williams
Herbie.......................John Tyrrell
Tony..........................Fred Graff
Capt. Murray............Addison Richards
Lieut. Freitas.............William Forrest
Brille.........................Tex Harding
Peterson.....................Loren Tindall
Sparks.......................Bob Meredith
Nana..........................Ida Moore
O'Toole..................Blackie Whiteford

This knock-down, drag-out "B" film, dedicated to an unheralded unit of the armed forces, the Army engineers' port repair service, is a neat dualler.

"Rough, Tough and Ready" stars Victor McLaglen and Chester Morris in the type comedy that the former, teamed with Edmund Lowe, made famous. However, this one doesn't pack the punch of yesteryears' top-flighters in any respect.

Yarn finds the male duo quite chummy, until McLaglen falls for a gal, with Morris stepping in as a rival. That splits them up in a swirl of fisticuffs. Sent to the Pacific for combat duty, they become reunited again when Morris saves McLaglen's life.

Supporting cast includes Veda Ann Borg, Jean Rogers and Amelita Ward. Performances are forthright, with director Del Lord putting the thesps through their paces capably.   *Sten.*

Una Mujer Sin Importancia
("A Woman of No Importance")
(ARGENTINE-MADE)

Argentine Exhibitors' Cooperative release of EFA production. Directed by Luis Bayon Herrera. Adapted by Arturo B. Mom from Oscar Wilde's famous play. Stars Mecha Ortiz and Santiago Gomez Cou; features Lidia Denis, Hugo Pimentel, Golde Flami, Blanca Vidal, Sara Barrie, Yolanda Alexandrini, Carlos Enriquez. At Gran Rex, Buenos Aires, March 1, 1945. Running time, 90 MINS.

Oscar Wilde transported to an Argentine locale and atmosphere, with the epigrams whittled away and dated melodram left in its place, represents riotous entertainment. Should do nicely, especially in neighborhoods and rural areas. It looks extremely limited for U. S. market excepting in foreign language spots.

The Wilde plot has been transferred to the hill province of Cordoba, and the cast moved from England to Argentine high life at a summer villa. "Mrs. Arbuthnot" has been transformed into the manager of a Cordoba curio shop, and her son, Gerald, clerks in the local bank.

The only slight change in the actual plot is that after 20 years Mecha Ortiz finds difficulty in resisting her seducer. Miss Ortiz gives a restrained interpretation of the role of Mrs. Arbuthnot. Santiago Gomez Cou is stilted as Lord Illingworth, and Hugo Pimentel as Gerald, is uneven.   *Nid.*

Miniature Reviews

"The Corn Is Green" (WB). Bette Davis for b.o. impact in the Ethel Barrymore stage hit.

"The Horn Blows at Midnight" (WB). Benny name will assure fair returns for this lightweight fantasy.

"Counter-Attack" (Col). Paul Muni in Russ-Nazi war drama headed for fair b.o.

"Identity Unknown" (Rep). Excellent topical theme, very well done. Looks like a sleeper.

"Cisco Kid Returns" (Mono). Duncan Renaldo stars in okay outdoor dualer.

"Castle of Crimes" (PRC) (British). Whodunit for duals.

"Fashion Model" (Mono). Good murder-mystery comedy, for duals.

The Corn Is Green

Warner Bros. release of Jack Chertok production. Stars Bette Davis; features John Dall, Joan Lorring, Nigel Bruce, Rhys Williams, Rosalind Ivan, Mildred Dunnock. Directed by Irving Rapper. Based on play of same name by Emlyn Williams; adaptation, Casey Robinson and Frank Cavett; editor, Frederick Richards; camera, Sol Polito. At Hollywood, N. Y., starting March 29, '45. Running time, **114 MINS.**

Miss Moffat..........Bette Davis
The Squire..........Nigel Bruce
Mr. Jones..........Rhys Williams
Mrs. Watty..........Rosalind Ivan
Miss Ronberry..........Mildred Dunnock
Will Davis..........Arthur Shields
Sara Pugh..........Gwyneth Hughes
Old Tom..........Thomas Louden
Idwal..........Billy Roy
Llwellyn Powell..........Brandon Hurst
Will Hughes..........Tony Ellis
Glyn Thomas..........Elliott Dare
John Owen..........Leslie Vincent
Dai Evans..........Robert Cherry
Eddie..........Ralph Cathey
The Groom..........Jock Watt
Gwilym Jones..........Gene Ross
Rhys Norman..........Robert Regent
Tudor..........Jack Owen

And Introducing
John Dall and Joan Lorring
(Morgan Evans) (Bessie Watty)

Not the type of screen material that ordinarily has general appeal, "Corn Is Green" has been well produced by Jack Chertok and the boxoffice draught of the Bette Davis name insures it at the gate. It was a big Broadway legit hit with Ethel Barrymore as its star.

The performances, not only of Miss Davis but of two newcomers to the screen, John Dall and Joan Lorring, together with those of Nigel Bruce and others, capture attention and admiration far and above that of the story itself, which is somewhat slow in the first half. Several sequences could have been edited more sharply. While the exteriors of the Welsh countryside with appropriate photography are almost entirely dreary and depressing, they reflect not only able production effort, but also the mood of the Emlyn Williams play and its locale.

Miss Davis, doing the emotional and serious-minded school mistress of the story, whose sociological ideals spur her to untiring efforts in raising the I. Q. of lowly Welsh mining folk, is cast in the kind of role she does well. It's one of her best to date and one of great sympathetic impact. Dall, her protege, who's difficult to handle, is much less an admirable character, though audience interest stays with him all the way. He's presently appearing in the legit, "Dear Ruth," on Broadway, but under contract to Warners, same as Miss Lorring. The youthful Miss Lorring is also a very intriguing type. As the trollop Bessie Watty, she is particularly socko in the final reel, when returning to the village with the news that she has borne Dall's illegitimate child. This development, from which Miss Davis has sought to shield Dall, so that it would not interfere with his going to Oxford, ends the picture on a rather tragic note for the schoolmistress, who agrees to adopt the baby so that Dall may go on with the future she has planned for him. The parts played by Dall and Miss Lorring, incidentally, are those done originally on Broadway by Richard Waring and Thelma Schnee.

Except for Miss Davis, heavy Welsh and English accents figure in the speech of most members of the cast. These accents, at first a little difficult to become accustomed to, may serve as a deterrent in the hinterlands, at least.

Bruce, playing a stuffed-shirt squire; Rhys Williams and Mildred Dunnock, teaching associates of Miss Davis, and Rosalind Ivan, a Cockney housekeeper, are all in the groove on the accents. They, as well as lessers, acquit themselves very creditably.

There are a number of the cast who are repeating for the screen roles they created on the stage, namely, Williams, Misses Ivan, Dunnock and Gwyneth Hughes. *Char.*

The Horn Blows at Midnight

Hollywood, March 30.

Warner Bros. release of Mark Hellinger production. Stars Jack Benny, Alexis Smith; features Dolores Moran, Allyn Joslyn, Reginald Gardiner, Guy Kibbee, John Alexander. Directed by Raoul Walsh. Screenplay, Sam Hellman and James V. Kern, based on idea by Aubrey Wisberg; camera, Sid Hickox; special effects, Lawrence Butler; editor, Irene Morra; music, Franz Waxman. Tradeshown L. A. March 29, '45. Running time, **80 MINS.**

Athanael..........Jack Benny
Elizabeth..........Alexis Smith
Fran..........Dolores Moran
Osidro..........Allyn Joslyn
Archie Dexter..........Reginald Gardiner
The Chief..........Guy Kibbee
Doremus..........John Alexander
Sloan..........Franklin Pangborn
Miss Rodholder..........Margaret Dumont
Junior..........Bobby Blake
Lady Stover..........Ethel Griffies
Thompson..........Paul Harvey
Radio announcer..........Truman Bradley
Humphrey Rafferty..........Mike Mazurki
Lew..........John Brown
Tony..........Murray Alper
Clerk..........Pat O'Moore

This one will have to lean heavily on Jack Benny to draw. It's a lightweight comedy that never seems able to make up its mind whether to be fantasy or broad slapstick. There are some good laughs but generally "The Horn Blows at Midnight" is not solid. The pace wavers, a portion of the plot is in questionable taste, and the finished product is not substantial, either for entertainment or boxoffice.

Benny works hard for his laughs and some come through with a sock, but generally the chuckles are dragged in and overworked. Biggest howls are the scenes depicting Benny and others dangling from atop a 40-story building. Sennett, Harold Lloyd and the other yesteryear comics explored this laugh-suspense trick pretty thoroughly decades ago and that it's necessary to use the old stunt here indicates story weaknesses.

Benny plays third trumpet in a radio station orch. Falling asleep during reading of dreamy commercials, Benny dreams he's an angel, third class, in Heaven—and still playing third trumpet. The Big Chief, disgusted with conditions on the planet earth, dispatches Benny to earth to destroy it. The angel is to blow his special horn promptly at midnight, the blast to do away with the earth. Benny flunks his first blasting try when he stops to save a girl from jumping off the building. He's given another chance and muffs that too when the horn is stolen, recovered and he almost falls off the building. Dream ends there with Benny back in the radio station orch. Heaven, as depicted, is certainly not a very soul-satisfying spot. Its portrayal as a satire on government and the many bureaus and sub-bureaus, etc., may disturb some audiences.

Alexis Smith, as secretary to heaven's Big Chief and with an angelic yen for Benny, hasn't too much to do in the plotting. Same goes for Dolores Moran as hotel cigaret girl who has a yen for super-crook Reginald Gardiner. Latter, along with Allyn Joslyn and John Alexander, two fallen angels, whip over some of the picture's funniest moments. Guy Kibbee is the Chief and Mike Mazurki aide to Gardiner's skullduggery.

Raoul Walsh's direction is not as forte as the pace and punch he displays when handling an action story. Special effects are dealt out with lavish hand for Heaven fantasy portions. *Brog.*

Counter-Attack

Columbia production and release. Stars Paul Muni; features Marguerite Chapman, Larry Parks. Directed by Zoltan Korda. Screenplay, John Howard Lawson, from play by Janet and Philip Stevenson, based upon the Russian original by Ilya Vershinin and Mikhail Ruderman; camera, James Wong Howe; editors, Charles Nelson and Al Clark; music, M. W. Stoloff. Previewed, N. Y., March 30, '45. Running time, **90 MINS.**

Alexei Kulkov..........Paul Muni
Lisa Elenko..........Marguerite Chapman
Kirichenko..........Larry Parks
Galkronye..........Philip Van Zandt
Colonel Semenov..........George Macready
Kostyuk..........Roman Bohnen
Ernemann..........Harro Meller
Vassilev..........Erik Rolf
Stillman..........Rudolph Anders
Ostrovski..........Ian Wolfe
Weiler..........Frederick Giermann
Krafft..........Paul Andor
Grillparzer..........Ivan Triesault
Mueller..........Ludwig Donath
Huebsch..........Louis Adlon
Petrov..........Trevor Bardette
General Kalinev..........Richard Hale

Ibee, in his "Variety" review of the Broadway opening of the play "Counter-Attack" in February, 1943, observed, "War plays have found the going difficult...and while this one is timely, having a Russian-Nazi background and is very well performed, its chances are limited. Impression is it will be better as a film." The latter hope is never fulfilled wholly despite Paul Muni's role portrayed so capably by Morris Carnovsky in the stage play. Only moderate boxoffice indicated.

In the first place, the scope of this drama has not been widened from its legit limitations of one-setting, majority of footage taking place in the blocked-by-debris cellar of a factory on the eastern front. Secondly, the picturization lacks the imagination and skill that such an important subject (Russ-Nazi psychological and battlefield warfare) should have. Somebody missed the boat on this one, although Columbia should not suffer too much financially, since the film obviously was produced at a minimum of overhead.

After several brief sequences leading up to the destruction of a Nazi-captured factory by Russian paratroopers, who were wiped out, Muni and his co-guerrilla Marguerite Chapman cower seven Nazi soldiers in the basement of the factory. From this point on the film bogs down into a study in characterizations, Muni intent on ekeing information from his captives, latter intent on getting the pair to give up the ghost and become their captives. It all is done with dialog, of course, except for some asides showing the Reds building a bridge slightly under the waterline right under the noses of the enemy across a river, and their consequent surprise counter-attack that pushes the Nazis back.

Muni's simulation of drowsiness because of lack of sleep leads his German captives into revealing the important battle information he is seeking. The Nazis, always the stubborn supermen, are convinced they will be rescued by their comrades. Finale, as in the play, finds the rescuers clearing away enough debris to enter the cellar. Latter are first heard chatting in German, which proved to be a trick.

The star gives forthright treatment to his role, as does Miss Chapman, who has many opportunities to display her histrionic ability and comes through surprisingly well. Harro Meller, as the Nazi officer, who is weeded out from the others through Muni's diligence and spills the beans, supplies the venom and arrogance to his part, which was built up to importance for the picture. Larry Parks is seen briefly, though capably, along with a large supporting cast.

Zoltan Korda's direction lacked the finesse and thoughtfulness that might have placed this screen dish on the top rungs of the entertainment ladder. *Sten.*

Identity Unknown

Republic release of Walter Colmes and Howard Bretherton production, directed by Colmes. Stars Richard Arlen, Cheryl Walker; features Roger Pryor, Bobby Driscoll, Lola Lane, Ian Keith. Original, Robert Newman; screenplay, Richard Weil; camera, Ernest Miller; editor, John Link. Tradeshown, N. Y., March 30, '45. Running time, **71 MINS.**

Johnny March..........Richard Arlen
Sally MacGregor..........Cheryl Walker
Rocks Donnelly..........Roger Pryor
Toddy Loring..........Bobby Driscoll
Wanda..........Lola Lane
Major Williams..........Ian Keith
Joe Granowski..........John Forrest
Mrs. Anderson..........Sara Padden
Mr. Anderson..........Forrest Taylor
Frankie..........Frank Marlowe
Harry..........Harry Tyler
Colonel Marlin..........Nelson Leigh
Auctioneer..........Charles Williams
Needles..........Charles Jordan
Spike..........Dick Scott
Nurse..........Marjorie Manners
Motor Cop..........Eddie Baker

This picture is socko from every angle, from the original story to the production, direction, acting and editing, and to the very timing of the release on a topical subject that concerns the friends and relatives of every GI who's been wounded or killed in this war. On all scores, it appears to be a sleeper.

Richard Arlen is the soldier returned from the French warfront without knowing who he is. He takes the temporary name of Johnny March and starts out over the USA to try to establish his own identity. In his travels he visits what comes close to being a cross-section of American homes—the home of a former truckdriver in Connecticut; the home of a former architect in West Virginia; a tough, young kid who works for a gambling syndicate in Chicago; and finally the home of a farmer couple in Iowa.

Wherever he goes, Arlen helps the people he visits understand more intimately, in the terms of their own family's dead, why the war was fought, why it is their job to carry on normal activities, and how they will perpetuate the life of their loved one by working toward a happier U.S.A. in a peaceful world.

Book is of a kind which, in less skillful hands, could have become a heavy sermon, sort of a super-preachment issued by OWI. But the story has suspense, it embodies a very natural love angle, it works on the tear ducts without becoming over sentimental, and ends on a note which makes Arlen symbolic of every demobilized soldier and of all his buddies who lost lives, limbs or health because of the war. When Johnny finally is aided toward self-identification, as the film ends and he gets the gal, the two lovers emerge as the embodiment of the hopes of the war generation for a world that will feel the sacrifices made were worthwhile.

It's a credit to everybody who had anything to do with the film, from the original yarn to those who timed the distribution for the period coinciding with the San Francisco security powwows. Although film is a low-budgeter, production is smooth and easy throughout, direction shows concern for precise detail, acting is superb. Arlen and Cheryl Walker are excellent as Johnny March and the widow of a man killed in France. And Bobby Driscoll, who mistakes

Arlen for his dead GI father, proves himself as not merely a cute kid but also a real little actor.

Cisco Kid Returns

Monogram release of Philip N. Krasne production. Stars Duncan Renaldo; features Roger Pryor, Martin Garralaga, Cecilia Callejo. Directed by John P. McCarthy. Screenplay, Betty Burbridge; camera, Harry Neumann; editor, Marty Cohen. At New York, N. Y., week of March 28, '45, dual. Running time, **64 MINS.**

Cisco....................Duncan Renaldo
Pancho....................Martin Garralaga
Rosita....................Cecilia Callejo
Harris....................Roger Pryor
Conway....................Anthony Warde
Padre....................Fritz Leiber
Mrs. Page....................Vicky Lane
Jeanette....................Jan Wiley
Nancy....................Sharon Smith
Jennings....................Cy Kendall
Tia....................Eva Puig
Sheriff....................Emmett Lynn

"Cisco Kid Returns" has romance, hard-riding action, comedy and mystery in sufficient quantity to please hoss opera audiences. A low-budget "B" for the duals.

Duncan Renaldo is starred in this one, having succeeded Ceasar Romero, now in the Navy. He enacts the outlaw samaritan in neat fashion, with the aid of Martin Garralaga, who supplies comedy relief as Pancho, and Cecilia Callejo, as the gal. Rest of the cast gives fair support.

Yarn finds Renaldo proving he is not the kidnaper of a young child, having taken her in protective custody to prevent her death at the hands of the same gent who murdered her father.

Settings are in the usual outdoor, western groove, and camera work is proportionately clear-cut. Direction and script have loose ends, but not enough to hinder the picture's chances. *Sten.*

Castle of Crimes
(BRITISH-MADE)

PRC release of Walter C. Mycroft production. Stars Kenneth Kent; features Diana Churchill, Belle Chrystall. Directed by Harold French. Screenplay, Doreen Montgobery, based on book by A. E. W. Mason; camera, Walter Harvey; editor, E. B. Jarvis. At New York, N. Y., week of March 28, '45, dual. Running time, **58 MINS.**

Inspector Hanaud....................Kenneth Kent
Betty Harlowe....................Diana Churchill
Ann Upcott....................Belle Chrystall
Jim Frobisher....................Peter Murray-Hill
Maurice Thevenet....................Clifford Evans
Madame Harlowe....................Louise Hampton
Francine Rollard....................Catherine Lacey
Giradot....................Aubrey Dexter
Boris Raviart....................James Harcourt
Jean Cladel....................Ivor Barnard

A British production, being released in this country by PRC, "Castle of Crimes" is an uninteresting whodunit geared for the duals.

There's not much mystery as to who murdered the wealthy spinster. Latter is obsessed with the thought that her relatives are just waiting for her to die so they can inherit her money.

Film is too wordy and it's hard for American audiences to understand much of the dialog because of the accents. Acting is stilted, although Kenneth Kent, as a police inspector, gives a fairly strong performance, better than anyone else in the cast. Dreary lighting impedes much of the values. *Sten.*

Fashion Model

Monogram release of William Strohbach production. Features Robert Lowery, Marjorie Weaver, Tim Ryan, Lorna Gray, Dorothy Christy. Directed by William Beaudine. Story by Victor Hammond; screenplay, Tim Ryan and Victor Hammond; camera, Harry Neumann; editors, Dan Milner and William Austin. At Brooklyn Strand, N. Y., week of March 30, '45. Running time, **59 MINS.**

Jimmy O'Brien....................Robert Lowery
Peggy Rooney....................Marjorie Weaver
O'Hara....................Tim Ryan
Yvonne....................Lorna Gray
Mme. Celeste....................Dorothy Christy
Grogan....................Dewey Robinson
Marie....................Sally Yarnell
Shiftless....................Jack Norton
Harvey Van Alyn....................Harry Depp
Jessica....................Nell Craig
Duval....................Edward Keane
Davis....................John Valentine
Jeffries....................Cedric Stevens

This is a murder mystery in which there are three murders, yet it's all pleasant, good-humored and not at all in the chiller style. A good light comedy for a dualler.

Story centers in a fashionable dressmaking establishment where two of the slayings take place, one victim being a model and the second the secret owner of the place. Suspicion centers on the stock boy, played by Robert Lowery, whose girl friend is another model, Marjorie Weaver. A number of characters are involved, and the boy is suspected of all three murders. But his girl friend helps him get out of the clutches, coming close to becoming the fourth victim.

Competent acting is turned in by all concerned, and direction is smooth enough to iron out wrinkles in a story that comes close to being complicated at times. There's one particularly funny sequence, excellently done by Lowery, Miss Weaver and Jack Norton as a near-sighted drunken window-dresser.

Watchtower Over Tomorrow
(DOCUMENTARY)

War Activities Committee of the Motion Picture Industry release of Jerry Dressler production. Features Secretary of State Edward R. Stettinius, Lionel Stander, Grant Mitchell, Jonathan Hale, Miles Mander, George Zucco. Screenplay by Ben Hecht; script by Karl Lamb. Directed by John Cromwell and Harold Kress; camera, Lester White; narrator, John Nesbitt. Previewed in N. Y. March 27, '45. Running time, **15 MINS.**

Although some of the top names in the film industry cooperated in making of "Watchtower Over Tomorrow," this 15-minute documentary explaining workings of the Dumbarton Oaks Conference emerges as a heavy-handed treatment that will cause much of its important content to miss its mark. Film was made with little imagination. It pontificates.

Only worthwhile achievement here is the explanation of the practical plan evolved at Dumbarton Oaks for preservation of the peace. But it's done in such a way as to inspire a lack of confidence in the plan.

Technique used here is to have Lionel Stander, as a workman, and Grant Mitchell, in a scholarly role, bandy the problem while riding a subway. John Nesbitt commentary intervenes to give an illustrated lecture on the conference. Ben Hecht's writing isn't too impressive on this matter.

Acting honors are carried off by photogenic Secretary of State Stettinius, who delivers the prolog calling attention to the importance of the conference. *Jose.*

Miniature Reviews

"Salome, Where She Danced" (U-Wanger) (Songs; Color). Beautifully filmed drama headed for strong b.o.

"Diamond Horseshoe" (Musical; Color) (20th), Betty Grable-Dick Haymes starred in socko filmusical.

"The Valley of Decision" (M-G). High caliber drama for carriage and trolley trade. Heading for lush b.o. coin.

"A Medal For Benny" (Par). Dorothy Lamour and Arturo de Cordova in neat entertainment.

"Murder, He Says" (Par). Broad comedy with good box-office prospects.

"Scared Stiff" (Par). Light weight comedy mystery, fair dualer.

"The Bullfighters" (20th). Routine Laurel and Hardy comedy for twin bills.

"Leave It To Blondie" (Col). New "Blondie" entrant up to dual standard.

"Fog Island" (PRC). A chiller and good dualler.

"The Town Went Wild" (PRC). A lesser dualler.

"Hollywood And Vine" (PRC). Superior comedy for double bill.

Salome, Where She Danced
(Songs)
(TECHNICOLOR)

Universal release of Walter Wanger (Alexander Golitzen) production. Stars Yvonne de Carlo; features Rod Cameron, David Bruce, Walter Slezak, Albert Dekker, Marjorie Rambeau, J. Edward Bromberg. Directed by Charles Lamont. Screenplay, Laurence Stallings from original by Michael J. Phillips; camera, Hal Mohr, W. Howard Greene; editor, Russell Schoengarth. Tradeshown N. Y., April 10, '45. Running time, **93 MINS.**

Salome....................Yvonne de Carlo
Jim....................Rod Cameron
Cleve....................David Bruce
Dimitrioff....................Walter Slezak
Von Bohlen....................Albert Dekker
Madam....................Marjorie Rambeau
Professor Max....................J. Edward Bromberg
Dr. Ling....................Abner Biberman
General Lee....................John Litel
Bismark....................Kurt Katch
Bartender....................Arthur Hohl
Panatela....................Nestor Paiva
Henderson....................Gavin Muir
Sheriff....................Will Wright
Henry....................Joseph Haworth
Lafe....................Matt McHugh

Salome Girls: Poni Adams, Barbara Bates, Daun Kennedy, Kathleen O'Malley, Karen Randle, Jean Trent, Kerry Vaughn.

Notable for many gorgeous scenes in Technicolor, plus the introduction of Yvonne de Carlo, a gal whom Walter Wanger discovered after a nationwide search for a lead, "Salome, Where She Danced" has strong entertainment value. Aided by good exploitation it should do well at the boxoffice in all situations, although there is a no-name cast.

Despite the fact that the story-line and screenplay contain several disjointed attributes, the picture impresses because of the settings, color and money that obviously was put into it by Wanger. Miss de Carlo, a looker with lots of talent, should go far with more experience and the buildup which Universal is currently giving her. She formerly played bit parts in several Hollywood lesser productions. She makes capital of her big chance, however. She emotes well, dances and sings capably, and the camerawork of Hal Mohr and W. Howard Greene do her justice at all times. Supporting cast of Rod Cameron, as a roving newspaperman; David Bruce, as the one whom she loves above all the others; Walter Slezak, as the wealthy Russian; Albert Dekker, as the Prussian military official, and Marjorie Rambeau and J. Edward Bromberg gives fairly impressive performances.

Story takes reporter Cameron from the final surrender of General Lee in the Civil War to Berlin where he meets Salome. After she helps him find out the starting date of the German-Austrian war, the Germans discover that she is a spy, but she flees to America before they can capture her. On the way across the desert, the reporter, her music teacher (Bromberg) and Salome run out of funds and she gives a performance in a mining town, only to be robbed by bandits who had been preying on the town. Leader of the bandits falls for her, returns the money and, at last, she winds up in San Francisco where she becomes the toast of the town through the good offices of Russian moneybags Slezak. Then comes the denouement.

Picture is replete with action and the usual western accoutrements. However, there is romance and other sequences which will please the women. It's got everything that makes for good b.o. except a strong story-line. Art directors John B. Goodman and Alexander Golitzen (latter is also associate producer) had a field day in bringing this one through, since the strings were off the bankroll and they made the best of it. Four tunes are oldies of the Civil War era, couple of which have lived through the years. *Sten.*

Diamond Horseshoe
(MUSICAL; TECHNICOLOR)

20th-Fox release of William Perlberg production. Stars Betty Grable, Dick Haymes; features Phil Silvers, William Gaxton, Beatrice Kay, Carmen Cavallaro, Willie Solar, Margaret Dumont. Directed and written by George Seaton. Suggested by play of John Kenyon Nicholson, produced by Chas. L. Wagner; songs, Mack Gordon-Harry Warren; dances, Hermes Pan; music, Alfred Newman, Chas. Henderson; arrangements, Herbert Spencer; editor, Robt. Simpson. Tradeshown April 5, '45. Running time, **104 MINS.**

Bonnie Collins....................Betty Grable
Joe Davis, Jr....................Dick Haymes
Blinky Walker....................Phil Silvers
Joe Davis, Sr....................William Gaxton
Claire Williams....................Beatrice Kay
Specialties....................{Carmen Cavallaro / Willie Solar}
Mrs. Standish....................Margaret Dumont
Harper....................Roy Benson
Pop....................George Melford
Carter....................Hal K. Dawson
Dance Director....................Kenny Williams
Interne....................Reed Hadley
Clarinet Player....................Eddie Acuff
Grogan....................Edward Gargan
Wardrobe Woman....................Ruth Rickaby

"Diamond Horseshoe" should be plenty lucky for everybody. This Technicolored filmusical has everything for the b.o.—flash, glamour, stars, tunes and entertainment.

It's a cinch to hasten the saloon cycle which is already underway with Paramount's "Stork Club," Metro's "Weekend at the Waldorf," not to mention the assorted ideas of building pix around other w.k. bistros such as the Copacabana and Latin Quarter, and hostelries like the Astor and Plaza.

After Sherman Billingsley sees what 20th-Fox did for Billy Rose's West 46th street (N. Y.) cabaret, he should give back the $100,000 Buddy de Sylva is supposed to have paid for the "Stork Club" title. And that goes for Rose and the 76G he's supposed to have gotten for his rights. They should pay Hollywood. Wotta trailer!

But, basically, none of these ideas is any good if the production values miss. Producer Bill Perlberg and scripter George Seaton, who is also making his debut as a director, made sure of everything.

For one thing, the basic story is solid. You could call the Diamond Horseshoe the Creep Club and Billy Rose might be Joe Blow for all that matters. True, it lends an authenticity and realism which are undeniable. But more potent are the plot components. It builds a solid heart story in a manner which is enough of a switch on the backstage formula to make it different.

Betty Grable and Dick Haymes are costarred and this, of course, puts the crooner over solidly as a film juvenile. William Gaxton plays Haymes' father, the lead at the Horseshoe, forever squabbling with Miss Grable, the No. 1 cheesecake. Haymes gives up medicine for a stage career, and while Miss Grable starts out under a cloud she emerges the noble influence to get him back to his M.D. studies, an objective in which Gaxton fails and for which he had blamed his son's romantic vis-a-vis.

Interlarded is convincing dialog as Seaton contrived it and also directed so well. Phil Silvers does a convincing stagemanager, Beatrice Kay (from radio) is the lovelorn old gal, featuring her yesteryear songs; and Gaxton is completely convincing as the over-intense father of the boy, bent on keeping him clear of show business. Willie Solar reprises his standard specialty, realistically out of one of Rose's Diamond Horseshoe revues. Carmen Cavallaro has an OK albeit somewhat wasted specialty in what is supposed to be a nondescript Village spot.

Mack Gordon and Harry Warren have handtailored a set of songs which bolster the libretto handily, and dance stager Hermes Pan has done tricks with his material. Apart from the usual ballad contenders, and there are two good ones in "I Wish I Knew" and "The More I See You," there's imaginative staging and costume-setting, as in "The Mink Lament" (dream sequence); a gay and colorful "Acapulco," an old-fashioned melody vs. jive number, capped by a good rhythmic tune, "A Nickel's Worth of Jive."

Per cinematic custom, some of these so-called cabaret revue numbers could happen only in Madison Square Garden, but this again is accepted Hollywood license by now. On the other hand, the Diamond Horseshoe decor and policy are sometimes so faithful it's startlingly familiar, even unto a lyrical ad for the joint, such as the line, "Two shows every night (without a cover)".

The opening and closing flash numbers are dandy. Gaxton, as the showman-chef who dishes up the entertainment menu, opens with a mixture of spices, and ends with "dessert," an imaginative chapeaux display that will probably give John-Frederics, Sally Victor, Walter Florell, et al. ideas.

The kaleidoscope of cocktailery and nitery fun in which the stellar pair engage is compactly done with a series of shots. The funniest is not too broad a satire on one of those dance-on-a-dime, jampacked jam session joints on 52d St. There's also a good running gag about "the show must go on," and the spectacled Phil Silvers is solid in one satirical obligato to "Climb the Highest Mountains." He also ad libs a clarinet solo via an offstage mike which is strong for laugh returns.

While Haymes looks a shade too adolescent as Miss Grable's romance interest, which is no unchivalrous reflection on the highly photogenic femme, he overcomes that as the footage progresses. Per usual Miss Grable handles her song-and-dance-ology for socko results, and Haymes' crooning, always acceptable, is played down and his dramatic role is accented. He should click in pix, evidencing nice ability with lines. As for Gaxton, this is perhaps his best screen performance to date, in a solid believable assignment. *Abel.*

The Valley of Decision

Hollywood, April 10.

Metro release of Edwin H. Knopf production. Stars Greer Garson, Gregory Peck; features Donald Crisp, Lionel Barrymore, Preston Foster, Marsha Hunt. Directed by Tay Garnett. Screenplay, John Meehan, Sonya Levien; based on novel by Marcia Davenport; camera, Joseph Ruttenberg; score, Herbert Stothart; special effects, A. Arnold Gillespie, Warren Newcombe; editor, Blanche Sewell. Tradeshown Los Angeles, April 6, '45. Running time, 118 MINS.

Mary Rafferty.................Greer Garson
Paul Scott.....................Gregory Peck
William Scott..................Donald Crisp
Pat Rafferty..............Lionel Barrymore
Jim Brennan..................Preston Foster
Constance Scott..............Marsha Hunt
Clarissa Scott...............Gladys Cooper
McCready...................Reginald Owen
William Scott, Jr...............Dan Duryea
Louise Kane....................Jessica Tandy
Delia.........................Barbara Everest
Ted Scott................Marshall Thompson
Kate Shannon.................Geraldine Wall
Mrs. Callahan...............Evelyn Dockson
Giles........................John Warburton
Mr. Laurence Gaylord........Russell Hicks
Julia Gaylord.......................Mary Lord
Callahan......................Arthur Shields
Paulie........................Dean Stockwell
Mrs. Laurence Gaylord........Mary Currier

"The Valley of Decision" is certain boff boxoffice. There is a human quality to its drama, brought out by Tay Garnett's skillful direction and the high calibre trouping, that means most favorable word-of-mouth to strengthen the value of the marquee names headed by Greer Garson. While emotional quality will particularly appeal to the femme trade, there's plenty of meat to hold the male patron as it unfolds.

The Marcia Davenport novel of the same title contained enough material for any number of pictures, and scripters John Meehan and Sonya Levien have made wise choice on what they plucked from the tome as a basis of the film. There are a few changes in characters and twisting of events but no reader of the book will be able to quarrel with the film's results. It's a class attraction from any angle as delivered under the production supervision of Edwin H. Knopf.

Plot picks up the Scott clan, a Pittsburgh pioneer steel family, at the time Irish Mary Rafferty comes to join it as in-between-maid. The tale of unfulfilled love between the servant girl and young Paul Scott, one of the family's sons, is beautifully and movingly dealt with by performance, direction and writing. Mary rises to post of family confidante, succors the young daughter through trying love affairs, and generally manages the Scotts whom she has grown to love as her own. It's all told so credibly there is little of make-believe about it and therein lies the strength of its drama and potential word-of-mouth draw. Mary carries the family through minor and major crises and in the end saves the beloved steel plant for Paul Scott when less-interested members of the family would sell out. Story ends on that note with only the promise that she and Paul, although unable to marry, will find happiness in unconsummated love.

Music score by Herbert Stothart sets an unobtrusive background mood for the individual performance gems. Casting is of uniform excellence, topped by Greer Garson's superb work. It is only in the initial scenes that Miss Garson, physically, doesn't quite fit the picture of the young Irish girl, but as characters and the story mature she rises to every demand. Gregory Peck, playing opposite as Paul Scott, is standout. He has the personality and ability to command and hold attention in any scene.

Donald Crisp, the senor Scott; Lionel Barrymore, Mary's mentally and physically crisppled father; Preston Foster, steel workers' union leader, and Marsha Hunt, as Constance Scott all give assured performances. Character of Constance has been given a happier English marriage than in the book, and John Warburton as her husband is a cast asset. Gladys Cooper (Mrs. Scott), Reginald Owen (McCready), Dan Duryea (Willie Scott), Jessica Tandy (Louise Kane), Marshall Thompson (Ted Scott), and Barbara Everest (Delia) are each factors in the playing that add to the credit side. Others, too, are worthy.

Production appurtenances measure up to the usual top Metro quality, with fine camera work by Joseph Ruttenberg and special effects. *Brog.*

A Medal for Benny

Hollywood, April 4.

Paramount release of Paul Jones production. Stars Dorothy Lamour and Arturo de Cordova; features J. Carrol Naish and Mikhail Rasumny, Fernando Alvarado and Frank McHugh. Directed by Irving Pichel. Screenplay, Frank Butler, with additional dialog by Jack Wagner, based on story by John Steinbeck and Jack Wagner; camera, Lionel Lindon; special effects, Gordon Jennings; music, Victor Young; editor, Arthur Schmidt. Reviewed in projection room, April 4, '45. Running time, 79 MINS.

Lolita Sierra..............Dorothy Lamour
Joe Morales.............Arturo de Cordova
Charley Martin..............J. Carrol Naish
Raphael Catalina..........Mikhail Rasumny
Chito Sierra.............Fernando Alvarado
Zack Mibbs..................Charley Dingle
Edgar Lovekin...............Frank McHugh
Toodles Castro...............Rosita Moreno
Pantara's Mayor............Grant Mitchell
The General.............Douglas Dumbrille

Paramount not only has a real sleeper in "A Medal For Benny," but also a picture that lifts two players to new histrionic heights. They are Dorothy Lamour and J. Carrol Naish. The performance turned in by Arturo de Cordova is also one that will not pass unnoticed. Film should do good biz on the singles when once the word-of-mouth gets around.

"Benny" runs only 79 minutes, but it is 79 minutes packed with fast-moving entertainment, outstanding performances and true-to-life mounting.

"Benny" is backgrounded against the Mexican fisherman wharves adjacent to any California city from San Diego to Monterey. Benny, who never appears on the screen, is the settlement's bad boy, yet one of whom his aged father (Naish) is proud. Ruled out of the locale by the courts, Benny is not heard from for months; then, suddenly, the Chamber of Commerce is notified that a hometown boy has been awarded the Congressional Medal of Honor for having killed, single-handed, 100 Japs in the Manila area, before being extinguished by a sniper's bullet.

From there on out, it is Sinclair Lewis' "Main Street," with press-agents, bankers and city officials, all of whom in the past brushed off old Charley, trying to seek his favor. Naish's speech, as he finally accepts the posthumous award on behalf of his boy, is something memorable.

Miss Lamour, loyal to Charley, because she was long betrothed to Benny, and the ne'er-do-well Joe (de Cordova) are in love, but Joe enlists in the Army instead of marrying her in the final fade, because, he too, doesn't want to ruin Charley's illusions. *Moak.*

Murder, He Says

Hollywood, April 10.

Paramount release of E. D. Leshin production. Stars Fred MacMurray; features Helen Walker, Marjorie Main. Directed by George Marshall. Screenplay, Lou Breslow; story, Jack Moffitt; camera, Theodor Sparkuhl; special effects, Gordon Jennings, Paul Lerpae; editor, LeRoy Stone; score, Robert Emmett Dolan. Tradeshown Los Angeles, April 6, '45. Running time, 89 MINS.

Pete Marshall.............Fred MacMurray
Claire Matthews...............Helen Walker
Mamie Johnson...............Marjorie Main
Elany Fleagle..................Jean Heather
Mr. Johnson.......................Porter Hall
Mert Fleagle...................Peter Whitney
Grandma Fleagle..................Mabel Paige
Bonnie Fleagle...............Barbara Pepper

This one tosses logic out the window and devotes itself to broad slapstick. Laughs clock heavily and pace moves so swiftly audiences won't have a chance to discover it is a lot of to-do about nothing and thinly premised until it's well over. It's strictly escapist fare that will play hilariously as top material in all situations. Fred MacMurray's name on the marquee will also help the boxoffice along.

Vigorous, but certainly not subtle, direction by George Marshall punches the many sight gags and physical comedy to gloss over fact that main characters are thinly disguised portraits of a number of sordid midwest bad boys and girls. They are all strictly "Tobacco Road" in actions and dress and only fact that they are played for broad laughs keeps them from being repulsive. Script piles on the corn thickly in detailing story of the weird Fleagle family, outlaw hillbillies, and what happens to a Trotter Poll man, collecting rural data, when he crosses the Fleagles' path.

MacMurray is the Trotter man, sent into a mountain district to find out what has happened to previous Trotterites polling the section. It seems they have done okay until approaching the Fleagles, who don't like strangers and calmly bump them off. The Fleagles are searching for $70,000 in loot hidden by Bonnie Fleagle (a facsimile of the midwest's cigar-smoking femme bandit, Bonnie Parker). Latter is in the jug for her crimes and rest of the family is trying to pull a doublecross with the coin. Helen Walker is also on the scene, seeking the money to save her father, a bank teller falsely accused of stealing it.

Continuous chases, fights, etc., keep the issues in a mad shambles before MacMurray and Miss Walker barely escape with their lives and the odd characters are rounded up by the law. A funny sight gag is phosphorescent effect achieved on some of the players who are being slowly poisoned by Porter Hall, the wacky husband of Ma Fleagle.

MacMurray and Miss Walker do creditably by their assignments. Marjorie Main finds role of Ma Fleagle little different from her usual uncouth blowsy parts and gives it her usual treatment. Peter Whitney does twin assignment as the not-very-bright Fleagle boys, and Barbara Pepper comes on late as Bonnie, escaped from jail and wanting her hidden loot. Mabel Paige completes the weird family as Grannie.

Production dress, photography, etc., are expert for plot background. *Brog.*

Scared Stiff

Hollywood, April 10.

Paramount release of Pine-Thomas production. Associate producer, Maxwell Shane. Stars Jack Haley, Ann Savage. Directed by Frank McDonald. Screenplay, Geoffrey Homes and Maxwell Shane; camera, Fred Jackman, Jr.; editor, Howard Smith. Tradeshown Los Angeles, April 5, '45. Running time, 65 MINS.

Larry Elliot.........................Jack Haley
Sally Warren......................Ann Savage
Deacon Markham...........Barton MacLane
Flo Rosson.....................Veda Ann Borg
Emerson Cooke..........Arthur Aylesworth
Mink.......................George E. Stone
Charles Waldeck..........Lucien Littlefield
Preston Waldeck..........Lucien Littlefield
Sheriff................................Paul Hurst
Prof. Wisner........Robert Emmett Keane
Mrs. Cooke.......................Elly Malyon
Oliver Waldeck..................Buddy Swan
Richardson.......................Roger Pryor

"Scared Stiff" is a thinly spaced programmer about a milquetoast chess player who turns reporter. It's never believable but does manage to inject a few chuckles around Jack Haley's antics. Strictly dual product that's not up to the standard of previous Pine-Thomas small-budgeted features.

Haley is seen as a dope who doesn't know news, even when it knocks him down. After fumbling all assignments he's given one more chance, only because the rest of the paper's staff are out chasing an escaped gangster. Sent to cover an annual wine festival in a nearby town, the dope goes to the wrong place. En route a man on the bus is murdered and Haley's suspected. Bus passengers are confined in an old inn and winery while waiting arrival of a slow-moving sheriff.

Long arm of coincidence has placed Haley's girl friend, Ann Savage, a femme detective, Veda Ann Borg, and sundry characters on the same bus. Miss Savage wants to buy a set of antique, jeweled chess men from the twin brothers operating the inn. Miss Borg is seeking to recover them for a client, from whom they were stolen by Barton MacLane, the escaped gangster. He, in turn, had sold them to the twins and now wants them back for getaway coin. For good measure, script also tosses in a child prodigy to further confuse the issues. Barton shows up at the inn and from then on it's one long, overdone chase. Haley finally captures the gangster and the murderer, but the dope still doesn't know he has a story and only apologizes for muffing the grape-squeezing celebration.

Cast tries hard and there's nothing particularly wrong with its work, but the way it all jells leaves it still pretty shaky. *Brog.*

The Bullfighters
(ONE SONG)

20th-Fox release of William Girard production. Stars Stan Laurel and Oliver Hardy; features Margo Woode, Richard Lane, Carol Andrews, Diosa Costello. Directed by Mal St. Clair. Screenplay, W. Scott Darling; camera, Norbert Brodine; editor, Stanley Rabjohn. Tradeshown in N. Y. April 6, '45. Running time, **61 MINS.**

Laurel and Hardy....................Themselves
Tangerine....................Margo Woode
Hot Shot Coleman....................Richard Lane
Hattie Blake....................Carol Andrews
Conchita....................Diosa Costello
El Brillante....................Frank McCown
Muldoon....................Ralph Sanford
Mr. Gump....................Irving Gump
Vasso....................Ed Gargan
Spanish Girl....................Lorraine De Wood
Prosecutor....................Emmett Vogan
Master of Ceremonies....................Roger Neury
Judge....................Gus Glassmire
Hotel Clerk....................Rafael Storm
Luis....................Jay Novello
Bullfighters.....Guy Zanetto, Robert Filmer
Attendant....................Max Wagner
Waiter....................Jose Portugal
Texan....................Hank Worden
Mexican Policemen....................Joe Dominguez, Stevan Darrell

Newest adventure of Laurel & Hardy finds the pair in Mexico City with the little guy winding up an unwilling matador. "The Bullfighters" sticks close to the accepted L&H formula and should do no better and no worse than previous films starring the duo. A dualer.

The comics and director Mal St. Clair have added nothing novel to the exasperation, etc., routines on which Laurel & Hardy have been cashing in with result that, except for locale, "Bullfighters" differs little from earlier efforts. Supporting cast, with little to do, does it acceptably enough.

Fiery Diosa Costello gets a chance to display her cooch rhumba in a cafe song-dance specialty, "Bim Bam Boom," and cashes okay. Sequence gave lots of evidence that shears had been used plenty to reduce the temperature of the dance routine. Margo Woode and Carol Andrews are easy on the eyes during their brief chances and Richard Lane and Ralph Sanford, as the bullfight impresarios, handle themselves acceptably.

Interspersed in the final action centered on Laurel's unhappy experience in the bullring are several excellent shots of actual bullfights highlighted by one or two topnotch examples of exciting cape work by bona-fide exponents of the Spanish pageantry. There also are a couple of exciting crowd shots with fighting bulls running wild through a crowd of aficionados.

"Bullfighters" will deliver its share of laughs but not much more. *Donn.*

Leave It to Blondie
(SONGS)

Columbia release of Burt Kelly production. Features Penny Singleton, Arthur Lake, Larry Simms. Directed by Abby Berlin. Screenplay, Connie Lee; camera, Franz F. Planer; editor, Al Clark. At Paramount, Brooklyn, week of April 5, '45. Running time, **74 MINS.**

Blondie....................Penny Singleton
Dagwood....................Arthur Lake
Alexander....................Larry Simms
Rita Rogers....................Marjorie Weaver
J. C. Dithers....................Jonathan Hale
Eddie Baxter....................Chick Chandler
Alvin....................Danny Mummert
Cookie....................Marjorie Ann Mutchie
Mrs. Meredith....................Eula Morgan
Mr. Fuddle....................Arthur Space
Mailman....................Eddie Acuff
Henry....................Fred Graff
Ollie....................Jack Rice
Magda....................Maude Eburne
Daisy....................Herself

Columbia has a staple neighborhood or duals commodity in the "Blondie" series, so that it was a good idea to renew it after a two-year layoff. "Leave It to Blondie" holds to the acceptable average of the series.

The story is a little hard to take, but the film has the usual agreeable small-town situations and typical mild comedy bits. In addition, it has a couple of songs for novelty and some very amusing moments when the bewildered hero, Dagwood Bumpstead, develops a cold and tries some home-made remedies.

The Bumpstead household has entered a songwriting contest. Dagwood and Blondie are in it because they rashly issued separate large checks for charity and can't cover. The kids are in it to help out the folks. Dagwood's boss is in it to land a real estate deal. There's a dark-haired woman real estate prospect and a brunet singing teacher, both of them complicating Dagwood's existence and arousing Blondie's jealousy. Dagwood, as usual, blunders his way out of it all.

Penny Singleton and Arthur Lake carry out familiar roles with ease, with young Larry Simms in strong support. Direction is smooth and production adequate for this modest budgeter. *Bron.*

Fog Island

PRC release of Leon Fromkess production. Stars Lionel Atwill, Jerome Cowan, George Zucco; features Veda Ann Borg, Sharon Douglas. Directed by Terry Morse. Screenplay, Pierre Gendron, based on original story by Bernadine Angus; camera, Ira Morgan. At New York, N. Y., week of April 9, '45. Running time, **70 MINS.**

Leo Grainger....................George Zucco
Alec Ritchfield....................Lionel Atwill
Kavanaugh....................Jerome Cowan
Gail....................Sharon Douglas
Sylvia....................Veda Ann Borg
Jeff....................John Whitney
Emiline Bronson....................Jacqueline DeWit
Dr. Lake....................Ian Keith
Allerton....................George Lloyd

A chiller with strictly stock situations, this picture is nevertheless done well throughout. A good dualler.

Story revolves around a man once rich who had served a prison term for embezzlement, and his efforts to avenge not only his conviction but also the murder of his wife. On his foggy island estate for a weekend are gathered the group of men and women he suspects of having been responsible for his downfall. Other characters are there, including a former cellmate of the ex-convict, an escaped lifer who somehow turns up as butler, the vengeful man's stepdaughter, and her college sweetheart.

When the doings are over, all involved in the plotting and counterplotting had met their just deserts, and the sweethearts go back to the mainland presumably a happy couple. George Zucco plays the principal role for all it's worth, and is given excellent support by the others, principally Lionel Atwill, Ian Keith and George Lloyd. Good acting is supplemented by smooth production, combining to lift a murder story that's not too subtle into a picture that's above the mediocre.

The Town Went Wild

PRC release of Roth-Greene-Rouse production. Stars Freddie Batholomew, James Lydon; features E. E. Horton, Tom Tully. Directed by Ralph Murphy. Screenplay, Bernard R. Roth, Clarence Greene, Russell Rouse; camera, Philip Tannura. At Brooklyn Fox, N. Y., week April 4, '45. Running time, **78 MINS.**

David Conway....................Freddie Bartholomew
Bob Harrison....................James Lydon
Everett Conway....Edward Everett Horton
Henry Harrison....................Tom Tully
Carol Harrison....................Jill Browning
Marian Harrison....................Minna Gombell
Lucille Conway....................Ruth Lee
Millie Walker....................Roberta Smith
Judge Bingle....................Maude Eburne
Mr. Tweedle....................Charles Halton
Mr. Walker....................Ferris Taylor
Justice of the Peace....................Jimmy Conlin
The Public Defender....................Monte Collins
The District Attorney....Charles Middleton
Doctor Hendricks....................Fred Burton
Judge Schrank....................Will Wright
The Watchman....................Emmett Lynn
Nurse Reeves....................Dorothy Vaughn

This picture has a fair story which could have been good comedy. But it peters out into tiresome obviousness. Strictly a lesser dualler.

Story centers about two feuding next-door neighbors, played by Edward Everett Horton and Tom Tully. Each has a son, and one has a daughter too. Two neighboring youngsters are in love, elope, and discover in process of getting marriage license that legal documents indicate they may be brother and sister. In due time, legal tangles are unsnarled, the lovers are united and the battling fathers become closest of pals.

The complications could have been funny. But direction had Horton and Tully act as if they were burlesqueing whole theme, which story does not call for; while Freddie Bartholomew, who is the lover, acts merely embarrassed. Chances are many customers will be too.

Hollywood and Vine

PRC release of Leon Fromkess production. Stars James Ellison, Wanda McKay; features Franklyn Pangborn and Ralph Morgan. Directed by Alexis Thurn-Taxis. Screenplay, Edith Watkins and Charles Williams from original story by Miss Watkins, Williams and Robert Wilmot; camera, Ira Morgan. At New York, N. Y., week of April 9, '45. Running time, **59 MINS.**

Larry....................James Ellison
Martha....................Wanda McKay
Gloria....................June Clyde
B. B. Benton....................Ralph Morgan
Reggie....................Franklyn Pangborn
Cedric....................Leon Belasco
Pop....................Emmett Lynn
Fanny....................Vera Lewis
Ann....................Karin Lang
Jenkins....................Robert Greig
Chick....................Charlie Williams
Tex....................Ray Whitley
Mug....................Dewey Robinson
Attorney Hudson....................Cy Ring
Attorney Wilson....................Grandin Rhodes
Joe (newsboy)....................Billy Benedict
Assistant Director....................Donald Kerr
Abigail....................Lillion Bronson
Judge....................John Elliott
Gateman....................Jack Raymond
Cop....................Charles Jordan
Doctor....................Lou Crocker
Casting Director....................Hal Taggart

As the title implies, this film is about Hollywood. Aimed at satirizing the picture capital, it achieves considerable success resulting in a well produced comedy on an adult level. Decidedly a superior item for a double bill.

The satirical barbs are aimed at the commander of a big movie studio who has a dozen members of his family working for him, a brasshat eccentric producer, and the industry in general which is shown capable of making a star out of almost anybody or anything. In this instance, the fabulous film concern makes a star out of a dog, and the takeoff results in some genuinely funny business.

Best in the piece, in addition to the dog which really deserves top billing, are James Ellison as the writer newly plucked from the sidewalks of New York and ordered to do a script about Hollywood; Wanda McKay, who is cast as the gal who has made her way to Hollywood in the hopes of becoming a star; and Emmett Lynn as the owner of a hamburger stand who rises to heights as landlord of valuable Hollywood real estate. Lynn's performance is socko, topping that of all others for genuineness and real fun. *Cars.*

Behind the Enemy Lines
(Newsreel Documentary)

Globe Film Co. (James N. Jovan) release of captured Nazi and Jap films. Edited and compiled by Maj. Ross Duff Whytock; narration, Bud Pollard; score, Edward Craig. At Monroe, Chicago, April 4, '45. Running time, **65 MINS.**

As the name indicates this captured footage gives the American public a view of the war from the eyes of Nazi and Nip cameras. Much of the stuff was shot in the early days of the conflict, both on the European and Pacific fronts and was apparently meant as propaganda to prove to the Jap and German home fronts that their armies and navies were invincible. That was when things were going their own way.

German scenes take you back to the rape of Poland, conquest of the Low Countries and early days on the Russian front showing wanton destruction everywhere. Jap shots picture the sneak attack on Pearl Harbor; the shelling of Hongkong; the bombing of Shanghai; the surrender of Corregidor and the taking of unfortified villages of China. Some of the film has been seen in newsreels but the majority of the footage is new. Although there aren't many shots of either of the Axis partners on the defensive there are enough to show how the tide has turned. Germans are seen retreating from the Russian blows and one of the high points of the picture shows the burning of Berlin and what it brought to Berliners. Another view shows our airmen bombing Tokyo. Lack of shots showing the Axis getting a licking is probably due to being too busy at the time to take any pictures.

Film has good exploitation possibilities. Although Maj. Whytock could have done a better job of editing it probably will not be noticed much by the public. Bud Pollard's narration and Edward Craig's musical score are tops and do a lot to make the subject interesting. *Morg.*

Miniature Reviews

"Patrick the Great" (Musical) (U). Diverting romantic item that should do well at b.o.

"Two O'Clock Courage" (RKO). Amnesia mystery; for the duals.

"I'll Remember April" (Songs) (U). Passable dualler.

"Flame of Barbary Coast" (Rep.) (Songs). Well made western.

"Hitchhike to Happiness" (Rep.). Mild show biz comedy; for the duals.

"Madame Sans Gene" (Sono). Argentine-made version of French revolution story; mild U. S. boxoffice.

"Zoya" (Russian). OK for specialty houses only.

"Livet Pa Landet" (Scandia). Swedish-made country story with Edward Persson starred; okay for foreign-language spots.

Patrick the Great

(MUSICAL)

Universal release of Howard Benedict production. Stars Donald O'Connor, Peggy Ryan; features Frances Dee, Donald Cook, Eve Arden. Directed by Frank Ryan. Story, Jane Hall, Frederick and Ralph Block; adaptation, Bertram Millhauser and Dorothy Bennett; songs, Sidney Miller, Inez James, Charles Previn, Charles Tobias, David Kapp; editor, Ted J. Kent; camera, Frank Redman. At State, N. Y., week April 12, '45. Running time, **88 MINS.**

Pat Donahue, Jr.	Donald O'Connor
Judy Watkin	Peggy Ryan
Lynn Andrews	Frances Dee
Pat Donahue, Sr.	Donald Cook
Jean Mathews	Eve Arden
Max Wilson	Thomas Gomez
Prentis Johns	Gavin Muir
Sam Bassett	Andrew Tombes
Mr. Merney	Irving Bacon

Donald O'Connor and Peggy Ryan as a song-and-dance team with romantic ups and downs help mightily to make "Patrick the Great" a diverting musical. It's not the tops in entertainment but with several listenable songs and a pleasing little story the chances to do well at the boxoffice are quite bright. The running time of 88 minutes may be considered a little more than was necessary but no serious slowness of action has resulted.

The story is built around Donald Cook, a musical comedy star, and young O'Connor as his stagestruck son, plus Miss Ryan who, in addition to having theatrical ambitions, is also plenty sweet on O'Connor. Virtually all of the action takes place at a mountain lodge where O'Connor mistakenly thinks Frances Dee, an authoress, has fallen in love with him. Meantime, Miss Ryan is bleeding her heart out but in the end everything rights itself while the kid's father, Cook, hits it up with Miss Dee.

In between are the several songs and dance numbers, a couple of a production nature, and the comedy relief. A particularly inviting song is "For the First Time" (Charles Tobias-David Kapp) which serves as a single for O'Connor. "Don't Move," "When You Bump Into Someone You Know," and "Ask Madam Zam" turned out by Sidney Miller and Inez James, are others which score nicely. They are doubles for O'Connor and Miss Ryan. A Latin-type number is "The Cubacha," also by Miller-James.

The cast supporting O'Connor and Miss Ryan fit well into the pattern of the story. Both Miss Dee and Cook give well-turned performances. Eve Arden plays secretary to Miss Dee and herself commands attention as a somewhat hardboiled blonde. Gavin Muir and Andrew Tombes are Broadway producers who favor young O'Connor over his father for the lead in a new show. Good character is Thomas Gomez, manager for Cook, while for a few laughs there's Irving Bacon, a professional type of fellow who is trying to get a rest in the mountains and doesn't.

Howard Benedict's production is adequate and the direction of Frank Ryan steady. *Char.*

Two O'Clock Courage

RKO-Radio release of Ben Stoloff production. Stars Tom Conway, Ann Rutherford; features Richard Lane, Bettejane Greer, Jean Brooks. Directed by Anthony Mann. Screenplay, Robert E. Kent; based on story by Gelett Burgess; camera, Jack Mackenzie; editor, Philip Martin, Jr. At Rialto, N. Y., week April 13, '45. Running time, **66 MINS.**

The Man	Tom Conway
Patty	Ann Rutherford
Haley	Richard Lane
Mark Evans	Lester Matthews
Maitland	Roland Drew
Brenner	Emory Parnell
Helen	Bettejane Greer
Barbara	Jean Brooks
O'Brien	Edmund Glover
Dilling	Bryant Washburn

"Two O'Clock Courage" has less guts than its title. Film is a slow-paced, drab mystery about an amnesia victim. Situations are obvious, the dialog routine. A modest budgeter, it's strictly nabe duals stuff.

Yarn concerns a man found wandering in the streets by a femme cab-driver, the man uncertain who he is, but implicated by his clothes in a series of murders. Cabbie and man make the rounds of various suspects, following newspaper leads, until the mystery of the murder of a theatrical producer and subsequent homicides are cleared up, and the amnesia victim absolved.

Tom Conway and Ann Rutherford, in the leads, give film some story strength, but overall effect is sowhatish. *Bron.*

I'll Remember April

(SONGS)

Universal release of Gene Lewis production. Features Gloria Jean, Kirby Grant, Milburn Stone, Edward S. Brophy, Samuel S. Hinds, Jacqueline de Wit, Hobart Cavanaugh. Directed by Harold Young. Screenplay by M. Coates Webster, from story by Gene Lewis, based on "Amateur Nights" by Bob Dillon; music director, Edgar Fairchild; camera, Jerome Ash. Tradeshown in N. Y., April 11, '45. Running time, **63 MINS.**

April	Gloria Jean
Dave Ball	Kirby Grant
Winchester	Milburn Stone
Shadow	Edward S. Brophy
Garfield	Samuel S. Hinds
Whisper	Jacqueline de Wit
Billings	Hobart Cavanaugh
Police Inspector	Addison Richards
Dr. Armitage	Pierre Watkin
J. C. Cartright	Clyde Fillmore
Mrs. Barrington	Mary Forbes
Childs	Morgan Wallace
Popolopolis	Paul Porcasi

Among items forgotten by those responsible for "I'll Remember April" are a clear story line to back up good production, and top singers to work with Edgar Fairchild's good band. An outstanding song or two might also help. As it stands, however, picture is just a passable dualer.

Story starts out to be tale of the singing daughter of a rich man gone broke. The gal is out to replenish the family coffers and tries to land on radio. But she becomes involved in a feud between two famous radio commentators, one of whom seems like a caricature of a real-life radio gabber. Then the story goes from a murder, its solution and then through the collaboration of the same two guys.

Gloria Jean's singing is not particularly distinguished, and Kirby Grant's is ditto, although latter acts well, as does Milburn Stone. As for the songs, only one that seems possible of catching on is a novelty number called "Hittin' the Beach Tonite," with music and lyrics by Marty Roberts and Chic Dornish. This number is done by a quartet whose members are not identified. *Cars.*

Flame of Barbary Coast

(SONGS, MUSIC)

Republic release of Joseph Kane production, directed by Kane. Stars John Wayne, Ann Dvorak; features Joseph Schildkraut, William Frawley, Virginia Grey, Russell Hicks, Jack Norton, Paul Fix, Manart Kippen. Screenplay, Borden Chase; music, Morton Scott; orchestration, Dale Butts; dances, Larry Ceballos; camera, Robert DeGrasse. Tradeshown N. Y., April 12, '45. Running time, **91 MINS.**

Duke Fergus	John Wayne
Flaxen Tarry	Ann Dvorak
Tito Morell	Joseph Schildkraut
Smooth Wylie	William Frawley
Rita Dane	Virginia Grey
Cyrus Danver	Russell Hicks
Byline Conners	Jack Norton
Calico Jim	Paul Fix
Dr. Gorman	Manart Kippen
Martha	Eve Lynne
Disko	Marc Lawrence
Beulah	Butterfly McQueen
Headwaiter	Rex Lease
Cabby	Hank Bell
Horseshoe Brown	Al Murphy

Republic evidently put much effort into this western but in spite of competent handling, excessive footage militates against it. A better-than-average dualler.

A Montana cattleman comes to scoff at the pre-earthquake Barbary Coast of San Francisco and stays to like it; a "gentleman" gambler runs the most successful joint in the district until the guy from the tall grass decides to take over; and the gambler's singer-sweetheart is also the toast of the town's haute monde.

Through dialog, songs and music that's distinguished chiefly for the fact that it sounds like 1945 instead of 1906, the story winds a tortuous path until the earthquake breaks things up and propels the pretty dame into the arms of the cowboy without a horse. But there is never any suspense in the piece, there is no juxtaposition of characters, no inner logic. One is conscious constantly of the dragging proceedings.

Despite picture's lack of character the songs sound good, the scoring is pleasant, the photography is excellent in one spot (earthquake sequence), and the acting is tops. Kane does a better job as director than as producer. John Wayne handles himself very well in the role of the man from the plains. Ann Dvorak not only sings well but looks and acts the part of the nitery queen, Joseph Schildkraut as the gambler is socko. Good support is turned in by the entire cast, especially by Virginia Grey as Miss Dvorak's rival and William Frawley is OK as another gambler. *Cars.*

Hitchhike to Happiness

(SONGS)

Republic release of Donald H. Brown production. Stars Al Pearce; features Dale Evans, Brad Taylor. Directed by Joseph Santley. Screenplay, Jack Townley; based on original by Manny Seff, Jerry Horwin; camera, Jack Marta; editor, Fred Allen. At Republic, N. Y., April 14, '45. Running time, **71 MINS.**

Kipling "Kippy" Ellis	Al Pearce
Alice Chase	Dale Evans
Joe Mitchell	Brad Taylor
Sandy Hill	William Frawley
Tony Riggs	Jerome Cowan
Ladislaus Prenska	Willy Trenk
Dolly Ward	Arlene Harris
Joan Randall	Joyce Compton
Mrs. Randall	Maude Eburne
Dennis Colby	Irving Bacon
Romer Twins	Lynn and Jeanne Romer

"Hitchhike to Happiness" is a mild comedy-drama about a budding songwriter and an aspiring playwright, with stock situations and a pretty familiar story. Broad-jowled Al Pearce, radio comic, ambles gently through the principal's role, and there are a few pleasant songs attractively sung by Dale Evans. On this basis, "Hitchhike" rates a ride through the duals.

Pearce plays a Broadway waiter with a yen to write plays, whose ambish is a standing joke among show biz folk patronizing his restaurant. That is, all except Brad Taylor, thumping the piano as he waits for someone to buy his first song, and Dale Evans, who left the restaurant a nobody to become a Hollywood radio songstress.

Miss Evans, on visit to New York, is needed by a show-producing trio to make their new play a success. The trio, incidentally, are practical jokers, palming the waiter off to a foreign producer as a successful Broadway playwright. She takes the waiter's part, promises to appear in a show he's written, to which the young tunesmith's songs are added, and makes the show a success by her efforts.

Miss Evans has looks as well as a voice, and Taylor is handsome as romantic lead opposite. Pearce's easy-going comedy would register more with some needed material. William Frawley and Willy Trenk add a little more comedy, with Jerome Cowan for the heavy. *Bron.*

Madame Sans Gene

(ARGENTINE-MADE)

Buenos Aires, March 15.

Argentina Sono Film production and release. Stars Nini Marshall; features Eduardo Cuitino, Adrian Cuneo, Luis A. Otero, Homero Carpena, Herminia Franco, Julio Renato, Delfy de Ortega, Olimpio Bobbio and Tato de Serra. Directed by Luis Cesar Amadori. Adapted by Conrado Naxle Rolo from the Victorien Sardou play. Camera, Roque Giacobino. At Premier, Buenos Aires, starting March 15, '45.

(In Spanish; No English Titles)

This picture was first released in Mar del Plata, the big Atlantic coast resort, last January 27, to open the new Ambassador theatre operated there by Joaquin Lautaret. Its chief claim to distinction are the lavishness of period settings and costuming and the scope of its action, unusual for an Argentine director. It seems to prove how quickly the Latin-Americans are learning their stuff. Scenes of the French Revolution and later at the Emperor Napoleon's court are extremely well done. Chances in U. S. look better than most Argentine films.

Director Amadori has turned out another picture of quality, but the wisdom of a semi-parody on Sardou's play might be questioned. Nina Marshall wins laurels in her first attempt at a more or less straight comedy, although she tends to overdo the famous French laundress who became Dutchess of Dantzig but continued an "enfant terrible." She certainly carries the audience with her, both in comic and serious moods. Eduardo Cuitino, who adds prestige of Argentina's National Comedy Theatre to this, is a vivid Napoleon while Homero Carpena also turns in a very good performance as the sinister Fouche.

Picture cashes in on the wave of pro-French sentiment which swept Argentina when Paris was liberated. Should do well in this market.

Nid.

El Intruso

("The Intruder")

(MEXICAN MADE)

Film Mundiales production and release. Stars Domingo Soler; features Narciso Busquets, Marta Elba, Carlos Grellana. Directed by Mauricio Magdaleno. At Belmont, N. Y., week of April 6, '45. Running time, **75 MINS.**

Juan Manuel Ramirez	Domingo Soler
Alberto	Narciso Busquets
Matilde	Marta Elba
Lavalle	Carlos Grellana
Gaspar	Agustin Isunsa
Tona	Lolita Camarillo

(In Spanish; No English Titles)

This is a dull drama lacking boxoffice appeal even for Spanish-speaking audiences in this country, because of its odd theme, talkiness and poor acting.

Yarn deals with the nasty treatment received by an illegitimate youth from his father, despite fact the boy is a cripple. In the end, though, the father repents and changes his attitude toward the lad.

Settings are average. Camerawork is not outstanding. Domingo Soler gives a fairly creditable performance, but remainder of the cast fails to impress. *Sten*

Zoya
(RUSSIAN-MADE)

Artkino release of Soyuzdet (Moscow) production. Stars Galina Vodianitskaya. Directed by Lev Arnshtam. Screenplay, Arnshtam and Boris Chirskov; English narration and dialog, Howard Fast, narrated by Donna Keath; music, Dmitri Shostakovitch; camera, A. Chelenkov, I. Chen. At Stanley, N. Y., week of April 14, '45. Running time, 86 MINS.

Zoya	Galina Vodianitskaya
Zoya as a Child	Katia Skvortsova
Her Mother	Xenia Tarasova
Her Father	Nikolai Ryzhov
Her Teacher	Tamara Altzeva
Boris Fomin	Alexander Kuznetsov
The Owl	Boris Poslavsky
Komsomol Secretary	Victor Volchek
German Officer	Boris Podgorny
German Soldier	Roman Pliatt

(English Titles and Narration)

During the dark days of the war, when the Nazis were close to the Russian capital, an 18-year-old Moscow girl became one of Russia's epic war heroines. She worked with the partisans behind the enemy lines, was caught and tortured by the Germans, refused to squeal about her confederates, and was hanged. On this factual material the Russian film makers based the picture bearing this femme's name, "Zoya." But on the screen, the picture has too slow a pace, judged by American film standards, and the story goes off into details about the gal's political development in which most Americans would not be interested. Decidedly fit only for houses specializing in Russian pix.

The girl's life story is developed through a long flashback pieced out with blurred news shots showing historic Russian scenes like the funeral of Lenin. There is some good acting by one of her school teachers, played by Boris Poslavsky, but most of the rest of the cast does its job routinely. The star herself is O.K.

Dmitri Shostakovich's music provides appropriate background, but rises to beauty in one long passage which, however, is accompanied on the screen by photography of a particularly stilted kind. On the other hand, photographic montages occurring in spots are excellent. Howard Fast wrote a sensitive narration in English, and it is done well by Donna Keath. *Cars.*

Livet Pa Landet
("Life in the Country")
(SWEDISH-MADE)
(With Songs)

Scandia Films production and release. Stars Edvard Persson. Directed by Bror Bugler. Based on Fritz Reuter's story; camera, Sven Thermanius. At 48th St. Cinema, N. Y., starting April 1, '45. Running time, 105 MINS.

Braslg	Edvard Persson
Frans von Rambos	George Fant
Axel von Rambow	Bror Bugler
Frida von Rambow	Brigitta Valberg
Haverman	Ivar Kage
Louise	Ingrid Backlin
Frits	Willy Peters
Carl Brockman	Kolbjorn Knudsen
Fru Brockman	Dagmar Ebbesen
Brolin	Albert Stahl

(In Swedish; English Titles)

"Life in the Country" is sturdy Swedish film fare because the whole picture is built around Edvard Persson, an outstanding screen star in Sweden. Without this talented player it would be just another foreign production with the by-now familiar, excellent Swedish camera work counter-balanced by an elongated, trite story and a more trite title. Stout entry for foreign-language and some arty houses.

Persson clowns in his usual sly style, doing several monologs, playing a corpulent Cupid part of the time and part of time warbling folk songs. It's fundamentally a story about a count who wants to modernize the farm that's left him by his dad, with Persson, as the retired overseer, eventually making the obstinate count see the error of his ways. It takes smart work by Persson to prevent the obdurate count from losing his huge estate while attempting to eliminate old farming methods.

Screenplay fashioned around Fritz Reuter's story is just one of those things that's been done countless times before on the screen. But with Persson present to make things move, the rather inane plot takes on added zest. "Life in the Country" is well produced with down-to-earth humor dotting the better scenes. The country background is so well reproduced that it is likely to make one want to visit Sweden.

Supporting the clever Persson are George Fant, Birgitta Valberg, Bror Bugler, Ingrid Backlin, Ivar Kage and Willy Peters. Bugler also does the creditable direction, but the unlisted editor has permitted earlier sequences to run far too long. *Wear.*

Miniature Reviews

"The Wonder Man" (Color; Songs) (RKO-Goldwyn). Danny Kaye's second pic, good b.o.

"Son of Lassie" (color) (M-G). Sentimental dog story. Will cash in on previous "Lassie" yarn, to which it is sequel.

"Betrayal From the East" (RKO). OK topical piece headed for good b.o.

"Escape In the Desert" (WB). Poor remake for the duals.

"Blithe Spirit" (Brit.). Slick British adaptation of the Noel Coward play, made-to-order for sophisticated audiences.

"Eve Knew Her Apples" (songs) (Col). Acceptable dualler.

"Song of the Sarong" (songs) (U). William Gargan and Nancy Kelly in musical adventure opus okay for the dualers.

"Te Quiero Para Mi" (Mex). Neat comedy for Spanish-speaking audiences; no English titles.

The Wonder Man
(SONGS; COLOR)

RKO release of Samuel Goldwyn production. Stars Danny Kaye; features Virginia Mayo, Vera-Ellen, Donald Woods, S. Z. Sakall, Allen Jenkins, Edward Brophy. Directed by Bruce Humberstone. Screenplay, Don Hartman, Melville Shavelson, Philip Rapp; adaptation, Jack Jevne and Eddie Moran; original story, Arthur Sheekman; song, Leo Robin and David Rose; special music and lyrics, Sylvia Fine; music director, Louis Forbes; orchestrated and conducted by Ray Heindorf; editor, Daniel Mandell; dances, John Wray; camera, Victor Milner and William Snyder; special effects, John Fulton. Tradeshown in N. Y. April 23, '45. Running time, 95 MINS.

Edwin Dingle	Danny Kaye
Buzzy Bellew	
Ellen Shanley	Virginia Mayo
Midge Mallon	Vera-Ellen
Monte Rosson	Donald Woods
Schmidt	S. Z. Sakall
Chimp	Allen Jenkins
Torso	Edward Brophy
Ten Grand Jackson	Steve Cochran
District Attorney	Otto Kruger
Assistant D. A.	Richard Lane
Mrs. Hume	Natalie Schafer
Sailor	Huntz Hall
Sailor's Girl Friend	Virginia Gilmore
Policeman in Park	Ed Gargan
Prima Donna	Alice Mock
Mr. Wagonseller	Grant Mitchell
Mrs. Schmidt	Gisela Werbiseck

All the productional finery that Samuel Goldwyn could muster has gone into his latest Danny Kaye starrer, "The Wonder Man," and the boxoffice should react accordingly. This is Kaye's second pic—his first, also for Goldwyn, was "Up in Arms" —and it will more firmly establish the Broadway comedian in the upper pix ranks.

The script is something that might well have emerged from a Thorne Smith story. Some of the ramifications of the Smith technique may be absurdly projected, but there's no denying the story deficiencies are insufficient to handicap Kaye's boff salesmanship. It's the type of yarn that enables him to give way to the inhibitive and distinctive style of comedy that has sent him soaring to stardom.

Niftily Technicolored and expensive-looking all the way, "Wonder Man" finds Kaye in a dual role, as twins, one being a nitery performer bumped off by yeggs because of information he was going to give the district attorney; the other as a mild-mannered, studious type who, after his brother's slaying, is belabored by the latter's "spirit" into taking his place and thus help run down the thugs.

The complications, notably on the romance, frequently get too unwieldy for comfort. Several of the comedy situations are rewrites of oldies, but Kaye makes them capital. There is, in particular, a final-reel scene, in which Kaye, trying to escape the gunmen, seeks refuge as a costumed singer during the midst of an operatic performance. It's boilerplate comedy but Kaye makes it belly-laugh fun.

Sylvia Fine (Mrs. Kaye) has contributed some original material for Kaye's unique gibberish style of lyricizing, and there's at least one, the "Otchi Tchornya" number, which Kaye has been doing in the varieties for a number of years.

If this sounds like all Danny Kaye, there's no mistaking that without him this film would be decidedly commonplace. He has a good supporting cast, namely the beauteous Virginia Mayo, as the main romantic link, and Vera-Ellen, out of the Broadway musicals, who is the secondary love interest. The blonde Miss Mayo screens like the couple of millions that are indicated to have been spent by Goldwyn on the pic; and Vera-Ellen is a fine young hoofer who can handle lines well, too. S. Z. Sakall, Donald Woods, Edward Brophy and Allen Jenkins are other support who contribute prominently.

Direction by Bruce Humberstone is aimed for broad laughs, and gets 'em. *Kahn.*

Son of Lassie
(COLOR)

Hollywood, April 20.

Metro release of Samuel Mark production. Stars Peter Lawford, Donald Crisp. Features June Lockhart, Nigel Bruce, William "Billy" Severn, Leon Ames, Donald Curtis, Nils Asther, Robert Lewis, Lassie and Laddie. Directed by S. Sylvan Simon. Story and screenplay, Jeanne Bartlett; based on some characters from book, "Lassie Come Home" by Eric Knight; camera, Charles Schoenbaum; special effects, A. Arnold Gillespie, Warren Newcombe, Danny Hall; editor, Ben Lewis; score, Herbert Stothart. Tradeshown L.A., April 19, '45. Running time, 100 MINS.

Joe Carraclough	Peter Lawford
Sam Carraclough	Donald Crisp
Priscilla	June Lockhart
Duke of Rudling	Nigel Bruce
Henrik	William "Billy" Severn
Anton	Leon Ames
Sergeant Eddie Brown	Donald Curtis
Olav	Nils Asther
Sergeant Schmidt	Robert Lewis
Joanna	Fay Helm
Willi	Peter Helmers
Karl	Otto Reichow
Hedda	Patricia Prest
Thea	Helen Koford
Arne	Leon Tyler
Old Woman	Lotta Palfi
Washwoman	Elly Malyon
and	
Lassie and Laddie	

"Son of Lassie" will get favorable b.o. reaction from the same type of audience that responded to "Lassie Come Home," Metro's initial sentimental dog story. This one adds 10 minutes' running time to length of previous entry and would benefit by at least 20 minutes' trimming. It's a slow starter, offers a surfeit of varied-hued scenery and its adventures have all the appearance of a 15-episode chapterplay condensed into a feature-length film. Nevertheless, it's good old sentimental hokum built around a dog that usually proves profitable at the ticket windows.

Theme is the same dog's-devotion-to-master that motivated "Lassie Come Home," only this time it's Lassie's son, Laddie, who follows his young master into the war and a high-adventure trek across Nazi-occupied countries back to England after their plane is shot down. Suspense elements hit high peaks at times, offsetting the sticky sentiment, and flambuoyant adventures carry sufficient interest to move it along. Picture bases some characters on those from Eric Knight's book, and Donald Crisp and Nigel Bruce are holdovers from the first casting.

When Joe Carraclough, grown to a young man, is off for training in Britain's air force, Laddie makes a nuisance of himself by continually showing up at the air field. Dog makes himself a passenger on Joe's last flight, and when plane is hit over Norway, parachutes down with his master. Joe, stunned by the fall, is left alone while dog seeks assistance. He reappears with two Nazi soldiers, finds his master gone. From then on it's a long chase as the dog seeks Joe, with the Nazis trailing, and Joe beats his way via underground back towards England. Dog and master get together occasionally and each time it results in Laddie betraying his owner's whereabouts to the Nazis. They make their final escape good after incredible incidents.

Peter Lawford plays excellently and with restraint the character of Joe, whose younger version was portrayed by Roddy McDowall in "Lassie Come Home." Donald Crisp is again seen as Joe's father, also excellent, and Nigel Bruce repeats his Duke of Rudling characterization to good effect. June Lockhart is believable as the Duke's granddaughter and romantic interest with Joe. Nils Asther, Leon Ames and others are seen to advantage.

Samuel Marx, who produced "Lassie," also expertly handled reins on this. Color photography by Charles Schoenbaum occasionally dazzles with the wealth of outdoor scenic values. *Brog.*

Betrayal From the East

RKO release of Herman Schlom (Sid Rogell) production. Stars Lee Tracy, Nancy Kelly; features Regis Toomey, Richard Loo, Abner Biberman, Addison Richards. Directed by William Burke. Screenplay by Kenneth Gamel, Audrey Wisberg, based on book by Alan Hynd; epilog by Drew Pearson; camera, Russell Metty. At RKO Palace, N.Y., week of April 24, '45. Running time, 82 MINS.

Eddie....Lee Tracy
Peggy....Nancy Kelly
Tanni....Richard Loo
Yamato....Abner Biberman
Scott....Rgis Toomey
Kato....Phillip Ahn
Capt. Bates....Addison Richards
Purdy....Bruce Edwards
Araki....Hugh Hoo
Omaya....Sen Young
Kurt....Roland Varno
Marsden....Louis Jean Heydt
Hildebrand....Jason Robards
Epilog: Drew Pearson

Pointing up Japanese duplicity and cruelty in the period just preceding Pearl Harbor, this one is a sock topical picture which should hypo boxoffices that exploit the product sensibly and tie it in with the war in Pacific and San Francisco plans for future peace.

Story revolves around efforts of Japanese to get Panama Canal defense plans in preparation for war, late in 1941. Lee Tracy, a happy-go-lucky and broke guy, who used to be a U.S. soldier, is contacted by the Jap spy gang who think he'll do anything for dough. He lets them think so, trying to doublecross them and turn them over to Army intelligence. G-2 also has a pretty counter-spy, acted by Nancy Kelly, working on case. When the swift action is over, Tracy and Miss Kelly had succeeded in putting the Japs on the spot, but at the cost of own lives. That's where Drew Pearson's neat little epilog comes in. He wraps up the whole thing, pointing up the lesson that America mustn't be caught unawares again.

None-too-expensive production is, however, entirely adequate, lavishness in case being out of character. Direction is very good, and acting is tops. Richard Loo, Abner Biberman and Philip Ahn are o.k. as the leaders of the sinister gang of Nips; Tracy and Miss Kelly are tops in their roles. Latter is particularly convincing and realistic in her final scene, when enemy agents find she's working for the USA. *Cars.*

Escape in the Desert

Hollywood, April 24.

Warner Bros. release of Alex Gottlieb production. Features Jean Sullivan, Philip Dorn, Irene Manning, Helmut Dantine, Alan Hale. Directed by Edward A. Blatt. Screenplay, Thomas Job; adapted by Marvin Borowsky from play by Robert E. Sherwood; camera, Robert Burks; editor, Owen Marks; music, Adolph Deutsch. Tradeshown L. A. April 18, '45. Running time, 79 MINS.

Jane....Jean Sullivan
Philip Artveld....Philip Dorn
Mrs. Lora Tedder....Irene Manning
Captain Becker....Helmut Dantine
Dr. Orville Tedder....Alan Hale
Gramp....Samuel S. Hinds
Hank Albright....Bill Kennedy
Lieut. Von Kleist....Kurt Kreuger
Hoffman....Rudolph Anders
Klaus....Hans Schumm
Danny (10 years old)....Blayney Lewis

Minor dualler for the action houses where patrons aren't particular. An attempt to remake Robert E. Sherwood's "Petrified Forest," the venture is an unhappy one on all counts. It's a patchwork conglomeration of thrill melodrama, propaganda, forced comedy and general hoke that has nothing to offer the top situations.

Sherwood's gangsters have been dressed in Nazi uniforms (which is certainly a badge of gangsterism), but the desert locale and the plot setup vary little from his original play. There's the lonely desert wanderer, this time a Hollander seeing America before going into action in the Pacific war area; the girl who wants to escape the desert and the lonely inn, and sundry other characters. Into this setup come a group of escaped prisoners of war, making their way to Mexico. They hide out at the inn while awaiting opportunity to obtain transportation and gas to take them nearer the border, keeping the inn's occupants prisoners by force. Some slight interest and suspense is developed in efforts of the inn's people to get word to the outside or escape from the Nazis; but there is too much wordy propaganda byplay in between the action to maintain proper pace.

Entrance of Alan Hale and Irene Manning into the plot as a credit dentist and his wife who stop at the inn has all the earmarks of a production afterthought to try to leaven heavy doings with some comedy. The Hale character will rate a few chuckles but doesn't save the picture.

Philip Dorn does the wandering Hollander, at first mistaken for one of the escaped Nazis, and Jean Sullivan is the girl who's tired of desert lift. Samuel S. Hinds' gramp role is an excellent characterization. Helmut Dantine is the Nazi leader who tries to make the most of the menace.

Alex Gottlieb's production guidance and Edward A. Blatt's direction can't rate much credit for this one and the script is equally undeserving. *Brog.*

Blithe Spirit
(Technicolor)
(BRITISH-MADE)

London, April 10.

General Film Distributors' release of Two Cities-Noel Coward-Cineguild production. Directed by David Lean. Features Constance Cummings, Kay Hammond, Margaret Rutherford, Rex Harrison. Adapted by Havelock Allen, David Lean, Ronald Neame from stage play by Noel Coward; camera, Ronald Neame. At Odeon, London, April 9. Running time, [illegible] MINS.

Charles Condomine....Rex Harrison
Ruth Condomine....Constance Cummings
Elvira....Kay Hammond
Madame Arcati....Margaret Rutherford
Dr. Bradman....Hugh Wakefield
Mrs. Bradman....Joyce Carey
Edith....Jacqueline Clarke

Given a sophisticated audience this one can't miss. But it is far too slick for hick audiences, in this country or in the States.

Incidentally, whether Noel Coward's name as author and producer had anything to do with it or not, the censor has been more than lenient in allowing the dialog to get nearer the knuckle than any flick has dished up since the talkies began. It's a shame to do American customers out of any of these bedroom cracks by this advance tipping off to the Will Hays office, but if that outfit runs true to form it's a cinch several nitties will land on the cutting room floor.

Oddly enough, inasmuch as this is largely a photographed copy of the stage play, the camera work is outstandingly good and helps to put across the credibility of the ghost story more effectively than the flesh and blood performance does. Technicolor does wonders in making Kay Hammond's Elvira an alluring pastel green siren from the grave, her scarlet mouth and finger nails to match adding oodles of oomph to her seductiveness. Both in interior and exterior shots the soft pedal on color has been judiciously used.

Acting honors go to Margaret Rutherford as Mme. Arcati, a trance medium who makes you believe she's on the level. There is nothing ethereal about this 200-pounder. Her dynamic personality has all the slapdash of Fairbanks, Sr., in his prime. Of course, a better part was never handed an actress, but Miss Rutherford gets her teeth into it in a way to make you convinced no one else could ever be as good. Kay Hammond, as dead Wife No. 1, brings to the screen a faithful repetition of the performance she has been giving in the flesh for nearly four years. As a spoiled darling with murder in her heart for Wife No. 2, she is as much a smiling menace as she is wistfully wraithlike.

As Ruth, the very much alive Wife No. 2, Constance Cummings more than holds her own in an altogether capable cast—until she, too, is smeared with the pastel green following her death in the automobile accident engineered by Elvira. As a ghost Miss Cummings is not at all convincing. Perhaps, in the jocose vein which permeates the flick, one may infer she is too fresh out of the grave to have lost her earthly blood-and-fleshness. As Charles Condomine, twice married novelist, Rex Harrison repeats his stage performance, which is so flawless as to merit some critics' charge of under-acting. But such critics are overlooking an important fact. When it comes to condescension, nobody in the English theatre has anything on Noel Coward. For Harrison to have the nerve to give an impression of condescending to play a Noel Coward lead would seem to be just about tops in the matter of guts.

Direction by David Lean is workmanlike, but in several spots faulty cutting undoes some of his most cleverly contrived situations. Time and again priceless lines are lost through characters not waiting for surefire laughs to subside. This is the less excusable in view of audience reactions during the long run of the stage play.

With this said, "Blithe Spirit" can safely be counted on to help J. Arthur Rank in his campaign to create a place for British-made films in American picture houses. *Talb.*

Eve Knew Her Apples
(SONGS)

Columbia release of Wallace McDonald production. Stars Ann Miller; features William Wright, Robert Williams, Ray Walker. Directed by Will Jason. Screenplay E. Elwin Moran; camera, Burnett Guffey. At Brooklyn Strand, N.Y., week of April 19, '45. Running time, 64 MINS.

Eve Porter....Ann Miller
Ward Williams....William Wright
Steve Ormand....Robert Williams
George McGrew....Ray Walker
Joe Gordon....Charles D. Brown
Walter W. Walters, II....John Eldredge
Roberts....Eddie Bruce

Ann Miller's singing and William Wright's acting help this item put into the class of an acceptable dualler.

A thin, trite story is built about Miss Miller as a radio singer who seeks a vacation away from her manager, press agent and fans—and falls in love with a newspaper reporter who has more romantic appeal than journalistic savvy. On stage and off, sitting in a bus, lying on a haystack and in other improbable situations, Miss Miller does four songs. One of them, "Someone to Love," by Bob Warren, makes for swell listening, and the others are done pleasantly too.

Ward Williams is the ne'er-do-well mugg who finally gets the gal after a lot of ninny business (like never kissing the jane who's alone in a field with him and literally throws herself at him) which will probably make a deacon laugh. Direction is that way, on the super-puritanical level throughout, and production is decidedly on the nether side of the budget. But Wright and Miss Miller are good, as far as script and business at hand will let them. There is one sequence in which Eddie Bruce, in a minor role as a smalltown wise guy, turns in a very good performance. *Cars.*

Song of the Sarong
(SONGS)

Universal release of Gene Lewis production. Features Nancy Kelly, William Gargan, Eddie Quillan, Fuzzy Knight, George Cleveland. Directed by Harold Young. Original, Gene Lewis; camera, Maury Gertsman; editor, Fred R. Feitshans, Jr.; songs, Don Kaye, Gene De Paul, Stephen Foster, Jack Brooks. Previewed in N. Y. April 19, '45. Running time, 65 MINS.

Sharon....Nancy Kelly
Drew....William Gargan
Tony....Eddie Quillan
Pete....Fuzzy Knight
Kalo....George Dolenz
Beemis....George Cleveland
Mahu....Mariska Aldrich
Adams....Morgan Wallace
Potter....Larry Keating
Jolo....Robert Barron

This is one of those harum-scarum adventure films, with a dash of sarong maidens and slapstick tossed in for good measure. It never makes pretensions of being anything but a "B" feature, and, as such, suffices for the twin bills.

Story of William Gargan, who takes all sorts of wild-goose chase jobs, and his ventures on an uncharted isle of the South Seas, turns out a peculiar conglomeration in its attempt to be different. Gargan follows his rep for taking strange jobs when he agrees to seek a fortune in pearls for a million dollars. Main catch to his successful accomplishment of getting the pearls is that the gems are zealously guarded by poison-spear-carrying natives.

Plot switches from outright adventure to a slight musical. Then it swings over to old-type hoke comedy, and finally winds up on a serious note. Last mentioned transpires when the odd-job adventurer is saved from burning at the stake when Nancy Kelly, white queen of the island, and his sweetheart, prays for him. Result is a downpour that blots out the flames. There are several production numbers, best being the one where the native femmes start hip-weaving and Miss Kelly does a vigorous solo dance. The native dances are torrid but trimmed to well-spaced flashes.

Most of music is only so-so though Gargan, Eddie Quillan and Fuzzy Knight, latter the two pals of Gargan in his quest for the gems, sing lustily whenever given an excuse. Best tune they do is "Pied Pipers From Swingtown." "Lovely Luana," warbled by Miss Kelly and gals, is also okay. Gargan duets with Miss Kelly on the Stephen Foster oldie, "Camptown Races," in lively fashion.

Gargan is fairly good when he has a chance as the adventurer while Eddie Quillan and Fuzzy Knight are saddled with all the slapstick of the film. Miss Kelly is capable enough in her love episodes with Gargan, and wears her sarong and scanty garb effectively. She's best in the ceremonial dance and ballading. George Cleveland plays the oldtimer who tries to dissuade Gargan to quit his pearl-hunting venture with skill and ease.

Harold Young's direction is better than the story itself, which was whipped up by Gene Lewis, who also produced. His production job is far superior to the yarn. Maury Gertsman's photography is classy. *Wear.*

Te Quiero Para Mi

("I want You For Myself")
(MEXICAN MADE)

Clasa Mohme release of Felipe Gerely-, Vincent Sempere production. Stars Jose Nieto, Isabel de Pomes, Antonio Casal. Directed by Ladislas Vajda from novel by Maria Luisa Linares. At Belmont, N.Y., week of April 20, '45. Running time, 92 MINS.

Heredia .... Jose Nieto
Lil .... Isabel de Pomes
Don Caesar Guzman .... Antonio Casal
And Maria Bru, Jose Isbert, Manuel Arbo, Antonio Plan.

(In Spanish; No English Titles)

This romantic comedy easily could get more business in U.S. film houses by addition of English titles, since it has the ingredients for better-than-average attention among audiences which patronize class houses.

As currently released the film is embellished with a clever story-line, several fine performances and other strong production values. Yarn deals with romantic advances made by a high school principal to a young lady who informs him she prefers his associate. However he gets her to accept through the promise of a large dowry, only to have the applecart upset during the film's denouement.

Three top players in the cast are new to U.S. Spanish-speaking audiences. Jose Nieto, a good-looking young Mex actor, gives neat portrayal in the romantic leading role. Isabel de Pomes is a pert miss who will gain favor, while Antonio Casal does a neat job as the principal and third member of the triangle.

Settings are average, dialog is witty and seems to hold the interest of the audience throughout, and camerawork above average. *Sten.*

Miniature Reviews

"Blood on the Sun" (Cagney-UA). James Cagney and Sylvia Sidney teamed in anti-Jap drama headed for strong biz.

"The Southerner" (UA-Loew-Hakim). Zachary Scott-Betty Field in morbid, unlikely boxoffice entry.

"The Brighton Strangler" (RKO). Good psychological feature for twin horror shows.

"Zombies on Broadway" (RKO). Bela Lugosi, Wally Brown, Alan Carney in comedy chiller-diller. Oke dualer.

"Swing Out, Sister" (Songs) (U). Lightweight opus with pleasant musical interludes.

"A Guy, a Gal and a Pal" (Col) A light comedy.

"Great Day" (RKO). British-made yarn about Eleanor Roosevelt's visit to England looks thin for U.S.

Blood on the Sun

United Artists release of Willaim Cagney production. Stars James Cagney, Sylvia Sidney; features Wallace Ford, Robert Armstrong, John Emery. Directed by Frank Lloyd. Screenplay by Lester Cole, based on story by Garrett Fort; camera, Theodor Sparkuhl; editors, Truman Wood, Walter Hanneman. Previewed Loew's 72d St., N.Y., April 24, '45. Running time 98 MINS.

Nick Condon .... James Cagney
Iris Hilliard .... Sylvia Sidney
Ollie Miller .... Wallace Ford
Edith Miller .... Rosemary De Camp
Col. Tojo .... Robert Armstrong
Premiere Tanaka .... John Emery
Hijikata .... Leonard Strong
Prince Tatsugi .... Frank Puglia
Capt. Oshima .... Jack Halloran
Kajioka .... Hugh Ho
Yamamoto .... Philip Ahn
Hayashi .... Joseph Kim
Yamada .... Marvin Mueller
Joseph Cassell .... Rhys Williams
Arthur Bickett .... Porter Hall
Charley Sprague .... James Bell
Amah .... Grace Lem
Chinese Servant .... Oy Chan
Hotel Manager .... 3George Paris
Johnny Clarke .... Hugh Beaumont

"Blood on the Sun" has an anti-Jap theme, somewhat familiar, but nevertheless timely, with an excellent screenplay that gives it terrific impact. Exploitation stunts galore are in its 98 minutes of running time. With James Cagney and Sylvia Sidney for the marquee, this picture can't miss doing topflight business in all situations.

Second indie production by William Cagney was piloted by director Frank Lloyd to get the most out of the newly-styled practice of shorter features. And this situation helps put the picture over. There was a lot of ground to cover in less time, so the frills were omitted, the values pointed up, and the total spells boxoffice.

Cagney portrays an American editor of a Tokyo newspaper who dares to print the story of the world-conquest plan formulated by Jap militarists. Naturally, the fur flies when the sheet hits the street—the police confiscating the papers, the Jap secret police demanding a retraction from his publisher, and the editor threatening to walk out if the latter does so. Quickly, Cagney finds himself in the midst of a dual murder committed by the Japs upon a U. S. newspaper pal and his wife, who were leaving Japan to bring to America the document describing the world-conquest plot in detail. The secret police frame Cagney, planting the story that he wound up in jail for the night after a wild party with a couple of gals. But not before the editor contacts Miss Sidney, who is playing both ends of the spy routine in an effort also to get the plan out to the rest of the world. Of course, it all winds up okay.

The stars of this picture are given plenty of opportunity to display their histrionics. Cagney is the same rough and tumble character he's always been, ready to tell the Jap bigshots off at the drop of a hat. Miss Sidney, back after a too-long hiatus from Hollywood, is gowned gorgeously and photographs ditto. The makeup job on the actors such as Robert Armstrong, John Emery and the others in supporting roles who portray Jap characters, is realistic indeed. And the acting in this film is topflight from the smallest to the top roles.

Several scenes are memorable. One, showing Cagney beating the yellow lowlifes at jiu-jitsu, lingers, and the other a rough and tumble, drag-out fight with a police officer, using boxing to finally trounce his opponent, will score strongly too. True, there are a couple of overdramatic sequences, but they just add to the tension of whether they're going to get the envelope with the plot out of the country, or not. Camerawork by Theodor Sparkuhl and settings are classy, but the important factor that will please audiences after the names of Cagney and Miss Sidney on the marquee get them into the theatres, is the fine screenplay evolved by Lester Cole from a story by Garrett Fort. *Sten.*

The Southerner

United Artists release of Loew-Hakim production. Stars Zachary Scott, Betty Field; features Beulah Bondi. Directed by Jean Renoir. Screenplay, Jean Renoir, based on novel by George Sessions Perry; editor, Gregg Tallas; camera, Lucien Andriot; music, Werner Janssen. Previewed in N.Y. April 27, '45. Running time, 91 MINS.

Sam .... Zachary Scott
Nona .... Betty Field
Granny .... Beulah Bondi
Daisy .... Bunny Sunshine
Jot .... Jay Gilpin
Harmie .... Percy Kilbride
Ma .... Blanche Yurka
Tim .... Cahrles Kemper
Devers .... J. Carroll Naish
Finlay .... Norman Lloyd
Doctor .... Jack Norworth
Bartender .... Nelson Psiva
Lizzie .... Estelle Taylor
Party Girl .... Dorothy Granger
Becky .... Noreen Roth

There is something distressing about the haphazards of the soil's human migrants, and all the squalor that one associates with their condition has been brought to "The Southerner." An adaptation from the George Sessions Perry novel, "Hold Autumn in Your Hand," this film conjures a naked picture of morbidity that should be the strongest factor to limit its boxoffice chances. It may be trenchant realism, but these are times when there is a greater need. Escapism is the word.

"The Southerner" creates too little hope for a solution to the difficulties of farm workers who constantly look forward to the day when they can settle forever their existence of poverty with a long-sought harvest—a harvest that invariably never comes.

This is, specifically, the story of Sam and Nona, and their struggle to cultivate the rich earth of their midwest farm. It is a farm beset by liabilities, of which lack of money and food are no small factors. Their home is a patchwork of sagging planks and misguided faith.

Because Sam has no money for fresh vegetables and milk, their youngest child, Jot, is stricken with the "spring sickness" (pellagra). Despite this and the near-death of the boy, Sam and Nona continue to take their chances on the cotton crop though they could insure food for their brood by Sam going to work in a factory.

Zachary Scott and Betty Field give fine performances, as do Beulah Bondi, the grandmother; Percy Kilbride, Charles Kemper and J. Carrol Naish. Estelle Taylor, star of the silents, is in a brief barroom brawl scene in which she's photographed and directed badly.

Jean Renoir generally directed with a feel for character, but the continuity and situational development are frequently unsteady. The film, practically all outdoors, appears to have been completed, from a straight production standpoint, on a comparatively modest budget.

"Southerner" marks the producing debut, as a team, of David L. Loew and Robert Hakim. *Kahn.*

The Brighton Strangler

Hollywood, April 27.

RKO release of Herman Schlom (Sid Rogell) production; features John Loder, June Duprez, Michael St. Angel, Miles Mamler, Rose Hobart. Directed by Max Nosseck. Original screenplay, Arnold Phillips, Max Nosseck; added dialog, Hugh Gray; camera, J. Roy Hunt; special effects, Vernon L. Walker; editor, Les Millbrook; music, Leigh Harline. Tradeshown, Hollywood, April 26, '45. Running time, 67 MINS.

Reginald .... John Loder
April .... June Duprez
Bob .... Michael St. Angel
Allison .... Miles Mander
Dorothy .... Rose Hobart
Dr. Manby .... Gilbert Emery
Shelton .... Rex Evans
Inspector Graham .... Matthew Boulton
Banks .... Olaff Hytten
Mrs. Manby .... Lydia Bilbrook
Mayor .... Ian Wolfe

This is a neatly grooved psychological melodrama for teaming on so-called horror programs. It's well enacted, directed and produced, and considerably above level of usual offerings aimed at the chiller exploitation market. Will show profitable returns.

Plot concerns actor who, after long run as lead in a horror play, assumes character's identity and homicidal traits when suffering head injury during London air raid. He carries on the play's plot in screen life, strangling victims who correspond to characters in the play. Plot is familiar to followers of radio and book thriller material and a standard in the shock-'em field.

Mood is well-sustained in building to climax and Max Nosseck's direction restrains the playing for realistic effects. John Loder's lead spot is excellently treated, character maintaining sympathy despite wanton killings. Also excellent in the casting are June Duprez, WAAF who almost falls victim to the strangler, Miles Mander, Rose Hobart, Gilbert Emery, Rex Evans, Michael St. Angel, Lydia Bilbrook and others.

Photography and music play important parts in furthering atmospheric tension set up under Herman Schlom's production guidance. Sets and special effects also add to mood. *Brog.*

Zombies on Broadway

RKO release of Ben Stoloff production. Stars Wally Brown, Alan Carney, Bela Lugosi; features Anne Jeffreys, Sheldon Leonard. Directed by Gordon Douglas. Original, Robert Faber, Chas. Newman; screenplay, Lawrence Kimble; camera, Jack Mackenzie; editor, Philip Martin, Jr. At Rialto, N. Y. week April 27, '45. Running time, 70 MINS.

Jerry Miles .... Wally Brown
Mike Strager .... Alan Carney
Prof. Renault .... Bela Lugosi
Jean La Dance .... Anne Jeffreys
Ace Miller .... Sheldon Leonard
Gus, His Henchman .... Frank Jenks
Benny .... Russell Hopton
Joseph .... Joseph Vitale
Prof. Hopkins .... Ian Wolfe
Walker .... Louis Heydt
Kalaga .... Darby Jones

The "zombie" horror film swings over to the funny side with this picture. "Zombies on Broadway" turns out to be a ghost comedy, with about half of it punched hard for laughs, some of which fail to materialize. A letdown for those taking their chiller-dillers straight, but stout dual fare.

Wally Brown and Alan Carney are teamed as pressagents who think it would be original if they'd have a real live "zombie" at the opening of a nightclub, which coincidentally is called "The Zombie." Owner Sheldon Leonard things it's a good idea, only he insists that the two boys go scouting a tropical isle for said "walking dead." Remainder of story follows the accepted "zombie" formula, excepting that Brown and Carney go into a string of obvious comedy tricks plus a wealth of patent slapstick.

Darby Jones, the original "zombie" of the first in this cycle, is back talking for Bela Lugosi. Latter is as menacing as ever, again a mad medico intent on trying to create "zombies" by giving live folks a shot in the arm. Only trouble is that the victims have a habit of dying after the hypo wears off. That is until the producers decide the picture needs a laugh finish.

Anne Jeffreys is a lively nightclub entertainer trying to get off the tropical island, and picked as first victim for Lugosi's experiments. Picture moves faster than previous entries in the "zombie" cycle, with Gordon Douglas' direction mainly responsible. It's lots better than the script.
Wear.

Swing Out, Sister
(SONGS)

Universal release of Bernard W. Burton production. Features Rod Cameron, Frances Raeburn, Arthur Treacher, Fuzzy Knight, Billie Burke, Jacqueline De Wit. Directed by Edward Lilley. Screenplay, Henry Blankford, from original by Eugene Conrad, Edward Dein; camera, Paul Ivano. Previewed N. Y., May 1, '45. Running time, 60 MINS.

Geoffry	Rod Cameron
Jessica	Billie Burke
Chumley	Arthur Treacher
Donna	Frances Raeburn
Pat	Jacqueline De Wit
Rufus	Samuel S. Hinds
Clutch	Fuzzy Knight
Tim	Milburn Stone
Motorcycle Cop	Edgar Dearing
Mr. Bradstreet	Sam Flint
Mrs. Bradstreet	Constance Purdy
Organ Specialty	Selika Pettiford
	Leo Diamond Quintet

Lightweight material, but with no pretense of being anything else, this pic provides a few pleasant musical interludes to pad out a story that folds before it unfolds.

Tale is based on gal singer who makes her family think she's studying for a longhair concert career whereas she's really starring as vocalist in a Broadway nitery. Her boyhood sweetie is the prominent conductor of a symphony orch who, however, has a secret yen to shine as a hot horn player. Each is attended by a stooge who's also musically equipped. After the couples had sung, played and cought their way through a half dozen trite situations, the two pairs of lovers end up before a magistrate ready to tie the knot.

However, since the music's the thing and the running time is short, there is a fair amount of enjoyment in the singing and music. Frances Raeburn and Rod Cameron do the leads well, and Arthur Treacher is okay as the No. 2 swain courting screwballish Jacquelin De Wit. Only outstanding musical number is an organ specialty dragged into a night club sequence, done in socko form by Selika Pettiford. Production is on low budget. Direction is good, making most of the material at hand and pacing the whole thing so that it seems even shorter than the hour allotted.
Cars.

A Guy, a Gal and a Pal

Columbia release of Wallace MacDonald production. Features Ross Hunter, Lynn Merrick, Ted Donaldson. Directed by Oscar Boetticher, Jr. Screenplay, Monte Brice, based on story by Gerald Drayson Adams; camera, Clen Gano; editor, Otto Meyer. At Brooklyn Strand, April 26, '45. Running time, 62 MINS.

Jimmy Jones	Ross Hunter
Helen Carter	Lynn Merrick
Butch	Ted Donaldson
Granville Breckenridge	George Meeker
Norton	Jack Norton
Barclay	Will Stanton
Porter	Sam McDaniel
Mayor	Alan Bridge
Annette Perry	Mary McLeod
Mrs. Breckenridge	Mary Forbes
General	Russell Hicks
General's Wife	Nella Walker

Columbia gave this one a quick brushoff. It's strictly a filler for duals.

Yarn deals with the familiar routine of a gal undecided whether to go for a serviceman or a civilian, finally deciding in favor of the former. In reaching this world-shaking decision audiences are subjected to 62 minutes of familiarly-themed, boy-meets-gal, boy-chases-gal, the other guy got the same idea, routine.

There is some comedy, and the acting is not bad as done by Ross Hunter, as the Marine who scores; Lynn Merrick, as the gal; George Meeker as the civilian, and Ted Donaldson, who goes along as chaperon for the unmarried couple. Camerawork is average, and settings, such as they are, are unpretentious, to say the least.
Sten.

Great Day
(BRITISH-MADE)
London, April 14.

RKO production and release. Stars Flora Robson, Eric Portman. Directed by Lance Comfort. Screenplay by John Davenport from play by Lesley Storm; camera, Erwin Hillier. At Empire, London, April 13. Running time, 82 MINS.

Captain Ellis	Eric Portman
Mrs. Ellis	Flora Robson
Margaret Ellis	Sheila Sim
Lady Mott	Isabel Jeans
John Tyndale	Walter Fitzgerald
Geoffrey Winthrop	Philip Friend
Mrs. Mumford	Marjorie Rhodes
Miss Tyndale	Margaret Withers

This story of Eleanor Roosevelt's visit to an English village had scant success as a legit play. This film version has much to commend it, yet is not wholly satisfying. Looks mild for the U. S.

The lives of small community members center around the Women's Institute as it prepares for the great event. This provides the background for the slight story. Main interest concerns a neurotic ex-army captain clinging to his last war rank, cadging drinks, borrowing from all and finally caught pilfering from a woman's purse in the local inn. The film saves him from a watery grave where the stage tactfully deposited him after his useless, shiftless life reaches this climax.

Sheila Sim is fresh and natural as his young daughter, a country girl who almost weds her wealthy employer for the sake of the security which her mother never had. Flora Robson and Eric Portman are excellent as the unhappy parents, disillusioned products of the war's aftermath.

Many of the amusing and pathetic side issues of the story have been omitted on the screen, but most of the odd assortment of characters are there to give local color.

Picturesque country scenes are given full treatment by the camera. Makes for pleasing entertainment of the second-feature class.
Clem.

Miniature Reviews

"See My Lawyer" (U) (Musical). Olsen-Johnson starrer; weak b.o.

"The Sister Lieutenant" (Mexican-Made) (Clasa). Lower-drawer stuff for foreign houses; no English titles or dialog.

See My Lawyer
(MUSICAL)

Universal release of Edmund L. Hartmann production. Stars Olsen & Johnson; features Alan Curtis, Grace McDonald, Noah Beery, Jr., Franklin Pangborn, Edward S. Brophy, Richard Benedict, Lee Patrick, Yvette, The Cristianis, Carmen Amaya Co., Hudson Wonders, King Cole 3, Rogers Adario 3, 4 Teens and 6 Willys. Directed by Eddie Cline. Screenplay, Edmund L. Hartmann and Stanley Davis, from Broadway stage play by Richard Maibaum and Harry Clork; songs, Milton Rosen, Everett Carter, Irving Kahal, Sammy Fain; music direct., H. J. Salter; editor, Paul Landres. At Loew's State, N. Y., May 3, '45. Running time, 69 MINS.

Ole	Ole Olsen
Chic	Chic Johnson
Charlie	Alan Curtis
Betty	Grace McDonald
Arthur	Noah Beery, Jr.
B. J. Wagenhorn	Franklin Pangborn
Otis Fillmore	Edward S. Brophy
Joe	Richard Benedict
Sally	Lee Patrick
Winky	Gus Schilling
Judge	William B. Davidson
Willie	Stanley Clements
Mrs. Fillmore	Mary Gordon
O'Brien	Ralph Peters

Vaudeville, which was believed to have been in various states of putrefaction these many years, is being given a shot in the arm by Universal Pictures in what is, ostensibly, a musicomedy. "See My Lawyer" is only vague entertainment, mostly by way of the specialty numbers that intersperse this Olsen & Johnson opus.

In converting the Richard Maibaum and Harry Clork Broadway stage comedy of some seasons ago the film scripters have belabored the original straight play with a distorted conglomerate. There is still present the basic comedy premise wherein a firm of young, penniless lawyers attempts to salvage its shoestring biz, with Olsen & Johnson as the roistering fulcrums for their conniving activities.

Notably supporting the stars in the straight narrative part of "Lawyer" are Alan Curtis, Grace McDonald, Noah Beery, Jr., Franklin Pangborn and Edward Brophy, and they do as well as the limited story permits them.

The specialty performances are not too artfully blended into the story, though a number of the individual specialists go over strongly. Yvette, the blonde songstress looker from radio and the varieties, screens well in her pic debut, singing two numbers, one of which—the by-now standard "I'll Be Seeing You"—is done particularly socko. Such standard turns as the Cristianis, Carmen Amaya, King Cole Trio and the Six Willys round out the film's specialty outstanders. But, by and large, the whole thing does a grave injustice to all the performers. They oughta see their lawyers.
Kahn.

The Sister Lieutenant
(MEXICAN-MADE)

Clasa production and release. Stars Maria Felix; features Jose Cibrian, Angel Garasa, Delia Magana, Consuelo De Luna. Directed by Emilio Gomez Muriel. Screenplay by Marco Aurelio Galindo; camera by Raul Martinez. At Belmont, N. Y., week of May 4, '45. Running time, 83 MINS.

Catalina	Maria Felix
Don Alonzo	Maria Felix
Roger	Angel Garasa
Don Juan	Jose Cibrian
Elvira	Delia Magana
Don Cesar	Jose Pidal
Dona Ursula	Fanny Schiller
Miguel	Paco Fuentes
Lucinda	Consuelo De Luna

(In Spanish; no English Titles)

This pic based on a story that's been told 1,000 times in countless Spanish romances; it's produced at a minimum cost; yet the actors are, for the greater part, doing a top job within the limitations of script. Decidedly lower-drawer stuff. Since there's no English dialog or titling, it's strictly for the language trade anyway.

The beautiful Mexican daughter (Maria Felix) of a rich family has her dower stolen by a wicked aunt, runs away to Peru to search for her father's will, gets shipwrecked, poses as a man, finds her lover, who also turns up in Peru, and in the end all's well.

Miss Felix, however, gives a sock performance, and Jose Cibrian is good throughout. Miss Felix is a looker, knows how to strut before the camera (which this role demands often) and would grace any film in Hollywood. Direction is adequate.
Cars.

Miniature Reviews

"Pillow to Post" (WB). Ida Lupino - William Prince-Sydney Greenstreet in moderate boxoffice comedy.

"That's the Spirit" (Musical). (U). Breezy and entertaining musical with a different story background.

"Big Show-Off" (Rep). Light budget comedy with music, starring Arthur Lake and Dale Evans.

"Bells of Rosarita" (Songs) (Rep.). Well-produced western; looks like good b.o. for its class.

"Scarlet Clue" (Mono). Another fair Charlie Chan whodunit with Sidney Toler.

"Goranssons Pojke" (Swedish). Good drama with English titles.

"Like All Mothers" (Mexican). Lightweight yarn about mother love, not for U.S. except in Spanish-language spots.

Pillow to Post

Warner Bros. release of Alex Gottlieb production. Stars Ida Lupino, William Prince, Sydney Greenstreet; features Stuart Erwin, Johnny Mitchell, Ruth Donnelly, Louis Armstrong's orch. Directed by Vincent Sherman. Screenplay, Charles Hoffman, from stage play by Rose Simon Kohn; editor, Alan Crosland, Jr.; music, Frederick Hollander; music director, Leo F. Forbstein. Previewed N. Y. May 11, 45. Running time, **91 MINS.**

Jean Howard	Ida Lupino
Col. Otley	Sydney Greenstreet
Don Mallory	William Prince
Capt. Jack Ross	Stuart Erwin
Slim Clark	Johnny Mitchell
Mrs. Wingate	Ruth Donnelly
Mrs. Kate Otley	Barbara Brown
Taxi Driver	Frank Orth
Mrs. Mallory	Regina Wallace
Lucille	Willie Best
Mr. Howard	Paul Harvey
Loolie	Carol Hughes
Wilbur	Bobby Blake
Mrs. Bromley	Ann O'Neil
Wilbur's Mother	Marie Blake
Charlotte Mills	Victoria Horn
Jerry Martin	Lelah Tyler
Doris Wilson	Sue Moore
Archie	Don McGuire
Gertrude Wilson	Joyce Compton

Louis Armstrong Orchestra

Rose Simon Kohn's comedy about Army marital manners, which Brock Pemberton produced briefly on Broadway a season or so ago, has been given an extensive treatment for the screen by Warners. The result is not nearly as imposing as the film's budget would indicate. "Pillow to Post" (the "Pillow" was originally "Pillar" in the play) has the benefit of some good performances headed by Ida Lupino, William Prince and Sydney Greenstreet, but its boxoffice prospects should reach only moderate proportions because of an uncertain story based on a weak premise.

This is the yarn of the gal who, in order to get lodging at a camp catering exclusively to servicemen and their wives, must first, naturally, secure a husband. She picks on a young lieutenant as her mate of the moment, her intention being, of course, to use him as a decoy in order to get admittance to a bungalow dwelling, where she intends to rest from an arduous trek as a saleswoman for her father's oilwell-supply firm. Her scheme with the lieutenant is a desperate effort after all other means for lodging had been denied her elsewhere. And circumstances that follow their initial meeting, when he gives her a lift in his car, necessitate his going through with the plan, though it all winds up with a near-courtmartial and the usual misinterpretations when it's learned they aren't husband and wife.

Miss Lupino stresses her flair for comedy as the girl; William Prince is the lieutenant. Greenstreet is the colonel around whom much of the story revolves. Willie Best, as a colored porter, contributes some of the funny moments. Stuart Erwin, as an army captain who becomes a father of quads, and Ruth Donnelly contribute to the comedy fol-de-rol.

Direction emphasizes speed all the way, and there isn't much more that the screenwrights could have done with the original play. In fact, the original title, "Pillar to Post," is at times more appropriate. The story that way. *Kahn.*

That's the Spirit

(MUSICAL)

Universal release of Michael Fessler-Ernest Pagano production of their own story. Stars Jack Oakie and Peggy Ryan; features Johnny Coy, Gene Lockhart, Andy Devine, Arthur Treacher, June Vincent, Irene Ryan, Buster Keaton, Victoria Horne. Directed by Charles Lamont. Songs, Inez James, Sidney Miller, Jack Brooks, Richard Wagner, Hans J. Salter; editor, Fred R. Feithans, Jr.; camera, Charles Van Enger and John P. Fulton; dances, Carlos Romero. Previewed in N. Y. May 11, '45. Running time, **85 MINS.**

Sheila	Peggy Ryan
Steve	Jack Oakie
Libby	June Vincent
Jasper	Gene Lockhart
Martin, Jr.	Johnny Coy
Martin	Andy Devine
Masters	Arthur Treacher
Bilson	Irene Ryan
L. M.	Buster Keaton
Patience	Victoria Horne
Abigail	Edith Barrett

"That's the Spirit" is a breezy, diverting musical with a story of somewhat different cast, several good songs, a couple eyeful production numbers and a group of troupers who move with ease and impressively through the 85 minutes it takes to wind the works up.

A foreword which immediately plants the time of the story during the mauve decade says cutely, "This is New York when a little flower was a petunia and not a mayor." Getting into the story, Gene Lockhart is quickly typed as a pious banker with terrific local pull who rules his household with an iron hand. A rebellious daughter, played by June Vincent, induces her cousin (Vicki Horne) to dare the dangers of going into the Majestic, a vaudeville of the cheaper type. Here Jack Oakie, with his flute, is doing a novelty turn and singing "The Fella With the Flute."

In what amounts to a shotgun wedding due to circumstances involved, Oakie marries the banker's daughter but about the time he is about to become a father, he's wafted away and turns up in Heaven where Buster Keaton is in charge of the complaint department. After serving many years there, Keaton permits Oakie to go back to earth to see his daughter, now 18. His spirit moves through the picture from there on, being unseen and unheard by everybody except Peggy Ryan, his offspring. This spirit angle provides many interesting and amusing moments in between the various song and dance numbers.

Johnny Coy, a dancing typhoon, and Miss Ryan are paired romantically and do several snappy dance numbers together. On first coming before the camera, Coy executes a hardshoe tap single that is terrific. He also sings one number, the oldie "How Come You Do Me Like You Do." "Baby, Won't You Please Come Home" is another from an old catalog that's used, this being a solo for Miss Ryan.

New songs are "Fella With the Flute," "Oh, Oh, Oh," "Evening Star" and "No Matter Where You Are." Tops among these is "Star." Exceptional among production numbers is the Rockettes-like dance routine, done in silhouette fashion against a black background.

Miss Ryan dominates all scenes in which she appears and scores strongly in her song and dance numbers. Oakie, now plenty corpulent, fits into the proceedings nicely, while the girl he marries, Miss Vincent, is a highly sympathetic and appealing type. Lockhart, the straightlaced banker, is also well cast. Others, all giving good performances, include Arthur Treacher, a butler; Irene Ryan, housemaid; Miss Horne, part of the Lockhart household, and Andy Devine, also now plenty obese, who is the operator of the Majestic theatre. *Char.*

The Big Show-Off

(SONGS)

Republic release of Sydney M. Williams production. Stars Arthur Lake, Dale Evans; features Lionel Stander, George Meeker, Anson Weeks orch. Directed by Howard Bretherton. Original screenplay by Leslie Vadnay and Richard Weil; camera, Jack Greenhalgh. At Brooklyn Fox, N. Y., week of May 14, '45. Runing time, **69 MINS.**

Sandy Elliott	Arthur Lake
June Mayfield	Dale Evans
Joe Bagley	Lionel Stander
Wally Porter	George Meeker
The Devil	Paul Hurst
Mitzi	Marjorie Manners
Boris the Bulgar	Sammy Stein
Muckenfuss	Louis Adlon
Announcer	Dan Toby
Hobo	Emmett Lynne
Dr. Dinwiddie	Douglas Wood

Anson Weeks and His Orchestra

Arthur Lake teams up with Dale Evans in this tale of a night-club pianist who tries to score with the gal by stating he is the unknown masked wrestler. "The Big Show-Off" is a briefie that has its moments. Three tunes in this pic are not weighty, but help to liven the proceedings. Anson Weeks and his orch supply the musical background for the vocals of Miss Evans, who has a nice voice and handles her role in neat style, also. Lionel Stander is seen as the nitery owner for whom both Lake and Miss Evans work, and who is instrumental in bringing them together. Remainder of the cast go through their chores in good fashion.

Settings, while not lavish, suffice, and the camerawork is average. Of the tunes, "Cleo From Rio" and "Hoops My Dear" were written by Dave Oppenheim and Roy Ingraham, while Miss Evans gets credit for composing "Only One You." *Sten.*

Bells of Rosarita

(SONGS)

Republic release of Eddy White production. Stars Roy Rogers; features George "Gabby" Hayes, Dale Evans, Adele Mara, Grant Withers, Janet Martin, Robert Mitchell Boychoir, Bob Nolan and Sons of the Pioneers, Wild Bill Elliott, Allan Lane, Donald Barry, Robert Livingston, Sunset Carson. Directed by Frank McDonald. Screenplay, Jack Townley; music director, Morton Scott; camera, Ernest Miller. Tradeshown N. Y., May 11, '45. Running time, **68 MINS.**

Roy Rogers	Roy Rogers
Gabby Whittaker	George "Gabby" Hayes
Sue Farnum	Dale Evans
Patty Phillips	Adele Mara
William Ripley	Grant Withers
Rosarita	Janet Martin
Slim Phillips	Addison Richards
Maxwell	Roy Barcroft
Themselves	Robert Mitchell Boychoir
Themselves	Bob Nolan and the Sons of the Pioneers

Republic Guest Stars: Wild Bill Elliott, Allan Lane, Donald Barry, Robert Livingston, Sunset Carson, and Trigger.

Republic has thrown the works into this western, and the result is kind of fare that should be eaten up by fans of this particular type of entertainment.

The daughter of an ex-circus man is about to be cheated out of her inheritance by her dead dad's former partner (Grant Withers). To the rescue come Roy Rogers and Bob Nolan, two Republic stars playing themselves in a Republic picture being produced on the gal's ranch. Rogers rings in a lot of other Republic stars, who play themselves and show that the guys who make a living out of the westerns can help a dame in distress in "real" life.

Out of this "play-within-a-play" comes a melange of fast riding, quick shooting, the pursuit and capture of the gang, and the usual crop of well-done songs by Rogers, Dale Evans, Bob Nolan and the Sons of the Pioneers. The Robert Mitchell boychoir is an extra attraction, doing some nice harmonizing. Production is somewhat more elaborate than most pix of kind, and direction meets the demands of the situation. Rogers is as nimble and pleasant as usual. George "Gabby" Hayes looks cleaner than in most of his pix, but is still the same trite but well-grooved character. *Cars.*

The Scarlet Clue

Monogram release of James S. Burkett production. Stars Sidney Toler; features Benson Fong, Mantan Moreland, Helen Devereaux. Directed by Phil Rosen. Original screenplay, George Callahan, based on character by Earl Derr Biggers; camera, William A. Sickner; editor, Richard Currier. At Brooklyn Strand, N. Y., week of May 10, '45, dual. Running time, **65 MINS.**

Charlie Chan	Sidney Toler
Tommy Chan	Benson Fong
Birmingham Brown	Manton Moreland
Diane Hall	Helen Devereaux
Capt. Flynn	Robert Homans
Mrs. Marsh	Virginia Brissac
Ralph Brett	Stanford Jolley
Wilbur Chester	Reid Kilpatrick
Willie Rand	Jack Norton
Sergt. McGraw	Chas. Sherlock
Gloria Bayne	Janet Shaw
Herbert Sinclair	Milt Kibbee

Somewhat on a better plane than prior attempts by Monogram to capitalize on its Charlie Chan series, "The Scarlet Clue" is a whodunit that should please fans of this type film fare.

Picture actually has suspense, and the well-written script keeps viewers guessing as to the actual murderer. Acting, too, is better than average, probably because main members of the cast have better material than in several previous pix. Sidney Toler, as Chan, plods along to a successful solution of the killings, with able support from Benson Fong, in the role of his son, and Mantan Moreland, who supplies the comedy relief. Helen Devereaux handles her role capably as do the other supporting actors.

Yarn deals with plot to steal radar plans from the Government, causing the death of several people by remote control. Chan and his aide center their activities in the radar plant which is also in the building where a radio station is located. Film gathers momentum and the denouement actually catches the viewers off guard. *Sten.*

Goranssons Pojke

("Goransson's Boy")
(SWEDISH-MADE)

Scandia Films release of Weyler Hildebrand production: Stars Weyler Hildebrand, Tom Olsson; features Emmy Hagman, Eric Abrahamson. Directed and written by Hildebrand, based on Charlie Chaplin's "The Kid"; camera, J. Julius; settings, Arne Akermark. At 48th St. Playhouse, N. Y., week of May 11, '45. Running time, **84 MINS.**

Goransson	Weyler Hildebrand
Pelle	Tom Olsson
Anna	Emmy Hagman
Sudden	Eric Abrahamson
Aunt Brink	Hilda Borgstrom
Karin	Gaby Stenberg
Junk-John	Sigge Furst
Snobben	Magnus Kesster
Balalaika	Kotti Chave
Clergyman	Carl Strom
Wholesaler	Arthur Fischer

(In Swedish; English Titles)

A high-class production in line with other recent Swedish films which have reached these shores from that nation, "Goranssons Pojke" embellished with English titles, should do well in class houses.

Yarn, based on the old Charlie Chaplin pic, "The Kid," deals with the hard life faced by a junk dealer and a waif whom he shelters, only to lose him to his mother who claims him after the junk dealer had learned to love the youth.

Weylar Hildebrand, of course, is no Chaplin, but he nevertheless gives a convincing performance in the role of the vagabond-at-heart, while Tom Olsson, as the abandoned youngster, is excellent in his portrayal of the role created by Jackie Coogan. Remainder of the cast does right by Hildebrand's writing and direction.

Settings are fairly impressive. The film is in surprisingly good condition, and the camerawork is far above par. *Sten.*

Like All Mothers

("Como Todos Las Madres")
(MEXICAN-MADE)

Grovas production and release. Stars Sagra Del Rio, Fernando Soler, Joaquin Pardave. Directed by Fernando Soler. At Belmont, N. Y., week May 11, '45. Running time, **105 MINS.**

Rosario....................Sagra Del Rio
Coronel Rivera..............Fernando Soler
Don Feliciano..............Joaquin Pardave
Dorotea....................Lolita Camarillo
Aurora....................Pituka de Foronda
Lalo.......................Manolin Fabregas
Enrique....................Victor Velasquez

(In Spanish; No English Titles)

"Like All Mothers" is supposed to be a story of mother love, and one of Mexico's 1944 prize plays, but it certainly does not measure up to the latter classification. Its mother-love angle is badly mangled before the conclusion is reached. Film won't create much of a boxoffice ripple even at Spanish-language spots despite the cast which includes Fernando Soler and Sagra Del Rio. Biggest drawback is its wordiness.

Entire production crew of picture appears to be wrapped up in the delight of having the actors talk. It becomes a 6-cylinder monolog, with the mother-love theme lost in the welter of chatter. The mother of this opus (Sagra Del Rio) is a widow with two boys and one daughter. She passes up Fernando Soler, an Army colonel, because she fears her children would not be happy with him around the house. That probably was the worst mistake the producers made—keeping Soler out of most of the story. Soler directs with an even, if unoriginal pace, but apparently his directorial chores kept him away from doing much before the cameras.

Plot is the familiar one about the good son and the erring one, except that there is too much unessential claptrap, and it's hard to tell when to laugh and when to be serious. Maybe a literal translation into English titles would have helped.

Sagra Del Rio as the mother looks more like a cafe hostess than a parent in earlier footage, wearing one of those off-the-forehead coiffs. Later she looks like a worn-out dressmaker, which she is, with the final scenes forcing her into a goshawful looking wig. She's remarkably comely but shallow histrionically. Soler is okay while in the yarn, which is not enough. Joaquin Pardave tries hard to be funny, and sometimes is. Lolita Camarillo in a lesser role looks promising if given proper direction and makeup. *Wear.*

Miniature Reviews

"Where Do We Go From Here?" (Musical; Color) (20th). Tiptop fantasy with MacMurray-Leslie-Haver for big b.o.

"Thrill of a Romance" (Musical; Color). Van Johnson, Esther Williams wrapped up in boxoffice bofferoo.

"They Met in the Dark" Brit.). Exciting British spy meller, stout for twin bills in U. S.

"A Place of One's Own" (Eagle-Lion). British-made about spirits, haunted house, looms thin for U. S.

Where Do We Go From Here?

(MUSICAL; COLOR)

20th-Fox release of William Perlberg production. Stars Fred MacMurray, Joan Leslie, June Haver; features Gene Sheldon, Anthony Quinn, Carlos Ramirez, Alan Mowbray, Fortunio Bononova, Herman Bing, Howard Freeman. Directed by Gregory Ratoff. Screenplay, Morrie Ryskind from story by Ryskind and Sig Herzig; songs, Ira Gershwin and Kurt Weill; dances, Fanchon; camera, Leon Shamroy, Fred Sersen; editor, J. Watson Webb; music, Emil Newman, Chas. Henderson, David Raksin, Maurice de Packh. Tradeshown May 17, '45. Running time, **77 MINS.**

Bill.......................Fred MacMurray
Sally.........................Joan Leslie
Lucille.......................June Haver
Genie (Ali)................Gene Sheldon
Indian Chief.............Anthony Quinn
Benito......................Carlos Ramirez
General George Washington..Alan Mowbray
Christopher Columbus..Fortunio Bononova
Hessian Colonel..............Herman Bing
Kreiger.................Howard Freeman
Benedict Arnold..............John Davison
Old Lady.......................Rosina Galli
Attorney.........................Fred Essler

When Morrie Ryskind and Sig Herzig contrived their highly imaginative tale, whereby a 1945 4F is whisked back, through the medium of a genial genie out of an Aladdin's lamp, into the periods of Washington, Columbus and Nieuw Amsterdam, it augured well for possibly a new era in filmusicals. That still goes. The fantasy will pay off. It holds too much, from marquee to production values, not to insure against any boxoffice pitfalls.

The "if" in this somewhat qualified review is the pity that it doesn't quite ring the bell all the way. Perhaps the idea, thrice-repeated, militates against a wholly satisfactory sum total. More likely the shortcoming lies in the sameness of the comedy.

Fred MacMurray is the 4F, stuck on khaki-wacky June Haver and blind to Joan Leslie's charms. It's a USO Canteen setting and the best patriotic job he can do, after gumming up the dishwashing, is to collect junk. One of the contributed pieces to the scrap drive is an antique from which emerges the genie, capitally done by Gene Sheldon. Thus, in a series of wishes, MacMurray is whisked back to the Valley Forge USO where George Washington Coffee, Martha Washington Candy, etc., are served. The 18th century USO hostesses go through their cotillions but the 20th century MacMurray—thinking in the present despite the powdered-wig era—breaks it up with a jitterbug routine.

Punctuations of the modern with the historical make for a pleasant sequence, especially with the sundry bits of business. Throughout, MacMurray keeps recalling what his history teacher, Miss Hockheimer of the Bronx High School, had taught him and thus he knows that when he assures Washington at Valley Forge that he will beat the Hessians and warns him of Benedict Arnold; or tells Columbus that that's Cuba (not America) he's discovered; or goes through the $24 "badger game" sale with a not so honest Injun for the purchase of Manhattan island, he's merely encoring the history he had learned.

In all three episodes, whether he's making teepee with the Indian maiden; or the Cuban conga line, when Columbus finally sights land in the western world; or the hocus-pocus with the not-so-dumb Dutchman who give him the real-estate works, the same femme vis-a-vis appear. Misses Leslie and Haver play virtually the same counterparts in the triangle throughout albeit under different names and different eras. The genie is also convenient in the clutch.

The finale is a fantasy effect of "you are now leaving the 17th century," then the 18th, 19th and finally into "you are now entering the 20th century," and for an extra fillip one cloud effect transplants them into "20th Century-Fox."

Finale wish, of course, has MacMurray granted his desire to be accepted for GI service, and the topper sees Ali, the genie, marching along with him.

Gregory Ratoff has directed "Where Do We Go From Here" with good humor and intelligence, well fortified by a lavish production under Bill Perlberg's expert aegis. The Ira Gershwin lyrics to Kurt Weill's pleasant melodies are literate and enhance the story, at no time intruding on the Ryskind script.

MacMurray handles himself well, as do the Misses Leslie and Haver, but the outstander is Gene Sheldon, former deadpan vaudeville panto-banjoist who seems to have finally found himself for pix. A Harry Langdonesque comic, he eschews the panto for dialog and handles the omnipotent genie role with authority and a fine sense of comedy values. The rest are adequate but not too impressive save for Herman Bing's characteristic German-comic impression of a Hessian colonel; Alan Mowbray as Washington; Fortunio Bononova as Chris Columbus; and Carlos Ramirez who tenors "The Pinta, the Nina, the Santa Maria" to good results. The Technicolor, per usual, is lavish and some of the trick lens effects above par. *Abel.*

Thrill of a Romance

(MUSICAL; COLOR)

Metro release of Joe Pasternak productions. Stars Van Johnson, Esther Williams; features Lauritz Melchior, Frances Gifford, Carleton G. Young, Tommy Dorsey orch. Directed by Richard Thorpe. Original, Richard Connell and Gladys Lehman; musical adaptation, direction, Georgie Stoll; songs, Ralph Freed, Sammy Fain, Axel Stordahl, Paul Weston, Sammy Cahn; camera, Harry Stradling; editor, George Boemler. Tradeshown projection room, N. Y., April 18, '45. Running time, **105 MINS.**

Major Thomas Milvaine.......Van Johnson
Cynthia Glenn..............Esther Williams
Maude Bancroft.............Frances Gifford
Hobart Glenn.................Henry Travers
Nona Glenn..................Spring Byington
Mr. Nils Knudsen........Lauritz Melchior
Robert G. Delbar.......Carleton G. Young
Mrs. Fenway..................Ethel Griffies
K. O. Karny.................Donald Curtis
Lyonel..........................Jerry Scott
Julio.....................Fernando Alvarado
Susan........................Helene Stanley
Oscar..........................Vince Barnett
Tommy Dorsey and His Orchestra

Metro pulled no punches in trying to score a boxoffice knockout with this one. It's got everything a lavish musical should have — delightful songs, gorgeous Technicolor, enough of a storyline to sustain interest in the proceedings, and Van Johnson, who is among the hottest attractions right now. It can't miss doing big biz.

As if Johnson wasn't enough to get them in, Esther Williams is co-starred, with Tommy Dorsey and his orch having plenty to do, and Lauritz Melchior, the Metropolitan star in his first film role, flitting in and out with his bombastic vocal gymnastics dressed up to please the masses. Besides, Metro has invested a barrel of dough in giving the production added values such as beautiful costuming for the entire cast, decor that is eye-filling to say the least, plus a lot of little things like camera tricks pointing up Miss Williams' chassis and swimming ability, as well as the comedy spots built around Vince Barnett.

Richard Thorpe's direction of the original screenplay by Richard Connell and Gladys Lehman allows for enough of a plot to saunter in and out of the production numbers without permitting it to spoil the lightness of the entertaining aspects.

Miss Williams, of course, displays her abilities as a swimmer, a diver and a teacher with a musical background of lilting melodies. Melchior, in the role of the chaperone who does his best to keep the romance between the soldier (Johnson) and the gal alive, gives forth with several appropriate light-opera tunes, backed by a small combo and Dorsey's full crew, as well. "Please Don't Say No," already recipient of a big radio plug, is given several renditions in this picture, including the finale where Johnson moves his lips, but Melchior actually does the singing, resulting in a funny sequence and the final clinch between the young star and his vis-a-vis. Georgie Stoll's musical adaptation and direction is especially commendable, but it seems that he (or the cutters) could have found time to give the song "I Should Care" more footage and sound. *Sten.*

They Met in the Dark

(One Song)
(BRITISH-MADE)

English Films release of Marcel Bellman production. Stars James Mason, Joyce Howard; features Tom Walls, Phyllis Stanley, David Farrar, Karel Stepanek. Directed by Karel Lamac. Screenplay by Anatole de Grunwald and Miles Malleson from story by Anthony Gilbert; camera, Otto Heller; editor, Terrence Fisher; dialog direction, Basil Sydney; song, Moira Heath, Ben Frankel. Previewed in N.Y., May 22, '45. Running time, 96 MINS.

Commander Heritage..............James Mason
Laura Verity.......................Joyce Howard
Christopher Child.....................Tom Walls
Lily Bernard......................Phyllis Stanley
Mansel.............................Edward Rigby
Carter...............................Ronald Ward
Commander Lippinscott..............David Farrar
Riccardo..........................Karel Stepanek
Fay....................................Betty Warren
Charlie...........................Walter Crisham
Pawnbroker.......................George Robey
Bobby................................Peggy Dexter
Max...............................Ronald Chesney
Merchant Captain....................Finlay Currie
Inspector Burrows...................Brefni O'Rorke
Lady with Dog...................Jeanne De Casalis
Mary, Manicurist........................Pat Medina
Benson, Illusionist......................Eric Mason
Van Driver..........................Herbert Lomas
Pub Owner...........................Charles Victor
Petty Officer Grant................Robert Sansom
Beothby, Radio Announcer..............Alvar Lidell

This meller of wartime England is British screen intrigue at its best. Despite an all-British cast, little known to U. S. audiences, "They Met in the Dark" is palatable fare for most American audiences. It needs selling by the average exhib. and will find its top income on twin bills, particularly circuit houses. Picture is a surefire pleaser for those who like their melodrama piled on thick and put across in slick manner by a capable cast and via superb production.

Producer Marcel Hellman and director Karel Lamac have taken a not-too-novel story of enemy agents thefting British admiralty sailing orders and punched it up into exciting spy-sleuth action. Yarn spots James Mason as the British naval officer who's bilked by the spy ring, and dismissed from the service when ships are sunk because of leak on sailing dates. He decides to unravel the mystery and break up the Nazi spy ring.

His venture takes him into the odd hideout of the gang—a nightclub and an adjoining dancing school for sailors. It also brings Joyce Howard, new arrival from Canada to join the British WRENS, into his life, as she accidentally stumbles onto the ring's latest femme victim. There's a hypnotist who strangles his victims when he gets the needed info from them, a magico, and a theatrical booker, who uses his agency as a blind for spy operations. There's the inevitable pay-off without a single war scene as Mason finally rounds up spies.

Director Lamac has kept his suspense at high pitch without letting the numerous characters clutter up the main theme.

James Mason, a cross between Clark Gable and John Garfield, plays the dishonored commander to the hilt although the audience suspects all along that British navy headquarters "breaks" him to help catch the spies. Joyce Howard appears a find as the frightened Canadian femme who becomes involved in the spy chase. Phyllis Stanley, a nightclub singer on the other side, is cast as the nitery warbler, doing the lone song, "Toddle Along," with polish although tune is far from smash.

Tom Walls, as the heavy, portrays the spy gang leader, but Karel Stepanek, as his gunman, steals the villain laurels. David Farrar, Pat Medina, Edward Rigby and Ronald Ward head the strong supporting cast of English players, all strangers to American audiences.

The Anatole de Grunwald-Miles Malleson screenplay is a skillful adaptation of Anthony Gilbert's story. Camera job by Otto Heller is topnotch. While Terrence Fisher's editing probably fits British theatre needs, part of earlier footage could be trimmed for American houses and make for a tighter film. *Wear.*

A Place of One's Own

(BRITISH-MADE)

London, May 5.

Eagle-Lion release of Gainsborough picture. Stars Margaret Lockwood, Barbara Mullen, James Mason. Directed by Bernard Knowles. Adapted by Brock Williams from story by Sir Osbert Sitwell. At Plaza, London, May, 4, Running time, 97 MINS.

Annette	Margaret Lockwood
Mr. Smedhurst	James Mason
Mrs. Smedhurst	Barbara Mullen
Dr. Selbie	Dennis Price
Mrs. Manning Tuthorn	Helen Haye
Major Manning Tuthorn	Michael Shepley
Sarah	Dulcie Gray

For lovers of the occult, this will prove interesting entertainment; others probably will scoff tolerantly. Eerie story from the pen of Osbert Sitwell of a house haunted by the spirit of a young girl, who takes possession of the body of another and almost causes a repetition of her own tragic end. Despite Margaret Lockwood's presence in cast, it looks mild for U.S. market.

James Mason is splendid as a retired tradesman, who buys an old mansion, empty for 40 years, ignorant of its sinister reputation. His wife, nicely portrayed by Barbara Mullen, engages a girl as companion who soon becomes betrothed to a local doctor. She is apparently psychic and the personality of the unquiet spirit gradually invades her being until she is at death's door. And she is only saved by the visitation from another guest of the other world. Margaret Lockwood does her best with a difficult role. Support is excellent.

Production is all that could be desired, but doubtful if film will enjoy popular appeal. *Clem.*

Miniature Reviews

"Nob Hill" (20th). (Color; Musical). Production lavishness doesn't overcome lightweight, familiar story. Moderate b.o.

"Back to Bataan" (RKO). Solid war drama paying tribute to Filipinos. Sturdy commercially.

"Twice Blessed" (M-G). Lightweight "B."

"Blonde Ransom" (Songs) (U). Well-paced piece based on trite tale but resulting in acceptable product for some houses.

"China Sky" (RKO). Mild version of Pearl Buck's novel; ditto boxoffice.

"I Live in Grosvenor Square" (Brit.). Timely British-made story of U.S. troops in wartime London; okay for U.S.

"We Accuse" (Indie). Atrocity documentary showing Nazi's brutal treatment of Russians; mild for most spots.

"Det Brinner En Eld" ("There Burns a Fire") (Swedish). Fine, stirring invasion story. English sub-titles.

"They Were Sisters" (GFD). Fine British-made version of Dorothy Whipple's book looks dubious U.S. boxoffice.

Nob Hill

(COLOR; SONGS)

Hollywood, May 29.

20th-Fox release of Andre Daven production. Stars George Raft, Joan Bennett, Vivian Blaine, Peggy Ann Garner; features Alan Reed, B. S. Pully, Emil Coleman, Edgar Barrier. Directed by Henry Hathaway. Screenplay, Wanda Tuchock and Norman Reilly Raine from story by Eleanore Griffin; camera, Edward Cronjager; songs, Jimmy McHugh and Harold Adamson; dances, Nick Castle; incidental music, David Buttolph; arrangements, Gene Rose; editor, Harmon Jones. Tradeshown May 24, '45. Running time, 95 MINS.

Tony Angel	George Raft
Harriet Carruthers	Joan Bennett
Sally Templeton	Vivian Blaine
Katie Flanagan	Peggy Ann Garner
Dapper Jack Harrigan	Alan "Falstaff Openshaw" Reed
Joe	B. S. Pully
At the Piano	Emil Coleman
Lash Carruthers	Edgar Barrier
Specialty	Joe Smith & Charles Dale
Rafferty	George Anderson
Fighting Bartender	Don Costello
Headwaiter	Joseph J. Greene
Cabby	J. Farrell MacDonald
Specialty	The Three Swifts
Big Tim	William Haade
Chinese Servants	Beal Wong, George T. Lee
Jose	Frank McCown
Butler	Robert Greig
Chips Conlon	Charles Cane
Show Girls	Helen O'Hara, Dorothy Ford
Luigi	Nestor Paiva
Housekeeper	Anita Bolster
Ruby	Jane Jones
Swedish Sailors—	Otto Reichow, Hugo Borg, George Blagoi

20th-Fox has lavished considerable production coin on "Nob Hill," dressing it up with musical numbers. Technicolor and other elegant appurtenances. The fascinating San Francisco's colorful history seems to have for fictioneers is evidenced by the frequency with which yarns of the Barbary Coast and birth pains of early Pacific slope society hit the screen. Hence "Nob Hill's" script bears a familiar stamp, despite attempts at new twists.

Three new tunes and three oldies are spotted through the score, and all are presented in music hall style as befits the picture's period. Musical portions have been given the usual 20th-Fox lavishness, and register interest. Plot tells of a Barbary Coast saloon operator (George Raft) with a heart of gold who falls for a Nob Hill society girl (Joan Bennett) while overlooking the qualities of his star entertainer (Vivian Blaine).

The well-worn story groove leads him to fancy a society marriage, he spurned, takes to the bottle to forget, and is finally rescued from despair by Miss Blaine. Peggy Ann Garners' role of a little Irish girl taken in by Raft when she comes to the States looking for her uncle is a tear-jerker which adds something new to the plot. Cast toppers are uniformly good, but can't make any of it believable.

Miss Blaine vocals the McHugh-Adamson tunes, "I Walked In," "I Don't Care" and "Touring San Francisco," as well as the older numbers in the score. She reprises "I Don't Care" twice. Numbers are all easy listening, and the incidental background music by David Buttolph is fine.

Technically, all departments, including photography, music, settings, etc., hit a high standard. *Brog.*

Back to Bataan

RKO release of Robert Fellows production. Stars John Wayne; features Anthony Quinn, Beulah Bondi, Feli Franquelli, Richard Loo, Philip Ahn, J. Alex Havier. Directed by Edward Dmytryk. Screenplay, Ben Barzman and Richard H. Landau; story by Aeneas MacKenzie and William Gordon; camera, Nicholas Masura; special effects, Vernon L. Walker; music, Roy Webb; editor, Marston Fay. Tradeshown at Los Angeles, May 25, '45. Running time, 95 MINS.

Colonel Madden	John Wayne
Captain Bonifacio	Anthony Quinn
Miss Barnes	Beulah Bondi
Dalisay	Fely Franquelli
Major Hasko	Richard Loo
Colonel Kuroki	Philip Ahn
Sgt. Biernesa	J. Alex Havier
Maximo	"Ducky" Louie
Lt. Commander Waite	Lawrence Tierney
General Homma	Leonard Strong
Jackson	Paul Fix
Jap Captain	Abner Biberman
Senor Bello	Vladimir Sokoloff

"Back to Bataan" is a sturdy war film that lends itself to lots of exploitation. It emphasizes deserved tribute to the fighting history of the Filipinos throughout, particularly the part played by native guerrillas in aiding the return of General McArthur to the islands, without overlooking any of the aspects that pay off at the boxoffice.

Events that transpire are based on fact, according to foreword, and clips of several U. S. fighting men released from Jap prison camps with the return of MacArthur's army are used both at beginning and end. Plot spans time from fall of Bataan and Corregidor to the Yank landings on Leyte, and depicts adventures of John Wayne as a colonel leading Filipino patriots in undercover sabotage against the islands' temporary conquerors.

The desperate deeds of men, women and children, fighting against overwhelming odds to hold the people together and harass the Jap, garner big attention as they unfold. Wayne is detailed to organize guerrilla warfare after the fall of Bataan and takes to the jungles to carry on the work. Lacking arms, food and other equipment of war, the little band sustains itself and carries on its objectives despite Jap propaganda and bullets, paving the way for MacArthur's return.

Love interest is given over to Anthony Quinn, portraying the descendant of the Filipino hero, Bonifacio, and Fely Franquelli, Manila contact for the band of heroes who does Nip propaganda broadcasts to get her information out. Quinn does a particularly outstanding job, as does Miss Franquelli. Wayne makes a stalwart leader for the guerrillas, commendably underplaying the role for best results. J. Alex Havier, as a Filipino scout; Beulah Bondi, American school teacher; "Ducky" Louie, Paul Fix, Vladimir Sokoloff, Richard Loo, Philip Ahn, Leonard Strong, Abner Biberman—last four seen as Japs—are among others whose playing is a measurable aid.

Edward Dmytryk's direction is strong on action and maintaining of interest. Photography and special effects are major factors in the production values. *Brog.*

Twice Blessed

Metro release of Arthur L. Field production. Features Preston Foster, Gail Patrick, Lee Wilde, Lyn Wilde. Directed by Harry Beaumont. Screenplay, Ethel Hill; camera, Ray June; editor, Douglas Biggs. Reviewed in projection room, N. Y., May 18, '45. Running time, 76 MINS.

Jeff Turner	Preston Foster
Mary Hale	Gail Patrick
Terry Turner	Lee Wilde
Stephanie Hale	Lyn Wilde
Senator John Pringle	Richard Gaines
Kitty	Jean Porter
Jimmy	Marshall Thompson
Mickey Pringle	Jimmy Lydon
Alice	Gloria Hope

Ethel Smith at the Organ

The Wilde twins have been playing small parts in Metro musicals for the past couple of years but this is their first opportunity to display their straight acting ability. But their effervesence doesn't help this lightweight "B."

Yarn finds the gals, offspring of a divorced couple, cast as twins with directly opposite personalities, Lee as a normal teen-ager, while Lyn has the highest I.Q. in the nation five years running. Each parent has one child, and the kids, looking so much alike, change off from one parent to the other merely by trading clothes. It's not very confusing because the writing of the screenplay keeps the thing clearly defined. Naturally, the twins accomplish their goal of bringing their pop and mom together again.

Preston Foster and Gail Patrick, as the parents, perform their roles in rather stilted fashion. On the other hand, the twins work hard throughout. Jimmy Lydon, in his first role for Metro, briefly but capably plays one of the boyfriends, along with Marshall Thompson.

Why Ethel Smith is in this film is hard to ascertain. She does one number on the organ, a Brazilian samba, "Lero, Lero," localed in the dancehall where the jitterbugs headquarter. It's an incongruous bit. Settings are substantial, but far from outstanding. Direction lacks even pace. *Sten.*

Blonde Ransom

(SONGS)

Universal release of Gene Lewis production. Features Donald Cook, Virginia Grey. Directed by William Beaudine. Screenplay, M. Coates Webster from story by Robert T. Shannon; songs, Jack Brooks, Norman Berens, Al Sherman; music, Frank Skinner; camera, Maury Gertsman. Previewed N.Y., May 29, '45. Running time, 66 MINS.

Duke	Donald Cook
Vicki	Virginia Grey
Pinky	Pinky Lee
Sheba	Collette Lyons
Uncle William	George Barbier
Larson	Jerome Cowan
Forbes	George Meeker
Oliver	Ian Wolfe
Bender	Joe Kirk
McDaily	Charles Delaney
Judge	Frank Reicher
Police Captain	Bill Davidson
Clerk	Chester Clute
Gypsy Dancer	Janina Frostova

Based on a familiar story, this pic nevertheless has good pace, some decent if unexciting singing, and will likely find itself acceptable on bills that don't mind some tinseled mediocrity.

The featured talent, Donald Cook and Virginia Grey, are respectively the owner of a Broadway bistro and niece of a rich, crotchety old fraud with a heart of gold. The boniface is about to lose his joint to a group of gangsters who had taken him for $63,000 with the aid of a phoney deck. When the gal fails to interest the uncle in buying a piece of the nitery, she fakes a kidnapping. Old fellow comes through, the bad boys are trapped, and the wedding at the end is a double feature, including a pair of stooges who had sung and cavorted through the piece. Latter are Pinky Lee, whose "Hinky Dinky Pinky" number is not only screwballish but really funny, and flashy Collette Lyons.

Undistinguished and lightweight production is given direction that moves the trite story along at good tempo, and all the principals acquit themselves as well as the unhefty material demands. *Cars.*

China Sky

RKO release of Maurice Geraghty production. Stars Randolph Scott, Ruth Warrick, Ellen Drew; features Anthony Quinn, Carol Thurston, Richard Loo. Directed by Ray Enright. Screenplay by Brenda Weisberg, Joseph Hoffman; based on novel by Pearl Buck; camera, Nicholas Musuraca; editor, Gene Milford; technical adviser, Wei Fan Hsueh. At Palace, N. Y., starting May 24, '45. Running time, **78 MINS.**

Thompson....................Randolph Scott
Sara....................Ruth Warrick
Louise....................Ellen Drew
Chen Ta....................Anthony Quinn
Siu Mei....................Carol Thurston
Col. Yasuda....................Richard Loo
"Little Goat"....................''Ducky'' Louie
Dr. Kim....................Philip Ahn
Chung....................Benson Fong
Magistrate....................H. T. Tsiang
Charlie....................Chin Kuang Chow

Too much attention paid to the love affairs in "China Sky" and too little to the actionful story from Pearl Buck's book militate against its boxoffice potentialities. Moderate boxoffice indicated.

Miss Buck's tale of the tenacity of Chinese guerrillas who harass the Japanese advance, and the American medico who runs the hospital in the key Chinese village, turns out far from the spectacular production it might have been. The guerrilla and fighting angle is played down, while stress is laid on interior sets and romantic conflict. As often happens, this lack of action wears the interest thin.

Scripters and director are so concerned with the triangle between Randolph Scott, as the American doctor, his devoted hospital coworker, Ruth Warrick, and his wife, Ellen Drew, that they neglect the story's movement. There finally is a bangup battle at the end between Jap paratroopers and the guerrillas as a wounded Jap officer wangles info out to his forces, but it's too late.

Ray Enright's direction is never especially inspired, although he helps bring out several excellent characterizations of Chinese natives. Best of these is by Philip Ahn as the Chinese doctor, who aids the wounded Jap when angered by his fiancee, Carol Thurston. Latter is okay as the native nurse. The role of guerrilla leader, which one might expect to be outstanding, is sluffed off by the story. Anthony Quinn does well by what lines are given him, but, given a better chance, he'd have registered even stronger.

Randolph Scott is routine as the hospital head. Ruth Hussey is superb, but her role of the doctor's assistant is not sufficient to carry the whole load. Ellen Drew makes a satisfactory portrayal of the wife, albeit a distateful one. Richard Loo is villainous enough as the wounded Jap colonel. *Wear.*

I Live in Grosvenor Sq.

(BRITISH-MADE)

London, May 16.

Pathe Pictures release of Associated British Picture. Stars Anna Neagle, Dean Jagger, Rex Harrison, Robert Morley. Directed by Herbert Wilcox. Screenplay, Maurice Cowan. At Palace theatre, London, May 15, '45. Running time, **114 MINS.**

Lady Patricia Fairfax........Anna Neagle
Sergeant John Patterson.......Dean Jagger
Major David Bruce............Rex Harrison
Duke of Exmoor...............Robert Morley
Mrs. Catchpole...............Irene Vanbrugh
Lieut. Lutyens...............Michael Shepley
Mrs. Wilson....................Nancy Price
Vicar....................Walter Hudd
Sgt. Benj. Greenburgh...Pfc. Elliott Arluck
John's Mother....................Jane Darwell

Every G. I. who visited Piccadilly's Rainbow Corner will want to see Grosvenor Square. In fact, every Yank who's ever been in London likely will try to see this. It is the best bet on Anglo-American relations buildup the screen has yet offered. Timely story of U. S. troops in wartime London looks okay for American market, with names of Anna Neagle, Robert Morley and Jane Darwell giving picture a boost. [No U.S. distrib set although director Herb Wilcox, now in N. Y., has mentioned WB.]

Anna Neagle gives her most convincing performance to date. Dean Jagger's love scenes, though a trifle long, were played with the subtlety one would expect in an American sergeant's diffidence towards a duke's grand-daughter. Rex Harrison as the major looks sure to impress American femmes in the service, even though the heroine jilts him.

Story by British newspaperman Maurice Cowan is based on the real-life events—that of the Air Corps crew sacrificing themselves to save inhabitants of an English village.

Of the other players, Jane Darwell gives a lesson in how to play a bit part so it won't be forgotten. Herbert Wilcox's direction is perfect. Even the Rainbow Corner hostesses look like real Rainbow Corner hostesses, and the girls the troops dance with do not look like extras.

An outstanding scene is that of Private Elliott Arluch, as the Brooklyn Sergeant, explaining to the Duke (Robert Morley) the difference between being a Dodger fan and merely a baseball game spectator.

It's to Wilcox's credit that he has screened Maurice Cowan's intelligent story in such a way that it comes through as a vital phase of American life in wartime London. It is paradoxically terrific boxoffice because yarn never tries to be commercial.

We Accuse

Irvin Shapiro production and release. Narration by Everett Sloane from script by John Bright; editor, Joseph Gluck; supervised by Joseph H. Zarovich. Running time, **71 MINS.**

Originally submitted to the Hays office in rough-cut version as "Atrocities," this fails to measure up to its advance bally. "We Accuse" tries too hard, needs pruning—not necessarily of the gruesome scenes, if the production staff wants to repeat—and lacks the continuity of its predecessors in the documentary field. As a feature, even in that classification, this film looks only a mild entry.

Alongside the powerful job done by all five American newsreels in covering the Nazi murder mills and brutal treatment of prisoners recently, this suffers by comparison. And it fails to hammer home its point as the newsreels did.

Main theme is the trial of three German officers and a traitor to Russia at Karkov, which the narrator describes as "one of the cities dominated longest by the enemies." It was here, he further narrates, the Soviets saw the "foulest deeds of the Master Planners." The four are found guilty, condemned to death and hung simultaneously as the climax to the film. Details of this trial, which of necessity require translation from the Russian and German (by the narrator), are prolonged and the most tiresome part of the picture.

It is when action on the battlefield or of the marching Nazi minions are shown that the pace quickens. Some of the battlefront scenes are thrilling although most of them appeared previously in newsreel and Russian-made films, and are marred by murky photography. The whole idea of the master race, brutality of the Nazis and how the marching Germans planned to dominate the world has been done previously in other documentaries and U.S. features. Here it's called the "master plan," with the story development pointing up the enslavement and bestiality of the Nazis as final stages of this proposition.

A seemingly never-ending string of dead bodies, including women and children, in various postures after they have met death by every conceivable means provides the gruesome portion. Constant repetition of the same gruesome scenes at different parts of the picture seem uncalled for, as do the repeat shots of the persons on trial. Nearly 20 minutes could have been trimmed from the production to snap up its entertainment value. No fault can be found with the gruesome scenes, since important to the story. The most judicious scissoring is needed on the dull scenes and repeats of certain battle stuff.

John Bright's script is a bit transparent although it gains strength from constant repeating of the same idea. Everett Sloane's narration is forthright and fits the wordage nicely. Credit is given to Artkino Pictures for scenes of the Karkov trial and the Soviet army included. Apparently, the trial portion of the production originally was made into a picture released in Great Britain.

The picture has no Hays office code seal, and probably won't have until the completed version is passed on. *Wear.*

Det Brinner En Eld

("There Burns a Fire")

(SWEDISH)

Scandia Films release of Svensk Filmindustri production. Stars Victor Seastrom, Inga Tidblad, Lars Hanson. Directed by Gustaf Molander, Story by Karl-Ragnar Gierow. At 48th St. theatre, week May 24, '45. Running time, **100 MINS.**

Theatre Manager..........Victor Seastrom
Harriet....................Inga Tidblad
Col. Lemmering..............Lars Hanson

Gerd Hagman, Lauritz Falk, Tollie Zellman, Erik Faustman, Stig Jarrel, Hugo Bjorne, Georg Funquist, Gabriel Alw.

(In Swedish; English Titles)

"Det Brinner En Eld" ("There Burns a Fire") is a fine, stirring drama of a peaceful country invaded by a bullying foreign power. Swedish-made, and reportedly a big hit at home, it has a universally attractive theme as well as a fine production to be a big draw in the foreign-film houses here. Yet, excellent film that it is, it is also suspect.

Although no names are given or a swastika shown, the invaded country is undoubtedly Norway, and the ruthless invader Germany. The peaceful, idyllic life of a simple northern folk is limned beautifully, and the unannounced attack of the oppressor is shown in its stark brutality. Yet because the film was made during the war, and by a neutral Sweden evidently careful not to rile the diplomatic feelings of an all-powerful neighbor, it hits one bad, dangerous note.

The story centers about a repertory company at the National theatre that is doing a Shakespearean cycle, and a foreign attache who is a warm friend of the group and in love with the leading lady. When invasion comes, the attache takes over the city as commandant and tries to have the theatre continue its activities as a sign of collaboration. The attempt fails, as do other such endeavors, the people resisting, fighting back in hopes of regaining their freedom.

The cast is uniformly good, with Inga Tidblad a poignant figure as the actress, Victor Seastrom a noble figure as the theatre manager, and Lars Hanson in a fine performance as the attache.

The film is persuasive because it is so well played. It has a good deal of quiet charm and appeal, with no false heroics. The contrast between the days of peace and war is effectively set forth. Yet the film has the same failing as the American John Steinbeck's "The Moon Is Down." It paints the commandant as a sympathetic figure, in love with the people and regretful of having been a party to the invasion, a gentleman whose family and military traditions go back 500 years, and who therefore presumably couldn't be at heart a ruthless, traitorous Nazi.

And that's dangerous propaganda these days, when the Nazi military is being corralled left and right, and all claim to be German gentlemen, not Nazis. If that point of view gains strength, the military who planned the wars of the last five centuries will be around for the next one. *Bron.*

They Were Sisters

(BRITISH-MADE)

London, May 18.

General Film Distributors' release of Gainsborough production. Stars Phyllis Calvert, James Mason. Directed by Arthur Crabtree. Adaptation from novel by Dorothy Whipple, by Katherine Strube; screenplay, Roland Pertwee. Camera, Jack Cox. At Gaumont theatre, London, May 17, '45. Running time, **155 MINS.**

Lucy....................Phyllis Calvert
Charlotte....................Dulcie Gray
Vera....................Anne Crawford
Geoffrey....................James Mason
Brian....................Barrie Livesey
Margaret....................Pamela Kellino
Terry....................Hugh Sinclair
William....................Peter Murray Hill
Judith....................Ann Stephens
Stephen....................John Gilpin

An efficient adaptation of Dorothy Whipple's book. Could do with a little judicious cutting, but is well produced. Whether the ultra-English accents will be palatable to U. S. patrons is another story, but its success on this side is undoubted.

Interest centers on the devotion of three sisters in the middle-class midlands. Their marriages, joys and tragedies form the background of the yarn. First to wed is Charlotte, the meekest, who takes on a swaggering show-off who so humiliates her that she takes to drink and is killed by an automobile. This portrayal by Dulcie Gray is picture's tops with no over-dramatics.

Vera, the haughty beauty of the family, reluctantly marries an adoring husband and then acquires a string of lovers. She is convincingly played by Anne Crawford while Phyllis Calvert portrays feelingly the only happy one of the trio, with a comfortable understanding husband.

James Mason is thoroughly at home as the brutish, persecuting husband who is finally denounced by his avenging sister-in-law at the inquest following his wife's death. Pamela Kellino handles skilfully the difficult role of the adolescent daughter who is the only person for whom the father evinces any real affection. Supporting cast is excellent. *Clem.*

Miniature Reviews

"Out of This World" (Musical) (Par). Entertaining musical; should do very well at b.o.

"The Great John L" (Songs) (UA). Boff from start to finish, with Greg McClure as Sullivan an absolute find.

"Within These Walls" (20th). Actionful prison yarn that shapes up as moderately good entertainment; should do okay.

"West of the Pecos" (RKO). Okay western.

"Don Juan Quilligan" (20th). William Bendix-Joan Blondell-Phil Silvers in absurd comedy, unlikely for big boxoffice.

"Penthouse Rhythm" (Songs) (U). Musical melange on a low budget with no names.

"Steppin' In Society" (Rep). E. E. Horton and Gladys George in lightweight comedy.

"Vampire's Ghost" (Rep). A "B" thriller with few thrills.

"Phantom Speaks" (Rep). Fair chiller starring Richard Arlen.

"Phantom of 42nd Street" (PRC). Whodunit with backstage locale geared for moderate grosses.

Out of This World
(MUSICAL)

Paramount release of Sam Coslow production. Stars Eddie Bracken, Veronica Lake, Diana Lynn; features Cass Daley, Parkyakarkus, Donald McBride, Florence Bates, Bing Crosby's Kids, Carmen Cavallaro, Ted Fiorito, Henry King, Ray Noble, Joe Reichman, Don Wilson. Directed by Hal Walker. Based on stories by Elizabeth Meehan and Sam Coslow; adaptation, Walter DeLeon and Arthur Phillips; songs, Johnny Mercer, Harold Arlen, Ben Raleigh, Bernie Wayne, Sam Coslow, Felix Bernard and Eddie Cherkose; dances, Sammy Lee; editor, Stuart Gilmore; camera, Stuart Thompson. Previewed at Paramount, N. Y., June 4, '45. Running time, **96 MINS.**

Herbie Fenton.............Eddie Bracken
Dorothy Dodge.............Veronica Lake
Betty Miller.............Diana Lynn
Fanny, the drummer.............Cass Daley
Gus Palukas.............Parkyakarkus
J. J. Crawford.............Donald MacBride
Harriet Pringle.............Florence Bates
Radio Announcer-M.C.............Don Wilson
Mrs. Robbins.............Mabel Paige
Charlie Briggs.............Charles Smith
Irving Krunk.............Irving Bacon

Bing's kids: Gary Crosby, Phillip Crosby, Dennis Crosby, Lin Crosby.

Glamourette Quartet: Osga San Juan, Nancy Porter, Audrey Young, Carol Deere.

Piano Maestros: Carmen Cavallaro, Ted Fiorito, Henry King, Ray Noble, Joe Reichman.

"Out of This World" is an entertaining musical with a strong cast headed by Eddie Bracken, Veronica Lake and Diana Lynn who are billed above the title. Boxoffice prospects are very promising.

Film is built along novel lines and pulls plenty of laughs. A unique stunt is having Bracken play a croon-swooner, which he isn't, with Bing Crosby's voice dubbed in to fit Bracken's singing lip movements. Crosby isn't seen at any point but his four young boys, Gary, Phillip, Dennis and Lin, appear in a bit shortly after the opening and are responsible for a couple cute cracks when they hear their father's voice coming from Bracken. There are numerous other little scenes and bits which land the laughs and give good pace to the action. Very funny is the sequence in which Miss Lynn and Cass Daley try to keep Bracken from appearing at a benefit show by getting him down with a cold. They partly undress him, steam him in a bathroom and then sit him on a piece of ice.

Action opens in a small town where Miss Lynn, who conducts a girl's band, is putting on a benefit show. Bracken accidentally gets pushed into it and sings a song, being Bing's voice, of course. Arrangements have been made to plant some bobby-soxers in the audience to go all out for Bracken. As result of what occurs, the band and the supposed crooner-killer get a lot of publicity. Miss Lynn takes him over and in order to get back to N. Y. sells shares in him to several persons. However, they make the mistake of selling 125% of shares, a situation which creates plenty of trouble.

Production contains seven song numbers. They are "Out of This World," "June Comes Around Every Year," "A Sailor with an Eight-Hour Pass," "All I Do Is Beat That Goldarn Drum," "I'd Rather Be Me," "Ghost of Mr. Chopin," and "It Takes a Little Bit More." On the whole they listen well but are not particularly outstanding. "Goldarn Drum" is comical, done by Miss Daley, drummer in Miss Lynn's band. She also does "Eight-Hour Pass." "I'd Rather Be Me," which is reprised by Bracken at the finish, looks to be tops among the picture's songs.

A production number toward the finish includes a slick sequence with five leading pianist-bandleaders, Carmen Cavallaro, Ted Fiorito, Henry King, Ray Noble and Joe Reichman, which is nicely staged.

Performances by the three stars of the picture are clickful, while Miss Daley, among the featured players, also registers strongly. Parkyakarkus is a smalltown merchant who has taken shares in Bracken. There isn't enough of him, however. Florence Bates is another Bracken investor. Don Wilson, not named on the screen, is a radio announcer and m. c. Donald McBride stands out sharply as a talent agent.

Sam Coslow, who figures on the story end and on several of the songs, injected good production value into the picture, while Hal Walker's direction is smooth.

Char.

The Great John L.
(SONGS)

United Artists release of Bing Crosby (Frank R. Mastroly and James Edward Grant) production. Stars Linda Darnell, Barbara Britton; introduces Greg McClure; features Otto Kruger, Wallace Ford. Directed by Frank Tuttle. Screenplay by Grant; fight contests staged by John Indrisano; editor, Theodore Bellinger; musical director, Victor Young; songs, Johnny Burke and James Van Heusen; camera, James Van Trees. Previewed N. Y., May 31, '45. Runing time, **96 MINS.**

John L. Sullivan.............Greg McClure
Anne Livinstone.............Linda Darnell
Kathy Harkness.............Barbara Britton
Mickey.............Lee Sullivan
Richard Martin.............Otto Kruger
McManus.............Wallace Ford
John Flood.............George Mathews
Billy Muldoon.............Robert Barrat
Father O'Malley.............J. M. Kerrigan
Monsieur Claire.............Simon Semenoff
Michael Sullivan.............Joel Friedkin
Arthur Brisbane.............Harry Crocker
Maura Sullivan.............Hope Landin

In his first independent production, Bing Crosby comes out with both fists swinging through a dramatization of the life of John L. Sullivan. When the pic is released, it should be a great day all around, for the Irish as well as for the houses that run it. It's straight boff from start to finish.

James Edward Grant has written a story that takes John L. from his early youth as the Boston strong boy, through his great victories here and abroad, into the days of drunken disillusionment, and finally to the mature man, no longer a champ with his fists, who becomes the exponent of clean living. It's a thoroughly credible story which gave the producers an opportunity of recreating the rowdy '80s with all their nostalgic appeal. Through sets that look authentic, dialog in character at all times, songs that flavor of the period, and sock boxing contests, the job has been done well. Result: Everyman's John L. Sullivan, a believable, human and warm character going through a play that's entertaining and at times gripping.

All this, of course, could not have been accomplished without careful casting and directing, especially since the real star of the film is a man who had never done anything in pictures except as an extra on the Warner lot. And that man is a find. His name is Greg McClure. He not only looks the part of the Great John L. He acts the part, and grows with it, even as the subject himself grew, from a boastful youngster who conquers a world and loses it, to the man who regains respect when he finds that he can fight another battle where heart counts for more than muscle. McClure was a day laborer, longshoreman, and a player in a little theatre when Crosby discovered him. He's in the Army now—having gone in as soon as he finished this picture. But he'll never be an unknown again. Crosby has signed him to a term contract and, like John L. himself, McClure should win many more plaudits before he's through.

But if it's McClure who carries the greatest burden, the rest of the cast is right there with him at all times. The two women in his life, played by Linda Darnell and Barbara Britton, are done effectively. J. M. Kerrigan does Sullivan's parish priest sensitively and without lush sentimentality. Lee Sullivan as the champ's boyhood pal and singer, Richard Martin as the suave man of the world who loses his woman to the fighter, George Mathews as the dumb ex-champ who becomes John L.'s sparring partner and friend, and Simon Semenoff as the French *la savotte* expert, add to the general sense of perfection.

There are a number of outstanding scenes that audiences will remember. One is excruciatingly funny. That's when Semenoff (who is a ballet dancer) fights the American pug in a Parisian bistro, using his *la savotte* skill in kicking. It's the first time this feet-fighting has been in a film. Another comes near the end of the picture, when Sullivan suddenly decides to stop drinking. That's when McClure really comes through, as a superb actor.

Cars.

Within These Walls

20th-Fox release of Ben Silvey production. Stars Thomas Mitchell, Mary Anderson, Edward Ryan; features Mark Stevens, B. S. Pully, Roy Roberts, John Russell, Norman Lloyd, Edward Kelly, Harry Shannon. Directed by Bruce Humberstone. Story, Charles Trapnell and James R. Fisher; adaptation, Eugene Ling and Wanda Tuchock; camera, Glen MacWilliams and Clyde De Vinna; editor, Harry Reynolds. Tradeshown N. Y., June 1, '45. Running time, **71 MINS.**

Michael Howland.............Thomas Mitchell
Anne Howland.............Mary Anderson
Tommie Howland.............Edward Ryan
Steve Russel.............Mark Stevens
Harry Bowser.............B. S. Pully
Martin Deutsch.............Roy Roberts
Rogers.............John Russell
Pete Moran.............Norman Lloyd
Tommy Callahan.............Edward Kelly
McCaffrey.............Harry Shannon
Hobey Jenkins.............Rex Williams
Pearson.............Ralph Dunn
Station Agent.............Dick Rush
Collins.............William Halligan
Stunt Guard.............Freddie Graham

Actionful film, ably produced and directed, "Within These Walls" is a prison story that rates as moderately good entertainment in its line and should do satisfactorily at the boxoffice.

Picture is built around Thomas Mitchell, a tough penitentiary warden who lives to regret the stern policies he placed in force, and his two adolescent children, a son and daughter. The story opens on demands by Mitchell, then a judge, for measures to curb riots which have been occurring at the prison of an unnamed state. He's nominated for the job of warden by the govenor and takes over with a vengeance, laying down very stiff rules.

Meantime, as Mitchell plays the part, the warmth of affection which he has for his daughter and a son, latter a ne'er-do-well, is accentuated though his paternal rigidness, on the other hand, finally estranges him from his boy. Finally the son is brought to the prison following conviction of a crime, with the father-warden making no exceptions for him.

Ultimately the lad figures in an attempted jail break and is shot by a fellow convict. This leads to a very tense scene in which the father himself shoots it out with the murderer within the prison walls. This sequence is excellently done and sustained for several minutes.

On the finish the warden softens when a new group of prisoners is brought before him, among them a young chap who reminds him of the son he lost and which taught him to temper discipline with kindness.

Mitchell gives an excellent performance, one that is partly sympathetic and partly not. His son is played effectively by Edward Ryan, while the daughter is Mary Anderson, youthful and refreshing type. She is paired romantically, but not with emphasis, with a model convict who becomes the warden's trusted chauffeur. The daughter has learned that the convict, played well by Mark Stevens, is serving a short term after having taken the rap on an embezzlement charge for his married brother. Tops among the numerous convict characters is Roy Roberts. Harry Shannon does well as assistant warden.

Char.

West of the Pecos

RKO release of Herman Schlom production. Features Robert Mitchum, Barbara Hale, Richard Martin, Thurston Hall, Rita Corday. Directed by Edward Killy. Screenplay, Norman Houston from novel by Zane Grey; camera, Harry J. Wild. Tradeshown N. Y., June 1, '45. Running time, **66 MINS.**

Pecos.............Robert Mitchum
Rill.............Barbara Hale
Chito Rafferty.............Richard Martin
Colonel Lambeth.............Thurston Hall
Suzanne.............Rita Corday
Jeff Slinger.............Russell Hopton
Tex Evans.............Bill Williams
Clyde Morgan.............Bruce Edwards
Brad Sawtelle.............Harry Woods
Sam Sawtelle.............Perc Launders
Dr. Howard.............Bryant Washburn
Marshall.............Philip Morris
Don Manuel.............Martin Garralaga

For fans of the great outdoors who like their Zane Grey without too many fancy frills, this pic is a natural. It's a western that should draw audiences who go for the type.

Story centers about Barbara Hale as the niece of a rich Chicago packer who goes out to his Texas ranch on orders of his doctor. Period is of the wild, lawless days. The party meets up with a quick-shootin', honest cowhand (Robert Mitchum) who rides well and knows how to handle bandits as well as the gal. Latter poses as a boy for a time, with some scenes promising luscious developments, but propriety is maintained. At end, the girl from Chicago had ditched her lawyer-fiance, and is ready to marry the cowboy at the nearest mission church.

Mitchum, with the help of Richard Martin, does the riders of the range proud. Miss Hale plays the rich girl well, and Rita Corday is okay also as the maid who's straight from Paree. Rest of the cast is adequate for the business at hand. Production is none too lavish but good enough, and direction is smooth.

Cars.

Don Juan Quilligan

20th-Fox release of William Le Baron production. Stars William Bendix, Joan Blondell, Phil Silvers. Directed by Frank Tuttle. Screenplay, Arthur Kober and Frank Gabrielson, from original by Herbert Clyde Lewis; editor, Norman Colbert; camera, Norbert Brodine; music, Emil Newman. Tradeshown N. Y., June 1, '45. Running time, **75 MINS.**

Patrick Quilligan.............William Bendix
Marjorie Mossrock.............Joan Blondell
Mac Denny.............Phil Silvers
Mrs. Rostigaff.............Anne Revere

Ed Mossrock	B. S. Pully
Lucy	Mary Treen
Howie Mossrock	John Russell
Beattle	Veda Ann Borg
Judge	Thurston Hall
Sales Girl	Cara Williams
Defense Attorney	Richard Gaines
Mr. Rostigaff	Hobart Cavanaugh
Annie Mossrock	Rene Carson
District Attorney	George Macready
Mrs. Blake	Helen Freeman
Artie Mossrock	Charles Cane
One-Eyed Fagan	Anthony Caruso
Customer	Eddie Acuff
Judge	Joel Friedkin
Court Clerk	Charles Marsh
Minister	Emmett Vogan
Police Sergeant	James Flavin
Usher	John Albright
Police Inspector	Charles D. Brown
Police Stenographer	Lee Phelps
Bartender	Tom Dugan
C.P.O	Carey Harrison
Doager	Genevieve Bell
Clerk, Marriage Bureau	Jimmy Conlin

Despite William Bendix, Joan Blondell and Phil Silvers for the marquee, "Don Juan Quilligan" is no boxoffice sock. It's a familiar yarn punctuated with the usual Bendix malaprops, Flatbush variety.

Bendix plays a Brooklyn barge captain with a mother complex, though she's been dead for 10 years. Seemingly everything he does is governed by the omniscient spirit of the old gal. He even marries bigamously because of it—one because she laughs like his mother; the second because she cooks as well. And the circumstances surrounding the marriages, including a gangland murder for which he almost takes the rap, reach so far afield that there's bound to be little audience restraint left when the courtroom finale comes.

Bendix is Bendix. As the title character, he's a deadpan dumb type with an inordinate capacity for committing lingual homicide. Miss Blondell is outstanding, physically; her dialog is unimportant, relatively. Most of the remainder of the cast is there for atmospheric purposes.

Arthur Kober, an invariably facile writer at this sort of dialog, and Frank Gabrielson are credited with the screenplay, from an original by Herbert Clyde Lewis. William Le Baron produced on what seems like a modest budget. There's little that Frank Tuttle could have done with the direction.

Brooklyn—and a certain tree—will have trouble living this one down.

Kahn.

Penthouse Rhythm
(SONGS)

Universal release of Frank Gross production. Features Kirby Grant, Lois Collier, Edward Norris. Directed by Eddie Cline. Screenplay, Stanley Roberts, Howard Dimsdale from story by Roberts and Min Selvin. Musical director, Edgar Fairchild; camera, William Sickner; editor, Russell Schoengarth. Tradeshown N. Y., June 4, '45. Running time, 60 MINS.

Dick	Kirby Grant
Linda	Lois Collier
Junior	Edward Norris
Maxie Rosenbloom	Maxie Rosenbloom
Ferdy Pelham	Eric Blore
Taffy	Minna Gombel
Bailey	Edward S. Brophy
Patty	Judy Clark
Irma	Marion Martin
Brewster	Donald McBride
Joe	Henry Armetta
Jack	Jimmy Dodd
Johnny	Bobby Worth
Bill	Louis Da Pron
Nick	George Lloyd
Sergeant	Paul Hurst
Tim	Harry Barris
Dance Specialty	Velasco and Lenee

Universal apparently has had success with the fluffy-type quickie musical fare and this one is in that category.

Story-line is not especially weighty; cast goes through its paces tongue-in-cheek; songs are just fair, and the whole picture is thrown together in an off-hand sort of way.

Yarn deals with the troubles four youngsters of a musical quartet have getting started in show biz. The way they finally reach their goal tests the credulity of the audience, since it is strictly the script writer's idea of how to become a hit.

None of the songs rate listing, three composed by Jack Brooks and Norman Berens; one, Berens teamed with Seymour Kramer, and other by Inez James and Sidney Miller. Acting and vocalizing by those in the cast showcases couple of good voices, notably Kirby Grant and Judy Clark, latter a lightweight edition of Betty Hutton. Remainder of the rather lengthy list of supporting actors do their best to liven up the proceedings, but fail in most cases because of material.

Sten.

Steppin' in Society

Republic release of Joseph Bercholtz production. Features Edward Everett Horton, Gladys George. Directed by Alexander Esway. Screenplay, Bradford Ropes, from novel by Marcel Arnac; editor, Harry Keller; camera, Reggie Lanning. At Fox, Brooklyn, N.Y., week of June 1, '45, dual. Running time, 72 MINS.

Judge Avery Webster	E.E. Horton
Penelope Webster	Gladys George
Lola Forrest	Ruth Terry
Montana	Robert Livingston
Bow Tie	Jack LaRue
The Duchess	Lola Lane
Jenny the Juke	Isabel Jewell
George	Frank Jenks
Cookie	Paul Hurst
Ivory	Harry Barris
Shirley	Iris Adrian
Hilliard	Tom Herbert

Idea of a jurist, who had a rep for throwing the book at malefactors appearing before him, being forced to take refuge in a questionable roadhouse run by and infested with lawless characters, may have presented possibilities on paper. Somehow it got lost in the shuffle. Result is lightweight comedy that will have to depend upon marquee draw of Edward Everett Horton and Gladys George, co-featured, to snare 'em.

"Steppin' in Society" has its moments but unfortunately does not sustain a rollicking pace throughout. Story sags and laughs are too widely spaced. Horton and his frau, Miss George, seek refuge in the Jungle Club after being caught in a storm. Underworld characters therein are leery of the strangers but one of the mob pegs the judge for a racketeer and he plays along with them. Everything's jake until a gunmoll (Isabel Jewell) cases him as the judge who ruined her love life by retiring her boy friend in durance vile for a long stretch. He is subjected to a "Kangaroo Court" trial in which he not only outsmarts the wise guys and gals but has them all converted to the straight and narrow at the fadeout.

Horton gives his usual good performance as the judge. Miss George is splendid as his wife. Miss Jewell is also standout as the jail-widow. Remainder of cast do okay in respective roles. Direction by Alexander Esway is as well as can be expected with material at hand.

Edba.

The Vampire's Ghost

Republic release of Rudolph E. Abel production. Features John Abbott, Charles Gordon, Peggy Stewart, Grant Withers. Directed by Lesley Selander. Screenplay, John K. Butler, Leigh Brackett from original story by Brackett; camera, Bud Thackery, Robert Pittack; editor, Tony Martinelli. At Brooklyn Strand, week of May 31, '45, dual. Running time, 59 MINS.

Webb Fallon	John Abbott
Roy Hendrick	Charles Gordon
Julie Vance	Peggy Stewart
Father Gilchrist	Grant Withers
Lisa	Adele Mara
Thomas Vance	Emmett Vogan
Jim Barrat	Roy Barcroft
Simon Peter	Martin Wilkins
The Doctor	Frank Jaquet
The Bum	Jimmy Aubrey

Republic endeavored to wrap this one up as economically as possible, and encase within the 59 minutes running time enough thrills to give the picture some semblance of respectability.

Whether associate producer Rudolph E. Abel succeeded is another matter entirely. Yarn deals with a vampire who rules the underworld of a plantation town on the west coast of Africa. He overpowers a plantation owner, who finally is saved through the reasoning power of a priest, in time to rescue the damsel from the clutches of the dastard.

John Abbott, as the vampire, along with Charles Gordon, Grant Withers and Peggy Stewart, go through their paces in stilted fashion. Script, settings and camerawork just so-so.

Sten.

The Phantom Speaks

Republic release of Donald H. Brown production. Stars Richard Arlen; features Stanley Ridges, Lynne Roberts, Tom Powers. Directed by John English. Original, John K. Butler; camera, Willaim Bradford; editor, Arthur Roberts. At Brooklyn Strand, week of May 31, '45, dual. Running time, 58 MINS.

Matt Fraser	Richard Allen
Dr. Paul Renwick	Stanley Ridges
Joan Renwick	Lynne Roberts
Harvey Bogardus	Tom Powers
Cornelia Willmont	Charlotte Wynters
Owen McAllister	Jonathan Hale
Charlie Davis	Pierre Watkin
Betty Hanzel	Marian Martin
Louis Fabian	Garry Owen
Frankie Teel	Ralf Harolde
Mary Fabian	Doreen McCann

This one is a spine-tingling sadistic chiller that has its odd moments, and on the whole does not test the credulity of the audience. With Richard Arlen as star, it will please those who enjoy this type film fare.

Arlen, as a reporter who outguesses the police throughout, aids in adding to the suspense of the proceedings. Phantom, played by Tom Powers, proves to be a convicted murderer who returns to the earth after dying and imposes his will on a scientist, latter carrying out the former's dastardly slaughters without realizing it.

Entire cast which, besides Arlen and Powers, includes Stanley Ridges and Lynne Roberts in the major roles, enact their parts in fairly good fashion. Settings and camerawork, too, are above par.

Sten.

Phantom of 42nd Street

PRC release of Martin Mooney and Albert Herman production, directed by Herman. Features Dave O'Brien, Kay Aldridge, Alan Mowbray, Frank Jenks. Screenplay, Milton Raison, from story by Jack Harvey and Raison; editor, Hugh Winn; camera, James Brown. At New York, N.Y., week of May 29, '45. dual. Running time, 58 MINS.

Tony Woolrich	Dave O'Brien
Claudia Moore	Kay Eldridge
Cecil Moore	Alan Mowbray
Romeo	Frank Jenks
Janet Buchanan	Edythe Elliott
Lt. Walsh	Jack Mulhall
Ginger	Vera Marshe
Reggie Thomas	Stanley Price
John Carraby	John Crawford
Roberts	Cyril Delevanti
Timothy Wells	Paul Power

Likeable whodunit woven around the theatre and members of "the royal family of that era" looks geared for moderate grosses in the duals. Although theme is somewhat old-hat, it zips along at a merry pace that arrests attention from outset and sustains it throughout.

Kay Aldridge is making her Broadway debut in a new play. Preem is snafued by murder of her wealthy uncle backstage. Alan Mowbray, the actress' father, is suspected. Although starring in a current hit, he's known to be short of coin. Being next of kin he'll naturally inherit his brother's estate.

Dave O'Brien, drama critic, muffs the murder yarn for his sheet, but later teams with Jack Mulhall, head of the homicide squad, to crack the case. This and two other murders are pinned on Mowbray's dresser.

O'Brien gives neat portrayal of the critic turned gumshoe. Miss Aldridge lends both personal charm and talent as the young actress, with Mowbray, Mulhall and Frank Jenks also turning in neat accounts. Latter, as a stage-struck taxi-jockey, sustains the comedy element of the yarn. Milton Raison has contributed compact script which Albert Herman has directed in proper tempo.

Edba.

Miniature Reviews

"Incendiary Blonde" (Par). (Musical; color)—Life of Texas Guinan. OK b.o.

"Junior Miss" (20th). Rollicking comedy, following legit version faithfully. Boff b.o.

"Conflict" (WB). Meldodrama with Bogart again in role of heavy. Strong b.o.

"Along Came Jones" (RKO-Int'l). Gary Cooper-produced and starred (with Loretta Young) western; moderate b.o.

"A Thousand and One Nights" (Color) (Songs) (Col). Brisk, comedy adventure for strong boxoffice.

"One Exciting Night" (Par). OK comedy whodunit.

"Bedside Manner" (UA). John Carroll, Ruth Hussey, Chas. Ruggles, Ann Rutherford, in well-done frothy comedy; okay b.o.

"Jungle Captive" (U). A real chiller for adults only.

"Ten Cents a Dance" (Songs) (Col). Lightweight but diverting comedy should bring moderate returns.

"The Frozen Ghost" (U). Another in the Inner Sanctum series starring Lon Chaney; fair whodunit.

Incendiary Blonde

Hollywood, June 1.

Paramount release of Joseph Sistrom production. Stars Betty Hutton, Arturo de Cordova; features Charlie Ruggles, Barry Fitzgerald. Director, George Marshall. Screenplay, Claude Binyon and Frank Butler; camera, Ray Rennahan; editor, Archie Marshek; music, Robert Emmett Dolan; vocal arrangement, Joseph J. Lilloy; music associate, Troy Sanders; dances, Danny Dare. Tradeshown Hollywood, June 1, '45. Running time, 113 MINS.

Texas Guinan	Betty Hutton
Bill Kolgannon	Arturo de Cordova
Cherokee Jim	Charlie Ruggles
Cadden	Albert Dekker
Mike Guinan	Barry Fitzgerald
Bessie Guinan	Mary Phillips
Tim Callahan	Bill Goodwin
Nick, the Greek	Edward Ciannelli
The Maxelles	Themselves
Maurice Rocco	Himself

"Incendiary Blonde" is sound musical drama based on the life of Broadway's Texas Guinan. Colorful incidents in the "hello sucker" girl's career lend themselves to film treatment, and added value of Technicolor, music and marquee strength indicate healthy business in all situations.

Screen story is packed with so much color, music, comedy and drama that its foundation in tragedy never becomes heavy. Script picks up the Guinan career in Texas in 1909 when she first joins a wild west show to aid her financially busted father. It carries her through to success in that field, on to Broadway musicals, to Hollywood and early-day western films and finally back to New York night clubs and death at the peak of success. Picture uses the flashback device to get started and wisely knows when to come to a conclusion.

Production injects considerable spectacle into the early wild west show sequences but allows too much footage to be spent in the telling, giving picture a slower start than necessary. Her switch to Broadway musicals to escape an unhappy love affair and then desertion of the White Way for Hollywood films to resume the affair are spanned more quickly. When misunderstandings again chill love, she returns to Broadway and launches her night club career. The part racketeering and kindred Prohibition ailments of the nation played in her life are all shown and these give dramatic wallop and tenseness to the concluding portions of the story.

Through it all run nostalgic tunes

and verve of the era pictured, with Betty Hutton extending herself in song to sell the musical spots. Her success in handling of the dramatic portions is equally potent and entrenches her firmly as an actress of ability. Arturo de Cordova plays opposite as the wild west operator, gangster and love of Miss Guinan's life, and registers solidly through-out.

Barry Fitzgerald throws his ability into portrayal of Miss Guinan's Irish father, a dreamer of fantastic financial schemes. Bill Goodwin is effective as Tim Callahan, the man who launched her Broadway career and served briefly as her husband. Charlie Ruggles, Albert Dekker, Mary Phillips and Edward Ciannelli all figure importantly in furthering the script by Claude Binyon and Frank Butler.

George Marshall's direction does a creditable job of welding the wealth of material together, in staging the outdoor spectacles and the musical production numbers in the Joseph Sistro production. A highgear laugh sequence is Miss Hutton's workout with the acrobatic Maxellos. Equally on the entertainment side is the spot given over to Maurice Rocco and his piano.

Whether or not film license has been taken with Miss Guinan's career will not matter to the majority of audiences viewing this one. Story has all the essentials for screen entertainment, whether fictionized or not. *Brog.*

Junior Miss

20th Century-Fox release of William Perlberg production. Stars Peggy Ann Garner; features Allyn Joslyn, Michael Dunne, Faye Marlowe, Mona Freeman, Sylvia Field, Stanley Prager, John Alexander. Directed by Geroge Seaton. Screenplay by Seaton from stage play by Jerome Chodorov and Joseph Fields based upon the stories by Sally Benson and produced upon the stage by Max Gordon; editor, Robert Simpson; camera, Charles Clarke. Previewed N.Y., June 8, '45. Running time, 94 MINS.

Judy Graves .... Peggy Ann Garner
Harry Graves .... Allyn Joslyn
Uncle Willis .... Michael Dunne
Ellen Curtis .... Faye Marlowe
Lois .... Mona Freeman
Grace Graves .... Sylvia Field
Fuffy .... Barbara Whiting
Joe .... Stanley Prager
J.B. Curtis .... John Alexander
Hilda .... Connie Gilchrist
Haskell Cummings, Jr. .... Scotty Beckett
Haskell Cummings, Sr. .... Alan Edwards
Mrs. Cummings .... Dorothy Christy
Merrill Feuerbach .... William Frambes
Donald Parker .... Ray Klinge
Tommy Arbuckle .... Mickey Titus
Albert Kunody .... Eddy Hudson
Sterling Brown .... Mel Torme
Maid .... Lillian Bronson
Sign Painter .... Tommy Mack
Barlow Adams .... William Henderson
Doctor .... Howard Negley
Saleslady .... Ruth Rickaby
Rheba .... Ruby Dandridge

"Junior Miss," that rollicking comedy of juve effects upon family life and woes, comes ingratiatingly to the screen with all the freshness of a moppet on her first date. Despite the fact that it was 'way back in November, 1941, that the legit version preemed on Broadway, the piece is as fetching now as it ever was. The fact that the story line was thin then is still true now. But there is over an hour and a half of good, healthy fun in the film version, sock production and top acting, and picture-goers will worry no more about the absence of genuine plot than did the audiences who flocked to this success in N. Y. and on tour. It's boff stuff.

Except for the wider range of the camera which can get off the set that limited the stage version, "Miss" sticks to the play faithfully. The same set of animated young maniacs that made life at times miserable but never uninteresting for their parents, and friends go through the same capers on the screen as in the original play.

George Seaton was sensible in not trying to improve upon a good thing when he did the screenplay, and he showed further competence in his direction. The production never yields to the temptation of gilding the lily, leaving a close approximation of the stage play's apartment setting as the mainstay among the scenes. The cast was chosen for its appropriateness to the action involved, and Seaton knew just how to put them through their paces most effectively.

Peggy Ann Garner as the amiable, imaginative 13-year-old bane of the Graves family's existence, is tops in her part, and her maniadversions are capably supported by that other moppet, Fuffy, played by Barbara Whiting. Allyn Joslyn as the harassed father, Sylvia Field as his wife, John Alexander as the humorless ham who's Joslyn's boss, and Faye Marlowe as the latter's daughter who disproves the Dorothy Parker maxim about gals who wear glasses, carry their roles with sufficient authority and skill. Michael Dunne is okay as Uncle Willis whose absence from the family fold fires young Judy Graves' imagination. Mona Freeman does the part of the family's senior daughter with good taste for the subtleties of her role. And the parade of Mona's swains is as funny—and no more—in the film version as it was on the stage.

Some of the scenes, such as the one involving the junior's acquisition of her first real fur-collar coat and high heels, don't come off too well, but will probably please the audiences who'll recall the touching equivalents from the stage version with something akin to nostalgia. One bit which was gratuitous on the stage—about the pompous young man who exhibits his new cigaret case and lighter—is just as superfluous now. But even these facts point up the screen's faithfulness to a play that's become part of American urban humor. The film is a splendid job all around. *Cars.*

Conflict

Hollywood, June 9.

Warners release of William Jacobs production. Stars Humphrey Bogart, Alexis Smith; features Sydney Greenstreet, Rose Hobart, Charles Drake, Grant Mitchell, Pat O'Moore, Ann Shoemaker. Director, Curtis Bernhardt. Screenplay, Arthur T. Horman and Dwight Taylor; original, Robert Siodmak and Alfred Neumann; camera, Merritt Gerstad; editor, David Weisbart; music, Frederick Hollander. Tradeshown June 8, '45. Running time, 85 MINS.

Richard Mason .... Humphrey Bogart
Evelyn Turner .... Alexis Smith
Dr. Mark Hamilton .... Sydney Greenstreet
Kathryn Mason .... Rose Hobart
Prof. Norman Holdsworth .... Charles Drake
Dr. Grant .... Grant Mitchell
Det. Lieut. Egan .... Pat O'Moore
Nora Grant .... Ann Shoemaker
Robert Freston .... Frank Wilcox
Phillips .... Ed Stanley
Det. Lieut. Workman .... James Flavin
Mrs. Allman .... Mary Servoss

"Conflict" is a convincing study of a murderer driven to revealing his crime by psychological trickery. Melodrama addicts will find it to their liking and the Humphrey Bogart drawing power assures sturdy business in all situations. A tight mood is sustained by direction and playing, holding interest in the events despite some obviousness in the eventual outcome of the plot.

Bogart, married to Rose Hobart, is in love with her younger sister, Alexis Smith. When his wife, aware of misplaced affection, begins to nag, Bogart plots her murder and nearly accomplishes the perfect crime. He hides her body and car on a lonely mountain road and establishes an airtight alibi. Sydney Greenstreet, psychiatrist and family friend, spots Bogart's only error in describing his wife's appearance as he last saw her.

A series of incidents, all aimed at making Bogart believe his wife is alive, slowly drive him to desperation and eventually he returns to the scene of his crime to convince himself that she is really dead. He finds Greenstreet and the police waiting and goes off to jail.

Bogart's return to a heavy role after more romantic assignments makes a good change of pace and he gives it a convincing reading. Miss Smith also lends interest to the sister role, a girl who is attracted by Bogart's court but holds back due to family loyalty. Greenstreet is creditably restrained in his assignment and Miss Hobart does well by her part.

Studied effect of Curtis Bernhardt's direction and the production backing by William Jacobs build and hold the suspenseful mood. Background music, photography and settings also play an important part in shaping the melodramatic events, although photography, costumes and hairdressing for Miss Smith make her somewhat less than the glamour girl type she has heretofore appeared to be. *Brog.*

Along Came Jones

RKO release of International (Gary Cooper) production. Stars Cooper and Loretta Young; features William Demerest and Dan Duryea. Directed by Stuart Heisler. Screenplay, Nunnally Johnson, from original by Alan Le May; editor, Thomas Neff; camera, Milton Krasner; music score, Arthur Lange. Previewed N.Y., June 9, '45. Running time, 90 MINS.

Melody Jones .... Gary Cooper
Cherry De Longpre .... Loretta Young
George Fury .... William Demarest
Monte Jarrad .... Dan Duryea
Cherry's Brother .... Frank Sully
Her Father .... Russell Simpson
Sheriff .... Arhtur Loft
Luke Packard .... Willard Robertson
Gledhill .... Don Costello
Ira Waggoner .... Ray Teal

For his first independent production, Gary Cooper has, in "Along Came Jones," turned out a better-than-average western that should do moderately good biz. Cooper is not only the producer but also the star, along with Loretta Young.

Without Cooper and Miss Young "Jones" would be just another horse opera, despite the production credits, Nunnally Johnson for the screenplay from an original story by Alan Le May. It should draw the action fans.

Cooper plays a mild-mannered cowpoke who drifts into a small town with his sidekick (William Demarest), thus precipitating a situation in which he's mistaken for a notorious road agent because of a similarity in physique and circumstantial evidence. Cooper, actually, can't even handle a gun, but the inevitable result finds him the unwitting and indirect cause of the hold-upman's slaying. And, of course, he gets the latter's girl (Miss Young), who, incidentally, is forced to make a quick decision and actually drills the gunman right between the eyes just as Cooper is himself about to be polished off by the former.

Cooper plays his usually languid self impressively, while Miss Young is decorative and photographed well. Demarest is in for some comedy relief, of which there is too little, while Dan Duryea is properly menacing as the killer. Rest of the cast to a considerable extent has been recruited from Hollywood's western stock companies. *Kahn.*

Thousand and One Nights

(COLOR; SONGS)

Columbia release of Samuel Bischoff production. Features Phil Silvers, Adele Jergens, Evelyn Keyes, Cornel Wilde. Directed by Alfred E. Green. Screenplay, Wilfrid H. Pettitt, Richard English and Jack Henley from Pettitt's original; camera, Ray Rennahan; editor, Gene Havlick; process photography, Ray Cory; Music, Martin Skiles. Previewed N.Y., June 11, '45. Running time, 92 MINS.

Aladin .... Cornel Wilde
The Genie .... Evelyn Keyes
Abdullah .... Phil Silvers
Princess Armina .... Adele Jergens
Novira .... Dusty Anderson
Sultan Kamar Al-Kir
Prince Hadji .... Dennis Hoey
Grand Wazir Abu-Hassan .... Philip Van Zandt
Jafar .... Gus Schilling
Kahim .... Nestor Paiva
Giant .... Rex Ingram
Kofir, the Sorcerer .... Richard Hale
Ali, the Tailor .... John Abbott
Camel Driver .... Murray Leonard
Handmaiden .... Carole Mathews
Handmaiden .... Pat Parrish
Handmaiden .... Shelley Winter

"A Thousand and One Nights" is solid amusement. It possesses the color, witticisms and action to make 92 minutes of fascinating fare. The producers have a valuable property that will satisfy all types of audiences, not only the juveniles. Picture's measure of boxoffice success, whether it does okay or strong to smash business, will depend largely on how well it is sold.

Featured are Phil Silvers, Adele Jergens, Evelyn Keyes and Cornel Wilde, who will make most of the public know that this is not just another sumptuous Arabian nights adventure. Actully, it's a streamlined fantasy of old Arabia with some likely to scream at the liberties taken, especially when Phil Silvers swings into action. Often it's played with tongue-in-cheek attitude.

Basically, this is the story of Aladdin, the love crooner of his day some 1,000 years ago, and his daring quest for the hand of the untochable princess. Scripters have pictured Cornel Wilde, as Aladdin, winning the princess' (Adele Jergens) heart but getting the heave-ho from the palace guards. It takes an accidental encounter with a hermit's yen for the Aladdin lamp to set Wilde back into the palace. Yarn goes far afield as it shows the faithful Genie as the curvaceous, red-haired Evelyn Keyes, who falls for Aladdin and thwarts the marriage.

Novel twists, bright dialog and modern slants help throughout. Phil Silvers, for example, seldom lapses into ancient verbiage. When slowed up in his itchy fingers work, he tosses a mean pair of ivories to accomplish the same results. Silvers' kibitzing on a gim-rummy game is terrific. Payoff to his long string of humorous moments is when the Genie gives him a break and switches him into a crooner to the delight of the screeching harem femmes.

Excellent color has been helped by the all-round production given by Samuel Bischoff. Alfred E. Green's direction always is smart, nicely paced and never dull. The script is keen. *Wear.*

One Exciting Night

Hollywood, June 1.

Paramount release of Pine-Thomas (maxwell Shane) production. Stars William Gargan and Ann Savage; features Leo Gorcey, George Zucco, Paul Hurst. Director, William C. Thomas. Original, David Lang; camera, Fred Jackman, Jr.; editor, Henry Adams. Tradeshown Hollywood, June 1, '45. Running time, 63 MINS.

Pete Willis .... William Gargan
Sue Gallagher .... Ann Savage
Clutch .... Leo Gorcey
Max Hurley .... Don Beddoe
Murphy .... Paul Hurst
Miggs .... Charles Halton
Jelke .... George Zucco
Cop .... Robert Barron
Joe Wells .... George E. Stone

This is another comedy-mystery entry from the Pine-Thomas stable that will prove okay on the dual bills. It deals out plenty of suspense and comedy for light amusement and is suitably mounted for the market.

Plot's antics are laid against a background of a wax museum and concerns the corpse of a gangster which continually plays hide-and-go-seek. William Gargan and Ann Savage, as rival reporters, do most of the juggling in their efforts to keep an exclusive on the story of the killing. The murderer, George Zucco, is also hot after the corpse, which he wants to disappear permanently so his crime and theft of a fortune in jewels won't be revealed. Between the three, there's little rest for George E. Stone as the stiff. Lighter moments in the yarn concern the characters played by Charles Halton, harassed operator of the wax museum, and his first assistant, Leo Gorcey.

Bill Thomas, co-producer with Bill Pine, tries his hand at directing and does okay for a starter. He mixes in considerable suspense, in the best whodunit manner, and handles the lighter moments for general chuckles. Overall credit rates him a note for his initial effort.

Production appurtenances, photography, etc., are standard backing for the mixture of mystery and comedy unfolded in this one. *Brog.*

Bedside Manner

United Artists release of Andrew Stone production, directed by Stone. Stars John Carroll, Ruth Hussey; features Charles Ruggles, Ann Rutherford. Screenplay by Frederick Jackson and Malcolm Stuart Roylan from Satevepost story by Robert Carson; editor, James Smith; camera, James Van Trees, John Mescall. Tradeshown N.Y., June 8, '45. Running time, 79 MINS.

Morgan Hale	John Carroll
Hedy Fredericks	Ruth Hussey
Doe Fredericks	Charles Ruggles
Lola	Ann Rutherford
Tanya	Claudia Drake
Stella	Renee Godfrey
Gravitt	Esther Dale
Mr. Pope	Grant Mitchell
Tommy Smith	Joel McGinnis
Dick Smith	John James
Harry Smith	Frank Jenks
George	Bert Roach
Mary	Vera Marsh
Elmer Jones	Sid Saylon
Mr. Perkins	Earl Hodgins
Mrs. Livingston	Mary Currier
Mrs. Moriarty	Constance Purdy
Mrs. Pringie	Mrs. Gardner Crane
Head Waiter	Joe Devlin
Waiter	Dimitrios Alexis
Good-Looking Stranger	Don Brody

"Bedside Manner" is a well-contrived, streamlined comedy of the overworked medico profession in wartimes. At least that is the clothes-rack on which is strung a ludicrous romance between a femme doctor and a war worker. It looks okay if not boff boxoffice.

Plot pits Dr. Chas. Ruggles against his niece, Ruth Hussey, another medico, in the former's frantic effort to have her stay in a war-boom town and assist him with his overworked practice (she's en route to Chicago to do research work). This central motive is speeded along by the romance between Miss Hussey and John Carroll, the airplane test pilot, to an almost wacky degree. It's his faked head injury, after getting concussions earlier in a plane crash, that brings on his phoney pantaphobia which keeps medico Hussey in town helping her uncle. And also hastens the anticipated love affair.

Production gets off to a smart start in the episode where Dr. Hussey picks up three marines while driving to Chi. These pickups are spotted between opening titles, with real action starting as soon as intro titles have appeared. The three leathernecks figure neatly in the yarn, one falling for Claudia Drake, the Russian looker sent to check on a new military plane. Another goes for Ann Rutherford and takes her off Carroll's hands. Third also finds a heart interest so that all three don't mind spending their furlough in this war town instead of Chicago.

Andrew Stone has accorded trim all-round production a strong directorial job. Only in the passages where Carroll affects being a bit tetched and afraid of his own shadow has he permitted the yarn to get a little out of hand. Stone has developed the jealousy slant showing the femme doctor becoming insanely jealous of Carroll just when he appears to have won her.

Carroll is effective but Miss Hussey steals the picture as the woman medico, proving a neat combo of femme charm and professional crispness. Miss Rutherford chips in with one of her better screen roles as the haughty sweetheart who finds one of the Marines more intriguing. Charles Ruggles, as usual, lends infectious humor to the role of overworked physician.

James Van Trees and John Mescall have done a bangup job of camera-ing, outstanding being the traveling shot of two careening autos as occupants exchange repartee. Scripting by Frederick Jackson and Malcolm Stuart Boylan of the Robert Carson original is sturdy. *Wear.*

Jungle Captive

Universal release of Morgan B. Cox production. Stars Otto Kruger, Vicky Lane; features Amelita Ward, Phil Brown, Jerome Cowan. Directed by Harold Young. Screenplay, M. Coates Webster and Dwight V. Babcock from original by Babcock; camera, Maury Gertsman; editor, Fred R. Freitshans, Jr. Tradeshown N. Y., June 11, '45. Running time, 63 MINS.

Dr. Stendahl	Otto Kruger
Ann Forrester	Amelita Ward
Don Young	Phil Brown
Harrigan	Jerome Cowan
Moloch	Rondo Hatton
Bill	Eddie Acuff
Jim	Ernie Adams
Fred	Charles Wagenheim
Motorcycle Cop	Eddy Chandler
Detective	Jack Overman
Paula, the Ape Woman	Vicky Lane

Universal didn't pull any punches in trying to build this chiller into one of the starkest mellers of the year. Pic was made on an obviously low budget, but has a mad, sadistic theme.

Yarn deals with the delving of biochemist Otto Kruger into experiments resulting in returning life to an Ape Woman. With the aid of gruesome Rondo Hatton, in the role of his assistant, Kruger uses the blood of a gal lab technician who works in his office. The assistant, in order to aid the chemist in his experiments, thinks nothing of killing a couple of people to achieve his objective. In the end, the Ape Woman is killed, but not before she had turned on the chemist.

Acting by all members of the cast is just average. Kruger's suave performance standing out. Settings and camerawork, as well as direction and screenplay, endeavor to keep viewers in the thrilling mood upon which the story is based, and rather successfully, too. *Sten.*

Ten Cents a Dance
(SONGS)

Columbia release of Michel Kraike production. Features Jane Frazee, Jimmy Lloyd, Robert Scott, Joan Woodbury. Directed by Will Jason. Screenplay, Morton Grant; asst. director, Ivan Volkman; editor, James Sweeney; camera, Benjamin Kline. At Strand, Brooklyn, N.Y., week of June 7, '45 dual. Running time, 60 MINS.

Jeannie Hollis	Jane Frazee
Billy Sparks	Jimmy Lloyd
Ted Kimball, III	Robt Scott
Babe	Joan Woodbury
Breezy Walker	John Calvert
Bits	George McKay
Joey	Edward Hyans
Sadie	Dorothea Kent
Marge	Carole Mathews
Glad	Muriel Morris
Vi	Pattie Robbins
Mae	Marilyn Johnson
Pat	Jewel McGowan
Rocky	Billy Nelson

Fairly diverting comedy, with songs, is woven around the Rodgers-Hart song of same title which Ruth Etting introduced in a yesteryear "Ziegfeld Follies." Although thin of plot, it has its entertaining moments and should do moderately well.

Jane Frazee warbles torchers when not participating in the bunion derby in John Calvert's dime-a-dance joint. Jimmy Lloyd and Robert Scott, a coupla GIs on a 36-hours pass, wander into the dancery. Latter is heir apparent to a fortune but keeps status subrosa so as not to prejudice fortune-hunting gals in his favor. Instead he lets Lloyd scatter it around.

Prompted by Calvert Miss Frazee and Joan Woodbury, taxi dancer, go on the make for the lads in hope of inveigling them into a card game with Calvert and henchmen so that latter can win $500 to pay for operation on another taxi-dancer, who has been victim of hit-and-run driver. But it doesn't come off after Miss Frazee falls for Lloyd. Miss Woodbury pairs off with Scott.

All four of the featured players give good account in respective roles, with Miss Frazee handling most of the vocals and also registering solid in this department. Calvert turns in creditable performance as the tinhorn dancehall operator. Others of cast are adequate in the lesser roles.

In addition to titular number there are three other songs. Will Jason has directed in breezy tempo and Ben Kline's cameraing is okay, too. *Edba.*

The Frozen Ghost

Universal release of Will Cowan production. Stars Lon Chaney; features Evelyn Ankers, Martin Kosleck, Milburn Stone. Directed by Harold Young. Screenplay, Bernard Schubert and Luci Ward from original by Harry Carter and Harry Sorber; adaptation, Sucher; camera, Paul Ivano. Tradeshown N.Y., June 11, '45. Running time, 61 MINS.

Alex Gregor	Lon Chaney
Maura Daniel	Evelyn Ankers
George Keene	Milburn Stone
Inspector Brant	Douglas Gumbrille
Rudi Poldan	Martin Kosbeck
Nina Condrean	Elena Verdugo
Skeptic	Arthur Hohl

Lon Chaney enacts the role of a mentalist who becomes scared of his own powers when a person whom he hypnotizes dies right in front of an audience. From that point on "The Frozen Ghost" becomes more involved by the minute. Its climax, however, is surprising enough to please whodunit fans.

Based upon the Inner Sanctum mystery stories, this yarn finds Chaney's business agent steering him into a wax museum, run by one of their mutual woman friends to rest his nerves following the incident. However, the aide of the museum owner, jealous of Chaney's way with women, connives with the business agent to drive him mad. When the duo actually find out one of the women whom they've tried to put to sleep actually dies, they become panicky and fall into the trap which ends the film.

Chaney gives a forthright performance, as do Evelyn Ankers, as his vis-a-vis, and Milburn Stone, as his business agent. Remainder of cast aids in giving suspense to the proceedings. Harold Young's direction keeps things moving. *Sten.*

Miniature Reviews

"A Bell For Adano" (20th). Honest version of Pulitzer best-seller will do good business.

"Story of GI Joe" (Cowan-UA). Sock production starring Burgess Meredith. Boff b. o.

"Captain Eddie" (20th). Fred MacMurray as Eddie Rickenbacker in dramatic story of First World War's ace; smash box-office.

"Bewitched" (M-G) Psycho drama, written and directed by Arch Oboler, with limited but interesting b.o. prospects.

"The Naughty Nineties" Musical) (U). One of the lesser Abbott-Costello comedies; moderate b. o.

"Those Endearing Young Charms" (RKO). Robert Young in frothy romance; better than moderate b.o.

"The Woman in Green" (U). Another fair Sherlock Holmes mystery.

"The Way to the Stars" (UA). British-made yarn of American Air Force in England; looks okay for most U. S. houses.

A Bell for Adano

20th-Fox release of Louis D. Lighton and Lamar Trotti production. Stars Gene Tierney, John Hodiak, William Bendix. Directed by Henry King. Screenplay by Lamar Trotti and Norman Reilly Raine, based on novel by John Hersey; camera, Joseph La Shelle; editor, Barbara McLean; music, Alfred Newman. Tradesshown N. Y., June 14, '45. Running time, 103 MINS.

Tina	Gene Tierney
Major Joppolo	John Hodiak
Sergeant Borth	William Bendix
Lieut. Livingstone	Glenn Langan
Nicolo	Richard Conte
Sergeant Trampani	Stanley Prager
Captain Purvis	Henry Morgan
Guiseppe	Montague Banks
Commander Robertson	Reed Hadley
Colonel Middleton	Roy Roberts
Father Pensovecchio	Hugo Haas
Zito	Marcel Dalio
Gargano	Fortunio Bononova
Errante	Henry Armetta
Erba	Roman Bohnon
Cacopardo	Louis Alberni
Mayor Nasta	Eduardo Ciannelli
Tomasino	William Edmunds
Francisca	Yvonne Vautrot
Captain Anderson	John Russell
Rosa	Anna Demetrio
Lt. Col. Sartorius	James Ronnie
Mercurio Salvatore	Charles La Torro
Alfronti	Charles Judels
Basile	Frank Jaquot
Zapulla	Gino Corrado
Craxi	Peter Cusanelli
General McKay	Minor Watson
Edward	Grady Sutton
Capello	Joseph "Chef" Milani
M. P.	Edward Hyans

"A Bell for Adano" has been made into an interesting film. The simple virtues of the Pulitzer prize-winning novel and the stage play have been retained. Film has certain uneven qualities but in the main reflects the care and respect that have gone into its production. On the basis of book and play, as well as marquee draw (with an up-and-coming John Hodiak, and a high-riding Gene Tierney and William Bendix), film should do good business.

John Hersey's story of an American major's administration of a town in Sicily, and his attempts to return it to its peaceful prewar status, has not been tampered with or elaborated upon. The simplicity of the story has been faithfully observed. The film begins quietly to set the simple keynote, has some very beautiful, inspired moments, and finishes off with several scenes of emotional brilliance.

In the middle the film sags, part of the fault being the episodic quality of the story. But there are many fine moments. The opening scenes, as the U. S. forces take the town over while the natives creep slowly back to watch; the scene in the fisherman's home, as three oddly-assorted couples sit eating torrone candy; the attempted lynching of the former fascist mayor in the public square; the return of the released Italian prisoners of war; presentation to the major of his portrait by a grateful community; the party in honor of the major—these are superb moments for any story.

John Hodiak, in the difficult role of Major Joppolo, presents the right hardboiled type of civil affairs officer, determined to bring spiritual rebirth (through the return of its city-hall bell) to the community. Gene Tierney, too, as the blonde fisherman's daughter, has a certain quiet grace without always bringing sufficient poignancy to the role.

William Bendix, as the major's orderly, plays the part in properly subdued fashion for the most convincing portrayal of the three leads, rising superbly to his one big scene at the end. Here Bendix goes roaring drunk from bitterness at learning that the major is to be displaced; he breaks down and cries when failing in his attempts to keep the news from the major until after the civic ceremony in the latter's honor is over.

There are some fine bits among subordinate characters. Roman Bohnen's scene as the cart-driver trying to explain why he innocently obstructed an Army convoy, and Richard Conte's description of the death of a fellow-prisoner are two of the individual highspots. They indicate the mood of honesty and deep-feeling pervading the whole film.

Henry King's direction has captured the story's mood superbly, and his was a job particularly well done because of his ability to instill the thought of movement frequently where no action actually existed.

Bron.

Story of G.I. Joe

United Artists release of Lester Cowan production; associate producer, David Hall. Stars Burgess Meredith. Director, William A. Wellman. Based on writings of the late Ernie Pyle; screenplay, Leopold Atlas, Guy Endore, Philip Stevenson; score, Ann Ronell, Louis Applebaum, Louis Forbes; camera, Russell Metty; editors, Otho Lovering, Albrecht Joseph; assistant director, Robert Aldrich. Tradeshown N. Y., June 15, '45. Running time, **109 MINS.**

Ernie Pyle .... Burgess Meredith
Lieutenant Walker .... Robert Mitchum
Sergeant Warnicki .... Freddie Steele
Private Dondaro .... Wally Cassell
Private Spencer .... Jimmy Lloyd
Private Murphy .... Jack Reilly
Private Mew .... Bill Murphy

For the Combat Correspondents

Don Whitehead .... AP
George Lait .... INS
Chris Cunningham .... UP
Hal Boyle .... AP
Sgt. Jack Foisie .... Stars and Stripes
Bob Landry .... Life Mag
Lucien Hubbard .... Reader's Digest
Clete Roberts .... Blue Net
Robert Reuben .... Reuters

From where the civilian sits, this seems the authentic story of GI Joe—that superb, slugging, human machine, the infantryman, without whom wars cannot be won. Add to authentic story handling a production that's superb, casting and directing that's perfect, a sock star supported by a flawless group of artists—and you have boff b.o.

It's sad to reflect that Ernie Pyle didn't live long enough to see the picture as a whole (he had been shown rough cuts only). For Ernie undoubtedly would have liked it, since he'd have found it a genuine tribute to the infantrymen whom he loved so.

From the moment the infantrymen are picked out by the camera at "blanket drill" in the African desert until the last shot on the open highway to Rome, it's the foot-slogging soldier who counts most in this film. Pyle is there, very much. He is ever present. But as conceived by the scripters, directed by William A. Wellman, and acted by Burgess Meredith, Pyle is not the war but a commentary on it—which is as it should be.

Meredith, playing the simple little figure that's Pyle, is felt in every scene, his impact carrying over from the preceding sequences. So skillfully does he do his role that he becomes a peripatetic, one-man Greek chorus, wandering through the drama, giving a rationale to the slaughter and suffering before you, making sense out of what seems so often like futility and chaos. Meredith as Pyle is right all the way through. He's a lonesome man even among his host of friends, yet never pathetic, never anything but lovable. Meredith as Pyle is memorable.

But without support, Meredith for all his worth could not have made this the great picture it is. Robert Mitchum is excellent as the lieutenant who, in the film, grows to a captaincy, maturity, and finally martyrdom. Freddie Steele is tops as the tough sergeant who finally cracks up when he hears his baby's voice on a disc mailed from home. Wally Cassell as the Lothario of the company, and all the others—professionals as well as real-life GIs who helped make the pic—are excellent.

As indicated, the story starts with the North African campaign, and ends after the capture of Cassino in Italy. Ernie Pyle is seen joining an infantry company for a tour to the desert front in the beginning. From time to time, as the war progresses, he keeps returning to this one company. At the end, when Capt. Walker (Mitchum) had been killed, and is bid farewell by his comrades, Ernie and the soldiers walk off on the highway to the Italian capital. That terrif scene is a fitting climax to the picture. In the body of the dead captain left against a stone wall, in the figures of Pyle and the soldiers, the sacrifices and the hopes of the entire war are symbolized.

To make sure that they were presenting authentic Pyleana, the producers lined up a number of war correspondents with combat experience to act as technical consultants. Result is that smallest details seem—at least to one who hasn't been in combat—correct. Apparently the combat correspondents think so, for some of them are being employed on the exploitation of the pic.

Nothing was spared in the production to make the film a fitting tribute to Pyle and GI Joe. Sensitive and sensible direction, fine camera work have combined with the other factors to make an absorbing drama that will hold audiences tense for its entire length. It's quite possible that, in perspective, this film may be judged the greatest non-documentary to come out of the war.

Cars.

Captain Eddie

20th-Fox release of Winfield R. Sheehan production; associate producer, Christy Walsh. Stars Fred MacMurray; features Lynn Bari, Charles Bickford, Thomas Mitchell, Lloyd Nolan, James Gleason, Mary Phillips, Darryl Hickman, Spring Byington, Richard Conte. Directed by Lloyd Bacon. Screenplay by John Tucker Battle; camera, Joe MacDonald; editor, James B. Clark; special effects, Fred Sersen. Tradeshown N.Y., June 15, '45. Running time. 147 MINS.

Edward Rickenbacker .... Fred MacMurray
Adelaide .... Lynn Bari
William Rickenbacker .... Charles Bickford
Ike Howard .... Thomas Mitchell
Lieut. Whittaker .... Lloyd Nolan
Tom Clark .... James Gleason
Eline Rickenbacker .... Mary Phillips
Eddie Rickenbacker (boy) ...... Darryl Hickman
Mrs. Frost .... Spring Byington
Private Bartek .... Richard Conte
Sgt. Reynolds .... Charles Russell
Capt. Cherry .... Richard Crane
Col Adamson .... Stanley Ridges
Jubez .... Clem Revans
Lester Thomas .... Grady Sutton
Lacey .... Chick Cahndler
Louis Rickenbacker .... Swayne Hickman
Mary Rickenbacker ...... Nancy Jane Robinson
Emma Rickenbacker .... Winifred Glyn
Dewey Rickenbacker .... Gregory Muradian
Albert Rickenbacker .... David Spencer
Bill Rickenbacker .... Elvin Field
Lieut. De Angelis .... George Mitchell
Mr. Frost .... Boyd Davis
Sgt. Alex .... Lon Carner
Mrs. Westrom .... Mary Gordon
Dinkenspiel .... Joseph J. Greene
Census Taker .... Olin Howtin
Mr. Foley .... Robert Malcolm
Mrs. Foley .... Leila McIntyre
Simmons .... Harry Shannon
Flo Clark .... Virginia Brissac
Charlie .... Peter Michael
Freddie .... Peter Garey
Professor Montagne .... Fred Essley
Mme. Montagne .... Lotte Stein

"Captain Eddie," the Eddie Rickenbacker picture, turns out an opus of American fortitude and faith in the future. More than that, it's a tear-jerker and, most important to exhibitors, smash boxoffice. Film does not expound any causes, being fundamentally a smalltown-boy-makes-good yarn.

Picture may have been a bit shorter than its 107 minutes, yet some of the seemingly extraneous footage carries incidents that will appeal to various groups. As for instance, the sequences of Columbus (O) in the horse-and-buggy age are sure to register well with the older folks. Producer Winfield R. Sheehan actually has made the life story of Rickenbacker, renowned auto-racing driver and the No. 1 American ace of World War I, a veritable Americana of the U. S. from the horseless-carriage era through the World War to that point in the current world conflict where Rick survived the 19-day ordeal in the Pacific when the Army transport he was on is forced down mid-ocean.

Any external forces regarding the Yank war ace count for naught here since the entertainment values measure any film's b.o. worth. And they are here, in abundance, plus the fact that exhibs will have Fred MacMurray, Lynn Bari, Thomas Mitchell, Lloyd Nolan and Richard Conte among others with which to decorate their marquees.

Story is done by means of flashbacks after Rickenbacker is shown floating in an Army rubber boat after the crash in the Pacific. Yet it never becomes episodic.

Some may find the earlier, somewhat prolonged sequences a bit tedious, but they are obviously there to stress the pioneering spirit of adventurer Rickenbacker. Always a tinkerer with machinery, the disastrous attempt to emulate an airplane off the roof of a family barn, his crack-up while spending $5 of his hard-earned auto factory coin to ride in a new-fangled airplane, and his ability to solve the early flaws in an automobile, are made deft highlights of his early life. These form a sturdy background for his later ventures as a racetrack contestant and his ascendancy to fame as a daring first World War pilot when a man's skill in handling a plane spelled the difference between victory and his own death.

Throughout, producer Sheehan and director Lloyd Bacon have pointed up his mother's love and the single romance in Eddie's life. In fact, they have managed to give an original twist to the love affair between MacMurray (as Eddie) and Lynn Bari, as Adelaide. They have implanted the idea of Addie's complete faith in Rickenbacker's ability to come through his Pacific ocean ordeal the same as he survived the Atlanta airplane crash. Incidentally, this is strictly historical, since Mrs. Rickenbacker never abandoned hope of Rick's return from the Pacific.

MacMurray is a happy choice for the title role, measuring up in all respects. Darryl Tickman makes a likeable juvenile Rickenbacker. Miss Bari is the modest Addie who shyly falls in love with the mechanically-minded Eddie, and then waits until he returns from his aerial combat over France to wed him. She makes it a standout role.

Mary Philips, as his mother; Thomas Mitchell, as the pioneer auto manufacturer; Lloyd Nolan, as co-pilot of the plane which crashes in the Pacific ocean; James Gleason, as the auto salesman, later identified with Eddie in business, and Richard Conte, as the seriously injured member of the party floating in rubber lifeboats mid-ocean are all standout.

Camera work of Joe MacDonald is tops, while Fred Sersen's special photographic effects measure up. Sound recording job, with special bows to Eugene Grossman and Harry H. Leonard, is an outstanding one. "Captain Eddie" is one of director Bacon's finest.

Wear.

Bewitched

Metro release of Jerry Bresler production. Stars Edmund Gwenn, Phyllis Thaxter; features Kathleen Lockhart, Henry H. Daniels, Jr., Horace McNally. Directed by Arch Oboler. Adaptation by Oboler from his original story, "Alter Ego"; camera, Charles Salerno, Jr.; music, Bronislau Kaper; editor, Harry Komer. Tradeshown, N.Y., June 6, '45. Running time, **65 MINS.**

Doctor Bergson .... Edmund Gwenn
Joan Alris Ellis .... Phyllis Thaxter
Bob Arnold .... Henry H. Daniels, Jr.
John Ellis .... Addison Richards
Mrs. Ellis .... Kathleen Lockhart
Dr. George Wilton .... Francis Pierlot
Small Girl .... Sharon McManus
Glenda .... Gladys Blake
Mr. Herkheimer .... Will Wright
Eric Russell .... Horace McNally
Captain O'Malley .... Oscar O'Shea
Governor .... Minor Watson
Governor's Wife .... Virginia Brissac

One of the oddest films to come out of Hollywood in many months, "Bewitched" is strictly adult fare. It will get word-of-mouth and critic okay to such an extent that it may well be one of the sleepers of the year.

Produced on a low budget, with a sterling cast of actors' actors, this picture just oozes with class because of the excellent adaptation and direction it has been given by radio's Arch Oboler, author of the story, "Alter Ego," on which the film is based. Climax follows climax, strong performance follows strong performance in this thrilling psychopathic study of a girl obsessed by an inner voice that drives her to murder.

Phyllis Thaxter carries the major burden in this one, and Oboler's direction guides her to new dramatic heights. She's in fast company here, with Edmund Gwenn, co-starred in the role of a psychiatrist who endeavors to drive out the troubled girl's obsessions, registering tellingly and the supporting actors each playing their parts to the hilt.

Yarn is told in flashbacks, an eerie musical score by Bronislau Kaper adding to the suspense. Set to wed, Miss Baxter hears a voice which she cannot drive away. She flees to another city, tries to escape her "tormentor," even goes out with another man, a lawyer. But little words dropped at the most unexpected moments bring the voice back. It tells her to kill her hometown boy friend who came to take her home. Just as she is about to be acquitted for the killing, she screams in the courtroom that she is guilty. Her lawyer-friend endeavors to pull strings, succeeding in getting to the governor to sit through an ordeal wherein psychiatrist Gwenn would endeavor to cure her of the obsession. The denouement will linger in the minds of the audience.

Entire production consists of stock sets, narration being depended upon to do the work. Oboler, in a way, uses radio technique in pictures. He definitely has something different to offer Hollywood. His talents may come to mean something at the cinematic boxoffice with proper conditioning of the public.

Sten.

The Naughty Nineties
(MUSICAL)

Universal release of Edmund L. Hartmann and John Grant production. Stars Abbott & Costello. Directed by Jean Yarbrough. Screenplay, Hartmann, Grant, Edmund Joseph and Hal Fimberg; additional comedy, Felix Adler; camera, George Robinson; editor, Arthur Hilton; songs, Harry Von Tilzer, Jack Brooke, Edgar Fairchild, Will A. Heelan, Thomas R. Allen, Junie McCree, Albert Von Tilzer. Previewed in N. Y., June 15, '45. Running time, **76 MINS.**

Dexter .... Bud Abbott
Sebastian .... Lou Costello
Crawford .... Alan Curtis

Bonita	Rita Johnson
Captain Sam	Henry Travers
Caroline	Lois Collier
Bailey	Joe Sawyer
Cropier	Joe Kirk

The names of Abbott & Costello will have to carry "The Naughty Nineties." It's one of their average musicomedies, containing considerable of the standard material, either straight or rewrite, with which they've been identified for years.

This time the pair are associated with a showboat—the setting presumably is in the Gay '90s—and the story concerns their efforts to extricate the showboat's captain from the scheming of a gambling trio to whom the cap is on the verge of losing the boat.

The comedy is belabored, and some of the situational funny stuff is much too prolonged in addition to being familiar. However, the stars keep the pace fast, which is what will probably satisfy. Alan Curtis, Rita Johnson, Henry Travers, Lois Collier and Joe Sawyer are in for the prominent support.

Songs are mostly standards. Production itself looks fairly impressive from a budget standpoint. *Kahn.*

Those Endearing Young Charms

RKO release of Bert Granet production. Stars Robert young, Lorraine Day; features Ann Harding, Bill Williams. Directed by Lewis Allen. Screenplay by Jerome Chodoroy basecupon play by Edward Chodoroy; camera, Ted Tetzlaff; editor, Roland Gross. At Palace, N.Y., week of June 19, '45. Running time. 86 MINS.

Hank	Robert Young
Helen	Laraine Day
Mrs. Brandt	Ann Harding
Captain Larry Stowe	Marc Cramer
Suzanne	Anne Jeffreys
Young Sailor	Glenn Vernon
Haughty Floor Lady	Norman Varden
Ted	Lawrence Tierney
Dot	Vera Marshe

Introducing Bill Williams as Jerry

"Those Endearing Young Charms" is a frothy romantic drama, with Laraine Day and Robert Young starred, that should score better than moderately at the boxoffice in all situations.

The film sticks closely to the play, written by Edward Chodorov and produced on Broadway by Max Gordon in June, '43. Entire plot evolves about four characters, a middle-class gal, the Army pilot, her mother, played by Ann Harding, and the gal's hometown boyfriend, portrayed by newcomer Bill Williams. Miss Day and Young give topflight performances, but somehow Miss Harding and Williams lack feeling, depth and understanding. In a picture which takes 81 minutes to unwind, much depends upon the latter duo, and they don't quite register.

Story finds Williams introducing his gal friend to flyer Young, and the suave routine handed out by the latter soon has the femme doing nip-ups. Unbeknownst to her, the Army pilot is just trying to make haste quickly, until, just when it looks like he scored a missout, he has a change of character from being an unscrupulous heel to become the marrying type. As indicated, some of the scenes are talk-bound. But bright dialog, especially in the love scenes, enhance the film.

Bert Granet has given "Charms" several worthwhile production values. The piloting of Lewis Allen, which bogs the proceedings down at times, could have guided Miss Harding and Williams, who is a likeable lad, but somehow appears to be miscast in this one. He bespeaks of possibilities as a juvenile which are almost wholly hampered here by script and direction. *Sten.*

The Woman in Green

Universal release of Roy William Neill production, directed by Neill. Stars Basil Rathbone, Nigel Bruce; features Hillary Brooke, Henry Daniell. Screenplay by Bertram Millhauser, based on characters created by Sir Arthur Conan Doyle; camera, Virgil Miller; editor, Edward Curtis. Tradeshown, projection room, N. Y., June 14, '45. Running time, 68 MINS.

Holmes	Basil Rathbone
Watson	Nigel Bruce
Lydia	Hillary Brooke
Moriarity	Henry Daniell
Fenwick	Paul Cavanaugh
Inspector Gregson	Matthew Boulton
Maude	Eve Amber
Onslow	Frederic Worlock
Williams	Tom Bryson
Crandon	Sally Shepherd
Mrs. Hudson	Mary Gordon

As usual Basil Rathbone is cast as Sherlock Holmes and Nigel Bruce as his friend, Dr. Watson, in still another of the long line of pix based upon the characters created by Sir Arthur Conan Doyle.

This one, an original screenplay by Bertram Millhauser, finds the pair tracking down a blackmail, murder syndicate headed by Henry Daniell. Latter has as his associate a hypnotist, portrayed by Hillary Brooke. And in order to catch the connivers at work, Holmes even goes so far as to permit himself to be mesmerized.

Acting by entire cast is fairly substantial. Production and direction by Roy William Neill is in the familiar light-budget whodunit groove, along with the settings and camerawork. *Sten.*

The Way to the Stars
(BRITISH-MADE)

London, June 6.

United Artists release of Two Cities Films production. Stars Michael Redgrave, Douglass Montgomery, John Mills, Rosamund John. Directed by Anthony Asquith. Screenplay by Terence Rattigan from story by Terence Rattigan and Anatole de Grunewald. At Pavilion, London, June 5, '45. Running time, 107 MINS.

David Archdale	Michael Redgrave
Peter Penrose	John Mills
Johnnie Hollis	Douglass Montgomery
Joe Friselly	Bonar Colleano
Miss Todd	Rosamund John
Iris	Renee Asherson
Mr. Palmer	Stanley Holloway
Tiny Williams	Basil Radford
Miss Winterton	Joyce Carey
Squadron Leader Carter	Trevor Howard
Rev. Charles Murray	Felix Aylmer

The worst thing about this American Air Force picture is its title. "My British Buddy" would have been more like it if Irving Berlin hadn't used it for that Anglo-American get-together song hit. Aside from title, this straight tale of what happened to an RAF airdrome when it was taken over by the 8th U. S. AAF is outstanding. It's the nearest thing to a Yank's letter home from wartime England ever to reach the screen. And it looks okay for most U. S. spots despite an all-British cast.

Not the least interesting thing is the camera technique. Instead of many aerial shots, the camera is grounded entirely. Except for a few necessary runway shots and equally necessary snatches of formation flying as seen from the ground, the camera concentrates on how the forces lived their lives on terra firma.

Despite technically perfect performances by the three male principals—Michael Redgrave, John Mills and Douglass Montgomery—Rosamund John actually walks away with the acting honors in a part as devoid of glamor as it is rich in femme charm. She reminds of Ruth Chatterton of the New York stage. If there were any English Oscars to be handed out, this London Cockney girl would get a dozen of 'em for this one performance.

When the Yank flyers first take a gander at her, as manageress of the village pub near the airfield, they decide she is just another of those English sour pusses, complete with spectacles. But they wind up worshiping at her feet when, little by little, they discover she has as much guts as any of them, and possibly more understanding. For instance, when closing time comes and they're yelling for one last drink, the way she handles them is a caution. From her earlier muted-string pianissimo she suddenly tops the bedlam with "Get the hell out of here." And one never has a moment's doubt about their getting out.

Several sequences showing the British aces imitating the Yanks, and the Yanks imitating the Englishmen, are guaranteed belly laughs on both sides of the ocean.

Direction by Anthony Asquith is underlined with sincerity and imagination. Production is unostentatious but redolent of English village life. Cooperation of officers of the RAF and the AAF gives the film authenticity in all the sequences on Halfpenny Airfield. The ending is the best in ages here. Script by Terence Rattigan is strong, and up to the high standard set by his "Love in Idleness," which the Lunts are taking to New York at the end of their long London season in that smash hit.

Not in any way comparable with any earlier flying pictures, this one rates tops as a gripping drama of British and American fighters in their hours on the ground. Its great virtue is its simple reproduction of exactly what boys from all over the States have experienced on this side during the past two years. *Talb.*

Miniature Reviews

"Rhapsody in Blue" (Musical) (WB). Plenty of b.o. black due from Gershwin's "Rhapsody in Blue," a tuneful boxoffice barrage.

"Blonde From Brooklyn" (Songs) (Col.). Modest radio romance for family trade.

"The Missing Corpse" (PRC) Comedy whodunit that should do moderately well.

"The Lady Confesses" (Songs) (PRC). Mary Beth Hughes tracks down killer to save her man; should do better than average.

"Crime, Inc." (PRC). Title, in view of apparent demand for gangster stuff, may carry this tiresome one across.

"Muggs Rides Again" (Mono). East Side Kids in satisfactory racetrack yarn.

"The Ural Front" (Artkino). Undramatic fare of doubtful value even to special houses.

"The Last Hill" (Artkino). Melodramatic material unlikely of acceptance.

"La Dama Duende" (San Miguel). Argentine-made costume drama, but dubious U. S. entry.

Rhapsody in Blue

Warner Bros. release of Jesse L. Lasky production. Stars Robert Alda, Joan Leslie, Alexis Smith, Chas. Coburn; Al Jolson, Oscar Levant, Paul Whiteman, George White, Hazel Scott, Anne Brown play themsleves. Directed by Irving Rapper. Story, Sonya Levien; screenplay, Howard Koch, Elliot Paul, Saga of George Gershwin naturally reprises Gershwin's music (lyrics by Ira Gershwin, Buddy deSylva, Irving Caesar. Camera, Sol Polito, Merritt Gerstad, Ernest Haller, James Leicester, Roy Davidson, Willard Van Enger; editor, Folmer Blangsted; dances, Leroy Prinz; arrangements, Ray Heindorf, Ferde Grofe ("Rapsody"); vocal arrangements, Dudley Chambers; "Rapsody" conducted by Paul Whiteman; "Rapsody" and "Concerto in F" piano solo recordings, Oscar Levant; other piano solos, Ray Turner; music, Leo F, Fothstein; asst. director, Robt. Vreeland. Opened June 26, '45, at Hollywood, N.Y. Running time, 130 MINS.

George Gershwin	Robert Alda
Julie Adams	Joan Leslie
Christine Gilbert	Alexis Smith
May Dreyfus	Charles Coburn
Leo Gershwin	Julie Bishop
Professor Frank	Albert Basserman
Poppa Gershwin	Morris Carnovsky
Momma Gershwin	Rosemary De Camp
Himself	Oscar Levant
Himself	Paul Whiteman
Himself	Al Jolson
Himself	George White
Herself	Hazel Scott
Herself	Anne Brown
Ira Gershwin	Herbert Rudley
Commentator	John B. Hughes
George Gershwin (as a boy)	Mickey Roth
Ira Gershwin (as a boy)	Darryl Hickman
Mr. Kast	Charles Halton
Mr. Milton	Andrew Tombes
Mr. Katzman	Gregory Goluhoff
Mr. Muscatel	Walter Soderling
Buddy De Sylva	Eddie Marr
Foley	Theodore Von Eltz
Herbert Stone	Bill Kennedy
American Man	Robert Shayne
Ravel	Oscar Loraine
Dancer	Johnny Downs
Otto Kahn	Ernest Golm
Jascha Heifetz	Martin Noble
Walter Damrosch	Hugo Kirchhoffer
Rachmaninoff	Will Wright

Warner Bros., which has always clicked with musicals and biographicals, has a surefire parlay in "Rhapsody in Blue," the filmusical biog of George Gershwin. It will play a tuneful boxoffice barrage at any exhibitor's wicket. It has everything for the film fan.

Those who knew Gershwin and the Gershwin saga may wax slightly vociferous at this or that miscue, but as cinematurgy, designed for escapism and entertainment, no matter the season, "Rhapsody in Blue" can't miss.

Forgetting the historical, there are sometimes such corny lapses in the Sonya Levien-Howard Koch-Elliot Paul script as to make one wonder how producer Jesse L. Lasky and the

Warnerites didn't see it. Contrasted to Oscar Levant's brittle dialog—incidentally he must have written much of that himself, and he has easily the best lines of the script—it's all the more pointed up. Those off-the-cob lines about a penthouse, etc., are almost embarrassing.

But "Rhapsody," which runs well over two hours, holds so much more that this can easily be glossed over. For one thing, take Gershwin's music—period. That's plenty easy to take. The years have certainly lent enhancement to his music, and the glib interplay of names such as Otto Kahn, Jascha Heifetz, Maurice Ravel, Walter Damrosch and Rachmaninoff (all of whom are impersonated) lend conviction to the basic yarn of the New York east side boy whose musical genius was to sweep the world.

Fundamentally it's an Alger story. Robert Alda plays Gershwin and makes him believable. Herbert Rudley as Ira Gershwin is perhaps more believable to the initiate, looking startlingly like the famed lyricist-brother of the composer, but young Alda, a newcomer, makes his role tick as the burningly ambitious composer who is constantly driving himself.

The musical highlights, of course, are authentic, and in real-life hands. Thus Al Jolson plays himself, introducing "Swanee," Gershwin's first hit which he wrote with Irving Caesar (who, incidentally, is not personated, whereas the now ailing Buddy de Sylva, another lyricist collaborator, is shown briefly, played by Eddie Marr). Jolson at the Winter Garden, first shown blacking-up when music publisher Max Dreyfus (Charlie Coburn) phones him, is a thrill. Still among the world's greatest single entertainers, Jolson in blackface is out of the memory-books and once again celluloided for posterity.

Levant as Levant can't miss, and he doesn't here. He has the meatiest, brittlest lines and whams over the titular "Rhapsody in Blue" and "Concerto in F" with virtuosity and authority as befits a real-life confidante of the late composer. Incidentally, Ray Turner (borrowed from Paramount) deserves more than the casual screen credit for the expert Steinwaying he does throughout.

Then there is Paul Whiteman who first introduced the "Rhapsody." Ferde Grofe, who first scored that now famous work, gets rightful billing for his arrangement. George White, for whom Gershwin composed several "Scandals," plays himself, chiefly in a Turkish bath scene with Coburn as Dreyfus (the head of the Chappell-Harms music firm). Incidentally, Coburn makes quite a robust Dreyfus, considering that venerable music publisher's slightness of stature, but the fans won't know the diff.

The two other real-life characters are Hazel Scott and Anne Brown. Former is discovered in a Paris boite—a sort of combo Bricktop and Josephine Baker—who has been seen to better photogenic avantage. Basically very attractive, Miss Scott packed some extra poundage when she Burbanked in this film, and the white decollatage doesn't help the illusion. Miss Brown recreates her "Porgy and Bess" and other Gershwin classics. Unbilled, but announced, is Tom Patricola, who reprises "Somebody Loves Me" as he did in a "Scandals."

Story almost borders on the Benny Davis "and then I wrote" idiom, but just as it gets overboard it segues out of the musical medley and the plot progresses. It wasn't an easy one to lick, especially with such an embarrassment of musical riches. But Joan Leslie is always resurrected as the patient ingenue who first met Gershwin when he was songplugging for Remick and who flits in and out of musical shows. Alexis Smith is the moneyed other woman.

References to Chico Marx as the best pianist in the neighborhood; to Lee Gershwin, Ira's wife; poppa and momma Gershwin, capitally played by Morris Carnovsky and Rosemary De Camp (he's especially good) all form an authentic pattern. So do some of Levant's cracks that "an evening with Gershwin is a Gershwin evening," etc. It's principally via the Levant dialog that the late, great composer's w.k. egoism is projected although never is it objectionable. Gershwin's self-centered intensity, of course, was born of his boundless ambition and desire to do more and more, greater and greater things. There's enough of this suggested in the film to satisfy the hep fans, and it won't bother anybody else.

The Remick music house; the peripatetic songplugging caravanseries, off the back of trucks; the backstage rehearsals; the Broadway, London and Paris atmosphere; the general movement of the action; Albert Basserman as the benevolent and understanding professor who was Gershwin's music mentor; the Jolson stuff backstage at the Winter Garden; Pops Whiteman with the "Rhapsody"; Damrosch interrupting his NBC broadcast of the "Rhapsody" to announce the composer's death, and Levant the piano soloist, deadpan continuing in the-show-must-go-on tradition—all these, and more, are fine, punchy touches in a fertile musical career.

There are shortcomings also. "Blue Monday Blues," from the 1927 "Scandals," was certainly allowed plenty of footage to prove how big a flop this one was for Gershwin when dialog could have covered it. The bedded Basserman listening to the "Rhapsody" from Aeolian Hall, via radio, is an historical anachronism, of course, considering the 1924 period.

Musically, it's an ingenuous job. "An American in Paris" is well cameraed and imaginatively montaged. Ditto the "Cuban Overture," the Concerto in F and Miss Scott's handling of "I Got Rhythm," "The Man I Love," "Fascinating Rhythm" and "Yankee Doodle Blues." And in all the large orchestral numbers (Whiteman and Damrosch) the lensers have done right well by their assignments with exciting camera angles and groupings.

Directorially, Irving Rapper has properly projected the career of a turmoiled youth whose genius sends him from his native shores to Paris, and coincidentally a quondam art career (Gershwin was no mean amateur painter), and ultimately to Hollywood, after "Porgy and Bess" has clicked in New York. *Abel.*

The Lady Confesses
(SONGS)

PRC release of Alfred Stern production. Stars Mary Beth Hughes; features Hugh Beaumont, Edmund MacDonald, Claudia Drake, Emmett Vogan. Directed by Sam Newfield. Screenplay, Helen Martin from original by Irwin R. Franklin; asst. director, Harold E. Knox; music, Lee Zahler; songs, Robert Unger, Al Seaman, Cindy Walker, Smith, Kuhstos and Blonder; editor, Holbrook Todd; camera, Jack Greenhalgh. At New York theatre, N. Y., week of June 19, '45, dual. Running time, **58 MINS.**

Vicki McGuire..........Mary Beth Hughes
Larry Craig..............Hugh Beaumont
Lucky Brandon........Edmund MacDonald
Lucille Compton.............Claudia Drake
Capt. Brown................Emmett Vogan
Harmon.......................Edward Howard
Steve.........................Dewey Robinson
Marge..........................Carol Andrews
Gladys..............................Ruth Brande
Norma Craig................Barbara Slater
Manager..........................Jack George
Bill..................................Jerome Root
Stand-In....................Edwina Patterson

"The Lady Confesses," starring Mary Beth Hughes, is likeable mystery melodrama with more twists and turns than a scenic railway, projecting good cast performances and sparked direction by Sam Newfield.

Yarn is woven around gal (Barbara Slater), wedded to Hugh Beaumont, who walks out on matrimony. After seven years spouse becomes romantically attached to Miss Hughes. He's about to invoke Enoch Arden proceedings to have wife declared legally dead, so he can marry Miss Hughes, when the former shows up. She is subsequently murdered and husband is suspected. Miss Hughes turns sleuth, hires out as cigaret gal in a nitery and gets the goods on the owner, Edmund MacDonald, as the killer. He gets hep and is about to polish her off when the police break in and nab him.

Miss Hughes gives a charming, well-balanced portrayal of the crime detector. Hugh Beaumont does well as romantic opposite. Claudia Drake looks charming and handles several songs neatly in the nightclub sequence, although the tunes are undistinguished, with others also adequate in respective assignments. *Edba.*

Crime, Inc.
(SONGS)

PRC release of Martin Mooney production. Stars Leo Carrillo, Tom Neal, Martha Tilton; features Lionel Atwill, Grant Mitchell, Sheldon Leonrd. Directed by Lew Landers. Based on book by Martin Mooney; adaptation, Ray Shrock; songs, Jay Livingston and Ray Evans; editor, Roy Livingston; camera, James Brown. At Rialto, N. Y., week June 22, '45. Running time, **82 MINS.**

Tony Marlow........................Leo Carrillo
Jim Riley..............................Tom Neal
Betty Van Cleve..............Martha Tilton
Pat Coyle.........................Lionel Atwill
Wayne Clark...................Grant Mitchell
Captain Ferrone............Sheldon Leonard
Commissioner Collins........Harry Shannon
Bugs Kelly......................Danny Morton
Trixie Waters...................Virginia Vale
Dixon..............................Don Beddoe
Barry North...................George Meeker
Lucas...............................Rod Rogers
Sgt. Hayes..........................Ed Cronley
Stecker............................Jack Gordon
Convict......................Monk Friedman

"Crime, Inc." is a rather tiresome gangster item dealing with the juicier Prohibition days of hoodlumism but its title, a paraphrase on Murder, Inc., coined by a N. Y. newspaper during cleanup of Brooklyn mobsters, will probably have some marquee value. Since the public seems to be in a mood for this type of fare, picture may do well in spite of itself.

Martin Mooney, former N. Y. newspaper reporter, whose book on gangsterism, called "Crime, Inc.," is the associate producer. The role of the newshound, played by Tom Neal, presumably is autobiographic. There is nothing more inconceivable than this reporter, however, who plays around with gangsters, knows their every move, and walks into the Police Commissioner's office without even knocking. The manner in which he is taken into confidence is utterly unbelievable.

Story is built around a crime syndicate whose chairman is supposedly a respected citizen and, at the moment, foreman of the grand jury. Numerous killings figure but, on the whole, the action is very routine and to some extent dated.

Paired with Neal for romantic interest is Martha Tilton, who sings two numbers, neither very impressive. They are "I'm Guilty" and "Lonely Little Camera Girl," both done in nitery sessions. Both players are ordinary in their performances but Leo Carrillo, Lionel Atwill, Grant Mitchell, Sheldon Leonard, Harry Shannon acquit themselves creditably. *Char.*

Muggs Rides Again

Monogram release of Sam Katzman and Jack Dietz production. Features Leo Gorcey, Huntz Hall, Billy Benedict. Directed by Wallace Fox. Screenplay, Harvey Gates; camera, Ira Morgan; editor, William Austin. At Fox, Brooklyn, June 21, '45. Running time, **68 MINS.**

Muggs................................Leo Gorcey
Glimpy...............................Huntz Hall
Skinny.........................Billy Benedict
Danny.........................Mendie Koenig
Sam................................Bud Gorman
Scruno.............................John H. Allen
Squeegie.......................Johnny Duncan
Gaby Dell.....................Bernerd Thomas
Mrs. Brown....................Minerva Urecal
Elsie Brown...............Nancy Brinckman
Dollar Davis....................George Meeker
Mike Hanlin....................Stanford Jolley
Joe English.....................Michael Owen
Dr. Fletcher......................Pierre Watkin
Nurse.............................Betty Sinclair
Veterinarian....................Milton Kibbee

The East Side Kids series takes a new lease on life in this film by transplanting the gang from city to country—to the racetrack, to be precise. Rough and tumble antics of Muggs, Glimpy, Danny and the others, plus some obvious humor, are dished up in an acceptable yarn to please ESK fans.

Story has the kids as track employees, with Muggs and Danny as jockeys. Muggs, a somewhat plump rider by the way, is barred from the track when his crooked employer frames him. The kids go back to New York, Muggs taking with him an aging horse given him by another indigent owner as security for a loan. Just when the kids run afoul of the law for keeping the nag in their clubhouse the owner reappears to redeem horse, release the boys, and hire them for a big race.

Rest of yarn concerns further efforts of Muggs' former employer to dope his rival's nag; revelation of the man's crookedness and Muggs' honesty, and winning of the big race by Muggs on the discarded nag he and the other kids have trained.

Scenes around track and stables are authentic, and two horseraces add excitement to film. Nancy Brinckman and Bernerd Thomas add romantic touch, and George Meeker is satisfactory villain. Budget is light but not skimpy. *Bron.*

Blonde From Brooklyn
(SONGS)

Columbia release of Ted Richmond production. Features Robert Stanton, Lynn Merrick, Thurston Hall, Mary Treen. Directed by Del Lord. Screenplay, Erna Lazarus; camera, Burnett Guffey; editor, Jerome Thoms. At Fox, Brooklyn, June 21, '45. Running time, **65 MINS.**

Dixon Harper.................Robert Stanton
Susan Parker.....................Lynn Merrick
"Col." Hubert Fransworth..Thurston Hall
Diane Peabody......................Mary Treen
W. Wilton Wilbur........Walter Soderling
Daniel Frazier........................Arthur Loft
Mrs. Frazier....................Regina Wallace
Harvey Branson..............Byron Foulger
Miss Quackenfish...........Myrtle Ferguson
Bartender................................John Kelly
Curtis Rossmore......................Matt Willis
Rickie Lester.......................Eddie Bartell

"Blonde From Brooklyn" has a familiar formula—the unknown singer getting a chance break at the mike and becoming a radio hit—but it also adds a pleasant romance, and songs to make up an entertaining film for the family trade. Film also kids Southern traditions—the old plantation, deep-South idea—for a little extra fun.

Story concerns a song-and-dance man released from the Army, who meets a jukebox singer, and plans teaming with her in a song routine. Meeting a Southern "Colonel," they adopt Southern accents, and win a place on a radio program pushing a Dixie-atmosphered coffee. Complications develop when the girl, under her assumed Southern name, is judged the heiress of an old plantation fortune, and the coffee sponsors publicize the connection. Girl breaks up the radio combine to run away, the boy finding her back at her old jukebox stint. This time they start again, on the level, and win success on another airer.

Lynn Merrick and Robert Stanton (formerly known as Bob Haymes, Dick's brother) make an attractive romantic pair, and sing nicely. Thurston Hall has a field day as a rascally pseudo-Southern "Colonel," and Mary Treen has some pert lines as the plain girl-friend. Songs and radio production numbers are pleasant, with film on a modest budget. *Bron.*

The Missing Corpse

PRC release of Leon Fromkess-Martin Mooney production. Features J. Edward Bromberg, Isabel Randolph. Directed by Albert Herman. Screenplay, Ray Schrock, from original by Harry O. Hoyt; music, Karl Hajos; editor, W. Donn Hayes; camera, James Brown; asst. director, William A. Calihan, Jr. At New York theatre, N. Y., week June 19, '45, dual. Running time, 54 MINS.

Henry Kruger........J. Edward Bromberg
Mrs. Kruger..............Isabel Randolph
James Kruger..................Eric Sinclair
Hogan..........................Frank Jenks
McDonald....................Paul Guilfoyle
Jeffry Dodd........................John Shay
Phyllis Kruger..............Lorell Sheldon
Joe Clary........................Ben Welden
Egbert....................Charles Coleman
Trigg......................Michael Branden
Desmond........................Eddy Waller
Miss Ames....................Elayne Adams
Madge.............................Mary Arden
Draper.........................Charles Jordan
Mrs. Swanaker................Anne O'Neal
Marie...........................Jean Ransome
Motor Cop.......................Ken Terrell
Miss Patterson..............Isabel Withers

"The Missing Corpse" is another of those whodunits, with a comedy switch, that should get over in the intermediate houses. It has pace, sufficient laughs and performances by cast which, if anything, enhance story content.

J. Edward Bromberg portrays a publisher who is feuding with a business rival. He blows his top after heated argument and threatens to erase the latter, one way or another. Paul Guilfoyle, the rival, is found dead. Naturally finger of suspicion points at Bromberg, who has a merry time of it trying to hide the stiff, with aid of his wisecracking auto jockey, Frank Jenks. Of course, the audience knows Ben Welden, an ex-con whom Guilfoyle had "framed," knocked him off, but Bromberg doesn't find out until denouement. Isabel Randolph gives good account as wife of Bromberg and all of above mentioned give splendid performances.

Director Al Herman has injected pace that sustains suspense throughout. James Brown's camera work okay, too. *Edba.*

Wildfire

(CINECOLOR)

Screen Guild Productions release of Action Pictures (William B. David) production. Directed by Robert Tansey. Screenplay by Frances Kavanaugh from story by W. C. Tuttle; camera, Marcel Le Picard; editor, Charles Hinkel. Previewed in Chicago, June 21, '45. Running time, 59 MINS.

Happy Hay..........................Bob Steele
Alkali.....................Sterling Holloway
Pete Fanning.......................John Miljan
Judge Polson................William Farnum
Judy Gordon..................Virginia Maples
Aunt Agatha......................Sarah Padden
Johnny Deal........................Eddie Dean
Moose Harris...............Wee Willie Davis
Buck Perry.....................Rocky Camron
Steve Kane........................Al Ferguson
Ezra Mills........................Francis Ford

First release of the newly formed Screen Guild Productions is strictly for the small towns as a secondary feature. Done in Cinecolor, the low-budgeted oater is slow moving, despite it's 59 mins., with a minimum of action. With the exception of a few scenes it's lacking in the usual amount of hard riding and gunplay expected in a western.

Yarn concerns the activities of a band of land-grabbing horse thieves, led by John Miljan, who have led the ranchers to believe that Wildfire, a wild horse, is responsible for their missing stock. Bob Steele and Sterling Holloway, horsetraders, meandering on the scene, get mixed up in the activities, discover skulduggery afoot, and manage to put the culprits to rout.

Acting by the entire cast is just about average. One of the bright spots is the warbling of Eddie Dean, a new singing cowboy. Camerawork is outstanding, Marcel LePicard having achieved some beautiful pictorial effects. *Morg.*

The Ural Front

(RUSSIAN-MADE)

Artkino release of Mosfilm production. Features Tamara Makarova and Vladimir Dobrovolsky. Screenplay and direction by Sergein Gerasimov; English titles, Charles Clement; camera, Vladimir Yakolev. At Stanley, N. Y., week of June 6, '45. Running time, 80 MINS.

Anna Sviridova.........Tamara Makarova
Yegor Sviridov..........Vladimir Solovyov
Kozyryev..........................Mark Bernes
Anikeyev...........Vladimir Dobrovolsky
Kostya.........................Peter Aleinikov
Kostya's Sweetheart.......Vera Altaiskaya
Sviridov's Mother.........Sofia Khalyutina
A Urals Worker..............George Kovrov
Engineer }
Kurochkin }..............Nikolai Konovalov
Prikhodko.......................Sergi Blinnikov

(In Russian; English Titles)

Filmwise, the war seems to have almost crippled the Soviet picture makers. While they do well in documentaries, there is no doubt that they have fallen down on dramatic pix, and "The Ural Front" is only one more instance of that downward trend. If the Russian film industry is still producing good pictures, then those in charge of recent export to the U.S.A. have certainly shown bad judgment. This film is doubtful fare even for special houses.

"Front" tells the story of a factory moved from the Nazi-threatened front, during the dark days of the war, to a safer spot behind the Ural mountains. But ordinary newspaper stories in the American press have told that tale with greater dramatic effect. Undoubtedly, that movement of industry eastward was a grave test and a great triumph in the Soviet way of fighting a winning war. But the moviegoer will see no hint of anything but pedestrian yarn-weaving and uninspired acting in this example on the screen. *Cars.*

The Last Hill

(RUSSIAN-MADE)

Artkino release of Tbilisi production. Directed by Alexander Zarkhi and Josef Heifitz. Screenplay from Boris Voyetekhov's "The Last Days of Sevastopol," by Zarkhi and Heifitz; music, A. Balanchivadze; camera, Arcady Kalzaty; English titles, Charles Clement. At Stanley, N. Y., week June 22, '45. Running time, 86 MINS.

Comdr. Boris Likhachev.Nikolai Kriuchkov
Maria Perventseva.....Marina Pastukhova
Major Zhukovsky..........Boris Andreyev
The Vice-Admiral..........Anton Khorava
Sergeant Sizov..............Nikolai Dorokhin
Sailors: Feodor Ischenko, Nikolai Gorlov, Evgeni Preov, Yegor Tkachuk, Zurab Lezhava.

(In Russian; English Titles)

For some reason the Russians seemed to have lost or mislaid the know-how of picture-making, since the war started. "The Last Hill" was written and directed by Alexander Zarkhi and Josef Heifitz, a team that a few years ago was responsible for one of Russia's film greats, "The Baltic Deputy." But this time, though their material was smash, what came finally to the screen was melodrama entirely out of key with the importance of the theme. The film, consequently, will probably find no acceptance.

Theme of the picture is the temporarily losing battle by the Russians to save Sevastopol, the 250-day siege which added up to one of the most heroic episodes of the entire war. Such heroism should have cued an epic film. Instead, a girl is introduced increditably amidst all the shooting, a naval officer raves his speeches, and even the camera work is never above the mediocre.

There is a fairly long sequence of fine acting as a group of Russian sailors carries on suicide raids against Nazi tankers. One knows from authentic war dispatches that, melodramatic as such action seems, it did take place in real life. But then the pretty gal finally stands high up on the ramparts, a target for the Nazi machine guns, and signals for artillery fire at her post—and lives through it. No Russian critic of the cinema would ever allow a Hollywood western to get away with such shoddy material without contemptuous laughter. But here, the Russians are doing that kind of stuff.

One hopes that, now the shooting is over for them, some of the fine Soviet film people may get back to dramatic work of importance. Meanwhile, they'd do their film reputation more good by keepnig stuff like "Hill" at home, instead of exporting it. *Cars.*

La Dama Duende

("The Ghost Lady")

Buenos Aires, May 17.

San Miguel production and release. Stars Delia Garces; features Antonia Herroro, Enrique Alvarez Diosdado, Ernesto Vilches, Paquita Garzon, Alejandro Maximino, Francisco Lopez Silva, Amelia Sanchez Arino. Directed by Luis Saslavsky. Screenplay by Maria Teresa Leon and Rafael Alberti from story by Don Pedro Calderon de la Barca; camera, Jose Maria Beltran. Opened in Buenos Aires, May 17, '45.

Action of this ambitious production takes place in Spain in the 18th century and picture contains much picturesque costuming and big scenes. Looks an excellent moneymaker, and started off at admission scales equal to highest placed on Hollywood films. Because the picture can't become dated, it should make coin for many years. It's dubious for the U. S. market.

Story is based on the ventures of the youthful widow of a Peruvian viceroy. To overcome the rigid etiquet of Spanish mourning, she poses as a ghost and so lures a young army captain, accidentally lodged in her castle, as her second spouse. Delia Garces is vivacious as the "Ghost Lady" and does well teamed with Enrique Diosdado, as the gallant captain.

Many scenes recall the best of Goya's paintings. *Nid.*

Miniature Reviews

"You Came Along" (Songs) (Wallis-Par). OK b.o. romance, with Lizabeth Scott, an arresting new personality.

"The Cheaters" (Rep). Joseph Schildkraut starrer should please in all situations.

"Waltz Time" (Anglo-Am.). Elaborate but faulty British-made musical; sans players known to U. S. patrons lessons chances.

"El Canto Del Cisne" (Lumiton). Argentine-made meller is distinct disappointment; thin entry for American market.

"La Cabalgata Del Circo" (San Miguel). Argentine-made showboat musical looks mild for U. S.

You Came Along

(SONGS)

Paramount release of Hal Wallis production. Features Lizabeth Scott, Robert Cummings, Don DeFore, Charles Drake. Director, John Farrow. Screenplay, Robert Smith and Ayn Rand, from Smith's original; camera, Daniel L. Fapp, Farciot Edouart; music, Victor Young; editor, Eda Warren. At Paramount, N. Y., opening July 4,' 45. Running time, 103 MINS.

Bob Collins..............Robert Cummings
Ivy Hotchkiss..................Lizabeth Scott
Shakespeare.....................Don DeFore
Handsome......................Charles Drake
Joyce Heath........................Julie Bishop
Frances Hotchkiss..............Kim Hunter
Bill Allen........................Robert Sully
Helen Forrest............................Herself
Col. Stubbs...................Rhys Williams
Hotel Clerk..............Franklin Pangborn
Uncle Jack.......................Minor Watson
Middle-aged Man.........Howard Freeman
Second Man.................Andrew Tombes
Chairman....................Lewis L. Russell
Bellboy............................Frank Faylen
Col. Armstrong..................Will Wright
Gertrude..........................Cindy Garner
Carol Dix..............Marjorie Woodworth
Gloria Revere......................Ruth Roman
Capt. Taylor......................Crane Whitley

Hal Wallis, in his second indie release for Paramount, has a winner in "You Came Along." Also a possible new star in Lizabeth Scott, who is appropriately introduced as a new screen personality. She makes the grade. Film, in toto, combined with the glamour ballyhoo attendant to the new femme, is destined for solid boxoffice returns.

Story is out of current events. It's authentic, rings true, is nicely played, never maudlin and sound all the way. The three flyers are shown for what they are—women-chasing, fast-drinking, realistic guys but with a strong bond among them, especially as concerns Robert Cummings, a victim of leukemia. Don DeFore is Shakespeare, the academic one, and Charles Drake is Handsome, the gentle ex-pug. They're on a bond barnstorming tour and I. V. (nee Ivy) Hotchkiss (Miss Scott) has been designated by the Treasury Dept. as their guide. She's efficient and slightly mannish at first but the boys soon sense her personable femininity and love develops according to plan.

The devil-may-care Cummings, despite his baffling disease which has numbered his days, takes his fun where he can find it. This is sharply contrasted to the real love when he falls for Miss Scott. The title song strain, "You Came Along (From Out of Nowhere)" is well integrated into the plot progression in the sundry cafe and pub scenes, and nicely emphasizes the romantic mood throughout.

Realistic impatience with stuffy committees, bond spiels, autograph-hounds and the like all ring true. The three wolves give out with a huba-huba-huba at the drop of a dirndl, but in between Shakespeare and Handsome keep tender watch on their Major (Cummings) and his mysterious ailment. The scenes with Helen Forrest chirping "Kiss the Boys Goodbye"; the historic Mission Inn at Riverside, Cal., a favorite

Gretna Green for flyers and their brides; the serious flight surgeon who orders Cummings into the Walter Reed hospital while he frames a series of letters from a London "drop," in order not to worry his bride—all these jell in this brisk, well-directed and well-scripted romance. Even the finale is realistic, with the major-hero's inevitable death, while his two buddies console the young widow.

Miss Scott, who understudied Tallulah Bankhead in legit, will suffer comparison to Lauren Bacall because of her personality, but she suggests more the young Garbo. She has a sonorous speaking voice and an intriguing manner. She is given excellent histrionic buoyancy by Cummings, DeFore and Drake as the omnipotent three musketeers of the skyways. The rest of the cast is competent but relatively unobtrusive.

Robert Smith's original plays well, especially as he and Ayn Rand have screenplayed it. John Farrow has directed with authority. *Abel.*

The Cheaters

Republic release of Joseph Kane production, directed by Kane. Stars Joseph Schildkraut; features Billie Burke, Eugene Pallette, Ona Munson, Raymond Walburn, Ann Gillis, Ruth Terry, Robert Livingston. Screenplay, Frances Hyland from original by her and Albert Ray; music, Walter Scharf; editor, Richard L. Van Enger; camera, Reggie Lanning. Previewed N. Y., June 29, '45. Running time, 87 MINS.

Mr. M....................Joseph Schildkraut
Mrs. Pidgeon....................Billie Burke
Mr. Pidgeon....................Eugene Pallette
Florie....................Ona Munson
Willie....................Raymond Walburn
Angela....................Anne Gillis
Therese....................Ruth Terry
Stephen Bates....................Robert Livingston
Reggie....................David Holt
MacFarland....................Robert Greig
St. Luke's Choristers

Republic should hit the jackpot with this one. Aside from standout performances of Joseph Schildkraut and supporting cast, its story content and nifty direction by Joseph Kane, dualling as producer-director, and with such names as Billie Burke, Ona Munson, Ray Walburn and Eugene Pallette for additional cast hypo, it should bring many happy returns at the b.o.

Yarn is woven around the wacky Pidgeon family who, although of the upper strata for years, are about to crash upon rocks of reverses due to the scatterbrained extravagance of the financier's wife. Their only hope is in the death of the tycoon's uncle, currently taking the count in Denver. Latter outfoxes them by leaving his coin to an actress whom he had seen, as a boy, as Little Eva in a rep troupe production of "Uncle Tom's Cabin." There had been some correspondence through ensuing triple decade but never a meeting.

Incidental to learning the bad news, the Pidgeons acquiesce to plea of their daughter to invite a "charity case" to spend Xmas with them. It arrives in the person of Mr. M., a fallen star of the theatre, who imposes himself and hammy machinations upon the screwy householders. He, however, agrees to assist in locating the missing actress and possibly make a deal with her to everybody's mutual advantage. They locate the gal, add her to the merry assemblage through selling her the idea that she is related to them. Romantic attachment springs up between actress and Mr. M., whom she recognizes. She attempts to wean him away from booze for a comeback. He gets drunker and when all are gathered around the Xmas tree he contribs enough of Dickens' "Christmas Carol" to penetrate the consciences of the cheaters, who apprise the actress of their attempt to cop her rightful inheritance. The gal takes it all standing up and agrees to split the $5,000,000 inheritance with the Pidgeons and everybody's happy at fadeout.

Schildkraut gives one of the best performances of his career as the magnificent refugee from Thespis. He brings artistry, poise and tongue-in-cheek sense of humor throughout.

Miss Munson, as the slangy, good-natured gal who inherits the pot of gold; Pallette, as the near financially embarrassed tycoon, and Miss Burke, as the giddy, extravagant spouse, all contribute splendid performances. Walburn also does nicely as the ne'er-do-well brother-in-law. Ruth Terry and Robert Livingston are likeable as the younger romantics, with other good performances by Ann Gillis, David Holt and Robert Creig. St. Luke's Choristers warble Xmas Carols incidental to the holiday setting.

Kane has turned out a production warranting the free rein given him on budget. He also directed in good tempo for top results. *Edba.*

Waltz Time
(BRITISH-MADE)
(With Songs)

London, June 20.

Anglo-American Film Corp. release of British National Film production. Features Carol Raye, Patricia Medina, Peter Graves, Richard Tauber. Directed by Paul Stein. Screenplay by Montgomery Tully, Henry C. James from idea by Karl Rossler. Music by Hans May. Starting at Palace, London, June 20, '45. Running time, 98 MINS.

Empress Maria....................Carol Raye
Count Franz Von Hofer....................Peter Graves
Cenci Prohaska....................Patricia Medina
Count Prohaska....................John Ruddock
Count Rodzanka....................Harry Welchman
Stefan Ravenne....................Thorley Walters
Vogel....................George Robey
Josef....................Wylie Watson
Gypsy Troubadours....................Ann Ziegler
Troubadour....................Webster Booth
Orchestra Leader....................Albert Sandler
Shepherd....................Richard Tauber
Augustine....................Toni Edgar Bruce
Minister of War....................Hay Petrie

This is a big disappointment. But it goes further than that. This film is proof of British picture makers' ignorance of fundamentals that make a film musical. Production-wise, "Waltz Time" is terrific. The tunes are okay and mainly adequately sung. Orchestration is top-notch and effectively handled both by visual bands and also background music. But it is no go, mainly because of faulty scripting and direction.

Can you picture a booking agent back in the days of the Keith Circuit teaming up Pat Rooney and Caruso—with the hoofer half of the act singing Pagliacci and the tenor trying to tap? It's a fair comparison with what happens in this very-English attempt to go gay Viennese. After almost an hour of warbling by Webster Booth and Ann Ziegler, Carol Raye, Patricia Medina and Peter Graves, suddenly for no reason, there's a cut to a hill-top cabin in which Richard Tauber, all by himself, gives out with a song welcoming the dawn. This sort of stuff does much to knife the whole flicker.

To make it worse, Tauber is back a second time near the end, and again The Voice (no resemblance to Sinatra) spells murder for the other singers. In this sequence, set in a huge cathedral, Tauber is in the center of a boy choir. He wears a white robe but still he puts in all the zip and gestures of a concert soloist's repertoire.

The producers went the limit in giving this great backgrounding and costuming. Coin for players also looks hefty. For instance, George Robey, the English music hall's Prime Minister of Mirth, has only a bit. Albert Sandler, leading BBC orchestra conductor and violin virtuoso, leads a gypsy band.

But why will Wardour Street try to do what the past has proved can't be done? After all, Chaplin never tried crashing the screen with "Hamlet". Lately the British film industry has produced some really great pictures. But when it comes to musicals, well, this is an example of what can happen, and usually does. *Talb.*

El Canto Del Cisne
("SWAN SONG")

Buenos Aires, April 30.

Lumiton production and release. Directed by Carlos Hugo Christensen. Stars Mecha Ortiz and Roberto Escalada; features Nelly Daren, Nicolas Freygues, Miguel Gomez Bao. Directed by Carlos Hugo Christensen. Story by Cesar Tiempo. Starting April 27, '45, at Gran Cine Palace, Buenos Aires. Running time, 105 MINS.

Carlos Christensen, one of youngest Argentine film directors who showed real promise in his first productions, is disappointing with this melodrama. Technique often dates back to the old silent days, and action crawls. It looks very thin for U.S. market.

Story concerns the last lave of an older woman for a man much younger than herself, a young composer whom she steals from her younger sister. Haunted by the prospect of fading beauty, and tormented by jealous suspicions, she grows exacting and morbid, hating even his work, which she had first inspired. Eventually she suicides while he is conducting his symphonic work, "The Swan Song," at the Colon Opera, Buenos Aires.

Photography reveals poor quality of celluoid. But the early scenes show the beauties of the Argentine southern lake region and are the best part of picture, with the exception of the music.

Mecha Ortiz photographs unflatteringly and struggles hard against the limitations of the story. Roberto Escalada is wooden but shows signs of improvement. Miguel Gomez Bao, as the fatherly old Colon Opera director, steals the picture. *Nid.*

La Cabalgata Del Circo
("The Circus Parade")
(ARGENTINE-MADE)

Buenos Aires, May 30.

San Miguel Studios release. Stars Libertad Lamarque, Hugo del Carril. Features Jose Olarra, Orestes Caviglia, Juan Jose Miguez, Evita Duarte, Ilde Pirovano, Armando Bo. Screenplay by Francisco Madrid, Mario Soffici. Directed by Mario Soffici. At Gran Cine Palace, May 30, '45. Running time, 90 MINS.

This picture has all the ingredients for success. Although it looks strong boxoffice here, it cannot be classed as a standout because of uneven direction and faulty photography. Libertad Lamarque, one of the lookers of the Argentine screen, shows to bad advantage at times, although her warbling is always socko, for those who like Argentine tango. Chances in U. S. are obviously mild.

It is the first attempt at telling the Argentine show-folk story, following a trend which has been so popular in Hollywood musicals. Trek of a circus caravan across the vast Pampa is used to show the country, its corny towns and its peasantry.

Cast was well chosen to give an idea of the development of Argentine popular music. Libertad Lamarque and Hugo Del Carril are tops among local tango warblers and acquit themselves well. They would make a romantic team and it seems a pity to cast them as brother and sister. Del Carril, usually a wooden actor, seems relaxed and natural as the scion of the traveling circus family who reaches stardom as a tango warbler. Story has some resemblance to "Show Boat." The Gaucho audiences are entertained by lurid melodrama based on their own folk tales.

Evita Duarte, who plays a small supporting role in this her first picture, does not reveal much screen talent, but is given small chance, due to poor lighting and unattractive make-up. *Nid.*

Miniature Reviews

"Her Highness and the Bellboy" (M-G). Nifty comedy romance, exceptionally well acted that should do nicely at b.o.

"And Then There Were None" (20th). Dull film version of the stage play, "10 Little Indians." Spotty b.o.

"On Stage Everybody" (Musical) (U). Pleasant little musical based on the radio program of same name.

"Road to Alcatraz" (Rep). Just another light-budgeted whodunit.

"I'll Be Your Sweetheart" (GFD) (With Songs). Margaret Lockwood, Vic Oliver and Michael Rennie in period musical; limited b.o. appeal even in Britain for this British-made.

Her Highness and the Bellboy

Metro release of Joe Pasternak production. Stars Hedy Lamarr, Robert Walker, June Allyson. Directed by Richard Thorpe. Story and adaptation. Richard Connell and Gladys Lehnian; editor, George Boemler; camera, Harry Stradling. Tradeshown N.Y. June 27, '45. Running time, 108 MINS.

Princess Veronica....................Hedy Lamarr
Jimmy Dobson....................Robert Walker
Leslie Odell....................June Allyson
Baron Zoltan Faludi....................Carl Esmond
Countess Zoe....................Agnes Moorehead
Albert Weever...................."Bags" Ragland
Paul MacMillan....................Warner Anderson

"Her Highness and the Bellboy," following a familiar format and style, is a diverting romantic item with pleasing comedy relief that should do well at the boxoffice but could have been trimmed, particularly in the earlier stages of the action.

What contributes immensely to the enjoyment of the picture are the performances, notably of Hedy Lamarr, Robert Walker and "Rags" Ragland. Playing a smartcracking bellhop, Walker is terrif in his role, while Ragland, his porter pal at the hotel, is particularly likeable. Miss Lamarr plays the princess of a mythical European kingdom who visits N. Y. and is still hotly in love with a columnist who had met her in Europe some years before but chilled on her. She is mistaken for a maid by Walker and the two regard each other warmly except that Walker, on learning her real identity, again makes the mistake of thinking she's in love with him after having been appointed her personal attendant.

Meantime, Walker chills on June Allyson, playing an invalid who's very much in love with him. In the end, of course, he realizes that dreams of royalty are nothing more than dreams and makes for the happy fade with Miss Allyson. She comes close to stealing the picture in a difficult bedridden role.

Warner Anderson acquits himself creditably as the columnist for whom the princess, suddenly become queen of her country, abdicates the throne, while also very good is Carl Esmond, as the baron on the make for the princess. Agnes Moorehead, as a countess, is excellent.

Joe Pasternak's production backgrounds are impressive, particularly one scene depicting a fairy tale dream of Miss Allyson's. Direction of Richard Thorpe leaves nothing to be desired except for some portions, especially at the beginning, that are a bit slow. *Char.*

And Then There Were None

Hollywood, July 10.

20th-Fox release of Harry M. Popkin production. Stars Barry Fitzgerald, Walter

Huston, Louis Hayward; features Roland Young, June Duprez, C. Aubrey Smith, Judith Anderson, Mischa Auer, Richard Haydn, Queenie Leonard, Harry Thurston. Directed by Rene Clair. Screenplay, Dudley Nichols from the Satevepost story and play, "10 Little Indians," by Agatha Christie; camera, Lucien Andriot; editor, Harvey Manger. Tradeshown L. A. July 6, '45. Running time, 97 MINS.

Judge Quineannon....................Barry Fitzgerald
Dr. Armstrong....................Walter Huston
Philip Lombard....................Louis Hayward
Blore....................Roland Young
Vera Claythorne....................June Duprez
General Mandrake....................Sir C. Aubrey Smith
Emily Brent....................Judith Anderson
Prince Starloff....................Mischa Auer
Rogers....................Richard Haydn
Mrs. Rogers....................Queenie Leonard
Fisherman....................Harry Thurston

This screen version of Agatha Christie's stage play and magazine story is a dull whodunit. Cast gives some marquee strength but none of the top names are at their best. It's all strictly ho-hum and will play to spotty business.

The Christie mag yarn was a fair mystery story and a Broadway hit as a stage adaptation, called "10 Little Indians," but the film version adds no laurels to the original. Plot concerns itself with 10 assorted characters, each with a bad spot in his past, who are marooned on a lonely island off the English coast. Like the nursery rhyme, the number is decimated by sudden death until only two leave the island alive. Victims are mysteriously gathered in the spot by a mad judge who fancies himself a dispenser of justice. Picture rarely rises to moments of suspense and despite the killings it gives the appearance of nothing ever happening as directed by Rene Clair.

Barry Fitzgerald is only fair as the killer. Walter Huston, Louis Hayward, Roland Young, June Duprez, C. Aubrey Smith and others appear equally out of place.

Production is first venture by Harry M. Popkin, burlesque and film theatre operator and doesn't get him off to a good start in the new field. Photography and other technical factors are expert, with exception of the music score. *Brog.*

On Stage Everybody
(MUSICAL)

Universal release of Warren Wilson (Lou Goldberg) production. Stars Peggy Ryan, Johnny Coy, Jack Oakie. Directed by Jean Yarbrough. Screenplay, Warren Wilson and Oscar Brodney; camera, Chas. Van Enger; music, Milton Rosen; editor, Philip Cahn; asst. director, Seward Webb. Tradeshown July 6, '45. Running time, 75 MINS.

Molly Sullivan .... Peggy Ryan
Danny Rogers .... Johnny Coy
Michael Sullivan .... Jack Oakie
Vivian Carlton .... Julie London
James Carlton .... Otto Kruger
Ma Cassidy .... Esther Dale
Emmet Rogers .... Wally Ford
Fitzgerald .... Milburn Stone
Tom .... Stephen Wayne
Dick .... Jimmy Clark
Themselves .... King Sisters
Skater .... Jean Richey

Winners of Radio Show Contest

Billy Usher, Georgiana Bannister, Ilene Woods, Bob Hopkins, June Brady, Cyril Smith, Ronnie Gibson, Jean Hamilton, Beatrice Fung Oye, Ed (Strawberry) Russell.

Fearful that the radio program idea would develop into a cinematic talent hunt, Universal reversed its field completely and played down "On Stage Everybody" to the degree it's only a minor component of the film version. In toto, a pleasant little musical.

Lou Goldberg's Blue Network radio program had to do with a new-faces idea, but this becomes but a segment of the plot which focuses around Jack Oakie and his vaudeville partner-daughter, Peggy Ryan. Oakie is a vaude diehard and violently anti-radio until he eventually sees the microphonic light, becomes a convert, auditions a new-talent radio show idea (see the film title) and clicks.

Much of the sentiment in which U execs Nate Blumberg, Cliff Work, et al. are steeped—and that goes also for Oakie, of course—is manifest in the vaude-radio motivation. True, some of it is rather ridiculous, especially when the central characters are supposedly literally starving.

There's a rich uncle in the background who has a soft spot for Peggy Ryan. Otto Kruger is the unk who gets the obstreperous Oakie out of jams and has a private Pinkerton always looking after their welfare.

Also ridiculous is that sequence where Miss Ryan acts stuffily "high society" when she visits her rich cousin, and is saved from being the complete jackass only when Johnny Coy comes to her rescue. Latter, incidentally, is picking up where Donald O'Connor left off before he went into service.

Interspersed is song-and-dance (Gus Sun-calibre) in the pre-radio vaude days; modern s. and d. around the swimming pool, and a host of other specialities, including the "On Stage Everybody" radio program.

The stellar trio do well by themselves, and Julie London has some promise as an ingenue despite that over-abundance of sweater-girl camera angles allotted her. The rest are adequate.

Of the specialties, the King Sisters jive "Stuff Like That There"; Beatrice Fung Oye does a modern rhythm tune despite her Chinese getup; Ronnie Gibson chirps; Ilene Woods, who has a voice, is wasted in an around-the-piano bit; Bob Hopkins socks with radio imitations, and the dusky Ed (Strawberry) Russell, to self-guitar accomp, also clicks. Georgiana Bannister, who suggests photogenic qualities, like Miss Woods, also gets a fast Fuller (or slight brushoff as they used to say).

Despite the brief 75 mins., there are 13 song numbers, more or less. *Abel.*

Road to Alcatraz

Republic release of Sidney Picker production. Stars Robert Lowery, June Storey; features Grant Withers, Clarence Kolb. Directed by Nick Grinde. Screenplay, Dwight V. Babcock and Jerry Sackheim from original by Francis K. Allen; camera, Ernest Miller; editor, Richard L. Van Enger. At Brooklyn Strand, week of July 6, '45, dual. Running time, 60 MINS.

John Norton....................Robert Lowery
Kit Norton....................June Storey
Inspector Craven....................Grant Withers
Phillip Angreet....................Clarence Kolb
Gary Payne....................Charles Gordon
Charles Cantrell....................William Forrest
Louise Rogers....................Iris Adrian
Dorothy Stone....................Lillian Bronson
House Manager....................Harry Depp
Servant....................Kenne Duncan

"Road to Alcatraz" is another one of those light-budget whodunits, wherein the wrong guy gets the finger until he proves his own innocence.

Yarn finds youthful lawyer Robert Lowery suspected by police of the murder of his law partner. He isn't sure of his own innocence, however, because, as later proved, he was drugged by the actual killer, and couldn't recall his activities on the night of the crime. However, he solves the whole thing by the finding of a fraternity pin belonging to his best friend, the actual culprit.

Film script does not waste much footage, keeping the action moving right along. But the cast, especially the stars, Robert Lowery and June Storey, who plays his wife, give rather stilted performances. To the picture's credit, though, is the suspense of how Lowery would eventually squirm out of the charge, and director Nick Grinde pilots it all fairly capably. *Sten.*

I'll Be Your Sweetheart
(Songs)
(BRITISH-MADE)

London, June 28.

General Film Distributors' release of Gainsborough production. Stars Margaret Lockwood, Vic Oliver. Directed by Val Guest; Screenploy, Val Guest, Val Valentine; camera, Phil Grindrod. At Gaumont theatre, London, June 27, '45. Running time, 104 MINS.

Edie Story....................Margaret Lockwood
Sam Kahn....................Vic Oliver
Bob Fielding....................Michael Rennie
Jim Knight....................Peter Graves
George le Brunn....................Moore Marriott
Pacey....................Frederick Burtwell
Mrs. Jones....................Maudie Edwards
Wallace....................Garry Marsh
T. P. O'Connor....................George Merritt
Mrs. le Brunn....................Muriel George
Kelly....................Jonathan Field
John Friar....................Eliot Makeham
Dresser....................Ella Retford

For professionals who remember when 28th Street was Tin Pan Alley, this period musical will revive bitter-sweet memories. Outside of that handful, Americans generally will probably count "I'll Be Your Sweetheart" as just another one of those things they can do without. Even so the picture is noteworthy because Michael Rennie, tall, dark and handsome screen newcomer, is likely Hollywood material.

This dominating personality, in the list of featured players, makes one wonder why Margaret Lockwood and Vic Oliver are starred. Of course, Miss Lockwood has all there is of femme interest as the Music Hall queen of the early 1900's, but it is Rennie, as the Yorkshire lad storming London with an ambition to make a fortune publishing song hits at sixpence (a dime), who walks away with the acting honors. As for Vic Oliver, the material provided him would make Joe Miller weep.

As a demonstration of the way songwriters were gypped by pirate publishers—until Tay Pay O'Connor came to their rescue with a Parliamentary Act—"I'll Be Your Sweetheart" faithfully reproduces the state of affairs in England 45 years ago. Two quid (10 bucks) was reckoned a fair price for a song hit, but even so the publisher who got it at that figure had to be lucky to break even on printing costs. Within hours of the appearance of a new popular ditty, a pirate version was being hawked up and down Charing Cross for tuppence (4 cents) a copy.

Production-wise the film is mounted more lavishly than the average run of British studio products, the Blackpool sequence with panoramic shots from the top of the Blackpool Tower being especially effective. The old Tivoli is also brought to life realistically with its chorus-singing audience of belted earls and costers.

Direction is adequate especially the fight scenes. The first roughhouse, when the hungry song writers wreck Berwick Market where pirate versions of their hits are being sold, takes the edge off the climactic value of the final sequence where the crook behind the pirates is traced to his hideaway printing establishment and beaten up by Rennie and his pals.

Anyhow, Gainsborough gets credit for "introducing" the best bet in the way of a new male star to have come out of a British studio in many years. Rennie not only has a lot on the ball as a straight lead, he knows the value of visual tricks. Femmes will go for him in a big way.

In this country, as well as in the U. S., the appeal of "I'll Be Your Sweetheart" would seem to be confined to too limited a section of old timers. Although many musical numbers are still popular (all are superbly orchestrated and put over) it is too much to expect even British picturegoers of 1945 to react sympathetically to scenes of starving songwriters. *Talb.*

Miniature Reviews

"Anchors Aweigh" (Musical; color). (M-G). Will grab hefty business.

"Our Vines Have Tender Grapes" (M-G). Simple, moving story of American farm life with strong family appeal.

"Christmas in Connecticut" (WB). High-gear farce about girl-meets-boy. B.o. hefty.

"The Caribbean Mystery" (20th). Murder meller in the programmer class that should do satisfactory if properly spotted.

"The Beautiful Cheat" (Songs) (U). OK light comedy starring Bonita Granville and Noah Beery, Jr.

"Johnny Frenchman" (Eagle Lion). British-made pic good for big U. S. b.o.

Anchors Aweigh

Hollywood, July 14.

Metro release of the Pasternak production. Stars Frank Sinatra, Kathryn Grayson, Gene Kelly; features Jose Iturbi, Dean Stockwell, Pamela Britton, "Rags" Ragland, Billy Gilbert, Henry O'Neill, Carlos Ramirez, Edgar Kennedy, Grady Sutton, Leon Ames, Sharon McManus. Director, George Sidney. Screenplay, Isobel Lennart; suggested by a story by Natalie Marcin; camera, Robert Planck and Charles Boyle; music, Georgie Stoll; dances, Gene Kelly; songs, Jule Styne-Sammy Cahn; orchestrations, Axel Stordahl; editor, Adrienne Fazan. Tradeshown L.A. Running time, 138 MINS.

Clarence Doolittle .... Frank Sinatra
Susan Abbott .... Kathryn Grayson
Joseph Brady .... Gene Kelly
Jose Iturbi .... Himself
Donald Martin .... Dean Stockwell
Girl from Brooklyn .... Pamela Britton
Police Sergeant .... "Rags" Ragland
Cafe Manager .... Billy Gilbert
Admiral Hammond .... Henry O'Neill
Carlos .... Carlos Ramirez
Police Captain .... Edgar Kennedy
Bertram Kraler .... Grady Sutton
Admiral's Aide .... Leon Ames
Little Girl Beggar .... Sharon McManus
Radio Cop .... James Flavin
Studio Cop .... James Burke
Hamburger Man .... Henry Armetts
Iturbi's Assistant .... Chester Clute

"Anchors Aweigh" is solid musical fare for all situations. The production numbers are zingy; the songs are extremely listenable; the color treatment outstanding. It's a showmanly package of entertainment cut to order for hefty boxoffice returns.

Two of the potent entertainment factors are the tunes and Gene Kelly's hoofing. Jule Styne and Sammy Cahn cleffed five new numbers, three of which are given the Frank Sinatra treatment for boff results. Kelly joins Sinatra on the other two and pair also wrap up parody on "If You Knew Susie." Sinatra ballads are "I Fall in Love Too Easily," "The Charm of You" and "What Makes the Sunset."

In the dance department Kelly sells top terping. There is a clever "Tom and Jerry" sequence combining Kelly's live action with a cartoon fairy story. Kelly also combines three Spanish tunes into another sock number executed with little Sharon McManus. His third is a class tango using rhythms of "La Cumparsita," "Espana Carri" and a tango by Carmen Dragon.

Kathryn Grayson, one of the three co-stars, figures importantly in the score with her vocalling. Her top numbers are "My Heart Sings" and "Jalousie." Both register solidly. Jose Iturbi plays and conducts "The Donkey Serenade," "Piano Concerto" and "Hungarian Rhapsody No. 2" for additional potent musical factor.

Script by Isobel Lennart is suitable framework upon which to hang the music and dancing, and George Sidney's direction welds the material together smartly.

Sinatra and Kelly are sailors on liberty. They come to Hollywood. Sinatra is a shy Brooklynite who's being instructed in the art of pickups by Kelly, the traditional gob with a gal in every port. Boys' romancing is stalled while they rescue a little boy who wants to be a sailor. They meet the youngster's aunt, Miss Grayson, and both fall hard. In between trying to make good a promise to get Miss Grayson an audition with Iturbi, the romances become mixed and Sinatra ends up happily with a Brooklyn-born waitress and Kelly gets Miss Grayson. There's plenty of comedy in the script and Sidney's direction makes the most of it.

Standing out in the supporting cast is little Dean Stockwell as the kid who wants to be a sailor. Youngster has plenty of appeal and assurance for his age. Also appealing is Sharon McManus, the tyke who works a dance number with Kelly. Pamela Britton is excellent as the Brooklyn hashslinger who gets the Voice. Others are uniformly good with short footage.

Joe Pasternak's production guidance has given lavish mounting to entertainment values. There's nothing brassy about the color as photographed by Robert Planck and Charles Boyle. In the music department, ace contributors are Georgie Stoll for direction; Axel Stordahl for the Sinatra orchestrations, and Earl Brent's arrangements of Miss Grayson's numbers. Film runs two hours and 18 minutes but it's all entertainment. *Brog.*

Our Vines Have Tender Grapes

Hollywood, July 14.

Metro release of Robert Sisk production. Stars Edward G. Robinson, Margaret O'Brien; features James Craig, Frances Gifford, Agnes Moorehead, Morris Carnovsky, Jackie "Butch" Jenkins. Directed by Roy Rowland. Screenplay, Dalton Trumbo, based on book by George Victor Martin; camera, Robert Surtees; score, Bronislau Kaper; special effects, A. Arnold Gillespie and Danny Hall; editor, Ralph E. Winters. Tradeshown L. A. July 13, '45. Running time, **105 MINS.**

Martinius Jacobson....Edward G. Robinson
Selma Jacobson..........Margaret O'Brien
Nels Halverson..................James Craig
Viola Johnson..............Frances Gifford
Bruna Jacobson...........Agnes Moorehead
Bjorn Bjornson..........Morris Carnovsky
Arnold Hanson....Jackie "Butch" Jenkins
Mrs. Bjornson.......................Sara Haden
Mrs. Faraassen.............Greta Granstedt
Ingeborg Jensen.............Dorothy Morris
Pete Hanson.....................Arthur Space
Kola Hanson..............Elizabeth Russell
Mr. Faraassen............Louis Jean Heydt
Kurt Jensen.............Charles Middleton
Ivar Svenson.......................Arthur Hohl
Minister........................Francis Pierlot
Circus Driver...................Johnnie Berkes

"Our Vines Have Tender Grapes" is heart-warming Americana, simply and movingly told. It has the names of Edward G. Robinson and Margaret O'Brien for b.o. value and returns will be good. Simplicity with which the episodic story of routine rural life and American youth is projected strikes home and will awaken a keen response. It is this virtue of simplicity in writing, direction, production and playing that holds the picture together and compels interest.

Background is laid in a small Wisconsin farming community, peopled with Scandinavian-descended soil-tillers whose only wealth is the ability and fortitude with which they meet the everyday problems of being good farmers and good Americans. Interest centers on young Miss O'Brien, daughter of Robinson, and Agnes Moorehead, and her deadpan youthful playmate, Jackie Jenkins. The wistfulness and yearnings of childhood have an excellent exponent in Miss O'Brien and the small adventures and tragedies of youth trying to grow up carry a wealth of chuckles and heartbreak.

Robinson gives a deft study of the farmer, an inarticulate, soil-bound man whose greatest dream is for a new barn. His groping for answers to his daughter's questions, and drawing on parallels from farm life for explanations make emphatic points to script's philosophy of simplicity.

Roy Rowland's direction neatly ties together the episodes in the Dalton Trumbo script, based on George Victor Martin's book of the same title. Plot carries through the seasons, depicting the generosity, kindliness, meanness and narrowness found in all groups of people, rural and urban. Romance is capably carried by James Craig editor of the small-town paper, and Frances Gifford, schoolteacher from the city. Both impress. Agnes Moorehead gives a solid reading to the role of Miss O'Brien's mother. Morris Carnovsky, as the farmer whose life's work is tied up in his new barn; Dorothy Morris, the village simpleton; Arthur Space, Sara Haden, Charles Middleton and others lend topnotch support.

Robert Sisk's production mounting is authoritative in supporting the mood of the story, as is Robert Surtees' camera work, the special effects, and musical score by Bronislau Kaper. *Brog.*

Christmas in Connecticut

Hollywood, July 12.

Warners release of William Jacobs production. Stars Barbara Stanwyck, Dennis Morgan; features Sydney Greenstreet, Reginald Gardiner, S. Z. Sakall, Robert Shayne. Director, Peter Godfrey. Screenplay, Lionel Houser and Adele Commandini; original, Aileen Hamilton; camera, Carl Guthrie; music, Frederick Hollander; editor, Frank Magee. Tradeshown Hollywood, July 12, '45. Running time, **102 MINS.**

Elizabeth Lane..........Barbara Stanwyck
Jefferson "Jamaica" Jones..Dennis Morgan
Alexander Yardley....Sydney Greenstreet
John Sloan.............Reginald Gardiner
Felix Bassenak.....................S. Z. Sakall
Dudley Beecham.............Robert Shayne
Nora...............................Una O'Connor
Sinkewicz..............................Frank Jenks
Mary Lee..........................Joyce Compton
The Judge..............................Dick Elliott
Mr. Higgenbottom...............Charles Arnt

Laugh-paced farce that does an excellent job of entertaining. Smoothly-cut production, strong names for the marquee point to gratifying grosses in all situations. Story is lightweight but well-polished situations, direction and playing keep it in high gear most of the way for nifty returns. Some of the gags cut rather close to the Haysian frown, but since they spring from nature are good for solid roars.

Plot deals with the problems of a lady writer of home articles for a housekeeping mag in producing a husband, child, farm and a well-cooked meal out of thin air in order to please a stern, truth-loving publisher. Difficulties start when the publisher gets a letter asking that the femme scribe take in a sailor for the Christmas holiday. Mag man invites himself along, not knowing that the girl has none of the things she writes about in her articles. She can't even cook.

In order to save her job, Barbara Stanwyck, the writer, does a hasty roundup of the required ingredients to maintain the farce. Early arrival of the guests at the farm of Reginald Gardiner prevent her hasty wedding to him, whom she likes but does not love. From then on it's a merry chase; Gardiner trying to get married, Miss Stanwyck trying to avoid it because she's falling for the sailor, and the gob's efforts to be the gentleman with what he believes is another man's wife. Circumstances eventually are revealed to the publisher after some hectic footage and the sailor and the girl get together happily.

Miss Stanwyck and Dennis Morgan make a delightful team as the writer and sailor, giving the proper delivery to dialog in the Lionel Houser-Adele Commandini script for laugh response. Sydney Greenstreet is excellent as the publisher. Excellent comedy credits go to Reginald Gardiner as the would-be groom and S. Z. Sakall, Miss Stanwyck's chef friend. Robert Shayne, Una O'Connor, Frank Jenks, Joyce Compton, Dick Elliott and Charles Arnt are among others who count.

Peter Godfrey's direction overlooks no bets in pointing the laughs. Situations are never prolonged and the pace is fast. William Jacobs has given it topnotch production mounting. Photography and editing are expert. *Brog.*

The Caribbean Mystery

Twentieth Century-Fox release of William Girard production. Features James Dunn, Sheila Ryan, Edward Ryan, Jackie Paley, Reed Hadley, Roy Roberts, Richard Shaw, Daral Hudson, William Forrest, Roy Gordon. Directed by Robert Webb. Based on novel, "Murder in Trinidad," by John W. Vandercook; adaptation, W. Scott Darling; editor, John McCafferty; camera, Clyde De Vinna. Tradeshown N. Y. July 13, '45. Running time, **65 MINS.**

Mr. Smith.............................James Dunn
Mrs. Jean Gilbert...................Sheila Ryan
Gerald McCracken...........Edward Ryan
Linda Lane............................Jackie Paley
Rene Marcel.........................Reed Hadley
Capt. Van den Bark...........Roy Roberts
Capt. Bowman Hall........Richard Shaw
Hartshorn........................Daral Hudson
Colonel Lane...................William Forrest
McCracken, Sr.....................Roy Gordon

"The Caribbean Mystery" is a medium-budgeted programmer which has compactness, running time being only 65 minutes, and, if properly booked, should do well. Picture stacks up nicely as a secondary feature on more important runs and will be okay singly on performance in "B" houses.

Based on a novel, "Murder in Trinidad," by the radio commentator, John W. Vandercook, action concerns the mysterious disappearance of numerous men who have ventured into the jungles of a Caribbean locale in search of oil. Story is compounded of many incredible plot elements but holds the interest all the way, maintains suspense and carries a light romantic interest but no comedy relief.

James Dunn, who staged an impressive comeback in "A Tree Grows in Brooklyn," plays a former Brooklyn copper who has been assigned as special investigator for an oil company to try to find out what has happened to geologists on the payroll who have been seeking oil deposits. Much of the action concerns the lack of cooperation from local authorities and suspicion of intrigue pointing in many directions. Dunn finally tracks down the murderer of the jungle who disposes of any strangers coming near his island retreat where treasure is being collected, together with the higher-up in government service who's the man behind the scenes.

Paired for romantic interest are Eddie Ryan and Jackie Paley but both are only of passing importance. Sheila Ryan, a better known member of the cast, plays a hotel hostess who gets bumped off because of information she tries to depart to Dunn. Hers is a comparatively unimportant part. Dunn turns in a familiar but steady performance, while lessers doing all right include Reed Hadley, Roy Roberts, Richard Shaw, Daral Hudson, William Forrest and Roy Gordon. *Char.*

The Beautiful Cheat

(SONGS)

Universal release of Charles Barton production, directed by Barton. Stars Bonita Granville, Noah Beery, Jr.; features Margaret Irving, Sarah Selby, Carol Hughes, Irene Ryan, Milburn Stone. Screenplay, Ben Markson, from original by Manny Seff and Fritz Rotter; added dialog, Elwood Ullman; dialog director, Eacha Bledsoe; editor, Ray Snyder; camera, Woody Bredell. Tradeshown N. Y. July 12, '45. Running time, **59 MINS.**

Alice.............................Bonita Granville
Prof. Haven.....................Noah Beery, Jr.
Olympia.........................Margaret Irving
Athena..................................Sarah Selby
Miss Kent...............................Irene Ryan
Dolly.................................Carol Hughes
Lucius Haven......................Milburn Stone
Cassidy..................................Tom Dillon
Manager.........................Edward Gargan
Harley...........................Lester Matthews
Dr. Pennypacer..............Edward Fielding
Jimmy..................................Tommy Bond

Universal has an OK light comedy in Charles Barton's produced-directed "Beautiful Cheat." Story good and ditto performances of Bonita Granville and Noah Beery, Jr.

Juve delinquency theme is timely and Barton hasn't missed a bet in transferring the albeit wacky affair to the screen for a bright dualer entertainment.

Yarn revolves around Beery, serious-minded sociologist, commissioned by his publisher to do a tome on juve delinquency. His psychologist pal, Edward Fielding, figures it would be splendid if they could borrow the worst case from local reformatory to bring into the home for closeup study. Upon finding that much red tape would have to be cut before gaining such permission from authorities, Fielding cuts corners by inducing Miss Granville, beauteous secretary at the reform school, to masquerade as the miscreant.

Payoff comes when she invades the solitude of the prof's menage, presided over by his maiden sisters, Margaret Irving and Sarah Selby, and his middle-aged secretary, Irene Ryan. Trio are horrified at behavior of the imp and order her out. However, the prof has paternal leaning towards his little guinea pig and dispatches Milburn Stone, legal member of family to arrange for gal's adoption. This, too, is stymied since law does not permit unmarried male to adopt minor female.

Besides the above, Carol Hughes, nifty looker with pleasant voice, handles a brace of vocals in the nitery sequence.

Ben Markson has kept screenplay compact and punched up with solid dialog of Elwood Ullman. *Edba.*

Johnny Frenchman

(BRITISH-MADE)

London, July 11.

Eagle-Lion release of Ealing Studios-Michael Balcon production. Stars Francoise Rosay, Tom Walls, Patricia Roc. Directed by Charles Frend. Screenplay, T. E. B. Clarke; music composed by Clifton Parker and played by London Philharmonic Orchestra; camera, Roy Kellino. At Leicester Square theatre, London, July 10. Running time, **112 MINS.**

Lanec Florrie...............Francoise Rosay
Nat Pomeroy.........................Tom Walls
Sue Pomeroy....................Patricia Roc
Bob Tremayne...............Ralph Michael
Yan Kevarec.......................Paul Dupuis
Zecky Penrose..............Frederick Piper
Steve Matthews.........Arthur Hambling
Jane Matthews....................Judith Furse
Joe Pender....................James Harcourt
Jerome...............................Paul Bonifas
Theo.................................Marcel Poncin
Mayor of Lanec................Pierre Richard
Charlie West...................Richard George
Dick Trewhiddle....................Bill Blewitt
Mrs. Tremayne...............Beatrice Varley
Miss Bennett......................Drusilla Wills

Any Los Angeleno will tell you San Francisco needs fumigating, and San Francisco's opinion of the City of the Angels makes a snake's belly an Alpine height. You have to listen to a Detroiter to discover what a tenth-rate burg Cleveland is, and to a Clevelander to realize Detroit is a paradise of 5-and-10-cent stores. All a new play has to do to be a flop on Broadway is to be a hit in Chi—and vice worser—the Windy City is prepared to tell the world Manhattan out-Sodoms Gomorrah.

Which may be a southpaw way of reviewing this flick, but the outstanding point about it is it drives home the silliness of such parochial spites and jealousies—and winds up with a convincing kind of reconciliation between two communities of grand battlers. Hardly less important, tradewise, "Johnny Frenchman" is the answer to the English critics' prayer for just one British film company to make one pic of local color before Hollywood grabbed the theme and screened it first.

Altogether aside from its considerable merit as gripping drama (played for the most part by real fishermen and villagers who never before faced a camera), "Johnny Frenchman" has a good chance of clicking with American audiences everywhere if only because its theme and backgrounds have until now been seemingly untouched by anybody. Eagle-Lion is to be congratulated for having this one as its first release under its deal with Ealing Studios, distribution both here and in the States appearing to be a cinch.

In the first few hundred feet establishing the locale—a fishing port in Cornwall—you discover there is only one set of humans on earth Cornishmen hate more than they do "Froggies," their prize hatred being reserved for the men of Devon, the neighboring county. It is only incidental, and no stress is laid on it, but because it happens to be hard fact it rings true.

Tom Walls as Harbor Master of Mevagissy, having spent the greater part of his life fighting French fishermen "poaching" in his waters, is frustrated time and again by the impudent daring of Francoise Rosay, skipper of a smack from the Breton fishing colony of Lanec. Dominating her flea-bitten crew of rascally "Froggies" with all the toughness of Jack London's Sea Wolf, she raids the Cornish crab pots and scoops up seines-full of red mullet close inshore—and then turns heel and gets back to France with scuppers awash by the poached cargo.

Second only to her in nose-thumbing cockiness is her son, Yan, himself skipper of the trawler given him to command. Paul Dupuis, as Yan, appears by arrangement with the Canadian Broadcasting Corp. and is —presumably—a French Canadian. (Ealing Studios offer no dope on him.) Allowing for the fact the part is fat, and awake to the fatuity of drawing conclusions from a single performance, this brand new newcomer to the screen gives every indication of having plenty on the ball. As a daredevil leader of the Free French resistance movement and as a suitor for the hand of Tom Walls' daughter, he never puts a foot wrong.

Patricia Roc, as the very English fiancee of the very English Ralph Michael, makes you believe she really does know what love means for the first time—when the Froggie takes her in his arms. In scenes with her irate father, defending herself against the crime of being unfaithful to the Englishman fighting in the navy in favor of a non-fighting Froggie. Miss Roc more than holds her own. Similarly Dupuis breaks even in his scenes with Mlle. Rosay—acclaimed here as the finest screen actress ever to have migrated from her native France—when he convinces her even a Cornish woman can become a worthy mother of French sons and daughters.

Except for these principals the balance of the long cast is composed entirely of natives of Cornwall and emigrees from Breton, together with a number of members of the Free French resistance movement whose escape from occupied France is vouched for by the British Admiralty.

Mickey Balcon, producer, and Charles Frend, director of the pic, are deserving of praise for having done something unique. "A Yank at Oxford," like "National Velvet," to mention two of dozens of Hollywood-made flicks which (according to the wailing London critics) should have come out of British studios, may have been nearly enough the real thing to score hits with American audiences. "Johnny Frenchman," because it is the real thing, ought to hit the bull's eye in big and little towns from Coast to Coast. *Talb.*

Miniature Reviews

"Weekend at the Waldorf" (Songs) (M-G). Big b.o. with Ginger Rogers, Lana Turner, Walter Pidgeon, Van Johnson.

"Over 21" (Col). Comedy, adapted from the stage hit, with hefty marquee names, insures bright b.o.

"Guest Wife" (UA-Skirball). Claudette Colbert-Don Ameche in weak comedy triangle.

"The Hidden Eye" (M-G). Lightweight whodunit.

"Falcon in San Francisco" (RKO). One of the lesser entries in the Falcon mystery series.

"Jealousy" (Rep). John Loder-Jane Randolph co-starred in OK whodunit.

Weekend at the Waldorf

(MUSICAL)

Metro release of Arthur Hornblow, Jr., production. Stars Ginger Rogers, Lana Turner, Walter Pidgeon, Van Johnson; features Edward Arnold, Phyllis Thaxter, Keenan Wynn, Robt. Benchley. Directed by Robert Z. Leonard. Screenplay, Sam and Bella Spewack; adaption, Guy Bolton; suggested by Vicki Baum's play; music, Johnny Green, Ted Duncan, Kay Thompson; dances, Chas. Walters; camera, Robt. Planck, Warren Nowconbe; editor, Robt. J. Kern. Tradeshown July 18, '45. Running time, **130 MINS.**

Irene Malvern....................Ginger Rogers
Bunny Smith....................Lana Turner
Chip Collyer....................Walter Pidgeon
Capt. James Hollis....................Van Johnson
Martin X. Edley....................Edward Arnold
Cynthia Drew....................Phyllis Thaxter
Oliver Webson....................Keenan Wynn
Randy Morton....................Robert Benchley
Henry Burton....................Leon Ames
Juanita....................Lina Romay
Mr. Jessup....................Samuel S. Hinds
Bey of Aribajan....................George Zucco
Xavier Cugat and His Orchestra

Ginger Rogers, Lana Turner, Walter Pidgeon, Van Johnson and Xavier Cugat for the marquee—how can it miss? Besides, it's a good picture.

The origin of "Weekend at the Waldorf" in "Grand Hotel" is apparent from the start. In fact, with tongue-in-cheek one of the characters reprises a scene from the Vicki Baum play, and Ginger Rogers recognizes it as being from "Grand Hotel"—and says so as part of the dialog.

Everything happened during this particular weekend at the famed Park Ave. hostelry. Bob Benchley's scottie had pups; a benevolent tycoon let a honeymooning couple utilize his apartment while he weekended in the country; Edward Arnold tried to gyp a visiting Egyptian bey (who, to nobody's great surprise, suddenly spoke an excellent Oxford English, after only parlez-vousing in French or through an Arabic interpreter); stenographer Lana Turner fell in love with the war-wounded Van Johnson (the Walter Reed experts gave him a good chance to survive a delicate heart operation); Phyllis Thaxter solved her own romance; Keenan Wynn, reporter (this time sober), got his scoop; and movie star Ginger Rogers and cynical war correspondent Walter Pidgeon found a throbbing romance.

Never a dull moment in this weekend. In between, Van Johnson lands a coast-to-coast plug for a pal's song from Xavier Cugat. The Starlight Roof puts on a little floor show that would do credit to the Roxy; Cugie acts sage and handles lines as well as his baton.

The Spewacks and Guy Bolton have done a good adaptation from Vicki Baum's "Grand Hotel" that's such a terrific trailer for Lucius Boomer's hotel that all the innkeepers the world over will start to scheme their own little movie sequels. Unlike past pix deals for the Stork Club, Billy Rose's Diamond Horseshoe, and the like, the Waldorf swapped its plug for the cinematic rights. It pays off OK for both sides.

Only two songs, "And There You Are" (Sammy Fain-Ted Koehler), which is the number supposed to be written by the GI buddy, and Cugat's productioning of "Guadalajara." Charles Walters and Kay Thompson masterminded the accompanying dance and choral routines under Johnny Green and Ted Duncan.

Productionally, Arthur Hornblow, Jr., gave it everything—perhaps a little too much so, both as regards the 130 mins. running time and the general hors d'oeuvres The Waldorf's p. a., Ted Saucier, was technical director, and he rates a bonus from the hotel for the feature-length trailer on behalf of the hostelry. The footage takes in everything from impeccable catering, telephonic and general service, to three-sheeting the hostelry's private police force.

Histrionically, Ginger Rogers suffers from the camera. In some angles it's particularly harsh. The plot at no time is anything into which the cast can sink its full force, but Pidgeon, Johnson and Miss Turner make the most of it, along witht Edward Arnold as the menace The rest are adequate. *Abel.*

Over 21

Hollywood, July 21.

Columbia release of Sidney Buchman production. Stars Irene Dunne, Alexander Knox, Charles Coburn; features Jeff Donnell, Loren Tindall, Lee Patrick, Phil Brown, Cora Witherspoon, Charles Evans. Director, Charles Vidor. Screenplay, Sidney Buchman, adapted from play by Ruth Gordon (stage-produced by Max Gordon); camera, Rudolph Mate; music, Marlin Skiles; editor, Otto Meyer. Previewed at the Pantages, Hollywood, July 19, '45. Running time, **104 MINS.**

Paula Wharton....................Irene Dunne
Max Wharton....................Alexander Knox
Robert Gow....................Charles Coburn
Jan Lupton....................Jeff Donnell
Roy Lupton....................Loren Tindall
Mrs. Foley....................Lee Patrick
Frank MacDougal....................Phil Brown
Mrs. Gates....................Cora Witherspoon
Colonel Foley....................Charles Evans
Joel I. Nixon....................Pierre Watkin
Mrs. Dumbrowski....................Anne Loos
Mrs. Clark....................Nanette Parks
Mrs. Collins....................Adelle Roberts
Mrs. Greenberg....................Jean Stevens

"Over 21" is a bright film comedy, just as it was a sparkling stage laugh piece. Its story is still as sketchy and erratic, but the lines and business that made it click in legit are equally as potent on celluloid.

It's a picture that depends a great deal on trouping and direction, and the Columbia production has top quality in both of these. Added factor in the name value is the curiosity many will have in seeing Alexander Knox in a role other than Wilson. He does a good job of interpreting the somewhat uneven character of the fortyish newspaper editor competing with youth at OCS.

There's a message to be found in the comedy and Sidney Buchman's scripting points it up. How to make a new and better world for everybody is a seemingly incongruous point to find in a slapstickish comedy, but it's there and put over without too much interference with the laughs—in fact, the leadup to it belts over some nifty situations.

Plot of the Ruth Gordon play (in which she also starred as a legit piece) takes a top femme writer and her editor-husband and pitches them into the crowded frenzy of a town near an Army base. Housing shortages and makeshift living are a substantial part of the comedy. Knox (a thinly disguised real-life publisher), feels the urge to acquire first-hand knowledge of the war for future editorializing and goes to OCS to try for a lieutenancy. He finds the competition tough among the youngsters and isn't helped by frantic efforts of his former boss to get him back on the job. Irene Dunne is the wife who puts up with haphazard housing and living to be near her husband. As with the others, the character is slightly superficial, but in Miss Dunne's hands comes out as a choice job of miming. Charles Coburn also is first rate as the grumpy publisher and belts over some prime dialog for roars.

Jeff Donnell and Loren Tindall, an Army couple, fit handily into the laughs. Charles Evans, the colonel; Lee Patrick, the colonel's lady, and Cora Witherspoon, her mother, are stinging satires on upper Army circles. Pierre Watkin, film producer, and others are good.

Charles Vidor's direction is top quality in gearing the comedy for audience reaction, and Buchman's production is smartly valued. Photography and other technical factors measure up to the high production standard. *Brog.*

Guest Wife

United Artists release of Jack Skirball production. Stars Claudette Colbert, Don Ameche; features Richard Foran. Directed by Sam Wood. Screenplay, Bruce Manning and John Klorer; editor, William M. Morgan; camera, Joseph Valentine; asst. director, John Sherwood; music, Daniele Amfitheatrof. Previewed at Normandie theatre, N.Y., July 20, '45. Running time, **90 MINS.**

Mary....................Claudette Colbert
Joe....................Don Ameche
Chris....................Richard Foran
Worth....................Charles Dingle
Detective....................Grant Mitchell
Susy....................Wilma Francis
Urban Nichols....................Chester Clute
Nosey Character....................Irving Bacon
Dennis....................Hal K. Dawson
Arnold....................Edward Fielding

The invariable triangle has been given a comedy twist by producer Jack H. Skirball, and the result is "Guest Wife," in which Claudette Colbert, Don Ameche and Richard (nee Dick) Foran are the principals. Its boxoffice value can be measured only in terms of the personal marquee lure of the stars.

The fault of "Guest Wife" lies basically in the screenplay, which has its own lend-lease arrangement, dealing with a convenient borrowing of a wife by the husband's best friend for the purpose of continuing a subterfuge. Miss Colbert is the wife, Foran the husband and Ameche the friend, a world-famous newspaper correspondent who for rather shallow reasons must play husband to Miss Colbert in order to deceive his publisher.

The major result of it all is that Miss Colbert shows how really excellent an actress she is, despite the trite story, though the same cannot be said of Ameche or Foran. It's just that neither can meet normal thespian standards against the weight of this script.

There has been a rehash of the inevitable situations involving a comedy triangle, no less of which is the housing under one roof of the trio, with the friend and wife being required to share the same bedroom in order to continue the deception. And the discomfort through it all of the friend, while the wife and husband are more or less complacent, is motivated poorly and unconvincingly. There's even the usual house detective, suspicious and unduly observing, to round out the collection of stock stuff.

Charles Dingle and Grant Mitchell, as the publisher and house detective, are most prominent among the remainder of the cast.

Sam Wood has managed to garner some laughs with his direction. Production is top-grade. *Kahn.*

The Hidden Eye

Hollywood, July 14.

Metro release of Robert Sisk production. Features Edward Arnold, Frances Rafferty, Ray Collins, Paul Langton, Friday (canine). Director, Richard Whorf. Screenplay, George Harmon Coxe and Harry Ruskin; story, Coxe; based on characters created by Baynard Kendrick; camera, Lester White; score, David Snell; editor, George Hively. Tradeshown, Culver City, July 11, '45. Running time, 70 MINS.

Capt. Duncan Maclain	Edward Arnold
Jean Hampton	Frances Rafferty
Phillip Treadway	Ray Collins
Barry Gifford	Paul Langton
Marty Corbett	Wm. "Bill" Phillips
Inspector Delaney	Thomas Jackson
Ferris	Morris Ankrum
Stornvig	Robert Lewis
Kossovsky	Francis Pierlot
Helen Roberts	Sondra Rodgers
Gibbs (Chauffeur)	Theodore Newton
Louie	Jack Lambert
Arthur Hampton	Ray Largay
Alistair	Leigh Whipper
Burton Lorrison	Byron Foulger
Polasky	Lee Phelps
Whitey	Eddie Acuff
Sergeant Kramer	Bob Pepper
Rodney Hampton	Russell Hicks

Friday played by himself

"The Hidden Eye" makes the grade as supporting material but doesn't rise above that classification due to unsteady direction and some lightweight performances. Whodunit factors fail to develop much suspense as directed by Richard Whorf, and interest goes mainly to the dog, Friday, who acts as the seeing eye for the yarn's blind detective.

This latest entry in Metro's features dealing with the adventures of Capt. Duncan Maclain, blind dick, portrayed by Edward Arnold, has the sleuth solving three murders and preventing a fourth. Killings apparently draw their motive from an old association in Sumatra and scene of the crime always has a noticeable fragrance of an Oriental perfume. It doesn't take Arnold long to figure out that the obvious is phoney and he fastens the crimes on the family lawyer, who has been thefting funds left in his care. Finale features hand-to-hand combat between the criminal and Arnold, with the detective the winner due to his special training to overcome handicap of blindness.

Arnold is at his customary ease in the lead role. Frances Rafferty and Paul Langton carry off slight romance, with latter as principal suspect of the police. Others are adequate.

Production appurtenances are expert for release intentions on this one. *Brog.*

Falcon in San Francisco

RKO release of Maurice Geraghty production. Stars Tom Conway; features Rita Corday, Sharyn Moffett. Directed by Joseph H. Lewis. Screenplay, Robert Kent and Ben Markson; original, Kent; camera, Virgil Miller and William Sickner; editor, Ernie Leadlay. At Rialto, N. Y., week of July 20, '45. Running time, 66 MINS.

Tom Lawrence	Tom Conway
Joan Marshall	Rita Corday
Goldie	Edward S. Brophy
Annie Marshall	Sharyn Moffett
Doreen Temple	Faye Helm
DeForrest	Robert Armstrong
Itt-Key	Carl Kent
Dolman	George Holmes
Peter Vantine	John Mylong

Lacking suspense and punch, the latest in RKO's series, "Falcon in San Francisco," is a disappointing whodunit.

Obviously produced on a low budget, it should wind up on the right side of the financial ledger as some better than average acting by star Tom Conway and moppet Sharyn Moffett hold the picture together, since the storyline and scripting job fail to jell. Conway gives a fine performance, while little Miss Moffett proves that she is capable of bigger things. Remainder of the cast is stilted.

Yarn finds the Falcon accused of kidnapping the kid while he is trying to track down the killer of her nurse. He is freed of the charge and warned indirectly to drop the case. Ignoring the warning, he finally finds the murderer, exposing a racketeer believed long dead. *Sten.*

Jealousy
(ONE SONG)

Republic release of Gustav Machaty production, directed by him. Stars John Loder, Jane Randolph; features Karen Morley, Nils Asther, Hugo Haas. Screenplay, Arnold Phillips and Machaty from original by Dalton Trumbo; theme song, "Jealousy," Rudolf Friml; editor, John Link; camera, Henry Sharp. Tradeshown in N. Y., July 20, '45. Running time, 71 MINS.

Dr. David Brent	John Loder
Janet Urban	Jane Randolph
Dr. Monica Anderson	Karen Morley
Peter Urban	Nils Asther
Hugo Kral	Hugo Haas
Melvyn Russell	Herbert Holmes
Shop Owner	Michael Mark
Bob	Maurita Hugo
Secretary	Peggy Leon
Nurse	Mary Arden
Expressman	Noble "Kid" Chissell

This whodunit, while not new in premise, has several twists that make it an OK entry. It also has sturdy performances by John Loder and Jane Randolph, co-starred, and Karen Morley, Nils Asther and Hugo Haas in support.

Yarn is spun around a refugee-novelist, impoverished by the war, who cannot reconcile himself to mundane employment. Unwarranted jealousy makes him unappreciative of wife's efforts to salvage union by hiring out as a taxi-jockey. She (Jane Randolph) picks up Loder and a friendship develops. The murder follows which police list as suicide. The rest of the footage is the story.

Besides Loder and Miss Randolph, Nils Asther is menacingly okay as the novelist, and Karen Morley is charming as the femme heavy. Hugo Haas turns in neat performance as the friend. Others are adequate in lesser roles. Scripting, direction and cameraing okay too. *Edba.*

La Casa Esta Vacia
(The House Is Empty)
(CHILEAN-MADE)
Santiago, Chile, July 9.

Sociedad Cinematografica Band y Sales release of Chile Films production. Stars Ernesto Vilches, Alejandro Flores and Maria Teresa Squella; features Horacio Peterson, Chela Bon. Directed by Carlos Schlieper. Screenplay, Jorge Jantus; music, Helmut Helfritz; camera, Ricardo Yunis. At Teatro Real, Santiago, Chile, July 8, '45. Running time, 84 MINS.

Daniel	Ernesto Vilches
Carlos	Alejandro Flores
Ruth	Maria Teresa Squella
Jorge	Horacio Peterson
Maria Cristina	Chela Bon

This item from studios of Chile Films has b. o. lure in Ernesto Vilches, who is known all over Spanish-speaking world, and Alejandro Flores, leading Chilean actor with admirers in Argentina as well as Chile. Production on the whole is up to high standard studio set for itself in previous films. For Latin America and Spanish-language houses it should be solid.

Action is located in unidentified country and opens with artist painting delapidated old house. Elderly character, Daniel, comes along and when storm drives them indoors for shelter, he unfolds story of the house and its inhabitants in a series of flashbacks. Carlos was cursed with ungovernable temper, and when young, had unwittingly been the cause of his sister's death because of it. Brooding develops, and his father consigns to his especial care newly born brother, Jorge, to ease him out of it. Scheme is apparently successful and brothers grow up together, swearing eternal devotion to each other. Jorge goes away to do military service and Carlos, feeling lonely, meets Ruth, much younger than himself, and forgets oath of allegiance to Jorge. When latter, who is more of an age with Ruth, returns the inevitable triangle is completed. Carlos finds them together and the temper he thought he had dominated flares up again. He shoots at Ruth, kills Jorge, and disappears, leaving the house as mute witness of tragedy.

Despite sad theme and almost complete absence of comic relief, attention of audience is held throughout by the fine work of Vilches and Flores. Maria Teresa Squella is of pleasing appearance. Horacio Peterson is a juvenile new to pictures whose slight stiffness is offset by his vital personality. He should go far. Other characters are adequately portrayed.

Direction by Carlos Schlieper, is excellent, camera-work is first rate and sets and sound indicate conscientious production. *Nid.*

Miniature Reviews

"**Capt. Kidd**" (Bogeaus-UA). OK pirate actioner with Chas. Laughton, Randolph Scott, Barbara Britton.

"**George White's Scandals**" (Musical) (RKO). Okay combination of tunes and comedy with John Davis-Jack Haley.

"**Johnny Angel**" (RKO). George Raft-Claire Trevor-Signe Hasso in moderate box-office sea drama.

"**Mama Loves Papa**" (RKO). Lightweight comedy okay for neighborhood family trade.

"**Man From Oklahoma**" (Songs) (Rep.). OK oater.

"**Easy to Look At**" (Musical) (U). Program tuner for the family trade.

Captain Kidd

United Artists release of Benedict Bogeaus production (Rowland V. Lee-Carley Harriman-Arthur M. Landau associates), directed by R. V. Lee. Stars Chas. Laughton, Randolph Scott, Barbara Britton; features John Carradine, John Qualen, Wm. Farnum, Gilbert Roland, Sheldon Leonard, Abner Biberman, Reginald Owen. Original, Robt. N. Lee; screenplay, Norman Reilly Raine; camera, Archie Stout, Lee Zavitz; editor, Jos. Smith; asst. dir., Jos. Depew. Tradeshown July 27, '45. Running time, 89 MINS.

Captain William Kidd	Charles Laughton
Adam Mercy	Randolph Scott
Lady Anne Falconer	Barbara Britton
Cary Shadwell	Reginald Owen
Orange Povy	John Carradine
William Moore	Gilbert Roland
Bert Blivens	John Qualen
Boyle	Sheldon Leonard
Blades	Abner Biberman
Lord Albemarle	Ian Keith
Ranson	William Farnum
King William III	Miles Mander
Michael O'Shawn	Ray Teale

"Capt. Kidd" is a swashbuckler which will please generally, despite its minimum of feminine appeal. Barbara Britton, who is costarred with Charles Laughton and Randolph Scott, could phone her stuff into the celluloid for all its impact, coming on past midsection of the footage, but it's sufficiently adequate to inject a modicum of romance.

Story in the main focuses around the piratical rogues of the late 17th century when Captain Kidd (Laughton) freebooted the Spanish Main on the route of ships from England to fabulously rich India. When the king enlists Kidd as a loyal subject of the empire to give safe escort to treasury-laden vessels belonging to the crown, Kidd's doublecrossing leads him to the gallows. The hour-and-a-half footage in between is replete with piratical skullduggery.

Laughton is capital as the ruthless brigand of the seas, ruling his equally villainous rogues (Carradine, Roland, Qualen and Leonard) with stern cruelty. Somehow Randolph Scott is introduced as a fellow-brigand only to miraculously escape Davey Jones' locker, bring Laughton to justice, and give the film a romantic conclusion via Miss Britton, whose father, a British ambassador, fell another victim to Kidd's chicanery.

Cast, production, scripting and direction are top-standard. *Abel.*

George White's Scandals
Hollywood, July 28.

RKO release of George White production; executive producers, Jack J. Gross and Nat Holt. Stars Joan Davis, Jack Haley; features Philip Terry, Martha Holliday, Ethel Smith, Margaret Hamilton, Glenn Tryon. Director, Felix E. Feist; screenplay, Hugh Wedlock and Howard Snyder, Parke Levy and Howard Green; from original by Wedlock and Snyder; camera, Robert de Grasse; songs, Jack Yellen-Sammy Fain, Leigh Harline, Lew Brown, Ray Henderson; dances, Ernst Matray; special effects, Vernon L. Walker; editor, Joseph Noriega. Tradeshown Hollywood, July 27, '45. Running time, 94 MINS.

Joan Mason	Joan Davis

Weight of the Joan Davis-Jack Haley names will carry this one along. Its backstage story doesn't always project interest, but clowning of Davis-Haley team bats out plenty of hefty chuckles for general audiences. Production puts plenty of emphasis on the musical side, spotting 12 numbers, including a ballet, and has additional advantage of Gene Krupa's drumming.

George White works in "Life Is Just a Bowl of Cherries" number from his "Scandals of 1931" for an interesting look into the past. Spot uses Beverly Wills, Joan Davis' daughter, to portray mama singing the tune, but Miss Davis furnishes voice for stint. There's an uproarious skit tagged "Who Killed Vaudeville?" written by Jack Yellen and Sammy Fain, with Miss Davis and Haley burlesquing the answer to the question. A standout is the ballet number by Leigh Harline, "Bouquet and Lace," danced by Martha Holliday and chorus.

Backstage yarn develops several plot angles. One has Miss Davis and Haley stymied in their love match by Haley's stern sister, Margaret Hamilton. Another brings in a British society gal, who crashes the show by mistake, and her up-and-down romance with Phillip Terry, aide to White. Miss Holliday plays the girl and she and Terry are both on the pleasant side despite obviousness of their roles.

Krupa's orch has five tunes, winding up with a topnotch presentation of "Bolero." Ethel Smith plays "Liza" and "Os Pintinhos No Perreiro" (samba) for her two organ specialties. Another specialty among the musical numbers is Rose Murphy at the piano doing "Wishing," the Buddy de Sylva tune.

There was plenty of directorial coordinating needed to whip together the tunes and story and Felix E. Feist achieved okay results. White's production is never lavish but numbers show up well for presentation. Camera work and other technical factors are good. *Brog.*

Johnny Angel
(ONE SONG)

"Johnny Angel" is another in the seemingly never-ending series of maritime intrigues involving murder and lust. George Raft, Claire Trevor and Signe Hasso are starred in this sea drama. It is slow and plodding, with poor story development. Its boxoffice prospects are only moderate.

Raft plays a sea captain who becomes involved in the mystery of what happened aboard the ship of his father, also a captain, after the vessel is found adrift, with no one aboard, in the Gulf of Mexico. Involved, too, are the wife of Raft's boss, who is infatuated with Raft; a French girl stowaway who was apparently the only witness as to what actually happened aboard the ship; a whimsical taxi-driver, and the steamship line's owner. They're all seemingly fugitives from a road company of a Jack London sea yarn or perhaps something out of Hemingway. It's that typed.

Raft is his invariably glowering self as a guy who really handles his mitts—and the dames—while Miss Trevor and Hasso are the romantic interests along with Raft. Rest of the cast is weighted down too much by the story, though of the feature performers, Hoagy Carmichael, the composer, as in the Bogart-Bacall "To Have and Have Not" for Warners, plays the character of whimsy with tongue in cheek. He and Paul Webster have teamed for the pic's lone tune, "Memphis in June," which is strongly atmospheric. *Kahn.*

Mama Loves Papa
Hollywood, July 30.

Family comedy with the familiar Leon Errol antics to help it along in supporting spots. Running time is short, making it easy to book, and Errol fans will approve formula proceedings.

Locale is 1905, and juicy six-pound prime roasts costing 17c a pound, cheap eggs and butter, is a certain groan-arouser for present-day audiences. Errol is a milksop employee of a furniture company until his wife, Elisabeth Risdon, buys a book on how to help a husband be a success. The pressure she puts on him to dress differently, ask for a raise, gets him in plenty of hot water. Through mistake, he becomes a park commissioner when a politician sees a chance to use him to land a big contract to manufacture playground equipment. Invited to the country for the weekend, Errol has his first adventure with champagne, which gives reason for his famous rubber-legs stunt, has a misunderstanding with his wife, kills the politician's deal. Windup has Errol's old boss offering him a new job and the wife forgiving all.

Situations are all formula but okay for release intentions as directed by Frank Strayer. Edwin Maxwell is a neat caricature of a grumpy boss and Paul Harvey makes a smooth politician. Lawrence Tierney, better known for his Dillinger characterization for another company, occupies a small spot as Harvey's henchman. Charlotte Wynters, Charles Halton and others are good.

Ben Stoloff's production framework is adequate for budget, as are camera and other technical aides. *Brog.*

Man From Oklahoma
(SONGS)

In its category this western is what the fans like it. It should draw nifty b.o. returns from audiences devoted to Roy Rogers and his usual supporters—George "Gabby" Hayes, Dale Evans, Bob Nolan and the Sons of the Pioneers, not to mention that horse, Trigger. Pic's play on name of state popularized by the Rodgers-Hammerstein "Oklahoma!" shouldn't hurt either.

The story is the same as usual, casting Rogers in the role of hard-ridin', heart-of-gold guy from the wild prairee who comes to the rescue of the gal, Miss Evans. This time, a feminine counterpart is given Hayes in the person of Maude Eburne, who does a wild-western grandma who can tote a shotgun and exchange maledictions with Hayes himself.

Some of the fancy riding is done by teams hitched to wagons, reenacting the wild rush of settlers into the newly opened territory of Oklahoma, and there is some good photography in those sequences. Aside from those scenes, realism is at a premium—but then who expects such things among the devotees of the western?

Better than the usual run, however, is the music. "I'm Beginning to See the Light" leads off a number of pops, and "The Martins and the Coys" is good satirical ribbing of hillbilly themes about feuding backwoodsmen. But no effort is made to exploit any of the numbers. The picture goes its even, traditional way to the traditional end, but there is no doubt that its audiences will enjoy it to the last shot. *Cars.*

Easy to Look At
(Songs)
Hollywood, July 26.

Another in Universal's small-budgeted, lightweight program musicals that will fare no better or worse than similar product from that studio. Okay for supporting bookings although slowly paced. Musical moments—and there are eight tunes in the picture—fill up running time, as does the plot.

Gloria Jean is seen as ambitious costume designer who comes to New York to win fame. She meets up with the lowly watchman in a swank establishment, finds he's a former great in the designing field. One of her sketches attracts attention of a musical comedy star, but credit goes to watchman, giving him a new start which Miss Jean abets. Head of the swank designing emporium falls for Miss Jean but, just as they declare their love, circumstance makes her appear a design thief. Before it's all over, she and the watchman are acclaimed and the romance is saved.

Miss Jean, growing up into quite a young lady, gives pleasant singing to four numbers. Kirby Grant tries hard as the slightly dopey guy who falls for her. George Dolenz, eccentric designer; J. Edward Bromberg, the watchman; Eric Blore, musical producer, and others deliver stilted performances under Ford Beebe's direction. Production dress by Henry Blankfort is okay for budget. He also authored the original. *Brog.*

Miniature Reviews

"Pride of the Marines" (WB). Socko celluloid saga of Marine-hero Al Schmid: a fine entertainment, surefire b.o.

"Lady on a Train" (U). (Songs). Nifty comedy mystery with farce treatment, plus three songs by Deanna Durbin; ok b.o.

"Uncle Harry" (U). Fair murder-meller that must depend on lure of George Sanders, Geraldine Fitzgerald and Ella Raines.

"Radio Stars on Parade" (Songs) (RKO). Topnotch b.o. revue starring Frances Langford and other radio headliners.

"Dangerous Partners" (M-G). Weak "B" melodrama lacking in action.

"Why Girls Leave Home" (PRC) (Songs). Fair combination of music and murder; mild b.o.

"In Old New Mexico" (Mono). Duncan Renaldo as "Cisco Kid" in okay b. o. western for nabes.

"Gangs of the Waterfront" (Rep.) Gangland yarn that will need heavy support in most situations.

"The Shanghai Cobra" (Mono). Charlie Chan whodunit, talky and slowly-paced.

"Military Secret" (Artkino). Well-paced and well-acted. Russian-made whodunit that should please.

Pride of Marines

Warner Bros release of Jerry Wald production. Stars John Garfield, Eleanor Parker, Dane Clark. Directed by Delmer Dayes. Screenplay, Albert Maltz; adaptation, Marvin Borowsky from Roger Butterfield's story; music, Franz Waxman; camera, Peverell Marley, L. Robt. Burks; editor, Owen Marks; arrangements, Leonid director, Chuck Hansen. Tradeshown Aug. 3, '45. Running time, 119 MINS.

Al Schmid ..... John Garfield
Ruth Hartley ..... Eleanor Parker
Lee Diamond ..... Dane Clark
Jim Merchant ..... John Ridgely
Virginia Pfeiffer ..... Rosemary DeCamp
Ella Merchant ..... Ann Doran
Lucy Merchant ..... Ann Todd
Kebabian ..... Warren Douglas
Irish ..... Don McGuire
Tom ..... Tom D'Andrea
Doctor ..... Rory Mallinson
Ainslee ..... Stephen Richards
Johnny Rivers ..... Anthony Caruso
Capt. Burroughs ..... Moroni Olsen
Red ..... Dave Willock
Second Marine ..... John Sheridan
Lieutenant ..... John Miles
Corporal ..... John Compton
Lenny ..... Lennie Bremen
Corpsman ..... Michael Brown

"Pride of the Marines" is a two-hour celluloid saga which should inspire much pride for many. As an entertainment film with a forceful theme, so punchy that its "message" aspects are negligible, it is a credit to all concerned. It's a cinch for boxoffice. And transcending the basic economic equation, there is much therein for which any American may well be proud.

The simple story of Al Schmid, real-life marine-hero of Guadalcanal, is the story of American patriotism and heroism which is unheroic in its simple forthrightness; American pride in defending our way of life; American guts; and also a distorted sense of foolish pride, born of stubbornness, when the blinded Al Schmid rebels at returning to his loved ones because he "wants nobody to be a seeing-eye dog for me."

With our more than 1,000,000 casualties affecting nearly every American family, the many wounded survivors and all their intimates—family, sweethearts and not forgetting former employers—are bound up in Jerry Wald's tiptop production job.

As such this is a significant film. Yes, even one with some social significance underneath its hard-hitting, biting and frequently bitter unfolding. It lays scalpel-clean the GI-in-the-street's concern about his post-war future, with memories of their fathers' apple-selling, bonus-marches and all the other post-World War I ills. In that San Diego Navy hospital scene, in staccato, punchy dialog the Marines sound off on GI Bill of Rights, their future, general security, reemployment, reactions to civilians, and the like.

An excellent foil is Rosemary DeCamp as the synmpathetic nurse, as each airs his gripes, while the brooding, blinded Marine-hero, Al Schmid, spurns his Philadelphia sweetheart (Eleanor Parker) and curses his fate.

Director Delmer Daves has paced his charges with clearcut crescendos, and from the climactic peaks he levels off only to volplane to another emotional impact.

As unfolded it's a heart-tugging, sentimentally heroic tale. John Garfield as the brittle Al Schmid, ex-machinist now Marine-hero, albeit blinded, gives a vividly histrionic performance that will not be easily forgotten. He is buoyed plenty by Dane Clark and Anthony Caruso, with Eleanor Parker as the No. 1 femme and Ann Doran, little Ann Todd and John Ridgely realistically the happy little middle-class family. All the casting is topnotch. Rory Mallinson, as the medico, suggests a good new face.

The craftsmanship behind the lens is of highest order, not the least of which is Franz Waxman's fine dramatic score which heightens the emotional pitch and movement so effectively. *Abel.*

Lady on a Train

(SONGS)

Hollywood, Aug. 4.

Universal release of Felix Jackson production. Stars Deanna Durbin; features Ralph Bellamy, David Bruce, George Coulouris, Allen Jenkins, Dan Duryea, Edward Everett Horton, Patricia Morison, Elizabeth Patterson, Maria Palmer, Jacqueline de Wit. Directed by Charles David. Screenplay. Edmund Beloin and Robert O'Brien; original story by Leslie Charteris; camera, Woody Bradell; musical score, Miklos Rozsa: editor, Ted Kent. At Warners Beverly. Beverly Hills, Aug. 3, '45. Running time, 96 MINS.

Nicki ..... Deanna Durbin
Jonathan ..... Ralph Bellamy
Haskell ..... Edward Everett Horton
Mr. Saunders ..... George Coulouris
Danny ..... Allen Jenkins
Wayne Morgan ..... David Bruce
Joyce ..... Patricia Morison
Arnold ..... Dan Duryen
Margo ..... Maria Palmer
Aunt Charlotte ..... Elizabeth Patterson
Mr. Wiggam ..... Samuel S. Hinds
Sergeant Christie ..... William Frawley
Miss Fletcher ..... Jacqueline de Wit
Joseph Waring ..... Thurston Hall
Cousin ..... Clyde Fillmore
Maxwell ..... Ben Carter
Cousin ..... Mary Forbes
Cousin ..... Sarah Edwards
Woman with Umbrella ..... Nora Cecil
Drunk ..... Hobard Cavanaugh

"Lady On a Train" is a mystery comedy containing plenty of fun for both whodunit and laugh fans. It's a top-of-the-bill feature backed with smart production values and the Deanna Durbin draw for sturdy boxoffice outlook. Melodramatic elements in the Leslie Charteris original are flippantly treated without minimizing suspense, and the dialog contains a number of choice quips that are good for hefty laughs as screenplayed by Edmund Beloin and Robert O'Brien, both former Jack Benny air scripters.

Miss Durbin sings three tunes as well as handling herself excellently in the comedy role. Songs are all delivered against a background of menace. This makes her "Silent Night" particularly potent. Actress is a bit too cute with "Give Me a Little Kiss, Will You Huh?", "Night and Day" is sock vocally but unbecoming hairdo and garish makeup worn during number are distractions.

Actress is seen as a murder mystery addict who witnesses a murder from her train window while arriving in Grand Central station. Police discount her story and she turns to David Bruce, mystery writer, for help. Her pursuit of the writer to enlist his aid is good funning and accounts for some hilarious sequences. Recognizing the murdered man from a newsreel clip, she gets mixed up with his heirs, is mistaken for the old gent's nightclub songstress sweetie, and has many strange adventures before unmasking the killer. The amateur detectives are never very smart and their blunders make for chuckles. Writer character played by Bruce pokes fun at whodunit scribblers, and other standard mystery characters are given the farce treatment to keep laughs coming.

Charles David's direction of the Felix Jackson production sustains pace throughout and smartly spots the laughs. Players are uniformly expert in keeping things on the move. Camera work takes advantage of the excellent settings and editing is good. *Brog.*

Uncle Harry

Universal release of Joan Harrison productions. Stars George Sanders, Geraldine Fitzgerald, Ella Raines; features Sara Aligood, Moyne Maggill, Harry Von Zel. Directed by Robert Siodmak. Screenplay, Stephen Longstreet: adapted by Keith Winter from stage drama, "Uncle Harry," by thomas Job; camera, Paul Ivano; editor, Arthur Hilton. Previewed in projection room. N.Y., Aug. 6, '45. Running time, 80 MINS.

Harry Quincy ..... George Sanders
Lettie Quincy ..... Geraldine Fitzgerald
Deborah Brown ..... Ella Raines
Nona ..... Sara Allgood
Hester ..... Moyna Maggill
Dr. Adams ..... Samuel S. Hinds
Ban ..... Harry Von Zell
Mrs. Nelson ..... Ethel Griffies
Helen ..... Judy Clark
John Warren ..... Craig Reynolds
Mr. Nelson ..... Will Wright
Mr. Follinsbee ..... Arthur Loft
Mrs. Follinsbee ..... Irene Tedrow
Biff Wagner ..... Coulter Irwin
Joan Warren ..... Dawn Render
Matron ..... Ruth Cherrington
Joe ..... Rodney Bel

As a stage play "Uncle Harry" was given adult treatment both by author Thomas Job and the cast headed by Joseph Schildraut and Eva Le Gallienne. However, in the film there has been a loss of much of the suspense and stark melodrama that gave the play the punch to run a full season on Broadway. **The picture version is just fair, and will have to depend upon its three stars—George Sanders, Geraldine Fitzgerald and Ella Raines—to score at the boxoffice.**

Unlike the play, which was enacted in flashback, the film version carries the action right through as it occurs. But the film is too leisurely rather than excitingly dramatized. The pic's ending is both unreal and unbelievable.

The title character, played neatly by George Sanders, is a designer in a fabric mill, and resides with two spinster sisters—Lettie (Geraldine Fitzgerald) and Hester (Moyna Maggill). Deborah (Ella Raines) meets Harry while on a visit from the N.Y. office of the milling concern, and they soon plan to be married. The younger sisters breaks that up, and when Harry finds out, he plans to poison her, but the cup of cocoa he had poisoned is mistakenly switched, so that the elder sister is killed. There's a trial, and the younger sister is convicted.

Miss Fitzgerald underplays her role too much as the younger sister. Miss Maggill neatly portrays the older sister. Remainder of cast is satisfactory. *Sten.*

Radio Stars on Parade

(SONGS)

RKO release of Ben Stoloff production. Stars Frances Langford, Wally Brown, Alan Carney; features Ralph Edwards, Don Wilson, Skinny Ennis and band. Directed by Leslie Woodwins. Screenplay, Robert E. Kent and Monty Brice, based on original by Kent; camera, Harry Walker; editor, Edward W. Williams; songs, Harold Adamson-Jimmy McHugh, Johnny Mercer-Harold Arlen, Arthur Amsden, Clifford Grey, Sonnie Miller, Jack Waller, Joseph Tunbridge, Jack Rock. Tradeshown N.Y., Aug. 1, '45. Running time, 69 MINS.

Jerry Miles ..... Wally Brown
Mike Strager ..... Alan Carney
Sally Baker ..... Frances Langford
Don Wilson ..... Don Wilson
Romano ..... Tony Romano
Pinky ..... Rufe Davis
Danny ..... Robert Clarke
Maddox ..... Sheldon Leonard
George ..... Max Wagner
Steve ..... Ralph Peters
"Truth or Consequences" with Ralph Edwards and Co.
Skinny Ennis Band
Town Criers
Cappy Barra Boys

"Radio Stars on Parade" proves to be an entertaining revue held together in slapstick fashion by the comical, though corny, lines and antics of Wally Brown and Alan Carney. Film should do better than average business.

Picture obviously started out as a low-budgeter and producer Ben Stoloff was kept within stringent monetary limitation to bring it in. However, Frances Langford (who is photoged throughout better than ever before) and Ralph Edwards and his "Truth or Consequences" radio troupe aid its entertainment values considerably, so that several of the other all-too-plain accoutrements wrapped up in this film are overlooked. Edwards & Co. should capture still wider audiences among their followers who have not seen them in action before, while those who have will laugh at their antics here just the same. He's a gracious m.c. who keeps things moving right along when he is on the screen, as he does on the air.

Yarn finds Carney and Brown subbing for an agent who had to leave town due to his non-payment of a gambling debt. In their efforts to get Miss Langford work, they cross the path of her suitor, a N. Y. gangster, whom she refuses to see. She gets the job of singing with the Skinnay Ennis band, but not before the comic pair are practically annihilated by the mobsters.

Don Wilson, Rufe Davis, Town Criers, Cappy Barra boys and Tony Romano are others in the cast who have been featured on the networks. Romano does a fine bit of guitar accompaniment to Miss Langford in one scene. Seven tunes in this picture have been showcased originally elsewhere, but the excellent vocal job Miss Langford does on "Don't Believe Everything You Dream," "Couldn't Sleep a Wink" and couple of others make them come to life all over again.

Production values aren't worth mentioning since they're in the low-budget vein. Camerawork and settings are just average, but there is lots of good family fun in this 69 minutes of film. *Sten.*

Dangerous Partners

(ONE SONG)

Metro release of Arthur J. Field production. Stars James Craig, Signe Hasso, Edmund Gwenn. Directed by Edward L. Cahn. Screenplay by Marion Parsonnet, from adaptation by Edmund L. Hartman, based on story by Oliver Weld Bayer; camera, Carl Freund; song by Earl Brent; editor, Ferris Webster. Tradeshown in N. Y., July 26, '45. Running time, 74 MINS.

Jeff Caighn ..... James Craig
Carola Ballister ..... Signe Hasso
Albert Richard Kingby ..... Edmund Gwenn
Lili Roegan ..... Audrey Totter
Marie Drumman ..... Mabel Paige
Clyde Ballister ..... John Warburton
Duffy ..... Henry O'Neill
Jonathan ..... Grant Withers

Dealing with a Nazi agent who

tries to get out of the U. S. by picking up enemy funds left with Americans, "Dangerous Partners" falters. Its boxoffice value is negative.

Picture lacks a comprehensive story-line and proper characterizations. James Craig and Signe Hasso, conniving to get funds willed to another man (Edmund Gwenn), are unbelievable in their transition to patriotism. However, as always, Gwenn gives a good performance.

It all deals with the finding of a briefcase, at the scene of a plane crash, with four different wills in it. Craig and Miss Hasso team when her husband is mysteriously killed on a train in an effort to nab the money from those to whom it is willed. However, just when they believe they have succeeded in their plan, they are caught up with by Gwenn, who reveals that he is a top Nazi agent trying to escape to his homeland—just in time to bring the picture to an end with his capture, the money being turned over to the government agents.

Production is uneven. *Sten.*

Why Girls Leave Home

(SONGS)

PRC release of Sam Sax production. Features Lola Lane, Sheldon Leonard, Elisha Cook, Jr., Constance Worth, Pameal Blake, Paul Guilfoyle, Claudia Drake. Director, William Berke. Screenplay, Fanya Foss Lawrence and Bradford Ropes: camera, Mack Stenler: songs, Jay Livingston and Ray Evens: asst. director, William A. Calihan, Jr. At Gotham, N.Y., Aug. 3, '45. Running time, 70 MINS.

Irene	Lola Lane
Chris Williams	Sheldon Leonard
Diana Leslie	Pamela Blake
Jimmie Lobo	Elisha Cook, Jr.
Steve Raymond	Paul Guilfoyle
Flo	Constance Worth
Marien	Claudia Drake
Mrs. Leslie	Virginia Brissac
Reilly	Thomas Jackson
Alice	Evelynne Eaton
Peggy Leslie	Peggy Lou Bianco
Ted Leslie	Fred Kohler
Wilbur Harris	Walter Baldwin
Ed Blake	Robert Emmett Keane

Title is misleading. Instead of being a juve delinquency story, film is a murder thriller. The footage has its share of thrills, but plot development is thin. Boxoffice will depend largely on the title, and that isn't much.

Story sets out to prove that all that glitters is usually brass, most of which is accomplished via throwback technique. Ambitious girl, unhappy about status quo of life with her parents, kid sister and big brother, wants the glamour life of nightclubs. After family squabble, she leaves home and walks practically into job as songstress in a nightclub with the stereotyped double-barreled background. Because she learns too much about the ruthless operators, they want to erase her and make it look like suicide. However, film is kept reeling through perseverance of a reporter who brings culprits to justice. The only cliche the film surprisingly lack is any love interest.

While the direction and script are mediocre, it's obvious that the performers are more than adequate. Lola Lane gets top billing as nightspot operator, but Pamela Blake, as the runaway, is povital character. However, Constance Worth, in a sympathetic sister role, is bound for bigger stakes. Songs are very unoriginal.

In Old New Mexico

(ONE SONG)

Monogram release of Philip N. Krasne production (Dick L'Estrange, associate). Features Duncan Renaldo, Martin Garralaga, Gwen Kenyon. Directed by Phil Rosen. Camera, Arthur Martinello: screenplay, Betty Burbridge, based on characters created by O. Henry; music, David Chudnow; song by Hershey Martin and Mayris Chaney. At Strand, Brooklyn, N.Y., week Aug. 2 '45, dual. Running time 62 MINS.

Cisco Kid	Duncan Renaldo
Pancho	Martin Garralaga
Ellen	Gwen Kenyon
Hastings	Norman Willis
Belle	Donna Day
Dolores	Aurora Roche
Sheriff	Lee White
Cliff	Kenneth Terrell
Brady	John Laurenz
Doc Wills	Richard Gordon
Padre	Pedro de Cordoba
Printer	Harry Depps

"In Old New Mexico," another in the long-running series of "Cisco Kid" pix, is okay for the kid trade, with enough gunplay to offset slow direction.

Duncan Renaldo proves a worthy successor to the role created by Warner Baxter. He imparts the proper Latin flavor and enacts the part of the Mexican Robin Hood with sufficient authority.

The Cisco Kid contrives to clear a girl of a murder charge, after kidnapping her from a stage coach. He traps the murderer and, with cooperation of the sheriff, stages a phoney shooting which tricks the culprit into a confession.

Romantic interest is supplied by Gwen Kenyon in a routine characterization, while Martin Garralaga does creditably as Cisco's assistant. Also prominently cast are Aurora Roche as a song-and-dance gal in a border saloon, Norman Willis and Richard Gordon.

Outdoor camera work of Arthur Martinello and music by David Chudnow are outstanding. *Jose.*

Gangs of the Waterfront

Republic release of George Blair production. Features Robert Armstrong and Stephaine Bachelor. Directed by Blair. Screenplay, Albert Beich, based on original story by Sam Fuller; camera, Marcel Le Picard; editor, Fred Allen; music Richard Cherwin. At Strand, Brooklyn, N.Y., week of Aug. 2, '45, Jual. Running time, 55 mins.

Dutch Malone and Peter Winkly	Robert Armstrong
Jane Rodgers	Stephanie Bachelor
Anjo Ferranti	Martin Kosleck
Rita	Marian Martin
District Attorney Brady	William Forrest
Commissioner Hogan	Wilton Graff
Miler	Eddie Hall
Ortega	Jack O'Shea
Dr. Martin	Davison Clark
Chief Davis	Dick Elliott

Republic's cops-and-robbers epic of the waterfront jars credibility, but "Gangs of the Waterfront" unfolds a fast story, with the proper amount of gunplay to please nabe payees.

"Gangs" tells of a taxidermist, a double for a notorious gangster, anxious to avenge his brother's death during a mob battle. The gangster having been injured in an auto accident, the animal stuffer is carefully coached in the mobsman's mannerisms and, with the connivance of the D. A., assumes the baddie's job. He ultimately rounds up the mob.

Robert Armstrong does double duty as the hoodlum and taxidermist and gives it a perfunctory treatment, with Stephanie Bachelor doing well as the inheritor of the ships-supply business who won't pay "protection." In the mob roster, Marion Martin has little to do as the gang-moll, while Martin Kosleck is miscast as the gangster of Italian descent. George Blair's direction is spirited. *Jose.*

The Shanghai Cobra

Monogram release of James S. Burkett production. Stars Sidney Toler; features Benson Fong. Mantan Moreland. Directed by Phil Karlson. Screenplay by George Callahan and George Wallace Sayre from story by Callahan; camera, Vince Farrar. Previewed N.Y., Aug. 1, '45. Running time, 64 MINS.

Charlie Chan	Sidney Toler
Tommy Chan	Benson Fong
Birmingham	Mantan Moreland
Paula	Joan Barclay
Jarvis	James Flavin
Adams	Addison Richards
Davis	Walter Fenner
Ned Stewart	James Cardwell
Harris	Arthur Loft
Morgan	Gene Stutenroth
Lorraine	Janet Warren
Taylor	Joe Devlin
Fletcher	Roy Gordon

To the Charlie Chan addicts this may be par, but viewed as an ordinary whodunit it's just slow-paced, talky material wthout particular flavor.

The Chinese dick employed by the U. S. Government is put on a case which involves the killing of people who are bitten by a cobra. There is a lot of pointless walking and riding around to, from, and in the sewers underneath a bank where the Government has stored radium. There is a lot of chatter which is supposed to be amusing, but would bore anyone above the age of eight. In the end there is a surprise angle when it turns out that the bank guard is not a blackguard, but really a big innocent. But even that point is developed mechanicallly.

Sidney Toler seems tired as Charlie Chan, Benson Fong seems wasted as Charlie's son, while Mantan Moreland as "Birmingham" is just the stereotyped Negro chauffeur. *Cars.*

Half-Way House

(BRITISH-MADE)

A.F.E. Film Corp release of Michael Balcon (Ealing Studios) production. Stars Francoise Rosay. Directed by Basil Deardeu. Screenplay, Angus MacPhail and Diana Morgan. From play "The Peaceful Inn" by Denis Ogden: Camera, Wilkie Cooper: editor, Charles Haase. Previewed, Little Carnegie, N.Y., Aug. 3, '45. Running time, 78 MINS.

Alice Meadows	Francoise Rosay
Capt. Meadows	Tom Walls
Rhys	Mervyn Johus
David	Esmond Knight
Gweneth	Glynis Johns
Oakley	Alfred Drayton
Jill	Valerie White

British psychological drama, built around an assorted group of characters gathered in a rural inn for a weekend, is a pleasant though preachy allegory. Story is fairly obvious and reminiscent though it holds interest. Its pulpit quality, "foreign" feel and lack of "names" will give film only a limited appeal.

Story recalls two plays, "The Passing of the Third Floor Back" and "Outward Bound." The group assembled at the country inn includes an ailing symphony conductor, a cashiered Army officer, a black-market operator, a disgraced sea captain and his spiritualist-inclined wife, a couple about to be divorced, and another younger couple about to be married. All are beset with problems, which the innkeeper and his daughter straighten out for them.

Odd fact is that the inn had burned down the year before, after being bombed by a German plane. In the course of the yarn, the truth comes out—the innkeeper and daughter are dead, the inn has been rebuilt for this weekend only, and time has been set back a year for the benefit of the house-guests. Some of us, is the theme, have to stop still in time for a while to readjust ourselves to the problems and future that we face. After the innkeeper has lectured his guests on their various sins or omissions and psyched them back to normalcy, he sends them packing and the inn and keeper go up in smoke again.

Story moves along too slowly and evenly. Performances are well done, however. Francoise Rosay, former French star, does a poignant bit in her first English-speaking role as a grief-stricken captain's wife. Mervyn Johns as the ghostly boniface, and Glynis Johns as his daughter, are also good. Direction and scripting are intelligent. Scenes of English countryside are attractive. Film is modestly budgeted. *Bron.*

Military Secret

(Soviet-Made)

Artkino release of Soyuzdet (Moscow) production. Directed by Vladimir Legoshin. Screenplay by Leonid and Peter Tur and Leo Sheynin: camera, Sergei Uruseysky; music, Konstantin Korchmarev; English titles, Charles Clement. At Stanley, N.Y., Aug. 1, '45. Running time, 73 mins.

Col. Lartsev	Sergei Lukianov
Captain Bakhmetiev	Ivan Malishevsky
Secret Service Commissar	Alexei Gribov
Engineer Leontiev	Andrei Tutishkin
Weininger	Victor Byelokurov
Gestapo Colonel Kraschke	Omar Abdulov
Maria Zubova	Natasha Borskaya
Natalia Ossenina	Natalia Alisova

(In Russian; English Titles)

For the first time in many months the Soviet film-makers have sent to their New York showcase, the Stanley, a picture that need take no backseat. This whodunit is a good, competent job.

Script is a suspenseful story about an exchange of wits between Moscow's equivalent of our G-2 and the Nazi Gestapo. Latter has set out to capture alive the Russian inventor of a secret weapon, and has assigned one of its topflight espionage agents to the job. But Moscow's counter-espionage chief knows what the Nazis are doing. The climax comes as a surprise and the dramatic action evolved has plenty of mystery, a thrill or two, lots of intrigue and even a touch of romance. Furthermore, there is very good camera work involved.

Production, while low budgeted, is entirely suitable. Alexei Gribov as the Russian in charge of secret service work, Victor Belokurov as the Nazi spy, and the two principal women in the cast—Natasha Borskaya and Natalia Alisova—act in the better style of Russian restraint, and the whole was directed smoothly and paced expertly by Vladimir Legoshin. Miss Alisova, incidentally, is a looker whose screen presence should intrigue Hollywood's yen for fresh talent. *Cars.*

Miniature Reviews

"The Lost Weekend" (Par) Ray Milland in smash boxoffice drama about a drunk's rehabilitation.

"Ziegfeld Follies" (M-G) (Musical). All-star, super due for smash biz.

"I Love A Bandleader" (Col.) (Musical). Phil Harris-Rochester in slow musicomedy slated as second feature material.

"Tell It to a Star" (Rep) (Songs). Pretty good combination of music and comedy; okay b.o.

"Adventures of Rusty" (Col). Weak "B" boy-and-his-dog melodrama born of a bad script.

The Lost Weekend

Paramount release of Charles Brackett production. Stars Ray Milland and Jane Wyman; features Philip Terry, Howard da Silva. Directed by Billy Wilder. Screenplay, Charles Brackett and Billy Wilder, from novel by Charles R. Jackson; editor, Doane Harrison; musical score, Miklos Rozsa; camera, John F. Seitz; special photographic effects, Gordon Jennings. Previewed in N. Y., Aug. 10, '45. Running time, **101 MINS.**

Don Birnam....................Ray Milland
Helen St. James..............Jane Wyman
Wick Birnam...................Philip Terry
Nat, the Bartender.......Howard da Silva
Gloria.........................Doris Dowling
Bim............................Frank Faylen
Mrs. Deveridge.................Mary Young
Mrs. Foley....................Anita Bolster
Mrs. St. James..............Lillian Fontaine
Mr. St. James............Lewis L. Russell
Attendant at Opera............Frank Orth

The filming by Paramount of "The Lost Weekend" marks a particularly outstanding achievement in the Hollywood setting. The psychiatric study of an alcoholic, it is an unusual picture. It is intense, morbid—and thrilling. Here is an intelligent dissection of one of society's most rampant evils. Ray Milland and Jane Wyman are the stars. It is smash boxoffice.

This is no picture to serve as sheer entertainment, for herein is what may well be termed the heresy of film-making. A picture of doubtful entertainment value? Well, now.

"Weekend" hasn't any laughs. Or gams. Or crackling, smart dialog. It is startling in its manic-depression. It required courage for Paramount to violate cardinal boxoffice principles to film it. Yet, here is a pic that should snowball b.o. interest on the basis of word-of-mouth and intelligent, conservative exploitation. That is, if the original novel by Charles R. Jackson hasn't already developed that interest.

"Weekend" is the specific story of a quondam writer who has yet to put down his first novel on paper. He talks about it continuously but something always seems to send him awry just when he has a mind to work. Booze. Two quarts at a time. He goes on drunks for days. And his typewriter invariably winds up in the pawnshop. To get dough for you-know-what.

Involved in his struggle to fight alcoholism are a brother, upon whom he's dependent for subsistence, and the drunk's sweetheart. They plan cures for him, but it's no use. Depriving him of funds, or appropriating hidden bottles are out of the question. His twisted mind always seems to determine a way to get the stuff.

Of course, there's the inevitable barkeep, a philosophical sort of guy named Nat who's pretty mad at himself for being a barkeep when he has to sell liquor to guys like this Don Birnam. Nat, next to the sot, is the story's most trenchantly written character.

"Weekend" isn't a pretty story for more than one reason. Its moral, of course, crusades against alcoholism, but to casual readers of the book and patrons of the picture there may well be a wholesale condemnation of the suppliers of spirits. Laymen aren't apt to be so perceptive as to determine for themselves that here is a film that doesn't condemn drinking, as such, but only seeks to illustrate the evils of over-imbibing.

"Weekend," filmed entirely in New York, is frequently terrifying in its realism. It atom-bombs in depicting a Bellevue hospital alcoholic ward. A d.t., for instance, who must be straight-jacketed and given a "treatment"; he "sees" beetles swarming all over him. And there's Birnam lurching from pawnshop to pawnshop—only to find them all closed because of a holiday. He wanted to hock his typewriter and satisfy a maddening craving. And he's sunk low enough, too, to accept money from a prostitute, to buy booze. And there's a particularly pathetic scene wherein he suddenly finds a bottle—one whose hiding place he had forgotten, in a drunken stupor. And, finally, where he himself becomes deeteed. He imagines a mouse trying to squeeze through a crack in the wall, only to have a nondescript bird swoop down on it. His warped brain is terrified (and so is the audience) as he imagines the rodent's blood streaming down the wall.

Ray Milland has certainly given no better performance in his career. His portrayal will have to be reckoned with when filmdom makes its annual awards. Drunks may frequently excite laughter, but at no time can there be even a suggestion of levity to the part Milland plays. Only at the film's end is the character out of focus, but that is the fault of the script. The suggestion of rehabilitation should have been more carefully developed.

Jane Wyman is the girl, Philip Terry the brother. They help make the story overshadow the characters. The entire cast, in fact, contributes notably. And that goes especially for Howard da Silva as the bartender.

Billy Wilder's direction is always certain, always conscious that the characters were never to over-state the situations. Throughout it is manifest that here is a story whose prime asset is in the telling rather than in the people who portray it. Which stands the test of any fine yarn. Charles Brackett produced, and he and Wilder teamed on the screenplay. They have teamed well. Suspiciously well. *Kahn.*

Ziegfeld Follies

Boston, Aug. 10.

(MUSICAL; COLOR)

Metro release of Arthur Freed production. Stars Fred Astaire, Lucille Ball, Lucille Bremer, Fanny Brice, Judy Garland, Kathryn Grayson, Lena Horne, Gene Kelly, James Melton, Victor Moore, Red Skelton, Esther Williams and William Powell; features Edward Arnold, Marion Bell, Bunin's Puppets, Cyd Charisse, Hume Cronyn, William Frawley, Robert Lewis, Virginia O'Brien, Keenan Wynn. Directed by Vincente Minnelli. Camera, George Folsey and Charles Roshner; songs, Harry Warren and Arthur Freed, George and Ira Gershwin, Ralph Blane and Hugh Martin, Kay Thompson and Roger Edens; dances, Robert Alton; music, Lennie Hayton; orchestrations, Conrad Salinger, Wally Heglin; editor, Albert Akst. Previewed in Boston. Running time, **116 MINS.**

Looking down from a very lush heaven, as Florenz Ziegfeld (William Powell) does in prolog of this film super, the Great Ziggy would be dazzled by color, sets and routines far above the capacities of his day. But despite the glory of Technicolor, borrowing of music by Gershwin, Friml, Herbert and Kern, and the various technical achievements from soap bubbles to underwater ballet, Ziegfeld would have missed his nudes, his pleasantly risque interludes and a certain heart-warming which came with the old productions.

Technicolor, in other words, does not replace the human touch in "Ziegfeld Follies." Nevertheless, it's a great spectacle after the Ziegfeld tradition, no expense spared even if some holds are barred in deference to Will Hays philosophy. It should do smash biz.

Those shining above all others in the generous cast of Metro stars are Fred Astaire, agile and gay; Judy Garland, who has perfected an ironic touch; sultry Lena Horne, graceful Esther Williams, comic Fanny Brice and sweet-warbling Lucille Bremer.

Pic opens with dreamland set out of which Powell emerges, apparently comfortably fixed in celestial heights a la Ziegfeld. As the great producer, he reflects on his successes—"Rosalie," "Rio Rita," "Showboat," the various "Follies." Puppets spring to action in beautiful array. He thinks of Eddie Cantor, Marilyn Miller, Will Rogers, and others impersonated in miniature. He wonders what he could do with a new "Follies" down on earth.

Thus, the new "Follies" swings into tuneful life. Lucille Ball, supported by a chorus on a merry-go-round, does a pink number, "Bring on the Beautiful Girls," largely distinguished for flesh and feathers, with the less obvious epidermis carefully concealed.

A touch of the classics comes with arias from "Traviata," sung adequately by James Melton and Marian Bell, supported by a well-devised, mixed ballet chorus. Carrying out the old Ziegfeld idea of a series of episodic spectacles relieved by humor, Keenan Wynn glorifies a wrong-number phone routine that wows.

Miss Williams' one-gal underwater ballet is a feat of grace and loveliness, cleverly pieced together to give her the appearance of a mermaid who could stay submerged forever. Another dash of humor comes when Victor Moore and Edward Arnold stage the oldie skit in which Moore is arrested for a subway violation but tries to evade a $2 fine. Court action, with various appeals, brings cost to skies, all of which, due to star's plaintive request for Arnold's payment of $2, gets zip laughter. Miss Brice also whizzes with Hume Cronyn and William Frawley in a mixup over who really has a winning sweepstakes stub.

One of the most colorful numbers is a ballroom scene in which Astaire, a swank dip, extracts jewels from Miss Bremer after paying her court. No need to look for subtle story here but dancing, support, sets and lighting are superb.

Miss Horne in a Negro cabaret bit could not look more seductive, or be in more torrid voice, with effective acting as well. Her song, "Love," amply paces the piece. Red Skelton provides more comedy by impersonating a looped television announcer, turn he did in vaudeville before he went into pix.

"Limehouse Blues," subtly staged with much atmospheric effect, finds Astaire and Miss Bremer in a theme somehow reminiscent, but there's some fine dancing here, with the ballet as seen through a dying man's vision. As a mistress of irony as well as dance and song, July Garland wows in "Great Lady Has an Interview." Ziegfeld never produced better satire than this.

Astaire and Gene Kelly trip gaily through what is hailed as hitherto-unseen Gershwin piece, "The Babbitt and the Bromide." Lyrics by Ira and music—good, too—by George. Moral is you can't cure banality. Finale is a fantastic number, replete with chorines emerging from soap-bubble mists. Here Kathryn Grayson sings "Beauty."

It's all supendous, terrific, colossal, practically everyone would agree. Even Zieggy. *Dame.*

I Love a Bandleader

(SONGS)

Columbia release of Michel Kraike production. Stars Phil Harris, Rochester (Eddie Anderson) and Leslie Brooks; features Walter Catlett and Frank Sully. Directed by Del Lord. Screenplay, Paul Yawitz; story, John Grey; camera, Franz F. Planer; editor, James Sweeney; musical direction, M. R. Bakaleinikoff, Paul Sawtell; songs, Sammy Cahn and Jule Styne; Phil Harris, Pinky Tomlin. At Strand, Brooklyn, Aug. 9, '45, dual. Running time, **70 MINS.**

Phil Burton.........................Phil Harris
Newton H. Newton.....................
Edward "Rochester" Anderson
Ann Carter.....................Leslie Brooks
B. Templeton Jones........Walter Catlett
Dan Benson....................Frank Sully
Gibley..........................James Burke
Dr. Gardener..................Pierre Watkin
The Jordan Sisters............The Four V's
Edwin............................Robin Short
Bill........................Philip Van Zandt
Willie Winters..................Nick Stewart

There are a few good spots to "I Love a Bandleader," although it adds up to an inexpensively budgeted comedy attempt which never really comes off, with a few songs thrown in for good measure. Mild boxoffice, with Rochester and Phil Harris drawing 'em.

Harris' personality and singing are the film's main attributes, with Rochester (Eddie Anderson) having too little to do though he shares top billing, sings one number, "Eager Beaver," and has a few comic scenes with Harris. Rest of film is devoted to slowly-paced story of an enamoured housepainter who gets amnesia and thinks he's a bandleader. Leslie Brooks, as the love interest opposite Harris, does nicely enough and shows promise in voice department.

Tell It to a Star

(SONGS)

Republic release of Walter H. Goetz production. Stars Ruth Terry, Robert Livingston; features Alan Mowbray, Franklin Pangborn, Isabel Randolph, Eddie Marr, Adrian Booth, Aurora Miranda. Directed by Frank McDonald; screenplay, John K. Butler; from original by Gerald Drayson Adams and John Krafft; camera, Ernest Miller; songs, Shirley Botwin, Gus Kahn, Walter Donaldson, Sammy Cahn, Jule Styne, Ary Barroso; dances, Aida Broadbent; special effects, Howard Lydecker; editor, Arthur Roberts. Previewed in N. Y., Aug. 10, '45. Running time, **67 MINS.**

Carol Lambert....................Ruth Terry
Gene Ritchie...............Robert Livingston
Col. Ambrose Morgan.......Alan Mowbray
Horace Lovelace........Franklin Pangborn
Mrs. Arnold Whitmore....Isabel Randolph
Billy Sheehan.....................Eddie Marr
Mona St. Clair................Adrian Booth
Augustus T. Goodman..........Frank Orth
Ed Smith........................Tom Dugan
Al Marx....................George Chandler
Miss Dobson..................Mary McCarty
Brannigan............William B. Davidson
Specialty by...............Aurora Miranda

This is one musical package, if properly publicized, that should prove good b.o. at the lesser houses at which it's aimed. It's the usual Cinderella story but it's all done in such a clean, tongue-in-cheek fashion that the multi-told plot will have the audience smiling with it.

The setting is a ritzy Florida hotel, and the story centers around a gal (Ruth Terry) who sells cigars but aspires to be a vocalist with bandsman Robert Livingston. However, she's getting the brushoff. Her impoverished but always resourceful uncle (Alan Mowbray) arrives on scene, discovers her vocability and decides to present himself at hotel as a notable "Colonel." Niece gets singing opportunity; from there in complications ensue. Uncle's fraud is discovered and niece's professional attainment and love routine almost nosedive, with the usual last-minute interception.

Title number, "Tell It to a Star," is most exploitable of the tunes. Other numbers are fair, specialty featuring Aurora Miranda in a Mexican routine is pretty good. Miss Miranda's gyratory exhibition of "A Batucada Comecou" (Ary Barroso) doesn't flatter her photographically.

Mowbray's performance is by far the best, with Isabel Randolph, as the inane hotel operator, okay, too. Miss Terry and Livingston as romantic leads are suited, and rest of cast do their perfunctory bits as well as the script allows. For most part, John K. Butler's script is smooth. Frank McDonald's direction was competent. Women's gowns are unattractive, but they're not obtruse enough to harm picture's chances.

Adventures of Rusty

Columbia release of Rudolph C. Flothow production. Features Ted Donaldson, Margaret Lindsay, Conrad Nagel, Gloria Holden, Ace, the Wonder Dog. Directed by Paul Burnford. Screenplay, Aubrey Wisberg; original story by Al Martin; camera, L. W. O'Connell; editor, Reg Browne. At Paramount, Brooklyn, N. Y., Aug. 9, dual. Running time, 69 MINS.

Danny Mitchell....Ted Donaldson
Ann....Margaret Lindsay
Hugh Mitchell....Conrad Nagel
Louise Hover....Gloria Holden
Will Nelson....Robert Williams
Psychiatrist....Addison Richards
Tausig....Arno Frey
Ehrlich....Eddie Parker
Henry....Bobby Larson
Billy....Douglas Madore
Herbie....Gary Gray
Mrs. Nelson....Ruth Warren
and
Ace, the Wonder Dog

"Adventures of Rusty" is B fare for the nabes. Plot sags too frequently.

Story is about a boy and his attempt to tame a vicious German police dog. The action wanders also to his difficulty in adjusting himself to a new stepmother. All old stuff with no new twist. There is a little comedy, but the acting, action and dialog are weak and awkward.

Ted Donaldson does well as the boy. Ace, the dog, captures whatever other honors there are. Conrad Nagel and Margaret Lindsay recite their dialog with as much warmth as a choppy script allows. Production is uneven.

Miniature Reviews

"State Fair" (20th) (Songs; Color). Smash b.o. remake, with Rodgers-Hammerstein songs.

"Love Letters" (Par-Wallis). Jennifer Jones and Joseph Cotten in stirring boxoffice drama.

"Duffy's Tavern" (Par) (Songs). Radio program draw, plus Par's list of stars, will make this good b.o.

"Paris Underground" (UA). Over-long film which should, nevertheless, garner okay b. o. returns.

"Abbott and Costello in Hollywood" (M-G). Lively comedy headed for good biz.

"Follow That Woman" (Par). William Gargan, Nancy Kelly in lightweight whodunit.

'Boston Blackie's Rendezvous' (Col). Well-paced, well-acted killer-thriller that should please.

"Dos Angeles Y Un Pecador" (Sono Film). Argentine-made comedy holds small interest for U. S. market.

State Fair
(SONGS; COLOR)

20th-Fox release of Willaim Perlberg production. Stars Jeanne Crain, Dana Andrews, Dick Haymes and Vivian Blaine; features Charles Winninger, Fay Bainter, Donald Mock, Frank McHUgh, Percy Kilbride and Henry Morgan. Directed by Walter Lang. Songs, Richard Rogers and Oscar hammerstein II; screenplay, Hammerstein from novel by Phil Stong; adapted by Sonya Levien and Paul Green. Tradeshown N.Y., Aug 16, '45. Running time, 100 MINS.

Margy Frake....Jeanne Crain
Pat Gilbert....Dana Andrews
Wayne Frake....Dick Haymes
Emily....Vivian Blaine
Abel Flake....Charles Winninger
Melissa Flake....Fay Bainter
Hippenstahl....Donald Meek
McGee....Frank McHugh
Miller....Percy Kilbride
Barker....Henry Morgan
Eleanor....Jane Nigh
Marty....Willaim Marshall
Harry Ware....Phil Brown
Hank....Paul Burns
Eph....Tom Fadden
Pappy....Willaim Frambes
Barker....Steve Olson
Mrs. Metcalfe....Josephine Wittell
Simpson....Paul Harvey
Announcer....John Dehner
Judges....Harlan Briggs, Will Wright, Alice Fleming
Farmer....Walter Baldwin
Police Chief....Ralph Sanford

A dozen years ago, Fox reduced the alfalfa and the rustic to terms of smash boxoffice when it produced "State Fair," the Phil Stong novel. Today, 20th-Fox has added some sock Rodgers and Hammerstein songs and given the remake a superb Technicolor production. Coupled with an excellent cast, "Fair" retains the old charm and yet adds some of its own. It is an excellent entertainment and should do boff b.o.

The original will be recalled as having Will Rogers, Janet Gaynor, Lew Ayres, Sally Eilers and Norman Foster in the leads; the latest version is no less distinctive with Charles Winninger, Dana Andrews, Jeanne Crain, Dick Haymes and Vivian Blaine.

The Stong story, which Oscar Hammerstein II has authored for the latest screen version, is still a boy-meets-girl yarn that has lost none of the flavor of the years. And notably distinctive in the telling is the frequent punctuation of the story by the Rodgers-Hammerstein tunes. There are six of the latter in the film; at least three are exploitable and two are likely smash hits.

Otherwise, the yarn is still the one of midwest rustication, concerning mainly the hoopla attendant to the farmers' annual state fair, at which their products, from pickles to hogs, are displayed for judging and prizes.

Charles Winninger has the original Rogers role, that of Abel Frake, the farmer whose intensity for hogs and his wife's brandied mincemeat is greater than an interest in the romantic complications of his two offspring.

Miss Crain and Haymes are the Frake progeny, and Andrews is the newspaper reporter who covers the fair and is the other half of the Crain romantic attachment. Haymes and Miss Blaine handle the other romantic situation. Fay Bainter is the mother.

The film's top tune is "That's for Me," featured by Miss Blaine in a bandstand sequence. It's a sock ballad that should become a hit. Not too far behind is another likely hit, "It Might as Well Be Spring," sung by Miss Crain. "It's a Grand Night for Singing," by Haymes, is another potential. The tunes are whammo from both lyrical and melody content. The care exercised in the film's overall production is made particularly evident by the allotment of one sock tune to each of the three singing principals.

The film has beauty and the refreshing quality that goes with abounding youth. The Misses Crain and Blaine are beauts for whom Technicolor is a smart foil, and their voices are excellent for the Rodgers-Hammerstein type of composition. Haymes, of course, has by now become a standard in 20th-Fox musicals, with his fine voice, modest manner and an improving acting ability. Andrews properly underplays the reporter. Winninger is his usually expostulative self, supplying some of the comedy relief, while Miss Bainter is excellent as the mother. *Kahn.*

Love Letters

Paromount release of Hal Wallis production. Stars Jennifer Jones and Joseph Cotten; features Ann Richards, Cecil Kellaway and Gladys Cooper. Directed by William Dieterle. Screenplay, Ayn Rand, from novel by Chris Massie; editor, Anne Bauchens; camera, Lee Garmes; music score, Victor Young; special photographic effects, Gordon Jennings. Tradeshown in N. Y. Aug. 17, '45. Running time, 101 MINS.

Singleton....Jennifer Jones
Alan Quinton....Joseph Cotten
Dilly Carson....Ann Richards
Helen Wentworth....Anita Louise
Mack....Cecil Kellaway
Beatrice Remington....Gladys Cooper
Derek Quinton....Bryon Barr
Roger Morland....Robert Sully
Defense Attorney....Reginald Denny
Bishop....Ernest Cossart
Jim Connings....James Millican
Mr. Quinton....Lumsden Hare
Mrs. Quinton....Winifred Harris
Bishop's Wife....Ethyl May Halls
Judge....Matthew Boulton
Postman....David Clyde
Vicar....Ian Wolfe
Dodd....Alec Craig
Jupp....Arthur Hohl

Let the tears fall where they may—"Love Letters' is that type of story. Warm and appealing, sentimental and emotional, this Hal Wallis production is potentially a big boxoffice winner, with Jennifer Jones and Joseph Cotten for the marquee.

It is a slowly developed story, of necessity, to achieve its mood. At its conclusion there isn't apt to be a dried eye in the theatre. Its appeal for the women is boundless.

In a couple of scenes "Letters," Ayn Rand's adaptation from Chris Massie's novel, fails to achieve a proper distinction between theatrical artifice and reality, but by and large there is so much stature to the film that those few moments are only for serious consideration by the more captious. Also, the first couple of reels could have been edited better; the continuity has too static a quality in the opening minutes.

This is an unusual story. It's the yarn of two British army officers on the Italian front, one of whom writes beautiful love letters for his friend to the latter's fiancee in England. The friend is a shallow egocentric, but in England the girl falls in love with the letters, and in turn with the man whom she thinks has written them. On a furlough in England the friend marries the girl, and she soon learns it wasn't he who wrote the letters but the fellow officer whom she's never met. And she becomes disillusioned by her husband's manner, which is utterly unlike that suggested by his letters. In a moment of drunkenness he beats her and, to save her, the girl's foster mother stabs him to death. The girl, shocked at the tragedy, becomes an amnesiac, while the older woman suffers a stroke that renders her speechless. The former is tried for the murder and sentenced to a year in prison, being unable to offer any defense because of the failure of her memory to respond to court questioning. From thereon it's the story of the girl and the other officer, who has learned of his friend's mysterious death and, meeting the wife, falls in love with her and marries her. Rest of the yarn concerns the return of her memory and the happiness that had been shrouded by the tragedy.

"Letters" is excellently performed, particularly by the stars. Miss Jones gives to the part of the girl an elfin quality that at times reaches sheer brilliance in performance. Cotten, as the writer of the letters, gives a fine, quietly restrained characterization, while Robert Sully is the officer-scoundrel she marries, a more-or-less bit part that he handles satisfactorily. Gladys Cooper is the foster mother, a modest part but one she performs impressively. Cecil Kellaway, as a man-of-all work, is likewise satisfactory. Ann Richards, another focal character, lends quiet dignity to the drama.

"Letters" has been given a grade A production, and that includes a fine directional job by William Dieterle and music score by Victor Young. *Kahn.*

Duffy's Tavern
(SONGS)

Paramount release of Danny Dare production. Stars Ed Gardner, Bing Crosby, Betty Hutton, Paulette Goddard, Alan Ladd, Dorothy Lamour, Eddie Bracken, Brian Donlevy, Sonny Tufts, Veronica Lake, Barry Fitzgerald, Cass Daley, Victor Moore, Marjorie Reynolds, Charles Cantor, Eddie Green, Ann Thomas. Directed by Hal Walker. Screenplay, Melvin Frank and Norman Panama; based on characters by Ed Gardner. Sketches: George White, Eddie Davis, Matt Brooks, Abram S. Burrows, Barney Dean, Frank and Panama. Songs: Johnny Burke and James Van Heusen, and Bernie Wayne and Ben Raleigh. Dances, Billy Daniels; music direction, Robert Emmett Dolan. Camera, Lionel Lindon; editor, Arthur Schmidt. Previewed in N. Y., Aug. 20, '45. Running time, 97 MINS.

Himself....Bing Crosby
Herself....Betty Hutton
Herself....Paulette Goddard
Himself....Alan Ladd
Herself....Dorothy Lamour
Himself....Eddie Bracken
Himself....Brian Donlevy
Himself....Sonny Tufts
Herself....Veronica Lake
Himself....Arturo de Cordova
Bing Crosby's Father....Barry Fitzgerald
Herself....Cass Daley
Herself....Diana Lynn
Michael O'Malley....Victor Moore
Peggy O'Malley....Marjorie Reynolds
Danny Murphy....Barry Sullivan
Archie (Himself)....Ed Gardner
Finnegan....Charles Cantor
Eddie....Eddie Green
Miss Duffy....Ann Thomas
Himself....Robert Benchley
Himself....William Demarest
Heavy....Howard da Silva
Doctor....Billy de Wolfe
Director....Walter Abel
Dancer....Johnny Coy
Dancer....Miriam Franklin
Ronald....Charles Quigley
Gloria....Olga San Juan
Masseur....Robert Watson
Himself....Gary Crosby
Himself....Phillip Crosby
Himself....Dennis Crosby
Himself....Lin Crosby

"Duffy's Tavern"—like most film extravaganzas, or saloons—has a lot of ingredients. Pic's first half is a stock comedy built around the w.k. radio program; second half is a vaudeville show enlisting practically every star on the Paramount lot. Marquee names of the latter, engaged in some hilarious sequences, plus the radio program's draw, will offset the film's draggy early sequences to put it over. Pic should do good business.

Ed Gardner's etherized booze-and-beef joint—"where the ay-leet meet to eat"—has the characters and situations to make a passable film plot. But Par has missed out on it. Utilizing the four principals of the air show, Archie, Eddie, Finnegan and Miss Duffy, the scripters have turned out a trite story of the quartet involved in a scheme to put some ex-servicemen to work, running the first 15 minutes of the film primarily as a vehicle for one Ed Gardner gag or malapropism after another. What sounds good in a half-hour radio show goes stale on celluloid.

Luckily, half-way in the film, the studio has thrown the plot out of the window, to concentrate on some rib-tickling burlesque where star after star does a specialty or lets his hair down. And the result is a funfest. Sonny Tufts, Brian Donlevy and Paulette Goddard do a funny variation on the triangle of boy-friend-finding-lover-in-girl's-apartment. Robert Benchley tells the four Bing Crosby children a fantastic Horatio Alger story of the boyhood of their father, with Bing, Barry Fitzgerald and Dorothy Lamour enacting the idyll, the scene seguing into a takeoff of the "Swinging on a Star" sequence from "Going My Way," with Der Bingle using a dozen Par stars as his "kid choir."

Betty Hutton throws herself out of joint singing "The Hard Way," and Cass Daley turns her face inside out warbling "You Can't Blame a Gal for Tryin'." Veronica Lake gets her face pummeled by Howard da Sylva. But highlight of the shenanigans is a burlesque of a western, with Eddie Bracken playing the double of a cowboy hero, taking successively a beating by a bandit mob, a water dunking and some pies in his face, all constituting a nostalgic throwback to the good old Mack Sennett days and as hilarious a sequence as one will find in any film-comedy.

Vaudeville show—which also includes some fancy dancing by Johnny Coy—is roped into the film on strength of a block party which Archie and his pals arrange to get themselves out of a financial jam. It seems that open-hearted Archie, as manager of Duffy's, has put about 14 ex-servicemen on the payroll as waiters because the next-door phonograph factory where they previously worked, had shut down, so that Duffy's books now show a sweet deficit of $1,200.

Matter is complicated by the fact that Victor Moore, as owner of the factory, can't get credit to buy the shellac needed to reopen his plant. Barry Sullivan, returned from the war, takes over to raise the money to open the factory, while Archie gets his block party on to save his own skin.

Pic's early scenes, with Archie discussing his financial woes with his pessimistic waiter Eddie or moocher Finnegan, contain most of the word-blunders for which Archie is air-famous. Although some are good, as when Archie soulfully refers to his dream-girl as the kind you want to place on a "pedestrian," most of the malapropisms tire after a while. Action drags, only the presence of Victor Moore being a saving grace. Latter, especially in a drunk scene, is tops.

Pic, skedded for release simultaneous to return of air show, is unique in presenting celluloid characterizations of radio figures who actually look the part.

Film is lavishly budgeted in its production scenes and block party numbers, with direction satisfactory for the plot limitations. *Bron.*

Paris Underground

United Artists release of Constance Bennett production (Carley Harriman, exec. asst. prod.). Directed by Gregory Ratoff. Stars Miss Bennett, Gracie Fields, Kurt Kreuger, Eily Malyon, Charles Andre, Leslie Vincent; features Richard Ryen, Harry Hays Morgan, Roland Varno, Andre Charlot, Adrienne D'Ambricourt, Gregory Gaye, George Rigaud. Screenplay by Boris Ingster and Gertrude Purcell, based upon original story by Etta Shiber in collaboration with Anne and Paul Dupre and Oscar Ray; camera, Lee Garmes; editor, James Newcom. Tradeshown N. Y., Aug. 17, '45. Running time, **97 MINS.**

This over-long film has promise of good but not exciting b.o. returns, part of its fault being the excessive time, 97 minutes, and part the fact that audiences will very likely find development of main theme as being too slow. Except for these flaws, however, and for one more, pic has good, solid story content once it gets going, enough suspense, and is pro-duced, directed and acted with a fine appreciation of the action involved.

Story, adapted from Etta Shiber's novel, is tale of two women in Nazi-infested France, one a gay American married to an official of the old French foreign office, the other a sedate, middle-aged Britisher who runs an antique shop in Paris. Constance Bennett and Gracie Fields, in those respective roles, come through competently; each in her own big scene is magnificent—Miss Bennett when she hides in the coalbin of her apartment house while the Gestapo is searching for her, and Miss Fields when she returns home after killing a Nazi spy planted among the French undergrounders.

Supporting cast is good all the way, with particularly nifty jobs by Kurt Kreuger as the Gestapo captain and Gregory Gaye as the French baker who helps the underground. George Rigaud, who is introduced to American films herewith as the husband of the American gal, is okay but undistinguished except for an appearance that comes close to his looking like Gen. DeGaulle.

After its slow start, the film gets into a fair enough pace. But within the last few minutes, the picture does a fold. In one sequence, the two women are in the hands of the Nazis, their underground activities broken up and they're probably about to be shot or tortured to death. Suddenly, in the very next shot, the U. S. Army liberators, like the Texas Rangers in an old western, come to the rescue. There's no effort made to bridge the gap. It looks like the fault's with the cutting. *Cars.*

Abbott and Costello in Hollywood
(SONGS)

Metro release of Martin Gosch production. Stars Bud Abbott and Lou Costello; features Frances Rafferty, "Rags" Ragland, Mike Mazurki. Directed by S. Sylvan Simon. Screenplay, Nat Perrin and Lou Breslow, based on an original by Perrin and Gosch; songs, Ralph Blane and Hugh Martin; camera, Charles Schoenbaum; editor, Ben Lewis. Previewed at Loew's Orpheum, N. Y., Aug. 20, '45. Running time, **83 MINS.**

Buzz Kurtis	Bud Abbott
Abercrombie	Lou Costello
Claire Warren	Francis Rafferty
Jeff Parker	Robert Stanton
Ruthie	Jean Porter
Norman Royce	Warner Anderson
"Rags" Ragland	By Himself
Klondike Pete	Mike Mazurki

An Abbott and Costello picture may not be an artistic triumph, but the duo certainly try hard enough to make audiences laugh. Their latest, "Abbott and Costello in Hollywood," is no exception; it should do fairly good business.

For their final effort at Metro the studio has embellished this A&C production with several sequences that run into important dough. Henceforth they will make pictures solely for their original studio, Universal.

Besides "On the Midway," Ralph Blane and Hugh Martin have composed two other okay tunes, "As I Remember You" and "I Hope the Band Keeps Playing." Bob Stanton, youthful newcomer, sings all three and acts capably, too. Others in the cast are seen briefly, serving as foils for A&C.

Duo portrays the role of barber and shineboy in a tonsorial establishment, who get the yen to be actors' agents when they see the easy life one of the latter has. When the agent turns down a youngster with a nice voice, they take him on, and before the film unwinds they have him set in a picture, but not before they almost wreck the studio and upset the personnel therein.

Despite the 83 minutes running time, this one moves rapidly, aided by direction of S. Sylvan Simon. *Sten.*

Follow That Woman

Paramount release of Pine-Thomas production. Stars William Gargan, Nancy Kelly; features Regis Toomey, Ed Gargan, Byron Barr, Don Costello. Directed by Lew Landers. Screenplay by Winston Miller, Maxwell Shane; based on story by Ben Perry; camera, Fred Jackman; editor, Henry Adams. Previewed in N. Y. Projection Room, Aug. 21, '45. Running time, **70 MINS.**

Sam Boone	William Gargan
Nancy Boone	Nancy Kelly
Butch	Ed Gargan
Barney Manners	Regis Toomey
Nick	Don Costello
John Evans	Byron Barr
Mr. Henderson	Pierre Watkin
Marge	Audrey Young

This inexpensive whodunit, which leans on the lighter side to keep it rolling, is okay for the lower rung of dualers. Wandering plot is the chief weakness.

Scripters have tried to use the old formula of a detective's wife trying to help her mate solve a murder mystery. Here the Sherlock is a private sleuth, about to be inducted into the Army. Fact that he goes into the Army soon after the slaying is the reason for aforesaid wife trying to become a femme detective.

Lew Landers, vet comedy director, strives hard to make Nancy Kelly funny as the sleuth's wife who attempts Sherlocking. But Miss Kelly is no great shakes as a comedienne. Yarn jumps about from one locale to another, with the sequences sometimes confusing. Of course, William Gargan as the private dick gets a seven-day leave, though just in the Army, to solve the baffling slaying.

The Pine-Thomas unit has given it nice production for this type of film. William Gargan makes a satisfactory private sleuth while Nancy Kelly is okay as his wife, although given a bad break by the cameraman many times. She's been in better roles. Ed Gargan, as the partner of the master detective, does well, while Regis Toomey, Pierre Watkin and Don Costello head the support. *Wear.*

Boston Blackie's Rendezvous

Columbia release of Alexis Thurn-Taxis production. Features Chester Morris, Nina Foch, Steve Cochran, Richard Lane, George E. Stone. Directed by Arthur Dreifuss. Screenplay, Edward Dein; original story by Fred Schiller; camera, George B. Meehan, Jr.; musical direction, M. R. Bakaleinikoff; editor, Aaron Stell. At Fox, Brooklyn, N. Y., Aug. 9, '45, dual. Running time, **64 MINS.**

Boston Blackie	Chester Morris
Sally Brown	Nina Foch
James Cook	Steve Cochran
Inspector Farraday	Richard Lane
The Runt	George E. Stone
Mathews	Frank Sully
Martha	Iris Adrian
Arthur Manleder	Harry Hayden
Patricia Powers	Adelle Roberts
Steve Caveroni	Joe Devlin
Hotel Clerk	Dan Stowell

Columbia has an okay, medium-budgeted programmer in "Boston Blackie's Rendezvous," ninth in the Boston Blackie series. Picture has compactness, the running time being only 64 minutes. Story and cast are good, with laurels too for Arthur Dreifuss' direction.

This time Blackie, elusive ex-crook turned private detective, searches for a homicidal maniac impersonating him. Latter has a bad habit of strangling people. He has escaped from a sanitarium and left a trail of dead lookers on the way. Blackie, of course, knocks him off.

In addition to some convincing fast action, film also packs laughs aplenty. George E. Stone is noteworthy as Runt, Blackie's aide. Chester Morris is in good form in the title role, with Steve Cochran doing a convincing job as the killer. Meriting mention are the numerous minor roles and bit parts, all done well.

Smart use of lights and shadow heighten tension. Pace and production are smooth.

Dos Angeles y un Pecadór
("Two Angels and a Sinner")
(ARGENTINE-MADE)

Buenos Aires, Aug. 14.

Argentina Sono Film production and release. Stars Zully Moreno and Pedro Lopez Lagar. Directed by Luis Cesar Amadori. Screenplay by Sixto Pondal Rios and Carlos Olivari; camera, Alberto Etchebehere. At Gran Cine Palace, July 4, '45. Running time, **42 MINS.**

This somewhat original story covers the borderline between fantasy and reality with excellent humor and continued suspense. The story material and direction are far superior to the acting, although Fanny Navarro, as a guardian angel, gives a winsome performance and Pedro Lopez Lagar is also more at ease than usual. Zully Moreno seems overcome by the sumptuousness of her costumes. Picture has small interest for U. S. audiences.

Lopez Lagar is cast as the gay millionaire whose guardian angel (Fanny Navarro) grants him a few hours' grace on this earth, after he has been killed in an auto accident. This is done to enable him to complete a mission, that of buying off the latter's girl friend so that he can wed another. The rake falls for the girl friend and decides to spend the few hours granted to him in her company so as to console her. When she is accused of the murder of her faithless lover, Lopez Lagar takes the blame in order to save her. Eventually the "murder" proves to be suicide.

When the millionaire's last minutes on earth are up, the guardian angel finds that through an oversight, Heaven was never notified of his "passing," so as he's not expected up there he can continue on earth for a happy ending. Sequence where the various guardian angels wait their charges at the millionaire's wild party is especially good, particularly as the guests couple up for further late night activities, much to the boredom of the angels. Photography is good and settings lavish, if not tasteful. Story material is good enough to warrant attention from Hollywood. *Nid.*

Miniature Reviews

"Swingin' On a Rainbow" (Rep). (Songs). Low cost musical for lower-half of dualers.

"They Knew Mr. Knight" (GFD). British-made version of Dorothy Whipple novel hasn't a chance in U. S.

"La Senora de Perez Se Divorcia" (Lumiton). Argentina-made version of Sardou play shows no promise for American market.

Swingin' on a Rainbow
(SONGS)

Republic release of Eddy White production. Stars Jane Frazee and Brad Taylor; features Harry Langdon, Minna Gombell, Amelita Ward, Tim Ryan, Paul Harvey. Directed by William Beaudine. Songs, Kim Gannon, Walter Kent and Jack Elliott; screenplay, Olive Cooper and John Grey, from story by Olive Cooper; camera, Marcel LaPickard; editor, Fred Allen. Previewed N. Y., Aug. 24, '45. Running time, 72 MINS.

Lynn Ford	Jane Frazee
Steve Ames	Brad Taylor
Chester Willoby	Harry Langdon
Minnie Regan	Minna Gombell
Barbara Marsden	Amelita Ward
Huston Greer	Tim Ryan
Thomas Marsden	Paul Harvey
Radio Announcer	Wendell Niles
Jimmy Rhodes	Richard Davies
Myrtle	Helen Talbot

Unoriginal story is handicapped by cliches, but may pass on the lower rung of dualers.

Story line is a complicated but unamusing affair about a girl who tries to collect $1,000 from a bandleader who has plagiarized her song. He leaves town to dodge her; she bluffs her way into living in his apartment during his absence. Here she also carries on a banging-on-the-wall feud with a neighbor with whom she is then unaware, she's been collaborating on songs.

Jane Frazee is satisfactory, but, with the script being what it is, few of the others have a chance. Film looks lightly budgeted.

They Knew Mr. Knight
(BRITISH-MADE)
London, Aug. 14.

General Film Distributors' release of G.H.W. production. Features Nora Swinburne, Joyce Howard, Alfred Drayton, Mervyn Johns. Directed by Norman Walker. Adapted by Victor MacClure from novel by Dorothy Whipple. Camera, Erwin Hillier. At Leicester Square, London, Aug. 13, '45. Running time, 93 MINS.

Thomas Blake	Mervyn Johns
Celia Blake	Nora Swinburne
Freda Blake	Joyce Howard
Ruth	Joan Greenwood
Mr. Knight	Alfred Drayton
Mrs. Knight	Olive Sloane
Coggy Selby	Kenneth Kove
Grandma	Marie Ault
Carrie Porritt	Joan Maude
Douglas Blake	Peter Hammond
Edward	Frederick Cooper
Isabel	Grace Arnold
Mr. Berry	Frederick Burtwell

In the old days at Hammerstein's Victoria, one of the outstanding features of Bert Williams' single act was his snail-like shuffle from wings to center. As compared with the pace of "They Knew Mr. Knight" Williams' amble was fast. Film hasn't a chance for the U. S.

Starred in this one, Mervyn Johns, Alfred Drayton, Nora Swinburne, Joyce Howard and Joan Greenwood all have a certain amount of pull with British audiences, but their best friends will steer clear of watching them struggle through this impossible story. Dorothy Whipple's novel of the same title may be enjoyable reading, but the screen adaptation makes it doubtful. To blame either Norman Walker, director, or the cast would be unfair. The scenario offers little either for cast or director.
Talb.

La Senora de Perez Se Divorcia
("Mrs. Perez and Her Divorce")
(ARGENTINE-MADE)
Buenos Aires, Aug. 28.

Lumiton production and release. Stars Mirtha Legrand, Juan Carlos Thorry, with Miguel Gomez Bao, Felisa Mary, Tito Gomez, Diego Martinez, Maria I. Notar, Teresita, Thilda Thamer and Juan Corona. Directed by Carlos Hugo Christensen. Adapted by Cesar Tiempo from Sardou play, "Divorcons." Camera, Alfredo Traverso. At Gran Cine Premier. Running time, 100 MINS.

Sardou's play is witty and ingenious. This screen adaptation is vulgar, banal and illogical, with little wit. Costly decorations, gaudy costumes and the combination of two stars as a romantic team proved excellent boxoffice here, are insufficient to lift this one out of the doldrums. Picture is a sequel to the previous production with the same cast, "Young Mrs. Perez," and it should get by on its previous box-office showing. U.S. chances are very slim.

Very bad treatment has been given to the Sardou plot. Young Mrs. Perez decides on a divorce after finding young Dr. Perez in the arms of a vamping patient. Dr. Perez in turn becomes jealous of his wife's ex-suitor lawyer, but his assumed indifference to a divorce reconquers the attention of Mrs. Perez. Mirtha Legrand is good on the eye and might learn to act under efficient direction and training. At present her inane giggle is becoming exasperating even to her most ardent bobby-sox fans. The dreariness of extras in nitery crowd scenes are surprising in a picture on which so much seems to have been spent in other ways.
Nid.

Miniature Reviews

"Shady Lady" (Songs) (U). Comedy with music and plenty of b.o. assets, including Ginny Simms and Charles Coburn.

"First Yank Into Tokyo" (RKO). Timely budgeter with new spy angle concerning atom bomb. Due for good returns.

"Perfect Strangers" (M-G). Robert Donat, Deborah Kerr in Alexander Korda British-made demobilization drama; looks only modest click in U. S.

"Come Out Fighting" (Mono). East Side kids in entertaining dualer.

"The Fatal Witness" (Rep). Secondary murder mystery; modest b.o.

"Song of Old Wyoming" (PRC) (Songs). Weak western.

"Girl No. 217" (Artkino). (Soviet). Russian-made drama of Nazi treatment of captured Russian civilians; mild b.o. for U. S.

"Youth Aflame" (Continental). N.g. juve-delinquency quickie.

"The Echo Murders" (Anglo-Am.). British-made whodunit hasn't a chance in U. S.

Shady Lady
(SONGS)

Universal release of George Waggner production. Stars Charles Coburn, Ginny Simms and Robert Paige; features Alan Curtis and Martha O'Driscoll. Directed by Waggner. Screenplay by Curt Siodmak, Gerald Geraghty and M.M. Musselman; camera, Hal Mohr; editor, Edward Curtiss; Songs, Waggner, Milton Rosen, Edgar Fairchild. Otto Harbach, Karl Hoschan. Previewed in projection room, N.Y., Sept. 4, '45. Running time, 94 MINS.

"Colonel" Appleby	Charles Coburn
Bob Wendell	Robert Paige
Lee	Ginny Simms
Marty	Alan Curtiss
Gloria	Martha O'Driscoll
Butch	Kathleen Howard
Crane	James Burke
Rappaport	John Gallaudet
Tramp	Joe Frisco
Bowen	Thomas Jackson
Fred	Billy Wayne
Clarence	William Hall
Warren	Bill Hunt
Proprietor	Erno Verebes
Card Player	George Lynn
Card Player	Bert Moorehouse
McNeil	Stuart Holmes
Norton	Billy Green
Porter	Emmitt Smith
Carlson	Chuck Hamilton

"Shady Lady" is a well-written screenplay, and while it hasn't strong name power, it should do well at the boxoffice. Credit the script to Curt Siodmak, Gerald Geraghty and M. M. Musselman, plus added dialog from Monty Collins.

Ginny Simms thus has a vehicle worthy of her latent abilities in this, her first starrer for Universal. Charles Coburn gives a witty, adroit touch to his performance, while Robert Paige, though stilted at times, comes through neatly as the other half of the love interest with Miss Simms.

Yarn finds Miss Simms, a singer, niece of newly-sprung gambler and cardsharp, Coburn, endeavoring to keep the latter on the straight and narrow. When the couple arrives in Chicago, where the singer is booked into a smart nitery-gambling casino. Coburn plans to make a killing. Meanwhile, Miss Simms becomes romantically involved with the assistant to the state's attorney, who is intent on nabbing the nitery boss with the gambling goods. Story winds up with everybody in the clear, except the nitery proprietor.

Supporting cast, led by Alan Curtis as the nightclub owner, and Martha O'Driscoll, as Paige's sister, whom Curtis double-crosses by refusing to marry after promising to do so, is substantial. A bit where

Paige and Miss Simms, sitting on a park bench, are disturbed by a bum, is notable. Joe Frisco, as the bum, in giving advice to the lovelorn couple, leaves out the suffering this time and comes close to stealing the picture. He's only on for a few minutes but supplies plenty of laughs.

None of the songs will catch on, the production numbers built around them in the nitery, fail to impress because of budgetary limitations. Miss Simms, however, handles the tunes well.
Sten.

First Yank Into Tokyo

RKO release of J. Robert Bren production. Features Tom Neal, Barbara Hale, Marc Cramer, Michael St. Angel, Keye Luke, Leonard Strong, Richard Loo. Directed by Gordon Douglas. Story by J. Robert Bren and Gladys Atwater; camera, Harry J. Wild; editor, Philip Martin, Jr. Previewed in projection room, N.Y. Aug. 30, '45. Running time, 82 MINS.

Major Ross	Tom Neal
Abby Drake	Barbara Hale
Jardine	Marc Cramer
Colonel Okunura	Richard Loo
Haan-Soo	Keye Luke
Major Nogiea	Leonard Strong
Captain Tanaho	Benson Fong
Major Ichibo	Clarence Iang
Captain Sato	Keye Chang
Captain Andrew Kent	Michael St. Angel

Timely angles in this picture make it a natural for heavy exploitation, but it will have to lean almost entirely on bullyhoo to get real money. There isn't a name that means much to the average theatre marquee.

Since "First Yank Into Tokyo" was produced before the atom bomb secret was released to the public, it takes an unidentified narrator's spiel and newsreel clips of the bomb in action to bring the picture up to date. The plot concerns a mystery bomb of atomic proportions, with a fancy spy twist as the Army seeks the missing link to the bomb's formula from a captured U. S. engineer in camp near Tokyo.

Ace Army pilot, Tom Neal, on furlough, is called in by a special Washington board and told that it's necessary to get this missing information from captured Capt. Michael St. Angel. Because Neal lived in Japan at one time, knew their customs, etc., a special surgery job is done on his face in order to send him into Japan as a spy. There he contacts the captain and ultimately smuggles him and Neal's sweetheart to a waiting submarine.

In between, Director Gordon Douglas and Producer J. Robert Bren, who's responsible with Gladys Atwater for the fanciful yarn, manage to build high suspense. Payoff is when the Nip colonel, played by Richard Loo, discovers Neal is his old college chum from California. Brutalities committed against Yank prisoners also provide a highlight. There are few expensive sets, but the direction helps cover this gap.

Neal makes something of his dual role. Barbara Hale is effective as his sweetie, an Army nurse captured at Bataan and held in the prison camp. Keye Luke does a fine job as a Korean underground operative, while Loo is the suave, villainous Nip colonel, a good job. Other standout roles are played by Leonard Strong, as a thieving Jap major; Marc Cramer, St. Angel and Benson Fong. The final scene seems too affected. It shows Neal staying in Japan to fight off Nip troops while his sweetheart and St. Angel get away. Narrator explains that he gave his life so that the atomic bomb could be perfected—an exaggeration, of course —and then newsreel shots from Pathe cover the atom bomb in action.
Wear.

Perfect Strangers
(BRITISH-MADE)
London, Aug. 31.

Metro release of Alexander Korda production. Stars Deborah Kerr, Robert Donat.

Directed by Alexander Korda. Screenplay by Clemence Dane. At Empire, London, Aug. 30, '45. Running time, **100 MINS.**

Robert Wilson	Robert Donat
Catherine Wilson	Deborah Kerr
Dizzy Clayton	Glynis Johns
Elena	Ann Todd
Richard	Roland Culver
Mrs. Hemmings	Eliot Mason
Mr. Staines	Eliot Makeham
Mr. Hargrove	Brefni O'Rorke
Petty Officer	Henry Longhurst
Webster	Billy Shine
Commander	Allan Jeayes
Charlie	Edward Rigby
Essex	Billy Thatcher

"Perfect Strangers" is a perfect stranger to modern technique, real life and smooth running. It appears too much like a museum piece to click in the U. S.

The story is that of a young worker and his suburban wife, who find themselves respectively in the Royal Navy and the Wrens with the war's outbreak. Both benefit physically and mentally from the change. Donat shaves his moustache; Deborah Kerr puts on lipstick. Neither expects to like the other when they meet again, but they do.

It's the type of yarn that will be seen again and again during the coming months and years of demobilization. It offers many possibilities of drama and situation, but all have been missed in this film. First you see Donat getting fit; then you see Deborah Kerr getting fit. Then you see Donat dancing; then you see Deborah Kerr dancing. Then you hear Donat telling his friends how dreary Deborah Kerr is; then you hear Deborah Kerr telling her friends how dreary Robert Donat is. It seems to go on and on like this.

This picture will be a blow to British motion picture hopes of successful American showings. It suggests that "The Way Ahead," "In Which We Serve" and "Way to the Stars" were flashes in the pan. "Perfect Strangers" may do fairly well in England, but not in the U. S.

This is Sir Alexander Korda's first full-length production since "Lady Hamilton." As far as direction is concerned, Lord Nelson would have been quite at home in it. *Grav.*

Come Out Fighting

Monogram release of Sam Katzman-Jack Dietz production. Stars Leo Gorcey; features Huntz Hall, Billy Benedict, Gabriel Dell. Directed by William Beaudine. Screenplay, Earl Snell; camera, Ira Morgan; editor, William Austin. At New York theatre, N.Y., Aug. 29, '45, dual. Running time, 62 MINS.

Muggs	Leo Gorcey
Glimpy	Huntz Hall
Skinny	Billy Benedict
Pete	Gabriel Dell
Lane	June Carlson
Rita	Amelia Ward
Mr. Mitchell	Addison Richards
Henley	George Meeker
Gilbert	Johnny Duncan
Mr. McGinnis Sr.	Fred Kelsey
Mayor	Douglas Wood
Police Chief	Milton Kibbee
Little Pete	Pat Gleason
Riley	Robert Homans
Mrs. McGinnis	Patsy Moran
Whitey	Alan Foster
Officer McGowan	Davidson Clark
Jake	Meyer Grace

"Come Out Fighting," 15th in the East Side Kid series, is entertainingly constructed and should provide a diverting hour as the supporting feature in duals.

Pic deals with the police commissioner countermanding an order closing the gang's clubroom. Gang wants to show its appreciation by "making a man" out of his ballet-dancing son. Son gets involved with gamblers who are out to ruin his dad, at which point the Kids come to the rescue.

In addition to being the happy medium for Leo Gorcey, picture spotlights Huntz Hall as his sidekick; the pair pick up a lot of laughs as they go along with elemental comedy and mugging. Balance of cast okay.

The Fatal Witness

Republic release of Rudolph E. Abel production. Features Evelyn Ankers, Richard Fraser, George Leigh, Barbara Everest, Barry Bernard, Frederic Worlock. Directed by Lesley Selander. Screenplay by Jerry Sackheim; adaptation by Cleve F. Adams, from story by Rupert Croft-Cooke; camera, Bud Thackery; editor, Ralph Dixon. At Strand, Brooklyn, Aug. 31, '45. dual. Running time, 69 MINS.

Priscilla Ames	Evelyn Ankers
Inspector Trent	Richard Fraser
John Bedford	George Leigh
Lady Ferguson	Barbara Everest
Scoggins	Barry Bernard
Sir Humphrey Mung	Frederick Worlock
Martha	Virginia Farmer
Sir Malcolm Hewitt	Colin Campbell
Butler	Craufurd Kent
Gracie Hallet	Peggy Jackson

Topping off an otherwise mediocre murder mystery is a surprise ending that helps salvage this one to some extent. It's strictly for the nabes, as a secondary dualer.

Rich dowager (Barbara Everest) gets bumped off and playboy nephew (George Leigh) falls under suspicion. Scotland Yard inspector who falls for victim's niece (Evelyn Ankers) is played by Richard Fraser. Murderer gives himself away to audience in middle of picture, but suspense hangs on.

As the heavy, Leigh does well. He performs with ease despite spotty scripting. Miss Ankers turns in a smooth performance while Barry Bernard, as the murderer's accomplice, contribs some fine acting.

Song of Old Wyoming
(SONGS)

PRC release of Robert Emmett production. Stars Eddie Dean; features Jennifer Holt, Ian Keith, Al La Rue, Sarah Padden. Directed by Robert Emmett. Screenplay Frances Kavanaugh; camera, Marcel Le-Picard; musical direction, Carl Hoefle; editor, Hugh Winn; songs, Ralph Rainger, Leo Robin, Eddie Dean, Milt Mabie, Carl Hoefle. Tradeshown in N.Y., Aug 31, '45. Running time, 66 MINS.

Eddie Reed	Eddie Dean
Ma Conway	Sarah Padden
Cheyenne Kid	Al La Rue
Vickey	Jennifer Holt
Uncle Ezra	Emmett Lynn
Slim	Ray Elder
Buck	John Carpenter
Landow	Ian Keith
Waco	Lee Bennett
Dixon	Bob Barron
Meeks	Horace Murphy
Ling	Pete Katchemaro
Ringo	Rocky Camron
Tex	Bill Lovett
Hodges	Richard Cramer
Bank Clerk	Steve Clark

"Song of Old Wyoming" is a lightweight western strictly for the stix. Plot is tired, being the story of a cowboy imported by the town villain to sabotage an elderly gal's ranch. Guy turns out to be her long-lost son.

There are no laughs and little excitement. Cast for the most part is postured and stereotyped. Eddie Dean has a pleasant singing voice but his acting is uncertain. Sarah Padden tries but the ragged story presents too great a challenge. Other characterizations are generally dull, production rough.

Worthy of note is PRC's use of cinecolor, a process that requires a single camera with a single film strip. Similar in appearance to Technicolor, it is easy on the eyes.

Girl No. 217
(RUSSIAN-MADE)

Artkino release of Mosfilm and Tashkent studios production. Stars Elena Kuzmina. Directed by Mikhail Romm. Story by Eugene Gabrilovich, Mikhail Romm; camera, Boris Volchek, Era Savelyeva; English titles, Charles Clement. At Stanley, N.Y., starting Sept. 1, '45. Running time, 91 MINS.

Tanya	Elena Kuzmina
Klava	Anastasia Lissianskaya
The Scientist	Vassili Zaichikov
Prisoner No. 225	Gregory Mikhailov
Johann Krauss	Tania Barisheva
Lotta	Ludmilla Sukbarevskaya
Rudolph Peschke	Peter Suthanov
Kurt Kahger	Gregory Greif

Soviet production is another indictment of Nazi slave-labor methods, showing the Russian idea of what happened to their countrymen when communities were overrun by the Germany army. Film is too somber and action-less, by American standards, to mean much at the American boxoffice. Picture follows too many other U. S. films covering the same subject, and with more melodramatic, better-done stories.

Film is aided by several sterling performances, nice direction and a superb score. No-name cast, tedious plot and superimposed titles also blight its chances here.

Pic concerns a girl sold to a typical German middle-class family. The girl, labeled No. 217, is handed over to a German housewife for 15 marks. Main portion of the story concerns the drudgery, mental torture and menial tasks she must perform.

Original score of Alexander Khatchaturian is particularly worthy of mention.

Of the several notable performances, that contributed by Ludmilla Sukharevskaya, as the German grocer's daughter, is especially strong. Elena Kuzmina, as Tanya (No. 217), is disappointing. Vassili Zaichikov, as a captured scientist, and Vladimir Vladislavsky, the German grocer, are excellent. *Wear.*

Youth Aflame

Continental release of J. D. Kendis production. Features Joy Reese, Warren Burr, Kay Morley. Directed by Elmer Clifton. Screenplay by Clifton, from story by Helen Kildy; editor, George Merrick; camera, Jack Greenhalgh. At Gotham, N. Y., week of Aug. 31, '45. Running time, 61 MINS.

Katy	Joy Reese
Frank	Warren Burr
Larry	Kay Morley
Al	Michael Owen
Lester	Rod Rogers
Harry	Edwin Brian
Peggy	Julie Duncan
Helen	Shelila Roberts
Father	Edward Cassidy
Mrs. Clark	Mary Arden
Tom	Duke Johnson

Another in a line of films supposedly geared to aid the fight on juvenile delinquency, "Youth Aflame" is just repetitious, an apparent quickie. Boxoffice values are negative.

Themed to prove that there really is no such thing as a delinquent child, but that parents are actually to blame, picture's message is crude. Dialog is reminiscent of that from other similar films, and delivery by the players is listless. *Sten.*

The Echo Murders
(BRITISH-MADE)

London, Aug. 24.

Anglo-American Film release of British National Strand Film. Features David Farrar, Pamela Stirling. Directed by John Harlow. Adapted from Sexton Blake stories by John Harlow. At Rialto, London, Aug. 23, '45. Running time, 80 MINS.

Sexton Blake	David Farrar
Dick Warren	Dennis Price
Stella Duncan	Pamela Stirling
James Duncan	Julian Mitchell
Rainsford	Dennis Arundel
Beales	Kynaston Reeves
P. C. Smith	Cyril Smith
Dr. Grey	Patric Curwen
Purvis	Johnnie Schofield
Marat	Paul Croft

With story and technique about as modern as a reissue of "Perils of Pauline," this adaptation of another in the seemingly unending Sexton Blake series injects a batch of Nazi bad eggs into the plot in a vain effort to cover up the cobwebs. Not good enough even for lesser runs in America.

Produced by British National Films, the pic is obviously pointed at whodunit fans. Incidentally, a record-breaking list of screen credits includes mention of the Amalgamated Press, the big mag factory founded by Lord Northcliffe, publisher of more than 75 different weeklies which grind out the Sexton Blake serials.

Dick Farrar as Sexton Blake gives a good imitation of all his predecessors in Sherlock Holmes parts, and emerges unscathed from beatings and various forms of Nazi tortures without losing face.

John Harlow's direction of his own script is workmanlike, but his too frequent use of long shots is made less excusable by out-of-focus camera defects. *Talb.*

Miniature Reviews

"The House on 92d Street" (20th). FBI-Nazi spy meller that should do biz based on exploitation possibilities.

"Pardon My Past" (Col). Slick comedy slated for nifty boxoffice.

"Kiss and Tell" (Col). Shirley Temple in boxoffice farce, adaptation from stage hit.

"Men In Her Diary" (Songs) (U). Light drama starring Peggy Ryan, Jon Hall and Louise Allbritton; fair b.o.

"Isle of the Dead" (RKO). Boris Karloff in slow horror film; moderate b.o.

"Three's a Crowd" (Rep). Diverting whodunit that should do moderate biz.

"River Gang" (U). Gloria Jean in feeble whodunit.

"Bargekeeper's Daughter" (French-made). Prewar French farce OK for arty spots.

"Fall of Berlin" (Artkino). Soviet-made documentary won't mean much at American b.o. because of length.

"Love, Honor and Goodbye" (Rep). Minor domestic farce.

The House on 92d St.

20th-Fox release of Louis de Rochemont production. Features William Eythe, Lloyd Nolan, Signe Hasso, Gene Lockhart, Leo G. Carroll, Lydia St. Clair, William Post. Directed by Henry Hathaway. Screenplay, Barre Lyndon, Charles G. Booth and John Monks, Jr., based on story by Booth; editor, Harmon Jones; camera, Norbert Brodine; music, David Buttolph; music director, Emil Newman. Tradeshown in N. Y., Sept. 10, '45. Running time, 85 MINS.

Bill Dietrich....William Eythe
Inspector George A. Briggs....Lloyd Nolan
Elsa Gebhardt....Signe Hasso
Charles Ogden Roper....Gene Lockhart
Colonel Hammersohn....Leo G. Carroll
Johanna Schmedt....Lydia St. Clair
Walker....William Post, Jr.
Max Coburg....Harry Bellaver
Adolphe Lange....Bruno Wick
Conrad Arnulf....Harro Meller
Gus Huzmann....Charles Wagenheim
Adolph Klaen....Alfred Linder
Luise Vadja....Renee Carson
Admiral....Rusty Lane
Dr. Arthur C. Appleton....John McKee
Major-General....Edwin Jerome
Freda Kazel....Elisabeth Neumann
Franz Von Wirt....Salo Douday
Sergeant....Paul Ford
Customs Officer....William Adams
Policeman....Lew Eckles
Intern....Tom Brown
Frank Jackson....George Shelton
Col. Felix Strassen....Alfred Zlesler

Twentieth-Fox, employing somewhat the technique of "The March of Time," has parlayed the latter with facilities and files of the FBI in arriving at "The House on 92d Street." It doesn't matter much whether it's east or west 92d—the result is an absorbing documentation that's frequently heavily-steeped melodrama. This film will do biz because of its excellent exploitation possibilities. The FBI, in peace as in war, is still a pretty good boxoffice bet.

"House" is comprised of prewar and wartime footage taken by the FBI, and it ties together revelations of the vast Nazi spy system in the United States. Woven into this factual data, along with what the foreword reveals is a thorough cooperation of the FBI in making the film, are the dramatic elements inserted by Hollywood in general and 20th-Fox in particular.

Lloyd Nolan is the FBI inspector in charge of ferreting out the espionage on a secret formula sought by the Nazis; William Eythe is the young German-American sent to Germany, by U. S.-located Nazis (and the FBI), to learn espionage and sabotage; Signe Hasso plays a key link to the Nazi system in this country. Other principals are Gene Lockhart, Leo G. Carroll, Lydia St. Clair and William Post. They play characters, wholly or composites, right out of the FBI indices.

Recently, it was revealed by 20th-Fox that it had a film which would be the first full-length feature to tell of the atomic bomb. "House" is purportedly that film. It tells of a certain secret formula—a Process 97. But the atomic bomb? One surmises that Process 97, which was a term applied to the pic by the FBI, must have dealt with the bomb. There obviously could be no mention of the atom in this film because of its secrecy at the time "House" was made. *Kahn.*

Pardon My Past

Hollywood, Sept. 8.

Columbia release of Mutual Production. Directed by Leslie Fenton. Stars Fred MacMurray; features Marguerite Chapman, Akim Tamiroff, William Demarest, Rita Johnson. Story, Patterson McNutt and Harlan Ware; screenplay, Earl Felton and Karl Kamb; camera, Russell Metty; editor, Richard Heermance; musical score, Dimitri Tiomkin. Previewed in projection room, Hollywood, Sept. 8, '45. Running time, 89 MINS.

Eddie York }
Francis Pemberton }....Fred MacMurray
Joan....Marguerite Chapman
Jim Arnold....Akim Tamiroff
Chuck....William Demarest
Mary....Rita Johnson
Grandpa Pemberton....Harry Davenport
Uncle Wills....Douglass Dumbrille
Stephani....Karolyn Grimes
Plainsclothesman....Dewey Robinson
Mr. Long....Hugh Prosser
Plainclothesman....Tom Moffatt
Butler....Herbert Evans
Thug....Frank Moran
Cab Driver....George Chandler
Clothes Salesman....Charles Arnt

"Pardon My Past" is a topnotch comedy packing plenty of fun for all types of audiences. There's production polish and slick direction by Leslie Fenton to give its boxoffice outlook a rosy hue, and there's the Fred MacMurray name for the marquee.

It's a comedy of mistaken identity and frustration. MacMurray and William Demarest are just-discharged G.I.'s enroute to Wisconsin to start a mink farm with their service savings. MacMurray is mistaken for a rich playboy by a gambler who tries to collect an old debt. MacMurray and his partner go to the playboy's home to explain mixup and recover coin but are again mistaken for the playboy, who's supposedly in Mexico.

Complications are hilariously written by Earl Felton and Karl Kamb from the Patterson McNutt-Harlan Ware original, and cast toppers make the most of the situations. MacMurray finds the playboy is a spineless heel who's been persuaded to divorce a loving wife and give control of his estate to a conniving uncle. The would-be mink farmer falls in love with a poor relative while temporarily at the playboy's estate, straightens out the latter's life, and also squares things with the gambler. While essentially written for laughs, script also has occasional flashes of heart that make the antics more convincing.

MacMurray's dual role is deftly handled so that the two characters he portrays never actually meet on the screen, which makes for a more satisfactory solution of the old double-exposure problems. Actor contributes an ace performance in his best style under Fenton's smart direction. Dry wit and dumbness of the Demarest character are also good for many a chuckle. Harry Davenport, as the grandfather soured on his worthless kin, is also topnotch. Marguerite Chapman is particularly good as the poor relative. Akim Tamiroff contributes an excellent gangster, aided by henchmen Hugh Prosser and Frank Moran. Rita Johnson shines as the divorced wife, accounting for genuine dramatic moments. Others who are expert include Douglass Dumbrille, the uncle; Karolyn Grimes, the child; Dewey Robinson, Herbert Evans and Charles Arnt, latter a sour clothing store clerk.

The editing bolsters the pace. The production design by Bernard Herzbrun is handsome and the musical score composed and conducted by Dimitri Tiomkin a definite contribution. *Brog.*

Kiss and Tell

Columbia release of George Abbott production (Sol C. Siegel, associate producer). Stars Shirley Temple; features Walter Abel, Katharine Alexander, Jerome Courtland, Robert Benchley, Mary Philips, Porter Hall, Virginia Welles. Directed by Richard Wallace. Screenplay, F. Hugh Herbert, from his own stage play; editor, Charles Nelson; camera, Charles Lawton, Jr.; music, Werner R. Heymann; music director, M. W. Stoloff. Previewed in projection room, Sept. 7, '45. Running time, 90 MINS.

Corliss Archer....Shirley Temple
Dexter Franklin....Jerome Courtland
Mr. Archer....Walter Abel
Mrs. Archer....Katharine Alexander
Uncle George....Robert Benchley
Mr. Franklin....Porter Hall
Mrs. Franklin....Edna Holland
Mildred Pringle....Virginia Welles
Mr. Pringle....Tom Tully
Mrs. Pringle....Mary Philips
Raymond Pringle....Darryl Hickman
Private Jimmy Earhart....Scott McKay
Lenny Archer....Scott Elliott
Louise....Kathryn Card

George Abbott's long-run Broadway production of F. Hugh Herbert's comedy, "Kiss and Tell," has also been produced for the screen by Abbott, and the screenplay has likewise been scripted by the play's author. Under those circumstances, it seems hardly likely that the screen version can miss the boxoffice mark.

Shirley Temple has the lead role of Corliss Archer in the picture edition, and Miss Temple is still having her growing pains not only as an adolescent but also in performance. It is in her characterization of Corliss Archer, the teen-aged brat who does more than her share to upset several households, that the film suffers most though certainly not with sufficient dire results to minimize the b.o. value of "Kiss." It is still an excellent farce for entertainment purposes though lacking, somewhat, the spark and pace that distinguished the Broadway stage play.

The story will be recalled as that which finds the central character involved in a situation that binds her to secrecy. Her brother, an army lieutenant overseas, has secretly married his neighborhood sweetheart, and the news cannot get out; the families of both principals are feuding because of some inconsequential reason. The young wife is pregnant, and because Corliss is so tightly linked with the secret, she must allow herself, because of extenuating circumstances, to be thought of as the enceinte one. The major laughs come in when, to carry out the lie, she names her next-door sweetheart, a 17-year-old, as the prospective father. Which makes it all as it was in the stage play, excepting for certain little touches which screen latitude can permit.

Walter Abel is capital as the irate father of Corliss, and Katharine Alexander, Robert Benchley, Porter Hall, Jerome Courtland, Virginia Welles and Mary Philips handle the other lead roles well.

Production is top-grade, and direction by Richard Wallace is paced for laughs. *Kahn.*

Men in Her Diary
(SONGS)

Universal release of Howard Welsch production. Stars Peggy Ryan, Jon Hall and Louise Allbritton; features Ernest Truex, Virginia Grey, William W. Terry. Directed by Charles Barton. Screenplay, F. Hugh Herbert and Ellwood Ullman based on original story by Kerry Shaw; camera, Paul Ivano; editor, Paul Landres. Tradeshown in projection room, N. Y., Sept. 11, '45. Running time, 73 MINS.

Doris Mann....Peggy Ryan
Randolph Glenning....Jon Hall
Isabel Glenning....Louise Allbritton
Williams....Ernest Truex
Diane Lee....Virginia Grey
Tommy Burton....William W. Terry
Douglas Crane....Alan Mowbray
Florist....Eric Blore
Judge Morgan....Samuel S. Hinds
Marjorie....Jacqueline de Wit
Moxie....Maxie Rosenbloom
Mme. Irene....Sig Ruman
Cavanaugh....Addison Richards
Pat Mann....Lorraine Miller
Stella....Robin Raymond
Mrs. Braun....Minerva Urecal
Attorney Reynolds....Arthur Loft
Linda....Vivian Austin
Whitman....Lorin Raker

With Peggy Ryan in her first straight acting role, and Jon Hall and Louise Allbritton as added marquee strength, "Men in Her Diary" should do fairly well at the boxoffice. It's a rather mixed-up screenplay, having some silly dialog from which even a strong all-around supporting cast has difficulty untangling themselves.

Yarn deals with the dreamy writings of a teen-age secretary (Peggy Ryan) concerning her allegedly romantic escapades with several men, including her boss. Unfortunately, the boss' wife gets hold of the diary and files suit for divorce. Star of a show the boss is backing, in love with him, convinces Miss Ryan she should dress smartly, "to aid her morale," day she takes the stand during the divorce suit. Naturally, despite all the double-dealing, everything comes out alright in the end.

Hall, as the innocent employer, gives a good performance. Miss Ryan portrays her role capably. Miss Allbritton, as Hall's wife, while getting star billing in this picture, is seen briefly as compared to the other major members of the cast. However, she, too, does creditably. Support, comprising some of the best character actors in Hollywood, do the best they can. William Terry, who scored strongly in "Stage Door Canteen," practically cops the picture as the press agent for the show, who tries to straighten things out between the backer and his frau. He winds up wed to Miss Ryan.

Direction by Charles Barton is uneven. Production values, including settings and photography, are above par. Two songs delivered briefly by Virginia Grey, who plays the star of the show not too impressively, fail to register. They are "Makin' a Million" and "Keep Your Chin Up," by Everett Carter and Milton Rosen. *Sten.*

Isle of the Dead

RKO release of Val Lewton production. Stars Boris Karloff; features Ellen Drew, Marc Cramer. Directed by Mark Robson. Screenplay, Ardel Wray and Josef Mischel; camera, Jack Mackenzie; editor, Lyle Boyer. At Rialto, N. Y., Sept. 7, '45. Running time, 72 MINS.

General....Boris Karloff
Thea....Ellen Drew
Oliver....Marc Cramer
Mrs. St. Aubyn....Katherine Emery
Kyra....Helene Thimig
St. Aubyn....Alan Napier
Albrecht....Jason Robards
Dr. Drossos....Ernst Dorian
Robbins....Skelton Knaggs
Colonel....Sherry Hall

"Isle of the Dead" is a slow conversation piece about plagues and vampires on an eerie Greek island. It's better handled and directed than most of the so-called "horror" films though thriller fans will still find its lack of action a drag and its suspense only mildly interesting. Even Boris Karloff fans will note the tired way he rambles through it all.

Yarn is a psychological drama of an assorted group of people gathered on the island, when a plague breaks out and death takes one of them. Precautions are taken but others are seized. A doctor is sure only a south wind can blow away the plague; a superstitious native is as positive that one of the guests is a vampire, carrying the plague's spirit within her. A couple of murders help to decimate the group until only a couple are left when the plague runs its course.

Some good sets, acting and moody atmosphere give the yarn a better backing than it deserves. Karloff, as a Greek general trying to keep the plague from reaching his troops, is more paternal than menacing. Ellen

Drew lends poignancy as a misunderstood nurse, and she and Marc Cramer present an attractive romantic couple. *Bron.*

Three's a Crowd

Republic release of Walter H. Goetz production. Features Pamela Blake, Charles Gordon, Gertrude Michael, Pierre Watkin, Virginia Brissac. Directed by Lesley Selander. Screenplay, Dane Lussier, from novel by Mignon G. Eberhart; editor, Tony Martinelli; camera, William Bradford. At Strand, Brooklyn, Sept. 7, '45, dual. Running time, **58 MINS.**

Diane Whipple	Pamela Blake
Jeffrey Locke	Charles Gordon
Sophie Whipple	Gertrude Michael
Marcus Pett	Pierre Watkin
Cary Whipple	Virginia Brissac
Jacob Waite	Ted Hecht
Willy Devaney	Grady Sutton
Grayson	Tom London
Ronald Drew	Roland Varno
Mamie	Anne O'Neal
Detective	Bud Geary
Madame Francine	Nenette Vallon

Diverting whodunit should do moderately well on double bills despite absence of potent names. Story, although not new, has sufficient twists to sustain interest.

Pamela Blake plays an heiress who's rushed into a hasty marriage, somewhat reluctantly, with Charles Gordon after a former suitor has been murdered. Finger of suspicion points at the bridal couple inasmuch as both visited the victim on night of the murder.

Miss Blake gives good performance. Gordon ditto. Pierre Watkin, Virginia Brissac, Ted Hecht, and Gertrude Michael are likewise okay. Direction by Lesley Selander is smooth. Cameraing by William Bradford okay too. *Edba.*

River Gang

Universal release of Charles David production. Stars Gloria Jean; features John Qualen, Bill Goodwin, Keefe Brasselle, Shelden Leonard, Bob Homas, Gus Schilling, Vince Barnett. Directed by David. Screenplay, Leslie Charteris, from story by David and Hugh Gray; camera, Jerome Ash; editor, Saul A. Goodkind. Previewed in N. Y., Sept. 10, '45. Running time, **64 MINS.**

Wendy	Gloria Jean
Uncle Bill	John Qualen
Mike	Bill Goodwin
Johnny	Keefe Brasselle
Peg Leg	Shelden Leonard
Dopey Charley	Gus Schilling
Organ Grinder	Vince Barnett
Police Captain	Bob Homans
Goofy	Jack Grimes
Butch	Mendy Koenig
Fatso	Rocco Lanzo
Slug	Douglas Croft

Universal mixed too many ingredients in this one. Modest-budgeted whodunit is a corny yarn about a Dead-endish gang, with Gloria Jean thrown in as a pawnshop assistant addicted to fairy tales. Miss Jean sings once, briefly, a little folk tune. Film has little other appeal.

Yarn concerns a pawnshop keeper, Miss Jean's uncle, who keeps the girl secluded from the crude outside world and fills her mind with fantastic fairy tales—while he's acting as boss of a gang of thieves, with the shop as hideout for loot.

Uncle's attempts to keep niece away from the neighborhood boys backfires. A valuable violin stolen from a murdered composer finds its way to the pawnshop, and another murder is committed (by the uncle, who also threatens to kill his niece) before the boys unearth the mystery and unmask the uncle to the police.

Yarn nowhere shows any originality or brightness, with suspense just as lacking. Miss Jean is a winsome heroine, but her fans will be disappointed that she doesn't sing more than she does. John Qualen handles the uncle role passably, but the neighborhood kids are as unreal as all getout, and Bob Homans and Bill Goodwin are caricatures as cops. Sheldon Leonard looks villainous enough as a one-legged piratical character, and Keefe Brasselle suits as the boys' chief. Direction is so-so. *Bron.*

Barge-Keeper's Daughter

("Education du Prince")

(FRENCH-MADE)

Famous International Film Co. release of C.I.C. production. Features Louis Jouvet, Alerme, Elvire Popesco, Robert Lynen. Directed by Alexander Esway. Screenplay by Carlo Rim. English titles, H. G. Weinberg. At 55th St. Playhouse, N. Y., starting Sept. 5, '45. Running time, **72 MINS.**

Cerdeux	Louis Jouvet
Sofia	Elvire Popesco
Chautard	Alerme
Prince Sascha	Robert Lynen
Barge-Keeper	Charpin
Barge-Keeper's Daughter	Josette Day

(In French; English titles)

Despite its mild title and the fact that pic was made before the war, "The Barge-Keeper's Daughter" should do well in U. S. arty spots. It's droll comedy, typically French, with some torrid scenes that seemingly were more so before the N. Y. state censor saw it.

Plot concerns the impoverished royalty, in exile in France, and the newly rich. There's the wealthy baron who has so much coin he wants to help bring back the young prince from exile and place him on the throne. The prince has grown up in Paris while in exile and doesn't want to be king, one reason being that his sweetheart is the daughter of a barge-keeper. Final scene has the prince marrying the poor gal after he has vetoed all others.

Direction by Alexander Esway is okay though the costumes date some scenes. Louis Jouvet and Alerme are the two who want the king restored, with the former the rich baron who's footing the bill. Others who are effective include Elvire Popesco, Robert Lynen, as the prince; Charpin and Josette Day, as the gal the prince finally weds. *Wear.*

The Fall of Berlin

(SOVIET-MADE)

Artkino release of Soviet Central Documentary Film Studios production. Produced and edited by Yuri Reisman. Previewed in N. Y. projection room, Sept. 6, '45. Running time, **70 MINS.**

This historical film document, covering some of the Russian campaigns leading to the downfall of the Nazis, and the actual drive on Berlin and fighting in the German capital's streets, is okay newsreel footage. But it's far too long and contains too much extraneous matter for U.S. audiences. Artkino held back this feature until "The True Glory" was released, and this, too, will hurt "Fall of Berlin" chances at the American boxoffice.

While most of the photography is on-the-scene material, Soviet documentary does not by any means measure up to most U. S. and British efforts in the same field. Scoring, the use of maps and commentary by William S. Gailmor are disappointing.

Some remarkable pictures of the firing of huge guns (all pointed Berlin-ward) at night make one startling sequence. The carnage inside Berlin is also mute testimony of the city's leveling. There are several unusual scenes taken from a fighter plane, showing the effect of strafing by Russo gunners. *Wear.*

Love, Honor and Goodbye

(SONGS)

Republic release of Harry Grey production. Stars Virginia Bruce and Edward Ashley; features Victor McLaglen, Nils Asther, Helen Broderick, Veda Ann Borg and Jacqueline Moore. Directed by Albert S. Rogell. Story, Art Arthur and Albert S. Rogell; adaptation, Arthur Phillips, Lee Loeb and Dick Irving Hyland; songs, Jack Strachey, Holt Marvell, Harry Link, Walter Scharf and Ned Washington; editor, Richard L. Van Enger; camera, John Alton. At Gotham, N.Y., week Sept. 7, '45. Running time, 86 MINS.

Roberta Baxter	Virginia Bruce
William Baxter	Edward Ashley
Terry	Victor McLaglen
Tony Linnard	Nils Asther
Mary Riley	Helen Broderick
Marge	Veda Ann Borg
Sally	Jacqueline Moore
Charles, the Butler	Robert Greig
Miss Whipple	Victoria Horne
Detective	Ralph Dunn
Miss Hopkins	Therese Lyon

An incredible domestic farce which drags throughout its 86 minutes and produces only a few mild moments of laughter, "Love, Honor and Goodbye" is strictly for minor time.

Virginia Bruce and Edward Ashley are starred. The former is a stage-struck wife who walks out on her husband in a huff, suspecting him of infidelity. Ashley plays an attorney who apparently spends little time in his office or in court, yet lives sumptuously in a penthouse.

When his wife walks out on him, Ashley takes into his home a dime-museum tattoo artist and his child ward under circumstances that are highly implausible. Then the wife, posing as a French nurse for the child, disguising herself, tries to compromise hubby in order to gain evidence that he's untrue. It adds up to ennui.

Miss Bruce and Ashley give very routine performances, while Victor McLaglen also fails to impress. Nils Asther plays a ham actor, and does a better job than the others. The little girl orphan, Jacqueline Moore, has possibilities.

There are two songs in the picture, both sung by Miss Bruce, "These Foolish Things" and "Close Those Eyes." *Char.*

Miniature Reviews

"That Night With You" (Songs) (U). Pleasant comedy with music that will do biz.

"The Enchanted Forest" (Color) (PRC). Edmund Lowe, Harry Davenport, Brenda Joyce in colorful fantasy; okay boxoffice.

"The Girl of the Limberlost" (Col). Modestly budgeted screen version of Gene Stratton Porter novel okay for double bills.

"Dead of Night" (Eagle-Lion). Collection of Grand Guignol spine chillers with strong cast make this sturdy U. S. entry.

"Behind City Lights" (Songs) (Rep). Entertaining light dualer.

That Night With You

(SONGS)

Hollywood, Sept. 18.

Universal release of Fessier-Pagano production. Stars Franchot Tone, Susanna Foster, David Bruce, Louise Allbritton; features Buster Keaton, Irene Ryan, Jacqueline De Wit. Directed by William A. Seiter. Screenplay, Michael Fessier and Ernest Pagano from story by Arnold Belgard; camera, Charles Van Enger; songs, Jack Brooks, J. J. Salter; editor, Fred R. Feitshans, Jr.; dances, Leslie Horton. George Moro, Louis Dapron. Previewed L. A., Sept. 18, '45. Running time, **84 MINS.**

Paul Renaud	Franchot Tone
Penny	Susanna Foster
Johnny	David Bruce
Sheila Morgan	Louise Allbritton
Blossom Drake	Jacqueline De Wit
Sam	Buster Keaton
Prudence	Irene Ryan
Wilbur	Howard Freeman
Clarissa	Barbara Sears
Tenor	Tony N. Caruso
Concertino Player	Julio Rivero
Bingo	Teddy Infuhr

Franchot Tone and Susanna Foster names will carry this gay comedy, which producers Michael Fessier and Ernest Pagano have packed with solid production values. Film can stand on its own merits as quality entertainment and should hit high grosses for Universal market. William A. Seiter, in his direction, has invested action with a lilting swing and picture is a showcase for Miss Foster's voice.

Situation comedy is based on her frantic efforts to become a star. In this pursuit, she invades apartment of Franchot Tone, musical-comedy producer, on claim she is his daughter, and very nearly gets away with it, when Tone's former wife, Jacqueline De Wit, to whom he was married briefly when very young, shows up and bears out girl's claim. for reason of her own. Story winds up on fanciful note, with Miss Foster getting her wish to sing on Broadway and later bear David Bruce the six children he wants after their marriage. Tone is at his comedy best in the role of confirmed bachelor who suddenly finds "fatherhood" a refreshing role. Miss Foster warbles five numbers to excellent effect. Bruce in smaller part stacks up favorably with his co-stars, and Louise Allbritton, as Tone's secretary, is good for some comedy moments. Rest of cast is comparable, with Buster Keaton in for a solid bit.

There are several novel musical numbers in a church wherein Miss Foster figures, outstanding among these being an adaptation of "Figaro" from "Barber of Seville" to a beauty shop routine, cleverly done with Edward Ward doing arrangement and Jack Brooks the lyrics. Musical numbers throughout have been turned out imaginatively, with technical department all of high standard. *Brog.*

The Enchanted Forest

(Music)

(CINECOLOR)

PRC release of Jack Schwartz production. Features Edmund Lowe, Brenda Joyce, Harry Davenport, Billy Severn. Directed by Lew Landers. Screenplay by Robert Lee Johnson, John Lebar and Lou Brock from original story by Lebar; camera, Marcel LePicard; editor, Roy Livingston; animals trained by Curley Twiford, Earl Johnson; music, Albert Hay Malotte; color, W. T. Crespinel. Previewed N. Y. Sept. 14, '45. Running time, **82 MINS.**

Steven Blaine....................Edmund Lowe
Anne..............................Brenda Joyce
Jackie............................Billy Severn
Old John.......................Harry Davenport
Henderson...........................John Litel
Gilson...........................Clancy Cooper
Blackie..................."Jim" the Crow

"The Enchanted Forest" is PRC's prestige picture, undoubtedly the top production effort of this company. It's a colorful fantasy, in the Disney manner, concerning an old hermit and his life in the outdoors, association with denizens of the forest, etc. Picture is a natural for youngsters and should hold considerable charm for grownups. How it will shape up at the wickets will depend largely on the way it's sold. PRC is unwrapping the b.r. to put it over. Its Cinecolor is excellent and goes far in making the production stand out. Story is no great shakes, yet director Lew Landers has guided it with an eye for detail, making it a brilliant-hued closeup of forest denizens. While some may find some fault with the rather tedious first few reels in spotting Harry Davenport, as Old John, in his outdoor abode and his daily contact with numerous forest pals (crow, watchdog, mountain lion, squirrel, etc.), it would have the spectator believe he hears sounds, woodland music and voices that the average person cannot distinguish. It shows him constantly moving deeper into the wooded glades as he retreats before the ex-swinging loggers for a lumber company.

Edmund Lowe adds dignity to the role of the medico who regains his health in the forest, and wins a bride, Brenda Joyce. As the child's mother, latter is okay in a difficult part. Davenport makes a fairly plausible old man of the forest while Billy Severn is excellent as the youngster. John Litel, as the lumberman and Clancy Cooper, as the conniving woodchopper boss, head the support. All the animals, including a remarkable police dog and "Jim, the crow," figure importantly and do well in their respective roles.

Marcel LePicard's cameraing is topflight while laurels go to W. T. Crespinel for his color supervision. Score by Albert Hay Malotte adds the necessary charm to the simple story. *Wear.*

The Girl of the Limberlost

Columbia release of Alexis Thurn-Taxis production. Features Ruth Nelson, Dorinda Clifton, Gloria Holden, Ernest Cossart, Vanessa Brown, James Bell. Directed by Melchor G. Ferrer. Screenplay, Erna Lazarus, based upon novel by Gene Stratton Porter; editor, Al Clark; camera, Burnett Guffey. At Fox, Brooklyn, week of Sept. 14, '45, dual. Running time, **60 MINS.**

Kate Comstock.....................Ruth Nelson
Elnora Comstock................Dorinda Clifton
Pete Reed.........................Loren Tindall
Miss Nelson......................Gloria Holden
Roger Henley....................Ernest Cossart
Helen Brownlee..................Vanessa Brown
Wesley Sinton........................James Bell
Margaret Sinton.....................Joyce Arling
Hodges..............................Charles Arnt
Chester Hopple......................Warren Mills
Amy Thurston......................Gloria Patrice
Miss Blodgett....................Lillian Bronson
Jessie Reed......................Peggy Converse
Bob Stewart.........................Jimmy Clark
Carrie..............................Carol Morris

Modestly budgeted film version of Gene Stratton Porter's yesteryear bestseller can hope for little better than moderate returns since cast fails to project any name lure for the marquee. For most part it must rely upon those who read the novel and may be intrigued to make comparison with screen version. Brief running time is an asset for programming.

Screen version has captured the tearjerker elements of the novel and should provide a field day for femme audiences who may enjoy weeping through the trials and tribulations of the backwoods gal whose mother hated her before birth—all because she blamed the approaching motherhood for inability to rescue her husband when latter met death in a quagmire.

Ensuing sequence depicts the mother carrying on her vicious campaign of hate, making practically a recluse of the girl and would deny her an education. A neighboring farm-boy and other friends finally get her off to school. Her happiness in her new surroundings is complete when her mother, finding out that her husband had been unfaithful, repents and becomes the devoted mother she should have been.

Dorinda Clifton turns in a good performance of the titular role, bringing to it refreshing touches that win and hold sympathy all the way. Ruth Nelson is sufficiently menacing as the mother. Ernest Cossart does neatly as the friendly school principal, and Loren Tindall does nittily as the boy friend. Vanessa Brown, Gloria Holden and James Bell are also okay in support roles.

Direction is at times spotty but cameraing is okay. *Edba.*

Dead of Night
(BRITISH-MADE)

London, Sept. 5.

Eagle-Lion release of Ealing Studios production. Features Michael Redgrave, Googie Withers, Basil Radford, Naunton Wayne. Directed by Cavalcanti, Charles Crichton, Basil Dearden, Robert Hamer. Screenplay by John V. Baines, Angus MacPhail. Based on original stories by H. G. Wells, E. F. Benson, John Baines, Angus MacPhail; camera, Jack Parker, J. Julius. At Gaumont theatre, London, Sept. 4, '45. Running time, **104 MINS.**

Maxwell Frere..................Michael Redgrave
Joan Cortland....................Googie Withers
Walter Craig.......................Mervyn Johns
Eliot Foley.......................Roland Culver
Mrs. Foley........................Mary Merrall
Dr. Van Straaten................Frederick Valk
Sally O'Hara....................Sally Ann Howes
Joyce Grainger.......................Judy Kelly
George Parratt....................Basil Radford
Larry Potter.....................Naunton Wayne
Mary Lee...........................Peggy Bryan
Maurice Olcott.....................Allan Jeayes
Beulah..........................Elisabeth Welch
Sylvester Kee.....................Hartley Power
Hugh Grainger...................Anthony Baird
Mitzi................................Magda Kun

Remember "If I Had a Million"? In "Dead of Night," Michael Balcon seems to have a winner every bit as big as that Hollywood hit. Certainly for every type of audience in this country, and almost as surely in the case of American moviegoers, this collection of Grand Guignol spine chillers has real entertainment appeal. Looks like a big U.S. grosser.

Intelligence stamps the whole production, with each of the five interpolated stories receiving topnotch direction. Faultless scripting in linking the narrative keeps the audience always centering their interest on the seven principal characters to whom the camera swings back between the unfolding of the episodic story. Gruesome and eerie as the injected sequences are, the gradual buildup of impending tragedy of the main drama makes for rare sustained suspense.

There's little to choose between the four directors, Cavalcanti, Chas. Crichton, Basil Dearden and Robert Hamer. Each of them handles his individual job with sure touch. Like the script writers, John V. Baines and Angus MacPhail, they had the best of it because the main plot is based on a story by E. F. Benson with one episode an adaptation of an H. G. Wells' yarn.

It's hard to pick the outstanding performances from the 24 principals. They're not only all good, but in most instances they turn in performances better than they've ever done before.

It is not because the directing, scripting or acting of "The Ventriloquist's Dummy" sequence is better than anything else in the film that it is specifically mentioned. It's only because the idea of the dummy's assuming mastery over his master is an unusual twist. As the victim of the inanimate wooden doll, Michael Redgrave reaches new heights. Hartley Power, as rival Yank ventriloquist, holds his own with Redgrave in a series of hair-raising clashes.

The H. G. Wells' contribution is his famous "Golfing Story," in which Naughton Wayne and Basil Radford fool their way through 15 minutes of absurdities. It's strong comic relief.

Mervyn Johns, as the architect whose nightmare forms the basis of the story, never misses a bet in a role as long as Hamlet. By canny underplaying each stage of his mounting murderous passion, he subtly suggests the inevitability of the long withheld climax when, against his will he strangles the sceptic psychiatrist played superbly by Frederick Valk.

Since Eagle-Lion took over distribution of the Ealing Studios' product, the West End has rated "Johnny Frenchman" as a boxoffice hit. "Dead of Night" looks in the same category. *Talb.*

Behind City Lights
(SONGS)

Republic release of Joseph Bercholz production. Features Lynne Roberts, Peter Cookson, Jerome Cowan, Esther Dale. Directed by John English. Screenplay, Richard Weil; adapted by Gertrude Walker; editor, Fred Allen; camera, William Bradford; music, Richard Cherwin; songs, Jule Styne, Harold Adamson, Frank Loesser. Tradeshown N. Y., Sept. 14, '45. Running time, **68 MINS.**

Jean Lowell......................Lynne Roberts
Lance Marlowe...................Peter Cookson
Perry Borden.....................Jerome Cowan
Sarah Lowell.......................Esther Dale
Ben Coleman......................William Terry
Daniel Lowell......................Victor Kilian
Curtis Holbrook....................Moroni Olsen
Detective Peterson..............William Forrest
Jones.............................Emmett Vogan
Gab Carson.....................Joseph J. Greene
Charles Matthews..................Frank Scannell
Andrew Coleman.....................Tom London
Doctor Blodgett..................George Carleton
Fred Haskins.........................Bud Geary

"Behind City Lights" is O.K. entertainment for the dualers, containing the proper blend of laughs, thrills and sentiment to give a young shape to an old plot.

Story is a typical tale of the farmer's daughter (Lynne Roberts) who craves big city life and, through a series of unique circumstances, eases out of wedding a country lad in time to visit New York. Here she is blissfully happy in the company of her romantic dream-man (Peter Cookson) and his companion, unaware that the pair are notorious jewel thieves. All's well until Cookson, charmed by her simplicity and sincerity, decides to take the straight and narrow. A chase and a couple of crime-doesn't-pay devices chases the gal back to the young farmer.

Direction by John English, satisfactory histrionics by Miss Roberts and Cookson with especially good support received from Jerome Cowan, Esther Dale and Victor Kilian assist materially. Tunes are oldies and add nothing.

Miniature Reviews

"The Dolly Sisters" (Color; Musical) (20th). Betty Grable-June Haver-John Payne costarrer in boxoffice filmusical.

"Man Alive" (RKO). Slapstick comedy, only fair outlook.

"Wanderer of the Wasteland" (RKO). Mild western fare.

"Sunset in El Dorado" (Songs) (Rep). Fair western.

"Forever Yours" (Songs) (Mono). Pretentious but weak medico-drama. Medium b.o.

"Arson Squad" (PRC). Robert Armstrong, Frank Albertson in arson-gangster thriller; strong for dual support.

"Flame of the West" (Mono). Johnny Mack Brown, Raymond Hatton in typical western.

"Bluebeard's Six Mothers-In-law" (Lumiton). Argentine-made fantasy not geared for U. S. audiences.

Dolly Sisters
(TECHNICOLOR; MUSICAL)

20th-Fox release of Gerge Jessel production. Stars Betty Grable, John Payne, June Haver; features S. Z. Sakall, Reginald Gardiner, Frank Latimore, Gene Sheldon, Sig Ruman, Trudy Marshall. Directed by Irving Cummings. Original screenplay, John Larkin and Marian Spitzer; dances, Seymour Felix; camera, Ernest Palmer, Fred Sersen; music, Alfred Newman, Chas. Henderson, Gene Rose; new songs, Max Gordon, James V. Monaco; editor, Barbara McLean. Tradeshown Sept. 20, '45. Running time, **114 MINS.**

Jenny..............................Betty Grable
Harry Fox...........................John Payne
Rosie................................June Haver
Uncle Litsie.......................S. Z. Sakall
Duke..........................Reginald Gardiner
Irving Netcher...................Frank Latimore
Professor Winnup...................Gene Sheldon
Tsimmis..............................Sig Ruman
Leonore..........................Trudy Marshall
Flo Daly..........................Collette Lyons
Jenny (as a child)..................Evon Thomas
Rosie (as a child)...............Donna Jo Gribble
Hammerstein..................Robert Middlemass
Dowling..............................Paul Hurst
Morrie Keno.........................Lester Allen
Stage Manager........................Frank Orth

"The Dolly Sisters" is another in the nostalgic cycle. Big boxoffice looms. It's George Jessel's first production for 20th-Fox. In Technicolor, with Betty Grable and June Haver in the title roles, and John Payne marking his return to the marquee since leaving the Army, these are major factors on the plus side.

As with many another yesteryear show biz figure—the boff Texas Guinan picture, "Incendiary Blonde," for instance—historical, chronological and biographical accuracy takes to the Hollywoods when the main intent is to entertain. This seems to be the case more where show biz personalities are involved than when films essay the more staid biographicals of the Disraeli-Rothschild-Pasteur-Dr. Ehrlich-Zola pattern.

Those who recall some of the more intimate aspects of the Guinans, the Nora Bayeses and the Dollys can best understand the necessity for a switch or qualification, and undoubtedly the same holds true for the biographicals of the savants and the industrialists. But it does seem that sometimes, perhaps, the change is too sharp.

As for instance the Dollys, known for their raven bobbed coiffures—so here they're glamorous blondes, and their looks-alike is startling. Undoubtedly the surviving Rosie Dolly (Mrs. Irving Netcher)—who, naturally, must have okayed things long ago—and certainly her estranged sister, were she alive, would have no cause for complaint as Betty Grable and June Haver play them. They're certainly a pair of super-glam babes.

Regardless of biographical authenticity, this film resurrects a golden era of the theatre and the international set of the early 1900s. The manner in which the benign S. Z.

Sakall cons Oscar Hammerstein into giving the pseudo-Budapest pets, Jansci and Rozsicka (Jenny and Rosie) Dolly, a date at the famed Hammerstein's Victoria, and their rise to international stardom thereafter, is a pleasant saga. It's no sock as a biographical but the kaleidoscope of the Ziegfeld Roof, the Folies Bergere in Paris, gay life in London, Paris and the Riviera, etc., is a good background to the basic romance between Jenny (Miss Grable) and Harry Fox (John Payne). Later the Rosie Dolly (June Haver)-Irving Netcher (Frank Latimore) romance is introduced.

But it's dominantly a boy-loses-and-recaptures-girl story with Miss Grable and Payne as Harry Fox, songwriter and song-and-dance man. Perhaps the major biographical shortcoming is in ascribing "I'm Always Chasing Rainbows" to Fox's (Payne) authorship, considering that Harry Carroll (and the late Joe McCarthy) long vaude-toured and spotlighted himself as the composer thereof. The real-life Harry Fox, obviously lacking a sufficiently socko song hit to have it re-created in this film version, thus is endowed with another contemporaneous songwriter's work. Jean Schwartz, another songsmith, whom Rosie Dolly first married, is never mentioned.

"Rainbows" is the romantic musical key of the film, with Mack Gordon and Jimmy Monaco having contributed only two newies. "I Can't Begin to Tell You" (very okay) and "Don't Be Too Old-Fashioned (Old-Fashioned Girl)," both of which get plenty of reprise. There's a nostalgic cavalcade of mid-1920 ditties such as "The Vamp," "Carolina in the Morning," "Darktown Strutter's Ball," "Oregon," "Dear Old Pal of Mine," "Give Me the Moonlight, Give Me the Girl," "Frenchy," "Oo, La, La," and others which are made part of the song-and-dance vaude routines, production numbers in Broadway and Paris, gang songs in World War I, and the like.

Productionally, Orry-Kelly's costumes, Seymour Felix's imaginative dance staging, Irving Cummings' direction and producer George Jessel's own well-seasoned and veteran showmanship and background have combined to cook up a number of eyefilling routines. The "Lipstick" number for Ziegfeld; the flash routines at the Folies Bergere; some lavish interiors to accent the Dollys' fabulous success; the scenes at the Monte Carlo casinos, and the like, all add up to b.o. And considering limitations, the original screenplay by John Larkin and Marian Spitzer is OK.

There are nostalgic touches throughout which, by suggestion or otherwise, give the effect of Cantor, Will Rogers, Sam H. Harris, Frank Tinney, et al. The old Knickerbocker hotel on 42d and Broadway, Charlie Cochran, Hammerstein's and the rest of it are tied into a big panorama.

The love that was lost, because of too much foreign success for the Dolly Sisters, is interrupted first by Fox enlisting. The Dollys' popularity with royalty and merchant princes, which took them from London to Paris to the Riviera, is a fast whirl. Intertwined with "Chasing Rainbows" is "I Can't Begin to Tell You," which serves as the musical link until the climactic welcome-back to Broadway, following Rosie's auto accident (which in real life estranged the sisters, ending with Jenny's suicide in Hollywood in 1941).

The stellar trio hold it all together, along with the homely charm of S. Z. Sakall, their klabiasch-addicted uncle and manager. Reginald Gardiner is the moneyed suitor, always on the scene; Gene Sheldon, as an ex-seal-trainer, is a good comedy foil to Payne; Trudy Marshall is a looker, with class and cinematic authority, who should travel faster than she has, and acquitting herself well here as Fox's vis-a-vis. Collette Lyons makes a good femcee, a raucous but effective comedienne. Frank Latimore as Netcher is adequate if undistinguished, Robert Middlemass makes Oscar Hammerstein a vivid impresario, and Lester Allen does one fast-talking bit which is standout.

Abel.

Man Alive

Hollywood, Sept. 22.

RKO release of Robert Fellows production. Stars Pat O'Brien, Adolphe Menjou, Ellen Drew; features Rudy Vallee, Fortunio Bonanova, Joseph Crehan, Jonathan Hale, Minna Gombell, Jason Robards, Jack Norton. Directed by Ray Enright. Screenplay, Edwin Harvey Blum, based on an original story by Jerry Cady and John Tucker Battle; music, Leigh Harline; camera, Frank Redman; editor, Marvin Coil. Tradeshown at Pantages theatre, Hollywood, Sept. 19, '45. Running time, 70 MINS.

Speed.............................Pat O'Brien
Kismet.........................Adolphe Menjou
Connie...............................Ellen Drew
Gordon Tolliver....................Rudy Vallee
Professor Zorada........Fortunio Bonanova
Doc Whitney...................Joseph Crehan
Osborne.......................Jonathan Hale
Aunt Sophie....................Minna Gombell
Fletcher.......................Jason Robards
Willie the Wino.................Jack Norton

"Man Alive" is slated for spotty runs in most situations. Sheer frenzy of its broad, slapstickish plot will force a number of chuckles and give it some chance in the lesser runs before neighborhood audiences. Additional help will come from names of Pat O'Brien and Adolphe Menjou on the marquee.

Ray Enright's direction isn't helped much by the flimsy script in telling yarn of a man believed dead who returns to haunt his widow and prevent her marriage to an old family friend. Characters are slimly drawn, and puckish quality that could have given it a lift fails to come through in the development.

O'Brien depicts successful garage owner, grown stouter than in his college days, who fancies his wife is in love with Rudy Vallee, a rah-rah brother who has maintained his waistline. In a huff he leaves home for the nearest bar, gets drunk, changes clothes with a tramp and when his car goes into the river is believed to have been killed. Instead, it's the tramp's body, and O'Brien, rescued by a river showboat, is puzzled how to tell his wife she's not a widow. Menjou, showboat busybody, becomes his advisor and continually leads him from one jam to another before it's all straightened out. Plot depends upon business and situation for what chuckles it will draw rather than substantially thought-out writing.

Ellen Drew is the flighty wife. Fortunio Bonanova, Joseph Crehan, Minna Gombell, Jack Norton, latter the funny drunk tramp, and others in the cast do as well as possible with material in the Robert Fellows production. Camera and other appurtenances are okay.

Brog.

Wanderer of the Wasteland

Hollywood, Sept. 25.

RKO release of Herman Schlom production. Features James Warren, Richard Martin, Audrey Long. Directors, Edward Killy and Wallace Grissell. Screenplay, Norman Houston, from novel by Zane Grey; camera, Harry J. Wild; music, Paul Sawtell; editor, J. R. Whittredge. Tradeshown Hollywood, Sept. 14, '45. Running time, 67 MINS.

Adam Larey.......................James Warren
Chito.............................Richard Martin
Jean Collingshaw................Audrey Long
Uncle Collinshaw..............Robert Barrat
Jay Collinshaw..................Robert Clarke
Guerd Elliott.....................Harry Woods
Mama Rafferty................Minerva Urecal
Papa Rafferty..................Harry D. Brown
Chito (boy).......................Tommy Cook
Adam (boy).......................Harry McKim
Dealer...........................Jason Robards

This latest version of Zane Grey's novel doesn't offer much for fans of western action and virility. It's a slowly paced oater, despite excellent physical production appurtenances, and doesn't stack up too well in comparison with the more swiftly paced, regular western film fare. It can't expect much more than general spotting in the houses regularly catering to the Saturday matinee fan.

Plot depicts a young man carrying on a search for the killer of his father. The hero is a mild type as portrayed, which doesn't help the action, and there's little adult punch or interest in the development. Hero is saved, as a lad, by an Irish-Spanish family, and when he gets a few years on him, starts his search for revenge. He finally catches up with the killer, but foregoes revenge as he's fallen in love with the murderer's niece. The uncle is killed, the hero is blamed but finally saved at the last minute so romance can get in its fadeout clinch.

Direction was divided between Edward Killy and Wallace Grissell, which may account for the lack of pace. James Warren's performance as the hero is too mild. More fitting to the Grey plot is Richard Martin as the Irish-Spanish friend of Warren. Audrey Long's heroine and other characters are adequate.

Photography by Harry J. Wild takes full advantage of outdoor scenery and picture has been well-mounted physically in all departments.

Brog.

Sunset in El Dorado
(SONGS)

Republic release of Louis Gray production. Stars Roy Rogers; features George "Gabby" Hayes and Dale Evans. Directed by Frank McDonald. Screenplay, John K. Butler; based on original by Leon Abrams; camera, William Bradford; editor, Tony Martinelli. At Republic, N. Y., Sept. 24, '45. Running time, 66 MINS.

Roy Rogers.........................Roy Rogers
Gabby..................George "Gabby" Hayes
Lucille Wiley........................Dale Evans
Cecil Phelps...................Hardie Albright
Aunt Dolly...................Margaret Dumont
Buster Welch.....................Roy Barcroft
Sheriff Gridley....................Tom London
Lyle Fish..........................Stanley Price
Curley Roberts......................Bob Wilke
U.S. Marshal.......................Ed Cassidy
Maisie.........................Dorothy Granger
Bob Nolan and Sons of Pioneers

Despite a weak script, fair direction, several so-so songs, the competent cast should make this one perform boxoffice-wise. There's enough shooting and fighting to satisfy the Roy Rogers fans.

Briefly, story opens up with the heroine itching to leave her job with a bus company to go out to get her fill of adventure. She does, and lands in El Dorado, where her grandmother reigned generations ago as the glamorous Kansas Kate. Via the dream sequence, Kansas Kate's reign is relived, with the case of the original heroine's era doing a double take.

Dale Evans plays the heroines who fall in love with Roy Rogers. George "Gabby" Hayes is the innocent victim of circumstances. Margaret Dumont plays the aunt who wants her niece to marry the affluent operator of the Golden Nugget, but the gal choses the man the audience will approve of, respect and worship.

Between the chases and the mauling moments, the pace is very slow, although the music and dance routines of the gold-mining days help to fill the gulches. Music is listenable, if not memorable.

Forever Yours
(SONGS)

Monogram release of Jeffrey Bernerd production. Stars Gale Storm; features Sir Aubrey Smith, John Mack Brown, Frank Craven, Conrad Nagel, Mary Boland, Billy Wilkerson, Johnny Downs. Directed by William Nigh. Screenplay, Neil Rau and George Sayre; songs, Harry Brown and Robert Watson, Al Jaxton and Neil Rau; camera, Harry Neumann; editor, Ray Curtiss. At Paramount, Brooklyn, week of Sept. 20, '45; dual. Running time, 83 MINS.

Joan Randall.........................Gale Storm
Grandfather..................Sir Aubrey Smith
Tex..........................John Mack Brown
Uncle Charles.....................Frank Craven
Dr. Randall......................Conrad Nagel
1st Soldier.....................Billy Wilkerson
Aunt Mary...........................Mary Boland
Ricky...........................Johnny Downs
Marthe......................Catherine McLeod
Williams.......................Selmer Jackson
Alabam..............................Matt Willis
2nd Soldier....................Russ Whiteman
Leo Diamond and His Harmonaires

This is an ambitious Monogram venture, well-budgeted with talent and production numbers, but with a weak story that will keep erturns down. Cast has eight names, most of them draws for film fans. Pic is spotted as well with several specialty numbers, the whole thing forming a confusing motley of song, dance, nightclubs, hospital wards and crippled children. What starts out as a musical romance winds up as a psychological drama and tear-jerker.

Yarn gives Gale Storm (as Joan Randall) the solo spot as a society deb addicted to horse-riding as well as song and dance appearances at niteries, utilizing the latter talents to aid in charity work for disabled vets and crippled kids. Over-exertion helps bring on infantile paralysis to Joan herself, which her doctor-father (Conrad Nagel) and ditto-medico grandparent (Sir Aubrey Smith) can't cure. An Army major (John Mack Brown), doing experiments as result of his wa rwork, thinks he can operate to cure Joan; he wins over a reluctant family to let him try, restoring Joan to health and winning her heart in the process. Family scenes are long, drawn-out and a little maudlin.

Film's early scenes have some interesting music sequences, with Miss Storm and Johnny Downs in dance routines and femme singing two attractive members, "Close Your Eyes" (Al Jaxton-Neil Rau) and "You're the Answer" (Harry Brown-Robert Watson). Sir Aubrey acts his crotchety self and Mary Boland simpers a little too much. The late Frank Craven carries the humorous load satisfactorily as a tipsy uncle. Brown is a little too stiff and solemn as the Army medico, while Downs enacts well the role of sacrificing swain.

Direction is satisfactory while camera work is quite commendable, especially the montage sequences showing Joan's delirium dreams about the nightclub.

Bron.

Arson Squad

PRC release of Arthur Alexander production. Features Robert Armstrong, Frank Albertson. Directed by Lew Landers. Screenplay, Arthur St. Claire; camera, Ben Kline; editor, Holbrook Todd. At New York, N.Y., Sept. 19, '45. dual. Running time, 66 MINS.

Tom Mitchell...................Frank Albertson
Capt. Joe Dugan.............Robert Armstrong
Judy Mason........................Grace Gillern
Amos Baxter......................Byron Foulger
Samuel Purdy.....................Chester Clute
Cyrus Clevenger...................Arthur Loft
Mike Crandall.....................Jerry Jerome
Bill Roberts....................Stewart Garner
Chief O'Neil....................Edward Cassidy

This is a surprisingly well-made meller. It has Robert Armstrong and Frank Albertson, in the leads, turning in expert jobs. Film is a sturdy programer.

This is the story of a big city's arson squad and its efforts to stamp out a wave of mysterious warehouse fires. They uncover an insidious ring that collects heavy sugar for such jobs. Film contains vivid night fire scenes, nice suspense and bangup direction by Lew Landers.

Armstrong is the persistent Joe Dugan, captain of the arson squad. Albertson makes a vigorous insurance salesman who digs into the mysterious blazes on his own and with startling results. Grace Gillern is the decorative heart interest. Chester Clute, as the insurance adjuster who's in on the arson racket, turns in a good performance.

Wear.

Flame of the West

Monogram release of Scott R. Dunlap production. Stars Johnny Mack Brown; features Raymond Hatton, Joan Woodbury, Douglas Dumbrille, Lynne Carver. Directed by Lambert Hillyer. Screenplay, Adele Buffington; camera, Harry Neumann; editor, Danny Milner. At New York, N. Y., Sept. 19, '45, dual. Running time, 71 MINS.

John Poore	Johnny Mack Brown
Add	Raymond Hatton
Poppy	Joan Woodbury
Nightlander	Douglas Dumbrille
Abbie Compton	Lynne Carver
Wisdon	Harry Woods
Compton	John Merton
Midland	Riley Hill
Hendricks	Steve Clark
Pircell	Bud Osborne
Knott	Jack Rockwell
Rocky	Raphael Bennett
Ed	Tom Quinn
Slick	Jack Ingram

Pee Wee King and His Golden West Cowboys

"Flame of the West" follows the usual western formula of law and order winning out. It's okay for followers of wildwest dramas.

Johnny Mack Brown plays a medico branded a coward by Lynne Carver, his sweetheart. Actually, it's a case of Brown dedicating his life to healing instead of killing. Payoff comes when Brown suddenly decides that rapid manipulation of a six-shooter is the only medicine that'll cure certain tough hombres. Cold-blooded murder of the new marshal (Douglas Dumbrille) prompts the doctor to abandon his medicine case and go after some crooked gamblers with a set of .45's. He wipes out the gang and then resumes his practice as medico.

Brown is satisfying. Raymond Hatton, as his aide, provides the needed comic relief. Joan Woodbury and Miss Carver carry the femme interest. Pee Wee King and the Golden West Cowboys, from the "Grand Old Opry" radio program, contrib instrumentals and singing. *Wear.*

Las Seis Suegras De Barba Azul

("Bluebeard's Six Mothers-in-Law")
(SPANISH-MADE)

Buenos Aires, Sept. 1.

Lumiton production and release. Directed by Carlos Hugo Christensen. Stars Pepe Arias; features Guillermo Battaglia, Alberto Contreras, Diego Martinez, Maria Santos, Amalia Sanchez Arino, Herminia Mancini, Raquel Notar, Olga Casares Pearson, Gloria Ferradis, Olimpio Bobbio, Ivonne Lescaut, Susana Freyre, Monica Val, Rita Juarez, Olga Zubarry and Monica Inchauspe. Original screenplay by Cesar Tiempo. At Gran Palace, Aug. 9, '45. Running time, 90 MINS.

Apart from the weight of comedian Pepe Arias' name, not to mention that of the director, the title here alone should prove sufficient draw at the boxoffice. Holds no value for U.S. audiences.

This is a whimsical farce of a bearded stranger who takes over a country castle and by his moroseness freightens a whole village into believing him to be Bluebeard in person. Amado Marmol (Arias) is the timid, sentimental victim of a lugubrious fate. Six times a widower, he lives among portraits of his departed spouses and in the company of six mothers-in-law who rule him with an iron rod. On one journey he falls in with touring act of seven sisters, and returns with them to the castle, determined to wed the eldest, to the chagrin of the mothers-in-law and horror of the villagers. But the truth shows "Bluebeard" as a hero. Not only had he taken care of six mothers-in-law, but it seems his six wives had died of too much love.

The six mothers-in-law are overplayed but Arias and the seven sisters are naturals in their roles, the girls being real lookers. This is Carlos Hugo Christensen's second venture into a realm of fantasy in a short time, and a credible one. Story material is worth looking into. *Nid.*

Miniature Reviews

"Mildred Pierce" (WB). Potent drama bringing Joan Crawford back to screen. Boff lure for femme trade with important b.o. prospects.

"The Spanish Main" (Technicolor) (RKO). Swashbuckling high-adventure melodrama. B.O. prospects sturdy.

"Colonel Effingham's Raid" (20th). Charles Coburn, Joan Bennett and William Eythe in comedy-drama good for okay returns.

"Query" (Anglo-Am.). Murder thriller with too much British flavor to rate much U. S. boxoffice; no cast also a handicap.

"Apology for Murder" (PRC). Good murder meller in the lightbudget vein.

"Stagecoach Outlaws" (PRC). Formula sagebusher.

Mildred Pierce

Hollywood, Sept. 26.

Warner Bros. release of Jerry Wald production. Stars Joan Crawford; features Jack Carson, Zachary Scott, Eve Arden, Ann Blyth, Bruce Bennett. Directed by Michael Curtiz. Screenplay, Ranald MacDougall, based on novel by James M. Cain; camera, Ernest Haller; music, Max Steiner; editor, David Weisbart. Tradeshown Sept. 26, '45. Running time 109 MINS.

Mildred Pierce	Joan Crawford
Wally	Jack Carson
Monte Bergaron	Zachary Scott
Ida	Eve Arden
Veda Pierce	Ann Blyth
Bert Pierce	Bruce Bennett
Mrs. Biederhof	Lee Patrick
Inspector Peterson	Moroni Olsen
Miriam Ellis	Veda Ann Borg
Kay Pierce	Jo Ann Marlowe
Mrs. Forrester	Barbara Brown
Mr. Williams	Charles Trowbridge
Lottie	Butterfly McQueen
Mr. Jones	Chester Clute
Dr. Gale	Manart Kippen
Ted Forrester	John Compton

"Mildred Pierce" returns Joan Crawford to the screen in a b.o. drama. It's potent vehicle earmarked for important boxoffice in all situations and justifies Miss Crawford's two-year wait for the proper story. Picture packs terrific appeal for adult audiences, particularly the women, though it has a tendency to be overlong and draggy.

At first reading James M. Cain's novel of the same title might not suggest screenable material, but the cleanup job has resulted in a class feature, showmanly produced by Jerry Wald and tellingly directed by Michael Curtiz. It skirts the censorable deftly, but keeps the development adult in dealing with the story of a woman's sacrifices for a no-good daughter. High credit goes to Ranald MacDougall's scripting for his realistic dialog and method of retaining the frank sex play that dots the narrative while, at the same time, making the necessary compromises with the blue-pencillers.

Story is told in flashback as Mildred Pierce is being questioned by police about the murder of her second husband. Character goes back to the time she separated from her first husband and how she struggled to fulfill her ambitions for her children. She turns waitress first, graduates to owning her own typical California drive-in and then a chain of eateries. Despite her success, she's not able to hold her selfish and snobbish daughter and in one high dramatic moment they part. Mildred then marries a worthless Pasadena socialite to gain a social standing that will bring her daughter back. The husband and the daughter carry on a love affair started at the time the playboy was also conducting an affair with Mildred before her marriage. In the driving climax Mildred discovers the truth, the daughter kills the husband, and the mother tries her last sacrifice in attempting to assume the blame. It doesn't work and ending indicates Mildred will try again with her first husband.

The dramatics are heavy but so skillfully handled by Curtiz's direction and the gifted work of the cast that they never cloy. Miss Crawford reaches the peak of her acting career in this pic. Ann Blyth, as the daughter, scores dramatically in her first genuine acting assignment. Zachary Scott makes the most of his character as the Pasadena heel, a talented performance. Lighter moments are sterlingly handled by Jack Carson, on the make for Mildred or anything else in skirts, and Eve Arden, as Mildred's friend and business associate. Bruce Bennett makes effective the quieter, restrained character of the first husband.

Jo Ann Marlowe, the young daughter; Moroni Olsen, a believeable detective-lieutenant; Butterfly McQueen, Mildred's maid with the surprise voice; Chester Clute, Lee Patrick, and others in the cast ably back up the fine work of the principals.

Jerry Wald's production is smartly devised to display every value in the dramatics and is an ace job of supervision. Ernest Haller's photography is fine. The score by Max Steiner, settings, art direction and other contributions are distinct aids in making this one something the public will flock to buy. *Brog.*

The Spanish Main

(COLOR)

Hollywood, Sept. 22.

RKO release of Robert Fellows (Stephen Ames) production. Stars Paul Henreid, Maureen O'Hara, Walter Slezak; features Binnie Barnes, John Emery, Barton MacLane, J.M. Kerrigan, Fritz Leiber. Directed by Frank Borzage. Screenplay, George Worthing Yates and herman J. Mankiewicz; original, Aeneas MacKenzie; camera, George Barnes; music, Hanns Eisler; special effects, Vernon L. Walker; editor, Ralph Dawson; technical director, Capt. Fred Ellis, Ret. B.M.M. Tradeshown Pantages, Hollywood, Sept. 20, '45. Running time, 101 MINS.

Laurent Van Horn	Paul Henreid
Francisca	Maureen O'Hara
Don Alvarado	Walter Slezak
Anne Bonny	Binnie Barnes
Du Bilar	John Emery
Captain Black	Barton MacLane
Pillery	J.M. Kerrigan
Bishop	Fritz Leiber
Lupita	Nancy Gates
Lieutenant Escobar	Jack LaRue
Swaine	Mike Mazurki
Captain Lussan	Ian Keith
Santa Madre Captain	Victor Kilain
Paree	Curt Bois
Commandante	Antonio Moreno

Robust saga of swaggering pirates and beautiful girls. Technicolor dressing and colorful action in production and direction earmark it for lusty boxoffice in majority of situations. Story concentrates on action melodrama but occasionally takes a satirical slant on such high adventure doings, thus bringing nifty chuckles. Red-blooded action will find male favor, as will charms of Maureen O'Hara displayed in color. Romantic aspects offer plenty of interest for femme audiences.

Plot concerns a group of Dutchmen whose ship is wrecked by a storm on the shore of Spanish-held Cartagena. Spanish governor orders the survivors into slavery and the ship's captain to be hung. The captain and several others escape and take up piracy against all Spanish ships. One ship seized is carrying the governor's betrothed, daughter of Mexico's viceroy. The captain-turned-buccaneer forces the girl into marriage but reckons not of jealousy and treachery among his fellow pirates who fear marriage will result in Spaniards arising in force against Tortuga, the buccaneer colony. They return the girl to the governor but by now she's willing to remain a pirate's bride and aids her lover to complete a swashbuckling rescue.

Frank Borzage's direction has packed a multitude of realistic fight scenes into the sea and land clashes, as well as maintaining high interest in the tale's other factors. Robert Fellows' production gives showmanly and colorful backing to the ingredients, and photography and special effects add to the overall top-notch job.

Familiar names of Paul Henreid and Maureen O'Hara offer marquee bait. Henreid does well by the dashing Dutchman who becomes the Spaniards' sea-scourge and will please his following. Miss O'Hara, as usual, hasn't much opportunity to show off her acting ability but fulfills the role's other requirements with lush beauty. Walter Slezak's cruel Spanish governor character is showy. Binnie Barnes, femme pirate, John Emery, J. M. Kerrigan, Mike Muzurki, Curt Bois, Antonio Moreno, Fritz Leiber are among others who show up well. *Brog.*

Colonel Effingham's Raid

20th-Fox release of Lamar Trotti production. Stars Charles Coburn, Joan Bennett and William Eythe; features Allyn Joslyn, Elizabeth Patterson, Donald Meek and Frank Craven. Directed by Irving Pichel. Screenplay, Kathryn Scola, based on novel by Barry Fleming; camera, Edward Cronjager, Fred Sersen; score, Cyril J. Mockridge; music director, Emil Newman; editor, Harmon Jones. Tradeshown N. Y., Sept. 28, '45. Running time, 70 MINS.

Colonel Effingham	Charles Coburn
Ella Sue Dozier	Joan Bennett
Al	William Eythe
Earl Hoats	Allyn Joslyn
Emma	Elizabeth Patterson
Doc Buden	Donald Meek
Dewey	Frank Craven
Mayor	Thurston Hall
Clara Meigh	Cora Witherspoon
Alsobrook	Emory Parnell
Jimmy Economy	Henry Armetta
Ed Bland	Michael Dunne
Capt. Rampey	Roy Roberts
Bibbs	Boyd Davis
Tignor	Charles Trowbridge
Wild Man	Frank Orth
Ninety-Eight	Nicodemus Stewart
Pete	Robert Dudley
Wishum	Ferris Taylor
Bill Silk	Oliver Prickett
Major Hickock	Grant Mitchell
Engineer	Clyde Fillmore
Sadie	Carol Andrews
Park Commissioner	George Melford
Box Smith	Harry Hayden
Young Man	Charles Wagenheim
Painter	Olin Howlin

A couple of years ago Barry Fleming's novel, "Colonel Effingham's Raid," was a Book of the Month Club selection, and now 20th-Fox has given a fairly literate adaptation to this story of patriotic fervor and small-town politics. It should do well at the boxoffice.

This is a yarn about a retired Army officer, Col. Effingham, who returns to his home town and attempts to bring reform to it through a column he writes in a local paper. The column, ostensibly, is supposed to be about military matters but in it he wields his pen as he would a bolo knife—and no one escapes, from the mayor down. Linked with the major story line is the lesser one of a young newspaper reporter who becomes imbued with the spirit of the oldster and, just when it looks like the crooked City Hall has the colonel whipped, the youngster comes through in the breach, via a patriotic gimmick, to win out.

Charles Coburn is the elderly colonel and William Eythe the reporter. Joan Bennett is the film's third starring link, the latter two forming the pic's romantic team. The performances are good, especially that of Coburn. Others who do well are Allyn Joslyn as the paper's editor; Elizabeth Patterson, the late Frank Craven and Thurston Hall as the mayor.

Irving Pichel has directed for pace, and Lamar Trotti's production is adequate. *Kahn.*

Query

(BRITISH-MADE)

London, Sept. 19.

Anglo-American Film Corp. release of

British National Film production. Features Billy Hartnell, Chili Bouchier, Jimmy Hanley. Directed by Montgomery Tully. Screenplay by Montgomery Tully from story by "Seamark." Camera, Ernest Palmer. At Palace, London, Sept. 18, '45. Running time, **90 MINS.**

Tom Masterick	Billy Hartnell
Peter Rogers	Jimmy Hanley
Doris Masterick	Chili Bouchier
Fred Smith	John Slater
Sullivan	Brefni O'Rourke
Jill Masterick	Dinah Sheridan
Jill (child)	Petula Clark
Crossley K.C.	Kynaston Reeves
Blake K.C.	John Salew
Spike	Edward Rigby
Docker	Ben Williams
Mrs. Green	Ethel Coleridge
Mrs. Moore	Maire O'Neill

This British National thriller, if and when it hits Broadway, will awaken memories of the stage hit of the early '20s, "It Is the Law." In most respects, "Query" follows the underlying plot of the Elmer Rice play as closely as did the silent film version made by Fox. "Query" has the earmarks of a fair-sized hit with British audiences. Lack of names and the unfamiliar workings of British courts of law would seem to minimize its chances in the U. S., but it is distinctly above the level of a Hollywood second feature.

Seamark was the nom de plume of a well-known Fleet Street character who committed suicide some 10 years ago. If, in fact, he wrote the story on which "Query" is based, he yanked the arm of coincidence clear out of its socket or grabbed boldly the plot of "It Is the Law" and embellished it with different non-essentials.

The film moves swiftly and smoothly to an effective and grim climax, direction and cutting of a higher-than-usual quality for this type of English pix helping. Billy Hartnell, who shoulders the job of making plausible the legal right of a man to commit murder, is excellent as a tough young stevedore and also as a prematurely aged ex-convict.

Of the others in a cast of unknowns to American patrons, John Slater, as an especially nasty heavy, and Kynaston Reeves, as an eminent K.C., are outstanding. Chili Bouchier does what she can with a sordid role as a faithless wife and mother, and Brefni O'Rourke contributes an authoritative touch as a London newspaper editor.

Production is adequate. Lime House slums and pubs being more like the real thing than the usual run of studio sets with the murder trial at the Old Bailey being especially realistic.

But, first and foremost, it is the query propounded by "Query"—is it really legally possible for a guy to have a murder coming to him—which will line 'em up at the boxoffice over here. *Talb.*

Apology for Murder

PRC release of Sigmund Neufeld production. Features Ann Savage, Hugh Beaumont, Russell Hicks, Charles D. Brown. Directed by Sam Neufeld from original by Fred Myton; camera, Jack Greenhalgh; editor, Holbrook N. Todd. At New York theatre, N.Y., week Sept. 27, '45, dualled. Running time, 67 MINS.

Toni Kirkland	Ann Savage
Kenny Blake	Hugh Beaumont
Ward McGee	Charles D. Brown
Kirkland	Russell Hicks
Craig Jordan	Pierre Watkins
Caretaker	Bud Buster
Allen Webb	Norman Willis
Maid	Eva Novak
Paul	Archie Hall
Rancher's Wife	Elizabeth Valentine
Warden	Henry Hall
Minister	Wheaton Chambers
Lt. Edwards	George Sherwood

Considering that "Apology for Murder" is obviously a small budgeter, this murder meller serves its purpose.

There is enough suspense, good scripting and acting in this film to provide an interesting hour or so of guessing for mystery fans as to how the thing will wind up. Unfortunately, however, the denouement

is too drawn out, proving a disappointment.

Ann Savage portrays the role of a gal who wants to be freed from her husband, who is older than she is. Hugh Beaumont is a reporter who falls in love with her and succumbs to her plan to kill in order to get her husband's money. They both give solid performances, along with some good thesping by a supporting cast led by Charles D. Brown, as Beaumont's city editor, who tracks down the murderers.

Original story and screenplay by Fred Minton is given neat direction by Sam Newfield. Settings are substantial enough, and camera work is fair. *Sten.*

Gaslight Follies
Hartford, Sept. 28.

Embassy Pictures release of Maxwell Finn and Joseph Levine production. Edited by Nathan Cy Braunstein; supervised by Walter Bilbo; commentaries by Ben Grauer, John B. Kennedy, Milton Cross and Ethel Owen. At E. M. Loew's theatre, week of Sept. 28, '45. Running time, 110 MINS.

A resuscitation of movie museum pieces, this production, by Maxwell Finn and Joseph Levine, is a welding of silent era films and clips. It is a documentation of the advance of motion pictures. It's also a nostalgic bit for oldtimers whose memory dates back plus or minus 40 years. Picture is strictly for laughs and is successful in eliciting response in that department.

Divided into four sections—so it can play either as four shorts or one complete feature—this film is a good historical review for students of the cinema. First section has same title as tag of show and contains series of sequences of Hollywood names who have been relegated to the movie hall of fame. Here grotesqueness of costumes and makeup is a dynamic spur to laffs. Commentary by Ben Grauer is ably presented. Number of oldtimers brought back to screen is numerous and includes Valentino, William S. Hart, Jackie Coogan, Chaplin, Marie Dressler, Mack Sennett, Pickford, Arbuckle, etc.

Second section is named "Time Marches Back," splicing of series of newsreel clips dating back to 1899, the Jeffries-Fitzsimmons fight, etc. Several shots are presented, with a bathing beauty contest of 1908 drawing laffs from femme department. Ethel Owen dubbs in an able description of woman's fashions in pictorial review styles of 1905. Also strong on femme hilarious reaction. John B. Kennedy on tap to commentate of news events.

The "Drunkard" fills in the third slot of this production. With the original Los Angeles company (now in its 13th year) cast, this is the only modern bit of the lengthy show. Modern as far as new techniques of cinema are concerned. High voltage in the guffaw department, this carries many moments of high hilarity. Originally produced as a full-length picture now cut to 31 minutes.

With Milton Cross and Ethel Owen dubbing in the commentary, "East Lynne," tearjerker meller of the gaslight days, is also good for laughs. Asides and crossfire patter of the duo help activities along with the script job for commenting done in excellent fashion. *Eck.*

Stagecoach Outlaws

PRC release of Sigmund Neufeld production. Stars Buster Crabbe; features Al St. John, Frances Gladwin. Directed by Sam Newfield from original by Fred Myton; camera, Jack Greenhalgh; editor, Holbrook N. Todd. At New York theatre, N. Y., week of Sept. 27, '45, dualled. Running time, 58 MINS.

Billy Carson	Buster Crabbe
Fuzzy Jones	Al (Fuzzy) St. John
Linda	Frances Gladwin
Jed	Ed Cassidy
Steve	Stanford Jolley
Vic	Kermit Maynard
Joe	Bob Cason
Matt	Robert Kortman
Sheriff	Steve Clark

An average oater. "Stagecoach Outlaws" is suitable fare for audiences who enjoy outdoor pictures.

This one has the usual amount of footage involving fast riding, free-for-all fisticuffs, gunplay and romantic interest. Yarn deals with the conniving tactics, including an attempted holdup that doesn't quite come off, used by a gang of outlaws led by a gambler. Their purpose is to take over a stagecoach line illegally.

Buster Crabbe is seen as the cowpuncher who breaks up the gang, aided by comedian Al St. John, who has been cast in this type horse opry for, lo. these many years. Frances Gladwin, as the daughter of the stagecoach-line operator, provides the pulchritude to the formula. Sets seem to be wearing out. Maybe PRC ought to get some new ones now that the war is over. Production lacks finesse, as do the direction and script jobs. *Sten.*

Miniature Reviews

"Stork Club" (Songs) (De-Sylva-Par). Tiptop Cinderella musical, geared for lush box-office.

"Kitty" (Par). Costume drama of 18th Century loves with Goddard - Milland names for marquee.

"The Spider" (20th). Well-enacted whodunit for the supporting market.

"The Fighting Guardsman" (Col). Film version of Dumas' novel, "Companions of Jehu." okay for cops-and-robbers trade.

"Scotland Yard Investigator" (Rep). Good murder thriller.

"Sunbonnet Sue" (songs) (Mono). Fair Gay 90s item.

The Stork Club
(SONGS)

Paramount release of B. G. deSylva (Harold Wilson) production. Stars Betty Hutton, Barry Fitzgerald, Don DeFore; features Andy Russell. Directed by Hal Walker. Screenplay, B. G. deSylva, John McGowan; camera, Chas. Lang, Jr., Farciot Edouart; editor, Gladys Carley; music, Robt. Emmett Dolan; Troy Sanders; dances, Billy Daniels; technical advisor, Leonard MacBain; songs, Jule Styne, Sammy Cohn; Hoagy Carmichael-Paul Francis Webster; Webster-Harry Revel; Jay Livingston-Ray Evans. Tradeshown N. Y., Oct. 4, '45. Running time, 98 MINS.

Judy Peabody	Betty Hutton
J. B. Bates	Barry Fitzgerald
Danny Wilton	Don DeFore
Jim	Andy Russell
Tom Curtis	Robert Benchley
Sherman Billingsley	Bill Goodwin
Gwen	Iris Adrian
Mrs. Bates	Mary Young
Fiske	Charles Coleman
Tom (Band)	Pepe Launders
Coretti	Mikhail Rasumny

Sherman Billingsley's famed Stork Club in New York has finally hit the screen as a filmusical background, along with Billy Rose's Diamond Horseshoe and Lucius Boomer's Waldorf-Astoria, and the batting average is still 1.000. Buddy deSylva has turned out a tiptop Cinderella story for Paramount and, is a cinch for comparable profit.

Actually it's not as elementary as the fundamentals may sound. True, even after the canny Barry Fitzgerald literally confesses that he's the mysterious benefactor of the Stork Club coatroom girl (she had saved his life), the plot could fall apart if taken too literally, but somehow the audiences will accept it for what it is—a pleasant 98 minutes of Cinderella romance against a glamorous background.

Much on the plus side is the fact that story is not restricted to being another Grand Hotel theme in a nitery setting. In fact, at one time one wonders what happened to the Stork Club part of the tale, since so much of the misunderstanding, the band rehearsals, etc., occur in the penthouse apartment where Miss Hutton has been mysteriously ensconced.

Interspersed is a blighted romance between the oldster Fitzgerald and Mary Young, his wife of 40 years, who had walked out on the eccentric Irish millionaire in disgust over his Scotch (pecuniary, not liquid) habits.

Robert Benchley is the deadpan lawyer who fronts for his eccentric client, further complicating the plot by not disclosing the facts when a romantic crisis occurs between the poor-but-honest checkroom gal (Miss Hutton) and her bandleader-ex-Marine (Don De-Fore), who properly enough can't cope out her unaccustomed affluence. Fitzgerald's paternal presence on one side and Bill Goodwin (as Billingsley) on the other mix up the juvenile leads for the proper footage until it's all straightened out. In between, Billingsley's now familiar generosity and credo as a host get plenty of spotlighting, along with a plentitude of Stork Club trademarks (from the main titles down to the insignia on the club's attaches). The femme star does four tiptop special songs; bandleader DeFore "auditions" for Billingsley; and crooner Andy Russell uncorks a couple of ballads.

Miss Hutton's "Doctor, Lawyer, Indian" is her first peppery delivery, backed by a neat male quartet. Russell, as the pseudo-drummer in the band, doubles with her on "I'm a Square in the Social Circle." "If I Had a Dozen Hearts," and "Love Me the Way I Love You," which are reprised in the band rehearsal, the audition and the Stork Club nitery performances. "Shade of the Old Apple Tree" is interpolated as the romantic theme of Fitzgerald and his estranged spouse. This is utilized to point up Billingsley's rule against no waltzes at the Stork; just fast continuous music to keep 'em pepped up. (It's not explained, of course, that the host's reason therefore is that fast music also stimulates faster bar tabs.)

As part of the plot a "Locke's (Saks) 5th Avenue" charge account for Miss Hutton is excuse for a fashion show. It's here that scripters deSylva and Jack McGowan plausibly reprise the oldie that the benefactor "wants to make her happy, but not hysterical," as she orders three or four minks for herself and her fellow-cloakroom checker, Iris Adrian. In the Stork setting, a natural for maitre d'hotel Mikhail Rasumny is another revival gag about cautioning the busboy to "be extra nice to the waiters; we can always get customers."

Miss Hutton is capital throughout, vocally and histrionically. Fitzgerald is superb; almost steals the picture from everything and everybody. His is another top performance as the alternatingly dour and generous, harassed and lovelorn millionaire of eccentric manner (old clothes, etc. in a mansion background). Don DeFore is convincing as the juve. Andy Russell shines better vocally but manifests good lens consciousness. Bill Goodwin is particularly good as Billingsley. Besides looking like the Stork Club's host, the radio announcer-actor works with authority and conviction. Miss Adrian makes a lot of her comedy opportunity as the heroine's pal.

The scripters have not overplayed the local color. There's but one reference to Winchell, and plausible; and Billingsley's reference to the "only three women in my life" (Mrs. B. and their two daughters) —in the portion where Miss Hutton suspects he might be her mysterious benefactor—is not too sticky.

Stork Club atmosphere, of course, is almost photographic in authenticity. Director Hal Walker has done right by producer deSylva on his first indie pic for Par (Harold Wilson aided him on the production), and the script and song writing credits are expert. The songsmiths who fashioned the clever "Square in a Social Circle" are worth watching.

Abel.

Kitty

Hollywood, Oct. 6.

Paramount release of Mitchell Leisen (Darrell Ware-Karl Tunberg) production, directed by Leisen. Stars Paulette Goddard, Ray Milland; features Patric Knowles, Cecil Kellaway, Reginald Owen, Constance Collier. Screenplay by Ware and Tunberg; from novel by Rosamond Marshall; camera, Daniel L. Fapp, Gordon Jennings, Farciot Edouart; music, Victor Young; settings and costumes designed by Raoul Pene du Bois; editor, Alma Macrorie. Tradeshown L.A., Oct. 5, '45. Running time, 103 MINS.

Kitty	Paulette Goddard
Sir Hugh Marcy	Ray Milland
Earl of Carstairs	Patric Knowles
Duke of Malmunster	Reginald Owen
Thomas Gainsborough	Cecil Kellaway
Lady Susan Dewitt	Constance Collier
Jonathan Selby	Dennis Hoey
Old Meg	Sara Allgood
Dobson	Eric Blore
Sir Joshua Reynolds	Gordon Richards
Prince of Wales	Michael Dyne
Earl of Campton	Edgar Norton
Elaine Carlisle	Patricia Cameron
Doctor Holt	Percival Vivian
Nanny	Mary Gordon
Nullens	Anita Bolster
Lil	Heather Wilde
Majordomo	Charles Coleman
molly	Mae Clarke
Madame Aurelie	Ann Codee

"Kitty" is an opulent period production that will have the curiosity of the book-lovers to start it off. Celluloid version of the book of the same title, produced with all the pomp of the period, is overlong and has a tendency to drag, but names of Paulette Goddard and Ray Milland will aid in generating good business. Femme audiences, in particular, will favor theme of self-sacrifice for love and the settings and costumes.

Plot tells of an 18th century easy lady who rose from the London slums to high position in court society—a society that was no better than that from which she rose; it only dressed better. The Kitty depicted in the film is a petty thief and beggar who gets a start towards a cleaner life after becoming a model for Gainsborough's portrait of a lady. The portrait and Kitty attract the attention of several society fops. One, an impoverished nobleman with few scruples, takes her into his home, gives her a fictional background and plots her marriage to a duke. Script carries her through two marriages, the birth of a child and sundry adventures, all to aid her poor nobleman—a prize heel—and make him realize her love for him.

Paulette Goddard credibly depicts Kitty in the various phases of the slum girl's rise in station. Ray Milland has the more difficult task of keeping the unpleasant, foppish character of Sir Hugh Marcy, Kitty's beloved, consistent and does well by it. Reginald Owen and Cecil Kellaway deliver character gems. The first is the doddering Duke of Malmunster, who strives to keep his faded youth revived with port wine. The other is Gainsborough, the painter who discovers Kitty. Patric Knowles is good as the Earl of Carstairs who loves Kitty. Constance Collier, Milland's gin-sodden aunt, Sara Allgood, Dennis Hoey, Eric Blore, Mary Gordon are among others who show up well.

Mitchell Leisen's direction has garbed the drama in fancy clothes and spectacle in telling the story, getting all the pomp and much of the pomposity of the era into the picture. Production is elegant in settings, associate producers Darrell Ware and Karl Tunberg having used lavish hand in providing the framework for their screenplay. Musical score by Victor Young is an aid and Daniel L. Fapp's camera work is skillful.

Brog.

The Spider

Hollywood, Oct. 5.

20th-Fox release of Ben Silvey production. Features Richard Conte, Faye Marlowe, Kurt Kreuger, John Harvey, Martin Kosleck, Mantan Moreland, Walter Sande, Cara Williams. Director, Robert Webb. Screenplay, Jo Eisinger and W. Scott Darling; based on play by Fulton Oursler and Lowell Brentano; camera, Glen MacWilliams; music, David Buttolph; editor, Norman Colbert. Tradeshown L. A., Oct. 5, '45. Running time, 61 MINS.

Chris Conlon	Richard Conte
Lila Neilson	Faye Marlowe
Garonne	Kurt Kreuger
Burns	John Harvey
Barak	Martin Kosleck
Henry	Mantan Moreland
Lt. Castle	Walter Sande
Wanda	Cara Williams
Lt. Tonti	Charles Tannen
Jean	Margaret Brayton
Bartender	Harry Seymour
Florence Cain	Ann Savage
Dutrelle	Jean Del Val
Mrs. Dutrelle	Odette Vigne
Johnny	James Flavin
Picket	Roy Gordon
Police Inspector	William Halligan
Radio Cops	Lane Chandler, Eddie Hart
Pretty Girl	Margo Woode

Uniformly good performances keep this whodunit moving and make it figure as okay for secondary bookings. Script fails suitably to explain why the villain started his series of murders but otherwise maintains casual interest in the melodramatic developments.

It's a yarn about a private detective who gets involved with murder and the police while trying to aid an attractive client. Richard Conte, private eye, is approached by Faye Marlowe, performer with a magic show, to see if he can discover whether or not her long-absent sister has been murdered. Conte's double-crossing partner, Ann Savage, has obtained the evidence but is mysteriously bumped off before turning it over to him. Police put the finger on Conte for the killing but he manages to duck the charge. Another victim turns up, shortly after Conte has talked to him. Police really turn the heat on the dick then but denouement turns up the real killer, who had turned strangler to conceal fact that he had actually done in Miss Marlowe's sister years ago.

Conte does an excellent job of the male lead and Miss Marlowe makes attractive her assignment. Skullduggery is contributed by Kurt Kreuger and Martin Kosleck is the chief red-herring suspect. Mantan Moreland injects some comedy as Conte's reluctant Negro helper.

Robert Webb's direction keeps the pace consistent and Ben Silvey's production furnishes standard appurtenances.

Brog.

The Fighting Guardsman

Columbia release of Michel Kraike production. Features Willard Parker, Anita Louise, Janis Carter, John Loder, Edgar Buchanan, George Macready. Directed by Henry Levin. Screenplay, Franz Spencer, Edward Dein, based on novel by Alexandre Dumas; camera, Burnett Guffey; music, Paul Sawtell; editor, Viola Lawrence. At Ambassador, N.Y., week Oct. 5, '45. Running time, 84 MINS.

Roland	Willard Parker
Amelie de Montreval	Anita Louise
Christine Rouault	Janis Carter
Sir John Tanley	John Loder
Pepe	Edgar Buchanan
Gaston de Montreyel	George Macready
King Louis XVI	Lloyd Corrigan
Mme. de Montrevel	Elisabeth Risdon
Berton	Jan Wolfe
Albert	Ray Teal
Montebar	Victor Kilian
Hyperion Pieot	Charles halton
Edouard	Maurice Tauzin
Abbe	Charles Waldron

Although "The Fighting Guardsman" has the elegant sets and garb of the Louis XVI period, film is a modestly budgeted item with little in the way of marquee lure. Alexandre Dumas' minor masterpiece, "Companions of Jehu," forms the basis of this piece. Film, despite its period setting, is an overdressed cops-and-robbers opera with plenty of flintlock and saber play to provide the major source of interest. The hackneyed Robin Hood theme has Willard Parker in the role of Baron Francois de Sainte Hermaine, who hobnobs with the aristocracy but who is convinced of the corruption of the royal set and consequently has gathered a band of revolutionaries to rob the King's tax-collectors and coaches carrying royal bullion for distribution among the deserving poor.

Expected complications in the plot arise from the fact that Parker must continually justify his leadership among his cohorts because of the fact that he's in love with an aristocrat (Anita Louise) whose brother's life he spares in a duel. Ultimately the French revolution clears the path for continued romance with the lady of his choice.

Henry Levin's direction strives too hard for swashbuckling effects and, while the film goes at a fast clip, it falls too easily into hokey lines. Attempts to set off Parker as a superman capable of taking on a dozen adversaries simultaneously often brings titters.

Acting is routine with Parker and Miss Louise trying to bring a degree of conviction to their parts. John Loder as the emissary of the English bankers from whom the King attempts to float a loan does a convincing job, while Lloyd Corrigan as the bloated highness, Janis Carter as his mistress who passes on vital information to the revolutionaries, Edgar Buchanan as Parker's Friday, and George Macready as the monarch's loyal aide, carry out their assignments in routine manner.

Jose.

Scotland Yard Investigator

(BRITISH-MADE)

Republic release of George Blair production, directed by Blair. Stars Sir Aubrey Smith, Erich Von Stroheim. Screenplay, Randall Faye; editor, Fred Allen; camera, Ernest Miller, William Bradford. Tradeshown, N. Y., Oct. 4, '45. Running time, [illegible] MINS.

Sir James Collison	Sir Aubrey Smith
Carl Hoffmeyer	Erich Von Stroheim
Tony Collison	Stephanie Bachelor
Sam Todworthy	Forrester Harvey
Ma Todworthy	Doris Lloyd
Mary Collison	Eva Moore
Inspector Cartwright	Richard Fraser
Jules	Victor Varconi
Col. Brent	Frederic Worlock
Henri	George Metaxa
Professor Renault	Emil Rameau
Waters	Colin Campbell

Here's a case where a mediocre, yet successful script, is made to appear like a well-polished project, simply because it was excellently cast, shrewdly directed and competently produced. "Scotland Yard Investigator" won't be the worse for half of a double fare.

Sir Aubrey Smith plays the conscientious curator of the National Art Gallery in London, where the Mona Lisa has been hidden away until now. The war concluded, two Frenchmen posing as representatives of the Louvre, call for the painting and are given it because they have proper credentials. However, their leader, Erich Von Stroheim, realizes after thorough inspection that the stolen portrait is only a fine reproduction. The original is in the hands of another man, equally ruthless and cunning, who runs an antique shop as a decoy for his illegitimate operations. The plot is literally filled with corpses after this point: Von Stroheim eradicating anybody who would prevent him from possessing the painting which he desires to hang in his personal gallery along with the other stolen masterpieces. The money-hungry antique dealer, played by Forrester Harvey, just wants to sell the painting back to the gallery at his own price, in order that he and his wife may retire for the rest of their lives. But Sir Aubrey Smith is betwixt and between, because his reputation is at stake, should word of the painting's loss leak out. All ends well, of course.

Charles Thompson's set decorations really contribute an air of authenticity to the production.

Sunbonnet Sue

(SONGS)

Monogram release of Scott R. Dunlap production. Stars Gale Storm, Phil Regan; features George Cleveland, Edna Holland, Alan Mowbray, Charles Brown. Directed by Ralph Murphy. Screenplay, Paul Gerard Smith, Bradford Ropes; editor, Richard Currier; camera, Harry Neumann; music, Eddie Kay; asst. directors, Bobby Ray, Eddie Davis. Tradeshown in N. Y., Oct. 8, '45. Running time, 89 MINS.

Sue	Gale Storm
Danny	Phil Regan
Casey	George Cleveland
Mrs. Fitzgerald	Minna Gombell
Joe Feeney	Raymond Hatton
Jonathan	Alan Mowbray
Milano	Charles Judels
Flaherty	Billy Green
Father Hurley	Chas. D. Brown
Julia	Edna Holland
Masters	Gerald O. Smith
Burke	Jerry Franks

"Sunbonnet Sue" has enough political squabbles, love scenes and a dash of social significance to make it a fair dual entry. However, it's too long for what it contains.

Business at a saloon (circa 1890) is keeping its pace, until the pedigree-minded aunt who lives on Fifth Avenue realizes that, if her niece continues to sing and dance in her father's Bowery saloon, the aunt's background will be discovered and her social future will be spoiled. It is during the local political elections that she conceives the idea of perpetrating a brawl in the tavern, thereby influencing the police to close it. Circumstances demanding, the daughter is forced to leave her father's home to live luxuriously at her aunt's home. However, the aunt's motive is soon discovered, after much more brawling, and all live happily after.

The film has some effective philosophical notes and manages never to hit them too hard. It supports the theory that, despite a Bowery background, one can attain the avenue of avenues, if he perseveres, etc.

The acting in this film is creditable. Particularly good are George Cleveland as the jovial tavern owner; Minna Gombell as the wise and successful wife of the governor, although formerly a Boweryite herself; Charles Brown, who intelligently underplays the role of Father Hurley. Dance routines fair, but help to convey the nostalgia of the Gay Nineties. None of the new songs is outstanding; the oldies are background themes.

L'Invite De La IIme Heure

("The Eleventh Hour Guest")

Paris, Oct. 2.

Produced and distributed by Eclair-Journal. Directed by Maurice Cloche. Starring Jean Tissier. Featuring Roger Pigault and Blanchette Brunoy. At Normandie, Paris.

Jean Tissier only came out as a star comparatively recently when his nonchalant manner gave him a following. In this crime meller he first plays the part of a journalist who later passes himself off as a detective to finally turn out as the criminal.

The story shows Tissier crashing an invitation to stay overnight at the country house of a scientist who has already invited several guests. The scientist has made a discovery which is apparently very much of the atomic style, and secret. During the night he is found in the hall, apparently dead. Tissier appears to proceed to a police investigation, his real object being to steal the secret, when finally the scientist who was supposed to have died, causes the death of the thief.

Even if the story is somewhat involved, direction is good and action faster than in most local films. But love interest is thin. Neither the crime investigation nor the scientific background will suffice to make this picture enhance Tissier's rating.

Maxi.

Miniature Reviews

"Yolanda and the Thief" (Color; Musical); (M-G). Fred Astaire, Lucille Bremer and Frank Morgan in moderate b.o. musical.

"People Are Funny" (Par). Secondary comedy kidding the radio industry.

"She Went To The Races" (M-G). James Craig and Frances Gifford in screwball comedy; okay as support on duals.

"George White's Scandals" (Musical) (RKO). Slow musical; running time too long.

"Senorita From The West" (Songs) (U). Pallid radio romance, with Allan Jones. Mild b.o.

"Journey Together" (RKO). R.A.F.-U.S. Film Service thriller of England's triumph via air power. Looks sturdy for U.S. b.o.

"Divorce" (Mono). Kay Francis' first independent production an okay dualer.

"Marie La Mirere" (Radio-Cinema). Odd French-made picture means little for U. S. audiences.

"Le Mystere de Saint-Val" CCFS. Fernandel in French spook comedy may do fairly well in arty American houses despite age of film.

Yolanda and the Thief

(COLOR; MUSICAL)

Metro release of Arthur Freed production. Stars Fred Astaire, Lucille Bremer and Frank Morgan; features Mildred Natwick and Leon Ames. Directed by Vincente Minnelli. Screenplay, Irving Brecher, based on story by Jacques Thery and Ludwig Bemelmans; songs, Arthur Freed and Harry Warren; music director, Lennie Hayton; dances, Eugene Loring; camera, Charles Rosher; editor, George White; special effects, A. Arnold Gillespie and Warren Newcombe. Previewed at Loew's 72nd St., N.Y., Oct. 9, '45. Running time, 108 MINS.

Johnny Parkson Riggs	Fred Astaire
Yolanda	Lucille Bremer
Victor Budlow Trout	Frank Morgan
Aunt Amarilla	Mildred Natwick
Duenna	Mary Nash
Mr. Candle	Leon Ames

Metro has come up with a musical story of virtue and the Divine in "Yolanda and the Thief," but the result is not all it might have been. Arthur Freed has produced (in Technicolor) with lavishness, and the casting, topped by Fred Astaire, Lucille Bremer and Frank Morgan, has been done with an eye towards marquee values, but the basic yarn hasn't lent itself toward the screen. It should do moderately well at the boxoffice.

The screenplay by Irving Brecher, from a story by Jacques Thery and Ludwig Bemelmans, too frequently is extraneous in its detail, although the Brecher flair for comedy dialog is always apparent. The songs by Freed and Harry Warren are employed mostly for background purposes.

This is the story of a Latin-American heiress who, after being brought up in a convent, assumes charge of her fortune upon coming of age. Her childhood, naturally one that saw her sheltered from the outer world, makes her easy prey for a fraud that a young American and his elderly confederate would play upon her to relieve her of her millions. The principals in this comedy-drama are played by Miss Bremer, Astaire and Morgan.

The ruse is to make Miss Bremer believe that Astaire is her guardian angel, and he succeeds easily—much too easily, in fact, from an audience viewpoint, despite the girl's convent background. But there's a suspicious-looking chap by the name of Mr. Candle who always seems to be around at inopportune moments (Leon Ames). At the film's end he's revealed as the real guardian angel sent to protect the heiress from such schemes as the American. It all winds up okay for the girl and the Yank when the latter has a change of heart and falls for the girl. Of course, the romance has the blessing of Mr. Candle.

There's an idea in this yarn, but it only suggests itself. It becomes too immersed in its musical background, and the story is too leisurely in pace. A musical production number attempts to be symbolic but only serves to waste too many moments of the over-long film. And the story itself, the way it's done, strains credibility.

Miss Bremer is a beaut who has a good friend in the cameraman. But sometimes there's a too-obvious attempt to show off the actress' looks, so replete is the photographic try to reveal her from all angles. Astaire, on the other hand, gets no such camera treatment, and some of the closeups are particularly unflattering. But his performance, as usual, is casual and sure despite the script, and the same holds true of Morgan. Mildred Natwick ably supplies some of the comedy, and Ames is likewise satisfactory.

Kahn.

People Are Funny

(SONGS)

Paramount release of Pine-Thomas production (Sam White, associate producer), directed by White. Features Jack Haley, Helen Walker, Rudy Vallee, Ozzie Nelson, Phillip Reed, Art Linkletter, Frances Langford, The Vagabonds. Screenplay, Maxwell Shane and David Lang, from story by Lang; based on John Guedel's "People Are Funny" radio program; additional dialog, Dorcas Cochran; songs, Duke Ellington-Don George, Don Reid-Henry Tobias, Pepe and Tito Guizar, Jay Livingston-Ray Evans, Archie Gottler, Jay milton-Walter Samuels, Rudy Vallee, Allan Roberts-Doris Fisher, Jimmy McHugh-Dorothy Fields; camera, Fred Jackman; editor, Henry Adams; dance, Jack Crosby; music director, David Chudnow. Previewed at Paramount theatre, N.Y., Oct. 12, '45. Running time, 93 MINS.

Pinky Wilson	Jack Haley
Corey Sullivan	Helen Walker
Ormsby Jamison	Rudy Vallee
Leroy Brinker	Ozzie Nelson
John Guedel	Philip Reed
Luke	Bob Graham
Aimee	Robert Roche
Himself	Art Linkletter
Herself	Frances Langford
Grandma	Clara Blandwick
Mr. Pippensiegal	Roy Atwell
Themselves	The Vagabonds

"People Are Funny" is a radio-backgrounded comedy that attempts to take advantage of the current interest in the audience-participation stunt in radio. It has some amusing moments, being geared for secondary houses.

"People," whose basis is an actual Coast-originated airer, is about the rivalry among radio producers, though it seems hardly to exist as indicated in this film. It deals specifically with the race by two producers to put on an audience-participation program, "People Are Funny," in which the show's emcee makes the participants do ridiculous things—much in the manner, incidentally, of Ralph Edwards' "Truth or Consequences" program. The pace is fast, but the scripting at times uncertain in the plot development.

Rudy Vallee plays a sponsor, Ozzie Nelson one of the producers, and Philip Reed the other, with Helen Walker as a radio writer mixed up in the shenanigans. Jack Haley is a hick whose program is the source of the assorted goings-on. Their performances satisfy the requirements.

There are a flock of pop songs punctuating the film, practically all standards. Frances Langford is in for one song sequence.

Kahn.

She Went to the Races

Metro release of Frederick Stephani production. Features James Craig, Frances Gifford, Ava Gardner. Directed by Willis Goldbeck. Screenplay by Lawrence Hazard; based on story by Alan Friedman and De Vallon Scott; camera, Charles Salerno; editor, Adrienne Fazan. Tradeshown in N.Y., Oct. 11, '45. Running time, 85 MINS.

Steve Confiled	James Craig
Dr. Ann Wotters	Frances Gifford
Hilda Spotts	Ava Gardner
Dr. Pecke	Edmund Gwenn
Dr. Gurke	Sig Ruman
Dr. Pembroke	Eginald Owen

Lacking marquee names, this mediocre racetrack comedy looks set as a supporting feature on twin bills.

Story is about two femmes wagering for James Craig, a racing sportsman, without his knowing that he's the main stake in the big race. Included is the twist of three professors doping the outcome of two crucial races on a scientific basis.

Craig makes a fairly effective racehorse owner with no visible means of support. Frances Gifford, as the feminine professor who herds her elderly associates along on the crazy venture, is satisfactory, and Ava Gardner is the rich gal with an eye for the ponies. Edmund Gwenn, Sig Ruman and Reginald Owen go far in lending credence to the screwball developments. A number of unlisted supporting players fill in capably.

Wear.

George White's Scandals

(MUSICAL)

RKO release of George White production. Stars Joan Davis, Jack Haley; features Philip Terry, Martha Holliday, Ethel Smith, Margaret Hamilton, Glenn Tryon, Bettejane Greer, Gene Krupa orch. Directed by Felix E. Feist. Story and adaptation, Hugh Wedlock, Howard Snyder, Parke Levy, Howard J. Green; songs, Jack Yellen and Sammy Fain; ballet, Leigh Harline; editor, Joseph Noriega; camera, Robert de Grasse, Vernon L. Walker. At Palace, N. Y., week Oct. 10, '45. Running time, 95 MINS.

Joan Mason	Joan Davis
Jack Williams	Jack Haley
Tom McGrath	Philip Terry
Jill Martin	Martha Holliday
Swing Organist	Ethel Smith
Clarabelle	Margaret Hamilton
George White	Glenn Tryon
Billie Randall	Bettejane Greer
Maxine Manners	Audrey Young
Hilda	Rose Murphy
Montescu	Fritz Feld
Joan, as a child	Beverly Wills

Gene Krupa and His Band

The George White "Scandals" legit musicals, Ziegfeld's "Follies" and Earl Carroll's "Vanities," date back to the prohibition era and the current picture under consideration, produced by George White, also dates back in that it is reminiscent of the backstage musicals of the early talker days. Though there are a few moments that hit home, on the whole the picture is a drawn-out affair. Boxoffice potentialities not good.

Joan Davis and Jack Haley, starred, yeomanly try to overcome the assignments handed them, as do others, but the net result is still very negative. One of the drawbacks is the padding to 95 minutes and the dreary routine concerned with planning a George White's "Scandals" show, the auditioning, the picking of chorines, costuming, etc.

Story, a weak one, concerns two romances in connection with the staging of a "Scandals." Miss Davis and Haley being paired on the one side and Martha Holliday and Phillip Terry on the other. Haley's romantic difficulties finally brook the interference of an old maid sister who herself finally capitulates to the marital yoke, while Miss Holliday, dancer set for the "Scandals," who's a little titled lady unbeknownst to others, goes AWOL just before the show's opening but reports in time to do her stuff and also fall into the arms of the casting director, played by Terry.

Miss Holliday, specialty dancer, is featured in the ballet number, music for which was written by

Leigh Harline and is called "Bouquet and Lace." A brief session of the lyrics are heard from offstage. Shortly after the opening there's a production sequence of "Life Is Just a Bowl of Cherries" from the 1931 "Scandals," written by Lew Brown and Ray Henderson. The 12-year-old daughter of Joan Davis, billed as Beverly Wills, sings the melody, backed by a line of choristers.

"I Wake Up in the Morning and It's You" is a novelty double done by Miss Davis and Haley in twin beds. Starring team works smoothly together, with a session toward the end called "Who Killed Vaudeville?" the nearest thing to a scream the picture contains. Being a burlesque, among other things, it includes a terrific impression by Miss Davis of a sputtering motor boat.

Gene Krupa orch is in and out of the picture but not given too much prominence though clicking when in action. "I Want to Be the Drummer in the Band" is one of his numbers, while "E.H.S." and "Leave Us Leap" are others, latter two being Krupa's own. Finale, "Bolero in the Jungle," features chorus and GK.

Ethel Smith, swinging it at the electric organ, scores strongly with "Liza" and a samba, while Rose Murphy, playing a colored maid, has a short, agreeable stint at the piano. Terry and Miss Holliday make a good team, while Margaret Hamilton is tops as Haley's spinster sister. Glenn Tryon, light comic of the old silent days, plays George White.

Char.

Senorita From the West

Universal release of Philip Cahn production. **Stars Allan** Jones, Bonita Granville; **features Jess Barker**, Oscar O'Shea, George **Cleveland, Fuzzy** Knight, Renny McEvoy, **Spade Cooley orch.** Directed by Frank **Strayer. Screenplay**, Howard Dimsdale; **camera, Paul Ivano**; editor, Paul Landres; **songs, Kim Gannon**, Walter Kent, Jack **Cardens, Mark Levant**, John Blackburn, **Les Huntley, Everett** Carter, Milton Rosen, **Buddy Pepper, Inez** James, Ray Sinatra. **Tradeshown, N. Y.,** Oct. 10, '45. Running time, **63 MINS.**

Phil Bradley....................Allan Jones
Jeannie Blake....................Bonita Granville
Tim Winters....................Jess Barker
Justice of Peace....................Olin Howlin
Kid....................Danny Mummert
Producer....................Emmett Vogan
Dusty....................Oscar O'Shea
Cap....................George Cleveland
William Wylliams....................Renny McEvoy
Rosebud....................Fuzzy Knight
Elmer....................Bob Merrill
Taxi Driver....................Billy Nelson
Motor Cop....................Jack Clifford
Spade Cooley and His Orchestra

"Senorita From the West" is a pretty feeble romance about the aspiring kid who comes to N. Y. and overnight becomes a radio star. It repeats a trite yarn with little originality and less humor. Despite some neat singing by Allan Jones and Bonita Granville, pic is a minor item.

Story gets off to a poor start with a corny situation badly hoked up—a trio of gold-miners who struck it rich are still mining their gold by hand and sweat, so's not to let their ward (Bonita Granville) know she's wealthly and fall for some fortune-hunting slicker. The little lady has a mind of her own, however, and it's set, not on marrying a hometown Lochinvar the guardians have chosen, but on a singing career in N. Y. So off the damsel goes—to fall for a slicker (Jess Barker) who learns about her wealth even if she doesn't. Said slicker is fronting as a famed crooner for a bashful singer (Allan Jones) afraid of mikes and bobbysox fans. The yarn is a little further confused as the guardian trio visit N. Y. to protect their ward; Jones falls for Miss Granville, and saves her from Barker.

Production and direction have the same makeshift quality of the story, and acting of some of the cast, particularly the guardian trio, is a caution. Jones and Miss Granville perform creditably enough, and warble pleasantly some acceptable, reminiscent tunes like "Am I in Love" and "What a Change in the Weather" (by Jones) and "Loo-Loo-Louisiana" (by Miss Granville). Spade Cooley and his orchestra are in for a neat specialty number.

Bron.

Journey Together

(BRITISH-MADE)

London, Oct. 2.

RKO release of Royal Air Force and U.S. Service Film production. Directed by John Boulting. Story by Terrence Rattigan. Camera, Stanley Sayer, Harry Waxman. At Ministry of Information projection room, London, Oct. 1, '45. Running time, 95 MINS.

Dean McWilliams.........Edward G. Robinson
David ....Sgt. Richard Attenborough
Adjutant ....Hugh Wakefield
Group Captain ....Ronald Squire
Flight Commander ......Flt. Lt. Arthur Macrae
Commanding Officer ......Ft. Lt. Reginald Tate
Squadron Leader Marshall ....
Flt. Lt. Sebastian Shaw
Commanding Officer ....
Commander Ronald Adam
Flt, Lt. Mander ....P. Waddington
A.C. 2 Jay ..........L.A.C. Bromley Challoner
Smith ....Flying Officer D. Tomlinson
Mary McWilliams.................Bessie Love

This one merits superlatives. If it doesn't out-gross many of the biggest foreign films in the U.S., it will contradict most of the London correspondents of American dailies who saw the film here. However, opening as a part of dual bill here, indicates it will get the same treatment at most spots in the U.S.

This war epic is so terrific in its simplicity and heart gripping story it makes everything previously screened look like cheap heroics. "Journey Together" may mark the end of all war films for a long time.

The screen calls it "a story dedicated to the few who trained the many." It's a convincing tribute to the last war aces (Yanks as well as British) and to grounded veterans of the Battle of Britain who took the rawest of raw material and made good airmen out of them.

The production was written, directed, photographed and produced by members of the R.A.F., some of them vets of the film biz, but all of them honest-to-God fliers. Also the cast, with four exceptions, was recruited from R.A.F. personnel.

Ronald Squire and Reginald Beck, in minor roles, and Edward G. Robinson and Bessie Love are the four pros who figure in the cast. Excellent as the work of this foursome is (Robinson has never done anything better), it is equalled by every performer in the long cast.

Flight Lieutenant Terence Rattigan wrote the script, and it tops anything this playwright has done before. In speed of action and in economy of dialog the film moves with a mounting pitch of tension guaranteed to glue one to his seat.

From a production angle this one has about everything. Film covers a wide range of territory, from the cloistered halls of Cambridge University to Falcon Field in Arizona, from the Canadian Navigation School to the blazing inferno of bomb-plastered Berlin. But it is the aerial camera work in "Journey Together" that sets a new high. Most of final 15 minutes are shot inside a bomber with a degree of great skill. The crash in the ocean, with which the film ends, is the real thing, or so it appears.

Except for the brief appearance of Bessie Love, as the understanding wife of Robinson, who makes a habit of "adopting" the English boys in training at the Arizona station, there is not a femme in the picture.

Talb.

Divorce

Monogram (Trem Carr) release of Jeffrey Bernerd-Kay Francis production. Stars Kay Francis, Bruce Cabot; features Helen Mack, Jerome Cowan, Craig Reynolds. Directed by William Nigh. Screenplay, Sidney Sutherland, Harvey Gates, from original story by Sutherland; camera, Harry Neumann; editor, Richard Currier, Dave Milton; music, Edward J. Kay. At Paramount, Brooklyn, week Oct. 11, '45. Running time, 71 MINS.

Diane Carter....................Kay Francis
Bob Phillips....................Bruce Cabot
Martha Phillips....................Helen Mack
Jim Driscoll....................Jerome Cowan
Bill Endicott....................Craig Reynolds
Liz Smith....................Ruth Lee
Joan Endicott....................Jean Fenwick
Ellen....................Mary Gordon
Michael Phillips....................Larry Olsen
Bobby Phillips....................Johny Calkins
Judge Conlon....................Jonathan Hale
Plummer....................Addison Richards

First independent production of Kay Francis, "Divorce" brings to the fore one of America's pressing moral problems. Film presents many exploitation angles and Miss Francis and Bruce Cabot on the marquee don't hurt, but a lack-lustre script grooves it for the duals.

Action moves slowly, with denouement apparent to the audience before the second reel. It opens in a divorce court where the judge (Jonathan Hale) is granting Miss Francis her fourth alimony-paying decree. Interesting scene has the judge lecturing the courtroom audience on the foibles of divorce, with the camera closing in on Hale so that he is lecturing directly to the theatre audience.

After the divorce Miss Francis returns to her home town where she sets her hooks for Bruce Cabot, her childhood sweetheart. Angered and disappointed, Cabot's wife (Helen Mack) sues for divorce and is granted an interlocutory decree, including custody of the children. In Chicago on a pleasure trip, Cabot and Miss Francis are caught in a gambling raid. Worried that the scandal may affect a real estate deal that he has put over with Miss Francis' financial backing, Cabot discovers that she plans to sell the project at a profit and leave town with him. Understanding that she is trying to buy him, Cabot returns to his family. When Miss Francis overhears him tell his children that he deserted them without cause, she leaves the home town alone.

Miss Francis and Miss Mack turn in creditable performances but Cabot appears to have lost his usual spark. The supporting cast does good work, top honors going to Ruth Lee as Miss Mack's best friend. Sets are disappointing, and the lack of comedy also detracts from the picture's merits.

Marie La Misere

("Destitute Mary")
(FRENCH-MADE)
(One Song)

Paris, Oct. 9.

Radio-Cinema release of Vedis production. Stars Madeline Sologne, Pierre Renoir; features Raymond Pellegrin, Jean Mercanton, Paul Meurisse, Jacques Pills. Directed by Jacques de Baroncelli. Adapted from stage play by Jean Felise. At Portiques, Paris, Running time, 105 MINS.

A Spanish version, which was made at the same time as this French version, will come in handy in covering production costs on this. It's a rather unconvincing story. The music contest in the picture, in which Jacques Pills plugs a song, "Against My Cheek," will help its boxoffice because of Pills' name. Film's chances in the U.S. are thin.

The story spots Pierre Renoir as a big business man, patron of young Madeleine Sologne, but who is too busy to give her attention as well as support. She leaves him to live with a young but poor musician, whom she leaves too when Renoir anonymously gives him a fat contract. It's all in hope that the girl will tire of this musician. Instead of returning to Renoir, she goes to yet another man. Again it's because Renoir repeats arranging for them to have enough money to cease interesting the girl, who only enjoys life in poverty. She finally returns to the musician who, his contract having expired, is poor again.

The repetition of three times breaking up a young couple is monotonous, and a weakness of the picture.

Le Mystere De Saint-Val

("St. Val's Mystery")
(FRENCH-MADE)

Paris, Oct. 9.

C.C.F.S. release of Harrispuru production. Stars Fernandel; features Alexandre Regnault, Pierre Renoir, Viviane Gosset, Arlette Guttinger. Directed by Rene le Haff. Story by Jean Manse and Albert Bessy. At Marivaux, Paris. Running time, 105 MINS.

This looks a sure bet locally due to Fernandel's following. Contrary to his usual habit, he does not sing in this picture. French star also is known in the U.S. and this may help this comedy to some popularity in America.

Fernandel, a clerk in his uncle's life insurance office, makes a nuisance of himself by trying to become a Sherlock Holmes. To cure him, his uncle sends him on a wild chase, an investigation of the death of one of his clients who lived in an isolated castle. The inmates have been tipped off to create a spook atmosphere. Result is that Fernandel nearly goes crazy himself. Finally, wanting to surrender to gendarmes, they find that apart from the joke on Fernandel, he has unwittingly put them on the track of a thief who used the place to hide his loot.

Plot and action follow the usual slapstick pattern, best laughs coming from Fernandel's mannerisms.

Direction keeps the tempo reasonably fast. Picture was produced several years ago.

Miniature Reviews

"Fallen Angel" (One Song) (20th). Alice Faye, Dana Andrews and Linda Darnell in okay b.o. murder meller.

"This Love of Ours" (U). Merle Oberon, Charles Korvin and Claude Rains starred in good boxoffice drama.

"Don't Fence Me In" (Songs) (Rep). Roy Rogers in ultra musical western.

"Strange Holiday" (Elite). Fair Arch Oboler item, about American people's lethargy.

"L'Extravagante Mission" (French). Weak French languager.

Fallen Angel
(ONE SONG)

20th-Fox release of Otto Preminger production, directed by Preminger. Stars Alice Faye, Dana Andrews, Linda Darnell; features Charles Bickford, Anne Revere, Bruce Cabot, John Carradine, Percy Kilbride. Screenplay, Harry Kleiner, based on novel by Marty Holland; camera, Joseph La Shelle; music, David Raksin; music director, Emil Newman; song, Raksin and Kermit Goell; editor, Harry Reynolds; special effects, Fred Sersen. Tradeshown N. Y., Oct. 16, '45. Running time, 97 MINS.

June Mills	Alice Faye
Eric Stanton	Dana Andrews
Stella	Linda Darnell
Mark Judd	Charles Bickford
Clara Mills	Anne Revere
Dave Atkins	Bruce Cabot
Madley	John Carradine
Pop	Percy Kilbride
Joe Ellis	Olin Howlin
Johnson	Hal Taliaferro
Mrs. Judd	Mira McKinney
Hotel Clerks	Jimmy Conlin, Gus Glassmire
Bank Clerk	Leila McIntyre
Waiter	Garry Owen
Sheriff	Horace Murphy
Maid	Martha Wentworth
Detective	Paul Palmer
Newsman	Paul Burns
Plain Clothes Man	Herb Ashley
Shoe Shine Boy	Stymie Beard
Bus Drivers	William Haade, Chick Collins
Store Keeper	Dorothy Adams
Policeman	Harry Strang
Bartender	Max Wagner

Twentieth-Fox has made an honest attempt to fill filmdom's almost complete void in murder melodrama with an interesting and frequently entertaining mystery entitled "Fallen Angel." With Alice Faye, Dana Andrews and Linda Darnell heading the cast, "Angel" should do strongly at the boxoffice.

There are lapses in "Angel" from the story viewpoint and character development, but these are few and unlikely to militate against the film's over-all entertainment values. Pic deals with a trollop (Miss Darnell) who gets a flock of guys on the string, then gets bumped off. The yarn revolves around which of her admirers committed the deed. Linked to the plot is the story's basic romantic tieup between Miss Faye and Andrews, the former as a respectable, wealthy small-town gal who is ripe for the takings, and Andrews is the guy who starts out to do the taking, even marrying her to do it, his idea being to get enough moola so he can cop the other gal.

This is Miss Faye's first straight dramatic part and she handles herself well, generally, though her one dramatic scene could have gotten better direction. Andrews remains one of the Coast's better young dramatic actors in this film though his character is not always too clearly defined in the writing. Miss Darnell looks the trollop part and plays it well.

Charles Bickford, as a dick; John Carradine, in a more or less bit part, as a phoney psychic; Anne Revere, Bruce Cabot and Percy Kilbride head the able support.

Preminger has both produced and directed. The film's pace could have been speeded in several spots, but generally this film has enough of what it takes to command audience interest. *Kahn.*

This Love of Ours

Universal release of Howard Benedict (Edward Dodd) production. Stars Merle Oberon, Charles Korvin, Claude Rains; features Sue England, Harry Davenport. Directed by William Dieterle. Screenplay, Bruce Manning, John Klorer, Leonard Lee; from play by Luigi Pirandello; camera, Lucien Ballard; editor, Frank Gross; music, H. J. Salter. Tradeshown N. Y., Oct. 23, '45. Running time, 90 MINS.

Karin	Merle Oberon
Tuzac	Charles Korvin
Targel	Claude Rains
Uncle Robert	Carl Esmond
Susette	Sue England
Chadwick	Jess Barker
Dr. Wilkerson	Harry Davenport
Dr. Lane	Ralph Morgan
Dr. Bailey	Fritz Leiber
Tucker	Helen Thimig
Housekeeper	Ferike Boros
Dr. Barnes	Howard Freeman
Dr. Melnik	Selmer Jackson
Dr. Dailey	Dave Willock
Anna	Ann Codee
M. Flambertin	Andre Charlot
Vivian	Doris Merrick
Jose	William Edmunds
Mrs. Dailey	Barbara Bates
Ross	Leon Tyler
Woman	Cora Witherspoon
Evelyn	Maris Wrixon
Call Boy	Robert Raison
Nanette	Evelyn Falke

Borrowing a story from Italian playwright Luigi Pirandello and a director (William Dieterle) from David O. Selznick, Universal added almost $2,000,000 of its own to this surefire combo and came up with a pic that should do well at the boxoffice. Merle Oberon, Charles Korvin and Claude Rains are starred.

Most commendable feature is the plot's originality. Korvin plays a famous doctor whose young daughter (Sue England) has sanctified the memory of her presumably-dead mother. Visiting a Chicago nitery while attending a doctors' convention, Korvin meets Miss Oberon who, it turns out, is his "dead" wife. She is working as accompanist for Claude Rains, an artist who does flash sketches of the bistro's patrons. She tries suicide after the meeting and Korvin saves her through an intricate operation. Then, via flashback, it's revealed that he had left her with his daughter 10 years previously after gossips convinced him his wife was cheating on him. He later realized his mistake but couldn't find her.

Back to the present, Korvin convinces the still-unforgiving Miss Oberon that the daughter needs her and, against the advice of Rains, she consents to return to his home as his "new" wife. Daughter, not knowing the true relationship, refuses to accept Miss Oberon as her mother. All comes out right, however. Picture fades with the thought that eventually the daughter will be told Miss Oberon is her real mother.

Film could have been a trite tearjerker but Dieterle's expert handling prevented that. Korvin seems to be just what the doctor ordered for the lonely-hearts club, and both he and Miss Oberon do well with their roles. Supporting cast is outstanding, with Rains and the diminutive Miss England as the sensitive daughter, especially commendable. H. J. Salter's music adds much to the mood of the picture.

Don't Fence Me In
(SONGS)

Republic release of Donald H. Brown production. Stars Roy Rogers, George 'Gabby" Hayes, Dale Evans; features Robert Livingston, Moroni Olsen, Bob Nolan and Sons of Pioneers. Directed by John English. Screenplay, Dorrell McGowan, Stuart E. McGowan; camera, William Bradford; editor, Charles Craft; music, Morton Scott, Dale Butts; dances, Larry Ceballos; songs, Cole Porter, Milton Shore & Zeke Manners, Jack School & M.K. Jerome, Billy Hill, Larry Markes, Dick Charles, Eddie Delange, Freddie Slack, F. Victor, R. Herman, Bob Nolan. Tradeshown N.Y., Oct. 19, '45. Running time, 71 mins.

Roy Rogers	Roy Rogers
Gabby Whitaker	George "Gabby" Hayes
Toni Ames	Dale Evans
Jack Chandler	Robert Livingston
Henry Bennett	Moroni Olsen
Cliff Anson	Marc Lawrence
Mrs. Prentiss	Lucille Gleason
Cartwright	Andrew Tombes
The Governor	Paul Harvey
The Sheriff	Tom London
Gordon	Douglas Fowley
Tracy	Stephen Barclay
Chief of Police	Edgar Dearing
Bob Nolan and Sons of Pioneers	

Republic must have dug deep into its budgetary sock for this ultra western, with a resultant lavishness that grooves it for better-than-average trade. Credible story, together with currently-popular songs and a leggy chorus line, slant it for the adult, as well as kid audiences, although the producers continue to solicit the Parent-Teacher backing of Roy Rogers by restricting his romancing to a mild peck on the cheek now and then.

Script pokes plenty of fun at hoary western plots and is a good construction job, keeping the pace fast and sustaining interest.

Story is about a nervy femme picture-magazine photographer from Manhattan (Miss Evans), assigned to dig up the facts about Wildcat Kelly, a six-gun western bad man who allegedly was shot and buried 40 years before. At a dude ranch run by Rogers, Miss Evans meets an oldtimer (Gabby Hayes), who claims to have known Kelly when. After complicated goings-on, in which Hayes is shot by gangsters and plays dead to decoy the culprits into the open, it turns out that Hayes is Wildcat Kelly and that a former sheriff, in collaboration with the gang leader, buried another body in Wildcat's grave to collect the state's reward. Interspersed, of course, are the rough-and-tumbles and wild chases through the sagebrush to catch the villains of the piece.

John English's direction keeps the action and comedy moving rapidly. Rogers, Hayes and the curvaceous Miss Evans do creditably in the leads, and the supporting cast, notably Moroni Olsen, Douglas Fowley and Lucille Gleason, are top-notch. Besides Cole Porter's title song, Rogers with Bob Nolan and his Sons of the Pioneers, give out with such popular western ballads as "Last Roundup" and "Tumbling Tumbleweeds." Miss Evans, who also sings for her supper over the ether, renders the current Hit Parader, "Kiss Goodnight," in pleasant fashion.

Strange Holiday

Elite Pictures release of Arch Oboler production, written and directed by Oboler, distributed by Mike J. Levenson. Stars Claude Rains; features Gloria Holden, Helen Mack, Martin Kosleck; editor, Fred Feirshans; camera, Robert Surfees; montage, Howard Anderson, Ray Mercer; music, Gordon Jenkins; asst. director, Sam Nelson. At Rialto, N.Y., week Oct. 19, '45. Running time, 61 MINS.

John Stephenson	Claude Rains
John Jr.	Bobbie Stebbins
Peggy Lee	Barbara Bate
Woodrow	Paul Hilton
Mrs. Jean Stephenson	Gloria Holden
Sam Morgan	Milton Kibbee
Farmer	Walter White
Truck Driver	Wallie Maher
Examiner	Martin Kosleck
Betty	Priscilla Lyon
Boyfriend	David Bradford

Here's an instance where a theatre audience could close its eyes and swear it was listening to a radio show—which is to be expected, since Arch Oboler, one of radio's top creative writers, penned, produced and directed "Strange Holiday." And where the script might have gone over via the ether, Oboler has put too many words and not enough action into it to make it top screen entertainment.

Film was originally produced in 1940 for General Motors which shelved it. Oboler then sold it to Metro, where the picture received the same treatment until the writer, together with Claude Rains, bought it back and released it through the independent Elite Productions.

Picture is the screen version of what Oboler has been doing on the air during the last year—striving to awaken America's interest in domestic and world affairs. Story has

Claude Rains as a typical postwar American, believing that "we won the war; what do I care now what happens to Germany and the Germans?" Returning from a holiday at an isolated north woods spot, Rains discovers that American Nazis, taking advantage of this lethargic attitude, have gained control of the country. Follows some melodramatics in which Rains is beaten senseless after his Nazi "examiner" boasts that the Americans caused their own downfall. Denouement has Rains shouting through his cell bars that America "must fight to regain its freedom," followed by a montage shot of typical American landscape with President Roosevelt's voice enunciating the Four Freedoms.

Oboler achieves remarkable suspense during the first 15 minutes but the picture thereafter falls flat. Rains practically carries the plot and does a fine job, with ample support from the rest of the cast but the picture's faults, coupled with the very lethargy against which Oboler is fighting, will make it a tough one to sell to the public. Typical comment from a sailor, overheard at the Rialto after the show caught, bears out the author's thesis: "I just came back from winning the war—I don't want to see this kind of stuff after that."

L'Extravagante Mission
("The Queer Assignment")
(FRENCH-MADE)

(Paris), Oct. 10.

National release of Sacher Gardine production. Stars Jean Tissier and Henri Guisol; features Marcel Vallee, Jean Paredes, Denise Grey, Mona Goya, Simone Valere, Marthe Carrol. Directed by Henri Caleb. Screenplay, Pierre Carel; camera, Claude Renoir; music by Cocatrix. At Etoile and Eldorado, Paris.

It takes the quota and resulting absence of opposition to understand the possibilities, if any, of this type of production. Some burlesqued antics and some jokes may draw a few laughs in the sticks; but direction is remindful of penny arcade days, photography so poor that the girls' faces are often blurred. And sound is bad. Jean Tissier does only a minor part, that of a ship doctor, with Henri Guisol on the screen from start to finish.

Action mostly takes place on a liner, which Guisol boards thinking he has been commissioned by a banker to impersonate a rich marquis and thus carry safely to the Far East some important papers. The girls on board pester him. He eventually discovers that he has been used by a crook to carry some stolen money away. He finds it difficult to get rid of to escape arrest, but finally succeeds, also wins a girl.

Entertainment value is supposed to come from Guisol's attempts to get rid of the stolen money; treatment of the story make these attempts look like a series of detached comic sketches. *Maxi.*

Miniature Reviews

"Spellbound" (Selznick-UA). Psychological mystery drama, starring Bergman, Peck, directed by Hitchcock, good b.o.

"Pursuit to Algiers" (Songs) (U). This OK Sherlock Holmeser further distinguished by four songs.

"The Seventh Veil" (British). Ann Todd and James Mason in British-made boxoffice click; okay for U. S.

"Latin Quarter" (British). British-made drama that'll go only in England, if there; no names for U. S.

"Skeppar Jansson (Swedish). Good Svensk film, should do well in arty houses.

Spellbound

United Artists release of David O. Selznick production. Stars Indrid Bergman, Gregory Peck; features Leo G. Carroll, John Emery, Steven Geray, Pul Harvey, Erskine Sanford, Jean Acker. Directed by Alfred Hitchcock. Screenplay, Ben Hecht, based on novel by Francis Beeding; camera, George Barnes; music, Miklos Rosza; dream sequence, Salvador Dali; production designer, James Basevi; editor, William Ziegler; asst. director, Lowell Farrell. Opens Oct. 31, '45, at Astor, N.Y., two-a-day. Running time, 116 MINS.

Dr. Constance Peterson	Ingrid Bergman
J.B.	Gregory Peck
Matron	Jean Acker
Harry	Donald Curtis
Miss Carmichael	Rhonda Fleming
Dr. Fleurol	John Emery
Dr. Murchison	Leo G. Carroll
Garmes	Norman Lloyd
Dr. Graff	Steven Geray
Dr. Hanish	Paul Harvey
Dr. Galt	Erskine Sanford
Norma	Janet Scott
Sheriff	Victor Killan
Stranger (Hotel Lobby)	Wallace Ford
House Detective	Bill Goodwin
Bellboy	Dave Willock
Railroad Clerk	George Meader
Policeman (R.R. Station)	Matt Moore
Gateman	Harry Brown
Lt. Cooley	Art Baker
Sgt. Gillespie	Regis Toomey
Dr. Alex Brulov	Michael Chekboy
Secretary (Police Station)	Clarence Straight
J.B. (as a boy)	Joel Davis
J.B.'s Brother	Teddy Infuhr
Police Captain	Addison Richards
Ticket Taker	Richard Bartell
Dr. Edwardes	Edward Fielding

David O. Selznick has devised unique production values for this Alfred Hitchcock-directed version of a psychological mystery novel with the result that top grosses should be assured, especially in the first-runs. Ingrid Bergman and Gregory Peck on the marquee are plus factors also.

The story, employing as it aoes psychiatry and psychoanalysis in a murder mystery, would not lend itself for anything but a skillfully blended top budget production. Even though these terms, and those more clinical, flow through the dialog, don't let the scientific words fool you. While an adult picture all right, beautifully played and photographed, it's still for the women patrons, containing all the suspense and characterization made to order for them.

The science of analysis during mental illness has been touched on before in "Lady in the Dark," but never the scientifically. "Spellbound" is based on the novel, "The House of Dr. Edwardes," written by Hilary St. George Saunders in collaboration with Leslie Palmer, and published under the pseudonym of Francis Beeding. Alfred Hitchcock worked with eminent English psychoanalysts before the adaptation was turned over to Ben Hecht for the screenplay.

Gregory Peck, suffering from amnesia, believes that he committed a murder but has no memory of the locale or circumstances surrounding the crime. Ingrid Bergman as a psychiatrist in love with Peck tries desperately to save him from punishment for the crime she is certain he could not have committed, and in doing so risks her career and almost her life. Both Peck's identity and the solution to the mystery are discovered by psychoanalysis and the most important solution stems from the analysis of one of Peck's dreams.

Salvador Dali designed the dream sequence with all the aids of futurism and surrealism in his sets. These sets, chairs and tables have human legs and roofs slope at 45-degree angles into infinity. This is a new screen treatment for the solution of a murder mystery by the scientific interpretation of dreams, and the customers should be greatly intrigued.

Some of the concluding action takes place on a ski run where the suspense and accompanying musical score create such a tension that the audience at the preview was literally bound as by a spell.

Miss Bergman as the female psychiatrist gives a beautiful characterization of the scientist who discovers her heart really rules her in treating the mental ills of the strange youth she blindly defends. Peck handles the suspense scenes with great skill and has one of his finest screen roles to date. An outstanding performance is scored by Leo G. Carroll as the doctor who is a victim of the ills he treats in his patients, and his closing scene is one to bring the fans to the edge of their seats. John Emery and Michael Chekhov turn in fine performances as the associate doctors.

Alfred Hitchcock has handled his players and action in suspenseful manner and, except for a few episodes of much scientific dialogue, maintains a steady pace in keeping the camera moving. Photography is of the highest, as are the sets commented upon above.

Pursuit to Algiers

(SONGS)

Universal release of Roy William Neill production, directed by Neill; executive producer, Howard Benedict. Stars Basil Rathbone, Nigel Bruce. Screenplay, Leonard Lee, based on characters created by Sir Arthur Conan Doyle; camera, Paul Ivano; editor, Saul A. Goodkind; music, Edgar Fairchild; dialog director, Raymond Kessler; asst. director, Seward Webb; songs, Jack Brooks-Milton Rosen, Everett Cutler-Rosen. At Rialto, N.Y., week Oct. 26, '45. Running time, 65 MINS.

Sherlock Holmes	Basil Rathbone
Dr. Watson	Nigel Bruce
Sheila	Marjorie Riordan
Agatha Dunham	Rosalind Ivan
Mirko	Martin Koslek
Jodri	John Abbott
Prime Minister	Frederic Worlock
Sanford	Morton Lowry
Nikolas	Leslie Vincent
Kingston	Gerald Hamer
Gregor	Rex Evans
Restaurant Proprietor	Tom Dillon
Johanssen	Sven Hugo Borg
Gubec	Wee Willie Davis
Clergyman	Wilson Benge

Latest Sherlock Holmeser from Universal will not disappoint albeit slightly below par for the course.

Introduction of four songs adds a novelty note in the detective meller series. Marjorie Riordan sings three of 'em and Nigel Bruce clears his throat with "Loch Lomond" for acceptable chuckles.

Action takes place for the most part on ship bound for Algiers and since this setting limits the action somewhat there are lapses where the yarn becomes too wordy. Production values of ship sequence very good, however. Naturally Rathbone and Bruce are the focal points so the tepid romance between Marjorie Riordan and Leslie Vincent is secondary.

Basil Rathbone is expert as Holmes and Bruce continues to blunder along as the amiable Dr. Watson. Marjorie Riordan is the thrush from Brooklyn, an unwilling agent for jewel thieves. Vincent is heir to a mythical kingdom. Rosalind Ivan has a comedy characterization of an athletic female passenger and chief among the conspirators who board the steamer at Lisbon is Martin Kosleck.

Production, direction and camera work are all okay within limitations of story, and suspense is maintained until last footage.

The Seventh Veil

(BRITISH-MADE)

London, Oct. 19.

General Film Distributors release of Sydney Box-Ortus production. Stars Ann Todd, James Mason. Directed by Compton Bennett. Story by Muriel and Sydney Box; camera, Reginald Wyer, Bert Mason. At Leicester Square theatre, London, Oct. 18, '45. Running time, 94 MINS.

Nicholas	James Mason
Francesca	Ann Todd
Dr. Larsen	Herbert Lom
Peter Gay	Hugh McDermott
Maxwell Leyden	Albert Lieyen
Susan Brook	Yvonne Owen
Dr. Kendall	David Horne
Dr. Irving	Manning Whiley
Conductor	Arnold Goldsborough
Conductor	Muir Mathieson
Nurse	Grace Allardyce
Parker	Ernest Davies
James	John Sinter

Bobbysox swoonatra fans and jive hounds—beware! For here—magnificently and intelligently done—is an exposition of the way English kids are put and kept in their place. It's due for good b.o. on both sides of the Atlantic.

In adult American eyes the merciless discipline to which a teen-age, sensitive orphan girl is subjected by a grim bachelor guardian will doubtlessly smack of sadism. In England "The Seventh Veil" should arouse no such audience reaction. Caning of kids of both sexes by school teachers is an everyday occurrence in Britain, and in the home the iron subjection of youth to age is also plenty rigorous. So this pic would be of major importance if for no other reason—and there are plenty—than it brings into sharp contrast a fundamental difference between the two countries.

Presented by General Film Distributors as a Sydney Box-Ortus production, directed by Compton Bennett, and scripted by Muriel and Sydney Box, "Veil" has for its b.o. appeal only the names of its two stars, Ann Todd and James Mason. But the results of the team of technicians should make them all assume a greater stature.

Apart from the engrossing story as it surges swiftly to its tremendous climax, there is a feast of harmony by the London Symphony Orchestra, conducted by Muir Mathieson, accompanying an unidentified piano virtuoso—ostensibly Miss Todd.

Title refers to the screen every human uses to hurdle his innermost thoughts. Like Salome, ordinary people will remove one or two—or more—veils for the benefit of friends, sweethearts, spouses. But, unlike Salome, nobody ever sheds the seventh veil. How Miss Todd is made to do this is the backbone of the pic—and its achievement is filmed magnificently.

Although primarily Miss Todd's pic, without in any way detracting from her superb performance it must be said that she has no monopoly of the acting honors. Herbert Lom, the young Czech spotted a year ago as a potential Valentino, gives to the role of the psychiatrist—who induces Miss Todd to cast aside the seventh veil and bare her mind to him—a degree of great authority. Mason does more than hold his own.

Talb.

Thunderbolt

(TECHNICOLOR)

War Activities Release of 18th Army Air Force base unit (Motion Picture unit) film produced under command of Lt. Gen. Ira C. Eaker. Directed by Lt. Col. Willaim C. Wyler. Edited by Capt. John Sturges; script by M/Sgt. Lester Koenig; music, Cpl. Gail Kubik; narrated by Eugene Kern and Lloyd Bridges. Previewed N.Y., Oct. 26, '45. Running time, 43 MINS.

"Thunderbolt," distribution of which is still to be decided by the War Activities Committee of the Motion Picture Industry, seems anticlimactic in view of the fact that tactical procedure depicted in the film has lost much of its timeliness with the end of the war. However, film can serve the practical purpose of acquainting the lay strategist with a little known phase of operations, and, more important, serve as a reminder anew that war is not a pretty thing.

Film, itself, is a superior production made in Technicolor from a 16 mm. original photographed by automatic cameras installed in various parts of the combat Thunderbolts used by the 57th Fighter Group based in Corsica. Documentary concerns the air operations surrounding the American and British advance in Italy. The ground troops were stymied at Cassino after air assaults leveled the city. The fighter command then decided that air-power was not used correctly and decided to bomb enemy supply lines behind the Gustav line. Thunderbolts equipped with 500 lb. bombs then made bridges, railroads, roads and shipping their targets, until enemy was weakened by lack of supplies, and thus effectively paved the way for a 250-mile advance by the ground troops.

Graphically the film can stand on its own as a supporting film. Col. Wyler, now a civilian, directed so that human interest was not lost, despite accent on the combat operations. Production spends a lot of time with the clean-cut kids comprising the fighter group, as a subtle means of saying, "Don't let it happen again."

Jose.

Latin Quarter

(BRITISH-MADE)

London, Oct. 17.

Anglo-American Film Corp. release of British National Film. Stars Derrick de Marney. Directed and written by Vernon Sewell; produced by Louis M. Jackson. Based on "T. Augoise" a play by Pierre Mills and C. Vylars; camera, Gunther Kramph, Gerald D. Moss. At Palace theatre, London, Oct. 16, '45. Running time, 85 MINS.

Charles Garrie	Derrick de Marney
Dr. Krasner	Frederick Valk
Minetti	Beresford Egan
Christine	Joan Greenwood
Lucille	Joan Seton
Maria	Lily Kaun
Prefecture of Police	Valentine Dyall
Morgue Keeper	Martin Miller
Ballet Master	Espinosa
Ballet Mistress	Margaret Clarke
Specialist	Anthony Hawtrey
Police Sergeant	Kempinski

Lacking in name values for the U. S. "Latin Quarter" will hit a good number of British provincial screens. But this is no meritorious addition to native product.

Derrick de Marney, starred, is also associate producer. Production is adequate. Opposite him—as a homicidal maniac sculptor—is tall, cadaverous, very English-looking Beresford Egan, who makes no attempt whatever to live up to the name of the character—Minetti. He suggests an Italian about as much as a glass of pale ale. Frederick Valk, in his usual role as an omniscient psychiatrist — although this breed hadn't hit the headlines in 1893, period of the pic—turns in a workmanlike performance, sorely handicapped as he is by dialog studded with cliches. Joan Greenwood, as the ballet dancer who turns model only to be strangled by the sculptor, is easy to look at.

Direction by Vernon Sewell matches the script of his authorship. Except for two utterly extraneous sequences—a long, drawn-out ballet rehearsal and a hysterical masquerade party in which nearly-nude girl guests are carried about on the shoulders of semi-nude young souses—the director's tempo is funereally slow.

Talb.

Skeppar Jansson

("Skipper Jansson")
(SWEDISH-MADE)

Produced and distributed by Scandia Films, Inc. Stars Sigurd Wallen, Douglas Hage. Directed by Wallen; screenplay, Wallen and Sven Gustafson; music, Erik Baumann and Nathan Gorling. At 5th Ave. Playhouse, N.Y., week of Oct. 24, '45. Running time, 90 MINS.

Jansson	Sigurd Wallen
Lonnman	Douglas Hage
Sjoblom	Arthur Rolen
Rune Sjoblom	Olof Bergstrom
Westerlund	Artur Fischer
Lilly	Gunnel Brostrom
May Westerlund	Margareta Eahlen

(In Swedish with English Titles)

"Skeppar Jansson" is the gay story of a conniving old sea-dog who returns from the seven seas just long enough to set things straight in his little native village—and then sets sail again. Written, directed and starred in by Sigurd Wallen, noted Swedish character actor, it's one of the best new Swedish films and should do top biz in the arty houses. Picture is filled with the salty humor of the Swedish archipelago's fisherfolk and where the English subtitles leave much to be desired, excellent acting makes the simple plot easy enough to follow.

Story revolves around Skipper Jansson (Wallen), an almost legendary character to his native villagers because of his reputed exploits on the high seas. Returning to the village after having allegedly discovered buried treasure in Bermuda, Jansson finds the two families to whom he's related feuding over the deed rights to a field connecting their two farms. Naturally, the son of one family loves the daughter of the other family and naturally, too, both families play up to Jansson, hoping some day to get a cut of his money. It turns out, however, that what the skipper has brought back from his travels is not pirate treasure but some simple philosophy and the ownership deed to the disputed field, both of which he uses in pursuading his relations finally to "skoal" each other over a Swedish schnapps.

Wallen is excellent in the lead role and his skillful direction keeps the pace consistently fast. Douglas Hage, lending just the right touch to his portrayal of the skipper's sentimental old crony, runs him a close second for top acting honors. The sweeping panoramas of the Swedish island and fjords are an eye-treat. Good bet for Hollywood; winsome Gunnel Brostrom, doing a fine job as the gal from Stockholm, who tries to lure the fisher-boy away from his hometown sweetheart.

Miniature Reviews

"Confidential Agent" (WB). Charles Boyer-Lauren Bacall will have to carry this one.

"Crimson Canary" (Songs) (U). Fair murder thriller.

"Dakota" (Rep). Action melodrama with okay prospects. John Wayne name will aid.

Confidential Agent

Warner Bros. release of Robert Buckner production. Stars Charles Boyer, Lauren Bacall; features Katina Paxinou, Peter Lorre, Victor Francen, George Coulouris, Dan Seymour. Directed by Herman Shumlin. Screenplay, Robert Buckner; from novel by Graham Greene; editor, George Amy; camera, James Wong Howe; dialog director, Jack Daniels. Tradeshown in N.Y., Oct 25, '45. Running time, 113 MINS.

Denard	Charles Boyer
Rose Cullen	Lauren Bacall
Licata	Victor Francen
Else	Wanda Hendrix
Capt. Currie	George Coulouris
Contreras	Peter Lorre
Mrs. Melandey	Katina Paxinou
Neil Forbes	John Warburton
Lord Benditch	Holmes Herbert
Mr. Muckerji	Dan Seymour
Chauffeur	Art Foster
Brigstock	Miles Mander
Lord Fetting	Lawrence Grant
Dr. Bellows	Ian Wolfe
Detective Geddes	George Zucco

The auspices under which "Confidential Agent" was produced—and the marquee values involved—are certain to insure a certain amount of boxoffice activity for this melodrama about the Spanish civil war. Charles Boyer and Lauren Bacall are the stars, and Warners (Robert Buckner) is the producer. The rest of the cast, headed by Katina Paxinou and Peter Lorre, must share the measure of respect that this cast commands. Period. The entertainment values are something else again.

The story is dated for these times, though it attempts to show, and doing it rather ambiguously, how in 1937 the success of Franco adherents was to become the prelude to an even greater conflict. The yarn's development is inept, and the link of the romance with the basic story is too pat, at the expense of the major story line.

Boyer plays a Spanish concert musician who has given up his career to fight the fascists. He's detailed by Spanish republicans to go to England and outbid the Francoites for British coal. The coal can be the difference between victory and defeat. The plot specifically deals with the obstacles that confront him, including the British fascists, and secondary to this is the romance that evolves between a British coal tycoon's daughter and Boyer.

The screenplay is uncertain all the way and, surprisingly, so is the direction by Herman Shumlin. However, the latter difficulty can mostly be blamed on the script, which is over-written and flimsy.

Boyer, as usual, underplays to gain an effect as adequate as possible under the circumstances. Miss Bacall, with more dialog than in her first pic, "To Have and Have Not" (her second, unreleased as yet, is "The Big Sleep," and "Agent" is her third), suffers from a monotony of voice and an uncertainty of performance. Her s.a., however, is still plenty evident. Between the two stars there should be enough to put this picture over for both sexes.

Miss Paxinou, invariably a fine actress, is inclined towards too-obvious melodramatics at times, while Lorre has one good scene in a characterization that is comparatively insignificant. Dan Seymour, Victor Francen, George Coulouris and Wanda Hendrix contribute satisfactory lesser performances.

Kahn.

Crimson Canary

(SONGS)

Universal release of Bob Faber production. Features Noah Beery, Jr., Lois Collier, Josh White. Directed by John Hoffman. Screenplay, Henry Blankfort, Peggy Phillips, based on story by Miss Phillips; camera, Jerome Ash; music, Edgar Fairchild; editor, Paul Landres. Tradeshown N.Y., Oct. 31, '45. Running time, 64 MINS.

Danny	Noah Beery, Jr.
Jean	Lois Collier
Johnny	Danny Morton
Quinn	John Litel
Anita	Claudia Drake
Vie	Steven Geray
Chuck	James Dodd
Hillary	Steve Brodie
Singing Specialty	Josh White
Esquire All-American Band Winners—	
Coleman Hawkins, Oscar Pettiford	

Audiences will take to this musical murder-thriller. While some of the performances lack variety, and direction is a little monotonous, neither overcomes the suspenseful overtones conveyed by the Peggy Phillips-Henry Blankfort script.

Five jazz bandsmen are about to depart from a smalltown nightspot for San Francisco for more affluent pastures when the femme vocalist has been mysteriously murdered. Two of the bandsmen are suspect from the start: Danny Morton who is found drunk and unconscious in the same room with her, but his mind a blackout when revived; Noah Beery, Jr., who is seen leaving the room with a dented trumpet. From here on it's under separate cover for all until it's supposed to blow over. However, the situation thickens as guilt favors Beery who unwittingly hocks his trumpet and the like, only to keep the detectives on his clue-ful heel. Fini, however, finds the nitery owner guilty—he was in love with the dead singer, and bashed her head in because she threatened to leave town with the jazz-makers.

Jazz sessions with the band provide some very diverting moments in the film, with due credit to the Esquire All-American band winners, Coleman Hawkins and Oscar Pettiford, who also appear in film. Josh White, of Cafe Society (N. Y.) distinction, renders "One Meat Ball" and "Jericho" in his inimitable technique.

Performances of Noah Beery, Jr., and Lois Collier are adequate. They were statically directed.

Dakota

(ONE SONG)

Los Angeles, Nov. 2.

Republic release of Joseph Kane production, directed by Kane. Stars John Wayne, Vera Hruba Ralston, Walter Brennan; features Ward Bond, Mike Mazurki, Ona Munson. Screenplay, Lawrence Hazard; original story. Carl Foreman; adaptation, Howard Estabrook; camera, Jack Marta; special effects, Howard and Theodore Lydecker; song Andrew Sterling and Harry Von Tilzer; music. Walter Scharf; editor, Fred Allen. Previewed Hollywood, Nov. 1, '45. Running time, 81 MINS.

John Devlin	John Wayne
Sandy	Vera Hruba Ralston
Captain Bounce	Walter Brennan
Jim Bender	Ward Bond
Bigtree Collins	Mike Mazurki
"Jersey" Thomas	Ona Munson
Mrs. Stowe	Olive Blakeney
Marko Poli	Hugo Haas
Nicodemus	Nicodemus Stewart
Carp	Paul Fix
Slagin	Grant Withers
Lieutenant	Robert Livingston
Devlin's Driver	Olin Howlin
Wexton Geary	Pierre Watkin
Mr. Stowe	Robert H. Barrat
Col. Wordin	Jonathan Hale
Little Boy	Bobby Blake
Captain Spotts	Paul Hurst
Stagecoach Driver	Eddy Waller
Mrs. Plummer	Sarah Padden
Suede	Jack LaRue
Mr. Plummer	George Cleveland
Dr. Judson	Selmer Jackson
Wahtonka	Claire DuBrey
Poli's Driver	Roy Barcroft

Republic has dressed up a familiar land-grab story with sufficient production to give this outdoor epic more than formula values. It has draw value in the John Wayne name to aid in the action market and returns will prove okay.

Action isn't always robust, but there are a number of knock-down fights to help carry it along. Plot has Wayne, a gambler, and his bride, treking to Dakota to make their fortune. Couple is aware that the railroad will soon go through land they hope to acquire, but a gang of crooks are also hep to coming events and are swindling wheat farmers of land. Two factions have their ups and downs before farmers realize what is happening and climax comes when villains set fire to vast wheat acreage in a last desperate attempt to have things their way.

Wayne runs through his assignment under Joseph Kane's direction with his customary nonchalance. Vera Hruba Ralston, femme lead, comes through a river ducking, the fire and fights with every hair in place and not a single wrinkle. Walter Brennan, a river boat captain, and his dusky aide, Nicodemus Stewart, supply several lighter moments. Ward Bond and Mike Mazurki head up the choice heavies in satisfactory fashion and others in the large cast do well. Ona Munson is wasted in a part little more than a bit. Photography and other technical appurtenances are workmanlike.

Brog.

Miniature Reviews

"Danger Signal" (WB). Average melodrama with modestly good b.o. possibilities.

"Hold That Blonde" (Par). Eddie Bracken and Veronica Lake in fair comedy, despite too much slapstick.

"Cornered" (RKO). Firstrate thriller. Packs plenty of suspense. B. o. outlook substantial.

"Strange Confession" (U). Routine murder mystery.

"My Name Is Julia Ross" (Col). No-name cast but tense melodrama should do okay.

"Sing Your Way Home" (Songs) (RKO). Fair musical romance. Jack Haley's name may lift out of routine biz.

"Marie - Louise" (Praesens). Excellent Swiss film should do well at U. S. box-offices.

"Outlaws of the Rockies" (Songs) (Col). Charles Starrett in a routine western.

"I Know Where I'm Going" (GFD-British). British-made, sock b.o. drama with Wendy Hiller and Roger Livesey; made by Powell-Pressburger.

"Girls of the Big House" (Rep). Prison meller will do for dual houses.

Danger Signal

Hollywood, Nov. 13.

Warners release of William Jacobs production. Stars Faye Emerson, Zachary Scott; features Dick Erdman, Rosemary DeCamp, Bruce Bennett, Mona Freeman, John Ridgely. Directed by Robert Florey. Screenplay, Adele Commandini and Graham Baker; from novel by Phyllis Bottome; camera, James Wong Howe; editor, Frank Magee; music, Adolph Deutsch. Tradeshown at Los Angeles, Nov. 13, '45. Running time, **77 MINS.**

Hilda Fenchurch............Faye Emerson
Ronnie Marsh..................Zachary Scott
Bunkie Taylor..................Dick Erdman
Dr. Silla..................Rosemary DeCamp
Dr. Andrew Lang............Bruce Bennett
Anne Fenchurch.............Mona Freeman
Thomas Turner.................John Ridgely
Mrs. Fenchurch.................Mary Servoss
Katie........................Joyce Compton
Mrs. Crockett....................Virginia Sale
Investigator...............Addison Richards

"Danger Signal" is an average melodrama turned out on a medium budget. Several exploitation factors will aid in selling and assure okay returns in general bookings. Running time is briefer than majority of features coming off studio assembly lines, which will be an advantage in double bill spotting. Zachary Scott gives another of his prize heel characterizations to carry majority interest in the plot and is well on his way to making himself the most hissable heavy on the screen.

Plot mixes in a little psychology but never rates classification as a psychological melodrama. In fact, the psychiatric explanations for behavior of characters only creates some confusion. Suspense is created in ultimate justice to be meted out to the Scott character but when doom does come it is so abrupt it lacks punch.

Script by Adele Commandini and Graham Baker is based on the novel of the same title by Phyllis Bottome and depicts a suave, dishonest heel who smooths his way through life with an oily tongue and a way with women. Scott gives a strong portrayal of the character. Implicated in the death of another man's wife, Scott flees across the country to California. He inveigles his way into the home of Faye Emerson, public stenographer, by a sympathy ruse and proceeds to charm both the girl and her mother. Romance is the first for Miss Emerson and when her younger sister returns home and begins to receive Scott's attention, it's a shock.

Miss Emerson handles herself capably as the femme lead but the camera doesn't always do her justice. Mona Freeman, as the younger sister, shows up well, as does Rosemary DeCamp, a femme psychiatrist. Bruce Bennett's role of the friendly doctor is a thankless part but well-handled. Other parts are small.

Robert Florey directed the William Jacobs production but doesn't always achieve the best results. *Brog.*

Hold That Blonde

Paramount release of Paul Jones production. Stars Eddie Bracken, Veronica Lake; features Albert Dekker, Willie Best. Directed by George Marshall. Screenplay by Walter DeLeon, Earl Baldwin, E. Edwin Moran, from play by Paul Armstrong; editor, LeRoy Stone; camera, Daniel L. Fapp, Gordon Jennings. At Paramount, N. Y., starting Nov. 7, '45. Running time, **76 MINS.**

Ogden Spencer Trulow III..Eddie Bracken
Sally Martin..................Veronica Lake
Inspector Callahan..........Albert Dekker
Willie Shelley......................Willie Best
Mr. Phillips......................Frank Fenton
Pavel Sorasky...................George Zucco
Mr. Kratz...................Donald MacBride
Mr. Henry Carteret.......Lewis L. Russell
Mrs. Henry Carteret.........Norma Varden
Mr. Reddy.........................Ralph Peters
Edwards, a butler.........Robert Watson
Tony.................................Lyle Latell
Victor................Edmund MacDonald

Paramount's latest method of getting one of its ace comics and one of its more enticing femme stars to the screen adds up to a fair film despite virtually every time-proven piece of slapstick being utilized. That the film is successful at all is due completely to Eddie Bracken, as a rich kleptomaniac, wringing everything possible from the assignment, although occasionally guilty of overplaying.

In building their story, from an old Paul Armstrong play, the adaptors apparently had trouble making the comedy and love angles jibe. They nicely lay the foundation for the latter idea when a psychiatrist tells Bracken that the cure-all for his sticky fingers lies in digging up a romance, but from there the development of his attachment to Veronica Lake is left to infrequent declarations by Bracken that come as a surprise and an interruption to the comedy theme.

As the weak yarn unwinds, Miss Lake is the femme portion of a gang of thieves out to make off with the Romanoff necklace. Bracken seeks to prevent her from participating in the snatch and that's about it. The fill-in, revolving around the gang's suspicion that Miss Lake is double-crossing them, and their attempts to knock him off, comprise the "action."

In between, there's all sorts of Mack Sennett gags. Chases up and down hotel corridors, disguises, even a rather long sequence in which Bracken, in getting away from the gang's trigger man, winds up on the ledge of a high building (shades of Harold Lloyd!) gets spotted as a peeping tom, and winds up hanging from a flag pole with a drunk bent on saving the inadvertently peeped-at gal. They both crash into the floor below when the pole breaks, and the drunk starts mistakingly belaboring the occupant of that room. That's real slapstick.

Willie Best gets in a few good laughs as Bracken's unwilling servant-companion attempting constantly to shield Bracken from his kleptomania. Albert Dekker has comparatively little to do as a police inspector, though he's given featured billing. As for Miss Lake, just about all she's called upon to do is look pretty. *Wood.*

Cornered

Hollywood, Nov. 9.

RKO release of Adrian Scott production. Stars Dick Powell; features Walter Slezak, Micheline Cheirel, Nina Vale, Morris Carnovsky, Edgar Barrier, Steven Geray, Jack LaRue, Gregory Gay. Directed by Edward Dmytryk. Screenplay, John Paxton; story and adaptation, John Wexley; camera, Harry J. Wild; music, Roy Webb; editor, Joseph Noriega. Tradeshown Pantages, Hollywood, Nov. 7, '45. Running time, **102 MINS.**

Gerard.........................Dick Powell
Incza..........................Walter Slezak
Mme. Jarnac............Micheline Cheirel
Senora Camargo..................Nina Vale
Santana................Morris Carnovsky
DuBois.........................Edgar Barrier
Senor Camargo..............Steven Geray
Diego..............................Jack LaRue
Marcel Jarnac..................Luther Adler
Perchon........................Gregory Gay

Suspenseful thriller with excellent boxoffice prospects. Marks second film for Dick Powell away from his musical characterizations and has all the good points of his first venture into melodramatics. Thriller fans will find it to their liking. Mounting is good and direction first rate.

It's the story of the relentless post-war hunt of a Canadian flier for the collaborationist who was responsible for the death of his French bride. Directed and played strictly for suspense and thrills, search gets underway in France, switches to Belgium, Switzerland and then Argentina, where most of action takes place. While all evidence points towards the death of the collaborationist, Powell believes the man still alive. His search reveals hibernation of pro-Nazis in the Argentine, where they are waiting to rise again in the future, and the efforts of good Argentinians to smoke them out.

Cast has many suspects weaving in and out to conceal identity of the mysterious "Marcel Jarnac" whom Powell seeks, and finale has a definite surprise in store for audiences who might believe they have guessed his assumed character. Edward Dmytryk's direction makes the most of the suspense and concealment, building a mood that never lets down in carrying the manhunt to a successful conclusion.

There are a number of character gems, in addition to the strong portrayal by Powell. Walter Slezak, as an opportunist who slyly cultivates both Powell and the group latter is seeking, does a standout job. Morris Carnovsky, Edgar Barrier and Jack LaRue, as good Argentinians, show up well.

Nina Vale is a sexy, unscrupulous femme menace among the pro-Nazi set. Michael Cheirel depicts an unwilling collaborationist who eventually leads Powell to the man he wants. Luther Adler is a bit too flamboyant in his portrayal. There are also a number of uncredited but importantly done, small roles.

Adrian Scott's production supervision furnishes proper backing for the John Paxton script, from story by John Wexley. Harry J. Wild's photography and Roy Webb's musical score are important contributions in furthering the pace and mood. Editing is concise except at opening of film, where motivation is choppily established. *Brog.*

Strange Confession

Universal release of Ben Pivar production. Stars Lon Chaney; features Brenda Joyce, J. Carrol Naish, Lloyd Bridges, Addison Richards, Mary Gordon. Directed by John Hoffman. Inner Sanctum mystery, based on story by Jean Bart; adaptation, M. Coates Webster; editor, Andrew J. Gilmore; camera, Maury Gertsman. At Rialto, N. Y., week Nov. 8, '45. Running time, **61 MINS.**

Jeff.................................Lon Chaney
Mary.............................Brenda Joyce
Graham.......................J. Carrol Naish
Stevens.........................Milburn Stone
Dave.............................Lloyd Bridges
Dr. Williams...............Addison Richards
Mrs. O'Conner.....................Mary Gordon
Harper.......................George Chandler
Tommy......................Gregory Muradian
Brandon..........................Wilton Graff
Hernandez..................Frances McDonald
Boarder.............................Jack Norton
Mr. Moore......................Christian Rub

This picture features a 13-year-old South American ringtail monkey. And not bad, this monk. The rest of the cast, headed by Lon Chaney, turn in performances that are routine albeit quite as natural as Bebe's and, under fairly able steering by director John Hoffman, manage to produce a murder mystery item that should do fairly.

Another in the Inner Sanctum mystery series, "Strange Confession" is done in flashback. Opening on the plea of a chemist to get a college chum, now a famous attorney, to represent him in a murder case, the action goes back to recount the events and incidents which led him to a killing. Story, with accompanying dialog that fails to impress, concerns a racketeering drug manufacturer who markets an unfinished formula without the knowledge of the chemist and, sending latter to South America on experiments, rides herd on the guy's wife meantime. The killing is the result.

Chaney plays the chemist and Brenda Joyce his dutiful wife. J. Carrol Naish is the racketeering drugman, while others are Milburn Stone, Lloyd Bridges, Addison Richards and Mary Gordon. All, as aforesaid, are routine. *Char.*

My Name Is Julia Ross

Columbia release of Wallace MacDonald production. Features Nina Foch, Dame May Whitty, George Macready, Roland Varno, Anita Bolster, Doris Lloyd. Directed by Joseph H. Lewis. Screenplay, Muriel Roy Bolton, from novel by Anthony Gilbert; camera, Burnett Guffey; editor, James Sweeney; music, M. W. Bakaleinikoff; asst. director, Milton Feldman. At Ambassador, N. Y., week Nov. 9, '45. Running time, **64 MINS.**

Julia Ross..........................Nina Foch
Mrs. Williamson Hughes.Dame May Whitty
Ralph Hughes.............George Macready
Dennis Bruce..................Roland Varno
Sparkes.........................Anita Bolster
Mrs. Mackie.......................Doris Lloyd
Peters.........................Leonard Mudie
Bertha........................Joy Harrington
Alice.......................Queenie Leonard
Robinson...............Harry Hays Morgan
Mrs. Robinson..............Ottola Nesmith
Reverend Lewis..................Olaf Hytten
Dr. Keller.......................Evan Thomas

Minus names for marquee, "Julia Ross" is an obvious B though far better as entertainment than a casual survey of production credits would indicate. Mystery melodrama with a psychological twist runs only 64 minutes but it's fast and packed with tense action throughout. Acting and production (though apparently modestly budgeted) are excellent. It should easily get back its cost though there's great need for exploitation to get its full boxoffice value.

New face is Nina Foch, who has looks and talent, while rest of cast is backed notably by Dame May Whitty, George Macready and Roland Varno.

Story is of gal hired fraudulently as secretary to wealthy English dowager. Purpose of hiring is to impose a murder scheme in which the dowager's son is implicated. The story has its implausibilities, but general conduct of pic negates those factors for overall click results.

Dame Whitty gives creditable performance, so does Macready as her psychiatric son. Others in support acquit themselves well. Joseph H. Lewis directed for pace, and he achieve it all the way. *Kahn.*

Sing Your Way Home

(SONGS)

RKO Radio release of Bert Granet production. Stars Jack Haley, Marcy McGuire, Glenn Vernon, Anne Jeffreys; features Donna Lee, Patti Brill, Nancy Marlow, James Jordan, Jr., Emory Parnell, David Forrest, Ed Gargan. Directed by Anthony

Mann. Screenplay, William Bowers; original story, Edmund Joseph, Bart Lytton; editor, Harry Marker; camera, Frank Redman; dialog director, Leslie Urbach; musical director, C. Bakaleinikoff; songs, Herb Magidson, Allie Wrubel. Tradeshown in N. Y., Nov. 9, '45. Running time, **72 MINS.**

Steve........................Jack Haley
Bridget........................Marcy McGuire
Jimmy........................Glenn Vernon
Kay........................Anne Jeffreys
Terry........................Donna Lee
Dottie........................Pattie Brill
Patsy........................Nancy Marlow
Chuck........................James Jordan, Jr.
Captain........................Emory Parnell
Windy........................David Forrest
Jailer........................Ed Gargan

If one accepts this unconvincing story, with coincidence taking the place of logical plot development, then the antics of the young musical charges of comedian Jack Haley will prove entertaining. But before an audience of returned vets the scenes on shipboard may well invite skepticism because seemingly no transport ever had such a passenger list.

Haley strives to rise above the confining role of the big-headed war correspondent en route to New York after V-J Day in charge of an adolescent group of hepcats supposedly trapped in Europe by the war and awaiting transportation for four years. Some of the gals and boys must have been 13 when they first went over to entertain, judging from their appearance.

The youngsters play at the drop of a hat which is doffed every few minutes but really get in the groove with the broadcast performance from sea. The musical section of story is well rendered and class-A entertainment but the romantic scenes between Haley and Anne Jeffreys as the nightclub singer never seem to be more than adequate.

Climax of story revolves around message Haley has one of youngsters send to his editor in "love code" to evade censorship restrictions. But nightclub singer interested in Haley misunderstands purpose of intercepted message and adds closing lines of her own which informs N. Y. bosses that Haley's peace plans are accepted by Allies. This brings in State Dept. and complications including prison spell for Haley. He is sprung by singer in some mysterious manner not clearly explained.

Marcy McGuire is outstanding as one kid entertainer and scores in several numbers, notably "I'll Buy That Dream." Miss Jeffreys is given two musical numbers, notably "Heaven Is a Place Called Home." Donna Lee with "The Lord's Prayer" and Miss McGuire and Glenn Vernon contribute individual performances that have fine entertainment value.

Marie-Louise

(SWISS-MADE)

Praesens Films release of L. Wechsler production. Stars Josiane and Heinrich Gretler; features Margrit Winter and Anne-Marie Blanc. Directed by Leopold Lindtberg. Screenplay, Richard Schweizer; camera, Emil Berna; editor, Herman Haller; music, Robert Blum; English titles, Herman Weinberg. Distributed by Mayer-Burstyn. Tradeshown in N. Y., Nov. 12, '45. Running time, **93 MINS.**

Marie-Louise........................Josiane
Mr. Ruegg........................Heinrich Gretler
Anna Ruegg........................Margrit Winter
Hedi Ruegg........................Anne-Marie Blanc
Mr. Banninger........................Armin Schweitzer
Paula........................Mathilde Danegger
Scheibli........................Fred Tanner
Schwarzenbach........................Emil Gerber
Andre........................Bernhard Ammen
Mme. Fleury........................Germaine Tournier
And French children

(In French; English Titles)

Billed as the first Swiss-made picture to be distributed in this country, "Marie-Louise" is a promise that, if all Swiss films are as well-done, then some fine entertainment is in store for the American public. Even though the story treats directly of the war, the customers will go for a war picture if well-made, and "Marie-Louise" is that kind of picture. It should be a natural for the arty houses, and, given the right type exploitation to overcome the average fan's resistance to foreign-language pix, it would do well generally.

Locale is laid in both France and Switzerland, hence both French and Swiss patois dialog. Action is good enough to carry the plot, however, and the English subtitles are adequate for American audiences. Story deals with a young French girl, Marie-Louise, one of a group who is evacuated to Switzerland for three months to escape the Nazi occupation of her home city of Rouen. Picture was begun during the occupation and the Swiss producers chose an actual French refugee, Josiane, for the title role. The girl handles the difficult part in gem-like fashion and it's her sensitive underplaying of the emotional scenes that prevents the picture from becoming a common tear-jerker.

As a child who has forgotten how to smile, Marie-Louise is taken into the home of Mr. Ruegg, a wealthy Swiss manufacturer, and his two daughters. There, under the family's ministrations, she regains confidence in life until one day the sight and sound of two passing airplanes so terrify her that she suffers a breakdown and has to be taken to a hospital. Her story gets around the manufacturer's factory and the workers, unable to afford to keep one of the French children themselves, decide to work 15 minutes' overtime daily to raise enough money to rent a chalet in the mountains for the accommodation of many more children.

Marie-Louise, meanwhile, has recovered and back in the Ruegg home, she is spoiled to such an extent that she refuses to return to France. It is decided then that it would be better if she went to the chalet with the other children. And when the time comes for her to start for home again, Marie-Louise is ready, with her comrades, to face the future.

Picture has its minor faults, of course, such as a tendency to drag during the last few reels, but the production, direction and acting are as good as in any foreign-made film to reach the American screen. Although overshadowed by the diminutive star of the piece, the supporting cast also contributes some fine work with Heinrich Gretler, as the autocratic, but kindly Mr. Ruegg, especially good. Panoramic shots of the Swiss mountains are breathtaking and Robert Blum's excellent score goes hand-in-hand with the film's all-round quality.

Outlaws of the Rockies

(Songs)

Columbia release of Colbert Clark production. Stars Charles Starrett; features Tex Harding, Dub Taylor, Carole Mathews. Directed by Ray Nazarro. Screenplay by J. Benton Cheney; camera, Geroge Kelley; editor, Aaron Stell. At New York, N.Y., dual. week Nov 9, '45. Running time, 54 MINS.

Steve Williams........................Charles Starrett
Tex Harding........................Tex Harding
Cannonball........................Dub Taylor
Jane Stuart........................Carole Mathews
Dan Chantry........................Philip Van Zandt
Ace Lanning........................I. Stanford Jolley
Bill Jason........................George Chesebro
Potter........................Steve Clark
Sheriff Hall........................Jack Rockwell
Carolina Cotton
Spade Cooley

"Outlaws of the Rockies" is a weak western. A low-budgeted film, lack of originality and poor attempts at humor groove it for the grade-school kids.

Songs, too, lack punch, the music by Spade Cooley and his band being of the nasal twang variety, with Carolina Cotton providing some cow-hand yodeling for those that go for it. Cooley is billed as the "King of Western Swing," but any swing attached to his music is somehow missing from the soundtrack.

Filled with more than the usual quota of chases and six-shooters that can fire 50 or so shots before reloading, plot concerns outlaws who roamed the range back in the gold-rush days. Charles Starrett, a sheriff who is accused of being a member of the outlaw gang when he helps his friend (Tex Harding) break jail is really the masked "Durango Kid," Robin Hood of the west. Two of them set out to capture the gang and, after some routine shenanigans, succeed in rounding up the outlaws and proving their innocence.

Chief asset of the picture, aside from its comparatively short running time, is heroine Carole Mathews whose talent and looks should get her a break in better films. Harding, too, is suited for better roles. Hero Charles Starrett, on the other hand, provides nothing out of the ordinary.

I Know Where I'm Going

(BRITISH-MADE)

London, Oct. 31.

General Film Distributors release of Archers Production. Stars Wendy Hiller, Roger Livesay. Written, produced and directed by Michael Powell, Emeric Pressburger. Music by Allan Gray; camera, Erwin Hillier. At Leicester Square theatre, London, Oct. 30, '45. Running time, 91 MINS.

Joan Webster........................Wendy Hiller
Mr. Webster........................George Carney
Torquil MacNeil........................Roger Livesay
Capt. Lochinvar........................Capt. Duncan McKechnie
Hunter........................Walter Hudd
Catriona........................Pamela Brown
Sir Robert Bellinger........................Norman Shelley
Cheril........................Petula Clark
Ruairdh Mor........................Finaly Currie
Colonel Barnstaple........................Capt. C.W.R. Knight
Mrs. Robinson........................Catherine Lacey
Mr. Robinson........................Valentine Dyall
Mrs. Crozier........................Nancy Price
Iain........................Ian Sadler
Kenny........................Murdo Morrison
Bridie........................Margo Fitzsimons

Like "Johnny Frenchman," this Archers production should click with American audiences keen to add to their stock of info about relatively unknown corners of this tight little isle. Story, stars and production—all of them above average—are of less importance than the performances by the men, women and children who people the wild, gale-swept Hebrides. Here is the real thing.

"I Know Where I'm Going" sets the seal of success on England's most workmanlike film-production pair, Michael Powell and Emeric Pressburger, who, between them, wrote, produced and directed the pic. It has all the values of a documentary as a foundation for the fictional tale of a girl who is sure she knows where she is going until she gets sidetracked—and likes it.

As the girl Wendy Hiller repeats her convincing portrayal of character development which made "Pygmalion" a personal triumph for her. Hard as nails in the opening sequences, when she tells her father, a band manager, she is off to the Island of Mull to marry the multi-millionaire boss of a great chemical combine, she dismisses his objections to the May-December misalliance by insisting her fiance is no older than her father—"and you're rather nice, daddy."

It is only when a gale prevents her from reaching the island and her waiting bridegroom-to-be she finds her heartless ambition to marry money becoming less attractive, the process of disillusionment aided and abetted by her proximity to a young navy officer, Roger Livesey, who begins by telling her what he thinks of gold diggers generally, and winds up by walloping her in the best-approved Cagney fashion. All of which, of course, makes the final clinch a cinch.

In support, Pamela Brown, as an unconventional native of the desolate, forbidding region, is outstanding. But it is the real people of the district who do most to make this pic stand out as something more than just another flick. In the celebrations of a native couple's diamond wedding, for instance, the dancing and singing of wild, folklore songs bring to sound track and screen something really new. Incidentally, top marks to the Glasgow Orpheus Choir, under Sir Hugh Robertson.

In next-to-the-closing sequence, when the girl, as much to escape from yielding to her own desires as to keep her promise to make the loveless wedding, bribes an 18-year-old boy to brave the storm and get her to the island, she and he are saved from certain death when the navy officer puts off with them. Nothing more terrifying than the seascapes—churning seas boiling into whirlpools from which there seems no escape—has seemingly ever been shot. *Talb.*

Girls of the Big House

(TWO SONGS)

Republic Pictures release of Rudolph E. Abel production. Features Lynne Roberts, Virginia Christine, Marian Martin, Adele Mara, Richard Powers, Geraldine Wall, Tala Birell, Norma Varden, Stephen Barclay. Directed by George Archainbaud. Screenplay, Houston Branch; editor, Arthur Roberts; camera, John Alton; songs, Jack Elliott, Sanford Green, June Carroll; score, Joseph Dubin; musical director, Morton Scott. Tradeshown in N. Y., Nov. 7, '45. Running time, **68 MINS.**

Jeanne Crail........................Lynne Roberts
Bernice........................Virginia Christine
Dixie........................Marian Martin
Harriet........................Adele Mara
Barton Sturgis........................Richard Powers
Head Matron........................Geraldine Wall
Alma Vlasek........................Tala Birell
Mrs. Thelma Holt........................Norma Varden
Smiley........................Stephen Barclay
Dr. Gale Warren........................Mary Newton
Professor O'Neill........................Erskin Sanford
Dormitory Matron........................Sarah Edwards
Mother Fielding........................Ida Moore
District Attorney........................William Forrest
Agnes........................Verna Felton

Action drama of life behind the walls in a State prison for women is handled well by the nearly all-girl cast and has several musical interludes with two song numbers in the recreation hall of the prison. However, lack of top names and locale of modestly budgeted story limit its appeal to dual bills where it should do nicely.

Starting out with the familiar story of the small-town girl framed in the big city by a nightclub acquaintance; the story moves behind bars and points up the prison hatreds that force the older inmates to take sides against the newcomer. Old-fashioned melo is invoked to account for a prison murder over a character named "Smiley," who is triple-timing three of the gals.

The framed girl, played effectively by Lynne Roberts, is finally released through the efforts of her home-town lawyer. Prison scenes authentic-looking and action-full with competent performances turned in by Virginia Christine, Marian Martin, Adele Mara, Tala Birell as inmates.

Two songs sung by the girls in prison rec hall are "There's a Man in My Life," by Jack Elliott, and "Alma Mater," by Sanford Green and June Carroll.

George Archainbaud got all he could out of the story with familiar meller cliches.

Miniature Reviews

"Saratoga Trunk" (WB). Gary Cooper - Ingrid Bergman - Edna Ferber a surefire boxoffice parlay for boffo biz.

"They Were Expendable" (M-G). High-budget war film, marking return to films of Robert Montgomery; big b.o.

"What Next, Corporal Hargrove?" (M-G). Hilarious boxoffice comedy sequel depicting a soldier's adventures in Europe.

"Too Young to Know" (WB). Appealing story of young love against war background that carries general interest.

"San Antonio" (Color; Songs) (WB). Lavishly produced western built along traditionally-hoary lines; will probably sell.

"Mexicana" (musical) (Rep). Mildly diverting tune film with Latin background; Will do okay biz.

"The Daltons Ride Again" (U). Solid boxoffice western.

"The Last Chance" (Swiss-made) (Metro-Praesens). Excellent foreign film should do well at all U. S. b.o.'s.

"Border Badmen" (PRC). Routine Buster Crabbe western.

"Dangerous Intruder" (PRC). Fair thriller item for the dual market.

"Shadow of Terror" (PRC). Well-paced meller about the atomic bomb.

Saratoga Trunk

Warner Bros. release of Hal B. Wallis production. Stars Gary Cooper, Ingrid Bergman; features Flora Robson. Directed by Sam Wood. Edna Ferber's novel adapted by Casey Robinson; music, Max Steiner; camera, Ernie Haller, Lawrence Butler; editor, Ralph Dawson; sets, Fred MacLean; music director, Leo F. Forbstein; asst. director, Phil Quinn. Opens indef run today (Nov. 21, '45) at Hollywood, N. Y. Running time, **135 MINS.**

Col. Clint Maroon....Gary Cooper
Clio Dulaine....Ingrid Bergman
Angelique....Flora Robson
Cupidon....Jerry Austin
Bartholomew Van Steed...John Warburton
Mrs. Coventry Bellop....Florence Bates
Augustin Haussy....Curt Bois
Roscoe Bean....John Abbott
Mme. Clarissa Van Steed....Ethel Griffies
Mrs. Porcelain....Maria Shelton
Mrs. Nicholas Dulaine....Helen Freeman
Charlotte Dulaine....Sophie Huxley
Monsieur Begue....Fred Essler
Raymond Soule....Louis Payne
Miss Diggs....Sarah Edwards
Grandmother....Adrienne D'Ambricourt
Guilia Forosini....Jacqueline DeWitt

"Saratoga Trunk" packs plenty of b.o. shekels for everybody. A cinch for the exhibitors, it is made-to-order film fare at a time when pure escapism is worth its weight in marquees. With Gary Cooper, Ingrid Bergman, Flora Robson in the Edna Ferber bestseller, it's a surefire boxoffice parlay.

Story has color, romance, adventure, and not a little s.a. Miss Bergman is the beautiful albeit calculating Creole, and Gary Cooper is very effective in the plausible role of a droll, gamblin' Texan who has the romantic hex on the headstrong Creole. Flora Robson is capitally cast as her body-servant and Jerry Austin does a bangup job as the dwarf who, with the mulatto servant, make a strange entourage.

The 1875 period, and the New Orleans and Saratoga locales, combine into a moving story as Miss Bergman returns from Paris to avenge her mother's "shame." That this is a spurious sentimentality, considering she was born out of wedlock, and her father's family sought to banish her virtually to France, is beside the point. Miss Bergman, as fetchin a brunet (wig), as in her natural lighter tresses, takes command in every scene. She sparks the cinematurgy, a vital plus factor considering Cooper's laconic personation, and the sultry reticence of her two curious servants.

Despite the longish footage (135 mins.), Casey Robinson's adaptation and the Sam Wood's direction have injected pace and gusto. For one thing, the Ferber yarn is meaty and moving. The two major geographical segments—her native N. O. and the fertile Saratoga, during the July-August season, where Miss Bergman comes to snare a tycoon (but winds up with Cooper, of course)—are replete with basic action and never pall.

Long before Hal Wallis left Warners to become an independent producer (Par), he put "Saratoga Trunk" into the can. This is another of the several big WB pix which our GIs have seen overseas as long ago as two years. The wisdom of the Warner plant in timing its general entertainment release now, after all the war-themed, patriotic and the other purposeful pix were first released, is fully manifest. "Trunk" is timeless; in fact, the clever sets and costumes do much to re-create a period for the postwar film fan which is highly refreshing.

While the top quartet dominate, Wallis and Wood have done a corking job with the other roles, ranging from the hard-bitten New Orleans clan to the dilettante Saratoga set, not forgetting the showdown fisticuffs for the strategic Saratoga trunkline which climaxes the melodramatics. *Abel.*

They Were Expendable

Metro release of Capt. John Ford Production. Stars Robert Montgomery and John Wayne; features Donna Reed, Jack Holt, Ward Bond, Marshall Thompson, Paul Langton, Leon Ames, Donald Curtis, Arthur Walsh, Harry Tenbrook, Charles Trowbridge and Robert Barrat. Directed by Ford and Capt. James C. Havens, USMCR: associate producer, Cliff Reid; based on book of same name by William L. White; adaptation, Frank Wead, Comm., USN (Ret.); editors, Frank E. Hull and Douglas Biggs; camera, Lt. Comm. Joseph H. August, USNR; special effects, A. Arnold Gillespie. Previewed in N.Y. Nov. 7, '45. Running time, 135 MINS.

Lt. John Brickley....Robert Montgomery Comd. U.S.N.R.
Lt. (j.g.) "Rusty" Ryan....John Wayne
Lt. Sandy Davyss....Donna Reed
General Martin....Jack Holt
"Boats" Mulcahey, C.R.M....Ward Bond
Ens. "Snake" Gardner....Marshall Thompson
Ens. "Andy" Andrews....Paul Langton
Major James Morton....Leon Ames
Seaman Jones....Arthur Walsh
Lt. (j.g.) "Shorty" Long....Donald Curtis
Ens. George Cross....Cameron Mitchell
Ens. Tony Aiken....Jeff York
"Slug" Mahan T.M. 1c....Murray Alper
"Squarehead" Larsen, SC 2c..Harry Teabrook
"Doc"....Jack Pennick
"Benny" Lecoco, ST 3c....Alex Havier
Admiral Blackwell....Charles Trowbridge
The General....Robert Barrat
Elder Tompkins, M.M. 2c....Bruce Kellogg
Ens. Brant....Tim Murdock
"Ohio"....Louis Jean Heydt
"Dad" Knowland....Russell Simpson
Army Doctor....Vernon Steele

"They Were Expendable," dealing with the Japs' overrunning of the Philippines, primarily concerns the part played by the U. S. torpedo boats in their use against the Japs. Produced and photographed excellently, it's highly interesting if too long. Regardless of any actual or supposed reaction against war films, this one is virtually certain to go over big. It has as a boxoffice asset the fact that the book on which it's based was a bestseller. Also, it's the first pic for Robert Montgomery since he was mustered out of the Navy, with which he served as a lieutenant-commander.

Metro acknowledges the cooperation it received from the Navy, Army, Coast Guard and Office of Strategic Services in producing "Expendable."

Montgomery and his buddy, John Wayne, are naval lieutenants in command of P-T boats. Montgomery from the start has faith in the little destroyers but Wayne is slow to appreciate the value of "a piece of soap in a tub of water," as he terms them.

While the squadron of P-T tubs stationed at Manila Bay prior to Pearl Harbor were looked upon doubtfully by naval officers there, invasion by the Japs gave them their chance to show what they could do. Most of the rest of the picture vividly portrays the big job the little boats did, winding up with orders to Montgomery and Wayne, plus two P-T ensigns, to return to the U. S. to train other P-T crews for the bigger job that was ahead.

The battle scenes in which the P-T's go after Jap cruisers and supply ships were exceptionally well directed and photographed. Capt. John Ford of the U. S. Naval Reserves was aided by James C. Havens, captain of the U. S. Marine Corps Reserves, on the direction. Running time of 135 minutes could have been cut way down.

Love interest is built around Wayne and an Army nurse, played appealingly by Donna Reed. It develops at an early stage in the running but then is dropped as Wayne and Miss Reed lose each other through assignments that separate them.

Montgomery and Wayne dominate among cast members, of which there are many, most important of the support being Jack Holt, Ward Bond, Marshall Thompson, Paul Langton, Donald Curtis, Harry Tenbrook, Charles Trowbridge, Robert Barrat and Russell Simpson. *Char.*

What Next, Corporal Hargrove?

Hollywood, Nov. 14.

Metro release of George Haight production. Stars Robert Walker and Keenan Wynn; features Jean Porter, Chill Wills, Hugo Haas, Wm. "Bill Phillips. Directed by Richard Thorpe. Story and screenplay by Harry-Kurnitz; based on characters created by Marion Hargrove; camera, Henry Sharp; editor, Albert Akst; special effects, A. Arnold Gillespie and Warren Newcombe; technical advisor, Richard L. Tryon, Capt., Field Artillery, A.U.S. Tradeshown at Village Theatre, Westwood, Cal., Nov. 9, '45. Running time, 95 MINS.

Corp. Marion Hargrove....Robert Walker
Pvt. Thomas Mulvehill....Keenan Wynn
Jeanne Ouidoc....Jean Porter
Sergeant Cramp....Chill Wills
Mayor Ouidoc....Hugo Haas
Bill Burk....Wm. "Bill" Phillips
Marcel Vivin....Fred Essler
Joe Lupot....Cameron Mitchell
Curtis....Ted Lundigan
Neilson....Dick Hirbe
Ellerton....Arthur Walsh
Gilly....Maurice Marks
Captain Drake....Paul Langton
Sergeant Hill....James Davis
Lieutenant Morley....John Carlyle
Major Kingby....Walter Sande
Captain Parkson....Theodore Newton
Lieutenant Dillon....Robert Kent
Sergeant Staple....Matt Willis
Chaplain Mallowy....Richard Bailey

Central characters that sparked Metro's original "Hargrove" feature have been brought back for another round of laugh-making in "What Next, Corporal Hargrove?" This venture takes Hargrove and his buddies overseas to Europe to make a shambles of regulations and discipline for the mirth of film audiences. Business prospects are solid in all situations.

Robert Walker and Keenan Wynn are again teamed as Hargrove and the larceny-minded Mulvehill, respectively. Although the background is war, there's nothing serious about the antics, even if there is an occasional bit of pathos. Richard Thorpe's direction plays it strictly for broad chuckles and punches them home. First rate production mounting is dealt out by George Haight.

Walker and Wynn, the incorrigibles of their artillery division, run the scale from garbage detail to heroes—and back to their original positions. Walker, wearing his corporal stripes seriously, although precariously, is in charge of an artillery truck stranded in the mud of France. Boys try a shortcut to catch up with their unit. They enter a French village as the first American soldiers and become heroes of the villagers. With that adventure resolved successfully, the next mixup finds them in Paris by error, with resulting M.P. trouble. Wynn's glib tongue saves the day, temporarily, but busts up the team's friendship until Walker and the tough top sergeant combine to save Wynn from charge of desertion as the unit prepares to move on without him. Boys wind up again in the ditch to bring the film to a close on its original situation.

The Harry Kurnitz script, based on the original Marion Hargrove characters, is full of little incidents, dialog, etc., that are calculated to maintain full interest. Another production achievement is in the casting. The actors portraying soldiers look like GIs and not like actors.

Jean Porter makes a pert French mayor's daughter with a yen for Walker. Chill Wills is excellent as the top sarg. Hugo Haas, the mayor; Wm. "Bill" Phillips, Fred Essler, Cameron Mitchell, Paul Langton, John Carlyle, Walter Sande, Theodore Newton, Robert Kent, Richard Bailey and others turn in expert support.

Camera work, special effects and other technical functions are first rate. *Brog.*

Too Young to Know

Hollywood, Nov. 13.

Warner Bros. release of William Jacobs production. Stars Joan Leslie, Robert Hutton; features Dolores Moran, Harry Davenport, Rosemary DeCamp. Directed by Frederick de Cordova. Screenplay, Joe Pagano from story by Harlan Ware; camera, Carl Guthrie; music, R. Roemfield; editor, Folmer Blangsted. Tradeshown at studio Nov. 9, '45. Running time, 86 MINS.

Sally Sawyer....Joan Leslie
Ira Enright....Robert Hutton
Patsy O'Brien....Dolores Moran
Judge Boller....Harry Davenport
Mrs. Enright....Rosemary DeCamp
Mrs. Wellman....Barbara Brown
Johnny Cole....Robert Lowell
Mr. Enright....Arthur Shields
Major Bruce....Craig Stevens
Lieut. Yates....Don McGuire
Tommy....Dick Erdman
Jimmy....Robert Arthur
Lieut. Beal....Johnny Miles
Transport Pilot....Larry Thompson
Mary....Dorothy Malone
Party Guests....Angela Greene, Ramsay Ames, Betty Brodel, Pat Clark, John Compton, John Sheridan, Sid Chatton, Larry Rio

"Too Young to Know" is a warm, appealing picture with a cast of young names. Boxoffice drag, while not sock, will be good, particularly in situations outside the few top key spots. Playing is excellent, the production well-mounted, and the direction smooth, all of which adds to the credit side. Pic marks film directorial bow of Frederick de Cordova, former stage director and lately film dialog director. He garners a good first credit.

Timely background is used to display plot of the misunderstandings of young love. Story is often moving and always warm as directed by de Cordova and played by the cast, headed by Joan Leslie and Robert Hutton. Both leads fit their assignments well and troupe to advantage.

Story opens just prior to Pearl Harbor with the marriage of Miss Leslie and Hutton, both teen-agers. Adjustment difficulties make life together a series of battles before Hutton walks out in anger. Three years later Hutton, now an AAF captain fighting Japs over China, runs into a friend of his former wife, finds there has been a divorce and the birth of a son. He also learns his wife had given the child up for adoption immediately after birth. He returns home on leave, intent on finding his son. An understanding judge finally brings the couple together again and helps them regain custody of the child.

Dolores Moran shows up well as the shallow girl friend of Miss Leslie. Harry Davenport does his usual dependable work as the judge. Rosemary DeCamp and Arthur Shields, as Hutton's parents, Robert Lowell, Craig Stevens, Don McGuire and others turn in excellent support.

William Jacobs' production supervision has given good mounting for his medium budget allotment to the Jo Pagano script, adapted from Harlan Ware's Satevepost story of same title. Camera work of Carl Guthrie, special effects by Edwin DuPar and other technical functions are craftsmanly. *Brog.*

San Antonio
(COLOR; SONGS)

Warner Bros. release of Robert Buckner production. Stars Errol Flynn, Alexis Smith; features S. Z. Sakall, Victor Francen, John Litel. Directed by David Butler. Screenplay, Alan LeMay, W. R. Burnett; music, Max Steiner; color director, Natalie Kalmus; editor, Irene Morra; camera, Bert Glennon. Tradeshown N. Y., Nov. 15, '45. Running time, **110 MINS.**

Clay Hardin........................Errol Flynn
Jeanne Starr......................Alexis Smith
Sacha Bozic..........................S. Z. Sakall
Legare..........................Victor Francen
Henrietta........................Florence Bates
Charley Bell..........................John Litel
Roy Stuart...........................Paul Kelly
Capt. Morgan....................Robert Shayne
Pony Smith...........................John Alvin
Cleve Andrews......................Monte Blue
Colonel Johnson..................Robert Barrat
Ricardo Torreon.............Pedro de Cordoba
Lafe McWilliams.......................Tom Tyler
Hymie Rosas...................Chis-Pin Martin
Sojer Harris.....................Charles Stevens
Stage Coach Driver.......Poodles Hanneford
Entertainer......................Doodles Weaver
Joey Simms............................Dan White
Rebel White...........................Ray Spiker
Al Hill................................Hap Winters
Hawker...........................Harry Cording
Poker Player...................Chalky Williams
Tip Brice............................Wallis Clark
Roper..................................Bill Steele
Henchmen...Allen E. Smith, Howard Hill
Specialty Dancer...................Arnold Kent

Here's a picture that will probably make dough. It's a western in the old, old tradition. Its story has been told many a time before but the prairie schooners that tickled the vets of World War I, when those heroes were very young, never had fetching Technicolor. Nor did they have fetching Alexis Smith in gorgeous costume. For that matter, those oldies never cost a fraction of the million or so that this one must have set the Warner Bros. back. So it's fair to assume that the oldtimers will come to see it with a feeling of nostalgia, the kids will eat it up, and the in-between generations will have a refresher course in pure, unadulterated grass-root stuff for auld lang syne.

In forsaking both modern social significance and art for this excursion into days of yore, the story-tellers cooked up what might well be some genuine history about the way in which one lone, honest hombre defeated the hordes of evil gathered in San Antonio (Texas) during the middle of last century. Errol Flynn looks and acts right handsome as that hero. Paul Kelly and Victor Francen earn their villainous hisses. Miss Smith walks through the business beautifully. S. Z. "Cuddles" Sakall is funny as the luscious dame's manager, and the furniture in that saloon at San Antonio, where the final battle starts, gets smashed with breath-taking thoroughness.

Old Texans may flinch and think their shrine was desecrated when some of the shooting is taken smack into the Alamo. But the producers were riding hard and couldn't stop to think of every nuance—at least not until an hour and 50 minutes had passed on the screen. By that time it's all over—and the Warners can count the shekels on the black side of the ledger. *Cars.*

Mexicana
Hollywood, Nov. 17.

Republic release of Alfred Santell production. Stars Tito Guizar and Constance Moore; features Leo Carrillo, Howard Freeman, Steven Geray, Estelita Rodriguez, Jean Stevens. Directed by Alfred Santell. Screenplay, Frank Gill, Jr.; camera, Jack Marta; editor, Arthur Roberts; songs, Gabriel Ruiz and Ned Washington; orchestral arrangements, Joseph Dubin; musical director, Walter Scharf. Previewed in RCA projection room, Hollywood, Nov. 16, '45. Running time, **83 MINS.**

"Pepe" Villarreal.....................Tito Guizar
Alison Calvert...............Constance Moore
Esteban Guzman....................Leo Carrillo
Lupita........................Estelita Rodriguez
Beagle.........................Howard Freeman
Laredo..............................Steven Geray
Bunny................................Jean Stevens
St. Luke's Choristers
Peter Meremblum Junior Orchestra

"Mexicana" can expect okay returns. Republic has backed production numbers with lavish budget, giving the 11 tunes a dressy background. As usual with a musical, story counts for little, but there's enough chuckles sprinkled in between the songs to keep the pace fairly diverting and an audience amused.

The score contains eight original numbers and three that have been out for some years. Majority of singing falls to Tito Guizar and Constance Moore, both doing excellently. Miss Moore takes three songs and Guizar five. A mixed chorus does a travelog piece tagged "See Mexico"; the St. Luke Choristers "The Children's Song," while remaining number, a fiery piece titled "Lupita," goes to Estelita Rodriguez. Ned Washington and Gabriel Ruiz did the cleffing on seven of the originals and Walter Scharf collabbed with Washington on the eighth, "Somewhere There's a Rainbow."

Standout among the production numbers is the silhouet dance performed as a backdrop for Miss Moore's vocalling of "Heartless." Other dressup values grab an "A" rating also under Nick Castle's musical staging.

Story reveals Guizar as the Sinatra of Mexico, beset by Latin bobbysockers. He plots a phoney marriage to make his fans ease off, and picks Miss Moore, American musical comedy star who is to star with him in a Mexican musical. Gal decides he's a conceited crooner and their antagonism and misunderstandings create the plot complications. It's all trite but sufficient to carry things along.

Main comedy interest goes to Leo Carrillo and Howard Freeman, as the managers of the two stars; Jean Stevens as Miss Moore's companion, and Estelita Rodriguez, Latin singer-dancer who has a yen for Guizar. Steven Geray enacts role of a conductor to complete the small cast. *Brog.*

The Daltons Ride Again
Hollywood, Nov. 14.

Universal release of Howard Welsch production. Features Alan Curtis, Lon Chaney, Kent Taylor, Noah Beery, Jr., Martha O'Driscoll, Jess Barker, Thomas Gomez, John Litel. Directed by Ray Taylor. Screenplay by Roy Cahnslor and Paul Ganglin; added dialog by Henry Blankfort; camera, Charles Van Enger; editor, Paul Landres. Previewed at Univeral City, Cal., Nov. 13, '45. Running time, 72 MINS.

Emmett Dalton........................Alan Curtis
Bob Dalton...........................Kent Taylor
Grat Dalton.........................Lon Chaney
Ben Dalton......................Noah Beery, Jr.
Mary..........................Martha O'Driscoll
Jeff....................................Jess Barker
McKenna........................Thomas Gomez
Graham..........................Milburn Stone
Bohannon...............................John Litel
Wilkins...............................Walter Sande
Sheriff.........................Douglas Dumbrille
Mrs. Walters....................Virginia Brissac

Action-packed outdoor melodrama has plenty to offer fans who like film entertainment rough and raw with a western flavor. Pic has enough production values and robust elements to give it a good rating for any but the de luxe situations, and should play well all down the line. Action emphasis and neat results make up for lack of boxoffice weight among the cast names, although all are familiars.

Footage contains spectacular chases and gunfight. Plot makes no attempt to glorify the criminal exploits of the Dalton brothers, but does offer an explanation for the cause of the outside-the-law adventures with which the film is concerned.

There's a romance angle carefully handled between Martha O'Driscoll, daughter of a western publisher, and Emmett Dalton, played by Alan Curtis. She and Curtis meet while the boys are preparing to renounce a life of crime and make their future way in the Argentine. Standard western formula enters when boys stop over to aid an old friend, about to be the victim of a land-grab plot. The railroad's coming through the valley and a land company, with advance notice, is foreclosing on all property. Company makes it difficult for ranchers to meet their notes and those that can are rubbed out. The Daltons save the widow of their friend, hide out and are accused of assorted depredations which are the work of the land company gang. Curtis, with Miss O'Driscoll's promise to wait, decides to give himself up and get square with the law. Additional crimes with which he and his brothers are accused put him on the spot but they dig up evidence against the other crooks and Curtis is ready to accept whatever the law hands out so his romance can have smooth sailing.

Curtis, Lon Chaney, Kent Taylor and Noah Beery, Jr., make a sturdy foursome as the brothers. Miss O'Driscoll also appears to advantage. Others helping along include Jess Barker, Thomas Gomez, as the drunkard who's really the brains of the land-grab; John Litel, Milburn Stone, Walter Sande, Douglass Dumbrille and Virginia Brissac.

Ray Taylor's direction gears every element for forthright action, and Howard Welsch's production backs it with good values. Camera work by Charles Van Enger and editing are equally good. *Brog.*

The Last Chance
(SWISS-MADE)

Metro International release of L. Wechsler (Praesens) production. Stars E.G. Morrison, John Hoy, Ray Reagan; features Luisa Rossi, Romano Calo, Therese Giehse. Directed by Leopold Lindtberg. Screenplay, Richard Schweitzer; camera, Emil Berna; editor, Herman Haller; score, Robert Blum; English titles, Herman Weinberg. Tradeshown in N.Y., NOv. 14, '45. Running time, 105 MINS.

Major Telford......................E.G. Morrison
Liet. Halliday..........................John Hoy
Sergt. Braddock......................Ray Reagan
Tonina...............................Luisa Rossi
An Innkeeper....................Odeardo Mosini
A Carrier........................Giuseppe Gaieati
Priest...............................Romano Calo
Muzio..................................Tino Erler
Swiss Lieutenant..................Leopold Biberti
Military Doctor....................Sigfrit Steiner
Frontier Guard......................Emil Gerber
Frau Wittels......................Therese Giehse
Bernard, her son.................Robert Schwarz
Madame Monnier...............Germaine Tournier
Hillel Sokolowski.................M. Sakhnowsky
Chanele, his niece..............Berthe Sakhnowski
The Professor........................Jean Martin
The Professor.....................Rudolf Kampf
A Dutchman..........................Jean Martin
A Dutchwoman...................Gertrudien Cate
A Yugoslav Worker...............Carlo Romatko

The Swiss have turned out another fine picture in "The Last Chance." Second in the list of Swiss-made films released in this country ("Marie-Louise," the first, also via L. Wechsler, and reviewed last week), it demonstrates that the knack of excellent picture-making isn't confined to Hollywood. Lack of marquee names, plus the foreign dialog, will prove a drawback in most runs but word-of-mouth should help considerably at the boxoffice.

Purchased by Metro International, Metro execs thought "Chance" so good that M-G is giving it nationwide distribution by including it in one of the regular blocks. Film has all the elements of fine acting, production and direction demonstrated by producer L. Wechsberg in "Louise," and Metro's hopes for its value for all houses should pay off.

Story deals with a group of central European refugees who are led from Italy to safety in Switzerland by three escaped Allied prisoners. Latter, one American and two Britishers, are actual Allied fliers who were shot down over Switzerland during the war and interned, acting in the film to help pass their time. Dialog, although predominantly English, also includes German, French, Yiddish, Serbian and Italian, with English titles adequate for American audiences.

Although far from a documentary, the film sets out to prove that the war-ravaged earth is really one world in which all people can live peacefully, and does so in a most convincing, albeit entertaining, fashion. Refugees, no two of whom are from the same country, are thrown together by their common danger and, although complete strangers who don't even speak the same language, work in harmony toward their goal of haven. Good illustration: one of the Allied prisoners, an American sergeant, starts singing in English an oldtime roundelay. Faces of the other refugees light up and each joins in on a chorus, singing in his own language.

Action gets off to a fast start as the American and a British officer escape from an enemy train carrying prisoners from Italy to Germany. They find refuge with an Italian priest who has been harboring another British officer and the refugee. The Italian guide, who was to lead the refugees across the mountains into Switzerland, is killed when the Germans attack the village and the priest, before he is captured and executed, talks the prisoners into looking after the civilians, who include a German widow and her young son, an old Jewish tailor and his orphaned niece, and two Frenchwomen.

Realizing they cannot leave the civilians behind, even though it means added danger for them in getting to Switzerland, the prisoners begin the long trek across the Alps. Advancing through the mountain snows, they succeed in eluding the pursuing German patrol and finally reach Switzerland in a rousing climax to the picture.

Predominantly amateur cast is surprisingly good, with John Hoy, one of the British fliers, particularly outstanding. M. Sakhnowsky, the old Jewish tailor; Giuseppe Galeati, the Italian priest, and Therese Giehse, the German hausfrau, are all actual refugees and bring to their roles all the tragedy brought into their lives by their Nazi persecutors. Ray Reagan, the American sergeant who has just returned to his home in Laurel Springs, Md., is no Hollywood find, however.

Director Leopold Lindtberg keeps the pace rapid and Robert Blum's score is another factor adding to the general quality of the film.

Les Caves Du Majestic
("Majestic Hotel Cellars")
(FRENCH-MADE)
Paris, Nov. 6.

Domaines (Public Property Office) release of Continental production. Stars Albert Prejean; features Suzy Prim, Jacques Baumer, Denise Grey, Jean Marchat, Gabriello, Gina Manes, Florelle, Charpin. Directed by Richard Pottier. From a novel by Georges Simenon; screenplay by Charles Spaak. Music by Sylviano. At Normandie, Paris. Running time, **95 MINS.**

Commissaire Maigret..........Albert Prejean
Murdered Woman..................Suzy Prim
Hotel Cook...................Jacques Baumer
Secretary...........................Denise Grey
Dead Woman's Husband......Jean Marchat
Detective...............................Gabriello
Hotel Guest................................Florelle
Judge.......................................Charpin

No screen mention is made of either producer or distrib, due to the picture having been made under German auspices during occupation and having been since seized by

Public Property authorities. If despite those conditions an export visa can be obtained, it might be worth trying in other territories. Charles Spaak has written a fair screenplay from the novel by Simenon, w.k. here as a detective story author. Production has not been stinted, cast is good and locally it is a sure click.

Whodunit shows the police hesitating to trace the murder of a woman to her husband or to a cook in the hotel where they were staying, finally nabbing an outsider. The murder is shown flashback fashion just before the end.

Albert Prejean leads the hunt as Inspector Maigret, a permanent character in Simenon's novels. His brainwork gets comedy relief by Gabriello, who docs his assistant and whose large bulk helps to draw laughs. Suzy Prim appears only in the first few sequences, except for the flashback at the end. Jean Marchat is the husband suspected on account of an affair with his secretary. Denise Grey. Jacques Baumer, as the cook wrongly accused, gives an excellent performance, with Florelle staging a comeback on the screen. Charpin gets laughs as the judge.

Direction is good, with an especially good scene when Prejean stages a dinner party, inviting both suspects to decide who is guilty and should be adjudged the father of the dead woman's child.

Tempo is reasonably fast and technique is good. *Maxi.*

Border Badmen

PRC release of Sigmund Neufield production. Stars Buster Crabbe; features Al (Fuzzy) St. John. Directed by Sam Newfield. Screenplay, George Milton; camera, Jack Greenhalgh; music, Frank Sanucci; editor, Holbrook N. Todd. At New York, N.Y., week Nov. 15, '45, dual. Running time, 58 MINS.

Billy Carson	Buster Crabbe
Fuzzy Jones	Al "Fuzzy" St. John
Helen	Lorraine Miller
Merritt	Charles King
Deputy Spencer	Ralph Bennett
Gillan	Archie Hall
Evans	Budd Buster
Roxie	Marlyn Gladstone
Mrs. Bentley	Marin Sais

Most that can be said about "Border Badmen" is that it's just another low-budgeted Buster Crabbe western, lacking originality. Kids will probably go for the usual type of western chases and the too-obvious humor inserted by Al St. John, Crabbe's perennial stooge in this series of horse operas, meaning the film should fill the bill on the family dualers.

Uninspired plot has St. John as a distant relative of a big silver magnate who has just died. He and Crabbe go to claim his share of the inheritance, only to find that a group of heavies in the town, including the mayor and deputy sheriff, are killing off all the legal heirs as they turn up in order to fake a claim to the several million-dollar legacy for themselves. Action then deteriorates into the usual Western sequences.

Pretty girl, the old man's closest relative, is kidnapped by the thugs and released by Crabbe and St. John after a tussle in a cabin hideout. Pair then return to the town and succeed in rounding up the heavies after more free-for-alls. Flat climax has the will being read, with each heir getting a substantial sum until the attorney reaches the last name, that of St. John, who, as a 32d cousin, finds he has inherited a dollar bill and a sheaf of debts the old man forgot to pay before he kicked off.

Acting in the film is so-so, with Crabbe and St. John carrying the bulk of the plot in their usual routine manner. Director Sam Newfield, with little to work with in the way of a script, keeps the pace fairly rapid.

Dangerous Intruder

PRC release of Martin Mooney production. Stars Charles Arnt, Veda Ann Borg; features Richard Powers, Fay Helm. Directed by Vernon Keays. Screenplay, Martin M. Goldsmith from original by Philip Macdonald and F. Ruth Howard; camera, James Brown; editor, Carl Pierson; music, Karl Hajos. At New York theatre, N.Y., week of Nov. 15, '45, dual. Running time, 58 MINS.

Max Ducane	Charles Arnt
Jenny	Veda Ann Borg
Curtis	Richard Powers
Millicent	Fay Helm
Foster	John Rogers
Jackie	JoAnn Marlowe
Mrs. Swenson	Helena P. Evans
Freckles	Roberta Smith
Holt	George Sorel
Dr. Bascom	Forest Taylor
Chauffeur	Eddie Rocco

"Dangerous Intruder," until the last reel, has all the necessary ingredients of suspense, fast action and good acting to make it an above-average thriller but then falls flat because of a routine denouement. Modestly budgeted, picture emerges as a fair entry.

Plot concerns a stranded showgirl (Veda Ann Borg), who is convalescing in the home of a wealthy art fancier (Charles Arnt), after having been struck by his car while hitching a ride back to New York. She is frightened during the night by piercing screams but Arnt's little stepdaughter (Jo Ann Marlowe) explains that it's her ill mother. Miss Borg notices that Arnt shows an almost insane obsession about his ancient art masterpieces and realizes that all is not well when she discovers that the family got its wealth only recently through inheritance from a spinster aunt.

Arnt overplays the villain role with too much mugging. Miss Borg (a looker) and the supporting cast do creditably, with the precocious Miss Marlowe especially good. Director Vernon Keays achieves suspense at the start but is stymied by the final letdown.

Shadow of Terror

Prc release of jack Grant Production. Stars Richard Fraser, Grace Gillern; features Cy Kendall, Emmett Lynn. Directed by Lew Landers. Screenplay, Arthur St. Claire from original by Sheldon Leonard. At New York theatre, N.Y., dual, week of Nov. 9, '45. Running time, 64 MINS.

Jim	Richard Fraser
Joan	Grace Gillern
Maxwell	Cy Kendall
Elmer	Emmett Lynn
McKenzie	Kenneth McDonald
Walters	Eddie Acuff
Sheriff	Sam Flint

PRC's venture into the atomic bomb film cycle, "Shadow of Terror," is further proof that this company is gradually rising out of the minor leagues. While lack of marquee-names still keeps this picture in the double-bill category, it is a well-paced mystery meller that should get favorable boxoffice reactions.

Story gets off to a fast start as the hero is slugged in his train compartment and thrown off the moving train into the desert after heavies make off with his papers. Found unconscious by the gal, the conk on his noggin has brought about amnesia. Recuperating at the gal's ranch, more assaults, kidnapings, etc., disclose the young scientist has the secret of atomic energy. The gang boss wants to capitalize on this before the scientist turns it over to the Government. More slugging and he regains his memory, he and the gal escape and, after a desert chase, are saved by the sheriff.

Richard Fraser, newcomer with a nice personality, makes a fairly effective lead, and Grace Gillern shows promise as the ingenue. Production and direction, while not of top calibre, are adequate.

Miniature Reviews

"Bells of St. Mary's" (RKO-Rainbow). Boff boxoffice, with Bing Crosby and Ingrid Bergman.

"A Walk in the Sun" (20th) (one song). Dana Andrews is lone name in GI war yarn.

"Vacation from Marriage" (M-G). Expert English-made comedy drama with excellent prospects for American market.

"Getting Gertie's Garter" (UA). Mild farce that shapes okay for double-bill situations.

"A Game of Death" (RKO). A chillerdiller for horror film fans, geared for double bills.

"The Lost Trail" (Mono). Johnny Mack Brown, Raymond Hatton in a so-so western.

"The Wicked Lady" (Eagle-Lion). Margaret Lockwood, James Mason, Patricia Roc in vivid English picture; costume meller not rated strong enough for American first-runs.

"Sensation Hunters" (Mono). Weak melodrama.

"Brief Encounter" (Eagle-Lion). Noel Coward playlet and production effort make this a top-bracket British vehicle; a likely U. S. entry.

The Bells of St. Mary's
(SONGS)

Hollywood, Nov. 24.

RKO release of Rainbow Productions, produced and directed by Leo McCarey. Stars Bing Crosby, Ingrid Bergman; features Henry Travers, William Gargan, Ruth Donnelly, Joan Carroll, Martha Sleeper, Rhys Williams, Dickie Tyler, Una O'Connor. Screenplay, Dudley Nichols from story by McCarey; camera, George Barnes, Vernon L. Walker; editor, Harry Marker; score, Robert Emmett Dolan; songs, Douglas Furber-A. Emmett Adams, John Burke-James Van Heusen, Grant Clarke-George W. Meyer. Tradeshown Los Angeles, Nov. 20, '45. Running time, 126 MINS.

Father O'Malley	Bing Crosby
Sister Benedict	Ingrid Bergman
Bogardus	Henry Travers
Patsy's Father	William Gargan
Sister Michael	Ruth Donnelly
Patsy	Joan Carroll
Patsy's Mother	Martha Sleeper
Dr. McKay	Rhys Williams
Eddie	Dickie Tyler
Mrs. Breen	Una O'Connor

"The Bells of St. Mary's" is boxoffice for all situations. Warmly sentimental, it has a simple story that hits home, is leavened with many laughs and, on all counts, bears comparison with "Going My Way," last season's b.o. winner. It has the name value of Bing Crosby and Ingrid Bergman to assure a fast start at the b.o. and entertainment plus to keep the ticket sales strong all down the line. Leo McCarey, who demonstrated his ability to combine wholesome sentiment into a potent attraction with "Going My Way," duplicates that ability as producer-director on this one.

Bing Crosby's Father O'Malley is the same priest character seen in "Way," and "Bells" tells of his new assignment as parish priest at the parochial school, St. Mary's. Plot opens with a chuckle as he's warned that he will be surrounded with nuns and moves swiftly through laughs and tears to the completion of his assignment. Story tells of how he aids the nuns' prayers for a new school building with a more practical application of guidance; steers a young girl through an unhappy domestic situation, and brings the parents together again. It's all done with the natural ease that is Crosby's trademark.

Ingrid Bergman again demonstrates her versatility as the sister in charge of the parochial school. Her clashes with Crosby—all good-mannered—over proper methods of educating children and authority, her venture into athletics, and coaching of a youngster to return a good left hook instead of the other cheek, are delightful moments that will have an audience alternately laughing and sniffling.

Dudley Nichols scripted from the McCarey story, and plot tells of the nuns' efforts, through prayer, to convert a crabby business man into a benefactor. He has erected a modern building next to the school and wants to take over the parochial property for a parking lot for his employees. The nuns believe that he intends to give them his building for use as a school. Neat air of suspense is injected around this premise as neither knows what the other is about. Father O'Malley deftly switches the situation to come out the perfect answer for the prayers.

Picture is packed with many simple scenes that tug at the heart and loosen the tears as directed by McCarey and played by the outstanding cast. The impromptu Christmas play staged by a group of children is socko for appeal. Crosby's singing of "Adeste Fidelis," the title song, and "O Sanctissima" with a children's choir, and his solo work on "Aren't You Glad You're You" and "In the Land of Beginning Again" is another bright spot. William Gargan and Martha Sleeper are standouts in their brief scenes as the separated parents of Joan Carroll.

Henry Travers, the grumpy millionaire; Ruth Donnelly, a nun; Rhys Williams, a doctor; Dickie Tyler, who learns the art of fisticuffs from Miss Bergman, and Una O'Connor, his mother, are among the others in the cast who contribute to the genuineness of the picture.

George Barnes' camera work is outstanding, as is Robert Emmett Dolan's music score. Other technical functions are on the same high level in helping to measure this one to top boxoffice standard. *Brog.*

A Walk in the Sun

20th-Fox release of Lewis Milestone production, directed by Milestone. Stars Dana Andrews; features Richard Conte, George Tyne, John Ireland, Lloyd Bridges, Sterling Holloway, Norman Lloyd, Herbert Rudley, Richard Benedict. Screenplay, Robert Rossen, from novel by Harry Brown; songs, Millard Lampbell and Earl Robinson; score, Fredric Efrem Rich; editor, Duncan Mansfield; camera, Russell Harlen. Previewed in N. Y., Nov. 23, '45. Running time, 117 MINS.

Sgt. Tyne	Dana Andrews
Rivera	Richard Conte
McWilliams	Sterling Holloway
Friedman	George Tyne
Windy	John Ireland
Porter	Herbert Rudley
Tranella	Richard Benedict
Archimbeau	Norman Lloyd
Sgt. Ward	Lloyd Bridges
Carraway	Huntz Hall
Hoskins	James Cardwell
Rankin	Chris Drake
Tinker	George Offerman, Jr.
Trasker	Danny Desmond
Cousins	Victor Cutler
Judson	Steve Brodie
Johnson	Al Hammer
Sgt. Halverson	Matt Willis
Lt. Rand	Robert Lowell
Giorgio	Anthony Dante

Ex-GI Harry Brown has achieved somewhat of a reputation during the past war years as a writer to be reckoned with, as his books, "Pfc. Artie Greengroin" and "A Walk in the Sun," have indicated. Add to that his first play, "A Sound of Hunting," which last week received some commendable notices when it opened on Broadway. But as a film, "Walk" is not so sunny.

"Walk," like his other works, is distinguished for some excellent, earthy GI dialog, but the author has failed to achieve a proper fusing of dialog and situation. Too frequently he is given to spieling the colorful talk of the enlisted man, and thus allows his yarn to flounder. He is content, seemingly, to allow GI talk to encompass all else. Coupled with the fact that this pic has little feminine interest—there isn't a gal in the film

—and the fact that it's evading an escapism from war themes that audiences in these times are likely to seek, boxoffice chances of "Walk" are limited. Dana Andrews is the film's only name.

Film concerns an operation by a platoon of American soldiers after they hit the beach at Salerno. They're detailed to wipe out a farmhouse and its Nazi occupants. That's the major element of the story, such as it is, and the rest of the pic is mostly concerned with reactions of the GI's to the conditions under which they're fighting, their thoughts, and so forth.

Almost two hours of talk is a lot of talk. While much of it cannot be questioned from the standpoint of realism, the pic, because of the excessive dialog, occasionally becomes tiresome. Stories with "colorful" gab of the enlisted man have long since become part of the scenarist's schedule of vital statistics.

Andrews gives one of his invariably forthright performances as a sergeant, and the rest of the impressive cast know their way around a script. And that holds particularly true of Richard Conte, who, perhaps, has the best lines.

Lewis Milestone has both produced and directed well. Millard Lampell and Earl Robinson have written a war-themed, catchy ballad that punctuates the unspooling at intervals, via an off-screen baritone voice.

The author is certainly one still to be heard from at his best. Right now his formula of well-written characters and dialog is at the expense of his story. And the play's still the thing. *Kahn.*

Vacation From Marriage

(BRITISH-MADE)

Hollywood, Nov. 24.

Metro release of Alexander Korda production (M-G-M-London Films)). Stars Robert Donat; features Deborah Kerr, Glynis Johns, Ann Todd, Roland Culver. Produced and directed by Alexander Korda. Screenplay, Clemence Dane and Anthony Pelissier; camera, George Perinal, Percy Day; editor, E. B. Jarvis; score, Clifton Parker. Tradeshown Nov. 20, '45. Running time, **92 MINS.**

Robert Wilson..................Robert Donat
Catherine Wilson..............Deborah Kerr
Dizzy Clayton..................Glynis Johns
Elena..........................Ann Todd
Richard........................Roland Culver
Mrs. Hemmings..................Elliot Mason
Mr. Staines....................Eliot Makeham
Mr. Hargrove...................Brefni O'Rorke
Chemist........................Ivor Barnard
Petty Officer..................Henry Longhurst
Webster........................Billy Shine
Essex..........................Billy Thatcher
Gordon.........................Brian Weske
Irene..........................Rosamund Taylor
Bill...........................Harry Ross
Charlie........................Edward Rigby
Minnie.........................Muriel George
A.R.P. Warden..................Vincent Holman
Commander......................Allan Jeayes
Stripey........................Leslie Dwyer
Scotty.........................Caven Watson
Jeannie........................Jeanne Carre
Meg............................Molly Munks

"Vacation From Marriage" is first of the Metro-London Films productions slated for release in this country. It's a good example of film entertainment using best points of Hollywood and British picture-making and should find a ready spot in the U. S. market. Produced and directed in London by Sir Alexander Korda, film's excellent cast is headed by Robert Donat to aid the marquee values, and it points its entertainment for general appeal in all situations.

The plot has a war background but deals less with fighting than it does with the change wrought in a rather stuffy British couple after three years of wartime living. Donat is a milquetoast English clerk whose young dreams of travel and adventure have been smothered under columns of figures. Deborah Kerr is his femme counterpart. Donat becomes a member of His Majesty's navy, and his wife, seeking escape from her humdrum existence, becomes a Wren. They are separated for three years and during that period gradually change into human beings, eager for life. After sea-fighting, shipwreck and heroism, Donat returns to London to meet his wife. Neither can see a life together with the other, not realizing that each has changed for the better. In these scenes, as each journeys towards London and mentally strengthens himself to ask for a divorce at the first meeting, Korda has put plenty of warmth in the comedy and the leads play it to the hilt.

Script skillfully blends comedy and drama with no undue emphasis on either, and Korda keeps the pace considerably faster than usually found in English films. Donat's character delineation is a smoothly turned job that creates plenty of interest. Outstanding also is Deborah Kerr as his mild wife who becomes a pinup girl—English version. Glynis Johns makes her role of the Wren friend to the dowdy wife a joy, and Ann Todd has an outstanding sequence as the nurse who advises Donat. Also good is Roland Culver, a sailor friend.

Production is never seemingly lavish and lends a natural background for the screenplay by Clemence Dane and Anthony Pelissier. Georges Perinal's photography, the score and editing are all of high technical order. *Brog.*

Getting Gertie's Garter

Hollywood, Nov. 23.

United Artists release of Edward Small production. Stars Dennis O'Keefe, Marie McDonald; features Barry Sullivan, Binnie Barnes, J. Carrol Naish, Sheila Ryan, Jerome Cowan, Vera Marshe. Directed by Allan Dwan. Adaptation and screenplay by Dwan and Karen De Wolf from play by Wilson Collison and Avery Hopwood; added dialog, Joe Bigelow; camera, Charles Lawton, Jr.; editors, Walter Hannemann and Truman K. Wood. Previewed Nov. 21, '45. Running time, **73 MINS.**

Ken............................Dennis O'Keefe
Gertie.........................Marie McDonald
Ted............................Barry Sullivan
Barbara........................Binnie Barnes
Patty..........................Sheila Ryan
Charles (butler)...............J. Carrol Naish
Billy..........................Jerome Cowan
Anna (maid)....................Vera Marshe
Clancy.........................Donald T. Beddoe
Winters........................Frank Fenton
Dr. Clark......................Richard Le Grand

Broad farce with laughs for general audiences. This remake of the old stage farce of same title has been given considerable production polish by Edward Small and expert casting to make it fit well for the double bill situations.

Plot is no more plausible on the screen than it was on the stage but bedroom touches and sheer frenzy of the slapstick comedy are certain for chuckles. Allan Dwan's direction keeps it moving fast and comedy ability of Dennis O'Keefe as the absent-minded scientist is a distinct aid.

O'Keefe is seen as the now-married scientist seeking to recover a jeweled garter which he had given a pre-marriage sweetie. The ex-love, about to marry O'Keefe's best friend, decides she should keep the garter—just in case—and her concealment, plus the scientist's frenzied efforts to recover, without his wife finding out, keeps the young man in continual hot water. Comedy is emphasized by the many compromising situations the search leads to and the misunderstandings that develop.

Marie McDonald matches O'Keefe in the comedy as Gertie. Her work indicates plenty of promise. Sheila Ryan also is seen to advantage as the wife who misunderstands her husband's antics. Barry Sullivan shows well well as the fiance. Other cast stalwarts include Jerome Cowan, Binnie Barnes, J. Carrol Naish and Vera Marshe.

Edward Small's production guidance has shaped the picture expertly for the market, giving it a topnotch dressing. Camera work, sets, editing, etc., are first rate. *Brog.*

Appointment in Tokyo

"Appointment In Tokyo," story of the entire Pacific campaign from MacArthur's flight from Bataan to the surrender ceremonies in Tokyo Bay is as tense and exciting a documentary as this reviewer has witnessed. A graphic portrayal of the glorious fight back, it strikes out with dramatic suddenness with no preliminary warmup, to keep one frozen in one's seat for 54 minutes of awe-inspiring warfare on film.

Naval blasting, jungle attack, street fighting, plane strafing, the bloody landing on Leyte, the malicious burning of Manila, the cruel murder of civilians—all is vivid panorama from Army film, map diagrams, captured Jap newsreels and brilliant screen montage. And the effect is stunning. A surging musical score heightens the effect.

Film is so exciting, so punching, so like the thriller of Hollywood, but with all the grim reality added, that one forgets to marvel at the magnificent filming, correlating and editing job that the Army Pictorial Service of the Signal Corps, the Army Air Forces and the Navy, have done. There are absolutely unforgettable moments—the faces of the various soldiers before the Philippine landing; planes struck at sea; dropping bombs filmed from the plane carrying them; the Leyte beachhead.

There are also one or two false moments, such as a sentimental flashback before a battle, or the final two minutes when an unseen choir hymns that the fight must go on. Such moments aren't needed in a story that speaks so eloquently for itself. Perhaps exception might be taken to the frequent shots of MacArthur—but this was MacArthur's battle, with his name as the symbol. These faults are minor in a thrilling documentary that mirrors history in the making.

The hundreds of Signal Corps combat cameramen, who did leonine work in this filming, rate warmest admiration. Praise is due, too, to the War Dept. for presenting, and Warners for distributing. *Bron.*

A Game of Death

RKO release of Herbert Schlom production. Features John Loder, Audrey Long, Edgar Barrier, Russell Wade. Directed by Robert Wise. Screenplay, Norman Houston from story by Richard Connell; music, Paul Sawtell; editor, J. R. Whittredge; camera, J. Roy Hunt. At Rialto, N. Y., week Nov. 23, '45. Running time, **72 MINS.**

Rainsford......................John Loder
Ellen..........................Audrey Long
Kreiger........................Edgar Barrier
Robert.........................Russell Wade
Whitney........................Russell Hicks
Captain........................Jason Robards
Pleshke........................Gene Stutenroth
Carib..........................Noble Johnson
Helmsman.......................Robert Clarke

"A Game of Death" is a remake of "The Most Dangerous Game," filmed by RKO in 1932 from Richard Connell's short story of same title and basic format of screenplay. Despite implausibility of yarn, it has expert direction and some good acting to make it a juicy horror cantata that should do moderately well.

Edgar Barrier portrays a big game hunter who becomes surfeited by his expertness in bringing down beasts of the jungle and has a maniacal desire to hunt humans instead. He appropriates an island, where he and two servants are the sole inhabitants, and then plots shipwrecks to bring his human quarry to the island. After putting them up at the menage for several days, he scares them into the rushes, then embarks on a manhunt to polish them off with his bow and arrow. John Loder, hunter-novelist, is washed in from a wreck and soon penetrates the madman's scheme. Audrey Long and Russell Wade, refugees from previous wreck, are also guests, with the latter selected as next victim of the manhunt. Loder is unable to frustrate Wade's killing but does manage to outwit the maniac and rescue Miss Long.

Loder and Barrier carry the picture with excellent portrayals of implausible roles. Miss Long is okay as the harassed gal, and Wade turns in a neat performance as her brother. Rest are adequate in lesser roles. Robert Wise has directed in a tempo that sustains suspense and accentuates the chillerdiller motif. *Edba.*

The Lost Trail

Monogram release of Charles J. Bigelow production. Stars Johnny Mack Brown; features Raymond Hatton, Jennifer Holt. Directed by Lambert Hillyer. Original screenplay, Jess Bowers; camera, Marcel LePicard; editor, Danny Milner. At New York, N. Y., dual, week Nov. 21, '45. Running time, **53 MINS.**

Nevada.........................Johnny Mack Brown
Sandy..........................Raymond Hatton
Jane Burns.....................Jennifer Holt
Ned Turner.....................Riley Hill
John Corbett...................Kenneth MacDonald
Hall...........................Lynton Brent
Bailey.........................John Ince
Dr. Brown......................John Bridges
Bill...........................Eddie Parker
Joe............................Frank McCarroll
Ed.............................Dick Dickinson
Zeke...........................Milburn Moranti
Janes..........................Frank Larue
Mason..........................Steve Clark

A so-so western, "The Lost Trail" features the usual amount of gunplay, chases through the sagebrush, etc. With Johnny Mack Brown and Raymond Hatton for the marquee, picture should fill the bill in the usual slot.

Wells-Fargo express franchise, subject of innumerable westerns in the past, is revived in this one. Action gets off to a fast start in the first sequence as Brown stops a runaway express coach and finds that a gang of outlaws have killed the driver, wounded his aide and made off with the gold shipment. Driving the stagecoach back to town, Brown discovers the line is operated by a young girl, who is having trouble keeping the franchise because of the many holdups.

Hatton then enters the scene as a comic character who is appointed sheriff by the town's bigshot, in reality leader of the outlaw gang, who wants to secure the Wells-Fargo franchise for himself. Denouement has Brown and Hatton revealed as U.S. marshals who round up the gang in a good shooting fray and unmask the leader. With the outlaws subdued, the miners return their shipping contracts to the girl and all ends well.

Brown has developed a noticeable paunch since his all-American football days at the U. of Alabama but still carries off his role as a western hero in convincing fashion. Hatton does well as Brown's foil and Jennifer Holt, daughter of Jack, also shows up to advantage. Lambert Hillyer achieves the necessary rapid-fire pace in direction.

The Wicked Lady

(BRITISH-MADE)

London, Nov. 16.

Eagle-Lion Distributors release of Gainsborough production. Stars Margaret Lockwood, James Mason, Patricia Roc. Directed by Leslie Arliss. Screenplay by Leslie Arliss from novel, "The Wicked Lady Skelton," by Magdalen King-Hall; additional dialog by Gordon Glennon, Aimee Stuart. At Studio One, London, Nov. 15, '45. Running time, **103 MINS.**

Barbara Worth..................Margaret Lockwood
Captain Jackson................James Mason
Caroline.......................Patricia Roc
Sir Ralph Skelton..............Griffith Jones
Henrietta Kingsclere...........Enid Stamp-Taylor

Kit Lockaby	Michael Rennie
Hogarth	Felix Aylmer
Martin Worth	David Horne
Cousin Agatha	Martita Hunt
Lord Kingsclere	Francis Lister
Aunt Doll	Amy Dalby
Aunt Moll	Beatrice Varley
Mistress Betsy	Helen Goss

Producers claim that this story is "set in the days of Charles II." Sets, costumes and a comely bunch of femmes bear out the claim. But the period atmosphere is not convincing.

No question about Gainsborough having spent a lot of coin on this one. Also the cast is unusually strong on names that are known in the U.S. as well as here.

James Mason as a Robin Hood type highwayman manages to suggest the swaggering love-'em-and-leave-'em rascal of an earlier day. He scores in spite of the weak script. The other performance lending credibility to the period comes from Felix Aylmer as an old retainer who tumbles to the villainy of Margaret Lockwood in the title role, and dies at her fair hands.

"The Wicked Lady" as a title is a characteristic English understatement. The way Miss Lockwood shoots, poisons and betrays all who get in her way make that taboo name a modest one. Between murders she steals the fiance of her best girl friend, and then grabs the bridal chamber for herself.

Patricia Roc, the jilted bride, is co-starred because of her work in "Johnny Frenchman." With Griffith Jones, Enid-Stamp-Taylor and England's newest femme star, Michael Rennie, also in the distinguished cast, "The Wicked Lady" will do big business on this side. Its chances in first-run houses in America appear limited.

In a way, "The Wicked Lady" serves a useful purpose. For years London critics have lambasted Hollywood for picturizing England as forever fog-bound, for staging fox hunting in mid-summer, or for showing the Grand National run against a background of waving palm trees. Now a British outfit does a film which distorts 17th century England no less grotesquely.

One can't overlook those buxom beauties who figure in this film. That is unless the U. S. censors use the shears. *Talb.*

Sensation Hunters

(SONGS)

Monogram release of Joseph Kaufman production. Stars Robert Lowery, Doris Merrick; features Eddie Quinlan, Constance Worth, Isabell Jewell. Directed by Christy Cabanne. Screenplay, Dennis Cooper from original story by John Faxon; camera, Ira Morgan; editor, Martin Cohn; songs, Jack Kenney and Lewis Bellin; dances, Phyllis Avery. At New York, N.Y., dual, week Nov. 21, '45. Running time, 62 MINS.

Danny Burke	Robert Lowery
Julie Rodgers	Doris Merrick
Ray Lawson	Eddie Quillan
Irene	Constance Worth
Mae	Isabel Jewell
Helen	Wanda McKay
New Davis	Nestor Paiva
Mark Rogers	Byron Folger
Agent	Vince Barnett
Edna Rodgers	Minerva Urecal

A picture that makes much ado about practically nothing, "Sensation Hunters" is a weakie. Film got laughs in the wrong places from the action fans at the house.

Story concerns a pretty young factory-worker who falls in love with a handsome heel. Thrown out of her home by irate papa when she is innocently caught in a gambling raid, the gal goes to the nightclub where the heel hangs out and talks her way into a chorus job. Rest of plot deals with her rapid degeneration until, when her boyfriend finally throws her over for her best friend, she pulls a gun on him and they are both killed in the subsequent struggle.

Robert Lowery and Doris Merrick try hard with their chores but never had a chance; ditto Eddie Quillan and Isabel Jewell. Faltering direction adds nothing to the trite yarn.

Brief Encounter

(BRITISH-MADE)

London, Nov. 14.

Eagle-Lion release of Noel Coward-Cineguild production. Stars Celia Johnson, Trevor Howard. Directed by David Lean. Adapted by Noel Coward from his playlet, "Tonight at 8:30." Camera, Robert Krasker, B. Francke. At Studio One, London, Nov. 13, '45. Running time, 85 MINS.

Laura Jesson	Celia Johnson
Alec Harvey	Trevor Howard
Albert Godby	Stanley Holloway
Myrtle Bagot	Joyce Carey
Fred Jesson	Cyril Raymond
Dolly Messiter	Everley Gregg
Beryl Walters	Margaret Barton
Stephen Lynn	Valentine Dyall
Mary Norton	Marjorie Mars
Stanley	Dennis Harkin

Even Brooklyn may be willing to overlook Noel Coward rather than miss this intelligent, gripping treatment of the eternal triangle. Based on his play of the same name, "Brief Encounter" does more for Noel Coward's reputation as a skilled film producer than "In Which We Serve." His use of express trains thundering through a village station coupled with frantic, last-minute dashes for local trains is only one of the clever touches masking the inherent static quality of the drama. Coward name and strong story spells nice U. S. chances.

Celia Johnson as the small-town mother whose brief encounter with a doctor, encumbered with a wife and kids, plunges her into a love affair from which she struggles vainly to escape, is terrific. Co-starred with her, Trevor Howard, as the doctor, gives a performance calculated to win the sympathy of femmes of all ages. As for the dumb husband whose idea of marital happiness is summed up in his parrot-like iteration, "Have it your own way, my dear," Cyril Raymond manages to invest the stodgy character with a lovable quality which makes the happy ending of the near-tragedy less unconvincing than it would be otherwise.

Direction by David Lean is generally of a high standard, and Jack Harris has done a better-than-usual job of cutting. Interiors and exteriors should have especial interest for GI's who came to know small towns during their stay in England. Laurels go to Coward for these production values.

"Brief Encounter" may strike some exhibitors as being too brief, but every one of its 85 minutes is packed tight with interest-compelling incident.

A notable contribution to the growing list of British-made pictures qualified to appeal to world audiences. *Talb.*

Miniature Reviews

"Road to Utopia" (Par). Wacky and fast Crosby-Hope-Lamour release in the "Road" series, fourth to date. Big b.o.

"Masquerade In Mexico" (Par) Fair story made okay by fine acting work of Dorothy Lamour, Ann Dvorak, Arturo de Cordova.

"A Letter for Evie" (M-G). Neat comedy-drama with familiar cast of names for twin-bill bookings.

"Frontier Gal" (Color) (U). Lusty western feature satire in Technicolor. Stout b.o. possibilities.

"Tokyo Rose" (Par). Well-paced action drama about the femme Jap propaganda radio announcer, looks okay for b.o.

"House of Dracula" (U). A money horror opus combining U's Dracula, the Wolfman and Frankenstein Monster.

"An Angel Comes to Brooklyn" (musical) (Rep). Fairly diverting musical programmer.

"White Pongo" (PRC). Poorly-executed jungle meller; weak b.o.

"Rake's Progress" (Eagle-Lion). Rex Harrison, Lilli Palmer in British production likely to go over strongly in America.

Road to Utopia

(SONGS)

Paramount release of Paul Jones production. Stars Bing Crosby, Bob Hope, Dorothy Lamour; features Bob Benchley, Hillary Brooke, Douglas Dumbrille, Jack LaRue, Robert Barrat, Nester Paiva. Story and adaptation, Norman Panama and Melvin Frank; songs, Johnny Burke, James Van Heusen; editor, Stuart Gilmore; camera, Lionel Lindon, Gordon Jennings, Farciot Edouart. Previewed N.Y., Nov. 14, '45. Running time, 90 MINS.

Duke Johnson	Bing Crosby
Chester Hooton	Bob Hope
Sal	Dorothy Lamour
Kate	Hillary Brooke
Ace Larson	Douglass Dumbrille
Le Bec	Jack LaRue
Sperry	Robert Barrat
McGurk	Nestor Paiva
Narrator	Robert Benchley

The highly successful Crosby-Hope-Lamour "Road" series under the Paramount banner comes to attention once again in "Road to Utopia," a zany laugh-getter which digresses somewhat from pattern by gently kidding the picture business and throwing in unique little touches, all with a view to tickling the risibilities. Very big boxoffice results assured.

Picture is the fourth with the Crosby - Hope - Lamour combination and the first to be released since "Road to Morocco" in October, 1942. Behind that were "Zanzibar" and "Singapore," respectively, April, 1941, and February, 1940.

Though this one is rich in laughs and fast, the songs turned out for it are not of heavy caliber. Crosby and Hope's "Put It There Pal" is on the novelty side and cute. Crosby single, "Welcome to My Dreams" and Miss Lamour's number in a saloon setting, "My Personality," is nothing to get excited over. Quite good, however, is her "Would You."

Late Bob Benchley is cut into an upper corner of various shots making wisecracks, first being that "this is how not to make a picture." Others are in the same groove, while additional off-the-path gags include Hope and Miss Lamour in a kissing scene, topped by Hope's aside to the audience: "As far as I'm concerned this picture is over right now." Another is a guy walking across a scene asking Crosby and Hope where Stage 8 is. Even the familiar Paramount trademark with the stars is thrown around a mountain, with Crosby looking up and cracking, "That's my bread and butter."

Action is laid in the Klondike of the gold rush days. On their way there, scrubbing decks because they'd lost their money, Crosby and Hope come upon a map leading to a rich gold mine. It had been stolen from Miss Lamour's father by two of the toughest badmen of Alaska. Miss Lamour goes to the Klondike in search of them.

Meantime, in a scuffle with the map's thieves, Crosby and Hope subdue them, switching clothes and also assuming the names of the team. Thus, on arriving in the Klondike they become the prey of not only Miss Lamour, but of sharpshooting saloon owner who also wants the goldmine map. Ultimately, Miss Lamour gets her map, learning Crosby and Hope were not the baddies who slew her dad to get it.

Technically picture leaves nothing to be desired. Paul Jones, producer, and Hal Walker, who directed, make a fine combination in steering and in the production value provided. Performances by supporting cast are all good. They include Hillary Brooke, Douglass Dumbrille, Jack LaRue, Robert Barrat and Nestor Paiva. *Char.*

Masquerade in Mexico

(SONGS)

Paramount release of Karl Tunberg production. Features Dorothy Lamour, Arturo de Cordova, Patric Knowles, Ann Dvorak. Directed by Mitchell Leisen. Screenplay, Karl Tunberg, from original by Edwin Justus Mayer and Franz Spencer; music, Victor Young; camera, Lionel Lindon, Gordon Jennings, Farciot Edouart; editor, Aliua Macrovic; dancer, Billy Daniels. At Paramount, N.Y., commencing Nov. 28, '45. Running time, 96 MINS.

Angel O'Reilly	Dorothy Lamour
Manolo Segovia	Arturo de Cordova
Thomas Grant	Patric Knowles
Helen Grant	Ann Dvorak
Boris Cassall	George Riguad
Irene Denny	Matalie Schafer
Pablo	Mikhail Rasumny
Rico Fenway	Billy Daniels

Guadalajara Trio

Beautifully mounted, well edited tale studded with excellent make-believing from start to finish, it should do OK.

Dorothy Lamour is the top name and she turns in a good job, first as the unwitting tool of a jewel thief and then the deliberate means of breaking up a triangle. However, her performance is easily topped by several of her assistants, notably Ann Dvorak with an excellent portrayal of a philandering wife. Arturo de Cordova also comes through as a Mexican bullfighter who does do all his fencing outside of boudoirs. There are also several small parts so excellently worked as to make the 96 minutes pleasant and enjoyable. Foremost among them is the individual touch given the role of a lowly cab driver by Mikhail Rasumny.

Producer Karl Tunberg and his assistants went far beyond the power of the story in mounting, the production. From the looks of every scene a substantial amount of money was poured into the making. One ni[illegible] Miss Lamour warbles, "Adios, Mariquita Linda," and others depicting the country home of Miss Dvorak and her husband, played by Patric Knowles, cut deeply into the exchequer. This expensive touch runs the length of the film.

Basic story, by Edwin Justus Mayer and Franz Spencer, is the weakest ingredient in the affair. It pictures Miss Lamour unwittingly carrying from the U. S. into Mexico a diamond stolen by her prospective mate. She discovers it on the plane and drops it into the pocket of a nearby passenger (Knowles) who's nabbed at the border. In Mexico, Miss Lamour fluffs her b.f. as a thief and winds up penniless in a strange town. Up pops Knowles, who figured her out as the culprit on the plane and, under threat of turning her over to the police, brings her into his home as the phoney Condesa de Costa Mora for the purpose of luring the attentions of de Cordova from his wife to herself.

From there the fun begins. Cordova immediately taking the bait and Miss Dvorak launching a sparkling bit of acting in the unusual position of a wife being brushed by a lover while her husband stands by to push the situation along. There are scenes between Lamour and Dvorak in which the audience can almost feel the rake of the claws each gal spreads for action. For this, director Mitchell Leisen rates plaudits since that is what carries the story.

Wood.

A Letter to Evie

Hollywood, NOv. 28.

Metro release of William H. Wright production. Features Marsha Hunt, John Carroll, Hume Cronyn, Spring Byington, Pamela Britton, Norman Lloyd. Directed by Jules Dassin. Screenplay, De Vallon Scott and Alan Friedman, based on story by Blanche Brace; camera, Karl Freund; editor, Chester W. Schaeffer; music, George Bassman. Tradeshown Nov. 27, '45. Running time, 88 MINS.

Evie O'Connor.................Marsha Hunt
Edgar "Wolf" Larsen.............John Carroll
John Phineas McPherson........Hume Cronyn
Mrs. McPherson..............Spring Byington
Barney Lee....................Pamela Britton
Dewitt Pyncheon...............Norman Lloyd
Mr. McPherson...............Percival Vivian
Captain Budlow...............Donald Curtis
Mrs. Edgewaters..............Esther Howard
Eloise Edgewaters............Robin Raymond
Mrs. Jackson...................Therese Lyon
Miss Jenkins...................Lynn Whitney

"A Letter for Evie" is a neatly concocted comedy-drama. Marquee values are light and head it for the twin bill houses, but it's soundly put together entertainment that will get favorable audience reaction. Production, direction and writing point the material for enjoyment and cast comes through in fine style to keep pace swift.

Plot is based on what happens to a girl when she writes a letter to an unknown soldier. Missive is placed in the pocket of a size 16½ army shirt and finds its way to John Carroll, a wolfish GI. He doesn't follow up the play. Instead, Hume Cronyn, his pint-sized buddy, starts the correspondence, building himself into a big, outdoors man. By the time the soldiers hit New York, the girl, Marsha Hunt, has developed romantic urge for her fictional 16½ shirt-size GI. Cronyn, to make illusion perfect, has sent her snapshot of Carroll and has to resort to subterfuge to see his dream girl without giving the deception away. Complications become difficult when Carroll gets wise to what's going on and appears on the scene. Cronyn's desperate attempts to protect his dream girl from Carroll's wolfishness build up to a neat ending and carry plenty of chuckles and heart tugs.

Jules Dassin's direction is understanding, playing up the situations and cast for best presentation. Marsha Hunt does a delightful job of the girl seeking romance. Hume Cronyn is a standout in his assignment as the shy GI, and Carroll fits his character perfectly. Pamela Britton is good for laughs, as is Norman Lloyd. Spring Byington and others show up well.

Production values marshalled by William H. Wright are excellent, and photography, editing and other technical functions measure up to budget standards.

Brog.

Frontier Gal

(COLOR)

Hollywood, Nov. 30.

Universal release of Michael Fessier-Pagano production; executive producer, Howard Benedict. Stars Yvonne De Carlo and Rod Cameron; features Andy Devine, Fuzzy Knight, Sheldon Leonard, Andrew Tombes, Beverly Simmons. Directed by Charles Lamont. Original screenplay by Fessier-Ernest Pagano; camera, George Robinson, Charles P. Boyle, John O. Fulton; editor, Ray Snyder; music, Frank Skinner, H.J. Salter; songs, Jack Brooks and Edgar Fairchild. Previewed Nov. 29, '45. Running time, 84 mins.

Lorena Dumont.......................Yvonne De Carlo
Johnny Hart...............................Rod Cameron
Big Ben.......................................Andy Devine
Fuzzy..Fuzzy Knight
Judge Prescott...........................Andrew Tombes
Shoulders..................................Sheldon Leonard
Abagail.......................................Clara Blandick
Mary Ann..................................Beverly Simmons
Cherokee...................................Frank Lackteen
Gracie..Claire Carleton
Baliff...Eddie Dunn
Baliff......................................Harold Goodwin
Buffalo..Jack Overman
Sheila..Jan Wiley
Henchman..Rex Lease
Henchman....................................Jack Ingram
Henchman...............................George Eldredge
Henchman..............................Joseph Hayworth
Dealer.......................................Lloyd Ingraham
Dealer...................................Joseph E. Bernard
Dealer.......................................Douglas Carter
Dealer...Paul Bratti
Dealer...................................Edward M. Howard
Hostess..Joan Fulton
Hostess..Jean Trent
Hostess......................................Kerry Vaughan
Hostess.......................................Karen Randle

High action and comedy satire dressed up in Technicolor, "Frontier Gal" pokes plenty of fun at its western contemporaries and gears itself for both thrills and laughs. The returns at the boxoffice should be as handsome as the production mounting. Film is a scenic display of rugged exterior and lavish interior, brings sex to the western formula plot and, at all times, has its eye on commercial payoff. Yvonne De Carlo, remembered for her visual treat in "Salome," and Rod Cameron head the excellent cast.

Writers Michael Fessier and Ernest Pagano scripted and produced this one and realize on the commercial values to be found in western satire. Latter is often developed in a ten-twent-thirt style of dramatics but also has its subtle moments in which audiences will delight. As a topper for the surefire elements, producers bring in a kid actress to take the play away from the adult cast in all her scenes. Standard western chases, fist fights and gunplay are used for thrills, topped by the old height-scare stunt of having the kid dangling over a deep gorge on a shaky log. Lensing of sequence make trick exposure obvious but, nevertheless, stunt grabs intended audience reaction.

Rod Cameron is the dashing hero, escaping from a posse. He rides into Red Gulch, site of a fancy saloon conducted by Yvonne De Carlo. Hero goes for the heroine and she thinks he means marriage. When she discovers otherwise she forces a shotgun wedding and then turns him over to the law. He again escapes, seizes his bride and rides off for a one-night honeymoon. Returning six years later, he finds he has a daughter, just past five years of age. From here on the plot and the kid work to bring the parents together again and eliminate the heavy, Sheldon Leonard, also a suitor for Miss De Carlo's favors.

Miss De Carlo garners more attention as a sultry personality than as an actress, but former is enough to assure her a following without the latter. Cameron is perfect as the tall personification of the typical, dashing western hero, and Leonard makes an okay villain. Comedy falls to Andy Devine, Fuzzy Knight and Andrew Tombes. Special mention goes to little Beverly Simmons as the youngster. Her kid appeal and smile register big.

Miss De Carlo sings "Set 'Em Up, Joe," and "What Is Love" against the saloon background, and Fuzzy Knight does "Johnny's Comin' Home."

Charles Lamont's direction makes the moppet's scenes highlights, but doesn't overlook plenty of scope in the rough action and more subtler portions. George Robinson and Charles P. Boyle photographed to catch rugged outdoor backgrounds and lush settings. Other technical appurtenances are capable.

Brog.

Tokyo Rose

Paramount release of Pine-Thomas production. **Features** Byron Barr, Osa Massen, **Don Douglas**, Keye Luke. Directed by **Lew Landers**. Screenplay by Geoffrey Homes and Maxwell Shane, based on original by Whitman Chambers; camera, Fred Jackman, jr.; editor, Henry Adams. Tradeshown in N. Y., Dec. 3, '45. Running time, **70 MINS.**

Tokyo Rose......................Lotus Long
Pete Sherman....................Byron Barr
Greta Swanson..................Osa Massen
Timothy O'Brien..............Don Douglas
Colonel Suzuki..................Richard Loo
Charlie Otani......................Keye Luke
Soon Hee..........................Grace Lem
Wong..............................Leslie Fong
Chung Yu.......................H. T. Tsiang
Jack Martin......................Larry Young
Mike Koyak...................William Challee
Frank..............................Chris Drake
Al Wilson......................James Millikan
Mel......................................Al Ruiz
Joe...............................Blake Edwards

It's too bad that Paramount couldn't have readied "Tokyo Rose" for release several months ago, when the Nipponese femme's unique contribution to the Japanese war effort was still fresh in the minds of Americans. By not trying to rush the shooting schedule, however, producers Pine & Thomas have come up with a well-paced action drama in which the title's timeliness still provides a good exploitation springboard for exhibs to capitalize on. Title itself should make up for the lack of marquee names. Boxoffice potentialities look okay.

Plot is a little far-fetched, dealing with an escaped GI prisoner's attempt to kidnap "Rose" from her Tokyo Radio studios—and from right under the Nips' noses, too—and spirit her away to the States aboard an American submarine. Background information on the Japanese sorceress is plenty authentic, however, with recordings of some of Rose's broadcasts to the GIs in the Pacific area that might have been monitored on the spot.

Story has Pete Sherman (Byron Barr) as one of a group of American prisoners selected by the Japs to be interviewed on Rose's program for propaganda purposes. Since his buddy was killed indirectly through one of her broadcasts, however, he has a special hate for the gal and, during an air raid, succeeds in wrecking the broadcasting studio. He escapes during the subsequent commotion and is rescued by an Irish newspaper correspondent, who leads him to the Japanese underground. Still wanting to have it out with Rose before he leaves Japan, he convinces one of the underground leaders (Keye Luke) to cooperate in the kidnapping venture. After a series of exciting sequences, the two outwit the Japs and take Rose to a meeting place on the coast, where a boat is waiting to row them out to the surfaced submarine.

Story leaves a few loose ends, such as the fate of Pete's fellow-prisoners who also escaped during the air raid but the customers will be too interested in the outcome to question these minor points until after they leave the theatre. Cast is okay, with Barr, Luke and Richard Loo, who turns in another good job as a nefarious Japanese officer, carrying most of the film. Lotus Long, in the title role, doesn't appear until the last reel but turns out to be almost as pretty as her voice.

House of Dracula

Hollywood, Nov. 28.

Universal release of Paul Malvern (Joe Gershenson) production. Features Lon Chaney, Martha O'Driscoll, John Carradine, Lionel Atwill, Onslow Stevens, Glenn Strange, Jane Adams, Ludwig Stossel. Directed by Erle C. Kenton. Original, Edward T. Lowe; camera, George Robinson; editor, Russell Schoengarth, John P. Fulton; music, Edgar Fairchild. Previewed Nov. 25, '45. Running time, 67 mins.

Talbot...Lon Chaney
Dracula.................................John Carradine
Miliza..............................Martha O'Driscoll
Holtz...Lionel Atwill
Nina...Jane Adams
Edelman...................................Onslow Stevens
Zeigfried....................................Ludwig Stossel
Monster.......................................Glenn Strange
Steinmuhl...................................Skelton Knaggs
Brahms...................................Joseph E. Bernard
Villager.......................................Dick Dickinson
Gendarme......................................Fred Cordova
Gendarme.....................................Carey Harrison
Villager..Harry Lamont
Johannes................................Gregory Muradian
Mother..Beatrice Gray

Universal has brought all of its terror figures—Dracula, the Wolfman and Frankenstein's Monster—together in a nifty thriller for the chiller trade. "House of Dracula" plays its gruesome plot straight and manages considerable effectiveness. Production is well-mounted and direction strong. Profits will be good.

Plot twist has two of the monster heavies taking a sympathetic angle. Each comes to a doctor for help in curing their strange afflictions. First to appeal for help from Onslow Stevens is John Carradine, the centuries-old vampire. Next is Lon Chaney, the werewolf, who wants the doctor to relieve his madness. Stevens is successful in his experiments with Chaney but the vampire curing backfires. The good doctor eliminates Dracula by letting the sun's rays fall on his sleeping body but finds he, himself, has acquired the blood-letting urge.

In his newly-acquired madness he revives Frankenstein's monster, found in sea caverns near the doctor's castle, kills a faithful servant and finally dies with the monster in flames—that is until Universal's horror experts revive them again for another boxoffice winner. Just how they will solve the problem of again injecting Chaney with the wolf madness is something else again, since plot has him definitely cured, but studio madmen are ingenious.

Cast turns in generally firstrate work in roles that have become more or less standard. Femme spots go to Martha O'Driscoll and Jane Adams as assistants to the doctor. Lionel Atwill is seen briefly as the village police chief. Glenn Strange donned the garb of the monster, instead of Chaney, who would have found it difficult to double between his werewolfing.

Paul Malvern's production guidance furnishes proper settings for such a tale and Erle C. Kenton's direction of the material in Edward T. Lowe's original script is forthright. Settings, music, photography all contribute to necessary atmospheric mood. Editing is concise.

Brog.

An Angel Comes to Brooklyn

(MUSICAL)

Hollywood, Nov. 30.

Republic release of Leonard Sillman production; supervising producer, Armand Schaefer. Features Kaye Dowd, Robert Duke, David Street, Barbara Perry, Charles Kemper, Marguerite D'Alvarez, Bob Scheerer, Alice Tyrrell, June Carroll, Rodney Bell, Betzi Beaton. Directed by Leslie Goodwins. Screenplay, Stanley Paley and June Carroll from original story by Miss Carroll and Lee Wainer; camera, Jack Marta; editor, Tony Martinelli; songs, Sanford Green and June Carroll; arrangements, Dale Butts. Previewed Nov. 30, '45. Running time, **69 MINS.**

Karen James......................Kaye Dowd
David Randall...................Robert Duke
Paul Blake.......................David Street
Barbara.........................Barbara Perry
Phineas Aloysius Higby....Charles Kemper
Madam Della........Marguerite D'Alvarez
Bob..............................Bob Scheerer
Susie..............................Alice Tyrrell
Kay................................June Carroll
Oscar............................Rodney Bell
Tiny...............................Betzi Beaton
Miss Johnson...................Jay Presson
Joe...................................Joe Cappo
Rosie..............................Sherle North
Theresa........................Billie Haywood
Cliff...................................Cliff Allen
Sir Henry Bushnell.....C. Montague Shaw
Olga Ashley.......................Eula Morgan
Sarah Gibbons....................Gladys Gale
Michael O'Day......................Harry Rose
Brian Hepplestone............Frank Scannell
Shadow Dancer..............Jack McClendon
Rodney Lloyd......................Wilton Graff
Cornelius Terwillinger........Jimmy Conlin
Sgt. O'Rourke.......................Ralph Dunn

Mildly amusing musical comedy that will serve okay for secondary bookings in general situations. Production isn't elaborate but works in for ensemble numbers and plenty of songs. Comedy is of the screwball fantasy type played against a plot that is basically formula. Cast is made up largely of unknowns so there's no marquee weight to aid the selling.

Story concerns group of unknown youngsters 'trying to make Broadway and a plaintive angel sent down from actor's heaven to aid them attain their goal. Charles Kemper, as the angel, points up main laughs as he goes ineptly about his good deeds. He uses his powers to get a producer interested in the staging of a show with the young talent but incurs displeasure of the boss man in actors' heaven while doing so. It all works out to the obvious conclusion—the angel's pleased, the talent recognized, etc.

Kaye Dowd sings and dances as femme lead and Robert Duke makes best male appearance opposite her as artist and designer. David Street sings two of the score's six tunes and car..ies off slight heavy part. Among the talent lineup for singing-dancing are Betzi Beaton, Sherle North, Alice Tyrrell, June Carroll (also co-writer and cleffer on script and songs), Barbara Perry, Billy Haywood and Cliff Allen. All do their specialties in okay fashion.

Leslie Goodwins directed the Leonard Sillman production and does good job of combining fantasy, comedy and music. Photography is standard. *Brog.*

¡Peloton D'Execution

("Firing Squad")
FRENCH-MADE

Paris, Nov. 20.
Cine-Selection production and release. Stars Lucien Coedei, Yvonne Gauleau, Pierre Renoir; features Robert Dalban, Louis Eymond, Pierre Magnier, Marcel Lelaitre, Georges Lannes, Abel Jacquin. Directed by Andre Berthomieu. At Max Linder, Paris, from Oct. 31, '45. Running time, 105 MINS.

Haus	Lucien Coedel
Francoise	Yvonne Gaudeau
French Colonel	Pierre Renoir
Intelligence Officer	Abel Jacquin
Schmitt	Robert Dalban

Made shortly after the Germans left and looks more heavily budgeted than the reported $180,000. It's the Gestapo-type of story and may be strong with French audiences not yet satiated with the type of warfilm. Realistic scenes of ill treatment of French prisoners by the Germans and of their execution in batches of four may help put this over with some audiences. Direction and tempo are fair. Thin hopes for American market.

Lucien Coedel is more of the heavy than the conventional leading man. He wears a German uniform in the role of a patriotic Alsatian working for the French. Despite his Gestapo rank, he does not overact. He is supported by Yvonne Gaudeau, well cast as the patriotic French girl who takes chances in the underground work. Pierre Renoir, co-starred, has only a secondary part. Robert Dalban, who does the true German officer, and Abel Jacquin, as the French intelligence officer, are both good. *Maxi.*

White Pongo

PRC release of Sigmund Neufeld production. Stars Richard Fraser, Maris Wrixon; features Lionel Royce, Al Eben. Directed by Sam Neufield. Screenplay and original story, Raymond L. Schrock; camera, Jack Greenhalgh; editor, Holbrook, N. Todd. At New York, N.Y., dual, week Nov. 27, '45. Running time, 77 MINS.

Bishop	Richard Fraser
Pamela	Maris Wrixon
Van Doorn	Lionel Royce
Kroegert	Al Eben
Sir Harry	Gordon Richards
Carswell	Michael Dyne
Baxter	George Lloyd
Dr. Kent	Larry Steers
Gunderson	Milton Kibbee
Old Doctor	Egon Brecher
Mumbo Jumbo	Joel Fluellen

"White Pongo" is the story of a safari's long trek through the Belgian Congo in search of a white gorilla supposed to be the missing link. With action revolving around a band of extras dressed in monkey suits who snort, beat their breasts and act just like Hollywood extras dressed in monkey suits, the film is a drawn-out affair.

Plot strains credulity all the way, with stock shots of jungle beasts having no bearing on the story thrown in at random. In the middle of the jungle, the safari guide and several of his riflemen mutiny, kidnap the daughter of the British scientist who heads the expedition, and leave the rest of the party stranded without supplies while they set off to find a fabulous gold field. White gorilla then follows the mutineers, strangles the guide and takes the gal off to his jungle cave. He gets into a poorly-staged fight with a black gorilla just as the stranded party, who have followed, arrive in the nick. As the albino dashes his adversary over a cliff, the riflemen wound him with two shots and put him in a cage to take him back alive to England, where the scientist hopes to prove he is the missing link.

Excepting Richard Fraser and Maris Wrixon in the leads, both of whom deserve better treatment, rest of the cast constitute some of the most wooden-faced actors seen on the screen. Faltering direction keeps the action to a snail's pace and a better job of editing would have helped things. Film editor, however, probably didn't have much to work with in the first place.

The Rake's Progress

(BRITISH-MADE)

London, Nov. 23.
Eagle-Lion release of Individual Production. Stars Rex Harrison; features Lilli Palmer, Godfrey Tearle, Griffith Jones. Directed by Sidney Gilliat. Screenplay by Sidney Gilliat, Frank Launder from original story by Val Valentine. Camera, Wilkie Cooper, Jack Asher. At Studio One, London, Nov. 22, '45. Running time, 110 MINS.

Vivian Kenway	Rex Harrison
Rikki Krausner	Lilli Palmer
Colonel Kenway	Godfrey Tearle
Sandy Duncan	Griffith Jones
Jennifer Calthrop	Margaret Johnston
Fogray	Guy Middleton
Jill Duncan	Jean Kent
Lady Parks	Marie Lohr
Sir Hubert Parks	Garry Marsh
Sir John Brackley	David Horne
Burgess	John Salew
Edwards	Alan Wheatley
Bromhead	Brefni O'Rorke

The extent of Hollywood's gain in obtaining Rex Harrison and Lilli Palmer will be appreciated here when patrons get an eyeful of this, probably one of the finest films to come out of a British studio. Superb as these two players are, their individual performances are equalled by many others in the big cast. The script, racy in dialogue, is as good as many that Hollywood has produced. This solid entry should go big in the U. S. For this country, such vets as Godfrey Tearle, Marie Lohr, it looks terrific. Same can be said of the younger players, Griffith Jones, Margaret Johnston and Jean Kent, each being handed material by the script writers that's rich in possibilities.

Direction by Sidney Gilliat who, with Frank Launder, also wrote and produced the picture, is virtually flawless. Production values are far above the general run of British features.

Interesting part about this is that it is the first to reach the screen from a new outfit. The new independent company was formed by Gilliat and Launder when these two experienced script writers got tired of working for a salary and threw up their jobs with Gainsborough.

"The Rake's Progress" has everything it takes, for the most sophisticated audiences down to small-town ones. To see Harrison's technique with glamorous girl after glamorous girl is to make one wonder where he's been all these years.

In a word, this is a "Must," Maine to California—and then some. *Talb.*

Miniature Reviews

"**Miss Susie Slagle's**" (Par). Drama of medical students with average boxoffice outlook.

"**Prison Ship**" (Col). Secondary melodrama about Jap atrocities; okay dualer.

"**Pillow of Death**" (U). Program murder mystery, okay for supporting brackets and chiller fans.

"**South of the Rio Grande**" (Mono). Cisco Kid in a standardized western; okay for the action fans.

"**Along the Navajo Trail**" (Songs) (Rep). Newest Roy Rogers western an OK b.o. entry.

"**Naïs**" (Gaumont). Fernandel in Marcel Pagnol adaptation of Emile Zola novel; has some possibilities for American market.

"**Rome, Open City**" (Minerva Film). Italy's first bid for postwar foreign market; looks extremely mild entry for U. S.

"**Peach Blossom**" (Grovas). Mexican-made boasts Fernando Soler, Esther Fernandez. Has some U. S. theatre possibilities.

"**Johansson Gets Scolded**" (Swedish). Dull importation; weak b.o.

"**Pink String and Sealing Wax**" (Eagle-Lion). Fable of Victorian period in England not likely to mean much in U. S.

Miss Susie Slagle's

Hollywood, Dec. 1.
Paramount release of John Houseman production. Stars Veronica Lake, Sonny Tufts, Joan Caulfield; features Billy DeWolfe, Ray Collins, Bill Edwards, Pat Phelan, Renny McEvoy, Lillian Gish. Directed by John Berry. Screenplay by Anne Froelick and Hugo Butler; additional dialog, Theodore Strauss; adaptation, Anne Froelick and Adrian Scott; from novel by Augusta Tucker; camera, Charles Lang, Jr.; editor, Archie Marshek; score, Daniele Amfitheatrof; technical adviser, Dr. Benjamin Sacks. Tradeshown Nov. 28, '45. Running time, 88 MINS.

Nan Rogers	Veronica Lake
Pug Prentiss	Sonny Tufts
Margaretta Howe	Joan Caulfield
Dr. Elijah Howe	Ray Collins
Ben Mead	Billy De Wolfe
Elijah Howe, Jr.	Bill Edwards
Elbert Riggs	Pat Phelan
Miss Susie Slagle	Lillian Gish
Dean Wingate	Roman Bohnen
Dr. Fletcher	Morris Carnovsky
Clayton Abernathy	Renny McEvoy
Silas Holmes	Lloyd Bridges
Irving Aaron	Michael Sage
Mrs. Johnson	Dorothy Adams
Dr. Metz	E. J. Ballantine
Dr. Boyd	Theodore Newton
Hizer	J. Lewis Johnson
Otto	Ludwig Stossel
Mr. Johnson	Charles E. Arnt

"Miss Susie Slagle's" is a clinical study of how medical students are turned into young doctors. Pace is often ambling but sufficient interest is maintained in the various characters to offset the slowness. Star trio offers enough marquee value to insure average boxoffice intake, but picture hasn't the calibre to rate more. Period costumes and mounting are tastefully conceived.

Veronica Lake, Sonny Tufts and Joan Caulfield share star billing, but principal footage goes to Tufts and Miss Caulfield. Latter, newcomer from legit, displays pert personality and charm in the romantic spot opposite Tufts. Miss Lake has a more dramatic assignment as a student nurse whose romance with Pat Phelan, interne, ends in tragedy. She gives it subdued playing. Tufts is stiff as the medical student in love with Miss Caulfield and his coming surgical career.

Screen adaptation of the Augusta Tucker novel deals with group of young men who live at Miss Susie Slagle's boarding house while studying medicine. Miss Slagle is as much an institution as the medical school, and plot points up fact she gives the lads the inspiration to become fine doctors. Center of interest is on Tufts, his studying and valiant efforts to overcome a fear of his patients dying. Romance with Miss Caulfield, daughter of a former Slagle boarder, has its ups and downs due to Tufts' attention to his lessons and lack of funds but is finally resolved in a neat climax. Scattered interest is shown in problems of the other students and the boning necessary before being entitled to the M.D. suffix.

Direction by John Berry manages interest in tying together the varied characters and incidents, but because of the many sub-plots wasn't able to generate a fast pace. John Houseman supervised as associate producer, giving material excellent mounting. Charles Lang Jr.'s camera work is topnotch. *Brog.*

Prison Ship

Columbia release of Alexis Thurn-Taxis production. Features Nina Foch, Robert Lowery, Richard Loo. Directed by Arthur Dreifuss. Screenplay, Josef Mischel, Ben Markson; editor, Aaron Stell; camera, Philip Tannura; music, Mischa Bakaleinikoff. At Strand, Brooklyn, dual, week Dec. 5, '45. Running time, **60 MINS.**

Anne Graham....Nina Foch
Tom Jeffries....Robert Lowery
Captain Osikawa....Richard Loo
Professor....Ludwig Donath
Hal Trevor....Robert Scott
Jim Priestley....Barry Bernard
Jan Van Steen....Erik Rolf
Chan Kwan....Moy Ming
Frenchie....Louis Mercier
Steve Huntley....David Hughes
Winnie DeVoe....Barbara Pepper
Danny....Coulter Irwin
First Mate....Key Chang

"Prison Ship" is a modestly-budgeted item that follows the steadily-growing list of similar films showing Japanese atrocities of American GIs and civilians. Picture packs plenty of action but its lack of marquee names and hackneyed script set it as a supporting feature on twin bills.

Story deals with a Jap ship supposedly carrying prisoners from a Pacific island to Tokyo. Prisoners notice that the ship, carrying very small crew, is lit up like a Christmas tree and become panic-stricken when they realize it's a decoy for American submarines. They stage a revolt, which is defeated and results in the shooting of 30 women and children by the Japs for revenge. When the prisoners learn that a U.S. sub actually is following them, however, they break into the radio room and signal it before they're again subdued. Sub surfaces and begins firing at the ship and, in the ensuing fight, the prisoners overcome the Jap guards, wave a white flag to let the sub know they're friendly and are rescued.

Despite the picture's familiar plot, good direction and production technique keep it moving at a rapid pace and provide sufficient melodrama for the thrill fans. Robert Lowery and Nina Foch, as leaders of the prisoners, top an okay cast that includes Robert Loo, who must be plenty tired by this time of playing Jap officers in various stages of sadism.

Pillow of Death

Hollywood, Dec. 8.

Universal release of Ben Pivar production. Features Lon Chaney, Brenda Joyce, Clara Blandick, Rosalind Ivan, J. Edward Bromberg, George Cleveland, Bernard Thomas. Directed by Wallace Fox. Screenplay by George Bricker; camera, Jerry Ash; editor, Edward Curtis. Previewed Dec. 8, '45. Running time, **65 MINS.**

Wayne Fletcher....Lon Chaney
Donna Kincaid....Brenda Joyce
Belle Kincaid....Clara Blandick
Amelia Kincaid....Rosalind Ivan
Julian Julian....J. Edward Bromberg
Sam Kincaid....George Cleveland
Bruce Malone....Bernard Thomas
Detective McCracken....Wilton Graff

"Pillow of Death" measures up to the program murder mystery market demands and is an okay supporting feature. Production mounting is adequate and direction unfolds plot of psychopathic killer in good fashion.

Lon Chaney is seen as lawyer in love with his secretary, Brenda Joyce. When his wife is found mysteriously smothered to death with a pillow, suspicion falls on him but lack of evidence permits him to remain free. Next victim of the secret killer is George Cleveland, kindly uncle of Miss Joyce. A third victim is Miss Joyce's aunt, Clara Blandick, and before a fourth can be added to the killer's string he is exposed by the mumbo-jumbo, phoney psychic adviser. While Chaney is suspected there are enough other suspects to keep audiences betting on the wrong horse until final scenes when Chaney's dual personality is revealed.

Chaney and Miss Joyce deliver in okay fashion. Cleveland is excellent, as are Clara Blandick, Rosalind Ivan, J. Edward Bromberg and Wilton Graff. Bernard Thomas has thankless spot as the boy next door in love with Miss Joyce.

Photography aids the mystery elements, as do score and sound effects. *Brog.*

South of the Rio Grande

(SONGS)

Monogram release of Glenn Cook production. Stars Duncan Renaldo; features Martin Garralaga, Armida. Directed by Lambert Hillyer. Screenplay, Victor Hammond, Ralph Bettinson; editor, William Austin; camera, William Sickner; music, Edward J. Kay. At Strand, Brooklyn, dual, week of Dec. 5, '45. Running time, **62 MINS.**

Cisco....Duncan Renaldo
Pancho....Martin Garralaga
Pepita....Armida
Sanchez....George J. Lewis
Dolores....Lillian Molieri
Torres....Francis McDonald
Sebastian....Charles Stevens
Luis....Pedro Regas
Mama Maria....Coledad Jimenez
Manuel....Tito Renaldo
The Guadalajara Trio

Latest in the "Cisco Kid" series, "South of the Rio Grande" is a loosely-woven western that offers only its Mexican setting to distinguish it from other outdoor mellers. With appeal limited to the kids and action fans, it's grooved for the lower dualers.

With less than the standard number of gun brawls and chases, story has the Kid and his ever-present sidekick, Pancho, on the trail of a district officer whose racket is shooting Mexican rancheros under the pretext that they're all cattle thieves and then expropriating their property for himself. Rounding up the remaining ranchers, the Kid poses as a district inspector to get the goods on the heavy, whom he kills in a gun fight. Rest of the gang close in on the hero but he signals the waiting ranchers who arrive in the nick. Picture fades out with the Kid riding off to new adventures.

Duncan Renaldo is a satisfactory Cisco Kid and will probably build up an okay following. Rest of the cast, topped by Armida as a nitery entertainer, and Martin Garralaga, as the Kid's foil, is good enough for the purpose. Photography is a bit hazy in spots and the entire production evidences low budgeting.

Along the Navajo Trail

(SONGS)

Republic release of Edward J. White production. Stars Roy Rogers; features George Hayes, Dale Evans, Estelita Rodriguez, Douglas Fowley, Nestor Paiva, Bob Nolan. Directed by Frank McDonald. Screenplay, Gerald Geraghty, based on novel by William C. MacDonald; songs, Larry Markes-Dick Charles-Eddie De Lange, Charles Newman-Arthur Altman, Bob Nolan, Gordon Forster, Jack Elliott; camera, William Bradford; editor, Tony Martinelli. Previewed N. Y., Dec. 7, '45. Running time, **66 MINS.**

Roy Rogers....Roy Rogers
Gabby Whittaker....George "Gabby" Hayes
Lorry Alastair....Dale Evans
Narita....Estelita Rodriguez
J. Richard Bentley....Douglas Fowley
Janza....Nestor Paiva
Breck Alastair....Sam Flint
Roger Jerrold....Emmett Vogan
Dusty Channing....Roy Barcroft
Lani....David Cota
Sheriff Clem Wagner....Edward Cassidy
Bob Nolan and Sons of the Pioneers

Republic's newest Roy Rogers pic is an amiable horse-opera that is sure to please the singing cowboy's growing list of westerns fans. A little slow in action, the story nevertheless combines some hard riding and fast shooting with some good music for a pleasant feature. Rogers' substantial musical contributions are augmented by a nifty singing-playing cowboy troupe and by an attractive gypsy dancing ensemble for further contrast and effect.

The film, which is carefully directed and produced with attention to style and detail, has eye-catching gypsy scenes as well as some fine ranch and mountain range shots for background. Pic nevertheless appears not too lavishly-budgeted, so that the sure-thing b.o. returns will be doubly sweet.

The music occupies an important part, with two song numbers that belong or are already in the hit brackets. The Markes-Charles-De Lange title song, which Rogers sings in his usual ingratiating style, was a hit before bought by Republic, and a honey of a specialty number, Bob Nolan's "Cool Water," is done by Nolan and his Pioneers in a tricky arrangement for boff effect. "How're You Doing in the Heart Department" (Newman-Altman), which Dale Evans sings smartly, is another above-average tune.

Story has Rogers, as a U. S. deputy marshal, investigating the murder of another Govt. official on the prairie. Trail leads to the Ladder A ranch where Rogers, posing as a wandering cowboy-minstrel, gets a job as ranch-hand. The ranch is being sought by a syndicate, which brings strong-arm methods to bear to get the owner to sell out. Rogers' investigations unearth the fact that the ranch right-of-way is needed for an all-important oil pipeline through the area. Story winds up in a gunfight between syndicate and ranchers.

Meantime, a group of traveling gypsies who help unseat the syndicate, offer opportunity for colorful dancing and some neat vocalizing by Estelita Rodriguez. Rogers wanders his amiable way through the proceedings, with attractive blond Dale Evans competing with brunet Estelita for romantic interest. George "Gabby' 'Hayes handles the comedy dept., which is weak *Bron.*

Nais

(FRENCH-MADE)

C.P.L.F. Gaumont release of a Films Pagnol production. Stars Fernandel; features Jacqueline Bouvier, Raymond Pellegrin, Henri Poupon, Arius, Blavette and Germaine Kerjean. Directed by Raymond Leboursier. Camera, Charles Suin. Story by Marcel Pagnol from Emile Zola novel. Opened at Gaumont Palace, Paris, Nov. 24, '45. Running time, **130 MINS.**

Antoine....Fernandel
Nais....Jacqueline Bouvier
Her Lover....Pellegrin
Micoulin....Henri Poupon
Lover's Father....Arius
The Engineer....Blavette
Lover's Mother....Germaine Kerjean

A considerably shortened version of this will be released in the States by the Siritzkys, and the picture can stand it. Because some sequences have been made either to satisfy the Zola heirs or Fernandel. Most of the picture was actually directed by Marcel Pagnol, who did the story though credit is given to Raymond Leboursier. It is a typically Pagnol picture with a Mediterranean setting. Like his previous pictures, it looks a success locally.

Fact that this is a Pagnol picture with Fernandel starred gives it a chance for reasonable returns in some U.S. theatres, especially if trimmed as has been done by the Siritzkys for America.

Direction as is usually the case when it's done by Pagnol differs from usual Hollywood type. Director Pagnol leans over backwards trying to create the Mediterranean atmosphere without which the film would be nearly meaningless.

Fernandel is the hunchback who hopes to win the love of Nais, a farmer's daughter, despite his handicap. Later he is pictured as realizing all he can do is protect her and her lover from the girl's infuriated father when he becomes enraged at learning of her seduction by the profligate son of her father's employer. Story has Fernandel carrying out this devotion by even causing the death of the murder-inspired father and then convincing the boy's mother that the girl, who is about to become a mother, should be accepted as a daughter-in-law.

Picture is overboard in dialog, especially the initial sequences. Jacqueline Bouvier (Mrs. Marcel Pagnol in private life) makes a personable country girl about whom the whole plot revolves. But chief laurels go to Fernandel as the self-sacrificing cripple. Music is incidental, and he never sings. Pellegrin is excellent as young man who ultimately wins the girl's love and weds her.

Rome, Open City

("Roma, Citta Aperta")

Rome, Nov. 20.

Minerva-Film release of Excelsa-Film production. Stars Aldo Fabrizi, Anna Magnani; features Vito Annicchiarico, Nando Bruno, Harry Feist, Giovanna Galletti. Directed by Roberto Rosselini; screenplay, Sergio Amidei; music, Renzo Rosselini; camera, Ubaldo Arata. Previewed in Rome, Nov. 1, '45. Running time, **90 MINS.**

Don Pietro....Aldo Fabrizi
Pina....Anna Magnani
Marcello....Vito Annicchiarico
The Sexton....Nando Bruno
Bergmann....Harry Feist
Ingrid....Giovanna Galletti
Francesco....Francesco Grandjacquet
Manfredi....Marcello Pagliero
Police Sergeant....Passarelli
Marina....Maria Michi
Lauretta....Carla Rovere
Chief of Police....Sindici

This is Italian film industry's first bid for postwar foreign market. It is a human, credible story of the fine behavior of the "little people" during the German occupation of Rome. But still looms a mild U.S. entry. Climax to series of intrigues and adventures of these little people in getting money and information and other assistance to the underground comes during a Gestapo raid on a block of workingmen's houses. Gestapo agents carry off the key underground leader, and shoot his girl as she runs after the truck that takes him off to prison. There is a nasty torture scene at prison. A stock conception of a brutal Prussian officer and sadistic German female agent who can see people suffer and think meanwhile mostly of her fur coat is given.

This much of the film is standard hero and villain stuff. But what makes picture good is the story of other characters involved in the tragedy. Aldo Fabrizi does superb job of portraying the understanding priest who carries money bound in scholarly-looking volumes across the lines, smuggles ammunition under his priest's robes and inspires the hero with courage in the final ordeal. For this last act of defiance the priest is executed, and he dies blessing a little band of neighborhood children who stand outside the prison whistling a tune to give him comfort. One of these neighborhood kids is played by one of Rome's real street urchins—one of the "shoe-shine" boys that the GIs have come to know so well. He plays the role convincingly.

Top performance is turned in by Anna Magnani as Pina, the hero's girl. She is certainly not a heroine in the Hollywood conception, as she is not only homely, but even quite slovenly and rather ordinary.

Despite grimness of plot, there are several little touches of humor. Much of the humor in Italian dialects will be lost in dubbing, which will hurt the film's chances in America.

Flor De Durazno

("Peach Blossom")
(MEXICAN-MADE)
(In Spanish)

Mexico City, Nov. 23.

Grovas Films-Miguel Zacarias production and release. Stars Fernando Soler and Esther Fernandez; features David Silva. Adapted from Hugo Wast's novel. Directed by Miguel Zacarias. At Cine Magerit, Mexico City, Nov. 23, '45. Running time, **93 MINS.**

This sad, sweet mixture of melancholy Argentinian philosophy and deft Mexican treatment and acting plus the colorful locale of Mexico is "Flor de Durazno." Producciones Grovas and Producer Miguel Zacarias, who also megged, have fared rather well by taking the tragic tale by Hugo Wast, prolific Argentinian author and father, and adapting it to 1945 Mexico. Has U. S. possibilities.

Picture's dominant note is the poignant grief of a widower and his daughter, an only child. The lonely old man and his unworldly young daughter are shown on a little ranch.

"Flor de Durazno" is lifted above being mere fare for the handkerchief brigade by superior performances by Fernando Soler, head of the family known as the Barrymores of Mexico, and Esther Fernandez, spiritual and comely. Soler is excellent as the grieving rancher. Fernandez teams perfectly with him as the unsophisticated yet dutiful daughter who flees to Mexico City from her drab surroundings and becomes an unwed mother. The Wast tale is given a happy ending. That helps.

Var Herr Luggar Johansson

("Johansson Gets Scolded")
(SWEDISH-MADE)

Produced ond distributed by Scandia Films, Inc. Stars Sigurd Wallen, directed by Wallen. Screenplay, Erik Lundegard; music, Erik Baumann and Nathan Gorling. At 5th Ave. Playhouse, N. Y., week Nov. 21, '45. Running time, **101 MINS.**

Johansson....................Sigurd Wallen
His Wife....................Dagmar Ebbesen
Olle....................Anders Ek
Lena....................Bojan Westin
Ake....................Hans Lindgren

(In Swedish; English Titles)

"Johansson Gets Scolded" is one of the most mediocre importations in many a screening.

The story of a small-time manufacturer and the uninteresting fricasse he and his family get into, because of unwarranted expansion of his business, is a very dull venture any way you look at it. The ill-contrived situations, despite a good cast, make for very weak b.o.

There's Johansson's wife who goes beyond her financial means to keep up with the Petersons, the son who's considered guilty of a robbery because he lacks an alibi, etc.; the wizened, matriarchal grandmother who comes to live with them and spout philosophical advice, etc.; all of which adds up to a tour-de-cliches.

Performances attempt to overcome the script's shortcomings, but to no avail. Settings, direction and camera shots are all on the debit side.

Pink String and Sealing Wax

(BRITISH-MADE)

London, Nov. 23.

Eagle-Lion release of Earling Studios-Michael Balcon production. Features Mervyn Johns, Googie Withers, Gordon Jackson, Sally Ann Howes. Directed by Robert Hamer. Screenplay by Diana Morgan based on play by Roland Pertwee. Camera, Richard S. Pavey, R. Julius. At Studio One, London, Nov. 22, '45. Running time, **95 MINS.**

Mr. Sutton....................Mervyn Johns
Mrs. Sutton....................Mary Merrall
David....................Gordon Jackson
Peggy....................Sally Ann Howes
Pearl....................Googie Withers
Miss Porter....................Catherine Lacey
Joe....................Garry Marsh
Dan....................John Carol
Victoria....................Jean Ireland
Mrs. Webster....................Maudie Edwards
Police Inspector....................Valentine Dyall

Gin and whiskey figure prominently in this screen adaptation of the West End stage hit. Incidentally it says something for Micky Balcon's daring at a time when this Socialist Government is in the saddle. It's chances in the U. S. are not so hot.

Bringing the England of the Victorian period to life is the best thing "Pink String and Sealing Wax" accomplishes. The black, high-necked, rustling Sunday-best bombazines which the church-going women wear contrast violently with the billowing cleavages of the bad women. The unrelenting tyranny of the lord and master of the respectable family is offset by the free-and-easy beatings-up the naughty gals receive at the hands of Cagney-ish husbands and sweethearts. In giving this side of English life, the picture is tops.

With Mervyn Johns, Googie Withers, Gordon Jackson and Sally Ann Howes starred there's no question about this one's clicking with British audiences. Faulty direction by Robert Hamer, whose insistence on giving Miss Withers, as the poison-administering harlot-wife, all the best of it destroys the drama's balance, and will hurt its U. S. lure.

Characteristic of the new order of things in British pictures, the bit players turn in performances so bright one wonders how come they aren't in the top billing. Catherine Lacey as a gin drunkard is superb. John Carol's warned-off jockey who loves 'em and leaves 'em without batting an eye is as smooth as the greasy cowlick draped over his forehead. Garry Marsh as the booze hound proprietor of the pub whom Miss Withers rubs out with strychnine is Bill Sykes come to life.

Where the pic disappoints is in its denying little Miss Howes and both Johns and Jackson their chances of scoring. *Talb.*

Boule De Suif

("Grease Ball")
(FRENCH-MADE)

Paris, Nov. 20.

Consortium Francais release of Artis Film production. Stars Micheline Presle; features Louis Salou, Alfred Adam, Brochard, Berthe Bovy, Denys d'Ines, Mona Doll, Louise Comte, Roger Carl, Suzet Mais, Palau, Marcel Simon, Georges Tourraill. Directed by Christian-Jacque. Screenplay by Henri Jeanson from short story by Guy de Maupassant. At Paramount, Paris, starting Oct. 17, '45. Running time, **105 MINS.**

Boule de Suif....................Micheline Presle
Fifi....................Louis Salou
Cornudet....................Alfred Adam
M. Loiseau....................Brochard
Wife of Hostage....................Berthe Bovy
Priest....................Denys d'Ines
Madame Loiseau....................Suzet Mais
M. Carre Lamandou....................Palau
Le Comte....................Marcel Simon
German Officers..Roger Carl and Tourraill

This is a much better picture than recently made by French producers. Performances by Micheline Presle and Alfred Adam are excellent. Looks good for French audiences, but may hit censor trouble in U. S. Yarn of the Franco-German war in 1870 is given a modern twist.

The story concerns Boule de Suif, a little prosty, who is widely known in Rouen, a small town. But she is patriotic and flees from German occupation via a stage coach. Traveling in the same coach are an aristocrat, an industrialist and a wine merchant, and their wives. At one village, a German officer billeted there makes it a condition that Boule de Suif shall spend the night with him if the coach is to proceed. She refuses at first, hating Germans, the others cajole her into accepting, after which they snub her. Later the coach is again stopped by German soldiers and the four women, irrespective of social standing are forced to be the guests of German officers in a chateau. The bad girl shows her spunk by knifing a German officer.

In spite of the 1870 uniforms and dresses, the audience reacts exactly as if the story was one of the recent war. *Maxi.*

Miniature Reviews

"Adventure" (M-G). Clark Gable, Greer Garson, Joan Blondell, Thomas Mitchell in smash love story; big biz and long runs.

"Doll Face" (Musical) (20th). Routine filmusical about burlesk queen that will do better in the nabes.

"Dick Tracy" (RKO). Fast action meller based on comic strip of same name for supporting spots.

"The Crime Doctor's Warning" (Col). Warner Baxter in a good whodunit, okay for the family trade.

"Woman Who Came Back" (Rep). Horror melodrama, sturdy fare for chiller trade.

"Strange Voyage" (Signal). Okay first venture for ex-serviceman film company. Shapes up as supporting material in action houses.

"The Strange Mr. Gregory" (Mono). Satisfactory meller for duals.

"Frontier Feud" (Mono). First-rate western starring Johnny Mack Brown.

"Girl With Grey Eyes" (Minerva). French-made given no chance in America despite Fernand Ledoux's fine performance.

Adventure

Metro release of Sam Zimbalist production. Stars Clark Gable, Greer Garson; features Joan Blondell, Thomas Mitchell, Lina Romay. Directed by Victor Fleming. Screenplay by Frederick Hazlitt Brennan, Vincent Lawrence; adaptation, Anthony Veiller, William H. Wright; based on novel by Clyde Brion Davis; camera, Joseph Ruttenberg; editor, Frank Sullivan; special effects, Warren Newcombe. Previewed in Projection Room, N. Y., Dec. 17, '45. Running time, **130 MINS.**

Harry Patterson....................Clark Gable
Emily Sears....................Greer Garson
Helen Melohn....................Joan Blondell
Mudgin....................Thomas Mitchell
Gus....................Tom Tully
Model T....................John Qualen
Limo....................Richard Haydn
Maria....................Lina Romay
"Old" Ramon Estado....................Philip Merivale
Dr. Ashlon....................Harry Davenport
"Young" Ramon Estado....................Tito Renaldo

With Gable's initial pic since returning from the service, Greer Garson costarred, and a supporting cast headed by Joan Blondell and Thomas Mitchell, this one can't miss. Sock boxoffice and extended runs, despite a rather inane title and a story that often is none too flattering to Gable, are assured. The co-stars turn in brilliant performances.

Metro picked the usual lusty role for the virile Gable. He's bos'n mate on a Merchant Marine vessel, and as tough as the toughest sailor on board. Handy with his dukes, he has a femme in every port. That is until he meets Greer Garson, the librarian, who finally decides that the venturesome traits displayed by Gable are just what she has been missing in life. So, it's a hurried wedding, a honeymoon in Reno. Then the romance collapses on the pair. He decides the sea is still for him and she decides on a divorce. The payoff is trite—the baby arrives only a few steps behind the return of Clark, but this climax is made to pack a real wallop.

Film shows a new Gable. He has many of the old mannerisms, but director Victor Fleming made him overly boisterous and stubborn, a seafaring man who would toss aside his new bride of a few days like she was another girl in port. That's a bit difficult to stomach, especially when the girl is Greer Garson. Nonetheless it's a solid bit of acting despite the directorial emphasis on possibly wrong angles.

Miss Garson, the librarian who at first abhors the rowdy Gable, dominates every scene even when being browbeaten by the obstinate mate. She effects the transition from the prim, standoffish office gal into a life-loving femme who refuses to let her man get away.

Joan Blondell, as her girl friend, who likes Gable from the start, and even better after a drinking session, seems almost a reborn actress in this role. Thomas Mitchell, who is the God-fearing sailor and particular pal of Gable, has a powerful characterization, and does it up brown. Lina Romay, as the latest gal Gable has found in a new port, does well with an unsympathetic part. She also sings superbly a couple of Latin tunes. Stout support is headed by Tom Tully, John Qualen, Harry Davenport and Richard Haydn.

Taken from the Clyde Brion Davis novel, the Anthony Veiller-William H. Wright adaptation and screenplay by Frederick Hazlitt Brennan and Vincent Lawrence both deserve laurels. Victor Fleming's direction always is topflight, his handling of tearjerker scenes being especially strong. Sam Zimbalist's production is A-1, with cameraing by Joseph Ruttenberg good. Frank Sullivan's editing has permitted this to run overly long. *Wear.*

Doll Face

(MUSICAL)

20th-Fox release of Bryan Foy production. Stars Vivian Blaine, Dennis O'Keefe, Perry Como, Carmen Miranda; features Martha Stewart, Michael Dunne, Reed Hadley. Directed by Lewis Seiler. Screenplay, Leonard Praskins; adaptation, Harold Buchman; from play by Louise Hovick; songs, Jimmy McHugh and Harold Adamson; dances, Kenny Williams; camera, Joseph La Shelle; editor, Norman Colbert. Tradeshown N. Y., Dec. 13, '45. Running time, **80 MINS.**

Doll Face....................Vivian Blaine
Mike Hannegan....................Dennis O'Keefe
Nicky Ricci....................Perry Como
Chita....................Carmen Miranda
Frankie Porter....................Martha Stewart
Gerard....................Michael Dunne
Flo Hartman....................Reed Hadley
Aides....................Stanley Prager, Charles Tannen
Stage Manager....................George E. Stone
Peters....................Frank Orth
Lawyer....................Donald McBride
Dancing Partner....................Ciro Rimac
Hotel Clerk....................Hal K. Dawson
Drug Store Clerk....................Charles Williams
Soho....................Edgar Norton
Bennett....................Boyd Davis
Harold (Soda Jerk)....................Alvin Hammer
Coast Guardsman....................Alex Barker

"Doll Face" is a run-of-the-mine filmusical with familiar backstage theme and stock situations. Its marquee names also lack strength. Biz in subsequents and nabes, however, should offset not too pretentious budget for satisfactory returns on outlay.

Pic could be exploited by use of the fact that Gypsy Rose Lee wrote the stage play, "The Naked Genius," on which the script is based, and also by fact that film has an autobiographical tinge in its story of a burlesque queen who writes the story of her life. But 20th, presumably fearing a boomerang, credits neither play nor authoress' w.k. stage-name, **merely listing pic as based on "a** play by Louise Hovick" (Miss Lee's real name).

The pic has some good music, well sung by personable leads. Idea of a burleycue queen hitting Broadway by writing her autobiog is original for a film. But from there on the treatment is routine, with the book slow and comic relief light. Pic lacks smartness and taste.

Story deals with the pride-and-joy of a downtown burlesk house, who yearns for respectability and class of the bigtime. Turned down at an audition by a legit manager, she and her manager-boy friend concoct idea of an autobiography, ghost-written, as a springboard to Broadway. Book brings the needed publicity, so that the whole burlesque troupe plans the uptown invasion. Crimp comes when the ghost-writer falls for the lady, and boy friend misunderstands and breaks up with her. He even holds up the Broadway premiere in his huff, until matters are smoothed over by Providence and Carmen Miranda, in equal parts.

Miss Miranda, for a surprise, takes a comic-dramatic role as understanding girl-friend, which she does well. Finally sings a song, the "Chico-Chico" tune in a lavish Porto Rican number worth the wait. Vivian Blaine makes an attractive heroine, and handles several vocals nicely. Dennis O'Keefe carries the torch manfully as her boy-friend, with Michael Dunne as satisfactory other-guy. Perry Como does some choice warbling, in solo or duet. Martha Stewart, as a jealous understudy for Miss Blaine, looks a find—a cute singer with oomph and personality. She's from the niteries; this is her debut pic.

Production numbers are full and handsome, with a couple of burlesk numbers that look like the Ziegfeld. Jimmy McHugh and Harold Adamson's tunes are the pic's strong part, with "Somebody's Walkin' in My Dreams" and "Here Comes Heaven Again" as two prime ballads, and "Dig You Later," a smart rhythm number. *Bron.*

Dick Tracy

Hollywood, Dec. 13.

RKO release of Herman Schlom (Sid Rogell) production. Features Morgan Conway, Anne Jeffreys, Mike Mazurki, Jane Greer, Lyle Latell, Joseph Crehan, Mickey Kuhn. Directed by William Berke. Original, Eric Taylor; based on cartoon strip by Chester Gould; camera, Frank Redman; music, Roy Webb; editor, Ernie Leadlay. Tradeshown Dec. 10, '45. Running time, **61 MINS.**

Dick Tracy....................Morgan Conway
Tess....................Anne Jeffreys
Splitface....................Mike Mazurki
Judith Owens....................Jane Greer
Pat Patton....................Lyle Latell
Chief Brandon....................Joseph Crehan
Tracy, Jr....................Mickey Kuhn
Professor Starling....................Trevor Bardette
Steven Owens....................Morgan Wallace
Deathridge....................Milton Parsons
Mayor....................William Halligan
Mrs. Caraway....................Edythe Elliott
Dorothy Stafford....................Mary Currier
Manning....................Ralph Dunn
Radio Announcer....................Edmund Glover
Sergeant....................Bruce Edwards

Nifty action melodrama for supporting positions. Chester Gould's comic strip of same title lends itself handily to screen melodrama. It's all aimed for satisfaction of the action fan. Pace is fast and production mounting good. Cast is excellent and bring the Gould characters alive without the grotesqueness that features the newspaper strip.

Morgan Conway takes on the title role, while Anne Jeffreys is seen as Tess, the detective's girl friend. Both add plenty of movement to the plot and may have inherited series jobs if RKO decides to make additional "Tracy" thrillers. Other familiar strip characters are Pat Patton, played by Lyle Latell; Chief Brandon, done by Joseph Crehan, and Tracy, Jr., portrayed by Mickey Kuhn.

Plot has Tracy chasing down a crazy killer tagged Splitface, so called because of a hideous scar running diagonally across his face. Mike Mazurki, as Splitface, is seeking revenge on those who sent him to prison years before, and manages to do in three victims before Tracy calls a halt. Plot is conventional murder melodrama, and is played straight to get over. It ends with Splitface, Tess and Junior, whom he has kidnapped, hidden in an abandoned boat. Tracy follows clues left by Junior, and arrives in the nick.

Jane Greer, as daughter of Morgan Wallace, an intended victim; Trevor Bardette, a screwy astrologist; Milton Parsons, an undertaker; William Halligan, the frightened mayor, and others show up well in the cast.

William Berke's direction keeps the pace fast all the way, and generally shapes the film for good reception. Herman Schlom produced, handling the values expertly for release intentions. Camera, editing, etc., measure up. *Brog.*

La Fille Aux Yeux Gris
("Girl With Grey Eyes")
(FRENCH-MADE)

Paris, Dec. 11.

Minerva release of a B.C.M. production. Directed by Jean Faurez. Stars Fernand Ledoux and Claude Genia; features Jean Paqui, Paul Bernard, Line Noro, Blondeau. From an original story by Maurice Cloche. Adapted by Jean Faurez and Le Chanois. At Francais, Paris, Nov. 26. Running time, **97 MINS.**

Dr. Bernard....................Fernand Ledoux
The Quack....................Blondeau
Quack's Daughter....................Claudia Genia
Dr. Bernier....................Jean Paqui
The Druggist....................Paul Bernard
Mrs. Bernard....................Line Noro

Picture is bad in every respect except the acting by Fernand Ledoux, whose performance is one of the best seen on the French screen recently. Maurice Cloche's original story has been so poorly adapted and dialogued that even good direction could not save it. Picture drags, and draws laughs in the wrong places. Naturally, it has no hope for U. S. market.

Fernand Ledoux plays the part of an old country doctor who has taken to drink and has sold his practice in an isolated mountain district to a young doctor, Jean Paqui. When latter arrives, he encounters opposition from a quack medico whose daughter really is Ledoux' offspring. Paqui falls in love with the girl, and after her father's death, succeeds in winning her.

Ledoux, who at the beginning of the picture just plays the plain drunkard, builds up interest in his character by revealing little by little what makes him stick to the place via minute changes in his attitude. From a human wreck, he winds up a sympathetic character. *Maxi.*

Frontier Feud

Monogram production and release. Stars Johnny Mack Brown; features Raymond Hatton, Dennis Moore, Christine McIntyre. Directed by Lambert Hillyer. Story, Charles N. Heckelmann; adaptation, Jess Bowers; editor, Dan Milner; camera, Harry Neumann. At New York, N. Y., dual, week Dec. 13, '45. Running time, **54 MINS.**

Nevada....................Johnny Mack Brown
Sandy....................Raymond Hatton
Joe....................Dennis Moore
Blanche....................Christine McIntyre
Don Graham....................Jack Ingram
Murphy....................Edwin Parker
Chalmers....................Frank La Rue
Bill Corey....................Steve Clark
Sheriff Clancy....................Jack Rockwell
Sarah Moran....................Mary MacLaren
Moran....................Edmund Cobb
Si Peters....................Lloyd Ingraham

Firstrate western built around two feuding ranchers and murders which point in the direction of both. Has plenty of action and speed, running time being held down to 54 minutes, shorter than for most hoss operas.

Johnny Mack Brown, by now a veteran in the saddle, plays a U. S. marshall who, with the aid of another Federal, Raymond Hatton, gets at the bottom of the murders, rounding up one rancher and his henchmen who are responsible. The other ranchowner (Dennis Moore) is freed of suspicion and makes off at the end with Christine McIntyre. Love interest is played down severely, however. *Char.*

Britain's 'Burma' Pic Anti-Climatic

A little less than a year ago Warner Bros. released its fictional "Objective, Burma." It drew the ire of Britain by its implications. Errol Flynn, the Britishers protested, along with what seemed purely an American operation, was responsible for the Burma victory over the Japs.

"Burma Victory" (62 mins.), produced by the British Army Film Unit, from material taken by British, Indian and American cameramen, might well be Britain's answer to American film audiences of what actually transpired in those exhausting days of 1943-44, during the combined operation to maintain the Allied lifeline to China. It is an occasionally exciting documentary that distributes equitably the credits for the Burma campaign. It is a film that emphasizes how the combined resources of the British, Australians, Americans, Chinese, among others, were responsible for the victory.

Warners has elected to distribute "Burma Victory" (on a straight selling basis) in the U. S., and it's to its credit that it hasn't chosen to ignore a "mistake" that found "Objective" forced to withdraw from Britain.

The release in the U. S. of the British pic is apt to be anti-climactic. "Burma Victory," seemingly, cannot compete with such "peacetime" pursuits as the General Motors strike, the atomic bomb controversy and the Brooklyn crime wave. *Kahn.*

Crime Doctor's Warning

Columbia release of Rudolph C. Flothow production. Stars Warner Baxter; features John Litel, Dusty Anderson, Coulter Irwin. Directed by William Castle. Original story and screenplay, Eric Taylor; camera, L. W. O'Connell; editor, Dwight Caldwell. At Strand, Brooklyn, dual, week Dec. 12, '45. Running time, **69 MINS.**

Dr. Ordway....................Warner Baxter
Inspector Dawes....................John Litel
Connie Mace....................Dusty Anderson
Clive Lake....................Coulter Irwin
Frederick Malone....................Miles Mander
Jimmy Gordon....................John Abbott
Nick Petroni....................Edward Ciannelli
Mrs. Wellington....................Alma Kruger
Robert MacPherson....................J. M. Kerrigan
Joseph Duval....................Franco Corsaro

Fifth in Columbia's series based on CBS' Dr. Ordway character, "The Crime Doctor's Warning," has Warner Baxter in the title role mixed up with three murders in this one. Picture is a natch for the whodunit fans. Baxter and ex-cover girl Dusty Anderson are the sole marquee values, but it should hold up well on any twin bill.

Scripter Eric Taylor has thrown together enough suspense, built around a strange corpse and a strange killer, to put the analyzing logic of the customers to a real test. Story, dealing with a group of Latin Quarter artists and models, gets off to a fast start with the murder of one of the pose-holders. After artist Clive Lake (Coulter Irwin) calls on Dr. Ordway for help, telling him that he suffers from memory lapses during which he can't be responsible for his actions, Lake's own model and sweetheart, Connie Mace (Dusty Anderson) is found strangled.

Famed psychologist then sets out to solve the crime. Suspense builds nicely as one after another of the suspects is ruled out and the crime doctor gets into the usual number of tight scrapes and adventures, including the murder of a blackmailer and the discovery of a third model's dead body in a plaster cast of a statue. All turns out well, of course, with the doctor finally unmasking the killer in a boff ending.

Despite its probable low budgeting, the film has been given good production mountings, and director William Castle gets the most out of the well-turned script. Baxter doesn't miss a trick in his Ordway portrayal, and Miss Anderson, although no wow as an actress, is at home as a bathing beauty model. Rest of the cast fills in capably.

Woman Who Came Back

Hollywood, Dec. 14.

Republic release of Walter Colmes production, directed by Colmes. Stars John Loder, Nancy Kelly, Otto Kruger; features Ruth Ford, Harry Tyler, Jeanne Gail, Almira Sessions. Screenplay, Dennis Cooper and Lee Willis; story, John Kafka; suggested by Phillip Yordan; camera, Henry Sharp; score, Edward Plumb; editor, John Link. Previewed Dec. 14, '45. Running time, **68 MINS.**

Dr. Matt Adams....................John Loder
Lorna Webster....................Nancy Kelly
Rev. Stevens....................Otto Kruger
Ruth Gibson....................Ruth Ford
Noah....................Harry Tyler
Peggy Gibson....................Jeanne Gail
Bessie....................Almira Sessions
Sheriff....................J. Farrel McDonald
Dr. Peters....................Emmett Vogan

Witchcraft and superstition combine to make "Woman Who Came Back" nifty fare for the horror bills. Picture is well turned out in all departments and contains a maximum of thrills and chills for patrons of goose-bump melodrama. Familiar names of the leads lend marquee values.

Story departs from the usual horror formula, in that it attempts a finale explanation for the weird doings that nearly drive a girl to suicide and the citizens of a small New England village to mob violence. Plot fails to clear up several points, but this won't fret the customers too much.

Nancy Kelly is returning via bus to the New England village where her family has lived for generations. She believes she is bewitched, the curse having come down for 300 years as result of a clerical ancestor framing an old crone for witchcraft. A mysterious old lady on the bus lends credence to the girl's fear, and subsequent events, such as a little girl falling ill, a phantom dog that terrorizes villages, storms and other calamities further strengthen belief.

It is not until the girl is stoned and throws herself in the lake that her doctor fiance, John Loder, and the village minister, Otto Kruger, are able to find evidence clearing her of the curse and showing her ancestor as an old witch-burning fanatic. There is a particularly hair-raising sequence in which the dog attacks Kruger. Other thrill moments, plus music score and photography, all point mood for suspense.

Miss Kelly, Loder, Kruger, Ruth Ford, Harry Tyler, Jeanne Gail and others deliver effectively under Walter Colmes' direction. Colmes also gives picture excellent framework as associate producer. Henry Sharp did the good lensing and Edward Plumb wrote the score for the Dennis Cooper-Lee Willis script. *Brog.*

Strange Voyage

Hollywood, Dec. 14.

Signal Pictures presentation of Louis B. Appleton, Jr., production (no release set yet). Stars Eddie Albert; features Forrest Taylor, Ray Teal, Matt Willis, Martin Garralaga, Elena Verdugo, Bobby Cooper. Directed by Irving Allen. Original screenplay by Andrew Holt; camera, Jack H. Greenhalgh, Jr.; editor, Irving A. Applebaum; music, Lucian Moraweck. Previewed at California Studios, Hollywood, Dec. 12, '45. Running time, 67 MINS.

Chris Thompson...............Eddie Albert
Skipper.....................Forrest Taylor
Capt. Andrews...................Ray Teal
The Hammer...................Matt Willis
Manuel....................Martin Garralaga
Carmelite....................Elena Verdugo
Jimmy.......................Bobby Cooper
The Sportsman.............Clyde Fillmore
Ben..........................Daniel Kerry
The Father..................Henry Orosco

"Strange Voyage" is first production for Signal Pictures, formed by group of ex-servicemen who were formerly in the industry. Signal has not yet set a release for 'Voyage' or product to follow. Producer, director, cameraman, star, writer ad assistant director make up the ex-servicemen heading Signal.

Initial venture is a leisurely account of a search for buried treasure in Lower California. Story is told in straightforward fashion to aid realism, and, while results are not exactly orthodox film-making, picture will be able to fill supporting brackets in many situations. It has the Eddie Albert name as star to help the selling.

Plot is told in flashback, opening when Clyde Fillmore attempts to charter the ketch owned by Forrest Taylor. Latter then details that boat is being held for Albert, who plans to resume an ill-fated treasure hunt in which the ketch had previously figured. Taylor tells Fillmore of the voyage that took place, of how Albert and his odd crew sailing for a deserted spot on the Mexican coast to search for a vast store of hidden gold. Sailors' superstitions, the dangers of the seas and the desert where the loot has been buried for years are depicted for plot interest.

Among film's thrills are underseas shots of a fight between a shark and an octopus, underwater spear fishing by Albert and young Bobby Cooper, a stowaway on the voyage, and a sandstorm on the desert. Irving Allen's direction makes a good try for realism and avoids hokum theatrics to a great extent. Production values shaped by Louis B. Appleton, Jr. are good throughout. Camerawork by Jack Greenhalgh, Jr., is the particular standout. The seascapes showing the ketch underway, the desert scenes and other lensing are tops.

Albert is excellent in the lead role. Elena Verdugo graces brief femme spot. Bobby Cooper, Forrest Taylor, Ray Teal, Matt Willis, Martin Garralaga, Daniel Kerry and others in cast show up well. *Brog.*

The Strange Mr. Gregory

Monogram release of Louis Berkoff production. Stars Edmund Lowe and Jean Rogers; features Don Douglas, Frank Reicher. Directed by Phil Rosen. Story, Myles Connolly; adaptation, Charles S. Belden; editor, Seth Larson; camera, Ira Morgan. At New York, N. Y., dual, week Dec. 13, '45. Running time, 63 MINS.

Gregory.....................Edmund Lowe
Ellen Randall..................Jean Rogers
John Randall.................Don Douglas
Riker.......................Frank Reicher
Sheila Edwards.........Marjorie Hoshelle
District Attorney....Robert Emmett Keane
Blair.......................Jonathan Hale
Inspector Hoskins.............Frank Mayo
Detective Lefert..............Fred Kelsey
Drunk.......................Jack Norton
Maid.......................Anita Turner
Judge....................Tom Leffingwell

"The Strange Mr. Gregory" is an utterly fantastic murder mystery about a murder that was never committed but it moves at a nice pace, holding the interest well, and should pan out all right as a supporting feature on double bills.

Edmund Lowe plays a magician who is supposed to have been killed and then, in order to further his romantic means, poses as a brother who, of course, doesn't exist. The idea is to pin the faked murder on the husband of the gal with whom he's fallen in love, that he may be free to take a lease on her. A friend

of hers, however, uncovers evidence of the hoax and Lowe finally is shot by police when he tries to escape.

Opposite Lowe is Jean Rogers, who plays the wife of Don Douglas, the man convicted of the phoney murder. Frank Reicher, Marjorie Hoshelle and Robert Emmett Keane in the cast also perform with ease and conviction. *Char.*

Miniature Reviews

"Voice of the Whistler" (Col). So-so whodunit of its type.

"The Tiger Woman" (Rep). Fair murder meller fare.

"Lightning Raiders" (PRC). Buster Crabbe, Al St. John in an okay western.

"It Happened at the Inn" (Metro - Int'l). French - made comedy - drama outstanding; strong boxoffice at arty theatres.

"Once There Was a Girl" (Russian-made) (Artkino). Moving story but slow and not for average U. S. audience despite English titles.

Voice of the Whistler

Columbia release of Rudolph C. Flothow production. Stars Richard Dix; features Lynn Merrick, Rhys Williams, James Cardwell, Tom Kennedy. Directed by William Castle. Screenplay by Wilfred H. Pettitt, William Castle; story by Allan Radar; suggested by CBS program, "The Whistler"; camera, George Meehan; editor, Dwight Caldwell. At Fox, Brooklyn, dual, week Dec. 19, '45. Running time, 60 MINS.

John Sinclair..................Richard Dix
Joan Martin.................Lynn Merrick
Ernie Sparrow..............Rhys Williams
Fred Graham................James Cardwell
Ferdinand.....................Tom Kennedy
Paul Kitridge................Donald Woods
Dr. Rose.....................Egon Brecher
Bobbie........................GiGi Pirreau

Despite the eerie buildup, "Voice of the Whistler" isn't as haunting as ballyhooed. A minor item.

The story opens in the champagne surroundings of Richard Dix's menage. He decides, after many years of hard work, to take a long-needed vacation. Given only six months to live, he asks the beautiful nurse whom he has known briefly to marry him for the short duration of his life, declaring all his fortune to her in exchange. Envisioning wealth for her struggling interne-fiance, she consents after promising to return to said fiance in a half year. They go to live in a luxuriously refurbished lighthouse, but seven months after their deal was made, Dix is healthier than ever, in love with his wife and vice versa. But the fiance-in-waiting enters the scene to reclaim his love, which Dix resents. The interne plans to kill him, but is killed instead. Her husband electrocuted and her lover murdered, the heroine shuts herself in the lighthouse, self-punishment for what she believes herself responsible.

Best portions of the pic are the interesting camera shots in the lighthouse and the coastal scenes. Dix as the selfish kingpin, Lynn Merrick as the bewildered and scheming wife, and James Cardwell as the avenging interne, turn in competent performances. The story itself leaves much unfinished, giving audiences a few bad steers. Opening as it does, like its predecessors, with the shadow of the philosophizing Whistler, the pic starts off with suspense, but the effect is lost after about a third of the film.

The Tiger Woman

Republic release of Dorell and Stuart E. McGowan production. Features Adele Mara. Directed by Phillip Ford. Screenplay, George Carleton Brown; based on radio play by John A. Dunkel; camera, Ernest Miller; editor, Fred Allen; special effects, Howard and Theodore Lydecker. At Strand, Brooklyn, dual, week Dec. 19, '45. Running time, 57 MINS.

Sharon Winslow...............Adele Mara
Jerry Devery...............Kane Richmond
Stephen Mason............Richard Fraser
Phyllis Carrington.........Peggy Stewart
Inspector Leggett..............Cy Kendall
Constance Grey..............Beverly Loyd
Joe Sapphire................Gregory Gay
Sylvester.....................John Kelly
Mr. White................Addison Richards
Rosie Gargan.................Donia Bussey
Coroner.....................Frank Reicher
Bartender....................Garry Owen

Except for her billing as a "tiger woman" in the nitery where she

sings, the title is a misnomer. It's a fair story that will get along on a co-featured basis.

Adele Mara, the cafe trush, bumps off her husband for the insurance. When her lover gets cold feet, she bumps him off, also. But the shrewd, handsome dick is on her heels right along. She connives to do away with him but it ends with a confession from her own lips just before she's about to pull the trigger on him. She's saved by the split-timely arrival of his aides.

Although the pic is well supplied with clues, there are many the writers themselves just forgot to pick up, in addition to much incredulity throughout. It is all obvious before half the film has unreeled.

Cast does an adequate job. Kane Richmond looks like another Alan Ladd. He resembles him and has enough of his swagger for the femmes.

Lightning Raiders

PRC release of Sigmund Neufeld production. Stars Buster Crabbe, Al "Fuzzy" St. John. Directed by Sam Newfield. Original story and screenplay, Elmer Clifton; camera, Jack Greenhalgh; editor, Holbrook N. Todd. Tradeshown N.Y., Dec. 21, '45. Running time, 60 MINS.

Billy Carson...............Buster Crabbe
Fuzzy.................Al "Fuzzy" St. John
Jane.......................Mady Laurence
Wright.......................Henry Hall
Hayden.....................Steve Darrell
Kane.....................Stanford Jolley
Murray.....................Karl Hackett
Phillips......................Roy Brent
Mrs. Murray..................Marin Sais
Lorrin.....................Al Ferguson

Latest of the Buster Crabbe-Al "Fuzzy" St. John starrers, "Lightning Raiders" is a run-of-the-mill western but with enough action, gun fights and juvenile comedy to satisfy the customers who go for this type of thing. Two stars have built up quite a following for themselves and their names on the marquee should make the film do okay in its usual spot on a weekend dualler.

Only novel factor in the picture is that the action begins in the very first sequence, the first shot fading in on a stagecoach robbery. Since the script for the previous film in the series had the robbers steal the gold, it's their turn now to make off with the mail. St. John, expecting an important letter, becomes suspicious of the motive for the robbery and calls in his pal, Crabbe, a roving cowhand. Investigating, they trail the bandits to a deserted shack, where they stage a rough-and-tumble to get back the mail.

Subsequent events prove that the cowtown's leading citizen is the brains behind the gang, using the stolen mail to get an inside on the citizens' business doings so he can crack down with mortgage foreclosures, etc. After getting into the usual scrapes with the sheriff and the heavies, Crabbe and his sidekick finally bring the gang to justice and everything winds up on a peaceful note.

Two stars of the piece do well in the riding, roping and shooting sequences, with St. John trying hard to inject some humor into his antics. Rest of the cast is adequate with the exception of Mady Laurence, the femme lead whose heavy gestures and eyebrow-lifting were passe several decades ago. Production mountings are okay and director Sam Newfield keeps tempo fast.

It Happened at the Inn

("Goupi Mains Rouges") (FRENCH-MADE)

Metro-International release of Minerva Productions picture. Stars Fernand Ledoux, Maurice Schutz, Georges Rollin, Blanchette Brunoy; features Arthur Devers, Germaine, Albert Remy. Directed by Jacques Becker. Screenplay, Pierre Very; English titles, Marjorie Adams. At 55th St. Playhouse, N.Y., starting Dec. 21, '45. Running time, 96 MINS.

"Red Hands"...............Fernand Ledoux
"The Emperor"............Maurice Schutz
"Monsieur"..................Georges Rollin

"Primrose" .... Blanchette Brunoy
"Penebpenny" .... Arthur Devere
"The Law" .... Guy Faviere
"Ten Drops" .... Germaine Kerjean
"Ditto" .... Rene Genin
Marie .... Lino Noro
Jean .... Albert Remy
"Chatterbox" .... Marcella Hainia
"Brigadier" Jerome .... Marcel Peres
Maurice, the Carpenter .... Pierre Labry

(In Frenchs English Titles)

This first new French feature to be shown in N.Y. since the war is in the best French tradition. It has the realism, grim humor and horrifices that recall how far French film productions had progressed before the war halted production. Why Metro chose this French-made comedy-drama to place on its program of foreign-mades for dubbing into English is easy to see. Production rates the brightest French cinematic efforts.

"It Happened at the Inn" is being synchronized into English for general release, and it's obvious how much more effective the picture will become when the countless passages of French wit are translated into Americanese. Even as is, picture is a strong entry for arty and foreign-language theatres of the U.S. because Metro has given it nice production and sparkling screen titling. It takes its place alongside the finest French screen vehicles of this type.

"Inn" is the fable of a greedy, old group of peasants who operate a country tavern and store in the back country several hundred miles from Paris. It seldom moves swiftly, usually concentrating on character studies. Family group is known as the Goupis, and they go in for nicknames. There's "Red Hands," the family prankster. There's "M'sieu," so dubbed because this young handsome youth has clicked in Paris. He's been called home by the threatened passing of his granddad, "The Emperor." Latter is only 106.

Sudden stroke of "The Emperor," the theft of some money he was making away with when stricken, plus the slaying of "Ten Drops," the irascible medicine-taking member of the family, builds to a strong climax. Then there's the romance between M'sieu and Primrose for added interest.

Probably the best known of the cast is Fernand Ledoux, who is the alert prankster, "Red Hands." He gives his usual superb performance. Standout, however, is Maurice Schutz as "The Emperor." Not far behind is a bright characterization by Georges Rollin as "M'sieu." Other finished portrayals are contributed by Blanchette Brunoy, Arthur Devere, Germaine Keriean, as "Ten Drops"; Line Noro, Albert Remy and Marcel Peres.

Direction by Jacques Becker is splendid, while Pierre Very's story is okay if a bit unoriginal. Production niceties include several traveling shots, nice use of closeups and superb sound. Metro has brightened up the introduction by employing cartoon reproductions of main characters so that the audience can spot different characters readily. Marjorie Adams' English titles are intelligent and much more easy to follow than usually found on a foreign production.

Once There Was a Girl
(RUSSIAN-MADE)

Artkino release of Soyuzdet (Moscow) production, directed by Victor Eisimont. Screenplay by Vladimir Nedobrovo; English titles, Charles Clement; camera, George Garibian. At Stanley, N. Y., week of Dec. 22, '45. Running time, 71 MINS.

Nastenka .... Nina Ivanova
Katla .... Natasha Zashipina
Nastenka's Mother .... Ada Voytsik
Katla's Mother .... Vera Altaiskaya
Tonia .... Leda Shtykan
Makar Ivanovich .... Alexander Larinov
Nastenka's Father .... Nikolai Korn

(In Russian; English Titles)

To the Soviet film-makers, the grim business of war needs nothing but stark war realism. That was evident again in "Once There Was a Girl." It's a slow picture, developing its theme with the monotony of war itself. To the average American film audience, it has little appeal. Which is merely a commentary about American remoteness from genuine suffering.

Story concerns the way in which two Leningrad girls took everything that the long Nazi siege of that Soviet city forced upon the town's residents. After many privations, and coming close to death in an air raid, the kids come through to celebrate the liberation, of course. It's stark realism, moving at times in a slow, funereal manner. Nine-year-old Nina Ivanova is superb, and moppet Natasha Zashipina, only 5 years old, literally steals the show. Both are great little actresses, and a Hollywood fortune could be assured to the younger of the two. *Cars.*

1946

Miniature Reviews

"Caesar and Cleopatra" (Eagle-Lion). Pascal's (Rank) Shavian epic disappointing despite opulence.

"The Harvey Girls" (Musical; Color) (M-G). OK filmusical with Judy Garland, John Hodiak, Ray Bolger, certain for big b.o.

"Leave Her to Heaven," (Technicolor) (20th). Lush color values and highly exploitable theme gear for heavy femme trade.

"Scarlet Street" (Diana-U). Okay b.o. melodrama with some lead trio that headed 'Woman In Window" (RKO) last season.

"The Sailor Takes a Wife" (MG). Smooth comedy about young love, based on stage play. B.o. outlook good.

"Up Goes Maisie" (MG). Typical "Maisie" comedy with plenty of laughs.

"One Way To Love" (Col). Fair comedy that should do okay.

"Snafu" (Col). Uninspired screen version of last year's legiter.

"I Ring Doorbells" (PRC). Mild melodrama for the dual situations.

"The Red Dragon" (Mono) (Song). Dull Charlie Chan whodunit.

"Allotment Wives, Inc." (Mono). Good cast in fair meller.

"Trojan Brothers" (Anglo-Am.). British-made comedy looks mild for U. S.; lacks names for marquee.

"The Old Clock at Roenneberga" (Swedish). Well produced Svensk pie, but too long.

Caesar and Cleopatra

(Technicolor)
(BRITISH-MADE)

London, Dec. 12.

Eagle-Lion release of Gabriel Pascal production, directed by Pascal. Stars Vivien Leigh, Claude Rains. Scenario and dialog from his own play by Bernard Shaw. Music by Georges Auric; decor and costumes by Oliver Messel; camera, F. A. Young, Robert Krasker, Jack Hildyard, Jack Cardiff. At Odeon Marble Arch, London, Dec. 11. Running time, **135 MINS.**

Caesar	Claude Rains
Cleopatra	Vivien Leigh
Appollodorus	Stewart Granger
Fatateeta	Flora Robson
Pothinus	Francis L. Sullivan
Ruffio	Basil Sydney
Ptolemy	Anthony Harvey
Lucius Septimius	Raymond Harvey
Britannus	Cecil Parker
Achillas	Antony Eustrel
Theodotus	Ernest Thesiger
Bel Affris	Leo Genn

Deplorable as is London critics' savage delight in damning the work of native artists—the while they hail with fulsome praise anything and everything of Russian or French origin—today's newspaper excoriation of this $6,000,000 spectacle is justified. Scripted by Shaw himself the actual lines are exactly as written in the original stage version, but perhaps because of the overpowering opulence of the screen settings the Shavian brilliance of 1898 sounds corny to 1945 ears.

To those on both sides of the Atlantic who realize the importance of more extensive distribution of British films in America, "Caesar and Cleopatra," intended to be the spearhead of J. Arthur Rank's pic invasion, will come as a disappointment. In spite of its prodigal magnificence, indeed because of its production values, such vague story interest as it has is hopelessly swamped.

Claude Rains' Caesar—thanks to Shaw and Gabriel Pascal, director—is accurately and succinctly pinpointed by Vivien Leigh as Cleopatra when she calls him "a nice old gentleman." As for her portrayal of the Queen of Queens—again the responsibility of author and director—Rains calls the turn when he tells her with justifiable incredulity she is not Queen of Egypt, but a queen of the gypsies. So they each establish the other's characterization at their first meeting—in the desert, under the stars, between the paws of a "kitten" sphinx. And so they go on for two-and-a-quarter hours — Caesar a flabby old appeaser, Cleopatra a petulant child-woman who does everything to disprove her royal birth except chew gum.

Mystery and the Sphinx have furnished a plethora of cliches down through the ages, but this Shavian yarn as presented in this pic poses another mystery. Anybody who can tell you what it is all about when the final fade comes, and you go back over it sequence by sequence, will have to be a super Gunga Din.

Sketchy references to an earlier visit of a young Roman "with strong round, gleaming arms" elicit his identification by Caesar as being Marc Antony. And at the end of the flick, as the Emperor departs in his trireme for Rome, Cleopatra is left with his promise to send Antony back to her. Apart from this vague, soft-pedal reference to the possibility of her knowing what passion means, Miss Leigh's Cleopatra is as lacking in sex consciousness as the boy actor (Anthony Harvel) who plays the part of her brother, Ptolemy, whose throne she seizes.

If her characterization did not show her to be utterly unmoral and capricious — ordering murder done between changes of gowns without batting an eye—excuse might be found for her sexlessness on the grounds of her loyalty to the far distant Marc. But there is nothing in the script to suggest she would be loyal—even if she were in love with Antony, as to which you are left more than somewhat in doubt.

Seemingly just to make things more irritating there appears halfway through the pic Stewart Granger as Apollodorus, a Sicilian with flashing eyes, dazzling white teeth and a torso of burnished bronze which, by contrast, makes tubby old Caesar remind you more than ever of an especially easy going President Taft. On his first meeting with Cleopatra all the femmes at the preview sat up straight, and took a new interest in the screen. Here at last was what they'd been waiting for. But nix on anything like that, says Mr. Shaw. So Cleopatra passes Granger up as if he were a dirty deuce—instead of being what he so obviously, so vibrantly is, a grand chunk of three-quarters nude male s.a.

In a cast of more than 100 of Britain's finest stage actors individual performances of bits are all flawless. To individualize would be to do injustice to those unnamed. But for the pic to have a chance in America, one of these supporting actors ought to be cut bodily out of the many sequences in which he figures in the present version as comic relief.

This is not to say anything disparaging of Cecil Parker's performance as Britannus. As a Dundreary-mustached, ladidah Englishman with an Oxford accent and a deeprooted disapproval of Caesar's gorgeous (Technicolor) trappings, Parker cuts a mildly amusing figure in English eyes. To Yanks dragging in this character—even if it may be historically accurate—it will be distasteful, and definitely unfunny. Doubtless, Shaw idolators will appreciate the Shavian irony implicit in Britannus' protesting against Caesar's having tete-a-tetes with Cleopatra—unchaperoned—but ordinary people will regard it as an unwarrantable intrusion of a Briton into Cleopatra's Egypt.

Genuine disappointment will be felt by those who have the best good of Hollywood and Wardour Street at heart if "Caesar and Cleopatra" proves to be the flop the London notices would seem to make certain. For at long last, in the person of J. Arthur Rank, a British film producer has arisen with daring enough to spend money as lavishly as his predecessors have scrimped penuriously. And make no mistake about it, the prodigality of this one makes Griffith and De Mille and Von Stroheim look like niggards. *Talb.*

The Harvey Girls

(MUSICAL; COLOR)

Metro release of Arthur Freed production; associate producer, Roger Edens. Stars Judy Garland, John Hodiak; features Ray Bolger, Angela Lansbury, Preston Foster. Directed by George Sidney. Screenplay by Edmund Beloin, Nathaniel Curtis, Harry Crane, James O'Hanlon, Samson Raphaelson; story by Eleanore Griffin and William Rankin, based on book by Samuel Hopkins Adams; additional dialog, Kay Van Riper; camera, George Folsey, Warren Newcombe; songs, Johnny Mercer and Harry Warren; dances, Robert Alton; music, Lennie Hayton; ochestrations, Conrad Salinger; vocals, Kay Thompson; editor, Albert Akst. Tradeshown N. Y., Dec. 26, '45; running time, **101 MINS.**

Susan Bradley	Judy Garland
Ned Trent	John Hodiak
Chris Maule	Ray Bolger
Em	Angela Lansbury
Judge Sam Purvis	Preston Foster
Alma	Virginia O'Brien
Terry O'Halloran	Kenny Baker
Sonora Cassidy	Marjorie Main
H. H. Hartsey	Chill Wills
Miss Bliss	Selena Royle
Deborah	Cyd Charisse
Ethel	Ruth Brady
Marty Peters	Jack Lambert
Jed Adams	Edward Earle
Rev. Claggett	Morris Ankrum
First Cowboy	Wm. "Bill" Phillips
John Henry	Ben Carter
Second Cowboy	Norman Leavitt
"Goldust" McClean	Horace McNally

"The Harvey Girls" owes its prime b.o. heft to its beautiful Technicolor and its hit song, "Atchison, Topeka & Santa Fe." The way that this Johnny Mercer-Harry Warren tune gets a plugfest would make any Lindy's songplugger do nipups with envy. These factors, plus Judy Garland, John Hodiak and Ray Bolger for the marquee, are enough insurance for fancy wicket takings.

As a story, "The Harvey Girls" is a curious blend of Technicolor wild-westernism, frontier town skullduggery and a troupe of Harvey restaurant waitresses who deport themselves in a manner that's a cross between a sorority and a Follies troupe. The prim Fred Harvey gals are pictured as trailblazers who bring civilization to the wild, wild west. They have the esprit of Vassarites on a picnic and the pulchritude of a Ziegfeld line.

In the "Oklahoma!" idiom—in fact "The Harvey Girls" would have made an even better legit musical—Miss Garland is a correspondence bride, hoaxed by the boss gambler (Hodiak) who has been doing a John Alden for Chill Wills, the town drunk. The manner in which Miss Garland tells off the gaming-house owner, upsets the crooked judge (Preston Foster), brings religion back to the New Mexico pioneer town, and the rest of it are of familiar but palatable pattern.

Hodiak is a curious casting in a musical of this nature. Miss Garland, however, makes much of it believable and most of it acceptable.

Angela Lansbury is prominent as the Mae West of the casino, Hodiak's No. 1 flame until Miss Garland, Virginia O'Brien, Cyd Charisse, Selena Royle and Marjorie Main appear on the scene. Bolger is an itinerant dancer; Kenny Baker is the gambling hall perfessor at the piano (who also writes songs on the side), a good vis-a-vis for Miss Charisse, newcomer who impresses. Baker's "I Shall Be Loving You" is a good solo, while Miss O'Brien deadpans "Wild Wild West" in standard style.

There's the usual fol-de-rol such as hijacking all the good steaks; snakes in the Harvey gals' closets; incendiary tactics, and the like.

Climax is a dance given by the Harvey Girls which the saloon dolls can't break up, proving that virtue is triumphant and that for the first time in the history of Sandrock, N. M., the forces of good have prevailed. The story, obviously, is one of those things but under the lush Metro production auspices, along with the color, the fine scoring, director George Sidney's megging and the rest of it, the film more than sustains itself. *Abel.*

Leave Her to Heaven

(TECHNICOLOR)

Hollywood, Dec. 22.

20th-Fox release of William A. Bacher production. Stars Gene Tierney, Cornel Wilde, Jeanne Crain; features Vincent Price, Mary Philips, Ray Collins, Gene Lockhart, Reed Hadley, Darryl Hickman, Chill Wills. Directed by John M. Stahl. Screenplay, Jo Swerling; based on novel by Ben Ames Williams; music, Alfred Newman; camera, Leon Shamroy, Fred Sersen; editor, James B. Clark. Previewed Carthay Circle, Hollywood, Dec. 19, '45. Running time, **111 MINS.**

Ellen	Gene Tierney
Richard	Cornel Wilde
Ruth	Jeanne Crain
Russell Quinton	Vincent Price
Mrs. Berent	Mary Philips
Glen Robie	Ray Collins
Dr. Saunders	Gene Lockhart
Dr. Mason	Reed Hadley
Danny Harland	Darryl Hickman
Leick Thome	Chill Wills
Judge	Paul Everton
Mrs. Robie	Olive Blakeney
Bedford	Addison Richards
Catterson	Harry Depp
Carlson	Grant Mitchell
Medcraft	Milton Parsons
Norton	Earl Schenck
Lin Robie	Hugh Maguire
Tess Robie	Betty Hannon
Nurse	Kay Riley

Sumptuous Technicolor mounting and a highly exploitable story lend considerable importance to "Leave Her to Heaven" that it might not have had otherwise. Theme offers heavy magnet for the femme trade and grosses should be correspondingly big. Added importance is being given film by 20th-Fox with a strong exploitation campaign. Starring personalities have draw value to aid the selling.

Script by Joe Swerling, based on Ben Ames Williams' bestseller, has emotional power in the jealousy theme but it hasn't been as forcefully interpreted by the leads as it could have been in more histrionically capable hands. This is not likely to make much difference in film's draw nor will its inclination towards talkiness and directorial slowness by John M. Stahl.

Essentially woman's story tells of a girl whose possessive jealousy smothered her father and destroyed her husband's infatuation. Gene Tierney, as the girl, meets Cornel Wilde while en route to the Western home of Ray Collins. Wilde, an author, resembles Ellen's late father and she falls madly in love. His infatuation for her leads her to rush into marriage. Jealousy takes over when Wilde and bride visit former's young brother, recovering from infantile paralysis. Trio go to Wilde's Maine lodge where she connives the death of the youngster by drowning. Her next murder is that of her unborn child. To round out her crimes Miss Tierney, discovering she has lost her husband, commits suicide in a manner to make her foster-sister, whom Wilde now loves, be accused of murder.

Story is told in retrospect by Ray Collins, family attorney, and film opens with Wilde returning to Maine and his waiting love, Jeanne Crain, after serving a prison term for concealing Miss Tierney's crimes. Latter and Wilde use their personalities in interpreting their dramatic assignments. Miss Crain's role of the foster-sister is more subdued but excellently done. Vincent Price, as the discarded lover, gives a theatrical reading to the courtroom scenes as the district attorney.

Top performances are turned in by the supporting players. Mary

Philips, as the mother; Darryl Hickman, particularly fine as the young brother; Gene Lockhart, seen briefly; Reed Hadley, Chill Wills and others make the most of their assignments.

William A. Bacher's production guidance furnished a lush frame for the outstanding color photography by Leon Shamroy. Mounting is exceptionally eye-appealing and lensing is of the highest quality. Among other production distinctions are special photographic effects by Fred Sersen and Alfred Newman's music, latter proving considerable aid to direction and playing in developing the mood. ***Brog.***

Scarlet Street

Hollywood, Dec. 20.

Universal release of Diana production. Stars Edward G. Robinson and Joan Bennett; features Dan Duryea, Jess Barker, Margaret Lindsay, Rosalind Ivan, Samuel S. Hinds. Produced and directed by Fritz Lang. Screenplay, Dudley Nichols; based on novel and play, "La Chienne," by George de la Fouchardiere (in collaboration with Mouezy-Eon); camera, Milton Krasner; editor, Arthur Hilton; musical score, H. J. Salter; special photography, John P. Fulton. Previewed in Hollywood, Dec. 20, '45. Running time, **98 MINS.**

Christopher Cross.....Edward G. Robinson
Kitty ....Joan Bennett
Johnny ....Dan Duryea
Millie ....Margaret Lindsay
Adele ....Rosalind Ivan
Charles Pringle...........Samuel S. Hinds
Janeway ....Jess Barker
Dellarowe ....Arthur Loft
Pop Lejon..................Vladimir Sokoloff
Patcheye ....Charles Kemper
Hogarth ....Russell Hicks
Mrs. Michaels...................Anita Bolster
Nick...................Cyrus W. Kendell
Marchetti ....Fred Essler
Policeman ....Edgar Dearing
Policeman ....Tom Dillon
Chauffeur ....Chuck Hamilton
Employee ....Gus Glassmire
Employee ....Ralph Littlefield
Employee ....Sherry Hall
Employee ....Jack Statham
Barney ....Rodney Bell

"Scarlet Street" has all the earmarks of getting Diana Productions off to an excellent boxoffice start. Star and production values gear it for top position in all situations. Extra exploitation value is offered through star names being same as headed the successful "Woman in the Window" (RKO). Melodrama is presented by Walter Wanger for Universal release.

Fritz Lang's production and direction ably project the sordid tale of the romance between a Milquetoast character and a gold-digging blonde. Script is tightly written by Dudley Nichols and is played for sustained interest and suspense by the cast. Edward G. Robinson is the mild cashier and amateur painter whose love for Joan Bennett leads him to embezzlement, murder and disgrace. Two stars turn in top work to keep the interest high, and Dan Duryea's portrayal of the crafty and crooked opportunist whom Miss Bennett loves is a standout in furthering the melodrama.

Robinson is partied for his 20 years of faithful service as a clothing store cashier. Miss Bennett believes he's a distinguished artist although actually his amateurish painting is for his own amusement. She and Duryea plot to milk Robinson for money and persuade him to finance an apartment. Duryea seeks to sell some of Robinson's unsigned daubs. The paintings become a hit but not until after the cashier has embazzled cash from his firm to satisfy the gal's demands for money. Theft is discovered; Robinson turns to her for comfort but finds her in Duryea's arms. He kills her with an icepick and manages to send Duryea to the electric chair for the crime. Finale has Robinson a drifting derelict, unable to convince anyone he's not crazy when he tries to give himself up for his crimes.

Featured cast capably carries out the mood of the piece. Jess Barker, art critic; Margaret Lindsay, as the girl's roommate; Rosalind Ivan, Robinson's shrewish wife; Samuel S. Hinds, Charles Kemper and others are expert. Production mounting is good. Melodramatics are aided considerably by the excellent camera work of Milton Krasner; H. J. Salter's musical score and editing by Arthur Hilton. ***Brog.***

The Sailor Takes a Wife

Hollywood, Dec. 28.

Metro release of Edwin H. Knopf production. Stars Robert Walker, June Allyson; features Hume Cronyn, Audrey Totter, Eddie "Rochester" Anderson, Reginald Owen. Directed by Richard Whorf. Screenplay by Chester Erskine, Anne Morrison Chapin, Whitfield Cook; based on play by Erskine; camera, Sidney Wagner; score, Johnny Green; special effects, Warren Newcombe; editor, Irvine Warburton. Tradeshown at Los Angeles, Dec. 27, '45. Running time, **92 MINS.**

John........................Robert Walker
Mary..........................June Allyson
Freddie.......................Hume Cronyn
Lisa...........................Audrey Totter
Harry.........Eddie "Rochester" Anderson
Mr. Amboy.................Reginald Owen
Butler.................Gerald Oliver Smith

"The Sailor Takes a Wife" stage play has been given light, broad screen treatment to head it for good returns in all situations. Production by Edwin H. Knopf isn't elaborate but has polish, the direction is smooth, and the cast gets the best from the comedy situations.

Robert Walker and June Allyson heading the funning, making the antics and complications around which the plot revolves delightful. Story is on the light side and laughs are mostly situation, but Richard Whorf's direction keeps it on the move for audience interest. Plot deals with a sailor and a girl who meet and marry, all in one evening, and subsequent efforts to adjust themselves to marital status.

Bride's first disappointment comes when her husband is dicharged almost immediately, leaving her with a civilian instead of the hero she expected. Further complications develop when Walker, searching for a job, becomes entangled innocently with a romantically-inclined foreign femme menace, brightly played by Audrey Totter. The husband also gets his chance to misunderstand when Hume Cronyn, as Miss Allyson's former boss, continues his pursuit of the bride. Situations contrive to keep bride and groom from consummating their marriage right up to the final footage. It's all broad farce with bedroom implications that will keep audiences amused.

In addition to the top foursome of players, Eddie "Rochester" Anderson rates considerable chuckles as handy man in the apartment house occupied by the newlyweds. Reginald Owen has one neat scene as Miss Totter's rich boy friend.

Production appurtenances are excellent, including camera work by Sidney Wagner, the editing by Irvine Warburton and Johnny Green's score. ***Brog.***

Up Goes Maisie

Hollywood, Dec. '28.

Metro release of George Haight production. Stars Ann Southern and George Murphy.; features Hillary Brooke, Horace McNally, Ray Collins, Jeff York. Directed by Harry Beaumont. Story and screenplay, Thelma Robinson; based on the character created by Wilson Collison; camera, Robert Planck; editor, Irvine Warburton; score, David Snell; special effects, A. Arnold Gillespie. Tradeshown at Los Angeles, Dec. 27, '45. Running time, 90 mins.

Maisie Ravier..............................Ann Southern
Joseph Morton..........................George Murphy
Barbara Nuboult.........................Hillary Brooke
Tim Kingby.............................Horace McNally
Mr. Hendrickson.............................Ray Collins
Elmer Saunders...................................Jeff York
Mr. J.G. Nuboult...........................Paul Harvey
"Mitch"......................................Murry Alper
Bill Stuart....................................Lewis Howard
Jonathan Marbey...............................Jack Davis
Miss Wolfe.....................................Gloria grafton
Benson..John Eldredge

Continuing the screen adventures of "Maisie," Metro's comedy character portrayed by Ann Sothern, film hits consistent pace throughout most of its footage and averages out as excellent chuckle material. It has been given good production mounting to back up performances. George Murphy's name as co-star with Miss Sothern lends additional marquee value.

Plot has the brash femme leaving war work and seeking a place in civilian business now that hostilities are over. She lands a job with Murphy, inventor of new type helicopter with an automatic pilot control. Romance develops between Maisie and the boss and before film can come to successful conclusion, Maisie is instrumental in saving Murphy's brainchild from a rival plane company; makes it possible for him to demonstrate it to a west coast industrial giant.

Development gets rather broad at times, a typical feature of the usual "Maisie" film, and plays up Miss Sothern's amateur piloting when she flies the helicopter away from the rivals, after it had been stolen, as principal thrill sequence. Harry Beaumont's directorial pacing is good with exception of couple of scenes that could have been tighter.

Menace is provided by Hillary Brooke, Horace McNally and Paul Harvey in the plot. Jeff York and Murray Alper show up well as loyal supporters of Murphy's experimental work, and Ray Collins is expert as the industrial production magnate.

George Haight produced. Robert Planck's photography is good. Particular aid to thrill sequence is special effects by A. Arnold Gillespie. ***Brog.***

One Way to Love

Columbia release of Burt Kelly production. Features Willard Parker, Marguerite Chapman, Chester Morris, Janis Carter, Hugh Herbert. Directed by Ray Enright. Screenplay by Joseph Hoffman, Jack Henley from original by Lester Lee, Larry Marks; editor, Richard Fantl; camera, Charles Lawton, Jr. Tradeshown N.Y. Dec. 26, '45 Running time, 83 MINS.

Mitchell Raymond..............................Willard Parker
Marcia Winthrop....................Marguerite Chapman
Barry Cole......................................Chester Morris
Josie Hart...Janis Carter
Eustace P. Trumble............................Hugh Herbert
Captain Henderson.........................Dusty Anderson
A.J. Gunther....................................Jerome Cowan
Train Conductor..................................Irving Bacon
Hobie Simmons..................................Roscoe Karns
Hopkins...Frank Sully
Jensen...Frank Jenks
Roger Winthrop.................................Lewis Russell

"One Way to Love" is an amusing little piece of escapist comedy with a capable cast, nice production mountings and plenty of gags that follow each other in rapid succession. Film misses, however, because of an overlong script that gives the impression the scripters got so entangled with their story they didn't know where to stop. **This fact, plus the dearth of any top marquee names, sets the film as a supporting feature on twin bills, where it should hold up okay.**

Plot, most of which takes place on a Chicago-Hollywood train, would have been much better if the film had ended several reels earlier. Chester Morris is a Chi radio writer who's reduced to writing singing commercials when his partner, Willard Parker, walks out on him to take a job with his fiancee's father. Duo's agent lines up a $1,000 per week show in Hollywood but the contract calls for the two to collaborate on the script. Morris and his secretary-sweetheart, Janis Carter, inveigle Parker onto a California-bound train, with Marguerite Chapman, the fiancee, pursuing to lure Parker back to Chi.

Aboard the train the foursome meets the president of the firm for whom they're to write the show (Jerome Cowan) and also Hugh Herbert, presumably an eccentric millionaire, who offers them twice the dough if they'll work for him. After they accept Herbert's offer, two private investigators pick up the latter as an escaped lunatic and the boys promptly try to re-sign with Cowan. Arriving in Los Angeles, however, it turns out that Cowan is really the lunatic while Herbert is the McCoy, so the foursome boards the train again to chase Herbert back to Chi.

Featured players all turn in competent comedy bits, with the supporting cast filling in capably. Director Ray Enright keeps the tempo fast and the gags timed nicely, but the entire proceedings are stymied by the looseness of the script.

Snafu

Columbia release of Jack Moss (George Abbott) production, directed by Moss. Features Robert Benchley, Vera Vague, Conrad Janis, Nanette Parks. Screenplay, Louis Solomon and Harold Buchman of their own play; camera, Frank F. Planer; editor, Aaron Stell. At Ambassador, N. Y., week Dec. 25, '45. Running time, **82 MINS.**

Ben Stevens..................Robert Benchley
Madge Stevens.....................Vera Vague
Ronald Stevens....................Conrad Janis
Laura Jessup.....................Nanette Parks
Kate Hereford.....................Janis Wilson
Danny Baker.......................Jimmy Lloyd
Aunt Emily..........................Enid Markey
Josephina.................................Eva Puig
Detective..............................Ray Mayer
Martha.......................Marcia Mae Jones
Colonel West...................Winfield Smith
Taylor...............................John Souther
Phil Ford...........................Byron Foulger
Dean Garrett................Kathleen Howard

When "Snafu" opened on the stage of the Auditorium, Rochester, N. Y., in October, 1944, the VARIETY review said that "it may be that the play has greater possibilities in the broader treatment for the screen than in the confines of the single setting." Despite that prediction, however, the screen version has emerged as a poor facsimile. Film has all the ingredients that made the stageplay a hit but falls short because of faulty direction and slow pace. Names of the late Robert Benchley and Vera Vague may help on the marquee but boxoffice prospects are tepid.

"Snafu," the title is taken from the GI's contraction of "situation normal—all fouled up," which almost describes the film. Most of the plot revolves around the difficulties of an under-age soldier hero in readjusting himself to civilian and family life after his parents succeed in getting him honorably discharged when his true age is discovered. Louis Solomon and Harold Buchman, who wrote the screenplay from their original legit show, have incorporated most of the same wacky dialog and tragi-comic incidents but the film is stymied by director Jack Moss' uninspired direction and its faltering pace. Tightening of the script and the maintaining of a more sock tempo could have done much to bolster the picture.

Competent cast is also hampered by these same faults, with the exception of Conrad Janis as Ronnie, the young soldier. Janis was allegedly snatched from the Broadway cast of "Dark of the Moon" for the role and shows up well, especially in the scene where he tries to explain to his father the facts of life as he learned them in the Army. Benchley, in one of the last films he made before his untimely death, tries hard to project his usually excellent humor as the father, but the role isn't suited to his talents and his efforts fall short of the mark.

Miss Vague, as Benchley's wife, is also miscast, the semi-serious role a far cry from her usual zany acting. Rest of cast is adequate, with Enid Markey shining in the role of Aunt Emily, which she also portrayed in the stage production. Moss has lined the film with good production settings, which bring in the "broader treament" referred to above," but the picture still winds up on the deficit side.

I Ring Doorbells

Hollywood, Dec. 28.

PRC release of Martin Mooney production. Stars Anne Gwynne, Robert Shayne; features Roscoe Karns, Pierre Watkin, John Eldredge, Harry Tyler, Doria Caron. Directed by Frank Strayer, Screenplay by Dick Irving Hyland, based on book by Russell Birdwell, adapted by Hyland and Raymond L. Schrock; camera, Benjamin H. Kline; music, Erdody; editor, George McGuire. Previewed Dec. 26, '45. Running time 67 MINS.

Brooke	Anne Gwynne
Dick	Robert Shayne
Stubby	Roscoe Karns
G. B. Barton	Pierre Watkin
Shannon	Harry Shannon
Ransome	John Eldredge
Tippy	Harry Tyler
Yvette	Doria Caron
Helen	Jan Wiley
Clyde	Joel McGinns
The Inspector	Charles Wilson
Mr. Bradley	Hank Patterson
O'Halloran	Eugene Stutenroth
Willie	Roy Darmour

Screen adaptation of Russell Birdwell's book. "I Ring Doorbells" comes out as program material of short running time that will adapt itself to the lesser dualers. Production manages considerable effect for small budget and plot mixes up newspaper background with a murder mystery to offer slight interest to the paying customers.

Direction isn't very steady in unfolding yarn of high pressure newshawk, his romance with a femme feature writer and his accidental solving of a murder. Robert Shayne and Anne Gwynne make personable leads and contrive to help things out considerably while Roscoe Karns supplies his usual comedy as a newsphotog.

Plot has Shayne returning to his old reporting job after flunking as a playwright and puts him through various adventures as a star reporter. Murder melodrama enters into scheme of things when his publisher has him trying to get the goods on a gold-digging blonde out for the old man's son. Antics involving Shayne's courtship of the blonde's French maid so he can stash a camera in the girl's apartment are tiresome and contain few chuckles. The blonde is bumped off. Shayne produces his film of the crime and breaks alibi of the killer, who turns out to be the newspaper's drama critic.

Camera work, score, editing and other production credits are standard for release intentions. *Brog.*

The Red Dragon
(ONE SONG)

Monogram release of James S. Burkett production. Stars Sidney Toler; features Fortunio Bonanova, Benson Fong. Directed by Phil Rosen. Original screenplay, George Callahan; camera, Vincent Farrar; editor, Ace Herman. At New York, N. Y., Dec. 27, '45. Running time, 64 MINS.

Charlie Chan	Sidney Toler
Luis	Fortunio Bonanova
Tommy Chan	Benson Fong
Alfred Wyans	Robert E. Keane
Chattanooga Brown	Willie Best
Marguerite Fontan	Carol Hughes
Countess Irena	Marjorie Hoshelle
Joseph Bradish	Barton Yarborough
Edmond Slade	George Meeker
Charles Masack	Don Costello
Prentiss	Charles Trowbridge
Josephine	Mildred Boyd
Iris	Jean Wong
Dorn	Donald Dexter Taylor

Monogram has entered the atomic-bomb pix race with a stock detective trifle involving the vet Asiatic sleuth Charlie Chan. Pic isn't a serious threat, the yarn being a draggy, obvious whodunit that will suit only for nabe support.

Story involves attempts to steal a scientist's plans for an atomic bomb, with various mysterious characters gathered in Mexico City to lift the loot. One by one the assorted grifters are shot, with killer or weapon mysteriously absent. Chan finally discovers that the shots are fired by remote control from a launching device, and nabs the murderer, while ending the threat to the precious formula.

A cosmopolitan cast goes through the motions. Sidney Toler enacting Chan in his usually placid way; Fortunio Bonanova playing a Mexican inspector; Benson Fong, Chan's irrepressible son, and Willie Best, the comic relief as servant. Marjorie Hoshelle, as a nitery singer-suspect, handles a song well.

Production budget is modest and direction so-so. *Bron.*

Allotment Wives, Inc.

Monogram release of Jeffrey Bernerd-Kay Francis production. Stars Kay Francis, Paul Kelly, Otto Kruger. Directed by William Nigh. Screenplay, Harvey H. Gates, Sidney Sutherland; original by Sutherland; editor, William Austin; camera, Harry Neumann. At Fox, Brooklyn, dual, Dec. 28, '45. Running time, 80 MINS.

Sheila	Kay Francis
Major Pete Martin	Paul Kelly
Whitey Colton	Otto Kruger
Gladys Smith	Gertrude Michael
Connie	Teala Loring
Spike Malone	Bernard Nedell
Agnew	Anthony Warde
General Gilbert	Jonathan Hale
Deacon Sam	Selmer Jackson
Ann Farley	Evelyn Eaton
Grey	Pierre Watkin
Madame Gaston	Marcelle Corday

"Allotment Wives, Inc." should make the grade on double bills with its strong name cast and its title exploitation (a bit belated) of a widespread and tragic war phenomenon. The film solemnly dedicates itself to the armed services, opens promisingly into a newsreel documentary of the Office of Dependency Benefits, but quickly slips back into the routine groove of the conventional Monogram meller. "Wives" is just another twist to the Govt. agent vs. crime syndicate formula tested and tried by this pix outfit again and again.

If the budget hadn't splurged so heavily on talent and so lightly on story, much dullness and waste could have been avoided. Kay Francis, Otto Kruger, Paul Kelly and other competent actors are set in a fantastic yarn about an organized bigamy racket of women who marry several service men apiece for their allotment checks.

Miss Francis, being cast with increasing frequency as a heavy, walks through her well-gowned but incredible part in a not too convincing fashion. Adequate for straight duties, she fails to express the high-key emotions sometimes demanded of her. In the midst of one tragically maternal tantrum, the customers commented with a snicker. Kelly is grim, tough, handy with his dukes and lightning on the draw. His portrayal is solid and, given the script, nothing more could be asked except a sense of humor. Kruger is smooth and self-assured and goes through his paces in standard form.

Trojan Brothers
(BRITISH-MADE)

London, Dec. 25.

Anglo-American Film Corp. release of British National Film. Features Patricia Burke, David Farrar, Barbara Mullen, Bobby Howes. Directed by Maclean Rogers. Screenplay by Erwin Reiner, Maclean Rogers from novel by Pamela Hansford Johnson. Camera, Ernest Palmer, Moray Grant. Running time, 85 MINS.

Betty Todd	Patricia Burke
Sid Nichols	David Farrar
Benny Castelli	Bobby Howes
Maggie Castelli	Barbara Mullen
Ann Devon	Lesley Brook
Cyril Todd	David Hutcheson
W. H. Maxwell	Finlay Currie
Stage Manager	Wylie Watson
Old Sam	George Robey
Tom Hockaby	Bransby Williams
Frank	Gus McNaughton

The most unfortunate aspect of this unpretentious adaptation of Pamela Hansford Johnson's novel so far as British audiences are concerned is the complete overshadowing of Bobby Howes, top notch West End stage star, by David Farrar, little known to theatregoers. With due allowance made for the inferiority of the south end of a horse going north it seems a pity to have cast a comedian of Howe's calibre in a role offering nothing but the worst.

To American audiences this miscasting will mean nothing, neither will Howes or Farrar, or the film itself. But the way the scripters have treated "The Trojan Brothers," a pair of small-time hoofers who tell each other they're "pals and partners" in and out of the horse's hide, it's the front end of the act which dominates the picture.

Co-starred with the two comics are Patricia Burke and Barbara Mullen, the former a cheating society dame who drives Farrar nuts by giving him the gate when she tires of him. The latter is the drab wife of the rear half of the act. Here again the fat role goes to Miss Burke while Miss Mullen, a bigger name on this side, gets small chance.

Production values, considerably above average for this type of picture, bring kudos to Louis Jackson. Maclean Rogers' direction for the most part is adequate, but irritating pauses in cross talk between Howes and Farrar need tightening up by better cutting.

Final moments of film show Farrar, mind unhinged, cornering the woman who has passed him up, deliberately strangling her. This is a gripping five-minute sequence. *Talb.*

Klockan Pa Ronneberga
("The Old Clock at Roenneberga")
(SWEDISH-MADE)

Scandia Films release of Svensk Filmindustri production. Features Lauritz Falk, Vibeke Falk. Directed by Gunnar Skoglund. Screenplay, Herbert Grevinius. At 5th Ave. Playhouse, N. Y., week Dec. 26, '45. Running time, 90 MINS.

Lennart Heijken	Lauritz Falk
Viveka Langenfelt	Vibeke Falk
Sara	Hilda Borgstrom
Henrik Heijken	Oskar Ljung
Brolin	Sten Lingdren
Johansson	Gosta Gustafsson

"The Old Clock," if given less time, may find an audience in the U. S. Photography and performances throughout are deftly handled, but "Clock" takes too long to wind up.

One and a half hours are too long to tell the story of a rich landowner whose elation over the birth of his only son prompts him to purchase a huge clock for the purpose of carving on its door all the happy events that befall junior's life. Date by date, the tale and clock follow the youngster up until the time when he's graduated from school and his dad expects him to learn how to operate the estate. But the son wants a military career and gets it. While at it, he meets the gal and they soon wed. Returning to his home after their honeymoon, they learn of his parents' death in a train accident.

Forced to assume the responsibilities of the estate, he goes his befuddled way trying to supervise the vast farm, while she spends all her time partying and horseback riding. Soon the inevitable happens: mismanagement of the farm, plus his wife's extravagance, force them to sell all. Then they go off to live in a confining five-room house. He becomes a drummer, while she feels sorry for herself because they're poor and she has to do the cooking and take care of their infant son.

At this point, a former, persistent suitor calls upon her while hubby is away and fills her with tales of the Riviera, sunny Italy, the Nile, etc. After much emoting and vacillating, she deserts hubby for the Nile. The ending shows the aged husband pining as he looks at the deserter's picture. Downstairs in his son's ballroom, the old clock mischimes at 9:15 p.m., the cue for the old gent to die quietly. This is the second time the clock has mischimed, the first being when he entered the house with his new bride, forwarning him of her unfaithfulness.

Lauritz Falk plays the disillusioned and abandoned husband with much charm. But the author has forgotten to show him in his scenes of remorse, disappointment and bitterness, thus making him a one-dimensional character. He has similarly forgotten to give the telling brushstrokes to his runaway wife. The audience never sees her after she has left him. Others in the pic, even though they are stock characters, are well done, especially Hilda Borgstrom's portrayal of the faithful housekeeper. She has the quality of Maria Ouspenskaya.

Miniature Reviews

"My Reputation" (WB). Psychologal drama should do well with femme trade.

"Whistle Stop" (UA). George Raft and Victor McLaglen command marquee attention in this heavy meller.

"Because of Him" (Songs) (U). Deanna Durbin, Laughton, Tone, in good comedy for lush returns.

"The Spiral Staircase" (RKO). Smart murder thriller, with Dorothy McGuire, George Brent, Ethel Barrymore.

"Abilene Town" (Songs)— (Levey-UA). Randolph Scott, Ann Dvorak in spectacular western meller; strong b.o.

"A Week's Leave" (Minerva). Italian-made love story not good for U. S.; a glorified tour of Rome.

My Reputation

Warner Bros. release of Henry Blanke production. Stars Barbara Stanwyck; features George Brent, Warner Anderson, Lucile Watson, John Ridgely, and Eve Arden. Directed by Curtis Bernhardt. Screenplay by Catherine Turney from novel by Claire Jaynes; editor, David Weisbart; camera, James Wong Howe; music, Max Steiner; Previewed N.Y., Jan. 4, '46. Running time, 93 mins.

Jessica Drummond	Barbara Stanwyck
Scott Landis	George Brent
Frank Everett	Warner Anderson
Mrs. Kimball	Lucille Watson
Cary Abbott	John Ridgely
Ginna Abbott	Eve Arden
"Hank" Hawks	Robert Shayne
Anna	Esther Dale
George Van Orman	Jerome Cowan
Kim Drummond	Scotty Beckett
Keith Drummond	Bobby Cooper
Bette Van Orman	Leona Maricle
Mary	Mary Servoss
Mrs. Thompson	Cecil Cunningham
Baby Hawks	Nancy Evans
Gretchen Van Orman	Ann Todd
Penny Boardman	Janis Wilson
"Droopy" Hawks	Darwood Kaye

With the emphasis on a woman's struggle within herself over the ethics of behavior following her husband's death, the target for this WB dramatization of the Clare Jaynes novel of a few years ago, "Instruct My Sorrows," is clearly the femme ticketholders. It should do okay with the matinee weep-trade and okay generally on strength of the Barbara Stanwyck tag.

Pic's greatest difficulty is getting started, scripter Catherine Turney and megger Curtis Bernhardt taking such pains to build up their characterizations that it is 35 minutes before George Brent hits the screen and causes the pace to pick up a bit. On the other hand, there's a well-architected buildup to a dramatic blowoff that's certain to have a lot of handkerchiefs moist when the lights go up.

Story emphasis is on psychological conflict rather than action. It attempts to picture the dilemma in the mind of an attractive young widow (Miss Stanwyck) as she balances the demands of community and family convention against her desire to live her life as she sees it—namely, an affair with a rather attractive wolf in wolf's clothing. With her two boys and her mother and friends tugging one way and the charms of George Brent pushing her the other, she satisfies the audience by leaning to the Brent side and the Johnston (Hays) office by properly bowing out when the real payoff comes.

Unfortunately, the script fails to demonstrate the deftness which is necessary to present a conflict like this. It takes extreme skill to make all the needed points with a minimum of footage and to keep things moving on the screen. While there are a number of engrossing moments, the story is too unsubtle in the telling and doesn't offer sufficient action to compensate.

Miss Stanwyck, with a justifiable rep for handling tear-jerking moments, goes through this with her usual skill. Supporting players likewise turn in neat jobs, particularly Eve Arden and Warner Anderson, although director Bernhardt tends to overstylize several of the roles, particularly that of Lucile Watson as Miss Stanwyck's too-too-stuffy mother. Direction otherwise is marked by a number of unusual tricks and camera angles, which don't always add anything.

Max Steiner's music is intelligently used to heighten effects without being obtrusive. *Herb.*

Whistle Stop

Hollywood

United Artists release of Seymour Nebenzal (Philip Yordan) production. Stars George Raft; features Ava Gardner, Victor McLaglen, Toni Conway, Jorja Curtright. Directed by Leonide Moguy. Screenplay by Philip Yordan from novel by Maritta M. Wolff; camera, Russell Metty; special effects, R.O. Ringer; score, Dimitri Tiomkin; editor, Gregg Tallas. Previewed Hollywood, Jan. 4, '46. Running time, 84 mins.

Kenny	George Raft
Mary	Ava Gardner
Gitlo	Victor McLaglen
Lew	Tom Conway
Fran	Jorga Curtright
Josie	Jane Nigh
Mom	Florence Bates
Ernie	Charles Drake
Pop	Charles Judels
Estelle	Carmen Myers
Barber	Jimmy Conlin

Heavy melodrama, which has the marquee weight and release to head it for top position in majority of situations, was adapted from the Maritta M. Wolff novel of same title. Characters have been changed to meet with more favor from the censors, but it is still somber melodrama, vignetting a seamy side of life in a small town. Production and playing are excellent and the direction strong, although latter is given to occasional arty tone, reminding of the foreign school.

Characters are all little people, and not very nice. Story opens with Ava Gardner returning to the whistle-stop town of Ashbury to renew her romance with the shiftless George Raft. Pair had broken off two years previous because he refused to change his habits. Pair fight continually, and romance is getting nowhere until a prosperous rival, Tom Conway, owner of the town's hotel and saloon, starts to move in. Raft is nearly talked into a theft and murder by his bartender friend, Victor McLaglen, but is saved by Miss Gardner, and decides to go to work. Conway then frames a killing, pointing towards Raft and McLaglen; pair flee, but McLaglen returns later to even accounts with Conway and clear Raft. Film ends on happy note.

Under Leonide Moguy's direction Raft does a capable job of the small-timer. Miss Gardner displays her best work to date as the girl who must have her man. McLaglen hits top form as the not too bright bartender, and Conway is smooth as the heavy. Jorja Curtwright makes her film debut in featured spot as one of Raft's casual romances, and shows plenty of promise. Other players hold up their end. Carmel Myers, off the screen for a long time, returns for brief sequence in final footage, doing excellently.

Philip Yordan did the screenplay and also served as associate producer under Seymour Nebenzal. Production mounting aptly fits the story's locale, as does the camera work. Score is an aid in projecting the somber mood. *Brog.*

Because of Him

(SONGS)

Universal release of Felix Jackson production. Directed by Richard Wallace. Stars Deanna Durbin, Franchot Tone, Charles Laughton; features Helen Broderick, Stanley Ridges. Screenplay, Edmund Beloin from original story by Beloin, Sig Herzig; camera, Hal Mohr; score, Miklos Rozsa; editor, Ted Kent. Tradeshown, N.Y., Jan. 3, '46. Running time, 100 MINS.

Kim Walker	Deanna Durbin
Paul Taylor	Franchot Tone
Sheridan	Charles Laughton
Nora	Helen Broderick
Charlie Gilbert	Stanley Ridges
Martin	Donald Meek
Mr. Dunlap	Charles Halton
Head Nurse	Regina Wallace
Samuel Happgood	Douglas Wood
Martha Manners	Lynn Whitney

Here's the picture Deanna Durbin fans have been waiting for since the star left the protective wing of Joe Pasternak. Film is a merry melange of music, comedy and drama with a good story and a top cast. Names of Miss Durbin, Franchot Tone and Charles Laughton will have the customers lined up and once inside the theatre, they'll have no kicks coming. Boxoffice looks lush.

Miss Durbin, despite the fact that she portrays a stage-struck waitress through most of the plot, is gowned to perfection and looks ditto. Music plays a minor part in the film, with the star's vocal efforts limited to three songs, but seldom has she been in finer voice. She registers solidly with the Lorenz Hart-Richard Rodgers' oldie "Lover" and shines equally well with Tosti's "Goodbye" and "Danny Boy."

Plot revolves around Miss Durbin's attempt to inveigle her way into a top Broadway production, and director Richard Wallace gets the most out of the consequent wacky proceedings. Faking a letter of intro from Laughton, top legit actor, the star gets in to see producer Stanley Ridges, who's convinced she's just the gal for the lead in Sheridan's new show. Playwright Franchot Tone objects, however, and pulls his name off the credits when Laughton also goes for her. Comes opening night and Tone, unable to resist, stands in the wings as Miss Durbin scores a success. Spotting him there, Laughton does a last-minute change with the production's lines to send Miss Durbin into Tone's arms in view of the entire audience.

Laughton grabs the acting honors in a sterling portrayal of the actor whose every gesture would look well between two slices of rye. Way he poses for the newspaper photogs, goes into lengthy quotes from his stage successes, etc., should bring the house down. Miss Durbin does well, also, and proves that she doesn't have to rely on her voice alone to carry a show, although it's too bad she doesn't get more songs to put over. Tone turns in his usual soft-spoken nonchalant acting and shines in several comedy sequences with Miss Durbin. Supporting cast is topnotch.

Producer Felix Jackson has lined the film with expensive mountings that help set it off as a high-budgeted production. Miklos Rosza's score highlights several of the comedy scenes and blends well with the film.

The Spiral Staircase

RKO release of Dore Schary production. Stars Dorothy McGuire, George Brent, Ethel Barrymore; features Kent Smith, Rhonda Fleming, Gordon Oliver, Elsa Lanchester, Sara Allgood, Rhys Williams, James Bell. Directed by Robert Siodmak. Screenplay by Mel Dinelli, based on novel "Some Must Watch," by Ethel Lina White; camera, Nicholas Musuraca; editors, Harry Marker, Harry Gerstad. Tradeshown N.Y. Jan. 3, '46. Running time, 83 MINS.

Helen	Dorothy McGuire
Professor Warren	George Brent
Mrs. Warren	Ethel Barrymore
Dr. Parry	Kent Smith
Blanche	Rhonda Fleming
Steve Warren	Gordon Oliver
Mrs. Oates	Elsa Lanchester
Nurse Barker	Sara Allgood
Mr. Oates	Rhys Williams
Constable	James Bell

This is a smooth production of an obvious though suspenseful murder thriller, ably acted and directed. Mood and pace are well set, and story grips throughout. Marquee strength of Dorothy McGuire, Ethel Barrymore and George Brent will clinch it for excellent boxoffice returns.

Mel Dinelli has done a tight, authentic-sounding script of a mass-murder story set in a small New England town of 1906. Director Robert Siodmak has retained a feeling for terror throughout the film by smart photography, camera angles and sudden shifts of camera emphasis, abetted in this job by a choice performance of his cast. Film lacks the leaven of a little humor, but interest never wanes.

Dorothy McGuire's stature as actress will be increased by her performance as a maidservant bereft of speech by a shock since childhood, and Ethel Barrymore's list of pic-portraits will get another goldframer from her role of bedridden wealthy eccentric. Miss McGuire's portrayal of a tongue-tied girl in love; the pathos of her dream wedding-scene; her terror when pursued by the murderer—are all etched sharply for unforgettable moments. Miss Barrymore's awareness from her bedchamber of the insanity and murder going on about her is also acutely set, to give distinction to her part.

Miss Barrymore plays an invalid widow, living in a huge mansion with her two sons, one a stepson who is a professor, another her real son who is a ne'er-do-well. The mute maidservant attends her. The town has been upset by several mysterious murders—all of them of girls suffering from some affliction. Pattern of murders suggests some fiend is despatching such girls on the warped premise that the world has no room for the imperfect.

The widow suggests that her mute servant leave her, and the town, to prevent any harm coming to her. A young country doctor who has fallen in love with the girl also wants her to leave; he feels he can cure her of her speech-loss. Before the servant can get away, a murder has been committed in the house, and her life too is threatened. Final moments of film are stark terror, with the climax a vivid finish as the invalid mother stalks out onto the staircase to shoot the murderer.

Brent plays a difficult role well as the stepson who has cared for the widow during her long illness. Kent Smith has the right rural quality for the simple country doctor, and Gordon Oliver plays the ne'er-do-well brashly. Minor roles are all good. *Bron.*

Abilene Town

(SONGS)

United Artists release of Jules Levey production. Stars Randolph Scott, Ann Dvorak; features Edgar Buchanan, Rhonda Fleming, Lloyd Bridges. Directed by Edwin L. Marin. Screenplay by Harold Shumate from novel by Ernest Haycox; camera, Archie J. Stout; editors, Otho Lovering, Richard Heermance; songs, Fred Spielman, Kermit Goell; dances, Sammy Lee. Previewed in N.Y. Projection Room. Running time, 91 MINS.

Dan Mitchell	Randolph Scott
Rita	Ann Dvorak
Bravo Trimble	Edgar Buchanan
Sherry Balder	Rhonda Fleming
Henry Dreiser	Lloyd Bridges
Big Annie	Helen Boice
Ed Balder	Howard Freeman
Charlie Fair	Richard Hale
Jet Younger	Jack Lambert
Doug Neil	Hank Patterson
Ryker	Dick Curtis
Hazelhurst	Earl Schenck
Hannaberry	Eddie Waller

"Abilene Town" is another saga of a western town, patterned along the same lines as "Dodge City," "Union Pacific" and "Virginia City." Film depicts a hellraising, Kansas pioneer community located at the end of the long cattle trail from Texas. It's a ripsnorting, spectacular meller calculated to do strong biz many places and sock where solidly sold. Picture has Randolph Scott and Ann Dvorak for marquee luster, which hints just how much showmanship will be needed to attract initial audiences.

But word-of-mouth likely will snowball this when given proper advance bally. It's that sort of picture.

Fundamentally a story about the violent conflict of interests between the cattlemen and newly arrived homesteaders. "Abilene" focuses interest on the evolution of this Kansas village from the familiar reckless cowboy town into a more peaceful community. Abilene is located where the Chisholm Trail ends. It's where cattle were placed on trains for the packing-house cities. This was the habit back in the early '70s, with the plot pointing up that the business men, with stores there, felt that without this cattle business and the periodical visits of the cattlemen, after their 90-day drive from Texas, the town would die. Arrival of homesteaders proved how wrong they were.

With this background, producer Jules Levey and his smart staff, headed by director Edwin L. Marin, have packed action upon action, spectacular sequence on thrilling episode and still manage to maintain a nice balance between the melodramatic and the humorous. There's the inveterate fan-tan playing sheriff and his drinking bouts, the sly wardrobe femme at the bigtown saloon to contrast with the fisticuffs of the quick-on-the-trigger town marshal.

Much of the yarn follows western pattern, but the tight screenplay of Harold Shumate never permits the action to become too implausible or hackneyed. Result is that it becomes a vivid account of this likeable town marshal and a few other hardy men who bring the high-handed cattlemen to account.

Randolph Scott chips in with one of his best western characterizations as the marshal, a law officer who really whips the community into line. Ann Dvorak clicks as the dancehall entertainer, equally adept at warbling and stepping. Scott's her sweetheart but this affair is kept fairly undercover until final scenes. Switch of Scott's affections from the nice gal to the supposedly wicked saloon belle certainly does not fit in with good, all western film tradition, but it's a welcome change. Lloyd Bridges, a comparatively new youngster on the screen, does a solid bit of work as the vigorous, youthful leader of the homesteaders. He should be heard from more favorably. Rhonda Fleming is the nice gal, daughter of the town's biggest storekeeper and political leader. At times, she's excellent. Edgar Buchanan makes a droll character out of Sheriff Bravo, the officer who could duck responsibility as easily as he could play cards or drink. Helen Boice makes lots of the lesser role of wardrobe mistress and fan-tan partner of the sheriff. Sturdy supporting cast is headed by Howard Freeman, Jack Lambert, Dick Curtis, Hank Patterson and Richard Hale.

Miss Dvorak sings all three songs by Fred Spielman and Kermit Goell, best being "I Love It Out Here in the West" and "Every Time I Give My Heart." Third, "All You Gotta Do," is routine and quaintly familiar. This looks to be one of director Marin's best jobs to date. Camera work by Archie J. Stout is topflight.
Wear.

A Week's Leave

("Un American in Vacanza")
(ITALIAN-MADE)

Rome, Dec. 18
Minerva Film release of Lux Film production. Stars Valentina Cortese, Leo Dale; featuresd Elli Parvo, Adolfo Celi, Andrea Chechci, Paolo Stoppa. Directed by Luigi Zampa; screenplay, Luigi Castrianano; camera, Vich. Previewed in Rome, Dec. 10, '45. Running time, 90 mins.
Maria..........................Valentina Cortese
Dick..................................Leo Dale
Tom.................................Adolfo Celi
Elena..................................Elli Parvo
Roberto...........................Andrea Chechci
Coachman............................Paolo Stoppa

This is the love story of Dick, a G I, and a young Italian schoolteacher, Maria. Maria leaves her country school in a village to go to Rome on a mission. This is to find the local rich man's son who disappeared from home to have a good time in the city, and also to get food and other help for her village from the Vatican. Not especially strong for the U. S.

On the way to Rome, Maria's old auto breaks down, and Dick comes along in a 5th Army jeep. Thereafter Dick follows Maria around in Rome, and in the course of their courtship they manage to cover most of the highlights of the Eternal City. This part will please veterans returning from the Mediterranean theatre who want to recapture their Roman experiences.

Maria returns to the country, not only having accomplished her double mission but also having been a good girl. Quite a point is made of her goodness, in contrast to wolf habits of other G I contacts. Dick finally comes to say goodbye to her, and leaves his diary to send home in case he is killed.

Both Valentina Cortese and Leo Dale do well in their roles. Film is pathetic and gay, with humor predominating.

Miniature Reviews

"**Tomorrow Is Forever**" (RKO). Emotional family-war drama, starring Claudette Colbert, Orson Welles and George Brent. Will do well.

"**Breakfast in Hollywood**" (UA) (Songs). Groovey for air audience of the Tom Breneman ABC program.

"**Tars and Spars**" (Col). Musical). Slow but moderately pleasant tuner starring Alfred Drake and Janet Blair.

"**Shock**" (20th). Vincent Price, Lynn Bari in horror meller; only moderate boxoffice.

"**Behind Green Lights**" (20th). Weak whodunit with tepid b.o. prospects.

"**Riders of the Dawn**" (Mono), (Songs). Minor westerner with heavy musical accent.

"**Le Jugement Dernier**" (Minerva). French-made semi-propaganda, patriotic story; slim chance in U. S. market.

Tomorrow Is Forever

RKO release of International Pictures (David Lewis) production. Stars Claudette Colbert, Orson Welles and George Brent; features Lucile Watson, Natalie Wood, Richard Long and Joyce Mackenzie. Directed by Irving Pichel. Screenplay, Lenore Coffee, from novel by Gwen Bristow; camera, Joseph Valentine; editor, Ernest Nims. Previewed at Normandie theatre, N. Y., Jan. 14, '45. Running time, 102 MINS.
Elizabeth Hamilton......Claudette Colbert
Erich Kessler and John MacDonald
..................................Orson Welles
Larry Hamilton...............George Brent
Aunt Jessie..................Lucile Watson
John Andrew (Drew)........Richard Long
Margaret.....................Natalie Wood
Cherry......................Joyce Mackenzie
Brian..........................Sonny Howe
Drew.........................Michael Ward
Dr. Ludwing..................John Wengraf
Charles Hamilton............Douglas Wood
Norton...........................Ian Wolfe
Pudge.........................Tom Wirick
Hamilton's Secretary........Lane Watson
Butler.......................Henry Hastings

International Pictures takes its audience through a deep emotional bath in this moving filmization of Gwen Bristow's magazine serial and novel. It's strong stuff and will suffer somewhat at the b.o. on the basis of its morbid war theme, but the star names, fine acting and excellent direction will insure it good grosses in virtually all situations. It'll be especially strong with the gals who measure the good time they're having by the quantity of tears they shed.

Yarn is a variation on the "Enoch Arden" theme. It goes back to World War I, with Orson Welles and Claudette Colbert virtual newlyweds when the bugle's note separates them. Badly disfigured and crippled, Welles allows himself to be mistakenly declared dead and makes a new life for himself in Austria under another name. Miss Colbert, meantime, marries George Brent and is happily married until shortly before World War II, when Welles returns to the States to work as a chemist in Brent's plant and he and Miss Colbert again come face-to-face. The struggle within each of them to determine whether the twice-wed wife shall go on with her children in the comfortable life they have known for more than 20 years, or cause a tremendous emotional split all around, comprises the latter part of the story, with the additional theme of Miss Colbert's fight to keep her air-minded son from the second World War.

First half of the film goes from one heart-shaking sequence to another, but, unfortunately, Lenore Coffee in her screenplay has been unable to build to great climaxes. She finally just runs out, and the latter portion of her script, which

should be a gripping unfolding of the emotional battle of her principal characters, becomes pedestrian in the telling. Were the film able to transfer fully those feelings to the screen, it would be an unqualified sock b.o. entry.

Cast is solid throughout, director Irving Pichel even holding his children pretty well in check on precocity. Miss Colbert gives the kind o' honest and sincere performance on which she has won her reputation, while Welles, with beard, limp, cane and cough, has a tailored role for his brand of thespics. He certainly doesn't underplay the part, but neither does he push it too heavily, and results are satisfying. Brent is convincing, while Richard Long and Natalie Wood, in roles of the children, show restraint and considerable promise.

Pichel's admixture of his ingredients keeps the proceedings moving well in most instances, although he is unable to overcome that letdown after the heavy emotionalism at the start. Production is unstinting, and musical background standard with theme tune. "Tomorrow Is Forever," by Max Steiner and Charles Tobias.
Herb.

Breakfast in Hollywood
(SONGS)

Hollywood, Jan. 12
United Artists release of Golden Pictures production. Stars Tom Breneman; features Bonita Granville, Beulah Bondi, Edward Ryan, Raymond Walburn, Billie Burke, ZaSu Pitts, Hedda Hopper, Andy Russell, Spike Jones and City Slickers, King Cole Trio. Directed by Harold Schuster. Original story and screenplay, Earl W. Baldwin; camera, Russell Metty; editor, Bernard W. Burton; musical supervision and direction, Nat. W. Finston; songs, Lou Alter and Marla Shelton, Nat Cole, Bob Levinson and Howard Leeds, Spike Jones and Jack Elliott. Previewed at Hawaii theatre, Hollywood, Jan. 11, '46. Running time, 90 MINS.
Tom Breneman.....................Himself
Dorothy Larson............Bonita Granville
Annie......................Beulah Bondi
Ken Smith......................Eddie Ryan
Mr. Cartwright........Raymond Walburn
Mrs. Cartwright.............Billie Burke
Elvira Spriggens..............ZaSu Pitts
Hedda Hopper...................Herself
Andy Russell....................Himself

"Breakfast in Hollywood" is a pretty faithful copy of the spirit that marks Tom Breneman's ABC air show. Ether program's reputed 7,000,000 daily listeners will find it just as comfortable old-shoe and natural as the five-times-weekly airing. Based on its possible draw from the air audience alone, film has substantial boxoffice prospects, as it gives the Breneman faithful a chance to see their favorite in action. For general film audiences, sufficient interest is maintained to carry it off in okay fashion, although it's overlong.

Of particular interest to "Breakfast" air fans will be Breneman's film appearance. For the record, Breneman is Breneman, making a natural, easy appearance. He wears silly hats, steers elderly ladies relays corny gags and generally lives up to his air reputation in top form. A smart performance all around.

Plot is built around a day in the life of Breneman, showing him staging his daily show, straightening out romance of a sailor and a girl, and participating in sundry other "good-deed" efforts designed for heart appeal and humanizing of a radio voice. A stalwart cast backs up the slim plot with smooth performances, and Director Harold Schuster guides the doings with considerable know-how.

Robert S. Golden's production has mixed in some musical highlights, performed by Andy Russell, the King Cole Trio and Spike Jone's City Slickers. His mounting and general guidance are all calculated to appraise correctly showmanship and marketable values. As "guest star," Russell reprises the tune ul, "If I Had a Wishing Ring," by Lou Alter and Marla Shelton, twice, and also comes through with his popular "Amor." King Cole Trio appears twice and does standout work on "It's Better to Be by Yourself," by Nat Cole, Bob Levinson and Howard Leeds. Jone's City Slickers also have two numbers, one a standard and a second novelty tagged "Hedda Hopper's Hats."

Young romance is portrayed by Bonita Granville and Edward Ryan. Both are excellent, with Ryan particularly appealing as the lonesome sailor. Beulah Bondi turns in the top work as the 82-year-old lady who wins an orchid and a bus from Breneman. Greatly aiding film are ZaSu Pitts and her screwy hats; Raymond Walburn and Billie Burke, and Hedda Hopper, as herself. Miss Hopper's goldfish bowl hat creation is good for a solid laugh.

The camera work by Russell Metty, music supervision by Nat W. Finston, and other technical contributions measure up to good standard.

Brog.

Tars and Spars

(MUSICAL)

Columbia release of Milton H. Bren production. Stars Alfred Drake, Janet Blair and Marc Platt; features Sid Ceasar and Jeff Donnell. Directed by Alfred E. Green. Screenplay, John Jacoby, Sarett Tobias and Decla Dunning, from story by Barry Trivers; songs Jule Styne and Sammy Cahn; camera, Joseph Walker; editor, Al Clark. Previewed in New York, Jan. 9, '46. Running time, 86 mins.

Christine Bradley	Janet Blair
Howard Young	Alfred Drake
Junior Casady	Marc Platt
Penny McDougal	Jeff Donnell
Chuck Enders	Sid Caesar
Lieutenant Scully	Ray Walker
Chief Bosun Mate Gurney	James Flavin

Columbia tuner is fair enough as long as it sticks to melody and terping, but it slows to waltz tempo where the story is involved. It's destined for mediocre biz, with b.o. considerably better in the nabes than in more sophisticated spots.

Marc Platt's extra-special ballet work and the tunes of Jule Styne and Sammy Cahn are the pic's principal pick-me-ups. Megger Alfred Green's pioneering with ballet as a means of advancing the story line, similar to what has been done in Broadway musicals, also rates a blossom. It does with surprising pleasantness and a minimum of footage what the pic's dialog otherwise handles awkwardly and slowly.

Film takes its title—and that's all—from the Coast Guard show, "Tars and Spars," which toured during the war and featured Coast Guardsman Victor Mature. Story is the merest skeleton on which to hang the song and dance work. Alfred Drake plays a seaman who can't get to sea, but mistakenly gets himself labeled as a hero. His effort and those of his pal, Sid Caesar, to square the rap with his gal, Janet Blair, when she tags him for a phoney, comprise the yarn.

Drake, who scored neatly in "Oklahoma!" on Broadway, doesn't measure up in this pic. He'll have no soxers swooning on either the looks or the voice department, his larynx work being pleasant but far from outstanding as it comes from the screen. Miss Blair registers well on physiognomy and personality. Caesar, working opposite Jeff Donnell for the comedy section, suffers from the similarity of his work to that of Danny Kaye and the over-liberality of the producers with footage for his specialties. He's a laugh-winner, though.

Alfred E. Green's direction makes the most of all that he has to work with.

Herb.

Shock

20th Century Fox release of Aubrey Schenck production. Stars Vincent Price, Lynne Bari; features Frank Latimore, Anabel Shaw. Directed by Alfred Werker. Screenplay, Eugene Ling; based on story by Albert deMond; camera, Glen MacWilliams, Joe MacDonald; editor, Harmon Jones; Tradeshown in N.Y., Jan. 10, '46. Running time, 70 mins.

Dr. Cross	Vincent Price
Elaine Jordan	Lynn Bari
Lt. Paul Stewart	Frank Lattimore
Janet Stewart	Annabel Shaw
Stevens	Michael Dunne
O'Neill	Reed Hadley
Mrs. Hatfield	Rene Carson
Dr. Harvey	Charles Trowbridge
Mr. Edward	John Davidson
Dr. Blair	Selmer Jackson
Hotel Manager	Pierre Watkin
Miss Penny	Mary Young
Clerk	Charles Tannen

"Shock" should have the psychiatrists screaming. It does them an injustice from several angles. With Vincent Price and Lynn Bari as principal boxoffice bait, it should take a big selling job to put this picture over.

Story is of a nerve-wrought wife being further unstrung by witnessing a slaying from her hotel window. An eminent psychiatrist has done the killing. Anabel Shaw, the wife, is jumpy because her Army-aviator husband has been delayed in returning after being held in a Jap prison camp. When she accidentally witnesses the quarrel and slaying of the psychiatrist's wife by the medico, Price, she goes completely haywire. The returned soldier finally shows up and places his wife in the hands of the doctor, the actual slayer. From then on it's only a question of time until the psychiatrist attempts to knock her off. Heavy suspense is built up as another doctor arrives just in time to save the soldier's wife.

Scripter Eugene Ling and Director Alfred Werker have failed to provide enough action for this horrific tale.

Price makes a sufficiently deadly menace, but Miss Bari is somewhat unconvincing as the nurse who lures him on. Frank Latimore makes an excellent Air Corps lieutenant, but one wonders why he permits the mental medico to go so far without further consultation with another doctor. Miss Shaw, as his wife, emotes through most of the picture in a hospital bed. She suggests possibilities in a more palatable role.

Reed Hadley makes something of the investigator from the D.A.'s office, while other supporting parts are well handled by Michael Dunne, Renee Carson and Charles Trowbridge. Werker's direction is overflowing with closeups and dearth of action. However, he maintains some suspense.

Wear.

Behind Green Lights

20th Century Fox release of Robert Bassler production. Directed by Otto Brower. Features Carole Landis, William Gargan, Richard Crane, Mary Anderson. Screenplay, W. Scott Darling and Charles G. Booth; camera, Joe MacDonald; editor, Stanley Rabjohn. Tradeshown in N.Y., Jan. 11, '46. Running time, 64 mins.

Janet Bradley	Carole Landis
Sam Carson	William Gargan
Johnny Williams	Richard Crane
Nora Bard	Mary Anderson
Detective Engelhofer	John Ireland
Arthur Templeton	Charles Russell
Max Calvert	Roy Roberts
Flossie	Mabel Paige
Ruzinsky	Stanley Prager
Ames	Charles Tannen
Zachary	Fred Sherman
Dr. Yager	Don Beddoe
Bard	Bernerd Nedell
Metcalfe	Tom Moore
Kaypee	Harry Seymour
King	Jimmy Cross
Wintergreen	Charles Arnt
Brewer	Lane Chandler
Radio Operator	Russ Clark
Webster	Jack Davis
Dr. Halliday	William Forrest, Jr.
Morgue Attendant	Steve Olsen
Ambulance Officer	Larry Blake
Crematorium Attendant	Harry Tyler

Stilted dialog is a major fault of "Behind Green Lights," one of the poorer whodunits. With most of the action centering around the press room of a police station, the film bears a slight resemblance to "Front Page," but any further similarity to that erstwhile top farce ends there. Names of Carole Landis and William Gargan will help brighten the marquee but b.o. prospects remain tepid.

The killer is easily identifiable several reels before he is unmasked. Film moves at a boresome pace, its basic theme involving a police officer torn between devotion to duty and the chance to grasp a dishonest political promotion. The idea has been used many times before.

Gargan does well as the copper, and Miss Landis, who spends most of the film sitting in Gargan's anteroom, waiting for him to decide whether she's guilty, looks decorative. Newcomer Richard Crane, as the cub reporter instrumental in solving the crime, is slated for better roles. Mary Anderson does a deadpan job as the murdered man's wife. Mabel Paige tops the supporting cast as a garrulous "Apple Annie" character.

Riders of the Dawn

(SONGS)

Monogram release of Oliver Drake production. Stars Jimmy Wakely; features Lee White, Johnny James. Directed by Oliver Drake. Screenplay, Louis Rousseau; camera, William Sickner; editor, William Austin. At New York, N. Y., Jan. 8, '46. Running time, 57 MINS.

Jimmy Wakely	Jimmy Wakely
Lasses	Lee "Lasses" White
Dusty	Johnny James
Melinda	Sarah Padden
Sheriff	Horace Murphy
Penny	Phyllis Adair
Doc	Jack Baxley
Bob	Bob Shelton
Dad Pickard	Himself
Arthur	Arthur Smith

Wesley Tuttle and His Texas Stars

This western is bogged down in music. Lacking in action and suspense, it's an obvious story that will appeal only to the kids.

Considerable of the brief running time is filled with an assortment of cowboy crooning, yodelling, acrobatic fiddling and the like. What's left is the old chestnut of a travelling cowboy troupe which happens across an infant whose rancher parents were murdered in a scheme to get oil deposits on their land. After lots of hard riding and shooting, Jimmy Wakely brings the villains to book.

Wakely handles his singing assignments with a pleasing voice but he doesn't click as a fighting cowhand. Johnny James, as his supporting sidekick, is awkward, while Lee White in the comedy role can't do much with his uncomic lines.

Le Jugement Dernier

("The Last Judgment")

Minerva production and release. Stars Michele Martin, Jean Davy; features Sandra Miloyanof, Brochard, Raymond Bussieres, Michel Vitold, Louis Seigner, Jean Desailly, Paul Oettly, Gromoff, Tino Grica. Directed Rene Chanas; story by Henri Jeanson; camera, Nicolas Toporkoff, A.S.C. At Max Linder and Cesar, Paris, Dec. 22, '45. Running time 105 MINS.

Milia	Michele Martin
Stephan	Jean Davy
Madame Swoboda	Sandra Milovanoff
Kroum	Raymond Bussieres
Vassili	Michel Vitold
Bora	Louis Seigner
Kyril	Jean Desailly
Yahova	Paul Oettly
Mietchek	Gromoff
Swoboda	Brochard

Russian influence is strongly seen in this picture. Good direction by Rene Chanas and fine camera work by Nicolas Toporkoff give the first half realism with the uprising of the patriots against the last remaining Germans in an occupied imaginary mid-European state. The second half, introducing romance, becomes an unconvincing meller.

Michele Martin, as the patriotic girl participating in the fighting to avenge her dead father, gives a good performance. She is well supported by the male cast.

Jeanson has been careful to avoid anything that might give the picture a clearly defined locale in his dialog. This possibly was done with a view of getting Soviets to okay it for release.

Maxi.

Miniature Reviews

"Life With Blondie" (Col). Another okay comedy in series based on the Chic Young cartoon strip.

"A Guy Could Change" (Rep). Well-paced meller with poor script; geared for minor grosses.

"Detour" (PRC). Fair meller that looks okay as supporting dualer.

"Night Boat To Dublin" (Pathe). Capable cast wasted in this British-made spy meller; mighty lukewarm for U. S.

"Prairie Rustlers" (PRC). Buster Crabbe in dual role as both hero and villain in a fair western.

"Six Gun Man" (PRC). Bob Steele in a watery formula westerner; even the addicts won't like it.

"Club Havana" (PRC). Feeble meller with w.k. Latin-American songs.

"The Flying Serpent" (PRC). Horror stuff that may get the kids but n.g. for adults.

Life With Blondie

Columbia production and release. Stars Penny Singleton, Arthur Lake, Larry Simms; features Marjorie Kent, Jonathan Hale, Ernest Truex, Marc Lawrence, Veda Ann Borg. Directed by Abby Berlin. Screenplay, Connie Lee, based on comic strip created by Chic Young; camera, L. W. O'Connell; editor, Jerome Thoms. At Fox, Brooklyn, N. Y., dual, week Jan. 18, '46. Running time, **69 MINS.**

Blondie	Penny Singleton
Dagwood	Arthur Lake
Alexander	Larry Simms
Cookie	Marjorie Kent
J. C. Dithers	Jonathan Hale
Theodore Glassby	Ernest Truex
Pete	Marc Lawrence
Hazel	Veda Ann Borg
Ollie	Jack Rice
Tommy Cooper	Bobby Larson
Blackie Leonard	Douglas Fowley
Cassidy	George Tyne
Dog Catcher	Edward F. Gargan
Simon Rutledge	Francis Pierlot
Anthony	Ray Walker

Invariably one of the better minor comedy bets, this entry in Columbia's "Blondie" series meets all requirements. Employing most of the comic strip's standby gags, plus the development of Daisy as a trick dog, film holds its own and draws plenty laughs.

The yarn twist has Daisy, the family dog, elected as the Navy's pinup pooch, which brings about her status as the Bumstead breadwinner due to her demand as a photographic dog model. Ensuing complications involve Dagwood's competing efforts with the dog for his head-of-the-house standing and eventual "dog-napping" angle which brings in gangsters, rescue of the dog and family readjustments.

Direction makes most of good supporting cast with comedy well distributed. Ernest Truex as the ad man, Jonathan Hale as Dithers, and Douglas Fowley as the gangster all register strongly and provide necessary hypo for the film. Penny Singleton and Arthur Lake, as Blondie and Dagwood, do their standard stuff right up to par as well as Larry Simms and Marjorie Kent in the kid parts.

A Guy Could Change

Republic production and release. Stars Allan Lane, Jane Frazee and Twinkle Watts; features Wallace Ford, Adele Mara, Eddie Quillan. Directed by William K. Howard. Screenplay, Al Martin, from story by F. Hugh Herbert; camera, John Alton; editor, Harry Keller. Reviewed in N. Y., Jan. 18, '46. Running Time, **65 MINS.**

Mike Hogan	Allan Lane
Barbara Adams	Jane Frazee
Nancy Hogan	Twinkle Watts
Alan Schroeder	Bobby Blake
Bill Conley	Wallace Ford
Bernice	Adele Mara
Grace Conley	Mary Treen
McCarthy	Joseph Crehan
George Cummings	Eddie Quillan
Eddy Raymond	Gerald Mohr
Gus	George Chandler
Hank Krane	Wm. Haade
Information Girl	Betty Shaw

Precise editing has neatly trimmed this story down to essentials. But otherwise the film falters, with a poor script tripping up the whole production. Matters aren't helped either by the too-precocious eight-year-old Twinkle Watts.

Yarn centers around Allan Lane, a newspaperman who loses his wife in childbirth. Lane rejects the kid, Twinkle Watts, until he falls for Jane Frazee, who lashes him for neglecting the child. He makes up to his daughter and is about to wed the girl when a prison-break springs a convict who was sent up on Miss Frazee's testimony. Gerald Mohr, the convict, stalks the girl and is set to shoot her when Lane crashes in. A knockdown fight takes place in which neither contestant loses his hat, and the picture fades in a blaze of gunplay.

Lane suffers from a dead pan which doesn't vary in expression whether he's grieving over a dead wife or joking with his boss. The only creditable performances are given by Wallace Ford and Adele Mara, who are able to squeeze the maximum laughs from their marital squabblings. Jane Frazee is a good-looker in a minor assignment.

Detour

PRC release of Martin Mooney production. Stars Tom Neal, Ann Savage; features Claudia Drake, Edmund MacDonald. Directed by Edgar G. Ulmer. Screenplay and original story, Martin Goldsmith; camera, Benjamin H. Kline; editor, George McGuire; musical score, Ordody. At New York, N. Y., dual, week of Jan. 16, '46. Running time, **67 MINS.**

Roberts	Tom Neal
Vera	Ann Savage
Sue	Claudia Drake
Haskell	Edmund MacDonald
Gus	Tim Ryan
Hedy	Esther Howard
Dillon	Roger Clark

Based on a novel story idea that could have raised this film out of the run-of-the-mill category, "Detour" falls short of being a sleeper because of a flat ending and its low-budgeted production mountings. Uniformly good performances and some equally good direction and dialog keep the meller moving, however, and make it figure as okay for the duals.

Theme is the buffeting that man gets from the fates. Story revolves around Tom Neal as a down-and-out young pianist hitchhiking his way to the Coast. Director Edgar G. Ulmer achieves some steadily-mounting suspense as the pianist becomes implicated in two murders, neither of which he's committed. Circumstantial case against him is so strong, however, that he realizes he wouldn't stand a chance in court, so he begins hitchhiking his way back east. His last pickup is—a ride in a police car. Story is told by Neal in flashback.

Neal, who's been kicking around for some time in these minor items, does well with a difficult role that rates him a break in something better. Ann Savage is convincing as a tough girl of the roads and gets off some rough lines that drew wolf-howls from the audience at the show caught. Claudia Drake and Edmund MacDonald are adequate in the principal supporting roles.

Benjamin H. Kline contributes some outstanding camera work that helps the flashback routine come off well. Ordody's score, revolving around some Chopin themes, aids in backing up the film's grim mood.

Night Boat to Dublin
(BRITISH-MADE)

London, Jan. 9.

Pathe release of Associated British Picture. Stars Robert Newton. Directed by Lawrence Huntington; scenario by Lawrence Huntington. At Palace theatre, London, Jan. 8, '46. Running time, **91 MINS.**

Captain David Grant	Robert Newton
Paul Faber	Raymond Lovell
Captain Toby Hunter	Guy Middleton
Marion Decker	Muriel Pavlow
Keitel	Herbert Lom
Bowman	John Ruddock
Professor Hansen	Martin Miller
Sir George Bell	Valentine Dyall
Frederick Jannings	Marius Goring
Mrs. Coleman	Olga Lindo
Lily Leggett	Brenda Bruce
George Leggett	Leslie Dwyer
Naval Surgeon	Derek Elphinstone
Inspector Emerson	Gerald Case

Its atom bomb theme makes comparison of this one with "The House on 92nd Street' inevitable, and unfortunate. This lacks any intercutting of newsreel shots. Instead, it is corny melodrama. Not for U.S. market generally.

After the recent batch of really first-class pictures from British studios, the glaring faults of this plot-heavy spy hunt bring to light many of the flaws of the old days of English film production. Once again miscasting, a banal script and third rate direction give the star and featured players all the worst of it. The few bright spots which bring the screen to life emanate from the bit actors, notably in the Dublin hotel sequence where the rich brogue of clerk, porter and page boy smacks of the real thing.

Robert Newton, widely acclaimed as one of the best of West End stage actors, has little opportunity to prove it in the starring role. Equally barren of chance to score is Muriel Pavlow, looker suggesting latent ability, as the Austrian refugee. Of the other featured players, Herbert Lom is wasted as a master Nazi spy, and Guy Middleton as Newton's assistant Intelligence officer struggles manfully with a stooge-like role.

The little appeal "Night Boat to Dublin" has for American audiences is to be found in above-average production values. Boat sequences, like those in the Dublin hotel, should intrigue Irish-Americans. As a second feature in small towns here, patrons probably will sit through this one without much beefing. *Talb.*

Prairie Rustlers

PRC release of Sigmund Neufeld production. Stars Buster Crabbe, features Al "Fuzzy" St. John. Directed by Sam Newfield. Original story and screenplay, Fred Myton; camera, Jack Greenhalgh; editor, Holbrook N. Todd. At New York, N. Y., dual, week of Jan. 16, '46. Running time, **53 MINS.**

Billy Carson	Buster Crabbe
Fuzzy Jones	Al "Fuzzy" St. John
Helen	Evelyn Finley
Dan Foster	Karl Hackett
Matt	Stanford Jolley
Bart	Bud Osborne
Vic	Kermit Maynard

Latest of the Buster Crabbe-Al "Fuzzy" St. John westerns, "Prairie Rustlers" provides everything that the outdoor film fan wants—plenty of chases, gunplay, mild humor and romance. And, for an added twist, this one has Crabbe in a dual role of hero and villain, in which he knocks himself out in a rough-and-tumble fight with himself in the last reel. Crabbe-St. John duo has garnered a sizable following for the series, and this one should do well at the b.o.

As the hero of the piece, Crabbe is blamed for a murder committed by his cousin, which he also plays. Climax is reached when the hero Crabbe catches up with the villainous Crabbe, knocks him out in a neat bit of trick photography, and so clears himself of the charge. Western star kids his way through the picture with a tongue-in-cheek attitude, but is convincing enough for the kids and other action fans.

St. John, bewhiskered and confused, supplies the comedy throughout the film, and is a neat foil for the star. Comedian revives his trick bicycle act that once made him a feature of the old vaudeville circuits for good results. Remainder of the cast is composed of familiar faces that always seem to play the same parts in the westerns, with Kermit Maynard, brother of onetime cowboy star Ken, showing up well as one of the bad guys.

Six Gun Man

PRC release of Arthur Alexander production. Stars Bob Steele. Directed by Harry Fraser. Screenplay, Fraser; camera, Jack Greenhalgh; editor, Roy Livingston. Previewed in N. Y., Jan. 17, '46. Running time, **59 MINS.**

Bob Storm	Bob Steele
Syd McTavish	Syd Saylor
Tim Hager	Jimmie Martin
Laura Barton	Jean Carlin
Matt Haley	I. Stanford Jolley
Ed Slater	Brooke Temile
Sam Elkins	Bud Osborne
Joe Turner	Budd Buster
Lon Kelly	Stanley Blystone
Slim Peters	Roy Brent
Sheriff Jennings	Steve Clark
Mrs. Barton	Dorothy Whitmore

Four fistfights, three gun battles and a stage holdup, all crowded into 59 minutes, aren't enough to make this formula westerner into anything pulse-quickening. Lacking imagination or skill, these affrays tend to run one into another, with the effect of tedium rather than excitement. Moreover, the story, the usual thing about cattle hijackers and the superman U. S. marshal, creaks too much to help.

Bob Steele as the marshal woodenly performs the wonders of his trade. Syd Saylor, as comic buddy to Steele, has his hooks out for the laughs, but the stilted lines and unfunny situations have burdened him with an impossible task. Performances by the rest of the cast add nothing. Even the deep-dyed addicts won't go for this one.

Club Havana
(SONGS)

PRC release of Leon Fromkess production (Martin Mooney, associate producer). Features Tom Neal, Margaret Lindsay, Don Douglas, Isabelita, Dorothy Morris, Ernest Truex, Rene Riane, Gertrude Michael. Directed by Edgar G. Ulmer. Screenplay, by Raymond L. Schrock, based on original story by Fred Jackson; musical director, Howard Jackson; camera, Benjamin N. Kline; editor, Carl Pierson. At Strand, Brooklyn, dual, week Jan. 18, '46. Running time, **62 MINS.**

Bill Porter	Tom Neal
Rosalind	Margaret Lindsay
Johnny Norton	Don Douglas
Isabelita	Isabelita
Lucy	Dorothy Morris
Willy Kingston	Ernest Truex
Mrs. Cavendish	Renie Riano
Hetty	Gertrude Michael
Jimmy	Eric Sinclair
Rogers	Paul Cavanagh
Joe Reed	Marc Lawrence
Charles	Pedro De Cordoba
Myrtle	Sonia Sorel
Iris and Pierre	Played by Themselves
Carlos Molina Orch	

"Club Havana" attempts a serious note that succeeds only in being heavy and unconvincing. Exclusively for the short end of dualers.

Camera is focused variously on a scramble of characters unfolding love, hate, and death problems during an evening in a fashionable Latin nitery. Margaret Lindsay and Don Douglas figure as the love interest. Miss Lindsay, as a divorcee, attempts suicide after learning she is to be discarded by her companion for another love. Tom Neal, a young doctor out on his first call, is there for the emergency and is instrumental in the lovers' reconciliation. Gertrude Michael appears inconsequentially as a powder-room maid.

Carlos Molina orch. plus vocals by Isabelita, who sings "Tico Tico" and "Besame Mucho," show up as relief. Ditto a samba dance performed by Iris and Pierre.

Cast manages to make the most of its material, which is feeble at best, and comedy sequences, with the exception of those involving Ernest Truex, fall flat.

The Flying Serpent

PRC release of Sigmund Neufeld production. Stars George Zucco and Ralph Lewis; features Hope Kramer and Eddie Acuff. Directed by Sherman Scott. Screenplay, John T. Neville; camera, Jack Greenhalgh; editor, Holbrook N. Todd. Previewed in N. Y., Jan. 17, '46. Running time, 59 MINS.

Prof. Forbes.......................George Zucco
Richard Thorpe.......................Ralph Lewis
Mary Forbes.......................Hope Kramer
Jerry Jones.......................Eddie Acuff
Lewis Havener.......................Wheaton Chambers
Dr. Lambert.......................James Metcalf
Billy Hayes.......................Henry Hall
Hastings.......................Milton Kibbee
Coroner.......................Bud Buster
Bennett.......................Terry Frost

This picture could have been the curdling meller it set out to be if its instrument of horror, a winged serpent, did not resemble an oversized hawk rather than the lethal, blood-sucking monster intended. As it is, "The Flying Serpent" may provide a few uneasy moments for the kids but will fail to garner thrills from the incredulous adult. Suspense, fatally lacking, could well have been used to spike the picture. It's headed for minor biz.

Story relates the connivings of a crazed archeologist to protect his discovery of a fabulous Aztec treasure hidden in New Mexico. George Zucco, the professor, uses the serpent, originally posted by the Aztecs in the treasure room on sentry duty, as the instrument to murder a number of innocents who threaten to stumble on the professor's find. The murders out when a young radio newscaster sent to cover the story unravels the far-from-tangled skien.

Zucco physically fills his part well and performs satisfactorily in poorly motivated role. Ralph Lewis plays the conventional infallible sleuth in unimaginative manner. As the love interest, Hope Kramer is stiff and awkward as the professor's stepdaughter and intended victim. Sherman Scott's direction is only so-so with several good opportunities for dramatic buildup badly muffed.

Miniature Reviews

"Diary of a Chambermaid" UA - Bogeaus - Meredith). Star-studded meller geared for strong grosses on name value.

"The Virginian" (Par). Flavorsome revival of Owen Wister novel in Technicolor. Will do okay.

"Three Strangers" (WB). Fine performances mainly recommend this one.

"The Blue Dahlia" (Par). Suspenseful murder thriller, with strong marquee pull in Alan Ladd, Veronica Lake and William Bendix.

"The Well-Groomed Bride" (Par). Mild comedy will be mildly dependent upon Ray Milland-Olivia De Havilland tags on the marquee.

"Terror By Night" (U). Standard for the Sherlock Holmes mystery series.

"The Mask of Diijon" (PRC). So-so horror meller for dualers.

"They Made Me a Killer" (Par). Action film featuring Bob Lowery and Barbara Britton, aimed for the nabes with fair b.o. prospects.

"The Navajo Kid" (PRC). Routine western okay for Bob Steele fans.

Diary of a Chambermaid

United Artists release of Benedict Bogeaus-Burgess Meredith production. Stars Paulette Goddard, Burgess Meredith, Hurd Hatfield, Francis Lederer; features Judith Anderson, Florence Bates, Irene Ryan and Reginald Owen. Directed by Jean Renoir. Screenplay, Burgess Meredith, adapted from novel by Octave Mirbeau and play by Andre Heuse, Andre De Lorde and Thielly Nores; editor, James Smith; camera, Lucien Andriot; special effects, Lee Zavitz. Previewed in N. Y., Jan. 25, '46. Running time, 86 MINS.

Celestine.......................Paulette Goddard
Mauger.......................Burgess Meredith
Georges.......................Hurd Hatfield
Joseph.......................Francis Lederer
Mme. Lanlaire.......................Judith Anderson
Rose.......................Florence Bates
Louise.......................Irene Ryan
Marianne.......................Almira Sessions
Lanlaire.......................Reginald Owen

It is interesting to note the experiment of Benedict Bogeaus and Burgess Meredith in their initial joint production venture, "Diary of a Chambermaid." "Diary" is interesting from several angles, no less of which is its adaptation from the original French. The transition is certainly the most important factor in drawing a line on its entertainment values. This is an odd yarn, the type done so well by the French—and so falteringly by almost anyone else. "Diary" in its American form has not nearly the intrigue, nor the color, suggested by the original French version, but it has names and an interest all its own to recommend it for the boxoffice.

To casual filmgoers unversed in a tendency of the French to measure their successful films in terms of stark realities, "Diary" is inclined to be too morbid, especially in these days, when "escapism" is still a term bandied about by the Hollywood cinemoguls. And especially, too, when the pic hasn't the trenchant quality of, say, a "Lost Weekend."

It is the yarn of a chambermaid who, tiring of her station in life, vows to achieve wealth whoever the man. The men in her life aren't too sharply defined, nor especially interesting. Nor is the murder of the aging captain by the valet, so he can get money to marry the chambermaid, committed with any degree of climactic excitement, a factor that's also true when the murderer is himself routed and killed by an angry mob. There is seldom any sense of impending tension.

There is Paulette Goddard, as the chambermaid with a gold glint to her orbs; Meredith, a psychopathic, aging army captain; Hurd Hatfield, the sensitive consumptive whom the girl loves, and Francis Lederer, the glowering valet-murderer. Then there are Judith Anderson, as the mistress of the household, and Reginald Owen, her weakling husband, among others. That's really a parlay of names—and performances, too.

Totaling these factors is director Jean Renoir, who knows his way about this sort of yarn, for he, in other days, when French pix were the delights of arty Americans, was responsible for many of them coming to these shores.

If Renoir has failed to establish his characters, as he might have with French performers, lay the blame upon a cast that is expert in its own way—its Hollywood way—but not clearly defining the nuances and sharp touches that are seemingly to be found only on the Continent. This is, after all, very much the Continental type of yarn, and occasionally there arises the thought that here are performers who can't, through no fault of their own, quite meet the occasion. One doesn't, conversely, expect the French to epitomize the old American west in their own picture-making.

Meredith not only is star and coproducer, but is billed as author of the screenplay. The script is occasionally uneven and lacking in proper motivation, but the production is Grade A. *Kahn.*

The Virginian

Paramount release of Paul Jones production. Stars Joel McCrea, Brian Donlevy, Sonny Tufts, Barbara Britton; features Fay Bainter, Tom Tully, Bill Edwards, William Frawley, Paul Guilfoyle, Marc Lawrence, Vince Barnett. Directed by Stuart Gilmore. Screenplay, Frances Goodrich, Albert Hackett; adaptation, Howard Estabrook; based on novel by Owen Wister and play by Wister and Kirk La Shelle; camera, Harry Hallenberger; editor, Everett Douglas; music score, Daniele Amfitheatrof. Reviewed in N. Y., Jan. 29, '46. Running time, 85 MINS.

The Virginian.......................Joel McCrea
Trampas.......................Brian Donlevy
Steve.......................Sonny Tufts
Molly Wood.......................Barbara Britton
Mrs. Taylor.......................Fay Bainter
Mr. Taylor.......................Henry O'Neill
Honey Wiggen.......................William Frawley
Sam Bannett.......................Bill Edwards
Judge Henry.......................Minor Watson
Nebraska.......................Tom Tully
Baldy.......................Vince Barnett
Spanish Ed.......................Martin Garralaga
Shorty.......................Paul Guilfoyle
Pete.......................Marc Lawrence
Andy Jones.......................James Burke
The Sheriff.......................Al Bridge
Mrs. Wood.......................Nana Bryant

"The Virginian" stands up pretty well over the years. First filmed in 1914 for the silents, then in '29 (by Par), the present version of the Owen Wister novel is still a pleasant, flavorsome western, with much of the old charm of a daguerreotype. Filmed for first time in Technicolor, pic's gaudy setting, as well as cast and story, will round 'em up again at the b.o.

Although story is a little dated as well as a mite slow, the yarn is still a satisfactory romance, with enough shooting and suspense to offset the plodding pace. Yarn hasn't been changed much, still being the story of the little schoolmarm from Vermont and the cowboy from Virginia, who meet in Montana and wed, after the hero has disposed of a few troublesome cow rustlers.

Costumes of the eastern '70s, the early-type railroads, the horse riding and cow roundups, the rolling Montana hills, all help in the nostalgic flavor. Direction, set to the even pace, is good, while camera work, especially in such matters as rustling and stampede scenes, is excellent. Tinted outdoors, too, is handsome.

Joel McCrea follows soundly in footsteps of Dustin Farnum and Gary Cooper as The ("When You Call Me That, Smile") Virginian, with a straightforward characterization. Barbara Britton is pert and pretty as the schoolteacher. Brian Donlevy, as the rustler, and Sonny Tufts, in his first western role as a misguided cowhand, head an okay supporting cast. *Bron.*

Three Strangers

Warner Bros. release of Wolfgang Reinhardt production. Stars Sydney Greenstreet, Geraldine Fitzgerald and Peter Lorre; features Joan Lorring, Robert Shayne, Marjorie Riordan, Arthur Shields, Rosalind Ivan, John Alvin, Peter Whitney and Alan Napier. Directed by Jean Negulesco. Story and adaptation, John Huston and Howard Koch; editor, George Amy; camera, Arthur Edeson. Previewed in N. Y., Jan. 24, '46. Running time, 92 MINS.

Arbutny.......................Sydney Greenstreet
Crystal.......................Geraldine Fitzgerald
West.......................Peter Lorre
Icy.......................Joan Lorring
Fallon.......................Robert Shayne
Janet.......................Marjorie Riordan
Prosecutor.......................Arthur Shields
Lady Rhea.......................Rosalind Ivan
Junior Clerk.......................John Alvin
Gabby.......................Peter Whitney
Shackleford.......................Alan Napier

"Three Strangers" carries a rather complicated, episodic plot, depending mostly on the fine cast performances to carry it. Boxoffice prospects range from average to good.

Not only the three stars, Sydney Greenstreet, Geraldine Fitzgerald and Peter Lorre, but various supporting players command special attention. Greenstreet overplays to some extent as the attorney who has raided a trust fund, but he still does a good job. Lorre is tops as a drunk who gets involved in a murder of which he's innocent, while Miss Fitzgerald rates as the victim.

Along with Greenstreet and Lorre, Miss Fitzgerald has an equal share in a sweepstakes ticket. They are strangers. All three win on the ticket but Greenstreet murders the girl in a fit of rage, in Lorre's presence, thus leaving latter, also a loser, since he cannot risk trying to cash the ticket because it would involve him in the killing.

Story jumps around uncertainly. Backgrounds and production reflect credit to Wolfgang Reinhardt, while Jean Negulesco's direction is satisfactory.

Outstanding among the lesser performers are Joan Lorring and Peter Whitney. Others, all good, include Robert Shayne, Marjorie Riordan, Arthur Shields and Rosalind Ivan. *Char.*

The Blue Dahlia

Paramount release of George Marshall production. Stars Alan Ladd, Veronica Lake, William Bendix; features Howard da Silva, Doris Dowling, Tom Powers, Hugh Beaumont, Howard Freeman, Will Wright. Produced by John Houseman. Directed by Marshall. Screenplay, Raymond Chandler; camera, Lionel Lindon; editor, Arthur Schmidt; music, Victor Young. Tradeshown, N. Y., Jan. 25, '46. Running time, 96 MINS.

Johnny Morrison.......................Alan Ladd
Joyce Harwood.......................Veronica Lake
Buzz Wanchek.......................William Bendix
Eddie Harwood.......................Howard da Silva
Helen Morrison.......................Doris Dowling
Capt. Hendrickson.......................Tom Powers
George Copeland.......................Hugh Beaumont
Corelli.......................Howard Freeman
Leo.......................Don Costello
"Dad" Newell.......................Will Wright
The Man.......................Frank Faylen
Heath (Gangster).......................Walter Sande

Smooth, suspenseful murder thriller has good performances by its trio of leads, Alan Ladd, Veronica Lake and William Bendix, to heighten natural boxoffice appeal and offset improbabilities in story structure. Sharp quality of the few tough fight scenes will also increase interest, for good word-of-mouth praise.

Ladd's fans, awaiting his first screen appearance since his stint in the armed service, won't be disappointed by his return. Playing a discharged naval flier returning home from the Pacific first to find his wife unfaithful, then to find her murdered and himself in hiding as the suspect, Ladd does a bangup job.

Performance has a warm appeal, while in his relentless track down of the real criminal, Ladd has a cold, steel-like quality that is potent. Fight scenes are stark and brutal, and tremendously effective.

Story gets off to a slow start, but settles to an even pace that never lets down in interest. Audience may guess the killer, as the story follows several alleys of suspects, but pic always has suspense, with sufficient variations in mood. Ladd is one of trio to return from the wars, others being Bendix and Hugh Beaumont. Ladd's path crosses Veronica Lake's, latter being separated wife of a nightclub owner who is one of the killer-suspects. Scenes between Ladd and Miss Lake are surprisingly sensitive, with an economy of dialog and emotion doubly appealing.

Miss Lake's performance is free of mannerisms and quietly appealing. Bendix, playing a tailgunner suffering occasionally from shellshock, brings a gruff, hearty quality to his role that is excellent contrast to Ladd's. Howard da Silva, as nitery owner, is menacing without exaggerating the part. Doris Dowling is sometimes unconvincing as the cheating wife. Tom Powers plays an intelligent police captain, and Howard Freeman an icily ruthless gangster.

Writing is taut and dialog terse and believable. Direction has similar economy of movement and action, which heightens the suspense. Production-wise, film stacks up creditably. *Bron.*

The Well-Groomed Bride

Paramount release of Fred Kohlmar production. Stars Olivia DeHavilland, Ray Milland and Sonny Tufts; features James Gleason, Constance Dowling and Percy Kilbride. Directed by Sidney Lanfield. Screenplay, Claude Binyon and Robert Russell from original by Russell; camera, John F. Seitz; editor, William Shea. Previewed at Normandie theatre, N. Y., Jan. 25, '46. Running time, 75 MINS.

Margie	Olivia DeHavilland
Lt. Briggs	Ray Milland
Torchy	Sonny Tufts
Captain Hornby	James Gleason
Rita Sloane	Constance Dowling
Mr. Dawson	Percy Kilbride
Wickley	Jean Heather
Mitch	Jay Norris
Buck	Jack Reilly
Goose	George Turner

One bottle of champagne—even in magnum size—is too frothy a concoction on which to float 75 minutes of screen time, as the Paramount mixologists have attempted here. Result is only a moderately amusing comedy, which will be mainly dependent on the marquee values of the Olivia DeHavilland-Ray Milland tags and the full-size production for fair grosses.

Screenwriters Claude Binyon and Robert Russell have stretched to the snapping point the single gag on which the pic is suspended. That's the effort of Milland, a Naval lieutenant, to get hold of the only magnum of French champagne in San Francisco for the launching of a carrier. Said bubbly is the property of Miss DeHavilland, who's hanging on to it for celebration within a few hours of her marriage to Sonny Tufts, playing a lummox Army officer. That Milland is going to get both the king-size bottle and the gal is so abundantly evident from the very first minute that it would take a much heavier pile of powerful gags than here evident to sustain top interest and laughs. There are nevertheless quite a few giggles contrived out of the situations.

Expert comedy playing by Milland and Miss DeHavilland must be credited with successfully bringing off as much mirth as there is. Tufts suffers from the broad and preposterous manner in which the would-be groom character he plays is written. He milks it for fairish results. Percy Kilbride, a vet comedy scenestealer and chuckle-winner, handily maintains that rep. James Gleason

is standard as the hard-shelled skipper who sets Milland off on the champagne-getting mission.

Director Sidney Lanfield is unable to rise above the script itself, with the action ankling along in wholly-anticipated and ordinary fashion. It's a smooth job he's done, however, and he gets his players over the weak spots quickly enough.

Producer Fred Kohlmar has given the film adequate production values. *Herb.*

Terror By Night

Hollywood, Jan. 24.

Universal release of Roy William Neill production. Stars Basil Rathbone and Nigel Bruce; features Alan Mowbray, Renee Godfrey, Dennis Hoey, Billy Bevan. Directed by Neill. Screenplay, Frank Gruber; from original story by Sir Arthur Conan Doyle; camera, Maury Gertsman; editor, Saul A. Goodkind. Previewed in projection room, Universal City, Jan. 22, '46. Running time, 60 MINS.

Sherlock Holmes	Basil Rathbone
Dr. Watson	Nigel Bruce
Major Duncan Bleek	Alan Mowbray
Inspector Lestrade	Dennis Hoey
Vivian Vedder	Renee Godfrey
Lady Margaret	Mary Forbes
Train Attendant	Billy Bevan
Professor Kilbane	Frederic Worlock
Conductor	Leyland Hodgson
Ronald Carstairs	Geoffrey Steele
McDonald	Boyd Davis
Mrs. Shallcross	Janet Murdoch
Sands	Skelton Knaggs

This one follows the usual production pattern of previous Sherlock Holmes mysteries from Universal. It is standard for the series and will pay off in okay style. Roy William Neill, as producer-director, has given it good mounting for the budget and nice pacing.

Action is all played on an English train, enroute to Scotland. Basil Rathbone, as Holmes, is guarding a fabulous diamond against jewel snatchers. With Holmes, to both help and hinder in his assignment, are Dr. Watson (Nigel Bruce) and Inspector Lestrade, of Scotland Yard (Dennis Hoey). There are several murders before Holmes decides that killer is hiding in a double-bottom coffin and the brains is masquerading as a dumbwitted passenger.

Rathbone's performance is a shade under his usual portrayal of the intrepid sleuth, but still satisfies. Bruce has a good hold on the bumbling Dr. Watson characterization. Renee Godfrey is interesting as a suspect, and others measure up. Script by Frank Gruber, based on the Sir Arthur Conan Doyle story, holds together well. Neill's direction wraps up all loose ends in finale as Holmes prepares for another adventure. *Brog.*

The Mask of Diijon

(SONGS)

PRC release of Max Alexander and Alfred Stern production. Stars Erich Von Stroheim. Directed by Lew Landers. Screenplay, Arthur St. Claire and Griffen Jay, based on original story by Arthur St. Claire; camera, Jack Greenhalgh; editor, Roy Livingston; musical director, Lee Zahler. Previewed in N. Y., Jan. 24, '46. Running time, 73 MINS.

Diijon	Erich Von Stroheim
Victoria	Jeanne Bates
Tony Holiday	William Wright
Sheffield	Edward Van Sloan
Danton	Mauritz Hugo
Denise	Denise Varnac
Fleming	Robert Malcolm
Mrs. McGaffey	Hope Landin
Guzzo	Shimen Ruskin
Mark Lindsay	Roy Darmour
Alex	Antonio Filauri

An involved and somewhat pretentious story, "Mask of Diijon" aims for deep dramatics which fail to register. Film, however, with its morbid theme involving mesmerism could pass as a so-so horror meller.

Erich Von Stroheim plays an ex-magician discovering hypnotic powers within himself. The role, incredible from the first, is aided by the Von Stroheim sour countenance in spite of momentary ridiculous sequences. Competent supporting performances are given by William

Wright, Edward Van Sloan and Joan Bates.

Horror element of story is the use of hypnotism by Von Stroheim in an experimental murder for the purpose of killing his wife's suspected lover (William Wright). The hypnotist is foiled by a fluke arrangement in which his hypnotized wife, Jean Bates, intended by Von Stroheim to kill Wright, selects a gun loaded with blanks to carry out the mesmeric will. Final death battle with the law has Von Stroheim barricaded in a magician's shop, where he meets his end via an illusionist's guillotine.

Songs are "White Roses," by Carroll K. Cooper and Lee Zahler, and "Disillusion," by Lou E. Zoeller and Billy Austin. Both are in the somber mood of the film.

They Made Me a Killer

Paramount release of Pine-Thomas production. Features Robert Lowery, Barbara Britton, Frank Albertson, Lola Lane. Directed by William C. Thomas. Screenplay, Geoffrey Homes, Winston Miller and Kae Salkow, from story by Owen Francis; camera, Fred Jackman, Jr.; editor, Henry Adams. Previewed in N. Y., Jan. 24, '46. Running time, 65 MINS.

Tom Durling	Robert Lowery
June Reynolds	Barbara Britton
Al	Frank Albertson
Betty	Lola Lane
Frank Chance	James Bush
Jack Chance	Edmund McDonald
Steve Reynolds	Byron Barr
Ma	Elizabeth Risdon
Roach	Ralph Sanford
Lafferty	John Harmon
District Attorney	Paul Harvey

A series of scarcely-credible escapes and plenty of gunplay lend "They Made Me a Killer" the superficial appeal designed to draw action fans. The more critical will certainly find fault with the ease with which a supposedly widely hunted man can float around the countryside in search of his framers. B.o. prospects are fair for action houses.

Bob Lowery as the escaped victim of a gang of bank rollers endows his role with the requisite masculinity and brawn. Enlisted in his aid is Barbara Britton, who seeks to clear her brother, killed in a bank hold-up, of suspicion as a conspirator. Together, the two confront the gangsters in their hideout. Two cops, who show remarkable and unprecedented acumen in deducing the perilous situation of Lowery and Miss Britton, help in the rescue.

Lowery and Miss Britton satisfactorily meet the minor demands on histrionic ability. Lola Lane, in the minor role of gun moll and temptress, performs convincingly. As gangsters, James Bush and Edmund McDonald fill their roles with the necessary sinister gyrations.

Dialog is stilted and unconvincing. In a film such as this, however, the fault is not necessarily fatal since so much stress is placed on action. Several bangup fist fights are well directed by William C. Thomas, although he doesn't appear to have gotten the maximum out of all the action sequences.

The Navajo Kid

PRC release of Arthur Alexander production. Stars Bob Steele; features Syd Saylor, Edward Cassidy, Caren Marsh. Directed by Harry Fraser. Screenplay, Harry Fraser; camera, Jack Greenhalgh; editor, Roy Livingston. At New York, N. Y., Jan. 23, '46. Running time, 59 MINS.

Navajo Kid	Bob Steele
Happy	Syd Saylor
Sheriff Roy Landon	Edward Cassidy
Winifred McMasters	Caren Marsh
Matt Crandall	Stanley Blystone
Bo Talley	Edward Howard
Lee Hedges	Charles King, Jr.
Abe Murdock	Bud Osborne
Pinky	Budd Buster
Dr. Cole	Henry Hall

Poured out of the same mold that has done service for countless other westerns, "The Navajo Kid" calls for two parts murder and revenge, spiced lightly with humor and stir-

red by long arm of coincidence. But since the shooting, riding, fisticuffs, and jailbreaks follow through from start to finish without scenic or romantic breathers, the outdoor addicts should buy this one without trouble.

Performances are par with pat script and story. Bob Steele, as the adopted Indian who tracks down the killers of his foster-father, makes up for lack of thespic finesse with rugged sincerity and acrobatic dash. Steele is a hard, clean fighter graded as a hero in any kid's book. Syd Saylor is an experienced hand at riding a comic line and, as the frog trainer and Steele's sidekick, he delivers the assigned laughs. Unintended laughs are earned by Edward Cassidy, the town sheriff, who quite fantastically turns up to be Steele's real father.

Miniature Reviews

"Sentimental Journey" (20th) (One Song). Maureen O'Hara-John Payne - William Bendix, plus moppet Connie Marshall, in big b.o. weeper.

"The Hoodlum Saint" (M-G). Revival of the miracle reformation theme, with name cast to aid selling. Average b.o.

"Bad Bascomb" (M-G). Wallace Beery and Margaret O'Brien in tale of pioneer western days; strong boxoffice.

"Ambush Trail" (PRC). Formula western with Bob Steele, but lacking in slugging and gunplay.

"Idea Girl" (U). Clever, small-budgeted tunefilm offering plenty of entertainment. Above average b.o.

"Six P. M." (Artkino). Russian-made musical okay for houses using this type of film.

"Fedora" (Variety). Italian-made version of Sardou's stage success; strong for arty and Italian-language houses.

Sentimental Journey
(ONE SONG)

20th-Fox release of Walter Morosco production. Stars John Payne, Maureen O'Hara and William Bendix; features Sir Cedric Hardwicke, Glenn Langan, Mischa Auer, Kurt Kreuger, Trudy Marshall, Ruth Nelson and Connie Marshall. Directed by Walter Lang. Screenplay, Samuel Hoffenstein and Elizabeth Reinhardt, based on story by Nelia Gardner White; song, Bud Green, Les Brown and Ben Homer; editor, Kay Nelson; camera, Norbert Brodine; special photographic effects, Fred Sersen. Previewed in N. Y., Feb. 1, '46. Running time, **94 MINS.**

Bill	John Payne
Julie	Maureen O'Hara
Donnelly	William Bendix
Dr. Miller	Sir Cedric Hardwicke
Judson	Glenn Langan
Lawrence Ayres	Mischa Auer
Hitty	Connie Marshall
Wilson	Kurt Kreuger
Ruth	Trudy Marshall
Mrs. McMasters	Ruth Nelson
Martha	Dorothy Adams
Agnes	Mary Gordon
Miss Benson	Lillian Bronson
Mrs. Deane	Olive Blakeney
Detective	James Flavin
Bus Driver	William Haade
Chaperon	Mary Field
Clerk in Toy Shop	Byron Foulger
Toy Hawker	George E. Stone
Floorwalker	John Davidson

Sentiment and heart-rending emotions have become particularly popular commodities during these past wartime years; and there seems to be enough left of that public fancy to warrant the high acceptance of "Sentimental Journey." It's the weeper to end all weepers, the film that may well be responsible for the five-cornered handkerchief. The current one doesn't seem large enough for the Niagara of tears that must surely flow into this bath of emotionalism.

"Journey" may not be for the critics—but who are critics? Just a lot of Joes with passes. It's the public that still counts. And "Journey" is strongly geared for public consumption.

Here is a story that seems certainly to have recalled all the old cliches. And it will hardly matter at all at the boxoffice. It is a yarn built around an orphaned youngster whose foster mother dies leaving her wavering amidst the widower's uncertainty and grief. There it is. There's hardly little else, except fill-in details, all spread out over more than an hour and a half.

Specifically, "Journey" deals with a famous stage actress and her producer-husband. The actress has a heart condition. She falls in love with an orphan, and adopts the child, so that her husband won't be left lonely—just in case. The wife suffers a fatal attack, and the film then resolves into the child's attempts to take her foster-mother's place as the one upon whom the widower can depend for moral guidance.

It's plodding and sometimes too premeditated, with a particularly uncertain ending.

"Journey" is notable for the first screen appearance of a youngster who seems slated to be starred before long; little Connie Marshall plays the orphan with a remarkable degree of understatement and lack of precocity. Maureen O'Hara is the stage star; she remains one of filmdom's most beautiful lookers in addition to being a better actress than her script permits. John Payne is her husband, and performs creditably, while William Bendix, though also starred, is pretty much lost in the shuffle. Sir Cedric Hardwicke, as a medico, is his usually forthright self in a comparatively relegated part.

Walter Lang has apparently trained his sights on the youngster in his direction, and he has done well, though possibly at the expense of the film's overall pace and character development. Then, again, the script is, by its very nature, contributory to a pic that drags too frequently on its own.

The hit tune, "Sentimental Journey," serves as background music throughout, being consistent with the lachrymal tenor of the picture.

Perhaps that hankie should have six corners. *Kahn.*

The Hoodlum Saint
(SONGS)

Hollywood, Feb. 2.

Metro release of Cliff Reid production. Stars William Powell, Esther Williams,; features Angela Lansbury, James Gleason, Lewis Stone, Rags Ragland, Frank McHugh, Slim Summerville. Directed by Norman Taurog. Screenplay by Frank Wead and James Hill; camera, Ray June; editor, Ferris Webster; musical score, Nathaniel Shilkret. Tradeshown in Culver City, Feb. 1, '46. Running time, 92 mins.

Terry Ellerton O'Neill	William Powell
Kay Lorrison	Esther Williams
"Dusty" Millard	Angela Lansbury
"Sharp"	James Gleason
Father Nolan	Lewis Stone
"Fishface"	Rags Ragland
"Three-Finger"	Frank McHugh
"Eel"	Slim Summerville
Father O'Doul	Roman Bohnen
Cy Nolan	Charles Arnt
Mike Flaherty	Louis Jean Heydt
Uncle Joe Lorrison	Charles Trowbridge
Lewis J. Malbery	Henry O'Neill
Dave Fernby	William "Bill" Phillips
Father Duffy	Matt Moore
Rabbi Meyerberg	Trevor Bardette
Rev. Miller	Addison Richards
Buggsy	Tom Duggan
Maggie	Amma Dunn
Trina	Mary Gordon
Sam	Ernest Anderson
Ed Collner	Charles D. Brown

Name values assure okay but not sock returns for "The Hoodlum Saint." It's a drama laid in the period just after World War I up through the 1929 stock market crash and deals with the power of belief in St. Dismus, the good thief, to reform all hoodlums. Film gives Esther Williams fans a chance to see their favorite in something other than a musical, and her name, coupled with those of William Powell, Angela Lansbury and others will prove an initial draw.

Cliff Reid has given it plenty of production dress, and Norman Taurog's direction points up the characterizations, but unfoldment is never exciting. There's no feeling of struggle in the development of the plot, everything coming too easily to the characters—love, riches, poverty and eventual belief in St. Dismus' power for good. Quietness of movement is occasionally quickened by a sharp line of earthy dialog, and there are laughs spotted here and there to help.

Plot concerns disillusionment of a returning Army major. He finds ideals rapidly pushing him towards the corner applestand, and determines to garner all the coin possible, no matter how. He first uses a girl, tosses her off when he sees bigger opportunity. After accomplishing his money goal, he wants love but finds the girl can't stand his new character. The stockmarket crash wipes out his wealth and illness turns him to St. Dismus, whom he had originally wished off on some old poolroom pals to keep them out of his new life.

Powell is his usual assured self as the opportunist, delivering a topnotch characterization. Miss Williams thoroughly pleases as the girl who loves but spurns Powell until his morals improve. Angela Lansbury puts sex emphasis on her assignment as sideline romance for Powell and also sings several pop standards of the period. James Gleason wallops over his part as an old Powell sidekick who gets religion. Other poolroom cronies are in the capable hands of Rags Ragland, Frank McHugh and Slim Summerville. Lewis Stone, sharing featured billing, has only a small bit as Father Nolan. Charles Arnt, Charles Trowbridge, Henry O'Neill, Emma Dunn and Mary Gordon stand out among the many others.

Camera work by Ray June; musical score, and other technical credits are of the usual high Metro standard. *Brog.*

Bad Bascomb

Metro release of Orville O. Dull production. Stars Wallace Beery, Margaret O'Brien; features Marjorie Main, J. Carrol Naish. Directed by S. Sylvan Simon. Screenplay, William Lipman and Grant Garrett, from original story by D. A. Loxley; camera, Charles Schoenbaum; editor, Ben Lewis; special effects, Warren Newcombe. Previewed in N. Y., Jan. 28, '46. Running time, **111 MINS.**

Zeb Bascomb	Wallace Beery
Emmy	Margaret O'Brien
Abbey Hanks	Marjorie Main
Bart Yancey	J. Carrol Naish
Dora	Frances Rafferty
Jimmy Holden	Marshall Thompson
Elijah Walker	Russell Simpson
Luther Mason	Warner Anderson
John Fulton	Donald Curtis
Annie Fremont	Connie Gilchrist
Tillie Lovejoy	Sara Haden
Lucy Lovejoy	Renie Riano
Hannah	Jane Green
Governor Winton	Henry O'Neill
Elder Moab McCabe	Frank Darien

Despite a lack-lustre title, "Bad Bascomb" looks destined for strong boxoffice. Starring combo of Wallace Beery and Margaret O'Brien is a happy choice for entertainment and marquee purposes.

Beery's role is reminiscent of his outlaw in "The Bad Man" (1941), while O'Brien moppet is likewise clicko. Picture has solid production. Scripters William Lipman and Grant Garrett have taken D. A. Loxley's story of the notorious Zeb Bascomb gang and developed a strong human interest yarn revolving around the "good bad man," Bascomb (Beery) and the little orphan (Margaret O'Brien).

Director S. Sylvan Simon has paced the convincing tale about how the rough-and-tumble Beery slowly develops a real affection for the little tot. This angle has been developed without becoming maudlin, as the O'Brien youngster works a complete reformation of the bandit and killer to his involuntary leadership of a Mormon band treking to Utah. Picture is highlighted by a spectacular Indian attack, rescue by the cavalry and the hair-raising river-crossing in the covered wagons.

J. Carrol Naish, as Beery's partner, makes the renegade white adequately villainous. Marjorie Main, again in a typical shrewd role for her, is the overbearing grandmother who looks after the orphan. Marshall Thompson is effective as a rebellious member of the outlaws. Support is headed by Frances Rafferty, Russell Simpson, Donald Curtis, Connie Gilchrist and Sara Haden.

Simon's direction is excellent. Camera work of Charles Schoenbaum is front-rank. Ben Lewis' editing is fine. Sound job is outstanding. *Wear.*

Ambush Trail

PRC release of Arthur Alexander production. Stars Bob Steele. Directed by Harry Fraser. Screenplay, Elmer Clifton; camera, Jack Greenhalgh; editor, Roy Livingston. Previewed in N. Y., Jan. 23, '46. Running time, **60 MINS.**

Curley Thompson	Bob Steele
Sam Hawkins	Syd Saylor
Hatch Bolton	I. Stanford Jolley
Alice Rhodes	Lorraine Miller
Al Craig	Charles King
Ed Blane	Bob Carson
Jim Haley	Budd Buster
Walter Gordon	Kermit Maynard
Frank Owen	Frank Ellis
Marshal Dawes	Edward Cassidy

Comparatively gentle spread of strongarm and gunplay stuff in this formula western makes the film negative for even youngsters. Too many speaking lines, plus unimaginative story, mellow the usually fast-moving Bob Steele to routine minor b.o.

The hackneyed yarn of foiling the heavy in his attempt to ruin the local ranchers is filled with stilted performances. Steele, as the stranger in town, does the good deeds with the aid of Sid Saylor, who is in for the comedy.

Idea Girl
(SONGS)

Hollywood, Feb. 2.

Universal release of Howard Welsch production (associate producer, Will Cowan). Features Jess Barker, Julie Bishop, Alan Mowbray, Joan Fulton, Arthur Q. Bryan, Charlie Barnet orch. Directed by Will Jason. Screenplay, Charles R. Marion; adaptation, Elwood Ullman; original, Gladys Shelley; camera, George Robinson; editor, Otto Ludwig; songs, Jack Brooks and Edgar Fairchild. Previewed in Universal City, Feb. 1, '46. Running time, **60 MINS.**

Larry Brewster	Jess Barker
Pat O'Rourke	Julie Bishop
Wilfred Potts	George Dolenz
J. C. Crow	Alan Mowbray
Mabel	Joan Fulton
Cynthia	Laura Deane Dutton
Evelina	Virginia Christine
Plain Clothes Man	Lane Chandler
Commissioner	Arthur Q. Bryan

This one is good entertainment, well above the level of the usual program offering. Its musical numbers are introduced logically, the chuckles are hearty. Slick writing of a good idea, smooth direction and solid playing all point it for popular reception. Mounting is above average and other production factors offer excellent values in shaping it for the market.

Plot concerns femme song plugger who hypoes an amateur tune contest and other stunts that put firm on top but give song publishers plenty of headaches. Situations are broad and brightly dialoged to keep laughs coming in the writing contributed by Charles R. Marion, Elwood Ullman and Gladys Shelley. Score contains three new numbers, "I Don't Care If I Never Dream Again" and "I Can't Get You Out of My Mind," both by Jack Brooks and Edgar Fairchild, and "Xango," by George Waggner and Fairchild. "I Don't Care" is best and is reprised several times for easy listening. Vocaling is by Laura Deane Dutton and could have been better.

Will Jason's direction cleverly utilizes mobile camera. He gets considerable punch out of the lines and situations, keeps the pace fast and displays the players to advantage. Associate producer Will Cowan makes his supervision a good job of blending songs, laughs and story.

Julie Bishop shapes up in fine style as the songplugger and romantic antagonist of Jess Barker, one of the harassed publishers. Latter also punches over his part for equal honors. Alan Mowbray, the wolfish other partner; George Dolenz, amateur songwriter; Joan Fulton, a luscious secretary; Virginia Christine, Arthur Q. Bryan and others round out the expert cast.

Camera work by George Robinson, Frank Skinner's musical direction, the editing and other technical contributions aid in keeping this one above average for small-budgeted product. . Brog.

Six P.M.
(RUSSIAN-MADE)
(SONGS)

Artkino release of Mosfilm Studios production. Stars Marina Ladynina, Eugene Samoilov, Ivan Lubeznov. Directed by Ivan Piriev. Story, Victor Gusev; music by Tikhon Khrenikov; camera, Valentin Pavlov; English titles, Charles Clement. Previewed in N. Y., Jan. 25, '46. Running time, 65 MINS.

Varya Pankova	Marina Ladynina
Lt. Kudriashev	Eugene Samoilov
Lt. Demidov	Ivan Lubeznov
Fenia	Anastasia Lysak
Aunt Katia	Elena Savitskaya

(In Russian, English titles)

Film strives to fit the grim background of the late Russian struggle against the Nazis to tuneful music. But it never quite makes the fit. When the characters are singing folk tunes or love duets the picture is gay and enjoyable. But when the effort is made to dovetail such gaiety with the firing line the film becomes haphazard. "Six P.M." likely will do well in Soviet-film houses in the U. S. Otherwise, it's thin for American consumption.

Fine music, excellent ballading and choral work are wasted through inept direction and story projection. Promise of two sweethearts, both comrades under the Soviet colors, to meet "at 6 p.m." after the war on a Moscow bridge provides the title.

Marina Ladynina is a blonde beaut with a real voice. Opposite her is Eugene Samoilov, who also sports nice vocal chords. Ivan Lubeznov, his pal in arms and rival, for a time, for the same gal, is equally good as a singer. Both are fairish sort of actors, with thespian laurels going to Miss Ladynina.

Music by Tikhon Tikhon Khrenikov is for the most part of the lilting type. Victor Gusev's story is strictly one of those things. Charles Clement has done well with his English titling. Cameraing of Valentin Pavlov is solid, but print is bad.
. Wear.

Fedora
(ITALIAN-MADE)

Variety Films release of Consorzio I.C. A.R. Generalcine production. Stars, Luisa Ferida, Amedeo Nazzari. Directed by Camillo Mastrocinque. Story by Antonio Rossi, based on play by Victorien Sardou; camera, Giuseppe La Torre; musical score by and under direction of Umberto Giordano; English titles by Russell Spalding. At Giglio theatre, N. Y., starting Jan. 14, '46. Running time, 97 MINS.

Fedora	Luisa Ferida
Loris	Amedeo Nazzari
Vladimir	Osvaldo Valenti
Olga	Rina Morelli
De Ciricux	Sandro Ruffini
Prince Yariskine	Memo Benassi
Gretch	Augusto Marcacci
Boroff	Annibale Betrone
Cirillo	Guido Celano

(In Italian; English Titles)

"Fedora," Sardou's famous tragedy, in this Italian-made version reaches new heights for screen production out of Rome's studios. While lacking stars familiar to U. S., film patrons, picture shapes up as surefire in the U. S. for arty and Italian-language houses.

Pretentious production has a strong cast and uniformly fine direction. Tragedy is backgrounded neatly with music that goes far in overcoming the few story lags.

Luisa Ferida, leading Italian actress, is superb as Fedora. Amedeo Nazzari, as the Russian painter with whom she falls in love, also is excellent. He looks somewhat like Errol Flynn. Osvaldo Valenti does well as the wastrel count who is slain before he weds Fedora. Augusto Marcacci tops the strong supporting cast.

Direction by Camillo Mastrocinque is outstanding. He has avoided the laborious pace so common with many foreign-made pictures. Antonio Rossi's production and story are topflight as is photography by Giuseppe La Torre. Wear.

Miniature Reviews

"Cinderella Jones" (WB) (Songs). Funny escapist film with musical slant, headed for good returns.

"Riverboat Rhythm" (RKO). Mediocre comedy starring Leon Errol.

"Lawless Empire" (Col) (Songs). Tangy outdoor stuff for westerns fans.

"Tarzan and the Leopard Woman" (RKO). Disappointing Tarzan film though with fair b.o. prospects.

"Deadline at Dawn" (RKO). Pretentious Clifford Odets whodunit, unlikely as strong b.o. puller.

"Live Wires" (Mono). Gets new Bowery Boys (nee Eastside Kids) series off to excellent start in fast-moving program feature.

"Romance of the West" (PRC) (Color). Adequate western that gets lift from Cinecolor.

"The Face of Marble" (Mono). John Carradine in another persuasive horror-film.

"Whirlwind of Paris" (Hoffberg). French-made musical with Ray Ventura band; mild entry for foreign-language spots.

Cinderella Jones
(SONGS)

Hollywood, Feb. 8.

Warners release of Alex Gottlieb production. Stars Joan Leslie and Robert Alda; features S. Z. Sakall, Edward Everett Horton, Julie Bishop, William Prince. Directed by Busby Berkeley. Screenplay, Charles Hoffman; from story by Philip Wylie; camera, Sol Polito; songs, Jule Styne and Sammy Cahn; musical score, Frederick Hollander; orchestral arrangements, Ray Heindorf and Frank Perkins; editor, George Amy. Tradeshown in Los Angeles, Feb. 8, '46. Running time, 90 MINS.

Judy Jones	Joan Leslie
Tommy Coles	Robert Alda
Gabriel Popik	S. Z. Sakall
Keating	Edw. Everett Horton
Camille	Julie Bishop
Bart Williams	William Prince
Minland	Charles Dingle
Cora Elliott	Ruth Donnelly
Oliver S. Patch	Elisha Cook, Jr.
George	Hobart Cavanaugh
Mahoney	Charles Arnt
Krencher	Chester Clute
Riley	Ed Garzan
Bashful Girl	Margaret Early
Soldier	Johnny Mitchell
Singer	Mary Dean
Jailer	Monte Blue
Manicurist	Marianne O'Brien
Burlesque Queen	Marian Martin

Current popularity of screwball, escapist features gives 'Cinderella Jones" excellent prospects. It has name values to assure business, and offers plenty of fun. Production by Alex Gottlieb has a musical slant, picture going almost musical-comedy on several occasions, but doesn't actually need these touches.

Plot deals with a girl who wants to inherit $10,000,000 but has to find a husband with a Quiz Kid brain to collect. She figures an exclusively male technology institute is the proper place to find such a husband, and action revolves around her attempts to enroll in the school to find her man. All the time her current boyfriend, a bandleader, is a Quiz Kid, too, but she doesn't discover this until the finale.

Around that basis scripter Charles Hoffman has fitted fast dialog and situations that pay off in chuckles. Busby Berkeley's direction generates plenty of speed in the unfolding, maintaining a pace that deftly points the laughs. On the musical side, though, he misses, staging one large production midway that only proves a pace-stopper. Tunes are not particular standouts but make for okay

listening, best being "When the One You Love."

Joan Leslie makes a delightful dumb dame who malaprops all over the place before wising up to the worth of her bandleader, both mentally and as a big hunk of man. Robert Alda gives the baton-waver role plenty of life to add to his film stature. Backing up the plentiful comedy are S. Z. Sakall, Edward Everett Horton, Julie Bishop and William Prince in the featured spots. Also laugh contributors are Charles Dingle, Chester Clute and Charles Arnt, a trio of nutty lawyers; Elisha Cook, Jr., Ruth Donnelly; Hobart Cavanaugh and others.

Gottlieb's production supervision has shaped the picture for popular reception and given it topnotch mounting. Aiding production dress are the camera work by Sol Polito, art direction, music score, etc.
Brog.

Riverboat Rhythm

RKO release of Nat Holt production. Stars Leon Errol; features Glenn Vernon, Walter Catlett, Marc Cramer, Jonathan Hale, Joan Newton, Dorothy Vaughan, Carter and Moreland and Frankie Carle orch. Directed by Leslie Goodwins. Story, Robert Faber; adaptation, Charles Roberts; editor, Marvin Coil; camera, Robert de Grasse. Previewed in New York, Feb. 7, '46. Running time, 65 MINS.

Matt Lindsey	Leon Errol
John Beeler	Glenn Vernon
Mr. Witherspoon	Walter Catlett
Lionel Beeler	Marc Cramer
Edward Beeler	Jonathan Hale
Midge	Joan Newton
Belle Crowley	Dorothy Vaughan
Carter & Moreland	
Frankie Carle Orchestra	

"Riverboat Rhythm" is very corny and slapsticky, being a series of dull incidents concerning the operator of a showboat on the Mississippi. It's weak boxoffice.

Leon Errol plays the financially-embarrassed captain of a riverboat which becomes grounded on property belonging to a resort hotel. Thus, the action shifts between the showboat, on which no show is ever given, and the resort, which provides background for the Frankie Carle orch. There are no song or dance numbers despite what the title would indicate.

The pitch for laughs, which at best are only mild, is based on the playing of two characters in clown fashion by Errol. He switches from a Yankee showboatman to a southern colonel with a Dixie accent. As the former he's avoiding a sheriff, as the latter trying to keep out of the way of feuding Kentucky family out to get the man he's impersonating.

Nat Holt's production is suitable and the direction by Leslie Goodwin's adequate, but photography of Robert de Grasse leaves much to be desired except for the scene, effectively lit, in which Carle plays "Carle Boogey," his own piano composition. Carle is featured in another session at the ivories in the earlier proceedings.

Supporting Errol, who's starred, is a small and unimpressive cast, including Glenn Vernon, Walter Catlett, Marc Cramer, Jonathan Hale, Joan Newton and Dorothy Vaughan. Catlett is best of the group. Miss Newton, nice to look at, may be on the way to better things. Colored team of Carter and Moreland likewise can be used to better advantage.
Char.

Lawless Empire
(SONGS)

Columbia release of Colbert Clark production. Stars Charles Starrett; features Tex Harding, Dub Taylor, Mildred Law, Bob Wills and Texas Playboys. Directed by Vernon Keays. Screenplay, Bennett Cohen; story, Elizabeth Beecher; camera, George Meehan; editor, Paul Borofsky. At New York theatre, N. Y., Feb. 7, '46, dual. Running time, 58 MINS.

Steve Random	Charles Starrett
Rev. Tex Harding	Tex Harding

Cannonball....Dub Taylor
Vicky....Mildred Law
Marty Foster....Johnny Walsh
Blaze Howard....John Calvert
Duke Flinders....Ethan Laidlaw
Doc Weston....Forrest Taylor
Jed Stevens....Jack Rockwell
Lenny....George Chesebro
Skids....Boyd Stockman
Mr. Murphy....Lloyd Ingraham
Mrs. Murphy....Jessie Arnold
Sam Enders....Tom Chatterton
Bob Wills and His Texas Playboys

There's nothing novel or startling in this horse-opera, but the combination of hard-riding, shooting, sheriff-vs.-outlaws story, suspense and insertions of music, makes a pleasant enough confection for western fans.

Story deals with frontier days when rustlers raided cow herds and ran settlers off their property, and concerns the Durango Kid's (Charles Starrett) attempts to clean the varmints out. Simple story is handled straight. A little gun dueling and a cow stampede add to the excitement, while some good mountain exteriors also contribute flavor.

Starrett has another he-man role as the Kid, which he handles acceptably, with a little fancy saddle-work to intrigue the city-folk. Tex Harding is good support as a fighting reverend, determined to erect a church in the lawless territory. He also contributes a neat vocal bit as solo in an attractive cowboy tune, "Farther Along." John Calbert, as the heavy; Mildred Law, as romantic element, and Dub Taylor, for laughs, are also okay.

Bob Wills and his Texas Playboys, a smooth strings combo, in addition to neat handling of "Along," go to town in two swingy tunes, "Stay a Little Longer" and "Devilish Mary." *Bron.*

Tarzan and the Leopard Woman

RKO release of Sol Lesser production. Stars Johnny Weissmuller, Brenda Joyce, Johnny Sheffield; features Acquanetta. Directed by Kurt Newmann. Story and screenplay, Carroll Young; camera, Karl Struss; editor, Robert O. Crandall; dances, Lester Horton; score, Paul Sawtell. Tradeshown N. Y., Feb. 8, '46. Running time, **75 MINS.**

Tarzan....Johnny Weismuller
Jane....Brenda Joyce
Boy....Johnny Sheffield
Lea....Acquanetta
Lazar....Edgar Barrier
Kimba....Tommy Cook
Commissioner....Dennis Hoey
Mongo....Anthony Caruso
Corporal....George J. Lewis
Zambesi Maiden....Iris Flores
Zamberi Maiden....Lillian Molieri
Zambesi Maiden....Helen Gerald
Zambesi Maiden....Kay Solinas
Superintendent....Doris Lloyd

Tarzan is growing old. After all these years of swinging through the trees and giving out with an occasional blood-curdling yell to thrill the kids in the front row, he's finally showing signs of age. Latest Tarzan film is bogged down by stock situations, unimaginative production and direction, indicating Sol Lesser, producer of the series since he purchased the rights from Metro, is having difficulty keeping up the standard. Names of Tarzan and Johnny Weissmuller on the marquee still look good to the action fans, however, signifying fair b.o. returns.

Carroll Young's original story and screenplay possess none of the illogical but entertaining fantasy that made the original Tarzan pix b.o. naturals. Story has Tarzan out to break up a belligerent tribe of natives who dress up in leopard skins with iron claws—the situation found in quickie serials. Apeman doesn't give out with his famous call once during the picture and, instead of bringing in the herd of elephants that used to get Tarzan out of trouble in the old days, story falls back on another cliche to let the hero free himself in the nick.

Brawny Weissmuller still makes a presentable Tarzan but he, too, shows signs of age, with a growing waistline and a minimum of athletic antics. Brenda Joyce is a decorative Jane, and little Johnny Sheffield does some good work as Boy. Acquanetta wears a beautiful sarong as the high priestess of the leopard clan. Acting honors, if there are any, go to little Cheeta, the amazing chimp whose intelligence is almost unbelievable.

Lesser's attempt to work with a small budget is revealed in the production. Leopard men's dances, staged by Lester Horton, resemble a high school gym class warming up. Karl Struss' camera work and Paul Satwell's score, however, belong on the credit side.

Deadline at Dawn

RKO release of Adrian Scott production. Stars Susan Hayward, Paul Lukas, Bill Williams; features Joseph Calleia, Osa Massen, Lola Lane, Jerome Cowan. Directed by Harold Clurman. Screenplay, Clifford Odets, based on novel by William Irish; camera, Nicholas Musuraca; music, Hanns Eisler; editor, Roland Gross. Previewed in N. Y., Feb. 11, '46. Running time, **83 MINS.**

June....Susan Hayward
Gus....Paul Lukas
Alex....Bill Williams
Bartelli....Joseph Calleia
Helen Robinson....Osa Massen
Edna Bartelli....Lola Lane
Lester Brady....Jerome Cowan
Sleepy Parsons....Marvin Miller
Collarless Man....Roman Bohnen
Man with Gloves....Steven Geray
Babe Dooley....Joy Sawyer
Mrs. Raymond....Constance Worth
Lieutenant Kane....Joseph Crehan

Combine of playwright Clifford Odets and director Harold Clurman, two onetime N. Y. Group Theatre stalwarts, should have produced a more plausible murder melodrama of Manhattan than this one. Marquee names won't be strong enough to pull pic out of the rut, and grosses will disappoint.

Film has an arty approach to an otherwise plain whodunit, and is shot through with phoney bits of story and dialog. Performances are of a mixed quality, some good, some bad, although in justice to some of the cast it must be said that even a Duse couldn't make some of the lines sound convincing. Film is slow for the most part, and only in its final reels picks up in momentum to hit a mood of tension and suspense.

Story concerns a naive gob on leave in New York, who wanders into a cafe to be fleeced in a card game, and who wanders out with a dame to—of all things—fix a radio in her home. A few drinks under his belt, and he remembers nothing—how he came to be one-stepping with a gal in a dime-a-dance joint, how he came to have a huge roll on him, or how the dame whose radio he fixed was murdered. But the gob feels incriminated and wants to give himself up. The dancer feels sympathy for him and tries to help him find the murderer.

Rest of film recounts the efforts of the two to track down the clues they find, the meanwhile involving a gangster, a taxi-driver, a shoestring theatrical producer, a blind pianist and a couple of two-timing gals.

Why a disillusioned, physically-fatigued dancehall gal, at 2 a.m., pokes her nose into a murdered woman's apartment in the first place, instead of running to the police, or just plain running, isn't made clear. The romance between gob and gal that develops also has a phoney ring. The Samaritan-like character of taxi-drivers, who here are depicted as either Spinoza-spouting philosophers or indulgent foster-fathers, is something to marvel at by a mugg who has ridden through mid-Manhattan.

The speech of other characters, especially the gullible gob who talks bookish English as if out of Shakespeare, hardly ever rings true. Undoubtedly scripter and director planned deliberately to set a mood or a symphony of moods, but in this case flubbed.

Production is of good quality while camera work is excellent, with several original angles and unusual shots to pique interest. Susan Hayward handles the dancehall girl well, while Paul Lukas is similarly persuasive as one of the several unusual cabbies. Bill Williams apparently finds the dialog and situations insuperable, although still appearing a wholesome, pleasant gob. Joseph Calleia is sturdily brutal as a gangster, while other bit parts vary in execution. Roman Bohnen, appearing in a brief sequence, adds another ex-Group Theatreite to the roster.

Live Wires

Hollywood, Feb. 8.

Monogram release of Jan Grippo-Lindsley Parsons production. Stars Leo Gorcey; features Huntz Hall, Mike Mazurki, Bobby Jordan, Billy Benedict, William Frambes, Pamela Blake. Directed by Phil Karlson. Screenplay by Tim Ryan and Josef Mischel; original story, Jeb Schary; camera, William Sickner; editor, Fred Maguire. Previewed at Campus theatre, Hollywood, Feb. 7, '46. Running time, **64 MINS.**

Slip....Leo Gorcey
Sach....Huntz Hall
Bobby....Bobby Jordan
Whitey....Billy Benedict
Homer....William Frambes
Mary....Pamela Blake
Patsy Clark....Mike Mazurki
Jeanette....Claudia Drake
Sayers....John Eldredge
Barton....Robert E. Keane
Mabel....Patti Brill
Girlfriend....Nancy Brinckman
Boyfriend....Bill Christy
Barker....Earle Hodgins

Better production and featured casting values distinguish the first of the new Bowery Boys features from its predecessors, the Eastside Kids series. These factors, plus the popularity enjoyed by the former series, give the replacement group excellent prospects in the Monogram market. Top-cast lineup is still virtually the same, with Leo Gorcey headlining, aided by Huntz Hall, Bobby Jordan and Billy Benedict. Jan Grippo, film agent turned producer, will deliver series for Monogram, and received production aid on first from Lindsley Parsons.

Plot throws most of the emphasis to Gorcey, who's seen as a tough mug handy with his firsts. Fisticuffs lose him one job after another, to the despair of his sister, until he lands with a process-serving outfit. This work fits his pugilistic tendencies and shapes story line for general roughhouse and broad comedy by the Bowery Boys. Phil Karlson's direction keeps the action fast to milk the situations, and generally points film for good reception.

There's less mugging by Gorcey in this, but still sufficient to please his following. Major teamwork falls to Hall, leaving Bobby Jordan, Billy Benedict and a new mug, William Frambes, little to do except appear as atmosphere. Pamela Blake, the sister; Mike Mazurki, a comedy gangster; Claudia Drake, songstress; John Eldredge and Earle Hodgins, latter as a pitchman, lend plenty of featured strength.

Tim Ryan-Josef Mischel script, from story by Jeb Schary, gives standard plotting good lines. Editing is tight and camera work by William Sickner takes full advantage of added production values. *Brog.*

Romance of the West

(Color)

(SONGS)

Hollywood, Feb. 7.

PRC release, produced and directed by Robert Emmett. Stars Eddie Dean; features Emmett Lynn, Joan Barton, Forrest Taylor. Screenplay by Frances Kavanaugh; camera, Marcel LePicard; color supervision, W. T. Crespinel; music director, Carl Hoefle; songs, Zamenick; Sam Franklin; Bob Nolan, Bernard Barnes and Carl Winge; editor, Hugh Winn. Previewed in Hollywood, Feb. 4, '46. Running time, **58 MINS.**

Eddie Dean....Eddie Dean
Melodie....Joan Barton
Ezra....Emmett Lynn
Father Sullivan....Forrest Taylor
Matthews....Robert McKenzie
Marks....Jerry Jerome
Rockwood....Stanley Price
Chief Eagle Feather....Chief Thundercloud
Little Brown Jug....Don Reynolds
Chico....Rocky Camron
Hadley....Lee Roberts
Miss Twitchell....Lottie Harrison
Brent....Don Williams
Smithers....Jack Richardson
Wildhorse....Matty Roubert
Comm. Wright....Forbes Murray
Marshall....Jack O'Shea

This western passes muster due to use of Cinecolor in the filming. Otherwise, it's stilted outdoor fare with little to interest the kiddies. Cinecolor photography gives a well-hued display of the scenic backgrounds, is never glaring or garish. Robert Emmett produced and directed as the second of the natural-color oaters on his schedule for PRC.

Scripting is slipshod in saga of a bunch of bad white men trying to stir up an Indian war so they can grab some valuable silver land. Eddie Dean, Indian agent and the hero, lacks camera experience but pleases vocally with three numbers, "Indian Dawn," "Ridin' the Trail to Dreamland," and "Love Song of the Waterfall." Emmett Lynn, Dean's saddle-pard, is good for several laughs, and Joan Barton supplies romantic interest as a schoolteacher.

Above-standard photography was contributed by Marcel LePicard, and the musical direction by Carl Hoefle is also on the credit side. *Brog.*

The Face of Marble

Monogram release of Jeffrey Bernard production. Stars John Carradine; features Claudia Drake, Robert Shayne, Maris Wrixon, Willie Best, Thomas E. Jackson, Rosa Rey. Directed by William Beaudine. Screenplay, Michael Jacoby; original, William Thiele, Edmund Hartmann; camera, Harry Newmann; editor, William Austin. At New York theatre, N. Y., Feb. 7, '46, dual. Running time, **72 MINS.**

Prof. Randolph....John Carradine
Elaine....Claudia Drake
David Cochran....Robert Shayne
Linda....Maris Wrixon
Shadrach....Willie Best
Norton....Thomas E. Jackson
Marika....Rosa Rey
Jeff....Neal Burns
Photographer....Donald Kern
Photographer....Allan Ray

Typical horror film has a confusing story but a plausible, serious treatment to make it acceptable. Good camera work, a well-chosen cast and a lot of pseudo-scientific and medical gadgets and palaver give pic more solid substance than it rates. It'll do well enough at the boxoffice in lesser situations.

Yarn concerns a brain surgeon (John Carradine) and his assistant (Robert Shayne), who are surreptitiously experimenting in bringing recently-died persons to life. Setup is complicated by surgeon's young wife (Claudia Drake), who is interested in the assistant, and the wife's Haitian maid (Rosa Rey), who invokes voodoo charms to bring the two people together.

Surgeon's experiments on a drowned sailor, which turns latter to marble, bring in the law and eventually lead to the death of all concerned through a fantastic set of circumstances.

Carradine is glib, as usual, as the surgeon; Miss Drake is very attractive as the wife, and Shayne acceptable as the assistant. Miss Rey suggests the jungle hoodoo. Willie Best adds a but weak comedy. *Bron.*

Whirlwind of Paris

("Tourbillon de Paris")

(FRENCH-MADE)

(With Music)

Jay Hoffberg release of Les Filmes Albert Lanzin production. Stars Ray Ventura Orchetra. Directed by Henri Diamant-Berger. Story by Andre Hornez; music by Paul Misraki; English titles, Herman G. Weinberg. At Fifth Avenue Playhouse, starting Feb. 9, '46. Running time, 88 mins.

Ray Ventura....Himself
His Orchestra....Themselves

Charbonnier..........Charpin
Mme. Charbonnier..........Marguerite Pierry
Marie-Claude..........Mona Goya
Paul..........Paul Misraki
Rosales..........Jean Tissler
Mony..........Mila Pitoeff
Coco..........Coco Asian
(In French, English titles)

Supposed to be initial new French musical film since the war, this is a disappointment. Film leans too heavily on Ray Ventura's band and also spots members of that outfit in important roles. It's doubtful for even arty houses.

Yarn is about students at a French school preparing for France's West Point. Not quite clear to the average spectator, but at any rate Ventura's band members, doubling as students, pop up as a small cafe orchestra. Later they disrupt an opera performance, go to Paris for their final exams and wind up in the local bastile when the headmaster loses the money for their exam fees while playing roulette. There's the usual blowoff when band makes good and wins a big contract.

When the story rings in sly Gallic humor it is best, but the scenario by Andre Hornez is strictly one of those things; being too involved.

Ventura is satisfactory as m.c. in several scenes and has a first-rate band. But when the band members try to act they merely prove they're good musicians. Charpin is solid as the headmaster, while Paul Misraki, who composed the tuneful music, does nicely as the juvenile who figures in the slight romance with Mona Goya. Coco Aslan provides the best comedy as the student who's always the goat. *Wear.*

Miniature Reviews

"Dragonwyck" (20th). Gene Tierney heads strong cast in big boxoffice version of bestseller.

"Young Widow" (UA). Jane Russell - Louis Hayward starrer disappointing, with modest b.o. indicated.

"The Bandit of Sherwood Forest" (Col) (Color). Technicolor swashbuckler, with name strength to see it through.

"The Catman of Paris" (Rep). Horror meller that will sell okay.

"Murder In the Music Hall" (Rep). Musical whodunit with production values and other factors to give it good payoff.

"The Madonna's Secret" (Rep) (Song). Interesting whodunit, well-handled, should do okay.

"A Close Call for Boston Blackie" (Col). Good "B" detective comedy.

"Drifting Along" (Mono) (Songs). Fairish western.

"Christina" (Sono). Argentina-made meller shapes as dull entry in Latin-America; slim chance for U. S. bookings.

Dragonwyck

20th-Fox release of Darryl F. Zanuck production. Stars Gene Tierney; features Walter Huston, Vincent Price, Glenn Langan, Anne Revere, Spring Byington, Connie Marshall and Henry Morgan. Directed by Joseph Mankiewicz. Screenplay, Mankiewicz, from novel by Anya Seton; camera, Arthur Miller; music, Alfred Newman; editor, Dorothy Spencer. Tradeshown in N. Y., Feb. 14, '46. Running time, 103 MINS.

Miranda..........Gene Tierney
Ephraim Wells..........Walter Huston
Nicholas Van Ryn..........Vincent Price
Dr. Jeff Turner..........Glenn Langan
Abigail..........Anne Revere
Magda..........Spring Byington
Katrine..........Connie Marshall
Bleecker..........Henry Morgan
Johanna..........Vivienne Osborne
Peggy O'Malley..........Jessica Tandy
Elizabeth Van Borden..........Trudy Marshall
Count De Grenier..........Reinhold Schunzel
Tabitha..........Jane Nigh
Cornelia Van Borden..........Ruth Ford
Obadiah..........David Ballard
Tom Wells..........Scott Elliott
Tompkins..........Boyd Irwin
Countess De Grenier..........Mava Van Horn
Mr. MacNabb..........Keith Hitchcock
Doctor..........Francis Pierlot

Anya Seton's "Dragonwyck," the bestseller, has been given a lucid, often-compelling transition to the screen. Backed by the book's reputation, and a cast of performers headed by Gene Tierney, its boxoffice chances are assured. It is one of Darryl F. Zanuck's invariably grade-A productions, in every detail.

"Dragonwyck" has been given a literate adaptation and is in the metier of a type of film that has consistently emerged from the 20th-Fox studios. It's a psychological yarn, its mid-19th century American-feudal background being always brooding, with never a break in its flow of morbidity. Yet, it is always interesting if somewhat too pointed at times in its fictional contrivance.

This Joseph Mankiewicz screenplay, which the latter also directed, concerns the feudal system passed down through the generations by the old-Dutch families on the Hudson. The story specifically concerns one Nicholas Van Ryn who exacts tribute from tenant farmers on his vast estate (the year is 1844). Van Ryn has a wife and daughter whom he dislikes, and his pet anathema is his failure to have a son to carry on the baronial tradition. When a distant relative is invited to be governess to the child, and he falls in love with her, he poisons his wife, thus leaving him free to marry the other girl. The latter bears him a son, but the infant dies. Van Ryn remains a brooding, pathological case, and a drug addict, to boot, it's later revealed. The denouement comes when a young medico uncovers the first wife's murder and upsets plans for the elimination of the second.

Gene Tierney plays the governess, and it is one of her most sympathetic roles. Miss Tierney is photographed attractively, and paced well, too, in the direction, as are all the others. Vincent Price is the psychiatric Van Ryn. It is one of his best roles to date, and he handles it for all its worth. A comparative newcomer, Glenn Langan, as the young doctor, plays the other focal part in the triangle, and he gives an always understated, clear characterization. Langan, a big, handsome juvenile type, is slated for bigger things.

Walter Huston, Anne Revere, moppet Connie Marshall and Jessica Tandy are most prominent in the rest of the cast, and each lends c[illegible] to the story. *Kahn.*

Young Widow

United Artists release of Hunt Stromberg production. Stars Jane Russell and Louis Hayward; features Faith Domergue, Marie Wilson, Kent Taylor and Penny Singleton. Directed by Edwin L. Marin. Screenplay, Richard Macaulay and Margaret Buell Wilder, with added dialog by Ruth Nordlc, from novel by Clarissa Fairchild Cushman; camera, Lee Garmes; editor, James Newcom. Previewed in N. Y., Feb. 18, '46. Running time, 100 MINS.

Joan Kenwood..........Jane Russell
Jim Cameron..........Louis Hayward
Gerry Taylor..........Faith Domergue
Mac..........Marie Wilson
Peter Waring..........Kent Taylor
Peg Martin..........Penny Singleton
Aunt Cissie..........Connie Gilchrist
Aunt Emeline..........Cora Witherspoon
Willie..........Steve Brodie
Sammy..........Norman Lloyd
Bill Martin..........Richard Bailey
Bob Johnson..........Robert Holton
Navy Lieutenant..........Peter Garey
Marine Lieutenant..........Bill Moss
Army Lieutenant..........Bill "Red" Murphy

It's taken almost four years to get Jane Russell off the shelf. And now that she's down, it's not in her initially-made "Outlaw," which is still muddled up with the censors, but in a Hunt Stromberg modest-budgeter, "Young Widow." Pic will no doubt do a bit of business on curiosity engendered by the long publicity buildup, but at best can be figured on for only modest grosses.

Neither Hughes' "Outlaw" nor the present pic has any playdates as yet, but it's virtually certain the latter will be seen first by the public despite the longtime lapse between the two Russell starrers. "Outlaw," according to reviews of the film when it played a single roadshow date in San Francisco more than two years ago, does nothing to enhance Miss Russell's thespic rep. And "Widow" reinforces that opinion. Gal is frequently embarrassing as an actress, particularly in a dramatic role, such as the present, and one in which the character is sympathetic. If Miss Russell has any forte, those bitter downturned corners of her mouth and sinister eyes indicate it's as a heavy.

Picture itself, of course, gives the neophyte star no break. Story is thin, dialog often sufficient to make an audience squirm, and direction slow and pedestrian. Dragging this all out to 100 minutes is beyond reason.

Despite all this, yarn is not entirely without appeal, although the fact that it's another sobby war story is one more strike against it at the b.o. Miss Russell is pictured as a young newspaperwoman widowed by the war. She strikes up a chance acquaintance with Louis Hayward, a freshy pilot. Her resistance to his ardor, as she lives with the memory of her dead husband, and her anticipated final enthralment with him comprise the story. Woven choppily into this are a number of passing incidents which, instead of creating the character as part of the film, merely serve to indicate it.

The role is obviously a highly-sympathetic one and, as has been pointed out, Miss Russell is an unfortunate choice to play it, even were it lucidly written and her acting ability up to playing it. And only when she turns on that bright smile is she particularly easy on the glims; otherwise those drooping corners to her mouth are particularly distracting.

Remainder of the cast is standard in standard roles, although they all have trouble at times getting over the hurdle of some of those lines. Hayward does a convincing job, although that thick British accent he sports is at times disconcerting. Kent Taylor, as the big-hearted and gentlemanly would-be lover, is unimpressive. Penny Singleton and Marie Wilson perform in their normal fashion, while Faith Domergue suffers through an unreal bit.

Director Edwin L. Marin seems unable to weave smoothly together the disjointed material with which he's frequently confronted. And, of course, some obvious padding; among other things, makes it almost an impossible strain to maintain pace. Production is very modest but adequate. *Herb.*

The Bandit of Sherwood Forest
(COLOR)

Hollywood, Feb. 16.

Columbia release of Leonard S. Picker-Clifford Sanforth production. Stars Cornel Wilde; features Anita Louise, Jill Esmond, Edgar Buchanan, Henry Daniell, George Macready, Russell Hicks, John Abbott, Lloyd Corrigan, Eva Moore. Directed by George Sherman and Henry Levin. Screenplay by Wilfrid H. Pettitt and Melvin Levy; story by Paul A. Castleton and Pettitt, based on novel, "Son of Robin Hood," by Castleton; camera, Tony Gaudio, William Snyder, George Meehan, Jr.; editor, Richard Fantl; music score, Hugo Friedhofer. Previewed at studio auditorium, Hollywood, Feb. 15, '46. Running time, 85 MINS.

Robert of Nottingham (Son of Robin Hood)..........Cornel Wilde
Lady Catherine Maitland..........Anita Louise
The Queen Mother..........Jill Esmond
Friar Tuck..........Edgar Buchanan
The Regent..........Henry Daniell
Fitz-Herbert..........George Macready
Robin Hood..........Russell Hicks
Will Scarlet..........John Abbott
Sheriff of Nottingham..........Lloyd Corrigan
Mother Meg..........Eva Moore
Little John..........Ray Teal
Allan-A-Dale..........Leslie Denison
Lord Mortimer..........Ian Wolfe
The King..........Maurice R. Tauzin

Technicolor spectacle of high adventure in the Sherwood Forest. Name of Cornel Wilde in star spot gives enough marquee weight to push business into the higher brackets in general release. It's a costume western, in effect, offering the fictional escapades of the son of Robin Hood, a hard-riding, hard-loving hombre who uses his trusty bow and arrow to right injustice and tyranny back in the days of feudal England.

There is considerable ineptness in writing, production and direction but it still stands up as okay escapist film fare for the not-too-critical. Dual producer and director credits are shared by Leonard S. Picker and Clifford Sanforth, and George Sherman and Henry Levin, respectively. There is a concentration of chases and "they-went-thata-way" flavor about the doings that hints at the western feature training of producers and directors. All that indicates feature will find the most favor among juvenile patrons, with Wilde in to lure the more adult.

Plot has the son of Robin Hood coming back to Sherwood Forest to save England's Magna Charta and young king from the cruel plotting of a wicked regent. With his long bow, sword and trusty horse, Wilde proves himself more than a match for the villain, saves the young king's life, the Magna Charta and wins true love and knighthood. Concocting the script, full of dialog cliches and ten-twent-thirt dramatics, were Wilfrid H. Pettitt and Melvin Levy, working from story by Paul A. Castleton and

Pettitt, based on the novel, "Son of Robin Hood," by Castleton.

Wilde is properly swashbuckling as the hero, and probably had himself a time enacting the dare-and-do. Anita Louise makes a beautiful Lady Catherine, also entering into the spirit of the fun. Edgar Buchanan, as Friar Tuck, and John Abbott, as Will Scarlet, aren't given enough opportunity for comedy. Russell Hicks is fine as the elder Robin Hood. Henry Daniell makes a melodramatic heavy.

Outdoor scenes and castle interiors have been photographed in topnotch style by Tony Gaudio, William Snyder and George B. Meehan, Jr., and Richard Fantl's editing holds the running time down to a tight 85 minutes. Other credits do well in furnishing lavish background apropos of the historical period. *Brog.*

The Catman of Paris

Republic release of Marek M. Libkov production. Features Carl Esmond, Lenore Aubert, Douglass Dumbrille, Gerald Mohr and Fritz Feld. Directed by Lesley Selander. Screenplay, Sherman L. Lowe; camera, Reggie Lanning; editor, Harry Keller. Previewed in N. Y., Feb. 14, '46. Running time, **65 MINS.**

Charles Regnier.................Carl Esmond
Marie Audet.....................Lenore Aubert
Margurite Duval.................Adele Mara
Henry Borchard........Douglass Dumbrille
Inspector Severen...............Gerald Mohr
Prefect of Police...............Fritz Feld
Paul Audet......................Francis Pierlot
Guillard........................George Renavent
Devereaux.......................Francis McDonald
Paul de Roche...................Maurice Cass
Maurice Cacaignac........Alphonse Martell
Jules...........................Paul Marion
Georges.........................John Dehner
Raoul...........................Anthony Caruso
Philippe........................Carl Neubert
Blanche de Clermont.........Elaine Lange
Yvette..........................Tanis Chandler
Concierge.......................George Davis

"Catman of Paris" is a cross between a garden-variety whodunit and a Jekyll-Hyde horror-meller, a breed that taxes belief to the breaking point. But customers preferring to check credulity at the boxoffice will okay this film for its rolling pace, sustained tension and competent cast. Neat direction succeeds in focussing interest on the catman's homicidal urges, while the makeup can be expected to earn balcony shrieks at the denouement. Added hypoes for rapid pulses are a well-staged tavern brawl and a cross-country chase a la the far west. Settings have solid mahogany look but the script only has a literate veneer.

Carl Esmond, in the lead part of the amnesia victim and killer-suspect, turns in a distraught and sympathetic, although occasionally stiff performance. Esmond especially suffers by comparison alongside Douglass Dumbrille who, as the hero's patron devil, goes through his paces in polished and eloquent form. The crime experts, Gerald Mohr and Fritz Feld, play effective counterpoints as skeptic and mystic, with Mohr showing distinct capabilities for earning heavier roles in the future. Lenore Aubert is pretty and pleasant but nothing special in the dramatic department.

Murder in Music Hall

(MUSICAL)

Hollywood, Feb. 15.

Republic release of Herman Millakowsky production. Stars Vera Hruba Ralston, William Marshall; features Helen Walker, Nancy Kelly, William Gargan, Ann Rutherford, Julie Bishop, Jerome Cowan. Directed by John English. Screenplay, Frances Hyland and Laszlo Gorog; original story, Arnold Phillips and Maria Matray; camera, Jack Marta; ice sequences photographed by John Alton; editor, Arthur Roberts; songs, Gannon and Kent, Ohman and Washington; musical director, Walter Scharf; ice numbers directed by Fanchon. Reviewed at Hollywood Paramount, Feb. 14, '46. Running time, **84 MINS.**

Lila....................Vera Hruba Ralston
Don.....................William Marshall
Millicent...............Helen Walker
Mrs. Morgan.............Nancy Kelly
Inspector Wilson........William Gargan
Gracie..................Ann Rutherford
Diane...................Julie Bishop
George Morgan...........Jerome Cowan
Carl....................Edward Norris
Bruce Wilton............Jack LaRue
Henderson...............Frank Orth
Singer..................Fay McKenzie
Hobarth.................Paul Hurst
Mr. Winters.............James Craven
Mom.....................Ilka Gruning
Waitress................Mary Field
Mission Worker..........Anne Nagel
Policeman...............LeRoy Mason
Ryan....................Tom London

Specialty Ice Stars: Condon and Bohland, Red McCarthy, Patti Phillippi, John Jolliffe, Henry Lie.

Whodunit factors and title are backed up with excellent production values to make this one marketable. Returns will be good. Murder mystery is combined in virtually a backstage story, with ice numbers and songs for audience interest. It all comes off acceptably.

Atmospheric mood is sustained by John English's direction of the Herman Millakowsky production, and former receives a major assist from the featured players. Story of murder, a multitude of suspects and eventual solution is unfolded in span of three hours. When a blackmailer is bumped off in an apartment next to the Music Hall, five gals in the ice show are suspect. Show's orchestra leader, in love with the ice star, turns amateur dick to clear his sweetie. Both he and the police are stumped until the solution falls in their lap when the killer unconsciously gives herself away.

Co-stars are Vera Hruba Ralston and William Marshall. Latter displays possibilities of developing into a screen personality. There's a strong group of featured femmes who back up the melodramatics in fine fashion. They are Helen Walker, Nancy Kelly, Ann Rutherford and Julie Bishop. William Gargan gives a smart portrayal of the police inspector, and Jerome Cowan is seen briefly as a columnist.

Miss Ralston takes to the ice in three skating numbers, and other specialty stars in the production numbers are Condon and Bohland, Red McCarthy, Patti Phillippi, John Jolliffe and Henry Lie. Songs go to Fay McKenzie, as a cafe singer, and she makes numbers show up despite their backgrounding more melodramatic doings.

Camera, editing and other productional functions are good. *Brog.*

The Madonna's Secret

(SONGS)

Republic release of Stephen Auer production. Stars Francis Lederer, Gail Patrick, Ann Rutherford, Edward Ashley; features Linda Stirling, John Litel, Leona Roberts, Michael Hawks. Directed by William Thiele. Original screenplay, Bradbury Foote and Thiele; camera, John Alton; editor, Fred Allen; musical score, Joseph Dubin; song, Al Newman, Richard Cherwin, Ned Washington. Previewed N. Y., Feb. 15, '46. Running time, **79 MINS.**

James Harlan Corbin.....Francis Lederer
Ella Randolph...........Gail Patrick
Linda "Morgan" North....Ann Rutherford
John Earl...............Edward Ashley
Helen North.............Linda Stirling
Lieutenant Roberts......John Litel
Mrs. Corbin.............Leona Roberts
Hunt Mason..............Michael Hawks
Mr. Hadley..............Clifford Brooke
District Attorney.......Pierre Watkin
The Riverman............Will Wright
Miss Joyce..............Geraldine Wall
Lambert.................John Hamilton

An interesting whodunit, "Madonna's Secret" combines mood, suspense and surprise in satisfying ingredients. Good performances by a well-chosen cast, and a careful production, will more than offset some obvious situations, occasional drab dialog and slow pace, so that pic will do o.k. biz generally.

Story has a habit of wandering, and is a little repetitive, but treatment gives close thought to detail in settings as well as script. Direction is intelligent, while the camera catches some unusual, even macabre, shots.

Yarn centers on a New York portrait painter with a strange penchant for using one face in all his paintings—that of a model he once had in Paris who was later found drowned in the Seine under mysterious circumstances. Returned to America, living with an adoring mother, the artist gets romantically involved with one of his models, who in turn also meets her death by drowning under strange circumstances similar to the Paris incident. The painter has an airtight alibi this time, too.

But when another woman who is attracted to him is also found dead, the case against the artist seems complete. A sister of the dead N. Y. model has come ostensibly to pose for him but in reality to spy on him in an effort to pin the guilt on him. Instead, the sister falls in love with the artist, encourages him when things look blackest, and is innocently the means of clearing him and finding the murderer.

Suspense is kept up very well throughout the story, with the twist at the end a bit of a surprise. Pic throughout, though slow, has a good brooding atmosphere that suits. A few macabre touches—such as that of a nitery chanteuse singing a moody ballad while a knife-throwing partner is etching her in blades against the wall—add a strange relief to the tension.

Francis Lederer gives an excellent performance as the painter, tortured by hallucinations and the fear that he may somehow have been guilty of the crimes of which he's accused. Linda Stirling and Ann Rutherford are attractive and winning as the sister models, while Gail Patrick, although coming into the film late, holds the spotlight in her scenes as an acquisitive patroness. Edward Ashley is too much the dandy to be a convincing N. Y. drama critic, carrying the brunt of the pic's weak characteristics. John Litel, as a police lieutenant, and Leona Roberts, as the artist's possessive mother, head a good supporting list. *Bron.*

A Close Call for Boston Blackie

Columbia release of John Stone production. Stars, Chester Morris; features Len Merrick, Richard Lane, Frank Sully, George E. Stone. Directed by Lew Landers; screenplay, Ben Markson, Based on story by Paul Yawitz; camera, Bernet Guffey; editor, Jerome Thoms. At Brooklyn Strand, N.Y., Feb. 14, '46, dual. Running time, 68 mins.

Boston Blackie.................Chester Morris
Geraldine Peyton...............Lynn Merrick
Inspector Farraday.............Richard Lane
Sargent Matthews...............Frank Sully
The Runt.......................George E. Stone
Mamie Kirwin...................Claire Carlton
Smiley Slade...................Erik Rolf
Hack Hagen.....................Charles Lane
John Peyton....................Robert Scott
Coroner........................Emmett Bogan
Harcourt.......................Russell Hicks

On par with others of this Columbia series, film uses all the tried tricks of the mystery detective formula, with comedy as the objective. Chester Morris as the detective does well with the material, which includes all the gimmicks, even to disguises. Quickly paced, film is an adequate "B" for commensurate biz.

With killings tossed off lightly, story tells of how Morris wrangles his way out of a murder rap on which he's been framed. George E. Stone, plays Morris' pal and aide. Lynn Merrick, although unconvincing as a menace, is decorative. Richard Lane as the Inspector and rest of cast are strong support.

Drifting Along

(SONGS)

Mongram release of Scott R. Dunlap production. Stars Johnny Mack Brown; features Raymond Hatton, Douglas Fowley, Lynn Carver. Directed by Derwin M. Abrahams. Screenplay, Adele Buffington; camera, Harry Neumann; editor, Carrol Lewis; music director, Edward Kay. At New York, N.Y. Feb. 13, '46. Running time, 65 mins.

Steve..........................John Mack Brown
Pat McBride....................Lynne Carver
Pawnee.........................Raymond Hatton
Jack Dailey....................Douglas Foley
Himself........................Smith Ballew
Zeke...........................Milburn Morante
Pedro..........................Thornton Edwards
Lou Woods......................Steve Clark
Slade..........................Marshall Reed
Sherriff Devers................Jack Rockwell
Joe............................Lynton Brent
Gus............................Terry Frost
Red............................Leonard St. Lee
Ed.............................Ted Mapes

Curt Barrett and the Trailsmen

Western interspersed with rancho songs, but not wanting in the brawn department, makes this film presentable biz-getter in the lesser blood-and-thunder class. Johnny Mack Brown heads the cast neatly, remainder of cast and formula rustler story all lagging far behind him.

Raymond Hatton and Milburn Morante, who handle the comedy element, aid Brown in clearing up a rustler conspiracy to covet a ranch owned by Lynne Carver. Proceeding involves a rough and tumble affair in which Brown singlehandedly flattens a flock of heavies. The shindig has Smith Ballew, playing himself, singing "Dusty Trails" and "You Can Bet Your Boots and Saddles," while Curt Barrett and His Trailmen, ranch-hands in the cast, do their western guitar and fiddle stints.

Christina

(Argentine-Made)

Argentina Sono Film production and release. Stars Zully Moreno and Esteban Serrador; features Alberto Clossas, Blackie, Berta Moss, Juan Jose Pineiro. Directed by Francisco Mujica. Screenplay by Sixto Pondal Rios and Nicolas Olivari; camera, Antonio Merayo. At Monumental, Buenos Aires, Jan. 18, '46. Running time, 85 mins.
(In Spanish)

Billed as the first release of the year, this Argentina Sono Film production was given unusual advance publicity. And it needs plenty of bally because it is distinctly disappointing. The importance of the cast as far as coin goes, past achievements of this major studio and an excellent writing team led to high hopes, but it just doesn't jell. Its chances in the U. S. are nil.

The story is the trite, out-of-date one of the smalltown girl who leaves for the big city to "live and find herself." There is the usual struggle to get ahead, the fascinating socialite who steals her heart, but proves to be a heel; and the old friend from home who is patiently standing by to pick up the pieces. There isn't a single good feature to relieve the conglomeration.

Photography leaves much to be desired, being especially hard on Alberto Closas, new juve lead, who may have possibilities but gets small chance in this first venture. Esteban Serrador, a clever player, seems perpetually surprised at the inanity of the whole thing. Blackie injects some personality into the few scenes in which she has a part, but is not photogenic. *Nid.*

Miniature Reviews

"From This Day Forward" (RKO). Story of young married love with veteran rehabilitation angle. Joan Fontaine name for sturdy boxoffice.

"Meet Me on Broadway" (Songs) (Col). Secondary bookings.

"Little Giant" (U). Boffo Abbott and Costello comedy.

"Open City" (Mayer - Burstyn). Italian-made story of resistance to Nazi rule in Rome will appeal to arty houses.

"Junior Prom" (Mono) (Musical). First in Mono's new teen-ager series shapes up as excellent for younger filmgoers.

"Four Hearts" (Artkino). Russian-made comedy suited only as moderate entry at Russ-language spots.

From This Day Forward

(ONE SONG)

Hollywood, Feb. 23.

RKO release of William L. Pereira production (Jack L. Gross), executive producer). Stars Joan Fontaine; features Mark Stevens, Rosemary DeCamp, Henry Morgan, Wally Brown, Arline Judge. Directed by John Berry. Screenplay, Hugo Butler; adaptation, Garson Kanin; based on novel, "All Brides Are Beautiful," by Thomas Bell; additional scenes by Edith R. Sommer and Charles Schnee; camera, George Barnes; special effects, Vernon L. Walker; editor, Frank Doyle; music, Leigh Harline; song, "From This Day Forward," by Mort Green and Harline; orchestral arrangements, Gil Grau. Tradeshown at Hollywood Pantages, Feb. 21, '46. Running time, 95 MINS.

Susan	Joan Fontaine
Martha Beesley	Rosemary DeCamp
Hank Beesley	Henry Morgan
Jake Beesley	Wally Brown
Margie Beesley	Arline Judge
Charlie Beesley	Renny McEvoy
Timmy Beesley	Bobby Driscoll
Alice Beesley	Mary Treen
Mrs. Beesley	Queenie Smith
Barbara Beesley	Doreen McCann
Higgler	Erskine Sanford

and introducing
Mark Stevens as Bill Cummings

There's plenty in "From This Day Forward" to attract the femme-trade. This factor, coupled with the Joan Fontaine name and the interest certain to develop in Mark Stevens, new leading man, indicates excellent boxoffice possibilities. Direction by John Berry evidences plenty of understanding of human qualities in presenting problems of young married love, and William L. Pereira's production backs it all up with values that remain true to the life presented.

Story unfolds in flashback. This makes it sometimes difficult to follow as a whole, but there can be no quarrel with the merit of presentation and acting of the individual sequences. Plot deals with marriage of a young couple, fear for their security, the draft and the husband's return to establish himself again. Scenes show a soldier's mind as he goes through the redtape of Government employment centers for the veteran.

Miss Fontaine and Stevens are the young couple. Under Berry's direction they make real the courtship, marriage and marital existence of the two young people. Their romance and marriage also projects humor and high dramatics, made all the better by the capable playing and directing.

Stevens is a screen bet. Personable, talented and with an appeal that will find wide favor, he's sure of important stature with proper vehicles. Miss Fontaine displays herself as an assured actress, capable of projecting emotions that carry an audience along with her.

Rosemary DeCamp and Henry Morgan shine as sister and brother-in-law of Miss Fontaine, victims of job scarcity in pre-war days. Queenie Smith also stands out as a miserly mother-in-law. Juve interest falls to young Bobby Driscoll and Doreen McCann. Erskine Sanford does a deft character bit as a dirty-minded writer of under-the-counter books. Wally Brown, Arline Judge, Mary Treen and some uncredited players make their footage count.

Realistic settings and art direction have the advantage of George Barnes' camera work, and Pereira's production guidance, under the executive supervision of Jack L. Gross, has assured top quality in all other technical aspects. Hugo Butler rates smart credit for his scripting job, working from adaptation by Garson Kanin, based on Thomas Bell's novel, "All Brides Are Beautiful." *Brog.*

Meet Me on Broadway

(MUSICAL)

Hollywood, Feb. 22.

Columbia release of Burt Kelly production. Features Marjorie Reynolds, Fred Brady, Jinx Falkenburg, Spring Byington, Allen Jenkins, Gene Lockhart, Loren Tindall. Directed by Leigh Jason. Screenplay, George Bricker, Jack Henley; story, Bricker; camera, Burnett Guffey; editor, James Sweeney; songs, Saul Chaplin and Eddie Delange, Allan Roberts and Doris Fisher. At Guild, Hollywood, Feb. 20, '46. Running time, 77 MINS.

Ann Stallings	Marjorie Reynolds
Eddie Dolan	Fred Brady
Maxine Whittaker	Jinx Falkenburg
Bob Storm	Loren Tindall
Sylvia Storm	Spring Byington
John Whittaker	Gene Lockhart
Deacon McGill	Allen Jenkins
Dwight Ferris	William Forrest
Grannis	Jack Rice

Okay musical for secondary positions. There's better than average cast values but it's short on entertainment. Production has spotted in a number of songs and dance routines in the backstage plot, and direction manages to spot a few chuckles along the way.

Plot concerns an arrogant young musical director's efforts to hit Broadway. He tosses all his chances out the window by his attitude and ends up staging club bookings with amateurs, aided by his girl friend and a tunesmith pal. Majority of footage deals with a country club production, with the would-be bigshot playing up to a rich gal in a try to get backing. It all ends with the director winning his production coin and still keeping his old girl.

Most of the production numbers are introduced as rehearsals, although several of the country club routines are reprised for finale. Vocal work of Marjorie Reynolds and Jinx Falkenburg fails to impress. Fred Brady, male lead, and Loren Tindall, a rival, are adequate in their spots. Allen Jenkins as the songwriter; Spring Byington, and Gene Lockhart try hard for laughs.

Songs do not stand out. Best display is made of "She Was a Good Girl," by Allan Roberts and Doris Fisher, in the Burt Kelly production. Camera, editing and other technical functions are standard. *Brog.*

Little Giant

Hollywood, Feb. 22.

Universal release of Joe Gershenson production. Stars Bud Abbott and Lou Costello; features Brenda Joyce, Jacqueline de Wit, Elena Verdugo, Mary Gordon, George Cleveland. Directed by William A. Seiter. Screenplay, Walter De Leon; original story, Paul Jarrico and Richard Collins; camera, Charles Van Enger; editor, Fred R. Feitshans, Jr.; music score and direction, Edgar Fairchild. Previewed at Warner's Forum, Feb. 22, '46. Running time, 91 MINS.

John Morrison and Tom Chandler	Bud Abbott
Benny Miller	Lou Costello
Ruby	Brenda Joyce
Hazel	Jacqueline de Wit
Uncle Clarence	George Cleveland
Martha Hill	Elena Verdugo
Mom Miller	Mary Gordon
President Van Loon	Pierre Watkins
Pullman Conductor	Donald MacBride
Gus	Victor Kilian
Mrs. Hendrickson	Margaret Dumont
O'Brien	George Chandler
Secretary (Miss King)	Beatrice Gray

Popularity of Bud Abbott and Lou Costello will get a big lift from "Little Giant." It's a wow comedy, giving a new slant to their laugh talents and making proper use of it for the fun market. Showmanly production supervision by Joe Gershenson has surrounded comics with top values, strong story and extremely competent direction.

Story pits country bumpkin against city slicker in a formula reminiscent of the type character that shoved Charles Ray to success in silent days. It's credibly developed all the way in scripting by Walter De Leon from original by Paul Jarrico and Richard Collins. Humor is solid, depending more on building to laugh situations for punch than the previously established A&C gag routines. Footage also includes some of the latter.

Most of the play goes to Costello as a not-too-bright farm lad who journeys to the city after completing a mail-order salesmanship course. He encounters Abbott, first a sharp sales manager for a vacuum cleaner company and then manager of a company branch office. Both comics are in there pitching all the way. Costello creates plenty of sympathy in his role, keeping the audience with him as he strives to be a salesman despite the villainy of Abbott. Of the many standout hilarity points in the footage, probably the best is the sight of Costello trying to undress in an upper berth. It's a socko, sustained howl situation for any audience.

Directorial skill of William A. Seiter has made the most of his actors and story, and he rates the major credit for giving the comics a new lease on screen life. Brenda Joyce, Jacqueline de Wit and Elena Verdugo capably furnish necessary romantic interest for the leads, and George Cleveland, Mary Gordon, Pierre Watkins, Donald MacBride and others live up to character assignments.

Technical appurtenances include excellent camera work by Charles Van Enger, editing, scoring, etc. *Brog.*

Open City

(ITALIAN-MADE)

Mayer-Burstyn release of Excelsa production. Directed by Roberto Rossellini. Screenplay by Sergio Amidei and F. Fellini, from story by Amidei; camera, Ubaldo Arata; English titles, Pietro Di Donato and Herman G. Weinberg. Previewed in N. Y., Feb. 23, '46. Running time, 102 MINS.

Don Pietro	Aldo Fabrizi
Pina	Anna Magnani
Manfredi	Marcello Pagliero
Marcello	Vito Annicchiarico
The Sexton	Nando Bruno
Bergmann	Harry Feist
Ingrid	Giovanna Galletti
Francesco	Francesco Grandjacquet
Police Warden	Passarelli
Marina	Maria Michi
Lauretta	Carla Revere
Chief of Police	G. Sindici
Hartman	Van Hulzen
The Austrian	A. Tolnay

(In Italian; English Titles)

Among the excellent films that have arrived in this country from abroad since the end of the war, "Open City" must rank high. It is a fictionalization that is virtually a documentary in the simplicity and fidelity with which it tells the story of the resistance movement in Rome. It will have appeal for the think-trade that patronizes the arty houses, but the grim story, with no punches pulled on the brutality of the occupying Nazi forces, will provide b.o. limitations on theatregoers aiming for escapism or frothy entertainment.

Pic was made in Rome shortly after American GIs pushed the Germans out, with U.S. Army Signal Corps technicians giving strictly unofficial aid to the Italian producers. Production, as might be expected, is very fundamental in nature, but the simplicity of sets, camerawork and lighting add rather than detract, blending with the inornate story itself to heighten the feeling of integrity, the idea that this was Rome as it actually was under the Nazi rule. The English titles which have been provided are rather ordinary, but still further carry out the impression of lack of affectation. Film's principal defect, as it now stands, is overlength for those who must depend on a few words of subtitle to cover frequent big chunks of Italian talk.

Story line in early reels is not hewed sharply enough to avoid spectator confusion, but clarifies as it continues. It discloses, via a small group of people, the cross-currents of the Nazi occupation and various reactions to it. Plotting against the Germans by the partisans is matched by betrayal of the resistors for finery, dope and dubious love, by a weakling Italian girl. And the horrible brutality of the SS men, in their efforts to make the patriots talk, is counterbalanced by the tenderness of true-to-life love and many minor and intimate aspects of family living. Sergio Amidei, who provided the original story and collaborated on the screenplay, missed very little, even providing a few exciting chases.

Topping the cast is Aldo Fabrizi as the neighborhood priest who gives his life to aid the resistance groups. Anna Magnani, as a widow engaged to marry one of the resistors, and Marcello Pagliero, as leader of the movement, likewise garner thespic laurels, as does an eight-year-old moppet, Vito Annicchiarico.

Since it has no playdates in major houses requiring the Production Code Administration seal, pic has not been presented for approval to the Johnstonites. It's got plenty to make them blanch if and when it is shown them, although the New York State censor board okayed it with but insignificant scissorings. Principal sympathetic femme character speaks openly of her pregnancy, although she's not wed, and the traitoress who leads to the capture and death of the partisans betrays them for a combination of cocaine and the love of a lesbo German spy. That's just a sample of the angles for the PCA to mull, while the handling of the priest will no doubt make the Legion of Decency gulp hard, although the film has been okayed by the Vatican. *Herb.*

Junior Prom

(MUSICAL)

Hollywood, Feb. 22.

Monogram release of Sam Katzman production (Maurice Duke, associate producer). Features Freddie Stewart, June Preisser, Judy Clark. Directed by Arthur Dreifuss. Story and screenplay, Erna Lazarus and Hal Collins; camera, Ira Morgan; editor, William Austin; music director, Abe Lyman; musical supervisor, Lee Zahler; dance director, Dean Collins; musical arrangements, Herschel Gilbert and Joe Sanns; songs, Sid Robin, Don Raye, Harold Rome and Jamblan Kerpin, Maury Lazar and Stanley Cohen, Eddie Heywood. Previewed in Hollywood, Feb. 21, '46. Running time, 69 MINS.

Freddie	Freddie Stewart
Dodie	June Preisser
Addie	Judy Clark
Betty	Noel Neill
Jimmy	Jackie Moran
Roy	Frankie Darro
Lee	Warren Mills
Tiny	Murray Davis
Mrs. Rogers	Mira McKinney
Miss Hinklefink	Belle Mitchell
Prof. Townley	Milt Kibbee
Mr. Forrest	Sam Flint
Uncle Daniel	Charles Evans
Tony	Hank Henry

Also Abe Lyman Orch., Eddie Heywood Orch., Harry (The Hipster) Gibson, The Airliners.

Young talent and smooth, well-balanced production aim "Junior Prom" for good reception in its market. Melange of songs, dances and groovy music by featured orchs assure the juve appeal, but it is also pleasant enough to get by with the oldsters. Freddie Stewart, Abe Lyman orchestra and others offer nice marquee bait to aid the selling. This is first of new teen-agers series Sam Katzman and associate, Maurice Duke, will deliver for Monogram.

Juve talent displays showmanship and ability in the musical portions, and youngsters also get by satisfactorily on the acting end. Plot of the Erna Lazarus-Hal Collins script is backgrounded in a high school and has adequate framework for exhibition of the musical highlights. Story struggle deals with class elections and play being made by a rich boy for the presidency. Other youngsters campaign for their candidate with music, all of which leads up to the flash finale.

Stewart does well vocally. Highlights are Eddie Heywood's orch doing special arrangement of "Loch Lomond" and "Keep the Beat" as wrapped up by Harry (The Hipster) Gibson. Lyman's band figures importantly in the music scoring as another creditable attraction. Among score's songs are "Teen Canteen," "It's Me, Oh Lawd," "My Heart Sings," and "Trimball for President," latter tying in with plot.

June Preisser's flashy acrobatic dancing, and Judy Clark's singing get over, and gals also do okay as femme leads. Older screen juveniles are seen in the person of Jackie Moran and Frankie Doran, both of whom have grown a little beyond their assignments in this. Noel Neill, Warren Mills, and others in the cast perform well.

Arthur Dreifuss' direction has tied the material together expertly. Production framework is excellent. Photography, musical arrangements, dance staging and other factors all click. *Brog.*

Four Hearts

(RUSSIAN-MADE)

Artkino release of Mosfilm Studios production. Features Valentina Serova, Eugene Samoilov, Ludmilla Tselikovskaya, Peter Springfield. Directed by Konstantin Yudin. Story, Anton Faiko; camera, Nikolai Vlassov; English titles by Charles Clement. At Stanley, N. Y., starting Feb. 22, '46. Running time, **80 MINS.**

Galina Murashova........Valentina Serova
1st Lieut. Peter Kolchin..Eugene Samoilov
Shura Murashova....Ludmilla Tselikoskaya
Gleb Zavartsev............Petef Springfield
The Mother...........Lisa Dmitrievskaya
The Manicurist...........Elena Murzayeva
Private Yeremeyev.........Vassily Sanayev

(Russian; English titles)

"Four Hearts" is a slight, romantic Soviet-made comedy that may fit into Russ-language theatres without creating much excitement. But not in any other U.S. spots.

This production about measures up to the quality of recent product from Moscow, but Soviet comedy producers have much to learn. Film has all the familiar gags that were time-worn in American pictures years ago.

Story is supposed to be the hilarious one about two youngish sisters who fall in love with each other's boyfriends. Just who's in love with whom is clear only to the director for reels and reels. One youth is an Army cadet; the other is a slap-happy-looking professor. There's much chatter about comrades, commissars, etc.

Eugene Samoilov, who impressed in recent Russ pictures, is the manly officer, in love with the more comely gal in the cast. Valentina Serova, femme favorite in "Six P.M.," recent Russian melodramatic musical, does better in this one as the chief heart interest. She also sings two slight, unidentified tunes from the pen of Yuri Milliutin. Ludmilla Tselikovskaya is the other femme but gets small chance here. Peter Springfield is the youngish but wooden professor. Nikolai Vlassov's camera work is not up to Russian par. *Wear.*

Miniature Reviews

"Two Sisters from Boston" (Songs) (M-G). OK b.o. via topflight chirping by Kathryn Grayson, Lauritz Melchior and Durante's low comedy.

"Tangier" (U). Hokum melodrama of spy intrigue. Enough action and marquee values to rate average b.o.

"Capt. Tugboat Annie" (Rep). Fair comedy and pathos; a dualer.

"Smooth as Silk" (U). Nifty budget melodrama that offers plenty of entertainment for secondary positions.

"Lisbon Story" (Brit.). Richard Tauber in topflight British musical from stage hit; strong American entry.

"The Poor in Paradise" Poorly made comedy; slim for U. S.

"Loyal Heart" (Brit.). Story of sheep dog; meagre chances in America.

"Murder Is My Business" (PRC). A well done Michael Shayne detective comedy meller for dualers.

2 Sisters From Boston

(SONGS)

Metro release of Joe Pasternak production. Features Kathryn Grayson, June Allyson, Jimmy Durante, Lauritz Melchior, Peter Lawford. Directed by Henry Koster. Original, Myles Connolly; additional dialog, James O'Hanlon and Harry Crane; operatic sequences adapted by Charles Previn (who also conducts) and Wm. Wymetal; dances, Jack Donohue; songs, Sammy Fain-Ralph Freed; camera, Robt. Surtees; editor Douglas Biggs. Tradeshown N. Y., March 4, '46. Running time, **112 MINS.**

Abigail Chandler..........Kathryn Grayson
Martha Canford Chandler.....June Allyson
Olstrom ....Lauritz Melchior
"Spike" ....Jimmy Durante
Lawrence Patterson, Jr......Peter Lawford
Wrigley ....Ben Blue
Aunt Jennifer.................Isobel Elsom
Uncle Jonathan..............Harry Hayden
Lawrence Patterson, Sr.....Thurston Hall
Mrs. Lawrence Patterson, Sr..Nella Walker
Ossifish ....Gino Corrado

"Two Sisters from Boston" is both an operatic and a low comedy treat, hence surefire boxoffice.

Kathryn Grayson and Lauritz Melchior carry the straight chirping. Jimmy Durante is at his peak with an equally legit role in that—akin to the manner in which he foiled for Jose Iturbi in "Music for Millions" last year—he's an integral character in the plot. As result, that's Metro's best insurance as regards the Great Schnozzola's b.o. durability. Then, too, the studio appears to have something in Peter Lawford, newcomer juve, somewhat of a stick in this assignment, but bespeaking potentialities. June Allyson is the other sister from Hubtown, good running mate to her impetuous cinematic kin, Miss Grayson.

Latter tees off as "High C Susie," a hotsy chirper who's quite a click in a Bowery joint until her staid Back Bay family descends on N. Y. and, with the somewhat outlandish assistance of Spike (Durante), the diamond-in-the-rough pianist-impresario of the Bowery bistro, does make the Met. That's where Melchior's legitimate operatics come in with his Liszt and Mendelssohn, making for a happy blend of high tenoring, higher sopranoing—and Durante's low comedy. Which isn't a bad parlay in anybody's picture house.

Starting in the Bowery atmosphere where, for the insiders, Durante does a touch of "The Americans!" (shades of Club Durante), and where drummerboy Jack Roth and sidekick Eddie Jackson are rung in (albeit anonymously), it segues into staid Boston. Thence the pyrotechnics to keep Miss Grayson's shame from her family, until she makes good on her own in the Met. In between Melchior indulges in temperamental outbursts. There's a closeup on what now seems the prehistoric method of His Master's Voice recording (old phonograph horn, etc.), a great sequence; and also some good turn-of-the-century song hokum, viz., "There Are Two Sides to Every Girl," to carry the action along.

The operatic didoes with Melchior, and Miss Grayson's near-comedy chase, are lavishly mounted in the best Culver City tradition. Ben Blue does a good comedy butler. Miss Grayson soloes "Take a Chance With Romance" rousingly. Miss Allyson's three-time pass-out, fainting away in mortification, is another good running gag.

The fine hand of the vet Henry Koster-Joe Pasternak team is manifested throughout. Koster's direction is sure and pitches the segments properly, and Pasternak has given it all fine production. *Abel.*

Tangier

(SONGS)

Hollywood, March 2.

Universal release of Paul Malvern production (executive producer, Joe Gershenson). Stars Maria Montez, Robert Paige, Sabu; features Preston Foster, Louise Allbritton, Kent Taylor, J. Edward Bromberg. Directed by George Waggner. Screenplay, M. M. Musselman and Monty F. Collins; original story, Alice D. G. Miller; camera, Woody Bredell; special photography, D. S. Horsley; editor, Edward Curtiss; music, score and direction, Milton Rosen; song, George Waggner and Gabriel Ruiz. Previewed in Universal City, March 2, '46. Running time, **74 MINS.**

Rita...............................Maria Montez
Col. Jose Artiego............Preston Foster
Paul Kenyon....................Robert Paige
Dolores....................Louise Allbritton
Ramon.............................Kent Taylor
Pepe ....Sabu
Alex Rocco..........J. Edward Bromberg
Fernandez.................Reginald Denny
Dmitri.....................Charles Judels
Sanchez...............Francis McDonald
Capt. Cartiaz..................Erno Verebes
Lieutenant..................George Lynn
Rocco's Girl.................Rebel Randall
Maid....................Dorothy Lawrence
Servant..........................James Linn
Mike..............................Billy Green
Elevator Boy....................Phil Garris

"Tangier" is spy melodrama with plenty of hokum. It should fare okay with the intrigue fans. It's not a good example of dialoging or direction but thrill ingredients make it acceptable. Cast names offer marquee value, and production framework supplies sufficient dress to show up the action.

Plot brings together a discredited war correspondent, on the track of an international yarn that will get him reinstated, and a Spanish dancer, who is seeking a Latin quisling. Locale is Tangier, North Africa. Denouement reveals the quisling has been disguised as the military governor of Tangier. He meets his end in a thrilling elevator crash that almost makes up for the dialog cliches and hit-and-miss direction that precede the finale.

Maria Montez and Robert Paige, particularly the latter, spark the lead roles as much as possible. Sabu, as a native guide and aide to Paige, supplies some chuckles and the vocal moments on "She'll Be Comin' 'Round the Mountain," "Polly Wolly Doodle," and "Love Me Tonight," latter cleffed by George Waggner, film's director, and Gabriel Ruiz.

Preston Foster manages quite a Latin air to his role of the masquerading villain. Louise Allbritton, responsible for the heavy's death, and Kent Taylor are seen as Miss Montez' dance partners. They do their best with impossible characters. J. Edward Bromberg, Reginald Denny and others are adequate.

Running time has been trimmed to a tight 74 minutes. Camera work and other factors are standard. *Brog.*

Captain Tugboat Annie

Republic release of James S. Burkett production. Stars Jane Darwell; features Edgar Kennedy, Charles Gordon, Mantan Moreland, Pamela Blake, Hardie Albright, H. B. Warner, Saundra Berkova. Directed by Phil Rosen. Screenplay, G. Callahan, based on characters created by Norman Reilly Raine; camera, Harry Neumann; editor, Martin G. Cohn. At Strand, Brooklyn, N. Y., dual, week Feb. 28, '46. Running time, **70 MINS.**

Tugboat Annie....................Jane Darwell
Captain Bullwinkle.........Edgar Kennedy
Terry........................Charles Gordon
Pinto.......................Mantan Moreland
Marion............................Pamela Blake
Johnny Webb...................Hardie Albright
Judge Abbott...................H. B. Warner
Susan......................Saundra Berkova
Shiftless...........................Jack Norton
Missouri...................Barton Yarborough
Pucci.................................Fritz Feld
Jake..........................Anthony Warde
Severn..............................Joe Crehan
Dr. Turner.....................Pierre Watkin
Fred.............................Cyril Delevanti
Jenkins.........................Guy Wilkerson
Detective Franklyn............Robert Elliott
Cop...............................Kernan Cripps
Man.................................Harry Lang
First Nurse...................Marion McGuire
Second Nurse....................Betty Sinclair
Harper..............................Eddie Earle
Swenson...............................Vic Potel
Fire Chief..............................Sam Flint
Cab Driver.........................Ralph Linn
Motor Cop.......................Eddie Chandler
Mike.................................Harry Depp

This film must depend almost wholly on performance strength of Jane Darwell in the title role. It's overloaded with would-be pathos, but has fair comedy intentions. A dualer.

Story involves everything from a child violinist to the mistaken adoption of a paroled convict by Jane Darwell, and shifts from one situation to another during the tugboat clan feuds. Horseplay and comedy is handled on opposing end by Edgar Kennedy as Capt. Bullwinkle. The tugboat factions vieing for big contract come to final clash when serious waterfront fire brings them together for amicable finale. Various situations attached to yarn concern Charles Gordon as the paroled convict and Pamela Blake, tugboat office secretary who engineers his rehabilitation and provides the boy-girl need.

Saundra Berkova, child violinist, is weaved into the yarn as a waif under the wing of Tugboat Annie. A concert in which the child excellently plays Sarasate's "Zigeunerweisen" serves as windup of film along with all around amnesty of tugboat teams.

Long list of players, all with bit speaking parts, tend to unnecessary distractions. Comedy has some moments, best humor being scored by Fritz Feld in brief sequences as the eccentric symphonic conductor.

Smooth As Silk

Hollywood, March 1.

Universal release of Jack Bernhard production (executive producer, Howard Welsch). Features Kent Taylor, Virginia Grey, Jane Adams, Milburn Stone, Danny Morton, John Litel, Charles Trowbridge. Directed by Charles Barton. Screenplay, Dane Lussier and Kerry Shaw; original story, Florence Ryerson and Colin Clements; camera, Woody Bredell; editor, Ray Snyder; music, Ernest Gold. Previewed in Universal City, Feb. 28, '46. Running time, **64 MINS.**

Mark Fenton......................Qent Taylor
Paula.........................Virginia Grey
Susan..........................Jane Adams
John Kimble.................Milburn Stone
Stephen Elliott......................John Litel
Dick Elliott.....................Danny Morton
Fletcher Holliday......Charles Trowbridge
Louise......................Theresa Harris
Wolcott......................Harry Cheshire
Detective....................Bert Moorhouse
Detective.......................Ralph Brooks

Neatly contrived murder melodrama that's well above average for its budget classification, thanks to snappy pace, good performances, writing and direction. It should do well.

Charles Barton's direction makes convincing and meller ingredients of the plot. In the leads are Kent Taylor and Virginia Grey, both delivering topnotch performances. Taylor is a sharp criminal lawyer, in love with Miss Grey, a cold, ambitious actress. When the latter tosses the attorney aside for a big producer, Taylor plots to murder the new sweetie and cast the blame on Miss Grey. How he gets away with the killing is unfolded with interest.

Strong support comes from Jane Adams, Milburn Stone, Danny Morton, John Litel, Charles Trowbridge and others. Morton shows up particularly well as a young drunk who is almost tricked into suicide by Taylor.

Camera, editing and other behind-the-camera functions are all expert.
Brog.

The Lisbon Story
(Musical)
(BRITISH-MADE)

London, Feb. 22.

Anglo-American Film Corp. release of British National Film production. Features Patricia Burke, Richard Tauber, David Farrar, Walter Rilla. Directed by Paul L. Stein. Screenplay by Jack Whittingham based on the play by Harold Purcell. Music by Harry Parr-Davies. Camera, Ernest Palmer, Gerald D. Moss. At Palace theatre, London, Feb. 21, '46. Running time, 100 MINS.

Gabrielle Girard	Patricia Burke
David Warren	David Farrar
Carl von Schriner	Walter Rilla
Andre Joubert	Richard Tauber
Michael O'Rourke	Lawrence O'Madden
Major Lutzen	Austin Trevor
Stephan Gorelle	Paul Bonifas
George Duncan	Harry Welchman
Dr. Cartier	Allan Jeayes
Lisette	Joan Seton
Journalist	Martin Walker

This is the best musical yet to be turned out by a British studio. Starring Patricia Burke, David Farrar and Walter Rilla, "Lisbon Story" should gross plenty in America although this trio of names may not mean much in the U. S. It's a big opportunity for Richard Tauber, being the first break this tenor has had on the screen.

Walt Disney's "Whistle While You Work" has nothing on one of Tauber's numbers, a recitative against a background of all male voices, with the tenor repeating the refrain. All the music, composed by Harry Parr-Davies, is well above the usual film-musical standard. Harold Purcell's lyrics are not less outstanding, and an exceptionally well-trained chorus helps.

Apart from Tauber, a featured player, Lawrence O'Madden, as a devil-may-care Irishman, is solid. If Wardour Street Americans don't grab O'Madden for Hollywood, they'll be overlooking a big bet. He's got everything.

Production by Louis H. Jackson is super. Paul L. Stein's direction is intelligent. The capable editing keeps the melodramatic story moving swiftly and smoothly. Based on the play which had a long run at the Hippodrome here, "Lisbon Story" has been skillfully adapted by Jack Whittingham.

Stress on the hits scored by Tauber and O'Madden does not discount the admirable work by the three stars. In a trying role Miss Burke, as Gabrielle Girard, French diseuse, is as charming in her stage and cabaret numbers as she is convincing in her offstage moments as a woman in love. Farrar, as a British spy, holds his own in scenes with Rilla, as Karl von Schriner, one of Goebbels' propaganda chieftains.

This picture should break records in England, and should be boxoffice tonic in America.
Talb.

Les Gueux Au Paradis
("Poor in Paradise")
(FRENCH-MADE)

Paris, Feb. 26.

C.P.L.F. release of Gaumont-Alcina production. Directed by Rene le Henaff. Stars Raimu and Fernandel; features Alerme and Armand Bernard. Screenplay and dialog by Andre Obey from stage play by G. M. Martens. At Gaumont Palace, Paris. Running time, 85 MINS.

St. Antoine	Raimu
St. Nicolas	Fernandel
The Undertaker	Armand Bernard
St. Peter	Alerme
The Virgin	Gaby Andreu

(In French; no English Titles)

The marquee draw of the Raimu-Fernandel combo won't save this picture. It lacks entertainment value. Even the old gag of having men supposedly dead perfectly conscious of what is going on around them, which gets laughs, won't help rescue this. Poor direction and camera work mar the film. Picture doesn't mean a thing for American market.

Film follows the stage play closely. It opens in a small town during the Louis XV regime and shows Raimu, inn-keeper, and his friend, Fernandel, garbed as two saints at a masquerade. Run over by a carriage, they take a trip to Hades and then Paradise after being killed. Plot shows the pair coming back to life in time to see the undertaker attempting to make love to Raimu's wife.

Strong cast is wasted here. There are no production values. Scenes on earth are stagey, and the heaven-and-hades sequences are poor makeshift. Raimu, who rewrote some of dialog, hasn't a suitable vehicle, and Fernandel does not get full play. Armand Bernard is good as the undertaker.
Maxi.

Loyal Heart
(British-Made)

London, Feb. 22

Anglo-American Film Corp. release of British National Film. Features Harry Welchman, Percy Marmont. Directed by Oswald Mitchell. Screenplay by Oswald Mitchell from novel "Beth and the Sheepdog" by Ernest Lewis; additional scenes and dialogue by George Cooper; camera, Arthur Grant, Gerald Gibbs. At Studio One, London, Feb. 22, '46. Running time, 75 mins.

Sir Ian	Harry Welchman
John Armstrong	Percy Marmont
Mary Armstrong	Eleanor Hattam
Burton	Beckett Bould
Alice Burton	Valentine Dunn
Joan Stewart	Patricia Marmont
Doctor	Mac Harry Pieton
Blinkers	Alexander Field
Nurse	Dorothy Dark
Sheepdog	Fleet

Screen patrons who like dog screen heroes may hail "Fleet." British entry, as a possible boxoffice favorite. Except for "Fleet" and impressive backgrounds of the mountainous grazing lands, "Loyal Heart" has little to recommend it either here or in the U. S.

A trite story, uninspired direction, and inexpert cutting defeat the efforts of such capable actors as Harry Welchman and Percy Marmont. It is only when "Fleet" has the screen to himself, whether rounding up sheep or winning the All-England championship at the sheep dog trials, that the picture comes to life. *Talb.*

Murder Is My Business

PRC release of Sigmund Neufeld production. Stars Hugh Beaumont; features Cheryl Walker, Lyle Talbot, George Meeker. Directed by Sam Newfield. Screenplay by Fred Myton, based on original characters and story by Brett Halliday; camera, Jack Greenhalgh; editor, Holbrook N. Todd. Previewed in N.Y., March 4, '46. Running time, 67 mins.

Michael Shayne	Hugh Beaumont
Phyllis	Cheryl Walker
Duell Renslow	Lyle Talbot
Carl Meldrum	George Meeker
Mr. Ramsey	Pierre Watkins
Tim Rourke	Richard Keene
Ernst Ramsey	David Reed
Mona Tabor	Carol Andrews
Dorothy Ramsey	Julia McMillan
Mrs. Ramsey	Helen Heigh
Pete Rafferty	Ralph Dunn
Joe Darnell	Parker Garvie
Dora Darnell	Virginia Christine

Attentive production and good casting makes this detective meller a par whodunit. Holds the interest from beginning to end. Although patterned closely after the routine private dick formula, creditable performances and good direction make the film a good entry for any dual program.

Hugh Beaumont, playing the Michael Shayne role, is convincing and registers as a strong performer. He carries the story involving murder and blackmail into an acceptable yarn with subtle humor injections that overshadow the standard dumbcop comedy also used.

Lyle Talbot and George Meeker as the heavies make the most of their parts, as do the rest of the cast.

Miniature Reviews

"**The Green Years**" (Songs) (M-G). Excellent screen transformation of A. J. Cronin novel will register strong b.o.

"**The Strange Love of Martha Ivers**" (Par). Socko adult melodrama with husky b.o. potential.

"**To Each His Own**" (Par). Solid emotional drama with strong femme appeal. Good boxoffice outlook.

"**Our Hearts Were Growing Up**" (Par). Excellent comedy sequel to "Our Hearts Were Young and Gay," should bring top returns in all situations.

"**Hot Cargo**" (Par). Pine-Thomas meller should do okay in the usual action slot.

"**The Notorious Lone Wolf**" (Col). Comedy whodunit with able cast and high-polished routine material.

"**Song of Arizona**" (Songs) (Rep). Better than average Roy Rogers oatuner, with plenty songs and gunplay.

"**Gentlemen With Guns**," (PRC). Poor western.

The Green Years
(SONGS)

Metro release of Leon Gordon production. Stars Charles Coburn and Tom Drake; features Beverly Tyler, Hume Cronyn, Gladys Cooper, Dean Stockwell, Selena Royle, Jessica Tandy. Directed by Victor Saville. Screenplay, Robert Ardrey and Sonya Levien, from novel by A. J. Cronin; camera, George Folsey; editor, Robert J. Kern; music, Herbert Stothart. Previewed N. Y., March 6, '46. Running time, 127 MINS.

Alexander Gow	Charles Coburn
Robert Shannon (young man)	Tom Drake
Alison Keith (young woman)	Beverly Tyler
Papa Leckie	Hume Cronyn
Grandma Leckie	Gladys Cooper
Robert Shannon (child)	Dean Stockwell
Mama Leckie	Selena Royle
Kate Leckie	Jessica Tandy
Jason Reid	Richard Haydn
Saddler Boag	Andy Clyde
Adam Leckie	Norman Lloyd
Murdoch Leckie	Robert North
Jamie Nigg	Wallace Ford
Alison Keith (child)	Eilene Janssen
Gavin Blair (young man)	Hank Daniels
Gavin Blair (child)	Richard Lyon
Canon Roche	Henry O'Neill
Blakely	Henry Stephenson
Mrs. Bosomley	Norma Varden

Metro, with the skill it has so often demonstrated in transforming a best-selling novel to a best-selling picture, turns the trick again with this filmization of A. J. Cronin's "The Green Years." Combination of the pre-sold audience created by the book and the artistic charm of the characterizations will go a long way in compensating for lack of upper-run b.o. names and assures the picture's strength at the b.o.

Since this is essentially a yarn built on careful development of its various characters, a major contribution is in giving new stature and audience appeal to virtually every player in it. That's true all the way from vet Charles Coburn, who evidences his virtuosity in a new type role for him, to moppet Dean Stockwell and Beverly Tyler, both making their second screen appearances.

Ten-year-old Stockwell is the particularly bright spot in the well-turned cast, as well as a top addition to the list of Hollywood juve players. Kid, whose father, Harry Stockwell, is known to Broadway for leads in "Marinka" and the Chi company of "Oklahoma!," first appeared in Metro's "Anchors Aweigh." In the present film he gets real opportunity to demonstrate a sensitivity and true dramatic poignancy that definitely set him off from the usual studio moppets. He has the ability to translate the most subtly-shaded nuance without at any time evidencing the precocity that so often makes audiences waver at the prospect of being forced to see a new child screen find.

Young Stockwell plays an orphan boy in this Scottish-located story of ambitious youth and amusing old age. The oldster, of course, is Coburn, as Dean's great-grandfather, a man of large heart and large desires for the native brew. While this not-so-venerable, but thoroughly enjoyable, citiizen is getting himself into one minor scrape after another, the youth (later played by Tom Drake) goes through the process of growing up, going to school and falling in love. What he wants most is to go to college, a desire which, unfortunately, is only achieved through the insurance resulting from the old man's death.

The two principals are set against a household full of characters. Hume Cronyn wreaks every bit of tight-fistedness and little man-meanness out of the role of head of the house that takes the small boy in. Selena Royle plays Cronyn's wife, Gladys Cooper his mother, Jessica Tandy his daughter. Each characterization, naturally, isn't so well developed as the boy and the old man, but there's nevertheless a nice sense given to their thoughts and feelings and the place they hold in relation to the tyrant running the household.

Miss Tyler and Drake play the teen-aged romance. Gal is adequate thespically, but shines in warbling of four pop Scottish tunes. Drake exhibits developing ability in handling emotions of youthful joy and disappointment.

Robert Ardrey and Sonya Levien show integrity and feeling in the screenplay they fashioned from Dr. Cronin's novel. Victor Saville's direction demonstrates restraint and subtle ability to translate mood and characterization to the screen. Unfortunately, there's a tendency to overlength which makes for an occasional slowness, but that's not too important in the otherwise topdrawer production. *Herb.*

Strange Love of Martha Ivers

Hollywood, March 9.

Paramount release of Hal Wallis production. Stars Barbara Stanwyck, Van Heflin, Lizabeth Scott; features Kirk Douglas, Judith Anderson, Roman Bohnen, Darryl Hickman. Directed by Lewis Milestone. Screenplay, Robert Rossen; original, Jack Patrick; camera, Victor Milner, Farciot Edouart; score, Miklos Rozsa; editor, Archie Marshek. Tradeshown March 8, '46. Running time, **115 MINS.**

Martha Ivers	Barbara Stanwyck
Sam Masterson	Van Heflin
Toni Maracek	Lizabeth Scott
Walter O'Neill	Kirk Douglas
Miss Ivers	Judith Anderson
Mr. O'Neill	Roman Bohnen
Martha (child)	Janis Wilson
Sam (child)	Darryl Hickman
Walter	Mickey Kuhn
Detectives	Charles D. Brown and James Flavin
Hotel Clerk	Frank Orth
Secretary	Ann Doran

Tense, exciting melodrama, it has entertainment value and marquee strength to command hefty returns. Production and direction used an adult approach in the making and gave it a polish that will pay off. Names of Barbara Stanwyck, Van Heflin and Lizabeth Scott add extra luster for selling.

Story is a forthright, uncompromising presentation of evil, greedy people and human weaknesses. Characters are sharply drawn in the Robert Rossen script, based on Jack Patrick's original story, and Lewis Milestone's direction punches home the melodrama for full suspense and excitement. Production guidance by Hal B. Wallis is showmanly, making the picture a class entry in the meller field.

Prolog opening establishes the murder of a bullying aunt by her young niece. Deed is witnessed by the son of the girl's tutor, but is blamed on an unknown prowler. Coverup moves the tutor and son into a position of power in the girl's household. Story then picks up 18 years later with the accidental return to the town of another of the girl's childhood friends. Return panics Barbara Stanwyck and Kirk Douglas, now grown up and married, who fear the friend was also a witness of the early killing. Gripping suspense, building to a socko climax, is generated as the couple seek to chase Van Heflin, the friend, from town, but only arouse his suspicions and bring about their downfall.

Character portrayed by Miss Stanwyck is evil and she gives it a high calibre delineation. Douglas, comparative newcomer, makes his weakling role interesting, showing up strongly among the more experienced players. Best performance honors, though, are divided between Heflin and Miss Scott, latter as a Heflin pickup. Heflin, recently out of service, returns to the screen with a bang in a fine piece of work. Miss Scott grabs herself a stronger film foothold with her performance as the pushover who goes for Heflin.

Opening sequences are dominated by young Janis Wilson, playing Miss Stanwyck as a girl. Darryl Hickman, as the young Heflin, and Mickey Kuhn as the younger Douglas, are good. Judith Anderson shows up in the small assignment of the cruel aunt. Others are capable.

Music score by Miklos Rozsa helps considerably in socking over the mood, and Victor Milner's camera work is another expert contribution in furthering the melodramatics. *Brog.*

To Each His Own

Hollywood, March 8.

Paramount release of Charles Brackett production. Stars Olivia De Havilland; features John Lund, Mary Anderson, Roland Culver, Phillip Terry, Bill Goodwin. Directed by Mitchell Leisen. Screenplay, Charles Brackett and Jacques Thery; from story by Brackett; camera, Daniel L. Fapp; special photographic effects, Gordon Jennings; process photography, Farciot Edouart; music score, Victor Young; editor, Alma Macrorie. Tradeshown in Hollywood, March 7, '46. Running time, **122 MINS.**

Miss Norris	Olivia De Havilland
Corinne Piersen	Mary Anderson
Lord Desham	Roland Culver
Alex Piersen	Phillip Terry
Mac Tilton	Bill Goodwin
Liz Lorimer	Virginia Welles
Daisy Gingras	Victoria Horne
Mr. Norris	Griff Barnett
Belle Ingham	Alma Macrorie
Griggsy (5½ years)	Bill Ward
Babe	Frank Faylen
Dr. Hunt	Willard Robertson
Mr. Clinton	Arthur Loft
Mrs. Clinton	Virginia Farmer
Miss Pringle	Doris Lloyd
Mr. Harkett	Clyde Cocke
Miss Claflin	Ida Moore
Mrs. Rix	Mary Young
and introducing	
Captain Cosgrove	John Lund

Paramount will rate a handsome payoff on this class emotional drama. Femme appeal and marquee pull point it for solid boxoffice. It's another retrospect story, but has been so smoothly turned out that interest is sustained all the way. Direction and production deftly get the unwed-mother angle past the censors without offending.

Charles Brackett, who wrote and produced, injected a human quality in the script, and Mitchell Leisen makes full use of it in his direction. Start and finish of story are laid against a wartime London background, but flashes back to World War I and a small-town locale. It depicts the love and sacrifices of an unwed mother for her son, born out of a one-night romance with a war hero in 1918. It carries her through the years to London where, the relationship still unacknowledged, she waits to catch a brief glimpse of the young man as he comes to town on leave. Finale strikes a happy note when the son recognizes his mother and she is given a chance at new happiness.

Artistry of Olivia De Havilland as the mother is superb. From the eager, young girl whose first romance ends when her hero is killed before marriage, through to the cold, brusque business woman, her performance doesn't miss a bet. Playing opposite, first as her lover and then as her grown son, is John Lund, a screen newcomer, from Broadway legit, who has the ability and personality to assure film success.

Strong performances by others include those of Mary Anderson, as the mother who adopts the nameless child; Phillip Terry, her husband; Bill Goodwin and Victoria Horne, Miss De Haviland's friends and business associates; Roland Culver, doing a sock job of the Englishman who helps the mother realize her final happiness; Griff Barnett, Virginia Welles and Willard Robertson. Particular mention goes to Bill Ward, playing the Lund character as a child. Youngster's performance has little of the artificial air that usually marks moppet acting.

Jacques Thery collaborated with Brackett on the fine script. Musical score provided by Victor Young is a major aid in making the dramatics felt. Camera work by Daniel L. Fapp and other credits are topflight. *Brog.*

Our Hearts Were Growing Up

Paramount release of Daniel Dare production. Stars Gail Russell, Diana Lynn, Brian Donlevy; features James Brown, Bill Edwards, William Demarest, Billy De Wolfe. Directed by William D. Russell. Screenplay, Norman Panama and Melvin Frank from story by Frank Waldman; camera, Stuart Thompson; editor, Doane Harrison. Tradeshown N. Y., March 7, '46. Running time, **83 MINS.**

Cornelia Otis Skinner	Gail Russell
Emily Kimbrough	Diana Lynn
Tony Minnetti	Brian Donlevy
Avery Moore	James Brown
Dr. Tom Newhall	Bill Edwards
Peanuts Schultz	William Demarest
Roland Du Frere	Billy De Wolfe
Suzanne Carter	Sharon Douglas
"Dibs" Downing	Mary Hatcher
Miss Dill	Sara Haden
Bubchenko	Mikhail Rasumny
Mrs. Southworth	Isabel Randolph
First Federal Agent	Frank Faylen

This is one of the gayest little film comedies in years, and one of the few sequels that's better than a successful original. Film has Gail Russell and Diana Lynn as Cornelia Otis Skinner and Emily Kimbrough, respectively, carrying on with the madcap antics they began in "Our Hearts Were Young and Gay." Picture offers exhibs plenty of opportunities to trade in exploitation-wise on the original, and it's also the kind of story that should get top word-of-mouth advertising. Will do well in all situations.

Chief ingredient of the film is its nostalgic quality. Adapted by Norman Panama and Melvin Frank from an original by Frank Waldman, the picture takes the two heroines through their college days during the roaring '20s. With a tongue-in-cheek attitude all the way, producer Danny Dare doesn't miss a bet in ringing in the humorous angles of the era, from raccoon coats and pre-flapper clothes to the wealthy society matrons who order their liquor undercover from tough bootleggers. Several added effects, such as the background playing of "Hearts and Flowers" each time girls have a lovers' tiff with their boy-friends and swear off men "forever," all provide for audience snickers.

Misses Russell and Lynn, along with the rest of the cast, milk the tightly-written script for all the comedy possible. Two girls are duly hammy in keeping with the film's mood but are also appealing in their love scenes and the film's rare serious moments. Brian Donlevy is excellent as the tough but gold-hearted bootlegger who takes the girls under his wing and throws his weight around to bring their boyfriends back to them.

Billy DeWolfe, as the perennially hungry bohemian from New York's Greenwich Village, reveals heretofore hidden talents in an hilarious solo comedy bit. William Demarest plays his usual role of a tough, stupid lug for good results. James Brown and Bill Edwards, the opposite side of the love interest, do good work as the college boys of the period. Another good comedy bit is turned in by Mikhail Rasumny as Bubchenko, another Village character.

Dialog maintains a sure-hit pace throughout, with some quotable gags that should be making the rounds after the picture plays. William D. Russell's direction gets the most out of the cast and situations and exhibits some subtle techniques. Sets and rich production mountings are in conformity with the picture's topdrawer quality. *Stal.*

Hot Cargo

Paramount release of Pine-Thomas production. Stars William Gargan, Jean Rogers, Philip Reed; features Larry Young, David Holt. Directed by Lew Landers. Screenplay, Geoffrey Homes; camera, Fred Jackman, Jr.; editor, Henry Adams. Tradeshown in N. Y., March 7, '46. Running time, **57 MINS.**

Joe Harkness	William Gargan
Jerry Walters	Jean Rogers
Chris Bigelow	Philip Reed
Warren Porter	Larry Young
Matt Wayne	Harry Cording
Tim Chapman	Will Wright
Mrs. Chapman	Virginia Brissac
Pete Chapman	David Holt
Frankie	Dick Elliot

"Hot Cargo" is a fair meller that manages to sustain interest through most of its 57 minutes. Cast and direction are okay, and the story, revolving about two ex-GIs who help the family of a slain buddy, will appeal. With names of William Gargan, Jean Rogers and Philip Reed as marquee lure, "Cargo" should do okay in the usual action slot.

Story concerns the two ex-tank corpsmen who, before returning to civilian life, stop off in the redwood country of California to bring a last message to the family of their buddy who was killed in action. Finding the family in financial trouble, they decide to stay awhile and help with their log-trucking business. Rival trucksters, out to shut off their competition, cause the death of the family's younger son before the two ex-soldiers, in a rough-and-tumble finale, set things right.

Gargan and Reed, as the samaritans, do a nice job, dishing out enough light banter to balance some of the film's grimmer moments, and mixing it up with the bad boys in realistic fashion. Jean Rogers, returning to the screen after several years' absence, is beauteous as ever as the dead soldier's girlfriend who falls for Reed. Supporting cast is competent.

Producers Pine and Thomas probably didn't sink too much moola into the film, some of the sets being obvious makeshifts. Cameraman Fred Jackman, Jr., however, got in some beautiful shots of the California timber country, with nature more than making up for the scenic designers. Director Lew Landers kept the pace up to the action-film standards.

The Notorious Lone Wolf

Columbia release of Ted Richmond production. Stars Gerald Mohr, Janis Carter; features Eric Blore, John Abbott, Don Beddoe, Adelle Roberts, Robert Scott. Directed by D. Ross Lederman. Screenplay, Martin Berkeley and Edward Dein from story by William J. Bowers, based on original characters by Louis Joseph Vance; camera, Burnett Guffey; editor, Richard Fantl. At Strand, Brooklyn, March 7, '46, dual. Running time, **64 MINS.**

Michael Lanyard	Gerald Mohr
Carla Winter	Janis Carter
Jameson	Eric Blore
Lal Bara	John Abbott
Inspector Crane	William Davidson
Stonely	Don Beddoe
Rita Hale	Adelle Roberts
Dick Hale	Robert Scott
Harvey Beaumont	Peter Whitney
Prince of Rapur	Olaf Hytten
Adam Wheelright	Ian Wolfe
Olga	Edith Evanson
Asst. Hotel Manager	Maurice Cass

Jones.............................Eddie Acuff
Lili.............................Virginia Hunter

Patterned after the slick "Thin Man" style, this comedy whodunit, fused with above-par casting and good direction, registers well in that category. Gerald Mohr, a newcomer, plays the suave ex-jewel-thief-turned-detective role with ample conviction and gets by on his own, although he's a ringer for William Powell. Good light comedy touch holds on throughout and makes film eligible dual material.

Lone Wolf Mohr, after his service in the armed forces, is rejoined with his valet-chum Eric Blore, and becomes involved in a museum jewel theft of which he is innocent. Predicament has Mohr reluctantly parted from girl friend Janis Carter on the eve of his return to solve the mystery and clear himself. Sole twist from routine yarn has pair disguised as beturbaned high potentates. Glib repartee and polished maneuverings, while official foreign emissaries are held captive, restores the jewel in spite of blundering police and lawbreakers are brought to justice.

Good support in cast is dominated by Blore doing his standard gentleman's gentleman stuff and garnering major laughs.

Song of Arizona
(SONGS)

Republic release of Edward J. White production. Stars Roy Rogers; features George "Gabby" Hayes, Dale Evans, Lyle Talbot. Directed by Frank McDonald. Screenplay, M. Coates Webster from original by Bradford Ropes; songs, Jack Elliott, Ira Schuster, Larry Stock, J. Cavanaugh, Mary Ann Owens, Bob Nolan, Gordon Forster; camera, Reggie Lanning; editor, Arthur Roberts. Previewed in N. Y. March 6, '46. Running time, 68 MINS.

Roy Rogers.....................Roy Rogers
Gabby Whittaker.. George "Gabby" Hayes
Clare Summers.................Dale Evans
King Blaine....................Lyle Talbot
Chip.........................Tommy Cook
Clarence...................Johny Calkins
Dolly Finuccin............Sarah Edwards
Jimmy........................Tommy Ivo
Cyclops.................Michael Chapin
Bart.........................Dick Curtis
Sheriff.....................Edmund Cobb
Tom.........................Tom Quinn
Jim.........................Kid Chissell
Themselves......Robert Mitchell Boy Choir
Bob Nolan and Sons of Pioneers

A streamlined oatuner which incorporates a nitery sequence, production numbers, "Boy's Town" theme, along with all the regular elements of gunplay, iron fists and finale chase. Roy Rogers, as a fave, holds on well and makes the film an all-around good bet. Click western and novelty songs well delivered by Rogers remain the better assets of his films.

Eight numbers occupy appreciable part of running time but are worked in nicely. "Round and Round—The Lariat Song," is done in nitery setting by Dale Evans and Rogers, who is there seeking Miss Evans as separated sister of orphaned youngster, one of gang of homeless boys sheltered by Gabby Hayes on an Arizona ranch. The boy, Tommy Cook, in possession of stolen bank money by his outlaw father, Lyle Talbot, who is killed off by the sheriff, attempts to save the ranch from foreclosure. Heavies, cohorts of Talbot, harass the kid and finally steal the cash to create the blood and thunder finale chase, restoration of money and cancellation of ranch mortgage as reward by bank.

Rogers' numbers, mainly done in duets with Miss Evans, include "Did You Ever Get That Feeling in the Moonlight" and "Will Ya Be My Darling." Sons of the Pioneers handle novelty stuff well with "Michael O'Leary, O'Bryan, O'Toole" as standout. Other numbers are "Song of Arizona," "Half a Chance Ranch," "Way Out There," and "Mr. Spook Steps Out," which is handled as a production number at ranch shindig.

Gentlemen With Guns

PRC release of Sigmund Neufeld production stars Buster Crabbe; features Al St. John. Directed by Sam Newfield. Screenplay, Fred Myton; camera, Jack Greenhalgh; editor Holbrook N. Todd. Previewed in N.Y. March 11, '46. Running time, 53 mins.

Billy.........................Buster Crabbe
Fuzzy..........................Al St. John
Matilda.......................Patricia Knox
McAllister....................Steve Darrell
Slade.......................George Chesebro
Justice of the Peace............Karl Hackett
Sheriff.......................Budd Buster
Cassidy......................Frank Ellis

Overload of fist fights, gun battles and long distance chases fail to help this hoss opry opus which even the kids will find hard to take. Hasty takes and forced humor give the film a negative standing in the lowest category.

Vintage story has Buster Crabbe handling the muscle stuff, and he makes most of material. Negligent production, however, uses such boners as a scene with Crabbe stumbling awkwardly on his mount. Crabbe with his pal, Al (Fuzzy) St. John, do the heavies out of their plan to absorb their ranch in a series of incidents injected with hapless humor. St. John's slapstickery dates back to silent films.

Miniature Reviews

"**The Kid from Brooklyn**" (Color; Songs). (Goldwyn-RKO). D a n n y Kaye in a lush Sam Goldwyn musical comedy opus, for top grosses.

"**The Postman Always Rings Twice**" (M-G). James M. Cain novel of lust and murder slated for plenty b.o. and talk.

"**The Bride Wore Boots**" (Par). Fair comedy that will be helped along by cast name strength.

"**Gilda**" (Songs) (Col). Rita Hayworth pic will do biz in anybody's theatre.

"**Johnny Comes Flying Home**" (20th). Run-of-the-mill action film of ex-Army flyers setting up as civvy air freighters.

"**Symphonie D'Amour**" (Musical) (French). Fernand Gravet in a stilted story; weak for U.S.

"**Gun Town**" (U). Fair western.

"**Out of the Depths**" (Col). Routine war meller set in a submarine.

"**Dark Is the Night**" (Artkino). Drama of war-torn Russia. Big for foreign-language and arty theatres.

"**Blonde Alibi**" (U). Routine whodunit.

"**The Spider Woman Strikes Back**" (U). Fair meller for dualers.

The Kid From Brooklyn
(Songs)
(COLOR)

RKO release of Samuel Goldwyn production. Stars Danny Kaye; features Virginia Mayo, Vera-Ellen, Walter Abel, Eve Arden, Steve Cochran, Fay Bainter, Lionel Stander. Directed by Norman Z. McLeod. Adapted by Don Hartman, Melville Shavelson, from screenplay by Grover Jones, Frank Butler, Richard Connell, based on play by Lynn Root, Harry Clork; camera, Gregg Toland; editor, Daniel Mandell; dances, Bernard Pearce; music, Sylvia Fine-Max Liebman, Jule Styne-Sammy Cahn. Tradeshown, N. Y., March 19, '46. Running time, 114 MINS.

Burleigh Sullivan.............Danny Kaye
Polly Pringle................Virginia Mayo
Susie Sullivan..................Vera-Ellen
Speed McFarlane............Steve Cochran
Ann Westley....................Eve Arden
Gabby Sloan....................Walter Abel
Spider Schultz.............Lionel Stander
Mrs. E. Winthrop DeMoyne....Fay Bainter
Mr. Austin..................Clarence Kolb
Photographer.................Victor Cutler
Willard ....Charles Cane
Fight Announcer............Jerome Cowan
Radio Announcer.............Don Wilson
Radio Announcer...........Knox Manning
Matron ....Kay Thompson
Master of Ceremonies......Johnny Downs
The Goldwyn Girls

Samuel Goldwyn-Danny Kaye combine has outdone itself in "The Kid from Brooklyn," topping the two highly successful previous efforts in almost every phase of production. Based on the old Harold Lloyd starrer, "The Milky Way" (originally the late Hugh O'Connell's legit play), the film is aimed straight at the bellylaughs and emerges as a lush mixture of comedy, music and gals, highlighted by beautiful Technicolor and ultra-rich production mountings. Looks certain to bring in top grosses wherever played.

Kaye is spotted in almost three-fourths of the picture's sequences, but the audience will be clamoring for more at the final fadeout. Zany comic clicks with his unique mugging, song stylizing and antics, but still packs in plenty of the wistful appeal.

Kaye's double-talking song style is limited to one number, easily as good as anything he's done. Coming just before the sock climax, "Pavlova," written by Sylvia Fine and Max Liebman, is a mirthful laugh-getting takeoff on modern ballet. It's one of his nitery era specialties. Kaye gets

a chance to mouth some of the difficult Russian names in his usual rapidfire pace, and his satire on Martha Graham and her "six crackers" should bring the house down. Number is set against a rich outdoors scene and winds up in a gag finish that's socko.

With a top cast and screenplay to work with, director Norman Z. McLeod gets the most out of each situation. Story has Kaye as a mild-mannered milkman who gets involved with a prizefight gang when he accidentally knocks out the current middleweight champ. With the champ's publicity shot to pieces, his manager decides to capitalize on the situation by building Kaye into a contender and then cleaning up on the title bout. Series of setup fights gives Kaye the idea he's a real killer and, through the stupidity of Lionel Stander, the champ's handler, he wins the title, Virginia Mayo and a partnership in the dairy business.

Kaye's supporting cast does uniformly fine work, keeping their sights trained on the comedy throughout. Miss Mayo, as the love interest, serves as a beautiful foil for Kaye's madcap antics and sings two ballads in acceptable fashion. Vera-Ellen gets in ably on the comedy and does some spectacular terpsichore in two equally spectacular production numbers. Walter Abel, as the harassed fight manager, turns in one of his best comedy shots and Stander is equally outstandish as the tough, but stupid handler. Eve Arden, Steve Cochran, Fay Bainter and Clarence Kolb all add to the fun.

Musical numbers, highlights of the picture, are interspersed unobjectionably into the script. Two songs are almost certain to join the hit parade and the others should be close runners-up. Tops are "You're the Cause of It All," one of Miss Mayo's ballads, and "Hey, What's Your Name?", novelty number that serves as the background for one of Vera-Ellen's dance sequences. "The Sunflower Song," a gag number done by the beautiful Goldwyn girls, is also tops.

Film's accessories are all in conformity with the richness evidenced throughout. Gals wear gowns that should panic the femmes and Goldwyn's sets are something to talk about. Gregg Toland gets some excellent effects with his color camera.
Stal.

The Postman Always Rings Twice

Hollywood, March 16.

Metro release of Carey Wilson production. Stars Lana Turner and John Garfield; features Cecil Kellaway, Hume Cronyn, Leon Ames, Audrey Totter, Alan Reed. Directed by Tay Garnett. Screenplay by Harry Ruskin and Niven Busch; based on novel by James M. Cain; camera, Sidney Wagner; editor, George White; score, George Bassman. Tradeshown Los Angeles, March 13, '46. Running time, 113 MINS.

Cora Smith....................Lana Turner
Frank Chambers............John Garfield
Nick Smith.................Cecil Kellaway
Arthur Keats...............Hume Cronyn
Kyle Sackett...................Leon Ames
Madge Gorland..............Audrey Totter
Ezra Liam Kennedy..........Alan Reed
Blair ....Jeff York

"The Postman Always Rings Twice" is a controversial picture. The approach to lust and murder is as adult and matter-of-fact as that used by James M. Cain in his book from which the film was adapted. The subject matter, the star values and release are a boxoffice combination that assure sock returns, but pic seems almost certain to be marked with controversy over such a frank display of adultery and the murder to which it leads.

Production guidance by Carey Wilson is showmanly. It was boxoffice wisdom to cast Lana Turner as the sexy, blonde murderess, and John Garfield as the foot-loose vagabond whose lust for the girl made him stop at nothing. Each give to the assignments the best of their talents. Development of the characters makes Tay Garnett's direction seem slowly paced during first part of the picture, but this establishment was necessary to give the speed and punch to the uncompromising evil that transpires.

As in Cain's book, there will be little audience sympathy for the characters, although plotting will arouse moments of pity for the little people too weak to fight against passion and the evil circumstances it brings. The Harry Ruskin-Niven Busch script is a rather faithful translation of Cain's story of a boy and girl who murder the girl's husband, live through terror and eventually make payment for their crime. The writing is terse and natural to the characters and events that transpire.

Cecil Kellaway, the husband, is a bit flamboyant at times in interpreting the character. Hume Cronyn is particularly effective as the attorney who defends the couple for murder. Leon Ames is splendid as the district attorney. Audrey Totter again demonstrates her ability to take a brief bit and make it something to remember. Alan Reed, the blackmailing detective, and others are equally good.

Camera, background music and other behind-the-scenes credits are carefully calculated to further the somber mood and the inevitable conclusion. *Brog.*

The Bride Wore Boots

Hollywood, March 15.

Paramount release of Seton I. Miller production. Stars Barbara Stanwyck, Robert Cummings, Diana Lynn; features Patric Knowles, Peggy Wood, Robert Benchley, Willie Best. Directed by Irving Pichel. Screenplay, Dwight Mitchell Wiley from story by Wiley and play by Harry Segall; camera, Stuart Thompson, Gordon Jennings; editor, Ellsworth Hougland; score, Frederick Hollander. Tradeshown Hollywood, March 14, '46. Running time, **85 MINS.**

Sally Warren..............Barbara Stanwyck
Jeff Warren..............Robert Cummings
Mary Lou Medford..............Diana Lynn
Lance Gale..............Patric Knowles
Grace Apley..............Peggy Wood
Tod Warren..............Robert Benchley
Joe..............Willie Best
Carol Warren..............Natalie Wood
Johnny Warren..............Gregory Muradian
Janet Doughton..............Mary Young

"The Bride Wore Boots" is never as funny as its makers intended. There's enough marquee weight to lure initial customers, but little else to keep them coming. It has prospects for only average business, and that due to strength of top cast names. The production dress is fancy enough and the players capable, but film's attempts at broad comedy aren't too successful. It is only in the final 10 minutes or so when story casts off all restraint and goes slapstick with a vengeance that comedy rates a genuinely hearty response.

Barbara Stanwyck and Robert Cummings are seen as married couple with divided interests. Miss Stanwyck loves horses, in fact, operates a breeding farm. Cummings is an author and hates horses. The wife hates the stuffy Civil War relics wished off on her husband by adoring Confederate Dames societies. The Dwight Mitchell Wiley plot saunters through petty misunderstandings, divorce, etc., and then brings the couple together again for the finale. It remains for the unbilled equine playing "Albert," a horse in love with Cummings, and a screwball steeplechase featuring Albert's antics as he valiantly tries to keep Cummings astride long enough to win the cup, to give a solid windup to the silly proceedings that went before.

Irving Pichel's direction had the advantage of the top talents of Miss Stanwyck, Cummings, Diana Lynn and others in which to make the fable a success, but it never quite comes off as anticipated. Star trio, which has Miss Lynn as a young southern vamp, make frantic efforts to put the material over, but often fail. Patric Knowles has a thankless spot as near-rival for Miss Stanwyck's attention. Peggy Wood and the late Robert Benchley team for more adult chuckles and Willie Best is good as Cummings' handy-man. Natalie Wood and Gregory Muradian are seen as the obnoxious offspring of the married couple.

The Seton I. Miller production supplied excellent technical backing, but should have exercised stronger supervision on story development. Stuart Thompson's lensing and other credits are expert. *Brog.*

Gilda
(SONGS)

Columbia release of Virginia Van Upp production. Stars Rita Hayworth; features Glenn Ford, George Macready, Joseph Calleia. Directed by Charles Vidor. Screenplay, Marion Parsonnet, from story by E. A. Ellington; adaptation, Jo Eisinger; songs, Allan Roberts and Doris Fisher; camera, Rudolph Mate; editor, Charles Nelson; music directors, M. W. Stoloff and Marlin Skiles. At Radio City Music Hall, N. Y., opening March 14, '46. Running time, **110 MINS.**

Gilda..............Rita Hayworth
Johnny Farrell..............Glenn Ford
Ballin Mundson..............George Macready
Obregon..............Joseph Calleia
Uncle Pio..............Steven Geray
Casey..............Joe Sawyer
Captain Delgado..............Gerald Mohr
Gabe Evans..............Robert Scott
German..............Ludwig Donath
Thomas Langford..............Don Douglas
German..............Lionel Royce
Little Man..............S. Z. Martel
Huerta..............George J. Lewis
Maria..............Rosa Rey

Practically all the s.a. habiliments of the femme fatale have been mustered for "Gilda," and when things get trite and frequently far-fetched, somehow, at the drop of a shoulder strap, there is always Rita Hayworth to excite the filmgoer. When story interest lags, she's certain to shrug a bare shoulder, toss her tawny head in an intimately revealing closeup, or saunter teasingly through the celluloid. She dissipates the theories, if any, that sex has its shortcomings as a popular commodity. Miss Hayworth will do business.

The story is a confusion of gambling, international intrigue and a triangle that links two gamblers and the wife of one of them. The setting is Buenos Aires. Sneaking in somehow is the subplot of a tungsten cartel operated by the husband, who also runs a swank gambling casino. A couple of Nazis are thrown in also.

It seems that the younger gambler and the wife had been sweethearts before her rebound marriage, but now they hate each other oh-so-much. For some reason the scripters don't reveal the cause of this hate. When the husband apparently suicides in an ocean plane crash, after his cartel machinations are found out by the police, the younger man and the wife marry in what looks like a patchup of their feud. But no. He's still mad. He's married her only to get even. And there she is wearing gowns down to here and waiting futilely for him every night. And looking oh-so-beautiful! And never more beautiful than in her hapless plight. Just a lot of impractical madness.

Of course, they finally get together. A cop who wends his philosophical way through the picture breaks down the guy's resistance. That's where the pic really winds up on its cartel.

Miss Hayworth is photographed most beguilingly, an undoubted envy for the femmes and an excitement for the men. The producers have created nothing subtle in the projection of her s.a., and that's probably been wise.

Glenn Ford is the vis-a-vis, in his first picture part in several years, after his release from service. He's a far better actor than the tale permits. And there are times, despite the script, when he's able to give a particularly creditable performance. George Macready plays the older gambler with some plausibility, and Steven Geray believably portrays the casino attendant.

There are a couple of songs ostensibly sung by Miss Hayworth, and one of them, "Put the Blame on Mame," piques the interest because of its intriguing, low-down quality.

"Gilda" is obviously an expensive production—and shows it. The direction is static, but that's more the fault of the writers. But this is another pic where the professional critics—those guys with passes—can't do enough to detour the paying public. *Kahn.*

Johnny Comes Flying Home

20th Century Fox release of Aubrey Schenck production. Stars Richard Crane, Faye Marlowe, Martha Stewart, Charles Russell, Henry Morgan; features Roy Roberts, Charles Tannen. Directed by Banjamin Stoloff. Screenplay, Jack Andrews and George Bricker, from story by Andrews; camera, Harry Jackson; editor, John McCafferty. Tradeshown N.Y., March 14, '46. Running time, 65 mins.

Johnny Martin..............Richard Crane
Sally..............Faye Marlowe
Ann Cummings..............Martha Stewart
Miles Carey..............Charles Russell
J.P. Hartley..............Roy Roberts
Joe Patillo..............Henry Morgan
Harry..............Charles Tannen
Peggy-Lou..............Elaine Langan
Jennie..............Marietta Canty
Butch..............Anthony Sydes
Dr. Gunderson..............Selmer Jackson
Metters..............John Hamilton
Grigsby..............Harry Tyler
Motorcycle Officer..............Frank Meredith
Watchman..............Tom Dugan
Mrs. Bixler..............Grayce Hampton
Engineer..............Hugh Beaumont
Technician..............Bernie Sell
Henry..............Walter Baldwin
Foreman..............Will Wright

A much too obvious dramatization of what may be one of the minor problems of returned vets is "Johnny Comes Flying Home." While spiked with some of our latest gadgets, including a jet plane performance, the film never revs up to anything more than low horsepower action. Without marquee attraction it adds up to a routine business-getter.

The celluloid, for the most part, is taken up with the efforts of a trio of discharged fliers to build up a going air freight concern with a C-47 plus flying experience. Dick Crane has been ordered grounded by a medico because of a mysterious (to the audience) nervous ailment garnered during combat. Love enters by way of a decorative mechanicess, Martha Stewart, who doubles as repair gal and sparring partner to Crane in a series of teapot tempests.

Plot winds its way through a string of tribulations which Crane and his partners, Charles Russell and Henry Morgan, meet in battling their way out of the red. They seize their own plane after it has been impounded for an unpaid repair bill in order to rescue a potential millionaire customer who has cracked up in inaccessible country. To make the rescue, Russell hits the silk. Here, as in other sequences, the situation is handled with so little imagination and freshness that what might have proved exciting ends in being only torpid.

Final scene muffs in the same way. In financial desperation Russell undertakes the dangerous job of test diving a new jet plane for a handsome fee. Crane through stratagem locks Russell in a telephone booth and takes the plane up despite his ailment. The successful trial run neatly ties the package with money in kick for the business and Crane a proven flier again. Unfortunately, with the suspense factor lacking and camera treatment mediocre, the scene is not the sock finish it was meant to be.

Crane, Russell and Morgan as the musketeering trio meet the moderate thespian requirements of their roles pleasantly enough. Miss Stewart does well as the attractive plane fixer even when, at times, her lines do her dirt. Faye Marlowe plays wife to Russell competently. Direction and story manipulation is where the picture misses fire most.

Symphonie D'Amour
(Musical)
(FRENCH-MADE)

Andre E. Algazy release of Algazy production. Stars Fernand Gravet; features Jacqueline Francell, Alerme, Jeanne Aubert. Directed by Robert Slodmak. Screenplay, Yves Mirande; camera, Harry Stradling; music, Werner Heymann; English titles, Henry G. Weinberg. At Fifth Avenue Playhouse, N.Y., week of March 9, '46. Running time, 80 mins.

Panard..............Fernand Gravet
His Girl..............Jacqueline Francell
Music Publisher..............Alerma
His Mistress..............Jeanne Aubert
The Marquis..............Signoret
The Bum..............Aimos
The Film Director..............Jeanne Tissler

Latest French pre-war film to be distributed in the U. S., "Symhonie D'Amour" holds practically nothing to interest American audiences. Judging from the garb of the actresses, the film was probably made in the early '30s and the production techniques are of similar vintage. Box-office prospects for this country look tepid in even the arty houses.

Story's a routine affair that's been recreated on the American screen several times. Fernand Gravet, a struggling young composer, gives up music when he can't click, turning to whatever kind of job he can get. His amie, a bit actress, persuades a rich marquis to stage a musical built around Gravet's theme and is cast in the ingenue lead. Theatre's publicity staff, to hypo interest, hands out the story the composer committed suicide. Comes opening night, the show's a solid hit and Gravet, unshaven and unkempt, turns up at the stage door to set things right again with his girlfriend and the world.

Gravet, who's turned in much better performances, is still the only member of the cast to make his role seem plausible. Rest of the actors, stymied by the things called for in the script, appear as caricatures rather than live beings. Director Robert Siodmak, now in Hollywood, evidently tried hard to get the right shades of acting from the cast, but he, too, never had a chance.

Producer Andre E. Algazy limned the film with rich settings, especially in the musical numbers, but production aspects of the film otherwise fall flat. Actors are too heavily made up, there's a noticeable lack of synchronization between the sound track and Gravet's hands as he plays a piano, and the picture's theme song, by Werner Heymann (long since gone Hollywood) sounds like a poor imitation of "Swanee River." English subtitles by Herman G. Weinberg are scarcely adequate, with long passages of vociferous French dialog ensuing between the few skimpy English words the American audience can tag on to.

Picture's chief redeeming feature is some outstanding camera work by Harry Stradling. Cameraman gets in some good superimpositions, dissolves, etc., in the film's dream sequence and manages to catch the right lighting to heighten the mood of various scenes. *Stal.*

Gun Town
(SONGS)

Hollywood, March 16

Universal releae of Wallace W. Fox production, directed by Fox. Features Kirby Grant, Fuzzy Knight, Claire Carlton, Lyle Talbot, Louis Currie. Original screenplay, William Lively; camera, Manry Gertsman; editor, Ray Snyder; songs, Everett Carter-Milton Rosen. Reviewed at Hitching Post Theatre, Hollywood, March 15, '46. Running time, 55 mins.

Kip..............Kirby Grant
Ivory..............Fuzzy Knight

Lucky Dorgan....Lyle Talbot
Belle Townley....Claire Carlton
"Buckskin" Jane Sawyer....Louise Currie
Davey Sawyer....Gene Carrick
Joe....Dan White
Nevada....Ray Bennett
Sheriff....Earle Hodgins
Townsman....Bill Sondholm
Townsman....George Morrell

Mild western fare. Too much talk and stock footage dim the action heroics more than necessary. It will rate no more than a fair reception from the Saturday matinee trade. Oater has above-average western production dressing, but long gab sessions make the action more pace than gallop.

Kirby Grant is comparative newcomer to westerns and does okay as a grim, dashing Indian Agent hero who foils formula villany perpetrated by Lyle Talbot. Latter is better than average casting for a prairie saga and is a help. Femme interest supplied by Louise Currie and Claire Carleton also is on the upgrade for oaters. Miss Carleton wraps up film's two tunes as a saloon canary and aide to Talbot's heavy work.

The William Lively plot, as produced and directed by Wallace W. Fox, concerns efforts of Talbot and his henchmen, acting for an eastern syndicate, to foil Miss Currier's stage-coach franchise plans. Tossed in is some stock footage and Indians to build up chases and other action. Fuzzy Knight tries hard with comedy material handed him without too much success.

Lensing by Maury Gertsman and other technical functions are standard. *Brog.*

Out of the Depths

Columbia release of Wallace MacDonald production. Features Jim Bannon, Ross Hunter, Ken Curtis, Loren Tindall, Robert Scott, Frank Sully. Directed by D. Ross Lederman. Story, Aubrey Wisberg; screenplay, Martin Berkeley and Ted Thomas; editor, Paul Borofsky; camera, Philip Tannura. At Strand, Brooklyn, dual, March 15, '46. Running time, **61 MINS.**

Capt. Faversham....Jim Bannon
Clayton Shepherd....Ross Hunter
Buck Clayton....Ken Curtis
Pete Lubowsky....Loren Tindall
"Pills" Wilkins....Robert Scott
Speed Brogan....Frank Sully
Lt. Ito Kaida....George Khan
Sparks....Coulter Irwin
Ten-to-One Ryan....George Offerman, Jr.
Mike Rawhide....Rodric Redwing
First Officer Ross....Robert Williams
Charlie Anderson....William Newell
Eddie Jones....Warren Mills
Bailey....John Tyrrell

"Out of the Depths" is a routine war picture that fumbles the dramatic elements inherent in a story about submarine operations. Film shoves off at a smart pace with promise of fast action and sharp character definition of the crew. But about two reels out of port, the film takes on heavy ballast in the form of milk-sop sentiment and leaden comedy that sends it to the bottom. Lack of marquee strength will also clip selling power although snappy exploitation of submarine theme could push it along in the nabes on male appeal basis.

Film opens with clever flashback technique thumbnailing backgrounds of four survivors from a U.S. sub which was sent into Jap waters on a secret mission. But yarn quickly switches over into the stock situation of a Yank sub foiling the plot of a Nip aircraft carrier to launch a Kamikaze attack upon the American fleet. Climactic scene of the sub ramming the carrier fails to achieve even a modicum of realism with its obvious process shots. One long, maudlin sequence of a sailor writing a farewell letter to his unborn son makes the customers squirm with embarrassment, while the comedy by-play is crude and pointless. The all-male cast try hard to bring their characters alive despite confusion of purpose by both script and direction.

Dark Is the Night
(RUSSIAN-MADE)

Artkino release of Erevan Studios production. Stars Irina Radchenko, Ivan Kuznetsov, Boris Andreyev, Alexei Yudin. Directed by Boris Barnet. Story by Fedor Knorre; camera, Sergei Gevorkian; English titles, Charles Clement. Previewed N. Y. March 15, '46. Running time, **70 MINS.**

Varya....Irina Radchenko
Artankin....Ivan Kuznetsov
Viatkin....Ivan Kuznetsov
Christophorov....Boris Andreyev
The Grandfather....Vladimir Leonov
The School Principal....Alexei Yudin
The German Sergeant....Alexei Yudin
The German Commandant....Boris Barnet
The Doctor....Nikolai Viazemsky
The Old Woman....Olga Goreva

(In Russian; English Titles)

This is one of the strongest pictures to come out of Moscow since before the war. "Dark Is the Night" is stark melodrama marked by several of the finest performances to be wrapped up by Russian actors in one picture. Film is a natural for foreign-language houses and arty theatres. It might also do fair to good biz in other U. S. spots, with a bit of editing.

Framed in the ruins of battle-scarred Stalingrad, story makes virtually a psychological study of a Russian schoolgirl, Irina Radchenko, as she is transformed into a courageous fighter for Russia. However, director Boris Barnet and scripter Fedor Knorre wisely have stressed the melodramatic phases of the story. As a result the picture becomes a powerful meller rather than a tedious portrayal of a girl's mind. This in no way detracts from the outstanding performance turned in by Miss Radchenko as the school miss.

Plot shows this girl befuddled by the victorious advance of the Nazi hordes but regaining control of herself in time to hide two wounded Russo aviators. After that her main purpose in life is to nurse them back to health, help them escape from the war-torn city and get back into the Soviet fighting ranks.

The shell-wrecked city that serves as a background is naturally more realistic than anything reproduced in a studio. For instance, the hiding place of the two flyers is in the attic of a tall, partly shattered apartment house. To reach it, the girl must climb a long series of stairs that are the only part remaining in that portion of the shell-riddled structure. A highlight of the picture is the chase of the Nazi officers, led by a German police dog, up these stairs only a few feet behind the girl.

Two other tense scenes are those where the girl first manages to conceal the presence of the wounded Russ; and the other where citizens, assembled by the Nazis at a circus, are mowed down when they cheer the anti-German speech of the town's school principal. Latter is developed to a high melodramatic peak, because fellow townspeople supposed the teacher had turned collaborationist.

Besides Miss Radchenko's powerful portrayal, Ivan Kuznetsov and Boris Andreyev, as the wounded aviators, are excellent. Former plays a dual role, doubling into a lesser characterization. Alexei Yudin is superb as the little schoolmaster who denounces the Germans at the crucial moment. He also doubles up, appearing in alternate scenes as the snooping Nazi sergeant trying to ferret out hidden Russo troops. Boris Barnet, who also directed with marked skill, makes a thoroughly despicable German commandant who shoots down any person displeasing him. Entire supporting cast, headed by Vladimir Leonov, deserves laurels for fine performances.

While Fedor Knorre's story is not highly original, he has given it enough new twists to make it jell. Sergei Gevorkian's cameraing is top-flight. English titling by Charles Clement is good. *Wear.*

Blonde Alibi

Universal release of Ben Pivar production. Features Martha O'Driscoll, Tom Neal, Donald MacBride, Robert Armstrong, Samuel S. Hinds. Directed by Will Jason. Screenplay, George Bricker; original, Gordon Kahn; camera, Maury Gertsman; editor, Edward Curtiss. Tradeshown N. Y. March 15, '46. Running time, **62 MINS.**

Marian Gale....Martha O'Driscoll
Rick Lavery....Tom Neal
Inspector Carmichael....Donald MacBride
Williams....Robert Armstrong
Professor Slater....Samuel S. Hinds
Sam....Elisha Cook, Jr.
Lt. Melody Haynes....Peter Whitney
Pat Tenny....Oliver Blake
Louie Carney....John Berkes
Lane....Matt Willis

This routine whodunit hasn't much to commend it. A familiar yarn about a murder, with circumstantial evidence pointing to the wrong suspect, is stretched out to a full-length pic with little originality or excitement. It's marked for only modest returns.

Situations are trite, with the solution obvious long before the finis. Dialog is pretty pat, and comedy relief weak and juvenile. Much of the comedy, for instance, is built around the dumb cop and long-suffering inspector routine, which long ago wasn't funny.

Film does have some amusing moments, supplied by John Berkes in his portrayal of a sneak thief named Louie. Scene in which Louie is picked up for questioning is good cinema, while the third-degree sessions in which the coppers vainly try to make Louie talk have real humor and sparkle.

Otherwise cast and director go through the motions, with camera lagging along. Martha O'Driscoll is pretty and static, as the sweetheart of an aviator accused of murder, while Tom Neal, as the boyfriend, gives the nearest semblance of verity to any performance. Peter Whitney is the imbecilic dick (with his name, of all things, Melody). Donald MacBride can't keep from looking foolish as the long-suffering inspector, while Samuel S. Hinds is just as unhappy as the near-sighted gent whose testimony incriminates an innocent man. Robert Armstrong helps to enliven the third-degree scenes. *Bron.*

The Spider Woman Strikes Back

Universal release of Howard Welsch production. Features Brenda Joyce, Gale Sondergaard. Directed by Arthur Lubin. Screenplay, Eric Taylor; camera, Paul Ivano; editor, Ray Snyder. Previewed in N. Y. March 13, '46. Running time, **59 MINS.**

Jean....Brenda Joyce
Zenobia....Gale Sondergaard
Hal....Kirby Grant
Mario....Rondo Hatton
Moore....Milburn Stone
Mr. Stapleton....Hobarth Cavanaugh
Tom....Norman Leavitt
Molly Cervin....Eula Guy
Sam Julian....Tom Daly
Jinnie Hawks....Lois Austin
Mrs. Wentley....Ruth Robinson
Martha....Adda Gleason

Far on the negative side concerning the horror element implied by the title, this film, although loaded with exploitation possibilities, is dimmed with too-obvious material. Able performances of principals Brenda Joyce and Gale Sondergaard, however, make pic adequate filler for duals.

Story builds well enough in preliminary footage. Miss Joyce is employed as companion to Miss Sondergaard, a respected menace playing blind in her conniving to regain property by mysterious cattle destruction via poison. Ghoulish angles are contributed by Rondo Hatton, mute car[illegible]r and Miss Sondergaard's accomplice, who looks the part but fails to convince.

Miniature Reviews

"So Goes My Love" (U). Nostalgic comedy-drama, good b.o. draw.

"The Wife of Monte Cristo" (PRC). Plume-and-saber hoss opera with Gallic accent will draw business.

"Suspense" (Mono). Ice musical melodrama a class production entry; entertainment for all.

"Mysterious Intruder" (Col.). Nicely paced whodunit with Richard Dix.

"The Caravan Trail" (Color) (PRC). Standard western photographed in Cinecolor.

"Thunder Town" (PRC). Fast moving knuckle and gun western of the old school.

"Danny Boy" (PRC). Boy-and-his-dog story, strictly for juve trade.

So Goes My Love

Hollywood, March 23

Universal release of Jack H. Skirball-Bruce Manning production. Stars Myrna Loy, Don Ameche; features Rhys Williams, Bobby Driscoll, Richard Gaines. Directed by Frank Ryan. Screenplay, Bruce Manning and James Clifden; based upon "A Genius in the Family," by Hiram Percy Maxim; camera, Joseph Valentine; music, score and direction, H.J. Salter; editor, Ted J. Kent. Previewed March 22, '46. Running time 88 mins.

Jane....Myrna Loy
Hiram....Don Ameche
Magel....Rhys Williams
Percy....Bobby Driscoll
Josephus....Richard Gaines
Garnet....Molly Lamont
Bridget....Sarah Padden
Emily....Renie Riano
Mrs. Meade....Clara Blandick
Theodore....John Gallaudet
Raymond....John Phillips
Weldon....Bruce Edwards
Willis....Howard Freeman
Committee Man....Wheaton Chambers
Committee Man....Pierre Watkin

"So Goes My Love" deals out nostalgic period comedy-drama in full measure for audience entertainment. Family appeal is wide and picture will be a certain pleaser for all types of trade. It's a mixture of laughs and tears with a hokum slant, based on the story, "A Genius in the Family," by Hiram Percy Maxim. There's no dull account of Hiram Maxim's many inventions, story being grooved for homey chuckles in telling of the domestic life of the Maxims and Brooklyn of the latter 1860s.

Production guidance by Jack H. Skirball realizes fully on the humor inherent in the plot and smartly sets it off with realistic mounting. Casting of Myrna Loy and Don Ameche in top roles adds marquee values that will aid the payoff. Under Frank Ryan's able direction, the pair make the most of the material. Dialog scripted by Bruce Manning and James Clifden has a natural sparkle and the screenplay unfolds with a natural ease that sustains attention.

Don Ameche is delightful as the temperamental, unconventional inventor, making it one of his most effective assignments. Miss Loy lends charm to her portrayal of Ameche's wife, giving the role a standout. Juvenile honors are captured by young Bobby Driscoll, as the couple's son. Youngster is so natural, with none of the too often obnoxious moppet mannerisms, that his work will be remembered. It's an honest, convincing piece of work adding measurably to the film's entertainment. Rhys Williams, a screwball artist; Richard Gaines, Molly Lamont, Sarah Padden, Renie Riano, Clara Blandick and others in the smart cast contribute generously to the chuckles.

Film is initial Jack H. Skirball-Bruce Manning production for Universal and gets them off to an excellent start. Choice of Frank Ryan as director proved wise, based on the top results he gets from the script and players. Joseph Valentine contributed topnotch lensing, and the settings, music score by H. J. Salter, editing and other technical functions are worthy. *Brog.*

The Wife of Monte Cristo

PRC release of Leon Fromkess production. Stars John Loder, Lenore Aubert; features Charles Dingle, Fritz Kortner, Eduardo Cianelli, Martin Kosleck, Fritz Feld. Directed by Edgar G. Ulmer. Screenplay by Dorcas Cochran from original by Franz Rosenwald and Edgar G. Ulmer, based on story by Alexander Dumas; camera, Adolph Kull; editor, Douglas Bagier. Tradeshown N. Y., March 20, '46. Running time, 83 MINS.

De Villefort....................John Loder
Haydee....................Lenore Aubert
Danglars....................Charles Dingle
Maillard....................Fritz Kortner
Antoine....................Eduardo Cianelli
Counte of Monte Cristo.....Martin Kesleck
Bonnet....................Fritz Feld
Mme. Maillard....................Eva Gabor
Baptisto....................Clancy Cooper
Abbe Faria....................Colin Campbell

"The Wife of Monte Cristo," PRC's top-coin effort to date, is a period piece set in la belle France, circa 1832, but despite the frilly dress and melange of foreign accen's it unreels as a hoss opera with a Gallic accent.

Westerners basic formula remains immutable, with the accent placed solely on derring-do adventure and mayhem, and no patience for such matters as internal story consistency or character delineation. But in the PRC tradition this film shapes up as a fast action thriller with higher than usual b.o. play to be expected as result of a widespread bally campaign in the fan mags and exhibitor exploitation of the plume-and-saber Monte Cristo theme. While marquee values are not outstanding, cast names assure solid performances to cine-shoppers.

Yarn, allegedly based on the Alexander Dumas' romance, in fact is an unrelated chronicle of villainy and vengeance spun out of the more prosaic fantasy of the studio scripters. The Count of Monte Cristo, as masked chieftain of an underground resistance movement in Paris, leads repeated raids against profiteers battening upon the people's misery. Suspected by the corrupt police prefect, the Count thwarts attempts to trap him by having the wife pinch-hit for him during several escapades. Plot affords plentiful chances for cross-country pursuits, daring jail-breaks, and odds-on fighting, all of which are seized. A long, superbly staged fencing match between the count and the prefect, in which virtue and love gain the inevitable triumph, climaxes the film.

John Loder, starring as a heavy, performs neatly as the police chief offering the part just enough cynicism and humor. Martin Kosleck, usually cast as a nasty little Gestapo agent, plays the count's role with suitable intensity and bounce although the heroic feats accomplished by such a slight build reduces his credibility. Lenore Aubert, in the prominent role of the wife, is the weak link of the cast. Her personality and thesping are undistinguished and her accent sounds foreign without being exotic. The others go through their paces with uniform competence.

Production is mounted handsomely with careful attention paid to interior settings and costuming. Director Edgar Ulmer successfully slants the film for pure action although many situations are too crudely contrived. Musical and camera effects par the general production level.

Suspense

Hollywood, March 23.

Monogram release of Maurice and Frank King production. Stars Belita, Barry Sullivan, Bonita Granville, Albert Dekker, Eugene Pallette. Directed by Frank Tuttle. Original screenplay, Philip Yordan; camera, Karl Struss; music, Daniele Amfitheatrof; songs, Miguelito Valdes, Dunham and Dan Alexander, Tommy Reilly; skating sequences, Nick Castle; editors, Ortho Lovering, Dick Heermance; special effects, Jack Shaw and Ray Mercer. Previewed March 21, '46. Running time, 103 MINS.

Roberta Elva....................Belita
Joe Morgan....................Barry Sullivan
Ronnie....................Bonita Granville
Frank Leonard....................Albert Dekker
Harry Wheeler....................Eugene Pallette
Max....................George E. Stone
Nora....................Edit Angold
Pierre....................Leon Belasco
Miguelito Valdes
Bobby Ramos and His Band

Ice extravaganza and melodrama are combined in "Suspense." Film is most expansive to come from Monogram and certainly the best vehicle yet handed the studio's skating star, Miss Belita. Ice numbers are showy and offer Miss Belita ample opportunity to display dazzling blade technique. Meller factors blend in neatly to carry sufficient interest for all audiences. Elastic bankroll handed Maurice and Frank King is reflected in production values obtained, the brothers having provided top talent in all departments to justify hefty coin outlay.

Frank Tuttle's direction had to exercise plenty of agility in weaving musical and dramatic portions together. His skill brings it off expertly. The Philip Yordan original script concerns a tough, ambitious young man who slugs his way up without regard for others. Locale is an ice palace run by Albert Dekker and his skating star-wife, Miss Belita. Barry Sullivan, the toughie, loses no time declaring himself in on the business as well as the wife. Suspense starts when Dekker plots Sullivan's murder but is supposedly killed himself, and the mood continues to heighten with Dekker's return from the dead and his murder by Sullivan. Finale has Sullivan's past catching up with him in the person of Bonita Granville, a cast-off sweetie, who bumps him off in the best "Frankie and Johnnie" style.

Ice palace background makes introduction of Miss Belita's numbers logical. She takes to the skates with ease, performing breath-taking routines that will fully capture audience fancy. She also gives a better account of herself on the story end than heretofore. Production numbers, staged by Nick Castle, include "East-Side Boogie" and "Ice Cuba," plus reprised solo sword routine by Miss Belita. Miguelito Valdes, Afro-Cuban singer, is featured in "Ice Cuba," chanting his own tune, "Cabildo."

Sullivan does a potent portrayal of the male lead, walking over the unsympathetic role with a fan-winning style that commands plenty of interest. Dekker is good as the ice impresario, as is Eugene Pallette as his handy man. Miss Granville, George E. Stone, Edit Angold and others also work well.

Bobby Ramos and his orchestra spot tune, "With You in My Arms," neatly, with Ramos handling the vocal. Number was cleffed by Dunham and Alexander. Tommy Reilly wrote "East-Side Boogie."

Fine lensing is contributed by Karl Struss; Daniele Amfitheatrof score is excellent, and art direction, setting, etc., measure up good standard set by production. *Brog.*

Mysterious Intruder

Columbia release of Rudolph C. Fothow production. Stars Richard Dix; features Barton MacLane, Nina Vale, Regis Toomey, Helen Mowery, Mike Mazurki. Directed by William Castle. Story and screenplay, Eric Taylor; camera, Philip Tannura; editor, Dwight Caldwell; asst. director, Carl Hiecke. At Strand, Brooklyn, N. Y., dual, week March 21, '46. Running time, 62 MINS.

Don Gale....................Richard Dix
Detective Taggart....................Barton MacLane
Joan Hill....................Nina Vale
James Summers....................Regis Toomey
Freda Hanson....................Helen Mowery
Harry Pontos....................Mike Mazurki
Elora Lund....................Pamela Blake
Detective Burns....................Charles Lane
Edward Stillwell....................Paul Burns
Rose Denning....................Kathleen Howard
Brown....................Harlan Briggs

Fifth in the Columbia series based on radio's "Whistler" programs, this film paces itself with a nicety that should prove attractive to the meller fans. With its surprise ending, frequent plot twists and generally excellent casting, "Mysterious Intruder" provides a consistently entertaining hour's performance.

Story relates sundry underhand doings, including a brace of homicides, behind efforts to secure a secret treasure which turns out to be two purportedly original recordings of Jenny Lind. It would appear that a handsome price has been offered for the records by a Swedish millionaire. General outline of the plot is conventional in pattern with Richard Dix as a private dick engaged in an argument with the cops while both chase the elusive murderer.

Despite the routine idea, the story clicks because the plot doubles up on its own tracks enough to keep the addicts guessing. Several of the scenes are well handled for suspense with one in which Dix gropes his way through a house in search of the killer, particularly good. A sprinkling of well placed laughs eases the tension at the right spots.

Dix, heading the cast, handles his part deftly with a pat touch of lightness that makes for a smooth portrayal. Net result is the creation of a hardboiled character who still is pleasant and casual enough for the audience to warm up. Mike Mazurki, a reconstructed heavyweight wrestler, gives the right rough-hewn tone to his part. Helen Mowery, Nina Vale, Regis Toomey and Barton MacLane are uniformly expert in supporting roles.

Direction of William Castle is nicely done. He keeps the action moving at a lively pace and the audience edged forward on their seats. Camera work and sound track obbligato are above par.

The Caravan Trail

(SONGS)
(COLOR)

PRC release of Robert Emmett production, directed by Emmett. Stars Eddie Dean; features Al La Rue, Emmett Lynn. Screenplay, Frances Kavanaugh; camera, Marcel LePicard; color supervision (Cinecolor), Arthur Phelps; editor, Hugh Winn; music, Carl Hoefle; songs, Billy Hill, Peter DeRose, Eddie Dean, Lewis Hersher, Lew Porter, Johnnie Bond. Previewed N.Y., March 22, '46. Running time, 53 mins.

Eddie Dean....................Eddie Dean
Ezra....................Al La Rue
Cherokee....................Emmett Lynn
Paula Bristol....................Jean Carlin
Jim Bristol....................Robert Malcolm
Joe King....................Charles King
Reno....................Robert Barron
Silas Black....................Forrest Taylor
Killer....................Bob Duncan
Poker Face....................Jack O'Shea
Bart Barton....................Terry Frost

Photographed in Cinecolor, this standard western is lifted above par somewhat with advantageous outdoor scenes and good incidental vocalizing by Eddie Dean. Color photography, however, although consistently in good taste, fails to cover hackneyed hoss opry yarn which is further hampered by stilted and camera-shy performances by most of the cast. Dean sings the standard "Wagon Wheels" as theme song but number suffers in awkward sound perspective. Other songs are "You're Too Pretty to Be Lonesome" and "Crazy Cowboy Song" in straight oatune style. Will do for dualers.

Story includes plenty fist fights and gun battles which evolve into an embarrassing number of killings even for a western. Dean accepts a marshal's job in the hope of squaring the murder of his friend and restoring to the homesteaders land which has been illegally usurped by the heavies. He and comic sidekick Al La Rue, aided by befriended outlaw, Emmett Lynn, do the good deed in a series of mad dashes, killings and escapes which wind up in finale showdown where remaining villains bite the dust.

Jean Carlin, the heart interest, is posed in colorful costuming.

Thunder Town

PRC release of Arthur Alexander production. Stars Bob Steele; features Syd Saylor. Directed by Harry Fraser. Screenplay, James Oliver; camera, Robert Cline; editor, Roy Livingston. Previewed N.Y., March 22, '46. Running time, 52 mins.

Jim Brandon....................Bob Steele
Utah McGirk....................Syd Saylor
Betty Morgan....................Ellen Hall
Chuck Wilson....................Bud Geary
Bill Rankin....................Charles King
Dunc Rankin....................Edward Howard
Sheriff Matt Warner....................Steve Clark
Henry Carson....................Bud Osborne
Peter Collins....................Jimmy Aubrey

Fast moving, eventful and jammed with lusty knuckle and gun scrapes, all cleanly spaced, makes this oater a fairly-rating western of the old school. Good direction and attentive twists in yarn resurrection click the action stuff and shows off saddle vet Bob Steele to best advantage along with Syd Saylor, handling the comedy chore.

The flying fists and six-shooters are spliced in the variegated story, having Steele returned to his ranch town as a paroled convict bent on clearing himself of a framed robbery. Browbeaten by heavies as an ex-con, Steele brings the heels to justice via newly discovered ballastic tests and a half dozen rough-and-tumble muscle melees, aided by Syd Saylor as his faithful chum. Femme decor is handled by Ellen Hall, who is rescued at the last minute from a forced marriage to provide a near-clinch finale with Steele.

Danny Boy

PRC release of Leon Fromkess production (Martin Mooney, associate producer). Stars Robert "Buzzy" Henry. Directed by Terry Morse. Screenplay, Raymond L. Schrock; story, Taylor Caven; camera, Jack Greenhalgh; editor, George McGuire. At New York theatre, N.Y., dual, March 20, '46. Running time, 53 mins.

Jimmy Bailey....................Robert "Buzzy" Henry
Joe Cameron....................Ralph Lewis
Mrs. Bailey....................Helen Brown
Margie Bailey....................Sybil Merritt
Mrs. Johnson....................Eve March
Mr. Johnson....................Tay Dunn
Lafe Dunkell....................Joseph Granby
Grumpy Andrews....................Walter Soderling
Judge Carter....................Richard Kipling
Pudgie....................Michael McGuire
Hal....................Myron Wilton
Louis....................Charles Bates
Rinky....................Bobby Valentine
Tuffy....................Larry Dixon
Jackie....................Eric Younger
Danny Boy....................Ace (Dog)

Devoid of much productional background, this film relies exclusively on juve appeal delivered by flock of camera-conscious kids in their reactions over a returned marine war dog. Stilted performances and overworked tear-fetching angles crowd out the cinch boy-and-his-dog theme, resulting in a negative affair strictly for nabe dualers.

The dog is kidnapped by neighborhood heavies whom the canine attacks after making his escape. Ensuing court trial has it sentenced to gas chamber. Ralph Lewis, a veteran and pal to Robert "Buzzy" Henry, dog's master, rescinds the death verdict in favor of firing squad, as befitting a marine. The animal is saved in the nick of time by evidence obtained by the kids that incriminates the kidnappers.

Henry stands out among the kids, who occupy the major footage along with the dog. Latter's frequent lack of cooperation shows conspicuously.

The Peoples Choice

Hollywood, March 26.

Jack Seaman's Planet Productions aroused more than novelty interest with the premiere of "The People's Choice," first showing of a 16m film feature in a public theatre against standard-gauge pictures. Opening at Hollywood's Marcal theatre last week proved that minnies can be projected successfully on any screen through intensified projectors, can fill a normal size screen, and present images clearly. Average picture patron will be quite unaware he is witnessing other than a regular full-width film.

Those were chief hurdles that had to be overcome and over which there had been doubt frequently expressed by sideline observers. Minnies can win showings on technical merit, about which even the most critical exhibs can't carp too much. Smallies could be produced to rival B and C product on duals, underbilling at a cost almost infinitesimal compared to the normal low budgeters.

"People's Choice" didn't prove a particularly auspicious piece to preem idea, farce being produced on a budget that must have been no more than a two-reel slapstick saga, but with what they were handed, producer Ray Collins and director Harry Fraser squeezed to dregs possibilities of effectiveness. In stock role of a slowly turning worm, Drew Kennedy milked the part. Opposite, as the ever-believing gal, Louise Arthur put spirit and sly good humor into what might have been a dull role. Film veterans George Meeker, Rex Lease, Fred Kelsey and Ernie Adams weighed in strongly, in support. Richard Hill Wilkinson's script is breezy, but bogged several sequences by inclusion of ancient wheezes which should have been eliminated. Ten minutes could have been sliced from the 68 running time to good, tightening effect. Tinted by Kodachrome, result is all right, not as eyefilling and delicate as some of the other color forms, but Eastman's isn't nearly so expensive, either.

Planet has set its own distribution, and major studios here are watching with undisguised interest this opening march of the minnies.

Foreign Films

(Unlikely for Anglo-American Market)

"Bataille Du Rail" ("Railroad Fight") **(FRENCH).** CineUnion release of Cooperative Generale Francaise du Cinema production; directed by Rene Clement; features Jean Daurand, Tony Laurent, Calrieux, Desagneaux, Jean Rozena, Mauleon, Leray; screenplay by Rene Clement; dialog, Colette Audry; reviewed in Paris. Running time, **106 MINS.**

This cooperative effort of French railroadmen to glorify the part they played in fooling the Germans in their efforts to use French railroads effectively during the war has small entertainment value, but patriotic French will enjoy it. Film stresses how the French railway workers prevented reinforcement trains from reaching Normandy after Allies landed. Film starts like an educational. Railroaders play many of the parts. Not a chance in U.S.

"Jericho" (FRENCH). Corona release of Sacha Gordine production; directed by Henri Calef; stars Pierre Brasseur; features Larguey, Santa Relli, Palau, Louis Seigner, Pasquali; screenplay, Claude Heyman; dialog, Charles Spaak; reviewed in Paris. Running time, **120 MINS.**

This is a war picture showing how timely the bombing of the Amiens prison by the RAF proved since saving the lives of 50 French hostages. Actual RAF footage of this bombing are highlights of the film. The French do not appear tired of war epics, so this likely to do well in France. Similar stories have been done many times before by U.S. producers hence film holds little for American audiences.

"2 x 2" (HUNGARIAN). Sarlo production; features Emmy Buttykay, Zoltan Varkonyi, Artur Somlay, Zoltan Maklary. Directed and story by Janos Manninger; reviewed in Budapest.

This feature was started in spring of 1944. After the war it couldn't be released because the hero was a pro-Nazi actor who escaped to Germany and is barred from the Hungarian screen. All his scenes had to be retaken, but after all these adventures, "2 x 2" is not a success. Janos Manninger, vet Hunnia lenser, of Hungarian films in the last 10 years, also wrote the story and directed it himself. His film is a series of beautiful stills with many good ideas, but it is not a good picture.

"Blood Och Eld" ("Blood and Fire") **(SWEDISH).** Europa Film production and release; directed by Anders Hendrikson. Stars Anders Hendrikson, Sonja Wigert; features George Fant, Inge Waern; screenplay, Bertil Malmberg; camera, Harold Berglund; reviewed in Stockholm. Running time, **100 MINS.**

A dramatic story about the Salvation Army and its work in Sweden. Anders Hendrikson, male star in film, was named the finest actor in the world here after this film, which is mentioned as the best Swedish production of 1945. Despite all this, its appeal in the U.S. is obviously limited.

"Blajackor" ("Sailors") **(SWEDISH).** Wivefilm release of S.A.G. Swenson production; directed by Rolf Husberg. Stars Nils Poppe, Annalisa Ericson; features Karl-Arne Holmsten and Cecile Ossbahr; screenplay, Nils Poppe and Rolf Botvid, based on musical show by Louis Laitai; reviewed in Stockholm. Running time, **105 MINS.**

This is probably the best Swedish comedy in several years. Nils Poppe ranks high among Swedish comedians. Although this has great popular appeal among local audiences, it looks only good for foreign-language spots in America.

"Fram for Lilla Marta" ("Go On, Little Martha") **(SWEDISH).** Terrafilm release of Hasse Ekman production; directed by Hasse Ekman; stars Stig Jarrel, Elsie Albiin; features Hasse Ekman, Agneta Lagerfeldt. Running time, **78 MINS.**

This Swedish variation of "Charley's Aunt" will be a click throughout Sweden. Comedy has Stig Jarrel as a sax player faking a woman's disguise for a flock of laughs. Rated among top Swedish productions of year but only good for a few foreign-language houses in U.S.

Miniature Reviews

"Devotion" (WB). Drama of Bronte Sisters with strong cast names to lure customers.

"The Dark Corner" (20th). Lucille Ball, Clifton Webb, William Bendix in ok meller.

"Gay Blades" (Rep). Okay action-comedy aimed at pleasing in secondary billings.

"Wanted For Murder" (20th) (British-made). Chiller with limited U. S. appeal.

"Night Editor" (Col). William Gargan in unexciting sleuth meller.

"Black Market Babies" (Mono). Timely theme should set this one for moderate returns on double bills.

"Behind the Mask" (Mono). Fair comedy-melodrama for secondary spotting.

"Border Bandits" (Mono). Below-par westerner; lacks action.

"Fear" (Mono). Taut melodrama on crime and punishment theme; solid entertainment.

Devotion

Hollywood, March 30.

Warners release of Robert Buckner production. Stars Ida Lupino, Paul Henreid, Olivia de Havilland, Sydney Greenstreet; features Nancy Coleman, Arthur Kennedy, Dame May Whitty, Victor Francen. Directed by Curtis Bernhardt. Screenplay, Keith Winter; original story, Theodore Reeves; camera, Ernest Haller; special effects, Jack Holden, Jack Oakie, Rex Wimpy; music, Erich Wolfgang Korngold; editor, Rudi Fehr. Tradeshown at Warners Beverly theatre, Beverly Hills, Cal., March 26, '46. Running time, **108 MINS.**

Emily Bronte....................Ida Lupino
Arthur Nicholls....................Paul Henreid
Charlotte Bronte.......Olivia de Havilland
Thackeray..................Sydney Greenstreet
Anne Bronte....................Nancy Coleman
Branwell Bronte..............Arthur Kennedy
Lady Thornton............Dame May Whitty
Monsieur Heger..............Victor Francen
Mr. Bronte......................Montagu Love
Aunt Branwell..................Ethel Griffies
Sir John Thornton..............Edmond Breon
Madame Heger....................Odette Myrtil
Mrs. Ingham.........................Doris Lloyd
Tabby..............................Marie DeBecker
Miss Thornton.......................Elly Malyon
Hoggs..........................Forrester Harvey
Draper...................................Billy Bevan
Seton...............................Geoffrey Steele

Warners has stacked the deck on this one with a very hefty cast. There's considerable lure for the femmes in the story of the Bronte sisters, but picture is not as complete an exploitation of the characters as it could be. It's all well-done make-believe without ever reaching point of reality. Because of the draw names, such as Ida Lupino, Paul Henreid, Olivia de Havilland, Sydney Greenstreet and others, it can be figured to show a substantial return at the b.o.

Production manages to catch a seemingly authentic picture of the Yorkshire village background of the Brontes before they rose to fame as authors of the 1830's. Individual performances are expert, with a few standouts, in miming the situations in the script by Keith Winter, but it fails to stir more than a modest response. Script, taken from an original story by Theodore Reeves, is not substantial, and dialog switches confusingly from the modern to the prose of the period.

Plot depicts the Brontes in the village of Haworth, Yorkshire, opening in the period just before they found fame as authors. Shown are the love triangle between Ida Lupino, as Emily; Olivia de Havilland, as Charlotte, and Paul Henreid, as the curate who aids the girls' father in the parish; the brief stay of Emily and Charlotte in Brussels, and latter's romance with a schoolteacher, Victor Francen; Charlotte's popular success as writer of "Jane Eyre" and Emily's lesser, but more solid, fame as authoress of "Wuthering Heights." As filmed there are a number of story points not clearly developed, particularly dealing with Emily's fatal illness and neurotic visions, and the love fancies of Charlotte.

Misses Lupino and de Havilland are expert as the two older sisters, while Nancy Coleman as the younger Anne Bronte has her moments. Henreid's portrayal is excellent. Greenstreet is good as Thackeray, a role that is almost a bit. Arthur Kennedy's performance as the drunken poet-painter brother of the sisters is a standout. Dame May Whitty, Francen, Montagu Love, the suffering father; Ethel Griffies and others in the cast lend capable support.

Curtis Bernhardt's direction of the Robert Buckner production never quite overcomes the handicap of an unreal story in the overall effect, although punching home a number of scenes and performances in telling style. Buckner's production guidance catches the flavor of the period without exercising enough strength on script to make the characters live. Of high order are the lensing by Ernest Haller, the score by Erich Wolfgang Korngold and other technical contributions. *Brog.*

The Dark Corner

20th-Fox release of Fred Kohlmar production. Stars Lucille Ball, Clifton Webb, William Bendix: features Mark Stevens, Kurt Kreuger, Cathy Downs. Directed by Henry Hathaway. Screenplay, Jay Dratler. Bernard Schoenfeld, based on story by Lee Rosten; camera, Joe Mcdonald; editor, J. Watson Webb; score, Cyril Mockridge. Tradeshow N.Y., April 1, '46. Running time, 102 MINS.

Kathleen..Lucille Ball
Cathcard.....................................Clifton Webb
White Suit................................William Bendix
Bradford Galt...............................Mark Stevens
Tony Jardine..................................Kurt Kreuger
Mari Catheart.................................Cathy Downs
Lt. Frank Reeves..............................Reed Hadley
Mrs. Kingsley..........................Constance Collier
Lucy Wilding..................................Molly Lamont
Mr. Bryson...................................Forbes Murray
Mrs. Bryson..................................Regina Wallace
Butler....................................John Goldsworthy
Foss....................................Charles Wagenheim
Mother...Minerva Ureal
Daughter..Raisa
Milk Man...Matt McHugh
Scrubwoman.....................................Hope Landin
Mrs. Schwartz................................Gisela Verbisek
Newsboy.......................................Vincent Graeff
Frau Keller..Frieda Stoll
Major Domo...................................Thomas Martin
Cashier..Mary Field
Maid...Ellen Corby
Saleswoman......................................Eloise Hardt
Barker..Steve Olsen

Eddie Heywood Orchestra

Although "The Dark Corner" has all the ingredients of sock, hard-fisted melodrama, an overlong and loosely-woven script, and a scarcity of action where it would help most, militate a bit against it. Names of Lucille Ball, Clifton Webb and William Bendix will help generate business, and picture should do okay in most situations.

Better editing, job, clipping about 20 minutes off the running time, would have aided considerably. Starting off as another slambang private investigator story, the first few reels are set at a fast pace. Stymied by an overabundance of dialog, however, the tempo gradually subsides and moves slowly to a so-so climax that misses because of the preceding draggy quality.

Story has Miss Ball as secretary to private detective Stevens. Latter's just set up shop after serving time in San Quentin on a trumped-up manslaughter charge instituted by Kurt Kreuger, his former partner. Kreuger, an unscrupulous lothario, sets out to snare the wife of Webb, socialite art collector, for her money. Knowing the cops think Stevens is out to get Kreuger for revenge, Webb hires Bendix, a tough gunman, to kill Kreuger and plant the blame on Stevens, then gets rid of Bendix. After much talk, Stevens and Miss Ball track down Webb and the boss marries his secretary.

Cast, steered in the right direction by director Henry Hathaway, does much to keep the picture running as smoothly as it does. Miss Ball is decorative and pleasantly emotional as the secretary. Webb's role, that of a socialite killer, is similar to that with which he made his screen debut in last year's "Laura," and he does equally well with it. Bendix's work as the unmoral gunman is a far cry from his recent comedy parts but it's outstanding.

Stevens, evidently being groomed by 20th-Fox for star roles, is creditable as the tough private dick. Kreuger is sufficiently sardonic and handsome, and the beauteous Cathy Downs is okay as Webb's wife. Eddie Heywood and his orch get spot billing in the cast but are seen in only one flash sequence.

Producer Fred Kohlmar has lined the picture with good accoutrements. Joe McDonald, with emphasis on trick mirror shots, gets in some top-drawer camera work, and Fred Sersen's trick camera sequence of Bendix hurtling through the air from a skyscraper window is one for the books. Sets by Thomas Little are in keeping with the story, and Cyril Mockridge's score helps heighten the picture's mood. *Stal.*

Gay Blades

Hollywood, March 28.

Republic release of George Blair production. Stars Allan Lane, Jean Rogers, Edward Ashley; features Frank Albertson, Anne Gillis, Robert Armstrong, Paul Harvey, Ray Walker, Jonathan Hale, Russell Hicks. Directed by Blair. Screenplay by Albert Beich; adapted by Marcel Klauber, from magazine story by Jack Goodman and Albert Rice; camera, William Bradford; musical direction, Morton Scott; editor, Tony Martinelli; special effects, Howard and Theodore Lydecker. Previewed in Hollywood, March 27, '46. Running time, **67 MINS.**

Andy Buell	Allan Lane
Nancy Davis	Jean Rogers
Ted Brinker	Edward Ashley
Frankie Dowell	Frank Albertson
Helen Dowell	Anne Gillis
McManus	Robert Armstrong
J. M. Snively	Paul Harvey
Bill Calhoun	Ray Walker
Whittlesey	Jonathan Hale
Buxton	Russell Hicks
Doctor	Emmett Vogan
Bartender	Edward Gargan
Gary Lester	Nedrick Young

"Gay Blades" will pay off in the comedy-action classification. It's neatly paced, well-played, with adequate production backing. Picture slants a bit more to the comedy side than it does to the action, and is occasionally a stinging satire on Hollywood.

George Blair produced and directed yarn of a hockey star who nearly succumbs to Hollywood's stardom lure. Plot motivation in the Albert Beich script, based on Marcel Klauber's adaptation of a mag story by Jack Goodman and Albert Rice, is a talent hunt staged by Jean Rogers to find a big hunk of man suitable to title role in a film tagged "The Behemoth." Search leads her to New York and Allan Lane, ice-hockey star. Balance of footage works in some exciting hockey games, the usual hokum as boy and girl resist each other and then come together. There's a nifty slapstick finish with twist that has the girl giving up Hollywood to be a hockey star's wife.

Two leads team neatly to get the best from their assignments. Miss Rogers is easy on eyes and pert in comedy delivery, with Lane equally expert. Edward Ashley, as Miss Rogers' assistant on the talent hunt; Frank Albertson, Anne Gillis, Robert Armstrong, Ray Walker, Jonathan Hale and Russell Hicks showing up among the others. Paul Harvey is particularly effective in broad role as head of Mammouth Studios, giving it a capital satirical touch.

Camera, settings, editing and other technical aids give good backing for release intentions of this one. *Brog.*

Wanted for Murder

(BRITISH-MADE)

London, March 28.

20th Century-Fox release of Excelsior Film-Marcel Hellman production. Stars Eric Portman, Dulcie Gray. Directed by Lawrence Huntington. Screenplay by Percy Robinson, Terence de Marney from story by Emeric Pressburger, Rodney Ackland. Camera, Max Greene, R. Frankie. At 20th-Fox projection room. Running time, **103 MINS.**

Victor Colebrooke	Eric Portman
Anne Fielding	Dulcie Gray
Jack Williams	Derek Farr
Inspector Conway	Roland Culver
Sergeant Sullivan	Stanley Holloway
Mrs. Colebrooke	Barbara Everest
Florrie	Kathleen Harrison
Jeannie McLaren	Jenny Laird
Detective Ellis	Bill Shine
Corporal Mappolo	Bonor Colleano
Walters	John Salew
Miss Willis	Moira Lister

Idea behind this chiller is that you are unlucky if your great-grandfather made his living as a professional hangman. Anyhow it's the alibi offered for Eric Portman's doing privately what Queen Victoria's government paid his ancestor to do publicly. Despite some nice performances, this has extremely thin possibilities for the U. S. market.

Film deserves credit for one thing, if nothing else. That is that a Scotland Yard inspector is given a chance to prove coppers aren't all dead from the neck up. Incidentally, Roland Culver, as the sleuth, walks away with acting honors, with Stanley Holloway as his assistant, a close second. Dulcie Gray, who is co-starred with Portman, does what she can with a stereotyped role.

As happens too often in British films, inept casting results in Miss Gray's having to face comparison with two femmes, playing bits, each with both okay chassis and comeliness. One of them, Moira Lister, as Portman's secretary, is not only easy on the eye but also displays some ability as an actress. She looks to be a future bet for more important parts.

Marcel Hellman's production is first-class, shots in London's underground railway being more than usually effective. Direction by Lawrence Huntington is adequate despite a script lacking in originality. Doubtful if this one will hit the West End except for quota requirements. As a second feature here the draw of Portman's name may satisfy the distributors. *Talb.*

Night Editor

Columbia release of Ted Richmond production. Features William Gargan, Janis Carter, Jeff Donnell. Directed by Henry Levin. Screenplay, Hal Smith from story by Scott Littleton, based on radio program of same name by Hal Burdick; camera, Burnett Guffey, Philip Tannura; editor, Richard Fantl. At Rialto, N. C., March 29, '46. Running time, **65 MINS.**

Tony Cochrane	William Gargan
Jill Merrill	Janis Carter
Martha Cochrane	Jeff Donnell
Johnny	Coulter Irwin
Crane Stewart	Charles D. Brown
Ole Strom	Paul E. Burns
Captain Lawrence	Harry Shannon
Douglas Loring	Frank Wilcox
Doc Cochrane	Robert Stevens
Benjamin Merrill	Roy Gordon
Doc (as a boy)	Michael Chapin
Max	Robert Emmett Keane
Tusco	Anthony Caruso
Chief of Police Barnes	Edward Keane
District Attorney Halloran	Jack Davis
Necktie	Lou Lubin
Swanson	Charles Marsh

"Night Editor" comes close to being the most cockeyed police-sleuth meller in months. It's an instance of a good idea gone haywire via slipshod production and faulty direction. Even the initial sequence in a daily paper's newsroom is phoney, and most of what follows is likewise a minor dualer.

Basically it starts out to be a news editors' recital of how a homicide squad lieutenant went wrong because of his affair with a wealthy society dame. Said ed is doing all this to snap a reporter out of a drinking spree. The newspaper is supposed to be a New York daily and so is the police department. Neither are even close to being reasonable facsimiles.

Recital of the sleuth's dereliction is surprisingly dull until he accidentally is eye-witness to a killing. Rather than admit that he, a married man, was out with the socialite when this happens, he remains silent. But when an innocent man is about to be found guilty he tracks down the real culprit. There's much to do about the spell this femme holds over the copper and how he breaks loose from her charms, but the plot never makes the charm reasonable or why he suddenly decides to go pure.

William Gargan is the hopeless police lieutenant. Janis Carter, the wealthy femme, manages to look enticing although given a thankless role. Paul E. Burns makes the Swedish police officer a worthwhile characterization although minor Jeff Donnell plays the copper's wife in make-believe fashion. Support is weak. But the main difficulty is with the story and direction. *Wear.*

Black Market Babies

Monogram release of Jeffrey Bernerd production. Features Ralph Morgan, Kane Richmond, Marjorie Hoshelle, George Meeker. Directed by William Beaudine. Story, George Morris; adaptation, George W. Sayre; editor, William Austin; camera, Harry Neumann. At Gotham, N.Y., week March 30, '46. Running time, 71 mins.

Dr. Jordan	Ralph Morgan
Eddie Condon	Kane Richmond
Evelyn Barret	Teala Loring
Donna Corbett	Marjorie Hoshelle
Anthony Marco	George Meeker
Doris Condon	Jayne Hazard
Barney	Dewey Robinson
Jake	Alan Foster
Mr. Andrews	Selmar Jackson
Mrs. Andrews	Nana Bryant
Helen Roberts	Maris Wrixon
Hamilton	Addison Richards
Paul Carroll	Parker Gee
Sam	Terry Frost

Timeliness of theme and several good performances by the featured players should bring fair returns on double bills. It's an exploitation picture.

Story, a new switch on rackets, has a former hoodlum, renegade medico and shady lawyer, operating a baby farm where illegitimate offspring may be parked after the unfortunate mothers sign their babes away for adoption. On the surface it's legal and philanthropic but gimmick is that when childless couples come to adopt the babes they are bilked for heavy coin, either as a donation or an assist to the unfortunate mothers. Racket does big until the usual slip-up and investigation by the authorities. The hood tries to make the old doc take the rap for everything but the latter polishes him and beats the murder rap.

Ralph Morgan is splendid as the bibulous M.D. who had been blackmailed into fronting for the racket. Kane Richmond is convincing as the gangster. George Meeker, as the mouthpiece, and Marjorie Hosheile, as the latter's gal, also contribute good performances. William Beaudine has directed neatly, maintaining good tempo of suspense throughout. *Edba.*

Behind the Mask

Hollywood, March 30.

Monogram release of Joe Kaufman production (Lou Brock, assoc. producer). Stars Kane Richmond and Barbara Reed: features George Chandler, Joseph Crehan, Pierre Watkin, Dorothea Kent, Joyce Compton, Marjorie Hoshelle, June Clyde, Robert Shayne. Directed by Phil Karlson. Screenplay, George Callahan; original story, Arthur Hoerl; based on "The Shadow," radio character; camera, William A. Sickner; editor, Ace Herman. Previewed in Hollywood, March 28, '46. Running time, 67 MINS.

Lamont Cranston	Kane Richmond
Margo Lane	Barbara Reed
Shrevvie	George Chandler
Cardona	Joseph Crehan
Weston	Pierre Watkin
Jennie	Dorothea Kent
Lulu	Joyce Compton
Mac Bishop	Margorie Hoshelle
Edith Merrill	June Clyde
Brad Thomas	Robert Shayne
Marty Greane	Lou Crosby
Dixon	Edward Gargan
Copy Boy	Bill Christy
Jeff Mann	James Cardwell
Susan	Nancy Brinckman
Head Waiter	Dewey Robinson
Girl	Marie Harmon
Dowager	Ruth Cherrington
Reporter	James Nataro

"Behind the Mask" has trouble deciding whether to be comedy or melodrama. Otherwise, it will prove acceptable secondary product. Meller factors are excellent, but comedy, introduced frequently, is too contrived and obvious. Production gives adequate backing to plot that tells of how the "Shadow" breaks up a bookie ring, a blackmailing racket, puts the finger on a murderer and gets rid of an impersonator, all in 67 minutes.

Phil Karlson's direction launches the melodrama with a bang to set the scene but isn't as adept at comedy. Kane Richmond, as the "Shadow," is called upon to solve murder of a columnist, presumably by the Shadow himself. Trail to the killer leads him to a phony nightclub, operated to clip the customers; a juke joint, which covers up a bookie ring, and finally to the newspaper office, where the city editor is the brains behind a shakedown racket. Richmond is hampered in his manhunt by a jealous sweetie, Barbara Reed. Both work hard with the light touches, as do George Chandler and Dorothea Kent, but with only fair success. Scripting by George Callahan, as filmed, doesn't help much, either.

Best of the cast is Marjorie Hoshelle, who rings true as the bookie queen and victim of Robert Shayne, blackmailing columnist. Joseph Crehan, Pierre Watkin, Joyce Compton, June Clyde and others try hard.

Camera, editing, etc., are standard for budget. *Brog.*

Border Bandits

Monogram release of Scott R. Dunlop production. Stars Johnny Mack Brown. Directed by Lambert Hillyer. Screenplay, Frank H. Young; camera, William A. Sickner; editor, Carroll Lewis. At New York, N.Y., dual, March 27, '46. Running time, 57 mins.

Nevada	Johnny Mack Brown
Sandy	Raymond Hatten
Steve Halliday	Riley Hill
Celia	Rosa Del Rosario
Spike	John Merton
Pepper	Tom Quinn
John Halliday	Frank La Rue
Doc Bowles	Steve Clark
Jose	Charles Stevens
Nogales	Lucio Villegas
Dutch	Bud Osborne
Cupid	Pat. R. McGee

Pace of this film is far too leisurely for the average action fan. Formula story of sheriff vs. badmen unwinds without any finesse to make up for fatal deficiencies in the fisticuff and gunplay departments. Too much celluloid of this short feature, moreover, is wasted on aimless galloping back and forth across a monotonous scenic background. Even kids will demand something more substantial than flying hoofs to hop up their pulse rates.

Johnny Mack Brown, an established saddle-sitter by now, plays the role of the U. S. marshal tracking down some ornery characters in an easy if somewhat quiet manner. Raymond Hatton, however, tries hard to inject some vitamins into the production. Rest of the cast contribute very little.

Fear

Monogram release of Lindsley Parsons production. Star, Warren William; features Peter Cookson, Anne Gwynne. Directed by Alfred Zeisler. Original screenplay by Zeisler and Dennis Cooper; camera, Jackson Rose; editor, Ace Herman. At New York, N.Y., dual, March 27, '46. Running time, 68 mins.

Captain Burke	Warren William
Eileen	Anne Gwynne

Larry Crain....................................Peter Cookson
Ben..James Cardwell
Schaefer.......................................Nestor Paiva
Morton Stanley.................................Francis Pierlet
Al...William Moss
Mrs. Williams..................................Almira Sessions
Chuck..Darren McGavin
Steve..Henry Clay
Painter..Ernie Adams
John...Johnny Strong
Doc..Charles Calvert
Magician.......................................Fairfax Burger

"Fear" is a solid fistful of entertainment that packs a wallop way out of its class. Set within the modest framework of a dualer, this film draws its strength from a combination of literate scripting and tight direction that keep the story elements in high gear from start to finish. Underlying idea is far from original, the scripters having been deeply influenced by Dostoevski's novel, "Crime and Punishment." But old and simple as the idea is, the well-executed drama of a guilt-laden conscience betraying itself retains more vitality than the most novel and complex twist of the usual whodunit. "Fear" definitely hits it off and word-of-mouth praise should give it a big lift at the b.o.

With Warren William in the lead, the cast, while not in the heavyweight division, is made to toe the mark in highly creditable fashion by director Alfred Zeisler. Peter Cookson carries the heaviest load in the role of the brilliant medical student driven by poverty to the murder-for-money of a usurious moneylender. Tripped up by fear, crushed by his burden of guilt-feelings, Cookson finds his only escape is surrender to the police.

William does a smooth job as the town sleuth who, though short on clues, is long on insinuations that seem to enmesh his victim in a web of evidence. Warren and Cookson play effectively at cat-and-mouse to mount the film's dramatic conflict on a straight upward line. Competent performances are also put in by Anne Gwynne, the romantic interest, and Francis Pierlot, as the loan-shark.

A tagged-on sequence at the finish, revealing the crime and punishment to be merely a fitful dream of the med student, is the one sour note of the production. This device of achieving a happy ending rebounds as a ruinous mechanism that unsprings audience tension and leaves them feeling cheated.

Miniature Reviews

"Easy to Wed" (Songs-Color) (M-G). Lush production and name cast pegs this one as a b.o. winner.

"The Cat Creeps" (U). Noah Beery, Jr. and Fred Brady in a strong whodunit thriller.

"Night in Paradise" (Color) (U). Gorgeously dressed film fantasy with plenty of escapist entertainment for general audiences.

"Joe Palooka, Champ" (Mono) Comic-strip prizefighter yarn okay for secondary spots.

"She-Wolf of London" (U). Weak horror meller.

"Home on the Range" (Songs-Color) (Rep). Fair oatuner in color.

"The Captive Heart" (Eagle-Lion). Semi-documentary about British troops in Nazi war camps; doubtful as U. S. entry.

"Song of Old Wyoming" (Songs-Color) (PRC). Standard musical western with Eddie Dean; color adds little.

"Devil Bat's Daughter" (PRC). Suspenseful horror-meller will satisfy the fans.

"The Years Between" (GFD). Daphne du Maurier's current London hit likely okay for sophisticated U. S. audiences.

Easy to Wed
(SONGS; COLOR)

Hollywood, April 5

Metro release of Jack Cummings production. Stars Van Johnson, Esther Williams, Lucille Ball, Keenan Wynn; features Cecil Kellaway, Carlos Ramirez, Ben Blue, Ethel Smith. Directed by Edward Buzzell. Adapted by Dorothy Kingsley from screenplay "Libeled Lady," by Maurine Watkins, Howard Emmett Rogers, George Oppenheimer; camera (Technicolor), Harry Stradling; music score and direction, Johnny Green; dances, Jack Donohue; orchestration, Ted Duncan; songs, Ralph Blane and Johnny Green, Pedro Galindo, Osvaldo Farres, Raul Soler, Ary Barroso; editor, Blanche Sewell. Tradeshown March 28, '46. Running time, 109 mins.

Bill Stevens Chandler..........................Van Johnson
Connie Allenbury...............................Esther Williams
Gladys Benton..................................Lucille Ball
Warren Haggerty................................Kennan Wynn
J.B. Allenbury.................................Cecil Kellaway
Carlos Ramirez.................................By Himself
Spike Dolan....................................Ben Blue
Ethel Smith....................................By Herself
Babs Norvell...................................June Lockhart
Homer Henshaw..................................Grant Mitchell
Mrs. Burns Norvell.............................Josephine Whitell
Farwood..Paul Harvey
Hector Boswell.................................Jonathan Hale
Joe..James Flavin
Farwood's Secretary............................Celia Travers
Receptionist...................................Sybil Merritt
Attendant......................................Sondra Rodgers

Metro has refurbished the old "Libeled Lady" script with brilliant color, plenty of fun and assured box-office stars. It all adds up to top-notch entertainment that will get big returns. Accent is on comedy with an occasional song in the new treatment, and Jack Cummings' production gives it a light treatment to make it sell with all types audiences. Marquee names of Van Johnson, Esther Williams, Lucille Ball, Keenan Wynn cinch customer lures.

Eddie Buzzell's direction emphasizes lightness and speed, despite picture's long footage, and draws the best from Dorothy Kingsley's adaptation of the "Libeled Lady" script by Maurine Watkins, Howard Emmett Rogers and George Oppenheimer. Plot, briefly, concerns a newspaper faced with a libel suit by a rich playgirl and how the sheet brings in a great lover to compromise the gal so suit can be forgotten. Around that premise are built delightful lines and situations, plus some prime broad comedy playing by several of the principals that keeps the interest high all the way. Music and production numbers are introduced logically into the plot, although dance numbers are so much added flash that isn't needed.

Van Johnson as the great lover and Esther Williams, the libeled lady, team romantically for fan favor and acquit themselves effectively in the plot development. Lucille Ball is a standout on the comedy end, particularly her sequence where she indulges in an inebriated flight into fantastic Shakespeare. Keenan Wynn's deft comedy work also presses hard for solid laughs as the newspaper's manager who concocts the schemes designed to save the sheet's bankroll. He's a certain pleaser. Cecil Kellaway, Miss Williams' father; Ben Blue, Johnston's valet; Paul Harvey, publisher; June Lockhart, Jonathan Hale and others are excellent.

What will probably prove the biggest laugh-getter in the film is an unbilled canine—a sad-eyed springer spaniel—who figures in a sequence wherein he undertakes to instruct neophyte Johnson into the art of duck-hunting. Buzzell's direction carefully plays up the canine expression of disgust and hopelessness at the situation for guaranteed audience reaction.

Carlos Ramirez' vocal ability isn't given the best display on "Acercate Mas." Lucille Ball, backed by dance troupe, gets over "The Continental Polka," by Ralph Blane and Johnny Green. Ethel Smith is spotted for two organ numbers, both of which will be well received. They are "Toca Tu Samba" and "Boneca De Pixe."

Cummings marshalled topflight technical aides to furnish backing for the fun. Harry Stradling's lensing of the tinter gives a beautiful display of the colorful settings. Musical score, supervision and direction by Johnny Green and orchestrations by Ted Duncan are both on the credit side. *Brog.*

The Cat Creeps

Universal release of Howard Welsch production. Features Noah Beery, Jr., Fred Brady, Paul Kelly. Directed by Erle C. Kenton. Screenplay by Edward Dein and Jerry Warner from original by Gerald Geraghty; camera, George Robinson; editor, Russel Schoengarth. Previewed, N.Y., April 4, '46. Running time, 58 mins.

Flash..Noah Beery, Jr.
Gay Elliot.....................................Lois Collier
Ken Grady......................................Paul Kelly
Tom McGalvey...................................Douglas Dumbfille
Terry Nichols..................................Fred Brady
Connie Palmer..................................Rose Hobart
Walter Elliot..................................Jonathan Hale
Cora Williams..................................Vera Lewis
Kyra Goran.....................................Iris Clive
Editor...William Davidson
Publisher......................................Arthur Loft
Polich...Jerry Jerome

Never pretending to be anything more than a lesser feature, "The Cat Creeps" turns out to be nearly an hour of gripping mystery. Capable cast headed by Noah Beery, Jr., and Fred Brady, puts across Gerald Geraghty's original story glibly with an obvious assist from director Erle C. Kenton. Picture is a sprightly dualer.

Idea of having a reporter solve a suicide of 15 years ago when it's topped as an actual murder is not exactly new. Nor is the tieup with a pending election with one of the candidates involved in the murder case. But Geraghty's original follows few of the familiar lines and the Edward Dein-Jerry Warner scripting is crisp enough to fit a longer vehicle. In fact, much of the dialog and situations measure up to the "A" mark.

Unlike so many Sherlock-spook chillers having animals in the plot, the black cat in this plays a vital role in solving the mystery. The number of people bumped off before reporter Brady unravels the mess is astounding. Actual killer is skillfully concealed until the climactic fight and revelation of the missing $200,000.

Picture is virtually a screentest for Fred Brady, as the reporter, and this personable young actor turns it into a starring vehicle for himself. He'll be heard from in the future. Noah Beery, Jr., as the photog assigned to the case, cashes in on his humorous role and proves excellent foil for Brady.

Jonathan Hale is excellent as the political candidate on whom the newspaper is trying to pin the murder rap. Lois Collier is better than usual as his daughter, in love with the reporter. Iris Clive makes the mystery girl, a bit role, stand out. Paul Kelly, Douglas Dumbrille, Rose Hobart and Vera Lewis head the stout support.

George Robinson contributes a skillful cameraing job, while Russell Schoengarth's editing is well above par. *Wear.*

Night in Paradise
(COLOR)

Hollywood, April 6

Universal release of Walter Wanger production (Alexander Golitzen, associate producer). Stars Merle Oberon, Turhan Bey; features Thomas Gomez, Gale Sondergaard, Ray Collins, Ernest Truex, George Dolenz, Jerome Cowan. Directed by Arthur Lubin. Screenplay, Ernest Pascal; adaptation, Emmet Lavery; from novel "Peacock's Feather," by George S. Hellman; camera (Technicolor) Hal Mohr and W. Howard Greene; special photography, John P. Fulton; musical score and direction, Frank Skinner; editor, Milton Carruth; title song, Jack Brooks and Frank Skinner. Previewed April 5, '46. Running time, 84 mins.

Dalarai..Merle Oberon
Aesop..Turhan Bey
Croesus..Thomas Gomez
Attossa..Gale Sondergaard
Leonides.......................................Ray Collins
Frigid Ambassador..............................George Dolenz
Archon...John Litel
Scribe...Ernest Truex
Scribe...Jerome Cowan
High Priest....................................Douglass Dumbrille
Cleomenes......................................Paul Cavanaugh
Scribe...Marvin Miller
High Priest....................................Moroni Olsen
Lieutenant.....................................Richard Bailey
Salabaar.......................................Wee Willie Davis
Marigold.......................................Roseanne Murray
Priest...Hans Herbert
Palace Maiden..................................Ruth Valmy
Palace Maiden..................................Karen X. Gaylord
Palace Maiden..................................Kathleen O'Malley
Palace Maiden..................................Karen Randle
Palace Maiden..................................Kerry Vaughn
Palace Maiden..................................Daun Kennedy
Palace Maiden..................................Julie London
Townswoman.....................................Eula Morgan
Townsman.......................................Art Miles
Townsman.......................................Al Choals
Palace Maiden..................................Patricia Alphin
Singing Specialty..............................Juli Lynne
Delarai Messenger..............................James Hutton
Palace Maiden..................................Barbara Bates
Iris...Jean Trent
Lotus..Poni Adams

This film fable out-Aesop's Aesop, and in doing so offers plenty for customer amusement. It's a tinter fantasy of love and adventure in the court of King Croesus. The richness of the Croesus court gives excuse for lush production trappings and Walter Wanger's guidance makes the most of the background in splendor and settings, costumes, etc. It's all designed to fill the eye with color and entertain, and registers on both counts. Marquee values are good to stimulate initial sales.

Direction by Arthur Lubin guides the players through the plot at a good pace, manages a number of sharp suspense sequences and lends an overall effect that will hold attention. Picture is best when treating itself seriously, but moments when modern dialog slang and tongue-in-cheek action creep in are good for chuckles. The Ernest Pascal script occasionally gets on a soapbox to propagandize that big countries shouldn't pick on small neighbors, but otherwise adheres strictly to furthering commercial entertainment aims. Emmet Lavery adapted from the George S. Hellman novel, "Peacock Feathers."

Merle Oberon plays Princess Delarai, who aims to marry King Croesus for his gold. The golddigger romance is all set until Turhan Bey, as Aesop, appears on the scene. Bey had long ago learned that the world won't listen to wisdom from a youth so runs around disguised as an old, crippled man. Plot development concerns Aesop's efforts to win the princess and keep Croesus amused and his neck intact. He wins the girl, saves his small country of Samos from destruction and the couple live happily ever after, all in the best airy tale manner.

Miss Oberon and Bey are an effective team romantically. Costumes of the femme lead are eye-filling, capably filled by Miss Oberon. Love scenes between the two are done with a realistic warmth that adds to appeal. Bey is properly dashing as the fable-teller, appearing to advantage in the clinches and as bearded wise man. Thomas Gomez shows up excellently as the rich, miserly and slightly mad Croesus. Gale Sondergaard, the sorceress Attossa who also wants to marry Croesus, has only one scene with others in the cast, making the rest of her appearances in trick photography as she seeks vengeance on Croesus. Ray Collins, rascally chamberlain; George Dolenz, John Litel, Ernest Truex, Jerome Cowan and others expertly aid the development.

Color lensing by Hal Mohr and W. Howard Greene takes full advantage of gorgeous mounting. Trick camera work by John P. Fulton adds to the interest. Editing keeps film to a tight 84 minutes. Music score by Frank Skinner is an effective part of the background. *Brog.*

Joe Palooka, Champ

Monogram release of Hal E. Chester production. Features Leon Errol, Elyse Knox, Joe Kirkwood, Jr., Eduardo Ciannelli. Directed by Reginald Le Borg. Screenplay, George Moskov and Albert De Pina; original, Hal E. Chester, based on Ham Fisher cartoon strip; camera, Ken Kline. At Victoria, N.Y., April 15, '46. Running time, 72 mins.

Knobby Walsh	Leon Errol
Anne	Elyse Knox
Joe Palooka	Joe Kirkwood, Jr.
Florini	Eduardo Ciannelli
Lefty	Joe Sawyer
Eugene	Elisha Cook, Jr.
Smoky	Sam McDaniel
Brewster	Robert Kent
Mom Palooka	Sarah Padden
Pop Palooka	Michael Mark
Al Costa	Lou Nova
Curly	Russ Vincent
Aladar	Alexander Laszlo
Mrs. Oberlander	Carole Dunne
Mrs. Van Praag	Carlos Hughes
Mrs. Stafford	Betty Blythe
Freddie Wells	Phil Van Zandt
Referee	Jimmy McLarnin

Monogram's "Joe Palooka, Champ" will draw Ham Fisher's comic-strip fans, while the many boxing-ring shots will attract fisticuff followers. Pic will do all right for itself in modest quarters.

Fight fans, though, may feel a little cheated at the come-on gimmick of Joe Louis, Manuel Ortiz, Ceferino Garcia, Henry Armstrong and other ring greats being advertised on the billboards, while being shown only fleetingly in passing on the screen.

Average public will find pic just another ring romance of the young unknown discovered by a promoter, developed into a contender, and successfully battling for the championship despite connivings of gangsters. The society gal who falls for the fighter and is his inspiration will also have a familiar ring (no pun intended).

Pic is modestly budgeted. Dialog and direction are routine but okay, while camera work, especially in ring shots, is good. Vet comic Leon Errol has an appealing role as Knobby, gruff, sentimental promoter and Palooka's manager. Joe Kirkwood, Jr., passably fills the bill of the handsome, earnest young fighter, and Elyse Knox is decorative as the girl-friend. Eduardo Ciannelli is sufficiently menacing as the gangster chief. Prizefighters Lou Nova, as the champ, and Jimmy McLarnin, as a referee, add some color in bit parts. *Bron.*

She-Wolf of London

Universal release of Ben Pivar production. Features Don Porter, June Lockhart, Sara Haden, Jan Wiley. Directed by Jean Yarbrough. Screenplay, George Bricker, based on original by Dwight V. Babcock' camera, Maury Grestman; editor, Paul Landres. At Rialto, N.Y., week April 5, '46. Running time, 61 mins.

Harry	Don Porter
Phyllis Allenby	June Lockhart
Martha Winthrop	Sara Haden
Carol	Jan Wiley
Inspector Pierce	Dennis Hoey
Latham	Lloyd Corrigan
Hannah	Eily Malyou
Dwight Severn	Martin Kosleck
Constable	Frederic Worlock
Mrs. McBroom	Clara Blandick

"She-Wolf of London" is a minor meller that misses because it never quite makes up its mind whether it's to be a straight whodunit or a horror film. Fence-sitting attitude cuts deeply into whatever suspense it might have had. Scarcity of name talent in the cast will make for a lack-lustre marquee, grooving the film for the dualers.

Dwight V. Babcock, who wrote the original story, attempted to inject a hint of the supernatural by basing his story on a "wolf spirit" curse plaguing an aristocratic London family. Idea is glossed over by scripter George Bricker after its initial introduction, however, and the picture winds up as a guessing game for the audience to figure out who's been committing all the were-wolf murders. Babcock has thrown too many clues into the story to give the audience much trouble.

Young girl, last remaining descendant of the ill-fated family, believes the curse has fallen on her when a series of murders by a wolf-like creature are committed in the vicinity of her home. Obsessed with the idea she's committed the murders under the spell of the curse, she breaks her engagement to a lawyer. Events move slowly to a tepid climax when she gives herself up to the police who then reveal the real killer.

June Lockhart, daughter of actors Gene and Kathleen, is appealing and sympathetic as the heroine but her constant underplaying of the horror motif helps negate the film's attempt to be a shocker. Don Porter, as the lawyer who helps unmask the killer to win the gal, is a little too foppish to win favor as the hero. Sara Haden is outstanding as the girl's aunt and Jan Wiley turns in a nice performance as the cousin. Eily Halyon shines in a bit role as the maid of the family.

Producer Ben Pivar furnished the film with rich mountings of London at the turn of the century. Jean Yarbrough's direction, although spotty, helps keep the film going at as rapid a pace as the loosely-woven script will allow. Maury Gerstman aids the film's mood with some lurid camera shots of the murders in a London fog. *Stal.*

Home On the Range

(SONGS; COLOR)

Republic release of Louis Gray production. Stars Monte Hale, Adrian Booth. Directed by Robert Springsteen. Screenplay, Betty Burbridge; story Betty Burbridge and Bernard McConville' camera, (Magnacolor), Marcel LePicard; editor, Charles Craft; musical director, Morton Scott; songs, Gordon Forster, Ken Carson, Glen Spencer. Tradeshown N.Y., April 4, '46. Running time, 55 mins.

Monte Hale	Monte Hale
Bonnie Garth	Adrian Booth
Grizzly Garth	Tom Chatterton
Cub Garth	Bobby Blake
Dan Long	LeRoy Mason
Clint Baker	Roy Barcroft
Slim Wallace	Kenne Duncan
Sheriff Cutler	Budd Buster
Benson	Jack Kirk
Statesman	John Hamilton

Bob Nolan and Sons of Pioneers

This oatuner, embellished with color photography and endowed with a message on wild life preservation, makes acceptable nabe fare although story registers negatively.

Monte Hale, in his first mustanger, carries himself well with a substantial set of pipes, and looks convincing in the muscle and gunplay stuff. He warbles material in standard style as do Bob Nolan and the Sons of Pioneers who are conspicuously costumed and part of acting cast.

Interspersed with fist fights and gun battles, the yarn deals with plans for the preservation of wild life on a zoned ranch. With Hale at the helm, LeRoy Mason is the heavy coveting this particular ranch land, but foiled by Hale's detective work. Adrian Booth plays a hard riding femme rancher who finally sees the light and teams with Hale in the wild life cause.

Slotted songs, exclusively westerns, are solid on the sound track but suffer frequently by poor synchronization. They include "Happy-Go-Lucky Cowboy," "Down at the Old Hoe Down," "Over the Rainbow Trail," and "Take Your Time."

The Captive Heart

(BRITISH-MADE)

London, March 27.

Eagle—Lion release of Ealing Studios—Michael Balcon production. Stars Michael Redgrave. Directed by Basil Dearden. Screenplay by Angus MacPhail, Guy Morgan from story by Patrick Kirwan. Camera, Douglas Slocombe, Jack Parker. At Odeon theatre. Running time, 108 mins.

Captain Karel Hasek	Michael Redgrave
Celia Mitchell	Rachel Kempson
Mr. Mowbray	Frederick Leister
Private Evans	Mervyn Johns
Mrs. Evans	Rachel Thomas
Corporal Horsfall	Jack Warner
Mrs. Horsfall	Gladys Henson
Lieut. Lennox	Gordon Jackson
Mrs. Lenox	Elliot Mason
Com. Robert Narsden	Robert Wyndham
Major Ossy Dalrymple	Basil Redford
Captain Jim Mason	Guy Middleton
Private Matthews	Jimmy Hanley
Forster	Karl Stapenek
Lieut. Harley	Derek Bond
Caroline Harley	Jane Barrett
Elspeth McDougall	Margot Fitzsimmons
Mr. McDougall	David Keir
Beryl Curtiss	Meriel Forbes

First film to be made in occupied Germany, this combination of documentary and suspenseful drama ought to knock them cold over here. Whether Americans will like this story, showing the effect on English, Scotch and Welsh women of the imprisonment of their husbands, sweethearts and sons in German wartime compounds, is something else again. Its length and general theme makes this a doubtful entry in the U. S.

Second only to the unrelieved grim reality of life as it was lived in Stalags, the outstanding merit of "The Captive Heart" is the number of superlatively good performances turned in. To Michael Balcon as producer must go chief credit for the newsreel fidelity of the prison camp sequences. For the brilliant portrayals of diverse characters, director Basil Dearden should take the bows. Both owe a lot to exceptionally fine scripting by Angus McPhail and Guy Morgan.

Michael Redgrave, as a Czech, educated in England and fleeing from the Gestapo, takes on the identity of a dead English army officer and is jailed in a Stalag with British soldiers. He escapes lynching only to find himself marked down for a visit to a Nazi gas chamber. Even when he convinces the British of the truth of his story, and after he has won freedom through repatriation, he's up against the task of squaring himself with the wife of the dead man whose identity he has assumed. The fact that this final sequence holds one's attention says something for the writing, acting, and directing.

Mervyn Johns, Basil Radford, Jimmy Hanley and Jack Warner also deserve praise. The femme roles are necessarily bits with Rachel Kempson best as the deceived widow. *Talb.*

Song of Old Wyoming

(SONGS; COLOR)

PRC release of Robert Emmett production, directed by Emmett. Stars Eddie Dean; features Jennifer Holt, Ian Keith, Al La Rue, Sarah Padden. Original screenplay by Frances Kavanaugh; songs, Ralph Rainger, Leo Robin, Eddie Dean, Milt Mabel, Carl Hoefle; camera (Cinecolor), Marcel LePicard; editor, Hugh Winn. At New York, N.Y., dual, April 3, '46. Running time, 65 mins.

Eddie Reed	Eddie Dean
Ma Conway	Sarah Padden
Cheyenne Kid	Al La Rue
Vickey	Jennifer Holt
Uncle Ezra	Emmett Lynn
Slim	Ray Elder
Buck	John Carpenter
Landow	Ian Keith

"Song of Old Wyoming" is a run-of-the-mill western glossed over with some lukewarm Cinecolor tints. Use of color process misses the point entirely in this film since the camera fixates on the dullest elements on the set without any panning to point up the varied splendors of the natural background. Story material is played out strictly according to the oatuner's Hoyle with enough knuckle-scraping and six-shooting spaced throughout to win over the fans.

Pleasantest aspect of the pic is Eddie Dean's performance as a casual, peace-loving cowhand who, in a pinch, knows how to use his dukes or warble a song. Dean appealingly croons three standard saddle tunes with some excellent choral support.

Yarn concerns the efforts of a patriotic old lady, Sarah Padden, to drive a gang of spoilers out of Wyoming and make the territoty a part of the Union. The Cheyenne Kid, Jennifer Holt, is imported into town to rub her out but the long arm of coincidence gets a good workout and the Kid turns up to be old gal's long-lost son. Dean, cast as a ranch foreman working for Padden, heads a competent roster of performers.

Devil Bat's Daughter

Hollywood, April 3

PRC release of Frank Wisbar (Carl Pierson) production, directed by Wisbar. Features Rosemary La Planche, John Ames. Screenplay, Griffin Jay from story by Wisbar and Ernst Jaeger; camera, James S. Brown, Jr.; editor, Douglas W. Bagieri; score, Alexander Steinert. Previewed April 2, '46. Running timne, 67 mins.

Nina	Rosemary La Planche
Ted	John James
Morris	Michael Hale
Ellen	Molly Lamont
Dr. Elliot	Nolan Leary
Myra	Monica Mars
Sheriff	Ed Cassidy
Apt. House Mgr.	Eddie Kane

Patently for the duals, this horror effort comes off well in the metier for which it was designed. "Devil Bat's Daughter" is never quite as lurid as its title, is well weighted with suspense and will give the horror fans enough gasps to satisfy 'em.

There's nothing for the marquee in the manner of magnetism, but exploitatively it's open for time-tried buildups and on its merits as film fare will keep customers' eyes front.

Frank Wisbar rates a bow for his work as producer-director and partial story scribbler. Unpretentiously produced, all possibilities have been drained. Sprinting off to good start, pace is maintained and suspense tightly built most of footage save for sag midway when time-out is called so romantic angle can be inserted.

Yarn recounts trials and tribs of gal living in dark fear that her dead father, a scientist-specialist in gland-growths, was a vampire. Coming from England to upstate N. Y. village she takes her troubled dreams to psychiatrist, who is tiring of wife he married for money. Her wild dreams seem to increase under care of the mind-kneader and suddenly it seems she's murdered his wife. However, not before Cupid has brought her together with son of slain woman, who heartily hates his stepfather. Windup is achieved punchily and logically.

Rosemary La Planche, in title role, doesn't accomplish any miracles o' character-delineation, but at bottom it's a tough part. John James makes of the juve a brisk, forthright fellow who helps keep pace driving. Michael Hale's psychiatrist tops the cast; in great measure his acting lends film much of its credulity and interest. Molly Lamont is softly attractive as his wife and Nolan Leary scores as village medico. Monica Mars, as a big blonde, over-emotes.

On a lower-racket budget, embellishments are okay for the piece. James S. Brown's camera cleverly calculates the mood sought. Terse dialog keeps plot constantly in rein. Background music also helps intensify effects.

The Years Between

(BRITISH-MADE)

London, April 4.

General Film Distributors' release of Sydney Box production. Stars Michael Redgrave, Valeria Hobson, Flora Robson. Directed by Compton Bennett. Screenplay by Muriel and Sydney Box from play by Daphne du Maurier. Camera, Reginald H. Wyer, Bert Mason. At Leicester Square theatre. Running time, 100 mins.

Michael	Michael Redgrave
Diana	Valerie Hobson
Nanny	Flora Robson
Richard	James McKechnie
Sir Ernest Foster	Felix Aylmer
Jill	Dulcie Gray
Robin	John Galpin
Venning	Wylie Watson
Alice	Yvonne Owen
Postman	Edward Rigby
Effie	Esma Cannon
Mrs. May	Muriel George

The draw of Daphne du Maurier's name in the U. S. may be enough to attract the cash customers to this adaptation of the current London stage hit. Anyhow, American audiences won't be bothered (British audiences undoubtedly will be) by Michael Redgrave's running a bad third to his co-stars Valerie Hobson and Flora Robson. Because likely to go best only with sophisticated patrons in the U. S., its boxoffice chances in America may be limited by the size of such an audience.

This fault lies with scripters Muriel and Sydney Box. Almost half of the film deals with events preceding the start of the stage original, by which time all the interest centers on the love affair between Miss Hobson and James McKechnie, neighboring farmer. So Redgrave's resurrection from the grave halfway through the action is an irritating interruption to what has given promise of being a satisfying second attempt at marital happiness. How a star of Redgrave's calibre could have been persuaded to play a part as subordinate as it is unsympathetic is not explained.

Production values are considerably above average, sequences in the House of Commons being by far the most effective yet done in a studio. Compton Bennett's direction is smooth and intelligent. But it is primarily Valerie Hobson's picture, and she makes the most of her big chances.

This looks a certain click in England. *Talb.*

Miniature Reviews

"Make Mine Music" (Musical-Color) (Disney-RKO). A must-see for all Disney fans.

"A Night in Casablanca" (Songs) (Loew-UA). Marx Bros. comedy will do business.

"Do You Love Me" (Musical-Color) (20th). Maureen O'Hara, Dick Haymes and Harry James in OK musical.

"Ding Dong Williams" (Songs) (RKO). Pleasing comedy headed for okay reception in dualers.

"Strange Conquest" (U). Man-vs.-microbe theme garners fair interest.

"The Falcon's Alibi" (RKO). Nifty murder-mystery in the "Falcon" series for supporting brackets.

"Caravan" (GFD). British-made meller, with Stewart Granger starred, looks solid American entry.

"Terrors on Horseback" (PRC). Buster Crabbe western of static pattern; for lesser duals.

"Badman's Territory" (RKO). Robust western, solid for adut and juve trade.

"Without Dowry" (Artkino). Broad Russ satire on Czarist-day marriages is amusing but slow. For specialized audiences.

Make Mine Music

(MUSICAL-COLOR)

RKO release of Walt Disney production. Musical fantasy in 10 parts combines following live actors with the cartoons: Benny Goodman, Sterling Holloway, Dinah Shore, Tatiana Riabouchinska and David Lichine, Nelson Eddy, Andrews Sisters, Andy Russell, Jerry Colonna, Ken Darby's Chorus, Pied Pipers, King's Men. Production and supervision, Joe Grant; direction, Jack Kinney, Clyde Geronimi, Hamilton Luske, Bob Cormack, Josh Meador; story, Homer Brightman, Dick Kelsey, Roy Williams, Jesse Marsh, Duck Huemer, Jim Bodrero, Cap Palmer, Erwin Graham; corps of animators, effects, layout and background cartoonists; music, Chas. Wolcott; music associates, Ken Darby, Oliver Wallace, Edward Plumb; songs, Bobby Worth, Allie Wrubel, Eliot Daniel, Ray Gilbert; process effects, Ub Iwerks; sound, S. O. Slyfield. Tradeshown April 10, '46. Running time, **75 MINS.**

"Make Mine Music" is a 75-minute Walt Disney treat. You can call it a big short which, technically, is just what it is—10 items pieced together in one "musical fantasy" as it is billed—but it entertains all the way and must please. Besides, with Benny Goodman, Dinah Shore, Nelson Eddy, Andrews Sisters, Andy Russell, Jerry Colonna and others for the marquee, it won't chase 'em.

Disney's blend of cartoonic color is almost celluloid portraiture. And the blending of broad cartoon comedy with ballads and ballets, jive and opera, whimsy and whamsy, are surefire entertainment.

Pic tees off with an interesting cinematurgical treatment of "The Martins and the Coys," chirped off-screen (as is everything done by the live talent with the exception of the ballet team) by the King's Men.

"Blue Bayou," with its everglades pastels, features another vocal group, Ken Darby's Chorus (Darby is prominent throughout in much of the vocalisthenics), giving way to Benny Goodman's "All the Cats Join In." The Disney imagination runs riot in this sequence, visualizing some of the animation as he projects his bobbysox and rugcutting kiddies in a sweet-swing jazzique which gives the footage plenty of lift at this point.

"Without You," ballad done well by Andy Russell, next is contrasted by "Casey at the Bat," cleverly conceived caricature in the Currier & Ives motif, with Jerry Colonna commentating the plight of Mudville's infamous hero. The color is particularly striking in the Russell chirping of his "Ballad in Blue."

"Two Silhouettes" is the nearest thing to human suggestion as the sketched reincarnations of Tatiana Riabouchinska and David Lichine are made to do terpsichorean marvels against peripatetic backgrounds which are a feast for the eyes. Dinah Shore does the vocal to the ballet pair's pyroterps. Incidentally it's the ballet pair's screen debut, even if only in effigy.

This gives way to a clever visualization of Sergei Prokofieff's "Peter and Wolf" in rich hues with some fine new Disney characters, which should become great kiddie toys and novelties, notably Peter, Sonia the Duck, Ivan the Cat and Sasha the Bird. The Wolf himself is an austere and forbidding menace. Sterling Holloway is capital as the narrator, warmly and dramatically interpreting each musical nuance. This excerpt, incidentally, may well do as much for Russo-American amity as the UN.

Goodman's Yankee jazz is a good contrast to Prokofieff's Russian whimsy, as the maestro's licorice stick, aided and abetted by Teddy Wilson's piano, Cozy Cole's traps and Sid Weiss' string bass, engage in a jazz challenge which would delight any lammister from 52d Street. The way they kick around "After You've Gone" really sends. It's a riot of imaginative color.

One of the cutest spots is the saga of "Johnny Fedora" and "Alice Blue Bonnet," flirtation skimmers in next-door shop-windows, which are torn asunder but finally reunited on the ears of a drayhorse. Disney and his corps of animators (there are so many they're not all listed in the above already fulsome credits) have weaved a warm romance about the male and female chapeaux, which the Andrews Sisters vocally interpret in usually tiptop manner.

And the finale, "The Whale Who Wanted to Sing at the Met," is as imaginative a conceit as Disney ever essayed. Willie the Whale, fished out of the briny, runs the gamut of familiar operatic excerpts as VARIETY records "Whale Wows Met." Audiences are set on their ears as Willie (yclept Nelson Eddy, who sings all three voices, tenor, baritone and bass; and, through scientific alchemy, is made to sing a trio with himself) truly wows the musical world. Willie the Whale will crowd Sonia the Duck for popularity in the Disney stable. Shapeless as the behemoth mammal is, the Disneyites have endowed Willie with a strange sympatico.

There is so much in "Make Mine Music"—the animation, color and music, the swing versus symph, and the imagination, execution and delineation—that this Disney feature (two years in the making) may command widest attention yet. The blend of cartoon with human action has been evidenced before; here Disney has retained all his characters in their basic art form, but endowed them with human qualities, voices and treatments, which is another step forward in the field where cartoons graduate into the field of the classics. But, above all, since after all this is fundamentally a film, he has concocted a socko b.o. entertainment.

Abel.

A Night in Casablanca

(ONE SONG)

United Artists release of David L. Loew production. Stars the Marx Bros.; features Chas. Drake, Lisette Verea, Dan Seymour; Lois Collier, Sig Ruman, Lewis Russell. Directed by Archie Mayo. Original screenplay, Joseph Fields, Roland Kibbee; camera, James Van Trees; editor, Gregg C. Tallas; song by Bert Kalmar-Harry Ruby-Ted Snyder. Tradeshown N. Y., April 12, '46. Running time, **85 MINS.**

Ronald Kornblow	Groucho Marx
Rusty	Harpo Marx
Corbaccio	Chico Marx
Beatrice Reiner	Lisette Verea
Pierre	Charles Drake
Annette	Lois Collier
Capt. Brizzard	Dan Seymour
Galloux	Lewis Russell
Emil	Harro Mellor
Kurt	Frederick Gierman
Count Pfefferman	Sig Ruman

A Marx Bros. picture is ripe for public consumption, and while this isn't the best they've made it's a pretty funny farce. It's replete with Groucho's madcap antics, along with the standard panto by Harpo Marx, including latter's characteristic harp specialty and Chico's pianolog solo. It'll do satisfactory if not smash business.

Postwar Nazi intrigue in Casablanca is the theme, having to do with the handsome French flyer who is under a cloud because of Nazi skullduggery dealing with European loot cached in the Hotel Casablanca.

When three of the hotel's managers get bumped off in rapid succession, Groucho gets the nod. Chico runs the Yellow Camel Co. and Harpo is his mute pal who later breaks the bank in the hotel's casino and between stumbling on the Nazi gold through a mishap with the lift.

In characteristic manner Groucho leers at and becomes victim of Lisette Verea's Germanic charms. She's in cahoots with Sig Ruman who is periodically made hors d'combat when he loses his toupee, the Westmore being snagged by Harpo's errant vacuum cleaner. The two pseudo-waiters are also Nazi conspirators; Charles Drake is the flyer in love with Lois Collier.

Against the desert background of French provincial political bungling and Nazi chicanery the Marxes get off some effective comedy, and some of it not so. The brighter spots are the clown fencing duel; the frustrated tryst between Groucho and Miss Verea, running from suite to suite, with portable phonograph, champagne cooler, etc.; the sequence with the packing cases and clothes closet, prior to the getaway; and finally the air-autotruck chase, winding up back in the same jail from whence all escaped, but finally ending happily.

The 85 minutes don't lag and while the Marxian madcap motif of pantomimicry appears somewhat trademarked it is appealing to the fans familiar with their style and will be wholly new to the new generation.

Cast plays everything broadly, perforce subordinated to the comedy, but Miss Verea is a looker as the femme accomplice who, when learning of a doublecross, turns on the Nazi conspirators. Drake impresses as a promising juve although hasn't much opportunity. Ruman is properly Teutonic as the arrogant Count Pfefferman. The one song, Bert Kalmar-Harry Ruby-Ted Snyder's oldie, "Who's Sorry Now?", is sung in French and English in the hotel dancery scene by Miss Verea.

Abel.

Do You Love Me?

(MUSICAL-COLOR)

20th Century-Fox release of George Jessel production. Stars Maureen O'Hara, Dick Haymes, Harry James; features Reginald Gardiner, Richard Gaines, Stanley Prager, Harry James' Music Makers. Directed by Gregory Ratoff. Story, Bert Granat; adaptation, Robert Ellis and Helen Logan, with additional dialog by Dorothy Bennett; camera (Technicolor), Edward Cronjager, with special photographic effects by Fred Sersen; songs, Jimmy McHugh, Harold Adamson, Herbert Magidson, Matty Malneck, Harry James, Lionel Newman, Charles Henderson and Harry Ruby; dances, Seymour Felix; editor, Robert Simpson. Previewed New York, April 12, '46. Running time, **91 MINS.**

Katherine Hilliard	Maureen O'Hara
Jimmy Hale	Dick Haymes
Barry Clayton	Harry James
Herbert Benham	Reginald Gardiner
Ralph Wainwright	Richard Gaines

Dilly....................Stanley Prager
Taxi Driver....................B. S. Pulley
Earl Williams....................Chick Chandler
Mrs. Crackleton....................Alma Kruger
Harry James' Music Makers

A thoroughly entertaining musical. A little slow to get rolling but picking up good pace about midway, "Do You Love Me?" is another George Jessel-produced musical for 20th-Fox, his second ("Dolly Sisters" was the first), that will do well. It's not a big pic but the cast is good, the color job excellent, and there are a couple strong tunes, all of which together with a pleasing little story makes the picture quite acceptable although very lacking in the comedy.

Jessel's production and the fine backgrounds couple with the direction of Gregory Ratoff and the fine costuming to provide much for the eye; while the songs, in addition to the generally good dialog, take care of the ear. "Do You Love Me?," both the title and theme number, reprised several times, is a knockout, while "Moonlight Propaganda," done in a park setting with dance specialties accompanying, also rates strongly. Two other numbers, lesser in importance but carrying weight, are "As If I Hadn't Enough On My Mind" and "I Didn't Mean a Word I Said." Throughout the proceedings they are done at various times by both Dick Haymes and Harry James, latter, of course, with his trumpet and orchestra.

Story background is simple but holds interest. It deals with the bespectacled dean of a straight-laced school of music, engaged to an equally serious-minded official of the school, who on a trip to New York gets bitten with the swing bug and on the romantic end is tossed between Haymes and James, former winning. Various complications figure for intriguing results, although obvious comedy opportunities are lacking.

Miss O'Hara, Haymes and James make a good team. Decked out in some nifty costumes, she commands visual attention, while Haymes does very well for himself, including the songs rendered, and James, with and without his trumpet, acquits himself very creditably. In fact, James proves quite an actor. His poise can't go unnoticed, and in closeups he's particularly at ease. James' various band numbers register, but the symphonic sequence toward the end, first legit, then in swing fashion, is a bit long. A jam session earlier clicks well.

In addition to the starring trio, cast includes Reginald Gardiner, excellent as a symphonic conductor; Ralph Wainwright, music school official who suffers from unrequited love, and various lessers, including Chick Chandler as a columnist.

Originally called "Kitten on the Keys," picture was held back for remakes and emerges a winner.

Char.

Ding Dong Williams

(SONGS)

Hollywood, April 13.

RKO release of Herman Schlom production. Features Glenn Vernon, Marcy McGuire, Felix Bressart, Anne Jeffreys, James Warren, William Davidson, Bob Nolan and Sons of Pioneers, Richard Korbel. Directed by William Berke. Screenplay, Brenda Weisberg and M. Coates Webster from Collier's mag stories by Richard English; camera, Frank Redman; musical direction, C. Bakaleinikoff; orchestral arrangements, Gene Rose; songs, James McHugh and Harold Adamson, Bob Nolan. Tradeshown at Alexander, Glendale, April 9, '46. Running time, **61 MINS.**

Ding-Dong....................Glenn Vernon
Angela....................Marcy McGuire
Hugo....................Felix Bressart
Vanessa....................Anne Jeffreys
Steve....................James Warren
Saul Dana....................William Davidson
Zang....................Tom Noonan
Zing....................Cliff Nazarro
Laura Cooper....................Ruth Lee
Kenmore....................Jason Robards
Bob Nolan & Sons of the Pioneers
Richard Korbel

Pleasing comedy with music is slated for okay reception by the juvenile and family trade. Film is exceptionally mounted for budget, spots in three pop tunes and two on the longhair side, and is directed and played with enthusiasm to get the best from the comedy. Cast carries no particular weight for the marquees but performances are uniformly good and will please in general supporting bookings.

Plot is pointed to mix laughs with music. It concerns a studio music director, stuck for a film score, who signs up a hot clarinetist to do the cleffing. Licorice stick guy only takes the job because he'll get a chance to meet the lot's western star. Plot complications are created when it's discovered the musician can't read or write notes and does his tooting strictly from inspiration. Efforts to get his modern noodling down on paper and into a sound track keep the chuckles flowing. Setup is spiced with some nifty satirical lines on Hollywood and film-making, but these will have more meaning for show trade than interlands.

Glenn Vernon, as the western-loving musician, delivers neatly. Marcy McGuire gets over comedy part of the music director's secretary and Vernon's love interest. Felix Bressart, the studio maestro; William Davidson, producer; Tom Noonan and Cliff Nazarro, wacky songsmiths, and others do their part in furthering the light fun.

Musical portion introduces Richard Korbel, 11-year-old pianist, who gives excellent interpretation to the Grieg Piano Concerto and Fantasie Impromptu by Chopin. Youngster is an added entertainment value who shows up well. Miss McGuire sings "I Saw You First," and Anne Jeffreys handles vocals on "Candlelight and Wine," both tunes by James McHugh and Harold Adamson. "Cool Water," western number, is a standout as done by Bob Nolan and the Sons of the Pioneers.

Herman Schlom's production gives suitable framework, getting good results for budget. William Berke's direction is on the credit side in keeping pace fast and showing off the players in the Brenda Weisberg-M. Coates Webster script, taken from the Collier's mag stories by Richard English. Frank Redman's lensing, editing and other technical functions are topnotch.

Brog.

Strange Conquest

Columbia release of Marshall Grant production. Features Jane Wyatt, Lowell Gilmore, Peter Cookson, Julie Bishop. Directed by John Rawlins. Screenplay, Roy Chanslor; story by Lester Cole and Carl Dreher; camera, Charles Van Enger; editor, Philip Cahn. Tradeshown in N. Y., April 10, '46. Running time, **63 MINS.**

Dr. Mary Palmer....................Jane Wyatt
Dr. Paul Harris....................Lowell Gilmore
William Sommers....................Peter Cookson
Virginia Sommers....................Julie Bishop
Bert Morrow....................Milburn Stone
Dr. A. L. Graves....................Samuel S. Hinds
Molugi....................Abner Biberman

"Strange Conquest" garners a fair amount of interest in its story of man's war against tropical fever. Avoiding for most part the patent cliches of the ordinary dualer, the film makes a serious bid to satisfy adult tastes. But somewhere en route, an artificial plot device sours up the production. Cast, though it squeezes the utmost out of the script, lacks marquee heft to counterbalance the light story.

An authentically designed jungle setting is the locale for the quietly unfolding story of two scientists competing against each other to discover the serum for a deadly disease. One of the medicos, played by Peter Cookson, thinking his own experiments fumbled and those of his rival valid, offers himself as a human guinea pig to test the remedy. Cookson dies just as he learns that his own investigations were on the right track.

At this point the film does a jackknife into incredibility. The other scientist, Lowell Gilmore, for some unexplained reason, assumes the identity of Cookson in order to complete the latter's unfinished work. The masquerade leads to some awkward complications with Jane Wyatt, Gilmore's romance, and Julie Bishop, Cookson's wife. The tangle is unsnarled in a very limp windup.

In the heaviest stint, Gilmore, who closely resembles the late Leslie Howard in both looks and style, acquits himself in completely engaging manner. Cookson puts over a solid performance though he tends to be over-grim. Miss Wyatt appears only in the latter part of this hour-long film, playing with competence.

The Falcon's Alibi

(SONGS)

Hollywood, April 12

RKO release of William Berke production. Features Tom Conway, Rita Corday, Vince Barnett, Jane Greer, Elisha Cook, Jr., Emory Parnell, Al Bridge, Esther Howard. Directed by Ray McCarey. Screenplay, Paul Yawitz; story by Dane Lussier and Manny Seff; based upon characters created by Michael Arlen; camera, Frank Redman; musical director, C. Bakaleinikoff; editor, Phillip Martin, Jr. Tradeshown in Hollywood, April 9, '46. Running time, 63 mins.

Falcon....................Tom Conway
Joan....................Rita Corday
Goldie....................Vince Barnett
Lola....................Jane Greer
Nick....................Elisha Cook, Jr.
Metcalf....................Emory Parnell
Inspector Blake....................Al Bridge
Mrs. Peabody....................Esther Howard
Baroness....................Jean Brooks
Alex....................Paul Brooks
Beaumont....................Jason Robards
Bender....................Morgan Wallace
Baron....................Lucien Prival

Neatly plotted whodunit will fare well as supporting material. It figures as better than average for "The Falcon" series in all departments. William Berke's production achieves topnotch values for budget expenditure, and direction by Ray McCarey unfolds the intrigue at a brisk pace. Cast, headed by Tom Conway, is capable.

Script by Paul Yawitz gives good lines and characters to the standard situations. Conway does an interesting job of his Falcon interpretation. He and his handyman, Vince Barnett, are called on to aid a fair damsel in distress, who fears she might be blamed for some missing jewelry. Three murders and added thefts carry along the suspense elements before the Falcon uncovers the crook, a radio disc jockey who uses a canned version of his air spiel to alibi him while he does his dirty work. Racetrack and hotel background add to production dress. Locale in the story, by Dane Tussier and Manny Seff, is Los Angeles.

Barnett is capable on the comedy end. Rita Corday does okay in the somewhat colorless role of the girl in distress. Femme honors go to Jane Greer, nitery canary and one of the victims. Miss Greer wraps up two pop songs in fine style and registers strongly on acting end in dramatic scenes with Elisha Cook, Jr. Latter, as the disc jockey, gives a corking display of thesp talents, making the role a standout among the smooth cast performers. Emory Parnell, Al Bridge, Esther Howard, Paul Brooks and others show up well.

Lensing by Frank Redman aids the sight values furnished by production. Editing is concise to speed unfoldment.

Brog.

Caravan

(BRITISH-MADE)

London, April 11.

General Film Distributors' release of Gainsborough production. Stars Stewart Granger, Jean Kent, Anne Crawford, Dennis Price. Directed by Arthur Crabtree. Screenplay by Roland Pertwee from novel by Lady Eleanor Smith. Camera, Stephen Dade. At Leicester Square theatre. Running time, **122 MINS.**

Richard....................Stewart Granger
Oriana....................Anne Crawford
Rosal....................Jean Kent
Francis....................Dennis Price
Wycroft....................Robert Helpmann
Don Carlos....................Gerard Hinze
Suiza....................Arthur Goullet
Diego....................John Salew
Manoel....................Julian Somers
Juan....................Peter Murray
Jose....................Josef Ramart
Tweeny....................Merle Tottenham
Camperdene....................David Horne
Marie....................Sylvie St. Clair
Betty....................Patricia Laffan
Bandit....................Joseph O'Donohue

Another sure sockeroo for Gainsborough, this picture should come close to duplicating the record business done by "The Wicked Lady." If this is held back until "Caesar and Cleopatra" opens in the U. S. (in that, Stewart Granger is billed next to Claude Rains and Vivien Leigh), audiences which may like him in the Shaw opus will be pleased with his work in this film. Looks solid for U. S. market.

Whatever merits Lady Eleanor Smith's novel may have had, the screen adaptation of "Caravan" suggests a Horatio Alger scripting since one melodramatic situation is piled on another. But strong direction, brilliant individual performances and production values far above the usual run of British films are enough to offset this type of plot.

As a penniless writer in love with the squire's very English daughter, Granger has a role made to order for him, especially when the locale shifts to Spain. There circumstances legitimize his displaying his bare chest in love scenes with Jean Kent, a gypsy dancer who vamps him with a degree of ardor amazing to find in an English femme. Anne Crawford, as the unemotional lady of the manor, has a tough task in her scenes with the sinuous gypsy, but she holds her own in the duel for Granger's permanent affections.

Dennis Price, as a titled skunk, has his villainies aided and abetted by Robert Helpmann. Latter's portrayal of a cringing coward bent on murder is a vivid characterization. The British screen has seldom offered in one picture anything more effective than the work of these five principals.

This production augurs well for the J. Arthur Rank organization. It looks to gross twice its production cost in Britain alone.

Talb.

Terrors on Horseback

PRC release of Sigmund Neufeld production. Stars Buster Crabbe; features Al (Fuzzy) St. John. Directed by Sam Newfield. Story and screenplay, George Milton; camera, Jack Greenhalgh; editor, Holbrook N. Todd. Previewed New York, April 12, '46. Running time, **55 MINS.**

Billy Carson....................Buster Crabbe
Fuzzy....................Al (Fuzzy) St. John
Roxie....................Patti McCarty
Grant Barlow....................I. Stanford Jolley
Wagner....................Kermit Maynard
Doc Jones....................Henry Hall
Ed Sperling....................Karl Hackett
Mrs. Bartlett....................Marin Sais
Sheriff Bartlett....................Bud Buster
Jim Austin....................Steve Darrell
Cliff Adams....................Steve Clark

"Terrors on Horseback" is a modest-budgeter that's little more than a run-of-the-mine galloper which again teams Buster Crabbe and Al (Fuzzy) St. John as the stalwarts who bring the dastards of the cow-country to justice.

This time the team clear up a stagecoach robbery in which all riders were massacred by the gunmen. After some nifty galloping and plenty fisticuffs between Crabbe and the bad men, the last of the bandits, who has polished off his partners, gives up and is delivered to the sheriff in the nick.

Unusual slant to this one is absence of love interest and only two femmes in cast—Marian Sais, as sheriff's wife, and Patti McCarty, as gambling hall siren, at whom nobody makes passes.

Crabbe turns in his usual neat

performance but St. John, usually pitched for comedy roles in these mustangers, doesn't have the laugh material in this one. Story is so-so. Sam Newfield directs at required racy pace. Cameraing of Jack Greenhalgh is up to par, particularly in some of the chase shots.　　Edba.

Badman's Territory

Hollywood, April 13.

RKO release of Nat Holt production. Stars Randolph Scott, Ann Richards, George "Gabby" Hayes; features Ray Collins, James Warren, Morgan Conway, Virginia Sale, John Halloran, Andrew Tombes. Directed by Tim Whelan. Original screenplay, Jack Natteford and Luci Ward; additional sequences, Clarence Upson Young and Bess Taffel; camera, Robert de Grasse; editor, Philip Martin, Jr.; music, Roy Webb. Tradeshown at RKO Hillstreet, Los Angeles, April 11, '46. Running time, 97 MINS.

Mark Rowley..............Randolph Scott
Henryette Alcott............Ann Richards
Coyote............George "Gabby" Hayes
Colonel Farewell...............Ray Collins
John Rowley.................James Warren
Bill Hampton.............Morgan Conway
Meg..........................Virginia Sale
Hank McGee.................John Halloran
Doc Grant................Andrew Tombes
Ben Wade...................Richard Hale
Hodge.......................Harry Holman
Chief Tahlequah.......Chief Thundercloud
Jesse James.............Lawrence Tierney
Frank James..................Tom Tyler
Bob Dalton.................Steve Brodie
Grad Dalton..................Phil Warren
Bill Dalton.................William Moss
Sam Bass...................Nestor Paiva
Belle Starr.................Isabel Jewell

Western feature with plenty to entertain the adult trade. Solid action is backed up with strong production, direction and dialog to give a lift to the standard hoss opry plot. Cast names offer sturdy marquee lures to attract busines*, and payoff should be handsome.

Expansion of the western plot into feature length has been capably handled in the original script by Jack Natteford and Luci Ward, with additional sequences by Clarence Upson Young and Bess Taffel.

Locale of yarn is a strip of land near Oklahoma, not yet taken into the Union, which is used as a hangout for the west's early-day bad men. Likeable villains that roam through the plot include such shoot-'em-up characters as the James Boys, the Daltons, Sam Bass and Belle Starr. Script doesn't try to whitewash the baddies and makes use of them in furthering story about a Texas sheriff who rides into Badman's Territory to find his younger brother. He also finds romance, with an attractive femme editor of the town's gazette, and plenty of heroics to keep him busy. Action reverts to formula on a couple of occasions when the principals seem to waste lead, but otherwise does a fast ride in keeping with its feature classification.

Randolph Scott makes a sturdy outdoor hero as the sheriff who meets with traditional western baddies in friendly truce in the territory. It's one of his better performances in a role tailored to his measure. Ann Richards is the comely editor trying to bring law and order to the town of Quinto, and gives a perfect account of herself. George "Gabby" Hayes is up to his usual trick of grabbing every scene in which he appears as the bearded pal of outlaws and sheriff. Despite presence of so many bad men, real villain of piece is Morgan Conway as political-minded U. S. marshal who stirs up continual trouble.

Ray Collins, Virginia Sale, Andrew Tombes, James Warren, Harry Holman and Chief Thundercloud are among others giving expert depictions of western characters. Steve Brodie makes comparatively small spot as Bob Dalton register big. Lawrence Tierney as Jesse James. Nestor Paiva as Sam Bass, and Isabel Jewell as Belle Starr also are effective, particularly Miss Jewell.

Robert de Grasse's camera makes the most of the action, and music by Roy Webb helps to sustain interest. Editing and other credits measure up to overall topnotch standard.　　Brog.

Without Dowry
(RUSSIAN-MADE)

Artkino release of Soviet Film Agency production. Direction and script by Yuri Protozanov; based on play by Alexander Ostrovsky. Music, P. I. Tchaikovsky; Russ folksongs arranged by David Blok; camera, Mark Magidson; English titles, Tom Jay Bell. At Stanley, N. Y., April 15, '46. Running time, 90 MINS.

Ogudolova....................Olga Pyshova
Larisa......................Nina Alisova
Paratov....................Alexei Ktorov
Robinson....................Vassili Popov
Knurov.....................Misha Klimov
Vozhevatov..................Boris Tenin
Karandishev................Victor Balikhin
Yefrosinia...............Valentina Pyzhova

(In Russian; English Titles)

Broad satire on corrupt social customs of middle-class Czarist Russians is interesting but slow-moving. Pic will attract specialized groups, but has no general audience appeal.

Foibles of bourgeois Russians are depicted amusingly, with pic containing many of the rich character types so prevalent in Russ films. Russ predilection for self-pity, and habit of tearing one's heart to tatters openly all over the place, are held up to proper scorn. Incidents, however, are somewhat episodic and therefore a little confusing. Pic is marred, too, by frequent bad lighting, to spoil some of the unusual shots.

Pic mocks at the dowry system of marrying off a daughter, specifically telling the tragedy of a girl whom a wealthy shipowner jilts and whom a mother betroths to a vain, impoverished government clerk. Such scenes as the wedding dinner, a picnic by the Volga, and moments on board ship as when a couple of drunks play at bowling with melons and wine-bottles, are standouts.

Film has nice atmospheric shots of the Volga, and many unusual angle shots as well. Some of the portrayals are fine—Olga Pyshova as the mother; Vassili Popov as a drunk; Victor Balikhin as the clerk, and Valentina Pyzhova as his aunt. Nina Alisova and Alexei Ktorov, as the romantic leads, have a tendency to posture and overact.

Russ folk songs, and passages from Tchaikovsky's "Pathetique" lend attractive musical background. English subtitles are simple and to the point, but imprint of them on white backgrounds frequently makes them indistinct.　　Bron.

Foreign Films

"Le Capitan" (FRENCH). Cine-Selection release of C.C.F.C.-Thery production; directed by Robert Vernay; stars Aime Clarion, Jean Paqui, Huguette Duflos, Lise Delamare, Pierre Renoir, Jean Tissier; features Alexandre Rignault, Thommy Bourdelle, Claude Genia, Sophie Desmarets, Maurice Esconde, Robert Manuel, Lucas Gridoux, Gabrielle Robine, Georges Marny, Lurville Serge Emrich, Francoise Moor, Pierre Magnier, Sylvette Sauge; camera, Artenise; screenplay, Robert Zimmer, Robert Vernay based on novel by Michel Zevaco; reviewed in Paris. Running time, 200 MINS.

A highly budgeted costume film which was originally meant to be released as a two-part serial, each running 100 minutes. Swashbuckling in character, the story takes place in 1600 and shows Jean Paqui as the nobleman who foils a plot against King Louis XIII. Lengthiness seriously hurts the film in spite of fair performances. With production values far below Hollywood standards, film is an unlikely bet for America except for exclusive French patronage.

"Roger La Honte" (FRENCH). Gray Film release of A. d'Aguire production; directed by Andre Cyatte; stars Lucien Coedel, Maria Cazares, Paul Bernard; features Jose Conrad, Louis Salou, Jean Tissier, Rene Devilliers, Gabriello, Jean Debucourt, Rellys, Paulette Dubost, Leonce Corne, Charles Lemonthier, Valther; based on a period novel by Jules Mary; camera, A. Thirard; reviewed in Paris. Running time, 100 MINS.

Above par casting and photography make this period film adequate for local consumption. It is the first part of a two-part serial, second half not being finished. Story deals with an industrialist of the early 1900s, who's sent to jail after being convicted of a killing which he did not commit. Lucien Goedel and Jean Tissier are cast standouts. Slow pace plus serial treatment gives film little chance in the U. S.

"L'Espione" (FRENCH). C.F.D.F. production and release; directed by Maurice de Canonge; stars Jany Holt, Pierre Renoir, Jean Davy; features Roger Karl, Jean Yonnel, Raymond Cordy, Fernande Fabre; screenplay, Simon Gantillon; reviewed in Paris. Running time, 105 MINS.

First of two stanzas in a serial extolling the work of the French intelligence service during the war which goes well with patriotic audiences here but is not likely for America because of uninspired direction and story material. Pierre Renoir plays the intelligence chief involved in a series of unconvincing adventures.

"120 Rue De La Gare" (FRENCH). Sirius release of Lucien Masson production; direction and screenplay by J. Daniel Norman; stars Jean Davy, Sophie Desmarets; based on a novel by Leo Malet; camera, Henry Triquet; reviewed in Paris. Running time, 95 MINS.

Poorly-made detective meller employing slapstick which is good only for nabe houses in France. Not a chance in the U. S.

"La Tentation de Barbizon" (FRENCH). Consortium du Film release of Consortium de Production picture; directed by Jean Stelli; stars Simone Renan, Francoise Perier, Larquey; features Daniel Genin, Juliette Faber, Myno Burney; screenplay, Andre Paul Antoine; dialog, Marc Gilbert Sauvageon; reviewed in Paris. Running time, 105 MINS.

Although poor in production and direction, this film hints potentially good comedy story material. Flavor is lost, however, in inadequate treatment here, giving it little chance excepting locally. U. S. producers might remake it into something. Done in phantasy, story deals with a young couple honeymooning. Daniel Gelin and Juliette Faber play the couple. They are thrown into a series of intrigues by the reincarnations of an angel and a devil. Cast suffers from poor direction.

"Fils De France" (FRENCH). Vog release of Sigma production; directed by Pierre Blondy. Stars Jean Mercanton, Jimmy Gaillard, Ginette Baudin; features Emile Genevois, Jean Daurand, Gaven, Jacques Famery, Florencie; screenplay, Pierre Lestdinguez; camera, Andre Germain. March 26. Running time, 90 MINS.

A quickie using considerable footage from French army newsreels to show the life of a tank crew. Story is built around the French army advance on the Rhine. Negative in technique and interest, appeal is strictly limited to patriotic audiences in France.

"Monsu' Travet" (ITALIAN). Lux Pan production and release; directed by Mario Soldati; stars Carlo Campanini, Vera Carmi, Gino Cervi; features Luigi Pavese, Paola Veneroni, Laura Gore, Alberto Sordi; from the play by Vittorio Bersezio; running time, 95 MINS.

This film was chosen to represent the Italian industry at Milan International Film Festival. It looks a good choice. Monsu' Travet, a minor employee of Royal Italian Government in the 80's, is still alive today. His domestic life, his struggles in office, have been and still are shared by millions in Italy, and this is the picture's main appeal. Plot is not worth mentioning because nothing more than scenes from the daily life of a bureaucrat. Several good performances help. It's chances in America are dubious except in Italian-language theatres.

Miniature Reviews

"Henry V" (UA) (Color). Technically excellent, but will require extra-special handling to get biz.

"Her Kind of Man" (Songs) (WB). Sturdy meller of Prohibition era.

"Heartbeat" (One Song) (RKO). Light comedy, with misleading title, has the Ginger Rogers name to help draw.

"Bedlam" (RKO). Boris Karloff in superior horror-film with historical background.

"The Truth About Murder" (RKO). Mild melodramatic programmer.

"Partners in Time" (RKO). Corn-fed Lum & Abner opus; for the sticks.

"Gaiety George" (Musical) (WB). British-made musical has small chance for big U.S. biz.

"Blondie's Lucky Day" (Col). Up to standard Dagwood and Blondie comedy for dualers.

Henry V

(Color)
(BRITISH-MADE)

United Artists release of Two Cities (Laurence Olivier-Dallas Bower) production, directed by and starring Olivier; features Robert Newton, Esmond Knight, Leslie Banks, Felix Aylmer, Renee Asherson, Leo Genn. Screen adaptation by Olivier, Alan Dent and Reginald Beck from the play by William Shakespeare; camera (Technicolor), Robert Krasker and Jack Hildyard; score, William Walton, conducted by Muir Mathieson and played by London Symphony Orchestra; text editor, Dent; film editor, Beck; art, Paul Sheriff; costumes, Roger Furse. Previewed N. Y., April 17, '46. Running time, 127 MINS.

King Henry V..........Laurence Olivier
Ancient Pistol..........Robert Newton
Chorus..........Leslie Banks
Princess Katharine..........Renee Asherson
Fluellen..........Esmond Knight
Constable of France..........Leo Genn
Archbishop of Canterbury..........Felix Aylmer
Mountjoy..........Ralph Truman
King Charles VI..........Harcourt Williams
Alice..........Ivy St. Helier
French Ambassador..........Ernest Thesiger
The Dauphin..........Max Adrian
Duke of Orleans..........Frances Lister
Duke of Burgundy..........Valentine Dyall
Duke of Bourbon..........Russell Thorndike
Capt. Gower..........Michael Shepley
Sir Thomas Erpingham..........Morland Graham
Court Soldier..........Brian Nissen
Earl of Westmoreland..........Gerald Case
Queen Isabel of France..........Janet Burnell
Duke of Exeter..........Nicholas Hannen
Bishop of Ely..........Robert Helpmann
Mistress Quickly..........Freda Jackson
Williams..........Jimmy Hanley
Capt. Jamie..........John Laurie
Capt. MacMorris..........Niall MacGinnis
Sir John Falstaff..........George Robey
Lieut. Bardolph..........Roy Emerton
Earl of Salisbury..........Griffith Jones
Bates..........Arthur Hambling
Corporal Nym..........Frederick Cooper
Duke of Gloucester..........Michael Warre
Governor of Harfleur..........Frank Tickle
Boy..........George Cole
English Herald..........Vernon Greeves
French Messenger..........Jonathan Field
A Priest..........Ernest Hare

As prexy Ed Raftery exclaimed during the initial screening of "Henry V" for United Artists execs: "Boy, can you imagine this in Chillicothe!" The answer is definitely "No." You can't imagine it. Not at Warner's Sherman theatre in Cillicothe, anyway. On the other hand, in the proper setting in a nearby big city, exhibition of the British-made "Henry V" seems perfectly plausible.

Which means that UA has hit the formula precisely for most successful possible merchandising in this country of Laurence Olivier's striking Technicolor filmization of the Shakespearean drama. UA's intention, which it has already put into practice in Boston, is to two-a-day the picture in small houses, preferably legiters, and make a determined pitch for the school and longhaired trade to whom a fine, artistic interpretation of the Bard is a really meaningful event.

Distributing company is treating the film as a stage play, even to the extent of tieing up with the Theatre Guild for merchandising via its subscription lists in some 20 cities. Openings are being widely spaced to allow the huzzahs which the film is getting in the academic trade to seep around the country. UA has only five prints and intends to make no more, although it is talking of a gross in excess of $1,000,000. That'll take time, of course, lots of time. But, on the merits of the picture for the special audience to which it appeals, it is by no means impossible with the nursing UA is giving it.

Erudite critics have testified, since the pic preemed in London in 1944, to the integrity and great artistry of the film. So there's little need to further gumbeat on that point. Suffice it that production cost ran to about $2,000,000 and every cent of it is evident on the screen. The color, the sets, the expanse and the imaginative quality of the filming are unexcelled.

"Henry V" as a picture, however, requires that the spectator take more with him into the theatre in the way of mental preparedness than mere curiosity. And, certainly, it is no film to be dropped in on by a casual passerby.

That Elizabethean English-time of the play is 1415 and it was first enacted in 1599—is just so much double-talk to the average audience. It has a way of going right over one's head and leaving him wondering what the devil's going on. Shakespeare's renowned verse, except in occasional instances, is just so much overrated abacadabra to the kid from Brooklyn or the average filmfan in Birmingham or Seattle. You must be thoroughly familiar with the plot and speeches before ever going near the theatre to derive much meaning from the picture.

Story is considerably simpler than the boys from Hollywood turn out. Henry's a British king, hardly more than a moppet, when, with the aid of a couple clergymen, he cons himself into believing that he ought to muscle his way into France and stake his royal claim there on the basis of ancestry. So he loads some 30,000 men and their horses on the 15th century version of LSTs and hies across the channel. He lays siege to a town named Harfleur, which apparently gives in without much pain, and it looks like Henry has his foot nicely inside the Gallic vestibule.

But Charles VI, of France, although an a.k. and a weakling, resents the intrusion and determines to toss the British out. Henry starts withdrawing his troops to Calais, only to find his way blocked by a French army that many times outnumbers his. The ensuing battle of Agincourt—with some 10,000 French killed to a mere 500 British—is the high point of the picture. Henry, of course, cops the stakes and immediately turns to wooing the French princess, Katharine. Their marriage sews up the French and British royal families.

There are many interesting scenes and one really exciting one—the battle. With thousands of horses, knights in armor and longbowmen in colorful costumes, it's a Technicolor setup. There's a bit of difficulty in telling who's who during the melee, but the blood is spilled in fulsome and satisfying fashion. Strong contrast is made between the overstuffed French warriors in armor so heavy they have to be lowered onto their horses with block and tackle, and the British, who won the battle with the atom bomb of the day, the longbow, used by men afoot and unhindered by iron pants.

Memorable for their deft humor and poignancy are both scenes in which Renee Asherson, as Princess Katharine, appears. Even Olivier is put well back into the No. 2 spot in the scene in which he woos her. And her liquancy in another sequence in which she is trying to learn English is a warming comedy bit that few films have equalled.

Unfortunately, there's not much other comedy. Humor is allegedly there and Shakespearophiles will probably get the intended laugh from it, but, like so much else, it will go right over the average audience.

Treatment is interesting and adds much to the general effect. Picture opens with the camera panning over London and coming into the Old Globe theatre. Heralds' horns announce the opening of the play as the camera gets to the stage—and the show is on. Performance for the first few minutes is held to the artificial limitations of the theatre. Full panorama is soon opened up, however, to provide a performance the scope of which Shakespeare could never even have imagined. There's a reversion, naturally, at the end to the Globe stage and its audience.

Acting, at the beginning, is in the stylized pattern of the 16th century and it doesn't get far away from that even when the camera is given full sweep after the Old Globe has been left behind. Sets throughout also give a feeling that you haven't left the theatre, for while tri-dimensional close to the camera, they fade into purposely obvious painted scenics in the background. Result of both that and the stylized acting is to give a sense of integrity to Shakespeare that is in keeping with the whole motif of the picture.

Olivier, who produced, directed and starred, will undoubtedly take on a new stature as the result of the job. In each category he rates superbly. As for the other players and technicians, same must be said for virtually all of them. Special words should go to William Walton, who composed the music, and the London Symph, which played it. It's the perfect counterpoint to the action on the screen.

UA has experimented a bit with the film in different lengths. Version being used in Boston currently and screened for tradepapers in New York is two hours and seven minutes. Except for purposes of being faithful to the Bard, it well could stand cutting. Since Shakespeare wrote his drama in scenes with virtually no integration, scissoring is an easy matter. However, with the appeal strictly to the scholar department anyway—and other filmgoers not likely to be interested if "Henry V" were trimmed to the length of a Mickey Mouse—there seems good justification for leaving it as Olivier made it. *Herb.*

Her Kind of Man

(SONGS)

Hollywood, April 20.

Warner Bros. release of Alex Gottlieb production. Stars Dane Clark, Janis Paige, Zachary Scott, Faye Emerson; features George Tobias, Howard Smith, Harry Lewis, Sheldon Leonard. Directed by Frederick de Cordova. Screenplay, Gordon Kahn and Leopold Atlas; original, Charles Hoffman and James V. Kern; camera, Carl Guthrie; editor, Dick Richards; music, Franz Waxman. Tradeshown April 16, '46. Running time, **80 MINS.**

Don Corwin..........Dane Clark
Georgia King..........Janis Paige
Steve Maddux..........Zachary Scott
Ruby Marino..........Faye Emerson
Joe Marino..........George Tobias
Bill Fellows..........Howard Smith
Candy..........Harry Lewis
Bender..........Sheldon Leonard

"Her Kind of Man" revives the old Prohibition era in a punchy melodrama. It's not a big-budgeted feature but carries plenty of weight for situations outside the key de luxers. It will be particularly forte in houses catering to meller trade. Cast has familiar if not hefty names and delivers capably. Production and direction are aimed at getting the most from the cops-and-robbers yarn. Three pop tunes of the period are spotted in for added interest.

Story is told in flashback, hitting latter part of the Roaring Twenties and carrying through to the day Roosevelt administration wiped out Prohibition. It deals with the rise and fall of a Broadway hotshot gambler and bad guy, the girl who loves him, and the man who loves her. Characters are consistent, although story is rather loosely woven, and there is sufficient amount of nostalgia about the period mixed in with the melodramatics to register with older filmgoers. Gordon Kahn and Leopold Atlas scripted from the original by Charles Hoffman and James V. Kern.

Frederick de Cordova's direction gives the story a good play for the money, ladling out suspense and punch in proper dosage to maintain interest. Cast response to guidance is excellent. Dane Clark has the sympathetic spot of a Broadway columnist in love with Janis Paige, and makes his role show up, despite the more colorful characters in the plot. Miss Paige wraps up her assignment capably, plus strong rendition of "Something to Remember You By," "Speak to Me of Love" and "Body and Soul." Zachary Scott displays another of his forthnight heel portrayals, a sharp performance that places him in danger of type casting. Faye Emerson does well by smaller part of Scott's sister and wife of George Tobias. Latter is excellent, as are Howard Smith, a detective; Harry Lewis, particularly good as a baby-faced killer; and Sheldon Lewis.

Production by Alex Gottlieb spends budget coin wisely in shaping film for good returns. It's well-mounted in all departments. Notably the low-key lensing by Carl Guthrie and music score by Franz Waxman. *Brog.*

Heartbeat

Hollywood, April 20.

RKO release of Robert and Raymond Hakim production. Stars Ginger Rogers; features Jean Pierre Aumont, Adolphe Menjou, Melville Cooper, Mikhail Rasumny, Eduardo Ciannelli, Mona Maris, Henry Stephenson, Basil Rathbone. Directed by Sam Wood. Adaptation, Morrie Ryskind; based on original screenplay by Hans Wilhelm, Max Kolpe and Michel Duran; added dialog, Roland Leigh; camera, Joseph Valentine; music, Paul Misraki; song, Misraki and Ervin Drake; editor, Roland Gross. Tradeshown April 18, '46. Running time, **100 MINS.**

Arlette..........Ginger Rogers
Pierre..........Jean Pierre Aumont
Ambassador..........Adolphe Menjou
Roland Medeville..........Melville Cooper
Yves Cadubert..........Mikhail Rasumny
Baron Dvorak..........Eduardo Ciannelli
Ambassador's Wife..........Mona Maris
Minister..........Henry Stephenson
Prof. Aristide..........Basil Rathbone

Fluffy Continental comedy with Ginger Rogers' name to spark box-office response. Title is misleading and extra selling is needed to point it up as light, escapist film fare with average gross possibilities. "Pygmalion" theme lends itself to Miss Rogers' talents and strong performances by others in the cast are on the credit side. These factors do considerable in glossing over production and story weaknesses that otherwise might militate against film's chances.

Continental flavor of Paris locale is maintained by Sam Wood's direction in unfolding story of a girl who becomes an apprentice in a pickpocket school, goes to an embassy ball and finds romance after she learns how to be a lady. Plot opens with the school conducted by Basil Rathbone and how he lures new pupils in. After preliminary schooling, Miss Rogers fluffs here first assignment, is forced by ambassador Adolphe Menjou to lift a watch from Jean Pierre Aumont at the ball. Antics up to this point are amusing if not always clear, but story hits a stock pattern afterwards as it carries Aumont and Miss Rogers through misunderstanding but without any doubt of the eventual finale clinch.

Aumont is interesting as the

young diplomat who falls for the femme purse-snatcher. New romance gets him out of a lightly established previous affair with Mona Maris, Menjou's wife. It is the character performances by others in the cast though that give a lift to proceedings. Menjou is expert. Melville Cooper as a cadgering lush is good for chuckles. Mikhail Rasumny as a pickpocket friend to Miss Rogers is delightful. Rathbone's professional performance furnishes laughs. Eduardo Ciannelli, Henry Stephenson and others do well.

Production by Robert and Raymond Hakim does not offer the top physical backing usually displayed for a star of Miss Rogers' calibre. Lensing by Joseph Valentine is not up to his usual standard. Miss Rogers sings score's one tune, "Can You Guess?" cleffed by Paul Misraki and Ervin Drake. Tighter editing is needed on a number of overlong sequences in the film, which was adapted by Morrie Ryskind from an original script by Hann Wilhelm, Max Kolpe and Michel Duran.
Brog.

Bedlam

RKO release of Jack J. Gross production. Stars Boris Karloff; features Anna Lee. Directed by Mark Robson. Screenplay, Carlos Keith and Robson; suggested by William Hogarth painting; camera, Nicholas Musuraca; editor, Lyle Boyer. At Rialto, N.Y., April 19, '46. Running time, 78 mins.

Master Sims.................Boris Karloff
Nell Rowen.................Anna Lee
Lord Mortimer.................Billy House
The Gilded Boy.................Glenn Vernon
Oliver Todd.................Jason Robards
Dorothea.................Joan Newton
Hannay.................Richard Fraser
Sidney Long.................Ian Wolfe
John Wilkes.................Leland Hodgson
Mistress Sims.................Elizabeth Russell

"Bedlam" is a horror-film in a more actual sense of the phrase than most of the tame concoctions advertised in that category. Touching on the mistreatment of the mentally sick in 18th century London, film is morbid and depressing, but fascinating as the same time. It should do business with the shocker audiences, and have a wider pull.

Pic is built around the infamous London institution, St. Mary's of Bethlehem, more widely known as "Bedlam," immortalized in Hogarth's bitter painting. Inmates, misunderstood and mistreated, were a joke and a spectacle, London citizenry paying two pennies admission to come and see them. Although RKO's picturization touches on the sociological question lamely and superficially, film succeeds in its avowed purpose—to shock.

Costumes and sets of the period seem to have been arranged with care and fidelity, so that pic has more real atmosphere than most such films. Camera minimizes real scenes of suffering, but suggests sufficient misery in those it depicts. Camera catches good shots of party scenes, frivolous nobility, degraded poor. Acting and direction are also superior to usual horror pix.

Boris Karloff plays the sadistic chief of the asylum with great finesse, his intellectual leanings and poesy adding sharper contrast to his physical brutalities with the inmates. Anna Lee, as the frivolous actress who deserts her aristocratic friends to aid the afflicted at "Bedlam," also makes hers a vivid, telling characterization.

Billy House, as a foppish Lord, and Richard Fraser, as a Quaker, are strong figures in the supporting cast.
Bron.

The Truth About Murder

Hollywood, April 13.

RKO release of Sid Rogell (Herman Schlom) production. Features Bonita Granville, Morgan Conway, Rita Corday, Don Douglas, June Clayworth, Edward Norris. Directed by Lew Landers. Original screenplay, Lawrence Kimble, Hilda Gordon, Eric Taylor; camera, Frank Redman; editor, Edward W. Williams; music, Leigh Harline. Tradeshown April 10, '46. Running time, 63 mins.

Chris Allen.................Bonita Granville
Les Ashton.................Morgan Conway
Peggy.................Rita Corday
Paul Marvin.................Don Douglas
Marsha Crane.................June Clayworth
Bill Crane.................Edward Norris
Johnny Lacka.................Gerald Mohr
Hank.................Michael St. Angel
Jonesy.................Tom Noonan

Mild little program melodrama that will have moderate success in the supporting market. It's well enough furbished in production values for the budget, but is never able to to quite overcome story confusion that prevents okay classification. Cast names are familiar, but without much marquee strength.

Plot concerns rivalry of a district attorney and his attorney girl friend in chasing down murderer of an amorous lady photographer. That's a switcheroo on the usual formula and helps somewhat, but rest of tale doesn't live up. Photog is kissing off her husband while making plenty of hay with assortment of other males until she's found dead in her studio. The husband is accused and, having been blind drunk over the kiss-off, can't establish an alibi. The d.a. believes he's guilty, but the galfriend doesn't. The two cross paths plenty before solution hits them in the face. Rivalry doesn't prevent an occasional clinch between the two principals nor the fadeout bundling.

Morgan Conway and Bonita Granville do their best with the lead spots. June Clayworth shows up well as the murder victim. Rita Corday, Don Douglas, Edward Norris, the suffering husband; Gerald Mohr and others run through standard parts in the original screenplay by Lawrence Kimble, Hilda Gordon and Eric Taylor.

Lew Landers' direction manages a number of good moments in the development, but never quite overcomes story handicaps. Herman Schlom produced for executive producer Sid Rogell. Lensing by Frank Redman, editing and other productional functions are oke.
Brog.

Partners in Time

RKO release of Jack W. Votion production (Ben Hersha, associate producer). Stars Chester Lauck, Norris Goff; features Pamela Blake, John James, Teala Loring, Danny Duncan. Directed by William Nigh. Original screenplay, Charles E. Roberts; camera, Jack Mackenzie; editor, S. Roy Luby. Tradeshown in N.Y., April 17, '46. Running time, 71 mins.

Lum.................Chester Lauck
Abner.................Norris Goff
Elizabeth.................Pamela Blake
Tim.................John James
Janet.................Teala Loring
Grandpappy Spears.................Danny Duncan
Constable Spears.................Danny Duncan
Cedric Weehunt.................Grady Sutten
Caleb Weehunt.................Grady Sutten
Squire Skimp.................Dick Elliott
Abagail.................Phyllis Kennedy
Miss Thurston.................Ruth Lee
Gerald Sharpe.................Charles Jordan
Josie.................Ruth Caldwell

This newest Lum 'n' Abner pic is strictly for the milk routes. A low-budgeted affair, it runs through the motions of a hackneyed small-town romance in the most appallingly corn-fed fashion, to hark back to the dark days of the early silent cinema. It will draw Lum-Abner radio fans in the outlands, but that's about all.

Lum 'n' Abner, after 40 years, are still running their general store in Pine Ridge, Arkansas. There is a dispute over ownership of their property. There is also a spat between two young lovers. Lum 'n' Abner set out to righten both problems, the film then taking them in flashbacks to their own youth, with a solution found in reminiscences of their yesteryears.

When the pic shows Pine Ridge in 1906, with its first gasoline buggy, the box socials, the square dance, it has a certain amount of lavender-old lace flavor. But otherwise, for 1946, it's a caricature. Tipoff to the film is such dialog as this from an attractive country maid, spoken straight: "I declare, them city folk is a caution." What radio serials are just getting around to, an adult film world dropped years ago. There ought to be a law.

Performances, all played straight, are stock in character, and the direction is routine to match. Camera work and sets are as matter-of-fact.
Bron.

Gaiety George

(BRITISH-MADE)

(Songs)

London, April 16.

Warner Bros. production and release. Stars Richard Greene, Ann Todd. Directed by George King. Screenplay by Katherine Strueby from story by Richard Fisher, Peter Creswell. Music by George Posford; lyrics by Eric Maschwitz. Camera, Otto Heller, Gus Drisse. At Palace theatre. Running time, 105 mins.

George Howard.................Richard Greene
Kathryn Davis.................Ann Todd
Carter.................Peter Graves
Morris.................Morland Graham
Elizabeth.................Hazel Court
Collier.................Charles Victor
Miss de Courteney.................Daphne Barker
Hastings.................Jack Train
Mrs. Murphy.................Marie O'Neill
Grindley.................Frank Pettingell
Lord Mountsbury.................David Horne
Lieut. Travers.................Patrick Waddington

Odious as comparisons may be, this Warner Bros. opus coincidentally previewed during the current West End run of "Ziegfeld Follies" can't escape comparison. Both films have the same central theme, glorification of a dead man as his country's greatest musical comedy producer. But whereas Hollywood makes no bones about the identity of the central character, Warner Bros., for some reason or other, have elected to call George Edwardes, in the Britain of his time a bigger name than possibly Ziegfeld was in the U. S., George Howard. It looks highly dubious as a strong entry in the U. S.

The real Georges Edwardes and the Gaiety theatre were as tightly linked as ham and eggs, even if he was never dubbed "Gaiety George." His chorus girls married titles by the gross. In "Gaiety George" peers storm the stage door and beg the pseudo chorines to be measured for coronets. Edwardes acquired a racing stable; the film impresario contents himself with buying one horse. The death of the real George Edwardes was accelerated by years of internment in a German concentration camp in the first World War; same thing happens to the film's hero. Where the film departs woefully from reality is in the dozen or more very sad stage sequences.

When "Gaiety George" concerns itself with the life drama of Edwardes, it is brilliant. But the moment the camera shifts to stage ensembles, many too long drawn out and terrible to talk about, this effort goes haywire.

Ruthless slashing of the stage sequences in "Gaiety George" would improve this British offering to a great extent. After such cutting there would still be left an hour of effective drama, skillfully portrayed.

Richard Greene, in the title role, shows the value of his Hollywood training. As his loyal wife, Ann Todd, is superb despite just about the toughest introduction a femme star ever had to live down as a cheap music hall soubrette of the 90's. It's a corny routine. Dazzling cameos, in supporting parts, are the performances of Peter Graves as a columnist, Ursula Jeans in the Edwardian London equivalent of Lillian Russell's heyday, and Morland Graham as an English Abe Erlanger.

George King's production and direction, so far as the off-stage sequences are concerned, are adequate. But the same can't be said for Freddie Carpenter and Leontine Sagan, who are responsible for the stage sequences.

Reverence and love of tradition being deeply ingrained in the British, "Gaiety George" will undoubtedly appeal to those who are left of the hansom cab era. Otherwise its chances, even on this side, are not so hot.
Talb.

Blondie's Lucky Day

Columbia production and release. Stars Penny Singleton, Arthur Lake, Larry Simms; features Marjorie Kent, Robert Stanton, Angelyn Orr, Jonathan Hale. Directed by Abby Berlin. Original screenplay, Connie Lee; based on comic strip created by Chic Young; camera, L. W. O'Connell; editor, Aaron Stell. At Fox, Brooklyn, N. Y., dual, week April 18, '46. Running time, **69 MINS.**

Blondie.................Penny Singleton
Dagwood.................Arthur Lake
Alexander.................Larry Simms
Cookie.................Marjorie Kent
Jonathan Butler, Jr.................Robert Stanton
Mary Jane McDermott.................Angelyn Orr
J. C. Dithers.................Jonathan Hale
Jonathan Butler, Sr.................Paul Harvey
Ollie.................Jack Rice
Tommy Cooper.................Bobby Larson
Mayor Denby.................Charles Arnt
Mary.................Margie Liszt
Salesman.................Frank Orth
Postman.................Frank Jenks
Daisy.................Herself

Despite use of all the worn comedy gimmicks drawn from the Chick Young strip, as in others of the series, "Blondie's Lucky Day" stands up as good entertainment for any dual bill. Variegated little in the duped and reduped sequences, the film, concentrated on the disarmingly absurd technique, is grooved in the proven pattern that satisfies. Cast, practically institutionalized and dominated by Penny Singleton as Blondie, performs in standard quality and is augmented ably for script variation by Angelyn Orr, Robert Stanton and Paul Harvey.

The Bumstead household in this one is disrupted through Arthur Lake (Dagwood) taking over executive duties at his office in the absence of the boss. Placing a discharged WAC, Angelyn Orr, on the payroll brings on complications evolving in the major departure from usual scripting. He is fired along with the WAC and the family is made to set up their own business leading to a reconciliation with former employer and conventional finale.

Strong cast support by Jonathan Hale as Dithers, Paul Harvey, Angelyn Orr and others round out the needed pace for the film without which the repetitious qualities of the series could scarcely hold up.

Foreign Films

"Etoile Sans Lumiere" ("Star Without Light") **(FRENCH).** Lux release of BUP production; directed by Marcel Blistene; stars Mila Parely, Marcel Herrand, Edith Piaf; features Jules Berry, Yves Montand, Serge Reggiani; reviewed in Paris. Running time, **105 MINS.**

Uninspired direction and poor camera work mar this feeble yarn involving personalities in the transition of silent films to talkies. Voice of Edith Paif, used secretly to cover up for a silent film star, played by Mila Parely, is worked up into an unconvincing tragedy. Technical shortcomings bar any chance for American showings.

"Le Pays Sans Etoiles" ("Land Without Stars") **(FRENCH).** Vog release of SPC production; directed by Georges Lacombe; stars Jany Holt, Pierre Brasseur, Gerard Philippe; features Jeanne Marken, Boverio, Helene Tossy, Jean D'Yd, Sylvie; screenplay by Georges Lacombe, based on novel by Pierre Very; reviewed in Paris. Running time, **105 MINS.**

This is an arty effort with limited appeal because of poor technique and incoherent story treatment. Cast principals double in parallel yarn, one at present time and the other a century ago, with melodramatic plot overdone. Too frequent flash-backs jumble the proceedings al-though the cast is fair. No hope for U. S. market. *Maxi.*

Miniature Reviews

"Cluny Brown" (20th). Charles Boyer-Jennifer Jones in smasheroo b.o. comedy.

"A Stolen Life" (WB). Bette Davis starrer has strong femme appeal and hefty b.o. potentiality.

"Boys' Ranch" (M-G). Pleasant youth drama of rehabilitation of juvenile delinquents with exploitation value.

"Rendezvous 24" (20th). Mild "B" thriller on the atom-bomb; for the duals.

"Portrait of a Woman" (French-made) (Mayer-Burstyn). Excellent film for arty houses; prospects elsewhere are questionable.

"In Old Sacramento" (Songs) (Rep). Handsomely mounted westerner with songs.

"The Glass Alibi," (Rep). Good murder-meller of its type.

"Days and Nights" (Artkino). Soviet-produced history (fictionalized) of the Stalingrad defense; strong pull in the foreign houses.

Cluny Brown

20th-Fox release of Ernst Lubitsch production, directed by Lubitsch. Stars Charles Boyer and Jennifer Jones; features Peter Lawford, Helen Walker, Reginald Gardiner, Reginald Owen, Richard Haydn, Sir C. Aubrey Smith, Margaret Bannerman, Sara Allgood, Ernest Cossart, Una O'Connor. Screenplay, Samuel Hoffenstein and Elizabeth Reinhardt, from novel by Margery Sharp; camera, Joseph La Shelle; editor, Dorothy Spencer; special effects, Fred Sersen. Tradeshown N. Y., April 18, '46. Running time, 100 MINS.

Adam Belinski	Charles Boyer
Cluny Brown	Jennifer Jones
Andrew Carmel	Peter Lawford
Betty Cream	Helen Walker
Hilary Ames	Reginald Gardiner
Sir Henry Carmel	Reginald Owen
Col. Duff Graham	Sir C. Aubrey Smith
Wilson	Richard Haydn
Lady Alice Carmel	Margaret Bannerman
Mrs. Maile	Sara Allgood
Syrette	Ernest Cossart
Dowager	Florence Bates
Mrs. Wilson	Una O'Connor
Weller	Queenie Leonard
Uncle Arn	Billy Bevan
John Frewen	Michael Dyne
Master Snaffle	Christopher Severn
Guest Piano Player	Rex Evans
Mrs. Tupham	Ottola Nesmith
Mr. Snaffle	Harold De Becker
Mrs. Snaffle	Jean Prescott
Rollins	Al Winters
Walter	Clive Morgan
Constable Birkins	Charles Coleman
Latham	George Kirby
Dowager's Son	Whitner Bissell
Girl at Party	Betty Fae Brown
Author's Wife	Mira McKinney
Policeman	Philip Morris
Woman in Chemist's Shop	Betty Fairfax
Mr. Tupham	Norman Ainsley

Apart from its whammo entertainment and boxoffice aspects, "Cluny Brown" can be recorded as glamorizing the first of a clan. A lady plumber. And a looker, no less. The kind for whom stopped-up pipes are a pleasure.

Jennifer Jones is the girl, Charles Boyer her anti-Nazi refugee vis-a-vis, Ernst Lubitsch produced and directed. With that combo, plus the fact that Margery Sharp's bestselling novel is the basis for this picture, "Cluny" is a comedy with unlimited b.o. appeal, let alone an interest for the ladies auxiliary of the United Assn. of Plumbers.

"Cluny" is in the best Lubitsch tradition of subtle, punchy comedy, and his two stars make the most of it. It is a satire on British manners, with bite and relish. The insipidity of a specific family is the mirror through which is reflected Miss Sharp's tale of British pre-war aristocracy and the middleclass. None of it is treated seriously, of course, "Cluny" dealing particularly with a cockney gal who, on occasion, can wield a wrench, and does.

When Cluny isn't cleaning stopped-up pipes, she's a maid in the home of the aforementioned aristocrats. The family's bowing acquaintance with world events is confined, for example, to the knowledge that an Austrian named Hitler had written a book, or something. Reginald Owen is the aristocratic squire, Margaret Bannerman his wife, and Peter Lawford their son. Boyer plays a writer fleeing the Nazis from his native Czechoslovakia.

"Cluny" is replete with typical Lubitschian double entendre, along with other bits of business that have long since become associated with his technique in direction. Never, however, are the comedic aspects allowed to get out of hand into outright travesty. Notable, too, is the projection of even lesser characters to points where their performances can be indelibly recalled even long after the pic's fadeout. And speaking of that fadeout, it's a clincher that will not only get sock laughs but is something that will draw plenty of comment for its artful contrivance and imagination.

Boyer and Miss Jones are excellent. Their performances are notable because comedy to them has been something foreign in view of their association with straight drama. The long list of supporting players is likewise strong, and outstanding of these are Lawford, Helen Walker, Reginald Gardiner, Owen, Sir C. Aubrey Smith, Richard Haydn, Miss Bannerman, Sara Allgood and Ernest Cossart.

The nifty screenplay is by Samuel Hoffenstein and Elizabeth Reinhardt. *Kahn.*

A Stolen Life

Hollywood, April 27.

Warners release of B. D., Inc. production. Stars Bette Davis; features Glenn Ford, Dane Clark, Walter Brennan, Charlie Ruggles, Bruce Bennett. Directed by Curtis Bernhardt. Screenplay, Catherine Turney, adapted by Margaret Buell Wilder from a novel by Karel J. Benes; camera, Sol Polito and Ernest Haller; special effects, William McGann, E. Roy Davidson, Willard Van Enger, Russell Collings; music, Max Steiner; editor, Rudi Fehr. Tradeshown April 26, '46. Running time, 109 MINS.

Kate Bosworth	
Patricia Bosworth	Bette Davis
Bill Emerson	Glenn Ford
Karnok	Dane Clark
Eben Folger	Walter Brennan
Freddie Linley	Charlie Ruggles
Jack Talbot	Bruce Bennett
Deidre	Peggy Knudsen
Mrs. Johnson	Esther Dale
Lucy	Joan Winfield
Martha	Clara Blandick

Bette Davis is a triple-threat proposition in "A Stolen Life." In addition to portraying the dual role, actress makes her producer debut with this. B. D., Inc., is her company. It's a femme story of heartache, unrequited love and the usual ingredients that go into this type of yarn. Opulent production values, marquee strength of Miss Davis' name and appeal story will have for femme audiences add up to hefty returns.

Story unfolds leisurely in telling of a sister who assumes her twin's identity in order to find love. Pace is slow because of lengthy establishment of character difference between sisters, but there are plenty of moments of high interest to help overcome this for the women's trade. Miss Davis appears as a sweet, sincere, artistic girl and as this girl's man-crazy sister. When the latter, by trickery, marries man with whom former has fallen in love and is later drowned in a boating accident, the sweet girl takes on her sister's identity in a try for happiness. Fake role doesn't jell but finale clears the way for true love. Script by Catherine Turney, spends a great deal of footage establishing life in New England summer resorts. Since it is a woman's story, dialog hands plenty of cliches to

male players, particularly to Glenn Ford as the man in love with both sisters. Curtis Bernhardt's direction gives Miss Davis and others competent guidance and gets the feel of the locale.

Dane Clark appears briefly in role of rude artist. Role is difficult and not a fortunate one for Clark in view of his rising popularity. Walter Brennan gives a good character reading to his part of a salty old down'easter. Charlie Ruggles, Bruce Bennett, Peggy Knudsen, Esther Dale, Joan Winfield and Clara Blandick round out the cast, all competent.

Special photography for dual role played by Miss Davis is the best yet. At no time is double exposure or other tricks used to bring the characters together in scenes apparent. Credit for trick work goes to Willard Van Enger and Russell Collings, both lensers, while other special effects were directed by William McGann and E. Roy Davidson. Regular lensing by Sol Polito and Ernest Haller gives a fine display to the physical production properties. *Brog.*

Boys' Ranch

Hollywood, April 26.

Metro release of Robert Sisk production. Features Jackie "Butch" Jenkins, James Craig, Skippy Homeier, Dorothy Patrick. Directed by Roy Rowland. Original story and screenplay, William Ludwig; camera, Charles Salerno, Jr.; editor, Ralph E. Winters; score, Nathaniel Shilkret. Tradeshown April 24, '46. Running time, 97 MINS.

"Butch"	Jackie "Butch" Jenkins
Dan Walker	James Craig
Skippy	Skippy Homeier
Susan Walker	Dorothy Patrick
David Banton	Ray Collins
Hank	Darryl Hickman
Mary Walker	Sharon McManus
Mr. Harper	Minor Watson
Mrs. Harper	Geraldine Wall
Mr. O'Neill	Arthur Space
Druggist	Robt. Emmet O'Connor
Judge Henderson	Moroni Olsen

Basically "Boys' Ranch" is familiar stuff, but gains added interest because its theme is reformation of juvenile delinquents. Formula used for the fight against delinquency is solid, giving film good exploitation value. Locale is the Texas ranch near Amarillo where teen-agers are given a new start in life. Film takes up too much time in telling its story, making for footage padding, but makes clever use of young Jackie "Butch" Jenkins' personality to appeal to majority of audiences.

Original story and script by William Ludwig depicts how a baseball player gets a group of Texas ranchers interested in a project to give sidewalk urchins a new lease of life through fresh air, sunshine, farm work and proper guidance. The formula is sound and naturally lends itself to good hoke. Villian of the piece is Skippy Homeier, a young delinquent who takes a lot of reforming before he realizes honesty and good sportsmanship pay off—even if it takes longer. Fictionizing is formula and makes a play for proper amount of pathos in spinning out the tear-jerking sequences.

Roy Rowland's direction makes the most of the material, displaying knowledge of keeping simple things simple and balancing heavier moments with lightness. Bratish cuteness of young Butch Jenkins is played up. In the plotting he's spotted for comedy, not as a delinquent, and his every appearance is a guaranteed chuckle. James Craig, adult male lead, does okay by assignment of the ballplayer who launches the ranch. Dorothy Patrick, as Craig's wife, has only a few scenes. Other adults in the cast also play second fiddle to the juves.

Skippy Homeier, Darryl Hickman, little Sharon McManus are among the younger players who prove very effective in projecting the story.

Robert Sisk's production guidance furnishes excellent physical accuments. Lensing by Charles Salerno, Jr., takes advantage of outdoor scenery and other credits measure up. *Brog.*

Rendezvous 24

20th-Fox release of Sol M. Wurtzel production. Features William Gargan, Pat O'Moore, Maria Palmer, Herman Bing. Directed by James Tinling. Story and screenplay by Aubrey Wisberg; camera, Benjamin Kline; editor, William F. Claxton. Tradeshown N. Y., April 25, '46. Running time, **70 MINS.**

Larry......................William Gargan
Timothy......................Pat O'Moore
Kleinheldt......................David Leonard
Greta......................Maria Palmer
Becker......................John Bleifer
Heligmann......................Kurt Katch
Mannfred......................Henry Rowland
Leopold......................Paul Kruger
Herr Schmidt......................Herman Bing
Frau Schmidt......................Ilka Gruning
Carstairs......................Boyd Irwin
Sinclair......................Evan Thomas
Clark......................Leslie Denison

This modest-budgeted morsel won't have any earth-shaking consequences. A B-grade thriller built around the atom-bomb theme, pic is a tame spy story with no particular distinction. It will pay off in the duals, but that's about all.

Film, when originally announced as an important contribution to the atomic energy question, brought down on producer Sol Wurtzel's head the denunciation of the Federation of American Scientists, who resented a world-shaking theme being made the subject of a B-grade melodrama. Although Wurtzel defended seriousness of pic's treatment, it's noticeable that claims to film's scientific importance have since been played down.

Aside from the fact that atom fission is dragged in as just a new angle in a mystery story, pic is further routine in that its plot structure and situations are duplications of dozens of similar spy yarns. Story is synthetic and slow, as well as obvious from the start.

In a secret lab in Germany's Harz mountains, a group of Nazi scientists are working on development of atomic explosions by remote radio control, despite the fact that the war is over. Their aim is to blow up cities like Paris and New York from their mountain fastness, and need only some data from a German scientist in America to complete their plans.

Film is the story of the tracking down of the plotters by an American and his British assistant, with lovely German spies, and murderous Nazi gunmen, involved in the proceedings. Of course the American hits on the German hideaway just in the nick, arriving at the secret lab one minute before Paris is to be blown up.

Gunplay as usual is plentiful for these formulae-fixed confections, and there is also interest in the chase angle. But pic never really stands up. Acting is as perfunctory as scripting and direction. William Gargan looks handsome and harmless as the prying American, and Maria Palmer is as superficial as the traitress Hun. Pat O'Moore is satisfactory as the English agent, and Kurt Katch is plausible as a German ringleader. Herman Bing contributes some obvious, feeble comedy. *Bron.*

Portrait of a Woman
(FRENCH-MADE)

Mayer-Burstyn release of Jacques Feyder production, directed by Feyder. Stars Francoise Rosay; features Henry Guisol, Jean Nohain, Ettore Cella. Screenplay by Feyder, based on novel by Jacques Viot; camera, Jacques Mercanton, Adrien Porchet; editor, John Oser; English titles, Herman G. Weinberg. At Little Carnegie, N. Y., April 27, '46. Running time, **80 MINS.**

Cast: Francoise Rosay, Henry Guisol, Jean Nohain, Ettore Cella, Claire Gerard, Yva Belle, Claude Alain, Florence Lynn.

(In French; English Titles)

"Portrait of a Woman," one of the better French films exported since the war, revives the excellent French finesse that made "Un Carnet du Bal" and "Baker's Wife" classics in this country. With Francoise Rosay, star of "Carnet," in the lead and with direction by Jacques Feyder, winner of several French Oscars, the film should rate strongly with arty American audiences. Boxoffice prospects for run-of-the-mill American houses, however, are questionable.

Film was made during the war in Switzerland, where Mme. Rosay and Feyder, her husband, fled during the occupation. Similarity of the French and Swiss terrains, however, make the location shots authentic. Fact that the film was shot in Switzerland probably aided it also in that the same studio facilities that were used for "The Last Chance" and "Marie-Louise" were available.

Feyder wrote the screenplay to display the unusual versatility of his wife, and Mme. Rosay, consequently, carries the entire picture on her very capable shoulders. She portrays four different women, each dissimilar to the others, and each done in top fashion. Story has her first as an opera star, who commits suicide over fear that she's losing her hold on her audience.

Her body is found, lacking identification. Answering police inquiries, four people appear, each believing the body to be that of a friend or relative who's disappeared. As the bereaved tell their stories via flashback, Mme. Rosay gets a chance to show her wares as an old peasant woman, a genteel schoolmistress and the lusty wife of a bargekeeper. Latter role gives her the opportunity to indulge in some raucous comedy and is probably the best-drawn, but all are excellently done.

While Mme. Rosay walks off with the acting honors, rest of the cast is uniformly good. Jean Nohain lends deft touches to his role of the young farmer who thinks the dead woman is his old nurse and servant. Ettore Cella, as the bargekeeper, maintains the lusty pace set by the star in this sequence. Duo's French dialog with an Italian accent is something for the ears.

Fine camera work of Jacques Mercanton and Adrien Porchet spotlights the title motif with shots of Mme. Rosay through a mirror, in a photograph, etc., all resembling actual portraits. Feyder's subtle directorial techniques are evident throughout, adding much to the picture's consistently fast tempo. English titles by Herman G. Weinberg are more adequate than in most foreign-made pictures.

"Portrait" is preeming in this run with "Hymn of the Nations," three-reeler with Arturo Toscanini and the NBC Symphony Orch. Produced by the OWI and reviewed in VARIETY on March 3, '44, latter is being distributed domestically by Mayer-Burstyn on a non-profit basis. *Stal.*

In Old Sacramento
(SONGS)

Republic release of Joseph Kane production, directed by Kane. Stars William Elliott, Constance Moore; features Hank Daniels, Ruth Donnelly, Eugene Pallette, Lionel Stander, Jack LaRue, Grant Withers. Screenplay, Frances Hyland, based on original by Jerome Odlum; songs, Jean Lenoir-Bruce Sievier, Fred Gilbert, Will D. Cobb-Gus Edwards, Barney Fagan, Andrew B. Sterling-Charles Ward; music director, Morton Scott; camera, Jack Marta; editor, Fred Allen. Previewed N. Y., April 24, '46. Running time, **89 MINS.**

Johnny Barrett..............William Elliott
Belle Malone..............Constance Moore
Sam Chase..............Hank Daniels
Zebby Booker..............Ruth Donnelly
Jim Wales..............Eugene Pallette
Eddie Dodge..............Lionel Stander
Laramie..............Jack LaRue
Capt. Marc Slayter..............Grant Withers
Newsboy..............Bobby Blake
Marchetti..............Charles Judels
Stage Driver..............Paul Hurst
Ma Dodge..............Victoria Horne
Oscar..............Dick Wessel

Old Sacramento was never like this. In 1848 it used to be a brawling camp triple-decked with gold-dusters, gamblers and gunplay. This version is loaded with music, albeit mounted handsomely with elaborately furnished indoor settings, masses of extras and a strong supporting cast which won't hurt at the b.o.

Faltering on the story and script items, production-direction of Joseph Kane spins the yarn around the romance between a music hall belle, of rigid ethical standards, and a gentleman-gambler who doubles as a notorious stagecoach yegg by the name of "Spanish Jack." With the sheriff and vigilante closing in on her lover, the femme permits romance to surmount virtue and she alibis for him. But when a young prospector, who has fallen for the singer, is falsely accused of being the masked bandit, the genuine article gallantly reveals himself, is shot up for his trouble, and dies in the arms of his Belle.

William Elliott, who was featured in the Red Ryder western series, makes his bow as a more substantial romantic figure in the role of "Spanish Jack." The physical equipment is perfect, Elliott being tall and lean, with a strong chin and voice of deep masculine timber. Thesping is a bit uncertain, however, with some stiffness visible in the trying spots. Constance Moore, as the heart interest, is a looker with appealing personality. She also totes the heavy musical load with finesse, sings four oldies: "Speak to Me of Love," "Man Who Broke the Bank at Monte Carlo," "Can't Tell Why I Love You," and "Camp Town Races." A well-trained barber shop quartet handles the fifth number, "My Gal's a High Born Lady."

Roster of supporting players includes reliables like Eugene Pallette, Ruth Donnelly, Lionel Stander and Jack LaRue, all of whom make the most of their lines.

The Glass Alibi

Republic release of W. Lee Wilder production, directed by Wilder. Stars Paul Kelly, Douglas Fowley, Anne Gwynne; features Maris Wrixon, Jack Conrad. Original screenplay, Mindred Lord; camera, Henry Sharp; editor, Asa Clark. Previewed N. Y., April 26, '46. Running time, **68 MINS.**

Max Anderson..............Paul Kelly
Joe Eykner..............Douglas Fowley
Belle Marlin..............Anne Gwynne
Linda Vale..............Maris Wrixon
Benny Brandini..............Jack Conrad
Dr. Lawson..............Selmer Jackson
Riggs..............Cyril Thornton
Red Hogan..............Cy Kendall
Coroner..............Walter Soderling
Gas Attendant..............Vic Potel
Bartender..............George Chandler
Nurse..............Phyllis Adair
Drug Clerk..............Ted Stanhope
Frank..............Dick Scott
Connie..............Eula Guy
Charlie..............Forrest Taylor

Infused with good direction, performance and refreshing twists, this murder meller clicks despite lack of cast names. Although somewhat too involved in story material, film is well paced and holds interest. Most of the load is carried ably by Douglas Fowley as the central interest. From the ranks as an oater heavy, Fowley is subordinated in this one by Paul Kelly playing the homicide cop. Styled unpretentiously, "Alibi" will register strongly on any dual bill.

Able direction focuses otherwise commonplace sequences into sustained interest for the story which is located in southern California. Fowley, as a reporter with criminal bent, inveigles a wealthy Santa Monica resident, played by Maris Wrixon, into marriage on learning she is to die because of heart ailment. His ambitions, spurred by the other gal, Anne Gwynne, fill in the middle footage with smooth suspense leading to the murder climax. Unknowing of her death because of heart failure, Fowley shoots his wife in accordance to carefully laid out murder plans. Due to his own schemed alibi, conviction and justice follow for the finale with Paul Kelly withholding the technical facts that would clear him.

Film is given excellent productional attention and is interspersed with well-set outdoor shots.

Days and Nights
(RUSSIAN-MADE)

Artkino release of Mosfilm Studios production. Stars Vladimir Soloviev, Anna Lisyanskaya, Dmitri Sagal, Yuri Liubimov, Lev Sverdlin, Mikhail Derjavin, Vassili Kliucharev, Andrei Alexeyev. Directed by Alexander Stolper; screenplay by Konstantine Simonov from the novel by same author; camera, Eugene Andrikanis; English titles, Charles Clement. Previewed in N. Y., April 26, '46. Running time, **88 MINS.**

Capt. Saburov..............Vladimir Soloviev
Vanin..............Dmitri Sagal
Lieut. Maslennikov..............Yuri Liubimov
Anya Klimenko..............Anna Lisyanskaya
Colonel Alexander Protsenko..Lev Sverdlin
General Matveyev..............Mikhail Derjavin
Colonel Sergei Remizov..Vassili Kliucharev
Petya..............Andrei Alexeyev

(In Russian; English Titles)

The defense of Stalingrad, the stand that broke the Nazis' back in the east, comes in for some grim and relentless treatment in the Soviet-produced "Days and Nights" now preeming at Artkino's first-run Stanley theatre. Adapted from Konstantine Simonov's novelized eyewitness report which copped a book-of-the-month spot, the film, in a sense, explains the surprising Teutonic upset by recounting the part played by a lone company. And in doing so, it develops a life-sized portrayal of the men who fought and won.

For the nonce, the Russians have come out with a war picture which omits depiction of a single enemy soldier. Instead of the usual black-and-white characterizations that mar more than help, the camera spends full-time on the Russian side of the story. The resulting vast improvement should pay off in b.o. receipts.

Entire action was reportedly lensed in Stalingrad's ruins with the film opening and closing with some familiar newsreels of the campaign. Related is the Volga crossing of the company as it first enters battle, its capture of three strategic buildings and the ensuing 70 days of desperate fighting which stopped the Nazis. Towards the close, the strategy of the counterattack which trapped the German army is glimpsed in a scene at g.h.q.

Sentimentality of the Russians is played up as a counterpoint to the grape and cannister scenes. In several sequences, with slight provocation, one or more of the players burst into nostalgic melody. The singing, typically Slavic, is rich, strong and good. One scene in which a colonel toasts his native Ukraine in song is a trifle unbelievable and altogether unmilitary to western eyes. But it would be captious to say the film loses out by the stress on melody.

Central role of a heroic captain who crosses the enemy lines three times to deliver vital messages is played to the hilt by Vladimir Soloviev. His solid performance gets across the nerve-wracking, unending fatigue of constant warfare. Soloviev duets with Anna Lisyanskaya in the role of nurse, on a love theme sufficiently muted so as not to interfere with the history of the battle. Lev Sverdlin is a standout in his bit as the robust and determined battalion colonel. Direction by Alexander Stolper is consistently excellent.

Miniature Reviews

"Blue Sierra" (Color) (M-G). Sentimental dog yarn, for moderate b.o. draw.

"Somewhere in the Night" (20th). Strong melodrama with punchy suspense, bespeaks healthy b.o.

"Without Reservations" (RKO). High-calibre escapist comedy with rosy b.o. outlook.

"Strange Triangle" (20th). Fast gaited meller an above average dualer.

"Rainbow Over Texas" (Rep.). Up to standard Roy Rogers oatuner.

'Sinfonia De Una . Vida" (Clasa). Mexican-made feature has slim chance in U. S. despite Julian Soler heading cast.

Blue Sierra
(COLOR)

Metro release of Robert Sisk production. Features Frank Morgan, Elizabeth Taylor. Directed by Fred M. Wilcox. Original screenplay, Lionel Houser; camera (Technicolor), Leonard Smith; editor, Conrad A. Nervig; co-director of animal sequences, Basil Wrangel. Tradeshown N. Y., May 1, '46. Running time, **93 MINS.**

Kathie Merrick...........Elizabeth Taylor
Harry MacBain..............Frank Morgan
Sergeant Smitty................Tom Drake
Mrs. Merrick..................Selena Royle
Judge Payson.............Harry Davenport
Old Man..................George Cleveland
Alice Merrick...Catherine Frances McLeod
Farmer Crews..............Morris Ankrum
Gil Elson...................Mitchell Lewis
Mrs. Elson.......................Jane Green
Pete Merrick.....................David Holt
Sergeant Mac.............William Wallace
Sheriff Ed Grayson..........Minor Watson
Charlie.......................Donald Curtis
Casey.........................Clancy Cooper
First Youth.......Carl "Alfalfa" Switzer
Second Youth...............Conrad Binyon
Lassie as Bill

This slow, sentimental story of a girl and a dog will attract the kids and canine lovers. Otherwise, pic lacks distinction to have more than moderate b.o. draw.

Pic is overlong for one thing, and the shots of outdoors and wild animals are a little familiar. So, too, is the story of a girl finding a wounded pup and nursing it back to health again. What distinguishes this pic from the others is the added angle of a dog gone to war, although even here the plot situations are hardly new and rather pat.

Film, with its mountain and lake backgrounds, its sheep herds and ranges, has a dreamy idyllic flavor, enhanced by its being in color. Camera, as well as color work, is very fine. Though pic isn't heavily budgeted, it has a rich air about it. Some of the outdoor shots and settings are strikingly beautiful. And close-ups of wild animals and birds, at beginning of film, are unusual for their natural quality and ease.

Story opens very slowly with a collie pup deserted in a wilderness, escaping snares of coyote, bear and skunk, only to be wounded by bird-hunters. Nursed to health by a girl (Elizabeth Taylor), aided by a kindly sheep rancher (Frank Morgan), pup grows into a fine sheep dog. While herding a flock across a road, dog is hit by a truck and carried by the driver into a nearby city, to a vet. Recovered but unclaimed, animal is sent to Army dog training center.

Training scenes, though brief, are interesting. Dog is shipped off with a unit to the Aleutians, goes through battle, and saves his group pinned down by a Jap barrage. Sent back to the States with shattered nerves, dog escapes, makes its way back to the mountain range, and to the girl. Dog is accused of raiding chicken farms, but is let off as a temporary shock case, after an impassioned plea by Morgan based on dog's war record.

Elizabeth Taylor has a charming naturalness as the girl who befriends the dog, and Morgan is appealing as the rancher, with his big moment the last-reel courtroom scene. *Bron.*

Somewhere in the Night
(ONE SONG)

Hollywood, May 2.

20th-Fox release of Anderson Lawler production. Stars John Hodiak and Nancy Guild; features Lloyd Nolan, Richard Conte, Josephine Hutchinson, Fritz Kortner, Margo Woode, Sheldon Leonard, Lou Nova. Directed by Joseph L. Mankiewicz. Screenplay, Howard Dimsdale anad Mankiewicz; adapted by Lee Strasberg from story by Marvin Borowsky; camera, Norbet Brodine; music, David Buttolph; special effects, Fred Sersen; editor, James B. Clark. Tradeshown April 30, '46. Running time, **110 MINS.**

George Taylor.................John Hodiak
Christy ....Nancy Guild
Lt. Donald Kendall............Lloyd Nolan
Mel Phillips................Richard Conte
Elizabeth Conroy.....Josephine Hutchinson
Anzelmo......................Fritz Kortner
Phyllis.......................Margo Woode
Sam.......................Sheldon Leonard
Hubert...........................Lou Nova
Marine Captain..............John Russell
Conroy.................Housely Stevenson
Little Man....................Charles Arnt
Cab Driver.........................Al Sparlis
Technical Sergeant........Richard Benedict
Medical Attendant............John Kellogg
Navy Doctor..............Phil Van Zandt
Bartender..................Whitner Bissell
Executive....................Forbes Murray
Bank Teller.........................Jeff Corey
Nurse..............................Paula Reid
Miss Jones..................Mary Currier
Bank Guard.........................Sam Flint
Swede.......................Henry Morgan
Hotel Clerk.................Charles Marsh
Attendant..................Clancy Cooper
Dr. Grant..........................Jack Davis
Brother Williams............Louis Mason
Headwaiter..................Henri De Soto
Baggage Room Attendant......Harry Tyler

Zingy melodrama, tightly-knit, earmarked for excellent b.o. returns. It's a good example of thoughtful coordination of production, direction, writing and playing into gripping meller entertainment for all. Footage is packed with new angles on the amnesia theme and will hold audiences despite nearly two hours running time.

Plot deals with a man in search for himself. John Hodiak is seen as a Marine stricken with amnesia after battle injuries. He conceals his condition so he can get a discharge and start finding out about himself. A letter from a girl makes him fear he's not a nice character, hence reluctant to reveal amnesia. Yarn quickly segues into his civilian status as he picks up a clue here and a clue there. Search directs itself towards an unsavory private detective character, who disappeared some time previous, and reveals sundry groups looking for $2,000,000 in Nazi loot that has vanished also. Hodiak is beaten, shot at and threatened but he keeps up the hunt. Finale reveals he is the missing dick, the Nazi loot is recovered. Trials and tribulations give the Marine a new slant on life and reformation leads to romance with the girl who has aided his search.

Howard Dimsdale and Joseph L. Mankiewicz contributed handsome script that proves a solid foundation for Mankiewicz's direction. Novel technique is used in hospital sequences where Hodiak is unable to speak because of injuries. Camera becomes his eyes and attendants look directly into the lenses when speaking to the Marine. Film is jammed with plenty of other realistic touches, all designed to create shock and suspense and keep an audience thrilled and chilled.

Hodiak delivers a strong performance in the lead role, making every scene count and giving character plenty of punch. Film introduces Nancy Guild as a new star. There's no quarrel with her performance as a newcomer but it carbon-copies too many other film lookers to stand out individually. Otherwise it is a wholly acceptable delivery and experience should sharpen her personality. Lloyd Nolan wraps up assignment as a casual policeman. Richard Conte effectively walks off with part of a smoothie who turns heavy for the finale. Standout sequence in the film is commanded by Josephine Hutchinson. Role of love-starved old maid was difficult but handled to perfection by Miss Hutchinson. Among others rating mention are Fritz Kortner, Margo Woode, Sheldon Leonard, Charles Arnt, Whitner Bissell, Henry Morgan, Paula Reid.

Anderson Lawler has given the picture expertly-appointed production values, showmanly backing the gripping mood of the plot, which was adapted by Lee Strasberg from a story by Marvin Borowsky. Score by David Buttolph is also effective in furthering melodramatic air. One song, "Middle of Nowhere," is spotted; song by Miss Guild. Norbert Brodine's lensing is notable, as are special photographic effects by Fred Sersen and other appurtenances. *Brog.*

Without Reservations

Hollywood, May 7.

RKO release of Jesse L. Lasky-Walter MacEwen production. Stars Claudette Colbert, John Wayne; features Don DeFore, Anne Triola, Phil Brown, Frank Puglia, Thurston Hall, Dona Drake, Fernando Alvarado, Charles Arnt, Louella Parsons. Directed by Mervyn LeRoy. Screenplay, Andrew Solt; from the novel by Jane Allen and Mae Livingston; camera, Milton Krasner; special effects, Vernon L. Walker, Russell A. Cully, Harold Stine; music, Roy Webb; editor, Jack Ruggiero. Tradeshown May 6, '46. Running time, **107 MINS.**

Kit.....................Claudette Colbert
Rusty..........................John Wayne
Dink...........................Don DeFore
Connie.........................Anne Triola
Soldier..........................Phil Brown
Ortega.......................Frank Puglia
Baldwin....................Thurston Hall
Dolores........................Dona Drake
Mexican, Boy............Fernando Alvarado
Salesman....................Charles Arnt
Louella Parsons

Rollicking comedy tinged with slapstick that will pay off heftily. Claudette Colbert and John Wayne assure initial b.o. draft, and film's contents will keep them coming. Production framework furnished by Jesse L. Lasky and his associate Walter MacEwen, is smartly valued to further entertainment. It's escapist fare marked by bright dialog, direction and playing. Film runs longer than necessary, causing some slowness in spots.

Plot concerns what happens to a femme author when she meets the real-life counterpart of her tome's hero. The misadventures that befall her, her hero and his pal as they make a cross-country trip together are guaranteed hilarity. Miss Colbert, the writer, is tripping west to adapt her book to the screen. On a crowded train she is picked up by two Marine fliers, Wayne and Don DeFore. Without realizing her identity, boys proceed throughout the footage to impress her with how wrong the book's slant on life, love, returned heroes, etc., actually is. By the time the finale rolls around she's convinced that heroes aren't too interested in carving out a brave new world, being pretty satisfied to return to the old way of life, liberty and the pursuit of romance.

Around this theme scripter Andrew Solt, working from the Jane Allen-Mae Livingston novel, has built delightful scenes and characters that, despite their laugh intentions, are a great deal closer to actual reality than most more serious writing. Mervyn LeRoy's direction doesn't miss a bet in underlying the laughs with a solid feeling of reality, and the players troupe the roles to the hilt.

Miss Colbert and Wayne romp through to star spots for certain fan favor. Both prove particularly facile in building to a solid laugh. As writer and Marine ace they are hep to demands of the parts, and deliver in top form. Don DeFore doesn't take a back seat in the miming, measuring up to every demand as the good friend of both. Surprise of the film, which has a number of surprises in its casting, is the manner in which LeRoy's direction give full development to the number of character gems that weave in and out of the story. Performers in these brief spots, given a chance to show their wares, come through with a wallop.

Anne Triola will command a lot of attention for her delivery of a smarty hash-slinger who knows all about men. Performance is boff for howls. Phil Brown, pfc who tries to interest the writer; Frank Puglia, a proud Mexican who knows all about life and love; Dona Drake, his amorous daughter; Fernando Alvarado, his young son with old wisdom; Charles Arnt, a weepy character who crosses paths with the wandering trio; and Thurston Hall, satirical composite of hysterical Hollywood producers; are among those who make many standout moments in the film.

Surprise walkons are spotted in the footage, such as Jack Benny approaching Miss Colbert in a railway station and asking for an autograph; Cary Grant dancing with the writer; LeRoy himself dining with her. Louella Parsons plays herself as an air chatterer who breathlessly brings breathless news to fans about the doings of the novelist and Hollywood.

Backing up the top entertainment are lensing by Milton Krasner, special effects, editing, score and other technical functions. All factors combine into making it a show that will amuse all. *Brog.*

Strange Triangle

20th-Century Fox release of Aubrey Schenck production. Stars Signe Hasso, Preston Foster; features Anabel Shaw, John Sheppard, Roy Robert, Emory Parnell. Directed by Ray McCarey. Screenplay by Mortimer Braus adapted by Charles G. Booth from story by Jack Andrews; camera, Harry Jackson; editor, Norman Colbert; music, David Buttolph. Tradeshown N. Y., May 6, '46. Running time, **65 MINS.**

Francine Huber..............Signe Hasso
Sam Crane...................Preston Foster
Betty Wilson....................Anabel Shaw
Earl Huber..................John Shepperd
Harry Matthews...............Roy Roberts
Barney Shaefer.............Emory Parnell
Hilda Shaefer..................Nancy Evans

Tight direction weaving together some exciting, though improbable story material marks this film as a better than average "B." Although lacking in high-power marquee rating, the cast turns in uniformly solid performances that help ride over the weak spots in the script. The production is exceptionally well-mounted for a low-budgeter, with settings, music and camera work of top-drawer caliber. Pace is maintained at a high speed by means of some extremely close-to-the-skin scissor work.

Plot is concocted of some surefire ingredients with sex intrigue and coin embezzlement the dominant elements. Story, unfolding via flashback technique, opens in jail where a bank examiner is being held for the murder of another man's life. As it turns out, the slain woman emerges as an adventuress who drove several former spouses to the gaspipe and her current one, a bank manager, to illegally dip his hand into the till to keep her in sables. Her demise is retribution for her double-crossing ways with other men. Story becomes a bit difficult to take at the point where the bank examiner shows himself ready to take the rap for his pal, the manager.

Signe Hasso, as the femme fatale, fits the part down to a feline's whisker. She glides through the film with thespic polish, and while not a looker, has an exotic aura that should sell. Preston Foster, as the bank examiner, turns in a square-jawed performance up to his usual good standards. John Sheppard's portrait of the weakling husband also fits the bill as does the rest of the cast.

Rainbow Over Texas
(SONGS)

Republic release of Edward J. White production. Stars Roy Rogers; features George "Gabby" Hayes, Dale Evans. Directed by Frank McDonald. Screenplay by Gerald Geraghty, based on original by Max Brand; camera, Reggie Lanning; editor, Charles Craft; songs by Jack Elliott, Glenn Spencer, Gordon Forster. Previewed N. Y. May 3, '46. Running time, 65 MINS.

Roy Rogers	Roy Rogers
Gabby Whittaker	George "Gabby" Hayes
Jackie Dalrymple	Dale Evans
Kirby Haynes	Sheldon Leonard
Wooster Dalrymple	Robert Emmett Keane
Larkin	Gerald Oliver Smith
Mama Lolita	Minerva Urecal
Jim Pollard	George J. Lewis
Pete McAvoy	Kenne Duncan
Iverson	Pierce Lyden
Captain Monroe	Dick Elliott
Bob Nolan and Sons of Pioneers	

As with its predecessors, this Roy Rogers mustanger is given the necessary quality in production and direction which maintains the high standard set for the series. Although comparatively sparse in musical material, the song injections in this one neatly balance the scripting (generally too slurred for Rogers' vocalizing). Outstanding song, "Little Senorita," by Jack Elliott, is outside the oater class and well put over by Rogers and Dale Evans in a production sequence.

The scripting has Rogers, playing himself, on a personal appearance tour with his group, which includes Bob Nolan and Sons of the Pioneers. They are placed in Rogers' Texas hometown for the fist-and-muscle stuff. Action is spread over the local bad men conspiring against Rogers, who is to take part in a pony express race staged by the community. With 10-gallon hats and sixshooters blended in modern settings incorporating limousines, radio broadcasts and snappy niteries, the action plausibly unravels, aided by good performances and relieving musical interludes. Rogers, of course, beats them out in the race and emerges a hero in clearing the town of heavies.

Sinfonia De Una Vida
("Symphony of Life")
(MEXICAN-MADE)
Mexico City, April 23.

Clasa Films Mundiales release of a Miguel Salkind production. Stars Julian Soler. Features Pituka de Foronda and Tina Romagnoli. Directed by Celestino Gorostiza. At Cine Metropolitan. Running time, 91 MINS.

(In Spanish; No English Titles)

This is definitely no contribution to Mexico's list of good pictures. Credible biogs of celebs have been made previously in Mexican studios. But this one, life story of the late Maestro Miguel Lerdo de Tejada, beloved in Mexico and the U. S. for his music and as conductor of Mexican Typica orchestra, is much below these other efforts. Looks mild even in Mexico.

Either "Sinfonia" was badly cut or the producer was in a big hurry. Result is a series of snapshots that look amateurish in some respects. Julian Soler, well-known in Mexico, is much below his par in the lead. He can do high comedy but he refrains from this here although he has several chances to do it well. Support also is inferior. Only the two featured femmes, Pituka de Foronda, sightly blonde, and Tina Romagnoli, vital brunette, do reasonably well. La Romagnoli sings nicely, her pipes and personality helping.

Don't Be a Sucker

Paramount release of U. S. Army Signal Corps short. Features Paul Lukas, Felix Bressart; commentary by Lloyd Nolan. Running time, 18 MINS.

Vividly depicting Nazi Germany as a horrible example of intolerance, "Don't Be a Sucker" points up in vivid fashion the need for the U. S. to remain a liberty-loving country of unified peoples. Made by the U. S. Army Signal Corps for showing to American troops, it is being distributed gratis by Paramount to regular theatres. It's an exceptional short, putting across the intolerance message without being too heavy-handed.

Short starts out with the thesis that the world is full of suckers. One soldier falls for a rigged card game, another for a comely, shakedown gal in a barroom. Third, a former serviceman, is about to fall for a rabble-rouser until tipped by a refugee professor. Soapbox orator is trying to set minorities against one another, attack being against any foreign-born person. Ex-GI starts to see the light, however, when he attacks the Masons. The school prof then explains more explicitly.

Professor's story points up that the same sort of plea to set one group against another had been employed by Hitler to Nazify the Teutons. It takes a German Jew, a Catholic, a tradesman, an unemployed youth and shows how each one was swayed into thinking the other was a person to be despised or that he was superior to his fellow countrymen. Results are graphically illustrated, close being the professor's plea that Americans would be dumb to fall for such an alignment in this country.

Paul Lukas, as the professor, is excellent, while Felix Bressart does a realistic job as the typical discharged soldier. Despite the number of newsreel clips used, the whole short smacks of nice production. It has a place in today's theatres.
Wear.

Foreign Films

Desiderio ("Desire") (ITALIAN). Fincine production and release; directed by Roberto Rossellini; stars Elli Parvo, Carlo Ninchi; features Roswita Schmidt, Massimo Girotti, Francesco Grandjacquet. Reviewed in Rome. Running time, 90 MINS.

Under top-notch direction by Rossellini, this film, although banal in plot, is saved as an arty item. With few lurid details, story deals with a seduced hometown girl who abandons her family to become a model in the city and eventually a street walker. Reforming on anticipation of marriage, the girl returns home where she is forgiven and accepted. But her past life crops up and leads the girl to suicide. Several fairly good performances and okay direction may help this to get by in the U. S. Necessary censorship trims indicate the expurgated version for American audiences would not mean much.

En Ole Kreivitar ("Countess for a Night") (FINNISH). Suomen Filmiteollisuus production and release; directed by Hannu Leminen; stars Helena Kara; features Olavi Reiman, Thure Bahne; screenplay, Roy; camera, Marius Raichi; reviewed in Helsingfors. Running time, 95 MINS.

A fantasy done in the comic vein. Plot deals with the adventures of a young mannequin in an imaginative locale, Pomeranien. Helen Kara, favorite here, plays the lead, a departure from her usual serious roles. Although well directed, film will not get by in the U. S.

Un Ami Viendra Ce Soir ("A Friend Will Come This Evening") (FRENCH). Francinex release of Cie Generale Cinematographique production; directed by Raymond Bernard; stars Michel Simon, Madeleine Sologne, Paul Bernard, Louis Salou; features Saturnin Fabre, Marcel Andre, Jacques Clancy, Daniel Genin, Lily Mounet, Yvette Andreyor, Raoul Morco, Jeanne Marny; screenplay by Jacques Companeez, Yvan Noe; reviewed in Paris. Running time, 120 MINS.

In spite of implausible story of French underground activities carried on in a lunatic asylum by patriots posing as insane, cast names make this one a local draw. Paul Bernard, Michel Simon, Saturnin Fabre and Louis Salou perform well in a series of unconvincing episodes. Limited to French language houses, at best, for the U. S.

Vain Sinulle ("Only for You") (FINNISH). Suomen Filmiteollisuus production and release; directed by Hannu Leminen; stars Helena Kara; features Aino Lohikoski; camera, Felix Foraman; reviewed in Helsingfors. Running time, 90 MINS.

A sentimental love story, this boasts Helena Kara, one of the most popular Finnish actresses who does well here. Strongly directed by Hannu Leminen, film displays excellent understanding but appeal is limited to national appeal. Chances in U. S. are virtually nil.

Kris ("A Young Girl's Troubles") (SWEDISH). Svensk Filmindustri release of Harold Molander production; stars Inga Landgre, Stig Olin; features Marianne Loefgren, Allan Bohlin; directed by Ingmar Bergman; screenplay, Ingmar Bergmar; based on a play, "Moderdyret," by Leck Fischer; reviewed in Stockholm. Running time, 94 MINS.

Perhaps one of the top Swedish pictures for 1946, this is headed for strong returns here. Ably directed by Ingmar Bergmar, cast includes two newcomers in Inga Landgre and Stig Olin who reveal potentialities. While few Swedish films mean much in the world market, "Kris" looks to have a chance for usual modest returns obtained by strongest product from Sweden in the American market.

Nokea Ja Kultaa ("Soot and Gold") (FINNISH). Soumen Filmiteollisuus production and release; directed by Edvin Laine; stars Edvin Laine, Ansa Ikonen; features Uuno Laakso; camera, Felix Forsman; reviewed in Helsingfors. Running time, 102 MINS.

Edvin Laine, director and actor, has made two films that may land him a "Jussi" (Finlandian Oscar) for 1946. This film, a natural for the Finnish public via its sentimental story, is one of them. Fine casting helps place it in a high category. Well directed, the yarn concerns Laine as a drifter who is helped to start life anew through a young lieutenant in the Salvation Army played by Ansa Ikonen. Aided by Felix Forsman's excellent camera work, film will be strong at the Finnish boxoffice. It would be a dubious entry, however, for the American market.

Les Demons De L'Aube ("Dawn Devils") (FRENCH). C.P.L.F. release of Gaumont production; directed by Yves Allegret; stars Georges Marchal; features Andre Valmy, Davray, Lohu, Hernantier, Fernand Rene, Jacqueline Pierreux, Simone Signeret; screenplay, Jean Ferry, Maurice Auberge; reviewed in Paris. Running time, 98 MINS.

Dealing in French heroics, this film is negative in international appeal and is intended mainly to build up Georges Marchal for French productions. He gives a fair performance as a commando in the war. Story material, aimed strictly for French patriots, limits the film to French language houses only in the U. S.

Les J 3 (FRENCH). Roger Richebe release of Richebe production; directed by Roger Richebe; stars Gisele Pascal, Gerard Nery, Saturnin Fabre; features Tramel, Marguerite Deval, J. Aumant, J. P. Leroux, G. Riggy, M. Vallee; screenplay, Jean Aurenche, Jean Ferry; based on a play by Roger Fernand; reviewed in Paris. Running time, 95 MINS.

Based on a successful recent play in Paris, this film is set in a village school with troublesome students who are eventually tamed by a teacher. Gisele Pascal, as the teacher who falls in love with one of the students, and Saturnin Fabre, the headmaster, do well enough. Inferior production gives the film little chance and no hope in America.

Miniature Reviews

"Monsieur Beaucaire" (Songs) (Par). Bob Hope at his screwiest in slapstick version of the old costume adventure.

"The Searching Wind" (Par). Fine class film on Europe's political scene of last 25 years.

"One More Tomorrow" (WB). Remake based on "The Animal Kingdom" play. Theme and cast names assure good b.o.

"O.S.S." (Par). Alan Ladd in OK war-spy thriller.

"Swamp Fire" (Par). Johnny Weissmuller in routine melodrama. OK nabe and duals fare.

"She Wrote the Book" (U). Joan Davis - Jack Oakie in amusing farce; good returns on the dualers.

"Renegades" (Color) (Col.). Western feature with color and action to attract.

"Quiet Week-End" (Pathe). Typical sly English comedy looks strong boxoffice in U. S. market.

"Larceny In Her Heart" (PRC). Run-of-the-mill whodunit with a weak plot.

Monsieur Beaucaire
(SONGS)

Hollywood, May 4.

Paramount release of Paul Jones production. Stars Bob Hope, Joan Caulfield; features Patric Knowles, Marjorie Reynolds, Joseph Schildkraut, Cecil Kellaway, Reginald Owen, Constance Collier, Hillary Brooks. Directed by George Marshall. Screenplay, Melvin Frank and Norman Panama; based on novel by Booth Tarkington; camera, Lionel Lindon; special effects, Gordon Jennings, Farciot Edouart; songs, Jay Livingston and Ray Evans; score, Robert Emmett Dolan; editor, Artrur Schmidt. Tradeshown May 3, '46. Running time, **92 MINS.**

Monsieur Beaucaire	Bob Hope
Mimi	Joan Caulfield
Duc de Chandre	Patric Knowles
Princess Maria	Marjorie Reynolds
Count d'Armand	Cecil Kellaway
Don Francisco	Joseph Schildkraut
King Louis XV	Reginald Owen
The Queen	Constance Collier
Madame Pompadour	Hillary Brooke
Don Carlos	Fortunio Bonanova
George Washington	Douglass Dumbrille
The Duenna	Mary Nash
Rene	Leonid Kinskey
King Philip	Howard Freeman

"Monsieur Beaucaire" has the Bob Hope name to assure stout business.

Picture is a frantic, screwballish version of Booth Tarkington's costume novel of high adventure in the days of silk-stockinged heroes. As such it has plenty of giggles and a few solidly-premised laughs. Production appurtenances furnished by Paul Jones are of the most expensive but the glitter of such finery is lost to considerable extent in the black-and-white background used for the broadest type of slapstick farcing.

With the script handed him, George Marshall's direction measures up. Since it is apparent all bars were down in the interests of forcing the laughs, Marshall was a wise directorial choice. He knows his way around a broadly aimed gag or situation, and proves it by milking each to its limit. Therein lies a fault of "Beaucaire." Many sequences that could have played out on their own merits are unnecessarily embellished and eventually detract from the basically amusing yarn about a court barber forced to impersonate royalty.

Hope is Hope—and that's not bad. He's funny, but not as funny as when able to bolster a situation with sly Crosbyana. He plays the French barber, Beaucaire, with all stops out, waltzes through trying situations and varied romances with a bravado that is his particular forte. It's all fun, but could have been even more so if treated with a bit less broadness.

Plot of the Tarkington novel, scripted by Melvin Frank and Norman Panama, has Hope forced to substitute for a French nobleman who is betrothed to Spanish royalty. Hope's interested in a chambermaid, who's interested in working her way up the court social ladder. As the substitute nobleman, Hope goes to Spain to meet his intended bride, marriage with whom will avert war. He becomes the scapegoat in a plot to upset international unity while the real nobleman is finding pleasure with a gal who turns out to be the Spanish princess. The conclusion is obvious.

Joan Caulfield is the chambermaid. Despite her high ambitions she ends up with the razor-wielder and a baby that duplicates the father. Finale closeup of the baby carriage had preview audience tense, expecting to see Bing Crosby instead of a diapered Hope—and it would have been a boff close. Miss Caulfield does justice to one of the score's three credited songs, "Warm as Wine," used as background for action leading up to a violent slapstick duel between Hope and the villain. "A Coach and Four" and "We'll Drink Every Drop in the Shop" are the other tunes credited to Jay Livingston and Ray Evans.

Patric Knowles and Marjorie Reynolds do okay by nobleman and princess assignments. Joseph Schildkraut is the capable heavy. Cecil Kellaway, Reginald Owen, Constance Collier, Hillary Brooke and others measure up to the general clowning.

Robert Emmett Dolan's music score is an assist. Lensing by Lionel Lindon and other technical contributions are okay. *Brog.*

The Searching Wind

Paramount release of Hal Wallis production. Stars Sylvia Sidney, Robert Young, Ann Richards; features Dudley Digges, Douglas Dick, Albert Basserman. Directed by William Dieterle. Screenplay, Lilian Hellman, based on her stage play of same name produced by Herman Shumlin; score, Victor Young; camera, Lee Garmes; editor, Warren Low. Tradeshown N.Y., May 9, '46. Running time, 107 mins.

Alex Hazen	Robert Young
Cassie Bowman	Sylvia Sidney
Emily Hazen	Ann Richards
Moses	Dudley Digges
Count Von Strammer	Albert Basserman
Torrone	Dan Seymour
Sears	Ian Wolfe
Sophronia	Marietta Carty
Mrs. Hayworth	Norma Varden
Carter	Charles D. Brown
David	Don Castle
Ponette	William Trenk
Sam (as a boy)	Mickey Kuhn
Sarah	Ann Carter
Male Attendant	Dave Willock
Sam Hazen	Douglas Dick

Hal Wallis has produced a fine film from Lillian Hellman's Broadway success of two seasons ago, presenting a searching indictment of the weak-willed liberal, and appeasement policy of the U. S. from World War I till now. Film, however, is a class rather than a mass appeal pic. **A far too talky film (although every word of it is important), its 107 minutes of serious dialog are too infrequently relieved by light moments.** Pic isn't likely to hold the run-of-the-mine entertainment-goer looking for escapist stuff.

Pic will do good biz in keys and first-runs, but taper off in subsequents. Although not likely for sock returns, it should earn back its coin, however, for though well-mounted, it nevertheless doesn't appear too heavily budgeted.

The film is an improvement on the Broadway play (Miss Hellman scripted both) because it is more coherent, and better acted. Although the story is carried forward only till Mussolini's death, and much of it is a flashback to the days of the March on Rome in 1922, pic isn't dated.

Fact is, it's pretty pertinent. The spirit of appeasement, of laissez faire, is strong in the U. S. again. The lessons of the first and second World Wars are apparently forgotten. By recalling the mistakes agreed on, by calling attention (as the film does in the beginning) to President Roosevelt's words that "we failed once 25 years ago, and mustn't again," film may wake the U. S. up through its message.

Film's entertainment values, for the wide-awake citizen, are strong. Dialog is good, literate and witty. The trail of an American ambassador-at-large through the Europe of the last two decades, with its glimpses of a corrupt Italy, a degenerating Germany, is absorbing.

Pic is story of a bewildered diplomat, stationed in Europe to report the significance of changing events to the U. S. State dept., who fails to see importance of a Fascist takeover in Italy, the rise of Nazism in Germany, the Munich agreement, etc. His wife is mixing socially with the wrong people, the smug, satisfied set who are pulling the strings for these events, unaware of the cataclysmic results.

Tied up with the political is a personal story, the diplomat's marriage to the wrong woman and his constant love for the newspaper woman he should have wed. Where the love-story seemed confusing in the play, it has its proper focus in the film, showing similar devastating effects of appeasement in one's personal life as in the fate of nations.

Robert Young plays the diplomat with an honest sense of bewilderment and inadequacy towards forces he can't foresee or direct. Sylvia Sidney, as the prescient reporter, is not only unusually attractive in both present-day and flashback scenes, but a superior actress. Ann Richards, as the wife, is also good.

Dudley Digges, repeating his stage role as the cynical publisher who retired from the political scene to spend his days in querulous needling, is excellent, especially in the final scene with his soldier-grandson who must have a wounded leg amputated. Douglas Dick, as the disillusioned son of the diplomat, who ties various strands of the film together in his epitome of the newer generation which must learn and benefit from its elders' mistakes, does a poignantly fine job. Albert Basserman is good in the brief role of a Nazi envoy, as are several other supporting bits.

Camera work is good, production and direction matching. *Bron.*

One More Tomorrow

Hollywood, May 11.

Warner Bros. release of Benjamin Glazer production. Stars Ann Sheridan, Dennis Morgan, Jack Carson, Alexis Smith, Jane Wyman; features Reginald Gardiner, John Loder, Marjorie Gateson, Thurston Hall. Directed by Peter Godfrey. Screenplay, Charles Hoffman and Catherine Turney; added dialog, Julius J. and Philip G. Epstein; based on the play, "The Animal Kingdom," by Philip Barry; camera, Bert Glennon; music, Max Steiner; editor, David Weisbart. Tradeshown May 7, '46. Running time, **89 MINS.**

Christie Sage	Ann Sheridan
Tom Collier	Dennis Morgan
Pat Regan	Jack Carson
Cecilia	Alexis Smith
Franc Connors	Jane Wyman
Jim Fish	Reginald Gardiner
Owen	John Loder
Edna	Marjorie Gateson
Rufus Collier	Thurston Hall
Baronova (Joseph)	John Abbott
Illa Baronova	Marjorie Hoshelle
Diaduska	Sig Arno

"One More Tomorrow" poses a love triangle that lends itself to easy exploitation to lure the femme trade. Values of cast toppers are also forte, and it all adds up to good business prospects. Film is a second celluloid edition of Philip Barry's play, "The Animal Kingdom" and, while never quite ringing true, story is brightly dialoged and strongly played to maintain interest in unfoldment, and gets able production backing.

Peter Godfrey's direction gives a good display to the Charles Hoffman-Catherine Turney script, for which Julius J. and Philip G. Epstein furnished the added dialog. Script is modernized to the extent of bringing it up to wartime period but essentials are still the problems of a rich playboy involved with a poor but honest girl and a golddigging femme. It makes a few casual attempts to project moral that honest work is better than prodigal spending, but this element isn't allowed to get too strong a foothold even though the playboy reforms to a certain extent.

Dennis Morgan is likeable as the rich young man who turns to Alexis Smith, the golddigger, after Ann Sheridan, poor girl who leans to the radical, turns him down because of his coin and way of life. An unhappy marriage with Miss Smith results and when Morgan again crosses paths with Miss Sheridan she realizes she loves him despite his gold. Inevitable conclusion has the wife en route to Reno and the other principals looking forward to a happy future of honest labor and love.

There are plenty of star names for the marquees but principal story play goes to Morgan and Miss Sheridan, with former garnering most footage. Both are good. Jack Carson, Morgan's unorthodox butler and friend, and Jane Wyman, friend to Miss Sheridan, also rate attention in more limited parts. Miss Smith gives a good reading to the conniving cat character to which she was assigned. Reginald Gardiner, a lazy radical, John Loder, Marjorie Gateson, Thurston Hall and others work expertly.

Benjamin Glazer overseered production values, furnishing smart touches. Lensing by Bert Glennon and other factors measure up. *Brog.*

O.S.S.

Paramount release of Richard Maibaum production. Stars Alan Ladd, Geraldine Fitzgerald; features Patric Knowles. Directed by Irving Pichel. Screenplay, Richard Maibaum; camera, Lionel Linden; editor, William Shea. Previewed N. Y. Paramount, May 2, '46. Running time, **105 MINS.**

John Martin	Alan Ladd
Ellen Rogers	Geraldine Fitzgerald
Commander Brady	Patric Knowles
Bernay	Richard Benedict
Parker	Richard Webb
Gates	Don Beddoe
Gen. Donovan	Joseph Crehan
Marcel Aubert	Egon Brecher
WAC Operator	Gloria Saunders
Col. Meister	John Hoyt
Braun	Harold Vermilyea
Mme. Prideaux	Julia Dean
Gerard	Bobby Driscoll

"O.S.S." is a good spy thriller which, on basis of the Office of Strategic Services buildup and Alan Ladd's marquee draw, will do okay business.

Film, however, won't necessarily redound to OSS' credit. While suggesting something of the intelligence work and spy operations of the Army's secret-service branch in the recent war, pic really only brushes the surface. It rarely conveys a sense of the real importance of the OSS setup, in all its ramifications, variety and depth.

Pic is just another spy story, with its tense situations, miraculous escapes, clever agents, obtuse enemy, and patriotic fervor. Paramount rushed to get its version of OSS operations onto celluloid before the other studios, and the haste is evident in a plausible thriller, not too deeply thought out.

Brief training sequences at film's start are interesting, and story carries suspense throughout. Plot concerns a quartet of OSS operatives, prepped to go overseas during the Nazi occupation of France to gather information for the Allies and help the F.F.I. in sabotage. The first specific task assigned them is to blow up a railroad tunnel that the Air Force can't reach.

Group loses its leader soon after parachuting into France when the Gestapo nabs him, and Ladd is put in charge. An early antipathy to Geraldine Fitzgerald, lone femme member of the group, because of her sex, is dissipated as the team works closely together, outwitting the Nazis and laying plans for getting at the closely-guarded, highly strategic tunnel. Ladd and Miss Fitzgerald are successful in accomplishing the mission, although the third operative is killed.

Instead of being returned to the U. S., the team (by now in love with each other) is kept on to help gather information for the Normandy landings. Miss Fitzgerald is trapped by the Germans, because Ladd has to choose between passing on vital information to the Allies and saving her, and pays with her life for Allied success.

Stock story is well produced, the direction, camera work and production angles being above par. So, too, is the acting. Ladd suggests the intelligent, resourceful operative without resort to heroics, while Miss Fitzgerald is a good teammate in a quiet, intense style. Patric Knowles is fine as the naval commander in charge of OSS operations in France.

John Hoyt—the Broadway legiter and nightclub entertainer formerly known as John Hoysradt—makes his film debut in a good job, as a Nazi colonel. Another legiter in satisfactory film debut is Harold Vermilyea (from "Jacobowsky and the Colonel" and "Deep Are the Roots) as a Gestapo agent.   *Bron.*

Swamp Fire

Paramount release of William Pine-William Thomas production; Doc Merman, associate producer. Stars Johnny Weismuller; features Virginia Grey, Buster Crabbe, Carol Thurston. Screenplay, Geoffrey Homes; camera, Fred Jackman, Jr.; editor, Howard Smith. Tradeshown N. Y., May 9, '46. Running time, 68 MINS.
Johnny Duval.........Johnny Weismuller
Janet Hilton................Virginia Grey
Mike Kalavich..............Buster Crabbe
Toni Rousseau.............Carol Thurston
Captain Moise.............Edwin Maxwell
Tim Rosseau...........Pedro De Cordoba
Mr. Hilton.................Pierre Watkin
Grandmere Rousseau.......Marcelle Corday

Johnny Weismuller finally gets away from his Tarzan roles for an everyday part in "Swamp Fire." Pic is a sentimental melodrama about love and adventure among river pilots and trappers in the Louisiana bayous. Modestly-budgeted, filled with action from boat collisions and swamp fires to fist-fights, film should attract family trade in neighborhood and dual houses for ok returns.

A routine story isn't handled with particular originality or skill, and performances are of a piece. But film has a certain flavor from home scenes among the Cajuns, and from picturesque bayou and river scenes, to offset. Camera work on the water is good, especially in the fog scenes.

Story concerns Weismuller, a bar pilot in the treacherous waters at the mouth of the Mississippi, who went to war, had his ship sunk under him, and returns home with nerves gone. His rehabilitation to bar pilot through love of his French sweetheart is complicated by rivalry of a trapper and designs of a society dame. Before pic ends, Weismuller has swum a river, killed an alligator, fought the trapper, rescued his girl from a swamp fire, with sundry incidentals in between.

An oversize Weismuller moves somewhat woodenly through the picture. Virginia Grey is attractive and slinky enough as the predatory dame, and Carol Thurston is cute and convincing as the loyal sweetheart. Buster Crabbe is a satisfactory villain.   *Bron.*

She Wrote the Book

Universal release of Warren Wilson (Joe Gershenson) production. Stars Joan Davis, Jack Oakie; features Mischa Auer, Kirby Grant, John Litel. Directed by Charles Lamont. Original screenplay, Warren Wilson and Oscar Brodney; camera, George Robinson; editor, Fred R. Feitshans, Jr., Tradeshown N.Y., May 10, '46. Running time, 75 mins.
Jane Featherstone.............Joan Davis
Jerry Marlowe.................Jack Oakie
Boris (Joe)..................Mischa Auer

Eddie Caldwell...............Kirby Grant
Dean Fowler...................John Litel
Millicent...............Jacqueline de Wit
Phyllis Fowler..............Gloria Stuart
Van Cleve.................Thurston Hall
George Dixon.............Lewis L. Russell
Governor Kilgour..........Raymond Largay
Maid........................Victoria Horne
Mrs. Kilgour..................Verna Felton
Orchestra Leader.............Jack J. Ford
Elevator Boy.................Phil Garris

Here's an example of the way a light-budgeted film can be turned into solid entertainment via a good script, consistently good acting and top direction and technical work. Picture's a highly-amusing little farce that kids the book publishing business and the recent bevy of bestsellers based on the sex motif. With the names of Joan Davis and Jack Oakie to help brighten the marquee, the film should bring good returns.

Emphasis throughout is placed on the situation type of comedy and the two stars make the most of it. Miss Davis gets a chance to ham up her role with a portrayal for two-thirds of the film of a sedate calculus instructor in a hick midwestern college. Comedienne plays it well and is appealing in the more serious moments. Oakie, of course, is his usual boisterous, cigar-waving self.

Picture's a satire on the way the publishers capitalize on the publicity given their bestsellers when they're banned in cities like Boston. Wife of the dean of the university has written a lurid sex tale in the best "Amber" fashion, but anonymously. When Miss Davis has to travel to New York for an award by some scientific organization, the wife asks her to impersonate the authoress and pick up the royalty checks. Oakie, as the publisher's advertising chief, has a sock publicity campaign mapped out for the writer's arrival. Miss Davis gets socked on the head in a taxi accident and, when she comes to, is convinced she's the author and has actually lived the torrid love life. Rest of the film is given over to the way she goes glamorous, finally recovers her memory and, by tagging one of her newly-found admirers for some much-needed money for the college, succeeds in getting back into the faculty's good graces.

Miss Davis has one dance number, to which she gives all the zany antics that first brought her fame. Oakie is a good foil for her comedy and keeps in the running for top honors all the way. Mischa Auer is excellent as the fake Russian count who helps the authoress spend all her dough so that she'll have to write another book. Kirby Grant is sufficiently competent as Miss Davis' legitimate love interest. John Litel, Jacqueline de Wit and Gloria Stuart round out the leads, all good.

Charles Lamont's able direction keeps the picture moving rapidly from one laugh sequence to another. Warren Wilson and Oscar Brodney deserve credit for an original screenplay. George Robinson's camera work, though never outstanding, is adequate.   *Stal.*

Renegades

(COLOR)

Hollywood, May 11.
Columbia release of Michel Kraike production. Features Evelyn Keyes, Willard Parker, Larry Parks, Edgar Buchanan; with Jim Bannon, Forrest Tucker, Ludiwg Donath, Frank Sully, Willard Robertson, Paul E. Burns. Directed by George Sherman. Screenplay, Melvin Levy, Francis Edwards Faragoh; story, Harold Shumate; camera (Technicolor), William Snyder; score, Paul Sawtell; editor, Charles Nelson. Preview May 9, '46. Running time, 67 mins.
Hannah Brockway..............Evelyn Keyes
Dr. Sam Martin...............Willard Parker
Ben (Taylor) Dembrow..........Larry Parks
Kirk Dembrow...............Edgar Buchanan
Cash Dembrow..................Jim Bannon
Frank Dembrow...............Forrest Tucker
Jackorski...................Ludiwg Donath
Link..........................Frank Sully
Nathan Brockway.........Willard Robertson
Alkali Kid...................Paul E. Burns
Davy Lane....................Eddy Waller
Caleb Smart..................Vernon Dent
Eph..........................Francis Ford
Mrs. Jackorski..............Hermine Sterler
Janina Jackorski.............Eileen Janssen

Sarah Dembrow..............Virginia Brissac
Sheriff....................Addison Richards

Another example of recent Columbia entries that have been geared to show better returns than budget outlay would normally indicate. A factor is color, which dresses up the western fare. It's an actioner that puts a slightly more adult slant on the usual prairie hoke and payoff will prove okay all down the line. Production stretches footage sufficiently to rate it for top position on the double bills and cast names, headed by Evelyn Keyes, are familiar enough to warrant better than average attention on bookings.

George Sherman's experience in handling outdoor product assures planty of action, chases, gunplay, etc., for those who like their film fare to unfold at a gallop. Backing up the movement is sharp lensing by William Snyder, whose camera develops full tint values of scenic background and other production acruments furnished by Michael Kraike.

Plot angles of the Harold Shumate story, scripted by Melvin Levy and Francis Edwards Faragoh, differ from usual western formula by having heroine renounce the upright hero in favor of romance with one of the heavies. In the end, she's back with the hero but it takes continual dodging of the law and the birth of a baby to prove to her that excitement isn't always a good substitute for true, though prosaic, love.

Evelyn Keyes lends plenty of looks to her role as the girl who decides romance with Willard Parker, western medico, isn't as attractive as an outlaw existence with Larry Parks. Latter is a son of a notorious outlaw family who makes an attempt to go straight before succumbing to the thrills of life outside the law. Edgar Buchanan, the psalm-spouting pater of the bad boys. Jim Bannon and Forrest Tucker, the other two brothers, and sundry other members of the cast also do their share in keeping the excitement going.

Music score by Paul Sawtell is used to emphasize chases and clashes between the good and bad elements. Outdoor and interior settings show up well under the color treatment.   *Brog.*

The Pale Horseman

Two-reel documentary written and produced by Irving Jacoby; edited by Peter Elgar; music, Henry Brant; narration, Arnold Moss. Screened in N. Y., May 10, '46. Running time, 19 MINS.

This film rates the widest possible distribution for performing a vital public service. It packs into its two reels the full horror and meaning of World War II with its aftermath of famine and disease. The film is an open plea for well-fed America to share its bread with the starving world and the message is delivered in a way that tears at the heart.

Deadly matter-of-fact, without phony sensationalism, the camera picks its way through the vast garbage heap of Europe and Asia throwing up faces of hunger-twisted kids and of their agonized parents helpless before the chaos. It's a tragic document, movingly told, of a world in flight across a road stretching from China to France. The camera record could tell the story by itself with its unfailing eye for the relevant detail and its sense of the fitting mood. But the narration here adds to the film's impact by its quiet, and slightly bitter tone.

A small part of the film is devoted to the efforts of UNRRA and the allied armies to deal with the situation abroad. The film, however, doesn't pretend to give the answers; it does enough by posing the problem.

The OWI-produced film was screened at a special meeting of the Independent Citizens Committee of Arts, Sciences and Professions at

which ex-Gov. Herbert H. Lehman spoke on the problem of giving wide publicity to the needs of European relief. The documentary, which is available in 16m and 35m, is being distributed nationally by Brandon Films to private and community organizations. Commercial distribution is being negotiated with indie exhibitor groups.

Quiet Week-End

(BRITISH-MADE)

London, May 1.
Pathe Pictures release of Associated British Picture. Features Derek Farr, Frank Cellier, Marjorie Fielding, Barbara White. Directed by Harold French. Screenplay by Victor Skutezky, Stephen Black, T. J. Morrison, Warwick Ward from play by Esther McCracken. Camera, Eric Cross. At Palace theatre. Running time, 90 MINS.
Denys Royd...................Derek Farr
Adrian Barrasford...........Frank Cellier
Mildred Royd............Marjorie Fielding
Arthur Royd..................George Thorpe
Miranda Bute...............Barbara White
Rowena Hyde.................Helen Shingler
Sam Pecker...................Edward Rigby
Mary Jarrow.............Josephine Wilson
Marcia Brent..................Owen Whitby
Jim Brent.................Ballard Berkeley
Ella Spender..................Judith Furse
Sally Spender...................Pat Field
Police Sergeant............George Merritt
Bella.......................Helen Burls
Vicar...................Christopher Steele

Effective underplaying paired with a witty script make this a triumph of high comedy in the best English tradition. Perfect performances by a brilliant cast are coupled with direction as expert as any to come out of a British film studio lately. "Quiet Week-End" is what the doctor ordered for those who prefer Sheridan to Nick Carter. This looks big enough even to do biz in U. S. neighborhood theatres.

This successor to "Quiet Wedding" duplicated that smash hit in its record-breaking stage run, and will unquestionably equal the fabulous grosses of the earlier Esther McCracken opus. It is no detraction from the very clever acting to say top honors go to Harold French for his directorial skill which frequently hints a touch of near-genius. It is no wonder that Hollywood is angling for him.

Of the five featured players the one most likely to interest American talent scouts is Barbara White, whose portrayal of a young, hero-worshipping subdeb gives promise of future stardom. Up against the flawless performance of Derek Farr this new youngster holds her own in scenes in which a less gifted femme would be edged off the screen. She looks like a find.

Production could not be bettered. The week-end cottage with its antique plumbing and "mind your head" signs stuck beside low doorways is a miracle of illusion. Exteriors, too, are unusually lovely, the scripters having managed to take the camera far afield with a fine disregard for the limitations of the stage play.

Primarily a feast of fun for sophisticates, this one ought to be strong at the American boxoffice.   *Talb.*

Larceny In Her Heart

PRC release of Sigmund Neufeld production. Stars Hugh Beaumont, Cheryl Walker; features Ralph Dunn, Paul Bryar, Charles Wilson, Douglas Fowley. Directed by Sam Newfield. Screenplay, Raymond L. Schrock; original, Brett Halliday; camera, Jack Greenhalgh; editor, Holbrook N. Todd. Tradeshown N. Y., May 13, '46. Running time, 68 MINS.
Michael Shayne...........Hugh Beaumont
Phyllis....................Cheryl Walker
Sgt. Rafferty................Ralph Dunn
Tim Rourke...................Paul Bryar
Chief Gentry...............Charles Wilson
Doc Patterson...........Douglas Fowley
Burton Stallings.........Gordon Richards
Arch Dubler...............Charles Quigley
Lucille...................Julia McMillan
Helen Stallings.............Marie Harmon
Whit Marlow...................Lee Bennett
Dr. Porter...................Henry Hall
Joe Morell...................Milton Kibbee

Second in PRC's series of Michael Shayne stories with Hugh Beaumont playing the private dick, "Larceny in Her Heart" is run-of-the-mine fare for the whodunit addicts. Although breezily paced in running gag fashion, the story holds neither tension nor surprise, and the ending falls completely flat in trying to clear up the devious route by which the sleuth solves the murder. Biggest mystery of the film is the relation between story and title.

Yarn is a confused tangle concerning a corpse which turns up several times on Shayne's front porch. In an effort to shake off the police while investigating the case, Shayne meanders into some absurd situations, including a dipso institution. But while he follows his infallible intuition, everybody else is left completely in the dark during and after the picture.

Beaumont displays a winning personality in the detective's role and given a better script is capable of more creditable work. Cheryl Walker makes an attractive foil while Paul Bryar delivers some laughable comedy as Shayne's pal. Rest of the cast play their stock parts adequately.

Foreign Films

Riskiton Varjossa ("Hunting Shadows") (FINNISH). Suomen Filmiteollisuus production and release; stars Edvin Laine, Marvi Jervintaus; features Aku Korhonen, Yrjö Tuominen; directed by Edvin Laine; screenplay, Olavi Visisto; camera, Marius Raichi; reviewed in Helsingfors. Running time, 105 MINS.

When the best Finnish production this year is picked this looks like a real contender. Well directed story with a moral deals with Edvin Laine as an ex-convict faced with the problem of starting life over again. Mervi Jerventaus, a girl at odds with the law, also is involved. Although strong for Finland, its possibilities in the U. S. market are limited to a few foreign-language spots.

Mission Speciale (FRENCH). C.F.D.F. production and release; directed by Maurice de Canonge; stars Jany Holt, Jean Davy, Pierre Renoir; features Roger Karl, Jean Yonnel, Raymond Cordy, Maurice Salabert, Elisa Ruis; original screenplay, Simon Gantillon; reviewed in Paris. Running time, 105 MINS.

Second and last stanza of a serial depicting French underground activities during the German occupation. Good performance by Pierre Renoir doesn't help this one which is aimed exclusively at local patronage. Negative story material and technical treatment bar any international chance.

La Fille Du Diable ("The Devil's Daughter") (FRENCH). Pathe Consortium release of Pathe Cinema-Safia production; directed by Henri Decoin; stars Pierre Fresnay, Fernand Ledoux; features Andree Clement, Therese Dorny, Serge Andreguy, Albert Glado, Francois Patrice, Felix Claude, Henri Charrett; screenplay, Alex Joffe, Jean de Witte; dialog, M. G. Sauvageon; reviewed in Paris. Running time, 108 MINS.

Sketchy and unconvincing, this story has Andree Clement as a disillusioned village girl involved in intrigues which lead to her suicide. Although having a capable cast, substandard production limits the film to local consumption exclusively.

Asa-Hanna (SWEDISH). Europa Film production and release; directed by Anders Henrikson; stars Edvin Adolphson, Aine Taube; features Anders Henrikson, Hilda Bergstroem; screenplay, Barbro Alving, based on a novel by Elin Waegner; camera, Harold Berglund; reviewed at Saga, Waexlo Marts. Running time, 108 MINS.

Considered a possible best picture

for the year in Sweden, this somber story of a village family is deep in dramatics and aided by many good performances. Well directed by Henriksen, film looks only eligible for Swedish language or arty houses in the U. S.

Miniature Reviews

"The Stranger" (RKO-Int'l). Class melodrama, tops in thrills and chills with heavy b.o. potential.

"It Shouldn't Happen To a Dog" (20th). Sock comedy with Allyn Joslyn for solid b.o. returns.

"The Walls Came Tumbling Down" (Col). Okay whodunit about a N. Y. columnist.

"The French Key" (Rep). Okay murder-mystery programmer.

"Dressed to Kill" (U). Standard Sherlock Holmes whodunit that will please in its market.

"Talk About a Lady" (Songs) (Col). Good b.o. prospects in lesser runs.

"How Do You Do?" (Songs) (PRC). Comic whodunit for dual bill support.

"Spectre of the Rose" (Rep). Ben Hecht's pic has limited appeal but appeal to arty fans.

The Stranger

Hollywood, May 18.

RKO release of International Pictures (S. P. Eagle) production. Stars Edward G. Robinson, Loretta Young, Orson Welles; features Philip Merivale, Richard Long, Byron Keith, Billy House, Konstantin Shayne. Directed by Orson Welles. Screenplay, Anthony Veiller; story, Victor Trivas; camera, Russell Metty; editor, Ernest Nims. Tradeshown May 16, '46. Running time, 94 MINS.

Wilson	Edward G. Robinson
Mary Longstreet	Loretta Young
Prof. Charles Rankin	Orson Welles
Judge Longstreet	Philip Merivale
Noah Longstreet	Richard Long
Dr. Jeff Lawrence	Byron Keith
Mr. Potter	Billy House
Meinike	Konstantin Shayne
Sara	Martha Wentworth
Mrs. Lawrence	Isabel O'Madigan

"The Stranger" is socko melodrama, spinning an intriguing web of thrills and chills for all audiences. It's class from any angle and makes a strong entry from International for RKO to sell big all down the line. Star values are sturdy and the word-of-mouth will be equally potent. Fine production, strong direction and playing, and clever writing shape the ingredients to concentrate interest on as deadly a manhunt as has ever been screened.

Director Orson Welles gives the S. P. Eagle production a fast, suspenseful development, drawing every advantage from the hard-hitting script written by Anthony Veiller from the Victor Trivas story. Plot moves forward at a relentless pace in depicting the hunt of the Allied Commission for Prosecution of Nazi War Criminals for a top Nazi who has removed all traces of his origin and is a professor in a New England school. Edward G. Robinson is the Government man on his trail. Loretta Young is the New England girl who becomes the bride of the Nazi.

Story opens in Germany, where a Nazi is allowed to escape in belief he will lead the way to former head of a notorious prison camp. Chase moves across Europe to the small New England town where Welles is marrying Miss Young. When the escaped Nazi contacts him, Welles strangles him and buries the body in the woods. From then on the terror mounts as Robinson tries to trap Welles into revealing his true identity and at the same time protect the bride. Events pile up rapidly, building suspense and sheer terror to the boff climax.

A uniformly excellent cast gives reality to events that transpire. Each rates equal kudoes for exceptionally strong performances. The three stars, Robinson, Miss Young and Welles, turn in some of their best work, the actress being particularly effective as the mislead bride. Standing out

among supporting cast is Billy House, who adds the humor to an otherwise sober melodrama as true-to-type New England storekeeper. Philip Merivale, Richard Long, Byron Keith, Konstantin Shayne, Martha Wentworth and others figure importantiy with topnotch performances.

Photography by Russell Metty adds much to the spell of terror which the film weaves and other credits contribute measureably to general class tone of this one. *Brog.*

It Shouldn't Happen to a Dog

20th-Fox release of William Girard production. Stars Carole Landis, Allyn Joslyn; features Margo Woods, Henry Morgan, Reed Hadley, Jean Wallace, Roy Roberts, John Ireland, John Alexander. Directed by Herbert I. Leeds. Screenplay, Eugene Ling, Frank Gabrielson, based on story by Edwin Lanham; camera, Glen MacWilliams; editor, Fred J. Rode; score, David Buttolph. Tradeshown in N. Y., May 21, '46. Running time, 70 MINS.

Julia Andrews	Carole Landis
Henry Barton	Allyn Joslyn
Olive Stone	Margo Woode
Gus Rivers	Henry Morgan
Mike Valentine	Reed Hadley
Bess Williams	Jean Wallace
Mitchell	Roy Roberts
Bennie Smith	John Ireland
Joe Parelli	John Alexander
Glass	Charles Tannen
Mrs. James	Kathryn Card
Nick	Ralph Sanford
Sam Black	Jeff Corey
Madigan	Charles Cane
House Detective	Clancy Cooper
Police Lieutenant	James Flavin
Chinese Laundry Man	Lee Tung Foo
Crester Frye	Whitner Bissell
Cab Driver	Tom Dugan
Policeman	Pat Flaherty

This film is a solid package of chuckle material that is sure to be a wicket-spinner on basis of word-of-mouth. With Allyn Joslyn on the celluloid for the full running time, film is a fast mix of gay situations and bright gags with no letdown at any point. Pat story of a newspaperman in dutch with his editor is given a screwball twist by the highly competent scripters who place a dog at the center of the plot. The canine, a Doberman pinscher, closely heels Joslyn as a laugh-winner and besides has looks and menace to make its option a cinch to be picked up.

Adroit directional touches by Herbert Leeds milk each comic situation for maximum returns but without slowing down the rollicking pace. Camera work and background music effectively maintain the light mood and the production accoutrements, though in the medium budget class, par the general excellent quality of the film.

Joslyn plays a reporter victimized by an April fool's joke into scooping his rivals on a robbery that never took place. Stickup was allegedly performed by Carole Landis aided by the Doberman who terrorized a barkeep into forking over his receipts.

Although story is unfounded, Joslyn keeps up the gag for his editor's benefit, kidnaps the dog and becomes involved in a series of hilarious adventures with the pooch. Landis plays a femme cop on the trail of a black marketeer and when the plot lines cross at the climax, Joslyn, the dog, and Landis trap the gangster and emerge as loving heroes.

Joslyn gives full sway to his talents in this pic showing himself off as a maestro with the gag line. Using his unhandsome face to best advantage, Joslyn muggs and double-takes with a sense of timing that puts him in the top-draw class of comics. Carole Landis, appearing in only a few sequences, is okay and her name won't hurt on the marquee. The dog is great and the rest of the cast come through with performances that add up to firm support.

The Walls Came Tumbling Down

Columbia release of Albert J. Cohen production. Stars Lee Bowman, Marguerite Chapman; features Edgar Buchanan, George Macready. Directed by Lothar Mendes. Screenplay, Wilfrid H. Pettitt; based on novel by Jo Eisinger; camera, Charles Lawton, Jr.; editor, Gene Havlick; asst. director, Sam Nelson. Previewed N. Y., May 17, '46. Running time, **81 MINS.**

Gilbert Archer...............Lee Bowman
Patricia Foster.......Marguerite Chapman
George Bradford..........Edgar Buchanan
Matthew Stoker..........George Macready
Susan.........................Lee Patrick
Captain Griffin..............Jonathan Hale
Ernst Helms..........J. Edward Bromberg
Catherine Walsh..........Elisabeth Risdon
Dr. Marko...................Miles Mander
Bishop Martin...............Moroni Olsen
Mrs. Stoker...............Katherine Emery
Rausch........................Noel Cravat
Detective Regan..................Bob Ryan
Bianca....................Charles LaTorre

Whodunit about a Broadway columnist tracking down killers of an old priest-friend has several twists and angles, to hold interest throughout. Pic, modest-budgeted, should do okay in general situations.

Story is plausible, though stretched a bit thin at times. Plot has sufficient action, with a couple vicious fights to stir blood-pressure. Dialog is hep, with an occasional lapse into smart-chat. Acting is uniformly good, with direction to match. Camera work is okay, too.

Plot, though not too novel, never gives itself away. Story concerns a well-known Broadway chatter-writer whose friend, an aged priest, is found hanged in his rectory. Police thinks it is suicide; columnist suspects foul play. Determined to track down the murderers, the columnist finds the trail involving a socialite looker from Boston, an eccentric art dealer, a blustering lawyer, and a trio of pseudo-missionaries. All are interested in finding two Bibles and a painting, latter describing the fall of Jericho. Plots unravels nicely at close, with parts fitting in neatly.

Lee Bowman plays the columnist satisfactorily, while Marguerite Chapman is very appealing as the mysterious deb. George Macready is the deceptively honest-looking, vicious killer and Edgar Buchanan a fitting teammate as the crooked lawyer. J. Edward Bromberg does a good bit as the eccentric art dealer, and Jonathan Hale is believable as a police captain. *Bron.*

The French Key

Hollywood, May 18.

Republic release of Walter Colmes production, directed by Colmes. Stars Albert Dekker; features Mike Mazurki, Evelyn Ankers, John Eldredge, Frank Fenton, Selmer Jackson, Byron Foulger, Joe DeRita. Screenplay, Frank Gruber from own novel; camera, Jockey Feindel; score, Alexander Laszlo; editor, Robert Jahns. Previewed May 17, '46. Running time, **67 MINS.**

Jornny Fletcher.............Albert Dekker
Sam Cragg...................Mike Mazurki
Janet Morgan................Evelyn Ankers
John Holterman..............John Eldredge
Horatio Vedder...............Frank Fenton
Walter Winslow..............Selmer Jackson
Peabody.....................Byron Foulger
Fox............................Joe DeRita
Betty Winslow...........Marjorie Manners
Eddie Miller.................David Gorcey
Murdock...................Michael Branden
Percy.........................Sammy Stein
Madigan........................Alan Ward
George Polson.............Walter Soderling
Desk Clerk.................Emmett Vogan

"The French Key" isn't as good a screen whodunit as it was a mystery novel. Exploits of super book salesman Johnny Fletcher and his muscle-bound sidekick read better than they film. It's still okay program material, having enough cast strength to help the bookings. Physical production has good values and there are moments of topnotch suspense but otherwise the mystery elements get lost in a maze of complications that never become quite clear.

Albert Dekker and Mike Mazurki are locked out of their hotel room for non-payment of rent. French key used for the sealing gives rise to the title. Boys use fire escape, find a dead man in the room with a gold coin in his hand and to prevent murder being fastened on them set out to find the real killer. Trail gets them involved with night club singers, coin collectors, more dead men, etc., and just what it's all about is never clear to the audience. The solution is also a mystery.

Cast is full of hard workers, all of whom try to bring some light into script complications. Dekker is good as Fletcher and Mazurki furnishes some chuckles as his brawny partner. Evelyn Ankers is easy to look at, and others, including John Eldredge, Selmer Jackson, Frank Fenton and Joe DeAita show up competently. Walter Colmes produced and directed from a script by Frank Gruber, who adapted from his novel. Lensing, editing and other production credits measure up to expenditure. *Brog.*

Dressed to Kill

(ONE SONG)

Hollywood, May 17.

Universal release of Howard Benedict production. Stars Basil Rathbone, Nigel Bruce; features Patricia Morison, Edmond Breon, Frederic Worlock, Harry Cording, Mary Gordon. Produced and diected by Roy William Neill. Screenplay, Leonard Lee; adaptation, Frank Gruber from story by Sir Arthur Conan Doyle; camera, Maury Gertsman; song, Jack Brooks; editor Saul A. Goodkind. Previewed May 15, '46. Running time, **72 MINS.**

Sherlock Holmes............Basil Rathbone
Dr. Watson...................Nigel Bruce
Hilda Courtney...........Patricia Morison
Gilbert Emery...............Edmond Breon
Colonel Cavanaugh......Frederick Worlock
Inspector Hopkins.............Carl Harbord
Evelyn Clifford...........Patricia Cameron
Detective Thompson........Tom P. Dillon
Hamid.......................Harry Cording
Kilgour Child..................Topsy Glyn
Housekeeper..................Mary Gordon

Okay supporting film fare. It follows the accepted Sherlock Holmes series pattern for the bread-and-butter bookings. Like most of the Universal series it is expertly put together and excellently played by a cast familiar with technique necessary to keep the Holmes fans satisfied. Film gets good production and direction from Roy William Neill and plot is neatly contrived to hold interest.

Holmes and Dr. Watson are called upon to uncover whereabouts of some stolen Bank of England banknote plates. Chase interest centers on three prison-made music boxes, in which brook has hidden clue to hiding place of the plates so his confederates can recover them. Music boxes are sold at auction before gang can grab them, resulting in a two-way race between Holmes and the crooks to be first to recover boxes and obtain the loot. Several killings, the near-death of Holmes and other whodunit stunts are pulled off before the fictional detective beats the crooks at their own game.

Basil Rathbone is up to his usual competence in delivery of the Holmes characterization. Same goes for Nigel Bruce as the bumbling Dr. Watson. Patricia Morison, Frederic Worlock and Harry Cording are an expert trio of antagonists matching wits with Holmes. Edmond Breon and others hold up their end. There's one tune used, a novelty beerhall number titled "Ya Never Know Just 'oo Yer Gonna Meet," capably sung by Delos Jewkes.

Lensing, editing and other technical functions help in the production dress. *Brog.*

Talk About a Lady

(SONGS)

Columbia release of Michel Kraike production. Stars Jinx Falkenburg, Forrest Tucker, Joe Besser; features Trudy Marshall, Richard Lane, Jimmy Little, Frank Sully, Jack Davis, Robert Regent, Mira McKinney, Robin Raymond, Stan Kenton orchestra. Directed by George Sherman. Screenplay, Richard Weil and Ted Thomas; based on story by Robert D. Andrews and Barry Trivers; camera, Henry Freulich; editor, James Sweeney; songs, Allan Roberts, Doris Fisher, Oscar Hammerstein II and Ben Oakland. At Fox, Brooklyn, week May 16, '46, dual. Running time, **71 MINS.**

Janie Clark..............Jinx Falkenburg
Bart Manners...............Forrest Tucker
Roly Q. Entwhistle..............Joe Besser
Toni Marlowe...............Trudy Marshall
Duke Randall.................Richard Lane
Buffalo......................Jimmy Little
Rocky Jordan..................Frank Sully
Carleton Vane..................Jack Davis
Arthur Harrison..............Robert Regent
Letitia Harrison...........Mira McKinney
Peaches Berkeley..........Robin Raymond
Stan Kenton and His Orchestra

This film, paced by some easy warbling by Jinx Falkenburg and a quartet of pleasant songs, shapes up to a mite better than average program fare. Combo of strong music plus tomfoolery of Joe Besser, which draws hearty chuckles, outweighs an obviously contrived story. Pic should please in the lesser runs.

Plot is an oldie, simply put, that of the unspoiled country lass who comes to town and by pure goodness bests the hardened urban socialite. In this case, it's all brought about by a testamentary bequest which leaves Miss Falkenburg, the country gal, a nitery and some other assets totalling several millions. While battling it out with the disinherited socialite wife of the testator, Miss Falkenburg vocalizes Allan Roberts and Doris Fisher's "You Gotta Do Whatcha Gotta Do" and "I Never Had a Dream Come True" plus "A Mist Is Over the Moon," by Oscar Hammerstein II and Ben Oakland. "I Never Had a Dream Come True," tops in the sentimental ballad genre, is reprised several times. Score also includes Roberts-Fisher's "Avocado," played as are the others by Stan Kenton and his orch.

Besser in the role of amateur magician and godfather to Miss Falkenburg brightens the film at several points when the story threatens to get in the way. Effective broad clowning, a risible appearance and comic mannerisms blend into a performance that customers go for. Miss Falkenburg's thesping matches her singing. Rest of cast, including Forrest Tucker, Trudy Marshall, Richard Lane, Jimmy Little, Frank Sully and Jack Davis, are uniformly satisfactory.

George Sherman's directing, though smooth, in the main suffers from one flaw. No originality or freshness is displayed in introducing the musical numbers. Camera work of Henry Freulich, editing, sound recording and other technical contributions add up to a first-rate job.

How Do You Do

(SONGS)

PRC release of Harry Sauber production. Stars Bert Gordon; features Harry Von Zell, Cheryl Walker, Ella Mae Morse, Frank Albertson, Claire Windsor, Keye Luke. Directed by Ralph Murphy. Story and screenplay, Harry Sauber and Joseph Carole; songs, Hal Borne, Paul Webster; music direction, Howard Jackson; camera, Benjamin H. Kline; editor, Thomas Neff. At Strand, Brooklyn, dual, May 17, '46. Running time, **80 MINS.**

Bert Gordon.........................Himself
Harry Von Zell......................Himself
Cheryl Walker.......................Herself
Frank Albertson..............Tom Brandon
Ella Mae Morse......................Herself
Claire Windsor......................Herself
Keye Luke...........................Himself
Charles Middleton....................Sheriff
Thomas Jackson......................Himself
James Burke.........................Himself
Fred Kelsey.........................Himself
Matt McHugh..........................Deputy
Leslie Denison......................Himself
Francis Pierlot....................Proprietor
Sidney Marion...................Dr. Kolmar

Radio is radio and films are films, and it takes a lot of stretching to make the twain meet. This is an unpretentious effort in every respect, including budget. but in its own pedestrian manner, serves to further point up a couple of personalities who might develop into fair screen draws. As is a minor dualer.

Story concerns cast of a radio show who travel incognito to a desert resort. During their first night a hated radio agent is murdered by someone supposedly in show biz, and the radioites are exposed as Bert Gordon, Harry Van Zell, Ella Mae Morse, etc. Gordon wires screen detective friends to come down and solve the crime. Turns out that "victim" was under drug administered in experiment by his doctor. Story's end flashes aud back to screening room, where cast and director decide they don't like the climax. While the last hundred feet are re-run, Gordon "re-kills" the supposedly dead man. Script falls apart here like a matchstick house.

Ella Mae Morse shows promise as a comedienne, with all the cute mannerisms necessary. Smart scripting could make this gal. She handles her meagre vocal assignments well. Picture isn't Gordon's first, but gives him one of his better efforts.

Specter of the Rose

Republic release of Ben Hecht production (Lee Garmes co-producer), directed by same. Features Judith Anderson, Michael Chekhov, Ivan Kirov, Viola Essen, Lionel Stander. Story and screenplay by Hecht, based in part on the ballet, "Spectre de la Rose"; camera, Garmes; editor, Harry Keller; music, George Antheil; choreography, Tamara Geva. Previewed in New York, May 16, '46. Running time, **90 MINS.**

La Belle Sylph............Judith Anderson
Max Polikoff.............Michael Chekhov
Andre Sanine....................Ivan Kirov
Haidi............................Viola Essen
Lionel Gans...................Lionel Stander
Specs McFarlan...Charles "Red" Marshall
Kropotkin.....................George Shdanoff
Jack James.......................Billy Gray
Jibby...........................Juan Panalle
Mr. Lyons.........................Lou Hearn
Mamochka......................Ferike Boros
Alexis...........................Constantine
Giovanni....................Ferdinand Pollina
Olga.............................Polly Rose
Jimmy............................Jim Moran
Ballet dancers: Freda Flier, Miriam Schiller, Miriam Golden, Grace Mann, Allan Cooke, Alice Cavers, Nina Haven, John Stanley, Arleen Claire, Celene Radding.

Ben Hecht, to say the least, has done the expected by coming up with the unusual. Fact is, unusual probably will not be a strong enough word to express the opinion of a Republic account in, say, Xenia, O., where he opens the can and expects horses to come galloping out. There are definitely no oats in this. On the other hand, sophisticated audiences in more or less arty locations will **find "Specter of the Rose" interesting, at the very least. With careful booking and proper selling it will find patronage.**

There's a possible chance, too, that "Specter" will turn out to be a b.o. whiz in special key city engagements. It has plenty of elements of unusual dialog, direction and general treatment to give reviewers an opportunity to say, "This is art; this is what a picture should be. Its lack of typical Hollywood pretentiousness is refreshing." In that case, expect the intelligentsia to jump on the bandwagon and pump up grosses.

On the other hand, there's plenty of opportunity, too, for the newspaper and mag o.o.ers to hop on the picture's excessive talkiness, lack of unusual production values and occasional dragginess. In which case—that's all, brother. In any event, unless Rep does a special pitch job, best the film can expect will be the bottom of occasional double bills, since even in the name department the top that it offers is Judith Anderson and Lionel Stander.

Republic, of course, isn't destined to lose much, come what may, because it didn't spend much. It was obviously a conscious attempt by Hecht to prove on how small a budget he could produce an acceptable picture. Reports are that it cost in the neighborhood of $160,000. And certainly not much of that went for sets. The Civilian Production Administration definitely will have no squawk on excessive use of materials in "Specter." That, of course, doesn't matter. The serious defect productionwise is a general lack of polish that is at times disturbing.

Yarn, fitting in with current trend to psychiatric mellers, concerns a ballet troupe in which the top male dancer has gone berserk. Okay mentally for periods, he at times has hallucinations in which he hears music which forces him to dance the ballet, "Spectre de la Rose" and, while terpin, he gets a desire to slit his wife's throat. This he has already done to one wife when the picture opens. One of the ballerinas is nevertheless in love with him and is sure she can cure him. She marries him, his mind remains clear and the ballet goes on. But, as is expected, the hallucinations suddenly return and he's about to kill wife No. 2 when he's interrupted. Still in love with him and still certain she can cure him, she secretes him to a hotel room. She nurses him for days but finally falls asleep in exhaustion. The hallucinations again return, he begins to dance, touches a knife several times to the gal's throat, but ends up instead by making a great ballet leap through the window to his death in the street below. The ballerina returns to the troupe.

All this is against a serio-comic and satirical background of the ballet's company's travails, financial and otherwise, in staging a tour. Miss Anderson is the troupe's mentor, Anton Chekhov the comic impresario, and two actual ballet dancers, Ivan Kirov and Viola Essen, the boy and girl. Stander is a Greenwich Village poet who seems to be in the film for no other reason than to mouth Hechtisms.

Hecht's direction and dialog give the acting a stylized artificiality that grows on the spectator as the picture progresses. Satire of the characterizations makes many of the film's people virtually caricatures. In this framework, Kirov gives a performance that marks him as an interesting possibility for future roles. Miss Essen is likewise considerably more than adequate thespically, as well as in her ballet work.

Among aspects of the picture that is sure to bring forth comment is probably one of the most exciting love scenes ever put on film, despite the fact the participants never get closer than four feet. It's sharply done via dialog, camerawork and cutting. Hecht's dialog, incidentally, is often vivid, discerning and entertaining. Trouble is that there's too much of it and it's too frequently used in place of action. *Herb.*

Foreign Films

Sciuscia ("Shoeshine Boys") (ITALIAN) ENIC release of Paolo W. Tamburella production. Stars Rinaldo Smordoni, Franco Interlenghi. Features Carlo Ortensi, Aniello Mele and Emilio Cigoli. Directed by Vittorio De Sica. Screenplay by Cesare Zavattini, Sesare Giulio Viola, Sergio Amidei, and Adolfo Franci. Tradeshown in Rome. Running time, **105 MINS.**

"Sciuscia," with the shoe-shine boys of Rome's streets as background for this film, is a preachment on Italian juvenile delinquency. Producers used real shoe-shine boys and the absence of experienced actors works out okay. Scenes in Rome's jail emphasize the need for drastic reforms there. Two bootblacks are the principal characters, the film showing their change from honest lads into bitter juvenile gangsters. Paolo W. Tamburella, producer, and Vittoria De Sica, director, deserve bulk of praise for this. Okay for Italy. But theme and fact that American pictures already have treated with the same problem in the U. S. militate against its foreign b.o.

Les Clandestins ("The Underground") (FRENCH). Cine Selection release of Essor Cinematographique Francais produduction. Directed by Andre Chotin. Stars Suzy Carrier, Georges Rollin; features Samson Fainsilber, Andre Reybaz, Guillaume de Sax, Constant Remy. Screenplay by Pierre Lestringuez. Music by Walberg. Camera by Georges Million.

Reviewed in Paris. Running time, **98 MINS.**

The picture is one of the "underground" cycle, and shows German soldiers in a punitive expedition on a French village, with hangings and all, in a realistic way. As such, it is a sure local grosser. It is one of the few of this type where Germans are not made to overshout in a ridiculous manner. The love story between the girl who goes underground to the man she first met when he was trying to escape after being wounded is less important than the war horrors and heroics which, with good lenswork, may give it a chance for strictly French patronage. Best acting is by Samson Fainsilber as the Jewish medico who undergoes torture, and Constant Remy as the Catholic priest.

Messieurs Ludovic (FRENCH). Richebe release of Optimax-Films production. Directed by J. P. Lechanois. Stars Odette Joyeux; features Bernard Blier, Marcel Herrand, Jean Chevrier, Carette, Jules Berry, Palau. Based on legit "Ludo" by Pierre Seize. Camera, Jacques Lemare. Music by Joseph Kosma. Adapted and dialog by Lechanois. Reviewed in Paris. Running time, 105 MINS.

Neat photo and good acting may give it a chance in spots where exclusively French patronage will accept this sketchy adaptation from the legit play. It is the rather unplausible story of Odette Joyeux, as the hard headed girl who comes from her coal mining village to try the big town, torn three ways between jailbird Jean Chevrier, Bernard Blier as a dreamy and kindhearted engineer, and the tough and wealthy Marcel Herrand. Jules Berry has only a bit. Film opens with a sequence ghost-voiced by Carette, before switching to usual talker. *Maxi.*

Miniature Reviews

"Centennial Summer" (Color) (20th). Pleasant musical on Philadelphia Centennial of 1876. Good boxoffice prospects.

"Valley of The Zombies" (Rep). Horror stuff that's not too horror-full nor too strong.

"Appointment With Crime" (Anglo-Am.). Fast British meller likely to do well in America.

"Don't Gamble With Strangers" (Mono). Unsuspenseful murder meller for twin bills.

"Meet the Navy" (Anglo-Am). Sock British musical rated strong enough for big U. S. trade.

Centennial Summer
(MUSICAL-COLOR)

Hollywood, May 28.

20th-Fox release of Otto Preminger production. Stars Jeanne Crain, Cornel Wilde, Linda Darnell, William Eythe, Walter Brennan, Constance Bennett, Dorothy Gish; features Barbara Whiting, Larry Stevens, Kathleen Howard, Buddy Swan, Charles Dingle. Directed by Preminger. Screenplay, Michael Kanin, based on novel by Albert E. Idell; music, Jerome Kern; lyrics, Oscar Hammerstein II, Leo Robin, E. Y. Harburg; camera (Technicolor), Ernest Palmer; special photographic effects, Fred Sersen; musical direction, Alfred Newman; orchestral arrangements, Maurice de Packh, Herbert Spencer, Conrad Salinger; vocal arrangements, Charles Henderson; dances, Dorothy Fax; editor, Harry Reynolds. Tradeshown in Los Angeles, May 23, '46. Running time, 104 MINS.

Julia	Jeanne Crain
Philippe Lascalles	Cornel Wilde
Edith	Linda Darnell
Benjamin Franklin Phelps	William Eythe
Jesse Rogers	Walter Brennan
Zenina Lascalles	Constance Bennett
Harriet	Dorothy Gish
Susanna Rogers	Barbara Whiting
Richard Lewis, Esq.	Larry Stevens
Deborah	Kathleen Howard
Dudley Rogers	Buddy Swan
Snodgrass	Charles Dingle
Specialty	Avon Long
Trowbridge	Gavin Gordon
Mr. Phelps	Eddie Dunn
Mrs. Phelps	Lois Austin
Mr. Dorgan	Harry Strang
Mrs. Dorgan	Frances Morris
President Grant	Reginald Sheffield
Messenger Boy	William Frambes
Senator	Paul Everton
Bartender	James Metcalfe
Drunk	John Farrell
Attendant	Billy Wayne
Kelly	Robert Malcolm
Nurse	Edna Holland
Governor	Ferris Taylor
Governor's Wife	Winifred Harris
Master of Ceremonies	Rodney Bell
Carpenter	Glancy Cooper

"Centennial Summer" is pleasant musical filmfare, sparked by a lilting Jerome Kern score. For marquee lure it offers color and a seven-star cast, both factors indicating sturdy grosses in all situations. Several of the songs have already moved up among country's top tunes, which adds to exploitation value. Production dress is lavish to point up the period, and direction adopts a leisurely style in welding together the music and story ingredients. It's not a sock film, but easy to take and will please.

The Kern-Oscar Hammerstein II "All Through the Day" is exploited most often in the score, but workouts are also given to the Kern-Leo Robin numbers such as "Love in Vain," "The Right Romance" and "Up With the Lark." Film's weakness is lack of top voices to punch the numbers over, but quality of the cleffing makes them stand out regardless. Specialty spot goes to "Cinderella Sue," with lyrics by E. Y. Harburg and sung by Avon Long.

Script by Michael Kanin was based on Albert E. Idell's novel of the same title. Background is the Centennial celebration held in Philadelphia during the summer of 1876. Plot spreads itself over several angles, projecting both elderly and younger romantic complications that beset members of a Philadelphia railroading family. Papa makes a mild play for his wife's sophisticated sister, and the two girls of the family both chase the same man. Side issues are papa's desire to interest the railroad president in a newfangled clock he has invented, a young doctor's efforts to win the heart of one of the daughters, and the sophisticated aunty's maneuvering to make things add up right for the Rogers family.

Producer-director Otto Preminger gets the most from the material and players. Jeanne Crain and Linda Darnell are the sisters seeking to ensnare Cornel Wilde. Both are exponents of femme loveliness, but the color lensing gives Miss Darnell's lush charms the best display. Miss Crain handles most of the vocaling of the score's numerous tunes, with exception of "Up With the Lark," which is family round-robined several times. William Eythe as the doctor isn't given as much script play as the other younger cast members.

Walter Brennan wraps up a good characterization as the clock-inventing father. Dorothy Gish does well by the wife role. Constance Bennett stands out as the sophisticated aunty who charms the males. Charles Dingle gets in some menace as Brennan's immediate boss. Others in the cast work well.

Color work isn't up to the usual Technicolor standard, but otherwise lensing does expertly in displaying the many-hued costumes and settings of the period piece. *Brog.*

Valley of the Zombies

Republic release of a Dorrell & Stuart McGowan production. Stars Ian Keith, Robert Livingston, Adrian Booth; features Thomas Jackson, Charles Trowbridge. Directed by Philip Ford. Screenplay, the McGowans, from original by Royal K. Cole and Sherman L. Lowe; camera, Reggie Lanning; editor, William P. Thompson. Previewed N. Y., May 24, '46. Running time, 56 MINS.

Terry Evans	Robert Livingston
Susan Drake	Adrian Booth
Ormand Murks	Ian Keith
Blair	Thomas Jackson
Dr. Maynard	Charles Trowbridge
Fred Mays	Earle Hodgins
Hendricks	Leroy Mason
Tiny	William Haade
Dr. Garland	Wilton Graff
Inspector Ryan	Charles Cane
Lacy	Russ Clark
The Driver	Charles Hamilton

Billed as a horror story, this picture, which will never get out of the twin-bill B league, features an unzombie-like zombie and a fairly horrorless story, despite half a dozen murders. However, it's pretty fair Saturday matinee stuff.

Ian Keith plays a big-city zombie on a lost weekend for blood. He kills a doctor who had him committed in the past; his brother, the doctor's assistant, a psychiatrist, a cab driver, a gas station attendant, and others who never appear on the screen, meanwhile incriminating the doctor's young partner and the nurse, who provide love interest. They eventually clear themselves after passing through a number of stock situations, and the zombie falls off a building.

Photography is better than fair, and the inclusion of Ian Keith and a group of experienced supports brings thesping up to a good B level. Title is derived from one line, in which the zombie, who looks more like a mean college professor, says he got that way in the valley of the zombies, and still carries a shot of the stuff to prove it. Scripting features all the horror-whodunit cliches.

Appointment With Crime
(BRITISH-MADE)

London, May 15.

Anglo-American Film Corp. release of British National Films picture. Features William Hartnell, Robert Beatty, Joyce Howard. Directed by John Harlow. Screenplay by John Harlow from story by Michael Leighton. Music by George Melachrino; camera, James Wilson, Gerald Moss. At Palace theatre. Running time, 91 MINS.

Leo Martin	William Hartnell
Loman	Raymond Lovell
Inspector Rogers	Robert Beatty
Gregory Lang	Herbert Lom
Carol Dane	Joyce Howard
Noel Penn	Alan Wheatley
Sergeant Weeks	Cyril Smith
Mrs. Wilkins	Elsie Wagstaffe
Prison Governor	Ian Fleming
Joe Fisher	Wally Patch
Detective Mason	Ian McLean
Big Mike	Harry Lane
Winckle	Ken Warrington
Harry Millerton	Frederick Morant

Here's a honey in any man's language. Basically it's meller in the best Corse Payton tradition, but the acting and direction make one overlook this. The top that U. S. films have had to offer in gangster spine-chillers have nothing on this one for slickness and speed. The murder here is planned and carried out to the accompaniment of low-pitched, velvet-smooth speaking tones. Despite lack of players known in the U. S., it should do well in America.

There's little to choose between the three co-stars, William Hartnell, Robert Beatty and Joyce Howard, each of whom triumphs over characterization improbabilities which would hamstring less competent players. Raymond Lovell has an especially nasty bit, one of the several characters who wind up full of lead. He is such a sweet-scented, double-crosser one almost regrets his demise. It is Herbert Lom, the brains of the gang, who dominates every scene in which he appears. This 27-year-old Czech is due in Hollywood soon to work for 20th-Fox, and looks like a real screen bet.

Credit also is due Louis H. Jackson for his production. Really convincing are the sequences in a Palais de Dance and the scene in which Lom, cloaking his murderous activities as an art dealer, conducts his operations. Incidentally, a palm goes to the genius who made his chief assistant a piano-playing pansy.

John Harlow, who scripted and directed, has done a great job of both. From start to finish, there isn't a dull spot. *Talb.*

Don't Gamble With Strangers

Monogram release of Jeffrey Bernerd production. Stars Kane Richmond, Bernadene Hayes, Peter Cookson; features Gloria Warren, Charles Trowbridge, Frank Dae. Directed by William Beaudine. Screenplay, Caryl Coleman, Harvey Gates; camera, William Sickner; editor, William Austin; asst. director, Doc Joos. Previewed N. Y. May 23, 46. Running time, **67 MINS.**

Mike Sarno	Kane Richmond
Fay Benton	Bernadene Hayes
Bob Randall	Peter Cookson
Ruth Hamilton	Gloria Warren
Creighton	Charles Trowbridge
John Randall	Frank Dae
Pinky Lutz	Tony Caruso
Morelli	Phil Van Zandt
John Sanders	Harold Goodwin
Robert Elliot	Leonard Mudie
Harry Arnold	Bill Kennedy
Chief Broderick	Addison Richards
Michael Larson	Ferris Taylor
Mrs. Arnold	Mary Field
Swedish Maid	Edith Evanson
Tony	Steve Darrell
Pete	Bob Barron
Dealer	Sayre Dearing

Built around a gambling motif, this modestly budgeted whodunit rolls along on its obvious way until the audience becomes thoroughly confused. Then it ends, sans enough explanation to clear things up. Entertainment value, fair throughout, is hampered by sloppy production, chief fault of which are periods of protracted silence followed by spurts of conversation, with everyone talking at once. Enough is there, through adherence to a tried formula, to provide twin bill spotting.

Story, which makes a trite attempt at a surprise ending, leaves much unclear Sharks hook up as gambling partners and, posing as brother and sister, fleece a small-town banker. take over a gambling joint, and finally break up over the "other woman," at which point the guy gets knocked off on a "hell hath no fury . . ." note. Gal is accused, but exonerated when ballistics show another gambler did it.

Aud will have difficulty reconciling scenes wherein the pair continually meet in the same hotel room, with no intimation, until the very last, that the guy has a room of his own. Also, during denouement, police chief tells gal he has enough on her to keep her around for a couple of years. Film then segues into scene of her in the gambling room of a ship, for closing shot.

Charles Trowbridge is spotted in a good supporting job, while Kane Richmond and Bernadene Hayes do a workmanlike reading of stiffly scripted lines. Peter Cookson, with less to do, also okay. Writing and direction, n.s.h.

Meet the Navy

(BRITISH-MADE)

(With Songs)

London, May 17.

Anglo-American Film Corp. release of British National Film. Features members of Royal Canadian Forces. Directed by Alfred Travers. Screenplay by Lester Cooper, James Seymore from original story by Lester Cooper. Musical directors, Eric Wilde, Ronnie Munro. Camera, Ernest Palmer, Moray Grant. At Palace theatre. Running time, **85 MINS.**

Johnny	Lionel Murton
Midge	Margaret Hurst
Horace	John Pratt
Tommy	Bob Goodier
C.P.O. Oliver	Bill Oliver
Jenny	Phyllis Hudson
Cook	Percy Haynes
Gracie	Jeanette de Hueck
Fisherman	Oscar Naske
Dancers	Alan Lund, Billie Mae Richards

To say this is easily the best musical to come out of a British studio is to damn it with faint praise. In many respects it seems up to Hollywood's best standards. Its factual sequences achieve a degree of realism rarely found in a song and dance offering. Credit for this picture goes largely to Louis Silvers, musical director of the Lux Radio Theatre, who took care of the melody, and to Larry Ceballos who handled the ensemble numbers. Result is a fast-moving, ear-appealing and colorful spectacle so slick it's difficult to believe 90% of the cast were raw amateurs when they were "directed" to join the troupe. Film should click with all kinds of American audiences.

Entirely different from the stage show which was a hit at the Hippodrome here, the screen version shows how the revue was gradually built up and whipped into shape during its Coast-to-Coast Canadian tour before being shipped overseas to entertain Allied troops on the Continent. When the show reaches London, black and white gives way to Technicolor to glamorize the arrival of the King and Queen and Princesses at the Command Performance.

Of the cast, Oscar Naske, the young New Zealand bass, repeats before the camera the sensational triumph he scored in the stage version. If this lad doesn't soar to the heights, prophets here will be a dime a dozen. John Pratt, lugubrious comic whose one number, "You'll Get Used to It," stopped the stage show, has a dead-pan technique which registers as effectively on the screen as it did before the footlights. The preview audience burst into spontaneous applause at the end of the song, killing a whole minute of the ensuing dialog. Laurels also go to Lionel Murton, Bob Goodier, Bill Oliver and Alan Lund. Last named is an eccentric tap dancer who takes the stage in the Coney Island sequence in a whirlwind routine worthy of Fred Astaire.

Margaret Hurst and Phyllis Hudson are easy on the eye and do their stuff convincingly enough. But this goes for the Wrens in the chorus.

With the war over, "Meet the Navy" may have the disadvantage of being mistakenly put in the war film category. In point of fact it is as timely as today's paper, and is crammed with entertainment. *Talb.*

Foreign Films

"Un Uomo Ritorna" ("Man's Return") **(ITALIAN)** Zeus Film production and release. Original story by Mario Tomassini. Stars Anna Magnani, Gino Cervi. Features Luisa Poselli, Felice Romano, Aldo Silvani. Directed by Max Neufeld. Camera, Giuseppe La Torre. Running time, **102 MINS.**

Anna Magnani and Gino Cervi tackle the problem of the returning soldier in this film. A power plant engineer returns from war to find his factory in ashes, his sister consorting with foreign soldiers and his small brother supporting the family' by selling cigarettes in the black market. He finds his countrymen howling for vengeance on collaborationists, puffed up when they have jobs and helpless or criminal when they don't. His solution is to begin rebuilding without waiting for outside help. While he tries to put across a worthwhile story, it will mean little in the U. S. market.

"Jeux De Femmes" ("Women's Games") **(FRENCH)** D.P.F. release of E.D.I.C. production. Stars Jacques Dumesnil, Helen Perdriere; features Mila Parely, Saturnin Fabre, Jeanne Helbling, Henri Cremieux, Francois Joux, Pasquali. Directed by Maurice Cloche. Screenplay by Maurice Cloche and Maurice Griffe from story by Maurice Cloche. Previewed in Paris. Running time, **98 MINS.**

A good comedy idea but not likely as an American entry. It shows Jacques Dumesnil as a young man leading the gay life with Mila Parely and compelled to marry and settle down, failing which a rich uncle will cut him out of his will. Some friends arrange to publicize that he is engaged to Helen Perdriere, pretending that the girl has been supplied by an employment agency for the purpose. Dumesnil falls for her and finally discovers who she really is.

Miniature Reviews

"Anna and the King of Siam" (20th). Ace biographical drama headed for lusty b.o.

"Two Smart People" (M-G). Melodrama that tries too hard to be bright and gay. Cast names will aid selling.

"Little Mister Jim" (M-G). Sentimental hokum about Army-raised youngster; okay for family trade.

"Janie Gets Married" (WB). Mild marital mixups; mild b.o.

"Bedelia" (GFD). British-made murder thriller by Vera Caspary, with Margaret Lockwood. Ian Hunter; big for U.S.

"Perilous Holiday" (Col). Pat O'Brien in a nicely-paced comedy meller.

"The Runaround" (U). Light comedy fluff with Ella Raines.

"A Girl in a Million" (British (Lion). Sydney Box production of light English comedy; mild American entry.

Anna and King of Siam

Los Angeles, June 1.

20th-Fox release of Louis D. Lighton production. Stars Irene Dunne, Rex Harrison, Linda Darnell; features Lee J. Cobb, Gale Sondergaard, Mikhail Rasumny, Dennis Hoey, Tito Renaldo, Richard Lyon. Directed by John Cromwell. Screenplay, Talbot Jennings and Sally Benson; based on biography by Margaret Landon; camera, Arthur Miller; music Bernard Herrmann; editor, Harmon Jones; special photographic effects, Fred Sersen. Tradeshown in Los Angeles, May 31, '46. Running time, 128 mins.

Anna	Irene Dunne
The King	Rex Harrison
Tuptim	Linda Darnell
Kralahome	Lee J. Cobb
Lady Thiang	Gale Sondergaard
Alak	Mikhail Rasumny
Sir Edward	Dennis Hoey
Prince (as a man)	Tito Renaldo
Louis Owens	Richard Lyon
Moonshee	William Edmunds
Phya Phrom	John Abbott
Interpreter	Leonard Strong
Prince (as a boy)	Mickey Roth
Beebe	Connie Leon
Princess Fa-Ying	Diane von den Ecker
Dance Director	Si-Lan Chen
Miss MacFarlane	Marjorie Eaton
Mrs. Cartwright	Helena Grant
Mr. Cartwright	Stanley Mann
Captain Orton	Addison Richards
Phra Palat	Neyle Morrow
Government Clerk	Julian Rivero
Siamese Guard	Chet Voravan
Amazon Guards	Dorothy Chung, Jean Wong

Socko adult drama, "Anna and the King of Siam" is a rather faithful screen adaptation of Margaret Landon's biography, intelligently handled to spellbind despite its long footage. Standout performances, scripting, direction and production contribute to the full measure of success it will enjoy. With the type of exploitation and selling "Anna" is certain to be handed, it is a cinch for big and sustained grosses.

"Anna" is solid handling of a biog subject that, in its entirety, could have been just as boring as it is interest-sustaining. "Anna's" charm and appeal to audiences don't rely on deliberately built peaks of high action. Rather it tells a straight-forward narrative, bringing in the natural humor, suspense and other dramatic values of the story of an English widow who finds herself confronted with the many problems of educating the children and some of the wives of the King of Siam. The monarch, himself, needs some education, and Anna sees that he gets it.

Script builds fascinating adult interest without ever implying that relationship between teacher and pupil goes beyond the friendship stage. The manner in which film is turned out in all departments makes this substitution for romance entirely satisfactory. The carefully written screenplay by Talbot Jennings and Sally Benson is packed with delightful incidents, sly humor and intense dramatic moments. John Cromwell's direction makes the most of the solid script basis, skillfully playing with tears, chuckles and drama, and getting the most from the potent cast.

Irene Dunne does a superb enactment of Anna, the woman who influenced Siamese history by being teacher and confidante to a kingly barbarian. Rex Harrison shines particularly in his American film debut, making a notable success of a difficult role. It's a sustained characterization of the King of Siam that makes the role real. Linda Darnell, third star, has little more than a bit as one of the king's wives, who incurs his displeasure and is burned at the stake. She does well.

Standouts among the featured cast are Lee J. Cobb and Gale Sondergaard. Former, as the king's minister, and latter, as a cast-off wife sock over commanding performances. Mikhail Rasumny, Dennis Hoey, Tito Renaldo, Richard Lyon, Leonard Strong, Mickey Roth and Addison Richards are among the others who lend excellent service to making this top-flight film entertainment.

Louis D. Lighton's production has polish and reflects wise budget expenditure. Only thing that could have been added would have been color, the costumes and settings lending themselves to tint treatment. Arthur Miller's lensing complements the players and physical appurtenances of the production, and Bernard Herrmann's score is an effective aid to the mood. *Brog.*

Two Smart People

(ONE SONG)

Hollywood, June 4.

Metro release of Ralph Wheelwright production. Stars Lucille Ball and John Hodiak; features Lloyd Nolan, Hugo Haas, Lenore Ulric, Elisha Cook, Jr. Directed by Jules Dassin. Screenplay, Ethel Hill and Leslie Charteris; story, Ralph Wheelwright and Allen Kenward; camera, Karl Freund; music score, George Massman; song, Ralph Blaine, George Bassman; editor, Chester W. Schaeffer. Tradeshown in Los Angeles, May 29, '46. Running time, 92 mins.

Ricki Woodner....Lucille Ball
Ace Connors....John Hodiak
Bob Simms....Lloyd Nolan
Senor Rodriguez....Hugo Haas
Senora Maria Ynez....Lenore Ulric
Fly Fellett....Elisha Cook, Jr.
Dwight Chandwright....Lloyd Corrigan
Jacques Dufour....Vladimir Sokoloff
Jose....David Cota
Porter....Clarence Muse

"Two Smart People" is flippantly-treated melodrama. It's never as bright as it tries to be and as a consequence overall results fail to stack up to expectations. Name values rate it for okay bookings, film having Lucille Ball, John Hodiak and Lloyd Nolan.

Script of the basically okay plot has been packed with awkward dialog. Over-direction and under-editing are other handicaps. Plot concerns the five days allotted a confidence man before he has to start serving a jail term. In the company of a femme sharper and a detective, the crook starts a gastronomical tour of the country, determined to have an eating fling that will last him through his time in jail. His two companions are interested in snaring $500,000 in government certificates he has concealed. Some suspense is developed, as is a romance between the crook and the confidence gal, but it's all a bit too smooth to register honestly. Windup has love convincing them it's time to go straight and start an honest life after the debt to the law has been paid.

Miss Ball and Hodiak have some good moments in bouncing the plot around, but never quite overcome dialog handicap. Nolan has a better time of it as the detective who aims to make sure Hodiak picks up his jail reservation. Most of the menace comes from Elisha Cook, Jr., an outsider also after the loot. He does well. Others are good.

Jules Dassin's direction of the Ralph Wheelwright production often fumbles what could have been bright situations and isn't made to look better by the editing. Wheelwright also did the story with Allan Kenward, while Ethel Hill and Leslie Charteris scripted. Score spots one song, "Dangerous," by Ralph Blane and George Bassman. *Brog.*

Little Mister Jim

Los Angeles, May 25

Metro release of Orville O. Dull production. Features Jackie "Butch" Jenkins, James Craig, Frances Gifford, Luana Patten, Spring Byington, Chingwah Lee. Directed by Fred Zinnemann. Screenplay, George Bruce; based on novel "Army Brat," by Tommy Wadelton; camera, Lester White; music score, George Bassman; editor, Frank Hull. Tradeshown in Los Angeles, May 22, '46. Running time, 92 mins.

Little Jim Tukker....Jackie "Butch" Jenkins
Capt. Big Jim Tukker....James Craig
Jean Tukker....Frances Gifford
Missey Choosey....Luana Patten
Mrs. Starwell....Spring Byington
Sui Jen....Chingwah Lee
Mrs. Glenson....Laura La Plante
Chaplain....Henry O'Neill
Colonel Starwell....Morris Ankrum
Miss Martin....Celia Travers
Miss Hall....Ruth Brady
Elsie....Sharon McManus
Ronnie....Buz Buckley
Clara....Carol Nugent
Mary....Jean Van

A tearjerker, designed to showcase personality of Jackie "Butch" Jenkins, "Little Mister Jim" serves its purpose. It's inexpensively mounted and generally fulfills its program aims.

Story is sentimental hokum in large doses. For what it deals with, script is well written by George Bruce and handled equally well directorially by Fred Zinnemann. Plot concerns youngster being raised by his mother and officer father at an Army base. It hews to a fairly straight line until the mother dies. Then the father takes to drink in his sorrow, the kid is neglected and it takes a Chinese manservant to straighten things out again. There's some Chinese philosophy thrown in for good measure, and scenes between young Jenkins and Chingwah Lee, the servant, are effective, made so by latter's performance.

As adult leads, James Craig and Frances Gifford have little chance to stand out. Luana Patten, Spring Byington, Laura La Plante, Henry O'Neill, Morris Ankrum and others are adequate to what transpires. Orville O. Dull's production is okay for expenditure. Lensing and other technical credits measure up. Film is overlong for its worth and could stand considerable tightening. *Brog.*

Janie Gets Married

Warner Bros. release of Ale Gottlieb production. Stars Joan Leslie, Robert Hutton; features Edward Arnold, Ann Harding, Dorothy Malone, Hattie McDaniel, Dick Erdman. Directed by Vincent Sherman. Original screenplay, Agnes Christine Johnston; based on characters created by Josephine Bentham and Herschel V. Williams, Jr. in stage play "Janie"; music, Frederick Hollander; camera, Carl Guthrie; editor, Christian Nyby. Tradeshown N. Y., May 31, '46. Running time, 89 MINS.

Janie....Joan Leslie
Dick....Robert Hutton
Mr. Conway....Edward Arnold
Mrs. Conway....Ann Harding
Spud....Dorothy Malone
April....Hattie McDaniel
Scooper....Dick Erdman
Elsbeth....Clare Foley
Mr. Stowers....Donald Meek
Mrs. Van Brunt....Barbara Brown
Mrs. Angles....Margaret Hamilton
Paula....Anne Gillis
Bernadine....Ruth Tobey
Dead Pan....William Frambes

Warners' sequel to its screen version of "Janie," the Broadway success of two seasons ago about adolescents, suffers from the same trouble of most followups. The idea, the well of inspiration, ran out with the one shot, and all the king's men couldn't put a second-hand model together again. Lacking all around in scripting, direction and acting, this one is mainly for the nabes and subsequents.

The plot is the typical story of the first few months in a young couple's marriage, with servant trouble, in-law trouble, job trouble and best-friend trouble. Janie has married her boy just returned from the wars and has wangled a job for him on her father's newspaper. A WAC friend arrives to monopolize young hubby. A newspaper magnate shows up to buy the local newspaper. A few more assorted people appear on the scene, to involve the young people further in a series of trite situations.

Not only are the circumstances familiar and a little tired, but the telling is an uninspired, the dialog being full of cliches with rarely a bright spot. The film has also been carelessly edited, in keeping with the haphazard quality of the rest of it. In several scenes, the pesty kid sister appears with a prominent but unexplained shiner. In the final scene, the WAC leaves the house, carrying in her hand the hat of the newspaper magnate who has just arrived. Perhaps she's to bring it back in the sequel's sequel.

Pic is paced in a slightly frenzied tempo, which isn't necessarily a synonym for fun. Robert Hutton plays the young husband with much appeal and some conviction, and the late Robert Benchley is amusing in a smallish role as stepfather. Donald Meek, too, is a standout in a sub role as newspaper magnate. But most of the other actors seem a little uncomfortable in their roles, in the grip of a silly script. Joan Leslie and Edward Arnold appear particularly unhappy about it. *Bron.*

Bedelia

(BRITISH-MADE)

London, May 24.

General Film Distributors' release of John Corfield production. Stars Margaret Lockwood, Anne Crawford, Ian Hunter, Barry K. Barnes. Directed by Lance Comfort. Screenplay by Vera Caspary, Herbert Victor, I. Goldsmith from novel by Vera Caspary; additional dialog, M. Roy Ridley, Moie Charles. Camera, Frederick A. Young, Harold Julius. At Leicester Square theatre. Running time, 90 MINS.

Bedelia....Margaret Lockwood
Charlie Carrington....Ian Hunter
Ben Chaney....Barry K. Barnes
Ellen....Anne Crawford
Mary....Beatrice Varley
Hannah....Louise Hampton
Nurse Harris....Jill Esmond
Dr. McAfee....Julien Mitchell
Mr. Bennett....Kynaston Reeves
Mrs. Bennett....Olga Lindo
Alec Johnstone....John Salew
Sylvia Johnstone....Barbara Blair
Captain McKelvey....Claude Bailey

No matter how much this may differ from Vera Caspary's novel, it could scarcely be improved on for adaptation and scripting for the screen. If "The Wicked Lady" did well in the U. S., this one should achieve even bigger returns there, being penned by author of "Laura."

Margaret Lockwood is more wicked than in her previous roles in a more subtle manner. Her portrayal of a woman who in greed for money poisons three husband with an air of maidenly innocence, is Miss Lockwood at her best. She is only prevented from doing away with hubby No. 4 by the intervention of an investigator who has been trying to catch up with her in connection with collection of successive life insurance policies, paid after each death.

Opens in Monte Carlo, with a young painter scraping acquaintance with a honeymoon couple. Latter learns the wife possesses a priceless black pearl which he ostensibly wishes to buy. He persuades the husband to let him paint his bride. When business compels their return home, the artist is invited there to complete the portrait. Only then does it become apparent that the persistent young man is trailing along, but not from amorous motives as the girl imagined. The husband's sudden illness after a Christmas party causes the sleuth to take the doctor into his confidence. Faced with exposure, the trapped woman ends in taking poison herself, which the husband has left with her as a way out. His gradual realization of her guilt is a dramatic highlight.

This is John Corfield's first production under the J. Arthur Rank banner and is commendable from all angles. Ian Hunter, as the husband, makes a welcome reappearance in English films, rejuvenated from his Navy service. Supporting cast is excellent. Camera work is exceptionally good.

Although story is unpalatable, no actual murder scenes are shown. The only victim visible is the Siamese cat who succumbs to poisoned food intended to dispose of the sleuth. Film should prove real boxoffice especially in view of vogue for this type of screen vehicle. *Clem.*

Perilous Holiday

(MUSIC)

Columbia release of Phil L. Ryan production. Stars Pat O'Brien, Ruth Warrick; features Alan Hale, Edgar Buchanan, Audrey Long. Directed by Edward H. Griffith. Screenplay by Roy Chanslor, based on story by Robert Carson; camera, Charles Lawton, Jr.; editor, Viola Lawrence. At Rialto, N. Y., May 31, '46. Running time, 90 MINS.

Patrick Nevil....Pat O'Brien
Agnes Stuart....Ruth Warrick
Doctor Lilley....Alan Hale
George Richards....Edgar Buchanan
Audrey Latham....Audrey Long
Graeme....Willard Robertson
Senor Aguirre....Eduardo Ciannelli
Mrs. Latham....Minna Gombell
Manuel Perez....Martin Garralaga
Luigi....Jay Novello
Benny Lockner....Al Hill
Pedro....Pedro Regas
Eddie LeBaron Orchestra

Another in the cycle of secret agent mellers, "Perilous Holiday" trades more on its comedy aspects than its melodrama, emerging with a fair share of both. Excellent dialog and good direction that keeps things moving help gloss over the film's overlength and story weaknesses that might militate against it. Looks good for average grosses in the subsequent run houses.

Roy Chanslor's screenplay, adapted from a Collier's mag serial by Robert Carson, is well tailored to the talents of Pat O'Brien, who rambles through the film in his usual glib fashion. Repartee between him and Ruth Warrick is the brightest spot in the picture. Course of action, however, sloughs off the story, resulting in the picture's buildup to a flat letdown. It comes out as another cops-and-robbers tale, transplanted to a Mexico City locale.

O'Brien plays a T-man, sent to Mexico to break up a counterfeit ring run by Alan Hale and Edgar Buchanan. Miss Warrick turns up as a syndicated columnist whose father had been murdered by Hale back in the States. She's already forced him to flee to Mexico City after breaking the story of his rackets north of the border and has followed him for further revenge. Subsequent events have O'Brien and Miss Warrick falling for each other, although each distrusts the other's interest in Hale until the final reel, when they crack down on him together.

O'Brien does good work as the treasury dept. sleuth, fast with both his fists and his wisecracks. Couple of Irish ditties he runs through at a piano come off well. Film gives Miss Warrick her first good break since her film debut in "Citizen Kane." Bounteous wardrobe reveals her as one of the screen's top beauties and her acting is plenty adept. Hale is sufficiently sardonic as the counterfeit leader and Buchanan turns in a nice performance as his side-kick.

Eddie LeBaron and his orch get featured billing but are seen only momentarily in a night-club sequence. Same sequence features Amelita Vargas, a lush Latin dancer who outmaneuvers Diosa Costello in a fast samba. Supporting cast is okay.

Producer Phil L. Ryan nas lined the film with rich mountings that emphasize the tourist's version of Mexico City. Director Edward H. Griffith keeps the cast jumping through its paces and gets the most out of the film's good dialog. Charles Lawton's photography is on the credit side. *Stal.*

The Runaround

Universal release of Joe Gershenson production. Stars Rod Cameron, Ella Raines' features Broderick Crawford, Frank McHugh. Directed by CHarles Lamont. Screenplay, Arthur T. Herman, Sam Hellman; camera, George Robinson; music, Frank Skinner; editor, Ted J. Kent; asst director, William Tummel. Tradeshown N.Y., June 4, '46. Running time, 86 mins.

Kildane	Rod Cameron
Penelope	Ella Raines
Louis Prentice	Broderick Crawford
Wally Quayle	Frank McHugh
Norman Hampton	Samuel J. Hinds
Baby	Joan Fulton
Feenan	George Cleveland
Hutchins	Joe Sawyer
Mrs. Hampton	Nana Bryant
Billy	Dave Willock
Butler	Charles Coleman
Cusack	Jack Overman

A pleasant, relaxing fluff comedy that doesn't require deep thought, "The Runaround" should prove self-supporting at the boxoffice and able to stand on its own, with Ella Raines providing better than fair marquee draw.

Story carries with it faint reminiscences of scenes from "It Happened One Night," and who says that's bad? Concerns a private detective and his former boss who are competing for a valuable contract from a man whose daughter has run away to get married. Guy who brings her back unmarried gets the contract. Chase carries them from New York to San Francisco and back, fighting for custody of the femme. When the dick returns with the gal he finds the old man has deliberately put him on the wrong track, that he's brought back the secretary, and he's in love.

Production and photography obviously been done in a more painstaking manner than usual. Limited use of prop scenery in favor of the real thing adds quality. Versimilitude in the situations is neither asked nor expected. Musical score by Frank Skinner provides creditable opener.

Thesping is convincing for the most part, with the only exceptions those scenes wherein Miss Raines tries to cry or laugh hard and evidently can't. A couple of the battles are too patently fakes. Brod Crawford and Rod Cameron do well, and Frank McHugh puts in a top support role.

A Girl in a Million

(BRITISH-MADE)

London, May 24.

British Lion release of Sydney Box production. Stars Hugh Williams, Joan Greenwood, Basil Radford, Naunion Wayne. Directed by Francis Searle. Story and screenplay by Muriel and Sydney Box. Camera, Reginald H. Wyer, Bert Mason, Bernie Lewis. At Studio One. Running time, 86 mins.

Tony	Hugh Williams
Gay	Joan Greenwood
Prendergast	Basil Redford
Fotheringham	Naunion Wayne
Peabody	Wylie Watson
Col. Sultzman	Hartley Power
Molly	Yvonne Owen
General	Garry Marsh
Policeman	Edward Lexy
Pavilion Manager	James Knight
Dr. Peters	Julian D'Albie

This is last picture Sydney Box will do for outside companies before assuming control of Gainsborough Films for J. Arthur Rank this fall. Story is light, but has many laughs. Chances not bright for any real returns in U. S.

Concerns inventor-hubby (Hugh Williams) who is always annoyed by a nagging wife. She finally gets a divorce, with the judge congratulating hubby on his escape. Then the husband accepts War Office appointment in an isolated town, when he learns that there are no women nearby.

Things run smoothly till the arrival of an American colonel, Hartley Power, with his niece, Joan Greenwood. Williams soon falls victim and marries the gal. Couple are separated when she starts the same routine as his first wife. Reunion results when hubby becomes father.

Cast is adequate, with Miss Greenwood, in her first starring role, acquitting herself well. On the other hand, Williams at times appears too old for a juve lead. Basil Radford and Naunton Wayne play their usual silly Englishmen. *Rege.*

Foreign Films

"An Petit Bonheur" ("Happy Go Lucky") (FRENCH). Pathe Consortium Cinema release of Gibe production. Directed by Marcel L'Herbier. Stars Dainelle Darrieux, Andre Luguet, Francois Perier: features Paulette Dubose, Odette Talazac, Paul Olivier, Maupi Pasquali, Henri Cremieux. From legit play by Marc Gilbert Sauvajon. Screenplay by Marc Gilbert Sauvajon, Francoise Giroud. Reviewed in Paris. Running time. 105 MINS.

Marquee value of names for local fan faves and witty dialog in an amusing story will assure local grosses. For America, the chances appear limited to spots with French patronage because director Marcel L'Herbier, in an attempt to retain the dialog, has made the picture look like a stagey filmization of a legit. Also camera work is not even. It shows Danielle Darrieux as the jealous wife of Francois Perier making herself the unwanted guest of Andre Luguet who, having his own worries, was about to commit suicide. The cast is good and does well considering. *Maxi.*

"Donde Mueren Las Palabras" ("Where Words Fail") (SPANISH). AAA (Artistas Argentinos Associados) production and release. Directed by Hugo Freganese. Stars Enrique Muino; features Halo Bertini, Dario Garzay, Hector Mendez, Linda Lorena, Aurelia Ferrer, Rene Mujica, Pablo Cumo, Maria Hurtado, Jose Vazquez, Enrique Ferraro. Musical score by Juan Jose Castro; choreography by Margarita Wallman, "prima ballerina." Maria Ruanova. At Gran Rex. Buenos Aires, April 25. Running time, 76 MINS.

Hailed by producers and critics as an artistic effort, this is vastly disappointing. Story is weak and Enrique Muino, hampered by inexpert direction and story, fails to measure up to his previous screen work. This is Hugo Fregonese's debut as a picture director. His stage experience doesn't help his screen work. Juan Jose Castro, Argentina's ace conductor and composer, has provided a great musical score although more original scoring would have helped. Dario Garzay, a newcomer, is the juve lead and has possibilities. He's an adolescent pianist in this. There are no touches of humor to relieve the dreary story. Ballet sequences are too long although the most interesting part of the picture, and laurels, if any, are due to Margarita Wallman and Maria Ruanova. Although made on an ambitious scale, this is too lugubrious to have any interest for U. S.

Miniature Reviews

"Faithful in My Fashion" (M-G). Sentimental romance has femme appeal.

"Three Wise Fools" (M-G). Margaret O'Brien in fantasy tailored for family trade.

"Till the End of Time" (RKO). Earnest but overlong treatise on the vets' postwar problems.

"Lover Come Back" (U). Amusing comedy with strong marquee pull in George Brent, Lucille Ball.

"One Exciting Week" (Rep). (Songs) Cornbelt comedy with radio's Al Pearce for duals.

"Crime of the Century" (Rep). Weak melodrama with unknown cast.

"Colorado Serenade" (Songs-Color) (PRC). Standard oatuner starring Eddie Dean.

Faithful In My Fashion

Metro release of Lionel Houser production. Stars Donna Reed, Tom Drake; features E. E. Horton, Spring Byington, Sig Ruman, Harry Davenport, William Phillips, Margaret Hamilton, Hobart Cavanaugh, Warner Anderson. Directed by Sidney Salkow. Original screenplay, Lionel Houser; camera, Charles Salerno, Jr.; editor, Irvine Warburton; score, Nathaniel Shilkret. Tradeshown N. Y., May 27, '46. Running time, 81 MINS.

Jean Kendrick	Donna Reed
Jeff Compton	Tom Drake
Hiram Dilworthy	Edward Everett Horton
Miss Swanson	Spring Byington
Prof. Boris Riminoffsky	Sig Ruman
Great Grandpa	Harry Davenport
1st Barfly	Wm. "Bill" Phillips
Miss Applegate	Margaret Hamilton
Mr. Wilson	Hobart Cavanaugh
Walter Medcraft	Warner Anderson
Mrs. Murphy	Connie Gilchrist
Nikolai	Fred Essler
Mr. Stute	Wilson Wood
2nd Barfly	Jack Overman

Hokey story handled deadpan style with a thick spread of molasses stamps this film as a fair sentimental item for the femmes. Given stronger thespic material and Metro's quality production framework, "Faithful in My Fashion" could have baled out of the dualer division by being given lighter direction, playing it for laughs instead of sighs. Basic stymie is the unimaginative scripting which piles one cliche upon another and makes it very tough for the cast to be persuasive.

Plot concerns a soldier, home on a two-week furlough, who returns to his pre-war job hoping to find this small corner of the world unchanged. His romance, who used to be a stock clerk, has been upped, however, to an executive post and furthermore is affianced to another man. A quartet of co-worker do-gooders persuade the girl to masquerade for duration of the furlough, as her bit to make the homecoming a happy one. Like clockwork the expected happens; just as the girl again falls for the soldier he discovers the truth. They fall out in anger. The do-gooders heal the breach. They fall back in love at finis.

As a buildup for Tom Drake, film showcases his boyish charms to good advantage. Despite flat-footed lines he was given to read, Drake comes off as a warm and likeable juvenile. Donna Reed makes an appealing heart interest. Edward Everett Horton backs up in usual competent form although the comedy bits are pale stuff. Spring Byington and Sig Ruman round out the supporting cast.

Three Wise Fools

Los Angeles, June 11.

Metro release of William H. Wright production. Features Margaret O'Brien, Lionel Barrymore, Lewis Stone, Edward Arnold, Thomas Mitchell. Directed by Edward Buzzell. Screenplay, John McDermott and James O'Hanlon; story by McDermott, based on the Austin Strong play; camera, Harold Rossen; musical score, Bronislau Kaper; editor, Gene Ruggiero. Tradeshown in Los Angeles, June 5, '46. Running time, 89 mins.

Sheila O'Monohan	Margaret O'Brien
Dr. Richard Gaunght	Lionel Barrymore
Judge Thomas Trumbull	Lewis Stone
Theodore Findley	Edward Arnold
Terence Aloysius O'Tavern	Thomas Mitchell
Judge Watson	Ray Collins
Sister Mary Brigid	Jane Darwell
Paul Badger	Charles Dingle
The Ancient	Harry Davenport
Horace Appleby	Henry O'Neill
Rena Fairchild	Cyd Charisse
The O'Monoham	Warner Anderson
Dugan	Billy Curtis

Film fantasy leans heavily on youthful shoulders of Margaret O'Brien to carry it off. Shapes up as okay for general trade, particularly family audiences, due to moppet's bright play-acting. Able casting, direction and production are other bulwarks helping to sustain interest in the fairy tale.

Miss O'Brien, giving a faithful illusion of a young colleen intent on bringing love and happiness into the lives of three rich old men, walks off with the footage despite the presence of such capables as Lionel Barrymore, Lewis Stone, Edward Arnold, Thomas Mitchell and others. Pixie yarn has been ably directed by Edward Buzzell for fantasy flavor.

It concerns tale told a group of leprechauns by an ancient one to convince them there really are such creatures as humans. An Irish curse placed on three young men makes them realize all of life's ambitions but finds them old and without friends. The grandaughter of the curse-maker enters their lives, lifts the curse and sets about teaching them how to be human. The three are hard nuts to crack but Irish charm eventually wins them over. In so doing the girl finally sees the "little people" in which she earnestly believes and they, in turn see her, convinced at last that humans do exist.

There's more than a coincidence in the casting of Barrymore, Stone and Arnold in respective roles of doctor, judge and banker. Trio are known almost as well as Dr. Gillespie, Judge Hardy and Metro capitalist as by their real handles. Thomas Mitchell points up his assignment as Miss O'Brien's manservant, who is full of Irish whisky and brogue most of the time. Harry Davenport is the ancient story teller. Ray Collins, Jane Darwell, Charles Dingle, Cyd Charisse and others are capable in acting out the John McDermott-James O'Hanlon script, based on the Austin Strong play.

Production guidance by William H. Wright shapes the film neatly for intended results. *Brog.*

Till the End of Time

RKO release of Dore Schary production. Stars Dorothy McGuire, Guy Madison, Robert Mitchum, Bill Williams; features Tom Tully, William Gargan, Jean Porter, Johnny Sands, Loren Tindall, Ruth Nelson, Selena Royle, Harry Von Zell. Directed by Edward Dmytryk. Screenplay, Allen Rivkin based on novel by Niven Busch; camera, Harry Wild; editor, Harry Gerstad; asst. director, Ruby Rosenberg; score, Leigh Harline. Previewed N. Y., June 10, '46. Running time, 105 MINS.

Pat Ruscomb	Dorothy McGuire
Cliff Harper	Guy Madison
William Tabeshaw	Robert Mitchum
Perry Kincheloe	Bill Williams
C. W. Harper	Tom Tully
Sgt. Gunny Watrous	William Gargan
Helen Ingersoll	Jean Porter
Tommy	Johnny Sands
Pinky	Loren Tindall
Amy Harper	Ruth Nelson
Mrs. Kincheloe	Selena Royle
Scuffy	Harry Von Zell
Boy from Idaho	Richard Benedict

A well-oiled shears and some generous snipping might have turned this earnest but overlong and hesitantly paced film into a more absorbing study of a group of vets' uphill climb to civilian normalcy. As it is, despite a slow start and lengthy sequences, it's packaged brightly with Dorothy McGuire and Guy Madison for marquee lure.

Theme has timeliness and concentrated appeal to the army of vets now footloose in a competitive world. Attempt is made to mirror the problems of former servicemen, disabled and intact, in picking up the threads dropped at Pearl Harbor. But the pic trips itself up along the route with a series of repetitious incidents and comes to life only in a windup which screens a dazzling barroom fight, tops in direction.

Story focuses on a trio of ex-Marines and a girl who lost her husband during the war. While each character's problem is individual, the sum total is a fair cross-section of current postwar woes. Madison, who has emerged with skin intact, thinks he is too old for schooldays again and drifts restlessly from job to job. As the central figure, he doesn't dig deep enough into his part to explain convincingly the source of his discontent. Superficial performance deprives his characterization of the psychiatric overtones, which the script apparently marked out.

Miss McGuire, armed with her usual charm and elfin appeal, does a bangup job as the war widow. She does manage to get across the sense of loss which blocks her return to normal emotional responses. Her off-again-on-again amorous entanglements with Madison are a little hard to take at times but here the script errs and not the actress. When Madison sees the light and decides to stick it out rather than seek an impossible Shangri-La, their cure is mutual.

Robert Mitchum does well with the lesser role of a buddy suffering from a head injury. Actor lends the right touch of hard-cored gruffness as he fights off hospital treatment. He, too, finds himself after getting konked during the barroom brawl in which the ex-Marines join hands in fighting a phoney vet organization. Bill Williams, last of the problem subjects, plays the part of a legless vet whose loss of limbs has spelled a loss of faith in himself. Williams' self-reliance plus acceptance of artificial limbs is neatly restored in the same brawl. Rest of cast groove their performances smoothly to meet the film's demands.

Musical background is good with the theme song, "Till the End of Time," an adaptation of Chopin's Polonaise, nicely aimed for the romantic interludes. Camera work suffers from heavy-handed direction. It is in direction and script that the film loses out.

Lover Come Back

Universal release of Howard Benedict production. Stars George Brent, Lucille Ball, Vera Zorina; features Charles Winninger, Carl Esmond, Raymond Walburn. Directed by William A. Seiter. Original screenplay, Michael Fessier and Ernest Pagano; camera, Joseph Valentine; editor, Ray Snyder; score, Hans J. Salter. Tradeshown N. Y., June 10, '46. Running time, **90 MINS.**

Bill Williams	George Brent
Kay	Lucille Ball
Madeline Laslo	Vera Zorina
Pa	Charles Winninger
Paul	Carl Esmond
J. P. Winthrop	Raymond Walburn
Tubbs	Wallace Ford
Hotel Clerk	Franklin Pangborn
Martha	Louise Beavers
Ma	Elisabeth Risdon
Jimmy Hennessey	William Wright
Waiter	George Chandler
Janie	Joan Fulton

Universal went far afield for talent for this one, ringing in Lucille Ball, George Brent and Vera Zorina, all starring under the U trademark for the first time. Move was a wise one, because without such stars the picture would have emerged as something that's been done many times before. With them, it comes out as a frothy little comedy that may remind the customers of previous films but that will get by on its own merits. Should chalk up good grosses in most situations.

Scripters Michael Fessier and Ernest Pagano must have had some of the old Cary Grant-Irene Dunne starrers in mind and have built their situations on the same type of sophisticated comedy. Starring roles, however, fit the talents of Brent and Miss Ball like a glove, and the scripters brought the scene up to date by building the triangle around a returned war correspondent, his femme photog and his wife.

Characters in the story come from the upper fringes of society, the breed around whom most of these pictures are built. Miss Ball is the ace designer for a women's clothing outfit, married to Brent who's been away for two years as a correspondent. Trouble starts as soon as Brent returns when his wife discovers he hadn't been as lonely overseas as he'd led her to believe. Miss Ball sets out to reverse the wolfing process to make Brent jealous but things don't work out and she finally heads for a Las Vegas divorce. Brent follows and, after a series of zany situations, they reconcile. Picture ends with Brent winking lewdly to the audience as he closes a door behind him and Miss Ball.

Miss Ball turns in one of her best comedy performances to date, mulcting every line and antic to the limit. Brent also shines as the correspondent-husband in a role that's a far cry from his recent string of grim pix. Miss Zorina is miscast as the third angle of the triangle, lacking the deft comedy touches necessary to the role. Her best forte is still ballet. Charles Winninger is good as Brent's rakish father and Carl Esmond and Raymond Walburn do well as two of Miss Ball's cortege of admirers.

Production mountings lined up by Howard Benedict follow the general frilly mood of the film. Settings, costumes, etc., are lush and ostentatious. Hans J. Salter rates a nice bow for his amusing score. Camera work of Joseph Valentine is okay. *Stal.*

One Exciting Week

(SONGS)

Hollywood, June 8.

Republic release of Donald H. Brown production. Stars Al Pearce; features Pinky Lee, Jerome Cowan, Shemp Howard, Arlene Harris, Mary Treen. Directed by William Beaudine. Screenplay, Jack Townley and John K. Butler; based on original story by Dennis Murray; camera, John Alton; editor, William P. Thompson; songs, Don Rayeand Hughie Prince, John Pettis, Billy Meyers and Elmer Schoebel, Jack Lawrence; orchestral arrangements, Dale Butts; music director, Morton Scott. Previewed at RCA studios, Hollywood, June 7, '46. Running time, **69 MINS.**

Dan Flannery	Al Pearce
Itchy	Pinky Lee
Al Carter	Jerome Cowan
Marvin	Shemp Howard
Lottie Pickett	Arlene Harris
Mabel Taylor	Mary Treen
Helen Pickett	Lorraine Krueger
Jimmy Curtis	Maury Dexter
Otis Piper	Will Wright
Charlie Pickett	Arthur Loft
Mayor Teeple	Chester Clute

Fair light comedy that would have rated better with punchier direction. Al Pearce from radio heads up the corn. For extra measure, production includes four tunes and a dance number. Array of comics is stout and material good but better pacing is needed for zip. For supporting positions in majority of situations.

It's an amnesia yarn with twist that has the hero impersonating himself. Pearce, Merchant Marine hero, gets tangled with a trio of slick crooks just prior to leaving for a hometown celebration in his honor. In a fight with the crooks, he's conked on the head and develops amnesia. Slickers, finding the hometown is to award the hero $10,000, convince him he is a public enemy and they're his gang. So, as a bigshot criminal, Pearce assumes the seaman's identity to collect the small fortune. Songs and dance are brought in during the homecoming celebration, lending okay musical moments to the comedy. There are plenty of plot mixups before another sock on the head brings Pearce out of his daze.

Major comedy chores go to Pinky Lee and Shemp Howard. Latter is worth a number of chuckles as a punch-drunk ex-jockey. Jerome Cowan completes the crook trio. Arlene Harris, Mary Treen, Lorraine Krueger and other do acceptably. The Teen-Agers orch furnishes peppy rhythms. "Bounce Me Brother With a Solid Four," Don Raye-Hughie Prince tune, is vocaled by uncredited Chinese femme to show up best in the score.

William Beaudine directed the Jack Towney-John K. Butler screenplay. Okay production mounting and supervision were furnished by Donald H. Brown. Lensing and other credits are standard. *Brog.*

Crime of the Century

Republic release of Walter H. Goetz production. Features Stephanie Bachelor, Michael Browne, Martin Kosleck, Paul Stanton. Directed by Philip Ford. Screenplay, O'Leta Rhinehart, William Hagens, Gertrude Walker; original, Rhinehart, Hagens; camera, Reggie Lanning; editor, William P. Thompson. At Strand, Brooklyn, dual, June 7, '46. Running time, **56 MINS.**

Audrey Brandon	Stephanie Bachelor
Hank Rogers	Michael Browne
Paul	Martin Kosleck
Margaret Waldham	Betty Shaw
Andrew Madison	Paul Stanton
Agatha Waldham	Mary Currier
Jim Rogers	Ray Walker
Dr. Jackson	Tom London

"Crime of the Century" has an attractive title but otherwise shapes up as a below-par melodrama. Production values are unusually solid for a low-budgeter but by themselves can't surmount the weak plot structure. Over-close scissor-work, moreover, has nicked whatever story content there was to begin with, causing the film to unreel at such a breakneck speed that essential details were either omitted or left dangling. Collection of marquee unknowns add little to the overall quality and slot this film as bottom-end program fare.

Yarn is concerned with the machinations of an industrial tycoon who attempts to suppress the news of his associate's death for a few days in order to fix a board of directors' election. When a newshound sniffs out the corpse, he's put out of the way by a kidnapping. The reporter's brother gets on the trail and en route falls in love with a femme fatale who's working for the tycoon. Crime is unsnarled by the dead man's daughter who leads the brother to the corpus delicti. Picture contains one macabre sequence in which the dead man is shown lying in a bathtub encased up to his neck in ice cubes.

Michael Browne, as the reporter's brother, tries to dress up the part with a tough-guy style but the mannerisms are too broadly conveyed to be convincing. Stephanie Bachelor, playing the dangerous lady, gets over a sultry air in credible fashion, while Paul Stanton, as the magnate, and Martin Kosleck, as his aide, do their chores with customary polish.

Colorado Serenade

(SONGS—COLOR)

PRC release of Robert Emmett Tansey production, directed by Tansey. Stars Eddie Dean; features David Sharpe, Roscoe Ates. Original screenplay, Frances Kavanaugh; songs, Eddie Dean, H. L. Canova, Sam Armstrong, Carle Hoefle; camera (Cinecolor), Robert Shackelford; editor, Hugh Winn. Tradeshown N. Y., June 7, '46. Running time, **68 MINS.**

Eddie	Eddie Dean
Nevada	David Sharpe
Soapy	Roscoe Ates
Sherry	Mary Kenyon
Judge Hilton	Forrest Taylor
Duke	Dennis Moore
Lola	Abigail Adams
Dad Dillon	Warner Richmond
Mr. Trimble	Lee Bennett
Col. Blake	Robert McKenzie
Ringo	Bob Duncan

Newest of the Eddie Dean starrers, "Colorado Serenade," is strictly standard-cut out of the same pattern as his previous pix. In fact, this oatuner bears such a close resemblance to its predecessor, "Song of Wyoming," it looks like a reissue. Everything's the same, from the lukewarm Cinecolor tints slightly running into each other, to the familiar echoing saddle tunes and formula story of bad man vs. law-abidin' folks. Dastard, moreover, duplicates his trick of turning out to be the long lost son of the town's leading citizen.

Only novelty in the film is the debut of a tough-looking young hombre, David Sharpe, who plays the role of an undercover Government agent. Sharpe displays an acrobatic agility that injects his fisticuffs and guntotin' with the spirit of the westerner's golden era when Tom Mix and Hoot Gibson rode the plains. Eddie Dean looks a little pallid beside him although still a pleasing personality. Voice is excellent in his yodel-crooning of "Home on the Range," "Western Lullaby," "Riding Down to Rawhide" and "Riding to the Top of the Mountain."

Abigail Adams, as the town moll, is another performer showing promise. Femme, a striking looker, is well-poised before the lens. Roscoe Ates supplies his stuttering comics for a few laughs and rest of the cast play their stock parts adequately.

Foreign Films

"Monsieur Gregoire S'evade" (Mr. Gregoire Runs Away) **(French).** Dispa release of Bervia Films production; directed by Daniel Norman; stars Bernard Blier; features Jules Berry, Aime Clarione, Alexandre Rignault, Yvette Lebon, Gaby Andreu; story and dialog by Daniel Norman; camera, Toporkoff. Reviewed in Paris. Running time, **98 MINS.**

Tempo, direction, photography, and sound are above the average of recent French pix. Bernard Blier, in his first starring role, is the legit actor currently in "Aupres de ma Blonde" here. His characterization of the insurance clerk unwittingly compelled to become a tool of jewel thieves provides many gags. Comedy stems mostly from funny dialog which would lose much in translation. For French patronage, it looks big; for U. S., lukewarm except in arty spots. *Maxi.*

Miniature Reviews

"Smoky" (Songs-Color) (20th). Exceptionally fine color production of the classic story of a horse. B.o. potential solid.

"Deadline for Murder" (20th). Neatly packaged whodunit.

"The Bamboo Blonde" (Songs) (RKO). Mediocre musical with Frances Langford the only marquee lure.

"Inside Job" (U.). Routine crook meller; for the duals.

"My Pal Trigger" (Rep) (songs). Classy cowboy pic with Roy Rogers and Trigger to bring good boxoffice draw.

"Beware" (Songs) (Astor). All-Negro production starring Louis Jordan and band for top returns in its market.

"Crack-Up" (RKO). Mystery thriller located in art museum shapes up for average returns in general runs.

"Man From Rainbow Valley" (Color) (Rep). Western with story novelty and tunes. Good material for market.

"Stormy Waters" (French) (M-G). Jean Gabin and Michelle Morgan in French-made seafaring romance; strong entry.

"Rosa de America" (Panamericana). Argentine-made story of South America's patron saint fails to measure up to hopes; mild U. S. entry.

"Hello Moscow" (Russian) (Songs) (Artkino). N.s.h. semi-musical for very limited draw.

Smoky
(SONGS—COLOR)

Hollywood, June 15.

20th-Fox release of Robert Bassler production. Stars Fred MacMurray; features Anne Baxter, Burl Ives, Bruce Cabot, Esther Dale, Roy Roberts, J. Farrell MacDonald. Directed by Louis King. Screenplay, Lillie Hayward, Dwight Cummins, Dorothy Yost; based on novel by Will James; camera (Technicolor), Charles Clarke; special effects, Fred Sersen; music, David Raksin; arrangements, Arthur Morton; editor, Nick De Maggio. Tradeshown L. A. June 13, '46. Running time, 86 MINS.

Clint Barkley	Fred MacMurray
Julie	Anne Baxter
Bill	Burl Ives
Frank	Bruce Cabot
Gram	Esther Dale
Jeff	Roy Roberts
Jim	J. Farrell MacDonald

20th-Fox has come through with a splendid interpretation of the Will James classic story of "Smoky." It's honest, completely natural tale-spinning on celluloid that will charm any audience. There's a solid cast but interest naturally goes to the equine portraying the title role. He is a fine specimen of horseflesh, intelligently trained to carry off his trouping chores with honors.

A horse story, told in color against the magnificent background of the Utah landscape, it has cinch b.o. When it has received the kind of understanding treatment given "Smoky" the draw potential is even greater.

There's no sticky sentiment or false hokum connected with the telling of the story. Instead, all factors are developed with a casual charm under Louis King's direction and the players come through with easy, natural performances that maintain the casualness that sparks the development. The cast is small, but each has been handpicked to fit the characters. Fred MacMurray is a believable working cowpoke who captures and trains the wild horse that becomes known as Smoky. Anne Baxter, operator of a Utah horse and cattle ranch, rings true with no attempt at glamor.

The James novel was scripted by Lillie Hayward, Dwight Cummins and Dorothy Yost. There is never an unnecessary line of dialog, no stock western phrases or phony situations in the wrting. Story concerns the capture and training of Smoky, how he is stolen by cattle thieves, kills a man for mistreatment and then becomes a notorious rodeo outlaw bronco. He is the object of a long search by his original master and is finally found pulling a junk wagon in a small western town. Less expert production, direction and writing could have made a maudlin tear-jerker out of this premise, but nowhere does it go off-key.

Complementing the audience values are the native songs as played and sung by Burl Ives, troubador of American folksongs. Here again, production has wisely fitted the tunes naturally into the story. Ives' portrayal of a ranch blacksmith and waddie who fills idle moments with song is genuine. Score contains such numbers as "The Foggy, Foggy Dew," "Blue Tail Fly," "Woolly Boogie Bee" and cowboy ballads. Bruce Cabot adds expert villainy to the piece. Esther Dale's dry humor, Roy Roberts' work as the ranch foreman and J. Farrell MacDonald, cook, are other factors that count.

Practically all the production was confined to Utah location, where showmanly use was made of the scenery in Robert Bassler's production guidance. Color lensing by Charles Clarke is breath-taking, particularly the day and night-time outdoor shots. Scenery and animals come through better on the color register than do the human actors, but this is a minor fault probably lying in the preview print. Story is backed up by sharp deliveries from other credited factors to help measure it as a solid pleaser for all type audiences.

Brog.

Deadline for Murder

Los Angeles, June 15.

Twentieth-Fox release of Sol M. Wurtzel production. Features Paul Kelly, Kent Taylor, Sheila Ryan, Jerome Cowan, Renee Carson, Joan Blair, Marian Martin, Leslie Vincent. Directed by James Tingling. Story and screenplay, Irving Cummings, Jr.; camera, Benjamin Kline; editor, William F. Claxton. Tradeshown in Los Angeles, June 13, '46. Running time, 64 MINS.

McMullen	Paul Kelly
Millard	Kent Taylor
Vivian	Sheila Ryan
Lynch	Jerome Cowan
Zita	Renee Carson
Helen	Joan Blair
Laura	Marian Martin
Paul	Leslie Vincent
Johnny	Matt McHugh
Tiny	Jody Gilbert
Keller	Edward Marr
Charles	Thomas Jackson
Hudson	Larry Blake
Frank	Ray Teal
Gordon	Andre Charlot
Masseur	Emory Parnell
Stickman	Lester Dorr
Floorman	Eddie Kane
1st Player	William Newell
2nd Player	Jack Mulhall
3rd Player	Bruce Fernald
1st Poker Player	Joey Ray
2nd Poker Player	Ernest Hilliard
Waiter	Syd Saylor
Elevator Operator	Spec O'Donnell

Sturdy supporting fare. A mystery thriller that uses a casual, matter-of-fact manner to spin tale of murder and intrigue. It avoids extraneous dialog, plots its action for suspense and interest. Production backing by Sol M. Wurtzel gets best values for budget expenditure, and direction by James Tingling keeps melodramatic factors in hand all the way.

Story by Irving Cummings, Jr., concerns a bigtime gambler, but nice guy, who gets mixed up in murder and theft of valuable Government document while trying to do an old friend a favor. Kent Taylor walks off with the gambler assignment, making it believable in every scene. Paul Kelly does the same by his police detective part. Less believable, but still interesting, is the newspaper girl played by Sheila Ryan.

Yarn tells how Taylor breaks up plot by Jerome Cowan and Renee Carson to make off with Government document concerning foreign oil lands. Taylor is called in to aid Joan Blair, a friend whose stepson, Leslie Vincent, has given document to charmer Marian Martin. As each individual who holds the paper is bumped off, Taylor's job becomes more dangerous, but windup has Kelly stepping in to cinch murders on Cowan and wrap up a satisfactorily concluded case.

In addition to cast principals, other good performances include those by Matt McHugh, Jody Gilbert and Edward Marr. Lensing by Benjamin Kline takes advantage of good mounting and aids action, as do score and crisp editing.

Brog.

The Bamboo Blonde
(SONGS)

RKO release of Herman Schlom (Sid Rogell) production. Stars Frances Langford; features Ralph Edwards, Russell Wade, Iris Adrian. Directed by Anthony Mann. Screenplay, Olive Cooper and Lawrence Kimble from original story by Wayne Whittaker; songs, Mort Greene and Lou Pollack; camera, Frank Redman; editor, Les Millbrook; musical numbers, Charles O'Curran. Tradeshown, N. Y., June 13, '46. Running time, 68 MINS.

Louise Anderson	Frances Langford
Eddie Clark	Ralph Edwards
Patrick Ransom, Jr	Russell Wade
Montana	Iris Adrian
Jim Wilson	Richard Martin
Eileen Sawyer	Jane Greer
Shorty Parker	Glenn Vernon
Patrick Ransom, Sr	Paul Harvey
Mrs. Ransom	Regina Wallace
Marsha	Jean Brooks
Art Department	Tom Noonan
Mom	Dorothy Vaughan

"Bamboo Blonde" marks Frances Langford's return, and it's not a very auspicious return. Picture impresses as a tired affair in production, acting, story and music.

Miss Langford's experiences overseas seem to have left their mark and Frank Redman's camera work does nothing to improve matters. Her voice, however, retains its honey-smooth quality. Script doesn't call for too much thesping ability from any of the cast and she carries the title role in okay fashion.

Yarn, adapted by Olive Cooper and Lawrence Kimble from a story by Wayne Whittaker, is novel but doesn't hold much in the way of suspense or appeal. Audience will be able to call the ending midway in the first reel. Miss Langford plays a singer in a two-bit nitery who develops a romance with a B-29 pilot the night he shoves off for the Pacific. They don't even know each other's names, however.

On Saipan, the bomber crew swipes Miss Langford's photo and has her portrait painted on the plane, which they christen the "Bamboo Blonde." Crew immediately becomes the hottest in the air force. Back in New York, the nitery manager capitalizes on the publicity by billing Miss Langford as the original blonde. Crew is ordered home for a bond-selling tour and Miss Langford and the pilot discover it's the real thing. After unsuccessful attempts by the pilot's ex-fiancee to break up the romance, his wealthy parents accept Miss Langford into the family and all ends well

Supporting cast, on the whole, is adequate. Russell Wade, as the pilot, seems unsure of himself when it comes to the heavy thesping, but comes through okay. Ralph Edwards supplies some nice comedy as the dough-hungry but warm-hearted nitery owner and Iris Adrian does a fair bit as his gal friend. Jane Greer is sufficiently catty as the pilot's ex-fiancee.

Four songs by Mort Greene and Lou Pollack are standard and none seems headed for the big time. "Dreaming Out Loud," which is reprised most often, gets by best as a smooth ballad. Film's one production number is built around "Moonlight Over the Islands," just another Hawaiian song.

Film's low budget is evidenced by the mediocre sets and other mountings lined up by producers Herman Schlom and Sid Rogell. Anthony Mann's direction follows suit, never too good and never too bad. Camera work, with the exception of the unfair handling given Miss Langford, is okay, especially in the simulated sky-fighting scenes.

Stal.

Inside Job

Universal release of Ben Pivar (Jean Yarbrough) production, directed by Yarbrough. Stars Preston Foster, Alan Curtis, Ann Rutherford. Screenplay, George Bricker and Jerry Warner; original, Tod Browning and Garrett Fort; camera, Maury Gertsman; editor, Otto Ludwig. Previewed N. Y., June 13, '46. Running time, 65 MINS.

Bart Madden	Preston Foster
Eddie Norton	Alan Curtis
Claire Gray	Ann Rutherford
Captain Thomas	Joe Sawyer
Ruth	Joan Fulton
Dist. Atty. Sutton	Milburn Stone
Skipper	Jimmie Moss
Judge Kinkaid	Samuel S. Hinds
Mr. Wickle	Howard Freeman
Freddie	John Berkes
Pop Hurley	Harry Brown
Fenway	Joe Kirk

Routine crook meller won't cause much stir. Obviously aimed for the duals, job looks like a quick throw-me-together, with no particular care in scripting, direction or performance. Especially the script.

Plot drags in all manner of trite situation in its story of a young couple, anxious to go straight, and prevented from doing so by a gangster who knows their past. The duo, working in a dept. store, are forced to burglarize the place. In turn, they doublecross the big-shot. Latter is killed by a cop when he comes for the coin, and the couple gives up loot and themselves to satisfy society.

Situation and dialog are maudlin and corny, with such items as the copper's motherless son and his dog dragged in for sentimental reasons, and the whole business ringing phony from beginning to end.

Alan Curtis and Ann Rutherford, as the young couple, play the roles straight, while Preston Foster gives a half-hearted performance as the gangster. Jimmie Moss is the precocious kiddie.

Bron.

My Pal Trigger
(SONGS)

Republic release of Armand Schaefer-Frank McDonald production. Stars Roy Rogers, "Gabby" Hayes, Dale Evans, Jack Holt, "Trigger." Features Leroy Mason, Roy Barcroft. Directed by Frank McDonald. Screenplay, Jack Townley and John K. Butler; camera, William Bradford; special effects, Howard and Theodore Lydecker; musical director, Morton Scott; editor, Harry Keller. Tradeshown New York, June 13, '46. Running time, 79 MINS.

Roy Rogers	Roy Rogers
Gabby Kendrick	George "Gabby" Hayes
Susan	Dale Evans
Brett Scoville	Jack Holt
Carson	LeRoy Mason
Hunter	Roy Barcroft
Sheriff	Sam Flint
Croupier	Kenne Duncan
Auctioneer	Ralph Sanford
Storekeeper	Francis McDonald
Dr. Bentley	Harlan Briggs
Davis	Wm. Haade
Wallace	Alan Bridge
Walling	Paul E. Burns
Magistrate	Frank Reicher

Bob Nolan and Sons of Pioneers

First of Republic's new series of "Roy Rogers specials," designed to bring Trigger's rider up to the "A" plane, "My Pal Trigger" is a plenty swank hoss opry and should move its pair of stars up another rung on the popularity ladder. With the tremendous reserve of Rogers fans upon which it will call, plus flicker habitues lured by the promise of a class production, the film should better than hold its own at the boxoffice.

Esthetically speaking, "My Pal" is neither fish nor fowl; moppet fans might prefer six-guns, swinging saloon doors, and a chase scene to the modern gambling joint and speeding station wagon. More likely, however, that they just want Rogers and his indispensable catalyst, Trigger.

Cowpoke plays an itinerant horse trader who wants to marry his mare to the best Palomino in the country, owned by "Gabby" Hayes, who refuses. Jack Holt, playing a fine heavy, has the same idea. When Holt tries to steal the prize horse it escapes and trots off into the bushes with Rogers' mare. Loss is discovered and when he finds the horse, Holt kills it firing at a wild stallion. Rogers gets the blame, but jumps bail and leaves, with his mare. After a year of travail, the foal, Trigger, is dropped. Rogers returns with the full-grown horse and saves the Hayes ranch by winning a race on which "Gabby" had bet his property against gambling debts. Real horse-killer is discovered and all is well.

Camera work, scripting, direction, and general production of this film are of a high order, especially for an oatuner. Thesping is well-controlled. Sons of the Pioneers are spotted in good sagebrush songs, while Rogers turns some credible crooning with Dale Evans. Occasional narration by Rogers is handled with finesse. As usual, there is no smoking or drinking by the star, and the only kissing is done by the nags.

Beware
(ALL-NEGRO)
(Musical)
(Songs)

Astor release of R. M. Savini-Berle Adams production. Stars Louis Jordan, Valerie Black; features Emory Richardson, Frank Wilson, Milton Woods. Directed by Bud Pollard. Screenplay, John E. Gordon; camera, Don Malkames; music and lyrics, Morry Lasco, Fleecy Moore, Dick Adams, Claude Demetrius, Bill Tennyson, Bob Hilliard, Dick Miles, Wm. Davis, Duke Groner, Charles Stewart, Herman Fairbanks, Dick Watson, Louis Jordan, Irene Higginbotham, Dan Fisher, Ervin Drake, Lucky Millender, Jerry Black; editor, Bud Pollard; assistant director, Ed Kelly. Premiered June 14, '46, Hamilton theatre, N. Y. Running time, **64 MINS.**

Lucius Brokenshire Jordan	Louis Jordan
Professor Drury	Frank Wilson
Dean Hargraves	Emory Richardson
Miss Annabelle Brown	Valerie Black
Benjamin Ware 3rd	Milton Woods
Schoolboys—	
Harry	Joseph Hilliard
Donald	Tommy Hix
Robert	Charles Johnson
Joe	John Frant
Porter	Walter Earle
Stranger	Ernest Calloway
Long Legged Lizzie	Dimples Daniels
Tympany Band	
William Davis	Piano
Joshwa W. Jackson	Sax
Aaron Izenhall	Trumpet
Carl Hogan	Guitar
Jesse Simpkins	Bass
Eddie Byrd	Drums
The "Aristo-Genes" Girls Club	

Louis Jordan's first feature-length effort shows wise direction in that thesping was held to a minimum in favor of music. By ordinary standards, "Beware" might just rate a "B." However, with 600 theatres playing Negro films and the fact that the picture would not be cut of place in some ofay houses, maximum grosses for this type of film can be expected.

Jordan is a consummate showman and has been surrounded with a couple of fine thespers in Frank Wilson and Valerie Black, both of the "Anna Lucasta" legiter. Tunes, which pop up one after another, are some of the Tympany's top platter sellers, including "Don't Worry 'bout That Mule," "Beware," "Salt Pork, West Virginia," "You Gotta-Have a Beat," and others.

Story tells of a small college, out of funds due to book-juggling of its endower's grandson, which calls upon its alumni for help. All refused except Jordan, apparently, who never received the letter and who was never given a thought. Stranded by a washout on the way to a date at the Paramount, N. Y., Jordan rescues the college, whips the nasty heir, and makes off with the physical instructress, with whom he's been in love all the time.

Music is okay and direction fairish, but camera work is definitely mediocre, showing too many close-ups of Jordan singing. Maestro's rhythmic bouncing in front of the backdrop, in the close-ins, is annoying and painful to the eyes. Production features are not impressive at any time, although some montage shots give band's sheet and platter music, and house dates good plugs.

Crack-Up

Hollywood, June 15.

RKO release of Jack J. Gross production. Stars Pat O'Brien, Claire Trevor, Herbert Marshall; features Ry Collins, Wallace Ford, Dean Harens, Damian O'Flynn, Erskine Sanford, Mary Ware. Directed by Irving Reis. Story, John Paxton, Ben Bengal, Ray Spencer; suggested by story, "Marman's Holiday," by Fredric Brown; camera, Robert de Grasse; special effects, Russell A. Cully; music, Cegh Harline; editor, Frederic Knudtson. Tradeshown L. A. June 14, '46. Running time, **93 MINS.**

George Steele	Pat O'Brien
Terry	Claire Trevor
Traybin	Herbert Marshall
Dr. Lowell	Ray Collins
Cochrane	Wallace Ford
Reynolds	Dean Harens
Stevenson	Damian O'Flynn
Barton	Erskine Sanford
Mary	Mary Ware

Psychological thriller that adds up to average results. There's sufficient name strength in the cast and exploitable angles to assure okay payoff in general situations. It's an actioner that moves along at a fairly fast clip, has been given good production values. Pat O'Brien, Claire Trevor and Herbert Marshall should further aid the selling.

Basic idea on which script is premised adds up to good thriller material and comes off well enough as scripted, played and directed, even though never reaching suspenseful heights aimed at. Plot is wrapped around a museum art lecturer who is believed to have cracked up mentally when he insists he has been injured in a non-existent train wreck. After proper amount of heroics and action it resolves into a plot to steal museum's old masters by substitution of copies and crooks are trying to keep lecturer from using his skill to detect forgeries.

O'Brien is not too aptly cast as the lecturer, but gives the assignment his usual vigor. Claire Trevor as his girl friend fares better, giving role some good moments. Marshall, mysterious character who proves to be a Scotland Yard man in the windup, also shows up well. Ray Collins, art-mad doctor, who stages the dirty work; Wallace Ford, prolice detective, Dean Harens, Damian O'Flynn. Erskine Sanford and Mary Ware are others doing okay in the cast.

Irving Reis' direction of the Jack J. Gross production moves yarn along but lacks extra drive to punch the material over solidly. Lensing, editing and other factors are competent. *Brog.*

Man From Rainbow Valley
(SONGS-COLOR)

Hollywood, June 15.

Republic release of Louis Gray production. Stars Monte Hale, Adrian Booth; features Jo Ann Marlowe, Ferris Taylor, Emmett Lynn, Tom London, Bud Geary, Kenne Duncan, Doye O'Dell, Bert Roach, Sagebrush Serenaders. Directed by Robert Springsteen. Original screenplay, Betty Burbridge; camera (Trucolor), Bud Thackery; songs, Eddie Cherkose and Cy Feuer; Roy Rogers, Glenn Spencer; editor, Edward Mann. Previewed at RCA studio, Hollywood, June 12, '46. Running time, **56 MINS.**

Monte	Monte Hale
Kay North	Adrian Booth
Ginny Hale	Jo Ann Marlowe
Col. Winthrop	Ferris Taylor
Locoweed	Emmett Lynn
Healey	Tom London
Tracy	Bud Geary
Lafe	Kenne Duncan
Jim	Doye O'Dell
The Mayor	Bert Roach
Enright Busse / John Scott / Frank Wilder	Sagebrush Serenaders

Excellent western. Story has interest, is developed away from usual oater formula, and color lensing gives extra values. Will play okay in the market for which aimed. In addition to regular action, several prairie ballads are ably spotted for interest. It's a budget production adding up to neat 56 minutes of entertainment for Saturday matinee fans.

Original script by Betty Burbridge plots action against background of ranch owned by cartoon strip artist and concerns theft of his stallion, Outlaw, by rodeo operator. Horse, model for the strip, is wanted for exploitation with kid rodeo fans, and since it's never been branded and runs loose on the range, his owner cannot make a legal claim for his return. Instead, he resorts to tricking rodeo operator into a bet on his ability to ride the nag. All ends well; Outlaw is back on his home range, Monte Hale gets the girl as well, and kid followers of the cartoon strip are happy again.

Robert Springsteen keeps footage moving along with his direction. Hale and Adrian Booth do well by top romantic spots, former also singing "Ridin' Down the Trail" and "The Man in the Moon Is a Cowhand." The two other tunes are taken care of by the Sagebrush Serenaders, typical Western song group. Jo Ann Marlowe, moppet; Ferris Taylor, Emmett Lynn (in for laughs), Tom London, Bud Geary, Kenne Duncan and others work well.

Louis Gray's production does okay by the values for budget. Bud Thackery did the color lensing, getting in some natural effects in outdoor shots. Other credits are standard. *Brog.*

Stormy Waters
("Remorque")
(FRENCH-MADE)

Metro release of Sedis Films production. Stars Jean Gabin, Michele Morgan. Directed by Jean Gremillon. From Concourt prize novel by Rogue Vercel; screenplay by Jacques Prevert. At 55th St. Playhouse, N. Y., starting June 15, '46. Running time, **77 MINS.**

Laurent	Jean Gabin
Catherine	Michele Morgan
Yvonne	Madeleine Renaud
Tanguy	Blavette
Captain of "Mirva"	Jean Marchat
Bosco	Fernand Ledoux

(In French; English Titles)

Made in Paris and in the port of Brest shortly before the Nazis took over France, this well-made French production finally gets its preem in the U. S. under the aegis of Metro. Both Jean Gabin and Michele Morgan have appeared in American screen productions since being "discovered" in French films. While this is not Gabin's top French screen effort and hardly measures up to other work Miss Morgan has done in her native land, the pair team up well here in the romantic passages. As one of the foreign language pictures Metro plans handling in the English-speaking market, picture shapes up strongly with the initial French production, "It Happened at the Inn," which M-G is handling in like fashion.

This simple tale of an ocean salvage-boat captain proves gripping entertainment, particularly in view of the French language being conveyed via superimposed English titles and the story obviously required considerable scissoring. At times this pruning makes the story too episodic, with the connecting skeins left dangling. Despite this trimming to fit American moral standards, "Stormy Waters" turns out to be a typical Gaelic romance of the sea.

All the action is packed into opening reels as Gabin goes to the rescue of a floundering merchant vessel in storm-whipped seas. Skipper of the stricken ship is unscrupulous and cuts loose when nearing port to deprive Gabin of the rescue fee. During the height of the storm, Miss Morgan, wife of the cutthroat captain, goes by lifeboat to Gabin's ship where she is treated until port is reached. The affair between the two is complicated by Gabin's ailing wife. Climax finds him returning to the sea when his wife dies.

Both stars click and Madeleine Renaud is adequate as Gabin's wife. Capable support is headed by Blavette, Jean Marchat and Fernand Ledoux.

Jean Gremillon's direction is good, while the screenplay by Jacques Prevert covers nicely the possibilities offered by Roger Vercel's novel. Marjorie Adams has done a superb job of English titling. *Wear.*

Rosa de America
("Rose of America")
(ARGENTINE-MADE)

Buenos Aires, June 4.

Distribuidora Panamericana release of San Miguel Studios' production. Directed by Alberto de Zavalia. Stars Delia Garces in the title role, with Orestes Caviglia, Antonio Herrero, Elsa O'Connor, Enrique Alvarez Diosdado, Angelina Pagano, Domingo Sapelli, Francisco Lopez Silva, Rafael Frontaura, Ernesto Vilches and Elisardo Santalla. Screen story by Ulises Pettit de Murat and Homero Manzi; camera, Jose Maria Beltran. Running time, **103 MINS.**

(In Spanish; No English Titles)

Aside from the excellent settings and photography, this is a dragging, uneven production which needs considerable cutting. Telling the story of South America's patron saint gave Argentina's film industry a golden opportunity to do a picture of interest to all the Latin-American countries. But in spite of lavish care, they have muffed it again. The picture has been two years in production and this may count for the slow pace.

As a compliment to the Saint's Peruvian birth, it was preemed simultaneously in Lima, Peru, and at the Monumental theatre here. Crix tried not to throw brickbats at the home production, but their disappointment was obvious. As usual, the life of a saint is treated with dignity, but Argentine producers have yet to learn that humor is not incompatible with the higher plane. They cling to their melancholia despite knowing this is a mistake for a boxoffice film.

As Rosa de Lima, the high-born Peruvian lady, who became a saint, Delia Garces is overshadowed once more by the greater experience of the veteran cast around her. As in the "Ghost Lady," Antonia Herrera steals nearly all her scenes. Story is laid in the Peru of vice-regal days and reproduction of Lima's colonial architecture is the best part of the film. Potentially a magnificent subject to interest U. S. audiences, the heavy treatment has reduced its chances there.

Hello Moscow
(Songs)
(RUSSIAN-MADE)

Artkino release of Mosfilm production. Stars Anya Stravinskaya, Nikolai Leonov, Lev Pirogov, Oleg Bobrov; features Vassili Seleznev, Ivan Lubeznov, Andrei Shirshov, Sergei Philipov. Directed by Sergei Yetkevich. Screenplay, Mikhail Volpin, Nikolai Erdman; camera, Mark Magidson; music, Anatole Lemin; English titles, Charles Clement. At Stanley, N. Y., week June 15, '46. Running time, **89 MINS.**

Tania	Anya Stravinskaya
Kolia	Nikolai Leonov
Oleg	Oleg Bobrov
Fedia	Vassili Seleznev
Grandpa Nikanor	Lev Pirogov
The School Director	Ivan Lubeznov
Assistant Director	Andrei Shirshov
Brikin, the Accordionist	Sergei Philipov
The Scenario Writer	Boris Tenin

(In Russian; English Titles)

All things considered, meaning past performance, Soviet picture policy, and language difficulties, this Russian offering to American flicker audiences is still pretty weak. And few American payees will stop to consider any of these factors, let alone a cast the majority of which is amateur. Market-wise, "Hello Moscow" will sell to that group of perennial hopefuls who patronize any picture with the red star stamp.

What a weak plot-within-a-plot attempts to do is sell Russian industrial schools. Method 'employs a group of amateur youngsters playing students who are preparing for a musical show in Moscow. In rehearsals they run into a crochety old school director who attempts to stop them by hiding the piano, but they rent an accordian from a local pub. Turns out the squeezebox was stolen by the saloon musician from the old professor, who accuses the boys. Justice ultimately prevails and show goes on. Final scene switches rather pointlessly to mass calisthenics and the young hero making a speech about Russia's destiny.

Story is presented in a series of disjointed flashbacks with looseness emphasized by the language block. The music might be good, but singing and dancing is obviously amateurish. Camera work is erratic, sometimes good and other times pretty bad.

Foreign Films

"Estrange Destin" (Strange Fate) (FRENCH). Discina release of Andre Paulve-Celia Film production. Stars Renee St. Cyr and Aime Clariond; features Henry Vidal, Nathalie Mattier, Denise Grey. Directed by Louis Cuny; screenplay by Marcelle Maurette from short story, "Gisele et son destin," by Mrs. de Lacombe. Dialog by Jean Sarment. Reviewed in Paris. Running time, 110 MINS.

Henri Vidal, male star in this film, looks like a man but doesn't get a chance here. Director Louis Cuny misses every potentiality. Photography is poor. Story shows Renee St. Cyr marrying Henry Vidal, and thinking him dead when he had only lost his memory in the trenches. He lives with a nurse but latter dies to permit him to recover his memory and return to his devoted wife. Dialogue frequently draws guffaws. Looks a U. S. washout.

"Le Couple Ideal" (Ideal Couple) (FRENCH). Comptoir Francais du Film release of S.U.F. (Jean Clerc) production. Stars Raymond Rouleau, Helene Perdriere; features Denise Grey, Philippe Olive, Sinoel, Yves Deniaud, Jacqueline Pierreu. Directed by Bernard Roland. Story by Pierre Leaud; dialog. Michel Durand and Leaud. Camera, Claude Renoir; music, Georges van Parys; sets. Roland Quignon. Running time, 90 MINS.

Unlikely for America, except for French language spots. The funny story and multiple role played by the star probably explains the Metro purchase of story for remake. Entirely different from usual French productions and smacking of slapstick comedy, yarn shows Raymond Rouleau as a 1912 pix star due to appear at a gala attended by former President of France Armand Fallieres. Latter is burlesqued. Detained by the police, Rouleau must alibi himself and adopt many disguises to defeat a rival producer. He finally wins Helene Perdiere who does a femme pix star of the serial era. Skit on the old-time film industry is geared fairly fast and drew laughs. *Maxi.*

Miniature Reviews

"Her Adventurous Night" (U). Well-handled light comedy for the duals.

"A Boy, A Girl, and A Dog" (FC). Minor quickie piece strictly for the kid trade.

"Beware of Pity" (Eagle). Hardwicke, Lilli Palmer, Gladys Cooper, in British pic possible U. S. bet.

Her Adventurous Night

Univeral release of Marshall Grant (Charles F. Haas) production. Features Dennis O'Keefe, Helen Walker, Scotty Beckett. Directed by John Rawlins. Original screenplay, Jerry Warner; editor, Edward Curtiss; camera, Ernest Miller. Previewed in N.Y., June 23, '46. Running time, 75 mins.
Bill..Dennis O'Keefe
Constance...Helen Walker
Carter...Tom Powers
Cudgeons..Fuzzy Knight
Petrucie...Charles Judels
Junior...Scotty Beckett
Horace...Bennie Bartlett
Cop No. 1..Milburn Stone
Miss Spencer......................................Betty Compson

---

"Her Adventurous Night" shapes up as a well-constructed blend of action and humor for the dualers. Modestly budgeted item has been directed with a nice light touch to take the corn out of most of the standard and sometimes implausible situations.

Story centers about Scotty Beckett, a hyper-imaginative 14-year-old son of Dennis O'Keefe and Helen Walker, whose flights into improbability provide the key shenanigans for the film. Having been found with a pistol in his possession in school, he invents a story incriminating the principal which not only lands the pedagog in jail, but jugs his parents as well. He gets them all out of the scrape by solving a 15-year-old murder mystery.

Thespic burden in the film alternates between Miss Walker and O'Keefe, along with the moppet. This nice work division is made possible by some flashback sequences which gives the older folks a chance to be by themselves. Chief support is by Fuzzy Knight with a few comedy touches, while other assignments are handled with varied degrees of capability by Charles Judels and Tom Powers. *Jose.*

A Boy, A Girl, and a Dog

Film Classics release of W.R. Frank production. Features Jerry Hunter, Sharon Moffett, Harry Davenport, Lionel Stander. Directed by Herbert Kline. Screenplay, Maurice Clark, Irving Fireman from original by Leopold Atlas adapted by Kline; camera, Edward Hull; editor, Marguerite Francisco. At Brooklyn Paramount, dual, week of June 20, '46. Running time, 51 mins.
Kip..Jerry Hunter
Button..Sharyn Moffett
Gramps..Harry Davenport
Jim...Lionel Stander
Mr. Stone..Charles Williams
Mrs. Foster....................................Charlotte Treadway
Lieut. Stephens...............................Howard Johnson
Mr. Hamilton.......................................John Vosper
Mrs. Hamilton......................................Nancy Evans

---

This is a synthetic little quickie for adolescents, otherwise nothing but a dual filler. Production values are glaringly of the basement bargain variety with story, script and direction equally shoddy. Performances don't offer much of a lift, either, while the photography bathes the whole affair in one dark shadow.

Syrupy yarn centers around a stray pooch and its adoption by two tots. Being wartime, the kids volunteer the dog for the army's canine branch, where after a difficult time in training, the pooch practically singlefooted wins the war against the Nips. The battle scenes are processed out of some old newsreel clips and some inept studio shots. Decibel rating of the sound track is deafening with every rifle report sounding like an atomic explosion.

The two youngsters, Jerry Hunter and Sharyn Moffett, have natural appeal but too often are pushed into that affected precocity supposed to pass for cuteness. Grit-voiced Lionel Stander walks through his part as an Army sergeant without too much effort as does Harry Davenport in role of the boy's grandfather.

Beware of Pity

London, June 12.

Eagle-Lion release of Two Cities Film. Stars Lilli Palmer, Cedric Hardwicke, Gladys Cooper, Albert Lieven. Directed by Maurice Elvey. Screenplay by W. P. Lipscomb from novel by Stefan Zweig; dialogue by Elizabeth Baron, Marguerite Steen; camera, Derick Williams. At Leicester Square theatre, London. Running time, 105 MINS.
Baroness de Kekesfalva........Lilli Palmer
Lieut. Anton Marek..........Albert Lieven
Doctor Albert Condor....Cedric Hardwicke
Klara Condor..............Gladys Cooper
Ilona Domansky...........Linden Travers
Baron de Kekesfalva......Ernest Thesiger
Lieut. Joszi Molnar............Emrys Jones
Major Jan Nivak.......Gerard Kempinski
Major Sandor Balinkay......Ralph Truman
Colonel Franz Babencic.........John Salew
Captain Ferencz Hercaeg......David Ward
Lieut. Blannik...............Tony Dawson
Count Ferdinand Salm.....Geoffrey Parker
Kusma........................Peter Cotes
Josef................Frederick Wendhausen

Gripping story of a crippled baroness who falls in love with good-looking lieutenant only to learn that his constant attentions are purely sympathetic. Rumored engagement of couple which is strenuously denied by the lieutenant when taxed by his army comrades results in tragic suicide of the baroness. Sure coin-getter for England, this has possibilities for U. S., especially in view of cast.

Story is unfolded in form of flashbacks, with lieutenant citing his own past life to a soldier who finds himself in similar quandary. At times it halts and becomes ponderous, but on the whole it is actionful.

Role of Edith de Kekesfala, the paralyzed baroness, is played by Lilli Palmer, now in Hollywood, her first stellar role in British films. She wins sympathy in this part, acquitting herself well. The Lt. Anton Marek role also is a first starrer for Albert Lieven. He turns in a sensitive performance.

Cedric Hardwicke and Gladys Cooper, who were brought over from Hollywood to portray Doctor Albert Condor and his wife Klara, prove effective. Latter, who portrays a blind woman, is very good. Emotional scene between her and the lieutenant is one of highlights of the picture. Supporting cast, with few exceptions, is well chosen, with Gerard Kempinski as Mayor Jan Nivak, rating special mention.

Screenplay, adapted by W. P. Lipscomb from Stephan Zweig's best seller of same title, is expertly done, while Derek Williams' lensing is commendable. *Rege.*

Foreign Films

"Vive La Liberte" (FRENCH). Eclair Journal release of Metropolis Films production; directed by Jeff Musse; features Raymond Bussieres, Jean Darcante, Jeanne Manet, Charles Moulin, Santa-Relli, Jean Deat, Chaduc, Pierre Ringel; story by Pierre Forest and Pierre Corcal; reviewed in Paris. Running time, 90 MINS.

This supposedly authentic story of life with the French maquis under German occupation looks like a quickie and offers little for American audiences. Locally it rates only nabe houses, with best chances in spots where the maquis were active.

"L'Idiot" (FRENCH). Lux release of Sacha Gordine production; directed by Georges Lampin; stars Lucien Coedel, Gerard Philippe, Nathalie Nattier, Marguerite Moreno, Jean Debucourt, Tramel, Sylvie; screenplay by Charles Spack, based on Dostoievsky's novel; camera, Christian Matras; reviewed in Paris. Running time, 105 MINS.

The psychological interest in the novel, set in the period of Russia before the Soviets, makes it good reading but the screen adaptation boils down to a long and sombre story. Its American potentialities will lean to arty spots. Technically the picture is way above the local average. Edwige Feuillere, in the role of the well-meaning bad woman, gives a fine performance. She is well supported by Lucien Coedel as a realistic flour merchant, and Gerard Philippe in the title role. Nathalie Nattier is the jealous girl, but Marguerite Moreno's excellent thesping has not been properly exploited for comedy relief. *Maxi.*

Miniature Reviews

"Of Human Bondage" (WB). Remake of Somerset Maugham novel shapes up for nominal b.o. returns.

"The Undercover Woman" (Rep). Neatly-spaced comedy whodunit, good for lesser situations.

"Dead of Night" (U-Rank). Unusual British film may prove a sleeper in the U. S.

"Queen of Burlesque" (Songs) (PRC). Routine murder story with burlycue background good for exploitation selling.

"West of the Alamo" (Mono) (Songs). Mild western starring Jimmy Wakely.

"Vertigo" (Clasa). Maria Felix, Emilio Tuero and Lilia Michel fail to help this Mexican-made tragedy; not for the U. S.

Of Human Bondage

Los Angeles, July 2.

Warners release of Henry Blanke production. Stars Eleanor Parker, Paul Henreid, Alexis Smith; features Edmund Gwenn, Janis Page, Patric Knowles, Henry Stephenson. Directed by Edmund Goulding. Screenplay, Catherine Turney, from novel by Somerset Maugham; camera, Peverell Marley; music, Erich Wolfgang Korngold; editor, Clarence Kolster. Tradeshown in Los Angeles, July 1, '46. Running time, **106 MINS.**

Mildred Rogers.............Eleanor Parker
Philip Carey.................Paul Henreid
Nora Nesbit...................Alexis Smith
Athelny...................Edmund Gwenn
Sally Athelny.....................Janis Paige
Griffiths...................Patric Knowles
Dr. Tyrell................Henry Stephenson
Dunsford...................Marten Lamont
Mrs. Athelny.................Isobel Elsom
Mrs. Foreman...............Una O'Connor
Mrs. Gray........................Eva Moore
Emil Miller.................Richard Nugent
Landlady.........................Doris Lloyd

Heavy drama with enough femme interest to assure average returns in most situations, this is a remake of the Somerset Maugham novel, first screened 12 years ago. Exploitable angles are strong enough to make for okay b.o. possibilities, even though what transpires is never as gripping as it could have been. Story has been given excellent period mounting to fit early London background, is well-played and directed in individual sequences, but lacks overall smoothness.

Top roles go to Eleanor Parker, as the tart; Paul Henreid, the sensitive artist-doctor, and Alexis Smith, novelist. A third femme love interest is Janis Page. Three femmes represent various loves that enter life of Henreid, frustrated artist, but major interest is concentrated on character played by Miss Parker and how she affects Henreid's happiness. Softening of censorable angles in the Maugham novel to meet screen requirements has lessened adult interest considerably, script necessarily having to quibble at the facts of life in story development.

Edmund Goulding's direction of the Henry Blanke production hits some high points in individual scenes, screenplayed by Catherine Turney. He gets good work out of the cast generally and helps interest although most of major characters carry little sympathy. Miss Parker's work is excellent, as is Henreid's depiction of the self-pitying cripple. Miss Smith's role has been edited to a comparatively small part. Edmund Gwenn as the Bohemian shows up as one of the more interesting characters, and Miss Paige appeals as his daughter, who is the third and final love in Henreid's life. Patric Knowles, Henry Stephenson, Marten Lamont and others are good.

Lensing by Peverell Marley expertly displays settings and cast, and other technical credits measure up.
Brog.

The Undercover Woman

Republic release of Rudolph E. Abel production. Features Stephanie Bachelor, Robert Livingston, Richard Fraser, Isabel Withers, Edythe Elliott, John Dehmer. Directed by Thomas Carr. Screenplay, Jerry Sackheim, Sherman I. Lowe; adapted by Robert Metzler from story by Sylvia G. L. Dannett; camera, Bud Thackery; editor, Fred Allen. At New York theatre, N. Y., dual, June 26, '46. Running time, **56 MINS.**

Marcia Conroy..........Stephanie Bachelor
Sheriff Don Long.......Robert Livingston
Gregory Vixon...............Richard Fraser
Penny Davis..................Isabel Withers
Laura Vixon...................Helene Heigh
Mrs. Grey.....................Edythe Elliott
Walter Hughes..................John Dehner
Juanita Gillette...............Elaine Lange
Cissy Van Horn...............Betty Blythe
Lem Stone.......................Tom London
Simon Gillette...................Larry Blake

Snappy dialog helps this mystery dualer to please. A modestly budgeted whodunit, "Undercover Woman" subordinates plot aspects to bright gags and laughable situations. Mystery elements, however, provide a neat framework for the production, heightening the chuckles with well-sustained suspense. Performances, although handled by marquee lightweights, are uniformly fluent and witty. Direction, editing, and photography lend overall polish.

Story, with a dude ranch background, is late getting under way, with the first half lingering over some romantic byplay between Stephanie Bachelor and Robert Livingston. Former plays a private gumshoe on commission to collect evidence against a philandering cad whose wife wants a divorce. Playboy instead gets mysteriously killed, with several vacationers at the dude ranch suspected of having committed the deed. As expected, the most innocent person on the lot turns up to be guilty party after some complicated sleuthing by the femme detective and her boyfriend sheriff.

Miss Bachelor is a pleasing looker and walks through her part with assurance. Robert Livingston, as the sheriff, is adequate in the action spots, but a bit stiff as a sophisticated romancer. Standout comedy bits are offered by Betty Blythe, as Miss Bachelor's lily-livered aide, and John Dehner, a visiting newspaperman.

Dead of Night

(BRITISH-MADE)

Universal release of Michael Balcon (J. Arthur Rank-Ealing Studios) production. Stars Mervyn Johns, Michael Redgrave; features Frederick Valk, Roland Culver, Anthony Baird, Googie Withers. Directed by Cavalcanti, Basil Deardon, Robert Hamer. Screenplay by John Baines, Angus MacPhail, based on original stories by E. F. Benson, Baines, MacPhail; editor, Charles Hasse; camera, Jack Parker, H. Julius; score, Georges Auric—played by London Symphony Orch. Tradeshown, N. Y., June 27, '46. Running time, **75 MINS.**

Hugh Grainger..................Antony Baird
Joan Cortland...............Googie Withers
Maxwell Frere...........Michael Redgrave
Sally O'Hara.............Sally Ann Howes
Walter Craig...................Mervyn Johns
Eliot Foley.....................Roland Culver
Dr. Van Straaten...........Frederick Valk
Mrs. Foley......................Mary Merrall
Dr. Albury...............Robert Wyndham
Joyce Grainger......................Judy Kelly
Hearse Driver..................Miles Malleson
Mrs. O'Hara...................Barbara Leake
Jimmy Watson.................Michael Allan
Antique Dealer.....................Esme Percy
Beulah.....................Elisabeth Welch
Maurice Olcott.....................Allan Jeayes
Sylvester Kee..................Hartley Power
Harry Parker....................Garry Marsh
Mrs. Craig.........................Renee Cado
Peter Cortland..................Ralph Michael

"Dead of Night," latest Rank pic released in America by Universal, shapes up as another of those unheralded British pix that emerge as sleepers, a la "39 Steps," "Night Train," etc. Dealing in psychic phenomena and the super-natural, it's an unusual picture, very well-produced and well-acted. Its word-of-mouth should be excellent.

Film preemed at the Winter Garden, N. Y., Friday (28) to standee business and exhibs can probably best base their publicity on the line adopted by that house. Management took special ads in the N. Y. dailies, claiming that "if you like something different in your motion pictures, then we guarantee that you will like 'Dead of Night.' If you're expecting 'Dead of Night' to be the usual, conventional motion picture, please pass it up."

Some form of special publicity will have to be used since, with the exception of Michael Redgrave, there's not a name in the all-British cast that means anything to American audiences. Cast also has that "English accent," which has proved poison at the boxoffice.

Tightly-woven script tells the story of a man who has fore-knowledge of the future through his dreams. Summoned on business to a British estate, he's shocked to find that the place and people have all been in his dreams. When he tells his dream, one of the house-guests, a psychiatrist, scoffs at the story and attempts to find a scientific explanation for it all.

Other guests, however, are more sympathetic and each then tells of a strange, similarly psychic situation in which he's been involved. Left alone with the psychiatrist afterwards, the dreamer is driven by a strange compulsion to kill him. At that point he awakens to find it's all been just a nightmare. The phone rings. Voice on the other end invites him on business to the same British estate of his dreams.

Producer Michael Balcon turned each individual episode over to a different director and, told via flashback, they're equally good. Best is the one featuring Redgrave as a ventriloquist whose dummy seemed imbued with a human brain and soul. Redgrave turns in a masterful piece of acting as he's driven to "kill" the dummy and in so doing, is destroyed himself.

Film is well-edited, each director maintaining consistently the suspense built up early in the yarn. Georges Auric's score, as played by the London Symphony Orch, adds greatly to the picture's all-around quality.
Stal.

Queen of Burlesque

(SONGS)

PRC release of Arthur Alexander-Alfred Stern production. Stars Evelyn Ankers; features Carleton Young, Marion Martin, Craig Reynolds, Rose La Rose. Directed by Sam Newfield. Screenplay, David A. Lang; editor, Jack Oglivie; camera, Vincent J. Farrar; songs, Gene Lucas and Al Stewart. At New York, N. Y., dual, week June 27, '46. Running time, **68 MINS.**

Crystal McCoy..............Evelyn Ankers
Steve Hurley...............Carleton Young
Lola Cassell................Marian Martin
Joe Nolan..................Craig Reynolds
Blossom Terraine............Rose La Rose
Inspector Crowley..........Emory Parnell
Chick Malloy..............Murray Leonard
Doorman......................Nolan Leary
Straight Man Singer.........Gordon Clark
Annie.........................Alice Fleming
Dolly Devoe.............Jacqueline Dalya
Johnson.......................Red Marshall
Stage Manager Max..........David Frisco
Dugan.........................Charles King

Producers of "Queen of Burlesque" probably had one eye on the possibility of censorial tiffs which they must have encouraged with the view of making this film a controversial issue. It contains several sides of dialog of questionable taste plus a burlesque background. With the burley backdrop, film offers a routine murder story that can be sold along sensational lines to the former patronage of the strip-shops.

Cast sheet on the opus gives prominence to Rose La Rose, runway peeler with considerable experience, and there is other cheesecake for ballyhoo.

Yarn is built around a femme lead in a burlesquerie, Evelyn Ankers, and her newspaperman-fiance, Carleton Young. A series of murders occur backstage and Miss Ankers finds herself a prime suspect. Her b.f. hooks the guilty party.

Story line isn't strong, but it's sufficient to maintain interest. The song and dance sequences are in the tired traditions of the burlesque houses.

Principals do their work in a capable manner with Miss Ankers showing up nicely, while Young attempts a breezy characterization of a newspaperman. Marian Martin, Craig Reynolds, Alice Fleming, Jacqueline Dalya and Miss La Rose provide adequate support.
Jose.

West of the Alamo

(SONGS)

Monogram release of Oliver Drake production. Stars Jimmy Wakely; features Lee White, Iris Clive, Jack Ingram. Directed by Oliver Drake. Original screenplay, Louise Rousseau; camera, Harry Neumann; editor, William Austin; musical director, Frank Sanucci. At New York theatre, N. Y., June 26, '46, dual. Running time, **57 MINS.**

Jimmy ....Jimmy Wakely
Lasses................Lee "Lasses" White
Jane Morgan.......................Iris Clive
Clay Bradford..................Jack Ingram
Emmet ....Red Holton
Shotgun ....Budd Buster
Dean ....Eddie Majors

Another in the Jimmy Wakely series of oatuners, "West of the Alamo" is standard with the usual run. Addicts will find this pic mild, the action thrills being heavily diluted in a tunefest of half-a-dozen numbers. Warbling chore in hillbilly style is handled by Wakely and "Lasses" White, assisted by the Arthur Smith Trio and a crew of fiddlers. Story and script are strictly formula mixtures of villainy, gunplay, and hoofbeating, with a slight seasoning of romance and comedy.

Yarn has rangers Wakely and White, working incognito, solving a crime wave which has been launched as a sideline by the town's bank president. Financier has falsely implicated a couple of young sisters in the affair, which involves a bank theft and murder. But Wakely balks the foul play through some far-fetched sleuthing and brings the real culprits to book in a fisticuff climax.

As a crooner, Wakely rates okay, but he cuts a rather tepid figure as a two-gun totin' terror. White, as the crusty old sidekick, has comic appeal for the juves. Jack Ingram plays the heavy in typical unsubtle style.

Vertigo

("Dizziness")

(MEXICAN-MADE)

Mexico City, June 18.

Clasa Films Mundiales production and release, features Maria Felix, Emilio Tuero and Lilia Michel. Based on novel of the same name by Pierre Benoit. Directed by Antonio Momplet. Camera, Alex Phillips. At Cine Orfeon. Running time, **75 MINS.**

Three of Mexico's topflight screen players, Maria Felix, Emilio Tuero and Lilia Michel plus some nice camera work are all that save this tragedy. Production is definitely the sort that Latin-Americans like, having to do with death and dead love. Excepting for the talent and looks of the featured players, it's doubtful if this picture would have much appeal for most American film patrons because it is such total tragedy.

Miss Felix has some harrowing scenes and never gets a chance to exert her usual charm. Tuero, formerly a juvenile, now has become a lead reminscent of William Powell.

He is shown preparing to marry a comely girl and then falling for the same girl's youthful, widowed mother. Plot has him killing the daughter only to be slain by the widow.

Miss Felix is good as the mother and Lilia Michel is okay as the daughter.

Antonio Momplet does not better his rep as a director with this production. He misses many opportunities but admittedly the story gives neither him nor the cast much chance.

Miniature Reviews

"**Night and Day**" (Musical; Color) (WB). Cary Grant and Alexis Smith in sockeroo filmusical. Smash boxoffice certain.

"**A Scandal in Paris**" (One Song) (UA). Slow-moving period piece with Carole Landis, Signe Hasso, George Sanders.

"**Danger Woman**" (U). Dull program melodrama.

"**I See a Dark Stranger**" (GFD). Deborah Kerr in British-made spy whodunit; looks fair for U. S.

"**Life and Miracles of Blessed Mother Cabrini**" (Roma). Italian made documentary will appeal only to Catholic audiences.

"**Avalanche**" (PRC). Mediocre murder mystery localed in and around a mountain skiing lodge.

Night and Day
(MUSICAL-COLOR)

Warner Bros. release of Arthur Schwartz production. Stars Cary Grant, Alexis Smith; features Monty Woolley, Ginny Simms, Jane Wyman, Eve Arden, Carlos Ramirez, Donald Woods, Mary Martin. Directed by Michael Curtiz. Screenplay, Chas. Hoffman, Leo Townsend, Wm. Bowers; adaptation, Jack Moffitt; camera, Peverell Marley, Wm. V. Skall; dances, LeRoy Prinz; orchestral arrangements and production numbers, Ray Heindorf; musical director, Leo F. Forbstein; additional music, Max Steiner; vocals, Dudley Chambers; editor, David Weisbart; dialog director, Herschel Daugherty; special effects, Robt. Burke; asst. director, Frank Heath. Tradeshown, N. Y., July 8, '46. Running time, 128 MINS.
Cole Porter....................Cary Grant
Linda Lee Porter............Alexis Smith
Himself...............Monty Woolley
Carole Hill.................Ginny Simms
Gracie Harris................Jane Wyman
Gabrielle.......................Eve Arden
Anatole Giron..............Victor Francen
Leon Dowling.................Alan Hale
Nancy......................Dorothy Malone
Bernie.......................Tom D'Andrea
Kate Porter..................Selena Royle
Ward Blackburn............Donald Woods
Omer Porter............Henry Stephenson
Bart McClelland..........Paul Cavanagh
Wilowsky......................Sig Ruman
Specialty Singer..........Carlos Ramirez
Specialty Dancer.........Milada Mladova
Specialty Dancer..........George Zoritch
Specialty Team...Adam & Jayne Di Gatano
Specialty Dancer.........Estelle Sloan
Caleb.......................Clarence Muse
Petey...........................John Alvin
O'Halloran....................George Riley
Producer................Howard Freeman
Director..................Bobby Watson
1st Peaches................John Pearson
2nd Peaches............Herman Bing
Herself.....................Mary Martin

"Night and Day" is a smash. It will mop up from New England to New Zealand. It has everything.

So much for the boxoffice equation. But there are other elements about this filmusical, based on the career of Cole Porter, which warrant accenting. Primarily it is, perhaps, the best of the songsmith biographicals to date.

There's also this about "Night and Day"—it's the first biographical about a vibrantly alive and active showman-songwriter. While George M. Cohan lived to see his career immortalized in celluloid, he was an ailing man. Then, too, where other film biogs have had a tendency to barely touch salient details, the Porter yarn loses none of the songwriter's real-life impact.

A season hasn't gone by without some new set of Cole Porter songs, and the extent of his prolific and memorable catalog of hits well nigh staggers the auditor of this 128-minute cinematurgical unfolding.

It's to the credit of director Mike Curtiz, producer Arthur Schwartz and the combined scripters that they weighed the fruitful elements so intelligently, and kept it all down as much as they did. Many a complete routine and portions of others must have wound up on the cutting room floor. Wisely all steered clear of making this a blend of "and then I wrote" and a Technicolored song-plug unspooling.

Here's a guy to whom nothing more exciting happens than that he's born to millions and stays in a "rut" for the rest of his career by making more money. One of the script's dialogicians perhaps tried to cue the sophisticated film fan by having one of the theatrical manager characters observe that Porter's stuff is too sophisticated; perhaps he should have started poor on the East Side like so many of the other show biz personalities.

The plot, per se, therefore is static, on analysis, but paradoxically it emerges into a surprisingly interesting unfolding. A real-life ambulance driver in World War I, Porter is shown with the French army. Alexis Smith plays the nurse whom he marries; she's previously introduced as of an aristocratic family. And thereafter, save for a fall off a spirited steed which has caused Porter much real-life suffering because of broken legs which never set properly, the footage of "Night and Day" is a succession of hit shows and hit songs.

The tunes are chronologically mixed up a bit—a cinematic license with which none can be captious—and the romantic story line takes the accent principally in that Miss Smith seeks to get her husband away from the mad show biz whirl of London and Broadway. The plea to hide away in their villa on the Riviera plays better than it sounds. It's not stuffy. The aura is all of constant success and the atmosphere is lush for the major portion of the picture. The title song is properly insinuated as the personal theme song of Linda and Cole Porter's private lives.

The talents are socko even though their opportunities are limited. Firstly, Cary Grant as Cole Porter underplays and does his chores exceedingly well, especially as the film progresses. He's a bit old for a Yale undergraduate in the early sequences.

Ginny Simms fares best of the featured femmes, looking a bit like Ethel Merman and handling some of Miss Merman's show tunes—"Got You Under My Skin" (with Adam & Jayne Di Gatano standouts in the accompanying terps); "Just One of Those Things," "You're the Top" (with Grant) and "I Get a Kick Out of You." She's first introduced as a music demonstration counter chirper to Grant's piano-pounding, at the time when he refused help from his family and, with Yale professor-actor Monty Woolley (playing himself), tried to break into show business.

Woolley is capital as the bombastic, brash ex-Yale prof. as is Jane Wyman in her soubret role. Eve Arden gets much out of her chantoosey comedienne bit. Carlos Ramirez registers with "Begin the Beguine," as Milada Mladova and George Zoritch click with their dance specialty in one of the better LeRoy Prinz dance stagings. Incidentally, "Night and Day" may well be Prinz's best terp production job to date, blending popular values with good imaginative qualities.

Mary Martin gets a buildup for her "Heart Belongs to Daddy" polite strip, looking better as the sequence progresses, for the lens wasn't too kind to her in the forepart. Estelle Sloan clicks with a sensational tap routine which should catapult her to further attention. The rest are bits but solid such as French impresario Victor Francen, Selena Royle as Porter's mother, and Henry Stephenson is capital as his grandfather. Also Alan Hale, Donald Woods, Paul Cavanagh, among others.

Unseen but well heard stars of "Night and Day" are the musical artificers who have done a corking job of mixing the Porter music and serving it so palatably. Ray Heindorf rates particularly in this connection since he orchestrated and maestroed. All the music credits are above par.

"Night and Day" is Warner Bros. keynote production in connection with the company's current buildup campaign to celebrate the 20th anniversary of sound. As with "Don Juan," "Lights of New York" and "The Jazz Singer," which 20 years ago helped WB create a new film era, "Night and Day" takes its place with the screen's distinguished motion picture entertainments. Abel.

A Scandal in Paris
(ONE SONG)

United Artists release of Arnold Pressburger production; associate producer, Fred Pressburger; stars George Sanders, Signe Hasso, Carole Landis; features Akim Tamiroff, Gene Lockhart. Directed by Douglas Sirk. Screenplay, Ellis St. Joseph; based on the life of Eugene-Francois Vidocq; camera, Guy Roe; music, Hans Eisler; asst. director, Joe Depew; editor, Al Joseph. Tradeshown July 9, '46. Running time, 100 MINS.
Vidocq....................George Sanders
Therese......................Signe Hasso
Loretta....................Carole Landis
Emile.......................Akim Tamiroff
Richet.....................Gene Lockhart
Mimi.....................Jo Ann Marlowe
Marquise...................Alma Kruger
Houdon.....................Alan Napier
Uncle Hugo............Vladimir Sokoloff
Priest................Pedro de Cordoba
Modiste..................Leona Maricle
Painter.....................Fritz Leiber
Cousin Pierre.............Skelton Knaggs
Cousin Gabriel.............Fred Nurney
Aunt Ernestine.........Gisella Werbiseck
Little Louis................Marvin Davis

A picture whose physical assets in the person of Carole Landis may cause it to be tagged a second "Outlaw" emerges as pretty weak fare in spite of elaborate mountings.

Marquee value of the cast should afford good initial boxoffice, boosted by the title, although there is little to cause scandal as filmgoers know it.

Taking better than an hour and a half to unwind, "A Scandal in Paris" moves lethargically through the story of Eugene-Francois Vidocq, French criminal of the Napoleonic era who graduated from the underworld to become Paris' chief of police, and was reformed on the way by love. The cast, competent with few exceptions, has been handed a loosely strung-together, cliche-ridden scenario which too successfully manages to talk around situations that might have become exciting had they been filmed.

Pic is introed by George Sanders as Vidocq, narrating his early history. Story actually begins with Sanders in jail at 29, after a life of thievery and feminine conquest. He and cellmate Akim Tamiroff escape and begin a partnership in crime which ends abruptly as Sanders' love for Signe Hasso, the daughter of the man he had duped into appointing him police chief, causes him to turn honest. Plot takes Sanders and Tamiroff through a series of talky episodes to the final denouement.

Story's motivation is weak, characters poorly drawn, with few lines given Miss Hasso, and Miss Landis as the waterfront singer, carrying far more than her thespic talents can support. Latter's feminine points are thoroughly outlined during her sequences. Sanders is forced to a monotonous performance, being given none of the accoutrements necessary to a dashing outlaw, while the characters portrayed by Tamiroff and Gene Lockhart, the jealous husband, are resolved in froth. Precocity of baby sister Jo Ann Marlowe is tough to take.

Danger Woman
Hollywood, July 6.

Universal release of Morgan B. Cox production. Features Brenda Joyce, Don Porter, Patricia Morison, Kathleen Howard, Milburn Stone, Samuel S. Hinds. Directed by Lewis D. Collins. Original screenplay, Josef Mischel; camera, Maury Gertsman; editor, Russell Schoengarth. Previewed at the studio, July 3, '46. Running time, 59 MINS.
Claude Ruppert.................Don Porter
June....................Brenda Joyce
Eve Ruppert..............Patricia Morison
Gerald King.............Milburn Stone

Sears..........Samuel S. Hinds
Eddie..........Kathleen Howard
Lane..........Ted Hecht
Howard..........Leonard East
Inspector Pepper..........Charles D. Brown

Mild program melodrama with little entertainment to offer. Plot trics for timeliness by using atomic research as background but is never exciting enough to sustain audience interest. It's a budget production slated for lesser situations.

Wordy script and static situations militate against performances and direction fails to give proceedings a lift. Don Porter is a young scientist working on a formula for commercial use of the atom. Aiding is Brenda Joyce as his secretary. Romance between two is complicated when scientist's wife reappears after a three-year absence. She joins forces with crooked interests seeking to steal formula. A few murders and other standard meller formula material are tossed in but pace under Lewis D. Collins' direction moves slowly to the obvious conclusion without excitement. It has all the appearance of off-the-cuff film-making with little display of expert craftsmanship.

Patricia Morison tries hard with the wife role, proving okay as femme menace. Miss Joyce and Porter have thankless roles that never gain much color as written. Milburn Stone, Samuel S. Hinds, Kathleen Howard and others do their best with assignments in this Morgan B. Cox production. Maury Gertsman's lensing and other technical credits are standard for budget expenditure. *Brog.*

I See a Dark Stranger

(BRITISH-MADE)

London, July 4.

General Film Distributors' release of Individual Pictures production. Stars Deborah Kerr, Trevor Howard. Directed by Frank Launder. Screenplay by Frank Launder, Sidney Gilliat, Wolfgang Wilhelm. Camera, Wilkie Cooper, William Allan. At Odeon theatre. Running time, **112 MINS.**

Bridie Quiltie..........Deborah Kerr
David Baynes..........Trevor Howard
Miller..........Raymond Huntley
Captain Goodhusband..........Garry Marsh
Lieut. Spanswick..........Tom Macaulay
Danny Quiltie..........W. O'Gorman
Uncle Joe..........Harry Webster
Uncle Timothy..........Liam Redmond
Mrs. O'Mara..........Marie Ault
Michael O'Callaghan..........Brefni O'Rourke
Mrs. Edwards..........Olga Lindo
Terence Delaney..........Eddie Golden
Oscar Pryce..........David Ward

The Gilliat-Launder writer-producer team turns out a nice little comedy-thriller, strong in pictorial values, though whodunit fans may find some flaws. It should do fairly well in the world market, but it has no smash highlights. Instead it simmers along with a continuous flow of easy laughs. The big fight at the end, in a bathtub and a murderous chase in a tunnel are the only real punches in the picture, and this fight seems thrown in simply to provide a climax. Film looks a fair possibility for U. S., but title may have to be changed.

Anti-British cracks in the manner of Shavian comedy, and at least one anti-American crack, give a provocative air to the whole production. The story shows an increasing mastery of technique from the Gilliat-Launder boys. Dialog is natural.

Deborah Kerr, teamed with the personable Trevor Howard, is an Irish girl born in the bitterness of Black and Tan history and anxious to show Britain where she gets off. In Dublin, London, Devonshire and the Isle of Man, she gets involved with a Nazi spy gang headed by Raymond Huntley, hot on the trail of a D-Day invasion plan. Meetings in bookshops, tunnels, hotels and on the Irish border warm up to the escape of a spy under the noses of British Intelligence, the death of Huntley in an exciting tunnel chase at night and the gradual dawning on the colleen's mind that she is the victim of wicked Nazi conspirators. Also that her Irish blood has fooled her.

Weakness of the film is that Miss Kerr's stubborn anti-British cracks and dumb motivation are not sufficient to give her character reality. The defect is worked off in a spirit of engaging irresponsibility, with good old Irish blarney takes the place of common-sense. Maybe it will do because the heroine is attractive type despite her plain appearance. Deborah Kerr's performance registers well. Trevor Howard, supported by Garry Marsh and a host of comic Irish cronies, does extremely well and should increase his popularity. Moving in fresh and unusual backgrounds, this picture certainly should give Irish-Americans in the U. S. something to enjoy. *Ebet.*

Life and Miracles of Blessed Mother Cabrini

(ITALIAN-MADE)

Cldye Elliott release of Roma Films (feature documentary) production. Stars La Cheduzzi. Directed by Auerlio Battistoni. Commentary by Rev. Cletus McCarthy. Tradeshown, N. Y., July 5, '46. Running time, **70 MINS.**

Blessed Mother Cabrini..........La Cheduzzi
Sister Delfina..........Mila Lanza
Convict..........Luigi Badolati
Doctor..........Gennaro Quaranta

Biographical film of Mother Cabrini in feature-length documentary form is being released commercially in the U. S. to coincide with the canonization of the Chicago-born nun in Rome last Sunday (7). Picture is straight religious fare and its appeal outside the Catholic audiences is definitely limited. It will probably be played in the arty houses in key cities and as a one-day attraction in smaller towns where the exhib can cooperate with the Catholic church in his locality for best results.

Produced in Italy by Roma Films, religious pix outfit, the picture was probably not meant to have any entertainment value, as such. English dialog has been dubbed in, along with an English commentary prepared by Father Cletus McCarthy. Film suffers from a technically poor soundtrack, which, coupled with the Italian accents of the principals, makes it difficult to understand. Editing job also is n.s.g., the sequence of events being interrupted several times by newsreel shots that seem to have little relationship with that part of Mother Cabrini's life being depicted.

Picture traces the career of the nun, showing the events that the Catholic church has accepted as miracles and that led to her canonization. Her influence on the social development of both Chicago and New York is told in full, with scenes showing the schools, hospitals and boulevards bearing her name.

Acting by La Cheduzzi, as Mother Cabrini, and the other principals is stilted. Emphatic gestures and eye-rolling is reminiscent of the early Hollywood output. Many of the newsreel shots, taken in the early part of the century, are jumpy and the photography, on the whole, suffers from poor lighting. *Stal.*

Avalanche

PRC release of Pat Di Cicco production. Stars Bruce Cabot; features Roscoe Karns, Helen Mowery, Veda Ann Borg. Directed by Irving Allen. Story and adaptation, Andrew Holt; editor, Louis Sackin; camera, Jack Greenhalgh. At Rialto, N. Y., week July 5, '46. Running time, **68 MINS.**

Steve Batchellor..........Bruce Cabot
Red Kelly..........Roscoe Karns
Ann Watson..........Helen Mowery
Claire Jeremy..........Veda Ann Borg
Mrs. Carlton Morris..........Regina Wallace
Sven Worden..........John Good
Malone..........Philip Van Zandt
Mr. Carlton Morris..........Eddie Parks
Austin Jeremy..........Wilton Graff
Duncan..........Harry Hays Morgan
Jean..........Eddie Hyans
Sam..........Eddy Waller
Bartender..........Syd Saylor
Joe, the Raven..........As Played by Himself

The only reward—and not enough—for tolerating this tedious, routine murder mystery laid in and around a winter lodge in the hills of Idaho are the good outdoor backgrounds and the numerous scenes which feature expert skiing. As entertainment lasting 68 minutes picture is mediocre.

Bruce Cabot, starred, is an agent of the Treasury Department assigned to track down a tax evader who has taken refuge in a far western, remote mountain lodge, assisted by Roscoe Karns. Their technique leaves much to be desired in the light of how they go about their job as secret service men. Plot, in the main, revolves around several murders designed to lay hands on a large amount of money the tax evader is known to have with him. It's all very routine and drab, highlighted by a lot of talk and not much action.

Production values rate much higher than either the direction or the boilerplate story, an original by Andrew Holt which to a certain extent follows the Grand Hotel formula.

Cabot's performance is marred by lack of material, this also being true of Karns who in a couple minor instances is looked upon to supply comedy relief. It's not there. Love interest, never reaching a high pitch, is supplied by Helen Mowery, a guest at the skiing lodge. Others, none outstanding, include Veda Ann Borg, Regina Wallace, John Good and Philip Van Zandt. A tame raven who walks up and down a bar in the lodge, carrying empty glasses back to the barkeep, is also in the supporting cast. *Char.*

Foreign Films

"L'Homme Au Chapeau Rond" ("Man With a Round Hat") **(FRENCH).** C. P. L. F. Gaumont release of Alcina production. Stars Raimu; features Aime Clariond, Gisele Casadesus, Arlette Mery, Helena Manson, Lucy Valnor, Micheline Boudet, Jeanne Marken, Louis Seignier. Directed by Pierre Billon. Based on Dostoievsky's novel, "Eternal Husband"; adapted by Charles Spaak and Pierre Brice. Camera, Nicolas Toporkoff. Reviewed in Paris. Running time, **90 MINS.**

Raimu is shown as the drunken widowed father who lets his child, Lucy Valnor, die to spite Aime Clariond after discovering latter was his dead wife's lover. Raimu, strong local draw, gives a good performance. Juvenile Miss Valnor looks realistically unfortunate but Clariond is given to shouting. The solidly morbid Russian character study of a man's hate for another is not entertaining fare. Bluenoses might object to several scenes including the one where Raimu is shown in a brothel hiding a coin in his clothes so the girls will paw him to find it. Not much hope for U. S. market.

Miniature Reviews

"Sister Kenny" (RKO). Rosalind Russell, Alexander Knox in a top biographical film of the Aussie nurse; sure boxoffice.

"The Cockeyed Miracle" (M-G). Film fantasy, with chuckles and tears aplenty for general audiences.

"Home Sweet Homicide" (20th). Randolph Scott, Lynn Bari, Peggy Ann Garner for initial pull; good b.o.

"Lady Luck" (RKO). Strong cast and gambling theme will override weak story for OK b.o.

"Smithy" (Col.) (Australian). Sir Charles Kingsford-Smith's biog creates Australian milestone; good b.o. for British Empire.

"The Dark Horse" (One Song) (U). Satisfying dualer with ex-GI motif.

"Black Beauty" (20th-Alperson). Dawdling horse pic, lacking marquee names, will have b.o. trouble.

"Step By Step" (RKO). Melodrama as strong secondary feature.

"Night Train to Memphis" (Songs) (Rep). Minor lower-end dualer.

"Sunset Pass" (RKO) (Songs). Well-done small budgeted oattuner for duals.

Sister Kenny

RKO release of Dudley Nichols production, directed by Nichols. Stars Rosalind Russell, Alexander Knox; features Dean Jagger, Philip Merivale, Beulah Bondi, Charles Dingle. Screenplay, Nichols, Knox and Mary McCarthy, based on "And They Shall Walk," by Elizabeth Kenny in collaboration with Martha Ostenso; camera, George Barnes; editor, Roland Gross; score, C. Bakaleinikoff. Tradeshown, N. Y., July 11, '46. Running time, **110 MINS.**

Elizabeth Kenny..........Rosalind Russell
Dr. McDonnell..........Alexander Knox
Kevin Connors..........Dean Jagger
Dr. Brack..........Philip Merivale
Mary Kenny..........Beulah Bondi
Mike Kenny..........Charles Dingle
Medical Director..........John Litel
Dorree..........Doreen McCann
Mrs. McIntyre..........Fay Helm
Mr. McIntyre..........Charles Kemper
Agnes..........Dorothy Peterson

"Sister Kenny" stacks up as one of those infrequent biographical films that does full justice to the subject, while at the same time providing sock entertainment. Picture has all the ingredients of a good cast, story, production and direction to elicit top grosses in any situation.

With Elizabeth Kenny known throughout the world for her fight to have the medical profession accept her unorthodox method of treating infantile paralysis, RKO has a good bet for the international market as well as the U. S. Rosalind Russell's name on the marquee will also lure. Picture will undoubtedly stir up the same controversy that's revolved around the Aussie nurse since she first introduced the Kenny method some 35 years ago, which is all to the good of the boxoffice.

Miss Kenny's life story was a natural for pictures and Dudley Nichols and Alexander Knox, who collabbed on the screenplay, have made the most of it. Subordinated love story runs a nice counterpoint throughout the film to the dramatic events in the nurse's life, with the emphasis placed on Miss Kenny's scientific career and work. While the picture has the stuff that brings emotional lumps to the throats of the audience and depicts the juve victims of the dread polio, it never becomes a downright tearjerker, for which all plaudits to Nichols and Knox.

Miss Russell in the title role comes up with one of the best performances in her luminous film career and is given an able assist by Knox, as the

Scotch medico who bucks his die-hard confreres to gain recognition for her work, and by the late Philip Merivale as the most obdurate of her opponents. Miss Russell, with a role that's primed for overacting, shows remarkable restraint in her difficult portrayal of the nurse from her college days in 1909 up to the present. Knox is equally good in a difficult role and Merivale's thesping is a fitting eulogy to the late actor's ability.

Story picks up Miss Kenny as she graduates from nursing school at 22 and takes her through her early "bush-nursing" work in the Australian back country, where she first came into contact with polio and, through lack of knowledge and simple inspiration, evolved her cure. Condemned by the medical profession because her system isn't in the books, she forsakes her personal happiness via marriage to continue her work and fight against the medicos, until in 1940, she comes to the University of Minnesota to set up the Kenny Institute. Picture winds up as she gives her first lecture to the more enlightened doctors who've accepted her, even though an American medical committee has just ruled against her treatment.

Supporting cast backs up the principals nicely. Dean Jagger carries off his part well as the Aussie army officer who must give up Miss Kenny to her work. Beulah Bondi and Charles Dingle make nice parents for the nurse and Doreen McCann is fine as the moppet who becomes her first polio patient.

Nichols, in his triple role as producer-director-scripter, does well with all three. Makeup dept. deserves special mention for the make-up jobs on the stars. System of showing Miss Russell age in the film is one of the best seen and the final scenes, in which she's an elderly lady of 60, show her with a face and figure that's perfectly in keeping with the age. *Stal.*

The Cockeyed Miracle

Los Angeles, July 11.

Metro release of Irving Starr production. Features Frank Morgan, Keenan Wynn, Cecil Kellaway, Audrey Totter, Gladys Coouer, Marshall Thompson, Richard Quine, Leon Ames. Directed by S. Sylvan Simon. Screenplay, Karen De Wolf; based on play by George Seaton; camera, Ray June; musical score, David Snell; editor, Ben Lewis. Tradeshown in Los Angeles, July 10, '46. Running time, **82 MINS.**

Sam Griggs....................Frank Morgan
Ben Griggs....................Keenan Wynn
Tom Carter....................Cecil Kellaway
Jennifer Griggs...............Audrey Totter
Howard Bankson...............Richard Quine
Amy Griggs....................Gladys Cooper
Jim Griggs...............Marshall Thompson
Ralph Humphrey.................Leon Ames
Mrs. Lynne.....................Jane Green
Dr. Wilson...................Morris Ankrum
Amos Spellman................Arthur Space

Metro has taken an engaging fantasy idea and developed it for audience entertainment. "The Cockeyed Miracle" doesn't carry enough marquee weight to go it alone in top situations, but does offer good possibilities for general situations when coupled with a supporting feature. Cast names are mostly familiar and dependable, the production good and the direction neatly valued to get the best from the material.

Script is based on a George Seaton play that had a brief Broadway stay a couple of seasons ago. Lines and situations carry enough punch and spice to flavor fantasy basis. Lead role is cut to Frank Morgan's measure and he troupes it solidly. He's seen as a Maine shipbuilder whose wealth is measured in family love and friendship, inept investments having dissipated more material wealth. He dies suddenly of a heart attack on eve of recouping a little from his last gamble on fortune, but lingers around as a ghost long enough to see his family assured of future security.

That idea doesn't seem to have much humor at first glance, but nifty scripting by Karen De Wolf and pointed direction by S. Sylvan Simon push it home, with honors evenly divided between chuckles and tears. Most of the laughs spring from screwball character played by Keenan Wynn and Morgan's antics as a newly-initiated shade. Former makes his appearance upon Morgan's death at 62 years of age and plays latter's father, who died in his 30's. Incongruousness of the father being younger than the son breeds chuckles, as does the father's instruction to his son on how to be a proper spirit. This father-son team makes an entertaining pair.

Audrey Totter, heretofore seen mostly as an s.a. menace, is kept under wraps as Morgan's daughter except for sequence where the fun-loving spirits promote her romance with Richard Quine, young professor. Sequence adds some spice, although strictly on the Johnston office side. Gladys Cooper is fine as Morgan's wife, who rallies the family after his death. Marshall Thompson, Morgan's son; Cecil Kellaway, a double-crossing friend who is struck dead by spirit Wynn's manufactured lightning; Leon Ames, Morris Ankrum and others aid the story-telling.

Ray June's lensing and trick effects, and other contributions help overall excellent results obtained by Irving Starr's production guidance. *Brog.*

Home Sweet Homicide

20th-Fox release of Louis D. Lighton production. Stars Randolph Scott, Peggy Ann Garner, Lynn Bari, Dean Stockwell, Connie Marshall; features James Gleason, Barbara Whiting, John Shepperd. Directed by Lloyd Bacon. Screenplay, F. Hugh Herbert, based on novel by Craig Rice; camera, John Seitz; editor, Louis Loeffler. Tradeshown July 16, '46. Running time, **85 MINS.**

Dinah Carstairs.........Peggy Ann Garner
Lt. Bill Smith..............Randolph Scott
Marian Carstairs...................Lynn Bari
Archie Carstairs............Dean Stockwell
April Carstairs.............Connie Marshall
Sergeant O'Hare.............James Gleason
Polly Walker.................Anabel Shaw
Jo-Ella Holbrook..........Barbara Whiting
Mr. Sanford.................John Shepperd
Mr. Cherrington..............Stanley Logan
Luke...........................Olin Howlin
Housekeeper................Marietta Canty
Policemen.....Pat Flaherty, Phillip Morris

With everything in its favor, including simplicity, this film should bring good grosses everywhere, especially in neighborhood situations. "Home Sweet Homicide" is a whodunit with a "Junior Miss" slant (including Peggy Ann Garner and Barbara Whiting, both featured in the earlier film), and fine entertainment for all age brackets. Moppets will love it.

Three precocious children of a lady mystery writer become involved in a real murder with a thread of blackmail running through it. In their attempts to baffle the police so their mother can solve the crime, for which she has no desire, the kids almost catch the murderer, but in the end leave that to homicide lieutenant Randolph Scott who, with mother Lynn Bari, provides love interest.

Direction throughout is excellent, with Dean Stockwell, Connie Marshall and Peggy Ann Garner, the three youngsters, turning in sock performances as a result. Story moves fast and shows wise selection of unpretentious mountings. Scott, Miss Bari and James Gleason are more than competent, and entire production is thoroughly polished. Fact that the identity of the killer can be guessed with fair certainty might even help boxoffice, since it will give payees w.k. "I knew it all the time" feeling.

Lady Luck

RKO release of Warren Duff production. Stars Robert Young, Barbara Hale, Frank Morgan; features James Gleason, Harry Davenport, Teddy Hart, Don Rice. Directed by Edwin L. Marin. Screenplay, Lynn Root and Frank Senton, based on story by Herbert Clyde Lewis; camera, Lucien Andriot; editor, Ralph Dawson. Tradeshown in N. Y., July 12, '46. Running time, **97 MINS.**

Larry Scott....................Robert Young
Mary Audrey...................Barbara Hale
William Audrey..............Frank Morgan
Sacramento Sam............James Gleason
Eddie...............................Don Rice
Judge Martin..............Harry Davenport
Little Joe...................Lloyd Corrigan
Little Guy.......................Teddy Hart
Happy Johnson...............Joseph Vitale
Dan Morgan..............Douglas Morrow

Parlay of the ever-popular gambling motif, with a strong cast for marquee lure, should net "Lady Luck" good returns at the b.o., particularly in the nabes. Intrinsically, however, the film is only mild entertainment.

Frail story loosely rattles around in an over-sized running time which could easily be snipped by about 20 minutes. Whatever tension there might have been is lost in the pedestrian direction. Switches in plot are telegraphed way in advance, and many situations, which should have been accented for laughs, are derailed into deadpan romance. Dialog doesn't sparkle either, and the comic talents of Frank Morgan, James Gleason and Teddy Hart are hard put to deliver chuckles. Production is excellently mounted.

Yarn is spun around a femme, who, as a descendant from a long line of ill-fated gamblers, develops a blue-nose aversion to the species. While keeping an eye on her poker-playing grandfather, she falls for and marries a professional dice-thrower who promises to reform. On their honeymoon, the bride glimpses the groom innocently rolling the cubes in behalf of a sucker, but she misunderstands and leaves him. As a device to patch up the break, the ex-gambler's friends try to infect the gal with gambling fever. She goes overboard, breaking the house and opening a green-felt club of her own. But now the roles are reversed, with the husband an advocate of the poor but honest life. Windup has the granddad, playing for the girl, throwing a winning poker hand into discard in an effort to clean her out and make her come to her senses.

Robert Young and Barbara Hale make an engaging romantic duo although the latter is not convincing as the high-flying belle of the faro table. Morgan carries the film as the incurable poker-playing sharpster while Gleason is effective, as usual, as an easy-come, easy-go gambler. Hart gives a sock performance in his brief part as a dice-struck factory worker who winds up with a limousine. Rest of the cast deliver competently.

Smithy
(AUSTRALIAN-MADE)

Sydney, June 26.

Columbia release of Nick Pery production. Stars Ron Randell; features Muriel Steinbeck, John Tate, Joy Nicholls. Directed by Ken G. Hall. Original screenplay, Alec Coppel and Max Afford; camera, George Heath; editor, Terry Banks. At State, Sydney, June 26, '46. Running time, **118 MINS.**

Sir Charles Kingsford-Smith..Ron Randell
Lady Kingsford-Smith.....Muriel Steinbeck
Charles Ulm.....................John Tate
Kay Suttor.....................Joy Nicholls
Nan Kingsford Smith............Nan Taylor
Capt. Allan Hancock.......Alec Kellaway
Sir Hubert Wilkins.............John Dease
Stringer ....Joe Valli
Arthur Powell............Marshall Crosby
Right Hon. W. M. Hughes......In Person
Capt. P. G. Taylor...............In Person
John Stannage...................In Person

"Smithy" may well be the best Aussie-produced pic to date. It's a credit to Nick Pery, the producer, and Ken G. Hall, director, and high praise goes to Columbia for financing. The biog of the late Sir Charles Kingsford-Smith, the Aussie air ace, here, indeed, is a milestone in local film-making. It should do well at British Empire boxoffices, and has a good chance in America.

Ron Randell, who has been in Aussie legit and radio for some years, has the title role, turning in an excellent performance. He is good Hollywood timber.

Pic has lots in it for U. S. appeal. It was an American, Captain Allan Hancock, who backed Smithy's flight across the Pacific, and Hall has brought in several U. S. scenes, with an eye to the American market, naturally, all well done, carefully cast and acted by genuine Americans, something unknown before in local production when script called for a U. S. character.

Muriel Steinbeck, vet of local radio and legit, makes a good foil for Randell, bringing sympathy and understanding to a most exacting role. Joy Nicholls is finely cast as an American and is another strong Hollywood pic possibility. She's been in vaude for some time. Rest of cast is adequate.

Story follows the career of Kingsford-Smith, minus any flagwaving. The dialog at times is a bit stilted and in spots the pic drags, running time needs pruning, both for here and for overseas. But generally this film helps intrench Australian production more strongly than ever before. *Rick.*

The Dark Horse
(ONE SONG)

Universal release of Howard Welsch production (associate producer, Will Cowan). Stars Phillip Terry, Ann Savage; features Jane Darwell, Allen Jenkins, Donald MacBride. Directed by Will Jason. Screenplay, Charles R. Marion, Leo Solomon; camera, Paul Ivano; song, Will Jason; editor, Paul Landres. Tradeshown in N. Y. July 10, '46. Running time, **59 MINS.**

George Kelly.....................Phillip Terry
Mary Burton......................Ann Savage
Willis Trimble.................Allen Jenkins
Aunt Hattie.....................Jane Darwell
John Rooney...............Donald MacBride
Eustace Kelly...............Edward Gargan
Mr. Aldrich................Raymond Largay
Mrs. Aldrich.......................Ruth Lee
Mrs. Mahoney..................Mary Gordon
Old Man.............................Si Jenks
Mr. Hodges.................Arthur Q. Bryan
Maitre de....................Henri De Soto

Relaxing fare for the dualers, "The Dark Horse" satisfies. It limns the travails of a returning vet (Phillip Terry) who is pressured by the local political boss into running for alderman. When he rebels and exposes the phoney setup, he is elected anyway, on the strength of his honesty.

Terry is not always convincing as the reluctant candidate. Donald MacBride, as the politico, gives better than average reading to slightly hoked-up lines, while Jane Darwell shows her usual competence in the benevolent aunt role.

One thing ex-servicemen among the payees will recognize, and probably be amused at, is the unctuous pseudo-sympathy among civilians who treat every returned vet as a psychopathic problem.

Black Beauty

20th-Fox release of Edward L. Alperson (Alson) production. Features Mona Freeman, Richard Denning, Evelyn Ankers, Charles Evans, J. M. Kerrigan, Moyna Macgill, Terry Kilburn and Highland Dale as Black Beauty. Directed by Max Nosseck. Screenplay, Lillie Hayward and Agnes Christine Johnston, based on novel by Anna Sewell; music, Dmitri Tiomkin. Tradeshown N. Y., July 12, '46. Running time, **74 MINS.**

Anne Wendon..................Mona Freeman
Bill Dixon...................Richard Denning
Evelyn Carrington..........Evelyn Ankers
Squire Wendon..............Charles Evans
John.........................J. M. Kerrigan
Mrs. Blake.....................Moyna Macgill
Joe...........................Terry Kilburn
Skinner.....................Thomas P. Dillon
Terry..........................Arthur Space
Dr. White......................John Burton
Mr. Cordon....................Olaf Hytten
Auctioneer..................Leyland Hodgson
Veterinary...................Clifford Brooke
"Black Beauty"...............Highland Dale

"Black Beauty," another of the Hollywood equine species, is none too promising. It lacks marquee names and adult entertainment values, though it's the sort of item that the youngsters would relish. "Beauty" has been produced independently by Edward L. Alperson for 20th-Fox release.

Adapted from the novel by Anna Sewell, "Beauty," a standard among horse yarns, has been filmed twice before, once in sound. Dealing with a young girl's love for a colt that she rears, the story, backgrounded by the English countryside in the late 19th century, mostly concerns the heartaches that result when the animal, through circumstances, is forced into the hands of others and subsequently encounters the downtrail as a jobhorse. That finale, wherein the girl finally finds the beast amid the starkly melodramatic aura of a stable fire, fails to achieve the effect it might have with better direction and screenplay.

Mona Freeman plays the girl and Richard Denning the American with whom she teams romantically. Miss Freeman is properly impetuous and eager, while Denning is bedeviled by the script, as are all the others. Direction is frequently poor. Acting by some lesser characters is unusually bad.

Coming on the releasing heels of "Smoky," another horse pic, produced at 20th-Fox, "Beauty" suffers by comparison. There are marked story similarities between the Sewell narrative and "Smoky," Will James' likewise-standard horse yarn. *Kahn.*

Step by Step

Los Angeles, July 11.
RKO release of Sid Rogell production. Features Lawrence Tierney, Anne Jeffreys, Lowell Gilmore, George Cleveland, Jason Robards, Myrna Dell. Directed by Phil Rosen. Screenplay, Stuart Palmer; based on original story by George Callahan; camera, Frank Redman; music, Paul Sawtell; editor, Robert Swink. Tradeshown in Los Angeles, July 11, '46. Running time, 62 MINS.
Johnny....................Lawrence Tierney
Evelyn.........................Anne Jeffreys
Von Dorn....................Lowell Gilmore
Simpson................▲..George Cleveland
Bruckner.......................Jason Robards
Gretchen........................Myrna Dell
Senator Remmy.............Harry Harvey
Blackton....................Addison Richards
Jorgensen.......................Ray Walker
Captain Edmonds..........John Hamilton

Melodrama is considerably above general level of smaller-budgeted features in this category. Tight tale should be a pleaser for meller fans. It's one of Phil Rosen's best director credits. Production appurtenances are also well valued.

Plot opens against a Malibu Beach locale. Stuart Palmer's sound script backgrounds the action, and yarn moves along smoothly in depicting the adventures that befall a young couple involved in a plot to steal valuable government documents. Shenanigans make it appear that Lawrence Tierney, ex-Marine, and Anne Jeffreys, a senator's secretary, are the guilty parties. Couple is the object of an FBI and police hunt, as well as being sought by the real crooks. Before it winds up there are two murders, plenty of chases and other action sequences.

Tierney and Miss Jeffreys handle the leads capably. Lowell Gilmore, Jason Robards and Myrna Dell are the foreign agents, all good. Harry Harvey, Addison Richards, Ray Walker and John Hamilton do well. George Cleveland contributes sharp characterization as a motel-keeper who shelters the leads from the law; role counting for good lighter moments.

Lensing, editing and other credits are satisfactory. *Brog.*

Night Train to Memphis
(SONGS)

Hollywood, July 13.
Republic release of Dorrell and Stuart McGowan production; screenplay by same. Stars Roy Acuff; features Allan Lane, Adele Mara. Directed by Lesley Selander.

Camera, William Bradford; editor, Tony Martinelli; music, Morton Scott. Previewed July 12, '46. Running time, 66 MINS.
Roy............................Roy Acuff
Dan Acuff.....................Allan Lane
Constance.....................Adele Mara
Rainbow.....................Irving Bacon
Stevenson...................Joseph Crehan
Ma Acuff.......................Emma Dunn
Chad Morgan.................Roy Barcroft
Asa Morgan.................Kenne Duncan
Wilson........................LeRoy Mason
Porter....................Nicodemus Stewart
Maid...................Nina Mae McKinney
Doctor...................Francis McDonald
Smoky Mountain Boys

This Roy Acuff starrer, hillbilly-overtoned, is for those special situations where star and ridge-runner music can outweigh a mawkish, trite tale in sequences frequently too dull to arouse much audience interest. Pic obviously designed for lower line of shared marquee.

Slow pace of plot and lack-lustre lines militate against performances all around. Acuff is a Tennessee mountain lad who, between sessions of caroling in front of his hillbilly band, strives to untangle strained situation of the mountain folks hating the railroad. His brother alternately leads the fight against the choo-choos diverting folks' favorite fishing lake and pitches woo to r.r. prexy's daughter, whose identity is unknown to him. There's no novelty in the plot meanderings, and if the denouement came as surprise to cast, it certainly won't to customers who not only have seen it all done before, but infinitely better.

Acuff appears ill-at-ease frequently and shows enthusiasm only when musiking. As his brother, Allan Lane strives to inject life into part never clearly delineated by script. Irving Bacon comes off best as a shiftless mountain character; the vet thesp plays down many lines and muggs his way. Adele Mara is attractive as the only gal in yarn. Other roles are bits, adequately and standardly niched by such established character-players as Emma Dunn, Roy Barcroft, Joseph Crehan and Francis McDonald. Nicodemus Stewart and Nina Mae McKinney are teamed for Negro "character humor" that is decidedly sub-standard. Songs are all hillbilly standards, and the title tune, while not bad, is reprised to point of irritability.

No particular production values point up this low-budgeter, with top technical credit belonging to cameraman William Bradford, who finely framed outdoor sequences. Director Lesley Selander should have injected more spark of life and speeded the pace.

Sunset Pass
(SONGS)

RKO release of Herman Schlom production. Stars James Warren; features Nan Leslie, John Laurenz, Robert Clarke. Directed by William Berke. Screenplay, Norman Houston; from novel by Zane Grey; camera, Frank Redman; songs, Paul Sawtell; musical director, C. Bakaleinikoff; editor, Samuel E. Beetley. Tradeshown in N. Y., July 12, '46. Running time, 60 MINS.
Rocky........................James Warren
Jane...........................Nan Leslie
Chito..........................John Laurenz
Helen...........................Jane Greer
Curtis.........................Robert Barrat
Cinnabar......................Harry Woods
Ash...........................Robert Clarke
Slagle.........................Steve Brodie
Doab.........................Harry Harvey

This adaptation of a Zane Grey novel, lensed in top fashion by Frank Redman, has some nice thesping and thus adds up to better-than average hoss opry entertainment. Boxoffice of the cast names is negligible, however.

Story tells of a railway express officer's attempts to break up a series of robberies, during which he finds that the young brother of the girl with whom he's in love is involved in the crimes. Turns out youngster is held by gangleader's threat to implicate him in a murder of which he is innocent.

Simply scripted, "Sunset Pass" presents its story in straight fashion, with a couple of incidental songs. *Tomm*

Miniature Reviews

"Notorious" (RKO). Alfred Hitchcock production, starring Cary Grant and Ingrid Bergman, is assured of high b.o.

"Holiday in Mexico" (Color Songs) (M-G), Walter Pidgeon, Jose Iturbi, Ilona Massey, Jane Powell in lush musical; big b.o.

"Claudia and David" (20th). Sturdy "Claudia" sequel.

"The Unknown" (Col). Standard horror fare for the dualers.

"Canyon Passage" (Wanger-U) (Color-Songs). Beautifully Technicolored high-budget western geared for good boxoffice.

"Men Of Two Worlds" (Color) (GF-Rank). Costly British pic on tropical disease is honest but dull. Dubious U. S. boxoffice.

"Cuban Pete" (U). Program musical with scant entertainment values.

"Frenzy" (British). Spotty horror meller not up to usual English mystery standard, only fair b.o.

"Bowery Bombshell" (Mono). Okay Bowery Boys comedy-drama for supporting positions.

"Prairie Badmen" (PRC). Routine buckskin opera built for south end of a double-bill.

"Ghost of Hidden Valley" (PRC). Meagre boxoffice for this poor western meller.

"In Fast Company" (Mono). Leo Gorcey and The Bowery Boys in some nice clowning; solid dual fare.

Notorious

RKO release of Alfred Hitchcock production. Stars Cary Grant and Ingrid Bergman; features Claude Rains, Louis Calhern, Madame Konstantin, Reinholdt Schunzel, Moroni Olsen, Ivan Triesault and Alex Minotis. Directed by Alfred Hitchcock. Story and adaptation, Ben Hecht; editor, Theron Warth; camera, Ted Tetzlaff. Previewed in N. Y., July 18, '46. Running time, 101 MINS.
Devlin.........................Cary Grant
Alicia Huberman.........Ingrid Bergman
Alexander Sebastian.........Claude Rains
Paul Prescott...............Louis Calhern
Mme. Sebastian......Madame Konstantin
"Dr. Anderson".......Reinhold Schunzel
Walter Beardsley............Moroni Olsen
Eric Mathis...................Ivan Triesault
Joseph..........................Alex Minotis
Mr. Hopkins..................Wally Brown
Commodore.............Sir Charles Mendl
Dr. Barbosa..................Ricardo Costa
Hupka............Eberhard Krumschmidt
Ethel.............................Fay Baker

Production and directorial skill of Alfred Hitchcock combine with a suspenseful story and excellent performances to make "Notorious" force entertainment. It's a romantic drama of topnotch caliber that will pay off big.

The Ben Hecht scenario carries punchy dialog but it's much more the action and manner in which Hitchcock projects it on the screen that counts heaviest. Of course the fine performances by Cary Grant, Ingrid Bergman and Claude Rains also figure. The terrific suspense maintained to the very last is also an important asset.

Story deals with espionage, the picture opening in Miami in the spring of 1946. Miss Bergman's father has been convicted as a German spy. Yarn shifts quickly to Rio de Janeiro, where Miss Bergman, known to be a loyal American, unlike her father, is pressed into the American intelligence service with a view to getting the goods on a local group of German exiles under suspicion.

Inducted into espionage through Cary Grant, an American agent with whom she is assigned to work. Miss Bergman, because she loves Grant, doesn't want to go through with an assignment to feign love for Claude Rains, head of the Brazilian Nazi group. She finally does so under the mistaken notion Grant does not love her. She even goes so far as to marry Rains that she may get the desired information, which revolves around iranium ore deposits which have been discovered by Rains' gang in Brazil. When Rains and his mother discover that they have a spy under their roof, they go about poisoning her, but in a very dramatic final scene Grant rescues her.

This is Miss Bergman's best job to date. Opposite her Grant gives an excellent account of himself, while Rains is also tops. His mother is played very effectively by Madame Konstantin. Among members of the Rains ring, all of whom are well cast, are Reinhold Schunzel, Ivan Triesault and Alex Minotis. Louis Calhern acquits himself creditably as boss of the U. S. Intelligence force in Brazil.

Impressive sets and colorful backgrounds, as well as the music, give the picture outstanding production value. Photography, including special effects, is of the best. *Char.*

Holiday in Mexico
(COLOR—SONGS)

Metro release of Joe Pasternak production. Stars Walter Pidgeon, Jose Iturbi, Ilona Massey; features Roddy McDowall, Jane Powell, Xavier Cugat. Directed by George Sidney. Screenplay, Isabel Lennart, from original by William Kozlenko; camera, Harry Stradling; editor, Adrienne Fazan; music, Georgie Stoll; songs by Soler-Freed, Abraham and Ralph Freed, Farres-Skylar, Victor Herbert, others. Tradeshown, N. Y., June 25, '46. Running time, **127 MINS.**

Jeffrey Evans..............Walter Pidgeon
Jose Iturbi..........................Himself
Stanley Owen.............Roddy McDowall
Toni Karpathy................Ilona Massey
Xavier Cugat.........................Himself
Christine Evans..................Jane Powell
Angus.................................Hugo Haas
Baranga.................Mikhail Rasumny
Yvette Baranga.............Helene Stanley
Sam.....................Wm. "Bill" Phillips
Amparo Iturbi.........................Herself
Tonia Hero.............................Herself
Teresa Hero...........................Herself
Madam Baranga...........Marina Koshetz
Angel.......................Linda Christian
Margaret..........................Ann Codee
Sir Edward Owen............Paul Stanton
Cady Millicent Owen..........Doris Lloyd
Maria.......................Rosita Marstini

"Holiday in Mexico" offers ample proof that Metro producers have not yet adopted Louis B. Mayer's cost-slashing edict. Judging from the ostentatious sets, high-salaried cast, color photography and big production numbers, producer Joe Pasternak must have sunk quite a hefty bankroll into his latest opus. And despite a weak, trite story and a poor job of editing, the picture will probably draw top grosses in all situations. Film was caught at a sneak preview at one of Loew's N. Y. nabes, where audience reaction evidenced immense enjoyment.

Film revolves around Jane Powell as the sub-deb daughter of Walter Pidgeon, American ambassador to Mexico, and carries through her travails as she imagines herself in love with Jose Iturbi, in reality old enough to be her grandfather. Situation is ludicrous to the extreme and certainly doesn't hold enough water to maintain interest for more than two hours. Yarn is broken up by some good musical numbers and a side love-story between Pidgeon and Ilona Massey.

Youthful Miss Powell, despite the part given her, shows evidence of becoming another Metro star, and her association with Pasternak, who guided Deanna Durbin up through the ranks, will be of definite asset. Although her soprano pipes currently lack the warmth and richness of Miss Durbin's, she's an outstanding songstress and does well with her numbers, including Victor Herbert's "Italian Street Song," "Gounod's "Ave Maria," and Delibes' "Les Filles de Cadiz." She's also an ingratiating actress and handles her role capably.

Music is the best part of the picture. Besides Miss Powell, Miss Massey does capitally with two ballads, "And Dreams Remain" and "Someone to Love." Xavier Cugat and his orch are in for several Latin tunes. Iturbi renders Chopin's "Polonaise" and Rachmaninoff's Second Piano Concerto and surprises, as usual, with a straight jive rendition of some boogie-woogie, at which he pairs with his sister, Amparo, also a recognized concert pianist, at the second piano.

Yarn has a unique and amusing introduction involving the use of animated cartoon characters to set the stage. As soon as it segues into the live cast, however, the trouble starts. Miss Powell, feeling herself losing the affections of her widowed father to Miss Massey, builds up her compensatory romance with Iturbi, while shunning the natural puppy-love of Roddy MacDowall, scion of the British ambassador. When Pidgeon and Iturbi conspire to reveal the pianist's grandchildren to her to break up the "affair," the dialog and situation are so trite that the audience will probably be just as embarrassed as Miss Powell was supposed to feel in the picture.

Cast is uniformly good. Pidgeon is his usual suave self, credible as the father and playing his romance scenes with Miss Massey in a manner to make the femmes' hearts flutter. Miss Massey is competent and McDowall does well as a voice-changing adolescent. Iturbi and Cugat again prove themselves excellent with the repartee and comedy. Corking comedy bit is provided by Mikhail Rasumny as a vociferous French diplomat.

Pasternak's production mountings are lush as in any top-coin Metro musical. Sets and costumes are eye-openers and the musical production numbers are easy to take. Color photography by Harry Stradling is some of the best seen on the screen. Some of the shots, especially the angle effects on Iturbi's piano, look almost like paintings and the shading of hues in the Technicolor process is excellent.

Cast is guided through its paces as well as is possible with the story by director George Sidney. Withal, the picture would have been much easier to take if editor Adrienne Fazan had left about 30 minutes of it on the cutting-room floor. Faltering continuity evidences that she sheared plenty as it is. *Stal.*

Claudia and David

Hollywood, July 20.

20th-Fox release of William Perlberg production. Stars Dorothy McGuire and Robert Young; features Mary Astor, John Sutton, Gail Patrick, Rose Hobart, Harry Davenport, Florence Bates, Jerome Cowan, Else Janssen, Frank Twedell, Anthony Sydes. Directed by Walter Lang. Screenplay, Rose Franken and William Brown Meloney; adaptation, Vera Caspary; from stories by Rose Franken; camera, Joseph La Shelle; special photographic effects, Fred Sersen; music, Cyril J. Mockridge; editor, Robert Simpson. Tradeshown in Los Angeles, July 19, '46. Running time, **78 MINS.**

Claudia....................Dorothy McGuire
David..........................Robert Young
Elizabeth van Doren...........Mary Astor
Phil Dexter.......................John Sutton
Julia Naughton..................Gail Patrick
Edith Dexter....................Rose Hobart
Dr. Harry................Harry Davenport
Nancy Riddle..............Florence Bates
Brian O'Toole..............Jerome Cowan
Bertha...........................Else Janssen
Fritz.........................Frank Twedell
Bobby......................Anthony Sydes
Hartley Naughton..........Pierre Watkin
Mr. Riddle.................Henry Mowbray
Mrs. Barry..................Clara Blandick
Butler..............................Eric Wilton
Charlie...........................Frank Darien

Strong entertainment for femme theatregoers has been developed from adventures of the Rose Franken magazine characters, Claudia and David. Film is jammed with tears and chuckles, played and directed to realize fully on all values. It has been given smooth production supervision by William Perlberg to shape it as excellent entry for all situations, and payoff will be good.

Dorothy McGuire makes the scatterbrained Claudia believeable, and Robert Young backs her up with an equally good performance as her longsuffering husband, David. Miss Franken and William Brown Meloney scripted, cramming plot with drama, pathos and easy laughs to sustain interest. Walter Lang's direction gets the best from the material.

Plot generally concerns Claudia's susceptibility and strong love for her young son. Trouble starts when a phoney mindreader warns her husband he will have an accident if he takes a trip to California. Sudden illness of the son, which Claudia builds into a serious tragedy only to find out it's measles; her jealousy of her husband's professional attention to an attractive widow seeking his architectural advice; the attentions paid her by an attractive married man; and a serious auto accident in which David is injured are some of the more dramatic moments that are leavened with smart, earthy chuckles.

Mary Astor is the widow who gives Claudia concern, and John Sutton is the married man whose interest in Claudia makes David twinge with jealousy. Both are good, as are others in the cast. Anthony Sydes does a believeable moppet role as the couple's young son. Others showing well include Gail Patrick, Rose Hobart, Harry Davenport, Florence Bates, Jerome Cowan, Else Janssen and Frank Twedell.

Film has been given topnotch mounting, and Joseph La Shelle's camera takes full advantage of the settings. Editing has given picture a fast 78 minutes' running time. Other credits are in keeping with good standard set. *Brog.*

The Unknown

Columbia release of Wallace MacDonald production. Features Karen Morley, Jim Bannon, Jeff Donnell, Robert Scott. Directed by Henry Levin. Screenplay, Malcolm Stuart Boylan and Julian Harmon based on original story by Carlton E. Morse; adapted by Charles O'Neal, Dwight Babcock; camera, Henry Freulich; editor, Arthur Seid. At Rialto, week July 18, '46. Running time, **70 MINS.**

Rachel Martin.................Karen Morley
Jack Packard....................Jim Bannon
Nina Arnold......................Jeff Donnell
Reed Cawthorne...............Robert Scott
Richard Arnold...............Robert Wilcox
Doc Long................Barton Yarborough
Edward Martin......................James Bell
Ralph Martin....................Wilton Graff
Phoebe Martin...............Helen Freeman
Joshua....................J. Louis Johnson
Capt. Selby Martin............Boyd Davis

Based on the "I Love a Mystery" radio program, this film shapes up as effective spine-tingling fare for the horror hounds. All the usual scarifying gimmicks are thrown into the works including an antique mansion with subterranean passageways, demented inmates, a hooded shadow, and a couple of stabbings. Accent in the pic is less on the whodunit elements than on an out-and-out attempt to shock the patrons into frightened squeals. Background music fits the general mood okay but the photography is underlit making it tough at many points to see the action. Direction is well-paced and suspenseful while the thesping is uniformly competent.

Strictly formula story revolves around a contested will left by a tyrannical matriarch. With a granddaughter arriving on the scene to claim her share, attempts are made to put her out of the way. Except for the young girl, all the other heirs are twisted and deranged characters making foul play something to be expected. Identity of the unknown assailant at the end doesn't cause any surprise.

Marquee weight of the pic is frail with Karen Morley the only name. She handles her difficult psychotic role as credibly as the plot situation permits. Jeff Donnell, Jim Bannon and Robert Scott in the other featured roles back up in acceptable fashion.

Canyon Passage
(COLOR—SONGS)

Universal release of Walter Wanger production. Stars Dana Andrews, Brian Donlevy, Susan Hayward, Patricia Roc; features Ward Bond, Andy Devine, Hoagy Carmichael. Directed by Jacques Tourneur. Screenplay, Ernest Pascal, from novel by Ernest Haycox; songs, Hoagy Carmichael and Jack Brooks; camera, Edward Cronjager; music, Frank Skinner; editor, Milton Carruth. Previewed in N. Y., July 22, '46. Running time, **91 MINS.**

Logan Stuart..................Dana Andrews
George Camrose.............Brian Donlevy
Lucy Overmire.............Susan Hayward
Caroline Marsh.................Patricia Roc
Honey Bragg.......................Ward Bond
Ben Dance........................Andy Devine
Marta Lestrade..................Rose Hobart
Clenchfield................Halliwell Hobbes
Johnny Steele....................Lloyd Bridges
Jonas Overmire...........Standley Ridges
Mrs. Dance................Dorothy Petersen
Vane Blazier..........................Vic Cutler
Mrs. Overmire.....................Fay Holden
Asa Dance............................Tad Devine
Rushrod Dance..............Dennis Devine
Linnet....................Hoagy Carmichael

Technicolor and Walter Wanger have combined for the major responsibility in turning out a teeming, sprawling tale of pioneering Oregon a century ago, and "Canyon Passage" is the result. "Passage" has the more important ingredients of good boxoffice, including such marquee names as Dana Andrews, Brian Donlevy, Susan Hayward and the British newcomer to Hollywood, Patricia Roc, and the grosses should be commensurate.

The Ernest Haycox original novel has not been treated especially well in the Ernest Pascal adaptation to the screen, but there are enough other standard factors to warrant a consistently maintained interest for this Technicolored western. Speaking of Technicolor, it doesn't seem possible that Oregon could have been pioneered without benefit of Natalie Kalmus. The story of the northwest state has been helped immeasurably by the color camera.

"Passage" is a familiar story of conflicting loves and idealogies, weaving its web around one Logan Stuart (Dana Andrews), an adventurer. Donlevy plays the manager of the local express office with a weakness for other men's gold; Miss Hayward is Donlevy's affianced though in love with Andrews, and Miss Roc, obviously to take care of her British accent, plays a Briton to whom Andrews is linked romantically until the script conveniently disposes of Donlevy and Miss Roc, leaving the way open for Andrews and Miss Hayward.

It is basically the story of blood and lust, with hardly a twist in stories of this type. Donlevy steals depositors' gold to pay off gambling debts; Andrews, his friend, helps him pay off. When the former becomes involved in the murder of one of his depositors whose claim he's unable to pay when he asks for his gold, the story becomes involved, tying in with an Indian uprising whose firing of the settlers' homes, etc., must surely draw the ohs and ahs for its beautiful color emphasis rather than for the horror of the killings. And that's one of the faults of the pic—the color too frequently, by way of backgrounds, et al., is made to draw the audience interest rather than the story itself.

The cast is excellent, notably Andrews in a role that he underplays adroitly to make the lead character assume a conviction that might easily have been lost in what, without him and the other names, might well have been just another western. Donlevy's character doesn't always ring true, though he plays it competently, while Miss Hayward is photographed neatly. The same can't be said for Miss Roc, who is making her American debut in this pic after having achieved stardom in England. The latter is a competent performer, but her British accent in the pioneering Pacific northwest is certainly an oddity, as is that of Halliwell Hobbes in one of the lesser roles.

Hoagy Carmichael has composed

four prairie ballads for the pic (one with Jack Brooks), and he saunters through the pic singing them all as the typically vagrant character he's been playing in pix of late. "Buttermilk Sky" is the catchiest.

Ward Bond plays a wrong guy in the usually glowering fashion. Andy Devine, Rose Hobart, Dorothy Petersen, Lloyd Bridges and Stanley Ridges play lesser parts adequately. Devine's two young sons, incidentally, have bit parts.

The production is grade A all the way, but as far as the story itself is concerned, there is more the thought of impending action in this pic than the actual action itself.

Kahn.

Men of Two Worlds

(Color)

(BRITISH-MADE)

London, July 16.

General Film Distributors' release of Two Cities Film. Stars Phyllis Calvert, Eric Portman. Directed by Thorold Dickinson. Screenplay by Dickinson and Herbert W. Victor from original story by Joyce Cary, based on an idea by E. Arnot Robertson. Music by Arthur Bliss, some based on themes from Tanganyika collected by H. Cory; camera (Technicolor), Raymond Sturgess, Laurie Friedman. At Gaumont, London. Running time, **109 MINS.**

District Commissioner........Eric Portman
Dr. Catherine Munro.......Phyllis Calvert
Prof. Gollner................Arnold Marle
Mrs. Upjohn.............Cathleen Nesbitt
Orchestra Conductor..........George Coope
Concert Agent..................David Horne
Education Officer...........Cyril Raymond
Kisenga.......................Robert Adams
Magole.....................Orlando Martins
Chief Rafi..........................Sam Blake
Kisenga's Father.........Napoleon Florent
Kisenga's Mother..........Viola Thompson
Saburi......................Eseza Makumbi
Ali............................Tunji Williams
Abram....................Randolph Evans

This ambitious Two Cities production, which enters the $4,000,000 class of the Rank organization, is honest, dull and in Technicolor. With the best of intentions, it states the case for a scientific treatment of sleeping sickness among the African tribes as opposed to witchcraft and superstition. But it is a statement of the obvious.

Film was three years in production with delays that appear to have badly dented the screenplay. It began in 1943. Eght months were spent in Tanganyika choosing locations. On the way out a U-boat sank cameras and stock. Film unit was put ashore 1,000 miles from Lagos, where its only still camera was impounded. Slow convoys, bad weather, a strike of lab men in Hollywood, delays waiting for Technicolor equipment, all brought costly handicaps to the enterprise. Director Thorold Dickinson has done his best, but the result is a long stretch of mumbo-jumbo, unrelieved by imaginative treatment or pictorial thrills.

It's nearly two hours before the district commissioner (Eric Portman) bashfully calls Dr. Munro (Phyllis Calvert) "Catherine," and nothing comes of that either.

Randall, the district commissioner, plans to evacuate an African village to save the inhabitants from the man-killing tse-tse fly. His assistant is Kisenga, a noble savage who has risen from ancestral swamps, found culture in England and gone back to his tribe as a musician and composer. He takes Randall's side in the fight against sleeping sickness, but the power of black magic in the hands of the local witch doctor, Magole (played with remarkable force by Orlando Martins), is too much for him. Kisenga injects his dying father with serum in defiance of the whole tribe. The father dies, and strengthens the hatred of the natives and the cause of superstition. Magole, accepting a challenge, plunges a knife into Kisenga's blood and swears he will die.

It is the challenge of magic against science. Doctor and district commissioner, with all their instruments and serums, can do nothing. But Kisenga's music, sung by the children, brings him back to life. Art, rather than medicine, brings the final victory.

It is a strange story dipped in rather watery propaganda. A case is made out for leaving the natives alone and letting them live or die as they please. Equally, Western culture is snubbed by an interfering woman on a visit, who has no faith in beautiful English doctors and romantic district commissioners. Dickinson, in his anxiety to be just to two worlds, has fallen between them. He leaves his case suspended in mid-air.

The effect is to weaken both drama and entertainment, and the characters themselves, flat and uninspired, aren't sufficiently exciting to justify 109 minutes on the screen.

Tribal dances, burning of a dispensary by a maddened crowd, blood-letting and puncturing of bodies, swamps and rivers, beating of tom-toms, and all the paraphernalia of the jungle are conventional adjuncts to a story that doesn't begin to live, but is throughout animated by good intentions.

Prospects for America are doubtful, notwithstanding capable performances by Eric Portman, Phyllis Calvert, Cathleen Nesbitt and Robert Adams.

Ebet.

Cuban Pete

(MUSICAL)

Hollywood, July 18.

Universal release of Will Cowan production. Features Desi Arnaz, Joan Fulton, Beverly Simmons, Don Porter, Jacqueline De Wit, King Sisters (4), Ethel Smith. Directed by Jean Yarbrough. Screenplay, Robert Presnell, Sr., M. Coates Webster; original story, Bernard Feins; camera, Maury Gertsman; editor, Otto Ludwig; songs, Jack Brooks and Milton Schwarzwald, Bobby Collazo, Rafael Hernandez, Bill Driggs, Jose Norman, Al Stillman and Ernest Lecuona; musical director, Milton Rosen. Previewed in Hollywood, July 18, '46. Running time, **61 MINS.**

Desi Arnaz.......................Desi Arnaz
Ann..............................Joan Fulton
Brownie...................Beverly Simmons
Roberts..........................Don Porter
Lindsay..................Jacqueline de Wit
King Sisters....................King Sisters
Ethel Smith.....................Ethel Smith
Perez.......................Pedro de Cordoba
Dance Specialty..........Igor de Navrotzki
Dance Specialty..........Yvette von Koris

This light-budgeted musical programmer from Universal is also lightweight entertainment. It hangs eight tunes on implausible plotting, features dull pace and few chuckles in 61 minutes running time. Production values are better than the yarn but dressing can't carry off light plot.

Title number is reprised twice by Desi Arnaz, who also has three other typical Latin tunes. King Sisters sing two numbers and Ethel Smith does an organ solo for her only appearance. Arnaz tries hard, and his songs and music are an aid. He's seen as a Cuban orchestra leader, lured to New York to head a commercial radio show. Joan Fulton plays the blonde lure used to bait him away from his native heath. She's in the employ of advertising agency run by Don Porter, who must obtain Arnaz to keep Jacqueline de Wit's perfume account. Scripting is trite in dialog and situations, and Jean Yarbrough's diection doesn't give it a lift.

Little Beverly Simmons is given plot emphasis as niece of Arnaz. She works with a trained parrot in try for what few chuckles are present in the haphazard affair. Singing of King Sisters is good, as is Miss Smith's turn at the organ on "The Breeze and I." Other performances lensing and editing are standard for budget expenditure.

Brog.

Frenzy

(BRITISH-MADE)

Four Continents Films release of Louis Jackson-Derrick de Marney production. Stars de Marney, Frederick Valk, Joan Greenwood; features Joan Seton, Beresford Egan. Directed by Vernon Sewell. Screenplay, Sewell, from the play "L'Angoise," by Pierre Mills and C. Vylars; camera, At Ambassador, N. Y., week July 19, '46. Running time, **75 MINS.**

Charles Garrie..........Derrick de Marney
Dr. Krasner....................Frederick Valk
Christine.....................Joan Greenwood
Lucille..............................Joan Seton
Minetti.........................Beresford Egan
Maria................................Lily Kann
Prefect of Police...........Valentine Dyall
Morgue Keeper..................Martin Miller
Ballet Master..........................Espinoza
Ballet Mistress............Margaret Clarke

Evidently a bid for the growing boxoffice of English films, and especially those of the horror variety, "Frenzy" does not come up to the standard of the more recent British product, in spite of some top quality thesping, occasional tense moments and unusual photography. Film has no marquee names although Frederick Valk might be recognized from his stint in "Dead of Night," but it should be able to hold up well on the "different" angle, especially in arty houses. Also good dual material.

Chief fault of the film lies in its inconsistency, with sharp contrasts between periods of suspense and long dragging sequences that are seemingly non-stop. Following the European penchant for presentation of a story via straight narration, "Frenzy" is unrolled in a series of flashbacks which become slightly confusing toward the end but straighten out satisfactorily. Story centers around a sculptor, Derrick de Marney, in the Paris Latin Quarter toward the end of the 19th Century. He falls in love with the wife of another sculptor, who is in the advanced stages of paranoia. The madman learns of their plans to run away, kills his wife by plastering her up in a statue, and subsequently is arrested for the murder of his mistress. In an effort to learn the fate of the wife, de Marney becomes the victim of occult manifestations, which provide the pic's eerie quality.

Acting by all hands is excellent, with Lily Kann as the concierge doing a particularly good job; De Marney and Joan Seton, as the model, underplay well. As with most European films, supporting roles are skillfully handled, and frequently dull lines are given nice life. Production, however, has not the necessary finesse for good b.o., with suspense often being lost by dwelling too long on interim sequences. Photography is done with sock effect in some scenes, but blurs out to a pale wash in others, evidently due to plain clumsy handling. Sound track suffers occasional bumps, too.

Bowery Bombshell

Hollywood, July 20.

Monogram release of Jan Grippo-Lindsley Parsons production. Stars Leo Gorcey; features Huntz Hall, Bobby Jordan, Billy Benedict, David Gorcey, Teala Loring, Sheldon Leonard, James Burke, Vince Barnett. Directed by Phil Karlson. Original screenplay, Edmond Seward; added dialog, Tim Ryan; suggested by story by Victor Hammond; camera, William Sickner; editor, William Austin. Previewed in Hollywood, July 16, '46. Running time, **65 MINS.**

Slip..............................Leo Gorcey
Sach..............................Huntz Hall
Bobby.........................Bobby Jordan
Whitey.......................Billy Benedict
Chuck........................David Gorcey
Cathy Smith...................Teala Loring
Ace Deuce..................Sheldon Leonard
Maizie.......................Dawn Kennedy
O'Malley......................James Burke
Street Cleaner...............Vince Barnett
Moose McCall.............Wee Willie Davis
Biff............................William Ruhl
Mr. Johnson..................Emmett Vogan
Louie.......................Bernard Gorcey
Professor Schrackenberger..Milton Parsons
Feather-Fingers..................Lester Dorr
Dugan.......................William Newell
O'Hara...........................Eddie Dunn

Standard entry in Monogram's "Bowery Boys" series will sell in its intended market. Stock plot is sparked by Leo Gorcey's mugging antics. Directorial pace is good and production values give suitable framework for comedy-melodrama.

Rowdy action stems from fact that one of the boys is mistaken for a bankrobber and bunch sets out to trap real crooks so Huntz Hall can be cleared. Mixup comes when boys are trying to sell their old auto to aid a friend, attempted sale taking place in front of bank while robbery is going on.

Comedy gangsters dot the plot to give Boweryites a chance at the kind of rough-housing their fans like. Phil Karlson's direction keeps it all moving towards slambang finish. Bobby Jordan, Billy Benedict and David Gorcey are the other Bowery Boys. Sheldon Leonard makes a good gangster, aided in his dirty work by Vince Barnett, Wee Willie Davis and William Ruhl. Teala Loring lends femme touch as a photographer.

Lindsley Parons served with Jan Grippo on production end, team work achieving neat effect for money spent. Lensing by William Sickner and William Austin's editing are good.

Brog.

Prairie Badmen

PRC release of Sigmund Neufeld production. Stars Buster Crabbe, Al (Fuzzy) St. John. Directed by Sam Newfield. Screenplay, Fred Myton; camera, Robert Cline; editor, Holbrook N. Todd. Previewed in N. Y., July 18, '46. Running time, **55 MINS.**

Billy Carson.................Buster Crabbe
Fuzzy Jones............Al (Fuzzy) St. John
Linda Lattimer..............Patricia Knox
Cal...............................Charles King
Doc Lattimer.....................Ed Cassidy
Lon.........................Kermit Maynard
Steve.........................John L. Cason
Sheriff..........................Steve Clark
Thompson........................Frank Ellis
Don Lattimer...............John L. Buster

This prairie potboiler is a routine affair to give the Saturday matinee trade a modicum of excitement. Situations, generally, are hokey, and story doesn't stand too much scrutiny. Fortunately, film doesn't have too much dialog to burden the ungifted cast, and Sam Newfield's well-oiled pacing hides a lot of basic deficiencies.

Story concerns the travails of a traveling medicine show which is set upon by a group of bad men who learn of the proprietor's possession of a treasure-map. Fortunately Buster Crabbe and Al (Fuzzy) St. John hook up with the outfit to ultimately outwit the baddies.

Bright spot in the cast is Knight's comedics. He brings in some good bits of business to perk up the picture when the routine script bogs the proceedings down too heavily. Crabbe does an adequate job and Patricia Knox manages to stay out of the camera's way for long stretches, which is all to the good.

Jose.

Ghost of Hidden Valley

PRC release of Sigmund Neufeld production. Stars Buster Crabbe, Al St. John; features Jean Carlin, John Meredith. Directed by Sam Newfield. Screenplay, Ellen Coyle; camera, Art Reed; asst. director, Stanley Neufeld; editor, Holbrook N. Todd. At New York theatre, N. Y., July 18, '46. Running time, **50 MINS.**

Billy Carson..................Buster Crabbe
Fuzzy Jones........................Al St. John
Kaye.............................Jean Carlin
Henry.........................John Meredith
Dawson.........................Charles King
Tweedle.......................Jimmy Aubrey
Jed..............................Karl Hackett
Sweeney.......................John L. Cason
Stage Guard.....................Silver Harr
Arnold...........................Zon Murray

There are some flicker fans who will go anywhere to see a western, and those few will probably constitute the major portion of this film's boxoffice. In twin bill teaming, "Ghost of Hidden Valley" might barely pull its weight. Slapstick antics of former keystone cop Al "Fuzzy" St. John provide the keynote for the pic's production values, which belong to another era. Story, thesping, even settings, which are ordinarily a cinch for a passable rating in oaters, are all strictly second-rate.

Scenario tells of a young Englishman who comes to the wild west to take over his father's ranch, and of the attempts of cattle rustlers who have been using the land to move their stolen goods. Buster Crabbe, providing some marquee lure, and St. John's take the newcomer under their collective wing and defeat the criminals.

Film was evidently meant to have some sort of period setting, with a stagecoach in evidence, but even that's shattered when Jean Carlin, the love interest, cracks, "Boy, you sure missed the boat on that one." John Meredith, the young Englishman, is given only a few lines in which to sound off an accent that is either palpably phony or lost in inept thesping. Crabbe is okay with some pretty dull lines and St. John presents an over-hoked performance, with Jimmy Aubrey as the butler.

Support roles are not well-handled, and backgrounds look like they were filmed partly in a backyard and partly on someone's well-kept estate. Of the fights that occur, two are completely without motivation.

In Fast Company

Monogram release of Lindsley Parsons and Jan Grippy production. Stars Leo Gorcey; features Huntz Hall, Jane Randolph, Judy Clark, Bobby Jordan, Billy Benedict, David Gorcey, Douglas Fowley, Marjorie Woodworth. Directed by Del Lord. Screenplay, Edmond Seward, Tim Ryan, Victor Hammond, based on original story by Martin Mooney; camera, William Sickner; editor, Richard Currier. At Brooklyn Strand, dual, July 20, '46. Running time, 63 MINS.

Slip	Leo Gorcey
Sach	Huntz Hall
Marian McCormick	Jane Randolph
Mabel Dumbrowski	Judy Clark
Bobby	Bobby Jordan
Whitey	Billy Benedict
Chuck	David Gorcey
Steve Trent	Douglas Fowley
Sally Turner	Marjorie Woodworth
Father Donovan	Charles D. Brown
Patrick McCormick	Paul Harvey
Tony	Luis Alberni
Mrs. Cassidy	Mary Gordon
Louis	Bernard Gorcey
Officer	George Eldredge
Gus	William Ruhl
Pete	Dick Wessel
Tony	John Indrisano

Cavortings of Leo Gorcey and his Bowery Boys leaning but lightly on an unimportant and slight story feature Monogram's "In Fast Company." When viewed at the Brooklyn Strand, this comic-action opus garnered plenty of customer chuckles and knee-slapping. While not strong enough to carry on its own, as obligato to a bigger pic solid fare for the nabes.

Plot serves its purpose by setting up comic situations which Gorcey and the boys exploit with gusto and copious corn. The story centers about the racketeering efforts of the manager of a large cab company to drive independents out of business. Gorcey, et al pinch hit for an indie cabbie rendered hors de combat in an accident maneouvred by the marauding mobsters. Windup neatly ties the package via free-for-all fisticuffs in which the cab company's minious are routed and deposited in the clink.

But it's not as serious as it sounds. The situations are clowned consistently and the story comes in for more ribbing than respect. There's no scarcity of stock gags but, somehow, the verve and dash which Gorcey and his gang inject into their efforts take the curse off the venerable lines. And Gorcey's lingo-mangling is still good for audience response.

Judy Clark, Jane Randolph and Marjorie Woodworth, trio of femmes assisting the proceedings, are surprisingly effective in their roles. Balance of cast does nicely to keep the pic moving at a sharp clip. Del Lord's directing, aimed at a fast and light treatment, is skillful and satisfying.

Foreign Films

"Menneisyden Varjo" ("The Shadow from the Past" (FINNISH). Valio Filmi release and production, directed by Ville Salminen. Stars Tauno Palo, Ritva Arvelo; features Jaavo Jaenner, Jorma Nortimo, Terttu Soinivirta, Kaisu Leppanen, Tauno Majuri, ku Korhonen. Music, Harry Bergstroem. Reviewed in Helsingfors. Running time, 94 MINS.

Finnish public will go for this sentimental story, but no one outside. The film is a comeback for Tauno Palo and Ritva Arvelo, and features Aku Korhonen in a small role in one of his usual types.

The music, by Harry Bergstroem, is a standout. Excellent story, direction and acting.

"Nuoruus Sumussa" ("Lost Youngsters" (FINNISH). Suomen Filmiteollisuus production and release, directed by Toivo Sarkka. Stars Leif Wager, Topi Ruuth; features Hannen Hayrinen, Olavi Saarinen, Marjatta Uski, Toini Vartiainen, Kirsti Hurme, Assi Nortia, Uuno Laakso, Yrjoe Tuominen. Screenplay by Toini Aaltonen. Camera, Armas Hirvonen; music, Harry Bergstroem. Reviewed in Helsingfors. Running time, 112 MINS.

War-stories seem to be all that interests the Finnish public and producers today. This sentimental film with the war as back-ground, is built on a "Crime doesn't pay" Motif, although very well-done in acting and production, isn't likely to interest anyone out of the country.

"On Ne Meurt Pas Comme Ca" ("One Does Not Die That Way") (FRENCH). Vog release of Astra production. Directed by Jean Boyer. Screenplay by Ernest Neubach; dialog, Andre Tabet. Music, Jose Hajos. Stars Eric von Stroheim; features Anne Marie Blanc, Denise Vernac, Temerson, Georges Tabet, Georges Lannes, Sylvie, Sinoel, Marcel Vallee, Numes Fils. Reviewed in Paris. Running time, 95 MINS.

Spots catering to French patronage are likely to be the only ones to show this whodunit because the complicated plot requires full understanding of the dialog. Only special point of interest is good acting by Eris von Stroheim, who does a motion picture director. When directing a sequence showing the death of a character, who has really been poisoned, he claims the thesping is not realistic, hence the title. There is no outdoor shot, the whole thing taking place in a motion picture studio. Film holds no femme interest.

Miniature Reviews

"2 Guys from Milwaukee" (W-B). Jack Carson-Dennis Morgan comedy that should do okay despite spotty script.

"Slightly Scandalous" (U). Modestly-budgeted musical with plenty of entertainment for supporting positions.

"Blonde for a Day" (PRC). Mildish Michael Shayne sleuth whodunit, okay for lesser duals.

2 Guys from Milwaukee

Warner Bros. release of Alex Gottlieb production. Stars Dennis Morgan, Jack Carson; features Joan Leslie, Janis Paige, S. Z. Sakall, Patti Brady. Directed by David Butler. Original screenplay, Charles Hoffman and I. A. L. Diamond; editor, Irene Morra; camera, Arthur Edeson; dialog director, Felix Jacoves; assistant director, Jesse Hibbs; score, Frederick Hollander; music director, Leo F. Forbstein. At Strand, N. Y., July 27, '46. Running time, 90 MINS.

Prince Henry	Dennis Morgan
Buss Williams	Jack Carson
Connie Read	Joan Leslie
Polly	Janis Paige
Count Oswald	S. Z. Sakall
Peggy	Patti Brady
Happy	Tom D'Andrea
Nan	Rosemary DeCamp
Mike Collins	John Ridgely
Johnson	Pat McVey
Theatre Manager	Franklin Pangborn
Dr. Bauer	Francis Pierlot

The odds of performance against script aren't sufficient to surmount the obstacles encountered in "2 Guys from Milwaukee," in which Dennis Morgan and Jack Carson are the titular characters. The pic should do well enough at the boxoffice because of the film's value, though it's basically the comedy fol-de-rol of the male stars that give "2 Guys" whatever entertainment merits the pic possesses.

It's an obvious story with a familiarly concocted ending that nevertheless will draw laughs. Yarn concerns the visit to the U. S. of a European king and his strictly democratic desire to learn about the common people, and also to meet one Lauren Bacall. With this in mind, he scrams an official New York reception and becomes hooked up with the inevitable commoner from Brooklyn. That would be Carson, a cabbie from Flatbush. To maintain his disguise, he presumes to be from Milwaukee, which is also the original home of the loud-gabbing but sincere fender-bumper.

For a day or so he's able to carry off the subterfuge, which is mixed up with his romance with the cab-driver's girl, a manicurist, and, finally, the revelation that his country has failed to elect him in a plebiscite —which makes Morgan a commoner free to marry anyone he pleases, the least of whom would be the cuticle-stabber. And that's where the story really flounders. Just when it appears as if that romance is the mccoy, the yarn does a strange switch and she goes back to Carson, while Morgan planes to Milwaukee to take a job as a salesman with a brewer. And who does he find in the seat next to him? Yep—Lauren Bacall. A tap on his shoulder at this point makes his elation short-lived. A dour-pussed character claims Morgan's seat, but quick. Said character is a guy by the name of Bogart.

Neither Miss Bacall nor Bogart is billed, of course. Carson, as usual, draws plenty of laughs from what most frequently are lines that are read much better than they deserve. Morgan fits the regal character well, while Joan Leslie—who is, surprisingly, only featured instead of starred as the manicurist—is a better actress than her part permits her to be. Janis Paige has a lesser role in helping to maintain the romantic element, with S. Z. Sakall hypoing the comedy, as usual.

David Butler has directed for pace, and gets the most out of the situations. Production is high-grade.

Kahn.

Slightly Scandalous

(MUSICAL)

Hollywood, July 27.

Universal release of Stanley Rubin production. Stars Fred Brady, Sheila Ryan; introducing Paula Drew; features Walter Catlett, Isabelita, Louis Da Pron, Jack Marshall. Directed by Will Jason. Original screenplay, Erna Lazarus and David Mathews; added dialog, Joel Malone and Jerry Warner; camera, George Robinson; editor, Fred R. Feitshans; music, Jack Brooks. Previewed July 25, '46. Running time, 61 MINS.

Jerry, John and James	Fred Brady
Trudy Price	Paula Drew
Christine Wright	Sheila Ryan
Mr. Wright	Walter Catlett
Lola	Isabelita
Rocky	Louis Da Pron
Erwin	Jack Marshall
Mexican Duet	Nick Moro
Mexican Duet	Frank Yaconelli
Guadaljara Trio	Guadaljara Trio
Specialty Dancer	Dorese Midgley
Specialty Dancer	Georgann Smith

This program filmusical has been brightened considerably by new variations on a standard plot. It will serve neatly as supporting material in majority of situations. Songs are delivered nicely; score has crammed six tunes into the 61 minutes' running time without obvious crowding, and comedy rates many pleasant chuckles.

Production coin has been carefully spent by Stanley Rubin, associate producer, under executive supervision of Marshall Grant, to give film neat framework and backing for release intentions. Picture introduces Paula Drew, singer, and she does interesting work as star of television show being concocted by ex GI's. She handles three numbers, all by Jack Brooks, in a listenable style. Jack Marshall, vaude and nitery comic, brings his hat routine and two songs to the score for nice spotting. Isabelita goes south of the border for dance and song, "Negra Leona," that fits in well with musical portions.

Plot concerns Fred Brady's effort to put on a television show for a sponsor. He plays the ex-GI and also his twin but bashful brother who's tricked into supplying the production coin. Romantic complications concern Sheila Ryan, sponsor's daughter, Miss Drew, Isabelita and the twin brothers. Mixups provide the laughs and finale rings in a third Brady to make it triplets, the tele show is sold, and the brothers pair off properly with the right femmes.

Brady is slightly flamboyant as the brash producer, more subdued as the bashful twin. Miss Ryan is easy to look at and does well by her assignment. Walter Catlett and others measure up to demands of the original script by Erna Lazarus and David Mathews. Will Jason's direction does the best by the material, spotting bits of business and touches that sustain interest. Louis Da Pron, Dorese Midgley and Georgann Smith do good terp production number, and Guadalpara Trio, supplemented by Frank Yaconelli and Nick Moro, fit in. Lensing, editing and other technical functions measure up. *Brog.*

Blonde for a Day

PRC Pictures release of Sigmund Neufeld production. Features Hugh Beaumont, Kathryn Adams. Directed by Sam Newfield Screenplay by Fred Myton, from original story, "Michael Shayne, Detective," by Prett Halliday; camera, Jack Greenhalgh; editor, Holbrook N. Todd. Previewed in N. Y., July 26, '46. Running time, 67 MINS.

Michael Shayne	Hugh Beaumont
Phyllis Hamilton	Kathryn Adams
Pete Rafferty	Cy Kendall
Helen Porter	Majorie Hoshelle
Dilly Smith	Richard Fraser
Tim Rourke	Paul Eryar
Brenner	Mauritz Hugo
Henty	Charles Wilson
Muriel Bronson	Sonia Sorel

Bronson	Frank Ferguson
Minerva	Claire Rochelle

Another in the Michael Shayne detective series, "Blonde For a Day" follows same general pattern in this whodunit series, but it is not nearly as strong as most of those in group. This particular story has the makings of a more intriguing mystery but story lags too much. Film is okay for lower rung of dual combos in small spots.

Hugh Beaumont again plays the detective Shayne, while Kathryn Adams is his pert secretary. They work well as a team, pair actually being husband and wife. Yarn deals with Beaumont rescuing a police reporter when a bunch of gamblers get tough with the guy. Scribe had been exposing the gang as being linked to a series of slayings when they try to bump him off. The Sherlock unravels the mystery, which seems to have more blondes than detectives showing up in some sequences.

Topping support are Cy Kendall, Marjorie Hoshelle and Paul Bryar. Sigmund Neufeld has given the picture all the necessary production for a story of this sort. *Wear.*

Foreign Films

I Dodens Vantrum ("Waiting Room for Death") (SWEDISH). Terrafilm release of Lorens Marmstedt and Hasse Ekman production; stars Hasse Ekman. Viveca Lindfors; features Erik Berglund, Stig Jaerrel, Bengt Ekeroth, Sven Bertil Norberg, Ronald de Wolfe, Gaby Douillard; screenplay, Walter Ljungquist and Hasse Ekman from novel by Sven Stolpe; camera, Hilding Bladh. Reviewed in Stockholm. Running time, **96 MINS.**

This film gives a wonderful closeup of the mountains in Switzerland, with cameraman Hilding Bladh taking credit for this. It's a sentimental story laid in a Switzerland hospital. Cast is not standout excepting Viveca Lindfors and Stig Jaerrel. It's sure of success here, but chances in the U. S. are slim.

Miniature Reviews

"The Killers" (Hellinger-U). Socko melodrama loaded with suspene and tension, solid for all houses.

"Genius at Work" (RKO). Program comedy for subsequent bookings.

"Black Angel" (Songs) (U). Strong cast and costly mounting should get biz despite weak story.

"GI War Brides" (Rep). Pleasant triangle situation for good dualling.

"La Maja De Los Cantares" (Sono). Argentine-made picture starring Imperio Argentina; only limited appeal for U. S.

The Killers

(ONE SONG)

Hollywood, Aug. 6.

Universal release of Mark Hellinger production. Features Burt Lancaster, Ava Gardner, Edmond O'Brien, Albert Dekker, Sam Levene. Directed by Robert Siedmak. Screenplay, Anthony Veiller, from story by Ernest Hemingway; editor, Arthur Hillton; camera, Woody Bredell, D.S. Horsley; asst director, Melville Shyer; music, Miklos Rozsa; lyrics, Jack Brooks. Previewed Aug 6, '46. Running time, 103 mins.

Swede	Burt Lancaster
Kitty Collins	Ava Gardner
Riordan	Edmond O'Brien
Colfax	Albert Dekker
Lubinsky	Sam Levene
Packy	Charles D. Brown
Kenyon	Donald McBride
Nick	Phil Brown
Al	Charles McGrow
Jake	John Miljan
Max	William Conrad
Queenie	Queenis Smith
Joe	Garry Owen
George	Harry Hayden
Sam	Bill Walker
Charleston	Vince Barnett
Dum Dum	Jack Lambert
Blinky	Jeff Corey
Charley	Wally Scott
Lilly	Virginia Christine
Ginny	Gabrielle Windsor
Man	Rex Dale

Mark Hellinger tees off his first Universal production with a bang. "Killers" is sock film fare for all situations. Seldom does a melodrama consistently maintain the high tension that distinguishes this one. There's never a letup, all factors combining to keep audiences on edge of seats.

Taken from Ernest Hemingway's story of the same title, picture is a hard-hitting example of forthright melodrama in the best Hemingway style.

Performances without exception are top quality even though names do not have assured boxoffice. It's a handpicked cast that troupes to the hilt to make it all believable. Film introduces Burt Lancaster from legit. He does a strong job, serving as the central character around whom the plot revolves. Edmond O'Brien, insurance investigator who probes Lancaster's murder, is another pivotal character who adds much to the film's acting polish.

Robert Siodmak's direction is adroit in maintaining punchy proceedings. He has added touches that come through with a wallop, builds tension almost to breaking point, and gets the best from the players. Script by Anthony Veiller didn't miss a bet in shaping the Hemingway story into forceful screen material making for a very solid foundation for the playing. Plot opens with Lancaster's murder in a small town. O'Brien takes it from there, trying to piece together events that will prove the murder of smalltown service station attendant has more significance than appears on the surface. Story has many flashbacks, told when O'Brien interviews characters in Lancaster's past, but it is all pieced together neatly for sustained drive and mood, finishing with expose of a colossal double-cross. Every character has its moment to shine and does.

Ava Gardner, bad girl of the piece; Albert Dekker, her cohort in crime and murder; Sam Levene, a thoroughly believable cop; Charles McGraw and William Conrad, as menacing a pair of killers as yet shown on the screen; Vince Barnett, Jack Lambert, Jeff Corey, Virginia Christine, Donald McBride, Phil Brown, John Miljan, Queenie Smith and all the others in the cast deserve kudos for performances.

Hellinger assured a music score that would heighten mood of this one by using Miklos Rosza, and the score is an immeasurable aid in furthering suspense. There's also one pop number, "The More I Know of Love," by Jack Brooks and Rosza spotted by Miss Gardner. Low key lighting and natural settings are pointed up by Woody Bredell's standout lensing. Editing is tight despite 103 minutes running time. *Bron.*

Genius at Work

Los Angeles, Aug. 2.

RKO release of Herman Schlom production. Stars Wally Brown, Alan Carney; features Anne Jeffreys, Lionel Atwill, Bela Lugosi, Marc Cramer, Ralph Dunn. Directed by Leslie Goodwins. Original screenplay, Robert E. Kent, Monte Brice; camera, Robert de Grasse, Vernon L. Walker; editor, Marvin Coil. Tradeshown July 31, '46. Running time, **61 MINS.**

Jerry	Wally Brown
Mike	Alan Carney
Ellen	Anne Jeffreys
Marsh	Lionel Atwill
Stone	Bela Lugosi
Rick	Marc Gramer
Gilley	Ralph Dunn

Lighiweight slapstick comedy aimed for supporting market. Short running time makes it okay filler material for subsequent bookings but otherwise it's flimsy film fare with about equal mixture of chuckles and dullness.

Plot concerns team of radio detectives, Wally Brown and Alan Carney, who fumble through to an expose of Lionel Atwill as a notorious killer. Boys play detective, using air script written by Anne Jeffreys, whom Atwill, criminologist, aids with details of The Cobra's latest crime. Screenplay development is more hysterical than hilarious and every type of sight gag and situation is rung in to force the laughs. Aiding Atwill in his mad work is Bela Lugosi, equally as crazy.

Cast tries hard under Leslie Goodwins' direction and does achieve modest results occasionally. Production accoutrements marshalled by Herman Schlom under executive supervision of Sid Rogell measure 'p to budget. Lensing and other credits are okay. *Brog.*

Black Angel

(SONGS)

Universal release of Tom McKnight—Roy William Neill production; directed by Neill. Stars Dan Duryea, June Vincent, Peter Lorre; features Broderick Crawford, Wallace Ford, Hobart Cavanaugh, Constance Dowling, Freddie Steele, Ben Bard, John Phillips. Screenplay, Roy Chanslor, based on novel by Cornell Woolrich; songs, Jack Brooks, Edgar Fairchild; camera, Paul Ivano; editor, Saul A. Goodkind; score, Frank Skinner. Tradeshown in N. Y., July 31, '46. Running time, **80 MINS.**

Martin Blair	Dan Duryea
Catherine	June Vincent
Marko	Peter Lorre
Captain Flood	Broderick Crawford
Joe	Wallace Ford
Jake	Hobart Cavanaugh
Marvis Marlowe	Constance Dowling
Lucky	Freddie Steele
Bartender	Ben Bard
Kirk Bennett	John Phillips

Best assets in this film is on the marquee. The major drawback of a jumbled script otherwise interferes seriously.

Script confusion grows out of the problem: what to do with Dan Duryea? Intent was to give a romantic buildup to Duryea and at the same time cash in on the underlip snarl he made famous in "Woman in the Window" and "Scarlet Street." Result is a watered down characterization that's neither one thing nor the other.

Title of "Black Angel" stems from Duryea's gallant confession at the climax to clear a murder charge pinned on the husband of the woman he loves. Plot opens as a routine whodunit with the strangulation of a blackmailing femme, and the pointing of suspicion at several characters. A tight web of circumstantial evidence implicates June Vincent's husband, as the killer, but the wife, convinced of his innocence, sets out to find the guilty party.

En route, she teams up in the sleuthing with Duryea, a down-at-the-heels songwriter and husband of the murdered woman. In running down a clue, they're led to Peter Lorre, operator of a high class nitery, where they obtain a job as a singing, piano duo. Lorre, however, establishes an air-tight alibi, but just as matters begin to look hopeless for the condemned man, Duryea hits the bottle and in an alcoholic daze recalls that he did the killing himself in a previous drunken stupor.

Plenty of coin was laid out for the production mountings. The nitery sequences have a high gloss finish although the three top tunes mooned over by June Vincent are very Tin Pan Alley. Musical interludes, moreover, break up the story tension without any compensation in the way of quality tunes or standout warbling. Pace of the direction lacks that extra speed needed to give this type of film the desired sock. Photography is excellent throughout.

Only some superior thesping by Duryea saves his badly written role from being a complete washout. As the femme lead, June Vincent comes through in competent fashion, although the chirping burden is too heavy for her to carry. Lorre makes a neat menace, as usual, and Broderick Crawford, as the cop, gives a solid, credible performance. Rest of the cast back up in acceptable fashion.

GI War Brides

Republic release of Armand Schaefer production. Stars Anna Lee, James Ellison; features Harry Davenport, William Henry, Stephanie Bachelor. Directed by George Blair. Screenplay, John K. Butler; camera, Alfred Keller; music, Morton Scott; editor, Tony Martinelli. Tradeshown Aug. 6, '46. Running time, **69 MINS.**

Linda Powell	Anna Lee
Steve Giles	James Ellison
Grandpa Giles	Harry Davenport
Capt. Roger Kirby	William Henry
Elizabeth Wunderlich	Stephanie Bachelor
Beatrice Moraski	Doris Lloyd
Dawson	Robert Armstrong
Sgt. Frank Moraski	Joseph Sawyer
Kathleen Fitzpatrick	Mary McLeod
Joyce Giles	Carol Savage
Margaret Lee	Pax Walker
Ruth Giles	Helen Gerald
Harold R. Williams	Pat O'Moore
Sgt. Polly Williams	Maxine Jennings
Inspector Ramsaye	Russell Hicks
Mr. Wunderlich	Francis Pierlot
Editor	Pierre Watkin
Donnie	Eugene Lay
Miss Nolan	Lois Austin
Helen Mayo	Virginia Carroll

Novel plot twists to the eternal triangle provide main support for this small-budgeter, and although it just misses on the timeliness angle, "G.I. War Brides" has enough in the way of production mountings and smart editing of stock shots to carry its weight well in dual billings. Fast pacing of director George Blair adds nice snap.

Plot tells of a girl who trades places on a ship carrying English war brides to the United States with a wife no longer in love with her husband. A suspicious reporter realizes the facts, and waits while the girl pretends she's married to the unwanted husband to give immigration authorities the slip. She finds her boy friend no longer cares and is saved from deportation by her once-fake hubby, thanks to the reporter.

Comedy angles strain at the leash throughout but never quite break through, with the exception of occasional shots of some twin babies aboard the ship. Unusual twist is the fact that there is no heavy in the entire story; everyone, including Robert Armstrong, the reporter who reports the stowaway but eventually unsnafus things.

Thesping is fair enough, though not outstanding. James Ellison is lightweight. Anna Lee, Harry Davenport and William Henry turned in good stock performances, while Doris Lloyd and Stephanie Bachelor are better than average.

La Maja De Los Cantares
("The Songstress")
(ARGENTINE-MADE)

Buenos Aires, July 23.

Argentina Sono Film production and release. Stars Imperio Argentina; features Mario Gabarron, Carmelia Vazquez, Amadeo Novoa. Directed by Benito Perogo. At Cine Monumental theatre. Running time, **90 MINS.**

(In Spanish)

This is the first picture made by Spain's Imperio Argentina, who was born in Buenos Aires. As might be expected, the story, locale and atmosphere are entirely Spanish. For local patrons this makes for good entertainment, but for the world market it's a bit dubious.

Actually the songstress is a wooden actress, but her Flamenco singing is tops of its kind. The fact that she has been given a role that calls for Spanish repartee, geared for plenty of laughs, helps her a bit. There was considerable trouble in lining up a cast to accompany the Spanish star because local leading men begged off, not wanting to be coupled with her for ideological reasons. Mario Gabarron, another Spaniard, acquits himself very well. Benito Perojo does best in directing the crowd scenes and the dansapation, which fell to the Gema Castillo ballet and Laberinto and Terremoto, Spanish dancers.

Production is nicely done. Story is the weakest part of the picture, being illogical and giving the impression of having been lopped off in the middle. Film holds hope for a limited U. S. audience. *Nid.*

Miniature Reviews

"The Big Sleep" (WB). Strong detective melodrama with Humphrey Bogat and Lauren Bacall. Important boxoffice prospects.

"The Show-Off" (M-G). Light comedy geared for okay reception by Red Skelton fans.

"Shadow of a Woman" (WB). Lightweight melodrama with modest prospects.

"Criminal Court" (RKO). Tight melodrama that will maintain interest in supporting playdates.

"The Time of Their Lives" (U). Abbott & Costello highjinks in a spooky film tailor-made for the fans.

"Earl Carroll Sketchbook" (Musical) (Rep). Well-mounted extravaganza shapes up as good program fare.

"Down Missouri Way" (Songs) PRC). Good cast riding a zany script and upbeat score in an above-par mule opera.

"The Last Crooked Mile" (Rep). Donald Barry, Ann Savage in gangster meller geared for strong support on duals.

"Personality Kid" (Col). Small-budgeter for family appeal.

"Passkey to Danger" (Rep). Lightweight comedy whodunit nicely mounted for dual billing.

The Big Sleep

Los Angeles, Aug. 10.

Warner Bros. release of Howard Hawks production. Stars Humphrey Bogart, Lauren Bacall; features John Ridgely, Martha Vickers, Dorothy Malone. Directed by, Hawks. Screen play, William Faulkner, Leigh Brackett and Jules Furthman; from novel by Raymond Chandler; camera, Sid Hickox; editor, Christian Nyby; music, Max Steiner. Tradeshown in Los Angeles, Aug. 9, '46. Running time, **113 MINS.**

Phil Marlowe	Humphrey Bogart
Vivian	Lauren Bacall
Eddie Mars	John Ridgely
Carmen	Martha Vickers
Proprietress	Dorothy Malone
Mona Mars	Peggy Knudsen
Bernie Ohls	Regis Toomey
General Sternwood	Charles Waldron
Norris (Butler)	Charles D. Brown
Canino	Bob Steele
Harry Jones	Elisha Cook, Jr.
Joe Brody	Louis Jean Heydt
Agnes	Sonia Darrin
Capt. Cronjager	James Flavin
Wilde (Dist. Atty.)	Thomas Jackson
Carol Lundgren	Tom Rafferty
Arthur Geiger	Theodore Von Eltz
Owen Taylor	Dan Wallace
Taxicab Driver	Joy Barlowe
Sidney	Tom Fadden
Pete	Ben Welden
Art Huck	Trevor Bardette

There's plenty of boxoffice potential in "The Big Sleep." Star names and release, combined with the sexy melodramatics of the Raymond Chandler novel, point the way to large returns. Brittle Chandler characters have been transferred to the screen with punch by Howard Hawks' production and direction, providing full load of rough, tense action most of the way. Name of Humphrey Bogart, coupled with Lauren Bacall, furnishes marquee voltage for customer lure.

Bogart's portrayal of Phil Marlowe, Chandler's hard-living and loving private detective, has plenty o

down by Production Code demands. Miss Bacall comes through strongly as Vivian, Marlowe's chief romantic interest. They make a smooth team to get over the amatory play and action in the script. Hawks has given story a staccato pace in the development, using long stretches of dialogless action and then whipping in fast talk between characters. This helps to punch home high spots of suspense, particularly in latter half of picture.

Chandler plot, scripted by William Faulkner, Leigh Brackett and Jules Furthman, deals with adventures of Bogart when he takes on a case for the eccentric Sternwood family. There are six deaths to please whodunit fans, plenty of lusty action, both romantic and physical, as Bogart matches wits with dealers in sex literature, blackmail, gambling and murder. Before he closes his case he has dodged sudden death, been unmercifully beaten, threatened, fought off mad advances of one of the Sternwood females, and fallen in love with another.

Some good scenes are tossed to others in the cast. Dorothy Malone, a bookshop proprietress, has her big moment in a sequence shot with sex implications as she goes on the make for Bogart. Martha Vickers, as the crazy Sternwood girl, does excellently by the assignment. John Ridgely makes a convincing bigtime gambler. Regis Toomey, Charles D. Brown, Bob Steele, Elisha Cook, Jr., and Louis Jean Heydt, Sonia Darrin, Joy Barlowe and Trevor Bardette are among others showing up well.

Low-key lighting and lensing by Sid Hickox help to further the mood, and other production appurtenances have been well valued by Hawks. *Brog.*

The Showoff

Hollywood, Aug. 10.

Metro release of Albert Lewis production. Stars Red Skelton; features Marilyn Maxwell, Marjorie Main, Virginia O'Brien, Eddie "Rochester" Anderson, Leon Ames. Directed by Harry Beaumont. Screenplay, George Wells; adapted from the play by George Kelly; camera, Robert Planck; editor, Douglass Biggs. Tradeshown in Los Angeles, Aug. 7, '46. Running time, **83 MINS.**

Aubrey Piper	Red Skelton
Amy	Marilyn Maxwell
Mrs. Fisher	Marjorie Main
Hortense	Virginia O'Brien
Eddie	Eddie "Rochester" Anderson
Pop Fisher	George Cleveland
Frank Harlin	Leon Ames
Joe Fisher	Marshall Thompson
Clara Harlin	Jacqueline White
Horace Adems	Wilson Wood
Flo	Lila Leeds
Appelton	Emory Parnell

"The Show-Off" is light comedy that will fare best in the lesser situations and as supporting material. Red Skelton fans will enjoy it and others will find a good deal of chuckles scattered through this tale of a showoff who never learns his lesson. Production values are good, although modest.

Skelton is seen as a brash young man who gives out fanciful tales of his travels, friends, position, etc., all figments of a fertile imagination. The George Kelly play, from which George Wells adapted the screenplay, has Skelton falling in love with Marilyn Maxwell, to the disgust of her family. His big talk gets himself and everyone else into all sorts of mixups, but familiar story pattern has the showoff still on top at the finale, although fooling no one but himself.

Miss Maxwell is a lush foil to the Skelton clowning, showing up well as his beautiful bride who loves the dope despite his faults. Marjorie Main, as mother of Miss Maxwell, and George Cleveland, the father, account for good share of the laughs by virtue of their reaction to the unwelcome son-in-law. Leon Ames, Marshall Thompson and Jacqueline White are others in the family circle who show to the best advantage permitted by the story. Virginia O'Brien and Eddie "Rochester" Anderson, both with featured billing, have little to do but add some marquee value.

Harry Beaumont directed the Albert Lewis production. Lensing, editing and other technical functions are good. *Brog.*

Shadow of a Woman

Hollywood, Aug. 7.

Warners release of William Jacobs production. Stars Helmut Dantine, Andrea King; features Don McGuire, Dick Erdman, John Alvin, William Prince. Directed by Joseph Santley. Screenplay, Whitman Chambers, C. Graham Baker; from novel by Virginia Perdue; camera, Bert Glennon; special effects, Edwin DuPar; music, Adolph Deutsch; editor, Christian Nyby. Tradeshown L. A., Aug. 7, '46. Running time, **78. MINS.**

Dr. Eric Ryder	Helmut Dantine
Brock	Andrea King
Johnnie	Don McGuire
Joe	Dick Erdman
Carl	John Alvin
David MacKellar	William Prince
Genevieve Calvin	Becky Brown
Mrs. Louise Ryder	Peggy Knudsen
Emma	Lisa Golm
Philip Ryder	Larry Geiger
Police Lieutenant	Monte Blue
Freeman	Jack Smart
Mrs. Calvin.	Leah Baird
Sarah	Lottie Williams
Dr. Nelson Norris	Paul Stanton

"Shadow of a Woman" is heavy melodrama that packs little entertainment weight. It has only modest boxoffice possibilities. Stagey theatrics are told with a minimum of realism and will draw only slight interest from general audiences. There's not much marquee voltage in the cast names to aid the selling. Production values are okay, although bearing no evidence of lavish budget.

Plot concerns a young bride married to a doctor and the terror that grips her life as she gradually realizes he is a quack and a killer. Plot has received poor development in the scripting hands of Whitman Chambers and C. Graham Baker, who worked from the Virginia Perdue novel. Helmut Dantine, the doctor, is such an obvious villain that Andrea King gains little sympathy as the bride who should have suspected him at first meeting. Some poorly executed attempts are made to inject suspense but mood never quite comes off, even the fight at the finale where the villain gets his just deserts fails to make for a slam-bang windup.

Two stars give almost straight readings to their assignments. Joseph Santley's direction is lightweight, which doesn't aid balance of the cast. Others include William Prince, lawyer who gets the girl in the end; Don McGuire, Dick Erdman, John Alvin, Peggy Knudsen and Lisa Golm. *Bron.*

Criminal Court
(SONGS)

Hollywood, Aug. 8.

RKO release of Martin Mooney production. Stars Tom Conway, Martha O'Driscoll; features June Clayworth, Robert Armstrong, Addison Richards, Pat Gleason, Steve Brodie, Robert Warwick, Phil Warren, Joe Devlin. Directed by Robert Wise. Screenplay, Lawrence Kimble; based on story by Earl Felton; camera, Frank Redman; special effects, Russell A. Cully; music, Paul Sawtelle; editor, Robert Swink. Tradeshown Aug. 7, '46. Running time, **63 MINS.**

Steve Barnes	Tom Conway
Georgia Gale	Martha O'Driscoll
Joan Mason	June Clayworth
Vic Wright	Robert Armstrong
District Attorney	Addison Richards
Joe West	Pat Gleason
Frankie	Steve Brodie
Marquette	Robert Warwick
Bill Brannegan	Phil Warren
Brownie	Joe Devlin
Gil Lambert	Lee Bonnell
Dance Director	Robert Clarke

RKO has concocted a neat courtroom melodrama that will play well in the supporting positions. It maintains interest, has excellent pace. Production backing by Martin Mooney gets the most from the budget allotment, showing off plot ingredients smartly.

Cast troupes well, performances being headed up by Tom Conway and Martha O'Driscoll in the leads. Robert Wise's direction keeps a tight grip on events to make this one come out better than average for such budget films. Conway is a smart defense attorney, running for office of district attorney. Miss O'Driscoll is his fiancee, a night club singer.

Plot of the Lawrence Kimble script, based on a story by Earl Felton, has Conway called upon to defend his girl against a murder charge when he is really the guy who did the killing, even though accidental. Because of his flamboyant courtroom tricks in saving clients, law won't believe his confession of the killing of a notorious racketeer who has been trying to keep Conway from entering race for d.a.'s office. Instead, Miss O'Driscoll, who came across the bodly shortly afterwards, is charged with murder.

Situations develop logically, and dialog is a factor in making melodramatics believable right through to the finale, when Conway uncovers a heretofore unsuspected witness to the killing, saves the girl and goes free himself.

June Clayworth, the witness; Robert Armstrong, the racketeer; Addison Richards, prosecuting attorney; Pat Gleason, Steve Brodie and others of the cast deliver expertly. Frank Redman's lensing, editing and other factors contribute to keeping this one okay for the market. *Brog.*

The Time of Their Lives

Universal release of Joe Gershenson production. Stars Bud Abbott and Costello; features Marjorie Reynolds, Binnie Barnes, John Shelton, Gale Sondergaard, Jess Barker. Directed by Charles Barton. Original screenplay, Val Burton, Walter De Leon, Bradford Ropes; camera, Charles Van Enger; editor, Phillip Cahn; score, Milton Rosen. Previewed at Mayfair, N. Y., Aug. 12, '46. Running time, **82 MINS.**

Horatio .... Lou Costello
Dr. Greenway }
Cuthbert } .... Bud Abbott
Melody .... Marjorie Reynolds
Mrs. Prescott .... Binnie Barnes
Sheldon Gage .... John Shelton
Emily .... Gale Sondergaard
Tom Danbury .... Jess Barker
Major Putnam .... Robert H. Barrat
Lt. Mason .... Donald MacBride
Nora .... Anne Gillis
June Prescott .... Lynne Baggett
Connors .... William Hall
Sgt. Makepeace .... Rex Lease
Motorcycle Rider .... Harry Woolman

This one's a picnic for Abbott & Costello fans. Replete with trowelled-on slapstick, corned-up gags and farcical plot, "Time of Their Lives" won't shock the patrons with any unfamiliar novelties. Abbott is still playing straight to Costello and all's well at the b.o.

Story line is a broad burlesque takeoff on the spectral theme that was so fancifully spun by Rene Clair in "I Married a Witch." Shot by mistake as a traitor in the American Revolutionary War and doomed to remain an earthbound ghost until proved innocent, Costello turns up in 1946 still looking for the evidence. In a similar fix, Marjorie Reynolds floats through the film like a Sears-Roebuck model ghost, but Costello can't quite make the smoothie grade. It's good for laughs.

Abbott, who early in the picture plays a 1780 heel, turns up in modern times as a psychiatrist, house-guesting in the mansion Costello and his girl friend are haunting. Latter wreak their revenge via a series of invisible-man stunts that drive the brain specialist out of his mind. This gimmick is worked to the limit, and beyond.

With many of the gags double-tracking on themselves, film could be snipped at a few points for punchier comic effects. Direction is well-aimed at the belly-laugh level and the trick photography is handled with flawless technique. With production values okay in every other department, film sags only in the script, where A&C could use some fresh, bright material instead of the easy and tired way out.

Strong supporting cast is headed by Binnie Barnes, playing another house-guest in the colonial mansion, and Gale Sondergaard, a psychic housemaid. Donald MacBride's bit as the bewildered cop is played to the hilt for chuckles. Marjorie Reynolds, in the ingenue lead, makes a sweet-looking spook.

Earl Carroll Sketchbook
(MUSICAL)

Republic release of Robert North production. Stars Constance Moore, William Marshall; features Bill Goodwin, Vera Vague, Johnny Coy, Edward Everett Horton. Directed by Albert S. Rogell. Screenplay by Frank Gill, Jr., Parke Levy from original by Frank; songs, Jule Styne; Sammy Cahn, Harold Arlen-Ted Koehler; camera, Jack Marta; editor, Richard L. Van Enger. Tradeshown N. Y., Aug. 13, '46. Running time, **90 MINS.**

Pamela Thayer .... Constance Moore
Tyler Brice .... William Marshall
Richard Starling .... Bill Goodwin
Johnny .... Johnny Coy
Sherry Lane .... Vera Vague
Dr. Milo Edwards .... E. E. Horton
Lynn Stafford .... Hillary Brooke
Lola .... Dorothy Babb
Pop .... Robert Homans

Second in the annual series of Earl Carroll's "colossals" for Republic, "Sketchbook" is an ornate piece of pastry topped by a pleasant musical score and neat performances. Film unreels as a series of warbling solos and production dance numbers tied into a package by a light story thread. Conventional treatment in the pic plus the absence of solid marquee lures won't hypo the b.o. in the key spots, but for general situations it shapes up as a winner.

Constance Moore handles the lead with an airy thespic touch and appealing though not standout set of pipes. She does nicely with the Julie Styne-Sammie Cahn numbers, including "I Was Silly, Headstrong and Impetuous," and "What Makes You Beautiful, Beautiful?" in addition to three reprises of a ballad, "I've Never Forgotten." In an effectively staged number, she wails over the Harold Arlen-Ted Koehler tune of a 1932 Earl Carroll production, "I've Got the Right to Sing the Blues."

Highlight of the film are the fast-stepping terp numbers by Johnny Coy and Dorothy Babb. Against one of those typical elaborate backgrounds, the duo work over some eye-filling routines in Styne-Cahn's "The Lady With a Mop" and Arlen-Koehler's oldie, "Hittin' the Bottle." Republic's dancing line gives okay support in the production numbers.

Vera Vague and Edward Everett Horton are on briefly but their comedy bits spice up the film. William Marshall, in the male lead as the talented songwriter who sold out to compose radio jingles, is acceptable although his crooning is on the weak side. Bill Goodwin, as the producer of an Earl Carroll nitery extravaganza, goes through his paces casually and makes a strong third angle to the pic's triangle.

Down Missouri Way
(SONGS)

PRC release of Josef Berne production; directed by him. Stars Martha O'Driscoll, John Carradine, Eddie Dean, William Wright; features Roscoe Ates, Mabel Todd, Renee Godfrey, Eddie Craven. Original screenplay, Sam Neuman; songs, Kim Gannon, Walter Kent; music, Karl Hajos; camera, Vincent J. Farrar; editor, W. Donn Hayes. Tradeshown, N. Y., Aug. 9, '46. Running time, **73 MINS.**

Jane Colwell .... Martha O'Driscoll
Thorndyke P. Dunning .... John Carradine
Mortimer .... Eddie Dean
Mike Burton .... William Wright
Pappy .... Roscoe Ates
Gloria Baxter .... Renee Godfrey
Cindy .... Mabel Todd
Sam .... Eddie Craven
Professor Shaw .... Chester Clute
Professor Morris .... Will Wright
Professor Lewis .... Paul Scardon

Out of the rut of the motheaten oatuner formula and in the groove with an upbeat musical score, a zany laugh-getting script and a good cast, "Down Missouri Way" shapes up as one of PRC's best offerings to date. It's a hillbilly mule opera with a tongue-in-cheek treatment that should earn this pic better slotting than the usual westerner.

A total of eight numbers, all highly listenable and several of sock quality, are closely distributed throughout the film. Eddie Dean's sole chore is the handling of three standard saddle songs with the main vocal stint carried off in top form by Renee Godfrey and Martha O'Driscoll. Standout tunes in a city-slicker tempo include "Big Town Gal," "Just Can't Get That Guy" and "Never Knew That I Could Sing."

Cast is topped by John Carradine who's taken off the leash in his role of a Hollywood director and given plenty of space in which to deliberately ham up the screen. Performance is a perfect facsimile of the Armour brand of thesping made famous by John Barrymore during the latter's more flamboyant moods. Supplied with florid, well-cadenced lines, Carradine pays off with plenty of laughs.

Story line is some frothy nonsense concerning the attempt to find a hep mule for a motion picture role in a hillbilly operetta. Madcap angle is played up in the fact that the animal is matriculating as an experimental student in an agricultural college. Plot doesn't stand up under scrutiny but clever dialoging saves the situation. Direction and camera work are okay but the editing has left some rough transitions.

The Last Crooked Mile

Republic release of Rudolph E. Abel production. Stars Donald Barry, Ann Savage; features Adele Mara, John Miljan, Tom Powers. Directed by Philip Ford. Screenplay by Jerry Sackheim, based on radio play by Robert L. Richards; camera, Alfred Keller, Howard and Theodore Lydecker. Previewed in N. Y., Aug. 9, '46. Running time, **67 MINS.**

Tom Dwyer .... Donald Barry
Sheila Kennedy .... Ann Savage
Bonnie .... Adele Mara
Floyd Sorelson .... Tom Powers
Ed MacGuire .... Sheldon Leonard
Ferrara .... Nestor Paiva
Lieutenant Blake .... Harry Shannon
Haynes .... Ben Welden
Lieutenant Mayrin .... John Miljan
Detrich .... Charles D. Brown
Jarvis .... John Dehner
Charlie .... Anthony Caruso

This gangster whodunit varies from most mobster mellers in that interest centers in recovering the missing $300,000 snatched in bank holdup, rather than in solving a crime. Otherwise, it follows the accepted pattern, making "The Last Crooked Mile" palatable fare for lower rung of dual combos.

Picture spots Donald Barry as a private sleuth who undertakes to trace the missing coin when offered 10% for the recovered loot. This is only a slight switch from the Barry of a couple of years back, when he was moved from straight westerns to a Robin Hood type gangster. Here he's an energetic private Sherlock, who irritates the coppers, nearly gets himself arrested several times and never overlooks a comely dame.

The $300,000 has disappeared when the bank robbers are killed in their wrecked auto. Detective Barry decides that the strong interest shown over this robbery car is the solution to the mystery. Before he winds up the case though he has caught a bank official red-handed there are three murders and the master sleuth uncovers the real culprit via his latest romance.

There are several implausible developments in view of the final denouement but these are largely covered up by the smart scripting of Jerry Sackheim and expert direction by Philip Ford. Barry makes a typical flip private detective. Ann Savage plays the cabaret singer who supposedly is helping him in the case but who several times is nearly bumped off by mysterious gangsters also seeking the missing bank coin. Adele Mara is Barry's real sweetheart though overshadowed by Miss Savage, who gives out with one pop song, the oldie "The One I Love Belongs to Somebody Else." Tom Powers, as the unscrupulous banker, heads the support which includes John Miljan, Sheldon Leonard and Nestor Paiva in important roles. *Wear.*

Personality Kid

Columbia release of Wallace MacDonald production. Features Anita Louise, Michael Duane, Ted Donaldson. Directed by George Sherman. Screenplay, Lewis Helmar Herman, William B. Sackheim, from story by Cromwell MacKechnie; camera, Henry Freulich; music, Mischa Bakaleinikoff; asst. director, Thomas Flood; editor, Richard Fantl. At Strand, Brooklyn, week Aug. 10, '46. Running time, **62 MINS.**

Laura Howard .... Anita Louise
Harry Roberts .... Michael Duane
Davey Roberts .... Ted Donaldson
Mrs. Roberts .... Barbara Brown
Albert Partridge .... Bobby Larson
Officer O'Brien .... Oscar O'Shea
Mr. Howard .... Harlan Briggs
Mrs. Partridge .... Regina Wallace
Mrs. Howard .... Edythe Elliott
Mr. Partridge .... Paul Maxey
Melendez .... Martin Garralaga

Family film fare and especially good for moppets who nurse their nickels for Saturday's matinee, "Personality Kid" pulls a couple of well-tested stops for audience reaction. Obviously done on a wee budget, story's setting and tone are such that elaborate production is not a requirement. Should do okay with strong primary dualer.

Evidently going on the premise that animals and moppets are a surefire bet for nabe filmgoers, pic gives top billing to a boy and a donkey, with a returned vet thrown in for good measure. Doubtful that this type of film can provide general entertainment, especially for that large group of flicker fans who like to live adventurously through pictures. There are no thrills in this one.

Two threads of the story begin separately, with young Ted Donaldson trying to keep a burro for a pet, and his big brother trying to make a career for himself as a commercial photographer instead of returning to a soap factory job. Climax comes when pictures of the burro win a big contest, reuniting big brother Michael Duane with love interest Anita Louise.

Thesping by all concerned is far above the general B average, with Anita Louise and Ted Donaldson heading performances. Corn and hoke is held to a minimum, although the angle on rehabilitation of the returned vet should either have been eliminated or given sufficient strength to make it an important factor in the story.

Passkey to Danger

Republic release of William J. O'Sullivan production. Stars Kane Richmond, Stephanie Bachelor; features Adele Mara, Gregory Gay. Directed by Lesley Selander. Screenplay, O'Leta Rhinehart, William Hagens; camera, William Bradford; music, Richard Cherwin; editor, Harry Keller. At Strand, Brooklyn, week Aug. 10 '46. Running time, **58 MINS.**

Tex Hanlon .... Kane Richmond
Gwen Hughes .... Stephanie Bachelor
Renee Beauchamps .... Adele Mara
Mr. Warren .... Gregory Gay
Malcolm Tauber .... Gerald Mohr
Alex Cardovsky .... John Eldredge
Julian Leighton .... George J. Lewis
Bert .... Fred Graham
Gerald Bates .... Tom London
Jenny .... Donia Bussey
Mr. Williams .... Charles Williams
Police Sergeant .... Charles Wilson

Smoothly directed lightweight comedy whodunit, "Passkey to Danger" trots snappily through a plot that will tax the thinking powers of no one. A well-finished though small-budgeted pic, it sports no marquee names but should do well in dual situations.

Story, which takes a couple of unusual turns, moves an advertising executive turned unwilling detective through everything that could possibly befall a man who accidentally stumbles upon a brother trio of embezzlers, unknown to anyone else, and competes with a couple of thorough thugs for the privilege of doing the nasties in. Brothers are all named Spring, which leads them to believe ad exec's "Three Springs" fashion ad campaign is a blackmail attempt on his part.

Love interest is provided by Stephanie Bachelor, who seems to be slated as Republic's bellwether of the B's, with Adele Mara adding a nice femme fatale touch. Heavies, with which this film is amply stocked, are led by Gregory Gay. Low production expenses become less obvious when backed by class sets and photography which is good, without reaching for special effects.

Miniature Reviews

"Invisible Informer" (Rep). Lightweight mystery chiller for dualers only.

"Postmaster's Daughter" (French). Well-acted but poorly scripted adaptation of Pushkin story for arty houses.

Invisible Informer

Republic release of William J. O'Sullivan production. Features Linda Stirling, William Henry. Directed by Philip Ford. Screenplay, Sherman L. Lowe, from original story by Gerald Drayson Adams; camera, William Bradford; editor, Richard L. Van Enger. Previewed in N. Y., Aug. 16, '46. Running time, 57 MINS.
Eve Rogers..................Linda Stirling
Mike Reagan................William Henry
Marie Ravelle...............Adele Mara
Eric Baylor.................Gerald Mohr
Rosalind Baylor............Peggy Stewart
Eph Shroud.................Tom London
Grandma Shroud............Donia Bussey
Martha Baylor..............Claire DeBrey
David Baylor...............Tristram Coffin
Nick Steele................Charles Lane
Sheriff Ladeau.............Cy Kendall
Jules Ravelle.............Francis McDonald

A mystery chiller, "Invisible Informer" is too lightweight for anything but secondary dual spots. Linda Stirling and William Henry are the top names, which means exhibitors will have to do plenty of selling.

Yarn concerns a private detective agency which probes insurance claims for missing gems, with current case covering a necklace insured for $100,000 which a bankrupt family reports mysteriously missing. Miss Stirling and Henry try to solve the mystery, plus several sudden deaths and a suicide. The heavy eliminates his victims by strangling them or unleashing a vicious police dog on them.

Miss Stirling and Henry do all right as the private snoopers without creating much stir. Their romantic moments are few, with Gerald Mohr, killer and gem thief, spotted in the most torrid love scenes, either with her or Adele Mara, as a hotel clerk. Latter doesn't have much to do but does that exceedingly well.

Sherman L. Loew's screenplay does as well with William Bradford's original as could be done. *Wear.*

Postmaster's Daughter
(FRENCH-MADE)

VOG release of Lux production. Stars Harry Baur; features Jeanine Crispin, Georges Rigaud. Directed by V. Tourjansky. Screenplay, Jacques Companez and Theodore Robert, from novel by Alexander Pushkin; English titles, Harry L. Ober; music, Michel Levine. Running time, 75 MINS.
Virine....................Harry Baur
Dounia...................Jeanine Crispin
Lieut. Andre Minsky......Georges Rigaud
Col. Raditch.............Charles Dechamps
Captain..................Rene Dary
Olga.....................Gina Manes
Lisa.....................Christine Ribes
Doctor ....Sinoe
Stable Boy...............Labry
Businessman ....Paulais

(In French; English Titles)

This film should do well at the arty houses despite a poor adaptation, in which mixed French and Russian temperaments and viewpoints form an underlying thread of confusion running through the story. Late Harry Baur's name should prove a good draw at the highbrow b.o.s. especially in view of reports of his death in a German concentration camp. Film, incidentally, was confiscated by the Nazis.

It's Baur who holds film together with sock thesping throughout as the old postmaster. Acting by others in the cast follows the European standard of top performers usually shackled by light story material. The Pushkin story tells of an obsequious postmaster who runs a way station in Czarist Russia, and his daughter who falls in love with one of the

officers passing through. Officer has been sent by his colonel to effect a "working agreement" with the girl, but has to give up his commission so they can be married. Throughout, the father attempts to win his daughter away because she so resembles his dead wife. Unusual, for Russian stories, is the happy ending.

Camera work is okay, but direction could have added more pace. Fundamental story is obvious enough from pictures and titles, but dialog nuances will probably be missed by those who can't speak French. Pic will not sell in general market.

Miniature Reviews

"Two Years Before the Mast" (Par). Excellent action epic of men against the sea. Surefire b.o.

"No Leave, No Love"- (Songs) (M-G). Surefire combo of Van Johnson pull and Pasternak slickness headed for lush returns.

"If I'm Lucky" (Musical) (20th). Light musical with enough cast flash to sight fair returns.

"Mr. Ace" (Bogeaus - UA). George Raft, Sylvia Sidney in uninteresting tale about femme politicians. B.o. potentials mild.

"Under Nevada Skies" (Songs) (Rep). Clicko Roy Rogers saddler, with fights and songs good for solid grosses.

"Theirs Is the Glory" (GFD). British documentary of Arnhem campaign; dubious as big grosser in U. S.

"The Shadow Returns" (Mono). Trite whodunit for the duals.

"Piccadilly Incident" (Pathe). Anna Neagle in latest Herbert Wilcox British-made production; looks possible U. S. entry.

Two Years Before the Mast

Paramount release of Seton I. Miller production. Stars Alan Ladd, Brian Donlevy, William Bendix, Barry Fitzgerald; features Howard da Silva, Esther Fernandez, Albert Dekker, Darryl Hickman. Directed by John Farrow. Screenplay, Seton I. Miller, George Bruce, based on novel by Richard Henry Dana, Jr.; camera, Ernest Laszlo; special effects, Gordon Jennings, J. Devereaux Jennings; editor, Eda Warren; score, Victor Young. Tradeshown, N. Y., Aug. 22, '46. Running time, 96 MINS.
Charles Stewart...............Alan Ladd
Richard Henry Dana........Brian Donlevy
Amazeen, First Mate......William Bendix
Terence O'Feenaghty......Barry Fitzgerald
Capt. Francis Thompson..Howard da Sylva
Maria Dominguez........Esther Fernandez
Brown.......................Albert Dekker
Foster, Second Mate......Luis Van Rooten
Sam Hooper..............Darryl Hickman
Macklin....................Roman Bohnen
Mr. Gordon Stewart..........Ray Collins
Hayes....................Theodore Newton
Bellamer....................Tom Powers
Garrick...................James Burke
Hansen......................Frank Faylen
Mrs. Gordon Stewart....Kathleen Lockhart
Mercedes.....................Rosa Rey
Don Sebastian............Pedro de Cordoba
Sailor No. 1.................John Roy
Sailor No. 2................Bink Hedberg
Clark, Sailor No. 3.........Ethan Laidlaw
Sailor No. 4.............George Bruggeman
Sailor No. 5...............Clint Derrington
Bobson, Sailor No. 6....Robert F. Kortman
Sailor No. 7................Carl Voss
Sailor No. 8..John P. "Blackie" Whiteford
Sailor No. 9..................Mike Lally
Sailor No. 10.................Joe Palma
Sailor No. 11................Dave Kashner

Paramount has another boxoffice bonanza in "Two Years Before the Mast." Film is probably the best of its kind since Metro's "Mutiny on the Bounty," with direction, acting, production and all the accoutrements expertly blended to make it a can't-miss proposition. There are plenty of exploitation angles for the exhib, in addition to the potent marquee names of probably every male action star on the Par lot, including Alan Ladd, Barry Fitzgerald, Brian Donlevy, William Bendix, etc.

Chief credit for this one belongs to director John Farrow. Only recently discharged from the British and Canadian Navies, Farrow apparently brought much of his ship-learning into his work, and producer Seton I. Miller's choice of him to handle the megging was a wise one. With the emphasis on action throughout, Farrow keeps his cast thesping to the hilt and achieves several little bits of suspense that will keep the audience on the edge of its seats. Scene in which Albert Dekker ruthlessly slices the neck of another sailor in cold blood will have them talking for days. Other deft touches, such as the convulsions another murdered man goes through before kicking off, also reflect Farrow's expert handling.

Although Ladd and the other stars top the cast, it's Howard da Silva, as the pitiless ship's captain, who walks off with the blue ribbon. Da Silva first came into his own as the barkeep in "Lost Weekend" and his work in "Mast" should rate him Academy Award mention. He makes his character portrayal even more cruel than Captain Bligh in "Mutiny."

Rest of cast, from leads to minor bit parts, perform excellently. Ladd does a nice job as the fop who finds his regeneration while fighting to get human treatment for the merchant seamen of that day. Bendix gives a restrained reading to his role as the tough but necessarily-sympathetic first mate, and Fitzgerald adds the comedy touches as the ship's cook. Donlevy, as Richard Henry Dana, the man responsible for attracting Congressional attention to the mariners' plight, and Darryl Hickman, as the stowaway cabin boy, are equally good. Esther Fernandez, in the only important femme role, is adequate.

Pic is strictly fare for the men and, to offset this, the scripters injected a minor love theme. Therein lies the film's only major fault. Writers apparently didn't know what to do with the gal after she first makes her appearance and this part of the story ends abruptly, with the gal giving Ladd only a half-hearted promise that she'll wait for him.

Story, based on Dana's novel, moves rapidly all the way. Ladd, as the worthless scion of a rich merchant, is shanghaied onto one of his father's ships, along with Fitzgerald, Dekker, etc. Da Silva, dishonorably discharged from the Navy, rules his men with an iron hand, flogging them for the slightest offense in his effort to set another record for the trip. Feelings against the captain mount as several of the crew die of scurvy and he still refuses to put in for fresh supplies. Crew finally mutinies, killing the captain, and, instead of fleeing to the Orient, takes a chance on being hanged by sailing the ship back to the U. S. in order to fight their cause through Congress. Book penned by Donlevy, as Dana, gets the necessary attention and, while the men are pardoned, Congress passes the Merchant Seamen's act.

Production mountings all bear out the film's action theme. Camera work by Ernest Laszlo is topnotch and the added special effects by Gordon Jennings and J. Devereaux Jennings include some of the best miniature work yet seen. Suspense will probably keep the audience from paying too much attention to Victor Young's score, but the music is there in the background to heighten that same suspense. ***Stal.***

No Leave, No Love
(SONGS)

Metro release of Joe Pasternak production. Stars Van Johnson, Keenan Wynn, Pat Kirkwod, Edward Arnold; features Guy Lombardo, Marina Koshetz, Marie Wilson, Leon Ames, Selena Royle, Wilson Wood, Vince Barnett, Frank "Sugarchile" Robinson, Xavier Cugat orch. Directed by Charles Martin. Original screenplay, Charles Martin and Leslie Kardos; musical direction, Georgie Stoll; vocal arrangements, Kay Thompson; songs by Thompson-Blaine-Stoll; Freed-Fain; Charles Martin; Fleecie Moore; Morales-Comacho; Kharito - De Lange; editor, Conrad A. Nervig; camera, Harold Rosson, Robert Surtees. Previewed at Loew's 72d St. theatre, N. Y., Aug. 13, '46. Running time, **119 MINS.**

Sgt. Michael Hanlon	Van Johnson
Slinky	Keenan Wynn
Susan Malby Duncan	Pat Kirkwood
Guy Lombardo	Himself
Hobart Canford Stiles	Edward Arnold
Rosalind	Marie Wilson
Colonel Elliott	Leon Ames
Countess Strogoff	Marina Koshetz
Mrs. Hanlon	Selena Royle
Mr. Crawley	Wilson Wood
Ben	Vince Barnett
Boy Piano Player	Frank "Sugarchile" Robinson
Sledgehammer	Walter Sande
Nick	Arthur Walsh
Boy Drummer Specialty	Joey Preston

Xavier Cugat and His Orchestra
The Garcias

Tally on the credit side of the ledger a canny mixture of potent marquee pull led by Van Johnson, Keenan Wynn and Marina Koshetz, a bright new luminary that's here to stay, along with Joe Pasternak's usual slick production values and a covey of gay musical numbers. Then ink the debit half with too much of a trite story and its puerile radio broadcast windup. Tote up both sides, and "No Leave, No Love" still comes out ahead as a hot b.o. pic that's drawn a bead on lush returns.

Merits of the film far outweigh its failings. And the plus side of the ledger gets a real hypo from the gay and winning performance of the unheralded Miss Koshetz. Thoroughly at home as a warbling Russian countess, this new femme star who's the daughter of famed opera diva Nina Koshetz, romps through her comic role lending it the deceptive appearance of pure, casual fun. Her unstudied singing and thesping are solid; her appearance is attractive plus; and when caught by this reviewer, the patrons were audibly loving it.

Tale concerns itself with the carrying-ons of two discharged marines, returned from the South Pacific, and the efforts of a radio singer, Pat Kirkwood, to delay the arrival home of one of the vets, a Congressional medal winner, to marry his girl. Big point in plot complication is that the vet's gal has already spliced to someone else. Singer's tactics are aimed at keeping the returned hero away from home until his mother can arrive to break the news gently.

In the course of the yarn's developments, Johnson playing the medal wearer and Wynn as Slinky, his pal, give Metro a chance to get in its musical pitch via nitery and radio station tours. Comic snarls crop up following Slinky's efforts to corral some easy coin by renting his hotel room to the countess and the radio star's boss, Edward Arnold. It all straightens itself out before fadeout time when Johnson, now in love with the mike songstress, owns up to his sentiments over a major hookup.

Johnson's appeal continues on the same high level that has spelled heaps of coin so far. But the pic doesn't have to lean upon his charm alone. Wynn as the somewhat dumb and lupine soldier pal wines, dines and chases the femmes with rib-tickling fervor. His cavortings with Miss Koshetz and Arnold plus a particularly funny scene in which he luxuriates in a super-bubble bath brighten the film no end.

Miss Kirkwood, piping several numbers, including "All the Time" and "Isn't It Wonderful?" does very nicely opposite Johnson. Arnold, abandoning his usual virile slot, plays cut-and-out comedy in a knowing finished fashion. Sepian moppet Frank "Sugarchile" Robinson polishes off the ivories like an inspired little imp and adds more than a mite to the sum total of entertainment.

A brace of orch renditions are fashioned by Guy Lombardo, who's very OK, and as a final Latin sprinkle to the musical mix, Xavier Cugat's ensemble pours out a liquid broth, "Oye Negra," that's divertingly grooved.

Production mountings, settings and costumes are burnished with the Pasternak-Metro wealth and polish. Aside from a few draggy moments when the pic's length tells on itself, smart direction of Charles Martin rates curtain calls. Musical direction and vocal arrangements are way ahead of norm. Score this one for heavy attendance. *Wit.*

If I'm Lucky
(MUSICAL)

Hollywood, Aug. 26.

Twentieth-Fox release of Bryan Foy production. Stars Vivian Blaine, Perry Como, Harry James, Carmen Miranda; features Phil Silvers. Directed by Lewis Seiler. Screen play, Snag Werris, Robert Ellis, Helen Logan and George Bricker; camera, Glen MacWilliams; editor, Norman Colbert; songs, Josef Myrow, Edgar De Lange; musical director, Emil Newman. Tradeshown Aug. 26, '46. Running time, **78 MINS.**

Linda	Vivian Blaine
Allen Clark	Perry Como
Earl Gordon	Harry James
Michelle O'Toole	Carmen Miranda
Wally	Phil Silvers
Magonnagle	Elgar Buchanan
Conklin	Reed Hadley
Harry James' Music Makers	Themselves
Governor Quilby	Harry Hayden
Gargan	Harry Cheshire
Bixby	William Halligan
Dwyer	Frank Fenton
Gillingwater	Lewis Russell
Secretary	Charles Tannen
Police Captain	Charles Wilson

Average musical that will get selling aid from cast names. Six tunes are spotted, several of which are reprised, and the numbers are embellished to give a neat display. Production backing is good without being lavish. It's all on the light side but with enough weight to amuse modestly.

Perry Como holds the male lead and gets over via his personality and vocals. He wraps up three of the Josef Myrow-Edgar de Lange tunes to good results. Ballads, "If I'm Lucky" and "One More Kiss," are good listening and he also shows well with swingy "One More Vote." Vivian Blaine reprises the title tune twice and works with Carmen Miranda on novelty "Bet Your Bottom Dollar." Latin turns her personality loose on "Jam Session in Brazil," aided by Harry James. Latter also sells trumpet solo. Entire cast vocals "Follow the Band," which is also reprised at the finale.

Plot tells of how group of would-be musicians become ballyhoo outlet for campaigning politician. When the latter defends his political machine, Como is rung in as the candidate for governor and wins the election. Plot is peppered with usual cliches and misunderstandings, plus preachment for the common man and honesty in government.

There's nothing to boast about in the writing but it does serve as a sufficient framework for musical moments. Lewis Seiler's direction sends players through their paces in okay fashion. Phil Silvers, as the band's manager, is in for comedy but doesn't have too much of a chance. Edgar Buchanan, candidate for governor; Reed Hadley and Frank Fenton, crooked politicos, and others of cast are good.

Harry James' Music Makers give smart workout to the music. Bryan Foy's production gives expert blending to the music and story. Lensing, musical direction, etc., measure up. Film features two large production numbers, one a dream sequence for Como's vocals of "One More Vote." Other backs Miranda's "Jam Session" display. *Brog.*

Mr. Ace
(ONE SONG)

United Artists release of Benedict Bogeaus production. Stars George Raft, Sylvia Sidney; features Jerome Cowan, Sid Silvers, Roman Bohnen. Directed by Edwin L. Marin. Original story and screenplay by Fred Finklehoffe; camera, Karl Struss; editor, James Smith; song, "Now and Then," by Sid Silvers, Fred Finklehoffe; score, Heinz Roemheld. Tradeshown N. Y., Aug. 19, '46. Running time, **84 MINS.**

Eddie Ace	George Raft
Margaret Wyndham Chase	Sylvia Sidney
Toomey	Stanley Ridges
Alma	Sara Haden
Peter Craig	Jerome Cowan
Pencil	Sid Silvers
Chase	Alan Edwards
Professor Adams	Roman Bohnen

Here's a picture that's very much ado about nothing. With a good cast topped by George Raft and Sylvia Sidney and some lush sets and other mountings, "Mr. Ace" comes a cropper mostly because of a poor story.

Star billing would rate it a crack at the first-run houses but its boxoffice potential there looks doubtful.

Idea of the story, revolving around an unscrupulous woman politician who gets nominated for mayor but then undergoes a change of heart and withdraws, is a good one. Scripter Fred Finklehoffe, however, failed to take advantage of the idea and turned out a plot holding very little interest. Theme falls flat in the almost corny mentions of "religion," which hits the politician for no apparent reason and causes her to reform. Film goes out of its way to emphasize the dirty groundwork of political bosses and then goes suddenly idealistic without pointing up the reasons for the change.

Cast is capable enough, although the script doesn't give any of them a chance to shine. Miss Sidney makes the politician as believable as possible, while still getting in enough of the teary-eyed glances that have become her trademark. Raft is his usual laconic self as a political machinist, and the love scenes between him and Miss Sidney come off okay. Roman Bohnen tops the supporting cast as an idealistic college professor who backs the femme after her regeneration, and Jerome Cowan does a nice job as her pressagent. Sid Silvers is funny enough but isn't seen enough as Raft's chief lackey.

Story has Miss Sidney coming to make a deal with Raft to help her get nominated, but he turns her down under the belief that women have no place in politics. After getting the nomination when one of Raft's henchmen double-crosses him, she gets "religion" and withdraws. Idea is apparently infectious because Raft also gets the idea of wanting to do good instead of bad. He and the professor line up a new party, sweep the election for Miss Sidney and she and Raft fall into each other's arms for the hoopla ending.

Although the billing spots a new song, "Now and Then," penned by Finklehoffe and Silvers, the tune is sung only once, with the singers spotted so far out of camera-reach they can hardly be seen or heard. Melody is played throughout the film, though, and is catchy.

With the exception of the story, Benedict Bogeaus has done a nice production job on this. Director Edwin L. Marin puts the cast through its paces in acceptable fashion, and Karl Struss demonstrates competent camera technique. *Stal.*

Under Nevada Skies
(SONGS)

Hollywood, Aug. 23.

Republic release of an Edward J. White production. Stars Roy Rogers; features George "Gabby" Hayes, Dale Evans. Directed by Frank McDonald. Screenplay, Paul Gangelin, J. Benton Cheney, from original by M. Coates Webster; camera, William Bradford; music, Dale Butts; editor, Edward Mann; asst. director, Yakima Canutt. Previewed Aug. 23, '46. Running time, **70 MINS.**

Roy Rogers	Roy Rgers
Trigger	Himslf
Gabby Whittaker	George Hayes
Helen Williams	Dale Evans
Arthur Courtney	Douglas Dumbrille
Tom Craig	Leyland Hodgson
Dan Adams	Tristram Coffin
Alberti	Rudolph Anders
Marty Fields	LeRoy Mason
LeBlarc	George Lynn
Flying Eagle	George J. Lewis
Hoffman	Tom Quinn

Bob Nolan and Sons of the Pioneers

Fast-paced westuner with plenty of gunfights and rousing range action, this is one of Roy Rogers' better saddle offerings, solid mystery story certain to hold interest both of juve and adult audiences. Six songs are interwoven into plot, with star and Dale Evans delivering strongly on musical end and George "Gabby"

Hayes up to his customary brand of seasoned comedy.

Yarn concerns Rogers tracking down murderer of his friend, Leyland Hodgson, and recovery of a jeweled crest which contains secretly a map pointing to location of pitchblende deposit, knowledge of which will enable any nation to use it for uranium. Writers don't bother to explain who killed victim, but they've contrived neat bit of action in leading up to climax, with Rogers heading band of Indians in swooping down on heavies who have crest.

Frank McDonald's direction maintains logical motivation of plot and he keeps his characters ever on the move. Cast without exception enact parts well, with Rogers in there with fists swinging and guns blazing. Dale Evans pretty as usual as she warbles melodically, and Hayes effective with his comedy performance. Edward J. White's production values are there, too. Song numbers include the title song, "Anytime That I'm With You," "Ne-hah-nee," "I Want to Go West," and "Sea Goin' Cowboy."

Theirs Is the Glory

(Documentary)
BRITISH-MADE

London, Aug. 15.

General Film Distributors' production and release. At Leicester Square theatre. Running time, **82 MINS.**

This is a war documentary to end all war films. Made at Arnhem, by the boys who actually took part in that attack on the memorable Sept. 17, 1944, it depicts the struggles, tribulations and misery encountered by these unfortunate English and Amer-icans in their tragic attempt to hold that vital Arnhem Bridge.

Picture gives a clear idea of the incidents which led to the abandonment of this strategic position at a loss of 8,000 men out of 10,000 because reinforcements couldn't get through. Naturally it's the ordinary Tommy who gets away with the acting honors, with the brasshats jarring with their Oxford drawl.

Situations are not entirely devoid of comedy, with real guffaws resulting even in the actual battle scenes.

Film is being distributed by General Film Distributors and produced by Castleton Knight, who specializes in this type of picture. It was directed by Brian Desmond Hurst, with no credit given anyone, something of a novelty in itself. This required ten weeks to make, cost only about $320,000.

Direction and lensing are both high. *Rege.*

The Shadow Returns

Monogram release of Joe Kaufman (Lou Brock) production. Features Kane Richmond, Barbara Reed. Directed by Phil Rosen. Screenplay, George Callahan, based on Shadow Magazine stories; camera, William Sickner; editor, Ace Herman. At Strand, Brooklyn, dual, week Aug. 24, '46. Running time, **61 MINS.**

Lamont Cranston	Kane Richmond
Margo Lane	Barbara Reed
Shevvie	Tom Dugan
Inspector Cardona	Joseph Crehan
Commissioner Weston	Pierre Watkin
Charles Frobay	Robert Emmett Keane
Michael Hasdon	Frank Reicher
William Monk	Lester Dorr
Lenore Jessup	Rebel Randall
Breck & Yomans	Emmett Vogan
Robert Buell	Sherry Hall
John Adams	Cyril Delevanti

An unexciting whodunit, "The Shadow Returns" is a minor dualer.

Yarn deals with missing jewels spirited from an opened grave. Gendarmes investigate amid the usual flickering lights and eerie shadows. Meanwhile several suspects are mysteriously rubbed out, baffling Inspector Cardona who's taunted from time to time by The Shadow (Kane Richmond), due to his inability to make any progress on the case. Later The Shadow reveals the jewels actually contain a revolutionary plastic formula and, collaborating with sleuths, eventually collars the culprit.

Plot, on the whole, was accorded frequent yawns by the audience when caught. Richmond, as The Shadow, acquits himself as best he can under circumstances; Barbara Reed, his girl Friday, is on hand mostly for decorative purposes, while Tom Dugan contributes some fair comedy relief as The Shadow's chauffeur. Joseph Crehan is an okay inspector.

Production values are in keeping with the meager budget. Phil Rosen directed at a standard pace and George Callahan's original screenplay faithfully followed the cliches present in similar minor whodunits.

Piccadilly Incident

(BRITISH-MADE)

London, Aug. 23.

Pathe Pictures release of Associated British Pictures film. Stars Anna Neagle, Michael Wilding. Directed by Herbert Wilcox. Screenplay by Florence Tranter. Camera, Bryan Langley, Max Greene. Previewed at private theatre, London. Running time, **100 MINS.**

Diana Fraser	Anna Neagle
Captain Alan Pearson	Michael Wilding
Joan Draper	Frances Mercer
Virginia Pearson	Coral Browne
Sir Charles Pearson	A. E. Matthews
Bill Weston	Michael Laurence
Judd	Edward Rigby
Sally Benton	Brenda Bruce
Mrs. Milligan	Maire O'Neill
Sam	Leslie Dwyer

Herbert Wilcox has used a little-known flaw in British legal procedure as the basis for his latest film. If a man, thinking his wife dead, marries again, the child of the marriage will be illegitimate beyond all redress should his first wife prove not to have died after all. That's what the law says in Britain.

According to Wilcox, diving into musty records, some 200 cases of this kind exist at present. Question here of course, is whether one case can be made effective as screen fare. It appears to have possibilities in U. S. because of Anna Neagle - Herbert Wilcox combo.

Picture shows a judge giving judgment on a case and then goes into a flashback to tell the main story. A Wren and a Marine meet by chance in an air raid. They get married. Wren goes overseas, is posted as missing. After three years Marine marries again and a child is born.

Then the first wife returns, her death being a mistake. Wife No. 1, confronted by wife No. 2 plus a child, dies in an air raid.

After a good deal of to do with her pals on a desert island, Anna Neagle, as the Wren, emerges with a first-rate piece of dramatic acting. Romantic scenes with goodlooker Michael Wilding are well handled, though dialog is conventional and leaves the problem unsolved. Notwithstanding some scenes of Adam-and-Eve temptation on the island and the usual Wilcox polish, story could have been improved with a general tightening-up. Length of picture tends to handicap the suspense.

Film may do well because of its provocative theme, the pull of the Anna Neagle-Michael Wilcox team and an admirable all-around cast. *Ebet.*

Miniature Reviews

"3 Little Girls in Blue" (Musical) (20th). Spritely costume musical with eye appeal. Good b.o. returns slated.

"Gallant Bess" (Color) (MG). Unusual yarn based on true-life incident concerning horse found on a Pacific island; OK b.o.

"I've Always Loved You" (Borzage - Rep). Technicolor and musical classics will have to carry this one.

"London Town" (Eagle-Lion) (Color; Songs). Wesley Ruggles' British production misses fire with all-English cast.

"Little Miss Big" (U) (One Song) Schmaltzy tear-jerker without much b.o. pull. Femme trade stuff.

3 Little Girls in Blue

(MUSICAL—COLOR)

Hollywood, Sept. 3.

20th-Fox release of Mack Gordon production. Stars June Haver, George Montgomery, Vivian Blaine, Celeste Holm, Vera-Ellen, Frank Latimore; features Charles Smith. Directed by Bruce Humberstone. Screenplay, Valentine Davies; adapted by Brown Holmes, Lynn Starling, Robert Ellis and Helen Logan from play by Stephen Powys; camera (Technicolor), Ernest Palmer; songs, Mack Gordon and Josef Myrow, Harry Warren; arrangements, Charles Henderson; orchestration, Maurice de Packh and Edward Powell; music, Alfred Newman; dances, Seymour Felix; ballets, Babe Pearce; editor, Barbara McLean. Tradeshown Sept. 3, '46. Running time, **91 MINS.**

Pam	June Haver
Van Damm Smith	George Montgomery
Liz	Vivian Blaine
Miriam	Celeste Holm
Myra	Vera-Ellen
Steve	Frank Latimore
Mike	Charles Smith
Hoskins	Charles Halton
Mammy	Ruby Dandridge
Colonel	Thurston Hall
Ben	Clinton Rosemond
Head Clerk	William Forrest, Jr.
Maid	Theresa Harris

Pleasant musical filmfare with extra value of color. A costumer, "3 Little Girls in Blue" marks producer debut of tunesmith Mack Gordon. It's a good first try, making excellent use of stock musical ingredients for general entertainment. **Boxoffice prospects shape up well for majority situations. Score works in eight tunes, reprising three of them, and one lavish production number. Familiar star names add marquee lustre to aid the selling.**

Score tees off with hillbilly arrangement of title tune and number is later reprised by June Haver, Vivian Blaine and Vera-Ellen. Trio also handles "A Farmer's Life Is a Very Merry Life" and "On the Boardwalk," latter being score's best. Torchy "Somewhere in the Night" is vocaled by Miss Blaine, and Celeste Holm does a comic version of "Always a Lady." Vera-Ellen snares larger musical moments, handling "I Like Mike" plus a ballet specialty to tune, and also "You Make Me Feel So Young," background for lavish kiddie production piece. Tune also gets reprise at finale. All voices are lightweight but carry off numbers by Mack Gordon, Josef Myrow and Harry Warren acceptably.

Plot concerns three country girls who take a small inheritance and dash to Atlantic City to snare some millionaire husbands. One plays a rich girl while the two sisters serve as secretary and maid, respectively. They all get their men, but only one is rich. Background for the romantic chase is brilliantly displayed in the lensing. Particularly outstanding for hues are the Maryland fox-hunt scenes when chase moves south. Camera handling by Ernest Palmer adds measurably to entertainment values.

Bruce Humberstone's direction puts the players through their paces smartly to get best from the material in the Valentine Davies script. Yarn was adapted from a play by Stephen Powys by Brown Holmes, Lynn Starling and Robert Ellis and Helen Logan. George Montgomery and Frank Latimore show up well as male targets for June Haver and Vivian Blaine. Charles Smith has his good moments as Vera-Ellen's vis-a-vis, and Celeste Holm sharpens up some comedy scenes as a man-crazy southern girl.

Gordon's production guidance has injected a bit of everything to keep appeal as broad as possible. Pace is fast, appurtenances of first order. Seymour Felix staged dances and Babe Pearce the ballet. Costuming of the period piece is on the elegant side as are other decorations. *Brog.*

Gallant Bess

(COLOR)

Hollywood, Sept. 2.

Metro release of Harry Rapf production. Features Marshall Thompson, George Tobias, Clem Bevans "Bess" (equine). Directed by Andrew Marton. Original story and screenplay, Jeanne Bartlett; suggested by incident as told by Lt. Marvin Park, USNR; camera (Cinecolor), John W. Boyle; music, Rudolph G. Kopp; editor, Harry Komer. Tradeshown Aug. 29, '46. Running time, **99 MINS.**

Tex	Marshall Thompson
Lug	George Tobias
Smitty	Clem Bevans
Lt. Bridgeman	Donald Curtis
Johnny	Murray Alper
Mike	Wally Cassell
Harry	Jim Davis
C.P.O.	Chill Wills
"Shorty"	John Burford
Oakie	Johnny Bond
"Bess"	

"Gallant Bess" offers considerable in the way of entertainment, assuring healthy grosses. It's a tihter, with plot developed from World War II incident of a Seabee finding a horse on a small Pacific island. There's some battle action, but it doesn't enter in until latter half of film and is kept to a minimum. B.o. factors are the horsey plot and color, film marking first major production in Cinecolor. Strong points balance overlength and sometimes maudlin development. Tear-jerker elements are well-handled by Harry Rapf's production guidance, making for showmanly job all around. Cast is uniformly good but names aren't stout enough to be a selling aid.

Yarn is essentially story of a boy's love for his horse, a beautiful mare named Bess. First half deals with his attempts to launch a stock ranch with the mare. Youngster is fast-talked into joining the Seabees, goes off to the wars leaving his horse in foal. Mare dies, kid's broken up but snaps out of it when he finds another horse on the Pacific isle. Considerable color concerning the Seabee's work is injected as background for story of how horse brings Seabee group good luck. Script never pretends to be anything but a tear-jerker, playing it straight throughout. Because of that it develops plenty of interest. Jeanne Bartlett scripted from the Seabee incident as told by Lt. Marvin Park, USNR.

Andrew Marton's directorial guidance is effective in keeping central theme in the foreground and shows the players and the horse to best advantage. Marshall Thompson is the young male lead, doing clever work. George Tobias is another who makes his footage count importantly. A standout is the terse, mountain storekeeper character performed by Clem Bevans. Donald Curtis, Murray Alper, Wally Cassell, Jim Davis, John Burford and Johnny Bond are good. Chill Wills gives a lift to single spot as fast-talking recruiting C.P.O. who dazes Thompson with a glib, flagwaving spiel.

Practically all of film is outdoors and color is easy on the eyes with perfectly natural hues. There's none of the artificial brilliance of most color films. Credit for ace lensing is garnered by John W. Boyle. Music score, montages, etc., measure up, but editing could have been more concise in clipping unneeded footage.

Brog.

I've Always Loved You

(COLOR; WITH MUSIC)

Republic release of Frank Borzage production (Lew Borzage assoc. prod.). Directed by Frank Borzage. Features Philip Dorn, Catherine McLeod, Wm. Carter, Maria Ouspenskaya. Screenplay, Borden Chase, from his own story; piano recordings by Arthur Rubenstein; camera (Technicolor), Tony Gaudio; special effects, Howard & Theodore Lydecker; music by Rachmaninoff, Chopin, Beethoven, Mendelssohn, Wagner, Bach, conducted by Walter Scharf; editor, Richard L. Van Enger. Tradeshown N. Y. Aug. 29, '46. Running time 117 MINS.

Leopold Goronoff..............Philip Dorn
Myra Hassman...........Catherine McLeod
George Sampter.............William Carter
Madame Goronoff......Maria Ouspenskaya
Frederick Hassman..........Felix Bressart
Nicholas.........................Fritz Feld
Mrs. Sampter..........Elizabeth Patterson
Porky at Seventeen.........Vanessa Brown
Michael Severin.............Lewis Howard
Senorita Fortaleza.............Adele Mara
Porgy at Five.............Gloria Donovan
Redhead................Stephanie Bachelor
Mrs. Blythe..............Cora Witherspoon

Frank Borzage's romance of a couple of longhair personalities will have to rely on the classical music and the Technicolor for best impact. It's a disappointing Technicolor tee-off for Republic and Borzage's first independent package for Republic. The color and the cavalcade of Rachmaninoff, Chopin, Beethoven, Mendelssohn, Wagner and Bach—plus the Steinway virtuosity of Artur Rubinstein, who is title-billed as "the world's greatest pianist"—will be the most positive boxoffice factors. Lack of cast names headed by Philip Dorn and Catherine McLeod, is another marquee factor.

The story is thin, trite and frequently implausible. Whatever scenarist Borden Chase's original American magazine story, "Concerto," may have been in published form, it doesn't come off in celluloid. It is dragged out for two hours, almost a biographical cavalcade of the loves of "the maestro," played by Dorn, and his pupil, Miss McLeod. A second generation is represented by Vanessa Brown who, at 17, essays a Carnegie Hall recital with the same Rachmaninoff 2d Piano Concerto as the piece-de-resistance which proved the musico-climactic breach between her mother and the maestro a generation back.

The classical jam session is such that Dorn and Miss McLeod are almost constantly at the Steinway. And while the off-screen piano virtuosity of Artur Rubinstein is highly impressive, it's overdoing a good thing. Not counting, of course, the question of classical music's appeal to the average film fan. However, that's not the hazard it was several years ago in light of the "middle-brow music" conditioning of Jose Iturbi, with his boogie-woogie palliative in between legitimate concertizing; and the radio-conditioned "challenge" of the Wagnerian tenor, Lauritz Melchior, in his radio sorties versus Sinatra, and the like. Not forgetting the pioneering done by the Chopin saga, "A Song to Remember" (Columbia), a season back.

None the less, there is an over-abundance of classicism in this score, underlined by a story which is repetitive and trite. Lack of marquee names is a notable factor, most familiar faces being the supporting Felix Bressart, Maria Ouspenskaya, Fritz Feld and Elizabeth Patterson.

Borzage relied on new faces for his leads, with the exception of the Dutch-born Dorn, who is unconvincing as the awesome maestro. That goes for Miss McLeod, who looks better as a matured woman than as the starry-eyed pupil; while William Carter is a rather indeterminate juvenile. That finale, when Miss McLeod breaks off in her triumphant Carnegie Hall interpretation of the Rachmaninoff Concerto—which is the love theme of the film—and goes to her husband's (Carter) arms, spurning the lady-killing Dorn, adds to the plot's shortcomings.

Dialog is frequently inane, sounding more like a conversational Baedeker as Dorn reels off his scenes of past triumphs; interspersed with impulsive commands to his long-suffering but faithful aide (Fritz Feld) to "get me a concert in Rio," or "we go to Carnegie Hall," and the like, without plausibility of booking commitments. No matter how potent is this celluloid maestro's boxoffice, even Toscanini must take cognizance of dates and routes.

Production otherwise is ultra. The color is beautiful and the romantic direction sometimes in Borzage's most persuasive vis-a-vis manner, but fundamentally the script is against them. Walter Scharf rates a kudo for his musical scoring.

Abel.

London Town

(COLOR; SONGS)

London, Aug. 30.

Eagle-Lion (J. Arthur Rank) release of Wesley Ruggles production. Stars Sid Field; features Great Gynt, Sonnie Hale, Tessie O'Shea, Claude Hulbert, Mary Clare, Petula Clark, Kay Kendall. Directed by Ruggles. Screenplay, Elliot Paul and Sig Herzig, from original by Ruggles; songs, Jimmy van Heusen and Johnny Burke; camera, Erwin Hillier and Harold Hyson. At Leicester Square theatre, London, Aug. 29, '46. Running time, 120 MINS.

Jerry Sanford.......................Sid Field
Mrs. Barry.........................Greta Gynt
Peggy...........................Petula Clark
Patsy...........................Kay Kendall
Charlie..........................Sonnie Hale
Belgrave.....................Claude Hulbert
Mrs. Gates.......................Mary Clare
Tessie O'Shea.................Tessie O'Shea
George......................Jerry Desmonde
Paula............................Beryl Davis
Bill............................Scotty McHarg
Mike...............................W. G. Fay
Stage Manager...............Reginald Purdell

Wesley Ruggles has spared no expense, time or trouble on this big-budgeter, which opens, according to the new credits for Rank productions, with "Arthur Rank Presents" a yard high. It serves as the film introduction of the famous British variety comic, Sid Field, with various other new faces, and its all-out emphasis on sex appeal, clothes and showmanship, slate it as a big money-spinner in the key spots. But for a budget this size (reportedly $2,600,000), and for the year it took in production, it is a misfire. Its American appeal would lie in the Yank names associated with the production.

Opening shows Field, as Jerry, smalltime performer seeking the big-time in London with his small daughter, Peggy, played by a 15-year-old newcomer, Petula Clark.

Jerry is offered a fat comedy part by the sleek Mrs. Barry (Greta Gynt), producer of the "London Town" show, but finds himself assigned, instead, as understudy to Charlie, the real comic, who is an obvious ham and always ill. Some neat comedy touches arise from the traditional jealousy of star and understudy, and when, by means of a trick played on him by young Peggy, Charlie misses the show, Jerry goes on and scores the usual big success. The story, such as it is, fades out in favor of dazzling scenes, vocal acts, production numbers and the brilliant fooling of Field with his dressy stooge, Jerry Desmonde.

The film concentrates on eye appeal. Opening with a dream sequence, with Fields sailing over roofs to fame, it proceeds to a spacious production number of love among the daffodils in which the color is notably good, as it is throughout the picture. It is followed by massive scenes of revue, with a profusion of girls in vast, shiny interiors, a long boating sequence on the Thames, four acts which made the Field name in the late George Black's revue, "Strike a New Note," and a handsome finale on Hampstead Heath, with the Pearly Kings doing their traditional stuff in song and dance among the crowds.

Field should certainly register in a big way in America. He has remarkable gifts of mime, reminding one of Chaplin. His Cockney creation of Slosher Green, the immortal Londoner with hunched shoulders and outside overcoat, is great eccentric fooling. He uses a plummy voice with extraordinary effect, his vitality is amazing, and he grabs the attention instantly by his mastery of the comic medium and knowledge of audience reaction. He is supported by Greta Gynt, Kay Kendall (a good-looking newcomer and grand-daughter of the famous Marie Kendall), Tessie O'Shea, Sophie Hale, Claude Hulbert and Mary Clare. But none of them, except Miss O'Shea, have parts which add up to anything. Claude Hulbert has brilliant flashes of comedy from time to time. Beryl Davis, crooner, has a few dullish lyrics.

Miss O'Shea, whose two-ton avoirdupois is well known here from vaude, is given a good opening spot and winds up with a smashing cockney dance with Field and the Pearlies. Her tonnage brings some big laughs. Centre of the glamor are the Dozen and One Girls of London Town, a luscious lot, of whom Miss Kendall is one. They are seen in constant effusions of color but their voices are mediocre in the extreme, and most of their production numbers run on to the point of tedium.

Treatment of the film is thoroughly American, forcing the question why it should have been made in Britain at all. In every respect it apes the American model, and London, as the London Times points out, becomes a suburb of Hollywood. Most surprising of all is the quality of the musical items, which fail every time to stun the ear with haunting hits and lack good voices throughout.

Film had a splash premiere at the Leicester Square theatre, to which the Prime Minister and many other notables were invited, and was followed by a party at the Savoy. "London Town" is set for a four weeks' run.

Ebet.

Little Miss Big

(ONE SONG)

Universal release of Marshall Grant (Stanley Rubin) production. Stars Fay Holden, Frank McHugh; features Beverly Simmons, Dorothy Morris, Fred Brady. Directed by Erle C. Kenton. Screenplay, Erna Lazarus, rom story by Harry H. Poppe, Chester Beecroft, Mary Marlind; camera, Paul Ivano; music, H. J. Salter; asst. director, Charles S. Gould; editor, Russell Schoengarth. Tradeshown N. Y., Aug. 28, '46. Running time, 60 MINS.

Nancy Bryan.............Beverly Simmons
Mary Jane Baxter............Fay Holden
Charlie Bryan...............Frank McHugh
Eddie Martin...................Fred Prady
Kathy Bryan................Dorothy Morris
Father Lennergan............Milburn Stone
Wilfred Elliott...........Samuel S. Hinds
Sanford Baxter..............John Eldredge
Duncan.................Houseley Stevenson
Clancy...............................Jeff York
Ellen........................Peggy Webber
Detective Lieutenant.............Jim Nolan

Femme and family trade ought to eat this one up, with its lightweight story and sugary tale. With no marquee value, film will be held to seconary situations as a rider to bigger name product, but it should do fairly well, with women and children first at the boxoffice.

Care in mounting "Little Miss Big" is obvious from sets and other accoutrements. Especially good are mid-Victorian furnishings surrounding Fay Holden as a crochety old lady. Script and direction not up to this standard, however, and picture limps in several spots.

Story concerns a fabulously wealthy but ill-tempered old woman whose wastrel nephew, John Eldredge, schemes to have her put away in an insane asylum because of her love for her dog to make the fortune available to him. She escapes and is taken in by a poor barber's family who eventually get in and out of trouble for harboring her from the police. A new hearing proves her mentally okay and the barber's (Frank McHugh) family lives wealthily ever after.

Scenario and direction are strictly pedestrian, with opportunities for injection of color or laughs missed for the most part. McHugh underplays his few comic lines smartly, but in a couple of instances seems a little embarrassed by what he has to handle. Miss Holden does a trouper's job with her part, but did look a little incongruous climbing out of the nuthouse window on a sheet. Dorothy Morris and Fred Brady as the love interests are fair.

Erle Kenton's direction stalls in a couple of sequences; especially one in which the old matriarch is telling of a lost love while fingering "Peter, Peter, Pumpkin Eater" on the piano. This particular scene is signicant, because it's indicative of the entire film. Something always seems about to happen, but never does. Title refers to little sister Beverly Simmons who is supposed to reform Miss Holden, but has a tough time doing it with a weakly written part.

Foreign Films

"Tombe Du Ciel" ("Dropped from Heaven") (FRENCH). C.C.F.C. release of Societe Francaise de Cinematographie production; directed by E. E. Reinert; stars Claude Dauphin; features Jacqueline Gauthier, Gisele Pascal, Ouvrard; screenplay, Gerard Carlier. Reviewed in Paris. Running time, 100 MINS.

Although made for a reported cost of less than $120,000, this looks like a nice grosser in France because it gets plenty of laughs. Looks more like worth remaking than dubbing for U. S. Film shows a touring orchestra of four boys and a girl stranded on a country farm. They decided to break up the band but hold a farewell dinner at which the boys get drunk. All Claude Dauphin can remember later is that he spent the night in the same hayloft as the girl. Up to this point picture is so badly made it looks amateurish. Balance of story contains some brisk comedy passages built around Dauphin, the girl and a baby, which he is led to believe is his.

Maxi.

Miniature Reviews

"Cloak and Dagger" (WB). Spy melodrama, with Gary Cooper name to sell O. S. S. plot. Initial U. S. Pic for WB release.

"Bachelor's Daughters" (Songs) (UA). Good cast in entertaining farce; good boxoffice.

"The Thrill of Brazil" (Songs) (Col). Keenan Wynn, Evelyn Keyes in fair musical.

"Gallant Journey" (Col). Disappointing bio of an airplane pioneer; keyed for only moderate grosses.

"Her Sister's Secret" (PRC). Fair drama with plenty of femme appeal.

"The Inner Circle" (Rep). Minor whodunit slotted for the dualers.

"Little Iodine" (UA). Program comedy based on comic strip character okay for release intentions and family trade.

Cloak and Dagger

Hollywood, Sep. 5.

Warners release of Milton Sperling (United States Pictures) production. Stars Gary Cooper, Lilli Palmer; features Robert Alda, Vladimir Sokoloff, J. Edward Bromberg, Marjorie Hoshelle, Ludwig Stossel, Helene Thimig, Dan Seymour, Marc Lawrence. Directed by Fritz Lang. Screenplay, Albert Maltz, Ring Lardner, Jr.; original story, Boris Ingster, John Larkin; suggested by the book by Corey Ford and Alastair MacBain; camera, Sol Polito; editor, Christian Nyby; music, Max Steiner. Tradeshown L. A., Sept.4, '46. Running time, **105 MINS.**

Prof. Alvah Jesper....................Gary Cooper
Pinkie....................Robert Alda
Polda....................Vladimir Sokoloff
Trenk....................J. Edward Bromberg
Ann Dawson....................Marjorie Hoshelle
The German....................Ludwig Stossel
Katerin Lodor....................Helene Thimig
Marsoli....................Dan Seymour
Luigi....................Marc Lawrence
Col. Walsh....................James Flavin
The Englishman....................Pat O'Moore
Erich....................Charles Marsh
Introducing Lilli Palmer

This tale of the O.S.S. and its undercover work during the war serves as kickoff production for U. S. Pictures. Despite boxoffice value of Gary Cooper's name, film is the usual cops-and-robbers story. It will grab handsome returns, nevertheless, due to Cooper draw. Physical production furnished by Milton Sperling gives action good background. Fritz Lang's direction manages suspense and several top moments of gripping dramatic conflict, but otherwise fails to rise to sock levels.

Cooper is seen as atomic scientist drafted by O.S.S. to enter first Switzerland and then Italy just prior to close of the war to get a line on Nazi atomic developments. He encounters the usual femme spy in Switzerland, gets out of that episode with whole skin but only after death of Austrian scientist he was contacting, and then moves on to Italy and romance with an Italian partisan who is assigned to aid him contact a Nazi-held scientist. Film ends with Cooper's promise to return to his Italian love after the war is over but value of his mission is never clearly shown in the development of the Albert Maltz-Ring Lardner, Jr., script as filmed.

Cooper fits requirements of his role, turning in his usual topnotch job. A high moment of thrill is his hand-to-hand, silent battle with Marc Lawrence, Nazi agent, in an Italian hallway. It's one of the few top sequences. Film introduces Lilli Palmer, foreign actress, as Cooper's romance, and her performance promises bright Hollywood future. Robert Alda, Cooper's partisan guide, does excellently, as do Vladimir Sokoloff, J. Edward Bromberg, Marjorie Hoshelle, femme spy, Helene Thimig, Dan Seymour, Marc Lawrence and others.

Sperling's production offers good commercial possibilities at the boxoffice without rising above usual thriller level. Sol Polito's camera work is expert in furthering action and other credits are craftsmanly.

Brog.

The Bachelor's Daughters

(SONGS)

United Artists release of Andrew Stone production. Stars Gail Russell, Ann Dvorak, Claire Trevor, Adolphe Menjou; features Jane Wyatt, Billie Burke, Damian O'Flynn, John Whitney, Eugene List. Directed by Andrew Stone from original screenplay by Stone; asst. director, Aaron Rosenberg; camera, Theodore Sparkuhl; editor, Duncan Mansfield; songs, Fred Spielman, Kermit Goell, Jack Lawrence, Irving Drutman. Previewed N. Y., Sept. 6, '46. Running time, **88 MINS.**

Eileen....................Gail Russell
Cynthia....................Claire Trevor
Terry....................Ann Dvorak
Mr. Moody....................Adolphe Menjou
Molly....................Billie Burke
Marta....................Jane Wyatt
Schuyler Johnson....................Eugene List
Miller....................Damian O'Flynn
Bruce Farrington....................John Whitney
Dillon....................Russell Hicks
Dr. Johnson....................Earle Hodgins
Mrs. Johnson....................Madge Crane
Mr. Stapp....................Bill Kennedy
Mr. Johnson....................Richard Hageman
Dancer....................Igor Diega
Bill Cotter....................Clayton Moore

This Cinderella tale about four department store salesgirls who decide to put on a front to win rich hubbies is filled with expected implausibilities, but under Andrew Stone's deft production-direction (he also dreamed up the yarn), "The Bachelor's Daughters" jells nicely.

Film turns out swift-moving entertainment, with the exhibitor's toughest task the job of convincing his patrons they should see it. Marquee lure obviously is solid if unspectacular. Exhibs additionally have the name of Eugene List, concert pianist, who is okay in this, his first picture.

Story does nicely in showing the transition of Adolphe Menjou from the fussy, irritable male into the "father" of the family who's as much interested in seeing the girls win their men as they are themselves. Billie Burke becomes pseudo-mother of the tribe.

It's to Stone's credit that he has made this such effective entertainment, that he has not been prone to gag it up too much and that interest is so well-sustained in such an artificial setup.

List does surprisingly well in the slight acting role but naturally cleans up with his piano solos. Producers smartly have introed these into the plot without interfering or making dull spots. Miss Dvorak ballads in fine shape the two original tunes, "Where's My Heart?" and "Twilight Song," neither especially noteworthy, however.

Wear.

The Thrill of Brazil

(MUSICAL)

Columbia release of Sidney Biddell production. Stars Evelyn Keyes, Keenan Wynn, Ann Miller; features Allyn Joslyn, Tito Guizar, Veloz & Yolanda, Enric Madriguera orch. Directed by S. Sylvan Simon. Screenplay, Allen Rivkin, Harry Clork, Devery Freeman, camera, Charles Lawton, Jr.; editor, Charles Nelson; dances, Eugene Loring, Nick Castle; songs, Allan Roberts-Doris Fisher, Raphael Duchesne, Enric Madriguera-Albert Gamse. At Loew's State, N. Y., week Sept. 5, '46. Running time, **90 MINS.**

Vicki Dean....................Evelyn Keyes
Steve Farraugh....................Keenan Wynn
Linda Lorens....................Ann Miller
John Harbour....................Allyn Joslyn
Tito Guizar....................Himself
Veloz and Yolanda....................Themselves
Ludwig Kriegspiel....................Felix Bressart
Irkie Bowers....................Sid Tomack
Luiz....................Eugene Borden
Enric Madriguera Orchestra

Columbia enlisted the Metro lot for this one, borrowing Keenan Wynn and director S. Sylvan Simon to add to its list of regulars. Despite the additional names, however, "The Thrill of Brazil" stacks up as a so-so item. Pic has several good production numbers interspersed with a highly implausible story and a mess of oversophisticated dialog. It's an okay top dualer but first run exhibs will have to plug it to make it stand up alone.

Unlike most other musicals, in which the story stands merely as a framework on which to string the songs, producer Sidney Biddell apparently tried the novel experiment this time of subordinating his production numbers to the tale. He failed to achieve a happy medium. Story, revolving around the antics of an American theatrical impresario in Brazil and his attempts to win back his almost-divorced wife, is funny enough but too improbable. In addition, scripters Allen Rivkin, Harry Clork and Devery Freeman dressed up the plot with a bunch of original gag lines that follow one another in too rapid succession to have much sock effect. They emerge as cute rather than funny.

Cast, on the whole, is good. Wynn does a nice job as the impresario, getting as much as possible out of his lines and the situation comedy. Evelyn Keyes shows heretofore unrevealed talents as a comedienne as Wynn's estranged wife, backing him up effectively. Ann Miller is a superb tapster but no great actress, and the same can be said of Tito Guizar and his singing. Allyn Joslyn adds to the comedy as Miss Keyes' new boy friend, and Felix Bressart and Sid Tomack, in supporting roles, turn in some excellent bits.

Best song, and the one around which the best production is weaved, is "Man Is Brother to a Mule," sung by Ann Miller in a wicked hipshaking routine. Others, including the title song and "Custom House," are okay show tunes but have little chance of catching on. Latin music, including Guizar's rendition of "Linda Mujer" and Enric Madriguera's "Minute Samba," should go over with the rhumba crowd, although staging of the latter is a direct facsimile of the way Chopin's "Minute Waltz" has hit the screen in previous films.

Eugene Loring and Nick Castle, with a nice assist from the sets designed by James M. Crowe and Robert Priestley, get some fine three-dimensional effects in the production numbers. Camera work by Charles Lawton, Jr., is almost uniformly tops. Rich production mountings indicate that Biddell sank more than a medium-sized budget into the film.

Stal.

Gallant Journey

Columbia release of William A. Wellman production, directed by Wellman. Stars Glenn Ford, Janet Blair; features Charles Ruggles, Henry Travers, Jimmy Lloyd; Original screenplay, Byron Morgan, Wellman; score, Marlin Skiles; camera, Burnett Guffey, George B. Meehan, Jr., Elmer Dyer; editor, Al Clark. Previewed N. Y., Sept. 3, '46. Running time, **86 MINS.**

John Montgomery....................Glenn Ford
Regina Cleary....................Janet Blair
Jim Montgomery....................Charlie Ruggles
Thomas Logan....................Henry Travers
Dan Mahoney....................Jimmy Lloyd
Father Ball....................Charles Kemper
Father Kenton....................Arthur Shields
Zachary Montgomery....Willard Robertson
Mrs. Montgomery....................Selena Royle
Jim Montgomery (as boy).Robert DeHaven
Jim Logan....................Loren Tindall
John Logan....................Byron Morgan
Mrs. Logan....................Eula Morgan
Raymond Walker....................Michael Towne
Tony Dondaro....................Paul Marion
Cornelius Rheinlander......Henry Rowland
Dick Ball (boy)....................Robert Hoover
"Peacock" Fox....................Paul E. Burns
Pedro Lopez....................Chis-Pin Martin
Juan Morales....................Fernando Alvarado
Tom....................Bobby Cooper
Hep....................Rudy Wissler
Cutty....................Tommy Cook
Sharkey....................Buddy Swan
Snort....................Conrad Binyon

This is a slow, sentimental story about a comparative unknown, John J. Montgomery, who pioneered in designing and experimenting on airplanes. Story has been treated stodgily, with its dramatic possibilities insufficiently realized, so that it isn't likely to offset lack of familiarity with the person involved. And marquee names won't be strong enough to make film more than a moderate grosser.

Film is a disappointing effort by William A. Wellman, who here bit off too much as producer, director and co-scripter. Production has a mawkish quality, with false touches of sentiment throughout. Dialog is sometimes corny and in a few places patently anachronistic. Humor is of a stilted kind, and at times of questionable taste. Acting, too, is only fair, with Glenn Ford a little wooden as the inventor and Janet Blair too frenzied as his inspiration. Supporting cast is only fair.

Story tells the bitter life-story of Montgomery, who flew the first home-made glider in 1883. His boyhood experiments with engineless planes were laughed at. Success of his first flight brought him notoriety, without financial success. Money from a gold separator he invented was spent in defending himself against lawsuits for patent infringement. Vertigo attacks kept him from flying his planes and hastened his early death. His bitter story, alleviated by devotion of a loving mate and affection of the Santa Clara College Jesuits who helped him continue his experiments, should have made A-1 drama. As handled here, it's maudlin.

It doesn't seem likely that, back in the 1880's, expressions like "warmed up," "joint" (for home), "on the house," "it's a cinch," and "that wouldn't be kosher" were being used—especially by a priest, and it certainly doesn't seem proper for a man of the cloth, with a big belly, to use that belly to butt another person frequently for humorous effect.

Story is relieved by some fine photography, especially the aerial pictures of cameraman Elmer Dyer; an occasional homespun mood that is successful, and some good background music by Marlin Skiles.

Bron.

Her Sister's Secret

PRC release of Henry Brash (Raoul Pagel) production. Features Nancy Coleman, Philip Reed, Margaret Lindsay, Felix Bressart. Directed by Edgar G. Ulmer. Screenplay, Anne Green, based on novel by Gina Kaus; editor, Jack W. Ogilvie; camera, Frank F. Planer; ass't director, Edward C. Jewell; music, Hans Sommer. Previewed N. Y. Sept. 9, '46. Running time, **86 MINS.**

Toni....................Nancy Coleman
Renee....................Margaret Lindsay
Dick....................Philip Reed
Pepe....................Felix Bressart
Bill....................Regis Toomey
Mr. Dubois....................Henry Stephenson
Wine Salesman....................Fritz Feld
Billy....................Winston Severn
Guy....................George Meeker
Etta....................Helene Heigh
Matilda....................Frances Williams
Birdman....................Rudolph Anders

Poignant drama of a mother's love for her child born out of a wartime romance points up this PRC entry for the upper brackets of the duals and may be strong enough to solo. Basically a picture for the femmes, this should be exploited to the hilt.

Taken from Gina Kaus' novel, "Dark Angel," Anne Green's screenplay tended to stretch the story a bit too much which good editing could have made more cohesive. Despite lengthy tale, performances are generally too quality.

From a chance meeting at the New Orleans Mardi Gras, Nancy Coleman falls in love with Philip Reed, a soldier from a nearby Army camp. Desperate when she finds herself pregnant—with her lover overseas possibly never to return—her sister, Margaret Lindsay, arranges to bring up the child as hers. However, the inevitable question — will her husband find out?—plagues her for three or four reels. Solution has Miss Coleman relinquishing the child to her sister and fadeout brings her into a final clinch with Reed who's returned in the nick.

Though the story's a familiar one, this Henry Brash producton has been creditably directed by Edgar G. Ulmer and film in general has wide femme appeal. Miss Coleman contributes a moving performance as the unwed mother, Miss Lindsay registers as the sister, Philip Reed is a forthright GI, and Felix Bressart sparkles as the cafe owner. Production values are better than average and Hans Sommer's musical score plus Frank Planer's lensing also rate.

The Inner Circle

Republic release of William J. O'Sullivan production. Features Adele Mara, Warren Douglas, William Frawley, Ricardo Cortez. Directed by Phil Ford. Screenplay, Dorrell & Stuart E. McGowan from radioscript by Leonard St. Clair, Lawrence Taylor; camera, Reggie Lanning; editor, Tony Martinelli. At Brooklyn Strand, dual, week Sept. 5, '46. Running time, 57 MINS.
Gerry Travis................Adele Mara
Johnny Strange............Warren Douglas
Webb......................William Frawley
Duke York.................Ricardo Cortez
Rhoda Roberts.........Virginia Christine
Radio Announcer..............Ken Niles
Henry Bogen.................Will Wright
Mrs. Wilson..............Dorothy Adams
Anne Travis.........Martha Montgomery

"The Inner Circle" hasn't much to recommend it. Even whodunit addicts will turn a quizzical eyebrow at the tangled, illogical and crudely put-together story. With slipshod scenario, pedestrian direction, and a total lack of marquee power, the film is a minor dualer.

What story there is concerns the murder frameup of a private investigator by his pretty secretary, who is trying to protect her kid sister suspected of the crime. Efforts of the detective to unravel the mystery leads him through a series of misadventures with the local police and a tough nightclub mob. As a windup, in a scene notable only for its absurdity, he assembles all the suspects in a radio studio where the crime is reenacted and the guilty party is revealed. After the gumshoe explains his solution, the mystery remains as thick as ever.

Adele Mara and Warren Douglas play the romantic leads, doing the best they can with their listless lines. Vet actors William Frawley and Ricardo Cortez, police detective and nightclub menace respectively, give big assists, while other cast members perform adequately in stock parts.

Little Iodine

Hollywood, Sept. 7.

United Artists release of Buddy Rogers-Ralph Cohn (Comet) production. Features Jo Ann Marlowe, Marc Cramer, Eve Whitney, Irene Ryan, Hobart Cavanaugh. Directed by Reginald LeBorg. Original screenplay, Richard Landau; camera, Robert Pittack; score, Alexander Steinert; editor, Lynn Harrison. Previewed Sept. 5, '46. Running time, 56 MINS.
Little Iodine..........Jo Ann Marlowe
Marc Andrews...............Marc Cramer
Janis Payne................Eve Whitney
Mrs. Tremble...............Irene Ryan
Mr. Tremble...........Hobart Cavanaugh
Horace.....................Lanny Rees
Simkins...................Leon Belasco
Mr. Bigdome..............Emory Parnell
Mrs. Bigdome...............Sarah Selby
Grandma Jones............Jean Patriquin

"Little Iodine," based on Jimmy Hatlo's King Features cartoon strip, marks production debut for Comet Productions, headed by Buddy Rogers and Ralph Cohn. For its intentions, film gives team good start and will serve as basis for series if sales warrant. Production makes no pretense of being other than supporting material, works in considerable chuckles in dealing with escapades of the pen-and-ink title character, and generally serves up salable film.

Hobart Cavanaugh and Irene Ryan, as Mr. and Mrs. Tremble, parents of the cartoon brat, carry the picture along on capable shoulders, overshadowing youngsters by merit of performances. It's a typical Hatlo

plot as scripted by Richard Landau, showing Iodine generally raising cain and persecuting her miserable parents, through misguided good intentions. Situations are exaggerated but are close enough to reality to make for good laughs. Reginald LeBorg's direction is not always even, but generally manages a good display of the material.

Adult romance, which Jo Ann Marlowe, as Iodine, and Lanny Rees, as her chum, manage to mix up is carried by Marc Cramer and Eve Whitney. Emory Parnell shows well as Tremble's gruff boss, Mr. Bigdome, as does Sarah Selby as the boss' wife. Leon Belasco, salesman of recorded French lessons, whose pitch to Mrs. Tremble starts Iodine to building an imaginary romance for her father, gets in some comedy licks. Young Miss Marlowe and other moppets do not stand out particularly.

Editing has kept film down to quick 56 minutes. Lensing by Robert Pittack is good and other credits are in keeping with release aims. *Brog.*

Russia on Parade
DOCUMENTARY
(Color)
(RUSSIAN-MADE)

Artkino release of Central Studio of Documentary Films production. Directed by Vassili Belayev, Igor Posselsky, Ivan Vengher. Music, David Block; narration, Kurt Hirsch. Tradeshown in N. Y., Sept. 5, '46. Running time, 45 MINS.

Chief interest of this film lies in its introduction of the new Sovocolor process which has been highly touted. Although the secret Soviet process reproduces the full chromatic band with good fidelity, extravagant claims are not warranted, especially since the average color production out of Hollywood easily equals the effect attained in this pic. Quality of naturalness is achieved by subduing the high-toned colors into soft pastel shades that are easy on the eyes. But off-focus distortion of backgrounds, the major drawback of all color processes, is far from licked by Sovocolor.

In itself, the film is a dry mouthful to swallow even for the faithful and has a slim b.o. potential in this country. An elongated newsreel shot of the annual sports pageant held in Moscow's Red Square in 1945, the film's monotony is not overcome even by the kaleidoscopic color patterns made by the swirling flags and colorful costumes of the various Soviet nationalities. About two dozen shots of Stalin reviewing the parade are seen with a sliding frequency scale for other Soviet luminaries, in addition to two shots of General Eisenhower who was visiting. Editing of the film is crudely handled at many points and the English narration by Kurt Hirsch is drowned in the blaring band music.

Foreign Films

"Der Weite Weg" ("The Long Way") (AUSTRIAN). Soviet Export Film release of Donau Film production. Stars Rudolf Prack; features Hans Holt, Maria Andergast, Willi Danek; directed by Eduard Hoesch; screenplay, Karl Jantsch; camera, Anton Pucher. Reviewed in Vienna. Running time, 85 MINS.

Produced at the Russian-owned Rosenhuegel studios, "The Long Way" is the first post-war Austrian film to stem from reconstructed Austrian film industry. Plot deals with prisoners of war and their love affairs. Rudolf Prack, Maria Anderfast, Willi Danek do the best work in the leads. If picture is synchronized in other languages, it may have some chance. Film is doubtful for Germany since many remarks will displease the Nazis *Maass.*

"Las Tres Ratas" ("The Three Rats") (ARGENTINE). San Miguel studios production. Stars Mecha Ortiz, Amelia Bence, Maria Duval, Miguel Faush Rocha, Santiago Gomez Cou; features Ricardo Passano, Jr., Felisa Mary, Amalia Sanchez Arino, Florem Delbene; directed by Carlos Schlieper; adaptation, Samuel Eichelbaum, Ariel Cartazzo, Jorge Jantus based on Diez-Canseco's novel of same name; camera, Bob Roberts. Reviewed in Buenos Aires. Running time, 95 MINS.

Dreary story of three sisters, mortgage on the old estanzia and big city pitfalls which await country-bred gals. Fatal attraction of the second sister for a heel (Gomez Cou) affects the lives of all three. Acting honors go to Maria Duval, as the youngest and happiest of the three characters. No interest for U. S. *Nid.*

"La Dama de la Muerte" ("The Lady of Death") (CHILEAN MADE). Cinematografica Interamericana release of Chile Films production. Features Carlos Cores, Judith Sullan, Guillermo Battaglia, Juan Corona; directed by Carlos Hugo Christensen; adapted from Robert Louis Stevenson story, "The Suicide Club." Reviewed in Buenos Aires. Running time, 80 MINS.

Although made in Chile, cast and direction of this film is all Argentine. Though a creditable effort, the story fails through poor screen adaptation plus inability of cast to get going. Necessary atmosphere of suspense fails to develop due mainly to poor direction of Carlos Christensen. Heavy dialog also detracts from the action. Some sets deserve praise. No appeal for American audiences. *Nid.*

Miniature Reviews

"The Jolson Story" (Color-Musical) (Col). A mop-up musical

"Angel on My Shoulder" (UA). Bright comedy-fantasy with high entertainment quotient.

'The Devil's Playground" (UA). Hopalong Cassidy (Bill Boyd) returns to the release schedule in a good average oater.

"So Dark The Night" (Col). Above-par whodunit marred by weak screenplay. A "B" that has "A" quality.

"Blondie Knows Best" (Col). Staple fare for family trade.

"Crime Doctor's Manhunt" (Col). Minor murder meller with Warner Baxter for marquee.

"Roll On Texas Moon" (Songs) (Rep). Roy Rogers in solid outdoor actioner with songs.

"Landrush" (Songs) (Col). Program oater for thin b.o. returns from moppet appeal.

"It's Great to Be Young" (Musical) (Col). Minor musical cast with juve players; dualer.

"Shadows Over Chinatown" (Mono). Routine Charlie Chan whodunit pars the general run of the series.

The Jolson Story
(MUSICAL-COLOR)

Columbia release of Sidney Skolsky (Gordon Griffith) production. Features Larry Parks, Evelyn Keyes, Wm. Demarest, Bill Goodwin. Directed by Alfred E. Green. Screenplay, Stephen Longstreet; adaptation, Harry Chandler, Andrew Solt; dances, Jack Cole; production numbers, Jos. H. Lewis; camera (Technicolor), Joseph Walker, Lawrence W. Butler; music director, M. W. Stoloff; editor, Wm. Lyon; asst. director, Wilbur McGaugh; arrangements, Saul Chaplin, Martin Fried. Tradeshown N. Y. Sept. 12, 1946. Running time, 128 MINS.
Al Jolson...................Larry Parks
Julie Benson.............Evelyn Keyes
Steve Martin...........William Demarest
Tom Baron.................Bill Goodwin
Cantor Yoelson.........Ludwig Donath
Mrs. Yoelson...........Tamara Shayne
Lew Dockstader.........John Alexander
Ann Murray..........Jo-Carroll Dennison
Father McGee.............Ernest Cossart
Al Jolson (as a boy)......Scotty Beckett
Dick Glenn.............William Forrest
Ann Murray (as a girl).......Ann Todd
Oscar Hammerstein.......Edwin Maxwell
Jonesy.....................Emmett Vogan

"The Jolson Story" unofficially stars Al Jolson. Even as Jose Iturbi's off-screen artistry got around, as regards the Steinwaying of the Chopin hit parade in Columbia's "Song to Remember," so will Jolson's singing, but more so, prove the big excitement for this Technicolorful film biog of the great mammy-singer's career. Film is destined for smash grosses.

"The Jolson Story" joins the increasing cycle of show biz biographicals dealing with still-living personalities. And along with it comes a medley of Jolson songs that he first introduced and made famous.

As a personality for a show biz cavalcade Jolson is a natural, of course. It's axiomatic in show business that he ranks with Sir Harry Lauder and the late Albert Chevalier as one of the three greatest single men entertainers.

"The Jolson Story" emerges as an American success story in song. It might be called a Hebrew "Going My Way" but just as the Crosby picture made the church background incidental, there's even less of the synagog in this. That Al Jolson is Asa Yoelson, son of Cantor Yoelson, in his Washington hometown, is incidental to the upsurge of a great American show business personality around whom is focused a trend of events which even now the competitive Warner Bros. is ballyhooing anew as part of its 20th anniversary of sound. While "Don Juan" with a Vitaphone score keynoted the start of sound, the full fruition of sound didn't come into being until more than a year later, in 1927, when Jolson's "Jazz Singer" swept the world and revolutionized an entire industry.

This is but one of the segments of "The Jolson Story." The yearning to sing, to give generously of himself, cued by the still famed-in-showbiz catchphrase, "You ain't heard nothin' yet"; the Sunday nights at the Winter Garden, the birth of the runway as Jolson got closer to his audience, the incidental whistling in between vocalizing—all these are recaptured for the screen.

But there's lots more on and off the screen. As Evelyn Keyes plays Ruby Keeler — only she's called Julie Benson—in meticulous manner, she helps carry the boy-girl saga. Ziegfeld's "Show Girl" and the "Liza" (Gershwin) tune, to which Miss Keeler terped, are utilized for this purpose, as are Jolson's accidentally-on-purpose audience-interruptions as he sings from the customers' side of the footlights. (It's w.k. that as soon as Jolson stopped this pseudo-ad lib vocalizing the show collapsed; that a weak Ziegfeld musical was only sustained by its unofficial, unbilled star with his nightly vocal "interruptions").

The story, thus, is an average admixture of fact and fiction, perhaps a shade more factual than the average show biz subject. More important is that it captures, in its story line, the fruitful progression of an inspired trouper who was to taste the heights from minstrelsy to vaudeville, from Broadway musical comedy hitdom to the talkers, carrying along his dancer-wife to some pretty good heights all her own.

But the real star of the production is that Jolson voice and that Jolson medley. It was good showmanship to cast this film with lesser people, particularly Larry Parks as the mammy kid. That was an inspired casting but one wonders what audiences of another season may think when they hear Parks singing in his own style, sans the traditional and trademarked Jolson style. Be that as it may, he's the youthful reincarnation of the mammy-singer. It's quite apparent how he must have studied the Jolson mannerisms in black-and-white because the vocal synchronization (with a plenitude of closeups) defies detection.

As for Jolson's voice, it has never been better. Thus the magic of science has produced a composite whole to eclipse the original at his most youthful best. The pops are a nostalgic hit parade and, in this day and age of song revivals, a cinch for '46-'47 reaffirmation. The tunes include "Rosie You Are My Posy," "Mammy," "Sittin' On Top of the World," "You Made Me Love You (I Didn't Wanna Do It)," "Swanee" (on the Winter Garden runway), "The Spaniard Who Blighted My Life" (production number), "Liza" and "42d Street" incidentally in the Keeler stuff, "Waitin' for the Robert E. Lee," "Rockabye Your Baby With a Dixie Melody" and "April Showers" among others. In view of the since broadly travestied "Sonny Boy," the latter is out.

Columnist Sidney Skolsky, who engineered this Jolson package for a Columbia picture, and officiates as producer thereof, has done a tiptop job, in collaboration with Gordon Griffith, his associate producer, and director Alfred E. Green. The casting is excellent, the choice of song material on the beam, the pacing right, the theme honest and forthright. Besides the top romantic pair, Ludwig Donath as Cantor Yoelson and Tamara Shayne as Mrs. Yoelson are the cast's outstanders. William Demarest and Bill Goodwin as Jol-

son's general advisers are capital, and the rest of the cast competent. Scotty Beckett, who plays Jolson as a boy, also does a highlight job.

There's a scene in which Cantor Yoelson explains a VARIETY headline containing the word sockeroo to his wife. Sockeroo, he explains in a hep manner, means "a double socko." That's what "The Jolson Story" should be at the b.o.   Abel.

Angel on My Shoulder

Hollywood, Sept. 14.

United Artists release of Charles R. Rogers production. Stars Paul Muni, Anne Baxter, Claude Rains; features Onslow Stevens, George Cleveland, Hardie Albright, James Flavin. Directed by Archie Mayo. Screenplay, Harry Segall, Roland Kibbee; original story, Segall; camera, James Van Trees; photographic effects, Howard Anderson; music, Dimitri Tiomkin; editor, Asa Clark. Previewed Hollywood, Sept. 13. '46. Running time, 100 MINS.

Eddie Kagle	Paul Muni
Barbara Foster	Anne Baxter
Nick	Claude Rains
Dr. Higgins	Onslow Stevens
Albert	George Cleveland
Smiley	Hardie Albright
Bellamy	James Flavin
Minister	Erskine Sanford
Mrs. Bentley	Marion Martin
Chairman	Jonathan Hale
Jim	Murray Alper
Brazen Girl	Joan Blair
Scientist	Fritz Leiber
Warden	Kurt Katch
Agatha	Sarah Padden
Big Harry	Addison Richards
Shaggsy	Ben Welden
Mr. Bentley	George Meeker
Bailiff	Lee Shumway
Interne	Russ Whiteman
Gangster	James Dundee
Gangster	Mike Lally
Gangster	Saul Gorss
Gangster	Duke Taylor
Prison Yard Captain	Edward Keane
Kramer	Chester Clute

"Angel on My Shoulder" stacks up as nifty entertainment in serio-comic vein slated to please all. Values are there to rate good business and if given exploitation hypo returns should be sturdy. Word-of-mouth will be an aid. It's a fantasy, brightly polished by scripting, direction and playing, that punches over contents. Charles R. Rogers' production measures up to his best in showmanly values. Top cast names of Paul Muni, Anne Baxter and Claude Rains will aid draw.

Theme deals with Satan's efforts to best his Heavenly adversary at least once. He uses as a tool for the attempt a gangster who wants revenge on the pal who bumped him off. That doesn't sound like too hot a premise on which to base a picture but results are solid for entertainment. Large credit goes to Archie Mayo's deft direction in developing humor without offense and his guidance of players. Harry Segall and Roland Kibbee, scripting from Segall's original, have given plot punchy dialog and situations that click.

Paul Muni is the murdered gangster, turning in performance that measures up to past credits and giving film plenty of zip. Awakening in hell after being bumped, Muni wants out so he can get revenge on his killer. Claude Rains, as Satan, sees chance to even things with a crime-busting earthly judge who's the double for Muni. Old Nick offers Muni opportunity to get his killer if he'll queer to judge's political halo. It's a deal, the two take off for earth and the fun starts. Bowery lingo and gangster mannerisms of Muni are an ill-fit for the judge's body, which Muni is occupying temporarily with Satan's help. Things don't work out as the devil planned because Muni goes soft for the judge's fiancee and mixes up all revenge plans. Windup packs a certain laugh as Muni brushes off Satan's threats of torture with the threat to tell the Hades mob how the big boss was bested on earth.

Rains shines as the Devil, shading

the character with a likeable puckishness good for both sympathy and chuckles. Anne Baxter is excellent as the troubled fiancee. Onslow Stevens, the judge's psychiatrist, who makes some wrong guesses about his patient's strange behavior; George Cleveland, Hardie Albright, good as Muni's murdering pal; James Flavin, Marion Martin, Murray Alper, Kurt Katch and others turn in solid work to back up the leads.

Rogers and his associate producer, David W. Siegel, have furnished smart backing for the serio-fun that transpires and marshalled expert technical aides. James Van Trees' lensing and photographic effects by Howard Anderson on trick exposure point up fantasy elements. Music score by Dimitri Tiomkin furthers effect and other credits fit equally well.   Brog.

The Devil's Playground

United Artists release of Lewis J. Rachmil production. Stars William Boyd; features Andy Clyde, Rand Brooks, Elaine Riley. Directed by George Archainbaud. Screenplay, Doris Schroeder, based on characters created by Clarence E. Mulford; editor, Fred W. Berger; camera, Mack Stengler. Previewed at the Park, Narrowsburg, N. Y., Sept. 14. '46. Running time, 62 MINS.

Hopalong Cassidy	William Boyd
California Carlson	Andy Clyde
Lucky Jenkins	Rand Brooks
Mrs. Evans	Elaine Riley
Judge Morton	Robert Elliott
Sheriff	Joseph J. Greene
Roberts	Francis McDonald
Curly	Ned Young
Dan'l	Earle Hodgins
U. S. Marshal	George Eldredge
Wolfe	Everett Shields
Dwarf	John George

After a hiatus of more than a year since the last Hopalong Cassidy western, 57th in the series is about to be released by United Artists. Bill Boyd is still in the saddle and the formula remains pat, so there is no reason to believe that "Devil's Playground" will fare any less successfully than its respectably long line of predecessors. Fact is, Boyd is a fitting hero, the story is more than ordinarily engrossing for a hoss opry, and there's been no stinting on production values, as such things go in a western, so exhibs should find it a readily-acceptable booking.

Long delay since manufacture and release of the last Hopalong sees this one coming out under new production auspices. Boyd has become a partner in the unit with Carl Leserman, who handles the distribution end, and Lou Pennish, one of the proprietors of General Service Studios, who takes care of production and financing. Harry Sherman, under whose aegis Clarence Mulford created the character and who produced the great majority of the pix in the series, retains a percentage interest, but no production authority.

Ninety-hour shooting schedule on which Hopalongs are produced in no way reflect on the first-rate photography, excellent locations, unusually good musical backgrounds, liberal use of extras and other production factors which give the series an edge on much of the average western output. George Archainbaud's taut direction also is worth note.

Yarn is the usual affair in which Boyd and his pards, Andy Clyde and Rand Brooks, find a damsel in distress (Elaine Riley) and, in some 60 fast minutes, straighten everything out for her. This entails outsmarting the sheriff and the standard gang of leather-chapped cutthroats, led by Robert Elliott. Acting is routine, with Miss Riley earning a laurel (or the sagebrush equivalent thereof) for effective handling of her featured part.   Herb.

So Dark the Night

Columbia release of Ted Richmond production. Features Steven Geray, Micheline Cheirel, Eugene Borden, Ann Codee, Helen Freeman. Directed by Joseph H. Lewis. Screenplay by Martin Berkeley, Dwight Babcock based on story by Aubrey Wisberg; camera, Burnett Guffey; editor, Jerome Thoms; music, M. W. Stoloff. Tradeshown in N. Y., Sept. 16, '46. Running time, 71 MINS.

Henri Cassin	Steven Geray
Nanette Michaud	Micheline Cheirel
Pierre Michaud	Eugene Borden
Mama Michaud	Ann Codee
Dr. Boncourt	Egon Brecher
Widow Bridelle	Helen Freeman
Georges	Theodore Gottlieb
Commissaire Grande	Gregory Gay
Dr. Manet	Jean Del Val
Leon Achard	Paul Marion
Pere Cortot	Emil Ramu
Jean Duval	Louis Mercier

Working out of the "B" corner of Columbia's lot, producer Ted Richmond has created in "So Dark the Night" a film that barely misses the "A" tag. Unfortunately, in this case the miss is as good as a mile, since the pic's failure lies in the decisive province of the screenplay. In all other departments, however, the film has been handled with extraordinary artistry to equal or better Hollywood's highest-priced product. It is sure to earn praise for making so much out of so little but, given the flaw in the screenplay and the cast of unknowns, the film's impact at the b.o. will be softer than it deserves.

Around the frail structure of a story about a schizophrenic Paris police inspector who becomes an insane killer at night, a tight combination of direction, camera-work and musical scoring produce a series of isolated visual effects that are subtle and moving to an unusual degree. Paradoxically, the film seems to collapse under the weight of its technical niceties as director Joseph H. Lewis continuously takes time out to make his points through the indirection of cinematic imagery rather than directly through the spoken word. One sequence, for example, draws the relationship between the police inspector and an ambitious daughter of a provincial innkeeper through pure camera technique. Cutting quickly between the man and woman, the camera softly plays upon the girl's features then coldly shifts, not to the man, but to the chromium fixtures on his expensive car, the hubcaps, the door handles, the car's name, etc. The effect and meaning are startling in their clarity.

Settings for the pic, which unfolds in an obscure French village, are outstanding for their density and accuracy of detail. Despite the obvious budget limitations, the layout of the streets, interior decorations and landscape shots define France as it exists in our imagination. Also contributing to the "continental" touch, but detracting once again from the film's b.o. potential, is the presence of numerous actors with foreign accents. Story revolves around the ill-fated romance between a middle-aged Parisian detective and a young country girl who is already betrothed to a neighboring farmer. On the wedding eve, the farmer, in a well-portrayed dramatic encounter, threatens the detective and stalks out of the party, the girl following in a frenzy of mixed emotions. Several days later, both the girl and farmer are found to have been strangled to death. The detective, who is famous for his sleuthing ability, is unable to find any clues but the scripters, who were also stumped for an ending, solve the case through an unfitting and totally mechanical foray into the realm of psychopathology.

Together with everything else, casting for this film is highly unusual, with Steven Geray playing the lead role of tri-partite lover, detective and killer. With a firm directorial hand controlling the works, Geray gives a credible performance but fails to evoke the pathos of his situation. Micheline Cheirel, as the young girl, is a talented actress with clear promise for the future. Eugene Borden, Ann Codee, Paul Marion and Helen Freeman, in supporting roles, also add importantly to the overall sincerity of the film.

Blondie Knows Best

Columbia production and release. Features Penny Singleton, Arthur Lake, Larry Simms, Marjorie Kent, Steven Geray, Jonathan Hale, Shemp Howard. Directed by Abby Berlin. Screenplay by Edward Bernds, Al Martin from story by Bernds based on comic strip character by Chic Young; camera, Philip Tannura; editor, Aaron Stell. Tradeshown N. Y., Sept. 16, '46. Running time, **69 MINS.**

Blondie	Penny Singleton
Dagwood	Arthur Lake
Alexander	Larry Simms
Cookie	Marjorie Kent
Dr. Schmidt	Steven Geray
J. C. Dithers	Jonathan Hale
Jim Gray	Shemp Howard
Charles Peabody	Jerome Cowan
Alvin Fuddle	Danny Mummert
Dr. Titus	Ludwig Donath
Conroy	Arthur Loft
David Armstrong	Edwin Cooper
Ollie	Jack Rice
Mary	Alyn Lockwood
Gloria Evans	Carol Hughes
Ruth Evans	Kay Mallory

Saga of Blondie and Dagwood, as continued in this pic, is surefire family fare in all nabe situations. Following down the trail blazed by its predecessors, "Blondie Knows Best" is a fast mix of situation comedy and broad caricature served up in typical sprightly fashion. Although scripting for this series has been reduced to a formula known by rote to all filmgoers, all "Blondie" pix, including this one, manage to diffuse a charm that pays off at the boxoffice. Cinematic standards, moreover, have been kept at a consistently high level.

Story for this stanza revolves around Dagwood's bumbling attempts to impersonate his boss on an important contract assignment while, at the same time, trying to dodge a process server. Familiar situations of Dagwood in dutch with his wife, his boss, and the world in general, are squeezed for all their worth. In addition, the psychiatric fad is exploited through Dagwood's falling into the hands of a couple of doctors who are fast on the hypodermic draw. Dagwood's rescue makes for a rousing windup with Dagwood's whole family, including a half-dozen pooches of varying size, joining in the act.

Cast remains standard with Arthur Lake and Penny Singleton in the lead roles assisted by Jonathan Hale, playing the irate boss, and Larry Simms and Marjorie Kent, as the children. Shemp Howard, playing a near-blind process-server, has a fat part which he plays to the hilt for laughs in his low-comedy style.

Crime Doctor's Manhunt

Columbia release of Rudolph C. Flothow production. Stars Warner Baxter, Ellen Drew; features William Frawley, Frank Sully. Directed by William Castle. Screenplay, Leigh Brackett from story by Eric Taylor, based on radio program, "Crime Doctor," by Max Marcin; camera, Philip Tanura; asst. director, Carl Hiecke; editor, Dwight Caldwell. Tradeshown N. Y., Sept. 11, '46. Running time, **64 MINS.**

Dr. Robert Ordway	Warner Baxter
Irene Cotter	Ellen Drew
Inspector Manning	William Frawley
Rigger	Frank Sully
Ruby Farrell	Claire Carleton
Waldo	Bernerd Nedell
Sergeant Bradley	Jack Lee
Gerald Cotter	Francis Pierlot
Philip Armstrong	Myron Healy
Marcus Leblanc	Olin Howlin
Alfredi	Ivan Triesault
Tom	Paul E. Burns
Martha	Mary Newton
Herrera	Leon Lenoir

A potpourri of rare psychiatric symptoms forms a basis for this story and it's a wobbly foundation. Taken from radio's "Crime Doctor" series, film has Warner Baxter in the "Doctor" role for just about the whole of its marquee draw. Entertainment values are not strong enough to sustain it without heavy exhibitor exploitation.

Unexplained twists in the scenario provide most of the mystery, and they're still unexplained at the end. Script concerns a returned vet who visits the doctor for diagnosis of amnesia attacks, and is subsequently murdered by two hoods who get the same treatment from a mysterious gal, thought to be the sister of the vet's fiancee. Denouement reveals personality split in the fiance, Ellen Drew, causing her to assume dead sister's stronger personality. No one explained where the vet's amnesia attacks came from.

In spite of the limping script, "Crime Doctor's Manhunt" has some fair moments, but the entire production could have been jacked up by better editing and direction. One house-searching sequence is evidently supposed to build suspense, but does nothing but put the brakes on interest. In this instance, as well as in others, cutting would have added much-needed pace.

Casting of some experienced hands such as Baxter, William Frawley and Ellen Drew might have made director William Castle's job easier but he failed to capitalize on it. The two hoods were made to look not so tough, and Miss Drew, in portraying her weaker self, went to saccharine extremes.

Radio show's bally may help this series but as it stands the film is a borderline case.

Roll On Texas Moon
(SONGS)

Hollywood, Sept. 12.

Republic release of Edward J. White production. Stars Roy Rogers; features George "Gabby" Hayes, Dale Evans, Bob Nolan and Sons of Pioneers. Directed by William Witney. Screenplay, Paul Gangelin, Mauri Grashin; original story, Jean Murray; camera, William Bradford; music, Dale Butts; songs, Jack Elliott, Tim Spencer; editor, Les Orlebeck. Previewed Hollywood, Sept. 10, '46. Running time, **67 MINS.**

Roy Rogers	Roy Rogers
Trigger	Horse
Gabby Whittaker	George Hayes
Jill Delaney	Dale Evans
Cole Gregory	Dennis Hoey
Cactus Kate Taylor	Elizabeth Risdon
Steve Anders	Francis McDonald
Frank B. Wilson	Edward Keane
Brannigan	Kenne Duncan
Bert Morris	Tom London
Don Williams	Harry Strang
Tom Prescott	Edward Cassidy
Ned Barnes	Lee Shumway
Joe Cummings	Steve Darrell
Stuhler	Pierce Lyden

Bob Nolan & Sons of Pioneers

Solid western musical fare for the Roy Rogers fans, "Roll On Texas Moon" is a showmanly roundup of oater ingredients aimed at good returns in the established market for this type product. Action is fast and tunes are neatly integrated with plot. Production backing makes handy use of outdoors to lend values, generally shaping film for favorable reception.

Rogers vocals three of the tunes, working with Dale Evans on two and with the Sons of the Pioneers on third. Latter group spots comedy number to round out score. Best of tunes are "Wontcha' Be a Friend of Mine," by Jack Elliott, and "The Jumpin' Bean," Pioneers' comedy piece by Tim Spencer.

William Witney's direction keeps the plot concerning feud between cattlemen and sheepherders moving at swift clip and puts players through their paces in smooth style. Dialog in the Paul Gangelin-Mauri Grashin script minimizes stock western formula to make appeal more adult without overlooking interest for younger filmgoers. Story concerns Rogers as trouble-shooter for cattle combine who's assigned to prevent a range war between ranchers and sheepmen. War is being connived by villains who want to grab off profitable sheep ranch operated by Dale Evans. Around that theme there's plenty of fast riding, shooting and other thrills to sate action tastes with songs mixed in to bridge any gaps in movement.

Rogers is in good form, both actionwise and vocally. Same goes for Miss Evans in femme lead. George "Gabby" Hayes clicks with fire-eating comedy lead as tough cattleman. Heavy works is capably taken care of by Dennis Hoey, Francis McDonald, Kenne Duncan and other henchmen. Elizabeth Risdon is a crusty companion to Miss Evans.

Edward J. White's production furnishes good backing for picture. Lensing by William Bradford, editing and other technical credits up to standard. *Brog.*

Landrush
(SONGS)

Columbia release of Colbert Clark production. Stars Charles Starrett, Smiley Burnette; features Doris Houck, Ozie Waters. Directed by Vernon Keays. Screenplay, Michael Simmons; camera, George B. Meehan; songs, Smiley Burnette, Ozie Waters; asst. director, William O'Connor; editor, James Sweeney. Tradeshown N. Y., Sept. 11, '46. Running time, **53 MINS.**

Steve Harmon	Charles Starrett
Smiley	Smiley Burnette
Mary Parker	Doris Houck
Jake Parker	Emmett Lynn
Hawkins	Bud Geary
Caleb Garvey	Stephen Barclay
Sackett	Robert Kortman
Bill	George Chesebro
Sheriff Collins	Bud Osborne

Ozie Waters and Colorado Rangers

A program dualer, "Landrush" will probably excite weekend moppets. This one is modest in every respect, most of all on budget.

Film dishes up the usual accoutrements of hoss "thrillers," with chase scenes galore, a couple of mediocre brawls, and lotsa shooting. Added to which there is hillbilly singing by Ozie Waters and his corny crew, and slapstick comedy by Smiley Burnette. Camera work fails to dispel the ever-present feeling that an automobile had passed over the trail just before a scene was shot.

Story harks back to days when the Government was giving Indian territory away free. In this case, land is called the Spur, and, faintly reminiscent of Oklahoma's panhandle, is a refuge for baddies. When the squatters come the gang tries to scare them away. Charles Starrett, the Durango Kid, saves the newspaper editor and the land for the newcomers.

Starrett is still a stiff and stilted parallel to the Lone Ranger, complete with white horse and mask. Burnette draws well-spaced laughs, Waters and his Colorado Rangers come in with unconnected songs, and Doris Houck is just fair as a weak love interest. Kids who will enjoy almost anything will take this.

It's Great to Be Young
(MUSICAL)

Columbia release of Ted Richmond production. Features Leslie Brooks, Jimmy Lloyd, Jeff Donnell, Robert Stanton, Milton DeLugg and orch. Directed by Del Lord. Screenplay, Jack Henley based on story by Karen DeWolf; songs, Allan Roberts, Doris Fisher, Jack Finn; musical director, Saul Chaplin; camera, Henry Freulich; editor, Aaron Stell. At Brooklyn Fox, N. Y., dual, Sept. 13, '46. Running time, **69 MINS.**

Terry	Leslie Brooks
Ricky Malone	Jimmy Lloyd
Georgia Johnson	Jeff Donnell
"Spud" Winters	Robert Stanton
"Ivory" Timothy	Jack Williams
Jack	Jack Fina
Franklin Johnson	Frank Orth
Mrs. Johnson	Ann Codee
Anita	Pat Yankee
Burkett	Frank Sully
Ambrose Kenton	Grady Sutton
Pop	Vernon Dent

Milton DeLugg and His Swing Wing

Columbia has thrown together a group of juve actors into a tunefest potpourri but, although youth predominates in "It's Great to Be Young," the pic lacks the expected freshness and vitality. Stale story of stage-struck kids trying to break into the big time is dressed up in a mediocre score and played by performers bordering on the amateurish for a not very impressive result. It's slated for the smaller situations.

Six tunes are scattered through the film with the cleffing team of Allan Roberts and Doris Fisher responsible for the bulk. Numbers include "It's Great to Be Young," "A Thousand and One Sweet Dreams," "Five of the Best," "That Went Out With High-Button Shoes," "Frankie Boogie" and Bumble Boogie." Bob Stanton, brother of Dick Haymes, together with Leslie Brooks, Jeff Donnell and Jimmy Lloyd carry the chief thesping and singing burdens on their as-yet-undeveloped shoulders. Production numbers are unimaginatively handled with Milton DeLugg and his small swing combo providing the hot and noisy jazz obligato.

Story revolves around the efforts of a group of ex-GIs who want to get into showbusiness and land in the borscht circuit where they try out their talents. After running through the mill of heartbreaks, they stage a big show at the summer hotel where a Broadway producer is vacationing. Pic winds up with the usual finale production number earning the performers contracts for a Broadway run.

Children on Trial
(BRITISH-MADE)

London, Sept. 4.

Ealing Films release of Crown Film Unit. Directed by Jack Lee. Story by Jack Lee, Nora Dawson. At Academy theatre. Running time, **60 MINS.**

Aftermath of any war always has been an increase in crime and juvenile delinquency. As the last war was a total one including younger people so peace shows a bigger increase in crime among children in their teens.

Well-produced by Basil Wright and finely directed by Jack Lee, this film shows what government social services are doing to combat crime. Many appearing in film duplicate their real life roles—John Vardy, headmaster of Liverpool Farm School, plays headmaster, and Basil Henriques, chairman of a Juvenile Court, reenacts his part on the screen. The kids were chosen from schools in Liverpool and Birmingham. Only professional is Julia Lang as a girl delinquent.

Story shows what happens to a youngster brought up in the slums. The state gives him a final chance to learn to be a good citizen.

Film is timely, but dubious if there's any big market for such film in the U. S.

Shadows Over Chinatown

Monogram release of James S. Burkett production. Stars Sidney Toler; features Mantan Moreland, Victor Sen Young, Tanis Chandler, John Gallaudet, Paul Bryar. Directed by Terry Morse. Original screenplay, Raymond Schrock based on Earl Derr Biggers' stories; camera, William Sickner; editor, Ralph Dixon. At Brooklyn Strand, N. Y., dual, Sept. 13, '46. Running time, **64 MINS.**

Charlie Chan	Sidney Toler
Birmingham	Mantan Moreland
Jimmy	Victor Sen Young
Mary Conover	Tanis Chandler
Jeff Hay	John Gallaudet
Mike Rogan	Paul Bryar
Jack Tilford	Bruce Kellogg
Capt. Allen	Alan Bridge
Mrs. Conover	Mary Gordon
Joan Mercer	Dorothy Granger
Cosgrove	Jack Norton

Standard Charlie Chan fare. A slimly-budgeted film, "Shadows Over Chinatown" is cooked up from the familiar recipe of Oriental epigrams and occasional corpses which have been the trademark of this series since the late Warner Oland first quoted Confucius. Plot originality in this one is negligible but dialoging is snappy and film is well-paced.

As usual, Sidney Toler plays the sage slant-eyed sleuth with comedy support from his two fumbling aides, Mantan Moreland and Victor Sen Young. Story revolves around the efforts of the Chinese detective to crack an insurance racket outfit. Mixed up in the case is a missing girl, thought to be a torse-murder victim, but who is on the lam from the mobsters because of their plot against her fiance. Plot converges in San Francisco's Chinatown where Chan tracks down the leader of the gang.

Minor romantic interest is furnished by Tanis Chandler and Bruce Kellogg with John Gallaudet, Paul Bryar and Jack Norton giving okay support in stock parts. Straight camera work and musical effects par the general level of the production.

Miniature Reviews

"Blue Skies" (Musical-Color) (Par). Crosby - Astaire - Joan Caulfield in Irving Berlin's parlay. How can you lose?

"Nobody Lives Forever" (WB). Familiar meller of gangster who reforms for love; cast names augur good b.o.

"The Magic Bow" (Music) (GFD). British-made film, a likely U. S. entry.

"This Man Is Mine" (Col). British filmization of stage comedy hit "A Soldier for Christmas" looks strong U. S. entry.

"The Overlanders" (Eagle-Lion). Lack of marquee names militates against Aussie-made pic in U. S.

"Accomplice" (PRC). Lightweight whodunit for secondaries.

Blue Skies
(COLOR-MUSICAL

Paramount release of Sol C. Siegel production. Stars Bing Crosby, Fred Astaire, Joan Caulfield; features Billy DeWolfe, Olga San Juan. Directed by Stuart Heisler. Screenplay, Arthur Sheekman; adaptation, Allan Scott, based on original idea by Irving Berlin. Songs, Irving Berlin. Music, Robt. Emmett Dolan; arrangements, Jos. J. Lilley, Troy Sanders; dances, Hermes Pan; camera (Technicolor), Chas. Lang, Jr., Wm. Snyder; special effects, Gordon Jennings, Paul K. Lepae, Farciot Edouart; editor, LeRoy Stone. Tradeshown N. Y. Sept. 25, 1946. Running time, **104 MINS.**

Johnny Adams	Bing Crosby
Jed Potter	Fred Astaire
Mary O'Hara	Joan Caulfield
Tony	Billy DeWolfe
Nita Nova	Olga San Juan
Francois	Mikhail Rasumny
Mack	Frank Faylen
Martha, Nurse	Victoria Horne
Mary Elizabeth	Karolyn Grimes

"Blue Skies" is another in the show biz cavalcade cycle and it'll spell beaucoup blue skies and black ink for any exhibitor. With Crosby, Astaire and Joan Caulfield on the marquee, a wealth of Irving Berlin songs and lush Technicolor production values, this filmusical can't miss for terrific grosses.

The cue sheet on "Blue Skies" lists 42 different song items but some of it has been excised and the rest so skillfully arranged, orchestrated and presented that the nostalgic musical cavalcade doesn't pall. The songs are pleasantly familiar to the World War I generation and, for the youngsters, they are refreshing and solid, especially as Berlin has modernized them.

Result is that Astaire's "Puttin' On the Ritz" (originally written for Harry Richman) is the musical standout of the more than 30 items which have been retained. The flash production terp routines are especially eye-arresting. Not forgetting the climactic "Heat Wave" when, in a lush Martinique setting, Astaire does a dramatic fall off an elevated platform as result of alcoholic predilections induced by his torching for Miss Caulfield.

The story of "Blue Skies" is of familiar pattern and rather sketchily hung together by Astaire. He's cast as a present-day disk jockey stringing the cavalcade of Berliniana together by recounting the nostalgic episodes behind the success of the platters as they are miked. Starts with "Pretty Girl Is Like a Melody" and thereafter it's an extension of the Astaire vs. Crosby technique, first unfolded by them in "Holiday Inn," and given a re-do here.

Crosby is the romantic winnah throughout. Miss Caulfield is partial to the nitery troubadour (Crosby) whose unusual flair for opening and closing niteries is a plot keynote. Astaire is the suave dancing star and she's in the line of one of his shows. Astaire's romantic interest carries her along but Crosby's crooning charms her until they marry, have a baby and split up. Finally Astaire's disk-jockey nostalgia brings the graying but still lovely Miss Caulfield into the story for another clinch with the Groaner.

Interspersed is a deft dovetailing of sundry production values. Billy De Wolfe is capital as the ex-vauder turned waiter-captain (including his own original "Mrs. Murgatroyd" specialty for solid results). Olga San Juan, Latin eyeful who came to attention in a Par short, is DeWolfe's vis-a-vis and clicks on her own with "You'd Be Surprised" and other numbers. To the showwise, "Surprised" will remind of Helen Kane's boop-a-doop style, especially as Miss San Juan is coiffed.

Generally speaking, for the fans who manifest a little sophistication and inside stuff on their favorites, the dialog is inclusive of such tongue-in-cheek cracks as "I like kids even better than horses" (Crosby), along with other topical innuendos on Bing's bangtails penchant. It's in a rather corny scene with the baby that one of the three new Berlin numbers, "Running Around in Circles (And Getting Nowhere)" is done by Crosby to Karolyn Grimes, a rather self-conscious five-year-old. (Incidentally, of the other two new Berlin numbers, "You Keep Coming Back Like a Song" and "A Serenade to an Old-Fashioned Girl," the former is the most promising of all three new tunes).

It's to the credit of producer Sol C. Siegel and director Stuart Heisler that the Berlin cavalcade did not assume talker versions of the old-time illustrated song slides. When it does occur, as with the title song, the Technicolor pastels make for fine camera portraiture. This takes place in the pre-Niagara Falls scene.

The niteries which Crosby founds, hosts and then unloads to an omnipotent Greek by the name of Rakopolis trace the speakeasy era. The cavalcade rings in a touch of World War I with "Got My Captain Working for Me Now," references to flaming youth, the jazz age, "keep cool with Coolidge," the Wall St. debacle, and up to World War II with "Any Bonds Today," "This Is the Army, Mr. Jones" and "White Christmas" (Okinawa setting).

The Berlin catalog being what it is there is no wanting for variety, novelty and production ideas. Whether it's "C-u-b-a" for the Havana setting, "Heat Wave" for the Martinique number, the deliberately corny song-and-dance challenge routine, the new theme, "You Keep Coming Back Like a Song," which ties it all together; the overtones of "Always," "Remember" and "How Deep Is the Ocean"; the productional "Everybody Step," a good flash although thrown away because of other footage; the modern boogie-woogie overtone to that corking arrangement in "Heat Wave" — whatever the number, the basic values are there, and director Heisler makes much of his opportunities.

Mark Sandrich, who, with Berlin, Crosby and Astaire, whipped up "Holiday Inn" three years ago, was the key man in "Blue Skies" until his sudden death interrupted production plans for the pic. Then, too, there was the emergency substitution of Astaire for Paul Draper, but with it all this film emerges a boxoffice winner in every respect.

Certainly, for Astaire, it's perhaps a new triumph. If he ever seriously thought of retiring, "Skies" should postpone any such ideas. "Puttin' On the Ritz" is a kudo for him, director Heisler and dance-stager Hermes Pan, with the latter manifesting imagination and novelty in other production numbers. But "Ritz" is particularly noteworthy with its concerted 10 Astaires in background to Astaire up front, marking an unique male chorus for the dancing star. Then, by camera abracadabra he is made to dance counter-clockwise to himself, mirror-multiplied by 10, so that the double quintet seemingly does a contra-routine to himself up front. It's the same lens magic which has inured film audiences to accept the idea of seeing a Roxy theatre-type number put on in an intime boite, as occurs in this film.

Crosby is Crosby although a slightly heftier Bing. He's the same troubadour, chirping the ditties as only Crosby does even though his waistline is somewhat more generous than behooves a juve. As for Miss Caulfield, she's the photogenic answer to the Kalmuses' prayer as an ideal Technicolor subject. Technicolor brings out her blue-eyed blonde beauty like a portrait. In every respect Paramount, Siegel, Heisler & Co. have done right handsomely by the stars, the tunesmith and their assignment. *Abel.*

Nobody Lives Forever
(ONE SONG)

Hollywood, Sept. 21.

Warner Bros. release of Robert Buckner production. Stars John Garfield, Geraldine Fitzgerald; features Walter Brennan, Faye Emerson, George Coulouris, George Tobias. Directed by Jean Negulesco. Original screenplay, W. R. Burness; camera, Arthur Edeson; music, Adolph Deutsch; editor, Rudi Fehr. Tradeshown L. A. Sept. 20, 46. Running time, **100 MINS.**

Nick Blake	John Garfield
Gladys Halvorsen	Geraldine Fitzgerald
Pop Gruber	Walter Brennan
Toni	Faye Emerson
Doc Ganson	George Coulouris
Al Doyle	George Tobias
Chet King	Robert Shayne
Charles Manning	Richard Gaines
Bell Boy	Dick Erdman
Shake Thomas	James Flavin
Windy Mather	Ralph Peters
Telesfero	Alex Havier
Mission Attendant	William Edmunds
Ben	Ralph Dunn
Counterman	Grady Sutton

"Nobody Lives Forever" is melodrama in a familiar pattern. It has name strength, good production and sufficient interest to generate healthy boxoffice returns. It's the old gangster reformation theme, dressed up with timely interest in veteran rehabilitation, although latter is not likely to be used as a model for such programs.

John Garfield is seen as a drafted mobster being released after years in the service and with plenty of heroic medals to indicate his fighting ability. Original script by W. R. Burnett follows writer's bent for putting down on paper more melodramatic elements of U. S. gang life and conmen. Garfield, intent on a long vacation from war duties, is talked into taking a wealthy widow for a large slice of her inheritance. Plot moves along towards its objective with all the obviousness of such a theme. The gangster falls for the gal he's trying to take, turns honest and it all ends in a high-pitched finale that suspensefully portrays complete reformation and proper end for those of the mob who failed to try making an honest living.

John Garfield, as the war hero-gangster carries most of the weight of the story on capable shoulders. His performance gives picture considerable lift. Geraldine Fitzgerald, as the girl he tries to take, is not comfortable in the assignment but comes through with best character allows. George Tobias, Garfield's aide, injects considerable number of chuckles. Also good is Walter Brennan as a con down on his luck. Faye Emerson does well as a past love of Garfield's who almost ruins his new romance. George Coulouris is a psycho gangster who gives Garfield trouble. Others are okay.

Jean Negulesco's direction man-

ages to carry the story along in good fashion most of the way, although he is inclined to be over-obvious in some individual scenes. Robert Buckner furnishes excellent production background for events, cloaking action in smooth values that show up. Camera work by Arthur Edeson is keyed to meller developments, as is score by Adolph Deutsch. Editing would benefit by cropping of at least 10 minutes from footage.
Brog.

The Magic Bow

(With Music)

(BRITISH-MADE)

London, Sept. 18.

General Film Distributors release of Gainsborough Picture. Stars Phyllis Calvert, Stewart Granger; features Jean Kent, Dennis Price. Directed by Bernard Knowles. Screenplay by Roland Pertwee from novel "The Magic Bow" by Manuel Komroff. Camera, Jack Cox, Jack Asher. At Palace theatre. Running time, **106 MINS.**

Paganini....................Stewart Granger
Jeanne....................Phyllis Calvert
Bianchi....................Jean Kent
Paul de la Rochelle..........Dennis Price
Germi....................Cecil Parker
Countess de Vermond..........Marie Lohr
Count de Vermond........Henry Edwards
Antonio....................Frank Cellier
Teresa....................Mary Jerrold
Cardinal....................Ronald Speaight
Pasini....................Felix Aylmer
Landlady....................Betty Warren
Manager....................Anthony Holles

Swan song of executive producer Maurice Ostrer before quitting J. Arthur Rank's Gainsborough Productions, there can be little doubt that "Magic Bow" will be big boxoffice in England. Strength of marquee names like Stewart Granger, Phyllis Calvert, and Yehudi Menuhin cannot be underrated. Only snag in the over-boosting of Menuhin is that it stresses the fact that whenever Granger, posturing as Paganini, is playing the violin, he is just giving an excellent imitation of the bowing and fingering of a genius. For the U. S. market, this represents a big selling job. But it may go over if nicely exploited.

Honors are shared between Stewart Granger and Yehudi Menuhin, who plays all the violin solos. Rarely has such emphasis been laid on the musical side of a film. Backed by the London Philharmonic, Menuhin is heard in "The Devil's Trill" (Tartini), "La Ronde des Lutins" (Brazzini), "Campanella," "Caprice No. 20," "Violin Concerto No. 1," "Introductions et variations" (all by Paganini), last movement of Violin Concerto Opus 61 (Beethoven) and "Romance," a haunting melody by Phil Green based on a theme by Paganini.

For those who dote on good music and rave about Menuhin, this film is a veritable feast. For the Granger fans, here he has an unusual and attractive part. For those who know something of Paganini and who are now drawn to the theatre by Granger or Menuhin, this picture may disappoint because of its conventional story packed with cliches.

Granger is not to blame for this. Given the right material and approach he probably could have portrayed the strange being who is said to have inspired dread as being in league with the devil while at the same time being the darling of the ladies. There's little to show how this uncanny genius conquered a world.

The usual montage of a traveling coach and concert programs is a poor substitute for building up a character whose career was more strange and entertaining than fiction. Nor is the background wholly convincing. The Genoa at the beginning of the 19th century shown is too reminiscent of the studio.

Being unacquainted with Manuel Komroff's novel, it is impossible to say how much the scriptwriters are indebted to him, but the resultant story resolves itself into the too familiar one of a man loved by two women, one a socialite, the other a gutter graduate with a heart of gold. It tells how Stewart Granger (Paganini), before leaving Genoa for Parma to win a Stradivarius, is tricked by aristocratic Phyllis Calvert into assisting her father to escape from prison. In Parma, she invites Granger to play at her home, but disgusted by the bad behavior of her friends, he leaves after insulting her. Seeking distraction with Jean Kent, he gambles, loses, pawns his Strad, and has it redeemed by Miss Calvert, unknown to him, in time for his big concert. The gifted violinist falls in love with her.

Leading Napoleon's troops into Parma is Dennis Price, selected by the Emperor as husband for Miss Calvert. After the usual love complications, she renounces Granger on the eve of their elopement. But they meet again in Paris, a duel with Price results. The faithful Kent and the heartbroken Miss Calvert save the violinist's life in time, but Granger has lost all interest in playing. Climax comes when she engineers a Papal Command Performance in the Vatican (an imposing reproduction) and to the strains of "Romance," Price releases Miss Calvert so that she can marry Granger.

Within the limits of the script, Granger gives a fine performance. Running him close for acting honors, is Cecil Parker, who, as lawyer-manager for Granger, provides the comedy. Parker, who won laurels in "Caesar and Cleopatra," adds to his reputation.

Miss Calvert has little opportunity in her struggle with an anaemic part, and her attractiveness sometimes escapes the camera. Kent's portrayal of the singer who came from Genoa's gutter has the odor of Lambeth Road. Price is a picturesque, stuffy soldier.

Whatever failings the picture may have, there are many bally angles for the exhibitor. Even though Granger and Calvert may not yet be big marquee names in the U. S., Yehudi Menuhin should count for something.
Cane.

This Man Is Mine

(BRITISH-MADE)

London, Sept. 12.

Columbia British Pictures release of Marcel Varnel production. Stars Tom Walls, Glynis Johns, Jeanne de Casalis. Directed by Marcel Varnel. Screenplay by Doreen Montgomery, Nicholas Phipps, Reginald Beckwith, Mabel Constanduros, from Reginald Beckwith's stage play "A Soldier for Christmas." Camera, Phil Grindrod. At Studio One. Running time, **103 MINS.**

Philip Ferguson....................Tom Walls
Mrs. Ferguson............Jeanne de Casalis
Phoebe Ferguson............Nova Pilbeam
Brenda Ferguson..........Rosalyn Boulter
Millie ....Glynis Johns
Bill MacKenzie..........Hugh McDermott
Ronald ....Barry Morse
Lady Daubney........Ambrosine Phillpotts
Mrs. Jarvis....................Mary Merrall

Living up to Columbia's boast that this is its best British comedy to date, picture should register hefty grosses here, and should find a ready market in America, when trimmed about 15 minutes. Starts off with ripples of laughter and keeps up the gait.

Christmas of 1946 finds Bill Mackenzie, ex-Canadian soldier, enjoying his holiday in Saskatoon. Greetings cable signed "The Fergusons" is excuse to flashback across the Atlantic to an English village in 1942 where soldier was Christmas guest of the Fergusons. Home is in a pleasant state of turmoil, Brenda has left her husband because he couldn't supply a turkey, second daughter Phoebe can't make up her mind about boy friend Ronald, ex-maid Millie, now in uniform, arrives as a billette and MacKenzie, primed by his Colonel about Anglo-American relations, comes in time to sweep Millie and Phoebe off their feet. Both girls make a bee line for him, having decided that the gloves are off.

Story follows a familiar pattern, but complications including a mail robbery and Phoebe's visit to the soldier's bedroom, provide good fun. Final shot shows Millie preparing Christmas dinner for her Canadian husband Mackenzie.

Acting honors go to Edinburgh-born Irishman, Hugh McDermott, who is rapidly becoming a star. Glynis Johns makes a fine foil, but her speech becomes somewhat monotonous. Nova Pilbeam and Barry Morse are an acceptable pair of lovers while Jeanne de Casalis dithers delightfully. Veteran Tom Walls begins a second career here as a straight actor.

Direction by Marcel Varnel is slick and aimed to get maximum laughs.
Cane.

The Overlanders

(AUSTRALIAN-MADE)

London, Sept. 19.

Eagle-Lion release of Ealing Studios-Michael Balcon production. Stars Daphne Campbell, Chips Rafferty. Written and directed by Harry Watt; Australian associate, Ralph Smart; music by John Ireland. Camera, Osmond Borradaile. At Studio One. Running time, **91 MINS.**

Dan McAlpine....................Chips Rafferty
Bill Parsons........John Nugent Hayward
Mary Parsons............Daphne Campbell
Mrs. Parsons....................Jean Blue
Helen Parsons....................Helen Grieve
Corky....................John Fernside
Sailor Sinbad....................Peter Pagan
Charlie....................Frank Ransome
Manager....................Stan Tolhurst
Minister....................Marshall Crosby
Police Sergeant....................John Fegan

First big feature film to be made in Australia by a British firm, this should come as a breath of fresh air to audiences jaded with routine pictures. Based on fact, the story has legitimate fictional twists to give it audience appeal. The fact that a million American servicemen spent part of the war years Down Under should not be overlooked. Whether it can be sold as an epic westerner will spell its U. S. chances.

Producer Michael Balcon sent director Harry Watt to Australia with a mandate to make a picture representative of that continent. Watt spent five months soaking up the atmosphere. In the Federal Food Office, Controller Murphy explained of the greatest mass migration of cattle the world has even known to get them out of reach of a probable Jap landing. Across 2,000 miles of heat and dust, drovers had battled with 500,000 heads of cattle. Watt decided this would be the film's theme.

Story begins in 1942 at the tiny town of Wyndham, where meat works are destroyed, personnel evacuated, and Chips Rafferty, boss cattle drover, is told to shoot 1,000 head of prime beasts. He decides instead to overland them across 2,000 miles of tough going.

Epic trip lasts 15 months, and the adventures are graphic. Highlights are the breaking in of wild horses when their own had died from poison weed; the stampede with the men facing a charge of maddened cattle and the forced march across a mountain path with a sheer drop on one side. The cattle are delivered safe from the Japs, and Chips and his team go back north to help again.

Direction reflects credit on Harry Watt, who adds one more success to his record, which includes "Target for Tonight" and "Nine Men." Not only does he show something of the real Australia, but he also puts over tragedy, comedy and romance. His cast had few professional actors.

Tall, laconic Chips Rafferty is a natural for the head drover. Labelled Australia's Gary Cooper, his experience in "Rats of Tobruk" and "Forty Thousand Horsemen" helped him in this film. He is now in London playing a lead in Balcon's "The Loves of Joanna Godden." Other stage people include John Fernside, Peter Pagan, John Nugent Hayward and Jean Blue. For his leading lady, Watt chose 20 year old Daphne Campbell, nursing orderly in an Australian military hospital. She had never before faced a camera, but she makes a real outdoor girl in this picture.

Cameraman Osmond Borradaille deserves laurels for his work. The veteran of British music, John Ireland, was persuaded to do the film music, for the first time.
Cane.

Accomplice

Hollywood, Sept. 21.

PRC release of John K. Teaford production. Stars Richard Arlen; Veda Ann Borg, Tom Dugan, Michael Branden, Marjorie Manners, Earle Hodgins. Directed by Walter Colmes. Screenplay, Irving Elman and Frank Gruber from novel by Gruber; camera, Jockey Feindel; score, Alexander Laszlo; editor, Robert Jahns. Previewed Hollywood, Sept 20, '46. Running time, **66 MINS.**

Simon Lash....................Richard Arlen
Joyce Bonniwell............Veda Ann Borg
Eddie Slocum....................Tom Dugan
Sheriff Rucker............Michael Branden
Evelyn Price............Marjorie Manners
Jeff Bailey....................Earle Hodgins
Pete Connors....................Francis Ford
Jim Bonniwell....................Edward Earle
Vincent Springer........Herbert Rawlinson
Castleman ....Sherry Hall

Dull whodunit with little to recommend. Will serve best as program filler for the secondary situations. Inept direction defeats whatever merit cast and script might have. Physical production values are good for minor budget expenditure.

"Accomplice" is from the Frank Gruber novel, "Simon Lash, Private Detective," but Richard Arlen as the book-loving dick, has few chances to break into action needed to sustain interest. He's called in to solve disappearance of husband of an old love and there are four murders before case is cleared up. Gal and her husband are in cahoots to defraud bank by phoney disappearance. When complications set in, pair resort to murder to cover their trail, but developments never makes it very clear.

Walter Colmes' direction is repetitious and lacking in skill needed to point up interest in proceedings. Veda Ann Borg and Edward Earle are the plotters. Tom Dugan strives for some laughs as Arlen's handyman. Best characterizations are furnished by Earle Hodgins as a grafting small-town marshal, and Michael Branden an intelligent sheriff. **Lensing, editing and other technical aides are stock.**
Brog.

Miniature Reviews

"Undercurrent" (M-G). Heavy drama with femme appeal and star values for hefty boxoffice.

"The Dark Mirror" (U-I) Strong cast headed by Olivia de Havilland and Lew Ayres in a weakly scripted whodunit.

"Below the Deadline" (Mono). Good melodrama for supporting positions.

Undercurrent

Hollywood, Sept. 28.

Metro release of Pandro S. Berman production. Stars Katharine Hepburn, Robert Taylor, Robert Mitchum; features Edmund Gwenn, Marjorie Main. Directed by Vincente Minnelli. Screenplay, Edward Chodorov; based on story by Thelma Strabel; camera, Karl Freund; score, Herbert Stothart; editor, Ferris Webster. Tradeshown L. A. Sept. 27, '46. Running time, 114 MINS.

Ann Hamilton	Katharine Hepburn
Alan Garroway	Robert Taylor
Michael Garroway	Robert Mitchum
Prof. "Dink" Hamilton	Edmund Gwenn
Lucy	Marjorie Main
Sylvia Lea Burton	Jayne Meadows
Mr. Warmsley	Clinton Sundberg
Prof. Joseph Bangs	Dan Tobin
Mrs. Foster	Kathryn Card
George	Leigh Whipper
Justice Putnam	Charles Trowbridge
Henry Gilson	James Westerfield
Uncle Ben	Billy McLain

"Undercurrent" is heavy drama with femme appeal and hefty marquee voltage. Typical lush Metro production gives it plenty of eye-appealing dress as background for drama and stars carry off their assignments in top fashion. Boxoffice potential is solid by virtue of such names as Katharine Hepburn, Robert Taylor and Robert Mitchum.

Film is first for Taylor since his war service and he puts over a difficult characterization as the heavy, somewhat of an inovation from his usual hero roles.

Picture deals with psychology angle in which a weak, uncertain man uses lies, theft and even murder to obtain power and acclaim. Unfoldment has a curious static quality as directed by Vincente Minnelli which keeps it from ever being really believable but cast talent and performances hold the interest.

Appeal for femmes lies in romance between Miss Hepburn and Taylor and uncertainty as to how it will work out. Taylor, war-made industrialist, marries Miss Hepburn, daughter of a scientist, after a whirlwind courtship. After marriage, the bride begins to discover odd incidents in her husband's past, including his brother's mysterious disappearance and the fear that dogs and other animals have for the man. She develops almost an obsession over digging up facts about the brother and when she learns her husband has falsely charged him with theft and, also murdered an obscure scientist and stolen the invention which was basis for his fortune, the break comes.

Climax builds up considerable chills and thrills as Miss Hepburn seeks to escape Taylor. He tries to ride her over a cliff and then, as he's set to smash her skull with a boulder, his own horse stomps him to death. Edward Chodorov scripted in fine fashion from a Thelma Strabel story.

Miss Hepburn sells her role with usual finesse and talent. Mitchum, as the missing brother, has only three scenes but makes them count for importance. Edmund Gwenn, Marjorie Main, both in small spots, Jayne Meadows, Clinton Sundberg, Dan Tobin, Kathryn Card, Leigh Whipper and others give the stars very solid support.

Pandro S. Berman did a tasteful job of assuring lush production dress for the picture. Art direction and set decorations are particularly noteworthy and handled by Cedric Gibbons and Randall Duell, and Edwin B. Willis and Jack D. Moore, respectively. Karl Freund's lensing is expert and musical score by Herbert Stothart counts towards setting mood for drama. Picture is overlong and could stand further editing. *Brog.*

The Dark Mirror

Universal-International release of Nunnally Johnson production. Stars Olivia de Havilland, Lew Ayres, Thomas Mitchell; features Richard Long, Garry Owen, Lester Allen. Directed by Robert Siodmak. Screenplay, Nunnally Johnson, based on original by Vladimir Pozner; camera, Milton Krasner; editor, Ernest Nims; music, Dimitri Tiomkin. Tradeshown N. Y., Sept. 30, '46. Running time, 85 MINS.

Terry Collins }	
Ruth Collins }	Olivia de Havilland
Dr. Scott Elliott	Lew Ayres
Detective Stevenson	Thomas Mitchell
Rusty	Richard Long
District Attorney	Charles Evans
Franklin	Garry Owen
George Benson	Lester Allen
Mrs. Didriksen	Lela Bliss
Miss Beade	Marta Mitrovich
Photo-Double	Amelita Ward

"The Dark Mirror" runs the full gamut of themes currently in vogue at the boxoffice—from psychiatry to romance back again to the double identity gimmick and murder mystery. But, despite the individually potent ingredients, somehow the composite doesn't quite come off. Name strength of the cast and solid production values, however, should counteract the screenplay's vagaries.

Opening with a promising gait, the pic gets lost in a maze of psychological gadgets and speculation that slows it down. Olivia de Havilland, playing a twin role, carries the central load of the picture. She's cast simultaneously as a sweet, sympathetic girl and her vixenish, latently insane twin sister. A murder is committed and while one girl has been positively identified as coming out of the man's apartment on the night of the murder, the other establishes a fool-proof alibi. Police are stymied in making an arrest since they can't establish which sister is which. While the police carry on with an attempt to differentiate the twins, the script tips its mitt to the audience and the tension is lost.

Making a comeback after several years' absence from the screen, Lew Ayres is cast in his familiar role as a medico—a specialist on identical twins. Slightly older looking and sporting a mustache, Ayres still retains much of his appealing boyish sincerity. But in the romantic clinches, Ayres is stiff and slightly embarrassed looking. Copping thespic honors, despite a relatively light part, Thomas Mitchell plays the baffled dick with a wry wit and assured bearing that carries belief. Miss De Havilland, however, can't make her roles come to life. Saddled with lines that go from sticky sentimentality in one part to five-and-dime melodrama in the other, she winds up with two-ply wooden characterizations. It's an incredible role that can't be surmounted by Miss Havilland's proven talents. One of the difficulties she faced is the fact that the plot starts the twin roles off in closely similar emotional keys then suddenly, without warning or motivation, splits them into night and day.

Camera work is excellent, as is the score, which at several points in the production contributes neat humorous touches. Direction by Robert Siodmak is handled positively despite the dramatic looseness. *Herm.*

Below the Deadline

Hollywood, Sept. 28.

Monogram release of Lindsley Parsons production. Stars Warren Douglas, Ramsay Ames; features Jan Wiley. Paul Maxey, Philip Van Zandt, John Harmon, Bruce Edwards. Directed by William Beaudine. Screenplay, Harvey Gates, Forrest Judd; original, Ivan Tors; camera, Harry Neumann; editor, Ace Herman. Previewed Sept. 24, '46. Running time, 65 MINS.

Joe Hilton	Warren Douglas
Lynn Turner	Ramsay Ames
Vivian	Jan Wiley
Arthur Brennan	Paul Maxey
Oney Kessel	Philip Van Zandt
Pinky	John Harmon
Sam Austin	Bruce Edwards
Jeffrey Hilton	George Meeker
Nichols	Clancy Cooper
Blonde	Cay Forrester
Turner	Alan Bridges
Vail	George Eldredge
Welsh	William Ruhl

Fast-action melodrama that will play off okay in supporting positions. Production values are good for budget and playing and direction maintain interest in slight but satisfactory story. "Below the Deadline" tag has little connection with plot.

Warren Douglas, comparatively new film face, does an interesting performance as an embittered veteran out to get all he can. When his brother, bigshot gambler, is bumped off by a rival mob, Douglas takes over the business. He's a ruthless operator, determined to parlay a fortune to make up for his war years. Cash flows in, yet looks a cinch to reach his goal. He resists efforts of friends to get him out of the rackets, reformation doesn't come, a new mayor is elected, and the rival mob nearly succeeds in bumping him off.

Ramsay Ames does well by femme lead as Douglas' romance. Jan Wiley, Paul Maxey, Philip Van Zandt, Bruce Edwards, George Meeker and others lend okay support. Particularly good chore is turned in by John Harmon as Douglas' henchman.

William Beaudine's direction gives the melodrama good pacing and Lindsley Parsons' production supervision shows money well spent. Lensing and other technical factors measure up. *Brog.*

Foreign Films

"L'Insaissable Frederic" ("The Uncatchable Frederic") (FRENCH). Pathe Consortium release of Tellus production; directed by Richard Pottier; stars Renee St. Cyr, Paul Meurisse; screen play, Gerard Cartier, Carlo Rim; reviewed in Paris. Running time, 100 MINS.

Local audiences laugh over old gags about a reporter fooling a femme detective writer as to his own identity. She falls for him when he impersonates one of her book's characters, the uncatchable Frederic. Camera and sound are not up to par. Thin chance for U. S. market.

"Son Dernier Role" ("Her Last Part") (FRENCH). U.F.P.F. release of S.F.P. production; directed by Jean Gourguet; stars Gaby Morlay, Jean Debucourt; features Dalio and Jean Tissier; based on play by Louis de Zilahy; screenplay, J. P. Lechanois; reviewed in Paris. Running time, 90 MINS.

Despite a few outdoor shots, this is a stagey filmization of the legit play without any inspired direction. Sound is bad and camera below par. Jean Debucourt portrays the medico who falls for actress, Gaby Morlay, and courts her during the rest cure she takes before she returns to her author-lover, Dalio. Action is slow and only comedy relief comes from antics of Jean Tissier, as provincial hotel keeper. No dice in America.

"Gringalet" (FRENCH). Pathe-Consortium release of Pathe Cinema production; directed by Andre Berthomieu; stars Charles Vanel and Marguerite Deval; features Suzy Carrier, Jimmy Gaillard and Paul Vanderberghe; based on stage play by Vanderberghe; reviewed in Paris. Running time, 105 MINS.

Stagey filmization of the play with Charles Vanel as an industrialist who introduces his illegitimate son, Gringalet, played by Vanderberghe, to his unreceptive family which finally accepts him. Production is geared for local nabes but lacks sufficient mountings to make it an American entry. Marguerite Deval, as the grandmother, uses only her stage mannerisms.

Mari.

Miniature Reviews

"My Darling Clementine" (20th). Top name cast in a sentimental westerner headed for big play at the b.o.

"Traffic in Crime" (Rep). Melodrama with only modest possibilities as secondary filler.

"Fool's Gold" (UA). Topnotch outdoor action fare. Continues "Hopalong Cassidy" series starring William Boyd.

My Darling Clementine

20th-Fox release of Samuel G. Engel production. Stars Henry Fonda, Linda Darnell, Victor Mature; features Walter Brennan, Tim Holt, Cathy Downs, Ward Bond, Alan Mowbray. Directed by John Ford. Screenplay, S. G. Engel, Winston Miller, based on story by Sam Hellman from book by Stuart N. Lake; camera, Joe MacDonald; music, Alfred Newman; editor, Dorothy Spencer. Tradeshown N. Y., Oct. 7, '46. Running time, **97 MINS.**

Wyatt Earp	Henry Fonda
Chihuahua	Linda Darnell
Doc Holliday	Victor Mature
Old Man Clanton	Walter Brennan
Virgil Earp	Tim Holt
Clementine	Cathy Downs
Morgan Earp	Ward Bond
Thorndyke	Alan Mowbray
Billy Clanton	John Ireland
Mayor	Roy Roberts
Kate Nelson	Jane Darwell
Ike Clanton	Grant Withers
Bartender	J. Farrell MacDonald
John Simpson	Russell Simpson
James Earp	Don Garner
Town Drunk	Francis Ford
Barber	Ben Hall
Hotel Clerk	Arthur Walsh
Stage Driver	Ronald J. Pennick
Francois	Louis Mercier
Sam Clanton	Mickey Simpson
Ph..n Clanton	Fred Libby

Sentimental saga of the western plains, "My Darling Clementine" is loaded with enough marquee voltage to insure it heavy play at the box-office in all situations. Heavy stress on the romantic angle, with consequent less time for six-shooting and hoofbeating, may tag it as being a bit tame for the average outdoor fan; but added appeal for the femme trade will more than compensate.

Trademark of John Ford's direction is clearly stamped on the film with its shadowy lights, softly contrasted moods and measured pace, but a tendency is discernible towards stylization for stylization's sake without relationship to the screen material. At several points, the pic comes to a dead stop to let Ford go gunning for some arty effect. But, as usual in a Ford pic, the photography is brilliantly conceived, especially the black-and-white panoramic shots which equal in striking force anything done in color.

Major boost to the film is given by the simple, sincere performance of Henry Fonda. Script doesn't afford him many chances for dramatic action, but Fonda, as a boomtown marshal, pulls the reins taut on his part, charging the role and the pic with more excitement than it really has. Playing counterpoint to Fonda, Victor Mature registers nicely as a Boston aristocrat turned gambler and killer. Role starts him off as a blackguard but in the end Mature winds up on the side of the law, giving up both his life and gal for the sheriff. Improvement in Mature's thesping is marked by a degree of emotional expression and facial animation not seen in his former roles.

Femme lead is held down by Linda Darnell although Cathy Downs plays the title role. As a Mexican firebrand and dancehall belle, Miss Darnell handles herself creditably while the camera work does the rest in highlighting her looks. Miss Downs, in the relatively minor role of Clementine, a cultured Bostonian gal who is in love with Mature, is sweet and winning.

Story opens with the killing of Fonda's brother while they are en route to California on a cattle-herding job. Fonda is offered, and takes, the post of sheriff in a bad man's town in an effort to track down the killers. Crossing paths with Mature in a saloon, Fonda suspects him at first but both become very chummy as Mature is revealed to be a talented surgeon who escaped to a dangerous life because he suffered from consumption. Plot twists into Mature's love life with Miss Darnell, as his current flame, and Miss Downs, as an echo out of the past. Fonda plays Cupid until he unferrets the gang of rustlers who plugged his brother and the pic goes out in a smashing climax of blazing guns as Fonda levels culprit Walter Brennan and his four sons.

Excellent supporting cast is topped by Brennan, who turns in a solid portrayal of a crusty old horse thief and father of a gang of ne'er-do-wells. Other players showing up well include Alan Mowbray, J. Farrell MacDonald, Ward Bond, Tim Holt and Grant Withers. Score by Alfred Newman is superb in its variations of the underlying theme melody, "My Darling Clementine." *Herm.*

Traffic in Crime

Los Angeles, Oct. 8.

Republic release of Donald H. Brown production. Features Kane Richmond, Adele Mara, Anne Nagel, Wilton Graff. Directed by Les Selander. Screenplay, David Lang; original story, Leslie Turner White; camera, Bud Thackery; editor, Les Orlebeck. At the Million Dollar, Los Angeles, Oct 1, '46. Running time **54 MINS.**

Sam Wire	Kane Richmond
Silk	Adele Mara
Ann Marlowe	Anne Nagel
Nick Cantrell	Wilton Graff
Tip Hogan	Roy Barcroft
Murphy	Arthur Loft
Dumbo	Wade Crosby
Jake Schultz	Dick Curtis
Dan Marlowe	Harry V. Cheshire
Hogan's Driver	Bob Wilke
Cab Driver	Charles Sullivan

Budget crime thriller with only modest ability to fill supporting spot in lesser situations, "Traffic in Crime" is dull tale of gang-busting that lacks finesse and virility needed to put its melodramatics over. Production values reflect small expenditure. Direction gets little from wavering script.

Plot concerns undercover operations of a police spy out to break up two gambling syndicates in a small town. How a small west coast town with seasonal fruit-picking boom could support two gambling outfits is a script mystery. Kane Richmond is the undercover man pitting wits against heavies. Dialog and situations are mostly made up of standard cliches in keeping with static development. Finale has Richmond contriving to have the two gangs and crooked police rub each other out, saving everyone a lot of trouble.

Adele Mara does a gambler moll and Anne Nagel is the sweet heroine. Contributing to heavy work are Wilton Graff, Roy Barcroft and Dick Curtis. Les Selander directed the Donald H. Brown production in standard fashion. Bud Thackery's lensing fits budget quality. *Brog.*

Fool's Gold

Hollywood, Oct. 4.

United Artists release of Lewis J. Rachmil production. Stars William Boyd; features Andy Clyde, Rand Brooks. Directed by George Archainbaud. Original story and screenplay, Doris Schroeder; based on characters created by Clarence E. Mulford; camera, Mack Stengler; musical supervisor, David Chudnow; editor, Fred W. Berger. Previewed Oct. 4, '46. Running time, **63 MINS.**

Hopalong Cassidy	William Boyd
California Carlson	Andy Clyde
Lucky Jenkins	Rand Brooks
Professor	Robert Emmett Keane
Jessie	Jane Randolph
Bruce	Stephen Barclay
Duke	Harry Cording
Sandler	Earle Hodgins
Barton	Bob Bentley
Blackie	William Davis
Col. Landry	Forbes Murray
Lieutenant	Glen B. Gallagher
Sergeant	Ben Corbett
Speed	Fred "Snowflake" Toones

Sturdy action fare for the outdoor fans. Second in new series of "Hopalong Cassidy" westerns for United Artists release, "Fool's Gold" adds up to good entertainment in its field.

William Boyd's characterization of "Hoppy," range sleuth extraordinary, fits like a glove. This time he attempts to aid an Army friend to persuade latter's son to give up life of crime with a gang of sage gangsters. Disguising himself as a cattle-buyer, but letting crooks think he's an Army captain ducking the military, Hoppy enters badman's territory. Before his mission is marked completed he has not only saved the friend's son but wiped out the gang.

It's all told at level above usual oater, giving adult as well as juve interest. Much is made of musical score, and photographic values of the outdoor mountain scenery are fully realized by Mack Stengler's lensing.

Andy Clyde is seen as Hoppy's pal, California, capably taking care of comedy touches. Rand Brooks does young Lucky, another Hoppy pal. Chief villain, and doing an excellent job, is Robert Emmett Keane. Romantic interest is supplied by Jane Randolph and Stephen Barclay. Earle Hodgins draws another of his sharply defined small characters as an outpost guard of the outlaw's hideout. Others measure up to demands of western roles. *Brog.*

Foreign Films

"La Foire aux Chimeres" ("The Dream Fair") **(FRENCH).** National Films release of Cinema Productions production; directed by Pierre Chenal; stars Eric von Stroheim, Madeleine Sologne, Louis Salou; screenplay, Jack Companeez, Ernest Neubach; dialog, Louis Ducreux; reviewed in Paris. Running time, **107 MINS.**

Possible entry for French patronage spots in the U. S. and a likely grosser in France. Picture is said to have cost over $300,000, big for France. It belongs to the blind-girl-who-gets-her-sight-back cycle. Depressing, without comedy relief, it's well photographed and ably directed. Eric von Stroheim contributes a fine performance as the disfigured engraver who forges banknotes for the sake of the blind girl whom he found in a cheap circus act. Madeleine Sologne and Louis Salou also acquit themselves well in lesser roles.

"Petrus" (FRENCH). Gray release of Imperia production; features Fernandel, Simone Simon, Pierre Brasseur, Dalio, Abel Jacquin; directed by Marc Allegret; adapted by Marcel Rivet, Marc Allegret, from Marcel Achard's play; dialog, Achard; reviewed in Paris. Running time, **100 MINS.**

Sure grosser here even if mountings are not up to standard. Achard comedy takes place mainly in a nitery locale. Fernandel portrays the unsophisticated photographer who finally wins Simone Simon, a night-club line girl. **With plenty of comedy plus good acting all around, film looks like a good bet for a remake and should be okay in U. S. arty theatres.** *Maxi.*

Miniature Reviews

"Margie" (One Song; Color). (20th-Fox). Jeanne Crain heads young cast in sentimental comedy of schooldays; good b.o.

"The Chase" (UA). Meller slated for okay b.o. results.

"Vacation in Reno" (RKO). Lightweight family comedy for supporting positions.

"Nocturne" (RKO). Whodunit thriller. George Raft in hard-boiled police role for meller fans. B.o. prospects good.

"Child of Divorce" (RKO). Light budgeter carrying a surprisingly hefty sock.

Margie

(ONE SONG; COLOR)

20th-Fox release of Walter Morosco production. Stars Jeanne Crain; features Glenn Langan, Lynn Bari, Alan Young, Barbara Lawrence, Conrad Janis, Esther Dale, Hobart Cavanaugh. Directed by Henry King. Screenplay, F. Hugh Herbert, based on stories by Ruth McKenney and Richard Bransten; camera, Charles Clarke; song, "Margie," by Benny Davis, J. Russel Robinson and Con Conrad; music direction, Alfred Newman; editor, Barbara McLean; special effects, Fred Sersen. Tradeshown N. Y., Oct. 10, '46. Running time, **93 MINS.**

Margie	Jeanne Craig
Prof. Fontayne	Glenn Langan
Miss Palmer	Lynn Bari
Roy Hornsdale	Alan Young
Marybelle	Barbara Lawrence
Johnny	Conrad Janis
Grandma McSweeney	Esther Dale
Mr. McDuff	Hobart Cavanaugh
Joyce	Ann Todd
Cynthia	Hattie McDaniel
Boy Charlie	Don Hayden
Vi	Hazel Dawn
Wanda	Vanessa Brown
Senior	Diana Herbert
Jefferson	Milton Parsons
Matron	Margaret Wells
Arnold	Warren Mills
Debater	Richard Kelton
Salesman	Tom Stevenson
School Teacher	Cecil Weston

A sentimentalism of the late '20s, of Hoover, Vallee, flappers and flagpole-sitters, has been wrapped around a hit song of the period to emerge as an entertaining bit of taffee called "Margie." There's no particular pretense of "Margie" being anything of epochal proportions, but it has a homey quality whose word-of-mouth should be a factor to set it right for the boxoffice.

"Margie," the song, is constantly reprised throughout the film, but it is by no means the pic's outstanding quality. Producer Walter Morosco has surrounded the Ruth McKenney-Richard Bransten stories with some of 20th-Fox's sprightlier younger players, F. Hugh Herbert knows his way about in scripting a screenplay about the highschool clan, and added to this is some excellent Technicolor photography that enhances the overall expensively mounted production.

No small credit should go to Henry King for the direction. It is a pic of 1928, of coonskin coats, flivvers, senior proms and the like, and King has captured all this without ever suggesting the travesty it could easily have become in less experienced hands.

"Margie" is the yarn of how a high-school teen-ager married her French teacher. It could probably be summed up as briefly as all that. There are such details, also, of how all the girls at Central High swooned at the sight of Mr. Fontayne, the handsome, young French teacher; of Roy, the beau of Margie's own age; the next-door, typically flapperish girlfriend with the peroxide hair, rouged knees and rolled stockings; of the young school librarian who had also set her sights for the young French teacher.

Jeanne Crain heads the cast of youthful performers who carry this story, as Margie, and, as usual, she screens beautifully in Technicolor. Miss Crain also looks and acts the type in this flashback story of a mother's memories of her school days. Glenn Langan is the French teacher who becomes the principal; he handles his comparatively small role satisfactorily. Alan Young, the radio comedian, who is making his first appearince in films, is excellent as the mooning sweetheart of Miss Crain during her school days.

Lynn Bari is the librarian, a small part handled adequately; Barbara Lawrence the flapper with boys on her mind constantly, an eye-opener part for the youngster; Conrad Janis is the football-playing, coonskin-wearing kid with a yen for scrimmaging on the parlor sofa as well as the gridiron; Esther Dale plays Miss Crain's grandmother, and Hobart Cavanaugh her father, and it is around him that the pic's funniest situation, at the finish, is set up. It is a fine, uniformly good cast whose performance helps "Margie" emerge as a sweetly sentimental story of a period that must inevitably produce fond memories for any audience.

Kahn

The Chase

UA release of Seymour Nebenzal production. Stars Robert Cummings; features Michele Morgan, Peter Lorre, Steve Cochran. Directed by Arthur Ripley. Screenplay, Philip Yordan, based on novel by Cornell Woolrich; score, Michael Michelet; camera, Eugene Frenke; editor, Ed Mann. Tradeshown N.Y., Oct. 11, '46. Running time, 86 mins.

Chuck....................Robert Cummings
Lorna....................Michele Morgan
Gino....................Peter Lorre
Roman....................Steve Cochran
Johnson....................Lloyd Corrigan
Commander Davidson....................Jack Holt
Fats....................Don Wilson
Acosta....................Alexis Minotis
Madame Chin....................Nina Koshetz
Midnight....................Yolanda Lacca
Job....................James Westerfield
Manicurist....................Shirley O'Hara

Another case of a sure wirner folding just before the finish line. "The Chase" is a meller that's taut as sprung steel for 75 minutes of its running time then slackens limply into the commonplace. Cut off the last few sequences, which are tacked on with a style and mood unlike the main body, and the pic is a superior production in every department. Taken as a whole, it still rates above-par and with fairly strong marquee pull on the credit side, the film's potential at the b.o. seems bright enough.

Yarn concerns the attempt of a killer's wife and his chauffeur to make their getaway from his household and henchman. Through a series of adroit directorial strokes, in the Hitchcock tradition, the pic's momentum is made to mount in a steady, ascending line. Terror stalks the pair in their flight to Havana then explodes with the shocking stillness of a gun with a silencer on it.

In the film's standout scene, Michele Morgan drops to the floor of a crowded cafe, killed by a stiletto thrust in the midst of an embrace. Robert Cummings, as the chauffeur ,is then picked up by the Havana police under suspicion of murder. Under pressure of a tightening web of framed-up evidence against him he breaks loose from the cops and tries to clear himself. In another smashing sequence, Cummings is cornered by Peter Lorre, a gunman, who riddles him full of holes and then dumps him down some stairs where Cummings lands in a grotesque heap. Having no place to go from here, the screenplay resorts to the easy device of having the whole business take place in a dream.

Cummings handles himself nicely but, though he tops the cast, is overshadowed by the dominating personality and looks of a newcomer, Steve Cochran, who plays the killer. Cochran is handsome, suave, confident, and menacing in the manner of a Humphrey Bogart. Thesping talents are adequate for a strong buildup. Lorre, in one of his best roles, comes through with a solid assist as the killer's aide-de-camp. Miss Morgan registers nicely, although she isn't given much to do besides modelling a few flashy gowns.

Lensing is executed with finesse and the process shot in which the killer's limousine crashes into a racing locomotive is done with excellent technique. Musical score is also nicely blended to add to the overall effect.

Herm.

Vacation in Reno

Hollywood, Oct. 5.

RKO release of Leslie Goodwins production, directed by Goodwins. Stars Jack Haley; features Anne Jeffreys, Wally Brown, Iris Adrian, Morgan Conway, Alan Carney. Screenplay, Charles E. Roberts and Arthur Ross; based on story by Charles Kerr; camera, George E. Diskant; special effects, Russell A. Cully; music, Paul Sawtell; editor, Les Millbrook. Tradeshown Oct. 4, '46. Running time, **60 MINS.**

Jack Carroll....................Jack Haley
Eleanor....................Anne Jeffreys
Eddie Roberts....................Wally Brown
Bunny Wells....................Iris Adrian
Joe....................Morgan Conway
Angel....................Alan Carney
Mrs. Dumont....................Myrna Dell
Dumont....................Matt McHugh
Sally Beaver....................Claire Carleton
Sheriff....................Jason Robards
Hank....................Matt Willis

Helter - skelter supporting comedy that should play off okay in secondary positions. Antics of names, which are all familiar enough to aid possibilities, is slanted for the family trade and, while it's all frantic, there are enough laughs to help spin out the 60 minutes running time. Production values measure up to budget expenditure in good fashion.

Marital comedy deals with lovey-dovey couple who have first quarrel and the husband goes off to Reno—not for a divorce but to spend a two-week vacation looking for buried treasure. Naturally wife misunderstands and follows. Many bedroom complications slow their eventual get-together as husband becomes involved with trio of bank robbers whose loot he has found. When script dialog and situations can't develop a laugh, mechanical devices such as chattering telephones are thrown in to assure a chuckle. It's obvious that the husband will end up a hero and with a tidy reward for his fumbling efforts in bringing the bank-robbers to justice.

Jack Haley is the husband and Anne Jeffreys the wife. Both try hard and get through with sufficient laughs to rate a nod under Les Goodwins' direction. Latter gets the most possible from script by Charles E. Roberts and Arthur Ross, based on a story by Charles Kerr. Wally Brown and Claire Carleton are in on opening sequences as a quarrelsome couple who provoke trouble between Haley and Miss Jeffreys. Iris Adrian, Morgan Conway and Alan Carney form the crook trio for some laughs. Matt Willis, a dumb deputy sheriff, holds up his end of what fun there is. Also good for a lift are Myrna Dell and Matt McHugh.

Goodwins, who also produced, makes most of budget allotment under executive supervision of Sid Rogell. Lensing by George E. Diskant measures up as do other technical aides.

Brog.

Nocturne

(SONGS)

Hollywood, Oct. 12.

RKO release of Joan Harrison production. Stars George Raft, Lynn Bari; features Virginia Huston, Joseph Pevney, Myrna Dell, Edward Ashley, Walter Sande, Mabel Paige. Directed by Edwin L. Marin. Screenplay, Jonathan Latimer; based on story by Frank Fenton and Rowland Brown; camera, Harry J. Wild; music, Leigh Harline; songs, Harline and Mort Greene, Eleanor Rudolph; editor, Elmo Williams. Tradeshown L. A., Oct. 7, '46. Running time, **86 MINS.**

Joe Warne....................George Raft
Frances Ransom....................Lynn Bari
Carol Page....................Virginia Huston
Fingers....................Joseph Pevney
Susan....................Myrna Dell
Vincent....................Edward Ashley
Halberson....................Walter Sande
Mrs. Warne....................Mabel Paige
Torp....................Bernard Hoffman
Queenie....................Queenie Smith
Gratz....................Mack Gray

"Nocturne" is a detective thriller headed for good b.o. payoff. George Raft name adds to selling values. It has been well mounted by Joan Harrison as her first RKO production. Action and suspense are plentiful and hard-bitten mood of story is sustained throughout by Edwin L. Marin's direction. There's some confusion towards windup in pulling all threads of tale together but this is apparently due to editing problem in keeping footage to tight 86 minutes' running time.

Raft is seen as hardboiled detective lieutenant whose stubbornness leads to uncovering a murder previously tagged a suicide. He gives his usual, slow-paced, tough touch to assignment to make it thoroughly effective. Co-star Lynn Bari, a prime suspect through much of the footage, turns in a capable job. Virginia Huston is interesting as Miss Bari's song-stress sister and sings three tunes, "Nocturne," "Why Pretend," and "A Little Bit Is Better Than None." All are tuneful. Former is by Leigh Harline and Mort Greene, while Eleanor Rudolph cleffed other two numbers.

Plot is the Frank Fenton-Rowland Brown story, scripted by Jonathan Latimer, has Edward Ashley, composer, found dead in his swank Hollywood home, an apparent suicide. Police accept theory, all but Raft, who can't believe the Ashley character is type to shoot himself in middle of composing tune. Raft steps on a lot of toes during attempts to put over his theory and is finally tossed off police force. He still keeps up search and finds a murder, but not until he has been beaten and otherwise kicked around.

Joseph Pevney, as a mild piano-pounder in a nitery, is the killer and shows up well. Myrna Dell, sexy blonde housekeeper for Ashley, adds some spice to proceedings. Mabel Paige shines as Raft's mother. Bernie Hoffman is an outsize menace. Others are capable.

Both Miss Harrison and Edwin Marin maintain a matter-of-fact mood in development to command-attention. Leigh Harline's music score and lensing by Harry J. Wild contribute expertly to sustaining suspenseful atmosphere.

Brog.

Child of Divorce

RKO release of Lillie Hayward production. Features Sharyn Moffet, Regis Toomey, Madge Meredith, Walter Reed, Una O'Connor, Doris Merrick. Directed by Richard O. Fleischer. Screenplay, Lillie Hayward; based on the play, "Wednesday's Child," by Leopold L. Atlas; camera, Jack MacKenzie; music, Leigh Harline; editor, Samuel E. Beetley. Tradeshown N. Y., Oct. 1, '46. Running time, **62 MINS.**

Bobby....................Sharyn Moffet
Ray....................Regis Toomey
Joan....................Madge Meredith
Michael....................Walter Reed
Nora....................Una O'Connor
Louise....................Doris Merrick
Judge....................Harry Chesire
Dr. Sterling....................Selmer Jackson
Carrie....................Lillian Randolph
Linda....................Pat Prest
Freddie....................Gregory Muradian
Donnie....................George McDonald
Betty....................Patsy Converse
Peggy....................Ann Carter

"Child of Divorce," as the tag implies, is a pic with a message about broken homes. Theme is old hat but this film is a surprise. It says what it has to say sincerely, poignantly and economically. A small budgeter, this film has rolled up its modest production resources into a tight little fist and will sock hard in any dualer situation in which it's placed. Properly angled exploitation towards church groups and parent-teacher associations could boost this effort to unexpected levels.

Whole production is held together by the superlative thesping of 8-year-old Shirley Moffat. Moppet conducts herself with admirable restraint, skirting the fatal pitfall into cloying sweetness or precocity. Child's heart-break as she gets torn between her parents is portrayed with an inner agony that will moisten many a kerchief. Rest of the cast, topped by Regis Toomey as the father and Madge Meredith as the mother, perform with equal conviction.

Story unfolds with the directness of a documentary study. Without any twisting, turning or corny embellishments, the camera keeps a steady focus on the child through the domestic breakup, the divorce proceedings, her shuttling back and forth between two homes, and her pathetic windup in a boarding school. Screenplay, which is simple but honest, gives no balm at the fadeout as the child looks wistfully out of her schoolroom window and the chapel chimes ironically strike up "Home, Sweet Home."

Herm.

Toccata and Fugue in D Minor

(CINECOLOR)

UA release of David L. Loew (Musicolor) Production. Produced by Werner Janssen, conducting Janssen Symphony Orchestra of Los Angeles; camera, Alan Stensvold; orchestration, Lucien Caillet; sound, W. M. Dalgleish. Running time, **10 MINS.**

New series of musical classics shorts filmed with outdoor backgrounds, of which this is the first, looks like a good bet. Reverse switch of setting backgrounds to music, instead of music to the scene, while not new, is still novel. And this series apparently is being done with care, skill, taste and artistry.

Film is a 10-minute recording of the great D Minor Toccata and Fugue of Bach, orchestrated by Lucien Caillet (who got his training while in the Philadelphia Orchestra under the eyes of that ace of Bach transcribers, Leopold Stokowski). The unusual, impressive formations of Bryce Canyon, Utah, are filmed as screen accompaniment, the majestic natural beauty of canyon, rocks, forests, clouds and sky teaming perfectly with the inspiring strains of the Bach work. Change of scenes, of seasons, are used cleverly to suit style and rhythm changes in the music (bright sunlight on the cliffs for the toccata; snowstorm in the forest for the fugue, etc.). Scenically, the short is eye-filling, while musically, the Janssen Symphony under its conductor Janssen, performs the Bach music in smooth, finished style, with the various choirs well balanced.

Bron.

Foreign Films

"L'Affaire Du Collier De La Reine" ("The Case of the Queen's Necklace") **(FRENCH).** Pathe release and production; directed by Marcel L'Herbier; stars Viviane Romance; features Marion Dorian, Maurice Escande, Jacques Dacqmine, Pierre Bertin; reviewed in Paris. Running time, **78 MINS.**

Picture, said to have cost $500,000, originally was started by Ile de France productions and after budgetary trouble was completed by Pathe. Marcel L'Herbier is credited as director but since he was ill during much of the shooting, few scenes are worthwhile with the exception of the last sequence which shows Miss Romance whipped and branded for her part in a royal swindle. Actress portrays the part done by Marcelle Chantal in the pre-war version. This entry is not likely to cover its cost because handicapped with the Louis XVI story very formally scripted and acted.

Johansson Och Vestman
("Johansson and Vestman")
Stockholm, Sept. 17.

Svensk Filmindustry production and release. Stars Holger Loewenadler, Sture Lagervall, Wanda Rothgardt. Directed by Olof Molander. Screenplay by Rune Lindstrom from play by Karl Staaff; camera, Ake Dahlquist. At Skandia, Stockholm, starting Sept. 3. Running time. 90 MINS.

This is one of the better Swedish productions. Story has a social background with the crime-does-not-pay motif pointed up. But it is more than that because of the excellent screenplay by Rune Lindstrom plus the splendid direction of veteran Olof Molander. This backed by the fine camera work of Ake Dahlquist makes for fine realism.

Principal players also go far in making this a thoroughly convincing yarn. Some of featured roles are a bit overdone, however.

Picture looms as a splendid representative for the Swedish picture industry throughout the world. As such, it stacks up as having possibilities in the American market. *Win.*

Miniature Reviews

"Deception" (WB). Potent Bette Davis vehicle with solid appeal for femme patrons. Box-office outlook hefty.

"Never Say Goodbye" (WB). Fairly amusing comedy with Errol Flynn name for average grosses.

"Laughing Lady" (Songs-Color) (Anglo-Am.). Despite lack of names this Britisher may do well in America.

"High School Hero" (Songs) (Mono). Lightweight teen-age comedy for featherweight gross.

"The Brute Man" (PRC). Dull meller that's strictly double bill fodder.

"Spring Song" (Anglo-Am.). British-made romance of stage yarn; okay for duals in U. S.

"Amok" (French). Fighting the N. Y. State censors is not worth the trouble.

"Broken Love" (Italian-Made) (Songs). Beniamino Gigli in an oppressively-weak story offering little for U. S. market.

Deception
Hollywood, Oct. 19.

Warner Bros. release of Henry Blanke production. Stars Bette Davis, Paul Henreid, Claude Rains; features John Abbott, Benson Fong. Directed by Irving Rapper. Screenplay, John Collier and Joseph Than; based on play by Louis Verneuil; camera, Ernest Haller; editor, Alan Crosland, Jr.; original music and Hollenius' Cello Concerto by Erich Wolfgang Korngold. Tradeshown Oct. 16. '46. Running time. 111 MINS.

Christine Radcliffe............Bette Davis
Karel Novak...................Paul Henreid
Alexander Hollenius..........Claude Rains
Bertram Gribble...............John Abbott
The Manservant..............Benson Fong

"Deception," a story of matrimonial lies that builds to a murder climax, gives Bette Davis a potent vehicle. Plot is backed with lavish production, strong playing of a story loaded with femme interest, and bright direction to point it for hefty boxoffice returns. Cast is small but the names of Miss Davis, Paul Henreid and Claude Rains guarantee marquee voltage for all situations. Another credit adding to entertainment values is the music score, used both as plot motivation and as standout production moments.

Role given Miss Davis is less neurotic than most of her recent assignments. She plays it to the hilt, using full dramatic talent in the reading to please her large following. It's not all her show, though. Claude Rains as her elderly teacher and sponsor walks off with considerable portion of the picture in a fine display of acting ability. His role is a choice one and what he makes of it adds much to the quality of this production. By contrast, Henreid suffers although turning in a smooth performance in a role with not too much color.

Plot concerns deception practiced by Miss Davis to prevent husband Henreid from discovering that she had been the mistress of Rains before her marriage. Henreid, refugee cellist, is a jealous man whose temperamental instability is reason for the wife's deception. Plot suspense is carefully fostered in the excellent script by John Collier and Joseph Than, based on the Louis Verneuil play. Pickup to story comes with Rains' entrance and his mad jealousy over his desertion by his mistress. To him falls juicy plums in the form of dialog and situations that carry the story along. End comes as Henreid makes his debut as a concert cellist, playing a Rains composition after Miss Davis, fearing that her sponsor planned to reveal previous relation, kills him.

Only others credited in the small cast are John Abbott and Benson Fong. Former, as a rival cellist, makes the most of the spot and Fong gives good account to his footage as Rains' understanding houseboy.

Finesse and understanding insight of Irving Rapper's direction does much to point up the dramatic play and show off the players to the best advantage. Henry Blanke's production is lush and showmanly, abetted by fine art direction by Anton Grot and decorations by George James Hopkins so eyefully displayed by Ernest Haller's camera.

Music importance is emphasized by Erich Wolfgang Korngold's score and staging of orchestral numbers by LeRoy Prinz. Korngold's original music and the Cello Concerto are outstanding highlights that will be fully appreciated by concert lovers. *Brog.*

Never Say Goodbye
Hollywood, Oct. 19.

Warner Bros. release of William Jacobs production. Stars Errol Flynn, Eleanor Parker; features Lucile Watson, S. Z. Sakall, Forrest Tucker, Donald Woods, Peggy Knudsen, Tom D'Andrea, Hattie McDaniel, Charles Coleman, Patti Brady. Directed by James V. Kern. Screenplay, I. A. L. Diamond and James V. Kern; original story, Ben and Norma Barzman; adaptation, Lewis R. Foster; camera, Arthur Edeson; music, Frederick Hollander; editor, Folmer Blangsted. Tradeshown Oct. 18. '46. Running time. 96 MINS.
Phil Gayley...................Errol Flynn
Ellen Gayley................Eleanor Parker
Mrs. Hamilton..............Lucile Watson
Luigi.........................S. Z. Sakall
Corp. Fenwick Lonkowski..Forrest Tucker
Rex..........................Donald Woods
Nancy.......................Peggy Knudsen
Jack Gordon.................Tom D'Andrea
Cozy.......................Hattie McDaniel
Withers....................Charles Coleman
Introducing Patti Brady.

"Never Say Goodbye" is a matrimonial comedy dealing with a divorced couple. It manages to be fairly amusing and has sufficient cast strength to rate average b.o. Lightweight plot is backed up with good physical production values and cast works hard to get the antics over. Names of Errol Flynn and Eleanor Parker, plus other familiars, lend marquee weight to aid selling.

Plot deals with divorced couple who are still in love but unable to get together again. Flynn is seen as a famous artist of the calendar girl type whose eye for the girls originally broke up the marriage. Plot centers largely on efforts of couple's young daughter, Patti Brady, to get her parents together again. Film introduces young Miss Brady but she offers little more than the usual screen moppet ability talent-wise.

James V. Kern's direction works hard to put over comical angles of Flynn playing Santa Claus and bedroomish mixups between him. Eleanor Parker and Forrest Tucker. General audiences will be amused but many of laughs will come from impossibility of majority of the situations found in the Kern-I. A. L. Diamond script. Story eventually gets the couple together but not without plenty of complications.

Flynn's forte is not comedy. Miss Parker gives role s.a. but otherwise has little opportunity to display histrionic talent. Abetting chuckles is S. Z. Sakall as restaurant-owning friend of the couple. Forrest Tucker does well as an overgrown marine who gives Flynn jealousy pangs. Donald Woods does another of his stiff-necked characterizations. Lucille Watson, Peggy Knudsen, Tom D'Andrea, Hattie McDaniel and others are capable.

William Jacobs' production supervision assured glossy physical appurtenances for dress. Lensing by Arthur Edeson is expert. Art direction and decorations by Anton Grot and Budd Friend, respectively are well valued. Running time of picture could be trimmed to advantage. *Brog.*

Laughing Lady
(Songs—Color)
(BRITISH-MADE)
London, Oct. 16.

Anglo-American Film release of British National picture. Stars Anne Ziegler, Webster Booth; features Felix Aylmer, Francis L. Sullivan, Peter Graves. Directed by Paul L. Stein. Screenplay by Jack Whittingham. Music by Hans May. Camera, Geoffrey Unsworth. At the Palace theatre, London. Running time. 100 MINS.
Denise.......................Anne Ziegler
Andre.......................Webster Booth
Sir William Tremayne..Francis L. Sullivan
Prince of Wales...............Peter Graves
Louise........................Chili Bouchier
Sir Felix Mountroyal.........Felix Aylmer
Lord Mandeville.............Ralph Truman
Robespierre.................Charles Goldner
Lord Barrymore...............Jack Melford
Pierre.........................Paul Dupuis
Gilliat.......................John Ruddock
Tinville...................George de Warfaz
Lady Langley.................Mary Martlew
Jenkins..................Frederick Burtwell

To make a big-scale Technicolor costume musical in 63 days for $400,-000 must constitute something of a record these days here, but indie producer Lou Jackson has a fine knack of film budgeting. However, until he can get international stars, his pictures are of necessity aimed at home and Empire markets. This one should bring in a nice profit. Like his "Waltz Time," this should find a place in the U. S.

While the star names mean nothing in America, Webster Booth and Anne Ziegler are big concert and theatre attractions here, and will bring many additional customers. They have been given some nice numbers by Hans May.

Based on a radio play by Ingram d'Abbes, story is set in France and England during the French Revolution. While watching heads roll from the guillotine, Charles Goldner (Robespierre) offers to reprieve a duchess if her son, Booth, can bring back to France the "Pearls of Sorrow," a necklace given to his mother by Marie Antoinette and subsequently smuggled to England.

So he becomes a highwayman on the London-Brighton road, meets Miss Ziegler, celebrates with a love duet, and finds himself commissioned to paint her portrait—complete with necklace—by her rich future husband. As the necklace was given her by the Prince of Wales, and theft of it, for some obscure reason, would shame her, Booth prefers to return to France and sacrifice his own and his mother's life. Booth's servant, who has stolen the necklace, is made to return it to Miss Ziegler who, learing the truth, rushes to Paris and arrives just as the guillotine is about to descend on her lover's neck.

For their singing, Miss Ziegler and Booth rate top marks. But their acting sometimes leaves much to be desired. They are hardly cut out for heroic romantic leads. General level of acting is first rate, with notable work by Francis Sullivan, Paul Dupuis, Felix Aylmer and a fine characterization by Peter Graves. *Cane.*

Amok
(FRENCH-MADE)

Distinguished Films release of Carlyle production. Features Marcelle Chantel, Jean Yonnel, Vladimir Inkijinoff. Directed by Fedor Ozep. Adapted from Stefan Zweig short story. English titles, Walter Klee. Reviewed N. Y., Oct. 18. '46. Running time. 68 MINS.

(In French; English Titles)

William Brandt and Oliver Unger, partners in Distinguished Films, Inc., recently-established importing unit, have been battling the N. Y. censors over "Amok." Continuing their efforts to prove their case—in public opinion, at least—they held a special screening last week with the press as a "jury." If the newspaper and mag critics agree with the Regents, declared g.m. Martin Levine, Distinguished will abandon further appeals to the courts. While no actual vote was taken, consensus of the "jury" was fairly clear: regardless of the censorship angles, "Amok" isn't worth fighting for.

Since the whole motivation of the film concerns a married woman's demands upon a doctor to perform an abortion before her husband returns home from a year abroad and discovers she is pregnant, there is certainly something to be said on the side of the censors. On the other hand, the more liberal and reasonable viewpoint on a film like this would be to approve it, since, if it has any appeal at all, it obviously will be only to the small, select audiences that patronize art houses. The N. Y. Regents may have been fearful, though—and justifiably—that the picture would be advertised and exploited as lurid, which, actually, it is not.

Whole dispute, of course, goes back to basic concepts of freedom of speech and press and the right of any politically-appointed body to deign itself a keeper of public morals and monitor of what may be seen and what may not be seen. Necessity of having official ganderers to prevent pure obscenity from reaching the screen is recognized as a justifiable infringement on freedom of speech, but "Amok" is not in that category. Although the situation set up by the author is a basically immoral one, of course, the treatment of it in the film is in no sense obscene or objectionable—at least from a moral standpoint.

Leaving all that aside, the picture itself is poor and boresome. It is based on a famous short story by Stefan Zweig—and should have remained that. Stretching it to 68 minutes spreads the yarn much too thin.

Scene of the tale is an unnamed French colonial island in which natives occasionally are driven "amok" by the wet and torrid climate. After one such "amok" scene—which has nothing whatever to do with the principal theme—that's forgotten and the conflict is picked up between a French doctor there (Jean Yonnel) and a woman from the French colony (Marcelle Chantal). The medico at first refuses to perform the abortion she requests and then virtually goes "amok" himself in his desire to perform it. Her pride by that time won't permit her to allow him to operate and the picture concerns itself principally with his efforts to convince her, since he has fallen in love with her. She winds up by going to a native herb doctor and dying. In the meantime, her husband has returned and, to keep him from having an autopsy performed, the doctor dramatically cuts a cable permitting the coffin containing her body to fall into the sea, knowing full well the act will likewise plunge him to his death.

Technically, the film is atrocious. Direction and, particularly, cutting are in the manner of early silents. The performances and English titles are likewise in keeping with that tradition. All in all, the whole thing would best be forgotten. *Herb.*

The Brute Man

PRC release of Ben Pivar production. Features Tom Neal, Jane Adams, Jan Wiley, Donald MacBride, Rondo Hatton. Directed by Jean Yarbrough. Screenplay, George Bricker and M. Coates Webster from original story by Dwight V. Babcock; camera, Maury Gertsman. Previewed N. Y., Oct. 17, '46. Running time, **58 MINS.**

Hal Moffat....................Rondo Hatton
Helen....................Jane Adams
Clifford Scott....................Tom Neal
Virginia....................Jan Wiley

Semi-horror pic, originally produced on the Universal lot, was turned over to PRC for distribution a couple months ago in line with U's policy of no more B's. Singularly unexciting meller is suitable only for lower dualers.

Replete with chases and murders, yarn concerns the maraudings of a paranoic killer known as The Creeper (Rondo Hatton). Disfigured by acid in a college chem lab, he seeks vengeance upon his former schoolchums whom he believes responsible for his plight. Hatton's facial features, which run a close second to those of Frankenstein's monster, furnish the film's few chills.

Unwittingly sheltering The Creeper from the law, a blind piano teacher (Jane Adams) is promised financial aid from the murderer for an eye operation to restore her sight. In thefting jewels from ex-classmates, the Clifford Scotts (Tom Neal and Jan Wiley), he rubs out Scott and escapes with the ice. However, the sleuths discover the link between The Creeper and the piano teacher when she attempts to hock the jools. Anticipating his return to her home, they seize him in a trite finale.

Producer Ben Pivar, long U's keeper of the B's, has done little to make what may have been his last "B" to stand out from similar fodder. Scripting and acting are in keeping with the quality of the production. Film, incidentally, was Hatton's last pic before his death in Beverly Hills last February.

Spring Song
(SONGS)
(BRITISH-MADE)

London, Oct. 15.

Anglo-American Film Corp., release of British National Films picture. Stars Carol Raye, Peter Graves, Leni Lynn. Directed by Montgomery Tully. Screenplay by Montgomery Tully, James Seymour from original story by Lore and Maurice Cowan. Music by Hans May, lyrics by Alan Shanks. Camera, Ernest Palmer, Moray Grant. At the Palace, London. Running time, **90 MINS.**

Tony Winster....................Peter Graves
Janet Hill; Janet Ware........Carol Raye
Johnnie Ware..........Lawrence O'Madden
Vera Dale....................Leni Lynn
Lady Norchester............Netta Westcott
Sir Anthony....................David Horne
Mary Norchester........Diana Calderwood
Menelli....................Alan Wheatley
Carrington....................Peter Penn
Dresser....................Maire O'Neill
Hotel Manager..........Gerald Kempinski
Cobb....................Finlay Currie
Dancer ....Jack Billings

Louis H. Jackson, production chief of British National, biggest indie British producer who has his own well-equipped studios, makes films on a budget calculated to bring profit in the home market. Anything extra from abroad is added gravy. But this attitude leads to playing safe, and imaginative treatment of any theme is ducked because it might be more difficult to sell.

"Spring Song" could easily have been elevated in nostalgic charm like that of "Meet Me in St. Louis," but conventional handling has robbed the original story of any individuality.

Film cost a fraction of some recent British epics ($280,000). Never pretending to be more than a modest film, it gives real entertainment value. Should play to hefty grosses in this country. For America it may fit nicely into dual bills. Much of the action being backstage cries for technicolor, but wisely hackneyed vaudeville turns have been omitted.

A valuable brooch, heirloom of the Norchester family, links two periods 1911 and 1946, and two love stories, in which Carol Raye plays mother and daughter and Peter Graves uncle and nephew. Searching for the donor of the brooch to the Red Cross, Peter ends up at the stage door of a theatre, falls in love with Carol, is forbidden by her father to see her again, and the young lovers learn the near-tragic love story of 1911. But when Carol discovers that Tony is to risk his life trying out a new jet plane, she tears half across England to fall into his arms.

On her showing here, Miss Raye establishes herself as top newcomer in British films. She appears destined to be a big topliner. Hollywood is certain to take more note of her than British producers have so far. Never has she danced better, her number "Give Me a Chance to Dance" (with Jack Billings) winning big applause.

Peter Graves shows up as an important light comedian. May soon rank in popularity with David Niven, whom he slightly resembles. Lawrence O'Madden, grand character actor, wins great sympathy by his fine playing, and Leni Lynn displays her coloratura in a couple of songs that have been interpolated to show the range of her voice.

Musically Hans May earns praise for composition and direction. He has given the picture a fine melodic lilt, and numbers like "Spring Song," "Somewhere in This Great Big World" and "It's Love Again" should reap a rich harvest.

The jet plane scenes were flown by Geoffrey de Havilland, recently killed breaking the world's speed record. *Cane.*

High School Hero
(SONGS)

Monogram release of Sam Katzman (Maurice Duke) production. Features Freddy Stewart, June Preisser, Noel Neill, Ann Rooney. Directed by Arthur Dreifuss. Screenplay, Hal Collins, Arthur Dreifuss; camera, Ira Morgan; music, Edward Kay; editor, Ace Herman. At Fox, Brooklyn, dual, week Oct. 19 '46. Running time, **69 MINS.**

Freddie....................Freddie Stewart
Dodie....................June Preisser
Betty....................Noel Neill
Addie....................Ann Rooney
Jimmy....................Jackie Moran
Roy....................Frankie Darro
Lee....................Warren Mills
Townley....................Milt Kibbee
Miss Hinklefink..............Belle Mitchell
Chi-Chi ....Isabelita
Coach Carter..............Douglas Fowley
Mrs. Rogers..............Edythe Elliott
Prof. Farrell..............Leonard Penn
Governor Huffington.........Pierre Watkin
Mayor Whitehead..............Dick Elliott
Jan Savitt....................Jan Savitt
Freddie Slack..............Freddie Slack
Tiny....................Joe Derita

Freddie Slack Orchestra
Jan Savitt Orchestra featuring Isabelita

Monogram might well go into the advertising business on the strength of this picture. Cross-plugs come so fast that it's hard to keep up with them, going from Capitol Records to Koret Fashions, to Royal Crown Cola ad infinitum, all of which makes the exhibs' exploitation job somewhat simpler, but doesn't add a great deal to the picture's b.o. value.

Nevertheless, the final product emerges as fair divertissement for the junior coke crowd to which it is pitched with ever so slight a touch of accidental honesty. If the company is able to train early teensters to make this film series a habit, grosses will be helped, but adult trade will find it slightly boresome. Film is one of Mono's Teen-Ager series, all of which feature the same perennial highschoolers in the same situation settings. So, outside of payroll, film's budget was probably negligible.

Story probably happened before, but only on the screen. At least all the old gimmicks are used for the occasional chuckles that emerge. Two highschools have a big football game, but only one has a team worth mentioning and they're the heavies in the black jerseys. Poor white-sweatered Whitney High has two objects in mind; to win the game and have a show, in which they eventually succeed, after taking the audience through a succession of stock teenster troubles. High spots are provided by the musicating of Freddie Slack and Jan Savitt.

Thesping by the "kid" veterans is good throughout, except for one sequence wherein June Preisser makes an impassioned speech to save the gang from suspension. Camera work is extremely spotty, with attempts in one sequence to follow a drum majorette's batoneering leaving the audience a little dizzy.

Broken Love
('Cuore Infranto')
(ITALIAN-MADE)
(Songs)

Suprafilm release of Italafilm production. Stars Beniamino Gigli; features Emma Gramatica, Camilla Horn. Directed by Guido Brignone. Music, Giacomo Puccini. At Arena Cine Verdi, N. Y., week of Oct. 18, '46. Running time, **89 MINS.**

Luciano Riccardi............Beniamino Gigli
Letizia....................Emma Gramatica
Claudia Riccardi..............Camilla Horn
Corinna Delly..............Ruth Hellberg
Alberto Vieri..............Herbert Wilk

(In Italian; English Titles)

"Broken Love," featuring slick production mountings seldom equalled in an Italian-made film, offers ample evidence that the Italian industry is rapidly regaining its pre-war equilibrium and is, in fact, casting surreptitious glances at the American market. However, bogged down by a very weak story, incompetent acting and equally incompetent direction, the film appears to have very little to offer American audiences. It will probably do business in the Italian-language theatres but its value in even arty American houses looks doubtful.

Pic's chief claim to fame lies in the Puccini music, as sung by Beniamino Gigli, the former Met tenor who's still under a Fascist cloud. Gigli's age is apparent in both his appearance and voice. He's still one of the most robust tenors on the screen but his speaking voice is ultra-poor and his acting is hammy to the extreme. Music lovers, though, will go for his rendition of the death-bed scene from "La Boheme," the film's climax.

Story is an oppressive tear-jerker, supposedly adapted from the opera, with hardly a touch of comedy or anything light-veined to break the mood. Gigli is seen as the "world's greatest tenor," whose happiness in success is marred by the fact that his young daughter suffers from a weak heart. Latter falls in love with a young bank clerk and the duo is all set to marry when the boy's former mistress comes back from a concert tour and puts her foot down. Weak-charactered boy goes off with the mistress and the gal's heart condition gets worse. After another couple of reels devoted to practically nothing, the boy returns to her just before she dies, with the final scene cutting back and forth from the gal to Gigli singing "La Boheme" in order to point up the similarity between the two stories.

Supporting cast is only fair. Emma Gramatica as Gigli's maiden sister and Ruth Hellberg as the mistress take whatever honors can be passed out. Camilla Horn suffers nobly but weakly as the daughter and Herbert Wilk is good-looking enough but too willy-nilly as her vis-a-vis.

Story is set against a rich backdrop of Roman homes, the canals of Venice and Riviera gambling casinos, representing a heavy outlay of cash. Guido Brignone's direction is stultified, adding to the film's slow pacing. *Stal.*

Foreign Films

"Karlek Och Stortlopp" ("Love Goes Up and Down") (Swedish). Stars Sture Lagervall, Eva Dahlbeck; features Sigge Fyrst, Thor Modeen, John Botvid, Hjoerdis Pettersson, Agneta Lagerfeldt, Bullan Weijden; directed by Rolf Husberg; screenplay, Sven Bjorkman, Hasse Ekuan. Reviewed in Stockholm. Running time, **92 MINS.**

Swedish comedy with strong international appeal. Story is woven around a young author who's sent by a film company to the mountains to write a love story with a skiing background. While in the hills on this job he meets a femme correspondent who's also there getting material. Romantic tale will do well in Sweden although it's too slow for the U. S. market. *Wins.*

Miniature Reviews

"The Strange Woman" (UA). Strong marquee names and lusty story content augur sturdy b.o.

"Carnival" (GFD). Not likely to raise the quality average of recent British films; slim U.S. chances.

"Woman to Woman" (Anglo-Am). Third screen version of Michael Morton play by British looks sure boxoffice but only for duals in U. S.

The Strange Woman

Hollywood, Oct. 26.

United Artists release of Hunt Strömberg presentation, produced by Jack Chertok. Stars Hedy Lamarr, George Sanders, Louis Hayward; features Gene Lockhart, Hillary Brooke, Rhys Williams, June Storey, Moroni Olsen, Olive Blakney, Dennis Hoey, Alan Napier, Ina Keith. Directed by Edgar Ulmer. Screenplay, Herb Meadow; based on novel by Ben Ames Williams; camera, Lucien Andriot; score, Carmen Dragon; editors, John Foley and Richard G. Wray. Previewed Oct. 25, '46. Running time, 100 MINS.

Jenny Hager	Hedy Lamarr
John Evered	George Sanders
Ephraim Poster	Louis Hayward
Isaiah Poster	Gene Lockhart
Meg Saladine	Hillary Brooke
Deacon Adams	Rhys Williams
Lena Tempest	June Storey
Reverend Thatcher	Moroni Olsen
Mrs. Hollis	Olive Blakney
Tim Hager	Dennis Hoey
Judge Saladine	Alan Napier
Lincoln Pittridge	Ian Keith

"The Strange Woman" is set for top boxoffice. The highly dramatic theme, dealing with a lustful, sadistic femme schemer, augurs bright potentials. While not always the strong, smooth feature it should be, largely due to inept casting in a top male spot, nevertheless, the names of Hedy Lamarr, George Sanders and Louis Hayward are husky enough to insure initial pull.

Based on the Ben Ames Williams best-seller, story deals with strong-willed Jenny Hager who uses men for personal pleasure and as stepping stones to wealth. It's told against a background of Bangor, Maine, in the 1840s, itself a lusty, brawling town in the throes of growing pains. Settings and costumes present a seemingly authentic picture of the period and other production backing supplied by the Hunt Stromberg production, produced by Jack Chertok, is strong to carry off the story.

Miss Lamarr scores as the scheming Jenny Hager. Two-sided character obtains plenty of realism in her hands. Her capacity of appearing as a tender, administering angel and of mirroring sadistic satisfaction in the midst of violence bespeaks wide talent range. Not so adept are her male co-stars, although Hayward gets across the weakling son of Jenny Hager's first husband who is finally driven to suicide by the evil woman. Sanders is out of his depths as a shy, backwoods character who becomes Miss Lamarr's second husband. Portrayal is indifferent and makes for a weak link that holds film back from overall sock rating. Gene Lockhart, as a rich, aging Bangor merchant who becomes Jenny's first husband, does a standout piece of work. It's deftly shaded to get over his desire for the town beauty and at the same time protect his pocketbook. June Storey is another who shows up well in supporting roles, portraying a bosomy barmaid friend of Miss Hager's.

Plot concerns a girl, beautiful but willful, whose driving ambition is men and wealth. Novel's implication of mental incest between the drunkard father and daughter is only lightly touched but other sex motivations in the Williams' story, as scripted by Herb Meadow, are made full use of. Hillary Brooke is seen as the girl from whom Miss Lamarr steals Sanders. Rhys Williams, Moroni Olsen, Olive Blakney, good as a

housekeeper; Dennis Hoey, the sodden father; Alan Napier and Ian Keith, latter as a hellfire and brimstone-shouting travelling evangelist, measure up to all the demands of their roles. Moppets who portray stars as youngsters are uncredited but serve to establish characteristics of elders.

Edgar Ulmer's direction gets much from most of the cast. He displays much skill, particularly in Miss Lamarr's intense scenes, and generally points up dramatic contents. Lucien Andriot's lensing is fine. Production design and art direction by Nicolai Remisoff and the musical score by Carmen Dragon also are deserving of credit. *Brog.*

Carnival

(BRITISH-MADE)

London, Oct. 15.

General Film Distributors release of Two Cities film. Stars Sally Gray and Michael Wilding; features Stanley Holloway, Bernard Miles, Jean Kent. Directed by Stanley Haynes. Original story, Compton Mackenzie; Adaptation Eric Maschwitz. Camera, Guy Green; Ballet arranged by Freddie Carpenter. Reviewed at New Gallery, London, Oct. 15, '46. Running time 93 MINS.

Jenny	Sally Gray
Maurice Avery	Michael Wilding
Charlie Raeburn	Stanley Holloway
Trewhella	Bernard Miles
Irene Dale	Jean Kent
Florrie Raeburn	Catherine Lacey
Mrs. Trewhella	Nancy Price
May Raeburn	Hazel Court
Fuzz	Michael Clarke
Maudie Chapman	Brenda Bruce
Corentin	Anthony Holles
Jack Danby	Ronald Ward
Arthur Danby	Mackenzie Ward
Mr. Dutt	Bruce Winston
Studholme	Dennis Arundell
Barmaid	Phyllis Monkman
Aunt Fanny	Amy Veness
Mrs. Dale	Marie Ault
Elsie Crawford	Virginia Keiley
Madge Wilson	Pamela Foster
Vergo	Aspinosa
Ballerina	Bebe De Roland
Carpenter Corps De Ballet	

Second version of Compton Mackenzie's novel (first was made by Anthony Asquith as "Dance, Pretty Lady" in 1931), this will not raise the quality average of recent British films. Script and production troubles have resulted in a disjointed, dispirited picture. None of the principal characters, with the possible exception of roles done by Stanley Holloway and Michael Clarke appears credible. There's no sense to their behavior, and little evokes interest, much less sympathy. This is the key to the failure which, with a better script and more imaginative direction might have been a success. As it is, the medium star names may be drawn a little here, but chances of collecting in U. S. are slim. This looks like one for the debit side.

Story is set in London 1900 when no lady would enter certain music halls even where an innocent ballet was the top attraction. Born in the slums, Sally Gray graduates to the corps de ballet at the Orient.

Lengthy prolog leading up to this is unnecessary. Ignoring her mother's warnings, Miss Gay pursues her quest for a good time, confident she can take care of herself. She meets Michael Wilding, a sculptor, becomes his model, falls in love with him, but refuses to live with him.

He leaves her, and disillusioned and burdened with the care of a crippled sister, accepts an offer of marriage from a dour Cornish farmer. She gives up the stage and moves into a puritanical home with a bigoted man to whom she refuses to be a wife. Remorseful Wilding turns up in Cornwall, and the jealous husband spotting the two lovers talking by the seashore, kills his wife.

Miscast in the first place, Miss Gray can put little life into the puppet figure of Jenny, and Wilding is as unfortunate with the incomprehensive lover. Stanley Holloway, fine character actor, can only sketch

in his part as Jenny's shiftless father, while the hamming of Bernard Miles, as the farmer, is more comic than tragic. In toto, a picture of missed opportunities. *Cane..*

Woman to Woman

(BRITISH-MADE)

London, Oct. 23.

Anglo-American Films release of British National production. Stars Douglass Montgomery, Joyce Howard, Yvonne Arnaud, Adele Dixon. Directed by Maclean Rogers. Adapted by Marjorie Deans from screenplay by James Seymour; camera, James Wilson. At Palace theatre, London, Oct. 22, '46. Running time, 99 MINS.

David	Douglass Montgomery
Nicolette	Joyce Howard
Sylvia	Adele Dixon
Henrietta	Yvonne Arnaud
David Junior	Paul Collins
Dr. Gavron	John Warwick
Concierge	Lily Kahn
Pauline	Kay Young
De Rillac	Eugene Deckers
John Meredith	Alan Sedgwick
Postman	Martin Miller
Cafe Proprietor	Gerard Kempinski
Hotel Clerk	Marcel de Haes

An old silent picture success has been dusted off and refashioned into a hit. Third screen version of Michael Morton's play (1924, Betty Compson and Clive Brook; 1929, Betty Compson, George Barraud), has been brought up to date. Although there are no important marquee names, it is definitely a woman's picture and should benefit from mouth-to-mouth. Should find a good place on dual bills in the U. S., and sure to go big here.

Fine popular entertainment, it could have achieved distinction had a little more care been taken with some of acting, notably that of Douglass Montgomery. His overplaying occasionally throws the whole thing out of balance. Restraint in gesture and speech would have made a mighty difference in some of the scenes. Too often he confuses mumbling with emotion.

Rediscovery of the picture is Joyce Howard. Having gained something of a reputation in "Love on the Dole" and "The Gentle Sex," producers made little use of her obvious talents. Being cast as the French ballet dancer gives Miss Howard a real opportunity.

Outstanding as chief scene-stealer is Yvonne Arnaud, who gives a perfect study as a chaperone, and who has a fleeting moment to show her excellence as a pianist. Her rare appearances on the screen are a condemnation of British producers. Notable, too, is Eugene Deckers, stage recruit, who makes his screen debut. It is safe to surmise that some of Adele Dixon's best scenes were left on the cutting room floor, but she gets what she can out of the wife role.

Original versions had the hero unmarried when he meets the dancer in Paris, and gave great prominence to his amnesia before he again meets the girl. Present story begins in 1940 with Douglass Montgomery as a Canadian captain (to account for American accent) attached to Secret Service. Estranged from his cold socialite childless wife Sylvia he accepts a dangerous mission, goes to Paris to await zero hour, and falls in love with Nicolette, a talented dancer. When he leaves Paris and the Nazis arrive, she goes to London for the birth of their son.

Years pass and the soldier returns a hero minus an arm, searching for Nicolette. Eventually he finds her in London, where she is a magnetic star, but their happiness is short-lived. *Cane.*

The Turning Point

(SOVIET-MADE)

Artkino release of Lenfilm Studios production. Stars Mikhail Dershavin. Directed by Frederick Ermler. Screenplay, Boris Chirakov; camera, Arcady Kaltsatyi; music, Gregory Popov. English titles, Charles Clement. At Stanley, N. Y., Oct. 26, '46. Running time, 106 MINS.

Col.-Gen. Muravyev......Mikhail Derzhavin
Col.-Gen. Vinogradov.....Pavel Andrievsky
Comrade Lavrov...........Yuri Tolubeyev
Lieut.-Gen. Krivenko.....Andrei Abrikosov
Lieut.-Gen. Panteleyev...Alexel Zrashevsky
Minutka......................Mark Bernes
Stepan.......................Pavel Volkov

(In Russian; English Titles)

Winner of the Stalin prize and award recipient in the recent International Film Festival at Cannes, long Russian picture of a documentary nature purports to give the low-down on how the Russian high command plotted out the victory of Stalingrad. With judicious cutting to speed up action and narrative, film may make a possible entry for houses other than foreign-language situations.

Revealing a frankness that's rather startling for the Soviets, film shows that much dissension existed among top generals of the Red Army, who differed as to the choice of tactics necessary to defeat the besieging Nazi armies of Gen. von Klaus. Despite the brass' occasional lack of accord, story's underlying theme is the grim determination and inexorable will both of the Red Army and the workers themselves to crush the fascist hordes.

With the exception of a few graphic scenes of actual combat, pic is weak in action, with better part of footage devoted to staff conferences around map-strewn tables. Strategy for Russia's eventual victory began with appointment of Col.-Gen. Muravyev as supreme commander of the front, supplanting Col.-Gen. Vinogradov, who became his superior's chief of staff. New commander discloses his master plan before his associates who thresh out its chances of success with spirited discussion. On the whole film should be of great interest to students of military tactics.

Production values contribute little to the pic. Sound track is noisy while print itself appears to be in poor condition. Arcady Kaltsaty, reportedly the Soviet's top lensman, turned in only a fair job. Acting for the most part is of the typical Soviet school—stern-visaged characters speaking their lines in a stoic, deadly seriousness. Mikhail Derzhavin, as the supreme commander, does perhaps the best job. Frederick Ermler could have directed at a brisker pace.

Foreign Films

"Det Glada Kalaset" ("The Gay Party") (SWEDISH). Europa Film production and release. Stars Sicken Carlsson, Olof Winnerstrand; features Marianne Loefgren, Sven Lindberg, Alice Babs, Rut Holm, Dagmar Ebbesen, Douglas Hage, Allan Bohlin; directed by Bengt Ekeroth; screenplay, Sven Gustavsson; music, Eric Bauman and Nathan Goerling; songs, Alice Babs; camera, Harald Berglund; reviewed in Stockholm. Running time, 90 MINS.

Debut of former actor, Bengt Ekeroth, as director, finds him turning out a good comedy. Olof Winnerstrand and Sicken Carlsson do well in starring roles. Alice Babs, fave Swedish singer on jive disks, is excellent in a couple numbers. Lensing of Harald Berglund is also topflight. An okay grosser here, film looks likely for some arty spots in U. S.

"Montecassino" (Italian). Pastor production and release; stars Alberto C. Lolli, Ubaldo Lay; features Zora Piazza, Pietro Bigerna; written and directed by Arturo Gemmiti. Reviewed in Venice. Running time, 95 MINS.

Story deals with the siege of Cassino during that part of Italian campaign. Pitiful scenes of the sick and harried populace plus romance under

trying conditions in the shadow of the town's famous abbey looms as a doubtful entry in America. *Forn.*

"Det Ar Min Modell" ("My Model") (SWEDISH). Svensk Filmindustri production and release; stars Maj-Britt Nilsson, Alf Kjellin, features Marianne Loefgren, Olof Winnerstrand, Stig Jaerrel, Oscar Winge, Georg Funkquist, Sven Bergvall; directed by Gustav Molander; screenplay, Rune Lindstroem; camera, Ake Dahlquist; reviewed in Stockholm. Running time, 98 MINS.

Swedish comedy has young actress Maj-Britt Nilsson in her first good role. Film registers another success for scripter Rune Lindstroem. Yarn is about a sculptor, his model and a momument unveiling committee. Has fair appeal.

Miniature Reviews

"Song of the South" (Color-Songs) (RKO). Walt Disney's charming live-and-cartoon story good b.o.

"The Verdict" (WB). Whodunit in period setting with moderate b.o. chances.

"Dick Tracy vs. Cueball" (RKO). Strong action fare will have nice b.o. pull in dualer situations.

"Home in Oklahoma" (Songs) (Rep). Above-par oatuner starring Roy Rogers.

"Tumbleweed Trail" (Songs) (PRC). Mediocre Eddie Dean oatuner slated for action trade.

"Decoy" (Mono). Swiftly paced, smart direction makes this pic tops. Action fans will go for it.

"Plainsman and the Lady" (Rep). William Elliott, Vera Ralston in OK pony express opus.

"Strange Holiday" (PRC). Wartime product for General Motors employees now being given regular release by PRC; light b.o.

Song of the South

(SONGS—COLOR)

RKO release of Walt Disney production. Features Ruth Warrick, James Baskett, Bobby Driscoll, Luana Patten, Lucille Watson, Hattie McDaniel, Eric Rolf, Glenn Leedy, Mary Field, Anita Brown, George Nokes, Gene Holland, "Nicodemus" Stewart, Johnny Lee. Screenplay, Dalton Reymond, Morton Grant, Maurice Rapf, from original story by Reymond. Based on Uncle Remus Tales by Joel Chandler Harris. Camera, Gregg Toland; music director, Charles Wolcott; editor, William M. Morgan. Songs by Ray Gilbert-Allie Wrubel; Sam Coslow-Arthur Johnson; Johnny Lange-Hy Heath-Eliot Daniel; Robert MacGimsey; Foster Carling. Associate producer, Perce Pearce; cartoon director, Wilfred Jackson; film director, Harve Foster. Tradeshown N.Y., Oct. 31, '46. Running time, 95 mins.

Some of the immortal Uncle Remus "Brer Rabbit" stories have been set down with a great deal of charm by Walt Disney in this combined live-and-cartoon characterization. An idyllic story of a kid suffering from estranged parents and finding comfort in the simple joys of a southern plantation, is intertwined with three sprightly cartoon sequences concerning Brother Rabbit and his contretemps with Messrs. Fox and Bear. Film is sometimes sentimental, slow and overlong. But its many virtues more than balance. Film is a natural for kids, and will also have a big pull with femmes. It will do okay.

Some excellent Technicolor effects heighten the picture of an idealized romanticized South, with its plantations, stately manors, campfire meetings and colored mammies. Alternate live and cartoon stories are interwoven smartly, with the occasional combination of real and animated figures handled with imagination and skill. Most of the songs are above-average, with one, "Zip-adee-do-da," likely to be one of the season's favorites. The usual distinctive Disney touches are sprinkled throughout.

Story of misunderstood Johnny gets away to an ambling start, and only picks up—although it does that with a swoop—when the live Uncle Remus segues into the first cartoon sequence with his singing of "Zip-adee." The story of Johnny and his little friend Ginny is unaffected and appealing. Johnny's attempt to run away; the frog sequences with Toby and the puppy-dog and birthday party bits with Ginny; above all, the rapt story sessions with Uncle Remus—are excellent bits.

But the rest of the real story, the confused and insufficiently explained estrangement of the parents, over-balances the three cartoon sequences, and could be cut. Film would do

better with less incidents like the drawnout, maudlin sickroom scene near the close and with another "Brer Rabbit" fantasy.

These cartoon sequences are great stuff. Uncle Remus tells Johnny the tar-baby story, the fox-trap incident and the laughing-place story, and the three tales are told in lavish color, detail and wit. Cartoon animals with southern Negro accents; butterflies with girlish giggles; bees and birds alighting on a live person's shoulder—are only a few of the brilliant touches. One of the smartest bits is the scene of a cartoon bullfrog and a real Uncle Remus exchanging tobacco and smoking pipes on a river log, while the closing bit of actual kids and cartoon characters trotting off together, with old Uncle Remus running slowly after, is a classic.

Songs stand out, as Hattie McDaniel's kitchen ballad, "Sooner or Late," Brer Rabbit's "How Do You Do," and, of course, Uncle Remus' "Zip-adee." The actual kids, Bobby Driscoll, as Johnny and Luana Patten as Ginny, are two of the most natural and appealing youngsters to grace a screen in years. James Baskett's Uncle Remus, with his fat, round black face and scraggly white beard, is also as warming a portrait as has been seen in a long time. Lucile Watson, as the wise grandmother; Hattie McDaniel as the maid Tempy head a good (live) supporting cast. *Bron.*

The Verdict

Hollywood, Nov. 5.

Warner Bros. release of William, Jacobs production. Stars Sydney Greenstreet, Peter Lorre, Joan Loring; features George Coulouris, Rosalind Ivan, Paul Cavanagh, Arthur Shields, Morton Lowry, Holmes Herbert. Directed by Don Siegel. Screenplay, Peter Milne, from novel by Israel Zangwill; camera, Ernest Halier; music, Frederick Hollander; editor, Thomas Reilly. Tradeshown Nov. 4, '46. Running time, 86 mins.

Geo. Edw. Grodman..............Sydney Greenstreet
Victor Emmric...................Peter Lorre
Lottie.........................Joan Loring
Supt. Buckley..................George Coulouris
Mrs. Benson....................Rosalind Ivan
Clive Russell..................Paul Cavanagh
Rev. Holbrook..................Arthur Shields
Arthur Kendall.................Morton Lowry
Sir William Dawson.............Holmes Herbert
P.C. Warren....................Art Foster
Barbey Cole....................Clyde Cook
Sister Brown...................Janet Murdock
Jury Foreman...................Ian Wolfe

Stock mystery tale with period background, "The Verdict" shapes up to moderate returns, due principally to cast names which are familiar enough to aid the selling. Melodrama elements are capably displayed by William Jacobs' production and it's all aimed at generating suspense and thrills, succeeding modestly.

Sydney Greenstreet creates character of a Scotland Yard superintendent who is fired when he convicts and hangs a man on circumstantial evidence. To show up the Yard and the man who replaced him, Greenstreet commits the perfect crime. Only the conviction of an innocent man for the murder makes Greenstreet reveal how the killing was done and the reason for it. Script by Peter Milne, from a novel by Israel Zangwill, is peopled with the usual number of suspects in order to divert suspicion from the real killer and Don Siegel's direction does well with his material.

Peter Lorre, macabre artist friend of Greenstreet's, is the prime suspect and turns in a good job to match latter's performance. Joan Lorring, music hall performer, does one song and figures as a suspect adequately enough. George Coulouris, rival to Greenstreet as a Yard man, is expert. Rosalind Ivan gets over role of tippling housekeeper. Paul Cavanagh is good as suspect nearly hanged for Greenstreet's crime. Others are acceptable.

Ernest Haller's lensing adds much

to the effects obtained. Also aiding is the Frederick Hollander score. Other credits measure up. *Brog.*

Dick Tracy vs. Cueball

RKO release of Herman Schlom production. Stars Morgan Conway, Anne Jeffreys; features Lyle Latell, Rita Corday, Ian Keith. Directed by Gordon M. Douglas. Screenplay, Dana Lussier, Robert E. Kent from original story by Luci Ward based on Chester Gould comic strip "Dick Tracy"; camera, George E. Diskant; editor, Philip Martin; music, C. Bakaleinikoff. Tradeshown in N.Y., Nov. 4, '46. Running time, 62 mins.

Tracy	Morgan Conway
Tess	Anne Jeffreys
Patton	Lyle Latell
Mona Clyde	Rita Corday
Vitamin Flintheart	Ian Keith
Cueball	Dick Wessel
Priceless	Douglas Walton
Flora	Esther Howard
Brandon	Joseph Crehan
Little	Byron Foulger
Junior	Jimmy Crane
Higby	Milton Parsons
Rudolph	Skelton Knaggs

Hot action celluloid that's bang-up and bang-bang from start to finish, this "Dick Tracy" film should be a surefire b.o. item even beyond the wide circle of comic strip addicts. RKO, which assumed screen rights to Chester Gould's cartoon after Republic finished using is as basis for a serial, is turning out these hour-long features on the "B" corner of its lot, but is giving them first class production dress. Scripting is simply designed, but tightly welded while topnotch direction keeps the accelerator pedal pressed to the floor throughout.

Following the strip closely on essential points, the film is peopled with a rogue's gallery of grotesque cutthroats, degenerates and slick criminal masterminds who, of course, are outwitted and outslugged by the square-chinned dick. Film, because it's pointed most directly at the juve trade, may be leaving itself wide open for attack because of its unremitting flow of violence. Windup scene, in which Cueball gets his foot caught in a track switch with a freight train bearing down on him, has a bald shock value that'll induce nightmares.

Film opens with a jewel snatch and a murder and before the finish is marked by a half-dozen well-defined strangulations. Story revolves around Dick Tracy's efforts to sniff out a nest of jewel thieves operating through a blind of respectable dealers. Cueball, a brutal looking hombre who's been double-crossed by the gang, knocks off most of them himself with Tracy left only with the job of finishing Cueball.

Portrayal of Tracy by Morgan Conway is straightforward thesping with more emphasis on direct action than any facial expression. Dick Wessell makes an ominous strangler as Cueball while mild romantic interest of Tess Truehart is handled competently by Anne Jeffreys. Occasional comedy is furnished by Lyle Latell, playing Tracy's dumb cluck aide, and Ian Keith, in the deliberately hammed up role of Vitamin Flintheart. *Herm.*

Home in Oklahoma

(SONGS)

Republic release of Edward J. White production. Stars Roy Rogers; features George Hayes, Dale Evans, Carol Hughes. Directed by William Witney. Original, Gerald Geraghty; songs, Jack Elliott, Tim Spencer; camera, William Bradford; editor, Les Orlebeck. Tradeshown N.Y., Oct. 30, '46. Running time, 72 mins.

Roy Rogers	Roy Rogers
Gabby Whitaker	George "Gabby" Hayes
Connie Edwards	Dale Evans
Jan Holloway	Carol Hughes
Steve McClory	George Meeker
Luke Lowry	Lanny Rees
Devoria Lassiter	Ruby Dandridge
Sheriff Barclay	George Lloyd
Judnick	Arthur Space
Lawyer Cragmyle	Frank Reicher

One of the best Roy Rogers oaters to date, "Home in Oklahoma" is destined for good nabe biz. Formula action story line is given a neatly turned whodunit twist and filled out with a listenable, nicely integrated score. Scripting is also better than the usual run with dialog and comedy situations avoiding the bromidic touch. Soft-focus camera work lends an over-all production polish while positive direction keeps the action rolling at a good pace throughout.

Story revolves around efforts of Rogers, playing bumpkin newspaper editor, to track down the killers of a w.k. cattle rancher. Teaming up with Dale Evans, big city reporter, and "Gabby" Hayes, ranch foreman, Rogers tracks down the murderers after some tricky sherlocking and a couple of knuckle-scraping encounters. Pitched battle between the forces of the law and the killer's ranchhands is excellently staged as is the windup fight on a rolling freightcar between Rogers and culprit George Meeker.

With his horse Trigger playing only a minor role, Rogers registers strongly both as a gun-totin' cowboy and as crooner. Pic's standout tune is Jack Elliott's "Miguelito," which Rogers duets with Miss Evans. Latter comes through with solid support in the romance and comedy departments. Hayes adds his usual assist while the heavies are played with competence by Meeker and his girl friend, Carol Hughes. *Herm.*

Tumbleed Trail

(SONGS)

PRC release of Robert Emmett Tansey production, directed by Tansey. Stars Eddie Dean; features Roscoe Ates, Shirley Patterson, Johnny McGovern. Original screenplay, Frances Kavanagh; songs, Eddie Dean, Glenn Strange, Johnny Bond, Ernest Bond, Lou Wayne, Bob Shelton; camera, Ernest Miller; editor, Hugh Winn. Tradeshown N.Y., Oct. 31, '46. Running time, 58 mins.

Eddie	Eddie Dean
Soapy	Roscoe Ates
Robin Ryan	Shirley Patterson
Freckles Ryan	Johnny McGovern
Brad Barton	Bob Duncan
Alton Small	Ted Adams
Gringo	Jack O'Shea
Bill Ryan	Kermit Maynard
Judge Town	Bill Fawcett
Ranch Hands	The Sunshine Boys

Poured out of the same mold used for all the other Eddie Dean starrers, "Tumbleweed Trail" rates as standard fare for the oatuner trade. Pic is compounded out of the regular ingredients of obvious good guys vs. bad guys plot, gun and fist play, a speck of romance, and a flock of fair saddle tunes delivered by Dean with banjo obbligato. Production accoutrements, as usual, are held down to the barest minimum with scripting, thesping and camera work of mediocre calibre.

Dean plays an undercover agent for the law on the trail of a gang of cattle rustlers. With sidekick Roscoe Ates, still using the stuttering routine for laughs, Dean takes a ranchhand job with a cowgal whose father has been murdered. After lots of hard riding and devious schemes to trap the killer, Dean finally tags his man and makes everybody happy by bringing the so-called dead man out of hiding.

Dean is okay and won't disappoint his fans but comedy lines given Ates are old and tired. Pic's most refreshing item is in the pert thesping of juve actor Johnny McGovern who plays kid brother to Shirley Patterson. Gang of cutthroats, headed by Bob Duncan and Ted Adams, give crude performances in a strictly dated tradition. *Herm.*

Decoy

Monogram release of Jack Bernhard and Bernard Brandt production, directed by Bernahrd. Stars Jean Gillie, Edward Norris; features Robert Armstrong, Herbert Rudley, Sheldon Leonard, Marjorie Woodworth. Screenplay, Ned Young, based on original story by Stanley Rubin; camera, L.W. O'Connell; music, Edward J. Kay; editor, Jason Bernie. At Rialto, N.Y., week Nov. 2, '46. Running time, 70 mins.

Margot Shelby	Jean Gillie
Jim Vincen	Edward Norris
Frank Olins	Robert Armstrong
Dr. Craig	Herbert Rudley
Joe Portugal	Sheldon Leonard
Nurse	Marjorie Woodworth
Tommy	Phil Van Zandt
Waitress	Carole Donne
Al	John Shay
Bartender	Bert Roach
Ruth	Rosemary Bertrand

It's not plausible but it doesn't have to be. For some canny direction whips "Decoy" along at a jet-propelled pace so fast that the customers can't take time out for wondering. And without that chance for introspection, the action addicts are going to give this one action at the wickets.

Pace all the way makes this graph of a seamy grab for buried holdup loot by a wicked lady, a straight line from credits to finale. And for this, laurels go to Jack Bernhard, who knows how to tell a story without waste of celluloid. He's met the test because "Decoy" takes hold of you though there isn't a kopek's worth of plausibility for every dollar of direction.

Tautly told, "Decoy" depicts the contrivings of a femme fatale via flashback technique in searching out and pocketing the aforesaid coin. Before she p.e.d.s with her own demise the Hollywood must axiom that crime doesn't pay, her maneuvers have brought about the death of her three lovers. Piece-de-resisance in the fable is the successful revival of a felon after a gas chamber execution. It's a bit of business that's hard to take—if you're in a mood for quibbling.

Preeming in American pix is Jean Gillie, a Monogram importation from England, who fills her part as the unregenerate murderess with thespic mettle and verve. If a softly British accent isn't too snug a fit for a gunmoll role, that's not Miss Gillie's fault. Gowned becomingly in a low necklined ensemble that flirts narrowly with Breen-banned cleavage, Miss Gillie is giving the action fans more pulchritude than usual in the custom and usage of the trade.

All other roles are played several steps above the average as though Edward Norris, Robert Armstrong, Herbert Rudley, Sheldon Leonard and Marjorie Woodworth knew this one was going to be tops for Bs and wanted to do their stint. For Leonard, it's in spades. For he adds one more excellent portrayal of the hard-shelled, tough yet wise, detective to the list of that type which Hollywood has compiled over the years. *Wit.*

Plainsman and the Lady

Republic release of Joseph Kane production, directed by Kane. Stars William Elliott, Vera Ralston, Gail Patrick, Joseph Schildkraut; features Andy Clyde, Donald Barry, Raymond Walburn. Screenplay, Richard Wormser from original by Michael Uris, Ralph Spence; camera, Reggie Lanning; editor, Fred Allen; special effects, Howard and Theodore Lydecker; dances, Fanchon. Previewed N.Y., Nov. 1, '46. Running time, 87 mins.

Sam Cotten	William Elliott
Ann Arnesen	Vera Ralston
Cathy Arnesen	Gail Patrick
Peter Marquette	Joseph Schildkraut
Dringo	Andy Clyde
Feisty	Donald Barry
Judge Winters	Raymond Walburn
Michael Arnesen	Reinhold Schunzel
Senator Gwin	Russell Hicks
Mr. Russell	William B. Davidson
Al	Paul Hurst
Manuel Lopez	Charles Judels
Simmons	Byron Foulger
Sival	Jack Lambert
Pete	Hal Talliaferro
Matt	Stuart Hamblen
Wassac	Noble Johnson
Anita Lopez	Eva Puig
Indian	Henry Wills

William Elliott, horse opry vet, plays the wealthy cattleman-rancher who is handy with the six-shooter to push through the pony express enterprise. But before he does, Elliott overcomes the usual scheming of a dastardly stageline owner, latter not being adverse to using a beautiful married woman to carry out his scheme of throttling this new competition. He also cooks up the time-worn stunt of having his gunmen masquerade as redskins and also hiring a prize badman to bump off the hero.

Vera Ralston, as the comely society femme of circa 1859, is Elliott's chief heart interest, and is seen to excellent advantage whether in a party dress or riding togs. Incidentally, she has developed into a first-rate thespian. Elliott is very good as the courageous westerner. Gail Patrick is excellent also as the rich man's wife, tool of Joseph Schildkraut, the stageline owner, who chips in with one of better villainous jobs. Andy Clyde, as Elliott's Man Friday, helps with some needed comedy relief, while Donald Barry is the tough gunman to the hilt.

Aside from the main plot, the action allows for some inspiring outdoor scenery. Richard Wormser has worked up marvels with a none too original story.

Besides doing fine work in maintaining a splendid pace, director Joseph Kane also has supplied production background worthy of a much bigger picture, ballroom scenes being especially noteworthy. Reggie Lanning's fine cameraing has captured the sweep of several gripping outdoor scenes. *Wear.*

Strange Holiday

Holly, Nov. 1, '46.

PRC release of Elite poroduction., Stars Claude Rains; features Bobbie Stebbins, Barbara Bate, Paul Hilton, Gloria Holden, Milton Kibbee, Walter White, Jr., Wally Maher. Screenplay and directed by Arch Oboler. Camera, Robert Surtees; music, Gordon Jenkins; editor, Fred Feltshans, Jr. Reviewed at Mel-Van theatre, Hollywood. Oct. 30, '46. Running time, 55 mins.

John Stevenson	Claude Rains
John, Jr.	Bobbie Stebbins
Peggy Lee	Barbara Bate
Woodrow, Jr.	Paul Hilton
Mrs. Stevenson	Gloria Holden
Sam Morgan	Milton Kibbee
Farmer	Walter White, Jr.
Truck Driver	Wally Maher
Newsboy	Tommy Cook
Hegan	Griff Barnett
First Detective	Ed Max
Second Detective	Paul Dubov
Secretary	Helen Mack
Examiner	Martin Kosleck
Guard	Charles McAvoy
Betty	Priscilla Lyons
Boyfriend	David Bradford

"Strange Holiday" is a converted commercial film, turned out in wartime to boost morale of General Motors workers. It's a strange offering for regular theatres, and will turn only slight profit for PRC. Name of Claude Rains adds some value for situations.

Written and directed by Arch Oboler, film poses thought that America's liberty must be carefully guarded. Most of the burden falls on Rains' shoulders and he makes a good try at keeping piece alive. It's pure propaganda aimed at winning the peace now that the war is over but poses no method of how it's to be done. Message is hung on melodramatic plot that has Rains coming back to the city after a vacation in an isolated spot. He finds the Nazis have taken over and he's kicked around, beaten and subjected to other totalitarian stunts to draw contrast of how great it is to live in a free United States. Windup shows it all to be a dream. Oboler's direction is not always forte, but the subject matter is not too easy to get across. Heavy and lengthy dialog that falls to Rains keeps general pace slow with little interest around.

Gloria Holden plays Rains' wife. Seen as his two children are Bobbie Stebbens and Paul Hilton. Martin Kosleck is a brutal Nazi leader. Others in cast are acceptable. Lensing by Robert Surtees and score by Gordon Jenkins are favorable factors in the overall production. *Brog.*

Foreign Films

"A Son Is Born" (Australian). British Empire Films' release of Eric Porter production; stars Ron Randell, Muriel Steinbeck; features Peter Finch, John McCallum, Jane Holland, Kitty Bluett; directed by Porter; screenplay, Gloria Bourner; camera, Arthur Higgins; editor, James Pearson. At Victory, Sydney. Running time, **85 MINS.**

Low budgeter with more appeal in rural areas than urban spots. Maiden effort of Eric Porter, young Aussie producer, this is a trite domestic drama. Acting and sound are adequate but poor photography, bad cutting and lack of continuity hamper the film. Pic has no chance in America. Ealing Studios is reported to have bought the film for British distribution. *Eric.*

"Eugenie Grandet" (Italian). Minerva Film release of Excelsa production; stars Alida Valli, Gualtiero Tumiati, Giorgio de Lullo; features Giuditta Rissone, Pina Gallini, Mario Siletti; directed by Mario Soldati; screenplay, Aldo de Benedetti and Soldati. Reviewed in Venice. Running time, **95 MINS.**

Story of frustrated love appears to be unlikely film fare for U. S. Plot revolves around young Charles Grandet who's left penniless by the suicide of his bankrupt father. His cousin, Eugenie, aids him financially and he leaves for India, seeking his fortune and promises to return to wed her. After seven years, Charles is back and in love with a Marchioness. Hearing of Charles' ambition, Eugenie steps aside to a cloistered, lonely life. Probably okay for Italian market. *Forn.*

"La Symphonie Pastorale" (French). Pathe Consortium release of Gibe production; stars Michele Morgan, Pierre Blanchar; features Line Noro, Andree Clement, Rosine Luguet, Louvigny and Jean Delannoy; based on novel of same name by Andre Gide; screenplay, Jean Aurenche and Delannoy; camera, Armand Thirard. Reviewed in Paris. Running time, **115 MINS.**

Film version of Andre Gide's novel, at best a morbid soul analysis, has lost much via its screen treatment. Michele Morgan portrays a blind waif who grows to womanhood in the home of a Swiss village parson. Recovering her eyesight, she commits suicide when torn between the love of young Jean Desailly and that of his parson father. Acting is good with exception of Blanchar's performance. Lensing also shines. Despite bally and Miss Morgan's fine performance, film is unlikely to do big biz, and appears doubtful in U. S. because lacking entertainment values. *Maxi.*

"L'Assassin n'est pas Coupable" ("The Murderer Is Not Guilty") (FRENCH). Gaumont release of Siffra production; stars Jules Berry; features Albert Prejean, Rosine Derean, Jacqueline Gauthier, Sinoel; directed by Rene Delacroix; screenplay, Alex Joffe and Jean Leville; reviewed in Paris. Running time, **95 MINS.**

Only thing which makes this picture worth mentioning is the fact that Jules Berry, locally popular on stage and screen, has been cast to play himself. Story is a whodunit which takes place in a studio where Berry is the star of a film. During the production he is murdered. Obviously a cheap quickie with little appeal. *Maxi.*

"Saa Modes Vi Hos Tove" ("We Meet at Tove's") (DANISH). Asa-Film production and release. Stars Ilona Wieselmann, Inge Stender, Poul Reichardt; features Clara Osto, Gull-Mai Norin, Gudrun Ringheim, Tudlik Johansen, Betty Helmengreen, Anna Henriques Nielsen, Axel Frische; directed by Alice O'Fredericks and Grete Frische; screenplay, Miss O'Fredericks and Miss Frische. Reviewed in Copenhagen. Running time, **90 MINS.**

Here is a good story gone astray. Eight girls meet after 10 years of separation. While doubtlessly a splendid idea to make a film describing their lives over the past 10 years, bad screenplay ruins the story. Even so it may be a success in Denmark due to good acting. No dice for America. *Wins.*

Miniature Reviews

"Till the Clouds Roll By" (Musical-Color) (M-G). Jerome Kern biopic a surefire mop-up.

"White Tie and Tails" (U). Dan Duryea, Ella Raines, William Bendix in amusing comedy that should do okay.

"Matter of Life and Death" (GFD). British-made with David Niven. Raymond Massey, retitled "Stairway to Heaven" for U. S.

"The Devil's Hand" (French). Pierre Fresnay's presence fails to save this French-made horror film.

Till the Clouds Roll By
(MUSICAL—COLOR)

Metro release of Arthur Freed production. Based on the life and music of Jerome Kern. Stars June Allyson, Lucille Bremer, Judy Garland, Kathryn Grayson. Van Heflin, Lena Horne, Van Johnson, Tony Martin, Dinah Shore, Frank Sinatra and Robt. Walker. Directed by Richard Whorf. Story, Guy Bolton; adapted by George Wells; screenplay, Myles Connolly and Jean Holloway; musical direction, Lennie Hayton; orchestration, Conrad Salinger; vocal arr., Kay Thompson; Judy Garland's numbers directed by Vincente Minnelli; dances, Robert Alton; camera, Harry Stradling, George J. Folsey; editor, Albert Akst; special effects, Warren Newcombe; montages, Peter Ballbusch. Tradeshown N. Y. Running time, **120 MINS.**

Jerome Kern	Robert Walker
Marilyn Miller	Judy Garland
Sally	Lucille Bremer
Sally, as a girl	Joan Wells
James I. Hessler	Van Heflin
Oscar Hammerstein	Paul Langton
Mrs. Jerome Kern	Dorothy Patrick
Mrs. Muller	Mary Nash
Charles Frohman	Harry Hayden
Victor Herbert	Paul Maxey
Cecil Keller	Rex Evans
Hennessey	William "Bill" Phillips
Julia Sanderson	Dinah Shore
Band Leader	Van Johnson
Guest Stars	June Allyson / Angela Lansbury / Ray McDonald
Dance Specialty	Maurice Kelly / Cyd Charisse / Gower Champion
Orchestra Conductor	Ray Teal
Specialty	Wilde Twins
Frohman's Secretary	Byron Foulger

"Showboat" Number

Captain Andy	William Halligan
Ravenal	Tony Martin
Magnolia	Kathryn Grayson
Ellie	Virginia O'Brien
Julie	Lena Horne
Joe	Caleb Peterson
Steve	Bruce Cowling

Specialties

Kathryn Grayson
Johnny Johnson
Lucille Bremer
Frank Sinatra
Virginia O'Brien
Lena Horne
Tony Martin

With a cast that reads like Metro's contract list and the immortal Jerome Kern melodies for the settings, they could musicalize Lindy's menu and make it boffo boxoffice. Fortified as it is with sturdier values, "Till the Clouds Roll By" is surefire film fare anywhere. It'll mop up.

Another entrant in the current cycle of pic biogs based on famed songwriters' careers, its boxoffice appeal now becomes a matter of superlative relativity. Fundamentally the themes and subjects are naturals. If the masses didn't know or care much about Kern, Porter, Cohan, Gershwin, Bayes-Norworth, Jolson and others in the past, they certainly know their works and the songs with which they're identified. Under skillful Hollywood projection these musical cavalcades take on plus values which are surefire for any picture customer. Slicked up in lush Technicolor and given lavish production values, as here, how can it miss? Especially with Sinatra, Garland, Johnson, Shore, Walker, Grayson and others on the marquee?

Why quibble about the story? It's notable that the Kern saga reminds of the current Cole Porter ("Night and Day") release—both apparently enjoyed a monotonously successful life. No early-life struggles, no frustrations, nothing but an uninterrupted string of Broadway and West End show success. Nearest thing to travail is Kern's contretemps with turn-of-the-century Broadway impresario Charles Frohman, who was apparently a rabid Anglophile—"no good songsmith in America; the only good ones come from Europe."

This chases Kern to London where one of his earlier tunes, "How'd You Like to Spoon With Me," gets interpolated into a London musical. Frohman going down on the Lusitania is used as a springboard for a fictional episode that Kern luckily missed that ill-fated liner when he and his arranger-confidante sought to board the same boat and chase the capricious Frohman to London.

Van Heflin plays Jim Hessler, the arranger-composer-confidante, whose life story parallels Kern's in a Damon-and-Pythias plot. (Some real-life counterpart may be the veteran arranger, Frank Sadler).

In London he meets Eva (Mrs. Kern), sympathetically played by Dorothy Patrick. And the rest of the story is virtually a success-story flashback. Picture actually opens with "Show Boat," a 1927 whammo. There is virtually a tabloid version of that operetta utilized for the opener, a play-within-a-play, depicting Bill Halligan as Cap'n Andy; Tony Martin as Ravenal; Kathryn Grayson as Magnolia; Virginia O'Brien as Ellie; Lena Horne as Julie; Caleb Peterson as Joe; and Bruce Cowling as Steve. It's not just a case of just one song being done but, following the opening chorus, Martin and Miss Grayson duet "Only Make Believe"; Lena Horne renders "Can't Help Lovin' Dat Man"; and Caleb Peterson clicks with "Ol' Man River."

Following the Ziegfeld production's debut, the handsomely graying Kern (Robert Walker) pensively gravitates to a side-street, detouring from the Waldorf where there is the usual opening night success party, and in flashback memory there unfolds almost the major portion of the ensuing two hours' film. How his "Ka-Lu-A" was his first struggling hit; thence "Spoon," followed by such specialties as Dinah Shore's "They Didn't Believe Me," Miss Shore doubling as Julia Sanderson.

June Allyson and Ray McDonald's "Till the Clouds Roll By" is an excellent staging by Robert Alton, whose work incidentally is the highlight of the picture. The imaginative dance stager has done a capital job from start to finish and the title song presentation is but one of the several highlights. Another is the Memphis cafe scene where Van Johnson gets hotcha in a song-and-dance specialty with Lucille Bremer in "I Won't Dance." Miss Bremer as Sally, the willful daughter of Van Heflin, whom Kern has watched and loved from childhood, supplies the sole major struggle in the plot. While unbelievable that a girl working in smalltime vaudeville and niteries could dodge the Pinkertons so long, it's accepted for sake of the story. Topper is that she finally does it the hard way, gravitating from the dumps to Hollywood, just as Kern himself has finally harkened to the call of the films, as "Land Where the Good Songs Go" is used as a test for the newcomer (Miss Bremer). Incidentally, this luscious alumna of the Copacabana (N.Y.) nitery recreates her own real-life saga in a measure.

"Leave It to Jane" is a standout opportunity for June Allyson who hits a high mark personally with everything she does here. Miss Garland's "Look for the Silver Lining" in the "Sally" sequence is socko, and she repeats in "Sunny" with "Who."

Miss Shore again with "Last Time I Saw Paris"; Kathryn Grayson with "Long Ago (And Far Away)"; Virginia O'Brien with "Fine Romance"; Tony Martin's "All the Things You Are"; Lena Horne's click, "Why Was I Born", and Sinatra's capping "Ol

Man River"—each done in the best Culver City production tradition—make for eye-appealing, audience-arresting, surefire production.

In effect, each successive bit and number is a nostalgic cavalcade of Broadway, from the old Princess theatre intimate musicals (Comstock & Elliott's Bolton-Thompson-Kern musicals) through the Victor Herbert era, into the Ziegfeldian profligacy. And Metro, not to be outdone, makes a three-ring circus with elephants, acrobats 'n' everything for the "Sunny" sequence.

Of the basic cast, Robert Walker is completely sympathetic as Kern, and Heflin is potent as Hessler. Joan Wells stands out as Sally (child) and Lucille Bremer's adult Sally is likewise effective. Paul Langton does well by his role as Oscar Hammerstein 2d, Kern's collaborator; Dorothy Patrick is OK as Mrs. Kern; and the rest are competent bits such as Paul Maxey's Victor Herbert, Harry Hayden as Frohman, et al.

Considering the weightiness of the material all artificers have done handsomely by themselves. That goes for director Richard Whorf, producer Arthur Freed (who certainly stretched the elastic on Metro's bankroll); the Technicolor, and all the rest of it. And certainly in a musical cavalcade of this nature the downbeat and orchestration department had to be in expert hands, and Lennie Hayton, Conrad Salinger and Kay Thompson deliver handily on that count. *Abel.*

White Tie and Tails

Universal release of Howard Benedict production. Stars Dan Duryea, Ella Raines, William Bendix; features Richard Gaines, Frank Jenks, Donald Curtis. Directed by Charles T. Barton. Screenplay, Bertram Millhauser, based on "The Victoria Docks at 8," by Rufus King, Charles Beahan; camera, Charles Van Enger; editor, Ray Snyder; score, Milton Rosen. At Loew's State, N. Y., Nov. 7, '46. Running time, 75 MINS.

Charles Dumont....Dan Duryea
Louise Bradford....Ella Raines
Larry Lundie....William Bendix
Archer....Richard Gaines
Mrs. Laitmer....Barbara Brown
Mr. Arkwright....Clarence Kolb
Nate Romano....Donald Curtis
George....Frank Jenks
Mr. Bradford....Samuel S. Hinds
Mr. Latimer....John Miljan
Emil....William Trenk
Bill Latimer....Scotty Beckett
Betty Latimer....Nita Hunter
Cynthia Bradford....Patricia Alhpin
Virgie....Joan Fulton

"White Tie and Tails" is an unpretentious little picture, compounded of a good cast, amusing but unbelievable story and top direction, that will please those who see it. Film still lacks, nonetheless, the requirements for top "A" playing time but will do okay in most other situations.

Much of whatever success the film piles up will have to be attributed to the fine screenplay adaptation by Bertram Millhauser of a story by Rufus King and Charles Beahan. Plot is almost a direct throwback to the Cinderella-type fairytales and it wouldn't have been too far amiss to fade it in with one of the characters reciting "Once upon a time." Sparked by the subtle directorial touches of Charles T. Barton, the cast gets the most out of the situation comedy involved and the whole thing winds up on a "all lived happily ever after" note. It's sheer escapism, but good.

Story has Dan Duryea, in a role far removed from his usual sneering gangster parts, as the impeccable butler of a wealthy family. He sets out to play a "real gentleman" for 10 days while the family vacations in Florida and, by falling for Ella Raines, daughter of another wealthy family, gets mixed up with a bunch of racketeer gamblers to whom Miss Raines' sister owes 100G. Trying to play the big shot, he signs a check for the debt and the gang chief, William Bendix, then takes a couple of priceless paintings from his master's home as security. Rest of the plot is given over to Duryea and Miss Raines trying to make good the debt before the master returns and finds the paintings missing. But it all turns out okay.

Duryea does a nice job as the butler, with his suave manners and soft voice giving him a nice background for the role. Miss Raines gives him good support as his vis-a-vis. It's William Bendix, though, as the tough but soft-hearted gambler who cops the honors, walking away with about every scene he's in. Frank Jenks shines in a supporting role as the chauffeur and ace crap-shooter of Duryea's household. Rest of the cast is competent.

Producer Howard Benedict has mounted the film on some ostentatious sets, including a couple of mansions and the gambling club. Exteriors, however, are sometimes too obvious even to the untrained eye. Charles Van Enger's camera work is okay and editor Ray Snyder rates a nod for helping achieve the film's rapid pace by trimming it successfully to its short running time. *Stal.*

A Matter of Life and Death

('Stairway to Heaven')
(BRITISH-MADE)
(Color)

London, Nov. 1.

General Film Distributors release of Archers film. Stars David Niven, Roger Livesey, Raymond Massey; features Kim Hunter, Marius Goring. Written, produced and directed by Michael Powell and Emeric Pressburger; production designed by Alfred Junge; camera, Jack Cardiff; music by Allan Gray; special effects, Douglas Woolsey and Henry Harris. At Empire. Running time, 104 MINS.

Peter....David Niven
June....Kim Hunter
Bob....Robert Coote
An Angel....Kathleen Byron
English Pilot....Richard Attenborough
American Pilot....Bonar Colleano
Chief Recorder....Joan Maude
Conductor 71....Marius Goring
Doctor Reeves....Roger Livesey
Vicar....Robert Atkins
Dr. Gaertler....Bob Roberts
Dr. McEwen....Edwin Max
Mrs. Tucker....Betty Potter
Surgeon / Judge....Abraham Sofaer
Abraham Farlan....Raymond Massey

Greatest boxoffice asset of this picture is the fact that it was chosen for first Royal Command Film performance in this country, recognition equivalent here to six Oscars. Even so, it may leave many folk cold and bewildered. Will need special bally in spite of marquee voltage. Determination of executives here to have a home-made film for the great occasion narrowed field considerably, but many good judges will wonder if this film really represents British industry at its best. Looks definite U. S. entry but will need special selling. American release title: "Stairway to Heaven."

Like other Powell-Pressburger pictures, the striving to appear intellectual is much too apparent. And even American audiences will find their usual anti-British barbs too obvious. Less desire to exhibit alleged learning, and more humanity would have resulted in a more popular offering. The Powell and Pressburger team must learn that their characters should not merely be mouthpieces for their theories, but also living subjects for love and pity.

For the first 10 minutes, apart from some pretentious poppycock, the picture looks like living up to its boosting. This is real cinema, then action gives way to talk, some of it flat and dreary. Story is set in this world (graced with Technicolor), and the Other World (relegated to dyemonochrome) as it exists in the mind of an airman whose imagination has been affected by concussion. Returning from a bomber expedition, Squadron-Leader David Niven is shot up. Last of the crew, minus a parachute, and believing the end is inevitable, before bailing out talks poetry and love over the radio to Kim Hunter, American WAC on nearby air station. Miraculously Niven falls into the sea, is washed ashore apparently unhurt, and by strange coincidence meets Kim. They fall desperately in love.

Meanwhile in the Other World there's much bother. Owing to delinquency of Heavenly Conductor Marius Goring, Niven has failed to check in, and Goring is despatched to this world to persuade Niven to take his rightful place and balance the heavenly books. In his hallucinations, Niven alone sees Goring, argues with him, but though willing to die 24 hours ago, he now refuses to go to the Other World because he is in love with Kim. He gets permission to appeal in the High Court on the grounds that during "borrowed time" in this world, through inefficiency of Conductor, he fell in love. As defending counsel Niven can choose anybody from Plato to Lincoln, from Henry VIII to Madame Du Barry. Prosecuting counsel is Abraham Farlan (Raymond Massey), first American to die from an English bullet in the War of Independence.

Roger Livesey, diagnosing Niven's hallucinations, orders immediate brain operation, and climax comes when Livesey, going for ambulance, is killed, and Niven, undergoing the operation, imagines Livesey as Counsel for Defense in High Court. So, while surgeons fight for Niven's life in this world, Livesey battles for it in Other. There is much meaningless eloquence, much talk about no nation having any love for Britain, but Livesey sweeps away historical prejudice and makes love the issue. The operation is successful, love triumphs.

David Niven, acting with his accustomed charm gives a fine performance, possible his best to date, and Kim Hunter runs him a close race for honors. Marius Goring makes the most of his effective role, and Raymond Massey a trifle overbombastic is in nice contrast to the sound solid Roger Livesey.

Obviously experimental in many respects, the designs for the Other World are a matter of taste, but with all their ingenuity Powell, Pressburger, and Alfred Junge could only invent a heaven reminiscent of the Hollywood Bowl and an exclusive celestial night club where hostesses dish out wings to dead pilots. Camera work is good, transition from color to monochrome being expertly achieved. *Cane.*

The Devil's Hand

(FRENCH-MADE)

Distinguished Films release of Maurice Tourneur production. Stars Pierre Fresnay; features Josseline Gael, Palau. Directed by Maurice Tourneur. Story by Jean-Paul Le Chanois; music, Roger Dumas; camera, Arnaud Thirer. Previewed in N. Y. Nov. 8, '46. Running time, 89 MINS.

Roland....Pierre Fresnay
Irene....Josseline Gael
Small Man....Palau
Melisse....Noel Roquevert
Gibelin....Guillaume de Sax
Colonel....Andre Varennes
Denis....Antoine Balpetre
Mme. Denis....Rexiane
Perrier....Robert Vattier
Duval....Chamarat
Le Moine....Jean Coquelin
Musketeer....Andre Bacque
Rifleman....Jean Davy
Surgeon....Douking
Juggler....Rene Blancard
Painter....Garzoni
Boxer....Marcel
Angel....Jean Despeaux
Diner....Pierre Larquey

(In French; English Titles)

Pierre Fresnay is fairly well known in American arty cinemas, and the Maurice Tourneur name is also familiar, but this combo does not insure topnotch entertainment for "The Devil's Hand." Turned out during the Nazi occupation, "Hand" is moderate fare for arty and foreign-language theatres.

Story of a gifted left hand, and how it's handed down from one man to another, has been done from horrific angle. Mystery slants and hair-raising sequences, however, are smothered in endless passages of chatter or loud scenes. Yarn of an untalented painter (Fresnay), who buys the hand, achieves fame, happiness and love, ends with the artist striving to rid himself of the devil's mitt. This is accomplished only via supreme sacrifice.

Fresnay is only as good as the script and direction permit, which is not too good. His performance nearly overcomes both. Josseline Gael has looks and displays talent as his sweetheart. Palau gives an excellent interpretation of the devil's representative, who's always seeking the missing hand.

Tourneur's attention to production details is on a higher plane than his direction. Jean-Paul Le Chanois' script is one of those things, but Roger Dumas' background music is unusually fine.

Before film can be released in the U. S. something will have to be done with the print, one used at this preview being jerky and buckling on a number of occasions. *Wear.*

Foreign Films

"Brollopet Pa Solo" ("Wedding at Sun Island") (SWEDISH). Sandrew-Bauman release of Monark Film production; stars Adolf Jahr; features Rut Holm, Sig Britt-Carlsson, Sven Magnusson, Emy Hagman, Sten Lindgren; directed by Ivar Johansson; screenplay, Ivar Johansson and Eric Lundegard; camera, Eric Blomberg; reviewed in Stockholm. Running time, **88 MINS.**

Adolf Jahr, once the Swedish Errol Flynn, is a strong film comedian over here. In this film, his first in a year, he turns in an excellent performance. Sig Britt Carlsson, a newcomer, shows promise. Story concerning the archipelagoes in mid-eastern Sweden, should find big appeal here. Probable chances in America appear limited.

"Mote I Natten" ("Meeting in Night") (SWEDISH MADE). Europa film release of Hasse Ekman production, stars Ekman, Eva Dahlbeck; features, Hugo Bjoerne, Eivor Landstroem, Goesta Cederlund, Sigge Furst, Ulf Palme, Tord Bernheim; directed by Ekman; screenplay, Ekman and Torsten Floden; camera, Bertil Palmgren; reviewed in Stockholm. Running time, **102 MINS.**

Hasse Ekman is a busy young man. Producer, director, writer and male star in most of his films, this one is tabbed a "non-psychological" thriller. Basically the picture's an experiment with something new for Sweden, being a mixture of U. S. and Swedish. Ekman rates a bow for attempting something out of the ordinary. Good acting, direction and camera work help this thriller along. Appeal for U. S. market is rather dubious.

Miniature Reviews

"The Razor's Edge" (20th). Cut yourself a fancy slice of boxoffice with this one.

"Magnificent Doll" (U). Ginger Rogers, David Niven, Burgess Meredith in a fictionalized biog of Dolly Madison; top biz.

"Cross My Heart" (Songs) (Par). Fair light fare with Betty Hutton and Sonny Tufts toplining.

"My Brother Talks to Horses" (MG). Topnotch family comedy, loaded with humor, tenderness and nostalgia.

"The Perfect Marriage" (Par). Trite tract on squabbling spouses; mild b.o. prospects.

"The Mighty McGurk" (MG). Standard Wallace Beery filmfare with plenty to entertain his substantial following.

"Susie Steps Out" (Songs) (UA). Modest family comedy for secondary positions.

"That Brennan Girl" (Rep). Hackneyed "true confession" drama slated for ordinary returns.

"Boston Blackie and the Law" (Col). Chester Morris whodonut due for fair grosses on strength of series' popularity.

"Singin' in the Corn" (Songs) (Col). Corny comedy with Judy Canova singing.

"School for Secrets" (GFD). Ralph Richardson fails to save this one; needs plenty of bally to get by in U. S.

"Appassionata" (Saga). Swedish-made love story by Viveca Lindfors in femme lead; strictly for arty spots.

The Razor's Edge

20th-Fox release of Darryl F. Zanuck production. Stars Tyrone Power, Gene Tierney, John Payne, Ann Baxter, Clifton Webb, Herbert Marshall. Directed by Edmund Goulding. Screenplay, Lamar Trotti from novel by W. Somerset Maugham. Camera, Arthur Miller; music, Alfred Newman; editor, J. Watson Webb; dances, Harry Pilcer; special effects, Fred Sersen. Tradeshown N. Y., Nov. 18, '46. Running time, 146 MINS.

Larry Darrell	Tyrone Power
Isabel	Gene Tierney
Gray Maturin	John Payne
Sophie	Anne Baxter
Elliott Templeton	Clifton Webb
Somerset Maugham	Herbert Marshall
Mrs. Louisa Bradley	Lucile Watson
Bob MacDonald	Frank Latimore
Miss Keith	Elsa Lanchester
Kosti	Fritz Kortner
Joseph	John Wengraf
Holy Man	Cecil Humphreys
Specialty Dancer	Harry Pilcer
Princess Novemali	Cobina Wright, Sr.
Albert	Albert Petit
Police Inspector	Henri Letondal
Russian Singer	Noel Cravat
Specialty Dancer	Laura Stevens
Lawyer	Jean De Briac
Sea Captain	Eugene Borden
Footman	Leo Galitzine
Housekeeper	Helen Glere
Maid	Isabelle Lamore
Bishop	Andre Charlot
Nurses	Adele St. Maur, Frances Morris, Hermine Stoler
Sophie's Friend	Renee Carson
Abbe	Demetrius Alexis
Bartender	Ray De Ravenne
Police Clerk	Jean Del Val
Doctor	Dr. Ross Thompson
Mr. Maturin	Forbes Murray
Information Clerk	Paul De Corday
Cure	Joseph Eurlando
Flower Woman	Marie Rabasse
Chauffeur	Adolph Damotte
Butler	Walter Bonn
Singer	Robert Laurent
Priest	Robert Norwood

"The Razor's Edge" will cut plenty of fancy boxoffice takings in all markets. It has everything for virtually every type film fan.

The values are solid-Jackson in the best Hollywood tradition. Here's how they shape up: cast, story, romance, action and, for the truly discriminating, non-addicted filmgoers, a possible message of faith. Set all this against the background of two continents, not counting the hero's excursion to the Hindu mystic in the Himalayas; segue it from the turbulent times of post-World War I after Wall Street's memorable omelet, and it's a surefire parlay.

Fundamentally it's all good cinematurgy. It's a moving picture that moves. Despite the urbanity of its leading characters and the high-society (Chicago and Paris) of backgrounds of most of its cast, which calls for not a little fancy dialog, the action is more than compensatory. If some of the scripting is slightly meritricious few will argue with its lesser artificialities. Even Harry Pilcer's phoney Rue de Lappe (Paris' Apache quarter) hokum is the least of it as the action depicts the degradation of Sophie (Anne Baxter), who becomes a hopeless dipsomaniac, acquiring one of those stage-looking maqreaus as protector, and winds up in a reefer layout with a crude Corsican.

The romance is more than slightly on the sizzling side. Tyrone Power, as the flyer who can't find himself, is always seeking goodness (hence his quest to the Hindu holy man), and spurns the easy life offered him by the more than casually appealing Gene Tierney. It reaches a climax after they play the Paris nitery belt from Montmartre to Montparnasse, and when back in Chicago she loses sight of him and marries John Payne there is the unashamed confession of a lasting love which Power spurns. When he essays to marry the downfallen Sophie, who went completely dipso when her husband and baby were killed in an auto crash, it's Miss Tierney who leaves the inviting bottle exposed so as to throw her over the brink, just as she was successfully taking the cure under Power's strong and slightly mystic influence.

Against this panorama is Clifton Webb as the dilettante rich uncle, the epitome of international snobbery who, even in an effective yet somewhat theatrical deathbed scene, only achieves final peace when Power expedites (1) a desirable socialite invitation from a princess (Cobina Wright, Sr.) who was snubbing him, and (2) the Bishop himself comes to administer the last rites.

Herbert Marshall introduces a new cinematic technique—as it was in the original novel—of playing the author W. Somerset Maugham who thus integrates himself into the story by name identity instead of the conventional first-person (but invariably fictitiously identified) characterization. As Edmund Goulding and Lamar Trotti have done it, Marshall utilizes an off-screen commentary technique in the earlier footage but, thereafter, is an ubiquitous character, integrated into the cinematurgy as the story unfolds.

The casting is superb. Power is thoroughly believable as the youth who finally learns aloft a rugged Himalayan peak what he's always sought; that "the path to salvation is as hard to travel as the sharp edge of a razor" but having found "God's beauty...fresh and vivid to the day of our death" he is prime to return to his homeland.

For all its pseudo-ritualistic aura the film is fundamentally a solid love story. Miss Tierney is the almost irresistibly appealing femme and completely depicts all the beauty and charm endowed her by Maugham's characterization. Miss Baxter walks off with perhaps the film's personal hit as the dipso, rivaled only by Webb's effete characterization. That goes right down the line. Elsa Lanchester makes a kittenish old-maid secretarial role count for much. Henri Letondal as the pompous little French functionary is a gem of a characterization as the Toulon police inspector (who also has commissionaire cards for funeral parlors, restaurants and the like for which he shills). Frank Latimore, relatively new face, looks promising as the young husband who gets killed. Fritz Kortner makes his religioso-angry miner role stand out; ditto Noel Cravat as an oh-chi-chornia specialist; Renee Carson as the Apache protector of the degraded Miss Baxter. And not forgetting Harry Pilcer, who is in his element (1) as the Apache specialty dancer and (2) as the general terp stager of the atmospheric Rue de Lappe stuff.

This is a personal Darryl F. Zanuck production and he has given it the gun in every detail. Not the least of it is Alfred Newman's fine score and excellent lensing.

Sumptuously mounted and capably administered by director Goulding, the film lives up to one of the industry's best pre-sold products. As a showmanship footnote in this new scheme of pre-selling the bigger pictures, "The Razor's Edge" evidences how sharply this particular commodity cut itself into public consciousness. It's an advance buildup which must interpret itself for extra values, especially when the pre-campaign is matched by the boxoffice pull.

Abel.

Magnificent Doll

Universal release of **Skirball-Manning** production. Stars Ginger Rogers, David Niven, Burgess Meredith; features Horace McNally, Peggy Wood, Robert Barrat. Directed by Frank Borzage. Original story and screenplay, Irving Stone; camera, Joseph Valentine; editor, Ted J. Kent; score, H. J. Salter. Tradeshown N. Y., Nov. 15, '46. Running time, **93 MINS.**

Dolly Payne	Ginger Rogers
Aaron Burr	David Niven
James Madison	Burgess Meredith
John Todd	Horace McNally
Mrs. Payne	Peggy Wood
Amy	Frances Williams
Mr. Payne	Robert H. Barrat
Thomas Jefferson	Grandon Rhodes
Count D'Arignon	Henri Letondal
Senator Ainsworth	Joe Forte
Darcy	Erville Alderson
Jedson	George Barrows
Barber Jenks	Francis McDonald
Mr. Gallentine	Emmet Vogan

Skirball-Manning production outfit brushed over the pages of American history with a clean sweep of its fictionalized pen for "Magnificent Doll" and came up with an entertaining, albeit hardly authentic story of Dolly Madison's life.

Professional historians will probably squirm in their seats of learning when they see what the screen treatment has done to Dolly's biography, and the blatant flag-waving will probably rankle some audiences. There's no question, though, that the picture will do top business. Marquee-laden cast is topped by Ginger Rogers, David Niven and Burgess Meredith. Frank Borzage directed, and producer Jack Skirball doesn't seem to have spared much in the way of a top-heavy budget.

Dolly Madison has always been considerd one of the most colorful figures in thi scountry's early history and her true life story would probably have been a natural for films. It's difficult to understand, therefore, why Irving Stone, who's credited with both the original story and screenplay, went out of his way to slough off facts in favor of fiction. Incident in which Dolly salvaged important Government documents from under the noses of the British in the War of 1812, for example, is given a quick brushoff. In its place, Stone has substituted such obvious fiction as having Aaron Burr, with a crush on Dolly, give up his claims to the presidency just because Dolly talked him out of it.

Picture's chief graces result from the fine work of the cast under Borzage's competent direction. Miss Rogers gives expert handling to the title role, making the transition from one emotion to another in good fashion. It's difficult to believe that speeches on democracy and good government could sound so convincing coming from the lips of Fred Astaire's former dancing partner.

Niven plays the scoundrelly Burr, sneering when he has to and being tender in his love scenes with Miss Rogers. He hams up several sequences but he couldn't do otherwise with the script. Meredith shines as James Madison, making the idealistic president convincing enough. Horace McNally as Dolly's first husband and Peggy Wood and Robert Barrat as her mother and father score in less prominent roles.

Story is told by Dolly in retrospect, with her monolog bridging the gaps. It picks her up as a young girl on her father's plantation in Virginia, carries through her first unhappy marriage, then her love affair with Burr and eventual marriage to Madison. Picture ends with her as the first lady of the White House under Jefferson's presidency, with her husband still secretary of state and yet to become president.

Sets, costumes, etc., bring one touch of authenticity to the story and are laid on lavishly. Joseph Valentine's lensing supervision is capable throughout, and Ted J. Kent has wrapped the story neatly into its 93-minute running time. H. J. Salter's score serves as good background for the film's various moods. *Stal.*

Cross My Heart
(SONGS)

Paramount release of Harry Tugend production. Stars Betty Hutton, Sonny Tufts. Directed by John Berry. Screenplay, Tugend and Claude Binyon from play by Louis Verneuil and Georges Berr; additional dialog, Chas. Schnee; score, Robt. Emmett Dolan; songs, Johnny Burke-James Van Heusen; arrangements, Jos. J. Lilley; cameras, Chas. Lang, Jr., Stuart Thompson; editor, Ellsworth Hoagland. Tradeshown Nov. 15, '46. Running time, **85 MINS.**

Peggy Harper	Betty Hutton
Oliver Clarke	Sonny Tufts
Prosecutor	Rhys Williams
Eve Harper	Ruth Donnelly
Detective Flynn	Alan Bridge
Miss Baggart	Iris Adrian
Wallace Brent	Howard Freeman
Judge	Lewis L. Russell
Peter	Michael Chekhov

"Cross My Heart" is a fragment which Betty Hutton and Sonny Tufts, along with an energetic supporting cast, will have to carry. It's acceptable if not socko film fare, innocuous in its tongue-in-cheek playing, with which audiences will have to go along for best results. If they take it straight—as some of the provincial fans may be inclined—it will have trouble.

The screwball antics of the congenitally fabricating Miss Hutton, who "confesses" to a murder she didn't commit, as a means to spotlight her young attorney-fiance, are given bounce by the Harpomarxian wackiness of a "Hamlet"-happy Russo actor, Michael Chekhov.

Against the courtroom trial of the pseudo-murderess is projected a sort of Roxie Hart treatment of melodramatic jurisprudence, including a good job by Rhys Williams, as the distrait prosecuting attorney, and the lampooned browbeating by detective Alan Bridge. The neo-"Irish Justice" antics include "That Little Dream Got Nowhere," sung by Miss Hutton, including an applauding "jury" of which one femme member is a diehard holdout who can't make up her mind. Incidentally, there are two other Johnny Burke-Jimmy Van Heusen songs, "How Do You Do It?" and "Love Is the Darndest Thing," but "Dream"—already well plugged—is the most likely contender.

Cast does a good all-round job, including Tufts as the barrister-juvenile. As for Miss Hutton, her usual verve and bounce compensate for some of the unflattering camera angles allotted her. Chekhov, as the maniacal lammister from Shakespeare, plays his screwball assignment to the hilt.

Film's short footage and general tempo give the script and directorial shortcomings extra values. *Abel.*

My Brother Talks to Horses

Hollywood, Nov. 19.

Metro release of Samuel Marx production. Features "Butch" Jenkins, Peter Lawford, Beverly Tyler, Edward Arnold, Charlie Ruggles, Spring Byington. Directed by Fred Zinnemann. Story and screenplay, Morton Thompson; camera, Harold Rosson; editor, George White. Tradeshown Nov. 18, '46. Running time, **92 MINS.**

Lewie Penrose................"Butch" Jenkins
John S. Penrose..............Peter Lawford
Martha.......................Beverly Tyler
Mr. Bledsoe..................Edward Arnold
Rich. Pennington Roeder..Charlie Ruggles
Mrs. Penrose.................Spring Byington
Mr. Puddy....................O. Z. Whitehead
Mr. Gillespie................Paul Langton
Mr. Mordecai.................Ernest Whitman
Mr. Piper....................Irving Bacon
Psyche.......................Lillian Yarbo
Hector Damson................Howard Freeman
Mr. Gibley...................Harry Hayden

"My Brother Talks to Horses," and who's to deny that he didn't. Whether he did or not, the theme supplies the basis for a delightful family story that goes leisurely about its business of good, clean entertainment for general audiences. It's turned out with an eye to sustaining amusing interest, punching over the nostalgic flavor of early-day Baltimore.

A smooth-working cast, bolstered by understanding direction from Fred Zinnemann, makes the Morton Thompson story of his younger brother believeable. Occasionally the script gets talky, but they are lines that spring naturally in a slightly wacky family such as the Penroses. Little "Butch" Jenkins carries the title role as the pixilated nine-year-old who's fey for animals. His ability to talk to horses, particularly the Preakness steeds that domicile in and around Baltimore, gives him unusual interest for gamblers such as Charlie Ruggles. Kid socks over part, his gaping gums and freckles lending authenticity to the role of average adolescence.

Roles of Peter Lawford, the breadwinning brother, and Beverly Tyler, his romance, have lesser value among the proceedings but development and playing make them a delightful part of what transpires. It's young love in bloom, realistically portrayed, that adds plenty of flavor. Spring Byington, the mother of Jenkins and Lawford, turns in a gem of a performance. It's a part that's done to the hilt, wacky and primed with choice dialog that clocks plenty of laughs.

Charlie Ruggles, the gambler who strives for "Butch" Jenkins' favor and race tips, does a good selling job of the assignment. Another laugh character, short but sock, is O. Z. Whitehead as the young inventor who boards with the Penroses. Ernest Whitman accounts for strong job as the colored friend of the title character, and Edward Arnold is good as a rich horse owner. Others also are capable.

Samuel Marx's production accounts for realism that prevails. Two exciting horseraces, one the running of the Preakness, will almost have customers laying bets on the outcomes. Period settings and art direction supplied by Edwin B. Willis, Alfred D. Spencer, Cedric Gibbons and Leonid Vasion lend authentic background for story, and Harold Rosson's lensing takes advantage of it. *Brog.*

The Perfect Marriage

Paramount release of Hal Wallis production. Stars Loretta Young, David Niven; features Eddie Albert, Charlie Ruggles, Virginia Field, Rita Johnson, Zasu Pitts, Nona Griffith, Nana Bryant, Jerome Cowan, Louella Gear, Howard Freeman. Directed by Lewis Allen. Screenplay by Leonard Spigelgass; based on play by Samson Raphaelson; camera, Russell Metty; score, Frederick Hollander; editor, Ellsworth Hoagland. Previewed Nov. 15, '46. Running time, **87 MINS.**

Maggie Williams..............Loretta Young
Dale Williams................David Niven
Gil Cummins..................Eddie Albert
Dale Williams, Sr.........Charlie Ruggles
Gloria.......................Virginia Field
Mabel........................Rita Johnson
Rosa.........................Zasu Pitts
Cookie Williams..............Nona Griffith
Corinne Williams.............Nana Bryant
Addison Manning..............Jerome Cowan
Dolly Haggerty...............Louella Gear
Peter Haggerty...............Howard Freeman

Give a celluloid puff-ball a little breeze and it can keep going. But "The Perfect Marriage," translation of Samson Raphaelson's minor Broadway stint, gets no push from lines or plot. Consequently, burdened as it is by a story that doles out an unrelenting diet of marital bickerings, the sum-total is a pic which proves as dull and heavy as cheesecake on a 2 a.m. stomach.

Only fresh and lively writing could have transmuted this j'accuse duet of husband wife into entertaining fare. Obviously intended to tickle audience risibilities with a rehash of the familiar and petty differences that may, or may not, lead to the divorce court, the result is a failure which leaves the spectator with the uncomfortable feeling of the eaverdropper on marital spats that might well be left unsaid in Macy's window.

Curtain lifts on Mr. (David Niven) and Mrs. (Loretta Young) celebrating the 10th anniversary of a heralded perfect marriage. With little or no motivation, this apparently devoted duo pick their quarrels and slide into them with a fervor and eclat of two kids rushing the neighborhood candy counter. Misunderstandings and differences which the expression of a few commonsense words by either of the combatants would have ironed out, lead to the divorce court and further entanglements with anxious third parties.

Caught in the mixup is the young daughter of the match and the conventionally interfering in-laws. Film has nothing new to say about the dilemma of innocent children victims of their parents pigheadedness, but rather treats the problem in an offhand manner. Finale comes around with the inevitable reconciliation between the two feuding parents, the kissoff to the potential corespondents, and the presumption, dubious in this case, that all's going to be well with alliance from now in.

Thesping is better than the lightweight plot requires. Niven becomes a shade too whimsical at times but the script rather than the actor bears the onus. Miss Young is attractive if irritating in her part as the youthful matron with the dialectical twist on matrimony. Standout in other roles is Gloria Endicott as extra-curricular pal of Niven. She, alone, of all the participants has a few pithy remarks to make on the proceedings which are not without their humor. Eddie Albert, Nona Griffith, Charlie Ruggles and Rita Johnson give to their parts at least the little that picture demands. *Wit.*

The Mighty McGurk

Hollywood, Nov. 19.

Metro release of Nat Perrin production. Stars Wallace Beery; features Dean Stockwell, Edward Arnold, Aline MacMahon, Dorothy Patrick, Cameron Mitchell. Directed by John Waters. Original screenplay, William R. Lipman, Grant Garrett, Harry Clork; camera, Charles Schoenbaum; editor, Ben Lewis. Tradeshown Nov. 18, '46. Running time, **85 MINS.**

Roy "Slag" McGurk.........Wallace Beery
Nipper.......................Dean Stockwell
Mike Glenson.................Edward Arnold
Mamie Steeple................Aline MacMahon
Johnny Burden................Cameron Mitchell
Caroline Glenson.............Dorothy Patrick
Millbane.....................Aubrey Mather
Fowles.......................Morris Ankrum
Flexter......................Clinton Sundberg
First Brewer.................Charles Judels
Second Brewer................Torben Meyer

"The Mighty McGurk" varies little from the basic theme of all Wallace Beery starrers. He's still the overgrown Puck's bad boy, using mugging, braggadocio and tears in full measure to get across. The formula must be okay, it's been used for years and the boxoffice returns have been gratifying. Payoff on this one will be up to the standard.

Plot is played to a period background, laid in the Bowery during the 1890's. Beery carries it off with his usual style as a bragging ex-champion fighter and now saloon hanger-on and general no-good. John Waters' direction makes the unfoldment straightforward, the best way to treat hoke elements in the theme. Player reaction to roles is good and it all comes off neatly.

Contrasting the Beery role is little Dean Stockwell's part as English lad whom the ex-champ takes in on the hope of being rewarded by kid's uncle. There's a religion vs. saloon angle, too, as Edward Arnold, Beery's saloonkeeper boss, seeks to run the Salvation Army from the Bowery so he can set up a new shop in the regilious group's quarters. Between Dean Stockwell and Cameron Mitchell, Salvation Army leader in the Bowery, Beery undergoes the expected change and reforms. Finale has a swell street fight between right and wrong forces that packs plenty of action to please. Romance is carried between Mitchell and Dorothy Patrick, latter daughter of Arnold, who likes the Salvation Army leader. Aline MacMahon is Beery's long-suffering romance and that, too, comes out all right, in the end.

Nat Perrin handled the production, catching plenty of the flavor of the period. Settings and art direction merit credit for backgrounds pointed up by Charles Schoenbaum's camera. Editing holds feature to tight 85 minutes running time. *Brog.*

Susie Steps Out

(SONGS)

Hollywood, Nov. 16.

United Artists release of Buddy Rogers-Ralph Cohn (Comet) production. Selmer L. Chalif assoc. prod. Features David Bruce, Cleatus Caldwell, Nita Hunter, Howard Freeman, Grady Sutton, Margaret Dumont. Directed by Reginald LeBorg. Screenplay, Elwood Ullman; added dialog, Fred Freiberger; original story, Reginald LeBorg, Kurt Neumann; songs, Hal Borne, Eddie Cherkose; camera, Robert Pitack; editor, Lynn Harrison. Previewed Nov. 15, '46. Running time, 65 mins.

Jeffrey Westcott..............David Bruce
Clara Russell.................Cleatus Caldwell
Mr. Starr.....................Howard Freeman
Dixon.........................Grady Sutton
Mrs. Starr....................Margaret Dumont
Papa Russel...................Percival Vivian
Wilkins.......................John Berkes
Bailey........................Joseph J. Greene
Nita Hunter as Susie Russell

Glimpse of what television set owners are in for in the way of commercials is furnished by "Susie Steps Out." Those who have complained about radio sales ballyhoo "ain't seen nothin' yet." Otherwise "Susie" also fills its aim of secondary film material, with added value of cute young singer who takes on title role. Budget production values are good and direction and playing sufficent to see it through.

Young Nita Hunter is the canary who pipes both pop and classical scales for interest. She's not new to films or stage, having worked previously under tag of Juanita Alvarez as part of a sister act. Voice qualifications fit title assignment as a 15-year-old chirper with usual adolescent imagination. David Bruce and Cleatus Caldwell carry off older assignments. Bruce as romantic crooner and Miss Caldwell as his heart interest. Both prove okay.

Family comedy plot concerns two sisters, their cello-playing dad and necessity of making a living. Elder sister works for an advertising agency preparing a television show. A mixup with the boss' wife gets her fired, the dad gets sick and little sister poses as a nitery singer to help out. Reginald LeBorg's direction doesn't always shape interest, but the scripting by Elwood Ullman from an original by LeBorg and Kurt Neumann isn't much help. Tale resolves itself through cliches into finale that has little sister become the television star and Miss Caldwell and Bruce getting together.

What's in store for video set owners is exampled by tele show staged in picture. There's enough repetitious hammering of sales messages on the ear via radio. When the eyes supplement the ear with video's advent button-pushing temptation will be even greater if "Susie's" visual commercials are an example of what's to come..

Howard Freeman, Grady Sutton, Margaret Dumont, Percival Vivian and others in cast are adequate to assignments. Buddy Rogers and Ralph Cohn marshalled okay production values for release intentions. Selmer L. Chalif served as associate producer. Lensing by Robert Pittack is good. David Bruce is credited with vocal work on "When You're Near" and "When Does Love Begin," both by Hal Borne. Miss Hunter canarys "Bop-Bop-That Did It" by Borne and Eddie Cherkose, and "For the Right Guy" by Borne. *Brog.*

That Brennan Girl

Hollywood, Nov. 8.

Republic release of Alfred Santell production, directed by Santell. Stars James Dunn, Mona Freeman, William Marshall, June Duprez; features Frank Jenks, Dorothy Vaughan, Charles Arnt, Rosalind Ivan, Fay Helm, Bill Kennedy. Screenplay, Doris Anderson; from story by Adela Rogers St. Johns; camera, Jack Marta; score, George Antheil; editor, Arthur Roberts. Reviewed at Hollywood Paramount, Nov. 7, '46. Running time, **95 MINS.**

Denny Reagan..................James Dunn
Ziggy Brennan.................Mona Freeman
Mart Neilson..................William Marshall
Natalie Brennan...............June Duprez
Joe...........................Frank Jenks
Mrs. Reagan...................Dorothy Vaughan
Fred..........................Charles Arnt
Mrs. Merryman.................Rosalind Ivan
Helen.........................Fay Helm
Arthur........................Bill Kennedy
Miss Jane.....................Connie Leon
Miss Unity....................Edythe Elliott
Mrs. Graves...................Sarah Padden
Dottie........................Jean Stevens
The Florist...................Lucien Littlefield
Natalie's Girl Friend.........Marian Martin

Sentimental tear-jerker that follows a "true confession" pattern. "That Brennan Girl" is overlong and heavily dialoged in sticking consistently to its theme. Producer-director Alfred Santell tries hard to pull story together but forced dialog and loosely-connected plotting aren't always overcome.

Plot tells the story of a young girl brought up by her mother to disregard principles in obtaining material advantages. This lack of proper guidance has a sentimental approach that runs a full course of familiar formula in the hackneyed sob-sister style. Santell's direction gets a good performance out of Mona Freeman as the girl. She shows to advantage among the stilted doings as the pawn of bad upbringing who finally finds happiness when she reforms. James Dunn's role is illogical and he doesn't succeed in whipping it. He appears as operator of a van and storage racket who is reformed by an Irish mother and a prison sentence, becoming Miss Freeman's second husband. The first was killed in the war.

William Marshall appears briefly as the young first husband and June Duprez is acceptable as the mother who passes on her lack of principles to the daughter. Frank Jenks, taxi-driver; Dorothy Vaughan, Dunn's old-fashioned Irish mother, and others are standard characters in this Adela Rogers St. Johns story, scripted by Doris Anderson.

Camera makes much of the San Francisco locale, but productionwise the stage shots and actual location footage are not always carefully blended. The George Antheil score is good. Further editing is needed to tighten pace and shorten overlong footage. *Brog.*

Boston Blackie and the Law

Columbia release of Ted Richmond production. Stars Chester Morris; features Trudy Marshall, Constance Dowling, Richard Lane, George E. Stone. Directed by D. Ross Lederman. Screenplay, Harry J. Essex; camera, George B. Meehan; editor, James Sweeney. Previewed Nov. 18, '46. Running time, **69 MINS.**

Boston Blackie............Chester Morris
Irene....................Trudy Marshall
Dinah Moran..........Constance Dowling
Inspector Farraday.........Richard Lane
The Runt..................George E. Stone
Sergeant Matthews............Frank Sully
Lampau (Jani)..............Warren Ashe
Warden Lund..............Selmer Jackson

Not up to the usual standard but nevertheless good saleable twin-bill fare, "Boston Blackie and the Law" emerges from the cutting room as a vehicle for the now-famous magic tricks of Chester Morris. Film is a program comic whodunit that over-reaches on the slapstick gibes at the police force but comes up with a fair enough surprise finish, in spite of occasionally careless scripting.

Morris sticks to his conventional Blackie reading, adding some simple legerdemain for the film's story. Thesping by all in the pic is okay, with veteran George E. Stone coming through nicely as the film eye's perennial aide. The two of them get in a jam when a girl at the women's penitentiary uses Blackie's magic show to escape and take revenge on her former magician partner who let her take the rap for a crime they both committed. As it turns out she's egged on by the magico's new partner, who bumps them both in an attempt to get the loot. It's all solved handily by Blackie's recording machine, which takes down a confession and puts the amateur magician-amateur sleuth and former baddie back on the right side of the fence.

Camera work doesn't call for much in the way of the unusual but builds suspense fairly well in one or two spots. Strong point of the film, entertainment-wise, is its pace, while the success of the series means a pretty good take.

Singin' in the Corn
(SONGS)

Columbia release of Ted Richmond production. Stars Judy Canova; features Allen Jenkins, Guinn "Big Boy" Williams, Alan Bridge. Directed by Del Lord. Screenplay, Isabel Dawn, Monte Brice, from story by Richard Weil; camera, George B. Meehan; songs, Allan Roberts, Doris Fisher; editor, Aaron Stell. Previewed Nov. 15, '46. Running time, **64 MINS.**

Judy McCoy..................Judy Canova
Glen Cummings..............Allen Jenkins
Hank..........Guinn "Big Boy" Williams
Honest John Richards.........Alan Bridge
Obediah Davis.............Charles Halton
Gramp McCoy................Robert Dudley
Indian Chief..............Nick Thompson
Ramona........................Frances Rey
Texas......................George Cresebro
Silk Stevens.................Ethan Laidlaw
Medicine Man.............Frank Lackteen
The Singing Indian Braves

If Judy Canova hopes to hold her already well-set radio audience, she'd better steer clear of films like "Singin' in the Corn." Comedienne's radio popularity is not for pictures if this is a sample.

It's a tossup as to what comprises the majority of footage; stock shots or those turned out for the film. Quality-wise the stock shots win in a walk. Even the very competent Allen Jenkins is lost in a welter of insipid conversation. Mountings were so low-grade that a jeep was used instead of an automobile.

Story is about a carnival mind-reader and her pitchman-partner, and their misadventures after she inherits her uncle's estate, with the clause that she won't get any money until she returns a ghost town to the Indians. Alternate beneficiary is a baddie who tries to fail her philanthropic attempts by fooling the redmen. In the course of events the uncle's ghost comes to their aid through celestial wireless.

Editing out the chaff would have improved the film, but Aaron Stell showed remarkable lack of eagerness to cut footage. There is no pace with long dead spots between what passed for repartee. The few songs dragged in are unsensational; musical stuff is in line with the film's title.

School for Secrets
(BRITISH-MADE)

London, Nov. 6.

General Film Distributors' release of Two Cities Filippo del Giudice production. Stars Ralph Richardson. Written and directed by Peter Ustinov. Camera, Jack Hildyard. At Odeon theatre, London. Running time, **108 MINS.**

Professor Heatherville....Ralph Richardson
Professor Laxton Jones..Raymond Huntley
Dr. McVitie....................John Laurie
Dr. Dainty......................Ernest Jay
Mr. Watlington...........David Tomlinson
Sir Duncan Wilson Wills.....Finlay Currie
Jack Arnold.........Richard Attenborough
Mrs. Arnold...............Marjorie Rhodes
Mrs. Watlington.........Pamela Matthews
Mrs. Laxton Jones.......Joan Haythorne
Mrs. McVitie..................Joan Young
Mrs. Dainty....................Ann Wilton
Sir Desmond Prosser.........Edward Lexy
Squadron Leader Sowerby.David Hutcheson
Corporal Aspinall.....Patrick Waddington

Billed as "The Secret a Million Kept," picture will appeal to those who served in the Air Force, but ordinary audiences may find this yarn of scientific research on Radar technical and wordy. Air Ministry is anxious to put on record Britain's discovery and perfection of Radar and found Filippo del Giudice a willing producer. But his attempt to make a Preston Sturges out of a 25-year-old Peter Ustinov has been unsuccessful. Writing, directing and co-producing has been too much for him, and all three departments have suffered. Somewhere along the line, a human story must have been there at the beginning, but it has gone down the drain.

Beginning with the war, story tells of Britain's back-room scientists, developing miracle discovery of Radar. Highlights are scientists testing instruments in night fighting, in 1,000 bomber raid on Cologne, and capture of an enemy radio-location station on French coast.

Returning to the screen with an "Old Vic" halo, Ralph Richardson is given the center of the stage whenever possible, and tries every trick, mostly with success, to get laughs as a somewhat eccentric scientist.

Cast as a gay, young beauty is Pamela Matthews, an unknown, spotted by Ustinov when she was a stand-in. She looks like a bet on her performance here. Special mention is due to Raymond Huntley, John Laurie, Ernest Jay, David Tomlinson, Marjorie Brooks and Peggy Evans.

Every exploitation angle will be needed to put this one over in America. *Cane.*

Appassionata
(With Music)
(SWEDISH-MADE)

Saga release of Lux production. Stars Viveca Lindfors. Directed and written by Olaf Molander. Previewed N. Y., Nov. 15, '46. Running time, **93 MINS.**

Maria.......................Viveca Lindfors
Dahlhoff....................Georg Rydeberg
Erik...............................Alf Kjellin
Hellenius....................Georg Funquist

(In Swedish; English Titles)

For music lovers this is okay, especially if audiences are willing to overlook countless dull passages and stilted acting sandwiched in between piano solos. For arty theatre customers, "Appassionata" shapes as stout fare. Swedish pictures before the war always had a certain, if limited following in U. S. because of fine photography and infrequent bursts of vivid acting. This film has both strong camera work and occasional flashes of real thespian work; so it will do.

"Appassionata," already done by several other foreign producers since 1929, is the story of a 19-year-old gal who is torn between a concert pianist's passion for her and her love for a rising young musician, also a pianist and pupil of the concert genius. However, without the piano playing of the noted Polish pianist, W. Witkowsky, this would be just another screen love triangle. And even with his playing and the Stockholm Philharmonic doing "Symphony No. 7," this picture does not measure up to American standards. Witkowsky, who never appears in the picture, doing the piano work Georg Rydeberg is supposed to perform in the production, plays "Appassionata Sonata," "B Flat Minor Piano Concerto," "Polonaise in A Flat," and "Etude in E Minor" among other tunes.

Viveca Lindfors, the heart interest of the two musicians in this, is now working for Warners in Hollywood. This film shapes as a screen test for her because the comely Swedish girl appears in innumerable closeups to the point of irritation. If she does as well in Hollywood as in this vehicle Miss Lindfors should be around for some time in American productions. She does well in the few dramatic or love scenes she's given. Rydeberg is convincing as the vivid concert pianist, while Alf Kjellin makes a reasonable young musician. Olof Molander's direction is never quite as good as his scripting, which, too, could stand pruning. *Wear.*

Miniature Reviews

"Abie's Irish Rose" (Crosby-UA). Embarrassing remake of a dated story.

"The Best Years of Our Lives" (Goldwyn-RKO). A boxoffice bonanza.

"The Yearling" (Color) (M-G). Sensitive version of Pulitzer prize novel for wide appeal.

"Lady in the Lake" (Metro). Robert Montgomery, Audrey Totter in Raymond Chandler detective story. Surefire b.o.

"Wake Up and Dream" (Color-Songs) (20th). Overboard on fantasy, underweight on story, slow pace for family trade. Stars, color might draw.

"Betty Co-ed" (Songs) (Col). N.s.g. treatment of campus snobbery plus Jean Porter singing several notches above.

"Sioux City Sue" (Songs) (Rep). Gene Autry's first post-war oatuner is standard western.

"Bringing Up Father" (Songs) (Mono). Adaptation of George McManus' King Features strip for fair nabe b.o.

"The Return of Monte Christo" (Col). Dumas pays off again. Swashbuckling adventure piece with plenty of b.o.

"Affairs of Geraldine" (Rep). Jane Withers in a so-so programmer that's handicapped by poor story.

"Wild West" (Songs — Color) (PRC). Cowboy opera in Cinecolor of superior grade.

"Sweetheart of Sigma Chi" (Musical) (Mono). Collegiate musical with hep tunes for listening pleasure. Good b.o.

Abie's Irish Rose

United Artists release of Bing Crosby Producers, Inc., production. Stars Joanne Dru, Richard Norris; features Michael Chekhov, J. M. Kerrigan, George E. Stone. Directed by A. Edward Sutherland. Screenplay, Anne Nichols, from her play. Camera, William Mellor; score, John Scott Trotter. Tradeshown Nov. 22, '46. Running time, **96 MINS.**

Rosemary.........................Joanne Dru
Abie............................Richard Norris
Solomon Levy.............Michael Chekhov
Patrick Murphy..............J. M. Kerrigan
Isaac Cohen...............George E. Stone
Mrs. Cohen......................Vera Gordon
Father Whalen..............Emory Parnell
Rabbi Samuels....................Art Baker
Rev. Mr. Stevens............Bruce Merritt
Hotel Manager.....................Eric Blore
Hotel Clerk............Harry Hays Morgan

Last week 1,200 people of all faiths gathered in the ballroom of New York's Hotel Astor to pay tribute to Paramount's Barney Balaban at a dinner under auspices of the Anti-Defamation League. Speakers of all denominations stressed the fine interfaith work being done by the ADL. On Sunday (24) a "Thanks to Thanksgiving" dinner at the Waldorf-Astoria, under auspices of the National Conference of Christians and Jews, made recognition of the contribution to American national life by the five media of public information—press, stage, radio, films, advertising. Two weeks hence, specifically Dec. 6, again at the Waldorf, an entertainment industry luncheon, and again under auspices of the National Conference of Christians and Jews, will jointly honor Irving Berlin, Robert Sherwood and Spyros Skouras for their work in interfaith relations.

These are of-the-moment capsule highlights of the awareness of show business towards the national and international need for understanding. It is because of its harsh contrast to that fact that a picture such as this remake of "Abie's Irish Rose" stands out. "Abie's Irish Rose" was spawned in an era when the world was at ease and, as a play, it enjoyed full success. None is better aware of "Abie's" b.o. appeal than VARIETY. Its multi-touring companies from Azusa to Australia, from South Carolina to South Africa, made Anne Nichols' property an all-time box-office champion whose record in many respects may never be shattered.

A play about Abie Levy who marries Rosemary Murphy that can become a $10,000,000 industry has every right to inspire showmen to refurbish it anew for successive generations. Whether it's "Life With Father," "Over the Hill," "Way Down East" or a Tom show—successive generations have found something in these and kindred entertainments to merit support. Unquestionably that was the logic of the production staff. But one thing has a bearing here which has no parallel in any of the other show biz perennials. Many "Hebe comics" once enjoyed applause and approbation. The Tad comic and "Irish Justice" were surefire and potently valuable for laughs. But circumstances have long since altered the situation. When minorities become political footballs, when all the energies of postwar rehabilitation seem to focus on an effort for better understanding, when the very premise of the clannish Poppa Levy and the bejabers Murphy militates against the popular thinking of the day—when all these factors loom so large in the public consciousness, it just doesn't figure that this screen version of "Abie's Irish Rose" will make popular entertainment.

The essence of film fare is obviously to entertain. This one doesn't. It can't, when the fundamentals are as meretricious as unwind in these hokey 96 minutes. Nor does it suffice to dismiss it as merely hokum. There is commercial hoke and there is spurious buncombe. This celluloid concoction, for all its elementary plot development, is untimely.

No longer is it a case of love conquers all. No longer is it the plot of Rabbi Samuels and Father Whalen standing benignly in the background, as the old codgers, Solomon Levy and Patrick Murphy, react explosively when they learn of the marriage of Abie and Rosemary. No longer is it just a happy finale around a Christmas tree as the twins, a boy and girl for the unwilling grandfathers, bridge the religious chasm between the two families. It is the overtones and the exaggerated byplay, the bits of business and gargoyle histrionics which display what may have been intended as pleasantries but which turn into unpleasant scenes. Michael Chekhov plays papa Levy in a manner to rebuff instead of amuse an audience. And no ambulance chaser could be the reincarnation of George E. Stone's version of the family lawyer.

Fundamentally the story has become a topical misfit. It opens with ultra-modern young Abie Levy meeting USO-Camp Shows entertainer Rosemary Murphy in a V-E Day London mixup, resulting in their marriage by an Army chaplain (incidentally Protestant, so as to get in all the three faiths, which didn't exist in the original play). Papa Levy is patently a prosperous Bronx department store owner; his place of business, his household and his friends bespeak prosperity. But thereafter this premise falls apart for he has the prejudices of a pushcart peddler, and barrister Isaac Cohen (Stone) and Mrs. Levy (Vera Gordon) who, somehow, manages a slightly more restrained characterization) are depicted as narrow-minded nitwits.

Many people seem certain to object to some of the dialog. Such phrases as "Rosemary—what a name for a nice little Yiddisha girl!" (with marked horror) offends non-Jews as others will wince at Chekhov's needless philosophy about all the skill that goes into a fine piece of cloth (business of fingering the texture and quality). A line about "get nice kosher food" is as unpalatable as Chekhov's whole characterization. All the cliches of shoulder shrugging, upturned palms, and Papa Levy complaining about paying "$100 for a suit I could hire for $3 and save $97"; all the oi-oi's, and the snide cracks by Papa Levy that "Sure I'm sure she ('Rosie Murphyski') is Jewish—that's why I love her!" are in. And more—since there is the other side. For instance, Patrick Murphy's steady pugnaciousness, the constant harrangues which include a scoffing at "that Jew person," the APA, an Orange-man and "I'd die of shame" (by Murphy).

As love conquers all, towards the belabored hour and half of unspooling, there emerges the fact that this $550,000 budgeter at least may prove a good screen test for Joanne Dru and Richard Norris, the titular Rose and Abie. Both impress as personable and for screen potential are in inverse ratio to their vehicle. Bruce Merritt, as an Army chaplain, is another good face. J. M. Kerrigan does a saner job as the Irish father than does the kosher hamming of Michael Chekhov. Emory Parnell and Art Baker give a semblance of balance to their roles as priest and rabbi.

It is understood that certain changes already have been made via editing and, of course, as is the ordinary trade practice, the picture industry's recognized trade organizations—the Eric Johnston office, etc.—along with the usual theological "technical advisers" undoubtedly have given this '46 remake of "Abie" more than casual attention. But whatever the master-minding back of the camera, the film emerges as a disturbing feature of nebulous entertainment value in this day and age.

Abel.

Best Years of Our Lives

RKO release of Samuel Goldwyn production. Stars Myrna Loy, Fredric March, Dana Andrews, Teresa Wright; features Virginia Mayo, Cathy O'Donnell, Harold Russell, Hoagy Carmichael. Directed by William Wyler. Screenplay, Robert E. Sherwood from MacKinlay Kantor's novel, "Glory for Me." Asst. director, Jos. Boyle; camera, Gregg Toland; editor, Daniel Mandell. Tradeshown Nov. 21, '46. Running time, **163 MINS.**

Milly Stephenson..............Myrna Loy
Al Stephenson..............Fredric March
Fred Derry..............Dana Andrews
Peggy Stephenson..............Teresa Wright
Marie Derry..............Virginia Mayo
Wilma Cameron..............Cathy O'Donnell
Butch Engle..............Hoagy Carmichael
Homer Parrish..............Harold Russell
Hortense Derry..............Gladys George
Pat Derry..............Roman Bohnen
Mr. Milton..............Ray Collins
Cliff..............Steve Cochran
Mrs. Parrish..............Minna Gombell
Mr. Parrish..............Walter Baldwin
Mrs. Cameron..............Dorothy Adams
Mr. Cameron..............Don Beddoe
Woody..............Victor Cutler
Bullard..............Erskine Sanford
Luella Parrish..............Marlene Aames
Rob Stephenson..............Michael Hall
Prew..............Charles Halton
Thorpe..............Howland Chamberlin

Samuel Goldwyn's "The Best Years of Our Lives" is one of the best pictures of our lives. It's the type of film production which belies Goldwyn's own well-publicized interview of last week that the British would soon seriously challenge America as pacemakers in motion picture production because of what he terms the Britishers' more realistic approach to films.

Ballyhooey or otherwise, Goldwyn fundamentally doesn't need any spurious spotlighting on his "Best Years." In the MacKinlay Kantor novel, as dramatist Robert E. Sherwood has transmuted into a screenplay and director William Wyler has vivified it, the producer has a fundamental story which will sell around the world. As the postwar saga of the soda jerk who became an Army officer; the banker who was mustered out as a sergeant; and the seaman who came back to glory minus both his hands, "Years" is right out of your neighbors' lives. Or, maybe, even your own.

Inspired casting has newcomer Harold Russell, a real-life amputee, pacing the seasoned trouper, Fredric March, for personal histrionic triumphs. But all the other performances are equally good. Myrna Loy is the smalltown bank veepee's beauteous wife. Teresa Wright plays their daughter, who goes for the already-married Dana Andrews with full knowledge of his wife (Virginia Mayo, who does a capital job as the cheating looker). Both femmes in this triangle, along with Andrews, do their stuff convincingly.

Cathy O'Donnell, newcomer, does her sincerely-in-love chore with the same simplicity as Harold Russell, the $200-a-month war-pensioned hero, who, since he has lost his hands in combat, spurns Miss O'Donnell because he never wants to be a burden. That scene, as he skillfully manages the wedding ring, is but one of several memorable high spots.

March's forthright stance as banker, father and free-and-easy bourbon drinker makes his performance easily one of the year's cinematic outstanders. Given a v.p. title and a returning war hero's salary boost as the bank's officer in charge of small loans to GIs, he tells off the smug doubletalking bankers about "secure collateral" by exercising innate judgment, predicated on human values and faith in the American future. In a couple of scenes which by their very underplaying hit hard he scores a single-handed thespic triumph.

Then there is Hoagy Carmichael as the laconic piano-playing tavern-keeper who teaches the amputated ex-seaman how to play the ivories with those trick lunch-hooks. The songsmithing actor has become quite a trouper. Gladys George does well as blowsy stepmother to Dana Andrews, whose pop (Roman Bohnen) lives in frowzy gin-reeking existence down by the railroad tracks, only suddenly awakening to the boy's military prowess which has made the kid from the wrong side of the tracks emerge an officer. It takes Andrews a little longer to find himself but he does in that telling final scene which augurs well for him and Miss Wright.

The pace of the picture is a bit leisurely. Almost a full hour is required to set the mood and the motivation, but never does it pall. Not a line or scene is spurious. The people live; they are not mere shadow etchings on a silver sheet. The realism is graphic; the story compelling; the romantic frailties and the human little problems confronting each of the group are typical of the headlines in stressing the impact of postwar readjustment and faith in the future.

Abel.

The Yearling
(COLOR)

Metro release of Clarence Brown (Sidney Franklin) production, directed by Brown. Stars Gregory Peck, Jane Wyman; features Claude Jarman, Jr. Screenplay by Paul Osborn, based on novel by Marjorie Kinnan Rawlings; score, Herbert Stothart conducting, utilizing themes by Fred'k Delius; camera (Technicolor), Charles Rosher, Leonard Smith, Arthur Arling; editor, Harold F. Kress; 2d unit directed by Chester M. Franklin. Tradeshown N. Y., Nov. 24, '46. Running time, **134 MINS.**

Penny Baxter..............Gregory Peck
Ma Baxter..............Jane Wyman
Jody Baxter..............Claude Jarman, Jr.
Buck Forrester..............Chill Wills
Pa Forrester..............Clem Bevans
Ma Forrester..............Margaret Wycherly
Mr. Boyles..............Henry Travers
Lem Forrester..............Forrest Tucker
Gabby Forrester..............Matt Willis
Millwheel Forrester..............Dan White
Pack Forrester..............George Mann
Arch Forrester..............Arthur Hohl
Fodderwing..............Donn Gift
Eulalie Boyles..............Joan Wells
Oliver..............Jeff York
Twink Weatherby..............June Lockhart
Doc Wilson..............B. M. "Chick" York

Marjorie Kinnan Rawlings' 1938 Pulitzer prizewinning novel has taken almost all this time to be transmuted to the screen and a fine job it is. Film, like story, will command wide attention because of its surefire basic ingredients, the heart-warming story of good earth, family ties and the love of the 11-year-old Jody Baxter for the faun which he is compelled to put out of life as it becomes a yearling.

The Florida scrub country is the locale of the Baxters, and the story focuses about Gregory Peck and Jane Wyman (starred) in the fight for their very existence, while raising meagre patches of crops and also their offspring Jody (Claude Jarman, Jr.). The lad becomes a man, for all his meagre years, in a great love and effort to ward off destruction of his pet yearling, albeit it be at the kindly hands of his parents. But when the constantly destructive deer—with whom Jody has learned to scamper through the woods unafraid—even scales the barricade which the boy single-handedly built as a supposed protection against another destruction of the crops, the yearling's die is cast. When the mother's poor marksmanship wounds the faun, and the crippled Peck is unable to kill it himself, the lad must fire the fatal shot to put the animal out of misery.

Against this simple background is projected the struggling existence of a slightly-better-than-Tobacco-Road family; the tilling of the soil which gives them the bare necessities; the height of ambition which is focused around getting the toil-worn mother a well right outside her window, so that she need not tote the water many yards down the road.

All done in a minor key, the underplaying is sometimes too static but, just as the interest lags, director Clarence Brown injects another highlight. The underlying power is impressive. The sentiment and the dramatic grip of the simple elements are undeniable. The primitiveness of it all is arresting. The admixture of family love, the good earth and the love of the boy for his pet deer are a sure-fire combination for any audience. Then, too, there are a couple of shockers like the battle of the bear with the dogs; or when Pa Baxter (Peck) is bit by a rattler. He is compelled to kill a doe so that its innards become a primitive antitoxin to the snake bite. It's that startled doe whose faun is adopted by Jody and when it becomes a yearling it becomes the climactic punch of the story.

Back of the camera the elements are the ultimate in almost portrait Technicolor photography, technical detail and, above all, casting. Claude Jarman, Jr., is a find as the lad, trouping his chore naturally and sincerely to such a degree that the realistic impact eclipses the awareness that here's a highly talented newcomer. The rangy, bony Peck and the stoic Miss Wyman are capital as his parents. The rest are relative bits, but all vivid. Donn Gift as the crippled neighbor lad, Chill Wills, Margaret Wycherly, Forrest Tucker, Clem Bevans, Henry Travers and Chick York being especially outstanding.

Producer Sidney Franklin and director-producer Clarence Brown have successfully captured all the warmth and appeal of the book and, save for the need for some cutting, since the 135-min. pic could stand excising, it's one of the better contributions to the screen.

Abel.

Lady in the Lake

Metro release of George Haight production. Stars Robert Montgomery, Audrey Totter; features Lloyd Nolan, Tom Tully, Leon Ames. Directed by Robt. Montgomery. Screenplay, Steve Fisher, based on novel by Raymond Chandler; camera, Paul C. Vogel; editor, Gene Ruggiero; score, David Snell. Tradeshown N. Y., Nov. 20, '46. Running time, **103 MINS.**

Phillip Marlowe........Robert Montgomery
Adrienne Fromsett..........Audrey Totter
Lt. DeGarmot.................Lloyd Nolan
Capt. Kane.....................Tom Tully
Derace Kingsby.................Leon Ames
Mildred Havelend..........Jayne Meadows
Chris Lavery................Dick Simmons
Eugene Grayson............Morris Ankrum
Receptionist.....................Lila Leeds
Artist.....................William Roberts
Mrs. Grayson............Kathleen Lockhart
Chrystal Kingsby..............Ellay Mort

"Lady in the Lake" proves, more than any film in recent years, that the capabilities of Hollywood for fresh, new, imaginative techniques have not yet been reached. Film in-stitutes a novel method of telling the story, in which the camera itself is the protagonist, playing the lead role from the subjective viewpoint of star Robert Montgomery. New idea comes off excellently, transferring what otherwise would have been a fair whodunit into socko screen fare.

Revolutionary system has never been tried before by any American company and Metro rates a hefty nod for attempting it on a big-budgeted production. Idea will pay off through plenty of word-of-mouth advertising. Coupled with the marquee lure of Montgomery's name and the fact that audiences are already acquainted with the detective in Raymond Chandler's novels (Dick Powell in "Murder, My Sweet" and Humphrey Bogart in "The Big Sleep"), this will make the film a top draw in any situation.

Credit for the excellent inauguration of the subjective camera goes equally to Montgomery for his direction, Paul C. Vogel for his lensing and the entire cast for handling the difficult assignment so capably. Montgomery starts telling the story in retrospect from a desk in his office, but when the picture dissolves into the action, the camera becomes Montgomery, presenting everything as it would have been seen through the star's eyes. Only time Montgomery is seen thereafter is when he's looking into a mirror or back at his desk for more bridging of the script.

Camera thus gets bashed by the villains, hits back in turn, smokes cigarettes, makes love and, in one of the most suspenseful sequences, drives a car in a hair-raising race that ends in a crash. Vogel does a capital job with the lensing throughout, moving the camera to simulate the action of Montgomery's eyes as he walks up a flight of stairs, etc. Because it would be impossible under the circumstances to cut from Montgomery to another actor to whom he's talking, the rest of the cast was forced to learn much longer takes than usual. Fact that Montgomery is heard but not seen will probably rankle audiences for the first reel or so but after that they'll be drawn into the plot in a way they seldom have before.

Steve Fisher has wrapped up the Chandler novel into a tightly-knit and rapidly-paced screenplay. Montgomery plays private detective Phillip Marlowe, who's dealt into a couple of murders when he tries to sell a story based on his experiences to a horror story mag. Audrey Totter, as the gal responsible for it all, looms as another major star on the Metro horizon. She's fine in this, in both her tough-girl lines and as the love interest. Leon Ames is okay as the publisher and Lloyd Nolan turns in a nice job as the tough city detective out to get Montgomery. Jayne Meadows overacts in an important role, but Tom Tully scores as the detective captain.

Producer George Haight has mounted the picture on rich-looking sets and follows through in all ways on the requirements for the subjective camera technique. Interesting thing to note from here in is what use Hollywood will make of the new system in the future. *Stal.*

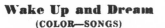

Wake Up and Dream
(COLOR—SONGS)

20th-Fox release of Walter Morosco production. Stars John Payne, June Havoc; features Charlotte Greenwood, Clem Bevans, Connie Marshall, John Ireland. Directed by Lloyd Bacon. Screenplay, Elick Moll from novel by Robert Nathan; songs, Harry Ruby, Rube Bloom; camera, Harry Jackson; music, Emil Newman; editor, Robert Fritch. Tradeshown Nov. 21, '46. Running time, **92 MINS.**

Jeff.............................John Payne
Jenny...........................June Haver
Nella......................Connie Marshall
Henry Pecket..................Clem Bevans
Sara March..........Charlotte Greenwood
Howard Williams............John Ireland
Lt. Coles...................Charles Russell
Mr. Agrippa.....................Oliver Blake
Toll-keeper.................George Cleveland
Lt. Commander.........Charles D. Brown

Even beautiful Technicolor photography and top musical backing will have a difficult time bringing more than fair grosses for "Wake Up and Dream."

Action drags after a promising beginning. In a production where music has a secondary position, the songs and background, orchestra, vocal and whistling effects in "Dream" are outstanding. One of the tunes, "Give Me the Simple Life," has already had its vogue and will probably get an additional hypo when the film is released. Likewise, the color shots under Harry Jackson's direction show the process at its best.

But these, as the only good points offered by the film, are not strong enough. "Wake Up and Dream" too often wobbles over that thin line demarcating fantasy and the ludicrous. John Payne, whose presence in the film might have afforded more action, was seen for about a reel and a half, just as he was leaving for the war (remember, this film is vintage 1943) and then at the close, when he returns. Charlotte Greenwood, given feature billing, was also given plenty of slicing. June Haver is only adequate while carrying the heaviest burden of lines. Connie Marshall is stumped by bad scripting.

Story is built around the "little child shall lead them" theme. It opens with Payne, a backward farm boy in love with the local waitress, going off to war, and leaving his little sister with a cousin. The little gal runs away and comes back to Clem Bevans, an old man who dreams of the sea and has built a ketch in his landlady's backyard, 300 miles from the nearest water. She has a wire from the Government saying that Payne is missing, and wants the old man to sail to an "island" they've dreamed about, where she knows her brother is waiting. After the landlady, Charlotte Greenwood, sells the tub in a fit of anger, a storm comes up and, with Bevans and Misses Haver and Marshall aboard, the boat gets loose and sails down the road. This begins a series of dull peregrinations, during which they pick up a wayward discharged pharmacist's mate and run aground in some semi-tropical river. They started from Maine. An old hermit keeps them alive until the Coast Guard comes, during all of which Payne returns. In spite of all the maneuvering the film follows a snail's pace.

Lloyd Bacon's direction is dilatory and Robert Fritch's editing limited. Neither could have done much with the script material offered. Cast is handicapped by the lines put into their mouths.

Betty Co-ed
(SONGS)

Columbia release of Sam Katzman production. Stars Jean Porter; features Shirley Mills, William Mason, Rosemary LaPlanche, Jan Savitt orchestra. Directed by Arthur Dreifuss. Screenplay, Dreifuss and George H. Plympton; camera, M. A. Anderson; editor, Henry Batista; songs, Allan Roberts and Doris Fisher, J. P. Fogarty and Rudy Vallee. Previewed Nov. 22, '46. Running time, **68 MINS.**

Joanne Leeds......................Jean Porter
Gloria Campbell...............Shirley Mills
Bill Brewster...............William Mason
Glenda Warren.......Rosemary LaPlanche
Louise Morgan...................Kay Morley
Ted Harris.....................Jackie Moran
Peggy Wilson......................Jane Isbell
A. J. A. Woodruff......Edward Van Sloan
Plimpton ....George Meader
Joyce Lee.......................Patsy Moran
Michael Leeds..................Ray Bennett

When "Betty Co-ed" forgets its pitch and lets Jean Porter take to song, this pic pokes its head above the level of tiresome puerilities that it's burdened with and makes a fair bid to entertain. Unfortunately, this happens only infrequently and what remains to harass the customers is a juvenile and boring tirade against sorority snobbery amongst the textbooks. As such, its lure on the patrons is in reverse.

Pity of it is that Miss Porter can deliver the merchandise when she's asked to beat out a vocal tune. Her two cantos, "Put the Blame on Mame" and "You Gotta Do What You Gotta Do," are handed flashy treatment and do, for the nonce, pump life into flagging celluloid. But this alone is short change for poorly drawn situations, childish lines and unbelievable characterizations.

There may be cinematic ore in fraternal abuses but "Betty Co-ed" hasn't hit the vein. Its fable relates the mishaps of a carnival singer (Miss Porter) who's been accepted by a hoity-toity co-ed mill under the misapprehension of hailing from a first Virginia family. Bulk of the footage relates her duel with the sorority prez: her near-departure under a cloud; and her vindication and acceptance into the select group, now happily reformed. What's hardest to take is the conversion to sweetness and light of the aforesaid prez (Shirley Mills), as thoroughly an obnoxious character, pictorally, as black-and-white brush strokes have painted in many a day.

Lines are not well written and direction suffers from painfully depicting the obvious, in obvious ways. Performances are satisfactory and certainly worthy of better scripting. Hollywood cameras can do better than this with a college campus. *Wit.*

Sioux City Sue
(SONGS)

Republic release of Armand Schaefer production. Stars Gene Autry; features Lynne Roberts, Sterling Holloway, Richard Lane, Ralph Sanford. Directed by Frank McDonald. Original screenplay, Olive Cooper; camera, Reggie Lanning; editor, Fred Allen; songs, Jimmy Hodges, Dick Thomas, Gonzale Roig, Jack Sherr, A. Rodriguez, John Rox, Sosnik Adams. Tradeshown N. Y. Nov. 26, '46. Running time, **69 MINS.**

Gene Autry......................Gene Autry
Sue Warner.................Lynne Roberts
Nelson "Nellie" Bly.....Sterling Holloway
Jefferson Lang...............Richard Lane
Big Gulliver.................Ralph Sanford
Jody.............................Ken Lundy
Miss Price...................Helen Wallace
G. W. Rhodes.................Pierre Watkin
Themselves..............Cass County Boys

First in the postwar cycle of Gene Autry starrers following the saddle-swooner's recent exit from the armed services. "Sioux City Sue" doesn't blaze any new trails in horse opry production. It's standard Autry fare slated for his regular fans who have been fed on almost two dozen Autry reissues since his induction into the Army in 1942. Following the fixed formula, pic combines a dash of action seasoned with romance, with the story acting as a peg for an armlong musical score of pleasant oatunes.

Except for a few shots of Autry jockeying his horse Champion in a hard gallop across the open plains, most of the celluloid is taken up with his crooning. Pic features six songs, two of which are reprised no less than three times, with Autry handling the full works. His vocalizing is okay, according to taste, while the score features only one firstrate number, "Sioux City Sue," by Dick Thomas. Other tunes are "Someday You'll Want Me to Want You," "Yours," "Ridin' Double," "You Stole My Heart," and "Chisholm Trail."

Story concerns a femme film scout who tricks Autry into coming to Hollywood by promising him a star role in a western. But all they want from him are song transcriptions to be used in an animated cartoon for a donkey part. Everyone gets burned until the whole thing is squared by the girl warning Autry that a couple of varmints are preparing to blow up a dam and drown his cattle. Process shot of the torrent pouring down the mountain pass highlights the production.

Pic is also marked by a strong cast of supporting players headed by Sterling Holloway, as a studio songwriter, and Richard Lane, as a madcap producer. Lynne Roberts, as the mild heart throb, registers nicely. Production mountings are good while direction and camera work par the general standard. *Herm.*

Bringing Up Father
(SONGS)

Monogram release of Barney Gerard production. Stars Joe Yule, Renie Riano; features June Harrison, Tim Ryan, Wallace Caldwell, George McManus. Directed by Eddie Cline. Screenplay, Jerry Warner from original by Barney Gerard, Eddie Cline; songs, Barney Gerard, Eddie Cline, Edward Kay; camera, L. W. O'Donnell; editor, Ralph Dixon. Premiered Laffmovie, N. Y., Nov. 20, '46. Running time, **68 MINS.**

Jiggs...............................Joe Yule
Maggie.........................Renie Riano
Himself..................George McManus
Dinty Moore........................Tim Ryan
Nora..........................June Harrison
Danny.....................Wallace Chadwell
Murphy.........................Tom Kennedy
Mrs. Kermishaw...........Laura Treadwell
Junior Kermishaw.......William Frambes
Dugan...............................Pat Goldin
Norton...........................Jack Norton
F. Newson Kermishaw......Ferris Taylor
Hod Carrier.......................Tom Dugan
Casey...............................Joe Devlin
Tom...............................Fred Kelsey
Frank.......................Charles Wilson
Jenkins.......................Herbert Evans
Groghарty..........................Dick Ryan
Jerry....................Mike Pat Donovan
Pianist...........................Bob Carleton
Fogarty.....................George Hickman

Whatever draw this film has will be solely on the power of the popularity of George McManus' King Features comic strip, from which "Bringing Up Father" is obviously adapted. Neighborhood trade, mostly moppet, will comprise the bulk of grosses.

In spite of occasional amusing moments, this picture averages out to something less than B product, largely because of a weak story. Casting of Joe Yule and Renie Riano in the Jiggs and Maggie roles is excellent, even to physical resemblance, while the occasional sudden appearances of cartoonist George McManus adds laughs.

Story revolves around a crooked tycoon's attempt to usurp plans of Dinty Moore's architect-son to rebuild a 10th Avenue neighborhood, and raze Dinty's restaurant in the process. In trying to put the plan across for the young architect, Jiggs unwittingly has everyone sign a petition to close Dinty's. Meanwhile Maggie falls for the tycoon's social lustre. Everything unwinds in a hurry at the end, as the petition is nullified by another petition.

"Father" is paced in fits and starts, and could have done with more of Yule's vaudevillisms which were especially effective under the direction of Barney Gerard, vet burlesque man in his first attempt as a single producer. **Gerard's parody of a folk ballad, "When the Mush Begins to Rush Down Father's Vest," sung straight by a barroom quartet, gets across very well. Laughs are strictly from low humor, reverting to slapstick most of the time, but will draw**

plenty of guffaws from younger trade.

Technical credits are only so-so, with the film given a purely New York locale. Even some of the jokes are localisms which might not be understood outside the city. With the help of King Features and Hearst paper backing "Father" should get good outside promotion to help b.o.

The Return of Monte Cristo

Columbia release of Edward Small-Grant Whytock production. Stars Louis Hayward, Barbara Britton; features George Macready, Una O'Connor, Henry Stephenson, Steven Geray, Ray Collins, Ludwig Donath. Directed by Henry Levin. Screenplay, George Bruce, Alfred Neumann from original by Curt Siodmak, Arnold Phillips; camera, Charles Lawton, Jr.; editor, Richard Fantl; music, Lucien Moraweck; musical director, Lud Gluskin. Previewed N. Y., Nov. 22, '46. Running time, 92 MINS.

Edmond Dantes............Louis Hayward
Angele Picard..............Barbara Britton
Henri De La Roche.......George Macready
Miss Beedle..................Una O'Connor
Professor Duval.........Henry Stephenson
Bombelles ....Steven Geray
Emil Blanchard.:...............Ray Collins
Judge Lafitte.............Ludwig Donath
Major Chavet..............Ivan Triesault
Pinot.........................Jean Del Val
Jacques ....Eugene Borden
Duree ....Crane Whitley
Guard ....John Cory

Alexandre Dumas can still be mined cinematically with profit as Edward Small has discovered in neatly piecing together a swashbuckling, colorful and consistently entertaining adventure based on the Frenchman's Monte Cristo legend. For in "The Return of Monte Cristo," which carries the saga into the third generation, a slick melange of potent action and well-spaced amour will edge the patrons forward in their seats. Rack this one up as a sure-thing in the side pocket for strong b.o. favorable comment.

Here, the moving picture is in its element—with plot manipulation, stratagem and counter-stratagem, conflict and merger, fitted snugly to the footage in a fashion that should appeal to both junior and his elders. To this is added a covey of freshly conceived situations, canny suspense buildup and a bit of gaudy thesping by Louis Hayward who gallops through a string of disguises, a la Muni of yore. If the series of counterfeit facades which Hayward dons in achieving vendetta is reminiscent of the Scarlet Pimpernel and his deeds, there's still gold in them hills.

Related in the film is the renewed struggle for the Monte Cristo fortune, with Hayward playing the French grandee's grandson while Barbara Britton, his antagonist, is the innocent pawn of a seamy trio of scoundrels. Actor, at the outset, is framed and dispatched to Devil's Island from whence he escapes along with a fellow inmate (Steven Geray), prominent performer in the clink for republican activities.

Back in France and hidden in the French version of Cain's warehouse, Hayward turns beaver specialist to track his enemies and claim his fortune. Tension mounts as he renders his foes, singly hors d'combat and winds up in spades with a rough - and - tumble fracas in a darkened theatre. Fortune and clinch ice the cake as finale.

Acting is slotted for top grade. Hayward's is particularly versatile with his disguise sequences fashioned for laurels. Miss Britton in a lesser part which puts no strain on her talents has the needed combo of attractiveness and grace aimed for the Graustarkian approach. All the others fill the bill handsomely.

Camera, direction and sound track accoutrements are excellent. Musical score of Lucien Moraweck is soundly conceived and brilliantly executed. The score enhances the action's effect while sufficiently muted to keep out of the story's way.

Wit.

Affairs of Geraldine
(SONGS)

Republic release of Armand Schaefer production. Stars Jane Withers, James Lydon; features Raymond Walburn, Donald Meek, Charles Quigley, Grant Withers. Directed by George Blair. Screenplay, John K. Butler based on story by Lee Loeb and Arthur Strawn; camera, John Alton; music, Morton Scott; arrangements, Dale Butts; editor, Tony Martinelli. Previewed N. Y., Nov. 22, '46. Running time, 68 MINS.

Geraldine Cooper.............Jane Withers
Willy Briggs...................James Lydon
Amos Hartwell..........Raymond Walburn
Casper Millhouse..............Donald Meek
J. Edmund Roberts........Charles Quigley
Henry Cooper................Grant Withers
Wayne Cooper..............William Haade
Charlie March............Michael Branden
Danny.........................Johnny Sands
Percy McBride.................David Holt
Liza Jane...................Tanis Chandler
Judge Fricke............Harry V. Cheshire
Belle Walker...........Josephine Whittell
Mrs. Hutchinson............Donia Bussey
Mrs. Eddington...........Edith M. Griffith
Lawyer Darnell............George Carleton

A surprisingly buxom Jane Withers appears in this lightweight programmer as a small-town heiress who lams from her native surroundings to seek a husband and finds herself, incongruously enough, assuming the role of "Madame L'Amour" in a matrimonial club. Far-fetched story offers few entertainment values aside from an excuse as a vehicle for Miss Withers.

Seeking to fulfill their mother's dying request to "get a husband for Gerry" (Jane Withers), brothers Grant Withers and William Haade promote some boy friends for the kid sister in a crude sort of way. However, most of the hometown boys don't go for Jane and Jimmy Lydon, who's really genuinely smitten, is spurned by her.

Feeling she should cast out on her own, Jane entrains to the city and acting upon the advice of fellow traveler Donald Meek, finds herself a job as secretary to Raymond Walburn who heads the Hartwell Matrimonial Club. Later as "Madame L'Amour," she thinks she's finally found true love in suave Charles Quigley who's eventually exposed as a three-time bigamist in the nick of time by Lydon and Walburn. Fadeout finds Jane and her hometown swain, Lydon, facing wedded bliss together. Sandwiched within the reels are two songs, "Rip Van Winkle" and "In the Middle of May," which Miss Withers warbles in acceptable fashion.

Competent cast struggles with John K. Butler's dull screenplay which stems from an equally fatuous story by Lee Loeb and Arthur Strawn. George Blair's direction is undistinguished in this Armand Schaefer production which boasts an extraordinary number of stock shots of moving railroad trains.

Wild West
(COLOR-SONGS)

PRC release of Robert Emmett Tansey production; directed by Tansey. Stars Eddie Dean; features Roscoe Ates, Al Larue, Robert "Buzzy" Henry, Sarah Padden. Screenplay, Frances Kavanaugh; camera, (Cinecolor), Fred Jackson, Jr.; editor, Hugh Winn; songs, Dorcas Cochran, Charles Rosoff, Eddie Dean, Ruth and Louis Herscher; musical director, Karl Hajos. Previewed N. Y., Nov. 25, '46. Running time, 78 MINS.

Eddie Dean.........................Eddie Dean
Soapy ....Roscoe Ates
Stormy ....Al Larue
Skinny ....Robert "Buzzy" Henry
Carrio ....Sarah Padden
Florabelle ....Louise Currie
Mollie ....Jean Carlin
Butler ....Lee Bennett
Drake Dawson.................Terry Frost
Judge Templeton........Warner Richmond
Capt. Rogers....................Lee Roberts
Chief Black Fox..........Chief Yowlachie
Rockey ....Bob Duncan
Doctor ....Frank Pharr
Halfbreed Charlie..........Matty Roubert
Constable ....John Bridges
Kansas ....Al Ferguson
Cactus ....Bud Osborne

Production of "Wild West" indicates that it's one of PRC's more ambitious efforts in which the producers were overly careful with detail at the expense of plot development in terms of action. Gaudy Cinecolor protography and frequent inclusion of songs slow up the movement considerably, but hastening process toward the close of the film compensates for earlier lapses, and "Wild West" winds up as one of the better westerns that will keep the Saturday matinee trade happy.

Big item in the film is Eddie Dean whose buildup as nag-epic boxoffice is gaining with each picture. He has one of the better set of pipes among the cowboy Carusos and once he gets rid of his self-conscious delivery, his top billing will carry more value at the b.o. Al Larue, also has potentialities in westerns. He impresses as likely to develop as boxoffice in this type film.

Story is along usual lines. Plot deals with a trio of Rangers who have come to assist an engineer laying cable for a telegraph. Villains attempt to stymie this procedure as rapid communications will play havoc with their lucrative rackets. Eventually Dean, Larue and Roscoe Ates overcome the opposition with a last-minute rescue by a large force of U. S. Rangers providing a valuable assist.

The Cinecolor photography registers well in the outdoor scenes, but loses much effect on the cast. For instance, it's said that one of the femme leads, Jean Carlin, is a redhead, but that can't be proved by the color camera. Direction of Robert Emmett Tansey hits a fast stride, once the film's songs are disposed of. Tunes, incidentally, are above par for this type film.

Jose.

Sweetheart of Sigma Chi
(MUSICAL)

Hollywood, Nov. 23.

Monogram release of Jeffrey Bernerd production. Stars Phil Regan, Elyse Knox, Phil Brito, Ross Hunter; features Slim Gaillard Trio, Frankie Carle Orchestra. Directed by Jack Bernhard. Screenplay, Frank L. Moss; original, George Waggner; camera, L.W. O'Connell; musical director, Edward J. Kay; songs, Sammy Cahn and Jule Styne; Byron Stokes and F. Dudleigh Vernor; Slim Gaillard and Lee Ricks; Merle Maddern and Lanier Darwin; Will Jason and Val Burton; Eddie Seiler, Sol Marcus and Al Kaufman; editor, William Austin. Previewed at Warners' Forum, Los Angeles, Nov. 20, '46. Running time, 76 mins.

Lucky Ryan...Phil Regen
Betty Allan..Elyse Knox
Phil Howard...Phil Brito
Ted Sloan..Ross Hunter
Coach...Tom Harmon
Frankie..Paul Guilfoyle
Sue..Anne Gillis
Arty..Edward Brophy
Bill Ryan..Fred Colby
Mike Mitchell..................................Alan Hale, Jr.
Tommy Carr.......................................David Holt
Margie......................................Marjorie Hoerner
Charlie..............................William Beaudine, Jr.
Emmett................................Emmett Vogan, Jr.
Ruth...Ruth Allen
Harry Townsend..............................Robert Arthur
Fred......................................Fred Datig, Jr.

Slim Gaillard Trio
Frankie Carle Orchestra

"Sweetheart of Sigma Chi" manages plenty of musical entertainment and will pay off in its market. Outside of tunes there's not much of an offering but former are forte enough to assure audience interest. Collegiate background has excellent production values and musical sequences are neatly meshed into the story under Jeffrey Bernerd's production guidance.

Tune-selling is in capable hands of Phil Regan, Phil Brito, Slim Gaillard's Trio and Frankie Carle's orch. Foursome delivers strongly to please. Regan gets off an Irish ditty and "Penthouse Serenade" for good listening. Brito socks over title tune, "Five Minutes More," "It's Not I'm Such a Wolf, It's Just You're Such a Lamb" and "And Then It's Heaven." "Five Minutes" has already proven itself with public and other two have possibilities. Gaillard clicks with "Cement Mixer" and "Yep Roc Heresi." Carle's orch backs songs and he also sells his "Bach Meets Carle" piano solo for smooth results.

Plot is slight but since music gives proceedings a lift, story is adequate framework. It concerns attempts of two crooks to fix a college rowing race so a big bet can be cashed. Thrown in without explanation is Elyse Knox's romantic chase of Ross Hunter and his resistance. Miss Knox does capable performance in a not so forte role but Hunter fails to fill demands of virile young rowing star and ex-GI back in college. A number of other younger players in cast could have filled assignment better, particularly Alan Hale, Jr.

Regan is Hunter's older brother, operating nitery near campus. Paul Guilfoyle and Edward Brophy are the crooks who attempt to fix the race. Both are good. Among student body showing up are Anne Gillis, Fred Colby, Hale, Jr.; David Holt, Marjorie Hoerner, William Beaudine, Jr.; Emmett Vogan, Jr.; Fred Datig, Jr., and others. Tom Harmon is in briefly as rowing coach.

Jack Bernhard's direction does well in musical portions but is not always smooth in story sequences. Frank L. Moss scripted from original by George Wagner. Edward J. Kay's musical direction, the lensing by L. W. O'Connell and other technical credits measure up.

Brog.

Foreign Films

"EL GRAN AMOUR de BECQUER" (Becquer's Great Love") (ARGENTINE-MADE). PYADA-ANDES production. Stars Delia Garces; features Estaban Serrador, Josefina Freyre, Susanna Freyre; directed by ALberto de Zavalia; story, Maria Teresa Leon and Rafael Alberti; camera, Pedro Narzialetti; reviewed at Ambassador, Buenos Aires. Running time, 80 mins.

Film's story is built around supposed loves of the Spanish poet Becquer. Although technically a great improvement on the ordinary run of local pictures, continuity and story construction are poor. Susana Freyre shows real promise while Delia Garces is wistfully appealing but far too static. No dice for U. S., and mild even here.

Nid.

"LAURACHA" (ARGENTINE-MADE). CADEC release of Pampa production. Stars Amelia Bence, Arturo Garcia Buhr; features Malisa Zini, Maria Santos, Ilde Pirovano; directed by Ernesto Arancibia; screenplay, Hugo MacDowall based on story by Otto Miguel Clone; camera, Pablo Tabernero; at the Ocean, Buenos Aires. Running time, 91 mins.

Long held up by raw stock shortage plus contractual difficulties of star Amelia Bence, film emerges as the story of a dominating and independent woman who is tamed by love. Her mate abandons her until he learns she is to have his child, when he, too, is tamed. Despite monotonous dialogue picture has a pecularly dramatic quality at times and looks okay down here. No appeal for U. S. audiences.

Nid.

"ROTAGG" ("Failure") (SWEDISH). Kungsfilm production and release; stars Stig Olin, Stig Jaerrel; features Marianne Loefgren, Arnold Sjoestrand, Elsie Albiin, Ingrid Backlin, Harrieth Phillipsson, Ingemar Pallin, Eric Berglund, Gunnar Bjoernestrand; directed by Arne Mattsson; screenplay, Eric Zetterstroem; camera, Sten Dahlgren; reviewed in Stockhom. Running time, 96 mins.

Dramatic story of a child of divorcement affords Stig Olin an actor's field day. Portraying the part of a spoiled young man who's been expelled from a Stockholm college, he's up to much deviltry with the story ending with an attempt at ravishment. Smartly directed, film introes many new names. An okay grosser here, it may find a market abroad if not hit by censor troubles.

"DISKRET OPHOLD" ("Discretion Wanted") (DANISH). Nordisk Films Kompagni production and release. Stars Grete Holmer, Lily Broberg, Lise Thompsen; features Ib Schoenberg, Betty Helsengreen, Preben Neergaard, Vera Geburh, Bjoern Watt Boolsen; directed by Ole Palsbo; screenplay, Leck Fischer, Fleming Lynge. Reviewed in Copenhagen. Running time, 118 mins.

Film is interesting since it marks Ole Palsbo's directorial debut. He does well. Ib Schoenberg and Betty Helsengreen portray a family, who because of economic difficulties, take in several unmarried girls. Pic generates some good comedy, though on the whole, running time could be trimmed to good advantage. It will be a success in Denmark for some time, and looks okay for other Scandinavian countries. But elsewhere it looms as a doubtful entry. *Wins.*

Miniature Reviews

"The Secret Heart" (M-G). Claudette Colbert, Walter Pidgeon, June Allyson in well-treated psychological drama. good b.o.

"Love Laughs At Andy Hardy" (M-G). Mickey Rooney's first postwar pic solid program fare.

"San Quentin" (RKO). Forthright melodrama that reaches near-documentary style in telling story of prison reforms.

"Dangerous Millions" (20th). Whodunit with familiar pattern slated for dualer situations.

"Carmen" (Italian - Made). Vivid, lusty dramatization of Merimee story, with opera music for background.

The Secret Heart

Metro release of Edwin H. Knopf production. Stars Claudette Colbert, Walter Pidgeon, June Allyson; features Lionel Barrymore, Robert Sterling, Marshall Thompson. Directed by Robert Z. Leonard. Screenplay, Whitfield Cook and Anne Morrison Chapin, based on original story and adaptation by by Rose Franken and William Brown Meloney; camera, George Folsey; editor, Adrienne Fazan; score, Bronislau Kaper. Tradeshown N.Y., Nov. 21, '46. Running time, 97 mins.

Lee Addams	Claudette Colbert
Chris Matthews	Walter Pidgeon
Penny Addams	June Allyson
Dr. Rossiger	Lionel Barrymore
Chase N. Addams	Robert Sterling
Brandon Reynolds	Marshall Thompson
Mrs. Stover	Elizabeth Patterson
Larry Addams	Richard Derr
Kay Burns	Patricia Medina
Miss Hunter	Eily Malyon
Penny, child	Ann Lace
Chase, child	Dwayne Hickman

"The Secret Heart" could probably best be described as Hollywood's answer to the British-made "Seventh Veil," based as it is on a psychological theme interwoven with classical music. Film is as good as "Veil" and should enjoy the same bountiful word-of-mouth. Marquee-laden cast topped by Claudette Colbert, Walter Pidgeon and June Allyson will boost the pic's pulling power, making it a good b.o. bet in any situation.

Although "Heart" ties in with the wave of psychological dramas to hit the screen in recent months, it's more than just a suspenseful thriller. Based on an original story by Rose Franken and William Brown Meloney, the film presents in honest fashion a tale of a young girl with a father fixation that might have been taken from an actual case history. Top teamplay between director Robert Z. Leonard and the cast converts what might have been a maudlin tearjerker into a touching but entertaining story. Femme fans will give their mouchoirs a heavy workout.

One of the picture's best factors is the subtlety woven into the script by screenwriters Whitfield Cook and Anne Morrison Chapin. Instead of hitting audiences over the head with an idea of what's going to happen next in the story, the scripters swing into it gradually. Everything turns out the way it should but the audiences will feel themselves absorbed into the story because of the way it's done.

Tale revolves around a rich widow and her two stepchildren, a boy just out of the Navy and a college-age girl. Latter, an excellent pianist, is in love with the memory of her father, who taught her to play. Her only interest, consequently, is to shut out the rest of the world by locking herself in a room and playing for him. On the advice of a psychiatrist, the widow takes her brood to the family farm where the father had committed suicide. There the girl begins to come out of her shell but then undergoes another deep emotional upset. Thoroughly disillusioned, she attempts to kill herself in the same way her father did. Story builds up from there to a suspenseful climax and then lets down gradually to the happy denouement.

Responsible to a large extent for the sympathetic handling of the story is Miss Allyson as the young girl. In a role that's a far cry from her usual song-and-dance parts, she gives out with what's undoubtedly the best emoting of her career. Miss Colbert is fine as the young widow, with her flair for comedy helping to lighten the film's heavy mood. Walter Pidgeon, as the guy she's been in love with all the time, is his usual suave, competent self. Robert Sterling, in his first role since checking out of the armed service, Lionel Barrymore, Marshall Thompson, Richard Derr and moppet Ann Lace score in supporting roles.

Film offers plenty of fine music via Miss Allyson's pianistics and Bronislau Kaper's excellent score. Usual rich Metro mountings are provided by producer Edwin H. Knopf, who rates a nod for giving Miss Allyson her big dramatic chance. George Folsey's camera work is professional. *Stal.*

Love Laughs at Andy Hardy

Metro release of Robert Sisk production. Stars Mickey Rooney, Lewis Stone; features Sara Haden, Bonita Granville, Lina Romay, Fay Holden, Dorothy Ford. Directed by Willis Goldbeck. Screenplay, Harry Ruskin, William Ludwig from original story by Howard Dimsdale; songs, Earl K. Brent; camera, Robert Planck; editor, Irvine Warburton. Tradeshown N.Y., Nov. 22, '46. Running time, 93 mins.

Andy Hardy	Mickey Rooney
Judge Hardy	Lewis Stone
Aunt Milly	Sara Haden
Kay Wilson	Bonita Granville
Isobel Gonzales	Lina Romay
Mrs. Hardy	Fay Holden
Coffy Smith	Dorothy Ford
Duke Johnson	Hal Hackett
Dane Kittridge	Dick Simmons
Haberdashery Clerk	Clinton Sundberg
Miss Geeves	Geraldine Wall
Mr. Benedict	Addison Richards

With Mickey Rooney back in mufti Metro has taken the most popular celluloid family off the shelf for another episode in the life and loves of Andy Hardy. This pic doesn't vary much from the basic formula used in the numerous predecessors in the Hardy family saga, but why should it? More than ever now in this era of atomic jitters, the secure, comfortable, middle-class dream world of the Hardy domicile is guaranteed a powerfully favorable and reaction. It's everyman's escape into adolescent nostalgia.

Rooney is a couple of years older but doesn't look it, and certainly doesn't act it. A diminutive dynamo, Rooney bounces through his paces with his usual zest, capering, mugging and energetically stealing every scene he's in—and he's in practically every one. In the standout laugh sequence, Rooney gets trapped into a teamup with a towering co-ed and flashes his top form in an hilarious jitterbug routine. Throughout most of the pic, Rooney is made to play a moonstruck kid, but even when purring over some lines from "Romeo and Juliet," he knows the difference between a deadpan and a serio-comic recitation.

Always a pillar of strength, Lewis Stone is back in his old stand as Judge Hardy, still playing the grave, distinguished, and ideally understanding dad. Other cast regulars in the series include Fay Holden, who does a convincing job as Andy's anxious mother, and Sara Haden, in a walk-on part as Aunt Milly. Ann Rutherford, who used to play Polly Benedict, is out, with her part being brushed off into an off-stage existence. Filling in as Andy's heart throb is Bonita Granville, who registers nicely as the campus siren but who had better watch her waist and chin line for the future.

Bowing to the fact that Rooney is growing older, if not larger, story line pushes him to the brink of a marital plunge. Back from the wars, Andy picks up his academic career as a college freshman and falls badly for Miss Granville, who trips him up by marrying someone else. Heartbroken, Andy is set to pack up for exile in South America until he's diverted back to normal by the chili wiles of Lina Romay, a south-of-the-border chick who happens to be visiting the town of Carvel. Latter chirps one number in okay style but otherwise has little to do.

Production trimmings measure up to the high standards set for this series. Thin plot is adroitly padded out with comic business by director Willis Goldbeck who keeps the film rolling at high speed. Camera work and musical scoring are competently handled, while the juve members of the cast, who play collegians, contribute a nice assist. *Herm.*

San Quentin

Hollywood, Nov. 27.

RKO release of Martin Mooney production. Stars Lawrence Tierney; features Barton MacLane, Marian Carr, Harry Shannon, Carol Forman, Richard Powers, Joe Devlin. Directed by Gordon M. Douglas. Original screenplay, Lawrence Kimble, Arthur A. Ross, Howard J. Green; camera, Frank Redman; music, Paul Sawtell; editor, Marvin Coil. Tradeshown Nov. 25, '46. Running time, 66 MINS.

Jim	Lawrence Tierney
Nick Taylor	Barton MacLane
Betty	Marian Carr
Warden Kelly	Harry Shannon
Ruthie	Carol Forman
Schaeffer	Richard Powers
Broadway	Joe Devlin
Marlowe	Tony Barrett
Carzoni	Lee Bonnell
Tommy	Robert Clarke
Torrance	Raymond Burr

"San Quentin" stacks up as a near-documentary with plenty of interest for the melodrama market. It is carefully produced, has a ring of authenticity and thoroughly fills its production aims of material for the action situations. Credit goes to Martin Mooney for the care with which he has expended a minor budget in shaping production values that are above the level of the usual budget thriller and the stamp of realism which he has given the picture.

Cast names are not assured b.o., but they all come through with performances that add to overall feeling under Gordon M. Douglas' showmanly direction. Douglas whips together this tale of reformation leagues within prisons with plenty of movement, spotting action and development without a slow moment. Lawrence Tierney, as a prisoner of San Quentin, now reformed and just discharged from honorable Army service, acquits himself capably, making role believeable all the way.

Plot frames its melodramatics around efforts of Harry Shannon, San Quentin warden, to keep his prisoners' welfare league going in the face of opposition. Taking a group of prisoners to San Francisco to speak to a newspaper club, Shannon is wounded and others killed when a supposedly reformed inmate arranges an escape. To clear the warden's plan and make life better for majority of prisoners Tierney goes on a manhunt for Barton MacLane, the killer. It's a long chase, but interest is sustained, and winds up in a free-for-all slugging match that will please the action lookers. Original script by Lawrence Kimble, Arthur A. Ross and Howard J. Green avoids as much as possible the usual cops-and-robbers cliches to keep it believeable.

MacLane turns in sturdy badman characterization. Shannon is good as the warden. Richard Powers is adequate as a detective who shadows Tierney. Joe Devlin is good for chuckles as Tierney's friend and Marian Carr shows well as femme interest. Same goes for Carol Forman, gangster moll. Neat smaller roles are contributed by Robert Clarke, Lee Bonnell, Tony Bartlett, Robert Clarke, Raymond Burr and several uncredited cast members.

There's plenty of San Quentin footage included in the Frank Redman lensing that is an aid. Music score by Paul Sawtell, tight editing by Marvin Coil and other technical factors are sturdy. *Brog.*

Dangerous Millions

20th-Fox release of Sol M. Wurtzel production. Features Kent Taylor, Dona Drake, Tala Birell, Leonard Strong. Directed by James Tinling. Original screenplay, Irving Cummings, Jr., Robert G. North; camera, Benjamin Kline; editor, William F. Claxton. Tradeshown N. Y. Nov. 29, '46. Running time, **69 MINS.**

Jack Clark	Kent Taylor
Elena Valdez	Dona Drake
Sonia Bardos	Tala Birell
Bandit Chieftain	Leonard Strong
Lance Warburton	Rex Evans
Hendrick Van Boyden	Robert Barrat
Jan Schuyler	Konstantin Shayne
Nils Otter	Otto Reichow
Rudolph Busch	Rudolph Anders
Alfredo Charles	Franco Corsaro

"Dangerous Millions" is standard whodunit fare for dualer situations. Pic is marked on the positive side by solid production dress, firstrate camera work and competent thesping corps to handle the main roles. Chief drawback is the old hat plot which is not enhanced by any novel twists in the scripting. Film will serve okay, however, for purposes intended.

Localed in China, story concerns the murderous shenanigans within a group of remotely related heirs who are laying claim to the fortune of a shipping tycoon allegedly dead. After two of the claimants have been disposed of, rest of the group is shanghaied to a mountain retreat by guerillas who want a cut of the inheritance takes. Plots and counterplots, escapes and additional corpses crowd the screen until the old shipping operator reveals himself and informs the remaining heirs that he devised the kidnapping to test their worthiness. Denouement comes only as mild surprise since this turn of events is telegraphed early in the film.

Kent Taylor, in the lead, registers well, as the debonair adventurer who's equally handy with dames or gats. As the romantic interest, Dona Drake comes through less successfully, badly mauling her emotions at the critical moments. Leonard Strong, as the Chinese bandit chieftain, plays the epigrammatic Oriental to the hilt, while Robert Barrat, as the shipper, is also good. Rest of the cast give adequate support. *Herm.*

Carmen
(ITALIAN-MADE)

Superfilm Distributing Corp. release of Scalera Film (Rome) production. Stars Viviane Romance; features Jean Marais, Marguerite Moreno, Julian Berteau. Directed by Christian Jaque. Adapted from Prosper Merimee story; music by Georges Bizet; camera, Ubaldo Arata; English titles, Herman G. Weinberg. At Ambassador, N. Y., Nov. 26, '46. Running time, **100 MINS.**

Carmen	Viviane Romance
Pamela	Elli Parvo
Dorotea	Margarite Moreno
Don Jose	Jean Marais
Lieutenant	Adriano Rimoldi
Lucas Escamillo	Julien Bertau
Garcia	Lucien Coedel
Romendado	Bernard Belier
Lillas Pastia	Jean Rochard

(In French; English Titles)

Prosper Merimee's novel about the temperamental gypsy cigaret-girl, Carmen, has a lusty retelling in this film. Its vitality and frankness, its attractive principals and intriguing story, the familiar Bizet opera music used for background, are all bound to appeal. Pic looks like an excellent grosser for the arty houses.

Filmed in Italy with a French cast, with French dialog (and English subtitles), pic is uninhibited, brutal and real. It tells a story of passion, intrigue, robbery and murder with absorbing honesty. The story is based on the Merimee original rather than on the sentimentalized operatic version which Bizet set to music.

Certain parts of the opera music—like the changing of the guards, smugglers march, or card scene episodes—are matched up with the film counterparts, while a good deal more is used for general background. But, although the music heightens the effect to anyone acquainted with the opera or music score, the picture could stand on its own without it. It's melodramatic, period stuff, but exceedingly well done.

Story describes the romance of Carmen and her dragoon friend, Don Jose; his murder of his lieutenant because of her, and his subsequent taking up with her smuggler-robber band; Carmen's desertion of Jose for a toreador, and her death at Jose's hands. Operatic characters like Micaela are omitted, without in the least affecting the story.

Story is filled with graphic incident, such as the fight in the factory between the two cigaret girls, a stagecoach holdup, the duel between Carmen's two lovers, Jose and Garcia, and the bullfight scene. Photography is of top grade, especially in such shots as of smugglers and horsepacks crossing the hills, or in the bandits' pursuit of the stage-coach. Dialog and love scenes are blunt and sexy without being offensive, while speech and action have an earthy, humorous touch throughout.

Performances are excellent. Viviane Romance makes an unusually attractive Carmen, with her acting suggesting the fiery, elemental gypsy, to striking effect. Jean Marais, as the taciturn Jose, is unusually handsome while making his stock character essentially real. Lucien Coedel, as the unscrupulous smuggler chief; Jean Rochard, the double-dealing innkeeper; Bernard Belier, as a smuggler, and Margarite Moreno, as a card-reading seer, bring rich flavor to their characterizations. Christian Jaque's direction is fluid, so that attention never lags. *Bron.*

Foreign Films

"Macadam" (FRENCH). Regina release of B.U.P. production. Stars Francoise Rosay, Andree Clement, Paul Meurisse; features Simone Signoret, Jacques Dacqmine; directed by Marcel Blistene; screenplay, Jacques Viot; camera, Louis Page; reviewed in Paris. Running time, **110 MINS.**

Stronger than most local product and sure here of hefty returns, this film's plot revolves around crooks, their mistresses and prostitutes in the Montmartre underworld. Direction of Marcel Blistene is top drawer; cast headed by Francoise Rosay, well known in U. S., is excellent. "Macadam' is a good bet for U. S. arty spots. *Maxi.*

"Ballongen" ("The Balloon") (SWEDISH). Svensk Filmindustri release of Nils Poppe production; stars Poppe; features Inga Landgre, Marianne Loefgren, Marianne Aminoff, Marianne Gyllenhammar, Ulla Norgen, Julia Caeser, Stig Olin, Sigge Furst; directed by Poppe; screenplay, Poppe and Gardar Sahlberg; camera, Martin Bodin; reviewed in Stockholm. Running time, **100 MINS.**

Nils Poppe scores again with a film that's headed for hefty returns in Sweden. This year he rated an extra Swedish Oscar for his acting in "Money." Now he's back with his second film which has cast him as a viking of the 8th century, a Turkish Caliph of the 13th century, a French King of the 17th, a clown of 1860 and a Swedish student of 1946. Long cast is chiefly female. Comedy may do fairly well in U. S. *Winq.*

"La Kermesse Rouge" ("The Scarlet Bazaar") (FRENCH). Ti. Breitz release of U.T.C. production. Stars Albert Prejean, Jean Tissier, Andree Servillanges; directed by Paul Mesnier; based on original story by Mesnier; reviewed in Paris. Running time, **90 MINS.**

Costume picture of the '90's is a long flashback of an old painter's life portrayed by Albert Prejean. Despite fact that cost of film was only around $100,000, it shows as much production values as the usual French pic budgeted at twice this amount. But film is obviously aimed at the French market, where big for nabes. No chance in U. S.

"Le Pere Tranquille" ("The Quiet Daddy") (FRENCH). Coronoa release of B.C.M. production; stars Noel-Noel; features Jean Varas, Dieudonne, Claire Olivier, Jose Arthur; directed by Rene Clement; screenplay, Noel-Noel. Reviewed in Paris. Running time, **105 MINS.**

Local Noel-Noel fans are likely to provide nice returns here. For America, it looks cued for foreign language spots. Theme is the over-played underground - fools - the Germans with Noel-Noel acting with finesse the role of a small town bourgeois who secretly is the head of the local underground. Rene Clement, who directed "Bataille du Rail" and won the director prize at the Cannes festival with it, did a neat job on what is primarily Noel-Noel's picture.

"La Belle et la Bete" ("The Beauty and the Beast") (FRENCH). Discina release of Andre Paulve production. Stars Jean Marais, Josette Day, Mila Parely; directed by Jean Cocteau; screenplay, Cocteau, based on short story by Mrs. Leprince de Beauveau; camera, Alekian; reviewed in Paris. Running time, **110 MINS.**

Unduly slow pace and repetitious use of trick sets hurts chances of this film. Story, a fairy tale in mediaeval costumes, shows Josette Day in a Cinderella part falling in love with a monster who turns into a Prince Charming upon death. Picture is geared more for the arty crowd than the masses. Offers little hope for American market.

"Les Chouans" ("The Royalists") (FRENCH). Corona release of Georges Legrand production; stars Jean Morais; features Madeline Robinson, Madeleine Lebeau, Marcel Herrand and Seigner; directed by Henri Calef; screenplay, Charles Spaak, based on novel by Honore de Balzac. Previewed in Paris. Running time, **95 MINS.**

Picture of the French Revolution period, this shows the last stand of the French Royalists in Brittany against the republican army and police. Direction is spotty. All the dialog has a decided red twist and picture does not compare well with the novel. Main interest for Americans is casting of Madeleine Lebeau who's familiar to some U. S. audiences for her work in "Casablanca," "Paris After Dark" and "French Touch." Light biz possibilities for America.

"Le Revenant" ("The Ghost") (FRENCH). Corona release of C.F.C.C. production; stars Louis Jouvet, Gaby Morlay, Francois Perier; features Ludmilla Tcherina, Marguerite Moreno; directed by Christian Jaque; story and dialog, Henry Jaenson. Reviewed in Paris. Running time, **90 MINS.**

Short on femme appeal, story deals with a ballet impresario who entices young Francois Perier from his native Lyons and wealthy family. Meanwhile impresario Louis Jouvet also revives the love Gaby Morlay had for him but jilts her at the last minute. Both Perier and Jouvet turn in okay performances. Marguerite Moreno shines in a minor role. Offers little for U. S. market.

"Patrie" (FRENCH). Regina release of Pierre O'Connel-Arys Nissotti production; stars Pierre Blanchar, Maria Mauban, Jean Desailly; directed by Louis Daquin. Reviewed in Paris. Running time, **100 MINS.**

Costume picture set in XVIth century Flanders under Spanish rule, this is based on Sardou's legit play. Story concerns Pierre Blanchar who heads a rebellion against Spanish rule. He pretends not to know that his chief aide, Jean Desailly, is having an affair with his wife so that rebels' chances may not be hurt. When rebellion is put down, execution scenes are among best of film. However, fair direction, stilted acting and lack of comedy relief prevents this from comparing with the old "Kermesse Heroique." No dice for U. S.

"91-An Karlsson" ("Private No. 91 Karlsson") (SWEDISH) AB Svea Film release of Film AB Imago production; stars Gus Dahlstrom, Stv Thulin; features Holger Hoeglund, Fritjof Billquist, Douglas Hage, Thor Modeen, Gustav Loewas; directed by Hugo Bolander; screenplay by Harry Iseborg based on story by Rudolf Pettersson. Reviewed in Stockholm. Running time, **88 MINS.**

Whole story suffers from faulty scripting. Billed as a comedy about military life, it's far from humorous. Little for any foreign countries and dubious even in Sweden. *Winq.*

"Il Suffit D'Une Fois" ("Once Is Enough") (FRENCH). Vog release of Sigma production; stars Fernand Gravet, Edwige Feuillere; features Henri Guisol; directed by Andree Feix; based on short story by Solange Terac; adaptation and dialog, Terac and M. G. Sauvageon; reviewed in Paris. Running time, **100 MINS.**

Local draw will come mostly from names and some amusing dialogue. Edwige Feuillere portrays sculptress who falls in love with explorer Fernand Gravey. Best performance is by Henri Guisol as an art dealer, a friend of both lovers who helps patch up their quarrels. Direction leans toward broad comedy. With different treatment, idea might make a good comedy. Film has dubious value for U. S. market. *Maxi.*

Miniature Reviews

"The Time, the Place and the Girl" (Color-Musical) (WB). Lavish color musical for general audience appeal.

"Unexpected Guest" (UA). Okay hybrid western-whodunit in Hopalong Cassidy series.

"Temptation" (U-I). Strong cast headed by Merle Oberon in slow moving murder meller.

"Swell Guy" (U-I). Off-the-beaten-path drama of a heel hero.

"The Falcon's Adventure" (RKO). Well-paced program whodunit for twin-bill trade.

"Out California Way" (Songs-Color) (Rep). Routine oatuner starring Monte Hale.

"Panique" (Regina). French-made Julien Duvivier production strong enough for big coin in France; chance for U. S. market.

"Mr. Hex" (Mono). Standard Bowery Boys fare that will pay off in its regular market.

"Spook Busters" (Mono). Slapstick dual fare with Bowery Boys for so-so b.o.

"The Taras Family" (Artkino). Soviet cycle of war films continued for those who like their history grim.

"Green for Danger" (British). Implausible whodunit heading for fair biz in Britain with slim U. S. prospects.

The Time, the Place and the Girl

(COLOR—MUSICAL)

Hollywood, Dec. 6.

Warner Bros. release of Alex Gottlieb production. Stars Dennis Morgan, Jack Carson, Janis Paige, Martha Vickers; features S. Z. Sakall, Alan Hale, Angela Greene, Donald Woods, Florence Bates, Carmen Cavallaro orch, Condos Bros., Chandra Kaly Dancers. Directed by David Butler. Screenplay, Francis Swann, Agnes Christine Johnston, Lynn Starling; original story, Leonard Lee; camera (Technicolor), William V. Skall and Arthur Edeson; dances, LeRoy Prinz; songs, Arthur Schwartz and Leo Robin; editor, Irene Morra. Tradeshown Dec. 6, '46. Running time, **105 MINS.**

Steven Ross	Dennis Morgan
Jeff Howard	Jack Carson
Sue Jackson	Janis Paige
Victoria Cassel	Martha Vickers
Ladislaus Cassel	S. Z. Sakall
John Braden	Alan Hale
Elaine Winters	Angela Greene
Martin Drew	Donald Woods
Madame Lucia Cassel	Florence Bates

Carmen Cavallaro Orchestra
Condos Bros.
Chandra Kaly & His Dancers

Warners has tossed a great deal of comedy and songs into this musical to give most any audience full measure of entertainment. "The Time, the Place and the Girl" is snappy tomfoolery, tunefully embroidered, that shapes up to stout b.o. potential. Cast names will brighten marquees and Alex Gottlieb's showmanly production has used color to display glittering costumes, musical number settings and femme beauty for sock eye appeal.

Score contains six numbers by Leo Robin and Arthur Schwartz. All are tuneful and four already are on the road to real hitdom: "A Rainy Night in Rio," "Oh But I Do," "Gal in Calico" and "Through a Thousand Dreams." Others are show tunes backing production numbers.

Dennis Morgan, Jack Carson, Janis Paige and Martha Vickers vocal the songs. A standout is Carmen Cavallaro's spot with "Thousand Dreams." Other high spots are furnished by Condos Bros. and the Chandra Kaly Dancers, both in specialty sequences that click. Most lavish of the six dance numbers staged by LeRoy Prinz are "Dreams" and "Rio."

David Butler's direction punches over the comedy, getting the most from bright lines and situations in the script. Plot is thin but neatly put together in the writing to carry through as support for musical sequences. Butler gives it broad treatment and cast responds for laughs.

Story line has Morgan and Carson trying to put on a musical show against the opposition of Florence Bates, oldtime opera star, and her priggish manager, Donald Woods. Morgan and Carson have enlisted aid of Miss Bates' husband, S. Z. Sakall, and granddaughter Martha Vickers, latter to be femme star. Around that plot has been built some beautiful production numbers, good tunes and plenty of corn, making for smooth, fast entertainment.

Morgan takes his straight assignment capably and Carson gets over many laughs. Janis Paige plays opposite latter, also adding to fun, while Miss Vickers holds up her end musically and on looks. Sakall rates chuckles for his usual comedy type. Alan Hale, bluff Texas oil man; Angela Greene, Woods, Miss Bates and others do well.

Dual lensing credit goes to William V. Skall and Arthur Edeson for expert color display of fancy production values. Editing and other technical contributions add to well-rounded production. *Brog.*

Unexpected Guest

United Artists release of Lewis J. Rachmil production. Stars William Boyd. Directed by George Archainbaud. Original story and screenplay, Ande Lamb; editor, Fred W. Berger; camera, Max Stengler. Tradeshown N. Y., Dec. 4, '46. Running time, **61 MINS.**

Hopalong Cassidy	Bill Boyd
Lucky Jenkins	Rand Brooks
California Carlson	Andy Clyde
Ruth Baxter	Patricia Tate
David Potter	John Parrish
Housekeeper	Una O'Connor
Ralph Baxter	Ned Young
Joshua Coulter	Earl Hodgins
Phineas Phipps	Joel Freidkin

This umteenth in the Hopalong Cassidy series stacks up as a hybrid oater and whodunit skillfully blended to insure a diverting hour for patrons of dual situations for which this opus is patently aimed. Hurdling the omnipresent cliches invariably found in all low budgeters, "Unexpected Guest" has a novel script treatment which keeps the customers guessing until the last frames of the footage.

Beneficiary in the will of his late cousin, Hiram Baxter, Andy Clyde heads his cayuse toward the Baxter ranch accompanied by his pals, Bill Boyd and Rand Brooks. They're harassed by a mysterious hooded figure who snipes a couple shells at 'em from a concealed position. Reading of the will by executor and family attorney, John Parrish, reveals that some six legatees are to share equally in the ranch and upon death of any of the beneficiaries, estate passes on to those remaining.

Suddenly obdurate cousin Joel Freidkin is rubbed out, following day Patricia Tate narrowly escapes a similar fate, shortly after cousin Ned Young is killed in the ranch house, etc. Murderer is finally nabbed by Boyd in a neat hand-to-hand encounter of the old school. Ranch house's spooky atmosphere accented by hidden passages, sliding panels and secret doors is heightened by the spiritual activities of housekeeper Una O'Connor who holds seances with departed souls in the family graveyard.

Producer Lew Rachmil rates bows for deftly reining the film into a top drawer programmer. George Archainbaud's direction took advantage of Ande Lamb's script values smartly pacing the thespers through a taut 61 minutes. Boyd, per usual, is standout as Hoppy, ably assisted by Brooks, Clyde, Miss Tate and Parrish. Miss O'Connor contribs a neat characterization of the superstitious housekeeper while Mack Stengler has done a bang-up job of lensing.

Temptation

Universal release of Internationl (Edward Small) production. Stars Merle Oberon, George Brent; features Paul Lukas, Charles Korvin, Lenore Ulric. Directed by Irving Pichel. Screenplay, Robert Thoeren from novel by Robert Hichens and play by James Bernard Fagen; camera, Lucien Ballard; editor, Ernest Nims; music, Daniele Amfitheatrof. Tradesrown N. Y. Dec. 10, '46. Running time, **98 MINS.**

Ruby	Merle Oberon
Nigel	George Brent
Baroudi	Charles Korvin
Isaacson	Paul Lukas
Marie	Lenore Ulric
Ahmed	Arnold Moss
Dr. Mueller	Ludwig Stossel
Smith-Barrington	Gavin Muir
Frau Mueller	Ilka Gruning
Hamza	Robert Capa
Don Gibbs	John Eldredge
Professor Dupont	Andre Charlot
Yvonne Dupont	Suzanne Cloutier
Jean McCormick	Gloria Lloyd
Mrs. McCormick	Mary Young
Dr. Harding	Aubrey Mather
Abdullah	Samir Rizkallah
Ibrahim	Egon Brecher

Final picture made under International's banner before its merger with Universal, "Temptation" is loaded with enough marquee punch to cinch good play at the wickets, despite its meandering pace. Production is well-stacked with solid values in every department except for the screenplay, which falls short in its attempt to stretch an unsubstantial story line over so long a running time.

Pulling the full weight of the pic practically single-handedly, Merle Oberon in the central role of the femme fatale scores a personal triumph. Gowned in a series of stunning creations that match her w.k. exotic looks, Miss Oberon runs the full gamut from diabolic caprice through tragic conflict to ultimate regeneration with delicate emotional shadings that lend solidity and credibility to her characterization. Femme trade will find special appeal in the actress' performance.

Two male vis-a-vis register less successfully. George Brent, playing the part-time husband and full-time Egyptologist, walks through his part with a wooden gait and frozen expression that fails to evoke the needed sympathy. Charles Korvin, as the Egyptian roue, complete with fez and corny romantic patter, lacks the polish and assurance for his role, and too frequently substitutes a sophomoric leer for heartbreak brutality. In a minor role as family doctor and adviser, Paul Lukas contributes heavily, as does Lenore Ulric as the lady's maid.

Story is localed in Egypt, where Brent, newly married to Miss Oberon, is engaged in a British museum expedition. Overcome by boredom while her husband is out digging for a mummy, Miss Oberon, already with a shady past containing several divorces, gets mixed up with an Egyptian dandy in a full-blown love affair. Down-at-the-heels and debt-ridden, her lover threatens to brush her off for an American heiress unless she kills her husband for the inheritance. Brent gets a slow-death-through-poison treatment until Miss Oberon awakens to the realization that her boy friend is a seedy, blackmailing blackguard. So she kills him instead, returns to her husband for a final embrace, and satisfies the crime-doesn't-pay code by arranging an accidental death for herself.

Direction by Irving Pichel, instead of using speed-up devices to pump up blood pressure, is cued to the leisurely tempo of the script. Photography and settings, which capture a genuine flavor of the Nile country, are first-rate but the editing could have improved on the film by additional judicious slicing. *Herm.*

Swell Guy

Hollywood, Dec. 6.

Universal-International release of Mark Hellinger (Edward A. Blatt) production. Stars Sonny Tufts, Ann Blyth; features Ruth Warrick, William Gargan, Thomas Gomez, Mary Nash, John Litel. Directed by Frank Tuttle. Screenplay, Richard Brooks; based on play by Gilbert Emery; camera, Tony Gaudio; music, Frank Skinner; editor, Edward Curtiss. Previewed at Academy Awards theatre, Dec. 3, '46. Running time, **86 MINS.**

Jim Duncan	Sonny Tufts
Marian Tyler	Ann Blyth
Ann Duncan	Ruth Warrick
Martin Duncan	William Gargan
Arthur Tyler	John Litel
Dave Vinson	Thomas Gomez
Steve	Millard Mitchell
Sarah Duncan	Mary Nash
Botsworth	Howard Freeman
Tony Duncan	Donald Devlin
Mike O'Connor	John Craven
Ray Link	Pat McVey
Sam Burns	Vince Barnett
Ben Tilwell	Charles Lane
Ernie	Gary Owen
Eddie	Frank Ferguson
Frank	David Clarke
Jackie	Eugene Persson
George	George Beban, Jr.

"Swell Guy" is an ironical handle for drama content of this Mark Hellinger production. Based on the old play, "The Hero," but with a modern background, picture deals with a heel hero who doesn't reform. Hellinger has given it smooth production polish, a number of noteworthy touches and a casting surprise. Sonny Tufts plays the title role, a departure from his usual casting. That he doesn't always fulfill demands of part doesn't diminish interest that casting twist generates. His name will aid customer draw. Also aiding are those of Ann Blyth, Ruth Warrick and William Gargan.

Story concerns stir caused in a small California town when a war correspondent comes to visit his family and how his lack of scruples and inability to do the right thing affect all he meets. Family and town characters are naturally displayed in the writing of the script by Richard Brooks, and Frank Tuttle's direction maintains that feeling.

Tufts, a hero to all but his mother and the correspondents who have worked with him, is taken to the town's heart. He soon starts taking the citizens in crap games; nearly wrecks the marriage of his brother and sister-in-law; and compromises the town's rich girl. At the finale, just as he is about to flee with funds collected in a GI veterans' drive, he meets death saving his young nephew.

Ann Blyth, co-starred, comes through with a highly effective performance as the spoiled rich girl who is taken in by the phoney hero. She has a bright film future. Ruth Warrick, the sister-in-law, is excellent. William Gargan does a natural job of the brother and Mary Nash, the mother who knows her son, is equally good. Thomas Gomez, as a correspondent, John Litel, Millard Mitchell, John Craven, Vince Barnett, Howard Freeman are among others who play their roles with ease. Young Donald Devlin makes his film debut as the nephew whose train tunnel adventure brings about the melodramatic finale.

An effective music score by Frank Skinner; the camera work of Tony Gaudio; the naturalness obtained by art direction and settings; are factors that contribute to the production polish maintained by Hellinger and his associate, Eddie Blatt. *Brog.*

The Falcon's Adventure

RKO release of Herman Schlom production. Stars Tom Conway; features Madge Meredith, Edward S. Brophy. Directed by William Berke. Screenplay, Aubrey Wiseberg and Robert E. Kent; camera, Harry Wild and Frank Redman; editor, Marvin Coll. Tradeshown N. Y., Dec. 9, '46. Running time, **61 MINS.**

Falcon	Tom Conway
Luisa	Madge Meredith

Goldie....................Edward S. Brophy
Sutton....................Robert Warwick
Doris....................Myrna Dell
Benny....................Steve Brodie
Denison....................Ian Wolfe
Helen....................Carol Forman
Inspector Cavanaugh..........Joseph Crehan
Geary....................Phil Warren
Paolo....................Tony Barrett
Duncan....................Harry Harvey
Lieut. Evans..............Jason Robards

A semblance of care seems to be all that's necessary to make a whodunit surefire program fare, and this latest in the "Falcon" series has that. Swiftly paced and competently mounted, "The Falcon's Adventure" moves fast enough so that the few inconsistencies probably will never be noticed. Should do well with the steady mystery fan trade.

Tom Conway, the lady-killing, British-accented Falcon, rescues a Brazilian gal from a kidnap attempt and falls into a plot to get her father's formula for synthetic industrial diamonds. After the old man is killed, for which Conway is blamed, the story moves to Florida, where another scientist is also gently disposed of and once again the blame falls upon the Falcon. With the police tailing him, Falcon manages to rescue the South American beauty from the yacht of the plotter, head of an industrial diamond syndicate who wants the formula destroyed. Action is well spiced with battles, in each of which the Falcon gets his lumps.

Pic's values are seemingly unhurt by the fact that victim of the second "murder" died of a heart attack, or that Conway, with the police after him for a killing, was able to leisurely hop a train to Florida.

Conway's thesping is fine, as is that of stooge Edward Brophy. Madge Meredith, as the Brazilian chick, looks like a steady comer. Others in the cast are veteran supports and hold up competently. Quick pace helps.

Out California Way
(SONGS—COLOR)

Republic release of Louis Gray production. Stars Monte Hale, Adrian Booth; features Bobby Blake. Directed by Lesley Selander. Screenplay, Betty Burbridge from original by Barry Shipman; songs, Paul Westmoreland, Foy Willing, Jack Meakin, Foster Carling, Tex Carlson, Jack Statham, Gus Snow, Eddie Dean, Hal Blair; camera (Trucolor), Bud Thackery; editor, Charles Craft. Tradeshown N. Y., Dec. 6, '46. Running time, **67 MINS.**

Monte....................Monte Hale
Gloria McCoy....................Adrian Booth
Danny McCoy....................Bobby Blake
Rod Mason....................John Dehner
George Sheridan....................Nolan Leary
Ace Carter....................Fred Graham
Johnny Archer....................Tom London
Jimmy Starr....................Jimmy Starr
E. J. Pearson....................Edward Keane
Assistant Director....................Bob Wilke
Cameraman....................Brooks Benedict
St. Luke's Choristers
Foy Willing & Riders of Purple Sage

A tame westerner, "Old California Way" will rate with fans who like their oatunes in concentrated doses. With the swooners firmly in the saddle these days, the wild and woolly sagas of the western plains are becoming as rare as buffaloes, and this pic is definitely part of the latter-day trend. More station wagons than stallions are used to get around here in addition to the usual swapping of gats for guitars. Only action feature in this film is a couple of fierce knuckle-scraping encounters involving a couple of varmints and Monte Hale, when the latter is not hitting the middle-C's.

Attempt is made to give an additional lift to this production through the use of color, but the process, trade-named Trucolor, only lends a hokey hue to the film with overtinting on the brown-orange and blue-green side. Makeup smear is clearly evident on the femme players. Another boosting technique is the use of Republic's galaxy of western stars for walk-on parts with Roy Rogers and Dale Evans during one number.

Although Hale wears chaps and sports a lariat, story is a behind-the-scenes conflict between a couple of lead players at a mythical Hollywood studio. Sandwiched into this plot-within-a-plot is the attempt of young Bobby Blake to get a part in a forthcoming westener for his educated nag, Pardner, whom he hopes will share cinematic glory with other top-billed equines like Trigger and Thunder. Six numbers are highlighted, including "Detour," "Rose of Santa Fe," "Hello Monte," "Out California Way," "Little Bronc of Mine" and "Boogie Woogie Cowboy," latter being the standout tune.

Hale registers as a likeable cowchanter, handling the vocals in easy, if not exceptional, style. Backing up nicely are young Blake, his big sister, Adrian Booth, the menace, John Dehner, and the hoss. Production accoutrements, scripting and direction are at the regular standards for low-budget westerns. *Herm.*

Panique
(FRENCH-MADE)

Regina release of Pierre O'Connel-Arys Nissotti production. Directed by Julien Duvivier. Stars Viviane Romance, Michel Simon and Paul Bernard. From a novel by Georges Simenon. Previewed in Paris. Running time, **95 MINS.**

Julien Duvivier, who has had Hollywood experience, has directed this picture expertly besides cooperating with Charles Spaak in adapting the police novel. This novel is more credible in book form than on the screen but the marquee names this picture has promise solid returns in Paris. Michel Simon handles the difficult part of the ugly, lonely suburbanite well. He foolishly falls in love with a girl who connives with her boy friend to have Simon framed for a murder, thus exonerating her guilty lover.

Direction of the sequence showing Simon pursued by the mob and trying to escape over the roofs is distinctly Hollywoodish, up to the point when the fleeing man finally falls and dies. Viviane Romance, as the crook's moll, and Paul Bernard, as her evil genius, give good performances. Minor parts look more authentic than is customary here. Film has some possibilities for the U. S. *Maxi.*

Mr. Hex
(SONGS)

Hollywood, Dec. 7.

Monogram release of Jan Grippo (Cyril Endfield) production. Stars Leo Gorcey; features Huntz Hall, Bobby Jordan, Gabriel Dell, Billy Benedict, David Gorcey, Gale Robbins, Ben Welden, Ian Keith, Sammy Cohen. Directed by William Beaudine. Screenplay, Cyril Endfield; original, Jan Grippo; camera, James Brown; music, Edward J. Kay; songs, Louis Herscher; editor, Seth Larsen. Previewed Dec. 4, '46. Running time, **63 MINS.**

Slip....................Leo Gorcey
Sach....................Huntz Hall
Bobby....................Bobby Jordan
Gabe....................Gabriel Dell
Whitey....................Billy Benedict
Chuck....................David Gorcey
Gloria....................Gale Robbins
Bull Laguna....................Ben Weldon
Raymond....................Ian Keith
"Evil-Eye" Fagin..........Sammy Cohen
Louie....................Bernard Gorcey
Mob Leader....................William Ruhl
Danny the Dip....................Danny Beck
Mazie....................Rita Lynn
Billy Butterworth....................Joe Gray
Blackie....................Eddie Gribbon
Spud....................Meyer Grace
Bill....................Gene Stutenroth
Referee....................John Indrisano
Truck Driver....................Dewey Robinson
Waiter....................Jimmy Aubrey

"Mr. Hex" settles into the Bowery Boys series groove capably, furnishing plenty of the antics liked by those who follow the doings of the rough-and-ready gang. Original story uses novel gimmick to spark chuckles, and the production values furnished by Jan Grippo get the most from budget expenditure.

Story pattern is developed around hypnotism, a device used by the Boweryites for their latest do-good action. When boys' favorite jukebox voice has to quit her job to take care of a sick mother, kids start looking for angles to raise coin so they can help. Leo Gorcey, as gang leader, learns trick of hynotizing Huntz Hall into believing he's strong as 10 men. Boys pit Hall in an amateur boxing contest in a try for prize money and through slapdash adventures they make the payoff. Grippo did original yarn and Cyril Endfield, who also serves as associate producer, scripted.

Film spots a number of surefire laugh touches such as gamblers employing an "evil-eye" character to counter-hex Hall and a pickpocket to snatch Gorcey's hynotizing coin. Hall, Bobby Jordan, Gabriel Dell, Billy Benedict and other Bowery Boys are up to their usual standards. Gale Robbins, the jukebox voice, appears to advantage and is credited with vocaling film's two tunes, "A Love Song to Remember" and "One Star-Kissed Night," both by Louis Herscher. Ben Welden, the gambler; Sammy Cohen, the "evil-eye"; Ian Keith, and others in cast are capable.

William Beaudine does neat job of directing, giving Gorcey and his mob chance for usual broad characterizations. Lensing by James Brown and other production factors measure up. *Brog.*

Spook Busters

Monogram release of Jan Grippo production. Stars Leo Gorcey; features Huntz Hall, Douglass Dumbrille, Bobby Jordan, Gabriel Dell, Billy Benedict. Directed by William Beaudine; assistant director, Eddie Davis. Screenplay, Edmund Seward, Tim Ryan; camera, Harry Neumann; editor, Richard Currier. At Brooklyn Strand, dual, Dec. 7, '46. Running time, **61 MINS.**

Slip....................Leo Gorcey
Sach....................Huntz Hall
Dr. Coslow..............Douglass Dumbrille
Bobby....................Bobby Jordan
Gabe....................Gabriel Dell
Whitey....................Billy Benedict
Chuck....................David Gorcey
Mignon....................Tanis Chandler
Dr. Bender....................Maurice Glass
Mrs. Grimm....................Vera Lewis
Stiles....................Charles Middleton
Brown....................Chester Clute
Ivan....................Richard Alexander
Louie....................Bernard Gorcey
Dean Pettyboff..........Charles Millsfield
Herman....................Arthur Mills

Film comedy, nurtured on slapstick, reverts to early childhood in "Spook Busters." Entire story, with all its attendant comedy business, reeks of gleanings from past productions long gone into the limbo of unremembered celluloid. There is the ever-present feeling of having seen all this somewhere before.

And yet spotty as the screen values are there are a lot of laughs among the hokum. Even the old business of two people, searching for something in the wall, and answering each other's knocks, is used. Overall, however, the film drags and is repetitious. It hasn't much appeal except to the grammar school level and weekend matinee business.

Story has the Bowery Boys graduated from an exterminating school and going out on their first job, which happens to be an old deserted mansion. But the joint's jumping with secret panels, sliding doors, magic tricks, flying axes, etc. And there, pulled right out of the story file, is a mad scientist who wants to transplant a human brain into that of a gorilla. Film is padded out to program length with many secret passages, lights on and off, disappearances, and other stunts which have been seen too many times before. One new angle is the mad doctor's television machine which enables him to see the goings-on in every room of the house; never did explain who panned the video camera around to follow action.

Leo Gorcey uses the vehicle for family employment, spotting his father and brother in feature roles. That the pacing holds up at all in the face of so much padding is a credit to editor Richard Currier and director William Beaudine. Dead end type thesping comes out like sausages out of a mill. Definitely a lower-strata dualer.

The Taras Family

Artkino release of Kiev Film Studios production. Stars Ambrosi Butchma; features Benjamin Zuskin, Daniel Sagal, Eugene Ponomarenko, Vera Slovina. Directed by Mark Donskov. Screenplay, Boris Gorbatov, from novel by Gorbatov; camera, Boris Monastrisky; music, Lev Schwartz; English titles, Charles Clement. Reviewed at N. Y. Stanley, Dec. 7, '46. Running time, **82 MINS.**

Taras....................Ambrosi Butchma
Dr. Fishman..............Benjamin Zuskin
Stepan....................Daniel Sagal
Andrei..............Eugene Ponomarenko
Nastya....................Vera Slovina
Antonina....................Maria Samosvat
Efrosinia..............Lubov Kartasheva
Valya..............Elena Osmyalovskaya
Vasilek....................Nikolai Zimovetz
Granddaughter..........Luda Lizengevich
Lonka....................Vadin Zakurenko
German Head..............Mikhail Visotsky

(In Russian; English Titles)

The overlong cycle of Russian films treating with Nazi brutality—and in this case, coupled with fierce demands for revenge—is followed through in "The Taras Family." Curiously out of joint with press reports of Russian efforts to win Germany over to communism, this film reiterates the black-and-white characterizations of the Teutons and Soviets, and, once again, tosses in some heavy-handed flagwaving sans ideology, for the nonce. It's earnest and elemental from cover to cover but reminiscent, too, in its preoccupation as heretofore with Russia's bitter struggle against Teutonic occupation.

"Taras" offers no quarter to the escapism school of thought. Unrelieved as it is by humor, pic is not a morsel for any but those who want their history grim and strong. Yet, dealing in elementals, the film is strangely lacking in dramatic build-up and wallop—to a sum-total that's episodic and non-climactic. In the dialectics of economics, it isn't b.o. except for those located more than a mite left of centre.

Heralded as the first Soviet film to dramatize the Nazi discriminatory policy against the Jews in German-occupied Russia, "Taras" actually focuses on a Russian family (Slavic) and Teutonic efforts to force reopening of an arms factory. Jewish question is treated in a few episodes, dramatically—the most effective in the film, one, a terrifying hunt for Jewish hideaways; the other, a brutal mass slaughter. The latter has impact despite some sloppy megging and camera work.

Acting is at the high level customary in major Soviet picturizing. This goes equally for the principles and the extras who combine interestingly diversified Slavic physiognomy with an honest touch of rustic earthiness. Hat doffing is particularly due to Ambrosi Butchma for his three-dimensional and consistently top-rate portrayal of father Taras. Trio of moppets who fill in as the Taras children also rate a plug—for doing their stint manfully without that precocious cloying quality that's tripped up more than one pic. *Wit.*

Green for Danger
(BRITISH-MADE)

London, Dec. 5.

General Film Distributors' release of Individual Picture. Stars Sally Gray, Rosamund John, Trevor Howard. Directed by Sidney Gilliat. Screenplay by Sidney Gilliat, Claud Curney from novel by Christianna Brand. Camera, Wilkie Cooper. At Gaumont-British, London, Dec. 5, '46. Running time, **91 MINS.**

Mr. Eden....................Leo Genn
Mr. Purdy....................Henry Edwards
Dr. Barnes....................Trevor Howard
Dr. White....................Ronald Adam
Sister Bates....................Judy Campbell

Nurse Sanson...............Rosamund John
Nurse Linley.................Sally Gray
Sister Carter.............Wendy Thompson
Nurse Woods................Megs Jenkins
Inspector Cockrill.............Alastair Sim
Sergeant Hendricks.....George Woodbridge
Joseph Higgins............Moore Marriott

This whodunit has the unusual setting of an emergency wartime hospital with the operating theatre as the scene of two apparently clueless murders. Wounded by a buzz-bomb, local postman is brought to hospital for a slight emergency operation, but dies under the anesthetic. Six people are present at the death—Leo Genn, Trevor Howard, Judy Campbell, Rosamund John, Sally Gray and Megs Jenkins. Judy Campbell finds evidence that the man was murdered and before she can inform the police she is stabbed to death.

Alastair Sim, unconventional detective from Scotland Yard, appears to enjoy the double murder case and has great fun annoying the suspects. He discovers each one had a motive, until an attempt on the life of Sally Gray reduces the number to four. To reconstruct the postman's death, the Inspector stages a mock operation. The suspects believe it to be serious and while they perform their normal duties, he unmasks the killer.

Messrs. Gilliatt and Launder, one-time masters of suspense, are losing their touch. The plot is too laboriously constructed, and the reason for the murders appears too incredible to be accepted by ordinary audiences. Nor is the wartime setting and the operating theatre likely to have much feminine pull. The acting is uniformly good without being outstanding, and Alastair Sim's unorthodox detective is welcome relief.

It should do fair business here on the cast and reputation of the producers, but it faces tough going in America. *Cane.*

Miniature Reviews

'13 rue Madeleine" (20th). Tiptop meller of the strategic services, starring Jimmy Cagney.

"California" (Par.) (Color-Songs). Milland-Stanwyck-Fitzgerald names assure hefty grosses.

"The Locket" (RKO). Well-made psycho melodrama with sturdy cast names.

"The Fabulous Suzanne" (Rep). Fair comedy for duals.

"Les Portes de La Nuit" (Pathe Consort). Jacques Prevert-Marcel Carne combo okay for U. S. arty houses.

13 Rue Madeleine

20th-Fox release of Louis de Rochemont production. Stars James Cagney; features Annabella, Richard Conte, Frank Latimore. Directed by Henry Hathaway. Screenplay, John Monks, Jr., and Sy Bartlett; music, Alfred Newman; music direction, David Buttolph; arrangements, Edward Powell; camera, Norbert Brodine (Fred Sersen); editor, Harmon Jones. Tradeshown N. Y., Dec. 16, '46. Running time, 95 MINS.

Bob Sharkey.................James Cagney
Suzanne de Bouchard...........Annabella
Bill O'Connell..............Richard Conte
Jeff Lassiter..............Frank Latimore
Charles Gibson.............Walter Abel
Pappy Simpson............Melville Cooper
Mayor Galimard.............Sam Jaffe
Duclois..................Marcel Rousseau
Psychiatrist............Richard Gordon
Emile..................Everett G. Marshall
Madame Thillot...........Blanche Yurka
Karl..................Peter Von Zerneck
Hains Feinke.................Alfred Linder
Hotel Clerk...................Ben Low
R.A.F. Officer.............James Craven
Joseph..................Roland Belanger
Burglary Instructor......Horace MacMahon
Briefing Officer........Alexander Kirkland
La Roche..............Donald Randolph

"13 rue Madeleine" is the type of film which will become increasingly interesting and boxoffice-valuable the longer history removes us from World War II. We're still too close to yesterday's headlines but even now, as the auditor views just one branch of today's scientific warfare, with its strategic services, the underground, secret radio transmitters, painstaking indoctrination, and all the rest of it, one is moved to realize how many facets went into the struggle for victory. As a film entertainment it's surefire.

Utilizing the same off-screen documentary exposition as he did in "The House on 92d Street," producer Louis de Rochemont, himself an alumnus of the Time-Life technique, reemploys the stentorian "March of Time" commentary to set his theme. Thereafter it evolves into a Nazi-Allies cops-and-robbers tale of bravery and bravado, honest histrionics and hokum. But it all adds up to an arresting film tale in its total unfolding.

What Jimmy Cagney endows the picture with in the way of marquee values is sometimes frequently dissipated by an unconvincing performance. When he is one of the strategic services' masterminds, on U.S. or British soil, he is effectively the mature training officer engaged in the important branch of the service having to do with strategy. When he essays the role of a brave young soldier-spy, to pit himself against Richard Conte, the crack Gestapo agent who had insinuated himself into the American espionage school as a means to learn our invasion plans, Cagney suffers comparison. But the hectic pace of the melodramatics is such that it will not bother the average fan too much.

The training methods, as indoctrinated into the plot's development, are arresting audience stuff. And it is more of this sort of celluloid cinematurgy, as the years roll away from today's peace parleys, that will take on greater values with the passing of time. We're still too close to it right now.

Conte as Bill O'Connell, nee Wil-

helm Kuncel of the Nazi espionage, emerges as the cast's outstander. Frank Latimore is the weakling U. S. espionage man who inadvertently tips off to the wily Conte that the invasion plans are purposely being made to appear it would be through Holland. That's when Cagney decides to parachute into France to capture a collaborator who has the key to the Nazis' rocket-launching sites. When Conte captures him and submits him to torture, to wrest the true plans from him, the Allied espionage in London executes superprecision bombing to obliterate the 13 rue Madeleine headquarters of this Normandy town as a means to make sure Cagney doesn't weaken under the Nazi lash, and coincidentally wipe out Conte and his Nazi intelligence staff. The fadeout is a wallop, with the tortured Cagney derisively laughing into Conte's face as the important D-Day secret perishes with all of them.

"Madeleine," incidentally, was shot wholly away from Hollywood, utilizing New England and Quebec sites in the main, but there is nothing about the film that doesn't indicate super-Hollywood standards. The support is good down the line. Even Annabella does more than look pretty, being cast here as a bilingual telegraphiste. Walter Abel as chief of American espionage, Melville Cooper in a prissy role, Sam Jaffe as the patriotic French provincial mayor, Marcel Rousseau as the collaborationist, and others, register. Direction by Henry Hathaway is taut, and Alfred Neuman's dramatic score doesn't hurt either. *Abel.*

California
(COLOR—SONGS)

Paramount release of Seton I. Miller production. Stars Ray Milland, Barbara Stanwyck, Barry Fitzgerald; features George Coulouris, Albert Dekker, Anthony Quinn, Frank Faylen. Directed by John Farrow. Screenplay, Frank Butler and Theodore Strauss, based on story by Boris Ingster; songs, E. Y. Harburg and Earl Robinson; score, Victor Young; arrangements, Ken Lane, Phil Boutelje; editor, Eda Warren; camera, Ray Rennahan, Gordon Jennings; asst. director, Herbert Coleman. Tradeshown N. Y., Dec. 13, '46. Running time, 97 MINS.

Jonathan Trumbo.............Ray Milland
Lily Bishop.............Barbara Stanwyck
Michael Fabian...........Barry Fitzgerald
Pharaoh Coffin...........George Coulouris
Mr. Pike..................Albert Dekker
Don Luis..................Anthony Quinn
Whitey...................Frank Faylen
Booth Pennock.............Gavin Muir
Pokey..................James Burke
Padre...................Eduardo Ciannelli
Colonel Stuart.............Roman Bohnen
Elvira..................Argentina Brunetti
Senator Creel..........Howard Freeman
Wagon Woman................Julia Faye

The big, sprawling western melodrama, which Paramount used to turn out so artfully, has again overtaken that company with "California," which, if one was to probe beyond the surface, is actually little different than dozens of other narratives of the war of the plains. But when peopled with such luminaries as Ray Milland, Barbara Stanwyck and Barry Fitzgerald, in what are "different" roles for them, and encased in shimmering Technicolor, "California" assumes a new aura. It is better acted than most westerns, it has better direction than most, and is better produced, too. Which makes it a decided boxoffice parlay.

The migration, in 1848, to California, and the factional differences that arose in the fight to permit the territory to join the Union, is the key to this story. And after that premise has been set there's little to tell beyond the additional background of the gold rush. But "California" has its share of fisticuffs, shooting and ingeniously contrived

double-dealers to achieve more than a modicum of interest.

The story is inclined to be too pat at times. Any kid with a beebee gun, for example, could tell that Miss Stanwyck would knock off the double-dealingest of 'em all at the final, critical moment. And that fadeout clinch between Milland and Miss Stanwyck, of course, is inevitable right from the beginning of the film —because, you know, she hates him, oh, so much!

Milland plays a deserter from the Union Army, who becomes enmeshed in the California sovereignty fight when he tries his pan-luck in the gold-rush trek. Miss Stanwyck is a poker-playing, steel-hearted dame of questionable repute. Fitzgerald, likewise, is also going a different film way, an itinerant farmer who would make his gold out of the soil one way or the other.

There is little that could be said of any of their performances, however far afield they may be, though each is certainly competent enough. Milland handles his drinking proclivities successfully, without being required to take any pledges, for a change. For a hero, though, he certainly gets kayoed frequently. And a knife-dueling sequence towards the end, where he surgically disposes of his vis-a-vis, is almost funny.

There's not too much sense to Miss Stanwyck's reasons for hating Milland, unless it's because she loves him, but when the script stops teasing her, and tells her which of the two to do, she manages to do it as only Miss Stanwyck can hate or love. Fitzgerald could make almost any part believable. George Coulouris is the menace, an over-written, too-obvious characterization. Other able actors, such as Frank Faylen, Anthony Quinn, Albert Dekker and Gavin Muir, help give whatever credence this story possesses.

E. Y. (Yip) Harburg and Earl Robinson have contributed a few atmospheric songs, two of which are purportedly sung by Miss Stanwyck, and at least one of them, "Lily-I-Lay-De-o," should get a play. *Kahn*

The Locket

Hollywood, Dec. 14.
RKO release of Bert Granet (Jack J. Gross) production. Stars Laraine Day, Brian Aherne, Robert Mitchum, Gene Raymond; features Sharyn Moffett, Ricardo Cortez, Henry Stephenson, Katherine Emery, Reginald Denny, Fay Helm. Directed by John Brahm. Screenplay, Sheridan Gibney; camera, Nicholas Musuraca; music, Roy Webb; editor, J. R. Whittredge. Tradeshown Dec. 11, '46. Running time, 85 MINS.

Nancy........................Laraine Day
Dr. Blair.....................Brian Aherne
Norman Clyde............Robert Mitchum
John Willis................Gene Raymond
Nancy (age 10)............Sharyn Moffett
Mr. Bonner.................Ricardo Cortez
Lord Wyndham..........Henry Stephenson
Mrs. Willis.............Katherine Emery
Mr. Wendell..............Reginald Denny
Mrs. Bonner..................Fay Helm
Mrs. Monks.............Helene Thimig
Mrs. Wendell..............Nella Walker
Woman Singer..........Queenie Leonard
Lady Wyndham.........Lillian Fontaine
Thelma..................Myrna Dell
Donald.....................Johnny Clark

"The Locket" is a case history of a warped mind and its effect on the lives of those it touches intimately. B.o. possibilities benefit from sturdy cast names and the public reception accorded well-made melodramas of this type. Interestingly told, carefully produced, pic measures up as a neat entry in the psycho field, able to carry off top position in any situation.

Vehicle is a strong one for Laraine Day and she does much with the role of Nancy, a girl with an abnormal obsession that wrecks the lives of four men who love her. Part is quite different from the typical femme lead usually played by Miss Day and she proves herself more than capable of seeing it through.

Story carries the flashback technique to greater lengths than generally employed. The writing by Sheridan Gibney displays an understanding of the subject matter and proves a solid basis for the able performances achieved by John Brahm's direction. Latter gears his scenes for full interest and carefully carries forward the doubt—and audience hope —that Nancy is not the villainess she is proven to be. This audience sympathy created by the Nancy character is a great element of appeal. It's premised without a false note and story avoids formula compromise while working to the inevitable conclusion.

Nancy is a young woman, marked in childhood by the cruel misunderstanding of a rich lady in whose home her mother is housekeeper. The misunderstanding, over a missing locket, influence Nancy to strange acts in her adult life. She kills a man, permits another to die for the crime; drives another to suicide and effectively wrecks the happiness of two others who dearly love her. Nancy goes about such unconscious evil with a clear heart and such innocent deception that, although she destroys her loves, they still remain under her spell.

Her story is told in various stages of flashbacks as Brian Aherne, one of her victims, seeks to prevent Gene Raymond's marriage to the schizophrenic Nancy. At the dramatic finale, Nancy goes into complete insanity during a suspense-laden wedding sequence, but film closes with the hope that love and care will eventually rid her of the childhood blight.

Top male leads add much to the film. Aherne is swell as a Nancy victim, deceived despite being a psychiatrist. Robert Mitchum makes real his role as the artist, Nancy's first love victim. Gene Raymond, her last love, makes a welcome return to films after service in the armed forces. Ricardo Cortez, seen too seldom in films of late, is excellent as the murder victim. Sharyn Moffett does standout work as the moppet Nancy. Others lending noteworthy performances to the drama include Katherine Emery, the rich lady; Fay Helm, Queenie Leonard, Reginald Denny and Myrna Dell.

Bert Granet, under the executive supervision of Jack J. Gross, has given a showmanly production touch to all phases of the film. The physical dress is smart, but never out of place, as conceived by art directors Albert S. D'Agostino and Alfred Herman. Nicholas Musuraca's lensing shows the players and settings to advantage. Roy Webb's music score is an important contribution. Editing by J. R. Whittredge, special effects and other production factors are in keeping with the overall standard of excellence. *Brog.*

The Fabulous Suzanne

(SONG)

Hollywood, Dec. 14.

Republic release of Steve Sekely production, directed by Sekely. Stars Barbara Britton, Rudy Vallee; features Otto Kruger, Richard Denning, Bill Henry, Veda Ann Borg, Iren Agay. Screenplay, Tedwell Chapman, Randall Faye; original, William Bowers and Chapman; camera, Henry Sharpe; editor, John Hoffman. Previewed Dec. 13, '46. Running time, 70 MINS.
Suzanne....................Barbara Britton
Hendrick Courtney, Jr......Rudy Vallee
Hendrick Courtney, Sr.......Otto Kruger
Rex......................Richard Denning
William Harris.................Bill Henry
Mary...................Veda Ann Borg
Ginette........................Iren Agay
Marstenson...................Grady Sutton
Mr. Tuttle................Frank Darian
Lawyer....................Harry Tyler
Hamburger Man.............Eddie Fields
The Little Man..............Al Hammer

There's nothing wrong with "The Fabulous Suzanne" that couldn't have been fixed by snappier direction and more decisive editing. Film lags so frequently that the okay story premise and lines seldom have a chance to lighten proceedings. For

budget expenditure values measure up to release intentions, without being particularly noteworthy in any department, but "Suzanne" lacks directional finesse and zip needed for its basic comedy content.

Steve Sekely served as associate producer and director. In the latter slot he is heavy-handed, lacking the glib touch needed to give the light material punch. Scenes are held too long and contents telegraphed. Instead of light editing on comedic sequences to heighten laugh material, scissoring is mostly on story connectives, which doesn't make for clear narrative.

Plot concerns a girl who picks winning horses by jabbing lucky pin into a race form. She's a waitress in a small pie shop and in love with the boss. Inheriting $7,000, girl offers to stake the boss in a better shop. He refuses and she, piqued, runs away to New York and tries her system in the stock market. It works and Suzanne acquires three suitors at the brokerage firm she patronizes. Her heart still belongs in the pie shop, however, and after sufficient footage and incident she finds happiness with the pie man.

Dull stretches overshadow better moments, despite valiant tries by Barbara Britton, in the title role; Rudy Vallee, Otto Kruger, Richard Denning, Bill Henry and others. Vallee has a laugh-provoking moment when, in his stuffy stockbroker character, he fires caustic criticism at Rudy Vallee, crooner, moaning "A Couple of Years Ago," tune by Bert Reisfeld and Larry Stewart. Best honors are carried off by Kruger, who benefits from experience.

Script by Tedwell Chapman and Randall Faye, from original by William Bowers and Chapman, wasn't helped by filming. Lensing and other credits are standard. *Brog.*

Les Portes De La Nuit
("The Doors of Night")
(FRENCH-MADE)

Paris, Dec. 10.

Pathe Contortium release of Pathe Cinema production. Stars Yves Montand and Nathalie Nattier; features Pierre Brasseur, Serge Reggiani, Jean Vilar. Directed by Marcel Carne; story and dialog by Jacques Prevert; camera, Philippe Agostini. Running time, 115 MINS.

A dismal failure of screenwriter Prevert and director Marcel Carne who had produced the Jacques costly but successful "Children of Paradise." Illustrating the current tendency of French scripters and directors to forget the producer's side of a picture, they gave free rein to their own propensities. Hailed in advance as a masterpiece, this is disappointing. However, may do in some U. S. spots. Originally budgeted at $400,000 it is reported to have cost twice that much, making it the most expensive French picture to date.

Despite their Pathe tieup, RKO refrained from co-financing. First snag came when Marlene Dietrich and Jean Gabin, expected to play the leads, backed out and had to be replaced by Nathalie Nattier (real name Natalia Balaieff) and Yves Montand, a newcomer to the screen.

Writer Prevert has mixed two stories, one showing Serge Reggiani as ex-militiaman unmasked by his former victim, Yves Montand, in post-liberation Paris. The other is a love affair between Montand and Nathalie Nattier. Result is a hodgepodge of frequently well-made sequences adding up to a very tedious picture, with dialog partly unsatisfactory.

Montand is fair but Miss Nattier is not sufficient to justify the dialog's claim that she is the most beautiful woman in the world. Reggiani is excellent but best acting is by Jean Vilar as a hobo with rare sight

who's able to tell what is going to happen in advance. Some sequences represent Carne's best direction and show Paris in a sufficiently realistic way to justify trying the picture in American arty theatres. Camera work by Philippe Agostini is great. *Maxi.*

Foreign Films

"Begar" ("Desire") (SWEDISH). Sandrew Bauman release of Monark production; stars Edvin Adolphson, Gunn Wallgran; features Olof Winnerstrand, Hilda Borgstroem, Sven Magnusson, Carl Deurell Person based on novel by Hans Severinsen; camera, Goeran Strindberg. At Olympia, Stockholm. Running time, 98 MINS.

Poor example of current Swedish film production, "Begar" is a story of spoiled marriages and a drunkard's life, but by no means a Swedish "Lost Weekend." Acting of Hilda Borgstroem and Olof Winnerstrand save the picture to some extent. However, poor direction and meagre production values are too heavy a burden to surmount. Film has done poorly in Sweden and probably will flop in the U. S. where it was booked prior to Swedish release. *Wins.*

Miniature Reviews

"It's a Wonderful Life" (Liberty-RKO). Socko Capra pic with James Stewart.

"The Man I Love" (Songs) (WB). Good romantic meller with Ida Lupino, Robert Alda, Andrea King and Bruce Bennett.

"Humoresque" (WB). Important Joan Crawford - John Garfield drama.

"The Beast with 5 Fingers" Out-of-the-ordinary whodunit, will get terrif word-of-mouth and please horror fans.

"Mr. District Attorney" (Col). Melodrama based on radio program of same title, for smaller first runs.

"Murder in Reverse" (Brit.)—Neat crime pic from England strong support in dualer situations in U. S.

"Stars Over Texas" (Rep). Fair oatuner in Eddie Dean series.

"Great Expectations" (GFD), British adaptation of Dickens' novel, with John Mills, Valerie Hobson, looks limited for U. S.

"Heldorado" (Songs) (Rep). Roy Rogers oatuner with plenty to please followers.

It's a Wonderful Life

Hollywood, Dec. 19.

RKO release of Liberty Films production, produced and directed by Frank Capra. Stars James Stewart, Donna Reed; features Lionel Barrymore, Thomas Mitchell; Henry Travers, Beulah Bondi, Ward Bond, Frank Faylen, Gloria Grahame. Story, Philip Van Doren Stern. Screenplay, Frances Goodrich, Albert Hackett, Capra; additional scenes, Jo Swerling; camera, Joseph Walker and Joseph Biroc; score, Dimitri Tiomkin; editor, William Hornbeck. Tradeshown Dec. 18, '46. Running time, 120 MINS.
George Bailey...............James Stewart
Mary Hatch..................Donna Reed
Mr. Potter..............Lionel Barrymore
Uncle Billy..............Thomas Mitchell
Clarence....................Henry Travers
Mrs. Bailey..................Beulah Bondi
Ernie.......................Frank Faylen
Bert..........................Ward Bond
Mr. Gower...................H. B. Warner
Violet Bick.................Gloria Grahame
Harry Bailey.................Todd Karns
Ruth Dakin................Virginia Patton
Pa Bailey...................Samuel S. Hinds
Cousin Tillie.................Mary Treen
Cousin Eustace.............Charles Williams
Sam Wainwright..........Frank Albertson
Mrs. Hatch.................Sarah Edwards
Mr. Martini................William Edmunds
Mrs. Martini............Argentina Brunetti
Annie......................Lillian Randolph
Little George.............Bobbie Anderson
Little Sam..................Ronnie Ralph
Little Mary..................Jean Gale
Little Violet.............Jeanine Ann Roose
Nick......................Sheldon Leonard
Potter's Bodyguard........Frank Hagney
Janie......................Carol Coomes
Zuzu.....................Karolyn Grimes
Pete.......................Larry Simms
Tommy......................Jimmy Hawkins

"It's a Wonderful Life" will enjoy just that at the b.o., and eminently deserves to do so. In the wake of the billowing ballyhoo which has preceded the first entry from Liberty Films, will come resurging word-o'-mouth to accelerate the whirring of theatres' wickets. After a somewhat clammy cycle of psychological pix and a tortured trend of panting propaganda vehicles, the April-air wholesomeness and humanism of this natural bring back vividly the reminder that, essentially, the screen best offers unselfconscious, forthright entertainment.

Frank Capra and James Stewart, in returning to films after long years in uniform, endow the pic with its most telling contributions. Herewith, Stewart touches the thespic peak of his career. He hasn't lost a whit of his erstwhile boyish personality (when called to turn it on) and further shows a maturity and depth he seems recently to have acquired.

Capra brought back to "Life" all

his oldtime craft, delicate devotion to detail and character delineation as well as his sure-footed feeling for true dramatic impact, as well as his deft method of leavening humor into right spots at right times. He again proves he can fashion what ordinarily would be homilizing hokum into gleaming, engaging entertainment for all brows—high, low or beetle. Capra may not have taken here the stride forward in film-making technique he achieved in "It Happened One Night," but no past Capra celluloid possessed any greater or more genuine qualities of effectiveness.

The tale, flashbacked, essentially is simple. At 30 a small-town citizen feels he has reached the end of his rope, mentally, morally, financially. All his plans all his life have gone awry. Through no fault of own he faces disgrace. If the world isn't against him, at least it has averted its face. As he contemplates suicide, Heaven speeds a guardian angel, a pixyish fellow of sly humor, to teach the despondent most graphically how worthwhile his life has been and what treasures, largely intangible, he does possess. The recounting of this life is just about flawless in its tender and natural treatment; only possible thin carping could be that the ending is slightly overlong and a shade too cloying for all tastes.

Stewart's lead is braced by a full fan-spread of shimmering support. In femme lead, Donna Reed will reach full-fledged stardom with this effort. As a Scrooge-like banker, Lionel Barrymore lends a lot of lustre. Thomas Mitchell especially is effective as lead's drunken uncle; as parents, Beulah Bondi and Samuel S. Hinds catch the spirit. Other standouts are H. B. Warner, Frank Faylen and Ward Bond; they make much more of small-town character roles than usually rather hackneyed parts receive. Two relatively new faces, Todd Karns and Gloria Grahame, score as youthful contemporaries of star.

Productionally, every value is milked. With the use of new technique, employing CO_2 base, snow is facsimilied far better than ever before. Bulwarking Capra, the cameras of Joseph Walker and Joseph Biroc caught all the flavor and nuances; latter is a newcomer who was elevated to lensing when former had to leave during shooting. Dimitri Tiomkin's score enhances, especially making more poignant the closing dramatic sequences. He has composed for most Capra pix and never more compellingly than in this. Jack Okey's art, especially in the exterior scenes, is fetchingly natural.

In working with the writing team of Frances Goodrich and Albert Hackett, Capra obviously helped inject the feel and spirit he wanted, while his partners' calm comedy sense frequently flavors. Jo Swerling's additional scenes, unidentified, patently parred the rest of the script.
Bert.

The Man I Love
(SONGS)

Warner Bros. release of Arnold Albert production. Stars Ida Lupino, Robert Alda, Andrea King, Bruce Bennett. Directed by Raoul Walsh. Screenplay, Catherine Turney; adaptation, Jo Pagano and Miss Turney, from novel by Maritta Wolff; camera, Sid Hickox; editor, Owen Marks; dialog director, John Maxwell; special effects, Harry Barndollar, Edwin DuPar; asst. director, Reggie Callow; songs, George and Ira Gershwin, Jerome Kern-Oscar Hammerstein 2d, Johnny Green, Henry Creamer-Jimmy Johnson; music adapted by Max Steiner; arrangements, Hugo Friedhofer; direction, Leo F. Forbstein. Tradeshown N. Y., Dec. 20, '46. Running time, **96 MINS.**

Petey Brown....................Ida Lupino
Nicky Toresca....................Robert Alda
Sally Otis....................Andrea King
Virginia Brown....................Martha Vickers
San Thomas....................Bruce Bennett
Riley....................Alan Hale
Gloria O'Connor....................Dolores Moran
Roy Otis....................John Ridgely
Johnny O'Connor....................Don McGuire
Joe Brown....................Warren Douglas
Johnson....................Craig Stevens
Tony Toresca....................William Edmunds
Jimmy....................James Dobbs
Buddy....................Patrick Griffin

Fortified by a good title (from the Hit Parader of the same name), a potent cast, a new personality in Bruce Bennett whom the gals (and boys) will talk about, an ultra-modern approach, and a few s.a. overtones which the Joe Breen offices gave the go-by, this is the sort of setup which can't miss at anybody's boxoffice.

It's one of those brittle, brash sex romances which, even if it leaves a few loose ends suspended, pans out as plenty of b.o. payoff. It presents Robert Alda as a new sort of he-man personality, away from the aesthetic Gershwin of the "Rhapsody In Blue" which first projected him. It spotlights Ida Lupino in a self-sufficient heroine (with a heart of gold) role which is vivid, vibrant and vital but, unfortunately, falls apart, as does the plot, towards the end. Then there is Bennett, a sort of Hoagy Carmichael character with loads of masculine s.a. who, if betimes a bit too mature to be a 52d St. jive kid, none the less impresses in one of those get-away-gals-you-bother-me chores which invariably have the reverse effect on their celluloid vis-a-vis—and the femme customers.

The loose ends are plot faults. Alda is a suavely tough Long Beach (Calif.) muscle guy, something out of the Little Caesar school, who has Andrea King's kid brother doing dubious chores for him. When their elder sister, Miss Lupino, comes on the scene, gets a singing job in Alda's nitery, rebuffs the boss, takes up with Bennett, the piano-playing fool, it evolves into a familiar but none the less arresting romance of unrequited love.

There are postwar overtones as Miss King copes with the problem of her shell-shocked husband (John Ridgeley); the sub-plot with the two-timing wife (Dolores Moran) and her trusting boob of a husband, Don McGuire; plus other detours as the battled-fatigued husband comes home for the happy ending, and the conniving nitery boniface-racketeer Alda meets his inevitable doom.

A good assortment of pops is deftly interspliced, including the George and Ira Gershwin title song; also their "Liza"; the Kern-Hammerstein "Why Was I Born?" and "Bill"; Johnny Green's "Body and Soul" and Creamer & Johnson's "If I Could Be With You (One Hour Tonight)" which isn't exactly a nursery rhyme, especially as the swoon-croon jivesters whip this up in the early a.m. It's in this scene, incidentally, when the threat of the muscle-man Alda to move in on the Long Beach-front bistro is one of several left-in-suspense situations.

Withal it shapes up as commercially good divertissement. Raoul Walsh's pacing is good; producer Arnold Albert has given it importantly-appearing investment, albeit it's by no means a costly production; the Turney-Pagano scripting is brittle (it's from the Maritta Wolff novel, "Night Shift"); and Max Steiner's musical treatment further enhances the over-all aura.
Abel.

Humoresque
(MUSIC)
Hollywood, Dec. 19.

Warner Bros. release of Jerry Wald production. Stars Joan Crawford, John Garfield; features Oscar Levant, J. Carrol Naish, Joan Chandler, Tom D'Andrea, Peggy Knudsen, Ruth Nelson, Craig Stevens, Paul Cavanagh. Directed by Jean Negulesco. Screenplay, Clifford Odets, Zachary Gold; based on story by Fannie Hurst; camera, Ernest Haller; music conducted by Franz Waxman; music advisor, Isaac Stern; editor, Rudi Fehr. Tradeshown Dec. 20, 1946. Running time, **123 MINS.**

Helen Wright....................Joan Crawford
Paul Boray....................John Garfield
Sid Jeffers....................Oscar Levant
Rudy Boray....................J. Carrol Naish
Gina....................Joan Chandler
Phil Boray....................Tom D'Andrea
Florence....................Peggy Knudsen
Esther Boray....................Ruth Nelson
Monte Loeffler....................Craig Stevens
Victor Wright....................Paul Cavanagh
Bauer....................Richard Gaines
Rozner....................John Abbott
Paul Boray (Child)....................Bobby Blake
Phil Boray (Child)....................Tommy Cook
Eddie....................Don McGuire
Hagerstrom....................Fritz Leiber
Night Club Singer....................Peg LaCentra
Orchestra Leader....................Nestor Paiva
Teddy....................Richard Walsh

"Humoresque" combines classical music and drama into a top quality motion picture. A score of unusual excellence gives freshness to standard classics and plays as important a part as Fannie Hurst's familiar story of a young violinist who rises to concert heights from the lower East Side of New York. Technically a remake (it was first produced in 1920) this version is virtually a new story, stripped of any racial connotations as was the case originally.

Picture is of the calibre to attract lush boxoffice in the top situations. It has the name strength of Joan Crawford and John Garfield to brighten marquees, thoughtful production guidance by Jerry Wald and strong direction by Jean Negulesco. Footage is long, running more than two hours, but does not drag because of the score potency and performance quality.

Integration of music and drama ties the two together so tightly there is never a separation. Classical lovers will hear special arrangements of such favorites as the orchestral suite from "Carmen," in which the violin becomes the vocal solo instead of the usual voice, and a smash violin solo of "Liebestod" from "Tristan and Isolde." Other musical standouts include the gypsy "Zigeunerweisen," another violin solo. Isaac Stern, violin virtuoso, acted as music advisor and dubbed the violin for the score, while Franz Waxman did the special arrangements and scoring.

Some 23 classical numbers are included, plus a number of pop pieces used as background for cafe sequences. Latter are played and sung by Peg LaCentra to good effect. Full symphony of 110 pieces is used for much of the recording and large viola section is used to back the "Carmen" melodies.

Principal footage goes to Garfield as the young violinist who, encouraged by his mother's interest, devotes his life to music. He turns in a distinguished, thoroughly believable performance. Adding to the effectiveness is the nigh-flawless fingering and bowing during the violin shots. Joan Crawford's role is an acting part, rather than a typical femme star assignment, and she makes the most of it. There's little sympathy connected with a dipsomaniac married woman who promotes Garfield's career but Miss Crawford's talent carries it off with top honors.

One of her best moments is the suicide scene in which she walks into the sea to the accompaniment of "Liebestod." It is an intense, dramatic moment, heightened by the stirring violin solo with full orchestral backing.

Oscar Levant's character of Sid Jeffers, Garfield's friend and accompanist, is a thinly-concealed Levant. He's in for quips, safe advice and generally to lighten the heavy dramatics. It is a good part, well done. J. Carrol Naish and Ruth Nelson contribute excellently as Garfield's parents. Tom D'Andrea and Peggy Knudsen have smaller spots as brother and sister. Minor romance is contributed by Joan Chandler. Garfield as a boy is skillfully performed by Bobby Blake. Paul Cavanagh, Richard Gaines, John Abbott and others are capable.

Clifford Odets and Zachary Gold gave Jean Negulesco a solid screenplay as basis for his strong direction. The careful production guidance by Jerry Wald has made a potent combination of music and drama to please the carriage trade, making each phase thoroughly effective in carrying out the class imprint. Lensing by Ernest Haller is fine, as are other contributions. *Brog.*

The Beast with 5 Fingers
Hollywood, Dec. 15.

Warner Bros. release of William Jacobs production. Stars Robert Alda, Andrea King; Peter Lorre. Directed by Robert Florey. Screenplay, Curt Siodmak, from story by William Fryer Harvey; camera, Wesley Anderson; special effects, William McGann, H. Koenekamp; editor, Frank Magee; dialog director, Jack Daniels; score, Max Steiner; arrangements, Hugo Friedhofer; music, Leo F. Forbstein; asst. director, Art Lueker. Tradeshown Nov. 19, '46. Running time, **90 MINS.**

Conrad Ryler....................Robert Alda
Julie Holden....................Andrea King
Hilary Cummins....................Peter Lorre
Francis Ingram....................Victor Francen
Ovidio....................J. Carrol Naish
Raymond Arlington....................Charles Dingle
Donald Arlington....................John Alvin
Duprex....................David Hoffman
Mrs. Miller....................Barbara Brown
Clara....................Patricia White
Antonio....................William Edmunds
Giovanna....................Belle Mitchell
Mr. Miller....................Ray Walker
Horatio....................Pedro de Cordoba

"The Beast with Five Fingers" is a weird, Grand Guignol-ish concoction that puts the customers strictly on their own. Till the last gasp, when J. Carrol Naish winks into the lens and gives out with a crack that "it could happen," it's in the continental groove, adding up to a whodunit that gives payees more credit for intelligence than the average thriller. Fate of the experimental item, therefore, is one that'll be decided by word-of-mouth more than via any other factor. It's strong enough from a productional standpoint. Warners having poured plenty into lush trappings, but the marquee pull is invested solely in Peter Lorre, Robert Alda and Andrea King.

Victor Francen, as a semi-invalid concert pianist, lives in a gloomy villa in northern Italy. His companions are his secretary, Lorre; his nurse, Miss King; a composer friend, Alda, and his attorney, David Hoffman.

A good deal of the plot is projected through Lorre's eyes, without any explanation of the switches from straight narration to scenes registered by Lorre's deranged mind. Best and most gruesome parts of the picture are when Lorre is alone with his vivid imagination. He chases a ghoulish hand around the library several times, catching it finally and hammering it down in a bloodcurdling scene reminiscent in mood of "The Cabinet of Dr. Caligari." Still it pursues him, escaping at last from the burning coals into which he has thrown it to strangle him also. Francen's mercenary relatives leave the unhappy place, glad to get out, and Alda and Miss King go off together to America.

Scenes in which the disembodied hand crawls around the room achieve a surrealistic effect and will surely be labeled among the most scary ever filmed. Photography here is remarkable, as it is throughout the William Jacobs projection, for which lensman Wesley Anderson and special effects William McGann and H. Koenekamp rate a deep bow. Robert Florey's direction of the tense Curt Siodmak screenplay is also impeccable. Editing, costuming, dialog and sets are all expert, and Leo Forbstein's handling of the Max Steiner score adds tremendously to the spine-tinglings.

Lorre's maniac is a masterly job. Also rating plaudits in the thesping dept. are Naish, Francen, Charles Dingle and Hoffman. Alda and Miss

King make an attractive pair of lovers, and the Italian villages and others in the cast ring the bell.
Mike.

Mr. District Attorney

Hollywood, Dec. 20.

Columbia release of Samuel Bischoff production. Stars Dennis O'Keefe, Adolphe Menjou, Marguerite Chapman, Michael O'Shea; features George Coulouris, Jeff Donnell, Steven Geray, Ralph Morgan, John Kellogg. Directed by Robert B. Sinclair. Screenplay, Ian McLellan Hunter; adaptation, Ben Markson; story by Sidney Marshall; based on the radio program, "Mr. District Attorney," created by Phillips H. Lord; camera, Bert Glennon; score, Herschel Gilbert; editor, William Lyon. Previewed Dec. 19, '46. Running time, **81 MINS.**

Steve Bennett..............Dennis O'Keefe
Craig Warren, D. A..........Adolphe Menjou
Marcia Manning......Marguerite Chapman
Harrington................Michael O'Shea
James Randolph..........George Coulouris
Miss Miller......................Jeff Donnell
Berotti.........................Steven Geray
Ed Jamison....................Ralph Morgan
Franzen........................John Kellogg
Longfield...............Charles Trowbridge
Peter Lantz....................Frank Reicher

"Mr. District Attorney" will benefit from popularity of radio program of same title. Familiar cast lends selling strength, and the exploitation values are good. These factors will help it through top positions in smaller first runs. Otherwise it is a rather haphazard film version of the ether whodunit with cloudy story line that will not always be clear to ticket buyers.

Samuel Bischoff's physical production values rate better than script but he hasn't given story tight supervision needed to point up melodrama elements. Plot concerns young assistant d.a. who resents his boss' interference in his private life and gets mixed up with a girl who will do anything, even murder, to obtain money and security. D.A. has the right idea about gal but his assistant is blinded by love. Before it all resolves itself the girl has bumped off two men and tries to do away with her lover in the finale when he won't accept her loot and charms.

Robert B. Sinclair's direction is uneven, mostly from script confusion in planting various story threads. Writing is obvious and often badly dialoged in the script by Ian McLellan Hunter. Ben Markson did the adaptation from a story by Sidney Marshall, based on the air show created by Phillips H. Lord.

Adolphe Menjou brings usual histrionics to the title role. Dennis O'Keefe is likeable as his assistant. Marguerite Chapman acquits herself well as the femme menace of piece and Michael O'Shea is dragged in as the d.a.'s wisecracking investigator. George Coulouris, Jeff Donnell, Steven Geray, Ralph Morgan, John Kellogg and others in the cast try hard to get a punch out of the material.

Lensing by Bert Glennon is skillful and other technical contributions measure up.
Brog.

The Story of the Pope

Chapel Films release of Bernard B. Brandt production. Written by John Meehan and Rev. John O'Connor; narration, Msgr. Fulton J. Sheen; music, Sistine Choir; editor, Walter Klee; sound, Edward Craig. Reviewed Dec. 19, '46, at Republic theatre, N. Y. Running time, **63 MINS.**

Market for this film may not be as limited as indicated by the title. March of Time didn't think so when it devoted an entire release to the Vatican Story some three years ago. Nevertheless, as a feature attraction "The Story of the Pope" is certainly not intended for general release. It's a straight documentary piece, with something less than popular interest. Too many factors militate against a religious subject limited to a single faith, and once in the theatre, the audience might be repelled by the occasional bits of doctrine that creep into Msgr. Fulton J. Sheen's narration, although that's held to a minimum.

Real interest of the picture lies in inside shots of Vatican grounds and the daily routine of Pope Pius XII. Some of the film is not new, and about 60% of it was lensed by Vatican photographers, but it presents a pretty good overall picture of what the spiritual leader of 340,000,000 Catholics does during a working day.

Film opens with a short introduction by Cardinal Francis Spellman of New York, and while that may add interest for the eastern crowds, it could have been dispensed with as so much padding. The Cardinal isn't a very good speaker, and suffers by comparison with the narration of the experienced Msgr. Sheen. The early career of the Pope is followed from his ordination as Father Pacelli to appointment as Papal Secretary of State and subsequent election as Pater Sanctus. Much of his time is shown spent in audiences with people ranging in station from Winston Churchill to Italian peasants.

Most impressive sequences are those showing tapestries and paintings by Raphael, and others of the ceremonies involved in creating 32 new Cardinals. Some of the latter scenes were overlong.

After the school and religious market is exhausted, best commercial chance for "Story of the Pope" lies in the possibility of its being edited down to short subject length, a task that shouldn't be too difficult.

Murder in Reverse

(BRITISH-MADE)

Four Continents Films release of Louis H. Jackson production. Stars William Hartnell, Jimmy Hanley, Chili Bouchier; features John Slater, Petula Clark. Directed by Montgomery Tully. Screenplay by Tully; based on story of "Seamark"; camera, Ernest Palmer; editor, Eve Catchpole; music, Hans May. Tradeshown N. Y. Dec. 20, '46. Running time, **80 MINS.**

Tom Masterick..............William Hartnell
Peter Rogers....................Jimmy Hanley
Doris Masterick..............Chili Bouchier
Fred Smith.........................John Slater
Sullivan.....................Brefni O'Rourke
Jill Masterick.................Dinah Sheridan
Jill Masterick (child)..........Petula Clark
Crossley K. C..............Kynaston Reeves
Blake K. C.........................John Salew
Spike..........................Edward Rigby
Docker..........................Ben Williams
Mrs. Green....................Ethel Coleridge
Mrs. Moore......................Marie O'Neill
The Tailor......................Wylie Watson

A unique climactic twist that'll keep audiences buzzing for minutes after the picture ends caps this overall fine effort from one of Britain's smaller production outfits. A modest budgeter by Hollywood standards, film is given plenty of cinematic heft by virtue of its superior screenplay, competent thesping and careful attention to realistic detail. Although its chances in the U. S. market will be limited to dualer situations because of a total absence of name values, film will have an increasing impact on the b.o. on basis of word-of-mouth. Dialog, despite a strong cockney burr in parts, will provide no special language barrier for American patrons.

Plot is an interesting variation from the run-of-the-mill crime pictures and will keep amateur legal brains working overtime trying to dope out a solution. Using flashback technique for the first half, story devolves upon a judicial mistake which sends a man up on a 15-year rap for murder that never took place. Coming out of jail after serving his time, the victim of the over-zealous prosecutor goes on an intensive manhunt to produce the man he allegedly killed. The man is found and in order to set the court records right, the innocent ex-con kills him before a dignified assemblage of England's leading legalites. Having paid for the crime in advance, could the murderer now be tried and sentenced over again? On this questioning note the pic fades out.

In the lead role of the stevedore unjustly accused of murder, William Hartnell runs the gamut from helpless indignation to cold vindictiveness in a solid portrayal. Chili Boucher, as his wife who set the stage for the circumstantial trap by two-timing him with another man, scores heavily as she goes downhill from being a dissatisfied wife to a decayed trollop. Light romantic interest is furnished nicely by Jimmy Hanley, reporter, and Dinah Sheridan, the boss' daughter. Rest of the cast perform with uniform competence.

Tight direction and editing keep the film rolling at a fast clip throughout. Photography is well-lighted and sharp and a good musical score lends to the general positive effect.
Herm.

Stars Over Texas

(SONGS)

PRC release of Robert Emmett Tansey (Jerry Thomas) production, directed by Tansey. Stars Eddie Dean; features Roscoe Ates, Shirley Patterson, Lee Bennett. Original story and screenplay, Frances Kavanaugh; songs, Dean, Hal Blair and Glen Strange; musical director, Karl Hajos; camera, Ernest Miller; editor, Hugh Winn. Tradeshown N. Y. Dec. 19, '46. Running time, **57 MINS.**

Eddie Dean.........................Eddie Dean
Soapy...............................Roscoe Ates
Terry Lawrence..........Shirley Patterson
Waco—Bert.......................Lee Bennett
Hank Lawrence.................Lee Roberts
Knuckles....................Kermit Maynard
Ringo Evans.....................Jack O'Shea
Tucker................................Hal Smith
Buggsy........................Matty Roubert
Two Horn.......................Carl Mathews
Judge Smith......................Bill Fawcett
Sunshine Boys..................Themselves

Shaping up as a moderately diverting oatuner, "Stars Over Texas" is an okay entry in PRC's Eddie Dean series and will probably satisfy most devotees of saddle song sagas in spite of a formula story and so-so acting. Three songs, which Dean cleffed, add to the pic's entertainment values.

Dealing with the nefarious scheming of neighboring ranch owner, Jack O'Shea who covets Lee Roberts' government contract, Dean, Roscoe Ates and Lee Bennett discover something's amiss when arriving at Roberts' ranch with a herd of cattle. Plenty of badly aimed lead bites the air through the ensuing reelage before O'Shea and his cohorts are brought to justice.

Dean, Ates and Bennett (who has a dual role) handle their thesping chores in creditable fashion while ingenue Shirley Patterson's chief talent lies in her appealing chassis. Title tune, "Stars Over Texas," "Sands of the Old Rio Grande" and "Fifteen Hundred and One Miles of Heaven" are better than average stirrup songs. Producer-Director Robert Emmett Tansey handled the reins on this low budgeter with finesse while other technical credits are standard.

Great Expectations

(BRITISH-MADE)

London Dec. 11.

General Film Distributors' release of Cineguild production. Stars John Mills, Valerie Hobson; features Bernard Miles, Francis L. Sullivan, Martita Hunt, Alec Guinness. Directed by David Lean. Adapted by David Lean, Ronald Neame from Charles Dickens' novel; camera, Guy Green. At Gaumont theatre, London, Dec. 10, '46. Running time, **118 MINS.**

Pip...................................John Mills
Estella.........................Valerie Hobson
Joe Gargery...................Bernard Miles
Jaggers...................Francis L. Sullivan
Magwitch.........................Finlay Currie
Miss Havisham.................Martita Hunt
Pip (as child)...............Anthony Wager
Estella (child)................Jean Simmons
Herbert Pocket...............Alec Guinness
Wemmick.........................Ivor Barnard
Mrs. Gargery..................Freda Jackson
Bentley Drummle............Torin Thatcher
Uncle Pumblechook...............Hay Petrie
Compeyson.....................George Hayes
Sarah Pocket...................Everley Gregg

Cineguild has earned an enviable reputation for its product, and this screen version of Charles Dickens' novel should equal in artistry the company's "Brief Encounter" and it may take its place alongside the best British pictures now being made.

No Dickens' story has been made in several years, and this may help "Expectations" at the boxoffice.

Only rabid Dickensians will find fault with the present adaptation, and paradoxically only lovers of Dickens will derive maximum pleasure from the film. For those who don't know Dickens, much bally will be needed. Dubious if it will amount to much in U. S.

To condense the novel into a two-hour picture meant sacrificing many minor characters. The period and people are vividly brought to life. But so particular have the producers been to avoid offending any Dickensian and every character is drawn so precise that many of them are puppets.

That's the great fault of the film. It is beautiful but lacks heart. It evokes admiration but no feeling. It would have been nice to obtain tear-jerker scenes from the tragedy of the noble-hearted Magwitch or from the heartless treatment of the hero by the callous girl he loves. But these folks, who should arouse deep feeling, are just illustrations to a correct but non-sentimental Dickens recital. This is true also of the humor.

With the exception of John Mills and Alec Guinness, only the secondary characters are entirely credible. Valerie Hobson, whose beauty is not captured by the camera, fails to bring Estella to life, and young Jean Simmons, who plays the role as a girl, is adequately heartless. Anthony Wager, making his film debut, plays well enough. Capital performances come from Francis L. Sullivan, repeating the role of Jaggers he played in Universal's 1934 version, Ivor Barnard, Bernard Miles and Finlay Currie.

This adaption tells how young Pip befriends an escaped convict, who, recaptured and transported to Australia, leaves Pip a fortune so he may become a gentleman with great expectations. Pip believes the unexpected fortune originated with the eccentric Miss Havisham at whose house he has met Estella the girl he loves. Years pass, and the ex-convict, returning to see if Pip has prospered, is recognized by an old enemy. Pip tries to smuggle him out of the country and in the resulting chase the ex-convict is fatally hurt. Before he dies he learns from Pip that the daughter he thought lost is Estella. Pip's illness follows. Then there's the usual love finale.
Cane.

Heldorado

(SONGS)

Hollywood, Dec. 23.

Republic release Edward J. White production. Stars Roy Rogers; features George "Gabby" Hayes, Dale Evans. Directed by William Witney. Original screenplay, Gerald Geraghty and Julian Zimet; camera, William Bradford; songs, Jack Elliott, Denver Darling, Roy Rogers, Bob Nolan; editor, Les Orlebeck. Previewed Dec. 23, 1946. Running time, **70 MINS.**

Roy Rogers..............................Himself
Gabby Whittaker..............George Hayes
Carol Randall......................Dale Evans
W. W. Driscoll...................Paul Harvey
Alex Baxter....................Barry Mitchell
Johnny...............................John Bagni
Sheriff.............................John Phillips
Bellboy..........................James Taggart
Charlie...............................Rex Lease
Mitch...............................Steve Darell
Ticket Taker......................Doye O'Dell
Ranger.............................Leroy Mason
Judte............................Charlie Williams
Shooting Gallery Attendant....Eddie Acuff
Bob Noland and Sons of Pioneers

Republic makes use of annual Heldorado Week in Las Vegas as background for another sleuthing chore by Roy Rogers. Film measures up to usual excellence of Cowpoke's series, flaunting extra production values, tunes and action to keep his large following in the saddle until finale. Plenty footage of Heldorado celebration and Las Vegas plugs should please this western hot spot's Chamber of Commerce.

Roger vocals four tunes but still finds time to romance lightly with Dale Evans and hunt down a gang of black market racketeers who are trying to unload their bankrolls through gambling houses without paying Uncle Sam his customary income tax. Parade and rodeo give Rogers' fave nag, Trigger, opportunity to show off education for kiddie pleasure. These spots also permit good introduction of songs without slowing action. Miss Evans joins Rogers in "Good Neighbor," written by Jack Elliott. Sons of Pioneers and Rogers work over the title number, also "My Saddle Pals and I" by Rogers. Roger solos "Silver Stars, Purple Sage, Eyes of Blue" by Denver Darling. All are effective for western setting.

Miss Evans is the rich girl who gets in Rogers' hair while he is trying to fasten bill-passing and murder on Paul Harvey. As amateur sleuth, Miss Evans keeps Rogers on the rescue continually and spots some chuckles. Dialoging is modern and occasionally slick in script and William Witney's direction is actionful to mesh all elements in the Edward J. White production. Lensing by William Bradford is expert for its outdoor job and editing is tight.

Foreign Films

"Unter den Bruecken" ("Under the Bridges") (GERMAN). UFA Film release of Terra Film production; stars Hannelore Schrot, Carl Raddatz; features Gustav Knuth, Ursula Grabley, Erich Dunskus, H. Helsig; directed by Helmuth Kautner; screenplay by Kautner; camera, Igor Oberberg. At Grand, Stockholm. Running time, 112 MINS.

Made in Germany during the last year of the war, this film has been distributed free by the Allied control commission. It's the first time a German picture has had its world preem in Sweden. This is a sentimental love story of river workers near Berlin. Good acting and fine direction of Helmuth Kautner hint good boxoffice for many markets though okay only for arty U. S. spots. Scripting and lensing are in keeping with film's top drawer production values.

1947

Miniature Reviews

"Duel in the Sun" (Color) (Selznick), Western with sex, cast names and tremendous box-office possibilities.

"Shocking Miss Pilgrim" (Color--Songs) (20th). Betty Grable, Dick Haynes and Gershwin score spell good b.o.

"Stagecoach to Denver" (Rep). Latest in Red Ryder series with Allan Dane up, okay for oater fans.

"Les Miserables" (French). Superb acting of Harry Baur, great story, good direction hold marathon-length film together for top arty b.o.

"La Otra" (Panamerican). Dolores del Rio in Rian James' yarn makes this loom as top Mexican-made this year.

"Queen For a Night" (Saga). Swedish-made operetta looks strong bet for arty theatres; Jussi Bjoerling starred.

Duel in the Sun

(COLOR)

Hollywood, Dec. 29.

Selznick Releasing Organization release of Vanguard (David O. Selznick) production. Stars Jennifer Jones, Gregory Peck, Joseph Cotten; features Lionel Barrymore, Lillian Gish, Walter Huston, Herbert Marshall. Directed by King Vidor. Screenplay by Selznick; adapted by Oliver H. P. Garrett; suggested by novel by Niven Busch. Second units directed by Otto Brower, Reaves Eason; camera, Lee Garmes, Hal Rosson, Ray Rennahan, Chas. P. Boyle, Allen Davey; score, Dmitri Tiomkin; editor, Hal C. Kern; dances, Tilly Losch, Lloyd Shaw. Previewed Dec. 29, '46. Running time, **134 MINS.**

Pearl Chavez	Jennifer Jones
Jesse McCanles	Joseph Cotten
Lewt McCanles	Gregory Peck
Senator McCanles	Lionel Barrymore
Mrs. McCanles	Lillian Gish
The Sinkiller	Walter Huston
Scott Chavez	Herbert Marshall
Sam Pierce	Charles Bickford
Helen Langford	Joan Tetzel
Lem Smoot	Harry Carey
Mr. Langford	Otto Kruger
The Lover	Sidney Blackmer
Mrs. Chavez	Tilly Losch
Sid	Scott McKay
Vashti	Butterfly McQueen
Gambler	Francis McDonald
Gambler	Victor Kilian
The Jailer	Griff Barnett
Ken	Frank Cordell
Ed	Dan White
Jake	Steve Dunhill
Capt. U. S. Cavalry	Lane Chandler
Caller at Barbecue	Lloyd Shaw
Engineer	Thomas Dillon
Bartender	Robert McKenzie
Sheriff Hardy	Charles Dingle

The familiar western formula reaches its highest commercialization in "Duel in Sun." It is raw, sex-laden, western pulp fiction, told in 10-20-30 style. It is pre-sold via advance exploitation and unusually strong marquee names. It has rough, rowdy and raucous action, factors that always have clicked at the boxoffice. "Duel" is a cinch for resounding ticket sales. Sex angle alone makes for boff b.o.

As a production it adds no class distinction to David O. Selznick but assures him a top commercial success. The star lineup is impressive. Vastness of the western locale is splendidly displayed in color by mobile cameras. Footage is overwhelming expansive, too much so at times considering its length.

Rarely has a film made such frank use of lust and still be cleared for showings. Features with much less open display of illicit sex have felt stern bluenose pressure. It's daring, even though all who love, when and where they can find it, meet production code punishment in the end.

While locale and plot are western, sensuality is the prime motivation. Development makes sure all action centers around sex. With that as a basis, producer Selznick has screenplayed a story of Texas cattle barons, encroaching railroads, wanton killings and other stock action of prairie thrillers. There are moments when the script leaves the bedroom and injects high spots of a different type of color and movement.

Single scenes that will stand out include Jennifer Jones' peril in riding bareback on a runaway horse, filmed against the vast scope of the western scene; Gregory Peck's taming of a sex-maddened stallion; the tremendous sweep of hundreds of mounted horsemen riding to do battle with the invading railroad. There are others, too, that will arouse thrill-seeking audiences. They are staged in a grandiose manner calculated to stimulate imagination.

Some of the more intimate dramatic scenes are likely to arouse different reaction, particularly among younger theatregoers. These sequences, played with melodramatic gusto and flamboyance, include Lillian Gish's death scene; Miss Jones' bawdy love dance; the sequence in which she pleads with Peck to take her on his flight from the law, and the finale when the two lovers kill each other only to cling together in death.

King Vidor's direction keeps the playing in step with production aims. He pitches the action to heights in the top moments and generally holds the overall mood desired. Sharing director credit on the mass sequences are Otto Brower and Reaves Eason.

Plot concerns a half-breed girl who goes to the ranch of a Texas cattle baron to live after her father has killed her adultress mother and lover. The baron's two sons fall for her but the unrestrained younger one captures her emotions. So strong is physical desire that he murders one man who wants to marry her and tries to kill the brother, shown in latter attempts to make the girl a lady. Finale is lovelorn depiction of the girl's determination to kill her master and then die in his arms. Majority of the principal roles are flamboyant, occasionally almost to the burlesque. Miss Jones as the half-breed proves herself extremely capable in quieter sequences but is overly meller in others. Same is true of Peck as the virile younger Texan, raised to love 'em and leave 'em. The role has no audience sympathy but will call a great fascination for the femmes. Contrasting is Joseph Cotten as the older son. Role in his hands is believable and never overdrawn. As the father, Lionel Barrymore uses the stock characterization of an irascible old man.

Lillian Gish is the suffering mother, doing a quiet job until her death scene. A brief, but fine, bit is played by Charles Bickford as the man who wants to marry Miss Jones. Same is true of Joan Tetzel as Cotten's fiancee. She contributes one of the few genuine emotional scenes. Herbert Marshall, Butterfly McQueen, Harry Carey, Walter Huston, Otto Kruger, Charles Dingle, Scott McKay, Sidney Blackmer and Tilly Losch are among others permitted to do not more than pad advertising credits.

Photography credits are multiple, and all contribute to the outstanding color lensing. It is a choice job, well done. Music score by Dmitri Tiomkin has an ear-shattering volume in mass scenes, distracting from the movement but otherwise proves an adequate bridge for dramatics. A catchy song, "Gotta Get Me Somebody to Love," by Allie Wrubel, is deftly planted for romantic interludes. *Brog.*

The Shocking Miss Pilgrim

(COLOR—SONGS)

Hollywood, Dec. 31.

20th-Fox release of William Perlberg production. Stars Betty Grable, Dick Haymes; features Anne Revere, Allyn Joslyn, Gene Lockhart, Elizabeth Patterson, Elisabeth Risdon, Arthur Shields. Written for screen and directed by George Seaton. From story by Ernest and Frederica Maas; songs, George and Ira Gershwin; camera, Leon Shamroy; dances, Hermes Pan; editor, Robert Simpson. Tradeshown Dec. 21, '46. Running time, **87 MINS.**

Cynthia Pilgrim	Betty Grable
John Pritchard	Dick Haymes
Alice Pritchard	Anne Revere
Leander Woolsey	Allyn Joslyn
Saxon	Gene Lockhart
Catherine Dennison	Elizabeth Patterson
Mrs. Pritchard	Elisabeth Risdon
Michael Michael	Arthur Shields
Herbert Jothan	Charles Kemper
Mr. Foster	Roy Roberts
Office Clerk	Tom Moore
Lookout in Office	Stanley Prager
Quincy	Ed Laughton
Peabody	Hal K. Dawson
Viola Simmons	Lillian Bronson
Mr. Packard	Raymond Largay
Sarah Glidden	Constance Purdy
Miss Nixon	Mildred Stone
Wendell Paige	Pierre Watkin
Mr. Carter	Junius Matthews

In stringing some George Gershwin tunes dug up out of the trunk a few years ago on a slim thread of a story, the William Perlberg-George Seaton team have gone about the whimsy in too heavy-handed a manner. As a result of which, except for a few flashes of the brilliant wit and tunefulness that inevitably made a show with a George and Ira Gershwin score a standout in the past, "The Shocking Miss Pilgrim" will have to rely on cast names—not to mention the gaudy Technicolor trappings—for its b.o. power.

Story concerns entry of Cynthia Pilgrim (Betty Grable) into Boston's "man's world" of commerce in the 1870's. Draped in fabulous Orry-Kelly gowns that belie her $8-a-week salary, Miss Grable wins her diploma in a New York business school and proceeds to shock Beacon Hill by applying for a job in the office of Dick Haymes' shipyards. She gets it only because of the pull exerted by Anne Revere, suffragette relative of Haymes. Gal makes good at the job, under great difficulties, but refuses to give up her fight for equal rights for women, upon which she has embarked with Miss Revere, when Haymes asks her to marry him. He finally realizes it's a losing battle, and they clinch.

Gag about Miss Grable being "a new typewriter" is okay the first few times, but carried throughout the picture it becomes tiresome. Other gags are belabored as well, and lines like "a woman's place is in the home" are sledge-hammered. Music is standout, most hummable tunes being "For You, for Me, for Evermore" and "Aren't You Kind of Glad We Did?" One that has all the flavor of the Gershwin freres' topmost sophisticated musicomedy stuff is "But Not in Boston." Others that listen well are "Changing My Tune," "Stand Up and Fight," and a fetching waltz.

Plenty of care has been taken that the Victorian drapings don't conceal too much of Miss Grable's figure, and the gal looks tops with a darker shade of blondine than usual. She also turns in a slightly more subdued thesping job than is her habit. Haymes looks and sounds good, too, dividing singing chores, which don't intrude too harshly, with Miss Grable. Support is tops, especially Miss Revere's suffragette, Elizabeth Risdon's not-too-Back-Bay-ish portrayal of Haymes' mother, and Gene Lockhart's sourpuss office manager.

Crackpot denizens of the boarding house at which Miss Grable stays, all of whom hate Boston, are Allyn Joslyn as a poet, Arthur Shields as a painter, Elizabeth Patterson as housekeeper, Lillian Bronson as a spinster who spends her time rewriting the dictionary, and Charles Kemper as a musician. All make their footage count plenty.

Leon Shamroy's camera work is slick. Music, as put together by Ira Gershwin, Kay Swift, Herbert Spencer and Edward Powell, comes through in a lush manner under Alfred Newman's baton. There isn't much dancing, but the waltzes staged by Hermes Pan make pleasant interludes. Sum total is a film that's easy on the eye and ear but not too bright. *Mike.*

Stagecoach to Denver

Hollywood, Dec. 27.

Republic release of Sidney Picker production. Stars Allan Lane; features Bobby Blake, Martha Wentworth, Roy Barcroft, Peggy Stewart, Emmett Lynn. Directed by R. G. Springsteen. Original screenplay, Earle Snell; based on cartoon strip, "Red Ryder," by Fred Harmon; camera, Edgar Lyons; editor, Les Orlebeck. Previewed Dec. 27, '46. Running time, **56 MINS.**

Red Ryder	Allan Lane
Little Beaver	Bobby Blake
The Duchess	Martha Wentworth
Big Bill Lambert	Roy Barcroft
Beautiful	Peggy Stewart
Coon-Skin	Emmett Lynn
Sheriff	Ted Adams
Duke	Edmund Cobb
Doc Kimball	Tom Chatterton
Dickie Ray	Bobby Hyatt
Blackie	George Chesebro
Felton	Edward Cassidy
Braydon	Wheaton Chambers
Matt Disher	Forrest Taylor

This saddle entry in Republic's Red Ryder series measures up as okay fodder for the Saturday matinee trade. There's plenty of action and Allan Lane as Ryder proves a bit more accurate with his six-shooter than the usual film cowpoke. Sidney Picker did better than average with production values considering budget and R. G. Springsteen keeps tight directorial hand to assure proper pacing and plenty of action.

Original script by Earle Snell contains more story development than expected in a western, lending interest to basic formula of a land grab that Ryder busts up. Plot concerns Ryder's efforts to find out why a stagecoach was wrecked, injuring a young protege and killing a land commissioner. Plot thickens when a new commissioner and the boy's aunt, latter rushing to kid's bedside, disappear and two phonies take their places. There are a lot of angles to resolve in 56 minutes running time but Ryder's range-sleuthing cleans them up, exposing town's bigshot as a land stealer and juggler of survey lines.

Lane makes a stalwart Red Ryder and Bobby Blake is excellent as Little Beaver. Chief heavy is Roy Bancroft, turning in expert skullduggery. Peggy Stewart, the phoney aunt; Bobby Hyatt, Ryder's protege; Emmett Lynn, Martha Wentworth and others show up well. Edgar Lyons' lensing is actionful and Les Orlebeck's editing concise. *Brog.*

Les Miserables

(FRENCH-MADE)

Distinguished Film release of Pathe Consortium Cinema-Raymond Borderie production. Stars Harry Baur, Josselyne Gael; features Charles Vanel, Jean Servait, Charles Dullin, Arane Demazis. Directed by Raymond Bernard. Screenplay, Raymond Bernard, Andre Lang, from novel "Les Miserables," Victor Hugo; camera, J. Kruger; music, Arthur Honneger. At Apollo, N. Y., Dec. 29, '46. Running time, **209 MINS.**

Jean Valjean	Harry Baur
Javert	Charles Vanel
Cosette } Fantine }	Josselyne Gael
Thernadier	Charles Dullin
Mme. Thernadier	Gaby Triquet
Marius	Jean Servait
Eponine	Arane Demazis
Gavroche	Emile Genevais

(In French; English Titles)

Any ordinary film, when loaded with the handicaps piled on "Les Miserables," would stagger and drop with a resounding flop. But this (actually it's two pictures) is no ordinary product, but two films, "Jean Valjean" and its sequel, "Cosette." Holding it all together is the thespic strength of the late great Harry Baur, who supports this spliced epic with a power strangely comparable to that of the Jean Valjean he played. It should do well in the arty houses despite short turnover due to the extreme length (209 mins.).

Neither of the films is new, both having been made some 10 years ago and then re-edited for a single presentation. Despite groaning length and the actual separateness of their production, continuity is excellent; a few short frames of annotation are used to bring plot forward the few years between the end of "Jean Valjean" and the beginning of its sequel, "Cosette."

Added to the three and a half hours' running time, "Les Miserables" labors under atrocious sub-titling, the poorer makeup and costuming of an earlier period of film-making, imperfect prints and occasional over-acting. And yet it's a fine picture. Baur is powerful, disciplined and moving in the lead role, while other lead and supporting players, Charles Dullin and Charles Vanel in particular, are far better than average. Raymond Bernard's sharp direction under productive supervision of Raymond Borderie is constantly in evidence.

Distrib's intention is to present the pic much in the same manner as "Gone With the Wind," a film of comparable length. Marquee pull of Baur's name alone is probably still strong enough to insure good arty-theatre returns.

Story is still essentially a moral essay, with Baur the reformed criminal who becomes the embodiment of good under constant flagellation of a scrupulous conscience. Film opens with his release from prison and metamorphosis through the kindness of a Bishop. He rises to mayoralty of a town and subsequent wealth, only to be forced by his conscience to declare his criminal identity, thereby saving another from prison. He escapes the police to carry out a mission to care for a dying woman's daughter (Josselyne Gael). There is a gap of eight years, where the second portion of the film takes up in 1832, following the Bourbon reaccession of the French throne. Miss Gael falls in love with a young revolutionary who mans the barricades against royalist troops. Although he disapproves, Baur finally effects their rescue and marriage, then dies.

Vanel, as Javert, the police inspector who constantly haunts Baur, is excellent; Dullin plays a scurrilous inn-keeper. Scenes of the abortive revolutionary attempts are outstanding, while camera work throughout is on a high plane. No credit line is given for the titling, which is just as well, since titles are misspelled and often laughable. *Tomm.*

La Otra
("The Other One")
(MEXICAN-MADE)

Mexico City, Dec. 17.

Panamerican Films release of Mauricio de la Serna production. Stars Dolores del Rio; features Agustin Irusta, Victor Junco and Jose Baviera. Directed by Roberto Gavaldon. Screenplay, Jose Revueltas and Gavaldon based on story by Rian James; camera, Alex Phillips. At Cine Olimpia, Mexico City. Running time, 93 MINS.

Of elegant simplicity, this Gallic-Latinesque tragedy starring Dolores del Rio shapes up as one of Mexico's top 1946 film offerings. Direction and photography are in keeping with the fine thesping of Miss del Rio who contributes one of the best performances of her career. Marquee lure of star's name alone should provide added pull in the U. S. market.

Hewing closely to the Rian James yarn, scripters have combined a melange of murders, morgues, cops and cemeteries into a taut tale with little comedy relief. Dialog is pointed and held to a minimum. Miss del Rio plays the dual role of two twin sisters, one who weds a millionaire and the other who ekes out a drab existence as a manicurist. Latter, rebelling from her station in life, murders her twin and carries on a masquerade which leads her into various jams including a 30-year rap for a murder she didn't commit.

Male support of Agustin Irusta, Jose Baviera and Victor Junco is top-flight. Miss del Rio, treasurer of the producing company which made the pic, shades the funereal tones of her role possibly a bit too darkly. Her costuming especially hits a macabre note with much of her garb resembling that of a femme undertaker. Director Gavaldon, whose technique is more of the best French school than Hollywood, rates laurels while the film's technical aspects are definite assets. *Grah.*

Queen for a Night
(Musical)
(SWEDISH-MADE)

Saga Films production and release. Stars Jussi Bjoerling. Directed by Willy Hildebrand. Screen story by Gardar Sahlberg from story by George Martens; music, Jules Sylvain; lyrics, Sven Olof Sandbergk, Karl-Ewert, Nils Thoren. Previewed N. Y. Dec. 27, '46. Running time, 91 MINS.

Madame La Grage..Gurli Lemon Bernhard
Pireo....................Jussi Bjoerling
Eva....................Inga Brink
Lars Hjelm..................Gosta Kjellertz
Gustaf III..................Torsten Winge
Count Hedencrona..........Hilding Gavle
Erik....................Ake Soderblom
Johansson....................Thor Modeen
Sergel....................Weyler Hildebrand

(In Swedish; English Titles)

This is Sweden's first screen operetta, and as such first-rate. Jussi Bjoerling, of the Metropolitan Opera Co., and some other excellent Swedish voices, including Gurli Lemon Bernhard, Gosta Kjellertz and the Royal Opera of Stockholm chorus, are all superb. Film looks like a first-rate bet for arty theatres in the U. S. but a bit too slow-moving and long for general American consumption.

Basically, this is a Cinderella story concerning a modiste who finds her lover drifting away when he falls for a French singer visiting Stockholm at a command performance in 1785. Their love affair appears headed for the rocks until Sweden's king accidentally overhears her at a masked ball and decides to bring the two together.

The Ballet of Venus, held outdoors before the royal party, is a highlight, although Miss Bernhard, clad in silken, revealing garb as Venus, does not measure up to Hollywood standards of streamlined beauty. Kjellertz bursts into song on the slightest provocation but is easily matched by Miss Bernhard's super vocalizing.

There are many closeups of buxom blonde femmes, some of them outdoing Jane Russell, but withal the story and sequences follow a routine operetta pattern. Acting is above par for a Swedish picture with laurels going to Miss Bernhard, Inga Brink, the little dressmaker who met a king; Bjoerling and Kjellertz. *Wear.*

Foreign Films

"Saltstaenk och Krutgubbar" ("Gay Old Time") (SWEDISH). Sandrew-Bauman release of Schamyl Bauman production; stars Sigurd Wallen; features Gull Natorp, John Elfstroem, Ludde Gentzel, Irma Christenson, Carl Hagman; directed by Schamyl Bauman; screenplay, Ragnar Arfvedsson, Eric Lundegard, Torsten Lundqvist, based on story by Albert Engstroem; camera, Sven Nyqvist. Reviewed in Stockholm. Running time, 112 MINS.

Swedish comedy paints some interesting and humorous pictures of island life not far from Stockholm. With thesping honors deftly handled by Sigurd Wallen, film's chances are enhanced by top lensing of newcomer Sven Nyqvist. Should do well in Sweden but U. S. appeal is negligible.

"Iris Och Lojtnantshjarta" (SWEDISH). Svensk Filmindustri production and release; stars Mai Zetterling, Alf Kjellin; features Ake Claesson, Holger Loewenadler, Margaretha Fahlen, Ingrid Borthen, Einar Axelson, Stig Jaerrel; directed by Alf Sjoeberg; screenplay, Sjoeberg; camera, Gosta Rosling. At Roda Kvarn, Stockholm. Running time, 96 MINS.

Better than average Swedish film due to fine direction and good scripting. Based on a best seller by Ollie Hedberg, story makes a fine vehicle for Alf Kjellin and Mai Zetterling. Incidentally, this was last one Miss Zetterling did here before joining J. Arthur Rank organization in England. Okay lensing enhances film's chances at U. S. arty houses.

"Odemarksprasten" ("The Country Priest") (SWEDISH). Sandrew-Bauman Film release of Anders Sandrew production; stars Olaf Widgren, Birgit Tengroth; features Arnold Sjoestrand, Carl Colbjorn Knudsen, Ake Claesson, Bjorn Berglund, Mona Ericsson; directed by Goesta Folke; screenplay, Rune Lindstrom, based on novel by Harald Hornborg; camera, Goeran Strindberg. At Grand, Stockholm. Running time, 98 MINS.

Topflight scripting of Rune Lindstrom has turned Harald Hornborg's novel into an okay vehicle for Olof Widgren and Birgit Tengroth. Goesta Folke's direction stands out. Film looms as a success in Scandinavian countries, but story hampers its possibilities in the U.S. *Wins.*

"Le Bataillon du Ciel" ("Sky Battalion") (FRENCH). Pathe Cinema release of C.I.C.C. production; stars Pierre Blanchar, Rene Lefevre, Janine Crispin; directed by Alexander Esway; screenplay, Joseph Kessel. Reviewed in Paris. Running time, 165 MINS.

Sure heavy grosser here and a good entry for arty theatres in the U. S. "Le Bataillon du Ciel" is an 18-reel epic of the French parachuters who dropped in Brittany at the time of the Normandy invasion. One of the biggest recent French productional efforts, cooperation of the R.A.F. and the French Army permitted use of planes and parachutes on a Hollywood scale. Acting is realistic but length of film along with fact that war heroics are getting dated will hurt the picture's chances for general release in America.

"Adieu Cherie" ("Goodbye Darling") (FRENCH). Osso release of Osso-Roitfeld production; stars Danielle Darrieux; features Gabrielle Dorzat, Salou, Larquey, Jacques Barthier; directed by Raymond Bernard; screenplay, Jacques Companeez. Reviewed in Paris. Running time, 115 MINS.

Film misses out because of unsatisfactory screen treatment and technique which has Danielle Darrieux portraying a role similar to that done by Michele Morgan in the pre-war "Taxi Girl." An adventuress, she tries and fails to be accepted as the bride of young Jacques Berthier in the respectable family headed by Larquey and Gabrielle Dorziat. Male lead is weak and poor direction fails to bring out capabilities of an able supporting cast. *Maxi.*

"Don Simon de Lira" (MEXICAN). Filmex release of Bracho Films production; stars Joaquin Pardave, Manuel Medel; features Elsa Aguirre; directed by Julio Bracho; based on Ben Jonson's "Velnone"; music, Raul Lavista; camera, Ezequiel Carrasco. At Cine Metropolitan, Mexico City, Dec. 18, '46. Running time, 118 MINS.

Though local crix have panned this, it has points of appeal. 'Don Simon de Lira' is a silly story about a rich old fool who's so stupid that one wonders how he ever got to be rich. Yarn is supposed to be based on Ben Jonson's sparkling comedy. Julio Bracho's direction is not up to his usual standard. Cancan dance sequence, one of best in picture, is cut to a mere flash. Looks strong for top spot here, and also may do for U. S. arty houses. *Grah.*

Miniature Reviews

"Ladies' Man" (Songs) (Par). Eddie Bracken holding up lightweight musical okay for general situations.

"Martin Roumagnac" (French). Marlene Dietrich-Jean Gabin, romantic drama, surefire with French audiences.

Ladies' Man
(SONGS)

Paramount release of Daniel Dare production. Stars Eddie Bracken, Cass Daley, Virginia Welles; features Spike Jones' City Slickers, Johnny Coy, Virginia Field. Directed by William D. Russell. Screenplay, Edmund Beloin, Jack Rose, Lewis Meltzer based on story by William Bowers, Robinson Holbert; songs, Jule Styne, Sammy Cahn; camera, Stuart Thompson; editor, Everett Douglas. Tradeshown N. Y. Dec. 26, '46. Running time, 91 MINS.

Henry Haskell....................Eddie Bracken
Geraldine Ryan....................Cass Daley
Jean Mitchell..................Virginia Welles
Johnny O'Conner....................Johnny Coy
Gladys Hayden..................Virginia Field
David Harmon..................Lewis Russell
Mr. Jones..................Georges Renevant
Phone Operator..................Roberta Jonay
Spike Jones & His City Slickers

"Ladies' Man" doesn't pack much punch but will serve as a palatable musical comedy creampuff for general situations. One of Paramount's lower cost items, film depends wholly upon the comic talents of Eddie Bracken to hold together a random assortment of specialty acts. Formula story of a rich yokel being taken for a ride in the big city is the peg for the musical score and comedy situations and is given a neat tongue-in-cheek treatment. But film is overlong for its purpose, and more decisive editing could cut between 10 and 15 minutes of running time for snappier results.

With Cass Daley and Spike Jones and His City Slickers acting as the chief supporting battery for Bracken's mugging and double-takes, plenty of raucous corn is to be expected. Miss Daley, in addition to a straight comedy part, does a vocal assault on "Mama ye quiere," while Spike Jones' combo hash up two of their best known numbers, "Holiday for Strings" and "Cocktails for Two." Johnny Coy registers solidly in two standout dance specialties. Bracken, in his screen's initial singing stint, does nicely on a couple of Jule Styne-Sammy Cahn tunes, "I Gotta Gal I Love" and "What Am I Gonna Do About You," and is backed up in a neat duet arrangement with Virginia Welles on the latter number.

Story concerns an Oklahoma oil king who comes to New York on a sight-seeing tour but gets tricked into acting as Prince Charming on a radio program contest. Bracken plays sucker as a beau geste towards Miss Fields, who leads him to believe that her job in an ad agency depends upon his cooperation. But disillusionment soon sets in together with the usual round of romantic difficulties against a background of niteries and behind-the-broadcast scenes. Throughout the proceedings, Virginia Field moves irrelevantly in a female Groucho Marx role of a phoney southern belle who sets her traps for Bracken.

Thesping by Bracken and supporting players is competent down the line. Direction is handled with an appropriately light touch although some of the specialty numbers are stretched out excessively. Musical score is okay, but nothing special in the way of hit tunes, while production dress and camera work is standard. *Herm.*

Martin Roumagnac
(FRENCH-MADE)

Paris.
Gaumont release of Alcina production. Stars Marlene Dietrich, Jean Gabin; features Margo Lion, Marcel Herrand, Jean d'Yd, Daniel Gelin, Michel Ardan, Marcelle Geniat, Paul Faivre, Lucien Nat, Jean Darcante. Directed by Georges Lacombe. Screenplay, Lacombe. Reviewed in Paris. Running time, 115 MINS.

Excellent casting of Marlene Dietrich and Jean Gabin, who turn in some top drawer thesping, makes this film a sure grosser here and likely b.o. wherever French pix are played. An adventuress, Miss Dietrich makes a play for small town contractor Jean Gabin. Falling heavily at first, he later gets wise to her true character and kills her in a fit of jealousy.

Packing more punch than most French-mades, pic is a fine vehicle for Gabin who is his usual authentic self in the part of the rough country guy unable to understand the sophisticated woman before it's too late. Miss Dietrich gives an interesting performance as the flighty woman, but disappears from the film three reels before the end.

Originally slated for leads in Pathe's "Night Doors," Gabin and Miss Dietrich turned it down, finding "Martin Roumagnac" more to their liking. Films' foreign rights have been acquired by Laudy Lawrence, film exec, formerly associated with Metro and Alexander Korda.
Maxi.

Foreign Films

"Det Regnar Pa Var Karlek" ("It Is Raining on Our Love") (SWEDISH). Nordisk Tonefilm release of Lorens Marmstedt production; stars Barbro Kollberg, Birgir Malmsten; features Goesta Cederlund, Ludde Gentzel, Douglas Hage, Hjoerdis Petterson. Directed by Ingmar Bergman. Screenplay, Bergman and Herbert Grevenius, based on play by Oskar Braathen. Camera, Hilding Bladh, Goerun Strindberg; music, Erland von Koch. Reviewed in Stockholm. Running time, 100 MINS.

Perhaps one of the best films any Swedish producer ever made, story's theme based on the premise that a man isn't a criminal just because he has erred once, develops into excellent entertainment chiefly due to fine scripting of Ingmar Bergman and Herbert Grevenius. Acting, lensing and direction are in keeping with other high production values. Looming as a top grosser in Sweden, picture should meet with worldwide b.o. success.

"Rumeurs" ("Allegations") (FRENCH). Consortium International release of C.A.P.A.C. production; stars Jacques Dumesnil, Jany Holt; directed by Jacques Daroy; screenplay, Simon Gantillon. Reviewed in Paris.

Poorly directed and photographed story that's very dreary. Shows Jacques Dumesnil as a small town garage proprietor who's wrongly suspected of the slaying of a prostitute. Preys on his mind and to relieve it he plans to commit a similar killing. Jany Holt is weak as the intended victim and whole production is below par. Mild for America.
Maxi.

"Om Kjaerligheten Synger De" ("The Song of Love") (NORWEGIAN). Apollo Film release of Oslo Film production; stars Harald Heide-Steen, Elisabeth Gording; features Alfred Solas, Edvard Drablos, Einar Vaage, Stig Egede-Nissen, Berit Brenne, Finn Bernhoft, Dagmar Myhrvold; directed by Olav Dalgard; screenplay, Dalgard, based on play by Nicolay Huggenvik; camera, Reidar Lund. Reviewed in Oslo. Running time, 80 MINS.

Dramatic Norwegian film about a hotel worker wrongfully accused of arson develops into a domestic tragedy which may prove okay in Scandinavia. However, picture is too sentimental to offer much appeal to U. S. audiences, despite good acting and fair screenplay.
Wins.

Miniature Reviews

"Sinbad the Sailor" (Color) (RKO). Color fantasy of Oriental adventure; Doug Fairbanks, Jr.; Maureen O'Hara insure b.o.

"Meet Me at Dawn" (British-Made). Romantic comedy provides good entertainment in this Marcel Helman - 20th - Fox pic.

"Hungry Hill" (British-Made). Disappointing adaptation of Daphne du Maurier's best-seller; tough sledding for the U. S.

Sinbad the Sailor
(COLOR)

Hollywood, Jan. 11.
RKO release of Stephen Ames production. Stars Douglas Fairbanks, Jr., Maureen O'Hara, Walter Slezak; features Anthony Quinn, George Tobias, Jane Greer, Mike Mazurki, Sheldon Leonard, Alan Napier, John Miljan, Barry Mitchell. Directed by Richard Wallace. Screenplay, John Twist; original, Twist and George Worthing Yates; camera (Technicolor), George Barnes; special effects, Vernon L. Walker, Harold Wellman; music, Roy Webb; editor, Frank Doyle. Tradeshown in Los Angeles, Jan. 9, '47. Running time, 116 MINS.
Sinbad..............Douglas Fairbanks, Jr.
Shireen.....................Maureen O'Hara
Melik........................Walter Slezak
Emir........................Anthony Quinn
Abbu........................George Tobias
Pirouze.........................Jane Greer
Yusuf..........................Mike Mazurki
Auctioneer..................Sheldon Leonard
Aga.............................Alan Napier
Moga...........................John Miljan
Muallin.....................Barry Mitchell

The sterling adventures of Sinbad as a sailing man and as a romancer have been garbed in brilliant color in this RKO production. The Oriental fantasy of "Sinbad the Sailor" should prove an apt escape valve for ticketbuyers, particularly among the very young and those who have passed the actively adventurous years. Boxoffice payoff should be handsome.

Cast values match production elegance. A return to pictures for Douglas Fairbanks, Jr., after war service, film has actor matching do-and-dare antics of his late father. He measures up to the flamboyance required to make Sinbad a dashing fictional hero. For the males, Maureen O'Hara lends shapely presence as the heroine. Role has little histrionic value but Miss O'Hara's comeliness graces period costumes and color to nth degree.

Story concerns Sinbad's mythical eighth adventure wherein he seeks a fabulously rich island and the love of an Arabian Nights beauty. Major production fault is that dialog and main story points are obscure, making intelligent following of plot difficult. Principal opponents to Sinbad's search are Walter Slezak and Anthony Quinn. Former's character is never clearly explained, and latter's role also is obscured in the writing. These are critical faults that are not likely to be too closely examined by theatregoers seeking pure escapism for film entertainment.

Richard Wallace's direction of the Stephen Ames production treats the adventuring with a light but actionful touch that pleases. Pageantry of the Oriental background lends itself handily to tints, and George Barnes' camera makes the most of the glorified production trappings. Special effects also contribute a large share to display as done by Vernon L. Walker and Harold Wellman.

George Tobias, as Sinbad's boon companion in adventures, doesn't have too much to do. Jane Greer is a comely maid-in-waiting to Miss O'Hara. Mike Muzarki, Sheldon Leonard, good in a single scene as an auctioneer; John Miljan and others fit the action.
Brog.

Meet Me at Dawn
(BRITISH-MADE)

London, Jan. 6.
20th-Fox presentation of Marcel Hellman production. Stars William Eythe, Hazel Court; features Margaret Rutherford, Basil Sydney, Stanley Holloway. Directed by Thornton Freeland; music by Mischa Spoliansky. Screenplay by Lesley Storm, James Seymour based on "Le Tueur," by Marcel Achard, Anatole Litvak. At Odeon theatre, London, Jan. 6, '47. Running time, 99 MINS.
Charles Morton............William Eythe
Emile...................Stanley Holloway
Gabrielle Vermorel............Hazel Court
Senator Renault............George Thorpe
Madame Renault.............Irene Browne
Margot..................Beatrice Campbell
Georges Vermorel...........Basil Sydney
Madame Vermorel.....Margaret Rutherford
Concierge......................Ada Reeve
Count de Brissac............Graeme Muir
News Editor.........Wilfred Hyde White
Doctor....................John Ruddock
Ambassador.............O. B. Clarence
Prefect of Police........Aubrey Mallalieu

It's a far cry from the psychopathic melodrama, "Wanted for Murder," to this airy romantic comedy, but producer Marcel Hellman has provided a good entertainment. To have been more than this it would have needed the finest romantic comedy couple, and William Eythe and Hazel Court are not yet in the Lunt-Fontanne class as artists. Eythe, lent by 20th-Fox, gives a performance that parallels his work in "A Royal Scandal," but director Thornton Freeland, conscientious as he is, lacks the one-time Lubitsch touch, and Eythe, competent actor, is minus the Gallic effervescence the part cries out for.

General level of acting is good, and production has a nice quality, particularly in the duelling scenes, which also owe something to the music of Spolianski. But absence of marquee names—Eythe means more in America than here—may handicap boxoffice, and picture will have to rely mainly on word-of-mouth.

Story is laid in Paris at the turn of the century, with Eythe as a professional duellist ready to take up anybody's quarrel for a financial consideration. Engaged by politicians to insult and wound a prominent senator who is to be put out of the way for a period, he uses Gabrielle as a pretext. The challenge becomes a sensation when a newspaper publisher, not knowing the mystery woman about whom the men are to duel is his own daughter, plasters his paper with lurid stories about "Madame X."

Meanwhile the couple have fallen in love and climax comes when the prospective father-in-law insults him publicly and the boy has to challenge him to a duel. Giving the father a fencing lesson during what appears to be a mortal combat, he turns the fumbling publisher into a hero and ends with the girl in his arms.

Introducing one of J. Arthur Rank's promising starlets in a leading part, producer Hellman took a big gamble which doesn't quite come off. Hazel Court has beauty, but to play such important roles she needs more training and experience. This is most apparent in her scenes with such seasoned troupers as Margaret Rutherford and Stanley Holloway. These two are scene-stealers par excellence and dominate the screen at every opportunity.
Cane.

Hungry Hill
(BRITISH-MADE)

London, Jan. 8.
General Film Distributors' release of Two Cities Film. Stars Margaret Lockwood, Dennis Price, Cecil Parker. Directed by Brian Desmond Hurst. Screenplay by Daphne du Maurier, Terence Young, based on Miss du Maurier's novel. Camera, Desmond Dickinson. At Studio One, London, Jan. 7, '47. Running time, 100 MINS.
Fanny Rose............Margaret Lockwood
Greyhound John..............Dennis Price
Copper John................Cecil Parker
Wild Johnnie.............Dermot Walsh
Henry Brodrick..........Michael Denison
Morty Donovan...........Arthur Sinclair
Jane Brodrick..............Jean Simmons
Barbara Brodrick.......Barbara Waring
Harry Brodrick.............Dan O'Herlihy
Bridget....................Eileen Crowe

Katherine...................Eileen Herlie
Young Johnnie............Anthony Wager
Sam Donovan.............Michael Golden
Old Tim.................F. J. McCormick
Young Tim................Shamus Locke
Denny Donovan................Tony Quinn
Dr. Armstrong...........Henry Mollison
Kate Donovan..........Siobhan McKenna

Sudden love for Irish backgrounds has prompted a spate of British productions set in Ireland, much to the benefit of Dublin's Abbey and Gate Theatres, which have been ransacked for talent.

Names of Lockwood, Price and du Maurier should draw customers here, but it will be hard going in America.

First film of the series to reach the screen is "Hungry Hill." Costing at least $1,500,000, this adaptation of Daphne du Maurier's best-seller is a sombre heavyweight created with care, but falling with a sad crash through absence of humanity and real feeling. For painstaking thoroughness the film deserves commendation, but with one or two exceptions the characters have no red blood in their veins and little interest is aroused in the fate of most of the principals. Cardinal failing, as with so many British films, is lack of heart. Too many British producers and directors appear to frown on emotion, and are becoming expert in creating screen puppets.

Story, beginning in 1840 and covering a period of 40 years, tells of the bitter feud between the Brodricks and the Donovans over the sinking of a copper mine on Hungry Hill by John Brodrick, owner of Clonmere Castle. Centuries before the Donovans owned the Hill, and inbred in the family is a hatred of Brodrick. Cursing him, old Morty Donovan declares that no Donovan will work at the mine which will bring nothing but bad luck to the Brodricks. To make his prophecy true, he invites the Irishman to riot, the mine is burnt to the ground, and Brodrick's eldest son is killed.

Next in succession to the Brodrick fortune is John, who has little interest in the mine, but having an affection for the Irish workers believes that mutual regard and understanding could banish hatred. After a hectic courtship he marries Fanny Rose, the much-courted and high-spirited local beauty; is a good husband, raises a family of four and dies. Fanny spoils her eldest son, who grows into a dissipated youth, and on the death of his grandfather, eagerly awaited by himself and his mother, he inherits the Brodrick fortune and the mine.

Realizing she is not wanted at Clonmere by her wild son, Fanny goes to London where she becomes a gambler and a drug addict, but Johnnie's hard heart is touched when he sees the lonely aging woman— he is in London while the scandal of his betraying a Donovan girl blows over. Mother returns happily to Ireland, but the mine soon takes its toll. In a brawl with the workers Johnnie is killed and Fanny charges one of the Donovans with murder. But her philosophical old servant changes her mind. She withdraws the charge, and the end comes with Fanny looking out over Hungry Hill believing that peace has come to the Brodricks and the Donovans.

It's a poor reward for Margaret Lockwood, England's most popular actress, to be given a part that calls for little more than posturing, acting as a clothes-horse, and adding some lines to her young face to denote age. Story of a woman who loses everything she loves should have touched one, but somewhere in the writing and direction the sentiment has been eliminated, and Miss Lockwood can do little with the puppet she plays. Instead of being a tragic figure as a gambler and drug addict, she is ludicrous. Nor, for some unaccountable reason, has the camera been kind to her.

Cecil Parker is monumental as old man Brodrick but his grief is soul-less. Dennis Price is the only one who is entirely credible. This is his best work to date, and he enhances a reputation earned by fine performances. Running him close is Dermot Walsh, product of the Gate Theatre, with his playing of Wild Johnnie. He shows much promise, and with his long-term contract from Rank may fill the gap left by James Mason.

F. J. McCormick, father of the present Abbey players, and his wife Eileen Crowe etch a couple of nice studies as faithful retainers. Jean Simmons, Rank starlet, is wasted, and Eileen Herlie (now under contract to Korda and slated for "Salome" with Orson Welles) makes a brief appearance.   *Cane.*

Foreign Films

"Desarroi" ("Distress") **(FRENCH).** C.F.C. release of Moulins d'Or production; stars Valentine Tessier, Jean Debucourt, Gabrielle Dorziat, Jules Berry; directed by Paul Robert Dagan; screenplay by Paul Achard based on play "Odette" by Victorian Sardou. Reviewed in Paris. Running time, 95 MINS.

Despite names and Paul Achard's expert streamlining of Sardou's old drama, poor direction and antiquated technique cue this one strictly for the local nabes. Story, a complicated romantic drama, wastes a capable cast. No dice for U. S.

"Reves d'Amour" ("Love Dreams") **(FRENCH).** Pathe Consortium release of Pathe production; stars Annie Ducaux and Pierre Richard Willm; directed by Christian Stengel based on legit play by Rene Fauchois. Previewed in Paris. Running time, 100 MINS.

This filmization of the legit deals with the love affair a century ago of pianist composer Franz Liszt and Comtesse d'Agoult. As a musical, it does not compare with the American product. Musical values are all in the incidental synchronized music with no singing. Aided by good thesping and marquee names of Annie Ducaux and Richard Willm, should do fairly well in France, but has doubtful values for America.

"Farrebique" **(FRENCH).** Ecran Francais release of Georges Rouquier production. Written and directed by Rouquier. Previewed in Paris. Running time, 95 MINS.

This picture, of a documentary nature, was considered sufficiently good to get a showing at the Cannes Festival. But it is too arty in its description of the life of French peasants. Farmers in the poor French southern country are the sole actors. Lensing is good and film might be improved by cutting into a two-reel documentary since the story itself is of no importance. As a feature "Farrebique" has no appeal for U. S. *Maxi.*

"Humo en los Ojos" ("Smoke in the Eyes") **(MEXICAN).** Filmex release of Producciones Rosas Priego production; stars Tona la Negra and Fernando Soto; features David Silva, Maria Luisa Zea, Mercedes Barba and Ruben Rojo; directed by Alberto Gout; camera, Alberto Carasco. At Cine Orfeon, Mexico City. Running time, 75 MINS.

Modest pic shapes up as fair entertainment largely because of music by Agustin Lara, Mexico's big romantic songsmith and warbling of buxom Tona la Negra. Story's a slow moving drama studded with gunplay. Okay acting, direction and lensing help it. Film should do well locally and may do for foreign language spots in the U. S. *Grah.*

"Le Visiteur" ("The Inspector") **(FRENCH).** Sirius release of Majestic production; stars Pierre Fresnay; features Balpetre, Michel Vitold, Debucourt, Charensol, Beauchamp, Simone Sylvestre; directed by Jean Dreville; screenplay, Jean Bernard-Luc. Reviewed in Paris. Running time, 90 MINS.

Despite Pierre Fresnay's marquee pull, this looms as a doubtful draw in any situation. Story deals with a shyster lawyer who commits murder and hides in an orphanage. There's little human interest and film's femme appeal is nil. No dice for U. S.

Miniature Reviews

"I'll Be Yours" (Songs) (U). Deanna Durbin starred in "Good Fairy" remake; okay boxoffice.

"The Macomber Affair" (UA). Gregory Peck, Joan Bennett and Robert Preston names needed to draw 'em to this African veldt safari.

"It's a Joke, Son!" (Eagle-Lion). Kenny Delmar as "Senator Claghorn" in Eagle-Lion's teeoff production; okay dualer.

"The Pilgrim Lady" (Rep). Romantic comedy, strictly for the duals.

"Man's Hope" (Lopert) (Spanish-Made). Andre Malraux film of own Spanish Civil war novel. Top arty b.o.

"Born to Speed" (PRC). Fair "B" actioner for the duals.

"Klockorna I Gamla Sta'n" (Swedish Made). First Swedish tinter will gross well in Scandinavia and stands U.S. chance.

I'll Be Yours
(SONGS)

Universal-International release of Felix Jackson production (Howard Christie, associate producer). Stars Deanna Durbin, Tom Drake and William Bendix; features Adolphe Menjou. Directed by William A. Seiter. Screenplay, Preston Sturges; based on play, "The Good Fairy," by Ferenc Molnar; translated and adapted by Jane Hinton; songs, C. C. S. Cushing, E. P. Heath, Emmerich Kalman, Augustin Lara, Jack Brooks and Walter Schuman; other music, Frank Skinner; music director for Miss Durbin, Walter Schuman; editor, Otto Ludwig; special photography, David S. Horsley; assistant director, William Holland. Tradeshown in in N. Y., Jan 16, '47. Running time, 93 MINS.

Louise Ginglebusher .... Deanna Durbin
George Prescott .... Tom Drake
Wechsberg .... William Bendix
J. Conrad Nelson .... Adolphe Menjou
Mr. Buckingham .... Walter Catlett
Barber .... Franklin Pangborn
Captain .... William Trenk
Blonde .... Joan Fulton
Usherette .... Patricia Alphin
Stagedoor Johnny .... William Brooks

Ferenc Molnar would probably recognize his former hit play, "The Good Fairy," in its current remake. "I'll Be Yours" more or less hangs on the framework of the Hungarian author's yarn, while Universal-International has added Deanna Durbin and several songs that the star sings engagingly. The result is a mildly pleasant little comedy that should do well enough at the boxoffice.

This version of the original Universal pic (1935), which starred Margaret Sullavan in a more literal Preston Sturges adaptation of the Molnar work, has assumed a modern-day New York aura instead of the original Continental atmosphere. Some of the Sturges satirical bite is still evident, while much of the situation comedy is obvious. With Miss Durbin a factor, though, there isn't much for the exhibitor to concern himself. The star's looks, lilting soprano and a charm she's carried over from her childhood thesp days are always sufficiently in evidence when the pic has a tendency to sag.

Miss Durbin plays a youngster who goes to New York from her small town, becomes an usher at what is supposed to be the Radio City Music Hall (though it's called the Buckingham). Then she becomes involved with an elderly millionaire roue chaser of the chaste. Complicating matters is a young, penniless lawyer, the other link in the romance. Difficulties are for the young lovers because of circumstances that rather innocuously involve the girl and the roue.

Miss Durbin solos three tunes neatly. It's doubtful if she's ever been in better voice. "Granada," the Augustin Lara tune, a standard in the Latin American catalogs, is done especially well, while the likewise standard "Sari Waltz" (C. C. S. Cushing-E. P. Heath-Emmerich Kalman) and "It's Dream Time" (Jack Brooks-Walter Schuman) are the other highly listenable numbers.

Tom Drake unassumingly plays the young lawyer, while William Bendix is the waiter, a part whose Jewish overtones are too obvious in a role where the semitisms as part of the character aren't even remotely necessary. This is strangely inconsistent; the Jewishness is only evident early in the pic—as if the producer had suddenly awakened to the role's tangent and then decided to cut it out without re-shooting the earlier reels. Adolphe Menjou plays the roue, which Frank Morgan played in the former pic. Herbert Marshall had the original part played now by Drake.

The pic has a sharp pace, having been directed by William A. Seiter, and the production is expensive-looking all the way. Miss Durbin is attractively garbed, but one frock, a dark affair with white lace collar, makes her look much too matronly, a factor pointed up because of her tendency to take on weight during the past couple of years. *Kahn*

The Macomber Affair

Hollywood, Jan. 20.

United Artists release of Benedict Bogeaus production. Stars Gregory Peck, Joan Bennett, Robert Preston; features Reginald Denny, Carl Harbord, Earl Smith. Directed by Zoltan Korda. Screenplay, Casey Robinson and Seymour Bennett, from adaptation of Ernest Hemingway story by Bennett and Frank Arnold; camera, Karl Strauss; editors, George Feld, Jack Wheeler; music, Miklos Roza. Tradeshown in Hollywood. Running time, **89 MINS.**

Robert Wilson.................Gregory Peck
Francis Macomber..........Robert Preston
Margaret Macomber.........Joan Bennett
Captain Smollet...............Reginald Denny
Coroner.........................Carl Harbord
Kongoni..........................Earl Smith

"The Macomber Affair," with an African hunt background, will get by principally through selling force of its cast toppers, Gregory Peck, Joan Bennett and Robert Preston. Story, while triangular in theme, isn't particularly pleasant in content, even though action often is exciting and elements of suspense frequently hop up the spectator. Certain artificialities of presentation, too, and unreal dialog are further strikes against picture, although portion of footage, that filmed in Africa, is as interesting as anything of the season.

Preston enacts role of Francis Macomber, a rich American with an unhappy wife (Miss Bennett), who arrives at Nairobi and hires Peck, a white hunter, to take him lion hunting. On the safari, this time in cars, Macomber can't stand up under a lion charge and his wife sees him turn coward. The white hunter kills the lion. Thereafter, Macomber broods over his shame, his wife falls for the hunter and finally she fires shot which kills her husband, ostensibly, as she levels her sights on a water buffalo charging her husband.

African footage is cut into the story with showmanship effect, and these sequences build up suspense satisfactorily. There are closeups of lions and other denizens of the veldt, and scenes in which lion and water buffalo charge, caught with telescopic lenses by camera crew sent to Africa from England, will stir any audience. These focal points of story out-interest the human drama as developed in scripters' enmeshing trio of stars.

Peck delivers a clear-cut delineation of the white hunter, a role in strange variance to his usual work. Miss Bennett doesn't fare so well with the stilted dialog, but scores as the shrewish wife. Preston, making his comeback after service in the Army, makes a neat impression in a difficult part. In bits, Reginald Denny and Jean Gillie acquit themselves satisfactorily.

"Affair" was co-produced by Benedict Bogeaus and Casey Robinson, latter also collabing with Seymour Bennett on adaptation of Ernest Hemingway's original story, "The Short and Happy Life of Francis Macomber." Plenty of values were inserted, which Zoltan Korda handled well enough in his direction. Camera work by Karl Strauss is above average, and George Feld and Jack Wheeler did bang-up job with the editing.

It's a Joke, Son!

Eagle-Lion release of Aubrey Schenck (Bryan Foy) production. Stars Kenny Delmar; features Una Merkel, June Lockhart, Kenneth Farrell. Directed by Ben Stoloff. Original screenplay, Robert Kent and Paul Gerard Smith; camera, Clyde de Vinna; editor, Norman Colbert; music, Alvin Levin. Tradeshown in N. Y., Jan. 15, '46. Running time, **63 MINS.**

Senator Claghorn.............Kenny Delmar
Magnolia Claghorn.............Una Merkel
Mary Lou.......................June Lockhart
Jeff Davis.....................Kenneth Farrell
Dan Healey..............Douglas Dumbrille
Senator Leeds..................Jimmy Conlin
Ace ....Matt Willis
Knifey ....Ralph Sanford
Daisy ....By Herself
Hortense ....Vera Lewis
Whipple Sisters .... Margaret McWade / Ida Moore

"It's a Joke, Son!" represents Eagle-Lion's first Hollywood-made production—and it's not a very auspicious entry. Film, evidently a modest-budgeter, sags through most of its length under a mess of slapstick that's laid on with a heavy trowel. Pic's only claim to prominence is the presence in the cast of Kenny Delmar, the "Senator Claghorn" of Fred Allen's radio show, which should be a good exploitation gimmick for enterprising exhibs. The picture's hardly strong enough to stand alone in first-run situations which, together with the fact that it runs only 63 minutes, would groove it for the duals.

Delmar tries hard to carry the film and, although he'll undoubtedly draw plenty of yocks in spots, his type of humor isn't strong enough for an entire feature. Story follows the theme of his radio work and funny though it may be, his constant play on the north vs. south angle seems almost in poor taste, what with the current trouble in the Georgia gubernatorial mansion, the Bilbo purge, etc. Guy's a fairly competent actor, however, and milks his particular type of dialog for all that's in it.

Original screenplay by Robert Kent and Paul Gerard Smith doesn't leave much to the imagination, and most audiences will be able to call the shots on each cliche long before the footage winds up. Delmar's a southern aristocrat, living on the glory of pre-Civil War days and little else, with his only income being from a mint bed. When his bossy wife is nominated for state senator by her Daughters of Dixie, the political bosses who've invaded from the north nominate Delmar to run against her and so split the party vote to leave the way open for their own minion. After much byplay, during which Delmar is kidnapped and arrives back at the courthouse just in time for the election, he wins the vote, takes over the pants-wearing in his family and cements the love affair between his daughter and her boyfriend.

Although they're overshadowed by Delmar, the rest of the cast come through okay under direction of Ben Stoloff. Una Merkel, as the senator's wife, is good, and June Lockhart, though no great shakes as an actress, is photogenic as the daughter. Kenneth Farrell, newcomer to the leading man ranks, is passable, and Douglas Dumbrille is on hand to provide the villainy. Daisy, the pup from the "Blondie" series, is excellent.

Producer Aubrey Schenck has mounted the film on authentic-looking sets but in keeping with the modest budget. Clyde De Vinna's camera work is good. *Stal.*

The Pilgrim Lady

Republic release of William J. O'Sullivan production. Features Lynne Roberts, Warren Douglas, Alan Mowbray, Veda Ann Borg. Directed by Lesley Selander. Original screenplay, Dane Lussier; camera, Reggie Lanning; editor, Arthur Roberts. Reviewed in N. Y., Jan. 17, '47. Running time, **67 MINS.**

Henrietta Rankin...........Lynne Roberts
Dennis Carter..............Warren Douglas
Clifford Latimer..............Alan Mowbray
Eve Standish...............Veda Ann Borg
Professor Rankin...........Clarence Kolb
Aunt Phoebe................Helen Freeman
Millicent Rankin.............Doris Merrick
Thackeray Gibbs.............Russell Hicks
Blackie Reynolds..............Ray Walker
Noel.........................Charles Coleman
Wayne Talbott, III..Carlyle Blackwell, Jr.
Dr. Bekins..............Harry V. Cheshire
Nell Brown................Dorothy Christy
Oscar.........................Paul E. Burns
Workman......................Tom Duggan
Hotel Clerk.......................Jack Rice
Cab Driver..................William Haade
Bellboy.....................William Benedict

A run-of-the-mill programmer. Story line is familiar, and despite adequate performances, it has little else.

Yarn is the oldhat saga of an inhibited femme university teacher, who has authored a daring novel pseudonomously and submitted it to a New York publisher. On latter's rejection it falls into the hands of a couple of embryonic publishers, who decide if the author is as glamorous as her yarn is sexy they might have something via a cheesecake buildup. Of course, auntie palms off her ugly duckling niece, who's not so bad sans glasses. Lads interest an influential radio commentator, who provides sponsorship for publication through having a yen for the gal.

What happens after that is the cliche wherein the pseudo authoress falls into the arms of the young publisher, wounds the vanity of her elder benefactor, while auntie finds romance with a middle-aged lecturer.

Alan Mowbray as the egocentric commentator practically has a field day via a juicy role which supplies most of the comedy. Lynne Roberts contributes a neat interpretation of the unwilling masquerader, while Helen Freeman turns in a nifty performance as the aunt. Warren Douglas does okay by the boyfriend-publisher role. Other good performances are contribbed by Veda Ann Borg, Clarence Kolb, Doris Merrick and Russell Hicks.

Lesley Selander has achieved pace in direction, with Reggie Lanning's cameraing okay. *Edba.*

Man's Hope
(SPANISH-MADE)

Lopert Films release of Andre Malraux producton. Stars Majuto, Nicolas Rodriguez, Jose Lado; features members of International Brigade. Direction and screenplay, Malraux, from his novel, "Man's Hope"; camera, Louis Page; assistant director, Denise Marion; music, Darius Milhaud. Previewed in N. Y. Jan. 17, '47. Running time, **78 MINS.**

Captain Munoz..........................Majuto
Pilot Marquez...........Nicolas Rodriguez
The Peasant.........................Jose Lado
And members of the International Brigade and Spanish peasants.

(In Spanish; English Titles)

Completely unique in treatment, utterly stirring in impact, "Man's Hope" has, if anything, gained strength from a strange odyssey which brings it to the screen almost eight years after production. In filming two incidents of the Spanish Civil War, both taken from his own novel, Andre Malraux has gained emphasis by deliberate understatement, and has underlined this entire screen work with bone-bare simplicity. Box-office value of "Man's Hope" is virtually assured in the art houses.

After being smuggled into France following the Franco accession and hidden there during the Munich era and German occupation, "Man's Hope" was first screened after the liberation. At that time it received the Louis Delluc award, French equivalent of the Hollywood Oscar.

For an audience accustomed to strict continuity of action and logical story progression, this film will require some digestion. "Man's Hope" tells its story by implication as much as by actual picturization. In the subtitling a lot of the dialog is literally left unsaid. But these are not the norms by which Malraux produced the film. He's obviously steered clear of any romanticizing of the Loyalist cause, although he fought with the International Brigade; instead, he paints a stark picture and leaves it to the audience for consideration.

Film opens on street scenes in Barcelona, with a sound background of monotonous machine-gun jabber and explosive light artillery. Not until a few minutes have passed does one realize that the sound is not dubbed in. It's the mccoy, but with no visual evidence of results. Pictures were made during the 1938 bombardment. Film, in near-essay form, then shows the efforts of the Spanish citizen army and the two-bomber Loyalist squadron to destroy a bridge. The culmination of those efforts comes quickly. A peasant breaks through to the squadron with the location of the new Franco airfield, which must be neutralized before the bridge can be bombed. Unable to read a map, the peasant is taken on the bombing ride, and suspense, while he's trying to spot the Franco airdrome, is excellent. After the bombing, the plane crashes in the mountains. The rescue funeral procession of peasants, with virtually no sound but the Darius Milhaud score, provides one of the most unusual endings ever filmed.

Flying sequences, actually taken in the cockpit of the old Potez which constituted the Red Air Force in that sector, are outstanding in dramatic quality. On only two occasions does Malraux give indication of his comparative inexperience with a camera. Thesping is near-perfect, mainly because it's natural. *Tomm.*

Born to Speed

PRC release of Marvin D. Stahl production. Features Johnny Sands and Terry Austin. Directed by Edward L. Cahn. Screenplay, Crane Wilbur, Scott Darling and Robert B. Churchill, based on original story by Churchill; editor, W. Donn Hayes; camera, Jackson Rose; music, Albert Levin. Reviewed in N. Y. Jan. 17, '47. Running time, **61 MINS.**

Johnny Randall.................Johnny Sands
Toni Bradley......................Terry Austin
Mike Conroy.......................Don Castle
Breezy Bradley...................Frank Orth
Mrs. Randall................Geraldine Wall
Duke Hudkins...................Joe Haworth

Turning to midget autos as story fodder, PRC has turned out a fair action film which should hold its own on double bills. Gripping lensing of racing scenes tends to offset the cliches of a none-too-original story.

Son of an oldtime racing driver killed plying his trade, Johnny Sands plays a chip-off-the-old-block, who teams with his dad's old mechanic (Frank Orth) and pilots a resurrected racing auto driven by his father. Spirited competition develops between him and his arch rival, Don Castle, another driver, both of whom compete for the affections of Terry Austin, who portrays Orth's niece. In a Frank Merriwell finish of the big race, Sands defeats Castle, wins Miss Austin and retires from the track much to the delight of his mother, Geraldine Wall, who feared he would have met an untimely end similar to that of his father.

Vivacious Miss Austin acquits herself nicely and deserves better parts. Sands is miscast. A bit too juvenile, his emotings lack conviction. Castle is adequate as the heavy, while Orth and Miss Wall do well. Handling production reins, Marvin Stahl squeezed as much entertainment as possible from the low budget, while Edward L. Cahn's direction was somewhat uneven. Jackson Rose rates kudos for his camera work.

Kloekorna I Gamla Sta'n

(The Bells in Old Town)
(COLOR)
(SWEDISH-MADE)

Stockholm, Jan. 10.

Europa Film production and release. Stars Edvard Persson, George Fant, Gunnel Brostrom, Elsie Albiin; features Goesta Cederlund, Marta Albin, Ulla Wikander, Axel Hoegel, Torsten Hillberg, Harry Ahlin, John Norrman. Directed by Ragnar Hylten-Cavallius. Screenplay by Hylten-Cavallius, based on idea by Bertil Malmberg; camera, Birgir Gottlieb; music, Alvar Kraft; color technicians, James B. Schakleford and Olle Nordemar. Made in Cinécolor. At Saga, Stockholm. Running time, **112 MINS.**

First Swedish tinter, aided by marquee value of comedian Edvard Persson and excellent lensing of Birgir Gottlieb, should reap hefty grosses in Scandinavia and has b.o. possibilities for many U. S. arty houses. Fine cast contribs okay thesping under Ragnar Hylton-Cavallius' smooth direction.

With the story centered in Stockholm's "Old Town," one of the most picturesque parts of the Swedish capital, locale lends itself to fine celluloid hues which technicians James B. Schakleford, borrowed from Paramount, and Europa's Olle Nordemar bring out to perfection. Idea could be called unoriginal, but smart scripting milks it for full entertainment values. *Wing.*

Foreign Films

"Jeg Elsker en Anden" ("I Love Another") **(DANISH).** Asa Film production and release. Stars Marguerite Viby, Ebbe Rode; features Ib Schoenberg, Ernie Arnesen, Bjorn Watt Boolsen, Betty Helsengreen, Else Colber, Astrid Holm, Henry Nielsen, Ebba Amfeldt, Ingeborg Pehrson. Directed by Lau Lauritzen. Screenplay, Grete Frische; camera, Rudolf Fredericksen; music, Svend Gyldmark. Reviewed in Copenhagen. Running time, **92 MINS.**

Sparked by Marguerite Viby's brilliant acting, this comedy is the Danish actress' first film in her homeland after years in Swedish studios. A good songstress, she warbles several numbers to good effect. With okay direction and lensing, pic looms as satisfactory film fare for Scandinavia, but chances in U. S. are dubious.

"Jag Alskar Dig, Argbigga" ("I Love You") **(SWEDISH).** Svea Film release of Ake Ohberg production. Stars Sonja Wigert, Aka Ohberg; features Margit Manstad, Rune Halvarsson, Naima Wifstrand, Henrik Schildt. Direction and screenplay by Ohberg. Reviewed in Stockholm. Running time, **90 MINS.**

Producer-writer-director Ake Ohberg apparently took too many chores on his hands and the result is a bad copy of a Laurel & Hardy comedy. Sonja Wigert, one of Sweden's best film comediennes, is cast as a strong-willed lass. She clashes with Ohberg who eventually tames her temperament. Chances out of Scandinavia are meager.

"To Liv" ("Two Lives") **(NORWEGIAN).** Kamera Film release of Dovre Film production. Stars Erling Drangsholt, Sigrun Otto; features Wenche Em Bugge, Jon-Lennart Mjoen, Rolf Christensen, Carl Struve, Frank Robert. Directed by Titus Vibe Mueller and Finn Bo. Screenplay based on play by Finn Bo. Camera, Kaare Bergstroem; music, Christian Hartman. Reviewed in Oslo, Dec. 26, '46. Running time, **112 MINS.**

Written when Norway was under German occupation, Finn Bo's drama, produced in November, 1945, is now a striking film about a youthful informer who comes as a "friend" to a family in Oslo. He contrives to send the son to jail and betrays the daughter. Finding her husband's life destroyed, the mother kills the informer. Jon-Lennart Mjoen is a realistic traitor, while other acting is equally good. Pic will do well in Scandinavian countries and may offer some appeal to the U. S. market.

"Le Village de la Colere" ("The Village of Wrath") **(FRENCH).** Cinema de France release of Participation du Film production. Stars Louise Carletti, Paul Cambo; features Micheline Francey, Marcelle Geniat, Jean Paredes, Raymond Cordy, Schultz. Directed by Raoul Andre. Screenplay, Jean Canolle. Previewed in Paris. Running time, **105 MINS.**

Poor direction and technique, as well as inexpert story treatment, bar this film from the bigger French spots and make it hardly a bet for America. Story, set in 1860, shows a young city slicker who moves to the country and falls in love with a gal of gypsy descent. Accusing her of being a witch, villagers want to toss the couple out of town but finally decide they're okay. Theme may be worth a Hollywood remake after suitable treatment.

"Stiliga Augusta" ("The Pleasant August") **(SWEDISH).** Wive Film release of Centrum-Rex Film production. Stars Ingrid Backlin, Ake Gronberg; features Emy Hagman, Bengt Logardt, Thor Modeen, Julia Caesar, Carl Hagman, Ann-Margret Bergendahl, Folke Hamrn, Naima Wifstrand. Directed by Elof Ahrle; screenplay based on play by Gustaf af Geiferstam. At Strand, Stockholm. Runnng time, **80 MINS.**

Film version of the w.k. play fails to improve upon the original despite an excellent cast which includes some of Sweden's best actors. Although stars Ingrid Backlin and Ake Gronberg are an interesting combination it's obvious that they will be seen to better advantage in a film of more merit than "Stiliga Augusta." With a fair run anticipated at Swedish theatres, comedy is too slowly paced to offer much interest for the U. S.

"Medan Porten var Stangd" ("While the Doors Were Closed") **(SWEDISH).** Europa Film release of Hasse Ekman production. Stars Ekman, Tollie Zellman, Olof Winnerstrand; features Goesta Cederlund, Douglas Hage, Hjoerdis Petterson, Marianne Loefgren, Gunn Wallgren, Gunnar Bjoernstrand, Inga Landgre. Direction and screenplay by Ekman. Camera, Harald Berglund. At Saga, Stockholm. Running time, **96 MINS.**

Reaching into the world-trade class, writer-producer-director-actor Hasse Ekman has turned out a creditable film dealing with varied characters in a house and what happened to them after the doors were closed. He does well as the star and shines in several scenes with young Inga Landgre. Lensing achieves same top-drawer standards as Ekman's direction and cast's thesping. A hit in Scandinavia, pic is a good bet for the U. S. as well.

Miniature Reviews

"Boomerang" (20th). Thrilling fact-fiction melodrama with high boxoffice content. Told in semi-documentary style.

"Songs of Scheherazade" (Songs; color) (U-I.) Costumer with music of Rimsky-Korsakoff for customer appeal.

"Dead Reckoning" (Col.). Satisfying whodunit with Humphrey Bogart, Lizabeth Scott; good boxoffice.

"The Shop At Sly Corner" (British-Lion). Picturization of London legit hit dubious b.o. factor for American market.

"Trail to San Antone" (Songs) (Rep). Routine Gene Autry fare.

"Wild Country" (PRC). Dull oatuner in the Eddie Dean series.

"I Live As I Please" (Superfilm) (Italian-made). Weak operatic film slated only for Italian-language patrons.

Boomerang

Hollywood, Jan. 25.

20th-Fox release of Louis de Rochemont production. Stars Dana Andrews; features Jane Wyatt, Lee J. Cobb, Cara Williams, Arthur Kennedy, Sam Levene, Taylor Holmes, Robert Keith, Ed Legley. Directed by Elia Kazan. Screenplay, Richard Murphy; based on an article by Anthony Abbot, published in Reader's Digest; camera, Norbert Brodine; music, David Buttolph; editor, Harmon Jones. Tradeshown in Los Angeles, Jan. 24, '47. Running time, **87 MINS.**

Henry L. Harvey	Dana Andrews
Mrs. Harvey	Jane Wyatt
Chief Robinson	Lee J. Cobb
Irene Nelson	Cara Williams
John Waldron	Arthur Kennedy
Woods	Sam Levene
Wade	Taylor Holmes
McCreery	Robert Keith
Harris	Ed Begley
Crossman	Philip Coolidge
Cary	Lester Lonergan
Whitney	Lewis Leverett
Sgt. Dugan	Barry Kelley
Mr. Rogers	Richard Garrick
Lt. White	Karl Malden
James	Ben Lackland
Annie	Helen Carew
Father Lambert	Wyrley Birch
Rev. Gardiner	Johnny Stearns
Cartucci	Guy Thomajan
Mrs. Lukash	Lucia Seger
Dr. Rainsford	Dudley Sadler
Mayor Swayze	Walter Greaza
Miss Manion	Helen Hatch
Mr. Lukash	Joe Kazan
Miss Roberts	Ida McGuire
O'Shea	George Petrie
Callahan	John Carmody
Judge Tate	Clay Clement
McDonald	E. J. Ballantine
Stone	William Challee
Coroner	Edgar Stehli
Bill	Jimmy Dobson
Sheriff	Lawrence Paquin
Warren	Anthony Ross
Herron	Bert Freed
Johnson	Royal Beal

"Boomerang" is gripping, real-life melodrama, told in semi-documentary style. It's the third such fact-fiction production by Louis de Rochemont for 20th-Fox release and carries plenty of entertainment punch for all situations. Based on a still unsolved murder case in Bridgeport, Conn., plot is backed up with strong cast and exploitation values to make it thoroughly saleable as suspenseful, thrilling whodunit.

Dana Andrews heads the convincing cast and furnishes a stout marquee name. His role is realistic and a top performance job. While carrying a fictional name as state's attorney, the role, in real life, has its counterpart in Homer Cummings, who went on from the state post to become Attorney-General of the United States. Case on which plot is based deals with murder of a Bridgeport priest and how the prosecuting attorney establishes the innocence of the law's only suspect. No attempt is made to fasten a phoney ending on tale, picture leaving case still unsolved as in real life.

Richard Murphy's script gives Elia Kazan's direction a solid foundation. All the leads have the stamp of authenticities. The dialog and situations further the factual technique.

Lee J. Cobb shows up strongly as chief detective, harassed by press and politicians alike while trying to carry out his duties. Jane Wyatt has only a few scenes as the wife of Andrews but makes them count. Arthur Kennedy is great as the law's suspect. Cara Williams, Sam Levene, Taylor Holmes, Robert Keith, Ed Begley and others reflect careful casting.

Lensing was done on location at Stamford, Conn., the locale adding to realism that features entire production. Credit for ace camera work goes to Norbert Brodine. Other contributions are in keeping with the general excellence. *Brog.*

Song of Scheherazade

(SONGS; COLOR)

Hollywood, Jan. 25.

Universal-International release of Edward Kaufman production (associate producer, Edward Dodds). Stars Yvonne DeCarlo, Brian Donlevy, Jean Pierre Aumont; features Eve Arden, Philip Reed, John Qualen, Charles Kullman. Written and directed by Walter Reisch. Story inspired by N. Rimsky-Korsakoff music; camera (Technicolor), Hal Mohr, William V. Skall; editor, Frank Goss; musical adaptation and direction, Miklos Rozsa; lyrics, Jack Brooks; choreography, Tillie Losch. Previewed in Hollywood, Jan. 24, '47. Running time, **105 MINS.**

Cara	Yvonne De Carlo
Captain	Brian Donlevy
Rimsky-Korsakoff	Jean Pierre Aumont
Madame de Talavera	Eve Arden
Prince Mischetsky	Philip Reed
Dr. Klin	Charles Kullman
Lorenzo	John Qualen
Lieutenant	Richard Lane
Lorin	Terry Kilburn
Pierre	George Dolenz
Fioretta	Elena Verdugo
Hassan	Robert Kendall
Sultan	Rex Ravelle
Orderly	Mickey Simpson
Giant	Sol Haines
Little Sister	Florene Rozen

Students: William Brooks, Leonard East, Edward Kelly, Russ Vincent, Peter Varney, Charles Robertson, Tom Skinner, Warren W. McCollum, Ernie Mishens, Marvin Press, Fred K. Hartsock, Gordon Arnold, Bill Cabanne, Don Garner, George Holmes

Basso	Milio Sheron
Native Girl	Patricia Alphin
French Girl	Joan Fulton

The music of N. Rimsky-Korsakoff and eye value of brilliant color give "Song of Scheherazade" entertainment elements not otherwise found in the fluffy, ineptly directed and played story. Production dress has plenty of sight appeal by virtue of magnificent color lensing by Hal Mohr and William V. Skall. Score contains 10 Rimsky-Korsakoff tunes, ably adapted to the screen by Miklos Rozsa. Three, with lyrics by Jack Brooks, get the benefit of Charles Kullman's fine tenor voice.

Basis for display of composer's music is his supposed escapades during a week in Spanish Morocco. Story has a comic-opera flavor, and Walter Reisch's direction of his own script often wavers in the treatment of plot elements and characters. Adding to ludicrous spots are a variety of accents, topped by the Broadway-ese and 20th century flippancy tossed into the 1865 period by Eve Arden. Plot purports to be based on an incident in Rimsky-Korsakoff's life, when he was a midshipman in the Russian navy, and is aimed at showing the influence the background had on his music.

Jean Pierre Aumont plays the young composer. Yvonne DeCarlo is the Spanish dancer with whom he falls in love during the week's adventuring. Miss DeCarlo has three dance numbers, terped to musical accompaniment of "Gypsy Song," "Fandango" and "Scheherazade." Latter is elaborately staged for the finale. Charles Kullman is seen as the ship's doctor who encourages the composer. Role gives him chance to highlight "Song of India," "Hymn to the Sun," both with new lyrics by Jack Brooks, and "Fandango."

Brian Donlevy does a chain-smoking captain of the training ship who tries to make his students the pride of the Russian navy. Philip Reed is a Russian prince and midshipman. Reed and Aumont are called upon to stage a whip duel, only spot of action in the footage, and not too exciting at that, over the favor of Miss De-Carlo. Miss Arden is Miss DeCarlo's wise-cracking mother, who lives a fashionable life while her daughter supports the family by dancing incognito in a waterfront cafe. Richard Lane, ship's lieutenant; John Qualen and others in the cast do their best with characters.

The Edward Kaufman production has been beautifully dressed.

Brog.

Dead Reckoning
(ONE SONG)

Columbia release of Sidney Biddell production. Stars Humphrey Bogart, Lizabeth Scott; features Morris Carnovsky, Charles Cane, William Prince, Marvin Miller, Wallace Ford. Directed by John Cromwell. Screenplay, Oliver H. P. Garrett and Steve Fisher, from adaptation by Gerald Adams and Sidney Biddell of story by Allen Rivkin; camera, Leo Tover; editor, Gene Havlick; song, Allan Roberts and Doris Fisher; musical score, Marlin Skiles. At Criterion, N. Y., Jan. 23, '47. Running time, 100 MINS.

Rip Murdock	Humphrey Bogart
Coral Chandler	Lizabeth Scott
Martinelli	Morris Carnovsky
Lieutenant Kincaid	Charles Cane
Johnny Drake	William Prince
Krause	Marvin Miller
McGee	Wallace Ford
Father Logan	James Bell
Louis Ord	George Chandler
Lt. Col. Simpson	William Forrest
Hyacinth	Ruby Dandridge

Humphrey Bogart's typically tense performance raises this average whodunit quite a few notches. Film has good suspense and action, and some smart direction and photography. Despite occasional slowdowns or a mawkish bit, pic will satisfy the mystery fans. It should do okay.

Columbia borrowed Bogart from Warners to play the role of a tough ex-paratrooper captain returning home with a pal to be honored by the War Dep't. for their achievements. When the pal jumps the D. C. train, to go home instead, the perplexed captain follows to find himself enmeshed in gangland, murders and romance. His pal, he learns, had enlisted under an alias because he was convicted of a killing. Two days after said pal arrives home, he gets bumped off.

Determined to solve the mystery and avenge his friend, the captain digs into his pal's haunts. He meets up with the nitery singer the pal loved, and with the tough club operator who has some mysterious hold on the girl as well as some vague part in the friend's disappearance. Bogart's interference brings about another death, several beatings to himself from the club-owner's gang, and a love-affair between singer and paratrooper, before the several mysteries are unveiled and the stories jelled. Gunplay and chase figure in the proceedings to heighten the interest. Script uses a flashback method for part of the telling, to add variety.

Bogart absorbs one's interest from the start as a tough, quick-thinking ex-skyjumper. Lizabeth Scott stumbles occasionally as the nitery singer, but on the whole gives a persuasive, sirenish performance. Morris Carnovsky is suavely unscrupulous as the gang chief, and Marvin Miller sufficiently sadistic as his somewhat shellshocked henchman. George Chandler and Charles Cane are realistic in supporting roles, while Wallace Ford makes a real portrait out of a safecracker bit.

John Cromwell's direction is sure and smooth, except where the script occasionally falters. Camera work of Leo Tover has some unusual shots and is uniformly good. Song,

"Either It's Love Or It Isn't," sung by Miss Scott, has the appealing, sultry quality to suit the film's mood.

Bron.

The Shop at Sly Corner
(BRITISH-MADE)

London, Jan. 23.

British Lion release of George King production. Stars Oscar Homolka, Derek Farr, Muriel Pavlow. Directed by George King. Music by George Melachrino. Screenplay by Katherine Strueby, from play by Edward Percy; additional dialog, Reginald Long. Camera, Hone Glendinning. At Studio One, London, Jan. 22, '47. Running time, 91 MINS.

Descius Heiss	Oscar Homolka
Robert Graham	Derek Farr
Margaret Heiss	Muriel Pavlow
Archie Fellowes	Kenneth Griffith
Corder Morris	Manning Whiley
Mrs. Catt	Kathleen Harrison
Major Elliot	Garry Marsh
Professor Vanetti	Jan Van Loewen
Ruby Towser	Irene Handl
Inspector Robson	Johnnie Schofield

Biggest boxoffice asset of this picture is fact that play, on which it is based, has run in London's West End for over two years. Absence of Oscar Homolka from screen for considerable period makes marquee value problematical. Picture will have to rely mainly on word-of-mouth and a 15-minute cut would speed up story and help considerably. Film gathers pace and is truly cinematic in the second half, but the first part is deadly slow and too explanatory without explaining much. More, too, should have been made of the romance between the two young lovers. This part of the story is unworthy of the talents of Derek Farr and Muriel Pavlow.

Homolka plays Heiss, the kindly old Frenchman, owner of an antique shop at Sly Corner, apparently interested only in beautiful things and the violin playing of his daughter. But now and again stolen jewels find their way to Sly Corner and Archie Fellowes, assistant in the shop, discovers that Heiss is an escaped prisoner from Devil's Island. Threatening to reveal this to the daughter, Archie systematically blackmails the old man, and climax comes when the young scoundrel decides he wants to marry the girl. Heiss strangles the blackmailed and, with the help of a friendly crook, dumps the body, which is discovered by the police. Scotland Yard takes up the chase, which ends in a box in a concert hall. Heiss commits suicide while his daughter is winning laurels playing the Mendelssohn Concerto.

Homolka gives an excellent performance as the shrewd, kindly fence. He makes real his love for his daughter and his passion for beautiful things. Kenneth Griffith reenacts his stage part and needs toning down for the screen. Derek Farr and Muriel Pavlow could do no more than they did with their nebulous parts, and two character gems come, as usual, from Kathleen Harrison and Irene Handl.

Direction is competent and production has a nice quality. Frederick Grinke was responsible for the violin playing of the Mendelssohn Concerto and Schubert's Ave Maria.

Picture should play to profitable business here, and may fit into dual spots in America where Homolka's name may draw.

Cane.

Trail to San Antone
(SONGS)

Republic release of Armand Schaefer production. Stars Gene Autry; features Peggy Stewart, Sterling Holloway, William Henry. Directed by John English; original screenplay, Jack Natteford, Luci Ford; songs, Deuce Spriggens, Sid Robin, Joe Burke, Marty Symes, Spade Cooley, Cindy Walker, Autry; camera, William Bradford; editor, Charles Craft. Tradeshown in N. Y., Jan. 24, '47. Running time, 67 MINS.

Gene Autry	Gene Autry
Kit Barlow	Peggy Stewart
Droopy Stearns	Sterling Holloway
Rick Malloy	William Henry
Ted Malloy	John Duncan
Cal Young	Tristram Coffin
The "Commodore"	Dorothy Vaughan
Sheriff Jones	Edward Keane
Sam	Ralph Peters
Themselves	Cass County Boys and Champion

"San Antone" is standard fare for the oatuner circuit. Made from the pat formula of Gene Autry vehicles, pic canters along a simple story line with a full quota of cow-crooning and a moderate amount of knuckle-scraping and hoofbeating. Photography is marked by some exceptional scenic shots but production dress in general is at the usual level for low-budgeters.

In this one, Autry plays a horse breeder who's concerned with the rehabilitation of a crippled jockey. Pic's villain is a wild stallion that breaks into the stables and leads astray the mare entry in the big race. Introducing a postwar note into westerners, Autry conducts his search for the horses via airplane and, in a climax that won't be believed even though seen, lassos the stray horse from the air. Windup is a stock racetrack sequence ending in a photo-finish for plenty of excitement. Hardly discernible thread of romance between Autry and a neighboring femme rancher never intrudes long enough to slow the action.

Autry registers okay in the action sequences and handles three vocals in his usual style, with the Cass County trio backing up nicely. Peggy Stewart as the heart interest is a looker but not given much to do. Sterling Holloway furnishes the comic angles in broad enough manner for easy absorption. Rest of the cast is adequate.

Herm.

Wild Country
(SONGS)

PRC release of Jerry Thomas production. Stars Eddie Dean; features Roscoe Ates, Peggy Wynn, Douglas Fowley. Directed by Ray Taylor. Screenplay, Arthur E. Orloff; camera, Robert Cline; songs, Dean, Hal Blair, Pete Gates; editor, Hugh Winn. Reviewed in N. Y., Jan. 22, '47. Running time, 60 MINS.

Eddie Dean	Eddie Dean
Soapy	Roscoe Ates
Martha Devery	Peggy Wynn
Clark Varney	Douglas Fowley
Rif Caxton	I. Stanford Jolley
Josh Huckings	Lee Roberts
Sam	Forrest Mathews
Spindle	Bill Fawcett
Marshall Thayer	Henry Hall
Brown	Charles Jordan
First Guard	Richard Cramer
Dilling	Gus Taute
The Sunshine Boys	Themselves

With a slow story and indifferent acting, the latest in the Eddie Dean series is considerably below the standard of its predecessors. Sagebrusher appears headed for the lower half of double bills.

Replete with such dialog gems as "they must've taken the short cut," "Wild Country" deals with Dean, a U. S. marshal, and his pal Soapy (Roscoe Ates), who track down Stan Jolley, an escaped convict who kills the sheriff responsible for his time in stir. Conniving with the local tavernkeeper (Douglas Fowley), Jolley conspires to knock off Peggy Wynn, daughter of the late sheriff, and take over her ranch, but Dean foils the thugs, of course. Trite story is not improved by three so-so tunes.

Acting of Peggy Wynn is amateurish. Dean and Ates are adequate while Fowley and Jolley register. Production values are in keeping with the low budget.

I Live As I Please
(ITALIAN-MADE)

Superfilm release of S. A. Grande Film production. Stars Ferruccio Tagliavini; features Silvana Jachino, Carlo Campanini, Margherita Seglin, Carlo Michelussi. Directed by Carlo Bugiani. Story, Mario Mat-

toli; camera, Rodolfo Lombardi. At Cinema Verdi, N. Y. Running time, 87 MINS.

(In Italian; English Titles)

Except for houses catering to Italian-language patrons, this pic is no b.o. factor in the U. S. Music lovers may derive some satisfaction from the highly-touted operatic tenor of Ferruccio Tagliavini, but that's the sole commendable aspect of this film.

Hackneyed story is framed within a primitive production that's marked by poor thesping, mediocre camera and just passable sound recording. English titles are adequate.

Tagliavini plays an operatically-inclined peasant who's made the victim of a practical joke by his brother and gets packed off to Rome, where he thinks an opera contract is awaiting him. He discovers the hoax but makes good regardless. Rich and famous, he returns to his native village and marries his erstwhile music teacher.

Herm.

Miniature Reviews

"The Late George Apley" (20th). Ronald Colman starred in boxoffice-puller, adaptation of stage hit.

"Smash-Up—the Story of a Woman" (Songs) (U-I). Susan Hayward as a dipso in lush Walter Wanger production; good b.o.

"Easy Come, Easy Go" (Par) Mild Irish comedy best suited for smaller family houses.

"Nora Prentiss" (WB). Dull melodrama with name of Ann Sheridan to help at boxoffice.

"Johnny O'Clock" (Col). Smart whodunit, with Dick Powell, should register at the b.o.

"The Brasher Doubloon". (20th). Mediocre whodunit based on Raymond Chandler novel.

"A Yank in Rome" (World Wide). Bi-lingual, Italian-made romantic comedy is okay entertainment; should do well.

"The Red House" (UA). Leisurely - paced psychological thriller with Edward G. Robinson. Fair b.o. draw.

"It Happened on 5th Avenue" (Songs) (Allied Artists). Comedy-drama launches upper-bracket Monogram co.; good b.o.

"Boy! What a Girl" (musical) (Herald). All-Negro tunepic strictly for houses catering to that type clientele.

The Late George Apley

20th-Fox release of Fred Kohlmar production. Stars Ronald Colman; features Vanessa Brown, Richard Haydn, Charles Russell, Richard Ney, Edna Best, Mildred Natwick, Percy Waram, Nydia Westman and Peggy Cummins. Directed by Joseph L. Mankiewicz. Screenplay, Philip Dunne, from Broadway play by John P. Marquand and George S. Kaufman, based on Pulitzer prize novel by Marquand; camera, Joseph La Shelle; editor, James B. Clark; music, Cyril J. Mockridge; music director, Alfred Newman; special photographic effects, Fred Bersen. Tradeshown in N. Y., Jan. 30, '47. Running time, **93 MINS.**

George Apley	Ronald Colman
Eleanor Apley	Peggy Cummins
Agnes	Vanessa Brown
Horatio Willing	Richard Haydn
Howard Boulder	Charles Russell
John Apley	Richard Ney
Catherine Apley	Edna Best
Amelia Newcombe	Mildred Natwick
Roger Newcombe	Percy Waram
Jane Willing	Nydia Westman
Wilson	Francis Pierlot
Margaret	Kathleen Howard
Julian Dole	Paul Harvey
Lydia	Helen Freeman
Chestnut Vendor	Theresa Lyon
Henry Apley	William Moran
Charles	Clifford Brooke
Manager of Modiste Shop	David Bond
Madame of Modiste Shop	Ottola Nesmith
Policeman	J. Pat Moriarity

John P. Marquand's story of Boston manners and high morals, which achieved a considerable success as a novel and later as a Broadway stage play, now emerges as humorous satire for the screen. "Apley" as a film, perhaps, has not the bite of the play and book, but it has enough to satisfy the boxoffice.

Marquand's yarn, which he and George S. Kaufman adapted for Broadway a couple of seasons ago, is basically the same as the book and play. And it's something of which Boston may well be conscious. For Marquand lampoons Bostonians, circa 1912, with a bite and relish that leaves them hanging on the ropes. Beacon street could never have been like this!

"Apley" deals with a Beacon street family of that name, whose paternal elder is more concerned with being elected to the Blue Hill Bird Watchers' directorate, or fighting the erection of a giant Grape-Nuts electric sign on the Common, than anything of a more radical nature. In short, nothing ever really happens to the Apleys.

George Apley does the same things his father did before him, and his father's father before him. And all staunch Harvard men. The family's horrors are Yale, Worcester and some foreign place called New York City.

The Apleys have a son and daughter, and the yarn's conflict arises when the boy is discovered to be secretly wooing a girl from, of all places, Worcester. As if it isn't bad enough that the daughter goes for a Yale instructor, it seems he's also from New York. However, since the Old Eli lad quotes freely from Emerson—George Apley's favorite—that partially vindicates him, and ultimately helps pave the way for the young lovers. The son is less fortunate; he has to wed a girl of his own class, thereby emphasizing the thought that he, too, will go on bird-watching and, probably, eating Post-Toasties because of that Grape-Nuts sign.

Ronald Colman is playing the Apley elder, the part created for the theatre by Leo G. Carroll. Colman is handling the role with less sharpness than Carroll, whose characterization produced a dryness that gave the caricature a particularly high comedy content. Peggy Cummins, in her first American film part, plays the daughter excellently. A piquant blonde looker with an elf-like figure, Miss Cummins performs with considerable vigor and authority. Richard Ney is the son, conveying the stodginess into which, as the picture unfolds, he's being relegated.

Lesser performances are all satisfactory, namely those of Edna Best, the mother; Richard Haydn, Vanessa Brown, Charles Russell, Mildred Natwick, and Percy Waram.

Joseph L. Mankiewicz has directed for pace; the Fred Kohlmar production accoutrements are all high-grade, both sharply emphasizing what occasionally verges on the burlesque. Yale men, no doubt.

Kahn.

Smash Up—The Story of a Woman
(SONGS)

Universal-International release of Walter Wanger production. Stars Susan Hayward, Lee Bowman; features Marsha Hunt, Eddie Albert, Carl Esmond. Directed by Stuart Heisler. Screenplay, John Howard Lawson, based on story by Dorothy Parker, Frank Cavett; camera, Stanley Cortez; editor, Milton Carruth; songs, Jimmy McHugh and Harold Adamson; Jack Brooks and Edgar Fairchild; music, Daniele Amfitheatrof. Tradeshown in N. Y., Feb. 4, '46. Running time, **103 MINS.**

Angie	Susan Hayward
Ken Conway	Lee Bowman
Martha Gray	Marsha Hunt
Steve	Edde Albert
Dr. Lorenz	Carl Esmond
Mr. Elliott	Carleton Young
Mike Dawson	Charles D. Brown
Miss Kirk	Janet Murdoch
Edwards	Tom Chatterton
Angelica	Sharyn Payne
Mr. Gordon	Robert Shayne
Emcee	Larry Blake
Wolf	George Meeker
Farmer	Erville Alderson

"Smash-up—The Story of a Woman" delineates the disintegration of a woman's character because of liquor and, as such, will undoubtedly be compared to "Lost Weekend." While it's not the classic that "Weekend" was, mostly because of a weaker story, it's still a highly-interesting and capable job that should do good biz in all situations. Marquee lure isn't too bright but exhibs will capitalize from good word-of-mouth, especially from the distaffers.

Just as Ray Milland achieved his greatest prominence because of "Weekend," Susan Hayward gets her biggest break to date in this one. Under the competent direction of Stuart Heisler, Miss Hayward handles a difficult thesping job with ease and assurance, faltering only where the story bogs down. Pixie quality and her beauteous looks enhance greatly her characterization of the gal who becomes a dipso to overcome an inferiority complex.

Any drawbacks to "Smash-Up" can be traced to John Howard Lawson's screenplay, based on an original story by Dorothy Parker and Frank Cavett. Tale has Miss Hayward as a successful nitery chanteuse who gives up her career to marry a struggling young singer. His break finally comes, and his popularity sprouts a la Sinatra but, in his effort to give his wife everything she wants, he takes away all her feeling of usefulness to him and their child. Already mildly addicted to drink because of stage-fright, she begins seeking constant refuge in the stuff until she's a good case for the alcoholic ward. Her misunderstanding husband finally sues for divorce. Near-tragedy snaps her out of the dipso stages and the two are reconciled.

Role of the husband, played by Lee Bowman, is overdrawn, since it's difficult to believe he could see his wife sink so low and not try to discover why. And several of the other characters are not too sharply defined. Cast, though overshadowed for the most part by Miss Hayward, does well. Bowman is miscast as the husband but gets as much as he can from the role. Eddie Albert is excellent as the understanding friend, and Marsha Hunt, as the other woman, handles an unsympathetic part nicely. Carl Esmond does okay as the medico.

Film introes three new songs by Jimmy McHugh and Harold Adamson, two of which are already known through records and radio. Duo, "Life Can Be Beautiful" and "Hush-a-Bye Island," are in the "Hit Parade" league. Third, "I Miss That Feeling," is equally good but is underplayed. There are also two cowboy songs by Jack Brooks and Edgar Fairchild.

Production mountings are up to Wanger's usual lush standards. Stanley Cortez' camera work is outstanding and the incidental music by Daniele Amfitheatrof excellent.

Stal.

Easy Come, Easy Go

Hollywood, Jan. 30.

Paramount release of Kenneth Macgowan production. Stars Barry Fitzgerald, Diana Lynn, Sonny Tufts; features Dick Foran, Frank McHugh, Allen Jenkins, John Litel, Arthur Shields, Frank Faylen. Directed by John Farrow. Screenplay, Francis Edwards Faragoh, John McNulty and Anne Froehlick, based on sketches by McNulty; camera, Daniel L. Fapp; process photography, Farciot Edouart; music, Roy Webb; editor, Thomas Scott. Tradeshown in Los Angeles, Jan. 31, '47. Running time, **77 MINS.**

Martin L. Donovan	Barry Fitzgerald
Connie Donovan	Diana Lynn
Kevin O'Connor	Sonny Tufts
Dale Whipple	Dick Foran
Carey	Frank McHugh
Nick	Allen Jenkins
Tom Clancy	John Litel
Mike Donovan	Arthur Shields
Boss	Frank Faylen
Harry Weston	James Burke
Gilligan	George Cleveland
Angela Orange	Ida Moore
Priest	Rhys Williams
Bookie	Oscar Rudolph

There's not too much reason for "Easy Come, Easy Go." As a consequence, it's not always amusing and will have to depend upon cast names to get by. Best reception will be recorded in smaller firstruns and from family trade.

It's an Irish caricature of a son of the auld sod who lives for the horses. Barry Fitzgerald's authentic Irish is a natural for the role, but most of the other players are padded in and mean little to the overall effect.

Kenneth Macgowan produced on an apparently modest budget, and John Farrow directed. As far as story values go, the team did an expert job. There are laughs, the running time is reasonable, and plot mildly interesting. Fitzgerald is a Third avenue Irishman who has to bet the ponies. He is always looking for the pot of gold at the payoff window. His multitude of creditors, continual borrowing of $2 bets and interference in his daughter's romance carry the light plot along.

Francis Edward Faragoh, John McNulty and Ann Froelick scripted, basing the screenplay of sketches by McNulty. Since racial caricatures are currently meeting with group displeasure there might be some minor squawks on "Easy Come, Easy Go," but the general effect is so mild that no offense should be taken.

Fitzgerald is good in his role. Diana Lynn, his long-suffering daughter, has some good moments. Sonny Tufts is a returned Seabee who dares love the daughter of Martin L. Donovan. Dick Foran, Frank McHugh, Allen Jenkins, John Litel, Arthur Shields, Frank Faylen and others have little to do.

Daniel L. Fapp's lensing measures up, and other credits are workmanlike jobs.

Brog.

Nora Prentiss
(SONGS)

Hollywood, Feb. 4.

Warners release of William Jacobs production. Stars Ann Sheridan, Kent Smith, Bruce Bennett; features Robert Alda, Rosemary DeCamp, John Ridgely, Robert Arthur, Wanda Hendrix. Directed by Vincent Sherman. Screenplay, N. Richard Nash; from story by Paul Webster and Jack Sobell; camera, James Wong Howe; editor, Owen Marks; songs, Jack Scholl, Eddie Cherkose, M. K. Jerome; music, Franz Waxman. Tradeshown in Los Angeles, Feb. 3, '47. Running time, **110 MINS.**

Nora Prentiss	Ann Sheridan
Dr. Richard Talbot	Kent Smith
Dr. Joel Merriam	Bruce Bennett
Phil Dinardo	Robert Alda
Lucy Talbot	Rosemary DeCamp
Walter Bailey	John Ridgely
Gregory Talbot	Robert Arthur
Bonita Talbot	Wanda Hendrix
Miss Judson	Helen Brown
Fleming	Rory Mallinson
Police Lieutenant	Harry Shannon
District Attorney	James Flavin
Doctor	Douglas Kennedy
Truck Driver	Don McGuire
Policeman	Clifton Young
Nurse	Adele St. Maur

"Nora Prentiss" is an overlong melodrama that will have to depend considerably on Ann Sheridan's draw value. It's a story of romance between a married man and a girl, which offers femme appeal angle as some boxoffice aid. But it's never quite believable. Miss Sheridan makes much of her role but the personal achievement isn't enough to balance general shortcomings. Production has unsympathetic slant for leads and a lack of smoothness. Background is San Francisco and New York, with authentic footage of both sites a physical aide.

Yarn concerns stuffy, middle-aged doctor who falls in love with a night-club singer. To follow his love to New York, the doctor fakes death, destroying the body of a patient who had died in his office and assuming latter's identity. This fact traps him later when he's arrested for killing himself, is convicted and sent to the death house without revealing true identity. While plot is supposedly based on actual insurance case history, script is full of holes that make for featherweight motivation.

Picture needs considerable editing to reduce overlong footage and sharpen draggy pace. Particularly in need of scissoring are repetitious scenes showing the doctor's gradual moral breakdown, which slow reelage to a walk.

Miss Sheridan is the singer, and has two tunes to warble, "Would You Like a Souvenir" and "Who Cares What People Say." Latter is best. Smith is okay dramatically in a part that doesn't hold much water. Bruce Bennett, co-starred, has little to do as a medico friend of Smith's. Robert Alda's role is equally short. Rosemary DeCamp, as Smith's wife, and others in the cast do their best with limited material.

Camera of James Wong Howe takes advantage of physical production appurtenances furnished by William Jacobs. *Brog.*

Johnny O'Clock

Columbia release of Edward G. Nealis production (Milton Holmes, assoc. producer). Stars Dick Powell, Evelyn Keyes; features Lee J. Cobb, Ellen Drew, Nina Foch. Directed by Robert Rossen. Screenplay, Rossen, from original by Milton Holmes; camera, Burnett Guffey; editors, Warren Low, Al Clark. Previewed in N. Y. Jan. 30, '47. Running time, **95 MINS.**

Johnny O'Clock	Dick Powell
Nancy Hobson	Evelyn Keyes
Inspector Koch	Lee J. Cobb
Nelle Marchettis	Ellen Drew
Harriet Hobson	Nina Foch
Guido Marchettis	S. Thomas Gomez
Charlie	John Kellogg
Chuck Blayden	Jim Bannon
Slatternly Woman	Mabel Paige
Hotel Clerk	Phil Brown
Turk	Jeff Chandler
Punchy	Kit Guard

This is a smart whodunit, with attention to scripting, casting and camera-work lifting it above the average. Pic has action and suspense, and certain quick touches of humor to add flavor. Ace performances by Dick Powell, as a gambling house overseer, and Lee J. Cobb, as a police inspector, also up the rating. Film will do biz.

Although the plot follows a familiar pattern, the characterizations are fresh and the performances good enough to overbalance. Dialog is terse and topical, avoiding the sentimental, phony touch. Unusual camera angles come along now and then to heighten interest and momentarily arrest the eye. Strong teamplay by Robert Rossen, doubling as director-scripter, and Milton Holmes, original writer and associate producer, also aids in making this a smooth production. Surprise, perhaps, is Cobb's excellent job as a tough, realistic cop, in an unusual portrait to point up the actor's versatility.

Plot concerns Powell's operation as a junior partner in S. Thomas Gomez's gambling joint, and his allure for the ladies, especially Ellen Drew, the boss's wife. A cop tries to cut into the gambling racket and is murdered. The hatcheck girl, sweet on the cop, is also killed. When the checker's dancer sister (Evelyn Keyes) comes to find out what happened to the girl, she steps into a round of mystery centering about Powell. More shootings and killings enliven the preceedings, as well as a romance between Powell and Miss Keyes, before copper Cobb unwinds the tangle.

Brief bits are etched in as carefully as large parts, as for instance the performance of Mabel Paige as a nosy slattern in the hatchecker murder scene. Camera angles of a group of gamblers, taken from a balcony, or the legs of a couple walking and discussing the mystery, stand out. Powell has a happy assignment as a wise-guy gambler and fills it neatly. Gomez, as his bullheaded superior, does a smooth job. Miss Keyes is attractive and appealing as Powell's sudden-found love, and Miss Drew sufficiently snaky as the faithless wife. Nina Foch, as the hatchecker, and John Kellogg, a bodyguard-valet, handle supporting roles well. Production has the right swank note. *Bron.*

The Brasher Doubloon

20th-Fox release of Robert Bassler production. Stars George Montgomery, Nancy Guild; features Conrad Janis, Roy Roberts, Fritz Kortner, Florence Bates. Directed by John Brahm. Screenplay, Dorothy Hannah; adaptation, Leonard Praskins, from Raymond Chandler novel; camera, Lloyd Ahern; editor, Harry Reynolds. Tradeshown N. Y., Feb. 3, '47. Running time, **72 MINS.**

Marlowe	George Montgomery
Merle Davis	Nancy Guild
Leslie Murdock	Conrad Janis
Lt. Breeze	Roy Roberts
Vannier	Fritz Kortner
Mrs. Murdock	Florence Bates
Blair	Marvin Miller
Morningstar	Houseley Stevenson
Sgt. Spangler	Bob Adler
George Anson	Jack Conrad
Eddie Prue	Alfred Linder
Manager	Jack Overman
Mike	Jack Stoney
Figaro	Ray Spiker
Coroner	Paul Maxey

Fourth and last of the Raymond Chandler novels to be picturized, "The Brasher Doubloon" is a whodunit based on the escapades of that indestructible private investigator, Philip Marlowe. Like its predecessors, this pic is loaded with enough cadavers, tough muggs and mayhem to sustain a modicum of excitement. But it's burdened by colorless scripting that has melted Chandler's tight style into watery prose and a thesping job in the central role that never attains credibility. Pic will be handicapped at the b.o., moreover, by the obscurity of the title.

George Montgomery suffers badly by comparison with the other celluloid Marlowes. Uneasy in his lines, Montgomery is slightly wooden where he should have been steely; for the gumshoe's dry wit and self-confidence, he substitutes cuteness and a boyish swagger. As the femme lead, Nancy Guild registers effectively as the distraught maid in distress despite her overwritten part. Rest of the cast, headed by Conrad Janis, Fritz Kortner and Florence Bates, are adequate in stock roles.

Pic's title refers to a rare coin which Marlowe is assigned to track down after it's been lifted from the collection of a rich old matron. While on its trail, the dick stumbles across the full quota of corpses of various gentry who were also interested in the numismatic sport, and is led into various bang-up encounters with a blackmailing gang.

Merged with the main plot line is the neurotic plight of Miss Guild, who is bonded to the old matron out of fear of being implicated in the murder of the latter's husband. Marlowe clears up the tangle by finding a newsreel shot which accidentally recorded the murder incident. In the complicated skein of events, not much logic is evident, with the pic relying almost exclusively upon a sadistic impulse to carry it along.

Production dress makes the most of a modest budget. John Brahm's direction is straightforward and the photography is good. Close editing keeps the film from lagging but one fight sequence unreels in bumpy fashion. *Herm.*

A Yank in Rome
(ITALIAN-MADE)

World Wide Film release of Lux Film production. Features Valentina Cortese, Leo Dale. Directed by Luigi Zampa. Screenplay, Aldo De Benedetti and Zampa, based on story by Gina Castrignano. At Squire, N. Y., Jan. 31, '47. Running time, **110 MINS.**

Maria	Valentina Cortese
Dick	Leo Dale
Tom	Adolpho Celi
Roberto	Andrea Checchio
Lor Augusto	Paolo Stoppa
Elena	Elli Parvo

(In English and Italian; English Titles)

Italian film industry's first bilingual picture is a compelling comedy romance deftly woven around two GIs who have a week's furlough in Rome. Despite a scanty plot, earnest efforts of one Italian-speaking soldier to win the affection of a shy schoolteacher in the Italian capital has the makings of first-rate entertainment. With 20 minutes judiciously scissored out of its 110 minutes' running time, "A Yank in Rome" should do well in arty houses as well as in theatres located in Italian-speaking situations. Satisfactory English titles clarify the Italian portion of the dialog.

Eager to aid in reconstructing her war-ravished town, schoolteacher Maria (Valentina Cortese) is en route to Rome on a mission to bring back ne'er-do-well Roberto (Andrea Checchi) to his father. If she's successful, his father will pay for the restoration of the town's school and church. GIs Dick and Tom (Leo Dale and Adolpho Celi) introduce themselves, and the former falls heavily for Maria's petite, blonde charms.

An elusive femme, Maria escapes several times in the city but Dick is a persistent suitor. Script cleverly merges a sightseeing tour of Rome with Dick's quest of Maria, and offers carriage driver Lor Augusto (Paolo Stoppa) some amusing lines. One striking scene brings Dick and Maria to St. Peter's, where the Pope himself is seen in the footage. Particularly poignant part is in the final reel, where Maria writes on the blackboard before her moppet class a quotation of Gen. Mark Clark, where he stated: "All we want of Italy is a piece of land to bury our dead."

Acting is generally good and is capped by the wistful, moving performance of Miss Cortese, while Dale registers as her pursuer. His companion, Adolpho Celi, typifies a GI on the loose with little on his mind besides women and liquor. Celi's use of an Italian-English conversational dictionary will be familiar to ex-GIs who have had the misfortune to be in a country where they were unable to understand the language. Rest of cast is adequate. Luigi Zampa's direction is forthright while film's production values are enhanced by fine shots of St. Peter's and other Roman landmarks.

The Red House

United Artists release of Sol Lesser production. Stars Edward G. Robinson, Lon McCallister; features Judith Anderson, Rory Calhoun, Allene Roberts, Julie London, Ona Munson, Harry Shannon. Directed by Delmer Daves. Screenplay by Daves, from novel by George Agnew Chamberlain; camera, Bert Glennon; editor, Merrill White; music, Dr. Miklos Rozsa. Tradeshown in N. Y., Jan. 31, '47. Running time, **100 MINS.**

Pete Morgan	Edward G. Robinson
Nath	Lon McCallister
Ellen	Judith Anderson
Meg	Allene Roberts
Tibby	Julie London
Teller	Rory Calhoun
Mrs. Storm	Ona Munson
Dr. Byrne	Harry Shannon
Officer	Arthur Space
Don Brent	Walter Sande

"The Red House" is an interesting psychological thriller, with its mood satisfactorily sustained throughout the pic. Film, however, has too slow a pace, so that the paucity of incident and action stands out sharply. Despite good performances by Edward G. Robinson, Judith Anderson, Allene Roberts, Lon McCallister and others, modest returns are indicated.

Film has a simple, rustic quality in scripting, setting and characterization. Sound effects are good, such incidents as the terror of a young man lost in mysterious woods being built up admirably. Music, too, is worthy of comment, as an important adjunct in building up and sustaining eerie moods. Outdoor shots are strikingly effective.

Pic, however, is built on a single thread, and takes too long in getting to its climax. It ends on something of a macabre note, and throughout it has several false touches—a muscle-brained young woodsman being in possession of $750; entrusting the money to a flighty girl to buy him a bond with it, etc.

This is the first picture of three in which Robinson is linked with Sol Lesser as (silent) co-producer. Robinson has supplied himself with a fat part that suits his talents and to which he gives his best efforts. He's cast as a farmer, living with a sister and an adopted daughter in an isolated area of a small community, further withdrawn from the community by his strange, gloomy moods. Part of his property is a wooded area to which no one can go; the farmer even employs a young woodsman to keep trespassers out by gunfire if necessary.

A young hired hand comes to work on the farm, is intrigued by the wooded area, and enters it, to meet with several mishaps. With the adopted daughter he finally stumbles on the mystery—a red house where two murders have been committed by the farmer. But solution is found only after the farmer's sister has met her death by trying to burn down the house (and save the brother's mind); the adopted daughter revealed as the child of the long-murdered couple, and the farmer committing suicide by driving his car into a water-pit.

Robinson portrays the quick-tempered, alternately kind and gruff farmer with care and conviction. Judith Anderson, as the sister who sacrifices her own life to stay with the mentally-troubled farmer, gives a strong performance. Allene Roberts is winsomely attractive and appealing as the adopted daughter, and Lon McCallister wholesome and engaging as the young hired hand. Production is modest but adequate. Camera work, especially in outdoor rustic scenes, is fine. *Bron.*

It Happened on 5th Ave.
(SONGS)

Hollywood, Jan. 31.

Monogram release of Allied Artists (Roy Del Ruth) production (associate producer, Joe Kaufman). Stars Don DeFore, Ann Harding; features Charlie Ruggles, Victor Moore, Gale Storm. Directed by Del Ruth. Screenplay, Everett Freeman and Vick Knight, from story by Herbert Clyde Lewis and Frederick Stephani; camera, Henry Sharp; songs, Harry Revel, Paul Webster; assistant director, Frank Fox; editor, Richard Heermance. Previewed Los Angeles, Feb. 1, '47. Running time, **116 MINS.**

Jim	Don DeFore
Mary	Ann Harding
O'Connor	Charlie Ruggles
McKeever	Victor Moore
Trudy	Gale Storm
Farrow	Grant Mitchell
Felton	Edward Brophy
Whitey	Alan Hale, Jr.
Alice	Cathy Carter
Hank	Edward Ryan, Jr.
Margie	Dorothea Kent
Brady	Arthur Hohl
Jackie	Anthony Sydes
Baby	Linda Lee Solomon

"It Happened on 5th Avenue" is the teeoff film for Allied Artists, upper-bracket production company slated to make and distribute Monogram's high-budget features. As an initialer it offers excellent entertainment and boxoffice values.

Film is Roy Del Ruth's first independent production and he realizes on it neatly. Picture is overlong and has some rough edges, but otherwise should be a solid pleaser for general audiences.

While cast names run to youth, it remains for oldtimer Victor Moore to carry the load. His role as a vagabond who uses the wealth of others to lead a life of ease will probably be termed the best yet he has had in films. He makes it a gem that thoroughly clicks in every facet. Another oldtimer, Charlie Ruggles, also makes a bright display of thespian experience, sharing honors with Moore as a sour-pussed rich man who learns that life offers more values than another million dollars.

Plot contains several basic themes that have been neatly correlated in the Everett Freeman script. Problem of housing, returned veterans and their future economic condition, and the evil of close concentration on riches are some of the themes explored. The preachments occasionally slow things down and make for overlength of footage, but it is all so well resolved under Del Ruth's direction that general entertainment is sustained.

Moore is seen as a tramp who moves into the 5th avenue home of Ruggles every winter when latter takes himself off to South Carolina. It's a life of luxury Moore leads.

wearing fine clothes, eating the best of foods, etc., all without the knowledge of the owner. Also, it's a life of no problems until he befriends Don De Fore, ex-vet who is homeless, and takes him into the millionaire's mansion. That slight break in routine has Moore also taking in Gale Storm, daughter of Ruggles but incognito; two GI families, and finally the millionaire and his ex-wife. It's not as confusing as it sounds but the masquerade being played by the rich characters adds much to the comedy.

Romantic angles lie between De Fore and Miss Storm, latter persuading her father and mother to join the masquerade so they will realize the young vet's worth. De Fore and Miss Storm make a strong team that will please. Ann Harding is the mother, whose adventure in honest living brings about a reconciliation with Ruggles. Grant Mitchell, Edward Brophy, Edward Ryan, Jr., Alan Hale, Jr., Abe Reynolds, Dorothea Kent, and others of the cast measure up fully to all demands.

Miss Storm sings three of the four songs included in the score. Numbers are "Speak, My Heart," "It's a Wonderful, Wonderful Feeling," both by Harry Revel, and "You're Everywhere," by Revel and Paul Webster. The ensemble joins in on "That's What Christmas Means to Me." Background vocals are contributed by the Kings Men. Good musical score was done by Edward Ward.

Henry Sharp's camera work is solid, making handsome display of elegant art direction by Lewis Creber and Ray Biltz, Jr.'s, set decorations. Joe Kaufman served as associate producer with Del Ruth on filming of the original story by Herbert Clyde Lewis and Frederick Stephani. Other technical credits are first rate. _Brog._

Boy! What a Girl

(MUSICAL)

Herald pictures release of Jack Goldberg production. Features Tim Moore, Elwood Smith, Duke Williams, Patterson & Jackson, Sheila Guyse. Directed by Arthur Leonard; story, Vincent Valentini; camera, George Webber; editor, Jack Kemp; songs, Walter Bishop, Walter Fuller, Mary Lou Williams, Deek Watson. Previewed in New York, Jan. 30, '47. Running time, 70 MINS.
Bumpsie (The Girl) .... Tim Moore
Jim .... Elwood Smith
Harry .... Duke Williams
Mr. Cummings .... Al Jackson
                                   Sheila Guyse
The Cummings Sisters .... Belli Mays
Madame Deborah .... Sybil Lewis
Mr. Donaldson .... Warren Patterson
The Gang: Slam Stewart, Deek Watson and His Brown Dots, Sid Catlett and Band, Ann Cornell and the International Jitterbugs.

The several hundred Negro film houses in this country have long been faced with a product shortage on race-films, and the newly formed Herald pictures will do something to alleviate the numerical relief. Initial release, "Boy, What a Girl," is along the song-and-dance lines, and, if only on the strength of its vaude and musical names, should provide sufficient playing time on the south end of doubleheaders.

This film is predominantly musical with a cliched, makeshift plot concerning two shoestring producers trying to win backing from a prospective angel with a wad of dough and two daughters. The showmen ultimately nab the coin as well as the girls.

Comedy is entrusted to Tim Moore, as a femme impersonator, while Elwood Smith and Duke Williams, together with Sheila Guyse and Betti Mays, take care of the romantic needs. The vaude and nitery team of Patterson and Jackson aids the comedy with respective characterizations of the angel and landlord, but efforts are generally weak. Forte of the film is its musical sequences.

with Slam Stewart trio, Sid Catlett orch, Ann Cornell and Deek Watson's Brown Dots.

Sets and production indicate the film's low budget. _Jose._

Foreign Films

Offering fair entertainment, this film concerning life in a small Swedish village has been nicely directed and acted. Lensing of Harald Berglund is okay. Should do well in Sweden and draw better than average grosses in U. S. arty houses.

Though this is graced by Mexico's top actress, Maria Felix at her best; has exceptional work by Eugene Rossi in his Mexican pic debut; good photography by Gabriel Figueroa, and high-grade megging by Emilio Fernandez, this story is more for Latin-American than Anglo-American trade.

Pic did sock biz, is setting new house records at the Cine Alameda and is in line for Mexico's best for 1946.

February 12, 1947

Miniature Reviews

"**The Sea of Grass**" (M-G) Marquee-laden cast in filmization of western-backgrounded novel certain for good b.o.

"**Suddenly It's Spring**" (Par). Very bright comedy with star values and entertainment worth. Gratifying b.o. a cinch.

"**The Arnelo Affair**" (M-G). Slick mountings, solid thesping, good marquee, and OK b.o.

"**Michigan Kid**" (U). Satisfactory Cinecolor western with Jon Hall, Victor McLaglen and Rita Johnson.

"**Odd Man Out**" (Two Cities). James Mason in big-prestige, fine-b.o. pic from England.

"**Calendar Girl**" (Musical) (Rep.). Mildly amusing musical.

"**Angel and the Badman**" (Rep). Solid western drama with plenty of appeal for ticketbuyers. B.O. potential stout.

"**Vigilantes of Boomtown**" (Rep). Okay western in the Red Ryder series.

The Sea of Grass

Metro release of Pandro S. Berman production. Stars Spencer Tracy, Katharine Hepburn, Melvyn Douglas, Robert Walker; features Phyllis Thaxter, Edgar Buchanan, Harry Carey. Directed by Elia Kazan. Screenplay by Marguerite Roberts and Vincent Lawrence, based on novel by Conrad Richter; editor, Robert J. Kern; camera, Harry Stradling; score, Herbert Stothart. Previewed in N. Y., Feb. 5, '47. Running time, 122 MINS.
Col. Jim Brewton .... Spencer Tracy
Lutie Cameron .... Katharine Hepburn
Brock Brewton .... Robert Walker
Brice Chamberlain .... Melvyn Douglas
Sarah Beth Brewton .... Phyllis Thaxter
Jeff .... Edgar Buchanan
Doc Reid .... Harry Carey
Selina Hall .... Ruth Nelson
Banty .... Wm. "Bill" Phillips
Floyd McCurtin .... Robert Armstrong
Sam Hall .... James Bell
Judge White .... Robert Barrat
George Cameron .... Charles Trowbridge
Major Harney .... Russell Hicks
Andy Boggs .... Trevor Bardette
Crane .... Morris Ankrum

With Spencer Tracy, Katharine Hepburn, Robert Walker and Melvyn Douglas for the marquee and a strong screen story against a western background. Metro's filmization of this Conrad Richter novel can't fail to drag 'em to the b.o. in large numbers. Because of some hackneyed and cliched writing and direction, it just misses being the real supergrosser it might have been.

Film is loaded with very superior acting and spectacular imaginative photography that are certain to bring strong audience response. Camera work by Harry Stradling is particularly breathtaking in the outdoor sequences for the sense of space and correct feeling it gives to this drama of the New Mexico prairielands.

One of the big hurdles the pic will have to get over, however, is its non-selling title, "The Sea of Grass." Richter's book was hardly well-enough known to merit weighting the film with that title. Be that as it may, it's a telling yarn of a man whose devotion and attachment to that "sea of grass," which makes up the rangeland, stubbornly transcends the true affection he feels for his wife and leads to family tragedy.

Story is built around the traditional American feud between cattlemen and farmers, with Tracy perfect as the iron-jawed leader in the ranchers' determined stand against the inevitable surge westward of the agriculturists whose hoes and fences cut into the ranges on which the huge herds are dependent. Despite the explosive possibilities of this background and the opportunities to

turn the yarn into a real western, the writers keep themselves always in check, never giving an inch in switching the story from family drama to hoss-opry. Had they just let the boys with the six-shooters and the fast mares get away for one good spree of gunpowder and leather-pounding, they could have undoubtedly widened audience-appeal considerably.

Miss Hepburn is pictured as a cultured St. Louis belle who goes to New Mexico to marry range-baron Tracy. His attachment is so great for the "sea of grass" that he has no understanding of his wife's feeling for the farm families whom he is forcing to starvation by illegally keeping them from the land. Douglas, as a lawyer and judge, not only has a feeling for the farmers, but for Miss Hepburn as well, and a natural amity grows between them.

Long arm of coincidence enters in when she finally leaves Tracy and runs into Douglas in Denver. In despair and confusion she gives herself up to him, only to turn remorseful the following day and decide to return to Tracy. A child is born and all concerned realize it is Douglas' not Tracy's. Tracy forces his wife to leave. He raises the boy and a girl that he and Miss Hepburn had previously had. They don't see each other for years. The lad grows into an appealing, but irresponsible young man (Robert Walker), with a great bond between him and Tracy. He gets himself into trouble, because of slurs on his parentage and escapes to the hills, only to be shot by the law. In the meantime, Miss Hepburn returns and, through intervention of the daughter (Phyllis Thaxter), gets together again with Tracy.

Edgar Buchanan as the ranch cook and Harry Carey as the cattle-country medico are as near perfection as the rest of the cast. Shortcoming of the film is the telegraphing ahead of the story and its habit of always falling into the expected pattern. There's never a surprise. Likewise, the cliched dialog is frequently hard to accept. Especially in that scene where Miss Hepburn first apprises Tracy he is to to a father. He puts his hand on her shoulder and says: "Good girl." Whereupon she puts her hand on his shoulder and says: "Good boy!"

Elia Kazan's direction keeps the story well-paced, after getting over some sinking spells during the first half in establishing characters and motivation. While much of the direction is tops for its simplicity and lack of pretension, there are other times when Kazan allows his cast to get perilously near the line between characters and caricatures.

Herbert Stothart's music and producer Pandro Berman's general mounting of the picture are noteworthily in keeping with the yarn itself. _Herb._

Suddenly It's Spring

Hollywood, Feb. 8.

Paramount release of Claude Binyon production. Stars Paulette Goddard, Fred MacMurray; features Macdonald Carey, Arleen Whelan. Directed by Mitchell Leisen. Screenplay, Claude Binyon, P. J. Wolfson; original story, Wolfson; camera, Daniel L. Fapp; score, Victor Young; editor, Alma Macrorie. Tradeshown Feb. 6, '47. Running time, 87 MINS.
Mary Morely .... Paulette Goddard
Peter Morely .... Fred MacMurray
Jack Lindsay .... Macdonald Carey
Floria Fay .... Arleen Whelan
Mary's Mother .... Lilian Fontaine
Harold Michaels .... Frank Faylen
Captain Rogers .... Frances Robinson
Lieut. Billings .... Victoria Horne
Major Cheever .... Georgia Backus
WAC Corp. Michaels .... Jean Ruth
WAC Sergeant .... Roberta Jonay
Porter on Train .... Willie Best

Socko escapist film fare that will please solidly. "Suddenly It's Spring" starts from foundation of a topnotch script, has been aptly cast and directed and given a production gloss that will pay off in all situations.

Names of Paulette Goddard and Fred MacMurray assure marquee brightness. As a film team, they leave nothing to be desired, trouping their slightly zany roles to the hilt for customer satisfaction.

Claude Binyon earns himself smart credits as both producer and collaborator on the script with P. J. Wolfson. In the writing they have projected sound comedy values in both situations and dialog and Mitchell Leisen's direction gives characters broad life for lusty laughs.

Story concerns marital team of lawyers, husband and wife, who had agreed to separate before the war. World strife delays the divorce and script picks them up again just as the WAC wife is returning from overseas. The husband already has his discharge, has fallen for another gal and wants the divorce pronto. His wife has new ideas since her Army service and would like to try again. Fun springs from MacMurray's prodding of Miss Goddard to get her to ink the necessary papers and her continual coy delay. Not unexpected in the finale when the pair decide maybe marriage should be given another try but the build-up to that point and the situations that bridge cram in hearty laughs.

What dialog an audience will be able to hear is strong with laugh content but so easily does situation and line dovetail that many a quip will be lost in audience response of loud guffaws. Adding to the merriment is Macdonald Carey, a wolfish client of MacMurray's who does his darndest to further the divorce so he can make hay with Miss Goddard. Another enjoyable role is that played by Arleen Whelan, the gal who wants MacMurray and nags him on about the signing of the papers. Lilian Fontaine, Frank Faylen, Frances Robinson, Victoria Horne, Georgia Backus, Jean Ruth, Roberta Jonay and Willie Best are others who lend plenty of spark to the proceedings.

Production complement lined up by Binyon turn in fine jobs. Victor Young has contributed a nifty musical score. Daniel L. Fapp's lensing glosses the production dress and the players. Miss Goddard and other femmes have been tastily costumed by Mary Kay Dodson and art direction of Hans Dreier and John Meehan rates a strong credit. *Brog.*

The Arnelo Affair

Metro release of Jerry Bresler production. Stars John Hodiak, George Murphy, Frances Gifford; features Eve Arden, Dean Stockwell, Warner Anderson. Directed by Arch Oboler. Screenplay, Arch Oboler from story by Jane Burr; camera, Charles Salerno; score, George Bassman; editor, Harry Komer. Tradeshown N. Y., Feb. 7, '47. Running time, **86 MINS.**

Tony Arnelo	John Hodiak
Ted Parkson	George Murphy
Anne Parkson	Frances Gifford
Ricky Parkson	Dean Stockwell
Vivian Delwyn	Eve Arden
Sam Leonard	Warner Anderson
Avery Border	Lowell Gilmore
Roger Alison	Michael Branden
Dorothy Alison	Ruth Brady
Maybelle	Ruby Dandridge
Claire Lorrison	Joan Woodbury

Arch Oboler, radio's master of suspense, has effectively transposed his technique into the visual medium with "The Arnelo Affair." Wisely, too, he's combined some of the best of both radio and film methods to build a mood of sustained tension in what may become one of this season's sleepers. Oboler leveled at the boxoffice battlements once before with "Bewitched" and failed even to make a dent; if the walls don't tumble for this one, it's only because the approach is too adult for the average filmgoer. John Hodiak, George Murphy and Dean Stockwell on the marquee will definitely help.

Strictly speaking, this is not a whodunit, nor can it be cataloged as a psychological suspense picture. Frances Gifford, a well-wedded Chicago wife on the eve of her 12th anniversary, finds herself attracted to John Hodiak, nitery owner with a disreputable background who is a client of her lawyer-husband, George Murphy. Subordinated by Murphy to his work, her almost hypnotic fascination for Hodiak drives her to see him daily. When another of Hodiak's amours turns up murdered, she is involved and he uses the situation as a means to bring her to him. A nick-of-time finish gets Hodiak and saves Miss Gifford from suicide.

There's never a question as to who committed the murder, but the crime is secondary to its effect on the characters involved. Until the film's very climax, no hint is given to the ultimate denouement. Only factor spoiling the suspense is the knowledge that the Johnston office will get Hodiak in the end. Dialog instills the feeling of action where none exists for much of the footage, and gab is excellent but for a couple of spots when Oboler gives vent to florid passages.

Credits for this film are about as good as they can get. Thesping of Miss Gifford, a horse opera graduate, marks her for a top dramatic slot in Metro's future book, while Hodiak smartly underplays the nitery op's vicious nature concealed by a genteel gloss. Murphy as the typical American husband, does all that's required, and young Dean Stockwell takes a long step closer to stardom. Surprise of the pic is the quiet, slow-talking detective, limned by Warner Anderson. It's unusual that the police are shown as anything but boobs, and Anderson, as the cop who knows the answer and is waiting patiently for a break, is fine.

Topping the production list is Charles Salerno's camera work. The authentic Chicago backgrounds are perfect and location shots blended well with the entire film. Sets also very good. *Tomm.*

Michigan Kid
(COLOR—SONG)

Universal release of Howard Welsch production. Features Jon Hall, Victor McLaglen, Rita Johnson, Andy Devine. Directed by Ray Taylor. Screenplay, Roy Chanslor, based on Rex Beach's "Michigan Kid"; additional dialog, Robert Presnell, Sr.; song, Jack Brooks and H. J. Salter; camera (Cinecolor), Virgil Miller; editor, Paul Landres; music, Hans J. Salter. Tradeshown N. Y., Feb. 10, '46. Running time, **69 MINS.**

Michigan Kid	Jon Hall
Curley	Victor McLaglen
Sue	Rita Johnson
Buster	Andy Devine
Mr. Porter	Byron Foulger
Sheriff	Stanley Andrews
Lanny	Milburn Splee
Steve	William Brooks
Soubrette	Joan Fulton
Dave	Leonard East
Sergeant	Ray Teal
Shotgun Messenger	Guy Wilkerson
Post Office Clerk	Eddy C. Waller
Sam	Karl Hackett
Hank	Tom Quinn
Rifleman	Bert Le Baron
Joe	Edmund Cobb

With Jon Hall, Victor McLaglen, Rita Johnson and Andy Devine on the marquee, Universal's Cinecolored "Michigan Kid" is a better than average cayuse carnival which should more than satisfy the payees in action situations. Hewing closely to the "Quick, paw! Call the sheriff, the outlaws are comin'!" school, sagebrusher nevertheless is a chase-packed opus which should earn its reward at the b.o.

Blending his ingredients nicely, producer Howard Welsch started this one off at a brisk pace with a diverting saloon scene where soubrette Joan Fulton warbles "Whoops My Dear," the film's only song, along with a line of girls. Mustered out of the Army after campaigning in an Indian war, Jon Hall bids farewell to his buddies William Brooks, Leonard East and Milburn Stone in a riotous free-for-all at the frontier tavern.

An ex-U.S. marshal, Hall hies himself to Rawhide, Arizona, where he plans to ranch it. Riding the stagecoach with driver Andy Devine and a rich passenger, Hall beats off an attack on the stage by road agents led by Victor McLaglen who vows revenge. Killed in the fight, passenger Prentice hides 50 grand in the bushes for his niece Rita Johnson and thereupon hangs a wellspring of jailbreaks, chases and plenty of six-shootin' before culprit McLaglen and his cohorts are brought to justice. A hard-ridin' posse-member succinctly summed things up in general by sagely observing, . . . "that's the trouble with these chases, you never know who's chasing whom."

Jon Hall, in one of his few appearances in hoss oprys, handles his role realistically, while burly Victor McLaglen is unexpectedly meek as the heavy. Rita Johnson, who runs Pearl White a close second in leaping into a roaring torrent, is an appealing heiress. Good-natured Andy Devine seems to be on the wrong side of the tracks as one of McLaglen's henchmen. Handling the directorial reins, Ray Taylor kept the plot moving at a fast pace, and cameraman Virgil Miller rates kudos for his lensing. Cinecolor process tints appear to be improving.

Odd Man Out
(BRITISH-MADE)

London, Feb. 1.

General Film Distributors release of Two Cities Film. Stars James Mason, Robert Newton. Directed by Carol Reed. Screenplay, F. L. Green, R. C. Sherriff, from F. L. Green's novel; camera, Robert Krasker. At Odeon, London. Running time, **116 MINS.**

Johnny	James Mason
Lukey	Robert Newton
Dennis	Robert Beatty
Shell	F. J. McCormick
Rosie	Fay Compton
Maudie	Beryl Measor
Pat	Cyril Cusack
Nolan	Dan O'Herlihy
Theresa	Maureen Delany
Granny	Kitty Kirwan
Alfie	Arthur Hambling
Kathleen	Kathleen Ryan
Head Constable	Dennis O'Dea
Tober	Elwyn Brook Jones
Father Tom	W. G. Fay
Fencie	William Hartnell
Cabby	Joseph Tomelty

With James Mason as marquee name and with the critical raves this film will receive, bigtown and discerning audiences will pay plenty to see it. More problematical is its fate in the sticks, where two hours of unrelieved gloom, with Mason in an unfamiliar character, might prove less acceptable. It will need plenty selling there.

Accent in this film is on art with a capital A.—No concessions to popular taste, no easy laughs to lighten the darkness. Carol Reed has made his film with deliberation and care, and has achieved splendid teamwork from every member of the cast. Occasionally too intent on pointing his moral and adorning his tale, he has missed little in its telling.

Story is set in a city in Northern Ireland and takes place between 4 p.m. and midnight on a winter's day. Johnnie, leader of an organization, sentenced for gun running, has broken gaol and is hiding with his girl Kathleen. He plans a hold-up on a mill to obtain funds, and although deprecating violence, he takes a gun. During the holdup he accidentally kills a man, is badly wounded himself, and the driver of the car panics, leaving Johnnie to fend for himself. Bleeding, he stumbles through the city trying to hide from the police. Some people befriend him, others plan to sell him to the police, who are now trailing Kathleen. She has planned to get Johnnie on board a ship and out of the country.

Visiting a priest to glean news of Johnnie, she gets information from an underworld character and finally contacts the former. But the two lovers are cornered outside the docks and, rather than have him taken by the police, she shoots it out. As midnight strikes two dead bodies are stretched on the street.

For Mason two-thirds of the film is silent. From the moment he is wounded he has few lines and has to drag himself along, a hunted man with a fatal wound. It is hardly his fault that, in this passive character that expresses little more than various phases of pain and occasional delirium, he is less effective than he could be. A scene or two in the early part of the picture should have made the audience realize Johnnie's right to be chief of the organization and what Kathleen meant to him.

Making her screen debut, Kathleen Ryan reveals undoubted ability and much promise. Graduate of the Abbey and Gate theatres, this 24-year-old redhead was "discovered" in Ireland by Reed, who coached and trained her for this part. Her second role is opposite Stewart Granger in "Captain Boycott," an indication that the Rank organization has much faith in her.

Most of the other parts are by the Irish players, as competent a crowd of scene-stealers as ever appeared on the screen. W. G. Fay, a co-founder with W. B. Yeats of the Abbey theatre, gives a fine study as a benevolent priest, and there is no finer acting than that of Cyril Cusack, Abbey actor-producer-manager, who plays the panicky car-driver. Praise too is earned by F. J. McCormick for his petty sneak, Dennis O'Dea as head constable, Joseph Tomelty as a cabby, and Maureen Delany as a stool pigeon.

Of the non-Irish players Robert Newton makes his appearance when the picture is more than halfway through, and Canadian-born Robert Beatty disappears far too soon. Newton gives a characteristic display as the eccentric, unshaven, hard-drinking painter, and Beatty enhances a rapidly-growing reputation with a grand performance as second-in-command to Mason. *Cane.*

Calendar Girl
(MUSICAL)

Hollywood, Feb. 4.

Republic release of Allan Dwan production, directed by Dwan. Stars Jane Frazee, William Marshall, Gail Patrick, Kenny Baker, Victor McLaglen; features Irene Rich, James Ellison, Janet Martin, Franklin Pangborn, Gus Schilling. Screenplay, Mary Loose, Richard Sale, Lee Loeb; original story, Loeb; camera, Reggie Lanning; editor, Fred Allen; musical director, Cy Feuer; orchestrations, Leo Arnaud; songs, James McHugh, Harold Adamson. Previewed Feb. 4, '47. Running time, **88 MINS.**

Patricia O'Neil	Jane Frazee
Johnny Bennett	William Marshall
Olivia Radford	Gail Patrick
Byron Jones	Kenny Baker
Matthew O'Neil	Victor McLaglen
Lulu Varden	Irene Rich
Steve Adams	James Ellison
Tessie	Janet Martin
Dillingsworth (Dilly)	Franklin Pangborn
Ed Gaskin	Gus Schilling
Captain Olsen	Charles Arnt
Clancy	Lou Nova
The Mayor	Emory Parnell

"Calendar Girl" is featherweight musical that strains for laughs and to put over its songs. Cast is able but encounters plenty of difficulties in trying to put over dull, talky script. Business indications are light.

James McHugh and Harold Adamson contributed seven songs, all listenable. Best two are the little number and "Have I Told You Lately?" Majority of vocal work falls to Jane Frazee and Kenny Baker. Both do a good job of selling tunes. William Marshall and Janet Martin also have vocal moments that listen well.

Plot is laid in New York at the turn of the century and brings central characters together in a boarding house operated by Irene Rich. It's the usual group of young hopefuls trying to win fame and fortune. Despite the many tunes, most of the action is resolved into much trite dialog that's not easy on the ears, as scripted by Mary Loos, Richard Sale and Lee Loeb from latter's original.

Title derives from work of James Ellison, rich young artist, who does calendar portrait of Miss Frazee. Art work and Ellison's character also cause conflict in the romance between girl and Marshall, a struggling composer, but everything comes out as expected in the finale. Best comedy work falls to Baker and Janet Martin. Miss Rich is good as the kindly landlady and Victor McLaglen displays two-fisted Irish fireman character. Gail Patrick has small spot as rich Boston society femme. Others come up to expectations.

As producer-director, Allan Dwan doesn't always display a sure hand. Dialog corn is directorial hindrance. Physical appurtenances are good. Lensing by Reggie Lanning and other technical credits are expert.
Brog.

Angel and the Badman
(ONE SONG)

(ONE SONG)
Hollywood, Feb. 8.
Republic release of John Wayne production. Stars John Wayne, Gail Russell; features Harry Carey, Bruce Cabot, Irene Rich, Lee Dixon. Written and directed by James Edward Grant. Second unit director, Yakima Canutt; camera, Archie J. Stout; editor, Harry Keller; score, Richard Hageman; music director, Cy Feuer. Previewed Feb. 5, '47. Running time, 100 MINS.
Quirt Evans ....John Wayne
Prudence Worth ....Gail Russell
Wistful McClintock ....Harry Carey
Laredo Stevens ....Bruce Cabot
Mrs. Worth ....Irene Rich
Randy McCall ....Lee Dixon
Johnny Worth ....Stephen Grant
Dr. Mangrum ....Tom Powers
Carson ....Paul Hurst
Bradley ....Olin Howlin
Thomas Worth ....John Halloran
Lila ....John Barton
Ward Withers ....Craig Woods
Nelson ....Marshall Reed

Big-time western drama has resulted from John Wayne's first production effort. "Angel and the Badman" is solid entertainment way above what might be expected on its western locale and characters. It's loaded with sharp performances, honest writing and direction. The grosses should be strong. Marquee lineup, headed by the Wayne name, offers plenty of strength for selling and entertainment values are broad enough to cover all types of situations.

On the production end, Wayne had paid particular attention to casting of the characters that people the James Edward Grant story. Latter, also a director, make the roles live in his writing. These factors set the pace for the honesty and realism that make "Angel" stand out. Wayne wins plaudits in his role as producer and star, as does Grant for dual function as writer and director.

Faith, religious or otherwise, provides the motivation for reformation of a badman. Picture equals worth of others that have depicted a religious faith and, essentially, is more honest in characterization. Story essentials deal with a hot gunman of the early west who is succored by a family of Quakers when he falls wounded on its doorstep. There is a gradual absorption of the family's formula for living by the bad man,

and in the end he turns to the soil and religion in a perfectly believable manner. Reformation is achieved not only through his love for the daughter of the Quaker family but through gradual realization that the faith of the Friends is a solid basis for achievement of happiness.

On the commercial side, pic overlooks none of the tried and found true formulas of lusty action. There are chases, high pitches of excitement and suspenseful plus beautiful love scenes. Climax is suspense-laden. The story and production pattern of "Angel" gives it flexibility for labeling. Picture can be called a western, a drama, a melodrama, or a love story and will satisfy the varied fans of each thoroughly.

Wayne does his best job since "Stagecoach" as the gunman. Gail Russell has never been seen to better advantage as the frank and honest Quaker girl who falls in love and actually pursues the gunman. Role is played with an intelligent interpretation of the attraction between the sexes. It should advance her career measurably. Harry Carey is another who turns in a performance gem. He makes his sheriff role a stout contributor to the general worth of this feature. Bruce Cabot is another "in character" badman who clicks. Attention to characterization also is the strong point of roles played by Irene Rich, Lee Dixon, Tom Powers, Paul Hurst, John Halloran, Olin Howlin, Stephen Grant, Joan Barton and others. Much credit for the writing and delineations achieved goes to Grant in his dual function as writer-director.

Film has been given production design by Ernst Fegte that makes for a natural background. Archie J. Stout's camera takes full advantages of the wide-open western scenery and other production dress. Music score by Richard Hageman is of mood importance. Film has one tune, "A Little Bit Different," by Kim Gannon and Walter Kent, which Joan Barton sings in saloon sequence.
Brog.

Vigilantes of Boomtown
Hollywood, Feb. 7.
Republic release of Sidney Picker production. Stars Allan Lane; features Bobby Blake, Martha Wentworth, Roscoe Karns, Roy Barcroft, Peggy Stewart, George Turner. Director R. G. Springsteen. Original screenplay, Earle Snell, based on Fred Harman's NEA cartoon "Red Ryder"; camera, Alfred Keller; editor, William P. Thompson. Previewed Feb. 7, '47. Running time, 56 MINS.
Red Ryder......................Allan Lane
Little Beaver..................Bobby Blake
The Duchess..........Martha Wentworth
Delaney..................Roscoe Karns
McKean.....................Roy Barcroft
Molly McVey..............Peggy Stewart
Corbett....................George Turner
Sparring Partner No. 1..Eddie Lou Simms
Dink....................George Chesebro
Sparring Partner No. 2.......Bobby Barber
Thug....................George Lloyd
Sheriff.....................Ted Adams
Bob Fitzsimmons.........John Dehner
Governor.................Earle Hodgins
Judge....................Harlan Briggs
Goff.......................Budd Buster
Referee....................Jack O'Shea

Republic has tossed just about everything into "Vigilantes of Boomtown." Latest entry in the Red Ryder series of oaters measures up for the juvenile trade, giving kiddies lessons not only in usual six-gun twirling and riding but in fisticuffs. Production by Sidney Picker is standard, as is R. G. Springsteen's direction, but both serve their purpose in keeping things on the move for 56 minutes. Plot is laid in early-day Nevada at the time of the Fitzsimmons-Corbett championship fight at Carson City. Earle Snell's script features a number of inaccuracies but the kiddies won't mind.

Allan Lane is Red Ryder and is called upon to match wits and guns with gang of baddies who are in town to rob the bank while the prize fight is underway. His upholding of law and order is not easy, as Peggy Stewart,

art, fiery heroine, does everything she can to prevent the championship match. These actions keep Red in hot water, climaxed by his being kidnapped by Miss Stewart's henchmen, who mistake him for Corbett. Ryder escapes in time to shoot it out with th eoutlaws and save the town's money.

Bobby Blake is Little Beaver. Martha Wentworth does the Duchess. Skullduggery is headed up by Roy Barcroft. George Turner does well by his characterization of Corbett, and Roscoe Karns gets in some comedy licks as the fighter's manager.

Alfred Keller's lensing is good and editing by William P. Thompson concise.
Brog.

Miniature Reviews

"The Beginning Or The End" (M-G). Atomic bomb story deserves and will get important boxoffice support.

"The Sin of Harold Diddlebock" (UA). Harold Lloyd's pic return in zany Preston Sturges production; top b.o.

"The Farmer's Daughter" (RKO). Sock romantic comedy fare starring Joseph Cotten and Loretta Young.

"Pursued" (WB). Second of U. S. Pictures adds up as strong period western fare slated for smart returns.

"My Favorite Brunette" (Par). Familiar hot water treatment for Bob Hope, with laughs crowding the screen. Surefire b.o.

"Dangerous Venture" (UA). Not up to previous Hopalong Cassidy caters. Ordinary western.

"That Way With Women" (WB). Mildly amusing, for lesser situations.

"Fear in the Night" (Par). Suspenseful melodrama with entertainment strength for dual bookings.

"Seven Were Saved" (Par.) Okay melodrama framed around work of Air-Sea Rescue Service in the Pacific.

"The Root of All Evil" (General Film) (British - Made). Tired femme emancipation drama, sparked by Phyllis Calvert. Limited appeal.

"Green Fingers" (Anglo-American) (British - made). Drama based on osteopathy; suitable for dual situations.

"Big Town" (Par). Program feature, based on the radio program of same title, lightweight entry.

"School for Danger" (UA) (British-Made). R.A.F. made film on sabotage; good selling possibilities.

"While the Sun Shines" (Pathe-British). Late Leslie Howard's son's pic debut; b.o. uncertain.

"We Lived Through Buchenwald" (Mage). Belgian-made documentary of the Nazi concentration camp.

"Before Him All Rome Trembled" (Superfilm). Woven around opera "Tosca," Italian-made film's appeal limited.

The Beginning Or the End

Metro release of Samuel Marx production. Stars Brian Donlevy, Robert Walker; features Tom Drake, Beverly Tyler, Audrey Totter, Hume Cronyn, Hurd Hatfield, Joseph Calleia, Godfrey Tearle, Victor Francen, Richard Haydn. Directed by Norman Taurog. Screenplay, Frank Wead; original, Robert Considine; camera, Ray June. Warren Newcomber, A. Arnold Gillespie, Donald Jahrus, Pete Ballbusch; editor, George Boemler; score, Daniele Amfitheatrof. Tradeshown N. Y., Feb. 13, '47. Running time, 110 MINS.

Maj.-Gen. Leslie R. Groves..Brian Donlevy
Colonel Jeff Nixon.........Robert Walker
Matt Cochran...............Tom Drake
Anne Cochran..............Beverly Tyler
Jean O'Leary..............Audrey Totter
Dr. J. Robert Oppenheimer..Hume Cronyn
Dr. John Wyatt............Hurd Hatfield
Dr. Enrico Fermi.........Joseph Calleia
President Roosevelt........Godfrey Tearle
Dr. Marre................Victor Francen
Dr. Chisholm.............Richard Haydn
Dr. Vannevar Bush.........Jonathan Hale
K. T. Keller...................John Litel
General Thomas F. Farrell..Henry O'Neill
Capt. Parsons, U.S.N....Warner Anderson
Colonel Paul Tibbets, Jr......Barry Nelson
President Truman...............Art Baker
Dr. Albert Einstein........Ludwig Stossel
Dr. Harold C. Urey.........John Hamilton

Dr. James B. Conant......Frank Ferguson
Dr. E. P. Wigner..........Tom Stevenson
Dr. Leo Szilard.............John Galiaudet
Grace Tully...................Nella Walker
Charles G. Ross.............Edward Earle
Dr. Arthur H. Compton......Moroni Olsen
Dr. Troyanski..............Norman Lloyd
Pilot at Tinian....................Jim Davis
Walter S. Carpenter, Jr..Chas. Trowbridge
Dr. W. H. Zinn.............Frank Wilcox
General Brehon Somervell......Henry Hall
Lieut.-Gen. W. D. Styer......Paul Harvey
Quaker Scientist..............Larry Johns
Dr. Rand...........Robert Emmett Keane
Dr. Ernest O. Lawrence.......James Bush
Clinic Doctor.............Trevor Bardette
Colonel John Lansdale....William Wright
C. D. Howe...............Damian O'Flynn

"The Beginning Or the End" is a story of our times. It dramatizes—in the comfort of one's favorite picture theatre—all the blood and sweat and tears, all the travail and fight for our very lives which Hitlerism brought to all of us. It tells the saga of America's one truly great secret weapon which not only turned the tide and won the war but, even now, is the crux of postwar power politics among the same Allies who were united in a common conquest of fascism. A moving unfolding of the top-secret story of World War II it's a tip-top cinematic entertainment. It's a credit of new proportions to the motion picture industry.

"The Beginning Or the End" tells its portentous tale in broad strokes of masterful scripting and production which the most casual film fan will recognize as achieving a stature far beyond the average celluloid standards. As the title tells it, the fictitious teime-capsule of the 25th century A.D. alone may fully unfold for our descendants of 500 years hence the answer to the wisdom of the atomic bomb. Whether this scientific splitting of the uranium atoms will work for good or evil ultimately is something "which only you in the 25th century will know THE END," as the fadeout title tells the auditor.

The showmanship device utilized for the unspooling of this film matches its sum total effort. Picture tees off with a pseudo-News of the Day (John B. Kennedy commentating) "news" clip, showing the burying of a time capsule, not to be opened until 2446 A.D. In the time capsule is placed a motion picture film which records "The Beginning Or the End." Thereafter is unfolded the nearly two-hour picture.

It brings to the most enlightened follower of world events a new appreciation of how science and big business were mobilized by America to achieve the Atomic Bomb even though President Roosevelt was told it would cost a billion dollars and possibly two billions. The daring and the diplomatic profligacy which apparently moved FDR to phone Winston Churchill in London, inviting the entire British scientific staff to come to America; the courage which inspired him to ask Congress to approve fantastically large funds for an anonymous (because it was so secret) war effort; the mobilization of big business and stout young scientists, to work with their more experienced elders; the rallying around Dr. J. Robert Oppenheimer (whom Hume Cronyn so expertly impersonates); the questioning by young Tom Drake whether he was doing the right thing, and the partial answer given by some of the scientists who tell the military and their co-savants that "this has now become a munitions project, hence we, as scientists, must resign" (from the further development of the world's most terrifying and destructive bomb)—these, and other facets, are skillfully integrated into Sam Marx's production which Norman Taurig so expertly directed from a tiptop Frank Wead-Bob Considine script.

Integrated also is a thin but pleasant—and obviously necessary—love story embracing Drake and his bride, Beverly Tyler, and Robert Walker cast opposite Audrey Totter for a secondary romance interest. Miss Totter personates the real-life Jean O'Leary, Major-General Leslie R. Groves' secretary, who was formally decorated by the U. S. Government for keeping the top war secret.

Brian Donlevy is capital as Gen. Groves, eclipsed only by Godfrey Tearle's extraordinary personation of President Roosevelt. A brother of the late Conway Tearle, w.k. in films, Terle incidentally makes his Hollywood debut although a standard lead in London films and legit.

The cast is replete with real names. Dr. Oppenheimer, who headed the atomic scientists; Dr. Albert Einstein (well done by Ludwig Stossel), Dr. John Wyatt, Dr. Enrico Fermi, Dr. Marre, Dr. Vannever Bush, Dr. James B. Conant, Dr. Harold C. Urey, Dr. Leo Szilard, Dr. Ernest O. Lawrence, General Brehon Somervell, Dr. Troyanski, Dr. E. P. Wigner, General Thomas F. Farrell, and other real-life savants and leaders in military affairs, give this film an aura of authenticity and special historical significance which must mark a step forward in the over-all motion picture industry. The full-front reenactment of FDR follows the tradition of personating past presidents; President Truman is shown only in rear silhouet, in keeping with the tradition of not depicting any living Chief Executive.

It's to the sum total credit of everybody concerned that the documentary values are sufficiently there without becoming static. Yet, wisely, none of it was given the brushoff. Whatever the abracadabra with ohms and neutrons, there is a sufficiently faithful reenactment of the laboratory excitement as the scientists stumble on one another in still another forward step in their exploration of the mystery and the magic of this new-found power from the atoms. The closely guarded subcellar laboratories, the evacuation of entire populations and developments from the northwest to the building of a new wonder city around Oak Ridge, Tenn., the experiments in Los Alamos, N. M., and all the rest of it are special tribute to the technical advisors who comprised Dr. H. T. Wensel, Dr. Edward T. Tomkins, Dr. David Hawkins, W. Branford Shank; and the military technical advisors, Col. William A. Consodine and Lt. Col. Charles W. Sweeney. Dr. Tomkins, of the consulting scientists enlisted for technical advice, incidentally, figures dramatically in this entire cinematic project, for it was his actress-pupil, Donna Reed, who helped motivate Metro into making this film. Miss Reed's agent-husband, Tony Owen, gets formal credit in the titles for his "cooperation" in having called on producer Sam Marx and furthered the idea of "The Beginning Or the End."

Performance-wise the trouping imparts a sense of realism beyond the average casting. The onlooker absorbs the idea that if it weren't for the real-life counterparts of all the characters unfolded on the screen they might very well not be here to view this film as an American film company produced it; in truth, had the Germans won the race for the secret weapon we might have been Hiroshimaed instead. Thus Brian Donlevy's performance as General Groves is highly impressive and that goes for the fictional integrations of the Robert Walker, Tom Drake, Beverly Tyler, Audrey Totter and other roles. Incidentally, Miss Totter impresses as an s.a. blonde who should be projected to new heights by this film, and that goes for Miss Tyler, winsome as an ingenue and no longer the teen-ager. *Abel.*

The Sin of Harold Diddlebock

United Artists release of California Pictures (Howard Hughes-Preston Sturges) production, written and directed by Sturges. Stars Harold Lloyd; features Jimmy Conlin, Frances Ramsden, Raymond Walburn, Edgar Kennedy, Rudy Vallee. Camera, Robert Pittack; editor, Tom Neff; music, Werner Richard Heymann. Tradeshown N. Y., Feb. 17. '47. Running time, 90 MINS.

Harold Diddlebock...........Harold Lloyd
Miss Otis...............Frances Ramsden
Wormy.......................Jimmy Conlin
J. E. Waggleberry......Raymond Walburn
Formfit Franklin........Franklin Pangborn
Flora...................Margaret Hamilton
Manicurist......................Arline Judge
Wild Bill Hitchcock..............Al Bridge
Jake.........................Edgar Kennedy
Mike..........................Frank Moran
Barber........................Torben Meyer
Prof. Potelle....................Victor Potel
James B. Smoke...............Jack Norton
Banker Blackston.............Arthur Hoyt
Bearded Lady................Georgia Caine
Snake Charmer.............Gladys Forrest
A Doorman.....................Max Wagner
Jackie, the Lion.................By Himself

Return to the screen of Harold Lloyd in almost any type of film vehicle would be a welcome note to film boxoffices, and when the particular brand of Lloyd slapstick is combined with the zany touch of producer-director Preston Sturges, as in "The Sin of Harold Diddlebock," boxoffice in almost all situations can be expected to do top biz.

Lloyd has appeared in several pictures since the advent of sound, but "Diddlebock" is his first since "The Milky Way" (Paramount) in 1936. Attired in what might be the same strawhat and black-rimmed specs that he wore in his early silent flickers, neither his person nor his comedy has changed much—which should be enough for any audience. As an added lure, Sturges has incorporated into the first 10 minutes of the film an actual sequence from Lloyd's "The Freshman," which the comedian made back in 1923 and which should be a certain word-of-mouth fillip.

Original screenplay, which Sturges handled along with his production and directorial chores, pegs directly onto the "Freshman" sequence, which shows the now-famous slapstick football game. Early print has been retouched nicely and shows well on the screen, with costumes of the femme football rooters and the slightly perky action the only throwbacks to the silent era. Lack of dialog is ably replaced by an hilarious score and Lloyd's antics should garner just as many laughs in 1947 as they did 24 years ago.

Film segues expertly from the "Freshman" footage to the new product, showing Raymond Walburn, as an enthusiastic alumnus now head of a top ad agency, promising Lloyd a job for having won the game. Lloyd takes the job after graduation but is stuck immediately into a minor bookkeeper's niche, where he remains forgotten for 22 years. Walburn finally remembers him long enough to fire him—which is where the fun starts. Lloyd, deep in the dumps, bumps into a racetrack tout who talks him into having his first drink. With a load on, he parlays a 15-1 bet into several hundred G's, throws his money around by buying hansom cab and a bankrupt circus and then wakes up to find he's broke. In some zany slapstick, he sells the circus at a neat profit and wins the seventh in a series of sisters he's been courting over the 22-year stretch.

Abetted by some excellent dialog from Sturges' pen, Lloyd handles his role in his usual funny fashion. One sequence, in which he dangles from a leash 80 stories above the sidewalk, with the other end of the leash tied to a nervous lion, is standout. The king of beasts is utilized for a number of other funny sequences. Rest of the cast, under Sturges' able direction, backs him capably. Vallee, Kennedy, Arline Judge, Franklin Pangborn and Lionel Stander, all familiar faces, are excellent in comparatively small roles. Vet vauder Jimmy Conlin, as his tout sidekick, makes his top impression in pix. Walburn also does well, and a deep bow is due the debut work of Frances Ramsden as the seventh sister whom Lloyd finally wins.

Production mountings are not too lush but are adequate for the picture. Robert Pittack's camera work is good, and the music, under direction of Werner Richard Heymann, is tops. *Stal.*

The Farmer's Daughter

RKO release of Dore Schary production. Stars Loretta Young, Joseph Cotton, Ethel Barrymore; features Charles Bickford, Rose Hobart, Rhys Williams. Directed by H. C. Potter. Screenplay, Allen Rivkin, Laura Kerr from play by Juhni Tervataa; camera, Milton Krasner; editor, Harry Marker. Tradeshown N. Y., Feb. 17, '47. Running time, 96 MINS.

Katrin Holstrom............Loretta Young
Glenn Morley.................Joseph Cotten
Mrs. Morley................Ethel Barrymore
Clancy.......................Chas. Bickford
Virginia.........................Rose Hobart
Adolph........................Rhys Williams
Dr. Sulven.................Harry Davenport
Nordick.........................Tom Powers
Ward Hughes...........William Harrigan
Olaf Holstrom.....................Lex Barker
Mr. Holstrom..............Harry Shannon
Sven Holstrom.................Keith Andes
Wilbur Johnson..............Thurston Hall
A. J. Finley.......................Art Baker
Einar..........................Don Beddoe
Peter Holstrom............James Aurness
Mrs. Holstrom.............Anna Q. Nilsson

This is a brightly wrapped celluloid package that can't miss at the boxoffice. With Joseph Cotton and Loretta Young as the top name players set in a witty variation of the poor-girl-meets-rich-boy theme, "The Farmer's Daughter" rolls irresistibly along in the light romantic comedy groove.

Appearance of Ethel Barrymore and Charles Bickford in supporting roles will help charge up the marquee voltage, and beyond that, the two vet thespers chip in a pair of sterling performances. One of the pic's chief assets is the political tilt given to the story line which, with its rapidly glossed over liberal democratic shibboleths, will give patrons a right-minded feeling in their hearts without disturbing their brain too much. Except to the lunatic fringe, political philosophy espoused in the film is completely inoffensive and non-partisan.

Loretta Young plays a Swedish country girl, complete with accent and rural garb who, upon coming to the big city, lands a second maid's job in the mansion of Cotten and his mother, Miss Barrymore. Latter pair are well-intentioned leaders of the local political machine which is embroiled in a hot fight with the opposition over the election of a Congressman.

The country lass, being naive and frank as well as an eyeful for Cotten, openly voices her disapproval of the compromise candidate chosen by her employers and heckles him at the nominating rally. And by a freak chance that never happened to any housemaid anywhere, but which is neatly put over in the film as a logical and credible development, she gets the nomination from the rival party. Politics being a grimy business, Miss Young is framed up on a morals rap on election eve. But the pic proves that honesty is greater than politics, and love is greater than both, as Cotten deserts his own party, smashes the fascist varmints within its ranks and rides his former housemaid into Congress on a landslide.

Although politicking is used only as a once-lightly-over excuse for the romantic bickerings and final clinch, director H. C. Potter slips in a few satirical barbs against the sacrosanct political practice of blarney and buncombe. In one montage, a rapid sequence of politicians shooting off their mouths fades out in pure jabberwocky of double-talk. Story is manipulated for laughs consistently and from all angles, including the romantic buildup between Cotten and Miss Young.

Difficulty with the Swedish accent, which occasionally collapses into straight Americanese, is the only flaw in Miss Young's performance. Otherwise she breezes through with finesse. Cotten adds to his rep as the slightly-confused but honest and charming politico. As the mother, Miss Barrymore walks through her part in the grand manner of a crusty matriarch but without overplaying her hand. Bickford's comeback is definitely established with this film. He registers solidly as the family butler and adviser and still retains that sense of brute power associated with his name.

Production is tastefully dressed throughout with a firstrate screenplay being given all the advantages of strong cast, positive direction, rich settings, excellent camerawork and good musical score. *Herm.*

Pursued

Hollywood, Feb. 17.

Warner Bros. release of United States Pictures (Milton Sperling) production. Stars Teresa Wright, Robert Mitchum; features Judith Anderson, Dean Jagger, Alan Hale, John Rodney. Directed by Raoul Walsh. Original screenplay, Niven Busch; camera, James Wong Howe; music, Max Steiner; editor, Christian Nyby. Tradeshown Feb. 17, '47. Running time, **100 MINS.**

Thor	Teresa Wright
Jeb	Robert Mitchum
Mrs. Callum	Judith Anderson
Grant	Dean Jagger
Jake Dingle	Alan Hale
Adam	John Rodney
Prentice	Harry Carey, Jr.
The Sergeant	Clifton Young
Jeb (age 8)	Ernest Severn
Adam (age 10)	Charles Bates
Thor (age 8)	Peggy Miller
The Callums	Norman Jolley Lane Chandler Elmer Ellingwood Jack Montgomery Ian MacDonald

"Pursued" is potent frontier days western film fare. Entertainment elements are put together solidly for assurance of audience reception and buildup of word-of-mouth exploitation. Marquee names are good, although not of top strength, and will aid the selling. It's the second production for U. S. Pictures, releasing through Warners, and returns should be gratifying.

Standout in picture is suspense generated by the Niven Busch original script and Raoul Walsh's direction. It builds the western gunman's death walk to high moments of thrill and action. Strong casting also is a decided factor in selling the action wares. Production makes use of natural outdoor backgrounds supplied by New Mexico scenery, lending air of authenticity that is fully captured by James Wong Howe's camera.

There are psychological elements in the Busch script, depicting the hate that drives through a man's life and forces him into unwanted dangers. Robert Mitchum is the victim of that hate, made to kill and fear because of an old family feud. His role fits him naturally and he mkes it entirely believable. Teresa Wright upholds the femme lead with another of her honestly valued, talented portrayals that register sincerity.

Plot motivation stems from feuding between the Callums and the Rands. Feud starts when Dean Jagger, a Callum, wipes out Mitchum's family because a Callum girl dared love Mitchum's father. Only a small son is saved, taken away by the Callum girl who raises him with her own family. He grows up to be Mitchum and as an adult is constantly put in jeopardy by Jagger's hate. In the finale, he finds true love with Miss Wright, a Callum, and Jagger is destroyed.

Among memorable moments is the stalking of Mitchum by the Callums as he spends his wedding night with a bride who also had just tried to kill him. Suspense developed by dialog absence and Max Steiner's music score is terrific. Another suspense-laden sequence occurs when Jagger eggs Harry Carey, Jr., into gunning for Mitchum over a fancied insult to Miss Wright.

Strong support to the stars comes from Judith Anderson, the Callum who dared to love a Rand and paid for her mistake; John Rodney, Miss Anderson's son who had been raised as a brother to Mitchum but hated him; Jagger, Alan Hale, Carey, Jr., and others. Ernest Severn, Charles Bates and Peggy Miller are good in portrayals of principals as children.

Milton Sperling's production makes smart use of showmanly values, giving the film backing that will pay off. *Brog.*

My Favorite Brunette

(ONE SONG)

Paramount release of Daniel Dare production. Stars Bob Hope, Dorothy Lamour; features Peter Lorre, Lon Chaney, John Hoyt, Reginald Denny, Jack La Rue. Directed by Elliott Nugent. Original screenplay, Edmund Beloin and Jack Rose; camera, Lionel Linden; editor, Ellsworth Hoagland; special photography, Gordon Jennings; assistant director, Mel Epstein; song, "Beside You," Ray Evans and Jay Livingston; score, Robert Emmett Dolan. Tradeshown N. Y., Feb. 9, '47. Running time, **87 MINS.**

Ronnie Jackson	Bob Hope
Carlotta Montay	Dorothy Lamour
Kismet	Peter Lorre
Willie	Lon Chaney
Dr. Lundau	John Hoyt
Major Simon Montague	Charles Dingle
James Collins	Reginald Denny
Baron Montay	Frank Puglia
Miss Rogers	Ann Doran
Prison Warden	Willard Robertson
Tony	Jack La Rue

Bob Hope, the sad sack would-be sleuth; Hope, the condemned prisoner, nerving out his imminent quietus with unhappy bravado; and Hope, the pushover, squirming uneasily under a chemical yen for the potent Lamour charms—it's familiar stuff but still grist for the yock mills. You can say Hope, like Kilroy, was here before but as long as the comic's fans want it that way—and there's enough of them around to swing the electoral college—Paramount's made its investment in a safe and sound formula. Score up the concoction for surefire b.o.

What's also traditional with the comic's celluloid antics is that the play's definitely not the thing. Employing the precedent of the Hope oldie, "My Favorite Blonde" and the "Road" series, Ed Beloin and Jack Rose have fashioned a plot that serves merely as a gadget to dip Hope into hot water up to his gilt-edged probiscis, then allow him free rein to founder with the peculiar brazen-timid capers in which the gagster excels. The story hardly stands inspection for either credibility or clarity—very probably its water-holding capacity wasn't ever considered.

One long flashback is the device employed. Credits segue into a scene depicting Hope as a condemned murderer being groomed for the gas chamber. To reporters gathered to record his early demise, Hope relates his tale of woe—which at the outset has him as a baby photographer whose frustrated urge towards gumshoeing has inspired the invention of a special keyhole camera.

When Hope's nextdoor neighbor, a private eye, leaves town requesting Hope to tend his office, the comic's usual pot of trouble rises to a simmer. He tangles with Dorothy Lamour in a fantastic snarl involving a mysterious map (concealed by Hope in a drinking cup container) and Miss Lamour's missing uncle who's been snatched by a gang of international criminals headed by that familiar lawbreaker, Peter Lorre.

Gags pile onto more gags in the intricate story development. Hope, the classically dumb dick, flees the gang's clutches in a wacky auto chase; lands back in their hands when lured to a sanitarium; gets himself framed for murder; traps a confession of the killing from the mobsters via a record player—and then dumbly loses the record. Hence, the murder rap. Throughout this melange, he drools ineffectually over Miss Lamour, wanting to run out of the dangerous mess but lured on by the urge to merge.

There's no execution, of course, since Hope is saved by an incredible last-minute discovery of a keyhole photo which exonerates him and convicts the gang. Curtain rings down on a solid rib. Hope's impatient executioner turns out to be—you guessed it—Bing Crosby. To which Hope cracks: "That guy will take any part." Another pretty conceit that comes off is the use of Alan Ladd in a bit part as the nextdoor detective whom Hope envies because he's panting to play the gumshoe a la "those hard muggs in the movies."

Miss Lamour is still the cinematic cutie whose attractiveness makes the Hope scramble plausible. Plot convolutions place no great strain on her thesping talents but she's still a hiltful in the classical role of the magnet which drags Hope into a snootful of trouble. Actress sings one number, "Beside You," which doesn't mean very much to the picture, one way or the other.

Lon Chaney, as a muscular and moronic sanitarium guard, rates for a risible replica of imbecility. Rest of the supporting cast put in their oars right skillfully. Direction by Elliott Nugent keeps the pace brisk and lively. *Wit.*

Dangerous Venture

United Artists release of Lewis J. Rachmil (Hopalong Cassidy) production. Stars William Boyd; features Andy Clyde, Rand Brooks. Directed by George Archinbaud. Screenplay, Doris Schroeder; camera, Mack Stengler; score, David Chudnow; editor, Fred W. Berger. Tradeshown Feb. 14, '47. Running time, **59 MINS.**

Hopalong Cassidy	William Boyd
California Carlson	Andy Clyde
Lucky Jenkins	Rand Brooks
Xeoli	Fritz Leiber
Dr. Atwood	Douglas Evans
Morgan	Harry Cording
Sue Harmon	Betty Alexander
Kane	Francis McDonald
Jose	Neyle Morrow
Talu	Patricia Tate
Stark	Bob Faust

Third in the new Hopalong Cassidy series has all the low-budget chemistry of the previous William Boyd productions but the mixing lacks one ingredient: story matter. Result is that the streamliner fails to jell and, perish forbid, even drags for portions of its 59 minutes.

For one thing this film is unique. It's a western without a single chase scene. A couple of gallopers might have added some needed spice. Story thread winds around a tribe of Indians isolated on a mesa, who are supposed to be direct descendants of the Aztecs. An archeological expedition headed by, of all things, a lovely gal, sets out to verify the Indian lineage. Suspicion is thrown on the redskins by a group of rustlers who dress like them on raids and leave planted evidence. Meanwhile, the assistant on the expedition gets ideas about the solid gold relics and ties up with the rustlers to raid the possessions buried with dead warriors. Through all of this rides Boyd with his sidekicks, ever eager to catch perpetrators of injustice, which he eventually does.

Camera work, as always in the Hoppy films, is tops, with filters fully are actually the best feature of the film. Thesping is ordinary but sufficient, as indicated by top credit going to Andy Clyde and his Keystone Kop bits of business. *Tomm.*

That Way With Women

Hollywood, Feb. 14.

Warners release of Charles Hoffman production. Stars Dane Clark, Martha Vickers, Sydney Greenstreet; features Alan Hale, Craig Stevens, Barbara Brown, Don McGuire, John Ridgely, Dick Erdman, Herbert Anderson, Howard Freeman. Directed by Frederick de Cordova. Screenplay, Leo Townsend; added dialog, Francis Swann; from a story by Earl Derr Biggers; camera, Ted McCord; editor, Folmer Blangsted. Tradeshown in Los Angeles, Feb. 13, '47. Running time, **83 MINS.**

Greg Wilson	Dane Clark
Marcia Alden	Martha Vickers
James P. Alden	Sydney Greenstreet
Herman Brinker	Alan Hale
Carter Andrews	Craig Stevens
Minerva Alden	Barbara Brown
Slade	Don McGuire
Sam	John Ridgely
Eddie	Dick Erdman
Melvyn Pfeiffer	Herbert Anderson
Dr. Harvey	Howard Freeman
L. B. Crandall	Ian Wolfe
Davis	Olaf Hytten
Desk Sargeant	Joe Devlin
Harry Miller	Charles Arnt
First Party Girl	Suzi Crandall
Alice Green	Janet Murdoch
Briggs	Creighton Hale
Hawkins	Philo McCullough
Deacon	Jack Mower
Angela	Jane Harker
MacPherson	Monte Blue

"That Way With Women" is a misnomer for this remake of the old George Arliss starrer, "The Millionaire." This version is a mild drama with comedy touches that will cause no great boxoffice stir, though the returns should be adequate.

Sydney Greenstreet, Dane Clark and Martha Vickers occupy starring spots and do about as well as might be expected considering the story. Greenstreet is an auto tycoon, put out to pasture on the Pasadena goldcoast. He hasn't lost his urge to work, though, so, in defiance of his medicos, he buys a partnership in a gas station with Clark. In between trouble with protection racketeers, the police and keeping his masquerade secret from his family, Greenstreet finds time to play cupid in promoting a romance between his daughter, Miss Vickers, and Clark.

Lending support to top trio are Alan Hale, Craig Stevens, Barbara Brown, Dick Erdman, Herbert Anderson, Howard Freeman and others. Frederick de Cordova's direction works hard to gloss over script contrivances, but characters are never real. Leo Townsend screenplayed with added dialog contributed by Francis Swann.

Physical production values measure up under Charles Hoffman's supervision, and lensing by Ted McCord gives them good display. *Brog.*

Fear in the Night

Hollywood, Feb. 14.

Paramount release of William Pine-William Thomas production. Features Paul Kelly, DeForest Kelley, Ann Doran, Kay Scott. Directed and written by Maxwell Shane. From story by William Irish; camera, Jack Greenhalgh; score, Rudy Schrager; editor, Howard Smith. Tradeshown Feb. 11, '47. Running time, **71 MINS.**

Cliff Harlan	Paul Kelly
Betty Winters	Kay Scott
Vince Grayson	DeForest Kelley
Lil Harlan	Ann Doran
Mr. Belnap	Robert Emmett Keane
Torrence	Jeff Yorke
Warner	Charles Victor

Tiptop job of projecting suspense makes "Fear in the Night" a nifty entry for dual bookings. It's a good psychological melodrama, unfolded at fast clip and will please the who-dunit-and-how fans. Production values reflect upped budget of the Pine-Thomas feature.

Maxwell Shane, who scripted from a William Irish story, also directed. It's his first directorial chore. He realizes on meller elements for full worth. Plot concerns young man who awakens one morning after dream that he has killed a man. Reality of dream is strengthened when he finds strange button and key in his pocket. He seeks aid from his detective brother-in-law and between the two they piece together enough evidence to assure that he had actually stabbed a man. Why and how takes further unravelling but unfoldment reveals he had been hypnotized into crime To get the goods on real villain young man goes through hypnotism again for fast action finale.

Paul Kelly is a believable cop who aids DeForest Kelley solve nightmare riddle. Latter also is good as bewildered young man. Ann Doran, his sister, and Kay Scott, his fiancee, do well. Robert Emmett Keane makes a smooth villain.

Suspense mood is furthered by Jack Greenhalgh's lensing and the score by Rudy Schrager. Editing and other production credits are equally expert. *Brog.*

Seven Were Saved

Hollywood, Feb. 14.

Paramount release of William Pine-William Thomas (L. B. Merman) production. Features Richard Denning, Catherine Craig, Russell Hayden. Directed by William H. Pine. Screenplay, Maxwell Shane; based on original story by Shane and Julian Harmon; camera, Jack Greenhalgh; editor, Howard Smith. Tradeshown Feb. 10, '47. Running time, **71 MINS.**

Capt. Allen Danton	Richard Denning
Susan Briscoe	Catherine Craig
Capt. Jim Willis	Russell Hayden
Mrs. Rollin Hartley	Ann Doran
Lt. Martin Pinkert	Byron Barr
Mr. Rollin Hartley	John Eldredge
Col. Yamura	Richard Loo
Smith	Keith Richards
Lt. Pete Sturdevant	Don Castle

Pine-Thomas have framed actionful melodrama around work of the Air-Sea Rescue Service, assuring "Seven Were Saved" an okay reception in action bookings. Plot use of ASRS garners interest on technical side depicting how the rescue of mishap victims is carried out. Footage is a bit overlength, particularly in life raft sequences, but general effect measures up to all demands of the market for which it is intended.

Story line sets up rescue technique by having a plane carrying principals crash in the Pacific. Assorted characters that survive crash are thrown together on a rubber life raft to battle elements while awaiting rescue. How common sense, along with aids provided in the rafts, will assure survival until the Air-Sea Rescue Service arrives is capably projected. Details of air search for victims are given, climaxing in dropping of powered rescue boat from a plane to carry survivors to safety.

Melodrama angles of plot as directed by William H. Pine strive for character studies of crash victim that don't always come off but general effect is okay. Among those awaiting rescue are three former victims of Jap prison camps, a high Jap war criminal en route to Manila for trial, a nurse, the plane pilot and two soldiers. Gradual breakdown of morale among the weaker and efforts of the stronger to hold the pitiful band together occupies considerable footage and sometimes becomes tedious.

Richard Denning, Catherine Craig, as pilot and nurse respectively, and Russell Hayden, rescue pilot, carry off the leads excellently. Ann Doran, Byron Barr, Richard Loo, John Eldredge, Keith Richards and an uncredited cast member make up others of the life raft group who are good. Don Castle has small spot as Hayden's co-pilot in the rescue work.

L. B. Merman served as associate producer to Pine & Thomas. Okay lensing contributed by Jack Greenhalgh. *Brog.*

The Root of All Evil

(BRITISH-MADE)

London, Feb. 6.

General Film Distributors' release of Gainsborough production. Stars Phyllis Calvert, Michael Rennie. Directed by Brock Williams. Screenplay by Williams from J. S. Fletcher's novel. Camera, Stephen Dade. At Studio One, London, Feb. 5. Running time, **110 MINS.**

Jeckie Farnish	Phyllis Calvert
Joe Bartle	John McCallum
Charles Mortimer	Michael Rennie
Farnish	Brefni O'Rourke
George Grice	Arthur Young
Albert Grice	Hubert Gregg
Lucy Grice	Pat Hicks
Rushie Farnish	Hazel Court
Bowser	George Carney
Perkins	Reginald Purdell
Scholes	Moore Marriott
Pam	Diana Decker

Final film of Maurice Ostrer, before bowing out of Rank organization, this will gain neither critical kudos nor much boxoffice trade. Pedestrian in production, it savors of those dramas of the twenties when feminine emancipation was quite a topic. Film never actually leaves the covers of the novel, and with suitable sub-titling and appropriate music it could have passed for a period piece.

Jilted by spineless Albert Grice, Jeckie becomes hard and embittered. When her father's farm is sold she determines to acquire money, and begins her fortune on a check for breach of promise settled out of court. Ruthlessly she gets what she wants and bumps into philandering Charles Mortimer, a mining engineer who has located oil in the neighborhood. Together they make a fortune, but all her wealth cannot buy Charles' true love. When the oil wells are fired by the aggrieved farmer who once owned the land, Jeckie stumbles back to the arms of humble farmer, Joe Bartle, who always loved her.

This shouldn't have happened to Phyllis Calvert. She plays the part as if she didn't believe in it for one moment. Michael Rennie, as the engineer, shows star potentialities. Given the right grooming and the proper parts—he is now under contract to Maurice Ostrer—he should become marquee value.

Rest of the cast is adequate, but with all their talents and all the goodwill in the world, they couldn't breathe life into the yarn. Phyllis Calvert will undoubtedly draw her quota of admirers in this country, but it will be tough going for American screens. *Cane.*

Green Fingers

(BRITISH-MADE)

London, Feb. 5.

Anglo-American release of British National production. Features Robert Beatty, Carol Raye, Nova Pilbeam, Felix Aylmer. Directed by John Harlow. Screenplay by Jack Whittingham from Edith Arundel's novel "The Persistent Warrior." Music by Hans May; camera, Ernest Palmer. At Palace, London, Feb. 4. Running time, **87 MINS.**

Thomas Stone	Robert Beatty
Jeannie Mansell	Carol Raye
Alexandra Baxter	Nova Pilbeam
Daniel Booth	Felix Aylmer
Dr. Baxter	Harry Welchman
Albert Goodman	Edward Rigby
Jones	Ellis Irving
Pickles	Moore Marriott
Mrs. Mansell	Olive Walters
Pamela	Felicity Deveraux
Angela	Doreen Lawrence
Joe Mansell	Charles Victor
Dr. Miles	Frederick Morant

Unlikely to please the medical profession, this picture is the biggest boost osteopathy has yet had, although it points out the dangers of the inexperienced dabbling in the art and science.

Thomas Stone, a fisherman, decides to become an osteopath. By hard work and study he has almost completed his four years at the Academy of Osteopathy. Jeannie, daughter of his landlady, is a cripple given up by the doctors. Stone treats and cures her, but instead of receiving praise from the deal, he is reprimanded for having laid hands on a patient before he is qualified. This is quackery, but the case receives such publicity that the ex-fisherman decides to set up in practice regardless of the academy or a degree.

He prospers, marries Jeannie, becomes a fashionable specialist, and finds he must choose between sophisticated Alexandra Baxter, a patient with whom he is having an affair, and his wife. He decides to break with the former, who commits suicide. The inquest discloses that Thomas had incorrectly diagnosed her illness and his treatment indirectly led to her death. He loses faith in himself, goes back to sea and only when, owing to an accident, his wife's paralysis recurs and doctors have despaired of a cure, does he yield to his wife's plea and use his "Green Fingers" again. She is healed and he recovers his faith.

John Harlow, who achieved success with "Appointment With Crime," has made a fair job of a not-too-convincing story. His failure is due to cliches and to lack of attention to detail. Nor has he been helped by the camera which has been particularly unjust to Carol Raye. Her good acting is often negated by indifferent photography.

Robert Beatty gives a good account of himself, and would have been helped considerably by better makeup. Nova Pilbeam looks like fulfilling the promise she revealed as a youngster a decade ago, and Felix Aylmer gives his usual polished performance.

Story should play to fair business here, and, with some cuts, may fit into dual situations in the States. *Cane.*

Big Town

Hollywood, Feb. 11.

Paramount release of William Pine-William Thomas production. Stars Phillip Reed, Hillary Brooke, Robert Lowery. Directed by William Thomas. Screenplay, Geoffrey Homes; original story, Homes and Maxwell Shane; based on radio program, "Big Town"; camera, Fred Jackman, Jr.; editor, Howard Smith; score, Darrell Calker. Tradeshown Feb. 10, '47. Running time, **59 MINS.**

Steve Wilson	Philip Reed
Lorelei Kilbourne	Hillary Brooke
Pete Ryan	Robert Lowery
Vance Crane	Byron Barr
Vivian LeRoy	Veda Ann Borg
Mrs. Crane	Nana Bryant
Mr. Peabody	Charles Arnt

Lightweight secondary feature that gets off to a promising start but bogs down too quickly. Based on ether's "Big Town," it looks like the start of a Pine-Thomas film series but other entries will have to be stronger if there's to be a survival.

Plot function is the establishment of Steve Wilson as the crusading editor of Big Town's illustrated Daily Press after getting burned by yellow journalism. Yarn gets under way with an actionful takeoff but soon slows down under the strain of carrying painfully unnatural dialog and improperly motivated situations. There's no city room authenticity to help, either. Geoffrey Homes scripted from an original by himself and Maxwell Shane.

Phillip Reed tries hard with the Steve Wilson role and would have given a better account of himself with worthier material. Same goes for Hillary Brooke as Lorelei and Robert Lowery as Pete Ryan, as well as others in the cast.

William Thomas' direction of the Pine-Thomas production isn't able to get much from the script. Lensing and other technical credits are standard. Music score has some good moments. *Brog.*

School for Danger

(BRITISH-MADE)

London, Feb. 5.

United Artists release of Central Office of Information film. Produced by R.A.F. Film Unit directed by Wing Commander E. Baird. Scenario, E. Baird and J. Woolaston; music, John Greenwood; camera, W. Pollard. Previewed Hammer, London. Running time, **68 MINS.**

Felix	Capt. Henry Ree
Cat	Jacqueline Nearne
Henri Pickard	E. Baird

Lapse of time since end of war, and Hollywood's efforts at depicting work of O.S.S., have blunted the edge of this exciting factual film which is a composite story of actual events. It features training and ultimate sabotage activities in Occupied France of two British agents, named for operational purposes Felix and Cat. Felix is an army officer, Cat an ordinary civilian. After extensive training they are parachuted into France for Felix to organize sabotage and underground resistance with Cat as wireless operator. Pickard is the connecting link in England.

Since Felix and Cat are reenacting their real life roles during the war and many of the actual agents appear in the production, there is a tendency to understate everything, thereby actually emphasizing the danger of these heroic folk.

The picture gives a much better idea of how underground resistance was organized than many fictional films could. With proper selling this should find a place. *Cane.*

While the Sun Shines

(BRITISH-MADE)

London, Feb. 1.

Pathe Pictures (Assocolated British Picture Corp.) release of International Screenplay Production. Stars Barbara White, Ronald Squire, Brenda Bruce, Bonar Colleano, Ronald Howard. Directed by Anthony Asquith. Screenplay, Terence Rattigan, Anatole de Grunewald, from Terence Rattigan's play; camera, Jack Hildyard. At Palace, London. Running time, **75 MINS.**

Lady Elizabeth Randell	Barbara White
Duke of Ayr	Ronald Squire
Mabel Crum	Brenda Bruce
Joe Mulvaney	Bonar Colleano, Jr.
Earl of Harpenden	Ronald Howard
Horton	Miles Malleson
Dr. Winifred Frye	Margaret Rutherford
Old Admiral	Cyril Maude
Daphne	Joyce Grenfell
Colbert	Michael Allan
Mr. Jordan	Garry Marsh
Mrs. Finckel	Amy Frank

Main interest in this adaptation of Terence Rattigan's London stage hit (it flopped on Broadway) is screen debut of Ronald Howard, 28-year-old son of the late Leslie Howard. Dead ringer for his famous father, except that he is taller, he has the same quiet voice, the same easy manner, and has inherited some of the talent. His natural flair for acting needs nursing, however. Like the Earl of Harpenden, whom he plays in the film, Howard served on the lower deck during the war before being commissioned. Pic has uncertain b.o. possibilities.

Story is set in wartime London on the eve of the Earl's marriage to Lady Elizabeth. She is an Air Force corporal and, traveling to London for the wedding, she meets one Colbert, who woos her with Gallic rapidity. By chance she meets Joe Mulvaney, an U. S. Army "loot," in Harpenden's rooms, and he, mistaking her for an accommodating girlfriend, sets a rapid pace. Complications ensue, but story ends happily with the loving couple paired off in church in the nick of time.

Possibly due to its stage origin, picture has a static quality, and efforts to make it adventurous and gay seem obvious. Only principal who is inherently funny is Bonar Colleano as Joe, and story lags when he's off the screen. *Cane.*

We Lived Through Buchenwald

(BELGIAN-MADE)

James Mage release of Belgian production. Directed by E. G. De Myest. Story, Herman Closson; music, Robert Pottier; dialog, Mary Dunton. Previewed in N. Y. Feb. 11, '47. Running time, **76 MINS.**

Evrard	Rene Herde
Fernand	Andre Gevrey
Jean Pierre	Werner Degan
Van Riel	Marcel Josz
Jules	Joseph Gevers
Janin	Maurice Auzat
Jacqueline	Sylviane Ramboux
La Fermiere	Anne Marie Ferrieres

While war's atrocities are being slowly dimmed by time, Belgian-made "We Lived Through Buchenwald" is a grim reminder of the frightful deeds of the Nazis. Dubbed into English by distributor James Mage, modest-budgeter tells of the miserable existence of Buchenwald's inmates, all in documentary style. Uneven story and poor editing, however, hamper the plot and b.o. possibilities.

Reportedly the "authentic" story told by the surviving inmates of the Nazi terror camp, film lacks a professional touch in the acting. Mage's first dubbing attempt is a good try at lip synchronization, but unfortunately some of the dubbed voices do not seem to match the screen characters.

Opening with a prolog, consisting of narrative and newsreel clips which trace the carnage wrought by the Germans, picture recounts the activities of several members of the Belgian underground seized by the Gestapo. Ultimately all find themselves at Buchenwald. Climax is reached with the arrival of American troops.

Before Him All Rome Trembled

(ITALIAN-MADE)

(Songs)

Superfilm release of Excelsa Film production. Stars Anna Magnani, Gino Sinimberghi. Directed by Carmine Gallone. Camera, Anchise Brizzi; music, Giacomo Puccini; conductor, Luigi Ricci; English titles, Armando V. Macaluso. Tradeshown N. Y. Feb. 13, '47. Running time, 110 MINS.

Ada	Anna Magnani
Franco	Gino Sinimberghi
Lena	Edda Albertini
Franz	Steffen Bode-Wab
Police Officer	Carlo Duse
Webb	Joop Von Hulzen
Doctor	Guido Notari
Mechanic	Tino Scotti
Stagehand	Guglielmo Sinaz
Stagehand	Guiseppe Varni

Cast for Opera "Tosca"

Floria Tosca	Elisabetta Barbato
Cavaradossi	Gino Sinimberghi
Scarpia	Tito Gobbi
Angelotti	Giulio Neri

(In Italian; English Titles)

An Italian import, "Before Him All Rome Trembled" is a long tale of the Italian underground woven around a performance of the opera "Tosca." The overlong plot could be speeded by judicious scissoring, especially in the first reel. Film's potential audience will largely be limited to music lovers.

Briefly story deals with Anna Magnani and Gino Sinimberghi, singers with Rome's Royal Opera. Latter, along with his teacher Franz (Steffen Bode-Wab) hide a wounded English agent, Joop Von Hulzen, in a cave near his country home. Paralleling the story of "Tosca" to some extent, jealous Miss Magnani suspects Sinimberghi of betraying her for another. Unwittingly this results in the Nazis' discovery of not only the Englishman's sanctuary but also leads to the arrest of the household staff. Though under suspicion, Sinimberghi is permitted to sing in the opera and with Miss Magnani effects a dramatic escape at the end of the finale.

A realistic prima donna, Miss Magnani registers as Ada. However, the voice of Elisabetta Barbato is dubbed in for the musical scenes. Tenor Sinimberghi handles his thespian chores in creditable fashion and is an acceptable "Cavaradossi" in the operatic sequences. Supporting cast is adequate. Direction and photography is satisfactory, while production accoutrements are better than the usual Italian import.

Miniature Reviews

"Ramrod" (Enterprise - UA). Above-average western with strong cast names for OK b.o. generally.

"Fabulous Dorseys" (Rogers-UA). OK filmusical for fair b.o.

"Private Affairs of Bel Ami" (UA). George Sanders, Angela Lansbury in denatured version of de Maupassant novel; OK b.o.

"Beat the Band" (Songs). (RKO). Lightweight musical.

"Danger Street" (Par). Mild melodrama with Jane Withers name to aid selling.

"The Devil Thumbs a Ride" (RKO). Exciting melodrama with plenty of appeal for the action market.

"I Cover Big Town" (Par). Good melodrama for supporting positions. Based on radio series, "Big Town."

"Jungle Flight" (Par). Standard adventure material for dual bills. Good aerial photography a feature.

"Trail Street" (RKO). Lusty pioneer western fare with hefty b.o. potential.

"Les Enfants du Paradis" (French). Expensive, ambitious film with high artistic aims but uneven attainment.

"Her First Affair" (Distinguish). Danielle Darrieux's first postwar French-made film; good for art houses but slim elsewhere.

"Angel and Sinner" (French). French pic on patriotic theme will have moderate b.o. success in art houses.

"Code of the West" (RKO). Taut western with moderate b.o. appeal.

"Hue and Cry" (General Film) British-made). So-so whodunit with kid angle.

"Praterbuben" (Sovexport). Action-less Austrian-made film built around famed Vienna Singing Boys.

Ramrod

United Artists release of Enterprise (Harry Sherman) production. Stars Joel McCrea, Veronica Lake, Donald Crisp, Don DeFore; features Preston Foster, Arleen Whelan, Charlie Ruggles. Directed by Andre de Toth. Story, Luke Short; screenplay, Jack Moffitt, Graham Baker, Cecile Kramer; asst. producer, Gene Strong; score composed and conducted by Adolph Deutsch; camera, Russell Harlan, Harry Pedmond, Jr.; editor, Sherman A. Rose; asst. director, Harold Godsoe; music director, Rudolph Polk. Tradeshown Feb. 20, '47. Running time, 94 MINS.

Connie Dickason	Veronica Lake
Dave Nash	Joel McCrea
Walt Shipley	Ian McDonald
Ben Dickason	Charles Ruggles
Frank Ivey	Preston Foster
Rose	Arleen Whelan
Red Cates	Lloyd Bridges
Sheriff Jim Crew	Donald Crisp
Annie	Rose Higgins
Dr. Parks	Chick York
Mrs. Parks	Sarah Padden
Bill Schell	Don DeFore
Curley	Nestor Paiva
Tom Peebles	Cliff Parkinson
Bailey	Trevor Bardette
Pokey	John Powers
Link Thomas	Ward Wood
Jess Moore	Hal Taliaferro
Virg Lee	Wally Cassell
Burma	Ray Teal
Bice	Jeff Corey

"Ramrod" is a good western with above-par cast names, a better-than-average romance appeal for the femmes, and hence a better-than-average grosser as outdoorers go.

It'll do plenty of key city business. Film marks the first from Enterprise via United Artists release although, fundamentally, it's Harry Sherman's production, which leaves Ent yet to make its real mark when "Arch of Triumph" is tradeshown.

The title stands for ranch foreman and Joel McCrea is the ramrod of Veronica Lake's ranch. The challenge starts when the cattlemen would stop sheepherding in this cowtown of the 1870s. Preston Foster runs the cow-country, with acquiescence of Charlie Ruggles whom his daughter (Miss Lake) defies when she throws the gauntlet to Foster. Arleen Whelan is the honest homespun seamstress to whom McCrea finally turns, and in between there is the volatile Don De-Fore as the hero's aide; Donald Crisp as the honest sheriff who is another victim of Foster's men; Nestor Paiva as the hero's hand who is fatally beaten; and other assorted characters on sides of law and the lawless.

The femme angles give more than ordinary substance to this western which otherwise has its usual assortment of gunplay, hard-riding, skull-duggery and the inevitable chase for the finale. Miss Lake is the predatory female who proves a wrongie although fundamentally she dares to challenge the marauding cattlemen. Miss Lake engages in such escapades as purposely stampeding her own cattle in order to throw the onus on Foster; while her ramrod (McCrea) is committed to the idea of fighting the varmints strictly according to the law. In this he has sheriff Donald Crisp's backing until the latter, too, is murdered.

Besides the good all-around cast, the film has other plus factors in a fetching outdoors lensing; a fine musical setting by Adolph Deutsch which does a lot to enhance the action; and lush production values in every respect. *Abel.*

The Fabulous Dorseys

(MUSICAL)

United Artists release of Charles R. Rogers (John W. Rogers) production. Stars Tommy and Jimmy Dorsey, Janet Blair; features Paul Whiteman, Wm. Lundigan. Directed by Alfred E. Green. Original screenplay, Richard English, Art Arthur, Curtis Kenyon; asst. director, Herbert T. Mendelson; music director, Louis Forbes; camera, James Van Trees; editor, George Arthur; music editor, Walter Hannemann; dances, Chas. Baron; photographic effects, Alfred Schmid; original songs, Don George-Allie Wrubel, Leo Shuken. Tradeshown N. Y., Feb. 24, '47. Running time, 88 MINS.

Himself	Tommy Dorsey
Himself	Jimmy Dorsey
Jane Howard	Janet Blair
Himself	Paul Whiteman
Bob Burton	William Lundigan
Mrs. Dorsey	Sara Allgood
Mr. Dorsey	Arthur Shields
Gorman	James Flavin
Eddie	William Bakewell
Foggy	Dave Willock
Young Tommy	Bobby Warde
Young Jimmy	Buz Buckley
Young Jane	Ann Carter
Walter	Tom Dugan
Joe	Jack Searl
Phil	James Taggart
Artie	Hal K. Dawson
Herself	Sherry Sherwood
Hotel Clerk	Edward Clark
De Witt	Andrew Tombes
Radio Station Attendant	Jack Roper

Specialties

Charlie Barnet	Stuart Foster
Henry Busse	Ray Bauduc
Mike Pingatore	Tommy Dorsey's
Ziggy Elman	Orchestra
Bob Eberly	Jimmy Dorsey's
Helen O'Connell	Orchestra
Art Tatum	

"The Fabulous Dorseys" emerges a pretty fair musical and may start a cycle of dance bandleaders' biographicals. Primed for the jive trade it tells the story of the scrapping freres who, longtime friendly enemies, were reunited with the passing of their father. Fortified by a band-show cavalcade of the top Jimmy and Tommy Dorsey arrangements it adds up to acceptable b.o. divertisement.

Story is simple, and, apparently, a pretty good approximation of real-life biography. Diskophiles and disciples of dansapation know that Tommy and Jimmy Dorsey came from the Pennsylvania coalmining territory, and Dorsey senior (Arthur Shields) is shown painstakingly persisting they raise themselves out of the soot and the grime of the Shenandoah poverty by adhering to their trombone and saxophone practice, even if he has to take their shoes off to keep them anchored indoors.

Janet Blair is the little hometown girl who grows up into loveliness to sing with the forever-scrapping Dorsey Bros.' band; keeps William Lundigan, pianist-composer with the band, on the hook because of her loyalty to the boys; and engineers the finale when Paul Whiteman reunites the brothers for a musical charity concert and features "The Dorsey Concerto" by an unknown "D. H. Smith," who turns out to be the juvenile lead, Lundigan. In between are shown the travails of a barnstorming band, the contempt of bands for early radio days, the call from the King of Jazz himself for both Dorseys to join the Whiteman ensemble, a jam session around Art Tatum's tricky pianology. Mom Dorsey (well played by Sara Allgood) utilizes the device of long-hand biographical notes, as if writing an informal diary, to tie the sundry scenes together from the days when the boys, in breeches, sit in with their father's band for the dance at Gorman's Hall, and TD starts to improvise on his slide trombone as he converts the turkey-trot and "When You and I Were Young Maggie" into a modern rhythmic arrangement.

Subsequently the boys unreel "Marie" (TD) and "Green Eyes" (JD), with Bob Eberly and Helen O'Connell featured in the latter, while Miss Blair works with TD. Specialties in the jam session and elsewhere bring in Charlie Barnet, Henry Busse, Mike Pingatore (with Whiteman), Ziggy Elman, Ray Bauduc and Stuart Foster. The action segues from Sands Point to the Island Casino, as it's called here (meaning Glen Island, N. Y., when the brothers really broke up in a hassle). The musical excerpts run the gamut from "Running Wild" to "The Object of My Affection," by Miss Blair, who also handles the only original ballad in the score, "To Me," a promising Don George-Allie Wrubel tune. The "Dorsey Concerto" is by Leo Shuken.

For what line-reading they must do, both Dorseys deport themselves well; ditto Whiteman, who plays himself in two brief sequences. Lundigan is okay as the romance interest opposite Miss Blair, who looks well and sings ditto (she's originally a band thrush, hence realistically recreates herself here). Bobby Warde and Buz Buckley play young Tommy and Jimmy Dorsey, and the rest are bits. Film has pace and tempo, under Alfred E. Green's direction, keeping itself to a brisk 88 minutes. *Abel.*

Private Affairs of Bel Ami

(ONE SONG)

United Artists release of David L. Loew (Loew-Lewin) production, directed by Albert Lewin. Stars George Sanders, Angela Lansbury, Ann Dvorak; features Frances Dee, John Carradine, Susan Douglas. Screenplay, Lewin, from novel by Guy de Maupassant; camera, Russell Metty; editor, Albrecht Joseph; music, Darius Milhaud; song, "My Bel Ami," Jack Lawrence-Irving Drutman. Tradeshown N. Y. Feb. 24, '47. Running time, 110 MINS.

Georges Duroy	George Sanders
Clotilde de Marelle	Angela Lansbury
Madeleine Forestier	Ann Dvorak
Marie de Varenne	Frances Dee
Charles Forestier	John Carradine
Suzanne Walter	Susan Douglas
Monsieur Walter	Hugo Haas

Rachel Michot	Marie Wilson
Jacques Rival	Albert Basserman
Laroche-Mathieu	Warren Williams
Madame Walter	Katherine Emery
Philippe de Cantel	Richard Fraser
Norbert de Varenne	David Bond
Paul de Cazolles	John Good
Potin	Leonard Mudie
Count de Vaudrec	Wyndham Standing
Laurine de Marelle	Karolyn Grimes
Hortense	Judy Cook
Mayor of Canteleu	Lumsden Hare
Commissioner	Jean Del Val
Lawyer	Charles Trowbridge
Keeper of the Seals	Olaf Hytten

Confronted with the old problem of cleaning up a classic novel to conform to strict censorhsip codes, the David L. Loew-Albert Lewin production outfit has come up with a scrubbed-face version of the complete scoundrel depicted in Guy de Maupassant's "Private Affairs of Bel Ami." Cleanup process, which denatured most of the story's original flavor, results in a fair picture which should go strongly with the femme trade but may be a little too talky for general audiences. Fact that it's a period piece will also militate against the film outside the keys. It's slotted for the first runs, though, where it should do satisfactory biz.

Lewin's screenplay adaptation of the de Maupassant novel has the title character pay for his sins by being killed in a duel which he brought on himself, in strict compliance with the Production Code's "crime doesn't pay" edict. Prosties, which had a feature part in the story, emerge as dancers of questionable character in the film, and other themes resembling the off-color are treated in the same fashion, none of which is Lewin's fault. Audiences will have to interpret the picture, consequently, via their own tastes and thinking.

Entire tempo of the story is slow-paced, which is carried out even in the dim lighting effects. Lewin's script builds up little sympathy for George Sanders, the "Bel Ami" of the piece, who climbs to the top of Paris social and political circles in the 1880's over the broken hearts of five women whom he uses to advance himself and then discards. Story picks him up as a down-and-out ex-soldier whose former comrade gets him a job on a Paris newspaper. Sanders marries the comrade's wife to further his career after the friend dies and then ditches her after getting half her inheritance. After nearing his goal by acquiring the title of a supposedly extinct noble family and proposing to the young daughter of his wealthy editor, he's brought up short when the last of the titled family appears on the scene and challenges him to a duel. Sanders naturally gets killed in the duel and the film fades out to mournful music.

Cast is exceptionally strong and, under Lewin's skilled direction, is mostly responsible for the film's merits. Sanders has one of the meatiest parts of his career and plays it with the correct hammy touch, leering nastily at the women, striking them when it suits his fancy and emoting with de Maupassant epigrams for sock effect. Angela Lansbury is beauteous and competent as the young widow with whom he's probably in love all the time. Ann Dvorak, Frances Dee, Susan Douglas, Katherine Emery and Marie Wilson all show well as the other women in his path. John Carradine, as the comrade, and Hugo Haas and Albert Basserman handle the male roles in okay fashion. Ex-star Warren William shows his old form in a feature role.

Production credits, under the able supervision of Loew, are for the most part standout. "My Bel Ami," feature song penned by Jack Lawrence and Irving Drutman, is a fair waltz which affords one of the picture's few light moments as background for an 1880 version of the dance terped in a Paris bistro by Sanders and Miss Lansbury. Painting of "The Temptation of Saint Anthony," by Max Ernst, which forms one of the focal points of the story a la "Dorian Gray," is flashed on the screen the first time it's shown in brilliant Technicolor for good effect.

Darius Milhaud's score is excellent and Russell Metty's camera work, spotlighting shadows and gas-lit interiors, is good. For an added innovation, set designer Edward G. Boyle carried out a vertical stripe theme in almost every scene, with the stripes appearing on floors, walls, ceilings and even the inside of hansom cabs. Reason behind this is unclear but the result is striking.

Stal.

Beat the Band
(SONGS)

RKO release of Michel Kraike production. Stars Frances Langford; features Ralph Edwards, Phillip Terry, Gene Krupa Orch. Directed by John H. Auer. Screenplay, Lawrence Kimble; adaptation by Kimble, Arthur Ross from play by George Abbott; songs, Leigh Harline, Mort Greene; camera, Frank Redman; editor, Samuel E. Beetley. Tradeshown N. Y. Feb. 19, '47. Running time, **67 MINS.**

Ann	Frances Langford
Eddie	Ralph Edwards
Damon	Phillip Terry
Willow	June Clayworth
Mrs. Peters	Mabel Paige
Professor	Andrew Tombes
Duff	Donald MacBride
Mrs. Rogers	Mira McKinney
Mr. Rogers	Harry Harvey
Harold	Grady Sutton

Gene Krupa Band

Lightweight filmusical spawned in the B corner of RKO's lot, "Beat the Band" is thin, obvious stuff intended for program filler in nabe situations. Except for Gene Krupa's intense skinbeating and some classy warbling by Frances Langford, pic has little to recommend. Scripting has an occasional bright spot but in the main is a conglomeration of cliched gags. Production mountings bespeak the budget limitations.

Musical score by Leigh Harline and Mort Greene is so-so but under stylistic treatment of Miss Langford has listenable qualities. Latter, not much in the straight thesping department, renders three tunes, including "Kissin' Well," "I'm in Love" and "I've Got My Fingers Crossed." Krupa and his orch are featured in two hot jive numbers with unusual camera angles giving them proportions of big productions.

Story, a fragile peg for the music, is concerned with a hick gal who comes to the big town for operatic lessons. She falls into the hands of Phillip Terry, a bandleader, who poses as a musical spaghetti slinger in order to get her money. Complicated bedroom gag of one man masquerading as another man's wife is provocation for most of the laughs.

Ralph Edwards, "Truth and Consequences" airshow star, plays comic sidekick to Terry, and while his super-volatile antics are bound to tickle, they're better suited for radio than films. He would do better to tone down the exaggerated mannerisms. Terry is okay as the romantic lead. Donald MacBride effectively registers for laughs while rest of the cast score par for the course.

Herm.

Danger Street

Hollywood, Feb. 20.

Paramount release of William Pine-William Thomas production. Stars Jane Withers, Robert Lowery; features Bill Edwards, Elaine Riley, Audrey Young, Lyle Talbot, Charles Quigley. Directed by Lew Landers. Screenplay, Maxwell Shane, Winston Miller, Kae Salkow; original, Miller, Salkow; camera, Benjamin H. Kline; editor, Howard Smith. Tradeshown Feb. 17, '47. Running time, **66 MINS.**

Pat Marvin	Jane Withers
Larry Burke	Robert Lowery
Sandy Evans	Bill Edwards
Cynthia Van Loan	Elaine Riley
Dolores Johnson	Audrey Young
Charles Johnson	Lyle Talbot
Carl Pauling	Charles Quigley
Smitty	Lucia Carroll
Veronica	Nina Mae McKinney
Turlock	Paul Harvey

Problems of operating a photo magazine and solving a murder at the same time set the pattern for light melodramatics in "Danger Street." It's secondary product from the Pine-Thomas unit at Paramount with name of Jane Withers to lend extra value.

Miss Withers and Robert Lowery team as heads of cooperatively run mag, taken over by employees when the publisher decides to unload. Pair lens compromising photo of a rich girl's fiance and sell it to another magazine for capital to get their own rag underway. Sale of pix results in murder of purchaser and leads become involved in amateur sleuthing to nail the killer. Before plot is washed up there's another killing but Miss Withers tricks killer into a confession and solves everything.

Lew Landers' direction carries plot along nicely, getting best from not too well based ingredients. Maxwell Shane, Winston Miller and Kae Salkow scripted from original by latter pair. Charles Quigley is the photoed heel who's trying to marry Elaine Riley for her money while Bill Edwards is the old friend who gets the gal in the end. Others are acceptable.

Photography by Benjamin H. Kline and other technical credits measure up.

Brog.

The Devil Thumbs a Ride

Hollywood, Feb. 21.

RKO release of Herman Schlom production. Stars Lawrence Tierney; features Ted North, Nan Leslie, Betty Lawford, Andrew Tombes, Harry Shannon. Directed by Felix Feist. Screenplay, Feist; based on the novel by Robert C. DuSoe; camera, J. Roy Hunt; music, Paul Sawtell; editor, Robert Swink. Tradeshown Feb. 20, '47. Running time, **63 MINS.**

Steve	Lawrence Tierney
Jimmy	Ted North
Carol	Nan Leslie
Agnes	Betty Lawford
Joe Brayden	Andrew Tombes
Owens	Harry Shannon
Jack	Glenn Vernon
Diane	Marian Carr
Capt. Martin	William Gould
Mother	Josephine Whittell
Pete	Phil Warren
Sheriff	Robert Malcolm

"The Devil Thumbs a Ride" depicts the dangers of giving a highway lift to strangers—and does a mighty good job of moralizing. It's strong melodrama with exploitation values that will play well in the action market.

Herman Schlom has given film good production backing to display melodramatics and Felix Feist's direction of his own script is an expert job. Lawrence Tierney does another of his uncompromisingly tough guys as the killer around whom the plot swings.

Story concerns Ted North, young salesman, returning to Los Angeles after attending convention in San Diego. Slightly drunk, he picks up Tierney, who has just held up and killed a theatre manager. Along the way, North also picks up two girls who are headed for San Pedro. A smart service station attendant puts the police on the trail of the killer. As police net tightens, Tierney talks North into avoiding road blocks because of drinking and foursome hole up at Newport in a friend's beach house.

Circumstance brings police manhunt closer to its goal and those with Tierney gradually realize what he is. One of the girls is killed as she tries to seek help and others are in jeopardy before a capture is effected. Script is taken from a novel by Robert C. DuSoe and builds plenty of suspense and thrills for meller addicts.

Nan Leslie and Betty Lawford are the two femme pickups, both good. Miss Leslie shows especially well as the girl who is bumped off. Andrew Tombes appears to advantage as a drunken night watchman at the beach, and Harry Shannon is a very believable policeman. Glenn Vernon, the smart service station attendant, clicks, and others in cast lend excellent support.

Lensing by J. Roy Hunt, Paul Sawtell's music score, the art direction and other credits do much to aid tight unfoldment of the production.

Brog.

I Cover Big Town

Hollywood, Feb. 20.

Paramount release of William Pine-William Thomas (Maxwell Shane) production. Stars Philip Reed, Hillary Brooke, Robert Lowery; features Robert Shayne, Mona Barrie, Vince Barnett, Louis Jean Heydt. Directed by William C. Thomas. Original screenplay, Whitman Chambers; based on the radio program, "Big Town"; camera, Jack Greenhalgh; score, Darrell Calker; editor, Howard Smith. Tradeshown Feb. 17, '47. Running time, **62 MINS.**

Steve Wilson	Philip Reed
Lorelei Kilbourne	Hillary Brooke
Pete Ryan	Robert Lowery
Chief Tom Blake	Robert Shayne
John Moulton	Louis Jean Heydt
Dora Hilton	Mona Barrie
Harry Hilton	Frank Wilcox
Norden Royal	Leonard Penn
Louis Murkil	Vince Barnett

"I Cover Big Town" is second in the Pine-Thomas series based on the "Big Town" radio program. It's a much stouter entry than initialer and will pay off in okay style in the supporting market. There's plenty of action and fast pace developed by William C. Thomas' direction and P-T production framing gets the most from budget.

News sleuthing of Philip Reed as Steve Wilson, and Hillary Brooke as Lorelei, prevents a man from being framed for murder, uncovers deal to bankrupt a building firm and brings a wanted crook to justice, all in the space of 62 minutes. Interlarded with the melodramatic ingredients are considerable chuckles to lighten proceedings. By-play in city hall pressroom when Lorelei takes over a police beat to resentment of diehard male reporters accounts for majority of lightness, blending well with more thrilling action in Whitman Chambers' original screenplay.

Reed and Miss Brooke do well by the leads and Robert Lowery is again seen as Pete Ryan. Robert Shayne does the police chief who is harassed by Reed. Frank Wilcox, accused of murder; Louis Jean Heydt, crook, and Vince Barnett, bail bond broker, give good support.

Maxwell Shane served as associate producer. Lensing, editing and other technical credits are expert for market intentions.

Brog.

Jungle Flight

Hollywood, Feb. 20.

Paramount release of William Pine-William Thomas production. Stars Robert Lowery, Ann Savage; features Barton McLane, Douglas Fowley, Douglas Blackley, Curt Bois, Duncan Renaldo. Directed by Peter Stewart. Screenplay, Whitman Chambers; original story, David Lang; camera, Jack Greenhalgh; aerial photography, Fred Jackman, Jr.; editor, Howard Smith. Tradeshown Feb. 17, '47. Running time, 67 **MINS.**

Kelly Jordan	Robert Lowery
Laurey Roberts	Ann Savage
Case Hagin	Barton MacLane
Andy Melton	Douglas Blackley
Tom Hammond	Douglas Fowley
Tony	Curt Bois
Police Captain	Duncan Renaldo

"Jungle Flight" bases its adventures on flying freighters and as a consequence the aerial photography is a chief production feature. It's standard material for filling out the twin bills and will show okay returns for modest budget.

Plot concerns freight line operated by Robert Lowery and Douglas Blackley, flying equipment and ore fore mine owned by Barton MacLane in a Latin-American country. Boys get over-anxious in effort to make sizeable stake and return to the States. As result Blackley is killed when his overloaded plane crashes. Yarn then segues into romantic phase when Lowery takes Ann Savage, flying from a crooked husband, to the mine as cook. Douglas Fowley, the husband, finally locates his missing frau, appears on the scene with the cops right after him. He's captured but plane crashes on return trip to civilization. Finale has Lowery flying to rescue victims, mixing in a violent slugfest with Fowley and getting the girl in the end.

Peter Stewart keeps the Whitman Chambers script on the move with his direction although pace would be helped by trimming another five minutes from footage. Lowery and Miss Savage carry off the leads okay. Curt Bois is in for some dialect comedy as a native who wants to fly.

Pine-Thomas production gets added value from air shots lensed by Fred Jackman, Jr. Other camera work is capably handled by Jack Greenhalgh. *Brog.*

Trail Street

(SONGS)

Hollywood, Feb. 20.

RKO release of Nat Holt production. Stars Randolph Scott, Robert Ryan, Anne Jeffreys, George "Gabby" Hayes; features Madge Meredith, Steve Brodie, Billy House, Virginia Sale, Harry Woods. Directed by Ray Enright. Screenplay, Norman Houston, Gene Lewis; based on the novel by William Corcoran; camera, J. Roy Hunt; music, Paul Sawtell; editor, Lyle Boyer. Tradeshown Feb. 19, '47. Running time, **83 MINS.**

Bat.......................Randolph Scott
Allen.........................Robert Ryan
Ruby........................Anne Jeffreys
Billy...............George "Gabby" Hayes
Susan.....................Madge Meredith
Maury.........................Steve Brodie
Carmody.......................Billy House
Hannah......................Virginia Sale
Larkin........................Harry Woods
Slim..........................Phil Warren
Mayor.......................Harry Harvey
Jason.......................Jason Robards

"Trail Street" is rough, tough western entertainment, geared to register heavily at the boxoffice. Nat Holt's production repeats the commercial factors he used in the successful "Badman's Territory" last season, and comparable success is a cinch.

Name values are strong for the action market, leading off with Randolph Scott and George "Gabby" Hayes. Locale is pioneer Kansas and the small trail's end town of Liberal. Against that background script and direction pitch fast movement that entertains. Scoring potently are Scott as Bat Masterson, famed western law man, and Hayes, a bewhiskered prairie veteran.

Action gets underway when Scott is brought in to clean up lawless element that is wrecking Liberal and the farmers who are trying to make the land fruitful. On the law man's side are Robert Ryan, young land agent who visions vast wheat fortunes for the farmers, and Hayes. Excitement rides high under Ray Enright's direction as story develops logically to the climax when the bad men are done in and Liberal settles down to be a peaceful wheat, instead of cow, town.

Action is leavened by Hayes' fine light comedy work. He gives a lift when needed and relieves tension at just the right moments. Scott makes his role a big success. Robert Ryan is excellent. Madge Meredith registers more favorably in the romantic spot with Ryan than does Anne Jeffreys. Latter's part is larger but not as clearly defined. Miss Jeffreys sings two tunes appropriate to the saloon background where she is entertainer. Steve Brodie and Billy House are the top heavies, but their henchman, Harry Woods, provides the most menace.

Expert lensing by J. Roy Hunt and purposeful music score by Paul Sawtell are extra values that help the punch. Nat Holt's production gives the screenplay by Norman Houston and Gene Lewis, based on William Corcoran's novel, showmanly treatment to make "Trail Street" pay off with large returns. *Brog.*

Les Enfants du Paradis

(Children of Paradise)

(FRENCH-MADE)

Tricolore Films release of Pathe (France) production. Stars Jean-Louis Barrault, Arletty; features Pierre Brasseur, Fabien Loris, Louis Salou, Etienne Decroux. Directed by Marcel Carne. Original screenplay, Jacques Prevert; music, Joseph Kosma, Maurice Thierte, Georges Mouque. At Ambassador, N. Y., Feb. 19, '47. Running time, **144 MINS.**

Baptiste Deburau ....Jean-Louis Barrault
Frederick Lemaitre ....Pierre Brasseur
Garance ....Arletty
Lacenaire ....Marcel Herrand
Jericho ....Pierre Renoir
Avril ....Fabien Loris
Anselme Deburau ....Etienne Decroux
Nathalie ....Maria Cassares
Madame Hermine ....Jeanne Marken
The Blind ....Gaston Modot
Count de Montray ....Louis Salou
Director ....Pierre Palau
Scarpia Barigni ....Albert Remy
Inspector of Police ....Paul Frankeur

(In French; English Titles)

The most ambitious French film, and certainly the longest, to cross the Atlantic since the Nazis were pushed back of the Seine, turns out to be a strange mixture of the beautiful, the esoteric and the downright dull. Some startling flashes of inspired mimicry and fresh Gallic humor are wedded to the not un-Hollywoodian concept of the femme fatale who, willy-nilly in this instance, leads men to their ruin in an uneven performance of writing and direction. A film, in short, which will do well in sureseater metropolitan situations where there are enough foreign pix fanciers for heavy traffic. In Chillicothe, its chances are in reverse.

"Les Enfants du Paradis" ("The Children of Paradise") borrows its title from the denizens (reminiscent of those old silents depicting mobs in French revolution scenes) who frequented the top gallery of a dreary little theatre in the Paris of the 1840s. Its poetical concept is to present the world's charade, in which the theatre's actors and actresses take part, with the Shakespearian view that life's a stage and those upon it poor players.

Much of its mood depends upon the wizardry of dialog—and here the film finds itself unhappily perched on the familiar horns of dilemma which beset subtitled pix. Choice had to be made between literal and copious subtitles or short, to-the-point ones which do not distract from the action. In taking the latter course, the transcriber merely sketched in lengthy, passionate exchanges—and the viewer has the irritated feeling, at times, of wondering what gives. An unwise choice, in this instance, because fixing of a mood is the sine qua non.

Covering a stretch of years in the lives of a players' troupe, the leisurely tale centers on a mimic (Jean-Louis Barrault) and his other-world passion for a demi-monde (Arletty) who moves through the seamy Parisian environs, bestowing her charms on those she likes—but not for coin. Arletty is also pursued by a flamboyant confrere of Barrault's (Pierre Brasseur); by a sinister cutthroat (Marcel Herrand); and an aristocrat (Louis Salou) whose attention is transfixed by Arletty's stage appearance.

Hanging on the fringe is Nathalie (Maria Cassares), hopelessly in love with Barrault. After considerable development of complex emotional cross-currents, Arletty cuts the knot by joining with the aristocrat in a continental tour of love. Interim of some half-dozen years is indicated in which Barrault turns to Nathalie for nuptials, consolation and devotion to his art.

Arletty returns and, surprisingly enough, discloses that her one permanent love is for Barrault. The latter, carried away by a relighting of the torch, deserts wife and family to rejoin her. In a final scene, Barrault loses her again in a carnival crowd after Arletty is moved to take a walk-out by the despairing pela of Barrault's wife.

Barrault is brilliantly effective as the sensitive, lovelorn mimic. His pantomining skill, portrayed in the stage sequences, is far and above anything that the screen's shown for a long time past. Hollywood should mark him down for future reference—and future acquisition, if that's in the cards.

Arletty has a beauty and allure that's pure feminine schmaltz. Her enigmatic smile, graceful carriage and magically appealing eyes have a worldly Gallic pull that goes far regardless of boundaries or language barriers. She, too, merits the attention of Hollywood's filmmakers. As to the other lead parts, their roles are sharply defined and maintained consistently in a film which is a peak of thespian artistry. *Wit.*

Her First Affair

('Premier Rendezvous')

(Songs)

(FRENCH-MADE)

Distinguished Films release of Henri Decoin production, written and directed by Decoin. Stars Danielle Darrieux, Louis Jourdan; features Fernand Ledoux, Jean Tissier. At 42d street Apollo, N. Y. Running time, **90 MINS.**

Micheline.................Danielle Darrieux
Henriette..............Jacqueline Desmarets
Angele.......................Rosine Luguet
The Directress...............Gabrielle Dorziat
Christophine.................Suzanne Dehelly
Marie...............................Eliza Ruis
Nicolas.......................Fernand Ledoux
Rollan...........................Jean Tissier
The Director..................Georges Mauloy
Pierre...........................Louis Jourdan

(In French; English Titles)

"Her First Affair" ("Premier Rendezvous") is Danielle Darrieux's first postwar film, which comes wrapped in all the Darrieux charm to give the art houses a happy tilt at the boxoffice. Whatever lure the French actress might have held with U.S. audiences, however, must have been dissipated during the war, so that chances for "Affair" elsewhere in the U.S. market look slim.

Of interest to U.S. audiences, though, is the introduction of Louis Jourdan, handsome juvenile whom David O. Selznick recently inked to make pix over here. Resembling a youthful edition of Charles Korvin, Jourdan seemingly has what it takes to make the grade. Pleasant but innocuous story of "Affair" doesn't give him too much chance to strut his thesping ability but he's the tall, dark type who will set the femmes agog and, with proper grooming in the DOS stable, he should make out well.

"Affair" was written, produced and directed by Henri Decoin, former spouse of Miss Darrieux, who made of the film a bright-enough little tale of a lonely orphan who seeks mental escape from her orphanage environment by answering a "lonely hearts" ad in the newspapers. Situation could have been made into one of the sprightly little comedies that made French pix famous but Decoin, by striving for novelty, gets snarled in an over-complicated plot that fails to rise above the ordinary.

By means of a ruse, Miss Darrieux gets to meet her secret pash but finds an a.k. college professor. Latter, however, reveals he's only subbing for the real "lonely heart," whom he describes as a young and handsome lad. Since it's too late to return to the orphanage, the professor takes Miss Darrieux home with him, where she moves in on a purely platonic basis. Since it's an all-boys' school, it presents the usual trouble of keeping her hidden. Younger man finally arrives, he and Miss Darrieux fall in love, but it's revealed that the professor had actually inserted the ad and he too loves the gal. In a mess of zany comedics, the boys at the school pool their dough to raise enough to adopt Miss Darrieux, she goes off with the younger guy and the professor gives them his blessings.

Miss Darrieux, although slightly above age to play a young and innocent orphan girl, turns in a sprightly performance and also handles her song assignments in good voice. Jourdan does well as the young guy who finally gets her but it's Fernand Ledoux, as the a.k. professor, who cops the acting honors with a smooth and subtle performance. Jean Tissier, as his wolfish colleague, is also standout.

Miss Darrieux has several songs and the boy students also sing several college tunes, none of which is outstanding. Decoin's direction is too heavy in spots for the comedy but he's mounted the film on well-designed sets, with the other production credits also good. *Stal.*

Angel and Sinner

(FRENCH-MADE)

AFE release of Louis Wips production. Stars Micheline Presle; features Louis Salou, Palau, Roger Karl, Marcel Simon. Directed by Christian-Jacque. Based on novel by Guy de Maupassant. Previewed N. Y., Feb. 21, '47. Running time, **84 MINS.**

Boule de Suif...............Micheline Presle
Lt. Eyrick (Fifi)..................Louis Salou
Carre-Lamadon ....Palau
La Major Falsborg.................Roger Karl
Le Comte........................Marcel Simon
Cornudet..........................Alfred Adam
Loiseau.........................Jean Brochard
Otto Grossling...................Michel Saline
Le Cure...........................Denis D'Ines

(In French; English Titles)

Latest entry from France is a melodramatic echo from World War II. Although taken from a de Maupassant novel based on the Franco-Prussian war of 1870, film draws a direct parallel to France's martyrdom and heroism during the recent Nazi occupation. Film is marked by a gallery of superlatively drawn characterizations, done in the best tradition of Gallic wit and candour; but a discursive screenplay and limp climax destines this effort to only moderate success in U.S. art houses.

Micheline Presle, in the star role of a modern Joan of Arc with a tarnished past, scores heavily on all counts—looks, talent and personality. Her playing of a fille de joie who refuses to share her charms with the Prussian conquerors is projected with simplicity and passion, skirting the pitfall of patriotic posturing. Generally appealing performance holds promise of a big future with U.S. audiences.

Surrounding her, without dimming her lustre, is a brilliant crew of character actors who depict the various layers of French society, the bourgeois, bureaucrat, aristocrat, and radical. Especially standout are Marcel Simon, Palau and Jean Brochard who, in portraying collaborationist elements, run the full gamut of emotions from craven fear to cunning back again to hysteria. Less accurate, psychologically, are the portrayals of the German officers which border on caricatures of brutality.

Story is concerned with a group of French citizens thrown together in a stagecoach while fleeing from the German-occupied zone around Paris. En route they are stopped by a nasty Prussian who makes it clear to the party that they cannot continue until Miss Presle walks the plank into his private chambers. Rest of the group cajole her into submitting to the officer as a patriotic duty. Bitterly disillusioned by scornful treatment she receives from her traveling companions for her immorality in finally submitting, she stabs another German officer who approaches her with the same deal as the first. She flees into the countryside and pic fades out with her happily tolling the church bells during the funeral of her victim.

English titles are adequate for fluent understanding of story development. Settings are good and camerawork is firstrate throughout. Excellent musical score underlines general production merits. *Herm.*

Code of the West

RKO release of Herman Schlom production. Features James Warren. Directed by William Berke. Screenplay, Norman Houston, based on Zane Grey's novel; music, Paul Sawtell; editor, Ernie Leadlay; camera, Jack Mackenzie. Previewed N. Y. Feb. 21, '47. Running time, 57 MINS.

Bob Wade	James Warren
Ruth	Debra Alden
Chito	John Laurenz
Saunders	Steve Brodie
Pepita	Rita Lynn
Harry	Robert Clarke
Milly	Carol Forman
Hatfield	Harry Woods
Carter	Raymond Burr
Stockton	Harry Harvey
Wescott	Phil Warren
Doc Quinn	Emmett Lynn

Despite a familiar story formula. "Code of the West" turns out to be a nicely paced galloper which should be acceptable fare for action situations. There's hard ridin', fightin' and mild romance packed in the film's 57 minutes.

Based on the Zane Grey tale, plot hangs on the efforts of James Warren and John Laurenz to homestead it on the Arizona strip circa 1880. Most strip claims have been optioned by gambler and tavern-keeper Raymond Burr who's had inside info that a railroad is to extend ultimately across the area. However, newly-arrived banker Harry Harvey refinances the settlers' loans. Thereupon Burr and his henchmen cook up plenty of skullduggery before they're all corralled by Warren and turned over to the law.

Thesping chores are well handled by a first-rate cast. James Warren turns in a credible and forthright performance as a champion of law and order. His partner, Laurenz, is vaguely reminiscent of Leo Carrillo. Burr is sinister as the heavy. Harry Harvey convinces as the banker, and Emmett Lynn's characterization of the Doc shines. Debra Alden and Rita Lynn acquit themselves favorably as the heart interest.

Despite the apparent low-budget, producer Herman Schlom has endowed this entry with better-than-average production values. Director William Berke milks Norman Houston's screenplay to advantage, while cameraman Jack Mackenzie's lensing is effective. Other technical credits are standard.

Hue and Cry
(BRITISH-MADE)
London, Feb. 5.

General Film Distributors' release of Ealing Studios production. Features Alastair Sim, Jack Warner, Valerie White. Directed by Charles Crichton. Screenplay by T. E. B. Clarke. Camera, Douglas Slocombe. At Studio ne, London. Running time, 82 MINS.

Felix Wilkinson	Alastair Sim
Rhona	Valerie White
Nightingale	Jack Warner
Joe Kirby	Harry Fowler
Mr. Kirby	Frederick Piper
Mrs. Kirby	Heather Delaine
Alec	Douglas Barr
Clarry	Joan Dowling
Fothergill	Alec Flinter
Norman	Ian Dawson
Dicky	Gerald Fox
Arthur	David Simpson
Wally	Albert Hughes
Sten	John Hudson
Dusty	David Knox

Reminiscent of the German classic "Emil and the Detective" (UFA, 1931), this film has neither its charm nor its wit. The stars, presumably the boxoffice magnets, have been woefully wasted, particularly Valerie White, uncommonly uncomfortable in an unsuitable part. Alastair Sim and Jack Warner, both with considerable followings in this country, will disappoint their public.

Lack of youthful charm and spontaneity, accents that will puzzle, are major failings. Principal actor is ex-news vendor Harry Fowler, who has played various cockney parts on the screen, but who fails to make the main character credible. And everything depends on believing in him.

Story revolves around a gang of crooks who use a serial story in "The Trump," a kids' weekly, as a means of communication. Joe Kirby, an imaginative youngster, spots this, and in spite of discouragement from his boss and an alleged detective, he perseveres, interests his pals, and brings off a great coup when boys of all ages flock to the bomb-ravaged wastes of dockland for a roundup of the criminals.

Director Charles Crichton has been conscientious, but queer camera angles and shadows can add little thrill when the original material lacks it. Film will need a lot of selling here, and is unlikely to weather Atlantic transportation. *Cane.*

Praterbuben
(Boys of the Prater)
(AUSTRIAN-MADE)
Vienna, Feb. 10.

Sovexport release of Vindobona Film production. Directed by Paul Martin. Screenplay by Hugo M. Kritz and Edmund Strzygowsky; music, Willy Schmidt-Gentner; sets, Julius V. Borsody; camera, Oskar Schnuerch; sound, Alfred Norkus. At Skala, Vienna, Feb. 6, '47. Running time, 105 MINS.

Schanagl	Fritz Imhoff
Marie	Pepi Kramer-Gloeckner
President	Alfred Neugebauer
Ferdinand	Herman Thimig
Semiramis	Rosy Werginz
Kaergli	Dorothea Neff
and the Vienna Singing Boys	

This third Austrian production has a paradoxical story. On the eve of the premiere, it was withdrawn, announcement being made that the Vienna Singing Boys were badly depicted as "bad boys playing Indians." Cuts were made. Film was then exported to Switzerland. Again there were cuts. Rumors spread about a political angle involved. Finally the Vienna premiere came and critics were practically unanimous that the picture was not worth the trouble and money expended.

Main objection is that film shows only the famous Austrian Singing Boys. There's very little action. One boy falsifies the signature of his father in order that a play of his friend can be produced. Father guarantees the eventual deficit. That is all. Reminiscences of old Viennese Prater with its amusement places are also not sufficient to warrant production. *Emil.*

Foreign Films

"L'Arche de Noe" ("Noah's Ark") (FRENCH). R.A.C. release of Productions Internationales Cinematographiques film. Stars Pierre Brasseur, Armand Bernard, Georges Rollin; features Alerme, Claude Larue, Jacqueline Pierreux, Armontel. Directed by Henry Jacques. Screenplay, Albert Paraz, based on his novel "Biru"; dialog, Pierre Laroche; camera, Henry Tiquet; music, Joseph Kosma. Reviewed in Paris. Running time, 97 MINS.

Poor direction and technique in every phase make this entry an unlikely bet for export, but the humorous story might provide material for a Hollywood remake. In France it's cued for the sticks and nabe situations where it will draw plenty of laughs. Title comes from a houseboat where most of the cast makes their home.

"Lykke Paa Rejsen" ("Lucky Journey") (DANISH). Palladium Film production and release. Stars Erling Schroeder, Ingeborg Brams; features Asbjorn Andersen, Peter Malberg, Maria Garland, Elsa Kourani, Greta Bendix, Vera Lindstroem, Valborg Neuchs. Directed by Christen Jul. Screenplay, Jul and Kirstine Andersen; camera, Einar Olsen; music, Sv. Erik Tarp. Tradeshown in Copenhagen. Running time, 88 MINS.

Good Danish comedy starring Erling Schroeder. Long absent from films, he handles his role with finesse. Story deals with a married man's journey to Paris and his amorous adventures there. Film will do well in Denmark and probably all over Scandinavia.

"L'Inspecteur Sergil" ("Inspector Sergil") (FRENCH). Constellation release of ATA production. Stars Paul Meurisse; features Liliane Bert, Rene Blancart, Vera Maxime, Andre Burgere, Florencie, Marc Valbel. Directed by Jacques Darcy. Screenplay by Darcy, based on novel by Jacque Rey. Reviewed in Paris. Running time, 95 MINS.

Poorly made whodunit has little to offer. Paul Meurisse, who portrayed the gangster in "Macadam," does the detective in this one supported by a very inept cast. Booked at the Marbeuf theatre to fill out its four-week quota, house's sophisticated patrons snickered at the picture's obvious amateurishness. What is intended for tragic suspense emerges as a comedy.

Miniature Reviews

"Carnegie Hall" (UA). Sock film presentation of musical greats of the famed showplace. Wide popular appeal.

"Blaze of Noon" (Par). Drama of pioneer days of airmail, interestingly unfolded. Good b.o. prospects.

"It Happened in Brooklyn" (Songs) (M-G). Sinatra, Grayson, Durante, Lawford in entertaining musical for top b.o.

"The Guilt of Janet Ames" (Col). Another psychological film Names plus exploitation values will help b.o.

"Undercover Maisie" (M-G). Maisie turns cop in a diverting comedy. Solid pleaser for Ann Sothern (Maisie) fans.

"Framed" (Col). Neat melodrama of unscrupulous woman slated for okay b.o. payoff.

"Blondie's Holiday" (Col.). Another episode in the Bumstead cycle. Good nabe fare.

"The Lone Hand Texan" (Col). Routine westerner aimed for juves.

"Temptation Harbor" (Pathe) Slow-paced British-made whodunit whose U. S. appeal is for the duals.

"A Cage of Nightingales" (French). Worthy French entry.

Carnegie Hall
Hollywood, Feb. 28.

United Artists release of Federal Films (Boris Morros and William LeBaron) production. Features Marsha Hunt, William Prince, Frank McHugh, Martha O'Driscoll, Hans Yaray, plus Carnegie Hall artists. Directed by Edgar G. Ulmer. Screenplay, Karl Kamb; original story, Seena Owen; camera, William Miller; musical advisor, Sigmund Krumgold; orchestration, Russell Bennett; songs, Sam Coslow, M. and W. Portnoff; Gregory Stone, Frank Ryerson and Wilton Moore. Hal Borne; editor, Fred R. Feltshans, Jr. Previewed Feb. 28, '47. Running time, 136 MINS.

Nora Ryan	Marsha Hunt
Tony Salerno, Jr.	William Prince
John Donovan	Frank McHugh
Ruth Haines	Martha O'Driscoll
Tony Salerno, Sr.	Hans Yaray
Anton Tribik	Joseph Buloff
Olin Downes	Himself
Henry	Emile Boreo
Tschaikowsky	Alfonso D'Artega
Walter Damrosch	Harold Dyrenforth
Katinka	Elola Galli

Guest artists: Walter Damrosch, New York Philharmonic Quintette, Bruno Walter, Philharmonic-Symphony Orchestra of N. Y., Lily Pons, Gregor Platigorsky, Rise Stevens, Artur Rodzinski, Artur Rubinstein, Jan Peerce, Ezio Pinza, Vaughn Monroe Orchestra, Jascha Heifetz, Fritz Reiner, Leopold Stokowski, Harry James.

The genius of its music and of the artists who present it makes "Carnegie Hall" a quality film presentation that will be a treat for any picture-goer. The trite story and direction are completely smothered by the finer points, making it capable of registering mightily at the boxoffice if sold properly.

Its lineup of name musical talent draws on the world's greatest artists and does them full justice in bringing them to a popular audience field. Standouts in a standout list are Ezio Pinza, singing the basso aria from "Simon Di Boccanegra" and the drinking song from "Don Giovanni"; Artur Rubinstein playing "Polonaise in A Flat" and "Fire Dance"; Jascha Heifetz's virtuosity on "Concerto for Violin and Orchestra in G Major"; Lily Pons' "Bell Song"; and Jan Peerce's solo of "O Sole Mio."

Each is given opportunity to sell classical music to the general public and is socko. Ranking with them are such artists as Gregor Piatigorsky, cellist, Rise Stevens, in a too short bit from "Carmen," and conductors like Fritz Reiner, Bruno

Walter, Artur Rodzinski, Walter Damrosch and Leopold Stokowski. In the more popular field are Vaughn Monroe, singing three pop tunes, and Harry James with a trumpet solo.

On the trite side is the script by Karl Kamb, loaded with cliche dialog and situations. Edgar G. Ulmer's direction does nothing with this part of the picture but, fortunately, the musical side is a heavy credit balance.

Plot covers an Irish girl who grows up in the service of the Hall and brings her son up to make his debut on its stage. Marsha Hunt surmounts an inane role to make the Irish girl part count. William Prince, the son, Frank McHugh and Martha O'Driscoll are others who almost overcome story burdens. A particularly bad performance is given by Hans Yaray as Miss Hunt's husband.

Producers Boris Morros and William LeBaron drew on the wealth of Carnegie Hall greats to assure quality artists to the picture but were careless on script and direction of the story. There is a magnificent sound recording job, lensing that is expert and other technical functions that play a major part in bringing top artistry of the musical world to the screen. These functions were under the supervision of Samuel Rheiner, who does a standout job.

Brog.

Blaze of Noon

Hollywood, March 4.

Paramount release of Robert Fellows production. Stars Anne Baxter, William Holden, Sonny Tufts, William Bendix, Sterling Hayden, Howard da Silva; features Johnny Sands, Jean Wallace, Edith King. Directed by John Farrow. Screenplay, Frank Wead, Arthur Sheekman; based on novel by Ernest K. Gann; camera, William C. Mellor; aerial photography, Thomas Tutwiler; special effects, Gordon and Devereux Jennings; score, Adolph Deutsch; editor, Sally Forrest. Tradeshown, March 3, '47. Running time, 90 MINS.

Lucille Stewart .... Anne Baxter
Colin McDonald .... William Holden
Roland McDonald .... Sonny Tufts
Porkie .... William Bendix
Tad McDonald .... Sterling Hayden
Gafferty .... Howard da Silva
Keith McDonald .... Johnny Sands
Poppy .... Jean Wallace
Mrs. Murphy .... Edith King
Reverend Polly .... Lloyd Corrigan
Sydney .... Dick Hogan
Mr. Thomas .... Will Wright

Early days of flying the airmail gets interesting treatment in "Blaze of Noon." Film has full star lineup for marquee strength, is well played and directed. It should fare particularly well as top feature in the general situations. Aerial sequences have authenticity and thrills.

Story concerns four flying brothers who leave their carnival stunting job to help carry the mails back in the early 1920's. Plot carries them through hazards of the pioneering, love, marriage, the death of two and the crippling of a third. Treatment is colorful, from opening sequences of carnival stunting right through air perils and gradual development of modern safeguards for pilots and planes.

John Farrow's actionful direction is backed with showmanly production values by Robert Fellows and a good script by Frank Wead and Arthur Sheekman, based on the Ernest K. Gann novel. Four brothers are well-played by William Holden, Sonny Tufts, Sterling Hayden and Johnny Sands. Principal role is filled by Holden as the likeable young pilot who marries Anne Baxter and is later killed.

Miss Baxter does a strong job as the wife, adding much to the general interest of the story. William Bendix rates laughs as screwball pilot and friend of the McDonald brothers. Howard da Silva underplays his role as shoestring airline pioneer for smart effect. Jean Wallace is in to carry off preliminary romance with Holden.

Standout aerial photography was contributed by Thomas Tutwiler, while chief pilot and aerial unit supervision was in expert hands of Paul Mantz. Regular lensing was given capable supervision by William C. Mellor. Editing is tight and other credits good.

Brog.

The Guilt of Janet Ames

Hollywood, Feb. 28.

Columbia production and release. Stars Rosalind Russell, Melvyn Douglas; features Sid Caesar, Betsy Blair, Nina Foch. Directed by Henry Levin. Screenplay, Louella MacFarlane, Allen Rivkin, Devery Freeman; based on story by Lenore Coffee; camera, Joseph Walker; score, George Duning; editor, Charles Nelson. Previewed at studio, Feb. 20, '47. Running time, 81 MINS.

Janet Ames .... Rosalind Russell
Smithfield Cobb .... Melvyn Douglas
Sammy Weaver .... Sid Caesar
Katie .... Betsy Blair
Susie Pierson .... Nina Foch
Walker .... Charles Cane
Carter .... Harry Von Zell
Junior .... Bruce Harper
Nelson .... Arthur Space
Joe Burton .... Richard Benedict
Danny .... Frank Orth
Sidney .... Ray Walker
Emmy Merino .... Doreen McCann
Frank Merino .... Hugh Beaumont
Police Sergeant .... Thomas Jackson
Surgeon .... Edwin Cooper
Susie's Father .... Emory Parnell

"The Guilt of Janet Ames" is a psychological fantasy that will have varied drawing appeal. Basic idea is good, the exploitation possibilities are strong, but overall effect just misses. Grossing potential is spotty. Names of Rosalind Russell and Melvyn Douglas give good marquee flash to help.

Plot takes an Ibsenesque angle of mental escape from surroundings but instead of using reality as framework for these mental venturings, production makes them ambiguous explorations into modernistic fantasy. It doesn't quite come off.

Miss Russell is the widow of a soldier killed in action when he flings himself on a grenade to save his five companions. Two years later the widow is trying to find the five men to see if any one is worthy of her husband's sacrifice. Subconsciously, she doesn't want to see them and when injured slightly in an accident, she develops hysteria paral- ysis and can't walk. Douglas, one of the men who has a guilt complex himself, undertakes to talk her out of her fixation. He does it by explaining how Ibsen took himself mentally out of prison and travelled the world. Her adventuring presents her to each of the ex-soldiers in a fanciful word-picture drawn by Douglas' neo-hypnosis. The cure works and she then applies it to Douglas to straighten him out for the finale.

The two stars give workmanlike performances under Henry Levin's direction, even though there is no lift to their portrayals. A standout spot is contributed by Sid Caesar, nitery entertainer who is on Miss Russell's list of names. With special material song written by Allan Roberts and Doris Fisher, Caesar draws a biting satire on the psychological film cycle that makes for a choice criticism of "Janet Ames" itself. Frank Orth is good as a bartender.

Louella MacFarlane, Allen Rivkin and Devery Freeman scripted from a Lenore Coffee story. There is no producer credit on film, but technical factors are expert in backing the tack taken in developing story.

Brog.

It Happened in Brooklyn

(SONGS)

Metro release of Jack Cummings production. Stars Frank Sinatra, Kathryn Grayson, Peter Lawford, Jimmy Durante; features Gloria Grahame, Marcy McGuire, Bobby Long. Directed by Richard Whorf. Screenplay, Isobel Lennart from original by John McGowan; camera, Robert Planck; editor, Blanche Sewell; songs, Sammy Cahn aend Jule Styne; piano solos, Andre Previn; dances, Jack Donohue. Previewed at Loew's Sheridan, N. Y., Feb. 18, '47. Running time, 103 MINS.

Danny Webson Miller .... Frank Sinatra
Anne Fielding .... Kathryn Grayson
Jamie Shellgrove .... Peter Lawford
Nick Lombardi .... Jimmy Durante
Nurse .... Gloria Grahame
Rae Jakobi .... Marcy McGuire
Digby John .... Aubrey Mather
Mrs. Kardos .... Tamara Shayne
Leo Kardos .... Billy Roy
Johnny O'Brien .... Bobby Long
Police Sergeant .... William Haade

About the only thing distinguishing "It Happened in Brooklyn" from the usual top-grade Metro musical is that it's filmed in black and white instead of Technicolor—and that's only probably because of the current Technicolor lab tieup. Pic is apparently budgeted lower than the usual tuners but it still has one big production number. In addition, it presents a star-studded cast, topped by Frank Sinatra, Kathryn Grayson, Peter Lawford and Jimmy Durante; an entertaining and uncomplicated story that should appeal to most audiences, and plenty of tuneful music. Withal a sock boxoffice entry.

Much of the lure will result from Sinatra's presence in the cast and the Voice presumably exerts as much pull now as he ever did. This is his first feature since "Anchors Aweigh" two years ago (except for a bit in "Till the Clouds Roll By") and he emerges in this one as a smooth, competent thesper. Guy's acquired the Crosby knack of nonchalance, throwing away his gag lines with fine aplomb. He kids himself in a couple of hilarious sequences and does a takeoff on Durante, with Durante aiding him, that's sockeroo.

Other stars also shine, although Durante has to struggle with some lines that don't do his particular brand of comedy too much good. As compensation, the comedian introduces a new voice-changing routine that's surefire and his songs are excellent. Miss Grayson is beauteous and appealing as the love interest but the sound recording doesn't do her singing any good. Lawford also makes out well and pulls a surprise with a jive rendition of a novelty tune, "Whose Baby Are You?", that will have the customers snickering.

Use of Brooklyn in the title should be an attraction and Metro wisely underplayed the Flatbush atmosphere in an apparent effort to please the sticks as well as Greenpernt. Isobel Lennart's nicely - handled adaption of an original story by John McGowan has Sinatra as a lonesome GI in London, thirsting for the Flatbush camaraderie. Before heading for home, he meets Lawford, young British nobleman whose longhair inclinations have made him a stuffed shirt, and tries to pull the Britisher out of his rut.

Back in Brooklyn, Sinatra returns to his old highschool to check with his draft board and meets Miss Grayson, the music teacher, plus Durante, the school's oldtime janitor. Unable to find a room, he moves in with Durante, and begins falling in love with Miss Grayson. Lawford appears on the scene, his grandfather having sent him over to try to acquire some of the Flatbush feeling from Sinatra, and also immediately falls in love with Miss Grayson. After Frankie and Durante succeed in breaking down Lawford's staid reserve, the quartet successfully puts over a concert to win a music scholarship for one of Miss Grayson's piano prodigies, Sinatra finds he's really in love not with the teacher but with an Army nurse from Brooklyn he met overseas, and all's well.

Interspersed in the story, none of which has any serious sociological tendencies, are a group of six new tunes from the able pianos of Sammy Cahn and Jule Styne. Of the ballads, "Time After Time" gets the most plugging, but "It's the Same Old Dream" sounds like a best Hit Parade possibility. "The Song's Gotta Come From the Heart" is strictly up the Durante alley and it's the one with which the comedian and Sinatra do their double takeoff. "Brooklyn Bridge" and "I Believe" look like other good novelties, with the latter serving as background for a fine bit of terping by Bobby Long, new Metro moppet. On the longhair side, Miss Grayson and Sinatra kid grand opera with an amusing version of "La Ci Darem La Mano" from "Don Giovanni," and Miss Grayson gives out with a straight rendition of the Bell Song from "Lakme."

Richard Whorf has directed the film with a light touch that gets the most out of the comedy situations. Four principals carry most of the film but the supporting cast shapes up well. There's one excellent bit by Gloria Grahame, as the nurse, which rates her further spotlighting. A real looker, the gal's also a fine comedienne. Production credits are all good, under producer Jack Cummings' aegis.

Stal.

Undercover Maisie

Hollywood, Feb. 28.

Metro release of George Haight production. Stars Ann Sothern; features Barry Nelson, Mark Daniels, Leon Ames, Dick Simmons, Clinton Sundberg. Directed by Harry Beaumont. Story and screenplay, Thelma Robinson; camera, Charles Salerno, Jr.; score, David Snell; editor, Ben Lewis. Tradeshown Feb. 28, '47. Running time, 98 Mins.

Maisie Ravier .... Ann Sothern
Lt. Paul Scott .... Barry Nelson
Chip Dolan .... Mark Daniels
Amor (Willis Farnes) .... Leon Ames
Guy Canford .... Clinton Sundberg
Gilfred I. Rogers .... Dick Simmons
Captain Mead .... Charles D. Brown
Mrs. Guy Canford .... Gloria Holden
Daniels .... Douglas Fowley
Mrs. Andrew Lorrison .... Nella Walker
Viola Trengham .... Gene Roberts
Isabelle .... Celia Travers
Parker .... Morris Ankrum

Latest in Metro's "Maisie" series is neat comedy, slanted for chuckles and excellent reception. Ann Sothern gives the title role plenty of bounce and furnishes marquee draw for general situations. Production dress has been expertly valued by George Haight to make "Undercover Maisie" one of the best in the group.

Plot concerns Maisie turning cop, joining Los Angeles police force as undercover operator. Interest is developed in the Thelma Robinson script by showing Maisie in training for her new characterization, when she goes on trail of a group of confidence people, and the varied adventures that have her almost taken for a real gangster ride before the case is washed up.

Harry Beaumont's direction keeps the pace fast and the chuckles hearty, displaying players and story to advantage. Miss Sothern sparks proceedings in her usual deft, flippant style. Dialog has plenty of snap and she makes the most of the lines. Barry Nelson capably handles top male spot as the young detective who persuades Maisie to join the force. Mark Daniels, another cop; Leon Ames, phony crystal-baller; Charles D. Brown, Clinton Sundberg, Dick Simmons, Gloria Holden, Nella Walker and others give expert backing to top performances.

Good lensing was contributed by Charles Salerno, Jr., to art direction and settings, and musical score lends good support to action and comedy.

Brog.

Framed

Hollywood, March 1.

Columbia release of Jules Schermer production. Stars Glenn Ford; features Janis Carter, Barry Sullivan, Edgar Buchanan, Karen Morley, Jim Bannon. Directed by Richard Wallace. Screenplay, Ben Maddow; story, Jack Patrick, camera, Burnett Guffey; score, Marlin Skiles; editor, Richard Fantl. Previewed at studio Feb. 27, '47. Running time, 81 MINS.

Mike Lambert .... Glenn Ford
Paula Craig .... Janis Carter
Stephen Price .... Barry Sullivan
Jeff Cunningham .... Edgar Buchanan
Mrs. Price .... Karen Morley
Jack Woodworth .... Jim Bannon

Bartender.....................Sid Tomack
Jane Woodworth.........Barbara Wooddell
Assay Clerk.................Paul E. Burns

Taut melodrama, another in the unscrupulous women cycle that will play off to okay business all down the line. It doesn't pack enough weight for the de luxe spots but as dual bill topper in other situations will carry itself well at the box-office. Productionally it has been given good mounting by Jules Schermer with story twists that add to melodramatic flavor.

Glenn Ford's name heads cast as out-of-work mining engineer who gets involved with beautiful blonde who's trying to steal $250,000. Script doesn't have too much finesse as written by Ben Maddow from Jack Patrick's story, but there's enough deftness to generate interest in unfoldment.

Ford is good as the young man who is supposed to be a murder victim and Janis Carter, the girl of the piece, does excellently. She is mistress of bank vice president and has plotted scheme to loot bank. Twist has girl falling for Ford, who is slated to be killed and become responsible for the theft. Girl kills her lover but Ford doesn't fall in with the scheme and finally brings her to justice after fast 81 minutes.

Backing leads under Richard Wallace's actionful direction is Barry Sullivan, Miss Carter's partner-in-crime until he becomes the victim, Edgar Buchanan, Karen Morley and Jim Bannon. Two smaller bits stand out, the bartender role of Sid Tomack and the assay clerk by Paul E. Burns. Barbara Woodell also is good in small spot.

Burnett Guffey adds to suspense with lensing and music score by Marlin Skiles fits the mood. Other credits are in keeping. *Brog.*

Blondie's Holiday

Columbia release of Burt Kelly production. Features Penny Singleton, Arthur Lake, Larry Simms, Marjorie Kent, Jerome Cowan, Grant Mitchell. Directed by Abby Berlin. Screenplay, Constance Lee; camera, Vincent Farrar; editor, Jerome Thoms. Tradeshown N. Y. Feb. 27, '47. Running time, 61 MINS.
Blondie ....Penny Singleton
Dagwood ....Arthur Lake
Alexander ....Larry Simms
Cookie ....Marjorie Kent
George Radcliffe............Jerome Cowan
Samuel Breckenbridge......Grant Mitchell
Pete Brody...................Sid Tomack
Mrs. Breckenbridge..........Mary Young
Paul Madison.................Jeff York
Alvin Fuddle................Bobby Larson
Cynthia Thompson............Jody Gilbert
Ollie ....Jack Rice
Mary ....Alyn Lockwood
Postman ....Eddie Acuff
Mike ....Tim Ryan
Bea Mason...................Anne Nagel
Tom Henley..................Rodney Bell

Misadventures of the Bumstead family in "Blondie's Holiday" continue to bounce along their methodically mad way for a solid hour of laughs. Pic is stamped from precisely the same general pattern that has been used for the numerous predecessors in this series, but impetus of a slightly new wrinkle in the situation comedy is enough to carry this film in audience favor. It will fit snugly into all nabe situations.

Once again it's trouble on all fronts for Arthur Lake and Penny Singleton. Problem of keeping ahead of the Joneses and appeasing his temperamental boss (Jerome Cowan) proves a brain-splitting job for the Bumsteads and lands them in a financial stew up to their ears. New twist in this pic is Lake's embroilment with a racetrack tout and a crowd of bookies ending in a trip to the clink. Situation is saved when the local bank president rewards Bumstead for having saved his pari-mutuel-addicted wife from being picked up in the police raid on the bookie joint.

Lake and Miss Singleton, aided by their celluloid family of juve actors

Larry Simms and Marjorie Kent and a kennel of puppy dogs, manage to mix up enough normalcy with their zaniness to be recognizable human beings. Cowan, newly added to this series as Bumstead's boss, is a good counterfoil for Lake's dim-wittedness. Rest of the cast turn in uniformly competent performances. *Herm.*

The Lone Hand Texan

Columbia release of Colbert Clark production. Stars Charles Starrett, Smiley Burnette; features Mustard & Gravy. Directed by Ray Nazarro. Screenplay, Ed. Earl Repp; camera, George F. Kelley; editor, Paul Borofsky. Tradeshown N. Y. Feb. 27, '47. Running time, 57 MINS.
Steve Driscoll..............Charles Starrett
Smiley......................Smiley Burnette
Mrs. Adams..................Mary Newton
Sam Jason...................Fred Sears
Mustard & Gravy.......Mustard & Gravy
Hattie Hatfield............Maude Prickett
Scanlon.....................George Chesebro
Boomer Kildea..............Robert Stevens
First Outlaw................Bob Cason
Strawboss...................Jim Diehl
Second Outlaw.............George Russell
Coachman....................Jasper Weldon

Straight action fare, "The Lone Hand Texan" is due to rouse some excitement for the Saturday matinee juve trade. Production, otherwise, is shaved to the bones of the western formula. Chief ingredient is a series of repetitious chases across a flat countryside, with a moderate quota of gunplay and fisticuffs. Pic dispenses entirely with such furbelows as romance and elementary logic.

Charles Starrett, as the Durango Kid, ranges down to the oil country where one of his old pardners is having a tough time bucking the local varmints scheming to get his land. After a round of potshots at him and an attempt to frame the Kid in a holdup, the gang is finally uncovered as working for an apparently kind old lady rancher.

Starrett operates okay behind a mask but in the open is awkward and wooden. Smiley Burnette is good as the comic relief and yodels a couple of hillbilly tunes with Mustard & Gravy in standard form. Mary Newton, as the femme villain, puts in a surprisingly polished performance that only puts into relief the surrounding mediocrity. *Herm.*

Temptation Harbor
(BRITISH-MADE)
London, Feb. 26.

Pathe Pictures release of Associated British Picture Corp. production. Stars Robert Newton, Simone Simon. Directed by Lance Comfort. Screenplay by Rodney Ackland, Frederick Gotfurt, Victor Skutezky from Georges Simenon's novel, "Newhaven-Dieppe"; music by Mischa Spoliansky; camera, Otto Heller. At Pathe, London, Feb. 27, '47. Running time, 102 MINS.
Mallinson...................Robert Newton
Camelia.....................Simone Simon
Brown.......................William Hartnell
Dupre.......................Marcel Dalio
Betty.......................Margaret Barton
Tatem.......................Edward Rigby
Mrs. Brown..................Joan Hopkins
Mabel.......................Kathleen Harrison
Reg.........................Leslie Dwyer
Gowshall....................Charles Victor
Mrs. Gowshall...............Irene Handl
Fred........................Wylie Watson
C.I.D. Inspector............John Salew
Frost.......................George Woodbridge
Mrs. Frost..................Kathleen Boutall

First of the Simenon thrillers to be filmed in Britain, this tells of the tragedy that enters the quiet uneventful life of an honest railway signalman. Mallinson, when, after witnessing a dockside murder, he comes into possession of $20,000. Battling with his conscience he decides not to hand it over to the police, and complications begin when he falls for a fairground "mermaid," Camelia, and is constantly pursued by Brown, the murderer, trying to retrieve the cash.

Climax is reached when, just before Mallinson has decided to skip the country with his daughter and the gold-digging "mermaid," he accidentally kills the murderer who is

tailing him. With the $20,000 tucked under his arm, Mallison gives himself up to police, emphasizing that it is impossible for an honest man to run away from his conscience.

Well acted and well produced, the picture fails to excite as it should because of its slow pace. Inclination to linger on unessentials, in order to create an "arty" atmosphere, has robbed the story of many of the thrills it should have had. Tightening in direction and dialog could have given the film a cleaner psychological twist.

Robert Newton, around whom most of the action pivots, gives a sound, thoughtful interpretation of the honest, distraught signalman. Cockney accent was a mistake, since the character gains nothing by it and does not help the boxoffice. Simone Simon, excellent in the fairground sequence, fails to keep the character vivid, and surprisingly fails to suggest the sexy side of the little trollop in spite of her scanty costumes.

Consistent good acting comes from Margaret Barton as Newton's teenage daughter. Only physical limitations prevent this young actress becoming a star, but as a character player she has few equals. William Hartnell, once again good as a crook, is in danger of becoming monotonously typed. He needs a change of part. Nice studies are contributed by Marcel Dalio, Charles Victor and a host of fine character players.

A cut of at least 10 minutes would improve its fair chances at the boxoffice here, but only hope in America is in dual situations. *Cane.*

A Cage of Nightingales
(La Cage Aux Rossignols)
(Songs)
(FRENCH-MADE)

Lopert release of Gaumont production. Stars Noel-Noel; features Micheline Francey, Georges-Biscot, Rene Genin, Rene Blancard. Directed by Jean Dreville. Screenplay, Noel-Noel, Rene Wheeler; dialog, Noel-Noel; music, Rene Cloerec; camera, Paul Cotteret; English titles, Edwin Denby. Previewed in New York, Feb. 27, '47.
Clement Mathieu.............Noel-Noel
Martine.....................Micheline Francey
Raymond.....................Georges Biscot
Maxence.....................Rene Genin
Rachin......................Rene Blancard
Madame Martine..............Marguerite Ducouret
The Chairwoman.............Marcelle Praince
Old Marie...................Marthe Mellot
Mr. Langlois................Georges Paulais
Mr. de la Prade.............Andre Nicolle
Mr. de Mazeres..............Richard Francoeur
New Director................Jean Morel
Academy Member..............Roger Vincent
Regent ....Jamin
Lequerec....................Michel Francois
Lauxler.....................Roger Krebs
And the Little Singers of the Wooden Cross

(In French; English Titles)

Life in a French reform school for boys is a holy-terror for the inmates, aged 10-14, and their instructors as well, until tutor Noel-Noel fires the youngsters with new hope by handling them with understanding and compassion. Told in flashback, "A Cage of Nightingales" is a worthy French entry whose minor story faults are overcome by fine direction and credible acting. Lending itself to exploitation, film's b.o. appeal should also build on word of mouth.

Noel-Noel writes of his experiences in the City Reform School in a novel aptly called "A Cage of Nightingales." With no takers and penniless, he ekes out a living shilling for pitchman Georges Biscot who sells toy airplanes. In a far-fetched ruse, Biscot plants the story in the Paris Telegram.

Micheline Francey, Noel-Noel's gal friend, is astonished to read the script in the paper. As she studies the first installment, the story flashes back to the authors initial entrance at the reform school. And shocking indeed is the situation. Branded as incorrigibles, the boys are brutally ruled by principal Rene Blancard. Touched

by the boys' mistreatment, and apparently a master of psychology, Noel-Noel brings out their latent good-behavior notably through the medium of a choral group.

Toward its closing moments, picture tends to become a shade too melodramatic by invoking lightning to destroy the school while principal Blancard is in Paris collecting plaudits for creating the choir. Children, fortunately, have been visiting a nearby carnival shepherded by Noel-Noel and are saved. Later their en masse escape to attend Noel-Noel's wedding to Miss Francey, cousin of one of their classmates, also rings implausibly.

However, Noel-Noel's scripting faults are minor and his portrayal of the schoolteacher is colored with honest realism and earnestness. Miss Francey as Martine is refreshingly beautiful while Blancard is genuinely severe as the cruel principal. Michel François and Roger Krebs, juvenile mischief-makers, do well in their moppet roles, and the Little Singers of the Wooden Cross further embellish the film with fine choral offerings.

Jean Dreville's direction paces the film nicely and his technique is especially evident in the reformatory scenes. Lensing of cameraman Paul Cotteret is also good as is Paul Cloerec's music. Particularly well done are Edwin Denby's English titles whose captions have ably caught the story's movement.

Foreign Films

"Ditte Menneskebarn" ("This Human Child") (DANISH). Nordisk Films Kompagni release and production. Stars Tove Maes, Karen Poulsen; features Rasmus Ottesen, Karen Lykkehus, Jette Kehlet, Edvin Tiemroth, Ebbe Rode, Kai Holm, Maria Garland, Mogens Wieth. Directed by Bjarne Henning-Jensen. Screenplay, Henning-Jensen; camera, Verner Jensen; music, Herma D. Koppel. Reviewed in Copenhagen. Running time, 108 MINS.

Based on Martin Nexoe's novel, picture introduces actress Tove Maes who does well in her debut. Dramatic story is also played to the hilt by a supporting cast of some 25 Danish actors. Fine scripting, direction and camera should make this film a success in Scandinavia and afford it a chance in the world market.

Miniature Reviews

"High Barbaree" (MG). Good dramatic tale that minimizes war background by flashbacks. Strong cast to aid b.o.

"Buck Privates Come Home" (UI). Zany Abbott & Costello comedy with good b.o. outlook.

"The Imperfect Lady" (Par). Teresa Wright, Ray Milland starrer due for moderate b.o.

"High Conquest" (Mono). Mountain-climbing drama considerably above Mono average; b.o. prospects good.

"Lost Honeymoon" (E-L). Better than average dualer buttressed with some neat directorial touches.

"Ivan the Terrible" (Artkino). Russian-made story of 16th century czar is okay Soviet fare but disappointing generally.

"Range Beyond the Blue" (PRC). Better than average oatuner in the Eddie Dean series.

High Barbaree

Hollywood, March 8.

Metro release of Everett Riskin production. Stars Van Johnson, June Allyson; features Thomas Mitchell, Marilyn Maxwell, Henry Hull, Claude Jarman, Jr. Directed by Jack Conway. Screenplay, Anne Morrison Chapin, Whitfield Cook, Cyril Hume; based on novel by Charles Nordhoff and James Norman Hall; camera, Sidney Wagner; editor, Conrad A. Nervig. Tradeshown March 5, '47. Running time, **91 MINS.**

Alec Brooke.....................Van Johnson
Nancy Fraser....................June Allyson
Capt. Thad Vail...............Thomas Mitchell
Diana Case...................Marilyn Maxwell
Lieut. Moore................Cameron Mitchell
Alec (age 14)...............Claude Jarman, Jr.
Dr. Brooke........................Henry Hull
Mrs. Brooke..................Geraldine Wall
Della Parkson.................Barbara Brown
John Case.........................Paul Harvey
Colonel Taylor.................Charles Evans

Flashback technique used in telling "High Barbaree" keeps it from being a war story, although its premise is laid in the Pacific during the recent fight against Japan. It has been movingly developed under Jack Conway's directorial skill and the strong production guidance by Everett Riskin. Picture carries top marquee strength in the names of Van Johnson, June Allyson, Thomas Mitchell and others to give it promising gross outlook.

Title derives from mythical island imagined by a seafaring uncle of a small boy in telling the youngster tall tales of life on the bounding main. It so captures the imagination of the kid that when his plane is downed in the Pacific he sets a course for the spot, little knowing that it is symbolic of death.

As the seaplane drifts towards High Barbaree, Van Johnson, the pilot, recounts his childhood to his only remaining companion, Cameron Mitchell. These flashbacks to civilian life are the means of keeping up morale for the two fliers and ring with genuine emotional appeal. Script by Anne Morrison Chapin, Whitfield Cook and Cyril Hume, based on novel of same title by Charles Nordhoff and James Norman Hall, is packed with lines and situations that punch over realism of family life.

Players do a sock job of making believeable the drama. Johnson gives an unusually good account of himself in the top male role. June Allyson is sincere and appealing as the childhood sweetheart grown up who brings Johnson back on the path of his destiny. Hers is a talent capable of moving an audience. Thomas Mitchell is fine as the uncle who periodically comes home from the sea with a new set of adventures. Marilyn Maxwell makes an attractive rival love interest. Moppets portraying leads in childhood are headed up by Claude Jarman, Jr., Cameron Mitchell, screen newcomer, impresses in his role with Johnson. Henry Hull, Geraldine Wall, Barbara Brown, Paul Harvey are among others showing well.

Picture has been given excellent lensing by Sidney Wagner, and other technical functions are of high standard. *Brog.*

Buck Privates Come Home

Hollywood, March 8.

Universal-International release of Robert Arthur production. Stars Bud Abbott and Lou Costello; features Tom Brown, Joan Fulton, Nat Pendleton, Donald MacBride, Beverly Simmons. Directed by Charles Barton. Screenplay, John Grant, Frederic I. Rinaldo, Robert Lees; based on story by Richard Macaulay and Bradford Ropes; camera, Charles Van Enger, David S. Horsley; music, Walter Schumann; editor, Edward Curtiss. Previewed March 6, '47. Running time, **77 MINS.**

Cpl. Slicker Smith..............Bud Abbott
Herbie Brown.....................Lou Costello
Bill Gregory.......................Tom Brown
Sylvia Hunter......................Joan Fulton
Sgt. Collins......................Nat Pendleton
Yvonne LeBru (Evey).....Beverly Simmons
Mr. Roberts.......................Don Beddoe
Captain...............................Don Porter
Police Captain............Donald MacBride
1st Lieutenant...................Lane Watson
2nd 1st Lieutenant.........William Ching
Steve........................Peter Thompson
Cal.........................George Beban, Jr.
Whitey..........................Jimmie Dodd
Hank.........................Lennie Bremen
Murphy................................Al Murphy
Stan.....................................Bob Wilke
Husband......................William Hande
Wife...........................Janna de Loos
New York Cop.............Buddy Roosevelt
New York Cop...............Chuck Hamilton

Back in 1941, Universal sent Abbott & Costello off to war in "Buck Privates." Six years and 18 pictures later, Universal-International brings them back to civilian life in "Buck Privates Come Home." The return is strong A&C film fare, geared for hearty risibility reaction and good boxoffice.

Fat and thin comics romp through familiar routines with few variations, but it's still strong laugh material with capacity to satisfy fans of rowdy slapstick. Picture opens with scene from the original "Buck Privates," getting things going with a sure laugh. Pace is maintained throughout by Charles Barton's direction which has plenty of punch to put over the crazy brand of comedy.

Sight gags, situations and chases that always feature Abbott & Costello comedies are strung on a story line that has the boys smuggling a little French girl into this country upon their return from overseas. Efforts to conceal the kid and prevent her deportation is frantic fun, climaxing in a hilarious chase that is socko. Chase has Costello taking off in a midget racing car with police after him and builds to hysterical peaks of audience gasps. Another high spot is version of the old heights situation wherein Costello dangles from a clothes-line between two high buildings.

Lending strong support to comedians is Nat Pendleton as the tough top kick who is driven frantic by antics. Romance angle is carried off by Tom Brown and Joan Fulton in satisfactory fashion, and Beverly Simmons is cute as the little French girl who causes all the trouble. Donald MacBride and others are good.

Robert Arthur has given excellent production values to the script by John Grant, Frederic I. Rinaldo and Robert Lees, based on a story by Richard Macaulay and Bradford Ropes. Lensing, background music, editing and other factors are expert. *Brog.*

The Imperfect Lady

Paramount release of Karl Tunberg production. Stars Ray Milland, Teresa Wright; features Sir Cedric Hardwicke, Virginia Field, Anthony Quinn, Reginald Owen. Directed by Lewis Allen. Screenplay, Tunberg based on story by Ladislas Fodor; camera, John F. Seitz; editor, Duncan Mansfield; score, Victor Young. Tradeshown N. Y., March 6, '47. Running time, **95 MINS.**

Clive Loring.......................Ray Milland
Millicent Hopkins............Teresa Wright
Lord Belmont.........Sir Cedric Hardwicke
Rose Bridges...................Virginia Field
Jose Martinez................Anthony Quinn
Mr. Hopkins.................Reginald Owen
Lord Montglyn..............Melville Cooper
Inspector Carston............Rhys Williams
Mr. Mallam....................George Zucco
Sam Travers...............Charles Coleman
Mr. Rogan.......................Miles Mander
Gladstone...................Gordon Richards
Lord Chief Justice..........Edmond Breon
Henderson...................Frederic Worlock
Malcolm Gadby................Michael Dyne
Lucy...............................Joan Winfield
Mrs. Gunner..................Lilian Fontaine

A galaxy of Paramount's top name players lends this pic a lustre that will pay off nicely at the wickets. "The Imperfect Lady," however, fails to measure up to the full b.o. possibilities afforded by its starring battery of Ray Milland and Teresa Wright chiefly because of a stunting screenplay and loose direction.

Pic is handicapped severely by the routine treatment given to the already familiar theme of an obscure showgirl surmounting obstacles of inferior social status and sullied reputation to win the love of an uppercrust English nobleman. Even the venerable melodramatic contrivance of a murder trial at the climax fails to rouse any tension due to director Lewis Allen's consistent habit of telegraphing far in advance every twist and turn in the plot.

Production mountings that have a solid mahogany illusion and a superb cast of lead and supporting players tend to counteract somewhat the negative effects of the inferior scripting. A period drama localed in England circa 1890, film gives enough of a glimpse into the life of the upper clawses which, together with the elaborate costumes, fancy dress balls and romantic heartaches, should stamp it as a good women's picture.

Miss Wright registers with an exceptionally appealing performance as the young ballerina who, while touring with her troupe, meets Milland in the midst of his election campaign for Parliament. Usual case of love at first sight, romance between the two is quickly blighted by the opposition of Milland's brother, Sir Cedric Hardwicke, a tradition-stuffed lord who persuades the gal to make an exit for the sake of Milland's promising career.

During this temporary romantic eclipse, Miss Wright gets mixed up in a jam with a hot-headed Spanish concert pianist (Anthony Quinn) and is forced to spend the night, in total innocence, at his rooms during a police roundup. Later, after Miss Wright and Milland get married over all family objections, Quinn is picked up on a false murder rap with Miss Wright's visit to his room the only alibi to prove his innocence. Dilemma of whether to reveal herself at the trial and risk the flood of innuendo or keep silent and see an innocent man condemned is resolved honestly and happily.

Milland puts in his usual polished performance, overcoming a series of stilted and cliched lines by using his native sense of humor to good effect. Hardwicke's playing of the English lord is to the manner born of a stiffnecked yet sympathetic aristocrat, his part being of standout brilliance in its full credibility. Other cast members who turn in credible performances are Virginia Field, as Miss Wright's ambitious cockney dancing partner; Reginald Owen, as the poor but honest father; Quinn, as the impetuous Spaniard, and Melville Cooper, in a brief characterization of a titled bon vivant. *Herm.*

High Conquest

Hollywood, March 8.

Monogram release of Irving Allen production, directed by Allen. Stars Anna Lee, Gilbert Roland, Warren Douglas; features Beulah Bondi, C. Aubrey Smith, John Qualen, Helene Thimig, Alan Napier. Screenplay, Max Troll; original story, Aben Kandel; based on novel by James Ramsey Ullman; camera, Jack Greenhalgh; exteriors photographed in Switzerland by Richard Angst and Tony Braun, score, Lud Gluskin; editor, Charles Craft. Previewed March 7, '47. Running time, **79 MINS.**

Marie...................................Anna Lee
Hugo Lannier..................Gilbert Roland
Jeffrey Stevens.............Warren Douglas
Clara Kingsley..................Beulah Bondi
Col. Hugh Banning....Sir C. Aubrey Smith
Peter Oberwalder..............John Qualen
Mama Oberwalder..........Helene Thimig
Thomas Donlin....................Alan Napier
Jules Koerber....................Eric Feldary
Young Peter.....................Mickey Kuhn
Franz Bitz.........................Louis Mercier
Guide.............................Richard Flato
Guide...........................Geza de Rosner
Guide...............................Al Mathews
Joel Hazlitt..........................John Good
Stefani...............................John Vosper
Douglaston.......................Wilton Graff
Walter............................Maurice Cass
Pastor................................Fritz Leiber
Steward...........................Eddie Parks
Miss Woodley................Minerva Urecal
Traveler..............................John Bleifer
Young Banning..............Douglas Walton
Miss Spencer..................Regina Wallace

"High Conquest" generates considerable interest as result of exterior footage being actually filmed in Switzerland. It's an expert blend of real mountain shots with studio-manufactured story points and the sum total is on the credit side. Film has production gloss well above usual Monogram standard and returns should be profitable in the company's market.

Plot, briefly, deals with a young man who returns to the Matterhorn site where his mountain-climbing father was killed many years before. Story is not always clear and its development of young man's reluctance to try to climb the mountain himself but overall effect is okay for sustaining some strong moments of suspense and action. These are aided by the good music score by Lud Gluskin, which helps to build excitement.

Story is taken from the James Ramsey Ullman novel of same title, as scripted by Max Troll. As producer-director, Irving Allen has made a nigh-perfect match between footage filmed in the Alps and studio sequences. Exterior shoots are compelling in showing the rugged, picturesque country of mountainous Switzerland and the peaks that annually attract human conquerors.

Anna Lee and Warren Douglas carry off leads as Swiss girl and the American boy who doesn't like mountains. Miss Lee is good but Douglas falls short in his interpretation, although script is no particular help in explaining his actions. Gilbert Roland shows well as the mountain guide. C. Aubrey Smith is in as narrator for some portions of the story. Better moments are contributed by John Qualen and Helene Thimig. Others in cast measure up.

Excellent location footage was lensed by Richard Angst and Tony Braun with Jack Greenhalgh's studio footage blending perfectly. *Brog.*

Lost Honeymoon

Eagle-Lion release of Bryan Foy (Lee Marcus) production. Stars Franchot Tone, Ann Richards, Tom Conway; features Frances Rafferty, Clarence Kolb, Una O'Connor, Winston Severn. Directed by Leigh Jason. Original screenplay, Joseph Fields; camera, L. W. O'Connell; editor, Norman Colbert; music, Irving Friedman. At Victoria, N. Y., March 5, '47. Running time, **71 MINS.**

Johnny Gray...................Franchot Tone
Amy Atkins.......................Ann Richards
Doctor Davis.......................Tom Conway
Lois Evans......................Frances Rafferty
Mr. Evans.........................Clarence Kolb
Mrs. Tubbs.....................Una O'Connor
Johnny, Jr....................Winston Severn
Joyce.........................Adele Davenport
Mrs. Jenkins.....................Sandra Roger
Major...................................John Wald

Eagle-Lion's second U. S.-produced release is a whipped-up bit of broth with entertainment values several rungs above average in the dual bracket. In it some neat pieces of business, cannily designed, are strung on a machine-made story. It should earn a respectable profit all around.

It's the icing on the cake that makes "Lost Honeymoon" despite that familiar pattern—the man afflicted with amnesia—who has (or has he?) married the gal while under its cinematic, if unmedical, spell. The sugar is in such gadgets as Franchot Tone struggling futilely to unwrap the cellulose packaging of his shirt; or seeking a return to amnesia by clunking his head against a street lamp, or, then again, pajama-clad, chasing along the midnight highways in quest of advice from a friend. These gather laughs and keep things lively. Poised against these creditable directorial foibles is a farce which fails to build up into punch finish.

His tongue-in-cheek portrayal of the harried swain and father is nicely tuned to the film's farcical intents. Ann Richards is effectively pert and likeable in her role as the unexpected visitor from across the seas. In slighter parts, Tom Conway, Frances Rafferty and Clarence Kolb amply meet the requisites. *Wit.*

Ivan the Terrible
(RUSSIAN-MADE)

Artkino release of Central Cinema production. Stars Nikolai Cherkassov; features Seraphima Birman, Nazvanov. Directed by Sergei Eisenstein. Screenplay, Eisenstein; camera, Edward Tisse, Andrei Moskvin; music, Sergei Prokofieff; English titles, Charles Clement. Previewed N. Y., March 6, '47. Running time, 96 MINS.

Ivan IV	Nikolai Cherkassov
Anastasia	Ludmila Tselikovskaya
The Boyarina Staritzkaya	Seraphima Birman
Vladimir Andreyevich	Piotr Kadochnikov
Prince Andrei Kurbsky	Nazvanov
Prince Fyodor Kolychov	Alex. Abrikosov
Nikola	Vsevolod Pudovkin
Malyuta Skuratov	Mikhail Zharov
Alexei Basmanov	Alexei Buchma
Fyodor	Mikhail Kuznetzov

(In Russian; English Titles)

Despite usual good Russian photography, a powerful score, a couple of nice performances and flashes of original direction, "Ivan the Terrible" will disappoint the average American picture patron. However, it is fairly palatable to those who go for Russian productions and appears good for sizable boxoffice in foreign-language and arty theatres.

Picture has so much that is tiresome, has so little action and becomes so involved that the average history student hardly will recognize this glorified Ivan. Additionally, it has the usual quota of Soviet propaganda that is so obvious it screams its meaning. Such blatant message material might have been forgiven if the result was outstanding entertainment. This isn't. These heavy-handed propaganda slugs include bows to the common folks, the merchants and tradesmen, pleas for a strong Russia, united to face the world and halt foreign intrigue.

Yarn makes Ivan virtually a saint, and at least the final saviour of his people. Story hardly depicts him as the man known in history, and seldom as one of action. Film starts out like this was to be the first of two or three super-productions. It never measures up to its initial premise or even its opening colorful coronation scene.

There's an impressive final scene where thousands of Ivan's friends follow him in the snow away from Moscow and his scheming enemies. But that sequence, like the battle scene and several others, never quite rises to its potentialities because of flighty direction or cutting, or a combination of both. Principal fault seems to lie in the fact that the producers fail to make up their minds as to whether it is a spectacle, a historical opus or a character study of Ivan.

Another "Ivan the Terrible" picture was made in silent version nearly 20 years ago. Understood that Eisenstein originally planned making this story in three pictures, each as long or longer than this one.

On the credit side is a splendid score by Sergei Prokofieff, fairly good if spotty direction by Eisenstein, fine camera work by Edward Tisse and Andrei Moskvin, and the superb character portrayal of Ivan by Nikolai Cherkassov. Besides Cherkassov's performance, Ludmila Tselikovskaya, Seraphima Birman and Nazvanov contribute the best thesping work. Charles Clement's English titling often is more vivid than the action on the screen.

Aside from the extreme wordiness and minimum of action, vehicle lacks humor of any sort. Even in the 16th Century, there must have been moments of levity. Apparently Eisenstein should have confined his efforts to directing because his script fails to be interest-sustaining. *Wear.*

Range Beyond the Blue
(SONGS)

PRC release of Jerry Thomas production. Stars Eddie Dean; features Roscoe Ates, Helen Mowery, Bob Duncan. Directed by Ray Taylor. Screenplay, Patricia Harper; songs, Eddie Dean, Bob Dean, Pete Gates, Hal Blair; music, Walter Greene; editor, Hugh Winn; camera, Robert Cline. Previewed N. Y. March 7, '47. Running time, 53 MINS.

Eddie Dean	Eddie Dean
Soapy	Roscoe Ates
Margie Rodgers	Helen Mowery
Lash Taggert	Bob Duncan
Henry Rodgers	Ted Adams
Kyle	Bill Hammond
Bragg	George Turner
Sneezer	Ted French
Kirk	Brad Slavin
Sheriff	Steve Clark
Sunshine Boys	Themselves

With plenty of gunplay, a fair plot and okay songs spotted in the right places, "Range Beyond the Blue" emerges as a better-than-average oatuner in the Eddie Dean series. Cayuse classic should find acceptance in most action situations.

Still operating as undercover investigators, Eddie Dean and pardner, Roscoe Ates, foil a stagecoach hold-up on a line owned and operated by Helen Mowery. Stage's gold shipments ostensibly are the loot sought by the road agents, but Dean suspects something else is behind the frequent attacks. Suspense built up by scripter Patricia Harper should hold an audience even though the film's denouement is rather obvious.

Climax is reached with the law's rout of the bandits led by Bob Duncan. Latter's a tool of Ted Adams, prexy of the local bank, who seeks to gain control of Miss Mowery's stage line. In the melee between the outlaws and a posse headed by Dean and Ates, there's plenty of six-shootin' before the badmen are rounded up and Adams bites the dust.

Thesping, direction and camera are relatively good in view of the low budget. Dean handles his chores in forthright fashion while Ates provides the comedy relief. Miss Mowery, a winsome blonde, doesn't quite ring true as a stagecoach operator. Supporting cast composed of Duncan, Adams, Ted French and others are adequate. Ray Taylor directed at a smooth pace.

Tales of Palestine
(BRITISH-MADE)
(Documentary)

London, Feb. 24.

Produced, written, and directed by Joseph Leytes. Stars Abraham Sofaer, Alexander Sarner. Music, Mischa Spoliansky; camera, Lipinski. At British Council, London, Feb. 24, '47. Running time, 50 MINS.

This is the best short yet made on Palestine. It has heart, soul and dignity. Not one reference is made to the troubled political situation, and can therefore be shown to any audience. Few people will remain unmoved by this simple story of converting sand and swamp and stone into a land fit for unwanted humans to live in.

Tieup with present-day situation is given by visit of few Palestinians of Jewish Brigade (including Abraham Sofaer) to Belsen. In conversation with a Hitler victim (Alexander Sarner), bereft of any hope, they tell him of Palestine. One soldier relates what his recent leave was like in his communal settlement; another tells how displaced and unwanted orphans were settled in Palestine; a third speaks of the River Jordan and the promise of harnessing the waters to bring life to the dead deserts of the South.

Most moving of all the episodes is that of the children, played by youngsters of a Palestine settlement. Brilliant is the performance given by the unnamed child playing Tamara, a girl more animal than human, transplanted from a concentration camp to a home in Palestine. This part of the film alone is worth myriads of pamphlets and volumes of speeches. Commentary is at all times simple and dignified.

Production reflects greatest credit on Joseph Leytes, onetime ace director in Warsaw. Spending six weeks in Palestine with a hand camera, raw stock of all makes collected from odd places, and recruiting locals from the settlements, he has made a grand moving picture. Sofaer and Sarner were the only professionals and they are admirable.

Spoliansky's music matches the mood of the picture and is some of the best he has composed. His "Jordan" theme has all the quality of a notable tone-poem. Camera work by Lipinski (who also won laurels in former Polish film industry) is worthy of highest praise.

Distribution has not yet been set here and political situation may militate against wide showing, but it should have nationwide screening in America and deserves it on its merits. *Cane.*

Miniature Reviews

"Stallion Road." (WB). Drama of love and horses in Southern California that will depend largely upon cast names to sell.

"Time Out of Mind" (UI). Dull dissertation of life and music of the Maine coast, despite tiptop photography and good music.

"Tarzan and the Huntress" (RKO). Moderately entertaining adventure film in the Tarzan series.

"Law of the Lash" (PRC). Introducing a new PRC film cowpoke; filler material for Saturday matinee trade.

"Bel Ami" (Filmex). Mexican-made version of de Maupassant tale, strong for Mexico market and a possibility in U. S.

Stallion Road

Hollywood, March 17.

Warners release of Alex Gottlieb production. Stars Ronald Reagan, Alexis Smith, Zachary Scott; features Peggy Knudsen, Patti Brady, Harry Davenport, Frank Puglia, Angela Greene. Directed by James V. Kern. Novel and screenplay, Stephen Longstreet; camera, Arthur Edeson; editor, David Weisbart. Tradeshown March 17, '47. Running time, 97 MINS.

Larry Hanrahan	Ronald Reagan
Rory Teller	Alexis Smith
Stephen Purcell	Zachary Scott
Daisy Otis	Peggy Knudsen
Chris Teller	Patti Brady
Dr. Stephens	Harry Davenport
Lana Rock	Angela Greene
Pelon	Frank Puglia
Richmond Mallard	Ralph Byrd
Ben Otis	Lloyd Corrigan
Chico	Fernando Alvarado
Joe Beasley	Matthew Boulton

"Stallion Road" manages to generate considerable interest for the general theatregoing public by virtue of its tale of a "Pasteur of the pasture." It's the story of a veterinarian who practices his trade among the wealthy Southern California horse-breeders. Horse doctor angle is sometimes a bit tediously developed and the dialog is strictly typewriter and not tongue, but overall, film has okay prospects in heading double bill situations outside of de luxe runs.

Main script fault is author Stephen Longstreet's indulgence in soporific speeches about horses and life. Speeches read okay in print but are cumbersome when spoken and strong cast never quite overcomes the monologs. Sex angles in the Longstreet novel are reduced by film censorship to minor items so principal interest to ticket-buyers will lie in the proud horseflesh displayed.

Strong interest is accounted for by horse-jumping scenes, each packing a thrill. There is also a socko fight sequence that rings with realism, and is well worth seeing although events leading up to it are hard to follow.

Plot premise deals with Ronald Reagan, horse doctor, who is visited by Zachary Scott, successful novelist. The saddle medico and the writer fall in love with Alexis Smith, femme horse breeder. Romance for Reagan goes smooth until he nixes help for his girl's prize horse to save a herd of cattle from anthrax. This gets all horsemen in the valley down on him, but there's a turnabout when anthrax hits the nags and the doc's serum saves them. Reagan falls ill from anthrax. Miss Smith injects him with his own serum and love wins out.

James V. Kern's direction packs a lot of punch in the few action sequences offered by the Longstreet script, but falls short on understanding necessary to develop characters that people the plot. Reagan, Miss Smith and Scott are as good as the script allows and even add a lift to the readings. Peggy Knudsen spots a bit of sex as the banker's wandering wife who's interested in the doctor. Patti Brady, moppet sister of Miss Smith's, and Angela Greene, who makes a brief, unexplained scene as a girl of light love, stand out. Harry Davenport, Frank Puglia and Fernando Alvarado also make their footage count.

Alex Gottlieb's production has given the picture top technical appurtenances and realistic backgrounds. Camera work of Arthur Edeson is fine and score by Frederick Hollander is a help. *Brog.*

Time Out of Mind

Hollywood, March 15.

Universal-International release of Robert Siodmak production, directed by Siodmak. Stars Phyllis Calvert, Robert Hutton, Ella Raines; features Eddie Albert, Leo G. Carroll, Helena Carter, John Abbott, Henry Stephenson, Olive Blakeney, Harry Shannon, Janet Shaw. Screenplay, Abem Finkel, Arnold Phillips; based on novel by Rachel Field; camera, Maury Gertsman; special photography, David S. Horsley; music, Miklos Rozsa, Mario Castelnuovo-Tedesco; editor, Ted J. Kent. Previewed March 14, '47. Running time, **86 MINS.**

Kate Fernald .... Phyllis Calvert
Christopher Fortune .... Robert Hutton
Rissa Fortune .... Ella Raines
Jake Bullard .... Eddie Albert
Captain Fortune .... Leo G. Carroll
Dora Drake .... Helena Carter
Max Lieberman .... John Abbott
Wellington Drake .... Henry Stephenson
Mrs. Fernald .... Olive Blakeney
Captain Rogers .... Harry Shannon
Penny .... Janet Shaw
Alfred Stern .... Emil Rameau
Dr. Weber .... Samuel S. Hinds
Aunt Melinda .... Lilian Fontaine
George .... Houseley Stevenson
Annie .... Maudie Prickett

This is a draggy celluloid version of Rachel Field's novel of a musician who finally escapes his seafaring family. It has technical achievements of Academy Award standards, particularly the photography, but falls short on entertainment.

Little interest is generated by the Abem Finkel-Arnold Phillips script to back strong physical production and camera values given the plot. As an American film debut for Phyllis Calvert, it doesn't display the British actress to advantage. Role could have been better in hands of a suitable Hollywood femme and would have meant more at the b.o.

Worthwhile standards in screen entertainment expected of Robert Siodmak, who has some top credits on his list as director, do not come through. He apparently has made an honest effort to spin a tale of frustration against a New England seafaring background but characters portrayed fail to arouse interest. Roles have a vagueness that prevents audience understanding of what is transpiring and characters carry no sympathy.

Robert Hutton is the musician-son of a New England sailing family whose composing complex is frustrated by his father's insistence he take to the sea. In the household is a servant girl who, with the boy's sister, pushes him towards his normal destiny in life. That eventually he makes it, after a period of unhappy marriage and dipsomania, is tepidly unfolded.

Miss Calvert is the servant girl and does not make a distinguished Hollywood debut. Neither does Ella Raines, the sister, come through with character clarity. Hutton tries hard with little success in his role. Eddie Albert, featured, has only a few minor scenes, all of which fail to register. Among femme contingent in supporting cast, Janet Shaw and Helena Carter make their footage count. John Abbott, as a music critic, also figures to advantage.

Standout lensing is given to the sterling settings by Maury Gertsman. It is camera work of the highest artistry that, unfortunately, isn't matched by story worth. There also is an excellent musical score by Miklos Rozsa and Mario Castelnuovo-Tedesco that is on the credit side. *Brog.*

Tarzan and the Huntress

RKO release of Sol Lesser (Kurt Neumann) production, directed by Neumann. Stars Johnny Weissmuller, Brenda Joyce, Johnny Sheffield; features Patricia Morison, Barton MacLane. Original story and screenplay, Jerry Gruskin, Rowland Leigh, based upon characters created by Edgar Rice Burroughs; camera, Archie Stout; editor, Merrill White; music, Paul Sawtell. Tradeshown, N. Y., March 12, '47. Running time, **72 MINS.**

Tarzan .... Johnny Weissmuller
Jane .... Brenda Joyce
Boy .... Johnny Sheffield
Tanya .... Patricia Morison
Weir .... Barton MacLane
Marley .... John Warburton
Smithers .... Wallace Scott
King Farrod .... Charles Trowbridge
Prince Suli .... Maurice Tauzin
Prince Ozira .... Ted Hecht
Monak .... Mickey Simpson
Cheta .... By Herself

Some 16 Tarzan films have ground through the hopper since First National broke the ice in 1918 with "Tarzan of the Apes." Sol Lesser, releasing through RKO, has turned out five of the jungle epics in the past four years. His latest, "Tarzan and the Huntress," while offering little interest to the more literate members of the picture-going fraternity, shapes up as a moderately entertaining adventure film whose commercial appeal rests largely in subsequent runs, the hinterland and abroad.

With Johnny Weissmuller in the title role per usual, apeman this time flexes his muscles to repel the depredations of a zoological expedition which seeks to capture scores of animals for various zoos. Huntress Patricia Morison is a leader of the safari along with Barton MacLane and John Warburton. Fauna quota set by native king Charles Trowbridge dampens the hunters' prospects.

MacLane, along with sinister Ted Hecht as Prince Ozira, a nephew of the King, arrange for the potentate's elimination in a hunting "accident." When it obviously appears that most of the jungle's four-footed inhabitants are well on their way to new homes, Tarzan saves the day, aided by an elephant herd. The expedition is put to flight and the King's rightful heir, Prince Suli, is restored to the throne.

Story's modeled after the countless plots found in any juvenile's library. Acting is also singularly undistinguished. Weissmuller's lines are confined to monosyllabic utterances and his still striking physique remains his top asset. Brenda Joyce is appealing as the apeman's helpmate while Johnny Sheffield as the youthful Boy is an adept vine-swinger. Miss Morison's talents are wasted in this tropic tale. As are those of Barton MacLane who's overly bombastic as the safari boss. Support of Warburton, Trowbridge, Hecht, et al, is adequate while thesping honors are chiefly carried off by the chimpanzee, Cheta, an exceptionally clever simian.

Jungle scenes are well lensed by cameraman Archie Stout who's realistically caught the flavor of the forest primeval. His animal shots are standouts. Production values of the Lesser-Neumann offering are high for an action film. Neumann, however, could have directed at a faster pace.

Law of the Lash

Hollywood, March 15.

PRC release of Jerry Thomas production; Stars Al "Lash" La Rue and Al "Fuzzy" St. John; features Lee Roberts, Mary Scott, Jack O'Shea. Director, Ray Taylor. Original screenplay, William L. Nolte; camera, Robert Cline; editor, Austin Bedell. Previewed March 3, '47. Running time, **53 MINS.**

Cheyenne .... Al "Lash" La Rue
Fuzzy .... Al "Fuzzy" St. John
Lefty .... Lee Roberts
Jane Hilton .... Mary Scott
Decker .... Jack O'Shea
Sheriff .... Charles King
Blackie .... Carl Mathews
Pee Wee .... Matty Roubert
Dad Hilton .... John Elliott
Bart .... Charles Whitaker
Smitty .... Ted French
Bartender .... Richard Cramer
Sam .... Brad Slavin

"Law of the Lash" is spotty western program fare that will have a varied effect upon its moppet ticket buyers. The idea of a hero who uses a whip as much as his sixguns is okay for the Saturday matinee trade, but the injection of corny psychological overtones fails to come off. It reads corny and is even more corny in the celluloid. Strictly for the minor kid trade in the western houses.

Plot spends a vague tale about a disguised U. S. marshal who is trying to clean up an evil-ridden western town. He works undercover as a prospector with a bearded pal, Al St. John. It takes no psychiatrist to know that the hero will triumph. He does and the town settles down to a dull life free of colorful outlaws.

Al "Lash" La Rue is a good prospect for the western film market. Only thing PRC has to watch is the psychological overtones with which scripter William Nolte and director Ray Taylor have burdened "Law of the Lash." On the comic side, Al St. John injects a few laugh moments for the kiddie trade. As the shy heroine, Mary Scott is sufficient, as are others in the cast, including such heavies as Jack O'Shea, Lee Roberts and others.

Production, lensing and other factors are standard for the minor budget. *Brog.*

Bel Ami
(MEXICAN-MADE)

Filmex production and release. Directed by Antonio Momplet. Features Armando Calvo, Gloria Marin, Patricia Moran, Emilia Guiu and Andrea Palma. Based on the Guy de Maupassant story. At Cine Metropolitan, March 8, '47. Running time, **102 MINS.**

(In Spanish; no English Titles)

This is another Bel Ami story, reputedly much the same as the United Artists' release but done in Spanish with the Latin touch visible both in the directing and acting. Chief interest here attaches to the excellent performance contributed by Armando Calvo, who is shaping up in Mexican pictures much the same as he did in films and on the stage in Spain, his native land. He has the lead in the Guy de Maupassant story.

Also U. S. picture patrons likely will pay considerable attention to the attractive costumes and beauty of the sets. Four femmes, Gloria Marin, Patricia Moran (Ethel Clark), an American; Emilia Guiu and Andrea Palma, are nice choices to wear the beautiful garb, and are the most fetching bits of femininity to be seen in Mexican pictures for a long time. Their thespian ability, however, does not measure up to Calvo's.

Antonio Momplet is reminiscent of Ernst Lubitsch with his direction. Camera work and sound are excellent. *Grah.*

Foreign Films

"La Rose de la Mer" ("The Sea Rose") **(FRENCH).** Sirius production and release. Stars Fernand Ledoux, Roger Pigault. Directed by Jacques de Baroncelli. Screenplay, Marc Gilbert Sauvageon, based on novel by Paul Vialar. Reviewed in Paris. Running time, **85 MINS.**

With Fernand Ledoux contributing an outstanding performance in a Wallace Beery-like role, film is a nautical melodrama which deals with the tough captain of a freighter on which most of the action takes place. He's bumped off by Rogert Pigault with the aid of the shady crew who had wind of the skipper's plot to scuttle the vessel and collect the insurance. Too crudely made in every respect for top bookings in France, film has no femme appeal and is of no interest to the U.S. market.

"Brevet Fra Afdode" ("Letter from the Dead") **(DANISH).** Palladium production and release. Stars Sonja Wigert, Eyvind Johan Svendsen, Gunnar Lauring features Inge Hvid-Moller, Axel Frische, Karin Nellemose, Liselette Bendix, Povl Woldike. Directed by Johan Jacobson. Screenplay, Arvid Muller; camera, Karen Andersen; music, Kai Moeller. Reviewed in Copenhagen. Running time, **92 MINS.**

Good drama introduces Norwegian-born Swedish actress Sonja Wigert in her first Danish film. Here she plays a girl who's a cocaine addict. Doctor Eyvind Svendsen attempts to force her to make love to him. When she refuses he tries to strangle her but is killed by Gunnar Lauring. Melodrama is nicely paced by director Johan Jacobsen. Other technical credits are also good. Picture's okay for Scandinavia.

"Driver Dagg Faller Regn" ("When the Rain Is Falling") **(SWEDISH).** Fribergs Filmbyra production and release. Stars Alf Kjellin, Mai Zetterling; features Sten Lindgren, Anna Lindahl, Hilda Borgstroem, Inga Landgre, Ulf Palme, Torsten Bergstroem, Hugo Hasslo, Ivar Hallbeck. Directed by Gustaf Edgren. Screenplay by Edgren and Gardar Sahlberg, based on novel by Margit Soederholm; camera, Martin Bodin. At Palladium, Stockholm. Running time, **112 MINS.**

Splendid film version of Margit Soederholm's prize-winning best-seller may prove as great a success as the book. Sentimental love story is helped by Gustav Edgren's perfect direction, latter wringing plenty of entertainment out of his own script. Enhanced by crisp acting, pic shapes up as a good prospect for U. S. art houses.

"The World Turns Backward" ("Die Welt Dreht Sich Verkehrt") **(AUSTRIAN).** Star Film release of J. A. Hubler-Kahla productnon. Stars Hans Moser, Karl Skraup, Alfred Neugebaur, Marianne Schonauer; directed by Hubler-Kahla. At Apollo, Vienna, Feb. 17, '47. Running time, **90 MINS.**

Pleasant small-scale production loaded with Viennese humor but with limited world appeal due to the broad Viennese dialect of Hans Moser, the Austrian W. C. Fields. Story deals with Moser's alcoholic reminiscences of the good old days.

"Tytto Onnen Ohjaksissa" ("Love and Fighting") **(FINNISH).** Fenno Filmi release of Bio Kuva production. Stars Sirkka Sipila, Esko Saha; features Kullervo Kalske, Assi Raine, Irja Ranniko, Hannes Hayrinen, Joel Asikainen. Directed by Yrjo Norta; screenplay, Tex Westerberg. Reviewed in Helsingfors. Running time, **90 MINS.**

Good Finnish comedy about prize-fighting and love. Cast, headed by Sirkka Sipila, turns in fine performances. Okay for Finland and film fans and Scandinavia in general, but chances in the U. S. are small.

March 26, 1947

Miniature Reviews

"The Egg and I" (U). Pleasing comedy picturization of the best-selling book should do well at the b.o.

"Carnival in Costa Rica" (Musical-Color) (20th). Bright color and rhythmic Latin tunes make for good entertainment.

"Love and Learn" (WB). Lightweight musical slated for moderate boxoffice returns.

"Backlash" (20th). Fair whodunit for the duals.

"Apache Rose" (Musical-Color) (Rep). Initial Roy Rogers musical oater in color gives extra value for marketing.

"Nicholas Nickleby" (GFD). British-made version of Dickens' story too slow, lacking marquee draw for big U. S. boxoffice.

"Untamed Fury" (PRC). Lightweight actioner for the duals.

"Turners of Prospect Road" (GN). Greyhound racing meller only good enough for dualers in England where produced.

The Egg and I

Universal release of Chester Erskine-Fred F. Finklehoffe (Leonard Goldstein) production. Stars Claudette Colbert and Fred MacMurray; features Marjorie Main, Louise Allbritton, and Percy Kilbride. Directed by Erskine. Screenplay, Erskine and Finklehoffe, from the book by Betty MacDonald. Editor, Russell Schoengarth; camera, Milton Krasner; music, Frank Skinner. Tradeshown N. Y., March 21, '47. Running time, **108 MINS.**

Betty.......................Claudette Colbert
Bob.........................Fred MacMurray
Ma Kettle....................Marjorie Main
Harriet Putnam..............Louise Allbritton
Pa Kettle....................Percy Kilbride
Tom Kettle...................Richard Long
Billy Reed.....................Billy House
Old Lady........................Ida Moore
Mr. Henty..................Donald MacBride
Sheriff...................Samuel S. Hinds
Mrs. Hicks.....................Esther Dale
Betty's Mother............Elisabeth Risdon
Geoduck.......................John Berkes
Crowbar..........................Vic Potel
Cab Driver...................Fuzzy Knight
Mrs. Hick's Mother.......Isabel O'Madigan
Maid......................Dorothy Vaughan

This picturization of Betty MacDonald's best-selling book is the initial big-budgeter to come from the Universal studios since the merger with International last fall that resulted in installation of Bill Goetz as production toppe:. There was naturally, therefore, every effort to make it a worthy teeoff for U-I's announced policy of nothing but important A's. While the result is not outstandingly auspicious, "The Egg and I" is a solid laugh-getter designed to hit the b.o. with good impact.

Claudette Colbert and Fred MacMurray in starring roles are only moderate boxoffice draws currently, so the picture must pretty well stand on its own feet, albeit plenty propped by the tremendous popularity of Miss MacDonald's bestseller. Fortunately, from that standpoint, most of the changes that have been made in adapting the yarn have been for the better and the book's vast audience should turn out en masse.

Screen story devised by Chester Erskine and Fred Finklehoffe tampers very little with the load of amusing situations Miss MacDonald gets herself into when her husband snaps her out of a Boston finishing school and takes her off to the modern-day frontier of the Pacific Northwest to embark on chicken farming. Femme knows nothing of housekeeping in general, let alone under conditions that include no indoor plumbing and no electricity, so the flock of incidents that enliven her life are hardly surprising. Picture takes them up, one after the other, with light-heartedness and good humor.

Shortcoming is in an evenness of treatment—partially in the writing but more importantly in Erskine's direction—that fails to suck the drama out of the situations presented in the book. Even the supposedly big scene where a forest fire licks down at all that the chicken-raising couple have in the world—their home, barn and henhouses—fails to achieve suspense or deep-seated emotional drama. For all that can be seen of the fire in the picture, it might be nothing more serious than a couple boy scouts rubbing sticks.

Likewise, through the film, all the mishaps are treated from the light and humorous angle, rather than occasionally from the dramatic, with the result that the humor is never pointed up and comes out as a series of chuckles instead of the belly laughs that result when an audience jumps on a bit of comedy as relief from a throat-gripping situation. Erskine and Finklehoffe seem to miss completely—as Miss MacDonald did somewhat in her book, too—the fact that great comedy must hew right up to that thin line that divides it from extreme pathos.

Miss Colbert is appealing but not entirely believable as the city gal who accepts so willingly out of wifely love the rugged life husband MacMurray lays out for her. MacMurray runs through his role in his routine, superficial fashion—which is unfortunately accentuated by the impassive manner of the telling of the story itself. Percy Kilbride and Marjorie Main, as the Kettles, the to-bacco-road-like neighbors of Miss Colbert and MacMurray, are literally tops as character players, accounting, by their feeling and understanding of their roles, for high points in the film every time they're on the screen. Billy House also scores in the character department as an itinerant merchant.

Louise Allbritton is telling in a role that will come as a bit of surprise to readers of the book. Added part is that of a sirenish widow, owner of a fancy farm down the road, who is out to snare MacMurray. Miss Colbert's suspicions of what goes on between Miss Allbritton and MacMurray, as matter of fact, lead her to leave him. The Allbritton characterization is a very acceptable addition to the original yarn.

Larded into the plentiful supply of chuckle-garnering scenes is at least one that should not go unheralded. It's probably one of the truly funniest in any recent comedy and director Erskine should get his full due. It finds Miss Colbert at her first country dance and under the impulsion of accepting the proffer of all-comers to a bit of terping, since that, she's told, is the polite thing to do. Assortment of partners and the director's technique of pointing up their idiosyncracies makes for a load of real yaks.

Also clever are the prolog and finale lines. Pic opens with Miss Colbert explaining to a dining car waiter—who has dropped an egg and refuses to take it seriously—what travail lies behind each of those elliptoid shell-pieces. For the curtain, Miss Colbert turns to the audience exasperatedly and declares: "I could write a book." Which is, of course, exactly what Miss MacDonald did.

Production as whole is plenty adequate, although not splashy, showing that Goetz was minding his budget. There's certainly no squawk about that, however, especially in view of the pleasing qualities of the picture as a whole. *Herb.*

Carnival in Costa Rica

(MUSICAL—COLOR)

Hollywood, March 22.

20th-Fox release of William A. Bacher production. Stars Dick Haymes, Vera-Ellen, Cesar Romero, Celeste Holm; features Anne Revere, J. Carrol Naish, Lecuona Cuban Boys. Directed by Gregory Ratoff. Original screenplay, John Larkin, Samuel Hoffenstein, Elizabeth Reinhardt; camera (Technicolor), Harry Jackson; music, Ernesto Lecuona; lyrics, Harry Ruby, with added lyrics by Sunny Skylar and Albert Stillman; dances, Leonide Massine; editor, William Reynolds. Reviewed at Grauman's Chinese, March 21, '47. Running time, **96 MINS.**

Jeff Stephens....................Dick Haymes
Luisa Molina......................Vera-Ellen
Pepe Castro.....................Cesar Romero
Celeste..........................Celeste Holm
Elsa Molina......................Anne Revere
Rico Molina..................J. Carrol Naish
Mr. Castro..................Pedro de Cordoba
Maria......................Barbara Whiting
Father Rafael...................Nestor Paiva
Clerk..............................Fritz Feld
Johnny Molina....................Tommy Ivo
Mrs. Castro.....................Mimi Aguglia
Lecuona Cuban Boys..........Themselves
Concha........................Anna Demetrio
Bell Boy........................Severo Lopez
Waiter.....................William Edmunds
Maid.........................Soledad Jiminez
Bartender.....................Alfredo Sabato
Cab Driver.................Martin Garralaga

"Carnival in Costa Rica" gains considerable from authentic footage filmed in the Central American coffee capital. The tunes are gay, the Technicolor beautiful and the story adequate. Sight appeal of production is excellent, the pace is sprightly. Three dance numbers are spotted with Vera-Ellen's terping a decided assist. She also appears to advantage on vocaling with Dick Haymes.

Gregory Ratoff's direction gets a lot of movement into telling rather ordinary story of a Latin boy and girl, betrothed to each other by their parents, but in love with someone else. The boy, Cesar Romero, has fallen for Celeste Holm, nitery singer, while the girl, Vera-Ellen, goes for Dick Haymes, coffee buyer. This plot, which moves steadily to the expected conclusion, is adequate framework for tunes and dances meshed in under William A. Bacher's production guidance.

"Another Night Like This," "I'll Know It's Love" and "Mi Vida" are standout songs, given strong presentation by Vera-Ellen and Haymes. Numbers are by Ernesto Lecuona and Harry Ruby. Additional lyrics for "In Costa Rica" and "Gui Pi Pia" were contributed by Sunny Skylar and Albert Stillman. There also are two instrumentals, "Maracas" and "Rhumba Bamba," played by the Lecuona Cuban Boys.

Vera-Ellen scores with choreography, particularly in the "Bridal Night" production number. She is given an assist on opening production dance by Leonide Massine, who staged dances. Celeste Holm sings "Gui Pi Pia," which is worked into large fiesta production number. Romance between Haymes and Vera-Ellen is pleasantly depicted and fares better than the Romero-Miss Holm story sequences.

Anne Revere is excellent as Vera-Ellen's mother. J. Carrol Naish and Pedro de Cordoba spot some frantic antic comedy as the two Latin papas. Nestor Paiva is a believable priest.

Much of the footage was taken in Costa Rica and is a sterling tourist plug, displaying scenic beauty and pageantry of fiesta time in coffee land. Ace camera work is by Harry Jackson, who obtained full tint values in his lensing. *Brog.*

Love and Learn

(MUSICAL)

Hollywood, March 25.

Warner Bros. release of William Jacobs production. Stars Jack Carson, Robert Hutton, Martha Vickers, Janis Paige; features Otto Kruger, Barbara Brown, Tom D'Andrea, Florence Bates, Craig Stevens. Directed by Frederick de Cordova. Screenplay, Eugene Conrad, Francis Swann, I. A. L. Diamond; adapted from story by Harry Sauber; camera, Wesley Anderson; songs, Charlie Tobias, M. K. Jerome, Jack Scholl, Ray Heindorf; score, Max Steiner; editor, Frank McGee. Tradeshown March 24, '47. Running time, **84 MINS.**

Jingles.........................Jack Carson
Bob Grant....................Robert Hutton
Barbara Wyngate..........Martha Vickers
Jackie..........................Janis Paige
Andrew Wyngate.............Otto Kruger
Victoria Wyngate..........Barbara Brown
Wells.......................Tom D'Andrea
Mrs. Davis..................Florence Bates
Willard......................Craig Stevens
Delaney.......................Don McGuire
William..........................John Alvin
Pete.......................Herbert Anderson
Receptionist....................Jane Harker
Marty............................Lou Nova

Moderately amusing musical comedy, "Love and Learn" offers little plot originality but stays on the pleasant side and has okay names for marquees. Outside of de luxe situations, it should rate adequate business as top side of dual bookings. It has little to offer the de luxers.

Songs are hung on a story formula that is tried and true. On one side of the plot is a songwriting team, trying to get a start in New York. On the other side is the poor little rich girl theme. Story brings two angles together, romance blossoms, gets a misunderstanding setback and then moves into the expected finale clinch. Film doesn't have a top budget, but William Jacobs' production supervision has given it okay physical appurtenances. Frederick de Cordova's direction makes the best of the material and does endow picture with good pace.

Tune lineup includes "Would You Believe Me," by Charlie Tobias, M. K. Jerome and Ray Heindorf, and "If You Are Coming Back to Me" and "Happy Me," by Jerome and Jack Scholl. Numbers are sung by Jack Carson and "Believe Me" is reprised by Trudi Erwin in dancehall sequence for okay results.

Martha Vickers is the rich girl who takes a fling at life by aiding the struggling tunesmiths, Carson and Robert Hutton. Her masquerade causes boys plenty of confusion and makes for misunderstanding between gal and Hutton that doesn't get cleared up until the final reel. Trio work hard for chuckles, as does Janis Paige, girl friend of Carson.

Otto Kruger, Miss Vicker's understanding papa; Craig Stevens, her stuffed shirt fiance, and others in cast are adequate to characters assigned. Trio of scripters on Harry Sauber's story added little. They were Eugene Conrad, Francis Swann and I. A. L. Diamond. Lensing and other technical factors are standard. *Brog.*

Backlash

20th-Fox release of Sol M. Wurtzel (Cliff R. Gans) production. Features Jean Rogers, Richard Travis, Larry Blake, John Eldredge, Leonard Strong. Directed by Eugene Forde. Story and screenplay by Irving Elman; camera, Benjamin Kline; editor, William F. Claxton. Previewed N. Y., March 19, '47. Running time, **66 MINS.**

Catherine Morland............Jean Rogers
Richard Conroy..............Richard Travis
Lt. Jerry McMullen.............Larry Blake
John Morland...............John Eldredge
The Stranger................Leonard Strong
James O'Neil.................Robert Shayne
Marian Gordon................Louise Currie
Red Bailey..................Douglas Fowley
Dorothy.........................Sara Berner
Det. Sgt. Tom Carey....Richard Benedict
Pat McMullen.................Wynne Larke
Maureen.......................Susan Klimist

Modest-budgeted whodunit is a fair mystery, with suspense sustained in large part. Slow action and commonplace dialog are hindrances, and lack of names is further indication of its slotting. It's fair product for the duals.

Film is a slightly involved story about a supposed murder, with a half dozen persons as likely suspects. Script is a succession of scenes wherein a police lieutenant interrogates the various suspects, and slowly works his way to solution of the mystery. Story weaves back and forth in brief flashbacks, which device wears thin after a time.

Larry Blake does a satisfactory job as a hard-working lieutenant, but Richard Benedict clowns too much as his assistant. Catherine Morland is attractive as the dame in the case. John Eldredge and Douglas Fowley handle the heavy roles okay, and Leonard Strong has a good bit as a hobo. *Bron.*

Apache Rose
(SONGS—COLOR)

Hollywood, March 22.

Republic release of Edward J. White production. Stars Roy Rogers; features Dale Evans, Olin Howlin. Directed by William Witney. Original screenplay, Gerald Geraghty; camera (Trucolor), Jack Marta; songs, Jack Elliott, Tim Spencer, Glenn Spencer; editor, Les Orlebeck. Previewed March 18, '47. Running time, 75 MINS.

Roy Rogers	Roy Rogers
Billie Colby	Dale Evans
Alkali Elkins	Olin Howlin
Reed Calhoun	George Meeker
Pete	John Laurenz
Carlos Vega	Russ Vincent
Felicia	Minerva Urecal
Hilliard	LeRoy Mason
Rosa Vega	Donna DeMario
Sheriff Jim Mason	Terry Frost
Dancer	Conchita Lemus
Likens	Tex Terry

Market value of color to a film should be proven with "Apache Rose." First tinter for Roy Rogers, picture lacks usual sterling action merit of his Republic oatuners but carries extra exploitation weight because of color lensing.

There's less adult appeal to "Apache Rose" than expected in a Rogers western but it contains plenty of juve interest. Tunes also fail to be more than adequate. Best song presentation comes from Dale Evans with singing of "There's Nothin' Like Coffee in the Mornin'." Rogers does well by "Wishing Well." Title tune, "Ride Vaquero," is reprised several times, and "Jose," sung by Sons of Pioneers, complete score.

Rogers is an oil wildcatter in this one and runs into some highly complicated skullduggery when he tries to get drilling rights on an old Spanish landgrant. To make the plot modern, there's a gambling ship anchored offshore, but that script concession doesn't lessen fact that it's the old formula land steal. Gamblers know about the oil and are seeking to take over the land by virtue of I.O.U.'s owed them by the ranch owner.

Dale Evans is a Tugboat Annie of the west and does well by the assignment. Olin Howlin is in for prairie comedy as Rogers' pal. Russ Vincent, the ranch owner; Terry Frost, sheriff; George Meeker, chief heavy; Minerva Urecal, Conchita Lemus, dancer, are among those giving Rogers good support.

William Witney's direction of the Gerald Geraghty original script spots some good action moments in the Edward J. White production. Color lensing by Jack Marta and other contributions are expert. *Brog.*

Nicholas Nickleby
(BRITISH-MADE)

London, March 12.

General Film Distributors release of Ealing Studios production. Stars Cedric Hardwicke, Stanley Holloway; features Alfred Drayton, Cyril Fletcher, Fay Compton, Bernard Miles, Sybil Thorndike, Derek Bond. Directed by Cavalcanti. Screenplay by John Dighton from Charles Dickens' novel. Music by Lord Berners, conducted by Ernest Irving. Camera, Gordon Dines. At Tivoli theatre, London. Running time, 108 MINS.

Nicholas Nickleby	Derek Bond
Ralph Nickleby	Cedric Hardwicke
Mrs. Nickleby	Mary Merrall
Kate Nickleby	Sally Ann Howes
Newman Noggs	Bernard Miles
Miss La Creevy	Athene Seyler
Wackford Squeers	Alfred Drayton
Mrs. Squeers	Sybil Thorndike
Fanny Squeers	Vida Hope
Wackford Squeers, Jr.	Roy Hermitage
Alfred Mantalini	Cyril Fletcher
Madame Mantalini	Fay Compton
Vincent Crummles	Stanley Holloway
Mrs. Crummles	Vera Pearce
Ned Cheeryble	}
Charles Cheeryble	} James Hayter
Frank Cheeryble	Emrys Jones
Tim Linkinwater	Roddy Hughes
Smike	Aubrey Woods
Phoebe	Patricia Hayes
Mr. Brey	George Relph
Madeline Brey	Jill Balcon
Mr. Gregsbury	Michael Shepley
Sir Mulberry Hawk	Cecil Ramage

Second in the present Dickens cycle, this inevitably will be compared with Cineguild's "Great Expectations." To make an entertaining film of this Dickens classic needed more courage than producer Michael Balcon has shown. He should have ignored the vociferous rabid clique of Dickensians and thought first of the millions who care little or nothing whether any particular character or episode is missing as long as the picture does no violence to the author and is entertaining. Long list of players known here may put this one over in England, but in U.S. it will need a lot of selling to get okay boxoffice.

The 52 characters of the original have proved too much for the scripwriter here. Some minor characters like Peg Sliderskew, Mr. Witterly, John Browdie and Brooker have been left out, and Gride has become amalgamated with Ralph at the end, but the screenplay is more in the nature of a condensation into a series of scenes. And that's the way it appears on the screen. There's a constant skipping from one character to another, from one scene to another, without that essential binding thread running right through.

Nicholas' adventures with the Crummles family has an old ham actor grandly played by Stanley Holloway. The stage scenes are amusing, but they do little to further the main story and, as an interlude, they slow up what action there might be. Scenes in Dotheboys Hall, which should have been among the most memorable, are slovenly, untidy and cramped. For some reason, Alfred Drayton, who otherwise gives a fine performance, makes Wackford Squeers a brutish Cockney thug. His forbidding consort, played by Sybil Thorndike, obviously comes from a slightly better family.

Casting any Dickens film is an unenviable chore because of the preconceived notions of a vast audience, and Balcon has made as good a job as most producers might have done. Derek Bond, ex-Guards officer, brings manly grace to the title role, but betrays inexperience. Nor does Sally Ann Howes, sweet and simple as Kate, rise to her big occasion when her wicked uncle uses her as a decoy to attract his unmoral clients.

Cedric Hardwicke, who journeyed from Hollywood to play Ralph, has the main role and gives whatever semblance of unity there is to the story. His villain is well played. Bernard Miles revels in his part as the downtrodden clerk. An impressive screen debut as Smike is made by Aubrey Woods, student of Royal Academy of Dramatic Art. An interesting debut is that of producer Balcon's daughter Jill, who, after stage work, became a broadcasting announcer, and has now returned to acting.

Direction by Cavalcanti, whose reputation rests mainly on documentaries, is pedestrian.

Biggest draw for this film is Dickens, for whom there appears to be a strong vogue at the moment. *Cane.*

Untamed Fury

PRC release of Danches Bros. (Ewing Scott) production, directed by Scott. Features Gaylord Pendleton, Leigh Whipper, Mikel Conrad, Mary Conwell, Althea Murphy. Screenplay, Taylor Caven and Paul Gerard Smith based on Scott's story, "Gator Bait"; camera, Ernest Miller; editor, Robert Crandall; music, Alexander Laszlo. Tradeshown N. Y., March 20, '47. Running time, 61 MINS.

Jeff Owen	Gaylord Pendleton
'Gator-Bait Kirk	Mikel Conrad
Uncle Gabe	Leigh Whipper
Judie Kirk	Mary Conwell
Patricia Wayburn	Althea Murphy
Sam Kirk	Jack Rutherford
Crane Owen	Charles Keane
Lige	Rodman Bruce
Swamper	Paul Savage
Pompano	E. G. Marshall
John Bradbury	Norman MacKay

Fairly writhing with alligators is this story of life deep in Florida's Okefenokee swamp region. Producer-director Ewing Scott filmed his own tale on location in the watery backwoods and while generating occasional suspense, picture's niche will be found in the lower half of the duals. With no cast names, exhibs will have to rely upon exploiting the film's background to draw 'em in.

Told in flashback, footage resolves itself into a feud between two swamp raised lads, Gaylord Pendleton and Mikel Conrad. College trained, former becomes a state engineer bent upon improving the lot of the Okefenokee dwellers while Conrad stays behind and emerges from boyhood as a typical swamp denizen. Balance of story is rather obvious. Conrad attempts to prevent any change in the Okefenokee and eventually realizes he had the wrong attitude.

Sandwiched in are some fair romantic scenes contributed by Mary Conwell and Althea Murphy. There are also some okay underwater swimming shots. Alligator sequences should garner a fair amount of interest. Generally thesping is in keeping with apparently low budget. Scott's direction is slow moving, while Ernest Miller's lensing adequately captures the swamp atmosphere.

The Turners of Prospect Road
(BRITISH-MADE)

London, March 13.

Grand National release of Maurice J. Wilson production. Stars Jeanne de Casalis, Wilfrid Lawson. Directed by Maurice J. Wilson. Screenplay, Patrick Kirwan, Victor Katona; camera, Freddie Ford. At Hamer theatre, London. Running time, 76 MINS.

Will	Wilfrid Lawson
Lil	Helena Pickard
Betty	Maureen Gwynne
Grandma	Amy Veness
Mrs. Webster	Jeanne de Casalis
J. G. Clarkson	Peter Bull
Mr. Webster	Leslie Perrins
Terence O'Keefe	Shamus Locke
Nicky	Desmond Tester
Magistrate	Christopher Steele
Jacqueline	Giselle Morlaix
Ruby	Joy Frankau
Andrew Carroll	Andrew Blackett
Knocker	Gus McNaughton
Jack	Charles Farrell

Greyhound racing, a sport that has millions of followers in this country, is the star attraction of this homey picture. It might pay to indicate this in the billing.

The Turner family comprises a philosophical grandma, a tired housewife, taxi-driver father and a nice schoolgirl. Father finds an unwanted greyhound pup in his cab and presents it to his daughter. She takes it to a track to be trained and it soon proves to be in the Derby class. An unscrupulous professional backer who has entered the favorite for the Derby makes an abortive attempt to buy the girl's dog. When her father refuses to sell, there's a drunken driving frameup with the usual payoff when the taxi-driver's friends deal out rough justice to the gang as the girl's dog wins the classic race.

No frills and an unaccountable lack of humor. For some reason Jeanne de Casalis, the featherbrained comedienne who gave the wonder dog away, is used only in two or three scenes. Acting throughout is competent without any noteworthy performance. Maureen Glynne, the 18-year-old, who has done broadcasting, makes her screen debut in this and shows some promise. Shamus Locke looks a good bet.

Picture will fit in nicely here in dualers but would not weather U. S. market. *Cane.*

Foreign Films

"Kultainen Kynttiläjalka" ("Golden Light") (FINNISH). Bio Kuva release of Fenno Filmi (Yrjoe Norta) production. Stars Edvin Laine, Mirjam Novero; features Mirjami Kuosmanen, Esko Saha, Jalmari Rinne, Paavo Jannes, Rauha Puntti, Hilja Jorma; directed by Edvin Laine; screenplay, Toivo Kauppinen; camera, Esko Toyri. Reviewed in Helsingfors. Running time, 80 MINS.

Starring the promising actress Mirjam Novero, this sentimental story about criminals is built on a strong idea, but unfortunately is ruined by a poor script and inept direction. Film has average chances in the Finnish market and elsewhere has nothing to offer.

Miniature Reviews

"The Other Love" (UA-Enterprise). Strong love story against sombre background will do satisfactory biz.

"Two Mrs. Carrolls" (WB). Heavy, talky melodrama, from stage play, needs Bogart and Barbara Stanwyck to aid selling.

"White Cradle Inn" (B-L). Madeleine Carroll, Ian Hunter in British-made story of Swiss Alps; mild U. S. entry.

"Buffalo Bill Rides Again" (SG). Barely passable western screen fare for juve matinee trade.

"Carnival of Sinners" (French). OK for arty trade.

"Bells of San Fernando" (SG). Dull costume drama of early California; dual filler.

"When You Come Home" (Butcher). Frank Randle slapstick comedy geared for British subsequents; no dice for U. S.

The Other Love

United Artists release of Enterprise (David Lewis) production. Stars Barbara Stanwyck, David Niven; features Richard Conte, Gilbert Roland, Joan Lorring, Lenore Aubert, Maria Palmer, Natalie Schafer. Directed by Andre de Toth. Screenplay, Harry Brown and Ladislas Fodor from short story by Erich Maria Remarque; camera, Victor Milner; score, Miklos Rozsa; special effects, Robert H. Moreland; editor, Walter Thompson. Previewed, New York, March 27, '47. Running time, **95 MINS.**

Karen Duncan..........Barbara Stanwyck
Dr. Antony Stanton..........David Niven
Huberta..................Maria Palmer
Celestine..................Joan Lorring
Paul Clermont..............Richard Conte
Prof. Linnaker..............Richard Hale
Richard Shelton............Edward Ashley
Dora Shelton...............Natalie Schafer
Yvonne....................Lenore Aubert
Pete.......................Jimmy Horne
Mme. Gruen.................Mary Forbes
The Florist..................Ann Codee
The Florist's Assistant..Kathleen Williams
A Croupier.................Gilbert Roland

This is the third film to be turned out on the new Enterprise lot and will be found a serviceable b.o. entry. With Barbara Stanwyck and David Niven starred in an Erich Maria Remarque yarn, which will appeal primarily to the femme trade, pic should do satisfactory biz.

Yarn is well-laden with interesting incidents and is handled by director Andre de Toth with tact and intelligence. Militating against its rising to anything more than ordinarily good b.o. proportions, however, is sombreness of the "Camille" theme against which its rather strong love story is backgrounded. Most of the action is in a sanitarium, and Miss Stanwyck dies at the finale of a lingering illness.

Producer David Lewis has done everything possible to overcome this initial handicap by providing handsome mountings (pic is laid in the Swiss Alps) and a highly-capable and appealing cast. Richard Conte, as a dashing boy-about-the-Continent, is a particular standout, topping even the excellent performances given by both Miss Stanwyck and Niven. Whatever results it otherwise achieves, the film will certainly have adde.. a notch to the stature of the cast and put Conte in line for top starring roles.

Shortcoming of the film, technically, lies in the patness of its plot. Remarque wrote the yarn as a short story, "Beyond" (as yet unpublished, and some of it autobiographical), and screenwriters Harry Brown and Ladislas Fodor haven't done much more than stretch it into a 95-minute film. Result is that the plot is completely telegraphed ahead from the very first scene. There are no surprises and, thus, despite all efforts of de Toth to hold up the pace, which he does rather effectively, there's still some inevitable slowness.

It takes little perspicacity to guess what's going to happen when Miss Stanwyck becomes a patient in the sanitarium where Niven is chief medico. Niven's cool professional attitude and the severe medical restrictions he imposes on Miss Stanwyck drive her into the arms of the more ardorous and dashing lover played by Conte. When she finds herself getting really ill, the femme retreats to true-love Niven, who marries her. Soon afterwards she dies.

There is a certain amount of universal interest in the dilemma faced by Miss Stanwyck: Shall she languish, perhaps for years, in the sanitarium, or shall she take a fling at life, come what may? Her trial of the latter leads to tragic results.

Flock of players are featured in the billing, although none has much in the way of roles, except Gilbert Roland and Joan Lorring. Roland is a sort of caricature of a heavy, playing a Monte Carlo croupier with wolfish designs on Miss Stanwyck. Miss Lorring is okay as another sanitarium inmate determined on a fling.

Miklos Rozsa's music is highly effective, while the art direction of Nathan Juran and set direction by Edward G. Boyle are standout.

Herb.

Two Mrs. Carrolls

Hollywood, April 1.

Warner Bros. release of Mark Hellinger production. Stars Humphrey Bogart, Barbara Stanwyck, Alexis Smith; features Nigel Bruce, Isobel Elsom, Pat O'Moore, Ann Carter, Anita Bolster, Barry Bernard. Directed by Peter Godfrey. Screenplay, Thomas Job, from stage play by Martin Vale; camera, Peverell Marley; music, Franz Waxman; editor, Frederick Richards. Tradeshown March 31, '47. Running time, **100 MINS.**

Geoffrey Carroll.........Humphrey Bogart
Sally.....................Barbara Stanwyck
Cecily Latham..............Alexis Smith
Dr. Tuttle..................Nigel Bruce
Mrs. Latham................Isobel Elsom
Charles Pennington...........Pat O'Moore
Beatrice Carroll...............Ann Carter
Christine...................Anita Bolster
Mr. Blagdon................Barry Bernard
MacGregor.................Colin Campbell
First Tout..................Peter Godfrey
Second Tout...............Creighton Hale

"The Two Mrs. Carrolls" will lean heavily on names of Humphrey Bogart and Barbara Stanwyck to get by. Adapted from the Martin Vale legiter, it's more stage play than motion picture. Overladen with dialog as action substitute, it talks itself out of much of the suspense that should have developed. There is some femme appeal, however, in the Bogart character as hero-villain, which will help its chances.

Production format hugs stage technique in settings and carrying out story. Backgrounds never seem realistic but rather appear as grouped on stage. Bogart, Miss Stanwyck and Alexis Smith feel the burden of dialog and unnatural characters but, under Peter Godfrey's direction, manage to give material an occasional lift.

Plot deals with married artist who meets a new love while vacationing in Scotland. He returns to London, murders his wife by methodical poisoning and marries the new flame. Second marriage works okay until another attractive girl appears. He is almost successful in again applying his poisoning technique but the wife gets wise just in time. Film's climactic peak gets an undeserved belting when principal characters are called upon to demand that doors be opened. Action ties in too closely with current popularity of the freak tune, "Open the Door, Richard," and serves to pull an untimely audience laugh just when suspense should be at its height.

Camera and music score help melodramatic air, overcoming to some extent the obviousness of development. Good lensing by Peverell Marley makes the most of players and settings and Franz Waxman did the score for the Mark Hellinger production. Competent support is lent the three stars by Nigel Bruce as a bumbling English doctor; Pat O'Moore, Ann Carter, Bogart's young daughter; Anita Bolster and Barry Bernard. Director Godfrey cut himself in for a bit as a racetrack tout. *Brog.*

White Cradle Inn
(BRITISH-MADE)

London, March 25.

British Lion release of a Peak production. Stars Madeleine Carroll, Ian Hunter, Michael Rennie. Directed by Harold French. Original story and screenplay by Harold French, Lesley Storm. Camera, Deric Williams, Erwin Hillier. At Palace theatre, London. Running time, **83 MINS.**

Magda...................Madeleine Carroll
Anton..........................Ian Hunter
Rudolph..................Michael Rennie
Louise...................Anne Marie Blanc
Roger......................Michael McKeag
Joseph......................Arnold Marle
Benno.........................Willi Fueter
Frederick....................Max Haufler
Maria.....................Margarete Hoff
President...............Gerard Kempinski

Picture signalizes the debut of Peak Films, new production company. About 50% of the film was shot on location in Switzerland, background of the story, and some of the photography is remarkable. But it looks like a fairly mild entry in the U. S.

White Cradle Inn, standing in a valley surrounded by mountainous grandeur, has been owned for generations by the family of Madeleine Carroll. Her husband, Michael Rennie, spends his time philandering and having a clandestine love affair with one of the maids at the inn. People in the valley have given refuge to French children, and Miss Carroll has become very attached to one of the orphans billeted with them. Rennie considers the boy a coward and dislikes him. The order comes for the children to return to France, but this one orphan escapes from the train and returns to Miss Carroll. Only chance of retaining the lad is official adoption, and Rennie refuses to sign the papers unless she makes over the inn to him. The boy has become so dear to her that she consents.

Determined to prove he is no coward, the lad persuades Rennie to take him on a perilous climb. A storm comes up, and finally after several narrow escapes, Rennie chooses death in order to save the boy's life.

A central theme in this story has a marked resemblance to that of "Marie Louise" (made by Praesens Films in Switzerland a couple of years ago). But those who made "White Cradle Inn" failed to inject the heart-interest found in the Swiss-made picture. The characters here rarely come to life, and it is difficult to conjure up sympathy for Miss Carroll, who looks beautiful as Magda but who cannot make us believe that her heart would really break without the orphan. Some of this fault may be laid to the director and some to Michael McKeag, the French lad, who fails to bring forth the tears. Actually it is only in the last 10 minutes that the picture and Miss Carroll really come to life.

Rennie strolls through his part as Rudolph without creating a real character, and Ian Hunter is stolid and sound as the local doctor. Most minor characters are good without being outstanding. This was the last picture Gerard Kempinski made before he died. Multiplicity of accents does not help, and it is difficult to understand why those characters, who speak perfect English, should adopt an accent for names.

Madeleine Carroll may prove something of a draw, but the picture will need plenty of selling both here and in America. *Cane.*

Buffalo Bill Rides Again

Hollywood, March 28.

Screen Guild release of Jack Schwarz production. Stars Richard Arlen; features Jennifer Holt, Lee Shumway, Gil Patrick. Directed by Bernard B. Ray. Original story and screenplay, Barney Sarecky, Fran Gilbert; camera, Robert Cline; editor, Robert Crandall. Previewed March 27, '47. Running time, **70 MINS.**

Buffalo Bill.................Richard Arlen
Lale Harrington..............Jennifer Holt
Steve........................Lee Shumway
Simpson.........................Gil Patrick
Sheriff......................Edward Cassidy
Morgan.......................Edmund Cobb
Sam............................Ted Adams
Young Bird....................Shooting Star
White Mountain............Charles Stevens
Chief Brave Eagle..........Many Treaties
Tom Russell..................John Dexter
Rankin.........................Hollis Baine
Hank.....................Frank McCarroll
Pete.......................Carl Matthews
Jeff..........................Clark Stevens
Mr. Smith...............George Sherwood
Mr. Dawson..................Fred Graham
Dawson's Daughter..............Paul Hill
Scratchy....................Philip Arnold
Senator....................Tom Leffingwell
Mr. Jordan.................Frank O'Conner
Mr. Howard.......................Fred Fox
Mrs. Dawson..............Dorothy Curtis

There's nothing to recommend "Buffalo Bill Rides Again." It's a meandering western overlength on footage and short of action. Strictly filler material for lowercase spots in minor situations.

Richard Arlen has title role in this land grab plot, which calls upon him to find out why someone is stirring up the Indians. It seems that there's oil under land settled by ranchers and a syndicate is trying to scare settlers off so heavies can benefit. Latter get the settlers and the Indians to fighting, and it takes Buffalo Bill to sort out the mess and bring peace to the ranch.

Dialog is loaded with cliches, the Bernard B. Ray direction actionless, and production mounting by Jack Schwarz hardly adequate. Arlen, Jennifer Holt, John Dexter and others in cast walk through uncomfortable 70 minutes. Technical credits, including lensing, editing, contribute little. *Brog.*

Carnival of Sinners
(FRENCH-MADE)

Distinguished Films release of Maurice Tourneur production, directed by Tourneur Stars Pierre Fresnay; features Josseline Gael, Pailaul. Screenplay, Jean-Paul Le Chanois; music, Roger Dumas; English titles, Charles Clément.

Roland........................Pierre Fresnay
Irene..........................Josseline Gael
Small Man................................Palau
Melisse....................Noel Roquevert
Gibelin..................Guillaume de Sax
Colonel.....................Andre Varennes
Denis......................Antoine Balpetre
Mme. Denis..........................Rexiane
Perrier.......................Robert Vattier
Duval...............................Chamarat
Le Moine....................Jean Coquelin
Musketeer....................Andre Bacque
Rifleman.........................Jean Davy
Surgeon...........................Douking
Juggler......................Rene Blancard
Painter..............................Garzoni
Boxer.................................Marcel
Angel........................Jean Despeaux
Diner........................Pierre Larquey

(In French; English Titles)

"Carnival of Sinners," originally titled "Le Main du Diable" ("The Devil's Hand"), is a worthy contribution to the art-house trade.

Macabre aspects of its basic theme and frequent use of symbolism make it unlikely for the run-of-mill film patronage. Pierre Fresnay, with staunch support from Josseline Gael, Noel Roquevert, Robert Vattier, Jean Coquelin and Guillaume de Sax, do well by their roles.

This Gallic dialog pic with English titles carries a variation of the Faust theme, and is reminiscent of "The Devil and Daniel Webster." Fresnay, an artist struggling to express his feelings on canvas and unable to win the affections of his model, Mlle. Gael, changes the pattern of his life with his purchase of a grisly talisman, consisting of a hand, purported to have been cut out of the grave of a medieval monk. While this ghoulish memento brings him everything he wants, it represents the sale of his soul to the devil, who comes around occasionally to see how his investment is faring. Fresnay is finally able to break the curse, at the cost of his life, by returning the hand to its original owner.

Direction by Maurice Tourneur is well paced, has its suspenseful moments, and carries with it a degree of symbolism. One scene in particular, in which Fresnay's predecessors in the possession of the hand are gathered at a banquet table, has a ballet-like quality that moves with poetic motion. Unfortunately, the English subtitles fail to capture that mood.

Photography occasionally shows a discernible flicker, and sound track frequently is blurred. But discounting occasional technical inferiority, "Carnival" is on par with the series of worthwhile French films that have been hitting the U. S. market.

Jose.

Bells of San Fernando

(SONG)

Hollywood, March 26.

Screen Guild release of James S. Burkett production. Features Donald Woods, Gloria Warren, Shirley O'Hara, Byron Foulger, Paul Newlan, Anthony Warde, Monte Blue. Directed by Terry Morse. Original story and screenplay, Jack Dewitt, Renault Duncan; camera, Robert Pettack; editor, George McGuire. Previewed March 26, '47. Running time, **74 MINS.**

Michael....................Donald Woods
Maria....................Gloria Warren
Nita....................Shirley O'Hara
Garcia....................Byron Foulger
Gueyon....................Paul Newlan
Mendoza....................Anthony Warde
Governor....................Monte Blue
Manta....................Claire DuBrey
Padre....................David Leonard
Enrico....................Gordon Clark
Perdido....................Gilbert Galvan
Mule Driver....................Felipe Turich

Dialog triteness and heavy-handed direction relegate "Bells of San Fernando" to strictly minor supporting classification. It's overlong on footage, slow in pace and dull in performance.

Plot is laid in early California during Spanish rule and concerns a cruel overseer of a valley rancho who keeps the natives in bondage. There's little that's picturesque about costuming or writing and Terry Morse's direction falls far short of breathing any life into unfoldment.

Gloria Warren is given one tune to warble, "Land of Make Believe," but recording doesn't display vocal ability. Otherwise she's the heroine pursued by the villain and only saved by the dare-and-do of Donald Woods, Irish seaman who has wandered into the valley.

Anthony Warde does the leering heavy. Shirley O'Hara is in as amorous native girl. Byron Foulger, Paul Newlan and others fare just as badly from material and direction. James S. Burkett produced, with Duncan Renaldo as associate producer. Lensing and other technical factors contribute little.

Brog.

When You Come Home

(BRITISH-MADE)

London, March 22.

Butcher Film Service release of Butcher Empire Production. Features Frank Randle, Leslie Sarony, Leslie Holmes. Produced and directed by John Baxter. Screenplay, David Evans, Geoffrey Orme; additional scenes and comedy dialog, Frank Randle. Camera, Faithfull. At Palace theatre, London. Running time, **95 MINS.**

Frank Randle....................Frank Randle
Maestro....................Leslie Sarony
Fingers....................Leslie Holmes
Paula....................Diana Decker
Mike O'Flaherty..........Fred Conyngham
Singer....................Linda Parker
Dormer Franklyn....................Jack Melford
Mrs. Ryngelbaum....................Lily Lapidus
Mr. Ryngelbaum....................Tony Heaton
Lady Langfield....................Hilda Bayley
Delia....................Lesley Osmond
Designer....................Gus Aubrey
Fireman....................Ernest Dale

With 40 years' experience in making pictures, Butchers are convinced that audiences want to laugh. Here they have starred a comedian, unknown to London's West End, whose following elsewhere in Britain exceeds that of any U. S. star. Frank Randle is as indigenous and as British to the North of England as is tripe. Without playing any of the big circuits his last five pictures are reported to have grossed $2,000,000. It won't mean much to West End deluxers, and has no chance in the American market despite this record.

Randle, downtrodden and kicked around, wins sympathy and laughs. Given the right sort of production and direction he could become a comic of distinction, but the Butcher's are content with short term policies. Many stars began their careers with this company. Among them were Clive Brook, Madeleine Carroll, Victor McLaglen, Walter Forde, George Formby and Emlyn Williams, but they all migrated from the unheralded modest-budget independent. "When You Come Home" has all the ingredients of a silent comedy. Custard pies hurtle through the air to land smack on the faces of the rich and snooty. Villainy is unmasked, virtue rewarded and true love comes into its own. It's that simple.

Story begins with Grandpa Randle disrupting his own birthday party reliving "The Charge of the Light Brigade" and brandishing his sword. Only thing to calm him is music of "When You Come Home" which leads to flashback to 1908 and the local vaudeville theatre, where Randle is general backstage factotum.

Everything in the film is sacrificed for laughs. It doesn't stand any chance in high-grade cinemas, but it will do well elsewhere in this country.

Cane.

Foreign Films

"Sangen Om Stockholm" ("Song of Stockholm") **(SWEDISH).** Sandrew-Bauman Film release of Ahrle-Film production. Stars Elof Ahrle, Bengt Logardt; features Alice Babs, Hilda Borgstroem, Douglas Hage, Marianne Gyllenhammer, Ake Groenberg, Carin Swenson, Sune Waldimir, Anders Boerje, Nils Ferlin. Directed by Ahrle. Screenplay, Sven Forsell, Arthur Spjuth. At Astoria, Stockholm. Running time, **92 MINS.**

Comedy-drama about musicians has a good chance in Scandinavia, but the story is perhaps too sentimental to go far in other markets. Bandleader Sune Waldimir plays himself and shows to advantage under Elof Ahrle's direction. Lensing is okay.

"Familien Swedenhielm" ("Sweden Hielm Family") **(DANISH).** ASA-Film release of Jens Dennow production. Stars Poul Reumert, Ebbe Rode, Mogens Wieth, Beatrice Bonnesen; features Lily Weiding, Maria Garland, Preben Neergaard, Mogens Brandt, Ib Schoenberg. Directed by Lau Lauritzen. Screenplay, Leck Fischer based on Hjalmar Bergman's play; camera, Rudolf Frederiksen. At World Cinema, Copenhagen. Running time, **84 MINS.**

Play by the late Swedish dramatist Hjalmar Bergman was filmed in Sweden prior to the war, was lensed in Germany during the conflict and now comes this Danish version. Plot revolves about a noted Swedish scientist who's awarded the Nobel prize. However, economic difficulties and domestic troubles make a thorny path for the savant before he meets success. Acting and lensing are okay but fail to balance poor script and direction. No dice in U. S.

"Ungdom I Fara" ("Youth's in Danger") **(SWEDISH).** Svensk Talfilm production and release. Stars Gunnar Sjoeberg, Barbro Hiort af Ornaes; features Karl-Henrik Fant, Nita Vaernhammar, Sven Eric Carlsson, Fylgia Zadig. Directed by P. G. Holmgren. Screenplay by Holmgren based on Bibi Rybrandt's radio play; camera, Walter Boberg. At Olympia, Stockholm. Running time, **84 MINS.**

Delinquent youth problem is analyzed in this film but offers no solution to the situation. Cast is replete with new talent. Market for this entry lies strictly in Scandinavia.

"Evig A Lankar" (Eternal' Links") **SWEDISH).** Lux Film production and release. Stars Anna-Lisa Ericsson, Ingrid Backlin, Margareta Fahlen; features Erik Berglund, Hjoerdis Pettersson, Hilda Boergstroem, Fritiof Billquist, Ingemar Pallin. Directed by Rune Carlsten. Screenplay, Adolf Schutsch, Paul Baudisch; camera, Karl-Erik Alberts. At Riviera, Stockholm. Running time, **76 MINS.**

Dealing with family life in Stockholm, this film is a fine comeback for Anna-Lisa Ericsson. Her acting is first-rate as is that of supporting cast. Okay direction, scripting and lensing afford this pic good chances here, but the story has no appeal to foreign markets.

"Onda Ogon" ("Bad Eyes") **(SWEDISH).** Wive Film release of Films production. Stars Anders Sjoestrand, Ingrid Backlin; features Sture Djerf, Stig Jaerrel, Goesta Cederlund, Arthur Fischer, Ake Claesson, Erland Colliander. Directed by Jaerrel. Screenplay, Ragnhild Prim; camera, Hilmer Ekdahl. At Skandia, Stockholm. Running time, **70 MINS.**

Stig Jaerrel makes his directorial debut in this dramatic story of love and jealousy. Arnold Sjoestrand's thesping helps bolster the feeble story. With Jaerrel turning in fine direction plus an excellent handling of a featured role, picture looks like a success here. It may be okay also in other markets.

Wins.

"Djurgardskvallar" ("Evening at the Djurgarden") **(SWEDISH).** Wive Film release of SAG Svensson production. Stars Adolf Jahr, Ingrid Bjork; features Emy Hagman, Nisse Ericsson, Lasse Krantz, Douglas Hage, John Botvid, Naima Wifstrand, Agneta Lagerfeldt. Directed by Rolf Husberg. Reviewed in Gothenburg. Running time, **82 MINS.**

This dull entry adds little to the prestige of Swedish film producers. Save for the work of Ingrid Bjork as a young debutante, this has nothing to offer. No dice for America.

Wins.

"Honkutuslintu" **(FINNISH).** Stars Laila Jokimo, Eino Laipanen; features Eero Levaluoma, Maire Karila, Joel Asikainen, Kalle Viherpuu, Irja Ranniko; directed by Roland af Hellstroem; screenplay, Viljo Hela; camera, Esko Toyri. Reviewed in Helsingfors. Running time, **78 MINS.**

Apparently limited for Finnish consumption is this dramatic story of an adventurous Helsingfors girl who attempts to break up the life of a couple in a small Finnish village. Camera and direction are good.

Win.

Miniature Reviews

"Dark Delusion" (M-G). Last of "Dr. Gillepsie" series should garner better than fair returns in all situations.

"Yankee Fakir" (Rep). Routine comedy mystery for dualer situations.

"The Man Within" •(GFD) (color). Michael Redgrave starred in British-made meller; some chance in U. S.

"That's My Man" (Rep). Richly dressed Frank Borzage film around racetrack theme slowly paced; fair b.o. outlook.

"The Bellman" (French). Meller looks sock for arty U. S. theatres.

"Violence" (Mono). Melodramatic story of undercover pressure groups with good chances in the Monogram market.

"Three On a Ticket" (PRC). Another Michael Shayne whodunit with good interest for supporting market.

"Shoot to Kill" (SG). Good melodrama for the supporting market.

Dark Delusion

Metro release of Carey Wilson production. Stars Lionel Barrymore, James Craig, Lucille Bremer; features Jayne Meadows, Warner Anderson, Henry Stephenson, Alma Kruger, Keye Luke, Art Baker, Lester Matthews. Directed by Willis Goldbeck. Original screenplay, Jack Andrews, Harry Ruskin; camera, Charles Rosher; music score, David Snell; editor, Gene Ruggiero. Tradeshown at Los Angeles, April 4, '47. Running time, **90 MINS.**

Dr. Leonard Gillespie.....Lionel Barrymore
Dr. Tommy Coalt....................James Craig
Cynthia Grace....................Lucille Bremer
Mrs. Selkirk....................Jayne Meadows
Teddy Selkirk....................Warner Anderson
Dr. Evans Biddle........Henry Stephenson
Molly Byrd....................Alma Kruger
Dr. Lee....................Keye Luke
Dr. Sanford Burson....................Art Baker
Wyndham Grace..........Lester Matthews
Sally....................Marie Blake
Gin Rummy Player....................Ben Lessy
Miss Rowland....................Geraldine Wall
Nurse Parker....................Nell Craig
Conover....................George Reed
Nurse Workman....................Mary Currier

It'll be ladies' night at the local cinema stands when this last in Metro's "Dr. Gillespie" (nee "Dr. Kildare") series opens, with a plot heavily, angled for femme tastes along the popular "psychological" story lines. "Dark Delusion" also marks the emergence of Lucille Bremer as a full-blown serious actress, steering her away from the musical fluff stuff and into a part that will heavily enhance her value as a screen property.

Despite the boxoffice value of the "Doctor" series, already established, Metro has indicated it will end it all on this film, which should bring better than fair returns in all situations, and particularly in the nabes. Emphasis has been segued, naturally, from the "Kildare" part formerly played by Lew Ayres, to the "Gillespie" role filled by Lionel Barrymore. In "Dark Delusion" James Craig plays the young doctor foil for Barrymore, and is excellent in his first film since receiving a service discharge.

A blunt young M.D., Craig is farmed out from the hospital to take over a rich private practice temporarily. While there he's called to cosign an order sending Miss Bremer, daughter of a wealthy father, to the insane asylum. Convinced that she's all right, Craig pleads for another chance for her and is almost successful, when circumstances convince the others she's really gone. Craig takes her away against the family's wishes, finds out what's wrong through narco-synthesis, operates on a blood clot, and everything turns out okay for everyone. There's a sub-plot concerning heart disease inter-twined skillfully, showing how it's possible to recover from heart ailments, contrary to popular belief.

All the standard characters of the old "Kildare" series, excluding Ayres and Nat Pendleton, hold up well in their usual roles, with Barrymore topping. As the crusty, but soft-hearted "Dr. Gillespie" he'll register well with all auds. Miss Bremer, as the psychopath, comes up with the juiciest part in her film career and interprets solidly. Femme's a looker in black-and-white as well as color. Production-wise, Carey Wilson bows out on a high note, while Charles Rosher's camera work and Willis Goldbeck's direction add nice snap.

Yankee Fakir

(ONE SONG)

Republic release of W. Lee Wilder production, directed by Wilder. Stars Douglas Fowley, Joan Woodbury, Clem Bevans; features Ransom Sherman. Screenplay, Richard S. Conway from story by Mindret Lord; song, J. Russel Robinson, Alexander Laszlo; camera, Robert W. Pittack; editor, Joseph B. Caplan. Tradeshown, N. Y., April 2, '47. Running time, **67 MINS.**

Yankee Davis..............Douglas Fowley
Mary Mason..............Joan Woodbury
Shaggy Hartley..............Clem Bevans
Professor Newton........Ransom Sherman
Randall..............Frank Reicher
Duke..............Marc Lawrence
Sheriff..............Walter Soderling
Mrs. Tetley..............Eula Guy
Mason..............Forrest Taylor
Jenny..............Elinor Appleton
Walker..............Peter Michael
Scrubwoman..............Elspeth Dudgeon
Charlie..............Ernest Adams
Tommy..............Tommy Bernard

Modest budgeted comedy mystery, "Yankee Fakir" will serve as lower-case fare for dualer situations. Film mismanages use of its central character, a snake-oil pitchman, with his natural colorful possibilities and gets derailed instead into a bog of whodunit cliches. General production values are par with the mediocre scripting with nothing special to commend in either its thesping, direction or camera work.

Yarn revolves around Douglas Fowley, an itinerant salesman, who wanders into a western town around the turn of the century and falls for the daughter of the sheriff. After latter is killed by a gang of smugglers, Fowley sets about tracking down the varmints through a complicated series of ruses that fill the footage, but have no relationship to the crime. Expose of the varmints in the end takes place when a local youngster simply identifies the killer and his boss who happens to be the town banker.

Fowley is adequate in the central role and gets okay comedy support from Ransom Sherman, his assistant in the pitchman routines. Clem Bevans, as a vagrant posing as a millionaire, also registers with a competent performance while Joan Woodbury, as the heart interest, is a nice looker, but not given much to do. Rest of the cast in stock parts do okay. Incidental song, "Caught Like a Rat in a Trap," is straight corn.

Herm.

The Man Within

(Color)
(BRITISH-MADE)

London, April 2.

General Film Distributors' release of Sydney Box production. Stars Michael Redgrave, Jean Kent, Joan Greenwood, Richard Attenborough. Directed by Bernard Knowles. Screenplay, Muriel and Sydney Box from novel by Graham Greene; camera, Geoffrey Unsworth. At Odeon theatre, London. Running time, **86 MINS.**

Carylylon..............Michael Redgrave
Lucy..............Jean Kent
Elizabeth..............Joan Greenwood
Andrews..............Richard Attenborough
Mr. Braddock..............Francis L. Sullivan
Priest..............Felix Aylmer
Cockney Harry..............Ronald Shiner
Sir Henry Merriman..............Basil Sydney
Farne..............Ernest Thesiger
Judge..............Allan Jeayes
Prison Interrogator..............Ralph Truman
Dr. Stanton..............David Horne
Hilliard..............George Merritt

First Technicolor picture to be made at Shepherd's Bush studios, and first one to come from Sydney Box since he took over Gainsborough production, this adaptation of Graham Greene's novel has much to commend it. Most glaring fault is amount of talk used. This is irritating when characters on the screen go through lip movements to accompaniment of running commentary. So much that should be acted is described, thus detracting from the excitement and suspense. Holds some promise for the U. S. market.

Story is told in flashback while Richard Attenborough is undergoing torture in prison. He relates how, as an orphan, he becomes the ward of Michael Redgrave, goes to sea with him and his crew of smugglers and is sharply disciplined because he is a poor sailor. He loathes the life and when he is flogged for an offense he did not commit, his love and admiration for his guardian turn to hate. He takes vengeance by giving him away to the customs men. In the ensuing fight one of the customs men is killed and several smugglers are arrested.

Attenborough flees, taking refuge in a lonely cottage the boy meets the step-daughter of the murdered man who approves his treachery and incites him to give evidence against his former shipmates. At the assizes he is suborned by the Crown Attorney's mistress, Jean Kent, with the promise of a love affair if he testifies against his guardian. He gives evidence against the sailors, but at the last moment he refuses to identify Redgrave as leader of the smugglers.

End of story is a trifle untidy but leaves one to assume that Attenborough goes to a happy life, while Redgrave remains in jail.

Most mature performance comes from Redgrave who plays the gentleman-smuggler with a sure touch. Attenborough, as the coward, who finds courage, has his moments, but Joan Greenwood, a promising Rank starlet, is somewhat handicapped by a slow genuine Sussex dialect as Attenborough's real love. Jean Kent is alarmingly modern as an 1820 vamp.

Redgrave and Sydney Box are good marquee names here. But it might be well to hold up this picture in U. S. until release of "The Secret Behind the Door," Fritz Lang film, in which Redgrave is co-starring with Joan Bennett.

Cane.

That's My Man

Republic release of **Frank Borzage** production, directed by **Borzage.** Stars Don Ameche, Catherine McLeod; features Roscoe Karns, John Ridgely, Kitty Irish, Joe Frisco, Joe Hernandez. Screenplay, Steve Fisher, Bradley King; camera, Tony Gaudio; editor, Richard L. Van Enger; score, Hans Salter. Tradeshown N. Y., April 3, '47. Running time, **104 MINS.**

Joe Grange..............Don Ameche
Ronnie..............Catherine McLeod
Toby Gleeton..............Roscoe Karns
Ramsey..............John Ridgely
Kitty..............Kitty Irish
Willie Wagonstatter..............Joe Frisco
Richard..............Gregory Marshall
Millie..............Dorothy Adams
Jockey..............Frankie Darro
Sam..............Hampton J. Scott
Secretary..............John Miljan
Monte..............William B. Davidson
Race Track Announcer..............Joe Hernandez

"That's My Man," Frank Borzage's second top money opus under Republic's banner, will pass muster at the boxoffice through proper exploitation of its horseracing theme and Don Ameche's name. Film, however, is an overlong saccharine nugget with slow pace, often lacking credibility. Only portions of the film that generate any interest or excitement are firstrate racetrack sequences, but these are brief and buried in the surrounding sentimental stuffing. Judicious snipping of about 15 minutes running time could sharpen this pic's appeal.

In tracing the rise and fall of a gambler, screenplay leans heavily upon a familiar pattern without adding any new embroidery to hide the basic triteness. Borzage's direction, instead of contending with this type of script with a tight, positive hand, tends to be diffuse and leisurely, adding to the overall prosaic quality of the film.

Yarn concerns Ameche's conflict, as the gambler, between his fascination for the pari-mutuel odds and the rolling dice and his marital duties as husband and father. After nursing a scrawny colt into a wonder bangtail and parlaying his bets into a bigtime bankroll, Ameche hits a snag with his wife whom he persistently neglects for other pursuits. Film belabors two old chestnuts in epitomizing this neglect; Ameche's card-playing on the night his wife has a baby and, later on, his truancy from a family Christmas eve party.

Following the pat formula, Ameche's gambling luck takes a nose-dive after the family splitup and his fortune is reduced to the ownership of his champion horse, Gallant Man, who finally is taken out of retirement to recoup the family losses and patch up the domestic breach. All the tear-jerking stops are pulled during the film including Ameche's choked-up recitation of a poem to his child who is hovering between life and death. But the hoke is so transparent that the emotional effect is entirely lost.

Ameche, handicapped throughout by the faulty script, walks through his paces in routine style, his own efforts adding nothing to the persuasiveness and motivation of the pic's key role. Catherine McLeod, as the over-loving wife, does nicely in a subordinated part that requires little thespic range. Vet trouper Roscoe Karns, as the family friend, registers effectively but his comedy lines are weak. Rest of the cast, including the horse, does okay.

Production is dressed in lavish style with richly draped interiors and realistic racetrack shots. Camera work is excellent but inferior editing has resulted in a film that is, at the same time, too long and too abrupt in its transitions. Background music is competently scored.

Herm.

The Bellman

(Sortileges)
(FRENCH-MADE)

Mage Films release of Moulin D'Or production. Stars Lucien Coedel; features Fernand Ledoux, Renee Faure. Directed by Christian Jaques. Screenplay by Jacques Prevert from Claude Boncompain's novel, "Horseman of Riouclare"; camera, Louis Page. At Studio 65, N. Y., starting April 5, '47. Running time, **95 MINS.**

The Bellman..............Lucien Coedel
Fabret..............Fernand Ledoux
Catherine..............Renee Faure
Marthe..............Madeleine Robinson
Pierre..............Roger Pigaut
Commandant of Gendarmes..............Georges Tourrell
The Old Woman..............Sinoel
The Village Outsider..............Pierre Labry

(In French; English Titles)

This French horror meller carries such a wallop that it easily rates as the strongest French-made picture to preem in the U. S. since the war. Made in 1945, "The Bellman" is reminiscent of those productions from France that attracted record crowds at arty N. Y. houses pre-war. Film seems certain of big biz at arty theatres in America, and should be okay in certain general houses. One thing that might help its boxoffice potential would be a new title to get across the horror, melodramatic angle, which also should be stressed in bally.

Claude Boncompain's story is about a bellman whose job is to sound a bell high in the French Alps and thereby assist travelers from becoming lost. The closeup of this fanatical character, Lucien Coedel, incorporates the cruelty of the man, his half-belief in witchcraft and a new-born yearning for money so he can get away from his isolated post. But it's the combination of Jacques Prevert's skillful adaptation of the original and Christian Jacques' smooth, smart direction that heightens all suspenseful moments. Work of this team plus remarkably strong camera work by Louis Page, especially the scenes in snow-swept high mountains, increase the potency of the more vivid passages.

Casual slaying of a wealthy horse trader, who's lost his way in the mountains, starts off the well-paced plot. Fernand Ledoux is the slightly demented father whose interest in his daughter's recovery from a long illness brings him into the grasp of the murderous Bellman. Fact that his Fabret character wanders from normalcy into insane moments makes him an easy dupe for the brutal Bellman. There's also a valuable trained horse who escapes the same fate as the horse trader and finally leads the gendarmes to uncover the crime.

Besides Coedel's magnificent portrayal and the fine characterization by Ledoux, Roger Pigaut also rates star billing. He's the romantic lead as the young woodcutter, an obvious comer in French films. Renee Faure, a looker who obviously shows strong theatre background, is Catherine, daughter of the slightly wacky peasant. She's superb. She also sings an untitled country ballad in effective style. Madeleine Robinson makes the rival girl, Martha, a strong character.

Wear.

Violence

Hollywood, April 5.

Monogram release of Jack Bernhard-Bernard Brandt production. Stars Michael O'Shea, Nancy Coleman; features Sheldon Leonard, Emory Parnell, Peter Whitney. Directed by Jack Bernhard. Story and screenplay, Stanley Rubin, Louis Lantz; camera, Henry Sharp; music, Edward J. Kay; editor, Jason Bernie. Previewed April 3, '47. Running time, **72 MINS.**

Ann Mason..............Nancy Coleman
Steve Fuller..............Michael O'Shea
Fred Stalk..............Sheldon Leonard
Joker Robinson..............Peter Whitney
True Dawson..............Emory Parnell
Ralph Borden..............Pierre Watkin
Pop..............Frank Reicher
Mrs. Donahue..............Cay Forester
Dr. Chalmers..............John Hamilton
Latimer..............Richard Irving
Bess Taffel..............Carol Donne
Joe Donahue..............Jimmy Clark
Mr. X..............William Gould

"Violence" is neat propaganda, warning veterans to beware of secret pressure organizations whose object is the spread of civic discord. Message is well-scripted and in addition, film contains plenty of suspense to carry out commercial melodramatic aims. Script and players combine to overcome lack of directorial finesse, giving picture punch that will put it over.

Production framework is expert under wing of Jack Bernhard and Bernard Brandt. Pair chose cast with care, and players deliver. Plot deals with operation of pressure group known as United Defenders, a front organization for all types of violence. Outfit makes a play for discontented vets, using them for the spread of discord under the cloak of patriotism.

Action concerns Nancy Coleman, undercover operator for a photo mag, out to bust United Defenders. To complicate plot, girl is made to suffer loss of memory as result of auto accident, a device that pitches heroine and Michael O'Shea, an investigator, into plenty of danger before denouement. Bernard's direction doesn't take the best advantage of the Stanley Rubin-Louis Lantz screenplay and consequently sense of reality isn't as strong as it might have been, but results still come off.

Chief heavies are capably performed by Sheldon Leonard, Peter Whitney and Emory Parnell, who match good work of Miss Coleman and O'Shea. Cay Forester and Jimmy Clark both spot good bits, and others in cast are acceptable.

Production has been given expert lensing by Henry Sharp, plus an Edward J. Kay music score that heightens meller factors.

Brog.

Three On a Ticket

Hollywood, April 1.

PRC release of Sigmund Neufeld production. Features Hugh Beaumont, Cheryl Walker, Paul Bryar, Ralph Dunn, Louise Currie, Gavin Gordon. Directed by Sam Newfield. Screenplay, Fred Myton; based on original characters and story by Brett Halliday; camera, Jack Greenhalgh; editor, Holbrook N. Todd. Previewed at Hollywood, April 1, '47. Running time, 62 MINS.

Michael Shayne	Hugh Beaumont
Phyllis Hamilton	Cheryl Walker
Tim Rourke	Paul Bryar
Pete Rafferty	Ralph Dunn
Helen Brinstead	Louise Currie
Pearson	Gavin Gordon
Kurt Leroy	Charles Quigley
Mace Morgan	Douglas Fowley
Trigger	Noel Cravat
Drunk	Charles King, Sr.
Jim Lacy	Brooks Benedict

Sturdy supporting film fare measuring up to market demands in all departments, "Three On a Ticket" has a good action whodunit story to tell and spins it off at smart clip that will please. Suspense is maintained by playing and direction and production mounting obtains values better than expected from budget expenditure.

Plot of this latest of PRC's Michael Shayne detective thrillers deals with the dauntless private eye's adventures while trying to outguess a choice bunch of doublecrossing crooks. Shayne and the sundry heavies are all after cache of bank loot hidden in a railroad storage locker. Ticket necessary to recover loot has been torn into thirds and holders all are trying to obtain parts held by others. Before the heroic finish, Shayne has been pushed around, beaten, etc., but comes through with expected flying colors to solve the case and make a nice fee for himself.

Hugh Beaumont is excellent as Shayne and his work is ably backed by Cheryl Walker, who gives considerable life to role of the private detective's smart secretary. Louise Currie makes femme heavy spot count in final results and other villains measuring up include Gavin Gordon and Douglas Fowley, Paul Bryar, Ralph Dunn and others in cast are good.

Sam Newfield has paced direction of the Fred Myton script to sustain interest, and the well valued production was furnished by Sigmund Neufeld. Lensing by Jack Greenhalgh, settings, and other production ingredients are expert. *Brog.*

Shoot to Kill

Hollywood, April 5.

Screen Guild release of William Berke production. Features Russell Wade, Susan Walters, Edmund MacDonald, Douglas Blackley, Vince Barnett, Nestor Paiva. Directed by Berke. Screenplay, Edwin V. Westrate; camera, Benjamin Kline; music, Darrell Calker; editor, Arthur A. Brooks. Previewed April 2, '47. Running time, 64 MINS.

George Mitchell	Russell Wade
Marian Langdon	Susan Walters
Lawrence Dale	Edmund MacDonald
Dixie Logan	Douglas Blackley
Charlie Gill	Vince Barnett
Gus Miller	Nestor Paiva
John Forsythe	Douglas Trowbridge
Jim Forman	Harry Brown
Al Collins	Ted Hecht
Mike Blake	Harry Cheshire
Ed Carter	Robert Riordan
Smokey	Joe Devlin
Bingo	Eddie Foster
Clem	Frank O'Conner
Blackie	Sammy Stein
Piano Player	Gene Rodgers

"Shoot to Kill" is good melodrama for supporting positions. It has been well cast, except for femme lead, the production gloss gets the best from small budget, and telling of its story leaves no loose ends.

Males in cast deliver consistently good performances in spinning yarn of crooked politicians and crooked gangs that operate under their shelter. Russell Wade makes a forthright, believable newspaperman who is instrumental in uncovering the operations. Edmund MacDonald is equally as good as the aspiring assistant d.a. who nurtures the crooks.

Story concerns MacDonald, supported by and supporting the villainous workings of Nestor Paiva, town gangster. Teamwork is going well until they frame a crook trying to muscle in. Latter's wife, working under cover, gets a job as MacDonald's secretary and obtains plenty of evidence, with Wade's help, to fix the heavies. Edwin V. Westrate script tells the plot in flashback and has only the common fault of having girl recount events in which she could not have figured.

Femme lead is played by Susan Walters in not too believable fashion. Paiva is good as one of the heavies. Douglas Blackley makes his footage count as the framed crook. Vince Barnett does neatly by small spot as courtroom janitor who is bumped off. Production touch adds Gene Rodgers, pianist, for two nitery instrumentals.

William Berke produced and directed, and got the most from budget and story. Benjamin Kline's camera work is good. *Brog.*

Miniature Reviews

"Monsieur Verdoux" (Chaplin-UA). Charlot will have to carry this one.

"Calcutta" (Par). Adventure thriller laid in Far East. Alan Ladd and others assure good boxoffice.

"Honeymoon" (Songs) (RKO). Dull romantic comedy of errors with strong pitch for Latin-American trade; dim b.o.

"A Likely Story" (RKO). Fast, fun-packed farce lively entertainment for all situations although light on marquee.

"Fun on a Weekend" (UA). Good quota of laughs with Eddie Bracken, Priscilla Lane for marquee.

"This Happy Breed" (Color) (British) (U). Noel Coward cavalcade-yarn with Celia Johnson, should do well at b.o.

"The Barber of Seville" (Music) (Italian). Static version of the Rossini opera, with limited b.o. appeal.

"Born to Kill" (RKO). Murder meller okay boxoffice in general situations.

"Banjo" (RKO). Family trade feature of femme moppet and her dog, in tear-jerker tradition.

"Twilight on the Rio Grande" (Rep). Gene Autry musical oater, not up to standard but with enough stunts to get by ok.

Monsieur Verdoux

United Artists release of Charles Chaplin production starring, directed, written by and music composed by Chaplin. Features Martha Raye, Isobel Elsom, Marilyn Nash, Robert Lewis. Associate directors, Robert Florey, Wheeler Dryden; camera, Roland Totheroh, Wallace Chewing; asst. director, Rex Bailey; editor, Willard Nico; music arranged and directed by Rudolph Schrager. At Broadway, N. Y., opening April 11, 47, combination grind run with reserved mezzanine seats, mats and eves, $1.80-$2.40. Running time, 122 MINS.

Henri Verdoux	Charles Chaplin
Mona	Mady Correll
Peter	Allison Roddan
Maurice Bottello	Robert Lewis
Martha	Audrey Betz
Annabella Bonheur	Martha Raye
Annette	Ada-May
Marie Grosnay	Isobel Elsom
Her Maid	Marjorie Bennett
Yvonne	Helene Heigh
Lydia Floray	Margaret Hoffman
The Girl	Marilyn Nash
Pierre	Irving Bacon
Jean	Edwin Mills
Carlotta	Virginia Brissac
Lena	Almira Sessions
Phoebe	Eula Morgan
Prefect of Police	Bernard J. Nedell
Detective Morrow	Charles Evans

Others in the cast: William Frawley, Arthur Hohl, Fritz Leiber, John Harmon, Barbara Slater, Vera Marshe, Christine Ell, Lois Conklin.

Chaplin will have to carry this one. And how. As the quintuple-threat combo producer, star, author, director and composer, Chaplin has the whole two hours' running time in his lap 500%. And it's not a happy sum total. Comedians who yen to do "Hamlet" usually wind up with neo-tragic results, and "Monsieur Verdoux" runs according to form.

Chaplin is an all-time great as a pantomimist. His yesteryear two-reelers are masterpieces of the art of slapstickery. Not for naught are they the treasured possessions of many home projectionists. Film museums and revival houses alike experience a bull market when the old Chaplin escapades are unmothballed. The sum and substance are that Chaplin and comedy are as much an affinity as ham and eggs, Pat and Mike, or Park & Tilford.

But now comes Chaplin in a Bluebeard story which, by its very premise, is a false note. Comedy based on the characterization of a modern Parisian Bluebeard treads danger shoals indeed. Even if the accent were more effective, the fundamentals are unsound when it's revealed that Chaplin has been driven to marrying and murdering middling mesdames in order to provide for his ailing wife and their son of 10 years' marriage.

Chaplin generates little sympathy. His broad-mannered antics, as a many-aliased fop on the make for impressionable matrons; the telltale technique, a hangover from his bankteller's days, of counting the bundles of francs in the traditional nervous manner of rapid finger movement; the business of avoiding Martha Raye at that garden party, when he finally woos and wins Isobel Elsom; the neo-"American Tragedy" hokum in the rowboat-on-the-lake scene with Miss Raye; the mixed bottles of poisoned wine [again Miss Raye, with oldtime musicomedy star Ada-May (Weeks) as the blowsy buxom blonde of a maid in support]; and all the rest of it is only spotty.

When Chaplin does a backward fall out the window in an early scene they laugh because they're hungry for a snicker. The forepart footage, incidentally, is on the stage-wait side for a considerable period. Foiled by the aggressively eager and amorous Miss Raye, these are some of the brighter moments. But here, too, the technique, from creative comedy to camera, seems disturbingly dated.

Marilyn Nash, the touted new femme, has yet to be sure of her dialog, but she looks well. The real looker of the film is a knockout of a natural blonde who plays the flower clerk in that scene where Chaplin is campaigning for the wealthy Miss Elsom. She's Barbara Slater, billed but not easily identified.

Chaplin's endeavor to get his "common man" ideology into the film militates against its comedy values. Story is rather strong sociological medicine with an allegorical basis throughout. Point that Chaplin is making, of course in exaggerated form, is that depressions in our economy force us into being ruthless villains and murderers, despite the fact we are actually kind and sympathetic.

Chaplin also rings in another of his favorite themes, his strong feelings against war. In one speech he forthrightly states that wars are brought on by big industrialists, who are the only ones who profit by them. Later he points out that while the murderer of one person is a villain, murderers of millions are heroes.

The scripting essays a touch of realism with news clips of the Hitlerian aggression, headlines about Spanish loyalists being bombed by Franco, clips of the 1929 Wall Street debacle, and the like. There is a questionable scene in the gaol preparatory to Chaplin's guillotining when he pointedly asks the padre "what can I do for you?", and further accents that by asking the cleric where would he (the padre) be if it weren't for sin.

The casting is all Chaplin, perhaps too much so, but William Frawley registers in one scene and Bernard J. Nedell is effective as the prefect of police. Robert Lewis, as the pharmacist-friend of the many-aliased Henri Verdoux, is telling in a couple of scenes, deadpanned by his buxom spouse, played by Audrey Betz.

Chaplin's direction (associate credits to Robert Florey and Wheeler Dryden) is disjointed also on occasion, although perhaps the natural enough result of a leisurely production schedule which ranged up to five years. Chaplin's score, however, is above par, fortifying the progression in no small measure. (Here, again, the producer-star-director-author-composer gives collaborative credit to Rudolph Schrager for arrangement and direction). *Abel.*

Calcutta

Hollywood, April 12.

Paramount release of Seton I. Miller production. Written by Miller. Stars Alan Ladd, Gail Russell, William Bendix; features June Duprez, Lowell Gilmore, Edith King. Directed by John Farrow. Camera, John F. Seitz; special effects, Gordon Jennings; score, Victor Young; editor, Archie Marshek. Tradeshown April 11, '47. Running time, **73 MINS.**

Neale Gordon	Alan Ladd
Virginia Moore	Gail Russell
Pedro Blake	William Bendix
Merina Tanev	June Duprez
Eric Lasset	Lowell Gilmore
Mrs. Smith	Edith King
Mul Raj Malik	Paul Singh
Inspector Kendricks	Gavin Muir
Bill Cunningham	John Whitney
Young Chinese Clerk	Benson Fong

Pulp fiction treatment gives "Calcutta" adventure flavor that should attract hefty action audience. Names are strong, led off by Alan Ladd and William Bendix, so returns should please in most situations.

Producer-writer Seton I. Miller lays action in the Far East and uses modern day airplane pilots whose characters closely parallel pop comic strip heroes. This is not a disadvantage for such high romance as film tells, and these production accoutrements give good backing to the adventuring.

There's enough in story, despite action aim, to attract the femmes. One cincher for distaff side is sequence in which Ladd slaps Gail Russell—not once but several times as she's exposed as baby-faced killer. Ladd is flying the air route between Calcutta and Chungking as one of trio of pilot pals. Sidekicks are Bendix and John Whitney. When latter is mysteriously killed, Ladd and Bendix take time off to track down murderer.

Plot carries them through plenty of dare-and-do before heroes are able to bring to justice Lowell Gilmore and Miss Russell, a smooth pair of jewel smugglers. Script has a cloudy beginning but interest gradually develops as audience finally gets wise that Miss Russell is not the nice girl she at first appears to be. Sprinkled through plot are a number of choice characters, principal of which is Edith King as a flowzy art shop dealer.

There's a double femme romance angle. Ladd is portrayed as love-'em hero who goes for both Miss Russell and June Duprez, nitery singer. Gavin Muir is good as police inspector and there is an uncredited hotel clerk role that helps fulfill directorial intentions of John Farrow. Latter handles players capably, showing them to advantage, and keeps story on the move.

John F. Seitz did expert lensing and Far Eastern motif is well carried out in art direction by Hans Dreier and Franz Bachelin. Editing is tight holding film to 73 minutes.

Brog.

Honeymoon

(SONGS)

RKO release of Warren Duff production Stars Shirley Temple, Franchot Tone, Guy Madison; features Lina Romay, Gene Lockhart, Corinna Mura, Grant Mitchell. Directed by William Keighley. Screenplay, Michael Kanin based on story by Vicki Baum; songs, Leigh Harline, Mort Greene; camera, Edward Cronjager; editor, Ralph Dawson. Tradeshown N. Y., April 11, '47. Running time, **74 MINS.**

Barbara	Shirley Temple
Flanner	Franchot Tone
Phil	Guy Madison
Raquel	Lina Romay
Prescott	Gene Lockhart
Senora Mendoza	Corinna Mura
Crenshaw	Grant Mitchell
Senor Mendoza	Julio Villareal
Registrar	Manuel Arvide
Doctor Diego	Jose R. Goula

Aimed directly at the Latin-American market, "Honeymoon" is a good neighbor taffypull that won't have any repercussions either diplomatically or boxoffice-wise. In catering to the presumed tastes of patrons south-of-the-border, film succeeds only in inverting the typical Hollywood formula by making all U.S. citizens inane and unreal and all Mexicans intelligent and equally unreal.

Story is a hair-thin, uninventive comedy of errors plodding through with a periodic repetition of identical situations and no buildup to any sort of climax. Pic ends by merely falling off the merry-go-round. It will take all the marquee lure of Shirley Temple, Franchot Tone and Guy Madison to give this effort any play at the wickets. Its brief running time of 74 minutes limits, in any case, its firstrun possibilities in the keys.

Overlarded with a heavy spread of Spanish dialog, yarn revolves around a U. S. consul in Mexico City who plays Cupid in trying to help join two American kids in love but divided by a series of legal barriers and personal misunderstandings. Consul, who is himself affianced to a high-born Mexican gal, runs through a mill of compromising situations that nearly break up his own affair before he brings his two charges together in a marital clinch.

Miss Temple, as a lightminded young jitterbug from the States intent upon romance with her soldier-boyfriend, or any eligible substitute, registers as a charming miss with a clear talent for comedy if given the chance which this pic rarely does. Her warbling, however, is only so-so and the numbers, "I Love Geraniums" and "Venaqui" are cut-and-dried pop tunes. Tone, a very good if somewhat neglected performer these days, is entirely miscast in a slapstick role of the U. S. consul but nonetheless accounts for all the high moments in the film. Madison, as the soldier, steams through his part in over-vigorous style, while Lina Romay does nicely as the aristocratic Mexican girl. Midway in the film a trio of visiting American Congressmen, headed by Grant Mitchell, appear on the scene with unintended farcical characterizations. What will Latin-Americans think when they get a load of their absurd caperings?

Production mountings are solid with good camera work and smooth editing.

Herm.

A Likely Story

Hollywood, April 15.

RKO release of Richard H. Berger production. Stars Barbara Hale; Bill Williams; features Lanny Rees, Sam Levene, Dan Tobin, Nester Paiva. Directed by H. C. Potter. Written by Bess Taffel; suggested by a story by Alexander Kenedi; camera, Roy Hunt; music, Leigh Harline; editor, Harry Marker. Tradeshown April 15, '47. Running time, **88 MINS.**

Vickie North	Barbara Hale
Bill Baker	Bill Williams
Jamie	Lanny Rees
Louie	Sam Levene
Phil Bright	Dan Tobin
Tiny	Nestor Paiva
Mr. Slepoff	Max Willenz
Tremendo	Henry Kulky
Ticket Girl	Robin Raymond
Little Old Lady	Mary Young

"A Likely Story" crams in a lot of fun to prove out as nifty escapist film fare for all audiences. Best playing level will be outside de luxe situations due to lightness of marquee names, but cast delivers strongly to keep farcing swift.

There's a load of fun developed from smart direction, playing and topnotch scripting, all elements combining to keep action fast and light. H. C. Potter peppers story with deft directorial touches that pay off and Bess Taffel's screenplay wraps amusing situations and dialog around essentially light story basis.

Plot chiefly concerns efforts of ex-soldier to die so a struggling femme artist and an ex-mobster can collect his insurance. Believing he has a fatal heart condition, soldier has talked gangster into insuring his life and giving girl some money immediately. Laughs spring from soldier's efforts, aided by mobsters, to bring about his early demise. Needless to say, he only gets healthier, love blooms and trick ending takes care of the gansters.

Barbara Hale and Bill Williams smartly fulfill all demands as artist and veteran, respectively. Miss Hale gets the best from assignment and Williams is solid as slightly pixilated vet. Backing young leads with strongest support is Sam Levene as contact man for ex-gangster Nester Paiva. Latter also shows up well. Lanny Rees, Miss Hale's young brother; Dan Tobin, would be suitor and insurance salesman, are capable and adds to laughs. Others rating mention include Max Willenz, Henry Kulky, Robin Raymond and Mary Young.

Richard H. Berger's production under executive supervision of Jack J. Gross has given film excellent appurtenances. Camera work by Roy Hunt lends gloss to good art direction by Albert S. D'Agostino and Field Gray and other technical ends are equally bright.

Brog.

Fun on a Weekend

United Artists release of Andrew Stone production directed and written by Stone. Stars Eddie Bracken, Priscilla Lane; features Tom Conway, Allen Jenkins, Arthur Treacher. Camera, Paul Ivano; editor, Paul Weatherwax; music, Lucien Caillet. Previewed N. Y., April 8, '47. Running time, **93 MINS.**

P. P. Porterhouse III	Eddie Bracken
Nancy Crane	Priscilla Lane
Van	Tom Conway
Joe Morgan	Allen Jenkins
B. O. Moffatt	Arthur Treacher
Quigley Quackenbush	Clarence Kolb
Mrs. Van Orsdale	Alma Kruger
John Biddle	Russell Hicks
Sergei Stronganoff	Fritz Feld
Mr. Cowperwaithe	Richard Hageman
Stooge at Lunch Counter	Lester Allen
Bill Davis	Bill Kennedy

Eddie Bracken's comedics put sufficient laughing matter into 'Fun on a Weekend" to lift an improbable yarn into a passable programmer. Opus will go well with the juve trade and will retrieve its keep in the nabes.

Yarn might have been catapulted into the class of satire, but lacks the necessary deftness. As it stands, it's a few shades above routine comedy.

Film is based on the get-rich-quick theme with Bracken cast as penniless milquetoast character with grandiose ideas. He meets Priscilla Lane who has sufficient gall to put Bracken's ideas into practice. They first exchange their clothing for bathing suits on the premise that in that type garb they can't be distinguished from wealthy socialites, and come near accomplishing their ends.

Andrew Stone's fast direction is instrumental in hiding many implausibilities in the plot. He succeeds in having Bracken clown his way out of situations where the slightest letdown in pace would have destroyed the logic of the story.

Miss Lane, who's been absent from films for some time, gives a good enough performance which should insure her work in more pictures. Tom Conway shapes up well as rival love-interest for Bracken, while further comedy is by Allen Jenkins and Arthur Treacher. Fritz Feld contributes a pair of laugh-provoking bits as an eccentric pianist as does Lester Allen, the former legit-comedian, unheard from in a long time.

Jose.

This Happy Breed

(Color)

(BRITISH-MADE)

Prestige Pictures (Universal) release of Noel Coward-Cineguild (Rank) production. Stars Robert Newton, Celia Johnson; features John Mills, Stanley Holloway. Directed by David Lean. Screenplay, Ronald Neame, David Lean, Anthony Havelock-Allan, from play by Noel Coward. Camera, Ronald Neame. At Little Carnegie, N. Y., April 12, '47. Running time, **110 MINS.**

Frank Gibbons	Robert Newton
Ethel Gibbons	Celia Johnson
Billy Mitchell	John Mills
Queenie Gibbons	Kay Walsh
Bob Mitchell	Stanley Holloway
Mrs. Flint	Amy Veness
Aunt Sylvia	Alison Leggatt
Vi	Eileen Erskine
Reg	John Blythe
Sam Leadbitter	Guy Verney
Edie	Merle Tottenham
Phyllis	Betty Fleetwood

The new-found American sweep-awaystakes—the lush U. S. market newly risen for better British films—has found another fine entrant in "This Happy Breed." The Noel Coward name, the presence of Celia ("Brief Encounter") Johnson, a message peculiarly apt to the restless present-day world, as well as an essentially superior production involving excellent story line and character portrayals, will make this pic a good b.o. draw.

Produced in London three years ago, but only shown in U. S. now because new releasing setup (Prestige Pictures-Universal) has been able to handle the new-found market, film has an added appeal for U. S. filmgoers it might not have had originally. Miss Johnson's work in "Brief Encounter" (released the past year in the U. S.) made her a candidate for an Oscar award and a draw with the public. The story of an average lower-class British family trying to find stability for itself during the troubled days between the two World Wars is of special interest today, as families everywhere try to hold anchor in an uncertain time which may also be a period between wars again.

Aside from that, the film stands on its own merits. Based on Noel Coward's London legit hit, it soundly captures the spirit of the twenties and thirties, reviving the era of the British general strike, the jazz dress style, the Charleston, and the depression. It touches on the troubled sphere of the class struggle and labor strife, although it has a dubious note once or twice, such as in an apparent defense of strike-breaking. But it is so much more the history of an average British family, with its pleasures and pains, whose counterpart lives everywhere, to make this the paramount interest.

Film is a bit episodic and choppy at the start, as it unwinds in cavalcadish fashion, but it settles down soon to an absorbing chronicle. Color work is handled deftly, to be of great help. Camera work is also superior, with some unusual shots and angles that stand out on their own, aside from the plot. Production is ample, although most of the story is contained within one house and garden ("an Englishman's home is his castle") in lower-class suburbs.

Film's excellence comes mainly in the performances. Celia Johnson, as the mother of three grown children and the rock around which the family revolves, presents a masterful, poignant portrayal. Her makeup and dress as a middle-class matron take away some of the smartness shown in "Encounter," so that at times she is plain, almost ugly. But an inner glow and warmth wash this away as a trifling interference.

Robert Newton, who has almost as important a role as the head of the house, is also a superb presentation as the steady, earth-bound but intelligent Britisher. Actor's versatility is the more marked when contrasted with his job as the cowardly braggart Pistol in "Henry V." Kay Walsh, as the flighty daughter dissatisfied with her lot; John Mills (hero of the forthcoming "Great Expectations") as the loyal sailor in love with the errant daughter; Amy Veness, as the crotchety grandmother; Alison Leggatt as the whining sister-in-law, and Stanley Holloway as the nextdoor neighbor, give fine support. The whole cast, in fact, is well chosen. Most of them are plain looking, with nary a typically pretty Hollywood face among them, but this plainness will impress the more because of its closeness to reality.

An unusual number of scenes

stand out for their humor, pathos or special interest, such as the riotous scene when the family quarrels just before going off to a wedding, or a simple kitchen scene of mother and daughter discussing their problems, or the highly emotional moment when an outraged mother breaks down and welcomes back a repentant, sinning child.

Best handled, perhaps, is the scene where a daughter breaks to the parents the news of the death of two other children, the set being absolutely empty for a few moments as the news is told offstage before the stunned parents come in. There is one perhaps unintentionally funny moment when a Britisher complains he can't make out what an American is saying (Charles King singing "Broadway Melody" from flash of the film of that name), when several times previously British characters have talked so fast it was difficult to make them out.

There's a lot in this film, direction, camera and production matching story and acting for a superior job.
Bron.

The Barber of Seville

(Music)
(ITALIAN-MADE)

Excelsior Pictures release of Tespi (Marie and Ugo Trombetti) production. Stars Ferruccio Tagliavini, Tito Gobbi, Nelly Cerradi. Directed by Mario Gosta. Opera by Gioacchino Rossini; libretto by Cesare Sterbini; story sequence, Deems Taylor; camera, Massimo Terzano; sets, Libero Petrassi; costumes, Giorgio Foeldes. Previewed N. Y., April 10, '47. Running time, 110 MINS.

Count Almavina	Ferrucio Tagliavini
Figaro	Tito Gobbi
Rosina	Nelly Corradi
Don Bartolo	Vito de Tarranto
Don Basilio	Italo Tajo
Berta	Natalia Nicolini
Fiorello	Nino Mazziotti

Rome Opera House chorus and orchestra under Guiseppe Morelli

(In Italian; English Titles)

"The Barber of Seville," Rossini's most tuneful of operas—a stage treat in N. Y. or Naples, at the Metropolitan or with a Miami High School senior class production—comes off as a distinct disappointment in its new Italian film version. Its boxoffice chances look limited.

Opera enthusiasts, who would be sold in advance on seeing the pic for its music, will be let down and hardly likely to help by word-of-mouth. The presence of Ferruccio Tagliavini, Metropolitan highly-touted tenor find, may draw some of the curious. But the general public will have to be sold heavily, and there aren't enough talking points to sell. Pic suffers from various production defects, and is at all times static and slow. In short, it's a big bore.

Pic is one of the rare instances of bringing a complete opera to the screen (although not the first time, as claimed). It is handsomely mounted, in costumes and sets, and peopled by some fine singers from the fount of opera, the Royal Opera House in Rome. Producers have been faithful to the letter in following the stage version for their film. Probably they've been too faithful. By photographing a stage production, not giving camera opportunity to roam and fill in an actionless story with outdoor or contiguous scenes, they've muffed an opportunity that wouldn't have spoiled the spirit of the show.

U. S. distribs have gone out of their way to help the film, but in reality have missed out. Film has ample English subtitles. But to insure the pic being completely comprehensible, Excelsior added Deems Taylor as an entr'acte commentator, to relate the plot of each act before its unfolding. This sounds like a good stunt, and Taylor's remarks are as literate and witty as they are informative. But his three appearances slow down a slow play that much more, to defeat the purpose. Subtitles alone are sufficient to tell the thin story.

The story, of course, is silly at best, showing how a Count in Seville disguises himself first as a drunken soldier, then as a music teacher, to get into his girl's house and woo her away from the pompous guardian who wants to marry her himself. Action is confined to the square in front of the house, and to two rooms inside, and what activity there is concerns itself with frantic runnings-around as soldiers, villagers and sundry kids bounce in and out of the house on the heels of the Count. The real moments of humor are so few that they stand out like beacons—a cockatoo expressing surprise at a soprano's aria, or the soprano flouncing behind a screen to change dress as she sings. The opera's libretto shows up feebly under a camera's cruel light.

Wooden acting by most of the participants, who are in reality opera singers first and actors theoretically after, doesn't help matters. Tagliavini is pretty stiff and expressionless. In fact, in singing as well as in acting, he has the show stolen from him by Tito Gobbi, playing the barber Figaro. Handsome, with a flair for the role, Gobbi brings style and sparkle to his acting, while in his great "Largo al Factotum" air, gives a brilliant vocal performance.

His singing (as is all the film's music) is marred by the sound track, which throughout suffers from being too shrill and grating. This piercing recorded quality is further affected by bad synchronization, it being too apparent from the indifferent vocal emotings that the singing had already been recorded before the filming. Photography at times is dark and indistinct.

On the credit side, in addition to Gobbi's acting and singing, are some choice vocal numbers by Tagliavini, and excellent presentation of the "Una voce poco fa" aria by Nelly Corradi. Latter is an unusually attractive Rosina, and one of the brightest figures in the film. Other characters look grotesque on screen, although being faithful reproductions of their stage versions. Italo Tajo, as Don Basilio, gives a rousing rendition of the Alumny Song. The cast in entirety, being star members of the Royal Opera House in Rome, lives up to its standards for vocal excellence. Recording spoils the effect, though. Guiseppe Morelli, conducting the Opera House's chorus and orchestra, does yeoman work throughout. The well-known overture, by the way, is noticeably cut. *Bron.*

Born to Kill

Hollywood, April 14.

RKO release of Herman Schlom (Sid Rogell) production. Stars Claire Trevor, Lawrence Tierney, Walter Slezak; features Phillip Terry, Audrey Long. Directed by Robert Wise. Based on novel by James Gunn; screenplay, Eve Green, Richard Macaulay; camera, Robert de Grasse; asst. director, Sam Ruman; editor, Les Millbrook; special effects, Russell A. Cully; music, Paul Sawtell; music director, C. Bakaleinikoff; dialog director, Anthony Jowitt. Previewed April 14, '47. Running time, 92 MINS.

Sam	Lawrence Tierney
Helen	Claire Trevor
Arnett	Walter Slezak
Fred	Phillip Terry
Georgia	Audrey Long
Marty	Elisha Cook, Jr.
Laury Palmer	Isabel Jewell
Mrs. Kraft	Esther Howard
Grace	Kathryn Card
Danny	Tony Barrett
Inspector Wilson	Grandon Rhodes

Murder melodrama for thriller fans is okay boxoffice in general situations although not of top calibre.

It presents Lawrence Tierney in another of his tough guy killer roles. Cast names surrounding Tierney also are stronger, with Claire Trevor and Walter Slezak co-starred to aid its chances. Film injects psychiatric overtones and a lot of plot, which means character motivation is not always clear. Otherwise it lives up to thriller intentions of depicting maniacal killer who cooly bumps off anyone who incurs his displeasure.

Role played by Miss Trevor is equally unscrupulous, script having been based on the novel, "Deadlier Than the Male," by James Gunn. Both stars are equal to the demands of their unsympathetic roles and get considerable out of them. Walter Slezak, shady private detective, is in keeping with unsavory mood of principals as developed by Robert Wise's direction.

Story opens in Reno where Miss Trevor is getting divorce. She comes on double murder shortly after Tierney has fled the scene. Pair meet on train to San Francisco and recognize kindred souls. She's out to marry Phillip Terry for his money, so Tierney marries her rich sister, Audrey Long. Slezak enters plot when he's hired privately to find the Reno murderer. Not too much suspense develops as he tracks down Tierney, which is one of the factors that keeps film from top classification. Tierney commits another murder before Miss Trevor turns on him and there's a shoot-'em-up finale in which both get their just deserts.

Script by Eve Greene and Richard Macauley loses ground by attempting to explain a little too thoroughly what motivates the two leads' actions and several other characters are on the vague side. Terry and Miss Long do their best with colorless spots. Elisha Cook, Jr., Isabel Jewell, Esther Howard and others try hard to make characterizations count.

Production by Herman Schlom under executive supervision of Sid Rogell gives film excellent mounting. Paul Sawtell's music score is good, as is lensing by Robert de Grasse.

Banjo

Hollywood, April 12.

RKO release of Lillie Hayward production. Stars Sharyn Moffett; features Jacqueline White, Walter Reed, Una O'Conner, Herbert Evans, Louise Beavers, Ernest Whitman, Banjo (Canine). Directed by Richard O. Fleischer. Original screenplay, Lillie Hayward; camera, George E. Diskant; music, Alexander Laszlo; editor, Les Millbrook. Tradeshown April 11, '47. Running time, 67 MINS.

Pat	Sharyn Moffett
Elizabeth	Jacqueline White
Dr. Bob	Walter Reed
Harriet	Una O'Conner
Jeffries	Herbert Evans
Lindy	Louise Beavers
Jasper	Ernest Whitman
Ned	Lanny Rees
Exodus	Theron Jackson
Genesis	Howard McNeely

"Banjo"

"Banjo" pulls all stops in living up to its tearjerker classification. Theme of little orphan girl and her dog is fully exploited for the general family trade.

Lillie Hayward produced from her own script and makes full use of weepy situations to show off decided talents of little Sharyn Moffett. Plot is loaded with tried and true cliches necessary to carry the story along. Miss Moffett is orphaned when her father is killed in fall from horse. She's sent from the Georgia plantation to her aunt in Boston. The aunt doesn't understand her or her setter, Banjo. The dog is sent back to Georgia and the little girl runs away. The aunt sees the light, takes chase and there's a weepy reconciliation when the dog saves his mistress from a dangerous swamp cat.

Performances of younger set and the dog aid in carrying the picture along. Miss Moffett makes excellent use of her talent as the young girl. Two Negro playmates come through cutely in the persons of Theron Jackson and Howard McNeely. Louise Beavers and Ernest Whitman are the intelligent, adult, true-to-life Negro servants on the old plantation. Script does a good job on these two roles, portraying them without caricature. Jacqueline White, the aunt, and Walter Reed, her doctor - fiance, handle older romance. Una O'Connor and Herbert Evans are caricature white servants on the Boston estate, Lanny Ross completes good credited cast.

Richard O. Fleischer's direction keeps script on the move and does expertly by its standard ingredients.
Brog.

Twilight on Rio Grande

(SONGS)

Hollywood, April 12.

Republic release of Armand Schaefer production. Stars Gene Autry; features Sterling Holloway, Adele Mara, Bof Steele, Charles Evans, Martin Gerralaga, Cass County Boys (3). Directed by Frank McDonald. Original screenplay, Dorrell and Stuart E. McGowan; camera, William Bradford; editor, Harry Keller; songs, Charles Tobias and Nat Simon, Smiley Burnette, Larry Marks and Dick Charles, Jack Elliott. Previewed April 10, '47. Running time, 71 MINS.

Gene Autry	Gene Autry
Pokie	Sterling Holloway
Elena Del Rio	Adele Mara
"Dusty"	Bob Steele
Henry Blackstone	Charles Evans
Mucho Pesos	Martin Garralaga
Jake Short	Howard J. Negley
Captain Gonzales	George J. Lewis
Torres	Nacho Gallindo
Joe	Tex Terry

Cass County Boys

"Twilight on the Rio Grande" amounts to filler product in the Gene Autry group. Burdened with complicated story, saving spots are sight stunts that will please the kiddies but tax adult credulity. Production crowds in six oatunes, including "The Old Lamplighter" and title number, for those who like guitar and vocals with outdoors heroics.

Plot concerns Autry's efforts to find out what's behind the murder of his ranch partner. Seems there's a plot by a border attorney to mulct refugees of family jools and then smuggle them into the U. S. from Mexico. Plot is mostly laid south of the border and presents an okay picture of Latin sleuthing. Before Autry is able to round up all the clues and bring justice to the wrongdoers he, and others, are targets of knives and other weapons.

Visual stunts used to help pick up pace include a number of running leaps on horses, jumping a horse into the bed of a racing truck and such that will draw favorable nod from juves. Otherwise there's too much plot mixup for Frank McDonald's direction to overcome. Autry sings title tune, "Lamplighter," "I Tipped My Hat and Slowly Rode Away" for his contributions to score. Cass County Boys (3) provide okay musical and vocal spots and Adele Mara does well by "Pretty Knife Grinder."

Sterling Holloway works hard at comedy chores and helps. Martin Garralaga shows up nicely as an undercover Latin insurance agent and George J. Lewis is good as Latin police captain. Miss Mara does as well as could be expected with her assignment as fiery singer but has shown to better advantage in other films.
Brog.

Miniature Reviews

"Dishonored Lady" (UA). Average b.o. for this film version of Katharine Cornell legit starrer.

"Cheyenne" (WB). Big, brawling western with broad appeal, augurs handsome boxoffice.

"The Woman on the Beach" (RKO). Unusual Jean Renoir film will depend on unpredictable word-of-mouth.

"Torment" (Oxford). Two Swedish finds, Alf Kjellin and Mai Zetterling, help make this Swedish film click; OK arty.

"Francis the First" (French-Made). Fernandel in costume comedy; mild even in arty houses.

"Courtneys of Curzon Street" (B-L). Anna Neagle in British-made Herbert Wilcox production; looks fairly good for U. S.

"Clockface Cafe" (Safia). French-made small-budget film shapes as too wordy, too long for big biz in America.

"Triumph of Love" (Mundus). Austrian-made version of "Lysistrata" holds little for U. S. market.

Dishonored Lady

Hollywood, April 19.

United Artists release of Hunt Stromberg (Jack Chertok) production. Stars Hedy Lamarr, Dennis O'Keefe, John Loder; features William Lundigan, Morris Carnovsky, Paul Cavanagh, Natalie Schafer. Directed by Robert Stevenson. Screenplay, Edmund H. North; based on play by Edward Sheldon and Margaret Ayer Barnes; camera, Lucien Andriot; score, Carmen Dragon; editor, John Foley. Previewed April 18, '47. Running time 86 MINS.

Madeleine Damien	Hedy Lamarr
Dr. David Cousins	Dennis O'Keefe
Felix Courtland	John Loder
Jack Garet	William Lundigan
Dr. Caleb	Morris Carnovsky
Victor Kranish	Paul Cavanagh
Ethel Royce	Natalie Schafer
District Attorney	Douglas Dumbrille
Mrs. Geiger	Margaret Hamilton
Defense Attorney	Nicholas Joy
Detective	James Flavin

This remake of the stage play has been weakened by censorship regulations but still has enough meat to attract femme audiences with proper exploitation. Production values are on the lavish side. Hedy Lamarr name figuring an aid in the selling.

Hedy Lamarr character is more psychological than immoral and the film approach, because of taboos, lessens interest and clarity. Miss Lamarr's work is strong, nevertheless, and will help to carry picture through to good grosses. Plot still gets in shadowy implications of character's promiscuous love life, mostly through dialog.

Edmund H. North did the screenplay, based on the Katharine Cornell stage play which Edward Sheldon and Margaret Ayer Barnes co-authored. It tells of editor of fashionable femme mag who's not getting the best out of life although apparently enjoying it. Mental desperation drives her to attempted suicide, a visit with a psychiatrist, and renunciation of old way of living. She meets a young doctor, falls in love, becomes involved in a murder but is eventually cleared for the happy finale.

Male co-stars are Dennis O'Keefe and John Loder as the young doctor and an old love, respectively. O'Keefe character isn't always even and Loder's role is a bit too smooth. William Lundigan, Morris Carnovsky (psychiatrist) Paul Cavanagh, (publisher) and Natalie Schafer are okay among other principals. Margaret Hamilton rates some chuckles in typical rooming housekeeper role.

The Hunt Stromberg presentation receives excellent physical values under Jack Chertok's production wing. Robert Stevenson's direction is sometimes heavy-handed. Camera work by Lucien Andriot is good, as is production design and art direction by Nicolai Remisoff. *Brog.*

Cheyenne
(SONGS)

Hollywood, April 22.

Warner Bros. release of Robert Buckner production. Stars Dennis Morgan, Jane Wyman, Janis Paige, Bruce Bennett; features Alan Hale, Arthur Kennedy, John Ridgely, Barton MacLane. Directed by Raoul Walsh. Screenplay, Alan LeMay and Thames Williamson; from story by Paul I. Wellman; camera, Sid Hickox; music, Max Steiner; songs, Steiner, Ted Koehler, M. K. Jerome; editor, Christian Nyby. Tradeshown April 21, '47. Running time, 99 MINS.

James Wylie	Dennis Morgan
Ann Kincaid	Jane Wyman
Emily Carson	Janis Paige
Ed Landers	Bruce Bennett
Fred Durkin	Alan Hale
Sundance Kid	Arthur Kennedy
Chalkeye	John Ridgely
Yancey	Barton MacLane
Pecos	Tom Tyler
Lucky	Bob Steele
Limpy Bill	John Compton
Single Jack	John Alvin
Timberline	Monte Blue
Miss Kittredge	Ann O'Neal
Charlie	Tom Fadden
Swamper	Britt Wood

"Cheyenne" carries a load of entertainment values that should give it a handsome wicket payoff. It's a lusty, brawling western, crammed with quick, hard action, crisp situations and good dialog. These factors, plus light sex dressing, insure its chances.

Sturdy cast names deliver strongly under Raoul Walsh's bold direction. Footage is fast, the action hard and realistic. Walsh contrasts action sequences with lightly played scenes between male and femme principals, an amatory detail that adds zip. Backing rugged movement are ace production values furnished by Robert Buckner, standout lensing by Sid Hickox and Max Steiner's music score.

Score has two pop numbers, "Going Back to Old Cheyenne," written by Steiner and Ted Koehler, and "I'm So In Love," by Koehler and M. K. Jerome. Both are put over solidly by Janis Paige with former showing best. Miss Paige's vocaling of "Going Back" is sock scene, made so as much by sexy barroom costume as by canarying.

Script by Alan LeMay and Thames Williamson is punchy, projecting smart lines and situations with adult flavor. Dialog avoids western cliches, using modern touch to heighten effect, and is particularly telling for both dramatic sequences and light love play between Dennis Morgan, Jane Wyman and Miss Paige. Based on a story by Paul I. Wellman, plot deals with adventurous gambler who takes on range detective chore for Wells Fargo. His assignment is to run down superbadman known as The Poet. Hampering his job is Miss Wyman, wife of the heavy, Bruce Bennett, an outlaw gang headed by Arthur Kennedy, and other standard western barriers to law and order.

Morgan does a forthright job of his heroics, tempering melodramatics with easy touch that helps. Miss Wyman's role is a bit more dour but well done and sweetens towards the end when she falls for Morgan. Miss Paige is a delight as saloon singer who figures in the final payoff. Bennett's role has minimum of footage, which he does well. Alan Hale, timid western sheriff, Kennedy, deadly killer, John Ridgely, Tom Tyler, Bob Steele and others in the outlaw gang, Barton MacLane are all good. Ann O'Neal, helps bit as western rooming house operator.

Much of exterior was filmed in Arizona to get proper Wyoming atmosphere for background. Art direction by Ted Smith does much to enhance rugged outdoor mood and other credits are in keeping to make this strong commercial western film fare. *Brog.*

The Woman on the Beach

RKO release of Jack Gross production. Stars Joan Bennett, Robert Ryan, Charles Bickford; features Nan Leslie, Walter Sande, Irene Ryan. Directed by Jean Renoir. Screenplay, Frank Davis and Renoir; adaptation by Michael Hogan from novel by Mitchell Wilson; camera, Leo Tover, Harry Wild; editor, Roland Gross, Lyle Boyer; music, Hanns Eisler. Tradeshown N. Y. April 16, '47. Running time, 71 MINS.

Peggy	Joan Bennett
Scott	Robert Ryan
Ted	Charles Bickford
Eve	Nan Leslie
Otto Wernecke	Walter Sande
Mrs. Wernecke	Irene Ryan
Kirk	Glenn Vernon
Lars	Frank Darien
Jimmy	Jay Norris

"The Woman on the Beach" is another original creation from the striking imagination of Jean Renoir, the transplanted French director who did "The Southerner" a few years back. Its boxoffice merits may be limited by its disturbing strangeness, but artistically, the film is a tour de force bound to provoke a hubbub of critical controversy.

Film is more mood than meaning. On the surface, it is a confusion of logic, a narrative drawn with invisible lines around characters without motivation in a plot only shadowily defined. But beneath, the cinematic elements are brilliantly fused by Renoir into an intense and compelling emotional experience. Patrons will sit through this one fascinated but wondering what it was all about at the finish.

Joan Bennett and Charles Bickford names will help push this pic off to a good starting b.o. momentum while unpredictable word-of-mouth reaction will decide from there. Thesping is uniformly excellent with the cast from top to bottom responding to Renoir's controlling need for a surcharged atmosphere. In subtle counterpoint to the film's surface vagueness, the settings are notably realistic in their size and quality. Choice camerawork sustains the film's overall impact while sweeping through the entire production is a magnificent score by Hanns Eisler which heightens all of the film's pictorial values.

Basically, the yarn is a variation of the eternal triangle theme but it unfolds elusively through implication and suggestion, only occasionally emerging to the level of full clarity. In the film's center, Charles Bickford plays the role of a blind artist, brutally strong and madly jealous of his wife. As the latter, Joan Bennett is a callous tart tied to her husband only through an obsession of guilt arising from her accidental blinding of Bickford early in their marriage. Third part is played by Robert Ryan, a Coast Guard officer stationed near the blind man's home in a desolate spot on the ocean front. He is recovering from a mental shock obtained in naval combat during the war.

Film's tension mounts with short, swift strokes as Ryan, doubtful whether Bickford is really blind at all, puts him to the test in order to free the woman. In a breath-taking sequence, the film's high point, Ryan walks Bickford to the edge of a cliff and abandons him to find his own way back. Renoir has modulated the whole film with periods of ominous silence followed by staccato violence. Only at the very end does the picture collapse into conventionality with an unreal, happy and moral solution.

Bickford comes the full way up the comeback trail with his performance in which he reestablishes his old pattern of he-man brutality and tenderness with more range and depth than he ever displayed before. Miss Bennett has been typed here in a part she has played before in "Woman in the Window" and "Black Angel" and she walks through her paces with ease and confidence. Ryan is a limited thesper but under Renoir's firm control, he registers with a sensitive, accurate portrayal. *Herm.*

Torment
(SWEDISH-MADE)

Oxford Film release of SF production. Stars Stig Jarrel, Alf Kjellin, Mai Zetterling. Directed by Alf Sjoberg. Screenplay, Ingmar Bergman; camera, Martin Bodin; English titles, Edward L. Kingsley. Previewed in N. Y. projection room, April 10, '47. Running time, 95 MINS.

Caligula	Stig Jarrel
Erik Widgren	Alf Kjellin
Bertha	Mai Zetterling
Headmaster	Olof Winnerstrand
Pippi	Gosta Cederlund
Doctor	Hugo Bjorne
Sandman	Stig Olin
Mr. Widgren	Olav Riego
Mrs. Widgren	Marta Arbin
Pettersson	Jan Molander
Widgren	Anders Nystrom
Police Officer	Nils Dahlgren

(In Swedish; English Titles)

It was the work of Alf Kjellin and Mai Zetterling, boy-girl romantic combo, in this picture that won them contracts in English-speaking films. Their performances easily tip why they were picked, former by Selznick and Miss Zetterling by J. Arthur Rank. "Torment" represents a big forward stride for Swedish-language productions and measures up to the prize-award classification won at the Cannes Film Festival last year. It should do unusually strong biz in U. S. arty theatres.

Picture shows what can be accomplished at Swedish studios if the producers there add pace and pointed direction to their familiar smooth thespian work and sparkling photography. Alf Sjoberg has whipped the Ingmar Bergman script into a gripping tale of the growing high school lad whose first violent love affair ends tragically.

This study of adolescent youth is full of more earthy episodes than U. S. audiences are accustomed to, but it's possibly more effectual because of this very fact. Scene where the college tart induces Kjellin, the high school student, into staying with her overnight pulls few punches. Even the deft shearing by state censors has failed to mar this sequence.

Plot has Kjellin, as the hard-studying, husky student, striving to learn his Latin and appease an almost sadistic professor while keeping up his affair with the college widow. How this comely femme, favorite of others at school, is found to be the secret sweetie of the same mad Latin prof and dies during one of their drunken orgies builds to a powerful climax. It's told with fine balance between lighter moments and melodramatic action. Unlike so many Swedish films, it is not weighed down with wordy passages.

Kjellin appears as a real find, and should need little grooming to win a spot on the American screen. Miss Ketterling also looks to be a future bet in England, her vampish college widow role here doing much to make this an unusual film. She manages to typify the gal who likes her liquor nearly as much as her men while at the same time showing that she had found real love in the high school lad.

Stig Jarrel, who's been in many Swedish pictures, has an unsympathetic part as the cruel, partying professor, and does it up brown. Olaf Winnerstrand, as head master of the school, and Gosta Cederlund, as the elderly professor, are excellent and top the excellent supporting cast.

Original score by Hilding Rosenberg helps stress the more dramatic episodes while Martin Bodin's cameraing is in the best Swedish tradition. Sjoberg's direction never falters and has surprisingly few dull moments. *Wear.*

Foreign Films

Francis the First
(FRENCH-MADE)

Noel Meadow-B. L. Garner release of Calamy production. Stars Fernandel. Directed by Christian-Jaque. Story by Paul Fekete. Previewed N. Y., April 18, '47. Running time, **85 MINS.**

Honorin	Fernandel
La Belle Ferronniere	Mona Goya
Henry VIII	Alexandre Rignault
Ferron	Henri Bosc
Jules (ghost)	Sinoel
Cascaroni	Genin
La Palice	Lemontier
Cagliostro	Mihalesco
Cascaroni's Son	Ferval
Innkeeper	Faivre
Bayard	Amato
Herald of Arms	Vitry
Lautrec	Marconi
Francis I	Aime-Simon Girard
Lady Alfredine	Alice Tissot

(In French; English Titles)

Despite having Fernandel, long a popular French comedian, in the principal role, this farce comedy is a disappointment. It seems to have been a mistake to cast the Parisian funster in a 16th century costume yarn even if the idea was to give him free rein to poke fun at the garb, customs and people. Comedy angles are so thin and threadbare that it would have taken a much more expert hand than Fernandel to make such a picture come off. The fact it is a Fernandel comedy gives it some slight possibilities in U. S. arty theatres.

Film shows Fernandel as a stage manager who aspires to be an actor in a dingy carnival repertory company. Disheartened by his failure to make good, he seeks relief from a hypnotist. Most of the remainder of story shows Fernandel as a renaissance gallant back in 1520, but still using his silly smile and droll mannerisms, and holding on to his pocket encyclopedia.

It's this book that helps him to fame in the court of Francis the First. He teaches the king and his court modern dancing and card games. Perhaps the most interesting scenes are the love episodes between Fernandel and Francis the First's mistress. Among the inane efforts to grab laughs is that ghost sequence.

Besides Fernandel's clowning, Mona Goya, a bit on the chunky side for pictures, makes a fascinating mistress of the king, while Aime-Simon Girard, as Francis I, and Alexandre Rignault, as Henry VIII, provide above-par support. Others worthy of mention are Henri Bosc, Sinoel and Mihalesco.

Story by Paul Fekete is one of those things, while direction by Christian-Jaque is uneven and uninspired. Chief flaw of the latter is that it permits too many slapstick incidents. *Wear.*

Courtneys of Curzon St.
(BRITISH-MADE)

London, April 11.

British Lion release of Herbert Wilcox production. Stars Anna Neagle, Michael Wilding. Directed by Herbert Wilcox. Screenplay by Nicholas Phipps from original story by Florence Tranter. Camera, Max Greene. At Curzon theatre, London. Running time, **120 MINS.**

Catherine O'Halloran	Anna Neagle
Sir Edward Courtney	Michael Wilding
Lady Courtney	Gladys Young
Valerie	Coral Browne
Edward Courtney	Michael Medwin
Cynthia	Daphne Slater
Teddy Courtney	Jack Watling
Mary Courtney	Helen Cherry
Mrs. L'Halloran	Ethel O'Shea
Colonel Gascoyne	Bernard Lee
Sir Frank Murchison	Percy Walsh
Louise	Alice Gachet
Pam	Terry Randall

Ignoring highbrow critics and their acid barbs, Herbert Wilcox continues his prosperous way by turning out boxoffice bonanzas. The super critical may argue that everything in this picture has been seen and said before and may cite Noel Coward's "Cavalcade" as a familiar predecessor, but the masses will flock to see this simple story of a man who married beneath him in the social scale and was darned lucky and happy he did so. Looks to be reasonably strong at U. S. theatres especially since Anna Neagle is no stranger.

Wilcox hasn't worried about any significant theme in this. He tells his four-generation story with smiles and tears, and that's where he's one up on many of alleged erudite British producers and directors who believe it's a crime to put heart and sentiment on the screen. Wilcox obviously enjoys seeing two people in love, he enjoys seeing them embrace, and so will the millions who pay for sentimental entertainment.

In addition, Miss Neagle (who makes her bow as co-producer) is as powerful a marquee name as there is over here. People here regard her as one of their own. Her co-star Michael Wilding is rapidly becoming a boxoffice bet.

As usual with Wilcox productions the supporting cast has been chosen with care, and newcomers Daphne Slater and Gladys Young make significant screen debuts. Miss Slater, 18-year-old gold-medalist of the Royal Academy of Dramatic Art, is signed to a long term contract with Wilcox, who has leased her to play Juliet in the Stratford Shakespeare Festival. Gladys Young has a following because of her radio success in England.

Story runs from 1900 to 1945. Michael Wilding plays the soldier son and heir of a baronet. He is in love with his mother's maid (Anna Neagle). Ignoring his mother's warning that he is risking social ostracism, he flouts tradition and marries the girl. Climax to society's persecution comes at a snobbish function with Queen Victoria present to hear first performance of Tchaikowsky's "Symphonie Pathetique." His wife, nervous, does not behave with conventional stoicism and has to listen to catty remarks about her lowly beginning.

Believing she is handicapping her husband's army career, the girl leaves him, disappears to Ireland to have her baby son, and reappears under another name on the London stage. Rising from chorus girl to star she is behind the lines in France (1914 war) singing to the troops when the two meet and are reconciled. From then on the story tells of the joys and sorrows of the Courtneys, ending in 1945 when their grandson brings home his girl who hopes her humble family won't object to her marrying into the aristocracy.

An accomplished musical score from "Soldiers of the Queen" to "Lily Marlene," marking the different years, is a decided asset to the picture and earns a bouquet for Tony Collins. A word of praise, too, for G. H. Mulcaster, unaccountably omitted from the cast list for a finely etched cameo.

Picture is undoubtedly set for boxoffice records here. No film more British in style and sentiment ever has crossed the Atlantic. It may call for a special brand of salesmanship. *Cane.*

Le Cafe Du Cadran
('Clockface Cafe')
(FRENCH-MADE)

Paris, April 5.

Safia and Dispa production and release. Stars Blanchette Brunoy, Bernard Blier, Aime Clariond. Directed by Jean Gehret. Screenplay by Pierre Benard and Henri Decoin from story by Benard; camera, Jacques Lemare. At Boulogne Studio. Running time, **101 MINS.**

Proprietor	Bernard Blier
His Wife	Blanchette Brunoy
The Fiddler	Aime Clariond
The Drunk	Felix Oudard

This small budgeter is much better than most current local films. Well directed, paced and acted, it needs but little editing to make it a bet for international release. Wordy passages may hurt for U. S.

Whole story takes place in the Cafe du Cadran, a bistro which actually exists on Avenue de l'Opera, opposite Cafe de Paris here, where newspapermen hang out. Low cost of film is explained by the one set used and also by the fact that director Gehret knows his costs since once a production manager.

Bernard Blier is excellent as proprietor who comes from the provinces and buys a Paris cafe which he begins operating with his provincial-looking wife. He tries to make her look more Parisian. When she buys finery on a scale he had not anticipated, he does not scold her until she falls for a musician. But once he gets jealous, he loses his mental balance and shoots her.

Blier's portrayal of the reliable husband, willing to work hard to keep his wife happy until forced to become bookmaker by her spending is one of the picture's strong points.

Blanchette Brunoy, as the wife, shows skill in changing from the simple provincial kid to the woman who learns to appreciate the finer things in life. Aime Clairiond, as the conceited fiddler who must try and show off before the young woman, is a bit stagey, but effective.

Credit is due Felix Ouvrard as the babbling drunk who does not realize his talk causes a lot of harm. Balance of cast is okay.

Benard shows a tendency to overdevelop the extraneous roles, which might well be scissored. But even as is, this is a vivid character study. Director Gehret, with Henri Decoin's suggestions, has been able to keep things moving fairly well in the small set so that its continuous use does not become boring. *Maxi.*

Triumph of Love
("Lysistrata")
(AUSTRIAN-MADE)

Vienna, April 1.

Vienna Mundus-Film production and release. Stars Judith Holzmeister, O. W. Fischer; features Hilde Berndt, Josef Meinrad, Paul Kemp, Inge Konradi, Mimi Shorp. Directed by Alfred Stoeger. Screenplay by Kasper Loser; camera, Oskar Sehnireh; editor, Anna Hollering; music, Alois Melichar. Previewed in projection room, Vienna. Running time, **116 MINS.**

(In German; No English Titles)

Many stage productions have been made of "Lysistrata," and the one on which Alfred Stoeger based this new film version fared okay when at the Insel theatre here last season. But in translating into a picture spectacle, the book has been extended and burdened with a sorry mess of new dialogue and an even heavier weight of highly modern, unmelodious music. As this stands, it has small chance in U. S. and does not figure to do much even here and in German-speaking territory.

There always will be laughs in the Greek's idea of a love strike to stop war. But pointedly modern allusions don't help the dialogue in this. Nor do whimsical costumes rather than the classical Greek ones make a fairly unattractive bunch of players look any better.

While the settings are of Athenian simplicity, though necessarily modest in cost for Vienna studios, the clothes, women's coiffures and other visual features are obtrusive to the point of interfering with concentration on the action. Length of picture plus long church-like choruses with poor diction and sound work obscuring what's being sung, slow things down even more.

One player, Inge Konradi, emerges as a young, fresh personality, giving considerable life and charm to the role of Lysistrata's servant. She's especially noticeable in contrast to Judith Holzmeister's wooden characterization of the title role. O. W. Fischer plays unresponsively in the male lead. *Isra.*

"Brollopsnatten" ("Wedding Night") (SWEDISH). Europa Film production and release. Stars Max Hansen, Sickan Carlsson, Lauritz Falk, Inga Langre; features John Botvid, Julia Caesar, Sten Hedlund. Directed by Bodil Ipsen. Screenplay by Sven Gustafsson based on play by Vivian Tidmarsh. At Saga, Stockholm. Running time, **85 MINS.**

Based on the play, "Is Your Honeymoon Really Necessary," this film shapes up as a fine comedy with good chances in the Swedish market, and some hope in the world market. Danish comedian Max Hansen handles his role well and Bodil Ipsen's direction is great.

"Harald Hondfaste" (SWEDISH). Lux Film production and release. Stars George Fant, Georg Rydeberg, Elsie Albiin; features Thor Modeen, Vera Valdor, Tord Stal, Hanny Schedin, Gunnar Olsson, Ragnar Falck. Directed by Hampe Faustman. Screenplay, Arne Bornebusch; camera, Felix Forsman; music, Jules Sylvain. Reviewed in Stockholm. Running time, **90 MINS.**

In George Fant, Sweden now has its own Errol Flynn. He does well in this 15th century adventure yarn. Acting direction and camera are all solid. Film looms as a long runner here although chances are dubious in the U. S.

"Kuudes Kasky" ("Sixth Commandment") (FINNISH). Suomen Filmiteollisuus production and release. Stars Ghedi Loennberg, Siiri Angerkoski; features, Tapio Rautavaara, Esko Vettenranta, Aku Korhonen, Aki Kosonen; directed by Orvo Saarikivi; screenplay, Toini Havu; camera, Armas Rirvonen; music, Heikki Aaltoila. At Rex, Helsinki. Running time, **96 MINS.**

Starring some of the best known Finnish talent, this film is based on the Bible's sixth commandment. Toini Havu's screenplay was adeptly scripted and technical credits are equally good. However, the sentimental story offers little interest outside of Finland.

"Kirkastuva Savel" ("Light Melody") (FINNISH). Suomen Filmiteollisuus production and release. Stars Kalle Ruusunen, Doris Hovimaa; features Rauha Rentola, Ruth Luoma-Aho, Veli Matti, Aku Korhonen, Uuno Laaski; directed by Edvin Laine; screenplay, Olavi Vesistoe; music, Heikki Aaltoila. At Astor, Helsinki. Running time, **104 MINS.**

Finnish opera singer, Kalle Ruusunen, makes his film debut in this musical opposite Doris Hovimaa. Score by Heikki Aaltoila along with some of Bizet's classics is fine, while direction and scripting are fair. Picture's chances are limited to Finland.

"Supe for Tva" ("Supper for Two") (SWEDISH). Terra Film release of Lorenz Marmstedt production. Stars Edvin Adolphson, Karin Ekelund; features Gaby Stenberg, Douglas Hage, Ragnar Arfvedsson, Mimi Pollack, Josua Bengisson; directed by Ragnar Arfvedsson; screenplay, Andre Paul Antoine, Jan Molander; camera, Felix Forsman, Hilding Bladh. At Grand, Stockholm. Running time, **88 MINS.**

French play and film "L'Inevetable M. Dubois," by Andre Paul Antoine, has been translated into an okay Swedish comedy starring Edvin Adolphson and Karin Ekelund. Made on the French Riviera and at studios in Finland, picture's thesping and technical credits are generally good. However, it looms as a poor entry for U. S.

Miniature Reviews

"Welcome Stranger" (Songs) (Par). Crosby-Fitzgerald team again in solid entertainment feature for sock b.o. potential.

"New Orleans" (Musical) (Levey; UA). Pleasant musical that should score okay in all stops.

"Homestretch" (Color) (20th). Cornel Wilde, Maureen O'Hara in Technicolored racetrack opus; should spin the wickets okay.

"Adventures of Don Coyote" (Color-Songs) (Comet-UA). Fast action slowed by lame romancing.

"Hit Parade of 1947" (Musical) (Rep). Satisfactory musical with trite story but marquee names should attract OK grosses.

"Philo Vance's Gamble" (PRC). Average whodunit with Alan Curtis and Frank Jenks for marquee decoration.

"West To Glory" (Songs) (PRC). Pleasant, slow oater, okay for the duals.

"The Little Martyr" (Italian-made). Domestic drama helped by child star, Luciano De Ambrosis; for Italian-languagers.

"Philo Vance Returns" (One Song) (PRC). Better than average in the series, but still for supporting situations.

Welcome Stranger

(SONGS)

Hollywood, April 29.

Paramount release of Sol C. Siegel production. Stars Bing Crosby, Joan Caulfield, Barry Fitzgerald; features Wanda Hendrix, Frank Faylen, Elizabeth Patterson, Robert Shayne, Larry Young, Percy Kilbride. Directed by Elliott Nugent. Screenplay, Arthur Sheekman; adaptation, Sheekman and N. Richard Nash; story, Frank Butler; camera, Lionel Lindon; songs, Johnny Burke and James Van Heusen; score, Robert Emmett Dolan; editor, Everett Douglas. Tradeshown April 28, '47. Running time, **106 MINS.**

Jim Pearson....................Bing Crosby
Trudy....................Joan Caulfield
Dr. Joseph McRory........Barry Fitzgerald
Emily....................Wanda Hendrix
Bill Walters....................Frank Faylen
Mrs. Gilley............Elizabeth Patterson
Roy Chesley................Robert Shayne
Dr. Ronnie Jenks.............Larry Young
Nat Dorkas................Percy Kilbride
C. J. Chesley...............Charles Dingle
Mort Elkins....................Don Beddoe
Congressman Beeker.........Thurston Hall
Miss Lennek..............Lillian Bronson
Secretary....................Mary Field
Mr. Daniels..................Paul Stanton
Ed Chanock....................Pat McVey

"Welcome Stranger" should find the boxoffice path easy treading. It's crammed with all the ingredients that make for popular entertainment. Names of Bing Crosby and Barry Fitzgerald together swing plenty of weight for marquees and film has been given strong production backing by Sol C. Siegel to insure top selling values.

While "Stranger" doesn't have the character novelty of "Going My Way," previous Crosby-Fitzgerald b.o. teaming, otherwise it fits the "Way" pattern of story-telling with sock human interest, comedy and drama, plus four tunes. Crosby and Fitzgerald take obvious pleasure in their friendly antagonist roles as young and old doctors, trouping parts to a fare-thee-well for audience response.

Elliott Nugent keeps it all moving at pace proper to best story unfoldment with his direction. He develops situations with humorous icing and makes plot command attention throughout. Dialog has a flip flavor that pleases, punching over gags that are laugh-getters. Tag of many of smart cracks will be lost in audience roars. Songs by Johnny Burke and James Van Heusen are well spotted and given the Crosby treatment vocally to pay off. Numbers are "Smile Right Back at the Sun," "My Heart Is a Hobo," "Country Style" and the ballad, "As Long as I'm Dreaming." Square dance sequence gives "Country Style" best production display to court audience favor.

Script by Arthur Sheekman concerns young doctor taking over village medical practice of older medico while latter vacations. Around that simple situation, story builds solid entertainment with a cast that gets the most from material. Sheekman and N. Richard Nash did the adaptation from a Frank Butler story. There is high humor in Fitzgerald's horror at modern, flip manner of young doctor who is to replace him. Drama is wrapped around the old doc's near loss of his hospital dream, an emergency operation and similar pat sequences, but overall emphasis is on comedy.

Femme star Joan Caulfield adds romance and comeliness as village school marm. An unusually natural, appealing performance is turned in by Wanda Hendrix as teen-ager who gets a crush on Crosby. It's a piece of work that stands out strongly in cast of assured troupers. Elizabeth Patterson and Percy Kilbride tickle risibilities with laconic humor as pair of New Englanders. Straight roles are contributed by Frank Faylen, Robert Shayne, Larry Young, Charles Dingle and others.

Village settings projected by art direction of Hans Dreier and Franz Bachelin carries interest and was lensed expertly by Lionel Lindon. Good music score is contributed by Robert Emmett Dolan. *Brog.*

New Orleans

(MUSICAL)

United Artists release of Jules Levey (Herbert J. Biberman) production. Stars Arturo de Cordova, Dorothy Patrick; features Marjorie Lord, Irene Rich, John Alexander, Richard Hageman, Louis Armstrong band, Billie Holiday, Woody Herman orchestra. Directed by Arthur Lubin. Screenplay by Elliot Paul and Dick Irving Hyland, from original by Paul and Biberman; songs, Eddie De Lange-Louis Alter, Cliff Dixon-Bob Carleton; editor, Bernard W. Burton; camera, Lucien Andriot. Tradeshown N. Y., April 24, '47. Running time, **89 MINS.**

Miralee Smith..............Dorothy Patrick
Mrs. Smith....................Irene Rich
Colonel McArdle...........John Alexander
Nick Duquesne..........Arturo de Cordova
Endie.....................Billie Holiday
Henri Ferber............Richard Hageman
Grace Voiselle..............Marjorie Lord

Louis Armstrong	Red Callendar
Kid Ory	Charlie Beal
Zutty Singleton	Woody Herman
Barney Bigard	Meade Lux Lewis
Bud Scott	

Jules Levey has come up with one of the pleasantest musicals of the season in this pseudo-historical tale of the genesis of jive. Even those for whom Louis Armstrong's trained horn ordinarily would hold no attraction will find a lift in the "jazz" with which "New Orleans" is liberally peppered. Those who are already partial to the Armstrong and Woody Herman brands of musicology will be in the bag for this, of course, so the pic looks certain of registering okay at the b.o.

Star names—Arturo de Cordova and Dorothy Patrick—won't mean a lot on the marquee, and some special sales effort is going to be required to draw audiences, outside the hep set, to whom the names of Armstrong, Herman and Billie Holiday would ordinarily be no magnet. Actually, as it turns out, "Satchmo" Armstrong is the star of the film, proving as solid in a generous dramatic role as he is on the trumpet.

Yarn finds de Cordova running a swank N. O. gambling den, with Miss Patrick from the set on the other side of the tracks. She falls for both de Cordova and this new brand of music that Armstrong and his crew privately give out with in the basement of the gambling house. Forced out of town, de Cordova opens in Chicago, where he finds the Armstrong music provides a profitable draw to his night spot without resorting to the gaming tables. Eventually, he winds up in New York running a big talent and booking agency for the new hot bands. Meantime, the family of Miss Patrick—who's forced into longhair concertizing—sees things her way about this newfangled jazz and there's the usual happy ending.

Gal breaks down the management of what's obviously Carnegie Hall, N. Y., for the jive music by introing it—and Woody Herman—in one of her concerts there. Tune she sings in this big production number finale is "Do You Know What It Means to Miss New Orleans," by Eddie De Lange aend Louis Alter. It's frequently reprised by Miss Patrick and Miss Holiday and is a certain best-seller. Other numbers include "Blues Are Brewin'" and "Endie," by De Lange and Alter, and "Where the Blues Are Born in New Orleans," by Cliff Dixon and Bob Carleton. They're all effectively done by a conglomeration of original ragtimers including Armstrong, Zutty Singleton, Barney Bigard, Kid Ory, Bud Scott, Red Callendar, Charlie Beal and Meade Lux Lewis.

Arthur Lubin's direction is generally well-paced to take advantage of the best aspects of the story and musical interludes. He gets a credit, too, for those lingering closeups of the expressive faces of the Negro musicians.

De Cordova's okay as the fast-money operator, although it is dubious that he'll ever register as a top marquee-draw in this country. He's a bit too old-looking for the heavy romance department. Miss Patrick, on the other hand, scores neatly on appearance and thespically. She'll be recalled as Mrs. Jerome Kern in Metro's recent biog of the composer, "Till the Clouds Roll By." Others in the cast include Irene Rich as the gal's mother, Richard Hageman as a jazz-addicted longhair, John Alexander as a reincarnation of "Senator Claghorn," and Marjorie Lord as the romantic threat.

Production gives evidence that Levey threw in plenty of coin without going overboard on being unnecessarily lavish. *Herb.*

Homestretch

(COLOR)

20th-Fox release of Robert Bassler producticeon. Stars Cornel Wilde, Maureen O'Hara; features Glenn Langan, Helen Walker, James Gleason. Directed by Bruce Humberstone. Original screenplay, Wanda Tuchok; camera, Arthur Arling; editor, Robert Simpson. At Roxy, N. Y., April 23, '47. Running time, **99 MINS.**

Jock Wallace....................Cornel Wilde
Leslie Hale................Maureen O'Hara
Bill Van Dyke...............Glenn Langan
Kitty Brant.................Helen Walker
Doc Kilborne...............James Gleason
Don Humberto Balcares..Henry Stephenson
Aunt Martha.................Ethel Griffies
Pablo.........................Tommy Cook
Ellamae Scott.........Margaret Bannerman

Latest Technicolor opus to be turned out by the 20th-Fox studios, "Homestretch," makes the most of a good cast, lush production trappings and the excitement engendered in watching the gee-gees thunder down the homestretch to compensate for a fairly entertaining but nonetheless trite story. Current popularity of Cornel Wilde and Maureen O'Hara, plus the topicality of the picture which should be released coincidentally with the racetrack season, should make the boxoffice register as snappily as the $2 window at any reputable parimutuel booth.

Wanda Tuchok's original screenplay spins a non-exciting tale about race enthusiasts and stable owners over 11 famous tracks from Jamaica to the Grand National in England, and therein lies the picture's chief selling point. Beautiful Technicolor photography shows the nags, the tracks and the brightly-costumed spectators in the stands as they've never been shown before and the neck-and-neck photo finishes furnish some of the most thrilling race sequences yet filmed. In addition, there are some torrid love passages between Wilde and Miss O'Hara that should excite almost as much interest as the horses.

Story has all been told before but Miss Tuchok lends it sufficient modernism and glow to sustain interest, although the audience will never be in doubt about the outcome. Wilde is seen as a happy-go-lucky guy with legitimate racing antecedents back in Maryland, but who's left all that to follow the international set in their trek from track to track. When Miss O'Hara, a staid Bostonian maid from Beacon Hill, is willed a thoroughbred by her uncle, Wilde buys the horse and, in so doing, the two fall in love. She forsakes her State Dept. fiance to marry Wilde, hoping that, despite his warnings, she'll be able to educate him to her way of life.

After much disappointment and green eyes caused by Helen Walker always being around, Miss O'Hara finally leaves Wilde to return to Boston, her fiance and a divorce. With a change of heart, Wilde stakes his last cent on his last thoroughbred at the Kentucky Derby with hopes of winning enough to rebuild his Maryland stables and so win back the gal. Her horse, of course, beats his out at the Derby in a photo finish but she returns to him and all's well. Interspersed with all this are the other races, plus some excellent color footage of the British coronation (story takes place before the war).

Cast, under the capable directorial touch of Bruce Humberstone, makes the story click. Wilde makes a handsome devil-may-care and plays his role with as much conviction as he can get into it. Miss O'Hara, with a beautiful wardrobe which amply sets off her looks, shows signs of increasing thesping ability. Glenn Langan and Miss Walker are okay as the other sides of the quadrangle, with Miss Walker rating more important roles on the basis of this performance. James Gleason is standout as the understanding trainer.

Production credits are in line with the picture's beauteous Technicolor, indicating producer Robert Bassler must have sunk a hefty budget into the film. Special nod is due camera director Arthur Arling for his handling of the racing footage. *Stal.*

Adventures of Don Coyote

(COLOR—SONGS)

United Artists release of Comet (Buddy Rogers-Ralph Cohn) production. Stars Richard Martin, Frances Rafferty; features Marc Cramer, Val Carlo, Benny Bartlett, Pierce Lyden. Directed by Reginald LeBorg. Screenplay, Bob Williams, Harold Tarshis, from original story by Williams; camera (Cinecolor), Fred Jackman. Tradeshown N. Y., April 25, '47. Running time, **65 MINS.**

Don Coyote..................Richard Martin
Maggie....................Frances Rafferty
Dave..........................Marc Cramer
Sancho...........................Val Carlo
Ted.........................Benny Bartlett
Big Foot.....................Frank Fenton
Felton.......................Byron Foulger
Joe..........................Edwin Parker
Jeff..........................Pierce Lyden
Steve......................Frank McCarroll

Cupid's bow takes equal billing with the sixshooter in this film's valiant effort to blanket an appeal over both oater habitues and the followers of l'amour toujours. Unfortunately for the formula, only the western end rings the bell while the romancing, burdened with stilted dialog and clumsy thesping, impedes more than helps. This Comet streamliner may be a step towards solving the dual problem, but it's only a step and not the whole trip.

In it, though, the western has come a long way. By a remarkable 180-degree switch, the forces of virtue are embodied in two hard-riding Mexicans (one of whom is also the romantic lead) whereas villainy is played Yankee across the board. This may do its mite for the Good Neighbor policy and by the same token its reception down Interstate circuit way should prove interesting—and maybe hotter than chile con carne.

Briefly put, the yarn concerns itself with the efforts of mobsters-in-chaps to drive off the rightful owners of a ranch so that they can take over. Gang's anxiety for the freehold is based on its pre-knowledge that the railroad intends extending rails plumb across the middle of the ranch. The duo of Mexicanos (Richard Martin and Val Carlo) as hired hands, in a string of riding and shooting sequences, fight off the gang and bring the ringleaders to heel.

Martin is effective enough in his action stints but he pokerfaces through his love chores like a guy with a full-house who isn't going to signal it. Frances Rafferty, the ranch owner and femme lead, is plenty cute in Cinecolor. Where Martin is wooden, however, she overmugs. Carlo helps the pic along considerably with his rich, tuneful singing of a brace of Spanish songs.

Pic is endowed with production values far above those ordinarily accorded oaters. *Wit.*

Hit Parade of 1947

(MUSICAL)

Republic release of Frank McDonald production, directed by McDonald. Stars Eddie Albert, Constance Moore, Joan Edwards; features Gil Lamb, Bill Goodwin, William Frawley. Screenplay, Mary Loos from original by Parke Levy; camera, John Alton; editor, Tony Martinelli; dances, Fanchon; songs, Jimmy McHugh and Harold Adamson, Tim Spencer, Jack Meakin & Foster Carling; musical director, Cy Feuer. Tradeshown N. Y., April 27, '47. Running time, 90 MINS.

Kip Walker....................Eddie Albert
Ellen Baker................Constance Moore
Joan..........................Joan Edwards
Eddie Paige.......................Gil Lamb
Rod Huntley...................Bill Goodwin
Harry Holmes...............William Frawley
Serial Director.................Richard Lane
Mr. Bonardi....................Frank Fenton
Small..........................Ralph Sanford
Sammy.........................Frank Scannell
Announcer.......................Knox Manning
Announcer.......................Del Sharbutt
Specialty Dancer.................Albert Ruiz
Cooper.........................Harland Tucker
Assistant in Radio Station....Chester Clute
Woody Herman Orchestra
Roy Rogers and Trigger
Bob Nolan and Sons of Pioneers

"Hit Parade of 1947" is a frothy little musical, much along the lines of its predecessors in the series. With a trite story used merely as a peg on which to hang the musical numbers, the picture manages to sustain continued interest. There's sufficient marquee lure in the names of Eddie Albert, Constance Moore, Joan Edwards and Gil Lamb to add a box-office fillip, in addition to which Roy Rogers and Woody Herman's orch get featured spotting for guest shots. In all, it should hold up fairly well in most situations.

Of prime interest is the screen debut of Miss Edwards, former star of radio's "Hit Parade," as well as nitery and vaude stages. Gal displays a nice personality and adequate thesping ability to get her across in a story such as this one. Carrying most of the vocal work with Miss Moore, she shines in her vocalistics and one of her solos, titled "It Could Happen to Me," is one of the best-done tunes in the film. With her looks, she should make out okay in future pix.

Mary Loos' screenplay from an original story by Parke Levy has been done so often before that the audience should be able to anticipate almost all of it. Albert is a struggling songwriter who teams with Lamb, Miss Moore and Miss Edwards in a nitery act that makes out well until he tries to inject sophistication in their material. After flopping miserably in an uptown Manhattan bistro, Miss Moore, already in love with Albert, is spotted by a Hollywood talent scout and succeeds in talking the guy into giving all four a contract. Other three get disgusted when they learn they've just been taken along for the ride and finally leave Hollywood while she becomes a star. Miss Edwards then makes radio bigtime, Lamb succeeding as a nitery comic and Albert gets his songs published. Then, in a trite denouement, Albert and Miss Moore are reconciled and go into the final clinch, echoed by Lamb and Miss Edwards.

Cast does adequately, with the four leads striving to make the whole thing authentic. Albert plays his usual wistful self and does well with the first vocalizing he's done in films. Miss Moore handles both her vocal and thesping activities neatly and wears costumes that should put her up front in the sweatergirl parade. Lamb, never a great actor, does best in his comedy routines and he and Miss Edwards carry out the second boy-girl material okay. William Frawley, as a soft-hearted agent, and Bill Goodwin, as the Hollywood talent exec, top the supporting roles.

Jimmy McHugh and Harold Adamson have cleffed seven good tunes for the picture, best of which are "I Guess I'll Have That Dream Right Now," a hummable ballad, and "It Could Happen to Me." One big production number, "Chiquita from Santa Anita," is staged unostentatiously by Fanchon. Roy Rogers, together with Bob Nolan and his Sons of the Pioneers, lasso onto two western tunes. Herman and his orch stick to their own recording material, in which xylophonist Red Norvo, although not billed, gets nice spotting.

Producer-director Frank McDonald, with his eye on achieving a realistic show biz atmosphere, tours the Repub studios in one sequence and shows the film makers actually at work. Other stunts, such as casting CBS announcer Del Sharbutt as a radio announcer, aid considerably. Production mountings for the film are okay, as is the technical work. *Stal.*

Philo Vance Returns

(ONE SONG)

PRC release of Howard Welsch production. Features William Wright, Terry Austin, Leon Belasco. Directed by William Beaudine. Screenplay, Robert E. Kent; camera, Jackson Rose; editor, Gene Fowler, Jr. Previewed in N. Y., April 23, '47. Running time, 62 MINS.

Philo Vance..................William Wright
Lorena Simms....................Terry Austin
Alexis............................Leon Belasco
Stella Blendon...............Clara Blandick
Virginia........................Ramsey Ames
Larry Blendon...............Damian O'Flynn
George Hullman................Frank Wilcox
Choo-Choo Divine.................Iris Adrian
Helen Sandman................Ann Staunton
Policeman.......................Tim Murdock
Maid...............................Mary Scott

"Philo Vance Returns" shapes up a few notches better than the average thus far attained in the formula-built Philo Vance series by PRC. Film shows a little more imagination in treatment of stock situations, but withal, it's still for supporting spots in most situations.

In this instance sleuth has the assignment of solving the murder of a playboy and prevent the extermination of his numerous ex-wives and former fiancees. The wildoater previous to his enforced demise had made a will leaving a huge trust fund to be shared with those previously involved in his lovelife. With that kind of will, it's advantageous to have the ex's liquidated, but Vance, as usual, selects the proper culprit after the regulation number of corpses are strewn about.

The character role in "Returns" is essayed by William Wright who does a creditable job, while humor is entrusted to Leon Belasco, as the theatrical manager who becomes the sleuth's assistant. Former bandleader's Russ dialect is productive of many laughs. Staunch support comes from the multitude of suspects and candidates for extermination in the persons of Ramsey Ames, Terry Austin, Iris Adrian, Ann Staunton and Clara Blandick.

William Beaudine gives the production good pacing job *Jose.*

West to Glory

(SONGS)

PRC release of Jerry Thomas production. Stars Eddie Dean; features Roscoe Ates, Dolores Castle, Gregg Barton. Directed by Ray Taylor. Screenplay, Elmer Clifton, Robert B. Churchill; camera, Milford Anderson; editor, Hugh Winn; songs, Eddie Dean, Hal Blair, Pete Gates. Tradeshown N. Y., April 23, '47. Running time, 60 MINS.

Eddie Dean........................Eddie Dean
Soapy.............................Roscoe Ates
Maria..........................Dolores Castle
Barrett..........................Gregg Barton
Cory.............................Jimmy Martin
Avery.............................Zon Murray
Juan.............................Alex Montoya
Don Lopez.........................Harry Vejar
Vincente.......................Carl Mathews
Sunshine Boys

PRC oater has no surprises, but the usual ingredients of songs, riding and shooting. Songs are pleasant, shooting ample and riding graphic. Lazy, slow story and corny humor won't hurt much. Oater will do for the duals.

Story has Eddie Dean as a U. S. sheriff unmasking a gang of crooks trying to steal gold and precious jewels from a Mexican rancher somewhere north of the border. Lame story, trite dialog don't excite, but accent is rather on romance and music. Dean warbles three cowboy ballads very pleasantly in a light, appealing lyric tenor, assisted by the Sunshine Boys, instrumental quartet.

Songs are above-average "Cry, Cry, Cry," "In the Shadow of the Mission," and "I'm Ridin' West," with first named the most appealing.

Lensing, direction stack up okay, with some good outdoor shots to catch the scenic-minded eye. *Bron.*

The Little Martyr

('Il Piccolo Martire')

(ITALIAN-MADE)

Superfilm Distributing Corp. release of Franco Magli production. Stars Luciano De Ambrosis. Directed by Vittorio De Sica. Story by Cesare G. Viola, Marguerite Maglione, Cesare Zavattini, Adolfo Franci, Gherardo Gheraradi, Vittorio De Sica; camera, Mario Benotti. At Arena, N. Y., starting April 25, '47. Running time, 91 MINS.

Andrew............................Emilio Cigoli
Prico.....................Luciano De Ambrosis
Nina................................Isa Pola
Roberto.........................Adriano Rimoldi
Agnese.........................Giovanna Cigoli
Nonna.............................Ione Frigerio
Mr. Uberti.......................Maria Gardena
Aunt Berelli......................Dina Pechellini
Giuliana.........................Nicoletta Parodi
Mrs. Berelli......................Tecla Scarano
Claudio.......................Ernesto Calindrini
Painter...........................Olinto Cristina
Doctor............................Mario Gallina
Paolina..........................Zaira La Fratta
Commendatore................Armando Migliari
Gigi Sbarlani.......................Guido Morisi

(In Italian; English Titles)

Only a bright performance by Luciano De Ambrosis, Italian child star, saves this from being only a passably good Italian-languager. Made in 1943, the film fails to measure up to the better pre-war Italian pictures. Main trouble appears to be that too many dabbled in the scripting, including director Vittorio De Sica taking a hand in whipping up the yarn. Despite these flaws, "The Little Martyr" should do well in Italian-language houses especially since few straight dramas have come over from Italy recently.

Little De Ambrosis easily steals the production, dominating every scene and figuring in each important development. It's the story of a sensitive 5-year-old child who is the victim of his mother's love affair. She falls for a youthful gigolo and despite the efforts of the youngster finally wrecks his home. The unfortunate youngster always has favored his mother until he finally sees what she has done to his father. His dad finally commits suicide after placing his son in a school, and the final scene shows the lad ultimately turning away from his mother.

Tedious pace maintained, with director De Sica's work not helping, goes far in deadening the plot. There is a surprising lack of action, and little in the dialog to overcome this fault.

Besides De Ambrosis, Isa Pola, as the mother, proves not only attractive but firstrate as a thespian. Emilio Cigoli is okay as the father though inclined to overact part of the time. Adriano Rimoldi is the young man who wrecks the home by making Miss Pola fall in love with him. *Wear.*

Philo Vance's Gamble

PRC release of Howard Welch production. Stars Alan Curtis, Frank Jenks, Terry Austin, Tala Birell. Directed by Basil Wrangell. Screenplay by Eugene Conrad, Arthur St. Clair from original by Lawrence Edmund Taylor; camera, Jackson Rose; editor, W. Donn Hayes; music, Irving Friedman. Previewed N. Y., April 23, '47. Running time, 62 MINS.

Philo Vance........................Alan Curtis
Laurian March....................Terry Austin
Ernie Clark.......................Frank Jenks
Tina Cromwell.......................Tala Birell
Oliver Tennant....................Gavin Gordon
Inspector Heath......................Cliff Clark
Geegee Desmond.....................Toni Todd
Lt. Burke..........................James Burke
Robert Butler......................Francis Pierlot
D. A. Stone.......................Joseph Crehan
Charles O'Mara...................Garnett Marks
Mr. Willetts........................Grady Sutton
Guy Harkness................Charles Mitchell
Norma Harkness..................Joanne Frank

Philo Vance's solution of a set of murders, in connection with a smuggled emerald, makes for a perfunctory whodunit that will serve its purpose on the south end of a dualler. Chief assets are fair pacing that will maintain a degree of interest, occasional touches of humor, and a vast amount of gunplay.

"Philo Vance's Gamble" has the sleuth drawn into a case in which a syndicate illegally acquires a huge emerald, and is about to peddle it when the chief thief is slain. Other murders follow in fairly rapid succession, and Vance finally lands the culprit.

Alan Curtis supplies an enactment with the necessary authority as Philo Vance, while humorous assignment is taken on by Frank Jenks as Vance's non-too-bright assistant. Gavin Gordon, Toni Todd and Dan Seymour constitute a choice batch of suspects that are later liquidated, while Terry Austin provides the near approach to love interest.

Basil Wrangell's direction helps overcome many of the cliched situations and dialog, while other of the film's components such as photography and music are in the so-so category. *Jose.*

Foreign Films

"Konsten att Elska" ("How to Love") **(SWEDISH).** Svenk Filmindustri production and release. Stars Wanda Rothgardt, Sture Lagervall, Lauritz Falk, Cecile Ossbahr; features Naima Wifstrand, Elsa Carlsson, Ake Engfeldt, Marianne Gyllenhammar, Kerstin Holmberg; directed by Gunnar Skoglund; screenplay, Eric Larsson-Lee; camera, Ake Dahlquist. At Spegeln, Stockholm. Running time, 76 MINS.

This fine Swedish comedy is helped by the strong acting of Wanda Rothgardt and Sture Langervall. Nice lensing helps the picture's chances in Scandinavia. Film also may have appeal in foreign marts.

"Dynamit" ("Dynamite") **(SWEDISH).** Svea Film release of Ake Ohberg production. Stars Bengt Ekeroth, Ake Ohberg, Birgit Tengroth; features Marianne Loewgren, Carl Stroem, Nils Hallberg, Eric Berglund, Hilda Borgstroem; directed by Ohberg; screenplay, Harald Beijer based on his novel; camera, Sven Thermaenius. At Astoria, Stockholm. Running time, 85 MINS.

Based on Harald Beijer's 1938 novel, this entry deals with a dynamite saboteur. Censor held up distribution for several months because of the activity of a real dynamiter known as the "Saturday Saboteur." Following his seizure here, the film preemed. Bengt Ekeroth turns in a fine performance as the saboteur. Picture should do well both in Scandinavia and possibly in world market. *Wins.*

Miniature Reviews

"Miracle On 34th Street" (20th). Sock human drama certain for word-of-mouth buildup.

"Hoppy's Holiday" (UA). Hopalong Cassidy western of usual type; okay where oaters are liked.

"Spoilers of the North" (Rep). Fair melodrama of salmon fishing and skullduggery in Alaska. For supporting positions.

"Black Narcissus" (Color) (G F D) (British-Made). Deborah Kerr, Sabu in colorful drama of nuns in Himalayas; needs big bally in U. S.

"Sarge Goes to College" (Songs) (Mono). Okay entry in Teen-Agers series.

"The Road Home" (Artkino). Russian-made meller of underground fight against Nazis shapes as stout boxoffice for arty spots.

Miracle on 34th Street

Hollywood, May 3.
20th-Fox release of William Perlberg production. Stars Maureen O'Hara, John Payne; features Edmund Gwenn, Gene Lockhart, Natalie Wood, Porter Hall, William Frawley, Jerome Cowan, Philip Tonge. Direction and screenplay by George Seaton. Story, Valentine Davies; camera, Charles Clarke, Lloyd Ahern; music, Cyril Mockridge; editor, Robert Simpson. Tradeshown April 30, '47. Running time, 95 MINS.

Doris Walker	Maureen O'Hara
Fred Gailey	John Payne
Kris Kringle	Edmund Gwenn
Judge Henry X. Harper	Gene Lockhart
Susan	Natalie Wood
Mr. Sawyer	Porter Hall
Charles Halloran	William Frawley
Thomas Mara	Jerome Cowan
Mr. Shellhammer	Philip Tonge
Dr. Pierce	James Seay
Mr. Macy	Harry Antrim
Mothers	Thelma Ritter, Mary Field
Cleo	Theresa Harris
Albert	Alvin Greenman
Mrs. Mara	Anne Staunton
Thomas Mara, Jr.	Robert Hyatt
Reporters	Richard Irving, Jeff Corey
Secretary	Anne O'Neal
Mrs. Shellhammer	Lela Bliss
Peter	Anthony Sydes
Dr. Rogers	William Forrest
Mara's Assistant	Joseph McInerney
Bailiff	Joseph McGuire
Drum Majorette	Ida McGuire
Santa Claus	Percy Helton
Mrs. Harper	Jane Green
Dutch Girl	Marlene Lyden

"Miracle On 34th Street" is one of the most appealing, heart-warming films to come out of Hollywood in many a day. Its word-of-mouth potential is the strongest and grosses should react bullishly when the word gets out on entertainment content.

So you don't believe in Santa Claus? If you want to stay a nonbeliever don't see "Miracle." Such a theme as whether or not there is a Kris Kringle seems hardly the thing for popular entertainment but George Seaton's scripting and direction sock it over with laughs, tears and all the other ingredients that spell ticket sales.

Film is an actor's holiday, providing any number of choice roles that are played to the hilt. Edmund Gwenn's Santa Claus performance proves the best in his career, one that will be thoroughly enjoyed by all filmgoers. Straight romantic roles handed Maureen O'Hara and John Payne as co-stars also display pair to advantage. Miss O'Hara has more opportunity to show acting talent and Payne makes a fine hero without a scowl.

Valentine Davies' story poses question of just how valid is the belief in Santa Claus. Gwenn, old man's home inmate, becomes Santy at Macy's Department Store, events pile up that make it necessary to actually prove he is the McCoy and not a slightly touched old gent. Gwenn is a little amazed at all the excitement because he has no doubt that he's the real article.

Before it's all over, ticket buyers are likely to believe he is, too, even without the difficult decision reached by Gene Lockhart, as New York supreme court judge who has to try the case, that Santa Claus does exist. Events build logically to get Gwenn into his legal jam and the plot is unfolded so realistically that it might actually have happened.

Gene Lockhart's performance as judge is a gem, as is Porter Hall's portrayal of a neurotic personnel director for Macy's. Surprise moppet performance is turned in by little Natalie Wood as Miss O'Hara's non-believing daughter who finally accepts Santy. It's a standout, natural portrayal. William Frawley spots solid bit as a shrewd politician. Jerome Cowan is good as the prosecuting attorney, and Philip Tonge registers as store executive. Others showing effectively include Alvin Greenman, James Seay, Harry Antrim, Theresa Harris.

Seaton's direction garners every possible bit of human drama, chuckles, heart-tugs and interest from the story and the cast. Film has been given top showmanly production values by William Perlberg. Art direction by Richard Day and Richard Irvine, the fine lensing by Charles Clarke and Lloyd Ahern (much of it actual New York footage), Cyril Mockridge's excellent score, editing and other credits lend strong backing to make this a thoroughly enjoyable screen treat.
Brog.

Hoppy's Holiday

United Artists release of Lewis J. Rachmil production. Stars William Boyd. Directed by George Archainbaud. Screenplay by J. Benton Cheney, Bennet Cohen and Ande Lamb from original story by Ellen Corby, Cecile Kramer, based on characters created by Clarence E. Mulford; editor, Fred W. Berger; camera, Mack Stengler. Tradeshown N. Y., May 2, '47. Running time, 70 MINS.

Hopalong Cassidy	William Boyd
California Carlson	Andy Clyde
Lucky Jenkins	Rand Brooks
Mayor Patton	Andrew Tombes
Danning	Leonard Penn
Jed	Jeff Corey
Gloria	Mary Ware
Sheriff	Donald Kirke
Ace	Hollis Bane
Jay	Gil Patric
Bart	Frank Henry

This is no better nor any worse than previous westerns in the Hopalong Cassidy series, music and comedy being an improvement but action too formula. It will do where the oats operas fill the bill.

In "Hoppy's Holiday," Bill Boyd and his two buddies, Andy Clyde and Rand Brooks, are on vacation when they uncover a new racket. Per usual Boyd leads the posse that captures the bank bandits. A horseless carriage (earliest-day motor vehicle) is employed by the robbers to escape the second time they get away with the bank loot. That's different but more implausible than usual even for a western.

Boyd again is his sturdy Cassidy self but appearing a bit older and overly jovial. Clyde contributes the principal comedy, at one juncture doing what amounts to be a monolog that's not too funny. Mary Ware, the only femme given cast credit, is decorative but there's no real romance, even such as found in a cactus meller.

George Archainbaud's direction is far from his best. Splendid musical score by David Chudnow enhances the more exciting moments, and this is made all the more evident because of a slick sound job. *Wear.*

Spoilers of the North

Hollywood, May 3.
Republic release of Donald H. Brown production. Features Paul Kelly, Adrian Booth, Evelyn Ankers, James A. Millican. Directed by Richard Sale. Original screenplay, Milton M. Raison; camera, Alfred Keller; special effects, Howard and Theodore Lydecker; editor, William Thompson. Previewed April 30, '47. Running time, 66 MINS.

Matt Garraway	Paul Kelly
Jane Koster	Adrian Booth
Laura Reed	Evelyn Ankers
Bill Garraway	James A. Millican
Moose McGovern	Roy Barcroft
Inspector Cal. Winters	Louis Jean Heydt
Joe Taku	Ted Hecht
Salty	Harlan Briggs
Pete Koster	Francis McDonald
Doctor	Maurice Cass
Johnny	Neyle Morrow

"Spoilers of the North" is a familiar title and should help in the selling of this one to action melodrama market. Film is a mixture of sex and salmon that will prove okay in supporting slots. Shots of salmon runs, fishing and canning are spliced in as backing for average melodramatics, adding interest for technical minded.

Paul Kelly is the ruthless northern lothario who uses skullduggery to trap both fish and women. He does the role well. Principal femme charmers are Adrian Booth and Evelyn Ankers, half-breed and femme exec, respectively. Manly heroics go to James A. Millican as Kelly's straitlaced brother.

Needing loan to finance fish cannery, Kelly charms Miss Ankers into advancing coin on his promise of a large salmon catch. To meet promise, Kelly charms Miss Booth into re-cruiting Indians for out-of-season fishing. His charm doesn't work as well on the brother, who's against law-breaking and rebels at aiding in the dirty work. Fate catches up with Kelly finally when Miss Booth harpoons him for cheating with Miss Ankers.

Cast works well under Richard Sale's direction of the Milton M. Raison original script. Roy Barcroft is chief heavy henchman to Kelly. Harlan Briggs spots neat character study as camp cook, and others are okay.

The Donald H. Brown production makes good use of outdoor shots, and Paul Youngblood furnished natural settings for action. Alfred Keller lensed. *Brog.*

Black Narcissus

(Color)
(BRITISH-MADE)

London, April 29.
General Film Distributors' release of Archers Production. Stars Deborah Kerr, Sabu, David Farrar, Flora Robson. Written, produced and directed by Michael Powell and Emeric Pressburger; adapted from Rumer Godden's novel; camera, Jack Cardiff. At Odeon, Leicester Square, London. Running time, 100 MINS.

Sister Clodagh	Deborah Kerr
The Young General	Sabu
Mr. Dean	David Farrar
Sister Phillipa	Flora Robson
The Old General	Esmond Knight
Sister Honey	Jenny Laird
Sister Ruth	Kathleen Byron
Sister Briony	Judith Furse
Kanchi	Jean Simmons
Con	Shaun Noble
Joseph Anthony	Eddie Whaley, Jr.
Mother Dorothea	Nancy Roberts
Angu Ayah	May Hallatt

Cynics may dub this lavish production, "Brief Encounter in the Himalayas," and not without reason. Stripped of most of its finery, the picture resolves itself into the story of two sex-starved women and a man. And since the women are nuns, there can be no happy ending, except perhaps in the spiritual sense. A difficult subject has been tactfully handled. As to its boxoffice, it looks good for theatres over here. In the United States, film will need plenty of bally to do business.

At the invitation of an Indian ruler, five sisters of an Anglo-Catholic order open a school and hospital in a remote Himalayan village. They occupy an ancient palace, once known as "The House of Women," built on a ledge 6,000 feet in the air. The nuns find their task overwhelming and Deborah Kerr, as the sister in charge, has to call for help on the cynical British agent, David Farrar, in spite of her instinctive antagonism.

To add to their worries, a native girl in need of a few months cloistering, is boarded with the nuns by Farrar. The peace of the convent is further disturbed when the young general heir to the ruler, enrolls as a pupil. Materially the work of the convent prospers, but Sister Kerr feels that spiritually most of the nuns are out of harmony. Her thoughts stray back to her girlhood sweetheart in Ireland. Another Sister is obviously thinking too much of Farrar and is taken to task. Sister Flora Robson, oldest and wisest, asks to be transferred. When another sister, against instructions, treats a dying child, and the child dies, none of the villagers will come near the convent. And the general, Sabu, having upset the calm of the place, with his fabulous jewels and his "Black Narcissus" perfume, runs away with the native girl.

Climax comes when one sister, having sent in her resignation, dresses herself in a frock she has secretly ordered and creeps out to Farrar's bungalow. He insists she return to the convent. Next morning as Sister Kerr is ringing the bell high above a parapet, the returning sister, crazed with jealousy, grabs her but falls to her death. The convent is closed, and the once cool, self-contained Sister Kerr returning to Calcutta, confesses to Farrar that she has learned spiritual humility.

Production has gained much through being in color. The production and camera work atone for minor lapses in the story, Jack Cardiff's photography being outstanding. There are cliches which film makers like Powell and Pressburger should have avoided. It seems unnecessary to employ the celestial choir with such frequency, the only criticism of an excellent score by Brian Esdaile. With less trimmings and more actual drama, the picture could have been improved immeasurably, and would have been more popular.

The cast has been well chosen, but Miss Kerr gets only occasional opportunities to reveal her talents. Largely she is keyed to one tone, an unemotional superior in command. Yet if she does nothing to enhance her reputation, she maintains it.

Most effective acting comes from Kathleen Byron who has the picture's plum as the neurotic half-crazed Sister Ruth. Old Vic graduate, this is her first big screen role, and she makes the most of it. Flora Robson gives her usual polished performance, and Jenny Laird and Judith Furse are good. It may not be Jean Simmons' fault that she does not live up to the novel's description of Kanchi, native girl. She has little to do as a native trollop who casts sidelong glances at Sabu, who plays the young general as though he were Sabu.

Farrar, having emerged from a series of indifferent roles, is superb as the British agent. Also excellent is eight-year-old Eddie Whaley. Doubtless the film will be shown in America after Miss Kerr's Hollywood debut as co-star of Clark Gable in "The Hucksters." It would be wise to do so. *Cane.*

La Forteresse
'(The Fortress')
(IN FRENCH; CANADA-MADE)

Eagle-Lion release of Quebec Productions Corp. production (George Marton and Paul L'Anglais), directed by Fedor Ozep. Stars Paul Dupuis, Nicole Germaine, Jacques Auger; features Henri Letondal, Mimi d'Estee, Henri Poitras, Arthur Lefebvre, Armande Lebrun, George Alexander. Screenplay, Rian James and Leonard Lee, from original by George Zuckerman and Michael Lennox; camera, Guy Roe; editor, Douglas Bagler; music, Jean Deslauriers. Previewed in Toronto, May 3, '47. Running time, **103 MINS.**

Michel Lacoste....................Paul Dupuis
Albert Frederic..................Jacques Auger
Marie Roberts..................Nicole Germaine
Edward Durant.................Henri Letondal
Mother Superior..................Lucie Poitras
Renee Brancourt...............Armande Lebrun
Blanche Lacoste..................Mimi d'Estee

(In French; No English Titles)

Toronto, May 3.

This is the first film made in Canada with an all-Canadian French-speaking cast, this totalling 32 players who get screen credits. "Forteresse" has such top-drawer appeal that the J. Arthur Rank organization will give it world-wide distribution and it should prove an international threat to Hollywood product in French-language areas. The film was made, leap-frog fashion, in French and English by Quebec Productions Corp., both troupes using the same interiors and exteriors in Quebec; but the French-Canadian cast acts rings around their opposites in the English-language version and "Forteresse' should have a telling effect on the foreign market. Even the direction of Fedor Ozep and the photography angles and lighting of Guy Roe and Harry Sundberg seem to enhance the Continental flavor. As a mystery-thriller, it is not exactly revolutionary, but "Forteresse" should do hefty business overseas.

Story deals with a wealthy Quebec lawyer and patron of the arts (Jacques Auger), who has killed his best friend in order to inherit the estate, discovers that a girl reporter (Nicole Germaine) has discovered a diary that will blast his life of respectability, and blackmails a young composer-protege (Paul Dupuis) into eliminating the girl when the lawyer discovers that the composer's wife has committed suicide by taking an overdose of sleeping pills and convinces the composer, who had been on a binge, that the piano-pounder was responsible for her death, but the great lawyer will defend him.

Important to the foreign market, the film will introduce Montreal-born Paul Dupuis, who was "discovered" in Britain as a war correspondent for the Canadian Broadcasting Corp. and placed, postwar, under long term contract by Rank. But more important, it marks the screen debut of Nicole Germaine, a young French-Canadian radio actress whose convincing appearance as the girl-reporter is as refreshing as the opening of a window on a spring day.

Whispering City
(CANADA-MADE)

Eagle-Lion release of Quebec production (George Marton and Paul L'Anglais). Stars Paul Lukas, Helmut Dantine, Mary Anderson; features John Pratt, Joy Lafleur, George Alexander, Arthur Lefebvre, Mimi d'Estee, Henri Poitras. Directed by Fedor Ozep. Screenplay, Rian James and Leonard Lee, from original by George Zuckerman and Michael Lennox; camera, Guy Roe; editor, Douglas Bagler; music, Jean Deslauriers. Previewed in Toronto May 3, '47. Running time, **95 MINS.**

Michel Lacoste..............Helmut Dantine
Mary Roberts..................Mary Anderson
Albert Frederic....................Paul Lukas
Mons. Durant........................John Pratt
Blanche Lacoste....................Joy Lafleur
Police Inspector............George Alexander
Renee Brancourt..................Mimi d'Estee
Asst. Police Inspector..........Henri Poitras

Toronto, May 3.

"Whispering City" is a cops-and-killer melodrama that, apart from its three imported stars, is the first film to be made in Canada with a Canadian cast. Turned out by Quebec Productions Corp. at a reputed cost of $600,000, the film is deemed of sufficent merit as to be taken over by the J. Arthur Rank organization for worldwide distribution.

Absorbing chronicle deals with a wealthy lawyer whose world of respectability is about to topple when a girl reporter gets the deathbed confession and diary of the famous actress-wife of the lawyer's best friend whom the solon has allegedly murdered. The problem is to liquidate the girl reporter before she writes the story. When the lawyer's protege, a young composer, discovers that his wife has committed suicide while he himself was on a binge, with the usual lapse of memory, his legal pal promises to get him out of the mess if the composer will knock off the girl reporter.

For the plot romance, the two youngsters, of course, fall in love and form a partnership to trap the killer. Their procedure makes for a dramatic and exciting story that builds to the big action-crammed climax of an unconventional plot.

Paul Lukas, as the lawyer and connoisseur of the arts, plays the role with his usual careful intensity; Helmut Dantine is as distraught and detached as composers are supposed to be, and Mary Anderson plays the reporter a little too flippantly and sexily. Excellent performances are given by several of the lesser players and the fact that they are unknown and not stock players adds piquancy and conviction. For once, the atmosphere of a newspaper office is authentic.

The intelligent direction and cutting keeps the story on the move, and a word should be said for the excellent camera work of Guy Roe, formerly with Cecil B. DeMille. With lack of marquee strength, "Whispering City" will have to be ballyhooed plenty for the North American and Empire markets, but it is an absorbing killer-thriller with solid production and performance values.

Sarge Goes to College
(SONGS)

Hollywood, May 3.

Monogram release of Will Jason production, directed by Jason. Features Freddie Stewart, June Preisser, Frankie Darro, Warren Mills, Noel Neill, Arthur Walsh, Alan Hale, Jr., Russ Morgan, Jack McVea. Screenplay, Hal Collins; original, Henry Edwards; camera, Mack Stengler; editor, Jason Bernie; songs, Will Jason-Henry Nemo, Buddy Kaye-Billy Reid; Val Burton, Sid Robin, Dick Howard, Bob Ellsworth, Russ Morgan, Mack David, Jack McVea, Dusty Fletcher, John Mason, Dan Howell. Previewed April 30, '47. Running time, **63 MINS.**

Freddie Trimball...........Freddie Stewart
Dodie Rogers.................June Preisser
Roy Donne...................Frankie Darro
Lee Watson...................Warren Mills
Betty Rogers.......................Noel Neill
Arthur Walsh.................Arthur Walsh
Sarge.............................Alan Hale, Jr.
Russ Morgan.................Russ Morgan
Dean McKinley..............Monte Collins
Prof. Edwards..................Frank Cady
Miss Koregmeyer.........Margaret Brayton
Capt. Handler...............Selmer Jaskson
Eddie............................Earl Bennett
Mrs. Rogers..................Margaret Burt
Mr. Rogers......................Harry Tyler
Landlord..........................Pat Goldin
Col. Winters..............William Forrest
George.........................Irwin Kauffman
Russ Morgan Orchestra
Jack McVea Orchestra

Nine tunes and three orchestras leave little time for story in "Sarge Goes to College," latest entry in Monogram's Teen-Agers series. Film has better production values than previous entries in group and will prove okay for its release intentions.

Music is carried by Russ Morgan and orchestra, with specialties coming from Jack McVea and an all-star group made up of Wingy Manone, Candy Candido, Abe Lyman, Les Paul, Jess Stacy, Joe Venuti and Jerry Wald. Those names add values for teen-age ticket buyers.

Freddie Stewart handles vocals on three of numbers, "Two Are the Same as One," "I'll Close My Eyes" and "Penthouse Serenade." Songs register well as piped by Stewart. "Blues in B Flat" is a standout as delivered by the all-star group, and Morgan gives "Somebody Else Is Taking My Place" slick treatment. Freak "Open the Door, Richard" has the McVea orch acting out the knocking.

Plot is stretched pretty thin in telling of Marine sergeant who is sent to college for relaxation before facing critical operation. There's the usual college show in preparation, puppy-love misunderstandings and prissy teachers as framework for songs and antics. Will Jason, as producer-director, manages interest in telling the slight story through spotting of tunes and handling of players.

Stewart, producer of school show, June Preisser, Frankie Darro, Warren Mills, Noel Neill, Arthur Walsh, make up the junior college set and will please their fans. Alan Hale, Jr., does well by title role as dumb Marine. Mack Stengler's lensing is good and other credits aid in lending production polish. *Brog.*

The Road Home
(RUSSIAN-MADE)

Artkino release of Leningrad-Riga Film production. Stars Oleg Zhakov and Anna Smirnova. Directed by Alexander Ivanov. Screenplay, Feder Knorre; camera, Ivan Goldberg, Alexander Zavialov; English titles, Charles Clement. At Stanley, N. Y., starting May 1, '47. Running time, **89 MINS.**

Yanis..............................Oleg Zhakov
Ilga, his wife................Anna Smirnova
Voldemar, his brother.....Nikolai Chibbius
The Miller........................Vassili Vanin
Milda, miller's daughter...Anna Petukhova
Karlis, the mechanic.....Victor Merkuriev
Christina, his wife.Ludmilla Sukharevskaya
Partisan Leader..........Gregory Michurin
Col. Grabbe............Vassili Politseimako
Lt. Brenner..................Georgi Spiegel

(In Russian; English Titles)

The Soviet film-makers have whipped up a fast-moving melodrama of the partisan underground operations in "The Road Home." Because this picture combines a passable story and action with some above-par performances, it looks to do smart biz at Russian arty houses in the U. S. Certainly it is a vast improvement over several recent laborious Russian cinematic efforts.

This is from the Riga and Leningrad studios of Russo's vast film industry and bespeaks the strides taken by these plants as compared with some other Soviet studios. Despite this being basically another war story, "Road Home" incorporates enough newness to the familiar underground fighter plot to whet interest. Starts off showing a Russian trying to escape from a train bearing citizens to a German concentration camp in his effort to see his home and family again. From this it swings into somewhat familiar scenes as the partisans try day and night to hamper the hated invading Nazis.

Idea of the one daring former prisoner trying to battle the German troops single-handed in a small Latvian village develops two exciting manhunts. Director Alexander Ivanov has smartly stressed the melodramatic phases, employing unusual lighting and camera work to highlight the more dramatic passages.

Oleg Zhakov, as the persistent peasant who is always ducking the enemy Nazis, and Anna Petukhova, as his brother's sweetheart, almost theft the film. Anna Smirnova, a looker, as his wife, is given star billing but has too little to do. What little she figures in the plot is well done. Victor Merkuriev, the expert mechanic who pretends being friendly to the Germans though the key figure in the underground movement, is especially good in a minor role. Nikolai Chibbius, as the escaped prisoner's brother, chips in with a clear portrayal despite his unsympathetic part as the lad who joins up with the Germans.

Camera work of Ivan Goldberg and Alexander Zavialov is remarkably fine. *Wear.*

Miniature Reviews

"Cynthia" (M-G). Appealing drama of youth carried out in simple, effective style to rate good b.o. returns.

"Desperate" (RKO). Steve Brodie in gangster meller of "B" stature; for twin bills and where they go for gang films.

"Thunder Mountain" (RKO). Sturdy western with plenty of action.

"Northwest Outpost" (Songs). (Rep.). Nelson Eddy, Ilona Massey in pleasant musical romance about early California. Will do biz.

"Dick Tracy's Dilemma" (RKO). Okay entry in the cartoon series with enough chills and thrills to carry it in supporting slots.

"Take My Life" (Cineguild-British). Potboiler whodunit.

"Hi-de-Ho" (States Rights). Cab Calloway musical should do okay in Negro houses.

"Killer Dill" (SG). Program comedy of Prohibition era.

"The Brothers" (Box-British). Patricia Roc in a grim meller for discriminating audiences.

Cynthia

Hollywood, May 13.

Metro release of Edwin H. Knopf production. Stars Elizabeth Taylor, George Murphy, S. Z. Sakall, Mary Astor; features Gene Lockhart, Spring Byington, James Lydon, Scotty Beckett. Directed by Robert Z. Leonard. Screenplay, Harold Buchman, Charles Kaufman; based on play by Vina Delmar; camera, Charles Schoenbaum; score, Bronislau Kaper, Johnny Green; editor, Irvine Warburton. Tradeshown May 12, '47. Running time, **97 MINS.**

Cynthia Bishop	Elizabeth Taylor
Larry Bishop	George Murphy
Professor Rosenkrantz	S. Z. Sakall
Louise Bishop	Mary Astor
Dr. Fred I. Jannings	Gene Lockhart
Carrie Jannings	Spring Byington
Ricky Latham	James Lydon
Will Parker	Scotty Beckett
Fredonia Jannings	Carol Brannan
Miss Brady	Anna Q. Nilsson
Mr. Phillips	Morris Ankrum
McQuillan	Kathleen Howard
Stella Regan	Shirley Johns
Alice	Barbara Challis
J. M. Dingle	Harlan Briggs
Gus Wood	Will Wright

"Cynthia" has a simplicity that projects warmth and feeling, particularly for family audiences familiar with the teen-age problems posed by its plot. A highly interesting performance delivered with veteran assurance by young Elizabeth Taylor, tasteful production values and the homey quality of the action promise well for boxoffice returns. The story is a familiar one in general outline and footage is a bit longer than necessary to tell it but overall it commands favorable interest for film-goers.

Miss Taylor breathes plenty of life into the title role as a sheltered young girl who has never had a date or other fun generally accepted as matter-of-fact by teen-agers. Plot builds to her first romance and first high school dance while depicting the myriad details of family life in a small town. Paternal frustration also is a factor in the yarn and is made believable by George Murphy and Mary Astor, the parents who were prevented from carrying out their dreams for the future by Miss Taylor's birth.

Robert Z. Leonard's direction is strong, using simple style to make the drama effective and displays an understanding of the young that gives the picture its appealing warmth. Story line of the Vina Delmar play is given good treatment in the script by Harold Buchman and Charles Kaufman.

Murphy and Miss Astor make an excellent team to carry the adult load. Particularly good is Miss Astor as the understanding mother, and Murphy socks over several punchy scenes. Miss Taylor raises voice in song for school numbers to round out a talent display that registers strongly. S. Z. Sakall gives one of his standard characterizations as the high school music professor. Gene Lockhart and Spring Byington team as Cynthia's uncle and aunt effectively. James Lydon, Miss Taylor's first love, is very good. Carol Brannan and Scotty Beckett rate chuckles as typical highschoolers. Harlan Briggs, Kathleen Howard and others give sturdy backing.

Edwin H. Knopf's production guidance is showmanly, furnishing quality appurtenances in keeping with story background. Camera work by Charles Schoenbaum, the music score by Bronislau Kaper, numbers by Johnny Green, and other factors are excellent. *Brog.*

Desperate

RKO release of Michel Kraike production. Features Steve Brodie, Audrey Long. Directed by Anthony Mann. Screenplay by Harry Essex, based on story by Dorothy Atlas, Anthony Mann; camera, George E. Diskant; editor, Marston Fay. Tradeshown N. Y., May 9, '47. Running time, **73 MINS.**

Steve Randall	Steve Brodie
Anne Randall	Audrey Long
Walt Radak	Raymond Burr
Pete	Douglas Fowley
Reynolds	William Challee
Ferrari	Jason Robards
Shorty	Freddie Steele
Joe	Lee Frederick
Uncle Jan	Paul E. Burns
Aunt Klara	Ilka Gruning

"Desperate" is a ripsnorting gangster meller, with enough gunplay, bumping off of characters and grim brutality to smack of pre-code days. Absence of players familiar to patrons of this type of fare is a handicap. Otherwise, this film fits nicely into the gangster groove, and okay for houses catering to this sort of crime fare.

Yarn is strictly one of those things, and not unfamiliar. Steve Brodie, honest truckdriver, becomes involved innocently in a fur warehouse robbery and cop slaying. He's beaten up by the mobsters when they realize he tipped off the police. Brodie flees with his wife, fearing gangster vengeance since the mobster's brother is captured and charged with murder. From then on, picture becomes more or less a continuing flight of Brodie and his wife, Audrey Long, both from the gendarmes and the gangsters.

Surprise ending gives film a lift. Anthony Mann's direction mainly stresses suspense, being done skillfully. However, he permits several corny incidents to creep in that should have been edited out. Suspense is accentuated by George E. Diskant's photography.

Brodie is okay as the honest truckman who gets into one jam after another. Miss Long, as his wife, shapes up nicely; at times she resembles Ginger Rogers. Too many closeups look like they might have been screen tests. Jason Robards as the relentless sleuth, does a good job but has too little to do. Support is strictly humdrum. *Wear.*

Thunder Mountain

Hollywood, May 13.

RKO release of Herman Schlom production. Stars Tim Holt; features Martha Hyer, Richard Martin, Steve Brodie, Virginia Owen. Directed by Lew Landers. Screenplay, Norman Houston; based on novel by Zane Grey; camera, Jack MacKenzie; music, Paul Sawtell; editor, Philip Martin. Tradeshown May 13, '47. Running time, **60 MINS.**

Marvin Hayden	Tim Holt
Ellen Jorth	Martha Hyer
Chito Rafferty	Richard Martin
Chick Jorth	Steve Brodie
Ginger Kelly	Virginia Owen
Trimble Carson	Harry Woods
James Gardner	Jason Robards
Lee Jorth	Robert Clarke
Johnny Blue	Richard Powers
Sheriff Bagley	Harry Harvey

With Tim Holt in the saddle, "Thunder Mountain" is sturdy western fare, carrying plenty of action to please the outdoor fan. Production makes good use of rugged background scenery caught by the Jack MacKenzie camera to dress up sight values, and other appurtenances furnished by Herman Schlom's production make it easily saleable for action houses.

Zane Grey plot has been given a tight script by Norman Houston, and Lew Landers' direction is always actionful. Young Holt rides easy, uses fists authoritatively and generally is a stalwart saddle hero. Story concerns his return to the old homestead just in time to save the ranch from the villains, who know a Government dam will increase land values. Heavies use old feud between Holt and the Jorth family as cover for their dirty work but in the end get their just desserts.

Martha Hyer, Steve Brodie and Robert Clarke are Holt's feuding neighbors, all measuring up to demands of assignments. Richard Martin is good for chuckles as Holt's pal and heavy work is in capable hands of Harry Woods, Richard Powers and Harry Harvey. Jason Robards does well by spot as drunken attorney who sides with Holt, and Virginia Owen is comely dancehall femme. *Brog.*

Northwest Outpost

(SONGS)

Republic release of Allan Dwan production. Stars Nelson Eddy, Ilona Massey; features Joseph Schildkraut. Directed by Dwan. Screenplay by Elizabeth Meehan, Richard Sale, from original story of Angela Stuart adapted by Laird Doyle. Original music score, Rudolf Friml; lyrics, Edward Heyman; musical director, Robert Armbruster. Camera, Reggie Lanning; editor, Harry Keller. Previewed N. Y., May 7, '47. Running time, **91 MINS.**

Capt. James Laurence	Nelson Eddy
Natalie Alanova	Ilona Massey
Count Igor Savin	Joseph Schildkraut
Princess Tanya	Elsa Lanchester
Prince Nickolai Balinin	Hugo Haas
Baroness Kruposny	Lenore Ulric
Volkoff	Peter Whitney
Olga	Tamara Shayne
Kyril	Erno Verebes
Baron Kruposny	George Sorel
Dovkin	Rick Vallin

and American GI Chorus

"Northwest Outpost" is a rather familiar musical romance, but it has flavor and charm. Nelson Eddy-Ilona Massey combo are personable and attractive here, and will draw. Pic will do biz.

Plot setting is fresh and novel enough to offset the frequently stilted dialog and familiar situations. The story is set in the 1830's in the little-known times when Russia held part of California. Scene is a trading fort, governed by a Russian prince (Hugo Haas), whose soldiery is under the command of a former U. S. Army cavalry officer (Nelson Eddy). The Russians, trading for furs, and holding off Indian raids, know that eventually the Americans will come into possession of their land. The ex-U. S. officer is there, unofficially, to help pave the way.

Idyllic scene is somewhat marred by constant sight of Russian convicts, in chains (sent here, as it were, to a sylvan Siberia), working roads, hauling lumber, etc. One of the convicts (Joseph Schildkraut) is a Russian count banished here for treason, who saved his skin by squealing on his fellow-conspirators. His wife (Ilona Massey, whom he forced into marriage as payment for his silence regarding the complicity of her titled father in the aforesaid conspiracy, comes to California to see what she can do for him.

Pic concerns itself rather placidly with the way the U. S. officer and titled Russian fall in love, the misunderstandings about her husband, the escape of the convict-husband and his subsequent death, and the reunion of the lovers.

Pleasant outdoor scenes, some fast riding, some fanciful court dresses and Russian peasant costumes, and some good music, help to enliven the slow-paced yarn. Eddy, who looks the part of a dashing frontiersman, also sings very well, in solo or duet with Miss Massey. Latter looks lovely, is gowned handsomely, and sings as appealingly. Songs aren't overdone, and fit in naturally into the story. The American GI Chorus, taking the part of the convicts, also sings well, particularly a mournful chant called, "Weary." Score, all by Rudolf Friml, has some pleasant tunes, as in "Nearer and Dearer," "Love Is The Time" and "Tell Me With Your Eyes."

Joseph Schildkraut, although too neatly got up for a convict, handles the role satisfactory. Hugo Haas and Elsa Lanchester do well with roles of Prince and Princess (in charge of the fort), and furnish some humorous moments. Lenore Ulric, vet legit actress, is good in a brief bit as a Baroness.

Photography is good, on outdoor horse-racing scenes, in a production number like the Russian Easter church scene, or in some neat touches like a conversation between officer and Princess shot through a lace curtain frame. Direction is okay. Production is adequately budgeted, though it doesn't seem to have been costly. Nothing seems stinted, however. *Bron.*

Dick Tracy's Dilemma

Hollywood, May 13.

RKO release of Herman Schlom production. Features Ralph Byrd, Lyle Latell, Kay Christopher, Jack Lambert, Ian Keith. Directed by John Rawlins. Screenplay, Robert Stephen Brode; based on cartoon strip created by Chester Gould; camera, Frank Redman; music, Paul Sawtell; editor, Marvin Coll. Tradeshown May 12, '47. Running time, **60 MINS.**

Dick Tracy	Ralph Byrd
Pat	Lyle Latell
Tess	Kay Christopher
The Claw	Jack Lambert
Vitamin	Ian Keith
Longshot Lillie	Bernadene Hayes
Sightless	Jimmy Conlin
Peter Premium	William B. Davidson
Sam	Tony Barrett
Fred	Richard Powers

This latest entry in RKO's "Dick Tracy" series draws on gruesome character of the Claw as menacing opponent of the pen-and-ink detective. Thrills are backed up with good budget production values by Herman Schlom and it's all aimed at satisfying demands of the Tracy fans as well as filling supporting bookings.

Ralph Byrd is an okay Tracy, with enough resemblance to the fictional character to carry off the role. Jack Lambert gives expert study to his role as The Claw, grotesque character right out of a Chester Gould strip. Plot moves along under John Rawlins' directorial wing to show how Tracy busts up a fur-stealing racket that's an insurance fraud and the chief heavy goes to glory in a typical Gould finish when his iron claw accidentally touches a high-voltage wire. Good script was furnished by Robert Stephen Brode.

Lyle Latell is the strip Pat. Kay Christopher is Tess and Ian Keith chews scenery as the flamboyant Vitamin Flintheart. Bernadene Hayes shows up well in brief spot as Longshot Lillie. Jimmy Conlin does an excellent character role as Sightless, pencil-peddler who aids Tracy, and others are okay.

Lensing by Frank Redman, Marvin Coil's editing and other credits are good. *Brog.*

Take My Life

(BRITISH-MADE)

London, May 8.

General Film Distributors' release of Cineguild Production. Stars Greta Gynt, Marius Goring, Hugh Williams. Directed by Ronald Neame. Screenplay by Winston Graham, Winifred Taylor; additional dialog, Margaret Kennedy; camera, Guy Green; music by William Alwyn. At Studio One, London, May 7, '47. Running time, **79 MINS.**

Nicholas Talbot.............Hugh Williams
Philippa Shelley.................Greta Gynt
Sidney Flemming.............Marius Goring
Prosecuting Counsel....Francis L. Sullivan
Inspector Archer.............Henry Edwards
Elizabeth Rusman.........Rosalie Crutchley
Mrs. Newcombe.................Marjorie Mars
Defending Counsel.........Maurice Denham
John Newcombe.......................Leo Britt
Leslie Newcombe..........David Wallbridge
Deaf, Man.........................Ronald Adam
Mike Grieve..................Herbert Walton

As a digression from making prestige pictures, Cineguild has tried its hand on a murder mystery, but there's nothing to differentiate it from ordinary potboiler. Attempts to create an arty atmosphere—narrative and flashbacks—merely result in making it tiresome. Film will do no more than fair here, and as just an average dualer in the U. S.

Ronald Neame in his first assignment as director has not distinguished himself, but as an ace cameraman he should have known that the prime essential of a pic is that it should move, and that talk is no satisfactory substitute for action. Nor is there any novelty in prolonged trial scenes, unnecessary flashbacks and exaggerated closeups.

It's hardly complimentary to Scotland Yard to discover that an opera singer, Philippa Shelley, making use of an obvious clue—a piece of written music—leads the police to the criminal. On the night of her big success, one of the violinists in the Covent Garden orchestra, Elizabeth, onetime flame of Nicholas, the star's husband-manager, is found murdered. Circumstantial evidence points strongly to the manager, and he is put on trial for his life. Only Philippa knows her husband is innocent, and through the snatch of a song she traces the real murderer, and saves Nick in the nick of time.

Marius Goring, as a fanatical criminal, makes a worthwhile impression. Greta Gynt, who has made much progress recently, is disappointing. The camera and the costumer have been unkind to her, and there's small scope for real acting. Hugh Williams as her husband has little to do but exhibit a crooked smile. *Cane.*

Hi-de-Ho
(MUSICAL)

Famous release of E. M. Glucksman production. Stars Cab Calloway; features Dusty Fletcher, Ida James, Jeni Le Gon, Peters Sisters, Miller Bros. & Lois. Directed by Josh Binney. Original story and screenplay, Hal Seeger; songs, Seeger, Calloway, Jack Palmer, Buster Harding, Elton Hill; camera, Don Malkames; editor, Louis Hess. At Squire, N. Y., week May 9, '47. Running time **72 MINS.**

Cab.............................Cab Calloway
Nettie.................................Ida James
Minnie.............................Jeni Le Gon
Sparks.........................Wiliam Campbell
His Fat Friend.................Virginia Girvin
Boss Mason...................George Wiltshire
Mo the Mouse................James Dunmore
Preacher......................Augustus Smith
Owner of Jive Club.........Edgar Martin
Ralph..........................Leonard Rogers
Owner of Brass Hat..........David Bethea
Police Sergeant..............Shepard Roberts
Head Waiter..............Frederick Johnson
Cab Calloway Orchestra
Dusty "Open The Door Richard" Fletcher
Peters Sisters
Miller Bros. & Lois

Working with an obviously low budget, producer E. M. Glucksman has turned out a fair negro musical which has Cab Calloway's name to furnish the b.o. draft. While such a film will receive meagre bookings in ofay houses, it's a natural for the 500-odd colored theatres throughout the U. S.

Calloway fans will find "Hi-de-ho" right up their alley as the stick-swisher appears in practically every scene. Using his lusty pipes in his own peculiar style, the Cab croons a half-dozen songs as well as leading his band in a number of sequences. Bolstering the marquee are Dusty Fletcher, Peters Sisters, and a top terp act, Miller Bros. & Lois.

Story is just one of those things. Calloway starts from scratch at the Brass Hat Club through the efforts of his femme manager, Ida James. His gal friend, Jeni Le Gon, disapproves of Miss James and in a fit of jealousy moves to have Boss Mason (George Wiltshire), operator of a rival spot rub Calloway out. Later, overcome with remorse, Miss Le Gon attempts to prevent the attack but is killed herself. Cab then weds Miss James.

Fletcher contribs his famed "Open the Door Richard" routine, which he's credited with having originated. Peters Sisters are solid with "A Rainy Sunday" and "Little Old Lady From Baltimore" while Miller Bros. & Lois do their standard tap routine atop built up blocks and stands. Of some three special tunes written for the pic, "I Got a Gal Named Nettie," by Calloway and Elton Hill is perhaps the best.

Calloway is natural enough as himself while the Misses James and Le Gon do as well as could be expected. Acting on the whole is static and Josh Binney's direction might have shown more results had the budget been larger. Production accoutrements and photography also reflects the low nut. "Hi-de-ho" is primarily an excuse for spotlighting some okay vaude acts on celluloid but the audiences it's aimed at will overlook the technical deficiencies.

Killer Dill

Hollywood, May 10.

Screen Guild release of Max M. King production. Stars Stuart Erwin; features Anne Gwynne, Frank Albertson, Mike Mazurki. Directed by Lewis D. Collins. Screenplay, John O'Dea; based on original by Alan Friedman; camera, William Sickner; editor, Marty Cohn. Previewed May 5, '47. Running time, **71 MINS.**

Johnny Dill......................Stuart Erwin
Judy...............................Anne Gwynne
Allen.............................Frank Albertson
Little Joe.........................Mike Mazurki
Maboose..........................Milburn Stone
Millie.........................Dorothy Granger
Louie..............................Anthony Warde
Moroni...............................Ben Welden
Gangster in Movie.................Will Orlean
Mushnose...........................Stanley Ross
Gloria..............................Shirley Hunter
Jack...............................Charles Knight
Mr. Jones.......................Stanley Andrews
Secretary..........................Julie Mitchum

"Killer Dill" goes back to the Prohibition era for its plot and proves fairly amusing for supporting bookings. Length is a bit unwieldy for lower half of bills but footage needs trimming so that can be easily fixed. Budget production values are good for expenditure.

Plot goes overboard and there are a number of script holes that faster direction would have skipped over. Story concerns misidentification of timid salesman as a public enemy who has bumped off a rival. Stuart Erwin handles role capably.

Lewis D. Collins' direction is spotty but overall effect is okay for release intentions. Frank Albertson, the attorney, is good and a number of excellent character spots are strongly filled by Mike Mazurki, Milburn Stone, Ben Weldon and Anthony Warde. Ann Gwynne has little to do as femme lead. Max M. King production was well lensed by William Sickner. *Brog.*

The Brothers
(BRITISH-MADE)

London, May 8.

General Film Distributors' release of Sydney Box production. Stars Patricia Roc, Will Fyffe, Maxwell Reed. Directed by David Macdonald. Adapted from L. A. G. Strong's novel by David Macdonald, Strong and Paul Vincent Carroll; camera, Stephen Dade; music, Cedric Thorpe Davie. At Odeon, London, May 7, '47. Running time, **98 MINS.**

Mary................................Patricia Roc
Aeneas McGrath....................Willie Fyffe
Fergus Macrae....................Maxwell Reed
Hector Macrae.....................Finlay Currie
John Macrae...................Duncan Macrae
Dugald...............................John Laurie
Willie McFarish..............Andrew Crawford
Angus McFarish..............Morland Graham
Angusina..........................Megs Jenkins
Priest...........................James Woodburn
George McFarish.............David McAllister
The Informer.....................Patrick Boxill

Starkly uncompromising is this Sydney Box version of L. A. G. Strong's novel. No attempt has been made to win favor of those who cannot stomach a grim story, and even the contemplated happy ending (not in the book) has been discarded in favor of one more logical. It will not be everybody's entertainment, and will do best with discriminating audiences here and in the U. S.

Drawing cards are a fine cast, good story, grand direction and splendid camera work and music score. Patricia Roc contributes her best performance to date, and newcomer Maxwell Reed establishes himself in a part that would have been a natural for James Mason. Reed, a protege of Box, is obviously destined for stardom. Only criticism is the sparing use made of that nifty character actor, Will Fyffe. He whams every moment he's on screen, but his importance in the novel has been whittled away in the adaptation.

Mention must be made of Duncan Macrae, John Laurie, Finlay Currie, Andrew Crawford and George MacDonald, an amateur Scottish actor (unnamed in the cast list), who etches a memorable cameo as a thrifty Scotsman bargaining about the marriage portion of his daughter.

Story is set in 1900, in a small remote island in the western isles of Scotland, where the Macraes and the McFarishes, farmers, carry on a feud of generations. To the Macraes comes Mary, a convent-bred orphan, to be a servant, causing the feud to flare again. It's resolved only when one of the boys takes the girl out in his boat, and neither returns. In the book he alone comes back. *Cane.*

Miniature Reviews

"Moss Rose" (20th). Well-made melodrama of murder against English costume background.

"Copacabana" (Songs) (Coslow-UA). Groucho Marx, Carmen Miranda in okay filmusical.

"The Ghost and Mrs. Muir" (20th). Slick romantic comedy headed for sock results in keys.

"Oregon Trail Scouts" (Rep). Standard Red Ryder entry for kiddie trade.

"Border Feud" (PRC). Fair western in the "Lash" La Rue, Al St. John series.

"Two Anonymous Letters" (Lux) (Italian). Another melodrama on the Italian resistance movement, but mild in b.o. effect.

"Road to Hollywood" (Songs) (Astor). Compilation of four two-reelers starring Bing Crosby; good double-bill filled.

Moss Rose

Twentieth-Fox release of Gene Markey production. Stars Peggy Cummins, Victor Mature, Ethel Barrymore; features Vincent Price, Margo Woode, George Zucco. Directed by Gregory Ratoff. Screenplay, Jules Furthman and Tom Read, adapted by Niven Busch from novel by Joseph Shearing; camera, Joe MacDonald; editor, James B. Clark; music, David Buttolph. Previewed Hollywood, May 19, '47. Running time, **82 MINS.**

Belle Adair.........................Peggy Cummins
Michael Drego.......................Victor Mature
Lady Margaret Drego...........Ethel Barrymore
Inspector Clinner....................Vincent Price
Daisy Arrow..........................Margo Woode
Craxton..............................George Zucco
Audrey Ashton....................Patricia Medina
Deputy Inspector Evans...........Rhys Williams
Liza.....................................Felippa Rock
Harriet..................................Carol Savage
Wilson..................................Victor Wood
George Gilby......................Patrick O'Moore
White Horse Cabby....................Billy Bevan
Asst. Hotel Manager...............Michael Dyne
Fothergill..............................John Rogers
Alf...............................Charles McNaughton
Mr. Bulke.................................Alex Frazer
Threadbard Little Man.................Harry Allen
Footmen.............Gilbert Wilson, Stanley Mann
Cassian...................................Alec Harford
Minister...........................John Goldsworthy
Maid......................................Sally Sheppard
Pub Owner...............................Paul England
Constable...................................Al Ferguson
Chemist...............................Clifford Brooke
Pompous English Colonel...........Stuart Holmes
Art Gallery Attendant..............Colin Campbell
Seamstress...............................Connie Leon
Coroner.................................Leonard Carey
Family Solicitor....................Major Sam Harris
Deputy Coroner......................Norman Ainsley

"Moss Rose" is good whodunit. Given a lift by solid trouping and direction, melodrama is run off against background of early-day England that provides effective setting for theme of destructive mother love. Gene Markey has provided film with strong production mounting and excellent casting.

Names of Peggy Cummins, Victor Mature and Ethel Barrymore have marquee value to aid selling. Gregory Ratoff's direction develops considerable flaver to the period melodramatics. He points up suspense factors to hold audience attention and get meticulous performances from players in keeping with mood of piece. Peggy Cummins' performance is unusually interesting and will boost her stock immeasurably. English pronunciation, at first broad and then becoming more educated, is a trick she uses to develop character of musichall girl who uses her knowledge of murder to satisfy a childhood desire. It's a well-rounded portrayal. Victor Mature handles his sombre character of a well-bred Englishman expertly and thoroughly pleases. Another strong performance is given by Ethel Barrymore, Mature's mother, whose fixation is responsible for the death of two girls loved by her son and the near-death of a third.

Jules Furthman and Tom Read did

the screenplay, adapted by Niven Busch from the Joseph Shearing novel. It's a sombre story of a mother who kills to keep from losing her son. First death comes to musichall girl romanced by Mature. Latter is seen leaving the girl's room by Miss Cummins, who protects Mature in turn for his taking her to visit his mother at a country estate. Next victim is Patricia Medina, Mature's proper fiancee. Then when Miss Cummins confesses her love, the mother attempts a third killing but is trapped. Melodramatic effect is heightened by low-key lensing by Joe MacDonald and the setting provided by Richard Day and Mark-Lee Kirk. David Buttolph's score also is strongly used for mood. *Brog.*

Copacabana

(SONGS)

United Artists release of Sam Coslow production. Stars Groucho Marx, Carmen Miranda, Andy Russell, Steve Cochran, Gloria Jean; features Louis Sobol, Abel Green, Earl Wilson. Directed by Alfred E. Green. Screenplay, Laslo Vadnay, Alan Boretz and Howard Harris, from original story by Vadnay; camera, Bert Glennon; editor, Philip Cahn; songs, Coslow, Edward Ward, Bert Kalmar, Harry Ruby; dances, Larry Ceballos. Previewed N. Y., May 16, '47. Running time, 90 MINS.

Lionel Devereaux............Groucho Marx
Carmen Novarro..........Carmen Miranda
Steve Hunt..................Steve Cochran
Anne...........................Gloria Jean
Liggett......................Ralph Sanford
Himself......................Andy Russell

"Copacabana" has all the ingredients of a successful filmusical, including an entertaining and lighthearted story, a group of okay songs, several good production numbers and a bevy of beautiful showgals. In addition, exhibitors have Groucho Marx and Carmen Miranda as marquee bait, plus the publicity inherent in the title, which is a famed New York nitery, known wherever syndicated Broadway columnists are read. Film should do okay in top situations throughout the country.

Story takes place almost entirely in the Copa, giving producer Sam Coslow a chance to show the rest of the country what Hollywood's version of a N. Y. nitery looks like—and the set naturally puts to shame the actual club, which is probably one of the most extravagantly-designed in the country. Picture also debuts Groucho Marx sans his Bros. Endowed with some hilarious gag lines by the scripters, he's zany as ever in the role of a fast-talking small-time Broadway agent and personal manager of Miss Miranda. Groucho has ditched his standard mustache and painted specs for most of the film in favor of standard horn-rimmed glasses and a small lip-adornment but returns with the props for his one specialty number, "Go West, Young Man," a Kalmar & Ruby oldie but excellent for his spot.

Miss Miranda, who's currently headlining the actual Copa floorshow, turns in what's probably the best performance of her career. Unable to get bookings as a double, Marx has her audition for the Copa boniface in her usual Brazilian routine. Boniface likes her but also wants a French chantoosey for the lounge, so Groucho throws a veil and a blonde coiff on Miss Miranda and she auditions for that also. Copa owner decides to take them both, but won't accept one without the other, so she's forced to work on a split-second schedule, dashing from the floorshow to the lounge and back again night after night.

Additional complications set in when the owner, still thinking she's two different gals, goes for the French version romantically. Groucho finally hits on the bright idea of staging a simulated fight behind closed doors between the two gals, with the French babe taking it on la lam after the Brazilian bombshell supposedly beats her up. When no trace of the chantoosey is found, though, the police are brought in and they charge Groucho with her murder. In a gag-some denouement, he and Miss Miranda finally convince everybody the French gal had never actually existed and all ends happily, with a Hollywood producer putting in a bid for the whole story.

Miss Miranda handles the semi-dual role neatly, shining in the comedy, as well as the French and Brazilian-staccato songs. Rest of the cast adds to the fun, under the light-handed direction of Alfred E. Green. Steve Cochran is an acceptable Copa boniface, but bears little resemblance to Monte Proser, owner of the club, or his greeter Jack Entratter. Gloria Jean, who's grown into an attractive ingenue, does nicely as his vis-a-vis and demonstrates she still has a good voice in the one number she sings. Andy Russell plays himself neatly, handling both his acting and vocalizing chores in good fashion.

As a promotion stunt, Coslow has N. Y. Journal-American columnist Louis Sobol, N. Y. Post columnist Earl Wilson, and VARIETY editor Abel Green play themselyes in one short sequence. Sobol handles his single line like an experienced newspaperman, and Wilson draws a big laugh as he brings out his tape measure when Copacutie Chili Williams drapes herself around his neck. As for Green, how honest can a mugg be in a review and still keep his job?

Nine songs, cleffed by Coslow, Edward Ward, Bert Kalmar and Harry Ruby, are okay, with "Stranger Things Have Happened," penned singly by Coslow, shaping up as the one with most commercial value. Bert Glennon's camera work and other technical credits are good. *Stal.*

Ghost and Mrs. Muir

Hollywood, May 17.

20th-Fox release of Fred Kahlmar production. Stars Gene Tierney, Rex Harrison, George Sanders; features Edna Best, Vanessa Brown, Anna Lee, Robert Coote, Natalie Wood, Isobel Elsom, Victoria Horne. Directed by Joseph L. Mankiewicz. Screenplay, Philip Dunne; from novel by R. A. Dick; camera, Charles Lang, Jr.; special effects, Fred Sersen; music, Bernard Herrmann; editor, Dorothy Spencer. Tradeshown May 15, '47. Running time, 103 MINS.

Lucy Muir.....................Gene Tierney
Ghost of Capt. Daniel Gregg..Rex Harrison
Miles Fairley..............George Sanders
Martha..........................Edna Best
Anna (Grown)..............Vanessa Brown
Mrs. Miles Fairley................Anna Lee
Combe........................Robert Coote
Anna..........................Natalie Wood
Angelica......................Isobel Elsom
Eva..........................Victoria Horne
Sproule.....................Whitford Kane
Inquiries.......................Brad Slaven
Bill.........................William Stelling
Author......................Helen Freeman
Scroggins....................David Thursby
Maid........................Heather Wilde

"The Ghost and Mrs. Muir" is delightful romantic comedy. It is told with distinctive results that mean sock b.o. in top situations. A lusty script, fine direction and solid production backing are given to the potent cast and players romp off with roles in manner that will stir ticket window interest. Handsome marquee values are furnished by names of Gene Tierney, Rex Harrison and George Sanders.

This is the story of a girl who falls in love with a ghost—but not an ordinary spook. As that girl, Miss Tierney gives what undoubtedly is her best performance to date. It's warmly human and the out-of-this-world romance pulls audience sympathy with an infectious tug that never slackens. In his role as the lusty, seafaring shade, Rex Harrison commands the strongest attention. It's a delightful puckish portrayal that boosts his talent sky-high.

Philip Dunne's script lards the R. A. Dick novel with gusty humor and situations that belie the ghostly theme. Dialog makes full use of salty expressions to point up chuckles. Joseph L. Mankiewicz gears his direction to get all values from script and cast, delivering a fine job in all phases. Plot, briefly, deals with young widow who leaves London at turn of century for a seaside cottage. The place is haunted by the ghost of its former owner, Capt. Daniel Gregg. The salty shade seeks to frighten the widow away but she's stubborn and stays. When her income is wiped out, the shade dictates to her his life story; she sells it as successful novel. Story carries over her life span when finally, an aged woman, she goes to join her ghostly lover.

George Sanders is in briefly, and effectively, as a married lothario who makes a play for the widow, much to Capt. Gregg's discomfort. Edna Best shows brightly as the widow's maid-companion. Natalie Wood, as the young daughter, is good, as is Vanessa Brown who becomes the grownup Anna. Robert Coote spots solid bit as English realtor. Anna Lee, Isobel Elsom, Victoria Horne, Whitford Kane and others back the principals with strong work.

Fred Kohlmar's production guidance is a telling part of the finished picture. He displays understanding showmanship in bringing imaginative tale to the screen, dressing it in authentic values. Playing decided part in flavor developed throughout is photography by Charles Lang, Jr., and the boff score by Bernard Herrmann. Art direction by Richard Day and George Davis is eye-satisfying, particularly the seaside cottage. Other credits are excellent. *Brog.*

Oregon Trail Scouts

Hollywood, May 17.

Republic release of Sidney Picker production. Stars Allan Lane; features Bobby Blake, Martha Wentworth, Roy Barcroft, Emmett Lynn. Directed by R. G. Springsteen. Original screenplay, Earle Snell; based on Fred Harman's NEA comic strip; camera, Alfred Keller; editor, Harold R. Minter. Previewed May 16, '47. Running time, 58 MINS.

Red Ryder........................Allan Lane
Little Beaver....................Bobby Blake
The Duchess............Martha Wentworth
Hunter........................Roy Barcroft
Bear Trap.....................Emmett Lynn
Jack..........................Edmund Cobb
Judge........................Earle Hodgins
Bliss........................Edward Cassidy
Running Fox................Frank Lackteen
Barking Squirrel...........Billy Cummings
Stage Coach Driver...............Jack Kirk

This latest Red Ryder western depicts how the stalwart oater hero picked up his moppet sidekick, Little Beaver. As such, it measures up to market demands for outdoor action houses and should please the juve trade. There is the standard amount of bad marksmanship by both hero and heavies, chases, prairie comedy and hard-riding action.

Allan Lane is a good Ryder, with physical ability to depict pen-and-ink character's dare-'n'-do for kiddie pleasure. Plot shows him as fur trapper, arranging treaty with Indians so he can set up operations within the territory. Heavies, led by Roy Barcroft, want fur rights also and try kidnapping chief's grandson. After proper amount of lead and footage has been expended, Ryder puts villains in their place and takes on Little Beaver as a saddle pal.

Bobby Blake does usual competent chore of the Indian moppet. Martha Wentworth is stormy Duchess and Emmett Lynn draws chuckles as fumbling Bear Trap. Others are up to standard as directed by R. G. Springsteen, who keeps footage on move. Sidney Picker's production furnishes adequate values for outdoor trade. *Brog.*

Border Feud

PRC release of Jerry Thomas production. Stars "Lash" La Rue, Al "Fuzzy" St. John; features Gloria Marlen, Ian Keith, Kenneth Farrell. Directed by Ray Taylor. Original screenplay, Joe O'Donnell, Patricia Harper; camera, Milford Anderson; editor, Joe Gluck. Tradeshown N. Y., May 15, '47. Running time, 55 MINS.

Cheyenne....................."Lash" La Rue
Fuzzy..................Al "Fuzzy" St. John
Barton.........................Bob Duncan
Jim Condon....................Brad Slavin
Bob Hart....................Kenneth Farrell
Carol Condon.................Gloria Marlen
Jed Young.................Casey MacGregor
Doc Peters.........................Ian Keith
Elmore.........................Mikel Conrad
Sheriff Steele....................Ed Cassidy

With plenty of gunfire and hard ridin', "Border Feud," the latest in the "Lash" La Rue-"Fuzzy" St. John series packs sufficient action to satisfy the average devotee of western drama. Under Ray Taylor's directorial reins, film moves at a nice pace and stacks up as okay fare to round out double bills in nabe situations.

The Hatfields and McCoys weren't the only mountain boys who vowed a struggle to the death. In this opus the Condons and Harts, co-owners of the Blue Girl Gold Mine, pour plenty of lead into each other unaware that their feud was stirred up by baddie Barton, who has designs upon the mine's rich ore. La Rue as Cheyenne, a U. S. Marshal, and St. John, as Sheriff, break up his plans. Usual skirmishes with the outlaws ensue and following the unmasking of Doc Peters (Ian Keith), as Barton's accomplice, film fades to a fast close.

La Rue is a forthright marshal whose moniker, "Lash" stems from his technique in handling a long whip which supplements his shootin' irons. St. John furnishes the comedy relief. As the heavies, Keith and Bob Duncan do well by their roles. In the only femme part, Gloria Marlen has little to do aside from looking petite at the right moments. Supporting cast is adequate. Milford Anderson's lensing incorporated some fine outdoor shots in this Jerry Thomas production. Other technical credits are standard.

Two Anonymous Letters

(ITALIAN-MADE)

Film Rights International release of Lux production. Stars Clara Calamai; features Andrea Checchi, Dina Sassoli. Directed by Mario Camerini. Story, Ivo Perilli; camera, Massimo Terzano. English titles by Herman G. Weinberg. At Times, N. Y., week May 17, '47. Running time, 90 MINS.

Gina.........................Clara Calamai
Bruno......................Andrea Checchi
Tullio...........................Otello Toso
Chevalier..................Armando Martelli
Rossini..........................Carlo Ninchi
Partisan........................Dina Sassoli

(In Italian; English Titles)

In their seeming efforts to achieve another "Open City," the Italian filmmakers continue to occupy themselves with the good fight of the resistance movement during the Nazi occupation. "Two Anonymous Letters" is the latest in the series to be brought over, but like the others fails to approach the near-classical "Open City." This Lux production has nothing for other than Italian-speaking audiences, who still get comfort from the reminders that their compatriots in the old country fought the Germans, too.

Pic succeeds at no time in rising above its simple story line. Tale is about a girl whose love for a soldier cools during his long absence in the army, and she weds another. Husband turns collaborationist, while she at the same time is won over by the underground. When he threatens the safety of her returned ex-sweetheart, who has also joined the movement, she bumps off her mate.

The dangers and terrors of the resistance movement are hardly more than suggested. There is none of the tenseness, the charged air and the excitement of "Open City."

Performances are pleasing, and agreeably free from the exaggerations of the usual continental troupe. Clara Calamai as the girl reminds strongly of Louise Rainer in her emotional moments. Otello Toso is the husband, and Andrea Checchi the soldier ex-lover. Photography and lighting are poor, a regular failing of Italian films. Herman G. Weinberg's English titles are satisfactory.

Road to Hollywood
(SONGS)

Astor Pictures release of compilation of four Educational-Mack Sennett shorts starring Bing Crosby. Producer, Robert M. Savini; director, Bud Pollard. Features Luis Alberni, Ann Christy. Screen adaptation, John E. Gordon and Charles P. Boyle; camera, Frank Good and George Unholz, with additional photography by Don Malkames; re-edited by Pollard. Reviewed in N. Y., May 7, '47. Running time, 55 MINS.

Astor Pictures has come up with what looks like a goldmine of an idea with its compilation of four old Mack Sennett-Educational two-reelers starring Bing Crosby into a feature-length production appropriately titled "Road to Hollywood." Shorts were bought by Astor prexy Bob Savini several years ago when Educational went bankrupt. Entire cost of this production is some $20,000 and, with the film already booked into several of the major circuits, Savini should realize several times that amount in profit.

Savini was aided in the compilation by Bud Pollard, prexy of the Screen Directors' Guild, eastern chapter, who re-edited and tied together the shorts with a live narration, in which he is seen on the screen seated in a director's chair. With Crosby's name as surefire marquee lure and with some zany Sennett slapstick for good word-of-mouth, the film should bolster double bill situations wherever played, if properly ballyhooed. It's not strong enough nor long enough to hold up by itself.

Savini and Pollard did a creditable job on editing the briefies, managing to integrate a faint story line with them. Opening with Pollard explaining to the audience that this is how Crosby got his start in Hollywood, the film fades into one of the shorts depicting the Groaner starting off to the Coast in a dilapidated jalopy (a stock Sennett trademark). Then, with Pollard bridging each gap with his explanatory narration, the other three shorts have Crosby in typical Sennett comedies, things which he probably wouldn't deign to do now. Stuff, besides being hilarious, has a certain nostalgic quality which should please any audience.

Interspersed with it all, of course, are eight oldtime faves sung by Crosby. There's been considerable speculation lately about whether his voice is as good now as it was several years ago and this picture proves, at least, how terrific he was when he first hit the Coast. He dishes out "I Surrender, Dear," "At Your Command," "Out of Nowhere," "Wrap Your Troubles in Dreams," "I'd Climb the Highest Mountain," "Just One More Chance," "Mine All Mine," and "When I Take My Sugar to Tea," all of which he almost single-handedly boosted to Hit Parade status. Sound track is free of fuzz, stacking up with present-day standards of recording. *Stal.*

The Great Betrayal
(DOCUMENTARY)

Screencraft release of Idea Film production. Story, Julia & Simon Singer; narration, William S. Gailmor; music, Paul Dessau; editor, Julia Singer. Previewed N. Y., May 8, '47. Running time, 73 MINS.

"The Great Betrayal," riding the crest of public interest in the year's hottest story, the Palestinian crisis, is a weak documentary that doesn't measure up to its catchpenny title. Containing little contemporary material, the film unreels more like an arty experiment in poetic photography than a vigorous political document.

Film is loosely draped around the story of a pioneering Jewish settlement's struggle to cultivate the desert soil of Palestine. Individual sequences achieve power through the imagery and pulsating rhythms evoked by an abstract camera technique. Taken as a whole, however, the film is nothing but a series of shots of flowing water, dancing machinery and heroic faces set against the horizon. These are repeated like musical variations on a theme but beyond that, the film is devoid of meaning.

During the last five minutes, some newsreel clips showing British mistreatment of Jewish refugees trying to enter Palestine are tagged on to stoke up the emotions. But because the film previously failed to define any of the issues involved in the dispute, this portion serves less as a concluding argument than as an artificially angry punctuation mark to a photographic ramble.

Narration by William S. Gailmor is also handled in semi-poetic style with an insistent straining for effect. Like the cinematic content, the narration repeats a couple of simple ideas over and over in a narrow range of variation. Gailmor, in stressing the need for a Jewish homeland, goes to town on the British but skirts taking sides with any factional group within Palestine. Film is scored with superb music by Paul Dessau. *Herm.*

Foreign Films

"Sankt Hans Fest" ("St. Hans Celebration") **(NORWEGIAN).** Snorre Film release of Toralf Sandoe production. Stars Tore Foss, Johs Eckhoff, Jon Lennart Mjoen; features Erling Drangsholt, Sigrun Otto, Sigurd Magnusson, Else Merete Heiberg, Toralf Sandoe. Directed by Sandoe. Screenplay based on novel by Alex L. Kielland; camera, Per G. Jonsen. Reviewed in Oslo. Running time, 86 MINS.

Good Norwegian film after an 1887 novel by Alex L. Kielland introduces Else Merete Heiberg. Story deals with a tyrranical priest who seeks to rule all human souls. Tore Foss does nicely as the priest. Well-made, with good direction and lensing, picture may find a market in Scandinavia but its chances are doubtful elsewhere.

"Stackars Lille Sven" ("Poor Little Sven") **(SWEDISH).** Fribergs Filmbureau production and release. Stars Nils Poppe, Annlisa Ericsson; features Douglas Hage, Hjoerdis Pettersson, Hilding Gavle, Ake Engfeldt, Marianne Gyllenhammer, Elisaweta von Gersdorff, Ake Jensen, Helge Mauritz. Directed by Hugo Bolander. Screenplay, Poppe and Rolf Botvid based on British operetta, "Mr. Cinders"; camera, Goesta Roosling; music, Sven Gyldmark and E. Eckert Lundin. At Skandia, Stockholm. Running time, 90 MINS.

Resembling an old Buster Keaton comedy, this film is based on an English operetta. It could have been much better. Nils Poppe, known as the "Swedish Chaplin," fails to enhance his rep in this one. Film's b.o. prospects in Scandinavia will be helped by Poppe's name as well as some top-drawer color lensing by Goesta Roosling. No dice for U. S. *Wins.*

Miniature Reviews

"The Perils of Pauline" (Color-Songs) (Par). Solid for entertainment seekers. Socko fun, geared for top grosses.

"Dear Ruth" (Par). Slick film version of hit stage comedy. Strong entertainment for all situations.

"The Unfaithful" (WB). Drama built around modern problem. Strong femme appeal and hefty b.o. potential.

"Long Night" (RKO). Grim yarn of returned vet who goes berserk. Mild b.o. prospects.

"Jewels of Brandenburg" (20th). Formula jewel robbery meller heading for fairish biz in duals.

"The Web" (U). Straight forward crime melodrama with quality presentation and hefty audience interest.

"Repeat Performance" (E-L). Joan Leslie, Louis Hayward, Richard Basehart in neat fantasy; should do okay.

"Winter Wonderland" (Rep). Charming romance kept fresh on ice; should give strong dual support.

"The Patient Vanishes" (British) (FC). James Mason in a weak, early effort; tepid box-office in dual situations.

"Bells of San Angelo" (Songs) (Rep). Satire intrudes here, which may add some adult fans to the host of young Roy Rogers admirers.

"Thunder in Hills" (General). Standout Czecho screen story of resistance movement in that country; solid for arties.

Perils of Pauline
(SONGS—COLOR)

Hollywood, May 24.

Paramount release of Sol C. Siegel production. Stars Betty Hutton, John Lund; features Billy de Wolfe, William Demarest, Constance Collier, Frank Faylen. Directed by George Marshall. Screen play, P. J. Wolfson, Frank Butler; based on story by Wolfson suggested by incidents in life of Pearl White and Charles W. Goddard's original serial, "The Perils of Pauline"; camera (Technicolor), Ray Rennahan; score, Robert Emmett Dolan; songs, Frank Loesser, Charles McCarron-Raymond Walker; vocal arrangements, Joseph J. Lilley; dances, Billy Daniels; editor, Arthur Schmidt. Tradeshown May 23, '47. Running time, 93 MINS.

Pearl........................Betty Hutton
Mike..........................John Lund
Julia....................Constance Collier
Timmy......................Billy de Wolfe
Mac.....................William Demarest
Gurt........................Frank Faylen

William Farnum, Chester Conklin, Paul Panzer, Snub Pollard, James Finlayson, Creighton Hale, Hank Mann, Francis McDonald, Bert Roach, Heinie Conklin.

When nostalgia is combined with belly laughs the results are pretty surefire. "Perils of Pauline" is just such a combo. It's top entertainment for any situation and will register resoundingly at the boxoffice. The socko fun is backed by beautiful color and other showmanly production touches by Sol C. Siegel and cast romps through it all solidly.

Betty Hutton is tiptop in the title role, giving distinction to antics of early day picture-making and four bright tunes. It's a funfest for the actress and she makes the most of it. Top song of group is "Poppa Don't Preach to Me," and Miss Hutton sells it strongly. She also gives her special touch to "I Wish I Didn't Love You So," "The Sewing Machine" and "Rumble, Rumble, Rumble," all by Frank Loesser; fifth tune is the oldie "Poor Pauline," by Charles McCarron and Raymond Walker, sung by a male quartet.

Pointing up many solid laughs are sequences depicting old open-air stages on which all variety of entertainment was ground out side by side in utter confusion. George Marshall draws heavily on his long picture experience to make it all authentic and garners himself a top credit for surefire direction.

Screenplay by P. J. Wolfson and Frank Butler purports to show how Pearl White, early-day serial queen, got her start in silent films. Scripters carry her from a New York sweatshop to a traveling stock company and then into pictures with credible writing. Romance angle is the only apparent hoke factor in script but it, too, blends well with overall high entertainment level.

John Lund co-stars with Miss Hutton as a ham stock actor who is loved by the cliffhanger queen. Choice performances are delivered by Constance Collier, as the character actress, and William Demarest, as the silent director. Latter milks many a laugh in depicting the puttee-attired megaphoner who gave Pearl White her chance at film fame. Billy de Wolfe, Frank Faylen, William Farnum, Chester Conklin, Paul Panzer, Snub Pollard, James Finlayson, Creighton Hale, Hank Mann, Francis McDonald, Bert Roach and Heinie Conklin are among some of the early day names who again strut their talent. Providing backing for the fun is Robert Emmett Dolan's music score and the beautiful color lensing by Ray Rennahan. Art direction, costuming, makeup, editing and other production credits give strong support to entertainment aims. *Brog.*

Dear Ruth

Hollywood, May 27.

Paramount release of Paul Jones production. Stars Joan Caulfield, William Holden; features Edward Arnold, Billy De Wolfe. Directed by William Russell. Screenplay, Arthur Sheekman from play by Norman Krasna; camera, Ernest Laszlo. Tradeshown May 26, '47. Running time, 94 MINS.

Ruth Wilkins..................Joan Caulfield
Lt. William Seacroft.......William Holden
Judge Harry Wilkins.......Edward Arnold
Mrs. Edith Wilkins...........Mary Philips
Miriam Wilkins..............Mona Freeman
Albert Kummer...............Billy De Wolfe
Sgt. Chuck Vincent......Kenny O'Morrison
Martha Seacroft.............Virginia Welles
Dora, the maid...............Marietta Canty

The solid comedy that made "Dear Ruth" a stage hit has been turned into rollicking film entertainment by Paramount. It's socko fun and should rate handsomely at the ticket windows. Although basis from which comedy springs has a war date on it, the laughs themselves are ageless since such things as uniformed, two-day leaves and the like are only incidental to principal aim of keeping the customers roaring. Production has been well polished by Paul Jones to point film for top drawer bookings.

William Holden and Joan Caulfield click as the principal couple around whom the chuckles are built. Holden does a sturdy piece of work as the love-eager soldier with a two-day leave and amatory urge. Miss Caulfield graces the title role niftily, making it count strongly among the potent cast.

William Russell's direction is sure-handed and points the comedy brightly. Pace is crisp and knowingly developed under his guidance. Standout performance is turned in by Edward Arnold as the fun-loving father of Ruth. His lines are surefire family humor, tossed off uproarishly by the actor who seemingly enjoys the assignment. As foil for the adult fun, Mary Philips registers well as the mother. Billy deWolfe rates handsome credit for potent work as the prissy suitor of Ruth who has to stand by while the soldier gets in his licks. Mona Freeman, the brash brat who causes all the trouble, is a delight, giving the juvenile character a generous display of talent.

Arthur Sheekman's screenplay closely follows the play by Norman

Krasna, and the broader screen scope gives Krasna's plot added interest. Story concerns a young soldier flying in for a quick romance with the girl with whom he's been corresponding for two years. Unknown to couple is fact that younger sister had done the letter writing, using the elder girl's name and picture. Ruth, just engaged to a banker, tries to carry serviceman along for the two-day period but nature intrudes and a new love blooms. It's infectious hilarity that hits hard at risibilities.

Strongly supporting entertainment aims are the camera work by Ernest Laezlo, art direction, music score, editing and other production credits.

Brog.

The Unfaithful

Hollywood, May 27.

Warner Bros. release of Jerry Wald production. Stars Ann Sheridan, Lew Ayres, Zachary Scott; features Eve Arden, Steven Geray, Ann Hoyt. Directed by Vincent Sherman. Original screenplay by David Goodis and James Gunn; camera, Ernest Haller; editor, Alan Crosland, Jr.; score, Max Steiner. Tradeshown May 26, '47. Running time, **109 MINS.**

Chris Hunter........Ann Sheridan
Larry Hammaford........Lew Ayres
Bob Hunter........Zachary Scott
Paula........Eve Arden
Prosecuting Attorney........Jerome Cowan
Martin Barrow........Steven Geray
Detective-Lt. Reynolds........John Hoyt
Claire........Peggy Knudsen
Mrs. Tanner........Marta Mitrovich
Reger........Douglas Kennedy
Martha........Claire Meade
Agnes........Frances Morris
Joan........Jane Harker

"The Unfaithful" gears its drama to a modern day social problem and comes through as potent screen material for top situations. Strong cast names of Ann Sheridan, Lew Ayres, Zachary Scott and others promise plenty of customer interest.

Backing drama is fine quality production by Jerry Wald and understanding direction by Vincent Sherman. Problem posed by well written script has to do with a married woman who, through unusual circumstance, cheats on her husband while he is overseas. The David Goodis - James Gunn screenplay makes a plea for understanding and forgiveness rather than divorce. Such dramatic content has been potently presented by the writers and the appeal to femmes is great.

Problem is brought to light a year later when the wife, returning to her home late at night, kills an attacker. Through slight flaws in her description of incident and police suspicion, it is gradually revealed the dead man was the one with whom she had an affair. High suspense and interest is developed by Sherman's direction in keeping characters and events entirely believable. He displays understanding that makes yarn increasingly engrossing as it unfolds through wife's trial for murder, separation from husband and eventual reconciliation.

Miss Sheridan clicks strongly as the wife, giving a performance that rings true and that will earn her most favorable mention. Scott also is very good as the husband, turning in a creditable job that boosts his stock. Ayres, family friend and attorney who brings the couple together again, lends his role a quiet assurance that is effective.

Among others in cast who register strongly are Eve Arden, Jerome Cowan, Steven Geray, Art Dealer, whose sly blackmailing helps build the drama; John Hoyt, believable detective, and Marta Mitrovich, wife of the death victim.

Accentuating mood is Ernest Haller's lensing and the music by Max Steiner. Art direction and settings are important production factors.

Brog.

The Long Night

Hollywood, May 27.

RKO release of Anatole Litvak, Robert and Raymond Hakim production, directed by Litvak. Stars Henry Fonda, Barbara Bel Geddes, Vincent Price, Ann Dvorak; features Howard Freeman, Moroni Olsen. Screenplay, John Wexley, based on story by Jacques Viet; camera, Sol Polito; editor, Robert Swink; music, Dimitri Tiomkin. Tradeshown May 26, '47. Running time, **97 MINS.**

Joe........Henry Fonda
Jo Ann........Barbara Bel Geddes
Maximilian........Vincent Price
Charlene........Ann Dvorak
Sheriff........Howard Freeman
Chief of Police........Moroni Olsen
Frank........Elisha Cook, Jr.
Janitor's Wife........Queenie Smith
Bill........David Clarke
Policeman........Charles McGraw
Peggy........Patty King
Freddie........Robert A. Davis

"Long Night" is a sullen brooding film about vet of World War II who goes on killing spree when his girl takes up with another guy. There's some good, challenging writing that indicts a society in which a guy can kill legally in war and get it in the neck if he does it in peace, but it's cinematic stuff that others may pounce on. Brilliant thesping jobs are turned in by Henry Fonda, Barbara Bel Geddes (making her film bow), Vincent Price and others, but despite the good cast, picture is too grim to achieve top b.o. results.

Film opens with bang-bang as Fonda shoots Price. Squad car arrives and crowd gathers as Fonda resolves to shoot it out with cops. Via flashbacks, Miss Bel Geddes' meeting with Price and subsequent tragic events are revealed. Price is a magician working in smalltown niteries with assistant Ann Dvorak, tough-as-nails gal with a heart of gold. He meets Miss Bel Geddes in an Ohio industrial town, breaks up her affair with Fonda, and she goes completely under his hypnotic influence. When Fonda tries to break it up Price claims it's strictly paternal. He tells lie after fantastic lie, until finally Fonda lets him have it.

Yarn moves from present to past and back cleverly, winding up where it started. As Fonda takes potshots at cops, Miss Bel Geddes braves gunfire and tear gas to talk him out of it. He surrenders on note that justice will eventually be done.

Fonda is never out of his depth in unusual—for him—role. While far from pretty, in the accepted Hollywood style, Miss Bel Geddes registers solidly as a potent film personality, fulfilling in every way the promise she gave in "Deep Are The Roots." Price is properly evil. Miss Dvorak, while a trifle too literate for the role of a gadabout showgirl, turns on some top histrionics and displays her elegant gams to good effect. Queenie Smith stands out in support as landlady.

Robert and Raymond Hakim-Anatole Litvak production has received a top direction job from Litvak. Mob scenes outside the apartment building are especially outstanding. Other credits rating high are Sol Polito's lensing, the magnificent scoring and conducting job by Dimitri Tiomkin, and Eugene Lourie's stark settings.

Mike.

Jewels of Brandenburg

20th-Fox release of Sol M. Wurtzel production. Stars Richard Travis; features Micheline Cheirel, Leonard Strong, Carol Thurston, Lewis Russell, Louis Mercier, Fernando Alvarado. Directed by Eugene Forde. Original screenplay, Irving Elman, Irving Cummings, Jr., Robert G. North; camera, Benjamin Kline; editor, William Claxton, Frank Baldridge. At Rialto, N. Y., week May 23, '47. Running time, **64 MINS.**

Johnny Vickers........Richard Travis
Claudette Grandet........Micheline Cheirel
Marcel Grandet........Leonard Strong
Carmelita Mendoza........Carol Thurston
Roger Hamilton........Lewis Russell
Pierre........Louis Mercier
Pablo........Fernando Alvarado
Miguel Solomon........Eugene Borden
Koslic........Ralf Harolde
Paul Rosholt........Otto Reichow
Frillman........Harro Meller

Producer Sol M. Wurtzel has reached for a worn formula in fashioning "Jewels of Brandenburg," an undisturbing who-stole meller. It's no gem in the hackle-raising department nor is it sufficiently high tempoed to keep the patrons edging forward. Nonetheless, there's enough verve and deftness in lines and acting to pick up most of the slack and make this film fair game for dual operations.

With Lisbon as locale, pic unreels the surprisingly unstrenuous efforts of a U. S. agent (Richard Travis) to recover the pile of purloined valuables which, at the war's fadeout, are in the mitts of Nazi mobsters. Posing as a jewel smuggler, Travis contacts the band and wangles his way into their confidence. After much to-do, he tracks down the hiding place of the jewels and recaptures the baubles. Pic ends in a burst of rod work that peps up an otherwise lagging development.

Travis detours the pitfalls of taking the yarn seriously. Obviously not playing for keeps, he skips through his part working more for the yocks than otherwise. Also plussing in the light touch is Carol Thurston who patly depicts a jealous senorita. Leonard Strong as the villainous, gun pumping Hitlerian gets enough menace into thin-lipped role to satisfy the action fans while Micheline Cheirel, as his wife, is svelte and sexacious.

Pic could be toned up by sharper pacing and added suspense buildup. On that score, directing is only fair to middling. Camera work also creaks in mediocrity.

Wit.

The Web

Hollywood, May 22.

Universal-International release of Jerry Bresler production. Stars Edmond O'Brien, Ella Raines, William Bendix, Vincent Price; features Maria Palmer, John Abbott, Fritz Lieber. Directed by Michael Gordon. Screenplay, William Bowers, Bertram Millhauser from story by Harry Kurnitz; camera, Irving Glassberg; editor, Russell Schoengarth; music, Hans J. Salter. Tradeshown May 20, 47. Running time, **87 MINS.**

Noel Faraday........Ella Raines
Bob Regan........Edmond O'Brien
Lieut. Danito........William Bendix
Andrew Colby........Vincent Price
Martha Kroner........Maria Palmer
Charles Murdock........John Abbott
Leopold Kroner........Fritz Leiber
James Nolan........Howard Chamberlain
Emilio Caneta........Tito Vuolo
District Attorney........Wilton Graff
Newspaper Librarian........Robin Raymond

There are no Freudian angles cluttering up "The Web's" melodrama. Picture presents a crook who kills because he wants money and power and not because of some psycho-quirk springing from a past incident. Film has a freshness in dialog and situations that project strong interest for audiences and will rate good boxoffice payoff all down the line.

Topnotch performances by majority of cast carry the melodramatics along in forthright style. The pace is tight and fast, accentuating intrigue and excitement. Standout is Edmond O'Brien as the hero who becomes enmeshed in Vincent Price's scheme to hold on to a stolen million dollars. He walks off with his assignment with a performance that will build his following. Another honor-garnerer is William Bendix as an honest cop whose lack of faith in things being as they appear is responsible for eventual downfall of Price. Latter gives a compelling reading to the role of a treacherous, suave big-business man. Ella Raines co-stars as heroine and secretary to Price who awakens romantic interest in O'Brien.

The sharp screenplay by William Bowers and Bertram Millhauser, based on a story by Harry Kurnitz, is loaded with clever dialog that sparks light feeling as antidote to heavier moments and accounts for freshness in plot development.

Plot deals with efforts of a young attorney and the police to trap Price into confession of two murders and theft of the million bucks. How it's done has plenty of punch and thrills to hold interest tight. As his first screen directing chore, former stage director Michael Gordon definitely establishes himself in films. It's an effective first try that gets the best from the suspense ingredients.

Firstrate supporting performances back up the principals. Maria Palmer, in a short bit, is very good. John Abbott, Fritz Leiber, Howland Chamberlin, Robin Raymond and others make short footage count. Production dress, marshalled by Jerry Bresler, is top showmanly mounting. Camera work and music score are effective suspense factors and film has been given smart art direction and set decorations to further quality flavor in physical values. Editing is good.

Brog.

Repeat Performance

Eagle-Lion release of Bryan Foy (Aubrey Schenck) production. Stars Joan Leslie, Louis Hayward, Richard Basehart; features Virginia Field, Tom Conway, Natalie Schafer, Benay Venuta. Directed by Alfred Werker. Screenplay, Walter Bullock, based on novel by William O'Farrell; camera, Lew W. O'Connell; editor, Louis H. Sackin; music, George Antheil. Reviewed N. Y., May 22, '47. Running time, **91 MINS.**

Barney Page........Louis Hayward
Sheila Page........Joan Leslie
William Williams........Richard Basehart
Paula Costello........Virginia Field
John Friday........Tom Conway
Eloise Shaw........Natalie Schafer
Bess Nichols........Benay Venuta
Mattie........Ilka Gruning

"Repeat Performance" represents Eagle-Lion's first stab at the bigtime via a top-budgeted production made on its home lot. That in itself would not rate it A playing time but the film has the proper ingredients to do good biz in most first-run situations. Novel story, a fantasy affair, is well-paced and well-acted and the names of Joan Leslie and Louis Hayward should help brighten the marquee. E-L has already teed off a boff ballyhoo campaign with its world preem last week in Zanesville, O., which will probably pay off.

"Performance" marks the first picture done by Miss Leslie since she ankled the Warners' lot after her lengthy litigation with that company. She gets a chance at a meaty, serious role and makes out okay in it, although a little more restraint would have helped erase the starry-eyed ingenue for which audiences have come to accept her. Film also marks the screen debut of Richard Basehart, whom E-L signed after he won the N. Y. Drama Critics' award for his Broadway performance in "Hasty Heart." He emerges in this as an intelligent thesper who should do well in films if given the right roles.

Story, scripted by Walter Bullock from a novel by William O'Farrell, leaves a few loose ends dangling at the final fadeout but nonetheless represents a neat treatment of a difficult assignment. On a New Year's Eve in 1947, Miss Leslie, a Broadway star, murders her alcoholic husband. On the way to seek advice from her friendly producer, she makes the wish that she could have the year to live over again so that she could make certain things worked out differently. Through some unexplained reason, her wish is granted and, when she reaches the producer's apartment, she discovers it's New Year's Eve in 1946.

Then, although she knows what will happen during the ensuing year, events prove that no human can meddle with fate. She tries to change the pattern of things that led up to the shooting but, though several events happen differently, comes New Year's Eve again and she's once more confronting her husband with a gun when he tries to kill her. Several shots ring out and he falls dead, but this time she finds it was an insane friend who'd just escaped from an asylum who shot from behind her. Moral to the tale, if there is one, is summed up in his words that destiny "doesn't care about the pattern as long as the result is the same."

Cast, for the most part, is competent under the guilding hand of director Alfred Werker. Louis Hayward tends a bit to over-emoting as the alcoholic husband but manages to convey the right mood to the part. Basehart shines as the friend who goes insane, although unfortunately the story doesn't clarify the reasons. Virginia Field, Tom Conway and Natalie Schafer carry out the supporting roles well. Musicomedy songstress Benay Venuta also makes her screen bow in "Performance" in a straight dramatic part and carries off her assignment capably.

Production credits are good, with the lush sets and costumes evidencing that producer Aubrey Schenck sunk a hefty bankroll into the film. *Stal.*

Winter Wonderland

Republic release of Walter Colmes-Henry Sokal production. Stars Lynne Roberts, Charles Drake; features Roman Bohnen, Eric Blore, Renee Godfrey. Directed by Bernard Vorhaus. Screenplay, Peter Goldbaum, David Chandler, Arthur Marx, Gertrude Purcell, based on idea by Fred Schiller; camera, John Alton; editor, Robert Jahns. Previewed N. Y., May 22, '47. Running time, **71 MINS.**

Nancy Wheeler	Lynne Roberts
Steve Kirk	Charles Drake
Timothy Wheeler	Roman Bohnen
Luddington	Eric Blore
Betty Wheeler	Mary Eleanor Donahue
Phyllis Simpson	Renee Godfrey
Marge	Janet Warren
Seth	Harry Tyler
Mrs. Schuyler-Riggs	Renie Riano
Telephone Operator	Diana Mumby
Bellboy	Alvin Hammer

There are no marquee names in "Winter Wonderland," but the title of this Repub pic should be a hot-weather lure in itself. Repub's skating star, Vera Ralston, who might be expected to be in it because of all that ice and snow, isn't. Femme lead is Lynne Roberts, who's very appealing, and with Charles Drake in the stellar bracket she helps create a charming variation of the Cinderella yarn for the lower part of the duals.

"Wonderland" is almost wholly outdoor stuff. But the dazzling white backgrounds are never permitted to get monotonous. When the farmer's daughter and the ski instructor from the big lodge aren't developing their romance, the lodge owner is putting on skating exhibitions and ski events.

A ski ballet is a distinct novelty, and a ski race, proceeds of which are hoped to get the heroine out of a jam, is pulse-quickening stuff. John Alton's camera work here is striking. Results are in the best manner of the chase.

Everyone in the pic is pleasant, including Eric Blore, as the lodge owner; Mary Eleanor Donahue, as the heroine's young sister, and Roman Bohnen, as her old man. There are no villians. Even in the big race it's the hero and heroine who compete with each other, and the windup of that is a clinch.

The Patient Vanishes
(BRITISH-MADE)

Film Classics release of Pathe Pictures, Ltd., production. Stars James Mason; features Margaret Vynor, Gordon McLeod, Mary Clare, Terry Conlin. Directed by Lawrence Huntington. Screenplay, David Hume from original by Hume. At Victoria, N. Y., week May 22, '47. Running time, **73 MINS.**

Mick Cardby	James Mason
The Matron	Mary Clare
Mollie Lennett	Margaret Vyner
Detective Inspector Cardby	Gordon McLeod
Doctor Moger	Frederick Valk
Mrs. Cardby	Barbara Everest
Lena Morne	Barbara James
Lord Morne	G. H. Mulcaster
Al Messon	Eric Clavering
Detective-Sergeant Trotter	Terry Conlin
Mr. Eslick	W. G. Fay
Doctor Crosbie	Brefni O'Rorke
Nurse	Viola Lyel
Sir Wallace Benson	Anthony Shaw

This picture predates the era of British know-how in filmaking. Turned out in 1943 as a vehicle for James Mason and stashed away unplayed during the war, it now finds its way to American screens as an unmuscular carbon of Hollywood's forte—the hard-hitting, tightly scripted mysto-actioner which depends on pace, tussles and plot twists. Its boxoffice pull rests on the extent that Mason's hold on Yankee customers can overcome the red ink of halting construction, unfamiliar accents and the punch that's signalled.

Rivalry of father and son—the elder a Yard inspector, his junior a private gumshoe—over homicide and kidnapping is put through the wringer. They're both shooting at the same target—to save the daughter of an English swell from the gang without coughing up the ransom. The son (Mason) gets there first, after gunplay, hard blows and false leads are bandied. In the curtain scene, he's rescued from the blot-out in a gas chamber by pater and confreres with honors divided. Amorous hijinks, strictly muted, are ladled out in dalliances between the sleuther and his secretary and chief aide (Margaret Vyner).

The customers' ear trumpets are going to strain a bit on this pic. For that old bugaboo that's tied a can to many past British imports—gabbing that's hard to decipher at times—hurts the opus in several spots. Lack of costuming glamor is noticeable. If there are curves on the cuties, they're the light under the bushel.

Mason, looking considerably younger than the current edition, is definitely likeable as the brash, fumbling detective despite a discernible clumsiness in portraying the role. In this earlier era, his lovemaking has the hearty, smacking quality of British roastbeef with none of the "Seventh Veil" meanness which caught on big. Miss Vyner, her allure lampened by potato-sack tailoring, acts out her secretarial and amatory stints brightly.

Gordon McLeod, handling the inspector-father role, muddies his lines with a heavy British timbre that's hard to catch. Other parts are satisfactorily dished out. *Wit.*

Bells of San Angelo
(SONGS; COLOR)

Republic release of Edward J. White production. Stars Roy Rogers; features Dale Evans, Andy Devine, Bob Nolan, Sons of the Pioneers. Directed by William Witney. Screenplay, Sloan Nibley, based on story by Paul Ganglin; camera, Jack Marta; editor, Les Orlebeck; songs, Jack Elliott, Tim Spencer. Previewed N. Y., May 21, '47. Running time, **71 MINS.**

Roy Rogers	Roy Rogers
Lee Madison	Dale Evans
Cookie	Andy Devine
Rex Gridley	John McGuire
Mr. Lionel Bates	Olaf Hytten
Gus Ulrich	David Sharpe
The Padre	Fritz Leiber
The Old Timer	Hank Patterson
The Cook	Fred S. Toones
Bus Driver	Eddie Acuff

Bob Nolan and Sons of the Pioneers

A touch of satire lifts "Bells of San Angelo" out of the formula western. But while that may appeal to the more discriminating filmgoer, the kids may not like it. Roy Rogers is made to appear less omniscient than usual, and that's a bit of tarnish on an idol. However, when this Republic hayburner keeps going that away it rides hard and furious, and with plenty of gunplay, fisticuffs and gore. If the kids overlook the satirical implications, they should take this one to their sadistic young hearts as avidly as they have most of the Rogers epics.

For once, neither Rogers nor Trigger, screen-credited as "the smartest horse in the movies," outwits the baddies. That's the contribution of the gal, blonde Dale Evans. She's a scribbler of cowboy novels whose creations are snickered at by Rogers, a Mex border investigator. But when Rogers and Miss Evans find themselves in the climactic tight spot, it's a reenactment of the big scene from her current book that gets them into the clear.

Leading up to that is the customary dirty work at a silver mine touching on the border, where John McGuire is up to mischief with the aid of David Sharpe. Midway through Rogers' expose he takes a monumental shellacking from McGuire, Sharpe, et al., and, with the aid of the pic's Trucolor tinting, the gore literally runs red. The kids will especially like that.

Andy Devine and Olaf Hytten are in for some agreeable comic relief, former as a sheriff with a mysterious past, and Hytten as an Englishman come all the way from London for, among other things, a fox hunt.

Songs are pleasant, Rogers offering up "Cowboy's Dream of Heaven," and the femme lead delivering "I Love the West." Sons of the Pioneers do some thesping in addition to their melodic aid. Direction and camera adequate.

Nuremberg Trials
(Documentary)
(RUSSIAN-MADE)

Artkino release of Central Documentary Film Studios production. Directed by C. Svilov. Original narration, B. Gorbatova; cameramen, Roman Karmen, B. Makaseyev, S. Semyonov, V. Shtatiand; score, A. Grana; editor, A. Vinogradov. At Stanley, N. Y., week May 24, '47. Running time, 58 MINS.

"Nuremberg Trials" is a grim if slightly disjointed Soviet newsreel—documentary version of the trial of top Nazi war criminals. U. S. exhibitors long have contended that documentaries must be topflight if able to serve as regular screen fare. This hardly measures up to this classification. Furthermore, this one gives the Russians too much credit for winning the war.

Principally it's not the fault of the producers but rather the tough subject they were handling. Earlier newsreel and special Russian-made subjects on this trial indicated just how tough it was going to be making the Nuremberg Trial into any sort of documentary feature. Obviously, even the most skilled photography, which this has, showing closeups of the Nazi war leaders being tried for their countless wartime misdeeds, needed plenty of flash-backs to make the story jell. Soviet filmmakers have filled this picture with numerous cut-ins on old newsreel clips, including some seized German newsreel material. There are battle scenes, episodes showing the hideous concentration camps and mass slaughter, etc.

Here, when an individual is put on trial, three are earlier shots of the person when he was strutting around as an arrogant conqueror, as a jubilant victor or exhorting the misguided German people to further stinting. Then the camera returns to the courtroom and actual, tedious recital of testimony and introduction of documents. It appears that the documentary boys were overwhelmed with the stupendous task and import of the trial, and forgot about some of their earlier and better efforts with such type of screen vehicle. Constant switching from one scene to another calls for acumen of skill to grip an audience. And, unfortunately, such skill is largely lacking in this film.

Fact that the British-accent narrator tends to become tiresome also is no help. In a few passages, the strictly Soviet side of the trial and the war, is given. For example, in trying to explain how the Nazis finally were brought to terms, the narrator says "the Red Army struck and struck again until victory came." In another passage, laurels are tossed to Tito's warriors. *Wear.*

Thunder in Hills
(CZECHOSLOVAKIAN-MADE)

General Film release of O. Sedlacek production. Directed by Vaclav Kubasek. Screenplay, Joseph Mach, from original by Frantisek Gotz; camera, J. Strecka, J. Holpuch. At Squire, N. Y., week May 23, '47. Running time, **82 MINS.**

Tailor	J. Prucha
Tereza	M. Vasova
Informer	V. Repa
Jelena	Eva Klenova
Flier	H. Homola

(In Czechoslovakian; English Titles)

Initial Czechoslovakian resistance picture to be released in U. S., this measures high in dramatic appeal and superb performances. Even though a war picture, and possibly the last in a long line of screen yarns about the underground movement, "Thunder in Hills" looks a strong entry for arty and foreign language theatres. Selling job should build word-of-mouth.

Starts out like a routine yarn about the usual brutal occupation Nazie forces with a Czech-Moravian village under the heel of this ruthless conqueror. Spotlights activities of partisans in blowing up a vital bridge and then closeups on daring British aviator who's shot down during a single-handed attack. From there on it's an untiring search by the Nazis to corner the enemy airman and an equally daring resistance by the villagers to giving the man up.

Plot brings in a conventional love story between the aviator and the village tailor's daughter. The tailor and his pretty offspring hide the aviator, and by accident the former is suspected of being friendly with the Nazis because his false tip turns out true. There is much to-do about spies and counter-espionage, but story winds up with the tailor, falsely suspected of being a traitor, fully exonerated and forgiven on his deathbed.

Picture builds to a realistic, battle climax between the German troops and partisan-village forces. Vaclav Kubasek turns in a crack job of direction from Joseph Mach's nicely-paced screenplay. Camera work of J. Strecka and J. Holpuch is surprisingly good, particularly in closeups. Cast is excellent, with acting laurels so well split among leads that there's no standout. *Wear.*

Palestine
(BRITISH-MADE)

Eagle-Lion release of J. Arthur Rank's first "This Modern Age" series. Producer, Sergei Nolbandov; editor, George Ivan Smith; music, Muir Mathieson, London Symphony Orchestra. Tradeshown May 23, '47. Running time, **21 MINS.**

This is the first release in Canada of a monthly series of factual films on the style of "March of Time" but which will deal with British Empire contemporary themes. "Palestine" could not be more timely and is also scheduled for U. S. release.

Designed for global showing, "Palestine" pulls no punches but is objectively impartial in its narration. The two-reeler has a terrific dramatic impact and should make money for exhibitors on auxiliary advertising in the current headlines. It relates the story of the country from its days of Turkish rule, the building of the Suez Canal, the adjacent oil discoveries which made the area coveted by the great powers, the way in which the Jewish people have made the desert bloom with their communal settlements, their schools and universities.

"Palestine" points out that the Jews joined the Allies in the last war while the Arabs remained indifferent and that the Mufti escaped to Germany to stab Britain in the back.

One of the most dramatic sequences in "Palestine" includes captured German newsreel clips showing the Mufti fraternizing with the Nazi bigshots and inspecting Nazi troops.

The two-reeler then jumps into the present period of revolt and terrorism; the King David Hotel explosion where 91 were killed; the house-to-house searchings and curfews; the claim that terrorism is not only a threat to the Empire but to Zionism; the admission that Britain alone cannot supply the solution. While the film is intentionally impartial, the sympathy still seems to lie with the Jewish people.

No screen credits are given the cameramen or narrator but the literary editor is George Ivan Smith, formerly with the Australian Broadcasting Commission and then with the British Broadcasting Corp. until he joined the J. Arthur Rank organization when the war ended. Moscow-born Sergie Nolbandov, producer, was formerly in charge of production at Warner studios in Teddington, England. *McStay.*

Miniature Reviews

"**The Bachelor and the Bobby-Soxer**" (RKO). Bright farce comedy with hefty b.o. prospects.

"**Living in a Big Way**" (One Song) (M-G). Gene Kelly, Marie McDonald in entertaining comedy; strong b.o.

"**Possessed**" (WB). Joan Crawford and Van Heflin in solid psycho-meller for top b.o. results.

"**Under the Tonto Rim**" (RKO). Good western based on Zane Gray novel, for supporting situations.

"**Seven Keys to Baldpate**" (RKO). Standard comedy-mystery remake of venerable story and play, okay for dual bills.

"**That's My Gal**" (Songs-Color) (Rep). Weak filmusical slated for dualers.

"**Dear Murderer**" (GFD). British-made so stagey and gloomy that looks only okay as support to U.S. dualers.

"**Bush Christmas**" (GFD). J. Arthur Rank's first children's feature film, made in Australia; dubious appeal in U.S.

"**Hollywood Barn Dance**" (Musical) (SG). Rural comedy, loaded with 18 hillbilly tunes, okay for corn belt areas.

"**Killer at Large**" (PRC). Formula thriller, with the vet housing situation as a side-issue; for supporting situations.

"**Too Many Winners**" (PRC). Good supporting product projecting further screen adventures of Michael Shayne.

"**The King's Jester**" (Superfilm). Standout Italian melodrama based on "Rigoletto"; surefire for sureseaters.

The Bachelor and the Bobby-Soxer

Hollywood, June 3.
RKO release of Dore Schary production. Stars Cary Grant, Myrna Loy, Shirley Temple; features Rudy Vallee, Ray Collins, Harry Davenport, Johnny Sands. Directed by Irving Reis. Original story and screenplay, Sidney Sheldon; camera, Robert de Grasse, Nicholas Musuraca; music, Leigh Harline; editor, Frederic Knudtson. Tradeshown June 2, '47. Running time, 94 MINS.

Dick	Cary Grant
Margaret	Myrna Loy
Susan	Shirley Temple
Tommy	Rudy Vallee
Beemish	Ray Collins
Thaddeus	Harry Davenport
Jerry	Johnny Sands
Tony	Don Beddoe
Bessie	Lillian Randolph
Agnes Prescott	Veda Ann Borg
Walters	Dan Tobin
Judge Treadwell	Ransom Sherman
Winters	William Bakewell
Melvin	Irving Bacon
Perry	Ian Bernard
Florence	Carol Hughes
Anthony Herman	William Hall
Maitre d'Hotel	Gregory Gay

"The Bachelor and the Bobby-Soxer" is broad farce slated for strong reception as summer film fare. It will brighten hot weather boxoffices in all situations. Fun is slickly projected to keep entertainment light and fast, and cast troupes it to the hilt. Names of Cary Grant, Myrna Loy and Shirley Temple are sturdy lures and other values are equally strong.

Comedy aims are firmly backed by Dore Schary's production and the broad directorial treatment by Irving Reis. Punchy dialog and situations grab sock laughs and it's all done with deft timing that further glosses farce mood.

Solid script by Sidney Sheldon poses a plot easily adapted to fluffy situations. Tossed together are a lady judge, a playboy artist and an impressionable teen-ager. Grant, the artist, has already had a brush with the judge. Myrna Loy, so when the judge's kid sister, Shirley Temple, is found in the artist's apartment late at night, he's in plenty of trouble. Court psychiatrist proposes that, rather than make Grant a martyr in Miss Temple's eyes, he be assigned to escort her around until she gets over her crush.

Chuckles get heartier and heartier as adult Grant plays at being a juvenile at basketball games, school picnics, etc. It's done with slapstick touch that pays off. Romance switch with Miss Loy going for Grant and winning him in the finale is an obvious development but well done.

Starring trio wrap up assignments in firstrate fashion, pleasing mightily. Not to be discounted for comedy playing is Rudy Vallee as an assistant d.a. who has his romantic eye on the judge also. Ray Collins (as the psychiatrist), Harry Davenport, Johnny Sands, Miss Temple's juve boy friend, Don Beddoe, Lillian Randolph, Veda Ann Borg and others hold up their end of the fun capably.

Production dress is strong. Lensing by Robert de Grasse and Nicholas Musuraca, art direction and set decorations, editing, background music and other factors lend able backing. *Brog.*

Living in a Big Way

(ONE SONG)

Metro release of Pandro S. Berman production. Stars Gene Kelly, Marie McDonald; features Charles Winninger, Phyllis Thaxter, Spring Byington. Directed by Gregory LaCava. Screenplay, LaCava and Irving Ravetch, based on original by LaCava; editor, Ferris Webster; camera, Harold Rosson; dances, Kelly and Stanley Donen; song, "Fido and Me," by Louis Alter and Edward Heyman. Previewed N. Y., May 27, '47. Running time, 102 MINS.

Leo Gogarty	Gene Kelly
Margaud Morgan	Marie McDonald
D. Rutherford Morgan	Charles Winninger
Peggy Randall	Phyllis Thaxter
Mrs. Morgan	Spring Byington
Abigail Morgan	Jean Adair
Everett Hanover Smythe	Clinton Sundberg
Stuart	John Warburton
Schultz	William Phillips

"Living in a Big Way" represents more than anything else an attempt by Metro to reintroduce Gene Kelly to audiences after his absence in the Navy and, as such, it succeeds. Uninspired story serves chiefly as a peg on which Kelly can hang his inspired dance routines, demonstrate his affable acting and generally enjoy a tour de force such as is seldom given an actor. He gets nice support from Marie McDonald, Charles Winninger, Phyllis Thaxter and the rest of the cast but the picture is all his. It should do okay in most first-run situations.

Navy service apparently kept Kelly in good trim because he has never danced better. He does three outstanding numbers, staged by himself and Stanley Donen, best of which is one he terps with a live dog as partner to an original song, "Fido and Me." He demonstrates neat agility and tumbling technique in another routine in which he plays hopscotch with a bunch of moppets and then hops across the rafters of an unfinished house with the greatest of ease. Other number is a nifty bit of ballroomology, marked by the fact that Miss McDonald keeps up with Kelly's stepping all the way.

Screenplay by Gregory LaCava and Irving Ravetch, based on an original story by LaCava, is entertaining enough but most of it's been told before. Kelly is seen as an Army flier who marries Miss McDonald, an unassuming young miss, just a few hours before he heads overseas. He returns after his discharge to his unkissed bride but finds that her father coined a mint during the war and she's now a society belle who's interested only in divorcing him with the least amount of publicity. Rest of the tale revolves around his romancing his wife for inevitable success. Intermingled with the romance is a sub-theme based on the vets' housing shortage, in which Miss McDonald's now-wealthy family back Kelly's Army pals in building a new project.

In addition to his dancing, Kelly shines in his thesping chores, demonstrating a genial flair for comedy. Miss McDonald, whose acting improves with each picture, does okay as the gal, ably abetted by her pinup figure. Winninger and Spring Byington add to the fun as her nouveau-riche parents, and Phyllis Thaxter, as the widow of one of Kelly's Army buddies, contributes a neat touch of pathos. Clinton Sundberg turns in an outstanding bit as the family's outspoken butler, and Jean Adair is good as Miss McDonald's understanding grandmother. William Phillips also does a nice job as Kelly's sidekick.

La Cava handles the cast with a light touch for the best comedy results and the film is given adequate mountings by producer Pandro S. Berman. "Fido" song by Louis Alter and Edward Heyman hasn't much commercial potentiality but serves as a neat showtune for Kelly's terping. Camera work, under the supervision of Harold Rosson, is standout. *Stal.*

Possessed

Warner Bros. release of Jerry Wald production. Stars Joan Crawford, Van Heflin; features Raymond Massey. Directed by Curtis Bernhardt. Screenplay by Silvia Richards and Ranald MacDougall, based on story by Rita Welman; camera, Jos. Valentine; editor, Rudi Fehr. Tradeshown N. Y., May 22, 47. Running time, 108 MINS.

Louise Howell	Joan Crawford
David Sutton	Van Heflin
Dean Graham	Raymond Massey
Carol Graham	Geraldine Brooks
Dr. H. Willard	Stanley Ridges
Harker	John Ridgely
Dr. Ames	Moroni Olsen
Pauline Graham	Nana Bryant
Dr. M. Sherman	Erskine Sanford
Wynn Graham	Gerald Perreau
Elsie	Lisa Golm
Dr. Craig	Don McGuire
Jury Foreman	Douglas Kennedy
Norris	Monte Blue
Coroner	Griff Barnett

Jerry Wald, taking his licks at the psycho film cycle, has turned out a solid boxoffice item for Warners in "Possessed." Film could coast into the blue solely on the marquee lustre supplied by Joan Crawford, Van Heflin and Raymond Massey. But the basic wicket-power is oiled by a gripping screenplay that's been translated into celluloid with unusual frankness. It's a superlatively accoutred production but the story it tells of a woman disintegrating into extreme insanity is not pretty.

Miss Crawford, who's been tackling a series of difficult roles in her recent pictures, cops all thesping honors in this production with a virtuoso performance as a frustrated woman ridden into madness by a guilt-obsessed mind. Actress has matured into a self-assurance that permits her to completely dominate the screen even vis-a-vis such accomplished players as Heflin and Massey. During several sequences in which Miss Crawford teeters precariously on the outer edge of sanity, she projects with an intensity that's unpleasant and fascinating at the same time.

Heflin's part of a footloose engineer who romances his ladies with one eye on the railroad schedule is not drawn with equal sharpness. By sheer power of personal wit, however, Heflin infuses his role with charm and degree of credibility despite a lack of clear motivation for his behavior. Massey, as the unlucky husband of two mad women, is solemn, strong and dignified, his thesping in this case being marked by more polish than emotional power.

Despite its overall superiority, "Possessed" is somewhat marred by an ambiguous approach in Curtis Bernhardt's direction. Film vacillates between being a cold clinical analysis of a mental crackup and a highly surcharged melodramatic vehicle for Miss Crawford's histrionics. As pure psychiatry, film achieves a strong quality of directness up to the point where the melodramatic flourishes negate its scientific accuracy. As melodrama, the clinical approach interferes with the steady forward progression of the plot mechanism and makes the film lose that mounting line of tension.

Unfolding via flashback technique, film opens with a terrific bang as the camera picks up Miss Crawford wandering haggard and dazed through Los Angeles until she collapses. In the psychiatric ward of the local hospital, under narco-hypnosis, she relives the series of personal blows that ultimately reduced her to schizophrenia. Desperately in love with Heflin, who brushed her off, she married Massey whose first wife committed suicide. Already slightly unbalanced by Heflin's coldness, she becomes deluded with the idea that she murdered Massey's first wife. Her grip on reality becomes completely lost when she discovers that Heflin is set on marrying Massey's daughter and, after unsuccessfully trying to poison that relationship, she kills Heflin and flees to L. A. where the picture opens.

Geraldine Brooks, screen newcomer who tops the supporting cast as Massey's daughter, shows big promise on her small part with a combination of striking looks and controlled thesping talent. Rest of the players are all firstrate. *Herm.*

Under the Tonto Rim

RKO release of Herman Schlom production. Stars Tim Holt; features Nan Leslie, Richard Martin. Directed by Lew Landers. Screenplay, Norman Houston, based on novel by Zane Grey; camera, J. Roy Hunt; score, Paul Sawtell; editor, Lyle Boyer. Reviewed N. Y., June 3, '47. Running time, **61 MINS.**

Brad....Tim Holt
Lucy....Nan Leslie
Chito....Richard Martin
Dennison....Richard Powers
Juanita....Carol Forman
Patton....Tony Barrett
Sheriff....Harry Harvey
Capt. McLean....Jason Robards
Hooker....Robert Clarke
Andy....Jay Norris
Joe....Lex Barker
Curly....Steve Savage

The plus values in "Under the Tonto Rim" are contained in a good grade of production and exploitation values contained in Zane Grey's name upon which the film is based. Actionwise, "Tonto" meets the requirements of the western trade more than adequately. Pacing is fast, and picture contains a sufficient amount of gunplay. In addition, yarn is capable of maintaining interest.

Name value is contained in Tim Holt, cast as the owner of a stagecoach line which is victimized by a gang holdup in which his bosom buddy is killed. He consequently tracks down the gang, through fairly ingenious methods. First, he gets himself jailed with a member of the gang as a prison mate and escapes so that his fellow prisoner takes him to the gang hideout. Conclusion of the story is obvious after that.

The cast gives standard performances with Holt sufficiently impressive as hero of the piece. Nan Leslie is picturesque in a slight role in which she provides love interest and Richard Martin provides comedy relief. The baddies, Tony Barrett and Richard Powers, give routine characterizations.

Far above average for westerns is the photography by J. Roy Hunt. The long-range desert shots sometimes give an arty air to the proceedings, but never slow up the action. Lew Landers' direction allows little time for letup and Norman Houston's screenplay contains a minimum of cliches. *Jose.*

Seven Keys to Baldpate

Hollywood, June 3.

RKO release of Herman Schlom production. Features Phillip Terry, Jacqueline White, Eduardo Ciarnelli, Margaret Lindsay, Arthur Shields, Jimmy Conlin. Directed by Lew Landers. Screenplay, Lee Loeb; from novel by Earl Derr Biggers and the dramatization by George M. Cohan; camera, Jack MacKenzie; editor, J. R. Whittredge. Tradeshown June 3, '47. Running time, **68 MINS.**

Magee....Phillip Terry
Mary....Jacqueline White
Cargan....Eduardo Ciannelli
Connie Lane....Margaret Lindsay
Bolton....Arthur Shields
Hermit....Jimmy Conlin
Max....Tony Barrett
Bland....Richard Powers
Hayden....Jason Robards

"Seven Keys to Baldpate" is back for its fifth screen version and the third remake of venerable stage piece by RKO. This one shapes up only as supporting comedy-mystery, plot having lost much of its thrill over the years. Production and direction don't give it much freshness or zip to overcome age.

Phillip Terry and Jacqueline White head cast. Terry is only adequate as the mystery writer who seeks out-of-season Baldpate Inn to knock off another chiller in 24 hours to win a bet. Miss White appears to slightly better advantage as the secretary of the inn's owner, who has made the bet with Terry and is trying to frighten him off. Standard sliding panels, dead bodies, black cats and mysterious characters clutter up the scene without generating too much suspense or excitement.

Gang of jewel thieves, which has unaccountably sought the old inn as payoff place, furnish menace for piece. Eduardo Ciannelli heads the gang, with Margaret Lindsay, Tony Barrett, Richard Powers and Jason Robards as the other crooks. Arthur Shields is the undercover insurance detective who adds some mystery to proceedings and Jimmy Conlin is the addle-pated hermit who sticks his nose into the skullduggery.

Lew Landers' direction puts plot and cast through standard paces and Herman Schlom's production guidance is average for release intentions, as are other production credits. *Brog.*

That's My Gal
(SONGS—COLOR)

Republic release of Armand Schaefer production. Stars Lynne Roberts, Donald Barry; features Frank Jenks, Pinky Lee, Edward Gargan. Directed by George Blair. Screenplay, Joseph Hoffman; original story, Frances Hyland, Bernard Feins; songs, Jack Elliott; camera (Trucolor), Bud Thackery; editor, Arthur Roberts. Tradeshown, N. Y., May 28, '47. Running time, **66 MINS.**

Natalie Adams....Lynne Roberts
Benny Novak....Donald Barry
Harry Coleman....Pinky Lee
Louie Koblentz....Frank Jenks
Mike....Edward Gargan
Helen McBride....Judy Clark
Governor Thompson....Paul Stanton
Assemblyman McBride....John Hamilton
Danny Malone....Ray Walker
Pepper....Marian Martin
Joshua Perkins....Elmer Jerome
Judge....George Carleton

Jan Savitt and His Top Hatters
Isabelita
Guadalajara Trio
Four Step Bros.
St. Clair & Vilova
Dolores & Don Graham

"That's My Gal" is a lowercase filmusical that'll serve its intended purpose as program filler in nabe situations. Conventional plot centers around backstage antics of a shady crew of legit producers. Slight relief is supplied by a series of vaudeville acts sporadically thrown to the camera fore. Overall production values are on the modest side, but the Trucolor process stains the celluloid haphazardly.

Frail story concerns a group of big-town operators who swindle some goggle-eyed angels into over-investing in a burleycue show. Idea was to put on a cheap turkey with a quick fold and clean getaway for the producers. But after one of the suckers dies, the estate executor steps in to build the show into a smash hit. Some absurd political angles and romantic mooning between gal executor and the No. 1 easy-money guy fail to make the film percolate.

In lead roles, Lynne Roberts and Donald Barry give weak performances. Pinky Lee and Frank Jenks register better in secondary parts, doing their best with limp lines. Among specialty acts, the Four Step Bros. are most impressive with a snappy acrobatic dance routine. Jan Savitt's orch, Guadalajara Trio, Judy Clark and other acts are on briefly and do okay. Musical score has nothing to recommend. *Herm.*

Dear Murderer
(BRITISH-MADE)

London, May 29.

General Film Distributors' release of Gainsborough production. Stars Eric Portman, Greta Gynt; features Dennis Price, Jack Warner, Maxwell Reed. Directed by Arthur Crabtree. Screenplay, Muriel and Sydney Box, Peter Rogers from play by St. John Legh Clowes. Camera, Stephen Dade. At Marble Arch Odeon, London. Running time, **94 MINS.**

Lee Warren....Eric Portman
Vivien Warren....Greta Gynt
Richard Fenton....Dennis Price
Jimmy Martin....Maxwell Reed
Inspector Pembury....Jack Warner
Avis Fenton....Hazel Court
Sergeant Fox....Andrew Crawford
Rita....Jane Hylton
Prison Warder....Charles Rolfe
American Secretary....Judith Carol
Warren's Secretary....Valerie Ward

First of Betty Box's films under her new contract as producer, this adaptation of a popular stage drama should earn its cost in this country. Story has a novel angle, but is always plausible. It is played with conviction by a good all-round cast. American audiences may find it too stagey and too gloomy. Nor has it enough emotional momentum to make it universally acceptable. It may do as supporting fare in U. S.

Neither a whodunit nor a psychological study, picture tells a straight story of revenge and planning of a perfect crime. But the adaptors appear to have been obsessed by the limitation of the original stage play. For much of the film, duolog follows duolog, and the economy in lighting is very apparent.

With popular comic Jack Warner as a Scotland Yard detective, there should have been scope for some legitimate comedy. But he raises no laughs. To prove that he can play a straight part is a waste of good character comedian. Trouble taken in garbing and photographing Greta Gynt is well rewarded and shows how best use can be made of this promising actress. Eric Portman is again cast in a role with which he is becoming too closely associated. But he plays it well. It would be unfair to judge Maxwell Reed on his acting in this. Newcomer to stardom, he exhibits the necessary physical qualifications, but is cast as such a dull, unemotional lover that one wonders why Greta Gynt fell in love with him.

Yarn tells how a successful business man hurries home from America on suspicion that his wife has been unfaithful. Finding evidence in his apartment that a lawyer is one of her lovers, he calls on him and makes a so-called sporting offer. Husband has decided to murder him and has planned the perfect crime so as to look like a suicide. If the victim can find a loophole, the husband will let him go scot free. But the lawyer can see no way in which the murderer will incriminate himself and so pays the penalty.

Having committed the murder, the man discovers that his wife has a new lover, and he fakes the evidence so that everything points to this one as the guilty man. To complete his revenge, husband reveals to his wife that he is the murderer, and gloats over the arrest of her boy friend. But, deadlier than the male, the wife spins a cunning web around her husband, and ends up by poisoning him. Last shot sees her leaving with the police. *Cane.*

Bush Christmas
(AUSTRALIAN-MADE)

London, May 27.

General Film Distributors' release of Gaumont-British Children's Entertainment Film production. Stars Chips Rafferty, John Fernside. Directed by Ralph Smart. Camera, George Heath. At Gaumont-British theatre. Running time, **80 MINS.**

Long Bill....Chips Rafferty
Jim....John Fernside
Blue....Stan Tolhurst
Father....Pat Penny
Mother....Thelma Grigg
Old Jack....Clyde Combo
Narrator....John McCallum
Helen....Helen Grieve
Snow....Nicky Yardley
John....Morris Unicomb
Michael....Michael Yardley
Neza....Neza Saunders

Made in Australia under the direction of J. Arthur Rank's Children's Film Production Dept. this is the first feature film specifically produced for Rank's Children's Cinema Club. Shot in Blue Mountains of New South Wales, it has an all-Australian staff and cast. Ralph Smart, who was associate-producer on "The Overlanders," and George Heath, vet film cameraman in Australia, helped put over the picture. This may interest some U. S. exhibs who go in strongly for kid matinees but the accent likely will be a slight handicap.

"Bush Christmas" may attract the attention of Hollywood producers. There is nothing childish about this western, which should get real support from all those groups clamoring for better and more suitable films for juveniles.

Story is about a family of Australian children who, riding home from school for Christmas holiday, inadvertently give horse thieves information about their father's prize horses. The horses are stolen and the children track the thieves through the wild mountain country. Climax comes in a gold mining ghost town where the youngsters catch up with the robbers. Kids finally are rescued by the police.

There's no playing down to children in any way. Nor is instruction rammed down their throats. Every custom and every authentic touch is introduced in a natural manner. Tolerance is certainly one of the lessons taught here.

Acting of the professionals is first-rate, and that of the children natural. Film's success in England is a foregone conclusion. *Cane.*

Hollywood Barn Dance
(MUSICAL)

Hollywood, June 3.

Screen Guild release of Jack Schwarz production. Features Ernest Tubb, Lori Talbott, Helen Boyce, Earle Hodgins, Frank McGlynn, Phil Arnold, Red Herron, Pat Combs, Jack Guthrie. Directed by B. B. Ray. Adaptation and screenplay, Dorothea Knox Martin; original, Ray; camera, Jack Greenhalgh; music, Walter Greene; songs, Ernest Tubb, Zeb Turner, Henry Stewart, T. Texas Tyler, Sam Neuman & Michael Breen, Jimmie and Leon Short, Willis Bros., Al Clauser & Tex Hoepner, Bob Nolan, Johnnie Tyler, Helen Boice; editor, Robert Crandell. Previewed May 27, '47. Running time, **73 MINS.**

Ernie....Ernest Tubb
Helen....Lori Talbott
Ezzy....Helen Boyce
Cartwright....Earle Hodgins
Pa Tubb....Frank McGlynn
Toppitt....Phil Arnold
Pete Dixon....Larry Reed
Jack....Red Herron
Ma Tubb....Anne Kundi
Ma Perkins....Betty Mudge
Theatre Manager....Cy Ring
Hotel Clerk....Frank Bristow
Croupier....Albin Robeling
Roper....Dotti Hackett
Philharmonic Trio....Philharmonic Trio
Ernie (boy)....Pat Combs
Specialty Act....Jack Guthrie

Only resemblance "Hollywood Barn Dance" bears to the radio show is the title and generous load of prairie ballads. Strictly for the swing-yure-partner trade. The 18 tunes guarantee the square-dance fans plenty of listening in 73 minutes running time. Best asset is the music, which is good hillbilly, well done by Ernest Tubb and other professional exponents of guitar-gaited cleffing. Music offerings leave little room for story or other budget expenditure but those who go for this type entertainment will be more than satisfied.

Tubb has six of his solo compositions in the score, as well as a number of tunes written with others. Best display is given "Walking the Floor Over You" and "You Nearly Lose Your Mind." While all numbers will please, others showing up well include "Oakie Boogie," sung by Jack Guthrie; "Old Indians Never Die," by Jimmie and Leon Short; "Two Wrongs Don't Make a Right," "If It's a Dream" and "Only Teasing Me."

Only acting in the cast is delivered by Earle Hodgins, ham actor who takes the Ernest Tubb troupe under his managerial wing when the boys leave home to seek fame and fortune. Otherwise cast is strictly amateur excepting when vocalizing or guitar strumming. Dorothea Knox Martin scripted from an original by B. B. Ray who directed adequately enough. Plot has Tubb and his pals leaving farm settlement to earn money to replace village church which they had accidentally burned while practicing their tunes. It's a cross-country saga to Hollywood and fame with a return as heroes to the village.

Lori Talbott carries femme lead as canary with group. Helen Boyce injects some doubtful comedy. Frank McGlynn and Anne Kundi portray Tubb's parents and Pat Combs does the hillbilly artist as a lad. The Jack Schwarz production values are acceptable for market aims, as are lensing and other credits. *Brog.*

Killer at Large

PRC release of Buck Gottlieb production. Features Robert Lowery, Anabel Shaw. Directed by William Beaudine. Screenplay, Fenton Earnshaw, Tom Blackburn; camera, James Brown; editor, Harry Reynolds; music, Alvin Levin. Reviewed N. Y., May 29, '47. Running time, **61 MINS.**

Paul Kimberly............Robert Lowery
Anne Arnold..................Anabel Shaw
Vincent Arnold..............Charles Evans
Edward Denton............Frank Ferguson
Rand.........................George Lynn
Bull Callahan......................Dick Rich
Margo.........................Ann Stanton
Brent Maddux..............Leonard Penn
Clerk..........................Eddie Parks
Captain McManus.........Stanley Blystone
Whiteman................Howard Mitchell
Brandon.....................Jack Cheatham
Miss Riley.....................Hazel Kerner
Hatcheck Girl........Hildegard Ackerman
Bartender......................Charles King
Croupier...................Brooks Benedict
Taxi Driver......................Phil Arnold

The vet housing status could easily rate a thorough going-over in films, but not along the lines of "Killer at Large." PRC has turned this situation into a little better than routine meller in which a crusading newspaper reporter tracks down the head of a ring preying upon the GI need of shelter.

Just how the top man does the preying or how he gets his end of the loot isn't made clear exactly. It's just known that he's an evil force, has hirelings bump off recalcitrants in wholesale manner and causes the suicide of a housing administrator.

Newspaperman Robert Lowery then gets on the story and ultimately tracks down the top man. Other complications enter the yarn, such as the ring-chief, owner of the major stock in the newspaper, getting his daughter a job on that sheet. It's expected that Lowery falls for the gal which makes it all the more difficult to get to the topper. It's worked out by the end of the film.

Lowery as the reporter and Anabel Shaw as the love interest do perfunctory jobs. Charles Evans as the big shot and Leonard Penn assume the other major roles in satisfactory manner. Other aspects of the pic are okay with William Beaudine's direction setting a fast pace. The Fenton Earnshaw and Tom Blackburn story and dialog follow a conventional pattern. *Jose.*

Too Many Winners

Hollywood, June 3.

PRC release of John Sutherland production. Features Hugh Beaumont, Trudy Marshall, Ralph Dunn, Claire Carleton, Charles Mitchell, John Hamilton, Grandon Rhodes, Ben Welden. Directed by William Beaudine. Screenplay, John Sutherland; adaptation, Fred Myton, Scott Darling; based on original characters and story by Brett Halliday; camera, Jack Greenhalgh; editor, Harry Reynolds. Previewed at Hollywood, May 27, '47. Running time, **60 MINS.**

Michael Shayne............Hugh Beaumont
Phyllis Hamilton............Trudy Marshall
Rafferty..........................Ralph Dunn
Mayme Martin..............Claire Carleton
Tim Rourke.................Charles Mitchell
Payson.......................John Hamilton
Hardeman..................Grandon Rhodes
Madden..........................Ben Welden
Edwards........................Byron Foulger
Mrs. Edwards...................Jean Andren
Clarence....................George Meader
Joe..............................Frank Hagney
Punk.....................Maurice B. Mozelle

"Too Many Winners" carries on the screen adventures of Michael Shayne, detective, in okay style for supporting bookings. PRC series is aided measurably by excellent work and personality of Hugh Beaumont as the private eye whose heroics keep things moving. Latest entry has good production dress for budget and should be readily acceptable in its market.

This time crime threatens to halt duck-hunting vacation planned by Beaumont and his secretary, looker Trudy Marshall. He has to turn in a quick job of solving mystery of how winning pari-mutuel tickets are being counterfeited. John Sutherland script has the detective punched around plenty and a number of murders tossed in for extra measure to provide thrills while private eye is unraveling case. It doesn't take him long to spot the culprit as the race-track manager and case is closed with chief suspects and main heavy all bumped off.

William Beaudine's direction of the Sutherland production spots plenty of action for whodunit flavor. Ralph Dunn is the blustering cop. Claire Carleton adds some s.a. Charles Mitchell does bad job of Shayne's newspaper friend. John Hamilton, Grandon Rhodes, Ben Welden, Byron Fougler and others in cast deliver acceptably. Lensing, editing and other production factors are standard. *Brog.*

The King's Jester
(ITALIAN-MADE)

Superfilm release of Scalera Film production. Stars Michel Simon; features Rossano Brazzi, Maria Mercader, Paola Barbara, Doris Duranti, Elli Parvo, Carlo Ninchi, Juan De Lando. Directed by Mario Bonnard. Story and music from Guiseppe Verdi's opera, "Rigoletto"; camera, Ubaldo Arata; English titles, Armando V. Macaluso. Previewed, N. Y., May 28, '47. Running time, **105 MINS.**

Rigoletto ....Michel Simon
Francesco I.................Rossano Brazzi
Gilda ....Maria Mercader
Marchesa di Cosse............Paola Barbara
Margot ....Doris Duranti
Gypsy ....Elli Parvo
Count St. Vallier...............Carlo Ninchi
Sparafucile....................Juan De Lando

(In Italian; English Titles)

"The King's Jester" is a powerful melodrama executed with the full brilliance of continental artistry. With this achievement, Italian film makers will secure the beachhead which they established on the American market with "The Open City" more than a year ago. It's surefire for the sureseater trade and bids fair to spill over into more general exhibition channels despite the language barrier.

Adapted from Verdi's "Rigoletto," but retaining only some incidental music from the opera, the film has recreated the familiar story on a vast, elegantly brocaded canvas. The depth, solidity and splendor of the background settings make for striking work of art in themselves while the rich profusion of costuming detail on the immense gallery of players make it difficult to believe that such a film could be turned out of war-devastated Italy. Technically, the production is marked by clean, well-lighted camera work, fluid editing, excellent sound and competent English subtitling.

Equalling the physical setup in perfection, the players perform with the full sweep of grand emotion demanded by the operatic story. Topping the cast is Michel Simon who brings to the role of Rigoletto profound thespic resources of character mobility. Playing a hunchbacked buffoon, he ranges from acidity to tenderness and from arrogance to broken pathos with sure control. Simon is a superb actor and only lacks the gift of tears to make him preeminently great. As the young, dissolute medieval French monarch, Rossano Brazzi is a find. He's handsome, flashing and talented with the sensuous qualities of Rudolph Valentino. Main femme part is handled by Maria Mercader, as Rigoletto's daughter, with appropriate beauty and innocence, but Doris Duranti in a brief part as a gypsy femme fatale registers more graphically. Rest of the cast, playing the court's entourage, is uniformly excellent.

Screenplay unfolds with a mounting pace, the gears of melodrama meshing in high along the lines of court intrigue, love, dishonor, revenge and death. Rigoletto, jester to the profligate King Francis of Valois, is a notorious figure who eases the path of the noble ladies to his master's chambers. At the same time, he keeps his own beautiful daughter away from the king's clutches by secretly housing her at another part of town.

After the court cuckolds uncover Rigoletto's secret, they trick him into kidnapping his own daughter who is brought to the palace for the w.k. fate worse than death. Rigoletto swears revenge on the king and hires a gypsy assassin to do the job. The gypsy gal, however, falls for the king and when Rigoletto comes for his body, he's handed a sack with someone else's corpse. As Rigoletto is about to dump the sack into the river, he hears the king singing in the distance. Realizing he's been duped, he tears open the sack and finds the body of his daughter. *Herm.*

Miniature Reviews

"I Wonder Who's Kissing Her Now" (Color - Musical) (20th). Fine turn-of-the-century show biz filmusical. Strong b.o.

"Ivy" (UI). Joan Fontaine in lavishly produced mystery melodrama of lady killer. Should attract good femme trade.

"Riffraff" (RKO). Sturdy melodrama to carry top half of twin bills. Reaction will be good.

"Bob, Son Of Battle" (color) (20tn). Fine family film in Technicolor, should do well at B. O.

"Gunfighters" (Color) (Col). Confused plot mars Randolph Scott western, but okay for outdoor fans.

"Stepchild" (PRC). Minor supporting film on the problems of second marriages.

"Colonel Chabert" (Siritsky). Tedious French film starring Raimu inadequate for U.S. market.

"Matto Regiert" ("Madness Rules"). (Indie). Swiss-made whodunit by producers of "Last Chance," dubious U. S. draw.

I Wonder Who's Kissing Her Now
(COLOR—MUSICAL)

20th-Fox release of George Jessel production. Stars June Haver, Mark Stevens; features Martha Stewart, Reginald Gardiner. Directed by Lloyd Bacon. Original, Lewis R. Foster; additional dialog, Marion Turk; based on life and songs of Joseph E. Howard; songs, Howard-Will M. Hough-Frank R. Adams; special added songs, Jessel-Chas. Henderson; musical director, Alfred Newman; associate m.d., Chas. Henderson; camera (Technicolor), Ernest Palmer; musical settings, Joseph C. Wright; arrangements, Maurice de Packh; dances, Hermes Pan; special effects, Fred Sersen; editor, Louis Loeffler. Tradeshown N. Y., June 9, '47. Running time, **105 MINS.**

Katie..............................June Haver
Joe Howard....................Mark Stevens
Lulu Madison................Martha Stewart
Will Hough.............Reginald Gardiner
Fritzi Barrington............Lenore Aubert
Jim Mason..................William Frawley
Tommy Yale......................Gene Nelson
Martin Webb.................Truman Bradley
John McCullem.......... George Cleveland
Charley........................Harry Seymour
T. J. Milford...............Lewis L. Russell
Kassel...................John "Skins" Miller
Karl................................Lew Hearn
Anita...............................Eve Miller
Marie.........................Florence O'Brien
Harris.........................Emmett Vogan
Herman Bartholdy..........Charles Judels
Mr. Fennabeck..............Milton Parsons
King Louis...................Dewey Robinson
Pres. Theodore Roosevelt.....John Merton
Mr. Kurlinger.......Robert Emmett Keane
Stage Doorman...............John Sheehan
Chef...........................Sam McDaniel
Clerk............................John Arledge
Song Plugger....................Steve Olsen
Stage Managers.....Frank Scannell, Harry Cheshire
Bartender......................Joe Whitehead
Critic...............................Perry Ivins
Doorman......................Herbert Heywood
Cigarette Girl..................Claire Richards
Italian Barber.................Antonio Filauri
Stage Hands.....Eddie Dunn, Ralph Dunn

A special tongue-in-cheek introductory sets the plot theme of this filmusical which purports to deal with the life and loves and times of songwriter-entertainer Joe E. Howard; and, as producer George Jessel concludes in his signed foreword, "Gad, what a life!" Such is the spirit of "I Wonder Who's Kissing Her Now." With Mark Stevens personating Howard, and June Haver and Martha Stewart as the rest of the triangle, along with a lush Technicolor production, "Kissing" should make all the exhibitors smack their lips in glee.

The title song gives 20th-Fox a surefire trailer. "I Wonder Who's Kissing Her Now" has long been the topic of Tin Pan Alley discussion, the consensus being that it remains the No. 1 torch song of all time. Along with "Honeymoon,"

"Hello Ma Baby," "What's the Use of Dreaming?", "Ah, Gee, Be Sweet to Me Kid" and also a little interpolation of "Glow Worm" (not by Howard), all this gives this songwriter-backstage filmusical enough of a Hit Parade cushion to carry it anywhere. Fortified by a sturdy plot framework, such as Lewis R. Foster has supplied, skillfully directed by Lloyd Bacon, and with producer Jessel's vaudeville background knowhow, it's an undeniable collaboration.

Casting is expert and stresses that the Zanuck factory has for some time now had two cast finds. Stevens increases his stature as a promising juvenile, of star potentials, and exnitery songstress Martha Stewart, given a role with more brittleness than has been her lot, comes through like a vet. Miss Stewart formerly was cast in saccharine assignments but, instead of being the sweet young thing with the pleasant soprano, she's Lulu Madison, vaude headliner with a letch for the personable songsmith Howard.

Miss Haver is cast as his pseudo-kid sister whose resourcefulness in latching on to Stevens bothers little with the truth. Both are wards of a kindly uncle, so when Stevens hits the vaudeville routes with the headliner who first introduced his "Hello Ma Baby," she shows up on the Orpheum circuit with the story the uncle had "died" and she is bereft. The romantic chase discloses Miss Haver as a talented as well as resourceful lass, besting the chicanery of Miss Stewart and her manager (latter well played by Bill Frawley). Militating a bit against Miss Haver, however, is her blonde country bumpkin appearance at first; also her inclination to avoirdupois.

The turn-of-the-century backstage stuff is sufficiently fresh and a departure from the now familiar and-then-I-wrote plus the latterday backstage musicals, giving "Kissing Her Now" freshness and verve. There's a good climax when a flop Broadway musical becomes a mop-up show, while the vagabond Stevens (Howard) knocks around the country, playing the honkytonk pianos from Basin St. to the Barbary Coast. He's about to take the steamer for Alaska when the title song attracts his attention, and when told that a soubret was clicking with it at the local theatre he thus learns of Miss Haver's success in the tab show. Will Hough, expertly played by Reginald Gardner (the real-life co-lyricist on "Kissing Her Now," "Honeymoon," etc.) had turned impresario with the tab after the Broadway version flivved.

There is some good inside stuff which Jessel and director Bacon have broadly painted without punching it too hard, notably the jealous single women with their good-looking piano accomps; the on-the-make primas (Lenore Aubert does a good job here); the schooling that goes into making a good vaude turn; the petty jealousies over specialty spots by pianists which might eclipse the headliner's own iridescence; the old-school vaude managers, such as the Kohl & Castle counterparts as done by John "Skins" Miller and Lew Hearn.

All the components are good, from the Alfred Newman-Charles Henderson-Joe Wright-Maurice de Packh musical setting; Hermes Pan's authentic yesteryear vaude terp routines; the gaslight era show business, and the like. Of the vocal dubs, Stevens' voice sounds suspiciously like Buddy Clark's. If this be an out-of-trade "expose," those things no longer hold mystery apparently for the average fan since "The Jolson Story." *Abel.*

Ivy

Hollywood, June 7.

Universal-International release of Sam Wood (William Cameron Menzies) production. Stars Joan Fontaine, Patric Knowles, Herbert Marshall, Richard Ney; features Sir Cedric Hardwicke, Lucile Watson, Sara Allgood, Henry Stephenson, Rosalind Ivan. Directed by Sam Wood. Screenplay, Charles Bennett; based on novel, "The Story of Ivy," by Marie Belloc Lowndes; camera, Russell Metty; music, Daniele Amfitheatrof; editor, Ralph Dawson. Tradeshown June 6, '47. Running time, **98 MINS.**

Ivy.......................Joan Fontaine
Roger Gretorex.............Patric Knowles
Miles Rushworth.........Herbert Marshall
Jervis Lexton..................Richard Ney
Inspector Orpington...Sir Cedric Hardwicke
Mrs. Gretorex..............Lucile Watson
Martha Huntley...............Sara Allgood
Judge.....................Henry Stephenson
Emily.........................Rosalind Ivan
Lady Flora..................Lilian Fontaine
Bella Crail....................Molly Lamont
Mrs. Thrawn.................Una O'Connor
Miss Chattle.....................Isobel Elsom
Sir Jonathan Wright...........Alan Napier
Dr. Berwick..................Paul Cavanagh
Sir Charles Gage.........Sir Charles Mendl
Sergeant...........................Gavin Muir
Lady Crail......................Mary Forbes

"Ivy" is another entry in the murderous ladies cycle. First for Sam Wood's new Interwood Productions, releasing through Universal-International, picture has been handsomely mounted and interestingly photographed. It just misses being a thoroughly satisfying mystery melodrama, but has name values and a plot that should attract strong femme trade.

William Cameron Menzies' production has an off-the-beaten path design that halps generate the melodramatic mood desired. Sets are small and players and settings are lensed from close range. These production touches will stimulate. Suspense in story-telling is good but misses being tops by obvious direction and playing in some sequences. Wood's direction gets plenty of movement but setups for coming thrill moments are emphasized too much, preventing surprise shock that should have moved customers to edge of their seats.

Cast performances are good, but reflect directorial obviousness. Joan Fontaine, in the title role, portrays mercenary femme who doesn't mind murder if it will get her what she wants. Star is gorgeously gowned and period costumes permit plenty of eye-attracting cleavage. Patric Knowles, Ivy's lover; Herbert Marshall, wealthy man for whom she has set her cap, and Richard Ney, her husband whom she poisons, are the top male contingent, all performing up to demands.

Period of the Marie Belloc Lowndes novel, "The Story of Ivy," has been moved back to the turn of the century in England. Charles Bennett scripted the plot which opens with Ivy getting a hint of coming events from fortune-teller. Saddled with a lover and a husband, Ivy wants to be rid of both to take on a wealthy English gentleman. She poisons the husband and transfers blame to the lover. Latter is convicted but Ivy is finally made to reveal her guilt. Climax has lover getting last-minute reprieve and Ivy meeting her end by fall down elevator shaft.

Supporting performances are good. Sir Cedric Hardwicke, Scotland Yard inspector; Lucile Watson, Knowles' mother; Sara Allgood and Rosalind Ivan, maids; Una O'Connor, with one scene as fortune-teller; Lilian Fontaine, Paul Cavanagh and others are capable.

Score by Daniele Amfitheatrof is strong point in developing mood. General score is interwoven with harpsichord theme that backgrounds the fortune-telling sequence, the tinkle being used at various intervals to point up effectively Ivy's murderous intentions as story develops. Russell Metty's lensing stands out and there is special photography by David S. Horsley adding to effect. Believeable art direction by Richard H. Riedel, set decorations by Russell A. Gausman and T. F. Offenbecker and other production factors lend strong backing to sight values. *Brog.*

Riffraff
(ONE SONG)

Hollywood, June 6.

RKO release of Nat Holt production. Stars Pat O'Brien, Walter Slezak, Anne Jeffreys; features Percy Kilbride, Jerome Cowan, George Givot, Jason Robards, Marc Krah. Directed by Ted Tetzlaff. Original screenplay, Martin Rackin; camera, George E. Diskant; editor, Philip Martin. Tradeshown June 3, '47. Running time, **70 MINS.**

Dan..............................Pat O'Brien
Molinar........................Walter Slezak
Maxine.........................Anne Jeffreys
Pop.............................Percy Kilbride
Walter Gredson..............Jerome Cowan
Rues...............................George Givot
Dominques....................Jason Robards
Hasso................................Marc Krah

Tight adventure melodrama with Panama background. "Riffraff" spins actionful tale of intrigue, mayhem and romance that garners interest and packs enough weight to fill top spot capably in dual bookings. Marquee values are good, headed by Pat O'Brien, Walter Slezak and Anne Jeffreys.

Picture puts particular emphasis on lens work. It's loaded with camera angles whose unusualness add to interest and meller mood. Photography is by George E. Diskant, working under director Ted Tetzlaff, himself a former top lenser. Latter's direction is generally strong, aided by Martin Rackin's punchy script. Nat Holt's production guidance backs action with realistic values.

O'Brien is gimmick guy and fixer, with little private eye work thrown in, who's hired to find missing map that marks location of valuable wildcat oil wells. Several factions are after the piece of paper and spare nothing in drive to obtain it. First murder comes when a man is tossed out of a plane. Next, the tosser is done in and then O'Brien's employer. Hero, himself, takes considerable beating before villains are put in their proper places, and O'Brien comes out on top.

Walter Slezak heads up the dirty work as arty heavy. Anne Jeffreys, singer in Panamanian nitery, furnishes crisp romance angles with O'Brien. She also chirps one uncredited tune. Support is strong. Percy Kilbride injects his dry comedy as laconic taxi driver. Jerome Cowan is O'Brien client. George Givot is good as police officer. Others measure up.

Art direction and set decorations keep physical properties in tune with story-background for realistic effect. Roy Webb's music score, tight editing by Philip Martin and other factors are good. *Brog.*

Bob, Son of Battle
(COLOR)

20th-Fox release of Robert Bassler production. Stars Lon McCallister; features Peggy Ann Garner, Edmund Gwenn, Reginald Owen, Charles Irwin. Directed by Louis King. Screenplay, Jerome Cady, based on novel by Alfred Ollivant; camera (Technicolor), Charles Clarke; musical direction, Alfred Newman; editor, Nick de Maggio. Tradeshown N. Y., June 4, '47. Running time, **103 MINS.**

David M'Adam............Lon McCallister
Maggie...................Peggy Ann Garner
Adam M'Adam..............Edmund Gwenn
James Moore...............Reginald Owen
Long Kirby....................Charles Irwin
Samuel Thornton............Dave Thursby
MacKenzie.....................John Rogers
Ferguson.................Leyland Hodgson
Tammas..........................Harry Allen
Parson Leggy Hornbut.......Edgar Norton
Lady Eleanor................Norma Varden
Mrs. Moore....................Jean Prescott
MacIvor................Houseley Stevenson
Steward.......................Cyril Thornton
Court Judge................James Finlayson
Judges.........C. Montague Shaw, George Melford, Charles Knight
Doctor..........................George Kirby
Bailiff............................Ad Ferguson

Conversion of the children's classic, "Bob, Son of Battle," to the screen has resulted in a moving, tender film skillfully capturing the warm charm of Alfred Ollivant's novel. It's a top "family" picture embellished with Technicolor and exhibs should find it a moneymaker.

In this Robert Bassler production is assembled a competent cast that ably reenacts the saga of the McAdams, the Moores and other Scottish hill folk who lead an honest, crusty life as sheepherders. But primarily the film unfolds the story of two dogs, one gentle and the other shifty and a killer.

In his first starring role, Lon McCallister credibly plays Davy, the abused son of Adam McAdam (Edmund Gwenn). Latter, fresh from his triumph in "Miracle of 34th St.", adds to his laurels with a fine characterization of a selfish man whose wits are continually clouded with drink. Plot traces Gwenn's struggle to retain a trophy won in sheepdog competition by his red collie who's suspected of killing sheep of other herdsmen.

Owned by James Moore (Reginald Owen), "Bob, Son of Battle" is McAdams' dog's chief rival. In a lush, green valley whose natural pastoral **beauties are enhanced by some top** color lensing, the canines run through their paces for the cup, generating considerable suspense. Interwoven with the dogs' tournament is a secondary romance between McCallister and Peggy Ann Garner who wistfully portrays Owen's daughter.

At odds with his high-strung father, Davy seeks sanctuary at neighbor Moore's home. There romance blooms with Maggie (Miss Garner). Comes the final cup competition where "Bob" is pitted against "Red Wool," who's already won twice. In the meet father and son are matched against the other, each handling their respective dogs.

McAdam is heartbroken when adjudged the loser. Then, too, he's forced to kill his own dog when confronted with evidence that his canine is a sheep-killer. Later, however, Davy salves his emotional wounds by revealing his own disqualification in the contest, thereby giving his father permanent possession of the cup.

Owen is excellent as the expansive, understanding and forgiving James Moore. He, as well as Miss Garner, Gwenn and McCallister play their parts to the hilt. Supporting cast has also caught the flavor of the Scotch countryside. Louis King's direction realistically transmuted Jerome Cady's able script to celluloid. Charles Clarke lensed with finesse while Alfred Newman's musical score adds much to the film. Other credits also measure up.

Gunfighters
(COLOR)

Columbia release of Harry Joe Brown production. Stars Randolph Scott, Barbara Britton; features Dorothy Hart, Bruce Cabot, Charley Grapewin, Steven Geray, Forrest Tucker, Charles Kemper, Grant Withers. Directed by George Waggner. Screenplay by Alan LeMay, adapted from Zane Grey's novel, "Twin Sombreros"; camera (Cinecolor), Fred J. Jackman, Jr.; editor, Harvey Manger. Tradeshown N. Y., June 5, '47. Running time, **87 MINS.**

Brazos Kane...............Randolph Scott
Bess Banner.................Barbara Britton
Jane Banner....................Dorothy Hart
Bard Macky......................Bruce Cabot
Inskip.....................Charley Grapewin
Jose...............................Steven Geray
Hen Orcutt....................Forrest Tucker
Sheriff Kiscaden...........Charles Kemper
Deputy Bill Yount...........Grant Withers
Johnny O'Neil.....................John Miles
Banner...........................Griff Barnett

"Gunfighters" has the handle for a rootin'-tootin' westerner but, getting away from conventional direct story treatment, film gets lost in a foggy plot which is made even more confusing due to a haphazard editing job. Reliable names of Randolph Scott and Bruce Cabot, however, will help draw the outdoor addicts to the wickets despite story obstacles. Vivid, sharply defined color photography will also add a nice boost.

Most of film's action takes place as background to the credits where Scott, the best trigger man west of the Hudson, is shown gun-duelling with his best friend. Latter, who was itching to find out if he could beat Scott to the draw, gets scratched out and, as a result, Scott vows to hang up his holsters and earn a

peaceful living as a cowhand. Travelling to another locale via a spectacular scenic route, Scott comes upon his friend's ranch just as his pal is being rubbed out by hirelings of a neighboring cattle baron.

Scott, in tracking down the killers, gets mixed up with the cattleman's two beauteous daughters, one of whom is a sweet maid while the other is a neatly manicured but bad tomato. After shuttling between the two femmes in alternating romantic clinches, Scott finally gets down to settling scores with their father, his hired killers and a corrupt deputy sheriff.

Pic blazes into excitement only during a standout fight sequence between Scott and deputy Grant Withers and, at the very end, with a general burst of gunplay. Scott registers with usual effectiveness as square-jawed, tight-lipped, lean and leathery guardian of the right. Barbara Britton, playing femme heavy, turns in a straight performance, relying mostly on her looks as does newcomer Dorothy Hart in sister role. Solid bits of support are added by Cabot, Charley Grapewin and Withers with rest of the cast serving competently. *Herm.*

Stepchild

PRC release of Leonard S. Picker production. Features Brenda Joyce, Donald Woods, Terry Austin, Tommy Ivo, Gregory Marshall. Directed by James Flood. Screenplay, Karen De Wolfe from original by Jules Levine; camera, Jackson Rose; editor, Alfred DeGaetano; score, Mario Silva. Reviewed N. Y., June 9, '47. Running time, 70 MINS.
Dale Bullock..................Brenda Joyce
Ken Bullock..................Donald Woods
Millie Lynne..................Terry Austin
Jim Bullock..................Tommy Ivo
Tommy Bullock..........Gregory Marshall
Brian Reed..................James Millican
Burns ....Griff Barnett
Judge ....Selmer Jackson
Miss Brighton..............Ruth Robinson

PRC's excursion into problem drama with "Stepchild" comes out as a rehash of virtually every film discussion of second marriages. It's a picture that can't be taken seriously despite the dead earnestness with which it's played. Some of the moments of pathos are as hilarious as slapstick. It's a minor dualer.

"Stepchild" concerns itself with the second marital try of Donald Woods who, after divorcing Brenda Joyce, takes up with Terry Austin as a means of making a home for his two children. The scheming Miss Austin generally maltreats the kids once she hooks the guy and is ultimately found out after nearly tragic results. A reconciliation with his first mate follows.

Film and enactments are pretty elementary. Virtually every cliche has been written into it and cast is unable to handle its situations with the necessary delicacy. Consequently the sequences which should move audiences to tears will make metropolitan audiences howl. Miss Austin doesn't have the delicacy to take on assignments of this type; her portrayal of a stepmother is such that she makes the hackneyed dialog and situations even more corny. Woods and Miss Joyce do as well as the duped husband and first spouse as can be expected, while a note of cuteness is imparted by the two youngsters, Tommy Ivo and Gregory Marshall. *Jose.*

Colonel Chabert
(FRENCH-MADE)

Siritzky release. Stars Raimu; features Marie Bell. Directed by Rene Le Henaff. Screenplay, Pierre Benoit; based on novel by Balzac; camera, Robert Le Febvre; music, Louis Beydts. Previewed N. Y., June 6, '47. Running time, 90 MINS.
Colonel Chabert....................Raimu
Countess Ferraud..............Marie Bell
Also: Aime, Clariond, Jacques Baumer, Jacques Charon, Roger Blin, Andre Varenne, and Rene Stern.

(*In French; English Titles*)

"Colonel Chabert" is a tedious film destined for plenty of ho-hums at the art houses. Name of the late Raimu is the sole asset to this dated importation which could have served the cause of French films in the U. S. much better if it remained in the archives. But even Raimu's formidable talent is reduced to commonplace proportions in this cinematic context of a hair thin story stretched interminably to patience's breaking point.

Based on one of Balzac's minor novels, it relates the thickly tragic story of an army officer who, after being taken for dead, finds it impossible to reclaim his identity. Lacking incident with which to elaborate the theme, pic's director resorts to a repetition of sequences unfolding at a snail's pace in order to pad out the running time. Pic's frail substance finally collapses into a bogus pathos under combined weight of its heavy tone and heavier-handed treatment.

Coming back like a ghost from the Napoleonic wars, Raimu, as Colonel Chabert, seeks to recoup his social position and fortune from a wife who refuses to recognize his existence. Latter a treacherous woman who remarried into nobility during Raimu's presumed death, schemes to put him out of the way by committing him to an insane asylum. He escapes, only to experience another round of hard knocks which embitters him against all of society. In an exceedingly maudlin denouement. Raimu is placed into a poorhouse where he chooses to remain despite last minute evidence which proves his former high estate.

Following lead of Raimu, whose role compels him to hoke up his thesping in a most obvious style, rest of the cast gives stilted performances without credibility. Camera work is uneven with poor lighting marring several scenes. On positive side, film is marked by excellent period settings. *Herm.*

Matto Regiert
('Madness Rules')
(SWISS-MADE)

Zurich, May 30.
Praesens Film release of L. Wechsler production. Features Heinrich Gretler, Heinz Woester, Olaf Kubler, Elisabeth Muller, Emil Hegetschweiler, Johannes Steiner, Adolf Manz, Hans Kaes, Irene Naef, Mathilde Danegger, Walburga Gmur, Jakob Straull, Zarli Carigiet, Max Werner Lenz, Hugo Doeblin, Sigfrit Steiner, Otto Brefin, Hans Gaugler, Max Haufler, Emil Gerber, Armin Schweizer, Fritz Dellus, Enzo Ertini, Gody Buchi, Emil Gyr, Arnold Rita. Directed by Leopold Lindtberg. Screenplay by Leopold Lindtberg and Alfred Neumann from novel by Friedrich Glauser; camera, Emil Berna; editor, Herman Haller.

(*In German; No English Titles*)

This new screen effort by producers of "Last Chance" and "Marie Louise" is unlike its predecessors. It is a crime detective story based on the novel by Friedrich Glauser, Swiss novelist who died a few years ago. Whether a sleuth whodunit, done in Swiss style, will appeal to U.S. audiences is dubious despite nice direction and acting.

Glauser created the character of Sergeant Detective Studer, the title of novel he wrote before "Madness Rules," which also was made into a film by the same producing company as "Sgt. Detective Studer." Heinrich Gretler again portrays this principal character as he did in the other picture, and turns in an excellent job. Remainder of cast is well picked, and comes through in fine style.

Main action is in a Swiss insane asylum, with Sergeant Studer clearing up the slaying of a director of the place. Besides plenty of suspense and a logical story, there is a surprise ending.

Supporting Gretler in perhaps the best characterization is young Olaf Kubler, a patient in the asylum who is suffering from an inferiority complex. This is complicated by the fact that he's suspected of the murder. Elisabeth Muller, as the nurse, is not outstanding but provides nice heart interest in her romance with Kubler. *Mezo.*

Miniature Reviews

"Fiesta" (Color-Songs) (M-G). Colorful pic spec for OK b.o.

"A Lady Surrenders" (British) (U). Slow-footed pic with doleful yarn; tepid b.o. prospects.

"Brute Force" (Hellinger-U). Prison meller a strong boxoffice entry.

"Web of Danger" (Rep). Minor supporting entry for action market.

"News Hound" (Mono). Another Bowery Boys feature, among best of series.

"Saddle Pals" (Rep). Gene Autry oatuner, okay for market.

"Dual Alibi" (Pathe). British-made meller stars Herbert Lom, slated for U. S. films; only okay for dualers in America.

"The Vow" (Artkino). Soviet production on Stalin's life just misses, mainly because of war treatment; big for arty theatres.

Fiesta
(COLOR-SONGS)

Metro release of Jack Cummings production. Stars Esther Williams; features Akim Tamiroff, Ricardo Montalban. Directed by Richard Thorpe. Original and screenplay, George Bruce, Lester Cole; camera (Technicolor), Sidney Wagner, Chas. Rosher, Wilfrid M. Cline; score and arrangements, Johnny Green, assisted by Ted Duncan; "El Salon Mexico" by Aaron Copland; dances, Eugene Loring; editor, Blanche Sewell. Tradeshown N. Y., June 5, '47. Running time, 104 MINS.
Maria Morales..............Esther Williams
Chato Vasquez..............Akim Tamiroff
Mario Morales..........Ricardo Montalban
Jose "Pepe" Ortega............John Carroll
Senora Morales..................Mary Astor
Conchita ....Cyd Charisse
Antonio Morales........Fortunio Bonanova
Maximino Contreras............Hugo Haas
Maria Morales (Child)............Jean Van
Mario Morales (Child)........Joey Preston
Doctor ....Frank Puglia
The Basque Singers..........Los Bocheros
The Tourist..................Alan Napier

"Fiesta" is a Technicolorful trailer for Mexican-American goodwill. It's an eyeful of Esther Williams, alternating between a little of her familiar Jantzen symmetry and her pseudo-skill as a matador. It's also pleasant if not socko summer film fare. With the color, the cast presence of Akim Tamiroff, John Carroll, Mary Astor, Cyd Charisse, and Metro's ballyhoo "introducing a new personality, Ricardo Montalban," it has enough for solid business.

The new personality is a nice departure in that he's not the Valentino type, but on the other hand neither is he socko in any other direction. As a Mexican juvenile, however, he is a sympathetic vis-a-vis to Miss Williams, who plays his twin sister.

The film plot punches over the fact that "not all Mexicans are bullfighters." Leisurely the story unfolds with the birth of the twins, after the famed matador (well played by Fortunio Bonanova, who does a tip-top interpretation of the role) at first betrays his chagrin that his firstborn is a girl. But when her twin brother arrives 15 minutes later he schools the lad to follow in the bullfighter tradition, even though his penchant is music. Eventually the "Salon Mexico" suite by Aaron Copland (brilliantly orchestrated by Johnny Green) serves as the Mexican Symphony's means to project his virtuosity as a serious composer. Plot projects his doting twin sister (who also has manifested skill in the arena) to masquerade as her brother in order to recapture a distorted loss of family honor.

John Carroll is her romantic vis-a-vis and Cyd Charisse makes a fine impression with her terps and general line-reading as the romantic interest opposite Montalban, with whom she clicks in a couple of intricate native terp routines. Mary

Astor is a shade somnolent as the worried wife and mother, fearful of her matador-husband's life since marriage, and later for her son who, rather unwillingly, essays to follow in his father's bullfighting footsteps. Tamiroff, as the trusted friend of the family, and Hugo Haas, as the maestro who would become Montalban's musical mentor, are other cast standouts.

But the substance of "Fiesta"—a rather vacuous nomenclature—is the atmosphere and color of the country south of the Rio Grande. All characters are treated with dignity and authority. There is no accent on the peonage; emphasis on the culture of the country is personified through the highly respected maestro whom Haas so well portrays. This is in contrast to mass idolatry for the matador.

Production is lavish and the Technicolor lush. The situation where Montalban hears the first performance of his suite over the radio in a wayside cantina, and is inspired to play the piano solo accompanied by the full orchestra as it comes over the wireless, is one of the better dramatic moments. So is the situation where he heroically saves his sister from being gored by the bull. These arena scenes, if a bit full, are effective because of size and Richard Thorpe's expert direction. Green's excellent musical score and arrangements and Eugene Loring's dance stagings are other plus factors.

Abel.

A Lady Surrenders

(Original title—'Love Story')
(BRITISH-MADE)

Universal (Prestige) release of Gainsborough production. Stars Margaret Lockwood, Stewart Granger; features Patricia Roc, Tom Walls. Directed by Leslie Arliss. Screenplay by Arliss, Doreen Montgomery from short story by J. W. Drawbell; additional dialog, Rodney Ackland; music, Hubert Bath, played by National Symphony Orchestra, conducted by Sidney Beer; camera, Bernard Knowles. Tradeshown N. Y., June 16, '47. Running time, **102 MINS.**

Lissa	Margaret Lockwood
Kit	Stewart Granger
Judy	Patricia Roc
Tom	Tom Walls
Albert	Reginald Purdell
Carol	Moira Lister
Ray	Walter Hudd
Colonel Pitt Smith	A. E. Matthews
Mrs. Pitt Smith	Josephine Middleton
Susie	Dorothy Bramhall
Angus Rossiter	Lawrence Hanray
Miss Rossiter	Beatrice Varley

"A Lady Surrenders," intended for the more leisurely-paced British audiences, took a 10-minute speedup before being unleashed on Yank patrons but still suffers from dragging pace. Aimed in the main for art house operations by reason of its Prestige release, some sparkling bits of Anglo thesping allay a tortuous and involved story. By-and-large, however, this pic isn't up to the standards set by prior Prestige offerings and its boxoffice chances are that much less.

An attempt to cram in a double-barrelled dose of death and blindness faced by the two principals in the story is at the root of the pic's flounderings. The youthful concert pianiste (Margaret Lockwood) is confronted by early death from heart trouble while her vis-a-vis (Stewart Granger) has been advised that blindness is his almost certain lot. Yarn takes place during the late war on the Cornish coast where the pianiste has gone for a last fling as has Granger who's been recently discharged from the RAF.

Both seek to conceal their dilemmas from each other and plot convolutions stem from those efforts. While they gradually work out their salvation by a determination to face things out together, the film manages to squeeze in a number of fine bit characterizations and some fetching photography of sea and coast. It's the momentary focusing of camera off the main beam that gives the film its strongest bid for customer attention.

Neither Miss Lockwood nor Granger come through with an outstanding performance but that's more the story's fault than the players. Hampered to a much lesser degree by the doleful plot, Tom Walls gives a brittle and winning performance as an elder adviser and friend. Patricia Roc as the other gal is cute enough for the Granger sweepstakes to take the money—even if she doesn't.

The recipe for livening the gait of British entries needs some more working over judging from this latest offering. Scissoring applied, moreover, is all too apparent in spots where dialog was cut in mid-sentence.

Wit.

(Film was originally reviewed by VARIETY'S *Jolo from London in the Nov. 22, 1944, issue; that notice also deprecated its b.o. chances. New review is published herewith because of extensive cuts in the U. S. version and the protracted period between the date of the original review and film's release here.)*

Brute Force

Universal release of Mark Hellinger (Jules Buck) production. Features Burt Lancaster, Hume Cronyn, Chas. Bickford; Yvonne DeCarlo, Ann Blyth, Ella Raines, Anita Colby. Directed by Jules Dassin. Screenplay, Richard Brooks from story by Robt. Patterson; camera, Wm. Daniels; special effects, David S. Horsley; editor, Edward Curtiss; asst. director, Fred Frank; music, Miklos Rozsa. Tradeshown N. Y., June 17, '47. Running time, **94 MINS.**

Joe Collins	Burt Lancaster
Captain Munsey	Hume Cronyn
Gallagher	Charles Bickford
Gina	Yvonne De Carlo
Ruth	Ann Blyth
Cora	Ella Raines
Flossie	Anita Colby
Louie	Sam Levene
Soldier	Howard Duff
Dr. Walters	Art Smith
Warden Barnes	Roman Bohnen
Spencer	John Hoyt
McCollum	Richard Gaines
Ferrara	Frank Puglia
Freshman	Jeff Corey
Muggsy	Vince Barnett
Crenshaw	James Bell
Kid Coy	Jack Overman
Tom Lister	Whit Bissell
Calypso	Sir Lancelot
Jackson	Ray Teal
Hodges	Jay C. Flippen
Wilson	James O'Rear
Gaines	Howland Chamberlin
Bronski	Kenneth Patterson
Armed Guard in Drain Pipe	Crane Whitley
Andy	Charles McGraw
Roberts	John Harmon
Hoffman	Gene Stutenroth
Peary	Wally Rose
Strella	Carl Rhodes
Convict Foreman	Guy Beach
Bradley	Edmund Cobb
Machine Gunner No. 1	Tom Steele

"Brute Force" packs plenty of boxoffice wallop. It will inevitably be likened to "The Killers," Mark Hellinger's first for Universal-International, and this one compares favorably with that b.o.-getter. In addition it gives Burt Lancaster, who Hellinger debuted in "Killers," added marquee stature.

A closeup on prison life and prison methods, "Brute Force" is a showmany mixture of gangster melodramatics, sociological exposition, and sex. The s.a. elements are plausible and realistic, well within the bounds, but always pointing up the femme fatale. Thus Yvonne DeCarlo, Ann Blyth, Ella Raines and Anita Colby are the women on the "outside" whose machinations, wiles or charms accounted for their men being on the "inside."

Burt Lancaster, Charles Bickford, Sam Levene, Howard Duff, Art Smith and Jeff Corey, along with Hume Cronyn as the machinating prison captain (later warden), are the "inside" cast. With them are such capital troupers as John Hoyt (nee Hoysradt, when he was a nitery mimic) who clicks with his precise speech as a bucket-shop operator; Jack Overman as Kid Coy, a pug gone wrong; and Sir Lancelot as Calypso, the Trinidad lyricist, who gets plausible opportunities for his lyrical interludes.

Each of the more prominent criminals has a saga. The flashback technique shows how bookkeeper Whit Bissell embezzled $3,000 to give his ambitious wife (Miss Raines) that mink coat; how soldier Howard Duff (the "Sam Spade" of radio, and excellent) got jammed with the Military Police because of his love for his Italian bride (Miss DeCarlo) and through the sniveling skullduggery of her fascistic father; how the sympathetic Lancaster is in love with the invalided Ann Blyth. Anita Colby, the fourth femme on the "outside," is the one who hijacks the crapshooting Wall St. sharper (Hoyt).

Bristling, biting dialog by Richard Brooks, who did the screenplay, paints broad cameos as each character takes shape under existing prison life. Bickford is the wise and patient prison paper editor whose trusty, Sam Levene, has greater freedom in getting "stories" for the sheet. Both are awaiting their paroles until forced into the prison break. Art Smith, veteran character actor, comes to the fore in truly great style as the stir-crazy prison doctor, ringing the bell with his fine interpretation of a sort of penal institution beachcomber who, for all his freedom as a medico, is as much a lifer as any of the real criminals for the simple reason that the cause of his moral incarceration is booze.

Hume Cronyn is diligently hateful as the arrogant, brutal captain, with his system of stoolpigeons and bludgeoning methods. When outside attention is attracted because of the repeated insubordination by prisoners and abortive prison breaks, this is Roman Bohnen's undoing as the warden, a role which he portrays rather too abjectly and in too sniveling a method, whereas Cronyn's bullying and suave arrogance is more convincing.

"Brute Force" is by no means a man's picture solely. The prisoners, for all their unsavory backgrounds, are personable types with plenty of muscles which will get the femmes. Then, too, the vignettes of the vis-a-vis give it the proper romance tang. The aspect of an audience rooting for the prisoners plotting a jailbreak is given a sharp turn-about, at the proper time, to point up that brute force by prisoners is as wrong as the brute force exercised by their keepers.

Direction by Jules Dassin (an alumnus of Maurice Schwartz's Yiddish Art Theatre) is tight and well-paced, matching the scripting. Miklos Rozsa's score is an asset to a mood meller of this nature. Producer Hellinger looks like he has given the sum total big league production mounting without completely hocking his entire bankroll. His gamble with Lancaster as a potential star in "The Killers" is paying off in spades with "Brute Force." As a present-day production item it points up the economic conclusion that Hollywood can still turn out top grossers without breaking the bankers.

Abel.

Web of Danger

Hollywood, June 17.

Republic release of Donald H. Brown production. Features Adele Mara, Bill, Kennedy, Damian O'Flynn. Directed by Philip Ford. Original screenplay, David Lang, Milton M. Raison; camera, Alfred S. Keller; special effects, Howard and Theodore Lydecker; editor, William Thompson. Previewed June 10, '47. Running time, **58 MINS.**

Peg Mallory	Adele Mara
Ernie Reardon	Bill Kennedy
Bill O'Hara	Damian O'Flynn
Wing	Richard Loo
Sam	Victor Sen Yung
Monks	Roy Barcroft
Slim	William Hall
MacKronish	J. Farrell MacDonald
Ramsey	Michael Branden
Dolan	Ed Gargan
Customer	Chester Clute
Peterson	Ralph Sanford
Gallagher	Russell Hicks

"Web of Danger" makes a stab at the action market, but misses by a sizeable span. Too much talk and too little action stifles tale of bridge building and floods that could have been passable for release intentions. Stock footage takes care of flood scenes, and the bridge-building shots also bear a library stamp, although nicely spliced in with those studio-staged.

Cast makes an effort to breathe movement and interest into proceedings with little success. Philip Ford's direction is hampered by dialog, as are principals. Plot in the David Lang-Milton M. Raison script has Bill Kennedy and Damian O'Flynn as bridge-builders who would just as soon fight each other. There's a girl, Adele Mara, mixed up in it for romance. Rivalry is forgotten when bridge must be completed on short notice to get flock of flood refugees out of an innundated valley. It's formula all the way, but could have been brightened by better dialoging.

Donald H. Brown's production is adequate in physical values. Same goes for lensing and other credits.

Brog.

News Hounds

Hollywood, June 14.

Monogram release of Jan Grippo production. Stars Leo Gorcey; features Huntz Hall, Bobby Jordan, Gabriel Dell, Billy Benedict, David Gorcey, Christine McIntyre, Tim Ryan, Anthony Caruso, Bill Kennedy. Directed by William Beaudine. Screenplay, Edmond Seward, Tim Ryan; original story, Seward, Ryan, George Cappy; camera, Marcel LePicard; editor, William Austin. Previewed June 11, '47. Running time, **68 MINS.**

Slip	Leo Gorcey
Sach	Huntz Hall
Bobby	Bobby Jordan
Gabe	Gabriel Dell
Whitey	Billy Benedict
Chuck	David Gorcey
Jane Connelly	Christine McIntyre
John Burke	Tim Ryan
Clothes Greco	Anthony Caruso
Mark Morgan	Bill Kennedy
Dutch Miller	Ralph Dunn
Mame	Nita Bieber
Big Tim Dolin	John Hamilton
Little Boy	Terry Goodman
Mack Snide	Robert Emmett Keane
Louie	Bernard Gorcey
Copyboy	Buddy Gorman
Jimmy Gale	Russ Whiteman
Mallon	Emmett Vogan, Jr.
Judge	John H. Elliott
Sparring Partner	Meyer Grace

"News Hounds" adds up to one of the best of Monogram's Bowery Boys series. Playoff will be good in the market for which it's aimed. As title indicates, it's a newspaper story with Leo Gorcey as ambitious copyboy. Jan Grippo's production has given boys a plot to work over and that accounts for more substance than usually found in B.B. entries.

Gorcey wants to be a star reporter and around his efforts in that direction the antics are built. Working from script by Edmond Seward and Tim Ryan, William Beaudine's direction spins the tale at fast clip for pleasure of Bowery Boys followers. Gorcey becomes involved in sports fixing racket and when his unsubstantiated story is printed the paper is sued for libel. Last-minute recovery of some missing photos clears the sheet and Gorcey to make for okay finish.

Gorcey continues his garbled-word way for chuckles; his antics pleasing. Huntz Hall, Gorcey's dopey pal, backs up the fun strongly. Adult romance falls to Christine McIntyre and Bill Kennedy. Among the Bowery urchins are Bobby Jordan, Gabriel Dell, Billy Benedict and David Gorcey. Moppet Terry Goodman spots laugh-getting character. Okay heavy work falls to Anthony Caruso, Ralph Dunn, John Hamilton and others.

Lensing, editing and other production credits measure up for release intentions.

Brog.

Saddle Pals
(SONGS)

Hollywood, June 14.

Republic release of Sidney Picker production. Stars Gene Autry; features Lynne Roberts, Sterling Holloway, Irving Bacon, Damian O'Flynn, Charles Arnt, Jean Van, Cass County Boys (3). Directed by Lesley Selander. Screenplay, Bob Williams, Jerry Sackheim; original story, Dorrell and Stuart E. McGowan; camera, Bud Thackery; editor, Harry Keller; songs, Harry Sosnik and Stanley Adams; Ray Allen and Perry Botkin; Britt Wood and Hy Heath; Haldeman-Autry-Evans. Previewed June 18, '47. Running time, **72 MINS.**

Gene....Gene Autry
Shelly Brooks....Lynne Roberts
Waldo T. Brooks, Jr....Sterling Holloway
Thaddeus Bellweather....Irving Bacon
Brad Collins....Damian O'Flynn
William Schooler....Charles Arnt
Robin Brooks....Jean Van
Dad Gardner....Tom London
Leslie....Charles Williams
Sheriff....Francis McDonald
Dippy....George Chandler
Jailer....Edward Gargan
Cass County Boys

"Saddle Pals" is a bit below entertainment level usually achieved by Gene Autry but will get by in the oatuner market. Five songs, with Autry contributing three with a reprise, stretch out tune portion of production. Values are standard for outdoor trade as marshalled by Sidney Picker's production and Lesley Selander keeps direction on move.

Plot is dressed up western formula. This time heavies are trying to bankrupt wealthy landowner so they can buy the property cheap. Owner has little business sense but his smartest play comes when he gives Autry power of attorney and then takes to the woods for a vacation. Autry soon spots the trouble and sets about correcting it. There's little gunplay or chases to help point up action.

"You Stole My Heart," "I Wish I had Never Met Sunhsine" and "Amapola" are the three Autry-vocaled numbers. Cass County Boys, western trio, do "Which Way Did They Go" and "The Covered Wagon Rolled Right Along."

Autry's costumes are not as sharp in this one as he usually displays. Lynne Roberts does excellent job as heroine, making part count for much more than average western femme assignment. Moppet femme interest is Jean Van. Sterling Holloway, as the landowner, and Irving Bacon, lawyer with more interest in Izaak Walton than Blackstone, furnish comedy. Damian O'Flynn and Charles Arnt head up the dirty work.

Bud Thackerey's lensing, editing by Harry Keller and other credits are standard. *Brog.*

Dual Alibi
(BRITISH-MADE)

London, June 4.

Pathe Pictures' release of British National production. Features Terence de Marney, Herbert Lom, Phyllis Dixey, Ronald Frankau. Directed by Alfred Travers. Screenplay by Stephen Clarkson, Vivienne Ades, Alfred Travers from story by Renault Capes. Camera, James Wilson, R. Holmes. At Studio One, London, June 3, '47. Running time, **87 MINS.**

Jules de Lisles
Georges de Lisles....Herbert Lom
Mike Bergen....Terence de Marney
Penny....Phyllis Dixey
Vincent Barney....Ronald Frankau
French Judge....Abraham Sofaer
Ali....Harold Berens
M. Mangin....Clarence Wright
French Lawyer....Marcel Poncin
Loterie Nationale Official..Sebastian Cabot
Trapeze Act....Cromwell Brothers

Based on the old situation that twins could be so much alike that no one could tell them apart, "Dual Alibi" should return its comparatively modest cost in this country. It may return some coin via dual situations in the U. S. Writers and directors, while paying some respect for logic, were mainly concerned about making it a dual role for Herbert Lom (spotted by Ben Lyon for 20th-Fox contract). As twin Georges he is apparently impervious to the wiles of a woman, while as Jules he falls for a femme. As one he is rather dour and practical, as the other he has little thought for the future.

Brothers are a daring headline trapeze act, and are doing okay until Terence de Marney, an unscrupulous publicity man, learns they have won a million francs in the French lottery. Employing Phyllis Dixey, his equally unscrupulous sweetheart, to make love to the more susceptible twin, they finally filch the winning ticket. And collect the million in Paris.

The twins, learning of the theft go after de Marney. While one is doing a solo trapeze act, the other slays the publicity man. No witness, not even the girl, can rightly identify who committed the murder, and both are set free. They return to the circus, but one of them accidentally hangs himself during the act. The other, the actual murderer, years later has sunk to being a sandwichboard man.

With a little more expenditure on production and wiser casting, picture would have rated better playing time than it probably will receive. However, Herbert Lom's acting makes it acceptable drama. Greatest defect is the casting of Phyllis Dixey as femme lead. Notorious for a stage strip-tease act, she may have a certain following, but her screen debut is most uninspiring. Ronald Frankau, returning to films after a long absence, and Terence de Marney give valuable support. *Cane.*

The Vow
(RUSSIAN-MADE)

Artkino release of Tbilissi Film production. Features Mikhail Gelovani. Directed by Mikhail Chiaureli. Screenplay, M. Chiaureli and N. Pavlenko; camera, A. Kesuatov; score, A. Balanchivadze; English titles, C. Clement. Previewed N. Y., June 13, '47. Running time, **98 MINS.**

Stalin....Mikhail Gelovani
The Mother....S. Chiatsintova
Alexander....N. Bogoliubov
Sergei....D. Pavlov
Olga....S. Bogoliubova
Xenia....T. Makharova
Yermilov....N. Plotnikov
Ruzayev....V. Soloviev
Baklan....S. Blinnikov
Georgi....G. Sagardze
Tugunbayev....P. Ismatov
U. S. Correspondent....M. Shtraugh
British Correspondent....N. Chapligin
French Minister Bonnet....I. Nabatov

Soviet leaders played by A. Mansvetov, N. Konovalov, A. Gribov, N. Rizhov, G. Musheghian, R. Yurlev, V. Mironov, A. Khbilya, F. Blazhevich, M. Sidorkin, A. Sovolev, T. Belnikevich.

(In Russian; English Titles)

"The Vow," latest Soviet opus, just misses being a great picture, and also being one of the finest turned out by the Russians. This near-miss stems from the way that the late war is handled by Soviet producers in an overly long, vaguely done sequel to the main theme of the story. This part of the film leads one to believe that the Russians won the war. In fact, this war propaganda phase of the production is so blatantly done it will make the average American patron squirm. And it is unfortunate, because marring an otherwise superb production. But the film should do strongly at many foreign-language houses in the U. S. even despite this.

Story pays tribute to Lenin at the outset, showing how Stalin followed in his footsteps, carrying on where he left off, but more vigorously. Picture's title stems from the fact that Stalin pledges to let no one destroy Lenin and his legacy. Workers are seen working in all sorts of weather to build factories and make Moscow a reality as a manufacturing city as well as seat of the Stalin government. Only off-the-track reference is that in the titles that refer to "lies of the foreign press hitting us for 25 years."

An American newspaper correspondent is pictured as a hearty fellow, easy to get along with and able to handle his share of vodka.

One of the new tractor manufacturing plants burns down, this dramatic blaze being rather badly executed particularly a scene in which the blonde heart interest of what promised to be a real romantic development loses her life in a plunge into the flames.

Scene supposedly inside the Kremlin is impressively done, especially the banquet episode and bright twist when an aged Party Worker insists on dancing to show up the professional terp artists.

Yarn has the typical Russian mother going to Stalin to tell of her fears about a big war. The Soviet leader confirms her suspicions but says Russia will survive because the Soviets are accustomed to trials and hardships. A wild-eyed, bellowing Hitler is excellently depicted, sound of his exhortations being heard all through the Paris episode—a clever touch.

The producers have I. Nabatov, as French Minister Bonnet, refusing to meet the Russian delegation, with the Soviets saying "now we are alone to meet the enemy." Bonnet is painted as a frivolous Frenchman who prefers to dance with his sweetheart at a nightclub to conferring with the Soviets. He is pictured phoning Chamberlain. Also expressing the feeling that the Nazis will attack in the east and feeling safe in France.

Then there's a quick flash to a purported scene of the Russians being attacked in 1941. What has transpired in the war prior to that is omitted completely. The scenes centering about the defense of Moscow are first-rate. Titles cite that the absence of a second front produced the bloody onslaught on Stalingrad with its house-to-house defense.

The father, who figures most importantly in the story, along with his young son, is shot down by a Nazi firing squad after being captured defending his tank. But his mother manages to survive everything, is cheered by the triumphant Russian troops and by Party Workers in another brilliant Kremlin scene.

Mikhail Gelovani, as Stalin, is a standout naturally, but it's a credit to his acting ability that he does not overplay this vital role. His makeup speaks much for the Russian artists, especially in later scenes when he has grown older. S. Chiatsintova, as the typical Russian mother, nearly thefts the picture from him, while I. Nabatov is priceless in the highly burlesqued version of Bonnet.

Several of the Soviet leaders are recognizable, particularly Molotov, but none of the actors is identified as to characters they portray. N. Bogoliubov, D. Pavlov, T. Makarova and M. Shtraugh (the American correspondent) chip in with the next best performances. Picture boasts the biggest group of extras probably ever employed in a Russian production.

Mikhail Chiaureli turns in a splendid job of directing. In fact, he proves himself a better director than scripter. He and N. Pavlenko did the screenplay, and obviously had their troubles. Camera work of A. Kesmatov is on the uneven side but superb on the sweeping mob scenes. Score by A. Balanchivadze is one of the better features of the production, it being employed with telling effect in the more dramatic scenes. English titling by C. Clement is solid. *Wear.*

Miniature Reviews

"Crossfire" (RKO). Provocative whodunit against anti-Semitism framework. Will get plenty of b.o. attention.

"The Upturned Glass" (British) (Gen.). James Mason in stark medico drama. Looks good b.o.

"Frieda" (British) (Gen.) Good postwar drama of Britisher marrying German; will need exploitation.

"Black Gold" (color) (Mono). Interesting story of the 1924 Kentuck Derby winner, told in Cinecolor. Okay b.o.

"Shop Girls of Paris" (French). Emile Zola story adapted into okay film for art houses.

"The Loves of Joanna Godden" (British). Mild melo with sheep raising farm background; limited b.o. prospects.

Crossfire

RKO release of Dore Schary (Adrian Scott) production. Stars Robert Young, Robert Mitchum, Robert Ryan; features Gloria Grahame, Paul Kelly, Sam Levene. Directed by Edward Dmytryk. Screenplay, John Paxton, from novel ("The Brick Foxhole") by Richard Brooks; camera, J. Roy Hunt, Russell A. Cully; asst. director, Nate Levinson; dialog director, William E. Watts; music, C. Bakaleinikoff; editor, Harry Gerstad. Tradeshown N. Y., June 20, '47. Running time, **86 MINS.**

Finlay....Robert Young
Keeley....Robert Mitchum
Montgomery....Robert Ryan
Ginny....Gloria Grahame
The Man....Paul Kelly
Samuels....Sam Levene
Mary Mitchell....Jacqueline White
Floyd....Steve Brodie
Mitchell....George Cooper
Bill....Richard Benedict
Detective....Richard Powers
Leroy....William Phipps
Harry....Lex Barker
Miss White....Marlo Dwyer

"Crossfire" is a frank spotlight on anti-Semitism. Producer Dore Schary, in association with Adrian Scott, has pulled no punches. There is no skirting such relative fol-de-rol as intermarriage or clubs that exclude Jews. Here is a hard-hitting film whose whodunit aspects are fundamentally incidental to the overall thesis of bigotry and race prejudice. It deserves to do well at the boxoffice because of its message.

While the murder-mystery aspect is an exciting overall pattern, the RKO sales department must depend on the more serious thesis for b.o. Some keys may react in greater or smaller degree at the wickets but it would be to the demerit of the American film public should "Crossfire" fail to get b.o. support. If the recent hoopla about British pictures commanding attention because they're "different" holds true, then here is one Hollywood entry which is certainly unusual.

The unusualness embraces a number of intra-trade factors beyond the ken or concern of the average exhibitor and/or his customers. Yet the press may well seize upon "Crossfire" to the degree it will enhance the apparent values.

There are three Roberts (Young, Mitchum and Ryan) on the marquee, all giving capital performances. Young is unusual as the detective captain; Mitchum is the "right" sort of cynical GI; and Ryan a commanding personality, in this instance the bigoted soldier-killer, whose sneers and leers about Sam Levene and his tribe are all too obvious. There are other good performances—Gloria Grahame as a floozy who should get much audience (and RKO studio) attention; George Cooper as the sensitive, artistic GI, and William Phipps as the Tennessee hillbilly who is the key in helping spring the trap on Ryan.

Herein is emphasized that, even in these days, Hollywood can turn out punchy modest-budgeters. "Crossfire" hasn't been skimped upon, yet it has movement, intrigue, tempo and purpose. Here's an excellent sample of a film that punches over a contemporaneous thought without preaching.

The pic opens with the fatal slugfest in Levene's apartment, when his hospitality is abused and Ryan kills him. Director Edward Dmytryk has drawn gripping portraitures. The flashback technique is effective as it shades and colors the sundry attitudes of the heavy, as seen or recalled by the rest of the cast. The lensing effectively interprets the vague, distorted recollections of a hazy drunken evening as the detective attempts to reconstruct the crime. The bully compounds his crime by killing one of his buddies to further protect himself.

Through it all, as Young, the dick, puts the pattern together, are introduced sundry bits of frank dialog. There is the adult-looking Levene, discharged after Okinawa, but still subject to Ryan's cracks about draft-dodging, and Young recounts how his own grandfather was berated as an "Irish mick" and "priest-lover," and less than 100 years before was himself a victim of prejudice. The Tennessee kid, whom Ryan bulldozes in the barracks as a "hillbilly," is part of the same secret hate or derision by one American for another; the prejudices, born of ignorance, frequently are germinated by an unconscious fear of something he can't comprehend. Whatever the hate philosophy, it's punched over in staccato style by John Paxton's screenplay and effectively linked to the general action. *Abel.*

The Upturned Glass

(BRITISH-MADE)

London, June 18.

General Film Distributors' release of Sydney Box production. Stars James Mason, Rosamund John, Pamela Kellino. Directed by Lawrence Huntingdon. Screenplay, J. P. Monaghan and Pamela Kellino, from original story by J. P. Monaghan; camera, Reginald Wyer. At Odeon theatre, London, June 17, '47. Running time, **86 MINS.**

Michael Joyce	James Mason
Emma Wright	Rosamund John
Kate Howard	Pamela Kellino
Ann Wright	Ann Stephens
Clay	Morland Graham
Dr. Farrell	Brefni O'Rourke
Coroner	Henry Oscar
Miss Marsh	Jane Hylton
Lorry Driver	Howard Douglas
Girl Student	Sheila Huntingdon
U. S. Driver	J. Monaghan
Mobile Policeman	Maurice Denham
Junior Doctor	Cyril Chamberlain

Of the boxoffice merits of "The Upturned Glass," there can be no two opinions. It will rake in handsome profits for all concerned. But about the artistry of the film there will be much debate. Some will condemn the interminable narrative—that besetting sin of present-day picture makers—even though it's admirably spoken through clenched teeth by James Mason.

Some will dislike the unnecessary flashbacks and the actual repetition of one incident. Many will squirm at two operations performed on children, sparing the audience nothing, and not a few will shudder at the three principals strewing the stage as corpses.

But in the final analysis it all boils down to James Mason. He spells boxoffice, and "Upturned Glass" will sweep the b.o.'s of this country, and probably those in America, just as surely as "Seventh Veil" did.

Michael, a brilliant young surgeon, falls in love with Emma, whose child he has saved from total blindness. The husband is abroad and her sheltered life is disturbed only by a jealous, widowed sister-in-law, Kate. But Emma decides she cannot endanger the child's future nor shirk her responsibilities to her husband, and she and Michael agree to say goodbye.

Then with tragic suddenness Michael learns that Emma is dead, having fallen from a high window in her country house. Suspicious of foul play, his notions are confirmed at the inquest, and he realizes that Kate has killed her sister-in-law. He decided to murder Kate, begins an affair with her, eventually takes her to the house and the very room where Emma was killed and murders Kate in a similar manner, throwing her from the window.

To dispose of the evidence of his crime, Michael stuffs the body into his car and begins a drive on fog-ridden highways. A stranded doctor begs a lift on his way to a dying child and Michael, torn between the escape instincts of a criminal and those of a great surgeon, performs a miraculous operation and saves the child's life. But the doctor has stumbled on the other's secret and tells him he is suffering from paranoia. In fact, he tells Michael he is mad, and obsessed with this diagnosis, the surgeon flings himself over a cliff into the sea.

That's the skeleton of the story, and most of it is related by Michael to a class of students as the case history of an anonymous surgeon. There is nothing heroic about the tale and little that is moving. One can almost hear Mason saying through those tight-clenched jaws that sentiment must be avoided at all costs.

The end may leave some patrons too shattered to express an opinion, but exhibs can cash in on the angle of Mason committing murder and dying to revenge the woman he loves.

The part has been tailored to fit Mason, and he gives it complete credibility. Rosamund John has never looked better nor played better, and Pamela Kellino is the perfect shrew.

Brefni O'Rorke, in last part before his death, plays the other doctor very well, and all the minor roles are okay.

Production is good and dialog adult, although a little of it may be too much so for some audiences. *Cane.*

Discovery

(DOCUMENTARY)

Boston, June 19.

Discovery Pictures, Inc., release of Joseph E. Levine and James R. Irwin production. Features Adm. Richard E. Byrd. Running time, **80 MINS.**

"Discovery," despite the patchy quality of much of the film, stands as a piece of high—and authentic—adventure. This, coupled with the current news value of Adm. Byrd's recent south polar naval operation, should make it plenty worthwhile for the action market, especially if properly coupled.

Actually reverts back to Byrd's 1933-1935 expedition that resulted in Byrd's best sellers, "Discovery" and "Alone," and has no connection whatever with the recent Navy deal. Begins with shots of the departure of the Bear and the Ruppert from Boston and, after a few shots of Equatorial crossing gags on the ships, gets right down to business with scenes of terrific south Atlantic gales and shots of the birth of icebergs as colossal hunks of the Great Barrier topple fantastically into the sea.

There follows the general narrative of the expedition's search for the snow-buried Little America, its difficulties unloading the ships alongside the ice barrier, its ordeal in setting up for the incredible gales and temperatures of the south polar winter night. Narrative builds up to Byrd's solitary five-month stay 150 miles from the expedition's base, from which he was rescued near death by asphyxiation. Lighter moments are provided by antics of penguins, husky puppies, the expedition's cows, etc., but the main theme is steadily scientific and business-like with frequent thrill shots of everything from plane crashes to schools of killer whales thrashing in a blow hole in the ice.

Adm. Byrd handles most of the narrative, and does it well. Camera naturally dwells on the admiral, but he's photogenic enough to stand it. Occasional scenes, such as those in the winter quarters with the expedition's lieutenants deciding to make the rescue, seem staged and phoney, while the use of sound effects, as the dubbing-in of a male chorus a la a Romberg operetta when the rescue crew takes off with flaming torches over the snow, offer a jarring theatrical note. But the authenticity of the picture, even when the photography fails to maintain a professional pace, is never open to doubt. Could have been more carefully edited—and the theatricals omitted entirely—but nobody is likely to figure he didn't get his money's worth of thrills. *Elie.*

Frieda

(BRITISH-MADE)

London, June 20.

General Film Distributors' release of Ealing Studios-Michael Balcon production. Stars Mai Zetterling, Glynis Johns, Flora Robson, David Farrar, Albert Lieven. Directed by Basil Deardeb. Screenplay, Angus McPhail, Ronald Millar, from play by Ronald Millar; camera, Gordon Dines; music, John Greenwood. At Studio One, London, June 19, '47. Running time, 98 MINS.

Robert	David Farrar
Judy	Glynis Johns
Frieda	Mai Zetterling
Nell	Flora Robson
Richard	Albert Lieven
Mrs. Dawson	Barbara Everest
Edith	Gladys Henson
Tony	Ray Jackson
Alan	Patrick Holt
Merrick	Milton Rosmer
Jim Merrick	Barry Letts
Mrs. Freeman	Renee Gadd
Bailey	Eliot Makeham
Granger	John Ruddock
Herriott	D. A. Clarke-Smith
Beckwith	Garry Marsh

The thoughtful play that scored a fair success on the London stage has been turned into a thoughtful picture. "Frieda" poses the timely post-war question—would you welcome a German girl into your home as wife of your son whom she helped to escape from a prison camp? And that's the best angle for exhibs to exploit, a method being widely adopted here.

Story begins in April, 1945, in the bombed shell of a Polish Protestant church, when Robert, a British officer, marries Frieda, a Catholic German nurse who helped him escape. She loves him, but Robert is merely repaying a debt with a British passport and a trip to his home in a small English town.

Frieda gets a cool welcome. Robert's mother tries to be nice but Frieda is not the daughter-in-law she hoped for. His aunt expects Frieda to be a handicap to a political career. His young stepbrother, Tony, hates all Germans on principle. Only person to show any warmth is Robert's sister-in-law Judy, a war widow who loves Robert. Being the sixth year of the war, and the era of flying bombs, there is natural hostility among the townspeople. Peace comes, and gradually Frieda is accepted. The shy foreigner is now at home, and she accedes to Robert's request that their marriage be ratified by the Roman Catholic Church so that Frieda can really be his wife.

On the eve of the ceremony, brother Ricky arrives dressed as a Polish soldier. She soon discovers that beneath the uniform is a fanatical Nazi looking forward to the next war. In the local pub his identity is revealed by a British soldier whom Ricky tortured in a camp. Denying it in public he admits it in private to Robert, and claims falsely that Frieda knows and approves.

Realizing that Robert's faith in her is shaken, Frieda attempts to drown herself, but is rescued by Robert. Aunt is left to confess she is wrong, with the explosive tag line, "You cannot treat human beings as though they were less than human, without becoming less than human yourself."

Political implications constantly intruding on this tragic love story, as they are doubtless intended to do, hinder it being poignant and moving. The spark is missing. One reason may be that Frieda's ordeal in rescuing Robert from prison camp is not seen. A brief mention that she saved him does not register sufficiently. Pic is overladen with symbolism. It will need a campaign to sell it, and may rate a prestige pic for U. S.

To play the name part, Mai Zetterling (star of "Torment"), was imported from Sweden. No pin-up girl, and with a liking for the Veronica Lake hair-do, she has a strong personality. There's no doubt she's a fine actress, but she's given a limited opportunity to reveal her range.

Best performances come from Flora Robson and Albert Lieven, less handicapped by their parts than others in the competent cast. *Cane.*

Black Gold

(COLOR)

Hollywood, June 21.

Monogram release of Allied Artists production, produced by Jeffrey Bernerd. Stars Anthony Quinn; features Katherine DeMille, Elyse Knox, Ducky Louie, Kane Richmond, Moroni Olsen, Raymond Hatton. Directed by Phil Karlson. Screenplay, Agnes Christine Johnston; story, Caryl Coleman; camera (Cinecolor), Harry Neumann; editor, Roy Livingston. Previewed at Pan Pacific theatre, Hollywood, June 19, '47. Running time, **89 MINS.**

Charley Eagle	Anthony Quinn
Sarah Eagle	Katherine DeMille
Ruth Fraser	Elyse Knox
Davey	Ducky Louie
Stanley Lowell	Kane Richmond
Dan Toland	Moroni Olsen
Bucky	Raymond Hatton
Col. Caldwell	Thurston Hall
Senator Watkins	Charles Trowbridge
Schoolboy	Darryl Hickman

Commentary of the Kentucky Derby:
Clem McCarthy
Commentary of the Tijuana Race:
Joe Hernandez

"Black Gold" draws its title from the Indian-owned winner of the 1924 Kentucky Derby. Film is second Allied Artists production for Monogram and returns should be good. Racing scenes are exciting, the western scenery is beautiful and there's a family interest in the story that stands up despite a bit too much emphasis on pathos and soapboxing on tolerance.

The story of an Indian and his horse, it's played for slowly developing interest. Accounting principally for the audience tug is the standout work of Anthony Quinn as the Indian. Actor demonstrates that all he needs to pack a wallop is the proper role. He has it here and makes it socko. His fine work is strongly backed by that of Katherine DeMille as his educated wife, and Ducky Louie as the orphaned Chinese boy whom he adopts.

The Agnes Christine Johnston script, from an original story by Caryl Coleman, is commendable in that there is not a single Indian-uttered "ugh" in the dialog. Plot depicts Charley Eagle, uneducated redskin who loves nature, his horse and his wife. Eagle's life is relatively uncomplicated until oil is discovered on his land. He becomes a millionaire, dreams of his horse running and winning in the Derby, a fact not accomplished until after his death. Throughout script points up tear-jerker moments, and Phil Karlson's direction dwells on such sequences a bit too long. Otherwise, he gives measured movement to story unfoldment and handles the players for solid effect. Running of the Derby at finale is as exciting as a real race as directed by Reeves "Breezy" Eason.

There is a light romance between Elyse Knox, school teacher, and Kane Richmond. Raymond Hatton registers as Eagle's friend and horse trainer, as does Moroni Olsen as a racing rival.

Harry Neumann makes good use of his color camera in lensing outdoor settings. Tint process, while entirely satisfactory on exterior shots, still leaves more perfection to be desired of interiors. Jeffrey Bernerd has given production sturdy values that will pay off. *Brog.*

Shop Girls of Paris
(Au Bonheur Des Dames)
(FRENCH-MADE)

Mage Films release. Stars Michel Simon, Albert Prejean, Blanchette Brunoy; features Suzy Prim, Jean Tissier. Directed by Andre Cayatte. Screenplay, Cayatte and Andre Legrand, from story by Emile Zola. At Studio 65, N. Y., beginning June 21, '47. Running time, 83 MINS.

Baudu	Michel Simon
Mouret	Albert Prejean
Denise	Blanchette Brunoy
Mme. Desforges	Suzy Prim
Bourdoncle	Jean Tissier
Mellevadon	Juliette Faber
Pauline	Jacqueline Gautier
Jean	Andre Reybaz

(In French; English Titles)

"Shop Girls of Paris," although a juicy morsel for the art houses, doesn't have the stuff to be classed with some of the screen classics that have been exported from French studios. Interesting story, adapted from one of Emile Zola's lesser-known novels, is played to the hilt in the best tradition of French realism and the cast is known enough to French film frequenters to constitute a marquee lure.

Zola apparently wrote the tale to depict the tragedies faced by the little guys under the survival-of-the-fittest philosophy. In transferring the theme to the screen, however, scripters Andre Cayatte and Andre Legrand seem to have been confused over whether they were filming a tragedy or a comedy. Result is a strange mixture of both, with the lighter side predominant. Two climaxes, consequently, in which the little guys are knocked off, come with almost shocking surprise.

Tale revolves around a department store magnate in Paris who's out to make his store the largest in the world, regardless of the fact that the small neighboring competitors are forced out of business. One of these is an old man with a small dry-goods shop, who rallies the other indie entrepreneurs on the block to cut their prices to stay in the running. His orphaned niece, a country lass, has come to the big city and, since the old man doesn't have a job for her, goes to work in the large store.

After most of the other small shops are liquidated, the magnate buys out the old man through a ruse and finally succeeds in opening what must have been the forerunner of today's Gimbel's or Macy's. Old man, heart-sick, interrupts a party celebrating the large store's opening to tell off the magnate and, returning home through the streets, is run over and killed by a horse. His niece, unmindful of the tragedy meanwhile, accepts the store owner's offer of marriage as the film ends.

Cast is unanimously excellent under the guiding hand of Cayatte, who doubled on direction. Michel Simon turns in a moving portrayal of the old man, at times resembling the late Raimu in both appearance and heavy-handed thesping. Albert Prejean, as the young magnate, is fine and is teamed well with Blanchette Brunoy as the niece. Suzy Prim has a role tailored to her talents in the amorous widow on the make for Prejean both romantically and in business. Neat character parts are turned in by Jean Tissier, as the prissy and unscrupulous assistant manager of the department store, and Jacqueline Gautier, as the old man's ill-fated daughter.

Sets are confined to the two stores but the department store's lavish interior evidences a heavy budget, as does the extremely large group of extras. Camera work and lighting are good, and the symphonic score fits well into the picture's various moods. English titles are adequate but miss much of the lusty dialog. *Stal.*

Loves of Joanna Godden
(BRITISH-MADE)

London, June 10.

General Film Distributors' release of Ealing Studios-Michael Balcon production. Stars Googie Withers, John McCallum, Jean Kent. Directed by Charles Frend. Screenplay by H. E. Bates; adaptation by Angus McPhail from novel "Joanna Godden," by Sheila Kaye-Smith; camera, Douglas Slocombe; music, Vaughn Williams. At Odeon theatre. London, June 9, '47. Running time, 91 MINS.

Joanna Godden	Googie Withers
Ellen Godden	Jean Kent
Arthur Alce	John McCallum
Martin Trevor	Derek Bond
Harry Trevor	Henry Mollison
Collard	Chips Rafferty
Louise	Sonia Holm
Grace Wickens	Josephine Stuart
Peter Relf	Alec Faversham
Stuppen	Edward Rigby
Isaac Turk	Frederick Piper
Young Turk	Fred Bateman
Miss Luckhurst	Barbara Leake
Reverend Brett	Ronald Simpson

As a record of sheep farming in a corner of England in 1905, this picture may have its points. But as a story of a high-spirited, lovely young woman who inherits a farm and is expected to marry and let her husband do the job, the picture falls short of its intentions. So enamored did producer and director become with their location, that they were determined to teach audiences all they had learned about sheep breeding. And that doesn't ring a merry tune at the boxoffice.

Set against the background of the Romney Marshes in Kent, Joanna, impetuous and self-willed, is bequeathed one of the leading farms on the Marsh. A codicil in her father's will expresses the hope that she will marry neighbor-farmer Arthur Alce. Determined to defy the conventions of the time, she outrages the countryside by running the farm herself and by her experiments in cross-breeding and ploughing. Stinting herself and luxury, she sends her young sister, Ellen, to a finishing school, from which the girl returns an accomplished gold-digger.

Joanna has a mild affair with Collard, the man engaged to look after her sheep, before she falls for a local aristocrat, Martin Trevor. The banns are put up, but Martin is drowned. Meanwhile Ellen has bewitched Arthur Alce, Joanna's "old faithful," marries him, and deserts him for an old man with money. Which paves the way for Joanna and Arthur to fall into each other's arms.

Too much attention appears to have been lavished on the atmosphere of the English countryside, and too little on the story. Photography too, isn't out-of-the-ordinary. Googie Withers looks as attractive as she has ever done, but her characterization of the name part has a soporific monotony. She rings the changes on a couple of moods, and for the main part moons around like a wounded heifer. Jean Kent has outgrown the pigtail stage, and not all the magic of the camera can make her credible as a schoolgirl.

The men fare somewhat better, although John McCallum is given little to lighten his dourness. Derek Bond gives a natural and pleasant performance as Martin, and Chips Rafferty disappears far too early. Minor characters are extremely well played.

Picture has little marquee value here and must fight hard to win audiences. In the U. S. it may find a place in prestige theatres.

Miniature Reviews

"The Hucksters" (M-G). Surefire filmization of bestseller, fortified by Gable topping strong cast.

"Cry Wolf" (WB). Melodrama with Errol Flynn and Barbara Stanwyck furnishing marquee strength.

"The Romance of Rosy Ridge" (Songs) (MG). Strong drama of reconstruction days in Missouri following Civil War. Good b.o.

"The Crimson Key" (20th). Average modest-budgeted whodunit for dualer support.

"The Roosevelt Story" (Tola). Moving semi-documentary on the late President's career. Will draw.

"For the Love of Rusty" (Col.). Well-developed program feature for family trade, another in "Rusty" series.

"They Made Me A Fugitive" (British) (WB). Good gangster pic, with cockney lingo only drawback. Good grosser.

'Heartaches' (PRC). Moderately entertaining programmer.

"Pioneer Justice" (PRC). Fast-moving, low-budget western for outdoor addicts.

"Dancing With Crime" (British) (Par). So-so crook story; moderate draw.

"Dragnet" (SGP). Mystery melodrama with okay prospects in smaller situations.

The Hucksters
(ONE SONG)

Metro release of Arthur Hornblow, Jr., production. Stars Clark Gable, Deborah Kerr; features Sydney Greenstreet, Adolphe Menjou, Keenan Wynn, Ava Gardner, Edward Arnold. Directed by Jack Conway. From bestseller by Frederic Wakeman; screenplay, Luther Davis; adaptation, Edward Chodorov and George Wells; camera, Harold Rosson; editor, Frank Sullivan; special effects, Warren Newcombe, A. Arnold Hillespie. Tradeshown June 18, '47. Running time, 115 MINS.

Victor Albee Norman	Clark Gable
Kay Dorrance	Deborah Kerr
Evan Llewellyn Evans	Sydney Greenstreet
Mr. Kimberly	Adolphe Menjou
Jean Ogilvie	Ava Gardner
Buddy Hare	Keenan Wynn
Dave Lash	Edward Arnold
Valet	Aubrey Mather
Cooke	Richard Gaines
Max Herman	Frank Albertson
Georgie Gaver	Douglas Fowley
Michael Michaelson	Clinton Sundberg
Mrs. Kimberly	Gloria Holden
Betty	Connie Gilchrist
Regina Kennedy	Kathryn Card
Miss Hammer	Lillian Bronson
Secretary	Vera Marshe
Allison	Ralph Bunker
Kimberly Receptionist	Virginia Dale
Blake	Jimmy Conlin

"The Hucksters" is one of those ready-made screen properties which fundamentally is figured not to miss. And it doesn't. It will be a boxoffice mop-up although, in a large sense, it will be largely to the basic credit of the well-publicized bestseller, the automatic ballyhoo that goes with a film of this nature, and perhaps even from unsuspected sources, should the radio broadcasting industry and its attendant ad agency and sponsoritis adjuncts kick up a rumpus. A casus belli might well be fomented in the now traditional pix vs. radio situation. The b.o. payoff on that is obvious.

All these factors may very conceivably take precedence even above the fact that Gable is back and this time Deborah Kerr has got him. And so Metro's technique of quickly projecting a new personality, by exposing her to Gable's masculine charms, is surefire payoff.

Despite this pat showmanship there are reservations on the Gable-Kerr team. Somehow he just doesn't quite take hold of the huckster chore in signal manner. Same goes for Miss Kerr who is a shade prissy for her volatile romantic role. That's as much scripting shortcoming as her personation. She's cast as a very proper Sutton Place war hero-general's widow, with two children who go for Gable, as she does, to the extent of a quickie plane flight to his Bel-Air layout where he's cutting a new radio program for Beautee Soap, tycooned by the irascible and tyrannical Evan Llewellyn Evans. Sydney Greenstreet's portrayal of the soap despot emerges as the performance of the picture, as does Keenan Wynn, for what he does, as the ham ex-burlesque candy butcher gone radio comic. Ava Gardner is thoroughly believable (she does an incidental song, "Don't Tell Me") as the on-the-make songstress; Adolphe Menjou is the harassed head of the radio agency which caters to Evans' whilom ways because it's a $10,000,000 account. As for Edward Arnold, playing the head of the powerful talent agency, he takes hold of a bit part, and in that dramatic scene where Gable blackjacks him into releasing the comedian, he takes the play away from the star.

Gable looks trim and fit but somehow a shade too mature for the capricious role of the huckster who talks his way into a $35,000 job (and bonus), is a killer with the femmes, and when he has the soap tycoon in his corner throws him over because he sees himself fast getting typed among the ad agency cliches.

The intra-trade sidelights on radio-agency-sponsor ulcerous vagaries are a credit to technical adviser John Driscoll. It's right out of Madison avenue and Columbia Square. The book's wide sale, of course, has punched over most of the alleged real-life prototypes. The visual enactment by Greenstreet of all the sponsor's grossness and cruelties—suffered by a group of high-geared people only because he pays the bills so handsomely—is a cinematic-plus factor under visual enactment. The plush atmosphere of ad agency behaviorism, in and out of business, is socked over by the scripters, Jack Conway's direction, and the ultra production endowed it by Arthur Hornblow, Jr. *Abel.*

Cry Wolf

Hollywood, June 28.

Warner Bros. release of Henry Blanke production. Stars Errol Flynn, Barbara Stanwyck; features Richard Basehart, Geraldine Brooks, Jerome Cowan, John Ridgely, Patricia White, Rory Mallinson, Helene Thimig. Directed by Peter Godfrey. Screenplay, Catherine Turney; from novel by Marjorie Carlton; camera, Carl Guthrie; music, Franz Waxman; editor, Folmar Blangsted. Tradeshown June 27, '47. Running time, 83 MINS.

Mark Caldwell	Errol Flynn
Sandra Marshall	Barbara Stanwyck
James Demarest	Richard Basehart
Senator Caldwell	Jerome Cowan
Jackson Laidell	John Ridgely
Angela	Patricia White
Becket	Rory Mallinson
Marta	Helene Thimig
Davenport	Paul Stanton
Roberts	Barry Bernard

And Introducing
Geraldine Brooks as Julie Demarest

"Cry Wolf" is fair melodrama that gains some importance from strength of its star names, Errol Flynn and Barbara Stanwyck. Film starts tensely and promises plenty of suspense but sags considerably before running its course. Production values by Henry Blanke are in keeping with melodramatic background.

Plot builds mystery around supposed death of young man secretly married to Miss Stanwyck. She comes to his home to attend the funeral and senses that something is wrong. By pointed hints gradually inserted, Miss Stanwyck comes to believe that her husband is still alive and being kept a prisoner by his uncle, Flynn. There are several socko shock scenes that aid mystery flavor but interest is not sustained and ending falls flat when it is disclosed that the husband is crazy and Flynn's concealment is to prevent unflavorable publicity spoiling political ambitions of another relative. Windup is too contrived to be believable when husband is conveniently killed to clear way for romance between Flynn and Miss Stanwyck.

Peter Godfrey's direction of the Catherine Torney script, based on Marjorie Carleton's novel, is not always even, although, as noted, he does hit high spots of tension. Miss Stanwyck gives her usual polished talent to her role, and Flynn is completely different type of characterization, holds up his end. Richard Basehart has only two sequences as the mad husband. Geraldine Brooks makes an interesting and promising film debut as another member of the mad family who commits suicide. Jerome Cowan, Patricia White, John Ridgely, Rory Mallinson, Helene Thimig and others are good.

Art direction has furnished gloomy settings and atmosphere for story in keeping with melodrama aims and Carl Guthrie's camera makes the most of them. Editing is choppy, which doesn't help clarity of plot motivation. Franz Waxman's score is effective. *Brog.*

Romance of Rosy Ridge
(SONGS)

Hollywood, July 1.

Metro release of Jack Cummings production. Stars Van Johnson; features Thomas Mitchell, Janet Leigh, Marshall Thompson, Selena Royle, Dean Stockwell. Directed by Roy Rowland. Screenplay, Lester Cole; based on story by MacKinlay Kantor; camera, Sidney Wagner; new songs, Earl Robinson and Lewis Allan; score, George Bassman; editor, Ralph E. Winters. Tradeshown July 1, '47. Running time, **105 MINS.**

Henry Carson....................Van Johnson
Gill MacBean..............Thomas Mitchell
Lissy Anne MacBean.........Janet Leigh
Ben MacBean.........Marshall Thompson
Sairy MacBean..............Selena Royle
John Dessark..............Charles Dingle
Andrew MacBean.........Dean Stockwell
Cal Baggett......................Guy Kibbee
Emily Baggett..........Elisabeth Risdon
Badge Dessark....................Jim Davis
Dan Yeary...............Russell Simpson
Ninny Nat................O. Z. Whitehead
John Willhart....................James Bell
Mrs. Willhart..................Joyce Arling
Ad Buchanan.............William Bishop
Tom Yeary......................Paul Langton

"The Romance of Rosy Ridge" is good screen entertainment. A tale of reconstruction days following the Civil War, picture packs strong drama and interest. As its star, Van Johnson has his best role to date and gives a splendid performance. Film also introduces femme newcomer, Janet Leigh, whose work indicates a bright future. Boxoffice outlook is sturdy, film's contents helping to overcome awkward title.

Picture poses a tolerance plea that is a legitimate part of story motivation, thus very effective. Producer Jack Cummings and director Roy Rowland make the most of drama in the MacKinlay Kantor story, scripted by Lester Cole. They give it natural unfoldment against austere farming background in early-day Missouri. From such a simple thing as getting the hay in before the rains come, Rowland develops a tense, suspenseful sequence that packs an almost unbelievable wallop. Other scenes are equally effective in selling the drama.

Tolerance theme is exploited through ill-feeling among neighbors who fought on opposite sides in the war between states and who have brought their feuding into peacetime. Van Johnson's character is used to resolve intolerance in the Missouri valley and the story pitch registers strongly as written by Cole.

American folk music used in the good score and new songs that follow the folk tune pattern contribute interest. Also catching attention is the folk dance used in one sequence.

Plot brings Johnson, wandering ex-soldier, to farm of Thomas Mitchell, a fiery rebel, who bases his friendship on the color of a man's britches. Grey is God's color to him and blue means war. Attention is centered on struggle of hewing a living from the soil, the fear of the night raiders who burn barns and spread discord between neighbors, a romance between Johnson and Miss Leigh, Mitchell's daughter. Climax has a pitched battle between Johnson and leader of the raiders that is crammed with hard action.

Thomas Mitchell's performance rates among his finest. Selena Royle, as his wife, is another who grabs plenty of credit for talented work. Marshall Thompson, Charles Dingle, Dean Stockwell, Guy Kibbee, Elisabeth Risdon, Russell Simpson, O. Z. Whitehead are others showing up in the strong cast.

Sidney Wagner's camera makes much of the settings against which the story is displayed. Realistic, austere quality of the art direction and set decorations aid in lending credence to the picture. Other credits are in keeping. *Brog.*

The Crimson Key

20th-Fox release of Sol M. Wurtzel production. Features Kent Taylor, Doris Dowling, Dennis Hoey. Directed by Eugene Forde. Original story and screenplay, Irving Elman; camera, Benjamin Kline; editor, Frank Baldridge. Tradeshown N.Y. June 30, '47. Running time, **76 MINS.**

Larry Morgan......................Kent Taylor
Mrs. Loring....................Doris Dowling
Steven Loring....................Dennis Hoey
Heidi..............................Louise Currie
Peter Vandaman..............Iran Triesault
Fitzroy.........................Arthur Space
Dizzy................................Vera Marshe
Jeffrey Regan.....................Edwin Rand
Mrs. Swann................Bernadene Hayes
Miss Phillips..................Victoria Horne
Dr. Swann..........................Doug Evans
Purris Wood.........................Ann Doran
Wing.........................Victor Sen Yung
Hotel Clerk....................Chester Clute
Gunman..........................Ralf Harolde
Dr. Harlow....................Milton Parsons
Det. Sgt.........................Jimmy Magill
Petuna.........................Marietta Canty
Night Clerk...................Stanley Mann

Conventionally modelled whodunit, "The Crimson Key" will give average support in dualer situations. Twisting, turning, blood-soaked plot, based upon the familiar shenanigans of a know-all private eye, never becomes crystal clear, but there are enough corpses per cinema foot to appease the mystery addicts.

Film's cast, though not standout in marquee power, does a neatly competent job with Kent Taylor and Doris Dowling in the top spots. Production dress is standard for modest-budgeters. Main flaw is the screenplay which hews too closely to overworked lines and situations. Direction and tight editing do nicely in maintaining a steady pace with an assist from good camera work.

Taylor is a confidential gumshoe who's hired by a rich dame jealous of her doctor-husband's nocturnal roamings. Before he can count the down payment, both his client and her husband are killed by persons unknown. Taylor, after thumbing his nose at the w.k. dumb dick from official headquarters, wends his way through a couple of beatings to the parlor of a rich femme dipso who was being treated by the murdered medico. Plenty of suspicious characters divert his attention but he nabs the guilty culprit on schedule as expected.

Taylor registers pleasantly as the handsome, self-assured eye who can flip a hardboiled crack and take, as well as give, a crusher on the jaw. Doris Dowling, as the dipso, is an unusual looker who oozes enough femme fatale shadings to adequately fit the bill. Dennis Hoey plays well as her falsely-suspected husband while rest of cast turns in competent performances in lesser roles. *Herm.*

The Roosevelt Story
(SEMI-DOCUMENTARY)

Tola Productions release of Martin Levine and Oliver Unger (in association with Harry Brandt) production. Original script by Lawrence M. Klee. Editorial consultant, Elliott Roosevelt. Score, Earl Robinson; lyrics, Lewis Allan; music director, Jack Shaindlin; supervising editor and compiler, Walter Klee; editor, William Van Praag. Previewed N. Y., June 26, '47. Running time, **80 MINS.**

Cabbie (Voice of People)....Kenneth Lynch
Voice of Depression............Canada Lee
Voice of Opposition.............Ed Begley
Boy............................Gene Blakely
Girl...............................Kelly Flint

It is surprising how the editors of this motley collection of silent and talker newsreel shots, Army and captured enemy clips, and a few production bits, have managed to catch and sustain the heroic spirit of the late President. But catch and sustain it they did, for an unusual memorial to FDR. It will draw trade.

Put together very cleverly, with evident loving care, and supervised tastefully by Elliott Roosevelt, the President's son, this 80-minute semi-documentary is a moving tribute to a great man, as well as a fascinating chronicle of the troubled times of the past three decades. The film has certain mechanical and artistic flaws. Some of the clips—inevitably, perhaps—are bad, blurred or dark. The war section may be a little protracted. There is a little too much preachment in the running commentary, and a prolonged ending with the usual corny swelling chorus of voices rising to heaven.

But these are minor faults in the overall clever manipulation of a melange of material, that handled differently could have been drab and dated. Not only are the varied newsreels neatly spliced, but in themselves they dovetail perfectly with a commentary that tells the President's story and the story of the nation as well.

The films unroll to the running talk of a cab-driver, commenting on the scenes and their significance. His talk is slangy and colloquial, of the street. He quips about someone's odd dress, another's peculiar manner. But he points out, too, the significant bits—the crying populace when the President's casket goes by, the relief when Roosevelt takes hold in 1933, the far-sightedness of the President in the wake of the Fascist menace. There is a Voice of Opposition breaking in, now and then, to decry the President's acts, to play down the emergencies. There is also the Voice of Depression, describing what it was like to live through Hooverville days.

The film opens with the funeral cortege in 1945, moving slowly along D. C. streets while multitudes gaze in bereaved tribute. Then a flashback to a clip of 1904, of the newly wedded couple, Eleanor and Franklin D. Roosevelt (probably taken more for her sake, as niece of Theodore Roosevelt, than for an FDR still obscure). Other newsreel shots, when Roosevelt was Asst. Secretary of the Navy, when he campaigned for Wilson, when he as eagerly stumped for Al Smith, and so on down the years, to his own campaigns for the Presidency, the first, second, third and last.

In between, shots or other newsreel scenes for change of pace as well as background to the story—Times Sq., Coney Island, Hooverville shacks, closed banks, breadlines. Shots of Chamberlain and Churchill. War films from Germany, Italy, Japan. Meetings at Casablanca, Cairo, with Stalin, De Gaulle. A few production shots to tie them together, to keep the story flowing smoothly. And at the end, back to the simple, flag-draped caisson moving along a Washington street.

There are several outstanding shots, as the one during the campaign when the President denounces his political opponents for their attack on his dog, Fala, FDR dragging this one out with rich dry humor, running his hand over his mouth frequently in a gesture the filmgoer won't soon forget. A happy though crippled President playing waterball with the kids in his Warm Springs, Ga., foundation pool, and getting dunked. The inevitable aging of the President under the strain of office and handling of the war.

Film is a backward glance at history, bringing it up to the moment. The impact is startling. *Bron.*

For the Love of Rusty

Hollywood, June 28.

Columbia release of John Haggott production. Features Ted Donaldson, Tom Powers, Ann Doran, Aubrey Mather, Sid Tomack, George Meader, Mickey McGuire. Directed by John Sturges. Screenplay, Malcolm Stuart Boylan, based on characters created by Al Martin; camera, Vincent Farrar; editor, James Sweeney. At Pantages Hollywood, June 27, '47. Running time, **68 MINS.**

Danny Mitchell............Ted Donaldson
Hugh Mitchell..................Tom Powers
Ethel Mitchell...................Ann Doran
Dr. Francis Xavier Fay....Aubrey Mather
Moe Hatch........................Sid Tomack
J. Cecil Rinehardt.........George Meader
Gerald Hobble............Mickey McGuire
Hobble..........................Harry Hayden
Doc Levy..........................Fred Sears
Bill Worden.....................Dick Elliott
Frank Foley......................Olin Howlin
Tommy Worden...............Teddy Infuhr
Doc Levy, Jr............Dwayne Hickman
Squeaky.......................George Nokes
Sarah Johnson..........Almira Sessions
Rusty.......................................Flame

This latest in Columbia's series around a boy and his dog furnishes tiptop entertainment. Characters are well-developed, and film generally stands up above usual programmer level.

The Malcolm Stuart Boylan script draws motivation from misunderstanding between a boy and his father. The dad is too busy to take much trouble with his son. It remains for a dog and a traveling veterinary to bring the principals together. Plot has many heart-warming moments and good chuckles that will please family audiences.

Ted Donaldson is natural as the boy, and Flash, his dog, also garners interest. The kindly old vet as played by Aubrey Mather heads adult honors. Others who also are good include Tom Powers and Ann Doran, the father and mother; George Meaker, Sid Tomack and Almira Sessions.

John Sturges' direction takes plenty of care in developing the characters and scenes, a point that raises "For the Love of Rusty" above the usual "B" level. Production by John Haggott also demonstrates careful handling. Lensing by Vincent Farrar is excellent. *Brog.*

They Made Me a Fugitive
(BRITISH-MADE)

London, June 25.

Warner Bros. release of Alliance Production film. Stars Sally Gray, Trevor Howard, Griffith Jones. Directed by Cavalcanti. Screenplay by Noel Langley, from Jackson Budd's novel, "A Convict Has Escaped." Camera, Otto Heller; music, Francois Gaillard. At Warner, London, June 24, '47. Running time, **101 MINS.**

Sally Connor.......................Sally Gray
Clem Morgan................Trevor Howard
Narcy.......................Griffith Jones
Cora...............................Rene Ray
Aggy...........................Mary Merrall
Mrs. Fenshaw......................Vida Hope
Inspector Rockcliffe.......Ballard Berkeley
Olga.........................Phyllis Robins
Ellen...............................Eve Ashley
Curley......................Charles Farrell
Soapy....................Jack McNaughton

Hollywood, having for the time being foresworn gangster pix, British producers are now poaching on what were once sacred American preserves. British are in for a cycle of postwar gangster films, and "Fugitive" is the first of many that will be reminiscent of pix that have flourished on U. S. and British screens for decades.

"Fugitive" is tough and timely, with its own British flavor. It cashes in on topical headlines and should play to hefty grosses. Greatest handicap in U. S. market is cockney dialect of most of the players. Except for this, it would have been a good bet in dual siuations.

Clem Morgan, ex-soldier, finding Civvy Street dull and unexciting, joins Narcy, smooth-operating chief of a black-market gang. When Clem jibs at peddling dope, the other appropriates his girl, then frames him. Clem, serving 15 years in jail, is visited by Sally Connor, one time sweetheart of Narcy and now jealous of his new attachment. She goads him to escape and take his revenge.

After adventures which include a false murder charge against him, Clem reaches London and sets out to find Narcy, who has moved to a new hideout. With the help of the police, who for a change appear to know the true facts, Clem trails the other and his gang, catches up with them, and the inevitable fight leaves Narcy a corpse.

Only criticism of Noel Langley's well-written screenplay is the ending, which will leave most of the customers dissatisfied. One line by the detective could have set their minds at rest, without in any way interfering with the artistry of the pic. Similarly a line or two at the beginning, indicating why a decent ex-serviceman like Clem falls for a gangster's life, could have lifted the story to a higher sociological plane.

Having built his reputation on documentaries, Cavalcanti now proves that he can make a tough crime story with the best of them.

Acting is uniformly firstrate. Griffith Jones as the flashy gangster revels in the best part he has had in years. Trevor Howard, the quiet doctor of "Brief Encounter," does a fine job as a facetious lover and amateur crook, and Sally Gray takes full advantage of a good part. Only one false note mars an excellent performance by Rene Ray and that's the fault of the script. Praise is due to the minor part players, one or two of them like Cyril Smith being undeservedly robbed of credit.

Francois Gaillard contributes a noteworthy musical score. *Cane.*

Heartaches
(SONGS)

PRC release of Ben Stoloff (Marvin D. Stahl) production. Features Sheila Ryan, Chill Wills, Edward Norris, Ken Farrell. Directed by Basil Wrangell. Screenplay, George Bricker; original story, Monty F. Collins, Julian I. Peyser; songs, Kim Gannon, Walter Kent, John Klenner, Al Hoffman; camera, Jack Greenhalgh; editor, Charles Gross, Jr. Tradeshown N. Y., June 26, '47. Running time, 71 MINS.

Toni Wentworth.................Sheila Ryan
Jimmy McDonald..............Edward Norris
Boagey Mann.......................Chill Wills
Vic Morton.........................Ken Farrell
Lt. Armstrong.....................James Seay
Mike Connelly.....................Frank Orth
Sally ....Chill Williams
Pete Schilling...............Charles Mitchell
DeLong ....Al LaRue
Lila ....Phyllis Planchard
Anne Connelly..................Ann Staunton

Carrying a top revival tune as its title, "Heartaches" is a moderately entertaining whodunit, with songs, that emerges as suitable fare to round out double bills. Film's b.o. pull may be helped by the title; cast names offer little marquee draft.

With the story's locale centered about Hollywood, yarn deals with the career of a film crooner, portrayed by Ken Farrell. He's okay on looks, but his "voice" is actually that of Chill Wills, whose piping is dubbed in on the sound track. Of course, studio execs make every attempt to prevent a leak that Wills croons for Farrell. Complicating matters are a number of mailed threats on Farrell's life. Cops, as well as reporter Edward Norris, are inclined to discount them as publicity gags, but are convinced when a radio agent is rubbed out, followed by the shooting of the crooner's own rep, Frank Orth. Culprit is eventually rounded up and Norris wins Farrell's femme flack, Sheila Ryan.

Sandwiched in the footage are several songs, including the oldie, "Heartaches." plus a trio of new ones by Kim Gannon and Walter Kent. Best of these is "Can't Get That Gal." Thesping is not particularly outstanding.

As the crooner, Farrell contribs a credible portrayal while Miss Ryan is okay. Norris is so-so as the breezy news scribe, and Wills is a fair heavy. Others, headed by Orth, James Seay and Chili Williams, are adequate. Basil Wrangell's direction is inclined to be somewhat spotty. Film's production values are in keeping with the low budget. Jack Greenhalgh's camera work is good.

Pioneer Justice

PRC release of Jerry Thomas production. Stars "Lash" La Rue, Al "Fuzzy" St. John; features Jennifer Holt. Directed by Ray Taylor. Screenplay, Adrian Page; camera, Ernie Miller; editor, Hugh Winn. Tradeshown, N. Y., June 25, '47. Running time, 58 MINS.

Cheyenne ...."Lash" La Rue
Fuzzy.................Al "Fuzzy" St. John
Betty ....Jennifer Holt
Uncle Bob....................William Fawcett
Bill Judd...........................Jack Ingram
Criler ....Dee Cooper
Joe ....Lane Bradford
Sheriff ....Henry Hall
Al Walters..........................Steve Drake
Jackson ....Bob Woodward

For its purpose, "Pioneer Justice" serves well. It's a fast-moving, action-crammed film which, though lacking in finesse, will keep the kiddies on the edge of their seats. Scripting, thesping and production are strictly on a coin-saving standard but there's no stinting on the gunfighting, hoof-beating or knuckle-scrapting.

Yarn revolves around efforts of "Lash" La Rue and his crusty sidekick, Al St. John, to track down the leader of a group of varmints trying to drive the law-abiding ranchers out of the far west. Mild suggestion of romance is injected when Jennifer Holt becomes the gang's target. La Rue punches, shoots and whiplashes straight to the mark and collars a madman who fashions himself a Napoleon with spurs on.

La Rue, handling a long whip in Mark of Zorro style, makes for a tough-looking, straight-talking cowboy hero who should appeal to the junior-age film fans. St. John is okay as the comedy support although not given much to do. Miss Holt is a nice looker and turns in a pleasant performance. Rest of the cast grimace their way through stocks parts. *Herm.*

Dancing With Crime
(BRITISH-MADE)

London, June 25.

Paramount release of Coronet Film production. Stars Richard Attenborough, Sheila Sim, Barry K. Barnes. Directed by John Paddy Carstairs. Story by Peter Fraser; camera, Reginald Wyer. At Paramount, London, June 25, '47. Running time, 81 MINS.

Ted Peters...........Richard Attenborough
Paul Baker..................Barry K. Barnes
Joy Goodall............................Sheila Sim
Dave Robinson.............Bill Rowbotham
Inspector Carter..............John Warwick
Sergeant Murray..............Garry Marsh
Gregory..............................Barry Jones
Toni....................................Judy Kelly
Sniffy.......................Cyril Chamberlain
Pogson...............................John Salew
Johnny..............................Peter Croft

Second pic of the present gangster cycle, this is fashioned on formula lines. Ex-servicemen, one good, one bad; the inevitable chorus girl, and the black marketeers, all set in slum quarters relieved by a palais de danse. Unlike the U. S. variety, British gangsters don't aspire to penthouses.

Peters and Robinson are old Army pals. Former drives a taxi, latter lines his pockets with ill-gotten gains. Asking gangster chief Gregory for a larger cut, Robinson gets a bullet instead, fired by the gangster's aide, Paul Baker. Unknown to Peters, his pal dies in his taxi and Scotland Yard gets to work. But astute as the detectives may be, Peters and Joy, his girl friend, are one ahead of them, and succeed in doing what Scotland Yard is unable to do.

Story begins well, but goes to pieces before the end. It has a good tempo, but the director telegraphs his punches too far ahead for shock or surprise.

Acting is good, but picture would have gained a great deal if Richard Attenborough and Bill Rowbotham had changed roles. Smaller parts are particularly well played, and attention has been paid to detail.

Pic will have to rely a great deal on word-of-mouth as marquee strength is moderate, and cockney accent will be a handicap in most of the country. Should earn its money in England, but is doubtful export to U. S., even in dual situations.

Cane.

Dragnet

Hollywood, July 1.

Screen Guild release of Maurice H. Conn production. Features Henry Wilcoxon, Mary Brian. Directed by Leslie Goodwins. Screenplay, Barbara Worth, Harry Essex; original story, Conn; camera, James S. Brown, Jr. Tradeshown June 30, '47. Running time, 71 MINS.

Cast: Henry Wilcoxon, Mary Brian, Douglas Dumbrille, Virginia Dale, Douglas Blackley, Tom Fadden, Don Harvey, Maxine Semon, Paul Newlan, Ralph Dunn, Bert Conway and Allen Nixon.

"Dragnet" concerns itself with international jewel thieves and contains enough action and skullduggery to prove okay as a supporting feature. Production framing by Maurice H. Conn obtains okay effect for small budget.

Henry Wilcoxon, long absent from screen, pleases as a Scotland Yard man in this country to track down crooks responsible for London jewel robberies. He joins with New York police to help them solve puzzle of unidentified body found on beach. As teamwork puts clues together, dead man is revealed as phony diplomatic courier who smuggled in gems. Before pieces are wrapped up, Wilcoxon is generally pushed around but does the crooks in properly.

Conn did original plot and it is better than the scripting job by Barbara Worth and Harry Essex. Screenplay stumbles over itself in attempting too much talk, but mystery angles carry it along.

Mary Brian shares top spot with Wilcoxon as airline hostess who aids detective. She pleases. Douglas Dumbrille and Virginia Dale make up heavy team. Douglas Blackley and Ralph Dunn are standard pair of film cops. Maxine Semon injects corny comedy as dumb waitress. Lensing by James S. Brown, Jr., features low key lighting. Editing could be tighter. *Brog.*

Foreign Films

"Hedelmaton Puu" ("Tree Without Fruit") (FINNISH). Suomen Filmiteollisuus production and release. Stars Helena Kara, Rauli Tuomi; features Matti Aulos, Emma Vaaanen, Aino Lohikoski, Rauha Rentola, Joel Rinne, Salli Karuna. Directed by Unto Koskela. Based on novel by Unto Koskela. At Rex, Helsingfors. Running time, 96 MINS.

Best Finnish film in years may find its market limited by censor difficulties. Story concerns a marriage made childless by the husband's impotence. Wife leaves him for an affair with a student and eventually abandons her spouse, choosing to live only for herself and her child. It's a sure grosser in Finland, aided by Hannu Leminen's fine direction. Chances abroad are dubious.

"Synnin Jaljet" ("The Ways of Sin") (FINNISH). Suomin Filmiteollisuus production and release. Stars Ghedi Loennberg, Eeva-Karina Volanen; features Rauha Rentola, Kaija Suonio, Salli Karuna, Yrjoe Tuominen, Tauno Majuri, Siiri Angerkoski. Directed by Hannu Leminen. Camera, Kalle Peronkoski; music, Harry Bergstroem. Reviewed in Helsingfors. Running time, 100 MINS.

Finnish film about venereal disease has a good story and boasts a cast made up chiefly of femmes. Swedish version was also produced using same actors with a couple of exceptions. Picture may find a market in Scandinavia and has some chances abroad as well.

"Lovisa" (FINNISH). Suomi Filmi production and release. Stars Tauno Palo, Emma Vaananen, Kirsti Hurme; features Reino Hakala, Hilkka Helina, Toini Vartiainen. Directed by Valentin Vaala. At Kino Palatsi and Ritz, Helsingfors. Running time, 94 MINS.

Fair dramatic Finnish film with the usual heavily-sentimental story found in so many Finnish pix. Tauno Palo, Finland's top film actor, handles his role well as do other cast members, despite the inept script. Picture has meagre b.o. prospects in Scandinavia and chances overseas are nil.

"Una Mujer Sin Cabeza" ("The Headless Woman") (ARGENTINE). Argentina Sono Film production and release. Stars Nini Marshall; features Francisco Charmiello, Angelina Pagano, Perlita Mux, Tato de Serra, Pascual Pelliciotta, Carlos Lagrotta, Sulma Montes, Carlos Perrelli. Directed by Luis Cesar Amadori. Camera, Alberto Etchebehere, Roque Giacobino. At Cine Ocean, Buenos Aires. Running time, 105 MINS.

Weak on story, this picture is partly saved by Nini Marshall's liveliness. She still retains her ability to make audiences laugh, however, absurd the plot. As a gypsy who is the life and soul of a traveling circus, Nini has opportunities enough for getting laughter even though this film is not one of her best vehicles. It may do well locally but chances in the U. S. are nil. *Nid.*

"Pimeanpirtin Havitys" ("Devastation") (FINNISH). Suomi Filmi production and release. Stars Irma Seikkala, Tauno Palo, Urho Sommersalmi; features Marta Laurent, Aino Lohikoski, Arvi Tuomi, Unto Salminen, Paavo Jannes, Reino Valkama, Rauli Tuomi. Directed by Ilmari Unho. Based on novel by Maila Talvio. At Kino Palatsi and Ritz, Helsingfors. Running time, 90 MINS.

Film version of Maila Talvio's novel offer little with the exception of handling silent-screen star Urho Sommersalmi an opportunity to make a comeback. Direction by Ilmari Unho is good, but the sentimental story militates against the picture's prospects overseas. Domestically, pic may do business.

Miniature Reviews

"The Vigilantes Return" (Color) (U). Fast action formula westerner for nice support in nabe situations.

"The Trespasser" (Rep). Better - -than - average mystery film.

"Kilroy Was Here" (Mono). Neat comedy for general situations built around war-inspired Kilroy myth.

"Rustlers of Devil's Canyon" (Rep). Neat low cost western packing plenty of action.

The Vigilantes Return
(COLOR—ONE SONG)

Universal release of Howard Welsch production. Stars Jon Hall, Margaret Lindsay; features Paula Drew, Andy Devine, Robert Wilcox, Jonathan Hale. Directed by Ray Taylor. Original screenplay, Roy Chanslor; camera (Cinecolor), Virgil Miller; editor, Paul Landres; song, Jack Brooks and Milton Schwarzwald. At Rialto, N. Y., week July 1, '47. Running time, 67 MINS.

Johnnie Taggart	Jon Hall
Kitty	Margaret Lindsay
Louise Holden	Paula Drew
Andy	Andy Devine
Clay Curtwright	Robert Wilcox
Ben	Jack Lambert
Judge Holden	Jonathan Hale
Sheriff	Arthur Hohl
Bartender	Wallace Scott
Messenger	Lane Chandler
Ben's Girl	Joan Fulton
Henchman	John Hart
Henchman	Monty Montague
Henchman	Bob Wilke

"The Vigilantes Return" is a better-than-average, modest - budgeted outdoor opus that should give good support in nabe situations. Pic is marked by a solid production background, pleasantly tinted Cinecolor camera work, competent thesping and a script that puts the accent on stirring action down the line. There's no variation on the basic bad men vs. good formula but the kiddies won't care.

Jon Hall plays an undercover agent for law and order who's assigned to clean out a nest of varmints preying on the ranchers. Arrayed against him is the owner of the local ginmill and gambling joint who heads the gang of meanies. Margaret Lindsay, an old flame of Hall from way back in New Orleans, is a business partner of the gang leader but her sympathies are strictly on the side of law and love. After Hall gets framed on a murder rap, he escapes from jail with the connivance of his sidekick, Andy Devine, and organizes the vigilantes. In a rousing climax, the gang and the vigilantes shoot it out across the barricades with the inevitable result.

Hall is highly effective as the U. S. marshal, showing off some hard riding and fast draws. He's tough but modest and handles his role with the required amount of easy heroism. Miss Lindsay is standout as the dancehall belle and chirps one good pop song, "One Man Woman," with a lowdown blues style that sells. Devine plays in usual fashion with fair comedy results. Jonathan Hale, as the county judge, is polished. Gang of toughies, with Jack Lambert and Robert Wilcox in the lead, sneer with finesse and will provoke hisses. *Herm.*

The Trespasser
(ONE SONG)

Republic release of William J. O'Sullivan production. Features Dale Evans. Directed by George Blair. Screenplay, Jerry Gruskin; adaptation, Dorrell and Stuart E. McGowan; original story, Jerry Sackheim, Erwin Gelsey; camera, John Alton; song, Eddie Maxwell, Nathan Scott; editor, Arthur Roberts; musical director, Mort Glickman. Tradeshown N. Y. July 2, '47. Running time, 71 MINS.

Linda Coleman	Dale Evans
Danny Butler	Warren Douglas
Stevie Carson	Janet Martin
Bill Monroe	Douglas Fowley
Dee Dee	Adele Mara
Charles	Gregory Gay
Kirk	Grant Withers
Bruce Coleman	William Bakewell
Bartender	Vince Barnett
Channing Bliss	Francis Pierlot
Mary Lou	Joy Barlowe
Davis	Fred Graham
Hall	Dale Van Sickel
Jane	Betty Alexander
The Doctor	Joseph Crehan

Incorporating a new approach in the action-mystery field, Republic's "The Trespasser" is a well contrived yarn which packs an exciting punch. Suspense builds nicely in this William J. O'Sullivan production and b.o. returns should reflect the film's better-than-average quality despite the lack of marquee lure.

Scripters have spaded up comparative virgin territory in slanting the plot around a ring of rare book forgers. Starting with a newspaper office locale most of the story emerges as fairly logical stuff. However, the studio has an extraordinary fanciful conception of a newspaper editorial department, what with marble-lined corridors and individual plush sanctums for such staffers as the feature editor no less.

Janet Martin lands a job with a sheet helped by one of the paper's ace scribes, Douglas Fowley. Fresh from college, she's assigned to the morgue to work under Warren Douglas. In no time at all she stumbles on book reviewer William Bakewell's nefarious work in peddling phony "rare" tomes to publisher Francis Pierlot. With Fowley handling the investigating reins, the forgery ring is eventually rounded up with the aid of Miss Martin, Douglas and detective Grant Withers. There's a bit of romantic interest between Fowley and Dale Evans, who portrays a nitery warbler and Bakewells sister.

On the whole cast turned in a competent performance under George Blair's able direction. Miss Martin is credible as the morgue worker and amateur sleuth, Douglas does a neat characterization as her boss, while Fowley and Bakewell register in their roles. Withers is an okay detective. In a brief sequence Miss Evans chirps the film's sole tune, "It's Not the First Love," a so-so number. Otherwise her thesping measures up. In a minor bit Adele Mara lends sparkle to an office-worker part while Gregory Gay is sufficiently sinister as the heavy. Production accoutrements are above standard in view of the low budget. John Alton's lensing is good.

Kilroy Was Here

Hollywood, July 8.

Monogram release of Dick Irving Hyland-Sidney Luft production. Features Jackie Cooper, Jackie Coogan, Wanda McKay, Frank Jenks. Directed by Phil Karlson. Screenplay, Dick Irving Hyland; added dialog, Louis Quinn; original story, Hyland and Lee Wainer; camera, William Sickner; editor, Jodie Caplan. Previewed June 24, '47. Running time, 68 MINS.

John J. Kilroy	Jackie Cooper
Pappy Collins	Jackie Coogan
Connie Harcourt	Wanda McKay
Butch Miller	Frank Jenks
Elmer Hatch	Norman Phillips
Rodney Meadows	Rand Brooks
Prof. Shepherd	Barton Yarborough
First Cab Driver	Frank Scannell
Marge Connors	Patti Brill
First Soldier	Robert Coogan
Registrar	Joe Forte
Second Cab Driver	Allen Mathews
Third Cab Driver	Sidney Melton
Walter	Pat Goldin

The Kilroy legend, of that fabulous war character who popped up all over the Pacific, is basis for this amusing comedy which has plenty of exploitation possibilities. Yarn picks up Jackie Cooper, who plays Kilroy, in a Pacific outpost, then projects him to college, where events will keep average audiences entertained.

Cooper is co-starred with Jackie Coogan, who plays his pal and for that reason is forever getting Cooper —or Kilroy—into trouble. Pair make excellent teammates, and script by Dick Irving Hyland, based on his and Lee Wainer's original story, keeps the ball moving. There are moments when action at college becomes slightly sophomoric, but this is more than compensated by straightforward approach to a subject which has both charm and humor.

Cooper finds not all of college life enchanting. Under GI Bill he manages to get in, after first turned down because of lack of credits, due to his being the Kilroy Taken up by snooty frat, whose members want to acquire him because he is Kilroy, then want to drop him because of his taxi-driving friends, Cooper learns the hard way, but manages finally to get going on right path.

Two Jackies turn in excellent performances and have top support from such players as Wanda McKay, Norman Phillips, Barton Yarborough, Frank Jenks and Rand Brooks.

Producers Hyland and Sidney Luft made most of situation at hand, turning out a neat entertainment, aided by direction of Phil Karlson. William Sickner's expert use of cameras is interestingly displayed, with balance of technical credits okay. *Whit.*

Rustlers of Devil's Canyon

Republic release of Sidney Picker production. Stars Allan Lane; features Bobby Blake, Martha Wentworth, Peggy Stewart. Directed by R. G. Springsteen. Original screenplay, Earle Snell; camera, William Bradford; editor, Harry Keller. Tradeshown N. Y., July 3, '47. Running time, 58 MINS.

Red Ryder	Allan Lane
Little Beaver	Bobby Blake
The Duchess	Martha Wentworth
Bess	Peggy Stewart
The Doctor	Arthur Space
Blizzard	Emmett Lynn
Clark	Roy Barcroft
The Sheriff	Tom London
Tad	Harry Carr
Matt	Pierce Lyden
Doc Glover	Forrest Taylor

"Rustlers of Devil's Canyon" is one of the best in the Red Ryder series. Westerner has been neatly assembled out of standard ingredients, and tight, positive direction by R. G. Springsteen keeps film in high gear from start to finish. Plenty of action is packed into the pic's short running time with surrounding production dress making most of a low budget outlay.

Plot has Allan Lane in role of Red Ryder returning to his ranch at end of the Spanish-American war to find his territory honeycombed with rustlers. Meanwhile, some postwar homesteaders arrive in the area to settle down right in the crossfire between the rustlers and ranchmen. Three-cornered tug-of-war develops, with the local medico, secret head of the outlaws, adding fuel to the fires. At windup, Lane smokes out the doctor, smashes the gang of rustlers and establishes peace between the farmers and cattlemen.

Lane makes a straightforward cowboy hero. Young Bobby Blake, as an Indian kid, will appeal to the juves. Excellent performance is turned in by Peggy Stewart as femme leader of the homesteaders while Arthur Space does well as the heavy and Emmett Lynn registers effectively as venerable comedy sidekick to Lane. *Herm.*

Foreign Films

"Madame Bovary" (ARGENTINE). Pan-American release of San Miguel Studio production. Stars Mecha Ortiz, Roberto Escalada, Enrique Diosdado; features Alberto Bello, Angelina Pagano, Alejandro Maximino, Manolo Diaz, Graciela Lecube, Ricardo Galache, Maria Esther Podesta, Juan Carlos Altavista, Felix Gil. Directed by Carlos Schleper and Luis Mottura. Screenplay, Maria Luz Regas and Ariel Cortazzo; based on Gustave Flaubert's novel; camera, Bob Roberts; music, Isidro Maisteguii. At Cine Normandie, Buenos Aires. Running time, 85 MINS.

Carefully produced and heavily blue-pencilled in comparison with Flaubert's original, this version of "Madame Bovary" is left with nothing but the melodrama. It undoubtedly will prove a draw at the Argentine boxoffice. Story continuity suffers by elimination of the book's cruder aspects. Acting in general is uninspired save for thesping of teenager Graciela Lecuba who shows up well and gives promise for the future. Film has little appeal for the U. S. market.

Miniature Reviews

"Variety Girl" (Part Color) (Musical) (Par). All-star filmusical, surefire b.o. anywhere.

"Secret Life of Walter Mitty" (Color-Songs) (RKO-Goldwyn). Danny Kaye at his best in smash screenplay of Thurber story. Tremendous b.o.

"Slave Girl" (Color) (U-I). Lavishly produced broad farce with Oriental background; moderate b.o.

"Trouble With Women" (Par). Mild college-newspaper comedy, mostly as support on twin bills.

"Second Chance" (20th). Suspenseful cops-and-robbers yarn providing staunch fare in supporting situations.

"The Marauders" (UA). Good entry in the Hopalong Cassidy series with William Boyd.

"Lured" (UA). Strong cast in familiar murder mystery yarn should do OK b.o.

"So Well Remembered" (British) (RKO). John Mills, Martha Scott starring in James Hilton novel; should be big grosser.

"The Corpse Came C.O.D." (Col). Broadly played comedy-mystery with Hollywood studio locale. Okay.

"Last of the Redmen" (Color) (Col). Adaptation of "Last of Mohicans," in Vitacolor. Okay summer fare.

"Scared to Death" (Color) (SG). Mild melodrama with Bela Lugosi looms only minor interest for supporting market.

Variety Girl

(PART COLOR—MUSICAL)

Paramount release of Daniel Dare production. All-star Paramount cast includes Bing Crosby, Bob Hope, Gary Cooper, Ray Milland, Alan Ladd, Barbara Stanwyck, Paulette Goddard, Dorothy Lamour, Veronica Lake, Sonny Tufts, Joan Caulfield, Wm. Holden, Lizabeth Scott, Burt Lancaster, Gail Russell, Diana Lynn, Sterling Hayden, Robt. Preston, John Lund, Wm. Bendix, Barry Fitzgerald, Cass Daley, Howard DaSliva, Billy DeWolfe, Macdonald Carey, Arleen Whelan, Patric Knowles, Mona Freeman, Cecil Kellaway, Johnny Coy, Virginia Field, Richard Webb, Stanley Clements; also director-producers Cecil B. DeMille, Mitchell Leisen, Frank Butler, George Marshall; other specialties and bits by Roger Dann, Pearl Bailey, Jim & Mildred Mulcay, Spike Jones & City Slickers, 6 DeWaynes, Barney Dean, Mary Edwards, Virginia Welles, Nanette Parks, Wanda Hendrix, Andre Verne, Patricia White, June Harris, Rae Patterson, Mikhail Rasumny, George Reeves. Directed by George Marshall. Original screenplay, Edmund Hartmann, Frank Tashlin, Robt. Welch, Monte Brice. Special Puppetoon (Technicolor) sequences by Thornton Hee and Wm. Cottrell. Music score and direction, Joe Lilley; associate, Troy Sanders; arrangements, Van Cleave; Puppetoon score, Edward Plumb; special songs, Johhny Burke-James Van Heusen, Allan Roberts-Doris Fisher, Frank Loesser; editor, LeRoy Stone; dances, Billy Daniels and Bernard Pearce; asst. director, George Templeton; camera, Lionel Lindon, Stuart Thompson; special and process camera, Gordon Jennings, Farciot Edouart. Tradeshown N. Y., July 11, '47. Running time, **93 MINS.**

Catherine Brown	Mary Hatcher
Amber La Vonne	Olga San Juan
Bob Kirby	DeForest Kelley
Barker	William Demarest
Stage Manager	Frank Faylen
R. J. O'Connell	Frank Ferguson
Bill Farris	Glen Tryon
Mrs. Webster	Nella Walker
Headwaiter, Brown Derby	Torben Meyer
Busboy	Jack Norton
Cashier	Elaine Riley
Asst. to Mr. O'Connell	Charles Victor
Asst. to Assistant	Gute Taute
Manager, Grauman's Chinese	Harry Hayden
First Girl	Janet Thomas
Second Girl	Roberta Jonay
Girl with Sheep Dog	Wallace Earl
Dog Trainer	Dick Keene
Hairdresser	Ann Doran
Asst. Director	Jerry James
Makeup Man	Eric Alden
Director	Frank Mayo
Special Voice Impersonator	Pinto Colvig
Cop	Edgar Dearing

Producer Danny Dare could shoot the credits, as above, and come out a winner. How can it miss with Crosby, Hope, Cooper, Milland, Ladd, Stanwyck, Goddard, Lamour, and the rest of the glittering Par stable of personalities? To the credit of all concerned it comes out even better, because that type of all-star specialty sequencing brooks the constant danger of becoming a big short. "Variety Girl" skirts that and emerges a socko entertainment.

Primed as an exploitation picture, tied in with the Variety Clubs of America, that plot phase of it gets a once-over-lightly but sufficient to the purpose thereof.

Perhaps more to the point than the already established Par stars, or the socko specialists like Spike Jones, Pearl Bailey, the Mulcays, et al., is the unfolding of two new personalities to add to the Par stable. One is Mary Hatcher, a winsome ingenue, currently the femme lead in the Broadway company of "Oklahoma!", and the other is Olga San Juan who is less sultry and more a young Betty Hutton in this, her best opportunity as a comedienne. Incidentally, Miss Hutton is the only Par name not in "Variety Girl"—she was expecting at the time of production.

Story is one of those things. There's an opening and closing titular and dialog attempt to tie in the Catherine Variety Sheridan saga of the nameless waif whose discovery in John H. Harris' Sheridan theatre, Pittsburgh, 18 years ago gave birth to the Variety Clubs movement. Bob O'Donnell and Harris are "R. J. O'Connell" and "Bill Farris" in the cast. Played by Frank Ferguson and Glen Tryon they're the sparkplugs to the plot to give "Catherine" (Miss Hatcher) a screen test and an opportunity in Hollywood.

Miss San Juan plays the opportunistic brash antithesis to the trusting Miss Hatcher, and the action revolves chiefly around studio workings, harassed and temperamental producers and directors, and is capped by the Variety Club benefit show which Bob Hope emcees. It's herein that he and Crosby click with their "Harmony" routine, a socko number for all its paraphrasing of the "Friendship" routine out of "Du Barry Was a Lady" which Bert Lahr and Ethel Merman made famous.

Closeups on the Par studio, the Brown Derby, the obviousness of Hollywood aspirants, swimming pool parties, inside stuff on voice-dubbing for a George Pal "Puppetoon," Crosby's flip asides ("I don't want to run this 'Father O'Malley' routine into the ground"), Milland's bit with the phone on the chandelier (a la "Lost Weekend"), the subtle trailer for DeMille's upcoming epic, "Unconquered," a ditto trailer for "Perils of Pauline," the accent on DeMille's oft-spoken credo, the intro of Roger Dann, new French juve, in a test; and all the rest of it is a sort of visual closeup on Hollywood which, basically, is surefire fan appeal.

There are a couple of rather inane interludes which, with the mass of footage obviously excised, could also have gone into the cutting room heap. The O'Connell character, theoretically the head of the studio, is (1) the victim of an harassment running gag, having to do with falling into pools, or puddles, or being otherwise doused, that is strictly from Laurel & Hardy; and (2) DeMille's autocracy and autonomy are accented by showing him ordering the studio head off his set.

But in the main it's surefire. The Technicolor cartoon sequence depicting the technique of vocal dubbing, sound effects, etc., is fresh inside stuff. Frank Loesser's "Tallahassee" is already a hit, and Dorothy Lamour and Alan Ladd handle this like a Hit Parader. Pearl Bailey mops up with "Tired," good specialty for the sepia songstress although slightly overboard on footage. Bill Bendix bollixes up Miss San Juan's screentest in a socko sequence with the real-life George Marshall, who directed the entire production, playing himself in an obvious horseplay bit. The rest of the ribbing sequences are likewise authentic.

DeForest Kelley looms as a good new juvenile potential. He personates the sympathetic talent scout. The other players are bits, some with a more or less special appeal for insiders, such as Barney Dean playing himself; or that fine acrobatic-waiters specialty by the 6 DeWaynes, among many others. Tipoff on the amount of cut stuff is the large cast's meagre footage, quite a few in only fleetingly or completely axed.

Abel.

Secret Life of Walter Mitty

(COLOR—SONGS)

RKO release of Samuel Goldwyn production. Stars Danny Kaye and Virginia Mayo; features Boris Karloff, Fay Bainter, Ann Rutherford. Directed by Norman Z. McLeod. Screenplay by Ken Englund and Everett Freeman from short story by James Thurber. Camera (Technicolor), Lee Garmes; special effects, John Fulton; editor, Monica Collingswood; score, David Raskin; "Symphony for Unstrung Tongues" and "Anatole of Paris" by Sylvia Fine. Previewed at RKO 58th Street, N. Y., July 10, '47. Running time, **108 MINS.**

Walter Mitty	Danny Kaye
Rosalind van Hoorn	Virginia Mayo
Dr. Hollingshead	Boris Karloff
Mrs. Mitty	Fay Bainter
Gertrude Griswold	Ann Rutheford
Bruce Pierce	Thurston Hall
Tubby Wadsworth	Gordon Jones
Mrs. Griswold	Florence Bates
Peter van Hoorn	Konstantin Shayne
Colonel	Reginald Denny
Hendrick	Henry Corden
Mrs. Follinsbee	Doris Lloyd
Anatole	Fritz Feld
Maasdam	Frank Reicher
Butler	Milton Parsons

Goldwyn Girls

With the nation's boxoffices aching at this particular moment for a smash comedy, Samuel Goldwyn has stepped in with exactly the right prescription. Better medicine for a b.o. suffering from malnutrition of laughs can hardly be imagined than this combination of Danny Kaye and James Thurber. Throw in a topnotch Technicolor job, Virginia Mayo, Boris Karloff the Goldwyn Girls, a couple of the best songs Sylvia Fine has ever concocted for husband Danny, and any exhib will find an admixture that assures him fulsome relief from the b.o. blues.

Some of the deepest-dyed Thurber fans may squeal at the pic, since there's naturally been considerable change from the famed short story on which the screenplay is built. There's been a basic switch in the plot that has been concocted around the Mitty daydreams. Thurber's whole conception of Mitty was an inconsequential fellow from Perth Amboy, N. J., to whom nothing—but nothing—ever happened and who, as a result, lived a "secret life" via his excursions into daydreaming. In contrast, the picture builds a spy-plot around Mitty that is more fantastic than even his wildest dream.

Although some of the critics and the Thurber intelligentsia may register objection to this providing of Mitty with real-life adventure, the vast majority of those who plunk their coins on the boxoffice sill will find solid yaks all the way. As a matter of fact, many will get parlayed laughs out of the fantastic plot, which is actually a caricature of Mitty's dreams.

Kaye without a doubt has never been better. He reveals a greater smoothness and polish thespically and a perfection of timing in his slapstick than has ever been evident in the past. The role, of course, of the milquetoast who dreams of high adventure, is perfect for permitting him to run through a gamut of characterizations, from his true self to the most fanciful products of his imagination.

Exceedingly slick job is done on the segues from the real-life Mitty into the dream sequences. Transitions are not only exceptionally smooth, but also give opportunity to work in a pair of Kaye specialties by his wife, Miss Fine. Both numbers have been previous standbys for the comic. They are "Symphony for Unstrung Tongues" and "Anatole of Paris."

Mitty's fantasies carry him through sessions as a sea captain taking his schooner through a storm, a surgeon performing a next-to-impossible operation, an RAF pilot, a Mississippi gambler, a cowpuncher and a hat designer ("Anatole") They're all well-loaded with satire, as is the real-life plot with pure slapstick. Incidentally, screenwriters Ken Englund and Everett Freeman, with commendable restraint, give no effort at all toward making sense of their plot. If the literal-minded spectator is completely confused by it, let him go home and figure it out later. No use halting the laughs for explanations.

Miss Mayo is the beautiful vis-a-vis in both the real-life spy plot, and the dreams. She comes a commendable distance thespically, incidentally, in this picture. Ann Rutherford is depicted as Mitty's not-so-bright fiancee from whom he finally breaks away in a burst of self-declaration. Fay Bainter is Mitty's too-too-cautious mother, while Karloff is tied up with the international jewel thieves who push Mitty into the scalp-raising adventures that bother him only because they make him "late for the office." Karloff wins heftiest yaks in a scene in which he plays a phony psychiatrist convincing Mitty he's nuts.

Norman Z. McLeod's direction keeps the action relatively fast and sharp. Production in general is up to the usual top Goldwyn standard.

Herb.

Slave Girl

(COLOR)

Universal-International release of Michael Fessier and Ernest Pagano production. Stars George Brent, Yvonne De Carlo; features Broderick Crawford, Albert Dekker, Lois Collier, Andy Devine, Carl Esmond, Arthur Treacher. Directed by Charles Lamont. Original screenplay, Fessier & Pagano; camera (Technicolor), George Robinson; editor, William Fritzsche; choreography, Si-Lan Chen; music, Milton Rosen. Tradeshown N. Y., July 14, '47. Running time, **80 MINS.**

Francesca	Yvonne de Carlo
Matt Claibourne	George Brent
Chips Jackson	Broderick Crawford
Pasha	Albert Dekker
Aleta	Lois Collier
Ben	Andy Devine
El Hamid	Carl Esmond
Liverpool	Arthur Treacher
Yusef	Philip van Zandt
Tolok Taurog	Dan Seymour

"Slave Girl," despite its grim title, is a rainbow-colored spoof on previous cinematic epics which were drenched in the romance and intrigue of North Africa's Barbary Coast. Although the pic's treatment is spotty, there's enough chuckle material in this parody to push it over at the wickets.

Film unreels as broad farce with more stress laid on brilliant tints than brilliant lines. Dominant flaw of the pic, however, doesn't show up in its lack of subtlety but in the inconsistency of the director's approach. With some sequences handled in deadpan fashion and others in a Keystone Kop style, film varies too widely in mood for sock comedy results.

Chief laugh gimmick is a talking camel, with a Brooklynese drawl, which supplies a running commentary on the action. Popping in and out of the story at regular intervals, the camel is decked out with some fast lines that beat the patrons to the punch by pointing up all the intended (and unintended) absurdities in the film. In short, the camel saves the pic from itself. Intended or unintended, the pic also attains a quality of burlesque by virtue of its super-colossal background settings, its over-lavish Oriental costuming, its hyper-melodramatic action and some ham acting, all befitting to a top-budget takeoff on "A Night in a Turkish Harem."

Aside from the camel, cast performances rarely measure up to comedy requirements. George Brent, playing a U.S. diplomat in the early 1800s on a mission to a bandit Pasha who's holding 10 American seamen for ransom, walks through his paces without spark. Yvonne De Carlo, as a mystery gal who's up to her earrings in political intrigue, performs a couple of harem gavottes with appropriate cooch insinuations, but otherwise relies solely on her looks. Adequate support is given by Albert Dekker, who pours it on as the heavy, and Broderick Crawford, as Brent's bodyguard.

Story is a frank potpourri of the most venerable cliches on the Hollywood shelf. After Brent gets hijacked of his bullion by a gang of turbanned politicians who are trying to finance a revolution, he spends the rest of his time on a search for the missing coin. Replete with dancing girls, torture chambers, knockdown-and-drag-out free-for-alls, film finally winds up with Brent salvaging his coin and Miss De Carlo from the clutches of the cruel Pasha and the phony revolutionists. *Herm.*

The Trouble With Women

Paramount release of Harry Tugend production. Stars Ray Milland, Teresa Wright, Brian Donlevy; features Rose Hobart, Iris Adrian. Directed by Sidney Lanfield. Screenplay by Arthur Sheekman, based on story by Ruth McKenney, Richard Bransten; camera, Lionel Lindon; editor, Willam Shea; dances, Billy Daniels. At Globe, N. Y., week July 12, '47. Running time, **90 MINS.**

Professor Gilbert Sedley	Ray Milland
Kate Farrell	Teresa Wright
Joe McBride	Brian Donlevy
Dean Agnes Meeler	Rose Hobart
Ulysses S. Jones	Charles Smith
Dr. Wilmer Dawson	Lewis Russell
Rita La May	Iris Adrian
Geeger	Frank Faylen
Judge	Rhys Williams
Avery Wilson	Lloyd Bridges
Mrs. Wilmer Dawson	Norma Varden
Jeefe	James Milligan
Herman	Matt McHugh
Peanuts	Jimmie Smith

Biggest trouble with "Trouble With Women" is the story, the way in which it was adapted and produced. When an inept yarn and routine direction are given such capable stars as Ray Milland, Brian Donlevy and Teresa Wright even strong thespian efforts fail. Result is a mild comedy that will have to get most of its pesos from dual bills.

Milland does not fit into the absent-minded professor role too well, and he would be a lot happier if the lines were smarter and direction better. He's pictured an instructor of psychology at a midwest college, who's just finished a book about subjugation of women, and who feels that he's been misquoted in an interview in a local newspaper. In fact, so much misquoted that he's suing for $300,000.

In trying to squelch the lawsuit, city editor of the sheet, Donlevy, assigns the star gal reporter (who's authored the damaging article) to try and get something on Professor Milland. Per film custom, he falls in love with the gal (Miss Wright) although apparently engaged to wed Rose Hobart, femme dean.

But the various limbs on which story development is hung takes in one of those cinematic burlesque-theatre episodes in which the college tutor is photographed on the stage trying to brush away from half-clad chorines. There are several brighter moments near the end of the story, including the climactic comical courtroom scene, but by that time the production has gone over the dam.

Besides Milland's usual fine work in an effort to breathe some life into the college professor role, Donlevy is passably good as the city editor, despite a characterization that is not even a fairly close facsimile. Miss Wright, as the reporter, is much better in the love scenes but unfortunately they are few. Miss Hobart makes a prim college dean while Charles Smith is the wild-eyed student on which too much footage is wasted. Lewis Russell, Matt McHugh and Iris Adrian head the support. Latter does the gumchewing stripper in the burley house.

Sidney Lanfield's direction keeps at about the same level as the routine screenplay by Arthur Sheekman, who adapted it from story by Ruth McKenney and Richard Bransten. *Wear.*

Second Chance

20th-Fox release of Sol M. Wurtzel production. Features Kent Taylor, Louise Currie, Dennis Hoey, Larry Blake. Directed by James S. Tinling. Original story by Louis Breslow, John Patrick; screenplay, Arnold Belgard; camera, Benjamin Kline; editor, Frank Baldridge. Tradeshown N. Y., July 14, '47. Running time, **62 MINS.**

Kendal Wolf	Kent Taylor
Joan Summers	Louise Currie
Roger Elwood	Dennis Hoey
Detective Sgt. Sharpe	Larry Blake
Doris	Ann Doran
Conrad Martyn	John Eldredge
Nick	Paul Guilfoyle
Pinky	William Newell
Jerry	Guy Kingsford
Sam	Charles Flynn
Bart	Eddie Feteherston
Montclaire	Francis Pierlot
Mrs. Davenport	Betty Compson

"Second Chance," while devoid of any top marquee lures, has a better selling potential than many cops-and-robber yarns because of skillful construction and aura of suspense created around the identity of a police informant. However, despite the generally good quality of this film, its short running time and modestly budgeted production, it's unlikely that "Second Chance" will be used except in supporting situations.

Yarn concerns a newly-formed team of jewel thieves, Kent Taylor and Louise Currie, who hurriedly form a business partnership at a bauble atelier, when Miss Currie obligingly conceals a valuable diamond lifted by Taylor. Racket here is to resell the jewel to a detective hired by the insurance firm, but in each instance, police are a step ahead, presumably on information furnished by one of the partners. One of them is ultimately divulged to be in the employ of an indemnity firm. But by that time that bit of intelligence is no deterrent to the ensuing romance.

Cast is generally competent, with Taylor and Miss Currie giving mature accounts of themselves in the central roles, while Larry Blake carries himself well as the ubiquitous detective. Other featured role goes to Dennis Hoey as the head of a theft ring posing as a jewel merchant.

A smooth job of direction by James Tinling results in fast pacing and a maximum amount of suspense, and the writers have endowed the film with dialog that sounds reasonable at all times. *Jose.*

The Marauders

Hollywood, July 11.

United Artists release of Lewis J. Rachmil production. Stars William Boyd; features Andy Clyde, Rand Brooks. Directed by George Archainbaud. Original screenplay, Charles Belden; based on characters created by Clarence E. Mulford; camera, Mack Stengler; editor, Fred W. Berger. Tradeshown July 8, '47. Running time, 63 MINS.

Hopalong Cassidy	William Boyd
California Carlson	Andy Clyde
Lucky Jenkins	Rand Brooks
Black	Ian Wolfe
Susan	Dorinda Clifton
Mrs. Crowell	Mary Newton
Black	Harry Cording
Clerk	Earle Hodgins
Oil Driller	Dick Bailey

"The Marauders" projects William Boyd in his standard Hopalong Cassidy characters for good results. Saddle opera shapes as neat fare for the western market, having been well-paced by George Archainbaud's direction and given smart production values by Lewis J. Rachmil.

The Charles Belden plot has Cassidy pitting wits and gunplay against gang of heavies who are trying to tear down a church in a ghost town. Villains made mistake of challenging the oater hero, arousing his curiosity enough to do a little sleuthing to find what's behind the destruction. While outdoor drama, story injects plenty of comedy by Andy Clyde that will please and at same time keeps characters plausible. Heavies are after oil and Cassidy discovers that gang's leader is responsible for series of mysterious deaths and other calamity that drove settlers from the town.

Boyd is smooth and believable in the Hoppy role and Clyde and Rank Brooks make good saddle pals. Ian Wolfe is the sanctimonious heavy masquerading as church deacon. Dorinda Clifton is okay as femme lead, as is Mary Newton as her mother. Earle Hodgins is neatly spotted for chuckles and Harry Cording is convincing tough guy.

Production credits measure up to good standard of series. Lensing by Mack Stengler, tight editing by Fred W. Berger, music background and art direction all rate mention. *Brog.*

Lured

United Artists release of Hunt Stromberg production. Stars George Sanders, Lucille Ball, Charles Coburn, Boris Karloff; features Sir Cedric Hardwicke, Alan Mowbray, Joseph Calleia, George Zucco. Directed by Douglas Sirk. Screenplay, Leo Rosten; camera, William Daniels; editor, John M. Foley; music, Michel Michelet. Tradeshown N. Y., July 11, '47. Running time, 102 MINS.

Robert Fleming	George Sanders
Sandra Carpenter	Lucille Ball
Inspector Temple	Charles Coburn
Maxwell	Alan Mowbray
Julian Wilde	Sir Cedric Hardwicke
Officer Barrett	George Zucco
Dr. Moryani	Joseph Calleia
Lucy Barnard	Tanis Chandler
Artist	Boris Karloff

Handsome roster of players plus an equally handsome production should make this pic a positive factor at the b.o. "Lured," however, misses entry into the jackpot class because of its familiar and transparent scripting job. Murder mystery, instead of building tension with swift melodramatic strokes, unfolds diffusely with lots of complications and few surprises.

Story, based on the homicidal operations of a madman, is in the straight whodunit style without any psycho overtones, which may prove a welcome change. Localed in England, film is richly studded with London background detail, including Scotland Yard appurtenances and a bevy of English-accented thespers well-established with U. S. patrons. The slick production dress assisted by some neat camera handling, highly effective score and motionful direction by Douglas Sirk almost, but not quite, succeed in obscuring flaws in the underlying plot structure.

Story opens with the disappearance and presumable murder of the eighth of a series of susceptible females who were lured to their demise by a honey-voiced killer. Only clues that Scotland Yard chieftain Charles Coburn has on this operator are his prediliction for gaudy poetry, in which his murders are preambled, and his advertisements in the personal columns for lonely, but beauteous gals. One of the film's high points, not sufficiently followed through, is its spotlighting of "agony" ads which are good for solid laughs.

Lucille Ball, stranded in England by a legit turkey from the U. S., is enlisted by the bobbies to bait the trap for the amorous homicide. Answering one ad, she meets up with a demented courtier played in broad style by Boris Karloff. Sequence, an effective goose-pimpler in itself, is entirely irrelevant to the central action, and Karloff's stay on the screen is limited to little more than five minutes. Also during her police work, she cleans out a nest of white slavers headed by Joseph Calleia who trafficks between England and South America. But the killer is still at large.

Mystery starts rolling when Miss Ball crosses lines with a duo of night club operators in persons of George Sanders and Sir Cedric Hardwicke. Sanders, a devastating lady-killer with ambiguous character, sweeps the distaff copper off her feet with his soft chatter and champagne. With long arm of coincidence getting a big workout, evidence is found pointing to Sanders as the culprit just as he's about to marry Miss Ball. Pic, however, has already tipped its mitt regarding the guilty party, and the final moment, Hardwicke gets nabbed as the poet-strangler.

Performances are good down the line despite many obvious situations. Miss Ball registers best in comic bits as a wisecracking showgirl, and less effectively in the emotionally distraught scenes. Male contingent, headed by Sanders, Hardwicke and Coburn, perform with their usual finesse. In lesser roles, Alan Mowbray, as an easy-money butler, and George Zucco, as a Scotland Yard inspector, give highly capable support. *Herm.*

So Well Remembered

(BRITISH-MADE)

London, July 9.

RKO Radio release of Alliance (Adrian Scott) production. Stars John Mills, Martha Scott, Patricia Roc, Trevor Howard, Richard Carlson. Directed by Edward Dmytryk. Screenplay by John Paxton from James Hilton's novel; camera, Fred Young. At Odeon, London, July 8, '47. Running time, **114 MINS.**

George Boswell	John Mills
Olivia	Martha Scott
Julie	Patricia Roc
Whiteside	Trevor Howard
Charles	Richard Carlson
Mangin	Reginald Tate
Annie	Beatrice Varley
Channing	Frederick Leister
Spivey	Ivor Barnard
Wetherall	Julian D'Albie
Baby Julie	Juliet Mills
Morris	John Turnbull

For the first joint RKO Radio-Rank picture, aimed at American and world markets, the producers made no mistake in choosing James Hilton's best seller. Producer Adrian Scott and director Edward Dmytryk have translated it to the screen with an efficiency that should please their Anglo-American promoters.

An excellent piece of pioneering, it set a time record at Denham Studios (75 days) where it was made for $400,000 less than it would have cost in Hollywood. Whatever shortcomings the picture may have from a highly critical point of view, there is little doubt it will rake in big grosses and will more than satisfy general audiences.

Spotting of Martha Scott and Richard Carlson can only be justified by the desire to have an Anglo-American cast and on their marquee value in America, and RKO should know whether their journeys were necessary. Here their pull is slight, and John Mills will be the main star attraction, with Trevor Howard and Pat Roc running him close.

Story begins with a stormy meeting of the council of Browdley, a northern English cotton town, when the name of Olivia Channing is put forward as librarian. Her father, former mill-owner, has a prison record, but George Boswell, local editor and councillor, champions Olivia and secures her the job.

When her father is killed in a car accident, she marries George, determined to help him gain a political career. But he resigns his parliamentary candidacy when an epidemic sweeps the town, a warning George ignored when it was given him by his best friend, Whiteside, the local medical health officer. Olivia and George lose their baby son, and finding that her husband refuses to fight for social or political honors, she leaves him. Years elapse, mainly occupied by the bringing up of Julie, an orphan of the epidemic, adopted by Whiteside.

Comes the war. Olivia, widow of her second marriage, returns to Browdley to reopen the onetime family mills. She brings her flying officer son George, who meets Julie. They fall in love, but when he is disfigured by a flying accident he comes under the domineering influence of his selfish mother. George intervenes, unites the estranged lovers and in a showdown pays off old scores to Olivia.

For no very good reason, story is told in flashback on VE night, and for an equally invalid reason James Hilton indulges in yards of narrative. But these are failings likely to be forgiven by most audiences. What the British will find hard to take will be the excessive rain—unnecessary on most occasions—and the inexcusable behavior of a medical health officer. No English town would tolerate for one moment the drunken creature Whiteside is supposed to be. And this is doubly hard on Trevor Howard, who gives the best performance of his career. It is not his fault that he is a caricature. It is a triumph that he makes him at all credible.

John Mills plays the type of man Americans like and consider typically English. He gives a grand performance, mellowing nicely with age, and winning complete sympathy. If Martha Scott's portrait does not hold 100% attention it is not because of her acting but for a slight miscasting as the young Olivia. As she matures she gains tremendously.

Richard Carlson does all that is required of him and the performance of Pat Roc is a feather in Dmytryk's cap. She has never been as good or as natural. The smaller parts are played to perfection, but it would be ungenerous not to mention the cameo of Frederick Leister. It is a memorable etching.

Production is first rate. There are none of the usual Hollywood mistakes that creep into a picture set in England, and direction should enhance Dmytryk's rapidly-growing reputation.

The picture should be the forerunner of a profitable RKO-Rank series.

Cane.

The Corpse Came C.O.D.

(SONG)

Hollywood, July 12.

Columbia release of Samuel Bischoff production. Stars George Brent, Joan Blondell; features Adele Jergens, Jim Bannon, Leslie Brooks, John Berkes. Directed by Henry Levin. Screenplay, George Bricker, Dwight Babcock; based on novel by Jimmy Starr; camera, Lucien Andriot; score, George Dunning; song, Allen Roberts and Doris Fisher; editor, Jerome Thoms. At Vogue, July 10, '47. Running time, **86 MINS.**

Joe Medford....George Brent
Rosemary Durant....Joan Blondell
Mona Harrison....Adele Jergens
Detective Mark Wilson....Jim Bannon
Peggy Holmes....Leslie Brooks
Larry Massey....John Berkes
Detective Dave Short....Fred Sears
Fields....William Trenk
Mitchell Edwards....Grant Mitchell
Nora....Una O'Connor
Rudy Frasso....Marvin Miller
Lance Fowler....William Forrest
Felice....Mary Field
Emmett Willard....Cliff Clark
Maxwell Kenyon....Wilton Graff

"The Corpse Came C.O.D." is neat summer film fare. It's a comedy mystery with a broad treatment and gains interest from Hollywood studio locale. Names are familiar and will aid in selling. Film has been given plushy-appearing production dress by Samuel Bischoff to gear it for top spot on twin bills.

Henry Levin's direction points up fast pace and light touch to balance melodramatics. Audience interest is sustained in unfoldment and villain of piece concealed until the final reel. Emphasis is on chuckles in the script by George Bricker and Dwight Babcock, although thrill moments are not neglected. Yarn is based on novel of same title by Jimmy Starr and throws in all the standard mystery tricks. Dialog is light and niftily handled by the cast.

A femme film star receives a box of dress goods and a corpse, c.o.d., and calls in a newspaper friend to help her out of the mess. The reporter turns detective and chases down clues that finally tie up the dead man with a jewel-stealing ring. There was a load of hot ice in the box and with several crooked factions after the loot, reporter is hard put to keep himself whole until finale. Three killings pepper the plot as chase leads through studios, Beverly Hills and Hollywood, to wind up when real heavy is exposed as crooked police detective who has loot and revenge on his mind.

George Brent gives a good account of himself as the reporter, injecting light touch that foils perfectly with Joan Blondell's broadly treated character of rival reporter. Adele Jergens is whistle-bait as the glamorous film star and shows up exceedingly well. Jim Bannon is excellent as the heavy. Leslie Brooks is spotted only briefly. John Berkes, Fred Sears, William Trenk, Grant Mitchell, Una O'Connor, Marvin Miller and others are good.

"He's Got a Warm Kiss" is solo tune, spotted in nightclub sequence. Lense work by Lucien Andriot takes full advantage of values in art direction by Stephen Goosoon and George Brooks, and set decorations by Wilbur Menefee and James Crowe. Editing is tight.

Brog.

Last of the Redmen

(COLOR)

Hollywood, July 11.

Columbia release of Sam Katzman production. Stars Jon Hall, Michael O'Shea; features Evelyn Ankers, Julie Bishop, Buster Crabbe, Rick Vallin, Buzz Henry. Directed by George Sherman. Screenplay, Herbert Dalmas, George H. Plympton; adapted from "The Last of the Mohicans," by James Fenimore Cooper; camera (Vitacolor), Ray Fernstrom, Ira H. Morgan; editor, James Sweeney. At the Vogue, July 10, '47. Running time, **78 MINS.**

Major Heyward....Jon Hall
Hawk-Eye....Michael O'Shea
Alice Munro....Evelyn Ankers
Cora Munro....Julie Bishop
Magua....Buster Crabbe
Uncas....Rick Vallin
Davy....Buzz Henry
General Munro....Guy Hedlund
General Webb....Frederic Worlock
Bob Wheelwright....Emmett Vogan

James Fenimore Cooper's classic, "The Last of the Mohicans," has been dressed up in color and a new title. It's aimed at extracting summer vacation admission coin from the juves and as such should give an okay account of itself. More adult ticket buyers are likely to quibble at character and plot incongruities that dampen grownup interest.

Production gains value from use of Vitacolor hues, processed by Cinecolor. It's almost all exteriors, rugged scenery showing up well in tint as lensed by Ray Fernstrom and Ira H. Morgan. Other production values furnished by Sam Katzman make the most of budget expenditure.

Jon Hall and Michael O'Shea wear the characters of British Major Heyward and scout Hawk-Eye, respectively, with an uneasy air, but will get by with the kiddies anyway. More suited is Buster Crabbe as the treacherous Iroquois Indian Magua. Because of the presence of Crabbe and Hall, there are several swimming and water battle sequences tossed in for action touch. George Sherman's direction spots a number of other high action spots.

Script by Herbert Dalmas and George H. Plympton depicts struggle of Jon Hall to escort Evelyn Ankers, Julie Bishop and Buzz Henry, children of a British general, safely through Indian country. Danger is more often invited than avoided as scripted and only by aid of O'Shea and his sidekick, Rick Vallin as Uncas, the last of the Mohican Indians, is the party brought to its destination.

Femmes have little to do. Others in cast measure up to demands.

Brog.

Scared to Death

(COLOR)

Hollywood, July 9.

Screen Guild Productions release of William B. David production. Stars Bela Lugosi, Douglas Fowley; features Joyce Compton, George Zucco, Nat Pendleton, Roland Varno, Molly Lamont. Directed by Christy Cabanne. Original story and screenplay, W. J. Abbott; camera (Cinecolor), Marcel Le Picard; editor, George McGuire. At the Million Dollar, L. A., July 9, '47. Running time, **65 MINS.**

Leonide....Bela Lugosi
Terry Lee....Douglas Fowley
Jane....Joyce Compton
Dr. Van Ee....George Zucco
Raymond....Nat Pendleton
Ward Van Ee....Roland Varno
Laura Van Ee....Molly Lamont
Indigo....Angelo Rossitto
Lilybeth....Gladys Blake
Rene....Lee Bennett
Autopsy Surgeon....Stanley Andrews
Antopsy Surgeon....Stanley Price

"Scared to Death" never lives up to title or story premise. It's a dull, poorly put together melodrama that fails to generate goosepimples expected by a Bela Lugosi vehicle. Made some time ago in Cinecolor, picture is poor example of what that process has achieved recently, although tint does add modest value for marketing in smaller houses.

Plot uses secret panels, faces at windows and similar standard chiller appurtenances in an effort to arouse interest, but effect comes through seldom. It's a flashback yarn that tries to explain why and how a girl was killed without a mark. Title gives the answer, otherwise audiences would have trouble following badly edited W. J. Abbott script, which essentially was okay for this type film. Gal is not a pleasant creature and when her husband turns up to haunt her, the strain finally does her in.

About all Lugosi has to do is to stand around and look mysterious. George Zucco, another mysterious character, gets a shade better break. Douglas Fowley is a poorly portrayed reporter. Best of cast is Molly Lamont, the girl who's scared to death. Nat Pendleton and Gladys Blake team for a few chuckles. Others try hard.

Best of the William B. David production is art direction by Harry Reif, which obtains values for budget expenditure. Christy Cabanne directed with uneven hand and Marcel Le Picard lensed. Bad editing is credited to George McGuire.

Brog.

Miniature Reviews

"Song of Love" (M-G). Katharine Hepburn, Paul Henreid, Robert Walker in longhair tale of Schumanns and Brahms; surefire for top situations.

"Something in the Wind" (UI) (Songs). Good Deanna Durbin musical comedy, with added value of Donald O'Connor clowning, for good biz.

"Merton of the Movies" (M-G). Top comedy with Red Skelton's funning slanting remake for nifty grosses.

"Her Husband's Affair" (Col). Screwball comedy with a laugh-a-minute pace. Sturdy escapist entertainment.

"They Won't Believe Me" (RKO). Sound scripting and acting give this character study solid potentialities.

"Song of Thin Man" (M-G) (Song). William Powell, Myrna Loy in resumption of "Thin Man" sleuth yarns; strong b.o.

"Springtime in the Sierras" (Rep) (Color). Topnotch Roy Rogers oatuner in Trucolor. Will be a solid pleaser in its market.

"The Red Stallion" (Color) (E-L). Good outdoor pic of horse, boy and dog, with a bear as heavy; good grosser.

"Gas House Kids Go West" (PRC). Badly-made comedy melodrama.

Song of Love

Metro release of Clarence Brown production. Stars Katharine Hepburn, Paul Henreid, Robert Walker; features Henry Daniell, Leo G. Carroll, Else Janssen. Directed by Brown. Screenplay, Ivan Tors, Irmgard von Cube, Allen Vincent, Robert Ardrey, from play by Bernard Schubert and Mario Silva; camera, Harry Stradling; editor, Robert J. Kern; musical direction, Bronislau Kaper; M-G symphony orch conducted by William Steinberg. Tradeshown N. Y., July 16, '47. Running time, **117 MINS.**

Clara Wieck Schumann.Katharine Hepburn
Robert Schumann....Paul Henreid
Johannes Brahms....Robert Walker
Franz Liszt....Henry Daniell
Professor Wieck....Leo G. Carroll
Bertha....Else Janssen
Julie....Gigi Perreau
Felix...."Tinker" Furlong
Marie....Ann Carter
Eugenie....Janine Perreau
Ludwig....Jimmie Hunt
Ferdinand....Anthony Sydes
Elise....Eilene Janssen
Dr. Hoffman....Roman Bohnen
Haslinger....Ludwig Stossel
Princess Valerie Hohenfels......Tala Birell
Judge....Kurt Katch
King Albert....Henry Stephenson
Reinecke....Konstantin Shayne

"Song of Love" will have varying reactions in different situations. Story of the lives, loves and music of Robert and Clara Schumann and Johannes Brahms, it has a good cast, entertaining tale and the usual top Metro production mountings to make it a sure draw in the key-city first-runs. Its longhair aspects may militate against it, though, in subsequent-runs and in the hinterlands. But taking into consideration the general public's growing acceptance of long-hair music and grosses rolled up by such flims as Columbia's "A Song to Remember," this one has a good chance of doing well all down the line.

Picture offers a goldmine of thesping opportunities to its three stars, Katharine Hepburn, Paul Henreid and Robert Walker, all of whom play it to the hilt. All three, moreover, show a surprising adeptness at the pianistics, which is highly necessary despite the fact that Artur Rubinstein ghosted for them all. Camera at many points is moved in for a closeup of their playing, and the dubbing job is done so expertly that only a well-trained student could be wise to the fact that someone else provided the actual soundtrack music. Music itself comprises the best works of Schumann, Brahms and Franz Liszt. Because of the extreme classicism of the three composers, however, only a small part of it will be familiar to the majority of audiences.

Screenplay, based on a play by Bernard Schubert and Mario Silva, is overlong, with the result that there's a slowness of pace throughout. Four different scripters had a hand in the adaptation. A little preface warns audiences that "certain necessary liberties have been taken with incident and chronology," step probably being taken to ward off such complaints as followed Jerome Kern's biopic, "Till the Clouds Roll By," "The Jolson Story," etc. Picture, however, follows more closely the composers' lives than is customary in scripters' dreams.

Yarn picks up the young Clara Wieck as an already popular concert pianist in the early part of the last century, at the time of her marriage to Schumann, a struggling young composer. Duo promptly, by screen time, have seven children, for whose care Frau Schumann sacrifices her concert work. The young Brahms enters the household as a student and promptly complicates things by falling for Clara. Schumann, meanwhile, continues to struggle to gain recognition for his works, but without success. Strain and overwork affect his mind, and he's taken to a mental institution where he dies. Brahms, who's become one of the top composers in Europe, later proposes to Clara (seven kids and all), but she turns him down in favor of returning to the concert stage to perpetuate the works of her late husband. Time then jumps 40 or so years to show Madame Schumann in her farewell appearance, gaining kudos for her husband's compositions.

Miss Hepburn is fine as Clara, showing in her work touches of the expert direction of Clarence Brown. She progresses neatly from emotion to emotion and registers solidly in both comedy and pathos. Henreid is a little too austere as Schumann but comes off well in a role suited more to his talents than some of his recent films. Walker is surprisingly good as Brahms, underplaying the part and making it seem at all times authentic. Supporting cast is uniformly good, with Henry Daniell standout as Liszt and Else Janssen contributing a neat performance as the maid in the Schumann menage.

Brown doubled as producer. Sets and costumes are good and technical credits are excellent. Camera work, under the supervision of Harry Stradling, adds much to the film's varying moods; his final shot, in which the camera moves from a closeup of Miss Hepburn at the piano to an extremely long shot of an entire auditorium, is exceptionally good. Special nods are due Bronislau Kaper for his intelligent musical direction and to the Metro orch under the capable direction of William Steinberg. *Stal.*

Something in the Wind
(SONGS)

Hollywood, July 19.

Universal-International release of Joseph Sistrom production. Stars Deanna Durbin, Donald O'Connor, John Dall; features Charles Winninger, Jacqueline de Wit, Helena Carter, Margaret Wycherly, Jan Peerce. Directed by Irving Pichel. Screenplay, Harry Kurnitz, William Bowers; based on story by Fritz Rotter and Charles O'Neal; camera, Milton Krasner; special photography, David S. Horsley; music, composed and directed by Johnny Green; lyrics, Leo Robin; editor, Otto Ludwig. Tradeshown Hollywood, July 18, '47. Running time, 88 MINS.

Mary Collins	Deanna Durbin
Charlie Read	Donald O'Connor
Donald Read	John Dall
Uncle Chester	Charles Winninger
Clarissa Prentice	Helena Carter
Grandma Read	Margaret Wycherly
Tony	Jan Peerce
Aunt Mary Collins	Jean Adair
Singing Quartette	The Four Williams Brothers
Saleslady	Jacqueline de Wit
M. C.	William Ching
Model	Patricia Alphin
Beamis	Chester Clute
Masterson	Frank Wilcox

"Something in the Wind" affords Deanna Durbin a warmth and s.a. lacking in most of her previous vehicles. It also gives her opportunity to display vocal ability on six numbers, both popular and classic, so the appeal to her fans should be wide. Film is light musical comedy with a broad treatment and sufficient chuckles to augur okay b.o. return. Sales will be aided by draw of Donald O'Connor, co-starring.

Music and lyrics by Johnny Green and Leo Robin are very listenable and get strong selling by Miss Durbin. In the popular style are "The Turntable Song" and "You Wanna Keep Your Baby Lookin' Right." Latter, a gold-digger number, is punched over solidly by Miss Durbin, who gives it a sexy, blues treatment. Standout on classic end is teaming of Miss Durbin and Jan Peerce on "Miserere" from "Il Trovatore." The title tune, "It's Only Love," and "Happy Go Lucky and Free" are others pleasing the ear.

O'Connor sings and dances to "I Love a Mystery," a takeoff on ether chill shows, and also terps again in finale production number. Aiding vocals are the four Williams brothers and a mixed chorus. Quartet gives good note-blending to back Miss Durbin on title song.

Plot is on the thin side, but sufficient backing for the music and laughs. Irving Pichel's direction paces it well. Scripted by Harry Kurnitz and William Bowers, from a story by Fritz Rotter and Charles O'Neal, plot deals with mistaken identity and attempts of wealthy family to buy off a girl it believes was supported by the late head of the clan.

Miss Durbin, a disk jockey, is the girl. John Dall is the priggish scion of wealth. An antagonistic romance grows between two, aided and abetted by O'Connor, poor third cousin of the wealthy, and Charles Winninger, a poor uncle. Expected finale clinch brings lovers together after romantic trials and tribulations that aren't too well premised in the writing.

Picture has not been well-edited. Otherwise, Joseph Sistrom's production guidance has shaped it expertly. Cast handles characterizations deftly. Helena Carter does okay by small spot as Dall's fiancee, Margaret Wycherly is good as his snobbish mother, Jean Adair, Jacqueline de Wit, Chester Clute, Frank Wilcox and others are competent.

Miss Durbin has been attractively gowned by Orry Kelly and, as further treat for ladies, a style show is thrown in as background for the "Baby Lookin' Right" tune. Art direction provides lush settings, and Milton Krasner's camera takes full advantage of the production dress and players. Figuring on credit side are the orchestrations by Ted Duncan and George Siravo, and set decorations. *Brog.*

Merton of the Movies

Hollywood, July 12.

Metro release of Albert Lewis production. Stars Red Skelton; features Virginia O'Brien, Leon Ames, Gloria Grahame, Alan Mowbray. Directed by Robert Alton. Screenplay, George Wells and Lou Breslow; based on novel by Harry Leon Wilson and play by George S. Kaufman and Marc Connelly; camera, Paul C. Vogel; score, David Snell; editor, Frank E. Hull. Tradeshown July 9, '47. Running time, 83 MINS.

Merton Gill	Red Skelton
Phyllis Montague	Virginia O'Brien
Beulah Baxter	Gloria Grahame
Lawrence Rupert	Leon Ames
Frank Mulvaney	Alan Mowbray
Jeff Baird	Charles D. Brown
Von Strutt	Hugo Haas
Mr. Gashwiler	Harry Hayden
Marty	Tom Trout
Phil	Douglas Fowley
Chick	Dick Wessell

"Merton of the Movies" isn't a tailor-made vehicle for Red Skelton but his master clowning makes light of that fact and gears film as a winner on laughs. A burlesque on Hollywood that's been made before and also legit-staged, "Merton" should register heftily at the ticket windows in all situations. Albert Lewis' production slant makes appropriate use of Skelton's talents in shaping showmanly presentation that will pay off.

There may be a cycle of old-time flicker rebirths in the making as this is second in the current season featuring megaphone-and-puttees days, other being "Perils of Pauline." Such films are graphic examples of how far industry has come technically and artistically and at same time furnish sure laugh material in depicting scenery-chewing techniques practiced in the early days.

Robert Alton puts the players through their paces with sure directorial touch that milks comedy inherent in fable of smalltown, film-struck youth who battles Hollywood to win fame and fortune. The Skelton comedy has substance underneath that draws full audience sympathy. There's none of the brash, forward technique usually used by him in grabbing laughs and it adds up to a nifty pace switch.

Virginia O'Brien proves herself a capable leading lady without recourse to deadpan vocaling. Erstwhile canary doesn't have a number to chirp throughout and sells herself strictly on talent merits in the romantic lead opposite Skelton. Manner in which she delivers should further her career.

Plot of the old Harry Leon Wilson novel, scripted by George Wells and Lou Breslow, has Skelton, smalltown theatre usher, brought to Hollywood as publicity gag to aid career of fading film star portrayed by Leon Ames. He soon finds it's a quick brushoff but sticks around to carry out aims of being a dramatic star himself. Recognizing his comedy talents, Miss O'Brien sets him in film burlesquing Ames. Skelton plays it straight and winds up a new star with a happy romance.

Gloria Grahame has herself a time as an oldtime screen vamp. Ames is excellent as the fading star. Alan Mowbray, early-day director; Charles D. Brown, producer; Douglas Fowley, brash flack, and others come through with solid support.

Production has been given first-rate lensing by Paul C. Vogel, and art direction, settings, editing, music score and other credits are topnotch in backing fun intentions. *Brog.*

Her Husband's Affairs

Hollywood, July 18.

Columbia release of Cornell production (Raphael Hakim, associate producer). Stars Lucille Ball, Franchot Tone; features Edward Everett Horton, Mikhail Rasumny, Gene Lockhart. Directed by S. Sylvan Simon. Screenplay, Ben Hecht, Charles Lederer; camera, Charles Lawton, Jr.; editor, Al Clark. Previewed at the Pantages, Hollywood, July 17, '47. Running time, 84 MINS.

Margaret Weldon	Lucille Ball
William Weldon	Franchot Tone
J. B. Cruikshank	Edward Everett Horton
Professor Glinka	Mikhail Rasumny
Peter Winterbottom	Gene Lockhart
Mrs. Winterbottom	Nana Bryant
Governor Fox	Jonathan Hale
Dr. Frazee	Paul Stanton
Mrs. Josper	Mabel Paige
Vice-President Starrett	Frank Mayo
Vice-President Beitler	Pierre Watkin
Vice-President Brady	Carl Leviness
Vice-President Nicholson	Dick Gordon
Tappel	Douglas Wood
Slocum	Jack Rice
Window Washer	Clancy Cooper
Police Captain	Charles C. Wilson
Brewster	Charles Trowbridge
Judge	Selmer Jackson
District Attorney	Arthur Space

"Her Husband's Affairs" should come as a welcome relief to a box-office overrun with psychosis melodrama. It's zaney, well-premised fun that has a laugh a minute. There's production polish, sure direction and extremely deft performances that add up to pleasurable entertainment for any theatre. It should garner strong receipts if properly exploited.

As a comedy team, Lucille Ball and Franchot Tone excel. Despite comedy emphasis there are several pash romantic sequences between the two as husband and wife that raise the temperature. Tone is slightly screwball advertising-slogan genius while Miss Ball is his ever-loving wife who somehow always winds up with the credit for his spectacular stunts.

Unusual twists and strong planting of events feature the excellent original script by Ben Hecht and Charles Lederer. With his direction, S. Sylvan Simon brings the crackpot doings to life for strong audience reaction. His pace is perfect and he welds zaney situations into socko laughs. Motivation for much of the comedy comes from Tone's sponsorship of a screwball inventor and the products that he develops while searching for the perfect embalming fluid. Gentle fun is poked at advertising agencies and bigshot sponsors and public figures.

Mikhail Rasumny is the crazy inventor and wraps up the role for honors. Edward Everett Horton, Gene Lockhart, a business tycoon; Nana Bryant, his wife, and Jonathan Hale are among others who keep the laughs busy.

Raphael Hakim has given production polish in all departments. *Brog.*

They Won't Believe Me

RKO release of Joan Harrison production (Jack Gross, executive producer). Stars Robert Young, Susan Hayward, Jane Greer; features Rita Johnson, Tom Powers. Directed by Irving Pichel. Screenplay, Jonathan Latimer, based on story by Gordon McDonell; camera, Harry J. Wild; editor, Elmo Williams. At Palace, N. Y., week July 17, '47. Running time, 95 MINS.

Larry	Robert Young
Verna	Susan Hayward
Janice	Jane Greer
Gretta	Rita Johnson
Trenton	Tom Powers
Lt. Carr	George Tyne
Thomason	Don Beddoe
Cahill	Frank Ferguson
Judge Fletcher	Harry Harvey

A modest budgeter embellished with a soundly rounded pivot-role and scripting that sparkles, RKO's "They Won't Believe Me" drives another spike through the whilom gospel that you can only get out of a pic the coin you put in. To sell, it'll need high-tension exploitation, but word-of-mouth will help.

This film scores in its tri-dimensional portrayal of its chief characters—a male no-gooder and the three gals in his life. Unerring casting has them at the inside rail from the gun with some neat thesping and writing. Camera focuses on Robert Young in a practically continuous take. Playing a photogenic weakling who's caviar to the femmes, Young donates depth and perception to an intrinsically unsympathetic part. Susan Hayward, Jane Greer and Rita Johnson are the women in his life.

Credits segue into a courtroom where Young is on trial for homicide. Via flashbacks, he testifies in his own behalf and biogs the actions leading to the event. He's shown as a weak sister who marries one woman (Miss Johnson) for her shekels and is about to lam out with another (Miss Greer). Key to his character is deftly signalled early in the game when he drops his getaway idea because his wife baits him with a stockbrokerage partnership and a home on the Coast.

Brief matrimonial reformation tunnels into a second affair with his partner's secretary (Miss Hayward) and a second walkout move. Pic takes a melodramatic twist with the accidental death of Miss Hayward and the wife's suicide. He's tried on a charge of murdering his girl friend. Film skirts possible Breen code complications by a solution which is a touch too obvious in its irony.

Steady directorial hand of Irving Pichel is apparent throughout. Camera and script are above par. *Wit.*

Song of the Thin Man
(ONE SONG)

Metro release of Nat Perrin production. Stars William Powell, Myrna Loy; features Keenan Wynn, Ralph Morgan, Philip Reed, Jayne Meadows, Dean Stockwell. Directed by Edward Buzzell. Screenplay, Steve Fisher and Nat Perrin, from story by Stanley Roberts, based on characters created by Dashiell Hammett; additional dialog, James O'Hanlon, Harry Crane; camera, Charles Rosher; editor, Gene Ruggiero; song, "You're Not So Easy to Forget," by Herb Magidson, Ben Oakland. Previewed in N. Y., July 17, '47. Running time, **86 MINS.**

Nick Charles..............William Powell
Nora Charles..............Myrna Loy
Clarence "Clinker" Krause..Keenan Wynn
Nick Charles, Jr..............Dean Stockwell
Tommy Edlon Drake..........Philip Reed
Phyllis Talbin.............Patricia Morison
Mitchell Talbin..............Leon Ames
Fran Ledue Page.........Gloria Grahame
Janet Thayar..............Jayne Meadows
David I. Thayar.............Ralph Morgan
Jessica Thayar..............Bess Flowers
Buddy Hollis..............Don Taylor
Dr. Monolaw..............Warner Anderson
Phil Orval Brant...........Bruce Cowling
Bertha..............Connie Gilchrist
The Neem..............Henry Nemo
Al Amboy..............William Bishop
Helen Amboy..............Marie Windsor

Initial "Thin Man" picture since 1945, this new Dashiell Hammett detective thriller puts the Metro series right back in full stride. "Song of Thin Man" is one of the better William Powell-Myrna Loy pictures in the "Thin Man" grouping. It's likely to get top boxoffice.

Per usual, Powell, as Nick Charles, super sleuth, is persuaded to come out of retirement and solve a slaying on a big gambling ship. And, as usual, there are other killings before Powell rounds up the real culprit besides several attempts made on his own life. Scripters Steve Fisher and Nat Perrin have tossed in plenty of confusing details for the Stanley Roberts story but interest is never lost. Edward Buzzell has directed with a nice touch, keeping interest at high pitch.

As customary, Miss Loy, as Powell's wife, has a narrow escape from one of the murder suspects. Asta (their pet dog), not only supplies several comical moments but figures in the plot, and their own son becomes the object of the mobsters.

Powell and Miss Loy, as his always inquisitive wife, fit ideally into the starring roles. They've played these characters ever since Nick and Nora Charles were first projected on the screen in "The Thin Man." Dean Stockwell, as Nick Charles, Jr., also does well.

Keenan Wynn clicks as "Clinker" Krause, hep clarinetist who steers the detective into many hangouts of after-hour musicians in trying to locate a missing bandsman. It's nothing like anything Wynn has previously done. Jayne Meadows, as the society gal who elopes with the gambler (Bruce Cowling), looks like a comer, although overly dramatic in earlier scenes. Ralph Morgan, Gloria Grahame and Philip Reed top an unusually strong supporting cast.

Aside from Buzzell's slick direction and Charles Rosher's topflight photography, James O'Hanlon and Harry Crane have contributed some witty dialog. *Wear.*

Springtime in the Sierras
(COLOR; SONGS)

Hollywood, July 19.

Republic release of Edward J. White production. Stars Roy Rogers; features Jane Frazee, Andy Devine. Directed by William Witney. Screenplay, A. Cloan Nibley; camera (Technicolor), Jack Marta; editor, Tony Martinelli; musical director, Morton Scott; songs, Jack Elliott, Bob Nolan, Tim Spencer. Previewed in Hollywood, July 18, '47. Running time, **75 MINS.**

Roy Rogers..............Roy Rogers
Taffy Baker..............Jane Frazee
Cookie Bullfincher.............Andy Devine
Jean Loring.............Stephanie Bachelor
Bert Baker..............Hal Landon
Captain Foster..........Harry V. Cheshire
Matt Wilkes..............Roy Barcroft
Old Timer..............Chester Conklin
Old Timer..............Hank Patterson
Henchman..............Whitey Christy
Henchman..............Pascale Perry
Bob Nolan and the Sons of the Pioneers

"Springtime in the Sierras" makes a pitch against indiscriminate destruction of wild game in between the load of standard western action. The two combine neatly, giving Roy Rogers one of his best action vehicles. There are spectacular stunts, hard riding, fisticuffs and gunplay as red meat for the action fan, along with a story that hangs together nicely.

In this one, Rogers breaks up a ring dealing in fancy game killed out of season. In doing so he nearly ends up as a frozen stiff in the gang's meat-locker. Aiding his range detective work are the Sons of the Pioneers and Andy Devine, as a western photographer and clown.

Rogers, the Pioneers and Jane Frazee have been given total of six tunes to blend into the action. Rogers and the Pioneers work over the title number, "A Cowboy Has to Sing," and "The Quilting Party." Rogers and Devine do "Oh, What a Picture," while Miss Frazee teams with Rogers on "Pedro from Acapulco." Pioneers do "What Are We Gonna Do Then."

William Witney's direction sends the A. Sloan Nibley original screenplay through fast paces to keep the action on the run. Stephanie Bachelor heads the gang dealing in illegal game, with Roy Barcroft as chief henchman. When a game warden friend of Rogers is murdered by Miss Bachelor, cowpoke goes into action. It isn't long before he's able to backtrack the slaughtering to Miss Bachelor's ranch. Gang spot him and toss him into freezing room. Rogers finally gets loose and the cleanup is staged with swift action.

Trucolor print on this one gives faded hues to players and scenery and proves to be an eye distractor. Otherwise, the Jack Marta lensing is sharp. Editing by Tony Martinelli is good, and other production values lined up by Edward J. White give the picture expert framing. *Brog.*

The Red Stallion
(COLOR)

Eagle-Lion release of Bryan Foy production (Ben Stoloff, associate producer). Stars Ted Donaldson, Jane Darwell; features Robert Paige, Noreen Nash, Ray Collins, Guy Kibbee, Robert Bice, Pierre Watkin, Bill Cartledge. Directed by Lesley Selander. Screenplay, Robert E. Kent, Crane Wilbur; camera, Virgil Miller; editor, Fred Allen. Tradeshown N. Y., July 16, '47. Running time, 81 MINS.

Andy McBride..............Robert Paige
Ellen Reynolds..............Noreen Nash
Joel Curtis..............Ted Donaldson
Mrs. Curtis..............Jane Darwell
Barton..............Ray Collins
Dr. Thompson..............Guy Kibbee
Jackson..............Willie Best
Ho-Na..............Robert Bice
Richard Moresby..............Pierre Watkin
Johnny Stevens..............Bill Cartledge
Big Red..............Himself
Daisy..............Herself

Bryan Foy's medicine men have tossed together a canny mixture in "The Red Stallion," Cinecolored outdoor spectacular with broad appeal to all levels. It's a parlay of a horse, a boy and a dog, with a bear as the heavy. And the animal kingdom makes for fancy entertainment. The exhib should gallop home on "Stallion" with more than spurs a-jingling.

There aren't any potent marquee names in this pic but the exploitation angle is obvious. It's a buildup, mainly of a story about a mighty bear vs. horse that spells nifty climaxing. Credit the camera also with some pretty mountain country. Racing scenes play up the ponies nicely to clinch the appeal to horse lovers.

Dimming the film's lustre are some overly saccharine sequences revolving about the boy (Ted Donaldson) and his grandmother's (Jane Darwell) efforts to save the ranch from the traditional foreclosure. These scenes, especially an overlong prayer closeup, could stand judicious scissoring. First half of pic needs general pepping.

Once the camera moves into high to depict the bear-horse fracas and the race that follows, pace pickup is sharp and effective. For the story, simply, is how a boy finds a foal, falls in love with it, and trains it to be a great racer. And the prelims are loaded for the second-half explosion. In winning the race and thereby inducing a stable-tycoon to buy a share in the nag, it's obvious that the old homestead is saved.

Hardly secondary is the horse's hatred for bears and the vendetta that's liquidated in the epic battle. Noteworthy, also, is a Phi Beta Kappa dog, Daisy, which does some scene-larceny on its own. Donaldson as the boy is adequate.

Camera work is good. The animal scenes must have taken considerable doing. Direction wavers at first but finds itself in the closeout reels. *Wit.*

Gas House Kids Go West

Hollywood, July 14.

PRC release of Sam Baerwitz production. Features Carl "Alfalfa" Switzer, Bennie Bartlett, Rudy Wissler, Tommy Bond. Directed by William Beaudine. Screenplay, Robert E. Kent, Robert A. McGowan, Eugene Conrad; original story, Sam Baerwitz; camera, William Sickner; editor, Harry Reynolds. Previewed in Hollywood, July 14, '47. Running time, **62 MINS.**

Sgt. Casey..............Emory Parnell
Nan Crowley..............Chill Williams
Steve..............Vince Barnett
Jim Kingsley..............William Wright
Mrs. Crowley..............Lela Bliss
Pulaski..............Ronn Marvin
Corky..............Ray Dolciame
Alfalfa..............Carl Switzer
Orvie..............Bennie Bartlett
Scat..............Rudy Wissler
Chimp..............Tommy Bond

PRC's Gas House Kids series won't live long if others are as poorly turned out as "Gas House Kids Go West." There's nothing to recommend this one for any booking.

Original story by Sam Baerwitz offers okay premise for stringing together comedy and melodrama but, as producer, Baerwitz displays little knowledge. William Beaudine's direction also misses badly, and Robert A. Kent, Robert A. McGowan and Eugene Conrad, turned out a consistently bad screenplay.

Plot has gashouse gang heading west for vacation on a ranch, along with a policeman friend. They maneuver job of driving car to California, not knowing it's a hot job. They find ranch is being used by crooked foreman as hideout for hot cars and trap the gang and save the rancher's daughter from a marriage with foreman.

Dialog is crammed with cliches that will arouse audience groans. Cast does nothing to improve gags and situations. Lensing and other production credits are adequate. *Brog.*

Miniature Reviews

"Down to Earth" (Col) (Musical; Color). Rita Hayworth-Larry Parks in musical fantasy that disappoints.

"Desert Fury" (Color) (Par). Western beautifully photographed in color; exploitable values will aid b.o.

"The Unfinished Dance" (M-G). Presenting beautiful ballet in magnificent color, starring Margaret O'Brien.

"Deep Valley" (WB). Strong melodrama with top performances to put it over.

"Heaven Only Knows" (UA). Amusing fantasy of an angel visiting earth; should find good general acceptance.

"Sport of Kings" (Col). Minor programmer of southern horse racing.

"Ghost Town Renegades" (PRC). So-so oater in the "Lash" La Rue series.

"Wyoming" (Rep). Quality western that should do well at the b.o.

"Sepia Cinderella" (Herald) Musical). Negro musical solely for houses catering to colored clientele.

"Green Cockatoo" (British) (Devonshire). John Mills, Robert Newton in antiquated gangster film.

Down to Earth
(MUSICAL; COLOR)

Columbia release of Don Hartman production. Stars Rita Hayworth and Larry Parks; features Marc Platt, Roland Culver, James Gleason, Edward Everett Horton, Adele Jergens, George MacReady and William Frawley. Directed by Alexander Hall. Original screenplay by Hartman and Edwin Blum, with "Jordan" characters taken from play, "Heaven Can Wait," by Harry Segall; camera, Rudolph Mate; editor, Viola Lawrence; songs, Allan Roberts and Doris Fisher, with additional music by George Duning and Heinz Roemheld. Previewed in New York July 28, '47. Running time, **100 MINS.**

Terpsichore..............Rita Hayworth
Danny Miller..............Larry Parks
Eddie..............Marc Platt
Mr. Jordan..............Roland Culver
Max Corkle..............James Gleason
Messenger 7013.....Edward Everett Horton
Georgia Evans..............Adele Jergens
Joe Mannion..............George MacReady
Police Lieutenant.........William Frawley
Betty..............Jean Donahue
Dolly..............Kathleen O'Malley
Spike..............William Haade
Kelly..............James Burke
Orchestra Leader..............Fred Sears

A flock of exceptionally good tunes, an excellent cast and brilliant Technicolor production job should make this Columbia musical a strong potential at the b.o. That they *will* looks uncertain, however, as even the best of other attributes have an impossible time overcoming the slow, tiresome and unacceptable plot. Pic looks set for nothing better than comparatively mediocre grosses.

Cast names should help considerably, since this is Rita Hayworth's first since the highly successful "Gilda" and Larry Parks' initialer since "The Jolson Story." In addition, there's Marc Platt, a fine dancer but who, by some inexplicable reasoning, never gets a chance to dance.

Yarn is one of those tricky ideas that looks so much better on paper than celluloid. It picks up the characters from Harry Segall's play, "Heaven Can Wait," filmed by Columbia in 1941 as the tremendously successful "Here Comes Mr. Jordan," and puts them down in a new setting. "Mr. Jordan" was about an angelized prizefighter who comes back to earth in someone else's body. "Down to

Earth" is a typical backstage story —and putting it in the "Mr. Jordan" setting is certainly the hard way of getting a twist on the old, standard musical.

The first requisite of fantasy is that it be believable in its frame of reference and thus accepted by the audience. "Down to Earth" misses that entirely and as a result has an uphill battle all the way.

Not that it will matter much to the paying guests, but producer Don Hartman has carried out his cute idea to the extent of using some of the same cast as "Jordan." James Gleason is back as an agent and Edward Everett Horton is seen once again as the messenger who accompanies the spirit down to earth. Roland Culver subs for Claude Raines in the Mr. Jordan role, the guy who runs Heaven.

Miss Hayworth is pictured as Terpsichore, the Greek muse of the theatre. Looking down from Heaven she's unhappy over a Broadway musical about the nine muses, being done in jazz by producer Larry Parks. She makes a request to go down and help him so she can clean the show up. She lands in the star role and there's the usual falling-in-love with the vis-a-vis—in this case Parks—the disagreements and breaking up, and the return. Finally, she's recalled to Heaven, busting up her romance, but it's all patched up when Parks dies some years later and joins her above the clouds.

Explanation necessary to get all this across—and plenty not even attempted in the plot summary above—takes interminable time and constantly slows even the angels to a lazy walk. Making things worse is the fact that all the gags which should give the yarn a bit of pepper fall flat.

Definitely on the credit side are the five tunes provided by Allan Roberts and Doris Fisher. Certainly to be heard more of are "This Can't Be Legal," "They Can't Convince Me," and "Let's Stay Young Forever." Also creditable are the excellent color camera work on the cloud and theatre backgrounds, and in making the most of Miss Hayworth's natural attractions.

Parks sings one tune—a moment that many in the audience, remembering "Jolson," will be waiting for. It's definitely a letdown. He's okay on the acting, but when it comes to singing, Parks should always have Jolson. Miss Hayworth does better in the vocal department and, of course, is fine in the terp routines. Platt is pictured as a member of the legit musical's cast and does a number of routines with Parks and Miss Hayworth, but never gets away into one of his spectacular solos.

Alexander Hall's direction is spotty. The excess of lines is tough, but his megging does nothing to speed up the proceedings and ofttimes adds to the slowness. On the other hand, dance director Jack Cole practically goes frantic—and almost gets the audience that way—in an excess of zeal to give speed to the production numbers.

Overall effect is regret that so much potential b.o. value has been bogged down in a mass of plot and misguidance. *Herb.*

Desert Fury

(COLOR)

Hollywood, July 24.

Paramount release of Hal B. Wallis production. Stars Lizabeth Scott, John Hodiak, Burt Lancaster; features Mary Astor, Wendell Corey. Directed by Lewis Allen. Screenplay, Robert Rossen; from Collier's mag novel by Ramona Stewart; camera (Technicolor), Charles Lang, Edward Cronjager; music, Miklos Rozsa; editor, Warren Low. Tradeshown at Los Angeles, July 22, '47. Running time, **94 MINS.**

Eddie Bendix....................John Hodiak
Paula Haller....................Lizabeth Scott
Tom Hanson....................Burt Lancaster
Johnny Ryan....................Wendell Corey
Fritzie Haller....................Mary Astor
Claire Lindquist....................Kristine Miller
Judge Berle Lindquist....William Harrigan
Pat Johnson....................James Flavin
Mrs. Lindquist....................Jane Novak
Rosa....................Ana Camargo

"Desert Fury" has exploitation values and a Paramount release to assure it initial boxoffice attention. If backed with hypoed selling campaign, its grossing potentialities in key runs are okay.

As a Hal Wallis production, film reflects top-booking values, namely in the assists of growing marquee draw of its star names and the Technicolor hues in which its starkly beautiful western backgrounds have been photographed. And there's the added fillip of a sports-style parade by femme star Lizabeth Scott. But despite those b.o. exploitable values, the picture falls short of entertainment credits earned by Wallis in previous films.

Story characters carry little audience sympathy and there is a "so what" attitude about their eventual fate. Dramatic punch that could have been given to the plot resolution comes out only as a strictly cliche clinch that falls completely flat.

It's a confused development of characters whose motivations are indefinitely pointed out in explanatory dialog rather than action. Flashbacks would have gone a long way in clearing up the plot, which is filled with characters going through meaningless action. Final reels attempt to premise the previous doings but general audiences are not likely to sort out the psychological and physical reasons motivating the unsympathetic roles.

Robert Rossen's screenplay hews to an uncensorable development of Ramona Stewart's novel. Censorship angles take the punch out of whatever interesting factors the original mag story might have had. On that basis, Lewis Allen's direction has had to compromise. He often gets spectacular beauty in the staging of scenes but there is little reality for the average ticketbuyer in the characters he puts through their paces. There is an occasional lift in an individual scene because of playing and dialog, but the mood is not sustained.

Standing out among the players is Wendell Corey. He gives punch to his part as John Hodiak's mentor. In a few, bare scenes, Burt Lancaster is enabled by good, honest dialog to make them register strongly. Hodiak is a bit too brittle as the hideaway gambler who takes advantage of Lizabeth Scott's 19-year-old innocence. Miss Scott is a wonderful clotheshorse for the far-west outdoor costumes provided by Edith Head. Otherwise, the role of a frustrated daughter of a gambling "house" madame fails to project the interest or sympathy it should. Mary Astor is good as the madame who wants her daughter to grow up right. Others are bits.

Picture has been given magnificent color lensing by Charles Lang and Edward Cronjager. Raw western scenery, night shots and interiors are beautiful. Intense art direction by Perry Ferguson and the set decorations by Sam Comer and Syd Moore; the special effects by Gordon Jennings and editing by Warren Low are all first class. Miklos Rozsa's music score is effective. *Brog.*

The Unfinished Dance

(MUSICAL; COLOR)

Hollywood, July 26.

Metro release of Joe Pasternak production. Stars Margaret O'Brien, Cyd Charisse, Karin Booth, Danny Thomas; features Esther Dale, Thurston Hall, Harry Hayden, Mary Eleanor Donahue. Directed by Henry Koster. Screenplay, Myles Connolly; based on the story, "La Mort Du Cygne," by Paul Morand; camera (Technicolor), Robert Surtees; musical score, Herbert Stothart; associate, Lothar Perl; dance direction, David Lichine; editor, Douglass Biggs. Tradeshown in Hollywood, July 24, '47. Running time, **100 MINS.**

"Meg" Merlin....................Margaret O'Brien
Mlle. Ariane Bouchet....................Cyd Charisse
La Darina....................Karin Booth
Mr. Paneros....................Danny Thomas
Olga....................Esther Dale
Mr. Ronsell....................Thurston Hall
Murphy....................Harry Hayden
Josie....................Mary Eleanor Donahue
Phyllis....................Connie Cornell
Miss Merlin....................Ruth Brady
Fred Carleton....................Charles Gradstreet
Mme. Borodin....................Ann Codee
Jacques Lacoste....................Gregory Gay

"The Unfinished Dance" carries sock appeal to the eye and ear. With music taken from the best ballet scores of the past, plus a magnificent ballet staging of "Holiday for Strings" finale, picture carries class distinction. For general audience appeal there is a moppet human interest yarn dominated by little Margaret O'Brien. Joe Pasternak earns himself a showmanly credit for combining the varied interests and for backing the film with the plushiest of physical trappings.

The beautiful spectacles of ballet dance running through the picture have been given elegant color lensing by Robert Surtees. His is an eloquent camera that contributes full measure to the sight appeal and provides a mobility that is spectacular in some sequences. Climaxing the dance artistry is "Strings" ballet, which reaches breath-taking heights of beauty and movement as staged by David Lichine. Throughout film are ballet dance moments that add to interest, all tellingly done by Cyd Charisse. The effective music score that backs the entire production earns top credit for Herbert Stothart and his associate, Lothar Perl.

Commanding direction by Henry Koster gets the best from the tear-jerker story that surrounds the music and dancing. Well-written for human interest, story depicts a little girl who wants to be a ballerina. She fastens her affections on Miss Charisse and when she feels her mentor's success is threatened by a foreign ballet star she arranges an accident that cripples the latter. Motivation gives Miss O'Brien opportunity to run the full gamut of emotions, and she delivers for strong fan favor. There is a happy ending when she finds a new friend in the star she has crippled. Myles Connolly screenplayed from the Paul Morand story, "La Mort Du Cygne."

Miss Charisse handles herself well in the acting assignment but, naturally, shines best when displaying her dance magic. Karin Booth does a strong job as the rival star, making it a standout piece of work. She and Miss O'Brien rate additional credit for the manner in which they simulate toe work.

Film introduces Danny Thomas to picturegoers. He's no nightclub clown in this, delivering a semi-serious portrayal of the little girl's friend that has plenty of merit. Esther Dale, Thurston Hall, Harry Hayden and Gregory Gay are among other grownups giving excellent accounts of themselves. Mary Eleanor Donahue and Connie Cornell are among the good moppets.

There is class art direction by Cedric Gibbons and Daniel B. Cathcart; smooth editing by Douglass Biggs; fine set decorations by Edwin B. Willis and Hugh Hunt; beautiful costumes by Helen Rose under Irene's supervision and other potent production factors to back the picture with outstanding physical values. *Brog.*

Deep Valley

Hollywood, July 26.

Warners release of Henry Blanke production. Stars Ida Lupino, Dane Clark, Wayne Morris; features Fay Bainter, Henry Hull, Willard Robertson. Directed by Jean Negulesco. Screenplay, Salka Viertel, Stephen Morehouse Avery; from the novel by Dan Totheroh; camera, Ted McCord; music, Max Steiner; editor, Owen Marks. Tradeshown in Hollywood, July 24, '47. Running time, **103 MINS.**

Libby....................Ida Lupino
Barry....................Dane Clark
Barker....................Wayne Morris
Mrs. Saul....................Fay Bainter
Mr. Saul....................Henry Hull
Sheriff....................Willard Robertson

"Deep Valley" is first-class melodrama, marked by distinctive performances. It will thoroughly please audiences who shop for moody violence and strongly-motivated, unleavened action. Sustained mood, austere settings and other physical props are surely applied by Henry Blanke's production to make this one stand out in the melodrama market.

Film affords Dane Clark his first real acting opportunity in films and he comes through with a credible performance that boosts his stock considerably. His interpretation of an escaped convict, who finds temporary happiness with a girl as frustrated as he, is a fine job that should aid his future. Ida Lupino, the love-starved girl, chalks up one of the finest performances she has ever turned in, tellingly carrying audience sympathy and interest from her opening scene to the finale.

Story deals with girl who for 10 years has known no love in her family. In a convict working on a road gang constructing a new coast highway in the Big Sur country of California she recognizes a kindred soul. When the convict escapes during a rainstorm and landslide, she shelters him, first in a hideaway cabin, then in the loft of her father's barn, while posses comb the hills. The Salka Viertel-Stephen Morehouse Avery script builds tension and suspense in these scenes of manhunt and escape. Dialog is realistic and climax does not resolve off into a happy ending. When his hiding place is finally discovered, Clark makes a break, is gunned down and crawls away into the woods to die a violent but peaceful death in Miss Lupino's arms.

It's strong, uncompromising drama, and Jean Negulesco's direction punches it over forcefully. He sustains a mood of desperation and pending violence that carries the spectator along, and draws performances from the cast that click big.

Wayne Morris, construction superintendent on the highway, capably fills the third co-starring part. His role is not as colorful but he gives it competent delivery to hold his own. Fay Bainter and Henry Hull, as the hating parents, stand out strongly with characterizations that set the melodramatic pattern of frustration. Willard Robertson is effective as the sheriff who enjoys his work of hunting down criminals.

Max Steiner's music score punches over the dramatics with a terrific effect, playing an important part in maintaining tension. Very good are the camera work by Ted McCord, the art direction and other factors backing the production. *Brog.*

Heaven Only Knows

Hollywood, July 26.

United Artists release of Seymour Nebenzal production. Stars Robert Cummings, Brian Donlevy; features Marjorie Reynolds, Jorja Curtright. Directed by Albert S. Rogell. Screenplay, Art Arthur, Rowland Leigh; adaptation, Ernest Haycox; original story, Aubrey Wisberg; camera, Karl Struss; music score and direction, Heinz Roemheld; editor, Edward Mann. Previewed in Hollywood, July 25, '47. Running time, **97 MINS.**

Mike....................Robert Cummings
Duke....................Brian Donlevy
Ginger....................Marjorie Reynolds
Drusilla....................Jorja Curtright
Plumber....................Bill Goodwin
Sheriff....................Stuart Erwin
The Reverend....................John Litel
Speck O'Donnell....................Peter Miles
Jud....................Edgar Kennedy
Treason....................Gerald Mohr
Mrs. O'Donnell....................Lurene Tuttle
Freel....................Ray Gennett

"Heaven Only Knows" is an amusing fantasy done in an almost straight manner to give it credence. There are no astonishing miracles of heavenly power, no fantastic harps and wings to stretch the imagination too far. It's a tongue-in-cheek treatment that lends a lightness to what, otherwise, could have been rather heavy drama. Seymour Nebenzal's production has shaped it well for general release, and cast names, headed by Robert Cummings and Brian Donlevy, add to selling values.

Story concerns an angel visiting earth to rectify a heavenly bookkeeping error. He had permitted a man to run loose without a soul because his destiny hadn't been properly entered in the books. On earth, he finds the soulless creature just that. He's a ruthless killer operating a saloon in the Territory of Montana.

The angel's chore is to bring together the killer and the schoolmarm because, according to heaven's books, they should have been married for two years. Since the angel is not permitted to work any miracles, his job is not an easy one but he finally brings the killer and his soul together, and does a good job of playing cupid.

Robert Cummings plays the visiting angel with just the right touch. There's a refreshing naiveness in the angel's conduct in the tough western mining town; his openly friendly approach to his task and occasional chagrin when he encounters a situation where a miracle would have been a big help. Brian Donlevy, too, sparks his assignment as the man without a soul, changing from ruthless killer to bewildered tough guy to, finally, a contented man.

Jorja Curtright is the schoolmarm and demonstrates talent. Unfortunately, makeup, hairstyling and camera do not treat her kindly. Marjorie Reynolds portrays dancehall queen who goes for the angel, an uncomfortable situation for that heavenly person. Bill Goodwin is good as Donlevy's arch rival for power in the town. Gerald Mohr, Donlevy's gunman, gets the proper satanish inflection into the character. Stuart Erwin is permitted to overplay the sheriff role. Little Peter Miles is good as a kid, as is John Litel as the preacher.

Overall good effect is achieved by Albert S. Rogell's direction. He generally overcomes some script heaviness and shines best in getting lightness into what, otherwise, would have been very strong melodrama. Screenplay by Art Arthur and Rowland Leigh has good dialog for punch and interesting characters. Ernest Haycox did the adaptation from the Aubrey Wisberg original story.

Karl Struss' lensing, special photographic effects by Ray Binger, Edward Mann's editing, music score by Heinz Roemhold, art direction and set decorations all provide expert backing for the fantasy. *Brog.*

Sport of Kings

Hollywood, July 25.

Columbia release of William Bloom production. Features Paul Campbell, Gloria Henry, Harry Davenport, Mark Dennis, Harry Cheshire, Clinton Rosemond. Directed by Robert Gordon. Screenplay, Edward Huebsch; based on story by Gordon Grand; camera, Henry Freulich; editor, Aaron Stell. At Pantages, Hollywood, July 22, '47. Running time, **67 MINS.**

Tom Cloud	Paul Campbell
Doc Richardson	Gloria Henry
Major Denning	Harry Davenport
Biff Cloud	Mark Dennis
Theodore McKeogh	Harry Cheshire
Josiah	Clinton Rosemond
Bertie	Louis Mason
Judge Sellers	Oscar O'Shea
Alf	Ernest Anderson

"Sport of Kings" is a routine programmer. Film has an occasional lift, despite obvious marketing destination. There's a horserace finish that will excite bangtail followers, and some good performances to help put it over in supporting positions.

Plot is corncob affair with benefit of a new twist that isn't developed strongly enough. Robert Gordon's direction is as slow-paced as script by Edward Huebsch, based on story by Gordon Grand.

Yarn concerns two northern lads who inherit a Kentucky plantation, won by their gambling father from a southern horse-racing colonel. Deep-south prejudice against Yankees make the heirs' life tough until they hit on scheme to take in the original owner under guise he was left a trust fund by the father. The old colonel eventually finds out the scheme and is outraged but when Yanks enter his horse in the big race, and he wins, everyone's face is saved.

As to be expected, Harry Davenport lends a lift to proceedings by giving the southern colonel role some importance. Paul Campbell, the older heir; Mark Dennis, his younger brother; Gloria Henry, femme lead, and others are acceptable. Clinton Rosemond turns in dignified chore as the faithful old retainer.

William Bloom produced with minor budget, which shows in such things as Southern California racetracks substituting for greener hills and ovals of Kentucky. Technical functions are adequate. *Brog.*

Ghost Town Renegades

PRC release of Jerry Thomas production. Stars "Lash" La Rue, Al "Fuzzy" St. John; features Jennifer Holt, Jack Ingram, Terry Frost. Directed by Ray Taylor. Screenplay, Patricia Harper; camera, Ernest Miller; editor, Joe Gluck; music, Walter Greene. Tradeshown N. Y., July 24, '47. Running time, **57 MINS.**

Cheyenne	"Lash" La Rue
Fuzzy	Al "Fuzzy" St. John
Diane	Jennifer Holt
Sharpe	Jack Ingram
Flint	Terry Frost
Trent	Steve Clark
Johnson	Lee Roberts
Wace	Lane Bradford
Jennings	Henry Hall
Watson	William Fawcett

Well stocked with standard oater cliches, "Ghost Town Renegades" is a run-of-the-mill actioner in the "Lash" La Rue series. Picture's market will be limited to the nabes where juvenile patronage is partial to saddle sagas. Names of La Rue and Al "Fuzzy" St. John may help some in situations where they've built a following.

Yarn has La Rue in his customary role as an investigator for the U. S. marshal. With his partner, St. John, he tries to foil the plot of Jack Ingram to take over an abandoned mining town from its rightful owners. There's a rich gold vein on the premises, and if the proprietors are rubbed out, Ingram would clean up.

Script too often forces a halt in action, especially in a sequence where La Rue, St. John, plus two others are awaiting to trap the culprits. Much footage is wasted there on St. John's alleged comic antics.

Acting is so-so, with La Rue standing out. St. John creates a nice comedy change of pace when spotted correctly. Jennifer Holt, as one of the heirs, is adequate in the lone femme part while Ingram convinces as the heavy. Ray Taylor's direction is halting upon occasion in this Jerry Thomas production. Ernest Miller's lensing is good while other technical credits are fair.

Wyoming

Republic release of Joseph Kane production. Stars William Elliott, Vera Ralston, John Carroll; features George "Gabby" Hayes, Albert Dekker, Virginia Grey, Mme. Maria Ouspenskaya. Directed by Kane. Screenplay, Lawrence Hazard and Gerald Geraghty; camera, John Alton; music, Nathan G. Scott and Ernest Gold; musical director, Cy Feuer; editor, Arthur Roberts. Tradeshown N. Y., July 23, '47. Running time, **84 MINS.**

Charles Alderson	William Elliott
Karen	Vera Ralston
Glen Forrester	John Carroll
Windy Gibson	George "Gabby" Hayes
Duke Lassiter	Albert Dekker
Lila Regan	Virginia Grey
Maria	Mme. Maria Osupenskaya
Joe Sublette	Grant Withers
Ben Jackson	Harry Woods
Queenie	Minna Gombell
Ed Lassiter	Dick Curtis
Sheriff Niles	Roy Barcroft
Timmons	Trevor Bardette
Judge Sheridan	Paul Harvey
Karen (9 years)	Louise Kane
Jennings	Tom London
Wolff	George Chesebro
Karen (.. years)	Linda Green
Bartender	Jack O'Shea

Latest in the celluloid series glorifying the western states, Republic's "Wyoming" is a better-than-average giddyapper that should reap strong returns in action situations. With a story more logical than in most pictures of this type, along with good production values, film also has the names of William Elliott, Vera Ralston and John Carroll as marquee lures.

While the cast turns in generally capable performances under Joseph Kane's direction, presence of Miss Ralston and Mme. Maria Ouspenskaya in this mesa melange is somewhat of a mystery. Accent of the former, onetime skating star (Vera Hruba), is explained away by a long hiatus in European finishing schools while Mme. Ouspenskaya is obviously out of place as a nurse and family retainer out in the virgin Wyoming territory.

Yarn, scripted by Lawrence Hazard and Gerald Geraghty, deals with the rise of Elliott from a pioneer to a top rancher. His career progresses comparatively smoothly until Congress passes the Homestead Act. Albert Dekker uses the incoming nesters as a pawn in a rustling game carried on against Elliott.

There's plenty of hard riding, six shootin' and skullduggery before the law of the land prevails. Some fine fisticuffs are contribbed by Elliott and Dekker in a hotel brawl over the hostelry's operator Virginia Grey. Also lending romantic interest is Miss Ralston, who feels that her father, Elliott, is wrong in his "war" upon the homesteaders. She sides with his foreman, Carroll, who holds that everything can be worked out legally, and it is, after Dekker's game is exposed.

Elliott is effective as the wealthy rancher, Dekker is craftily sinister as the heavy and Carroll also convinces. Others, including the perennial George "Gabby" Hayes, Miss Grey, Miss Ralston and Mme. Ouspenskaya, turn in good thesping. Kane's direction is in keeping with the neat productional embellishments he's given the film, while John Alton's lensing is also first rate.

Sepia Cinderella
(SONGS)

Herald Pictures release of Jack Goldberg and Arthur Leonard production. Features Billy Daniels, Sheila Guyse. Directed by Leonard. Original story and screenplay; Vincent Valentini; editor, Jack Kemp; camera, George Webber; songs, Elaine & Leona Blackman. Deek Watson, Herman Fairbanks, Willie Best. Previewed in N. Y., July 16, '47. Running time, **70 MINS.**

Bob	Billy Daniels
Barbara	Sheila Guyse
Vivian	Tondeleyo
Barney	Ruble Blakey
Ralph	Jack Carter
Mooney	Dusty Freeman
Sonny	George Williams
Press Agent	Fred Gordon
M. C.	Harold Norton
Evelyn	Lora Pierre
Great Joseph	Emory Richardson
Mrs. Dryden	Gertrude Saunders
Mama Keyes	Hilda Offley Thompson
MacMilliam	Percy Verwayen
Chinaman	Al Young
Collins	Jimmy Fuller
Themselves	Apus & Estellita
Themselves	Deek Watson His Brown Dots
Themselves	Leonardo & Zolo
Preacher	Ray C. Moore
Walter Fuller's Orchestra	
John Kirby's Band	
Himself	Freddie Bartholomew

"Sepia Cinderella," designed for the race trade, retains the Herald Pictures formula of intertwining a series of vaude and musical acts with a slight and familiar story. Film, second in the Herald series, is worth its keep in the Negro houses, having marquee lure with well-known colored performers and offering a fair degree of entertainment.

Story is a frequently seen item centering about Billy Daniels, a struggling songwriter who, after striking it rich with a hit tune, strays from his true love, Sheila Guyse, but returns upon disillusionment with the more worldly-type femme, the singularly named Tondeleyo.

Film displays some entertaining moments in its musical interludes, including Ruble Blakey's songs, John Kirby's band offerings, and tunes by Deek Watson's Brown Dots. Miss Guyse and Daniels also contribute vocals for good overall effect, and varied specialties, such as the hoofing turn by Apus and Estellita, Fred Gordon's bit as a press agent, and comedy by Leonardo and Zolo hit the desired effect.

Freddie Bartholomew, brought in as a guest artist, reprises part of an act he does in vaudeville.

Arthur Leonard's directorial pace is okay, but much speed has been lost in the editing with inclusion of unnecessary dramatic sequences and running together of too many musical sessions at one time. *Jose.*

The Green Cockatoo
(BRITISH-MADE)

Devonshire Films release of William K. Howard production. Stars John Mills, Rene Ray; features Robert Newton, Charles Oliver, Bruce Seton. Directed by William Cameron Menzies. Screenplay, Edward O. Berkman, from novel by Graham Greene; music, Miklos Rozsa. At Rialto, N. Y., week of July 18, '47. Running time, **63 MINS.**

Jim Connor	John Mills
Eileen	Rene Ray
Dave Connor	Robert Newton
Terrell	Charles Oliver
Madison	Bruce Seton
Steve	Julian Vedey
Inspector	Allan Jeayes
Butler	Frank Atkinson

With British film-makers currently engaged in an all-out effort to secure more playing time for their product on U. S. screens, they should take steps to prevent the export of such pictures as "Green Cockatoo" to this country. "Cockatoo" is slated for low grosses even in "shootin' gallery" houses.

It's an obvious imitation of the gangster-type pictures produced by Hollywood during the last decade. As with all imitations made by those without the proper know-how, however, film, made before the war, emerges as more of a travesty than a carbon copy. Picture had the proper foundation in a story by Graham Greene, but whole thing collapses in a caricature of pseudo-thugs walking around with their hat-brims pulled down over their eyes, their hands continually in their pockets, etc.

Film's chief saving grace is the acting. John Mills does the best he can in a James Cagney-type role, even with the songs and dances. American gangster slang, though, just doesn't sound right coming from him. Robert Newton is good as Mills' no-account brother, around whom all the action revolves. Rene Ray is beauteous and has the right wide-eyed stare as the young country lass who unintentionally gets mixed up with all the big, bad gangsters in her first trip to London.

Film was produced by William K. Howard and directed by William Cameron Menzies. Both Americans, they should have known better how to treat the story. Score was composed by Miklos Rozsa, who won an Academy award for "Spellbound" in 1945. Soundtrack is so raspy, though, that the music often can't be heard. Camera work and other technical credits are nothing to brag about. *Stal.*

Miniature Reviews

"Singapore" (U-I). Slow adventure romance with Fred MacMurray and Ava Gardner; mediocre b.o.

"Wild Harvest" (Par). Star names, headed by Alan Ladd, will aid in putting over story of wheat harvesting.

"Blackmail" (Rep). Melodrama of private detective and his dubious clients. Fails to live up to action promised in title.

"Key Witness" (Col). Mild murder yarn suited for lower rung of twin bills.

"High Tide" (Mono). Okay action whodunit.

"I Know Where I'm Going" (British) (U-I). Michael Powell-Emeric Pressburger production. Surefire for sure-seaters.

"Twins" (Artkino) (Songs). Russian-made comedy a modest entry for foreign houses.

"A Man About The House" (BL) (British). Good whodunit limited by lack marquee names.

"Anything for a Song" (Italian) (Superfilm). May entice some opera fans, but otherwise for Italian-language fans.

"A Sangre Fria" ("In Cold Blood"). Tepid Argentine thriller with no appeal for U. S.

Singapore

Universal-International release of Jerry Bresler production. Stars Fred MacMurray, Ava Gardner; features Roland Culver, Richard Haydn, Spring Byington, Thomas Gomez, Porter Hall. Directed by John Brahm. Screenplay, Seton I. Miller and Robert Thoeren, based on original story by Miller; camera, Maury Gertsman; editor, William Hornbeck; music, Daniele Amfitheatreof. Tradeshown, N. Y., Aug. 5, '47. Running time, **79 MINS.**

Matt Gordon	Fred MacMurray
Linda	Ava Gardner
Michael Van Leyden	Roland Culver
Chief Inspector Hewitt	Richard Haydn
Mrs. Bellows	Spring Byington
Mr. Mauribus	Thomas Gomez
Mr. Bellows	Porter Hall
Sascha Barda	George Lloyd
Ming Ling	Maylia
Rev. Barnes	Holmes Herbert
Miss Barnes	Edith Evanson
Cadum	Frederick Worlock
Mr. Hussein	Lal Chand Mehra
Pepe	Curt Conway

"Singapore" is a slow-paced pic that will have to bank heavily on its fair marquee values and snappy exploitation of its intriguing title. A postwar adventure tale set against an Oriental background, film is short on action and too long on pedestrian romantic mooning between the principals, Fred MacMurray and Ava Gardner.

Producer Jerry Bresler, however, has limned this offering with a solid dress that manages to generate an authentic atmosphere of British-controlled Singapore. Firstrate supporting cast, well-defined camera work, smooth editing and a good musical score also help greatly. But the production fails to surmount towering obstacles presented by obvious directorial treatment of a formula screenplay tritely scripted.

MacMurray plays an ex-American sailor who returns to Singapore to continue his prewar job of smuggling pearls out of the territory. Via flashbacks, story establishes a previous romance between MacMurray and Miss Gardner, who presumably was killed in a Japanese air raid on their wedding night during the war years. Meantime, a gang of Singapore cutthroats tail MacMurray to take over a swag of pearls which he stashed away in a hotel room during the Japanese occupation.

While making the rounds of the Singapore niteries, MacMurray finds his gal still alive but wedded to another man and suffering from total amnesia. Film gets bogged in talk in trying to unravel the complications but finally solves them with pat meller devices that are handled without credibility. Windup has Miss Gardner getting kidnapped, with an heroic bang-up rescue by MacMurray and a tragic renunciation by her husband.

In central role of debonair adventurer, MacMurray walks through his paces in standard okay form. Miss Gardner, miscast as sweet, young item, has no chance to display her sultry charms and falters in the high-key emotive range. Solid performances are turned in by Porter Hall and Spring Byington, as visiting American tourists from Minneapolis; Roland Culver, as Miss Gardner's husband; and George Lloyd as a subtle pickpocket. *Herm.*

Wild Harvest

Hollywood, Aug. 1.

Paramount release of Robert Fellows production. Stars Alan Ladd, Dorothy Lamour, Robert Preston, Lloyd Nolan; features Dick Erdman, Allen Jenkins. Directed by Tay Garnett. Screenplay, John Monks, Jr.; camera, John Seitz; process photography, Farciot Edouart; music score, Hugo Friedhofer; editor, Billy Shea. Tradeshown Aug. 1, '47. Running time, **92 MINS.**

Joe Madigan	Alan Ladd
Fay Rankin	Dorothy Lamour
Jim Davis	Robert Preston
Kink	Lloyd Nolan
Mark Lewis	Dick Erdman
Higgins	Allen Jenkins
Mike Alperson	Will Wright
Rankin	Griff Barnett
Pete	Anthony Caruso
Long	Walter Sande
Nick	Frank Sully

"Wild Harvest" concerns itself more with harvesting of wheat than with virile action. As a consequence, there are long stretches of dull footage that take the edge off the action when it does come. Name values are strong and will help in arousing initial boxoffice interest, although take in the upper brackets is not likely to be sustained.

Film opens slowly and doesn't gear itself for wild and violent action until well past the halfway mark. Scenes of harvesting by gangs of reaper-wielders begin to pall after awhile. Tay Garnett's direction of the Robert Fellows production has considerable scope to cover in this apparently censor-softened story of a gang of adventurers who turn talents to wheat harvesting.

Garnett does wallop over some sequences of fisticuffs between Alan Ladd and Robert Preston. There's a good chase when angry farmers take after the gang but these highlights aren't backed up by other footage. There's a lack of tension that could have punched over the harvesting scenes, the battle against time and weather when the wheat is ripe. Sex-play, too, between Ladd and Dorothy Lamour, with Preston as third side of a triangle, has been watered down and fails to excite.

Ladd, Preston and Lloyd Nolan are good in top two-fisted roles, while Dick Erdman and Allen Jenkins appear okay in featured spots. Miss Lamour shares star billing, holding her own in a film that emphasizes muscled males. She's a no-good gal who tries to talk Ladd into taking her away from the farm. He passes up the chance, so she picks Preston, causing trouble in camp. Preston is swayed to highjack grain from farmers, resulting in more trouble. Final blowup has Ladd and Preston going at it in a knockdown, dragout fight that sends Miss Lamour packing and brings the buddies together again.

John Monks, Jr., scripted. Camera work by John Seitz is expert, and good process photography was contributed by Farciot Edouart. Hugo Friedhofer's music score is on the credit side. *Brog.*

Blackmail

Hollywood, Aug. 1.

Republic release of William J. O'Sullivan production. Stars William Marshall, Adele Mara, Ricardo Cortez; features Grant Withers, Stephanie Bachelor, Richard Fraser, Roy Barcroft, George J. Lewis. Directed by Lesley Selander. Screenplay, Royal K. Cole; added dialog, Albert DeMond; original story, Robert Leslie Bellen; camera, Reggie Lanning; editor, Tony Martinelli. Previewed in Hollywood, July 31, '47. Running time, **67 MINS.**

Dan Turner	William Marshall
Sylvia Duane	Adele Mara
Ziggy Cranston	Ricardo Cortes
Inspector Donaldson	Grant Withers
Carla	Stephanie Bachelor
Antoine	Richard Fraser
Spice Kelloway	Roy Barcroft
Blue Chip Winslow	George J. Lewis
Jervis	Gregory Gay
Pinky	Tristram Coffin
Mamie	Eva Novak
Gomez	Bud Wolfe

"Blackmail" never proves as exciting as its title would indicate. Actionless motion and dull talk keep interest at a minimum. Production dress is good but physical quality fails to make up for lack of punch.

Melodrama deals with another of those tough private detectives lately in fashion. The guy is called in by a rich playboy gambler to protect him from blackmailers. Detective's interference in the case apparently only results in the ante being boosted from original $50,000 tap to $150,000. A number of bumpoffs, several fisticuff encounters by the dick and sundry stock ingredients are padded in but only serve to further the confusion.

William Marshall isn't too convincing as the dick. Neither are the others, including Ricardo Cortez, the client; Adele Mara and Richard Fraser, the villains; Grant Withers, the police detective; Roy Barcroft, Stephanie Bachelor and George J. Lewis.

Lesley Selander's direction keeps the players in motion but it's not meller action. Mild script was furnished by Royal K. Cole from an original story by Robert Leslie Bellem. *Brog.*

Key Witness

Columbia release of Rudolph C. Flothow production. Features John Beal, Trudy Marshall, Jimmy Lloyd. Directed by D. Ross Lederman. Screenplay, Edward Bock, from story by J. Donald Wilson; camera, Philip Tannura; editor, Dwight Caldwell. At Rialto, N. Y., week starting July 29, '47. Running time, **67 MINS.**

Milton Higby	John Beal
Marge Andrews	Trudy Marshall
Larry Summers	Jimmy Lloyd
Sally Guthrie	Helen Mowery
Albert Loring	Wilton Graff
Martha Higby	Barbara Reed
John Ballin	Charles Trowbridge
Custer Bidwell	Harry Hayden
Smiley	William Newell
Edward Clemmons	Selmer Jackson
Officer Johnson	Robert Williams
Nurse Sibley	Victoria Horne

Exhibitor complaint nowadays is that the B's are so sad they can't get a dollar with them. Such a squawk applies to this film, a B which distributors would have been afraid to offer a few years ago. Lack of cast names is also a factor.

John Beal does fairly well as a much-harried inventor who is accidentally involved in the slaying of a girlfriend. Trudy Marshall is cast as his buddy's sweetheart, this looking like a fairly good screentest for the gal. Beal's buddy, Jimmy Lloyd, seems to have the best future possibilities of the whole cast. Lad has looks and can act, something that can't be said for many in this picture. However, one is inclined to blame both the director and editor for some of the absurd sequences and hammy entrances.

J. Donald Wilson's original story is okay but what Edward Bock, scripter, and D. Ross Lederman, director, didn't do to it, the cast did. All continuity and semblance of reasonable development appear to have been tossed aside at times. *Wear.*

High Tide

Hollywood, Aug. 1.

Monogram release of Jack Wrather production. Stars Lee Tracy, Don Castle, Julie Bishop, Anabel Shaw; features Regis Toomey, Douglas Walton, Francis Ford, Anthony Warde. Directed by John Reinhardt. Screenplay, Robert Presnell, Sr.; added dialog, Peter Milne; story, Raoul Whitfield; camera, Henry Sharp; musical score, Rudy Schrager; editor, Stewart S. Frye. Previewed in Hollywood, July 31, '47. Running time, **70 MINS.**

Hugh Fresney	Lee Tracy
Tim Slade	Don Castle
Julie Vaughn	Julie Bishop
Dana Jones	Anabel Shaw
Inspector O'Haffey	Regis Toomey
Clinton Vaughn	Douglas Walton
Pop Garrow	Francis Ford
Nick Dyke	Anthony Warde
Cleve Collins	Wilson Wood
Mrs. Cresser	Argentina Brunetti
Interne	George H. Ryland

"High Tide" is actionful whodunit that will serve capably. Turned out for Monogram by Jack Wrather, new to Hollywood production, film gives interesting fulfillment to its tale of mayhem against a newspaper background. Production quality is good for budget expenditure.

Cast is good in depicting various characters who try to make life tough for private detective Don Castle. Latter does well by assignment, as does Lee Tracy as the hard-boiled editor who is the cause of all the trouble, although not exposed until the end.

Behind the mystery is Tracy's efforts to take control of newspaper for which he is editor. He knocks off his publisher, attempts to get the detective he had called in to protect him from alleged threats, and does in an undercover operator for the publisher as well as his own gambler sidekick before the round of events catch up with him.

John Reinhardt's direction keeps the plot on the move and performances good. Julie Bishop and Anabel Shaw carry off the small femme leads okay, with Miss Bishop appearing to best advantage in unsympathetic spot. Regis Toomey is good as the police inspector and others measure up to requirements.

Lensing by Henry Sharp, editing, music score by Rudy Schrager and other productional functions furnished by Wrather and his associate, James C. Jordan, supply okay backing to the Robert Presnell, Sr., script, based on story by Raoul Whitfield. *Brog.*

I Know Where I'm Going

(BRITISH-MADE)

Universal-International (Prestige) release of Michael Powell, Emeric Pressburger (J. Arthur Rank) production. Stars Wendy Hiller, Roger Livesey; features Finlay Currie, Pamela Brown. Directed and written by Powell and Pressburger. Camera, Erwin Hillier; editor, John Seabourne; music, Allan Gray, with Glasgow Orpheus Choir. Tradeshown, N. Y., July 31, '47. Running time, **91 MINS.**

Joan Webster	Wendy Hiller
Torquil MacNeil	Roger Livesey
Ruairidh Mor	Finlay Currie
Catriona	Pamela Brown
Mr. Robinson	Valentine Dyall
Cheril	Petula Clark
Hunter	Walter Hudd
Mr. Webster	George Carney
Capt. Lochinvar	Capt. Duncan Mackechnie
Kenny	Murdo Morrison
Birdie	Margot Fitzsimons
Mrs. Corzier	Nancy Price
R.A.F. Sergeant	Graham Moffett
John Campbell	John Laurie
Postmistress	Jean Cadell

"I Know Where I'm Going" should be a natural for the arty houses. Turned out by Michael Powell and Emeric Pressburger, one of J. Arthur Rank's ace production units, the picture has in it all the charm and realism with which this team has successfully embellished a number of its other films released in the U. S. Slotted for distribution under the Prestige banner of Universal-International, the picture hasn't sufficient boxoffice draw to enable it to stand alone in general situations; with the tremendous word-of-mouth it's certain to amass, however, it can't miss for the sureseaters.

Film returns Wendy Hiller to U. S. screens after a long absence, and the actress scores as heavily in this as she did in "Pygmalion" and "Major Barbara," her two most noteworthy successes heretofore. Only other marquee names, even for the arty houses, are Roger Livesey and Pamela Brown, both of whom add to their laurels in this one. With most of the action taking place in northern Scotland, Powell and Pressburger evidently recruited some of the natives to add to the supporting cast. Result is a neat touch of realism, with the Gaelic language, used sparingly for effect, serving to build interest in the tale.

Title is taken from an old Scottish folktune, which runs sporadically through the film. Rapidfire sequences at the outset show Miss Hiller progressing from childhood to the point at which the story picks her up, continually building the impression that "she knows where she's going" — which, to her, means marrying money. She hooks a wealthy industrialist and leaves London to marry him on a tiny island in the Hebrides, which he's rented during the war. Just when she's in sight of the island, on the last lap of her journey, a sudden gale springs up and she's forced to stay on the mainland with the native Scots in the village.

She naturally meets and falls for a young navy lieutenant, actually a Scottish lord and the owner of the island, who's also trying to get there for some hunting while on leave. Rest of the picture shows her gradually losing faith in her ideas, under the combined blandishments of the lieutenant and the happy, but poor, Scotsmen. After making one last attempt to reach the island, in which she and the lieutenant are almost drowned, she finally realizes she's been wrong all the time and, in a logically-drawn denouement, throws over the old codger for the young Scotsman.

Story is an original by Powell and Pressburger. Production team's direction gives the film a leisurely pace that slows it down too much at times but the combined story line, acting and novel setting and characters build sufficient suspense. Production mountings are standout, from the unique method of presenting the credits to the suspense-laden climax. Allan Gray's score adds to the film's mood, with the Glasgow Orpheus Choir helping with some interesting Scottish airs. *Stal.*

Twins
(Russian-Made)
(SONGS)

Artkino release of Mosfilm Studios production. Stars Mikhail Zharov, Ludmilla Tselikovskaya. Directed by Konstantin Yudin. Screenplay, Y. Uluner, M. Vitukhnovsky; camera, A. Tarasov; songs, Boris Lasker; English titles, Charles Clement. At Stanley, N. Y., starting July 26, '47. Running time, **80 MINS.**

Yeropkin....................Mikhail Zharov
Luba..............Ludmila Tselikovskaya
Liza.............................Vera Orlova
Listopadov................Andrei Tutishkin
His Son..................Pavel Shpringfeld
Orlikov.........................Dmitri Pavlov
Gadalov...............Konstantin Sorotkin
Alla Broshkina............Irina Murzayeva

(In Russian: English Titles)

Striving hard to be funny, "Twins" is really only a mildly amusing Soviet pic. It should do just passably good biz in foreign-language houses.

Difficulty is that too much hokum was piled on a slim story. Only when it verges on the slapstick does it manage to generate genuine laughter.

Plot concerns a pair of unidentified baby twins who are adopted by a femme Soviet worker. First her roommate is annoyed by the babes. Then her landlady. Story ultimately drags in the head Commissar in her precinct, two sailors recuperating from wounds and, ultimately, the real parents. The babies are supposed to be war orphans and yarn mildly touches on the angle that Soviet citizens should adopt war orphans.

Mikhail Zharov chips in with a strong performance as food-loving chaser, while Ludmila Tselikovskaya is excellent as the comely party worker who adopts the kids. Dmitri Pavlov and Konstantin Sorotkin do okay as the two sailors who decide to help support the twins, with one falling in love with the gal. In fact, their comedy work far overshadows the silly yarn.

Konstantin Yudin directed but he's never surmounted the story handed him. Several untitled songs by Boris Lasker are fairly tuneful, especially when sung by Miss Tselikovskaya. Others in the cast break into song on the slightest pretext but the director, luckily, has confined this to a few late sequences. *Wear.*

A Man About the House
(BRITISH-MADE)

London, Aug. 1.

British Lion release of Edward Black production. Stars Margaret Johnston, Dulcie Gray, Kieron Moore. Directed by Leslie Arliss. Screen adaptation of novel by Francis Brett Young by J. B. Williams and Arliss. Music by Nicholas Brodzsky. Camera, Georges Perinal. At Palace, London, Aug. 31, '47. Running time, **95 MINS.**

Agnes Isit...............Margaret Johnston
Elein Isit........................Dulcie Gray
Salvatore.....................Kieron Moore
Sir Benjamin Dench........Guy Middleton
Ronald Sanctuary..........Felix Aylmer
Mrs. Armitage..........Lilian Braithwaite
Maria..............................Jone Salinas
Assunta.........................Maria Fimiani
Gita.............................Fulvia de Priamo
Antonio........................Nicola Esposito
Higgs..........................Reginald Purdell
Solicitor.....................Wilfred Caithness

Lack of marquee names is bound to have effect on pulling power of this picture, especially for America; and the best it can attain is the dualer spot. But with all its deficiencies, this John Perry screen adaptation of Francis Brett Young's best seller is good cinema, and should do well on its general release after its West End premiere, some time in September, at Metro's ace spot, the Empire.

Story is woven around two spinster sisters running a school in the Midlands in very straitened circumstances, but full of family pride, especially Agnes, the elder, who dominates the younger, Ellen.

As they are about to sell some old sticks of furniture to a local junk man, he draws their attention to an advertisement in a London paper asking for the whereabouts of a family Isit, a very uncommon name, wondering if it's meant for them. Gals investigate and find they have been left a legacy by their uncle—a beautiful villa south of Naples. They sojourn there with object of disposing of the property and returning to England.

On arrival they find the place is managed by Salvatore, their late uncle's general factotum. Agnes is bent on returning, but Ellen falls in love with the beauty and plentitude that abounds after their abject poverty. She also falls in love with Salvatore, in reality a man with a bad record. They are finally married and hubby makes up his mind to get rid of her by a slow poisoning process. His action is revealed by Sir Benjamin Dench, former sweetheart of Agnes, who has now fallen for the younger sister.

Dench forces a confession from Salvatore who, after a realistic fight, is killed falling over a cliff. His wife thinks it's an accident and is left in ignorance of real cause of death. Fadeout is departure of Dench and Ellen, off to get married in India, with Agnes staying behind to manage the estate, as her husband (whom she still cherishes as one of the finest men in the world) would have wished her to do.

Acting is good all around, with exception of Guy Middleton who, in two scenes, gives out with that plum-in-the-mouth accent which has been great hindrance to the popularity of some English pix in America. Kieron Moore, formerly known as Kieron O'Hanrahan when he was acting at the Abbey theatre, Dublin, is a find and should be in great demand.

Most of the outdoor shots were made in Genoa and are beautiful, while direction is pretty slick and workmanlike. *Rege.*

Anything for a Song
(SONGS)
(Italian-Made)

Superfilm Distributing Corp. release of S. A. Grandi production. Stars Ferruccio Tagliavini. Directed by Carlo Bugiani. Screenplay, Mario Mattoli; camera, Charles Suin; music, Cilea, Donizetti, Cardillo. Previewed in N. Y., Aug. 1, '47. Running time, **76 MINS.**

Mario Guadalucci......Ferruccio Tagliavini
Bodoloni.........................Carlo Romani
Anna...............................Luisa Rossi
Parcotti............................Tino Scotti
Cavoncelli.......................Aldo Silvani
Giulio........................Carlo Campanini
Elena...............................Vera Carmi
Conte...............................Luigi Cimara
Gualducci......................Virgilio Riento

(In Italian; English Titles)

Ferruccio Tagliavini, one of the Met Opera's prize importations of last season, is one of the more active voices in the renascent postwar Italian film industry because of his U. S. acclaim. He's attained considerable stature in name value in the music fields, but draw of this pic is confined to those circles, mainly because of meagre production surrounding him. Latest importation, "Anything for a Song," Italian picture with English subtitles, is mainly for the Italian-language houses, but with hefty exploitation of Tagliavini, film could get a play from longhair devotees.

Tagliavini does considerable singing in this film, running a wide range from opera to lighter Italian airs. He's seen in a far-fetched comedy as the son of an eggplant processor who rebels against the family trade in an effort to crash music. Opposition of his father stymies any attempt in that direction, and he ultimately returns to the family fold in order to procure enough money to restore the sight of a blind girl, even so far as intending to marry a girl his father has selected for him. However, his intended bride falls for another, and matters work out to Tagliavini's satisfaction.

Comedy is frequently naive. Performances are similarly lightweight, Virgilio Riento hitting a nice stride as the singer's father. Vera Carmi, as the love interest, and Luisa Rossi, the blind gal, play their roles adequately. Tagliavini is believable, but his major importance, naturally, lies in his song contributions. *Jose.*

A Sangre Fria
("In Cold Blood")
(ARGENTINE-MADE)

Buenos Aires, July 22.

Inter-Americana release of Luis Saslavsky production. Stars Amelia Bence; features Pedro Lopez Lagar. Directed by Daniel Tinayre. Story and screenplay, Saslavsky; camera, Alberto Etchebehere. At Gran Cine Ocean, June 6, '47. Running time, **95 MINS.**

Like other recent Argentine whodunits, this film is a tepid thriller tending to be boring rather than exciting. Picture has no appeal for U. S. audiences but may do well in small local houses. Yarn is built around the attempts on the life of a wealthy old lady. Her nephew expects to inherit her money and uses a servant to poison her. Pair are foiled and killed in a chase.

Only bright spot is Amelia Bence's performance, but she's handicapped by inept story. Other acting is generally poor. Lopez Lagar, once one of the better actors, seems more mystified with the plot than the audience.

Daniel Tinayre's direction is stodgy and unimaginative. *Nid.*

Miniature Reviews

"Body and Soul" (UA-Enterprise). John Garfield - Lilli Palmer starred in b.o. winner about boxing and the rackets.

"Kiss of Death," (20th). Hard-boiled action yarn, in semi-documentary style, a boxoffice natural.

"Stork Bites Man" (Comet) Lightweight comedy for dualers.

"Louisiana" (Songs) (Mono). Story of Jimmie Davis's rise from sharecropper to governor of Louisiana has strong rural appeal.

"Adventure Island" (Color) (Par.) Sturdy supporting product with enough weight to head the bill in some situations.

"Holiday Camp" (Gen.) (British). Interesting drama of Grand-Hotel doings at an adult summer camp.

"The Burning Cross" (SGP). Amateurish tale of Ku Klux Klan; okay for duallers if given right exploitation.

"Vienna Melodies" (Indie). Austrian-made musical shapes as a cinch for U. S. arty spots and possibly other playdates.

"Todo Un Caballero" (Every Inch a Gentleman) (Mexican-Made). Fair melodrama, aided by good thesping.

"Admirel Nakhimov" (Indie.) Russian-made war meller has too much Soviet bally; mild even for American arty theatres.

"Singing House" (Indie) Vienna-made pic brings no prestige to Danubian films; minor U. S. entry.

"In Those Days" (Indie). German-made pic turned out in British-occupied zone has slim chance of biz in America.

"Albeniz" (Indie). Argentine-made music-biography of composer Isaac Albeniz looks stout for U. S. arty theatres.

"The Great Dawn" (Italian) (Superfilm). Well-made, featuring longhair music and conventional plot; moderate b.o. at art houses.

"Shoe-Shine" (Lopert) Needlessly grim tone limits b.o. potential of this Italian entry.

Body and Soul

United Artists release of Enterprise production (Bob Roberts, associate producer). Stars John Garfield and Lilli Palmer; features Anne Revere, Hazel Brooks, William Conrad, Joseph Pevney and Canada Lee. Directed by Robert Rossen. Screenplay, Abraham Polansky; editor, Francis Lyon; camera, James Wong Howe; assistant director, Robert Akdrich; music director, Rudolph Polk. Previewed in N. Y., Aug. 7, '47. Running time, **104 MINS.**

Charlie Davis....................John Garfield
Peg Born..........................Lilli Palmer
Alice...............................Hazel Brooks
Anna Davis........................Anne Revere
Quinn............................William Conrad
Shorty Polaski.................Joseph Pevney
Ben Chaplin........................Canada Lee
Roberts...............................Lloyd Goff
David Davis..........................Art Smith
Arnold...............................James Burke
Irma..............................Virginia Gregg
Drummer.............................Peter Virgo
Prince..................................Joe Devlin
Grocer...........................Shimin Rushkin
Miss Tedder......................Mary Currier
Dan...................................Milton Kibbie
Shelton..................................Tim Ryan
Jack Marlowe.......................Artie Dorrell
Victor.......................................Cy Ring
Marine...................................Glen Lee
Referee..........................John Indresano
Fight Announcer......................Dan Tobey

A topical yarn obviously designed to take advantage of the recent New York inquiry into sports "fixing," with an emphasis on some of the crookedness manifest in professional boxing, "Body and Soul" has a somewhat familiar title and a likewise familiar narrative. It's the telling, however, that's different, and that's what will sell the film. John Garfield is the pic's only name to mean anything at the boxoffice, playing a champ governed by the dictates of a crooked gambler. Garfield's name, coupled to a potential exploitation hinging on a widely-ballyhooed N.Y. State Boxing Commission probe of bribery last winter, gives "Body" a strong boxoffice chance.

The story concerns a youngster with a punching flair who emerges from the amateurs to ride along the knockout trail to the middleweight championship. But to get himself a crack at the title he has to sell 50% of himself to a bigtime gambler with a penchant for making and breaking champs at will. At the finale, however, the champ, who's supposed to lose his title in a "fix," about-faces and kayoes the contender late in the fight when he realizes he himself has been doublecrossed by the gambler, all this after betting on himself to lose, too.

There are a flock of loopholes in this story, but interest seldom lags. Some of the "inside boxing" is authentic, but the "inside gambling" is another story in itself, which this pic doesn't tell. Garfield is convincing in the lead part, and the boxing scenes look the McCoy.

There is also considerable authenticity given to the pic by the appearance of Canada Lee, as the middleweight champ belted out for the crown by Garfield in what is purported to be a denouement of one method of crooked gambling operations; namely a fading champ supposed to be "carried" but, instead, is given the old double-x and punched into unconsciousness, incurring a head injury that ultimately results in his death. (Lee, now a name legit actor, will be recalled as a pretty fair middleweight title contender a dozen years back).

The pic has captured much of the background of what makes a pro fighter. This might have been the real-life story of any one of a flock of New York eastside or Brooklyn street fighters who hammered their way to, or close to, the top in the past couple of decades. Poolhall and beer stube environments are effectively captured to indicate the sordidness that backgrounds the early careers of most boxers, who turn to the ring because of a proficiency with their fists on the streetcorner.

This is the environment of Charlie Davis (Garfield), son of poor parents who operate a candy store in a poor neighborhood. When his father is killed accidentally in a gangland war, and his mother is forced to seek charity, Davis embarks on his fisticuff career. The trail to the crown is shown dotted with the usual on-the-make dame with an eye to sharing the spotlight with him; the sweetheart whom he never gets around to marrying; the easy-come-easy-go dough, and all the rest of it. It adds up to familiar but interesting telling.

Lilli Palmer is miscast as Garfield's sweetheart and inspiration, especially with a Continental accent that even the dialog can't properly clarify. She just doesn't look like a fighter's sweetie. Lee has a lesser part, but he handles it exceptionally well. Anne Revere, as the mother; William Conrad, as Garfield's manager; Joseph Pevney, the fighter's close friend and booster, and Lloyd Goff, the gambler, all contribute sturdy supporting performances.

The direction by Robert Rossen is pointed for sharp pace, and the other productional embellishments are consistent with the direction. *Kahn.*

Kiss of Death

Hollywood, Aug. 12.

20th-Fox release of Fred Kohlmar production. Stars Victor Mature, Brian Donlevy, Coleen Gray. Directed by Henry Hathaway. Screenplay, Ben Hecht and Charles Lederer; story, Eleazar Lipsky; camera, Norbert Brodine; editor, J. Watson Webb, Jr.; music, David Buttoleh. Tradeshown, Hollywood, Aug. 11, '47. Running time, **98 MINS.**

Nick Bianco .... Victor Mature
D'angelo .... Brian Donlevy
Nettie .... Coleen Gray
Tom Udo .... Richard Widmark
Earl Howser .... Taylor Holmes
Warden .... Howard Smith
Sergeant Cullen .... Karl Malden
Williams .... Anthony Ross
Ma Rizzo .... Mildred Dunnock
Max Schulte .... Mildred Mitchell
Blondie .... Temple Texas
Skeets .... J. Scott Smart
District Attorney .... Jay Jostyn

"Kiss of Death" is a boxoffice natural, being one of those hard-boiled, tough action stories that will thrill the men folks, plus also strong femme appeal. Story, though fiction, is given the same semi-documentary treatment that 20th-Fox used in its three fact dramas, "The House on 92nd Street," "13 Rue Madeleine" and "Boomerang."

Though those were good this one tops them in realism, suspense and dramatic interest. Theme of an ex-convict who sacrifices himself to gangster guns, to save his wife and two small daughters, will get the women. Pathos that will bring out the handkerchiefs is legitimate outgrowth from the grim cops-and-robbers yarn, and Henry Hathaway's real-life slant on direction brings the picture close to authentic tragedy.

Victor Mature, as the ex-convict, does some of his best work to date. Brian Donlevy and Coleen Gray also justify their star billing, Donlevy as the assistant district attorney who sends Mature to Sing Sing for a jewelry store robbery, and later makes use of him as a stool pigeon, Miss Gray as the girl Mature marries after being paroled. Taylor Holmes earns a big hand as a shyster lawyer hooked up with a gang of crooks. Balance of cast is uniformly excellent.

The acting sensation of the piece is Richard Widmark, who is just about the most shuddery menace of the year as the dimwit, blood-lusty killer.

Plot hook of the Ben Hecht-Charles Lederer script is the decision of Mature to turn stoolie when he learns that his wife has been driven to suicide by his pals, who had promised to care for her while he was in prison, and that his two children have been put in an orphanage. He fingers Widmark for a murder rap in return for parole, marries Miss Gray and starts a new home for his children, only to live in terror when Widmark is acquitted and set at liberty. Knowing that Widmark intends to take it out on Miss Gray and the children, he deliberately sets himself up as a target for the killer's bullets in order to deliver him to the police.

Producer Fred Kohlmar filmed the picture on actual settings in New York and has gotten top production values out of cast, crew and materials. Hathaway's direction gets utmost effect from players and script, and paces the action smartly. Norbert Brodine's photograph is of cameo sharpness and skillfully employed to heighten drama. *Fisk.*

Stork Bites Man

United Artists release of Comet (Buddy Rogers, Ralph Cohn) production. Stars Jackie Cooper; features Gene Roberts, Gus Schilling, Emory Parnell. Directed by Cyril Endfield. Screenplay, Endfield; adaptation, Fred Freiburger; original story, Louis Pollock; camera, Vincent Farrar; editor, Lynn Harrison. Previewed in New York, Aug. 11, '47. Running time, **67 MINS.**

Ernie .... Jackie Cooper
Peg .... Gene Roberts
Butterfield .... Gus Schilling
Kimberly .... Emory Parnell
Voice of the Stork .... Stanley Prager
Mrs. Greene .... Sarah Selby
Mabel .... Majorie Beckett

"Stork Bites Man" is lightweight comedy that'll serve for the dualers. Comic angles are based on topical problem of the housing shortage, which film occasionally turns into passable laugh material. But scripting is generally trite and frequently silly, with little compensation being offered by other production aspects. Direction, settings, camera-work and thesping are of typical modest-budget variety.

Yarn revolves around antics of an apartment house manager saddled with a baby-hating boss and a wife who's in a family way. After failing to keep fact of his upcoming paternity from his boss, and getting fired and evicted as a result, manager organizes a strike among the apartment house workers to force a change in policy. Manager, meanwhile, is being counselled by an invisible stork, which pops in and out of the soundtrack at frequent intervals. Eventually, under combined pressure of the strike and irresistible charm of the infant, boss reverses his anti-baby stand and gives the manager back his job and apartment.

Jackie Cooper registers pleasantly as the manager. Chief laugh lift is supplied by Gus Schilling, as a baby-supply salesman, with Emory Parnell also handing in good performance as the sour-faced boss. Rest of cast gives fair support. *Herm.*

Louisiana
(SONGS)

Hollywood, Aug. 8.

Monogram release of Lindsley Parsons production. Stars Jimmie Davis, Margaret Lindsay; features John Gallaudet, Freddie Stewart, Dottye Brown, Mollie Miller, Eddy Waller, Mary Field, the Sunshine Serenaders. Directed by Phil Karlson. Screenplay, Jack De Witt; added dialog, Vick Knight, Scott Darling; based on an original story by Steve Healey; camera, William Sickner; songs, Jimmie Davis, Charlie Mitchell, Floyd Tillman, Ekko Whelan, Lee Blastic, Vaughn Horton, Lloyd Ellis; editor, Ace Herman. Previewed Aug. 5, '47. Running time, **82 MINS.**

Jimmie Davis .... Jimmie Davis
Alvern Adams .... Margaret Lindsay
Charlie Mitchell .... John Gallaudet
Freddie Stewart .... Freddie Stewart
Laura .... Dottye Brown
Mollie Miller .... Mollie Miller
Jimmie Davis (as a boy).... Ralph Freeto
Fred Astor .... Russell Hicks
Old Timer .... Lee "Lasses" White
Steve .... John Harmon
Tomlins .... Tristram Coffin
Mr. Davis .... Eddy Waller
Mrs. Davis .... Mary Field
Neilson .... Joseph Crehan
McCormack .... Charles Lane
Dr. Dodd .... Raymond Largay
Ford Pearson .... Ford Pearson
The Sunshine Serenaders—Charlie Mitchell, Jimmy Thomason, Lloyd Ellis, Logan Conger, Gib Thompson, Slim Harbert.

The story of Jimmie Davis' Horatio Alger climb from poor farmer to the governor's mansion in Louisiana has been given documentary treatment by Monogram. Film is loaded with Davis' best songs, all delivered in his particular style of singing showmanship. Picture's prospects should be good in the rural sections, where the Davis songs are big sellers. Ticket-buying reaction elsewhere is likely to be spotty.

From production standpoint, picture stacks up as Lindsley Parsons' best job, although he could have slanted the treatment of Davis' life along less idolatrous line. Nobility becomes a bit sticky at times and decreases interest. Story of the Davis career stresses the man's simplicity and honesty in rising to governor, and the service he has rendered his state. Davis' performance is hard to evaluate from acting standpoint since he is playing himself, but there is a self-consciousness about the portrayal that has appeal. He bows to no one, though, when it comes to putting over his hillbilly type of song. There are eight of his numbers, including "You Are My Sunshine," "Nobody's Darling But Mine," "It Makes No Difference Now," "There's a New Moon Over My Shoulder," "Let's Be Sweethearts Again" and "You Won't Be Satisfied That Way." In addition, score has Mollie Miller playing the accordion and singing "Basin Street" and "Old Man Mose" as specialties for bright moments.

Story starts with Davis' life on the farm of his sharecropper father, points up his desire for education, carries him through college, his days as a professor in a femme school of higher learning and into politics, first as a fighting police commissioner, then state commissioner and finally governor of Louisiana. Davis' vote-getting ability via song has long been a proven fact.

Margaret Lindsay pleases as Davis' wife, doing a solid job. John Gallaudet, portraying Davis' real-life friend, Charlie Mitchell, is another strong point in the cast. Eddy Waller and Mary Field, as Davis' parents, are exceptionally good, and there are a number of smaller spots that are capably enacted. Ralph Freeto does Davis as a boy. The Sunshine Serenaders, including the real Charlie Mitchell, lend good musical backing to Davis' vocals.

Story development follows documentary style, with offstage narration to make plot points, and Phil Karlson's direction gets the most of the script by Jack De Witt. Steve Healey did the original story and added dialog was contributed by Vick Knight and Scott Darling. Camera work by William Sickner is good, and authentic backgrounds filmed in Louisiana, add production values. Editing is okay. *Brog.*

Adventure Island
(COLOR)

Hollywood, Aug. 8.

Paramount release of William Pine-William Thomas production. Stars Rory Calhoun, Rhonda Fleming, Paul Kelly; features John Abbott, Alan Napier. Directed by Peter Stewart. Screenplay, Maxwell Shane; based on "Ebb Tide," by Robert Louis Stevenson and Lloyd Osbourne; camera, (Cinecolor), Jack Greenhalgh; music score, Darrell Calker; editor, Howard Smith. Tradeshown Aug. 8, '47. Running time, **66 MINS.**

Mr. Herrick .... Rory Calhoun
Faith Wishart .... Rhonda Fleming
Capt. Lochlin .... Paul Kelly
Mr. Huish .... John Abbott
Mr. Atwater .... Alan Napier

Pine and Thomas have delivered tinted version of the Robert Louis Stevenson story, "Ebb Tide," that has a good payoff in sight. Under title of "Adventure Island," film offers nifty pulp fiction romancing for adventure-lovers. It packs enough weight to head the bill in situations outside the deluxe spots. Color is a selling aid, too.

South Seas setting neatly backgrounds tale of three men on a beach and how destiny changes their situation. Maxwell Shane's script takes advantage of plot's color, and direction by Peter Stewart moves the story along. There are a number of sea scenes that fill the eye with beauty, particularly those of a large schooner under full sail. Jack Greenhalgh's lensing is a major contribution to production values achieved by William Pine and William Thomas.

Rory Calhoun, Paul Kelly and John Abbott are the beachcombers. Their chance comes when Kelly, a discredited sea captain, is offered a job sailing a schooner to Australia. Enroute, trio plans to steal ship's cargo of champagne, discover it's really water and that the former captain's daughter is aboard. Next adventure comes when ship drops anchor off island to gather supplies. Principals, including Rhonda Fleming, become the unwilling guests of Alan Napier, mad Englishman, who has the natives thinking he is God. Windup has Napier falling into his own snakepit after killing Kelly and Abbott. Calhoun gets the heroine and sails off into the sunset. It's strictly pulp fiction but it's played straight for best results.

Cast performs well and Miss Fleming is eye-appealing in some scant costumes. Kelly's work is crisp, Abbott supplies some chuckles as a cockney and Calhoun makes an acceptable romantic hero. Editing has held film to proper amount of footage, and other production credits measure up. *Brog.*

Holiday Camp
(BRITISH-MADE)

London, Aug. 5.

General Film Distributors' release of J. Arthur Rank presentation of Gainsborough-Sydney Box production. Features Flora Robson, Dennis Price, Jack Warner, Hazel Court. Directed by Ken Annakin. Screenplay by Muriel and Sydney Box, Peter Rogers from story by Godfrey Winn; camera, Jack Cox. At Studio One, London, Aug. 5, '47. Running time, 97 MINS.

Esther Harman ....Flora Robson
Squad. Leader Hardwicke.....Dennis Price
Joe Huggett ....Jack Warner
Mrs. Huggett.............Kathleen Harrison
Joan Martin ....Hazel Court
Michael Halliday ....Emrys Jones
Angela Kirby ....Yvonne Owen
Jimmy Gardner ....Jimmy Hanley
Valerie Thompson....Jeannette Tregarthen
Elsie Dawson ....Esme Cannon
Camp Announcer ....Esmond Knight
Steve ....John Blythe
Charlie ....Dennis Harkin

This is a well-knit, true-to-life depiction of the varied characters and grades of society who spend their vacation at huge organized camps, whose stories are interwoven to a colorful and entertaining pattern. Drama and pathos are present, but never over-dramatized, and film should have popular appeal to the masses. For the U. S., perhaps less might have been left to the imagination, and the abrupt ending visually clarified.

Among the new arrivals seeking relaxation are a bus driver, his wife, son, and young widowed daughter with infant; a young, jilted sailor; a hunted murderer; a homely, boy-seeking maidservant; a couple of idlers; a pair of lovers unable to marry, fleeing from convention; a cultured, lonely spinster, and thousands of the annual holiday-makers of all ages who are a feature of these large summer resorts.

Among all the varied attractions provided for communal recreation, the problems and histories unfold: the maniac posing as an ex-RAF pilot (reminiscent of recent London murder case), who exudes charm and claims another victim before the law catches up with him; the busman who cleans out the crooks who have robbed his son at cards; the embittered sailor who finds consolation with the war widow; and the youthful pianist who must sacrifice his music to face up to family responsibilities with the young girl he has wronged.

All characters are splendidly contrasted, with the people looking real and down to earth and not glamorized, photogenic specimens. Flora Robson displays with gracious dignity the tragedy of a wasted youth as the lonely woman who discovers in the blinded camp announcer her lost love of World War I.

Pic is realistically directed, with asset of natural background and camp surroundings. Artistically and technically it is a commendable piece of work. *Clem.*

The Burning Cross

Screen Guild release of Walter Colmes production; directed by Colmes. Stars Hank Daniels, Virginia Patton; features Raymond Bond, Betty Roadman, Dick Rich. Original screenplay, Aubrey Wisberg; camera, Walter Strenge; editor, Jason Bernie. Tradeshown, N. Y., Aug. 7, '47. Running time, 77 MINS.

Johnny ....Hank Daniels
Doris ....Virginia Patton
Chester ....Raymond Bond
Agatha ....Betty Roadman
Lud ....Dick Rich
Charlie ....Joel Fluellen
Strickland ....Walden Boyle
Gibbons ....Alexander Pope
Tony ....John Fostini
Tobey ....John Doucette
Hill ....Jack Shutta
Kitty ....Mady Norman
Bubby ....Glen Allen
Dawson ....Matt Willis
Police Sergeant ....Tom Kennedy
Pelham ....Dick Bailey
Elkins ....Ted Stanhope

Screen Guild must be given an A for effort in filming this tale of the Ku Klux Klan but that's about all. Film has all the earmarks of a low-budgeted, amateurish production, including a static script and inept acting and direction. As a result, it will have to be sold on its exploitation value alone, which makes it okay for the dualers. It hasn't got what it takes, though, for any top first-run situations.

With several of the majors flirting with the idea of doing a picture on the Klan and then forgetting about it, Screen Guild followed through to take advantage of a topical situation. And that's about all "Burning Cross" has to offer. Story shows what happens to a demoralized ex-GI who follows the Klan leaders' spiel of "kicking out the foreigners and making America a place for Americans." With the recent Klan outbreaks in the south still fresh in the minds of the public, the film should do okay in B spots with the right kind of buildup.

Original screenplay by Aubrey Wisberg tries hard to get its point across to the public. Film's denouement can be guessed from events in the first reel, leaving no room for suspense. Some of the more pertinent points, morever, are lost in an overdose of flagwaving. And the Klansmen's initiation, though it might be authentic, resembles nothing so much as a highschool fraternity soiree.

Cast is lost in a maze of apparent inexperience, plus poor direction by Walter Colmes. GI, as played by Hank Daniels, never rings quite true, with Daniels muffing his big dramatic scenes by over-emoting. Virginia Patton falters, too, as his vis-a-vis. Raymond Bond and Betty Roadman also tend to overact as the GI's parents. Only one creating any semblance of reality is Dick Rich as the Klansman who does all the dirty organizing work.

Entire production lined up by Colmes, who doubled as producer, with low budget showing up particularly in the wrong places. Street scenes are too obvious facades on a studio lot and the score is standard cops-and-robbers stuff. Walter Strenge's camera work is okay. *Stal.*

Vienna Melodies
(Musical)
(AUSTRIAN-MADE)

Locarno, July 14.

Donau Film release of Eduard Hoesch production. Stars Elfie Mayerhofer, Johannes Heesters; features Fritz Gehlen, Hedwig Bleibtreu, Anton Gaugl, Elizabeth Markus, Fritz Imhoff, Rudolf Brix. Directed by Hubert Marischka and Theo Lingen. Screenplay by Kaspar Loeser; camera, Karl Hoesch; music by Frank Filip. At Locarno Film Festival. Running time, 95 MINS.

(In German; No English Titles)

A pleasant, unpretentious musical film, this is probably the first genuinely exportable postwar Austrian product. "Vienna Melodies" scores a personal success for Elfie Mayerhofer. Producer and director both have avoided the mistake of other Austrian postwar filmers and stuck to limitations of material, talent and story line indigenous to Vienna's musical charm. With English titles, "Melody" should have a definite future in the U. S. It's a cinch for the arty houses and could go a lot further. Johann Strauss and Schubert music, delightfully executed by Mayerhofer, add strength to film's modern numbers.

Screenplay is nothing strikingly original. But it doesn't get in the way of light handling of picture's story about twin sisters who are separated in infancy. One is adopted in Sweden, the other brought-up by her musician father in Vienna. Both sing and both start crossing trails and confusing their boy friends when the Swedish twin comes to Vienna for study and the local gal's cabaret and operetta appearances snarl things up.

Miss Mayerhofer plays the double roles with a feeling for subtle differences between twin Viktoria, whose upbringing is in wealthy Swedish home and Lily, whose poorer father helps her to a semi-pop singing career. When their respective suitors, Johannes Heesters and Fritz Gehlen, begin encountering their two girls in strange surroundings the usual complications pile up. But Heesters brings them together for a happy ending which includes some cleverly staged scenes with Miss Mayerhofer and an excellent duet of a Strauss waltz. She sings both parts. In an earlier church scene, she delivers an impressive Schubert-Gounod "Ave Maria."

Miss Mayerhofer, Jugoslavian born, is an engaging personality who hints U. S. potentialities after acquiring knowledge of English. She has sung in the Vienna State Opera and at Salzburg Festival. She is small but has a large and well-trained voice. She is not always photographed or dressed to best advantage in "Vienna Melodies," but these failings are inherent under current Vienna shooting conditions.

It's noteworthy that "Melodies," although most action is placed in present-day Vienna, makes no pleas for the beaten-up condition of Vienna or the Viennese. Scenes of the city are made with affection and charm, concentrating on blooming trees in the parks, handsome architecture and people who don't look as starved and depressed as most real Viennese. Even the scripters have avoided giving comics references to food shortages or bombings.

Direction and supporting players are more than adequate. But the film belongs to Mayerhofer. *Isra.*

Todo Un Caballero
("Every Inch a Gentleman")
(MEXICAN-MADE)

Mexico City, Aug. 1.

Ramex release of J. M. Noriega production. Stars Fernando Soler, Malu Gatica; features Gustavo Rojo, Julio Villarreal, Carolina Barrett. Directed by Miguel M. Delgado. Screenplay, Salvador Novo; music, Gonzalo Curiel. At Cine Alameda, Mexico City, July 30, '47. Running time, 93 MINS.

Conventional melodrama deals with a lad who's on trial for a murder that actually was a suicide. However, a clever lawyer clears everything up to the satisfaction of all concerned. Thesping is creditable while Miguel Delgado's direction is good on his first try of a script of this type. His other directing experience was confined to a film for Mexico's top comic, Cantinflas.

Role of an autumnal gentleman who renounces love is carried with professional grace by Fernado Soler, one of Mexico's best actors. He shows neat versatility and humor in the part. Malu Gatica, Chilean siren, in the femme lead contribs a fine performance and shows promise. Gustavo Rojo is an adequate juve while Carolina Barrett rather overplays her role of the romance-hungry woman who's beginning to get on in years. *Grah.*

Admiral Nakhimov
(RUSSIAN-MADE)

Locarno, July 5.

Mosfilm release of Poudovkino production. Stars A. Diky, E. Samoilov, V. Poudovkine, A. Khohlov, P. Gaidebourov. Directed by D. Vassiliev; screenplay, I. Loukovsky; camera, A. Golovnia and T. Lobova. At Locarno Film Festival. Running time, 95 MINS.

(In Russian; no English Titles)

Much of what is usually found in Russian pictures applies to "Nakhimov." It's rich in fine photography, gripping battle scenes and strong acting. And simultaneously it is about as dull a mouthful of Soviet ideology as might be forced on any audience. It's strictly for the arty houses, and not much for them, either.

As shown in Locarno, the all-Russian dialogue was relieved for the international audience only by short spots of French language commentary. These were so noisily blended and ineptly written as to be practically no help. Every entry and exit of the French voice was heralded by thumps and cracklings in the sound track. Usually the commentator said only what was simultaneously self evident on the screen. An unsatisfactory method as presented here.

"Nakhimov" sets out to glorify the naval hero of Sebastopol in the 1853 war against the British and French. Naturally the English, and secondarily the Turks are shown as nefarious and treacherous enemies. Audience can easily draw any present day parallels it wishes. It's made clear that Nakhimov lost his war only because rottenness of the Czarist regime behind him weakened his forces and English spies ratted on him.

After Admiral dies from a British rifle bullet on the ramparts of besieged Sebastopol, film's closing scenes go into brief and uninformative shots of modern Soviet war vessels plunging through high seas. Off-screen-voice explains that 20th century Soviet fleet and its sailors have inherited proud traditions of Nakhimov's bravery.

Performances are uniformly fine, with A. Diky turning in a strong depiction of a harassed but silent naval hero. No women are in the cast. R. Simonov, as a Turkish admiral, is likewise notable. Scenes of both land and sea battles are magnificently and lavishly staged with masses of extras and equipment. But in content it's still unrelieved borscht-bright Red. *Isra.*

The Singing House
("Das Singende Haus")
(GERMAN-MADE)
(Musical)

Locarno, July 16.

Kollektiv Film production and release. Features Herta Mayen, Hennelore Schroth, Susi Nicoletti, Paul Kemp, Kurd Jurgens, Hans Moser. Directed by Franz Antel. Screenplay by Aldo von Pinelli and Franz Antel; music, Peter Kreuder. At Second International Film Festival, Locarno, June 30, '47. Running time, 120 MINS.

(In German; No English Titles)

Another in the string of cheap and tasteless films which have emanated from the Vienna studios since the war's end, "Singing House" won't do much for itself or prestige of Danubian pix. In a futile attempt to bring out a comedy-revue combination, it's only near success is in providing a framework for bright new tunes by Peter Kreuder as well as a reprise of some of his oldies. Further to be considered in its export possibilities is the fact that director-author Franz Antel remains charged by three western occupation powers with wartime Nazi activities. Neither he nor film are cleared for showing except in the Russian zone since made under Soviet auspices in Moscow-seized Rosenhugel Studios, Vienna. Minor chances in U. S. arty houses.

Story is the chestnut about the gal whose father is a classical musician and doesn't approve of her falling in with some swing band boys. After customary tribulations gal (Herta Mayen) appears in a big revue singing and dancing with such success that dad is charmed out of his grouch. Almost all of first half of film is virtually all dialogue sans music. Whole show biz theme is dumped into closing half hour. Fuzzy sound job is no help.

Acting is only so-so, even including Hans Moser, only local marquee name. Moser needs strong direction and didn't get it here. *Isra.*

In Those Days
("In Jenen Tagen")
(GERMAN-MADE)

Locarno, July 10.

Mondial Film release of Helmut Kautner production. Features Bettina Moissi, Winnie Markus, Erika Kautner, Carl Radazz. Direction and screenplay by Kaurtner. At Second International Film Festival, Locarno. Running time, **95 MINS.**

(In German; No English Titles)

European films circles attached much interest to this first production from British-occupied zone of Germany. Reception at Film Festival was generally dissapointing. Little chance for it in U. S. Film is the story of an automobile. Using battered remains of a once-smart but unpretentious German car as the story book, it reveals the people who owned the jalopy from time it was purchased by the rich lover of an attractive femme (Winnie Markus). Shows how the car passes into widely assorted ownerships. In almost every case the owners fall victims, physically, intellectually or professionally, to the growth of Nazism.

While the original lovers are driving together they are stopped by the parade (1933) celebrating Hitler's accession as Reichschancellor. Another owner is a composer and pianist who may no longer appear in public because of non-'Aryanism.' A third has his business destroyed by Nazi hoodlums because of his Jewish wife. In the end, an SS officer using the car to flee the oncoming Allies is shot and the auto thoroughly smashed. Throughout the picture's action, cutbacks are punctuated with efforts of a couple of Wehrmacht veterans to salvage what's usable from the wreck.

Even with due allowances for material shortages (film was shot mostly in open air), starvation of actors and limitations of film shooting in postwar Germany, there's not much to be said in favor of "Jenen Tagen." Dialogue is windy and philosophical to the point where occasional dramatic developments are thoroughly snowed under. Acting is poor, and direction and photography even poorer. *Isra.*

Albeniz

Locarno, July 12.

Argentina Sono Films production and release. Features Pedro Lopez Lagar, Sabina Olmos, Amadeo Novoa, Guillermo Contreros, Marisa Regules, Carmelita Vasquez. Directed by Luis Cesar Amadori. Screenplay by Pedro Miguel Obligado; music by Albeniz; musical direction, Guillermo Cases. At Locarno Film Festival. Running time, **110 MINS.**

(In Spanish; English Titles)

First major Argentine production sent abroad for straight film distribution, "Albaniz" is qualified to stand on its own. It's a workmanlike, well-acted, handsomely mounted music-biography of the Spanish composer Isaac Albeniz. Strikingly fiery piano and orchestra playing of Albeniz compositions (better known in U. S. than his name) as well as some Mozart and other classics lend distinction to this worthy film. This should get better than average returns in U. S. arty theatres, and might even go further if English titles are improved. As they are now, some vary from literal translation to incogruous injection of what the writer thought were hot Americanisms.

Albeniz first is shown as a child prodigy who plays the piano so well at a recital that the audience charges an adult had done the playing from behind a curtain. The young composer-virtuoso is shown as the victim of a stern father whose tyranny drives him to South America and U. S. After lurid love affairs, including one with a castanet-clicking, cafe tramp (Carmelita Vasquez), Albaniz returns to Spain. Cafe interlude offers chance for socko Spanish heel routine by Carmelita Vasquez, a sultry Latin looker.

Back in Madrid the still youthful Albeniz breaks down resistance of Spanish King's secretary by playing an uninvited piano solo. This gets him a scholarship at the Brussels Conservatory where he's depicted neglecting studies for cafe life and girls. Nevertheless, he and some compatriots stage concerts in Paris which launch his bombshell musical career as pianist, composer and conductor. Concert presentations are magnificent. So are scenes with musical greats of the time.

Pic closes with Albeniz, incurably ill, receiving one of France's highest honors and peacefully dying.

Pedro Lopez Lagar, as Albeniz, does a colorful and convincing portrait of a doubting youth, an inspired musician and a fiery lover. Other performances are more than adequate. All that might be asked is a slight shortening of film to eliminate draggy moments. Musical interludes are frequent and good enough general to take up the slack. "Albeniz" disappointed none at its preem at Locarno. It should click with music-loving trade in U. S. *Isra.*

The Great Dawn
(ITALIAN-MADE)

Superfilm release of Scalera production. Stars Pierino Gamba; features Rossano Brazzi, Renee Faure, Giovanni Grasso, Michele Riccardini. Directed by G. M. Scotese. English titles, A. V. Macaluso. Previewed, N. Y., Aug. 6, '47. Running time, **90 MINS.**

Pierino Gamba.................Pierino Gamba
Renzo Gamba.................Rossano Brazzi
Anna Gamba.....................Renee Faure
Oreste Bellotti...............Giovanni Grasso
Don Terenzio...............Michele Riccardini
Daisy ....Yvonne Samson
Fausto ....Fausto Guerzoni
Cooky ....Loris Gizzi
Salesman ....Guglielmo Sinaz

(In Italian; English Titles)

Starring Pierino Gamba, Italy's nine-year-old musical prodigy, "The Great Dawn" will have moderate b.o. appeal for the art house trade. Film, which is scheduled to follow the grim "Open City" into the World theatre, N. Y., following a two-year run, Sept. 15, is built along more conventional lines with artificial plot, synthetic pathos and broad comedy. Although lacking in that continental touch of realism, this offering is marked by general production finesse highlighted by an excellently recorded score of longhair music.

Plot revolves around conflict between talents of young Gamba and more materialistic goals of his grandfather, an industrial tycoon who tyrannizes the boy. Latter, however, is secretly aided by a priest with a flair for music and comedy, who organizes a fullscale orchestra for the kid to conduct at an open-air concert. In background, child's parents are caught in a tragic swirl of events, with the father, an unsuccessful composer, taking a clown's job in Paris and the mother unable to support her son.

Melodramatic climax brings a sugar-sweet solution, with the grandfather finally accepting the child's musical career and the parents happily reunited as the moppet achieves a sensational success as a symphony orchestra conductor. Musical score, performed by the Theatro dell Opera orchestra of Rome, includes selections from Beethoven, Schubert and Rossini.

Thesping job by youngster devolves mainly upon his Stokowski-like antics on the podium, which seem slightly overdone for a tyke in kneepants. Solid supporting performances are turned in by Michele Riccardini, as the priest, and Giovanni Grasso, the grandfather. Renee Faure and Rossano Brazzi are both excellent in briefer roles, as the boy's parents, and strike with genuine force in one sequence where Brazzi, with his clown's grease paint still on, tenderly embraces Miss Faure upon an unexpected encounter. *Herm.*

Shoe-Shine
(ITALIAN-MADE)

Lopert Films release of Paolo W. Tamburella production. Stars Rinaldo Smordoni, Franco Interlenghi; features Aniello Mele, Maria Campi, Bruno Ortensi, Pacifico Astrologo, Francesco De Nicola. Directed by Cittorio De Sica. Screenplay, Sergio Amidei, Adolfo Franci, C. G. Viola, Cesare Zavattini; camera, Anchise Brizzi; English subtitles, Herman G. Weinberg. Previewed in N. Y. Running time, **93 MINS.**

Giuseppe ....Rinaldo Smordoni
Pasquale ....Franco Interlenghi
Raffaele ....Aniello Mele
Arcangeli ....Bruno Ortensi
Vittorio ....Pacifico Astrologo
Ciriola ....Francesco De Nicola
L'Abruzzese ....Antonio Carlino
Giorgio ....Enrico De Silva
Righetoo ....Antonio Lo Nigro
Siciliano ....Angelo D'Amico
Staffera ....Emilio Cigoli
Avv. Bonavino ....Giuseppe Spadaro
Commissario P S. ....Leo Garavaglia
Il Panza ....Luigi Saltamerenda
La Chiromante ....Maria Campi
La Mamma di Giuseppe...Irene Smordoni
Nannarella ....Anna Pedoni

(In Italian, English Titles)

A senselessly grim ending and the depiction of brutalities which seem more an exercise of the director's whim than an integral part of the story rob "Shoe-Shine" of its laurels. Otherwise, this Italian-made pic might well have garnered uniform critical hosannas for its superb acting and mature naturalism. Patrons who enjoy beating themselves may take a shine to it—but masochism as b.o. lure is a doubtful quantity.

It starts off, smartly enough, as a sprightly picture of the maneuvers of two Italian gamins to buy a horse for which they yen. In the near background are soldiers, Rome and sources of easy money as is their army's easily blackmarketed equipment. And for a reel or so, the complex repercussions of their presence on these gamins and their elders make for informative and entertaining fare.

But "Shoe-Shine" moves into the clink when the lads are picked up for handling stolen army merchandise and consigned to the local big house. When the iron doors clang shut, a general gloom settles over the pic as sufferings, harshness and misunderstandings drive the youngsters apart. Final, futile tragedy is the accidental death of one moppet at the hands of the other.

This pic makes a few feeble passes but fails completely to explain sensibly the needless brutalities inflicted on the jail's juvenile inmates. It might have been logically latched onto the war—but it isn't, and the net is another bighouse pic which could have localed any place in the world. As such it's inferior to Hollywood's more lavish inmate-and-keeper stints.

Rinaldo Smordoni and Franco Interlenghi are topnotch in the lead spots as the two youngsters. Maria Campi plays superbly a bit part as a dowdy fortuneteller in the best sequence in the film. All other roles have the magic touch.

Lighting is uncertain and flickery. Direction on details are surefooted and carry a ring of verisimilitude. The trees are okay; it's the forest that's wrong. *Wit.*

Pageant of Russia
(Documentary; Color)
(RUSSIAN-MADE)

Artkino release of Documentary Film Studios production. Directed by Sergei Yutkevitch. Camera, V. Bobronitsky, S. Semyonov. At Stanley, N. Y., Aug. 9, '47. Running time, **50 MINS.**

"Pageant of Russia," a drawn-out compilation of camera shots taken at one of the Soviets' physical culture demonstrations in Moscow, has an appeal limited only to adherents and Russophiles in general. Its chief interest for the U. S. trade lies in its superb color, a new process invented by Soviet technicians which tints the screen warmly.

Documentary has some impact as a brilliant spectacle with its mass processions and swirling flags of different Soviet nationalities; but basic lack of variety in material soon dulls the senses. Working from unusual angles, crew of cameramen have managed to squeeze all the eye-filling surprises out of mass gymnastic drills performed with remarkable precision. Propaganda point is made sharply by the narration which stresses "the health and happiness" of the population, and the film generally is a nationalistic display of martial strength. Cutting into the film's action are the inevitable, countless shots of Generalissmo Stalin smiling benignly on the participants. *Herm.*

Miniature Reviews

"Life With Father" (WB) (Color). Irene Dunne-William Powell in adaptation of record-run Broadway comedy; strong b.o. winner.

"Magic Town" (RKO). Amusing, sentimental yarn of average American town troubled by poll-takers, with James Stewart and Jane Wyman. Good b.o. entry.

"Mother Wore Tights" (20th). (Musical; Color.) Familiar filmusical with Betty Grable and Dan Dailey; moderate b.o.

"Fun and Fancy Free" (Disney) (Color: Songs). Cartoon-live action feature a disappointment.

"Frieda" (British) (U). Topically hot treatise on the Germans, ok for big urban centers, n.s.g. in nabes.

"The Pretender", (Rep). Gangster meller lacks action; strong dual support.

"Last Frontier Uprising" (Rep). (Songs; Color). Formula oatuner starring Monte Hale.

"Jassy" (British) (Gen). Margaret Lockwood, Patricia Roc in a good costume melodrama.

"Marshal of Cripple Creek" (Rep.) Allan Lane in strong entry of Red Ryder series; fine for spots where westerns are liked.

"The Murderer Lives at Number 21" (Mage) (French). Pierre Fresnay in French-made whodunit; slight b.o. at arty houses.

Life With Father
(COLOR)

Warner Bros. release of Robert Buckner production. Stars Irene Dunne and William Powell; features Elizabeth Taylor, Edmund Gwenn, ZaSu Pitts. Directed by Michael Curtiz. Screenplay, Donald Ogden Stewart, from original stageplay by Howard Lindsay and Russel Crouse (produced by Oscar Serlin); camera (Technicolor), Peverell Marley and William V. Skall; Technicolor director, Natalie Kalmus; editor, George Amy; dialog director, Herschel Daugherty; special effects, William McCann (directed by Ray Foster); music, Max Steiner; orchestral arrangements, Murray Cutter; music director, F. Forbstein; assistant director, Robert Vreeland. At Warner theatre, N. Y., opening Aug. 14, '47. Running time, 118 MINS.
```
Vinnie..................Irene Dunne
Father................William Powell
Mary................Elizabeth Taylor
Rev. Dr. Lloyd.........Edmund Gwenn
Cora.......................ZaSu Pitts
Clarence...............Jimmy Lydon
Margaret................Emma Dunn
Dr. Humphries..........Moroni Olsen
Mrs. Whitehead......Elizabeth Risdon
Harlan.................Derek Scott
Whitney..............Johnny Calkins
John.....................Martin Milner
Annie...............Heather Wilde
The Policeman..........Monte Blue
Nora...................Mary Field
Maggie..............Queenie Leonard
Delia................Nancy Evans
Miss Wiggins.........Clara Blandick
Dr. Somers..........Frank Elliott
```

A stage play that runs eight years can be awfully tough to follow. When those eight years have formed the links by which that play has set an alltime Broadway run record—that makes it particularly tough to follow. "Life With Father" holds both these distinctions. Which creates for its cinematic version the unenviable challenge of maintaining a great standard.

That "Father" the picture does not consistently maintain the standard of "Father" the play should thus create no unusual dismay. "Father" was, after all, a very unusual play with a very unusual success. But by retaining enough of its charm and substituting such stars as William Powell and Irene Dunne, plus a beautifully Technicolored production and the natural exploitation values accrued through the play's long run, Warners has turned out a film that can't miss at the box-office.

"Father" the play had a remarkable wit, charm and some truly wonderful performers in Howard Lindsay and Dorothy Stickney. Not to mention the intimacy of the theatre. That must be it—the intimacy of the theatre! That's where the underlying difference must be between the two media into which this story has been translated.

"Father" at its best on the stage was never more than a series of vignettes of a day in the life of the Days on New York's Madison avenue in the mauve decade. There was never any story, as such—merely a grouping of tintypes and situations. But the intimacy of audience and performer in the theatre gave to all these a closeup perspective that the broader scope of the screen has, somehow, managed to diminish to an appreciable extent. The little pieces of business that were sharp etchings on the broad comedy canvas of the stage lost their sharpness when brought into focus of the camera.

This can happen so easily in a show that is, by and large, no more pretentious than a series of character studies painted with broad strokes against a background of casual story values.

All this, of course, it must be emphasized, should not be construed as any particular disparagement of a picture that still retains considerable entertainment value. Enough entertainment, in fact, to escape the jaundiced eye of all except those with a particularly fond memory for a great stage entertainment. "Father," after all, as a play, comes along once in a lifetime. What, under those circumstances, can stand up under such a critical gaze? It is, perhaps, unfair to question a picture's boxoffice values on the basis of any such analogy. But "Father" as a film needn't concern itself about the b.o.; it will stand on its own.

Miss Dunne and Powell have captured to a considerable extent the play's charm, though, as bombastic Clarence Day, Powell must bow low to the part's creator, Lindsay, who with Russel Crouse adapted the stage version from the original New Yorker magazine stories. Miss Dunne compares very favorably with the Dorothy Stickney original role, exacting the comedy from the part without overplaying it.

The major humor of the story, based on Father's eccentric characteristics and Mother's continual mollifying of his tantrums, is still evident in the pic. The Day children are not as effectively projected as in the play, but this, too, has been shrouded by the lesser intimacy of the pic.

Elizabeth Taylor, as the vis-a-vis for Clarence Day, Jr., is sweetly feminine as the demure visitor to the Day household, while Jimmy Lydon, as young Clarence, is likewise effective as the potential Yale man. Edmund Gwenn, as the minister, and ZaSu Pitts, a constantly visiting relative, head the supporting players who contribute stellar performances.

It's a superlative production all the way, and no less important than any other single feature of the pic is the photography. Michael Curtiz' direction is excellent, though unable to achieve, because of the very nature of the pic, anything more than a pedestrian pace. *Kahn.*

Magic Town
(SONGS)

RKO release of Robert Riskin production. Stars James Stewart, Jane Wyman; features Kent Smith, Ned Sparks, Wallace Ford, Regis Toomey. Directed by William A. Wellman. Screenplay, Riskin, based on story by Riskin and Joseph Krumgold; camera, Joseph F. Biroc; editors, Sherman Todd, Richard Wray; music, Roy Webb. Songs, Mel Torme, Bob Wells, Edward Heyman. Previewed N. Y., Aug. 18, '47. Running time, 103 MINS.
```
Rip Smith..............James Stewart
Mary Peterman..........Jane Wyman
Hoopendecker...........Kent Smith
Ike Sloan..............Ned Sparks
Lou Dicketts..........Wallace Ford
Ed Weaver.............Regis Toomey
Mrs. Weaver...........Ann Doran
Mr. Twiddle..........Donald Meek
Moody................E. J. Ballantine
Ma Peterman........Ann Shoemaker
Nickleby............Howard Freeman
Hank Nickleby........Mickey Kuhn
Mayor................Harry Holman
Mrs. Frisby..........Mary Currier
Bob Peterman........Mickey Roth
Birch................Frank Fenton
Senator Wilton......George Irving
Mrs. Wilton..........Julia Deane
```

"Magic Town" is a smooth combination of comedy and hokum. Its smart dialog and superior direction will overcome a longwinded, sentimental story to register favorably with the cash customers, while James Stewart's loyal following won't be let down by another of his ingratiatingly boyish performances. Film's humor and performances will carry it through.

Robert Riskin has bitten off a huge chunk with this, his first independent picture, of which he is both producer and writer. Unusual freedom and authority had the natural tendency of Riskin spreading himself too much and overdoing a good thing. An editor's severe bluepencil would have helped to change a fairly good boxoffice entry into a surefire hit.

The story is a little complicated in starting out to be a yarn about an opinion-polling outfit and winding up as the life, death and rebirth of an average American town. It was time the films got around to kidding the various Gallup, Hooper and Nielson polls, and this pic does a good job of it. Whether the average filmgoer, despite the fact that he is constantly being polled for opinions on this or that subject, can get excited about a group of people testing an average town for its opinion on progressive education in America is debatable. But the story eventually veers away from this angle to study the attitude of a small town when national publicity goes to its head, and the filmgoer is on familiar ground again.

Stewart plays an enterprising researcher who plans to get rich quickly with what he calls his "mathematical miracle" method — finding one small town that thinks as the nation does, and by polling it constantly on various issues have a cross-section of American opinion at very small cost. He finds the town in Grandview. Posing as an insurance salesman planning to settle there, Stewart and his two cronies (Ned Sparks and Donald Meek) poke their noses into the affairs of the town, and upset plans a young newspaper editor (Jane Wyman) has for improving the place with a new civic centre.

When the editor finally learns of Stewart's scheme and exposes it in her newspaper, the town is publicized nationwide as America's average city, and the resultant onrush of cameramen, feature writers, sidewalk radio commentators, tourists and get-rich-quick gentry inflates the town mentally, physically and morally. Its opinion on anything is no longer worth much, and resultant polls make it ridiculous in the nation's eye. The boom collapses and the town faces economic as well as spiritual ruin. How Stewart and Miss Wyman save it is interesting stuff, even if it is highly far-fetched and unmitigated corn.

The film has a good deal of the charm of smalltown communal life, with constant warming touches. The comic incidents, however, are its brightest spot and its insurance for success. Sourpuss deadpan Ned Sparks, back on the screen after four years' absence, is excellent foil for Stewart's exuberance, while the late Donald Meek adds strong points. The comedy touches crop up constantly, especially when most needed. One of the hilarious bits has Stewart and Miss Wyman wandering into a schoolroom, remembering their respective childhoods, and bursting into recitation of the poems they loved best—Miss Wyman into "Hiawatha," Stewart into "Charge of the Light Brigade" — oblivious of each other, while an incredulous janitor finally is overcome enough to join in with some verse of his own.

The love scenes are gentle and tinged with good humor, to be very engaging, and the bit in the gym, when Stewart and Miss Wyman discover they love each other is excellent stuff. Homey touches, like Stewart's informal coaching of a boys' basketball team; the Mayor recording an interview into a dictaphone; the cordial sidewalk meeting of two men who don't even know each other; the three elderly newspaper "office boys" who speak as one; the drunk scene of Stewart and Sparks, are all cinema highspots.

Stewart's shy charm and eagerness pairs well with Miss Wyman's reticent affection. Latter looks especially attractive in this film with a boyish hairdo upsweep. Anne Shoemaker, Wallace Ford, Kent Smith, Regis Toomey and E. J. Ballantine add effective bits as various citizens of Grandview.

Riskin's humor and gags; Wellman's easy, slick direction, and Riskin's unstinted production efforts, are obvious assets to the trained eye. *Bron.*

Mother Wore Tights
(MUSICAL; COLOR)

20th-Fox release of Lamar Trotti production. Stars Betty Grable, Dan Dailey; features Mona Freeman, Connie Marshall, Sara Allgood, William Frawley. Directed by Walter Lang. Screenplay, Trotti, based on book by Marian Young; camera (Technicolor), Harry Jackson; editor, J. Watson Webb, Jr.; lyrics and music, Mack Gordon and Josef Myrow. Previewed in New York, Aug. 18, '47. Running time, 107 MINS.
```
Myrtle McKinley Burt.......Betty Grable
Frank Burt.................Dan Dailey
Iris Burt..................Mona Freeman
Mikie Burt.................Connie Marshall
Bessie.....................Vanessa Brown
Bob Clarkman...............Robert Arthur
Grandmother McKinley.......Sara Allgood
Mr. Schneider.............William Frawley
Miss Ridgeway.............Ruth Nelson
Alice Flemmerhammer.......Anabel Shaw
Roy Bivins................Michael Dunne
Grandfather McKinley....George Cleveland
Rosemary Olcott..........Veda Ann Borg
Papa.....................Sig Ruman
Lil......................Lee Patrick
Specialty................Senor Wences
Mrs. Muggins.............Maude Eburne
Papa Capucci.............Antonio Filauri
Mama.....................Lotte Stein
Mr. Clarkman.............William Forrest
Mrs. Clarkman...........Kathleen Lockhardt
Ed.......................Chick Chandler
Dance Director...........Kenny Williams
Withers..................Will Wright
Stage Doorman............Frank Orth
```

"Mother Wore Tights" is a familiarly styled Technicolor musical opus on the life and times of a song-and-dance team that knocked around the vaude circuits about the century's turn. Leisurely paced and loosely constructed as a series of undramatic vignettes, picture will appeal to patrons who prefer their nostalgia trowelled on thickly and sweetly. Marquee values are limited solely to Betty Grable's name, which will not be strong enough to pull this film out of the just-fair b.o. class.

Musical is severely limited by its long and mediocre score of tunes, which are presented without any visual imaginative touches. Numerous hoofing sequences featuring Miss Grable and her vis-a-vis, Dan Dailey, also fail to rate the heavy accent put on them by the footage. Chief drawback, however, is the rambling story, whose lack of both major and minor climaxes is made glaring by Walter Lang's deadpan direction and a script which pulls out all the stops in its use of cliches and sentimentalism.

Yarn, unfolding via simple flashbacks to the commentary of the hoofers' younger daughter, progresses through the various stages of the vaude team's career. Beginning with Miss Grable's highschool graduation, where she was named the class' top dancer, film wanders through her encounter with Dailey, their marriage, a couple of childbirths to a warmly happy ending. It's one of the most harmonious domestic pictures ever seen on land or celluloid.

Incidental trouble is met along the way when the elder daughter, getting some polish at a finishing school, is chagrined to learn that her parents have been booked for a one-night stand at a local theatre. Everything's ironed out quickly, however, when the whole school of swells comes out to cheer the duo's routine. Sample of the film's unreality is the daughter's protest against the language used by VARIETY in its marriage columns. Quote runs something like this: "Zippee! Daughter of Joe and Bertha Klotz, vaude hoofers, was married to son of the Ernest Smiths, noted acrobats. Whoopee!" [Ed note: VARIETY likewise protests.]

Brace of six numbers provided by Mack Gordon and Josef Myrow, none of which shows any hit parade class, include "Rolling Down Bowling Green," "Kokomo, Indiana," "You Do," "There's Nothing Like a Song," "This Is My Favorite City" and "Fare-Thee-Well, Dear Alma Mater." In addition to Miss Grable and Dailey, Mona Freeman, as the elder daughter, also warbles a few numbers, displaying nice but not distinctive pipes.

Main thesping chore is carried by Dailey, who, after five years in the Army, is getting a star buildup at 20th. Dailey shows nice form as a hoofer and patter singer, and his thesping reveals a comic talent that might go places given right lines and situations. Miss Grable and her gams are set off to best advantage, and while her singing and dancing are okay, her emoting is unpersuasive. Two daughters, played by Miss Freeman and moppet Connie Marshall, are among the film's standouts. Supporting cast, headed by Sara Allgood and William Frawley, is uniformly capable.

Lensing is executed in superb taste, with tints being warm yet realistic without any garish color contrasts. *Herm.*

Fun and Fancy Free

(Cartoon-Live Action)
(Color; Songs)

RKO release of Walt Disney production. Stars Edgar Bergen and Dinah Shore; features Charlie McCarthy, Mortimer Snerd, Luana Patten, Donald Duck, Mickey Mouse and Jiminy Cricket. Directors, Jack Kinney, W. O. Roberts, Hamilton Luske; live-action director, William Morgan. Story, Homer Brightman, Harry Reeves, Ted Sears, Lance Nolley, Eldon Dedini, Tom Oreb, with "Bongo," from an original by Sinclair Lewis. Songs by Ray Noble, Buddy Kaye, Bernie Benjamin, Arthur Quenzer, William Walsh, Bobby Worth and George Weiss; editor, Jack Bachom. Previewed in N. Y., Aug. 18, '47. Running time, **73 MINS.**

It is unfortunate that the economics of film distribution and exhibition make it all but impossible to show an adequate return on better-than-usual one and two-reel shorts. Result is that Walt Disney has long since discovered he can greatly enhance his chances of turning a profit by stringing several of his briefies together and offering them as a feature. That's what he's done here with two shorts—or what should be shorts. He's expanded them far beyond their potentialities and tricked a bit of dressing around them to bring the package up to the length of the conventional "B" feature. The result is a dull and tiresome film that even the most rabid Disney addicts will not find to their taste.

To be sure, the drawings and color work are up to the high Disney technical standard, and most of the producer's favorite characters are on hand, including Mickey Mouse, Donald Duck and Jiminy Cricket. To give an added fillip, and as marquee hypo, there are the live-action talents of Edgar Bergen, Charlie McCarthy, Mortimer Snerd and Luana Patten, and the offscreen voice in song and narration of Dinah Shore. Anita Gordon, Cliff Edwards, Billy Gilbert, Clarence Nash, The Kings Men, The Dinning Sisters and The Starlighters.

But all the fine technical work and all the names in the world can't compensate for lack of imagination. The whole combo is uninspired and belabored, completely unlike Disney. And at least 75% of the trouble appears to be from the efforts to make 73 minutes of running time out of what would be two good 10-minute shorts.

First of the pair of stories is "Bongo," from an original by Sinclair Lewis, which Disney once considered for a full-length feature on its own. Bongo is a unicycle-riding circus bear who tires of his artificial comforts and escapes to go native. He finds himself an unhappy stranger to forest ways until he meets a femme bear and her tough boy-friend-bear. After numerous trials, he defeats the gorilla-like chum, wins the gal and rules the domain.

Second yarn is "Mickey and the Beanstalk," a variation on the old familiar fairy tale. It attempts to tie together so many elements it does justice to none. It opens with a live-action Edgar Bergen entertaining Charlie McCarthy, Mortimer Snerd and blond-tressed little Luana Patten with the story of a place called Happy Valley. Tough times come when a magic singing harp is stolen and the peasants—Mickey Mouse, Donald Duck and Goofy—find their only possession some magic beans. From them result the beanstalk into which the trio climb into the land of Willie the Giant. After numerous adventures they rescue the harp and return to their valley.

The two stories are held together by Jiminy Cricket, who first turns on a phonograph to have the "Bongo" yarn told and then climbs into Bergen's house to hear the "Beanstalk" tale. Dinah Shore narrates "Bongo" and sings some of the tunes in it, all very creditably. Cliff Edwards neatly voices the cricket, whose principal number is the title song. Bergen and his dummies are unnecessary, with their dialog especially unfunny.

There are seven identifiable tunes, most of them as uninspired as the stories and the antics of the characters. It will take the most deft plugging by publishers Santly-Joy to get them anywhere. They include "Fun and Fancy Free," "Lazy Countryside," "Too Good to Be True," "Say It With a Slap," "Oh What a Happy Day," "I'm a Most Amazing Guy" and "In My Favorite Dream." *Herb.*

Frieda

Universal release of J. Arthur Rank production (Michael Balcon-Ealing Studios). Stars David Farrar, Mai Zetterling; features Glynis Johns, Flora Robson, Albert Lieven, Barbara Everest. Directed by Basil Dearden. Screenplay by Ronald Millar and Angus MacPhail from an original by Millar; camera, Gordon Dines; editor, Jim Morahan; music, John Greenwood. At Park Ave. theatre, N.Y., Aug. 15, '47. Running time, **97 MINS.**

Robert	David Farrar
Judy	Glynis Johns
Frieda	Mai Zetterling
Nell	Flora Robson
Richard	Albert Lieven
Mrs. Dawson	Barbara Everest
Edith	Gladys Henson
Tony	Ray Jockson
Alan	Patrick Holt
Merrick	Milton Rosmer
Jim Merrick	Barry Letts
Lawrence	Gilbert Davis
Mrs. Freeman	Renee Gadd
Hobson	Douglas Jefferies
Holliday	Barry Jones
Bailey	Eliot Makeham
Crawley	Norman Pierce
Granger	John Ruddock
Herriot	D. A. Clarke-Smith
Beckwith	Garry Marsh
Irvine	Aubrey Mallalieu
Latham	John Molecey
Post-boy	Stanley Escane
Polish Priest	Gerhard Hinze
First Official	Arthur Howard

The Briton's restrained and muted touch is turned to a topically hot potato in Michael Balcon's "Frieda," a surprisingly early plea for tolerance towards the Germans. In fashioning his opus, Balcon has made an earnest and adult treatise which still stitches in a goodly dose of dramatic impact. "Frieda" should do its share of the biz in major urban centers. Sans marquee allure for American box-offices, it promises a tepid performance in the nabes and smalltown flickeries.

Nicely lensed, soundly written and maturely handled, "Frieda" could ordinarily count its boxoffice battle half won by a friendly critical reception. But with the bones of Dachau scarcely buried, more than one crick is going to sniff Empire politics in the pic's premise. Rightly or wrongly, that suspicion may well decimate the huzzahs.

For Frieda (Mai Zetterling), a German nurse, is stand-in for the so-called decent Teuton who joined with the Nazis and then had his tardy repentance when victory and loot faded out. In the pic, she's married to an RAF officer (David Farrar), whose life she saved and by whom she's brought to a quiet British town, close on the war's end. Early refusal of Farrar's family and his home town to accept her and their subsequent conversion build the drama.

Film falters when it fails to reflect sympathetically the townspeople who refuse the face-value acceptance of a German after five years of vicious war with her tribe. It scores a point, however, when it contrasts the regeneration of Frieda with that of her brother (Albert Lieven), who turns up midway in the yarn still the hellion Hitlerite. Final footage moves swiftly as Frieda wins her place in the family while her brother is done in.

Excellent limning of both Miss Zetterling and Farrar help lend conviction to the story. Glynis Johns does standout work as the sister-in-law, and her low-keyed winsome voice should cop Hollywood's attention. Flora Robson, as an aunt whose chances of winning a Parliament seat are dimmed by her nephew's marriage, scores soundly.

Direction by Basil Dearden is adroit and sure. Particularly deft is his handling of one scene, in which the flier accuses his frau of remaining a Nazi by the simple device of dropping her brother's swastika medallion in her lap. Camera work is expert and polished. *Wit.*

The Pretender

Republic release of W. Lee Wilder production. Stars Albert Dekker; features Catherine Craig, Charles Drake, Alan Carney. Linda Stirling. Directed by W. Lee Wilder. Screenplay, Don Martin; added dialog, Doris Miller; camera, John Alton; editor, Asa Boyd Clark. At Rialto, N. Y., week of Aug. 11, '47. Running time, **69 MINS.**

Kenneth Holden	Albert Dekker
Claire Worthington	Catherine Craig
Dr. Leonard Koster	Charles Drake
Victor Korrin	Alan Carney
Flo Ronson	Linda Stirling
Fingers	Tom Kennedy
Charles Lennox	Selmer Jackson
Butler (William)	Charles Middleton
Butler (Thomas)	Ernie Adams
Mickie	Ben Welden
Hank Gordon	John Bagni
Stranger	Stanley Rosa
Dr. Stevens	Forrest Taylor
Margie	Greta Clement
Miss Chalmers	Peggy Wynne
Nurse No. 1	Eula Guy
Evelyn Cossett	Cay Forrester
Stephen	Peter Michael
Janitor	Michael Mark
Miss Michael	Dorothy Scott

Credit a polished performance by Albert Dekker wasted in a gangster meller simply because of belabored direction. He is a conniving Wall Street dealer whose juggling of accounts finally catches up with him largely because he fears the gangsters he has called in to eliminate a rival. Despite a somewhat laggard pace, "The Pretender" carries enough entertainment to provide strong dual support.

Dekker keeps meeting margin requirements of his broker by switching money from a large estate for which he is trustee. But a falling market forces him to plot marriage with Catherine Craig, heiress to the coin he's been mishandling. But she's about to announce her marriage to a young medico. In desperation, Dekker hires a gang to bump off the girl's fiance, but when Miss Craig suddenly tosses the medico overboard and elopes with Dekker, the complications come in heavy doses.

Don Martin's original is neatly concocted though ponderously directed.

Alan Carney also chips in with a realistic job as the gangster chief. Miss Craig makes an acceptable heiress while Linda Stirling shows promise as a gangster's moll. Tom Kennedy, as the righthand man to Carney, makes considerable of the chief supporting role. *Wear.*

Last Frontier Uprising

(SONGS; COLOR)

Republic release of Louis Gray production. Stars Monte Hale, Adrian Booth; features Foy Willing. Directed by Lesley Selander. Screenplay, Harvey Gates; original story, Jerome Odlum; camera (Trucolor), Bud Thackery; editor, Charles Craft; musical score, Mort Glickman. At New York theatre, N.Y., Aug. 14, '47. Running time, **67 MINS.**

Monte Hale	Monte Hale
Mary Lou Gardner	Adrian Booth
Vance Daley	James Taggart
Boyd	Roy Barcroft
Skillet	Tom London
Lyons	Philip Van Zandt
Sheriff Hanlon	Edmund Cobb
Sam Chisholm	John Ince
Rancher	Frank O'Connor
Texan	Bob Blair
Rancher	Doyle O'Dell
Themselves	Foy Willing and the Riders of the Purple Sage

"Last Frontier Uprising" is formula-baked fare for the oatuner trade. According to recipe, pic is a fast mix of knuckle-scraping, gun-shooting, hoofbeating and cowboy serenading with a slight speck of romance. Production dress is also standard, with celluloid tinted with Trucolor, a process that overhighlights greens and browns.

Yarn has a pre-Civil War date, with Monte Hale acting as Government agent commissioned to buy up some horses in Texas. Pic, which has absolutely no relation to the title, revolved around fight between a gang of southern horse-stealing varmints and Hale. Latter is framed on a murder charge but blazes his way out in a pitched battle between his boys and the gang.

Hale registers okay in lead both as fighting hero and saddle-crooner. As romantic interest, Adrian Booth gets by with nice looks. Couple of heavies, Roy Barcroft and Philip Van Zandt, play their stock parts adequately enough to earn hisses from the kids, while rest of cast turns in routine performances. *Herm.*

Jassy

London, Aug. 12.

General Film Distributors' release of J. Arthur Rank-Gainsborough production by Sydney Box. Stars Margaret Lockwood, Patricia Roc; features Dennis Price, Basil Sydney, Dermot Walsh. Directed by Bernard Knowles. Screenplay by Dorothy and Campbell Christie, Geoffrey Kerr from novel by Norah Lofts. Music by Henry Geehl; camera (Technicolor), Jack Asher. At Odeon, London, Aug. 12, '47. Running time, **102 MINS.**

Jassy Woodroffe	Margaret Lockwood
Dilys Helmar	Patricia Roc
Christopher Hatton	Dennis Price
Nick Helmar	Basil Sydney
Barney Hatton	Dermot Walsh
Mrs. Helmar	Linden Travers
Mrs. Hatton	Nora Swinburne
Stephen Fennell	Grey Blake
Woodroffe	John Laurie
Lindy	Esme Cannon
Elizabeth Twisdale	Cathleen Nesbitt

Sir Edward Follesmark .... Ernest Thesiger
Sedley .... Bryan Coleman

This is a colorful and dramatic story, smoothly and skillfully adapted from the bestseller. It should have general appeal, including chance in the U. S., where Margaret Lockwood and Patricia Roc are known.

In the early 19th century, when a gentleman had little to do but drink and gamble, Mordelaine, a stately country home, is sacrificed by its squire at the card table and he and his wife and son go to live on an humble adjoining farm. The father shoots himself, and Barney, his boy, lives for the day he can return to the home of his ancestors. He befriends a village girl tormented because of her gypsy mother and she becomes a servant at his farm when her father is killed heading a deputation to the new squire for higher wages.

Barney's mother, fearing propinquity will develop an undesirable attachment sends Jassy away to serve at a girl's school where she becomes popular for her gift of second sight and Dilys, the squire's daughter, enlists her help for a love tryst. Both are sent away in disgrace. Dilys takes the maid home as a friend, she becomes housekeeper, then wife to the squire. Jassy has tricked him into signing over the house to her as a condition but refuses to consummate the marriage, and glories in her revenge of her father.

Dilys, coquetting between Barney and a neighbor, marries the latter. Her father sustains severe injuries while riding and dies suddenly when considered convalescent. Jassy is charged with his murder, having every motive, and is condemned mainly because she refused any of the servants access to him. One, a mute half-wit devoted to her, was the sole exception and during the trial she becomes articulate, confesses she poisoned her master and expires dramatically in the dock.

Barney realizes how misplaced was his love for Dilys and when he finds Jassy has made over Mordelaine to him, they find the usual consolatory clinch.

The two girls are well contrasted, with honors even. Basil Sydney, as the drink-enflamed despot, is convincingly forceful and Dermot Walsh is an attractively manly lover. Dennis Price gives a grand performance as the ruined gambler, and minor roles are excellently portrayed by Nora Swinburne and Ernest Thesiger.

Production is in every way commendable with some of the most beautiful exteriors ever seen in a British film, and interiors correspondingly impressive. No doubt this is another winner for Gainsborough. *Clem.*

Marshal of Cripple Creek

Republic production and release. Stars Allan Lane; features Bobby Blake, Martha Wentworth. Directed by R. G. Springsteen. Screenplay, Erale Snell, based on Fred Harman's Red Ryder syndicated comic strip; camera, William Bradford; editor, Harold R. Minter. Previewed in N. Y., Aug. 15, '47. Running time, **58 MINS.**

Red Ryder .... Allan Lane
Little Beaver .... Bobby Blake
The Duchess .... Martha Wentworth
Tom Lambert .... Trevor Bardette
Baker .... Tom London
Link .... Roy Barcroft
Long John Case .... Gene Stutenroth
Dick Lambert .... William Self
Mrs. Lambert .... Helen Wallace

Latest in Republic's Red Ryder stories rates as one of best in series. Patterned after the NEA cartoon character, it follows the general style of the comic strip yarns. Main interest centers on Ryder, Little Beaver, youthful Indian, and the Duchess. This fits ideally into spots where they go for fast westerns.

"Marshal of Cripple Creek" has the mastermind of outlawry at a booming Colorado gold-mining town working right under the nose of the sheriff. Outlaw's pet stunt is hijacking the regular gold ore wagon-train.

Allan Lane, as Red Ryder, has personality and looks. Young Bobby Blake is okay while Martha Wentworth plays the duchess in cartoon tradition. Only other femme principal is Helen Wallace, as the middle aged wife of Trevor Bardette. The latter makes something of his character, the reformed crook who turns the tables on the outlaws.

R. G. Springsteen directed with an eye to action and suspense. *Wear.*

The Murderer Lives at Number 21
(FRENCH-MADE)

Mage Films release of Liote production. Stars Pierre Fresnay; features Suzy Delair, Jean Lissier, Pierre Larquey, Noel Roquevert. Directed by H. G. Clouzot. Screenplay, Clouzot and S. A. Steeman from novel by Steeman; camera, Armand Thirard; English titles, George Slocombe. At Studio 65, N. Y., Aug. 16, '47. Running time, **83 MINS.**

Wens .... Pierre Fresnay
Mila Malou .... Suzy Delair
Lalah-Poor .... Jean Tissier
Colin .... Pierre Larquey
Dr. Linz .... Noel Roquevert
Mme. Point .... Odette Talazac
Melle Cuq .... Maximilienne
Kid Robert .... Jean Despeaux
Vania .... Huguette Vivier

(In French; English Titles)

"The Murderer Lives at Number 21" is a comedy-mystery potboiler from France that'll make only a slight dent in the American sureseater market. Pic has several pleasant spots, but on whole hews too closely to the ready-made pattern of Hollywood's whodunit fashionists to rate as a novel item. Name of Pierre Fresnay will help at the b.o. although his role doesn't offer many openings for his formidable thespic talent.

Yarn is a carnival of cadavers handled in a tongue-in-cheek style without any insistence on plot details. In this production the proverbial Gallic touches of candor are frequently evident, with borderline between candor and coarseness not always observed. English titling, while competent, is restrained by code tabus from transplanting the spice. General production dress is good, with big lift furnished by excellent cast and well-defined camera work.

Fresnay plays a detective bent on collaring a homicide who keeps 'em dropping en masse. After tracing the murderer to a boarding house, Fresnay assumes the garb of a clergyman to better investigate activities of the residents, a collection of seedy, suspicious characters. Arrests follow each other, but with killings still taking place, and murderer hanging his calling card on the corpses, police are forced to release the suspects. Fresnay finally breaks case by brilliant deduction that the killer isn't one guy but three pranksters acting as a team.

Fresnay walks through his paces impassively, not giving any extra push to comedy situations. Other players, however, add more animation, with Suzy Delair, Jean Tissier, Pierre Larquay and Noel Roquevert turning in especially good performances.

Miniature Reviews

"Golden Earrings" (Par). Ray Milland and Marlene Dietrich in brisk anti-Nazi meller; solid b.o.

"Out of the Blue" (E-L). Screwball comedy with Virginia Mayo, George Brent. Fair b.o.

"Flashing Guns" (Mono). Routine action thriller for supporting situations.

"Master of Bankdam" (British) Gen). Saga of English milltown should be good boxoffice.

"The Hat Box Mystery" (SG). Creditable murder yarn designed for supporting situations.

Golden Earrings
(ONE SONG)

Paramount release of Harry Tugend production. Stars Ray Milland, Marlene Dietrich; features Marvyn Vye, Bruce Lester, Dennis Hoey, Quentin Reynolds. Directed by Mitchell Leisen. Screenplay, Abraham Polonsky, Frank Butler, Helen Deutsch from novel by Yolanda Foldes; camera, Daniel L. Fapp; editor, Alma Macrorie; music and lyrics; Victor Young, Jay Livingston, Ray Evans. Previewed at Normandie, N.Y., Aug. 25, '47. Running time, 95 MINS.

Col. Ralph Denistoun .... Ray Milland
Lydia .... Marlene Dietrich
Zoltan .... Murvyn Vye
Byrd .... Bruce Lester
Roff .... Dennis Hoey
Quentin Reynolds .... Himself
Professor Krosigk .... Reinhold Schunzel
Major Reimann .... Ivan Triesault

Parlay of Ray Milland and Marlene Dietrich in a well-paced meller makes "Golden Earrings" a solid boxoffice item. Despite its oldhat plot of the anti-Nazi fox vs. the Gestapo hounds, pic is dished up with enough suspenseful twists to give it a novel aspect. War theme, temporarily in shade of customer preferences, is neatly muted, with film putting fortissimo accent on perennial ingredients of straight action, heavy romance and light comedy.

Pic's surprise is Miss Dietrich, who blossoms forth here with new verve as a blackhaired, brownskinned Gypsy. Switch from henna to brunet not only puts the actress' looks in a distinctly favorable new light, but re-focuses attention on her whole personality. In many chances offered by her Gypsy role, she plays on all the emotive keys, from sultriness to tempestuousness and back again, from comedy to earnest pathos. She's rarely been in better form. Milland, as a British officer, is in a tailor-made part which he acquits with vigor and finesse.

Backing up the principals is a top coin production that's firmly buttressed in the story and scripting department. Mitchell Leisen's direction is positive, with alternation between the chase's excitement and the romance's heat merging into steady movement. Supporting cast, including Quentin Reynolds in a bit part playing himself, is uniformly excellent.

Yarn, which Milland unfolds to Reynolds on a plane trip from London to the continent, clears up the mystery of the former's pierced ears. Flashback sequence opens into 1939, with Milland, as a colonel in the British army, and Bruce Lester, his aide, on an espionage mission to Nazi Germany. After being caught and breaking out of the Gestapo's grasp, both Britishers plunge into the underbrush to carry on by themselves.

Milland meets Miss Dietrich en route and, as part of his plan to duck the police, he assumes a Gypsy's complexion and garb, hence, the pierced ears. Following a knockdown, drag-out fight with the caravan's chieftain and several close calls with his pursuers, Milland gets the poison gas formula and heads back to England, leaving his vagabond romance behind. Postwar windup, is naturally, happy with the lovers reunited on the same spot in Germany where they parted.

One number, "Golden Earrings," is intoned by Miss Dietrich in her customary rich, deep-toned style. Murvyn Vye, as the Gypsy king, also works over the same tune with a good baritone and registers with an overall effective performance. *Herm.*

Out of the Blue
(ONE SONG)

Boston, Aug. 20.

Eagle Lion release of Bryan Foy production. Stars George Brent, Virginia Mayo; features Turhan Bey, Ann Dvorak, Carole Landis. Directed by Leigh Jason. Screenplay, Walter Bullock, Vera Caspary, Edward Eliscu; based on story by Miss Caspary; camera, Jackson Rose; editor Norman Colbert; song, Will Jason, Henry Nemo. Previewed at Brighton, Boston, Aug. 18, '47. Running time, **90 MINS.**

Deborah .... Virginia Mayo
Mr. Earthleigh .... George Brent
David .... Turhan Bey
Olive .... Ann Dvorak
Mrs. Earthleigh .... Carole Landis
Singer .... Hedda Brooks
Dombry .... Alton E. Horton
Elevator Boy .... Charlie Smith
Miss Ritchie .... Julia Dean
Miss Spring .... Elizabeth Patterson
Noonan .... Richard Lane

A curious film to figure, not quite making the grade as a screwball item yet catching a good if spotty reaction through the incongruity of George Brent, Ann Dvorak and Turhan Bey working out as comedians. Chances are it'll appeal to the urban trade and do well enough outside if properly coupled, as the names will get them in, and they'll hardly know whether they liked it or not. It's got laughs, but overall impressions will be plenty mixed.

The yarn presents Brent as a frau-dominated and generally willynilly guy living in a Greenwich Village apartment down the terrace from Bey, an artist with a big dog and a bigger appetite for models. Feud between them is touched off when the dog buries a bone in Brent's zinnias and Brent's wife (Carole Landis, fairly unrecognizable) forces him to try and oust the artist from the apartment.

During the weekend absence of his wife, Brent is picked up by an interior decorator (Ann Dvorak) whose interior is already well decorated with brandies, and, in a fit of wickedness, he invites her to his apartment. When she passes out he thinks she is dead, and stuffs her onto Bey's terrace. Obviously she comes to, and Bey, using Brent's guilt as a stratagem to call off the landlords, forces Brent to go through with a mock burial. Criss-cross farce from one apartment to the other follows. Brent, finally caught by his wife, worms the turn in time-honored fashion.

Brent, who seldom gets a chance to show how accomplished he really is in light comedy, easily holds up his end, but it is Miss Dvorak who wows as the screwball interior decorator. Reveals an entirely new side to a public that, if it hasn't exactly forgotten her, never remembers her in this sort of thing. Had the others fitted as neatly into their roles, outcome might have been quite different, but it is very hard to accept Bey without a turban, while Virginia Mayo registers only when she simulates a tough babe. Miss Landis, in a neutral role, remains merely decorative. There's some nice character stuff by Julia Dean and Elizabeth Patterson.

Story, though basically as sound as any of this style and sometimes offering sock situations, never quite makes up its mind whether it's a sophisticated bedroom farce or an out-and-out slapstick job. Tries at times for Lubitsch touches, so-called, at others for Thorne Smitheries, and at still others for the general agitation of the windup of a two-reel comedy. So it's only when the situations themselves are in the slot that it clicks; the rest is by no means above the timber line.

Production, though okay, is plainly economical, the opening sequence itself (the dog Rabelais coming through a stagey reproduction of the arch at Washington Square) setting the tone. *Elie.*

Flashing Guns

Monogram release of Barney A. Sarecky production. Stars Johnny Mack Brown; features Raymond Hatton. Directed by Lambert Hillyer. Screenplay, Frank H. Young; editor, Fred Maguire; camera, Harry Neumann. Reviewed at New York theatre, N. Y., Aug. 21, '47. Running time, 57 MINS.

Johnny	Johnny Mack Brown
Shelby	Raymond Hatton
Ann	Jan Bryant
Longden	Douglas Evans
Ainsworth	James E. Logan
Ripley	Ted Adams
Sheriff	Edmund Cobb
Foley	Norman Jolley
Dishpan	Ken Adams
Duke	Gary Garrett
Stirrup	Ray Jones
Sagebrush	Jack O'Shea
Cannon	Steve Clark
Judge	Frank LaRue
Cassidy	Jack Rockwell

"Flashing Guns" is a routine Monogram contribution to the action trade.

The story centers around Johnny Mack Brown's fight to save a heavily mortgaged ranch owned by Raymond Hatton from a crooked banker aligned with the town's gambling elements. Robbery, marked decks and forgery virtually deliver the homestead to the banking interests, but Mack's firstrate gunplay eliminates most of the baddies and, by digging up sufficient evidence of foulplay by the banker, the family roost is retained.

Brown is properly virile, and Hatton does a competent job. Jan Bryant, as the love interest, retains the tradition of westerners by being as obsequious as possible, while Douglas Evans and James Logan stand out among the villains.

The script, however, gives the impression of having been improvised as shooting progressed. Unnecessary complications come in to detract from the straight story line. Lambert Hillyer's direction is well paced, and Harry Neumann's outdoor photography is okay. *Jose.*

The Master of Bankdam
(BRITISH-MADE)
London, Aug. 20.

General Film Distributors release of Holbein-NA Bronsten production. Stars Anne Crawford, Dennis Price, Tom Walls; features Stephen Murray, Linden Travers. Directed by Walter Forde. Screenplay and adaptation by Edward Dryhurst from novel by Thomas Armstrong; additional dialog, Moie Charles. Music, Arthur Benjamin; camera, Basil Emmott, Arthur Grant. At Odeon, London, Aug. 20, '47.

Annie Pickersgill	Anne Crawford
Simeon Crowther	Tom Walls
Joshua Crowther	Dennis Price
Zebediah Crowther	Stephen Murray
Lydia Crowther	Nancy Price
Young Simeon	Jimmy Hanley
Lancelot Crowther	David Tomlinson
Clara Baker	Linden Travers
Lemuel Pickersgill	Patrick Holt
Tom France	Herbert Lomas
Ezra Hoylehouse	Edgar K. Bruce
Edgar Hoylehouse	Nicholas Parsons
Handel Baker	Raymond Rollett
Dr. Clough	Frank Henderson

Lengthy films being in vogue, this adaptation of a 900-page best-seller should make the grade in public opinion. Only fault for the U. S. market, which so often detracts from value of British pics, is the dialect, which is strong Yorkshire, vintage 1854. Plenty of dramatic action and unleashing of violent passions supply current appetite for such fare.

Story is set in small Yorkshire town, showing three generations, opening with tenacious father and two sons building up their wool mill from humble to highest position in the district. Antagonism is thinly veiled between the boys and when Joshua, the younger, marries a weaver's daughter his mother turns against him and persuades her husband to keep him in a subordinate capacity. Later both are made equal partners.

Zebediah marries a calculating young social climber and becomes mayor through building new hospital wing at the expense of the firm. Rift between the brothers widens, culminating in a brawl, after which Joshua dies, with many others, in collapse of a mill. The elder had assured his father the upper floor was safe for looms, but his attempt to suborn an architect is discovered. The old man dies before he can disinherit the son and Zebediah remains in control.

Each son has an heir, Simeon a credit to his father, Joshua, and Lancelot, the pampered, idler product of his mother's snobbery. Zebediah makes his own boy managing director, knowing Simeon is the better man, and goes to Vienna for treatment for heart disease. Word reaches him of a strike and imminent ruin caused by his wife and son's criminal extravagance. Returning in time to see his nephew bravely facing a desperate mob, he declares he will make him the master of Bankdam.

Of a generally excellent cast, outstanding performances are by Tom Walls, as the old millowner; Stephen Murray, as his unscrupulously efficient son, and Dennis Price, as the younger brother. Only thing marring Price's usual competence is his erratic accent, often lapsing into straight London tones. Anne Crawford looks almost too refined for her humble origin as Simeon's wife, but is meticulous over her dialect. Nancy Price as the boys' mother is well in the picture as the hardened product of the child-slavery conditions of that era. Jimmy Hanley and David Tomlinson make the grandsons the requisite opposites of temperament and grit, and supporting roles all well characterized.

Direction is concise and unruffled and on its merits alone, apart from fame as best-selling novel, film should attract popular support. *Clem.*

The Hatbox Mystery

Screen Guild release of Carl Hittleman production. Features Tom Neal, Pamela Blake, Allen Jenkins, Virginia Sale. Directed by Lambert Hillyer. Screenplay, Don Martin, Hittleman from original story by Maury Nunes, Hittleman; camera, Jim Brown; editor, Arthur Brown; music, Dave Chudnow. Reviewed at New York theatre, N. Y., Aug. 21, '47. Running time, 44 MINS.

Russ	Tom Neal
Susan	Pamela Blake
Harvard	Allen Jenkins
Veronica	Virginia Sale
District Attorney	Ed Keane
Stevens	Leonard Penn
Flint	William Ruhl
Joe	Zonn Murray
Mrs. Moreland	Olga Andre

"The Hatbox Mystery," inspired by an actual incident in which a small package hiding a sawed-off shotgun was used in an attempted murder, is designed to meet lower-half dual requirements. Streamlined 44-minutes contains the usual excitement quota of mystery fare.

Story centers about Tom Neal's often-idle detective agency where secretary Pamela Blake takes an assignment from a van-dyked gent to take a picture of what she believes to be a philandering wife. Supposed camera is contained in a hatbox and contains a gun, with the result that she's held for a murder rap. Neal, however, ultimately finds the culprit who engaged her and why, not trusting her aim, shot the victim himself from a building across the street.

The film has a fair degree of lighter moments with Allen Jenkins, who plays Neal's not-too-bright assistant, and Virginia Sale, as Jenkins' fiancee. Leonard Penn as the head malefactor does right by his role.

Lambert Hillyer's direction is fairly rapid, but the altogether good effect of the film is somewhat marred by the unnecessary end, in which there's a round of explanations for what is already obvious to the audience. *Jose.*

Miniature Reviews
"Dark Passage," (WB). Humphrey Bogart-Lauren Bacall team in a gory, but effective thriller, for sure returns.

"The Devil's Envoys" ("Les Visiteurs du Soir") (French) (Superfilm). Heavy dramatic legend, moderate for foreign houses, but not for regular runs.

"La Casa De La Zorra" (House of the Fox) (Filmex). Mexican-made social drama. OK for Spanish-language houses.

Dark Passage

Warners release of Jerry Wald production. Stars Humphrey Bogart, Lauren Bacall; features Bruce Bennett, Agnes Moorehead, Tom D'Andrea. Directed by Delmar Daves. Screenplay by Daves, from novel by David Goodis; camera, Sid Hickox; editor, David Weisbart; music, Franz Waxman. Previewed N. Y. Aug. 29, '47. Running time, 106 MINS.

Vincent Parry	Humphrey Bogart
Irene Jansen	Lauren Bacall
Bob	Bruce Bennett
Madge Rapf	Agnes Moorehead
Sam (Cabby)	Tom D'Andrea
Baker	Clifton Young
Detective	Douglas Kennedy
George Fellsinger	Rory Mallison
Dr. Walter Coley	Houseley Stevenson

The Bogart-Bacall team is still box-office. Sterling, sultry performances by the duo in a grim story that has plenty of killings and suspense, will more than offset the frequent slow pace and highly implausible story. Clever directorial bits, and some tricky lensing will also carry the pic over the far-fetched hurdles, and bring it into the money.

The film has a sharp, brutal opening; macabre touches throughout, and a thick, gruesome quality. What starts out as a thriller switches en route into a sagging, psychological drama, but recovers in time to give out with the satisfying gory stuff. Miss Bacall's charm and Bogart's ruggedness count heavily in a strange treatment of a murder story, which if it doesn't withstand scrutiny, does sustain mood and interest.

Scripting is superior and dialog frequently crackles. Direction is smart, with suggestion of the impressionistic approach. What begins as an apparent imitation of the "Lady in the Lake" technique, with the central figure speaking but not being visible to the audience, explains itself part way into the film in a clever fashion. Bogart isn't shown at the start because he's supposed to look like someone else. When a doctor has done a plastic surgery job on him to hide him from the police, and he looks the familiar Bogart, the point of his late appearance in the film is evident.

First actual appearance of Bogart, his face completely swathed in white bandages so that he looks like a mummy, has its own macabre appeal. Such smart touches abound in the film—the shadowy old Bogart lurking in a darkened cab; the hands of the convict gripping the drum at the start of the pic; the montage effect as Bogart comes out of the face operation.

Pic is a story of a man imprisoned on circumstantial evidence for the murder of his wife, his escape from jail, and the efforts of a girl to help him, because her father similarly had suffered unjust imprisonment. The man, on the lam from the cops, is involved with all sorts of characters—a garrulous, altruistic cabbie; a small-time blackmailer; the woman who actually killed his wife (and also bumped off his friend), and the strange art student who hid him from the police and befriended him. There is little rhyme or reason to much of what goes on, but pic's mood and performances hold the audience in suspense, even over the dull moments.

Miss Bacall, in a simple, unglamorous pose at the start, even then has a pleasant appeal, that hypoes intensely as soon as the old, sultry makeup and sexy charm are turned on. Bogart is impressive in something of a lacklustre character for him. Agnes Moorehead is sufficiently vicious as the discarded femme who turns killer, giving the film some of its most vivid moments in her big scene at the close. Tom D'Andrea's eccentric cabby study has warmth, and Clifton Young's shakedown role is effective. Bruce Bennett's part as the other fellow is routine, with Rory Mallinson's bit as Bogart's pal more definite.

Outdoor shots, of the San Francisco bridge, of long steps up winding streets, of apartment entrances and facades, make good pictorial material. Franz Waxman's music helps greatly to sustain the mood. Production is ample in a yarn that doesn't call for lavish outlay. *Bron.*

The Devil's Envoys

('Les Visiteurs du Soir')

Superfilm release of Andre Paulve production. Stars Arletty; features Jules Berry, Marie Dea, Alain Cuny; Fernand Ledoux. Directed by Marcel Carne. Screenplay, Jacques Prevert and Pierre Laroche. At Ambassador, N. Y., starting Aug. 29, '47. Running time, **118 MINS.**

Dominique .... Arletty
Devil .... Jules Berry
Anne .... Marie Dea
Baron Hugues .... Fernand Ledoux
Giles .... Alain Cuny
Le Bourreau .... Gabriel Gabrio
Chevalier Renaud .... Marcel Herrand
Le Gros Seignor .... Pierre Labry

Although it was made late in 1944, after the liberation, "The Devil's Envoys" has some of the basic characteristics of much of the dramatic entertainment produced in France during the Occupation. That is, the story is romantic legend and the theme is classic morality. In this instance, however, there is little contemporary significance in the yarn about two damned souls who return to earth to corrupt the human race, but remain long enough for one to be saved by a girl's love.

"The Devil's Envoys" is an interesting picture, but probably a trifle puzzling for average American audiences, and too vague and slow-moving for general popularity. It's hardly promising fare for regular run houses, but may do moderately in the arty spots. The picture won't be easy to exploit, either, as it has only low-wattage love interest, no spectacular dramatic or topical idea and no names familiar to the U. S. public.

Film's story is based on an old French legend. It is a sort of love-conquers-all version of the Good-versus-Evil theme, but isn't too well pointed or paced in the script. The early scenes, in which the two Devil's disciples arrive at the castle in time to entertain the banquet guests and presently disrupt the household, are promising. Some of the Devil's later scenes are amusing, too. But the yarn itself is slow and the direction further retards it. Also, the picture's closing scenes, in which the Devil is outwitted by the mortal girl, wander and have a letdown quality. Technically, the picture is about average for a French-made.

"The Devil's Envoys" has the same writer-director-star combination as "Les Enfants du Paradis" ("Children of Paradise"). In this production, Arletty again plays an enigmatic femme fatale, handling the assignment with skill and poise suggesting Hollywood possibilities. Jules Berry, as Satan, gives a standout character-comedy performance, revealing excellent range, flexibility and personal impact. The others are less notable, though Alain Cuny is acceptable as the lost soul saved by a girl's devotion, and Marie Dea is dramatically satisfactory as the mortal heroine.

The film's running time, just two minutes short of two hours, would profit by severe cutting. *Hobe.*

La Casa de la Zorra

('House of the Fox')

(MEXICAN-MADE)

Filmex production and release. Stars Ricardo Montalban, Virginia Fabregas, Susana Guizar; features Andora Palma, Isabela Corona, Andres Soler. Directed by Juan J. Ortega. At Belmont, N. Y., starting Aug. 29, '47. Running time, **90 MINS.**

(In Spanish; No English Titles)

Ricardo Montalban, who by this time is a lot better known to American audiences than when this was made, is the male star of this extremely wordy social drama. He had one of the leads in "Fiesta," and those who watched him in that Metro picture hardly will recognize his work in this earlier Mexican opus. The picture is stolen by Virginia Fabregas, as the foxy mother. Despite its talkiness, this Mexican-made film is okay for Spanish-language houses and possibly for some arty theatres if and when English titles are added.

Story centers around the notorious gambling casino or house operated by an elderly woman who is the fox of picture. Plot has her most concerned with the philanderings of her handsome, indolent son. Returning home from years in school, he soon is off on a drinking and gambling spree. The lad, Montalban, also never overlooks a comely femme, jumping from one affair to another. His early discovery that the boss behind the scenes at the luxurious casino is his mother prompts him to spend even more freely.

Yarn becomes a bit involved as he apparently falls madly in love with girl after girl. It's only when his amours step on family ties that a showdown develops. His mother, who felt that he had found the girl he finally was going to marry, straightens the whole affair out by stopping payment on the check she had given him as a wedding gift even though Montalban temporarily winds up in jail. There is a terrific scene in which his mother, Virginia Fabregas, goes on a binge and wrecks her own gambling casino in disappointment over her son's love affairs.

Obviously, Montalban evidences enough acting ability in this rather loosely-knit production to see why Metro picked him for a role. He's the harum-scarum son who finds that money fails to bring him happiness. Miss Fabregas is excellent in the heavy mother role. Susana Guizar, Andres Siler, Andora Palma and Isabela Corona are best in the supporting cast.

Juan J. Oretega's direction is much better than the story. Not too much is spent on production values here, most of coin apparently going to an unusually large cast. *Wear.*

Miniature Reviews

"Robin Hood of Texas" (Songs) (Rep). Topflight Gene Autry musical western; solid for spots that go for his pictures.

"Along the Oregon Trail" (Color-Songs) (Rep). Sagebrush tinter okay for Saturday matinee trade.

"Captain Boycott" (British) (GFD). Exciting historical yarn Stewart Granger. OK b.o. anywhere.

"The Silver Darlings" (British) (Pathe). Romantic drama of Scottish fishermen limited in appeal.

"The October Man" (British) (GFD). Smooth Eric Ambler meller; hefty grosser internationally.

Robin Hood of Texas

(SONGS)

Republic release of Sydney Picker production. Stars Gene Autry; features Lynne Roberts, Sterling Holloway, Adele Mara, Cass County Boys. Directed by Lesley Selander. Original screenplay, John K. Butler, Earle Snell; camera, William Bradford; editor, Harry Keller; songs, Gene Autry, Carson J. Robison, Sergio De Karlo, Kay Charles. Tradeshown N.Y., Sept. 5, '47. Running time, 71 MINS.

Gene Autry .... Gene Autry
Virginia .... Lynne Roberts
Droopy .... Sterling Holloway
Julie Reeves .... Adele Mara
Duke Mantel .... James Cardwell
Nick Castillo .... John Kellogg
Lacey .... Ray Walker
Jim Preston .... Michael Branden
Ace Foley .... Paul Bryar
Capt. Danforth .... James Flavin
Mrs. O'Brien .... Dorothy Vaughan
Mr. Hamby .... Stanley Andrews
Sheriff .... Alan Bridge
Themselves .... Cass County Boys

This new Gene Autry musical western comes close to upsetting the premise that all oat operas are alike. Film is not overboard on instrumental music nor Autry's singing, and for the most part goes along in slickest Autry tradition. Director Lesley Selander keeps the story moving logically, concentrating on fast action rather than inane dialog. This is in the groove for Autry fans, his best since returning from the service.

Cowboy picture scripters many times have tried ringing in a gangster angle with usual cattle-rustling theme but generally with unhappy results. Here John K. Butler and Earle Snell make four bank robbers and their gunmoll dovetail into Autry's newly-opened dude ranch and the western atmosphere logically. After the initial bank stickup and Autry's gang being innocently involved, the whole action is in and about this Serenity (Texas) Rest ranch.

Yarn finally focuses on the search for missing $100,000 taken in the bank holdup, with Autry, per usual, riding headlong after two bandits who are making off with the coin in the last reel. This gives the warbling western star a chance to stage a fist fight with the pair as the wagon careens down the road. Topflight stuff for a western.

He's the Autry of old, singing better than ever. He's best with the sentimental ballad, "You're the Moment of a Lifetime" and "Goin' Back to Texas." Other rather lilting tune is "Merry-Go-Round-Up." Cass County Boys make with solid instrumental music and singing to background the musical sequences. Lynne Roberts provides the slight romantic touch in okay manner but Adele Mara, as femme foil for the gangsters, provides the more torrid love sequences as she goes on the make for Autry. Sterling Holloway, cast as the shoe clerk who's worried about his health, provides the comedy moments and o.k. Ray Walter makes a plausible western detective. *Wear.*

Along the Oregon Trail

(COLOR—SONGS)

Hollywood, Sept. 6.

Republic release of Melville Tucker production. Stars Monte Hale, Adrian Booth; features Clayton Moore, Roy Barcroft, Max Terhune, Will Wright, Foy Willing and Riders of Purple Sage. Directed by R. G. Springsteen. Screenplay, Earle Snell; added dialog, Royal K. Cole; camera (Trucolor), Alfred S. Keller; music, Mort Glickman; songs, Foy Willing; editor, Arthur Roberts. Reviewed Sept. 3, '47. Running time, **64 MINS.**

Monte Hale .... Monte Hale
Sally Dunn .... Adrian Booth
Gregg Thurston .... Clayton Moore
Jake Stoner .... Roy Barcroft
Max .... Max Terhune
Jim Bridger .... Will Wright
Tom .... Wade Crosby
John Fremont .... LeRoy Mason
Driver .... Tom London
Kit Carson .... Forrest Taylor
Foy Willing and Riders of Purple Sage

"Along the Oregon Trail" carries formula plot along at action pace to satisfy moppet western fans. Lensed in Trucolor, film uses the stock yarn of the heavy who plots to hew an empire out of the early west but there are enough chases and gunplay to keep it moving.

Monte Hale is an okay hero in the action, portraying protege of Kit Carson who's called upon to guide party of Fremont's men opening up a trail to Oregon. He also tries his hand at two traditional songs, "Pretty Little Pink" and "Sweet Betsy from Pike." Foy Willing and the Riders of the Purple Sage combine on "Oregon" and "Along the Wagon Trail."

Clayton Moore heads up the villainy as the ambitious empire-builder. Chief henchman for the dirty work is Roy Barcroft. Pair steal rifles to arm Indians for uprising but Hale gets in his licks before any serious damage is done. Adrian Booth, femme star, shows up well among the action. Max Terhune tries for comedy and others are okay.

R. G. Springsteen directed the Melville Tucker production and Alfred S. Keller lensed. *Brog.*

Captain Boycott

(BRITISH-MADE)

London, Aug. 27.

General Film Distributors release of Individual Sidney Gilliat-Frank Launder production. Stars Stewart Granger, Kathleen Ryan; features Alastair Sim, Mervyn Johns, Noel Purcell, Cecil Parker, Nial McGinnis. Directed by Frank Launder. Screenplay by Frank Launder, Wolfgang Wilhelm, from novel by Philip Rooney; additional dialog, Paul Vincent Carroll, Patrick Campbell; music, William Alwyn; camera, Wilkie Cooper, Oswald Morris. At Odeon, London, Aug. 26, '47. Running time, **93 MINS.**

Hugh Davin .... Stewart Granger
Anne Killian .... Kathleen Ryan
Captain Boycott .... Cecil Parker
Watty Connell .... Mervyn Johns
Father McKeogh .... Alastair Sim
Daniel McGinty .... Noel Purcell
Mark Killian .... Niall McGinnis
Lieut. Col. Strickland .... Maurice Denham
Mrs. Davin .... Maureen Delaney
Sean Kerin .... Eddie Byrne
Martin Egan .... Liam Redmond
Michael Fagan .... Liam Gaffney
Mrs. Fagan .... Bernadette O'Farrell
Sergeant Demsey .... Edward Lexy
Robert Hogan .... Harry Webster
Times Correspondent .... Ian Fleming
American Reporter .... Reginald Purdell

This story of troubled Ireland in 1880 is off from the beaten track. From Philip Rooney's historical romance Frank Launder and Sidney Gilliat have fashioned a first-rate film, although some of the changes from the novel appear unnecessary.

Part of the picture was shot in Ireland, and the locations and native extras were chosen with a care and judgment reflected in the quality of the film. In addition to the marquee pull of Stewart Granger and the growing prestige and popularity of Kathleen Ryan, the production should earn plenty of word-of-mouth publicity. Business on it should be good, and there should certainly be a market in the U. S. for a film dealing with the troubles caused by the British in the bad old Imperialist days.

Story centres round Captain Boycott, whose surname was coined into the English language. Land agent to the Earl of Erne's Mayo estates, it's his duty to exact rents for the absentee British landlord. His slogan is "pay the rent or be evicted," and he is unmoved by pity, threats, or violence. In the end he is beaten by a strategem devised by Parnell, who advises a form of moral banishment.

But before his defeat, Boycott stirs up a newspaper agitation and obtains military protection for his volunteer farm workers. But it is a pyrrhic victory. He is bankrupt unless he can find ready money and to do this he evicts Hugh Davin, buys his steeplechaser for $20, and rides him in the big race on which he bets himself heavily to win. Just as he nears the winning post the enraged villagers invade the course and it's curtains for Boycott. As he rides away from Ireland, ruined and ashamed, the local priest tells his people they no longer have need of violence. "If anyone offends against the community you can ostracise him, you can isolate him, you can boycott him."

Since scant attention has been paid to history it is a pity that a little more tension was not engendered between the estranged lovers. Granger has compensatory scenes, but Miss Ryan has been sadly neglected.

Picture should give Granger a much-needed fillip and please his multitude of fans. Cecil Parker makes Captain Boycott a most credible and understandable figure, and Ireland's leading comic, Noel Purcell, misses nothing as a fire-eating schoolmaster agitator. Good actor as Alastair Sim is, he is still a Scot, and his humor is not that of the Irish parish priest. *Cane.*

The Silver Darlings
(BRITISH-MADE)

London, Sept. 4.

Pathe Pictures release of Holyrood Film-Karl Grune production. Stars Clifford Evans; features Helen Shingler. Directed by Clarence Elder. Screenplay by Clarence Eder, from novel by Neil Gunn; camera, Francis Carver, Paddy Vinten. At Studio One, London, Sept. 3, '47. Running time, **93 MINS.**

Roddy....Clifford Evans
Catrine....Helen Shingler
Angus....Carl Bernard
Hendry....Norman Shelley
Mrs. Hendry....Jean Shepherd
Don....Simon Lack
Tormad....Norman Williams
Tormad's Mother....Phyllis Morris
Finn....Murdo Morrison
Finn (child)....Christopher Capon
Bo'sun....Stanley Jay
Lieutenant....Harry Fine
Una....Josephine Stuart
Una (child)....Carole Lesley
Kirsty....Iris Vandeleur
Skipper Bremner....Jack Faint

Much conscientious labor has gone to the making of this film, and it's evident in every foot of it. What was needed was a dash of inspiration and a little imagination to make this work of a couple of years more acceptable to general audiences. As a documentary it is too sketchy and as fiction it is too conventional and packed with cliches.

Story is set a century ago in the Hebrides. Tormad, a crofter dispossessed of his holding, makes a precarious living herring fishing. His wife hates the sea and sees her foreboding come true when her husband is shanghaied into the Navy. She decides to move to another part of the country and make her home with an aunt. Here she meets Roddy, skipper of a fishing boat. From now on the love story is punctuated by the newly setup herring industry, an outbreak of cholera, the determination of the woman's son to be a fisherman, a storm or two, all ending in the final lovers' clinch.

Ingredients for an exciting picture are present, but somewhere along the line it became lost in the desire to show the rugged scenery and grandeur of the Scottish coast. Only faintly implied is the courage and tenacity of the crofters, a people of mountains and glens who tried to win a livelihood from a sea that held terror and catastrophe for them.

Clifford Evans gives a nice performance as the hero and Helen Shingler, a comparative newcomer, has her moments as wife and lover.

In spite of need for British pictures, "Silver Darlings" (nickname for herrings) will find the going hard here and is not likely to win any market in U. S. *Cane.*

The October Man
(BRITISH-MADE)

London, Aug. 29.

General Film Distributors release of Two Cities Film-F. Del Giudice production. Stars John Mills, Joan Greenwood; features Edward Chapman. Directed by Roy Baker. Screenplay by co-producer Eric Ambler. Music, William Alwyn; camera, Erwin Hillier, Russell Thomson. At Studio One, London, Aug. 28, '47. Running time, **93 MINS.**

Jim Ackland....John Mills
Jenny Carden....Joan Greenwood
Mr. Peachey....Edward Chapmab
Molly....Kay Walsh
Mrs. Vinton....Joyce Carey
Miss Selby....Catherine Lacey
Godby....Frederick Piper
Dr. Martin....Felix Aylmer
Joyce Carden....Adrianne Allen
Harry....Patrick Holt
Mr. Pope....George Benson
Miss Parsons....Ann Wilton
Wilcox....Jack Melford
Miss Heap....Esme Beringer
Troth....John Boxer

Author of many thrillers, Eric Ambler makes his debut as producer of his own script, and a fine beginning it is. With John Mills in top form and a grand all-round cast, this pic is due for hefty grosses here and should be well received in America.

Unlike the usual Ambler story, this is not a whodunit or spy story. It's a study of the conflict in the mind of a mentally sick man, not absolutely certain that he hasn't committed murder.

John Mills plays Jim Ackland, an industrial chemist who suffers from a brain injury following an accident in which the child of a friend is killed. He blames himself for the child's death, and develops suicidal tendencies. Released from hospital, he is warned of a possible relapse unless he takes things easy. He returns to work and lives in a suburban hotel inhabited by a small cross-section of the community—retired business men, fussy old women, young people struggling for a job—some well meaning and some viciously stupid.

Molly, a fashion model, is being ruthlessly pursued by Peachey, a retired wolf. He is anxious to pay her hotel bill, but in a tight corner she borrows a check from Jim, who has only met her once. The following day Molly is found murdered and Jim is suspected. From then on it is the police versus Jim until, finally escaping arrest, he tracks down the murderer.

This bare outline, which omits the somewhat superimposed love affair between Jim and Jenny Carden (Joan Greenwood), can't do justice to the development and treatment of the yarn, nor to the unusual angles. The dialog is taut and adult, and the direction by Roy Baker, onetime assistant to Hitchcock, is imaginative. Only defect is the tempo. For a suspense pic it sometimes lacks pace.

As a man haunted by fear and a prey to nerves, Mills gives a splendid performance. He makes use of every opportunity provided him in a fine part. Co-starr Miss Greenwood is less fortunate. She seems to have been an afterthought in Ambler's mind and is too sparingly used. Photographed better than in previous productions, she still has a certain stiffness about her acting and in her speech.

All the minor characters are exceptionally well played, and special praise is due to Catherine Lacey, Joyce Carey and Edward Chapman.

Title, which can have little selling value until the book is published, has an astrological reference. Presumably people born in October have among other qualities, a love of life, and so find it difficult to commit suicide. And Mills is an October man. *Cane.*

Foreign Films

"Maria" (SWEDISH). Sandrew Bauman Film release of Anders Sandrew production. Stars Maj-Britt Nilsson, George Fant; features Elof Ahrle, Stig Jaerrel, Georg Skarstedt, Ake Claesson, Agneta Prytz, Nils Hallberg. Directed by Goesta Folke. Screenplay, Sven Bjoerkman, based upon novel by Gustav Sandgren; music, Hakon von Eichwald; camera, Goeran Strindberg. At Royal, Stockholm. Running time, **88 MINS.**

Fine scripting and especially brilliant lensing give this film excellent prospects in Scandinavia, and it should do well abroad. Yarn, based upon a best-seller, deals with a young girl from the country who comes to Stockholm seeking to become a picture star—and succeeds. Performance of Maj-Britt Nilsson in the title role is one of the top femme thesping portrayals of the year.

"Krigsmans Erinran" ("Soldiers Reminder") **(SWEDISH).** Svensk Filmindustri production and release. Features Elof Ahrle, Birgit Tengroth. Gunnar Bjoernstarnd, Harriet Philipsson, Ivar Kage, Bengt Eklund, Sven-Eric Carlsson. Directed by Hampe Faustman. Screenplay, Herbert Grevenius, based on his own play; camera, Gunnar Fischer. At Skandia, Stockholm. Running time, **80 MINS.**

Last year's most successful Swedish play has emerged as a film of dubious quality. Elof Jahrle as Jocke, a soldier in 1940, contributes a brilliant performance. but his fine work can't save the picture. Camerawork is okay. Young, promising Harriet Philipsson is deserving of better roles. Pic's chances overseas are nil. It's strictly for the Scandinavian market.

"Tosen Fran Stormytorpet" (The Girl from the Marshcroft **(SWEDISH)** Kungsfilm release and production. Stars Alf Kjellin, Margareta Fahlen; features Ingrid Borthen, Ceve Hjelm, Oscar Ljung, Carl Stroem, Goesta Cederlund, Erik Berglund, Sten Lindgren, Sven d'ailly, Lil Hermelin, Anna Lennmalm. Directed by Gustav Edgren. Screenplay, Oscar Rydquist and Edgren based on novel by Selma Lagerlof; camera, Martin Bodin. At Palladium, Stockholm, Aug. 18. Running time, **106 MINS.**

Based on the late Selma Lagerlof's noted novel, "Tosen Fran Stormytorpet" is a good film that's headed for long runs in Scandinavia. Story originally hit the screen some 30 years ago as a silent and scripters found it necessary to expand the yarn somewhat to conform with the needs of modern filmmaking. Thesping, led by Alf Kjellin, is generally good. Lensing of Martin Bodin is especially worthy of mention. Film has a good chance in the world film market.

Miniature Reviews

"The Unsuspected" (WB). Mystery drama done in the Michael Curtiz manner. Good b.o.

"Ride the Pink Horse" (U-I). Tough melodrama plot hides under creampuff title. Exploitable for good returns.

"Exposed" (Rep). Adele Mara, Robert Armstrong in lesser whodunit; minor dualer.

"The Marriage of Ramuntcho" (color-songs) (French. (DPF) Romantic drama sure b.o. for all Latin countries.

"The Case of the Baby Sitter" (SG). Weak detective yarn, running only 41 minutes.

"Russian Ballerina" (Songs) (Russian) (Artkino). Story of Leningrad ballet okay for art situations.

The Unsuspected

Hollywood, Sept. 13.

Warner Bros. release of Michael Curtiz (Charles Hoffman) production; associate, George Amy. Stars Joan Caulfield, Claude Rains, Audrey Totter, Constance Bennett, Hurd Hatfield, Michael North; features Fred Clark, Harry Lewis, Jack Lambert. Directed by Michael Curtiz. Screenplay, Ranald MacDougall; adaptation, Bess Meredyth; from a story by Charlotte Armstrong; camera, Woody Bredell; music, Franz Waxman; editor, Frederick Richards. Tradeshown Sept. 11, '47. Running time, **103 MINS.**

Matilda Frazier....Joan Caulfield
Alexander Grandison....Claude Rains
Althea Keane....Audrey Totter
Jane Moynihan....Constance Bennett
Oliver Keane....Hurd Hatfield
Steven Francis Howard....Michael North
Richard Donovan....Fred Clark
Max....Harry Lewis
Mr. Press....Jack Lambert
Donovan's Asistant....Ray Walker
Mrs. White....Nana Bryant
Justice of the Peace....Walter Baldwin

"The Unsuspected" marks the initial Michael Curtiz production for Warners via his own unit. Mystery drama has class production, interesting development and is loaded with thrills and suspence. Boxoffice outlook is good. Cast names are familiar and performances sturdy.

Curtiz has packed yarn with plenty of rugged action thrills, despite society setting. Two chase sequences are especially humdingers for audience chills. Story deals with suave mayhem, with murderer Claude Rains known from the opening crime. Directorial tricks, lighting and mobile camera are strong in maintaining the atmosphere.

Plot workings are not as clear as they could have been but motivation of principal characters is followable as scripted by Ranald MacDougall from a Bess Meredyth adaptation of the Charlotte Armstrong story. Rains is seen as radio narrator of murder mysteries who's not above making his stories actually true. An apparently suave, kindly soul, he's unsuspected in the death of his secretary, niece and latter's husband. He meets his downfall, though, when he attempts to kill another niece and her boyfriend.

Rains pulls out all his thesping tricks to sustain the character, and makes it believable. Joan Caulfield is good as the rich, troubled niece who believes in her uncle's goodness. Audrey Totter and Hurd Hatfield show up well as the murdered pair, and Constance Bennett peps up assignment as a radio producer.

Picture introduces Michael North under the Curtiz banner. Young actor is not new to films, having worked under another name prior to the war. He makes a good impression as Miss Caulfield's friend, whose suspicions of Rains are finally responsible for justice being served. Fred Clark, Harry Lewis, Jack Lambert and others round out the good cast.

Charles Hoffman draws producer credit on the Curtiz production, with George Amy as associate.

Mounting is handsome, with tasty art direction and set decorations that give Woody Bredell's standout lensing a smooth physical target. Franz Waxman's music score is good. *Brog.*

Ride the Pink Horse

Hollywood, Sept. 12.

Universal-International release of Joan Harrison production. Stars Robert Montgomery; features Wanda Hendrix, Andrea King, Thomas Gomez, Fred Clark, Art Smith. Directed by Robert Montgomery. Screenplay, Ben Hecht, Charles Lederer; based on novel by Dorothy B. Hughes; camera, Russell Metty; music, Frank Skinner; editor, Ralph Dawson. Previewed in Hollywood Sept. 9, '47. Running time, **100 MINS.**

Gagin....................Robert Montgomery
Pancho....................Thomas Gomez
Carla....................Rita Conde
Maria....................Iris Flores
Pila....................Wanda Hendrix
Mr. Edison....................Grandon Rhodes
Bellboy....................Tito Renaldo
Jonathan....................Richard Gaines
Marjorie....................Andrea King
Bill Retz....................Art Smith
Barkeeper....................Martin Garralaga
Locke....................Edward Earle
Red....................Harold Goodwin
Elevator Girl....................Maria Cortez
Hugo....................Fred Clark

"Ride the Pink Horse" hides its tough melodrama under an odd title. It's a suspense thriller that features unconventional casting and sturdy performances. Story lends itself to exploitation that will be needed to garner good ticket sales.

Production has given thriller story a background that heightens suspense, and Robert Montgomery, in dual function of star and director, takes every advantage of plotting to hold spectator interest. The Ben Hecht-Charles Lederer script is nifty melodrama writing, and lays its story of violence against colorful fiesta background in a small New Mexico town.

Getaway has Montgomery arriving in the town on trail of war-profiteer who has had former's buddy knocked off. What the shootin's all about is foggy at first but gradually clears. Montgomery has a cancelled check that ties up the heavy with illegal profits. He hopes to sell the check but, after being knocked around by the villain's strongarm crew, he turns the evidence over to the law for windup.

Socko performance is turned in by Wanda Hendrix, as young Mexican girl who befriends the hero. Miss Hendrix has an appealing personality and abundant talent that gives the character of the adolescent girl warmth and interest. Also registering big is Thomas Gomez, operator of the merry-go-round with the pink horse from which picture gets its title. He gives a sustained portrayal that clicks.

Fred Clark is an unconventional heavy, wearing a hearing aid and personifying the average citizen. Another casting off beaten path is the G-man role performed by Art Smith. Both are excellent. Andrea King, femme heavy; Grandon Rhodes, Richard Gaines, Martin Garralaga, Tito Renaldo, Rita Conde, Iris Flores and others deliver competently.

The Joan Harrison production has a topnotch music score by Frank Skinner. Another major production factor is lensing by Russell Metty. Art direction, set decorations and other credits are strong. *Brog.*

Exposed

Republic release of William J. O'Sullivan production. Features Adele Mara, Robert Scott, Adrian Booth, Robert Armstrong, Harry Shannon. Directed by George Blair. Screenplay by Royal K. Cole and Charles Moran from original by Charles Moran; camera, William Bradford; editor, Irving M. Schoenberg. Tradeshown N. Y., Sept. 12, '47. Running time, **59 MINS.**

Belinda Prentice....................Adele Mara
Wm. Foreeman, 3rd....................Robert Scott
Judith....................Adrian Booth
Inspector Prentice....................Robert Armstrong
Iggy Broty....................William Haade
Chicago....................Bob Steele
Severance....................Harry Shannon
Jonathan Lowell....................Charles Evans
Emmy....................Joyce Compton
Colonel Bentry....................Russell Hicks
Professor Ordson....................Paul E. Burns
Dr. Richard....................Colin Campbell
Big Mac....................Edward Gargan
Miss Keets....................Mary Gordon
Waitress....................Patricia Knox

Never pretending to be anything more than a lesser meller, this whodunit from the Republic stables is OK entertainment. Picture obviously lacks marquee names which relegates "Exposed" to lower rung of average dualers where a short picture is needed.

This tale of a private crime investigator (this time a femme operative) contains the usual ingredients intended to baffle the audience until the last five minutes of screen time. And it succeeds fairly well. There's the usual slaying. Adele Mara (Belinda the investigator) is about to do her first checking on mysterious goings-on in an apartment when her new client is bumped off. After that it's merely a question of how many will die before Miss Mara uncovers the actual slayer. In between a bit too much dialog are the gunplay and fisticuffs between her heavy assistant and the gang's torpedo lad. Plot has the odd twist of making Robert Armstrong, as chief police inspector, also the father of investigator Mara.

Miss Mara continues to show cinema promise. William Haade does right by his part of tough aide to the feminine Sherlock. Armstrong is acceptable as the police official. Bob Steele, generally in cowboy roles, is the hardboiled gunman. Robert Scott, closest approach to the male lead, looks well but is no signal actor. George Blair's direction is passable if seldom original. *Wear.*

Le Mariage de Ramuntcho
(The Marriage of Ramuntcho)
(Color—Songs)
(FRENCH-MADE)

Paris, Sept. 4.

DPF release of Films de France (Anet Badel) production. Stars Gaby Sylvia, Andre Dassary and Frank Villard. Directed by Max de Vaucorbeil. Original story, Pierre Apesteguy; screenplay, Ernest Neubach; dialog, Andre Tabet; camera, Raymond Cluny; music, Marc Lanjean. Franco-Alfa-Color process. Assistant producers, Maurice Refregier and Yves Ducygne. At Gaumont Palace and Rex, Paris. Running time, **83 MINS.**

Maritchu....................Gaby Sylvia
Ramuntcho....................Andre Dassary
George....................Frank Villard
Barbara....................Anne Bruslay
Bartender....................Jean Hebey
Old Larramendy....................Maupi
Puntamento....................Jean Jacques Rouff
Ramuntcho's Sister....................Monique Delavaud
Carlos....................Arsenio Freygnac
Priest....................Gustave Lacoste
Jail Warden....................Lucien Callamand
Customs Officer....................Jacques Lemoine
Mrs. Maupi....................Daisy
Louise....................Mona Dol

This is the first tinter made in France, and the color is excellent. Film was made in the Basque country, on the Riviera, and studios de la Victorine, Nice. Lab work was done at Laboratories Eclair, at Epinay, near Paris.

Produced against considerable difficulties, resulting from bad weather on location, running short of raw stock, and problems involving alleged color experts, the picture was made for about $520,000. It is an unquestionable success. In France, it's a smash, and due to the locale and story, as well as the tuneful songs, a decided bet for all Latin countries. For England it is handled by the General Distributors branch of the Rank organization.

Lab work was made possible here because the Germans, during the occupation, installed the necessary equipment in Epinay for their own use and forgot to take it away when they left. When the producers ran short of raw stock, they had to buy whatever they could at fancy prices, in odd lengths. Finally, after attempting to shoot on location in the Basque country, the bad weather made a switch to the Riviera necessary.

Despite this, Max de Vaucorbeil has turned out a picture which has everything—colorful story that's easily understood; plenty of beautiful outdoor shots; enough love interest; tuneful songs, and novelty of color.

Yarn shows Andre Dassary, popular singer here in musical comedies, as a man of the Basque country, who like most of the men on the Pyrenees Spanish border, is engaged in contraband. His love for comely Gaby Sylvia strikes a temporary snag when Frank Villard, a handsome painter, falls for her when he tours the country. To win her he mixes also in contraband but when the custom officers catch the gang, bad man Jean Rouff wounds one of them and Dassary takes the rap and is jailed. Of course, he finally gets cleared and gets his gal, while Villard consoles himself by painting the beautiful countryside.

Dassary, as Ramuntcho, has a part which permits him to warble plenty. Gaby Sylvia is a very personable Maritchu, and Frank Villard, as the third corner of the triangle, gives an excellent account of himself. Balance of the cast is very good. Besides Anne Bruslay, Maupi as the old countryman and Jean Hebey as the bistro owner have good character parts.

Rouff is very convincing as a bad hombre, and both priest and jail warden, respectively done by Gustave Lacoste and Lucien Callamand, provide plenty comedy relief, helped by Andre Tabet's witty dialog. Jacques Lemoine, as the officer, is suitably dumb to be taken in by the contraband experts, while Monique Delavaud, Mona Dol and Daisy, as the local females, provide local color.

Director de Vaucorbeil, under very trying circumstances, has managed to draw all there could be from the simple story which is mostly a pretense to have tuneful music sung amidst beautiful scenery well brought out by the color process. He has wisely refrained from detracting attention from the main fare and abstained from an arty direction or queer camera angles which would have not been in keeping with the material. This self-effacement insures the picture a maximum mass appeal.

A couple of composer Marc Lanjean's tunes are likely to become very popular here. *Maxi.*

Case of the Baby Sitter

Screen Guild release of Maury Neunes production. Stars Tom Neal, Allen Jenkins; features Virginia Sale, Pamela Blake. Directed by Lambert Hillyer. Screenplay by Carl K. Hittleman and Ande Lamb; camera, Jim Brown; editor, Arthur Brooks. At New York theatre, N. Y., week Sept. 10, '47. Running time, **41 MINS.**

Russ....................Tom Neal
Howard....................Allen Jenkins
Veronica....................Virginia Sale
Susan....................Pamela Blake
Duke....................George Meeker
Duchess....................Rebel Randall
Silk....................Keith Richards
Maxine....................Lona Andre
Moore....................Crane Whitley

"The Case of the Baby Sitter" has little to recommend even for the bottom end of dualer programs. Running time of 41 minutes makes it seem like an elongated short subject but without the usual production care given to the briefies. Pic has been crudely assembled with deficient lighting, inferior camera work, and bare settings framing a weak screenplay.

Yarn concerns a pair of jewel thieves who hire a detective agency to watch their swag under guise of guarding their baby. Another gang, meanwhile, is trying to hijack the jewels, and after a series of unlikely coincidences, the culprits are unmasked just as they're about to bump off the private eye's girl friend.

Cast does as well as expected under the circumstances with Allen Jenkins turning in an okay performance as a comedy aide to Tom Neal, who plays the gumshoe in standard style. Rest of the cast grimace through stock parts. *Herm.*

Russian Ballerina
(SONGS)
(RUSSIAN-MADE)

Artkino release of Lenfilm production. Features Maria Redina, Vladimir Kazanovich. Directed by A. V. Ivanovsky. Screenplay, A. Erlich and Ivanovsky; camera, A. Kalsatl; dances, V. Ponomarev; songs, M. Dudin and V. Pozhdestvensky. At Stanley, N. Y., week Sept. 17, '47. Running time, **75 MINS.**

Natasha....................Maria Redina
Alexei....................Vladimir Kazanovich
Olga....................Nadia Yestrebova
Ballet Teacher....................Olga Zhizneva
Lubomirsky....................Vladimir Gardin

(In Russian; English Titles)

Despite the fact that anything Russian is in disfavor in many sections of the U. S., "Russian Ballerina" can be exploited into good boxoffice in metropolitan art and language situations.

In the exhibitor's favor is the absence of any political propaganda. Film may be sold also on the strength of its ballet aspects. Major portions of appeal lies in the excellent musical and ballet sequences. Terp enthusiasts will go all-out for the well staged and lengthy passages from Tschaikowsky's "Swan Lake" with Galina Ulanova as premiere ballerina, and "Sleeping Beauty" with Maria Redina of the Leningrad ballet in the lead role. For added strength in its cultural appeal, lead male role is by Vladimir Kazanovich who impresses with fine tenor work.

Film falls down in the story line, which is too thin to sustain interest on its own. Yarn is a familiar tale of a ballerina and a singer who overcome a major misunderstanding based upon disappointments in their careers as artists.

English subtitles fail to give the audience some credit for intelligence. Any non-linguist knows that "da" means yes, but even with head-wagging accompaniment that gets literal translation.

Performances by Miss Redina and Kazanovich are creditable. Miss Redina giving a note of piquancy in her thesping. Nadia Yestrobova and Vladimir Gardin provide staunch support. *Jose.*

Power Behind Nation
(INDUSTRY DOCUMENTARY)

With the blessing of Eric Johnston, Motion Picture Assn. prexy, who appears in a Technicolored intro, and the backing of the MPA, this is the first of the industry-documentaries on current U.S. subjects. Warner-made subject is being sent out with MPA backing because the association felt it illustrated how productivity was the power that made the U.S. the great nation it is today. Short (20 mins.) strives to show what makes the U. S. tick as a democracy.

"Power Behind the Nation" certainly is an improvement over many of the wartime documentaries that were supposed to sell the public a message. This subject never drags. While at times it may appear to wander a bit, ultimately it slips home the point without using the sledgehammer. Picture is constantly on the move in pointing up how cooperation, workmanship and productivity has built America to its present greatness. Because it covers all the many ramifications of a nation's productivity, the film could well be shown in some other countries where production activity is at low ebb.

Technicolor cameras here obviously have made a grand tour of countless industries, U. S. commerce and its leading cities, its forests, fields, prairies, rivers, lakes and ocean fronts. Subject tries to condense American accomplishments from early days up to the present. There's an intelligent roundup at the finish, showing that America today is united, laborer and executive, all creeds and racial groups combining to make it click.

Technically this is not Gordon Hollingshead's best effort in this field. Perhaps that was because he attempted to show too much in the limited footage. In fact, there seems an excess in shifting of scene, and some of these do not appear to be closely related. Saul Elkins' written narration fits the subject matter nicely but Art Gilmore's narration is too much on the breathless side. Music by William Lava is superb as is the color. *Wear.*

Miniature Reviews

"Unconquered" (Color) (DeMille-Par). Prodigious size and cast insure strong boxoffice for this $4,000,000 spec.

"Bury Me Dead" (EL). Above-average supporting film. Fair grosser.

"Foxes of Harrow" (20th). Rex Harrison, Maureen O'Hara in filmization of Frank Yerb's novel; fairly sturdy boxoffice.

"My Father's House" (Indie). Palestine-made feature only mildly interesting.

"Schoolgirl Diary" (Indie) (Italian). Italian-made comedy-drama of a girls' school, with Valli starred; strong arty theatre entry.

"Marco Visconti" (Indie). Italian-made period meller with nice appeal for art house patrons.

Unconquered

Paramount release of Cecile B. DeMille production, directed by DeMille. Stars Gary Cooper, Paulette Goddard; features Howard DaSilva, Boris Karloff, Ward Bond, Cecil Kellaway. Screenplay, Charles Bennett, Fredric M. Frank, Jesse Lasky, Jr., based on novel by Neil H. Swanson; score, Victor Young; camera (Technicolor), Ray Rennahan; special photography, Gordon Jennings, Paul Perpae, Devereux Jennings, Farciot Edouart; asst. director, Edward Slaven; dialog director, Robert Foulk; editor, Anne Bauchens; dances, Jack Crosby. Tradeshown in New York, Sept. 18, '47. Running time, 135 MINS.
Captain Christopher Holden....Gary Cooper
Abby Hale................Paulette Goddard
Martin Garth..............Howard DaSilva
Guyasuta..................Boris Karloff
Jeremy Love................Cecil Kellaway
John Fraser...................Ward Bond
Hannah................Katherine DeMille
Captain Steele............Henry Wilcoxon
Lord Chief Justice.....Sir C. Aubrey Smith
Capt. Simeon Ecuyer.......Victor Varconi
Diana..........................Virginia Grey
Leach..........................Porter Hall
Dave Bone......................Mike Mazurki
Col. George Washington....Richard Gaines
Mrs. John Fraser........Virginia Campbell
Lieut. Fergus McKenzie......Gavin Muir
Sir William Johnson..........Alan Napier
Mrs. Pruitt................Nan Sunderland
Sioto.......................Marc Lawrence
Evelyn..........................Jane Nigh

Cecil B. DeMille's "Unconquered" is a $4,000,000 Technicolor spectacle which will make money on its size, epochal pretentiousness and strong cast headed by Gary Cooper and Paulette Goddard. It's a pre-Revolutionary western with plenty of Injun stuff which, for all the vacuousness and shortcomings, has its gripping moments. "Unconquered" is the type of film which, contradictorily, doesn't stand analysis and yet will get and interest the customers.

Paramount knows best of any that this "epic" requires plenty of selling. But that very selling—and an extensive exploitation campaign it is, too, from the intra-trade viewpoint—will get "Unconquered" over the hump. The producer-director is going out on the missionary campaign himself, and the Par ballyhooists are giving this one the all-out gun.

Like David O. Selznick's "Duel in the Sun," this one is so un-DeMille it's surprising. But, like "Duel," it will get business. As a spec it has sufficient size and scope to command plenty of b.o.

The redskins are ruthless scalpers and the British colonials alternately naive and brave, patriotic and full of skullduggery to give substance to the melodramatic heroics and knavery of the most derring-do school. When Cooper and Miss Goddard stay a death-dance ritual and escape over the treacherous falls, the customers will have to call forth their best Dick Tracy attitude. But when the brave colonials are hemmed in their stockades and surrounded by Comanches, Senecas and Pontiacs, there's nothing sweet-Sioux about those scenes.

Howard DaSilva is the arch-knave whose marriage to Injun chief

Boris Karloff's daughter (Katherine DeMille) puts him plenty in the black with the redskins on fur-trading and the like. Miss Goddard is the proud slave-girl whose freedom Cooper purchases on the British slaveship, only to cross paths with the heavy, DaSilva, and his No. 2 menace, Mike Mazurki.

It's not generally known that in that 1763 period English convicts had the alternative of being sold into limited slavery in the American colonies. Although a bond slave, Miss Goddard spurns DaSilva and sufficiently attracts Cooper to make for a romantic angle. All this is silhouetted against the siege of Fort Pitt, the daring pioneering of Cooper and the luscious-looking Miss Goddard, who conveniently finds party dresses in the Pennsylvania-Ohio jungles to properly scintillate when the king's birthday ball calls for a little sartorial splendor against the otherwise standard Daniel Boone backgrounds. In fact there's even a characteristic DeMille bath scene, albeit a bit on the road-company side, as she takes a primitive tub, but, none the less, the trademarked ablutions take place. Just for a little s.a. fillip, Cooper is the one who administers the bath.

Despite the ten-twent-thirt meller-dramatics and the frequently inept script, the performances are convincing, a great tribute to the cast because that dialog and those situations try the best of troupers.

Along with the hokey scripting the major fault revolves around the pace and tempo, which some judicious cutting could have solved. Some 2¼ hours of "chase," can be a little too much for the hardiest of city-slicker western addicts. *Abel.*

Bury Me Dead

Eagle Lion release of Charles F. Reisner production. Features Cathy O'Donnell, June Lockhart, Hugh Beaumont, Mark Daniels. Directed by Bernard Vorhaus. Screenplay, Karen deWolf, Dwight V. Babcock; based on story by Irene Winston; camera, John Alton; editor, W. Donn Hayes. Tradeshown N. Y., Sept. 22, '47. Running time, 68 MINS.
Rusty....................Cathy O'Donnell
Barbara Carlin.............June Lockhart
Michael Dunn.............Hugh Beaumont
Rod Carlin...................Mark Daniels
George Mandley............Greg McClure
Waters.......................Milton Parsons
Mrs. Haskins...........Virginia Farmer
Helen Lawrence.............Sonia Darrin
Archer.........................Cliff Clark

With "Bury Me Dead," Eagle Lion has a film that's several notches above the usual run of supporting situation film. It will also get a quota of word-of-mouth by virtue of a few sides of racy dialog. Despite a complicated method of story-telling, through a series of flashbacks and frequently unnecessary departures from the straight story line, there's a good degree of interest and excitement.

"Bury" is a break from the usual whodunit, starting witht June Lockhart's sudden appearance on the day of her funeral. With the aid of the family attorney, she intends to find out if someone attempted to murder her, and the identity of the one buried under her name. Virtually everyone in the cast, including her sister, Cathy O'Donnell, and Miss Lockhart's husband, Mark Daniels make for prime suspects, but eventually the hatchet man is correctly cased.

One item that will make audiences sit up is an amazingly frank bit of dialog in which Miss O'Donnell tells her sister's husband of her efforts to wreck their marriage. Explaining her attention to another man, she tells that the other party was only a transference — "You're the one that's locked deep down in my libido." Some added boxoffice usually results from such verbiage.

Cast is uniformly good with Miss Lockhart doing a competent job in the lead role, while Miss O'Donnell as the adolescent sister, on the verge

of being a psycho, does commendably. Mark Daniels lends a deal of warmth and considerable ease to the role of husband and Hugh Beaumont gives a good characterization as the family attorney. The slight comedy requirements are filled by Greg McClure.

Except for some intrusions of unnecessary flashbacks, film's pacing is good. Direction of Bernard Vorhaus gets around some implausible situations handily and hide some defects in the screenplay. *Jose.*

The Foxes of Harrow

20th-Fox release of William A. Bacher production. Stars Rex Harrison, Maureen O'Hara; features Richard Haydn, Victor McLaglen, Patricia Medina, Vanessa Brown, Gene Lockhart. Directed by John M. Stahl. Screenplay by Wanda Tuchock, based on novel by Frank Yerby; camera, Joe La Shelle; special effects, Fred Sersen; editor, James B. Clark. Tradeshown N. Y., Sept. 22, '47. Running time, 115 MINS.
Stephen Fox...............Rex Harrison
Odalie................Maureen O'Hara
Andre.....................Richard Haydn
Mike Farrel..............Victor McLaglen
Aurore....................Vanessa Brown
Desiree.....................Patricia Medina
The Vicomte................Gene Lockhart
Sean Fox....................Charles Irwin
Otto Ludenbach................Hugo Haas
Master of Harrow............Dennis Hoey
Tom Warren..................Roy Roberts
St. Ange..................Marcel Journet
Achille............Kenneth Washington
Zerline....................Helen Crozier
Josh.......................Sam McDaniel
Angelina...................Libby Taylor
Little Inch..................Renee Beard
Tante Caleen.............A. C. Bilbrew
Belle.......................Suzette Harbin
Etienne Fox.........William (Bill) Ward

"The Foxes of Harrow" is an elaborate filmization of Frank Yerby's novel. Invested with the polished direction of John M. Stahl, it builds into a powerful drama of an adventurer's rise to fame and fortune in New Orleans of the 19th Century. Exciting story has strong production, vivid developments and helped along with excellent pace most of the time. With the names of Rex Harrison and Maureen O'Hara as main marquee decoration, picture should do quite ok at the boxoffice.

Technically, "Foxes" runs too long. It contains passages at the outset and near the end that appear superfluous, and would have snapped up the action if liberally pruned. But because there are so many meaty scenes, even the more tedious ones overflow with nice performances.

Harrison, the child born out of wedlock, rises to the heights in New Orleans business even though his first money is won gambling. Plot shows Harrison being put off a Mississippi steamboat for cheating at cards but being rescued from a sandbar by Victor McLaglen, captain of a pigboat. Harrison's audacity both at cards and with women catapult him to riches. His main ambition is to build another Harrow estate like his mother had known in Ireland. He finally persuades Maureen O'Hara, daughter of one of New Orleans' aristocrats, to become his wife. A quarrel on their wedding night produces a bitterness that lasts for more than three years, even though Harrison and his wife adore their only child.

There is a background of voodooism that brings in a lot of extras and drumbeating but often is too forced and extraneous for real effectiveness. One passage where one of the slaves on Harrow's plantation declaims that her newborn is not going to grow up into slavery, but be a warrior son, is likely to run into difficulties in many Southern states.

Withal Miss O'Hara and Harrison build a powerful yarn about a twisted marriage that finds satisfactory solution only after the latter has lost everything in a financial crackup. Harrison is perfect as the suave gambler whose sole ambition is to rise to power and wealth, and have the comely Miss O'Hara as his wife. Latter carries the highly dramatic scenes with surprising skill, but it seems a pity that she is not permitted to smile more often.

Richard Haydn, as Harrison's first-found friend in New Orleans, is excellent as the southern dandy While Vanessa Brown does all right as Miss O'Hara's sister albeit having little to do. McLaglen is the rough-neck riverboat captain whose crew is largely to blame for starting Harrison's marriage off on a sour note. Patricia Medina makes an acceptable lady-of-the-evening. Gene Lockhart's portrayal of the aristocratic father also is outstanding. Renee Beard, small colored lad, makes something of a lesser role while Hugo Haas, Dennis Hoey and Roy Roberts top a long, well-picked supporting cast.

Aside from Stahl's fine direction, Joe La Shelle rates a bow for strong lensing. *Wear.*

My Father's House

(PALESTINE-MADE)

Independent release of Herbert Kline and Meyer Levin production, directed by Kline from screenplay by Levin. Camera, Floyd Crosby; editor, Peter Elgar. Previewed in N. Y., Sept. 17, '47. Running time, **85 MINS.**

David	Bonnie Cohen
Miriam	Irene Broza
Avram	Isaac Danziger
Abba	Herman Heuser
Yehuda	Joseph Pacovsky
Smulik	Zalman Leiviush
Walter	R. Klatchkin
Nahama	Miriam Laserson
Zev	I. Finklestein
Shulamith	Israela Epstein
Maccabee	Michael Cohen
Dvora	Naomi Salzberger
Weisbrod	P. Goldman
Jamal	Y. Adaki
Mustafa	Josef Saadia

First full-length feature ever to be completely shot in Palestine, "My Father's House" unfortunately is considerably more commendable in idea and effort than in finished product. It tells an excellent and compassionate fictionalized story against the background of the present-day Holy Land and the Jews' struggles and triumphs there. As it comes through, however, much of the considerable potential for emotional impact is lost in a welter of amateurish acting and directing. Its principal interest now lies in occasional scattered scenes.

Picture was partially financed by the Jewish National Fund, which is sponsoring its showing in this country. No release has been set, with the probability that distribution will be limited to spot bookings obtained by Albert Margolies, who is handling it for the JNF. It opens this week at the Ambassador, N. Y., under such an arrangement.

Film was shot with Hebrew-speaking actors, but has been very skillfully dubbed in English in Hollywood, where it was edited. It cost about $250,000 to produce, with Herbert Kline and Meyer Levin, who produced it, supplementing JNF coin with some of their own funds. Unless the JNF sponsorship can succeed in efforts to make block sales of tickets to Jewish groups, unions, lodges, etc., it appears to have scant chance of winning back its nut.

Although not planned that way, getting back its production cost probably would have been a secondary consideration had the film been a first-class propaganda job. As it is, it smears on so thickly the pleasant aspects of Palestinian life for the Jews that it becomes virtually unbelievable. The Jews all love each other, the Arabs love the Jews, the Jews love the Arabs, the British don't exist, and everybody's just having a dandy time. [Would it were so.]

Yarn by Levin is topnotch, as was evidenced by the splendid reviews by the literateurs over the weekend for the novel (of the same title) devised by the author from his original screenplay. It's the story of an 11-year-old refugee boy whose father tells him, before the family is dragged off to a Nazi camp, that they will meet again in Palestine. Lad finally gets to the Holy Land and, against the prevailing of adults fully aware his family is dead, insists on following one false lead after another in his search for "my father's house."

Actors are all amateurs or semi-pro. Kline, as director, has completely failed to get anything out of them but wholly amateur results. Rather than the asset of rugged realism which is occasionally obtained from untrained talent—such as in the current Italian pix, "Open City" and "Shoe Shine"—the acting here devoids the story of meaning.

Backgrounds and photography are generally excellent, with the editing spotty.

Two shorts have also recently been produced in Palestine and made available for U.S. bookings. They are "Home in the Desert" and "Assignment: Tel Aviv." Produced by Palestine Films, Inc., they're sponsored by United Palestine Appeal. *Herb.*

Schoolgirl Diary

(ITALIAN-MADE)

Film Distributor release of Manenti Film production. Stars Valli; features Irasema Dilian, Andrea Checchi, Giuditta Rissone, Carlo Campanini. Directed by Mario Mattoli. Story and screenplay, Mario Mattoli; camera, Jan Stallich; editor, Ferdinando Tropea. Previewed in N. Y., Sept. 19, '47. Running time, **91 MINS.**

Anna	Valli
Maria	Irasema Dilian
Prof. Marini	Andrea Crecchi
Principal	Giuditta Rissone
Miss Mattei	Ada Dondini
Campanelli	Carlo Campanini
Maria's Father	Sandro Ruffini
Campolmi	Nino Micheluzzi
Luisa	Bianca dell Corte
Miss Bottelli	Olga Solbelli
Marcella	Giuliana Pitti
Teresa	Tatiana Farnese
Music Teacher	Dedi Montano
Carla	Diana Franci

(In Italian; English Titles)

"Schoolgirl Diary," which won first prize at the Venice Film Festival, is one of the better productions to come from the Italian studios. Forthright direction and superb performance, not only by the stellar players but supporting cast, go far in overcoming a none-too-original story and a laggard pace. Film is a bet for arty theatres, and Italian-language houses.

Valli, who has one of the principal roles in this story of a girls' finishing school, has, since making this pic, been signatured by David O. Selznick. She appears a find but, oddly enough, Irasema Dilian, her rival in this vehicle, shapes up as having equally strong screen possibilities. Both contribute fine portrayals.

Valli is a selfish, domineering schoolgirl. As head of a select sorority, she makes her presence felt in every classroom. Fact that her father is a millionaire gives her sufficient assurance to bluster her way through many escapades. Flunking in Latin, mathematics and chemistry, she thinks up many ways to make life uncomfortable for Miss Dilian, who's unassuming but a smart student and willing to follow school rules without trying to dominate her classmates.

Plot ascends to a climax when Valli falls madly in love with Andrea Checchi, her chem professor, only to suspect that the Dilian girl is making more progress with her teacher. When Valli and her friends discover Miss Dilian in a man's arms out in the garden late at night, they suspect the professor. It's all straightened out but not before scripter Mario Mattoli has dragged in a blood-transfusion scene, with Valli donating to save her rival's life.

The scene in which the Dilian miss is pictured fleeing the school in a driving rainstorm is perhaps the only one in which skimpiness of production values is visible. The gal apparently passes the same spot nearly three times before she falls off a ledge and is seriously injured.

Checchi impresses with his clipped manner of speaking and general deportment as the instructor. Giuditta Rissone gives a smart performance as the principal, while Carlo Campanini chips in with a fine comic character role as the professor's assistant. Nino Micheluzzi, cast as Valli's talkative father, is outstanding among supporting characters.

Mattoli did considerably better as director than as original story writer and scripter. Appears to be a case of one man trying to do too many things on the production line, with the story suffering. Ferdinando Tropea failed to use the shears often enough in editing. *Wear.*

Marco Visconti

(ITALIAN-MADE)

Film Rights International release of Lux production. Stars Carlo Ninchi; features Mariella Lotti, Roberto Villa, Alberto Capozzi. Directed by Mario Bonnard. Based on novel by Thomas Grossi; camera, Mario Albertelli; music, Giulio Bonnard; English titles, Herman Weinberg. At Cinema Verdi, N. Y., week Sept. 19, '47. Running time, **110 MINS.**

Marco Visconti	Carlo Ninchi
Bice del Balzo	Mariella Lotti
Ottorino Visconti	Roberto Villa
Lodrisio Visconti	Alberto Capozzi
Oldrado del Balzo	Guglemo Barnabo
Tremacoldo	Ernesto Almirante
Pelagrua	Mario Gallina
Lupo	Augusto di Giovanni

(In Italian; English Titles)

Lavishly decked-out period melodrama, "Marco Visconti" will merit a nice draw in the foreign language theatre circuit. Film has an operatic plot based on medieval love and jealousy which is handled by a troupe of leading Italian actors in the grand style. Starting at leisurely pace, pic gathers momentum as it progresses to a powerful denouement. Slicing of about 15 minutes from the long running time would correct an uneven quality evident in the early reels. Otherwise, direction, photography, editing and background music are handled with deftness typical of best Italian postwar productions. English titles by Herman Weinberg suffice for fluent following of action.

Set in Milan during the Middle Ages, yarn revolves around conflict between Marco Visconti, leader of the Milanese militia, and his youthful cousin for the hand of a beauteous noblewoman. Twenty years earlier, Visconti had been in love with the girl's mother who was forced by her family to wed another. In background of this triangle, another cousin, scheming for political power, to a blinding hatred of his cousin who formerly was his protege.

Against this framework, film exploits its chances for drama and color to the hilt. Among the standout sequences is a jousting tournament in full array, between the two rivals which is executed with brilliant eye-appeal and emotional sock. In an exciting horse opera windup in which the gal is rescued from the villain's clutches in the nick of time, Marco Visconti, the real hero of the piece, is killed by his perfidious cousin and the young lovers are reunited.

Carlo Ninchi, as Marco, is responsible for most of the pic's credibility by virtue of a powerful performance. Mariella Lotti, as the girl, is sweet and pretty but Robert Villa, while turning in a good performance as the young cousin, lacks the stature for the role. Albert Capozzi, as the villainous relative, mugs slightly in the beginning, but as the plot unfolds, steadies into a solid portrayal. *Herm.*

Miniature Reviews

"Desire Me" (M-G). Postwar story, laid in Normandy, must depend upon Greer Garson and Robert Mitchum to draw.

"The Wistful Widow of Wagon Gap" (U). Abbott & Costello in western comedy with Marjorie Main. Good b. o. prospects.

"The Gangster" (Mono). Another psychological melodrama with fair prospects on strength of title.

"Dick Tracy Meets Gruesome" (RKO). Karloff and Ralph Byrd in new adventure of cartoon strip character; fair dualer.

"Le Diable Au Corps" (French). (U). Romantic tragedy surefire French click; controversial story may limit U. S. draw.

"Midnight in Paris" (Indie). Inferior French-made whodunit starring Raimu.

Desire Me

Hollywood, Sept. 25.

Metro release of Arthur Hornblow, Jr., production. Stars Greer Garson; features Robert Mitchum, Richard Hart. Screenplay, Marguerite Roberts and Zoe Akins; adaptation, Casey Robinson; from novel by Leonhard Frank; camera, Joseph Ruttenberg; score, Herbert Stothart;; editor, Joseph Dervin. Tradeshown Sept. 25, '47. Running time, **90 MINS.**

Marise Aubert	Greer Garson
Paul Aubert	Robert Mitchum
Jean Renaud	Richard Hart
Martin	Morris Ankrum
Father Donnard	George Zucco
Dr. Andre Leclair	Cecil Humphreys
Postman	David Hoffman

"Desire Me" has a doubtful box-office future. Returns will lean heavily on amount of exploitation given femme angles of story and the draw factor of the Greer Garson name. Growing b.o. importance of Robert Mitchum also will aid.

Against the technical excellence of mounting, a confused flashback plot is unfolded. Offered is a story of a wife who, after long years of faithful waiting, succumbs to lonesomeness on the eve of her supposedly dead husband's return from war. The husband kills his rival in a struggle and when the wife rids herself of the psychological barrier of her unfaithfulness the pair are again together for the finale. Locale is a small fishing village on the coast of Normandy and catches interest with colorful settings and seascapes.

Flashbacks within flashbacks make plot hard to follow as the wife talks over her story—and what caused it—with a doctor. There is no director credit, picture having had several during its long camera career, so kudos for some topnotch atmospheric effects, a number of strong, emotional scenes and occasional suspense go uncredited. George Cukor started it and Mervyn LeRoy finished it, but neither wants the credit apparently. Otherwise pace is slow and interest slack.

Miss Garson's role requires continual emotional stress that makes for a heavy job but she is capable. Mitchum has too little footage as the husband, appearing briefly in the beginning during a prison camp sequence and again in the final reel, but he makes every scene count. Richard Hart, the betrayer of the faithful wife, is permitted to overstress his designs where underplaying would have aided. George Zucco, a priest; Morris Ankrum, Cecil Humphreys and David Hoffman make up the other capable players.

The Arthur Hornblow, Jr., production has been strikingly photographed by Joseph Ruttenberg and effectively scored by Herbert Stothart. Other technical credits are in keeping. *Brog.*

The Wistful Widow of Wagon Gap

(SONG)

Hollywood, Sept. 27.

Universal release of Robert Arthur production. Stars Bud Abbott, Lou Costello, Marjorie Main; features George Cleveland, William Ching, Gordon Jones. Directed by Charles T. Barton. Screenplay, Robert Lees, Frederic I. Rinaldo, John Grant; based on story by D. D. Beauchamp and William Bowers; camera, Charles Van Enger; music, Walter Shumann; editor, Frank Gross. Previewed Sept. 26, '47. Running time, **77 MINS.**

Duke Egan.......................Bud Abbott
Chester Primm...................Lou Costello
Widow Hawkins...................Marjorie Main
Juanita Hawkins.................Audrey Young
Judge Benbow....................George Cleveland
Jake Frame......................Gordon Jones
Jim Simpson.....................William Ching
Phil............................Peter Thompson
Undertaker......................Olin Howlin
Mat Hawkins.....................Bill Clauson
Billy Hawkins...................Bil O'Leary
Sarah Hawkins...................Parmela Wells
Jefferson Hawkins...............Jimmy Bates
Lincoln Hawkins.................Paul Dunn
Sally Hawkins...................Djane Florentine
Hank............................Rex Lease
Lefty...........................Glenn Strange
Lem.............................Edmund Cobb
Squint..........................Wade Crosby
Miner...........................Dewey Robinson
Bartender.......................Murray Leonard

Abbott & Costello ride herd on plenty of laughs in "The Wistful Widow of Wagon Gap." Team makes the most of the funning and will please fan following, all of which makes boxoffice outlook shape up well. Aiding antics is Marjorie Main who gives added marquee strength.

There's a good plot premise on which to hang the comedy and as a result the high spots are more substantial. Story is woven around old Montana law that makes any person killing another in a duel responsible for the victim's dependents and debts. Script brings in all the western situation cliches for A&C to work over. There's the terse "when you say that, smile" and the gunman's long death walk down a deserted street, plus other familars. Sometimes, material gets out of hand but slow spots are few and overall pace maintained by Charles T. Barton's direction is good.

A&C, travelling salesmen in the early west, enter the lawless town of Wagon Gap. Costello gets involved in a killing and is made the guardian of the victim's widow, Marjorie Main, and her passel of kids. Because the widow is such a fright, the town's toughies steer clear of Costello for fear they might have to take her over if the guardian is bumped off. Costello is made sheriff and clears the town of the villains. After many hilarious adventures, Costello is finally freed of his obligation and takes off with his partner for California.

Comics have revived their socko frog-in-the-soup gag for results that register high on the laugh-meter. Costello's bravado as the strutting sheriff. Abbott's wily use of his partner's dumbness, Miss Main's blowzy appeal and brazen courting of the fat comic are all credit factors pointing up the fun. Audrey Young sings one song in saloon sequence but otherwise has little to do. George Cleveland, Gordon Jones, William Ching and others furnish good support.

Robert Arthur's production guidance lends neat touches. Lensing by Charles Van Enger, art direction and settings, editing and other credits are expert. *Brog.*

The Gangster

(SONG)

Hollywood, Sept. 26.

Monogram release of Allied Artists production, produced by Maurice and Frank King. Stars Barry Sullivan, Belita, Joan Lorring; features Akim Tamiroff. Directed by Gordon Wiles. Original screenplay, Daniel Fuchs, from his novel, "Low Company"; camera, Paul Ivano; music, Louis Gruenberg; editor, Walter Thompson. Previewed Sept. 24, '47. Running time, **82 MINS.**

Shubunka........................Barry Sullivan
Nancy...........................Belita
Dorothy.........................Joan Lorring
Nick Jammey.....................Akim Tamiroff
Shorty..........................Henry Morgan
Karty...........................John Ireland
Cornell.........................Sheldon Leonard
Mrs. Ostroleng..................Fifi D'Orsay
Mrs. Karty......................Virginia Christine
Oval............................Elisha Cook, Jr.
Swain...........................Theodore Hecht
Beaumont........................Lief Erickson
Dugas...........................Charles McGraw
Sterling........................John Kellogg

Title strength will go a long way in selling "The Gangster" to the melodrama trade just as did with the King Bros. previous "Dillinger." Otherwise film fails to live up to promise of violent action and proves a disappointment. Because it bears the Allied Artists label, it is due for extra push from Monogram in setting bookings but will need plenty of support to maintain a good pace. It has been given realistic settings for its tale of a smalltime mobster with a psychosis, production reflecting hefty budget expenditure.

Plot is a psychological study of a hood who has risen to some prominence in the rackets and wants to be liked for himself. Since he's a moody, sourpuss individual with an enlarged ego, he has scant success in the friendship line and this gives him a complex. There's a promise of violence when a rival mob moves in to take over his business but it tapers off to a mild ending, even though title character is shot down.

Barry Sullivan gives the lead some strength but is never able to make it believable because of script and directorial weaknesses. Daniel Fuchs' screenplay, from his own novel, is vague in establishing characters and plot premise. Best example is failure to explain sufficiently just what the gangster's rackets are that make him so disliked and feared. Action is mostly dialog instead of carried out physically. Stronger direction by Gordon Wiles would have helped build suspense and interest. He adheres too much to mood, neglecting forceful action needed to put over this type yarn.

Belita tries hard with vague character of the gangster's moll who turns on her boy friend in the end. She also sings the oldie, "Paradise," in night club scene. She is not treated kindly by the camera. Joan Lorring has small spot of nice girl who tells off the baddie and shows up in okay fashion. Akim Tamiroff, in the rackets with Sullivan, is good. Best played character is handled by Sheldon Leonard as Sullivan's rival. Attempts to inject lightness with characters of Henry Morgan and Fifi D'Orsay only result in strained comedy. John Ireland, Virginia Christine, Leif Erickson and others are okay with what they have to do.

Maurice and Frank King's production supervision has provided good physical polish. Paul Ivano's lensing is expert and the music score by Louis Gruenberg a factor. *Brog.*

Dick Tracy Meets Gruesome

RKO release of Herman Schlom production. Stars Boris Karloff, Ralph Byrd; features Anne Gwynne, Edward Ashley. Directed by John Rawlins. Story by William H. Graffis and Robert E. Kent; screenplay by Robertson White, Eric Taylor; based on cartoon strip "Dick Tracy" by Chester Gould; camera, Frank Redman; Editor, Elmo Williams. Tradeshown N. Y. Sept. 25, '47. Running time, **65 MINS.**

Gruesome........................Boris Karloff
Dick Tracy......................Ralph Byrd
Tess Truhart....................Anne Gwynne
L. E. Thal......................Edward Ashley
I. M. Learned...................June Clayworth
Pat Patton......................Lyle Latell
Melody..........................Tony Barrett
X-Ray...........................Skelton Knaggs
Dan Sterne......................Jim Nolan
Chief Brandon...................Joseph Crehan
Dr. A. Tomic....................Milton Parsons

Dick Tracy on the screen closely resembles the newspaper cartoon strip character; that is, he goes through one hair-raising experience after another. And always comes off triumphant. In his latest, Tracy traces down a band of bank robbers. "Dick Tracy Meets Gruesome" is a chiller-diller that will do biz where this sort of mellers have an audience, being given an added asset in that Boris Karloff heads the cast.

Plot has an odd-looking gang of bank looters using a mysterious chemical in miniature bombs, gimmick being that said bombs temporarily paralyze every person within close radius of same. Just why they fail to effect the bank robbers themselves or Tracy and his Girl Friday is not made clear. But this helps the yarn, since it enables the holdups to tackle a bank, and have the guards and everybody else helpless even before they come in the door.

Yarn casts Karloff as Gruesome, stalking through his familiar menacing scenes, pet stunt being to put his victims in a huge furnace for safe keeping. To give it a meller, poetic justice twist, story has Karloff escaping a similar fiery death only by last second intervention by Tracy (Ralph Byrd).

Karloff, per usual, thefts every scene in which he appears. Byrd is acceptable as Tracy, even to resemblance to the square-jawed detective. Anne Gwynne is feminine and gushy enough to make an okay Tess Truehart or Girl Friday. Lyle Latell is an effective Pat Patton. Support is headed by June Clayworth, Edward Ashley and Tony Barrett.

Director John Rawlins employs almost serial-type action but with surprisingly good results. Apparently this is what is needed for cartoon adventure yarns. *Wear.*

Le Diable au Corps

(Spirit of Devilry)
(FRENCH-MADE)

Paris, Sept. 16.

Universal International release of Paul Graetz production (Transcontinental Films). From the novel by Raymond Radiguet. Directed by Claude Autant Lara. Stars Gerard Philipe, Micheline Presle; features Denise Grey, Debucourt. Screen adaptation, Jean Aurenche and Pierre Bosc; camera, Voinquel; music, Rene LeCloarec. At Normandie, Olympia and Moulin Rouge, Paris. Running time, **122 MINS.**

Francois........................Gerard Philipe
Marthe..........................Micheline Presle
Francois' Father................Debucourt
Marthe's Mother.................Denise Grey
Francois' Pal...................Emile Francois
Schoolmaster....................Maxudian
Headwaiter......................Francoeur

Even before it was completed, this picture received tremendous publicity, due to production quarrels between producer and director which threatened to stop the work. Film is a smasheroo, getting raves from all sides after having been awarded a prize in Brussels during the International Film Festival in June.

Controversy as to the expediency of permitting the risque script to pass censor started the publicity ball rolling, due to the fact that the story shows a young college boy in an affair with the wife of a soldier while he is at the front. She becomes the mother of his chil whose birth causes her death while he is compelled to be a mere looker-on. Since then, the controversial theme has got more space in the press than any other picture.

With an eye to American distribution, a few of the scenes most likely to draw fire from bluenoses were shot in sapoliod form for foreign consumption. But the original version, as presented here, has nothing that cannot be paralleled in many other pictures, and doesn't contain the slightest bit of obscene or salacious material, even by implication.

The film is beautifully acted. Micheline Presle, as the young girl, is the embodiment of maidenly reserve. Her sex appeal, which registers heavy on the screen, is used by her in a totally different way than in "Boule de Suif," and makes the scene of her surrender not only understandable, but altogether satisfactory to the audience.

Opposite her, Gerard Philipe, whose work got him a prize for best screen actor, is equally exemplary as the young and irresponsible boy unable to cope with a major situation.

Balance of cast is also good. Debucourt, as the boy's father; Denise Grey, as the straightlaced mother; Emile Francois, as the lover's juvenile schoolmate, are excellently cast. Maxudian is suitably pompous as the school prof. Francoeur dignified as a headwaiter, and even the very minor parts are well acted.

Direction by Claude Autant Lara is top drawer. Helped by excellent lensework of Voinquel, he has projected the characters with finesse, and made graphically realistic without coarseness a touchy story. In handling the sexy and tragic sequences, he has shown considerable tact and restraint. The mob scenes are well done.

Film's only drawback for America is the publicity given it, which makes it, unjustifiably, a target for misinformed or prejudiced censors. Coarsely treated, it might have been questioned, but director and cast have vied in making it suitable screenfare for the most punctilious. *Maxi.*

Midnight in Paris

('Monsieur La Souris')
(FRENCH-MADE)

Distinguished Films release of Roger Richebe production. Stars Raimu. Directed by Georges Lacombe. Story, George Simoneon; editor, Walter Klee. Previewed in N. Y., Sept. 25, '47. Running time, **90 MINS.**

Monsieur La Souris..............Raimu
Simon Negretti..................Aime Clariond
Labord..........................Charles Granval
Osting..........................Gilbert Gil
Cupidon.........................Aimos
L'Inspecteur Lognon.............Bergeron
Le Commissaire Lucas............Paul Amiot
Muller..........................Pierre Jourdan
Lucille Boisvin.................Micheline Francey
Dora............................Marie Carlot

(In French; English Titles)

This is the sort of film which, if perpetrated too often, can put a quick and permanent damper on the popularity which quality foreign-language importations are justly enjoying. "Midnight in Paris," an evident potboiler which the French studio turned out many years ago under the title of "Monsieur La Souris," is a long, belabored and confused whodunit which has no appeal either for the mystery addicts or art house patrons. This film was resurrected from the vaults solely because of the late Raimu's name but even this formidable actor cannot salvage b.o. gold from dross.

Overlong running time of 90 minutes crawls tortuously through a threadbare plot which hasn't even the basic minimum of logic or credibility. Raimu plays a deteriorated petit-bourgeois who walks into the middle of a murder affair by reporting a corpse to the Paris gendarmarie. According to the whodunit's Hoyle, Raimu, plus a series of assorted characters, falls under suspicion until the windup reveals the culprit to be someone no filmgoing detective could ever have tabbed. But there's no effort to tie the loose threads together by an explanation, which isn't playing cricket.

As usual, Raimu delivers with an unusual characterization of the bum who's seen better days. Unfortunately, role doesn't provide much substance so he's forced frequently into hokey stage business. Aimos, w.k. French comic, as Raimu's sidekick, is wasted in a couple of irrelevant sequences. Aime Clariond, Gilbert Gil and Pierre Jourdan serve okay as the suspects with Bergeron turning in good performance as the Gallic version of the fumbling dick.

Herm.

Foreign Films

"La Navidad de los Pobres" ("The Poor People's Christmas") **(ARGENTINE).** Argentina Sono Film production and release. Stars Nini Marshall; features Tito Lusiardo, Irma Cordoba, Osvaldo Miranda. Directed by Manuel Romero. screenplay, Miss Marshall, based on Romero's story; camera, Alberto Etchebehere; songs, Paul Misraky. At Monumental, Buenos Aires. Running time, **95 MINS.**

This film sifts down to merely a vehicle for Nini Marshall whose role is that of a department store salesgirl. Hers is an excellent characterization punctuated with malapropisms, "refinement" and fundamental common sense. Picture should gross well in Argentina, Chile and Uruguay. It has a limited appeal for the U. S. mart. *Nid.*

"Ingen Vag Tillbaka" ("No Road Back") **(SWEDISH).** Sandrew-Bauman Film release of Carl Nelson-Monark Film production. Stars Edvin Adolphson, Gaby Stenberg; features Anita Bjoerck, Olof Bergstroem, Arnold Sjostrand, Hugo Bjoerne, Naemi Brise, Willy Peters, Aurore Palmgren, Julie Bernby, Nancy Dalunde. Directed by Adolphson. Screenplay, Ragnar af Geijerstam, based on novel by Hans Severinsen; camera, Hilding Bladh; music, Sune Waldimir. At Grand, Stockholm. Running time, **98 MINS.**

Based on a Danish novel, this film is hampered by an inept screen adaptation. Yarn deals with the Danish underground during the German occupation. Picture may find some acceptance in the Scandinavian market, but its chances abroad are doubtful.

"La Cumparsita" ("The Little Parade") **(ARGENTINE).** San Miguel production and release. Stars Hugo del Carril, Aida Alberti, Ernesto Vilches; features Jose Olarra, Nelly Daren, Florindo Ferrario, Felisa Mary, Carlos Castro, Maruja Pais. Directed by Antonio Momplet. Story, Alejandro Verbisky, Emilio Villalba Welsa; camera, David Altschuler. At Normandie, Buenos Aires. Running time, **35 MINS.**

This musical's principal theme is the glorification of the Argentine tango. Woven in the weak yarn is the alleged story of composer Mattos Rodriguez, writer of "La Cumparsita." Packed with showmanship, the picture is destined to do sock biz in the sticks. Hugo del Carril's warbling of tango favorites is also on the credit side although he's still as wooden as ever as an actor. Film has no U. S. value. *Nid.*

Miniature Reviews

"Where There's Life" (Par). Bob Hope at his funniest, which means solid business.

"This Time for Keeps" (Songs-Color) (M-G). Esther Williams, Melchior, Durante and Technicolor insure hearty b.o.

"Railroaded" (EL). Gangster meller with plenty of killings but no cast names; lower dualer.

"The Last Round-Up" (Col). Top-grade western, first of the new Gene Autrys from Columbia. Plenty to recommend it for the Autry market.

"The Wild Frontier" (Rep). Neat westerner for dual situations.

"The Spirit of West Point" (FC). Exploitable feature built around last season's Army gridiron greats, "Doc" Blanchard and Glenn Davis. Filled with actual news footage of season's top games.

"Blonde Savage" (E-L). Modest-budgeted jungle yarn for the dualers.

"White Stallion" (Astor). Westerner with Ken Maynard and Eddie Dean. Okay for supporting situations.

"Fame Is the Spur" (Gen.) (British). Excellent drama of a self-made politician, with U. S. appeal somewhat restricted.

"Farewell, My Beautiful Naples" (Italian). Overlong, average quality romance with music; little appeal byeond the Italian-speaking.

Where There's Life

Hollywood, Oct. 3.

Paramount release of Paul Jones production. Stars Bob Hope, Signe Hasso, William Bendix; features George Coulouris. Directed by Sidney Lanfield. Screenplay, Allen Boretz and Melville Shavelson; based on story by Shavelson; camera, Charles B. Lang, Jr.; special effects, Gordon Jennings; editor, Archie Marshek. Tradeshown Sept. 25, '47. Running time, **75 MINS.**

Michael Valentine	Bob Hope
Katrina Grimovitch	Signe Hasso
Victor O'Brien	William Bendix
Krivoc	George Coulouris
Hazel O'Brien	Vera Marshe
Paul Stertorius	George Zucco
Minister of War Grubitch	Dennis Hoey
Mr. Herbert Jones	John Alexander
Finance Minister Zavitch	Victor Varconi
Albert Miller	Joseph Vitale
Joe Snyder	Harry Von Zell

"Where There's Life" gives Bob Hope a tailor-made vehicle and adds up to nifty boxoffice. That old mythical kingdom fable has been brushed off and brightened up to furnish framework for a laugh-provoking melange of gags and situations. All involved make it register strongly. Production, direction and writing are smartly valued to display the Hope talents and he pops the maize handsomely.

Hope is seen as a happy New York disk jockey who doesn't know he's the heir-apparent to the kingdom of Barovia. The king is shot down by a bolshevik and a party is sent to America to bring back Hope. He doesn't take kindly to the idea as he's just about to marry Vera Marshe. He begins to change his mind, though, after being kidnapped and meeting Signe Hasso, the beautiful general in the party.

Plot is virtually one long chase as Hope and his kidnappers seek to avoid a group of murderous bolsheviks and at the same time dodge Miss Marshe's policemen brothers, headed by William Bendix, who want him for the proposed wedding. All the formula situations of the plot are milked dry for laughs in the swift scripting by Allen Boretz and Melville Shavelson. Dialog is punchy as tossed off by Hope and laughs often crowd laughs in unfoldment. Sidney Lanfield's direction is sure-handed in belting over the chuckles and keeping pace fast.

Miss Hasso brightens proceedings considerably as the fascinating general. Eye-appeal is strong and talent excellent, which makes the assignment count. Bendix rates laughs for work as the flat-foot brother of Miss Marshe, and George Colouris gets over as the principal heavy. Harry Von Zell is in briefly for chuckles as gag-playing announcer.

Production polish has been capably furnished by Paul Jones. Charles B. Lang used his camera expertly, and special photographic effects by Gordon Jennings aid laugh intent. Other credits measure up. *Brog.*

This Time for Keeps

(COLOR-SONGS)

Metro release of Joe Pasternak production. Stars Esther Williams, Lauritz Melchior, Jimmy Durante. Directed by Richard Thorpe. Screenplay, Gladys Lehman; story, Erwin Gelsey, Lorraine Fielding; camera (Technicolor), Karl Freund; special effects, A. Arnold Gillespie; music, Georgie Stoll; editor, John Dunning; dances and water ballet, Stanley Donen. Tradeshown N. Y., Oct. 6, '47. Running time, **105 MINS.**

Nora	Esther Williams
Richard Herald	Lauritz Melchior
Ferdi Farro	Jimmy Durante
Dick Johnson	Johnnie Johnston
Xavier Cugat	Himself
Grandma	Dame May Whitty
Deborah	Sharon McManus
Gordon Coome	Dick Simmons
Frances	Mary Stuart
Peter	Ludwig Stossel
Merle	Dorothy Porter
Tommy Wonder	Himself
Mrs. Allenbury	Nella Walker
Norman	Holmes Herbert

"This Time for Keeps" is a money picture. Esther Williams, Lauritz Melchior and the yeoman Jimmy Durante, who struts himself to a new personal hit, virtually insure it on marquee values alone. Couple the splendiferous Technicolor production with the s.a. splash of the bathing beauts and it's ideal entertainment anywhere.

Johnnie Johnston is projected as the juvenile, his usual blonde coif wisely denatured so that the color gives him a better camera perspective, but actually he is eclipsed by Dick Simmons (cast as the disappointed juve) who does a standout job. Miss Williams, besides the aquatic and pulchritudinous display, comes off above par on her personal histrionics. She handles her lines (dialog) almost as well as her other lines (Jantzen).

Melchior gets off a few arias including a rather operatic version of a Cole Porter oldie, "You Are So Easy to Love." He is cast as Johnston's doting dad. Latter is an ex-GI who is more jive than longhair in his vocal leanings and he displays them with a swing treatment of "Martha" after Melchior does it rousingly well as a legitimate aria.

Miss Williams is costarred with the comedic Durante in the Aqua-Caper show. Latter alternates between a mimic and a father confessor for the aquabelle whose grandmother (Dame May Whitty), an equestrian star on her own, generations back, watches over the brood. It's established that the pride of heritage that comes with an old theatrical family permits this grand dame of the circus to rule as arbiter of her favorite granddaughter's romantic, as well as professional, career.

The story is episodic as it flits from the Casa (Xavier) Cugat to the aquashow to the Mackinac Island (Wis.) locale where grandma is permanently domiciled. It thus becomes an on-location bally for the Mackinac resort, shifting from the tropical California locale to the Wisconsin winter-summer spot (both seasons are shown). In between, maestro Cugie batons his band with a tiny chihuahua pooch, in lieu of the baton. There are specialties by Tommy Wonder and others; Durante whams over a symphonic arrangement of "Inka Dinka" and a good comedy routine, "I Found the Lost Chord"; the marine ballet and other dance numbers are effective flashes as Stanley Donen staged them; "Piquita Amor" is interspliced as a promising theme, but the standard Porter number, "Easy to Love," snags the tune honors.

Joe Pasternak's production is ultra; director Richard Thorpe's pace good; and the swimming ensemble strictly orb-filling but done with restraint and consummate good taste. *Abel.*

Railroaded

Eagle Lion release of Charles F. Riesner production. Features John Ireland, Sheila Ryan, Hugh Beaumont, Jane Randolph. Directed by Anthony Mann. Screenplay by John C. Higgins from original by Gertrude Walker; camera, Guy Roe; editor, Louis Sackin. Tradeshown N. Y., Oct. 2, '47. Running time, **72 MINS.**

Duke Martin	John Ireland
Rosa Ryan	Sheila Ryan
Mickey Ferguson	Hugh Beaumont
Clara Calhoun	Jane Randolph
Steve Ryan	Ed Kelly
Captain MacTaggart	Charles D. Brown
Chubb	Clancy Cooper
Marie	Peggy Converse
Mrs. Ryan	Hermine Sterler
Cowie	Keefe Brasselle
Ainsworth	Roy Gordon

This is an old-type blood-and-thunder gangster meller that's better than its no-name cast would indicate. A ruthless mobster's trigger-happy mood is reflected by many killings and robberies, with payoff gun battle in nightclub reminiscent of gangster shockers before the strict code era. Fact that there are no names to brighten the marquee will militate against film's draw but it will do okay as under-half of some dualers, and possibly other spots where the exhibitor is smart enough to circus his bally.

Story starts out like a familiar cops-and-robbery, then disintegrates into a plot wherein police detectives misinterpret circumstantial evidence, and it finally winds up with yarn centering on a cold-blooded gangster who uses his gun whenever anybody gets in his way.

Probably the most suspenseful moment is built around said mobster's deliberate gun-blasting of his sweetheart after he overhears her tipping off the coppers. Even skillful cutting does not make this a nice episode particularly since he had pushed her around all through the picture. The cold-blooded slaying of his boss soon afterwards steeps this production in plenty of gore.

Anthony Mann has directed, for the most part, with real acumen in developing maximum of suspense. Earlier passages where a truck-driver is unjustly accused by the gendarmes and put through a vivid third-degree seems a bit extraneous. John C. Higgins' screenplay is okay even if the Gertrude Walker original story proves not so original.

Outstanding in the cast is Hugh Beaumont, as the conscientious detective. He tends to underplay which makes his work all the more effective. John Ireland is sufficiently menacing as the gangster killer. Jane Randolph does excellent work as the gunmoll while Sheila Ryan, comely dark-haired gal, shows promise as the heroine. *Wear.*

The Last Round-Up

(Songs)

Hollywood, Oct. 4.

Columbia release of a Gene Autry production, produced by Armand Schaefer. Stars Gene Autry; features Jean Heather, Ralph Morgan, Carol Thurston, Mark Daniels, Bobby Blake, Russ Vincent, The Texas Rangers. Directed by John English. Screenplay, Jack Townley and Earle Snell; story, Townley; camera, William Bradford; musical supervisor, Paul Mertz; editor, Aaron Stell. Previewed Oct. 2, '47. Running time, **76 MINS.**

Gene Autry	Himself
Carol	Jean Heather
Mason	Ralph Morgan
Lydia Henry	Carol Thurston

Matt Mason	Mark Daniels
Mike	Bobby Blake
Jeff Henry	Russ Vincent
Marvin	George "Shug" Fisher
Indian Chief	Trevor Bardette
Goss	Lee Bennett
Taylor	John Halloran
Jim	Sandy Sanders
Smith	Roy Gordon
Sam Luther	Silverheels Smith
Cora Luther	Frances Rey
Carter	Bob Cason

Gene Autry has teed off his new Columbia production slate with a top western entry. "The Last Round-Up" has everything a good, actionful western should have to make it click in the outdoor market. There's knowledgeable production, direction and writing to give the action plenty of substance. It's certain to please the many Autry fans and should attract some new ones.

Film bears evidence of higher than average oater budget. Because of that, extra sales efforts are called for to make sure the western market is completely covered, but picture is strong enough to back up any extra efforts taken.

"Round-Up" needs tighter editing in the beginning and on the finale for better pacing, but otherwise is practically minus faults. Although Jack Townley's solid script is laid in the modern west, there're Indians on the war path and other prairie action. It's all well premised, though, and the story holds water, a point not too common in westerns. Earle Snell collabed on script with Townley from latter's original.

John English's direction points up all of the plus factors, injecting little bits of business that add to overall merit. One instance is use of tune, "She'll Be Coming Around the Mountain," sung by Autry and classroom of Indian kids with gestures. Other Autry numbers are the title tune, "An Apple for the Teacher" by Johnny Burke and James Monaco; "You Can't See the Sun When You're Crying," by Allan Roberts and Doris Fisher, and "160 Acres" by David Kapp. All are nicely sold.

Plot deals with efforts of Autry to get the Indians to take new, fertile lands in exchange for barren acres through which an aqueduct is to be built. Between necessity of convincing the Indians, obtaining water rights from ranchers and blocking the villains' attempts to balk the deal, the hero has his hands full. Setup gives basis for a number of rough-and-tumble fistic displays, the Indian uprising promoted by the heavies, and general chases that make action swift.

Aiding Autry is a very competent cast, all registering strongly. Jean Heather, the heroine school teacher; Ralph Morgan and Mark Daniels, chief heavies; Bobby Blake, Carol Thurston and Russ Vincent, very believeable as educated Indians; George "Shug" Fisher, and others make for solid support.

Armand Schaefer, production head of the Autry company, selected film's backgrounds with care and exercised equal judgment on all phases. The action and outdoor backgrounds have been given wise attention by William Bradford's camera. Art direction, sets, Paul Mertz's musical supervision and other factors fit in perfectly. *Brog.*

The Wild Frontier

Republic release of Gordon Kaye production. Stars Allan Lane. Directed by Philip Ford. Screenplay, Albert DeMond; camera, Alfred S. Keller; editor, Les Orlebeck. Tradeshown N. Y. Oct. 3, '47. Running time, **59 MINS.**

Allan "Rocky" Lane	Allan "Rocky" Lane
His Stallion	Black Jack
Charles "Saddles" Barton	Jack Holt
"Nugget" Clark	Eddy Waller
Marshal Frank Lane	Pierre Watkin
Jimmy Lane	John James
Lon Brand	Roy Barcroft
Patrick MacSween	Tom London
Steve Lawson	Sam Flint
A Gunman	Ted Mapes
Sam Wheeler	Budd Buster
Doc Hardy	Wheaton Chambers

"The Wild Frontier" is a fast actionful westerner that won't disappoint the customers for whom it's intended. Pic, marking the demise of Republic's Red Ryder series and the start of another mustang cycle with Allan Lane playing himself, is cut from a familiar formula but with exceptional neatness. Director Philip Ford has paced this one-hour feature at a breakneck speed with no time out for even a hint of romance. There's not a femme to be seen which is probably okay for the juve trade who don't like to mix mushin' with murderin'.

Production standards for this new series are fixed at a solid level. Backing up Lane is a good roster of players headed by Jack Holt and Eddy Waller. Camera work is first-rate, especially in fisticuff sequences where the punches look very realistic. Editing job is tight but smooth with overall dress making this film appealing fare for dualer situations.

Yarn revolves around the sheriff vs. outlaw theme with Lane getting the law-and-order job after his father is killed by some rustlers. Plenty of hard riding and gunplay takes place before Lane uncovers the town's leading citizen as being head of the robber gang. Climax is a bangup shooting fray ending in a stiff hand-to-hand fight between Lane and Holt, playing the heavy.

In lead, Lane registers nicely as a cowboy hero, showing an adequate thesping talent besides the usual square jaw. Holt makes a creditable villain, albeit it's strange to see this upstanding guardian of the law in so many previous pictures in part of a cattle thief. Rest of the cast play competently in their stock roles. *Herm.*

The Spirit of West Point

Hollywood, Oct. 7.

Film Classics release of John W. Rogers-Harry Joe Brown production. Stars Felix "Doc" Blanchard, Glenn Davis; features Robert Shayne, Anne Nagel, Alan Hale, Jr. Directed by Ralph Murphy. Screenplay, Tom Reed; camera, Lester White; editor, Harvey Manger. Previewed Sept. 30, '47. Running time, **75 MINS.**

Felix "Doc" Blanchard	Himself
Glenn Davis	Himself
Ralph Davis	Glenn Davis
Col. Red Blaik	Robert Shayne
Mrs. Blaik	Anne Nagel
Oklahoma Cutler	Alan Hale, Jr.
Joe Wilson	George O'Hanlon
Mileaway McCarty	Michael Browne
Mrs. Davis	Margaret Wells
Mildred	Tanis Chandler
Mrs. Blanchard	Mary Newton
Mr. Blanchard	William Forrest
Cabot	Lee Bennett
Quarterback	Mickey McCardle
Ferriss	John Gallaudet
Young Doc Blanchard	Rudy Wissler

Bill Stern Harry Wismer Tom Harmon

Film Classics should garner fast return on "The Spirit of West Point" if releasing film during current football season. There's much actual footage of games that gave "Doc" Blanchard and Glenn Davis their reputation as the touchdown twins for Army, and presence of two pigskinners gives added exploitation material. Story is sketchy and film kudoes West Point and its traditions with plenty of flag-waving but authentic gridiron footage carries the ball satisfactorily.

Careers of football stars are picked up as they enter West Point and become members of the team in 1944. Their lives are sketchily and briefly dealt with, but there's enough to justify actual football footage, which, after all, is main contributor to the picture's salable values.

Quite a pitch is made on struggle of the two pigskinners to holdout against lucrative professional offers that flowed their way and how the Army was victorious in retaining its two new officers. Film was made while pair were on 60-day furlough between graduation and reporting for active duty as officers of the Army. Temptation is stressed through Mileaway McCarty departing West Point for better paying professional ball field.

Blanchard and Davis do an okay job of portraying themselves on the screen. Robert Shayne, as the coach, Col. Red Blaik, is excellent, as is Alan Hale, Jr., as Oklahoma Cutler. Anne Nagel, Mary Newton, Margaret Wells, Rudy Wissler and others are good under Ralph Murphy's direction in the John W. Rogers-Harry Joe Brown production.

New lensing and newsreel clips have been fitted together expertly by editor Harvey Manger. Other technical credits measure up. *Brog.*

Blonde Savage

Eagle Lion release of Ensign (Lionel J. Toll) production. Stars Leif Erickson, Gale Sherwood; features Veda Ann Borg, Douglas Dumbrille, Frank Jenks. Directed by S. K. Seeley. Original screenplay, Gordon Bache; camera, William Sickner; editor, Paul Landres. Previewed N. Y., Oct. 1. Running time, **62 MINS.**

Steve Blake	Leif Erickson
Meelah	Gale Sherwood
Connie Harper	Veda Ann Borg
Mark Harper	Douglas Dumbrille
Hoppy Owens	Frank Jenks
Berger	Matt Willis
Tonga	Ernest Whitman
Mary Comstock	Cay Forester
Joe Comstock	John Dehner
Stone	Arthur Foster
George Bennett	Alex Fraser
Clarissa	Eve Whitney
Inspector	James Logan

Initial filmmaking venture of Ensign Productions is a modest-budgeter whose distributional market will be confined to lower dualers. "Blonde Savage," an unpretentious African jungle yarn, is just passable entertainment for the action fans. Overworked is the use of the flashback technique, but occasional employment of narrative to outline the plot presents a novel touch.

Picture has inherent exploitation values in the "blonde savage" angle. Mystery of why a flaxen-haired damsel is living with a tribe of African aborigines is eventually explained, but even when Meelah (Gale Sherwood) first appears in the reel there's little suspense generated as to how she got there.

First scene has Leif Erickson in a powwow with an attorney in an African coastal town pondering the fates of a gal and man who are held on murder raps. Then comes the flashback. Erickson and his pal, Frank Jenks, operators of a plane transport firm, are hired by diamond mine owner Douglas Dumbrille to make an aerial search for a native village. Forced down in the wilds they encounter Miss Sherwood, a femme big wheel among the savages. It develops she is the daughter of Dumbrille's murdered partner.

Acting is generally mediocre. Erickson physically is a stalwart enough hero but as the footage unreels he fails to inject conviction into his role. Jenks' comedy relief is strained while Miss Sherwood does as best she can in an implausible part. Dumbrille and Matt Willis register as heavies and Veda Ann Borg is so-so as Dumbrille's wife who loathes her life in the jungle.

Gordon Bache's screenplay is reminiscent of the Tarzan tales. S. K. Seeley's direction is fair. Producer Lionel J. Toll made liberal use of stock shots and film's mountings reflect his care in disbursing the budget.

White Stallion

(SONGS)

Astor release of Walt Mattox production. Features Eddie Dean, Ken Maynard, Rocky Cameron, Max Terhune. Directed by Robert Emmett. Screenplay, Frank Simpson; editor, Fred Bain; camera, Edward Kull; music, Frank Sanucci. At New Yorker theatre, N. Y., Oct. 1, '47. Running time, **[illegible] MINS.**

Ken Maynard	Himself
Eddie Dean	Himself
Rocky Cameron	Himself
Max Terhune	Himself
U. S. Marshall Taylor	Glen Strange
Ann Martin	Ruth Roman
Pop Martin	Bob McKenzie
Jim Sorrell	Charles King
Tip	Bud Osborne
Red	Al Ferguson
Bronco	Dan White
Sleepy	Fred Gildart
Tex	Jerry Shields
Mr. Hodges	Hal Price
Sheriff	John Bridges

"White Stallion" is a routine western that's able to sustain itself in supporting situations. Picture is well-paced, has a certain marquee value with Ken Maynard and Eddie Dean, and there's a dab of comedy to heighten the interest.

Film makes some slight departure in that the cast toppers run through the film using their own names. Only obvious advantage in this procedure is the easy identification of the players. Otherwise there's the incongruity of having the rest of the cast fictionally labeled.

Maynard, Dean and Max Terhune work under Rocky Cameron in an effort to capture a group of bankrobbers. Heroics of this quartet ultimately break up the band and recover the loot.

Aside from chasing the baddies, Maynard, whose assignment has him posing as an entertainer with a medicine show, is afforded an opportunity to make with fancy roping and trick-shooting. Eddie Dean, ladles out his quota of songs and Max Terhune works a ventriloquist dummy for comedy effects. Further comedy is by Bob McKenzie as the medicine show operator, whose makeup and characterization is highly reminiscent of the late Walter Connolly. Ruth Roman is the minor love interest and villainy is by Charles King.

Robert Emmett's direction is fast and Frank Simpson's screenplay is good inasmuch as it uses a minimum of dialog. *Jose.*

Fame Is the Spur

London, Sept. 24.

General Film Distributors' release of Two Cities-F. Del Giudice film. Stars Rosamund John, Michael Redgrave. Directed by Roy Boulting. Screenplay by Nigel Balchin from Howard Spring's novel. Editor, Richard Best; music by John Woodridge; camera, Gunther Grampf, Harry Waxman, Stanley Pavey. At Studio One, London, Sept. 23, '47. Running time, **116 MINS.**

Hamer Radshaw	Michael Redgrave
Ann	Rosamund John
Tom Hannaway	Bernard Miles
Arnold Ryerson	Hugh Burden
Mrs. Radshaw	Jean Shepheard
Grandpa	Guy Verney
Suddaby	Percy Walsh
Lady Lettice	Carla Lehmann
Old Buck	Seymour Hicks
Lord Liskeard	David Tomlinson
Aunt Lizzie	Marjorie Fielding
Magistrate	Milton Rosmer
Pendleton	Wylie Watson
Boy Hamer	Anthony Wager
Boy Ryerson	Brian Weske
Boy Hannaway	Gerald Fox
Dai	Charles Wood

Few writers can give poverty such an air of adventure as Howard Spring, and in the Boulting Bros. he found the right producer and director. It was not an easy matter to translate Spring's workmanlike saga of a self-made politician to the screen, but the Boultings have done this with praiseworthy conscientiousness.

In these days, when British audiences are politically minded, this story of a lad from the slums, who rises to cabinet rank, although he has qualities everyone will condemn, should have a wide appeal. It lacks humor, and now and again is pedestrian, yet Michael Redgrave's playing of the principal part—a blend of many labor politicians with a strong dash of Ramsay MacDonald—is powerful enough to hold attention all through.

For American audiences it may be a revelation of what British workmen have suffered since 1870. It may explain to them Labor's uncompromising attitude today to many Tory ideas. But as a general entertainment it will most likely find its way into the arty pix theatres. With the exception of the woman's suffrage sequences, there is little to thrill the distaff side.

Having wisely discarded the flashback, the Boultings begin in 1870 when Hamer Radshaw, a lad in a north country slum, dedicates his life to better the lot of his fellow workers. The sword his grandfather picked up at Peterloo (1819), when soldiers cut down workers crying for "Bread and Liberty," becomes his talisman and symbol.

Attractive (uncannily like Mac-Donald in some shots), he becomes a grand rabble-rouser. With his sword he can incite men to their own death, all for the "cause," and as a Labor Member of Parliament he takes the line of least resistance, shedding old friends when necessary, making new ones if they can help, as long as it all leads to glory and power.

Only his wife, Ann, really knows him and is unblinded by her deep love. He resents her suffragist activities, but she is true to her ideals and goes to prison for them. Her treatment there accelerates her end and, on her deathbed, she reveals a little of her true self to the man-she loves.

When Labor comes to power he joins the Cabinet, and vanity and adulation is too rich a diet. Comes the day when Labor joins its opponents to form a National Government, and Hamer throws over any remaining principles to retain his high position. At the election he is rejected, and losing his seat in the Commons, he accepts a peerage and becomes Lord Radshaw.

Closing scenes show a pitiful old man addressing the Lord Mayor's banquet and, as some of the past flashes through his mind, doddering and failing to make sense. Film ends on the symbolic note of the old man struggling in vain to draw the sword from the scabbard in which it has rusted.

Michael Redgrave gives a grand performance as the earnest young idealist who becomes the vain selfish politician. It is a difficult part, but he makes it wholly credible. As his wife, Rosamund John chalks up her best performance to date, and reveals an acting ability hitherto only suspected.

Bernard Miles is more than competent as a shrewd moneymaker, to whom the end always justifies the means. Nice work comes from Hugh Burden, Seymour Hicks, David Tomlinson, Marjorie Fielding, Jean Shepheard and Anthony Wager as the boy Hamer.

Production and direction are firstrate, and for those who want a thoughtful adult picture, this can be recommended.   *Cane.*

Farewell, My Beautiful Naples
('Addio Mia Bella Napoli')
(ITALIAN-MADE)

Saturnia Film release of Ideal Films production. Directed by Mario Bonnard. Story, Ernesto Muolo; camera, Gabor Pogany and Tino Santoni. English titles, Armando Macaluso. Previewed N. Y., Oct. 1, '47. Running time, **100 MINS.**
Carlo Sanna................Fosco Giachetti
Roberta Sullivan...............Vera Carmi
Yvonne....................Clelia Matania
Michael....................Paolo Stoppa
Mother..............Bella Starace Sainati
Chaperone..............Giulietta de Riso
Off-Screen Voice.......Francesco Albanese

Italian-born audiences may find nostalgic appeal in "Farewell, My Beautiful Naples," and it may have a wallop for lovers of Neapolitan music, but the general public will hardly be drawn and probably wouldn't be much entertained by it. The film is a musical romance of the sort Hollywood does well, but this Italian-make is uneven dramatically, unimpressive musically and above all extremely attenuated.

The thin story of the early 1900's, is about the romance of a young composer, whose songs are the rage

of Naples, and an American heiress tourist. Some of the action occurs in a Neapolitan music hall, with Clelia Matania as a temperamental singer with a yen for the songwriter. Other scenes are in the Naples opera house (which a few GI's may recognize), the hotel, the composer's home overlooking the Mediterranean, and various sightseers' spots in and around Naples, Pompeii, Amalfi and Capri. Some of the latter provide effective scenic shots, but they're dragged out and repeated too much.

Fosco Giachetti is a handsome composer-hero, but his appearance is a bit mature and he's somewhat heavy-moving. Vera Carmi, the "American" heiress (whose grandfather was a Neapolitan and who speaks fluent Italian) is a blonde looker and a satisfactory actress. Much of the sparkle of Miss Matania's performance is obviously lost to non-linguists, since she plays a Neapolitan posing as a Parisienne. However, Paolo Stoppa gets sympathy and comedy into the part of an agent, Bella Starace Sainati is touching in the trite role of the composer's mother, and Giulietta de Risco combines dignity and gentleness as the heroine's chaperone.

Mario Bonnard's direction seems acceptable, but the photography is spotty and the music, despite the presentation of some famous Neapolitan songs, suffers from imperfect reproduction. As indicated, the film begs for drastic editing.   *Hobe.*

Miniature Reviews

"Forever Amber" (Color) (20th). How can it miss?

"Nightmare Alley" (20th). Tough drama about tough carnival people needs all its cast draw.

"The Exile" (Fairbanks-U). Douglas Fairbanks, Jr.'s first indie assured good grosses through star names and romantic action.

"Invisible Wall" (20th). Gangster meller, lacking any marquee names, for the dualers.

"The Lost Moment" (Wanger-U). Robert Cummings and Susan Hayward romantic meller, should do business.

"Bowery Buckaroos" (Mono). Bowery Boys in a satire on westerns. Should draw well in nabes.

"Furia" (Italian). Powerful film surefire for art houses.

Forever Amber
(COLOR)

20th-Century-Fox release of Darryl F. Zanuck (Wm. Perlberg) production. Stars Linda Darnell, Cornel Wilde, Richard Greene, Geo. Sanders; features Glenn Langan, Richard Haydn, Jessica Tandy, Anne Revere. Directed by Otto Preminger. Screenplay, Philip Dunne, Ring Lardner, Jr., adapted by Jerome Cady from Kathleen Winsor's novel. Score, David Raksin, conducted by Alfred Newman; arrangements, Maurice de Packh, Herbert Spencer; camera (Technicolor), Leon Shamroy; special effects, Fred Sersen; editor, Louis Loeffler. Tradeshown N. Y., Oct. 15, '47. Running time, **140 MINS.**
Amber......................Linda Darnell
Bruce Carlton...............Cornel Wilde
Lord Almsbury...............Richard Greene
King Charles II............George Sanders
Capt. Rex Morgan...........Glenn Langan
Earl of Radcliffe.........Richard Haydn
Nan Britton................Jessica Tandy
Mother Red Cap.............Anne Revere
Black Jack Mallard..........John Russell
Corinna......................Jane Ball
Sir Thomas Dudley............Robert Coote
Matt Goodgroome.........Leo G. Carroll
Countess of Castlemaine....Natalie Draper
Mrs. Spong.............Margaret Wycherly
Lady Redmond................Alma Kruger
Lord Redmond..............Edmond Breon
Landale.....................Alan Napier

"Forever Amber," the 17th century British road company of French postcards, was a lurid bestseller, and in Technicolor, it should likewise sell strongly. Can't miss boxofficewise.

A picture property with an advance campaign such as Kathleen Winsor's novel, which has been the subject of gags and the butt of wits in every form of colloquial communication, chiefly by comics over the air and on cafe floors, naturally becomes endowed with a buildup that's the pressagent's dream. Rarely does it kick back. That goes even for the Jane Russell and "Duel In the Sun" type of films.

And so with "Amber" which, despite its sundry shortcomings, is a surefire wicket-spinner. The exhibitor can hang up the shingle and get out of the way of the customers. Here is a $4,000,000 (and claimed to be more) picture that looks its cost. That goes even for the lost footage through mishap with Peggy Cummins, the original candidate until Linda Darnell replaced. And she does quite well—in fact, the sum total compels an intra-trade salute to the Zanuck factory for so successfully shadow-boxing with existing tabus and regulations, and coming up so satisfactorily with the finished product.

The lusty yarn is treated for what it is. Miss Darnell runs the gamut from romantic opportunist to prison

degradation and up again to being the king's favorite and finally a discarded mistress, grateful that the royal equerry invites her to supper after Charles II gives her the brushoff.

In between there's a wealth of derring-do, 17th century knavery and debauchery, the love of a good woman (Jane Ball), and the rest of a depraved court's atmosphere. It's solid escapology, particularly pat commercial stuff in this day and age of postwar world problems.

Cornel Wilde is the No. 1 juve, although Glenn Langan suggests he might have made an excellent choice for that role instead of a secondary swain. Richard Haydn plays his a.k. role well as the arrogant earl who Amber premeditatedly weds in order to gain a title. John Russell is convincing as the highwayman; Anne Revere is sufficiently despicable as a keeper of a thieves' den; Jessica Tandy does all right as Amber's maid; George Sanders turns a neat character when chiding Amber for thinking he could be played for a sucker in a supposedly compromising rendezvous with Miss Ball; and Richard Greene makes an effective pal for Wilde as a swashbuckling privateer in the king's service.

Miss Darnell manages her chameleon Amber character very well. Her blonde beauty shows off well in Technicolor, and she is equally convincing when she is thrown in a pauper's gaol.

While some of the color is in minor key, creating a too dim perspective, by and large the lensing expertly captures all the shadings of regal splendor, the devastating fire on London town following the bubonic plague, etc.

By attacking the story for what it is, without pandering to the sensitivities, the result is at least moderately convincing. There is no double-talk about the illegitimacy of Amber's lovechild; there are, in fact, two childbirth scenes, with reasonably well-cut closeups. The lechery and debauchery are effectively projected because they've given a quasi-historical delineation in the reign of Charles II, whose grants to privateers (slang for pirates who shared their loot with the crown) are no less virtuous than the illicit atmosphere generally pervading his court.

Certainly, 20th-Fox's bossman, Darryl Zanuck, didn't spare the hosses, and producer Bill Perlberg endowed the sum total with a wealth of props that must have exhausted the resources of the combined Western, Eaves and Brooks Costume Cos. It's that kind of a flash splash.
                                    Abel.

Nightmare Alley

Hollywood, Oct. 8.
20th-Fox release of George Jessel production. Stars Tyrone Power; features Joan Blondell, Coleen Gray, Helen Walker. Directed by Edmund Goulding. Screenplay by Jules Furthman, based on novel by William Lindsay Gresham; camera, Lee Garmes; editor, Barbara McLean. Tradeshown Oct. 7, '47. Running time, **110 MINS.**
Stan Carlisle...............Tyrone Power
Zeena....................Joan Blondell
Molly....................Coleen Gray
Lilith...................Helen Walker
Grindle..................Taylor Holmes
Bruno....................Mike Mazurki
Pete.......................Ian Keith
Mrs. Peabody.................Julia Dean
Hoatley..................James Flavin
McGraw...................Roy Roberts
Town Marshal..............James Burke

"Nightmare Alley" is a harsh, brutal story told with the sharp clarity of an etching. There isn't a really sympathetic or inspiring character in the show, but acting, direction and production values lift the piece to the plane of gripping drama. In spots it approaches the dignity of authentic tragedy. The picture will satisfy no demands for light entertainment, hence the boxoffice is problematical and largely conditioned on the femme draw of Tyrone Power in the lead.

The film deals with the roughest and most sordid phases of carnival life and showmanship. Despite the grim realism of its treatment, it has all the shuddery effect of a horror yarn.

Power's talent hits a new high in his depiction of Stan Carlisle, reform school graduate, who works his way from carney roustabout to big-time mentalist and finally to important swindling in the spook racket. Ruthless and unscrupulous, he uses the women in his life to further his advancement, stepping on them as he climbs.

Most vivid of these is Joan Blondell as the girl he works for the secrets of the mind-reading act. Coleen Gray is sympathetic and convincing as his steadfast wife and partner in his act and Helen Walker comes through successfully as the calculating femme who topples Power from the heights of fortune back to degradation as the geek in the carney. Ian Keith is outstanding as Blondell's drunken husband, and the balance of the supporting cast works hard and effectively.

The Jules Furthman screenplay keeps all the strength of a tough story and Edmund Goulding's direction points the drama to inspire pity for its unpalatable characters. *Fisk.*

The Exile

Hollywood, Oct. 13.

Universal release of Fairbanks (Douglas Fairbanks, Jr.) production. Stars Douglas Fairbanks, Jr., Maria Montez, Paule Croset; features Henry Daniell, Nigel Bruce. Directed by Max Opuls. Written by Douglas Fairbanks, Jr.; camera, Frank Planer; music, Frank Skinner; editor, Ted J. Kent; arrangements, David Tamkin; asst. director, Ben Chapman; special effects, David Horsley. Previewed Oct. 13, '47. Running time, **94 MINS.**

The Countess.................Maria Montez
Katie.........................Paule Croset
Col. Ingram.................Henry Daniell
Sir Edward Hyde...............Nigel Bruce
Pinner.......................Robert Coote
Jan...........................Otto Waldis
Seymour.......................Eldon Gorst
Wilcox.....................Milton A. Owen
Capt. Bristol..........Colin Keith-Johnston
Milbanke....................Ben H. Wright
Ross..........................Colin Kenny
Higson.........................Peter Shaw
Tucket........................Will Stanton
Cavalier Official..........C. S. Ramsey-Hill
Cavalier Guard................Gordon Clark
Roundhead Gen...............Lumsden Hare
Robbins....................Lester Matthews
Jasper....................Thomas P. Dillon
Footman....................William Trenk
Coach..........................Fred Cavens
Marie............................Alla Dunn
Sea Captain...................Torben Meyer
First Court Lady...........Grayce Hampton
Second Court Lady.............Mary Forbes
Painter.....................Charles Stevens
Charles Stuart......Douglas Fairbanks, Jr.

Douglas Fairbanks, Jr.'s first indie production, with himself starred, is of heroic measure in its approach to a romantic period in history when Charles II was in exile from England. Film is highly exploitable, particularly since it follows the type of costume action-drama the elder Fairbanks once was noted for. Response at boxoffice is assured by star names of Fairbanks and Maria Montez.

Too much time is consumed, however, in reaching its exciting stages, with a script which sometimes leans toward antiquated proportions. Interesting especially is a blonde newcomer, Paule Croset, who co-stars with Fairbanks and Miss Montez in her introductory role, an opportunity of which she acquits herself most adequately. Miss Croset garners as much interest as the male star, delivering a sock performance. She's a cinch for popularity.

She plays a young Dutch innkeeper and farm owner, on whose place the exile is in hiding. Plot concerns mostly efforts of Cromwell's Roundheads to catch up with exiled king and do away with him. Story would have benefited had they caught up with him sooner, rather than lot of more or less inconsequential action in the first half of the feature. Romantic spirit is achieved, however, by Fairbanks in his role and action points up this flavor.

Filmed in sepia, this gives the picture soft tones and fits in perfectly with the subject. It assays high in production values and, with Frank Planer handling the cameras, it's a beautifully executed piece of work. Production designing by Howard Bay and art direction by Bernard Herzbrun and Hilyard reach a high level of perfection, calculated to appeal to the eye. Max Opuls gave the film rugged direction, but at times was hampered by the screenplay written by Fairbanks. The star's producer efforts far overshadow his scripting.

While Fairbanks performs strongly in his role of the exiled King Charles, Miss Montez, though getting co-star credit, is in only one long sequence, and is not always understandable. Standouts in support are Nigel Bruce, as the king's chancellor; Henry Daniell, as the Roundhead sent by Cromwell to kill the king; Robert Coote, as an actor who masquerades as the fleeing king. Top talent completes the cast. *Whit.*

Invisible Wall

20th-Fox release of Sol M. Wurtzel production. Features Don Castle, Virginia Christine, Richard Gaines. Directed by Eugene Ford. Screenplay by Arnold Belgard; based on story by Howard J. Green, Paul Frank; camera, Benjamin Kline; editor, William Claxton. Tradeshown N. Y. Oct. 9, '47. Running time, **72 MINS.**

Harry Lane....................Don Castle
Mildred Elsworth........Virginia Christine
Richard Elsworth..........Richard Gaines
Hanford......................Arthur Space
Marty Floyd.................Edward Keane
Al Conway....................Jeff Chandler
Hamilton...................Harry Cheshire
Mrs. Bledsoe..................Mary Gordon
Detective Captain..........Harry Shannon
Alice Jamison.................Rita Duncan

Gangster meller, with uneven pace, is fairly entertaining despite absence of any name players to brighten the marquee. "Invisible Wall," which manages to become exciting towards the end, will have to be sold heavily as a gangland melodrama to amount to much. It will fit best into lower half of twin bills, and there only as a mild entry.

Yarn involves Don Castle, an ex-GI, who returns to handling payoffs for a west coast bookmaker when he gets back from the war. His yen for gambling leads him to squander half of the $20,000 which has been entrusted to him by his boss bookmaker. He'd been sent to the Flamingo hotel, Las Vegas, to pay off a racing bet, but $5,000 of this is invested, so Castle thought, in a sure-thing mining proposition. Complications follow.

Whole story is done via flashbacks which makes for a neat surprise ending that's done too sketchily. Film telegraphs its irregular direction by Eugene Ford but, one suspects, he struggled with too many story angles before this finally came out of the cutting room. Picture would have been lots better if held to 55 minutes.

Castle is outstanding and should be heard from in the future via more satisfactory stories. Virginia Christine is competent as the wife of the former con who later weds Castle. Gaines makes a smooth heavy while Edward Keane is excellent as the bookmaking king. Support is headed by Jeff Chandler and Arthur Space. *Wear.*

The Lost Moment

Universal release of Walter Wanger production. Stars Robert Cummings, Susan Hayward; features Agnes Moorehead, Joan Lorring, Eduardo Ciannelli, John Archer. Directed by Martin Gabel. Screenplay by Leonardo Bercovici; from novel, "The Aspern Papers," by Henry James; camera, Hal Mohr; music, Daniele Amfitheatrof; orchestrations, David Tamkin; editor, Milton Carruth. Tradeshown N. Y., Oct. 9, '47. Running time, **89 MINS.**

Lewis.....................Robert Cummings
Tina........................Susan Hayward
Juliana....................Agnes Moorehead
Amelia........................Joan Lorring
Father Rinaldo...........Eduardo Ciannelli
Charles.......................John Archer
Pietro.........................Frank Puglia
Maria.......................Minerva Urecal
Vittorio...................William Edmunds

A romantic melodrama with a Venetian locale and a schizophrenic heroine, "The Lost Moment" is a heavy but reasonably absorbing picture. It should draw moderately well, chiefly through word-of-mouth, since it lacks marquee strength.

Based on the Henry James novel, "The Aspern Papers," story is essentially a study of emotional maladjustment and a consequent retreat into the unreality of the past. As adapted by ex-radio writer Leonardo Bercovici and directed by ex-radio actor-director Martin Gabel, the emphasis is on romance and, as an obvious boxoffice element, the therapeutic value of love. Thus, the picture doesn't attempt a clear explanation of why the heroine's childhood in the grim old Venetian mansion unbalanced her emotional-mental makeup, but concentrates on the romantic aspects of her reaction to the unprecedented presence of a real-life young man.

The atmosphere of the centuries-old house, the 105-year-old blind woman and the lurid subject matter of the story, give the picture a sombre tone. This is partly relieved by a cafe scene of music, gayety and violence, and by a couple of meetings between the young American publisher and the Venetian priest who maintains a worried watch over the household. But the finale scenes, despite a seemingly contrived attempted murder and a fatal fire, are pleasanter.

Apparently due to the editing, the picture is cryptic in several places. For instance, the centenarian aunt's blindness is indicated by little more than a suggestion, and there are various undeveloped references in the story, such as the spot in the garden, where nothing will grow, apparently because the murdered poet was buried there (and the surface there is clay rather than topsoil). The direction has good tempo and builds suspense properly, but the occasional use of stream-of-consciousness speeches by the hero, possibly a vestigial device from radio, mars illusion.

As the U. S. publisher who seeks the long-dead poet's legendary love letters to the once-beautiful aunt, Robert Cummings is direct and believable. Susan Hayward, who played another psychotic character in "Crackup," also for Walter Wanger, is effective in both facets of the present part, but the contrast between them occasionally seems abrupt. Agnes Moorehead, with a major assist from the makeup man, has a character actor's splurge with the role of the guileful ex-belle, and Joan Lorring, Eduardo Ciannelli and John Archer are satisfactory in principal supporting parts. *Hobe.*

Bowery Buckaroos

Monogram release of Jan Grippo production. Features Bowery Boys. Directed by William Beaudine. Screenplay, Tim Ryan and Edmond Seward; camera, Marcel LePicard. At New York, N. Y., week Oct. 8, '47. Running time, **66 MINS.**

Slip.............................Leo Gorcey
Sach............................Huntz Hall
Bobby.........................Bobby Jordan
Gab............................Gabriel Dell
Whitey.......................Billy Benedict
Chuck.........................David Gorcey
Carolyn Briggs.................Julie Briggs
Louie.......................Bernard Gorcey
Blackjack.....................Jack Norman
Kate Barlow.................Minerva Urecal
Luke Barlow...............Russell Simpson

Lampooning the oaters, this low-budgeter hands the Bowery Boys free rein to lead their hosses from New York's east side water holes to the wild and wooly west. In changing their stamping grounds from the metropolis to the mesa, the boys dish out plenty of zanyisms charged with uninhibited corn, but the less discriminating filmgoer will find plenty of laughs in their antics. Picture should do well in the nabes—especially with the juve trade.

Plot is an inconsequential one of those things. But who cares when Leo Gorcey is getting off such gems of idiom as, "I'm goin' out and prosecute for gold." Scripters Tim Ryan and Edmond Seward pitched plenty of grist into the gag mill. Even an Indian comes up with incongruous lingo, e.g. his analysis of a peculiar situation, "This don't look kosher to me!" Otherwise the yarn concerns itself with the efforts of Gorcey, Huntz Hall, et al., to see that right is done by Julie Briggs who's been rooked of her share of a gold mine.

Bowery Boys register in their comic roles. Jack Norman, as Blackjack, is a credible heavy. Blonde Miss Briggs' chassis decorates the footage nicely and she displays a passable voice in warbling one tune. Minerva Urecal and Russell Simpson contrib okay bits as the U. S. marshal and deputy, respectively. William Beaudine directed at a swift pace in this Jan Grippo production. Marcel LePicard's lensing is satisfactory.

Furia

(ITALIAN-MADE)

Film Classics release of Franchini-AGIC production. Stars Isa Pola, Rossano Brazzi; features Gino Gervi, Adriana Benetti, Umberto Spadaro. Directed by Geoffredo Alessandrini. Screenplay, Alessandrini; editor and English titles by Herman Weinberg. Previewed in N. Y., Oct. 9, '47. Running time, **90 MINS.**

Clara.............................Isa Pola
Antonio....................Rossano Brazzi
Oreste..........................Gino Cervi
Marietta..................Adriana Bennetti
Rocco....................Umberto Spadaro
Priest.......................Camillo Pilotto
Priest's Sister........Bella Starace Sainati

(In Italian; English Titles)

Italian film producers, who've been plying the U. S. market with a parade of art house clicks such as "The Open City," "Shoe Shine" and "The King's Jester," have come up with another winner in "Furia."

Basically, its appeal stems from the candor with which the elemental drives of love, jealousy, hate and double-distilled lust are handled. The whole film is drenched in an aura of sexual craving that definitely removes it from the family-feature category and makes its chances in Boston seem a bit dubious. Several sequences are virtual shockers not only in their unprecedented cleavage exposure but for a voluptuous suggestiveness that'll make heating systems superfluous. Over-exploitation of this theme, however, is liable to do more damage than good if it rouses the bluenoses into action.

The film can get by, moreover, on its merits as a straight melodrama. Unfortunately, the second half of the pic fails to fulfill the promise of the opening reels. After a smashing midway climax, the film goes slightly astray in maze of plot complications that aren't fully clarified. These defects, however, are minimized by a superlative group of players and an overall solid production dress.

Center of the film is Isa Pola who plays the role of a blowzy, bored, slightly-aging and libidinous mate of a well-to-do horse breeder. Surrounding her are Rossano Brazzi, a stud-keeper with whom she engages in extra-curricular romancing; Gino Gervi, her husband, who suspects the worst; Adriani Benetti, the latter's beauteous young daughter by another wife; and Umberto Spadaro, a half-idiot stable hand with a furious yen for the mistress of the house.

The surging undercurrent of passion, the suspicions and the rivalry of the two women for Brazzi are manipulated for a terrific explosion as the husband schemes to uncover the clandestine lovers. He lays his traps but, at the decisive moment, the daughter substitutes herself for the wife in Brazzi's room in self-sacrifice to her father's happiness. After this confrontation, the story weakens. Brazzi marries the girl whom he loves but since his flesh is weak, he still carries on with the older woman. After many futile pledges of abstention, the habit is finally broken when the idiot strangles Miss Pola in a frenzy of desire.

Each of the principals does a standout job. Especially striking are Miss Pola for her remarkably modulated range of sensuality, and Brazzi [who is being brought to Hollywood by Eddie Small]. Spadaro, as the half-wit, also registers with a powerful impact in his recounting of the murder scene. *Herm.*

Woman Without Face
("Kvinna Utan Ansikte")
(SWEDISH-MADE)

Stockholm, Sept. 25.

Svensk Filmindustri production and release. Stars Alf Kjellin, Gunn Wallgren, Stig Olin, Ella Lindblom; features Anita Bjork, Marianne Lofgren, Georg Funkqvist, Ake Gronberg, Siv Ruud, Gun Adler, Olof Winnerstrand. Directed by Gustaf Molander. Screenplay, Ingmar Bergman; camera, Ake Dahlqvist. At Roda Kvarn, Stockholm. Running time, **110 MINS.**

Ruth....................Gunn Wallgren
Martin....................Alf Kjellin
Ragnar....................Stig Olin
Marie....................Ella Lindblom
Frida....................Anita Bjork
Charlotte....................Marianne Lofgren
Victor....................Georg Funkqvist
Sam....................Ake Gronberg
Magda....................Siv Ruud
Girl in Shop....................Gun Adler
Martin's Father........Olof Winnerstrand

A psychological study that emerges as a topdrawer artistic film, "Woman Without Face" looks as fine a Swedish talking picture as was ever made and should make an indelible impression upon the world market. As a further guarantee, this Scandinavian entry has Alf Kjellin, now a Selznick contract player, for marquee lure.

Youth's life and problems are deftly analyzed in this yarn, which principally is the story of Ruth, an artist whose emotional existence has been destroyed. Her companions comprise her close friend, Martin; the latter's chum, Ragnar, a promising author; Ragnar's gal friend, Marie, while Victor is the devil personified. These characters are realistically etched in the brilliant screenplay of Ingmar Bergman.

Power of evil and its hold on the masses is ably brought out in the footage by fine delineations of Kjellin and Gun Wallgren as Martin and Ruth, respectively. Ella Lindblom also shines in the role of Marie. But chief praise goes to scripter Bergman, who, incidentally, scripted "Torment," an earlier Kjellin starrer which made its mark on the foreign market. Gustav Molander's direction is firstrate; likewise Ake Dahlqvist's lensing. *Winq.*

Miniature Reviews

"Green Dolphin Street" (M-G). Spectacular values and a strong marquee insure good if not smash business.

"The Swordsman" (Color) (Col). Larry Parks in a Scotch-tinted swashbuckler that's assured good grosses.

"That Hagen Girl" (WB). Ronald Reagan and Shirley Temple in weakly scripted melodrama; mild b.o.

"Man About Town" (RKO) (French). Chevalier starrer, with English commentary by him; good for many U. S. theatres.

"The Blue Veil" (French). Gaby Morlay starrer of minor interest for U. S. audiences.

"On the Old Spanish Trail" (Color-Songs) (Rep). Moderately ambitious western starring Roy Rogers; fair entertainment.

"While I Love" (20th). British-made with Tom Walls, Sonia Dresdel is tale of reincarnation of souls; slim chance in U. S.

"Uncle Silas" (GFD). Two Cities meller made in England is not for export despite Katina Paxinou in a star role.

"The Girls in Smaland" (Songs) (Swedish). Mediocre Swedish comedy romance for mild b.o. in art situations.

Green Dolphin Street

Metro release of Carey Wilson production. Stars Lana Turner, Donna Reed, Richard Hart, Van Heflin; features Frank Morgan, Edmund Gwenn, Dame May Whitty, Reginald Owen, Gladys Cooper, Moyna MacGill, Linda Christian. Directed by Victor Saville. Screenplay, Samson Raphaelson; from novel by Elizabeth Goudge; camera, George Folsey; score, Bronislau Kaper; editor, George White; special effects, Warren Newcombe, A. Arnold Gillespie. At Criterion, N. Y., Oct. 15, '47. Running time, **140 MINS.**

Marianne Patourel............Lana Turner
Timothy Haslam..................Van Heflin
Marguerite Patourel...........Donna Reed
William Ozanne..............Richard Hart
Dr. Edmond Ozanne..........Frank Morgan
Octavius Patourel.............Edmund Gwenn
Mother Superior.........Dame May Whitty
Captain O'Hara.............Reginald Owen
Sophie Patourel.............Gladys Cooper
Mrs. Metivier.................Moyna Macgill
Hine-Moa.....................Linda Christian
Jacky-Poto.....................Bernie Gozier
Kapua-Manga.....................Pat Aherne
A Maori.............................Al Kikume
Sister Angelique...............Edith Leslie
Veronica...........................Gigi Perreau

Metro's thrown the full weight of its moneybags into "Green Dolphin Street," first of its contest-winning novels to be filmed, and if all that money can buy in the way of spectacular acts of God still queues them up, the investment is safe. To salvage the $4,000,000 or so that went into this epic, it must primarily count on the eminent saleability of earthquakes, tidal waves and native uprisings. Its curiously unreal story offers no help but the cast and the spec should pay off.

Surprising to note is that this Elizabeth Goudge novel, handpicked from hundreds of entries, should pop up as the weakest link in the celluloid chain. For the painstaking efforts, enormous production values and topflite cast poured into "Dolphin" would have endowed almost any modestly priced original with enough pulling strength to make the grade. As it is, the $200,000 yarn rarely catches on fire.

Flaws in the novel, which verbiage may have made less perceptible, sore-thumb their way through the pic. There's the weak dramatic dodge, for one instance, of the wrong sister being married because she was mistakenly named by the suitor in a letter of proposal to her parents. And it's nothing but a hokey have-your-cake-and-eat-it device to confer happiness on the other by retiring her to a religious order. That oldie, unless shrewdly handled, is a patent maneuver to comfort the customers.

On the other hand, there's frank femme appeal in "Dolphin's" double-ply premise that devotion and loyalty can finally worm a similar response from an unwilling spouse. Working that beat twice in the same opus lends a touch of corn—nonetheless, it's boxoffice stuff.

Alternately localed in primitive New Zealand and one of the French channel isles (circa 1840), pic details how Lana Turner, mistaken for her sister Donna Reed, makes the perilous sea voyage to the Antipodes to marry a deserter from the British navy. Once there, the camera really gets in its innings, sweeping over a horrendous earthquake and tidal wave, and a native Maori uprising that follows. Amidst these upheavals, her child is born.

Rather disconcertingly abrupt, camera flicks back frequently to the channel isle where Miss Reed, already beaten by the defection of her lover, takes the double blow of the loss of her parents. Years reel by and Miss Turner's drive and shrewdness win both fortune and amnesty for her husband. It's only upon reunion of the entire family that she discovers her hubby's initial blunder but Miss Reed pulls the strings for a curtain reconciliation.

When Victor Saville's direction focuses on nature's vengeance on man's works, the handling is superb. The toppling of giant trees, the shuddering of splitting earth and the sweep of a river rending everything in its path is simon-pure cinematology. Credit, too, the fetching grandeur of the New Zealand country.

Refusal by M-G's studioites to recognize the ravages of time and events on the human face hampers Miss Turner in depicting her exacting and pivotal role. All the same, hers is the best performance of the lot in portraying the scheming, domineering gal who sees the light in time.

As the gentler of the sisters, Miss Reed is bogged by the weight of the yarn. Patly performing in the early reels, she fails to turn the hazardous trick of making her later conversion credible. Richard Hart, Broadway importee who breaks into his second Hollywood role as the weak hubby, will have to do better. In the pinches, his thesping was wooden. Van Heflin comes a shade under his usually high level of thesping as a disappointed swain who remains a friend of the menage. Edmund Gwenn, Frank Morgan, Gladys Cooper et al., filling smaller parts, come up to snuff.

Musical score obtrudes too much at crucial points in the story. As previously noted, Metro hasn't stinted in its outlay on this one and sets, costumes, backgrounds have that solid gold glint. ***Wit.***

The Swordsman
(COLOR)

Columbia release of Burt Kelly production. Stars Larry Parks; features Ellen Drew, George Macready, Edgar Buchanan, Marc Platt. Directed by Joseph H. Lewis. Original screenplay, Wilfrid H. Pettitt; camera (Technicolor), William Snyder; editor, Al Clark; score, Hugo Friedhofer. Tradeshown N. Y., Oct. 15, '47. Running time, **81 MINS.**

Alexander MacArden..........Larry Parks
Barbara Glowan..................Ellen Drew
Robert Glowan...........George Macready
Angus MacArden..........Edgar Buchanan
Mac-Ian............................Ray Collins
Murdoch Glowan..................Marc Platt
Colin Glowan................Michael Duane
Lord Glowan................Holmes Herbert
Bruce Glowan..............Nedrick Young
Ronald MacArden..........Robert Shayne
Old Andrew..................William Bevan
Reverend Douglas..........Lumsden Hare
Gordon Glowan..............Tom Stevenson
Charles..............................Harry Allen

Take Columbia's "Bandit of Sherwood Forest" of last year, transfer its locale from England to the Scottish moors, dress its cast in plaid instead of forest green and there you have "The Swordsman." Film is primed with the same sort of swashbuckling romance, lush Technicolor and beauteous outdoor sets, all of which offers excellent escapism. Payees should pile in for this one, same as they did for "Bandit."

"Swordsman" has Larry Parks in his second starring role since "Jolson Story" (other was "Down to Earth"). As the scion of an aristocratic Scotch clan of the 18th century, he's definitely miscast. This probably represents Columbia's efforts to wean him away from the Jolson identification but the weaning has been done too rapidly. Considering his previous song-and-dance efforts, he still makes out surprisingly well, wielding his sword and making like an athlete generally. Audiences may still find themselves expecting him to get down on one knee and yodel "Mammy," but that's something only time and other dissimilar roles will erase.

Producer Burt Kelly tagged this one for sheer blood-and-thunder and that's the way scripter Wilfrid H. Pettitt and director Joseph H. Lewis have wrought it. Tale is naive to the extreme, representing nothing more than a standard western story fashioned to a Scottish Romeo and Juliet theme, but it's been endowed with enough action and romance to please. Parks is a MacArden and Ellen Drew is a Glowan and the two clans have been carrying on a Hatfield-Coy for generations. Two of them finally get the lords of the two families to sign a peace treaty but this is broken when a couple of hot-headed youngsters on both sides start the feud rolling again. As with any good western, the MacArden clan is ambushed by the unruly Glowans but the "vigilantes" arrive in the nick to set things right again. Parks and Miss Drew wed in the fadeout to make certain permanent peace has been cemented.

Entire cast is burdened with phony Scotch brogues and none of them makes his rolling r's come out right but this too can be passed off in favor of the derring-do. Miss Drew, with her first real part in years, has the only femme speaking role in the picture. She's sufficiently winsome to make her Scotch lassie acceptable. George Macready, as the insurgent Glowan scion, is as vicious and reprehensible a scoundrel as one could want.

Marc Platt, against whom Columbia seems to hold a grudge, is again woefully miscast. Possessor of one of the brightest pair of dancing feet in Hollywood, he still doesn't get a chance to terp, his only exercise coming in a javelin-tossing duel with Parks. Nice bits of thesping are turned in by Edgar Buchanan, Holmes Herbert and William Bevan.

With the exception of making the picture in obviously-identifiable California hills instead of in Scotland, producer Kelly hasn't spared the budget much. Sets and costumes, emblazoned in vivid Technicolor, lend the correct atmosphere. Director Lewis gets the maximum out of the corn and the cast, making both believable enough. Other production credits, including William Snyder's camera direction, Al Clark's editing and Hugo Friedhofer's score, are good. *Stal.*

That Hagen Girl

Warner Bros. release of Alex Gottlieb production. Stars Shirley Temple, Ronald Reagan; features Dorothy Peterson, Charles Kemper, Rory Calhoun. Directed by Peter Godfrey. Screenplay, Charles Hoffman; based on novel by Edith Roberts; camera,

Karl Freund; editor, David Weisbart. Tradeshown N. Y., Oct. 17, '47. Running time, **83 MINS.**

Mary Hagen....................Shirley Temple
Tom Bates....................Ronald Reagan
Minta Hagen....................Dorothy Peterson
Jim Hagen....................Charles Kemper
Ken Freneau....................Rory Calhoun
Sharon Bailey....................Jean Porter
Molly Freneau....................Nella Walker
Selma Delaney....................Winifred Harris
Cora....................Ruth Robinson
Julia Kane....................Lois Maxwell

"That Hagen Girl" will not perk up much boxoffice activity. Handicapped by a shopworn screenplay, pic must depend exclusively on the marquee boosts given by Ronald Reagan and Shirley Temple and heavy exploitation of the tearjerking angles that may give it some play among femme customers.

Miss Temple, looking much younger than her 18 years, is an evident casting problem, being too immature for straight romantic parts and too old for simple juve roles. As a result, she's been forced in this film to undertake the characterization of an anguished adolescent—the most demanding role of all. She won't add any stature to her rep because of this effort primarily as a result of an inept, all-thumbs scripting job that shows no comprehension of the problem.

Production is also guilty of a glaring slip-up in the handling of Reagan. At the outset of the pic, he's a young man of about 20, suspected of fathering an illegitimate child. Returning to the scene some 18 years later, he reveals absolutely no signs of aging despite the fact that his friends have grayed considerably. This is an obstrusive error that adds to the film's general incredibility.

Plot is chiefly concerned with the persecution of Miss Temple by a group of small town gossips who treat her as an outcast because of doubtful parentage. She's cheated out of the lead in her school's dramatic presentation of "Romeo and Juliet;" loses her boy friend, gets expelled just before graduation, and finally, in desperation, attempts to commit suicide.

In background, an apparent romance builds up between Lois Maxwell, a teacher sympathetic to Miss Temple, and Reagan, a successful lawyer and war hero. But, in a most sudden, surprising and inexplicable climax, Miss Maxwell bows out of the scene to let Reagan marry Miss Temple who is supposed to be young enough to be his daughter. Story doesn't give the slightest preparation for this windup.

Miss Temple registers with an ingratiating performance despite the hoked-up melodramatics foisted upon her by the script. Reagan walks through his role without conviction while Miss Maxwell shows promise in a secondary role. Rest of the cast turns in standardly competent jobs.

Alex Gottlieb has dressed this production neatly, despite elimination of expensive trappings. Expert lensing gives an important assist.

Herm.

In the Name of Life

(RUSSIAN-MADE)

Artkino release of Lenfilm production. Stars Victor Kokriakov, Katya Lepanova. Directed by Alexander Zarki, Joseph Heifits. Screenplay by Eugene Gabrilovich, Zarki, Heifits; camera, Vladimir Gardanov; English titles, Charles Clement. At Stanley, N. Y., starting Oct. 18, '47. Running time, **99 MINS.**

Dr. Vladimir Petrov......Victor Kokriakov
Dr. Alexander Kolesov..Mikhail Kuznetsov
Dr. Alexei Rojdestvensky......Oleg Zhakov
Lena....................Katya Lepanova
Vera....................Lydia Shabalina
Anyushka....................Margarita Gromyko
Attendant....................Nikolai Cherkassov

(In Russian; English Titles)

Despite a familiar plot, this Russmade yarn about the medical profession's battle against disease has been given a great lift through the superb direction of Alexander Zarki and Joseph Heifits and several excellent characterizations. Zarki and Heifits, who directed "Baltic Deputy," one of topflight Soviet productions, measure up to previous effort on this. Even though some of the vivisection scenes are far from appetizing, this latest Russian picture is a strong entry for language houses.

Soviet version about a trio of former soldiers who vow to give the remainder of their lives to find a nerve or paralysis cure becomes a tribute to medicos who fight against countless odds to gain success. It is Victor Kokriakov, of Moscow's Transport Workers Theatre, who wins out after many disappointing experiments while the other two ex-Army men carry on their research with less vigor.

There are too many shots of lab work on rabbits, monkeys, dogs and other dumb beasts with all the stops out. When a Russian film producer has a rabbit killed on the experimental table it's killed, but good. And then photographed as the limp body lies on the table.

Kokriakov contributes the ace performance even though this is supposed to be his first work before the camera. Katya Lepanova, also making her bow in pictures, is fairly good as the actress who figures in his life. Mikhail Kuznetsov and Oleg Zhakov are surprisingly fine in giving realism to the other two research medico roles. Nikolai Cherkasov, who's known to U. S. audiences for his work in "Ivan the Terrible" and "Alexander Nevsky," does something with a minor part.

Plot makes a point of citing how numerous scientists have been listed as discoverers in the world of science whereas Russians really should have been handed the laurels. Edison and Marconi are outstanding errors, according to the English title explanations in this film. Story also makes something of one of research trio being lured to U. S. because of his knowledge.

Lens job by Vladimir Gardanov is solid. Score for background music is unusually vivid, being done by Benedict Puskov. English titling by Charles Clement is above par.

Wear.

Man About Town

("Le Silence est d'Or")
(FRENCH-MADE)

RKO release of Rene Clair (French Pathe Cinema) production. Stars Maurice Chevalier; features Francois Perier, Marcelle Derrien. Directed by Clair from his own story; assistant in production and English adaptation, Robert Pirosh. English commentary spoken by Chevalier. Camera, Armand Thirard. Costumes, Christian Dior. Previewed N. Y., Oct. 16, '47. Running time, **89 MINS.**

Emile....................Maurice Chevalier
Jacques....................Francois Perier
Madeleine....................Marcelle Derrien
Lucette....................Dany Robin
Duperrier....................Robert Pizani
Curly....................Raymond Cordy
The Cashier....................Paul Olivier
Celestin....................Roland Armontel

(In French; English Commentary)

RKO and French Pathe have combined forces with Rene Clair to star Maurice Chevalier in a charming bit of Parisian froth that should earn almost as many dollars as laughs in the United States. By the clever device of having Chevalier speak an English commentary, instead of the usual printed subtitles, the potential American audience has been broadened tremendously beyond the usual expectations for a French dialog picture. It should run for weeks in the art houses and be successful in a considerable number of carefully-selected general audience theatres.

Leisurely Gallic pace is the principal factor militating against unrestricted playdating in the U. S., since the film otherwise has more of the elements for broad audience appeal than probably any Continental picture yet delivered here. Certainly, the Chevalier popularity in the U. S., as demonstrated by the success of his personal appearance tour last year, proves the star a b.o. power on anybody's marquee.

Film was made in Paris by French Pathe with RKO's blocked francs. Rene Clair, who wrote, directed and produced, apparently set out from the beginning to design the film for broadest appeal to American audiences and to make possible the easy adaptation to English on which Robert Pirosh was assigned to work with him. Their success could have been more complete only had they been able to make the pace equal that to which the average American filmgoer has become accustomed.

Adaptation device is highly ingenious. Picture was made all in French dialog under the title "Le Silence est d'Or." For the American version, first shot is a marquee advertising Chevalier and then a closeup of the performer in his familiar top hat, singing "Place Pigalle." When he's finished, a picture screen rolls down on the stage behind him and he announces that he's not only appearing in person, but in a film. This film, having been made in France, he explains, is subject to a peculiarity of the French people—they talk in French. But don't worry, he admonishes, because "I'll be right down here (standing at the side of the screen) to explain those little things you don't understand."

The titles of "Silence" shoot on the screen to a few covering wisecracks from Chevalier, with the camera then dollying down to eliminate him from the corner and take the picture itself full screen. Throughout the film, Chevalier's voice in English is intermittently heard, not generally giving a direct translation of dialog, but third-person explanation of the plot development. Usually, the English is inserted in what are apparently planned spaces in the French dialog, although sometimes the dialog is faded down to allow for the English. Also, occasionally, when Chevalier is turned back to the camera, so that no lip sync is necessary, he's made to speak his lines in English instead of French. It's all done so cleverly, it's entirely unobtrusive and frequently the audience doesn't actually realize whether it's hearing French or English.

Spacing of the English, of course, was a problem and overlong periods of straight French are partially responsible for the slow pace. It leaves you wondering at times not what's going on, which is always clear, but what's being said. The finis, incidentally, has a nice snapper, all in English.

Technique has attracted considerable trade attention in the U. S. as a possibility for broadening audience potential on other foreign films. There seems no reason why it shouldn't work, although not necessarily with the great success achieved in this case, since the whole setup here was planned to this end and all the elements are conducive, even to the very simple plot structure of the story itself.

Yarn pictures Chevalier as a 1906 Paris film producer and is a delightful burlesque all the way through of picturemaking of that era. There are a flock of Gallic Mack Sennett characters who have the sets cave in on them, earn a flood of laughs with a goat as mustachioed as they are and otherwise roll through a gamut of everything but custard pies.

Chevalier, from the very beginning, is wisely made to kid about his age—with his 59 years evident on the screen. He falls in love with one of his actresses (Marcelle Derrien), daughter of a friend. Because of the disparity in their ages, he makes her unhappy by refusing to ask her to marry him, until she falls in love with one of his young actors (Francois Perier), who is also Chevalier's best friend and whom he has been mentoring in techniques of lovemaking. Thus veins of tragedy and irony are lightly introduced to spice the comedy, although even the serious parts are semi-burlesqued. Sum total bears a pleasant reminiscence of early Chaplin.

Chevalier comes off much better as a song-and-dance man than as a serious thesper, with his native charm, however, fortunately overriding his shortcomings as an actor. Miss Derrien is a pretty newcomer to the screen, while Perier is a first-rate comedian. Minor characters are all expertly cast.

Photography is excellent, but the sound is not up to Hollywood standards. Production is amusingly kept to the primitiveness of the era depicted in motion picture development.

Herb.

The Blue Veil

(FRENCH MADE)
('Le Voile Bleu')

Leo Cohn release of Raymond Artus production for Compagnie Generale Cinematographique. Stars Gaby Morlay. Directed by Jean Stelli. Screenplay by Francois Campaux; camera, Rene Caveau; music, A. Theurer. At Studio theatre, N. Y., week of Oct. 1, '47. Running time, **90 MINS.**

Louise....................Gaby Morlay
Mona....................Alvire Popesco
Mme. Breuilly....................Marcelle Geniat
Ernest....................Alerme
Perrette....................Charpin
Antoine....................Larquey
Judge....................Aime Clariond
Doctor....................Rene Devillers

(In French; English Titles)

The slow pacing of "The Blue Veil," combined with its unabashed bid for lachrymose response, makes this French import a risky proposition even for the usual run of art houses. Film, designed as a tribute to child nurses, is too frequently repetitious, holds little sustained story telling power and save for the excellent performance of Gaby Morlay in the central role, offers little for U. S. audiences.

Yarn has Miss Morlay cast as a World War I widow whose child dies at birth, and consequently consecrates herself to the care of other peoples' children. She gets a succession of governess' jobs, and at one point even gives up a romantic attachment in order to be near her charge. Windup of the film is idealized with a reunion with all her previous wards.

There are some sequences in which the film gets a bit of movement. One of them is her loss of a child to his parents after latter left him in her charge for a number of years. Other is the sequence in which she sustains injuries while saving an infant. Otherwise, the static concept of the film is too much to take.

Other than Mlle. Morlay, the cast gives a uniformly adequate account. Most of the supporting players make too spasmodic appearances to distinguish themselves. The photography is okay and the titles are comprehensive.

Jose.

On the Old Spanish Trail

(COLOR-SONGS)

Republic release of Edward J. White production. Stars Roy Rogers, Tito Guizar; features Jane Frazee, Andy Devine, Estrelita Rodriguez. Directed by William Whitney. Screenplay, Sloan Nibley from original by Gerald Geraghty; camera (Trucolor), Jack Marta; music, Morton Scott; editor, Tony Martinelli. Tradeshown, N.Y., Oct. 17, '47. Running time, 75 MINS.

Roy Rogers....................Roy Rogers
Ricco....................Tito Guizar
Caudy Martin....................Jane Frazee
Cookie Bullfincher....................Andy Devine
Lola....................Estrelita Rodriguez
Harry Blaisdell....................Charles McGraw
Marco the Great....................Fred Graham
Al....................Steve Darrell
Gus....................Marshall Reed
Silas MacIntyre....................Wheaton Chambers
Bob Nolan and Sons of Pioneers

"On the Old Spanish Trail" is a simple musical western with a couple of variations. Except that it's in color and that its locale and situation involve a cowboy tentshow, it's the usual hard-riding, shootin' and sluggin' oater-with-songs. Within those limitations, it should get satisfactory business.

With plot is musical comedy stuff, not only because it supplies mild continuity for a series of song cues, but because its credibility doesn't bear severe scrutiny. However, in that respect it merely conforms to sagebrush traditions, which combines 1947 cars with 1880 frontier law, and invariably presents the most fantastic slugfests from which the principals emerge unmarked. As usual, what matters is not realism, but atmosphere, romance and action galore. On that basis, "On the Old Spanish Trail" qualifies.

In this case the picture has Roy Rogers, Tito Guizar, Jane Frazee and Estrelita Rodriguez, plus Bob Nolan's Sons of the Pioneers, to handle the vocal numbers. Most of the tunes are standard western ballads, but Guizar also sings a short excerpt from "Una Furtiva Lagrima" ("A Furtive Tear"), from Donizetti's "The Elixir of Love." In several instances the tentshow locale provides the setting for the songs.

Performance-wise, the picture is satisfactory. The singing is acceptable and the acting meets the modest standards of westerns. Most of the scenes are outdoor locations, which are fairly good, and the interior sets are realistic. The facial makeup, particularly on the girls, is too obvious. *Hobe.*

While I Love
(BRITISH-MADE)

London, Oct. 8.

20th-Fox release of Edward Dryhurst Productions picture. Features Tom Walls, Sonia Dresdel, Clifford Evans, Carol Raye, Patricia Burke. Directed by John Harlow. Screenplay John Harlow from play by Robert Bell; music, Charles Williams; camera, F. A. Young. Previewed Oct. 7, '47. Running time, **85 MINS.**

Nehemiah....................Tom Walls
Peter....................Clifford Evans
Sally....................Carol Raye
Christine....................Patricia Burke
Julia....................Sonia Dresdel
George....................John Warwick
Selby....................Edward Lexy
Sergeant Pearne....................Charles Victor
Olwen....................Audrey Fildes
Ruth....................Enid Hewit
Ambrose....................Ernest Butcher
Allie....................Johnny Schofield

For those who believe in reincarnation and transmigration of souls, this free adaptation of Robert Bell's play will be satisfying. Those who find this an insufficient theory or reason for the mysterious happenings may not go for it. Chances across the Atlantic are slim because the film has little marquee value even here. There are one or two femme angles that could be exploited. It is the first pic of new production company being made in Metro's British studios.

Story is divided into two parts. Sonia Dresdel and sister, Audrey Fildes, live in a house on the wild Cornish coast. Latter is finding difficulty ending a poem. One night the distraught girl, sleep-walking along the cliffs, falls to her death. After 25 years (1947), Dresdel, refusing to accept that her sister is dead, builds her life around memories of Fildes. The annual broadcast of the tone poem becomes a sacred ritual.

A strange girl wanders in, goes to the piano and plays the tone poem perfectly. She is Carol Raye, a journalist who has lost her memory and has wandered there from London. Miss Dresdel is convinced that Fildes has returned in another's body and decides to keep the stray woman. Also there is a husband who is searching for his lost wife. Every clue points to the Cornwall coast and there, after a repetition of the sleep-walking scene, husband and wife are reconciled on the cliff top.

Included in the story is a secondary love affair, and some "laying on of hands" by Tom Walls, an old retainer reputed to have second sight.

Story can stand little analysis, and direction is uninspired. This is virtually the screen debut of Miss Dresdel, from the stage, but she has to learn that the screen is not the stage. She needs discipline and direction. Miss Raye does what she can with her nebulous role, and Patricia Burke gives a forthright performance of one of the few credible characters. The picture only comes to life when the minor folk are on the screen.

Walls, who has begun a promising second career, is suitably impressive as Nehemiah. Clifford Evans, and John Warwick are dull as a couple of husbands.

Piano solo, composed by Charles Williams, and recorded by Betty Humphy-Beecham (wife of Sir Thomas Beecham) is melodious and reminiscent.

Well exploited, it may draw the women and prove a fair boxoffice success over here. *Cane.*

Uncle Silas
(BRITISH-MADE)

London, Oct. 9.

General Film Distributors' release of Two Cities Film production. Stars Jean Simmons, Katina Paxinou, Derrick de Marney. Directed by Charles Frank. Screenplay by Ben Travers from novel by Sheridan le Fanu; camera, Robert Krasker, Nigel Huke. At Odeon, London, Oct. 8, '47. Running time, **103 MINS.**

Caroline Ruthyn....................Jean Simmons
Madame Rougierre....................Katina Paxinou
Uncle Silas....................Derrick de Marney
Lord Richard Ilbury....................Derek Bond
Lady Monica Waring....................Sophie Stewart
Dudley Ruthyn....................Manning Whiley
Dr. Bryerly....................Esmond Knight
Austin Ruthyn....................Reginald Tate
Mrs. Rusk....................Marjorie Rhodes
Giles....................John Laurie
Branston....................Frederick Burtwell
Sleigh....................George Curzon
Rigg....................Frederick Ranalow
Mary Quince....................Patricia Glyn
Vicar....................O. B. Clarence

Only excuse for this blood-and-thunder meller appears to have been the desire to screen what is alleged to be one of the first thrillers. That Sheridan le Fanu's novel is still in public demand probably explains why over $1,000,000 was spent on a yarn that should have been allowed to stay on the shelf. This labored hokum can add little to British prestige. It's not for export.

Action is set in 1845, when a 16-year-old girl is left a rich ward of her unscrupulous Uncle Silas (Derrick de Marney). She learns to loath her ex-governess, Katina Paxinou, and her uncle's son, both being in league with the old man to murder Jean Simmons and grab her coin. Of course there's the doctor who distrusts Silas and the hero—who rides to the rescue.

It is difficult to understand why Miss Paxinou was asked to play the villainous, alcoholic hag, and more difficult to understand why she accepted. Miss Simmons is all-at-sea as the heroine, the 16-year-old ward. Derrick de Marney hams all over the place as Uncle Silas.

Picture has been given good production, and there's merit in some of camera work, but quaint angles are no compensation for a hopeless story. This is Charles Frank's debut as a director. While deserving sympathy, he at the same time shows promise.

Best hope for this is to exhibit it as a comic interpretation of a past era. As such it might draw here. *Cane.*

Flickorna I Smaland
("The Girls in Smaland")
(SWEDISH-MADE)

Scandia Films release of Sandrew-Bauman production. Stars Sickan Carlsson, Ake Gronberg. Directed by Schamyl Bauman. Screenplay by Rune Waldecrantz, Ragnar Arvedson, Bauman; camera, Hilmer Ekdahl; music, Gunnar Johansson. At 5th Ave. Playhouse, N. Y., Oct. 4, '47. Running time, **100 MINS.**

Christina Larson....................Sickan Carlsson
Gunnar Carlman....................Ake Gronberg
Foreman Algotson....................Sigge Fuerst
Laban....................John Elfstroem
Hanna....................Rut Holm
Forsman....................Carl Reinholds
Gypsy Emma....................Ruth Kasdan
Farmer Alfred Joensson....................Douglas Hage
Ottilia....................Carin Swenson
The Photographer....................Artur Rolen
Ester....................Ninni Loefberg
Maertha....................Ingrid Oestergren
Gypsy Mans....................Kolbjoern Knudsen
Gypsy Elias....................Nils Hallberg
Danjel ve korsgrinna....................Victor Haak

(In Swedish; English Titles)

This importation is a mediocre comedy romance not likely to cause any stir at the art house wickets. "Flickorna I Smaland" is limited by a trite story structure handled without distinctive touches. If there are any laughs imbedded in the Swedish dialog, neither the thesping nor the English titling relay that impression to Yank customers.

Points of appeal in the pic are the leisurely bucolic scenes of life on a farm and the musical score. Latter comprises only two numbers, both of which having a winsome folk song quality that should have earned a couple of reprises but didn't. Film is also marked by firstrate outdoor photography which almost succeeds in covering up the thin spots in the story.

Plot has been derived from the cliche of baseless suspicions between lovers. After a young knockabout settles down as a farmhand and wins the fancy of the femme owner of the establishment, usual misunderstandings set in when he's seen in the company of a gypsy gal. It's only a question of time before he establishes his honest intentions and marries the boss lady. In between, there's a melodramatic diversion in which the gypsy and her accomplices steal a horse from the farm and give the hero a chance to show his fighting stuff.

Performances by Ake Gronberg, as the farmhand, and Sickan Carlsson as his femme boss, are okay but show nothing exceptional. Miss Carlsson, however, is a looker with a promising voice who might have possibilities for Hollywood. Several players in minor roles register with creditable performances. *Herm.*

Quai Des Orfevres
(Goldsmith's Embankment)
(FRENCH-MADE)

Paris, Oct. 1.

Corona release of Majestic Films production. Stars Louis Jouvet; features Bernard Blier, Suzy Delair, Pierre Larquey, Simone Renant, Jeanne Fusier-Gir, Charles Dullin. Directed by Henri-Georges Clouzot. Screenplay and dialog by Clouzot and Jean Ferry, after the novel by S. A. Steeman. Music, Francis Lopez; camera, Armand Thirard. Previewed in Paris, Sept. 23, '47. Running time, **110 MINS.**

Police Inspector....................Louis Jouvet
Husband....................Bernard Blier
Torchsinger....................Suzy Delair
Taxidriver....................Pierre Larquey
Photographer....................Simone Renant
Hatcheck girl....................Jeanne Fusier-Gir
The banker....................Charles Dullin

"Quai des Orfevres" being for the French the equivalent of what "Scotland Yard" is for the British, indicates clearly that this is a detective meller. In every respect it is outstanding in French production and for acting, direction, tempo and all other phases compares very well to Hollywood product. For the French speaking countries, both on Henri-Georges Clouzot's name as director of "Le Corbeau" and for marquee pull of Louis Jouvet, it's a sure top grosser. An excellent bet for South America. If well dubbed, it might get distribution in U. S., or else it's worth remaking for America.

The murder on which the investigation hangs is but an excuse for the story, which combines a character study of a show business couple, detective work most realistically staged in authentic sets of police headquarters. Shows the French criminal investigation procedure with plenty of suspense at various stages of the plot, and no small amount of sex appeal. Also human interest.

Jouvet, as the star, does not enter the picture until it has rolled some time. It opens showing Suzy Delair, an ambitious smalltime torchsinger, making overtures to a banker who can star her overnight, despite the jealousy of her husband. Miss Delair is of the Mae West type, and sings a song, "Tralala," quite appropriate to her style, in a way to make her the most sirenish figure on the French screen. (Song is to lyrics by Andre Hornez, music by Francis Lopez).

Jouvet does his part of the poor but honest detective with his usual peculiar mannerisms, but in exemplary manner. Bernard Blier, as the weak husband whom jealousy makes a potential murderer, brings out everything in the character. Miss Delair is alluring as the woman who is ready to go a long way to get starred.

Simone Renant, as the photographer who is the couple's best friend, is very plausible. Charles Dullin, legit actor who specializes in character parts, is suitably repulsive as the picture-maker. Pierre Larquey is the honest taxidriver whom police methods compel to turn informant in spite of himself, and Jeanne Fusier-Gir is the blabbering woman who, through desire to place herself in the limelight (she has only a bit), starts the whole ball rolling.

Direction by Clouzot is of the best. He has taken full advantage of every possible opportunity to bring out character and has managed to keep the tempo at a fast clip all the time. He has had excellent support from cameraman Armand Thirard, one of the best French lensers. Sets of Max Douy are authentic. *Maxi.*

Monsieur Vincent
(FRENCH-MADE)

Paris, Oct. 1.

A. G. D. C. release of E. D. I. C. (Georges Maurer) and Union Generale Cinematographique production. Stars Pierre Fresnay. Directed by Maurice Cloche. Original story and screenplay by Jean Bernard Luc and Jean Anouilh. Dialog by Anouilh. Camera, Claude Renoir. Music by M. Grunewald. Previewed in Paris. Running time, **122 MINS.**

Saint Vincent de Paul....................Pierre Fresnay
Cardinal de Richelieu....................Aime Clairiond
Mr. de Gondi....................Jean Debucourt
Mme. de Gondi....................Lise Delamare
Anne d'Autriche....................Germaine Dermoz
Mme. Grousault....................Gabrielle Dorziat
Louise Marillac....................Yvonne Gaudeau
Abbe Portail....................Jean Carmet
Chancelier Seguier....................Pierre Dux
Mr. de Rougemont....................Georges Vitray
Hospital Supervisor....................Marcel Vallee

Depicting the life of Vincent de Paul, a humble cleric who incepted social work in France and was made a saint for his good works and exemplary life, this is less a picture with a story than with a message. In all Roman Catholic countries it will enjoy the enthusiastic backing of the church, which gave it its full endorsement from the start.

Saint Vincent de Paul was a poor peasant boy who was born in southern France in 1576, and died in 1660. His early life was not especially edifying, until he was caught by Algiers pirates and made a slave there for some years. After he was freed, he took to the cloth, and the misery he had seen when a slave as well as his inborn goodness turned him into a social worker whose success with the great and the poor alike brought him into the limelight.

From the picture angle, this is just a series of sketches in which Pierre Fresnay, in the title role, is the central figure. All other parts are incidental. Fresnay acquits himself masterfully, in a performance that got him the award for best acting at the Venice festival. There is neither plot nor suspense at any time in the film. Despite the long footage, however, the humanity which pervades the picture, Fresnay's acting and Maurice Cloche's direction save the picture from being boring.

Supporting cast, made up of names well known here, is adequate if somewhat stagey in places. The sets by Rene Renoux are adequately suggestive of the period. Camera work by Claude Renoir (brother of Jean and Pierre Renoir) is commendable.

Maxi.

Non Coupable
('Not Guilty')
(FRENCH-MADE)

Paris, Oct. 1.

Sirius release of Ariane production. Stars Michel Simon; features Jany Holt, Jean Wall, Jean Debucourt, Robert Dalban. Directed by Henri Decoin. Original screenplay, Marc Gilbert Sauvageon; camera, Jacques Lemarre; music, Marcel Stern. At Helder, Vivienne, Balzac and Scala, Paris. Running time, 102 MINS.

This unique film won its star, Michel Simon, the award for the best male acting at the Locarno festival. Psychological twist of the Marc Gilbert Sauvageon script shows an intelligent man committing "perfect murders." But when the police fail to detect his crimes, thus depriving him of the credit he thinks he's entitled, the murderer commits suicide. Story is an excellent idea. However, direction and lensing are too inconsistent to afford much of a market for "Non Coupable" in the U. S.

Yarn revolves around Simon, who portrays a provincial doctor. His professional reputation damaged because of his penchant for drinking, the physician's colleagues shun him. Later he has an affair with an expostoffice employee and makes his first excursion into crime by pulling a "hit-and-run" when his car accidentally kills a motorcyclist.

Series of killings ensues in rapid order when Simon by chance discovers his mistress has been cheating on him with a garage owner. He rubs him out and also does away with a surgeon who's given him the brushoff. Third murder comes about when the errant physician drives his gal friend to an apparently accidental death by drowning. Throughout these heinous acts Simon continuously seeks recognition for his intelligence in contriving the murders.

Failure of detective Jean Debucourt to solve the bloodshed provokes Simon's disgust. He then writes a confession and takes his life. Confession, incidentally, is designed to win him posthumous credit, but its purpose is frustrated when the missive is burned before authorities discover it. U.S. distribution rights have already been sold to Andre Lelarge.

Maxi.

Foreign Films

"Livet I Finnskogarna" ("Life in the Finn Woods") **(Swedish-made).** Sandrew-Bauman release of Rune Waldekrantz production. Stars Karl-Henrik Fant, Sighrit Carlsson; features Carl Jularbo, Naima Wifstrand, Bengt Logardt, Barbro Ribbing, Eivot Landstrom, John Elfstrom, Mirjami Kuosmanen. Directed by Ivar Johansson. Screenplay, Johansson and Waldekrantz; camera, Erik Blomberg; music Gunnar Johansson. At Olympia, Stockholm. Running time, **96 MINS.**

With "King of the Accordion" Carl Jularbo making his screen debut in film titled after one of his waltz compositions, picture should register good business throughout Scandinavia but offers doubtful appeal for the world market. Finnish actress Mirjami Kuosmanen is also making her bow in this entry—the first time in years that Finn talent has been used by the industry in Sweden.

"Lata Lena Och Bla Ogde Per" ("Lazy Lena and Blue-eyed Per") **(Swedish-Made).** Sandrew-Bauman release of Carl Nelson-Monark Film production. Features John Elfstrom, Rut Holm, Anna-Greta Krigstrom, Olof Bergstrom, Josua Benktsson, Gudrun Brost, Anders Frithiof, John Botvid. Directed by Lennart Wallen. Screenplay, John Elfstrom, based on play by Ernst Fastbom; camera, Sven Nykvist; music, Gunnar Johansson. At Astoria, Stockholm. Running time, **88 MINS.**

Remake of a Swedish comedy adapted from a classic appears to have little appeal for any market including the Scandinavian area. Originally filmed in 1932, picture was a flop then and there's no improvement in this edition. Gudrun Brost has essayed a comeback but fares badly in a poor role. Sven Nykvist's lensing helps, as does John Elfstrom's adaptation. However, nothing can save this hopeless film.

"Det Vackraste Pa Jorden" ("The Most Beautiful on the Earth") **(Swedish-Made).** Europa production and release. Stars Anders Henriksson, Inger Juel; features Marianne Lofgren, Der Oscarsson, Eerik Hell, Stig Jarrell, Irma Christensson, Ann Westerlund, Carl Henrik Fant. Directed by Henriksson. Screenplay, Bertil Malmberg; camera, Harald Berglund; music Herbert Sandberg. At Saga, Stockholm. Running time, **110 MINS.**

Brilliant story, scripting and musical direction have made this psychological study of an unfaithful wife a top quality picture suited for any segment of the world market. Yarn, however, may run afoul of the censors in some situations. Inger Juel chalks up a sterling performance as the erring wife. As her husband, Erik Hell also shines. Lensing is first-class.

"Skepp Till India-Land" ("Ship to India-Land") **(Swedish-Made).** Nordisk Tonefilm release of Lorens Malmstedt production. Stars Holger Lowenadler, Birger Malmsten; features Gertrud Fridh, Anna Lindahl, Lasse Krantz, Jan Molander, Erik Hell, Neami Brise, Hjordis Petterson, Douglas Hage, Ake Fridell, Peter Lindgren. Directed by Ingmar Bergman. Screenplay, Bergman, based on play by Martin Soederhjelm; camera, Goran Strindberg; music, Erland von Koch. At Royal, Stockholm, Sept. 22, '47. Running time, **100 MINS.**

Transition of the Martin Soederhjelm play into cellouloid has made a good film. Ingmar Bergman's crisp direction and scripting plus fine camerawork of Goran Strindberg are principally responsible for making this picture a crack tale of a salvage boat and four persons whose lives are tied up in the ship's destiny. Holger Lowenadler's portrayal of the captain is neat thesping and others in cast measure up to his standard. Okay for the U. S. mart.

"Immortal Face" ("Das Unsterbliche Antilitz") **(Austrian-Made).** Sascha Distributing release of Geza von Cziffra production. Stars Marianna Schoenauer, O. W. Fischer, Helene Thimig; features Siegfried Breuer, Attila Hoerbiger. Directed by Carl Hofer. Screenplay, Cziffra; camera, Ludwig Berger; music, Alois Melichar. At Apollo, Vienna. Running time, **110 MINS.**

Film version of the life of painter Anselm Feuerbach is a dramatic yarn with a new twist to an old plot. The artist's model elopes with another man but the unhappy denouement should be an audience pleaser nevertheless. Acting is generally good as is the camerawork. Alois Melichar's music lacks originality. Picture may have fair success in German-language situations in the U. S.

Miniature Reviews

"So Well Remembered" (British) (RKO-Rank). Mature, impressive adaptation of James Hilton's novel will draw.

"Killer McCoy" (M-G). Fast action melodrama of prize ring. Sturdy Mickey Rooney vehicle with good b.o. prospects.

"It Had to Be You" (Col). Fine farce with Ginger Rogers and Cornel Wilde that should please plenty.

"Christmas Eve" (UA). George Raft, George Brent, Randolph Scott, Ann Harding in overly-contrived episodic pic; so-so b.o.

"Road to the Big House" (SG). Dull melodrama of the pitfalls of crime; strictly for secondary houses.

"Linda Be Good" (Songs) (PRC). Lightweight comedy okay for lesser situations.

So Well Remembered
(BRITISH-MADE)

RKO release of Adrian Scott (J. Arthur Rank) production. Stars John Mills, Martha Scott, Patricia Roc, Trevor Howard, Richard Carlson; features Reginald Tate, Frederick Leister, Beatrice Varley. Directed by Edward Dmytryk. Screenplay, John Paxton, from novel by James Hilton; camera, Frederick A. Young; score, Hanns Eisler; musical director, C. Bakaleinikoff; editor, Harry Gerstad. Tradeshown N.Y., Oct. 27, '47. Running time, 113 MINS.

George	John Mills
Olivia	Martha Scott
Julie	Patricia Roc
Whiteside	Trevor Howard
Charles	Richard Carlson
Mangin	Reginald Tate
Annie	Beatrice Varley
Channing	Frederick Leister
Spivey	Ivor Barnard
Wetherall	Julian D'Albie
Baby Julie	Juliet Mills
Librarian	Roddy Hughes
Morris	John Turnbull
Mayor	Lyonel Watts
Woman	Kathleen Boutall
Narration	James Hilton

A mature, thoughtful story, plus intelligent, skilled and tasteful handling, make "So Well Remembered" an entertaining, impressive picture. It is likely to get favorable reviews, which, with the probable word-of-mouth recommendation, should pull good grosses in larger communities, particularly in first-runs and class neighborhoods. The lack of top marquee names and the absence of readily-exploitable romantic elements may limit appeal in smaller towns and subsequent-runs.

"So Well Remembered" is primarily a film for adults. Based upon James Hilton's novel of life in a Lancashire mill town between the two world wars, it is a flashback story of interplay of characters, an amalgam of varied personalities and emotions in a provocative basic situation. It has topical elements, some of which have interesting special values of the present highly-charged moment. But the picture is, above all, plausible story-telling and absorbing human drama.

The yarn's chief characters, representing the main opposing forces, are the quiet, earnest, liberal-minded, stubbornly idealistic local editor, and the possessive, ruthless, but pretty and deceptively appealing daughter of a notorious factory-owner. Stemming from opposite social and economic poles in the town, their lives meet, merge for a time and, as the highly charged circumstances bring out their contrasting characters, they separate and finally become deadly enemies.

At the finale, as they face each other in middle age, they represent not merely adversaries in a human drama, but the personifications of two eternally opposing social, economic, political, and, indeed, moral philosophies. Since the man, the sympathetic character, is triumphant, at least for the moment, over the woman, who is unsympathetic, the picture ends on a pleasant note, and will probably satisfy popular taste.

As adapted by John Paxton, the Hilton story is a skillful blend of apparently authentic English country atmosphere, believable characters, stimulative situations, steady pace and mounting suspense, without undue dramatic license. And, though the picture's lack of romantic emphasis and its concern with serious matters may limit its mass popularity, they add stature and depth.

From a directorial viewpoint, "So Well Remembered" might be a trifle less unhurried, but it is eloquently understated and its vital scenes are properly projected. The performances are unusually creditable for every one of the principals. John Mills has an expressive reticence as the editor and Martha Scott gives one of the top performances of her career as the possessive wife-and-mother, particularly in the unsympathetic latter scenes, when her American accent is less noticeable.

Trevor Howard is excellent in the juicy part of a drunken village doctor, and Patricia Roc and Richard Carlson are effective as the young love interest. Hanns Eisler's score, consisting chiefly of mood-setting scene bridges, is unobtrusive and occasionally seems to add dramatic dimension.

Hobe.

Killer McCoy

Hollywood, Oct. 24

Metro release of Sam Zimbalist production. Stars Mickey Rooney, Brian Donlevy, Ann Blyth; features James Dunn, Tom Tully, Sam Levene. Directed by Roy Rowland. Screenplay, Frederick Hazlitt Brennan; based on story and screenplay by Thomas Lennon, George Bruce, George Oppenheimer; camera, Joseph Ruttenberg; score, David Snell; "Swanee River" number by Stanley Donen: editor, Ralph E. Winters. Tradeshown Oct. 23, '47. Running time, 103 MINS.

Tommy McCoy	Mickey Rooney
Jim Caighn	Brian Donlevy
Sheila Carrson	Ann Blyth
Brian McCoy	James Dunn
Cecil Y. Walsh	Tom Tully
Happy	Sam Levene
Bill Thorne	Walter Sande
Johnny Martin	Mickey Knox
Father Ryan	James Bell
Mrs. McCoy	Gloria Holden
Mrs. Martin	Eve March
Waitress	June Storey
Danny Burns	Douglas Croft
Sailor Graves	Bob Steele
Pete Mariola	David Clarke

Metro has concocted a fast action melodrama in "Killer McCoy" to introduce Mickey Rooney to adult roles. It all comes off neatly and should give a good account of itself at the boxoffice. Sentimental hoke is mixed with prize ring action but never gets too far out of hand by virtue of Roy Rowland's careful direction and smart production guidance of Sam Zimbalist.

Rooney makes much of his tailor-made assignment in the title role. He's a tough kid who comes up to ring prominence after accidentally killing his friend, the ex-champ, who had started him on the road up. There's nothing that's very original with the story but scripting by Frederick Hazlitt Brennan has given it realistic dialog that pays off.

Plot develops from time Rooney and his sot of a father, James Dunn, become a song-and-dance team to pad out vaude tour being made by a lightweight champion. Through this association Rooney moves into the ring and after killing his friend ties up with a gambler to cash in on his fistic prowess. He falls in love with the gambler's daughter and quits the ring after a smash battling climax.

Highlights are "Swanee River" soft-shoed by Rooney and Dunn; sweet, sentimental courting of Rooney and Ann Blyth; and the fistic finale that features plenty of rugged action. In handling of the romance Roy Rowland's direction keeps it on a believable plane that registers strongly. He is equally at home in pulling all strings to keep action high and sentiment on the proper hokum level. Only fault is overlength in some top sequences, notably the finale fight.

Brian Donlevy gives strong touch to the gambler role and Miss Blyth gets the most out of every scene. Dunn hokes up assignment as the drunken actor-father with just the right amount of overplaying to stress "ham" character. Sam Levene as the trainer, Tom Tully, Mickey Knox, very good as the champ, Gloria Holden, Bob Steele, standing out as a fighter, Eve March and others turn in sturdy support. June Storey, in a single scene, makes it register big.

Sam Zimbalist production values are spotlighted by ace lensing of Joseph Ruttenberg, the art direction and settings. *Brog.*

It Had To Be You

Columbia release of Don Hartman production. Stars Ginger Rogers, Cornel Wilde; features Percy Waram, Spring Byington, Ron Randell, Thurston Hall, Charles Evans, William Bevan, Frank Orth. Directed by Don Hartman and Rudolph Mate. Screenplay, Norman Panama and Melvin Frank; story, Hartman and Allen Boretz; camera, Rudolph Mate and Vincent Farrar; editor, Gene Havlick; asst. director, Sam Nelson; music, M. W. Stoloff; asst. to the producer, Norman Deming. Previewed in N. Y., Oct. 17, '47. Running time, **98 MINS.**

Victoria Stafford..........Ginger Rogers
"George" / Johnny Elaine..........Cornel Wilde
Mr. Stafford..........Percy Waram
Mrs. Satfford..........Spring Byington
Oliver H. P. Harrington..........Ron Randell
Mr. Harrington..........Thurston Hall
Dr. Parkinson..........Charles Evans
Evans..........William Bevan
Conductor Brown..........Frank Orth
George Benson..........Harry Hays Morgan
Mr. Kimberly..........Douglas Wood
Mrs. Kimberly..........Mary Forbes

"It Had to Be You" is farce of the broadest genre. There are psychological and whimsical overtones in this comedy and if the customers accept it in that idiom they will get plenty of bellylaughs. It's a one-woman show for Ginger Rogers whose fine sense of comedy is ever to the fore; and for that matter, the entire cast, from Cornel Wilde, her co-star, to the rest of the act, it's a troupers' delight. Once Rogers-Wilde bring them in, it's certain to please.

This is one of those fantastic comedies which can't be taken deadpan. Critical endorsement and/or word-of-mouth will have decided influences in certain consumer markets. The Columbia studio, which has been partial to whimsy and fantasy (viz., "Mr. Jordan" and "Down to Earth"), was particularly adventurous with this one, but as Don Hartman & Co. have devised it pic it comes off in tiptop manner. As with Miss Rogers' histrionic dominance, so it is a one-man Hartman undertaking, since he officiates as producer, co-director and co-author of the original. In turn, his co-director, Rudolph Mate, also doubles as co-cinematographer with Vincent Farrar. In fact, somehow this blend of interlocking talents and credits points the way to something or other in future cinematurgy.

"It Had to Be You," incidentally, points up a thing or two as a Hollywood entry. It has a quality which smacks of the best of the French school. The male-Cinderella role, played by the proud fire laddie and quondam Injun, Cornel Wilde, is a refreshing idea. The Injun stuff goes back into Miss Rogers' childhood when a 6-year-old lad in an Indian suit was her first sweetheart. That's been her dreamlover through the years, and unwittingly the hurdle three times as she jilts her grooms-to-be at the altar. It's gotten so that the No. 4 prospect's father complains that "the boys at the club are laying 5-1 this one also won't go through."

Miss Rogers sculpts. Returning from a Maine hiatus, convinced she was going through with it, this dream-prince with the Indian sign on her is discovered in her compartment, and from then on it's a curious mixture of realistic dialog with psychologic overtones. Confused and screwball as it frequently is, the identities are always sharp, and before long it captures the auditor. The laugh results are frequently boffo.

Percy Waram, Spring Byington and Thurston Hall are capital as the distrait parents, and Ron Randell doesn't over-do his slightly sap assignment as the No. 4 to-be-jilted-at-the-altar. The rest are likewise expert.

Norman Panama and Melvin Frank have written some sprightly dialog to match the nicely tempoed action. The locales and atmosphere are otherwise of a modern mood and mode to keep everything in a romantically appealing groove. Camera values especially good. *Abel.*

Christmas Eve

United Artists release of Benedict Bogeaus production. Stars Ann Harding, George Raft, George Brent, Randolph Scott; features Joan Blondell, Virginia Field, Dolores Moran. Directed by Edwin L. Marin. Screenplay, Laurence Stallings, adapted from original stories by Stallings, Richard H. Landau; camera, Gordon Avil; editor, James Smith; music, Heinz Roembeld. Tradeshown N.Y., Oct. 23, '47. Running time, **90 MINS.**

Mario..........George Raft
Michael..........George Brent
Jonathan..........Randolph Scott
Ann..........Joan Blondell
Claire..........Virginia Field
Jean..........Dolores Moron
Aunt Matilda..........Ann Harding
Phillip..........Reginald Denny
Doctor..........Douglass Dumbrille
Psychologist..........Carl Harbord
Butler..........Dennis Hoey
Judge Alston..........Clarence Kolb
Harriett..........Molly Lamont
FBI Agent..........John Litel
Hood..........Walter Sande
Gimlet..........Joe Sawyer
Reichman..........Konstantin Shayne
Auctioneer..........Andrew Tombes
Dr.'s Wife..........Claire Whitney

"Christmas Eve" runs the gamut from a sentimental old lady who plays with her grownup kids' electric trains on the dining room table, to a rodeo cowboy, to the baby-adoption racket, to Nazis who escaped from Europe on the prowl for their hidden loot. And all that, plus much more, in 90 minutes. Result of the overcrowded conditions is a disjointed picture that will have to depend almost entirely on cast names for lure. B.o. prospects only fair.

"Eve" probably rates first run playdates on the basis of its star value, if nothing else. Story of three orphan boys who've been taken under the wing of a rich spinster, the picture has George Raft, George Brent, Randolph Scott and Ann Harding in the four leads. In addition, there are Virginia Field, Joan Blondell and Dolores Moran as the three vis-a-vis, respectively. Even with these names, though, the average exhib will have to do plenty of selling.

Producer Benedict Bogeaus probably had something like the episodic narration of "Tales of Manhattan" in mind when he assigned Laurence Stallings to the scripting job. While "Eve" has as much of a story line to tie the episodes together as did "Manhattan," it's the individual tales themselves that are so widely divergent that militate against the film's plausibility. Overflow of widely-separated themes will probably have the customers scratching their heads in confusion long before the tale is wrapped up in the last reel. Stallings probably deserves a vote of thanks for not having left any loose ends lying around, even though he did take an obvious short-cut in reaching the fadeout for several of the characters.

As the wealthy and eccentric old spinster, Miss Harding is beset by her stuffed-shirt nephew, Reginald Denny, to let him take over administration of the entire estate. She persuades a skeptical but friendly judge to desist until Christmas Eve, however, so that she can round up her three adopted sons to come to her aid. Tale then swings into her search for the trio and episodic stories of their activities since they went out to make their own in the world.

Brent is disposed of first as a ne'er-do-well playboy who's into Denny for 75G in rubber checks. Raft then takes over as a guy on the lam from the FBI, who's become a wealthy cafe op in South America. He's the one who gets tangled up with the bad Nazis. Scott enters the scene as a slightly dipso cowboy who's naively lured into a hassle with a couple of baby racketeers. Anyway, they all finally get together at the old lady's mansion on Christmas Eve, where it's revealed that Raft actually took the rap for Denny, who's both stupid and dishonest. The judge meets the boys, decides the old gal's okay and they all sit down to Christmas dinner. Sound confusing?

Director Edwin L. Marin must have had his hands full in covering such a wide range of characters but makes out okay in guiding them through their paces. Miss Harding, burdened with an ungainly makeup job, throws plenty of corn into her spinster's role and is seldom believable. Raft gets most of the action in a rough-and-tumble with the Nazis, playing the part in his usual deadpan. Brent and Scott, plus the three ingenues, make out okay with their share of the melodramatics. Supporting cast, though not standout, is capable.

Multiplicity of sets, some of which are fairly ornate, indicates Bogeaus must have spent a tidy sum on the picture. Technical credits are in line with the rest of the film, sometimes good and sometimes bad. *Stal.*

Road to the Big House

Hollywood, Oct. 28.

Screen Guild release of Somerset Pictures; Selwyn Levinson-Walter Colmes production, directed by Colmes. Features John Shelton, Ann Doran, Glinn Williams, Dick Bailey, Joe Allen, Jr. Original Screenplay, Aubrey Wisberg; camera, Walter Strenge; editor, Jason Bernie. Previewed Oct. 24, '47. running time, **74 MINS.**

Eddie..........John Shelton
Agnes..........Ann Doran
Butch..........Guinn Williams
Sutter..........Dick Bailey
Bates..........Joe Allen, Jr.
Fred..........Rory Mallinson
Kelvin..........Eddy Fields
Prosecutor..........Walden Boyle
Harvey..........Keith Richards
Collins..........Jack Conrad
Benson..........Charles Jordan
Judge..........C. Montague Shaw
Danny..........John Doucette
Case..........Mickey Simpson

"Road to the Big House" is trite melodrama, unfolded in uninteresting manner. It will get by only as filler product for secondary bookings. Production values marshaled by Walter Colmes show a short budget and his direction is inept in handling melodrama.

Story concerns a bank clerk who gets tired of being poor and lifts $200,000 from the vault. He hides coin and is jailed, figuring on paying debt to society and then getting out to enjoy his spoils. He's target of other cons in stir who are interested in money. There's an engineered jail break by an outside gang which wants the money but the clerk is captured. Finale has him a free man without his loot. His wife had found the hiding place and returned it to the bank.

John Shelton fights his way through corny dialog and situations to register fairly well. Ann Doran, his long-suffering wife, also is handicapped by triteness of lines in the Aubrey Wisberg script. Guinn Williams, a con, Dick Bailey, Joe Allen, Jr., Eddy Fields, and others get by in support.

Walter Colmes' production and direction doesn't build interest. Selvyn Levinson served as associate producer on the Somerset Pictures production. Lensing by Walter Strenge is adequate but film is way overlength at 74 minutes. *Brog.*

Linda Be Good
(SONGS)

Hollywood, Oct. 25.

PRC release of Matty Kemp production. Stars Elyse Knox, Marie Wilson, John Hubbard; features Gordon Richards, Jack Norton, Ralph Sanford, Sir Lancelot, Professor Lamberti. Directed by Frank McDonald. Screenplay, Leslie Vale, George Halasz; original, Dick Irving Hyland, Howard Harris; camera, George Robinson; songs, Charles Herbert and Jack Mason, Sir Lancelot; editor, Norman A. Cerf. Previewed Oct. 22, '47. Running time, **66 MINS.**

Linda Prentiss..........Elyse Knox
Roger Prentiss..........John Hubbard
Margie LaVitte..........Marie Wilson
Sam Thompson..........Gordon Richards
Jim Benson..........Jack Norton
Nunnally LaVitte..........Ralph Sanford
Mrs. LaVitte..........Joyce Compton
Eddie Morgan..........Frank Scannell
Sir Lancelot..........Sir Lancelot
Sergeant Hrubichka..........Lenny Bremen
Butler..........Gerald Oliver Smith
Myrtle..........Claire Carlton
Officer Jones..........Alan Nixon
Book Shop Owner..........Bryon Foulger
Frankie..........Edward Gargon
Maitre d'hotel..........Muni Seroff
Mrs. Thompson..........Myra McKinney
Professor Lamberti

"Linda Be Good" is fair comedy with music that will rate sufficient chuckles in lesser situations to get by. It hasn't been too skillfully put together and dialog is awkward but trojan efforts of Marie Wilson playing her dumb chorine character is a big help in spotting number of entertaining sequences.

Two calypso tunes written and sung by Sir Lancelot give some pep to the score. Numbers are "Old Woman with the Rolling Pin" and "Young Girls of Today." Miss Wilson sings "My Mother Says I Mustn't," by Jack Mason. Latter also collaborated with Charles Herbert on the title tune.

Frank McDonald's direction does its best with awkward script by Leslie Vale and George Halasz. Plot has authoress Elyse Knox joining a burlesque show to get color for a new novel. John Hubbard, her husband, is out of town and unaware of situation. Complications are introduced when the husband's boss and a friend date Miss Wilson, burley strip queen, and Miss Knox. Slapstick moves forward to keep the husband and wife in hot water while identities are mixed. Windup has Miss Knox blackmailing the boss into giving her husband a vice presidency so she won't squeal about burlesque adventures to his wife.

Miss Knox and Hubbard are okay as husband-wife team but it's Miss Wilson who sparks the piece. Gordon Richards, Jack Norton, Ralph Sanford, Lenny Bremen, Bryon Foulger and others make for acceptable support. Professor Lamberti spots a neat specialty.

Matty Kemp's production circumvents short budget adequately. Camera work by George Robinson is good and editing is tight. *Brog.*

Elixir of Love
(ITALIAN-MADE)

Film Rights International release of Lux Films production. Stars Margherita Carosio, Riberto Villa, Armando Falconi. Directed by Amleto Bettoni. Screenplay, L. Ronelli and G. Spellani; music, Gaetano Donizetti; camera, Scatrice; English titles, Samuel A. Datlowe. At Cinema Verdi, N. Y., Oct. 24, '47. Running time, **85 MINS.**

Adina..........Margherita Carosio
Dr. Dulcamara..........Armando Falconi
Belcore..........Carlo Romano
Notary..........Luigi Almirante
Panzanella..........Silvio Bacolini
Innkeeper's wife..........Carmen Navascues
Nemorino..........Roberto Villa
Giannetta..........Jones Salinas
Dolores..........Pina Renzi
Don Alvaro..........Olinto Cristina
Innkeeper..........Claudio Ermelli
Rosario..........Livia Minelli

(In Italian; English Titles)

Donizetti's opera, "L'Elisir d'Amore," is used as main support for this film, in the form of an extensive flashback. Voices of opera singers Ferruccio Tagliavini and Vincenso Bettoni are used for the chief arias sung, with former's name being counted on as a draw because of his present Metopera tieup. Film, however, is slow and static, its occasional amusing moments helping to give its simple story the aura of a lavender-and-old-lace chromo. Aside from Italian enthusiasts, it's unlikely that even other type opera-goers will go for it.

Story is the slim one of a traveling quack who helps a bashful village suitor to win his highstrung maid by the aid of a magic potion, an "elixir of love." Quack revisits a certain village, to be met by a youngster who recalls to the aged charlatan the time he brought the lad's parents together years ago. Which enables film to flash back into the opera setting of "L'Elisir," when the quack helped the lad's father out of pique against the latter's rival, who had crossed the doc.

Story is dramatized, with the principals only occasionally slipping into song, to present the opera's well-known arias. Voice dubbing is obvious, especially in the case of the hero, who is kept half-hidden in various shadows, or with his back to the camera, while his arias are being sung. It's difficult to tell whether leading femme is doing her own singing, due to faulty synchronization, although no femme singer is listed in supporting credits, as are Tagliavini and Bettoni.

A bad job of subtitling has been done on the film, the titles occasionally showing up twice, and sometimes obviously not being timed properly with the original dialog or with the action.

Film has some charm, while the singing is good and music well performed. Armando Falconi, playing the role of the likeable rascal, Dr. Dulcamara, gives it a meaty, engaging portrayal. Margherita Carosio is an attractive undecided Adina, and Roberto Villa a handsome bashful suitor. Carlo Romano as the braggart Sergeant Belcore, Luigi Almirante as the notary, Claudio Ermelli as the innkeeper, are good support. *Bron.*

Miniature Reviews

"Cass Timberlane" (M-G). Filmization of Sinclair Lewis novel has all the elements for b.o. strength.

"Escape Me Never" (WB). Errol Flynn, Ida Lupino, Eleanor Parker, Gig Young in good comedy meller; surefire b.o.

"The Fugitive" (RKO). Made-in-Mexico, this anti-Communistic religious theme should do fair business.

"Love from a Stranger" (EL). Routine version of the Bluebeard story for fair boxoffice pull.

"Song of My Heart" (Mono). Based on life and music of Tchaikovsky; interesting told with appeal to classical lovers.

"Roses Are Red" (20th). Neat meller for good support in dualer situations.

"Return of Rin Tin Tin" (Color) (E-L). Brings back canine film hero in okay adventure yarn.

"Driftwood" (Rep.) Walter Brennan, Ruth Warrick, Dean Jagger, Charlotte Greenwood, Natalie Wood in moppet-medico smalltown meller; nice boxoffice.

"Citizen Saint" (Indie). Based on life and miracles of Frances Cabrini; appeal limited but okay for religious screenings.

Cass Timberlane

Metro release of Arthur Hornblow, Jr., production. Stars Spencer Tracy, Lana Turner, Zachary Scott; features Tom Drake, Mary Astor, Albert Dekker, Margaret Lindsay. Directed by George Sidney. Screenplay by Donald Ogden Stewart, from an adaptation by Stewart and Sonya Levien of Sinclair Lewis' novel; camera, Robert Planck; editor, John Dunning. Tradeshown New York, Nov. 3, '47. Running time, **119 MINS.**

Cass Timberlane	Spencer Tracy
Virginia Marshland	Lana Turner
Bradd Criley	Zachary Scott
Jamie Wargate	Tom Drake
Queenie Havock	Mary Astor
Boone Havock	Albert Dekker
Chris Grau	Margaret Lindsay
Diantha Marl	Rose Hobart
Webb Wargate	John Litel
Avis Elderman	Mona Barrie
Lillian Drover	Josephine Hutchinson
Louise Wargate	Selena Royle
Gregg Marl	Frank Wilcox
Dennis Thane	Richard Gaines
Dr. Roy Drover	John Alexander
Eino Roskinen	Cameron Mitchell
Hervey Plint	Howard Freeman
Mrs. Higbee	Jessie Grayson
Herman	Griff Barnett
Alice Wargate	Pat Clark

Metro has accomplished a highly successful translation to the screen of Sinclair Lewis' bookstore boff. Larded heavily with the romantic elements that are never-fail with the matinee trade—and with Spencer Tracy and Lana Turner for the marquee—"Cass Timberlane" is a cinch to keep Metro's checking crews working overtime.

Miss Turner is the surprise of the picture via her top performance thespically. In a role that allows her the gamut from tomboy to the pangs of childbirth and from being another man's woman to remorseful wife, she seldom fails to acquit herself creditably. Tracy, as a matter of fact, is made to look wooden by comparison.

What fault the picture has is its overlong running time. Director George Sidney is unable to hold the pace for two hours and the film lags in the midsection. It's a customary complaint against Metro pix, so much so that even veteran sales chief Bill Rodgers took unguarded cognizance of it at a trade press confab two weeks ago. It's difficult to understand the studio's insistence, especially during these days of economy on turning out films, that exhibitors, the public and even M-G's own sales force would prefer in more abbreviated form. If the studio is going to do any more cutting, let it start with the length of pictures.

This is a love story all the way. Essentially, it's the tenderness of an older man—41, not too old, of course—for a young girl. Tracy, respected small-town judge, pays tender court to Miss Turner, who's strictly out of his class socially, as well as chronologically, until he wins her. She adapts herself to local society and the new life until she thinks she can stand it no more and then is off with the husband's gest-friend, Zachary Scott. Scott, of course, doesn't want her when he can have her and the remorseful femme is eventually back to roost on Tracy's understanding doorstep.

Tracy's meeting and early courting of the gal is difficult to accept, but once that's passed, the only misgiving is that the yarn telegraphs its punches so far ahead. It's got so much of the old schmaltz, however, that all of its shortcomings will be easily forgiven and forgotten by the femmes, from soxers to septuagenarians, who should comprise its principal audience.

In direction, Sidney has done a good job in keeping tight rein on his players, yet giving them sufficient leeway to get in plenty of emoting. An assortment of lesser players in the role of Tracy's socialite friends are particularly effective. They include Mary Astor, Albert Dekker, Margaret Lindsay and Selena Royle.

Production itself, while exhibiting no sign of undue opulence, shows customary Metro attention to quality. *Herb.*

Escape Me Never

Warner release of Henry Blanke production. Stars Errol Flynn, Ida Lupino, Eleanor Parker, Gig Young; features Reginald Denny, Isobel Elsom, Albert Basserman. Directed by Peter Godfrey. Screenplay, Thomas Williamson and Lenore Coffee, based on novel and play by Margaret Kennedy; camera, Sol Polito; editor, Clarence Kolster; dances, Leroy Prinz; music, Erich Wolfgang Korngold. Tradeshown N. Y. Oct. 31, '47. Running time, **101 MINS.**

Sebastian	Errol Flynn
Gemma	Ida Lupino
Fenella	Eleanor Parker
Caryl	Gig Young
Ivor MacLean	Reginald Denny
Mrs. MacLean	Isobel Elsom
Heinrich	Albert Basserman
Steinach	Ludwig Stossel
Landlady	Helene Thimig
Guide	Frank Puglia
Minister	Frank Reicher
Milada Mladova George Zoritch	Ballet Specialty

"Escape Me Never" represents the best break that the Warner factory has given Errol Flynn in a couple of seasons. Cast in a role vastly different from his usual assignment, he shows up remarkably well in an engrossing tale laid in Venice, London and the Italian Alps at the turn of the century. Film has a slightly longhairish tinge but that's proven an asset recently, not a boxoffice liability. Marquee-laden cast, with Ida Lupino, Eleanor Parker and Gig Young sharing the star honors with Flynn, should it make it a big grosser in all situations.

Flynn is given plenty of opportunity to flash the old charm but there's hardly a touch of the usual swashbuckling or boudoir romance activities in his role of a serious composer. Under the capable direction of Peter Godfrey, he turns in one of the best jobs of his career and "Escape" may well mark his arrival at maturity as a serious actor. Miss Lupino, although she's seldom been typed so much as Flynn, has a role here that she can really sink her teeth into and she demonstrates once more her versatility as a serious actress.

Story, scripted by Thomas Williamson and Lenore Coffee from a novel and play by Margaret Kennedy, is cut sharply in half between light romance and heavy drama and therein lies its only fault of note. Switch in mood is too keenly drawn, with no shading to ease the audience gradually from one theme to another.

Tale is imbued with much of the nostalgic flavor of pre-World War I Europe. It tees off in Venice where Young, a struggling young composer, wants to marry the wealthy Miss Parker. Through a misunderstanding, however, her parents think Young is living with Miss Lupino, a widowed waif with an infant son, and so rush Miss Parker off to a resort in the Alps. Seems, though, that it's been Flynn, Young's happy-go-lucky brother, who took Miss Lupino and child in off the streets. To set things right again, the two brothers, Miss Lupino and the moppet start off on foot through the Alps to find Miss Parker and explain the mistake to her.

When they finally catch up with her. Flynn meets her before realizing who she is and makes a pitch for her, getting inspiration thereby for a new ballet. When Miss Lupino threatens to leave him, though, he marries her and the two of them set up shop in a London garret where Flynn finishes the ballet. Still a philanderer, Flynn again goes after Miss Parker and is away with her on a rendezvous when the baby takes sick and dies. He finally realizes he's been a heel and, on the night of his ballet opening, he's reconciled with Miss Lupino while Young and Miss Parker also get together.

Although Flynn and Miss Lupino carry most of the picture, they're given plenty of assist from Miss Parker and Young. Former has seldom been seen to better advantage and Young makes his role of the dull, plodding brother highly believable. Reginald Denny, as Miss Parker's stuffed-shirt father; Isobel Elsom as her understanding mother, and Albert Basserman, as the sympathetic old music conductor, top the supporting cast.

Chief production assist is lent by Erich Wolfgang Korngold's score, with both the ballet and theme music standout. Ballet sequences are tastefully staged by Leroy Prinz and Milada Mladova sparkles in both terping and thesping as the prime ballerina. Entire film is a notable achievement for producer Henry Blanke, with all production credits a definite asset. *Stal.*

The Fugitive

RKO release of Argosy Pictures-John Ford and Merian C. Cooper production (Emilio Fernandez, associate producer), directed by Ford. Stars Henry Fonda, Dolores Del Rio, Pedro Armendariz; features J. Carrol Naish, Leo Carrillo, Ward Bond, Robert Armstrong, John Qualen. Screenplay, Dudley Nichols, based on novel, "The Labyrinthine Ways," by Graham Greene; camera, Gabriel Figueroa; score and musical direction, Richard Hageman; editor, Jack Murray. Tradeshown N. Y., Nov. 3, '47. Running time, **99 MINS.**

Fugitive	Henry Fonda
Indian Woman	Dolores Del Rio
Police Lieutenant	Pedro Armendariz
Police Informer	J. Carrol Naish
Police Chief	Leo Carrillo
El Gringo	Ward Bond
Police Sergeant	Robert Armstrong
Refugee Doctor	John Qualen
Governor's Cousin	Fortunio Bonanova
Organ Grinder	Cris-Pin Martin
Hostage	Miguel Inclan
Singer	Fernando Fernandes

Made in Mexico with Hollywood leads and native extras, "The Fugitive" tells how the government of one of the Mexican states, in a ruthless drive to stamp out religion, hunts down the last remaining priest, captures him by a cruel ruse and has him executed by a firing squad. The picture is rich in atmosphere and is sincerely done, but it is slow in spots and uneven in dramatic power. It lacks romantic appeal and the subject and locale are unfamiliar to most U. S. audiences. It should have moderate draw, but will get support from religious groups.

According to the opening screen narration, "The Fugitive" is a true story, with Biblical overtones and with "topical, timely and universal" qualities. It is apparently based on the efforts of the Mexican government 20-odd years ago to curtail the power of the Catholic church and control its priests.

But as the Soviet government similarly tried to wipe out religion in Russia, and presumably opposes it today in the countries it dominates, "The Fugitive" will probably be widely regarded as an attack on Communism. As such, it is vigorous, unlimited and arousing. And as such it has, as the screen narration says, topical and timely significance.

Parts of the story aren't clear. The government's drive against the church, for instance, isn't fully motivated. The only explanation offered is a rabid speech-from-horseback by the fanatical, callous police lieutenant, as he tries to coax the terrorized peons into betraying their village priest. Subsequently, this storm trooper-like character is shown as actually beset with qualms about his actions and torn by doubts of his anti-religious protestations.

In addition, there is a character of an American bandit-murderer in the story, whose function isn't satisfactorily established, but who risks his life in helping the fleeing priest to reach temporary haven, and later dies trying to prevent his ultimate capture. Also, the picture's fadeout, a miracle-suggestive scene in which a new priest arrives to serve the devout villagers, is insufficiently clarified.

"The Fugitive" is handsomely photographed, with colorful village scenes and impressive landscapes. Some of the sequences, such as the police squad's raid on the quiet village, or the military formations in the constabulary headquarters, are effectively done. But at other times the mounting suspense of the chase is dissipated in meandering action.

Henry Fonda is expressive in the subdued and somewhat static role of the priest. Dolores Del Rio is decorative and mutely impassioned as a devout victim of the law. Pedro Armendariz almost succeeds in resolving the zealous but slightly doubting lieutenant. J. Carrol Naish, Leo Carrillo, Ward Bond and Robert Armstrong are believable in principal supporting roles. *Hobe.*

Love From a Stranger

Eagle Lion release of James J. Geller production. Stars John Hodiak, Sylvia Sidney, Ann Richards; features John Howard, Isobel Elsom, Ernest Cossart, Phillip Tonge, Anita Sharp-Bolster, Frederic Worlock. Directed by Richard Whorf. Screenplay, Philip MacDonald; from play by Frank Vosper; based on story by Agatha Christie. Previewed N. Y., Oct. 80, '47. Running time, **80 MINS.**

Cecily Harrington............Sylvia Sidney
Manuel Cortez..................John Hodiak
Nigel Lawrence..................John Howard
Navis Wilson....................Ann Richards
Auntie Loo-Loo..................Isobel Elsom
Billings........................Ernest Cossart
Ethel..................Anita Sharpe-Bolster
Dr. Gribble....................Phillip Tonge
Inspector Hobday..............Fred Worlock

The old bluebeard story, staple of literature and drama for generations, is given standard treatment in "Love From a Stranger." The result is a fair thriller, without novelty or any particular "viewpoint," with little suspense, surprise or excitement, and only moderate boxoffice prospects.

There have been no vital changes in the story for this screen edition. There are a few additional minor characters, such as the heroine's gabby aunt, a sleuth from Scotland Yard and assorted bits like the postman, cab driver, railroad station attendants, etc.

Also, instead of being tricked into having a paralytic stroke, the murderer is now run over by a team of rampaging horses, climaxing a rock-'em, sock-'em fistfight with the detective and the heroine's devoted suitor. The final scene, incidentally, takes place in one of those synthetic thunderstorms customary for the climaxes of film whodunits. For no apparent reason, the whole picture is interspersed with shots of surf breaking over rocks and pounding across the shore.

Because of, or perhaps in spite of, all the standard plot and directorial devices, "Love From a Stranger" never seems plausible or particularly interesting and, of course, it never causes any spinal shivers. The sinister character of the stranger is indicated at the start, so there's no mystery.

John Hodiak plays the homicidal psychotic with a glowering sort of intensity that would tip off the most credulous wife or servant. That obviously complicates Sylvia Sidney's task of playing the wife, but she gives a direct and spirited performance. Ann Richards is acceptable in the straight part of the heroine's friend, while John Howard is believable as the earnest suitor and Isobel Elsom is effective as the dizzy aunt. Ernest Cossart, Anita Sharpe-Bolster, Phillip Tonge and Frederic Worlock are satisfactory in supporting parts.

As handled by Agatha Christie in the novel, "Love From a Stranger" is supposed to have built compelling atmosphere and a mounting terror, and the Frank Vosper dramatization was fairly successful in London, with the adaptor starred as the villain. The play flopped on Broadway, however, when Alex Yokel presented it in September, 1936, with the star in the same part. Subsequently, while Vosper was returning to England, he disappeared from the ship, and his battered body was later washed up on the French coast. *Hobe.*

Song of My Heart
(MUSIC)

Hollywood, Nov. 1.

Monogram release of Allied Artists presentation, produced by Nathaniel Finston and J. Theodore Reed. Stars Frank Sundstrom; features Audrey Long, Sir Cedric Hardwicke, Mikhail Rasumny, Gale Sherwood. Written and directed by Benjamin Glazer. Added scenes, Bernard Schubert; camera, Roland Totheroh; music director, Nathaniel Finston; music, Peter Ilyitch Tchaikovsky; songs, Janice Torre and Fred Spielman;; editor, Richard Heermance. Previewed Oct. 30, '47. Running time, **83 MINS.**

Peter Tchaikovsky..........Frank Sundstrom
Amalya.........................Audrey Long
Grand Duke..........Sir Cedric Hardwicke
Sergei-Stephan...........Mikhail Rasumny
Sophia.......................Gale Sherwood
Ivan..........................Serge Krizman
Jurgesen................Charles Trowbridge
Nurse..........................Kate Lawson
Lubenstein...................Lester Sharpe
Kolya...........................Drew Allen
Lieut. Sanderson..............Scott Elliott
Lieut. Julian.................Gordon Clark
Pfc. Murphy...................Jimmie Dodd
Rimsky-Korsakoff..........David Leonard
Czar........................John Hamilton
Cesar Cui....................William Ruhl
Aide in Uniform..............Steve Darrell
Borodin.....................Robert Barron
Housekeeper...................Elvira Curci
Ballet Master...............Maurice Cass
Doctor...................Grandon Rhodes
Doorman..................William Newell
Conductor..................Leonard Mudie
Policeman...................Lane Chandler
Manager....................Leonid Snegoff
Moussorgsky................Lewis Howard
Capt. Weatherly.............Stan Johnson
Mess Sergeant.....................Leo Kaye
Priest...........................Jack George
Evans........................Vernon Cansino
Sophia's Mother..................Nina Hansen

The career of Russian composer Peter Ilytich Tchaikovsky gets its first screen presentation in "Song of My Heart." It makes good use of his music in spinning an interesting, although fanciful, tale of the composer's life. Mounting is excellent, the score speaks for itself, although marred by poor sound projection at the preview, and values generally are geared to hold audience attention.

Film was produced by Nathaniel Finston and J. Theodore Reed under the banner of Symphony Films for presentation by Monogram's upper-bracket Allied Artists. "Song" rates the AA classification because of the manner of projecting score values as more than a background for story. Benjamin Glazer, directing from his own script, with added scenes by Bernard Schubert, develops interest with sensitive handling of the plot and players. Frank Sundstrom, Swedish actor, garners attention in the role of the composer. He handles himself capably, demonstrating understanding of the characterization. His piano work was dubbed by the uncredited Jose Iturbi.

Major credit for sparking the story goes to Mikhail Rasumny. His timing, facile comedy and facial expressions give the plot needed lifts to bridge dry spots. It is through his eyes, as the son of Tchaikovsky's man-servant, that the story is told. Rasumny plays the father and the son, and plays both to the hilt.

Composer's early and brief marriage is shown and his later sponsorship by an unknown lady. It is here that story departs from actuality to depict a moving love story between the composer and his sponsor, played by lovely Audrey Long. Their scenes together during a sojourn in Italy and at the finale when Tchaikovsky is fatally ill with cholera register big. Sir Cedric Hardwicke is in briefly as Miss Long's father, and Gale Sherwood shows well as the composer's young wife. She also sings "I Looked For Love." Others in the cast are good.

Roland Totheroh's lensing presents players and smart art direction and set decoration to advantage. Richard Heermance's editing, under the supervision of Otho Lovering, has held running time to crisp 83 minutes. *Brog.*

Roses Are Red

20th-Fox release of Sol M. Wurtzel production. Features Don Castle, Peggy Knudsen, Patricia Knight. Directed by James Tinling. Screenplay, Irving Elman; camera, Benjamine Kline; editor, Frank Baldridge. Tradeshown N. Y. Oct. 20, '47. Running time, **67 MINS.**

Thorne }
Carney }.........................Don Castle
Martha.....................Peggy Knudsen
Jill..........................Patricia Knight
Wall...........................Joe Sawyer
Locke.......................Edward Keane
Knuckle.....................Jeff Chandler
Duke.....................Charles McGraw
Lipton.......................Charles Lane
Cooley......................Paul Guilfoyle
Oliver........................Doug Fowley
Ray.........................James Aurness

Turned out on the B corner of 20th's lot, "Roses Are Red" is an unpretentious, but neatly paced meller that'll serve as firm support in nabe situations. There's not much logic in the yarn but this defect is adroitly covered up by snappy dialog, fast action and a series of sharp characterizations, especially in the minor roles. Production dress and camera work is standard for modest-budgeters.

Story is a formula takeoff on the double-identity stratagem with a cops-and-robbers twist. Don Castle, screen newcomer who bears a striking resemblance to Clark Gable, plays the dual role of an honest district attorney and an underworld character set to take the former's place in order to spring one of the local hoods. After a kidnapping and set of complications involving a crooked detective, the d.a. makes his escape and plays as his twin in order to get the goods on the racketeer mastermind. Director James Tinling draws the action with straight, broad strokes and leaves romantic play hushed in background.

In lead, Castle registers as likeable personality but reveals no adequate thesping range to step into tougher roles as yet. Casting oversight has paired Perry Knudsen and Patricia Knight as the only two femmes in the film. These two actresses look so much alike that, coupled with deliberate twin part of Castle, the pic becomes more confusing than necessary. In minor parts, Joe Sawyer, Jeff Chandler, Charles McGraw and Paul Guilfoyle turn in racy performances that establish basic atmosphere of the film. *Herm.*

Return of Rin Tin Tin
(COLOR)

Hollywood, Nov. 1.

Eagle Lion release of William Stephens production. Features Rin Tin Tin III, Donald Woods, Bobby Blake, Claudia Drake, Gaylord Pendleton, Earl Hudgins. Directed by Max Nosseck. Screenplay, Jack De Witt; original, William Stevens; camera (Vitacolor), Carl Berger; editor, Eddie Mann. Previewed Oct. 29, '47. Running time, **65 MINS.**

Father Matthew..............Donald Woods
Paul, the refugee lad.........Bobby Blake
Mrs. Graham.................Claudia Drake
Melrose ....Gaylord Pendleton
Joe ....Earl Hudgens
Rin Tin Tin III

"The Return of Rin Tin Tin" shapes up as good fare for the smaller situations and should be particularly sturdy in houses catering to moppet and family trade. It brings back to films the descendant of the educated canine known to most adult fans and indications are that new crop of kiddies will take to Rin Tin Tin, III.

William Stephens' production guidance has given picture smart outdoor values, a sentimental story and sufficient demonstration of canine intelligence to fill all release aims. There is no credit for the color process used but picture was filmed in Vitacolor and processed by Cinecolor. The hues are good, showing to advantage the Santa Ynez country and Santa Barbara coast line in California.

Plot hinges on the morale-saving value of the love between a dog and a refugee lad, mentally-scarred by the war in Europe. Bobby Blake is the boy, spending a summer at the Santa Ynez mission while Donald Woods, a kindly priest, seeks to help the lad find himself. It's a hopeless job until Rin Tin Tin, escaping from kennels in Santa Barbara, takes to the boy. From then on action centers on dog's efforts to keep away from his owner and stay with the boy. Finally, canine saves his owner from a mob of wild dogs and is given to Bobby Blake.

There's plenty of tense action in Rin Tin Tin's fight with a wild dog and other demonstrations of intelligence and training at the hands of owner-trainer Lee Duncan. Young Blake is good as the troubled refugee. Woods as the priest measures up. Gaylord Pendleton, kennel operator, Claudia Drake, guardian of the boy, and Earl Hudgins complete the okay cast.

Max Nosseck's direction does a good job with the Jack De Witt script. Lensing by Carl Berger and other credits measure up. *Brog.*

Citizen Saint
(SONGS)

Hollywood, Nov. 4.

State-rights release of Clyde Elliott production. Features Carla Dare, Julie Hayden, June Harrison, Clark Williams, Del Cansino. Directed by Harold Young. Screenplay, Harold Orlob; camera, Don Malkames; editor, Leonard Anderson; songs, Harold Orlob, Arthur A. Norris. Previewed Oct. 29, '47. Running time, **73 MINS.**

Mother Cabrini......................Carla Dare
Sister Delphina...................Julie Hayden
Dorine ....June Harrison
The Prisoner...................Clark Williams
Perry.............................Del Cansino
Cecchina ....Robin Morgan
Anton ....Maurice Cavell
Antonia Tordini...............Lucille Fenton
Sister Grace.....................Joy Bannister
Sister Chiera......................Ruth Moore
Father Vail................William Harrigan
The Peddler......................Ralph Simone
The Prison Guard...............Wm. Sharon
Archbishop ....George Kluge
Salesia ....Lauretta Campeau
Veronica ....Jane Dufrayne
The Baker........................Kurt Kupfer
Committee Chairman..........Alma Du Bus
Dr. Riley......................Richard Good
Landlord ....Boris Aplon

Attempt has been made to detail the life and miracles of Mother

Frances Cabrini but the results are sketchy and the appeal limited for commercial screenings. Film is to be sold through state-right distribution and was produced by Clyde Elliott at the RKO Pathe studios in New York. Best selling for film will come through tieups with religious. groups for sponsorships, otherwise "Citizen Saint" has little to attract ticket sales at the regular boxoffice.

Picture opens and closes with clips of the canonization of Mother Cabrini by the Pope in Rome. In between the Harold Orlob script, directed by Harold Young, works in a·few of the Sister's best miracles and manages general impression of her devotion to the church and a sense of humor that carried her through trying times.

Carla Dare plays the title role and does well by it. Best sequence is that in which she miraculously recalls Julie Hayden, as Sister Delfina, from death. Miss Hayden's experience gives a lift to the scene. June Harrison as the singer who regains her voice through belief in Mother Cabrini, sings "Saint Frances Cabrini," tune by Harold Orlob. A femme group do "Ave Maris, Stella," by Arthur A. Norris. Clark Williams portrays a prisoner saved from execution by Mother Cabrini's intervention. Photography by Don Malkames and other credits are okay.
Brog.

Driftwood

Republic production and release. Stars Ruth Warrick, Walter Brennan, Dean Jagger, Charlotte Greenwood, Natalie Wood; features H.B. Warner, Jerome Cowan, Margaret Hamilton. Directed by Allan Dwan. Original screenplay, Mary Loos, Richard Sale; camera, John Altou; editor, Arthur Roberts; special effects, Howard and Theodore Lydecker. Tradeshown N.Y., Oct. 30, '47. Running time, 88 MINS.

Susan	Ruth Warrick
Murph	Walter Brennan
Dr. Steve Webster	Dean Jagger
Mathilda	Charlotte Greenwood
Jenny	Natalie Wood
Mayor Snyder	Jerome Cowan
Rev. Hollingsworth	H.B. Warner
Essie Keenan	Margaret Hamilton
Judge Beckett	Hobart Cavanaugh
Abner Green	Francis Ford
Dr. Adams	Alan Napier
Hiram Trumbell	Howland Chamberlin
Sheriff Bolton	James Bell
Lester Snyder	Teddy Infuhr
Rev. MacDougal	James Kirkwood
Perkins	Ray Teal
Blaine	Zeke Holland

Homespun yarn about a small far-west town and its fight against spotted fever is backed up by fine performances of five stars and strong production. Fact that Walter Brennan, Ruth Warrick, Dean Jagger, Charlotte Greenwood and Natalie Wood provide solid marquee decoration should bring "Driftwood" nice boxoffice despite lack-lustre title. Diminutive Miss Wood is the youngster who won attention as the little refugee in "Tomorrow Is Forever," "Ghost and Mrs. Muir" and "Miracle on 34th Street."

Story centers about Miss Wood as the orphan girl who's left alone in a desert town when her grandfather dies. He was the minister in the ghost town, and the precocious miss' knowledge of the Bible leads her to constantly quote passages from it. Adopted informally by a young country medico in a nearby community, she manages to creep into the lives of many sedate figures in the typical village.

For the most part this tale has been told in a straightforward manner but the near-deathbed scenes have been permitted to become slightly hokey. This is too bad because Allan Dwan's direction and the original screenplay by Mary Loos and Richard Sale had carried through the story nicely up to that point.

Brennan contributes one of his rare if familiar characterizations as the village's pharmacist and town health officer. He is standout in every scene where allowed to have

much to do. Jagger makes a likeable young town medico anxious to combat spotted fever while Miss Warrick furnishes the heart interest as the schoolteacher with whom he's in love. Miss Greenwood, · usually strictly comedienne, has more or less a straight character as the homely aunt who's still waiting for the right man after 30 years.

The Wood girl, of course, is the orphan, and excellent although permitted to become a bit verbose at times. H. B. Warner is in only for a slight bit as the elderly minister who dies in the first reel. Jerome Cowan and Margaret Hamilton head a strong supporting cast. Shepherd dog that figures actively in plot gets no billing but is remarkably good.

Camera work of John Alton is unusually fine while editing job of Arthur Roberts has resulted in minimum of lesser passages. *Wear.*

Miniature Reviews

"Gentleman's Agreement" (20th). Film version of best-seller, should get critical raves and smash b.o.

"Road to Rio" (Songs) (Par). Another boxoffice winner in Paramount's "Road" series with Crosby, Hope and Lamour.

"Night Song" (Music) (RKO). OK drama of blind musician; marquee furnished by Dana Andrews, Merle Oberon, Artur Rubinstein and others.

"Pirates of Monterey" (Color) (U). Conventional historical adventure-romance of California in the 1840s.

"Fabulous Texan" (Rep.). William Elliott, John Carroll, Catherine McLeod in super-western; good b.o.

"Whispering City" (Canadian) (EL). Canadian-made meller with Paul Lukas, Helmut Dantine, Mary Anderson, looks OK.

"Comin' Thro' the Rye" (Advance). British-made documentary has no chance in U. S.; minor even for England.

"Ghosts of Berkeley Square" (Pathe). Robert Morley stars in this strange British sophisticated comedy; not for America.

"White Unicorn" (GFD). Margaret Lockwood as femme lead gives this British-made tear-jerker a chance in U. S.

"End of the River" (GFD). Sabu, Bibi Ferreira in British-made meller about Brazil; disappointing even for England.

Gentleman's Agreement

20th-Fox release of Darryl F. Zanuck production. Stars Gregory Peck, Dorothy McGuire, John Garfield; features Celeste Holm, Anne Revere, June Havoc, Albert Dekker, Jane Wyatt, Dean Stockwell. Directed by Elia Kazan. Screenplay, Moss Hart, from the novel by Laura Z. Hobson; music, Alfred Newman; orchestral arrangements, Edward Powell; camera, Arthur Miller; editor, Harmon Jones. Previewed N. Y. Nov. 7, '47. Running time, 118 MINS.

Phil Green	Gregory Peck
Kathy	Dorothy McGuire
Dave	John Garfield
Anne	Celeste Holm
Mrs. Green	Anne Revere
Miss Wales	June Havoc
John Minify	Albert Dekker
Jane	Jane Wyatt
Tommy	Dean Stockwell
Dr. Craigie	Nicholas Joy
Prof. Lieberman	Sam Jaffe
Jordan	Harold Vermilyea
Bill Payson	Ransom M. Sherman
Mr. Calkins	Roy Roberts
Mrs. Minify	Kathleen Lockhart
Bert McAnny	Curt Conway
Bill	John Newland
Weisman	Robert Warwick
Miss Miller	Louise Lorimer
Tingler	Howard Negley
Olsen	Victor Kilian
Harry	Frank Wilcox
Receptionist	Marlyn Monk
Maitre D	Wilton Graff
Room Clerk	Morgan Farley

The spectacular critical, popular and financial success of Laura Z. Hobson's "Gentleman's Agreement" as a novel should be repeated by Darryl F. Zanuck's brilliant and powerful film version. Just as the original story of the writer (character), who poses as a Jew to write a magazine series on anti-Semitism was a milestone in modern fiction, the picture is one of the most vital and stirring and impressive in Hollywood history. It should clean up at the boxoffice and bring deserved acclaim to its creators.

The film is, if anything, an improvement over the novel. This is not merely because the story has been better focused and somewhat condensed, without softening the treatment. It is also more graphic and atmospheric than the book and, more importantly, because it has

greater dramatic depth and force, and more personal, emotional impact. Even the least-informed and least-sensitive filmgoer can hardly fail to identify himself with the characters on the screen, and be profoundly moved. The picture provides an almost overwhelming emotional experience and thus is not only highly topical, but truly universal.

Moss Hart's screenplay has eliminated some of the book's secondary characters, such as the writer's bigoted sister, as well as a number of plot sequences, like the events at the winter resort. Also, obviously for censor-morality reasons, the intimate relationship between the writer and Kathy, as well as between Dave and Anne, is now merely inferential in the first case and completely eliminated in the second.

The basic elements of the Hobson work are not only retained, but in some cases given greater dimension and plausibility. This is true of the adaptation, direction and performances. Thus, the first meeting between Phil Green and Kathy is more understandable on the screen than it was on the printed page. Similarly, the couple's other scenes, especially the initial love scene, dramatize their irresistible mutual physical attraction, which overcomes their violent philosophic disagreements.

The picture is memorable for numerous other vivid, impelling passages. For instance, the breakfast scene, when Green tries to explain anti-Semitism to his innocent little son, stamps the picture's urgent theme on the spectator's mind virtually at once. Other unforgettable moments are when the youngster tells his father of being taunted by his playmates, Phil's childlike terror at his mother's heart attack, Kathy's reaction when Phil reveals the "angle" for his magazine series, Phil's helpless rage at the "restricted" resort hotel, the scene with Anne and the unconscious bigot in the cocktail bar, Dave's quiet account of the Jewish soldier's death and Dave's conversation with Kathy about her passive disapproval of "nice" anti-Semites.

There are many other fine ones, but the picture isn't perfect. There are also disappointing or confusing scenes. One is the party given by Kathy's sister, which remains as unresolved on the screen as in the book, and as lacking in realistic atmosphere. In the same scene, the stupid Connecticut dowagers seem exaggerated. Celeste Holm, with some of the film's most pungent lines, frequently reads them too fast for intelligibility. And the scene in which Phil's mother reads from his articles seems verbose and preachy, although her lines about "your father would have been pleased" are acutely touching.

Another measure of the success of "Gentleman's Agreement" as a picture is the distinguished quality of so many of its individual performances. As Phil Green, the magazine writer, Gregory Peck gives unquestionably the finest performance of his career to date. He is quiet, almost gentle, progressively intense and resolute, with just the right suggestion of inner vitality and turbulence.

Dorothy McGuire, too, is dramatically and emotionally compelling as Kathy, adding considerable scope and depth to anything she has done heretofore. The range from her somewhat flippant opening scene to the searing final one with John Garfield is impressive. Garfield is a natural in the part of Dave, giving it admirable strength and understated eloquence.

Except for her fault of diction noted above, Miss Holm is excellent in the likable part of Anne, while Anne Revere turns in another of her expressively terse portrayals as the mother. June Havoc as the anti-Semitic Jewish secretary, Albert Dekker as the red-blooded publisher, Jane Wyatt in the bit part of Kathy's sister, Dean Stockwell as the manly urchin, Nicholas Joy as the hypocritical doctor, and Sam Jaffe as the satirically philosophical scientist, are all excellent.

Hart's screen adaptation is masterful, and Elia Kazan's direction, added to his work on such films as "Boomerang," establishes him in the top rank in Hollywood. (He already is on the Broadway stage.) Arthur Miller's photography is outstanding, and the settings and special effects are exceptional. In sum, "Gentleman's Agreement" is more than a top-drawer adaptation of a successful book and a worthy treatment of a vital subject—it is a credit to the screen. *Hobe.*

Road to Rio

(Songs)

Hollywood, Nov. 11.

Paramount release of Daniel Dare production. Stars Bing Crosby, Bob Hope, Dorothy Lamour; features Gale Sondergaard, Frank Faylen, Wiere Bros. (3), Andrews Sisters (3). Directed by Norman Z. McLeod. Original story and screenplay, Edmund Beloin and Jack Rose; camera, Ernest Laszlo; songs, Johnny Burke, James Van Heusen; music, Robt. Emmett Dolan; editor, Ellsworth Hoagland. Tradeshown Nov. 10, '47. Running time, 100 MINS.

Scat Sweeney	Bing Crosby
Hot Lips Barton	Bob Hope
Lucia Maria De Andrade	Dorothy Lamour
Catherine Vail	Galo Sondergaard
Trigger	Frank Faylen
Tony	Joseph Vitale
Rodrigues	Frank Puglia
Cardoso	Nestor Paiva
Johnson	Robert Barrat

Stone-Barton Puppeteers
Jerry Colonna
Andrews Sisters

This celluloid junket along the "Road to Rio" should find smooth riding to sturdy boxoffice. The pattern established by other Paramount "Road" pictures is solidly followed by Daniel Dare's production to keep the laughs spilling and the paying customers satisfied. Background is laid in Latin-America, which furnishes reason for listenable tequilla score and pert new tunes by James Van Heusen and Johnny Burke.

There are no talking animals in this to prep uproarish see-hear gags, but a capable substitute is a trumpet that blows musical bubbles. Stunt pays off as one of a number of top, hard-punching laugh-getters. Norman Z. McLeod's direction blends the music and comedy into fast action and sock chuckles that will please followers of the Crosby-Hope-Lamour series.

Able song selling is given to "But Beautiful" and "You Don't Have to Know the Language" by Crosby. Miss Lamour tosses off "Experience" for listening pleasure. Two male stars combine on "Apalachicola, Fla.," for laughs as song-dance team, while the Andrews Sisters lend their special touch to "For What?" Score is further abetted by inclusion of five rhythmical Latin standards.

Crosby and Hope repeat their slap-happy characters in the Edmund Beloin-Jack Rose plot. Opening establishes the boys, as usual, in trouble and broke. When they set a circus on fire, pair escape by taking refuge on a ship heading for Rio. It doesn't take them long to discover a damsel in distress (Miss Lamour) and action centers around their efforts to save her from a wicked aunt and a forced marriage. Beloin and Rose pulled all stops in assuring generous supply broad gags, but wasted a lot of time finishing punch lines. Audiences start their roaring before a gag is finished so the tag is never heard.

Star trio is up to all demands and gives extra punch because of obvious enjoyment of playing roles. Aiding fun are the Wiere Bros., dopey trio of Latins picked up by Crosby and Hope. Gale Sondergaard heads up the menace as the wicked aunt who tries to marry off Miss Lamour so she can get her money, using hypnosis. Frank Faylen, Joseph Vitale, Nestor Paiva and others are capable. Jerry Colonna, the talking mustache, is cut in for a wacky finale in true "the Marines to the rescue" style.

Ernest Laszlo's camera work is an asset, as are art direction, settings, special photographic effects and Robert Emmett Dolan's musical direction. *Brog.*

Night Song

(MUSIC)

Hollywood, Nov. 11.

RKO release of Harriet Parsons production. Stars Dana Andrews, Merle Oberon, Ethel Barrymore; features Hoagy Carmichael, Jacqueline White, Donald Curtis, Walter Reed. Directed by John Cromwell. Screenplay, Frank Fenton, Dick Irving Hyland; adapted by DeWitt Bodeen from story by Hyland; camera, Lucien Ballard; score, Leith Stevens; song, Hoagy Carmichael, Fred Spielman, Janice Torre; editor, Harry Marker. Tradeshown Nov. 10, '47. Running time, 101 MINS.

Dan	Dana Andrews
Cathy	Merle Oberon
Miss Willey	Ethel Barrymore
Chick	Hoagy Carmichael
Connie	Jacqueline White
George	Donald Curtis
Jimmy	Walter Reed
Mamie	Jane Jones

Artur Rubinstein
Eugene Ormandy

"Night Song" packs some competent performances, both musical and thespian, to help its boxoffice. It's a drama of a musician saved from bitterness over sudden blindness by the love of a girl, and the top names in the cast carry marquee weight. Latter value will be an aid in pulling customers, indicating average grosses in most situations.

Physical values are good, the score registers on the ear, particularly Artur Rubinstein's piano performance of the Piano Concerto in C Minor, written for the film by Leith Stevens. Backing that assist is Eugene Ormandy conducting the New York Philharmonic Symphony Orchestra.

Dana Andrews as the composer generally accounts for a topnotch performance. His bitterness in the early part of the film is much too stern as directed to register realistically but carries feeling. After he's cured, character takes on a frivolous aspect but actor manages the transitions called for in plot with considerable skill.

Merle Oberon is extremely likeable and attractive as the rich girl who believes so much in Andrews' possibilities that she adopts a blind pose herself. Actress' role is entirely sympathetic and she skillfully carries an audience with her.

Balancing dramatics are lighter performances by Ethel Barrymore and Hoagy Carmichael. Former's light touch gives plenty of zip to lines furnished by the Frank Fenton-Dick Irving Hyland script. Carmichael, as Andrews' seeing-eye friend, brings a personality that stands out to the part. Also, he has opportunity to sing a typical Carmichael number, "Who Killed 'Er," written by himself in collaboration with Fred Spielman and Janice Torre.

John Cromwell's direction plunges the players into brittle, staccato situations as story gets underway. Abrupt breakoff of early scenes by script and direction makes establishment of feeling difficult and sympathy for characters thin. Dialog puts a bit too much emphasis on difference between wealth and poverty, but when off the soapbox tells an interesting story with both feeling and lightness.

Harriet Parsons' production guidance under the executive supervision of Jack L. Gross has invested picture with good physical background. Locale is San Francisco and New York and special effects blend well with studio lensing by Lucien Ballard. His camera graces players and settings furnished by art direction and set decorations. Leith Stevens' musical direction as well as his piano concerto are excellent. *Brog.*

Pirates of Monterey

(COLOR)

Universal release of Paul Malvern production. Stars Maria Montez, Rod Cameron; features Mikhail Rasumny, Philip Reed, Gilbert Roland, Gale Sondergaard. Directed by Alfred Werker. Screenplay, Sam Hellman and Margaret Buell Wilder; original, Edward T. Lowe and Bradford Ropes; camera (Technicolor), Hal Mohr and W. Howard Greene; music, Milton Rosen; editor, Russell Schoengarth. Tradeshown N. Y., Nov. 10, '47. Running time, 78 MINS.

Marguerita	Maria Montez
Phillip Kent	Rod Cameron
Pio	Mikhail Rasumny
Lt. Carlos Ortega	Philip Reed
Major De Roja	Gilbert Roland
Senorita de Sola	Gale Sondergaard
Filomena	Tamara Shayne
Governor	Robert Warwick
Sergeant Gomara	Michael Raffetto
Manuel	Neyle Morrow
Captain Cordova	Victor Varconi
Juan	Charles Wagenheim
Pirate	George J. Lewis
Doctor	Joe Bernard
Lieutenant No. 1	George Navarro
Thug No. 1	Victor Romito
Thug No. 2	Don Driggers
Pirate	George Magrill

"Pirates of Monterey" is a romantic adventure story of the California coast in the 1840s, when the area belonged to Mexico. Because of the scenic beauty of its locale, impressively reproduced in color, it is a handsome production. But when the outstanding appeal of an adventure film is the visual quality of its photography, it's a negative comment on its entertainment value. That's a fair estimate of the picture, however. It's merely a decorative dualler.

The story deals with an American soldier of fortune who takes a wagon train of the latest type rifles from Mexico City to a Mexican army detachment at the presidio in old Monterey. There are ambushes, wild rides, sword and gun fights, intrigue and fiesta scenes of dancing, singing, laughter and love-making.

Although every bit of the story could obviously have happened, it all seems incredible. The lines are stilted, the direction appears labored and the acting is hackneyed and frequently arch. The actual outdoor scenes are effectively photographed, particularly in their use of colorful costumes. But some of the sets and scenic effects are palpably synthetic. *Hobe.*

The Fabulous Texan

Republic release of Edmund Grainger production. Stars William Elliott, John Carroll, Catherine McLeod; features Albert Dekker, Andy Devine, Patricia Knight, Ruth Donnelly. Directed by Edward Ludwig. Screenplay, Lawrence Hazard and Horace McCoy, based on original by Hal Long; camera, Reggie Lanning; editor, Richard L. Van Enger; music, Anthony Collins. Tradeshown N. Y., Nov. 5, '47. Running time, 97 MINS.

Jim McWade	William Elliott
John Wesley Barker	John Carroll
Alice Sharp	Catherine McLeod
Gibson Hart	Albert Dekker
Elihu Mills	Andy Devine
Josie Allen	Patricia Knight
Utopia Mills	Ruth Donnelly
Bud Clayton	Johnny Sands
Reverend Barker	Harry Davenport
Doctor Sharp	Robert H. Barrat
Luke Roland	Douglass Dumbrille
Jessup	Reed Hadley
Standifer	Roy Barcroft
Wade Clayton	Russell Simpson
Shep Clayton	James Brown
Sam Bass	Jim Davis
Dick Clayton	George Beban
Sim Clayton	John Miles

Republic has apparently taken the advice of some of its major stockholders to forego attempts at making prestige films and sink its heavier budgets into the type of pictures it knows best how to make. "Fabulous Texan" is a western in every sense of the word and, as such, right down Republic's alley. It's obviously, too, an expensive job and, with the cast topped by William Elliott, John Carroll and Catherine McLeod, looks good for first runs, as well as the shootin' galleries.

Despite its opulence, "Texan" is beset by several obstacles that prevent it from being a standout film of its kind. Screenplay by Lawrence Hazard and Horace McCoy elicits plenty of interest by dealing with a phase of Texas history seldom touched upon heretofore in films. Cameras take full advantage of the beauteous terrain in which the film was lensed but then negate all the good work by rendering Miss McLeod and Patricia Knight, the second femme lead, anything but beautiful.

On the credit side of the ledger is the fine work turned in by Elliott and Carroll. Former is a western star in the best William S. Hart tradition, even slightly resembling the old master. He's got plenty of opportunity to demonstrate his thesping, as well as riding and shooting ability in this one, and emerges on top in all three departments. Carroll, too, is standout, although he's burdened by many of the trite phrases that were so unwisely injected into the screenplay. As for Miss McLeod, westerns definitely aren't her forte. Whatever acting ability she might possess is completely lost in a welter of overemoting and posing, much of which again is doubtless due to the screenplay.

Story has Elliott and Carroll as a couple of Confederate officers who return to Texas after the war only to find it over-ridden by carpetbaggers and despotic state police. To avenge the death of his father at the hands of the troopers, Carroll shoots it out with them and has to flee into the mountains. Elliott follows and the two start a crusade against the police. Elliott then decides they'd get better results by cooperating with the Federal government, and so is appointed a U.S. marshal.

Carroll meanwhile, has forsaken his Robin Hood career to rob a bank with his band, which makes him a Federal offender. Disillusioned populace then forms a band of vigilantes and, in a major gunfight, Carroll's the only one of his gang that escapes. Through a ruse, he learns the state police general is out to ambush Elliott. He gets there first, they shoot it out and both are killed. Peace and order are restored and Elliott marries Miss McLeod, with whom both he and Carroll had been in love.

Picture has a final sequence, incidentally, which will rank among the corniest ever seen unless Republic gets hep and trims it before "Texan" goes into general release. It shows Miss McLeod as an old grandmother, posing before a statue of her late husband and telling bystanders something about the fact he wasn't the only one who did a lot for Texas. Miss McLeod's gray wig and the painted backdrop are too obvious for comfort.

Supporting cast, topped by Albert Dekker, Andy Devine, Ruth Donnelly and Harry Davenport, handle their chores competently. Producer Edmund Grainger and director Edward Ludwig missed out on the script supervision but otherwise handled the film capably. Anthony Collins' score lends much to the picture's heavier dramatic moments. *Stal.*

Jens Mansson I Amerika

('Jens Monson in America')

(SONGS)

(SWEDISH-MADE)

Scandia Films release of Europa Film production. Stars Edvard Persson; features Stig Olin, Mim Persson, Bojan Westin. Directed by Bengt Janzon. Screenplay, Janzon and Carl-Adam Nycop; camera, Bertil Palmgren and Mack Stengler; music, Alvar Kraft. At 5th Avenue Playhouse, N. Y., Nov. 1, '47. Running time, 105 MINS.

(In Swedish; English Titles)

One of the better Scandinavian imports, this film stars veteran Swedish comedian Edvard Persson in a yarn that takes him on a Cook's tour of half the U. S. Picture has a natural appeal for Swedish-Americans and the word-of-mouth should help. It's bound to be a dependable grosser in the art situations.

Making his first visit to America last year, Persson was accompanied by several technicians. Through the group's collective efforts they shot some 40% of the footage which appears in "Jens Monson in America." Scenes of Niagara Falls, Chicago, parts of Texas, Hollywood, San Francisco and Oregon are logically introduced in the script. Especially emphasized as samples of Americana are the many-hued neon signs, concrete highways, drive-in eateries with their classy carhops and "cheap" automobiles.

Prime fault of the film is its extreme length. Story easily could have been ended 20 minutes earlier. Plot is built around Persson, a struggling farmer in Sweden. Informed he's inherited a farm in the U. S., he sails for America only to discover that he must find a missing brother before the property is his.

Cast's acting has a sincere ring to it. Persson is outstanding as the jovial farmer. He also shines with an occasional vocal, self-accompanied on the guitar. His man Friday, Stig Olin, handles his bi-lingual role well betraying only the suggestion of a Swedish accent. Mim Persson, the comic's screen and real life wife, along with Bojan Westin register in lesser roles. Direction and camera are okay.

Whispering City
(CANADIAN-MADE)

Eagle Lion release of Quebec Production Corp. production. Stars Helmut Dantine, Mary Anderson, Paul Lukas; features Mimi d'Estee, John Pratt, Joy LaFleur, Lucie Poitras. Directed by Fedor Ozep. Screenplay by Rian James, Leonard Lee from original story by George Zuckerman, Michael Lennox; camera, Guy Roe; "Quebec Concerto" by Andre Mathieu. Tradeshown in N. Y., Nov. 6, '47. Running time, **98 MINS.**

Michel Lacoste............Helmut Dantine
Marie Roberts..............Mary Anderson
Albert Frederick..............Paul Lukas
Renee Brancourt............Mimi d'Estee
Edward Durant..................John Pratt
Nun............................Lucie Poitras
Blanche Lacoste.............Joy LaFleur
Police Inspector..........George Alexander
Assistant Police Inspector....Henri Poitras

This first Canadian feature film to attract attention in the U.S. is a melodrama of considerable suspense unfolded with Quebec and Montreal as a background. Having Mary Anderson, Paul Lukas and Helmut Dantine in the cast, it will do well in U. S. theatres and exceedingly so in Canadian houses.

Besides a fairly intriguing murder yarn, done skillfully by Rian James and Leonard Lee from the George Zukerman-Michael Lennox original, production introduces an excellent concerto by Andre Mathieu. This theme figures in two rehearsal scenes and then the full-dress preem with a big symphony orchestra, latter being done as the picture moves to its crashing climax.

Plot has Miss Anderson, as a police reporter, trying to unravel an old mystery and becoming involved in a murder plot which seeks to have her bumped off. Scripters have cleverly worked in a suicide and an innocent husband coming under the thumb of an unscrupulous attorney, suspected of the old crime by the femme newspaper scribe. By doing this, the yarn brings this baffled male into a series of meetings with the gal reporter with the auditors led to believe he will take her life at any moment. He's been ordered to do this by the lawyer in order to save his own neck.

Fedor Ozep rates a bow for the way in which he has built suspense in several sequences. George Marton does creditably as production chief, with the scenic beauties of Canadian cities nicely worked into the story without slowing it up. Guy Roe does well enough in photographing his exteriors but is not so successful with his closeups, those of Miss Anderson often being far from flattering.

Lukas, as the wealthy attorney who becomes enmeshed in additional murder plottings in an effort to cover up his old crime, is superb although in an unflattering role. Miss Anderson plays the American-born police reporter with the minimum of implausible moments, being especially effective in the episodes where her life is in jeopardy. She provides the slight romantic angle with Dantine as the vis-a-vis.

He's the pianist-composer who comes under the evil influence of Lukas until his affair with Miss Anderson adjusts him mentally. His interpretation is solid. John Pratt makes an okay editor but Joy LaFleur overdoes the neurotic wife.

Wear.

Lucia di Lammermoor
(ITALIAN-MADE)

Grandi Film Distributors release of Opera Film Co. (Mario Trombetti) production. Stars Nelly Corradi, Italo Tajo. Directed by Piero Ballerini. Music, Gaetano Donizetti; libretto, Salvatore Cammarano, based on Sir Walter Scott novel; adapted by Ballerini and Pier Giuseppe Franci; camera, Mario Albertelli; editor, Virginia Genesi Cufaro; English titles, Walter Klee. At Cinema Dante, N. Y., Oct. 31, '47.. Running time, **108 MINS.**

Lucia............................Nelly Corradi
Lord Ashton........................Afro Poli
Sir Edgar................Mario Filippeschi
Lord Bucklaw...............Aldo Ferracuti
Raymond Bidebent...............Italo Tajo
Alisa.......................Loretta di Lelio
Norman...................Adelio Zagonara
Orchestra and chorus of Rome Opera Co.

(In Italian; English Titles)

Recent opera film imports have been of several categories. One type dramatizes the story on which an opera had been built, using the opera's music only incidentally (as in "Carmen"). Another tells a story with an opera used as background in flashback (as in "Elixir of Love"), and some of the opera's chief arias brought in. A third (as in the case of "The Barber of Seville" and the current "Lucia di Lammermoor") is a literal translation of the opera to the screen, with characters singing their roles as on stage, and the music continuing throughout as the main ingredient.

"Lucia," being a literal lensing, has all the drawbacks of such a treatment. It's static and stilted. There is no spoken dialog or recitative, and to make matters worse, the English titles are in stiff and unnatural verse. Actionless story and old-fashioned treatment make film curiously corny and slow, so that though the beautiful Donizetti music is appealing, film can be of only limited draw.

Direction is also pretty stodgy, the camera trying vainly to prove interesting while a long aria is in progress, and failing because of its unimaginative lensing of a fountain, a garden, a lake as alternative to the singer's countenance. Principals are singers, rather than actors, and perform woodenly, in the true tradition of grand opera. Dubbing, too, is unsatisfactory, it being apparent that voices were recorded at another time, and not too faithfully dubbed in.

Story is the familiar one of the Scotch lady who is loved by a member of a rival clan, enemy of her brother, and the tragedy that ensues. Singing is good, both in principals and chorus, while recording too is quite satisfactory. Nelly Corradi is a physically attractive Lucia, with an appealing lyric soprano. Afro Poli, as Lord Ashton, and Mario Filippeschi, as Sir Edgar, are quite wooden. Italo Tajo is distinctive as Raymond.

Bron.

Comin' Thro' the Rye
(BRITISH-MADE)

London, Oct. 30.

Advance Films production and release of documentary, biographical film of Robert Burns. Directed by Walter C. Mycroft. Screenplay, Gilbert McAllister, M.P. Camera, Cedric Williams; editor, Robert Hill. At House of Commons, Oct. 29, '47. Running time, **55 MINS.**

Robert Burns...........Terence Alexander
Jean Armour.............Patricia Burleigh
Clarinda.......................Beryl Bowen
Highland Mary.................Olivia Barley
Handsome Nell.................Sylvia Abbott

Previewed in the improvised cinema of a committee room in the House of Commons (scenarist Gilbert McAllister is a member of Parliament), this film was not seen to best advantage, particularly in the matter of sound. But even seen under ideal conditions, this story of Robert Burns' life has little to offer the commercial theatre. It is unbelievably amateurish and, with the exception of the singing, it is little better than the old lanternslide lecture.

The first time the screen has done a biog of this sort of poet's life and loves, it is mainly silent footage with continuous commentary. Completely devoid of action, the pictures "illustrate" in an almost childish way the narrator's words. For example when the song "My Love Is Like a Red Red Rose" is sung, pictures of roses are spattered all over the screen. Trefor Jones is outstanding among the singers and is responsible for five of the 19 songs.

It may have some appeal to the numerous Burns Societies but average audiences will find it tedious and old-fashioned. If Bing Crosby still plans to do a story of Robert Burns, this should in no way deter him.

Cane.

Ghosts of Berkeley Sq.
(BRITISH-MADE)

London, Oct. 30.

Pathe Pictures' release of British National production. Stars Robert Morley, Felix Aylmer; features Yvonne Arnaud, Claude Hulbert. Directed by Vernon Sewell. Screenplay by James Seymour from novel by Caryl Brahms, S. J. Simons; music, Hans May; camera, Ernest Palmer, Moray Grant. At Studio One. Running time, **85 MINS.**

General Burlap............Robert Morley
Colonel Kelsoe..............Felix Aylmer
Millie.......................Yvonne Arnaud
King's Equerry..........Robert Beaumont
Merryweather...............Claude Hulbert
Tex........................Ronald Frankau
Matron.....................Madge Brindley
Lottie............................Marie Lohr
Lady Mary....................Martita Hunt
Lettie........................Mary Jerrold
Disraeli..................Abraham Sofaer
General Bristow..........A. E. Matthews
Investigator...............Ernest Thesiger
Captain Dodds...............James Hayter
Croupier................Gerald Kempinsky
Brigadier....................Edward Lexy
Mortimer Digby............John Longden

Original novel, "No Nightingales," on which this is based, was a joke that could be taken in small doses. A chapter or two and one could put the book down. But this elaborate screen joke has to be taken in one, and obviously it won't suit every person. Not for America.

It's a story about a couple of pals in the days of Queen Anne. They are General Burlap and Colonel Kelsoe. They dislike Marlborough and the way he's running the war and plot to trap him in Berkeley Square. Testing the booby trap, they are killed. The Queen, incensed at their behavior, has them arraigned before a celestial court-martial whose verdict is that Burlap and Kelsoe must haunt the house until royalty visits it.

What might have been a short romp is extended into a long series of gags. There is straining to point parallels to the modern way of life, but what must have seemed funny in the conference room hardly raises a smile in the theatre. And the camera tricks, good as they may be, lose by repetition.

Robert Morley and Felix Aylmer, both first-rate character actors, had a tough assignment as the ghosts. Story that converts them into humans when they desire is likely to mystify audiences. Yvonne Arnaud is given little to do as the French countess but does it well. Direction and camera work are good and the music by Hans May is eerily appropriate.

priate.

Cane.

The White Unicorn
(BRITISH-MADE)

London, Oct. 30.

General Film Distributors' release of J. Arthur Rank-John Corfield production. Stars Margaret Lockwood, Ian Hunter, Dennis Price, Joan Greenwood. Directed by Bernard Knowles. Screenplay, Robert Westerby, A. R. Rawlinson, Moie Charles from novel by Flora Sandstrom; camera, Reginald H. Wyer; editor, Robert Johnson. At Odeon., Running time, **97 MINS.**

Lucy..................Margaret Lockwood
Lottie......................Joan Greenwood
Philip.............................Ian Hunter
Richard........................Dennis Price
Joan............................Eileen Peel
Fabey.....................Guy Middleton
Miss Cater................Catherine Lacey
Paul.............................Paul Dupuis
Alice Waters......................Joan Rees
Mrs. Madden...............Elizabeth Maude
Charles Madden..............Stewart Rome
Sir Humphrey Webster.......Noel Howlett
Norey..........Margaret Julia Lockwood
Storton....................Valentine Dyall
Nurse...................Mabel Constanduros

Following a "Love Conquers All" formula, this romantic melodrama will have rough handling by the highbrows, but should prove a box-office winner. Story is on hokey side but a tearjerker, and with Margaret Lockwood and Joan Greenwood in the two leads, it might do well in U. S.

Miss Lockwood is the well-to-do woman disappointed in marriage and robbed by death of her real love. Miss Greenwood is Lottie, an unwed mother who has learned the hard way about men and love. Former is warden of a home for delinquent girls to which she has been remanded pending her trial for attempting to kill her own baby. In trying to bring comfort to the derelict girl, the two exchange life stories via flashbacks. These are fairly well knit together.

Substuff yarn can hardly fail to wind up a potent mixture of ham and hokum for women, and an obvious tearjerker. Both women play with all the stops out, and perhaps Miss Greenwood has a slight advantage because of the nature of her role. But the camera flatters neither of them. Particularly it is unkind to Miss Lockwood in many sequences. Nor could Hunter be too happy over closeups made of him.

Dennis Price is good as the lover, and Guy Middleton meanders pleasantly about as a good-hearted bounder. Without being outstanding, the minor characters are well played. Miss Lockwood's own daughter, Margaret Julia, appears as her daughter in this.

Cane.

End of the River
(BRITISH-MADE)

London, Oct. 30.

General Film Distrib. release of J. Arthur Rank-Archers (Michael Powell-Emeric Pressburger) production. Stars Sabu, Bibi Ferreira; features Esmond Knight, Robert Douglas, Raymond Lovell. Directed by Derek Twist. Screenplay by Wolfgang Wilhelm from novel by Desmond Holdridge; camera, Christopher G. Challis; music by Lambert Williamson. At Odeon. Running time, **83 MINS.**

Mancel ....Sabu
Teresa.........................Bibi Ferreira
Dantos.....................Esmond Knight
Conceicao................Antoinette Cellier
Jones.......................Robert Douglas
Lisboa.......................Torin Thatcher
Harrigan...................Orlando Martins
Porpino.....................Raymond Lovell
Dona Serafina............Nicolette Bernard

Chico..........James Hayter
Defending Counsel........Maurice Denham
Maria Gonsalves..........Eva Hudson
Irgoyen..........Alan Wheatley
Raphael..........Charles Hawtrey
Feliciano..........Nino Rossini
Ship's Officer..........Basil Appleby
Judge..........Dennis Arundell

Judged by usual standards, this picture, with Brazil locale, has little to offer at the boxoffice. Nor does it rate for its artistry. It does not even measure up to previous efforts of Michael Powell and Emeric Pressburger. Sabu and Bibi Ferreira, latter publicized as the "First Lady of the Brazilian theatre," won't draw many customers. It will be very tough to sell in the U. S. Original story idea becomes hopelessly entangled, with the 60% shot on location difficult to justify.

Sabu plays Mancel, a young Arekuna Indian, on trial for murder in Brazil. Terrified, he refuses to speak to his lawyer and only murmurs "Kanaima" and "Mister." Obviously this cries for flashbacks and the film gets them. Sabu's family had been wronged by "Mister," a local chief. The boy was declared "Kanaima," an outlaw. He falls foul of a trade that sends him to a slow but certain death. Later he becomes involved in a political plot, with the staying of the mulatto in some way purging his soul.

There's little in the way this story unfolds to touch any emotion, and the acting by the stars calls for little comment. On her showing in this, her first picture, Miss Ferreira looks small addition to screenplayer ranks.

Minor parts are well played, particularly since getting little help from the script. For Derek Twist, directing his first feature, it was a tough assignment. *Cane.*

Return of the Lash

Eagle Lion release of Jerry Thomas production. Stars "Lash" La Rue, Al "Fuzzy" St. John; features Mary Maynard, Brad Slaven, George Chesebro. Directed by Ray Taylor. Original screenplay, Joseph O'Donnell; camera, Ernest Miller; editor, Hugh Winn. Previewed N. Y., Oct. 31, '47. Running time, 61 MINS.

Cheyenne..........."Lash" La Rue
"Fuzzy"..........Al "Fuzzy" St. John
Kay..........Mary Maynard
Grant..........Brad Slaven
Kirby..........George Chesebro
Clark..........Lee Morgan
Dave..........Lane Bradford
Pete..........John Gibson
Hank..........Dee Cooper

There's a new twist in "Return of the Lash," latest in the "Lash" La Rue sagebrush series—amnesia has been discovered by the westerns as a story element. It's a change of pace for the usual formulas but nevertheless the film's appeal lies in the nabe dualers and action situations. B.o. prospects should be substantially the same as those experienced by preceding pix in this chain.

La Rue's forte is his unerring ability with what resembles a long blacksnake whip. It cracks out frequently to foil the schemes of the "bad guys" who nefariously conspire to take over property of ranchers adjacent to the town of Sagebrush. In this most recent episode in the adventures of La Rue and his sidekick, Al "Fuzzy" St. John, the pair aid the ranchers who are led by Brad Slaven.

Plot is a variation on the old "water rights and railroad right-of-way" ingredients. George Chesebro is the heavy who seeks to rook the settlers. But La Rue and St. John hit upon raising some necessary cash for the ranchers by rounding up some six of the outlaws, all of whom have a stiff price on their heads. En route home with the coin, St. John falls from his hoss in a skirmish with the baddies and can't recall his identity nor what happened to the money. However, he regains his memory in a free-for-all fisticuff climax with Chesebro's men, which results in a complete victory for the ranchers and recovery of the reward cash.

La Rue turns in his customary forthright portrayal of Cheyenne Davis, the modern Robin Hood; St. John is okay as the comedy relief, while Mary Maynard is cast in the lone femme role as Slaven's sister. Other performances are adequate as is the lensing and direction in this Jerry Thomas production.

The Woman in the Hall
(BRITISH-MADE)

London, Oct. 29.

General Film Distributors release of J. Arthur Rank-Wessex (Ian Dalrymple) production. Stars Ursula Jeans, Jean Simmons, Cecil Parker. Directed by Jack Lee. Screenplay by Dalrymple, Lee, G. B. Stern, from novel by Stern; camera, C. Pennington Richards, H. E. Fowle; film editor, John Krish; music, Temple Abady. At Odeon, London, Oct. 28, '47. Running time, 93 MINS.

Lorna Blake..........Ursula Jeans
Jay..........Jean Simmons
Sir Halmar..........Cecil Parker
Molly..........Jill Raymond
Neil..........Edward Underdown
Susan..........Joan Miller
Toby..........Nigel Buchanan
Shirley..........Ruth Dunning
Baroness..........Lily Kann
Ann..........Terry Randal
Mrs. Maddox..........Barbara Shaw
Miss Gardiner......Dorothy Truman Taylor
Judge..........Martin Walker
Lady Clay..........Everley Gregg
Miss Mounce..........Alexis France
Mr. Walker..........Hugh Miller

Wessex Productions (Ian Dalrymple), a J. Arthur Rank subsidiary, makes an inauspicious debut with the first of G. B. Stern's novels to be screened. A story should have a beginning, middle and an end, and this story certainly has no end. And the ending is all important in this picture, as far as audiences are concerned. They will certainly come away dissatisfied.

Woman in the title, Lorna Blake, is an unprincipled cadger with a knack of telling a hard-luck story and getting money from soft philanthropists. Presumably she does this for her two daughters, but one of the girls, Jay, on finishing school, leaves home because she can't stand her mother's mode of life, and takes a job. Her notions of honesty are definitely warped and feeling it is better to give than to receive she forges a check and plays Lady Bountiful. She is caught and held for trial.

Meanwhile mother has hooked and married a rich victim, to whom she has told a string of lies. In the inevitable court scene mother tries to straighten things out for her daughter, but the husband, now aware of his wife's real character, insists on her going into the witness box, and there the story ends.

Somewhere in the film are a couple of tepid love stories that are completely uninteresting. Without a marquee name and with little word-of-mouth to help it, prospects for this one at the boxoffice appear none too rosy. It stands little chance in U. S.

Ursula Jeans struggles hard in the name part, but the story defeats her, and the only one of the principals to register is Cecil Parker as the husband, a role hardly worthy of his talents.

Production is lavish, camera work is good, as is the music, and Jack Lee's direction is competent. *Cane.*

La Vie de Boheme
('The Love Life of Mimi')
(FRENCH-MADE

Superfilm Distributing release of Andre Paulve production. Features Maria Denis, Suzy Delair, Gisele Pascal, Louis Jourdan. Directed by Marcel L'Herbier. Screenplay, Nino Frank, based on Henri Murger's operatic libretto, "La Boheme"; camera, Pierre Montazel; music, Giacomo Puccini; musical adaptation, Louis Beydts. Previewed in New York. Running time, 92 MINS.

Rudolphe..........Louis Jourdan
Mimi..........Maria Denis
Musette..........Gisele Pascal
Phemie..........Suzy Delair
Schaunard..........Alfred Adam
Colline..........Louis Salou
Le Viconte..........Jean Parades
Barbemuche..........Sinoel
Marcel..........Roussin

(In French; English Titles)

Based upon the libretto of "La Boheme," "La Vie de Boheme" is an overlong, chronological account of a quartet of 19th century Paris bohemians—their love life and their foiled financial ambitions. Puccini's music is a good selling point but unfortunately most of it is subordinated as background strains with the exception of a few arias. Picture should do moderately well in the art situations but is unlikely to receive acceptance beyond those houses.

Introductory scenes showing the transition of Musette from an environment of wealth to a penniless, carefree existence, carry an element of sparkle. Final reel is also charged with pathos when the dying Mimi slips away in the arms of her poet, Rudolphe. However, the intervening portion is a welter of noisy, pointless dialog which rambles on through a multitude of parties, romantic disappointments and graphic illustrations of poverty suffered by the bohemians.

It's a long, winding route that scripter Nino Frank takes in adapting the Henri Murger libretto. Film etches the lives of Rudolphe, painter Schaunard, philosopher Collins and painter Marcel, lightly and airily. All four are typical denizens of the Paris garret literary and easel set.

Acting is generally good. As Rudolphe, Louis Jourdan (now a Selznick contract player) plays Mimi's lover with elan. His emotions—from a gay suitor in spring and summer to abject sorrow at Mimi's winter demise—are finely drawn. Equally pungent is the work of Maria Denis as Mimi. Gisele Pascal's Musette captures the mood of a gal who knows the value of her blonde charms, while Suzy Delair's performance as Phemie is done in a similar vein. Louis Salou's characterization of Collins, faithful and loyal to his companions, also stands out.

Marcel L'Herbier's direction is good but a tighter script and judicious editing might have been the saving grace of this Andre Paulve production. Lensing is fair. Print at this screening showed signs of wear. Armando Macaluso's English subtitles satisfactorily interpret the story movement.

Antoine et Antoinette
(FRENCH-MADE)

Gaumont production and release. Stars Roger Pigaut, Claire Maffei. Directed by Jacques Becker. Original story and adaptation, Francoise Giroux, Becker and M. Griffe; assistant producer, C. F. Tavano; Camera, P. Momtozel. Previewed in Paris. Running time 98 MINS.

Antoine..........Roger Pigaut
Antoinette..........Claire Maffei
Roland..........Noel Roquevert
Juliette..........Annette Poivre
Barbelot..........Jacques Meyran
Father-in-law..........Emile Drain
Huguette..........Paulette Jan
Official..........Gaston Modot
Customer..........G. Oury
Bridegroom..........Francois Joux
Riton..........Pierre Trabaud
Bride..........Huguette Saget

Refreshing French-made picture turned out under the Gaumont banner won a grand prize at the Cannes Festival mostly because of its simplicity and change from most pix representing the masses. It is unquestionably a departure from the usual comedy because the light story is merely a pretense on which to hang authentic filming of work-people without trimmings. It may interest some in the U. S. because of backgrounds and closeups of French life, but even so its appeal will be very limited.

Jacques Becker, one of foremost French directors, has done a commendable job, although some scenes are questionable due to their extreme length. Acting is good throughout. Roger Pigaut carries lead role well while Claire Mattei as his wife looks to be a new find. Others in cast are unusually good down to the smaller bits. Noel Roquevert is an okay villain; Pierre Trabaud shines as a third-rate prize-fighter and Huguette Saget is funny as the bride who is called upon to sing at her wedding breakfast.

Story shows Pigaut as a foreman in a bookbinding works, and Miss Maffei, as his wife, a salesgirl in an easily recognizable Champs Elysees equivalent of a five-and-ten. She is a solid click. The young couple is involved in a story about a lost lottery ticket, with yarn having a simple, happy ending.

Appeal of the picture, lies in the fact that the French people are treated realistically. Camera work by Montazel is good and Jules Garnier has provided sets which are exactly what the homes of the French masses are like. In France, even without the Cannes Festival buildup, it's a sure top grosser. It might rate a remake for an American producer. *Maxi.*

Les Maudits
('The Accursed')
(FRENCH-MADE)

Discina release of Speva production. Stars Dalio, Henri Vidal, Florence Marly and Paul Bernard. Directed by Rene Clement. Scenario, J. Companez, V. Alexandrov; screenplay, Clement and Jacques Remy; dialog, Henri Jeanson; camera, Henri Alekan. At Normandie, Olympia and Moulin Rouge, Paris. Running time, 103 MINS.

Larga..........Dalio
Reporter..........Paul Bernard
Doctor..........Henri Vidal
Willy..........Michel Auclair
Hilde..........Florence Marly
Forster..........Jo Dest
U-Boat Captain..........Jean Didier
Ingrid..........Anne Campion
German General..........Kronefeld
His Assistant..........Karl Munch
Carosi..........Fosco Giachetti

This picture, directed by Rene Clement, who handled the big grosser, "Battle of the Rail," got one of the Cannes Film Festival awards. But it doesn't rate it.

Story centers on no one in particular, moves frequently at a slow pace, has a lot of dialog spoken in German, and depicts the adventures of a U-boat escaping the Allied blockade at the end of the war, when anything pertaining to the war is already practically outdated. It is technically well made, with some fine direction in several sequences and occasionally some praiseworthy lenswork, but it isn't likely to be one of the big grossers.

The various episodes depicted appear like so many sketches, permitting at times bits of fine acting. The women have comparatively secondary parts, and the episodes in which they appear leave the film an undecided mixture of adventure or psychology.

Acting is usually good, and the picture well cast. Dalio, as the South American who gets murdered, is exemplary, but appears only in a small part of the film. Michel Auclair, as the tool of the Gestapo chief, and Jo Dest as his boss, are excellent. Henri Vidal as the doctor has the only sympathetic part and acquits himself well. Paul Bernard, stage and screen star, is only given a minor part, though appearing in many sequences.

The sets are good and the open sea sequences look authentic. The production is good. *Maxi.*

Miniature Reviews

"Mourning Becomes Electra" (RKO). Faithful representation of the Eugene O'Neill drama will take heavy selling.

"The Bishop's Wife" (RKO). Class fantasy loaded with warmth and human appeal; potent boxoffice prospects.

"Big Town After Dark" (Par). Able entry in the "Big Town" film series. Capable supporting fare.

"Out of the Past" (RKO). Private detective melodrama in the modern, hard-boiled manner. Sturdy stuff for action fans.

"Check Your Guns" (EL). Moderately entertaining oatuner starring Eddie Dean.

"Wild Horse Mesa" (RKO). Another Tim Holt western, oke where they like cowboy films.

"Return, My Beloved" (Songs) (Indie). Old-fashioned Italian-made musical for limited situations.

Mourning Becomes Electra

RKO release of Dudley Nichols production (in association with The Theatre Guild). Stars Rosalind Russell, Michael Redgrave, Raymond Massey, Katina Paxinou, Leo Genn, Kirk Douglas; features Nancy Coleman, Henry Hull. Directed by Dudley Nichols from his own adaptation of the Eugene O'Neill play. Camera, George Barnes; film editors, Roland Gross and Chandler House; music, Richard Hageman; costumes, Travis Banton. Previewed in N. Y., Nov. 13, '47. Running time, 173 MINS.

Lavinia Mannon..........Rosalind Russell
Orin Mannon..........Michael Redgrave
Ezra Mannon..........Raymond Massey
Christine Mannon..........Katina Paxinou
Adam Brant..........Leo Genn
Peter Niles..........Kirk Douglas
Hazel Niles..........Nancy Coleman
Seth Beckwith..........Henry Hull
Landlady..........Sara Allgood
Dr. Blake..........Thurston Hall
Amos Ames..........Walter Baldwin
Mrs. Hills..........Elisabeth Risdon
Josiah Borden..........Erskine Sanford
Abner Small..........Jimmy Conlin
Reverend Hills..........Lee Baker
Joe Silva..........Tito Vuolo
Mrs. Borden..........Emma Dunn
Louisa Ames..........Nora Cecil
Minnie Ames..........Marie Blake
Ira Mackel..........Clem Bevans
Eben Nobel..........Jean Clarenden

Eugene O'Neill's classic drama opened at the Guild theatre on Broadway Oct. 26, 1931. It has taken 16 years to find a producer with enough economic fortitude to transcribe the grim, unmitigating tragedy to the screen. That's perfectly understandable. For while Dudley Nichols has made a tolerably good transposition, only by the most carefully planned and zealous selling can RKO anticipate favorable grosses.

O'Neill's post-Civil War version of the ancient Greek classic was at best "good for those who like that sort of thing." The success of the play proved that there were plenty who did—or who were drawn by the O'Neill name and/or a sense that they owed it to themselves aesthetically to see "Electra." That same group, of course, will be drawn by the picture. Average audiences will no doubt tend to shy away unless sufficiently sold on its importance.

Unfortunately, the picture—although still laden with tense drama—lacks much of the impact of the play. Nor are Rosalind Russell, Katina Paxinou and Michael Redgrave able to sustain the emotion with which Alice Brady, Alla Nazimova and Earle Larimore imbued the same roles. The five-hour play (plus an hour's intermission for dinner) seemed less long than the 2 hours and 53 minutes of picture, which is run without intermission.

Nichols, who produced, directed and wrote the adaptation for the screen, will rate a bow from the O'Neill lovers in that he has made no compromises. The picture is every bit as unrelenting in its detailing of family tragedy, brought on by the warping effect of Puritan conscience in conflict with human emotion, as was the play. Even the distorted Oedipus relationships are unflaggingly handled. Never is there concession to a smile or other relaxation from the hammering tragedy of murder, self-destruction and twisted, dramatic emotionalism.

RKO has chosen to handle the film on a true roadshow—two-a-day, reserved seat—basis. That's actually the only way it could be exhibited. As with United Artists' handling of "Henry V," pitches will have to be made for school and organizational trade. Outside of the bigger cities, only a minimum of off-the-street patronage can be expected.

As with "Henry," The Theatre Guild is tied in on the exhibition and its subscription list in 20 cities will give a tremendous head start to the film. Word-of-mouth won't be of any help in attracting the average layman. Guild got 2½% of the distributor's gross of "Henry" and is believed getting about the same on "Electra" in return for use of its list, its "The Theatre Guild Presents..." sponsorship and some minor consultation with Nichols on casting.

Wisely, RKO has held the production to a minimum, so that the type of specialized patronage anticipated may well be able to make it profitable. Miss Russell is the only "expensive" member of the cast in the Hollywood sense and the picture employs hardly more than the three sets of the original play. Almost the entire film is photographed on the low flight of steps in front of the Greek-columned New England house and in a large family parlor. The town itself is depicted via an uncamouflaged painted backdrop, which is slightly disturbing. The magnificent 1865 costumes, created by Travis Banton, appear to have taken as large a slice out of the budget as anything else.

O'Neill originally wrote "Electra" as a trilogy, "The Homecoming," "The Hunted," and "The Haunted." Nichols has eliminated the demarcations. The story, based on one of the many variations of an ancient Greek myth, is a psychological study of an overbred family, and its aborted and confused loves and hatreds of each other.

The legend has been set down in almost modern surroundings, and given the locale and speech, the morals and manners of Civil War New England. The central figure is the daughter of the family (Rosalind Russell). Her mother (Katina Paxinou) bears a deep hatred for her father (Raymond Massey), and while he is at war gives herself to the love of a sea captain remotely related to the family (Leo Genn).

The daughter, who hates her mother, partly because of her own romantic attachment to her father, confronts her with the fact she knows of the relationship. That results in the mother's murder of the father and the killing by the daughter and her brother (Michael Redgrave) of the mother's lover.

The brother bears more than a usual maternal love and a struggle ensues between mother and daughter for his confidence and affection. The daughter wins out with the resulting suicide of both mother and son. But the daughter, through it all, has brought about her own spiritual destruction and, as the only remaining member of the family, turns back into the desecrated home, there to await in solitude her own distant doom.

The first two-thirds of the film is made largely unbelievable by poor casting. While Miss Paxinou is a very able actress, she appears considerably too old to be acceptable as the great love of the much younger Genn. That he passes up the more youthful—and not too much so—Miss Russell for an unattractive old woman is hard to swallow.

Performances are uniformly good, although they never rise beyond the drama that is inherent in the situations themselves. Too often the emoting consists of Miss Russell, Miss Paxinou and Redgrave popping their eyes. Outstanding are Massey and Henry Hull, the latter in the secondary role of an aged retainer. Good are Nancy Coleman and Kirk Douglas as the would-be normal loves of Miss Russell and Redgrave.

Faced with a herculean directorial problem by his own determination to stick close to the original play, Nichols hasn't always succeeded. There are a series of strong emotional climaxes, but they fail to rise successively in a pattern or rhythm. Between them there results an inevitable slowness. There's no gainsaying, however, that the overall effect is to give the spectator a considerable and lingering emotional shaking up.

Photography is frequently disturbing in its shallowness of focus. Only occasional effort apparently was made to get a sharp image of anyone but the central character in a scene. Richard Hageman's music is once or twice obtrusive, but is sparsely used and generally heightens the heavy drama.

And heavy drama there is aplenty in this tale of a warped woman so beset by destiny that mourning is her only appropriate garb. *Herb.*

The Bishop's Wife

Hollywood, Nov. 15.

RKO release of Samuel Goldwyn production. Stars Cary Grant, Loretta Young, David Niven; features Monty Woolley, James Gleason, Gladys Cooper, Elsa Lanchester, Mitchell Boy Choir. Directed by Henry Koster. Screenplay, Robert E. Sherwood, Leonardo Bercovici; from novel by Robert Nathan; camera, Gregg Toland; music, Hugo Friedhofer; editor, Monica Collingwood. Tradeshown, Nov. 13, '47. Running time, 108 MINS.

Dudley..........Cary Grant
Julia Brougham..........Loretta Young
Henry Brougham..........David Niven
Professor Wutheridge..........Monty Wooley
Sylvester..........James Gleason
Mrs. Hamilton..........Gladys Cooper
Matilda..........Elsa Lanchester
Mildred Cassaway..........Sara Haden
Debby Brougham..........Karolyn Grimes
Maggenti..........Tito Vuolo
Mr. Miller..........Regis Toomey
Mrs. Duffy..........Sara Edwards
Miss Trumbull..........Margaret McWade
Mrs. Ward..........Ann O'Neal
Mr. Perry..........Ben Erway
Stevens..........Erville Alderson
Defense Captain..........Bobby Anderson
Attack Captain..........Teddy Infuhr
Michel..........Eugene Borden
First Lady in Michel's..........Almira Sessions
Second Lady..........Claire DuBrey
Third Lady..........Florence Auer
Hat shop proprietress..........Margaret Wells
Hat shop customer..........Kitty O'Neill
Hysterical mother..........Isabell Jewell
Blind man..........David Leonard
Delia..........Dorothy Vaughan
Policeman..........Edgar Dearing
Mitchell Boy Choir

This is a picture calculated to make an audience leave the theatre with a good feeling. It has a warmth and charm that makes believable the fantasy and has been put together with complete understanding by all involved. Samuel Goldwyn's marshalling of cast, director, writers and physical values stamps it with a class touch, assuring "The Bishop's Wife" a strong draw in all situations and plenty of boxoffice take.

While a fantasy, there are no fantastic heavenly manifestations. There's a humanness about the characters, even the angel, that beguiles full attention. Henry Koster's sympathetic direction deftly gets over the warm humor supplied by the Robert E. Sherwood-Leonardo Bercovici script, taken from Robert Nathan's novel of the same title.

Cary Grant is the angel of the piece and has never appeared to greater advantage. Role, with the exception of a minor miracle or two, is potently pointed to indicate character could have been a flesh-and-blood person, a factor that embellishes sense of reality as the angel sets about answering the troubled prayers of Episcopalian bishop, David Niven. Script and Koster's direction develop a strong sense of anticipation as story unfolds, greatly adding to picture's charm.

Plot, essentially, deals with Grant's assignment to make people act like human beings. In great need of his help is Niven, a young bishop who has lost the common touch and marital happiness because of his dream of erecting a massive cathedral. The wife, Loretta Young, seemingly draws much of the angel's attention to the bishop's discomfort but before it's all over. Grant has laid his heavenly touch on problems distressing the story's characters and has straightened them out.

Miss Young gives a moving performance as the wife whose life is touched by an angel without her knowledge of his heavenly origin. Niven's cleric character is played straight but his anxieties and jealousy loosen much of the warm humor gracing the plot. Featured and supporting players contribute strong performances to back sock work of principals. Monty Wooley, James Gleason, Gladys Cooper, Elsa Lanchester, Sara Haden, Karolyn Grimes, Tito Vuolo, Regis Toomey, Isabell Jewell are among those who impress.

Gregg Toland's camera work and the music score by Hugo Friedhofer, directed by Emil Newman, are ace credits among the many expert contributions. Mitchell Boy choir stands out with vocals on a religious piece. Score contains a harp solo, "Lost April," composed by Newman, and effect of Grant playing the string instrument has been cleverly inserted by special effects. Art direction by George Jenkins and Perry Ferguson, and the set decorations by Julia Heron lend authenticity to Victorian rectory and other settings. *Brog.*

Big Town After Dark

Hollywood, Nov. 15.

Paramount release of Pine-Thomas production. Stars Philip Reed, Hillary Brooke; features Richard Travis, Anne Gillis, Vince Barnett. Directed by William C. Thomas. Original screenplay, Whitman Chambers; based on radio program, "Big Town"; camera, Ellis W. Carter; editor, Howard Smith. Tradeshown Nov. 14, '47. Running time, 70 MINS.

Steve Wilson..........Philip Reed
Lorelei Kilbourne..........Hillary Brooke
Chuck LaRue..........Richard Travis
Susan Peabody..........Anne Gillis
Louie Sneed..........Vince Barnett
Monk..........Joe Sawyer
Jake Sebastian..........Douglas Blackley
Amos Peabody..........Charles Arnt
Wally Blake..........Joe Allen, Jr.
Marcus..........William Haade
Fletcher..........Arthur Space
Jimmy O'Brien..........Dick Keene
Harvey Cushman..........Sumner Getchel

"Big Town After Dark" is an able entry for supporting bookings. Its melodrama moves fast, story holds together and the playing is capable. Release aims more than fulfilled by production values obtained by William Pine and William Thomas.

Based on radio's regular "Big Town" program, this latest in the Paramount series takes a potshot at poker clubs, legal in some sections of the country. Involved in the plotting is the shakedown of the publisher of Big Town's newspaper through a phoney kidnapping and the daily's fight against racketeering poker clubs and the mobs that run them. It all works out to an action finale wherein the ends of justice are upheld and the crooks get their come-uppance.

Philip Reed handles character of fighting Steve Wilson, editor, in easy style and Hillary Brooke sparks her role as the police reporter known as Lorelei Kilbourne. Anne Gillis shows up well as the conniving femme menace who takes her publisher uncle for a shakedown. Capable heavies are headed up by Richard Travis and Vince Barnett rates chuckles with role of bailbond broker, a standard in the film series.

William Thomas' direction of the Whitman Chambers original script keeps a steady eye on action and melodramatic flavor. A good job. Ellis W. Carter's lensing is expert in dressing up physical values and the players, particularly the femmes.

Brog.

Out of the Past

Hollywood, Nov. 15.

RKO release of Warren Duff (Robert Sparks) production. Stars Robert Mitchum, Jane Greer; features Kirk Douglas, Rhonda Fleming, Richard Webb, Steve Brodie, Virginia Huston, Paul Valentine, Dickie Moore, Ken Niles. Directed by Jacques Tourneur. Screenplay, Geoffrey Homes; based on his novel. "Build My Gallows High"; camera, Nicholas Musuraca; editor, Samuel E. Beetley, score, Roy Webb. Tradeshown Nov. 13, '47. Running time, 95 MINS.

Jeff	Robert Mitchum
Kathie	Jane Greer
Whit	Kirk Douglas
Meta Carson	Rhonda Fleming
Jim	Richard Webb
Fisher	Steve Brodie
Ann	Virginia Huston
Joe	Paul Valentine
The Kid	Dickie Moore
Eels	Ken Niles

"Out of the Past" is a hardboiled melodrama strong on characterization. Considerable production polish, effective direction and compelling mood slot it for attention of ticket buyers who go for violence and help overcome tendency towards choppiness in story unfoldment. It's sturdy film fodder for twin bill situations.

Direction by Jacques Tourneur pays close attention to mood development; achieving realistic flavor that is further emphasized by real life settings and topnotch lensing by Nicholas Musuraca. Players groove themselves into the assorted characters with an easy naturalness that abets the melodrama.

Geoffrey Homes scripted from his novel titled "Build My Gallows High" and film plot depicts Robert Mitchum as a former private detective who comes to a violent end despite efforts to lead a quiet, small-town life. Good portion of story is told in retrospect by Mitchum when his past catches up with him. Hired by a gangster to find a girl who had decamped with $40,000 after shooting the crook, Mitchum crosses her path in Acapulco, falls for her himself and they flee the gangster together. He wises up to the dame when she kills his former detective partner and seeks a simple life as a gasoline station operator in a small town. Later he's discovered and tries to get himself clear but in the end is killed by his former love, after she has managed to bump off the other heavies. There are six killings to add to the blood and thunder.

Mitchum gives a very strong account of himself. Jane Greer as the baby-faced, charming killer is another lending potent interest. Kirk Douglas, the gangster, is believable and Paul Valentine makes role of henchman stand out. Rhonda Fleming is in briefly but effectively. Virginia Huston, Mitchum's village love; Steve Brodie; Richard Webb, and Ken Niles are good. Dickie Moore, former film moppet, wraps up part of deaf-mute friend of Mitchum's, garnering attention.

Warren Duff produced under executive supervision of Robert Sparks and gives film the proper backing to make its story effective. Aiding moody atmosphere is music by Roy Webb.

Brog.

Check Your Guns

(SONGS)

Eagle Lion release of Jerry Thomas production. Stars Eddie Dean; features Roscoe Ates, Nancy Gates, George Chesebro. Directed by Ray Taylor. Original screenplay, Joseph O'Donnell; songs, Pete Gates, Dean and Hal Blair; camera, Ernie Miller; editor, Joseph Gluck. Previewed, N. Y., Nov. 6, '47. Running time, 55 MINS.

Eddie	Eddie Dean
Soapy	Roscoe Ates
Cathy	Nancy Gates
Farrell	George Chesebro
Brad	Stan Jolley
Ace	Mikel Conrad
Slim	Lane Bradford
Sloane	Terry Frost
Rider No. 1	Mason Wynn
Rider No. 2	Dee Cooper
Judge Hammond	Bill Fawcett

Latest Eddie Dean oatuner is a moderately entertaining western that will prove acceptable fare for the action situations. Dean, who plays himself in the film, is the usual self-reliant Eddie, a constant champion of law and order. His fans will find his performance quite to their taste.

Standard story formula deals with a band of outlaws led by Stan Jolley who have jeopardized the safety of law-abiding citizens in Red Gap. In cahoots with a crooked judge, William Fawcett, they give Dean and his pardner, Roscoe Ates, a rugged tussle before the last reel unfolds. There's little originality in the yarn but plot works in plenty of shootin' and ridin'.

Picture's title stems from an ordinance established by Dean after he becomes sheriff replacing the murdered Ed Cassidy. Enforcing it, the star displays he's quick on the draw much to the chagrin of his nefarious adversaries. But a trifle ludicrous even in these hoss operas is the slow, determined walk affected by Dean preparatory to engaging in a six shootin' duel. Scene no doubt will elicit chuckles from hidebound western habitues.

Otherwise Dean is a forthright sheriff in this Jerry Thomas production. As the deputy, Roscoe Ates contribs okay comedy relief; Nancy Gates is a cloying femme decoration while Jolley, George Chesebro and Fawcett register as the heavies. Ray Taylor's direction is brisk and Ernie Miller's lensing stands out. Some three songs, sandwiched in the footage, are so-so with Dean crooning the lyrics.

Wild Horse Mesa

(SONGS)

RKO release of Herman Schlom production. Stars Tim Holt; features Nan Leslie, Richard Martin. Directed by Wallace A. Grissell. Screenplay, Norman Houston from Zane Grey story; camera, Frank Redman; editor, Desmond Marquette. Tradeshown in N. Y., Nov. 13, '47. Running time, 61 MINS.

Dave Jordan	Tim Holt
Sue Melbern	Nan Leslie
Chito	Richard Martin
Hod Slack	Richard Powers
Pop Melbern	Jason Robards
Jim Horn	Tony Barrett
Jay Olmstead	Harry Woods
Marshall Bradford	William Gould
Tex	Robert Bray
Rusty	Richard Foote

Another in the Tim Holt cowboy series, this is a bit above average, having been adapted from a Zane Grey story. Sufficiently strong to play in spots where they go for cactus epics, as support on twin bills.

Holt plays Dave Jordan, here shown helping the father of his sweetheart discover the hiding place of 2,000 wild horses. Per usual, there's the rival gang seeking the same hosses. Also a wild stallion that comes close to being the best thespian in the picture.

A cold-blooded murder and a hoss stampede are included in the action.

Holt is okay, while Nan Leslie makes an unusually neat-looking heart interest. Richard Martin, as a Mexican cowboy, supplies enough comedy relief to satisfy. He also strums a banjo and sings a couple of western standards. Jason Robards is effective as the girl's father, victim of the gang. Support is headed by Richard Powers, Harry Woods and William Gould.

Wallace A. Grissell chips in with a nice directorial job, while lens work of Frank Redman, largely outdoor shots, is markedly strong.

Wear.

Return, Most Beloved

(Italian-Made)
(SONGS)

Grandi Film release of S.A.F.A. production. Directed by Guido Brignone. Screenplay, Ettore Margadonna, Aldo Vergano, Gherardo Gherardi; English titles, Armand Macaluso. Previewed in N. Y., Nov. 12, '47. Running time, 90 MINS.

Maria Wernowska	Laura Adani
Dionisia Tesseri	Germana Paolieri
Francesco Paolo Tosti	Claudio Gora
Governante	Mercedes Brignone
S. A. R.	Carlo Lombardo
Conte Wernowska	Ernesto Sabatini
John	Mario Mina
Lord Hotham	Loris Gizza
Barbella	Ruggero Paoli
Paolo Michetti	Bruno Persa
Slawisky	Achille Majeroni

(In Italian; English Titles)

"Return, Most Beloved" is an old-fashioned tearjerker destined exclusively for Italian-language situations. Pic is cashing in on the popularity of Ferruccio Tagliavini, whose tenor voice is dubbed in for the vocal assignments. However, a fuzzy soundtrack negates the efforts of the talented tenor and his wife, Pia Tassinari, who also handles several numbers.

Production, otherwise, is a tediously slow and hammily-stilted meller in a style dating back to early film days. Both story and thesping lack conviction in the over-stuffed tragic proceedings. Framed within period settings of the 1890's, pic is marked by a plush mounting and some good scenic shots of Italy, but these assets have little bearing on overall effect.

Musical numbers are introduced via a fictionalized biog of the Italian songwriter, Francesco Paola Tosti, who was, according to this version, a combination Victor Herbert and Don Juan of his time. Story is focused on his affair with a Polish countess, for whom he deserted another mistress. Countess, however, stricken with a fatal, slow-working disease, heroically gives up her lover in order to allow him to continue with his musical career.

In central role, Claudio Gora is a handsome figure, but with limited acting range. Laura Adana, as the countess, over-emotes and is further handicapped by ludicrous makeup and hairdo. Germana Paolieri, as the mistress, registers as a competent actress.

Herm.

Zygmunt Kolosowski

(RUSSIAN-MADE)

Artkino Films release of Kiev Film Studios production. Stars Boris Dmochowski; features Stanislav Orlik, Waclaw Szyskin, Daniel Golubinski. Directed by Zygmunt Nawrocki and Dmochowski. Screenplay, Igor Lukowski. At Stanley theatre, N. Y., Nov. 12, '47. Running time, 90 MINS.

Zygmunt Kolosowski	Boris Dmochowski
Waclaw Szyszkin	Stanislav Orlik
Ludwig	Waclaw Oswiecimski
Fathern Jan	Daniel Golubinski
Stefan Muraszko	Piotr Skorochad
Julka Muraszko	Irena Murowa
Waclaw Wiencek	Dmitri Miliutenko
Gauleiter	George Klering
S.S. Lieut. Ratz	Andrei Tarszyn
S.S. Capt. Hauch	Nikolas Grodski

(In Polish; English Titles)

"Zygmunt Kolosowski" is touted as the first postwar Polish-language film to hit the States. Why it was chosen as the pathbreaker must remain a mystery. It would have been better if prudent second thoughts had stayed its trip. It is ineptly assembled, poorly produced and carries the burden of a disjointed and incredible story of derring-do. As such, the pic can bring no credit to nascent Polish filmmaking nor profit to Yank exhibs.

The impression is that this version had some mighty careless editing, plus flickering illumination, weak camera work and general tintype effects.

Action centers on a preposterous latter-day version of the Scarlet Pimpernel myth. The place is Poland rather than France this time, and the hokus-pokus occurs during the Nazi occupation of its eastern neighbor. There are no other differences. Kolosowski is the tag assumed by an escaped Polish poet, who spreads terror in Teuton ranks by incredible rescues, assassinations, sabotage and like devices. In the end, the Soviet armies appear on the scene and the new Polish nation is born.

Dmochowski is the whole works. He appears, in and out of disguise in almost every scene. His performance is uneven, much of it having the exaggerated quality of the old-time silents. Yet, when it comes to comedy, Dmochowski shows a real flair which should be put to use in something more digestible. As for the supporting cast, all they're called to do are bits. To that extent, subordinate portrayals are adequate.

Pic was filmed in Poland and Russia but has none of the feel of movement which a wandering camera might capture. Photography lacks clarity or sharpness of detail. There's a flickery milkiness of finish which has the audience reaching for its best pair of bi-focals.

Wit.

Miniature Reviews

"Captain From Castile" (Color) (20th). Sweeping action story in brilliant Technicolor with Tyrone Power; socko b.o.

"An Ideal Husband" (Brit.-Lion). Alexander Korda-London Film Technicolor picture with Paulette Goddard, C. Aubrey Smith. Okay b.o.

"Daisy Kenyon" (20th). High-powered melodrama surefire for the femme market.

"To Live in Peace" (Indie). Fine Italian-made war film for good sureseater b.o.

"Bush Christmas" (U). Aussie-made oater with mild b.o. appeal.

"The Crime Doctor's Gamble" (Col). Another of the medico's adventures, this time with Paris background. Okay dualer.

"Philo Vance's Secret Mission" (PRC). Okay whodunit for twin bills.

"Fighting Vigilantes" (EL). Run-of-the-mesa formula actioner starring "Lash" LaRue.

"Lone Wolf in London" (Col). Another Louis J. Vance story of fictional sleuth-gem manipulator; okay for dual support.

Captain From Castile
(COLOR)

20th-Fox release of Darryl F. Zanuck (Lamar Trotti) production. Stars Tyrone Power; features Jean Peters, Cesar Romero, Lee J. Cobb, John Sutton. Directed by Henry King. Screenplay by Trotti, from novel by Samuel Shellaberger; camera (Technicolor), Charles Clarke, Arthur E. Arling; editor, Barbara McLean; music, Alfred Newman; arrangements, Edward Powell. Tradeshown N. Y., Nov. 24, '47. Running time, **140 MINS.**

Pedro De Vargas	Tyrone Power
Catana	Jean Peters
Cortez	Cesar Romero
Juan Garcia	Lee J. Cobb
Diego De Silva	John Sutton
Don Francisco	Antonio Moreno
Father Bartolome	Thomas Gomez
Botello	Alan Mowbray
Luisa	Barbara Lawrence
Marquis De Caravajal	George Zucco
Captain Alvarado	Roy Roberts
Corio	Marc Lawrence
Manuel	Robert Karnes
Soler	Fred Libby
Dona Maria	Virginia Brissac
Coatl	Jay Silverheels
Cermeno	John Laurenz
Mercedes	Dolly Arriaga
Escudero	Reed Hadley
Donna Marino	Stella Inda
De Lora	John Burton
Hernandez	Mimi Aguglia

This is a b.o. bonanza. A surging, massive, spectacularly irridescent opus, "Captain From Castile" will line 'em up layers deep from the tanktowns to the key cities despite the upped admission scales which 20th-Fox has pinned on this offering.

Based on Samuel Shellaberger's 1945 best-selling historical novel, the cinema adaptation hews closely to the structure of the book, capturing the vast sweep of its story and adding to it an eye-stunning Technicolor dimension. In its sumptuous mountings, costuming, numberless horde of extras, name players and solidly packed running time of two hours and 20 minutes, this film is beyond doubt among the most elaborate ever turned out by a Hollywood studio. The coin poured into this production, reported to be around $4,500,000, is visible in every inch of the footage.

For this plume-and-sabre epic of 16th Century Spanish imperial conquerors, producer Lamar Trotti and 20th production chief Darryl Zanuck have assembled a group of thespers who, besides their high-powered marquee voltage, are cleanly tailored for the various parts. Led by Tyrone Power, who's rarely been shown to better advantage, the roster is buttressed by Cesar Romero, in a stirringly virile portrait of Cortez; Lee J. Cobb, as a fortune hunter; John Sutton, as a velvety villain, and newcomer Jean Peters, a buxom, appealing wench for the romantic byplay. Lesser parts are stocked by such solid standbys as Alan Mowbray, George Zucco, Thomas Gomez, Antonio Moreno and others who play their bit parts to the hilt.

The Technicolor, and the usages to which it is put in this film, is a brilliant achievement considered by itself. Like the British masterpiece, "Henry V," the tinting in "Captain From Castile" is something more than an added visual element, but is explored for its dramatic possibilities as an integral aspect of the action. Through staggering contrasts, subtle shadings and kaleidoscopic merging of color patterns into a dominant tone fitting to the sequence, the color is the most prominent single factor in this production's densely atmospheric quality.

Trotti's screenplay, like the book, has a headlong pace. Due to its pseudo-historical scaffolding, plot has a loose structure based on a succession of individually exciting episodes. From the opening reel to the closing, there's a stampede of action that rarely slows down long enough for the spectator to catch his breath.

From one viewpoint, this picture is constructed like a self-contained double feature. In the first half, the locale is Spain during the Inquisition, with Power and his family unjustly persecuted for heresy. (The Catholic Church's role in the witch-hunting atrocities of that time have been neatly muted to the satisfaction of the unofficial censorship bodies.) This passage is loaded with cross-country chases, jailbreaks and one superb duelling scene between Power and Sutton within a prison cubicle.

Escaping from Spain, Power finds himself during the second half in Mexico as a recruit in Cortez's expedition of plunder against the Aztec empire ruled by Montezuma. Also crammed with action, this section is notable for its handling of panoramic shots of the Spanish camp and the huge diplomatic delegations from Montezuma. Photographed on location in Mexico, many of the Aztec civilization relics are melded into the film, giving an authentic flavor to the pic. Whatever the historical validity of this depiction of the brutal, gunpowdered policy of Cortez towards the spear-armed Aztecs, this film builds and sustains a persuasive canvas of history-in-the-making.

There are, however, several soft spots in the story that interfere with credibility. There is, for instance, the fact that Power narrowly escapes death no less than three times under the most extreme circumstances. Sutton, likewise, cheats death two times despite his being stabbed through the heart with a foot of steel one time and near-strangled the next. But these are picayune considerations in a film that will satisfy all levels of taste in its elemental excitement and colossal size.

Performances are properly keyed, without exception, to the derring-do proceedings. Power, as a Spanish nobleman who becomes a captain in Cortez's army, is an intense, brooding and agile personality with all the emotional depth the part requires. Romero, breaking away from the fancy-dan type casting, draws a dominating portrait as Cortez which shades surrounding players while he's on the scene. Cobb turns in a sharply etched characterization as a fortune-hunter tormented in his lust for the revenge of his mother's death at Sutton's hands. Latter, playing a civilian inquisitor in false service to the faith, is superb in his aristocratic sadism. Miss Peters, as Power's plebian flame, is a flashy looker who handles the thesping needs competently. Other cast members are uniformly excellent.

Powerfully underscoring the driving tandem of the story and the color is a magnificent score by Alfred Newman. The music, which is not unobtrusive, adds heavily to the overall pulse-quickening tempo of the picture. *Herm.*

An Ideal Husband
(Color)
(BRITISH-MADE)

London, Nov. 13.

British Lion release of Alexander Korda-London Film production. Stars Paulette Goddard, Michael Wilding; features Hugh Williams, Diana Wynyard, C. Aubrey Smith, Glynis Johns. Directed by Alexander Korda. Screenplay by Lajos Biro from play by Oscar Wilde; Editor, Oscar Haffenrichter; music by Arthur Benjamin; camera, Dennis Coop. At Carlton theatre. Running time, **96 MINS.**

Mrs. Cheveley	Paulette Goddard
Viscount Goring	Michael Wilding
Sir Robert Chiltern	Hugh Williams
Lady Chiltern	Diana Wynyard
Earl of Caversham	C. Aubrey Smith
Mabel Chiltern	Glynis Johns
Lady Markby	Constance Collier
Mrs. Marchmont	Christine Norden
Lady Basildon	Harriette Johns
Phipps	Fred Groves
Mason	Johns Clifford

Great prestidigitator of the British screen, Alexander Korda, now pulls out of his Technicolor hat this fluffy, somewhat antiquated comedy-drama of Oscar Wilde. This version of the 1895 play, is given handsome mounting by Korda. Yet he could do little more than put the play on the screen, stage asides and all. Film should have great appeal to discriminating if limited audiences. For U. S. market, it has the name of Paulette Goddard. On the stage, Wilde's indolent way with all his characters always gave the effect that he was laughing not only at probity in politics but at morality. But this doesn't come over on the screen.

Story relates how Hugh Williams, under-secretary of the foreign office and marked for a Cabinet post, in his youth profited by selling a Cabinet secret about the Suez Canal, thereby founding his fortune and his political career. Arrival of Miss Goddard, an adventuress and old school friend of his wife complicates matters. She knows about Williams' misdeed and threatens him with exposure if he doesn't support a phony Argentine canal scheme in Parliament.

At first he agrees, but his wife, Diana Wynyard, persuades him to refuse. It looks like the end of his career and marriage, until his best friend, Michael Wilding, takes a hand. He was once engaged to Goddard and his astute handling of the blackmailing adventuress saves Williams, keeps intact his married bliss and earns for him the political promotion he sought.

This bare synopsis can do little justice to the Wilde epigrams, and to the pleasant trivialities of the love affair between Wilding and Glynis Johns.

It seems a brave experiment to cast Miss Goddard as the adventuress. But it doesn't quite come off, although bound to help the boxoffice. She gives the impression of reciting her lines as though just learned. Not a solitary epigram is thrown off with spontaneity, and her loveliness in gorgeous costumes is inadequate compensation. The contrast is striking when she has scenes with seasoned stage players like Williams, Wynyard and Wilding.

Williams hits the right note as the loving husband and ambitious politician, and he is admirably partnered by Miss Wynyard. Wilding turns in a fine performance as the trifler who can be serious when occasion demands. Aubrey Smith is unalloyed delight as the Earl of Caversham.

Korda's direction is straightforward, resulting in a rich, distinctive picture of the colorful nineties. *Cane.*

Daisy Kenyon

Hollywood, Nov. 21.

20th-Fox release of Otto Preminger production, directed by Preminger. Stars Joan Crawford, Dana Andrews, Henry Fonda; features Ruth Warrick, Martha Stewart, Peggy Ann Garner, Connie Marshall, Nicholas Joy, Art Baker. Screenplay, David Hertz; from novel by Elizabeth Janeway; camera, Leon Shamroy; music, David Raksin; editor, Louis Loeffler. Tradeshown Nov. 19, '47. Running time, **100 MINS.**

Daisy Kenyon	Joan Crawford
Dan O'Mara	Dana Andrews
Peter	Henry Fonda
Lucile O'Mara	Ruth Warrick
Mary Angelus	Martha Stewart
Rosamund	Peggy Ann Garner
Marie	Connie Marshall
Coverly	Nicholas Joy
Lucile's Attorney	Art Baker
Attorney	Robert Karnes
Mervyn	John Davidson
Marsha	Victoria Horne
Judge	Charles Meredith
Dan's Attorney	Roy Roberts
Thompson	Griff Barnett
Dino	Tito Vuolo
Walter Winchell	Himself
Leonard Lyons	Himself

"Daisy Kenyon" is a True Confessions yarn with a Vogue sheen. Producer-director Otto Preminger hasn't missed a trick in endowing 20th-Fox's version of the successful Elizabeth Janeway novel with glittering boxoffice accoutrements.

Triangle, in which Dana Andrews and Henry Fonda fight it out for the love of Joan Crawford, is basically a shallow lending-library affair, but it's made to seem important by the magnetic trio's slick-smart Stork Club-Washington - Hollywood - Cape Cod-Nassau backrounds — plus, of course, excellent direction, sophisticated dialog, solid supporting cast and other flashy production values. Tipoff on the film's ultra-ultra appeal is the brief appearance of Walter Winchell and Leonard Lyons in a faithful reproduction of Sherman Billingsley's 53d street swankery at a dramatic moment when the high-lifers cross paths.

Miss Crawford, a fashion illustrator living in a glamorized Greenwich Village walkup, plays Andrews' reluctant mistress. He's a wealthy, ruthless attorney who refuses to give up his wife, Ruth Warrick, and two kids, Peggy Ann Garner and Connie Marshall, to make an honest woman of Miss Crawford (in the title role). Fonda, an ex-soldier, but somewhat less of a he-man than Andrews, comes along and talks her into marrying him and going to live in a Cape Cod hideaway. But Andrews doesn't give up that easily.

After losing a civil rights lawsuit which he had taken on because he thought it would please her, Andrews turns to Miss Crawford again for sympathy. She spurns him, but Miss Warrick finds out about the intrigue they had kept under wraps so long and threatens to divorce Andrews, naming Miss Crawford as corespondent, unless he gives her custody of the kids. Now that he's really in trouble, Miss Crawford agrees to go through with a trial, although it might wreck her own marriage. Andrews keeps after her, of course, to leave Fonda and run away with him to Nassau and a new life.

Andrews breaks up the trial when he sees how tough it is on his light-o'-love, agreeing to the stiff payoff demanded by Miss Warrick, who still loves him. This makes Andrews out a martyr, and he arranges a showdown in which Miss Crawford is to choose between him and Fonda. She settles for Fonda, who has been playing along with his wife's "let-me-do-it-for-Andrews-for-old-time's-sake" deal. Andrews goes back to his family. Fonda is not such a weakling after all, it's revealed. "When it comes to modern combat tactics," says he, "both of you are pikers compared to me."

Women will be pushovers for the torrid love scenes, a violent sequence in which Miss Crawford musses up Andrews when he tries to break up her marriage, and the several scenes in which the three get together for "civilized discussions" of their affairs.

Charles LeMaire's wardrobe for the Misses Crawford, Warrick and Martha Stewart, playing Miss Crawford's girl friend, are knockouts.

Other positive factors are the pleasing David Raksin score, which boasts an ear-pleasing theme; Leon Shamroy's flattering lensing; the fine art direction, sets and special effects, and Louis Loeffler's intelligent editing.

Title role is a thesping plum, with the audience never knowing which guy "Daisy" is going to wind up with, and Miss Crawford really makes the most of it. Andrews, though a trifle young for the tycoon assignment, makes it a strong characterization. Fonda as the dreamer who develops into a man of iron is perfect for the part. The Misses Warrick and Stewart also make their footage count, and the Misses Garner and Marshall get across as completely believable children of the rich. Others who stand out are Nicholas Joy as Miss Warrick's father and Andrews' law partner, and Art Baker as Miss Warrick's counsel in the brilliantly handled courtroom scene. *Mike.*

To Live in Peace
(ITALIAN-MADE)

Times Film release of Lux-Pao production. Stars Aldo Fabrizi. Directed by Luigi Zampa. Screenplay, Suso Cecchi D'Amico, Fabrizi, Piero Tellini; camera, Carlo Montuori; English titles, Armando Macaluso. Previewed N. Y., Nov. 19, '47. Running time, 80 MINS.

Uncle Tigna	Aldo Fabrizi
Ronald	Gar Moore
Silvia	Mirella Monti
Joe	John Kitzmiller
Hans	Heinrich Bode
Corinna	Ave Ninchi
The Grandfather	Ernesto Almirante
Political Secretary	Nando Bruno
The Doctor	Aldo Silvani
The Priest	Gino Cavalieri
Franco	Piero Palermini
Citto	Franco Serpilli

(In Italian; English Titles)

"To Live In Peace" is a sincere and poignant film that will add to the growing prestige of Italian product in U. S. art houses. The film, while falling short of topranking caliber, attains superior rating through original treatment of its war theme, and its excellent cast of players headed by Aldo Fabrizi, best known in America for his role as the Catholic priest in "The Open City."

Some elements in the story fail to merge completely into the picture's simple design and folk mood, but these flaws are heavily overbalanced by a group of individual portraits impressive in their depth, honesty and consistency. Moments of great charm and pathos are struck in these characterizations of a mountain village people who, after several years of isolation, are dramatically thrust into the vortex of the war. It's unfortunate that otherwise steady direction allowed some mawkish romantic interludes and one protracted death-bed scene to mar the film.

Opening quietly in a remote Italian town with camera innocently picking up details of the locale, the film flares into excitement with introduction of two escaped American soldiers in the neighboring woods where they are hiding from the Germans. The two GIs, one of whom is a Negro, are picked up and harbored by Fabrizi's family with unfolding story based upon the conflict between the townspeople's anti-fascist sympathies and their fear of drastic reprisals by the Nazis.

Film is notable both for its treatment of the colored soldier and, in a lesser way, of an ordinary German soldier whose mission of checking on the town's activity furnishes the story tension. The Negro, played with the direct realism of an amateur by John Kitsmiller, is drawn as a full human being without prejudice and without patronizing glorification. The German, likewise, is drawn without the crude cliches that would tend to turn him into caricature.

In an uproarious sequence, the Negro and German, meeting each other in totally squiffed condition, embrace each other as comrades and parade through the town during the dead of night popping off their tommyguns in celebration. The villagers, believing the war is over, raid the German warehouse. Learning their mistake, they flee to the hills in hope that the besotted German soldier will not remember the events of the previous night. He does, but by this time the American armies are overrunning this section of Italy and the Germans beat a hasty retreat.

Brilliant performances are turned in by Fabrizi and Ave Ninchi, playing his pinched and distraught wife. Gino Cavalieri, as the local priest, and Nando Bruno, as the fascist political secretary, also contribute superbly drawn portraits. In lesser parts, Mirella Monti, who befriends the two Yanks, is sweet and sensitive but registers as too immature for the love interest. Gar Moore, as the other American soldier, does nicely but is stilted in part by an artificial romantic situation. *Herm.*

Bush Christmas
(AUSTRALIAN-MADE)

Universal (Prestige) release of J. Arthur Rank (Ralph Smart) production. Features Chips Rafferty, John Fernside, Stan Tolhurst, Pat Penny, Helen Grieve. Directed and written by Ralph Smart. Camera, George Heath. Previewed N. Y., Nov. 21, '47. Running time, 76 MINS.

Long Bill	Chips Rafferty
Jim	John Fernside
Blue	Stan Tolhurst
Father	Pat Penny
Mother	Thelma Grigg
Old Jack	Clyde Combe
Narrator	John McCallum
Helen	Helen Grieve
Snow	Nicky Yardley
John	Morris Unicomb
Michael	Michael Yardley
Neza	Neza Saunders

Ralph Smart, who was associate director on the highly-touted Australian-made "The Overlanders" last season, has taken over completely on this new Aussie-made pic, serving as producer-director-scripter. But aside from this fact, and the use of Chips Rafferty in a lead role, as well as some striking outdoor shots, there is little resemblance in the two films. Current production is a simple, obvious yarn about a group of kids helping to round up some horse rustlers that can only have mild boxoffice draw.

Diction in this pic is an improvement aurally on its predecessor. Acting has much of the same homespun, almost amateurish quality, except for the kids, who when left to themselves appear natural and appealing. Film has some unusual angles—the fact that Christmas in Australia comes in their midsummer; shots of Aussie bush, or wild mountain country; life among rural Australians, with kids born to horseback, to long camping trips by themselves, etc. There is one amusing scene in half-starved kids trying to eat a meal of broiled snakes.

But the plot, an elementary variation on the cops-and-robbers chase, isn't likely to hold much interest. Two rustlers make off with some prize horses belonging to a rancher. His children refuse to believe the thieves can get away with it, and follow their trail, over mountains and into bush country, bedevilling the crooks with tactics learned from native servants, and holding the thieves at bay until the police come.

Parts of the film have an attractive idyllic quality, and the outdoor shots have real pull. The chase, too, has some suspense. But overall effect is weak. Chips Rafferty, a striking performer in "Overlanders," has a secondary spot here as one of the rustlers. Helen Grieve, as oldest of the kids, and Nicky Yardley, as youngest, stand out in a quintet of appealing urchins.

Production is on a simple scale. Camera work is good, while direction and dialog are fair. *Bron.*

The Crime Doctor's Gamble

Hollywood, Nov. 22.

Columbia release of Rudolph C. Flothow production. Stars Warner Baxter; features Micheline Cheirel, Roger Dann, Steven Geray, Marcel Journet, Eduardo Ciannelli. Directed by William Castle. Screenplay, Edward Bock; story, Raymond L. Schrock, Jerry Warner; based on radio program, "Crime Doctor," by Max Marcin; camera, Philip Tannura; editor, Dwight Caldwell. Reviewed Nov. 21, '47. Running time, 65 MINS.

Dr. Ordway	Warner Baxter
Mignon	Micheline Cheirel
Henri Jardin	Roger Dann
Jules Daudet	Steven Geray
Jacques Morrell	Marcel Journet
Maurice Duval	Eduardo Ciannelli
Anton Geroux	Maurice Marsac
Louis Chabonet	Henri Letondal
Theodore	Jean Delval
Auctioneer	Leon Lenoir
Brown	Wheaton Chambers
O'Reilly	Emory Parnell
Paul Romaine	George Davis

"The Crime Doctor's Gamble" is okay supporter for twin bill situations. Filler product pits the wits of the radio fiction medico sleuth against some Paris sharpshooters for switch in backgrounds and results come off acceptably for the intended market.

William Castle's direction of the Edward Bock script could have been sharper to heighten excitement but otherwise is adequate. Warner Baxter, in title role, is vacationing in Paris when he becomes interested in a murder case. A young Frenchman is charged with killing his father but Baxter soon proves the old man was done in because a valuable painting he owned had been stolen and copy substituted. Crime doctor nearly gets his in finale clash with the real villain, who's not tracked down until two more killings have passed.

Cast is okay in filling demands of roles. Micheline Cheirel, Roger Dann, Steven Geray, Marcel Journet and Eduardo Ciannelli are among accented featured players who give foreign touch in keeping with Paris locale.

Rudolph C. Flothow's production uses montage and stock clips to round out budget physical values. Lensing, editing, and other credits are standard. *Brog.*

Philo Vance's Secret Mission

Hollywood, Nov. 21.

PRC release of Howard Welsch production. Stars Alan Curtis, Sheila Ryan, Tala Birell, Frank Jenks; features James Bell, Frank Fenton, Paul Maxey, Kenneth Farrell, Toni Todd. Directed by Reginald LeBorg. Screenplay, Lawrence Edmund Taylor; camera, Jackson Rose; editor, W. Donn Hayes. Reviewed Nov. 20, '47. Running time, 58 MINS.

Philo Vance	Alan Curtis
Mona Bannister	Sheila Ryan
Mrs. Phillips	Tala Birell
Ernie Clark	Frank Jenks
Harry Madison	James Bell
Paul Morgan	Frank Fenton
Martin Jamison	Paul Maxey
Joe, Photographer	Kenneth Farrell
Louise Roberts	Toni Todd

"Philo Vance's Secret Mission" is at no time very secretive, but secrets aren't necessary where there is plenty of action and a few murders to keep the house detectives wondering. Plot gets a bit involved with dead men who aren't dead and bodies that can't be found, but Lawrence Edmund Taylor's screenplay is good fare for double bill houses.

Film gets off to a quick start when detective magazine head Paul Maxey is murdered at his palatial home. Maxey had called Curtis in to write a novel concerning an unsolved murder for which, Maxey said, he could supply the ending. Curtis follows through, out of curiosity, and learns that Tala Birell's husband had been murdered seven years previous and that Maxey thought he had the answer. Curtis decides that he must first solve her husband's murder before he can solve Maxey's.

Howard Welsch's production remains at constant level for series while Reginald Le Borg's direction gets plenty of fast action out of Lawrence Edmund Taylor's script. Entire cast turns in a creditable performance. *Free.*

The Fighting Vigilantes

Eagle Lion release of Jerry Thomas production. Stars "Lash" LaRue, Al "Fuzzy" St. John; features Jennifer Holt, George Chesebro, Lee Morgan. Directed by Ray Taylor. Original screenplay, Robert B. Churchill; camera, Ernest Miller; editor, Hugh Winn; music, Walter Greene. Previewed N.Y., Nov. 14, '47. Running time, 61 MINS.

Cheyenne	"Lash" LaRue
Fuzzy	Al "Fuzzy" St. John
Abby	Jennifer Holt
Price Taylor	George Chesebro
Sheriff	Lee Morgan
Check	Marshall Reed
Shanks	Carl Mathews
Trippler	Russell Arms
Frank Jackson	Steve Clark
Old Man	John Elliot
Old Woman	Felice Richmond

"The Fighting Vigilantes" is a run-of-the-mesa formula actioner. "Lash" LaRue is spotted in his customary role as the U. S. Marshal who travels the range incognito. Al "Fuzzy" St. John provides the comedy relief. Picture has moderate b.o. prospects in the juvenile market and adult devotees of oaters no doubt will find the shootin' and ridin' ample enough.

Cast in the lone femme role of any importance, Jennifer Holt tees off this tale of life in the lawless west when she's held up by three riders while driving a chuck wagon loaded with grub. Later, it develops, she turns out to be the daughter of Steve Clark, who heads a group of law-abiding citizens known as "The Vigilantes." His organization is warring on George Chesebro, a provision dispenser who seeks to rub out competitors by a variety of foul means.

Smack into this intrigue come LaRue and his sidekick, St. John. The boys round up all the culprits including the crooked sheriff, Lee Morgan. Chesebro's aspirations in creating a monopoly on food sales are smashed. The price of beans and flour come down and peace once more reigns throughout Gravel Gulch or whatever the locale was called.

LaRue registers per usual as the champion of the law. The bearded St. John's childish buffoonery may find favor with the moppets but his comedy is pretty silly for those over 12. Miss Holt does not appear to be too enthusiastic about her chores, and other thesping is so-so. Ray Taylor's direction keeps things moving in this Jerry Thomas production. Camera and other technical credits are fair.

Mine Own Executioner

London, Nov. 19

London Films release of Alexander Korda production. Stars Burgess Meredith, Kieron Moore, Dulcie Gray. Directed by Anthony Kimmons. Screenplay by Nigel Balchin from his own novel. Music, Benjamin Frankel; camera, Wilkie Cooper; editor, Richard Best. At M.G.M., London, Nov. 18, '47. Running time, 108 MINS.

Felix Milne	Burgess Meredith
Patricia Milne	Dulcie Gray
Peter Edge	Michael Shepley
Barbara Edge	Christine Norden
Adam Lucian	Kieron Moore
Molly Lucian	Barbara White
Dr. Norris Pile	Walter Fitzgerald
Sir George Freethorne	Edgar Norfolk
Dr. James Garsten	John Laurie
Dr. Hans Tautz	Martin Miller
Robert Paston	Clive Morton
Julian Briant	Joss Ambler
Inspector Pierce	Jack Raine
Lady Maresfield	Helen Haye
Dr. Lefage	Lawrence Hanray

Add one more picture to the long list dealing with psychoanalysis, but in this instance it's a serious, thoughtful, adult contribution. Nigel Balchin strives to show that psychoanalysis is an experience shared by analyst and patient, and that when a man dedicates himself to what is perhaps the most difficult profession in the world, the demands made are almost superhuman.

For this country there is good marquee value in the all-round team of first class artists, and pic will appeal mostly to better class audiences. This will also apply to U. S., where the sticks should be bypassed.

This is well put over by director Anthony Kimmins, who has turned in a fine piece of work. Only failing (and here Nigel Balchin, author of the script play, must share responsibility) is that the technique of inference used in the novel is carried too far on the screen for ordinary audiences. A passage in the book can be re-read any number of times when more is inferred than is spoken or described. Not so with the screen.

Story tells how Felix Milne, immersed in his work as a psychiatrist, takes on the treatment of an ex-RAF pilot, Lucian, who is suffering from the effects of a crash in the Burma jungle, and subsequent imprisonment and torture. During a brainstorm he has tried to kill the wife he loves.

Milne is apparently obtaining satisfactory results, but during the treatment, Milne himself is experiencing a mental unrest making him intolerant of his wife and involving him in a serious flirtation with a married woman. Against his better judgment, Milne slackens somewhat in his treatment of the ex-pilot, with the result that Lucian kills his wife, escapes, and takes refuge on the perilous ledge of a tall building. Milne climbs up in a courageous but vain attempt to prevent the murderer's suicide.

Follows the inquest before a hostile coroner, when Milne is saved from professional ruin by the loyalty and support of a qualified colleague, and his rehabilitation is brought about by the sympathy and love of his wife.

These final scenes are something of an anti-climax because, for some unexplained reason, the author has omitted to screen or deal with the prolog of the story, in which Milne, a third-year medical student, decides against the best advice not to qualify as a doctor, but to devote himself immediately to psychoanalysis, thereby branding himself as a quack.

Production, direction and acting are first rate, although the tempo is often too deliberate. Burgess Meredith portrays with skill the complex psychoanalyst, and Kieron Moore gives a fine performance as the nerve-shattered pilot. The rest of the cast revolve around these two, and those particularly noteworthy are Barbara White as the pilot's wife, Dulcie Gray as the analyst's wife, Christine Norden as the sexy disturbance. John Laurie as the faithful colleague and Laurence Hanray, whose coroner is a gem.

Cane.

When the Bough Breaks

(BRITISH-MADE)

London, Nov. 20.

General Film Distributors release of J. Arthur Rank-Gainsborough-Sydney Box production. Stars Patricia Roc, Rosamund John; features Bill Owen. Directed by Lawrence Huntington. Screenplay, Peter Rogers; original story, Mole Charles, Herbert Victor; music, Clifton Parker; camera, Bryan Langley, Dudley Lovell. At Studio One, London, Nov. 19, '47. Running time, **81 MINS.**

Lily Bates....................Patricia Roc
Frances Norman..............Rosamund John
Bill..............................Bill Owen
Ruby Chapman...................Brenda Bruce
Robert Norman...................Patrick Holt
Jimmy..........................Cavan Malone
George..........................Leslie Dwyer
Nurse.............................Sonia Holm
Adams.........................Torin Thatcher
Almoner......................Catherine Lacey
Matron..........................Edith Sharpe
Doctor...........................Gerald Case
Judge............................Noel Howlett
First Landlady.................Muriel George
Second Landlady.....................Ada Reeve
Miss Brent.....................Joan Haythorne

First of a series of sociological studies to be produced by Sydney Box, picture packs a particular appeal for women.

Patricia Roc as Lily Bates, a young working girl nursing a newly born baby, learns that the child's father is a bigamist. Exit the father for good. Lily takes a job as a salesgirl, struggles hard to keep the babe, but finally allows Frances Norman, voluntary worker at a day nursery, to adopt the boy, notwithstanding Lily's refusal to make the adoption legal.

Eight years later the problem becomes acute. Lily has married but has no children, and yearns for her boy. Frances refuses to part with him, but the law decides against her, and the boy who knew no mother and father but Frances and her husband leaves a comfortable suburban home for a strange life with strange people.

Climax comes when the boy runs away to his former home, is brought back by Lily who, seeing the lad's misery, voluntarily gives him up to the people he loves. Happy finale shows Lily celebrating the birthday of her one-year-old son.

Production and direction are good and rarely is a false note struck. Main burden of the acting falls on Miss Roc. Rosamund John is much more appealing, and fine performances come from Bill Owen (formerly Bill Rowbotham), Brenda Bruce, Patrick Holt, Leslie Dwyer and Cavan Malone as the young boy. Screenplay by Peter Rogers has provided a good quota of comedy and tears.

Picture made on the usual modest Gainsborough budget should pay off handsomely here, and may appeal to specialized audiences in America.

Cane.

Lone Wolf in London

Columbia release of Ted Richmond production. Features Gerald Mohr. Directed by Leslie Goodwins. Screenplay, Arthur E. Orloff, based on story by Brenda Weisberg and Orloff; camera, Henry Freulich; editor, Henry Batista. At Rialto, N.Y., Nov. 22, '47. Running time, **64 MINS.**

Michael Lanyard....................Gerald Mohr
Ann Kelmscott....................Nancy Saunders
Jamison..............................Eric Blore
Iris Chatham.....................Evelyn Ankers
David Woolerton.................Richard Fraser
Lily............................Queenie Leonard
Monty Beresford....................Alan Napier
Garvey...............................Denis Green
Inspector Broome...............Frederic Worlock
Henry Robards....................Tom Stevenson
Sir John Kelmscott................Vernon Steele
Bruce Tang............................Paul Fung
Mitchum............................Guy Kingsford

Another in the series, "Lone Wolf in London" is one of those pictures that manages to be so baffling that it sometimes trips over its own involved entanglements. However, it will be okay as solid support on dualers despite this weakness.

Story of a reformed Michael Lanyard, the Lone Wolf, who's tabbed here as a former international gem thief, doubtlessly was a gripping tale in Louis J. Vance's original work but suffers in transference to the screen. Failure to follow through on vital story angles is a handicap for best results.

For a detective whodunit, this film is surprisingly slow getting started. Per usual, the Lone Wolf (Gerald Mohr) proves a better Sherlock than Scotland Yard. Although suspected of a daring gem theft, right from the safe of the Yard itself, he locates the costly missing jewels and captures the mastermind of the gem-stealing ring.

Mohr is fair as the Lone Wolf, but doesn't measure up to others who have done the same character on the screen. Eric Blore, as his butler, per usual thefts every scene if given half a chance. Evelyn Ankers is markedly strong as the femme lure while Nancy Saunders does okay as the British society damsel. Queenie Leonard is nicely cast as the bright maid for the old English family, hinting future possibilities.

The long line of assorted villains heading the support include Richard Fraser, Alan Napier and Tom Stevenson. Paul Fung makes a bit character stand out. Arthur E. Orloff's screenplay does not play as smoothly as the story he did originally with Brenda Weisberg. Leslie Goodwins' direction is inclined to be uneven.

Wear.

Det Kom En Gest

("A Guest Is Com'ng")
(SWEDISH-MADE)

Stockholm, Nov. 10.

Fribergs Filmbureau production and release. Stars Sture Lagerwall, Elsie Albiin; features Ivar Kage, Naima Wifstrand, Gerd Hagman, Karl-Arne Holsten, Erik Berglund, Anita Bjoerck, Olav Riego, Olga Appellof, Peter Lindgren, Erik Hell, Juli Caesar. Directed by Arne Mattsson. Screenplay, Stieg Trenter; camera, Martin Bodin; music, Nils Castegren. At Skandia, Stockholm. Running time, **98 MINS.**

Essman....................Sture Lagerwall
Eva............................Elsie Albiin
Clemens..........................Ivar Kage
Mrs. Clemens...............Naima Wifstrand
Christina.....................Gerd Hagman
Ragnar..................Karl-Arne Holmsten
Urban......................Erik Berglund
Siv..........................Anita Bjoerck
Dr. Hager......................Olav Riego

Swedish film producers in the past have been notoriously inept in turning out criminal mellers. But "Det Kom en Gest" is a genuinely brilliant thriller. Credit for the picture's quality goes to writer Stieg Trenter. One of Sweden's most able authors of detective novels, he's done a bit of commendable scripting. Film has excellent chances in the Scandinavian area as well as in the world market.

Yarn tees off when Sture Lagerwall, a stranger, enters the house of a family about to eat its Christmas night dinner, when a melodramatic set of incidents follows. Generally good acting helps the story with Lagerwall particularly sparkling as the stranger. Others scoring in fine characterizations are Elsie Albiin, as Eva; Gerd Hagman, as an insane girl; Ivar Kage, in the role of the count, and Naima Wifstrand as the countess.

Director Arne Mattsson contributes a neat job, while lensing of Martin Bodin also enhances the film's value. Musical score and other technical credits, too, rate kudoes.

Wing.

Foreign Films

"En Fluga Ger Ingen Sommar" ("One Swallow Does Not Make a Summer") **(SWEDISH-MADE)**. Europa Film release of Hans Ekman production. Stars Eva Henning, Hasse Ekman, Lauritz Falk, Sonja Wigert; features Olof Winnerstrand, Katie Rolfsen, Douglas Hage, Margitt Andelius, Gunnar Bjornstrand, Ulla Andreasson, Gull Natorp, Charlie Almlof. Directed by Ekman. Screenplay, Ekman; camera, Bertil Palgren; music, Nathan Goerling, Erik Bauman. At Anglais, Stockholm. Running time, **92 MINS**

Producer - writer - director - actor Hasse Ekman has turned out a fine romantic comedy in this entry. Ekman, playing husband to Eva Henning, elects to remain in Stockholm when his secretary-wife treks to Venice in the employ of Lauritz Falk. She falls for her chief there but meanwhile Ekman is dating Sonja Wigert. Both are reluctant to tell each other of their escapades. However, the truth comes out in a neat denouement. Acting is good and picture may have a moderate appeal in the U. S.

Winq.

"Jag Elskar Dig, Karlsson" ("I, Love You, Karlsson") **(SWEDISH - MADE)**. Kungsfilm release of Inge Ivarsson production. Stars Marguerite Viby, Sture Lagervall; features Olof Winnerstrand, Ib Schonberg, Lillebil Kjellen, Viveca Serlachius, Curt Masreliez, Linnea Hillberg, Astrid Bodin, Julia Kindahl, Solveig Lagstrom, Lau Lauritzen, Jr. Directed by Lauritzen and John Zacharias. Screenplay, Grete Frische and Gosta Stevens; camera, Rudolf Fredrikssen; music, Svend Gyldmark. At Astoria, Stockholm. Running time, **86 MINS.**

One of the better films made by a Swedish producer in a Danish studio, this picture is a comedy built around children. Cast includes several Danish players, among them Marguerite Viby, who registers well after a long absence from Swedish screens. Direction, camera and scripting are competently handled. Pic should have good b.o. prospects in Scandinavia but its chances overseas are negligible.

Winq.

"Fem Ar—Som Vi Saa Dem" ("Five Years—As We Saw Them") (Documentary) **(NORWEGIAN - MADE)**. Europa Film release of Per G. Johnson and Bredo Lind production. Narration, H. R. H. Crown Prince Olav. Direction and camera, Johnson and Lind; music, Jolly Kramer-Johansen. Reviewed in Oslo. Running time, **72 MINS.**

Season's first Norwegian film is a documentary dealing with the period between 1940-45. Picture is described as a "cavalcade of Norway and the Norwegian people's work in foreign countries" during the German occupation of their homeland. With Crown Prince Olav handling the narration on portions of the reel, this documentary affords an interesting view of the Norwegian government functioning in London as well as the activities of Norwegian troops. Filled with historical facts, film is well directed and lensed. It has a fair chance in the world market.

Winq.

"Her Kommer VI" ("Here We Are Coming") **(SWEDISH-MADE)**. Svensk Talfilm production and release. Stars Sture Lagervall, Gunner Bjornstrand; features Sigge Fyrst, Marianne Aminoff, Inga Brink, Fritiof Billquist, Gosta Cederlund, Magnus Kesster. Directed by Lagervall and John Zacharias. Screenplay, Torsten Lundquist; camera, Hilmer Ekdahl; music, Ernfrid Ahlin; songs, Roland. At Astoria, Stockholm. Running time, **88 MINS.**

This is a poor musical comedy about the military that will have small chances in the world market. Gunnar Bjornstrand offers some marquee pull in Scandinavia but the script offers him little opportunity to display his ability. Songs of Roland and Hilmer Ekdahl's lensing to some extent offset the film's general mediocrity.

Winq.

Miniature Reviews

"Good News" (Color-Songs) (M-G). Bright with color, songs and fun, pic has b.o. appeal that indicates hearty grosses.

"The Tender Years" (20th). Heartening story of faith and goodwill marks Joe E. Brown's screen return; okay family pic.

"Two Blondes and a Redhead" (Songs) (Col). Mild tuneful for twin bills and smaller situations.

"Shadow Valley" (EL). Fair western in the Eddie Dean series.

"Prairie Express" (Mono). Routine Johnny Mack Brown-Raymond Hatton oater.

"Pacific Adventure" (Australian) (Col). Poor biopic of the late Aussie airman, Sir Charles Kingsford Smith.

"It Always Rains on Sunday" (GFD). British-made underworld meller looks likely in U. S. only for limited audience.

Good News
(COLOR—SONGS)

Hollywood, Dec. 2

Metro release of Arthur Freed (Roger Edens) production. Stars June Allyson, Peter Lawford; features Patricia Marshall, Joan McCracken, Ray McDonald, Mel torme. Directed by Charles Walters. Screenplay, Betty Comden, Adolph Green; based on musical comedy by Lawrence Schwab, Lew Brown, frank mandel, B.G. DeSylva, Ray Henderson, additional material, Betty Comden, Green and Roger Edens; camera (Technicolor), Charles Schoenbaum; songs, DeSylva, Brown & Ray Henderson, Hugh Martin, Ralph Blane, Roger Edens; director, Lennie Hayton; arrangements, Kay Thompson; editor, Albert Akst. Tradeshown Dec. 1, '47. Running time, 92 MINS.

Connie Lane .... June Allyson
Tommy Marlowe .... Peter Lawford
Pat McClellan .... Patricia Marshall
Babe Doolittle .... Joan McCracken
Bobby Turner .... Ray McDonald
Danny .... Mel Torme
Peter Van Dyne, III .... Robert Strickland
Coach Johnson .... Donald MacBride
Pooch .... Tom Dugan
Prof. Burton Kennyone .... Clinton Sundberg
Beef .... Loren Tindall
Cora, the Cook .... Connie Gilchrist
Dean Griswold .... Morris Ankrum
Flo .... Georgia Lee
Mrs. Drexel .... Jane Green

This latest remake of "Good News" has an infectious appeal that should click with all type audiences. First turned out by Metro in 1930 after being a Broadway and hinterlands stage hit, "Good News" has the entertainment stuff that wears well with age. Its songs still make the foot pat, the comedy comes through with punch and the latest cast delivers in every respect.

Production is lavish with eye-appeal, the trappings appearing to advantage in Technicolor. Song and dance staging is a potent value in making it register and the players sock contents home under the very smart direction by Charles Walters. Arthur Freed knows his way about in furnishing a musical comedy with the proper production values and, aided by associate Roger Edens, he misses no trick in this one. In all, it's the answer to a considerable public clamor for light, carefree escapist entertainment.

Such pop standards as "Lucky in Love," "The Best Things in Life Are Free," "Varsity Drag," "Just Imagine," "Ladies Man" and the title tune are judiciously spotted in the original score by B. G. DeSylva, Lew Brown and Ray Henderson, and get over with all of their old appeal. Score has been lengthened by addition of two new tunes, "Pass the Peace Pipe" and "The French Lesson." Both are showy pieces that fit with older numbers and are strong additions. First was cleffed by Hugh Martin, Ralph Blane and Roger Edens, while latter came from the pens of Betty Comden, Adolph Green and Edens.

"Ladies Man" kicks off the extravagant music and dance, with Peter Lawford and Mel Torme spotlighted principally. Torme also comes through with "Lucky in Love." Joan McCracken gives the big lift to production number of "Good News," as well as the catchy new tune, "Peace Pipe." June Allyson displays seldom-used pipes on "Best Things" and works with Lawford on "French Lesson," giving vocal end a decided assist.

College backgrounded plot depicts Lawford as the football hero, Miss Allyson as the girl working her way through as a librarian, Patricia Marshall, the school vamp, and others as students. Familiar complications are ably wrapped around music and dance ingredients by scripters Betty Comden and Adolph Green. The dialog is spritely with some modernization from its 1920s origin, the fun clean and hearty as written. Walters' direction misses no bets in getting the most and the best from the excellent material.

Miss Allyson is most appealing as the heroine, lending considerable charm to her lead role. Lawford shows up strongly as the conceited gridiron hero who is finally straightened out on the right love path. Miss Marshall's college siren is exactly right and Miss McCracken shows the stuff that made her a success in legit musicals. Rounding out topnotch cast are Torme, Ray McDonald, Donald MacBride, Tom Dugan, Clinton Sundberg, Loren Tindall, plus others.

Art direction and set decorations furnish eye-catching backdrops and Charles Schoenbaum's color camera takes every advantage of them. Kay Thompson, recently a click in the night club field, is responsible for sharp vocal arrangements of the numbers. Lennie Hayton's musical direction is in same class, as are other credits. *Brog.*

The Tender Years

Hollywood, Nov. 29.

20th-Fox release of Edward L. Alperson-Jack Jungmeyer, Jr. (Alson) production. Stars Joe E. Brown; features Richard Lyon, Noreen Nash, Charles Drake, Josephine Hutchinson, James Millican, Griff Barnett. Directed by Harold Schuster. Screenplay, Jungmeyer, Jr., and Arnold Belgard; adapted by Abem Finkel from story by Jungmeyer, Jr.; camera, Henry Freulich; music, Dr. Edward Kilenyi; editor, Richard Farrell. Tradeshown Nov. 28, '47. Running time, 81 MINS.

Rev. Will Norris .... Joe E. Brown
Ted .... Richard Lyon
Linda .... Noreen Nash
Bob .... Charles Drake
Emily .... Josephine Hutchinson
Barton .... James Millican
Sen. Cooper .... Griff Barnett
Jeanie .... Jeanne Gail
Sheriff .... Harry V. Cheshire
Frank .... Blayney Lewis
Spike .... Jimmie Dodd

"The Tender Years" spins a tale with several morals and points itself as okay film fare for smaller key towns and family situations. Film has value as object lesson in right and wrong for youngsters—and adults—and poses that moral around the first fight to outlaw organized dog fighting back in the 1880s. Production values have a simplicity in keeping with the story told and the country locale used.

Joe E. Brown, in his first film role in some time, deserts his customary buffoon character to give an able and moving performance as a country preacher who believes in the value of faith, goodwill and honesty in conducting his daily life. Picture doesn't preach and pound over the thought, letting it unfold in simple fashion for the most effect. Brown teaches those tenets to his son and the members of his church, and extends them to cover treatment of animals when he becomes personally involved in a battle against the pit-fighting of dogs.

Harold Schuster's direction manages some tense scenes of fighting dogs that are so realistically shown they will have a chilling affect on audiences. Such sequences add to moral values of yarn scripted by Jack Jungmeyer, Jr., and Arnold Belgard. Writers have kept their story on a simple line with believeable dialog and situations.

Young Richard Lyon shows up strongly as the son of Brown, an unusually good moppet prformance. Josephine Hutchinson also impresses as Brown's understatnding wife. Charles Drake, Noreen Nash, carrying the slight romantic interest, are good. James Millican registers as the operator of pit fights. Jeanne Gail, Griff Barnett, Blayney Lewis and Jimmie Dodd are excellent support.

Film was produced for 20th-Fox release by Edward L. Alperson, with Jungmeyer, Jr., as associate producer. Latter also did the original story, adapted by Abem Finkel. Lensing by Henry Freulich, editing, music score and other credits measure up to all demands. *Brog.*

Two Blondes and a Redhead
(SONGS)

Los Angeles, Nov. 28.

Columbia release of Sam Katzman production. Features Jean Porter, Jimmy Lloyd, June Preisser, Judy Clark. Director, Arthur Dreifuss. Screenplay, Victor McLeod, Jameson Brewer; story, Harry Rebuas; camera, Ira H. Morgan; editor, Jerome Thomas; songs, Allan Roberts and Doris Fisher, Saul Chaplin. Reviewed Nov. 27, '47. Running time, 69 MINS.

Catherine Abbott .... Jean Porter
Tommy Randell .... Jimmy Lloyd
Patti Calhoun .... June Preisser
Vicki Adams .... Judy Clark
Freddie Ainsley .... Rick Vallin
Judge Abbott .... Douglas Wood
Miles Bradbury .... Charles Smith
Mrs. Abbott .... Regina Wallace
Melvin Lounsdale .... John Meredith
Miss Courtley .... Diane Fauntelle
Jeanette .... Joanne Wayne
Tony Pastor Orchestra

Program comedy with tunes that will satisfy sufficiently to get by in supporting bookings and smaller situations. "Two Blondes and a Redhead" spots four tunes, three of them new, plus a modest amount of comedy. Production background for slight story achieves okay values for budget expenditure, giving it better dress than usually seen in lesser features.

Jean Porter, aided by June Preisser, Judy Clark and Tony Pastor's orch, pipes several songs, for okay results, while Pastor gives his vocal interpretation of the oldie "Sunny Side of the Street."

Thin plot concerns small-town society girl who plays hookey from an exclusive school to try her hand at chorus line in a show. When show closes she invites two chorine chums to her hometown and there a number of complications are injected to pad out the story. Usual assortment of stuffy fiance, snobbish rich, etc., found in this type yarn add to mixups but don't cloud the inevitable finale.

Cast performs adequately under formula direction by Arthur Dreifuss. Miss Porter is the society girl who chums with June Preisser and Judy Clark. Jimmy Lloyd holds down male lead as a rich boy masquerading as a servant. Rick Vallin, Charles Smith and others measure up to demands.

The Sam Katzman production has been given capable lensing by Ira H. Morgan and other technical credits are standard. *Brog.*

Shadow Valley
(SONGS)

Eagle Lion release of Jerry Thomas production. Stars Eddie Dean; features Roscoe Ates, Jennifer Holt, George Chesebro. Directed by Ray Taylor. Screenplay, Arthur Sherman; camera, Ernest Miller; songs, Pete Gates. Previewed in New York, Nov. 20, '47. Running time, 61 MINS.

Eddie .... Eddie Dean
Soapy .... Roscoe Ates
Mary Ann .... Jennifer Holt
Gunnison .... George Chesebro
Foster .... Eddie Parker
Sheriff .... Lee Morgan
Bob .... Lane Bradford
Tucker .... Carl Mathews
Grimes .... Bud Buster
and
The Plainsmen: Andy Parker, Earl Murphy, Paul Smith, George Bamby and Charles Morgan.

Eddie Dean's screen adventures continue anew in a so-so yarn built around a goldmine. Exhibs won't mine more than usual in this series aimed for the Saturday matinee kiddies along with other action fans.

Dean is again matched against George Chesebro. Casting of the latter in the heavy's role, incidentally, has now become almost tradition. A trainrobber on the lam, he heads the outlaws while in the guise of an attorney. Jennifer Holt is the object of his schemings. He and his gang have already killed Miss Holt's father and uncle in an attempt to scare her into selling her ranch. Thar's gold in them thar hills, but Miss Holt doesn't know it.

In the nick of time comes Dean, mounted on his snowwhite charger, White Cloud. He puts the badmen to flight and saves the ranch with its valuable gold lode for Miss Holt. Interspersed in the footage are a trio of mediocre songs which make a fair attempt to capture the flavor of the mesa.

Picture's thesping fails to emerge beyond the quality usually found in these low-budgeters. Dean registers as the champion of the law, his chum, Roscoe Ates, supplies the comedy relief, Chesebro is sinister enough as the renegade, while Miss Holt is decorative in the lone femme role. Ray Taylor's direction and Ernest Miller's lensing are generally good in this Jerry Thomas production.

Prairie Express

Hollywood, Nov. 28.

Monogram release of Barney A. Sarecky production. Stars Johnny Mack Brown, Raymond Hatton. Directed by Lambert Hillyer. Screenplay, J. Benton Chaney and Anthony Coldoway; camera, William Sickner; editor, Fred Maguire. Reviewed Nov. 27, '47. Running time, 51 MINS.

Johnny Hudson .... Johnny Mack Brown
Faro Jenkins .... Raymond Hatton
Dave Porter .... Robert Winkler
Peggy Porter .... Virginia Belmont
Gordon Gregg .... William H. Ruhl
Barke .... Marshall Reed
Kent .... Gary Garrett
Lem .... Ted Adams
Langford .... Curly Gibson
Pete .... Ken Adams
Jarrett .... Steve Clark
Sheriff .... I. Stanford Jolley
Deputy .... Hank Worden
Collins .... Carl Mathews
Perry .... Boyd Stockman
Joe .... Bob McElroy
Blane .... Jack Hendricks
Torgo .... Artie Ortego

"Prairie Express" lopes along at casual pace through most of its 51 minutes, being pretty much average sagebrush fare which juveniles and other western fans will find mildly diverting. Latest of the Johnny Mack Brown-Raymond Hatton series, scripters didn't bother too much with a purposeful subject, with result audiences will find little of a romantic nature. Best it can hope for is lower-bracket billing.

Yarn, what there is of it, has to do with heavy trying to put small freighting oufit out of business, so that he may acquire ranch owned by brother and sister, who also operate hauling trick. Reason for all this, unknown to anybody but heavy, is fact the railroad is coming through and wants right-of-way through the ranch. Of course, heavy doesn't get property; of course, he gets his, in the end; and of course, hero Johnny triumphs and everybody is happy, except the heavy and his cohorts, 'cause they're dead, the rascals.

Brown pretty much walks through his role, although part of the time on his hoss, and Hatton seems to be lost in the shuffle. William H. Ruhl plays villain in static fashion, with Robert Winkler and Virginia Belmont, young ranchowners whom Johnny helps in saving their outfit and ranch. Lambert Hillyer might have drained more action out of his direction in this Barney A. Sarecky production. Technical credits are average. *Whit.*

Pacific Adventure
(AUSTRALIAN-MADE)

Columbia production and release. Stars Ron Randell; features Muriel Steinbeck. Directed by Ken G. Hall. Screenplay, John Chandler, Alec Coppel, based upon an adaptation by Hall and Max Afford; camera, George Heath; editor, Terry Banks. At New York theatre, N. Y., week Nov. 25, '47. Running time, **62 MINS.**

Sir Charles Kingsford Smith..Ron Randell
Lady M. Kingsford Smith.Muriel Steinbeck
Charles Ulm......................John Tate
Kay Sutton......................Joy Nichols
Nan Kingsford Smith..........Nan Taylor
Capt. G. Allan Hancock.....Alec Kellaway
Sir Hubert Wilkins............John Dease
Stringer..........................Joe Valli
Arthur Powell.............Marshall Crosby
Harold Kingsford Smith.......John Dunne
Beau Sheil.................Edward Smith
Tommy Pethybridge..........Alan Herbert
Rt. Hon. W. M. Hughes..........Himself
Captain P. G. Taylor.............Himself
John Stannage.....................Himself

An Australian import, "Pacific Adventure" unreels the story of pioneer Aussie airman, Sir Charles Kingsford Smith. The aviator's exploits might well have been filmed into a telling and forceful biopic, but this Columbia version is singularly dull. Picture's documentary style fails to build audience interest and the market for this entry obviously lies in the double bills.

In preparing exploitation and bally for "Adventure," exhibs would do well to emphasize the film is not a war picture. Kingsford Smith, as is generally known, chalked up a number of long-distance hops a score of years ago before flying to his death on one of them. Flight sequences, which occupy the bulk of the film, are worth pointing up in sales promotion.

Ron Randell, now in Hollywood for Columbia, is forthright and virile enough as Smith but poor direction and a faulty script fail to give him an opportunity to exhibit his true thesping prowess. Story tees off with Smith's discharge from the air force after the close of World War I.

Smith then makes a round-Australia flight and later, with government backing, flies the Pacific in the "Southern Cross." Starting his own domestic airline, he meets with reverses. In an attempt to win a British mail contract, he sails to London. Flying home in a final try for financial support, the airman is lost without trace.

Sandwiched in the flier's career is a brief romance with Muriel Steinbeck which blooms into marriage. Her role is not a particularly pleasant one inasmuch as she's continually pleading with her husband to abandon his flights. Her work is mediocre as is the acting of the balance of the cast. Photography is okay although there are numerous insertions of newsreel clips.

It Always Rains on Sunday
(BRITISH-MADE)

London, Nov. 26.

General Film Distributors release of Ealing Studios-Michael Balcon production. Stars Googie Withers, John McCallum, Jack Warner. Directed by Robert Hamer. Screenplay by Angus Macphail, Robert Hamer, Henry Cornelius from novel by Arthur la Bern; editor, Michael Truman; music, Georges Auric; camera, Douglas Slocombe, Jeff Seaholme. At Leicester Square, Nov. 25, '47. Running time, **92 MINS.**

Rose Sandigate..............Googie Withers
George Sandigate........Edward Chapman
Vi Sandigate....................Susan Shaw
Doris Sandigate............Patricia Plunkett
Alfie Sandigate..................David Lines
Morry Hyams.................Sydney Tafler
Sadie Hyams............Betty Ann Davies
Lou Hyams.......................John Slater
Bessie.........................Jane Hylton
Solly Hyams...............Meier Tzelniker
Tommy Swann..............John McCallum
Whitey ....Jimmy Hanley
Freddie ....John Carol
Sgt. Fothergill....................Jack Warner
Sgt. Leech.....................Frederick Piper
Mrs. Spry...................Hermione Baddeley
Slopey Collins................Michael Howard
Ted Edwards.........................Nigel Stock
Caleb Neesley.........................John Salew
Mrs. Neesley..................Gladys Henson
Mrs. Watson........................Edie Martin

Gloom, and more gloom creeps into every foot of this film. For those to whom misery and art are synonymous, this may be entertainment, but the average patron will feel no better for having spent 90 minutes watching Dead End folk living Dead End lives. In days when a British High Court jury has given legal sanction to anti-Semites, Fascists possibly will find some ready ammunition in this. In the U. S., film might win approval from a limited audience.

Story opens in London's East End on a wet Sunday. Normal routine to many of its inhabitants is upset by the news that a former resident, convict John McCallum, has escaped from jail. He makes for the house occupied by a former sweetheart, now married to an easy-going man, father of a couple of grown daughters.

Her love for the convict is reawakened, and she hides him until night. He deserts her when her complicity is discovered, and she attempts suicide. Meanwhile the police have thrown a cordon round the district, and a lengthy, unnecessary chase occurs until the convict is caught. Minor sequences deal with cheap gangsters and a couple of lukewarm love affairs. The escaped convict theme is becoming commonplace, but the labelling of wrongdoers with a religious tag, when such description has no real bearing on the story, looks dangerous. Production and camera work have merit and authenticity.

Googie Withers gives a sound performance as the harassed housewife in love with the convict, but the minor key in which everything is pitched tends to make her monotonous. Her husband, Edward Chapman, is in perfect harmony with his surroundings while McCallum gives the convict the necessary brutality.

Jack Warner is once again the cockney detective and the supporting cast is well chosen. Susan Shaw, as a rebellious daughter, hints distinct promise.

Film has too much against it to insure popularity, and will find it hard sledding to win audiences over here. *Cane.*

The Winner
(RUSSIAN-MADE)
(Songs)

Artkino release of Mosfilm Studios production. Features Ilya Perevertsev, Irina Cherednlachenko. Directed by Andrei Frolow. Screenplay, Sergei Vladimirsk, V. Yurenev; camera, V. Petrov; music, V. Affasiev; songs, Vladimir Lebedev-Kumach; English titles, Charles Clement. Previewed N. Y., Nov. 26, '47. Running time, **89 MINS.**

I. V. Privalov.............Vladimir Volodin
Mrs. Privalov..............Anastasia Zuyeva
Nikita Krutikov............Ilya Perevertsev
Nina Grekova.......Irina Cherednlachenko
Shishkin.....................Vassily Gribnov
Yuri Rogov..............Alexander Stepanov
Mrs. Rogov...............Tamara Govorkova
Koshalov........................Sergei Blinikov
Lubiago.........................Anton Byelov

(In Russian; English Titles)

In this musicomedy of Russia's fistic arena, the film's hero rides nearly two weeks on a train, and then goes into the ring seeking the boxing title. As expected, he gets kayoed. Which would seem to prove that it's impossible to become a champ athlete, even in Russia, without regular training. Main complaint over this amiable little film is that it takes so long to prove this point. Okay for Russo-language theatres, where it should be a relief from the usual diet of Soviet propaganda pix.

Soviet producers might be interested to know that in the matter of title fights, defeated aspirants have come back to win in the U. S. on several occasions. So that the idea of a worthy foe returning to seek the championship after one defeat is not exactly original.

Story has a husky Siberian athlete being developed into a heavyweight ring champ. There's much elaboration about a femme swimmer falling for him. Also, much hocus-pocus over whether he will stay in the fistic game and near his sweetheart, or return to his former home in Siberia. Persuaded to return to hunting big game in the Siberian woods, he rides, nearly to his destination and then back to Moscow before making up his mind. (Train ride, incidentally, is too long even in the picture). Naturally, he returns to seek the boxing champ title of Moscow.

Pic apparently marks Russo producers' discovery of the fight ring as possible film locale. That's the only feasible explanation for numerous pat pugilistic angles and patter that's been done countless times in U. S. pictures. The title fight scenes are surprisingly dull.

Andrei Frolow's direction is much better than the actual story. Camera work of V. Petrov, not including the wornout newsreel clips for some of the Moscow stadium scenes, is among the best to come from Soviet studios in months.

Pic marks the screen debut of Irina Cherednlachenko, blonde beaut, as the swimmer and all-round femme athlete. She's a first-rate thespian by Russo standards. The hero is impressively played by Ilya Perevertsev. He might possibly be a future bet—if he can cut down the length of his name. Vladimir Volodin, standby favorite in any Soviet musical, is excellent in the comedy role of fight manager. His singing, too, is the best of several efforts. *Wear.*

Miniature Reviews

"The Senator Was Indiscreet" (U). Fine satire, starring William Powell, which should do OK business.

"My Wild Irish Rose" (Color-Songs) (WB). Sparkling Dennis Morgan starrer on Chauncey Olcott's life geared for solid biz.

"Bandits of Dark Canyon" (Rep). Sturdy entry for the western market; plenty of action, etc., for kiddie fans.

"Devil Ship" (Col). Unimportant filler screen material with stereotype performances.

"Cheyenne Takes Over" (EL). Okay oater in the "Lash" LeRue series.

"Symphonic Fantastique" (Indie). Stilted French-made biog of Hector Berlioz for below-par sureseater results.

The Senator Was Indiscreet

Universal release of Nunnally Johnson (Gene Fowler, Jr.) production. Stars William Powell; features Ella Raines, Arleen Whelan, Peter Lind Hayes. Directed by George S. Kaufman. Screenplay, Charles MacArthur from story by Edwin Lanham; camera, Wm. Mellor; editor, Sherman A. Swartz; asst. director, Jack Voglin; special effects, David S. Horsley; music, Daniele Amfitheatrof; score, David Tamkin. Tradeshown N. Y., Dec. 8, '47. Running time, **88 MINS.**

Sen. Melvin G. Ashton.....William Powell
Poppy McNaughton............Ella Raines
Lew Gibson...............Peter Lind Hayes
Valerie Shepherd...........Arleen Whelan
Houlihan.........................Ray Collins
Farrell........................Allen Jenkins
Dinty.....................Charles D. Brown
Waiter.........................Hans Conried
Oakes............................Whit Bissell
Woman at Banquet.........Norma Varden
"You Know Who"..........Milton Parsons
Frank.......................Francis Pierlot
Helen........................Cynthia Corley
Indians..Oliver Blake, Chief Thunder Cloud, Chief Yowlachie, Iron Eyes Cody
Politicos..........Boyd Davis, Rodney Bell
Eddie............................Edward Clark
U. S. Officer.............William Forrest
University President.........Douglas Wood
Attendant-Stand...............Tom Dugan
Texan.......................George K. Mann
Ingred........................Claire Carleton
Book Dealer................Wm. J. Vedder
Girl in Elevator..................Nina Lunn
Broadcaster..................John R. Wald
Quiz Master..............Vincent Pelletier

With Hollywood and Congress a bad parlay these days one might wonder if Universal is indiscreet about releasing "The Senator Was Indiscreet." But tain't so, McGee. This is such a broadly humorous lampoon of politico goings-on that it would be foolhardy for the most thin-skinned of our lawmakers to think the shoe fits. Actually, this is tiptop entertainment of a type the audiences haven't had in a long time—and could stand. It will do good to smash business.

Film may even exceed expectations if it gets the press breaks that should naturally befall an effort from the allied typewriters and celluloid of such a combo as Nunnally Johnson (producer); George S. Kaufman, making his debut as a film director; scripter Charles MacArthur; and associate producer Gene Fowler, Jr. These behind-the-camera factors should command plenty of accentuated newspaper commentary, all of it good.

As for director, Kaufman manifests pace and polish in a fast-moving bit of fluff about a flannel-mouth solon whose presidential aspirations become complicated when he loses an incriminating diary wherein he had recorded every step taken by his political backers in the past 30 days. Twice the boys flash the hit-the-road call, the last time scattering the kiddies to Patagonia, Little America and other outposts with which the U. S. maintains no extradition treaties. Topper finds William Powell (in the title role) in native South Seas garb and his "queen" is the unbilled Myrna Loy—a frank takeoff on the

Crosby-Hope technique of "surprise" tongue-in-cheek fadeouts.

Powell does a fine job as the stuffy dimwit of a senator who was not stupid enough not to record his political machine's machinations. He uses that as a club over Charles D. Brown, who does a capital job as the bullying political boss. Ella Raines is the newspaper gal who rightly suspects Arleen Whelan got away with the diary as a favor to her beau, who too has political ambitions, in opposition to the senator. Peter Lind Hayes is highly believable as the p.a., playing his role with ease, mugging only a shade here and there, but in the right proportions, and impressing generally as a likely juve.

Casting is good down the line, and there are many nice little touches in the Johnson - Kaufman - MacArthur manner (such as that autographed, oversize postage stamp whereon George Washington "thanks" p.a. Hayes for "putting me on the stamp"). The satire is broad, such as the hokum Indian induction scene; the broad Communistic waiter character, and all the rest of the fine spoofery which, for all its sophistication, should appeal generally.

Abel.

My Wild Irish Rose

(COLOR—MUSICAL)

Warner Bros. release of William Jacobs production. Stars Dennis Morgan; features Arlene Dahl, Andrea King, Alan Hale, George Tobias, George O'Brien, Sara Allgood, Ben Blue, William Frawley. Directed by David Butler. Screenplay by Peter Milne, based on book by Rita Olcott; camera (Technicolor), Arthur Edeson, Wm. V. Skall; editor, Irene Morra; montages, James Leicester; dialog director, Charles Vance; special effects, Harry Barndollar; dances, Le Roy Prinz; orchestrations conducted by Ray Heindorf; score, Max Steiner; songs, Ted Koehler, M. K. Jerome. Tradeshown N. Y., Dec. 5, '47. Running time, **101 MINS.**

Chauncey Olcott	Dennis Morgan
Rose Donovan	Arlene Dahl
Lillian Russell	Andrea King
John Donovan	Alan Hale
Nick Popolis	George Tobias
"Duke Muldoon"	George O'Brien
Mrs. Brennan	Sara Allgood
Hoppe	Ben Blue
William Scanlan	William Frawley
Terry O'Rourke	Don McGuire
Foote	Charles Irwin
Joe Brennan	Clifton Young
Augustus Pitou	Paul Stanton
Capt. Brennan	George Cleveland
Pat Daly	Oscar O'Shea
Della	Ruby Dandridge
Brown	Grady Sutton
Brewster	William Davidson
Rawson	Douglas Wood
Stone	Charles Marsh

"My Wild Irish Rose" puts Warner Bros. back in the screen musical sweepstakes with a winner. Whether this pic, a first-rate production in every department except big marquee names, lands first money, place or show likely will depend on how well the distributor and exhibitor sell it. It's that sort of a picture. This handsomely mounted Technicolor musical on Chauncey Olcott's life needs to be smartly sold to land big openings because it will thrive on strong word-of-mouth. Film is the sort of vehicle that pleases right off the reel.

But just as "Rose" obviously has the ingredients for big returns, just as obviously this picture appears to need being judiciously put over with the public. A whale of an ad-exploitation outlay will be required. The selling should center about the Olcott-Lillian Russell angle. And, of course, this film is a natural for Americans of Irish extraction.

"Rose" surprises with its ability to tell a concise story, without too much dependence on the surefire Irish ballads or other Celtic angles. In many respects, the production becomes a swiftly moving panorama of the variety stage of Miss Russell's era, with a considerable leaning to the minstrel and musical division of show biz.

While Dennis Morgan is the chief name for lobby decoration, and measures up to star billing in the Olcott role, Arlene Dahl shapes as a brilliant newcomer in the chief romantic part. This titian-haired beaut is a terrific looker who displays okay thespian ability. But she needs selling.

Film comes at a time when bluenose fingerpointers have had certain recent pix under fire; but this success story, with its clean-cut romance, should be welcome to many exhibs. Furthermore, producer William Jacobs has made solid entertainment out of what could well have been a rather routine story. Actually, the title is the dullest part of this film although identifying one of Olcott's popular ballads.

Scripter Peter Milne has used the Rita Olcott story with some liberties to depict Chauncey Olcott's rise to fame via minstrel shows and musical comedies. Plot has Lillian Russell figuring vitally in his theatrical career from their first meeting when the Irish singer was trying to get away from his work on a tugboat in Buffalo, N. Y. Later she gives him a break by making him her leading man in a Broadway musical. In fact, it's the so-called newspaper romance with Miss Russell that brings the first rift between Olcott and his real heart interest, the daughter of a wealthy N. Y. alderman.

Director David Butler has maintained interest in this stylized plot, however, quickening the pace from the more leisurely moments by injecting exciting episodes such as the fight in the theatrical boarding house and the first time Olcott subs for the tiring Irish ballad-singing favorite, William Scanlan. Butler shows an Olcott who continues pushing forward, with the few obstacles in his rise to fame overcome with only slight effort. He's kept the colorful stages on which the Irish balladist rose to the heights constantly before the eye. Net result is that, even with the slow ballads, there's no letdown.

Morgan (or his vocal double) displays remarkably fine voice for the numerous songs, besides looking the part of a typical Irishman from N. Y. Miss Dahl is the Rose Donovan who finally weds him despite her father's objections. Andrea King's Lillian Russell is effective without being flamboyant. Alan Hale makes a typical alderman and dad to the Dahl girl.

Nick Popolis, the Greek hotel operator and backer of theatrical ventures, is nicely done by George Tobias, while George O'Brien makes a rugged strong man. William Frawley does William Scanlan in fitting fashion. Ben Blue furnishes fine comedy support as Olcott's little pal of early minstrel days. Latter's mother is portrayed in pat fashion by Sara Allgood. Heading the big supporting cast are Charles Irwin, George Cleveland and Don McGuire.

Besides the standard Irish ballads such as "Wild Irish Rose," "Called It Ireland" and "Mother Machree," the additional tunes by Ted Koehler and M. K. Jerome add modern twist to the musical end of the vehicle. Best of these are "Wee Rose of Killarney," "Miss Lindy Lou" and "There's Room in My Heart for Them All."

Le Roy Prinz's handling of musical numbers is in excellent taste, never being permitted to slow the action. He's also credited with the several nicely done dance ensembles. Outstanding dance specialties are provided by Three Dunhills and Lou Wills, Jr. Lensing of Arthur Edson and William V. Skall is topnotch throughout, and the Technicolor is a definite asset.

Wear.

Bandits of Dark Canyon

Hollywood, Dec. 6

Republic release of Gordon Kay production. Stars Allan "Rocky" Lane; features Bob Steele, Eddy Waller, Roy Barcroft, John Hamilton, Linda Johnson. Directed by Philip Ford. Original screenplay, Bob Williams; camera, John MacBurnie; editor, Les Orlebeck. Previewed Dec. 2, '47. Running time, 59 MINS.

Allan "Rocky" Lane	Allan "Rocky" Lane
Ed Archer	Bob Steele
Nugget	Eddy Waller
Jeff Conley	Roy Barcroft
Ben Shaw	John Hamilton
Joan Shaw	Linda Johnson
Billy Archer	Gregory Marshall
Horse Trader	Francis Ford
Farriday	Eddie Acuff
Guard	LeRoy Mason
Sheriff	Jack Norman

As fodder for the western action market, "Bandits of Dark Canyon" measures up to all requirements. The pace is fast, the action plentiful and it's all woven around better than usual plotting, which gives it extra interest for the oater fans. Production and camera take advantage of outdoor settings to advance action intrigue.

Allan "Rocky" Lane rides hard and shoots straight as the Texas Ranger who aids Bob Steele, escaped convict, straighten out a phony murder conviction. Philip Ford's direction keeps everything on the move and production by Gordon Kay backs up all departments.

Plot centers around efforts of Lane and Steele to chase down clues that will prove latter did not murder his mine foreman. When it's all unraveled in the Bob Williams script, the skulduggery is fastened on Steele's best friend and the supposedly murdered foreman is discovered very much alive and helping the "friend" steal Steele's gold.

John Hamilton and Roy Barcroft head up the dirty work. Linda Johnson fills the slight romantic interest and Gregory Marshall is okay as Steele's young son. Some chuckles are injected by Eddy Waller and Lane's stallion, Black Jack, shows off his tricks for kiddie pleasure.

Brog.

Devil Ship

Hollywood, Dec. 6.

Columbia release of Martin Mooney production. Features Richard Lane, Louise Campbell, William Bishop, Damian O'Flynn, Myrna Liles, Anthony Caruso. Directed by Lew Landers. Original screenplay, Lawrence Edmund Taylor; camera, Allen Siegler; editor, James Sweeney. Reviewed Dec. 5, '47. Running time, **61 MINS.**

Capt. "Biff" Brown	Richard Lane
Madge Harris	Louise Campbell
Sanderson	William Bishop
Red Mason	Damian O'Flynn
Jeanie	Myrna Liles
Venetti	Anthony Caruso
Mike	Marc Krah
Burke	Anthony Warde
Carl	Denver Pyle
Evans	William Forrest
Dolly	Marjorie Woodworth
Chum	Joseph Kim
Jerry	Sam Bernard

"Devil Ship" is a minor dualer, told in stereotype fashion and generating little interest. Production's budget values are padded out with sea clips. Cast names are minor.

Plot concerns itself with Richard Lane, captain of small tuna ship which hauls prisoners to Alcatraz in the San Francisco Bay, and the dull adventures which he encounters. Some library shots of tuna fishing, two big storms, a wreck and fisticuffs feature action division while Lane pushes his suit of widow Louise Campbell. The Lawrence Edmund Taylor script spreads itself thin and Lew Landers' direction isn't able to give it much lift.

Lane, Miss Campbell and William Bishop, in leads, are only adequate to demands. Damian O'Flynn, Anthony Caruso and Marc Krah are obvious heavies. Myrna Liles, moppet, and others, fill in.

Martin Mooney's production is standard for budget feature and lensing and other technical aides are okay. There's not much to recommend other than to pad out the bill in twin feature houses.

Brog.

Cheyenne Takes Over

Eagle Lion release of Jerry Thomas production. Stars "Lash" LaRue, Al "Fuzzy" St. John. Directed by Ray Taylor. Original screenplay, Arthur E. Orloff; camera, Ernest Miller; editor, Joe Gluck. Previewed New York, Nov. 28, '47. Running time, 58 MINS.

Cheyenne	"Lash" LaRue
Fuzzy	Al "Fuzzy" St. John
Fay	Nancy Gates
Dawson	George Chesebro
Delhaven	Lee Morgan
McCord	John Merton
Sheriff	Steve Clark
Anderson	Bob Woodward
Companion	Marshall Reed
Bostwick	Bud Buster
Messenger	Carl Matthews
Johnson	Dee Cooper
Bailey	Brad Slaven

Purely as a novelty, latest in the "Lash" LaRue series has a whodunit tinge. Story departs from formula, calling for the old water hole or railroad right-of-way angle, and instead of missing cattle the film has a missing body. However, "Cheyenne" still falls comfortably in the same dualer groove as its many predecessors in this oater series.

LaRue and his comic sidekick, Al St. John, dive into the plot early when they suspect something's amiss at a ranch hard by Rock Creek, Ariz. Sure enough, badman George Chesebro has killed the rightful heir to the property to seize the premises for himself. Saloon keeper Nancy Gates has witnessed the murder but she's afraid to inform the sheriff. After the usual moonlight search for the will, some hard ridin' and shootin', plus discovery of the body, Chesebro is exposed and the law triumphs.

Singularly enough, while LaRue wins his sobriquet of the "Lash" through his adept usage of a long whip, he fails to use the weapon once in this cayuser. Instead he relies on his dukes and six-shooter. St. John furnishes the comic relief and Miss Gates is amusingly petulant in the lone femme role. Chesebro contribs his usual standard characterization of the heavy. Lensing and Ray Taylor's direction are smooth in this Jerry Thomas production.

Symphonie Fantastique

(Music)

(FRENCH-MADE)

A. F. Films release of L'Atalier Francais production. Stars Jean-Louis Barrault. Directed by Christian Jacque. Screenplay by J. P. Feydeau and H. A. Legrand; camera, Armand Chirard; musical director, Maurice-Paul Guillot. At 55th St. Playhouse, N. Y., Dec. 6, '47. Running time, **90 MINS.**

Hector Berlioz	Jean-Louis Barrault
Marie Martin	Renee Saint-Cyr
Henriette	Lise Delamare
Schlessinger	Jules Berry
Charbonnel	Bernard Blier
Louis Berlioz	Gilbert Gil

(In French; English Titles)

"Symphonie Fantastique" is a ponderously slow and stilted long-hair musical destined for below-par results in arty situations. Based on the biog of Hector Berlioz, early 19th Century composer, film fails to capture the revolutionary excitement of his time, and, instead, is a static arrangement of tableaux elaborately dressed but without conviction.

Jean-Louis Barrault, talented star of 'Children of Paradise," plays Berlioz disappointingly with a series of agonized grimaces that frequently provoke laughs where they should be kindling sympathy. Rest of the cast also sags under the burden of a dull screenplay and uninspired direction. Camera work is okay but a scratchy sound track nearly ruins listenability of the symphonic and operatic selections from Berlioz's works which are played by the Conservatory Orchestra of Paris.

Story traces the rise of Berlioz from obscurity to fame with all the conventional devices. Artistic failure gives way to domestic travail until the composer is forced to desert his wife and son for another woman who succors his genius into fruition. Latter part of the film offers a maudlin portrait of Berlioz as an old man still suffering but on the pinnacle of success. For long-hair addicts, a liberal sprinkling of Berlioz's compositions are offered, including pieces from "Damnation

From Faust," "Requiem," "Benvenuto Cellini," "Symphonie Funebre at Triomphale" and "Symphonie Fantastique." But this great music doesn't make up for the surrounding inadequacies. *Herm.*

Two on a Vacation

('Pazzi Di Gioia')

(ITALIAN-MADE)

(One Song)

Hoffberg Productions release of Atlas production. Stars Vittorio Di Sica, Marie Denis, Umberto Melnati; features Enzo Biliotti, Paglo Stoppa, Rosetta Tofano. Directed by Carlo Ludovico and Bragalli. Original script by Vittoria Di Sica; camera, Anchise Brizzi, Rodolfo Lombardi; musical director, Giovanni Fusco. Previewed in N. Y., Dec. 3, '47. Running time, **82 MINS.**

Count Valli................Vittorio Di Sica
Lilliana.....................Marie Denis
Corrado....................Umberto Melnati

Also: Enzo Biliotti, Paglo Stoppa, Rosetta Tofano.

(In Italian; English Titles)

There's no attempt to "say" anything in "Two on a Vacation" ("Pazza Di Gioia"). This Italian picture isn't intended as another "Open City" or "Shoe Shine" of realism. It's merely an escapist romance more or less in the Hollywood manner of a decade or so ago. As such, it seems somewhat weak for average American audiences, but may appeal to Italian-born filmgoers.

The picture was scripted by Vittorio De Sica, who wrote and directed "Shoe Shine." He also co-stars in "Two on a Vacation" with Marie Denis and Umberto Melnati. There's one song in the picture, a sentimental ballad sung by De Sica, with lyrics translated via subtitles, during a brief daydream sequence.

The story is a fairly involved one about a young couple who take an auto trip through southern Italy. There are various mistaken-identity twists, a running farce situation dealing with two jilted swains, and a rather hackneyed happy ending as the girl learns her supposedly poor sweetheart is a wealthy count.

The picture is not expertly produced. The scripting seems guileless and fulsome. The direction is adequate, but the photography is somewhat stilted. De Sica is an acceptable romantic lead and Marie Denis is pretty as the girl, though not impressive dramatically. Some of the secondary parts, mostly comedy relief, are reasonably well played but suffer from seemingly unimaginative subtitling. *Hobe.*

Foreign Films

Nyckeln Och Ringen

("The Key and the Ring")

(SWEDISH-MADE)

Europa Film production and release. Stars Anders Henrikson, Aino Taube; features Lauritz Falk, Hilda Borgstrom, Eva Dahlbeck, Ulla Sallert, Olle Hilding. Directed by Henrikson. Screenplay, Bertil Malberg, based on novel by August Brunius; camera, Harald Berglund; music, Sune Waldimir. At Saga, Stockholm. Running time, **88 MINS.**

With some of Sweden's best film stars in this entry, "Nyckeln Och Ringen" looms as a good grosser in Scandinavia as well as having potentialities in the overseas market. Based on a novel by August Brunius, the comedy has been brilliantly directed by Anders Henrikson, who also handles a leading role.

Cast is uniformly good. Outstanding is Hilda Borgstrom. Bertil Malberg's screenplay is excellent, as is the camera work of Harald Berglund. On the whole the picture compares favorably with most American film comedies. *Winq.*

"Kronblom" (SWEDISH-MADE). Svea-film release of Sven Nygren-Imago Film production. Stars Ludde Gentzel, Dagmar Ebbesen; features Julia Caesar, Calle Reinholdz, Thor Modeen, Sigge Fischer, Sigge Fyrst, Arthur Rolen, Georg Skarstedt, John Norrman. Directed by Hugo Bolander. Screenplay, Torsten Lundqvist and Fischer based on a magazine serial by Elov Persson; camera, Hilmer Ekdahl; music, Gunnar Johansson. At Olympia, Stockholm. Running time, **110 MINS.**

Poor adaptation and direction spoil this comedy. Yarn is based upon "Kronblom," a comic figure sketched in one of the Swedish mags. As drawn in the publication the character is a humorous person who's invariably out of funds due to his dislike for work. But the film version presents him as a man of intelligence and sagacity. Picture offers little for the international trade. *Winq.*

"Foraummad Av Sin Fru" ('Neglected by His Wife") (SWEDISH-MADE). Sandrew-Bauman Film production and release. Stars Irma Christensson, Karl Arne Holmsten; features Agneta Prytz, Lars Kage, Carl Hagman, Ake Claesson, Arthur Cederbergh, Margit Andellus, Harry Ahlin, Barbro Flodqvist, Georg Skarstedt. Directed by Gosta Folke. Screenplay, Sven Bjoerkman; camera, Goran Strindberg, Hilding Bladh; music, Hakon von Eichwald. At Royal, Stockholm. Running time, **88 MINS.**

Good Swedish comedy, this film is the story of a femme journalist and her husband. Because of the nature of her work he seldom sees her at home. Plot has other amusing complications which point up plenty of audience laughs. Acting, direction and scripts are okay. Picture rates as having a fine chance in the Scandinavian market with possibility of breaking into the foreign marts. *Winq.*

Miniature Reviews

"High Wall" (M-G). Sturdy melodramatic film fare, backed by strong cast and production. B.o. outlook good.

"I Walk Alone" (Par). Suspenseful, hard-boiled melodrama with good b.o. prospects.

"Tycoon" (Color) (RKO). John Wayne, Laraine Day in over-long action tale of South American bridge-building; fair biz.

"T-Men" (EL). Documentary-type action film geared for strong grosses.

"Always Together" (WB). So-so zany comedy with mild b.o. appeal.

"Dangerous Years" (20th). Moderately entertaining meller about juve delinquency; adequate for dual bills.

"Mrs. Fitzherbert" (Pathe). No-name cast in British-made historical drama may get by on some U. S. dualers if cut down.

"The Eternal Return" (French). Brilliantly executed love story made in France; surefire for art houses.

"The Chinese Ring" (Mono). Fair programmer in Monogram's "Charlie Chan" series.

"The Story of Tosca" (Italian). Slow but interesting costume drama based on Sardou play, with Puccini background music. Good art house draw.

"Under Colorado Skies" (Color & Songs) (Rep). Good oatuner filmed in Trucolor.

High Wall

Hollywood, Dec. 13.

Metro release of Robert Lord production. Stars Robert Taylor, Audrey Totter, Herbert Marshall; features Dorothy Patrick, H. B. Warner, Warner Anderson. Directed by Curtis Bernhardt. Screenplay, Sydney Boehm, Lester Cole; suggested by story and play by Alan R. Clark and Bradbury Foote; camera, Paul Vogel; score, Bronislau Kaper; editor, Conrad A. Nerwig. Tradeshown Dec. 11, '47. Running time, **98 MINS.**

Steven Kenet...............Robert Taylor
Dr. Ann Lorrison..........Audrey Totter
Willard I. Whitcombe...Herbert Marshall
Helen Kenet...............Dorothy Patrick
Mr. Slocum..................H. B. Warner
Dr. George Poward.......Warner Anderson
Dr. Philip Dunlap............Moroni Olsen
David Wallace..............John Ridgeley
Dr. Stanley Griffin.......Morris Ankrum
Mrs. Kenet................Elisabeth Risdon
Henry Cronner..............Vince Barnett
Emory Garrison............Jonathan Hale
Sidney X. Hackle...........Charles Arnt
Tom Delaney.................Ray Mayer
Richard Kenet..............Bobby Hyatt

"High Wall" garners a high score as a strong entry in the psycho-melodrama cycle. Unfolded credibly and with almost clinical attention for detail, film holds the i n t e r e s t and punches all the way. Its boxoffice values are good, paced by Robert Taylor heading excellent cast names.

Robert Lord has given the melodramatics fine production polish and able handling to spotlight best features in story of a man who believes he has murdered his wife during a mental blackout. Curtis Bernhardt's direction misses no bets in guiding plot through high tension sequences and in getting the most from the capable cast.

Taylor is seen as a man believed homicidally insane, being treated at mental hospital pending trial for murder of his wife. His case seems hopeless until a femme doctor breaks down his reluctance to try treatment to penetrate details that occurred during the lapse of memory. Bit by bit, as the topnotch script by Sydney Boehm and Lester Cole reveals the facts, Taylor and his doctor become convinced of his innocence. Efforts to force a confession from the real

murderer, the manhunt staged when Taylor escapes to rout out the villain and other touches of action and intrigue reflect good writing and strong direction. On the latter score are sharply etched, brief glimpses of pathetic mental cases, interesting disclosures of hospital methods in handling the insane.

Taylor scores in his role, making it believable. Audrey Totter registers strongly as the doctor, displaying a marked degree of talent able to handle most any character. Herbert Marshall is another who clicks as the murderer who cloaks his sin behind the garb of a pious publisher of biblical tracts. H. B. Warner movingly creates a pathetic mental case. It's no more than a brief bit but will be remembered. Dorothy Patrick has short footage as the murdered wife, and Warner Anderson is a doctor interested in Miss Totter. Others are very able in making their roles realistic.

The Bronislau Kaper music score and Paul Vogel's lensing play a major part in pointing up the melodramatic mood. Settings, art direction and other production contributions are expert assists. *Brog.*

I Walk Alone

(SONG)

Hollywood, Dec. 13.

Paramount release of Hal B. Wallis production. Stars Burt Lancaster, Lizabeth Scott; features Wendell Corey, Kirk Douglas, Kristine Miller. Directed by Byron Haskin. Screenplay, Charles Schnee; adaptation, Robert Smith and John Bright; based upon an original play, "Beggars Are Coming to Town," by Theodore Reeves; produced on the stage by Oscar Serlin; camera, Leo Tover; music score, Victor Young; song, Ned Washington, Allie Wrubel; editor, Arthur Schmidt. Tradeshown Dec. 10, '47. Running time, **97 MINS.**

Frankie Madison............Burt Lancaster
Kay Lawrence..............Lizabeth Scott
Noll Turner.................Kirk Douglas
Dave......................Wendell Corey
Mrs. Richardson..........Kristine Miller
Maurice...................George Rigaud
Nick Palestro.............Marc Lawrence
Dan......................Mike Mazurki
Skinner...................Mickey Knox
Felix.....................Roger Neury

"I Walk Alone" is tight, hard-boiled melodrama developed from Theodore Reeves' short-lived stage play, "Beggars Are Coming to Town." It punches over its melodramatics and has been given bright polish by Hal B. Wallis that should pay off. Names values are good and talent ably fits characters to give them sense of reality.

A number of unusually tough sequences are spotted that will give ample satisfaction to the bloodthirsty. One, in particular, is bloody beating handed out to Burt Lancaster by a trio of bruisers who spare no punches. Another is the dark-street stalking and gore-tinged death meted out to Wendell Corey.

Element of suspense is high, broken into only occasionally by cryptic bursts of brittle dialog, but even these scenes become clear as plot moves on. Byron Haskin earns a top credit with his strong direction, which has all the strength needed to unfold gutty action and other red-meat ingredients.

There's a Rip Van Winkle angle to the plot wherein a gangster returns from 14 years in prison to find that his former cronies now wear the garb of respectability and are in such pseudo-legit rackets as used cars, n i g h t clubs, n y l o n s, etc. Charles Schnee's screenplay, from the adaptation by Robert Smith and John Bright, makes much of the basic story's flavor, although letting dialog run away with a few scenes.

Lancaster belts over his assignment as the former jailbird who returns from prison to find the parade has passed him by and that old friends have given him the double-cross. Melodrama develops as Lancaster plots to muscle in on Kirk Douglas' prosperous nitery. He finds that old strongarm methods no longer work, rackets are now run through legal corporate setups. Tension hits hard as the rough-tough guys play it all out and windup is cleverly handled.

Lizabeth Scott holds up her end capably as co-star, making role of nitery singer who falls for Lancaster after a cross from Douglas, believable. Douglas is a standout as the hood turned respectable and fighting a losing battle to hold his kingdom together against Lancaster's assault. Wendell Corey impresses, as do Kristine Knox, George Rigaud, Marc Lawrence, Mike Mazurki and Mickey Knox.

Among potent values backing the production are Victor Young's music score, the lensing by Leo Tover, and art direction. Lizabeth Scott reprises the single tune, "Don't Call It Love," listenable cleffing by Ned Washington and Allie Wrubel.

Brog.

Tycoon
(COLOR)

RKO release of Stephen Ames production. Stars John Wayne, Laraine Day; features Sir Cedric Hardwicke, Judith Anderson, James Gleason, Anthony Quinn. Directed by Richard Wallace. Screenplay, Borden Chase and John Twist, adapted from novel by C. E. Scoggins; camera (Technicolor), Harry J. Wilde, W. Howard Greene; editor, Frank Doyle; music, Leigh Harline. Tradeshown N. Y., Dec. 12, '47. Running time, **128 MINS.**

Johnny....................John Wayne
Maura....................Laraine Day
Alexander............Sir Cedric Hardwicke
Miss Braithwaite..........Judith Anderson
Pop....................James Gleason
Ricky....................Anthony Quinn
Fog....................Grant Withers
Joe....................Paul Fix
Chico..................Fernando Alvarado
Holden....................Harry Woods
Curly....................Michael Harvey
Senor Tobar..........Charles Trowbridge
Chavez..................Martin Garralaga

"Tycoon" could have been a standout action picture, but because of an ultra-slow, faltering script and injudiciously long running time it emerges as just another attempt at escapist fare. Bulwarked with a good cast, Technicolor and some expensive backgrounds, it rates top playing time. Whether it will get more than fair biz is problematical.

With both distributors and exhibitors asking for shorter films these days, it seems strange that producer Stephen Ames could have let "Tycoon" get so out of hand as to run 128 minutes—especially when there was no apparent reason for its longevity. Trimming as much as 30 minutes off the picture wouldn't have hurt the story and could have done much to bring the action sequences close enough together to maintain seat-edge interest throughout. As the picture stands, the slow pace creates enough disinterest to spoil the effect of the spectacular action in the final reel.

Story, which scripters Borden Chase and John Twist expanded too fully from C. E. Scoggins' novel, has John Wayne and Jimmy Gleason partnered in a contracting firm that's building a railroad through the South American Andes. With plenty of high mountains in California from which to choose, Ames could have done better than the desert site he picked. Mountain that Wayne and Gleason have to tunnel through doesn't look as tough as the picture tries to make out. Anyway, the two engineers would rather bridge a river for their railroad than cut through the mountain, but Sir Cedric Hardwicke, as the tycoon for whom the road's being built, says no.

Wayne's role as the rough-and-tough engineer is tailored to his style and he handles both the action and love scenes with Laraine Day (as Hardicke's daughter) in convincing fashion. Miss Day is beautiful in Technicolor and makes the most of an unconvincing role. Hardwicke's part as the austere father is beneath his talents but he makes it believable and Judith Anderson does the same in a minor role as Miss Day's governess. Gleason does his standard thesping job as Wayne's partner and Anthony Quinn, as Hardwicke's nephew, is good. Grant Withers, Paul Fix and Fernando Alvarado, latter the construction camp's moppet mascot, top a good supporting cast.

Director Richard Wallace handles both the thesping and action techniques neatly, but producer Ames hasn't fared too well with his production accoutrements. Technicolor lensing of Harry J. Wilde and W. Howard Greene is negative, with the colors looking smudged in most places. Leigh Harline's score is incidental, lending little to the film's atmosphere. Other production credits are similarly average.

Stal.

T-Men

Eagle Lion release of Edward Small (Aubrey Schenck) production; Turner Shelton, associate producer. Stars Dennis O'Keefe; features Jane Randolph, June Lockhart, Mary Meade, Alfred Ryder, Wally Ford, Charles McGraw. Directed by Anthony Mann. Screenplay, John C. Higgins, suggested by story by Virginia Kellogg; camera, John Alton; editor, Fred Allen; music, Irving Friedman. Tradeshown N. Y. Dec. 10, '47. Running time, **91 MINS.**

Dennis O'Brien............Dennis O'Keefe
Evangeline....................Mary Meade
Tony Genaro....................Alfred Ryder
Schemer....................Wally Ford
Mary Genaro....................June Lockhart
Moxie....................Charles McGraw
Diana....................Jane Randolph
Gregg....................Art Smith
Chief Carson....................Herbert Heyes
Brownie....................Jack Overman
Shiv....................John Wengraf
Lindsay....................Jim Bannon
Paul Miller....................William Malter

Producer Edward Small has taken a closed case out of the Treasury Dept. files, reenacted it in documentary fashion, and the result is "T-Men"—an entertaining action film geared for good grosses. March-of-Time technique in the early reels flavors the footage with pungent realism that builds up to a suspenseful finish at the final fadeout. What "House of 92d St." did for the FBI "T-Men" does for the Treasury agents.

Small and his associate producers, Aubrey Schenck and Turner Shelton, have embellished this entry with unusual production values. Location scenes in Detroit, Los Angeles and several of its beach suburbs, may have cost a little more but the effect they achieve in verity can't be denied. Of particular help is the capable lensing of John Alton.

Preceded by a brief foreword delivered by a Treasury official, plot unfolds at a slow pace in its early stages. Later, however, it's obvious why the opening scenes were so carefully and meticulously outlined. Solution of every crime depends upon the most minute clues. When assembled in the proper sequence there's a crashing denouement. And so it is with "T-Men." The final reel is a corker.

There's a new Dennis O'Keefe in this film. His characterization of the Treasury agent is finely drawn and is a complete contrast to some of his more recent roles—most of which were in musicals. He's almost Jimmy Cagneyish at times. Cast as his partner is Alfred Ryder. They're undercover agents assigned to break the "Shanghai Paper Case." Masquerading as mobsters they join a ring of liquor cutters in Detroit who are known to be using phony revenue stamps.

Performances are of uniform high quality. O'Keefe sparkles as the agent while his team-mate, Alfred Ryder, is also convincing. Wally Ford stands out in a neat portrayal of a onetime gangland big shot who's a victim of his own peculiar idiosyncrasies. Mary Meade lends a touch of realism to the part of a nitery photographer. Jane Randolph is a sinister moll while Charles McGraw, John Wengraf and William Malter shine as heavies. June Lockhart, heralded as a Broadway "find" by her current appearance in "Love or Money," is seen only fleetingly as Ryder's wife. Anthony Mann's direction is well done as is the scripting chore of John C. Higgins.

Always Together

Warner Bros. release of Alex Gottlieb production. Stars Robert Hutton, Joyce Reynolds; features Cecil Kellaway, Ernest Truex. Directed by Frederick De Cordova. Original screenplay by Phoebe and Henry Ephron, I. A. L. Diamond; camera, Carl Guthrie; editor, Folmer Blangstead; music, Werner Heymann. At Strand, N. Y., Dec. 10, '47. Running time, **78 MINS.**

Donn Masters....................Robert Hutton
Jane Barker....................Joyce Reynolds
Jonathan Turner............Cecil Kellaway
Mr. Bull....................Ernest Truex
McIntyre....................Don McGuire
Judge....................Ransom Sherman
Doberman....................Douglas Kennedy

With "Always Together," the series, which began so sparklingly with "Janie" and dimmed a bit in "Janie Gets Married," has come to the end of the line. The original cheekiness has faded into contrived comedy that pulls too hard for its laughs. Moderate marquee lure of the cast, moreover, makes this pic a dubious prospect for key firstruns and will demand solid support in nabe situations.

Director Frederick De Cordova has wrapped lots of cute tricks into this if-I-had-a-million story, some of which come off as intended. Several of the big stars on the Warner Bros. lot are used as comedy props in bit parts, a device usually surefire in its results. Among those appearing in hoked-up sequences of films within a film are Humphrey Bogart, Dennis Morgan, Jack Carson and Eleanor Parker and they make up the best portions of this production.

Surrounding story is a giddy concoction about the effect of a $1,000,000 gift on a young stenog who's married to an unemployed author. From seeing too many pictures, she thinks her husband will leave her if he finds out she's rolling in moola but, in reality, he loves the stuff. Meantime, the old guy who gave her the million in a death-bed gesture of generosity, recovers and tries to take it back. In playing Satan, he throws the marriage on the rocks, drives them to Reno and gets them mixed up in a jungle of absurdity out of which the pic never finally emerges.

In lead, Joyce Reynolds registers as a winsome gal for light comedy roles but packs only average thesping talent. Robert Hutton plays the vis-a-vis energetically but his lines offer him few chances. Two vet comics, Cecil Kellaway, as the eccentric millionaire, and Ernest Truex, as his two-timing lawyer, give sturdy performances in their usual fashion.

Production is good but modest, with sets, size of cast and running time held down to minimum. Camera work and editing are both handled expertly.

Herm.

Dangerous Years

20th-Fox release of Sol M. Wurtzel production (Howard Sheehan, associate producer). Features William Halop, Ann E. Todd, Scotty Beckett, Jerome Cowan, Richard Gaines, Anabel Shaw. Directed by Arthur Pierson. Story and screenplay, Arnold Belgard; camera, Benjamin Kline; musical score, Rudy Schrager; editor, Frank Baldridge. Previewed in N. Y., Dec. 10, '47. Running time, **60 MINS.**

Danny Jones....................William Halop
Doris Martin....................Ann E. Todd
Weston....................Jerome Cowan
Connie Burns....................Anabel Shaw
Edgar Burns....................Richard Gaines
Willy Miller....................Scotty Beckett
Leo Emerson....................Darryl Hickman
Judge Raymond....................Harry Shannon
Gene Spooner....................Dickie Moore
Jeff Carter....................Donald Curtis
Phil Kenny....................Harry Harvey, Jr.
Tammy McDonald.........Gil Stratton, Jr.
August Miller....................Joseph Vitale
Evie....................Marilyn Monroe
Miss Templeton....................Nana Bryant

Here, from appearances, is a picture that started with a sound idea but was apparently crimped by budget limitations and inadequate writing. As a result, "Dangerous Years" is a mildly interesting meller about juvenile delinquency, without the necessary plausibility, dramatic punch or marquee strength to draw heavy patronage. It's dual-bill fodder. Yet it has intrinsic merit and might have been made into a superior picture.

"Dangerous Years," as it's noted in the documentary-like soundtrack that sets the locale and basic situation, are the juve years, the teens. The yarn is set in a typical American small town, in which the popular schoolteacher who tries to encourage the kids in healthy recreation is killed by a young hoodlum who has ensnared them into criminal activities. A major portion of the film is devoted to the murder trial, with some of the action in the form of flashbacks.

The premise is plausible and the general plot outline is reasonably acceptable. But the picture never gets beneath the surface or comes to grips with essentials. The writing is frequently loaded with hokum, so certain scenes seem phoney, and the overall impression is disappointing. Thus, like many current radio shows, what purports to be a realistic treatment of a serious subject becomes merely a minor cops and robbers-courtroom meller with a contrived switched-identity orphan-parent denouement.

Under the circumstances, Arnold Belgard apparently deserves credit for the original story, but his screen treatment is inept. Arthur Pierson's direction is taut and propulsive, but possibly depends too much on aural, rather than purely visual, methods in the story-telling.

William Halop, having graduated from the "Billy" name of his Dead End Kids days, is properly restrained and yet vigorous as the killer. Anne E. Todd (not to be confused with Ann Todd, the British ingenue of "The Seventh Veil" and Selznick's "The Paradine Case"), is touching as a lonely, intense schoolgirl. Jerome Cowan is expressive as the shrewd, tolerant defense lawyer, Anabel Shaw is believable as the D.A.'s pretty daughter. Richard Gaines is competent as the conscientious prosecutor. And Harry Shannon is impressive as the judge. Various kids and several adults are convincing in supporting roles.

Hobe.

Mrs. Fitzherbert
(BRITISH-MADE)

London, Dec. 3.

Pathe Pictures release of British National production. Stars Peter Graves, Joyce Howard, Leslie Banks, Margaretta Scott. Directed by Montgomery Tull. Screenplay by Montgomery Tully from novel "Princess Fitz" by Winifred Carter. Music by Stanley Black; camera, James Wilson, Gerald Moss; editor, Charles Hasse. At M-G-M private theatre, London. Running time, **99 MINS.**

Prince of Wales....................Peter Graves
Maria Fitzherbert....................Joyce Howard
Charles Fox....................Leslie Banks
Lady Jersey....................Margaretta Scott
Duchess of Devonshire.........Mary Clare
King George III....................Frederick Valk
Sheridan....................Ralph Truman
Duke of Bedford....................John Stuart
Lady Sefton....................Helen Haye
Prince William....................Julian Dallas
Beau Brummel....................Barry Morse
Lord Southampton.....Lawrence O'Madden
Henry Errington..........Frederick Leister
Queen Charlotte....................Lily Kann
Caroline....................Wanda Rotha

Presumably this is the love affair which shook Georgian England, and there is just a little emphasis to parallel events in recent history. But pardonable whitewashing has converted the morganatic wife of the Prince Regent into a woman of great character and even made the dissolute Prince something. May find a place on U. S. twin bills if cut down.

It is in 1783 that the Prince (Peter Graves) and Joyce Howard meet by chance in the streets of London. The susceptible young man, who is adept in acquiring mistresses, falls under her spell and begins a determined chase. She eludes him, knowing that nothing more than friendship is possible.

But the Prince laughs at Acts of Parliament, and when she refuses to compromise herself he, in desperation, attempts suicide. His friends send for Miss Howard, and as the Prince's life is at stake, she agrees to a secret marriage. Wild tales circulate, the queen refuses to receive her at Court, pointing out that the marriage is illegal. When the matter is raised in Parliament, the Prince's friend denies the marriage ever took place. And when the Prince refuses to clear her name she retires to the country, in her humiliation, which is complete when his betrothal to Princess Caroline (Wanda Rotha) of Brunswick is announced.

All this is told in flash-back when the Prince dies.

Production on a modest budget is adequate for the slight story, but the greatest handicap is lack of marquee names although the cast is uniformly first-rate. It should play to fair business here.

As the Prince of Wales, Graves gives a nice performance. It's not his fault that the character is not true to history. Miss Howard has the difficult name role of Maria Fitzherbert, but is unable to bring the woman fully to life. Fine character studies are contributed by Frederick Valk, Lily Kann and Wanda Rotha, three continental artists who play with all the stops out. Direction is competent but uninspired. Not a picture for historians, but quite passable entertainment. *Cane.*

The Eternal Return
('L'Eternal Retour')
(FRENCH-MADE)

Discina International release of Andre Pauve production. Stars Jean Marais, Madeleine Sologne; features Yvonne DeBray, Jean Murat. Directed by Jean Delannoy. Original screenplay, Jean Cocteau; camera, Roger Hubert; music, Georges Auric; English titles, Herman G. Weinberg. Previewed in N. Y., Dec 11, '47. Running time, 103 MINS.
Patrice.....................Jean Marais
Nathalia...................Madeleine Sologne
Gertrude....................Yvonne DeBray
Marc..........................Jean Murat
Nathalia the 2nd............Junie Astor
Lionel.......................Roland Toutain
Achille..........................Pieral
Anne.......................Jeanne Marken
Amedee.......................Jean d'Yd
Le Morolt..............Alexandre Rignault

(In French; English Titles)

"The Eternal Return," written by the Parisian avant-garde poet, Jean Cocteau, who formerly dabbled in surrealist cinematics, is one of the great films that have come out of France and the rest of Europe in recent times. Powerful b.o. appeal will be generated by the pic's universal theme and the certain critical raves.

In a brief perface, Cocteau explains that "The Eternal Return" is a takeoff on the Tristan and Isolde legend, the original three-cornered love affair which is duplicated here in modern dress. Into this mythic mold, Cocteau has poured a tragic yarn which is familiar in outline but brilliantly conceived in detail. Imaginative direction, superlative camera work and a perfectly attuned musical score complete the parlay for a monumental payoff.

Unrolling with an unhurried but steady beat in the style of a romantic epic, story is anchored to a palatial country chateau where the three central characters, the uncle, his youthful wife, and the nephew, spell out the predestined pattern of their doom. Fatal cross-conflict develops as the wife and nephew are drawn together by a cosmic yen only to be discovered by the uncle, cast out, and separated from each other.

Forgiven by her husband, the wife returns to the chateau and declines into a lifeless melancholy. The boy, meantime, half tries an affair with another woman but is driven, in torment, to see his first love once again. In the attempt, he gets wounded mortally. Following the legendary pattern, the two lovers are finally brought together again in a powerfully moving death-bed embrace.

Despite the undercurrent of passion and sexual craving, the film has an austere, classic structure, unmarred by eroticism yet profoundly vibrant and disturbing in its total emotional impact. Through the device of a dwarf, one of the chateau residents who is played masterfully by Pieral, Cocteau has invented a concentrated symbol for the world's evil and conventional hypocrisy which is among the outstanding triumphs of this or any other film.

The cast is uniformly excellent. As the latter-day Tristan, Jean Marais is a strikingly blonde Adonis who plays with a vitality and intensity which carries conviction. He's a natural bet for Hollywood. As the wife, Madeleine Sologne, while not a remarkable looker by U. S. standards, establishes the credibility of her tragic role through the honesty of her thesping. Jean Murat plays the elderly uncle with requisite sombreness. Other players, including Yvonne DeBray as the dwarf's mother and Junie Astor as the second love, deliver with equally striking portraits. — *Herm.*

The Chinese Ring

Hollywood, Dec. 8.
Monogram release of James S. Burkett production. Stars Roland Winters; features Warren Douglas, Victor Sen Young, Mantan Moreland. Directed by William Beaudine. Screenplay, W. Scott Darling; based on character created by Earl Derr Biggers; camera, William Sickner; editor, Richard Heermance. Previewed in Hollywood, Dec. 8, '47. Running time, 67 MINS.
Charlie Chan...............Roland Winters
Sergeant Davidson.........Warren Douglas
Tommy....................Victor Sen Young
Birmingham................Mantan Moreland
Capt. Kong....................Philip Ahn
Peggy Cartwright...........Louise Currie
Armstrong..................Byron Foulger
Capt. Kelso.................Thayer Roberts
Princess Mei Ling.............Jean Wong
Lilly Mae.......................Chabing
Dr. Hickey...........George L. Spaulding
Sergeant........................Paul Bryar
Stenographer..........Charmienne Harker
Hotel Clerk...........Thornton Edwards
Butler.......................Lee Tung Foo
Hamishin.................Richard Wang
Chinese Officer............Spencer Chan
Chinese Boy...............Kenneth Chuck

As filler material for supporting positions, "The Chinese Ring" will get by. It's another in Monogram's series built around Charlie Chan, the fictional Chinese sleuth created by Earl Derr Biggers. This one draws only fair rating due to slow pace and story holes.

Roland Winters, who has donned garb of the Chinese supersleuth, a character worn by a number of other character actors in the past, doesn't quite measure up to role in appearance, but otherwise is okay. William Beaudine's direction cues the movement too slowly for suspense, a factor that goes against essentially adequate plot formula furnished by W. Scott Darling.

Wrapped up in this whodunit's story is a Chinese princess, in the U. S. to buy planes. When she is murdered in Chan's den, a chain of circumstances leads the detective, eventually, to pin that killing and two more on a bank manager who's trying to cut in on a large sum of money belonging to the princess. A couple of other doublecrossers, a not-too-keen police sergeant and an annoying femme reporter all manage to keep clues sufficiently befogged so that only Chan can wrap up the case.

Warren Douglas, the sergeant, and Louise Currie, the reporter, carry on a battling romance. Mantan Moreland spots some okay comedy. Victor Sen Young, Philip Ahn. Byron Fougler, Thayer Roberts and others round out adequate casting.

James S. Burkett has given production standard values for budget, and technical credits are also in keeping with the budget. *Brog.*

The Story of Tosca
(ITALIAN-MADE)

Superfilm release of Scalera-Era (Arturo Ambrosio) production. Stars Imperio Argentina, Michel Simon. Directed by Carlo Koch. Based on play by Victorien Sardou, with "La Tosca" arias and background music by Giacomo Puccini. Camera, Ubaldo Arata. English titles, Herman Weinberg. Previewed N. Y., Dec. 12, '47. Running time, 105 MINS.
Floria Tosca.............Imperio Argentina
Scarpia.......................Michel Simon
Mario Cavaradossi.........Rossano Brazzi
Marchesa Attavanti.........Carla Candiani
Angelotti..................Adriano Rimoldi

(In Italian; English Titles)

This is a slow but interesting version of the Victorien Sardou play on which Puccini based his wellknown opera. Arias and incidental music from the opera are used only sparingly, but story has sufficient drama and suspense to stand on its own. Film should draw at the art houses.

Sardou's play has much more incident, naturally, than the Puccini opera, and since the film follows the former, it makes for a palatable pic. The story concerns the revolutionaries in Italy in the time of the all-conquering Napoleon, when Italy was a collection of dictator-ridden principalities, and those citizens trying to change the political setup were termed Jacobins and traitors, and hunted down. Specifically, it relates the story of Tosca, the singer; Cavaradossi, her lover, and the way the two meet their fate at the hands of the police chief, Baron Scarpia, for harboring a Jacobin fugitive.

Pic is stilted and corny in large measure, but the suspense, the chase effect, carries it, as well as the performances. The pageantry of the Te Deum number in the cathedral and the court scenes are interesting, too. When the opera's orchestra music is used as background, it fits, but the few vocal numbers merely distract from the story. The arias are sung as if offstage, by unseen soloists. In this case, voices are those of Mafaldo Tavero and Ferrucio Tagliavini, who render the wellknown arias most creditably.

Undoubtedly, foreign film importers are cashing in on Tagliavini's current popularity since his sensational debut at the N. Y. Met last season, playing up his name even when his connection with a film, as in this case, is very minor and only incidental. Exploitation is legitimate, but it might irk the customers, if they hear his voice once or twice accompanying a film that might otherwise be bad.

Cast in this pic is quite good. Rossano Brazzi is a handsome Cavaradossi, with Imperio Argentina very attractive opposite him, and both fine actors. Michel Simon makes a menacing Scarpia. Adriano Rimoldi, as the fugitive Angelotti, and Carla Candiani, as his titled sister, give good support. Camera work is satisfactory, and direction adequate. *Bron.*

Under Colorado Skies
(COLOR-SONGS)

Republic release of Melville Tucker production. Stars Monte Hale, Adrian Booth; features Foy Willing and Riders of Purple Sage. Directed by R. G. Springsteen. Screenplay, Louise Rousseau; camera (Trucolor), Alfred S. Keller; songs, Bob Wills, Willing, Sid Robin; music, Mort Glickman; editor, Arthur Roberts. Previewed N. Y., Dec. 12, '47. Running time, 65 MINS.
Monte Hale...................Monte Hale
Julia.......................Adrian Booth
"Lucky" John Hawkins........Paul Hurst
Marlowe...................William Haade
Jeff..........................John Alvin
Faro........................LeRoy Mason
Sheriff Blanchard............Tom London
Clip........................Steve Darrell
Red..........................Gene Evans
Doc Thornhill................Ted Adams
Pony........................Steve Raines
Slim.....................Hank Patterson
Foy Willing & Riders of Purple Sage

Filmed in Trucolor, "Under Colorado Skies" reveals sets and atmosphere that rises above the ordinary oatuner. It should have bright b.o. prospects in the double bill situations. Instrumental group of the Riders of the Purple Sage may also mean something at the wicket.

While the mountings and production of this Republic entry reflect care, the casting comes a cropper in the selection of William Haade as the ringleader of the heavies. Physically he's well adapted to the role, but a Brooklyn accent in the Colorado territory circa 1873, can't be dismissed on the grounds of poetic license. Furthermore, it's given sharper contrast to the hero Monte Hale's authentic Oklahoma twang.

As screenplayed by Louise Rousseau, none too original plot tees off in Texas where Hale works part time in the local bank to finance a medical career. Haade's gang stages a holdup and Hale is suspected of complicity. Actually he's shielding John Alvin, brother of his fiancee, Adrian Booth. There are numerous gun fights with the outlaws before law and order prevails, resulting in Hale's vindication.

Hale is forthright in his portrayal of the would-be medico. Adrian Booth is pleasantly decorative as the heart interest. Paul Hurst lends realism to the part of a hotel proprietor. Alvin is okay as the youth gone wrong. Spotted in several sequences, Riders of the Purple Sage contrib several vocal harmonies among them such standbys as "San Antonio Rose." R. G. Springsteen's direction paces the film well while Alfred S. Keller's lensing dresses up the celluloid.

Miniature Reviews

"If Winter Comes" (M-G). Remake must depend on star names to attract.

"Intrigue" (Song) (UA). George Raft, June Havoc, in trite adventure story; should do okay.

"I Love Trouble" (Col). Neatly paced whodunit for top half of the bill.

"Bill and Coo" (Rep). Highly original all-bird film geared for the family trade.

"Heading For Heaven" (EL). Stuart Erwin, Glenda Farrell in farce; strong support for duals.

"A Woman's Vengeance" (U). Grim but engrossing melodrama of murder and revenge that should click with the femmes.

"Volpone" (French). Excellent French-made version of classic stage piece; solid sureseater fare.

"Beauty and the Beast" (French). Jean Cocteau fairy-tale should do well in art houses.

"For You I Die" (FC). Mild melodrama for supporting bookings.

"Cavalleria Rusticana" (Italian). Simple, appealing story based on w.k. opera yarn, good art house draw.

If Winter Comes

Hollywood, Dec. 20.

Metro release of Pandro S. Berman production. Stars Walter Pidgeon, Deborah Kerr, Angela Lansbury; features Janet Leigh, Binnie Barnes, Dame May Whitty. Directed by Victor Saville. Screenplay, Marguerite Roberts, Arthur Wimperis; based on novel by A. S. M. Hutchinson; camera, George Folsey; score, Herbert Stothart; editor, Ferris Webster. Tradeshown Dec. 17, '47. Running time, **96 MINS.**

Mark Sabre	Walter Pidgeon
Nona Tybar	Deborah Kerr
Mabel Sabre	Angela Lansbury
Natalie Bagshaw	Binnie Barnes
Effie Bright	Janet Leigh
Mrs. Perch	Dame May Whitty
Sarah, "Low Jinks"	Rene Ray
Rebecca, "High Jinks"	Virginia Keiley
Mr. Fortune	Reginald Owen
Mr. Twyning	John Abbott
Mr. Bright	Rhys Williams
Tony Tybar	Hugh French
Tiny Wilson	Dennis Hoey
Mr. Pettigrew	Nicholas Joy
The Coroner	Halliwell Hobbes
Mr. Fargus	Victor Wood
Freddie Perch	Hugh Green
Harold Twyning	James Wethered
"Uncle" Fonraker	Owen McGiveney

"If Winter Comes" shows its age and seems headed for mild box-office reception. First made by Fox in 1923, plot has been brought up to World War II, but still is localed in an English village. Pandro S. Berman has given it the usual Metro production polish but results will depend greatly on value of cast names, which will give it some initial momentum.

Static tale opens just before European hostilities and meanders through a story of the plight of Mark Sabre, a good man who is nearly destroyed because of his goodness. Only mild interest is generated by Victor Saville's direction of the Marguerite Roberts-Arthur Wimperis script and Walter Pidgeon's performance as Sabre is spotty. In lighter moments he pleases but when more dramatic scenes come he misses.

A. S. M. Hutchinson's novel is a long time getting to its main action and contrivances used fail to carry much punch. Climax is the coroner's hearing to establish whether the pregnant girl being cared for by Sabre committed suicide or was poisoned by the hero. Sabre, writer of school books, loses his good name, his job and a wife he doesn't love when he insists on caring for the girl, but goodness wins out in the end, indicating he will find happiness in another love.

Deborah Kerr, as Pidgeon's real romance, comes off okay in the histrionics. Angela Lansbury gives a consistent characterization that registers as Pidgeon's wife. Janet Leigh continues to show promise as the young girl who gets herself in trouble. Binnie Barnes, a village gossip, Dame May Whitty, Rene Ray and Virginia Keiley, two delightful servants, Reginald Owen, John Abbott and Rhys Williams are among others showing up capably.

George Folsey's camera work and the Herbert Stothart score lend some assistance. Editing is rough.

Brog.

Intrigue
(SONG)

United Artists release of Sam Bischoff (Star Films) production. Stars George Raft; features June Havoc, Helena Carter, Tom Tully. Directed by Edwin L. Marin. Screenplay, Barry Trivers and George Slavin, based on original by Slavin; camera, Lucien Andriot; editor, George Arthur; music, Louis Forbes. Tradeshown N. Y., Dec. 19, '47. Running time, **90 MINS.**

Brad Dunham	George Raft
Tamara Baranoff	June Havoc
Linda Parker	Helena Carter
Mark Andrews	Tom Tully
Ramon	Marvin Miller
Karidian	Dan Seymour
Lui Chen	Phillip Ahn
Mike	Jay C. Flippen
Nicco	Marc Krah
Hotel Clerk	Charles Kane
Miss Carr	Edna Holland
Captain Masters	Michael Visaroff
Newspaper Editor	Peter Chong
Ling	Maria San Marco

Producer Sam Bischoff must be a faithful reader of the "Terry and the Pirates" comic strip. "Intrigue," his latest George Raft starrer, has characters that might have come directly from the strip, including a sexy dragon lady, American fliers and a Chinese locale. In addition, though, the picture has most of the corny cliches usually associated with such adventure films. As a result, it will appeal to straight adventure fans of all ages, meaning that grosses should be fair in minor first run situations.

With the exception of Raft, who's still a good draw, "Intrigue" has little to offer in the way of marquee lure. Film has June Havoc in her second major screen assignment (first was "Gentleman's Agreement") but she's still more a legit than a film name. Miss Havoc, incidentally, has the dragon lady role as a White Russian leader of a black market outfit. Part is far beneath her talents as an actress and, while she handles it in good style, it's mostly an opportunity for her to parade across the screen in a series of ultra-revealing gowns. In other words, a one-woman fashion show.

Similarity between "Intrigue" and "Terry" doesn't necessarily mean that George Slavin, whose original story formed the basis of the screenplay, got his ideas from "Terry." Manner in which Bischoff cast and lensed the picture, however, is sure to conjure up remembrances in anybody who's ever read the strip. Story has a timely quality which partially compensates for its triteness, dealing as it does with the still-current black market in Shanghai.

Raft is seen as a former Army flier who was unjustly tossed out of the service on charges of flying contraband material during the war. Disillusioned, he joins forces with Miss Havoc to clean up in the black market, despite the pleas of his best friend, a newspaperman who's trying to expose the illegal crews. When the reporter puts the finger on Miss Havoc, she has him murdered, which brings Raft to his senses. He throws open the black market warehouse to the starving Chinese and, in an actionful climax, discovers it was Miss Havoc who stored the contraband on his plane during the war. She's killed accidentally and Raft winds up in the arms of a beauteous young social worker, who's been around the picture most of the time.

Under the uninspired direction of Edwin L. Marin, Raft is his usual wooden, laconic self even in some intended tender scenes with a group of Chinese orphans. His particular style of thesping, though, is okay for pictures such as this. Miss Havoc looks sufficiently sexy to lend the correct amount of intrigue to her role. Helena Carter makes a promising screen debut as the social worker, and Tom Tully as the newspaperman, makes the most of what are probably the corniest lines in the film. Marvin Miller and Dan Seymour are properly menacing as the insidious black marketeers, and former nitery comic Jay C. Flippen shows well in a minor role.

Bischoff handled the medium-budgeted production okay. Sets are neatly executed and look authentic. Lucien Andriot's camera work is good, as is Louis Forbes' score. Ann Wynn is spotted in one short sequence to sing the film's title song, whose writers are not identified. Other production credits are good.

Stal.

I Love Trouble

Hollywood, Dec. 20.

Columbia release of S. Sylvan Simon production, directed by Simon. Stars Franchot Tone, Janet Blair; features Janis Carter, Adele Jergens, Glenda Farrell, Steven Geray, Tom Powers. Screenplay, Roy Huggins from his novel, "The Double Take"; camera, Charles Lawton, Jr.; editor, Al Clark. At Vogue, Hollywood, Dec. 18, '47. Running time, **93 MINS.**

Stuart Bailey	Franchot Tone
Norma Shannon	Janet Blair
Mrs. Caprillo	Janis Carter
Boots Nestor	Adele Jergens
Hazel Bixby	Glenda Farrell
Keller	Steven Geray
Ralph Johnston	Tom Powers
Mrs. Johnston	Lynn Merrick
Reno	John Ireland
Martin	Donald Curtin
John Vega Caprillo	Eduardo Ciannelli
Lieut. Quint	Robert H. Barrat
Herb	Raymond Burr
Sharpy	Eddie Marr
Sergeant Muller	Arthur Space
Buster Buffin	Sid Tomack

"I Love Trouble" follows popular pattern for private detective heroes and spins its involved melodramatics at a good pace. Production polish is excellent and film will fulfill all aims in majority of situations as okay diversion.

S. Sylvan Simon produced and directed under the label of Cornell Productions. His handling of more or less standard ingredients of the whodunit gives it a lightness and fast pace that pleases, and wherever called for suspense is punched over.

Franchot Tone is the glib private eye seeking to trace background of a politician's wife for her husband. Roy Huggins' screenplay from his novel, "The Double Take," draws a lot of red herrings across the hero's path and hasn't taken too much care in putting all the factors together for the finale. Tone gives a pleasant air to his work that gets attention and aids in keeping things on the move as he sorts out the clues, suffers a couple of rugged beatings and makes eyes at the ladies.

Janet Blair is one of the nicer red herrings that Tone encounters as he tracks down an elusive femme. Janis Carter, Adele Jergens and Lynn Merrick are others making his work more pleasant, and more involved. Glenda Farrell, not seen often in films of late, gives welcome flip touch to her role as Tone's secretary. Steven Geray, John Ireland, excellent as tough hoods, Tom Powers, Tone's client, Sid Tomack are among others lending capable support.

Lensing by Charles Lawton, Jr., is topnotch and other physical values measure up. Film is a bit overlength at 93 minutes and could be trimmed.

Brog.

Bill and Coo
(COLOR-SONGS)

Republic release of Ken Murray production. Stars George Burton's Love Birds, Curley Twiford's Jimmy the Crow. Directed by Dean Riesner. Screenplay, Royal Foster and Riesner, based upon an idea from Ken Murray's "Blackouts"; camera (Trucolor): Jack Marta; songs, David Buttolph, Lionel Newman, Foster, DeSylva, Brown & Henderson; music, Buttolph; musical director, Newman; editor, Harold Minter. Tradeshown in N. Y., Dec. 22, '47. Running time, **61 MINS.**

Ken Murray
George Burton
Elizabeth Walters

"Bill and Coo" is easily the year's most novel film. With a cast composed entirely of birds, picture is charged with originality, sentiment and a compelling tenderness resulting in a top quality entry for the family groove. The kids will love it—and bring their mamas. Whether it will pull at the b.o. is a poser. Word of mouth should help and quite possibly will overcome resistance in the more sophisticated situations which may be too blase for an "all-bird" film.

Aside from a prolog in which producer Ken Murray and bird trainer George Burton appear briefly to explain the ensuing footage, picture is entirely confined to the activities of the feathered flock. But don't let Murray's amusing prefatory remarks of "we're making a picture with birds—it's murder!," mislead you. It may have abeen tough on the production end, but the finished product undeniably reflects painstaking care.

Wholehearted credit should be bestowed upon Burton for the admirable and realistic job he's accomplished in putting the birds through their paces. The warblers' thesping contributions are superb. Fred Malatesta's ingenuous sets also rate plaudits inasmuch as the film's entire yarn takes place in the village of Chirpendale, mounted on a 30 x 15 foot table.

Story's built around life in Chirpendale, a model village housing several hundred birds. It has its "birdway," a theatre, shops, hotels, etc. Feathered inhabitants' daily existence is threatened by an archfiend, Jimmy the Crow. He's a fearsome menace until lovebird Bill courageously bags him in a trap.

Best sequences are a fire scene where Bill, a volunteer fireman, mounts a ladder to rescue his vis-a-vis, Coo, from a burning hotel as well as a circus scene where dozens of birds show their skill in tight rope walking, the slide for life, aerial work, etc. Producer Murray accompanies the footage throughout with an explanatory narration. Jack Marta's expert Trucolor lensing dresses this ornithological achievement in firstrate fashion.

Heading for Heaven

Eagle Lion release of George Moskov production. Stars Stuart Erwin; features Glenda Farrell, Russ Vincent, Irene Ryan, Milburn Stone, George O'Haulon. Directed by Lewis D. Collins. Screenplay, Lewis D. Collins, Oscar Mugge; based on play by Charles Webb, Daniel Brown; camera, George Robinson; editor, Marty Cohn. Previewed in N.Y., Dec. 11, '47. Running time, 65 MINS.

Henry	Stuart Erwin
Nora	Glenda Farrell
Swami	Russ Vincent
Molly	Irene Ryan
Harding	Milburn Stone
Alvin	George O'Hanlon
Janie	Janice Wilson
Danny	Ralph Hodges
Wingate	Dick Elliot
Eddie	Charles Williams
Doctor	Selmer Jackson
Professor	Harry Tyler
Sam	Ben Welden
Lila	Betty West

"Heading for Heaven" is a fluffy

comedy that never pretends to be anything more than a lesser item. It's strong support for twin setups. Stuart Erwin and Glenda Farrell are the marquee lures.

Familiar story of a realtor's drive to develop a residential development. Stress is placed on a swami's crystal-balling and Erwin's fear that his days on earth are numbered. He gets a mistaken medico's report which predicts his death within three months. When his clothes are fished out of a creek, Erwin is erroneously mistaken for a suicide. High farcical moment comes when Erwin appears in the flesh at a seance to contact his departed spirit.

Erwin is fine as the realtor. Miss Farrell is convincing as his flighty wife who dotes on handsome swamis. Janice Wilson is attractive, while Irene Ryan makes something of a maid role. Best supporting parts are played by Russ Vincent, Milburn Stone and George O'Hanlon.

Lewis D. Collins' direction seldom permits the action to lag. *Wear.*

A Woman's Vengeance

Hollywood, Dec. 19.

Universal release of Zoltan Korda production, directed by Korda. Stars Charles Boyer; features Ann Blyth, Jessica Tandy, Sir Cedric Hardwicke, Mildred Natwick. Screenplay, Aldous Huxley; camera, Russell Metty; editor, Jack Wheeler; music, Miklos Rozsa. Previewed Dec. 15, '47. Running time, 95 MINS.

Henry Maurier	Charles Boyer
Doris	Ann Blyth
Janet Spence	Jessica Tandy
Dr. Libbard	Sir Cedric Hardwicke
Nurse Braddock	Mildred Natwick
General Spence	Cecil Humphreys
Robert Lester	Hugh French
Emily Maurier	Rachel Kempson
Clara	Valerie Cardew
Coroner	Carl Harbord
Prosecuting Counsel	Leland Hodgson
First Warder	Ola Lorraine
Maisey	Harry Cording
McNabb	

"A Woman's Vengeance" lives up to its title and should attract femme ticket buyers. It's a highly polished, talky melodrama that engrosses even without high tension suspense. Cast is very able and performances are top caliber, adding to interest in unfoldment of the grim tale of murder and revenge.

Production and direction by Zoltan Korda is smoothly valued to make the most of the Aldous Huxley story. Yarn is given a lift where needed, particularly in earlier sequences, and Huxley's philosophical platitudes do not bore because of capable handling by players and director.

Cast lineup, headed by Charles Boyer is hand-picked talent that answers every demand of the plot. Story concerns arrest and trial of Boyer for the poisoning of his invalid wife. Although innocent, the chain of circumstantial evidence places him in the shadow of the gallows from which he is reprieved by a last-minute breakdown of the real murderer.

Femme angles are strong, dealing as they do with a love-starved spinster willing to murder for romance and to send a man to the gallows when her love is unrequited. Jessica Tandy scores decisively as the femme who wreaks vengeance on Boyer when her love is spurned. It's a standout performance. Boyer is another who points up his work for most favorable reception. Ann Blyth clicks strongly as the young girl who marries Boyer after his first wife's death. Mildred Natwick, mentally warped nurse who's Miss Tandy's tool for vengeance, is good. Sir Cedric Hardwicke makes much of his assignment as the doctor who uses psychology to gain a confession of murder from Miss Tandy. Rachel Kempson, the invalid wife, Hugh French and others are good.

Korda has given film a polished mounting with realistic English lo-cale, ably lensed by Russell Metty. Latter's camera is a major aid in proceedings, as are settings and art direction. *Brog.*

Volpone
(FRENCH-MADE)

Siritzky release of Ile De France production. Stars Harry Baur, Louis Jouvet. Directed by Maurice Tourneur. Screenplay, Jules Romains and Stefan Zweig; adapted from Ben Johnson's play, "Volpone"; music, Marcel Delannoy. Previewed in N.Y., Dec. 18, '47. Running time, 105 MINS.

Volpone	Harry Baur
Mosca	Louis Jouvet
Corvino	Fernand Ledoux
Canina	Marion Dorian
Voltore	Jean Temerson
Leone	Alexandre Rignault
Corbaccio	Charles Dullin
Columba	Jaqueline Delubac

(In French; English Titles)

With typical yet always surprising lack of inhibition, the French have made this film version of "Volpone" as a broad and bawdy romp that will go over solidly with the sure-seater trade. Solely on the basis of the credit lines, this offering gets off to a flying start. A team of prominent novelists, Jules Romains and the late Stefan Zweig, has faithfully fashioned the adaptation from Ben Jonson's respected, but rarely played classic, while two of France's foremost actors, the late Harry Baur and Louis Jouvet, head the cast.

This film is played in tongue-in-cheek operatic style that has the cumulative effect of a running gag. The comic tone completely pervades the pic from the super-lush Venetian settings and costumes to the thesping, which is superbly balanced on that fine edge separating high theatre from ham. The cast is equal to the job.

With this farcical air, the pic gets away with lots of hijinks which in other contexts would appear in bad taste. There's an attempted rape scene, a dousing of a gondolier serenader with a chamber pot and other mentions of unmentionables, but it's all done in a spirit of good clean fun, Gallic style, that'll melt the cold tip of a bluenose. Unfortunately, the ribaldry is only dimly shadowed in the washed-out, atrociously spelled English subtitling (done in France).

The yarn is spun out of pure skullduggery, being an Elizabethan's comment on humanity's avarice and treachery. Volpone is a nouveau riche merchant of Venice who hasn't any scruples in adding to his fortune. With the help of his agile-minded flunkey, Mosca, he masquerades as being dangerously ill in order to collect gifts from a trio of equally disreputable characters who are being egged on by the illusory hope of becoming his heir.

Vying for the immense prize, the trio ply Volpone with guldens and trinkets, one of them even offering his virtuous wife as a playmate. The rape miscues, a furore follows and Volpone is pinched for violating a married woman. He pushes the intrigue too far, however, when he names Mosca as his heir and has himself declared dead in order to confound his enemies. Upshot is that Mosca stops playing flunkey and turns the legally dead Volpone into the street without a Venetian dime.

Baur, usually seen before his death in heavy tragic roles, exhibits here another range of his talents. As Volpone, his buffoonery and lechery mingle with an animal intelligence for a sharp portrait of a comic personality. Louis Jouvet, as Mosca, almost steals the picture with his smooth and enigmatic performance. As the trio of competitors for the inheritance, Fernand Ledoux, Jean Temerson and Charles Dullin are excellent. Two femmes, Marion Dorian, as a courtesan, and Jacqueline Delubac, as the bartered wife, add their charms to a film full of wit and surprises. *Herm.*

Beauty and the Beast
(FRENCH-MADE)

Lopert Films (in association with Discina Int'l) release of Andre Paulve production. Features Jean Marais, Josette Day. Screenplay and direction by Jean Cocteau, from story by Mme. Leprince de Beaumont. Music, Georges Auric; camera, Henri Alekan; English titles, Irving Drutman, Previewed N. Y., Dec. 10, '47. Running time, 90 MINS.

Avenant	
The Beast	Jean Marais
The Prince	
Beauty	Josette Day
The Merchant	Marcel Andre
Adelaide	Mila Parely
Felicie	Nane Germon
Ludovie	Michel Auclair

(In French; English Titles)

This Jean Cocteau French film is a fairy-tale—for grownups. It is slow-moving and quite obvious, but on the other hand it has the charm of simplicity, and a good deal of imagination. This version of the beauty-and-the-beast legend, and its Cinderella story switch, may be a little grisly at times for the kiddies, but adults will see its fine points. It's a good art house draw.

Cocteau doubles as director and scripter, in an original version of the wellknown story of the maid who transforms a beast into a prince by her love for him. Dialog is poetic, while English titles are sensitively transposed. Direction has style and mood, and a professional touch amidst the poesy.

The story has a simple maid going to live with a beast in a forest castle as sacrifice to save her father's life. Her ambitious sisters treat her like a slavey, but after she's become lady of the castle, try to get rich through her. The girl defeats their purposes, and regenerates the beast, through her love, and the young pair finally go off to be rulers in a magic land.

In the delicate hands of Cocteau and an excellent cast, this yarn becomes palatable. Early scenes in the forest castle are gruesome, with candelabra held out from the walls by human hands, with human heads breathing fire from statuary, with the beast wearing makeup that would scare the Hunchback of Notre Dame. But they are also fascinating, as well as in such moments when the maid visits the castle, and seems to float through it rather than walk. There are many other such intriguing or touching bits, to show Cocteau's clever or artistic hand.

Josette Day, who did such a nice job in "The Well-Digger's Daughter," does a better one here, and looks more beautiful. Jean Marais is excellent in a triple-threat role as beast, prince and the maid's country lover. Supporting cast is also good. Pic is a modest-budgeter. Camera work is artistic, in keeping with direction, plot and performance. *Bron.*

For You I Die

Hollywood, Dec. 13

Film Classics release of Robert Presnell, Sr. - John Reinhardt (Arpi) production. Stars Cathy Downs, Paul Langion; features Mischa Auer, Roman Bohnen. Directed by Reinhardt. Original screenplay, Presnell, Sr.; camera, William Clothier; editor, Jason Bernie. Previewed Dec. 12, '47. running time, 76 MINS.

Hope Novak	Cathy Downs
Johnny Coulter	Paul Langton
Alec Shaw	Mischa Auer
Smitty	Roman Bohpen
Georgie	Jane Weeks
Maggie Dillon	Marion Kerby
Louisa	Mannela Callejo
Gruber	Don Harvey
Jerry	Charles Waldron, Jr.
Mac	Rory Mallinson

"For You I Die" has all the elements needed to fulfill release intentions but misses cause of inept handling. It's a first try for Arpi Productions, releasing through Film Classics, and co-producers Robert Presnell, Sr., and John Reinhardt have achieved okay physical values for small budget and fast shooting schedule.

Reinhardt's heavy - handed direc-tion clouts over tearjerker elements and puts the players through their paces in ten-twent-thirt style. Presnell's screenplay poses problem of escaped convict who's reformed by love for a girl he meets at a tourist camp while hiding out. Basically, story is okay for the market but needs more dialog smoothness.

That Cathy Downs and Paul Langton in the leads, manage to generate some feeling under the stereotyped direction is credit to their talent. Youngsters show promise if backed up properly. Mischa Auer is in for some sad comedy that will strike an occasional chuckle by its sheer frenzy. Roman Bohnen is a short order cook and Marion Kerby has the ill-conceived character of hillbilly, hymn-singing camp owner. Jane Weeks is put through obvious sex parade as the blonde tramp inhabitant of the tourist camp. Don Harvey and others are adequate. William Clothier did the okay lensing. Editing is bad. *Brog.*

Cavalleria Rusticana
('Rustic Chivalry')
(ITALIAN-MADE)

Superfilm release of Scalera (Cesare Zanetti) production. Features Isa Pola, Carlo Ninchi, Leonardo Cortese. Directed by Amleto Palermi. Story, Giovanni Verga; camera, Massimo Terzano. English titles, Armando V. Macaluso. At Cinema Verdi, N. Y., Dec. 19, '47. Running time, 82 MINS.

Santuzza	Isa Pola
Compar Alfio	Carlo Ninchi
Gna Lola	Doris Duranti
Turiddu	Leonardo Cortese
Gna Nunzia	Bella Starace Salhati
Zio Brasi	Luigi Almirante
Bammulu	Carlo Romano

(In Italian; English Titles)

This is an appealing, unpretentious film, the story of open passions of simple, rustic folk. Film is based on the story by Giovanni Verga, which forms the basis for the well-known Mascagni opera of the same title. Pic uses songs and music from Sicilian folklore instead of the opera's music, and musical background is just as effective. Film has charm, and should prove a good art house draw.

Tale is that of a young tavern-keeper's son who returns from military service to find that the girl he loved has married someone else. She's a coquette and he pretty much a weakling. He makes love to another village maid, meanwhile having an affair with the married lady, who is very willing. The rejected maid informs the husband, who challenges the lad to a duel and kills him.

This Sicilian story of simple passion is told as simply, to make it an engrossing yarn. The workers in the fields, tilling wheat with antiquated methods; the market-place fair; the church processions and service—these form colorful background, with their costumes and customs. Little bits stand out—the biting of an ear to indicate challenge to a duel; a serenading trio under a lady's balcony; a card-playing scene in the tavern; street venders at the fair.

Performances are quite credible. Leonardo Cortese, as the weakling Turiddu; Isa Pola, as the rejected Santuzza; Carlo Ninchi, as the betrayed husband, and Doris Duranti, as the coquetting Lola, are all good. The two women are also quite beautiful. In smaller roles, Bella Starace Saihati as Turiddu's mother; Luigi Almirante as a farmer, and Carlo Romano as a family friend stand out. Especially the mother.

Direction is stark and straight, concentrating on the surging story. Camera work is good, with rural shots for intriguing backgrounds. Production is simple, but adequate. *Bron.*

The Great Glinka
(Musical)
(RUSSIAN-MADE)

Artkino release of Mosfilm production. Stars Boris Chirkov. Directed by Lev Arnshtam. Screenplay by Arnshtam; camera, Alexander Shelenkov, Yolanta Chen; musical arrangements, Vissarion Shebalin; choir and ballet of Bolshoy theatre; English titles, Nicholas Napoli, Charles Clement. At Stanley, N. Y., starting Dec. 20, '47. Running time, 100 MINS.
Glinka (child)..............Sasha Sobolyev
Glinka........................Boris Chirkov
His Wife.................Valentina Serova
Ulyanich..................Victor Merkuriev
Anna Kern...................Katya Ivanova
Katya Kern..............Lydia Lipskerova
Pushkin..................Peter Aleynikov
Czar Nicolas I...........Boris Livanov
Baron Rosen..............Nikolai Svobodin
Petrov....................Mikhail Mikhailov

(In Russian; English Titles)

Despite bits of excellent singing by Boris Chirkov, superb choral work by the Bolshoy Theatre choir and strong musical passages, "The Great Glinka" simmers down largely into a screen vehicle for students of Russian music. Film may hold considerable interest for lovers of Russian classical tunes, and as such should do stout business at Russo-language theatres. For general consumption in the U. S., it's lean pickings.

Supposedly a Soviet film biography of the noted 19th Century Russian composer who first placed Russian folksongs into concert form, this production becomes too much of a character study of Glinka (sometimes dubbed Mikkail Ivanovitch in picture). As such it gives full scope to his emoting, largely in closeups, and this is the weakest thing Chirkov does.

The overture to "Russlan and Ludmilla," which is best remembered in the concert and operatic repertory field, figures importantly in the musical end of the film. Rise of Glinka follows the familiar pattern of screen vehicles, with much footage devoted to preem of his first opera, "Ivan Susanin." In fact, the happiest moments of the picture are reproductions of these operatic launchings, with production values pointing up high expenditure of coin.

Glinka's unfortunate marriage, his close relationship with the poet Pushkin and final triumph as a composer lauded by the Czar, figures in the story. The composer's love affair introduces too much overacting by Chirkov, who really has a fine voice. His vocalizing and the work of the Bolshoy Theatre groups are standout.

Besides Chirkov, Sasha Sobolyev, who is Glinka as a boy; and Valentina Serova, his wife; and Lydia Lipskerova, his romance, contribute fairly good, if not unusual, bits of acting. As often is the case, Lev Arnshtam, faltered at times in directing the scenario he whipped up.

Some unusually smart English titling by Nicholas Napoli and Charles Clement salvages some of the more wordy episodes. *Wear.*

Miniature Reviews

"The Paradine Case" (SRO). A Selznick winner. High-potency star names in class melodrama.

"The Voice of the Turtle" (WB). Solid celluloid treatment of the long-lived stage comedy. Infectious mirth - maker with bright b. o. outlook.

"A Double Life" (U). A class film, marked by top calibre performances and story interest.

"Secret Beyond Door". (U). Psycho-meller looks headed for fairly nice returns.

"Glamour Girl" (Col). Gene Krupa musical looks primed only for dualers.

"Main Street Kid" (Rep). Al Pearce of radio fails to lift this above twin-bill rating.

"Just William's Luck" (UA). British-made kid pic of limited overseas interest.

The Paradine Case
Hollywood, Dec. 27.

SRO release of David O. Selznick production. Stars Gregory Peck, Ann Todd, Charles Laughton, Charles Coburn, Ethel Barrymore, Louis Jourdan, Valli; features Leo G. Carroll, Joan Tetzel, Isobel Elsom. Directed by Alfred Hitchcock. Screenplay, Selznick; adapted by Alma Reville and James Bridie from novel by Robert Hichens; camera, Lee Garmes; music, Franz Waxman; editor, Hal C. Kern; associate, John Faure. Previewed Dec. 27, '47. Running time. 131 MINS.
Anthony Keane..............Gregory Peck
Gay Keane......................Ann Todd
Lord Horfield.............Charles Laughton
Sir Simmon Flaquer.......Charles Coburn
Lady Horfield............Ethel Barrymore
Andre Latour................Louis Jourdan
Mrs. Paradine.......................Valli
Sir Joseph Farrell..........Leo G. Carrol
Judy Flaquer..................Joan Tetzel
Keeper at Inn...............Isobel Elsom

"The Paradine Case" is David O. Selznick's entry in the class film derby that is currently featuring the winter releasing season. From any angle it's a high-potency contender for major boxoffice grosses. Its returns will be particularly high in the de luxe situations and there is general popular appeal in its star names and its melodramatic content that will drawall down the line.

Even without the meticulous polish of production and the importance film will be given in the exploitation, "Paradine Case" would ride to top grosses on strength of the cast and the director. Combo of Alfred Hitchcock for melodrama, Gregory Peck as the attraction for femmes and superior performances by its other stars and featured players packs a punch that couldn't miss, boxoffice-wise.

Selznick introduces two new stars to the U. S. scene and both should have a bright future. Louis Jourdan, French actor, is a handsome, talented young man who will click with the femmes. Valli, Italian actress, is also comely and histronically able with an appeal that will be generally accepted.

Peck's stature as a performer of ability stands him in good stead among the extremely tough competition. As the barrister who defends Valli, charged with the murder of her husband, he answers every demand of a demanding role. Ann Todd delights as his wife, giving the assignment a grace and understanding that tugs at the emotions. Particularly honest is the feeling she achieves in romantic, wholesome, marital love byplay.

Hitchcock's penchant for suspense, unusual atmosphere and development get full play. There is a deliberateness of pace, artful pauses and other carefully calculated melodramatic hinges upon which he swings the story and players. Selznick wrote the screenplay, adapted

from the Robert Hichens novel by Alma Reville and James Bridie. It is a job that puts much emphasis on dialog and it's talk that punches. A very mobile camera helps give a feeling of movement to majority of scenes confined to the British courtroom as Hitchcock goes into the unfoldment of the highly dramatic murder trial.

Plot concerns murder of a blind man by his wife so she can marry her lover. Her attorney, believing in her not guilty plea, fights for her life. Himself infatuated with his client, the barrister plots and schemes to defeat justice but as dramatic events are brought out the truth is revealed. There are no flashback devices to clutter the trial and the audience gradually is let in on the facts as is the court as the hearing proceeds and emotions take hold.

Charles Laughton gives a revealing portrait of a gross, lustful nobleman who presides at the trial Charles Coburn packs all his experience into delivering some choice lines and Ethel Barrymore skillful imprints her performance as Laughton's half-crazed wife. Leo G. Carroll is socko as the prosecutor. Joan Tetzel come through with a strong performance as Laughton's inquisitive daughter. This young actress shows plenty promise. Isobel Elsom completes credited cast and is excellent in brief spot.

"The Paradine Case" offers two hours and eleven minutes of high dramatics. Because of the long running time and deliberate pace, it has slow spots but still maintains interest both for technical achievements and story content. The class photography is by Lee Garmes. Franz Waxman did a compelling score to carry the mood. J. McMillan Johnson's production design carries the stamp of authenticity as does art direction, set decorations and other behind-the-camera contributions. *Brog.*

The Voice of the Turtle
Hollywood. Dec. 24.

Sgt. Bill Page ....Ronald Reagan
Sally Middleton ....Eleanor Parker
Olive Lashbrooke ....Eve Arden
Comm. Ned. Burling ....Wayne Morris
Kenneth Barttlett ....Kent Smith
George Harrington ....John Emery
Storekeeper ....Erskine Sanford
Henry Atherton ....John Holland

Warner Bros. release of Charles Hoffman production. Stars Ronald Reagan, Eleanor Parker, Eve Arden, Wayne Morris; features Kent Smith, John Emery, Erskine Sanford, John Holland. Directed by Irving Rapper. Screenplay, John van Druten; from his stage play, produced by Alfred de Liagre, Jr.; camera, Sol Polito; music, Max Steiner; editor, Rudi Fehr. Tradeshown Dec. 19, '47. Running time, 103 MINS.

Warners has a nifty film package of fun in "The Voice of the Turtle." John van Druten's long-lived stage play has been extended in the celluloid treatment by the author and adds up to strong comedy entertainment. It's an infectious, fluffy mirth-maker with sturdy boxoffice prospects.

Film is a walkaway for Eleanor Parker who, despite the comparison with legit femmes who have played Sally Middleton, gives the character an individual interpretation that is sock. She's naive, exasperating, flighty, besides having plenty of s.a. and sells the role for top honors. Co-star Ronald Reagan doesn't miss any bets either in getting the most from the role of Sgt. Bill Page, the roomless soldier who is succored by the heroine.

In turning his legit piece to the screen, van Druten has added characters only spoken of on the stage. The buildup hasn't lessened the chuckles—in fact it helps spring the comedy—and Irving Rapper demonstrates solid ability to accurately pace a laugh. He's better known for direction of drama and this serves to establish his versatility. There

were production code limitations to overcome in adapting legit play to the screen, but barriers have been surmounted without losing any of the zing of the original. Association of van Druten, Rapper and Charles Hoffman, producer, was a happy one, judging from results obtained.

Eve Arden is the only other on-stage character. As Olive Lashbrooke, the wisecracking, man-conscious actress, Miss Arden registers importantly. Wayne Morris also gets over the offstage role of Comdr. Ned Burling, a sailor who has been to sea too long and wants to do something about it.

Adding zip to the four other credited assignments are Kent Smith, the legit producer; John Emery, playwright; Erskine Sanford, and John Holland, the amorous legit ham. Added characters give breath to the play and more firmly establish the light, fluffy to-do about a romantically inclined actress who has to be in love. Picture is filled with aptly timed bits of business that are as responsible for laughs as the flip dialog and situations.

Hoffman's production has glossed the script with topnotch values and lensing, background music score, editing and other factors are of the best. *Brog.*

A Double Life
Hollywood, Dec. 27.

Universal release of Michael Kanin production. Stars Ronald Colman; features Signe Hasso, Edmond O'Brien, Shelley Winters, Ray Collins, Philip Loeb, Millard Mitchell, Joe Sawyer. Directed by George Cukor. Written by Ruth Gordon and Garson Kanin; camera, Milton Krasner; music, Miklos Rozsa; editor, Robert Parrish. Reviewed at Guild Theatre, Hollywood Dec. 25, '47. Running time 103 MINS.
Anthony John..............Ronald Colman
Brita........................Signe Hasso
Bill Friend.................Edmond O'Brien
Pat Kroll.................Shelley Winters
Victor Donlan................Ray Collins
Max Lasker...................Philip Loeb
Al Cooley................Millard Mitchell
Pete Bonner....................Joe Sawyer
Stellini...................Charles La Torre
Dr. Stauffer................Whit Bissell
Stage Manager..............John Drew Colt
Asst. Stage Manager.......Peter Thompson
Gladys.....................Elizabeth Dunne
Rex........................Alan Edmiston
Wigmakers..........Art Smith, Sid Tomack
Dr. Mervin...................Wilton Graff
Oscar Bernard..............Harlan Briggs
Waitress..................Claire Carleton
Girls in Wig Shop......Betsy Blair, Janet Warren, Marjory Woodworth
"OTHELLO" SEQUENCES
Guy Bates Post....................Fay Kanin
Leslie Denison..........Frederic Worlock
David Bond.............Arthur Gould-Porter
Virginia Patton................Boyd Irwin
Thayer Roberts.............Percival Vivian
"A GENTLEMAN'S GENTLEMAN"
Elliott Reid....................Mary Young
Georgia Caine.............Percival Vivian

Everyone responsible for "A Double Life" can be proud. It's a nigh-perfect example of good theatre in story content, performances and direction. Film is drawing special roadshow engagement in Hollywood to qualify for Academy Awards nomination and offers competition to the other biggies to be entered in the annual Oscar race.

A presentation by Kanin Productions for release through Universal, "Life" is particularly distinguished for the manner in which the characters have been conceived and played. Each character rings true as the story goes into its play-within-a-play about actors and the theatre. There's murder, suspense, psychology, Shakespeare and romance all wrapped up into one polished package of class screen entertainment.

Plot poses an interesting premise—that an actor takes on some of the characteristics of the role he is playing if the run is long. In this instance Ronald Colman lives his roles without danger until he tackles "Othello." Gradually, as the play goes into a second year, he is dominated more and more by the character he creates on the stage. It finally leads him to murder a chance acquaintance in the same manner in which Othello snuffs out the life of Desdemona each night on the stage. When events finally catch up with him he takes his own life on the stage with Othello's dagger, much as Shakespeare wrote it.

Colman realizes on every facet of the demanding part in a performance that is flawless. It's a histronic gem of unusual versatility. Signe Hasso, his stage co-star and former wife, is a solid click, revealing a talent that has rarely been called upon in her other film roles. Her Desdemona is brillant and her interpretation of the understanding ex-wife perfect.

George Cukor's direction has found all of the merit in the characters written by Ruth Gordon and Garson Kanin. Each is developed with loving care to make them come alive on the screen and register with a sock. Edmond O'Brien, legit press agent, impresses strongly, as do Ray Collins, Philip Loeb, Millard Mitchell and Joe Sawyer. Particularly impressive is the work of Shelley Winters as the chance acquaintance whose easy virtue leads to her death. Same stamp of authority and excellence has been given the other roles in the playing.

The standout production job was performed by Michael Kanin. Filmed largely in New York at the old Empire theatre, it all rings with authenticity. There's a naturalness about the lensing by Milton Krasner that aids in the sense of reality that has been created. The editing is smooth, the music score good and other credits are of high order.

Brog.

Secret Beyond the Door

Hollywood, Dec. 29.

Universal release of Fritz Lang (Diana Pictures-Walter Wanger) production, directed by Fritz Lang. Stars Joan Bennett, Michael Redgrave; features Anne Revere, Barbara O'Neil. Screenplay, Silvia Richards, based on story by Rufus King; camera, Stanley Cortez; editor, Arthur Hilton; music, Miklos Rozsa. Tradeshown Dec. 29, '47. Running time, **98 MINS.**

Celia Lamphere	Joan Bennett
Mark Lamphere	Michael Redgrave
Caroline Lamphere	Anne Revere
Miss Robey	Barbara O'Neil
Edith Potter	Natalie Schafer
Intellectual Sub-Deb	Anabel Shaw
Paquita	Rosa Rey
Bob Dwight	James Seay
David	Mark Dennis

Heavy psycho-melodrama for the fingernail-biting addicts. Overall boxoffice will be spotty but returns should add up nicely in houses catering to suspense fans.

Film carries the Diana Productions label, a combo of Walter Wanger, Fritz Lang and Joan Bennett who have been responsible for several other Diana thrillers. It is arty, with almost surrealistic treatment in camera angles, story-telling mood and suspense, as producer-director Lang hammers over his thrill points. Sometimes it's a bit too obvious, but it builds mounting tension that pays off with this type film.

Co-starring with Miss Bennett is Michael Redgrave, English thespian. He disappoints as the man with an anti-woman complex who nearly murders his wife before finding out what his trouble is. Miss Bennett is good as the rich, useless society girl who finds a love so strong she would rather die than give it up. Mental complexities of the principals makes it sometimes hard to sort out the various motivations used to spin the tale. It's based on a story by Rufus King, scripted by Silvia Richards. Such psychiatric tricks as mental cases who recoil at locked doors, lilacs, or become oddly stimulated by physical combat and looks, are some of the suspense devices that will have the audience shuddering.

Anne Revere, a bossy sister; Barbara O'Neil, a sexually frustrated woman; Natalie Schafer, an idle rich gal; James Seay, and Mark Dennis, as the twisted boy, are among the characters contributing to the dark doings.

Stanley Cortez's lensing gives an odd pictorial beauty to many of the scenes, particularly the Mexican church and other Latin architectural creations. Miklos Rozsa's music score aids in building the thrill mood of this somber piece. Film is considerably overlength, as previewed, and could stand tightening to better pace the earlier sequences.

Glamour Girl
(SONGS)

Columbia release of Sam Katzman production. Features Gene Krupa orchestra, Susan Reed. Directed by Arthur Dreifuss. Screenplay, M. Coates Webster, Lee Gold; story, Gold; camera, Ira Morgan; editor, Charles Nelson; songs, Segar Ellis, George Williams, Jule Styne, Sammy Cahn, Allan Roberts, Doris Fisher; music director, Mischa Bakaleinikoff. At Loew's Metropolitan, week Dec. 24, '47. Running time, **68 MINS.**

Gene Krupa	Himself
Lorraine Royle	Virginia Grey
Johnny Evans	Michael Duane
Jennie Higgins	Susan Reed
Buddy Butterfield	Jimmy Lloyd
Ray Royle	Jack Leonard
T. J. Hopkins	Pierre Watkin
Luigi Tamarini	Eugene Borden
Aunt Hattie Higgins	Netta Packer
Gertrude	Noel Neill
Rosa	Jeanne Bell

Vocalist—Carolyn Grey

"Glamour Girl," despite its title, is anything but glamorous entertainment. Entry obviously was primed for dual classification.

Film is chiefly a vehicle for the antics of Gene Krupa and his band as well as spotlighting Susan Reed, her zither and her Irish harp. Plot is one of those tried and true affairs where writers M. Coates Webster and Lee Gold fashioned a script out of Gold's "from sticks-to-stardom" yarn. Band is centered in several sequences. Interpretation of "Gene's Boogie," by Segar Ellis and George Williams, is about the best of its efforts. Krupa, himself, also contribs one of his characteristic, spirited solos on the skins.

Susan Reed, who's played the New York nitery circuits, is a gal with a pristine demeanor. In this opus she's a songstress-zither plucker whose talents are buried in the wilds of Tennessee. Found by Virginia Grey, a performer scout for a platter firm, she's brought to Gotham. Her ability is unappreciated, and as a result, Miss Grey and her colleague, Michael Duane, start their own company. It goes without saying that Susan is the star.

In what may be her screen debut, Miss Reed shows an uncommonly wistful voice that's ideally adapted to warbling folk tunes of the "Molly Malone" category. Her self-accompaniment on the zither and harp is also a showmanly touch. With further experience her acting will be on par with her musical prowess. So-so performances are turned in by Miss Grey, Duane, and Jimmy Lloyd as the latter's assistant.

Other thesping, headed by Jack Leonard as a diskcrooner, Pierre Watkin, a recording company topper, and Carolyn Grey, in a brief vocaling stint, is adequate. Sam Katzman's production reflects a careful disbursement of the budget while Arthur Dreifuss' direction is standard for a film of this type. Jule Styne and Sammy Cahn contribbed "Anywhere" for the pic with the lone other tune, "Without Imagination," coming from Allan Roberts and Doris Fisher. Neither song is particularly meritable. Lensing of Ira Morgan is well done.

The Main Street Kid

Republic release of Sidney Picker production. Stars Al Pearce; features Janet Martin, Alan Mowbray, Adele Mara. Directed by R. G. Springsteen. Screenplay, Jerry Sackheim, based upon radio play by Caryl Coleman; additional dialog, John K. Butler; camera, John MacBurnie; editor, Tony Martinelli; music director, Morton Scott. At New York theatre, N. Y., Dec. 25, '47. Running time, **64 MINS.**

Otis	Al Pearce
Jill	Janet Martin
Martine	Alan Mowbray
Gloria	Adele Mara
Edie Jones	Arlene Harris
Max	Emil Rameau
Bud Wheeling	Byron S. Barr
Mark Howell	Douglas Evans
Torrey	Roy Barcroft
Riley	Phil Arnold
Mrs. Clauson	Sarah Edwards
Judge Belin	Earah Edwards
Sam Trotter	Dick Elliott

Based upon a homespun yarn with a small town locale, "The Main Street Kid" is unpretentious fodder for the duals. Al Pearce, billed as the star, may afford the entry some b.o. draft due to his radio background. Otherwise picture is relatively ordinary film fare with not much to offer as selling points.

Pearce, on the air for years with his own air show, has also made occasional film forays. In his latest celluloid venture, he's cast as a print shop operator in a whistle stop hamlet. Commendably stabbing at originality, scripter Jerry Sackheim has adapted a radio play dealing with "mindreaders" by Caryl Coleman. It all revolves about Byron S. Barr, youthful head of a publishing firm, who's in love with one gal and fancies he is with another.

Long sweet on his hometown g.f., Janet Martin, Barr is temporarily diverted by the wiles of ex-show girl Adele Mara. Already in cahoots with pseudomindreader Alan Mowbray, Miss Mara is approached by Barr's business associate, Douglas Evans. He seeks the presidency of the publishing company. Trio works out a deal to frame Barr. This conveniently is exposed by Pearce, father of Miss Martin.

Pearce has a bucolic way about him that, in some respects, is akin to Bob Burns. As the small town printer who has the gift of "reading minds" due to a blow on the head, but later loses the faculty, he handles his role well. Mowbray is credible as the fake mindreader. Miss Mara sparkles in the golddigger part while Barr is suitably shy and innocent as the publishing heir. Emil Rameau shines as Pearce's friend, a tobacco store proprietor. Other performances are adequate.

While acting in general is good, modest budget in this Sidney Picker production will, of necessity, groove the film in the lesser situations. R. G. Springsteen's direction is okay and average lensing is provided by John MacBurnie. Scripting is fair; other technical credits are standard.

Just William's Luck
(BRITISH-MADE)

London, Dec. 18.

United Artists release of Alliance-James Carter production. Features William Graham, Leslie Bradley, A. E. Matthews, Jane Welsh, Garry Marsh. Directed by Val Guest. Screenplay by Guest, based on Richmal Crompton's stories. Music, Robert Farnow; camera, Leslie Rowson. At Pavilion, London, Dec. 17, '47. Running time, **91 MINS.**

William	William Graham
Mr. Brown	Garry Marsh
Mrs. Brown	Jane Welsh
Robert	Hugh Cross
Ethel	Kathleen Stuart
The Boss	Leslie Bradley
The Tramp	A. E. Matthews
Emily	Muriel Aked
Ginger	Brian Roper
Douglas	James Crabbe
Henry	Brian Weske
Violet Elizabeth	Audrey Manning
Gloria Gail	Hy Hazell
Hubert Lane	Ivan Hyde

With an estimated circulation of over 6,000,000 "William" books and a radio audience in excess of 10.000,000, Richmal Chompton's juvenile hero should find a ready welcome in most theatres here. Whether adults will share the youngsters' enjoyment is questionable. It would have been wiser to have aimed primarily at grownups, but amusing as youngsters may find the film, the script leaves much to be desired.

Produced on a modest budget, with David Coplan, U. A. managing director here, taking screen credit for the first time, picture should have little difficulty earning its cost, particularly at this time of year. But it shouldn't be exported to America.

There are too many loose ends left trailing in midair. A schoolgirl, Violet Elizabeth, is introduced and promptly disappears. So does a film star who, presumably, was thought of as romantic bait. More important, Hubert and his cronies, the opposition to William and his gang, make a brief appearance and fade when, according to all exciting children's yarns, they should have provided a certain amount of tension, drama and comedy.

The picture gets off to a slow start. Everybody talks about William. He has stolen his sister's lipsticks to play Red Indians; he has broken a window; he has blown up the geyser; he has changed the shoe cream and shaving cream. William and his trio of pals decide to become Knights of the Square Table, and right wrongs. In their endeavors to find a home for a couple they want to see married the kids haunt a house, thereby uncovering a gang of crooks, and so earn the comendation of the police.

The last 10 minutes of the picture contain practically all the action. Formula isn't employed for the remaining 80. As a family picture, something to set alongside Hollywood's best, it is deficient, particularly in sentiment. But the Brown family is there, with a ready-made public, if only the right stories are written around them.

Production and acting are adequate, with Garry Marsh and Jane Welsh as acceptable parents, Muriel Aked as a maid of whom too little is seen, and William Graham as a likeable hero, who makes a pleasant if not significant screen debut.

Cane.

Atomic Physics
(Documentary)
(BRITISH-MADE)

London, Dec. 5.

Produced by Gaumont British Instructional. Previewed at G-B projection room, London, Dec. 4, '47.

Made primarily for the academic world, the implications of this documentary will not be lost sight of by any intelligent audience. It is the first authoritative film on the history and development of atomic energy and gives due credit to every person and nation who made any contribution. Many scientific institutions and world-famous scientists provided facilities and assisted in its preparation.

Film naturally falls into five parts, each of which is a complete story in itself. It first discusses the atomic theory as proposed by John Dalton in 1808 and outlines progress through the 19th century. Other parts deal with rays from atoms, nuclear structures of the atom, atom smashing and uranium fission, respectively.

An idea of the present day research into the peaceful uses of atomic energy is discussed in speeches by Dr. Cockcroft, head of British Research on Atomic Energy, and Prof. Albert Einstein. Copies of the film have been sent to the U. S., but it is unlikely that anyone but students will see it.

Cane.

1948

Miniature Reviews

"The Treasure of the Sierra Madre" (WB). Superlative film on a grim, brutal theme with all-male cast starring Bogart.

"King of the Bandits" (Mono). So-so western in the "Cisco Kid" series; okay as average filler for duals.

Treasure of Sierra Madre

Warner Bros. release of Henry Blanke production. Stars Humphrey Bogart; features Walter Huston, Tim Holt, Bruce Bennett. Directed by John Huston. Screenplay, John Huston; based on novel by B. Traven; camera, Ted McCord; editor, Owen Marks; music, Max Steiner. Previewed N. Y., Dec. 26, '47. Running time, **124 MINS.**

Dobbs	Humphrey Bogart
Howard	Walter Huston
Curtin	Tim Holt
Cody	Bruce Bennett
McCormick	Barton MacLane
Gold Hat	Alfonso Bedoya
Presidente	A. Soto Rangel
El Jefe	Manuel Donde
Pablo	Jose Torvay
Pancho	Margarito Luna
Flashy Girl	Jacqueline Dalya
Mexican Boy	Bobby Blake

If the boxoffice is currently ailing from an over-diet of films that look too much alike, then this production is what the doctor ordered. "The Treasure of the Sierra Madre" is not only radically different, but it's a distinguished work that will take its place in the repertory of Hollywood's great and enduring achievements.

The picture has a compelling honesty. It's a grim and brutal slice of life whose raw elements have been ordered onto the plane of tragedy through a terrific twist of irony. There's a magnificent joker hidden at bottom, but spectators will find it so grisly and so bitter that this film moves out of the class of simple entertainment into the realm of vivid experience. With Humphrey Bogart as the marquee lure, however, strong positive reaction at the wickets is even assured from rank-and-file filmgoers who insist upon their happy fadeouts.

"Sierra Madre," adapted from the popular novel by B. Traven, is a story of psychological disintegration under the crushers of greed and gold. But director John Huston, who also wrote the lean and brilliant screenplay, has completely avoided the cliched structure of the whilom psycho dramas. The characters here are probed and thoroughly penetrated, not through psychoanalysis but through a crucible of human conflict, action, gesture and expressive facial tones. Huston, with an extraordinary assist in the thesping department from his father, Walter Huston, has fashioned this standout film with an unfailing sensitivity for the suggestive detail and an uncompromising commitment to reality, no matter how stark ugly it may be.

Except for some incidental femmes who have no bearing on the story, it's an all-male cast headed by Bogart, Huston and Tim Holt. They play the central parts of three gold prospectors who start out for pay dirt in the Mexican mountains as buddies, but wind up in a murderous tangle at the finish. Lensed for most part on location, the film has, at least, a physical aspect of rugged beauty against which is contrasted the human sordidness. The location shots combine with the pic's realistic focus into a powerful authenticity, but director Huston skirts the documentary's trap of sacrificing depth for realism.

Bogart, who was getting tired in his repetitious assignment as the indestructible private eye, comes through with a performance as memorable as his first major film role in "The Petrified Forest" was in 1935. Bogart is no hero, which may prove disappointing to his fans. In this film, he's a surly panhandler with a moral fibre as run down as his heels. After the three prospectors strike gold, Bogart is the first to sink into a bog of fear, suspicion and hatred of his comrades. In a remarkably controlled portrait, he progresses to the edge of madness without losing sight of the subtle shadings needed to establish persuasiveness.

Walter Huston, as an old miner who guides Bogart and Holt out of a Tampico flophouse to the Sierra Madre's treasure, contributes a performance that would have stolen the picture if director Huston had not been so careful in marshalling all of the players into a superbly balanced team. But Huston's crusty characterization merges with the terrain as naturally as Mexican cactus. His energy and mobility are immense, and his warmth and humor provide the only pleasant spots of the film.

As the third fortune-hunter, Tim Holt also registers effectively in a simple but honest portrayal of a good-hearted Texan cowhand who finds himself in a nasty predicament. In a lesser part, Bruce Bennett, as a wandering prospector who strays onto the others' stake, shows a highly polished talent. Among the film's many notable qualities is the skill with which all of the bit roles are played by the anonymous Mexican and Indian personnel.

The plot mechanism winds up with a growing hatred between Bogart, on one hand, and Huston and Holt on the other. Bogart, after an attempted murder of Holt, makes off with all the piles of gold dust only to meet some Mexican bandits who kill him. The ironic jest is sprung with the bandits' ripping open of the saddle bags and finding only dirt instead of animal skins, scatter the gold to the winds. It's a sort of grim joke the film public will remember but won't laugh at.

Herm.

King of the Bandits

Monogram release of Jeffrey Bernerd production. Stars Gilbert Roland; features Angela Greene, Chris-Pin Martin, Anthony Warde. Directed by Christy Cbaanne. Screenplay, Bennett R. Cohen; original story, Cabanne, based on character created by O. Henry; additional dialog, Gilbert Roland; camera, William Sickner; editor, Roy Livingston. At New York theatre, N. Y., week Dec. 30, '47. Running time, **65 MINS.**

Cisco Kid	Gilbert Roland
Alice Mason	Angela Greene
Pancho	Chris-Pen Martin
Smoke Kirby	Anthony Warde
Mrs. Mason	Laura Treadwell
Capt. Mason	William Bakewell
Burl	Rory Mallinson
Pedro	Pat Goldin
Connie	Cathy Carter
Col. Wayne	Boyd Irwin
Padre	Antonio Filauri
U. S. Marshal	Jasper Palmer
Orderly	Bill Cabanne

Latest in Monogram's "Cisco Kid" series, "King o the Bandits," stacks up as passable entertainment for lower half of double bills. Marquee lure is confined to Gilbert Roland, who's starred in the title role.

Plot is relatively standard. Roland is sought for a string of stagecoach holdups, but in reality the jobs have been pulled off by Anthony Warde, who masquerades as the Cisco Kid. Seized by an Army detachment in the Arizona wilds, Roland is jailed. He later escapes and brings back Warde to the authorities to clear himself. There's a bit of romance sandwiched in the yarn, with Angela Greene furnishing the pulchritude.

Roland contribs a fair characterization as the bandit who has his share of Robin Hood qualities. Miss Greene is pleasantly decorative. Chris-Pen Martin, the Cisco Kid's sidekick, acceptably handled the comedy relief. Others adequate in their roles are Warde and William Bakewell, cast as an Army captain.

Jeffrey Bernerd gave this western better-than-average productional trimmings. Christy Cabanne's direction is standard while his story, screenplayed by Bennett R. Cohen, shows more originality than usually found in similar oaters. William Sickner's lensing is good.

Gilb.

Shakuntala
(SONGS)
(INDIAN-MADE)

Mayer-Burstyn release of V. Shantaram production, directed by Shantaram. Stars Jayashree. Screenplay, Dewan Sharar, from Indian classic of Kalidasas; camera, V. Avadhut; songs, Dewan Sharar and Pt. Ratanpiya. Previewed N. Y., Dec. 12, '47. Running time, **76 MINS.**

Shakuntala	Jayashree
Dushayant	Chandra Mohan
Kanva	Nimbalkar
Menaka	Zohra
Priyamvada	Shantarin
Anasooya	Vidya
Bharat	Kumar Ganesh
Madhav	Raja Pandit
Sharang	Villas
Gautami	Amina
Minister	Nana Palsikar
Sharadwat	Madan Mohan
Durvasa	Ratanpiya
Madan	The Deer

(In Hindustani; English Titles)

"Shakuntala" is different from other foreign pictures with music. But aside from its differentness and sufficient dramatic effort by Jayashree, rated India's top actress, to indicate possibilities, this will have to get its principal U. S. revenue from a few arty theatres. Because it lacks the action, humor and appeal to attract much of an audience in this country. This, however, does not detract from the fact that it is a worthy effort from the producers of India. It's simply that it fails to measure up with other product with which this will have to compete in the U. S.

The story of "Shakuntala," a play written by Kalidasas, Indian poet, is reputed to date 15 centuries before Shakespeare did "Romeo and Juliet." It is a play about an impoverished Indian maiden and her love for a king, with their brief marriage ending in a tragic separation. According to Indian lore, their son, born after the lovers split up, was the true founder of India.

Despite this simple tale, typical Indian music, some stilted, romantic scenes between the two lovers and unusual settings go a long way in lifting this out of the realms of an ordinary screen production. The native tunes have a peculiar chant and at times a strange lilt. Only difficulty that the very picturesqueness of the scenes and strangeness of the music wears out after about 30 minutes of it.

Photography by B. Avadhut, at times almost first-rate, for the most part is below par. V. Shantaram's direction is unoriginal and hardly out of the amateur class, indicating just how far behind in the film-making parade India producers are today.

Jayashree, as the poor girl who elopes with a king, is the principal bright spot of the vehicle. While her ideas of acting fail to measure up to American standards, she hints future possibilities. Heading the supporting cast are Chandra Mohan, Nimbalkar, Zohra and a diminutive deer named "Madan."

Wear.

Miniature Reviews

"Sleep, My Love" (UA). Neat melodrama with okay b.o. outlook. Sturdy cast names and exploitable angles.

"Relentless" (Color) (Col). Solid outdoorer with good characterization. Color an added b.o. inducement.

"Prince of Thieves" (Color) (Col). Sub-standard production, in Cinecolor, of an Alexandre Dumas Robin Hood yarn starring Jon Hall.

"The Flame" (Rep). Mild melodrama that should rate fair returns.

"Open Secret" (EL). Fair entry in the anti-Semitism cycle but can't play by itself.

"The Gay Ranchero" (Songs; Color) (Rep). Standard Roy Rogers oatuner for juve market.

"Women in the Night" (FC). Yarn of Nazi and Nip atrocities against women. Lends itself to strong exploitation.

"Jenny Lamour" (Indie) (French). Gallic-spiced whodunit with Louis Jouvet; solid art-house fare.

"Gun Talk" (Mono). Fast-paced Johnny Mack Brown western with good element of suspense.

Sleep, My Love

Hollywood, Jan. 10.

United Artists release of Charles (Buddy) Rogers-Ralph Cohn (Triangle) production, presented by Mary Pickford. Stars Claudette Colbert, Robert Cummings, Don Ameche; features Rita Johnson, George Coulouris, Hazel Brooks. Directed by Douglas Sirk. Screenplay, St. Clair McKelway, Leo Rosten; from the novel by Leo Rosten; camera, Joseph Valentine; music score, Rudy Schrager; editor, Lynn Harrison. Previewed in Hollywood Jan. 9, '48. Running time, **96 MINS.**

Alison Courtland	Claudette Colbert
Bruce Elcott	Robert Cummings
Richard Courtland	Don Ameche
Barby	Rita Johnson
Charles Vernay	George Coulouris
Daphne	Hazel Brooks
Mrs. Vernay	Queenie Smith
Jimmie	Keye Luke
Haskins	Fred Nurney
Jeannie	Maria San Marco
Sgt. Strake	Raymond Burr
Helen	Lillian Bronson
Dr. Rinehart	Ralph Morgan
Maid	Lillian Randolph

"Sleep, My Love" manages a fair share of suspense and adds up to okay melodrama. Exploitation angles are strong, which will help in getting it over to the public, and cast lineup commands marquee attention.

Film marks the first to carry the Mary Pickford name in about 12 years, she joining with Charles (Buddy) Rogers and Ralph Cohn in presenting this under the Triangle label through United Artists. Latter pair are new to higher-budgeted efforts, and inexperience shows occasionally. However, overall results are good and well-paced, assuring auditor interest throughout.

Plot gets off to a strong start and windup is high melodrama that brings off the finale on a fast note. Basic story is the familiar one of the man who wants to kill off his wealthy wife so he can marry the sexy trollop. Development, however, brings in some new angles.

Claudette Colbert is the healthy, wealthy wife who is being stealthily drugged by husband Don Ameche. Under drugged hypnosis, she is made to do strange things that indicate a mental crackup. Opener has her awakening on a train to Boston, unable to explain how it happened. Next she sees a strange, sinister character who gives her a phony psychoanalysis. Events continue to pile up and she is saved from a violent death in the nick of time by a new friend. Robert Cummings. Latter is responsible for the final denouement when he adds up the facts and rescues fair lady.

Three principals all turn in excellent performances, with Cummings managing good share of chuckles with his romantic pursuit of the lady. Rita Johnson sparks a mere bit as a gabby girl, and George Coulouris works well as the sinister character. Hazel Brooks is allowed to make her role too obviously sexy so that it becomes almost allegorical of all bad women but without the animal appeal it should have. Lillian Randolph scores in a standout scene as a maid who likes the comics. Queenie Smith and Raymond Burr sharpen their brief appearances. Keye Luke, Maria San Marco and others measure up.

Douglas Sirk paces his direction neatly in handling the not always smooth script by St. Clair McKelway and Leo Rosten. Joseph Valentine did the okay lensing, and other technical functions are competent.

Brog.

Relentless

(COLOR)

Hollywood, Jan. 10.

Columbia release of Eugene B. Rodney (Cavalier) production. Stars Robert Young, Marguerite Chapman; features Willard Parker, Akim Tamiroff, Barton MacLane, Mike Mazurki, Robert Barrat, Clem Bevans. Directed by George Sherman. Screenplay, Winston Miller; based on a story by Kenneth Perkins; camera (Technicolor), Edward Cronjager; music score, Marlin Skiles; editor, Gene Havlick. Previewed in Hollywood Jan. 8, '48. Running time, **91 MINS.**

Nick Buckley	Robert Young
Luella Purdy	Marguerite Chapman
Jeff Moyer	Willard Parker
Joe Faringo	Akim Tamiroff
Tex Brandow	Barton MacLane
Jake	Mike Mazurki
Ed Simpson	Robert Barrat
Dad	Clem Bevans
Jim Rupple	Frank Fenton
Bob Pliny	Hank Patterson
Len Briggs	Paul Burns
Nester	Emmett Lynn
Horse Dealer	Will Wright

Cavalier Productions has come through with strong offering in "Relentless," its first for Columbia release. Film has a solid story, backgrounded against the west, able production and direction, with added value of color to sharpen boxoffice attention.

There is an attention to detail, careful story and character development and other factors that heighten interest under Eugene B. Rodney's showmanly production guidance. Background scenery hasn't been filmed to death, and color lensing paints plenty of scenic beauty.

George Sherman's direction misses no bets in keeping the action lively. Plot, essentially, concerns itself with a cowboy's hunt for a man who can clear him of murder charges, and this basis and its ramifications have been soundly established in the script by Winston Miller, based on a story by Kenneth Perkins.

Robert Young, an actor at home in any kind of a background, makes the cowboy character real. It's an honest portrayal at all times, and intensely satisfying. Marguerite Chapman, proprietor of a travelling covered wagon store, pleases mightily as the girl who befriends the cowpoke. It's another character that rings true and helps to make this more than just a western.

Willard Parker, the relentless sheriff who's continually on Young's trail as latter stalks Barton MacLane, is good. MacLane turns in a strong bit as the villain, and Akim Tamiroff is consistent as a gambler who wants the gold mine that lies at the end of the long chase. Choice smaller spots are ably contributed by Mike Mazurki, Robert Barrat, Clem Bevans and Emmett Lynn.

Film offers a number of exploitable values to point up the selling for appeal to adult trade and the youngsters. The birth of a young colt and the death of its mother, which serve as springboard for the manhunt; a brush fire started to burn out Young, and the finale sequence where Young uses the burning desert sun and thirst to finally trap his man are all points that sharpen appeal. Edward Cronjager did the excellent color lensing.

Brog.

The Prince of Thieves

(COLOR)

Columbia release of Sam Katzman production. Stars Jon Hall; features Patricia Morison, Adele Jergens, Alan Mowbray, Michael Duane, H. B. Warner, Lowell Gilmore. Directed by Howard Bretherton. Screenplay, Maurice Tombragel; adaptation, Charles H. Schneer, based on novel by Alexander Dumas; camera (Cinecolor), Fred H. Jackman, Jr.; editor, James Sweeney; musical director, Mischa Bakaleinikoff. At Fox theatre, Brooklyn, week Jan. 5, '48. Running time, **71 MINS.**

Robin Hood	Jon Hall
Lady Marian	Patricia Morison
Lady Christabel	Adele Jergens
The Friar	Alan Mowbray
Sir Allan Claire	Michael Duane
Gilbert Head	H. B. Warner
Sir Phillip	Lowell Gilmore
Baron Tristram	Gavin Muir
Maude	Robin Raymond
Sir Fitz-Alwin	Lewis L. Russell
Little John	Walter Sande
Will Scarlet	Syd Saylor
Bowman	I. Stanford Jolley
Lindsay	Fredric Santley
Margaret Head	Belle Mitchell

This version of an Alexander Dumas yarn, based upon one of Robin Hood's fabled exploits, boils down to nothing more than a typical western transplanted to King Arthur's era. Despite the fact there's action aplenty, principal failing of "Prince of Thieves" is that the fantasy is never punched across. Picture is destined to hold down the secondary spot in the dualers.

Mountings and costumes in this Sam Katzman production reflect a heavier-than-average budgetary expenditure, and use of Cinecolor sets them off well with exception of some of the night scenes, which are none too well defined. Acting and scripting don't measure up to the film's physical properties. Jon Hall, cast in the title role, interprets his lines almost satirically as do most of his supporting players.

On the other hand perhaps the picture was intended as a burlesque. When caught last week at a Brooklyn downtown deluxer, audience gave Alan Mowbray, portraying Friar Tuck, the biggest laugh of the film when he admonished his opponents that anyone striking "his holy habit would be guilty of sin." Mowbray plays the part broadly, bordering on a slapstick vein.

Plot hinges on the efforts of Michael Duane to win Adele Jergens. During Duane's absence of some five years, the damsel's father, Lewis Russell, has pledged her to Gavin Muir, whom she does not love. With the aid of Hall and his colleagues the romance is adjusted, of course.

As the fair Ladies Marian and Christabel, respectively, Patricia Morison and Miss Jergens are on hand chiefly for decorative purposes. Duane manages to inject a note of authenticity into his part of a bold knight in quest of his lady love. Robin Raymond, hand-maiden to Miss Jergens, is saucily sexy in a role calling for just those qualities. Balance of cast is so-so.

Howard Bretherton's direction is able enough in the combat scenes but misses out on the film's dramatic import. Screenplay of Maurice Tombragel as well as Charles H. Schneer's adaptation unfortunately have exaggerated the spirit of Sherwood Forest and that of its denizens. Fred Jackman's Cinecolor lensing is admirably done with the exception of the few nocturnal sequences. On the whole, "Prince of Thieves" will find its best market in the juvenile trade on Saturday matinees.

Gilb.

The Flame

(SONG)

Hollywood, Jan. 8.

Republic release of John H. Auer production. Stars John Carroll, Vera Ralston, Robert Paige, Broderick Crawford; features Henry Travers, Blanche Yurka, Constance Dowling, Hattie McDaniel, Victor Sen Yung. Directed by Auer. Screenplay, Lawrence Kimble; based on story by Robert T. Shannon; camera, Reggie Lanning; music, Heinz Roemheld; editor, Richard L. Van Enger. Previewed in Hollywood, Jan. 6, '48 Running time **96 MINS.**

George MacAllister	John Carroll
Carlotta Duval	Vera Ralston
Barry MacAllister	Robert Paige
Ernie Hicks	Broderick Crawford
Dr. Mitchell	Henry Travers
Aunt Margaret	Blanche Yurka
Helene Anderson	Constance Dowling
Celia	Hattie McDaniel
Chang	Victor Sen Yung
The Minister	Harry V. Cheshire
Detective	John Nitjan
Detective	Garry Owen
Policeman	Eddie Dunn

Plushy production fails to cover up the contrived melodramatics and characters in "The Flame." Physical dressing is well polished, the acting good, but parts fail to register with punch. Grosses will be spotty, although film lends itself to high-pressure exploitation.

John H. Auer's production and direction get all there is to be gotten out of the Robert T. Shannon story, scripted by Lawrence Kimble. He establishes a mood that is good, uses the music score and camera effectively and generally creates a fair amount of suspense.

Where film misses is in lack of motivation for a number of key characters. Plot deals with John Carroll's scheme to gain possession of his brother's fortune. The brother, Robert Paige, supposedly has only a few months to live, so Carroll has his girl friend, Vera Ralston, marry the sick man. She learns to love her bridegroom, nurses him back to health, and when a blackmailer threatens her new happiness, Carroll suddenly reforms and has a fatal shooting match with the villain.

Carroll walks a sketchy tightrope between sympathy and deep-dyed villainy in the principal role. Miss Ralston shows considerable improvement in her work. Robert Paige makes the brother pleasant and would have endowed character with more strength had role been better established. Broderick Crawford is the most consistent character as the blackmailer. Constance Dowling injects s.a. that almost gets out of hand in her nitery scene while singing 'Love Me or Leave Me." Others are adequate.

Reggie Lanning did an excellent lensing job, working from good sets and art direction. Heinz Roemheld cleffed background music. Film is overlong at 96 minutes.

Brog.

Open Secret

Eagle Lion release of Marathon Pictures production (Frank Satenstein). Features John Ireland, Jane Randolph, Roman Bohnen, Sheldon Leonard. Directed by John Reinhardt. Screenplay, Henry Blankfort, Max Wilk; original story, Wilk and Ted Murkland; additional dialog, John Bright; camera, George Robinson; editor, Jason Bernie. Previewed in N. Y. Jan. 9, '48. Running time, **70 MINS.**

Paul Lester	John Ireland
Nancy Lester	Jane Randolph
Locke	Roman Bohnen
Mike Fronteili	Sheldon Leonard
Harry Strauss	George Tyne
Mitchell	Morgan Farley
Mrs. Locke	Ellen Lowe
Mrs. Tristram	Anne O'Neal
Carter	Arthur O'Connell
Ralph	John Alvin
Mace	Bert Conway
Hill	Rory Mallinson
Mrs. Hill	Helena Dare
Bartender	Leo Kaye
Fawnes	King Donovan
Bob	Tom Noonan

With "Crossfire" and "Gentleman's Agreement" blazing the trail for an anti-Semitism cycle, Marathon Pictures' "Open Secret" further spotlights an incident of racial prejudice. Unquestionably such a theme possesses the utmost merit but Marathan's interpretation lacks a finesse that a higher budget may well have provided. Controversial nature of the film will impart a moderate amount of b.o. stimulus, and its producers undoubtedly will realize a profit on their investment.

To illustrate the spread of prejudice in a community when sanctioned by a political heeler, picture employs a melodramatic yarn reminiscent of cloak-and-dagger stuff. Newlyweds John Ireland and Jane Randolph fall heir to the problems of a male friend who's disappeared while secretly attempting to expose a ring of hoodlums who prey on "foreigners." Much of the plot centers about the efforts of the schemers to recover candid shots of them participating in acts of violence and vandalism against those of the Jewish faith.

Instrumental in rounding up the gang which sought to emulate Hitler are Ireland, a police lieutenant (Sheldon Leonard) and a camera shop proprietor, (George Tyne). Latter sparkles as a victim who turns the tables on his persecutors. Other roles, neatly portrayed are those of Leonard, and Roman Bohnen, who not only is a gang member but a wife-beater and drunk to boot.

Cast as the lead, Ireland delivers a wooden performance. His conception of an ex-serviceman who helps break up the machinations of the conspirators is underplayed. Likewise, Miss Randolph offers little to the film aside from proving her prowess as a sweater gal. Rather puzzling is the emphasis on the sinister qualities of Ireland's landlady, Anne O'Neal. She reeks of villainy, yet no link develops to associate her with the gang.

Script, on which a quartet of writers worked, is a fairly good job, pulling no punches to show that anti-Semitism will receive short shrift under our form of government. John Reinhardt's direction paced the film well in most sequences while fine lensing of George Robinson is further embellished by use of exceptional lighting effects. Production reins, handled by Frank Satenstein, wrung maximum value out of the film's limited budget.

Gilb.

The Gay Ranchero

(SONGS; COLOR)

Republic release of Edward J. White production. Stars Roy Rogers, Tito Guizar; features Jane Frazee, Andy Devine, Estelita Rodriguez. Directed by William Witney. Screenplay, Sloan Nibley; camera (Trucolor), Jack Marta; editor, Tony Martinelli; songs, Abe Tuvim, Francia Luban, J. J. Espinosa, Harry Glick, Jimmy Lambert, Dave Olsen, Augustin Lara and Ray Gilbert. Previewed in N. Y., Jan. 9, '48. Running time, **72 MINS.**

Roy Rogers	Roy Rogers
Nicci Lopez	Tito Guizar
Betty Richards	Jane Frazee
Cookie Bullfincher	Andy Devine
Consuelo Belmonte	Estelita Rodriguez
Vance Brados	George Meeker
Mike Ritter	LeRoy Mason
Tex	Dennis Moore
Slim	Keith Richards
Reception Clerk	Betty Gagnon
Breezy	Robert Rose
Roberts	Ken Terrell

Themselves: Bob Nolan and the Sons of the Pioneers

"The Gay Ranchero" is standard outdoor fare made according to the simple recipe for past Roy Rogers oatuners. With Tito Guizar and Estelita Rodriguez in the cast, this pic is slightly flavored with chile for solid reception south-of-the-border. Otherwise, formula ingredients of hoofbeating, fisticuffs, gunplay and a brace of listenable tunes are assembled in familiar pattern. Tinting of this pic shows marked improvement in the Trucolor process towards greater definition and vividness.

Yarn revolves around efforts of a gang of varmints to gain control of an airport through mysteriously wrecking the planes. Rogers, as sheriff, undergoes usual complications in tracking down the thugs but not before plenty of corpses are strewn about. Odd mixture of airplanes with 1880 style of horse opera plot is handled in perfect deadpan fashion but the Saturday matinee juve trade won't mind the contradictions.

Musically, film is solidly buttressed with Guizar's strong tenor piping of "Granada" and "You Belong To My Heart," and Miss Rodriguez' vivacious rendering of "A Gay Ranchero" plus a neat terping routine. Rogers and Miss Frazee handle a nice tune, "Wait'll I Get My Sunshine in the Moonlight," competently. Cowboy chorus also contributes a couple of okay numbers. Thesping, direction and scripting are par for this type of production. *Herm.*

Women in the Night

Film Classics release of Lewis K. Ansell production. Features Tala Birell, William Henry, Virginia Christine. Directed by William Rowland. Screenplay, Robert St. Clair, Edwin Westry, based on story by Rowland. Editor, Dan Milner. Previewed in N. Y., Jan. 7, '48. Running time, **90 MINS.**
Yvette Aubert...................Tala Birell
Major Van Arnhelm.........William Henry
Claire Adams...............Virginia Christine
Col. Noyama....................Richard Loo
Col. Von Meyer...........Gordon Richards
Frau Thaler...............Bernadine Hayes
Chang........................Benson Fong
Li Ling......................Frances Chung
Helen James..................Kathy Frye
Sheila Hallett...............Helen Mowery
Prof. Kunioshi................Philip Ahn
Maria Gonzales.................Iris Flores

Purportedly based on United Nations Information Service files on crimes against women by the Nazis and Nips, "Women in the Night" should lend itself for good grosses where given wide exploitation. The exploitation possibilities are here.

"Women" is the initial effort of the newly-formed Southern California Pictures, headed by St. Louis exhibitor Louis K. Ansell. Despite the wealth of exploitation material, there's a good deal of naivete in the story. The writing and story line are fairly elementary, but direction by William Rowland helps overcome some of these deficiencies.

Yarn concerns itself with a group of women rounded up by the Nazi military in Shanghai in an attempt to find the murderer of a German officer. They're forced to entertain Jap and Nazi dignitaries in the Nazi officers' club. Between indignities, they work with the Chinese underground; eventual relief comes when an OSS man, played by William Henry, is flown in to forestall exchange of information between the Axis on a "cosmic ray" weapon.

Tala Birell, as the French girl who divides her loyalties but does all right finally by the Allied cause, does a creditable job, while Virginia Christine, as the wife of the OSS man, is competent. Gordon Richards, as the Nazi colonel; Richard Loo and Phillip Ahn, as Jap inquisitors, also do well. *Jose.*

Jenny Lamour
(SONGS)
(FRENCH-MADE)

Vog Films release of Majestic production. Stars Louis Jouvet; features Suzy Delair. Directed by Henri-Georges Clouzot. Screenplay, Clouzot, Jean Ferry; adapted from novel by S. A. Steeman; camera, Armand Thirard; editor, Charles Clement; songs, Francis Lopez and A. Hornez; English titles, Noel Meadow and Harry L. Ober. Previewed in N. Y., Jan. 7, '48. Running time, **102 MINS.**

Dora.......................Simone Renant
Jenny........................Suzy Delair
Maurice Martineau...........Bernard Blier
Brignon.....................Charles Dullin
Antoine.......................Louis Jouvet
Chief Inspector..............Rene Blancart
Paulo...........................Dauran
Taxi Driver................Pierre Larquey
Manon......................Claudine Dupuis
(In French; English titles)

"Jenny Lamour" is a salty entry from France that'll do nicely in foreign-language situations. Framed around a conventional whodunit yarn, pic avoids that familiar look through a parlay of wit, realism and expert thesping. Pace, however, is not fully sustained but slicing of about 15 minutes from the long running time would tighten the action.

With show people as the central characters, film has a music hall background which offers Suzy Delair openings for several neatly rendered pop tunes. The backstage life is handled without glamorization, obliquely giving Americans an idea of the hardships suffered in France due to lack of fuel by having everybody wear their overcoats even in the indoor sequences. Film's other major setting is the gendarmerie headquarters, where once again interest is kindled by the completely realistic treatment of the workovers received by criminals.

Plot revolves around the murder of a notorious film producer who insisted on pawing his females before pacting them. Miss Delair, a poor, talented but ambitious chanteuse, had made a play for him, but conked him with champagne bottle at the payoff rendezvous. Meanwhile, her frantically jealous husband breaks into the rake's chateau with murderous intentions but finds someone has already beaten him to the job.

Enter Louis Jouvet as the cynical dick from headquarters who begins to pick up a chain of clues pointing to the husband as the killer. Miss Delair believes, however, that she's the murderer and, just as her husband attempts suicide, makes a confession. But through a long and slightly incredible stretch of coincidence, some underworld character is picked up to get the rap and restore the domestic bliss.

As usual, Jouvet, one of France's great cinema actors, delivers a subtly shaded characterization of a bored detective with a distaste for his job. Miss Delair is graced with looks, vitality and a good set of pipes, while Bernard Blier, as her husband, registers with a competent performance. Charles Dullin, as the film producer, is appropriately repulsive, and Simone Renant, as a friend of the couple, shows a noble heart but impassive face.

Camera work is excellent, and the English titling is adequate for fluent understanding of the action. *Herm.*

Gun Talk

Monogram release of Barney Sarecky production. Stars Johnny Mack Brown; features Raymond Hatton, Christine McIntyre. Directed by Lambert Hillyer. Screenplay, J. Benton Cheney; camera, Harry Neumann; editor, Fred Maguire; music director, Edward Kay. At New York theatre, N. Y., week of Jan. 6, '48. Running time, **57 MINS.**
Johnny McVey........Johnny Mack Brown
Lucky Danvers...........Raymond Hatton
Daisy.................Christine McIntyre
Rod Jackson................Douglas Evans
June.........................Geneva Gray
Herkimer Stone.........Wheaton Chambers
Simpson........................Frank LaRue
Tim..........................Ted Adams
Pepper......................Carl Mathews
Nolan........................Zon Murray
Marshall Wetherby...........Cactus Mack
Burke........................Carol Henry
Joe...........................Bill Hale
Diggs......................Boyd Stockman
Bartender....................Roy Butler
Pete.......................Bob McElroy

With Johnny Mack Brown as the marquee lure, exhibs will find this fast-paced oater acceptable in action situations. "Gun Talk" shapes up as a taut combination of hard ridin' coupled with a fair amount of suspense.

Compressed into less than an hour's running time, story is a brisk variation of the old mine-steal formula. Tale tees off with Brown foiling an attempted stagecoach holdup. Saved from the bandits are mine-investor Raymond Hatton and youthful Geneva Gray, an eastern gal heading west to visit her sister, Christine McIntyre.

Villainy is furnished by Wheaton Chambers, an outlaw leader who poses as a barber, along with an underling, Douglas Evans. They try to seize Hatton's mine but justice, as meted out by Brown, triumphs in a swirl of fancy fisticuffs and six-shootin'. Yarn is familiar fodder but J. Benton Cheney's treatment has overcome its triteness to some extent.

Acting is average for films of this type. Brown who's getting a bit beefy, is fairly credible as the champion of the law. Mine owner Hatton contribs an okay characterization along with occasional comedy relief. Chambers and Evans are sufficiently sinister as the heavies. Miss McIntyre is adequate as the saloon queen while Miss Gray's obvious inexperience is not too evident in a role which calls for shyness and innocence.

Lambert Hillyer's direction shows the touch of a veteran in this Barney Sarecky production. Lensing of Harry Neumann is better than average for gallopers in the low-budget bracket. *Gilb.*

The Mark of Cain
(BRITISH-MADE)

London, Jan. 3.
General Film Distributors release of J. Arthur Rank-Two Cities Film Production. Stars Eric Portman, Sally Gray; features Patrick Holt, Dermot Walsh. Directed by Brian Desmond Hurst. Screenplay by Francis Crowdy, Christiana Brand; adaptation by W. P. Lipscomb from Joseph Shearing novel. Editor, Sydney Stone; camera, Erwin Hillier; music, Bernard Stevens. At Odeon, London, Jan. 1, '48. Running time, **88 MINS.**
Sarah Bonheur.................Sally Gray
Richard Howard.............Eric Portman
John Howard................Patrick Holt
Jerome Thorn..............Dermot Walsh
Sir William Godfrey.......Dennis O'Dea
Lord Rochford.............Edward Lexy
Sister Seraphine..........Therese Giehse
Daisy Cobb..............Maureen Delany
Mary.......................Helen Cherry
Jennie........................Vida Hope
Madame Bonheur...........Dora Sevening
Sylvia.......................Janet Kay
Dr. White..................James Hayter
Sir Jonathan Dockwra..Andrew Cruickshank
Lady Rochford..........Marjorie Gresley
Nurse Brand..............Beryl Measor
Mrs. White..............Mary MacDonald
Sally Howard............Susan English
Chemist.................Johnny Schofield

Basis of this story is presumably the notorious Maybrick murder case of about 50 years ago. But although much trouble has been taken with ornate settings and period detail, the screen version deviates a great deal from and lacks the suspense of the original story. It never comes to life. Long before the end, most audiences will hardly care if the innocent woman is hanged or escapes the gallows. There's a little boxoffice value in the star's names here, and U. S. draw will be limited to duals.

Scene is laid first in France, where Sarah Bonheur, fresh from a convent school, entertains at her chateau. Richard Howard has come from England to close a business deal. Egoistic and ingratiating, he is dominated by two emotions, love for Sarah and hatred of his brother, John. The feud between the brothers comes to a head when John arrives unexpectedly at the chateau, clinches the deal and makes Sarah his bride.

A few years elapse and Sarah is now a dutiful wife and mother in a grim Victorian mansion in Manchester. Discouraged by her failure to become a successful hostess, she makes Richard her confidant and he eggs her on to seek a divorce. But when a reconciliation takes place, Richard poisons his brother and plants the clues so that Sarah is arrested for the murder of her husband. Comes the inevitable trial —something of a farce for a British court—and the verdict of guilty. But just before she is to be hanged, Jerome Thorn, also in love with Sarah, forces the truth from Richard.

Atmosphere and trimmings are overdone at the expense of the story. With the exception of comparative newcomer Dermot Walsh as Jerome, all the principals behave in an incredible, melodramatic manner. *Cane.*

Miniature Reviews

"The Naked City" (UI-Hellinger). Mark Hellinger's last picture is money in the bank.

"Call Northside 777" (20th). Documentary based on 1932 Chicago murder case has moderate dramatic impact.

"To the Ends of Earth" (Col). Action meller with opium-smuggling theme; good b.o. helped by Dick Powell-Signe Hasso.

"You Were Meant For Me" (Songs) (20th). Nostalgic tunefest; hefty entertainment content for boxoffice.

"My Girl Tisa" (WB). Warm, human interest story about early-day immigrants, but no b.o. assurance in star names.

"Albuquerque" (Par). Stereotyped western, but with okay prospects due to cast names and color.

"Perilous Waters" (Mono). Modest programmer with okay entertainment values.

"Tenth Avenue Angel" (M-G). Trite tearjerker with pollyanna twist. Will get some attention from family trade.

"Mary Lou" (Songs) (Col.). Mediocre musical for dualers.

"Stage to Mesa City" (EL). Fair galloper, with "Lash" LaRue as the marquee lure for action trade.

"Fanny" (Indie) (French). Deeply moving French pic starring Raimu; surefire for sureseater trade.

The Naked City

Universal-International release of Mark Hellinger production (Jules Buck, associate producer). Stars Barry Fitzgerald. Directed by Jules Dassin (Fred Frank, assistant director). Screenplay, Albert Maltz and Malvin Wald, from story by Malvin Wald; camera, William Daniels; editor, Paul Weatherwax; music supervisor, Milton Schwarzfeld; music, Miklos Rozsa and Frank Skinner. Tradeshown in N. Y., Jan. 20, '48. Running time, **96 MINS.**

Lt. Dan Muldoon.........Barry Fitzgerald
Frank Niles..................Howard Duff
Ruth Morrison.................Dorothy Hart
Jimmy Halloran...................Don Taylor
Garzah.......................Ted De Corsia
Dr. Stoneman..............House Jameson
Mrs. Halloran.................Anne Sargent
Mrs. Batory..................Adelaide Klein
Mr. Batory................Grover Burgess
Detective Perelli...................Tom Pedi
Mrs. Hylton...................Enid Markey
Captain Donahue..............Frank Conroy

New York City can be a pretty exciting place in which to live, as Mark Hellinger told it. In "The Naked City"—the producer's last picture—Hellinger filmed a magnificently realistic kaleidoscope of the metropolis in action. Made entirely in New York, it lays bare a city caught with its haunts down. It can't miss at the boxoffice.

"Naked City" has only a single star, Barry Fitzgerald. Yet, its b.o. prospects are not to be measured in terms of stars. There's hardly a recognizable name in the cast—from a film b.o. viewpoint—but that doesn't matter. It is the unfolding of this story that must assume the stellar rating. The word-of-mouth on "City" should be phenomenal.

"Naked City" is a boldly fashioned yarn about eastside, westside; about Broadway, the elevated, Fifth avenue; about kids playing hop-skip-and jump; about a populace of 8,000,000 —about a blond beaut's mysterious murder in an upper-westside apartment house. It is the murder that forms the basic narrative for "Naked City," and whenever Hellinger dealt in blondes, homicide squads, newspapermen and thugs, he was always in his metier. "Naked City" has all of these.

Hellinger's off-screen voice carries the narrative. At the very opening he describes New York, with the aid of a mobile camera, and its teeming humanity. Kids at play. Subway straphangers. Street vendors on Orchard street. Then that blonde with a questionable background who is mysteriously murdered. The kind of a story that Hellinger, one of the great tabloid crime reporters of the bath-tub-gin era, used to write.

Through the pic the producer's voice punctuates and bridges the film's incidents.

The homicide squad running down infinitesimal clues, roundup of suspects, all the detail that goes with great crime-reporting — these have been told with painstaking detail by Albert Maltz and Malvin Wald in their screenplay.

In this pic there are no props. A Manhattan police station scene was photographed in the police station; a lower eastside cops-and-robbers chase was actually filmed in the locale; the ghetto and its pushcarts were caught in all their realism.

Throughout, despite its omniscient, stark melodrama, there has been no sight lost of an element of humor. Barry Fitzgerald, as the film's focal point, in playing the police lieutenant of the homicide squad, strides through the role with tongue in cheek, with Don Taylor as his young detective aide. They creditably handle the lead roles, while lesser performers who stand out are Howard Duff and Ted De Corsia. Most of the others are in for bit parts, all of the players, incidentally, excepting Fitzgerald, being recruited from New York legit or radio ranks.

The direction by Jules Dassin was crisp and sharply points up the dramatic content as does the excellent camera work of William Daniels. The music score by Miklos Rozsa an. Frank Skinner always helps activat.. the story.

Yes, New York has been made into a pretty exciting place by Mark Hellinger. "Naked City" can stand as a fitting memorial. *Kahn.*

Call Northside 777

20th Fox release of Otto Lang production. Stars James Stewart; features Richard Conte, Lee. J. Cobb, Helen Walker. Directed by Harvey Hathaway. Screenply, Jerome Cady, Jay Dratler; adaptation, Leonard Hoffman and Quentin Reynolds from articles by James. P. McGuire; camera, Joe MacDonald; editor, J. Watson Webb, Jr. Tradeshown N.Y. Jan. 19, '48. Running time, 111 mins.

McNeal.................................James Stewart
Frank Wiecek..........................Richard Conte
Brian Kelly................................Lee. J. Cobb
Laura McNeal..........................Helen Walker
Wanda Skutnik...........................Betty Garde
Tillie..................................Kasla Orzazewski
Helen Wiecek-Rayska...................Joanne de Bergh
Palmer..................................Howard Smith
Parole Board Chairman...................Moroni Olsen
Sam Faxon..............................John McIntire
Martin Burns..............................Paul Harvey
Sullivan...................................J.M. Kerrigan
Judge Charles Moulton..................Samuel S. Hinds
Tomek Zaleska............................George Tyne
Warden..................................Richard Bishop
Boris...Otto Waldis
Frank. Jr...............................Michael Chapin
Jan Gruska................................John Bleifer
John Albertson.......................Addison Richards
Larson..................................Richard Rober
Patrolman...................................Eddie Dunn
William Decker............................Percy Helton
Prosecuting Attorney.......................Charles Lane

Latest documentary from 20th-Fox, "Call Northside 777" has all the separate ingredients for a sock film but registers only with a mild impact due to a lack of integration. Although following the surface pattern of such clicks as "The House on 92nd Street" and "Boomerang," this pic has a faltering pace, an uneven realistic focus and only a thin dramatic point. Its potential at the wickets will hinge chiefly on its attractive title and cast names.

Among the film's principal drawbacks is James Stewart's jarring and unpersuasive performance in the key role. As a Chicago reporter who's assigned to dig up a human-interest angle out of an 11-year-old murder case, Stewart shuttles between a phoney cynicism and a sob-sister sentimentalism without ever jelling the portrait into a recognizable newspaperman. His over-theatrical flaws become even more glaring against the expertly controlled thesping of the other players.

Henry Hathaway's direction marks a retreat from the documentary form. Instead of consistent realism, he lapses into a hybrid technique with plenty of hokey melodramatic tones. His handling of the relations between the city editor and reporter, for example, is only a modified version of Hollywood's stereotyped glamorization of a newspaper office.

Based on a celebrated miscarriage of justice in 1932, when two innocent men were sentenced to 99 years apiece for killing a cop, the screenplay constructs a serviceable plot on the factual groundwork. Film, however, tends to wander aimlessly in an over-sized running time. Hathaway is forced to pad the pic with some highly interesting visual gimmicks, such as the operation of a lie detector machine, a photo facsimile unit, a photo-developing tank, etc. But while interesting in themselves, these digressions don't help to fuse the story elements into a tight structure.

Title is derived from a personal ad placed in the Chicago Times-Herald by the mother of one of the prisoners offering a $5,000 reward for information leading to the release of her son. Answering the ad, Stewart uses it as a peg for a series of human interest stories about the case. Initially skeptical, he's progressively drawn to a belief in the man's innocence and finally commits himself to plead the convict's case in his paper.

Plot swivels on Stewart's efforts to blast the testimony of the eyewitness who identified the killers. Finally, through a cute trick in which an old photo is blown up several hundred times in order to uncover a decisive clue, Stewart proves that a judicial error was committed and exonerates the man. For some unexplainable reason, the fate of the other innocent man is left in the dark. Maybe he never had a mother.

Richard Conte gives an intensely sincere performance as the young Polish-American who is railroaded to jail. As a broken-down ex-speakeasy operator, Betty Garde also draws a sharp portrait in a relatively brief role. Lee J. Cobb, as the city editor, is competent, as is the rest of the long roster of players.

Lensing is expert, maintaining a surface tone in the style of a newsreel. Editing is fairly smooth and the musical score lends an unobtrusive assist. *Herm.*

To the Ends of Earth

Columbia release of Sidney Buchman production. Stars Dick Powell, Signe Hasso; features Maylia, Ludwig Donath, Vladimir Sokoloff, Edgar Barrier, John Hoyt. Directed by Robert Stevenson. Screenplay, Jay Richard Kennedy; camera, Burnett Guffey; editor, William Lyon; music director, M. W. Stoloff. Previewed in N. Y., Jan. 16, '48. Running time, **104 MINS.**

Michael Barrows...............Dick Powell
Ann Grant.......................Signe Hasso
Shu Pan Wu..........................Maylia
Nicolas Sokim..............Ludwig Donath
Lum Chi Chow..........Vladimir Sokoloff
Grieg.........................Edgar Barrier
Bennett...........................John Hoyt
Commissioner Lariesier.....Marcel Journet
Alberto Berado..........Luis Van Rooten
Binda Sha......................Fritz Leiber
Commissioner Hadley........Vernon Steele
Mahmoud.......................Peter Virgo
Commissioner Amar Hassam.Lou Krugman
Chian Soo........................Eddie Lee
Naftalie Vrandstadter.......Ivan Triesault
Hernando......................Leon Lenoir
Joe..............................Peter Chong
Cassidy........................George Volk
Clark.....................Robert Malcolm
Comm. Harry J. Anslinger.........Himself

"To the Ends of Earth" is a fast-moving melodrama with okay boxoffice results to be expected from its marquee lures and snappy exploitation of its sensational theme. This is the pic that encountered heavy opposition from the Production Code Administration because of its opium-smuggling background. Scripter Jay Richard Kennedy, however, has juggled the theme into conventional whodunit patterns without any objectionable stress on the opium angle.

Film generates considerable interest from its shifting locales. As a U. S. government narcotics investigator, Dick Powell ranges over the whole globe, with major plot developments occurring in such widely scattered points as San Francisco, Shanghai, Egypt, Havana and the Atlantic Ocean off the New Jersey coast. Production and direction are neatly keyed to a realistic note, giving maximum credibility to the proceedings.

Beneath the documentary veneer, however, the film spins a fantastic yarn which, if factual, only proves once again that truth is stranger than fiction. Pic's major premise is based on the existence of an international ring of power-hungry fanatics aiming to subjugate the peoples of the world through the spread of dope.

Tale opens in 1935 with Powell making a routine check of an unchartered ship reported off the California coast. High point of the film's action is staged in the opening reel as the Japanese-manned steamer, racing to get beyond the 12-mile limit, jettisons 100 Chinese opium-plantation slaves to destroy all evidence. Unable to pin a rap on the captain, Powell picks up his trail in Shanghai and gets a scent on a notorious gang which has organized its smuggling activities into a fine science.

In China, the finger of suspicion points to enigmatic Signe Hasso, acting as governess to a Chinese girl orphan, as the gangleader. Powell continues his pursuit of the gang into Egypt, where it's growing the stuff, then heads for the shipment destination in Havana. Crossing paths once again with Miss Hasso here, Powell plays cagily in order to crack the gang's system of smuggling the smoke past the U. S. customs guards in New York. After some incredible guesswork, presumed to be brilliant deductions, Powell solves the riddle and nabs the real leader. Like most whodunits, she turns out to be the most innocent-looking character in the lot, the babyish, Chinese orphan, Maylia, who has actually been duping Miss Hasso.

Interlaced with the action, pic tries to put across a laudable one-world idea. Windup shows a session of the narcotics control commission of the United Nations organization at work trying to wipe out the opium trade. At several points, however, film gets bogged in some moralizing talk which is not attuned to this high adventure type of story.

Cast lineup, headed by Powell and Miss Hasso, does a uniformly competent job. Powell is adequately tough and taciturn while Miss Hasso uses her exotic looks to best advantage. Vladimir Sokoloff, as a Chinese official, and Ivan Triesault, as a Dutch opium smuggler, register with polished performances. Maylia, as the Chinese lassie, is burdened by an incredible role which she carries bravely.

Camera work is excellent throughout, contributing largely to the capture of the atmospheres in the various locales. Smooth editing and good score also lend able assistance. *Herm.*

You Were Meant for Me

(SONGS)

Hollywood, Jan. 17.

20th-Fox release of Fred Kohlmar production. Stars Jeanne Crain, Dan Dailey; features Oscar Levant, Barbara Lawrence, Selena Royle, Percy Kilbride, Herbert Anderson. Directed by Lloyd Bacon. Screenplay, Ellick Moll, Valentine Davies; camera, Victor Milner; musical direction, Lionel Newman; orchestral arrangements, Herbert Spencer, Earle Hagen; vocal arrangements, Charles Henderson; dances, Dan Dailey, Les Clark; editor, William Reynolds. Tradeshown in Hollywood Jan. 14, '48. Running time, **91 MINS.**

Peggy Mayhew....................Jeanne Crain
Chuck Arnold....................Dan Dailey
Oscar....................Oscar Levant
Louise Crane....................Barbara Lawrence
Mrs. Mayhew....................Selena Royle
Mr. Mayhew....................Percy Kilbride
Eddie....................Herbert Anderson

Framing itself around the still-listenable tunes of the 1929-30 crash era, "You Were Meant for Me" is pleasant entertainment that should do well at the boxoffice. Seven songs are given full treatment, and a number of others are interspersed briefly to round out the ear-and-foot-tickling score.

Music gives punch to the standard musical story plotting around which is depicted the days of 1929, the stock market crash and the depression that followed. Short-skirted flappers, spit-curls, hipflasks and wide-bottomed trousers will carry young oldtimers back to the days of the "chicken-in-every-pot" prosperity slogan.

Jeanne Crain charmingly portrays the '29 flapper. There is an infectious quality to her playing that takes a strong hold on the auditor. Dan Dailey socks over his spot as the band leader, a composite of several of that period. Vocal chore on the seven songs, plus terping, also falls his way. He scores in all departments.

In addition to the title tune, reprised several times, score has "Goodnight Sweetheart," "Crazy Rhythm," "Ain't Misbehaving," "If I Had You," "I'll Get By" and "Ain't She Sweet." Backing Dailey on vocals is male trio, and arrangements are of the era, which heightens nostalgia value.

Plot deals with marital ups and downs of Miss Crain and Dailey. Married on short acquaintance, the honeymoon is a series of one-night stands, and when "Wall Street Lays An Egg," Dailey can't adjust himself to hard times. A contrived splitup takes place but the maestro wises up in time to make for a happy finale. Lloyd Bacon's direction has pace, humorous touches and other showmanly handling to build the entertainment content to a pleasing level.

Oscar Levant does another of his sour-pussed characterizations — and that isn't bad. He also gives competent touch to Gershwin's "Concerto in F." Percy Kilbride and Selena Royle are amusing smalltowners. Barbara Lawrence, Herbert Anderson and others in cast fill in. Fred Kohlmar's production guidance points up atmosphere of the era with authenticity aided by capable art direction and set decorations. Good lensing was contributed by Victor Milner. Lionel Newman's musical direction has sharp orchestral and vocal arrangements by Herbert Spencer, Earle Hagen and Charles Henderson. *Brog.*

My Girl Tisa

(SONGS)

Hollywood, Jan. 16.

Warners release of Milton Sperling (United States Pictures) production. Stars Lilli Palmer, Sam Wanamaker; features Akim Tamiroff, Alan Hale, Hugo Haas, Gale Robbins, Stella Adler, Benny Baker. Directed by Elliott Nugent. Screenplay, Allen Boretz; based upon a play by Lucille S. Prumbs and Sara B. Smith; camera, Ernest Haller; music, Max Steiner; editor, Christian Nyby. Tradeshown in Hollywood Jan. 13, '48. Running time, **95 MINS.**

Tisa Kepes....................Lilli Palmer
Mark Denek....................Sam Wanamaker
Mr. Grumbach....................Akim Tamiroff
Dugan....................Alan Hale
Tescu....................Hugo Haas
Jenny Kepes....................Gale Robbins
Mrs. Faludi....................Stella Adler
Herman....................Benny Baker
Georgie....................Sumner Getchell
Binka....................Sid Tomack
Svenson....................John Qualen
Riley....................Tom Dillon
Theodore Roosevelt....................Sidney Blackmer
Prof. Tabor....................Fritz Feld
Otto....................John Banner

"My Girl Tisa" tells a warm, interesting story of American immigrants at the turn of the century. Handed colorful production in keeping with the New York background of that era, film has strong performances and direction to rate good word-of-mouth attention. Only sag in whole show is the hokum ending, but its fairytale flavor is held to short footage. There's no b.o. assurance in the star names to back up the obvious top-budget allotment.

Apparently, Milton Sperling's United States Pictures, releasing through Warners, has put a great deal of faith in capturing public fancy with a new male star, Sam Wanamaker. Exploiting of new star, the general strong effect of the picture and word-of-mouth are all factors that will help shape boxoffice returns.

Wanamaker is a young talent with a personality that builds. He makes an able partner with Lilli Palmer in depicting little people who have come from the old country to grow with America. Characters are graphically drawn in the scripting and portrayals.

Elliott Nugent achieves a telling effect with his direction. Particularly good characterizations are Akim Tamiroff's sweatshop operator, Hugo Haas' villainy as crooked travel agent who preys on the hopeful, Stella Adler's lusty boarding-house-keeper, Alan Hale's politician, and Benny Baker's beer-barrelled type of the day.

Allen Boretz scripted from an unproduced play by Lucille S. Prumbs and Sara B. Smith. Plot depicts Miss Palmer as middle-European slaving to get money so her father can come to the new country. Her plans are undisturbed until she falls for Wanamaker, ambitious would-be lawyer. Story carries them through romance and heartbreak, deportation proceedings instigated by Haas, and other tribulations with a fine flavor right up to the wishful ending when young love is rescued by the intervening hand of the President of the United States — Teddy Roosevelt. Final scenes don't compare in worth to genuineness of preceding footage.

Sperling has given film authentic production backing. Ernest Haller's camera work, the Max Steiner score, studded with oldtime and foreign tunes synonymous of the people and period; art direction, editing and other contributions are excellent. *Brog.*

Albuquerque

(COLOR)

Hollywood, Jan. 14.

Paramount release of William Pine-William Thomas (Clarion) production. Stars Randolph Scott, Barbara Britton, George "Gabby" Hayes, Lon Chaney; features Russell Hayden, Catherine Craig, George Cleveland. Directed by Ray Enright. Screenplay, Gene Lewis, Clarence Upson Young; from novel by Luke Short; camera (Cinecolor), Fred Jackman, Jr.; music score, Darrell Calker; editor, Howard Smith. Tradeshown Jan. 12, '48. Running time, **89 MINS.**

Cole Armin....................Randolph Scott
Letty Tyler....................Barbara Britton
Juke....................George "Gabby" Hayes
Steve Murkil....................Lon Chaney
Ted Wallace....................Russell Hayden
Celia Wallace....................Catherine Craig
John Armin....................George Cleveland
Myrtle Walton....................Karolyn Grimes
Sheriff Linton....................Bernard J. Nedell
Huggins....................Russell Simpson
Pearl....................Jody Gilbert
Jackson....................Dan White
Dave Walton....................Irving Bacon
Matt Wayne....................John Halloran
Judge....................Walter Baldwin

With all the basic ingredients to be exciting western filmfare, "Albuquerque" nevertheless misses. Initial boxoffice outlook, however, is okay, based on values of such outdoor sturdies as Randolph Scott, George "Gabby" Hayes and others. Color lensing also adds to ticket-selling possibilities.

Pine-Thomas, who have bee turning out successful string of bread-and-butter "B's" for Paramount release, have a sturdy physical framing in this pic, but story lacks punch.

Basically, the Luke Short story, from which Gene Lewis and Clarence Upson Young did their script, has all the tried and true ingredients necessary to appeal to the western action fan. The crooked sheriff, the town bigshot, stage holdups, pure sagebrush love and a strong, true hero are all there. Dialog and situations are awkward.

Scott and Hayes bolster doings considerably. Former is seen as nephew of town tyrant, George Cleveland, and steps in to help save a small wagon train line when the bigshot tries to kill off competition. There's never much doubt of the outcome and the hero eventually winds up the winner.

Barbara Britton and Catherine Craig are in for romance and are adequate to demands. Lon Chaney teams with Cleveland for the heavy work, and Russell Hayden is on the side of the hero. Others measure up.

Ray Enright directed in a not-always-satisfactory manner. Stronger helming could have put more sock into action. The excellent color photography is by Fred Jackman, Jr. Other technical aids are first class. *Brog.*

Perilous Waters

Monogram release of Jack Wrather production. Stars Don Castle, Audrey Long, Peggy Knudsen; features Samuel S. Hinds, Gloria Holden, John Miljan. Directed by Jack Bernhard. Screenplay, Richard Wormser, Francis Rosenwald, from Good Housekeeping story, "Search," by Leon Ware; camera, Henry Sharp; editor, Stewart S. Frye. At New York theatre, N. Y., week Jan. 13, '48. Running time, **66 MINS.**

Willie Hunter....................Don Castle
Judy Gage....................Audrey Long
Pat Ferris....................Peggy Knudsen
Dana Ferris....................Samuel S. Hinds
Mrs. Ferris....................Gloria Holden
Carter Larkin....................John Miljan
Franklin....................Walter Sande
Captain Porter....................Stanley Andrews
The Boss....................Cy Kendall
Fred....................Gene Garrick
Bart....................George Ramsey
Brooks....................Mike Kilian
Fisherman....................Julian Rivero

"Perilous Waters" is a modest programmer whose entertainment values are reinforced with liberal quantities of action and romance. While there's nothing particularly original about the story, film manages to generate enough interest to more than hold its own in the dualers.

Made on a budget said to have been around $225,000, picture reflects a good standard of acting, direction and production for that kind of coin. Cast is an able one headed by Don Castle, who bears a resemblance to Clark Gable. Exhibs would do well to stress the yarn's romantic angles in a bid for the femme trade. Audrey Long and Peggy Knudsen offer surefire eye appeal as contender's for Castle's affections.

Plot is a relatively simple one with most of it unreeling aboard a yacht underway for Mexico. Owner of the vessel is a newspaper publisher (Samuel S. Hinds). He's been on an anti-gambling crusade, and Castle ships aboard the craft to rub him out. But Castle, who's been hired to do the job for 10 grand, suffers a change of heart and fails to go through with his mission.

Also woven in the tale for more or less sinister effect are some small-time blackmailing and swindling which John Miljan attempts to pull off. In cahoots with Hinds' wife, Gloria Holden, he tries to shake him down as well as the publisher's secretary, Miss Long.

As a whole the acting is generally okay. Castle is stalwart enough as the hero, while roles of Hinds, Miljan and Miss Holden are capably handled along with those of the Misses Long and Knudsen.

Leon Ware's Good Housekeeping mag story, "Search," is the source of the film, scripters Richard Wormser and Francis Rosenwald having done a fair job in transplanting it to celluloid. Henry Sharp's lensing is adequate while direction of Jack Bernhard maintains a good pace in this Jack Wrather production.

Tenth Avenue Angel

Hollywood, Jan. 14.

Metro release of Ralph Wheelwright production. Features Margaret O'Brien, Angela Lansbury, George Murphy, Phyllis Thaxter. Directed by Roy Rowland. Screenplay, Harry Ruskin, Eleanore Griffin; based on story by Angna Enters and a sketch by Craig Rice; camera, Robert Surtees; editors, Ralph E. Winters, George Boemler. Tradeshown in Hollywood Jan. 7, '48. Running time, **74 Mins.**

Flavia Mills....................Margaret O'Brien
Susan Bratten....................Angela Lansbury
Steve Abbutt....................George Murphy
Helen Mills....................Phyllis Thaxter
Joseph Mills....................Warner Anderson
Blind Mac....................Rhys Williams
Al Parker....................Barry Nelson
Mrs. Murphy....................Connie Gilchrist
Daniel Oliver Madson....................Tom Trout
Jimmy Madson....................Dickie Tyler
Rad Ardley....................Henry Blair
Parole Officer....................Charles Cane
Street Vendor....................Richard Lane

"Tenth Avenue Angel" gives little Margaret O'Brien another chance to turn on the cinematic tears. As a weeper, film fulfills all aims, but the young actress' suffering is beginning to wear. She needs a change of pace. In situations where she and other familiars in the cast are favorites, film should have a modest success. Otherwise, its chances are slender.

Hokum plot lays the sob stuff on thick, and without too much interest, as the moppet suffers disillusionment and loses her faith in grownups. Plot hinges on child's interference in the lives of the adults who surround her. One of them is an ex-con trying to work out an honest future. Tearjerker ingredients put the principals through all types of tribulation to insure the emotional upsets.

Roy Rowland puts the players through their paces in okay style, considering the material in the Harry Ruskin - Eleanore Griffin script, based on a story by Angna Enters and a sketch by Craig Rice. Angela Lansbury and George Murphy carry the adult leads as sweetheart and ex-con, respectively. Phyllis Thaxter and Warner Anderson are the suffering parents of the moppet. Rhys Williams draws a good characterization of a blind news vendor. Barry Nelson and others do their best.

Lensing, editing and other behind-the-camera factors reflect standard craftsmanship. *Brog.*

Mary Lou

(SONGS)

Hollywood, Jan. 19.

Columbia release of Sam Katzman production. Features Robert Lowery, Joan Barton, Glenda Farrell, Frankie Carle Orch. Directed by Arthur Dreifuss. Screenplay, M. Coates Webster; camera, Ira H. Morgan; editor, Viola Lawrence; songs, J. R. Robinson, Abe Lyman, George Waggner, Allan Roberts, Lester Lee, Doris Fisher, Frankie Carle, Facundo Rivero, Ben Blossner. Previewed in Hollywood, Jan. 19, '48. Running time, **65 MINS.**

Steve Roberts....................Robert Lowery
Ann Parker....................Joan Barton
Winnie Winford....................Glenda Farrell
Mary Lou....................Abigail Adams
Mike Connors....................Frank Jenks
Murry Harris....................Emmett Vogan
Eve Summers....................Thelma White
Airlines President....................Pierre Watkin
Mortimer Cripps....................Charles Jordan
Mrs. Harris....................Leslie Turner
Cheever Chesney....................Chester Clute
and Frankie Carle's Orch

"Mary Lou" is a program musical

comedy for smaller situations; it should serve okay for supporting positions and in lesser houses.

Singing of Joan Barton and music played by Frankie Carle's orchestra are assists to trite story. Songs include title number, "Don't Mind My Troubles," "I'm Sorry I Didn't Say I'm Sorry," "That's Good Enough for Me," "Wasn't It Swell Last Night," "Carle's Boogie" and "Learning to Speak English," which is a lot of music to crowd into 65 minutes of film. Miss Barton makes the lyrics listenable and Carle's keyboard work pleases. Plot involves itelf with two femmes' fight over right to use handle of Mary Lou while singing with Carle's band. Handle has been taken over by Miss Barton when she becomes orch chirp after being fired as an air hostess for soothing passengers with song. Abigail Adams, rival canary, contests use of name but, after some contrived ups and downs, plot unwinds to expected conclusion.

Miss Barton impresses as femme lead and Robert Lowry shows okay as the leading man. Frank Jenks and Glenda Farrell toss around some comedy bits. Carle's music is good but he's no thespian. Miss Adams is competent, as are Thelma White, Charles Jordan and others. Sam Katzman's production gardnered expert values for low budget. Arthur Dreifuss' direction is only average. Lensing and other technical work are standard. *Brog.*

Stage to Mesa City

Eagle Lion release of Jerry Thomas production. Stars "Lash" LaRue, Al "Fuzzy" St. John; features Jennifer Holt, George Chesebro, Brad Slaven. Directed by Ray Taylor. Screenplay, Joseph F. Poland; camera, James Brown, Sr.; editor, Hugh Winn; music, Walter Greene. Previewed in N. Y., Jan. 16, 48. Running time, 52 MINS.

Cheyenne	"Lash" LaRue
Fuzzy	Al "Fuzzy" St. John
Margie	Jennifer Holt
Padgett	George Chesebro
Bob	Brad Slaven
Baxter	Marshall Reed
Ed	Terry Frost
Jim	Carl Mathews
Pete	Bob Woodward
Watson	Steve Clark
Stocker	Frank Ellis
Sheriff	Leo Morgan

A formula western, "Stage to Mesa City" is a fair galloper with "Lash" LaRue supplying the marquee lure. On the overall, film is just an average filler for the action houses.

As his latest mission, U. S. Marshal LaRue is scrutinizing the much-attacked Mesa City stage line. A lucrative mail contract is coming up and unknown outlaws are attempting to take over the line. Suspicion eventually falls upon the postmaster, George Chesebro. He's bagged by LaRue in a typical toe-to-toe slugging match.

LaRue turns in his usual brisk performance as the marshal. Al "Fuzzy" St. John handles the comedy while Chesebro is a so-so heavy. Jennifer Holt lends some pulchritude in the lone femme role. Supporting players are mediocre.

Scripting of Joseph Poland makes liberal use of the stock plot ingredients found in most films of this category. Ray Taylor's direction is satisfactory in this Jerry Thomas production. Lensing of James Brown, Sr., is okay, and Hugh Winn's editing neatly pared the footage to a snappy 52 minutes. *Gilb.*

Fanny
(FRENCH-MADE)

Siritzky International release of Marcel Pagnol production. Stars Raimu, Charpin, Pierre Fresnay; features Orane Demazis. Directed by Marc Allegret. Screenplay, Pagnol; English titles, H. G. Weinberg. Previewed in N. Y. Jan. 9, '48. Running time, 125 MINS.

Cesar	Raimu
Marius	Pierre Fresnay
Panisse	Charpin
Fanny	Orane Demazis
Honorine	Alida Rouffe
Mr. Brun	Robert Vattier

(In French; English Titles)

Producer-writer Marcel Pagnol and the late Raimu, France's great cinema team responsible for such classics as "The Baker's Wife" and "The Well-Digger's Daughter," reach the highest point of their collaboration in "Fanny." Like their other offerings, this film is deeply human in its perception of the way in which the tragic and comic elements of life reinforce each other. Its boxoffice appeal among the art house clientele is assured.

Once again, Pagnol plays variations on his favorite theme of the young maid's fall from virtue into pregnancy. The story of "Fanny," however, is secondary to the gallery of superlative portraits drawn by the cast members. Several long sequences are wholly discursive and even irrelevant to the plot's central axis. But the talk in these passages is so packed with earthy humor, and the characterizations of the middle-class types are so acute, that in reality they make up the substance of the film.

The story revolves around Fanny's plight after she's deserted by Raimu's son, her lover who leaves to become a sailor. Under pressure of her outraged mother, Fanny is forced into marrying Charpin, who's old enough to be her father. Raimu and Charpin, good friends, battle temporarily over the custody of the child but ultimately join hands against the young lover, Pierre Fresnay, who returns to claim his paternal rights.

Raimu delivers one of the best performances of his career, with the loose structure of the plot offering him chances to display the full range of his talents. As a barkeep who's brokenhearted over his son's departure, Raimu displays his rich comic vein with a delicacy that never shatters the poignant qualities underlying his role. Charpin also plays superbly, equalling Raimu in his ability to merge the pathetic, the sentimental and the comic into a unified mood.

As Fanny, Orane Demazis is slightly short on looks but more than compensates by her sensitivity and fragility. Fresnay, as the impulsive swain, is disappointing in a small part which he plays too theatrically. Brilliant performances are turned in by Alida Rouffe, as Fanny's mother, and Robert Vattier, one of Raimu's friends.

Chief defects lie in the lensing, which is uneven, and the editing, which causes several choppy transitions. English titling, however, achieves a rare success in capturing the body and spirit of the French dialog. *Herm.*

Miniature Reviews

"Anna Karenina" (Lion) (British). Tolstoy novel with Vivien Leigh, Ralph Richardson should be big grosser.

"Alias A Gentleman" (M-G). Medium-budgeted Wallace Beery starrer okay for nabe situations.

"Slippy McGee" (Rep). Meller about reformed safecracker, with Donald Barry, Dale Evans, Tom Brown; okay for twinners.

"Black Hills" (EL). Trite oatuner in the Eddie Dean series.

"Fighting Mad" (Mono). Good entry in Monogram's "Joe Palooka" series. Punchy fight sequences and okay plot.

"Campus Honeymoon" (Rep). Breezy comedy dualer of GI's at college.

"Angels Alley" (Mono). Okay entry in Monogram's "Bowery Boys" group.

"This Wine of Love" (Songs) (Indie). Well-made Italian version of Donizetti's opera.

"Panhandle" (Mono). Good outdoor actioner, filmed in sepia for added scenic beauty. Well-acted.

Anna Karenina
(BRITISH-MADE)

London, Jan. 23.

British Lion release of London Film-Alexander Korda production. Stars Vivien Leigh, Ralph Richardson; features Kieron Moore. Directed by Julien Duvivier. Screenplay by Jean Anouilh, Guy Morgan, Duvivier from Tolstoy's novel; editor, Russell Lloyd; music, Constant Lambert; camera, Henri Alekan, Robert Walker. At Leicester Square, London, Jan. 22, '48. Running time, 139 MINS.

Anna Karenina	Vivien Leigh
Karenin	Ralph Richardson
Count Vronsky	Kieron Moore
Stepan Oblonsky	Hugh Dempster
Dolly Oblonsky	Mary Kerridge
Princess Shcherbatski	Marie Lohr
Prince Shcherbatski	Frank Tickle
Kitty Shcherbatski	Sally Ann Howes
Levin	Niall Macginnis
Nicholm	Michael Gough
Princess Tversky	Martita Hunt
Countess Ivanovna	Heather Thatcher
Countess Vronsky	Helen Haye
Princess Nathalia	Mary Martlew
Countess Meskov	Ruby Miller
Colonel Vronsky	Austin Trevor
Princess Sorokina	Ann South
Prince Makhotin	Guy Verney
General Serpuhousky	John Longden

There should have been no "ifs" or "buts" about the record boxoffice value of this picture. Here are the ingredients—popular classic story, a rare cast headed by magnetic Vivien Leigh, an Alexander Korda production with no stinting of cash, and Julien Duvivier as director. Small wonder that everybody here was expecting it to be the picture of the year. But, fine as this fourth production of Tolstoy's novel is (Fox 1915, Metro 1927 and 1935), and well as it will do at the boxoffice, it misses greatness and has tedious stretches. Judicious cutting will help considerably.

That the picture will play to big grosses is certain. It has too many boxoffice values for any exhibitor to miss, and should, after a little careful pruning, find a ready audience in American theatres.

It would appear that far too much attention was paid to the sets and the artistic structure at the expense of the players. It would have been wise for Korda and Duvivier to realize that the story, for screen purposes, is frankly Victorian melodrama, and that there was always the danger of reducing the characters to puppets. Numerous lavish scenes and gigantic sets might arouse admiration for the producer, but unless one laughs and cries—and tears are particularly needed in this picture—there can be no complete entertainment or enjoyment.

It speaks volumes for Miss Leigh and Ralph Richardson that they are able to disentangle themselves from their overwhelming surroundings and become credibly human. Miss Leigh dominates the picture, as she rightly should, with her beauty, charm and skill. It isn't her fault that eyes remain dry and hearts unwrung when she moves to inevitable tragedy, as the neglected wife and discarded lover. It is a sad commentary on modern production to assert that with less expenditure on the film the Leigh-Duvivier cooperation would have achieved much more.

Richardson's portrayal of the priggish, unlikeable husband is masterly yet uneven. Sometimes he gives the impression of a Chinese philosopher with accent and staccato phrase. Incidentally, the multiplicity of pronunciations of "Karenina" by various people is a trifle distracting.

As the dashing lover, Count Vronsky, who deserts Anna, Kieron Moore, apart from his neat Irish brogue, is a trifle wooden. It may be Russian but it isn't popular cinema. He should have matched Miss Leigh's anguished love with a dash of fiery passion.

Of the minor characters in the long list of experienced players, Mary Kerridge is easily outstanding, closely followed by Sally Ann Howes, who reveals an unexpected maturity in her work.

Photography, sets, costumes and music all deserve their mead of praise. They all add up to a distinction which will not be lost on audiences. *Cane.*

Alias a Gentleman

Metro release of Nat Perrin production. Stars Wallace Beery; features Tom Drake, Dorothy Patrick, Gladys George. Directed by Harry Beaumont. Screenplay, William R. Lipman; based on story by Peter Ruric; camera, Ray June; editor, Ben Lewis. Tradeshown N. Y., Jan. 21, '48. Running time, 74 MINS.

Jim Breedin	Wallace Beery
Johnny Lorgen	Tom Drake
Elaine Carter	Dorothy Patrick
Madge Parkson	Gladys George
Matt Enley	Leon Ames
Capt. Charlie Lopen	Warner Anderson
No End	John Qualen
Harry Bealer	Sheldon Leonard
Jig Johnson	Trevor Bardette
Zu	Jeff Corey
Spats Edwards	Marc Krah
Carruthers	William Forrest

"Alias a Gentleman" is a moderately entertaining comedy meller that'll carry its weight in nabe situations. Built as a vehicle for Wallace Beery, pic accents that type of sentimental hokum which has been the vet actor's trademark. Production dress for this pic is trimmed down to medium-budget standards, with supporting cast, direction and scripting on a par level.

Unfolding with large dosages of cornfed gags, yarn revolves around an ex-jailbird who falls into a fortune when an oil company buys up his farm. Searching for his lost daughter, whom he hasn't seen in 15 years, Beery gets stuck with a phoney gal whom his former cronies ring in to get some information on the source of his income.

Denouement, with Beery becoming wised up to the identity of his so-called daughter, provides opening for some tearjerking. Pic, however, immediately slides into kidnapping complications, with the gal, who becomes fond of Beery, being snatched by the gang. Windup blazes out in a slambang shooting fray and slugfest, with the law intervening in the nick of time.

Beery registers okay in his familiar style of mugging malapropisms. As the young gal who turns virtuous after a bad start, Dorothy Patrick is a smart looker who shows thesping talent. Tom Drake, as an ex-con buddy of Beery, handles his role competently. Rest of the cast come through nicely in stock parts. *Herm.*

Slippy McGee

Republic release of Lou Brock production. Stars Donald Barry, Dale Evans, Tom Brown; features Maude Eburne, Harry V. Cheshire. Directed by Albert Kelley. Screenplay, Norman S. Hall and Jerry Gruskin; based on novel by Marie Conway Oemler; camera, John MacBurnie; editor, Les Orlebeck. Tradeshown in N. Y., Jan. 16, '48. Running time, **63 MINS.**

Slippy McGee..................Donald Barry
Mary Hunter....................Dale Evans
Father Shanley.................Tom Brown
Doctor Moore...........Harry V. Cheshire
Thomas Eustis..................James Seay
Red........................Murray Alper
Fred Appelby...................Dick Elliott
Mrs. Dexter..................Maude Eburne
John Hunter..............Raymond Largay
Charlie.....................Eddie Acuff
Al..........................Michael Carr
Tommy......................George Nokes

This modestly budgeted meller of a safecracker who goes straight is strong enough to provide underpinning on any twin bill. It's a bread-'n'-butter picture from this lot and is packed with suspense and thrills.

Donald Barry plays the title role. Yarn shows him being forced into idleness from his usual safebusting prowls with two robber pals due to a broken leg suffered when he rescues a youngster from the path of a speeding truck. A young priest (Tom Brown) goes out of his way to speed his recovery.

Story depicts the gradual reformation of the yegg. But not until after he has liquidated his own gang, recovered the money taken from the town's bank and unmasked a polite blackmailer who was trying to force his newly-found sweetheart into an unwanted marriage.

Director Albert Kelley has done well with these pat situations, getting a nice assist from a tight screenplay by Norman S. Hall and Jerry Gruskin. This compact meller also is helped by trim editing by Les Orlebeck and okay lensing by John MacBurnie.

Barry's portrayal of the yeggman is realistic. Per usual, he's in a rip-roaring fist fight at the end. Brown makes an acceptable priest, and Dale Evans is effective as the young country gal who falls for Barry. Maude Eburne, vet stage-screen character comedienne, neatly handles the lesser role of the priest's housekeeper. Harry V. Cheshire makes an affable country medico, but James Seay is too melodramatic as town's richest man who's willing to stoop to blackmail. *Wear.*

Black Hills
(SONGS)

Eagle Lion release of Jerry Thomas production. Stars Eddie Dean; features Roscoe Ates, Shirley Patterson, Terry Frost. Directed by Ray Taylor. Screenplay, Joseph Poland; camera, Ernie Miller; songs, Dean Hal Blair, Pete Gates; editor, Hugh Winn. Previewed in New York, Jan. 15, '48. Running time, **60 MINS.**

Eddie.......................Eddie Dean
Soapy......................Roscoe Ates
Janet.....................Shirley Patterson
Kirby......................Terry Frost
Larry......................Steve Drake
Chiquita....................Nina Bara
Tuttle.....................Bill Fawcett
Cooper....................Lane Bradford
Sheriff...................Lee Morgan
Allen....................George Cheesbro
The Plainsmen: Andy Parker, Earl Murphy, Paul Smith, George Bamby, Charles Morgan.

Another trite oatuner in the Eddie Dean series, "Black Hills" is pretty dull. Its b.o. prospects are meagre. Story is unimaginative and performances are indifferent.

A secret gold mine is the excuse for this one. The lode, discovered by ranch owner (Steve Drake), is the solution to the overdue mortgage. Dirty work comes in when a saloon keeper (Terry Frost) kills Drake in an effort to seize the ranch and the mine. He also knocks off George Chesebro, the mortgage holder. But before Frost can cash in on his crimes, Eddie Dean and his sidekick, Roscoe Ates, turn him over to the law amid the usual stagecoach chases, hand-to-hand fisticuffs and inaccurate six-gun shooting. Dean does a

so-so job as the champion of the law, Ates contribs his stock comic relief and Frost is a standard heavy.

Joseph Poland's script is well sprinkled with cliches. Ray Taylor's direction is ordinary, and Ernie Miller contribs average lensing. Three songs, "Black Hills," "Punchinello" and "Let's Go Sparkin'," offer little to the picture with the exception of interrupting the story. Producer Jerry Thomas would give the fans a treat by using a different set for the frontier town in the next Deaner. Same street in all these series is getting monotonous. *Gilb.*

Fighting Mad
(ONE SONG)
Hollywood, Jan. 22.

Monogram release of Hal E. Chester production. Stars Leon Errol, Joe Kirkwood; features Elyse Knox, John Hubbard, Patricia Dane, Charles Cane. Directed by Reginald LeBorg. Screenplay, John Bright; added dialog, Monte F. Collins; original story, Ralph S. Lewis, Bernard D. Shamberg; camera, William Sickner; editor, Roy Livingston. Previewed in Hollywood, Jan. 21, '48. Running time, **74 MINS.**

Knobby Walsh................Leon Errol
Joe Palooka.................Joe Kirkwood
Anne Howe...................Elyse Knox
Charles Kennedy.............John Hubbard
Iris March..................Patricia Dane
George Wendell..............Charles Cane
Archie Stone................Wally Vernon
Ralph.......................Frank Hyers
Jeff Lundy..................Jack Shea
Waldo.......................Jack Roper
Looie......................Horace McMahon
Truck Driver...............Jack Overman
Scranton....................Eddie Gribbon
Mom Palooka................Sarah Padden
Pop Palooka.................Michael Mark
Truck Driver's Wife.......Evelynne Smith
Hat Check Girl..............Geneva Gray
Referee....................Johnny Indrisano
Dr. MacKenzie..............Frank Reicher
Stevie.....................Jay Norris
Dr. Burman.................Paul Scardon
Nurse......................Virginia Belmont
Dr. Gray...................Larry Steers
Reporter...................Robert Conway
Reporter...................Herb Vigran
Fighter....................Dewey Robinson
Photographer...............Emil Sitka
Arthur Wild................Murray Leonard
Fight Announcer......Robt. C. McCracken
Commissioner...............Cy Kendall
Water Boy..................Bill McLean
Cop........................Jack Mower
Detective..................Paul Bryar
Bookmaker..................Sammy Wolfe
Radio Announcer..........Reid Kilpatrick
Sparring Partner...........Ted Pavelec

"Fighting Mad" carries interest for the smaller houses and neighborhood trade and will pay off well in that market. It further projects the screen adventures of the comic strip hero, Joe Palooka, and Joe Kirkwood has the physical appearance to back up the assignment.

Picture has some of the best production values yet achieved under the Monogram label. Settings are good and well-lighted, the lensing clear and other physical factors help to belie the budget. Story opens slowly but picks up pace under Reginald LeBorg's direction. Ring sequences are punchy, and plotting in the John Bright script makes for okay motivation.

Palooka, injured in a fight, goes blind. An operation restores his sight but he must lay off for a year. Meanwhile, Leon Errol as Knobby Walsh, buys a piece of another promising heavyweight to keep busy. Later Walsh wises up that gamblers are using the pug and Palooka comes back to the ring to save his manager from disgrace, even though it may mean a fatal eye injury. Naturally, the side of right comes through with flying colors and there's a happy tag for all.

Producer Hal E. Chester and his associate, Bernard W. Burton, have taken care that ring and training sequences are authentic, using tech advice of John Indrisano. Players answer all requirements of roles with Errol sparking piece. Elyse Knox, as Anne Howe, John Hubbard, Patricia Dane, who canaries "Don't Fall in Love" in a nitery scene; Charles Cane, the heavy; Wally Vernon, Horace MacMahon and others are good.

Expert lensing is by William Sickner. Art direction and set decorations were contributed by Dave Milton and Raymond Boltz, Jr., respectively. *Brog.*

Campus Honeymoon
(SONGS)

Republic release of Fanchon production. Features Lyn Wilde, Lee Wilde, Adele Mara, Richard Crane, Hal Hackett. Directed by Richard Sale. Screenplay, Richard Sale and Jerry Gruskin from original by Thomas R. St. George; camera, John MacBurnie; music, Richard Sale, J. P. Knight; editor, Arthur Roberts. Tradeshown in N. Y., Jan. 23, '48. Running time, **61 MINS.**

Skipper Hughes.............Lyn Wilde
Patricia Hughes............Lee Wilde
Bessie Ormsbee.............Adele Mara
Robert Watson..............Richard Crane
Richard Adams..............Hal Hackett
Busby Ormsbee..............Wilson Wood
Dean Carson...............Stephanie Bachelor
Junior Ormsbee.............Teddy Infuhr
Senator Hughes............Edwin Maxwell
Dr. Shumway................Boyd Irwin
Polly Walker...............Kay Morley
Benjie Briggs..............Charles Smith
Motorcycle Cop.............Edward Gargan
Waitress..................Maxine Semon
Messenger..................Wm. H. Simon, Jr.

Starting out like a typical Hollywood campus comedy, with the usual corn and hokum, "Campus Honeymoon" builds into a fairly amusing comedy. Despite lightweight marquee lure, it should serve as fine support on most twin bills. Lyn and Lee Wilde, as the two sisters who figure importantly in the story, help make it an attractive production.

Yarn concerns two war veterans who are striving to carry on their college work after getting out of the army. Plot has the two husky youths agreeing to fake marriage with the two sisters in order to obtain two homes in a veterans housing project. Friendly enemies despite this arrangement of fake wedded bliss (boys live in one unit and girls in another), the sisters fall in love with the ex-GI's, and vice-versa. There is the usual complication when the couples can't dig up marriage licenses when the inevitable crisis arises.

The two Wilde girls sing well, and Richard Crane and Hal Hackett are passable with the few notes they warble. Both gals photograph flatteringly and perform adequately. Crane and Hackett, as the former servicemen, are lightweight with their thespian efforts. Adele Mara is vivacious as a breezy ex-WAC sergeant, while Wilson Wood, as her hubby, does nicely and sings in solid style. Teddy Infuhr makes something of a brat kid role.

Fanchon has given this nice production, with a firstrate screenplay by Richard Sale and Jerry Gruskin helping. Of the several tunes by Richard Sale, "How Does It Feel to Fall in Love?" and "Who's Got a Tent For Rent?" shape as the catchiest. J. P. Knight also contributes "Rocked in the Cradle of the Deep." *Wear.*

Angels Alley
Hollywood, Jan. 16.

Monogram release of Jan Grippo production. Stars Leo Gorcey; features Huntz Hall, Billy Benedict, David Gorcey, Frankie Darro, Nestor Paiva, Nelson Leigh, Geneva Gray, Rosemary La Planche. Directed by William Beaudine. Screenplay, Edmond Seward, Tim Ryan, Gerald Schnitzer; camera, Marcel LePicard; editor, William Austin. Previewed in Hollywood, Jan. 14, '48. Running time, **66 MINS.**

Slip Mahoney...............Leo Gorcey
Sach.......................Huntz Hall
Whitey.....................Billy Benedict
Chuck......................David Gorcey
Ricky......................Gabriel Dell
Jimmie.....................Frankie Darro
Tony Lucarno...............Nestor Paiva
Father O'Hanlon............Nelson Leigh
Josie O'Neill..............Geneva Gray
Daisy Harris........Rosemary La Planche
District Attorney..........John Eldredge
Mrs. Mahoney...............Mary Gordon
Jockey Burns...............Richard Paxton
Andy Miller................Buddy Gorman
Boomer.....................Tommie Menzies
"Jag" Harmon...............Benny Bartlett
Moose......................Dewey Robinson
Magistrate.................John H. Elliott

Felix Crowe........Robert Emmett Keane
Brian Watson...............William Ruhl
Mike......................Wade Crosby
Welder....................Meyer Grace

"Angels Alley" measures up as okay comedy-melodrama for the Bowery Boys' fans. Sparked by Leo Gorcey and Huntz Hall, the antics fit into the accepted pattern for the series and returns should stack up with others in the group.

This time Gorcey turns his attention to busting up a car-stealing ring that is making bad boys out of his sidewalk buddies. Script has an occasional sparkle and plotting is good. Besides the comedy mugging of Gorcey and Hall, there's a serious moment thrown in now and then, and William Beaudine's direction keeps it all moving for fast 66 minutes.

Nestor Paiva contributes the heavy work as racketeer who draws his car-stealing recruits from among the probationers, who are being turned into good citizens by the district priest. He has successfully foiled the police until he steps on Gorcey's toes. Latter makes short work of gathering enough evidence to assure a long jail term for Paiva.

In the cast are series regulars such as Billy Benedict, David Gorcey, Gabriel Dell, Frankie Darro, Mary Gordon and Benny Bartlett. Nelson Leigh enacts the priest, and femme spots fall to Geneva Gray and Rosemary La Planche.

Jan Grippo's production supervision obtains good values for small budget. Lensing and other technical credits are standard. *Brog.*

This Wine of Love
(SONGS)
(ITALIAN-MADE)

Superfilm release of Prora Film production. Directed by Mario Costa. Adaptation by Costa and C. Castelli from opera by Gaetano Donizetti; camera, Mario Bava; editor, Otello Colangeli; English commentary, Milton Cross. Previewed in N. Y., Jan. 22, '48. Running time, **75 MINS.**

Adina......................Nelly Corradi
Giannetta..................Loretta Di Lelio
Belcore....................Tito Gobbi
Nemorino..................Gino Sinimberghi
Dulcamara..................Italo Tajo

(In Italian; English Titles)

Another in the cycle of picturized operas being produced by Italian studios, "This Wine of Love" ("L'Elisir D'Amore") is a neatly-rendered film that will do solidly with the Italian-language trade, and music lovers in general. Gaetano Donizetti's celebrated comic opera has wit, charm and basketful of tuneful arias to provide excellent groundwork for the film.

This film, while being a faithful replica of the original, gets away from the confining limitations of the opera stage and makes full use of the camera's mobility. The settings are large and deep, while direction cleverly stresses pace and action, letting the music take good care of itself. For English-language audiences, a commentary by Milton Cross is supplied at the opening and at the one-act curtain. This pic could be greatly improved if this addition was cut since the narration adds nothing except a pompous, artificial tone. Good English titling permits close following of the score.

Cast has that happy parlay of looks, vocal brilliance and thesping talent. As Adina, the young coquette who teases her lovers to distraction, Nelly Corradi is a delightful lyric soprano very easy on the eyes. Gino Sinimberghi as the cow-eyed lover whose inheritance successful substitutes for lack of social graces, has a mellow tenor and registers as a creditable actor. One of the standout operatic stars is Italo Tajo, a basso playing the role of the charlatan medicineman who dispenses the elixir which finally brings the lovers together. Rest of the cast are uniformly excellent. Important assists are also made by the chorus, informally assembled as townsfolk.

Film was apparently shot without sound, with voices dubbed in later. Minor defect of the pic is the lack of technical dexterity with which the dubbing was handled. *Herm.*

Panhandle

Hollywood, Jan. 23.

Allied Artists (Monogram) release of John C. Champion-Blake Edwards production. Stars Rod Cameron; features Cathy Downs, Reed Hadley, Anne Gwynne, Blake Edwards. Directed by Lesley Selander. Screenplay, Edwards and Champion; camera, Harry Neumann; music, Red Dunn; editor, Richard Heermance. Previewed in Hollywood, Jan. 20, '48. Running time, 84 MINS.

John Sands....................Rod Cameron
Dusty Stewart....................Cathy Downs
Matt Garson....................Reed Hadley
June O'Carroll....................Anne Gwynne
Floyd Schofield....................Blake Edwards
Elliott....................Dick Crockett
Sheriff....................Rory Mallinson
Barber....................Charles Judels
McBride....................Alex Gerry
Crump....................Francis McDonald
Doc Cooper....................J. Farrell MacDonald
Wells....................Henry Hall
Tyler....................Stanley Andrews
Jack....................Jeff York
Harland....................James Harrison
Juan....................Charles LaTorre
Regan....................Frank Dae

As a first production for two newcomers to film making, "Panhandle" registers well. It has plenty of strong action, an interesting story, although with some characters slightly incongruous to the western period, is expertly played and beautifully lensed in sepia tones. While not of top calibre, film will give sturdy support in most situations and can carry the weight in smaller houses.

John C. Champion and Blake Edwards produced from their original screenplay. In addition, Edwards plays one of the principal heavies and does a good job of it.

The plot deals with a reformed gunman who again dons his six-shooters to avenge the murder of his brother. Rod Cameron gives a strong performance as the avenger. He makes it a virile character that could believably go through the several solid fight sequences that point up the action. There are two heroines, and this time the hero grabs off the more lively of the pair instead of the sweeter—a nice switch. He is pitted against Reed Hadley, who has ambitions to control a western territory. Cameron shoots his way through the gang with unexpectedly accurate gunfire and gives the top heavy a fatal dose of lead for the finale.

Hadley does a firstrate baddie with a suavely menacing air that registers. Anne Gwynne, in the surprising role of the villain's secretary during an era when male clerks were the order, nevertheless pleases and gets the hero in the end. Cathy Downs also shows up well as the sweeter femme. Edwards is good as the baby-faced killer for Hadley, and others are okay.

Lesley Selander's direction keeps the plot on the move. Film, however, is not the usual western for the kiddies. The hero takes too many slugs of hard liquor and lavishes too many kisses on Miss Gwynne to be pure Saturday matinee filmfare.

Outdoor backgrounds and action are expertly photographed by Harry Neumann. Editing, music score, and other contributions give the picture neat values. *Brog.*

The Lucky Bride

(Color; Songs)

(SOVIET-MADE)

Artkino release of Mosfilm production. Story and direction, Igor Savchenko; songs, Sergei Potonky and Dmitri Fliangoltz; camera, Eugene Andrikanis. At Stanley, N. Y., Jan. 24, '48. Running time, 62 MINS.

Ivan Mordashov....................Makoim Shtraukh
His Daughter....................Elena Shvetsova
Maid....................Anna Lysianskaya
Lt. Fadeyev....................Nikolai Gritsenko
Faddei....................Sergei Stoltarov
Rich Aunt....................Alexandra Panova

(In Russian; English Titles)

"The Lucky Bride" is unadulterated escapist stuff. It's a costume romance with music, seasoned with slapstick comedy. It's moderately entertaining, but has little apparent boxoffice draw, except for Russian-speaking audiences, whose appreciation of the dialog was audible at the show caught.

The picture is localed in Moscow just after the defeat of Napoleon. The costumes of that era, plus the many panoramas of Moscow and the handsome indoor scenes, provide rich material for the color photography, which is effectively done. However, some of the outdoor settings are palpably synthetic.

The story is about a fat, middle-class widower who must marry off his daughter to someone with the initials A. F., so she can inherit the fortune of a rich aunt. It seems the latter was once engaged to a man with the same initials, so all her silverware, linens and personal possessions are thus marked, and she's determined they must go to someone appropriately named.

The girl, of course, falls in love with a man who happens to be suitably named, but there's the traditional amount of complication, misunderstanding, etc., before the surprise switch and somewhat puzzling (to anyone not understanding the language, for the titles don't make it quite clear) denouement and happy ending.

Elena Shvetsova and Nikolai Gritsenko are properly ardent as the romantic leads, and they have several pleasant songs together. Anna Lysianskaya and Sergei Stolarov are broadly comic as the supporting romantic leads, and also have song and dance numbers together. Makoim Shtraukh plays the pompous father comparatively straight, and Alexandra Panova gives a clowning portrayal of the coy aunt. *Hobe.*

Kings of the Olympics

(Documentary)

Westport International release. Editors, Joseph Lerner, Max Rosenbaum; narrator, Bill Slater. Previewed in N. Y., Jan. 23, '48. Running time, 60 MINS.

Lensed by some 600 cameramen at the 1936 Olympics in Berlin, this film has been cut from the original three-hour footage shown in the U. S. initially at the Museum of Modern Art, N. Y. Reports that several major companies are hankering to distribute this feature commercially are fully justified by its thrilling recapture of that last great international sports competition. Timeliness of the pic is heightened by worldwide preparations for the Olympic games this year.

This film is more than just a simple run-through of the various contests. It's a superbly photographed spectacle, full of heart-pounding excitement. Bill Slater's commentary is good, never tipping off the results while pointing out important details of the action. Excellent score contributes to the overall excitement.

Neatly edited for U. S. consumption, film accents the track and field contests in which such greats as Jesse Owens, Ralph Metcalfe, Earle Meadows, Ken Carpenter and others were supreme. Rarely has a sports picture captured the muscle tone, the facial tension and the grim will-to-win of athletes.

In the high jump competition, where the bar is shown going up two inches at a time, the audience will almost crack under the strain of the rivalry which narrowed down finally to Ken Carpenter of the U. S. and a Japanese. The latter's imperturbable face is shown clouded with indecision and fear just as he takes off on his final miss; then Carpenter hurtled over in a desperate lunge to win the event.

In the 1,500-meter race the hot fight between Jack Lovelace of New Zealand and Glenn Cunningham is recorded step by step. Jesse Owens, in the 100-meter run, and Ralph Metcalfe in the 800 meters are shown running away from the field.

Audience will get a kick out of seeing athletes with the Nazi swastika emblem across their chests being trounced by Owens and Metcalfe. Other events covered include the 400-meter run, running broad jump, javelin throw, discus throw, women's diving, boat races and four-oared and eight-oared shell races. *Herm.*

Design for Death

(Documentary)

Hollywood, Jan. 24.

RKO release of Theron Warth and Richard O. Fleischer production. Narrated by Kent Smith and Hans Conried. Written for the screen by Theodor S. and Helen Geisel; special effects, Russell A. Cully; montage, Harold Palmer; music, Paul Sawtell; film research, I. Kleinerman, John Stratford; editors, Elmo Williams, Marston Fay. Tradeshown in Holylwood, Jan. 22, '48. Running time, 48 MINS.

That war's a racket is well illustrated in "Design For Death." A documentary compiled from confiscated Japanese film, picture fastens war guilt on the Bushido and throws a thin whitewash over the ordinary Jap citizen. Footage also illustrates, uncomfortably, that the pattern for war has been followed by too many other nationalities for any one country to be completely exonerated.

The average filmgoer will brush aside picture's message, but there is an interest in the way producers Theron Warth and Richard O. Fleischer have cleverly handled the compilation. "Design" was put together from footage released in the public interest by the Alien Property Custodian. It all depicts Japanese history from before its feudal days right through to the atomic bomb.

It stresses the way the leaders duped the ordinary guy with force, propaganda, thought control, etc., to make him into a willing tool of aggression. Theodor S. and Helen Geisel have written a strong narration, and the reading by Kent Smith and Hans Conried is punchy. Music score, special effects, montage, editing and other credits are good.

Miniature Reviews

"A Miracle Can Happen" (UA-Bogeaus - Meredith). Whimsy with Goddard - Meredith - Stewart - Fonda - James - Lamour - Moore-MacMurray. How can it miss?

"Saigon" (Par). Sturdy adventure-romance, with names of Alan Ladd, Veronica Lake for marquee.

"If You Knew Susie" (Songs) (RKO). Eddie Cantor-Joan Davis in pleasant comedy that should do okay.

"The Sign Of the Ram" (Col). Leisurely-paced domestic drama for femme trade.

"Woman From Tangier" (Col). Adele Jergens in melodramatic whodunit; fine support on twinners.

"Black Bart" (Color) (U). Actionful western. Will give good account of itself.

"The Idiot" (French) (Lelarge-E.C.D.). Good adaptation of Dostoievsky classic, for okay art-house biz.

"Daughter of Darkness" (Par) (British). Taut psychological murder story. Good British draw; some U.S. appeal.

"The Hunted" (Mono). Dull melodrama for secondaries.

"Laugh, Pagliacci" (Songs) (Italian). Fine version of the Leoncavallo opera, with Alida Valli, Beniamino Gigli. Good arthouse draw.

"Western Heritage" (RKO). Tim Holt western with okay prospects in straight action houses.

"Smart Politics" (Songs) (Mono). Another of Monogram's Teenagers pix. Pleasant supporting fare.

"Passionnelle" (French). French-made meller has enough spice to make it first-rate for foreign-language spots.

"Brighton Rock" (ABP). British-made gangster meller should do mildly in U.S.

"Easy Money" (Rank) (British). Good English grosser on football pools; mild U. S. appeal.

"Bohemian Rapture" (Artkino). First big Czech production since end of war; disappointing; for foreign-language houses strictly.

"Les Jeux Sont Faits" (Pathe). French-made Jean Paul Sarte film of after-world good U.S. art-house draw.

A Miracle Can Happen

(SONGS)

United Artists release of Benedict Bogeaus-Burgess Meredith production. Stars Paulette Goddard, Burgess Meredith, James Stewart, Henry Fonda, Dorothy Lamour, Victor Moore, Harry James and Fred MacMurray; features William Demarest, Eduardo Ciannelli, Hugh Herbert, Charles D. Brown, Dorothy Ford, Carl Switzer, Eilene Janssen, Betty Caldwell, Frank Moran and David Whorf. Directed by King Vidor and Leslie Fenton. Screenplay, Laurence Stallings and Lou Breslow, from original story by Arch Oboler; James Stewart-Henry Fonda material by John 'Hara; camera, Edward Cronjager, Joseph Biroc, Gordon Avil, John Seitz; editor, James Smith; music, Heinz Roemheld; music supervision, David Chudnow and Skitch Henderson; songs, Skitch Henderson and Donald Kahn, Frank Loesser; arrangements, Henry Russell. Sneak-previewed at Warner theatre, N. Y., Jan. 29, '48. Running time, 107 MINS.

Oliver Pease....................Burgess Meredith
Martha Pease....................Paulette Goddard
Al....................Fred MacMurray
Elisha Hobbs....................Hugh Herbert
Slim....................James Stewart
Gloria Manners....................Dorothy Lamour
Ashton Carrington....................Victor Moore

Peggy Thorndyke	Eilene Janssen
Lank	Henry Fonda
Floyd	William Demarest
Lola	Dorothy Ford
An Editor	Charles D. Brown
Cynthia	Betty Caldwell
Sniffles Dugan	David Whorf
A Bookie	Frank Moran
Deputy Sheriff	Tom Fadden
Another Deputy	Paul Hurst

No matter what one might think of "A Miracle Can Happen," he'd be clamoring for the big man with the tight white coat if he said this pic couldn't do biz. All you have to do is take a gander at the list of names in the production credits. The fact that this attempt at whimsy doesn't always come off is incidental; the paying customers can read pretty well, and those names stand out pretty boldly.

Just look at 'em! The pic opens with a pair of surefire names like Goddard and Meredith—and in bed, too.

Then Stewart, Fonda, and Harry James. Plus Lamour and Victor Moore, in a Hollywood satire, or how the sarong became famous. Followed by Fred MacMurray and William Demarest. All in episodic sequences detailing what an inquiring reporter encounters when he seeks to have answered the question of how a child influenced the lives of a group of selected adults.

Meredith is the reporter, so-called. Actually he's only a classified-ad solicitor for a newspaper. But he's lied to his recent bride; he's told her he's the inquiring reporter. Through a subterfuge, however, he assumes the mantle of the paper's actual I.R., a longtime ambition, for just this one question. The film's story comprises a series of episodes telling of the reporter meeting his assorted public, their narratives being told in flashback.

"Miracle" has some amusing whimsy, namely one involving Dorothy Lamour and Victor Moore, in which each is shown as a Hollywood extra, the former later achieving stardom through her inadvertent use of a sarong in a test. The "child" who influences the change in her career was a moppet star who urged her director to give Miss Lamour a test.

James Stewart and Henry Fonda tell of a "child" influence in their lives—only this time it's a big "baby" —a twentyish beaut who, their story reveals, upset their applecart years before when they toured as musicians with a band. The details here are fairly amusing. Harry James works into this episode as a judge of a trumpet contest.

Least interesting is the episode involving Fred MacMurray and William Demarest in their encounter with a brat during their itinerant travels as con-men.

All of this wrapped up by the inquiring reporter for his paper and, of course, it's all so good that the editor actually gives him the job permanently. And the child's influence that is greatest is the one that his wife tells him will soon be their own.

The cast couldn't have been better. The story's execution falters because a scene here and there is inclined to strive too much for its whimsical effect. But Meredith responds capitally to the mood of the character he plays, being given more of a chance to do so than any of the other stars. Of the supporting players, there is Demarest for his usually competent performance along with other fine characterizations by young David Whorf, son of Richard Whorf, as the brat, and Charles D. Brown, the editor.

King Vidor and Leslie Fenton shared the direction, and it was no easy job to dovetail the individual sequences into a single entity. But this they achieved to a considerable degree. The fault lies in the failure of some of the episodes to achieve as plausible an acceptance as whimsy could permit under the circumstances. *Kahn.*

Saigon

Hollywood, Feb. 2.

Paramount release of P. J. Wolfson production. Stars Alan Ladd, Veronica Lake; features Douglas Dick, Wally Cassell, Luther Adler, Morris Carnovsky, Mikhail Rasumny. Directed by Leslie Fenton. Screenplay, P. J. Wolfson, Arthur Sheekman; based on story by Julian Zimet; camera, John F. Seitz; music score, Robert Emmett Dolan; editor, William Shea. Tradeshown in Hollywood Feb. 2, '48. Running time, **93 MINS.**

Major Larry Briggs	Alan Ladd
Susan Cleaver	Veronica Lake
Captain Mike Perry	Douglas Dick
Sergt. Pete Rocco	Wally Cassell
Lieut. Keon	Luther Adler
Alex Maris	Morris Carnovsky
Clerk	Mikhail Rasumny
Simon	Luis Van Rooten
Boat Captain	Eugene Borden

Alan Ladd fans and other followers of high adventure will like "Saigon." It's strictly pulp-fiction stuff but done with a flare for good characterizations and plenty of action. P. J. Wolfson, in his production and coscripting chore with Arthur Sheekman, has paid close attention to the little details that will catch audience interest.

Performers' characters are well-established and they know what to do with them under Leslie Fenton's able direction. Latter keeps the action high and the interest unflagging in telling the saga of three ex-Army fliers who go adventuring in Saigon with a beautiful blonde.

Script, based on a story by Julian Zimet, deals with a flier who has only a few months to live, the result of a crash. His two buddies keep the bad news from him and they all decide to take a last fling in the Orient. Trio, expecting to fly a rich man to Saigon, end up, instead, with his blonde secretary carrying a brief-case full of cash. The doomed man falls in love, another cross for his buddies to bear, and they force the femme, on threat of exposure to the police, to play along.

There's a load of menacing and mysterious characters, a plane crash, a jungle boatride and lushly backgrounded Saigon to point up action and intrigue before finale. Music score aids plotting, and camera work is sharp in depicting settings.

Ladd is at home as the ex-Army flier who, with Wally Cassell, tries to ease the last days of Douglas Dick. Cassell adds considerable as a happy-go-lucky air sergeant, selling plenty of chuckles. Dick equals the other two for honors. Miss Lake aptly fits the blonde siren role. Carefully valued character studies are turned in by Luther Adler, a detective; Mikhail Rasumny, hotel clerk; Morris Carnovsky, the rich man; Luis Van Rooten, gunman, and Eugene Borden, boat captain.

Editing holds picture to 93 minutes without leaving story holes. Photographic effects, process shots, costumes and other production details are excellent. *Brog.*

If You Knew Susie

(SONGS)

RKO release of Eddie Cantor production. (Jack J. Gross, executive producer). Stars Cantor and Joan Davis; features Allyn Joslyn, Charles Dingle and Bobby Driscoll. Directed by Gordon M. Douglas (Maxwell Henry, assistant director; screenplay, Warren Wilson and Oscar Brodney; additional dialog, Bud Pearson and Lester A. White; songs, B.G. de Sylva and Joseph Meyer, Jimmy McHugh and Harold Adamson, George Tibbles and Ramirez Idriss; musical score, Edgar "Cookie" Fairchild; musical director, C. Bakaleinikoff; camera, Frank Redman; editor, Philip Martin. Previewed at Normandie theatre, N.Y., Jan. 29, '48. Running time, 90 mins.

Sam Parker	Eddie Cantor
Susie Parker	Joan Davis
Mike Garrett	Allyn Joslyn
Mr. Whitley	Charles Dingle
Joe Collins	Phil Brown
Steve Garland	Sheldon Leonard
Zero Zantini	Joe Sawyer
Marty	Douglas Fowley
Marjorie Parker	Margaret Kerry
Handy Clinton	Dick Humphreys
Mr. Clinton	Howard Freeman
Grandma	Mabel Paige
Count Alexis	Sig Ruman
Chez Henri	Fritz Feld
Mrs. Clinton	Isabel Randolph

And Bobby Driscoll

With Eddie Cantor as both producer and star, "If You Knew Susie" should do well enough in the family houses. There's nothing here of really sock value, but the family aura of this comedy, in which Cantor and Joan Davis are co-starred, should help it do business.

There's little here that Cantor hasn't done in one form or another for many years, whether it's been in radio, musicomedy or pictures. However, there's a certain relish and zest with which he and Miss Davis go about their chores that help minimize its familiarity.

The yarn is about a vaudeville husband-wife team (Cantor and Miss Davis) who retire to settle down in their home town, a burg of snobbishness and who's who. But the ex-vauders and their two children, unable to live up to the supposed rep established by one of their Revolutionary forebears, are ostracized. There's the discovery, then, that the government owes the family billions of dollars via some rather complicated inheritance maneuver, but the complications all iron themselves out rather patly when Cantor disavows his monetary heritage because the money and its attendant publicity were breaching the family happiness. And, of course, their social standing is regained.

Cantor sings the title song, and other standards, plus rolling his eyes as usual; Miss Davis mugs as only she knows how—so what more can one ask? Unless it's such usual urbane fol-de-rol as the two principals being involved with some thugs in a Keystone Kops-type of chase, etc. Allyn Joslyn, Charles Dingle and little Bobby Driscoll handle lesser roles competently, as do Sheldon Leonard and Joe Sawyer, as a couple of plug-uglies. *Kahn.*

The Sign of the Ram

Columbia release of Irving Cummings, Jr., production. Stars Susan Peters, Alexander Knox, Phyllis Thaxter, Peggy Ann Garner, Ron Randell, Dame May Whitty, Allene Roberts; features Ross Ford, Diana Douglas. Directed by John Sturges. Screenplay, Charles Bennett; based on novel by Margaret Ferguson; camera, Burnett Guffey; editor, Aaron Stell; musical director, M.W. Stoloff. Tradeshown, N.Y., Jan. 30, '48. Running time 84 MINS.

Leah St. Aubyn	Susan Peters
Mallory St. Aubyn	Alexander Knox
Sherida Binyon	Phyllis Thaxter
Christine St. Aubyn	Peggy Ann Garner
Dr. Simon Crowdy	Ron Randell
Clara Brastock	Dame May Whitty
Jane St. Aubyn	Allene Roberts
Logan St. Aubyn	Ross Ford
Catherine Woolton	Diana Douglas
Emily	Margaret Tracy
Perowen	Paul Scardon
Reverend Woolton	Gerald Hamer
Mrs. Woolton	Doris Lloyd

Marking Susan Peters' return to the screen since she lost the use of her legs in a hunting accident several years ago, "Sign of the Ram" is a leisurely-paced meller slanted for the femme trade. Obscure title and middling marquee values, however, will limit the distaff b.o. reaction to just-fair levels.

Miss Peters showed lots of pluck in accepting a role that, far from stirring any sympathy, turns her into a malignant personality whose ultimate come-uppance is the pic's chief interest. Inadequate scripting job, however, lacks details for a plot buildup and fails to draw a consistent character in which the actress can feel wholly at ease. Monotone direction by John Sturges doesn't help either in generating a consistent tempo to grip attention.

Opening calmly in an apparently happy English household, yarn suddenly dips into psycho waters with suggestions that a well-disguised mad woman is ruling the roost. Miss Peters, wife of Alexander Knox and foster-mother to his three grown children, is confined to a wheelchair but through a powerful will exercises complete domination over the family. As explained by an amateur astrologist in the pic, she was born under the sign of the Ram, which means trouble.

As a benevolent tyrant, she breaks up a love affair involving one daughter and drives the son's fiancee to a suicide attempt. Gradually, the family becomes wised up to her true nature and escapes from her overloving clutches. Lonely and frustrated, she finally wheels herself over the cliffs.

As far as permitted by her lines, Miss Peters registers with a solid performance, shading with subtlety her transitions from sweetness to poisonous jealousy. As the husband, Knox draws a neat, credible portrait of a good-hearted fellow slightly baffled by events around him. Peggy Ann Garner carries off well a tough assignment as the youngest daughter twisted by the family atmosphere. Rest of the cast contribute important assists in lesser roles.

Production is also marked by excellent settings, clear, deep-focussed lensing and a good musical score that lends atmospheric quality. *Herm.*

Shades of Gray

(DOCUMENTARY)

U. S. Army Pictorial Service production (Frank J. Payne, producer). Directed by Joseph E. Henabery. Script, John B. Davenport and Mortimer Offner; camera, Gerald Hirschfeld: editor, Eric Lawrence; technical advisers, Dr. George Goldman, Lt. Col. M. C. Res., and Lt. Col. Frank Drake. Previewed at the U. S. Army Signal Crops Photographic Center, Astoria, L. I., Jan. 29, '48. Running time, **67 MINS.**

Cast: Sandy Campbell, Ed Kreisler, Paul Larson, Hal Vinson, John Leighton, Lewis Howard, Tom Nello, Bob Knight, Michael Higgins, Berton Tripp, Bill Hollandbeck, Ewing Mitchell, Neil McMahon, Hal Conklin, Ray Rahner, Harry Hennessy.

Army's treatment of officers and men who suffered neuropsychiatric breakdowns during World War II, as revealed through faithfully re-created case histories, is vividly shown in "Shades of Gray." The film was rushed to completion shortly before the end of 1947 to become the entry of the Army Pictorial Service for an Academy award in the documentary class. It's a worthy contender.

While the picture is ostensibly for showing to professional audiences, both in and out of the Army, and to special interest groups, it's no secret that it was also designed with an eye on possible regular theatrical release. Unfortunately, however, while extremely interesting and informative, the treatment of the theme is such that it seems hardly suitable for general theatrical showing. It no doubt, however, will find large appreciative lay audiences among special groups and perhaps in some limited art theatre exhibition.

Picture's possibility for widespread distribution is interesting because of its genesis. It came about as the result of a smashing film on Army psychiatry, "Let There Be Light," made at the end of the war by Holywood writer-director John Huston (then in the Army). It was produced solely for military professional use, but there was a clamor among civilians who saw it for general release.

Actual cases, however, were pictured. Inasmuch as the film could be construed by its unwitting actors as a serious invasion of their privacy and might do them tremendous harm if seen in hometowns where they are now living normal lives, Army nixed the idea of public release. As a result, it was decided to use professional players in a recreation of "Let There Be Light" and several other films made solely for Army personnel, primarily "Combat Psychiatry."

As might be expected, no re-enacte' film can have the power and sense of human drama inherent in the original. While "Light" was gripping to the point of being breathtaking, "Gray" is pedantic by unavoidable comparison, although considerable additional meritorious material has been added to it.

Title is pretty much an explanation of the film's aim. No one's mental or emotional balance, it succinctly demonstrates via animation, is 100% perfect. Nervous systems are all just a variation of a shade of gray between pure black and pure white. How much shock and upset they'll withstand hinges on a combination of the "shade of gray" to start with and the strain under which they are put.

One of the aspects in attaining a "light shade," or good emotional balance, is the mother's treatment of her offspring in infancy and early childhood to give him a sense of security and self-assurance. Lives of several boys are traced in the picture from infancy up to their Army experiences to show why one breaks down under simple anxieties, while the other doesn't suffer severe neuroses until he has been subjected to deadly fire in a lonely shellhole for days.

Treatment of the cases—undoubtedly idealized — by Army psychiatrists at the front and in various echelons back to large special hospitals in the U. S. is shown. Lay audiences will undoubtedly be amazed when they see right before their eyes cures effected by narcosynthesis (narcotic drugs), hypnotism, electro-therapy and simple psychiatry. Despite their medical veracity, undoubtedly some of these miracle cures will find disbelievers.

A major defect of the film is a grayness of its own in choosing its point and sticking to it. It's frequently too divergent from its "shades of gray" thesis and puts too much emphasis (certainly from an Army public relations standpoint) in that cures are effected merely to get a man back into the front line again. Greater emphasis rather should be on the theme that there is no reason for stigma to be attached to mental patients. It could happen to anyone. Application today should be to making good civilians out of the sufferers, rather than good combat soldiers.

With a few exceptions, acting is excellent throughout, especially by "patients" Sandy Campbell, Paul Larson, John Leighton, Lewis Howard and Tom Nello. Some of the actors are civilian professionals and some enlisted men assigned to the Photographic Center. Direction by Joseph E. Henabery, vet Hollywood and documentary director, is topnotch all the way for keeping a rapid pace and at the same time getting from his players the carefully-shaded emotional responses required. He directed the film on a contract basis. Also a civilian, but a fulltime Army employee, is producer Frank J. Payne, who does a firstrate job of bringing the difficult elements together to achieve drama, please the Army and stick rigidly to limitations imposed by psychiatrist-technical advisers.

Film was shot at the Army hospital at Northport, Long Island, and on the stages at Astoria. It is, technically, a thoroughly professional job all the way. *Herb.*

Woman From Tangier

Columbia release of Martin Mooney production. Features Adele Jergens, Stephen Dunne, Denis Green, Ian MacDonald. Directed by Harold Daniels. Screenplay, Irwin Franklyn; camera, Henry Freulich; editor, Richard Fantl. At New York, N. Y., starting Jan. 27, '48. Running time, 6[illegible] MINS.

Nylon........Adele Jergens
Ray Shapley........Stephen Dunne
Ned Rankin........Michael Duane
Capt. Graves........Denis Green
Rocheau........Ivan Tiesault
Purquit........Curt Bois
Paul Moreles........Ian MacDonald
Flo-Flo........Donna Demario
LeDeux........Anton Kosta
Martine........Maurice Marsac

"The Woman From Tangier," a moderate budgeter from Columbia, proves a lusty melodrama, played with all the stops out. It has some implausibilities but not enough to detract as fairly exciting fare. It's a cinch as a dual-bill backer-upper.

From the time a ship's captain, in harbor at Tangier, bumps off his purser over 50,000 pounds, the story is a succession of fast-moving events. Yarn has the chief crook parachuting from a plane after bumping off his pilot while 3,000 feet in the air. An insurance agent from N. Y., interested because of the theft from a boat insured by his firm, helps the native gendarmes solve the double slaying and robbery.

The woman in the case is a comely cafe entertainer who goes straight long enough to tip off the cops on the hideout for the brains of the gang. Adele Jergens plays this role with certainty. Ian MacDonald is a life-like tough gangster boss. Denis Green is smooth enough as the crooked British captain, while the supporting cast is headed by Stephen Dunne and Robert Taour.

Harold Daniels maintains a swift pace, directing to obtain a maximum of suspenseful moments. *Wear.*

Black Bart

(COLOR)

Hollywood, Jan. 31.

Universal release of Leonard Goldstein production. Stars Yvonne DeCarlo, Dan Duryea, Jeffrey Lynn; features Percy Kilbride. Directed by George Sherman. Screenplay, Luci Ward, Jack Natteford, William Bowers; original story, Luci Ward, Natteford; camera (Technicolor), Irving Glassberg; music, Leith Stevens; editor, Russell Schoengarth. Previewed in Hollywood, Jan. 27, '48. Running time, 80 MINS.

Lola Montez........Yvonne DeCarlo
Charles E. Boles........Dan Duryea
Lance Hardeen........Jeffrey Lynn
Jersey Brady........Percy Kilbride
Sheriff Gordon........Lloyd Gough
Lorimer........Frank Lovejoy
Clark........John McIntire
J. T. Hall........Don Beddoe
MacFarland........Ray Walker
Teresa........Soledad Jimenez
Mason........Eddy C. Waller
Mrs. Harmon........Anne O'Neal
Indian........Chief Many Treaties

Western plot of "Black Bart" has been given romantic trappings and beautiful color. It adds up to first-rate entertainment, and b.o. returns will be excellent, particularly outside the key-city firstruns. Film is first for Leonard Goldstein as a Universal - International producer, and he has delivered lushly mounted, actionful outdoor melodrama.

George Sherman got plenty of punch and suspense into his direction, making every scene move swiftly. Stars Yvonne DeCarlo, Dan Duryea and Jeffrey Lynn justify their top billing with sturdy performances. Script has taken standard western ingredients, given them a slightly sophisticated twist for adult interest, plus other intelligent use of the material to sustain attention.

For once, two male leads, both carrying audience sympathy, get their just desserts—a hot dose of lead —as a reward for their likeable, but lawless, ways. A reformation of either character would have been a letdown. Duryea, Lynn and Percy Kilbride make a neat trio of western hoods, taking their gold where they find it—even if it belongs to a buddy. Film opens with a hanging party, from which Duryea and Lynn are rescued by Kilbride. They part but meet again in California, where Duryea has established himself as a respectable rancher whose sideline is a yen for Wells Fargo gold which he steals under the guise of one Black Bart.

His former partners spot his Mr. Hyde character and figure to do some hijacking but windup has Kilbride safely behind bars and the two toughies on the losing end of a gun battle with the sheriff's posse. It's not all formidable, though. There's plenty of humor sprinkled around to spring an occasional chuckle, and Miss DeCarlo lends femme charm as Lola Montez, herself a gal who didn't mind a bag of gold dust, no matter how come by. She has two dance numbers that do not halt the action, and otherwise she fills all demands.

Kilbride injects his dry humor expertly. In supporting roles, Lloyd Gough, Don Beddoe, Ray Walker and others are capable. Irving Glassberg's camera captures scenic beauties. Music score by Leith Stevens ably backs the action. Editing and all other contributions are sturdy. *Brog.*

The Idiot

(FRENCH-MADE)

Andre Lelarge-E.C.D. release of Sacha Gordine production. *stars Gerard Philippe, Edwige Feuillere; features Marguerite Moreno, Lucian Coedel, Nathalie Nattier. Directed by Georges Lampin. Screenplay, Charles Spaak, based on novel by Dostoyevsky; camera, Christine Matras; music, Maurice Thiriet, V. deButzow. Tradeshown N.Y., Jan. 28, '48. Running time, 90 mins.

Muichkine........Gerard Philippe
Nastasia Philipovna........Edwige Feuillere
General's Wife,........Marguerite Moreno
Rogogine........Lucien Coedel
Aglae........Nathalie Nattier
Totsky........Debucourt
Ceneral Epantchine........Chambreuil
Gania........Michael Andre

(In French; English Titles)

Producer Sacha Gordine evidently lavished painstaking care on this adaptation of the Dostoievsky classic, imbuing it with a standout cast and some excellent production values. With Dostoievsky's name as the chief marquee lure, it'll do well in the art houses. Its chances for other audiences in the U.S., though, are practically nil.

Chief factor militating against "Idiot" is the belabored story involved in the novel itself. Scripter Charles Spaak managed to point up the Christ-like quality of Prince Muichkine, the lead character, and his effects on others in the story, but failed to crystallize sufficiently the religious theme of the novel—submersion of the good by the hypocrisy and evil of the bad. What should have been a dramatic climax, consequently, emerges as an uninspired denouement sans punch or reason.

Until the final reel, however, Spaak handled his adaptation job well. With the screenplay following the basic pattern of the novel, Muichkine is painted with subtle strokes as the youth whose mental illness has given him a naive simplicity, yet a deep perception. Returning from a Swiss institution to his Russian birthplace, he's dragged immediately into the intrigues of those with whom he comes in contact, all of whom consider him queer because of his insight into their innermost feelings.

Two women fall in love with him. The pure one he saves from a marriage fostered by her parents but loses her because of her innate human jealousy. The other one, who recognizes in him her only means of salvation, is killed at the hands of her jealous lover. Still a child mentally, he realizes that he doesn't inspire faith enough to overcome human foibles. Film closes with him sobbing at his now-realized futility.

Actors, with their work cut out for them, are uniformly excellent under the fine directorial touch of Georges Lampin. Gerard Philippe lends some finely-shaded thesping to his role of the prince and resembles the common conception of Christ sufficiently to leave no doubt as to his character. Edwige Fueillere, as the "fallen woman," is both fiery and subdued at the right places, managing to evoke considerable sympathy with a difficult part. Lucien Coedel, as the boorish tradesman lover, is excellent, as is Marguerite Moreno as the mother of the "pure woman." Nathalie Nattier is a little too saccharine in the latter role. Debucourt, as Totsky; Chambreuil, as the general, and Michel Andre, as the weakling secretary, are fine.

Despite the fact the film was produced last year in Paris in the midst of tremendous economic difficulties, Gordine limned it with lush-looking production accoutrements. Sets, particularly the exteriors, are neatly-executed. Christian Matras' camera work is consistently good, and the score, by Maurice Thiriet and V. de-Butow, ties in neatly with the film's varying moods. English titles are adequate but the editing job, sans film credit, has left the picture extremely choppy in spots. *Stal.*

Daughter of Darkness

(BRITISH-MADE)

London, Jan. 22.

Paramount release of Alliance Studio—Victor Hanbury production. Stars Anne Crawford, Maxwell Reed. Directed by Lance Comfort; screenplay, Max Catto from his play, "They Walk Alone." Editor, Lito Carruthers; music, Clifton Parker; camera, Bernie Lewis. At Carlton, London, Jan. 21, '48. Running timne, 91 mins.

Bess Stanforth........Anne Crawford
Dan........Maxwell Reed
Emmy Baudine........Siobhan McKenna
Larry Tallent........Grant Tyler
Julie Tallent........Honor Blackman
Robert Stanforth........Barry Morse
Mr. Tallent........George Thorpe
Saul Trevithick........Denis Gordon
Father Corcoran........Laim Redmond
Jacob........Arthur Hambling
David Price........David Greene
Parishoners........Nora O'Mahoney, Ann Clery

Max Catto's play, "They Walk Alone," produced in 1938, dealt with an unusual and difficult subject, a homicidal nymphomaniac. It took courage to attempt a screen version, but all concerned have come out with flying colors. The playwright converted his original work into a good script, and producer Victor Hanbury and director Lance Comfort have turned out a firstrate adult picture.

Picture grips from the first moment and holds throughout. It may be grim in days when the public is longing for laughs, but it should play to good business, more on word-of-mouth publicity than on any star values. With a little tightening up it should find a place in U. S. theatres catering to adult tastes.

The cast was chosen with particular care. Brunt of the playing falls on Siobhan McKenna. Graduate of Dublin's Abbey and Gate theatres, she made a fleeting appearance in "Hungry Hill," but registered well enough to be cast as the complex murderess who has to be alluring enough to attract men and demure enough to belie her true character. She gives a brilliant portrait of the strange, unbalanced creature about whom there's a fatal fascination.

As the woman who traps the murderess, Anne Crawford reveals true acting ability, and a newcomer, Honor Blackman, is excellent. Maxwell Reed gives his best performance to date, and Liam Redmond as an Irish priest and Nora O'Mahony and Ann Clery as two of his parishioners are memorable. Clifton Parker's music is a decided asset to the film.

Story opens in an Irish village where Miss McKenna works for a village priest. For all her simplicity, men find her irresistible, and the women, hating her, insist on the priest getting rid of her. Then follows a series of sordid adventures, with several of her lovers murdered, and the inevitable retribution. *Cane.*

The Hunted

Hollywood, Jan. 30.

Allied Artists (Monogram) release of Scott R. Dunlap production. Stars Preston Foster, Belita; features Pierre Watkin, Edna Holland, Russell Hicks, Frank Ferguson, Joseph Crehan. Directed by Jack Bernhard. Original story and screenplay, Steve Fisher; camera, Harry Neumann; music score, Edward J. Kay; editor, Richard Heermance. Previewed in Hollywood, Jan. 29, '48. Running time, 8[illegible] MINS.

Saxon........Preston Foster
Laura........Belita
Simon Rand........Pierre Watkin
Miss Turner........Edna Holland

Meredith	Russell Hicks
Harrison	Frank Ferguson
Police Captain	Joseph Crehan
Hollis Smith	Larry Blake
Sally	Cathy Carter
Detectives	Thomas Jackson, Charles McGraw, Tristram Coffin

"The Hunted" doesn't rate the Allied Artists releasing label. It's a dull, uninspired melodrama. With further trimming it will get by in the secondaries as supporting feature but otherwise will find the going tough. There is a try for production values with ice skating sequence by Belita. She's an eye-catcher on ice for grace and ability but single routine alone can't carry "Hunted."

Steve Fisher's original story had a good idea for a melodrama, but in the scripting, direction and playing it fails to come off. Pace is weary, as is the dialog, in telling of a detective who sends his fiance off to prison when she's framed for robbery. Out on parole, she's still pursued by him, and when she's framed again, this time for murder, he can't believe her innocent. It takes a knock on the head and a confession by the real murderer before he finally sees the light. Despite his bullheaded ways, he and the girl wind up in a finale clinch.

Jack Bernhard's direction doesn't have much to work with, and he fails to give it a lift. Scott R. Dunlap's production is stereotyped and often inept. Preston Foster as the detective walks through the role. Belita tries hard but only registers in the single ice scene. Others in the cast are adequate to demands.

Lensing and other technical functions are standard. *Brog.*

Laugh Pagliacci

(SONGS)

Continental release of Itala Films production. Directed by Guiseppe Fatigati. Stars Alida Valli, Banjamino Gigli. Story, Cesare Viola; music, Leoncavallo and Donizetti. Previewed in N.Y., Jan. 28, '48. Running time, 89 mins.

Julia	Alida Valli
Morelli	Benjamino Gigli
Canio	Paolo Hoerbiger
Leoncavallo	Carlo Romano
Valmondi	Dagny Servaes

'Pagliacci' Opera

Nedda	Adriana Perris
Canio	Benjamino Gigli
Tonio	Pacci
Silvio	Mario Boviello
Beppe	Adelio Zagonara

(In Italian; English titles)

This is one of the finer operatic-backgrounded films to come out of Italy. In story presentation, performances and camera work, film can very well stand on its own merits, even without the added lure of the presence of Alida Valli and Beniamino Gigli. Former will draw the curious, anxious to see the "Paradine Case" Valli on her home lot. Latter will attract the opera fans, especially those who remember Gigli from the Met. Pic should be an excellent arthouse draw.

Film was made before the war. It's interesting to observe what a femme fatale Hollywood has made out of the sweet-faced innocent who plays the girl in "Laugh, Pagliacci," and what tricks Coast makeup and coaching can do. Not that Miss Valli is anything but attractive in this film, as well as acting charmingly the part of a young society miss in love with her handsome soldier. Gigli will also satisfy the nostalgic who remember his brilliant work in America, his screen voice still retaining its unusual bell-like quality as he plays both a dramatic role and that of the betrayed operatic tenor.

Story is the well-known Leoncavallo tragedy of the traveling-troupe clown whose wife is unfaithful, but the film tells it in a very clever way. Film is the story of the clown, released from prison after a 20-year sentence for killing both wife and lover, who seeks his child to ask her forgiveness. Child has now been adopted by a wealthy lady and is to be married into the nobility; revelation of her father's relationship would ruin the match.

Dilemma is solved when the young composer, Leoncavallo, sets the clown's story to music, while keeping the father's identity secret. The young girl witnesses the opera's premiere and sympathizes deeply with the clown's actions, and the father goes off, satisfied.

The short opera is sung expertly and acted convincingly by Gigli, Adriana Perris and others. Paolo Hoerbiger, as the real Canio, or father, gives a poignant portrayal as a broken ex-convict, and Miss Valli emotes sensitively as the girl who senses something wrong but can never know. Dagny Servaes is very moving as the distraught foster-mother and Carlo Romano is appealing as the composer, Leoncavallo.

In addition the music during the opera sequence, the famous Prologue, is heard before the picture unfolds, and music other than Leoncavallo's is played intermittently during the dramatic sequences. There is an attractive ballet bit, and some good country and mountainside shots, as well as other neat camera bits. Production, direction and sets are all satisfactory. *Bron.*

Rossini

(ITALIAN-MADE)

Best Films release of Lux Studios production. Stars Nino Besozzi; features Greta Gonda, Paola Barbara, Armando Falconi. Directed by Mario Bonnard. Screenplay, Bonnard, Parsifal Bassi, Vittorio Novarese; camera, Mario Albertelli; music, Vittorio Gui. Previewed in N.Y., Jan. 28, '48. Running time, 90 MINS.

Gioacchino Rossini	Nino Besozzi
Isabella Colbran	Paola Barbara
Impresario	Camillo Pilotto
Ferdinando I	Armando Falconi
Teresa Coralli	Greta Gonda
Tottola	Paolo Stoppa
Beethoven	Memo Benassi
Col. Negri	Lamberto Picasso
Rosina	Gianna Pedersini
Don Basilio	Tancredi Pasero
Desdemona	Gabriella Gatti
Figaro	Mariano Stabile
Almaviva	Enzo De Muro Lomanto
Don Bartolo	Vito De Taranto
Otello	Piero Panli

(In Italian; English titles)

Ponderous and often dull, this pic biog fails to do justice to Rossini, the Italian composer. Aside from excerpts of his music from the "Barber of Seville" and "Otello," film offers little to generate interest of arty patrons. Its best market lies in the Italian-language field.

According to musical authorities, Rossini was not only a talented musician but also was famed for his wit. Had this facet been logically blended in the script along with his better compositions, the result would have been more in keeping with firstclass entertainment. But the yarn skims much of Rossini's career. Plot spotlights incidents in the composer's life in Naples, Vienna and Paris, spanning the years between 1815 and 1827. Portrayed by Nino Besozzi, the composer is shown writing his opera, "Queen Elizabeth," for eccentric King Ferdinando I while in Naples. Later he goes to Rome to create "Otello." In Vienna he visits Beethoven, and in Paris he's on the verge of writing "William Tell" when the film ends in a typical FitzPatrick travelog fadeout.

As Rossini, Besozzi is a listless maestro. He fails to catch the mood and spirit of the character. Paola Barbara is unimpressive in the role of contralto Isabella Colbran, who later becomes Rossini's wife. Greta Gonda, a ballerina, provides some heart interest while Armando Falconi is inclined to overplay the bombastic characteristics of the King. Other performances are so-so.

Writer Bonnard's direction was heavy-handed and uneven. Modest production mountings bear great resemblance to those used in other Italian-made films in the operatic cycle which preceded "Rossini" to the U. S. Mario Albertelli's photography is fair while other technical credits are standard. Picture's saving grace is its music. *Gilb.*

Western Heritage

(SONG)

Hollywood, Jan. 24.

RKO release of Herman Schlom production. Stars Tim Holt; features Nan Leslie, Richard Martin, Lois Andrews, Tony Barrett, Walter Reed, Harry Woods, Richard Powers. Directed by Wallace A. Grissell. Screenplay, Norman Houston; camera, Alfred Keller; music, Paul Sawtelle; editor, Desmond Marquette. Tradeshown in Los Angeles, Jan. 22, '48. Running time, 61 MINS.

Ross Daggett	Tim Holt
Beth Winston	Nan Leslie
Chito	Richard Martin
Cleo	Lois Andrews
Trigg	Tony Barrett
Joe Powell	Walter Reed
Arnold	Harry Woods
Spade	Richard Powers
Judge Winston	Jason Robards
Pike	Robert Bray
Sheriff	Perc Launders

Average prospects are in store for "Western Heritage." It's stock oater filmfare but with Tim Holt and Richard Martin to assure acceptance by the kiddies. The heroes are extremely poor marksmen but that's proverbial of the usual Hollywood western. Otherwise, pair go at it with the heavies in excellent style to keep the footage lively for 61 minutes.

Norman Houston has used the old Spanish land grant to stir up trouble in his script, and there's little that is new about the plotting. As usual, the grant is a phoney, forged by a clever penman. He's killed and the three gunmen who shoot him down try to take over a rich valley. Toll gates, prohibitive rents and other shenanigans keep the villains and the heroes mighty busy before Holt proves the falseness of it all and does the wrong guys in.

Nan Leslie fills the slight heroine footage and Lois Andrews has a spot as saloon canary, warbling "If You Happen to Find My Heart." Harry Woods, Tony Barrett and Richard Powers head up the boys handling the dirty work, and others are acceptable.

Wallace A. Grissell directed the Herman Schlom production with good pace. Alfred Keller lensed. Other credits are standard. *Brog.*

Smart Politics

(SONGS)

Hollywood, Jan. 31.

Monogram release of Will Jason production. Features Freddie Stewart, June Preisser, Frankie Darro, Warren Mills, Noel Neill, Donald MacBride, Gene Krupa orchestra, Cappy Barra Harmonica Boys. Directed by Will Jason. Screenplay, Hal Collins; original story, Monte F. and Hal Collins; camera, Mack Stengler; songs, Freddie Stewart and Hal Collins, Bobby Troup, Val Burton, Sid Robin, Will Jason; musical director, Edward Kay; editor, Will Austin. Reviewed in Los Angeles Jan. 30, '48. Running time, 65 MINS.

Freddie	Freddie Stewart
Dodie	June Preisser
Roy	Frankie Darro
Lee	Warren Mills
Betty	Noel Neill
Phineas Wharton Sr. } Phineas Wharton Jr. }	Donald MacBride
Martha	Martha Davis
Butch	Butch Stone
Joe	Don Ripps
Alvin	Candy Candido
Peabody	Harry Tyler
Dean McKinley	Monte F. Collins
Breezie	George Offerman, Jr.
Eddie	George Fields
Johnny	Dick Paxton
Murphy	Tommy Mack
Policeman	Billy Snyder

Gene Krupa Orchestra
Cappy Barra Harmonica Boys

"Smart Politics" is pleasant musical fare as projected by Monogram's Teenager group. Chuckles are plentiful, the tunes listenable, and the plot light. Good supporting material, particularly for the nabes.

Will Jason produced and directed, as well as having a hand in writing two of the tunes. He has done a neat job in all departments, projecting the fun to be found in the Hal Collins script, which latter adapted from an original written with Monte F. Collins.

Gene Krupa and his crew draw feature billing but are in for only short finale of "Young Man With a Beat." Freddie Stewart tenors "Sincerely Yours" and "Isn't This a Night For Love," while Martha Davis does some solid selling on "Household Blues" as well as taking chorus on "Young Man" with Stewart.

Plot has the Teenagers, headed by Stewart and June Preisser, launching project to build a youth center. They eye an old warehouse for the foundation, but the town's mayor also is anxious to corner the property. Two factions battle it out, with the youngsters winning both the fight and reforming the grasping city father.

Cast equals all demands and please. Donald MacBride, in dual role of mayor and the mayor's aged father, punches over plenty of chuckles. Candy Candido, as the dumb mayor's nephew, also gets into the act strongly. Frankie Darro, Warren Mills, Noel Neill and Harry Tuler are among others contributing expertly.

Lensing, musical direction, editing and other technical functions are good. *Brog.*

Passionelle

(FRENCH-MADE)

Distinguished Films release of Corona Films production. Stars Odette Joyeaux, Roger Blin; features Alerme, Sylvie, Raymond Galle. Directed by Edmond T. Greville. Screenplay, Edmond T. Greville and Max Joly, based on novel "Pour Une Nuit D'Amour," by Emile Zola; camera, Jacques Lemare; editor, Walter Klee. Previewed in N.Y., Jan. 29, '48. Running time, 86 mins.

Theresa	Odette Joyeaux
Baron de Musanne	Alerme
Mme. de Musanne	Sylvie
Julien	Roger Blin
Henri de Veteuil	Jacques Castellot
Pierre Colombel	Raymond Galle

(In French; English titles)

Emile Zola's "Pour Une Nuit D'Amour" still is a slightly spicy French melodrama, with even the censor scissors apparently failing to mar the more sexy episodes. Despite tedious early developments, "Passionnelle" should be okay at foreign-language houses in the U. S.

Story concerns a French miss, just out of a convent, who is about to be married off to a playboy heir. She's carrying on a mild flirtation with a musically-minded postal clerk but her real affair has been with the son of her serving maid. When he threatens to expose her just before her engagement is to be announced, she bumps him off.

The girl persuades the postal clerk into carrying away the body. The dreamy clerk dumps the body in the river, but is suspected of the murder as soon as the body is washed up on shore. Then the gal confesses all to her family, but they won't believe her. Instead the clerk gives himself up as a sacrifice.

There is one torrid rassling match between Raymond Galle and a slightly-clad (unbilled) miss that's reminiscent of American films pre-Code days. It's a scene, too, that will probably be lifted by censors in most states.

Odette Joyeaux gives a forthright performance as the convent miss. Roger Blin does well with the fantastic, almost unbelievable postal clerk role. Alerme, familiar French character actor, and Sylvie, as the girl's parents, are satisfying although the latter seems a trifle too bombastic. Galle is excellent as the despicable village fop—the son of the serving maid. Jacques Castellot, as the playboy heir, plays a rather insipid part nicely.

Edmond T. Greville and Max Joly have done fairly well in scripting from Zola's original novel. Jacques Lemare's camera job is uneven and prone to go in for countless and sometimes uncalled-for closeups. Greville, who also directed, goes in for odd lighting effects and strange camera angles but most of them add to the effectiveness of the yarn. Jean Wiener's background music accentuates the more dramatic moments.

Wear.

Brighton Rock
(BRITISH-MADE)

London, Jan. 8.

Associated British Picture Corp. release of Boulting Bros. production. Stars Hermione Baddeley, Richard Attenborough, William Hartnell. Directed by John Boulting. Screenplay by Graham Greene, Terrence Rattigan from novel by Graham Greene; camera, Harry Waxman, Gilbert Taylor; editor, Frank McNally. At the Warner, London. Running time, 92 mins.

Pinkie Brown	Richard Attenborough
Ida Arnold	Hermione Baddeley
Dallow	William Hartnell
Rose	Carol Marsh
Prewitt	Harcourt Williams
Spicer	Wylie Watson
Cubitt	Nigel Stock
Fred Hale (Kibber)	Alan Wheatley
Phil Corkery	George Carney
Colleoni	Charles Goldner
Judy	Virginia Winter
Frank	Reginald Purdell
Police Inspector	Campbell Copelin

At a time when Hollywood is frowning on gangster films, British producers are competing with each other in rushing mobster yarns to the screen. This tends to prove that Britain can turn out a gangster picture as brutal as any Hollywood has recently devised, and this likely will meet with serious objections from America's Production Code Administration. One other strike against this film is that it may arouse the ire of Catholics. Cockney accent also may hurt its chances in the U.S.

Picture will depend largely on its being a best-seller. Secondary marquee names won't help it any in the U. S.

With Graham Greene and Terence Rattigan responsible for the screenplay, something more exciting might reasonably have been expected. Some of blame goes to director John Boulting whose tempo is much too leisurely for this type of picture.

Story is laid in pre-war seaside resort Brighton, where two razor-slashing race gangs are feuding.

It is difficult to believe that any gang which included William Hartnell could be led by Richard Attenborough. Hartnell is so much more the gangster type than Attenborough that it is obvious that an exchange of parts would have made the film more credible.

Acting honors are collared by that seasoned actress, Hermione Baddeley. She steals every scene in which she appears, making Ida, the concert artist, a sympathetic character. Carol Marsh (formerly Norma Simpson) plays the waitress and gangster's wife with modesty. Well done performances are turned in by Harcourt Williams, Wylie Watson, Alan Wheatley, Virginia Water and the late George Carney.

Cane.

Easy Money
(BRITISH-MADE)

London, Jan. 21.

J. Arthur Rank presentation of Sydney Box-Gainsborough production. Stars Greta Gynt, Dennis Price, Jack Warner. Directed by Bernard Knowles. Screenplay by Muriel and Sydney Box, Arnold Ridley; editor, V. Sagovsky; camera, John Asher, D. Harcourt; commentary, E. H. V. Emmett. At Odeon, London, Jan. 20, '48. Running time, **94 MINS.**

Philip Stafford	Jack Warner
Ruth Stafford	Marjorie Fielding
Carol Stafford	Yvonne Owen
Dennis Stafford	Jack Watling
Jackie Stafford	Petula Clark
Grandma	Mabel Constanduros
Herbert Atkins	Mervyn Johns
Agnes Atkins	Joan Young
Cameron	Gordon McLeod
Pat Parsons	Greta Gynt
Joe Henty	Dennis Price
Mr. Lee	Bill Owen
Martin	Frederick Piper
Teddy Ball	Edward Rigby
Archie	Guy Rolfe
Mr. Cyprus	Raymond Lovell
Orchestra Director	Frank Cellier
Martin Latham	David Tomlinson

Having made a picture on mass-produced vacations ("Holiday Camp"), Sydney Box has chosen another popular pastime of the British public—the football pools. Every week during the football season millions of people fill in forms forecasting the results of major league games. With each form goes a money order, the amount varying according to the forecast, and each hopeful looks forward to winning anything up to $200,000 for an average outlay of 65c. It is legalized gambling in which millions of dollars are spent weekly.

With such a cast-iron subject, and using the formula of "If I Had a Million," the picture is set for good grosses in this country, and with some drastic clipping might find a place in dual bills in U. S. Pic will draw more on title and theme than marquee names.

Picture consists of four separate stories, each dealing with folk who win, or want to win, a fortune in the pools.

Graduate from the documentary school, Frank Bundy makes a good debut as a feature film producer, and direction by Bernard Knowles is competent but uninspired. Acting by a good all-round cast calls for no particular comment, with the exception of Edward Rigby, who is a standout.

Cane.

Bohemian Rapture
(CZECH-MADE)

Artkino release of National Film Studios (Prague) production. Features Jaromir Spal and Vlasta Fabianova. Directed by Vaclav Krska. Screenplay, Vaclav Krska; camera, Ferd Pecenka; symphony orchestra conducted by Otakar Parik; music, Frantisek Skvor. Tradeshown in N. Y., Jan. 29, '48. Running time, **88 MINS.**

Josef Slavik	Jaromir Spal
Frederik Chopin	Vaclav Voska
Nicolo Paganini	Karel Dostal
Anna Zasmucka	Vlasta Fabianova
Henrietta Astfeldova	Libuse Zemkova
Magdalenka	Jirinka Kreisova
The Unknown Woman	Marie Vasova
Baron Astfeld	Jiri Steimar
Coco Cavalleno	Karel Jelinek
Pavel Adam Lazansky	Eduard Kohout

(In Czechoslovakian; English Titles)

Coming at a time when American companies are on the lookout for strong foreign fare to handle in the U. S., this production is a distinct disappointment. "Bohemian Rapture" smacks too much of pre-war quality and even some of those early '30 German musicals. It's not for America.

Story of a struggling, temperamental musician has been done often. Picture's based on the life of the early 19th century Czech violinist and composer, Josef Slavik. It touches on the influence of Paganini and his friendship with Chopin. Story has him bitterly squabbling with Chopin when latter accuses him of stealing his mistress, Countess Anna Zasmucka. And there's Slavik's indecision, too, about whether he loves a country girl, a wealthy femme or Anna. Pic is vague about all three loves. In fact, vagueness crops up all through the recital. Every time Slavik is crossed up or belittled, he goes into a rage and wanders out into the wide-open spaces, where it's always raining.

Production is loaded with artistic touches, but few manage to jell.

Jaromir Spal is fairly good as the temperamental musician, but Vlasta Fabianova steals the picture as Anna. She's a trifle on the voluptuous side; otherwise, attractive, dark-haired girl might go places in U. S. films. Libuse Zemkova is fairly comely but no great shakes as an actress in the role of rich girl. Vaclav Voska does okay as Chopin.

Vaclav Krska's scripting is better than his direction. There are several good symphony orchestra sequences, with Otakar Parik taking bows for his direction of it.

Wear.

Les Jeux Sont-Faits
(The Game is Set)
(FRENCH-MADE)

Paris, Jan. 27.

Pathe release of Gibe-Nagel production. Directed by Jean Delannoy. Stars Micheline Presle, Michel Pagliero; features Marguerite Moreno, Dullin, Fernand Fabre, Jacques Irwin. Screenplay by Jean Paul Sartre. At Marignan, Paris, Jan. 20, '48. Running time, **95 MINS.**

Woman	Micheline Presle
Man	Michel Pagliero
Bookkeeper	Marguerite Moreno
Husband	Fernand Fabre
Worker	Jack Irwin

Jean Paul Sartre's notoriety as a writer and Micheline Presle's standout performance in "Boule de Suif" and "Diable au Corps" make a likely entry of a picture which is neither a raveroo nor as bad as the crix reported it to be when given a preview at the Cannes International Film Festival.

As a picture, Sartre's initialler may leave much to be desired, but nevertheless it remains a potential entry for U. S. foreign film houses on account of the marquee draw of b.o. names.

Film is extremely arty, with obvious interference of Sartre in the directing job, but it misses the finesse which has gone into other pictures featuring the world of the dead. Also some uses of flashback are not very judicious. Photography is good, and acting by the principals excellent. Miss Presle, however, has not been given full chance to emote and Michel Pagliero's choice is dubious because of his Galian accent.

Story concerns a Communist worker who gets killed during an uprising, and the wife of a militia man dying at the same time. They meet in the place of the dead, and fall in love. They then avail themselves of the permission given those who thus meet and think they would have been lovers, had they met on earth, to return there for a trial of a new love life, together. Their previous work and associations prevent making a go of it. They are doomed to a renewed and this time final death, and thus return where they were after their first demise.

Maxi.

Night Beat
(BRITISH-MADE)

London, Jan. 16.

British Lion production and release. Stars Anne Crawford, Maxwell Reed; features Ronald Howard, Christine Norden. Directed by Harold Huth. Screenplay by Guy Morgan, T. J. Morrison from original story by Morgan; additional dialog, Robert Westerby, Roland Pertwee; music, Ben Frankel; camera, Vaclav Vich. Previewed in London, Jan. 15, '48. Running time, **95 MINS.**

Julie Kendall	Anne Crawford
Felix	Maxwell Reed
Andy Kendall	Ronald Howard
Don Brady	Hector Ross
Jackie	Christine Norden
P. C. Kendall	Fred Groves
Nixon	Sidney James
Rocky	Nicholas Stuart
Magistrate	Frederick Leister
Sergeant Slack	Philip Stainton

Something went wrong in the making of this story. Original idea was topical and could have been the basis of a good drama, but barely is the story under way when cliche is piled on cliche and the audience knows every move before the director has made it. Soon the yarn degenerates into incredible melodrama full of ham and hokum. Marquee pull is small. Not likely set for America.

Story concerns two ex-Commandos, one who joins the police, the other who becomes a black marketeer, and the melodramatic problems that result.

Neither direction nor acting calls for any special comment. Artists who are near topliners could do little with the material given them. Ronald Howard still betrays signs of inexperience, but is rapidly improving, and Christine Norden has a lot to learn to become an accomplished nightclub entertainer.

Cane.

Valahol Europaban
("Somewhere in Europe")
(HUNGARIAN-MADE)

Budapest, Jan. 13.

MAFIRT distribution and release. Stars Arthur Somlay, Zsuzsa Banky, Miklos Gabor and Gyorgy Bardy. Directed by Geza Radvanyi. Written by Radvanyi and Bela Balazs. Musical score, Denes Buday; camera, Barna Hegyi. At Royal, Apollo, Atrium and Corvin, Budapest. Running time, **85 MINS.**

Pianist Peter Simon	Arthur Somlay
The Girl	Zsuzsa Banky
Hosszu	Miklos Gabor
Official	Gyorgy Bardy

Picture, fourth produced in Hungary since the war's end, and first in the past two years, is a good, artistic attempt. Crix gave it a warn. welcome. Pic will do good biz here, and would appeal in U. S. Also in a remake.

Geza Radvanyi, director who made many films in Italy during the war, has touched with great skill and ability on one of the most important problems of Europe, that of children who were lost in the welter of World War II.

Story starts a bit slowly, showing children of various origin forced to roam the highways. They form into a gang, and due to mistreatment, are forced to rob for food.

Kids find a ruined castle in the country and decide to live there. However, it's not deserted as they thought, an elderly pianist living there who too wants to escape from the world into this asylum. First they rob him, get drunk and want to hang him, but Hosszu, their leader, saves him. The artist later begins to lead them back to the right way, and battles local officials who want to get rid of them.

The actors give good portrayals and raise the picture to an artistic level. The kids are played by boys picked up on streets.

Camera work of Barna Hegyi is outstanding, while the musical score is good, too.

Gaal.

Brott I Sol
("Crime in the Sun")
(SWEDISH-MADE)

Stockholm, Jan. 2.

Terra Film release of Lorenz Marmstedt production. Stars Birger Malmsten, Margareta Fahleu, Gunnel Brostrom; features Ulf Palme, Curt Masreliez, Jan Molander. Directed by Goran Gentele. Screenplay, Gentele and Loulou Forssell, based on play by Staffan Tjerneld; camera, Sten Dahlgren. At Grand, Stockholm. Running time, **104 MINS.**

Harry	Birger Malmsten
Marguerite	Gunnel Brostrom
Eva	Margareta Fahlen
Rickard	Ulf Palme
Raoul Kessler	Curt Masreliez
Jojje	Jan Molander

Based on a stage mystery by Staffan Tjerneld, "Brott I Sol" is a fine picture that has good Scandinavian b.o. prospects and may do well in the foreign market. Unlike some celluloid versions of stage plays, this film follows its predecessor faithfully.

Told in flashback, story recalls a summer's romance involving six characters. Sprinkled in the footage are a number of torrid love sequences. Plot hinges on the amorous designs Curt Masreliez has on Margareta Fahlen, who actually is affianced to Ulf Palme. Triangular affair is climaxed with the murder of Masreliez.

Performances of the cast are excellent with Jan Molander registering in particular. Goran Gentele's direction, lensing of Sten Dahlgren and scripting of Gentele and Loulou

Forssell all measure up to a high standard. If censors are hurdled, film will be a good entry for the U.S. market. *Wing.*

Foreign Films

"Un Flic" ("A Cop") (FRENCH-MADE). Sirius production and release. Stars Lucien Coedel; features Suzy Carrier, Raymond Pellegrin, Michele Martin. Directed by Maurice de Canonge. Screenplay, Jacques Companeez; dialog, Michel Duran, J. J. Delvo-Dunan, Leo Laparra. At Balzac, Paris. Running time, **105 MINS.**

For the French market, "Un Flic" has some drawing power due to the fact the film is the last picture made by Lucien Coedel, who was recently killed in a fall from a train. He portrays a policeman who unsuccessfully attempts to prevent a weak brother-in-law from becoming a mobster. Poor scripting, antiquated direction and technique minimize the pic's chances even for foreign arthouse sureseaters. *Maxi.*

"Singing Angels" ("Singende Engel") (AUSTRIAN-MADE). Sacha Film release of Gustav Ucicky production. Stars Hans Holt, Gustav Waldau, Inge Konradi, Gusti Wolf. Story, Rolf Olsen and Ucicky; music, Willi Schmidt Gentner, based upon themes of Josef Haydn; sets, Prof. Otto Niedermoser, Walter Schmidt; musical director, Josef Krips. At Apollo theatre, Vienna. Running time, **120 MINS.**

Long film based on the classics will find its appeal largely limited to those fond of longhair music. Story revolves about the formation of the Vienna Singing Boys Society. Portions of the life of composer Josef Haydn are also outlined. Chances in the international market are slight. *Maas.*

"Come Persi la Guerra" ("How I Lost the War") (ITALIAN-MADE). Lux release of RDL production. Stars Macario; features Vera Carmi, Nando Bruno, Carlo Campanini, Piero Lulli. Directed by Carlo Borghesio. Story by Borghesio and Giannini; screenplay, Monicelli and Amendola; camera, Aldo Tonti; music, Nino Rota. Running time, **80 MINS.**

Macario, popular Italian revue star, is the only appeal of this trite comedy. It's obviously written and produced for his clownish personality. Cinema audiences haven't gone for him as much as stage fans, and this film, which is not his best, won't help.

Pic is a succession of amusing but inconclusive gags and sketches, without any plot connection. Macario, Carlo Campanini and Nando Bruno are good and Vera Carmi is attractive. Production and direction are average; camera work is okay. No value for U. S. market. *Quat.*

"Tva Kvinnor" ("Two Women") (SWEDISH-MADE). Wive Film production and release. Stars Eva Dahlbeck, Cecile Ossbahr, Gunnar Bjornstrand, Georg Rydeberg, Arnold Sjostrand; features Marianne Lofgren, Naima Wifstrand, Lasse Krantz, Nils Hallberg, Nils Orlin, Arthur Fischer, Viveca Linder, Tord Stahl. Directed by Sjostrand. Screenplay, Roger Richebe, Torsten Quensel; camera, Kari-Erik Alberts; music, Sune Waldimir. At Spegeln, Stockholm. Running time, **96 MINS.**

Adapted from an old French film, "Prison de Femmes," this Swedish version fails to match predecessor's quality. Story hinges on the theme that it doesn't matter what a person has done as long as he gets away with it. However, if jailed, he'll carry a lifelong stigma. Direction is okay although acting is rather spotty. Picture was submitted to the recent Cannes film festival with mediocre results. Not likely for the U. S.

Miniature Reviews

"Three Daring Daughters" (Songs-Color) (M-G). Jeanette MacDonald, Jose Iturbi in okay Joe Pasternak musical.

"The Pearl" (RKO). Mexican-made film of high artistry. Very exploitable for art houses and other selected situations.

"Half Past Midnight" (20th). Routine whodunit for dualers.

"Jiggs and Maggie in Society" (Mono). Broadly gagged comedy for secondaries.

"Paisan" (Mayer-Burstyn). Italian made, excellent for art houses and selected situations.

"This Was a Woman" (20th) (British). Story of power-crazed femme limited to art-house draw.

Three Daring Daughters
(SONGS; COLOR)

Metro release of Joe Pasternak production. Stars Jeanette McDonald, Jose Iturbi; features Jane Powell, Edward Arnold, Ann. E. Todd, Mary Eleanor Donahue. Directed by Fred M. Wilcox. Screenplay, Albert Mannheimer, Frederick Kohner, Sonya Levien, John Meehan; camera (Technicolor), Ray June; editor, Adrienne Fazan; "Dickey Bird Song," Howard Dietz and Sammy Fain. Previewed N.Y., Jan. 28, '48. Running time, 115 mins.

Louise Rayton Morgan	Jeanette McDonald
Jose Iturbi	Himself
Tess Morgan	Jane Powell
Robert Nelson	Edward Arnold
Dr. Cannon	Harry Davenport
Mrs. Smith	Moyna MacGill
Alix Morgan	Mary Eleanor Donahue
Ilka Morgan	Ann E. Todd
Michael Pemberton	Tom Holmore
Jonesy	Kathryn Card

"Three Daring Daughters," which marks Jeanette MacDonald's return to the screen, is a typical Metro-Joe Pasternak songfest. That means it probably won't be appreciated by the so-called sophisticates but will do well at the boxoffice. Film is subject to many of the plot failings of such product but it has plenty o. songs and it's in Technicolor. That should be enough to insure it okay grosses in all situations.

Miss MacDonald's soprano comes over as bell-like and clear-toned as ever, and she's lost none of her appealing beauty. Pasternak wisely cast her in a role suitable to her maturity, as the divorced mother of three precocious kids. Although she has the romantic lead, her vis-a-vis is the middle-aged Jose Iturbi and not some bright-eyed juvenile. In all, she turns in a neat job.

Iturbi, who usually is assigned a minor character role in these Metro musicals, has his most important part to date in "Daughters," and he does well enough with it. He won't get an Academy award for his thesping ability but he nonetheless sufficiently skims the surface of the various moods he's called on to portray to let the audience know what he's trying to put across. Piano playing, in which his noted sister, Amparo, joins him in a couple of numbers, is grooved niftily for pop audiences, no matter whether it's de Falla's "Ritual Fire Dance" or some hep boogie.

Highlight of the film is the emergence of a promising new moppet star in the person of Ann E. Todd. (The "e" is not an affectation but used obviously to distinguish her from the British actress o the same name.) Youngster resembles Judy Garland as a kid and has Miss Garland's same appeal and infectious quality in her acting. Miss Todd isn't the singer Miss Garland is (or was), but holds her own against the competition of Jane Powell, no slouch herself when it comes to giving out with the dulcet tones.

Story of "Daughters" would seem to prove the old saw about too many cooks, etc. Four scripters are credited with the original screenplay, and it won't reflect credit on any of them. The Misses Powell, Todd and Mary Eleanor Donahue, as the three daughters, are pictured trying to effect a reconciliation between Miss MacDonald, as their mother, and the father, whom the kids don't even remember. Miss MacDonald, unaware of their plot, meets Iturbi on a vacation in Cuba and marries him before returning home. When the kids learn of this, they're brokenhearted, figuring their own father got a raw deal, and so they refuse to accept Iturbi into the family. They're finally made to realize the error of their ways. Intertwined throughout the innocuous story are some overly-saccharine confabs between the mother and daughters, which are much too repetitive.

Cast, under the slow-paced direction of Fred M. Wilcox, does okay. Miss Powell and Miss Donahue are fairly cute as the other two daughters, with Miss Powell demonstrating an amazing soprano. Edward Arnold is brought in for some hefty laughs as the boss of the divorced father, and Harry Davenport plays his usual kindly family adviser. Moyna MacGill is okay as a flighty old gal who pitches for Iturbi herself.

Film has the usual lush Pasternak production mountings. Score has only one original, the "Dickey Bird Song" by Howard Dietz and Sammy Fain, which is already on the best-seller lists. Other songs are standards or classics. Larry Adler is spotted in one short sequence harmonicizing "Roumanian Rhapsody." Sets, painted in glaring Technicolor, appear costly under Ray June's color cameras. *Stal.*

The Pearl

Hollywood, Feb. 10.

RKO release of Oscar Dancingers (F.A.M.A.-Aguila) production. Features Pedro Armandariz, Maria Elena Marques. Directed by Emilio Fernandez. Screenplay, John Steinbeck, Emilio Fernandez, Jack Wagner; original, Steinbeck; camera, Gabriel Figueroa; music, Antonio Diaz Conde; editor, Glora Schoemann. Tradeshown in Los Angeles, Feb. 10, '48. Running time, 72 mins.

Kino	Pedro Armendariz
Juana	Maria Elena Marques
Buyer of Pearls	Fernando Wagner
Village Doctor	Charles Rooner
Godfather of Kino and Juana's Baby	Alfonso Bedoya
Sapo	Juan Garcia
Medicine Woman	Enadine Diaz De Leon

The tragedy of wealth visited on the poor, as explored in John Steinbeck's "The Pearl," has been given a moving, poetic treatment in the hands of Mexican film artists. It's not commercial entertainment in the accepted sense, yet film has the dramatic elements that make for good theatre. It is intensely moving and often excitingly suspenseful, done with superb artistry.

Picture calls for unusual exploitation selling—and lends itself to it—or playdates other than in the art houses. Audiences enticed to see this one will find themselves engrossed with the simplicity of the story telling, the fine photography, the compelling music and intelligent performances.

RKO is releasing this Mexican-made picture. Its locale is the west coast of Mexico. Story is laid in a simple village where the natives scratch out a bare existence by diving for shells in the Gulf of California. Steinbeck's gift for accurately mirroring little people in prose has been graphically brought to the screen by Oscar Dancinger's production and the direction by Emilio Fernandez.

Sudden wealth comes to one of the native families when a large, flawless pearl of fabulous value is discovered. The discovery awakens the greed in evil men and brings danger and death to the family before the pearl is cast back into the sea from which it came. Tale is allegorical, displaying the inability of the poor to cope with sudden wealth, the covetousness of man and the happiness to be found in a simple life. Steinbeck, Fernandez and Jack Wagner wrote the script.

Beautiful performance by Pedro Armendariz and Maria Elena Marques, as the suddenly rich family, compel high interest. The other performances are of equally high order under Fernandez' unerring direction. He has caught the mood of the Steinbeck original perfectly, balancing suspense and movement against the background of inevitable tragedy.

Gabriel Figueroa, who has attracted Hollywood attention for past lensing jobs, has done standout photographic work on "The Pearl." He treats the eye with vast vistas, intriguing use of light and shadow, and fluid scenes. Antonio Diaz Conde embroidered his score with colorful native Mexican music, making it tie story mood together carefully. Other credits are commendable. *Brog.*

Half Past Midnight

20th-Fox release of Sol M. Wurtzel production. Features Kent Taylor, Peggy Knudsen. Directed by William F. Claxton. Screenplay, Arnold Belgard; camera, Benjamin Kline; editor, Frank Baldridge. Tradeshown in N.Y., Feb. 9, '48. Running time. 69 MINS.

Wado Hamilton	Kent Taylor
Sally Parker	Peggy Knudsen
Joe Nash	Joe Sawyer
Mac	Walter Sande
Chick Patrick	Gil Stratton, Jr.
Cortez	Martin Kosleck
Hester Thornwall	Mabel Paige
Blosson	Jean Wong
Carlotta	Jane Everett
Murray Evans	Danien O'Flynn
Lee Gow	Richard Lee
Barker	Tom Dugan

"Half Past Midnight" is a routine item turned out on the B corner of the 20th lot. It'll serve in dualer situations. Pic has lots of action but little rhyme or reason in racing through its whodunit plot. Scripting passes minimum low-budget standard in furnishing a few corpses, a speck of romance and some simple-minded comedy touches. Other production accoutrements, including cast, direction and camera work, par the screenplay's level.

Kent Taylor, playing a debonair young man about town with a nose for trouble, picks up Peggy Knudsen at a nightclub where an adagio team is blackmailing her. Just as Taylor turns his back, a murder is committed and Miss Knudsen finds herself in a highly compromising position with the cops. The couple take it on the lam, and the rest of the yarn revolves around their pursuit of the killer and the cops' pursuit of them through an unexplainable tangle of complications. Tipping its mitt long in advance on the culprit's identity, the film winds up on a limp climax as the girl is cleared.

Taylor and Miss Knudsen perform competently in the lead roles, with some good support from Joe Sawyer and Walter Sande as the rival detectives. Mabel Paige, in a brief role as a broken-down ex-chorine, turns in a firstrate comedy performance that steals all honors. Rest of the cast do okay in stock parts. *Herm.*

Jiggs and Maggie in Society

Hollywood, Feb. 6.

Monogram release of Barney Gerard production. Stars Joe Yule, Renie Riano; features Dale Carnegie, Arthur Murray, Sheila Graham. Directed by Eddie Cline. Screenplay, Cline and Gerard; camera, L. W. O'Connell; editor, Ace Herman. Previewed in Hollywood, Feb. 3, '48. Running time, **65 MINS.**

Jiggs	Joe Yule
Maggie	Renie Riano
Dale Carnegie	Dale Carnegie
Arthur Murray	Arthur Murray
Sheilah Graham	Sheilah Graham
Dinty	Tim Ryan
Millicent	Wanda McKay
Van De Graft	Lee Bonnell
Dugan	Pat Goldin
Jenkins	Herbert Evans
Nora	June Harrison
Tommy	Scott Taylor
McGurk	Jimmy Aubrey

Boisterous slapstick that will find a ready payoff in its market. Second in Barney Gerard's film series based on George McManus' cartoon characters, "Jiggs and Maggie in Society" tickles the risibilities with broad antics that will amuse the family trade.

Some exploitation value is added by inclusion of such familiar names as Dale Carnegie and Arthur Murray, and otherwise Gerard's production gives the picture good gloss. Eddie Cline's direction isn't up to his best fast pace throughout, but when he does hit his stride the results are hilarious. Gerard and Cline did the original script, and McManus' characters come to life with expert fidelity in the hands of Joe Yule and Renie Riano as Jiggs and Maggie, respectively.

As title indicates. Maggie is trying to crash society with Jiggs suffering along with the idea. He's taught manners by Carnegie while Maggie learns proper terping from Murray. Thrown in is an air interview with columnist Sheilah Graham that comes off well. Plot also includes roundup of a gang of jewel thieves, Jiggs' apparent chasing of Wanda McKay, and finale has everyone happy over a plate of corned beef and cabbage.

In addition to cast mentioned, little Scott Taylor gets over as poker-faced youngster. Helena Drake as Maggie's sister; Lee Bonnell, shady character; Tim Ryan as Dinty; Constance Purdy, professional party-arranger who images Elsa Maxwell, and others measure up.

Lensing and other technical functions are good. *Brog.*

Paisan
(ITALIAN-MADE)

Mayer-Burstyn release of Roberto Rossellini production (made for Organizations Films International in collaboration with Foreign Film Productions). Directed by Rossellini. Screenplay, Alfred Hayes, Frederico Fellini, Sergio Amidei, Marcellea Pagliero and Rossellini; camera, Otello Martelli; music, Renzo Rossellini; American version prepared by Stuart Legg and Raymond Spottiswoode; English titles, Herman G. Weinberg. Previewed in N. Y. Feb. 4, '48. Running time, **120 MINS.**

Carmela	Carmela Sazio
Joe from Jersey	Robert Von Loon
Negro M. P.	Dots M. Johnson
Boy in Naples	Alfonsino
Francesca	Maria Michi
Fred	Gar Moore
Harriet, a Nurse	Harriet White
Renzo	Renzo Avanzo
Catholic Chaplain	Bill Tubbs
O.S.S. Man	Dale Edmonds
American and British soldiers and Italian Partisans

(English Titles)

Roberto Rossellini has again turned out a film that must rank near the great foreign pictures of all time. The young Italian writer-director-producer has, in "Paisan," even topped in some respects his own "Open City," which has exceeded in gross several times over any other foreign-language film shown in the U.S. "Paisan" lacks elements which gave its predecessor such phenomenal b.o. strength, but certainly can be counted on for boff returns in important art houses and selected general-audience theatres.

"Paisan" (meaning "fellow-countryman") comprises six episodes as Yank and British troops battled their way northward to push the Nazis out of Sicily and Italy. They are tied together in semi-documentary fashion by an off-screen narrator pointing out on an on-screen map the successive waves that took the Allies from Sicily to the valley of the Po. Sequences are otherwise unconnected.

They are unconnected, that is, except for having in common that indescribable something that Hollywood calls "heart"—that whatever it is that gives a film feeling, deep excitement and the sense of humanity that makes for greatness in the art of picture making. Part of it is in the eminent simplicity of the episodes themselves. They are like a well-done short story, which in a minimum of time and wordage catches the full breadth of the characters as it limns a relatively insignificant, but telling, incident.

Most of the film's quality must be credited, however, to Rossellini's feeling for people and his ability to put them in an atmosphere of reality. Aside from a director's sensitivity to his characters, Rossellini knows the technical tricks of getting desired effects with the camera, lighting, mood and location.

Forced by the sparsity of studio space and equipment, when he made "Open City" and "Paisan" in the early postwar period, to depend largely on location shooting, he uses it to give rugged honesty and realism to his pictures. Rossellini's cold gray photography most of all catches what ex-GI's who've seen Italy or France or China or Korea, after the enemy occupation, will particularly appreciate—a sense among the people of an urgency for living, a constant sub-surface excitement, a whole speedup of existence as they feverishly try to get themselves back to a norm that the destruction of war has decreed can never be.

Rossellini achieves part of his effect by the mingling of professional and non-professional actors in his cast in such a way that it's often impossible to tell which is which. In addition, the Italians speak Italian, the British speak English and the Yanks—well, they speak like Yanks. Subtitles on the American version are used, of course, only for the Italian dialog.

Initial episode, in Sicily, is the night of the landing there, with an American—Joe from Jersey (Robert Von Loon)—left by his squad leader to guard an Italian girl in a deserted castle. The short-lived relationship between them is marked by nothing more than Joe's effort to get over the barrier of language to win a word or smile of friendship from the distraught and reticent native.

In Naples, a Negro M.P. has his shoes stolen while he sleeps by an Italian urchin. When he finds the boy later and is led to his home—a mass of humans living in a cove—he is overwhelmed by the poverty and rushes off without the stolen shoes.

Rome sequence is the best of the lot. A prostitute (Maria Michi) picks up a GI (Gar Moore) and takes him to her room. He lies on her bed too drunk to do anything but babble of the fresh, sweet girl who befriended him with a drink of water when his tank burst into the city six months earlier. The girl recognizes the description of herself and tries to get the GI to return to her as he originally found her, but it doesn't work out.

In Florence there's a chase by an American nurse and a partisan through German lines. It's more tense and breathtaking than any staged by maestro Alfred Hitchcock himself. At the Gothic line, three chaplains—a Catholic, Protestant and Jew—are overnight guests in a Franciscan monastery. There's much humor and poignancy in the attitude of the monks, shut off from the world, to the Protestant and Jew in their monastery, but all are united by a common godliness.

Final sequence, in the Po Valley, has a group of OSS and British Intelligence men working with Partisans behind German lines. Caught in a desperate situation, they put up a hopeless fight, only to be mercilessly slain.

Stuart Legg, who has been responsible for many of the fine documentary shorts of the Canadian

Film Board, and Raymond Spottiswoode prepared the American version for distribs Mayer & Burstyn. The bridges which they have provided to link the episodes are the weakest part of the picture, being too prominent and thereby proving a distraction that breaks the mood. But that's small criticism of a film that is in most other respects a fine and moving human document. *Herb.*

This Was a Woman
(BRITISH-MADE)

Hollywood, Jan. 28.

20th-Fox release of Excelsior Film—Marcel Hellman production. Stars Sonia Dresdel, Barbara White. Directed by Tim Whelan. Screenplay by Val Valentine, from play by Joan Morgan; editor, J.B. Jarvia; music, Mischa Spolian-sky; camera, Gunther Krampf. Previewed in London, Jan. 27, '48. Running time, 104 mins.

Sylvia Russell	Sonia Dresdel
Arthur Russell	Walter Fitzgerald
Terry Russell	Emrys Jones
Fenella Russell	Barbara White
Valentine Christie	Julian Dallas
Austin Penrose	Cyril Raymond
Mrs. Holmes	Marjorie Rhodes
Effie	Celia Lipton
Sally	Lesley Osmond
Dr. Morrison	Kynaston Reeves
Chief Surgeon	Noel Howlett
Miss Johnson	Joan Hickson

It was in the play, "This Was a Woman," that comparatively-unknown Sonia Dresdel rose to stage stardom. Her part was a tour-de-force, and this applies to the present screen version. Actress dominates the film as she did the play. She has tremendous personality and great talent, but unfortunately she has been allowed to carry over to the screen certain annoying stage mannerisms. Pic's appeal is limited, but can do for U. S. art houses.

Miss Dresdel plays a woman who lusts for power. Regarding her husband as a mediocrity, she humiliates him on every possible occasion. She resents the marriage of her daughter to a doctor and sets about destroying their happiness. Only to her son does she give her complete love, taking an inordinate pride in his medical work.

Supporting Miss Dresdel is a good all-round cast. Walter Fitzgerald as ices sympathy as the henpecked husband and Cyril Raymond is credibly forthright as a friend. Barbara White shapes up as a promising young actress, and Celia Lipton shows talent. Emrys Jones registers sufficiently in his big scene, and Marjorie Rhodes is good in too few flashes. Marcel Hellman's production is okay, and Tim Whelan, after an absence of many years, has returned to direct. *Cane.*

The Lady is Fickle
(SONGS)
(Italian-Made)

Superfilm Distributing release of Minerva Films production. Stars Ferrucio Tagliavini. Directed by Mario Mattoli. Camera, Alverto Fusi; English titles, Armando Macaluso. At Cinema Verdi, N.Y., Feb. 6, '48. Running time, 82 mins.

Ferrucio Landini	Ferrucio Tagliavini
Rosetta	Fioretto Dolfi
Christopher	Carlo Campanini
Mr. Bonsi	Carlo Micheluzzi

(In Italian; English titles)

"The Lady Is Fickle" is a musical potboiler with an appeal strictly limited to Italian-language situations.

Sole excuse for this film is the presence of Ferruccio Tagliavini, Metropolitan Opera star, who lends his great singing voice and fair thesping talent. Beyond this, film is an entirely tasteless mixture of an absurd story and some ancient comedy that even a Keystone Kop would have found too slapsticky. Production dress is mediocre although a firstrate soundtrack captures the grandeur of Tagliavini's voice in several operatic and folk numbers.

Yarn revolves around the efforts of a provincial school teacher to break into grand opera via his friendship with the impresario's chauffeur. At the same time, Tagliavini runs into complications with his girlfriend, whom he accidently loses in a theatre lobby. Obvious windup brings the lovers together while getting the singer his big chance to prove his voice. Besides Tagliavini, there is no one else in the cast to recommend. *Herm.*

Foreign Films

"Preludio D'Amore ("Love Prelude")" (ITALIAN-MADE). CEIAD release of Albatros production. Stars Vittorio Gassman, Marina Berti, Maria Michi, Massimo Girotti, Claudio Gora; features Vira Silenti, Lauro Gazzolo. Directed by Giovanni Paolucci. Original story by Leopoldo Triests; screenplay, Triests and Paolucci; camera, Piero Portalupi; music, Valentino Bucchi. At Barberini, Rome. Running time, 85 mins.

This pic, dealing with juve delinquency and romance, is too simply and childishly treated. Set in Genoa, picture has many outdoor scenes neatly photographed by Piero Portalupi. Good performances by Maria Michi, seen in "Open City" and "Paisan;" Marina Berti, recently signed by Hal. B. Wallis; her husband, Claudio Gora; Massimo Girotti, and especially Vittorio Gassman, young Italian stage and screen actor, who looks like a good U. S. bet. Film has no export value. *Quat.*

Miniature Reviews

"Arch of Triumph" (UA-Ent). Big grosses assured via story buildup and cast headed by Bergman-Boyer.

"B. F.'s Daughter" (M-G). Plushy adult film with femme interest and top-calibre names for the marquees.

"The Big Clock" (Par). Speedy and suspenseful meller set to do big biz down the line.

"Adventures of Casanova" (EL). Rousing horse opera yarn in period dress.

"Speed to Spare" (Par). Good actioner about trucking industry for supporting bookings.

"The Challenge" (20th). Neat Bulldog Drummond pic for solid dualer support.

"Mr. Reckless" (Par). Standard action thriller for the secondary market.

"Caged Fury" (Par). Top-notch Pine-Thomas secondary feature about circus life.

"Tornado Range" (EL). Average western in the Eddie Dean series.

"My Brother Jonathan" (Pathe). British small-town medico melodrama, with some appeal for U. S.

"Voyage Surprise" (Indie). Fair French-made comedy minus marquee names.

Arch of Triumph

(ONE SONG))

United Artists release of Enterprise (David Lewis-Lewis Milestone) production, directed by Milestone. Stars Ingrid Bergman, Charles Boyer, with Charles Laughton, Louis Calhern, Ruth Warrick, Roman Bohnen, Ruth Nelson, Michael RomanoffScreenplay, Milestone and Harry Brown, from novel by Erich Maria Remarque; executive production manager, Jos. C. Gilpin; camera, Russell Metty; score, Louis Gruenberg, conducted by Morriss Stoloff; musical director, Rudolph Polk; asst. prod., Otto Klement; 2nd unit director, Nate Watt; editor, Mario Castenaro. Tradeshown N.Y. Feb. 16, '48. Running time, 120 mins.

Joan Madou	Ingrid Mergman
Dr. Ravie	Charles Boyer
Haake	Charles Laughton
Morosow	Louis Calhern
Kate Hergstroem	Ruth Warrick
Dr. Veber	Roman Bohnen
Alex	Stephen Bekassy
Madame Fessler	Ruth Nelson
Tatooed Waiter	Curt Bois
Hotel Manager	J. Edward Bromberg
Alidze	Michael Romanoff
Inspector	Art Smith
Col. Gomez	John Laurenz
Captain, Spanish	Leon Lenoir
Novarro	Franco Corsaro
Gen. Aide	Nino Pipitoni
Nugent	Vladimir Rasbevsky
Milan Porter	Alvin Hammer
Refugee Boy	Jay Gilpin
Russian Singer	Ilia Khmara
Roulette Croupier	Andre Marsauden
Sybil	Hazel Brooks
Policeman	Byron Foulger
Official	Bill Conrad
Polansky	Peter Virgo

"Arch of Triumph" has finally emerged as a triumphant grosser. The powerful cast, headed by Ingrid Bergman and Charles Boyer, assures marquee lure for the Remarque best-seller in its screen transition. It's a powerful parlay. Pre-World War I romance, laid in Paris, will do plenty of business.

The Remarque novel, by very suggestion of authorship and the Lewis Milestone association, conjures up analogy to the now classic "All Quiet," the post-World War I film, also from a Remarque work. The analogy ends there because the character of both differs strikingly. Current entry is a frank romantic item, laid in a setting of Paris intrigue just before open war with the western allies broke out, and as director Milestone has projected it, it makes for a minor key cinematurgy which has all the attributes of major boxoffice potency.

The surcharged atmosphere of pre-Polish aggression and its repercussions in the City of Light that suddenly grows into blackout is a dramatic background for the Boyer-Bergman romance. The very atmosphere of the boulevards, from the Eternal Light underneath the Arc d'Triomphe to the gaiety of the Sheherezade and kindred boites "on the hill" (Montmartre) make for surefire appeal.

Paris is the haven of all middle-European refugees whose lives are held cheaply because they are stateless men and women, for one reason or another. Boyer is the emigre medico who rescues Miss Bergman from obvious sucide attempt off one of the Paris ponts. Louis Calhern (capital in his interpretation) is the white Russian colonel whose relatively humble post as chasseur of the Franco-Russo nitery is ever eclipsed by his former Petrograd military station. He's Boyer's confidante. Set in the polyglot International Hotel which obviously houses knaves and knights of all nations, the aura makes for an exciting motivation. There is just enough of the Nazi brutality kaleidoscoped to keep that phase of shameful history fresh in memory.

Thereafter the romance between the stellar twain takes possession of the film which permits its historic overtones and significances to become subordinate to the pash idyll. That it ends on a note of sweet sorrow—as she succumbs to a jealous suitor's pistol wounds and he goes into concentration camp as a technical "alien," once war is declared—is but a climactic footnote.

In between Charles Laughton is rather wasted as a Nazi menace, obviously the victim of the cutting room shears, as was Ruth Warrick, the American dilletante. There is no question but that over $1,000,000 of this film's cost never shows on the screen. It's reported to have hit near the $4,000,000 negative cost.

"Arch" is the first of what must be more films to come to evince that, close as we still are to World War II, the background can be utilized for dramatic romantic values, away from the cops-and-robbers, cloak-and-dagger idiom.

David Lewis' production and Milestone's direction are matched by the many standout bits. These run from Mike Romanoff, playing himself, although this time as boniface of a pre-war Parisian boite; Feodor Chaliapin as the chief chef of the Sheherezade; Roman Bohnen as a sympathetic medico; Stephen Bekassy as the ill-fated swain who commits mayhem on Miss Bergman; and other tiptop hits by Curt Bois, J. Edward Bromberg, Art Smith, John Laurenz and Leon Lenoir.

Production values are highgrade, from the excellent Louis Gruenberg score to direction and general mounting. *Abel.*

B.F.'s Daughter

Hollywood, Feb. 14.

Metro release of Edwin H. Knopf production. Stars Barbara Stanwyck, Van Heflin, Charles Coburn; features Richard Hart, Kennan Wynn. Directed by Robert Z. Leonard. Screenplay, Luther Davis, based on novel by John P. Marquand; camera, Joseph Ruttenberg; musical score, Bronislazu Kaper; editor, George White. Tradeshown in Los Angeles, Feb. 11, '48. Running time, 107 mins.

"Polly" Fulton	Barbara Stanwyck
Thomas W. Brett	Van Heflin
B.F. Fulton	Charles Coburn
Robert S. Tasmin, III	Richard Hart
Martin Delwyn Ainsley	Keenan Wynn
"Apples" Sandler	Margaret Lindsay
Gladys Fulton	Spring Byington
The Sailor	Marshall Thompson
Eugenia Taris	Barbara Laage
Major Isaac Riley	Thomas E. Breen
Jan	Fred Nurney

Metro has given "B. F.'s Daughter" a plushy presentation and strong marquee names to stir initial ticket sales. It carries femme interest and has other recommendations to point it for good returns. The polished production supervision has been carefully handled by Edwin H. Knopf to give it the expected Metro gloss, and performances are of top calibre.

Script, however, makes an even more shallow exploration of the passing of a colorful era than did the John P. Marquand novel on which it is based. It's a boy meets girl story, backgrounded against the period from the early '30s into the war years. To catch the distaff eye, Barbara Stanwyck has been stunningly gowned and beautifully photographed. The art direction and set decorations add to elaborateness of production.

Miss Stanwyck and Van Heflin, as the two principal characters, wrap up the roles with smooth performances. Heflin gives an expressive interpretation as the poor, liberal college professor and lecturer who falls in love with and marries the daughter of an industrial giant. The marriage is wrecked when the girl uses her wealth to aid her husband, and only when she confesses a need of him does the happy ending occur.

Charles Coburn is his competent self as the industrialist. Richard Hart does well as the stuffy lawyer fiance who is tossed over for the poor prof. Keenan Wynn ably projects the opportunist newscaster. A gem of a small part comes to life in the hands of Barbara Laage. Margaret Lindsay, Spring Byington, Marshall Thompson and others are capable.

Robert Z. Leonard has guided the players through their parts with sure hands in filming the Luther Davis screenplay. Bronislau Kaper's music score, the lensing by Joseph Ruttenberg, Irene's costumes, and other production contributions are top drawer. *Brog.*

The Big Clock

Paramount release of Richard Malbaum production. Stars Ray Milland, Charles Laughton, Maureen O'Sullivan; features Elsa Lanchester, George Macready, Rita Johnson, Henry Morgan. Directed by John Farrow. Screenplay, Jonathan Latimer, from novel by Kenneth Fearing; camera, John Seitz' editor, Eda Warren; music, Victor Young. Previewed in N.Y., Feb. 4, '48. Running time, 95 mins.

George Stroud	Ray MIlliand
Earl Janoth	Charles Laughton
Georgette Stroud	Maureen O'Sullivan
Steve Hagen	George Macready
Pauline York	Rita Johnson
Louise Patterson	Elsa Lanchester
Don Klausmeyer	Harold Vermilyea
Roy Cordette	Dan Tobin
Bill Womack	Henry Morgan
Nat Sperling	Richard Webb
Tony Watson	Tad Van Brunt
Lily Gold	Elaine Riley
Edward Orlin	Luis Van Rooten
McKinley	Lloyd Corrigan
Second Secretary	Margaret Field
Sidney Kislav	Philip Van Zandt
Antique Dealer	Henri Letondal
Bert Finch	Douglas Spencer

Paramount has hit upon a top-speed formula and coupled it with a novel melodramatic twist to make "The Big Clock" one of the sure successes of the current year. What the doctor ordered is in this one—breathless pace after the first few feet, sharp plot convolutions, distinctly etched characterizations of the principles and a sock windup. It's the sort of film which will register from showcase to shooting gallery.

There are weaknesses lurking in this pic, namely a too-patly tailored yarn and some spotty acting, but these matter little. The pace is so red-hot that the customers are going to teeter on edge to follow the corkscrew story. There's no time or inclination, during the unfolding, to question coincident or misplaced mugging.

The story has something special for mellers. One part, though, that played by Charles Laughton, has a familiar touch. It's a fair enough approximation to Sydney Greenstreet's domineering tycoon in "The Hucksters" to make the similarity striking. Laughton, in this instance, is cracking the whip as the topkick in a gigantic publishing house.

Toiling under him is Ray Milland, editor of a crime mag, whose peculiar value is his ability to run down concealed felons and expose them in his sheet. Milland, it seems, is about to embark on a delayed honeymoon. Instead, he tiffs with boss Laughton, quits in anger, and then haplessly tangles with Laughton's girlfriend. In the course of the evening, he scoots from the gal's apartment as Laughton enters. Milland spots his employer without being seen by him. Goaded by insane jealousy, Laughton kills his mistress and scurries for cover. It's at this point that story's peculiar twist shoves it into high.

Laughton is aware that he's been sighted by his unknown rival. As he sees it, there's only one way out, and that's to locate the sole witness and either buy him off or cancel him in some other way. Milland, of course, is hired for that job, and his desperate efforts are directed towards covering his own tracks while pinning the goods on the real murderer.

The device of a man being assigned to hunt himself down—a peculiar switch on the manhunt theme—is a fortuitous choice, used as it is here with cumulative effect. As Milland's technique, developed in less-personal probes, brings in clue after clue pointing to Milland himself, film takes on frenetic suspense. Each situation is adeptly handled to distill the maximum impact with a sock climax adroitly maneuvered. Solution is neatly tied at the windup.

Milland turns in a workmanlike job, polished to groove to the unrelenting speed of the plot. Laughton, unfortunately, overplays his hand so that his tycoon-sans-heart takes on the quality of parodying the real article. The plot calls for a pretty unbelievable specimen, and understatement would have been the wiser of adding credibility.

All supporting roles are excellently handled. Elsa Lanchester (Mrs. Laughton), as a wacky portrait painter, is particularly superb. She can tinge a screwball giggle with real humor and draw the most out of unpredictable doings. Henry Morgan (not the radio comic) is properly lethal as a hired thug and bodyguard. Maureen O'Sullivan performs smartly as Milland's much-jilted spouse.

Production trimmings are plenty lush. John Farrow's direction is top-flight, pushing the action along at the crisp pace required for this sort of meller. Photography and editing reflect skillful treatment. *Wit.*

Adventures of Casanova

Eagle Lion release of Leonard S. Picker (Bryan Foy) production. Stars Arturo De Cordova, Lucille Bremer; features John Sutton, George Tobias, Noreen Nash, Lloyd Corrigan, Fritz Lieber, Nestor Paiva. Directed by Roberto Gavaldon. Screenplay by Crane Wilbur, Walter Bullock, Karen DeWolf; adapted from story by Wilbur; camera, John Greenhalgh; editor, Louis H. Sackin; music, Hugo Friedhofer. Tradeshown N. Y. Feb. 16, '48. Running time, 83 MINS.

Casanova	Arturo De Cordova
Lady Bianca	Lucille Bremer
Lorenzo	Turhan Bey
Count de Brissac	John Sutton
Jacopo	George Tobias
Zanetta	Noreen Nash
D'Albernasi	Lloyd Corrigan
D'Anneci	Fritz Lieber

Although its title might suggest a series of amorous episodes, "Adventures of Casanova" skips by romance for a rousing plume-and-sabre saga that'll be wholly acceptable to the family trade. Made in Mexico to cut the budget outlay, pic makes good use of colorful outdoor backgrounds and effectively integrates hordes of native extras into the action. Film's chief appeal, however, will be among the juves who'll appreciate the good horse opera yarn. Lack of strong marquee names may limit the pic's b.o. potential in key firstruns.

Set in Sicily in 1793 when Italy was under the Austrian yoke, film unfolds a tale of underground revolutionary activity full of hard riding, gunplay and dueling. Although plot can't stand too close an examination, it covers up all illogicalities by generating an elemental tension and excitement. Whole production, from screenplay to direction to thesping, is geared to sweeping action.

Getting off on a high note with scenes of guerrilla war, pic soon boils down to a conflict between Arturo De Cordova, leader of the Italian patriots with a legendary reputation as a lover, and John Sutton, smooth-tongued, black-hearted envoy of the Austrian emperor. Incidental romantic byplay between Casanova and the daughter of the quisling Sicilian governor is drowned in the derring-do proceedings climaxed by a superbly staged 10-minute dueling match between De Cordova and Sutton.

As Casanova, De Cordova carries the part on strength of his face and physique, although his voice and thesping talents fail to bring authority to the role. Sutton makes an accomplished heavy in the silken-gloved tradition. Turhan Bey, as Casanova's sidekick, registers okay in his portrait of an intense patriot. Femme support is managed competently by Lucille Bremer. In a brief part as a spy parading in clergyman's garb, George Tobias contributes some broad comedy touches.

On technical side, film is marked by expert lensing and smooth editing. Good background score adds to overall impact. *Herm.*

Speed to Spare

Hollywood, Feb. 14.

Paramount release of Pine-Thomas production. Stars Richard Arlen, Jean Rogers; features Richard Travis, Roscoe Karns, Nanette Parks. Directed by William Berke. Screenplay, Milton Raison; camera, Ellis W. Carter; editor, Monty Pearce. Tradeshown in Los Angeles, Feb. 13, '48. Running time, 57 mins.

Cliff Jordan.....Richard Arlen
Mary.....Jean Rogers
Jerry.....Richard Travis
Pete Simmons.....Pat Phelan
Jane Chandler.....Nanette Parks
Kangaroo.....Roscue Karns
Pusher.....Ian McDonald
Al Simmons.....Paul Harvey

"Speed to Spare" measures up to all demands of the action market. Fast pace and plenty of thrills insure good reception in the secondary field.

Story is standard plotting but freshened considerably, being capably played and directed. Richard Arlen is the daredevil auto-crasher who gives up that game for the trucking business with a friend. Script gives good idea of safety practices used by trucking concerns, negating idea that truck-drivers are bulging-muscled toughies. However, for sake of thrills, Arlen doesn't knuckle down too well to the safety formula, resulting in action that races along under William Berke's brisk direction.

There's fisticuffs, runaway trailers, high-explosives and chases, all with maximum of suspense staging. Arlen shows well in the lead and Richard Travis, as his sane friend, is excellent. Jean Rogers, costarred, has a minimum of footage. Roscoe Karns, Nanette Parks, Pat Phelan, Ian McDonald, the heavy who gives Arlen most of his trouble; and Paul Harvey round out the good cast.

William Pine and William Thomas have given film the kind of production supervision that pays off. Lensing by Ellie W. Carter is good, and Monty Pearce's editing holds film to tight 57 minutes. *Brog.*

The Challenge

20th-Fox release of Ben Pivar and Bernard Small (Reliance) production. Stars Tom Conway; features June Vincent, Richard Stapley. Directed by Jean Yarbrough. Screenplay by Frank Gruber, Irving Elman; adapted from original story by Sapper; camera, George Robinson; editor, Fred Feitshuns, Jr.; tradeshown N.Y. Feb. 16, '47. Running time, 68 mins.

Bulldog Drummond.....Tom Conway
Vivian Bailey.....June Vincent
Cliff Sonnenberg.....Richard Stapley
Algy Longworth.....John Newland
Kitty.....Eily Malyon
Seymour.....Terry Kilburn
Inspector McIver.....Stanley Logan
Sergeant Shubeck.....Leyland Hodgson
Blinky Henderson.....James Fairfax
Jerome Roberts.....Pat Aherne
Arno.....Oliver Blake
Capt. Sonnenberg.....Housely Stevenson

Another in the Bulldog Drummond series, "The Challenge" is a clean-cut, fast-moving whodunit that'll serve as solid support in dualer situations. Pic is buttressed by a cleverly written screenplay, a competent cast, positive direction cued for action and suspense, and a modest but neat production dress.

Yarn develops at least one novel twist to appease the mystery addicts. As a couple of killings take place to spice up a treasure hunt for a casket of gold, the finger of suspicion points in conventional manner to several assorted characters. Switch, however, occurs at windup when everybody, except for one femme, is found to be guilty.

Plot revolves around the conflict among a group of heirs to a hidden fortune left by an old sea-dog who's murdered by persons unknown. Needling Scotland Yard with his unofficial gumshoe activity, Drummond finds a clue to the mystery in a secret code sewn into the sails of a clipper model. After a couple of close scrapes, he corners the culprits in a trap and delivers the inheritance to its rightful owner.

Tom Conway, in his regular spot as Drummond, registers up to requirements as the strong, handsome, know-it-all amateur sleuth with a pleasantly mild British accent. June Vincent, as one of the heirs, uses her flashy looks and enigmatic personality to good advantage. In lesser roles, Richard Stapley, John Newland and Eily Malyon give sound performances with rest of the cast adding able assists. *Herm.*

Mr. Reckless

Hollywood, Feb. 12.

Paramount release of Pine-Thomas production. Stars William Eythe, Barbara Britton; features Walter Catlett, Minna Gombell, Lloyd Corrigan, Nestor Paiva. Directed by Frank McDonald. Screenplay, Maxwell Shane, Milton Raison; camera, Ellis W. Carter; editor, Howard Smith. Tradeshown in Los Angeles, Feb. 12, '48. Running time, 66 mins.

Jeff Lundy.....William Eythe
Betty Denton.....Barbara Britton
Joel Hawkins.....Walter Catlett
Ma Hawkins.....Minna Gombell
Gus.....Nestor Paiva
Hugo Denton.....Lloyd Corrigan
Pete.....James Millean
Jim Halsey.....Iam McDonald

"Mr. Reckless" is fair thriller that offers some tension for the secondary market. It wastes too much time on dialog and could have used smoother continuity, but is a bread-and-butter meller that will get by.

Plot gives a fast onceover to oil-well workers' occupation. Scripting is strictly stock. There are only a few high spots of action to give a lift to plot triteness. Yarn principally concerns a dashing digger of wells, William Eythe, who returns to scene of earlier romantic triumphs to find the gal he left behind is engaged to an older man. From then on it's just a question of how much time will be used up before the couple admit they're still in love.

Eythe does as well as could be expected with an uncomfortable character. Barbara Britton, femme lead; Paiva, Minna Gombell, Ian McDonald and James Millican are okay. In for comedy are Walter Catlett and Lloyd Corrigan.

Frank McDonald's direction of the Maxwell Shane-Milton Raison screenplay tries hard to smooth out the wandering material but succeeds only occasionally. William Pine and William Thomas have given picture okay mounting for the market, lensing and other technical credits measuring up. *Brog.*

Caged Fury

Hollywood, Feb. 13.

Paramount release of William Pine—William Thomas production. Features Richard Denning, Sheila Ryan, Buster Crabbe, Mary Beth Hughes, Frank Wilcox. Directed by William Berka. Screenplay, David Lange; camera, Ellis W. Carter; editor, Howard Smith. Tradeshown in Los Angeles, Feb. 12, '48. Running time, 60 mins.

Blaney Lewis.....Richard Denning
Kit Warren.....Sheila Ryan
Lola Tremaine.....Mary Beth Hughes
Smiley.....Buster Crabbe
Dan Corey.....Frank Wilcox

"Caged Fury" is among the best, if not the best, of the thrillers turned out by Pine-Thomas for Paramount release. It's an exciting circus story, complete with snarling lions, hand-to-hand combat, a fire and an auto chase. It will be a mighty pleaser in the market for which it is aimed and response should be unusually good for Saturday night, small-town trade.

William Berke's direction demonstrates that he knows his way around an action tale. David Lang's original script deals with a circus wild animal act in which the head man arranges fatal accident for his leading lady so he can take on a new love. Scheme works but when he then tries to get the other male member of the trio, he's uncovered, makes his escape and returns a year later for another try, which springs actionful finale wherein circus catches fire, animals escape, etc.

Richard Denning pleases in the male lead, as does Sheila Ryan as chief femme interest. Buster Crabbe is the sulking villain of the piece, and Mary Beth Hughes is his first victim. Frank Wilcox, and others work out well.

Production values are excellent and careful use has been made of circus montage and other action clips that give a gloss beyond budget expenditure. Capable lensing was by Ellis W. Carter, and Howard Smith did the tight editing. *Brog.*

Tornado Range
(SONGS)

Eagle Lion release of Jerry Thomas production. Stars Eddie Dean; features Roscoe Ates, Jennifer Holt, George Chesebro. Directed by Ray Taylor. Screenplay, William Lively; camera, James Brown, Jr.; songs, Dean, Curt and Alan Mussey; editor, Joseph Gluck. Previewed in N. Y., Feb. 11, '48. Running time, **56 MINS.**

Eddie.....Eddie Dean
Soapy.....Roscoe Ates
Mary.....Jennifer Holt
Lance.....George Chesebro
Jobby.....Brad Slaven
Wilson.....Marshall Reed
Thayer.....Terry Frost
Thorne.....Lane Bradford
Dorgan.....Russell Arms
Pop.....Steve Clark

Another in the Eddie Dean oater series, "Tornado Range" hews closely to the tradition of minor-league westerns. Dialog and plot are standard, and there are ample gunplay and fisticuffs to satisfy the more rabid hoss-opera devotees as well as the Saturday matinee juves. Overall, picture stacks up as an average filler for the action situations.

Yarn is woven around a "war" between homesteaders and ranchers. This particular story material, incidentally, is becoming threadbare. Dean has been assigned by the U. S. Land Office to bring about better relations between the two factions. With the usual intrigue sequences out of the way, the differences of both groups are worked out satisfactorily

Dean contribs an okay performance of hard-ridin' and hard-fightin', His sidekick, Roscoe Ates, supplies the comedy relief, while Jennifer Holt, as the daughter of the ranchers' leader, George Chesebro, furnishes the heart interest. Terry Frost registers as the leader of the outlaws, who seeks to profit by matching the homesteaders and cattlemen against the other.

Ray Taylor directed to advantage in this Jerry Thomas production. Lensing of James Brown, Jr., makes good use of the outdoor scenery.

Eternal Melodies
(Musical)
(ITALIAN-MADE)

Grandi Film release of E.N.I.C. production. Stars Gino Cervi, Conchita Montenegro. Directed by Carmine Gallone. Original story, Ernest Marischka; adaptation, Guido Cantini, Gallone; camera, Brizzi; editor, Nicola Lazzari. At Cinema Dante, N. Y., Feb. 13, '48. Running time, **93 MINS.**

Mozart.....Gino Cervi
Aloisia W. Lange.....Conchita Montenegro
Costanza Weber Mozart.....Luisella Beghi
Anna Maria Mozart.....Maria Jacobini
Nannina Mozart.....Jone Salinas
Signora Weber.....Margherita Bagni
Haibl.....Paolo Stoppa
Deiner.....Lauro Gazzolo
Leopoldo Mozart.....Luigi Pavese
Mozart as a child.....Carlo Barbetti

(In Italian; English Titles)

"Eternal Melodies" is a long-winded, sentimental biog of the great German composer, Wolfgang Amadeus Mozart. Despite an elaborate production facade, the film is a mediocre item that'll dampen the rising prestige Italian offerings are currently enjoying in the sureseater trade. Longhair addicts will be interested in the soundtrack recordings of snatches of Mozart's symphonic and operatic works.

Following a cliched tradition, yarn traces the tribulations of the musical genius through a series of romantic heartbreaks, illness and financial troubles. Film depicts Mozart as dashing off his greatest works in the flicker of a femme's eyelash, paying little attention to the historical facts concerning the composer's life. Plot chiefly revolves around the triangular affair among Mozart and the two Weber sisters, one of whom he loves and the other he marries.

As the composer, Gino Cervi gives a colorless portrait that generates neither credibility nor interest. Conchita Montenegro, as his faithless amour, registers effectively. Luisella Beghi does nicely as the sweet, adoring wife of Mozart. *Herm.*

My Brother Jonathan
(BRITISH-MADE)

London, Feb. 6.

Pathe Pictures release of Associated British Picture Corp.-Warwick Ward production. Stars Dulcie Gray, Michael Denison, Ronald Howard, Stephen Murray. Directed by Harold French. Screenplay by Leslie L. Landau, Adrian Alington from novel by Francis Brett Young. Editor, Charles Hasse; music, Hans May; camera, Derick Williams. At Studio One, London, Feb. 5, '48. Running time, **106 MINS.**

Jonathan Dakers.....Michael Denison
Rachel Hammond.....Dulcie Gray
Harold Dakers.....Ronald Howard
Dr. Craig.....Stephen Murray
Mrs. Dakers.....Mary Clare
Dr. Hammond.....Finlay Currie
Edie Martyn.....Beatrice Campbell
Sir Joseph Higgins.....Arthur Young
Eugene Dakers.....J. Robertson Justice
Tom Morse.....James Hayter
Tony Dakers.....Peter Murrey
Connie.....Jessica Spencer
Young Jonathan.....Desmond Newling
Young Harold.....Alan Goodwin
Alec Martyn.....Felix Deebank
Mr. Martyn.....R. Stuart Lindsell
Mrs. Martyn.....Avice Landone
Mrs. Perry.....Hilda Bayley
Bagley.....Wylie Watson

Adaptation of Francis Brett Young's grim novel is adult and entertaining. It is well acted and should play to good business, despite lack of marquee names. It will need trimming to suit U. S. theatres.

Story is set in England in the early 1900's. Since boyhood Jonathan has wanted to become a great surgeon and to marry Edie. He becomes a doctor but his father's sudden death and the desire to keep his mother in their former home and his younger brother Harold at the university, condemns him to a half share in a poor medical practice in a dreary industrial town. Further blow is Edie falling in love with Harold.

In the first world war Harold joins up and is killed, leaving Edie to bear their illegitimate child. Once again Jonathan proves his love for his brother by marrying Edie, although he is now deeply in love with another. Edie dies in childbirth, committing her baby son Tony to Jonathan's care. He marries Rachel, and they bring up Tony as their own son. Story is told in flashback when Tony, now a grown man, learns the truth.

In his first starring part, Michael Denison gives a good account of himself. Best acting comes from Dulcie Gray. She has no chance for histrionic fireworks, but she strikes the right sympathetic note and maintains it throughout. Ronald Howard (son of late Leslie Howard) gives his best performance to date, and Stephen Murray is good. As Edie, Beatrice Campbell plays her first important part, and is adequate.

Numerous smaller roles are played with distinction, including Mary Claire, Finlay Currie, J. Robertson Justice, Josephine Stuart, E. Stuart Lindsell, Avice Landone, Fred Groves, Beatrice Varley, Paul Farrell and James Hayter. It's the most important picture Harold French has yet directed, and with a little less restraint and improved camera work he might have turned a good film into a memorable one. The music by Hans May is commendable. *Cane.*

Voyage Surprise

(FRENCH-MADE)

Duke International release of Cooperative Generale du Cinema Francais-Synops production. Stars Sinoel and Martine Carol; features Maurice Baquet, Jacques Henri Duval and Rene Bourbon. Directed by Pierre Prevert. Screenplay, Claude Accursi, Jacques and Pierre Prevert; camera, Paul Paviot; music, Joseph Kosma. Previewed in N. Y. Feb. 12, '48. Running time, **80 MINS.**

Grim	Jacques Henri Duval
Teddy	Maurice Baquet
Grandpa Piuff	Sinoel
Baron Gregor	Vitsoris
Mikhail	Etienne Decroux
Renardot	Max Revol
Inspector Vaudor	Charles Lavialle
Grosbois	Rene Bourbon
Isabelle Grosbois	Martine Carol
Marinette	Annette Poivre
The Curate	Fernand Rene
Commandant Wagon	Orbal
Duroc	Lucien Raimbourg
Mrs. Duroc	Jeanne Dussole
Pierrot	Christian Simon
Mlle. Roberta	Therese Dorny
Barbizon	Caccia
Florence	Cecilia Paroldi
Richard	Robert Lombard
Gauthier	Peres
Mme. Marguerite	Claire Gerard
Boris	Nico Dakis
The Grand Duchess	Pierre Pieral

(In French; English Titles)

An amusing bit of Gallic humor, "Voyage Surprise" is a broad comedy that often borders on the fantastic. Nevertheless, its situations are so disarmingly trite and spontaneous in some instances that the film should rate at least a moderate reception in most art houses despite its lack of marquee names.

In authoring a takeoff on the tourist business, writers Jacques and Pierre Prevert, plus Claude Accursi, have utilized some amazingly bizarre scenes. Among them are an hilarious night in a defunct bagnio, an unintentional theatrical performance by a group of sightseers as well as several other equally absurd sequences.

Plot combines some of the best elements of a Hollywood "chase" film augmented with a goodly dash of intrigue supplied by "revolutionists." Picture's title stems from a tour promoted by a travel agent (Sinoel), whose customers are fascinated by the idea of taking pot luck on a vacation trip rather than going or a jaunt with a planned itinerary.

Performances are generally fair. Cast projects the film's satirical flavor with a gay Mardi Gras abandon. Sinoel sparkles as the irresponsible tour conductor. His grandsons and assistants, Maurice Baquet and Jacques Henri Duval, also convince, especially in the romantic passages. Martine Carol, daughter of rival tour promoter Rene Bourbon, is pleasantly decorative while Etienne Decroux is a sinister revolutionist constantly in quest of some crown jewels.

Direction of Pierre Prevert keeps the humor moving at a clumsy pace. Paul Paviot's lensing is good. Production mountings are quite modest. *Gilb.*

Il Diavolo Bianco

("The White Devil")
(ITALIAN-MADE)

Rome, Jan. 23.

Manenti Film release and production. Stars Rossano Brazzi, Annette Bach, Roldano Lupi; features Lea Padovani, Harry Feist, Mario Ferrari. Directed by Nunzio Malasomma. Original story by Gaspare Cataldo; screenplay, Cataldo and Malasomma; camera, Rodolfo Lombardi; music, Ezio Carabella. At Supercinema and Adriano, Rome. Running time **100 MINS.**

Prince Mdwani / The White Devil	Rossano Brazzi
Countess Olga	Annette Bach
Governor Alexis	Roldano Lupi
Katiousha	Lea Padovani
Col. Stanikow	Harry Feist
Professor Ilya	Mario Ferrari
Wassili	Armando Francioli
John	Vittorio Sanipoli

This is a big-budgeted costume melodrama, combining love, violence, intrigue and pageantry. Likely for Italian and Latin-American popular taste, it's too slow-moving and not lavishly enough mounted for large exploitation in U. S. However, picture has some values for the American market.

Set in the Caucasus, in 1850, action is concerned with a mysterious cavalier, the White Devil, who fights to deliver his province from the despotism of a cruel governor. When the outlaw finally takes off his white mask, people recognize Prince Mdwani, who seemed so obsequious to the tyrant and interested only in clothes and quadrilles.

As the White Devil, Rossano Brazzi, now under contract to David O. Selznick, lacks fire. Annette Bach is also miscast as Olga, the Prince's fiancee. Lea Padovani, promising young Italian actress, is very attractive as Katiousha, the governor's mistress, even though she's badly photographed. Roldano Lupi gives a solid characterization of Governor Alexis. *Quat.*

Den Glade Skraddaren

("The Happy Tailor")
(SWEDISH-MADE)
(Songs)

Scandia Films production and release. Stars Edvard Persson. Directed by Gunnar Olsson. Camera, Sven Thermaenious; music, Alvar Kraft. At Fifth Avenue Playhouse, N. Y., starting Feb. 7, '48. Running time, **92 MINS.**

Soren, the tailor	Edvard Persson
Boel, his wife	Mim Persson
Anne-Marie, their oldest daughter	Marianne Gyllenhammar
Anders Bengt, the miller	Ivar Kage
Hanna, his wife	Gurli Lindstrom
Gunnar, their son	Sture Djerf
Squire Sten	Sven Bergvall
Ingvar, his son	Ernst Wellton
The Innkeeper	Fritiof Billquist
The Chairman of the Council	Carl Deurell
Crazy Lars	Algot Larsson
The Minister	Josua Bengtsson

(In Swedish; English Titles)

Without Edvard Persson, chubby Swedish clown, this would be an insipid comedy. With the comic going through his familiar antics, it is fairly palatable judged by foreign screen comedy standards. Plenty of old, laborious slapstick is strutted out for this picture, but despite this Persson puts it over.

Story is one of those things. It has Persson as the amiable village tailor, who would like to make more money (since he has eight children) but never seems to get ahead or care if he does or not. He bids for a flour mill, and miraculously the town's richest man ultimately agrees to advance the money to swing the deal. There's much patter about the wealthy landowner forcing Persson to marry off his daughter to the former's son, but nothing comes of it.

Supporting cast is merely standard, with all acting laurels going to Persson. Camera work by Sven Themaenius is okay. Gunnar Olsson's direction is okay. *Wear.*

Rallare

("Railroad Workers")
(SWEDISH-MADE)

Svensk Filmindustri production and release. Stars Victor Seastrom, John Elfstrom, Gunnel Brostrom; features Bengt Eklund, Sven Magnusson, Birger Asander, Axel Hogel, Keve Hjelm, Inga Landgre, Ingrid Borthen. Directed by Arne Mattsson. Screenplay, Olle Laensberg, Rune Lindstrom, based on latter's novel, "Nordanvind"; camera, Martin Bodin; music, E. Eckert-Lundin. At Roda Kvarn, Stockholm. Running time, **108 MINS.**

Stora Ballong	Victor Seastrom
Valfrid	John Elfstrom
Viktoria	Gunnel Brostrom
Amos	Bengt Eklund
Dynamite	Sven Magnusson
Fabian Bred	Birger Asander
Calle-Ville	Ake Gronberg
Baptist-Anders	Axel Hogel
Natan	Keve Hjelm
Hildur	Inga Landgre
Black Bear	Ingrid Borthen
Stina	Svea Holst
Hager	Sven Bergvall
Blom	Harry Ahlin

One of the top Swedish b.o. pix of the year, "Rallare" is a fine film version of the Rune Lindstrom novel which dealt with an important phase in Swedish history—railway construction during the last century. Picture is a salute to the workers who were called "Rallare."

These men were untutored, with a liking for liquor and an eye for the women. Leading the husky giants are John Elfstrom and Victor Seastrom. Latter is seldom seen in films of late but when he does appear he invariably turns in a top performance. Story calls for few femme parts, but Gunnel Brostrom and Inga Langre lend pleasant decoration. Veteran cameraman Martin Bodin skillfully handled the lens. *Winq.*

Tant Gron, Tant Brun Och Tant Gredelin

("Aunt Green, Aunt Brown and Aunt Lilac")
(SWEDISH-MADE)
(COLOR)

Svensk Filmindustri production and release. Features Brita Brunius, Elsa Ebbesen, Irma Christensson, Einar Axelsson, Anders Borje, Ernst Brunman, Sigge Fyrst, Anders Andelius, Kate Elffors, Bjorn Naesund. Directed by Rune Lindstrom. Screenplay by Lindstrom, based on story by Elsa Beskow; camera (Technicolor), Gunnar Fischer; music, Lillebor Soderlundh. At Spegeln, Stockholm. Running time, **54 MINS.**

First Swedish film in Technicolor emerges as an entertaining nursery tale for children. While the picture probably is too short to offer much appeal overseas, domestic business will be excellent especially from the matinee trade.

Pictures made expressly for juvenile audiences are rarely undertaken in Swedish studios. However director Rune Lindstrom has done a first-class job in bringing his own screenplay to celluloid. Cast in the title roles are Brita Brunius, Elsa Ebbesen and Irma Christensson.

Excellent Technicolor enhances the film's story considerably. With a tint precedent now established, other Swedish filmmakers no doubt will rush to produce pictures in the same medium. This film, incidentally, reportedly will be entered in the Children's Film Festival scheduled to be held at the Bath Assembly, England, the end of April. Event is sponsored by the Rank Orranization. *Winq.*

Tappa Inte Sugen

("Don't Give Up")
(SWEDISH-MADE)

Svensk Filmindustri release of Fribergs Filmbyreau and Koniiska Teatern production. Stars Nils Poppe, Annalisa Ericsson; features Gaby Stenberg, Ulla Sallert, Karl-Arne Holsten, Sigge Fyrst, Stig Jarrel. Directed by Lars-Eric Kjellgren. Screenplay by Poppe, based on the Stanley Lupino operetta, "Lady Behave"; camera, Gunnar Fischer. At China, Stockholm. Running time, **94 MINS.**

Pelle	Nils Poppe
Gulli	Annalisa Ericson
Sonja	Gaby Stenberg
Ylva	Ulla Sallert
Allan	Karl-Arne Holsten
Albert	Sigge Fyrst
Valle	Stig Jarrel
Director	Nils Jacobsson
Manager	Folke Hamrin
Andre	Arne Lindblad
Secretary	Margit Andelius
Jack	Ernst Brunman

A Swedish filmusical, "Tappa Inte Sugen," will be a merry click at the Scandinavian b.o. and has great possibilities for the world market as well. Entire picture reflects the excellent work of Nils Poppe, who is starred in his own adaptation of the Stanley Lupino operetta, "Lady Behave."

Yarn is built around Poppe, whose role is that of a great actor. Script is chiefly an outline of his life, his marriage and career. As a sub-plot, several sequences are woven in around an unknown actress who wants to be a star. Performances deftly reflect the film's spirited pace under the neat direction of Lars-Eric Kjellgren, who made his megging debut with this picture.

Poppe acquits himself admirably as the male lead while his co-star, Annalisa Ericson, also scores as his wife. Gaby Stenberg as the unknown actress who strives to better her professional stature contributes a fine performance. Supporting players measure up. *Winq.*

Foreign Films

"Lo Sconosciuto di San Marino" ("The Unknown of San Marino") **(ITALIAN-MADE).** Generalcine release of Film Gamma production. Stars Anna Magnani. Directed by Vittorio Cottafavi. Story, Cesare Zavattini; screenplay, Zavattini and Cottafavi; camera, Arturo Gallea; music, Antonio Cicognini. At Splendore and Bernini, Rome. Running time, **82 MINS.**

Film produced in Milan, and story of a Nazi officer whose sadistic nature is transformed by illness, has little to commend it. Only Anna Magnani gives, as usual, a poignant performance. Not likely for U. S. Film deals with some prostitution scenes so realistically, it won't pass U. S. censor anyway. *Quat.*

"Natale al Campo 119" ("Christmas at Camp 119") **(ITALIAN-MADE).** Minerva Film release of Excelsa-Amato-De Sica-Fabrizi production. Stars Aldo Fabrizi. Directed by Pietro Francisci. Original story by Michele Galdieri; screenplay by Galdieri, Francisci, Fabrizi; camera, Mario Bava and Augusto Tiezzi; score, Francesco Lavagnino; songs, Bixio and Danzi. At Corso, Moderno and Margherita, Rome. Running time, **90 MINS.**

Episodic story, with flashback sequences in which seven Italian war prisoners, natives of different towns (Rome, Naples, Florence, Venice, Milan, Bologna and a small Sicilian village), remember, during one Christmas Eve, an episode of their civil life. Each episode, acted in a different town, is scored by a local folksong. Songs are fine, but plots are vapid and uninspired. Appeal is only for Italian-born audiences.

Pietro Francisci's direction is fair, but the photography, as the screenplay, often frustrates many of his efforts. The real strength of the picture is in the male cast, above all, with Aldo Fabrizi. His performance is highly vivid. Femmes are weak. *Quat.*

"La Gondola del Diavolo" ("Devil's Gondola") **(ITALIAN-MADE).** Scalera release and production. Features Loredana, Carlo Lombardi, Nino Pavese, Alfredo Varelli, Erminio Spalla. Directed by Carlo Campogalliani. Screenplay,

Marcello Pallieri; camera, Mario Albertelli; music, Renzo Rossellini. At Olympia and Odescalchi, Rome. Running time, 90 MINS.

Routine cloak-and-dagger melodrama set in ancient Venice. Scalera owns a small studio in Venice. Unlikely for U. S. but may do for Latin-American audiences. *Quat.*

"Hofrat Geiger" ("Counsellor Geiger") (AUSTRIAN MADE). Sacha Film Co. release of Willi Forst production. Stars Paul Hoerbiger, Hans Moser, Maria Andergast. Scenario, Martin Costa, Hans Wolff; music, Hans Lang; camera, Rolf Icsey, Ladislaus Szente. Directed by Wolff.

This makes excellent entertainment. Based on a play very successful in Vienna during the war, story depicts search of an elderly man for his lost daughter, of whose existence he learns through perusal of government documents. All ends happily, including his finding an old love. *Maass.*

"Sjatte Budet" ("Sixth Commandment") (SWEDISH-MADE). Kungafilm release of Stellan Claesson production. Features Esther Roeck-Hansen, Stig Jarrel, Ingrid Backlin, Lauritz Falk, Gosta Cederlund, Irma Christenson. Directed by Jarrell. Screenplay, Arne Mehrens; camera, Walter Boberg. At Rigoletto, Stockholm. Running time, 112 MINS.

Poor direction and camerawork spoil this drama. Dealing with some risque situations, film's story doesn't have much to recommend it in first place. Esther Roeck-Hansen, cast in the principal femme role, is badly photographed. "Sjatte Budet" may have a chance in Sweden as the result of an exploitation campaign, but its prospects in the foreign marts are nil.

"Jag Ar Med Eder" ("I Am With You") (SWEDISH-MADE). Svensk Film release of Studio Film Production. Stars Victor Seastrom, Rune Lindstrom; features Karin Cederstrom, Nils Dahlgren, Ake Fridell, Carl Strom. Directed by Gosta Stevens. Screenplay, Stevens and Lindstrom; camera, Ake Dahlquist. At Spegeln, Stockholm. Running time, 94 MINS.

Another film starring Victor Seastrom, with story dealing with the life of Swedish missionaries in Africa. Most of the picture was shot on location in Africa last fall. Camerawork of Ake Dahlquist stands out, especially in the outdoor scenes of Rhodesia and the Zambesi river. Film should do well in Sweden and has mild chances overseas. *Winq.*

"Le Beau Voyage" ("The Beautiful Trip") (FRENCH-MADE). CPLF release of Gaumont Gelia production. Stars Pierre Richard Willm, Renee Saint Cyr; features Andre Valmy, Laure Diana. At Paramount, Paris. Running time, 104 MINS.

Extremely weak in every respect, "Le Beau Voyage" is an amateurish tale of a pianist who meets a girl on shipboard. She's bound for Australia to marry an ex-convict who befriended her in her early struggles. Direction, photography and acting are of poor quality. Andre Valmy helps to some extent with a fair performance. French market is limited for this one and the overseas outlook is nil. *Maxi.*

"Loffe Pa Luffen" ("Loffe, the Tramp") (SWEDISH-MADE). Kungafilm production and release. Stars Elof Ahrle; features Viktor Andersson, Erik Berglund, Agneta Prytz, Lasse Krantz, Yngve Nordvall, Magnus Kesster. Directed by Gosta Werner. Screenplay, Arne Mehrens; camera, Karl-Erik Alberts. At Astoria, Stockholm. Running time, 86 MINS.

This is a story of a corporation head who believes his employees do their best to cheat the firm. He decides to use a tramp to expose the wrongdoers. He has faith in the tramp's honesty but views his own personal friends with distrust. While the idea may be good material for a comedy it just doesn't come off under Gosta Werner's direction. Film's chances are limited to the Scandinavian mart only.

Miniature Reviews

"All My Sons" (U). Powerful screen adaptation of the prize-winning Broadway play. Class drama, superbly done.

"The Bride Goes Wild" (M-G). Nifty comedy with good b.o. potential. Solid laughs sparked by antics of strong cast.

"Sitting Pretty" (20th). Outstanding comedy with great word - of - mouth potential for gross-building.

"Six-Gun Law" (Col). Okay Charles Starrett western

"The Westward Trail" (EL). Trite oatuner in the Eddie Dean series.

"The Raven" (Indie). Pierre Fresnay in complicated French-made whodunit.

"Against the Wind" (GFD). So-so British-made sabotage melo, suitable for U. S. duals.

"Call of the Blood" (BL). British-made period rama of limited appeal.

All My Sons

Hollywood, Feb. 20.
Universal release of Chester Erskine production. Stars Edward G. Robinson, Burt Lancaster; features Mary Christians, Louisa Horton, Howard Duff, Frank Conroy, Arlene Francis, Lloyd Gough. Directed by Irving Reis. Screenplay, Chester Erskine from play by Arthur Miller; camera, Russell Metty; music, Leith Stevens; editor, Ralph Dawson. Previewed Feb. 18, '48. Running time, 93 MINS.
Joe Keller..............Edward G. Robinson
Chris Keller................Burt Lancaster
Kate Keller................Mady Christians
Ann Deever.................Louisa Horton
George Deever................Howard Duff
Herbert Deever..............Frank Conroy
Jim Bayliss...................Lloyd Gough
Sue Bayliss.................Arlene Francis
Frank Lubey..............Henry Morgan
Lydia Lubey..............Elisabeth Fraser

"All My Sons" comes to the screen with a potent impact. Whatever message may have been in the stage presentation has been resolved to the more fundamental one of man's duty to man, and gains strength by that switch. It's a serious, thoughtful study, loaded with dramatic dynamite, that rates as a class attraction for the de luxers.

Chester Erskine's approach to the Arthur Miller play benefits from the broader movement permitted by the screen. It's an ace scripting and production job that carefully measures every value to be found in the plot. Irving Reis' direction never permits the story-telling to waver, underplaying rather than overplaying, the many intense scenes for telling effect.

Script makes the point that we all are our brother's keepers with a responsibility that can't be shunted aside for purely personal desires. Rather than hammering point over, it is gradually brought out in telling of a man who, in a desire for success, becomes responsible for the death of 21 fliers during the war. How retribution is visited on him, by his own hands, gives a solid finish to dramatic events that lead up to the climax.

Edward G. Robinson gives an effective performance as the small-town manufacturer who sends defective parts to the Army Air Forces. It's a humanized study that rates among his best and lends the thought behind the film much strength. Burt Lancaster, as his war-embittered son, shades the assignment with just the right amount of intensity. His love and belief in his dad, whom he must betray to right the wrong done, cloaks the role with that human touch that marks all of the characters.

Louisa Horton, debuting in films from legit, is a talented lass with personality. The love story (Lancaster is opposite) ably projected, carrying warmth and tenderness against a tragic background. Mady Christians scores as the understanding wife and mother who tries to protect her husband. Howard Duff points up his role as the son of Robinson's betrayed partner, Frank Conroy. Latter makes a brief prison scene stand out. Arlene Francis. Lloyd Gough, Henry Morgan and Elisabeth Fraser are others who shine.

Leith Stevens' score combines sound effects with musical theme for highly effective backing of the drama. Russell Metty's photography is a class work and other technical credits figure importantly in measuring this for top playing time. *Brog.*

The Bride Goes Wild

Hollywood, Feb. 21.
Metro release of William H. Wright production. Stars Van Johnson, June Allyson; features Butch Jenkins, Hume Cronyn, Una Merkel. Directed by Norman Taurog. Original screenplay, Albert Beich; camera, Ray June; score, Rudolph G. Kopp; editor, George Boemler. Tradeshown Feb. 18, '48. Running time, 97 MINS.
Greg Rawlings..............Van Johnson
Martha Terryton...........June Allyson
Danny.....................Butch Jenkins
John McGrath..............Hume Cronyn
Miss Doherly..............Una Merkel
Tillie Smith...............Arlene Dahl
Bruce Kope Johnson........Richard Derr
"Pop".....................Lloyd Corrigan
Mrs. Carruthers..........Elisabeth Risdon
Aunt Pewtie..............Clara Blandick
Aunt Susan..............Kathleen Howard

There's nothing subtle about the comedy in "The Bride Goes Wild." It's a broad, slapstickish ribtickler that's mighty pleasant to take. Audience reaction will be strong and the returns should be gratifying. Marquee flash is added by names of Van Johnson and June Allyson, both of whom demonstrate a flare for comedy that registers.

Plot is a belly-laugher about a character called "Uncle Bumps" who writes kiddie stories. The scribe is Van Johnson, a kid-hating young man who's inclined to be an irresponsible lush. Action is well-plotted and is carried swiftly along by Norman Taurog's firm direction. He has injected bits of business that click, makes the laughs spring easily from both the naturally funny situations and those that are frenetic sight gags. June Allyson is sheer delight as the artistically-inclined New England school teacher who wins a job as illustrator for Uncle Bumps' latest story. The two are brought together with a mistaken-identity gag that grows into an hilariously funny drunk scene played by Miss Allyson. Johnson also is sharp in grabbing the laughs. Plot is kept alive by antagonism between the pair even though there's never any doubt about the outcome. Albert Beich's original screenplay carries a load of standard physical gags that have been neatly dressed up and the dialog is smart, although not much of it will be heard because of audience reaction to sight stuff.

Butch Jenkins is his precocious self as the orphan who eventually gets the romantic principals together via adoption. It's a character that cloaks lonesomeness with a tough attitude against adults. He is responsible for the frantic uproar that breaks up the finale wedding by loosing a horde of ants on the guests. Hume Cronyn is the harrassed publisher of Johnson's literary outpourings, playing nursemaid and mentor to the young man and his troubles. It's a funny, well-played role. Una Merkel sparks laughs as his secretary. Arlene Dahl gets in some good licks as a vampish young lady and Richard Derr is the stuffy suitor of Miss Allyson's. Elisabeth Risdon and others play capable part in the fun.

William H. Wright's production garnishes the story with suitable physical values, backed by Ray June's excellent lensing, the Rudolph G. Kopp score, settings and art direction. *Brog.*

Sitting Pretty

Hollywood, Feb. 21.

20th-Fox release of Samuel G. Engel production. Stars Robert Young, Maureen O'Hara, Clifton Webb; features Richard Haydn, Louise Allbritton, Randy Stuart, Ed Begley, Larry Olsen, John Russell, Betty Ann Lynn, Willard Robertson. Directed by Walter Lang. Screenplay, F. Hugh Herbert, based on novel by Gwen Davenport; camera, Norbert Brodine; music, Alfred Newman; editor, Harmon Jones. Tradeshown Feb. 20, '48. Running time, 84 MINS.

Harry	Robert Young
Tacey	Maureen O'Hara
Lynn Belvedere	Clifton Webb
Mr. Appleton	Richard Haydn
Edna Philby	Louise Allbritton
Peggy	Randy Stuart
Hammond	Ed Begley
Larry King	Larry Olsen
Bill Philby	John Russell
Ginger	Betty Ann Lynn
Mr. Ashcroft	Willard Robertson
Tony	Anthony Sydes
Roddy	Roddy McCaskill
Mrs. Appleton	Grayce Hampten
Secretaries	Cara Williams, Marion Marshall
Mr. Taylor	Charles Arnt
Mr. McPherson	Ken Christy
Mrs. Ashcroft	Ann Shoemaker
Mrs. Maypole	Minerva Urecal
Mrs. Phillips	Mira McKinney
Cab Driver	Sid Saylor
Matron	Ruth Warren
Mrs. Frisbee	Isabel Randolph
Effie	Ellen Lowe
Mailman	Dave Morris
Mrs. Gibbs	Anne O'Neal
Maitre D'	Albin Robeling
Mrs. Hammond	Josephine Whittell
Librarian	Mary Field
Newsreel Man	Billy Wayne

Inherent humor in the baby-sitting profession has been slicked up into a surefire comedy. "Sitting Pretty" is the best of the mirthmakers to come from Hollywood in a long, long time. It has everything to point it for smart grosses. Socko values will have audiences boosting this one as much as the studio—a form of exploitation guaranteeing solid returns.

It kicks off with a chuckle and ends on a belly-laugh. In between is just about the smoothest package of fun possible. Picture gives you a baby sitter—but what a sitter. Just the thought of Clifton Webb following such a profession is cause enough for mirth, indicating the hilarity to be found in "Sitting Pretty." Samuel G. Engel's production hasn't overlooked a single bet in bringing this one to the screen, garbing it with showmanship that will pay off.

Dialog crackles in the husband-wife talk between Robert Young and Maureen O'Hara, reaches the heights of blase self-satisfaction when Webb explains he's a genius, and always is geared to making the characters entirely believable. The fun is of the type completely familiar to all parents with kids and baby-sitter problems. One of the big merits of the scripting job by F. Hugh Herbert from the Gwen Davenport novel is the fidelity with which family situations are portrayed without exaggeration, and subtle buildup of the other sequences to wham home a laugh.

Cast principals romp through their assignments with apparent enjoyment, lending infectious quality to what transpires under the surehanded direction of Walter Lang. Latter carefully builds each scene, milks every element of mirth, and then moves quickly into the next hilarious incident. It's a top job of direction for comedy.

Plot is located in the residential suburb of Hummingbird Hill, wherein dwell Robert Young, Maureen O'Hara and their three small sons. Life is not too hectic until the mother advertises for a baby-sitter and gets Clifton Webb. The self-styled genius is a jewel at his trade. His presence smooths complications —and adds them—to the suburb but the real blowup comes when he turns out to be an author who has faithfully recorded the peccadillos of the suburbanites in a best-seller.

Young, Miss O'Hara and Webb wrap up slick portrayals as the starring trio. Richard Haydn contributes a gem of performance as suburban snoop and prissy gossiper. Betty Ann Lynn clicks as a teenage baby-sitter. Larry Olsen, Anthony Sydes and Roddy McCaskill register as the three roughneck youngsters. Louise Allbritton and John Russell team as friends of the principals. Others give importance to smaller roles.

Backing the surefire entertainment are some topnotch technical credits. Norbert Brodine's lensing, the score by Alfred Newman, with orchestral arrangements by Edward Powell; art direction and set decorations, which are never too flossy for the couple's financial circumstances; and crisp editing are among factors aiding merriment.

Brog.

Six-Gun Law

Columbia release of Colbert Clark production. Stars Charles Starrett, Smiley Burnette; features Nancy Saunders, Paul Campbell, Hugh Prosser, Curly Clements, Rodeo Rangers. Directed by Ray Nazarro. Original screenplay, Barry Shipman; camera, George F. Kelley; editor, Henry DeMond. At New York theatre, N. Y., week Feb. 17, '48. Running time, 54 MINS.

Steve Norris	Charles Starrett
Smiley Burnette	Smiley Burnette
June Wallace	Nancy Saunders
Jim Wallace	Paul Campbell
Boss Decker	Hugh Prosser
Bret Wallace	George Chesebro
Crowl	Billy Dix
Larson	Bob Wilke
Ben	Bob Cason
Sheriff Brackett	Ethan Laidlaw
Jack Reed	Pierce Lyden
Barton	Bud Osborn
Bank Clerk Duffy	Bud Buster

There's ample shootin' and hard ridin' in "Six-Gun Law" which, in itself, will make this oater an audience satisfier in the action situations. While the budget obviously is modest, producer Colbert Clark also has endowed the film with an okay cast with technical support also measuring up. Henry DeMond's trim editing reels out the plot in a tight 54 minutes.

As the Durango Kid, Charles Starrett is a sterling example of law triumphant. He's framed by town boss Hugh Prosser into the delusion he's killed the sheriff. Upon Prosser's orders, Starrett then assumes the badge of office.

But far from being merely a stooge for the outlaw boss, Starrett assumes his disguise of the masked Durango Kid to foil the sinister schemes of the baddies. He succeeds in thwarting a bank robbery engineered by Prosser and as a climax bags his adversaries with the aid of a U.S. marshal he's summoned. Story, of course, is relatively standard but scripter Barry Shipman has injected several amusing twists.

Smiley Burnette ably supplies the comic relief and Prosser is adequate as the rascal. Nancy Saunders has the lone femme role, that of a rancher's daughter. Other performances are better than usually seen in hoss op'rys. Curly Clements and his Rodeo Rangers are spotted in the musical sequences. Ray Nazarro's direction is good and lensing of George F. Kelley is a creditable job.

Gilb.

The Westward Trail

Eagle Lion release of Jerry Thomas production. Stars Eddie Dean; features Roscoe Ates, Phyllis Planchard, Eileene Hardin. Directed by Ray Taylor. Original screenplay, Robert Alan Miller; songs, Pete Gates, Hal Blair and Dean; camera, Ernie Miller; editor, Hugh Winn. Previewed N. Y., Feb. 19, '48. Running time, 56 MINS.

Eddie	Eddie Dean
Soapy	Roscoe Ates
Ann	Phyllis Planchard
Mrs. Benson	Eileene Hardin
Tom	Steve Drake
Larson	Bob Duncan
Art	Carl Mathews
Sheriff	Lee Morgan
Stage Driver	Bob Woodward
Benson	Budd Buster
Bartender	Charles "Slim" Whitaker
Taggart	Frank Ellis

"The Westward Trail" is one of the poorer Eddie Dean oatuners. Film is handicapped by a triter than usual saddle saga. Entry is destined to wind up as a filler for the duals or as a pad-out on Saturday matinee screenings.

For this opus Dean is cast in his customary role as a representative of the U.S. marshal. He hides his identity through most of the footage but flashes the badge of office in time to win the confidence of Phyllis Planchard, who's on the verge of losing her newly-purchased ranch to the scheming Bob Duncan.

Dean contribs a standard performance doling out the fisticuffs where necessary. He also warbles several tunes of which the interminable "When Shorty Plays the Schottische" rates the dubious distinction of having almost as many choruses as "Casey Jones." Supporting players are mediocre. Ray Taylor's direction is ordinary while Jerry Thomas' production mountings are meagre. Ernie Miller's lensing is so-so as are other technical credits.

Gilb.

The Raven
(FRENCH-MADE)

Westport International release of Continental Films production. Stars Pierre Fresnay. Directed by Henri-Georges Clouzot. Screenplay, Louis Chavance, Clouzot; camera, Nicolas Hayer; English titles, Herman G. Weinberg. Previewed in N. Y., Feb. 19, '48. Running time, 90 MINS.

Dr. Germain	Pierre Fresnay
Dr. Vorzet	Pierre Larquey
Saillens	Noel Roquevert
Delorme	Antoine Balpetre
Bonnevi	Jean Brochard
Bertrand	A. Louis Seigner
DeMaquet	Robert Clermont
Mail Superintendent	Palau
Preacher	Marcel Delaitre
Denise	Ginette Leclerc
Laura	Micheline Francey
Marie	Helena Manson
Shopkeeper	Jeanne Fusier-Gir
Mother of "No. 13"	Sylvie
Rolande	Liliane Maigne

(In French; English Titles)

"The Raven" ("Le Corbeau") is a Gallic-style whodunit of uneven quality. Full impact of its salty details and sharply etched characters is weakened by an overlong screenplay that's barely able to extricate itself from a tangled web of complications. Good play at the art houses, however, will be assured by Pierre Fresnay's pulling power and from the mystery addicts who don't care what language they're baffled in.

Rarely has a nastier crew of personalities been assembled in one film. From a group of five-year old kindergarten tots up through all levels of a typical small French town, the collection includes peeping-toms, forgers, perverts, madmen and murderers with nary a pleasant face in the lot. Considerable force is derived by the story from these off-color characters but, unfortunately, they tend to meander a bit.

Yarn traces the rising fever chart of a town in which a diabolical poison-pen letter-writer is at work. Each official in turn is needled by revelations of some petty grafting of his own or some extra-curricular marital activity of his wife. Chief target of the letters, however, is a young doctor, Pierre Fresnay, with a mysterious past. After dark hints that Fresnay might be writing the letters himself, the finger of suspicion travels around the full circle until it stops at the least likely character.

Interwoven into this cliched plot is a series of graphic incidents involving Fresnay and Ginette Le-Clerc, a man-crazy voluptuary with a spine-chilling leg deformity that lends a new twist to horror and sensuality. Piling on to the morbid atmosphere, Liliane Maigne, a 14-year old, who sneaks around keyholes like an ideal reform school candidate.

Fresnay gives another one of his brilliant performances that goes a long way in making the incredible plausible. Miss LeClerc also fully captures the meaning of her part. As the town psychiatrist who turns out to be a psychopath, Pierre Larquey is highly competent. Rest of the cast also contribute with some expert thesping.

Camera work and editing are good while the English titles permit fluent understanding of the action.

Herm.

Against the Wind
(BRITISH-MADE)

London, Feb. 12.

General Film Distributors release of Ealing Studios-Michael Balcon production. Features Robert Beatty, Simone Signoret, Jack Warner. Directed by Charles Crichton. Adapted by Michael Pertwee from story by J. Elder Wills; added dialog, Paul Vincent Carroll; editor, Alan Osbiston; music, Leslie Bridgewater; camera, Lionel Banes, Paul Beeson. At Studio One, London, Feb. 11, '48. Running time, 96 MINS.

Father Philip	Robert Beatty
Michele	Simone Signoret
Cronk	Jack Warner
Duncan	Gordon Jackson
Picquart	Paul Dupuis
Julie	Giselle Preville
Emile	John Slater
Andrew	Peter Illing
Ackerman	James Robertson Justice
Malou	Sybilla Binder
Marie Beriot	Helene Hansen
Commandant	Gilbert Davis
Frankie	Andrew Blackett
Verreker	Arthur Lawrence
Marcel Van Hecke	Eugene Deckers
Balthasar	Leo de Pokorny
Carey	Rory MacDermot
Captain Parker	Kenneth Hyde
Abbot	Andre Morell

There is little fresh treatment in this story of sabotage organized in London during the war and carried out by the underground in Belgium. It takes 40 minutes for a couple of principal actors to disentangle themselves from the documentary aspect to initiate the first thrill. Although the film is well made, it can't hope to do more than average business here, and will only suit for duals in America.

Somewhere in London in 1943, various people are training for sabotage. One group consists of a Catholic priest from Montreal, a young Scot with a knowledge of explosives, a foreign girl anxious to forget a love affair, an elderly man who undergoes a facial operation as a disguise, a genial time-server willing to doublecross anybody for money, and others.

Having completed their training they are parachuted into Belgium. The two amusing characters now disappear—a girl who has fallen for the priest breaks her neck parachuting from the plane, and the incompetent doublecrosser is bumped off. Two main jobs for the group are destruction of the Records Office and the rescue of a keyman held by the Nazis. The Record Office goes up in flames, and the last part of the film resolves itself into familiar cops-and-robbers stuff.

This should have been a biting, gripping melodrama, but something went wrong with the treatment. Methods of sabotage are no longer screen novelty, and the documentary should have been reduced to a bare minimum. During the last 15 minutes there is a lot of bewildering conversation that doesn't help.

There's a lot of good acting in the picture. French actress, Simone Signoret makes a successful British screen debut. She has charm and ability, and her restrained love scenes with Gordon Jackson are extremely well played. Robert Beatty does all required of him as the priest, Paul Dupuis has his moments as the patriot turned Nazi, John Slater is good as the man with two faces, Peter Illing suffers nobly as the key man, James Robertson Justice makes the sabotage chief an intriguing and important figure, and the smaller ro'es are played very well.

Production is up to Ealing standard, and direction by Charles Crichton is firm. He did a good job, particularly in the unexciting moments.

Cane.

Call of the Blood
(BRITISH-MADE)

London, Feb. 13.

British Lion release of John Stafford, Steven Pallos (Pendennis) production. Stars Kay Hammond, John Clements, John Justin. Directed by Clements. Screenplay by Clements, Akos Tolnay from Robert Hichens 'novel; editor, Carmen Beliaeff; music, Ludovico Lunghi; camera, Wilkie Cooper, V. Arata. At Academy, London, Feb. 12, '48. Running time, 88 MINS.

Dr. Anne Lester............Kay Hammond
Julius Ikon..................John Clements
David Erskine................John Justin
Dr. Robert Blake...........Hilton Edwards
Gaspare.......................Robert Rietty
Salvatore......................Carlo Ninchi
Maddelena....................Lea Padovani
Sebastiano......................Jelo Filippo
Uncle..........................H. G. Stoker
Dr. Sabatier....................Keith Pyott
Lucretia.................Maresa Faclacani

Little entertainment in this outmoded adaptation of Robert Hichens' dated novel. B.o. draw won't be strong, with little market in America.

Story is set in 1900 when Anne, a pioneer doctor, decides to marry David. On their wedding day he receives as a gift a villa in Sicily left him by his mother. They honeymoon there and meet Ikon, an elderly dilettante. Latter's cynicism takes the form of lengthy dissertations on destiny and marionettes, and when Anne receives an SOS to help combat an epidemic in Tunis, Ikon deliberately maneuvers David into the arms of Maddalena, exotic daughter of a fisherman. Story ends in tragedy.

John Clements, as screenwriter, has handicapped Clements as director and actor. Motion pictures must move, and some motivation must exist for actions of people in a story. Film lacks both. Kay Hammond is only fair. John Justin struggles hard to make dialog and situations credible. Lea Padovani is suitably seductive as the Sicilian passion-flower, and other native players help give the film some atmosphere.

Cane.

Miniature Reviews

"The Miracle of the Bells" (RKO). Simple, moving story of faith. Certain of potent audience response. Strong b.o.

"Scudda - Hoo! Scudda-Hay!" (Color). (20th). Modern farming story excellent for general b.o.

"The Return of the Whistler" (Col). Fairish whodunit for supporting situations.

"The Hawk of Powder River" (EL). Poor western in the Eddie Dean series.

"Oklahoma Badlands" (Rep). Allan "Rocky" Lane in fast-paced western thriller; fine support on twinners.

"Blanche Fury" (Color) (British) (GFD). Stewart Granger in moody meller; likely only for prestige market in U.S.

Miracle of the Bells

Hollywood, Feb. 28.

RKO release of Jesse L. Lasky-Walter MacEwen production. Stars Fred MacMurray, Valli, Frank Sinatra; features Lee J. Cobb, Veronika Pataky, Philip Ahn, Harold Vermilyea. Directed by Irving Pichel. Screenplay, Ben Hecht, Quentin Reynolds; from novel by Russell Janney; camera, Robert DeGrasse; score, Leigh Harline; song (English lyrics), Jules Styne and Sammy Cahn; special bell effects, Liberty Carillons, Inc.; editor, Elmo Williams. Tradeshown Feb. 26, '48. Running time, 118 MINS.

Bill Dunnigan.............Fred MacMurray
Olga Treskovna..............................Valli
Father Paul.................Frank Sinatra
Marcus Harris...................Lee J. Cobb
Anna Klovna.............Veronika Pataky
Ming Gow......................Philip Ahn
Nick Orloff..............Harold Vermilyea
Father Spinsky...........Charles Meredith
Doctor........................Frank Wilcox

"The Miracle of the Bells" comes to the screen as a tremendously moving drama. Told with compelling simplicity and great heart, it will rate audience acclaim that counts for heavy grosses. As a goodwill messenger for Hollywood, film also is potent.

In telling the story of faith as narrated in Russell Janney's novel of the same title, Jesse L. Lasky and Walter MacEwen have strung their production on a chord of simplicity that registers with the widest appeal. The characters, locale and theme ring true.

Valli, introduced to American audiences in a previous Hollywood production ("Paradine Case"), justifies any acclaim with her performance in "Miracle." It's a portrayal of great sympathy, understanding and boff talent. Her marquee value should soar after this. She is not alone, though, with outstanding work. Her co-stars, Fred MacMurray and Frank Sinatra, top previous performances, and the featured and supporting players come through with characterizations that make the story live.

"Miracle" is not without its human chuckles, and never bears down with a dramatic weight that would make for heaviness or tediousness. Responsible for this smooth flow of interest is the direction of Irving Pichel, which makes the almost two-hour running time seem comparatively short.

Screenplay by Ben Hecht and Quentin Reynolds is always engrossing in development, takes hold early and never lets up in the realistic unfoldment. Script isn't patterned too closely in detail to the novel, but brings out the original's theme with all the scope possible in screen treatment.

Story is told partly in flashback as a hotshot press agent brings the body of an actress back to the small Pennsy mining town, in which she was born, for burial. The character of the girl, what she found in life and what she wanted to give to her people, is brought out as Fred MacMurray, the flack, recounts her story to the priest of a small, poor church. MacMurray's scheming to make her funeral a memorable event and, incidentally to use that fanfare to induce her producer to release her first and only picture, has a vivid reaction throughout the nation. Story subject seems morbid, but so tastfully is it handled, it never repels and the miracle of the bells created gets a strong grip on the imagination.

Miss Valli's performance conveys the impression of the poor Polish girl, ambitious for good, with a feeling that socks home. Her reading of Joan of Arc in the motion picture sequences is high artistry. MacMurray shades the p.a. character with just the right touch to win interest. Sinatra, the poor priest, is outstanding. It's a human, thoughtful portrayal. He also sings English lyrics to a Polish folksong, "Ever Homeward," for standout vocal moment.

Lee J. Cobb is a solid ambassador for Hollywood in his performance as the producer. It's a character that's more true to life than the popular fiction drafting of film makers as money-grubbers with no instinct for good or beauty. Veronika Pataky, a temperamental actress, clicks in a single scene. Philip Ahn lends dignity to performance as an aged Chinese, and Harold Vermilyea graphically gets over the smallness that afflicts too many persons in this world.

Leigh Harline's musical score, directed by Constantin Bakaleinikoff, is an ace job. Special bell effects and other background tones figure importantly. Robert De-Grasse did the top quality lensing and other credits are equally outstanding in measuring this one for attention.

Brog.

Scudda-Hoo! Scudda-Hay!
(COLOR)

Hollywood, Feb. 28.

20th-Fox release of Walter Morosco production. Stars June Haver; features Lon McCallister, Walter Brennan, Anne Revere, Natalie Wood, Robert Karnes, Henry Hull, Tom Tully. Direction and screenplay, F. Hugh Herbert. From novel by George Agnew Chamberlain; camera (Technicolor), Ernest Palmer; music, Cyril Mockridge; editor, Harmon Jones. Tradeshown Feb. 27, '48. Running time, 95 MINS.

Rad McGill.........................June Haver
Snug Dominy...............Lon McCallister
Tony Maule................Walter Brennan
Judith Dominy..................Anne Revere
Bean McGill...................Natalie Wood
Stretch Dominy...............Robert Karnes
Milt Dominy.......................Henry Hull
Roarer McGill......................Tom Tully
Ches.......................Lee MacGregor
Mrs. McGill..................Geraldine Wall
Sheriff Bursom..................Ken Christy
Judge Stillwell..................Tom Moore
Jim...........................Matt McHugh
Barber................Charles Wagenheim
Dugan....................Herbert Heywood
Ted..........................Edward Gargan
Elmer............................Guy Beach
Malone.......................G. Pat Collins
Jeff..........................Charles Woolf
Stable Hand.................Eugene Jackson
Girl Friend..................Marilyn Monroe

An eulogy to a mule doesn't sound like a good, commercial film idea, but "Scudda-Hoo! Scudda-Hay!" easily proves it is. Taken from the novel of the same title, which enjoyed a wide reading audience, plot has been adapted to celluloid in manner that carries appeal for most any theatregoer. Added value of Technicolor, a sound story of farm life, and general production showmanship augur well for boxoffice returns in most situations.

While theme of giving the mule his proper place in fame as a smart draft animal is thoroughly explored, elements of story that will hit a wider appeal have not been overlooked. Combination of the two has been developed with punch in F. Hugh Herbert's script and, as director, he overlooks no bets in pointing the ingredients for audience interest. A firstrate credit on both counts.

The mule, with no pride of ancestry and no hope for posterity, is shown for just what he is—a hybrid developed from mating of a horse to a jack—a proud animal, able to hold his own with the thoroughbreds for savvy, work ability, or contrariness. Film examples are a pair of striking animals, a large mule and a jenny.

Lon McCallister gives a sound portrayal as the young farm lad who acquires ownership of the mules on the time-payment plan and his adventures as he works and fights to retain them against odds posed by nature and man are engrossing. Left with a cruel stepmother and step-brother when his father returns to the sea, McCallister hires himself out to a blustering farmer neighbor. Hard work to meet his weekly payments on the team, his romance with the farmer's daughter, his friendship with an old muleskinner and other ingredients are told with interesting simplicity in the Herbert script.

June Haver, as romance opposite McCallister, justifies her starring role in one scene when she tells off her father for his plot to take away the boy's team. Otherwise, her role is more or less standard. Walter Brennan is skillful as the old muleskinner. Anne Revere and Robert Karnes are excellent as the menacing step-parents. Tom Tully gives a top account of himself as the loud-mouthed farmer and little Natalie Wood clicks as Miss Haver's kid sister. Henry Hull is seen briefly and effectively as McCallister's father. Geraldine Wall and others in the cast point up their playing well.

Walter Morosco garbed the production with topnotch outdoor values and gave the George Agnew Chamberlain novel intelligent screen interpretation. Ernest Palmer's color lensing milks every value from the outdoor and night scenery and other credits measure up in craftsmanship.

Brog.

Return of the Whistler

Columbia release of Rudolph C. Flothow production. Features Michael Duane, Lenore Aubert, Richard Lane. Directed by D. Ross Lederman. Original story, Cornell Woolrich, suggested by CBS program, "The Whistler"; screenplay, Edward Bock, Maurice Tombragel; camera, Philip Tannura; editor, Dwight Caldwell; music, Mischa Bakaleinikoff. At New Yorker theatre, N. Y., Feb. 25, '48. Running time, 63 MINS.

Ted Nichols.................Michael Duane
Alice Barclay..................Lenore Aubert
Gaylord Travers..............Richard Lane
John.........................James Cardwell
Mrs. Barclay..............Ann Shoemaker
Mrs. Hulskamp................Sarah Padden
Dr. Grantland.................Wilton Graff
Jeff Anderson....................Olin Howlin
Sam..............................Eddy Waller
Arnold........................Trevor Bardette
Sybil..............................Ann Doran
Hart...............Robert Emmett Keane
Captain Griggs..............Edgar Dearing

"The Return of the Whistler" misses because of obvious padding of an insufficient amount of story material. With some judicious editing, the film could have been a superior suspense thriller. However, there's an okay substitution of the chase and fisticuffs to provide the picture with the normal quota of excitement. Fair dualer.

There are times during the picture when the taut story lines of the Cornell Woolrich original are discernible. However, an undue amount of slow dialog and unnecessary flashbacks obscure the virtues of the original idea of presenting a crime with few clues to work on.

The story concerns the sudden disappearance of Michael Duane's would-be bride with Duane unable to provide any of her background that would lead to her return. From a few effects left behind, he's able to trace her whereabouts and finally affect a reunion after the customary chase and fisticuffs.

Central character of the CBS radio program, "The Whistler," has little if anything to do with the proceedings. Occasionally, the Whistler flashes across the screen with some dire forebodings that neither contribute nor detract from the general procedure.

The lead roles by Duane and Lenore Aubert, latter as the missing bride, are completely essayed, with staunch support by Richard Lane as the private eye who walks into the case. James Cardwell provides the major portion of the villainy.

Director D. Ross Lederman manages to infuse some excitement after the story padding is out of the way. Lensing by Philip Tannura is okay.

Jose.

The Hawk of Powder River

(SONGS)

Eagle Lion release of Jerry Thomas production. Stars Eddie Dean; features Jennifer Holt, Roscoe Ates, June Carlson. Directed by Ray Taylor. Original screenplay, George Smith; camera, Ernie Miller; songs, Dean, Hal Blair, Pete Gates; editor, Joe Gluck. Previewed N. Y., Feb. 26, '48. Running time, 54 MINS.

Eddie	Eddie Dean
Soapy	Roscoe Ates
Vivian	Jennifer Holt
Carole	June Carlson
Cochrane	Eddie Parker
Mitchell	Terry Frost
Cooper	Lane Bradford
Heavy	Carl Mathews
Heavy	Ted French
Bill	Steve Clark
Stage Driver	Tex Palmer

Film vaults evidently contributed in no small way to the footage of "The Hawk of Powder River." Number of scenes which had been used in previously released Eddie Dean oatuners are spliced into the plot of this entry. Picture is bound to produce a "haven't I seen this before" reaction among the action fans. B.o. prospects mild.

While the story formula remains basically similar to other films in this series, there's a slight switch in that Jennifer Holt is the leader of the outlaws. Her underlings kill her uncle who was on the verge of exposing her. She also plots to rub out her cousin, June Carlson, but the scheme is nipped by Eddie Dean. Usual chase sequences, fisticuffs and shooting sprinkle the reels.

Quartet of songs is sandwiched in at strategic points. Tunes all had been spotted in other Dean pix. Acting is so-so with Dean contributing his standard characterization of a U.S. Marshal on a secret mission. Miss Holt is a credible heavy while Miss Carlson shows the need of further experience. Roscoe Ates, as customary, supplies the comic relief. Others are adequate.

Ray Taylor's direction is fair. Producer Jerry Thomas drew the budgetary pursestrings a bit too tightly on "Hawk." Ernie Miller's camerawork is average. Joe Gluck rates a nod for editing the library clips in so adroitly.

Oklahoma Badlands

Republic release of Gordon Kay production. Stars Allan "Rocky" Lane. Directed by Yakima Canutt. Original screenplay, Bob Williams; camera, John MacBurnie; editor, Arthur Roberts. Tradeshown N. Y., Feb. 27, '48. Running time, 59 MINS.

Allan "Rocky" Lane	Allan "Rocky" Lane
Nugget Clark	Eddy Waller
Leslie Rawlins	Mildred Coles
Sanders	Roy Barcroft
Oliver Budge	Gene Stutenroth
Jonathan Walpole	Earle Hodgins
Sharkey	Dale Van Sickel
Ken Rawlins	Jay Kirby
Agatha Scragg	Claire Whitney
Sheriff	Terry Frost
Postmaster	Hank Patterson
Passenger	House Peters, Jr.
Stagecoach Driver	Jack Kirk

Allan "Rocky" Lane and his big stallion, "Black Jack," go far in helping put over this western thriller. Aside from this, Yakima Canutt, vet of many oat operas and former champ rodeo performer, has directed with a know-how that undoubtedly stems from long contact with this type of screen fare. Hence, it's a pat entry for spots where they go for these cactus mellers or to back up a No. 1 feature of many twin combos.

Film deviates from familiar wide-open spaces plot in that the cowboy hero fakes being the newly arrived ranchowner, a comely femme. This enables him to outwit the usual western outlaws and the familiar two-faced leaders, this time the latter being a western newspaper publisher. Besides painting him as thoroughly unscrupulous, yarn is inclined to poke fun at an out-of-work legit actor.

There's the usual note due on the ranch, the careening stagecoach, stickups, gunplay and rough-and-tumble fights. Last one is staged on the top of a racing stagecoach for a maximum of thrills.

Besides the fine job turned in by Lane and his hoss, Mildred Coles adds the necessary femme touch as the newly-arrived ranchowner. Eddy Waller adds some comedy touches as the hired hand at the ranch, Gene Stutenroth heads the support. Besides Canutt's fast direction, John McBurnie does nicely with his camera.

Wear.

Blanche Fury

(BRITISH-MADE)

(Color)

London, Feb. 19.

General Film Distributors release of A. Havelock-Allan (Rank-Cineguild) production. Stars Valerie Hobson, Stewart Granger. Directed by Marc Allegret. Screenplay by Audrey Lindop, Cecil McGivern from novel by Joseph Shearing. Editor, Jack Harris; music, Clifton Parker; camera, Guy Green, Geoffrey Unsworth. At Odeon. Running time, 95 MINS.

Philip Thorn	Stewart Granger
Blanche Fury	Valerie Hobson
Simon Fury	Walter Fitzgerald
Laurence Fury	Michael Gough
Major Fraser	Maurice Denham
Louisa	Sybilla Binder
Colonel Jenkins	Edward Lexy
Lavinia Fury	Suzanne Gibbs
Wetherby	Allan Jeayes
Calamy	Ernest Jay
Lord Rudford	Arthur Wontner
Mrs. Winterbourne	Amy Veness
Aimes	George Woodbridge
Jordan	Brian Herbert
Prosecuting Counsel	Cecil Ramage
Molly	Cherry London
Banks	Townsend Whitling
Mrs. Hawkes	Margaret Withers

This $1,500,000 Technicolor entry in the current Joseph Shearing cycle ("Moss Rose," "Mark of Cain," "So Evil My Love") is like all Shearing murder stories in that it's based on fact. This film is on the famous Rush murder in the 19th century, which caused a stir throughout England. It is a morose, moody tale of sex and unabashed villainy. Picture has been well produced although cool calculation is visible in every move of the picture. Pic should do well here, but may only find a prestige market in U. S.

French director Marc Allegret makes his English debut and his technique is evident throughout. He has used color to great advantage, while his settings and outdoor scenes have immense beauty. This should help put it over although principal b.o. pull will be Stewart Granger.

The suddenness with which the climax is reached, the amazing and not wholly explicable change in a loving woman and the seeming insanity in the man she loves are never satisfactorily explained.

Not one of the principals is sympathetic, which is hardly an asset. But that is the nature of the tale, and Blanche, played by Valerie Hobson (Mrs. Havelock-Allan), certainly dominates the picture. She has beauty that lends itself enchantingly to color. If she cannot register the depth such a woman should have had it perhaps is because it is asking too much of one person.

Stewart Granger, as Philip, is a curious mixture of degenerate nobility with melodramatic stableboy. His best moments are those of passion, but the camera and the script are occasionally less kind to him than it has been to his co-star. The lesser characters are played with skill. Camera work is good. Both contributed more than the usual share to a distinctive picture.

Cane.

Crime and Punishment

(SWEDISH-MADE)

(In Swedish; English Titles)

Film Rights International release of Terrafilm production. Stars Hampe Faustman. Directed by Faustman. Screenplay, Bertil Malmberg, Sven Stolpe; based on Dostoevsky novel; camera, Goran Strindberg. At Stanley, N. Y., Feb. 28, '48. Running time, 100 MINS.

Raskolnikov	Hampe Faustman
Sonia	Gunn Wallgren
Samiotov	Sigurd Wallen
Dunia	Elsie Albiin
Lusjin	George Funkquist
Modern	Tekla Sjoblom
Rasumikin	Toivo Pawlo
Aliona	Elsa Widborg
Marmeladov	Hugo Bjorne
Katarina	Lisskulla Jobs
Nataschka	Harriet Philipson

This Swedish version of "Crime and Punishment" is the latest and least successful cinematic try at the popular Dostoevsky novel. This one lacks the intensity of the French pic starring the late Harry Baur, and falls far short of the technical slickness of the American version with Peter Lorre. Full of irrelevant details and loaded with gab, the pic travels at a snail's pace with little to relieve the tedium. This entry will make only a slight dent in the sure-seater market.

Chief defect lies in the scripters' presumption to improve the novel by adding some original story details. As a result, the film frequently topples into a hokey mood completely at odds with the overall serious intent of the production. On credit side, film manages to generate that "old Russia" look through authentic settings and backgrounds, appropriate costuming and some darkly shadowed lensing.

Well-known yarn of a conscience-stricken murderer who's finally driven to confessing his crime is enacted by a group of thespers who make near-misses in their parts. As Raskolnikov, the pauperized intellectual with a Napoleonic complex, Hampe Faustman glowers strongly through his role but lacks the fine shadings necessary to project acute psychological suffering. As the detective who plays a cat-and-mouse game with his victim, Sigurd Wallen also misses the depth of irony needed as counterpart to the criminal's fake bravado.

The women come through a bit more effectively. Gunn Wallgren, as the religious streetwalker, registers with an honest and simple performance. Playing Raskolnikov's sister and mother, Elsie Albin and Harriet Philipson also deliver solid portrayals. Rest of the cast give good support.

Herm.

Love Life of Adolph Hitler

(DOCUMENTARY)

American Film Producers production. Narrators, George Bryan and Philip Stahl; editor, Jean Oser; music, Edward Craig. Previewed N. Y., Feb. 25, '48. Running time, 61 MINS.

Adolph Hitler	Himself
Eva Braun	Herself
Hermann Goering	Himself
Paul Joseph Goebbels	Himself
Julius Streicher	Himself
Heinrich Himmler	Himself
Benito Mussolini	Himself

And a supporting cast of other famous and infamous personages.

With the backing of the Navy Club of the U. S., an indie production outfit known as American Film Producers has compiled a chronological pictorial account of Hitler's rise and eventual slide to oblivion. Negotiations for theatrical distribution of the 61-minute film are in progress. Exhibitors will find the picture packed with exploitational qualities.

For the most part, "Love Life of Adolph Hitler" does not rank as a good documentary of the past war. Title chosen is cheap and lurid. No doubt it will stimulate interest of grind house patrons, but the better situations will shy away. Market for this one will be garnered by heavy bally plus the further attention of those who are morbidly curious as to how Eva Braun looked in a bathing suit.

Film's title is a misnomer inasmuch as the pic stresses Hitler's desire for power as his dominating trait rather than overly developing the top Nazi's occasional fondness for women. Most of the footage appears to be old newsreel vault stuff. However, the producers claim much of the film's running time represents clips seized from the Germans, especially the frequent sequences where Hitler's paramour, Eva Braun, is seen frolicking at Berchtesgaden.

Entire print is accompanied by narration of George Bryan and Philip Stahl. Summed up, their comments point out a moral by retracing the diabolical development of the Hitler military machine via the celluloid medium. Naturally, with the Navy Club sponsoring the picture, the moral is the "Navy is our first line of defense" and as such we must build it up to the extent where a similar threat to world peace cannot be made.

Editing and narration are fairly well handled, while the musical score is adequate.

Gilb.

Lost Happiness

(ITALIAN-MADE)

I.C.I. release and production. Stars Leonardo Cortese, Dina Sassoli. Directed by F. M. Ratti. At Cinema Verdi, N. Y., Feb. 27, '48. Running time, 78 MINS.

Giorgio Viglieri	Leonardo Cortese
Anna	Dina Sassoli
Franco	Manuel Roero
Sabastriaro	Giuseppe Porelli
Nicola	Aroldo Tieri
Maria	Adriana de Roberto

(In Italian; English Titles)

"Lost Happiness" is a minor offering with an appeal strictly limited to Italian-speaking audiences. Stilted and old-fashioned, pic dates way back to the ten-twent'-thirt' type of melodrama. Some newsreel shots of the recent war are interlaced into the story, but that's its only sign of modern vintage. Otherwise, pic is marked by uneven direction, corny yarn and florid thesping. Background music is damaged by a noisy soundtrack.

Plot concerns a fatal love triangle involving a famous violinist, his wife and accompanist. Latter is a heel who takes advantage of the wife's one moment of weakness to blackmail her into continuing the affair. Pushing his pique to rather extreme limits, he frames the husband to a 10-year jail sentence by planting fake evidence of his own murder. Choppy film suddenly ends as the culprit gets caught and killed by the violinist.

Dina Sassoli, as the wife, is a striking looker who also does as well as can be expected under the burden of her role. Leonardo Cortese, as the vilionist, shows some thesping promise, but Manuel Roero, as the accompanist, shows nothing but ham.

Herm.

Miniature Reviews

"I Remember Mama" (RKO). Irene Dunne in deeply moving version of the legit play; solid b.o. in all situations.

"Fort Apache" (RKO). Exciting saga of early west and fights between U. S. cavalry and Indians. Certain for important b.o.

"The 'Sainted' Sisters" (Par). Fair comedy, Veronica Lake, Joan Caulfield and Barry Fitzgerald to help the selling.

"Casbah" (Songs) (U). Romantic melodrama pic version of "Pepe Le Moko" set to music with Tony Martin singing solid tunes.

"April Showers" (WB). Standard backstage musical with vaude background in 1900's; stars Jack Carson and Ann Sothern.

"The Mating of Millie." (Col) Delightful comedy for the entire family. Glenn Ford and Evelyn Keyes for marquees.

"So Evil My Love" (British) (Par). Ray Milland, Ann Todd in overlong thriller. Good boxoffice.

"Smart Woman" (Mono). Well-made drama of femme lawyers, racketeers and murder. Okay programmer.

"Madonna of the Desert" (Rep). Good action programmer with misleading, but apt, title.

"Idol of Paris" (British) (WB). First indie Maurice Ostrer production looks too feeble for U.S.

"The Tioga Kid" (EL). Good Eddie Dean western for the action situations.

"Three Weird Sisters" (British) (Pathe). Horrific meller has little marquee pull; chances in America are slight.

I Remember Mama

RKO release of George Stevens (Dore Schary) production, directed by Stevens. Stars Irene Dunne, Barbara Bel Geddes, Oscar Homolka, Philip Dorn; features Sir Cedric Hardwicke, Edgar Bergen, Rudy Vallee, Barbara O'Neil. Screenplay by DeWitt Bodeen; based on play by John van Druten from Kathryn Forbes' novel, "Mama's Bank Account"; camera, Nicholas Musuraca; editor, Robert Morse; special effects, Russell A. Cully, Kenneth Peach; ass't director, John H. Swink; music, C. Bakaleinikoff; score, Roy Webb. Tradeshown N. Y. March 8, '48. Running time, **137 MINS.**

Mama.........................Irene Dunne
Katrin.................Barbara Bel Geddes
Uncle Chris.................Oscar Homolka
Papa...........................Philip Dorn
Mr. Hyde.............Sir Cedric Hardwicke
Mr. Thorkelson...............Edgar Bergen
Dr. Johnson....................Rudy Vallee
Jessie Brown................Barbara O'Neil
Christine...................Peggy McIntyre
Dagmar..........................June Hedin
Nels...........................Steve Brown
Aunt Trina.....................Ellen Corby
Aunt Jenny.....................Hope Landin
Aunt Sigrid..................Edith Evanson
Cousin Arne......................Tommy Ivo

With "I Remember Mama," RKO is spreading a layer of warm and deeply moving nostalgia that plucks at that special heart-string which echoes strongly at the cash register. Based on the John van Druten legiter (which is still touring in the U. S. hinterlands), the film encompasses those same broad, human values which lifted the play into the smash hit class. The ingredients are equally surefire on the screen.

DeWitt Bodeen's screenplay is a faithful adaptation of the original, adding only an extra dimension of background depth and story detail. In extending the scope, however, it doesn't blunt the impact of the yarn. This reminiscence of growth in a San Francisco Norwegian family is related in a simple and genuine manner. It's frequently sentimental but never hokey.

Irene Dunne, who played a New York mom in Warners' "Life With Father," is the central pillar of this production. In holding down the most demanding role of her career, she earns new honors as an actress of outstanding versatility. Her Norwegian dialect sounds queer for the first couple of minutes but soon establishes itself solidly as a natural part of her lingo. In general, her role is marked by a great strength and sympathy that makes her symbolize all mothers. That won't hurt the b.o., either.

Unfolding in flashbacks as the eldest daughter mulls over her memoirs, yarn brings into leisurely focus a series of domestic crises and tragedies. The mist of tears is relieved by plenty of laughs in the telling. There's the buildup of the maternal bank account which turns out to be mythical; the growing pains of the four appealing children; the sour aunts and the bluff uncle; the chloroformed cat, the graduation exercises and the rest of the anecdotes leading up to the heart-cracking finale. Against the story, the production neatly suggests a Frisco background in the 1910's.

The rest of the cast also do yeoman's service in draping this pic with a flesh-and-blood reality. Oscar Homolka, repeating his stage role of the uncle, contributes a massive and memorable performance. As the youngster who matures into an authoress, Barbara Bel Geddes plays a 15-year-old schoolgirl in a tour de force. Her portrait of adolescence is sensitive, compelling and authentic. Remaining kids are played appealingly by Peggy McIntyre, Steve Brown and June Hedin.

Surprise performances are turned in by Edgar Bergen and Rudy Vallee. Bergen, playing a milquetoast romeo to an aging spinster aunt, reveals a sharp comic talent that doesn't have to depend on gags for its effect. Vallee, in a bit part as the family doctor, delivers a straight dramatic role in first-rate style. As the father, Philip Dorn is slightly colorless but that's the part's fault and not his.

The three aunts from the old country are played superbly in a variety of comic styles by Ellen Corby, Hope Landin and Edith Evanson. Sir Cedric Hardwicke is on the screen only briefly as a mysterious boarder who leaves his literary inheritance with the family. Other players in lesser parts also deliver uniformly excellent support.

Dore Schary's production is ultra and George Stevens' expert direction is geared to the film's total mood. The long running time is caused by his lingering over the separate incidents, squeezing out of them the last drop of sentiment. Camera work and editing are handled with superb craftsmanship while the musical score also adds to the film's high quality. *Herm.*

Fort Apache

Hollywood, March 6.

RKO release of John Ford-Merian C. Cooper (Argosy) production, directed by Ford. Stars John Wayne, Henry Fonda, Shirley Temple, Pedro Armendariz; features John Agar, Ward Bond, George O'Brien, Victor McLaglen, Anna Lee, Irene Rich, Dick Foran, Guy Kibbee, Grant Withers, Miguel Inclan. Screenplay, Frank S. Nugent; suggested by story, "Massacre," by James Warner Bellah; camera, Archie Stout; score, Richard Hageman; editor, Jack Murray. Tradeshown March 3, '48. Running time, **127 MINS.**

Capt. York.......................John Wayne
Colonel Thursday.............Henry Fonda
Philadelphia..................Shirley Temple
Lt. O'Rourke......................John Agar
Beaufort..................Pedro Armendariz
Sgt. O'Rourke....................Ward Bond
Mrs. O'Rourke....................Irene Rich
Capt. Collingwood..........George O'Brien
Mrs. Collingwood..................Anna Lee
Sgt. Mulcahy.............Victor McLaglen
Sgt. of the Guard.............Dick Foran
Sgt. Shattuck..................Jack Pennick
Dr. Wilkins......................Guy Kibbee
Silas Meacham..............Grant Withers
Cochise.......................Miguel Inclan

"Fort Apache" undoubtedly will cause considerable critical pro and con because of the openly commercial approach John Ford has used on the subject. He has aimed the picture directly at the average theatregoer, bypassing non-profitable art effects. As a consquence, film has mass appeal, great excitement and a potent boxoffice outlook.

The important cast names, pointed up by John Wayne, Henry Fonda and Shirley Temple, among others, will give luster to any marquee, and that initial draw is backed up with super action entertainment.

Film captures the flavor of the early west, and whams over high-pitched, stirring scenes of U. S. Cavalry and Indians in action. For sheer, seat-edge attention, "Apache" is socko. Mass action, humorous byplay in the western cavalry outpost, deadly suspense, and romance are masterfully combined in the Ford-Merian C. Cooper production to stir the greatest number of filmgoers.

Integrated with the tremendous action is a superb musical score by Richard Hageman. Score uses sound effects as tellingly as the music notes to point up the thrills. In particular, the massacre scene wherein the deadly drumming of the Indian ponies makes more potent the action that transpires. Archie Stout's camera, too, plays a strong part in dressing up the rugged outdoor background against which the story and movement takes place. There's a breathless feeling of space in some of the shots, in fact, the scenic beauty occasionally distracts.

Cast is as tremendous as the scope achieved by Ford's direction and as a consequence, some of the roles are very short but all effective. Henry Fonda is the colonel, embittered because he has been assigned to the remote fort after a brilliant war record. His rule-book manners and inability to accept advice of officers experienced with the west and the Indians lead to a tragic, and unnecessary, death, by massacre for himself and the majority of his command.

John Wayne makes a virile cavalry captain, wise in the way of the Indian. Shirley Temple, the colonel's daughter, perks her sequences in romance with John Agar, West Point graduate. Latter impresses. Pedro Armendariz, Mexican film name, is excellent as a sergeant. Making up a group of tough topkicks that are responsible for the film's humor are Victor McLaglen, Dick Foran and Jack Pennick. Ward Bond, post's master sergeant; George O'Brien, a cavalry captain; Anna Lee, his wife; Irene Rich, Guy Kibbee, post medico; Grant Withers, crooked Indian agent; Miguel Inclan, the Indian chief, and others in the large cast all make their roles count.

Dick Foran demonstrates a voice seldom used in his films with singing of "Genevieve" during post horseplay. Good for laughs are sequences wherein the topkicks break in a new group of recruits. The Frank S. Nugent screenplay, suggested by James Warner Bellah's story, "Massacre," is expert framework for the action.

As tradeshown, "Fort Apache" is long, but length is not wearing although scissoring is indicated in a few of the sequences, particularly the opening. *Brog.*

The 'Sainted' Sisters

Hollywood, March 5.

Paramount release of Richard Maibaum production. Stars Veronica Lake, Joan Caulfield, Barry Fitzgerald; features William Demarest, George Reeves, Beulah Bondi. Directed by William D. Russell. Screenplay, Harry Clork, N. Richard Nash; adapted by Mindret Lord; based on story by Elisa Bialk and a play by Elisa Bialk and Alden Nash; camera, Lionel Lindon; music, Van Cleeve; editor, Everett Douglas. Tradeshown in Los Angeles, March 5, '48. Running time, **89 MINS.**

Letty Stanton................Veronica Lake
Jane Stanton..................Joan Caulfield
Robbie McCleary..........Barry Fitzgerald
Vern Tewilliger..........William Demarest
Sam Stoaks....................George Reeves
Hester Rivercomb.............Beulah Bondi
Will Twitchell......................Chill Wills
Jud Terwilliger.............Darryl Hickman
David Frisbee (8 yrs.).........Jimmy Hunt
Martha Tewilliger............Kathryn Card
Abel Rivercomb....................Ray Walker
Lederer..................Harold Vermilyea

"The 'Sainted' Sisters" a fair comedy about a pair of early-day confidence girls. Marquee value of cast names is on the sturdy side to help grosses but returns will be spotty. Veronica Lake and Joan Caulfield, in title roles, seem out of place but there is enough of the ridiculous in the situations to spring chuckles, and Barry Fitzgerald makes for a strong keystone to help carry this one along at a fair pace.

While undoubtedly the era portrayed had its ladies who played the shakedown trade, characters in "Sisters" do not ring true, so entertainment depends strictly on laughs that can be wrung from frenetic situations into which golddiggers are forced. Outside of the artificiality of the doings, William D. Russell's direction is good for material offered.

Fitzgerald's tricks of the trade stand him in good stead in pulling laughs from his character as a shrewd New Englander who turns his forced harboring of the sisters into a good thing for his small village. It's his role that principally carries the story.

Plot has the Misses Lake and Caulfield fleeing New York for Canada after shaking down a banker for $25,000. A storm forces them to take refuge in Fitzgerald's house and when latter discovers true circumstances he sees a way to aid the poor of the Maine border town. He forces the girls to dole out their ill-gotten swag in good deeds and eventually brings about their reformation.

William Demarest points up assignment as cagey sheriff who spends most of his time dodging disagreeable duties and the town's rich shrew, Beulah Bondi. George Reeves occupies romantic spot opposite Miss Lake. Chill Wills, Darryl Hickman, Jimmy Hunt and others are acceptable.

Lensing and other production credits are okay. *Brog.*

Casbah

(SONGS)

Hollywood, March 5.

Universal release of Nat C. Goldstone (Marston) production. Stars Yvonne DeCarlo, Tony Martin, Peter Lorre, Marta Toren; features Hugo Haas, Thomas Gomez, Douglas Dick, Katherine Dunham and her dancers. Associate producer, Erik Charell. Directed by John Berry. Screenplay, L. Bush-Fekete, Arnold Manoff; musical story, Erik Charell; based on novel, "Pepe Le Moko," by Detective Ashelbe; camera, Irving Glassberg; songs, Harold Arlen, Leo Robin; music director, Walter Scharf; editor, Edward Curtiss. Previewed March 2, '48. Running time, **93 MINS.**

Inez.......................Yvonne DeCarlo
Pepe Le Moko..................Tony Martin
Slimane...........................Peter Lorre
Gaby............................Marta Toren
Omar..............................Hugo Haas
Louvain......................Thomas Gomez
Carlo..........................Douglas Dick
Odette...................Katherine Dunham
Claude......................Herbert Rudley
Roland.........................Gene Walker
Maurice.........................Curt Conway
Willem............................Andre Pola
Max..........................Barry Bernard
Madeline....................Virginia Gregg
Beggar..............................Will Lee
Pierre.........................Harris Brown
Anton Duval............Houseley Stevenson
Ahmed.......................Robert Kendall

That romantic prince of thieves, Pepe Le Moko, is back again, this time with music. In "Casbah" Universal has a number of entertainment elements that indicate pleasing returns. The music is excellent, Tony Martin's singing is sock, and the Le Moko story has always been good, if familiar, screen fare. That the romantic melodrama doesn't always mesh too well with the musical story makes for a distraction, but on the whole, this Marston production is generally on the credit side. It'll do okay business.

Film introduces a new femme face to American audiences and the debut of Marta Toren, Swedish actress, augurs well for her Hollywood future. She has grace, beauty, talent and knows how to use those assets to the best advantage. Martin is good as the dashing thief whose elusive ways are the despair of the police. He makes full use of his s.a. vocalisthenics with the tuneful Leo Robin-Harold Arlen songs. "For Every Man There's a Woman" and "What's Good About Goodbye?" stand out, while "It Was Written in the Stars" and "Hooray for Love" are listenable.

Atmospheric values obtained by producer Nat C. Goldstone and his associate, Erik Charell, reflect lavish budget and give color to the melodramatics. Story plot hews closely to the original yarn about the thief who hides in the Casbah from the police but is finally lured to his death by a beautiful girl. Suspense and intrigue are forced to a halt by musical portions, making John Berry's direction seem ragged at times, but when film is telling the story the pace is expert. L. Bush-Fekete and Arnold Manoff scripted.

Yvonne DeCarlo is good as the native girl who loves Martin, but major femme interest goes to newcomer Marta Toren. Peter Lorre clicks strongly as the police inspector who finally gets his man. Hugo Haas sells his tourist guide character well and Douglas Dick scores as the informer. Thomas Gomez, harassed police chief, Gene Walker and others are capable. Katherine Dunham and her dancers appears too briefly, apparently on the cutting floor in the main.

The sharp lensing by Irving Glassberg, atmospheric art direction and set decorations, costumes and other factors are excellent production values. *Brog.*

April Showers

(SONGS)

Hollywood, March 9.

Warners release of William Jacobs production. Stars Jack Carson, Ann Sothern; features Robert Alda, S. Z. Sakall, Robert Ellis, Richard Rober, Joseph Crehan. Directed by James V. Kern, Screenplay, Peter Milne; suggested by a story by Joe Laurie, Jr.; camera, Carl Guthrie; new songs, Kim Gannon, Ted Fetter, Walter Kent; editor, Thomas Reilly. Tradeshown in Los Angeles, March 8, '48. Running time, **93 MINS.**

Joe Tyme....................Jack Carson
June Tyme....................Ann Sothern
Billy Shay....................Robert Alda
Mr. Curly....................S. Z. Sakall
Buster....................Robert Ellis
Al Wilson....................Richard Rober
Mr. Barnes....................Joseph Crehan
Mr. Barclay....................Ray Walker
Mr. Gordon....................John Gallaudet
Mr. Swift....................Philip van Zandt
Vanderhouten....................Billy Curtis

"April Showers" is an average backstage musical. This time the standard plotting deals with vaude hoofers shortly after the turn of the century, with the west coast as the locale. Names of Jack Carson and Ann Sothern will help spark okay returns in most situations. Entertainment quota in the familiar story has old songs and vaude routines to give it nostalgic value.

Title tune is reprised several times, and other oldies used as background for musical routines will carry older filmgoers down memory lane pleasantly. "Put On Your Old Gray Bonnet," "Carolina in the Morning," "Pretty Baby," "Cuddle Up a Little Closer," "Every Little Movement has a Meaing All Its Own," and "Mr. Lovejoy and Mr. Gay" are among those that will rate favor.

Two newer numbers, "World's Most Beautiful Girl," by Kim Gannon and Ted Fetter, and "Little Trouper," by Gannon and Walter Kent, are neatly spotted storywise, to gain added meaning. Carson gives them good vocal treatment. In addition to his songs, Carson rates a nod for excellent handling of hoofing sequences, working both with Miss Sothern and moppet Robert Ellis. Trio does much to inject a lift into the musical formula.

Carson and Miss Sothern are seen as hoofers never quite in the big time, but when their youngster deserts school to do the stage with his family the act becomes west coast bigtime. Act's Broadway chance is killed when blue-noses clamp down, with the Gerry Society movement forbidding kids under 16 from stage work. Carson takes to drink, while his wife and kid start over again in the more liberal west. Finale has the family back together again, and working, when Carson takes the pledge.

There's nothing much that's new in the Peter Milne script, suggested by a story by Joe Laurie, Jr., ex-vaude bigtimer, but directorial pacing of James V. Kern helps to give it some freshness. Dance numbers and the jokes have the quaintness of the era and are good for an occasional giggle. Miss Sothern displays just about the most shapely gams in films and appeals otherwise as the patient wife and mother. And Carson knows how to sell his wares. Young Ellis is talented and precocious, showing best in footwork routines. Robert Alda's role as impresario of a group of dancing femmes is rather thankless, but he manages to lift it. His near-finale knockdown and dragout fight with Carson is solid action stuff. S. Z. Sakall, theatrical hotel keeper, and others of the cast lend okay trouping.

William Jacobs' production supervision garbs the picture with all the necessary trappings to fit the period. Carl Guthrie's lensing is good, and musical arrangements and adaptations by Ray Heindorf are expertly cleffed to portray flavor of the entertainment era. Other credits measure up. *Brog.*

The Mating of Millie

Hollywood, March 6.

Columbia release of Casey Robinson production. Stars Glenn Ford, Evelyn Keyes; features Ron Randell, Willard Parker, Jimmy Hunt. Directed by Henry Levin. Screenplay, Louella MacFarlane, St. Clair McKelway; story, Adele Comandini; camera, Joseph Walker; score, Werner R. Heymann; editor, Richard Fantl. Previewed March 5, '48. Running time, **86 MINS.**

Doug Andrews....................Glenn Ford
Millie McGonigle....................Evelyn Keyes
Ralph Galloway....................Ron Randell
Phil Gowan....................Willard Parker
Madge....................Virginia Hunter
Tommy Bassett....................Jimmy Hunt
Mrs. Hanson....................Mabel Paige
Mrs. Thomas....................Virginia Brissac
Cookie....................Patsy Creighton
Harvey Willoughby....................Tom Stevenson

"The Mating of Millie" is solid fun, ladling out hefty laughs and schmaltzy heart tugs in just the right doses to keep audience interest high. It should click with all types of theatregoers and be particularly strong in rating attention of the younger set and family groups. Its stars, Glenn Ford and Evelyn Keyes, please mightily in projecting the fun to be found in this ace script.

The lively dialog and situations have been given strong directorial guidance by Henry Levin. He has injected deft bits of business and at all times realizes on entertainment aims of the punchy script by Louella MacFarlane and St. Clair McKelway, based on a story by Adele Comandini. The racy pace belies the running time.

Miss Keyes is seen as a business girl who wants to adopt an orphan. To do so she must get a husband, even though she doesn't like the idea of wedlock. A kindred free soul is Glenn Ford, who volunteers as coach to snare the right man. There's never any doubt of the outcome, but the way the inevitable conclusion is reached is sparked with plenty of fun, sharp writing, playing and direction. Dialog is particularly bright.

Performances by the principals delight. Ford and Miss Keyes make a sock team, able to broadly belt the risibilities or drop into a sincere touch when a heart tug is needed. Ron Randell registers strongly among the able performances, as does Willard Parker, both targets of Miss Keyes' matrimonial chase. Little Jimmy Hunt is an appealing orphan, the object of Miss Keyes' affections and others in the cast answer to all demands capably.

Casey Robinson's production guidance gives this one solid backing. Film is crammed with smooth touches, properly valued art direction and set decorations, a music score that aids the chuckles, and crisp editing. *Brog.*

So Evil My Love

(BRITISH-MADE)

London, March 4.

Paramount-British release of Hal Wallis production. Stars Ann Todd, Geraldine Fitzgerald, Ray Milland. Directed by Lewis Allen. Screenplay by Leonard Spigelgass, Ronald Millar, based on novel by Joseph Shearing. Camera, Max Greene; music, William Allwyne. Previewed London, March 3, '48. Running time, **112 MINS.**

Olivia Harwood....................Ann Todd
Mark Bellis....................Ray Milland
Susan Courtney....................Geraldine Fitzgearld
Kitty Feathers....................Moira Lister
Mrs. Courtney....................Martita Hunt
Henry Courtney....................Raymond Huntley
Jarvis....................Leo G. Carroll
Hattie Shoebridge....................Muriel Aked
Edgar Bellamy....................Raymond Lovell
Sir John Curle....................Roderick Lovell
Dr. Kyrlie....................Finlay Currie

Last of the present Joseph Shearing cycle ("Moss Rose," "Blanche Fury" and "Mark of Cain"), this Hal Wallis production is the best of the quartet, but can be vastly improved by further judicious editing. Like all Shearing murder stories—fictionalized versions of actual British murder cases during the 19th century—this has plenty of atmosphere and the usual trappings of the period. But Wallis has been almost as long as the original author in getting to the kill and the thrill. With Ray Milland and Ann Todd, boxoffice should be good, though the going may not be too easy.

There's no evidence in the pic that Wallis had all the disadvantages of a strange organization and of building up a production in a foreign country. Such failings as the film has aren't due to its being made over here. Best piece of fortune was getting Max Greene, ace cameraman, to look after the photography. Rarely has Ann Todd, a difficult subject, been photographed with such skill and sympathetic understanding. Camera work throughout is remarkably fine, and other assets are the splendid musical score and art work.

Story begins with the return to England from Jamaica of Olivia Harwood, widow of a missionary, and Mark Bellis, charming criminal of many aliases, wanted by the police of many countries. During an outbreak of malaria on the boat she nurses him, and he calls on her when she takes up residence in her suburban London villa where she keeps lodgers. Bellis moves in, sponges on her generosity, and pretends to fall for her.

Olivia renews acquaintance with Susan Courtney, her old school friend, who had sent Olivia some indiscreet letters before her marriage to a rich, stuffy lawyer. This is too good an opportunity for Bellis to miss, and soon Olivia is installed in a luxurious home indulging in a little blackmail. By now she is deeply in love with the worthless Bellis, and climax comes when Susan's husband gets the lowdown on Bellis. Olivia puts a liberal dose of antimony in the husband's medicine, arranges for the wife to administer it, and has just a qualm or two when the wife is arrested for murder.

Bellis by now is really in love with Olivia. The criminal pair decides to go abroad, arranges a rendezvous, and as Olivia is getting ready to leave she is visited by a flame of Bellis. She learns of his infidelity, keeps the rendezvous, and in the cab stabs him. Then she drives to the nearest police station.

It's not either principal's fault that the emotions are barely touched. The story gives scope for horror, pity, disgust and terror, and director Lewis Allen must share the blame with the wordy scripwriters. Style and atmospheric detail are no compensation for suspense, and if it is to be a psychological study of a good woman ruined by her love for a bad man, then Ann Todd should have been given a chance to harrow the soul. Within the scope of the story she gives a fine performance and the same goes for Ray Milland, but impression remains that the emotional scenes are phoney.

Geraldine Fitzgerald gives a competent performance as the unhappy and freightened dipsomaniac wife; Raymond Huntley is suitably stuffy as the husband, but Martita Hunt, the spiteful mother-in-law who looms large in the original novel, is wasted in a tiny part. Raymond Lovell and Leo G. Carroll contribute two excellent character studies. *Cane.*

Smart Woman

Hollywood, March 6.

Monogram (Allied Artists) release of Hal E. Chester production. Stars Brian Aherne, Constance Bennett, Barry Sullivan; features Michael O'Shea, James Gleason, Otto Kruger. Directed by Edward A. Blatt. Screenplay, Alvah Bessie, Louis Morheim, Herbert Margolis; adaptation, Adela Rogers St. Johns; original, Leon Gutterman, Edwin V. Westrate; camera, Stanley Cortez; music, Louis Gruenberg; editor, Frank Gross. Previewed March 4, '48. Running time, **93 MINS.**

Robert Larrimore....................Brian Aherne
Paula Rogers....................Constance Bennett
Frank McCoy....................Barry Sullivan
Johnny Simons....................Michael O'Shea
Sam....................James Gleason
Dist. Att. Wayne....................Otto Kruger
Mrs. Rogers....................Isobel Elsom
Rusty....................Richard Lyon
Mrs. Wayne....................Selena Royle
Dr. Jasper....................Taylor Holmes
Clark....................John Litel
Patty Wayne....................Nita Hunter
Joe....................Lee Bonnell
Sob Sister....................Iris Adrian
Porter....................Willie Best
Lefty....................Horace McMahon

"Smart Woman" has been given smart production garb, good story and playing to merit okay attention in smaller firstruns. An Allied Artists release through Monogram, picture fits into that distribution bracket neatly. Cast names aren't too hefty, boxoffice-wise, but are familiar.

Script adds some new twists to old formula and Edward A. Blatt's direction uses good story-telling technique to hold interest. Hal E. Chester's producer guidance gets top values for budget expenditure, giving film a dress that is expertly polished.

Constance Bennett plays the title role as a smart femme lawyer, earning an excellent credit. Opposite is Brian Aherne as a crusading special prosecutor who locks professional horns with Miss Bennett while carrying on an off-duty romance with the femme. Both do well by the assignments, as do Barry Sullivan, racketeer; Michael O'Shea, reporter; James Gleason, Aherne's aide, and Otto Kruger, crooked d.a.

Scripters Alvah Bessie, Louis Morheim and Herbert Margolis framed plot ingredients for best values, even giving the oft-used murder trial climax a new twist for dramatic emphasis. Finale has Miss Bennett, defending Sullivan against a murder charge, revealing that he is her former husband although admission may hurt her son and ruin her romantic future with Aherne.

Young Richard Lyon is good as the son. Isobel Elsom, Selena Royle, John Litel, Nita Hunter are others among the cast measuring up to demands. Stanley Cortez makes effective use of his camera in displaying players and settings. Louis Gruenberg's score adds to unfoldment. Miss Bennett has been smartly gowned by Adrian. *Brog.*

Madonna of the Desert

Hollywood, March 5.

Republic release of Stephen Auer production. Stars Lynne Roberts, Donald Barry, Don Castle, Sheldon Leonard; features Paul Hurst, Roy Barcroft, Paul E. Burns, Betty Blythe. Directed by George Blair. Screenplay, Albert DeMond; original story, Frank Wisbar; camera, John MacBurnie; editor, Harry Keller. Previewed March 2, '48. Running time, 60 MINS.

Monica Dale	Lynne Roberts
Tony French	Donald Barry
Joe Salinas	Don Castle
Nick Julian	Sheldon Leonard
Pete Connors	Paul Hurst
Buck Keaton	Roy Barcroft
Hank Davenport	Paul E. Burns
Mrs. Brown	Betty Blythe
Mama Baravelli	Grazia Narciso
Papa Baravelli	Martin Garralaga
Peppo	Frank Yaconelli
Mrs. Pasquale	Maria Genardi
Maria Baravelli	Renee Donati
Enrico	Vernon Cansino

Neat, cleancut melodrama that will hold up well in the programmer market. "Madonna of the Desert" plot is slightly off the beaten path, the pace is good and interest sustained.

Action contained in this one makes the title seem misleading but it is apt to the plotting, which concerns a statue of the Madonna to which is attributed miraculous powers. Statue is owned by rancher Don Castle and intrigue enters when two sets of crooks decide to steal the miracle lady. Sheldon Leonard smoothly heads up one group, which employs Lynne Roberts to do the job, while Donald Barry properly enacts the other crook.

George Blair's direction of the Albert DeMond script, from an original by Frank Wisbar, keeps the story continually on the move and makes the several apparent miracles that occur seem convincing. Through her powers, the good lady of the desert reforms the femme crook and has the others killing themselves off.

Leads are uniformly good and several character parts, headed by Paul Hurst, come off excellently. Production values obtained by Stephen Auer on a small budget are expert. Camera work by John MacBurnie, art direction and other technical contributions are good in shaping this one for neat playoff in its market. *Brog.*

Idol of Paris

(BRITISH-MADE)

London, Feb. 26.

Warner Bros. release of Premier (Maurice Ostrer) Production. Features Michael Rennie, Christine Norden, Beryl Baxter. Directed by Leslie Arliss. Adapted from Alfred Schirokauer's book, "Paiva, Queen of Love"; screenplay by Norman Lee, Stafford Dickens, Harry Ostrer. Music by Mischa Spoliansky; film editor, A. S. Bates; camera, Jack Cox. At Studio One. Running time, 106 MINS.

Hertz	Michael Rennie
Theresa	Beryl Baxter
Cora Pearl	Christine Norden
Offenbach	Miles Malleson
Antoine	Andrew Osborn
Prince Nicholas	Andrew Cruickshank
Emperor Napoleon	Keneth Kent
Empress Eugenie	Margaretta Scott
Bellanger	Patti Morgan
Barucci	Genine Graham
Lachman	Henry Oscar
Mrs. Lachman	Sybilla Binder
Count Paiva	Leslie Perrins
George Tremer	Campbell Cotts
George Tremer, Jr.	John Penrose
Countess de Molney	April Stride

This dates back 30 years when melodramatic saccharine and costume operas were the fashion. Maurice Ostrer, once producer for Gainborough, forgot that recent successful mellers leaned on stars for clicks with this first independent production. He boasts that the team that made his "Wicked Lady" has turned out this picture, but he has no James Mason and no Margaret Lockwood to carry the burden of an ill-written, corny script. Instead, he has comparative newcomers, who unfortunately do not merit leads in an ambitious picture. Its boxoffice prospects are dim. It would be a waste to export it to America.

Set in Russia and France of the 1860's the story tells how Beryl Baxter rose from a drab poverty-stricken home to become the toast of Paris, to acquire a reputation as the notorious demi-mondaine of her day, wealthy and powerful enough to snub the Emperor.

It was a tough assignment for young artists to cope with such a tedious mixture. Theresa, the new demi-mondaine of Paris, is quite outside the present scope of Beryl Baxter, who makes her screen debut in a role that would have taxed any star. Christine Norden as Cora, the early "queen of the half world," is unconvincing in speech and action. The part of Hertz, one of the lovers, is as unsuitable as any could be for Michael Rennie.

Only good professionals like Miles Malleson, whose Offenbach is quite a study, and Andrew Osborn and Margaretta Scott give superior reading to their lines. The music by Mischa Spoliansky is good enough to be worthy of a better film while the production is lavish. But to make sin entertaining by showing it as the pastime of the aristocratic is a job for experts. *Cane.*

The Tioga Kid

(SONGS)

Eagle Lion release of Jerry Thomas production. Stars Eddie Dean; features Roscoe Ates, Jennifer Holt, Dennis Moore. Directed by Ray Taylor. Screenplay, Ed Earl Repp; camera, Ernie Miller; songs, Dean, Johnny Bond, Pete Gates, Lewis Porter, Robert Tansey; editor, Hugh Winn. Previewed in N. Y., March 4, '48. Running time, 54 MINS.

Eddie	Eddie Dean
Soapy	Roscoe Ates
Tioga	Eddie Dean
Jenny	Jennifer Holt
Morino	Dennis Moore
Tucson	Lee Bennett
Tennessee	Bill Fawcett
Clem	Eddie Parker
Trigger	Bob Woodward
Sam	Louis J. Corbett
Ranger Captain	Terry Frost

"The Tioga Kid," newest Eddie Dean western, shows sharp improvement over some of its immediate predecessors. Production and entertainment values are good. On the overall, film rates as okay fodder for the action dualers and Saturday matinee-kid trade.

Yarn has Dean taking on a dual role, that of a Texas Ranger as well as a notorious outlaw, "The Tioga Kid." Latter's a lone wolf who attempts to muscle in on a band of rustlers led by Dennis Moore. Henchmen of the outlaw chieftain prey on horses of ranch owner Jennifer Holt and climax their crimes by stealing a federal payroll.

As the Texas Ranger, Dean credibly foils the bandits amid ample six-shooting and hand-to-hand combat. His portrayal of the "Tioga Kid," who's killed in the fadeout battle, is average thesping. Miss Holt handles her lines with finesse in the lone femme role. Moore scores as the rustlers' leader. Comedy, per usual, is furnished by Roscoe Ates.

Picture is helped by some apparently fresh scenery; frontier town, in particular, has a seemingly marked difference compared to the standard buildings and street employed in other Dean oatuners. Some three vocal numbers supply the musical background. Ernie Miller's lensing is good as is Ray Taylor's direction.

The Three Weird Sisters

(BRITISH-MADE)

London, Feb. 26.

Pathe Pictures release of British National production. Stars Mary Clare, Mary Merrall, Nancy Price. Directed by Dan Birt. Screenplay by Louise Birt, Dylan Thomas from novel by Charlotte Armstrong; adapted by David Evans; editor, Monica Kimick; camera, Ernest Palmer, Morlay Grant. At Studio One. Running time, 78 MINS.

Gertrude Morgan-Vaughan	Nancy Price
Maude Morgan-Vaughan	Mary Clare
Isobel Morgan-Vaughan	Mary Merrall
Claire Prentiss	Nova Pilbeam
David Davies	Anthony Hulme
Owen Morgan-Vaughan	Raymond Lovell
Thomas	Elwyn Brook-Jones
Waldo	Edward Rigby
Mabli Hughes	Hugh Griffith
Beattie	Marie Ault
Police Sergeant	David Davies
Minister	Hugh Pryse
Solicitor	Lloyd Pearson
Mrs. Proburt	Doreen Richards

There is more than the usual stock ingredients in this horror story. The dark doings in a rackety Welsh mansion are told intelligently and with suspense. There is a cumulative effect about it and the film is simple and satisfying in scripting and characterization. Although there is little marquee value, it may appeal to those who enjoy the macabre. As a dualer, it should provide a nice program here. Prospects in the U.S. are slight.

"Weird" is a mild word for the three mentally-befogged elderly Morgan-Vaughan spinster sisters. The eldest is blind and lusts for power, another is twisted physically and bitter, while the third is deaf and sly. To help them in a large house they cannot afford to keep up, is the idiotic Elwyn Brook-Jones and his tormented mother. They try to maintain appearances and pose as benefactors on an overdraft supplied by a half-brother Owen. Then the story develops into a sinister murder mystery.

The cast has been fairly well chosen, and the story is told nicely by three veterans, Nancy Price, Mary Clare and Mary Merrall. Raymond Lovell is good as the weak half-brother and Nova Pilbeam and Anthony Hulme do well with restrained romance as two of the few normal people in this film.

His first fictional assignment, Dan Birt shows directorial promise. *Cane.*

Henry IV

(ITALIAN-MADE)

Superfilm release of Minerva Films production. Stars Osvaldo Valenti. Directed by Giorgio Pastina. Screenplay, Pastina, Febrizio Sarazani, Stefano Landi, V. Brancati; based on play by Luigi Pirandello; camera, Carlo Montouri. Previewed in N. Y., March 3, '48. Running time, 92 MINS.

Count Enrico di Nolli (Henri IV)	Osvaldo Valenti
Frida Spina	Clara Calamai
Belcredi	Luigi Pavese
Professor Genoni	Enzo Biliotti
Mrs. Griotto	Rubi D'Alma
Giovanni	Lauro Gazzolo
Landolfo	Augusto Marcacci
Violante	Ori Monteverdi
Arialdo	Giorgio Piamonti
Bertaldo	Checco Rissone

(In Italian; English Titles)

"Henry IV," a pre-war Italian film based on a popular play by Luigi Pirandello, is an unusual psycho-meller that'll impress the art-house clientele. Pic has an uneven dramatic quality with several dull stretches but opens and closes with such a bang that the sagging center will be forgiven.

Yarn kicks off in deadpan historical style as Henry IV, German emperor circa the 11th century, is shown plotting war with his councillors against the Pope. Suddenly, with a violent directorial stroke, the film is wrenched out of its medieval framework into a modern setting, with Henry IV being revealed as a rich, modern-day count who's as mad as a hatter. His flunkeys were only pretending to be historic figures in order to humor him.

After this startling switch, the pic partially collapses into a conventional flashback story of a triangular love affair with an elusive fille de joie at the apex. In a joust between the two suitors, the count gets a knock on the head which results in his insanity. Yarn revives interest at the windup with the count regaining his senses 20 years later, stabbing his opponent and then relapsing into insanity as a matter of convenience to avoid the consequences.

Without the extraordinary bravura thesping of Osvaldo Valenti, as the mad nobleman, this offering might have badly misfired into farce. Valenti, however, carries the whole burden with a passionate and compelling performance full of wild, yet controlled, expression. Rest of the cast rates dimly by comparison, although sound portrayals are turned in by Clara Calamai, as the woman; Luigi Pavese, as the rival suitor; and Lauro Gazzolo, as the count's faithful retainer.

Film is marked by firstrate photography and smooth editing. English titles, however, are too sparse, leaving too much crucial dialog completely untranslated. *Herm.*

Miniature Reviews

"Summer Holiday" (Color-Musical) (M-G). Amusing musical based on the play, "Ah, Wilderness!" Fair names; good boxoffice.

"Hazard" (Par). Broad melodramatic comedy with Paulette Goddard, Macdonald Carey pacing good cast.

"Are You With It?" (Musical) (U). Screen version of the Broadway musical comedy slated for good returns.

"Corridor of Mirrors" (GFD) (British-Made). Disappointing mystery made by new indie producing firm.

"Docks of New Orleans" (Mono). Below-average programmer in the Charlie Chan series.

"Die Fledermaus" (Musical-Color) (Artkino). Strauss operetta in German, done in nice color, for arty spots.

"Devil's Cargo" (Film Classics). So-so detective yarn with John Calvert and Rochelle Hudson.

Summer Holiday
(COLOR-MUSICAL)

Metro release of Arthur Freed production. Stars Mickey Rooney, Gloria DeHaven, Walter Huston, Frank Morgan; features Butch Jenkins, Marilyn Maxwell, Agnes Moorehead, Selena Royle. Directed by Rouben Mamoulian. Adapted by Irving Brecher and Jean Holloway, from screenplay by Frances Goodrich and Albert Hackett, based on Eugene O'Neill's play, "Ah, Wilderness!" Songs, Harry Warren, Ralph Blane; musical direction, Lennie Hayton; orchestrations, Conrad Salinger; dances, Crarles Walters; camera (Technicolor), Charles Schoenbaum; editor, Albert Akst. Tradeshown, N. Y., March 3, '48. Running time, **92 MINS.**

Richard Miller	Mickey Rooney
Muriel	Gloria DeHaven
Nat Miller	Walter Huston
Uncle Sid	Frank Morgan
Tommy	Butch Jenkins
Belle	Marilyn Maxwell
Cousin Lily	Agnes Moorehead
Mrs. Miller	Selena Royle
Arthur Miller	Michael Kirby
Mildred	Shirley Johns
Wint	Hal Hackett
Elsie Rand	Ann Francis
Mr. McComber	John Alexander
Miss Hawley	Virginia Brissac
Mr. Peabody	Howard Freeman
Mrs. McComber	Alice MacKenzie
Crystal	Ruth Brady

Producer Arthur Freed has followed the example of Broadway in making a straight play success the basis for a period musical. And as director for the assignment he shrewdly picked Rouben Mamoulian, who staged the plays-into-musicals, "Porgy and Bess," "Oklahoma!" and "Carousel." In this instance it is Eugene O'Neill's only comedy, "Ah, Wilderness!" which has been made into an entertaining musical. It is a pleasant picture with few weak spots, and it should do well. Note the running time.

"Ah, Wilderness!" was originally produced by the Theatre Guild in the 1933-34 season, with George M. Cohan as the wise, kindly newspaper publisher, subsequently played by Will Rogers and Harry Carey. It was filmed by Metro in 1936, with Lionel Barrymore in the same part, Wallace Beery as tipsy Uncle Sid, Mickey Rooney as playful young Tommy and Eric Linden as the painfully adolescent son, Richard. Rooney is also in this musical remake, but now plays Richard. Frances Goodrich and Albert Hackett wrote the screenplay of the 1936 picture, from which Irving Brecher and Jean Holloway have adapted "Summer Holiday."

The O'Neill play, with its account of a turn-of-the-century smalltown New England family, provides admirable setting, story, color and mood for the musical numbers and script. The musical numbers, tastefully chosen and skillfully staged, are not spotted arbitrarily, but stem naturally from the situations. For example, the film is introduced by a song called "It's Our Home Town." Walter Huston sings the first chorus, as the newspaper publisher, with the other characters taking it up to identify themselves and plant the general story line.

Some of the tunes may have limited popularity, as they are evidently tailored to fit and advance the story. But at least a couple of the songs among "Afraid to Fall in Love," "All Hail Dannville High," "Stanley Steamer," "It's Independence Day" and "I Think You're the Sweetest Kid I've Ever Known," should be heard around.

The picture has tone and atmosphere in keeping with its background. That is true of the picturesque Connecticut exteriors, the costumes and such stylized sequences as the high school commencement, the youngsters' sleep-shattering July 4 celebration and the holiday picnics. And there are various diverting touches, such as tableaux imitating several of Grant Wood's period paintings.

For obvious boxoffice reasons the story emphasizes the puppy-love romance between the publisher's son and girl across the street. Respectively Rooney and Gloria DeHaven. Except for some laughable mugging by the former, they make an appealing pair, and their musical numbers are nicely done. In several scenes Rooney is quite effective as the bumptious teen-ager bitten by Omar Khayyam, Swinburne and Carlisle.

Huston is fine as the understanding Nat Miller, the boy's father. Frank Morgan achieves a nice blend of comedy and pathos as Uncle Sid, while Selena Royle and Agnes Moorehead are expert as Mrs. Miller and the pathetic spinster, Cousin Lily.

Butch Jenkins is amusing without being over-precocious as the moppet, Tommy, but Marilyn Maxwell overdoes the sinister strumpet, Belle, and does the "Sweetest Kid" tune as too much of a "number." Howard Freeman registers in the bit of a fatuous banker and John Alexander is believable as the stuffy father of the girl. Virginia Brissac is good as the proud school principal.

Mamoulian's direction has style, is well paced and, without sacrificing story credibility, makes the songs stand out. The two real production numbers, "Stanley Steamer" and "Independence Day," are effectively done, and the only dance routine, to "Afraid to Fall in Love," provides a bright moment. The film editing is exceptional in that it compresses the scenes and cuts them just as they seem about to drag. Which is sufficient reason why the 92 minutes running time is a pleasure. *Hobe.*

Hazard

Hollywood, March 12.

Paramount release of Mel Epstein production. Stars Paulette Goddard, Macdonald Carey; features Fred Clark, Stanley Clements, Frank Faylen, Maxie Rosenbloom. Directed by George Marshall. Screenplay, Arthur Sheekman, Roy Chanslor; based on novel by Chanslor; camera, Daniel L. Fapp; score, Frank Skinner; editor, Arthur Schmidt. Tradeshown March 8, '48. Running time, **94 MINS.**

Ellen Crane	Paulette Goddard
J. D. Storm	Macdonald Carey
Lonnie Burns	Fred Clark
Joe (Bellhop)	Stanley Clements
Truck Driver	Maxie Rosenbloom
Houseman	James Millican
Beady	Percy Helton
Chick	Charles McGraw
Oscar	Frank Faylen

"Hazard" cloaks its melodramatics with a broad comedy treatment that entertains. There's a lively air about it that augurs well for audience reception. Returns should please in majority of general situations. Material has been backed with good production values by Mel Epstein, assuring top playing time.

Story of a girl driven to desperate gambling through a psychological quirk is never permitted to take itself seriously under George Marshall's racy direction. He plays it broadly and strictly for fun, which is the proper treatment for psycho basis in the present film market. Arthur Sheekman and Roy Chanslor, scripting from novel by Chanslor, have kept the dialog flip and the situations broad, even slapstickish at times.

Paulette Goddard adapts herself to comedy aims easily as the gal who'll do anything for a chance to gamble. The yen was brought on by guilt complex over the death of a lover lost in the war. When gal loses a bet to a gambler she takes to her heels rather than go through with marriage to him. Private detective Macdonald Carey is hired to bring her back and the cross-country chase and the situations it brings about are good for some solid laughs. Carey gets his woman, both professionally and for the finale clinch, and while doing so demonstrates smooth talent that expertly values the role.

Fred Clark's interpretation of the gambler is smart and the bits of business given him by director Marshall reach broadly for good laughs. Stanley Clements injects a glib and pointed performance as the bellboy of whom Miss Goddard takes advantage in Chicago during the cross-country trek. Standing out sharply is the character of Beady as played by Percy Helton. Frank Faylen, Maxie Rosenbloom and others deliver capably.

Action is backed by Frank Skinner's competent music score and the lensing by Daniel L. Fapp. Other technical credits are expert. *Brog.*

Are You With It?
(MUSICAL)

Hollywood, March 13.

Universal release of Robert Arthur production. Stars Donald O'Connor, Olga San Juan, Martha Stewart, Lew Parker; features Walter Catlett, Pat Dane. Directed by Jack Hively. Screenplay, Oscar Brodney; based on musical comedy by Sam Perrin and George Balzer; camera, Maury Gertsman; songs, Sidney Miller, Inez James; music, Walter Scharf; dances, Louis Da Pron; editor, Russell Schoengarth. Previewed March 9, '48. Running time, **89 MINS.**

Milton Haskins	Donald O'Connor
Vivian Reilly	Olga San Juan
Bunny La Fleur	Martha Stewart
Goldie McGoldrick	Lew Parker
Jason Carter	Walter Catlett
Sally	Pat Dane
Mr. Bixby	Ransom Sherman
Bartender	Louis Da Pron
Terry	Noel Neill
Ann	Julie Gibson
Buster	George O'Hanlon
Herman Bogel	Eddie Parks
Mr. Mapleton	Raymond Largay
Mrs. Henkle	Jody Gilbert
Ed McNaughton	Howard Negley
Barker	Charles Bedell

Universal has given the Broadway musical, "Are You With It?", good screen treatment and playoff should show pleasant returns all down the line. Best reception likely will come from smaller first-runs and in family trade situations.

Donald O'Connor sparks the fun, delivering in both songs and dancing with talent that will rate neat response. Carnival background adds color and exploitation factors that are easily adapted to plugging this one to pep business.

Picture has been given an entirely new score by Sidney Miller and Inez James. Six tunes are strongly sold by O'Connor, Martha Stewart and Olga San Juan. Listening best are "Daddy, Surprise Me" and "What Do I Have to Do?" Two others, "I'm Looking for a Prince of a Fella" and "A Little Imagination" are combined in finale production number that is good but too elaborate for the carny locale. "Daddy" gets more fitting production treatment, as does "Down at Baba's Alley."

Jack Hively, in his first directing job since before the war, maintains a lively pace and capably combines the music with comedy. Oscar Brodney scripted the Sam Perrin-George Balzer stage musical of a brainy young man who leaves the insurance business to adapt his mathematical genius to the carnival. Antics are strung on a thin plot thread which concerns efforts of a pair of connivers to steal the carny only to be bested by the hero. Sawdust expressions pepper the dialog, even the title being a carny term.

Lew Parker repeats his stage role in the film, adding considerable to the laughs as glib carnival man. He works in dance routines with O'Connor, as does Louis Da Pron, also dance director on picture. Miss San Juan shares romantic angles with O'Connor while Martha Stewart is teamed with Parker. Pat Dane is a femme menace. Walter Catlett registers as the carnival owner. Noel Neill and Julie Gibson please the eye as a couple of carny lookers.

Robert Arthur's production supervision has measured the physical values excellently to dress up the show. Musical supervision by Milton Schwarzwald and music arrangement and direction by Walter Scharf are valuable assists. Maury Gertsman lensed and Russell Schoengarth contributed concise editing. *Brog.*

Corridor of Mirrors
(BRITISH-MADE)

London, March 11.

General Film Distributors release of Apollo Films Cartier-Romney production. Stars Eric Portman, Edana Romney. Directed by Terence Young. Screenplay by Rudolph Cartier, Romney, inspired by novel by Chris Massie. Music, Georges Auric; editor, Douglas Myers; camera, Andre Thomas. At Odeon, London, March 10, '48. Running time, **105 MINS.**

Paul Mangin	Eric Portman
Mifanwy Conway	Edana Romney
Caroline Hart	Joan Maude
Veronica	Barbara Mullen
Edgar Orsen	Alan Wheatley
Sir David Conway	Bruce Belfrage
Mortimer	Leslie Weston
Owen Rhys	Hugh Sinclair
Bing	Hugh Latimer
Defense Counsel	Valentine Dyall
Imogene	Lois Maxwell
Babs	Mavis Villiers
Psychiatrist	Noel Howlett
Charles	Christopher Lee
Brand	John Penrose
Prosecutor	Gordon Macleod
Old Woman	Thora Hird

It's the current fashion in British studios to have at least one murder in a picture, succeeded by the inevitable trial scene. And so this new company, having waited four years for the financial backing to produce this film, made in the old Buttes-Chaumont studios in Paris—there was no space here at the time—use the old ingredients none too skillfully. If any bouquets are to be handed out they should go to the art director, director of photography, and Georges Auric for a fine musical score.

There is little marquee value with Edana Romney, a newcomer, and Eric Portman, losing favor through repetitive playing in a series of pix of practically one character. But the lavish production and the novelettish story may draw its quota of patrons. It will be hard going to earn its cost in spite of an intensive campaign to popularize Miss Romney, who is wife of John Woolf, joint managing director of General, distributors of the film. An abbreviated version might find a limited public in America.

With a desire to be sensual but clean, story systematically shrouds itself with mystery and then proceeds cliche by cliche to unravel a disappointing yarn. Becoming obsessed in Italy by the 400-year-old painting of a girl, Paul Mangin believes he is the reincarnation of the girl's lover and that somewhere is the reincarnation of the girl.

Meeting Mifanwy, a judge's daughter, at a nightclub, Paul decides she is the reincarnation for whom he has been searching. She comes under Paul's spell, enjoys dressing up in period costume in the corridor of mirrors, accepts priceless gifts, but leaves when Veronica, the housekeeper, tells her Paul is a Bluebeard. Involved situations ensue.

Although South African Miss Romney, trained here, displays no impressive talents in her first major test, she does reveal latent ability coupled with a handsome presence. As the day-dreaming narcissist in love with his so-called renaissance incarnation, Portman moves around like a pan-faced actor in search of a part.

Remainder of the acting calls for no special comment, although Hugh Sinclair, one of the few male men in the pic, deserves sympathy for being so neglected. Former writer Terence Young makes his debut as director and has done quite well with his material. *Cane.*

Docks of New Orleans

Monogram release of James S. Burkett production. Features Roland Winters, Virginia Dale, Mantan Moreland. Directed by Derwin Abrahams. Screenplay, W. Scott Darling; camera, William Sickner; music, Edward J. Kay; editor, Ace Herman. At New York theatre, N. Y., week March 9, '48. Running time, **67 MINS.**

Charlie Chan........Roland Winters
Tommy........Victor Sen Young
Birmingham........Mantan Moreland
Capt. McNally........John Gallaudet
Rene........Virginia Dale
Lafontaine........Boyd Irwin
Nita Aguirre........Carol Forman
Pareaux........Howard Negley
Grock........Douglas Fowley
Henri Castернarc........Emmett Vogan
Swendstrom........Harry Hayden
Thompson........Rory Mullinson
Von Scherbe........Stanley Andrews
Dansiger........George J. Lewis
Mrs. Swendstrom........Dian Fauntelle
Dr. Dooble........Ferris Taylor
Mobile........Haywood Jones
Butler........Eric Wilton
Detective........Forrest Matthews
Chauffeur........Wally Walker
Doctor........Larry Steers
D. A. Man........Paul Conrad
Sergeant........Frank Stephens
Armed Guard........Fred Miller

An implausible plot and mediocre acting wont help "Docks of New Orleans" at the wicket. Latest in Monogram's Charlie Chan series shapes up as below average program filler with little to recommend it. Production values are meagre.

Yarn traces a complicated pattern liberally sprinkled with the standard Chinese philosophy of Chan, the famed Oriental detective. Latter is fairly well portrayed by Roland Winters, but the balance of the cast is relatively undistinguished. Better scripting by W. Scott Darling might have drawn the plot's loose ends together into a more logical tale.

Case which Winters tackles involves the shipment of chemicals from the New Orleans docks. There are the usual cliches about various individuals receiving threats from unkown parties. Several killings result and the cops are baffled how these murders were accomplished. Out of a welter of suspects, including a chap who claims he was swindled out of a "secret" formula by the head of the chemical firm, Winters gets his man.

Mantan Moreland and Victor Sen Young supply the comedy relief. Virginia Dale has little to do as secretary to Boyd Irwin, her uncle and chemical firm exec. Story incorporates too many characters in the footage and as a result no one has a chance to demonstrate thesping aiblity. Title itself is a misnomer as action on the waterfront is negligible.

Direction of Derwin Abrahams is only fair in this James S. Burkett production. William Sickner's camerawork is average while other production credits reflect the low budget.

Die Fledermaus
(MUSICAL-COLOR)
(GERMAN-MADE)

Artkino release of DEFA (Berlin) production. Features Willi Fritsch, Marte Harell, Johannes Heesters, Willi Dohm. Directed by Geza von Bolvary. Adapted from play, "Le Revelllon," by Meilhac and Halevy, and based on operetta of same title by Johann Strauss; musical arrangements by Alois Melichar; editor, Alice Ludwig; English titles, Charles Clement. At 55th St. Playhouse, N. Y., starting March 13. Running time, **96 MINS.**

Rosalinda Eisenstein........Marte Harell
Herbert Eisenstein........Johannes Heesters
Falke (Die Fledermaus)........Willi Dohm
Melzer, the Tenor........Haus Brausewetter
Adele, the Maid........Dorit Kreysler
The Warden........Willi Fritsch
Frosch, the Guard........Joseph Egger
Prince Orlovsky........Seigried Breuer

(In German; English Titles)

Odd spectacle of Artkino, Russia's official distributor in the U. S., releasing this German-made picture is explained by the fact that it is a picture seized by the Russians when they got into Berlin during the war. Its release under aegis of the Russian distrib agency appears smart business since "Die Fledermaus" looks like a real money-maker.

Geza von Bolvary, who directed "Two Hearts in Waltz Time," has done a good job. Johann Strauss' fine music, coupled with the fact that this is one of the first German pictures using the Afga color film process to be been in the U. S., is good showmanship. While not appearing to be quite up to Technicolor standards, tinting is effective and never tends to detract from the plot or the immortal score.

Aside from Willi Dohm's suave portrayal of The Bat, laurels are copped by Marte Harell and Dorit Kreysler, two comely blondes. Miss Harell, as the flirtatious wife, is fascinating in scenes where she's supposedly dyed her hair to become a redhead. Miss Kreysler, while apparently assigned to lesser role, is particularly appealing and has an excellent voice. She and Hans Brausewetter, as the tenor, contribute most of vocalizing.

Willi Fritsch, young vet of many German films, does nicely with the part of Warden while Johannes Heesters is okay as the husband with a roving eye. Joseph Egger clicks with the subordinated role of prison guard. Support is headed by Seigfried Breuer, as the prince.

Some of the cast had a collaborationistic cloud but the Russians took over the film, gave it a new tag and are salvaging on the lavish production. *Wear.*

La Bataille de L'Eau Lourde
(The Heavy Water Battle)
(FRENCH-MADE)

Paris, March 3.

Trident-French release of Trident and Hero-Film production. Directed by Titus Wibe-Muller. (Norwegian.) Supervised by Jean Dreville. Script, Jean Marin; screenplay and dialog, Jean Drefille, Marin, A. Felborg, Robertson, Kurt Haukelid, Poulsen. Commentary by Marin and Pierre Laroche. Music, Gunnar Songstevold. Camera, Bladh, Marcel Weiss. Previewed in Paris. Running time, 107 mins.

Picture, which depicts the sabotage of the Norwegian heavy water works on which Hitler depended to make atomic researches, has been made in several versions spoken in Norwegian, English and French, according to which country is to be played. Though it's meant to be an action picture, like "Battle of the Rail," it boils down to a big documentary. Though there is some action in it, it always remains rather static.

Pic has been given a lot of publicity, especially because it is a war picture, backed by all sorts of Resistance organizations, but for America it looks like a dualer unless stripped down to the strictly action scenes as a documentary.

Out-of-door scenes, and some of the studio work, have been reenacted by the men who actually took part in the action during the war. Not being actors, they frequently look less authentic than if their parts had been handled by screen talent.

Picture, besides the actual war episode, includes several sequences by scientists explaining the atomic value of heavy water and why it was desirable not to let the Germans use it. *Maxi.*

Devil's Cargo

Film Classics release of Falcon (Philip Krasne) production. Stars John Calvert; features Rochelle Hudson, Roscoe Karns. Directed by John F. Link. Screenplay, Don Martin, from original by Robert Tallman and Jason James; camera, Walter Strange; editor, Asa Clark. Previewed N.Y., March 11, '48. Running time, 61 mins.

Michael Waring........John Calvert
Margo........Rochelle Hudson
Mieutenant Hardy........Roscoe Karns
Morello........Lyle Talbot
Naga........Tom Kennedy
Bernie........Paul Regan
Tom Mallon........Theodore von Eltz
Ramon Delgado........Paul Marion

A lightweight whodunit, "Devil's Cargo" is passable entertainment. John Calvert and Rochelle Hudson head the cast of this low budgeter, obviously primed for the double bill field.

Appearing as the "Falcon," based upon the character created by Michael Arlen, magician John Calvert racks up a fair performance. Besides making like a detective he also works in some occasional sleight-of-hand via pulling ducks out of hats, etc.

Story is familiar stuff. Paul Marion supposedly has killed a racetrack operator in a dispute over the former's wife, Rochelle Hudson. The slayer enlists the aid of Calvert prior to surrendering to the cops. Later he dies of poisoning in his cell. Meanwhile a thug is killed by a bomb planted earlier by Marion. There are several suspects in the various murders including Miss Hudson. However, the Falcon nabs his man in a climax that most filmgoers won't find too difficult to anticipate.

Acting is generally uninspired. Miss Hudson automatically endows the footage with her natural charms but her delineation of the femme lead is a mechanical interpretation. Roscoe Karns is a standard police lieutenant while Theodore Von Eltz is okay as the heavy. Marion is acceptable as a guy who assumes the rap for murder committed by another.

Occasional drags in the action might have been speeded by director John V. Link through use of faster pacing. Producer Philip N. Krasne evidently held a close rein on costs, while lensing of Walter Strange is good. *Gilb.*

Ruy Bias

Discina release of Andre Paulve-Georges Legrande production. Stars Danielle Darrieux, Jean Marais, Adapted by Jean Cocteau from Victor Hugo's drama. Directed by Pierre Billon. Music, by Georges, Auric; camera, Voinquel, Michael Kelbes. At Marignan, Paris. Running time, 97 mins.

Queen........Danielle Darrieux
Ruy Blas........Jean Marais
Don Salluste........Marcel Herrand
Goleyzovsky........Alexandre Rignault
Duchess........Gabrielle Dorziat
Santa Cruz........Paul Amiot
Duke of Alba........Gilles Queant
Casilda........Ione Salinas
Giovanni Grasso........Curitan
Minister........Charles Lemontier
Archbishop........Lurville
Minister........J. Berlinz
Minister........P. Magnier

This cloak-and-dagger epic of 17th century Spain can't miss here. The popular classic, Jean Cocteau's rep, and the marquee draw of the stars would suffice in any case. It's a fair bet for export.

Picture has been well cast, and the adapter has kept it moving along at a tempo unusual here. The Wakhevitch sets are excellent, filmization having taken place in the Epinay studios near Paris, with location sequences made in Italy. But the Spanish atmosphere has been well rendered.

Jean Marais plays a double part, that of a nobleman turned bandit, and a young student. He handles the double role very well, both in the love scenes, which are very restrained as befits the strictness of the Spanish court, and in the action sequences.

Danielle Darrieux, as the queen, expresses her feelings by commendable underplay, and stages a real screen comeback. She is accompanied by a lady in waiting, Ione Salinas, who is worth watching. Marcel Herrand gives a very good impersonation of the unscrupulous politician who would compromise the queen rather than lose his job, while Gilles Queant does very well as the Duke of Alba. As the maintainer of court traditions, Gabrielle Dorziat is suitably stiffnecked and handles her part very commendably.

Neither direction nor technique are standouts, but the picture depends on story, action, atmosphere, supported by excellent sets, and stars. As such, it's one of the better French pix. *Maxi.*

Spring
(MUSICAL)
(SOVIET-MADE)

Artkino release of Mosfilm production. Stars Nikolai Cherkassov, Lubov Orlova. Directed by Gregory Alexandrov. Scenario, Gregory Alexandrov, A. Raskin, M. Slobodsky; music, Isaac Dumayevsky; lyrics, Vassili Lebedev-Kunach; camera, Yuri Yekelchik. At Stanley, N.Y., March 13, '48. Running time, 105 mins.

Irina Nikitina........Lubov Orlova
Vera Shatrova........Lobov Orlova
Arkady Gromov........Nikolai Cherkassov
Mukhin........Nikolai Konovalov
Nikolai Roschin........Mikhail Sidorkin
Nikitina's Housekeeper........Fenya Ranyevskaya

Corps de Ballet of the Bolshoy Theatre
under direction of K. Goleyzovsky

(In Russian; English Titles)

"Spring" is another frivolous musical comedy from the Soviet studios, which used to be noted for heavy dramas. And as usual nowadays, this picture is practically devoid of propaganda, whereas Moscow productions of several years ago were often almost buried under their "message."

For all its emphasis on pure entertainment, however, "Spring" is likely to be pretty heavy going for U. S. audiences, except for the few who understand the Russian language and can presumably appreciate the comedy dialog (which audibly amused a minority at the show caught). To most spectators, the film will seem overlong, frequently tedious and only occasionally diverting. The script and musical numbers are the sort Hollywood outgrew a decade ago, while the score, performances and production are undistinguished.

"Spring" is a romantic yarn based on a hackneyed version of the mistaken identity situation. It's about an eminent Soviet scientist and a Bolshoy theatre dancer who resembles her. The scientist is a chilly article with glasses, no makeup and no time for a personal life, while the dancer is a pert dish and a taste for adventure. When a film studio, planning a screen biog of the scientist, casts the dancer to play the part, the identity mixups begin, with the stereotype emotional consequences.

There's endless footage of musical production stuff, supposedly backstage at the Bolshoy theatre, numerous shots of glorified scientific laboratory mumbo-jumbo, and more than enough picture studio scenes. Virtually all of it is in the exaggerated idiom of musical comedy, and many of the dance production numbers are shot from various odd angles (as was a vogue in Hollywood once), but some of the song numbers show at least the rudiments of staging skill.

Lubov Orlova is acceptable in the dual part of the scientist and actress, and Nikolai Konovalov is worth a smile as the dimwit assistant film director, but the others are merely standard.   *Hobe.*

Der Prozess

(The Trial)

Zurich, March 6.

G. W Pabst production, directed by Pabst, produced by Oesterreicheische Wecheschau & Filmproduktions A.G., J.A. Heubler-Kahn & Co. (producer J.W. Beyer). Screenplay, Rudolf Braungraber, Jurt Heuser, Emmerich Robenz; score and direction, Alois Melichar; camera, Oskar Schuirch, Helmut Fischer-Ashely; editor, Anna Hoeltering; assistant directors, George Reuther, Hermann Lanske, Walter Meiners. World premiere, March 4, '48, Scala Cinema,   Zurich.
Dr. Eotvoes..............................Ewald Balser
Scharf..Ernest Deutsch
Moritz..Albert Truby
Baron Onody..............................Heinz Moog
Mrs. Sotymori...........................Marcia Ebs
Esther.,.....................................Aglaja Schmid
Egnessy......................................Ivan Petrovitch
Eoth...Gustav Diessl
Bary...Josef Meinrad
Salomon Schwarz...................Ladislaus Morgenstern
Wollmer......................................Ernest Waldbaum
Peezely......................................Frank Pfandler
Reszky.......................................Leopole Rudolf
Farkas..Herman Thimig
Prussian.....................................Otto Schmoele
Dr. Eoetvoes' Fiance............Marinanne Schoenauer
A Jew..Max Rood
Julca..Klaramaria Skala

World preem of controversia Pabst pic, with its ritual murder theme, took place in Zurich before release in Austria. Public reaction at the premiere seemed favorable but the press comment in local papers ranged from mediocre to bad. Critics say that the picture is too direct in spreading its thesis against anti-Semitism and too theatrical-like, which, in certain sequences of the film, is quite true. One paper compared it to "Crossfire," due to have its Swiss preem soon, opining that the American treatment of practically the same problem is much more convincing.

It cannot be denied that "The Trial," despite several faults and

exaggerations, is unusual. Pabst is still a film expert. Several sequences are potent and magnificently photographed. Unfortunately the closing scene is rather tasteless, showing some angels in white gowns singing hymns.

The story: In 1882, a young Hungarian peasant girl commits suicide. The inhabitants get the idea that the girl has been the victim of a ritual murder and they arrest all the Jews and arrange a great trial against them which stirs up the entire world. A liberal lawyer who fights for justice and unity of all religions takes the defense for the Jews and finally succeeds to win the trial, showing incontestable proof that the charge has not been justified. Based on the historic trial, the screenplay by Austrian writer Rudolf Brunngraber is very apt work. Photography is excellent, also the score by Alois Melichar, using several old Jewish melodies, one of which, in the synagog, is beautifully sung by famed Hungarian cantor Ladislaus Morgenstern.

The cast is well picked in general, but Ernst Deutsch, as the main defendant among the Jews, and the w.k. stage actor of the Burgtheater Vienna Ewald Balser are by far the best. Femme parts are rather inferior, featuring Burgtheater actress Maria Eis as the dead girl's mother who initiates the pursuit of the Jews, and Aglaja Schmid in the opening scenes as the girl. She gives a remarkable proof of dramatic talent. Heinz Moog, in the role of Baron Onody, the arch-anti-Semite, is too exaggerated and plays the villain in the good old "shouting" way.

One of the most positive points of this picture is its fight on anti-Semitism, which, more than ever, appears one of today's most delicate problems. ·   *Mezo.*

Apres L'Amour

Films Osso release of Emile Nathan production. Screenplay by Jean Bernard Luc from the Pierre Wolff-Henri Duvernois comedy. Directed by Maurice Tourneur. Stars Pierre Blanchar, Simone Renant and Giselle Pascal. Dialog, Jacques Natanson; music, Marc Lanjean; camera, A. Trirard. At Marivaux, Paris. Running time, 95 mins.
Francois Mexaule..............................Pierre Blanchar
Nicole Mezaule................................Simone Renant
Germaine...Giselle Pascal
Fournier...Fernand Fabre
Catou..Gabrielle Fontan
Sister...Germaine Ledoyen

Maurice Tourneur, who is now 72 and has had plenty of Hollywood experience, enjoys the rare distinction among French directors of never having one of his numerous pictures turn anything but a handsome profit to the producer. He is still the safest and soundest French director, and without going in for high falutin' stunts, makes celluloid a paying investment.

This is what makes this very modest budgeter well worthy of notice, because at a time when French producers as a body claim they are stymied by spiraling costs and can't operate anymore, this sure local grosser was made in five and a half weeks, under schedule, for 25,000,000 francs ($83,-000), at less than original budget. Tourneur's name is hardly visible on some of the publicity and doesn't even appear on the theatre front, which leaves him indifferent.

The 1900 style of story shows Pierre Blanchar as a literary mogul getting a Nobel prize. He has a wife (Simone Renant) whom he knows has cheated on him for a long time with a worthless newspaperman (Fernand Fabre). He

also had a mistress, long dead, done by Giselle Pascal.

When the wife discovers that her husband has another menage, with a child about the same age as hers, and that one of her sisters (Germaine Ledoyen) is taking care of the kid, she finally agrees to let her husband take him home. She'll mother him as well as her own, never realizing until the end that long ago the husband substituted one of the kids for the other, and that she is really taking home her own child.

Picture is the mushy, hackneyed type of story that the French proletariat loves. It may not have international appeal, but Tourneur played safe, but it's money in the bank from French-speaking territories.   *Maxi.*

Miniature Reviews

"State of the Union" (M-G) Frank Capra production, plus strong boxoffice names in Tracy, Hepburn, Van Johnson; socko b.o.

"Big City" (Songs) (M-G). Entertaining tear-jerker for general audiences. Good acting and heart-warming theme of neighborly tolerance.

"The Search" (M-G). Excellent semi-documentary type pic on Europe's displaced children should do fine.

"Ruthless" (EL). Disappointing drama told largely in flashback.

"The Inside Story" (Rep). Broad comedy on rural life during the depression; good b.o. in general situations.

"The Arizona Rangers" (RKO). Okay western co-starring Tim and Jack Holt.

"The Arizona Ranger" (RKO). Above par Tarzan adventure; strong twin-biller.

"The Enchanted Valley" (Color) (EL). Animal outdoor meller fine for kids on twin bills.

"Mr. Orchid" (French) (Lopert). Meller of French underground activities; strong for foreign-language spots.

State of the Union

Hollywood, March 20.

Metro release of Frank Capra (Liberty Films) production, directed by Capra. Stars Spencer Tracy, Katharine Hepburn, Van Johnson, Angela Lansbury, Adolphe Menjou, Lewis Stone; features Howard Smith, Charles Dingle, Maidel Turner, Raymond Walburn. Screenplay, Anthony Veiller (also associate producer) and Myles Connolly; based on play by Howard Lindsay and Russel Crouse; camera, George J. Folsey; score, Victor Young; editor, William Hornbeck. Tradeshown March 19, '48. Running time, 121 MINS.
Grant Matthews..................Spencer Tracy
Mary Matthews........Katharine Hepburn
"Spike" MacManus.........Van Johnson
Kay Thorndyke.........Angela Lansbury
Jim Conover..............Adolphe Menjou
Sam Thorndyke.................Lewis Stone
Sam I. Parrish.............Howard Smith
Bill Nolard Hardy........Charles Dingle
Lulubelle Alexandar........Maidel Turner
Judge Alexandar.......Raymond Walburn
Norah.......................Margaret Hamilton
Leith, Radio Announcer........Art Baker
Senator Lauterback..........Pierre Watkin
Grace Orval Draper.....●...Florence Auer
Buck Swenson..............Irving Bacon
Blink Moran................Charles Lane
Joyce Matthews..............Patti Brady
Grant Matthews, Jr.........George Nokes
Bellboy..........Carl "Alfalfa" Switzer
Waiter.......................Tom Fadden
Barber........................Tom Pedi

"State of the Union" should be an election year natural. It's sock entertainment, full of humor and drama. At the same time it projects a timely social message. It calls its shots about the political scene in a manner that should prod the voter's conscience, but without using soapbox oratory. Message is adroitly cloaked in good story theatrics that cleverly ladle out drama and humor to make the po'itical sales talk palatable.

Boxoffice-wise, "Union" is an important Frank Capra production that lends itself to the strongest kind of exploitation. It has star names for the marquees, timeliness of release and, above all, entertainment values that will hold the interest of a broad audience. It's not likely that such a parlay could miss.

The hit Broadway play by Howard Lindsay and Russel Crouse has been expanded somewhat in the screen adaptation by Anthony Veiller and Myles Connolly, a broadening that makes the best use of screen technique. Dialog has headline freshness, and a stinging bite when directed at politicians, the normal voter and the election scene. All the various power groups are soundly spanked as they pass through a writing wringer that has enough truth to hurt. It's satire with a sting, made stronger by serious, instead of slapstick treatment.

Cast is loaded with stalwarts who deliver in top form. The fact that it's pat casting only helps to insure the payoff. Spencer Tracy fits his personality to the role of the airplane manufacturer who becomes a presidential aspirant. It's a sock performance. Katharine Hepburn makes much of the role of Tracy's wife, giving it understanding and warmth that register big. Van Johnson shines as the columnist turned political press agent. It's one of his better performances.

Capra's direction punches over the pictorial expose of U. S. politics and candidate manufacturers, the indifference of the average voter, and the need for more expression of true public opinion at the polls. Plot deals with a powermad femme newspaper publisher who picks up a selfmade plane magnate and shoves him towards the White House to satisfy her own interests. The candidate begins to lose his commonsense when the political malarkey soaks in and only is saved by his frank and honest wife.

Angela Lansbury, outside of frequently unintelligible speech, gives a topnotch account of herself as the publisher with ambitions to be the power behind the White House. Adolphe Menjou draws a typical portrait of the political conniver who is used by the newspaper chain. Lewis Stone appears only briefly in an opening scene establishing Miss Lansbury's character, but makes it remembered.

Film is dotted with strong bits by capable lesser lights. Among these standing out is Howard Smith's crass big business man; Charles Dingle's labor leader; Maidel Turner's and Raymond Walburn's southerners; Margaret Hamilton's maid; Pierre Watkin's opportunist senator; Irving Bacon's butler; and Tom Fadden's waiter.

Capra and his associate producer, Anthony Veiller, have given the picture important production backing in all departments. The music score by Victor Young; George J. Folsey's lensing; special effects, art direction, settings and other contributors figuring expertly in measuring this one for the top market.

Brog.

Big City

(SONGS)

Hollywood, March 20.

Metro release of Joe Pasternak production. Stars Margaget O'Brien, Robert Preston, Danny Thomas, George Murphy, Karin Booth, Edward Arnold, Butch Jenkins; features Betty Garrett, Lotte Lehmann. Directed by Norman Taurog. Screenplay, Whitfield Cook, Anne Morrison Chapin; added dialog, Aben Kandel; based on a story by Miklos Laszlo, as adapted ny Nanette Kutner; camera, Robert Surtees; music, George Stoll; songs, Irving Berling, Fred Spielan and Janice Torre; Jimmy McHugh; Inez James and Sidney Miller; Walter Popp and Jerry Seelen; arrangements, Leo Arnaud; editor, Gene Ruggiero. Tradeshown March 17, '48. Running time, 103 mins.

Midge.................Margaret O'Brien
Rev. Andrews.................Robert Preston
Cantor Feldman.................Danny Thomas
Patrick O'Donnell.................George Murphy
Florence Bartlett.................Karin Booth
Judge Abercrombie.................Edward Arnold
Lewis Keller.................Butch Jenkins
"Shoe-Shoo" Grady.................Betty Garrett
"Mama" Feldman.................Lotte Lehmann
Martha.................Connie Gilchrist
Page Cavanaugh Trio

"Big City" pulls all stops in appealing to the sentimentalism of the average filmgoer. The tearjerker theme is wrapped around a load of music of all faiths and ranges from traditional to modern pop. It's schmaltz, but the kind that will rate okay returns, particularly in family trade theatre circles. Above its theme of neighborly tolerance, film is marked by several mighty solid performances that will do much to advance those players with picture fans.

Danny Thomas and Betty Garrett, two names better known in the nitery and musical stage fields, deliver outstandingly. Thomas' portrayal of the Jewish cantor in the big city sector of mixed faiths is a talented, sympathetic job. Working with a young male choir, Thomas gives feeling to "Sholem Aleichem" and "Kol Nidre." For variety he delivers "The Whiffenpoof Song," "What'll I Do" and "Yippee-O Yippee-Ay," in a more modern vein.

Miss Garrett registers big with vocals on "I'm Gonna See a Lot of You," "Don't Blame Me" and "Ok'l Baby Dok'l," and comes through with a veteran performance as a hard-knocks gal who goes straight for love. Queenly voice of Lotte Lehmann adds class to renditions of "God Bless America," Brahms' "Lullaby," "Traumerei" and "The Kerry Dance." A neat reprise of 'Ok'l' is wrapped delightfully by little Margaret O'Brien for an especially pleasing treat of precocity. Page Cavanaugh Trio ably intersperses itself into the pop musical end.

Plot in the script by Whitfield Cook and Anne Morrison Chapin deals with a foundling who is adopted by three young men of Jewish, Catholic and Protestant faiths, and raised in the Jewish home. There's little intolerance in the story and the lone basis for conflict is when the Catholic boy marries and wants to take over the youngster; and only a judge's wisdom and the kid's instinct straightens out the muddle.

Norman Taurog's direction puts the players through their paces with neat dispatch to point up the sentimental but is never too maudlin. Little Miss O'Brien pleases as the foundling. Robert Preston is good as the Protestant, and George Murphy makes on excellent Irish Catholic cop. Karin Booth and Miss Garrett are eyefuls as romantic interests for Preston and Murphy. Edward Arnold is an able judge and little Butch Jenkins, with a haircut, is a solid laugh-getter. Miss Lehmann does intelligent work as Thomas' mother.

Joe Pasternak backs the picture with excellent values that fit the story background. Technical credits rundown gives mention for expert work to Robert Surtees' lensing, musical direction by Georgie Stoll and orchestral arrangements by Leo Arnaud, art direction and other factors.

Brog.

The Search

Metro release of Lazar Wechsler production. Features Montgomery Clift, Aline MacMahon, Jarmila Novotna, Wendell Corey and Ivan Jandl. Directed by Fred Zinneman. Original screenplay by Richard Schweizer in collaboration with David Wechsler; additional dialog, Paul Jarrico; camera, Emile Berna; editor, Hermann Haller; score, Robert Blum. Previewed in N.Y., March 15, '48. Running time, 105 mins.

Ralph Stevenson.................Montgomery Clift
Mrs. Murray.................Aline MacMahon
Mrs. Malik.................Jarmila Novotna
Jerry Fisher.................Wendell Corey
Mrs. Fisher.................Mary Patton
Mr. Crookes.................Edward G, Robinson
Tom Fisher.................William Rogers
Karel Malik.................Ivan Jandl
Joel Makowsky.................Leopold Markowski
Raoul Dubois.................Claude Gambier

Swiss producer Lazar Wechsler, who proved his superior hand as a semi-documentary maker when he delivered "The Last Chance" to Metro two years ago, wins another palm for "The Search." And he once again proves that the quasi-factual film can be not only superb picturemaking, but can at the same time carry the medium to perhaps its highest mission, that of a force for a humane and less selfish world. Unfortunately, as in this case, however, truth is too often grim and the b.o. is unlikely to equal either the purpose or quality of the production. "The Search" can be expected to hit its peak potential only in selected big-city houses and via the hefty campaign that Metro is giving it.

This simple film was made in the American zone of Germany, principally in and around the rubbled remains of Nuremburg. Only four of its actors are professionals, the others having been recruited on the spot. It's probably that fact that gives the picture its warmest and deepest interest, for no actor could recreate the terror, the abjectness, the remnants of starvation that cameraman Emil Berna has so magnificently caught in the faces of Europe's lost children.

The story is the familiar one of a family torn apart by the Nazis. This time the family is Czech. Only survivors are the mother and a nine-year-old boy, who are separated. Unable to differentiate between the beatings suffered from the Germans and the good intent of UNRRA's displaced persons workers, the lad runs away. His cap is found by a river bank and it is assumed he has drowned. Actually, he lives amongst the rubble until hunger tempts him close enough to a GI for the soldier to catch him.

Beaten and starved so long he can't say anything but "I don't know" in German, the boy is finally tamed and taught a few words of English by his kind and patient GI guardian. In the meantime, his mother has started a round of children's camps, peering into the pinched faces, hoping to find her boy. She finally runs into a femme camp official who remembers the lad, breaks the news of his supposed death and then convinces her to find herself by working with the other children for a while.

The GI, finally ready for home and discharge, takes the boy to this same camp to leave him until he can arrange to bring him to America. The mother meantime has left the camp, but in a last-minute change of mind returns to be reunited with her son.

The picture is fine most of the way. It's in that last bit of business that it fails to ring the bell completely. It seems to make the solution to the problem of kid DP's all too easy. By putting a saccharine finale on a single case, there's an undue submergence of the fact that other millions of these pitiable youngsters are still in camps and have still failed to find their mothers and security. It's probably a necessary concession, however, to most audiences — and to the boxoffice—to picture the traditional "happy ending."

The four professionals in the cast are Montgomery Clift, as the GI, who is a Howard Hawks contract player making his film debut following a Broadway break-in; Aline MacMahon, as the camp official, and as typical a social worker as one could put a finger on anywhere; Jarmila Novotna, Metropolitan Opera singer and herself a Czech, who plays the mother, and Wendell Corey, a Hal Wallis contractee, who plays a friend of the GI.

Each of them shows a deep comprehension, giving a feeling portrayal that neatly catches the nuances of the situation. Thespic hero, however, is Ivan Jandl as the boy. Discovered while singing with an amateur group of kids on a Prague radio station, he reveals an enormous ability to fathom and interpret his difficult part in a manner that sharply profiles its full tragedy. Metro has reportedly offered him a studio contract, with the idea nixed by his parents.

Overall credit for the depth and naturalness of the characterizations, for the topnotch choice of players, both professional and non-professional, for the fast movement, for the realistic locations and the technical excellence throughout must go to director Fred Zinneman. He, incidentally, was dropped from the M-G contract lists while he was abroad making the picture last summer and fall. RKO signed him. Then Metro, following early screenings of "The Search," optioned him for another film at considerably more coin than he was getting originally.

Screenplay by Swiss writer Richard Schweizer (who also did "The Last Chance") is taut and natural, falling short only in the patness of an embarrassed denouement. David Wechsler collaborated on the script, with Paul Jarrico making a considerable contribution in the unstilted added dialog with which he is credited. Incidentally, it's all in English or immediately translated via the dialog of the screenplay itself.

Metro, if it maintains its present enthusiasm and drive on behalf of the film, merits a reward even more attractive than big boxoffice grosses would be at the moment. Films like "The Search" can be a decisive factor in causing the world to take a deep breath and give another thought to the fearful eyes of those children before it plunges itself off the present brink and into another international catastrophe.

Herb.

Ruthless

Eagle Lion release of Producing Artists (Arthur S. Lyons) production. Stars Zachary Scott, Louis Hayward, Diana Lynn, Sydney Greenstreet, Lucille Bremer, Martha Vickers. Directed by Edgar G. Ulmer. Screenplay, S. K. Lauren, Gordon Kahn, based on novel, "Prelude to Night," by Dayton Stoddart camera, Bert Glennon; editor, Francis D. Lyon; musical score, Werner Janssen. Tradeshown in N. Y., March 18, '48. Running time, 104 MINS.

Horace Vendig.................Zachary Scott
Vic Lambdin.................Louis Hayward
Martha Burnside / Mallory Flagg.................Diana Lynn
Susan Duane.................Martha Vickers
Buck Mansfield.................Sydney Greenstreet
Christa Mansfield.................Lucille Bremer
Mrs. Burnside.................Edith Barrett
Mr. Burnside.................Dennis Hoey
Pete Vendig.................Raymond Burr
Kate Vendig.................Joyce Arling
Bruce McDonald.................Charles Evans
Horace Vendig (as child).................Bob Anderson
Vic Lambdin (as child).................Arthur Stone
Martha Burnside (as child).................Anne Carter
Libby Sims.................Edna Holland
J. Norton Sims.................Fred Worlock
Bradford Duane.................John Good
Bella.................Claire Carleton

Despite a sextet of name players, "Ruthless" will have only a moderate b.o. draw. Picture is a victim of cliched and outmoded direction and of weary dialog to which no actor could do justice.

Long running time of 104 minutes is another negative factor. At least 15 minutes out would help the yarn considerably. Arthur S. Lyons, Hollywood agent turned producer, has rounded up an impressive list of players whose efforts might well have been put to better use.

Practically the entire yarn stems from the mental reflections of Louis Hayward. one-time partner of powerful financier Zachary Scott. Film tees off at a social gathering where Scott is awarding a large slice of his gains to charity. Comes then the first of many confusing flashbacks, reverting to the boyhood days of the two men. These early sequences show how Scott moved from a poor environment to a position of prestige and wealth by a "what-makes-Zachary-run" technique.

Picture boils down to a character study of Scott, finally illustrating the retribution which Joe Breen's Production Code Administration insists is invariably faced by pursuing greed. In delineating his role, the actor is on familiar territory, for he's frequently played similar heavies in recent years.

Performances are handicapped by the direction of Edgar G. Ulmer, which employs many cliches the profession cast aside long ago. Screenwriting job by S. K. Lauren and Gordon Kahn has made the adaptation from the Dayton Stoddart novel, "Prelude to Night," involved and confusing. Plot's denouement is also telegraphed long before the finale.

Hayward contribs a fair interpretation of Scott's associate, who eventually breaks from him. Diane Lynn, in a dual role, is wistful and appealing as a pawn in Scott's affections. Sydney Greenstreet, cast as a utilities magnate who's ousted by Scott from his power empire in a stock manipulation, tends to overact. Lucille Bremer, as Greenstreet's wife, and Martha Vickers, a gal with influential connections, are both adequate in depicting women who were foolish enough to aid Scott in achieving the heights but later realized their errors.

Production values are mediocre while camerawork and other credits fail to rise above the ordinary.

The Inside Story

Republic release and production. Stars Marsha Hunt, William Lundigan, Charles Winninger, Gail Patrick; features Gene Lockheart, Florence Bates, Allen Jenkins, Roscoe Karns, Hobart Cavanaugh, Robert Shaybe. Directed by Allen Dwan; screenplay, Mary Loos, Richard Sale; original story, Ernest Lehman, Geza Herczeg; camera, Reggie Lanning; editor, Arthur Roberts' musical director, Morton Scott. Trade shown N.Y. March 22, '48. Running time, 87 mins.

Francine Taylor	Marhsa Hunt
Waldo Williams	William Lundigan
Uncle Ed	Charles Winninger
Audrey O'Connor	Gail Patrick
Horace Taylor	Gene Lockhart
Geraldine Atherton	Florence Bates
Mason	Robert Cavanaugh
Eddy Hale	Allen Jenkins
Eustace Peabody	Roscoe Karns
TomO'Connor	Robert Shayne
Jay Jay Johnson	WIll Wright
Rocky	Wm. Haade
Eph	Frank Ferguson
Ab Follansbee	Tom Fadden

One of Republic's top budgeters, "The Inside Story" is an entertaining mixture of frothy plot ingredients and comic talents of a good cast. Pic is likely to stir only secondary interest in the key firstruns but will do very nicely in nabe and rural situations.

It's a folksy film about life in a small town brimming with cracker-barrel philosophy and homespun humor. Some of the gags are as broad as a barn wall but the pic none the less escapes from falling completely into the corn bin. Director Allen Dwan keeps action rolling, rarely letting the slapstick interfere with the pace. Chief credit, however, for keeping this pic afloat goes to a comedy combo consisting of Charles Winninger, Gene Lockhart, Allen Jenkins and Roscoe Karns.

Story kicks off on serious note with a flashback to the depression era of 1933. Setting is a whistle-stop burg in Vermont where the natives are beset with the familiar problem of raising enough coin to keep the sheriff from the door. After this ominous opening, story takes a sharp turn into farce when a New York visitor puts $1,000 into a hotel vault for safe-keeping.

The grand proves to be the town's salvation despite the fact that its circulation is strictly illegal. Beginning with the hotel owner who uses the money to pay off his creditors, the coin makes a complete cycle through the town's pocketbooks, restoring love and confidence to each of its owners. In the nick of time, however, it's restored to its proper place. The moral is hammered home: if you don't want another depression, keep your cash circulating.

Winninger, as the hotel owner's aide, gives a familiar portrait as a fumbling, absent-minded old man with a shrewd sense of humor. As the frantic hotel keeper, Lockhart contributed an energetic performance. Karns, as the New York wiseacre, and Allen Jenkins, as an honest safe-cracker, also add importantly to the pic's comedy atmosphere.

Subsidiary romantic interest is handled in neat style by Marsha Hunt and William Lundigan, both of them giving the love angle a once-lightly-over treatment. Gail Patrick and Robert Shayne, as a shaky marital team, also do okay.

Production dress is solid with good lensing and background score giving an overall polish to the film.

Herm.

The Arizona Ranger

RKO release of Herman Schlom production. Stars Tim Holt, Jack Holt; features Nan Leslie, Richard Martin. Directed by John Rawlins. Original screenplay, Norman Houston; camera, J. Roy Hunt; editor, Desmond Marquette; music, Paul Sawtell. Tradeshown N. Y. March 22, '48. Running time, 64 MINS.

Bob Wade	Tim Holt
Rawhide	Jack Holt
Laura Butler	Nan Leslie
Chito Rafferty	Richard Martin
Quirt	Steve Brodie
Ben Riddle	Paul Hurst
Nimino	Jim Nolan
Jasper	Robert Bray
Gil	Richard Benedict
Mac	William Phipps
Peyton	Harry Harvey

In "The Arizona Ranger," producer Herman Schlom has come up with a good western that's reinforced with some bang-up hand-to-hand combat as well as the usual six-shootin'. It should more than satisfy the action fans along with the Saturday matinee juve patrons.

Novel is the billing which costars Tim Holt and his father Jack. Both turn in creditable performances. Holt pere, of course, is an old hand at these oaters, and his son, Tim, measures up. Story, appropriately enough, has them portraying father and son roles.

Yarn, screenplayed by Norman Houston, is woven around the rivalry of the senior Holt, a powerful rancher, and his son who spurns a partnership on the ranch to accept a commission in the Arizona Rangers. Question of whether the law should be taken into one's own hands results in a further rift between the pair. But their differences are patched up before the finale.

Supporting players contrib some okay thesping under John Rawlins' able direction. Nan Leslie, in the lone femme role, generates audience sympathy as the wife of outlaw Steve Brodie. Latter registers as the heavy, while Richard Martin, the comic relief, would have done better had he not been handicapped by some unusually trite lines.

J. Roy Hunt embellished the film with some above-average outdoor lensing. Production values are good as is Desmond Marquette's editing which keeps the print down to a tight 64 minutes without impairing the pacing.

Tarzan and the Mermaids

RKO release of Sol Lesser production. Stars Johnny Weissmuller, Brenda Joyce; features Linda Christian. Directed by Robert Florey. Original story and screenplay by Caroll Young, based on characters created by Edgar Rice Burroughs' camera, Jack Draper, Gabriel Figueroa, Raul Martinez Solares; editor, Merrill White. Tradeshown N.Y., March 19, '48. Running time, 68 mins.

Tarzan	Johnny Weissmuller
Jane	Brenda Joyce
Mara	Linda Christian
Benji	John Laurenz
Varga	Fernando Wagner
Commissioner	Edward Ashley
Palanth	George Zucco
Luana	Andrea Palma
Tike	Gustavo Rojo
British Inspector-General	Matthew Bolton

"Tarzan and the Mermaids" is standard Johnny Weissmuller, differing only from other jungle epics in that this one was produced in Mexico. Also, it introduces Linda Christian to U. S. audiences and is faster-moving than others in the Tarzan group.

Robert Florey gets credit for keeping an implausible story moving swiftly with a minimum of dull, hokey interruptions. Sol Lesser moved his company into the Churubusco studios just outside of Mexico City to film the picture. They also went on location at Acapulco, Mexico's west coast watering resort, for many exteriors and the hair-raising high-diving shots. Newcomer Miss Christian, native-born Mexican, hints possibilities. She's comely and has the physical attributes to measure up for the screen.

This story is strictly one of those things about a forbidden island in mythical Aquatania where a white trader and his undercover cutthroat employ a fake tribal god to keep the natives subjugated in order to grab pearls. The crooks want Miss Christian as a bride for this god, but she has other ideas. Here's where Tarzan comes in, and where the film gets its tag. He fishes her out of the river accidentally and tells his wife he has bagged a mermaid. Tarzan ultimately unfrocks the phoney tribal priest and his helper but not until after the familiar exciting climax.

Weissmuller gets more chances than customary to show his prowess in the water. Brenda Joyce is his very attractive spouse. John Laurenz, as jungle mail carrier, is a pleasing addition with his guitar-strumming and warbling. George Zucco, as high priest, heads the support.

Two photographers, Gabriel Figueroa and Raul Martinez Solares, helped Jack Draper on the lensing. Result is some spectacular camera work, probably the best on any Tarzan film.

Wear.

The Enchanted Valley

(COLOR)

Eagle Lion release of Jack Schwarz production. Stars Alan Curtis; features Anne Gwynne, Charley Grapewin. Directed by Robert Emmett Tansey. Original screenplay, Frances Kavanaugh; camera, (Cinecolor), Ernie Miller; editor, George McGuire; Tradeshown in N.Y., March 19, '48. Running time, 77 mins.

Johnny	Alan Curtis
Midge	Anne Gwynne
Grandpa	Charley Grapewin
Timmy	Donn Gift
Chief Scott	Joseph Crehan
Buggsy	Joseph Devlin
Pretty Boy	Al Le Rue
Menelli	John Bleifer
Constable	Rocky Cameron
Gangster	Jerry Riggio

This is reminiscent of "Enchanted Forest," which PRC turned out in 1945. Story, characters and settings smack remarkably of the earlier picture. PRC will be recalled as the predecessor to Eagle Lion, which distributes "Enchanted Valley." The producer again has used Cinecolor to effective results. Pic should delight most juvenile patrons but it's strictly for twin bills.

As with the earlier production, the central character is a creature of the forest, a great lover of nature. In this case it is Donn Gift, as a crippled youth who likes the simple things in life. His tranquil existence with his grandad (Charley Grapewin) is sharply interrupted by the arrival of two payroll bandits and their femme companion. Their arrival is just in time to save the picture from becoming a rather dull study of outdoor animal life. After that all developments are telegraphed well in advance. The gangster chief reforms and goes straight through the ministrations of the crippled youngster.

Grapewin lends some fairly professional atmosphere to earlier passages, while Alan Curtis, as the fleeing thug, makes a passable gangster. Anne Gwynne is okay as his sweetheart, who also reforms in favor of the great outdoors. Joseph Devlin is acceptable as his assistant. Young Gift does well enough as the crippled youth.

Production is marred by some very mediocre acting in earlier passages. Curley Twiford, Earl Johnson and Byron Nelson should take bows for their animal-training stints. Ernie Miller's camera work is A-1 throughout.

Wear.

Mr. Orchid

(Le Pere Tranquille) (FRENCH-MADE)

Lopert Film release of B.C.M. production. Stars Noel-Noel. Directed by Rene Clement. Screenplay, Noel-Noel; music, Rene Cloeree. Previewed in N.Y., March 18, '48. Running time, 106 mins.

Mr. Martin	Noel-Noel
Monique Martin	Nadine Alari
Pierre Martin	Jose Artur
Madame Martin	Claire Olivier
Peltier	Jean Varas
Simon	Paul Frankeur
Charrat	Delaitre
Father Charles	Lemontier

(In French; English Titles)

A story of the French underground with Noel-Noel, French comic. in a dramatic role for a change. "Mr. Orchid" is a vivid character study of a typical French patriot under the Nazi heel. Noel-Noel turned out the script and did the dialog, so it's more or less tailor-made for him. There are several extraneous passages, but despite this "Orchid" shapes up as a strong entry for U.S. foreign-language theatres.

The star plays the easy-going chief of the underground. His hobby of raising orchids, so as to better hide his radio equipment and dynamite supplies, gives the film its tag. Nadine Alari is refreshing as his daughter, and Jean Varas and Paul Frankeur are superb as the two leading undercover operatives. Claire Olivier also is excellent as a typically French housewife constantly worried about her husband's health.

Rene Clement has directed in a fairly leisurely manner but still managed to sustain suspense. Rene

Cloerec's original score helps to stress the more exciting moments.
Wear.

"Master Detectiven Blomkvist" ("Blomkvist, Master Detective") (SWEDISH-MADE). Sandrew-Bauman release of Schamyl Bauman production. Features Ann-Marie Skoglund, Olle Johansson, Sven-Axel Carlsson, Bengt Callenbo, Ulf Torneman-Stenhammer, Roberto Gynther, Henrik Schildt, Bjorn Berglund, Gosta Johnsson, Solveig Hedengran, Sigge Fryst, Caile Reinholz. Directed by Rolf Husberg. Screenplay, Husberg, based upon novel by Astrid Lindgren; camera, Rune Ericsson. At Astoria, Stockholm. Running time, 88 mins.

Adapted from a novel written for youths by Astrid Lindgren, "Master Detektiven Blomkvist" emerges as a good Swedish film. Yarn revolves about a young boy who essays some sleuthing. Scandinavian business will be satisfactory on this one but film offers little appeal for the international mart.
Winq.

"L'Aventure Commence Demain" (Adventure Starts Tomorrow) (FRENCH-MADE). C.F.C. release of Tellus production. Stars Isa Miranda, Andre Luguet and Raymond Rouleau. Directed by Richard Pettier. At L'Hermitage, Paris. Running time, 101 mins.

Inept camera work and general amateurishness of technique including editing mar this picture which is well acted. Isa Miranda acquits herself well as an adventuress. She conspires with Raymond Rouleau to swindle explorer Andre Luguet who's found an inexhaustible ivory source in the African jungles. Film has scanty chance in France and none abroad.
Maxi.

"Mademoiselle S'Amuse" (Mademoiselle Has Fun) (FRENCH-MADE). Corona release of Hoche production. Stars Ray Ventura and band, Giselle Pascal; features Randall, Jeanne Fusier-Gir, Georges Lanne. Directed by Jean Boyer. Music, Paul Serge Veber; lyrics, Andre Hornez. At Paramount, Paris. Running time, 97 mins.

Dearth of French films suitable for quota weeks enabled this entry to hit the first-runs. A feeble effort, this is merely an exalted musical short plugging Ray Ventura's band. Musicomedy actress Giselle Pascal is the jazz-crazy daughter of Randall. She exacts from her father a promise to hire Ventura's outfit to play for her day and night. And don't they do it! Picture is a likely grosser in France, but is highly dubious export fare.
Maxi.

"Route Sans Issue" (Road Blocked) (FRENCH-MADE). Filmsonor release of CCC production. Stars Claude Dauphin, Helene Perdriere; features Armontel, Jane Marken, Lucienne Lemarchand, Georges Paulais, Jacques Castellot, Giselle Casadesus. Directed by Jean Stelli. Screenplay, Stelli and P. de Thomasot. At Cinema le Paris, Paris. Running time, 92 mins.

Mild quality picture in every respect except the cast which does as well as it can despite inexpert scripting and direction. Plot centers around the use of "ghost-voicing" to reveal the inner thoughts of Claude Dauphin, an architect who's unwittingly committed a murder. Results in loss of his girl because she feels he might have confided in her. Ineptly made, "Route Sans Issue" has small chance in the French market and none abroad.
Maxi.

"Nattvaktens Hustru" (The Night Watchman's Wife) **(SWEDISH-MADE).** Wive Film release of Centrum Film production. **Features** Ake Gronberg, Britta Holmberg, Sture Lagervall, Naima Wifstrand, Ake Classon, Douglas Hage, Allan Bohlin, Thor Modeen, Carl Strom, Linnea Hillberg, Hugo Bjorne. Directed by Bengt Palm. Screenplay, Torsten Floden and Sune Bergstrom; camera, Nils Dahlgren. At Esplanad, Stockholm. Running time, **82 MINS.**

Poor scripting and direction spoil this. Yarn deals with a country gal who comes to Stockholm without a job or shelter. Her problems are temporarily solved when she meets and marries a night watchman. Later she has some romantic escapades with a wealthy character, but the final reel finds her back with the watchman. Picture might have been acceptable if properly made. Biz prospects are meagre both here and in the U. S.
Winq.

"Far Jag Lov, Magistern?" (Shall We Dance, Mr. Teacher?) **(SWEDISH-MADE).** Europa Film production and release. Stars Stig Jarrel, Ulla Sallert, Agneta Lagerfeldt; features Katie Rolfsen, Hakon Westergren, Gull Natorp, Georg Funkquist, Carl-Gunnar Wingard, Arthur Fischer, Wiktor Andersson, Christian Bratt, Lars Sarri. Directed by Borje Larsson. Screenplay, Georg Eliasson and Sven Gustafsson based on an idea by Gynther Stiel; camera, Bertil Palmgren, Harald Berglund; music, Erik Bauman, Nathan Goerling. At Anglais, Stockholm. Running time, **86 MINS.**

A splendid comedy, "Far Jag Lov, Magistern?" is headed for good grosses in Scandinavia and has some appeal for the international market. Performances are first class, with Stig Jarrel a standout as a dancing instructor. He's involved in a number of amusing pranks while studying the modern dance in Stockholm. Scripting, direction and camerawork measure up.
Winq.

"Livet Pa Forsbyholm" ("Life at Forsbyholm Manor") **(SWEDISH-MADE).** Kungsfilm production and release. Stars Sickan Carlsson, Egon Larsson; features Nils Ericsson, Douglas Hage, John Botvid, Thor Modeen, Marianne Lofgren, Greta Liming, Sten Gester, Ulla Andreasson. Directed by Elof Ahrle. Screenplay, Henrik Hill; camera, J. Julius; music, Arthur and Seymour Ostervall. At Draken, Stockholm. Running time **86 MINS.**

Fine thesping of Sickan Carlsson and Egon Larsson coupled with the b.o. pull of their names will help this Swedish comedy in Scandinavia, but abroad the picture hasn't a chance.
Winq.

"Nittiotttan Karlssons Permis" ("Private Karlsson on Leave") **(SWEDISH-MADE).** Svea Film release of Imago Film production. Features Gus Dahlstrom, Helger Hoglund, Irene Soderblom, Fritiof Billquist, Douglas Hage, Thor Modeen, Julia Caesar, John Norrman. Directed by Hugo Bolander. Screenplay, Gosta Bernhard and Tage Holmberg; camera, Sven Thermaenius; music, Kai Gullmar and Georg Enders. At Lyran, Stockholm. Running time, **106 MINS.**

Based on "Private Karlsson," a magazine cartoon character, this comedy falls far short of equalling the original. Designed as a humorous takeoff on military life, "Nittioettan Karlssons Permis" shows army routines in an objectionable manner. Picture most likely will do well in Sweden due to the mag tieup, but overseas its chances are nil.
Winq.

Miniature Reviews

"Mr. Blandings Builds His Dream House" (SRO). Good cast names, headed by Cary Grant, to help comedy's grosses.

"The Pirate" (Color-Songs) (M-G). Sprightly musical with strong marquee names.

"To the Victor" (WB). Melodrama with peace message. Chase theme and good cast help but b.o. looks fair.

"Escape" (20th). New British version of John Galsworthy thriller, with Rex Harrison, should do good biz.

"Spring In Park Lane" (Lion). British-made light comedy with Anna Neagle, Michael Wilding is sure b.o.

"The First Gentleman" (Col.). British historical drama, with Jean Pierre Aumont, holds only prestige draw.

"The Lost One" (Col). Appealing Italian-made version of Verdis opera, "La Traviata," should do in art houses.

"Snowbound" (RKO). Satisfactory British thriller about buried Nazi gold, good as U. S. dualer.

"Confessions of a Rogue" (French). Nifty comedy, starring Louis Jouvet, for the arties and sureseaters.

"Last Days of Boot Hill" (Col). Another in the Durango Kid series. Okay oater for the Saturday matinee trade.

"Songs of Idaho" (Songs) (Col). Cornfed comedy will attract hillbilly fanciers.

"Money Madness" (FC). Poor programmer for the duals.

"Man From Texas" (EL). Johnnie Johnston, Lynn Bari, James Craig in implausible western; too lightweight.

Mr. Blandings Builds His Dream House

Hollywood, March 26.

Selznick release of RKO production, produced and written by Norman Panama and Melvin Frank. Stars Cary Grant, Myrna Loy, Melvyn Douglas; features Reginald Denny, Sharyn Moffett, Connie Marshall, Louise Beavers, Ian Wolfe. Directed by H.C. Potter. Based on novel by Eric Hodgins; camera, James Wong Howe; music, Leigh Harline; editor, Harry Marker. Previewed March 24, '48. Running time, 93 mins.

Jim Blandings	Cary Grant
Muriel Blandings	Myrna Loy
Bill Cole	Melvyn Douglas
Henry Sims	Reginald Denny
Joan Blandings	Sharyn Moffett
Betsy Blandings	Connie Marshall
Gussie	Louise Beavers
Smith	Ian Wolfe
W.E. Tesander	Harry Shannon
Zucca	Tito Vuolo
Joe Appollonio	Nestor Paiva
John Retch	Jason Robards
Mary	Lurene Tuttle
Carpenter	Lex Barker
Mr. BeDelford	Emory Parnell

"Mr. Blandings Builds His Dream House" is a mildly amusing comedy with strength enough in star names to pull through to satisfactory grosses. Cary Grant's boxoffice value will be an important aid in boosting initial ticket sales, and names of Myrna Loy, Melvyn Douglas and others are marquee familiars.

Eric Hodgins' novel of the trials and tribulations of the Blandings, while building their dream house, read a lot funnier than they filmed. Norman Panama and Melvin Frank come through with a glossy lustre in handling physical production, but failed to jell the story into solid film fare in their dual scripting.

Film's opening pulls some standard sight gags that register strongly, helped by the business injected through H. C. Potter's direction. Such elemental situations as a "Fibber McGee closet," the sight of a man trying to shave while his wife shares the basin, and other such familiar stunts are always good for a laugh response. Less funny is the sight of a man trying to make ends meet on $15,000 a year, especially to the average filmgoer who squeezes by on considerable less. Script gets completely out of hand when unnecessary jealousy twist is introduced, neither advancing the story nor adding laughs.

Grant is up to his usual performance standard as Mr. Blandings, getting the best from the material, and Myrna Loy comes through with another of her screen wife assignments nicely. Melvyn Douglas, the lawyer friend of the family, gives it a tongue-in-cheek treatment. Trio's finesse and Potter's light directorial touch do much to give proceedings a lift.

Reginald Denny, the architect, is good, as are Ian Wolfe, the sharp Yankee realtor; Louise Beavers, the maid; Harry Shannon, Tito Vuolo, Nestor Paiva and others. The Blandings' young daughters are played by Sharyn Moffett and Connie Marshall.

On the technical end, film has some class contributions. James Wong Howe's lensing is expert. Art directors Albert S. D'Agostino and Carroll Clark really dreamed up a dream house and the set decorations show it off. Leigh Harline's score, the editing and other factors are good.
Brog.

The Pirate

(SONGS—COLOR)

Hollywood, March 27.

Metro release of Arthur Freed production. Stars Judy Garland, Gene Kelly; features Walter Slezak, Gladys Cooper, Reginald Owen. Directed by Vincente Minnelli. Screenplay, Albert Hackett, Frances Goodrich; based on play by S. N. Behrman; camera (Technicolor), Harry Stradling; songs, Cole Porter; music, Lennie Hayton; dances, Robert Alton, Gene Kelly; editor, Blanche Sewell. Tradeshown March 24, '48. Running time, **101 MINS.**

Manuela	Judy Garland
Serafin	Gene Kelly
Don Pedro Vargas	Walter Slezak
Aunt Inez	Gladys Cooper
The Advocate	Reginald Owen
The Viceroy	George Zucco
Gaudsmith Brothers	Nicholas Brothers
Uncle Capucho	Lester Allen
Isabella	Lola Deem
Mercedes	Ellen Ross
Lizarda	Mary Jo Ellis
Casilda	Jean Dean
Eloise	Marion Murray
Gumbo	Ben Lessy
Bolo	Jerry Bergen
Juggler	Val Setz
Trillo	Cully Richards

Nicholas Brothers, Gaudsmith Brothers

"The Pirate" is escapist film fare. It's an eye and ear treat of light musical entertainment, garbing its amusing antics, catchy songs and able terping in brilliant color for certain audience response. Arthur Freed's production guidance gives it strong backing to show off the stars and entertainment content.

Gene Kelly and Judy Garland team delightfully in selling the dances and songs, scoring in both departments to make "Pirate" mighty pleasant to take. The Cole Porter score is loaded with tunes that get over to the ear and the foot. Miss Garland sells three of the numbers, **"Love of My Life," "Mack the Black"** and **"You Can Do No Wrong."** Kelly vocals **"Be a Clown"** and **"Nina,"** using both as dance introductions also.

In terp department, Kelly flashes his heels first in near-ballet routining for "Nina," then highspots a fire dance as biggest of the elaborate production pieces. Another highspot is his footwork with the Nicholas Bros. in the "Clown" number. For finale, Kelly and Miss Garland send them out with a laugh reprising "Clown" in full baggy-trouser makeup.

Vincente Minnelli's direction is light and seems to poke subtle fun at the elaborate musical ingredients and plot. The fact that "The Pirate" never takes itself too seriously adds to enjoyment, giving sharp point to some of the dialog in the Albert Hackett-Frances Goodrich script.

Adapted from the S. N. Behrman play, picture tells of the cloistered Latin girl about to fulfill an arranged wedding when she meets a travelling troupe of entertainers headed by Kelly. From then on its just a question of how much footage before the actor gets the girl and the old groom-to-be gets the noose. Title springs from fact that gal yearns for a fabulous pirate and sees him in the actor while all the time it's the old boy, who has given up blackguarding to settle down with a young wife.

Walter Slezak makes a nifty retired pirate. Gladys Cooper and Lester Allen are Miss Garland's fluttery relatives who arranged the wedding. George Zucco is good as the viceroy. Making up the travelling troupe are Ben Lessy, Jerry Bergen, Val Setz, the Gaudsmith Bros. and Cully Richards.

Film moves fast. Harry Stradling's color photography is both mobile and artful in displaying the gorgeous costumes and settings as well as the able dances staged by Robert Alton and Kelly. Lennie Hayton's direction of the music and Conrad Salinger's instrumental arrangements are creditable, as are all of the contributions. *Brog.*

To the Victor

Hollywood, March 30.

Warners release of Jerry Wald production. Stars Dennis Morgan, Viveca Lindfors; features Victor Francen, Bruce Bennett, Dorothy Malone, Tom D'Andrea, Eduardo Cianelli, Douglas Kennedy, Joseph Buloff, William Conrad. Directed by Delmer Daves. Screenplay, Richard Brooks; camera, Robert Burks; music, David Buttolph; editor, Folmar Blangsted. Tradeshown March 29, '48. Running time, 100 mins.

Paul	Dennis Morgan
Christine	Viveca Lindfors
Capt. Beauvais	Victor Francen
Henderson	Bruce Bennett
Miriam	Dorothy Malone
Gus	Tom D'Andrea
Firago	Eduardo Ciannelli
Steve	Douglas Kennedy
Bolyanov	Joseph Buloff
Farnsworth	William Conrad
Geran	Luis van Rooten
Pablo	Konstantin Shayne
Mikki	Anthony Caruso
Gabby	Joanee Wayne
Lestrac	John Banner
Zinzer	Henry Rowland
Victor	Felipe Turich

"To the Victor" has exploitation possibilities as an exciting chase melodrama. Otherwise it misses. Unfortunately, the pic's good elements have been confusingly put together and its message, the need for all to work together for peace, is sledge-hammered. There's no quarrel with the worth of the propaganda. The fault is with the manner in which it is presented.

Footage is mostly on postwar Paris as to locale and plot timing. Film practically gives a complete tour of the French capital and includes one impressive sequence on Omaha beach in Normandy with

closeups of the battered German forts and abandoned Allied ships and equipment. These shots are highly effective in themselves but not sufficiently integrated into the film's general development.

With this film, a promising new star in the person of Viveca Lindfors is introduced to American audiences. (Her first for Warner Bros., "Night Unto Night," is being held up for release to follow this one.) This girl has beauty and talent with a faint Swedish accent, a la Ingrid Bergman, which won't do any harm.

Story has her married to a traitor and collaborationist who's been brought back to France to stand trial for his war crimes. It is the efforts of the latter's henchmen to silence her that spring the chase. Dennis Morgan plays an American vet engaged in the Paris black market with a couple of unsavory Russians and Nazis. After taking the girl into his safekeeping, a romance develops and triumphs with Miss Lindfors testifying against her husband and Morgan reforming.

Flaw in the script, or maybe the editing, is an uneven continuity with several unexplained characters. Delmer Daves' direction manages good suspense, particularly in the opening scene wherein Miss Lindfors is stalked through the streets by a gunman.

Jerry Wald's production values gain strength from the footage filmed in Paris by Robert Burks with special effects by Marcel Grignon. Morgan plays well as the blacketeer, while Victor Francen makes his role of a French detective count heavily. Bruce Bennett walks through an unexplained bit *Brog.*

Escape

(BRITISH)

London, March 24.

20th-Fox release of William Perlberg production. Stars Rex Harrison, Peggy Cummins. Directed by Joseph L. Mankiewicz. Screenplay by Philip Dunne from John Galsworthy's "Escape." Editor, Alan L. Jaggs; music, William Alwyn; camera, Frederick A. Young, Russell Thomson. Previewed London, March 23, '48. Running time, 79 mins.

Matt Denant	Rex Harrison
Dora Winton	Peggy Cummins
Inspector Harris	William Hartnell
Parson	Norman Wooland
Grace Winton	Jill Esmond
Brownie	Frederick Piper
Mrs. Pinkem	Marjorie Rhodes
Girl in Park	Betty Ann Davies
Rodgers	Cyril Cusack
Car Salesman	John Slater
Constable	Frank Pettingell
Plain Clothes Man	Michael Golden
Judge	Frederick Leister
Defense Counsel	Walter Hudd
Crown Counsel	Maurice Denham
Phyllis	Jacqueline Clarke
Mr. Pinkham	Frank Tickle
Titch	Peter Croft
Farmer Browning	George Woodbridge
Sir James	Stuart Lindsel

For this remake of John Galsworthy's play (Radio 1930, Sir Gerald du Maurier and Edna Best) 20th-Fox imported two topnotchers in William Perlberg and Joseph Mankiewicz. Result, although not Galsworthy, is eminently satisfying, and will play to good business here and in U. S.

Galsworthy stated his theme in a matter-of-fact way — how would various people react to an escaped convict who had been a gentleman? With restraint he avoided anything sensational. There was no woman to fall in love with him, although a couple did sympathize. It was a straightforward story, coming to the only possible conclusion, an

ending fortunately retained in the present version. But the elimination of the fishing scene from the film betrays a lamentable ignorance of British psychology.

Picture has been brought up to date by making Rex Harrison, the escaped convict, an ex-RAF squadron leader, sentenced to three years for manslaughter for hitting and accidentally killing a policeman who was trying to arrest a prostitute in Hyde Park to whom the airman had been speaking. He is sent to Dartmoor. One foggy morning he escapes from jail and for a time dodges the police with the aid of a girl who has fallen in love with him, played by Peggy Cummins. Finally, to save a padre lying, he gives himself up, knowing he has the girl to come back to.

For those who do not know their Galsworthy the story will be perfectly satisfactory, although it will not, as Galsworthy hoped, produce in the audience "a mental and moral ferment." Rex Harrison is good as the convict, but Peggy Cummins is too shallow to make her love for him really convincing.

William Hartnell, for once on the side of the law, gives a first-rate, natural performance, and Norman Wooland is most effective as the parson. All the minor characters are well played. *Cane.*

Spring in Park Lane

(BRITISH)

London, March 18.

British Lion release of Herbert Wilcox production. Stars Anna Neagle, Michael Wilding, Tom Walls. Directed by Wilcox. Screenplay by Nicholas Phipps; music, Robert Farnon; camera, Max Greene, Bob Walker. Previewed London, March 17, '48. Running time, 91 mins.

Judy Howard	Anna Neagle
Richard	Michael Wilding
Joshua Howard	Tom Walls
Basil Maitland	Peter Graves
Mildred Howard	Marjorie Fielding
Marquis of Borechester	Nicholas Phipps
Perkins	G.H. Mulcaster
Lady Borechester	Catherine Paul
Kate O'Malley	Josephine Fitzgerald
Mr. Bacon	Nigel Patrick
Rosie	Lana Morris
Higgins	H.R. Hignett
Antique Dealer	Cyril Conway
Bates	Tom Walls, Jr.

Like a shaft of light piercing the prevalent gloom of the British screen comes this gay, irresponsible comedy, bringing joy to exhibs. Herbert Wilcox has done it again, and the boxoffice will react. Rich in entertainment, it has top marquee value in the country's most popular romantic team, Anna Neagle and Michael Wilding, and while she consolidates her position as screen's first lady, Wilding establishes himself as Britain's foremost light comedian.

Great merit of the story is that it seems like a happy improvisation. None of the elaborate and necessary scaffolding is apparent, and when Michael Wilding as a younger son of a noble family, needing money for a return trip to New York, becomes a temporary footman in a Park Lane mansion, he is immediately accepted as such by the audience. And since Anna Neagle plays a secretary in the same house, everybody knows it will be love at first sight and that sooner or later the two will march altarwards.

It's a story in which the trimmings and incidentals are all-important. The gay harmless fun poked at the film stars, the dinner party bore, the housekeeper to whom bridge is a religion, the

footman cutting in to dance or discussing art with his boss—incident upon incident carry merry laughter through the picture.

In addition to the two stars and Tom Walls, who are in top form, Wilcox has gathered some notable first-timers. Significant screen debuts are made by Nicholas Phipps, Lana Morris, Josephine Fitzgerald, Nigel Patrick and Catherine Paul, while Peter Graves proves triumphantly how sadly some producers have misused him for years.

Max Greene maintains his reputation as top camera specialist. Bill Andrews deserves a bouquet for his art work, and the musical score by Robert Farnon is appropriately impressive. In all, a rewarding picture for everybody. *Cane.*

The First Gentleman

(BRITISH)

London, March 25.

Columbia Pictures production and release. Stars Jean Pierre Aumont, Joan Hopkins, Cecil Parker. Directed by Cavalcanti. Screenplay by Nicholas Phipps, from play by Norman Ginsbury. Editor, Margery Saunders; music, Lennox Berkeley; camera, Jack Hildyard. At Studio One, London, March 24, '48. Running time, 111 MINS.

Prince Leopold	Jean Pierre Aumont
Prince Regent	Cecil Parker
Princess Charlotte	Joan Hopkins
Mr. Brougham	Ronald Squire
Miss Knight	Athene Seyler
Lady Hertford	Margaretta Scott
Edward, Duke of Kent	Jack Livesey
Dr. Stockmar	Gerard Heinz
Mrs. Griffiths	Joan Young
Sir Richard Croft	Anthony Hawtrey
Bishop of Salisbury	Hugh Griffith
Duke of York	George Curzon
Princess Elizabeth	Betty Huntly-Wright
Prince William	Tom Gill
Princess Augusta	Lydia Sherwood
Queen Charlotte	Frances Waring
Caroline	Amy Frank
Lord Eldon	Richard Shayne
Princess Sophia	Judy Beaumont
Princess Mary	Olwen Brookes
Lady Conyngham	Melissa Stribling

Hollywood has often been blamed for laying rude hands on British history, but nobody would have dared travesty a principal character as has been done here. In this adaptation of Norman Ginsbury's play, the Prince Regent (afterwards George IV of England), self-styled "First Gentleman of Europe," has been turned into a caricature. History records he was naturally gifted, had considerable taste, was a blend of polished gentleman and accomplished blackguard, but never a buffoon. And it is his cheap comicalities and his amours that dominate the picture, to the detriment of the boxoffice.

The rich elegance of the production should attract certain patronage, but with little marquee help it will be hard work to recoup the considerable outlay. With 20 minutes cut it may find a place in prestige theatres in America.

Story begins when George III, having lost his reason, is replaced, as Regent, by his son, George, Prince of Wales. Afraid of the popularity of his daughter, Charlotte, he plans to marry her to Prince William of Orange, but having fallen in love with Prince Leopold of Saxe-Coburg, she disobeys her father, and is virtually kept as a prisoner. To gain public favor, the Regent relents, allows Charlotte to marry the man she loves, but rejoicing turns to tragedy when she dies in giving birth to a stillborn son. Story ends with the Regent attending the baptism of his niece Victoria, future Queen of England.

Picture is elegantly mounted, but fails mainly through indecision of producer and director to make up their minds how to deal with the story. It is a lush pageant with too few dramatic highlights and an overlong deathbed scene.

Cecil Parker is too good an actor to have burlesqued the title role without instructions, and Joan Hopkins (stage understudy to Wendy Hiller in the part) is just adequate as Charlotte for whom Jean-Pierre Aumont makes a nice lover. Participating in the picture is a considerable cast of good players.

For the first time since 1935, when he conducted for the Mozart musical film "Whom the Gods Love," Sir Thomas Beecham directed the complete music score of a film. It isn't noteworthy. *Cane.*

The Lost One
('La Traviata')
(ITALIAN)

Columbia release of Gregor Rabinovitch (William Szekely) production. Stars Nelly Corradi, Gino Mattera. Directed by Carmine Gallone. Screenplay by Hamilton Benz, adapted from opera, "La Traviata," with music by Giuseppe Verdi and libretto by F. M. Piave, and from "La Dame aux Camelias," by Alexander Dumas, Jr.; camera, Arturo Gallea; editor, Niccolo Lazzari; musical adapter, Luigi Ricci; conductor, Ettore Panizza. At Golden, N. Y., March 29, '48. Running time, **84 MINS.**

Alexander Dumas, Jr......Massimo Serato
Giuseppi Verdi..............Nerio Bernardi
Violetta Valery...............Nelly Corradi
Alfredo Germont..............Gino Mattera
George Germont........Manfredi Polverosi
Flora Bervoix................Flora Marino
Baron Douphol..............Carlo Lombardi

(In Italian; English Narration)

Italian-made version of the Giuseppe Verdi opera, "La Traviata," filmed in Rome by Gregor Rabinovitch as first of six pictures scheduled for Columbia release, is several cuts above recent operatic imports from abroad. The irresistible Verdi score and sentimental though moving love story are backed by some fine casting and performances and superior production. But being essentially an adaptation of an opera, and following the opera closely, the film is fairly static and frequently very slow. It will appeal to opera-lovers and prove a good bet for the art houses, but little more.

It's evident that great care, and good taste, went into the production. Sets, costumes and general production are superior by far to most other opera films. Casting has been made with an eye to U. S. tastes, with a handsome Alfredo in Gino Mattera, 24-year-old Italian tenor find, and an eye-filling beauty for Violetta in Nelly Corradi. Not only is the lady a knockout visually, but she can act. Love scenes between the two, despite the artificial, mood-dispelling situation of having them flinging arias to each other in the tenderest of moments, are frequently poignant and of much beauty. Handsome couple do much to offset the dull spots.

It's obvious that the singing is dubbed (and someth... the dubbing isn't too perfectly synchronized). Credit goes to Onella Fineschi, Mattera, Tito Gobbi, Francesco Albanese and Arturo La Porta for the actual singing. But the singing is of high order, and the recording is exemplary, with the sound track superior to most such pix. Ettore Panizza, former conductor at the N. Y. Met, has handled singers, as well as supporting orchestra and chorus of the Rome Opera House, with skill and distinction. Camera work is fine, with some lovely outdoor shots.

Film follows the opera closely. Prolog has Dumas, the writer, and Verdi, the composer, standing by the grave of the noted Parisian courtesan, Alphonsine Plessis, in a Montmartre cemetery, discussing her life and loves. Then the film fades into the familiar opera tale of the lady who deserts her fast Parisian life for her new-found young love, their breakup and her tragic end. Most of the film is sung, and all in Italian.

The prolog is in English, and a running commentary throughout the film, done in English as if the heroine is reading her diary, explains the story perfectly to eliminate need for subtitles. The diary voice is a little confusing, the audience believing it is Violetta's, and being constantly surprised as spoken word in English is immediately followed by singing voice in Italian. Matter should have been cleared up a bit.

Film is also badly cut in a couple of places, especially at the beginning of one tenor aria, to make it jerky. Spoken dialog, as it's read from the diary, is somewhat stilted and corny at times, too. Pic is a good attempt at translating opera palatably for U. S. audiences, but by its very nature is limited in appeal. *Bron.*

Snowbound
(BRITISH)

London, March 24.

RKO release of J. Arthur Rank, Sydney Box-Gainsborough production. Features Robert Newton, Dennis Price, Herbert Lom. Directed by David McDonald. Screenplay by David Evans, Keith Campbell, adapted from "The Lonely Skier," by Hammond Innes. Music, Cedric Thorpe Davie; editor, Charles Knott; camera, Stephen Dade. At Odeon, Marble Arch, London, March 23, '48. Running time, 86 mins.

Derek Engles..............................Robert Newton
Neil Blair....................................Dennis Price
Keramikos..................................Herbert Lom
Stefan Valdini..............................Marcel Dalio
Joe Wesson...............................Stanley Holloway
Gilbert Mayne............................Guy Middleton
Carla Rometta..............................Mila Parely
Aldo..Willy Fueter
Mancini.......................................Richard Molinas
Emilia...Catherine Ferraz
Auctioneer...................................Massino Coen
Stelben.......................................William Price

Scene for this thriller is a skihut in the Alps, cache of Nazi gold buried when Germany was defeated. Like flies to a sugar-tart come an assortment of folk all searching for the hideout. It is a sure formula for a game of cops and robbers, and will find favor here with most audiences, although a little less doublecrossing would have made the story less complicated and more enjoyable. For U. S. it should fit into dual bills.

Main failing of the yarn is that situations do not thrill sufficiently, even when all the protagonists are snowbound in the hut and trigger-pulling, knife-throwing, and a raging fire become inevitable.

Robert Newton plays his usual self as an ex-British Intelligence officer. Dennis Price is a careless hero, Herbert Lom scowls suitably as a Nazi, Marcel Dalio is duly acceptable as a conspirator, Guy Middleton is effectively nonchalant as a British deserter, and Stanley Holloway contributes his quota of laughs as an innocent cameraman drawn into the hornets' nest. For corpses it rivals "Hamlet."

For the romantic interest Mila Parely was imported from Paris, an experiment difficult to justify by results. *Cane.*

Confessions of a Rogue
(FRENCH)

Distinguished Films release of Constellation Films production. Stars Louis Jouvet; features Suzy Delair. Directed by Constantin Geftman. Screenplay, Henri Jeanson from scenario by Jacques Companeez; camera, Jean Feyte; English titles, Walter Klee. At Pix, N. Y., March 26, '48. Running time, **84 MINS.**

Ismora..........................Louis Jouvet
Caroline..........................Suzy Delair
Charlotte....................Annette Poivre
Concierge......................Jane Marken
Mme. Charles.............Madeleine Suffel
Oscar...................Jean Jacques Delbo
Andre...........................Leon Lapara
An accomplice..................Jean Carmet
Laprune....................................Pally
M. Charles..................Henri Charrett
Peroni.....................Fernand Rauzena
Pauzat.......................Georges Cusin
Judge..........................Robert Seller

(In French; English Titles)

"Confessions of a Rogue" is a neat comedy item from France slated for solid returns in the sure-seater circuit. Taking the old Hollywood chestnut of a double identity mixup, this pic turns it into a tasty souffle of Gallic wit, slyness, sexiness and cynicism.

Louis Jouvet, France's most popular and, apparently, most active thesper who's also being seen hereabouts in "Volpone" and "Jenny Lamour," is a one-man show in this production. Playing a super-swindler, Jouvet assumes a half-dozen different roles with which to con his clientele and tickle his U.S. fans. A consummate artist, he's able to suggest a new personality through an eyebrow flick or a slight resetting of his chin.

First half of the film is a sparkling recital of Jouvet's technique of selling museums to gullible provincials. Complications set in midway with the introduction of the swindler's double, a mousy, honest clerk, who's picked up by the police for the other's crimes. The doubles finally team up to confound the cops, but through a sharp turnabout, the honest man comes out on top with the swindler's loot and mistress.

Principal support to Jouvet is delivered by Suzy Delair, a pert looker with a sharp sense of humor. Other thespers in minor roles also turn in good performances. English titling by Walter Klee is competent, but several important dialog bits are left untranslated. *Herm.*

Last Days of Boot Hill
(SONGS)

Hollywood, March 27.

Columbia release of Colbert Clark production. Stars Charles Starrett; features Smiley Burnette, Virginia Hunter, Paul Campbell, Mary Newton, Cass County Boys. Directed by Ray Nazarro. Original screenplay, Norman S. Hall; camera, George F. Kelley; editor, Paul Borofsky. Reviewed at Valley, North Hollywood, March 26, '48. Running time, **55 MINS.**

Steve Waring / The Durango Kid......Charles Starrett
Smiley Burnette.............Smiley Burnette
Paula Thorpe...............Virginia Hunter
Frank Rayburn..............Paul Campbell
Mrs. Forrest Brent...........Mary Newton
Reed Brokaw..........................Bill Free
Dan McCoy.............J. Courtland Lytton
Bronc Peters.......................Bob Wilke
Forrest Brent.....................Alan Bridge
The Cass County Boys

The Durango Kid rides again in "Last Days of Boot Hill" to bring six-gun justice to prairie evildoers. That most of his action takes place by flashback is unusual for this forthright series that draws a clear line between right and wrong. It's also production sleight-of-hand, permitting close shaving on the budget, but the Saturday matinee fans of western derring-do won't mind.

In between the action, four musical interludes are spotted with standard results. Charles Starrett walks through his assignment as the U. S. Marshal on the trail of $100,000 in gold stolen years before, adopting the Durango character to deal out the villains' just desserts. Smiley Burnette is his roly-poly undercover assistant, in between working with the Cass County Boys on oatunes such as "Texas Belle," "Lookin' Out, Lookin' In," "On My Way Back Home" and "Giddey-Ap."

Ray Nazarro's direction puts the players through their paces in okay style, although film could have used a few spectacular thrills outside of the tried-and-true chase and gun fight. Casting is standard, villains looking like villains and the good element in shining armor. Starrett's dual function as the law and the outlaw, saves Virginia Hunter's ranch from skullduggery by Mary Newton, Bill Free and J. Courtland Lytton. Standing by is Paul Campbell as romantic interest for the heroine.

Colbert Clark produced and George Kelley did the lensing in standard outdoor fashion. *Brog.*

Song of Idaho
(SONGS)

Hollywood, March 27.

Columbia release of Colbert Clark production. Features Hoosier Hot Shots, Kirby Grant, June Vincent, Tommy Ivo. Directed by Ray Nazarro. Original screenplay, Barry Shipman; camera, Vincent Farrar; editor, Aaron Stell. At Million Dollar, L. A., March 27, '48. Running time, **67 MINS.**

King Russell.....................Kirby Grant
Eve Allen.......................June Vincent
Junior.............................Tommy Ivo
Sara Mom...................Dorothy Vaughn
J. Chester Nottingham......Emory Parnell
Hash Brown......................Eddie Acuff
Millie........................Maudie Prickett
Hoosier Hot Shots
Sunshine Boys
Sunshine Girls
Starlighters

"Song of Idaho" is another of Columbia's light-budgeted rural comedies with music. It has plenty to please, particularly in the corn belt. A fast pace, able clowning by the Hoosier Hotshots, Kirby Grant's very listenable baritone, and other ingredients are all on the credit side.

Plot is the one about hillbilly singer trying to interest his sponsor in a renewal when show goes off the air. To get the sponsor's signature, program must please latter's young son, a little hellion. Antics center around Hot Shots' effort to win the youngster's favor and the kid's blackmailing of the foursome. Barry Shipman's script put the ingredients together neatly and pleasantly and Ray Nazarro's direction makes it all come out entertainingly for the audience at which it is aimed.

Kirby Grant reprises "Idaho" several times, gives solid vocal treatment to "Driftin'" and "Nobody Else But You" in a baritone that is good listening. Hot Shots sell several bucolic pieces for laughs. Others aiding musical portions are the Sunshine Boys, backing Grant's singing; the Sunshine Girls and the Starlighters.

June Vincent is a comely program analysist who mixes romance with her job. Tommy Ivo does a sharp job as the precocious youngster and Emory Parnell is good as his father. Dorothy Vaughn, Eddie Acuff and Maudie Prickett measure up to demands.

Colbert Clark's production furnish good values for the limited budget. Lensing and other credits are okay. _Brog._

Money Madness

Film Classics release of Sigmund Neufeld Production. Stars Hugh Beaumont and Frances Rafferty. Directed by Peter Stewart. Original story, Al Martin; editor, Holbrook N. Todd; camera, Jack Greenhalgh; musical director, Leo Erdody. Tradeshown in N. Y. March 25, '48. Running time, 73 MINS.

Steve Clark	Hugh Beaumont
Julie	Frances Rafferty
Donald	Harlan Warde
Cora	Cecil Weston
Mrs. Ferguson	Ida Moore
Rogers	Danny Morton
Dr. Wagner	Joel Friedkin
Policeman	Lane Chandler

A feeble programmer, "Money Madness" will find its market limited to the dualers and nabes. Small cast, lack of production mountings and a trite script reflect an all too-limited budget. Co-stars. Hugh Beaumont and Frances Rafferty are deserving of better roles.

Story's built around a supposedly ingenious scheme that bankrobber Beaumont has hit upon to spend a $200,000 haul without arousing suspicion of authorities. He weds Miss Rafferty, then poisons her aunt to make it appear the latter has hoarded the money to leave to her niece upon her demise. Miss Rafferty discovers too late that her husband is a crook. However, the law eventually catches up with him, thus satisfying the Production Code's retribution requirements.

Beaumont struggles with an unsympathetic part. Miss Rafferty does what she can, and Cecil Weston is okay as the carping, hypochondriacal aunt. Harlan Warde contribs a fair job as an attorney who sees through Beaumont's machinations.

Producer Sig Neufeld, an old hand at turning out modestly-budgeted program pix, failed to give "Money Madness" much help via production values. Al Martin's scripting is quite ordinary while Jack Greenhalgh's lensing as well as other technical credits are adequate. _Gilb._

Man From Texas
(SONGS)

Eagle Lion release of Joseph Fields production. Stars James Craig, Lynn Bari, Johnnie Johnston; features Una Merkel, Harry Davenport. Directed by Leigh Jason. Screenplay, Joseph Fields and Jerome Chodorov, from stageplay by E. B. Ginty; camera, Jackson J. Rose; editor, Norman Colbert; songs, Earl Robinson and Joseph Fields. Tradeshown in N. Y., March 25, '48. Running time, 71 MINS.

El Paso Kid	James Craig
Zoe Bixbee	Lynn Bari
Billy Taylor	Johnnie Johnston
Widow Weeks	Una Merkel
Jed	Wally Ford
Pop Hickey	Harry Davenport
Aunt Belle	Sara Allgood
Charles Jackson	Vic Cutler
U. S. Marshal	Reed Hadley
Jim Walsh	Clancy Cooper
Bob Jackson	Bert Conway
Sam	King Donovan

This western, with Johnnie Johnston, Una Merkel, Lynn Bari and James Craig for marquee lustre, is lightweight and has extremely limited chances.

Pic depicts Craig wavering between being a law-abiding citizen and an outlaw. In between the picture falls apart. At one juncture, Craig helps a poor widow (Una Merkel) lift the mortgage on her ranch and then turns arounds to rob a bank. After that it's a free-for-all as to whether Craig will reform or continue his bandit career.

Dialog is surprisingly corny. Craig strives hard to be an outlaw but with not much success. Lynn Bari plays his wife, but not one of her better performances. Johnnie Johnston adds little to his cinematic career as a guitar-strumming crooner who bursts into song on the slightest provocation. His choice of tunes also is questionable. Miss Merkel also falters as the widow, but maybe it's what she's asked to do and say. Reed Hadley is best of the support.

Jackson J. Rose's camera job is refreshing. Joseph Fields is credited with being producer and contributing the lyrics to several of the cowboy songs, plus teaming with Jerome Chodorov on the screenplay. _Wear._

20 Years of Academy Awards

RKO release of Academy of Motion Picture Arts and Sciences production. Narration by Carey Wilson. Tradeshown in N. Y. March 26, '48. Running time, 18 MINS.

Showing the Oscar winners and Academy Award pictures starting with 1928, and carrying through 1947, this novel two-reeler constitutes a swift-moving quickie close-up of the screen industry's triumphs over the past 20 years. It was produced by the Academy, with proceeds from showing of film to be used by the AMPAS in furthering constructive work on films. It should interest any audience.

Carey Wilson carries the running story to point up highlights. Mary Pickford and Warner Baxter are shown as first Oscar winners, for their work in "Coquette" and "In Old Arizona," respectively. There's also an excellent closeup of Al Jolson, given a special award for being star in the first talking picture ("The Jazz Singer," for Warners), there's one of Shirley Temple handed special mention when she was a child star, plus awarding of special small Oscars to Walt Disney.

Besides showing the Academy winners in the outstanding films which won them the laurels, each year also depicts top sequences from each year's best picture. Short carries through to include actual presentations to 1947 winners (awarded March 20) in Hollywood, with Darryl Zanuck, Loretta Young and Ronald Colman stepping up to receive the Oscars. Then typical scenes from "Gentleman's Agreement," 20th-Fox 1947 prizewinner, are given as well as sequences from "Farmer's Daughter," RKO picture for which Miss Young won her prize, and "Double Life," Universal film for which Colman won his.

Much of this short's effectiveness stems from Wilson's deft narration. Crisp editing also is a big factor. _Wear._

Miniature Reviews

"Homecoming" (MG). Socko drama with great femme appeal. Clark Gable at his best.

"Winter Meeting" (WB). Heavy, talky drama. Bette Davis name will help but gross outlook slow.

"Berlin Express" (RKO). Fast melodrama backed by solid cast and authentic European backgrounds; good b.o.

"The Noose Hangs High" (EL). Abbott and Costello up to their usual fun antics. Sturdy for A&C followers.

"Fury at Furnace Creek" (20th). Robust western with strong appeal for the action and outdoor minded.

"Old Los Angeles" (Rep). Fair western with average grosses in sight.

"Silent Conflict" (UA). Standard Hopalong Cassidy horse opera for regular action spots.

"Arthur Takes Over" (20th). Domestic comedy for lower rung of dualers.

"Close-Up" (EL). Slack-paced actioner heading for tepid returns.

"Buckaroo from Powder River" (Col). Okay oatuner in the Durango Kid series.

"Angelina" (Italian). Interesting Anna Magnani starrer with surefire returns due in art situations.

Homecoming
Hollywood, April 3.

Metro release of Sidney Franklin production (in association with Gottfried Reinhardt). Stars Clark Gable, Lana Turner, Anne Baxter, John Hodiak; features Ray Collins, Gladys Cooper, Cameron Mitchell. Directed by Mervyn LeRoy. Screenplay, Paul Osborn; adaptation, Jan Lustig; original story, Sidney Kingsley; camera, Harold Rosson; music. Bronislau Kaper; editor, John Dunning. Tradeshown March 31, '48. Running time, 113 MINS.

Ulysses Delby Johnson	Clark Gable
Lt. Jane "Snapshot" McCall	Lana Turner
Penny Johnson	Anne Baxter
Dr. Robert Sunday	John Hodiak
Lt. Col. Avery Silver	Ray Collins
Mrs. Kirby	Gladys Cooper
Sgt. Monkevickz	Cameron Mitchell
Sgt. McKeen	Marshall Thompson
Miss Stoker	Lurene Tuttle
Sarah	Jessie Grayson
Sol	J. Louis Johnson
Nurse Aldine Bradford	Eloise Hardt

"Homecoming" is the picture Clark Gable fans have been waiting for. A showmanly drama out of the top production drawer, film has its sights on solid grosses in all situations. Teaming of Hollywood's biggest s. a. names, Gable and Lana Turner, in a story that will appeal strongly to the femmes, gives "Homecoming" all the earmarks of being a natural.

Performances are of top quality all down the line, with Gable and Miss Turner pacing the playing. Story line makes a direct play for the tear ducts and has heart. These two factors overcome some patness in resolving plot's problems and direction shapes material for strong interest despite lengthy footage.

Gable portrays a successful surgeon, happily married, who joins the Army. Three years of patching up the wounded in close association with his nurse, Miss Turner, gradually changes the man's character from smug successfulness to an awareness of his obligations to others. There is a restrained romance with the nurse smoldering through most of the footage but it is tastefully and believably projected, and gives film one of its strongest exploitation factors.

Story, scripted by Paul Osborn from an original by Sidney Kingsley, is told in flashback and draws its title from the surgeon's return home after his great war love. The dialog and the characters are made real by the forceful playing. There is strong sympathy for the love between Gable and Miss Turner, even though the doctor's wife, Anne Baxter, awaits at home. Problem is resolved when the nurse dies of war wounds and Gable returns to tackle life again with his new philosophy.

A considerable portion of the footage is devoted to detailing heroic work done by doctors and nurses under fire at the front, but film does not class as a war picture. Combat medical scenes add punch.

Gable gives an assured, compelling performance and Miss Turner demonstrates a dramatic talent that definitely boosts her histrionic stock. Miss Baxter does a beautiful smooth job as the understanding wife and John Hodiak as a family friend scores in shorter footage. Ray Collins, Army doctor; Gladys Cooper, Miss Baxter's mother; Cameron Mitchell and others are very capable.

Sidney Franklin's production supervision, in association with Gottfried Reinhardt and Mervyn LeRoy's expert direction, have given the film realistic values. Topnotch technical credits go to Harold Rosson's photography, the musical score by Bronislau Kaper, art direction, special effects. _Brog._

Winter Meeting
Hollywood, April 3.

Warner Bros. release of Henry Blanke production. Stars Bette Davis; features Janis Paige, James Davis, John Hoyt. Directed by Bretaigne Windust. Screenplay, Catherine Turney; from novel by Ethel Vance; camera, Ernest Haller; music, Max Steiner; editor, Owen Marks. Tradeshown March 31, '48. Running time, 104 MINS.

Susan Grieve	Bette Davis
Peggy Markham	Janis Paige
Slick Novak	James Davis
Stacy Grant	John Hoyt
Mrs. Castle	Florence Bates
Mr. Castle	Walter Baldwin
Mr. Moran	Ransom Sherman

"Winter Meeting" fails to measure up as one of Bette Davis' better ventures into heavy drama. Her name on the marquee will aid some but it's a tediously talky drama, slowly paced, and rarely stirs sympathy for the principal characters.

There's a modest amount of appeal to femme audiences to help carry story along, but on the whole, plot and character motivation do not hold together strongly. Dialog is on the trite side. Henry Blanke's production supervision misses on pulling the story together entertainment-wise and Bretaigne Windust's direction isn't able to do much with material.

Miss Davis appears as a spinsterish girl of wealth with a tragic homelife background. She meets a returning war hero who also has a fixation. They fall in love and, with much dialog, talk out their respective mental troubles. Finale has them parting, the hero to become a priest and the girl to return to her family. Miss Davis plays the role skillfully and that it doesn't come alive is the fault of the essentially thin character. James Davis, the war hero, tries hard but fails to register strongly.

Janis Paige gets some life into her role as an amorous secretary to John Hoyt. Latter's elegant rich man character has the falseness of most of the roles. Florence Bates, Walter Baldwin and Ransom Sherman complete the small cast.

Technically, film is up to the usual high Warners standards. Ernest Haller's lensing, the art direction and settings, score and other contributions lending gloss to the production. *Brog.*

Berlin Express

RKO release of (Bert Granet) Dore Schary production. Stars Merle Oberon, Robert Ryan, Charles Korvin, Paul Lukas. Directed by Jacques Tourneur. Screenplay, Harold Medford from story by Curt Siodmak; camera, Lucien Ballard; editor, Sherman Todd; music, C. Bakaleinikoff. Tradeshown N. Y., April 1, '48. Running time, **86 MINS.**

Lucienne	Merle Oberon
Robert Lindley	Robert Ryan
Perrot	Charles Korvin
Dr. Bernhardt	Paul Lukas
Sterling	Robert Coote
Walther	Reinhold Schunzel
Lt. Maxim	Roman Toporow
Hans Schmidt	Peter von Zerneck
Kessler	Otto Waldis
Franzen	Fritz Kortner
Sgt. Barnes	Michael Harvey
Major	Richard Powers

With Berlin currently the focal point of international tension, this pic might ride the newspaper headlines into the boff b.o. class. "Berlin Express" is part of that incipient cycle of Hollywood pix which have been lensed for most part in European locales and deal with postwar problems. Although this yarn has many loose edges, it propels forward with an unflagging pace under Jacques Tourneur's adroit direction. Besides, its marquee values are solid.

Most striking feature of this production is its extraordinary background of war-ravaged Germany. With a documentary eye, this film etches a powerfully grim picture of life amidst the shambles. No newsreel or factual film has equalled this pic in describing the scope and depth of the shellacking which the Reich received. It makes awesome and exciting cinema.

Although the plot is fanciful melodrama, everything else in this film is keyed to straight realism. Tourneur has muted the thesping down to a matter-of-fact, casual, life-like tone that merges skillfully into the setting. German and French lingo is used extensively wherever it's naturally called for. Instead of disturbing the ordinary filmgoer, it'll undoubtedly add to the impact of authenticity.

Chief defect of the screenplay is its failure to break away from the formula of anti-Nazi films. The Nazis, now underground, are still the heavies but it's difficult to get excited about such a group of ragged hoodlums. Their motivation in the pic, moreover, is never explained satisfactorily as they set about kidnapping a prominent German democrat, played by Paul Lukas.

Starting out on the Paris-to-Berlin express to an Allied conference on the unification of Germany, Lukas gets waylaid in Frankfurt despite an over-elaborate scheme of guarding him. Symbolizing the Big Four powers, other passengers on the train include an American (Robert Ryan), a Frenchwoman (Merle Oberon), an Englishman (Robert Coote), and a Russian (Roman Toporow) plus a dubious character of unknown nationality (Charles Korvin).

As these five set out to find Lukas, the camera combs the underworld life of Frankfurt, acutely picking up details of starvation, blacketeering and general ruin. Finally, after a slambang climax, Lukas is rescued from the Nazi mob and Korvin is exposed as their ringleader. There's only a slight hint of romance between Ryan and Miss Oberon and it's wisely not followed through. The pic hews closely to its theme of international cooperation.

Ryan establishes himself as a firstrate actor in this film, demonstrating conclusively that his brilliant performance in "Crossfire" was no one-shot affair. He has ease, polish and the quality of sincerity. Miss Oberon holds her end up competently, sporting a faint French accent and doing without glamorization.

Lukas turns in an effective portrayal as an idealist. Korvin likewise registers well as the suave conspirator. In a lesser part, Roman Toporow, playing a Russian lieutenant, strikes a solid characterization of a distrustful and stern, but yet friendly visitor from behind the Iron Curtain. *Herm.*

The Noose Hangs High

Eagle Lion release of Charles Barton production, directed by Barton. Stars Bud Abbott, Lou Costello; features Joseph Calleia, Leon Errol, Cathy Downs, Mike Mazurki, Fritz Feld. Screenplay, John Grant, Howard Harris; adapted from screenplay by Charles Grayson and Arthur T. Horman; original story, Daniel Taradash, Julian Blaustein, Bernard Fins; camera, Charles Van Enger; editor, Harry Reynolds. Previewed April 1, '48. Running time, **77 MINS.**

Homer	Lou Costello
Ted Higgins	Bud Abbott
Carol	Cathy Downs
Mike Craig	Joseph Calleia
McBride	Leon Errol
Chuck	Mike Mazurki
Joe	Jack Overman
Psychiatrist	Fritz Feld

"The Noose Hangs High" gives Abbott & Costello full opportunity to display their fine slapstick art. The pair of buffoons deliver in great style. It's a funfest from start to finish, chockful of strong laughs for the A&C fans.

Routines, despite their age, have a freshness that wallops the risibilities in the artful hands of the comics. All of the gags are good with several that reach the acme of hilarious nonsense. Such a one is the on-and-off pants routine, a display of apt timing and high comedy talent. Another is the oldie, "you can't be here," played to top results.

A lot of writers had their hands in the plotting, but the story line is only a thread upon which to hang the A&C routines. Pic kicks off with window-washing setup that has the boys fumbling on a high window ledge. From there it moves into a mistaken-identity theme, involving comics with gambling syndicate and a missing $50,000 bet. Charles Barton gives it all ace directorial guidance to wring every situation of its humor, and it's his handling that counts measureably in making "Noose" sturdy stuff for the comedy market.

Backing the talents of A&C is a sharp supporting cast. Leon Errol, as a rich eccentric who never loses a bet, fits naturally into the antics and earns a strong credit. Joseph Calleia is good as a gambler. Cathy Downs perks her role as the girl who gets the $50,000 by mistake and becomes involved in the plotting. Mike Mazurki and Jack Overman are Calleia's henchmen.

Barton's production supervision places proper value on physical backing. Photography by Charles Van Enger is good, as are other technical contributions. Editing has held film to a tight 77 minutes. *Brog.*

Fury at Furnace Creek

Hollywood, April 1.

20th-Fox release of Fred Kohlmar production. Stars Victor Mature, Coleen Gray; features Glenn Langan, Reginald Gardiner, Albert Dekker. Directed by Bruce Humberstone. Screenplay, Charles G. Booth; added dialog, Winston Miller; suggested by story by David Garth; camera, Harry Jackson; music, David Raksin; editor, Robert Simpson. Tradeshown April 1, '48. Running time, **88 MINS.**

Cash	Victor Mature
Molly Baxter	Coleen Gray
Rufe	Glenn Langan
Captain Walsh	Reginald Gardiner
Leverett	Albert Dekker
Bird	Fred Clark
Peaceful Jones	Charles Kemper
General Blackwell	Robert Warwick
Judge	George Cleveland
Al Shanks	Roy Roberts
General Leeds	Willard Robertson
Appleby	Griff Barnett
Evans	Frank Orth
Pops	J. Farrell MacDonald
Artego	Charles Stevens
Little Dog	Jay Silverheels
Leverett Henchman	Robert Adler
Professor	Harry Seymour
Clerk	Harry Carter
Defense Counsel	Mauritz Hugo Howard Negley
Prosecutor	Harlan Briggs
Jury Foreman	Si Jenks
Court Clerk	Guy Wilkerson
Stranger	Robert Williams
Judge Advocate	James Flavin

"Fury at Furnace Creek" has a bold action air that points it for favorable reception in most situations. It's a western feature with all the story ingredients that please, and is told at a fast pace and with sturdy trouping. Rugged outdoor scenery, beautifully photographed, backgrounds the actional movement and lends ace production value. Sight appeal is strong.

Cast, with few exceptions, romps through assignments most ably under Bruce Humberstone's robust direction. Victor Mature sits easily in the hero's saddle and pleases mightily with his interpretation of the outdoor character. It's a forthright performance that adds credence to the melodramatic doings. Coleen Gray is a pert and pretty heroine with not too much to do.

Plot is based on white man's skulduggery that leads to an Indian massacre at old Fort Furnace Creek, where a cavalry troop is wiped out. The general who gave the order for re-routing reinforcements is courtmartialed and his estranged son, Mature, sets out to clear his father's record. Sagebrush detective work is interestingly handled by actor and denouncement fastens the blame on western silver tycoon Albert Dekker, who had connived the dastardly deed so he could gain possession of a rich mine.

Reginald Gardiner is good as a weak army officer used by Dekker for the skulduggery. Dekker is a menacing villain, as are his henchmen, Fred Clark, Roy Roberts and Charles Stevens. Glenn Langan is just adequate as Mature's stuffy brother. Sturdy comedy relief is supplied by Charles Kemper, making a light, bright spot in the heaving doings. George Cleveland, J. Farrell MacDonald and others measure up to all demands.

Fred Kohlmar has given the western story "A" values in production dress. The outstanding lensing is by Harry Jackson, with special photographic effects by Fred Sersen. Music score by David Raksin is excellent. *Brog.*

Old Los Angeles

(SONGS)

Republic release of Joe Kane production, directed by Kane. Stars William Elliott, John Carroll, Catherine McLeod, Joseph Schildkraut; features Andy Devine, Estelita Rodriguez. Screenplay, Gerald Adams, Clements Ripley, based upon latter's original story; camera, William Bradford; editor, Richard L. Van Enger; musical director, Morton Scott; songs, Aaron Gonzales, Nathan Scott, Quirino F. Mendoza y Cortes, Jack Elliott. Previewed in N. Y., April 5, '48. Running time, **87 MINS.**

Bill Stockton	William Elliott
Johnny Morrell	John Carroll
Marie Marlowe	Catherine McLeod
Luis Savarin	Joseph Schildkraut
Sam Bowie	Andy Devine
Estelita Del Rey	Estelita Rodriguez
Senora Del Rey	Virginia Brissac
Marshal Luckner	Grant Withers
Tonio Del Rey	Tito Renaldo
Clyborne	Roy Barcroft
Larry Stockton	Henry Brandon
Diego	Julian Rivero
Horatius P. Gassoway	Earle Hodgins
Miguel	Augie Gomes

One of Republic's typical westerns, "Old Los Angeles" is an overlong oatuner with a story that could have been told in a breezy 60 minutes instead of dragging out to almost an hour and a half. Film shapes up as only fair entertainment with average grosses in sight from the action spots.

Overworked are the musical sequences. Two or three vocals are okay in any hoss opera, but the songs are reprised entirely too often in this entry. As a result the plot postpones the more or less obvious finale. Some neat scissoring could speed up the yarn.

Cast is composed of standard Republic players most of whom are duplicating the same roles they've held down in other outdoor gallopers for the same studio. William Elliott again portrays a Sir Galahad-like warrior, handy with his dukes and six-guns, who makes a fearsome nemesis for renegades to face. Heavy is John Carroll, trodding familiar ground, having thesped similar stints previously.

On the romantic side, Catherine McLeod and Estelita Rodriguez supply the heart interest. Former poses as a singer in Joseph Schildkraut's cafe, but it later develops she's actually a government undercover gal. Both handle their lines satisfactorily as well as vocaling a quintet of tunes. "Ever Faithful" is perhaps the best of these. Schildkraut is an okay menace while Elliott's pardner, Andy Devine, has little to do. Grant Withers is fair as the crooked marshal. Supporting players are adequate.

Writers Gerald Adams and Clements Ripley did a fair job in scripting the screenplay from the latter's original. With omission of much of the unnecessary musical scenes, their story would have been much more to the point. Producer Joe Kane helps the film with some better than average production values and his direction tends to give the pic a fresh twist in some instances. William Bradford lensed in good fashion.

Silent Conflict

United Artists release of Lewis J. Rachmil (William Boyd) production. Stars William Boyd; features Andy Clyde, Rand Brooks. Directed by George Archainbaud. Original screenplay, Charles Belden; based on characters created by Clarence E. Mulford; camera, Mack Stengler; editor, Fred W. Berger. Tradeshown N. Y. April 2, '48. Running time, **61 MINS.**

Hopalong Cassidy	William Boyd
California Carlson	Andy Clyde
Lucky Jenkins	Rand Brooks
Rene Richards	Virginia Belmont
Doc Richards	Earle Hodgins
Speed Blaney	James Harrison
Randall	Forbes Murray
Clerk	John Butler
Yardman	Herbert Rawlinson
First Rancher	Richard Alexander
Second Rancher	Don Haggerty

Latest in the string of Hopalong Cassidy films, "Silent Conflict," is a formula westerner strictly for the juve and action trade. The title isn't too apt since this pic is somewhat short on conflict and a little long on talk. There's not a single fisticuff encounter and only two shots are fired, probably an all-time low for a modern horse opera. However, there's enough hard riding over the purple sage to keep the kids bouncing in their seats.

Plot is also on the unusual side with a hypnotist playing the key heavy role. One of Hopalong's cowhands falls under his sway and delivers to him a bag of coin that belong's to a cattlemen's combine. After a couple of false turns in tracking down the culprits, Hopalong finally catches up with the Svengali and turns him politely over to the law. Barely a brush of romance is hinted as developing between the hynotist's innocent niece and Hopalong's young sidekick.

Silver-haired Boyd continues to impress as a forceful cowboy hero. Rest of the cast performs according to Hoyle in stock parts with Earle Hodgins turning in a neat characterization as the herb selling hypnotist.

Production backgrounds and camera work measure up to this series' fairly high standards.

Herm.

Arthur Takes Over

20th-Fox release of Sol M. Wurtzel production. Features Lois Collier, Richard Crane, Skip Homeier, Ann Todd. Directed by Mal St. Clair. Story and screenplay, Mauri Grashin; camera, Benjamin Kline; editor, Roy Livingston. Tradeshown in N. Y., April 1, '48. Running time, **63 MINS.**

Margaret Bixby	Lois Collier
James Clark	Richard Crane
Arthur Bixby	Skip Homeier
Valerie Jeanne Bradford	Ann E. Todd
George Bradford	Jerome Cowan
Flora Bixby	Barbara Brown
Lawrence White	William Bakewell
Bert Bixby	Howard Freeman
Mrs. Bradford	Joan Blair
Mrs. Barnsfogle	Almira Sessions
Betty Lou	Jeanne Gail

"Arthur Takes Over" is unpretentious and strictly for the twin bills. Cast is lightweight for the marquee.

The old story about the doting mama who would marry off her daughter to an aristocrat has been dressed up slightly. In this one the daughter returns home wed to a sailor she met while serving as a hospital nurse. Proceedings grow so hectic in latter stages that only the tossing of custard pies appears to have been overlooked.

Lois Collier, who photos well, brings some realism as the much-sought after daughter. Skip Homeier, as the teen-age brother, makes up partly in enthusiasm for what he lacks in being a polished juvenile. Jerome Cowan, as father of the teen-age miss, has an absurd characterization but makes it click. Ann E. Todd, as his daughter, is spotty as is Richard Crane.

Howard Freeman heads the support nicely. Benjamin Kline's camera work stands out in this odd mixture of comedy and dizzy action.

Wear.

Close-Up

Eagle Lion release of Marathon Pictures production (Frank Satenstein, producer; Robert L. Joseph, assoc. producer). Stars Alan Baxter, Virginia Gilmore; features Richard Kollmar, Loring Smith, Phil Huston, Russell Collins, Wendell Phillips, Joey Faye. Directed by Jack Donohue. Screenplay by John Bright and Max Wilk; editor, Robert Klager; music, Jerome Moross; camera, William Miller. At Globe, N. Y., week April 3, '48. Running time, **72 MINS.**

Phil Sparr	Alan Baxter
Peggy	Virginia Gilmore
Beaumont	Richard Kollmar
Avery	Loring Smith
Gibbons	Phil Huston
Beck	Russell Collins
Harold	Wendell Phillips
Roger	Joey Faye
Rita	Marcia Walter
Fredericks	Michael Wyler
Cabby	Sid Melton
Jimmy	Jimmy Sheridan
Inspector Lonigan	Maurice Manson
Miller	Lauren Gilbert
Receptionist	Erin O'Kelly

"Close-Up" is touted by Marathon as the first film completely shot in New York during the past 10 years and, as such, it admittedly has the advantages of Gotham's solid backdrops, a touch of lavishness which no Hollywood low-budgeter could afford. Aside from its gift from Manhattan, the pic labors under a yarn shot full of holes, an overly-wordy pace and scripting that slips at times. Result should be tepid grossing in dual and nabe situations.

For one, "Close-Up" which is obviously intended as a zippy actioner, takes unconscionably long in getting started. Almost the first half of the film is spent in setting the scene, a process delayed by talky comic gags which come off infrequently. For another—and a strange device for a film dependent on action—a crucial scene involving the struggle of two men in a 12th floor office and the forcible ejection of one via the window, is narrated by one character but not depicted.

Story details the efforts of a w.k. Nazi (Richard Kollmar), to gain and destroy a newsreel clip, accidentally taken by cameraman Alan Baxter, which proves that the Hitlerite is hiding out in New York after the collapse of the fuehrer's government. Why he should persistently stick his neck out, once the police are on to his existence and why films deemed so valuable should be as carelessly kicked around as they are in this story are things never satisfactorily explained.

At any rate, Baxter mixes with a femme stooge of the gang (Virginia Gilmore); is captured with a negative of the films; makes his getaway only to be grabbed again. Meanwhile, the positive, after some mighty careless handling, reaches the police who stage a grand manhunt for the Nazi. Windup which has good, smart pace is a three-cornered gun battle among the Nazi, the cameraman and the Nazi's gangster henchman who's out to get his boss.

Thesping is adequate if not standout. Baxter meets his role's requirements though he's frequently embarrassed by weak lines. Miss Gilmore is fairish on delivery and cute in appearance. Kollmar has little to do but on that little registers well. Phil Huston, as the gangster, overmugs in spots.

Camera work is well handled, cagily cashing in on the New York locale. Direction is faulty in allowing the pace too much slack.

Wit.

Buckaroo From Powder River
(SONGS)

Columbia release of Colbert Clark production. Stars Charles Starrett, Smiley Burnette; features Eve Miller, Forrest Taylor, Paul Campbell. Directed by Ray Nazarro. Original screenplay, Norman Hall; camera, George F. Kelley; editor, Paul Borofsky. At New York theatre, N. Y., week March 30, '48. Running time, **55 MINS.**

Steve Lacey (Durango Kid)	Charles Starrett
Smiley Burnette	Smiley Burnette
Mollie Parnell	Eve Miller
Pop Ryland	Forrest Taylor
Clint Ryland	Paul Campbell
Tommy Ryland	Doug Coppin
Sheriff Parnell	Philip Morris
Dave Ryland	Casey MacGregor
Lon Driscoll	Ted Adams
Ben Trask	Ethan Laidlaw
McCall	Frank McCarroll

The Cass County Boys

"Buckaroo from Powder River" is a standard oatuner in Columbia's Durango Kid series. Charles Starrett shoots a mean pair of six-guns in a dual role adequately satisfying the action requirements while Smiley Burnette supplies the comedy and the Cass County Boys furnish a quartet of rural tunes. It's okay film fare for the action spots and Saturday matinee trade.

Formula plot contrived by scripter Norman Hall calls for Starrett to break up a trio of outlaws headed by Forrest Taylor. With his two sons he's pulled off many a bank job and is scheming to unload some phoney territorial bonds. His stepson, Doug Coppin, gets wise to the plotting and is marked for death. However, he's saved by the Durango Kid who poses as a hired killer. Law and order, per usual, prevail at the finale via a furious gun battle where the Kid subdues the evildoers.

Performances, in general, capably catch the mood of the mesa. Starrett scores as the champion of righteousness. Burnette is amusing for lovers of slapstick while Eve Miller is pleasantly decorative in the lone femme role. Taylor is plenty sinister as the bewhiskered bandit. Supporting players are adequate. Cass County boys are okay with the hillbilly rhythms. Ray Nazarro directed at a speedy pace. George F. Kelley's lensing incorporated some nice outdoor shots in this Colbert Clark production.

Gilb.

Angelina
(ITALIAN)

President Films release of Lux-Ora (Paolo Frasca) production. Stars Anna Magnani. Directed by Luigi Zampa. Screenplay, Suso Cecchi D'Amico, Piero Tellini, Luigi Zampa, Anna Magnani; camera, Paoli Craveri; English titles, Herman Weinberg. Previewed N. Y. April 1, '48. Running time, **90 MINS.**

Angelina	Anna Magnani
Pasquale	Nando Bruno
Carmela	Ave Ninchi
Cesira	Agnese Dubbini
Luigi	Ernesto Almirante
Callisto Garrone	Armando Migliari
Roberto	Vittorio Mittini
Mrs. Garrone	Maria Donati
Annetta	Maria Grazia Franci
Filippo Garrone	Franco Zefferelli
Libero	Gianni Glori

(In Italian; English Titles)

Filmed against a background of poverty and squalor, "Angelina" is a pictorial history of the struggles of the poor of an Italian slum for food, better housing, adequate transportation as well as improved sanitation. These oppressed people revolt against their exploiters under the leadership of housewife Anna Magnani, a modern-day Joan of Arc. Documentary styled picture is frank and raw in its indictment of the corrupt resulting in surefire b.o. at the art houses where it should reap strong word-of-mouth.

A secondary story theme, which comes close to overshadowing the main plot, is Miss Magnani's realization that in fighting for an uplift in her district's social conditions she has thoughtlessly neglected her husband and five children. Urged to run for office by her followers, she declines their support in a compelling address. The speech is beautifully delivered and ably sets forth her reasons for eschewing a political career for her home and family.

Direction of Luigi Zampa has neatly integrated the film. His fine technique not only is visible in the excellent performances of Miss Magnani and other principals but also is obvious in the well-done minor characterizations of shopkeepers, police sergeants and other types who mingle through the picture. Script, itself, is creditable with Zampa, Miss Magnani as well as Suso Cecchi D'Amico and Piero Tellini collaborating on it.

Writers attack their subject with the utmost candor reinforcing the plot with realistic sequences that occasionally exceed the censorial bounds of the American Production Code. However, no censor could justifiably scissor a foot on the grounds the public's morals were endangered. Acting is on par with the direction. It's crisp, pithy and catches the flavor of the story in every respect.

As the film's star, Miss Magnani appears in practically every scene. Her portrayal of an ordinary housewife who zealously battles against black marketers and dishonest contractors, with ultimate success, is done in the same spirited vein as her work in the now famed "Open City." Others who measure up include Nando Bruno as her policeman-husband who disapproves of his wife's interest in politics, but is appeased when she rediscovers the sanctity of the home.

Armando Migliari does okay as a crooked contractor who admittedly pocketed a government housing subsidy. In a minor romance are his son, Vittorio Mittini, and Miss Magnani's daughter, Ave Ninchi. Their association occasionally proves somewhat embarrassing to the campaign for civic improvement, but the scripters plausibly find a solution. Paoli Craveri's camerawork is good while producer Paolo Frasca made skillful use of what appeared to be location backgrounds employed for practically the entire footage.

Gilb.

Miniature Reviews

"Letter From an Unknown Woman" (U). Strong woman's picture with Joan Fontaine and new star Louis Jourdan.

"The Lady from Shanghai" (Col). Stylized melodrama with Rita Hayworth name to aid ticket sales.

"Shaggy" (Color) (Par). Boy and dog film in color aimed for juve and family trade.

"Here Comes Trouble" (Color) (UA). Hal Roach "Laff-Time" comedy about a cub reporter; deluxe slapstick geared for lower half of dualers.

"Miranda" (GFD). Amusing British farce about a mermaid in London; good boxoffice.

Letter from an Unknown Woman

Hollywood, April 10.

Universal release of Rampart (John Houseman) production. Stars Joan Fontaine, Louis Jourdan; features Mady Christians, Marcel Journet, Art Smith, Carol Yorke. Directed by Max Opuls. Screenplay, Howard Koch; from story by Stefan Zweig; camera, Frank Planer; score, Daniele Amfitheatrof; editor, Ted J. Kent. Previewed April 6, '48. Running time, 86 MINS.

Lisa Berndle....Joan Fontaine
Stefan Brand....Louis Jourdan
Frau Berndle....Mady Christians
Johann Stauffer....Marcel Journet
John....Art Smith
Marie....Carol Yorke
Herr Kastner....Howard Freeman
Lt. Leopold von Kaltnegger....John Good
Stefan, Jr....Leo B. Pessin
Porter....Erskine Sanford
Concierge....Otto Waldis
Frau Spitzer....Sonja Bryden

"Letter From An Unknown Woman" is a first for the new Rampart Productions, independent company organized by Joan Fontaine and William Dozier. Debut film is a distinguished offering, production-wise, giving Rampart a strong woman's picture for Universal distribution. If backed with exploitation playing up femme appeal and high production qualities b.o. returns should be gratifying.

Picture teams Miss Fontaine and Louis Jourdan, French actor, as co-stars and they prove to be a solid combination. Both turn in splendid performances in difficult parts that could easily have been overplayed.

Story follows a familiar pattern but the taste with which the film has been put together in all departments under John Houseman's production supervision makes it a valid and interest-holding drama. The mounting has an artistic flavor that captures the atmosphere of early-day Vienna and has been beautifully photographed.

Story unfolds in flashback, a device that makes plot a bit difficult to follow at times, but Max Ophuls' direction holds it together. He doesn't rush his direction, adopting a leisurely pace that permits best use of the story. Film is endowed with little touches that give it warmth and heart while the tragic tale is being unfolded. It concerns a young girl who falls in love with a neighbor, a concert pianst. She follows his career from the sidelines until one night they meet on the eve of his departure for a concert tour. His promise to return isn't kept and later she marries another man to give her son a name and home. Years later she again meets her only love but he fails to remember. Story is told as he reads a letter from the girl, written after the second meeting and just before she dies of typhus.

Supporting roles are brief but effectively handled in keeping with high quality of the entire picture. Mady Christians, Marcel Journet, Art Smith, Carol Yorke, Howard Greeman, John Good and others creditably supply the backing performances.

The ace lensing is by Frank Planer. Daniele Amfitheatrof's music score is topnotch and art direction, settings, costumes and other contributions earn the same rating. *Bart.*

The Lady from Shanghai
(SONG)

Hollywood, April 10.

Columbia release of Orson Welles production, direction and screenplay by Welles. Stars Rita Hayworth, Orson Welles; features Everett Sloane, Glenn Anders. Based on novel by Sherwood King; camera, Charles Lawton, Jr.; song, Allan Roberts, Doris Fisher; score, Heinz Roemheld; editor, Viola Lawrence. Previewed April 8, '48. Running time, 86 MINS.

Elsa Bannister....Rita Hayworth
Michael O'Hara....Orson Welles
Arthur Bannister....Everett Sloane
George Grisby....Glenn Anders
Sidney Broome....Ted De Corsia
Judge....Eskine Sanford
Goldie....Gus Schilling
District Attorney....Carl Frank
Jake....Louis Merrill
Bessie....Evelyn Ellis
Cab Driver....Harry Shannon
Li....Wong Show Chong
Yacht Captain....Sam Nelson

"The Lady From Shanghai" is okay boxoffice. It's exploitable and has Rita Hayworth's name for the marquees. Entertainment value suffered from the striving for effect that features Orson Welles' production, direction and scripting.

Script is wordy and full of holes which need the plug of taut story telling and more forthright action. Rambling style used by Welles has occasional flashes of imagination, particularly in the tricky backgrounds he uses to unfold the yarn, but effects, while good on their own, are distracting to the murder plot. Contributing to the stylized effect stressed by Welles is the photography, which features artful compositions entirely in keeping with the production mood.

Story tees off in New York where Welles, as a philosophical Irish seaman, joins the crew of a rich man's luxury yacht. Schooner's cruise and stops along the Mexican coast en route to San Francisco, furnish varied and interesting backdrops. Welles' tries for effect reach their peak with the staging of climatic chase sequences in a Chinese theatre where performers are going through an Oriental drama, and in the mirror room of an amusement park's crazy house. He has satirized human foibles in the courtroom scenes of the murder trial, getting a sting into depicting justice and the people who gather to watch human drama unfolded on the witness stand.

There's a complicated murder pattern involving Welles, Miss Hayworth, latter's husband, Everett Sloane, and Glenn Anders, crazy law partner of Sloane's. Plot is often foggy of purpose and confusing to follow, but apparently deals with Welles' yen for Miss Hayworth. That leads to his acceptance of scheme to stage a phony murder of Anders which turns into a real killing, a trial and final, poetic justice for the evildoers.

Welles has called on players for stylized performances. He used an Irish brogue and others depict erratic characters with little reality. Miss Hayworth isn't called on to do much more than look beautiful. Best break for players goes to Sloane, and he gives a credible interpretation of the crippled criminal attorney.

The excellent lensing is by Charles Lawton, Jr., in the mood of Heinz Roemheld's music score. There's also one song, "Please Don't Kiss Me," used in shipboard scene. *Brog.*

Shaggy
(COLOR)

Hollywood, April 9.

Paramount release of William Pine-William Thomas production. Features George Nokes, Brenda Joyce, Robert Shayne. Directed by Robert Emmett Tansey. Original screenplay, Maxwell Shane; camera (Cinecolor), Ellis W. Carter; editor, Howard Smith. Tradeshown, April 6, '48. Running time, 71 mins.

Laura Calvin....Brenda Joyce
Robbie Calvin....George Nokes
Bob Calvin....Robert Shayne
Tessie....Jody Gilbert
Fuzzie....Ralph Sanford
Mac....Alex Frazer
Gonnell....William Haade
Joe....Dan White
Shaggy....Himself

"Shaggy" is a familiarly laid-out story of a boy and his dog. It will serve okay for juve and family trade circles. Use of color adds to sales values, slotting it for good bookings in supporting position on two bills.

Plot gets off to a slow start, but gradually picks up to neat finale. It concerns a sheep dog that is branded a killer, although the real culprit is a mountain lion. Shots of the lion and its marauding among sheep flocks, its fights with a wolf and the dog hero are good excitement stuff that helps interest. Human angle in plot deals with boy's new stepmother and the antagonism that instantly develops when she is introduced to the ranch's wild life.

Robert Emmett Tansey's direction often has a naive flavor, in keeping with the story and generally does a good job of resolving all plot problems in acceptable fashion. Sheep dog hero and his juve master, George Nokes, project the usual appeal of such characters. Grownup leads are handled in okay style by Brenda Joyce and Robert Shayne. Others measure up to demands.

The William Pine-William Thomas production has been neatly dressed in outdoor scenic values that will interest type of audience at which film is aimed. Color lensing by Ellis W. Carter gives an excellent display of settings, and other technical credits are good. *Brog.*

Here Comes Trouble
(COLOR)

United Artists release of Hal Roach, Jr., production. Stars William Tracy, Joe Sawyer; features Joan Woodbury, Beverly Loyd, Betty Compson. Directed by Fred Guiol. Screenplay, George Carleton Brown, Edward E. Seabrook; camera (Cinecolor), John W. Boyle; editor, Arthur Seld. Tradeshown N. Y., April 9, '48. Running time, 55 MINS.

Dodo....Bill Tracy
Ames....Joe Sawyer
Winfield Blake....Emory Parnell
Martha Blake....Betty Compson
Stafford....Paul Stanton
Penny Blake....Beverly Loyd
Bubbles LaRue....Joan Woodbury
Dexter....Patti Morgan
McClure....Thomas Jackson

This is the third of Hal Roach's "Laff-Time" subjects, originally made to sell in pairs with each group of two pictures being sold as a single feature. However, with "Here Comes Trouble" and "Who Killed Doc Robbins," latter being listed as Part 2 of this group, distributor will sell either the two as a group or the exhib can buy either one separately. These are designed to fill out double-feature setups, and as such "Trouble" will help pad out the lower rung of many dualers.

This is far from being Roach's best comedy effort. It runs the full scale of inane hokum, none of which is done well by a fairly capable cast. Excellent Cinecolor appears wasted since every scene is pounded over with sledge-hammer force. It relates the ventures of a cub reporter with a photographic memory. Scripters and Fred Guiol, director, also seem to have retentive memories, many a hackneyed routine being included.

Idea of the blundering cub reporter being handed the tough police reportorial beat is merely the groundwork for introduction of such gags as the exploding cigars, spattering powder in face, drenching a damsel in a shower-bath, tossing a valuable diary around a la football, and a chase finish in the fly-loft of a theatre.

William Tracy, who's been in other Roach comedies, is the silly reporter just back from the war. As such he's not too bad. Joe Sawyer is his ex-buddy in arms, now on the police force, in his familiar flatfoot character. Joan Woodbury adds some zest to the zany proceedings as a burlesque vamp but she's pushed aside early in the quest for laughs.

Patti Morgan looks fetching in a secretary bit role, while Betty Compson, veteran of silent era, does nicely as the newspaper publisher's wife. Emory Parnell is the overly bombastic publisher. Beverly Loyd shows promise as the comely daughter. *Wear.*

Miranda
(BRITISH)

London, April 7.

General Film Distributors release of Gainsborough-Sydney Box production. Stars Glynis Johns, Googie Withers, Griffith Jones, John McCallum. Directed by Ken Annakin. Screenplay by Peter Blackmore from his stage play; additional dialog, Denis Waldock; editor, Gordon Hales; camera, Ray Elton, Dudley Lovell. At Odeon, London, April 6, '48. Running time, 80 MINS.

Miranda....Glynis Johns
Clare Marten....Googie Withers
Paul Marten....Griffith Jones
Nigel....John McCallum
Nurse Cary....Margaret Rutherford
Charles....David Tomlinson
Betty....Yvonne Owen
Isobel....Sonia Holm
Inn Landlord....Lyn Evans
Cocklestall Keeper....Maurice Denham
Manell....Brian Oulton
Secretary....Zena Marshall
Fisherman....Howard Douglas

Mermaids are in fashion and Sydney Box has piloted the first of the season past the popular winning post to considerable applause. Amusing and unpretentious, this farce-fantasy should play to good business here, and if shown in America before "Mr. Peabody" should earn some nice coin.

Danger of these stories is that the joke might wear thin very quickly, but Peter Blackmore, who adapted his own play, has sustained the fun to the right length of time. A trifle more imagination and a tender moment here and there would have added to its success.

Planning a holiday alone in Cornwall, Paul Marten, a fashionable doctor, is dragged out of his fishing boat to the sea bottom by Miranda, a lovely mermaid. Price for return to his home and wife is that he take Miranda to London. She arrives as a special patient, unable to walk, with lower part of body wrapped in blankets or long dresses, and soon causes disaster between two pairs of happy, engaged people. Men find her irresistible, and women find her "fishy." But the call of the sea becomes too strong for Miranda and she decides to go to warmer climes. Final shot shows her nursing a mer-baby at the bottom of the ocean.

Everything is rightly played for laughs and Glynis Johns makes the mermaid an attractive and almost credible creature. Griffith Jones is good as her serious sponsor. Googie Withers turns in a nice performance as his bewildered wife, and David Tomlinson and John McCallum do well as the lovestruck swains. As nurse to the mermaid, Margaret Rutherford gets plenty of laughs, but occasionally descends to unnecessary burlesque.

Direction by Ken Annakin is straightforward. Temple Abady has composed a helpful score, but the art direction wins no bouquets. Interiors are restless and devoid of personality. *Cane.*

L'Ebreo Errante

(The Wandering Jew)
(ITALIAN)

Rome, March 29.

Distributori Indipendenti release and production. Stars Vittorio Gassman, Valentina Cortese; features Noelle Norman, Inga Gort, Pietro Sharov, Harry Feist. Directed by Goffredo Alessandrini. Original story by G.B. Angioletti; screenplay, Alessandrini, Ennio De Concini, Anton Giulio Majano; camera, Vaclav Vich; music, Enzo Masetti. At Imperiale and Capranica, Rome. Running time, 97 mins.

Matthew Blumenthal....................Vittorio Gassman
Esther....................Valentina Cortese
Blumenthal's Mistress....................Noelle Norman
Sarah....................Inge Gort
Professor Epstein....................Pietro Sharov
Hans....................Harry Feist
David....................Armando Francioll
Doctor Schuster....................Hans Hinrich
German Officer....................Antonio Crast
Deschamps....................Amilcare Olivieri
Maquisard....................Egisto Olivieri

"The Wandering Jew" is one of the biggest-budgeted pictures produced here last year. This time the money was well spent. Film seems to have strong potential for export success, with particularly favorable reactions on American market. Its unique (and minor) defect is to mix legend with reality, reincarnating in the hero the Jew doomed by Christ to eternal wandering. The Divine curse is in fact recalled in a prolog, laid in ancient Jerusalem, which adds a pompous artificial tone to the real drama, which begins in 1940 when Germans enter Paris.

The young and wealthy Vittorio Gassman, who could and would collaborate with the invaders, realizes in time the treachery he's about to do against his own people, and prefers to go with all the others into a concentration camp. Having escaped with the girl he loves, while the Allies are approaching, he comes back to the camp, having known that Nazis will kill a number of prisoners if he doesn't surrender. Through death under the fire of machine-guns, the Wandering Jew finds in his sacrifice the deliverance from the curse.

Except for the symbolical angle, pic registers very well. It has plenty of strong action and impressive scenes and combines realism and poetry cleverly. Helped by an excellent cast, which is headed by Gassman and Valentina Cortese (latter now under contract to 20th-Fox), director Goffredo Alessandrini (who made "Furia") has handled story and cast with sharpness and frankness, rendering a gruesome story poignantly, without coarseness. Lensing by Vaclav Vich, sets by Arrigo Equini, costumes by Dario Cecchi, are all expert, and the music score by Enzo Masetti is adequate. Westport-International Films acquired U. S. distribution rights. *Quat.*

Gioventu Perduta

(Misled Youth)
(ITALIAN)
(ONE SONG)

Rome, March 30.

Lux Film release of Carlo Ponti production. Stars Jacques Sernas, Carla del Poggio, Massimo Girotti; features Nando Bruno, Diana Borghese, Franca Maresa. Directed by Pietro Germi. Original story by Germi; screenplay, Germi, Mario Monicelli, Bruno Valeri, Leopoldo Trieste; camera, Carlo Montuori; music, Carlo Rustichelli. At Metropolitan, Rome. Running time, **84 MINS.**

Stefano....................Jacques Sernas
Marcello....................Massimo Girotti
Luisa....................Carla del Poggio
Inspector....................Nando Bruno
Stefano's father....................Leo Garavaglia
Maria....................Franca Maresa
Torchsinger....................Diana Borghese

When "Misled Youth" first went before the censors, they wouldn't pass it. Decision, somewhat unusual here, caused protest from film directors and critics, giving the film much publicity. Pic finally received the greenlight in order to avoid political speculations, as Italian exhibs are generally leftist, while government is Christian-Democrat.

As a thriller, pic is a little disappointing. Most suspenseful sequence, showing a detailed robbery by a group of students at the Rome University, has been cut out. However, it can be kept in for exploitation abroad. Film offers a fine directorial job. Helped by a clever screenplay, Pietro Germi has turned out a vivid dramatization of the moral disorder which has taken hold of postwar Italian youth, especially the middleclass. He has given more stress to characters than to story. Plot revolves around the double life of Jacques Sernas, a student and leader of a gang of young bandits. Love and robbery form complications, with murder in the denouement.

Film is beautifully played. As Stefano, the wicked hero, young French actor Jacques Sernas is handsome and authoritative. He looks like a good U. S. bet. Massimo Girotti adds realism in the role of the investigator whose feigned love becomes true. Carla del Poggio does nicely as the devoted sister of Stefano, and Franca Maresa is adequate as Maria, the young victim.

Film was shot in authentic interiors, in the manner of Roberto Rossellini and Louis De Rochemont, but photography by Carlo Montuori is class A work, as if done in the studio. Carlo Rustichelli wrote the only song, "Hawaii," attractively sung by Diana Borghese. *Quat.*

Caccia Tragica

(Tragic Chase)
(ITALIAN)

Rome, March 30.

Titanus release of ANPI production. Stars Andrea Checchi, Vivi Gioi, Massimo Girotti, Carla del Poggio. Directed by Giuseppe De Santis. Original story by De Santis, Carlo Lizzani, Alberto Rem-Picci; screenplay, De Santis, Michelangelo Antonioni, Umberto Barbaro, Cesare Zavattini; camera, Otello Martelli; music, Giuseppe Rosati. At Europa and Galleria, Rome. Running time, **86 MINS.**

Alberto....................Andrea Checchi
"Lili Marlene"....................Vivi Gioi
Michele....................Massimo Girotti
Giovanna....................Carla del Poggio
Peasant....................Vittorio Duse
"The Lame"....................Umberto Sacripanti
Bandit....................Checco Rissone
Driver....................Folco Lulli

This film won the award for the best Italian pic at the last Venice exhibition. Produced by ANPI (National Assn. of Italian Partisans) its Communist purposes are obvious. Aside from the political angle, film is on technical and artistic side one of the best made here since liberation. In U. S. it may do well for arthouses and selected situations.

Story deals with bandits, fascists, and collaborationists against a peasant background. A truck, carrying millions of liras for agricultural works, is attacked by outlaws and the money stolen. Peasants form together to arrange a general chase of the bandits. After many ups and downs, bandits are finally besieged in their refuge. Personal elements are brought in as a pair of innocent lovers are involved, with further complications from the bandit chief and his mistress.

Although "Tragic Chase" is the first film made by Guiseppe De Santis, direction is absolutely unerring. Young director has balanced realism and refinement with masterly adroitness in an eleborate, intellectual work of extremely European taste. Characters, well projected, are rendered equally well by leading and supporting players. Otello Martelli's lensing is firstclass, as are sets by Carlo Egidi. Giuseppe Rosati's score backs the drama very effectively. *Quat.*

Music I Morker

(Music in Darkness)
(SWEDISH)

Stockholm, March 16.

Terra Film release of Lorens Marmstedt production. Stars Mai Zetterling, Birger Malmsten; features Olof Winnerstrand, Hilda Borgstrom, Naima Wifstrand, Douglas Hage, Bengt Eklund, John Elfstrom, Bibi Skoglund. Directed by Ingmar Bergman. Screenplay by Dagmar Edqvist, based on her novel, "Musik i Morker." Camera, Goran Strindberg; music, Erland von Koch. At Royal, Stockholm. Running time, **88 MINS.**

Ingrid....................Mai Zetterling
Bengt Vyldecke....................Birger Malmsten
The Priest....................Olof Winnerstrand
Mrs. Schroder....................Naima Wifstrand
Agneta....................Bibi Skoglund
Lovis....................Hilda Borgstrom
Kruge....................Douglas Hage
Klasson....................Gunnar Bjornstrand
Ebbe....................Bengt Eklund
A blind man....................John Elfstrom

Film version of Dagmar Edqvist's best-selling novel, "Musik I Morker," has emerged as one of the best Swedish pictures in years. It's a surefire grosser in Scandinavia and has good b.o. potential in the international market as well. Picture picks up added values in the fine performances of co-stars Mai Zetterling and Birger Malmsten.

Yarn relates the career of Malmsten as a blind pianist. He's a victim of a military training accident. After failing to gain admission to the musical academy in Stockholm he's forced to eke out a drab existence as an entertainer in a cheap cafe. But life takes on a brighter aspect when a former acquaintance (Miss Zetterling) realizes she loves him.

Picture's underlying romantic theme is ably pointed up in the well-written script by Miss Edqvist from her book. Unknown to the public only a year ago, Malmsten shows genuine promise in portraying the sightless musician. As his girl friend and later his wife, Miss Zetterling stands out in a meaty role. Supporting players are good, with John Elfstrom and Douglas Hage particularly registering in minor parts.

Ingmar Bergman has directed brilliantly while camerawork of Goran Strindberg and Erland von Koch's musical direction maintain a general excellence. Producer Lorens Malmstedt, long noted for his b.o. clicks, has delivered again in "Musik I Morker." *Wing.*

Rendezvous in Salzkammergut

(Songs)
(AUSTRIAN)

Sascha Film Distributing Co. release of Vienna Mundus Film production. Stars Herta Mayen and Inge Konradi; features Hans Holt, Josef Meinrad, Elisabeth Markus, Theodor Danegger, Harry Fuss. Directed by Alfred Stoeger. Screenplay, Aldo von Pinelli; camera, Ludwig Berger; music and musical direction, Robert Stolz; sets, Fritz Jueptner-Jonstorf. At Apollo, Vienna. Running time, **95 MINS.**

Catchy music of Robert Stolz is the saving grace of "Rendezvous in Salzkammergut." Picture's score is Stolz at his best with three of the numbers guaranteed to entrance audiences throughout the world. Trio includes "A Little Joddler," "You Need Only a Comrade" ("Du Brauchst Nur Einen Kameraden") and "Never Was the Night So Beautiful" ("Nie War Die Nacht So Schoen").

Story is an illogical yarn built around two girl secretaries who lose $9.50 at the races and are forced to walk all the way from Vienna to St. Gilgen. Scripters took some poetic license at this point for the sum lost wouldn't cover the fare for the six-hour railroad ride in the first place. Eventually the gals reach their destination falling in and out of love en route. Some of the scenes are admittedly amusing, but on the whole the plot is pretty far-fetched.

Stars Herta Mayen and Inga Konradi aren't particularly photogenic. Hans Holt and Josef Meinrad are adequate in their support. Ludwig Berger's camerawork is not up to par, nor is the sound either, for that matter. However, with careful editing and repairs the picture might appeal to some U.S. audiences. *Maas.*

"I Miserabili" ("Les Miserables") **(ITALIAN).** Lux release of Carlo Ponti production. Stars Gino Cervi, Valentina Cortese, Hans Hinrich; features Andreina Pagnini, Aldo Nicodemi, Luigi Pavese. Directed by Riccardo Freda. Screenplay, Mario Monicelli, Riccardo Freda and Stefano Vanzina from novel by Victor Hugo; camera, Rodolfo Lombardi; music, Alessandro Cicognini. At Supercinema and Odescalchi, Rome. Running time, **180 MINS.**

This seventh adaptation of Victor Hugo's classic has been produced with no stinting of cash, and in regard to sets, costumes and lensing is of the best continental standard. But yarn remains of doubtful interest, as it's too well known, and is without any attempt to adapt it to modern taste. Cast, besides, is generally unimpressive, except Hans Hinrich, who plays Javert with force.

Pic is divided into two episodes, "Caccio all'uomo" ("Manhunt") and "Tempesta su Parigi" ("Storm Over Paris"), each running 90 minutes. The second is the better. Export values are modest, because other pix of the same inspiration were produced in the last 15 years in France, U. S. and Mexico.

Quat.

"I Fratelli Karamazov" ("The Brothers Karamazov") (ITALIAN). Fincine release of Comiran production. Stars Fosco Giachetti, Elli Parvo, Mariella Lotti, Andrea Checchi; features Giulio Donnini, Lamberto Picasso, Franco Scandurra, Paola Veneroni. Directed by Giacomo Gentilomo. Screenplay, Gentilomo, Gaspare Cataldo, Alberto Vecchietti, Giorgio Pala from novel by Dostoievsky; camera, Giuseppe La Torre; music, Renzo Rossellini. At Fontana di Trevi, Rome. Running time, 116 MINS.

Adapted from Dostoievsky's novel, this film has dramatic and spectacular appeal to Italian and Latin - American audiences, but may find uncertain acceptance in the U. S. market. It isn't Russian enough for arthouse filmgoers and not popular enough for large exploitation. Cast is good, especially Giulio Donnini, who gives a highly impressive portrayal as Smerdiakov. Technical credits are average.

Quat.

Miniature Reviews

"Another Part of the Forest" (U). Strong drama which should click solidly, with Frederic March heading impressive cast.

"The Woman in White" (WB). Costume melodrama based on old novel. Old-fashioned but interesting mystery.

"Green Grass of Wyoming" (Color) · (20th). Sentimental horse story a strong bet for kid attendance; agreeable adult entertainment.

"French Leave" (Mono). Okay dualer, with Jackie Cooper, Jackie Coogan topping the cast.

"Lightnin' in the Forest" (Rep). Fair dualer overloaded with action.

"California Firebrand" (Color-Songs) (Rep). Monte Hale in fast-action cowboy thriller of high-rating for spots liking cactus mellers.

"Son of the Regiment" (Artkino). Poor Russian-made war film.

"Broken Journey" (GFD). Firstrate British melo of air crash will do biz.

"No Orchids for Miss Blandish" (Renown). Vapid, British-made gangster pic, with little b.o. draw.

"The Argyle Secrets" (FC). Mystery meller based on the Suspense radio show. Okay supporting material.

Another Part of the Forest

Hollywood, April 17.

Universal release of Jerry Bresler production. Stars Fredric March, Dan Duryea, Edmond O'Brien, Ann Blyth; features Florence Eldridge, John Dall, Dona Drake. Directed by Michael Gordon. Screenplay, Vladimir Pozner; from play by Lillian Hellman; camera, Hal Mohr; music, Daniele Amfitheatrof; editor, Milton Carruth. Previewed April 13, '48. Running time, 106 MINS.

Marcus Hubbard	Fredric March
Oscar Hubbard	Dan Duryea
Ben Hubbard	Edmond O'Brien
Regina Hubbard	Ann Blyth
Lavinia Hubbard	Florence Eldridge
John Bagtry	John Dall
Laurette Sincee	Dona Drake
Birdie Bagtry	Betsy Blair
Colonel Isham	Fritz Leiber
Jugger	Whit Bissell
Penniman	Don Beddoe
Sam Taylor	Wilton Graff
Clara Bagtry	Virginia Farmer
Coralee	Libby Taylor
Jake	Smoki Whitfield

"Another Part of the Forest" is backtracking 20 years from "The Little Foxes," picturization of Lillian Hellman's new play showing the same family of Hubbards, and how they got to be that way in "Foxes." Picture is sparked with list of top names headed by Fredric March who make this a field day for superb characterization, and from a production standpoint film is outstanding on all counts. It's cinch to clean up in city showings, and in smaller towns should likewise find ready response, accompanied by proper kind of exploitation.

"Forest" is the type of film audiences will leave theatre talking about, and continue pointing out as a prime example of how a highly dramatic piece may still spell entertainment. From bitter drama, pace frequently swings to near whimsical humor, with result spectator is left in constant state of expectancy, with never a dull moment.

Picture opens 15 years after close of Civil War, in a small southern town where the Hubbards dominate the community financially but still aren't accepted socially, due to Hubbard pere (March) having run salt at $8 a pound during the war to Confederates who badly needed the commodity. March heads his unsavory family—composed of two sons and a daughter, Edmond O'Brien, Dan Duryea, Ann Blyth, and his balmy wife, Florence Eldridge—and rules them completely with a harsh hand. Family is the same vicious, grasping group, with exception of mother, they turned out to be in "Foxes," and March makes life unbearable for them with his overbearing. All but the daughter who, without his knowing it, governs him.

These characters are put together, shaken up and emerge proponents of a plot which manages to grip. The degeneration of one son, the rise of the other as he takes over the family's fortunes from the father, after mother discloses that it was the father who betrayed his neighbors during the war and caused death of 27 young Confederate soldiers, sons of the community—these and other parts are definite standouts, either for their domination or weaknesses.

March delivers to tremendous effect as the father, and he has benefit of as fine a cast of co-stars and support as could be imagined. Miss Eldridge makes her portrayal count, particularly as the mother who in the end admits she dislikes every one of her children, because of their meanness. O'Brien, as the elder son who learns his father's long-held secret and threatens to expose him to a lynching if family fortune isn't turned over to him immediately, is seen in best role of his career. Duryea, the weakling son, who was seen in previous "Foxes" in same character, does a rare bit of character acting, and Ann Blyth, the daughter, is a vixen who elicits small sympathy as she makes up to her father for his favor until her brother takes over the household. Part is one of the best she has ever turned in.

In brief, but no less effective appearances, Dona Drake is the can-can girl with whom Duryea is in love; Betsy Blair, daughter of aristocratic family in need of funds, whose estate the elder Hubbard covets; John Dall, her cousin, who loves war and who spurns the Hubbard daughter to go to Brazil where there's a lovely war. Balance of cast, too, likewise scores.

Jerry Bresler evinced showmanship handling and holding producer reins, and Michael Gordon's direction is topflight, catching nuances of every scene at right pitch. Lillian Hellman's play was brought to the screen expertly by Vladimir Pozner, and Hal Mohr's camera work effectively points up every scene.

Whit.

The Woman in White

Hollywood, April 17.

Warner Bros. release of Henry Blanke production. Stars Eleanor Parker, Alexis Smith, Sydney Greenstreet, Gig Young; features Agnes Moorehead, John Emery, John Abbott. Directed by Peter Godfrey. Screenplay, Stephen Morehouse Avery; based on novel by Wilkie Collins; camera, Carl Guthrie; music, Max Steiner; editor, Clarence Kolster. Tradeshow, April 16, '48. Running time, 105 MINS.

Laura Fairlie	
Anne Catherick	} Eleanor Parker
Marian Halcombe	Alexis Smith
Count Fosco	Sydney Greenstreet
Walter Hartright	Gig Young
Countess Fosco	Agnes Moorehead
Frederick Fairlie	John Abbott
Sir Percival Glyde	John Emery
Louis	Curt Bois
Mrs. Vesey	Emma Dunn
Dr. Nevin	Matthew Boulton
Mrs. Todd	Anita Sharp-Bolster
Jepson	Clifford Brooke
Dimmock	Barry Bernard

Meticulous production, excellent performances and smooth direction help to make "The Woman in White" interesting. Film is based on the famous old mystery novel of same title, written nearly 100 years ago by Wilkie Collins. It has an old-fashioned air about it, but characters still register and b.o. outlook is okay.

Costume melodrama lends itself to elaborate settings and producer Henry Blanke has shot the works in obtaining sight values that are striking. Art direction and set decorations are particularly tasteful. Peter Godfrey's direction maintains mystery air throughout, making for a showmanly credit in pointing up tale's flavor for audience interest.

Eleanor Parker gets a crack at a dual role and comes through nicely. Strong character portrayals are delivered by Sydney Greenstreet, John Emery and John Abbott. Alexis Smith has a less colorful straight assignment, but also pleases, as does Gig Young.

Plot concerns scheme of Greenstreet and Emery to seize a young girl's fortune through marriage and title derives from costume favored by a mystery lady, who appears on the scene at intervals to warn of the evil scheme. Stephen Morehouse Avery has given the story smooth scripting for suspense elements, leaving no loose ends dangling at windup. Miss Parker's double assignment has her doing the girl tricked into marriage with Emery, and the mystery woman, who has escaped from a private asylum where she had been committed by Greenstreet. Young is an artist, who falls first for Miss Parker and then Miss Smith, and who eventually brings about downfall of the heavies.

Max Steiner's score fits the story's mood and the lensing by Carl Guthrie is an ace assist in displaying melodramatics and the striking settings. Other technical credits measure up in excellence.

Brog.

Green Grass of Wyoming
(COLOR-SONGS)

20th-Fox release of Robert Bassler production. Stars Peggy Cummins, Charles Coburn, Robert Arthur; features Lloyd Nolan, Burl Ives, Geraldine Wall. Directed by Louis King. Screenplay, Martin Berkeley, from novel by Mary O'Hara; Technicolor director, Natalie Kalmus; camera, Charles Clarke; musical director, Lionel Newman; music, Cyril Mockridge; editor, Nick DeMaggio. Previewed in N. Y., April 10, '48. Running time, 89 MINS.

Carey Greenway	Peggy Cummins
Beaver	Charles Coburn
Ken	Robert Arthur
Rob McLaughlin	Lloyd Nolan
Gus	Burl Ives
Nell McLaughlin	Geraldine Wall
Joe	Robert Adler
Jake	Will Wright
Storekeeper Johnson	Herbert Heywood
Old Timers	{ Richard Garrick
	{ Charles Hart
Veterinarian	Charles Tannen

This is another in Mary O'Hara's series of "Flicka" and "Thunderhead" horse stories, also produced in Technicolor by 20th-Fox. "Green Grass of Wyoming" is a handsome picture, providing an interesting and pleasant hour-and-a-half. It's a natural for juve audiences, but should also entertain adults.

The yarn is another sentimental blend or human and equine romance, with Peggy Cummins and Robert Arthur as the innocent juvenile sweethearts, and the stallion Thunderhead and a black mare as the devoted horses. Also, their shaky-legged white colt is introduced in the fadeout scene, doubtless as a promise of still more sequels.

The story of "Green Grass of Wyoming" is in two distinct parts, each with a different locale. The opening portion is about how a young rancher, played by Arthur, buys a sleek mare and how, after the outlaw Thunderhead lures her to the neighboring hills, the lad brings both horses docilely back to the corral. This part of the picture is crammed with stunning visual stuff, particularly the scenic shots taken in the hills.

For the concluding events the yarn shifts to Lancaster, O., where its trotting-race scenes were shot on location. Here the young rancher and his prized mare are finally nosed out for the Governor's Trophy by Charles Coburn, a Wyoming neighbor and harness racing veteran, who has gone on the wagon to make a comeback. As the old geezer is Peggy Cummins' grandfather, his victory doesn't mar the happy-ending quality of the picture, particularly when he reveals that the black mare faltered in the stretch of the final heat because she is going to foal.

There is colorful atmosphere to the race-meet scenes, and fairly good suspense to the races themselves. Earlier, the sequences on and about the ranch are skillfully handled so as to explain events to adult audiences but not suggest too much to moppets. There are several excellent song numbers by Burl Ives, mostly at a ranch dance.

Coburn handles the part of the tippling old harness driver with artful ease, and Miss Cummins and Arthur are agreeable as the puppy-love interest. Lloyd Nolan and Geraldine Wall are believable as the boy's understanding parents and, in addition to his singing, Ives is okay as a friendly ranch hand.

Louis King's direction has pace and a sense of relative story values. The color photography is, of course, a definite asset. *Hobe.*

French Leave

Monogram release of Sid Luft production. Stars Jackie Cooper, Jackie Coogan. Directed by Frank McDonald. Screenplay, Jameson Brewer and Jack Rubin; camera, William Sickner. At New York theatre, N. Y., week April 13, '48. Running time, 65 MINS.

Skitch	Jackie Cooper
Pappy	Jackie Coogan
Muldoon	Ralph Sanford
Marcel	Curt Bois
Mimi	Renee Godfrey
Pierre	William Dembrosi
Mom LaFarge	Claire DuBrey
Pop LaFarge	John Bleifer
Shultz	Larry Blake

Grist for the dualers is "French Leave," a modest low budgeter, with one-time child stars Jackie Coogan and Jackie Cooper cast in the lead roles. Picture's replete with brawls tinged with a goodly share of slapstick humor. Action situations and nabes will find the film an okay program filler.

Coogan and Cooper, both merchant seamen, are salty enough as two tars who shirk their work and have both eyes cocked for the ladies whenever ashore. Scripters Jameson Brewer and Jack Rubin pad out the plot by involving the lads in the machinations of a French black market ring which systematically loots ships' foodstuff cargoes on the Marseilles waterfront.

Whole yarn is played broadly with an obvious intent to reap maximum laughs from filmgoers. Two Jackies register well enough as the bungling, irresponsible sailors. Ralph Sanford realistically portrays a tough bos'n who has plenty of busy moments trying to keep his charges in line. Renee Godfrey furnishes the heart interest while other players capably maintain the film's mood.

Frank McDonald's direction moves the yarn along at a fast tempo while William Sickner's lensing is also good. Producer Sid Luft neatly stretched the budget for maximum values.

Lightnin' in the Forest

Hollywood, April 13.

Republic release of Sidney Picker production. Stars Lynne Roberts, Donald Barry, Warren Douglas; features Adrian Booth, Lucien Littlefield. Directed by George Blair. Original, J. Benton Cheney; screenplay, John K. Butler; camera, John MacBurnie; music, Mort Glickman; asst. director, Joe Dill; editor, Irving M. Schoenberg; special effects, Howard and Theodore Lydecker. Tradeshown April 13, '48. Running time, 61 MINS.

Jerry Vail	Lynne Roberts
Stan Martin	Donald Barry
Dave Lamont	Warren Douglas
Dell Parker	Adrian Booth
Joad	Lucien Littlefield
Martha	Claire DuBrey
Lieut. Bain	Roy Barcroft
Judge Waterman	Paul Harvey
Bud	Al Eben
Stinger	Jerry Jerome
Elevator operator	George Chandler
Police officer	Eddie Dunn
Valtin	Dale Van Sickel
Prichard	Bud Wolfe
Bartender	Hank Worden

"Lightnin' In The Forest" is overloaded with action and embellished with enough different plot lines to make up at least three more pictures. A fair dualler.

Characterizations by Lynne Roberts, Donald Barry and Warren Douglas are capable though Barry's voice doesn't carry underworld depth. Lucien Littlefield and Claire DuBrey featured in film roll up some good minutes with a bit of light humor and supporting cast projects well enough.

Douglas, a psychiatrist on vacation, is thrown together with Miss Roberts and her inexhaustible drive for excitement. He is blackmailed and, while in her company, runs the gauntlet from street brawls to romance. The excitement urge is cured in one last fling which involves the pair with Barry, for whom the police are searching.

Sidney Picker, at the production helm, runs on through a lot of ragged edges with little attempt at smoothing them out. George Blair handles the directional chores well enough.

California Firebrand

(COLOR—SONGS)

Republic release of Melville Tucker production. Stars Monte Hale, Adrian Booth; features Paul Hurst, Alice Tyrrell, Foy Willing and Riders of Purple Sage. Directed by Philip Ford. Screenplay, J. Benton Cheney and John K. Butler; adapted by Royal K. Cole; camera (Trucolor), Reggie Lanning; editor, Tony Martinelli; songs, Foy Willing and Sid Robin. Tradeshown N. Y., April 16, '48. Running time, 63 MINS.

Monte Hale	Monte Hale
Joyce Mason	Adrian Booth
Chuck Waggoner	Paul Hurst
Dulcey Waggoner	Alice Tyrrell
Jim Requa } Jud Babbit }	Tristram Coffin
Luke Hartell	LeRoy Mason
Lance Dawson	Douglas Evans
Granny Mason	Sarah Edwards
Gunsmoke Lowry	Daniel M. Sheridan
Zeke Mason	Duke York
Rick	Lanny Rees

Foy Willing and Riders of Purple Sage

The most profitable westerns today have three essential elements—dangerous action, a chase and a light touch of romance. "California Firebrand" has all three plus Trucolor and songs. Hence, it stacks up as a solid coingetter in spots where sagebrushers are appreciated.

Picture has the hero, Monte Hale, in physical trouble almost at the outset. Three times he's chased. once by the gold mining folks he's trying to befriend, and the other times by the film's baddies. Finally, Hale turns the tables and does some firstrate chasing of his own. The action gets into high gear as soon as he agrees to act as sheriff while masquerading as a two-gun killer. It pits him against two of the outlaws in a fist-fight almost as soon as the audience decides the Trucolor tinting job is okay. After that the action comes via a stagecoach near-holdup, a plunge through a window and a gun fight with this two-gun expert.

Minor romance has him falling for Adrian Booth and he almost rides away into the sunset at the finish, only here the camera fades out on him just as he's about to go into a clinch.

Director Philip Ford has done remarkably well, being helped by an efficient cast, with these pat ingredients. The color heightens many of the sweeping outdoor scenes without making the audience too aware of the tinting. Foy Willing and the Riders of the Purple Sage provide tuneful songs and instrumentation in their usual manner, with Hale joining in a couple of songs. The tune, "Trail to California," by Foy Willing and Sid Robin, is one of the better western ditties, and "Streets of Laredo," also shapes well.

Hale looks and acts like a healthy cowboy, and rides like one. This is a real asset especially since the lad can act, too. Miss Booth shows up unusually effectively in color, and is okay thespically. Paul Hurst, usually associated with screen gangster roles, is excellent as Monte's pal, providing the film's humor and fitting into this new characterization with surprising ease. Tristram Coffin, in the dual role of dumb Indian guide and the suave outlaw chief, makes something of his villain role. Alice Tyrrell and Douglas Evans head the support. Reggie Lanning's lensing is firstrate while Tony Martinelli has edited smartly. *Wear.*

Son of the Regiment

(RUSSIAN)

Artkino release of Soyuzdetfilm Studio production. Directed by Vassili Pronin. Screenplay, Valentin Katayev; camera, Gregory Garibyan. At Stanley, N. Y., April 17, '48. Running time, 73 MINS.

Vanya Solntsev	Yura Yankin
Captain Yenakiev	Alexander Morosov
Bidenko	Gregory Pluzhnik
Gorbunov	Nikolai Parfenov
Yegorov	Nikolai Yakhontov
Corporal Vosnesensky	Vova Sinev
Vasily Ivanovich	Pavel Volkov
Soboliev	Nikolai Yakhontov

(In Russian; English Titles)

This is another shallow patriotic film out of postwar Russia. Indicative of the declining quality of the Soviet studios, this crassly childish pic copped one of the top prizes from Stalin last year. By U.S. standards, however, it's a potboiler with a shoddy dress and hokey story. This offering's appeal is strictly limited to the Russophile circuit in this country.

"Son of the Regiment" is a Russian version of the Rover Boys at the front. Yarn concerns the adventures of a war-orphaned boy who is adopted by an artillery regiment as their mascot. After a stretch of sentimental episodes with the commander and a brief imprisonment by the crudely-depicted Germans, the kid finally earns his epaulettes. Grand climax of the film is a parade of goose-stepping Russian youngsters before the leader in Moscow square. Ideologically, this film is an unrestrained hymn to militarism.

Single merit of the film is the discovery of the child actor, Yura Yankin, an 11-year old with a wild and appealing personality. Adults in the cast walk through their mawkish roles in a half-embarrassed fashion. *Herm.*

Broken Journey

(BRITISH)

London, April 14.

GFD release of Sydney Box-Gainsborough production. Stars Phyllis Calvert. Directed by Kenneth Amakin; screenplay, Robert Westerby; camera, David Harcourt. At Odeon, London, April 14, '48. Running time, 89 MINS.

Mary Johnstone	Phyllis Calvert
Joanna Dane	Margot Grahame
Bill Haverton	James Donald
Perami	Francis L. Sullivan
Edward Marshall	Raymond Huntley
Jimmy Marshall	David Tomlinson
Richard Faber	Derek Bond
Fox	Guy Rolfe
Ann Stevens	Sonia Holm
John Barber	Grey Blake
Kid Cormack	Andrew Crawford
Harry Gunn	Charles Victor
Joseph Romer	Gerard Heinz
Lilli Romer	Sybilla Binder
Frau Romer	Amy Frank
Lieutenant Albert	Michael Allan
Mr. Barber	R. Stuart Lindsell
Mrs. Barber	Mary Hinton

Crash of an American Army Dakota in the Alps in November, 1946, and dramatic rescue of passengers and crew provided Sydney Box with the inspiration for this first-class entertainment. It's not a new story, but it has been made with imagination and holds from start to finish. With a fine all-round cast headed by Phyllis Calvert this should play to good business, and should find its place on U.S. screens.

Best picture director Ken Amakin ("Holiday Camp," "Miranda") has made to date, he used his location in the Haute Savoie to good purpose and was helped by expressive camera work.

Thirteen people of various types and temperaments flying over the Alps are crash-landed on a glacier slope and, radio batteries being damaged, are isolated from the outside world. There is a pampered film star (Margot Grahame) who panics while her boy friend (Derek Bond) finds new strength in the catastrophe. There is a vain opera singer (Francis L. Sullivan) who ruins his voice in a call for help. There is the love tragedy of a nurse (Sonia Holm) and her patient (Grey Blake) traveling in an iron lung, who makes the supreme sacrifice, giving his batteries to send out an S.O.S.

Two embittered brothers (Raymond Huntley and David Tomlinson) find the bond they need in adversity; a champion boxer (Andrew Crawford) fulfills a long desire to escape from his domineering manager (Charles Victor); a displaced person (Gerard Heinz), at last on the road to home and love, symbolically dies in finding help for others, and the air hostess (Phyllis Calvert), calming and helping passengers, replaces her love for a dead man by real love for a more worthy one (James Donald). Behavior of each person is credible and logical, and the story is expertly knit together right down to the moment when the survivors are safely landed.

Level of acting is high. Casting was skillful and every person, including those who contributed minute cameos, deserves praise. For Phyllis Calvert it is something of a comeback on the British screen, and the same goes for Margot Grahame. But it is the teamwork that makes it an enjoyable entertainment. *Cane.*

No Orchids for Miss Blandish
(BRITISH)
London, April 14.

Renown production and release. Stars Jack La Rue, Hugh McDermott, Linden Travers. Direction and screenplay, St. John L. Clowes. From novel by James Hadley Chase; editor, Manuel del Campo; camera, Gerald Gibbs. At Plaza, London, April 13, '48. Running time, 102 MINS.

Slim Grisson	Jack La Rue
Fenner	Hugh McDermott
Miss Blandish	Linden Travers
Eddie	Walter Crisham
Bailey	Leslie Bradley
Margo	Zoe Gail
Louis	Charles Goldner
Doc	MacDonald Parke
Mr. Blandish	Percy Marmont
Ma Grisson	Lilly Molner
Anna Borg	Frances Marsden
Flyn	Danny Green
Brennan	Jack Lester
Flagerty	Bart Norman
Johnny	Bill O'Connor
Olga	Irene Prador
Foster Harvey	John McLaren
Cabaret artists	{ Jack Durant { Halama & Konarski { Toy & Wing

A lurid bestseller has been converted into a deplorable picture. For years England has crusaded against Hollywood making films with phoney British settings. Now comes a chance for America to shriek with laughter at this picture of alleged gangsters. That is, if anybody across the Atlantic is unwise enough to import it, except as a joke. As a supposed American gangster thriller this film touches bottom in sadism, morbidity and taste. A good deal of money has been spent on it, and the only return can come from those who have read the book (publisher's figure: 500,000), those intrigued by the title or those who want to see how stupid, nasty and inane a film can be.

Set in the phoniest New York yet seen on the screen, it tells how Jack LaRue, boss of a gang, kidnaps Miss Blandish, daughter of a multi-millionaire, after her playboy fiance has been wiped out. Presumably Linden Travers reciprocates the gangster's love, and after the film has been punctuated with dead bodies, the police catch up with him, surround his hideout and pepper him with bullets. Miss Travers (plus orchid) jumps to her death out of a window. All this happens 102 minutes too late.

Participating in this tasteless parody of a film are a number of competent performers who deserve

---

sympathy. Charity forbids a detailed examination. Definitely no orchids—not even a carrot. *Cane.*

The Argyle Secrets
Hollywood, April 17.

Film Classics release of Eronel Productions, produced by Alan H. Posner and Sam X. Abarbanel. Features William Gargan, Marjorie Lord, Ralph Byrd, Jack Reitzen, John Banner. Directed by Cyril Endfield. Original screenplay, Endfield; based on "The Argyle Album" as presented on Suspense radio program; camera, Mack Stengler; editor, Gregg Tallas. Previewed April 16, '48. Running time, 63 MINS.

Harry	William Gargan
Marla	Marjorie Lord
Lt. Samson	Ralph Byrd
Panama	Jack Reitzen
Mr. Winter	John Banner
Miss Court	Barbara Billingsley
Jor McBrod	Alex Fraser
Scanlon	Peter Brocco
Pierce	George Anderson
Gil	Mickey Simpson
Pinky	Alvin Hammer
Nurse	Carole Donne
Mrs. Rubin	Mary Tarcai
Melvyn	Robert Kellard
Irving	Kenneth Greenwald
Dr. Van Selbin	Herbert Rawlinson

"The Argyle Secrets" adds up to okay supporting material. It's a mystery melodrama based on a Suspense radio presentation, and is the first production for Eronel, new indie outfit. Film is on the talky side, but has been well paced and has an interesting plot.

William Gargan portrays reporter on the trail of an album of documents that reveal treachery of big shots in secret dealings with the Nazis. Also trying for the album are two sets of blackmailers. Along the way are five murders and some close calls for the hero, all of which pepper doings with sufficient thrills to make for an okay payoff.

Cyril Endfield does a good job of direction, working from his original screenplay. He also authored the radio play. Gargan acts as narrator as well as the hero. Marjorie Lord is good as top femme, one of the blackmailers. Ralph Byrd is a police detective. Jack Reitzen, John Banner, Alex Fraser, Peter Brocco, Mickey Simpson are among the assorted heavies who deal out the dirty work.

Alan H. Posner and Sam X. Abarbanel share producer credit. Pair has given film neat physical values for small budget expenditure. Lensing by Mack Stengler could have used better set lighting. Gregg Tallas' editing is good. *Brog.*

Miniature Reviews

"**On an Island With You**" (Musical-Color) (M-G). Brightened by Jimmy Durant's Comedy; fair grosser.

"**Trapped By Boston Blackie**" (Col). Standard melodrama in the "Blackie" series; average grosses.

"**The Dude Goes West**" (AA). Crackerjack western satire bound to please in all situations.

"**The Strawberry Roan**" (Color-Songs) (Col). First color for Autry adds new lustre and greater exploitation value to star's series.

"**Crossed Trails**" (Mono). Fair western starring Johnny Mack Brown.

"**The Bold Frontiersman**" (Rep.). Solid action fare for the western market with Allan "Rocky" Lane.

"**One Night With You**" (GFD). Nino Martini, Patricia Roc in weak British-made romantic drama.

"**Dreams That Money Can Buy**" (Color) (Independent). Overlong surrealist pic, probably "interesting" for arty fans, but tedious for most.

"**Sins of the Fathers**" (Can.). Unsensationalized OK Canadian-made feature on VD.

"**Who Killed Santa Claus?**" (French) (Lopert). Harry Baur in firstrate French whodunit; strong biz in arty houses.

"**Day of Wrath**" (Danish) Extremely heavy story has practically nothing for the U. S.

On an Island with You
(COLOR-MUSICAL)

Metro release of Joe Pasternak production. Stars Esther Williams, Peter Lawford, Ricardo Montalban, Jimmy Durante; features Cyd Charisse, Xavier Cugat. Directed by Richard Thorpe. Screenplay, Dorothy Kingsley. Dorothy Cooper, Charles Martin, Hans Wilhelm; original by Charles Martin, Hans Wilhelm; musical direction, Georgie Stoll; songs, Nacio Herb Brown and Edward Heyman; dances and water ballets, John Donohue; camera (Technicolor), Charles Rosher; editors, Douglass Biggs, Ferris Webster. Previewed at Loew's 72d Street, N. Y., April 19, '48. Running time, 107 MINS.

Rosalind Reynolds	Esther Williams
Lt. Lawrence Kingslee	Peter Lawford
Ricardo Montez	Ricardo Montalban
Buckley	Jimmy Durante
Yvonne Torro	Cyd Charisse
Commander Harrison	Leon Ames
Penelope Peabody	Kathryn Beaumont
George Blaine	Dick Simmons

Xavier Cugat and Orchestra

The principal assets of this musical are several attractive personalities and performances, some striking dance and aquatic numbers and a visually stunning production. The book is weak, the music rather commonplace and the running time too long for the amount of entertainment involved. The picture should have moderate boxoffice draw.

"On an Island With You" is a film about a film. That is, it's about the romantic developments that occur when a Hollywood company goes to a semi-tropic resort (presumably Miami) to shoot a picture starring Esther Williams. Complications ensue when Peter Lawford, a Navy flier assigned to give technical advice, turns out to have an uncontrollable crush on the star, dating from her camp-show appearance at his training base during the war.

When she refuses to dance with him one night in the glittery ca-

---

sino, he kidnaps her in his Navy plane and takes her to a neighboring island and makes her give him the dance to the music of a portable radio set. Unfortunately, this sequence is handled with at least a pretense of seriousness. And, as in the rest of the picture, the production number interruptions are too infrequent and too short for the silly book.

Miss Williams is, as usual, a real dish in a bathing suit, and some of the outfits she wears are particularly choice in color. However, she isn't given as many individual swimming shots as she might be, and she fails to impress dramatically. As a frenzied assistant director, Jimmy Durante supplies the entertainment highlights of the film with a series of his standard numbers. He also gives needed drive and vitality to the story scenes in which he appears.

As the flier, Lawford is as believable as the part allows. Ricardo Montalban is acceptable dramatically as the star's leading man-fiance, and he teams with Cyd Charisse for some standout dance numbers. Miss Charisse is an electrifying dancer, a looker and handles her modest acting requirements satisfactorily.

Xavier Cugat portrays the leader of Xavier Cugat's band at the lavish nitery, Leon Ames is effective as Lawford's stern-but-amused superior, Kathryn Beaumont plays a hopeful moppet thesper, and Dick Simmons is okay as the film director. Of the various production numbers, the dances are generally best, with the water ballets limited slightly by the fact that Miss Williams has too little solo stuff. Except for Jimmy Durante's oldies, there are no memorable songs. *Hobe.*

Trapped by Boston Blackie

Columbia release of Rudolph C. Flothow production. Features Chester Morris. Directed by Seymour Friedman. Screenplay, Maurice Tombragel; story, Charles Marion, Edward Block, based upon character created by Jack Boyle; camera, Philip Tannura; editor, Dwight Caldwell; music, Mischa Bakaleinikoff. At New York theatre, N. Y., week April 20, '48. Running time, 67 MINS.

Boston Blackie	Chester Morris
Doris Bradley	June Vincent
Inspector Farraday	Richard Lane
Joan Howell	Patricia White
Igor Borio	Edward Norris
Runt	George E. Stone
Sergeant Matthews	Frank Sully
Sandra Doray	Fay Baker
Mr. Carter	William Forrest
Mrs. Carter	Sarah Selby
Mrs. Kenyon	Mary Currier
Dunn	Pierre Watkin
Louis	Ben Welden

For some seven years Columbia has been turning out the "Boston Blackie" series. As the 13th and latest in this action-mystery cycle, "Trapped by Boston Blackie" fits comfortably in the groove etched by its predecessors. Story formula is a familiar one and the film looks to be heading for average business in the double bill situations.

Lack of originality on the part of the trio of scripters is best revealed by the perennial disguises which at one point drape Chester Morris and George E. Stone in beards and Indian turbans while in another scene the pair pose as an elderly couple. This brand of plot technique is pretty much old hat to followers of the "Blackie" melodramas.

In the title role, per usual, Morris is involved in the theft of a "priceless" string of pearls. He and his sidekick, Stone, are hired as private detectives to guard the jewels, but when the sparklers are lifted the cops place both of 'em under suspicion. Balance of the footage is devoted to the efforts of the suspects to clear themselves with the authorities.

Performances are comparable to the thesping found in the average whodunit. Morris is forthright enough as a one-time crook gone straight. Stone is okay as his partner. Both point up their lines for laughs. Femme interest is supplied by June Vincent and Patricia White. They're capable in routine roles. Richard Lane contribs his standard characterization of a bungling inspector who frequently is outfoxed by Morris' cunning. Other players are adequate.

In making his first directorial effort, Friedman maintained a satisfactory pace for this Rudolph C. Flothow production. He previously was assistant director on Columbia's "To the Ends of the Earth." Philip Tannura's camerawork is good as are other technical credits. Mischa Bakaleinikoff's musical direction aids in sustaining the picture's mood. *Gilb.*

The Dude Goes West

Allied Artists release of King Bros. production. Stars Eddie Albert, Gale Storm; features James Gleason, Binnie Barnes, Gilbert Roland, Barton MacLane. Directed by Kurt Neumann. Original screenplay, Richard Sale, Mary Loos; camera, Karl Struss; music, Dimitri Tiomkin; editor, Richard Heermance. Previewed April 20, '48. Running time, **87 MINS.**

Daniel Bone	Eddie Albert
Liza Crockett	Gale Storm
Sam Briggs	James Gleason
Kiki Kelly	Binnie Barnes
Pecos Kid	Gilbert Roland
Texas Jack	Barton MacLane
Beetle	Douglas Fowley
Spiggoty	Tom Tyler
Horace Hotchkiss	Harry Hayden
Running Wolf	Chief Yowlachie
Mrs. Hallahan	Sarah Padden
Grandma Crockett	Catherine Doucet
Conductor	Edward Organ
Finnegan	Olin Howlin
Mr. Brittle	Francis Pierlot
J. J. Jines	Tom Fadden
Horse Trader	Si Jenks
Gambler	George Meeker
Whiskey Drummer	Dick Elliott
Harris	Charles Williams
Baggage Master	Lee White

"The Dude Goes West" has a premise which will tickle every spectator who catches it. Picture's a sleeper which can expect satisfactory returns wherever shown, a satire on western pictures made with tongue in cheek but emerging a class production notable for top values in every department. Producers haven't missed a bet in this one, as audiences will agree.

For Eddie Albert, co-star with Gale Storm, film is an individual triumph, but so is it for entire cast and all concerned with its making and one of top products Allied Artists has ever released. Albert plays a gunsmith, who leaves Brooklyn back in the '70s because he has read there's a nice little place called Arsenic City out in Nevada with lots of people who pack guns, and where there's guns there's business for him.

Practically everything that can happen to a man descends upon Albert as he makes his way westward to his destination, including his meeting Miss Storm who, it develops, is also going to Arsenic City in effort to locate gold mine her murdered father found. Albert has his difficulties with badmen, he and Miss Storm are captured by wild Piutes, he outshoots worst outlaws in state and what-have-you.

As mild-mannered gunsmith Albert is immense and Miss Storm is lovely in role of young femme who still doesn't trust him after he's gone all-out to show her his good intentions. James Gleason, an old desert rat, turns in standout comedy performance. Barton MacLane, outlaw leader who takes liking to easterner even though he steals his outfit, is tops in role and Gilbert Roland makes a colorful figure of another outlaw. Binnie Barnes is saloon-keeper who wants Gale's map showing location of mine, and is dashing in part.

Frank and Maurice King have done a bangup job in projecting this funfest on screen, and Kurt Neumann's direction lends itself admirably to catching spirit of piece. Dimitri Tiomkin's score likewise fits in perfectly with mood, while Karl Struss' photography assays top grade. *Whit.*

The Strawberry Roan
(COLOR-SONGS)

Hollywood, April 23.

Columbia release of Gene Autry (Armand Schaefer) production. Stars Gene Autry; features Jack Holt, Dick Jones, Gloria Henry, Rufe Davis, Pat Buttram, John McGuire, Eddy Waller, Redd Harper. Directed by John English. Screenplay, Dwight Cummins, Dorothy Yost; story, Julian Zimet; editor, Henry Batista; camera (Cinecolor), Fred H. Jackman; music, Paul Mertz. Previewed April 15, '48. Running time: 76 MINS.

Gene Autry	Himself
Connie Bailey	Gloria Henry
Walt Bailey	Jack Holt
Joe Bailey	Dick Jones
Hank	Pat Buttram
Chuck	Rufe Davis
Bud Williams	John McGuire
Steve	Eddy Waller
Andy	Redd Harper
Pete Lucas	Jack Ingram
Jake	Eddie Parker
Smitty	Ted Mapes
Dr. Nelson	Sam Flint

Gene Autry's bow in color is an event which will pay off handsomely. Picture spells boxoffice throughout, despite action which occasionally becomes too slowly-paced. Surefire story, however, makes it highly acceptable for juve and family market, and there is added attraction of some of most beautiful use of Cinecolor yet attained.

Story about a wild horse which Autry tames, blends with several song numbers warbled by star to excellent effect. Star, too, has benefit of a particularly able supporting cast. This is headed by Jack Holt, ranch owner for whom Autry is foreman and who is intent upon killing the roan; and Dick Jones, playing Holt's son, injured by horse in his first attempt to ride and break him, thereby causing Holt to vow vengeance on steed.

Real star of "Roan" is Champion, Autry's own horse in title part, beautifully photographed in shades which set off animal's beauty. Horse's training is demonstrated at every turn. Some of color work is unusually effective, which makes for new exploitation values in Autry's films.

Whole plot centers around Champion and Autry's efforts to save him from Holt's wrath. Autry is discharged, and when he tries to take the horse, staked out, with him, Holt charges him with rustling. Autry thus becomes a fugitive with a price on his head. It all ends happily, of course, when Autry, through the horse, is responsible for the ranchowner's son, who doesn't think he can ever walk again, climbing aboard Champion and finding life again.

Autry delivers one of his customary easy portrayals and balance of cast is topflight. Holt makes his role convincing. Jones, a newcomer, shows considerable promise as the son; Gloria Henry makes most of a role with plenty of meat to it; and Rufe Davis is in effectively for his impersonations.

Armand Schaefer as producer has tossed in plenty of class production and John English's direction is first-class. Fred H. Jackman's' photography is particularly noteworthy. *Whit.*

Crossed Trails

Monogram release of Louis Gray production. Stars Johnny Mack Brown; features Raymond Hatton, Lynne Carver. Directed by Lambert Hillyer. Original screenplay, Colt Remington; camera, Harry Neumann; editor, Fred Maguire; music, Edward J. Kay. At New York theatre, N. Y., week April 20, '48. Running time, 57 MINS.

Johnny	Johnny Mack Brown
Bodie	Raymond Hatton
Maggie	Lynne Carver
Hudson	Douglas Evans
Melissa	Kathy Frye
Curtin	Zon Murray
Mrs. Laswell	Mary MacLaren
Laswell	Ted Adams
Blake	Steve Clark
Judge	Frank LaRue
Anderson	Milburn Morante
Wright	Robert D. Woodward
Whitfield	Pierce Lyden
Stoddard	Henry Hall
Jury Foreman	Hugh Murray
Sheriff Cook	Bud Osborne

Action fans will find a fair amount of interest in "Crossed Trails." With Johnny Mack Brown packin' an accurate six gun and an unerring set of dukes, the outlaws come off second best in their age-old battle against frontier society. Picture's speed occasionally slows down to a canter, but on the overall the film rates as an okay filler for the dualers and situations catering to the Saturday matinee trade.

Colt Remington's (sic!) original deals with the nefarious attempts of Douglas Evans and Steve Clark to take over Kathy Frye's ranch inasmuch as the property controls the water rights for the entire area. When she and her guardian, Raymond Hatton, resist, the two frame him on a murder charge. However, Brown breaks up the baddies' plans by getting a rancher to prove that Hatton was not present at the killing. Simultaneously he cleans up the outlaws in hand-to-hand combat.

Picture runs a leisurely course in the earlier sequences and a trial scene especially drags. But when finally rolling, it fully measures up to preceding Brown cayuse pix. Cowboy star is a credible champion of the law. Hatton flavors his role with realism while Douglas Evans is sinister enough as the heavy. Lynne Carver lends a bit of pulchritude to this outdoor saga and Miss Frye scores as a tomboyish 13-year-old who loathes school. Balance of the cast handles its chores in okay fashion.

Direction of Lambert Hillyer is particularly effective in the action scenes. Harry Neumann's lensing brought in some nice outdoor shots. Producer Louis Gray endowed the entry with satisfactory production values despite an obviously low budget.

The Bold Frontiersman

Hollywood, April 23.

Republic release of Gordon Kay production. Stars Allan "Rocky" Lane, features Eddy Waller, Roy Barcroft, John Alvin, Francis McDonald. Directed by Philip Ford. Original screenplay, Bob Williams; camera, Ernest Miller; editor, Arthur Roberts. Previewed April 20, '48. Running time, 59 MINS.

Allan "Rocky" Lane	Himself
His Stallion	Black Jack
Nugget Clark	Eddy Waller
Smiling Jack	Roy Barcroft
Don Post	John Alvin
Adam Post	Francis McDonald
Smokey	Fred Graham
Morton Harris	Edward Cassidy
Pete	Edmund Cobb
Cowboy	Harold Goodwin
Rancher	Jack Kirk
Judd	Ken Terrell
Sam	Marshall Reed
Professor	Al Murphy

"The Bold Frontiersman" is a western that moves. Saddle fans will find this one right up their alley and reception will be strong in the oater market. Emphasis is on fast action and those spectacular stunts too often skipped in present-day westerns. Makes no difference that they're not credible, it's the kind of sight stuff that goes over big with the fans and helps to build new ones among the youngsters.

Allan "Rocky" Lane is a stalwart hero whose sixgun usually hits what he aims at, another feature not used enough in this day of croon-and-swoon oaters. There's no femme cluttering up the scenery, either. Lane's character lives up to the title as he goes about his business of protecting money raised by ranchers in a drought area to build a dam. Roy Barcroft is the heavy trying to sieze the gold but he and his henchmen meet their come-uppance at the hands of Lane as plot races through 59 minutes of slam-bang action.

Philip Ford's direction misses no bets in keeping this one on the move and the original script by Bob Williams dresses the western plotting neatly for interest.

Lane and his horse, Black Jack, made a sturdy lead team. Eddy Waller supplies comedy as a timid sheriff and Barcroft's dirty work is excellent. John Alvin, Francis McDonald and others in the cast come through expertly.

Gordon Kay's production supplies everything needed to have the Saturday matinee trade cheering the hero on. Camera work by Ernest Miller is exceptionally good for a budget western and editing is crisp. Other credits measure up to all demands of the market. *Brog.*

One Night With You
(BRITISH)

London, April 22.

GFD release of Josef Somlo (J. Arthur Rank-Two Cities) production. Stars Nino Martini, Patricia Roc. Directed by Shaun Terence Young. Screenplay by C. Brahms, S. J. Simon from original by Carlo Ludovico Bragaglia. Editor, Douglas Myers; music, Lambert Williamson; camera, Andre Thomas, Norman Warwick. At Odeon, London, April 21, '48. Running time, 92 MINS.

Giulio Moris	Nino Martini
Mary Santel	Patricia Roc
Piero Santellini	Bonar Colleano
Mr. Santel	Hugh Wakefield
Matty	Guy Middleton
Tramp	Stanley Holloway
Fogliati	Charles Goldner
Pirelli	Willy Fueter
Lina Linari	Irene Worth
Pirelli's Assistant	Christopher Lee
Script Writer	Stuart Latham
Second Script Writer	Judith Furse

Remake of the seven-year-old Italian picture, "Fuga a Due Voci," this was hardly worth the time, trouble and expense. As a first venture into stories with music for Two Cities by producer Josef Somlo, it is unfortunate and will earn no dividends. Marquee value is limited to those who know Nino Martini and to the special fans of

Patricia Roc, and their disappointment will be reflected in the boxoffice. Definitely not worth exporting to America.

Stories poking fun at the mechanics of filmmaking rarely find favor with audiences, and this attempt is no exception. Alleged smart-aleck lines about producers, stars and writers leave audience unmoved and weary, and what may look screamingly funny on paper is so often deadly dull on the screen. That can be the only explanation in this adaptation from the Italian. Nor does the multiplicity of accents presumably from one nationality help the audience.

Told as a flashback, the central theme of the story is the meeting of a famous tenor with an English girl, both stranded on a railway station, having lost their trains while he rescued her dog from a fight. Tramp steals the tenor's luggage, and is mistaken for the star. He is carried in triumph to the studio in Rome, but is dumb when asked to sing at a test.

Meanwhile tenor and girl, having to wait until morning for trains, sing for their supper, are arrested for passing a forged note, and are put in jail, while her father and a couple of lovers scour the country for her. Tenor and girl escape and arrive on set in time to save the situation.

Production, direction and acting call for little comment. Martini sings well but can do little with his part. Miss Roc is badly handicapped by the script and unkindly treated by the camera. A little of Bonar Colleano's comedy goes a long way—he is too overpowering to have in big doses. Charles Goldner overacts as the film producer, and a number of good artists do their painful ulmost to raise laughs. *Cane.*

Dreams That Money Can Buy

(COLOR)

Film Rights release of Hans Richter production, directed and written by Richter. From stories and ideas of Fernand Leger, Max Ernst, Marcel Duchamp, Alexander Calder, Man Ray; score, John Latouche, John Cage, Louis Applebaum, Paul Bowles, Darius Milhaud; musical accompaniment sung by Libby Holman and Josh White; camera (Kodachrome), Arnold Eagle. At 5th Ave. Playhouse, N. Y., April 23, '48. Running time, **99 MINS.**

Cast: Jack Bittner, Max Ernst, Julien Levy, Arthur Seymour, Miriam Raeburn, Jo Mitchell, others.

"Dreams That Money Can Buy" is frankly an experimental film about the subconscious. It is an attempt to find a new cinematic technique for expressing the abstract. It is surrealist and, according to a program note by its creator, Hans Richter, "You don't have to understand it to enjoy it."

Only a tiny segment of the public is likely to endorse that estimate of the picture. Most, including those who have seen more or less similar attempts dating back 20-odd years, may find "Dreams That Money Can Buy" neither as imaginative, skillful or entertaining as it should be. It is painfully attenuated and progressively tiresome.

Considering that the picture was produced in a Manhattan loft by recruits working on a share of the possible profits, and that the total budget was only $25,000, "Dreams" can be excused a lot. It was originally filmed in 16m. Kodachrome and then transferred to 35m. stock. As Richter himself recently said, "We created as an artist does, for his own responsibility and not for the audience."

The film consists of various episodes strung together in a loose continuity about a "heavenly psychiatrist" and the wish-fulfillment visions in the eyes of his patients. There are a number of erotic scenes (which may help popularize the picture somewhat), an occasionally humorous moment and an assortment of abstractions which could conceivably mean anything to anybody. As a whole, the film is visually unimpressive, particularly as to color, although there are a few effective shots. The score, written by different composers for the various episodes, is generally good.

The already limited appeal of "Dreams" isn't helped by its present showing at the 5th Ave. Playhouse. When it was caught opening day the operators must have been doping out their next day's horse bets, for the film was frequently projected clear off the screen and onto the theatre ceiling, in several instances continuing so until the audience began whistling and clapping. As always, the fact that the entrance and exit to the house is in the front repeatedly caused a distraction. And the policy of charging 25c. for programs (neither the giveaway program nor the screen credits is adequate), in addition to the 85c. admission, seems likely to arouse resentment. *Hobe.*

Sins of the Fathers

(CANADA)

Toronto, April 21.

Canadian Productions release of Larry Cromien (Cyril Strange) production. Stars Austin Willis, Joy LaFleur, John Pratt, Suzanne Avon, Mary Barclay. Directed by Phil Rosen and Richard J. Jarvis. Original screenplay, Gordon Burwash; camera, William Steiner; score, Morris C. Davis; conducted by Samuel Hersenhoren; editor, Richard J. Jarvis. Tradeshown April 21, '48. Running time, **98 MINS.**

Dr. Ben Edwards	Austin Willis
Patsy Curran	Joy LaFleur
Marty Williams	John Pratt
Daphne	Phyllis Carter
Leona	Suzanne Avon
Charlie Mitchell	Frank Heron
Ellen Carter	Mary Barclay
Higgins	Gerald Rowan
Shorty	Norman Taviss

"Sins of the Fathers" is the first feature-length film, dealing with the V. D. problem, to be written and produced in Canada. Canadian Motion Picture Productions, Ltd., has the cooperation of the Federal Department of National Health and Welfare, with animations and clinical scenes supplied by the Royal Canadian Air Force. The picture, financed by Toronto businessmen, cost $66,000 and was produced in 11 days.

The original script by Gordon Burwash avoids the usual sensationalizing treatment of the subject of venereal disease, as was the b.o. draw in such oldies as "The End of the Road" and "Damaged Goods." This time, the treatment is marked by commendable good taste and restraint; there are no clinical sequences of V. D. victims' faces and limbs falling off and the horror angle has been carefully skirted. The film, however, still packs a powerful wallop, its power even enhanced perhaps by the restrained treatment.

The Canadian backers were astute enough to import a Hollywood director, Phil Rosen, who used the current in-favor technique of the documentary and maintained the swift pace without any artiness. The script is literate and the theme timely, with whole undertaking a technical success on photography, background music and sound. Excellent acting jobs are turned in by Austin Willis as the young medical health officer attempting to clean up the town against the opposition of crooked politicians in the pay of local vice racketeers; Joy LaFleur as the councillor's daughter whose V. D. infection swings her father to the side of the reform element; John Pratt, late of the Canadian Navy Show, as the nightclub operator, and Mary Barclay as the "nice" girl.

With lack of marquee strength, "Sins of the Fathers" will need plenty of selling activity but the exploitation angles are all there and require only imagination and energy. *McStay.*

Who Killed Santa Claus?

(L'Assasinat Du Pere Noel)

(FRENCH)

Lopert Film release of Film Rights International production. Stars Harry Baur. Directed by Christian Jacques. Adapted from novel of Pierre Very by Charles Spaak; special music, Henry Verdun; camera, Armand Thirard. At Avenue Playhouse, N. Y., starting April 22, '48. Running time, **95 MINS.**

Cornusse ("Santa Claus")	Harry Baur
The baron	Raymond Rouleau
Catherine	Renee Faure
Mother Michel	Marie-Helene Daste
The school-master	Robert Le Vigan
The pharmacist	Jean Brochard
Kappel	Jean Paredes
The mayor	Fernand Ledoux
Marie Coquillot	Helena Manson

(In French; English Titles)

Produced some years ago, when French producers were turning out some of their outstanding pix, "Who Killed Santa Claus?," is a vivid meller of odd twists. It hasn't given the late Harry Baur, as many opportunities as usual but he has enough to do in the Santa Claus role to add to this picture's boxoffice. Film should be a strong foreign-language grosser, particularly if judiciously edited and, possibly, the title doctored.

Story points up how children of a small French village eagerly anticipate the town's Santa Claus, actually the community's toymaker. He always dolls up as Kris Kringle and visits with gifts Xmas eve. Early attention is focused on a costly ring used in Christmas eve church services and the return of a baron after an absence of 20 years. When the ring is stolen, the baron bound and tied up, an unknown man wearing the Santa Claus outfit is murdered, the mystery is off in high gear. Charles Spaak has deftly adapted the Pierre Very novel while director Christian Jacques keeps suspence at a high pitch until the actual thief and killer is apprehended.

Considerable has been made of a crippled lad who becomes gravely ill when Kris Kringle fails to arrive on time (because Kris was thoroughly soused from taking a nip at every home visited). Also, the director has injected a peculiar sort of romance by having the baron fall in love with Santa Claus' daughter and, in so doing, restores her wavering mentality.

Baur dominates every scene in which Raymond Rouleau is superb as the young baron. Renee Faure is the girl who lives in a dream world until she falls for the baron.

Marie-Helene Daste believably portrays a half-demented femme; Robert Le Vigan is the schoolmaster and Jean Brochard's village pharmacist is down-to-earth.

Besides Jacques' fine direction, Armand Thirard's lensing (especially of the vast, snow-covered outdoor scenes) deserves special mention. Technically this is one of the best films to come out of France in months. ***Wear.***

Day of Wrath

(DANISH)

George J. Schaefer Associates release of Carl Dreyer production. Stars Thirkild Roose, Lisbeth Movin; features Sigrid Neiiendam, Preben Lerdoff. Directed by Dreyer. Screenplay, Mogens Skot-Hansen, Poul Knudsen, Dreyer, from novel by Wiers Jenssens; camera, Carl Andersson; editors, Edith Schlussel, Anne Marie Petersen; music, Poul Schierbeck. Tradeshown, N. Y., April 21, '48. Running time **97 MINS.**

Absalon Pedersson	Thirkild Roose
Anne, his wife	Lisbeth Movin
Merette, his mother	Sigrid Neiiendam
Martin, son by his first marriage	Preben Lerdorff
The Bishop	Albert Hoeberg
Laurentius	Olaf Ussing
Herlofs Marte	Anna Svierkier

(In Danish; English Titles)

As the first Danish-made talking film to arrive in the U. S., "Day of Wrath" doesn't augur well for future film importations from Denmark. Hampered as it is by the unfamiliar speech, which slows the action despite adequate subtitles, the picture is tedious to the extreme. Any market, even for the art houses in this country, will lie strictly with the Danish-speaking population.

Film's chief trouble lies in the gratingly plodding pace. And the heavy story, unlightened by the slightest sign of comedy relief, will militate against the film's boxoffice potential here.

Producer-director Carl Dreyer has apparently taken his cue from Russia's famed Sergei Eisenstein in attempting to use certain camera techniques to help tell the story. But he is no Eisenstein. Camera moves slowly from scene to scene, with no apparent rhyme or season.

Story, set in 16th century Denmark, deals with the family of a town pastor. He's responsible for committing to death at the stake a woman accused of witchcraft. Before she dies, shes charges him with having spared another witch because he was in love with the witch's daughter, whom he subsequently married. Interwoven is a romance between the young wife and the pastor's grown son by a former marriage. As was to be expected, it all ends in a tragedy that rivals the most tragic tales of Shakespeare.

Cast does nothing to lighten the film's load. Romantic leads, in addition, are not overly attractive by mountings are in keeping with the American standards. Production film's darker aspects. *Stal.*

Miniature Reviews

"The Emperor Waltz" (Color - Songs) (Par). Bing Crosby and Joan Fontaine costumer for heavy boxoffice.

"Dream Girl" (Par). Broader and probably more popular edition of the Elmer Rice play; should pull heavy grosses.

"Silver River" (WB). Western drama of silver mining days. Errol Flynn and Ann Sheridan to spark b.o.

"Assigned to Danger" (EL). Gene Raymond in gangster meller; strong second feature for dualers.

"Waterfront at Midnight" (Par). Neat action melodrama for supporting position.

"Heart of Virginia" (Rep). Pleasant programmer dealing with horseracing.

"13 Lead Soldiers" (20th). Good "Bulldog Drummond" whodunit for supporting market.

"Good Time Girl" (GFD). Mild British meller on juve delinquency.

"I Wouldn't Be in Your Shoes" (Mono). Programmer whodunit for smaller situations.

"Who Killed 'Doc' Robbin" (Color) (UA). Hal Roach comedy in "Laff-Time" series; okay for lower half of dualers.

"Gelosia" (Italian) (Lux). Heavy Italian drama geared strictly for foreign-language spots; limited appeal.

The Emperor Waltz
(COLOR-SONGS)

Hollywood, April 30.

Paramount release of Charles Brackett production. Stars Bing Crosby, Joan Fontaine; features Roland Culver, Lucile Watson, Richard Haydn, Harold Vermilyea. Directed by Billy Wilder. Written by Brackett and Wilder; camera (Technicolor), George Barnes; music, Johann Strauss; score, Victor Young; songs, James Van Heusen, Johnny Burke; vocal arrangements, Joseph J. Lilley; editor, Doane Harrison. Tradeshown April 30, '48. Running time, **105 MINS.**

Virgil Smith....................Bing Crosby
Johanna Augusta.............Joan Fontaine
Baron Holenia.................Roland Culver
Princess Bitotska.............Lucile Watson
Emperor Franz Joseph......Richard Haydn
Chamberlain..............Harold Vermilyea
Dr. Zwieback....................Sig Ruman
Archduchess Stephanie..........Julie Dean
Chauffeur.......................Bert Prival
Inn Proprietress............Alma Macrorie
Chambermaid...............Roberta Jonay

"The Emperor Waltz" should solve any ticket buyer's entertainment problem. That's the only kind of problem it attempts to resolve, and the way it goes about it is strictly enjoyable. Such a natural parlay as Bing Crosby, Johann Strauss melodies, comedy, and gorgeous color, played against a breath-taking scenic background, is earmarked for the niftiest kind of grosses.

Film is a costumer laid "in the days" (sic) of Emperor Franz Joseph, and is played to the hilt by Crosby, Joan Fontaine and their supporting cast. Auditors will find little that's particularly surprising in the fable, but will be able to assume a relaxed position and concentrate on being amused. Picture has a free-and-easy air that perfectly matches the Crosby style of natural comedy. Costar Joan Fontaine, better known for heavy, serious roles, demonstrates adaptability that fits neatly into the lighter demands and she definitely scores with charm and talent as the Crosby foil.

One complaint likely to be made by audiences is that Crosby doesn't sing enough. What the crooner does deliver registers strongly, as to be expected, and there's a load of music otherwise to fill the sharp Victor Young score. Johnny Burke wrote special lyrics for three Johann Strauss melodies and teamed with James Van Heusen on cleffing one new tune.

Standouts in the music department is the Crosby touch on "I Kiss Your Hand, Madame," oldie by Fritz Rotter and Ralph Erwin; and "Friendly Mountains," number based on two old Austrian yodel songs. "Madame" is reprised several times and Crosby reached back into his groaner past to give it the extra special treatment of "boo-boo-bah-boo." In for romantic treatment is "The Kiss in Your Eyes," old Viennese tune with lyrics by Burke.

There's plenty of pageantry in the staging of the title number, using the colorful swirling of richly costumed dancers in the palace ballroom as eye-filling backdrop. "Friendly Mountains" has backdrop of processed Tyrol crags and valleys (actually Jasper National Park) filled with native yodelers and dancers.

Multiple functions of Charles Brackett and Billy Wilder on "Waltz" have given film an infectious quality that surmounts the gorgeously apt trappings against which is projected the fable of an American travelling phonograph salesman and his dog who crash the court of the Emperor, fall in love with a countess and her poodle, defy tradition and find happiness. Crosby uses his terrier to simulate the famed Victor "his master's voice" trademark — a strange trailer for Victor by a Decca recording artist, incidentally. The Brackett-Wilder dialog has zing, the pace is zippy and the results well worth 105 minutes of theatre time.

Crosby's romp into such lushness is directed at pleasing solidly and his yen for Miss Fontaine is understandable considering the picture she makes in Technicolor. Roland Culver delights as Miss Fontaine's impoverished father whose chief aim is mating her poodle with the Emperor's pet pooch. Richard Haydn registers strongly as the Emperor. Lucile Watson, Harold Vermilyea and others also click in their assignments.

George Barnes' camera takes every advantage of the sumptuous production backing furnished by the art direction and settings. Special photographic effects and process photography are firstrate production additions and all other technical functions rate a salvo.

Brog.

Dream Girl

Paramount release of P. J. Wolfson production. Stars Betty Hutton, Macdonald Carey; features Patric Knowles, Virginia Field, Walter Abel, Peggy Wood. Directed by Mitchell Leisen. Screenplay, Arthur Sheekman, from play by Elmer Rice; camera, Daniel L. Fapp; special photographic effects, Gordon Jennings; music score, Victor Young; musical numbers staged by Billy Daniels; costumes, Edith Head; art direction, Hans Dreier and John Meehan; editor, Alma Macrorie. Previewed in N. Y., May 4, '48. Running time, **88 MINS.**

Georgina Allerton..............Betty Hutton
Clark Redfield............Macdonald Carey
Jim Lucas....................Patric Knowles
Miriam Allerton Lucas......Virginia Field
George Allerton...............Walter Abel
Lucy Allerton..................Peggy Wood
Claire........................Carolyn Butler
George Hand................Lowell Gilmore
Music Teacher.........Zamah Cunningham
Antonio.........................Frank Puglia

Paramount has turned out a sure boxoffice winner in this film version of Elmer Rice's smash play of two seasons ago. The picture has strong comedy, with a few moving scenes. In has romantic appeal, lots of color and action, and a satisfying ending. The title and star names should also have ample marquee draw.

The screen treatment is naturally, and perhaps properly, broader than the original play. This results primarily from the production and Mitchell Leisen's direction rather than from the Arthur Sheekman adaptation. Thus, the film turns the play's humor into outright comedy and sometimes into slapstick. Possibly this will mean wider mass popularity and larger grosses, but it inevitably loses much of the subtlety and the ingratiating quality of the play.

This broadening treatment applies to practically every phase of the picture. For instance, the fact that the heroine is a chronic daydreamer isn't left to the yarn's title and the use of fade-into-reverie technique, but is put into explicit words by an off-screen voice, at the very start. Similarly, the heroine is no longer a young woman who merely clings to immature escapism, but is downright adolescent, if not bordering on the infantile.

The family is no longer ordinary middleclass, but obviously rich. The home is not a modestly comfortable one, as in the play, but is now a mansion, handsomely furnished and expensively servanted. The girl's mother, no longer philosophically resigned to her daughter's vagueness, is an ill-tempered scold. The sister is not an unhappy girl disappointed in marriage to a weakling, but a hard, selfish schemer.

This sledgehammer treatment provides some very funny scenes, as when the heroine daydreams her sister's wedding in terms of schoolgirl sentimentality, when she fancies herself a fallen woman committing suicide in a tawdry cabaret. It also provides one of the most moving sequences in the picture, when the heroine imagines herself doing a last-minute substitution for the prima donna in "Madama Butterfly" (with Metopera soprano Nadine Connor singing the famous "One Fine Day" aria from that opera).

As the self-preoccupied heroine, Betty Hutton gives one of her most skillful performances to date. Besides her familiar vitality and drive, she underscores the comedy in the part and does reasonably well dramatically. Although it may be merely an illusion, Miss Hutton at times seems to read lines with an intonation curiously reminiscent of Betty Field, who created the role brilliantly in the original Broadway play.

Macdonald Carey is likeable as the brash newspaperman, though he also gives the character broader dimension than intended by Elmer Rice. Patric Knowles is rightly stuffy as the no-account son-in-law, while Virginia Field is effectively enamel-coated as the chilly sister. Walter Abel is invariably plausible as the quiet father, whom his daughter always conceives in a protective role in her daydreams. Peggy Wood plays the unpleasant mother emphatically, and manages to give the part a touch of humor and warmth at the close. Lowell Gilmore is a believable cafe society wolf, and Zamah Cunningham does a laughable bit as an uninhibited vocal teacher.

The production is physically impressive, at least in supplying a toney background to the proceedings. Leisen's direction has helpful pace, though it takes the fine edge off the original story. There are some effective musical and dance shots as part of the heroine's daydreams. The musical score is excellent.

Hobe.

Silver River

Hollywood, April 30.

Warners release of Owen Crump production. Stars Errol Flynn, Ann Sheridan; features Thomas Mitchell, Bruce Bennett, Tom D'Andrea, Barton MacLane, Monte Blue. Directed by Raoul Walsh. Screenplay, Stephen Longstreet, Harriet Frank, Jr.; from novel by Longstreet; camera, Sid Hickox; music, Max Steiner; editor, Alan Crosland, Jr. Tradeshown at Los Angeles April 27, '48. Running time, **108 MINS.**

"Mike" McComb..............Errol Flynn
Georgia Moore...............Ann Sheridan
John Plato Beck...........Thomas Mitchell
Stanley Moore...............Bruce Bennett
"Pistol" Porter.............Tom D'Andrea
"Banjo" Sweeney.........Barton MacLane
"Buck" Chevigee...............Monte Blue
Major Spencer...............Jonathan Hale
Slade...........................Alan Bridge
Major Ross....................Arthur Space
Major Wilson......................Art Baker
President Grant..................Joe Crehan

"Silver River" isn't likely to be a bonanza for Warners, but b.o. returns will please. Ingredients of western background, some rousing action, and combo of Errol Flynn and Ann Sheridan sparking ticket sales indicate grosses will be on the good side. Production values are expensive, complete with mass spectacle and lavish settings.

Film is long, and there's too much footage devoted to talk. Opening sequences kick it off swiftly but as story develops, pace slows and leaves long waits between robust scenes. Raoul Walsh's direction shows an experienced hand at pointing up the action moments, and there are several sequences, such as the barroom fight between Flynn and Barton MacLane, and the mass clash between miners and villains, that come off with a wallop.

Film goes back to the early days of the west and the fight for control of the silver market. When Flynn is cashiered out of the Union Army he turns his face west to cash in on gambling opportunities. From there it's a mere step into banking, mining and dreams of a western empire that nearly come true. Character isn't sympathetic, mitigating against interest, but Flynn gives it a good reading.

Against the semi-historical story background is a romance between Flynn and Miss Sheridan. She's the wife of Bruce Bennett, miner, but Flynn starts his amatory chase from their first meeting, is eventually responsible for Bennett's death and finally marries the girl. While Miss Sheridan adds marquee advantages, she's not particularly at home in the role, but, nevertheless, gives a competent performance.

Thomas Mitchell carries off the top supporting role as the drunken lawyer who becomes Flynn's legal brains in big business and then turns to politics to aid the poor miners. Tom D'Andrea depicts soldier sidekick who follows Flynn through the various stages of fortune. Barton MacLane, Monte Blue, Jonathan Hale and others are capable.

Simplification of the Stephen Longstreet plot, scripted by author and Harriet Frank, Jr., would have helped. Owen Crump's production guidance furnishes strong physical values, which are enhanced by Sid Hickox' lensing but missed on insuring story tightness. Film could stand footage trimming.

Brog.

Assigned to Danger

Eagle Lion release of Eugene Ling production. Stars Gene Raymond, Noreen Nash. Directed by Oscar Boetticher. Screenplay, Eugene Ling, based on story by Robert E. Kent; camera, Lewis W. O'Connell; editor, W. Donn Hayes. Tradeshown in N. Y., April 23, '48. Running time, 65 MINS.

Dan Sullivan....................Gene Raymond
Bonnie.............................Noreen Nash
Frankie Mantell..................Robert Bice
Joe Gomez.........................Martin Kosleck
Joey..................................Gene Evans
Matty Farmer.....................Ralf Harolde
Biggie Kritz.......................Jack Overman
Evie..................................Mary Meade

Typical gangster film brings Gene Raymond back to the screen in a starring role that showcases him effectively. "Assigned to Danger" should furnish strong help on twinners.

As an insurance investigator checking on a daring payroll robbery, Raymond is kept busy trying to save his own hide because the thugs get the jump on him. Bulk of action occurs in an isolated inn, where the gangster chief's wife has arranged an ideal hideout. Main interest centers on the seriously wounded mobster chief's efforts to live and Raymond being forced to operate on him when mistaken for a medico. Director Oscar Boetticher has built continuing suspense around the chances of the gangster to recover and Raymond's efforts to get away and notify the sheriff.

Raymond and Noreen Nash, as the gangster's wife, do well enough in a number of romantic interludes. Statuesque beaut does enough to hint future possibilities even though she's a bit stilted in her first scenes. Raymond does well by a somewhat sterner role than he's been used to.

Praise should also go to cameraman Lewis W. O'Connell. Standard supporting cast is headed by Robert Bice and Gene Evans. *Wear.*

Waterfront at Midnight

Hollywood, May 4.

Paramount release of William Pine-William Thomas production. Features William Gargan, Mary Beth Hughes, Richard Travis, Richard Crane. Directed by William Berke. Screenplay, Bernard Girard; camera, Ellis W. Carter; editor, Howard Smith. Tradeshown in Los Angeles, May 4, '48. Running time, 63 MINS.

Mike Hanrohan.................William Gargan
Ethel Novack...................Mary Beth Hughes
Socks Barstow..................Richard Travis
Denny Hanrohan...............Richard Crane
Helen Hanrohan................Cheryl Walker
Hank Bremmer..................Horace McMahon
Woody...............................John Hilton
Joe Sargus.......................Douglas Fowley
Commissioner Ryan...........Paul Harvey
Loy..................................Keye Luke

The Pine-Thomas label on this one insures "Waterfront at Midnight" as a capable filler for dual bills. Neat action, good suspense and fast pace answer all demands of the market. Production has been given good mounting for budget, and William Berke's direction makes the most of actionful screenplay.

It's a cops-and-robbers yarn. William Gargan is the sturdy cop out to get the lowdown on Richard Travis, mobster who deals in stolen goods. Plot kicks off with cold-blooded killing by Travis and maintains meller pace throughout. Adding complications to Gargan's sleuthing is a kid brother (Richard Crane) who ties up with Travis so he can get rich fast. The Bernard Girard script brings in a few new angles to keep it moving and interesting, such as having Gargan believe he has shot down his own brother. Windup ties all story threads together neatly.

Cast is uniformly good, paced by Gargan, Mary Beth Hughes, Travis' moll; Travis, very good as the heavy; Crane, interesting as the kid brother; Cheryl Walker, Gargan's wife; Horace McMahon, John Milton and others all measure up.

Good lensing is by Ellis W. Carter, and Howard Smith did the tight editing. *Brog.*

Heart of Virginia

Hollywood, April 29.

Republic release of Sidney Picker production. Stars Janet Martin, Robert Lowery, Frankie Darro; features Paul Hurst, Sam McDaniel, Tom Chatterton, Bennie Bartlett. Directed by R. G. Springsteen. Original screenplay, Jerry Sackheim; added dialog, John K. Butler; camera, John MacBurnie; editor, Irving M. Schoenberg. Previewed April 28, '48. Running time, 60 MINS.

Virginia Galtry..................Janet Martin
Dan Lockwood..................Robert Lowery
Jimmy Easter....................Frankie Darro
Whit Galtry.......................Paul Hurst
"Sunflower" Jones............Sam McDaniel
Doctor Purdy....................Tom Chatterton
Breezy Brent....................Bennie Bartlett
Bud Landeen.....................Glen Vernon
Gas Station Attendant......Edmund Cobb

"Heart of Virginia" will get by as a programmer for lower half of the bill. Its 60 minutes running time, some good racetrack sequences and okay trouping help to overcome familiar plotting and obvious developments.

Principal cast weight is carried by Frankie Darro and he reads his jockey role capably, even offsetting stereotyped dialog. Plot concerns fear complex developed by Darro when he is responsible for the death of a jockey friend during a race. Saga finally gets him back on a horse when the daughter of his former employer demonstrates her faith in his ability.

Romance between Janet Martin and Robert Lowery is nicely carried off, even though they're rival horse owners. Pair team acceptably. Neat character jobs are handled by Paul Hurst, Sam McDaniel, Tom Chatterton and Bennie Bartlett.

Sidney Picker's production values show ingenuity in using small budget allotment and directorial pacing by R. G. Springsteen makes it all come off pleasantly, if not outstandingly. Good lensing by John MacBurnie and tight editing by Irving M. Schoenberg are assists. *Brog.*

13 Lead Soldiers

Hollywood, May 1.

20th-Fox release of Ben Pivar-Bernard Small (Reliance) production. Stars Tom Conway; features Maria Palmer, Helen Westcott, John Newland, Terry Kilburn. Directed by Frank McDonald. Screenplay, Irving Elman; adapted from original story by "Sapper"; camera, George Robinson; editor, Saul Goodkind. At Grauman's Chinese, Hollywood, April 30, '48. Running time, 64 MINS.

Bulldog Drummond...........Tom Conway
Estelle..............................Maria Palmer
Cynthia.............................Helen Westcott
Algy.................................John Newland
Seymour...........................Terry Kilburn
Coleman...........................William Stelling
Inspector McIver..............Gordon Richards
Vane.................................Harry Cording
Steadman.........................John Goldsworthy
Collier.............................William Edmunds

"13 Lead Soldiers," another "Bulldog Drummond" crime venture, aimed at the lower half of dualers, is fast and keeps to its business of solving some murders with a light but sufficiently suspenseful air.

Tom Conway gives the Drummond character necessary suaveness, while lighter touch of dumbness is supplied by John Newland. When an art collector is killed and two lead soldiers and an old parchment stolen, Conway takes over to discover why. It doesn't take him too long to find out that when the soldiers, with the 11 mates, are placed in the right position on a 900-year-old chimney heath in England a fabulous treasure will be revealed. Two assorted groups are after the loot and give Conway some tough complications before he wraps up the case for the police.

Maria Palmer is an intriguing mystery gal seeing the treasure, and Helen Westcott has a less-colorful spot as daughter of the murdered art collector. Terry Kilburn, William Stelling, the real villain; Gordon Richards, Harry Cording and others in the cast are acceptable.

Frank McDonald's direction of the Ben Pivar-Bernard Small production carries the story along at the proper clip. Mounting achieves good values for budget. Lensing; editing and other technical factors are okay. *Brog.*

Good Time Girl
(BRITISH)

London, April 28.

GFD release of J. Arthur Rank-Sydney Box production. Samuel Goldwyn, Jr., associate producer. Stars Jean Kent, Dennis Price, Flora Robson, Griffith Jones, Herbert Lom. Directed by David Macdonald. Screenplay by Muriel and Sydney Box, Ted Willis; editor, Vladimir Sagovsky; music, Lambert Williamson; camera, Stephen Dade. At Odeon, London, April 28, '48. Running time, 93 MINS.

Gwen Rawlings..................Jean Kent
Red Farrell.......................Dennis Price
Danny Martin....................Griffith Jones
Court Chairman.................Flora Robson
Max...................................Herbert Lom
1st Deserter......................Bonar Colleano
2nd Deserter.....................Hugh McDermott
Jimmy Rosso.....................Peter Glenville
Matron..............................Nora Swinburne
Mr. Pottinger.....................Elwyn Brook-Jones
Roberta.............................Jill Balcon
Mrs. Rawlings....................Beatrice Varley
Agnes...............................Margaret Barton
Lyla Lawrence....................Diana Dors
Mr. Hawkins......................Garry Marsh
Det. Sgt. Girton.................Jack Raine

Although this picture, based on Government reports, analyzes causes and seeks to find a solution to some aspects of juvenile delinquency among girls in London's underworld, it won't bring much kudos to Sydney Box. It has a fair list of near-stars who may help at the boxoffice, but the going won't be easy.

Story is mainly based on the "cleft-chin" murder committed here by an American GI deserter three years ago, but Sam Goldwyn, Jr. — in his first assignment as associate producer — should have known that an incident in real life becomes a generalization on the screen, and that showing a couple of U. S. gangster deserters robbing and murdering in London isn't good for Anglo-American relations, and is definitely poison for the U. S. boxoffice. If only on this account it can be ruled out for export across the Atlantic.

Jean Kent plays a slum girl who runs away from home because her father has undeservedly belted her. She gets mixed up with assorted racketeers. After a drunken party she drives a car, runs down a cop, kills him, but apparently is allowed to get away with it by the police. Meeting two GI deserters she joins forces to rob pedestrians, hijack taxidrivers and murder a car driver who, by a strange coincidence, is her former lover. She gets 15 years. This is told in flashback by Flora Robson as the juvenile court magistrate to a young girl who has run away from home. This gives a moral touch to a thoroughly unpleasant yarn.

Starring for the first time, Miss Kent has full opportunity to reveal a rather limited range. The gangsters are portrayed by screen experts in that line — Griffith Jones, Herbert Lom, Peter Glenville, Bonar Colleano and Hugh McDermott. Dennis Price, the one sympathetic underworld character, is credibly charming, and Jill Balcon, daughter of producer Michael Balcon, gives a good performance as a rebellious inmate of a reform school. Direction and production are average. *Cane.*

I Wouldn't Be in Your Shoes

Hollywood, April 28.

Monogram release of Walter Mirisch production. Stars Don Castle, Elyse Knox; features Regis Toomey, Charles D. Brown. Directed by William Nigh. Screenplay, Steve Fisher; from novel by Cornell Woolrich; camera, Mack Stengler; editor, Roy Livingston. Previewed April 26, '48. Running time, 70 MINS.

Tom.................................Don Castle
Ann.................................Elyse Knox
Judd................................Regis Toomey
Inspector Stevens.............Chas. D. Brown
Detectives.......................Rory Mallinson, Bill Kennedy
Shoe Shine Boy................Ray Dolciame
Police Lieutenant.............William Ruhl
Mrs. Finkelstein...............Esther Michelson
District Attorney...............Steve Darrell
Shoe Clerk........................Wally Walker
Judge...............................John Sheehan
Jury Foreman....................Herman Cantor
Lawyer.............................John H. Elliott
Grocer..............................Tito Vuolo
Tramp...............................Jimmy Aubrey
Salesman..........................John Shay
Vaudevillian......................Donald Kerr
Janitor..............................Joe Bernard
McGee...............................Stanley Blystone
Mrs. Alvin..........................Dorothy Vaughan
Kosloff..............................Robert Lowell
Prisoners..........................Matty Fain, John Doucette, Bill Walker, Dan White
Guards..............................Ray Teal, Paul Bryar
Announcer.........................Lou Marcelle
Priest................................Walden Boyle
Counterman.......................Hugh Charles
Mrs. Stevens......................Laura Treadwell

"I Wouldn't Be in Your Shoes" wears a clumsy but apt title. It's an okay whodunit for lesser situations. It has been given good mounting and casting for the budget.

Film gets off to an inept start, but after settling down to the main story telling, offers sufficient suspense to fulfill all aims. William Nigh's direction points up some individual scenes strongly, and has generally geared the pace with interest after the clumsy start.

Story concerns a young dancer who is convicted of robbery and murder after print of one of his dancing shoes is found at the scene of the crime. Only the continued belief in his innocence by his wife and her final tricking of the real culprit into a confession save the dancer from the chair. There's nothing particularly new about the devices used to project the yarn but good playing and direction make it all come off.

Don Castle and Elyse Knox team as the young couple. They take capable account of assignments, managing several moments of excellently valued emotional interest. Regis Toomey underplays the culprit role, his crime being masked by his guise as detective in love with Miss Knox. There are no knowing side glances or other stock-in-trade tricks used to show his true colors, a factor that helps interest. Charles D. Brown, detective inspector, Esther Michelson, Dorothy Vaughan, Robert Lowell and others supply nice support.

The Walter Mirisch production was given standard lensing by Mack Stengler and other technical credits are in keeping. *Brog.*

Who Killed 'Doc' Robbin
(COLOR)

United Artists release of Hal Roach production. Features Virginia Grey and Grant Mitchell. Directed by Bernard Carr. Screenplay, Maurice Geraghty, Dorothy

Reid; camera, John W. Boyle; editor, Arthur Seid; special camera effects, Roy W. Seawright. Tradeshown at Beacon theatre, N. Y., April 29, '48. Running time, 55 MINS.

Ann Loring....................Virgina Grey
Defense Attorney..............Don Castle
Doc Robbin....................George Zucco
Dan...........................Whitford Kane
Housekeeper...................Claire Dubrey
Judge.........................Grant Mitchell
Curley........................Larry Olsen
Betty.........................Eilene Janssen
Ardda.........................Ardda Lynwood
Dudley........................Gerald Perreau
Speck.........................Dale Belding
Dis...........................Renee Beard
Dat...........................Donald King

Recalling the Our Gang kid comedies, this 55-minuter is built around a new group of Hal Roach juveniles, and they help make this one jell into a fast comedy. Film rings in all the familiar gags of a haunted-house comedy. Pic is okay for lower rung of twin bills.

Current picture is the second part of the "Laff-Time" package, of which "Here Comes Trouble" was the first. Roach is selling either together or separately. This appears best suited to go with some No. 1 feature on a dualer rather than combined with "Trouble," since both are in the Roach comedy groove and both heavily gagged.

Disappearance of a mysterious scientist in a blast that wrecks a house on his estate starts a chase to uncover the suspected murderer. Gang of juve kids gets right into the middle of it because they seek to help their pal (Whitford Kane), the village's Mr. Fixit. To win his freedom they prowl the haunted mansion of the supposedly slain medico, played by George Zucco.

Bernard Carr directs for maximum of slapstick but manages to keep up breakneck pace. Lensing of John W. Boyle is good.

Standard cast also includes Virginia Grey, Don Castle and Grant Mitchell. But main interest focuses on the juveniles, namely Larry Olsen, Eilene Janssen, Ardda Lynwood, Gerald Perreau, Dale Belding, Renee Beard and Donald King. Last two are billed as "Dis" and "Dat," two small Negroes who steal the play whenever given the chance. Others do okay, especially the Olsen youngster. *Wear.*

Gelosia
(Jealousy)
(ITALIAN)

Lux Film release of Cinese-Universalcine production. Stars Luisa Ferida, Rolando Lupi, Elena Zareschi. Directed by Ferdinando M. Poggioli. Screenplay, adapted from novel by Luigi Capuana, Sergio Amidei; English titles, Carel Catalano. Previewed in N. Y., April 15, '48. Running time, 100 MINS.

Agrippina Solmo...............Luisa Ferida
Marquis di Roccaverdina.......Rolando Lupi
Zosima Munoz..................Elena Zareschi
Signora Munoz.................Elvira Betrono
Baroness di Lagomorto..Vanda Capodaglio
Aquilante Guzzardi............Franco Coop
Neli Casaccio.................Angelo Dessy
Agata Casaccio................Anna Arena
Dr. Meccio..............Andrea D'Amaniera
Mother Grazia.........Bella Starace Sainati
Don Silvio....................Ruggero Ruggeri

(In Italian; English Titles)

After "Furia" and "Open City" and, more recently, "Paisan," American film patrons may have come to expect strong fare from Italian studios. However, this is the sort of morbid story that has a limited appeal for Italian-language spots. It has a ponderous pace, wordiness and total lack of comedy relief, though containing several first-rate character portrayals.

Story depicts a marquis (Rolando Lupi) as a typical high-living Italian aristocrat who apparently can do no wrong until he tangles with religion. Scripter Sergio Amidei has painted him as a pleasure-loving individual who carries on an affair with one of his servants (Luisá Ferida) until he tires of her. Then he forces her into marriage with a man of his own choosing. Becoming jealous of her after she's wed, he kills her husband but manages to have an innocent man convicted of the crime.

It is only after his second marriage that he realizes Miss Ferida is still his real love. And it is along about this time that he denounces the Church and begins having wild dreams as his crime comes to haunt him. Yarn shows him a thoroughly demented man about to die at the conclusion.

There are plenty of acting lapses and sloppy scripting, but some powerful music backgrounding. Lupi is standout, indicating much greater possibilities in a better story and with stronger direction. Miss Ferida, who, since the pic was made has died, contributes an impressive portrayal as the servant. Elena Zareschi, as Lupi's second wife, manages several dramatic moments although she's too stilted in earlier passages. *Wear.*

La Vie en Rose
(Merry Life)
(FRENCH)

Paris, April 21.

UGC release of Raoul Plaquin production. Stars Francois Perier, Colette Richard, Louis Salou. Directed by Jean Faurez. Story by Rene Wheeler; script, Henri Jeanson; music, Georges van Parys; camera, Louis Page. At Madeleine, Paris. Running time, 90 MINS.

The Lover.....................Francois Perier
Schoolmaster..................Louis Salou
The Girl......................Colette Richard
Innkeeper's Daughter..........Simone Valere
Professor's Wife..............Claire Olivier

Sarcastically titled "Merry Life," this is the sad epic of a schoolmaster who commits suicide because not only can't he get the girl he loves but he's additionally victimized by less sensitive people and derided by schoolboys. Picture reminds of Noel-Noel's "Nightingale," due to locale, a boy's acedemy, but isn't geared for such heavy grosses. Marquee value will draw in France, but sombre theme will reduce foreign pull, with only moderate returns in U. S. in French patronage spots.

Direction is uneven, with some good scenes. Camera doesn't favor the gals nor enhance their s. a. Picture looks like the filmization of a psychoanalytical novel more than an original written for the screen. Louis Salou convincingly handles the poor simpleton who gets licked by the menace, Francois Perier, in his love attempt. Perier, as the heartbreaker, is decidedly authenic, while the boys handle their parts commendably. The sets are okay and the incidental music efficient support in places. *Maxi.*

Une Jeune Fille Savait
(A Girl Knew)
(FRENCH)

Paris, April 12.

P. C. release of Royalty (Maurice Lehmann) film production. Directed by Lehmann. Adapted by Michel Duran from play by Andre Haguet. Music by Philippe Pares. Stars Andre Luguet, Francois Perier, Dany Robin. At Marignan, Paris. Running time, 94 MINS.

Bernard Levaison..............Andre Luguet
Coco..........................Francois Perier
Jacqueline....................F. Christophe
Corinne.......................Dany Robin
Nurse.........................Suzanne Despres

The legiter on which this is based was written by Andre Haguet while in a German prison camp and produced without his seeing it. It was a hit, and the screen comedy is likely to gross heavily due to the excellent Luguet-Perier starring combo as well as to the human interest story.

Andre Luguet is introduced as a middle-aged matinee idol whose son Francois Perier is engaged to Dany Robin. When Luguet, a widower, is jilted by one of his friends, he sours on all women, and induces his son to wrong Miss Robin. Complex romantic scenes end, however, in a happy finish, with a repentant father. The story doesn't drag and builds up nicely to its climax. Acting is good.

Michel Duran's script has retained the best lines of the legiter. Bits handled by the supporting cast are in keeping with the leading player's work. *Maxi.*

Assunta Spina
(ITALIAN)

Rome, April 15.

Titanus release of Ora production. Stars Anna Magnani; features Antonio Centa, Eduardo and Titina De Filippo. Directed by Mario Mattoli. Screenplay, Eduardo De Filippo from play by Salvatore Di Giacomo; camera, Gabor Pogany; music, Renzo Rossellini; editor, Fernando Tropea. At Corso, Moderno and Margherita, Rome. Running time, 79 MINS.

Assunta Spina.................Anna Magnani
Michele Boccadifuoco...Eduardo De Filippo
Federico Funelli..............Antonio Centa
Emilia Forcinelli.........Titina De Filippo

Salvatore Di Giacomo's "Assunta Spina" got on to the Italian stage in 1910, first as a Neapolitan vernacular play, then turned into Italian by the author himself. It is now considered a classic of the Italian theatre. Filmization, handled by Mario Mattoli with care, takes on the importance of a celebration. In U. S., pic may do well for art houses and Italian-born audiences. For Latin-American market, its values are terrific.

Plot is built around a typical Neapolitan love vendetta. Blackmail, infidelity, murder, all figure in a story that has the elementary lines of a classic tragedy, but is quite understandable only to a Latin public. Its chief fault is a miscast Eduardo De Filippo. Considering Anna Magnani's maturity, the role of her jealous lover couldn't be assigned to a boy, but De Filippo is too aged and in spite of his thesping ability, lacks fire for such a torrid character.

Opposite him, Miss Magnani is superb. She wraps up the film with her tremendous personality, creating an intensely moving portrayal of a wretched woman. She's well photographed here, to look a real beauty. Titina De Filippo gives a colorful characterization of the go-between, and Antonio Centa plays the unpleasant role of the cheat cleverly.

Renzo Rossellini's score combines popular Neapolitan themes with dramatic musical effects. Camera work by Gabor Pogany, sets by Piero Filippone, costumes by Gino Sensani are okay. *Quat.*

Amanti Senza Amore
(Lovers Without Love)
(ITALIAN)

Rome, April 15.

Lux Film release of Carlo Ponti production. Stars Clara Calamai, Roldano Lupi, Jean Servais. Directed by Gianni Franciolini. Screenplay by Vittorio Novarese, Gianna Manzini, Guido Piovene, Antonio Pietrangeli and Gianni Franciolii from Tolstoy's "Kreutzer Sonanta"; camera, Carlo Montuori; music, Nino Rota. At Rivoli, Rome. Running time, 76 MINS.

Doctor Leonardi...............Roldano Lupi
Elena.........................Clara Calamai
Henry Miller..................Jean Servais

This modernized adaptation of Tolstoy's "Kreutzer Sonata" is a fine attempt to get Italian cinema away from the usual realism. It combines a risque psychological study with polemics on divorce. Film has many possibilities for good exploitation in art houses.

Pic is a story of an unhappy marriage. A reputed doctor (Rolano Lupi) kills his wife (Clara Calamai). Then, meeting with her lover, a well-known violinist (Jean Servais), he talks over the story with him, and what caused it—incompatibility, misunderstanding, and, above all, a love which was merely sensuality. His marriage with Elena was a blind alley, from which the woman tried to escape first by attempted suicide, and then through adultery. Film ends with doctor shooting himself near Elena's corpse. *Quat.*

Foreign Films

"Tuhottu Nuoruus' (Destroyed Youths) **(FINNISH-MADE).** Adams Filmi production and release. Stars Helena Kara, Kullervo Kalske; features Henny Valjus, Paavo Jannes, Lea Lampi, Sasu Haapanene, Sylva Rossi, Hannes Hayrinen, Enni Rekola. Directed by Hannu Leminen. Screenplay, Martta Salmela-Jarvinen; camera, Armas Hirvonen; music, George de Godzinsky. At Bio-Bio and Rex, Helsinki. Running time, 74 MINS.

Finland, as with other countries, has its juve problem. In this film the producers have tried to analyze some of them. With a social story as plot, picture has developed into one of the better Finnish pix made in several years. Acting and fine technical credits contrib greatly in upping the film's quality.

"Maaret, Tunturien Tyttö" ("Maaret, Daughter of the Mountains") **(FINNISH).** Suomi Filmi production and release. Stars Eila Pehkonen, Sakari Jurkka; features Ale Porkka, Ester Lindgren, Olavi Reimas, Hilkka Helina, William Markus. Directed by Valentin Vaala. Screen play, Usko Kempil; camera, Eino Heino. At Kaleva and Kino Palatsi, Helsinki. Running time, 82 MINS.

Excellent camera work in lensing some firstrate scenery of northern Finland boosts this Finnish film out of the Scandinavian mart and into the international field. Story is a romantic one which stems from Olavi Reimas' trip to the north country. He meets Eila Pehkonen and the couple are married. Supporting players turn in some good thesping. *Winq.*

"God's Angels Are Everywhere" ("Gottess Engel Sind Ueberall") **(AUSTRIAN).** Sacha Film Distributing Co. release of Unitas Film production. Stars Attila Hoerbiger, Heikie Eis; features Susi Niccoletti, Lotte Lang, Helene Thimig, Maria Eis, Gisa Wurm, Helli Servi, Ilse Hanel, Hans Putz. Directed by Hans Thimig. Screenplay, Peter Francke, Kurt Heuser; camera, Franz Hoffermann; editor, Henriette Bruensch; music, Anton Profes; sets, Werner Schlichting. At Apollo, Vienna. Running time, 90 MINS.

Well acted, this film is a pictorial account of a soldier's return to Vienna a few days before the end of the war. He encounters a young boy who also is bound for the same destination in search of his mother. It's a fine human interest plot which should garner interest of European audiences as well as filmgoers overseas. *Maas.*

Miniature Reviews

"The Iron Curtain" (20th). Timely and important expose of Soviet undercover activities; a cinch b.o. leader.

"Hamlet" (GFD). British-made classic, starring Laurence Olivier, is magnificent. Great prestige-builder and b.o.

"Fuller Brush Man" (Col). Red Skelton, Janet Blair in comic's best slapstick in years; okay boxoffice.

"So This New York" (UA). First pic for radio comic Henry Morgan is original, smart comedy for city slickers; good general b.o.

"Four Faces West" (UA). Joel McCrea, Frances Dee, Charles Bickford, Joseph Calleia in gripping western; strong b.o. entry.

"River Lady" (Color) (U). Outdoor meller of logging and gambling; average b.o.

"Port Said" (Col). Contrived melodrama of very modest interest. For fill-in bookings.

"Fighting Father Dunne" (RKO). Story of the St. Louis priest who made life easier for newsboys in the early 1900s. Pat O'Brien in title role; average b.o. outlook.

"Under California Stars" (Color-Songs) (Rep). One of the weaker Roy Rogers pix but still good for the oatune fans.

"Guns of Hate" (RKO). Action western with Tim Holt for Saturday matinee trade.

"Stage Struck" (Mono). Mild expose of fate awaiting stage-struck girls. Good story basis badly used. For secondaries.

"Sword of the Avenger" (Sepia) (EL). Sepiatone dressing to so-so cloak and dagger okay for duallers.

"Whirlwind Raiders" (Songs) (Col). Standard Charles Starrett oatuner in Durango Kid series; limited b.o.

"Campus Sleuth" (Mono). Moderately entertaining entry in Monogram's Teenager series. For secondary bookings.

The Iron Curtain

Hollywood, May 8.

20th-Fox release of Darryl F. Zanuck (Sol C. Siegel) production. Stars Dana Andrews, Gene Tierney; features June Havoc, Berry Kroeger, Edna Best, Stefan Schnabel, Nicholas Joy, Eduard Franz, Frederic Tozere. Directed by William A. Wellman. Screenplay, Milton Krims; based on the personal story of Igor Gouzenko, former code clerk, U.S.S.R. Embassy in Ottawa, Canada; camera, Charles G. Clarke; music from selected works of Soviet composers, Dmitri Shostakovich, Serge Prokofieff, Aram Katchaturian, Nicolas Miaskovsky; conducted by Alfred Newman; editor, Louis Loeffler. Tradeshown May 6, '48. Running time, **88 MINS.**

Igor Gouzenko....................Dana Andrews
Anna Gouzenko....................Gene Tierney
Karanova....................June Havoc
Grubb....................Berry Kroeger
Mrs. Foster....................Edna Best
Ranev....................Stefan Schnabel
Dr. Norman....................Nicholas Joy
Major Kulin....................Eduard Franz
Col. Trigorin....................Frederic Tozere
Bushkin....................Noel Cravat
Andrei..........Christopher Robin Olsen
Winikov....................Peter Whitney
Editor....................Leslie Barrie
Leonard Leetz....................Mauritz Hugo
Sergeyev....................John Shay
Captain Class....................Victor Wood
Helen Tweedy....................Anne Curson
Mrs. Kulin....................Helena Dare
Mrs. Trigorin....................Eula Morgan
Commentator....................Reed Hadley
Policeman....................John Ridgeley

The documentary screen technique reaches the heights of timeliness in "The Iron Curtain." Telling a true story with implications important to every American, film comes off as a boxoffice winner that should fill the tills of every theatre playing it. Factually dealing with Soviet undercover activities in Canada where atomic bomb secrets were thefted, picture is a corking spy melodrama. In fact, it would have rated a large b.o. payoff on that count alone, even without the timeliness and importance of its news story.

Footage is crammed with eye-opening details of Soviet treachery and the suspense mounts to tingling levels as the expose is unfolded. Story is the personal one of Igor Gouzenko, former code clerk in the U.S.S.R. Embassy in Ottawa. A devoted Communist when he arrives at his new post, Gouzenko is gradually aware of what it means to live without fear and, to help insure his son's future, exposes the Soviet spy network to the world in a story that filled newspapers' front pages in 1946. Gouzenko, his wife and son still live in Canada, under the protection of its government, but still in fear of Red reprisals.

High credit goes to all involved in filming this one. Sol C. Siegel's production realistically values the case history report on which Milton Krims based his screenplay and, at the same time, has insured showmanly qualities of the story, essentially a spy melodrama.

William A. Wellman's direction carries out documentary technique, pointing up factual material and the dramatic values by never permitting a scene to be overplayed. Stress on underplaying and the absence of obvious meller tricks goes a long way in adding to realistic air with which the film is imbued.

Dana Andrews does one of his best jobs as Gouzenko, making the character as real on the screen as it is in life. Gene Tierney is fine as his wife, who first becomes aware of the deadend that Communism leads to. June Havoc, Soviet spy, has little to do. Berry Groeger portrays the notorious Grubb, Red secret agent, and it is the only theatrical performance in the cast. Splendid work is contributed by Eduard Franz as the Soviet major who becomes sickened of his country's policies. Edna Best, Stefan Schnabel, Nicholas Joy, as the atomic scientist who aided the Commies; Frederic Tozere, Peter Whitney, Mauritz Hugo are among the others that help put the factual stamp on the picture. Wisely, there has been no attempt to have the dialog accented, contributing to reality.

The Darryl F. Zanuck presentation draws on the music of four Soviet composers to highlight the excellent score conducted by Alfred Newman. Charles G. Clarke's photography documents the story expertly. Exterior scenes were filmed on actual sites in Ottawa. Louis Loeffler's editing has held the picture to a crisp 88 minutes without sacrificing any story values.

Brog.

Hamlet
(BRITISH)

London, May 5.

GFD release of J. Arthur Rank-Two Cities production. Stars Laurence Olivier; features Basil Sydney, Eileen Herlie, Jean Simmons, Felix Aylmer. Directed by Olivier. Editor, Helga Cranston; music, William Walton; camera, Desmond Dickinson. At Odeon, London, May 4, '48. Running time, **155 MINS.**

Hamlet....................Laurence Olivier
The Queen....................Eileen Herlie
The King....................Basil Sydney
Horatio....................Norman Wooland
Polonius....................Felix Aylmer
Laertes....................Terence Morgan
Ophelia....................Jean Simmons
Osric....................Peter Cushing
Gravedigger....................Stanley Holloway
Francisco....................John Laurie
Priest....................Russell Thorndike
Bernardo....................Esmond Knight
Marcellus....................Anthony Quale
Sea Captain....................Niall Macginnis
First Player....................Harcourt Williams
Player King....................Patrick Troughton
Player Queen....................Tony Tarver

This is picture-making at its best, and its showing must be done with the dignity it deserves. Exhibs should profit from the handling of "Henry V" and should be warned that "Hamlet" is rich in qualities that don't readily blend with the usual ballyhoo. At a cost of $2,000,000 it seems incredibly cheap compared with some of the ephemeral trash that is being turned out, and it will earn profit as well as prestige for its makers.

Star-producer-director Laurence Olivier was the driving force behind the whole venture. His confidence and energy infected those around him and resulted in the teamwork which has produced one of the most memorable films ever to come from a British studio. Minor characters and a good deal of verse have been thrown overboard, and a four-and-a-quarter hour play becomes a two-and-a-half hour film. But this speeding and tightening has in no way impaired the artistic integrity of the play.

Pundits may argue that Rosencrantz, Guildenstern and Fortinbras shouldn't have been sacrificed, and that many familiar gems are missing. They will argue about the bewildering crossing and intercrossing of motives. Scholars may complain that this isn't Hamlet as Shakespeare created him, but one that Olivier has made in his own image. The multitude of questions will remain unanswered, but that won't prevent audiences from getting maximum enjoyment and an appreciation of a story that hitherto may have been obscure to millions.

In his interpretation of Hamlet, Olivier thinks of him as nearly a great man, damned, as most people are, by lack of resolution. He announces it in a spoken foreword as "the tragedy of a man who couldn't make up his mind." Olivier's "Hamlet" isn't in a class apart. He's neither a petulant poppycock nor a moody Dane suffering from an Oedipus complex. His dreams, his thoughts, his eternal questioning to which he can find no answer, are a natural part of the sensitive, educated man Olivier makes him.

Stage performances of "Hamlet" invariably succeed or fail on the interpretation of the title part, but this film—although naturally dominated by Olivier—will also be judged as a whole, and not merely on the star's great performance. Every character has been cast with meticulous care and for the most part the company of trained dramatic stage actors, with a capacity for wearing costume to the manner born, gives a perfect performance.

Special praise is due Eileen Herlie for her playing of the Queen. She has made the character really live. Her love for her son, the consciousness of evil-doing, her grief and agony, her death—made by Olivier to appear as sacrificing herself for Hamlet—make her a very memorable, pitiful figure. It was an experiment to cast Jean Simmons as Ophelia. This part, about which critics have wrangled for years, will still give cause for argument, but she does bring to the role a sensitive, impressionable innocence, perhaps too childlike.

Basil Sydney repeats his stage success as the King, of whom ambition and lust have taken possession, and rises to his greatest height in his soliloquy trying to pray and seeing himself accursed like Cain. Felix Aylmer is a tremendous Polonius, giving true value to his famous verses, and embodying the perfect busybody. As Laertes, Terence Morgan is the complete foil to Olivier's Hamlet; Norman Wooland is understandably Hamlet's best friend; Harcourt Williams represents the First Player as though in need of Hamlet's advice, and Stanley Holloway makes the Gravedigger human and humorous. Utterances of the Ghost are at times unintelligible.

Olivier's conception of "Hamlet" as an engraving has been beautifully executed by Roger Furse and Carmen Dillon. Sets have been planned as abstractions and so serve to point the timelessness of the period. The story takes place any time in the remote past. This conception has dominated the lighting and camera work and has made the deep-focus photography an outstanding feature of the film.

With no use for the static camera, Olivier has aimed for speed and action. The final duel scene is a masterpiece of production. The famous soliloquies—most of the lines represented as thoughts, here and there a line actually spoken—are spoken in movement. With bold use of crane shots Olivier moves the action about ancient Elsinore with technical skill. Everything was done in the Denham studios. Elsinore Castle was there, Ophelia died in the tiny stream of the studio grounds, yet the keynote is always grandeur and spaciousness.

Music of William Walton for his third Shakespearean film ("As You Like It," "Henry V") is inspired and dramatic, and always in sympathy with the story. He's made an integral contribution to the film.

Cane.

Fuller Brush Man

Columbia release of Edward Small production, produced and directed by S. Sylvan. Stars Red Skelton, Janet Blair; features Don McGuire, Hillary Brooke, Adele Jergens, Ross Ford. Screenplay, Frank Tashlin, Devery Freeman, based on story by Roy Huggins; camera, Lester White; editor, Al Clark; music, Heinz Roemheld. Previewed N. Y., April 20, '48. Running time, **92 MINS.**

Red Jones....................Red Skelton
Ann Elliot....................Janet Blair
Keenan Wallick....................Don McGuire
Mrs. Trist....................Hillary Brooke
Miss Sharmley....................Adele Jergens
Freddie Trist....................Ross Ford
Sara Franzen....................Trudy Marshall
Commissioner Trist....................Nicholas Joy
Gregory Cruckston....................Donald Curtis
Lieutenant Quint....................Arthur Space
Henry Seward....................Selmer Jackson
Detective Foster....................Roger Moore
Detective Ferguson....................Stanley Andrews
Jiggers....................Bud Wolfe
Skitch....................David Sharpe
Blackie....................Chick Collins
Herman....................Billy Jones
Chauffeur....................Jimmy Lloyd
Butler....................Jimmy Logan
Junior....................Jimmy Hunt

In "Fuller Brush Man," producer Edward Small has done for Red Skelton what Metro hasn't been able to accomplish in the last couple of years. Film marks the comedian's best offering since his early break-in days on the Culver City lot. It should do okay in almost any situation. Janet Blair's name on the marquee won't hurt either.

In addition to being highly entertaining slapstick from the Mack Sennett school, interlaced with a mild dose of murder mystery, the film also represents a terrific running commercial for Fuller brushes. That theme is carried to such an extent, in fact, that a brush turns up as the murder weapon in the picture.

S. Sylvan Simon, who produced and directed for Small, wisely

gave the comic a chance to strut almost every mugging trick and routine for which he's become known, and Skelton milked practi-cally every line and situation for maximum comedy. Result is a film that builds into a free-for-all finale that should have the customers guffawing. Tighter editing would help the first half of the picture considerably, but the slam-bang denouement more than compensates for the earlier mildness. Illustrative of the film's general zaniness is one sequence in which Skelton, as a door-to-door brush salesman, runs up against the nasty little "junior" character that he himself plays on his radio show.

Story, scripted by Frank Tashlin and Devery Freeman from an original by Roy Huggins, is divided almost perceptibly in half. First part attempts to delineate Skelton's attempts as a ne'er-do-well zany to prove he can make good at selling brushes to win the hand of Miss Blair. Film really generates steam, though, when it rolls into the second half, where Skelton is present in his brush-selling role at a society murder and gets tagged for the crime. Released, but still under suspicion, he and Miss Blair set out to track down the killers. Free-for-all comes in a hilarious finale, where the pair are trapped by the killers in a war surplus goods warehouse and run the thugs a wild chase through rubber rafts, camouflage sets, pre-fab houses, etc.

Although Skelton carries the film almost single-handedly, he's given a good assist by the rest of the cast, working under Simon's light directorial touch. Miss Blair makes a winsome heroine and works the helter-skelter finale neatly. Don McGuire is smoothly repugnant as the competition for Miss Blair's affections, and Hillary Brooke is beauteous as woman of mystery. Adele Jergens turns in a nice bit as a sexy customer for Skelton's brushes.

From the looks of the sets, the film is a medium-budgeter but nothing more spectacular is called for. Other production credits are all good. *Stal.*

So This Is New York

United Artists release of Enterprise (Stanley Kramer) production. Stars Henry Morgan; features Rudy Vallee, Hugh Herbert, Bill Goodwin, Leo Gorcey, Jerome Cowan. Directed by Richard O. Fleischer. Screenplay by Carl Foreman and Herbert Baker; based on novel "The Big Town," by Ring Lardner; camera, Jack Russell; editor, Walter Thompson; music, Dimitri Tiomkin. Tradeshown N. Y. May 6, '48. Running time, 79 MINS.

Ernie Finch....................Henry Morgan
Herbert Daley....................Rudy Vallee
Jimmy Ralston....................Bill Goodwin
Mr. Trumbull....................Hugh Herbert
Sid Mercer....................Leo Gorcey
Ella Finch....................Virginia Grey
Kate Goff....................Dona Drake
Francis Griffin....................Jerome Cowan
Willis Gilbey....................Dave Willock
A. J. Gluskoter....................Frank Orth
Western Union Clark....................Arnold Stang
Hotel Clerk....................William Bakewell

"So This Is New York" is a promising pushoff for the new production outfit, Screen Plays, headed by Stanley Kramer and George Glass. Pic (launched under the Enterprise studio banner after a complicated series of financial maneuvers) is a fast mix of subtle gags and brittle situations jelled by ingenious direction into a neat and novel comedy.

This offering may be a sleeper. But its novelty is likely to cut both ways with plenty of word-of-mouth in more sophisticated circles and plenty of wonderment about what's going on out in the hinterlands. Yet, even though this film's impact may be greater on the critics than at the boxoffice, it should garner good returns with a bright selling campaign.

The marquee strategy will have to be based almost exclusively on Henry Morgan, radio comic who hereby makes his debut as a film personality. He won't disappoint his air fans by his screen comedics. His drollery is still acid, varying between wryness and nastiness, and his nonchalance is left unperturbed by the cameras. Within a narrow range of demands, Morgan displays an expert thesping talent that warrants additional Hollywood tries. But Morgan sums up the pic's b.o. question mark. With the nation's dialers split into two irreconcilable camps of pro and anti-Morganites, the comedian's Hooperating may be a gauge of his drawing power. Currently, the rating is only fair.

Based on a Ring Lardner story about some hicks who are taken in the big city, pic's yarn is a wide-open scaffold for the New York misadventures of Morgan, his wife (Virginia Grey), and his marriageable sister-in-law (Dona Drake). Although strung together like gags in a radio script, the situations roll at top speed, sparkling with originality and only deftly dropping the laughs instead of hammering them.

Funniest sequence is set at a racetrack where some jockeys who have fixed the main event whip home the opposition horse. A brilliant touch is added as Morgan steps out of Grand Central upon his arrival and encounters a sample of New Yorkese from a local cabbie. Subtitles, translating the lingo into American, are printed underneath, a la the European films. Director Richard O. Fleischer has crammed the film with this type of suggestive comedy but doesn't belabor his points. Sometimes, it would have been wiser to have done so for the general run of filmgoers.

Although a medium-budgeter, the pic's coin was spent in the right places for script and thespers with only a minimum laid out for backgrounds and setting. Case in point is the firstrate group of supporting players for Morgan.

Rudy Vallee cuts another notch in his belt with a superlative portrait of a far-western track tycoon. Leo Gorcey, as a crooked jock, puts his "Dead End Kids" training to use for an hilarious drunk act. Hugh Herbert, Jerome Cowan and Bill Goodwin also score in brief roles. Arnold Stang, Morgan's sidekick on the radio, punches over the single scene in which he appears.

Editing job of integrating stock shots of New York circa 1920 is handled flawlessly. Camera work is top grade while Dimitri Tiomkin's score has a fanciful touch to match the film's outlook and quality. *Herm.*

Four Faces West

United Artists release of Harry Sherman production. Stars Joel McCrea, Frances Dee, Charles Bickford; features Joseph Calleia, William Conrad, Martin Garralaga, Raymond Largay. Directed by Alfred E. Green. Screenplay, Graham Baker and Teddi Sherman, from novel and Sat. Evening Post story, "Pasco Por Aqui," by Eugene Manlove Rhodes; adaptation by William and Milarde Brent; camera, Russell Harland; editor, Edward Mann; special effects, Robert H. Moreland. Tradeshown in N. Y., May 7, '48. Running time, 96 MINS.

Ross McEwen....................Joel McCrea
Fay Hollister....................Frances Dee
Pat Garrett....................Charles Bickford
Monte....................Joseph Calleia
Sheriff Egan....................William Conrad
Florencio....................Martin Garralaga
Dr. Eldredge....................Raymond Largay
Frenger....................John Parrish
Clint Waters....................Dan White
Burnett....................Davison Clark
Anderson....................Houseley Stevenson
Winston Boy....................George McDonald
Mrs. Winston....................Eva Novak
Storekeeper....................Sam Flint
Conductor No. 2....................Forrest Taylor

"Four Faces West" shapes up as a strong grosser in most spots. Literal adaptation of the novel, "Paso Por Aqui," makes for a highly satisfactory western meller, which gets a nice boxoffice boost from having Joel McCrea, Frances Dee, Charles Bickford and Joseph Calleia in the top roles. Add to that excellent production values, scripting and directing.

A cross-section of New Mexico pioneer days, yarn concerns itself with the reformation of a cowboy turned bank robber to help his father from losing a ranch. It has an neat blend of manhunt and romance.

McCrea is at home as the outlaw who's ultimately reformed.

Calleia, as the Mexican saloonkeeper, is outstanding though his is more or less a subsidiary character. Bickford plays an understanding U. S. marshal. Miss Dee (Mrs. McCrea in real life) contributes one of her better roles as the railway company nurse, sharing the romance with McCrea. William Conrad and Martin Garralaga top the big and capable supporting cast.

Russell Harland's camera has successfully taken in the broad sweep of the western plains. And editing by Edward Mann is sharp. *Wear.*

River Lady
(Color-Song)
Hollywood, May 7.

Universal release of Leonard Goldstein production. Stars Yvonne DeCarlo, Dan Duryea, Rod Cameron, Helena Carter; features Lloyd Gough, Florence Bates. Directed by George Sherman. Screenplay, D. D. Beauchamp, William Bowers; from novel by Houston Branch; camera (Technicolor), Irving Glassberg; music, Paul Sawtell; song, Walter Schumann, Jack Brooks; editor, Otto Ludwig. Previewed May 4, '48. Running time, 77 MINS.

Sequin....................Yvonne DeCarlo
Beauvais....................Dan Duryea
Dan Corrigan....................Rod Cameron
Stephanie....................Helena Carter
Mike....................Lloyd Gough
Ma Dunnigan....................Florence Bates
Mr. Morrison....................John McIntire
Swede....................Jack Lambert
Mrs. Morrison....................Esther Somers
Esther....................Anita Turner
Rider....................Edmund Cobb
Bouncer....................Dewey Robinson
Hewitt....................Eddy C. Waller
Limpy....................Milton Kibbee
Dealer....................Billy Wayne
Logger....................Jimmy Ames
Executive....................Edward Earle

"River Lady" is a brawling outdoor melodrama with average boxoffice returns in sight. A logging camp yarn, with a gambling boat thrown in for good measure, feature stresses outdoor muscle flexing by male cast toppers. Action is garbed in Technicolor, giving it added b.o. value, and production otherwise supplies good backing to make it satisfactory for the outdoor film fan.

Plenty of footage of forest logging activities, logjams and river shots are included for interest. These, coupled with some good hand-to-hand fight stuff, keep the emphasis on action. Latter is needed since story never builds too strongly on suspense angles.

Plot deals with rich gambling gal who tries to buy the love of an independent logger. She sets him up in business by a ruse and things look good for romance until he finds out. Piqued, he marries another girl and the gambling lady sets out to ruin him. She nearly succeeds but right triumphs. Yarn follows a fairly familiar formula but hard-working cast and George Sherman's direction keep it unfolding at fast pace.

Choicest role falls to Helena Carter as the gal whom Rod Cameron marries. Her character has zip and is brightly dialoged, and she whams it over with a style that gives plenty of lift to the proceedings. Yvonne DeCarlo has heavier going as the gambling lady but has been gorgeously costumed in period style for male appeal.

Rod Cameron makes a virile hero, handy with fists or lovemaking, and pleases. Dan Duryea turns in some strong villainry with accustomed assurance. Lloyd Gough is good as Cameron's sidekick and Florence Bates and John McIntire are among the capable supporting players.

A bright spot in picture is the score's single tune, "Louis Sands and Jim McGee" by Walter Schumann and Jack Brooks. Number has infectious beat and Miss DeCarlo gives the lumberjack jingle neat delivery. While without pop sale value, tune fits perfectly into the story. Leonard Goldstein's production guidance supplied excellent lensing by Irving Glassberg, tight editing and numerous sight values that help. *Brog.*

Port Said
Hollywood, May 8.

Columbia release of Wallace MacDonald production. Features Gloria Henry, William Bishop, Steven Geray, Edgar Barrier, Richard Hale, Ian MacDonald, Blanche Zobar. Directed by Reginald LeBorg. Screenplay, Brenda Weisberg; story, Louis Pollock; camera, Allen Siegler; editor, Richard Fantl. Reviewed at Guild, Hollywood, May 7, '48. Running time, 66 MINS.

Gila Lingallo / Helena Guistano....................Gloria Henry
Leslie Sears....................William Bishop
Alexis Tacca....................Steven Geray
The Great Lingallo....................Edgar Barrier
Mario Guistano....................Richard Hale
Jakoll....................Ian MacDonald
Thymesta....................Blanche Zohar
Bunny Beacham....................Robin Hughes
Taufik....................Jay Novello
Carlo....................Ted Hecht
Lt. Zaki....................Lester Sharpe
Hotel Porter....................Martin Garralaga

"Port Said" is a contrived melodrama that will find a modest payoff in lower rung bookings. Script is dull and isn't given much of a lift by production, direction or playing.

Picture concerns itself with search of a man and his daughter for the people responsible for death of the mother during war in Italy when the Nazis and Fascists ruled. Locale is the Egyptian port of the title but doesn't add a particularly colorful background, productionwise.

Gloria Henry plays both the good daughter and the femme heavy and she fares a bit better in the latter characterization. She and Edgar Barrier, as the father, come to Port Said to hunt down some pro-Fascist in-laws and William Bishop is drawn into the plot when a friend is murdered. Another friend is bumped off before Bishop can get the clues in proper order and disclose the villainous Miss Henry for the heavy she is, along with Steven Geray, Richard Hale and Ian MacDonald as cohorts in the dirty work.

Reginald LeBorg's direction is short on the action needed to bring off the melodrama. Best technical credit on the Wallace MacDonald production is camera work by Allen Siegler. *Brog.*

Fighting Father Dunne

Hollywood, May 8.

RKO release of Phil L. Ryan production. Stars Pat O'Brien; features Darryl Hickman, Charles Kemper, Una O'Connor, Arthur Shields, Harry Shannon, Joe Sawyer, Anna Q. Nilsson, Donn Gift, Myrna Dell. Directed by Ted Tetzlaff. Screenplay, Martin Rackin, Frank Davis; story, William Rankin; camera, George E. Diskant; music, Roy Webb; editor, Frederic Knudtson. Tradeshown May 6, '48. Running time, 92 MINS.

Father Dunne	Pat O'Brien
Matt Davis	Darryl Hickman
Emmett Mulvey	Charles Kemper
Miss O'Rourke	Una O'Connor
Mr. O'Donnell	Arthur Shields
John Lee	Harry Shannon
Steve Davis	Joe Sawyer
Mrs. Knudson	Anna Q. Nilsson
Jimmy	Donn Gift
Paula	Myrna Dell
Kate Mulvey	Ruth Donnelly
Danny Briggs	Jim Nolan
Tony	Billy Cummings
Chip	Billy Gray
Monk	Eric Roberts
Lefty	Gene Collins
Archbishop	Lester Matthews
Governor	Griff Barnett
Sonin	Jason Robards
Soloist	Rudy Whistler

"Fighting Father Dunne" is an inspirational piece dealing with the priest's work with St. Louis newsboys early in the 20th century. There's a lot of hoke, humor and heart tugs to make it an okay entry for general situations and the family trade, with average b.o. returns indicated.

Pat O'Brien does an excellent job of making the priest warm and human, and the story carries satisfactory interest in detailing how Father Dunne was inspired to better the lives of newsboys when he found one sick and freezing in a packing case home. Uphill fight for funds, the newsboys' fight for good corners, the inevitable bad boy who reforms at the finale, and other details are unfolded leisurely in the Phil L. Ryan production.

Interest is achieved mainly by the little tricks to which the priest resorts to carry out his aims, and the good hearts of most of the people he approaches. There's plenty of humor in the daily situations faced by Dunne and his boys and these chuckles are abetted by good work of Charles Kemper, Una O'Connor and Arthur Shields.

Darryl Hickman heads the younger troupe of players as the bad boy who finally turns to God on the eve of hanging for a murder he didn't mean to commit. Donn Gift is another who stands out among youngsters. Anna Q. Nilsson has one sharp scene that impresses. Myrna Dell, Jim Nolan, Harry Shannon, Joe Sawyer, Jason Robards are among others contributing capable performances.

Ted Tetzlaff's direction makes good use of the script material furnished by Martin Rackin and Frank Davis from a story by William Rankin, although pace is a bit on the leisurely side. Lensing by George E. Diskant, art direction, settings, and other technical credits are standard. *Brog.*

Under California Stars

(SONGS-COLOR)

Republic release of Edward J. White production. Stars Roy Rogers; features Jane Frazee, Andy Devine, Sons of the Pioneers. Directed by William Witney. Screenplay, Sloan Nibley and Paul Gangelin, based on original story by Gangelin; camera, Jack Marta; editor, Tony Martinelli. Tradeshown N.Y., May 5, '48. Running time, 70 mins.

Roy Rogers	Roy Rogers
Caroline Maynard	Jane Frazee
Cookie Bullfincher	Andy Devine
Jonas "Pop" Jordan	George H. Lloyd
Lye McFarland	Wade Crosby
Ted Conover	Michael Chapin
Ed	House Peters, Jr.
Sheriff	Steve Clark
Joe	Joseph Garro
Director	Paul Power
Announcer	John Wald

Bon Nolan & Sons of the Pioneers

Republic hasn't done right by Roy Rogers in this one. "Under California Stars" represents one of his weakest jobs though it's still okay for anybody's Saturday matinee trade, since Rogers' name continues to be a magic lure for the kids.

Film suffers mostly from poor camera and editing. Use of a double for Rogers' trick horsemounting is easily apparent, and use of a dummy to double for one of the villains kicked in the face by Trigger, Rogers' horse, is also easily discernible.

Otherwise, the film is the usual shootin' match, straining at credulity. This one has Rogers and his Double-R cowhands mixing it with a gang of rustlers, who kidnap the famous Trigger and hold it for $100,000 ransom. Crippled kid who Rogers befriends is apparently in cahoots with the rustlers, but in the end it's he who saves the day, and Rogers and Trigger are reunited.

Rogers plays the hero in his usual offhanded manner, handling the acting, fighting and singing chores neatly. Jane Frazee is a good replacement for Dale Evans (who's now Mrs. Rogers). Andy Devine is sufficiently funny for the comedy relief, and George H. Lloyd and Wade Crosby make a couple of dastardly bad guys. Bob Nolan and the Sons of the Pioneers are along to break into song at the slightest provocation. Trigger, along with some unidentified pooch, acquit themselves well.

Film was lensed in Republic's Trucolor, which doesn't show well in this one. Process runs too much to blues, which makes it tough on the eyes. *Stal.*

Guns of Hate

Hollywood, May 7.

RKO release of Herman Schlom production. Stars Tim Holt; features Nan Leslie, Richard Martin, Steve Brodie, Myrna Dell, Tony Barrett. Directed by Lesley Selander. Screenplay, Norman Houston, Ed Earl Repp; camera, George E. Diskant; editor, Desmond Marquette. Tradeshown May 3, '48. Running time, 61 MINS.

Bob	Tim Holt
Judy	Nan Leslie
Chito	Richard Martin
Morgan	Steve Brodie
Dixie	Myrna Dell
Wyatt	Tony Barrett
Sheriff	Jim Nolan
Ben Jason	Jason Robards
Rocky	Robert Bray
Mabel	Marilyn Mercer

"Guns of Hate" follows the expected pattern set by previous Tim Holt westerns and, as such, will fulfill release aims in the oater market. It has been given good production, story and direction to take care of outdoor action demands, but its many good points are neutralized to some extent by lack of spectacular stunts and some of the worst shooting yet demonstrated by a western hero.

An essential of western plots is a definite cleavage between good and bad and a hero that is a marksman without peer. Holt rides through this one aimlessly banging away like a kid playing cowboy and Indians in the street. The lack of marksmanship will be unfavorably noticed by moppet patrons.

Holt and his sidekick, Richard Martin, appear on the scene in time to be accused of murdering Jason Robards, discoverer of a long-lost goldmine. Heavies Steve Brodie and Tony Barrett did the killing to secure Robards' map to the treasure and the heroes are forced to break jail and dodge the sheriff while they attempt to link the baddies with the murder. After sufficient chases and much footage of aimless "bang-bang" Holt and Martin corner the killers and justice is done.

Holt makes a good appearance and chuckles are well taken care of by Martin as the amorous Chito. Nan Leslie and Myrna Dell supply slight romantic touches. Brodie and Barrett are excellent heavies, and Jim Nolan is a capable sheriff.

Lesley Selander directed the Herman Schlom production, keeping it on the move. Good camera work was turned in by George E. Diskant, displaying outdoor backgrounds for full value. *Brog.*

Stage Struck

Hollywood, May 8.

Monogram release of Jeffrey Bernerd production. Stars Kane Richmond, Audrey Long, Conrad Nagel, Ralph Byrd; features John Gallaudet, Anthony Warde, Pamela Blake. Directed by William Nigh. Screenplay, George Wallace Sayre, Agnes Christine Johnson; original story, Sayre; camera, Harry Neumann; editor, William Austin. Previewed, May 7, '48. Running time, 71 mins.

Nick Mantee	Kane Richmond
Nancy Howard	Audrey Long
Lt. Williams	Conrad Nagel
Sgt. Tom Rainey	Ralph Byrd
Benny Nordick	John Gallaudet
Mr. Barda	Anthony Warde
Janet Winters	Pamela Blake
Capt. Webb	Charles Trowbridge
Mrs. Howard	Nana Bryant
Mr. Howard	Selmer Jackson
Miss Lloyd	Evelyn Brent
Helen Howard	Wanda McKay
Ruth Ames	Jacqueline Thomas
Prof. Corella	Wilbur Mack

"Stage Struck" had a chance to be a sturdy expose of dangers lurking for girls yearning for stardom, but producer, director and writers failed to make the most of their opportunities. The results are dull, slating this one of lower billing in the secondaries.

Jeffrey Bernerd has achieved some good physical production values, but misses on guidance otherwise. William Nigh's direction paces it slowly and his development is never quite adequate for the melodrama demands. Scripting by George Wallace Sayre and Agnes Christine Johnston, from Sayre's original, fills players' mouths with trite, cumbersome dialog and completely fails to realize on okay essentials in the original yarn.

Plot deals with police efforts to track down the killer of a young girl who had taken her stagestruck ideas to Broadway in search of stardom. Police work gradually discloses a phony agency where stagestruck dreams are fattened, and a nightclub where girls eventually end up as customer conveniences. There are some complications when the dead girl's sister turns amateur detective but police put everything right for finale and turn to the next missing girl case.

Conrad Nagel and Audrey Long try very hard to give their assignments some lift but are often thrown by the clumsy dialog and situations. Kane Richmond and John Gallaudet share the heavy assignments and Ralph Byrd is Conrad's aide. Others are adequate, also.

On technical side, credits are good, from the lensing by Harry Neumann through art direction, settings and editing. *Brog.*

Sword of the Avenger

(SEPIA)

Eagle-Lion release of Sidney Salkow production, directed by Salkow. Stars Ramon Del Gado, Sigrid Gurie; features Ralph Morgan, Duncan Renaldo. Screenplay, Julius Evans; camera (sepia), Clyde DeVinna; editor, Mel Thorsen; music, Eddison von Ottenfeld. Previewed N. Y. April 29, '48. Running time, 72 MINS.

Roberto Balagtas	Ramon Del Gado
Maria Louisa	Sigrid Gurie
Don Adolfo	Ralph Morgan
Fernando	Duncan Renaldo
Ming Tang	Leonard Strong
Ignacio	David Leonard
Rodrigo	Tim Huntley
Miguel	Trevor Bardette
Aunt	Belle Mitchell
Duke of Herrara	Lee Baker
Count Velasquez	Cy Kendall

Sepiatone, an infrequently used print process, gives "Sword of the Avenger" its most distinguishing feature. Otherwise it's a routine cloak-and-dagger opera that can provide a decorative lower line to theatre marquees in most situations.

The story is virtually a direct rewrite of "Count of Monte Cristo" with no credit to the original. Except for a change in locale and a few other items, the story unfolds in the same manner of the famed Dumas classic.

Locale is the Spanish-dominated Philippine Islands in the early 1800s, when Castillian noblemen ran the islands in a manner that invited resurrection. Ramon Del Gado is depicted as a sailor who is falsely imprisoned for a political crime and allowed to languish for an interminable period in a dungeon. With the aid of Ralph Morgan and Trevor Bardette, they tunnel their way to escape, with Del Gado getting possession of a treasure map. He ultimately retrieves the hoard and makes his way back to Manila to get his revenge on those that betrayed him.

Sigrid Gurie does well as the love interest as the girl whose wedding is postponed by Del Gado's arrest, and who spends the intervening time leading a band of guerillas.

The sepiatone process, as used here, gives added dramatic values to the outdoor shots but otherwise tends to slow the action sequences.

Sidney Salkow's pacing is good, but has permitted the cast to overact. The sepia lensing by Clyde DeVinna is of top cut as it the musical scoring by Eddison von Ottenfeld. *Jose.*

Whirlwind Raiders

(SONGS)

Columbia release of Colbert Clark production. Stars Charles Starrett, Smiley Burnette; features Fred Sears, Nancy Saunders, Little Brown Jug, Doye O'Dell and Radio Rangers. Directed by Vernon Keays. Screenplay, Norman Hall; camera, M. A. Andersen; editor, Paul Borofsky. At New York theatre, N. Y., week of May 4, '48. Running time, 54 MINS.

Steve Lanning / The Durango Kid	Charles Starrett
Smiley Burnette	Smiley Burnette
Tracy Beaumont	Fred Sears
Claire Ross	Nancy Saunders
Tommy Ross	Little Brown Jug
Buff Tyson	Jack Ingram
Homer Ross	Philip Morris
Bill Webster	Patrick Hurst
Red Jordan	Edwin Parker
Slim	Lynn Farr

Doye O'Dell and the Radio Rangers

"Whirlwind Raiders," another oatuner in Columbia's Durango Kid series, shapes up tepidly compared to some of its predecessors. Standard hoss opera has only a fair amount of shootin' and ridin'. Market appears limited only to the Charles Starrett-Smiley Burnette fans plus the Saturday matinee juvenile trade.

Moppet attendance, incidentally, should receive a lift through the presence of 10-year-old thesp. "Little Brown Jug" (Don Kay). "Champ" rodeo rider has a meaty role climaxed by a bit where he foils the outlaws by recognizing their disguised leader. Formula story treats with depredations upon ranchers by dishonest Texas "State Police." Minions of the law are rounded up when the Texas Rangers return to power.

In his customary dual thesping assignment, Starrett adeptly carries out his mission of thwarting the evil-doers. Comedy is ably handled by Burnette. He also contribs a few vocals, supplementing the backwoods rhythms of Doye O'Deill and the Radio Rangers. Fred Sears is an okay bandit chief who hides his true status under the guise of a respectable banker. Nancy Saunders brightens the celluloid as a cattleman's daughter.

Other players are adequate. Vernon Keays does well enough with the direction while M. A. Andersen's camerawork is creditable. *Gilb.*

Campus Sleuth

(SONGS)

Hollywood, May 5.

Monogram release of Will Jason production. Features Freddie Stewart, June Preisser, Warren Mills, Noel Neill, Donald MacBride, Bobby Sherwood orch., Gerri Gallian. Directed by Jason. Screenplay, Hal Collins; story, Max Wilson, Collins; camera, Mack Stengler; songs Freddie Stewart, Will Jason, Sid Robin, Bobby Sherwood, Tony Beaulieu; editor, William Austin. Previewed May 3, '48. Running time, 57 mins.

Freddie Trimball	Freddie Stewart
Dodie Rogers	June Preisser
Lee Watson	Warren Mills
Betty Rogers	Noel Neill
Inspector Watson	Donald MacBride
Dean McKinley	Monte Collins
Winkler	Stan Rose
Bobby Davis	Bobby Sherwood
Ronnie Wallace	Billy Snyder
Coroner	William Norton Bailey
Dunkel	Charles Campbell
Houser	Paul Bryar
Officer Edwards	George Eldredge
Telegraph Girl	Dottye D. Brown
Husband	Harry Taylor
Wife	Margaret Bert
Police Officer	Lane CHandler
Joey	Joey Preston
Little Miss Cornshucks	Mildred Jorman
Boy in Wagon	Jimmy Grisson
Band Boy	George Fields

Bobby Sherwood and Orch.
Gerri Gallian

"Campus Sleuth" is a musical whodunit that will get by as supporting feature for the secondaries. It follows a formula groove in presenting its songs and mystery; the results are just adequate.

Score has three songs by Freddie Stewart, but tunes are poorly introduced and, consequently, lose value. They are "Baby, You Can Count On Me," "What Happened?" and "Neither Could I." Better presentation is given "Sherwood's Forest" by the Bobby Sherwood orch and Gerri Gallian's nifty keyboarding of "Jungle Rhumba."

Trite plot has Stewart, June Preisser, Warren Mills and Noel Neill mixed up in the campus murder of a mag photog. Plot stumbles along until evidence ties batoneer Sherwood to the killing.

Best lift to proceedings comes from Mills, who exerts good comedy talent to raise a few chuckles. Donald MacBride runs him a close second for laughs. Miss Preisser and others are adequate to demands made by Will Jason's direction and production guidance. Lensing and other technical contributions are standard. *Brog.*

Que Dios Me Perdone

(May God Forgive Me)
(MEXICAN)

Mexico City, April 30.

Peliculas Nacionales release of Filmex production. Stars Maria Felix, Fernando Soler; features Tito Junco, Julian Soler, Ernesto Vilches. Adapted (and directed) by Tito Davison from original by Jose Revueltas. Camera, Julio Bracho. At Cine Alameda, Mexico City. Running time, 101 mins.

This smoothie, one of the best of this year by Mexicans, has a good deal to recommend it to U. S. audiences. Star is Maria Felix, Mexico's highest-paid pic actress

and concededly Mexico's leading looker. She can act, too. She's outstanding in this mystery of a European refugee who has a child in a concentration camp. Opposite her is the dean of Mexican actors, Fernando Soler, in the role of bon vivant, a wealthy widower with a charming daughter, Carmelita Gonzalez.

Story stresses the languid Latin adoration of tragedy too much. But it's interesting as a slice of life among the Mexican elite during the unprecedented wartime prosperity. Story climaxes on Lake Patzcuaro, Michoacan State, with Soler and Tito Junco, an excellent heavy, in death grapple out in a skiff. Miss Felix inherits Soler's property, but renounces it in favor of her stepdaughter, a promising pianist, then suicides when word comes that her child couldn't survive the concentration camp horrors. *Grah.*

Foreign Films

"Olympiad I Vitt" ("Olympic Games in White") (SWISS-SWEDISH). Europa release of Svensk Journalfilm & Condor Film, Zurich. Directed by Torgny Wickman. Camera, Harry Persson, Rene Boeniger, Robert Garbade, Ernst Elsigen, George Alexath, J. Bart, Hans Jaworsky. At Aveny and Lorry theatres, Stockholm.

An interesting documentary, "Olympiad I Vitt" is the first film covering the winter Olympic games to be shown in Sweden. Produced by Svensk Journalfilm in cooperation with Swiss producer Condor Film, the pic is a sure moneymaker here principally due to the fine lensing of the cameramen. Sport shots have a worldwide appeal. *Winq.*

"Karlek, Solsken Och Sang" ("Love, Sunshine and Songs") (SWEDISH). Sandrew-Bauman production and release. Stars Ake Soderblom, Bengt Logardt, Anne-Marie Aaroe, Stig Jarrel; features Anders Borje, Gustaf Torrestad, Benkt Ake Benktson, Gull Natorp, Lena Cederstrom. Directed by Per Gunwall. Screenplay, Gunwall; camera, Curt Jonsson. At Astoria, Stockholm. Running time, 104 MINS.

With practically no plot at all, this entry boils down to merely a big variety show whose chief selling point is that it features some of Sweden's niftiest bathing beauties. Picture is best described as a Swedish "Hellzapoppin." Cast does a good job while direction and camerawork are okay. Film looms as a satisfactory grosser in Scandinavia and has mild chances abroad. *Winq.*

Miniature Reviews

"Wallflower" (WB). Delightful comedy for family audiences. Hokum loaded with chuckles.

"Melody Time" (RKO) (Musical-Color). Entertainment for all ages in the best Disney manner.

"Return of the Badmen" (RKO). Randolph Scott, Robert Ryan, George "Gabby" Hayes in OK western.

"Raw Deal" (EL). Fast gangster meller is solid program fare.

"Best Man Wins" (Col). Interesting family comedy-drama, warmly told. Nice dualer.

"I, Jane Doe" (Rep). Mildly entertaining melodrama, with spotty b.o. prospects.

"Jinx Money" (Mono). Good programmer in the popular Bowery Boys series headed by Leo Gorcey.

"The Cobra Strikes" (Mono). Dull lower rung murder mystery.

Wallflower

(SONG)

Hollywood, May 18.

Warner Bros. release of Alex Gottlieb production. Stars Robert Hutton, Joyce Reynolds, Janis Paige; features Edward Arnold, Barbara Brown, Jerome Cowan, Don McGuire. Directed by Frederick de Cordova. Screenplay, Phoebe and Henry Ephron; from stage play by Reginald Denham and Mary Orr; as produced by Meyer Davis; camera, Karl Freund; score, Frederick Hollander; editor, Folmar Blangsted. Tradeshown May 17, '48. Running time, 77 MINS.

Warren James	Robert Hutton
Jackie	Joyce Reynolds
Joy	Janis Paige
Mr. Linnett	Edward Arnold
Mrs. Linnett	Barbara Brown
Mr. James	Jerome Cowan
Stevie	Don McGuire
Mrs. James	Ann Shoemaker
Minna	Lotte Stein
Officer	Walter Sande
Miss Walsh	Angela Greene

A light, breezy comedy pace makes "Wallflower" altogether easy to take. It has a free and easy air about telling its situation comedy and is farced just enough to keep the essentially familiar plotting highly amusing.

Production is not lavish but Alex Gottlieb has spent the budget wisely to project showmanly values in keeping with the plot. Film should please thoroughly in majority of situations, particularly houses catering largely to family audiences.

Cast gives amusingly with antics demanded by the Phoebe and Henry Ephron script, based on the stage play by Reginald Denham and Mary Orr. Frederick de Cordova paces his direction to get maximum fun results, giving film decidedly effective handling to punch over chuckles.

Plot is the one about the ugly duckling who comes to life and wins the hero from her more glamorous sister. Sparking the piece are Joyce Reynolds in the title role and Janis Paige as the s.a.-laden but dumb sister. Girls make an effective team and Robert Hutton lends the masculine appeal as the objective of the femmes' affections.

Edward Arnold and Barbara Brown are teamed as the parents of the girls. They are expert at portrayals and add to comedy highlights in the family squabble over a date for the wallflower, the family conference on a forced elopement and other situations. Plot sequence dealing with a midnight swim builds to hilarious consequences when mischievous kids steal the bathers' clothes.

Included in film is chorus of "I May Be Wrong," oldie from the 1929 Broadway show, "Almanac." Setting is country club dance with Miss Paige taking the vocals. Background score by Frederick Hollander is good. Among cast members helping to put this one over are Don McGuire, a wolfish suitor; Jerome Cowan, Lotte Stein, with a very funnily conceived interpretation of a servant; and Walter Sande, a cop.

Expert lensing by Karl Freund, smart art direction and settings, and crisp editing are among other earned credits. *Brog.*

Melody Time

(COLOR-MUSICAL)

Hollywood, May 15.

RKO release of Walt Disney production. Stars Roy Rogers and Trigger; Dennis Day, Andrews Sisters, Fred Waring & Pennsylvanians, Freddy Martin, Frances Langford, Ethel Smith, Buddy Clark; features Bob Nolan & Sons of Pioneers, Dinning Sisters, Bobby Driscoll, Luana Patten. Production supervision, Ben Sharpsteen. Cartoon directors, Clyde Geronimi, Wilfred Jackson, Hamilton Luske, Jack Kinney. Story, Winston Hibler, Erdman Penner, Harry Reeves, Homer Brightman, Ken Anderson, Ted Sears, Joe Rinaldi, Art Scott, Bill Cottrell, Bob Moore, Jesse Marsh, John Walbridge. Hardie Gramatky; folklore consultant, Carl Carmer; live action photography (Technicolor), Winton Hoch; special processes, Ub Iwerks; musical direction, Eliot Daniel, Ken Darby; associate, Paul Smith; special arrangements, Vic Shoen, Al Sack; songs, Kim Gannon, Walter Kent, Ray Gilbert, Johnny Lange, Allie Wrubel, Bobby Worth, Benny Benjamin, George Weiss; editors, Donald Halliday, Thomas Scott. Tradeshown May 13, '48. Running time, 75 MINS.

The seven stories told in "Melody Time" should strike wide appeal. There's meat for all in varying degree, told with the resourceful interpretative skill of the Walt Disney organization. Film, essentially, is seven complete Disney-treated subjects, each with an appeal for a particular type of audience, but all with the element of interest for the most general theatregoer.

Youngsters will find the seven chapters filled with engrossing charm but, since the kiddies hold no corner on flights into fantasy, the grownups, too, will follow the varied entertainment with attention. Eleven tunes are presented with the artistry that has become the Disney trademark. From the opener, "Melody Time," which explains what is to come, through "Once Upon a Wintertime" and "Blue Shadows," they all have a melodic appeal to the eye and ear in the hands of the Disney staff.

Only two of the stories feature live action. First comes Ethel Smith and her organ romping through the hip-wiggling "Blame It on the Samba" with Donald Duck, Jose Carioca and the Aracuan Bird of Brazil. Vocal backing is supplied by the voices of the Dinning Sisters and the piece is an infectious combination of sound track and drawing that pays off. Ray Gilbert did the English lyrics to music by Ernesto Nazareth.

Other live-actioner is the finale "Pecos Bill," wherein Roy Rogers spins a folk tale of the old west for Bobby Driscoll and Luana Patten, with the aid of Bob Nolan and the Sons of the Pioneers. Standout in this chapter is the tune, "Blue Shadows." Otherwise it emphasizes comedy in the best Disney manner in depicting why coyotes howl at the full moon.

There's a greeting card daintiness about "Once Upon a Wintertime," telling of two lovers who go ice skating. The animation is beautiful and the vocals register strongly from the pipes of Frances Langford. "Bumble Boogie" chapter has Jack Fina's adaptation of the classic "Flight of the Bumble Bee" coming to cartoon life in an almost frightening animation of musical instruments, notes and the busy bee. Freddy Martin's backing is all that could be asked.

Dennis Day's voice and caricature carry off the imaginative treatment accorded folk tale of Johnny Appleseed. Chapter has three numbers sung by Day; "The Pioneer Song," the hymn, "The Lord Is Good to Me" and "Apple Song." The Appleseed legend of how the character spread the fruit to the pioneer borders of the land projects moral values tellingly while entertaining. "Little Toot," fable of a baby tugboat in New York harbor, is colorful and engrossing. Andrews Sisters give it popular vocal interpretation.

Full rein to imaginative artistry is used in telling the pictorial story of "Trees" as Fred Waring and His Pennsylvanians supply the musical lacework. There's a breathless beauty in the animation of the seasons. Introductory title piece is sung by Buddy Clark, who also acts as master of ceremonies for the chapters to come. Lyrics of tune establish the theme and Paul Smith's background score ties the episodes together neatly.

As to be expected, the technicians on the Disney staff have given this one a flawless stamp, technically perfect and artistically stimulating. Beautifully photographed in Technicolor, it's a show that rates all connected with its making a top credit. *Brog.*

Return of the Badmen

Hollywood, May 14.

RKO release of Nat Holt production. Stars Randolph Scott, Robert Ryan, Anne Jeffreys, George "Gabby" Hayes, Jacqueline White; features Steve Brodie, Richard Powers, Robert Bray, Lex Barker, Walter Reed, Michael Harvey, Dean White, Robert Armstrong, Tom Tyler, Lew Harvey. Directed by Ray Enright. Screenplay, Charles O'Neal, Jack Natteford, Luci Ward; story, Natteford, Ward; camera, J. Roy Hunt; music, Paul Sawtell; editor, Samuel E. Beetley. Tradeshown May 12, '48. Running time, **89 MINS.**

Vance	Randolph Scott
Sundance Kid	Robert Ryan
Cheyenne	Anne Jeffreys
John Pettit	George "Gabby" Hayes
Madge Allen	Jacqueline White
Cole Younger	Steve Brodie
Jim Younger	Richard Powers
John Younger	Robert Bray
Emmett Dalton	Lex Barker
Bob Dalton	Walter Reed
Grat Dalton	Michael Harvey
Billy the Kid	Dean White
Wild Bill Doolin	Robert Armstrong
Wild Bill Yeager	Tom Tyler
Arkansas Kid	Lew Harvey
Johnny	Gary Gray
Muley Wilson	Walter Baldwin
Emily	Minna Gombell
George Mason	Warren Jackson
Dave	Robert Clarke
Judge Harper	Jason Robards

"The Return of the Badmen" will measure up to all demands of the outdoor action fan. It fits carefully into the sturdy pattern set by previous feature westerns from RKO and boxoffice indications are good. Marquee value of such action names as Randolph Scott, Robert Ryan and George "Gabby" Hayes spark the cast lineup and add to grossing possibilities.

The brawling story goes back to the opening of the Oklahoma territory and throws in an assortment of w.k. western bad men to point up the action developed by Ray Enright's strong directorial guidance. The Daltons, the Youngers, Billy the Kid, the Sundance Kid, and others, people the script with enough heavies for several pictures, but their appearances have been handled in such a way film doesn't seem overcrowded.

Principal heavy interest is tossed to the Sundance Kid, and Ryan plays the character as a thorough menace. Plot mainly concerns conflict between Ryan and Scott, latter as a retired marshal who again takes up his guns when Ryan and the assorted outlaws that surround him launch a series of train and stage holdups in the territory.

Story develops two interesting femme characters and they are pleasingly portrayed by Anne Jeffreys and Jacqueline White. Former is seen as a rootin'-tootin', gunslinging daughter of the outlaw west who reforms for love of Scott, even though she doesn't get him. Miss White shades her heroine part neatly for interest, making it count for more than the usual femme assignment in westerns.

Scott turns in expected competent performance as a believeable hero, able with guns and fists to lay down the law when necessary. Ryan is capable opponent, playing assignment without sympathy to show up the western outlaw as a sadistic killer. Hayes is in for chuckles as a sagebrush banker, and more than holds his own.

Steve Brodie, as Cole Younger, and Robert Armstrong, as Wild Bill Doolin, have the best opportunities among the featured players. They give expert performances. Gary Gray, moppet; Minna Gombell, Walter Baldwin and Jason Robards are among the others in the large cast that show up well.

Nat Holt, responsible for previous RKO feature westerns under Jack J. Gross' executive supervision, has packed "Badmen" with all the ingredients that pay off in the action market. Enright's direction insures swift action despite the abundance of story material and makes it add up to neat filmfare. Much use is made of outdoor movement by J. Roy Hunt's lensing, and action is backed with good music score by Paul Sawtell. *Brog.*

Raw Deal

Eagle Lion release of Edward Small production. Stars Dennis O'Keefe, Claire Trevor, Marsha Hunt. Directed by Anthony Mann. Screenplay, Leopold Atlas and John C. Higgins; from story by Arnold B. Armstrong and Audrey Ashley; camera, John Alton; editor, Alfred De Gaetano; music, Paul Sawtelle. Tradeshown N. Y. May 14, '48. Running time, **79 MINS.**

Joe Sullivan	Dennis O'Keefe
Pat	Claire Trevor
Ann Martin	Marsha Hunt
Fantail	John Ireland
Rick Coyle	Raymond Burr
Spider	Curt Conway
Marcy	Chili Williams

"Raw Deal" is a fast-rolling gangster melodrama with a strong undercurrent of romance for an across-the-board customer appeal. Solid b.o. returns will come from the smaller firstruns and nabe situations where the pic can be backed with dualer support. Though a medium budgeter, pic is dressed tidily with a good production and some marquee weight furnished by Dennis O'Keefe, Claire Trevor and Marsha Hunt.

Story of a con who breaks out of jail with the aid of one gal and then falls in love with another unfolds within an exciting framework of a cross-country chase. Director Anthony Mann keeps the action taut from the opening esape to the slambang finale while, at the same time, integrating a torch theme into the yarn. Working in a familiar formula, scripters managed to avoid triteness with a hard-hitting style of dialog which is clever as well as tough.

O'Keefe registers as an authentic tough guy who's ready for any risk in his flight from the coop. Travelling with Miss Trevor after she sprung him, he kidnaps a social worker, Miss Hunt, for additional protection from the police. He finally breaks through the dragnet to a rendezvous with his gang chief only to discover that he's the object of a murderous double-cross. In a crashing climax, he finishes off his boss and dies in the arms of Miss Hunt while the other gal broken-heartedly looks on.

Miss Trevor gives a firstrate interpretation of a gangster moll, maintaining a steady sense of strain without going to pieces. Miss Hunt delivers competently in a glib thesping style. As the sadistic gang chieftan, Raymond Burr is reminiscent of the late Laird Cregar in bulk and manner but is deficient in a sinister quality. John Ireland, as a cynical hoodlum, gives a sharp portrayal.

Tense atmosphere of the film is supported by expert low-key lensing and an eerie musical background. *Herm.*

Best Man Wins

Hollywood, May 14.

Columbia release of Ted Richmond production. Features Edgar Buchanan, Anna Lee, Robert Shayne, Gary Gray, Hobart Cavanaugh, Stanley Andrews. Directed by John Sturges. Screenplay, Edward Huebsch; based on Mark Twain's "The Celebrated Jumping Frog of Calaveras County; camera, Vincent Farrar; editor, James Sweeney. At Grauman's Chinese, Hollywood, May 12, '48. Running time, **73 MINS.**

Jim Smiley	Edgar Buchanan
Nancy Smiley	Anna Lee
Judge Carter	Robert Shayne
Bob Smiley	Gary Gray
Amos	Hobart Cavanaugh
Sheriff Dingle	Stanley Andrews
Mr. Crow	George Lynn
Monty Carter	Bill Sheffield
Hester	Marietta Canty
Bartender	Paul E. Burns

Mark Twain's "The Jumping Frog of Calaveras County" furnishes the story idea for the effective little comedy-drama turned out at Columbia under the title of "Best Man Wins." It's a budget film for lower half of double bills and will please the family trade. Production backing, direction and playing fit it capably into the secondary bracket.

While pace is leisurely, there's a gentle humor about the way the plot is developed under John Sturges' direction and he gets excellent performances from the cast. Best showing among the players is made by veteran Edgar Buchanan and moppet Gary Gray. Former is the wandering gambler who returns to his home town to find his wife has divorced him and is about to marry another man. Buchanan finds his young son, Gary Gray, still on his side and, working through the moppet, gradually wins his wife back. For kiddie interest, there's the jumping frog owned by Buchanan and the training of dog for a big race.

Anna Lee makes a gracious wife and Robert Shayne, as the man she's about to marry, is good. Small town types are given good reading by Hobart Cavanaugh, Stanley Andrews, George Lynn, William Sheffield and others.

Ted Richmond's production guidance shows expert expenditure of light budget, making sure hokum was kept interesting. Edward Huebsch did the good script. There is neat lensing by Vincent Farrar, smooth editing by James Sweeney to back up other good points. *Brog.*

I, Jane Doe

Hollywood, May 15.

Republic release of John H. Auer production, directed by Auer. Stars Ruth Hussey, John Carroll, Vera Ralston; features Gene Lockhart, John Howard, Benay Venuta, Adele Mara, Roger Dann, James Bell. Screenplay, Lawrence Kimble; adaptation, Decla Dunning; camera, Reggie Lanning; music, Heinz Roemheld; editor, Richard L. Van Enger. Tradeshown May 11, '48. Running time, **85 MINS.**

Eve Meredith Curtis	Ruth Hussey
Stephen Curtis	John Carroll
Jane Doe / Annette DuBois	Vera Ralston
Arnold Matson	Gene Lockhart
William Hilton	John Howard
Phyllis Tuttle	Benay Venuta
Marga-Jane Hastings	Adele Mara
Julian Aubert	Roger Dann
Judge Bertrand	James Bell
Duroc	Leon Belasco
Horton	John Litel
Robert DuBois	Eric Feldary
Father Martin	Francis Pierlot
Marie	Marta Mitrovich
Reporter	John Albright

"I, Jane Doe" is a highly involved melodrama that generates only mild interest for general audiences. Grosses will be spotty with film's best chances in the secondary houses. Picture bears evidence of good budget allotment in its physical trappings but lacks sufficient excitement to be good entertainment.

Flashbacks and dissolves used by producer-director John H. Auer to tell his story contribute to confusion and make the 85 minutes' running time seem overlong. Majority of the cast wear their assignments uncomfortably, also mitigating against sustained interest.

Plot, essentially, tells the story of a French girl, wooed and won by a philanderer in uniform. After the war, the battle bride comes to the States to find her missing husband, only to discover he is already married. After he seeks to have her deported when tired of a seasick rendezvous, the girl goes into a mental fog and bumps him off. Story tries for novelty in telling the saga by flashback during her trial for murder, but the only twist that registers is the ludicrous courtroom technique. After a conviction, gal is found to be pregnant and the philanderer's widow undertakes her defense at a second trial.

Ruth Hussey tries hard as the legitimate widow and defense attorney. John Carroll, also, tries to bolster unhappy assignment as the playboy. Vera Ralston is impassive as the wronged French girl. Gene Lockhart is a blustering prosecutor. Benay Venuta is Miss Hussey's friend and John Howard has a thankless role.

A bright bit is contributed by Leon Belasco, French shyster lawyer, and Adele Mara spices brief sequence as a kept woman. Air clips used during battle scene are exciting. Photography, settings and other physical dressing are all good. *Brog.*

Jinx Money

Hollywood, May 15.

Monogram release of Jan Grippo production. Features Leo Gorcey, Huntz Hall, Billy Benedict, David Gorcey, Benny Bartlett, Gabriel Dell, Betty Caldwell, Sheldon Leonard, Donald MacBride. Directed by William Beaudine. Original screenplay, Edmond Seward, Tim Ryan, Gerald Schnitzer; from story suggested by Jerome T. Gollard; camera, Marcel Le Picard; editor, William Austin. Previewed May 12, '48. Running time, **60 MINS.**

Slip Mahoney	Leo Gorcey
Sach	Huntz Hall
Whitey	Billy Benedict
Chuck	David Gorcey
Butch	Benny Bartlett
Gabe	Gabriel Dell

Candy	Betty Caldwell
Lippy Harris	Sheldon Leonard
Capt. Broadderck	Donald MacBride
Lullaby Schmo	John Eldredge
Virginia	Wanda McKay
Tipper	Lucien Littlefield
Louie	Bernard Gorcey
Augie	Benny Baker
Benny "The Meatball"	Ben Welden
"Cold-Deck" Shapiro	Ralph Dunn
Officer Rooney	Tom Kennedy
Sgt. Ryan	William Ruhl
Bank President	Stanley Andrews
Tax Man	George Eldredge
Meek Man	William Vedder
Bank Guard	Mike Pat Donovan

"Jinx Money" is an easily salable Bowery Boys entry from the Monogram stable. Strictly for laughs, it has a slap-happy pace calculated to please any following built by the series, and payoff in that particular market will be good.

Plot combines comedy and melodrama effectively enough to show off the antics of the Boweryites, led by Leo Gorcey. Direction by William Beaudine paces the chuckles and thrills for best all-around reception, letting the Bowery gang have its head in frantic antics—a formula particularly pleasing to series fans.

A gambler wins $50,000 at cards and is murdered on the street while carrying away the loot. Gorcey and Huntz Hall find it and the fun develops in their trying to keep it against the onslaught of other gamblers and a killer. Boys out-trick the brains at every turn and there are five murders before the killer is brought to justice.

Boweryites backing Gorcey and Hall are capably depicted by Billy Benedict, David Gorcey, Benny Bartlett and Gabriel Dell. Adult comedy as an apoplectic detective is furnished by Donald MacBride, Lucien Littlefield is the killer and other heavies, all properly sinister, include Betty Caldwell, Sheldon Leonard, John Eldredge, Benny Baker, Ben Welden and Ralph Dunn. Comic malt shop proprietor is handled by Bernard Gorcey.

Jan Grippo has given the film good production backing for budget allotment, with lensing, editing and other factors measuring up to market demands. *Brog.*

The Cobra Strikes

Hollywood, May 14.

Eagle-Lion release of David I. Stephenson production. Features Sheila Ryan, Richard Fraser, Leslie Brooks, Herbert Heyes. Directed by Charles F. Riesner. Screenplay, Eugene Conrad; camera, Guy Roe; editor, Louis Sackin. Reviewed May 11, '48. Running time, 61 MINS.

Dale	Sheila Ryan
Mike Kent	Richard Fraser
Olga Kaminoff	Leslie Brooks
Dr. Damon Cameron }	
Ted Cameron }	Herbert Hayes
Capt. Monohan	James Seay
Hyder Ali	Richard Loo
Sgt. Harris	Lyle Latell
Atlas Kilroy	Pat Flaherty
Kasim	Philip Ahn
Franz Lang	Fred Nurney
Victor Devereaux	George Sorel

"The Cobra Strikes" is a dull uninspired tale welded together by a series of murders committed by Herbert Heyes in his greed for money. Film lacks character individuality thus creating a mass of milling players whose glances continually accuse one another leaving none unsuspected—with the exception of the police force. "Cobra" is poor booster material.

Film gets under way with the attempted assasination of a doctor (Heyes) who has just invented a medical instrument which can be a boon to mankind or, conversely, annihilate mankind. Heyes is relieved of his invention when shot and shortly after a series of murders occur. Newspaper columnist Richard Fraser tackles the case and is led to the criminal via a hoked up clue. Murderer, apprehended, reveals that he is after jewels unobtainable without murder.

Sheila Ryan and Fraser project fairly well through some bad dialog in a weak plot. Leslie Brooks' characterization of a novelist, complete with Russian dialect, is extremely unbelievable while Heyes and Richard Loo all look alike in character.

David I. Stephenson's production values are weak with screenplay by Eugene Conrad, direction by Charles F. Riesner and Guy Roe's lensing to match. *Free.*

Miniature Reviews

"The Time of Your Life" (UA-Cagney). Film version of Saroyan play okay, but will have to be sold hard outside of keys.

"Easter Parade" (Musical-Color) (M-G). Sock screen musical in Technicolor, certain for big business.

"Up in Central Park" (Musical) (U-I). Ornate romantic musical about the Boss Tweed era; moderate grosser.

"The Big Punch" (WB). OK dualer melodrama with Wayne Morris and introducing Gordon MacRae.

"Give My Regards to Broadway" (20th) (musical-color). Dan Dailey starred in neat little piece of show biz nostalgia; should do well.

"The Vicious Circle" (UA). Tedious pic with racial tolerance theme.

"The Gallant Legion" (Rep). Strong outdoor action entertainment for western fans.

"Big Town Scandal" (Par). Finale in the Pine-Thomas "Big Town" series. Mild dualer.

"King of the Gamblers" (Rep). Supporting feature dealing with gambling and fixed pro football.

The Time of Your Life

United Artists release of William Cagney production. Stars James Cagney, William Bendix, Wayne Morris, Jeanne Cagney; features Broderick Crawford, Ward Bond, James Barton, Paul Draper. Directed by H.C. Potter. Adapted by Nathaniel Curtis from play by William Saroyan; camera, James Wong Howe; editors, Walter Hannemann and Truman K. Wood. Previewed in New York May 19, '48. Running time, 108 mins.

Joe	James Cagney
Nick	William Bendix
Tom	Wayne Morris
Kitty Duval	Jeanne Cagney
Krupp	Broderick Crawford
McCarthy	Ward Bond
Kit Carson	James Barton
Harry	Paul Draper
Mary L.	Gale Page
Dudley	James Lydon
Willie	Richard Erdman
Arab	Pedro de Cordoba
Wesley	Reginald Beane
Blick	Tom Powers
A Tippler	John "Skins" Miller
Society Lady	Natalie Schafer
Society Gentleman	Howard Freeman
Blind Date	Renie Riano
Girl in Love	Nanette Parks
Nick's Mother	Grazia Marciso
"Killer"	Claire Carleton
Side Kick	Gladys Blake
Newsboy	Lanny Rees
Nick's Daughter	Marlene Ames

Were there an Oscar for contribution to the art of picturemaking via courage in bringing an off-the-trodden-path approach to the screen, James and William Cagney would be sure winners for this transmutation of William Saroyan's prize-garnering play. As it is, the partner-brothers certainly stand an excellent chance of copping at least a couple of the Academy figurines for the exceptional performances of virtually every player in this unusual film.

Whether exhibs will be as liberal with Oscars for b.o. performance is another question. It should be noted at once, however, that "The Time of Your Life" is as full of guffaw-type humor and entertainment as the frothiest of comedies. The catch is that it is presented in the unconventional and more-or-less formless pattern of Saroyan's stage writing. Whether exhibitors and audiences will accept this unfamiliar format is the question mark. Outside of major cities, grosses may be limited.

Realizing the difficulties, United Artists has adopted a well-designed distribution plan. Film will premiere tonight (Wednesday) in New York and San Francisco. No further dates will be taken for at least a month and the playoff throughout the country will be slow. Idea is to allow maximum hinterland seepage of the excellent criticism and controversial newspaper and magazine publicity that the picture is almost certain of getting.

The "snob appeal" which may thus be generated for the Saroyan epic is the major hope for making it a really big grosser.

Saroyan-lovers will find that the play, which won both the New York Critics Circle and Pulitzer prizes in 1940 (although the playwright refused to accept the Pulitzer award), has been tampered with to the minimum extent consistent with transference from one medium to another. The heavy Saroyan philosophy has been partly excised (not so much that the playwright's "I love the common people" theme doesn't remain perfectly clear) and the comedy has been pointed up. Latter has been effected not by rewriting or adding lines, but largely by the fact that the closeup lens can catch facial expressions and nuances that wouldn't be visible at all or would smell of the smokehouse in legit.

Major switch has been in the ending. After shooting a Johnston-office version of the original finale, it was discovered in sneak previews that it "didn't play." The heavy Saroyanism left audiences bewildered. As a result, $300,000 was added to the original $1,700,000 budget to retake the closing scenes. The result is a more pat and conventional fadeout, but one that retains much of the beauty of the original.

The difference between "Life" and the standard film is that this one has no story in the accepted sense of the term. It merely introduces, one by one, a series of "characters." It doesn't even delve deeply into what makes them tick, but presents their amusing exterior sides as they spout the Saroyan views on life and living.

Setting for this strangest assortment of people any play or film has ever latched together is Nick's bar in the toughest quarter of San Francisco. James Cagney, as an unexplained lover of the commonfolk, is the central character (created by Eddie Dowling in the legiter) around which the others more-or-less revolve. The second focal point is the barkeep, William Bendix) (he played a cop in the original, a part now held by Broderick Crawford).

Cagney's role is static but amusing. Bendix's is solid comedy most of the way. The other wayfarers bring laughs, pathos, philosophy and entertainment. They include James Barton as a tall-tale-telling Indian scout; Jeanne Cagney as a prostie who dreams of home; Wayne Morris is a lug-like handyman for Cagney; Paul Draper (Gene Kelly played the legit version) as a terper whose only yen is to dance—anyplace, anytime; Reginald Beane as a Negro piano player (he did the same role in the stage version), and a flock of others.

Strangely enough, the whole thing hangs tightly together, despite the absence of all plot but a bit of by-play introduced in the film between Morris and Miss Cagney. Henry C. Potter's direction starts leisurely, but the pace soon picks up and the film moves smartly most of the way. Adding to the entertainment level are the topnotch dancing of Draper (although there's a bit too much of it) and the keyboard work of Beane.

Barton and Bendix have probably never given better performances in their lives. Actually, however, there's not a single member of the cast who can't be handed thespic honors. Every part verges on ham and yet Potter has managed to keep all of his players on the right side of the fine line.

Like the stage play, the picture is virtually all in one set, but James Wong Howe's camera has a mobility that transcends the background. It completely catches the tender, human quality of the Saroyan writing and some of the warmth. It also emphasizes, however, one of the shortcomings of the film—the fact that its crew of characters is so strange and unknown that they permit the audience to make no identifications with themselves. That's one of the major factors that will militate against the film's b.o. chances in the sticks.

In any case, the Cagneys can take artistic pride in having successfully brought off a picture that some considered at the time "couldn't be made." *Herb.*

Easter Parade
(MUSICAL-COLOR)

Hollywood, May 25.

Metro release of Arthur Freed production. Stars Judy Garland, Fred Astaire, Peter Lawford, Ann Miller; features Jules Munshin, Clinton Sundberg, Jennie LeGon, Richard Beavers. Directed by Charles Walters. Screenplay, Sidney Sheldon, Frances Goodrich, Albert Hackett; original story, Goodrich & Hackett; camera (Technicolor), Harry Stradling; songs, Irving Berlin; musical direction, Johnny Green; orchestrations, Conrado Salinger, Van Cleave, Leo Arnaud; vocal arrangements, Robert Tucker; editor, Albert Akst. Tradeshown May 19, '48. Running time, **102 MINS.**

Hannah Brown....................Judy Garland
Don Hewes....................Fred Astaire
Jonathan Harrow, III..........Peter Lawford
Nadine Hale....................Ann Miller
Francois....................Jules Munshin
Mike, the Bartender..........Clinton Sundberg
Essie....................Jennie LeGon
Singer....................Richard Beavers

"Easter Parade" is a musical that will rate high customer enthusiasm in all situations. The lush and colorful 1912 Broadway background is embroidered with old and new Irving Berlin tunes and standout dance numbers to rate it sock screen entertainment.

Boxoffice advantages indicating top returns include Technicolor, the score, Fred Astaire's dancing, Judy Garland's singing and dancing, and Ann Miller in three big production numbers. It's all a treat for eye and ear, displayed for thorough enjoyment of its comedy, romance and spectacle.

The Berlin score includes 17 songs, seven new and 10 from his extensive catalog. They are all melodic Berlin, from the opening "Happy Easter" through to the finale "Easter Parade." Eight are used to point up that many class production numbers featuring exceptional terping of Astaire and the Misses Garland and Miller.

Astaire's standout solo is the elaborate production piece, "Stepping Out With My Baby," during which he does a slow-motion dance in front of a large chorus terping in regular time. It's a sharp blending of technical and artistic skills that will pay off with hefty word-of-mouth. Number uses three moods, light ballet, a sexy blues touch and jitterbug antics with as many partners before Astaire picks up his solo spot. "Drum Crazy" solo in a toy store has the Astaire rhythm, as does "When the Midnight Choo Choo Leaves for Alabam."

Highpoint of comedy is reached when Astaire and Miss Garland team for vocals and foot work on "A Couple of Swells." It's a show number that socks the risibilities and the pair go through their routines in full tramp regalia, complete even to Miss Garland's blacked-out tooth. They work together in another number in which Miss Garland slickly values the clumsiness of a dance tyro and also shine in a medley of three tunes, "I Love a Piano," "Snooky Ookums" and "Ragtime Violin."

Ann Miller's standout is "Shaking the Blues Away," in which she displays her shapely, sinuous limbs and body in a rapidfire dance of lightning taps. She lends poetic rhythm to "The Girl on a Magazine Cover," to a background of excellent baritoning by Richard Beavers, and in her teaming with Astaire on "It Only Happens When I Dance With You."

Miss Garland's pipes make easy listening of "Better Luck Next Time," a reprise of "When I Dance With You," and "I Wanna Go Back to Michigan," "I Love a Piano," "Easter Parade" and "A Fella With An Umbrella," the latter shared with Peter Lawford.

Arthur Freed's production guidance has set a perfect stage for the display of song and dance, a showmanly piece of work that demonstrates the top experience used all down the line in bringing this one to the screen. Charles Walters takes it away with his direction to make a solid blend of story and music that will pay off. High credit also goes to Robert Alton's direction of the musical numbers, Harry Stradling's photography, and the music direction by Johnny Green.

The light story by Frances Goodrich and Albert Hackett, scripted in conjunction with Sidney Sheldon, makes a perfect backing for the Berlin score and playing. Plot opens on Easter, 1911 and carries through to Easter, 1912. It deals with splitup of Astaire and Miss Miller as partners and recruiting of Miss Garland by the dancer, who is determined to make her outdraw his former hoofer. Lawford is in as a rich playboy who goes for both of the girls without success. Dialog comes off lightly and situations answer all demand for projection of music.

Among the few credited supporting players Jules Munshin registers as a film comedian of promise. His pantomime of preparing a salad and other briefly spotted routines rang the bell with preview audiences. Clinton Sundberg, as a philosophical bartender, also registers strongly.

Freed has garbed the picture with all the trappings that appeal to the eye. Lovely girls, beautiful costumes by Irene, rich art direction by Cedric Gibbons and Jack Martin Smith, and a lush dance to tions by Edwin B. Willis and his associate, Arthur Krams, add to brilliance. Tricky synchronization of Astaire's slow motion dance to sound track is a first by John Arnold's camera department. *Brog.*

Up in Central Park
(MUSICAL)

Universal release of Karl Tunberg production. Stars Deanna Durbin, Dick Haymes, Vincent Price; features Albert Sharpe, Tom Powers; Hobart Cavanaugh. Directed by William Seiter. Screenplay, Karl Tunberg; from musical comedy by Dorothy Fields and Sigmund Romberg; arranged and conducted by Johnny Green; choreography, Helen Tamiris; camera, Milton Krasner; special effects, David S. Horsley; editor, Otto Ludwig. Previewed N. Y. May 25, '48. Running time, **87 MINS.**

Rosie Moore....................Deanna Durbin
John Matthews....................Dick Haymes
Boss Tweed....................Vincent Price
Timothy Moore....................Albert Sharpe
Rogan....................Tom Powers
Mayor Oakley..........Hobart Cavanaugh
Governor Motley..........Thurston Hall
Myron Schultz..........Howard Freeman
Miss Murch....................Mary Field
O'Toole....................Tom Pedi
Big Jim Fitts....................Moroni Olsen
Dancers........Wm. Skipper, Nelle Fisher

"Up in Central Park," which ran 15 months on Broadway as a musical comedy, has much the same merits and faults in this Universal film version. That is, it's an overstuffed, sentimental, handsome tune-and-terp show with a so-so score, little pace and not enough period flavor. It should do moderate business.

Only two songs from Sigmund Romberg's original score are retained in the picture. They are "When She Walks in the Room," handled nicely by Dick Haymes, and "Carousel in the Park," which Deanna Durbin and he sing pleasantly in an actual merry-go-round scene. The show's click ballad, "Close As Pages in a Book," is not sung, but used merely as occasional theme music. However, Miss Durbin has a new song, "Oh! Say Can You See (What I See)," which is acceptable. There are several full-staged dance numbers, the most notable of which is the Currier & Ives skating ballet, restaged from the original show.

The story, adapted from the original by Herbert and Dorothy Fields, stresses the romantic interest between the spirited but innocent Irish immigrant and the muckraking N. Y. Times reporter, and turns Boss Tweed into a champagne-dispensing wolf. But although the greater scope of the screen provides unusual possibilities for turn-of-the-century New York atmosphere, particularly if it had been photographed in color, it is only partially utilized.

Within the limits of the stubborn material, William Seiter's direction has reasonable flexibility. Miss Durbin is forcefully agreeable as the curiously unaccented colleen and her singing is generally satisfactory, though she doesn't especially impress with the "Pace, Pace, Mio Dio" aria from Verdi's "Forza del Destino."

Haymes is vocally good as the Rover Boy reporter, and as believable dramatically as the part allows. Vincent Price seems a bit unctuous as Tweed, Albert Sharpe registers sharply as the guileless Irishman, Hobart Cavanaugh is amusing as the stooge Mayor, and William Skipper and Nelle Fisher click in the skating dance number, skillfully staged by Helen Tamiris. Howard Bay's settings and Mary Grant's costumes appear excellent, within the limitations of black-and-white reproduction. *Hobe.*

The Big Punch

Hollywood, May 25.

Warner Bros. release of Saul Elkins production. Stars Wayne Morris, Lois Maxwell, Gordon MacRae; features Mary Stuart, Anthony Warde, Jimmy Ames. Directed by Sherry Shourds. Screenplay, Bernard Girard; from story by George Carleton Brown; camera, Carl Guthrie; editor, Frank Magee. Tadeshown May 24, '48. Running time, **80 MINS.**

Chris Thorgenson..........Wayne Morris
Karen Long....................Lois Maxwell
Johnny Grant..........Gordon MacRae
Midge Parker....................Mary Stuart
Con Festig....................Anthony Warde
Angel Panzer....................Jimmy Ames
Milo Brown....................Marc Logan
Ed Hardy....................Eddie Dunn
Sam Bancroft..........Charles Marsh

Warners has come through with a medium budget feature that should show a neat return for its production outlay. "The Big Punch" offers a melodrama built around the prize ring and the pulpit. Two elements combine into a theme that is not always plausible but still manages sufficient interest to hold casual attention in general situations.

Picture serves to focus attention on Gordon MacRae, newcomer from radio and record fields, as a young man capable of adapting himself to camera demands. He should get along in films, presenting an easy personality and an ability to read lines credibly. He doesn't need vocalizing to sell himself.

Hero interest is divided between MacRae and Wayne Morris. Latter nixes a bid for bigtime boxing in favor of the pulpit, and in describing his reasons to a promoter, makes MacRae discontent with his lot as a "tanker" on the prize ring circuit. MacRae fails to take a dive as ordered, flees town. A nosey policeman is bumped off by the promoter and MacRae is framed for the killing. He seeks refuge with the minister and when his past catches up, it's the new found friends in the small town who prove his innocence.

Morris could have used a more experienced directorial hand in some of his scenes, but on the whole pleases as the minister ready to deal out the gospel, either mildly or sternly. He has been given some good pulpit lines by scripter Barnard Girard. Lois Maxwell has principal femme assignment as the parson's romance. Mary Stuart is in briefly as boxing days flame of MacRae's. Anthony Warde, crooked promoter, Jimmy Ames, his henchman, Eddie Dunn, Marc Logan and Charles Marsh complete the small cast.

"Punch" marks upping of Saul Elkins from shorts to feature producer and the promotion of Sherry Shourds from assistant director. Both have done a good first chore in putting the film together within budget limitations. Picture is okay material for twin bills, able to go on top or bottom according to demands of the situation booking it. Photography, settings and other technical functions are standard. *Brog.*

Give My Regards to Broadway
(SONGS-COLOR)

Twentieth-Fox release of Walter Morosco production. Stars Dan Dailey; features Charles Winninger, Nancy Guild, Charlie Ruggles, Fay Bainter, Barbara Lawrence. Directed by Lloyd Bacon. Screenplay, Samuel Hoffenstein, Elizabeth Reinhardt, based on story by John Klempner; camera, Harry Jackson; editor, William Reynolds; dances, Seymour Felix. Tradeshown N. Y. May 19, '48. Running time, **89 MINS.**

Bert....................Dan Dailey
Albert....................Charles Winninger
Helen....................Nancy Guild
Toby....................Charlie Ruggles
Fay....................Fay Bainter
June....................Barbara Lawrence
May....................Jane Nigh
Arthur Waldron, Jr..........Charles Russell
Dinkel....................Sig Ruman
Mr. Waldron..........Howard Freeman
Frank Doty..........Herbert Anderson
Wallace....................Pat Flaherty
Emcee....................Harry Seymour
Mr. Boyd....................Paul Harvey
Mrs. Boyd....................Lela Bliss
Mrs. Waldron..........Georgia Caine
Fan....................Matt McHugh

Twentieth-Fox has another boxoffice winner in "Give My Regards to Broadway." An unpretentious little film dressed up in Technicolor gladrags, it misses by a hair being as entertaining as "Margie," the previous 20th pic with songs that it most closely resembles. With Dan Dailey the only name of any marquee importance, "Broadway" will require a little extra plugging to get 'em up to the wickets. Once the word-of-mouth gets rolling, though, it should be all easy gravy.

Despite the mental images of lush production numbers that might be conjured up by the title, "Broadway" has none of that. Instead, it's a simple story about an old vaude family that lives in the hope that the Palace two-a-day will some time be revived. Film has plenty of the show biz nostalgia that's been welcomed by customers in other pictures. Most of the film's charm, though lies in the picturization of the family's life in the small New Jersey town where it awaits faithfully the return of vaude.

Although he's backed by a fine supporting cast that might otherwise steal his thunder, Dailey has a personal field day in "Broadway" and the film should enhance his boxoffice value considerably. He gets a full chance to demonstrate his amazing versatility. If vaude were actually to be revived, in fact, Dailey would be an almost certain headliner.

Story of such a vaude family's life, of course, has all been told before, but not with the new twist given "Broadway." Winninger and Fay Bainter comprise the husband-and-wife team who made the Palace in the opening slot but were never quite good enough to headline. When the props are knocked out from under their business, they move to the small town where Winninger takes a factory job, but only as a stopgap. Their three kids grow up imbued with the lure of show biz but the family also settles in the comfortable groove of small-town security. When the big chance finally comes, after a wait of more than 20 years, the family can't break away from their jobs and new friends and so pass up a chance for 16 straight weeks' booking.

In addition to Dailey, who's standout as the son, the cast is excellent under the leisurely directorial touch of Lloyd Bacon. Winninger does one of his neatest characterizations as the oldtimer who refuses to toss in the sponge, and Miss Bainter is fine as his understanding spouse. Nancy Guild is pretty and adequate as Dailey's vis-a-vis and Charlie Ruggles does his usual okay stint as the agent and lifetime friend of the family. Another standout is Barbara Lawrence as one of the daughters, who's moving rapidly into the star slot that 20th has grooved for her.

Title song, cleffed by the late George M. Cohan, runs through the film as its theme. Other numbers include "When Francis Dances With Me," terped by Dailey and Miss Lawrence, and several other oldies, including "Good Morning to All" and "Let a Smile Be Your Umbrella."

Production mountings, under the supervision of producer Walter Morosco, all add to the picture's show biz tenor. Particularly impressive are montage shots of oldtime vaude greats, which intro the story. Harry Jacksons' color photography is unostentatiously good and William Reynolds' editing job, while compact, is loose enough for the film's leisurely pace. *Stal.*

The Vicious Circle

United Artists release of W. Lee Wilder production, directed by Wilder. Stars Conrad Nagel; features Fritz Kortner, Reinhold Schunzel. Screenplay, Heinz Herald and Guy Endore based on play, "The Burning Bush," by Herald and Geza Herczeg; camera, George Robinson; editor, Asa Boyd Clark; music, Paul Dessau. Tradeshown N. Y. May 25, '48. Running time, 77 MINS.

Karl Nemesch....................Conrad Nagel
Joseph Schwartz....................Fritz Kortner
Baron Arady....................Reinhold Schunzel
Balog....................Philip Van Zandt
Miller....................Lyle Talbot
Samuel Schwartz....................Eddie Leroy
Presiding Judge....................Edwin Maxwell
Stark....................Frank Ferguson
Fisher....................David Alexander
Marton....................Robert Cherry
Mrs. Schwartz....................Nina Hansen
Herman....................Sam Bernard
Ethel Mihaly....................Rita Gould
Dr. Darosch....................Rudolph Cameron
Dr. Samosch....................Peter Brocco
Mrs. Horney....................Belle Mitchell
Constable....................Ben Welden
Mr. Horney....................Michael Mark

Latest in the Hollywood cycle on racial tolerance basic themes, "The Vicious Circle," is a well-intentioned production which fails as adequate screen entertainment. Pic is too solemn and static either to register at the boxoffice or to punch across the message of brotherhood. Lack of marquee names and a thin production dress mark it for dualer fare.

Except for a couple of brief sequences, the film unfolds within the frame of a simple courtroom setting. Yarn, which is allegedly based on records tracing back to 1882 in Hungary, is narrated exclusively via legal debates and testimony. Heavy accent on pedestrian verbiage unrelieved by any action whatsoever is this pic's recipe for tedium. Despite the serious ideas on which it's pegged, "Vicious Circle" is only a talkative whodunit. But the basic danger of unsuccessful films dealing with anti-Semitism is that they can provoke more irritation than right thinking.

Story concerns a murder frame-up of five Jewish farmers in Hungary by an unscrupulous landowner who wants to drive them out of his neighborhood. Corrupt prosecuting attorneys fake evidence and suborn witnesses to build a case which the defense counsel regularly tears down. Procession of surprise witnesses, long speeches and the usual cross-examination brilliancies are all discarded at the climax when the sister of the corpus delicti admits that it wasn't murder but suicide.

Fritz Kortner, as one of the defendants, contributed the sole persuasive and moving performance. Conrad Nagel, as the defense attorney, is stuffy in his idealism, while the opposition, led by Reinhold Schunzel, as the landowner, and Lyle Talbot and Philip Van Zandt, as the prosecutors, are caricaturized villains. *Herm.*

The Gallant Legion (SONGS)

Hollywood May 22.

Republic release of Joe Kane production Stars William Elliott, Adrian Booth, Joseph Schildkraut, Bruce Cabot; features Andy Devine, Jack Holt, Grant Withers, Adele Mara, James Brown, Hal Landon. Directed by Joe Kane. Screenplay, Gerald Adams; original story, John K. Butler, Gerald Geraghty; camera, Jack Marta; musical director, Morton Scott; editor, Richard L. Van Enger. Previewed May 19, '48. Running time, 88 MINS.

Gary Conway....................William Elliott
Connie Faulkner....................Adrian Booth
Clarke Faulkner....................Joseph Schildkraut
Beau Laroux....................Bruce Cabot
Windy Hornblower....................Andy Devine
Captain Banner....................Jack Holt
Wesley Hardin....................Grant Withers
Catalina....................Adele Mara
Tom Banner....................James Brown
Chuck Conway....................Hal Landon
Sgt. Clint Mason....................Tex Terry
Matt Kirby....................Lester Sharpe
Billy Smith....................Hal Taliaferro
Senator Beale....................Russell Hicks
Major Grant....................Herbert Rawlinson
Bowling....................Marshall Reed
Dispatch Rider....................Steve Drake
Lang....................Harry Woods

"The Gallant Legion" is a strong western for all patrons who buy brawling outdoor action. Its basic story is a familiar one but is sold with a wallop that keeps it constantly on the move.

Joe Kane's forte for putting this type of film together is solidly demonstrated in his production and direction. There's a load of mass spectacle in brawls between Rangers and outlaws, plenty of exciting hand-to-hand encounters, and the pace is always swift. Story's familiarity doesn't mitigate against interest. It has a solid base in semi-historical events that transpire, the dialog has an occasional brightness not expected in a western, and plot development follows a logical pattern.

Story is laid in the period just after Texas had been admitted to the union and lawless forces sought to divide the state. During a six-month tryout of the Texas Rangers, every effort is made to discredit the law-enforcement body and it strikes back with wits and guns to prove itself to anxious citizens.

William Elliott heads up the heroics with ease as a soldier of fortune who joins the Rangers after his kid brother is killed while riding with the renegades. Opposite is Bruce Cabot, whose ambition to become king of West Texas causes all the trouble. They make expert antagonists. Adrian Booth's character of femme news correspondent isn't believable but adds romantic interest. Adele Mara pertly handles the other femme interest, as a saloon canary, and pipes three public-domain tunes, "A Gambler's Life," "Lady From Monterey" and "A Kiss or Two."

Joseph Schildkraut, a crooked senator; Andy Devine, in for chuckles; Jack Holt, good as the forthright Ranger captain; Grant Withers, James Brown and Hal Landon are among others whose work rates mention.

The swift action, backgrounded against outdoor scenery, has been expertly captured by Jack Marta's camera, and other credits are in keeping with generally excellent production values. *Brog.*

Big Town Scandal

Hollywood, May 22.

Paramount release of William Pine-William C. Thomas production. Stars Philip Reed, Hillary Brooke; features Stanley Clements, Darryl Hickman, Carl "Alfalfa" Switzer, Roland Dupree, Tommy Bond. Directed by William C. Thomas. Original screenplay, Milton Raison; based on the radio program, "Big Town"; camera, Ellis W. Carter; editor, Howard Smith. Tradeshown at Los Angeles, May 21, '48. Running time, 61 MINS.

Steve Wilson....................Philip Reed
Lorelei Kilbourne....................Hillary Brooke
Tommy Malone....................Stanley Clements
Skinny Peters....................Darryl Hickman
Frankie Sneed......Carl "Alfalfa" Switzer
Pinkie Jones....................Roland Dupree
Dummy....................Tommy Bond
Louie Sneed....................Vince Barnett
Amos Peabody....................Charles Aunt
Wally Blake....................Joe Allen, Jr.
Marian Harrison....................Donna de Mario
Joe Moreley....................John Phillips
Cato....................Reginald Bilado

"Big Town Scandal" is mildly entertaining melodrama. It will be passable in lower-rung bookings for which it was intended. Film is finale in the Pine-Thomas "Big Town" series, adapted from air show of same title.

There's a try or two for comedy in telling a story of juvenile delinquency but it's clumsy, and the adult principals bow to younger members of the cast in the playing. Co-producer William C. Thomas also directed from an original script by Milton Raison, but achieved only fair results.

This time plot has fighting editor Steve Wilson going on a crusade to aid the unfortunate youths of Big Town, being pressured into the deal by star reporter Lorelei Kilbourne. A group of teen-agers is paroled to the editor and he sets up a youth center to reform them through sports. A smarty in the bunch, ably portrayed by Stanley Clements, plays with gamblers in betting on basketball games and in providing them with a place to hide stolen goods. Others wise up and, in trying to help Clements reform, one is killed. Ending promises better things for all when Clements fingers the adult heavies.

Philip Reed has tough going with the Wilson character, being called upon to act mighty juvenile for a bigtime editor. Hillary Brooke, as his star reporter, fares somewhat better. In addition to Clements, other juves turning in good performances include Darryl Hickman, Carl "Alfalfa" Switzer, Tommy Bond and Roland Dupree. Vince Barnett shows up nicely as a bail bond broker, and others are okay.

Film has been given standard production mounting for the series. *Brog.*

King of the Gamblers

Hollywood, May 22.

Republic release of Stephen Auer production. Stars Janet Martin, William Wright, Thurston Hall; features Stephanie Bachelor, George Meeker, Wally Vernon, William Henry, James Cardwell, Jonathan Hale. Directed by George Blair; original screenplay, Albert DeMond, Bradbury Foote; camera, John MacBurnie; editor, Robert Leeds. Previewed May 18, '48. Running time, 60 MINS.

Jean Lacey....................Janet Martin
Dave Fowler....................William Wright
"Pop" Morton....................Thurston Hall
Elsie Pringle....................Stephanie Bachelor
Bernie Dupal....................George Meeker
Mike Burns....................Wally Vernon
Jerry Muller....................William Henry
"Speed" Lacey....................James Cardwell
Sam Hyland....................Jonathan Hale
Judge....................Selmer Jackson
Jordon....................Howard J. Negley
Symonds....................John Holland
O'Brien....................George Anderson
Cassidy....................Ralph Dunn
Bartender....................John Albright

"King of Gamblers" probes superficially into racketeering on professional football games and has sufficient interest to get by as secondary feature. Film is loaded with implausible developments but playing is good and running time is confined to tight 60 minutes.

There are a few moments of excitement stirred up by George Blair's direction and his handling otherwise is adequate to demands of a story that follows an obvious path. Plot deals with tiein between a gambler and the publisher of a sporting sheet. When their gridiron stooge threatens to reveal thrown games, he's bumped off and the murder framed on another pro footballer. A crusading district attorney, stepson of the publisher, takes on the accused's defense, and windup court trial exposes gambling syndicate.

William Wright shows up well as the crusading attorney, and Thurston Hall makes a good appearance as his stepfather. Janet Martin hasn't too much to do as top femme, with more lines going to Stephanie Bachelor as one of the heavies. George Meeker and Wally Vernon, gamblers; James Cardwell and William Henry, the pro footballers; Jonathan Hale and others are capable.

Stephen Auer has expended budget dollar carefully in shaping physical values but could have exercised stronger story guidance. Creditable is John MacBurnie's lensing. *Brog.*

Miniature Reviews

"The Gay Intruders" (20th). Broad comedy on domestic bickerings of legit star team. Mildly amusing for supporting market.

"The Counterfeiters" (20th) Good melodrama for supporting positions, well put together.

"Carson City Raiders" (Rep). Good Allan "Rocky" Lane western to please sagebrush fans.

"Secret Service Investigator" (Rep). Good action melodrama for the duals.

"Daybreak" (GFD). Disappointing British thriller; limited at b.o.

"Bond Street" (British) (Pathe). Roland Young plus all-British cast unknown to U.S.; dim chances in America.

"The Fatal Night" (Col). Tepid British thriller; mild draw.

"The Calendar" (GFD). Moderate British horse-race yarn, limited in draw.

"Marius" (Siritzky). Standout French pic starring the late Raimu.

"They Are Not Angels" (French). War Film has melodramatic ingredients for general U. S. Market.

"Clandestine" (Indie). French-made film dealing with the underground. For arty situations only.

The Gay Intruders

Hollywood, May 29.

20th-Fox release of Frank N. Seltzer (Hugh King) production. Stars John Emery, Tamara Geva; features Leif Erickson, Roy Roberts, Virginia Gregg. Directed by Ray McCarey. Screenplay, Frances Swann; based on an original by Swann and McCarey; camera, Mack Stengler; editor, Bert Jordan. Tradeshown May 28, '48. Running time, 68 MINS.

John Newberry	John Emery
Maria Ivar	Tamara Geva
Dr. Harold Matson	Leif Erickson
Charles McNulty	Roy Roberts
Dr. Susan Nash	Virginia Gregg
Arthur	Si Wills
Ethel	Sara Berner
Male Secretary	Harry Lauter
Female Secretary	Marilyn Williams

As a lower rung dualer, "The Gay Intruders" will serve its purpose. It's a broadly farced domestic comedy of the private lives of a legit star team, generously hoked to spring its chuckles from frantic antics. Results are mildly entertaining.

Plot deals with an aging theatrical pair who, on stage, are romantic lovers but, off stage as husband and wife, are a team of temperamental bickerers. Roles offer plenty of opportunity for scenery-chewing and John Emery and Tamara Geva miss no bets under broad direction by Ray McCarey. There's no subtlety to the unfoldment and plenty of points are stretched in obvious try for giggles.

The Frances Swann script, based on her original written with director McCarey, has thespians' agent recommending psychiatric treatment for their troubles, but this only results in the psychiatrists becoming bickerers like their patients after moving in to give home study to the cases.

Leif Erickson and Virginia Gregg are okay as the mental medicos, as is Roy Roberts as the agent. Si Wills and Sara Berner are the couple's quarrelsome servants.

Frank N. Seltzer's production supervision has decked light story with suitable framework for release intentions, aided by Hugh King, associate producer. Lensing, art direction and other factors are standard. *Brog.*

The Counterfeiters

Hollywood, May 29.

20th-Fox release of Maurice H. Conn (Reliance Pictures) production. Stars John Sutton, Doris Merrick, Hugh Beaumont; features Lon Chaney, George O'Hanlon, Douglas Blackley, Herbert Rawlinson. Directed by Peter Stewart. Screenplay, Fred Myton, Barbara Worth; original by Maurice H. Conn; camera, James S. Brown, Jr.; editor, Martin G. Conn. At Grauman's Chinese, Hollywood, May 28, '48. Running time, 73 MINS.

Jeff MacAllister	John Sutton
Margo	Doris Merrick
Philip Drake	Hugh Beaumont
Louie	Lon Chaney
Frankie	George O'Hanlon
Tony	Douglas Blackley
Norman Talbot	Herbert Rawlinson
Carter	Pierre Watkins
Dan Taggart	Don Harvey
Piper	Fred Coby
Art Model	Joyce Lansing
Jerry McGee	Gerard Gilbert

As a cops-and-robbers melodrama dealing with bogus money trade, "The Counterfeiters' 'is a good entry for the secondary market. Its melodramatics have been given neat production framing, the pace is excellent, and playing measures up to all demands of supporting bills.

Plot deals with an international counterfeit ring, with the Treasury Department and Scotland Yard joining forces to run down the villains. International angles are rung in production-wise with opening montages and then action switches to the west coast where the cops and the bogus experts maneuver for possession of U.S. $20 plates and English pound notes.

Hugh Beaumont heads up the counterfeiters as chief pusher of the queer and makes a rough, tough villain. John Sutton is his chief antagonist, appearing as the Scotland Yard man who adopts crook's role to get his man. Another member of the gang who is not what she appears is Doris Merrick, daughter of the plate-maker who is trying to recover and destroy evidence so she can save her father.

Teaming for comedy are Lon Chaney as strong-backed and weakminded henchman for Beaumont, and George O'Hanlon, sharpie who wants to get into the racket. Douglas Blackley is convincing as a T-Man, working with Don Harvey and Fred Coby to round up the crooks, and others in the cast are capable.

Peter Stewart directed the Maurice H. Conn production with an able style to keep development of the Fred Myton-Barbara Worth script on the move. Conn did the original story. There are a number of good production touches that display expert use of budget coin. Backgrounds are good, the lensing excellent and other technical aids well valued. *Brog.*

Carson City Raiders

Republic release of Gordon Kay production. Stars Allan "Rocky" Lane; features Eddy Waller, Frank Reicher, Beverly Jons, Hal Landon, Steve Darrell. Directed by Yakima Canutt. Screenplay, Earle Snell; camera, William Bradford; editor, Tony Martinelli. Previewed in Hollywood, May 24, '48. Running time, 60 MINS.

Allan "Rocky" Lane	Allan "Rocky" Lane
His Stallion	Black Jack
Nugget Clark	Eddy Waller
"Razor" Pool	Frank Reicher
Mildred Drew	Beverly Jons
Jimmy Davis	Hal Landon
Tom Drew	Steve Darrell
Starkey	Harold Goodwin
Brennon	Dale Van Sickel
John Davis	Tom Chatterton
Sheriff	Edmund Cobb
Joe	Holly Bane
Ed Noble	Bob Wilke

"Carson City Raiders" adds up to snappy film fare for the western market. It has fast pace, strong heroics and stunts to catch the fancy of Saturday matinee ticketbuyers. Production and direction have condensed a lot of action into 60 minutes, and the plot tells a lively, if standard, oater story.

Allan "Rocky" Lane makes a stalwart hero, not afraid to inject some flamboyance into his tight-lipped heroics, a factor that pays off in the action field. This time, he's an express company agent riding into Carson City to put a gang of outlaws behind bars. Crooks are trying to grab control of a wagon freight outfit and blacken the name of a sheriff who at one time had been an outlaw. Ready and accurate sixguns, potent fists and wit bring Lane out on top.

Lane's stallion, Black Jack, which draws star billing in the series, gets an action scene in this one when he saves his master from ambush — another neat stunt for the western trade. Steve Darrell, the reformed sheriff; Eddy Waller and Hal Landon are among those aiding Lane establish law and order. Heading up the dirty work are Frank Reicher, as town barber; Harold Goodwin and Dale Van Sickel.

Gordon's Kay's production gives the Earle Snell script proper backing to please the outdoor fan, and Yakima Canutt's direction is always packed with action. Lensing by William Bradford and other technical aids give okay mounting. *Brog.*

Secret Service Investigator

Republic release of Sidney Picker production. Features Lynne Roberts, Lloyd Bridges, George Zucco, June Storey. Directed by R. G. Springsteen. Original screenplay, John K. Butler; camera, John MacBurnie; editor, Arthur Roberts; music, Mort Glickman. Tradeshown N. Y. May 28, '48. Running time, 60 MINS.

Susan Lane	Lynne Roberts
Steve Mallory }	
Dan Redfern }	Lloyd Bridges
Otto Dagoff	George Zucco
Laura Redfern	June Storey
Henry Witzel	Trevor Bardette
Benny Deering	John Kellogg
Herman	Jack Overman
Al Turk	Roy Barcroft
Inspector Crehan	Douglas Evans
Miller	Milton Parsons
Police Inspector	James Flavin
Teddy Lane	Tommy Ivo
Porter	Sam McDaniel
Counterman	Billy Benedict
Mrs. McGiven	Minerva Urecal

An okay melodrama, Republic's "Secret Service Investigator" emerges as solid program fare for the duals. In most cases the footage should satisfy the action fans for there's fisticuffs aplenty along with occasional mayhem.

While scripter John K. Butler has commendably peppered the yarn with several unusual story twists, the average filmgoer won't find it too difficult in figuring out the finale well in advance. A counterfeiting tale, the story revolves around jobless ex-G.I. Lloyd Bridges, who's hired for an impersonation stint by several crooks posing as Secret Service men. Later he gets wise to the thieves and succeeds in rounding them up with the aid of bona fide Treasury agents.

Bridges does well enough with his role, but somehow fails to make it as colorful as it should be. George Zucco, head of a bogus coin syndicate, contribs a neat characterization as the picture's top heavy. Lynne Roberts is so-so as the heart interest while June Storey capably portrays a frowzy gunmoll. Supporting performances are acceptable.

Producer Sidney Picker handed the film adequate production mountings. R. G. Springsteen came through with a brisk directorial job while Arthur Roberts edited the pic down to a trim hour's running time. Camerawork of John MacBurnie is refreshing and Mort Glickman's musical direction helps give the overall print a lift. *Gilb.*

Daybreak
(BRITISH)

London, May 18.

GFD release of J. Arthur Rank-Sydney Box production. Stars Ann Todd, Eric Portman; features Maxwell Reed. Directed by Compton Bennett. Original, Monckton Hoffe; screenplay, Muriel and Sydney Box. Editors, Helga Cranston, Peter Price; camera, Reginald H. Wyer. At Leicester Square, London, May 18, '48. Running time, 81 MINS.

Eddie	Eric Portman
Frankie	Ann Todd
Olaf	Maxwell Reed
Bill Shackle	Edward Rigby
Ron	Bill Owen
Doris	Jane Hylton
Mr. Bigley	Eliot Makeham
Mrs. Bigley	Margaret Withers
Superintendent	John Turnbull
Inspector	Maurice Denham
Governor	Milton Rosmer
Waterman	Lyn Evans

Recent government edict abolishing capital punishment should have provided some topical interest but, according to producer Sydney Box, the film has been mutilated by the British censor, accounting for the anaemic condition of the story. Box protests that his best scenes have been bowlerized, and even a quotation from a Parliament debate, which appeared in every national newspaper, has been snipped.

Based on Monckton Hoffe's play, "Grim Fairy Tale," made a couple of years ago and ran into plenty of bother in addition to censor trouble. Stars may draw some patronage, but word-of-mouth can hardly be encouraging. Unrelieved gloom, for 81 minutes, mostly conversational—due, no doubt, to censorial cuts—isn't likely to bring joy to the boxoffice. It isn't the best Box vintage. Prospects here are not bright, and there is little hope for it on U. S. screens.

Eddie, ostensibly a barber and then barge owner, is actually the public hangman. Meeting Frankie, an attractive waif, in a saloon bar, he marries her. Intends to quit his hanging job and, while waiting for a successor, he absents himself fairly regularly "on business," and gives Olaf, a Danish seaman, opportunities to force his attention on Frankie.

Returning unexpectedly from a trip the husband finds the couple in a compromising situation, fights Olaf and is knocked overboard. The seaman is charged with murder, Frankie commits suicide, but unknown to the police Eddie has dragged himself ashore and subsequently is called upon to officiate at Olaf's hanging. At the last minute revulsion sets in and Eddie reveals he is the man Olaf is accused of murdering. Story is told in flashback, leaving the finale of Eddie hanging in his barber shop.

Ann Todd and Eric Portman try hard to bring their characters to life. Maxwell Reed makes his Dane a musclebound, adenoidal sissy. Only the minor characters like Edward Rigby, Bill Owen and Jane Hylton give credibility to the yarn. Direction doesn't enhance reputation of Compton Bennet ("The Seventh Veil") but there again the censor may have been to blame. *Cane.*

Bond Street
(BRITISH)

London, May 12.

Pathe release of Associated British Picture Corp.-World Screenplays production. Stars Roland Young, Jean Kent. Directed by Gordon Parry. Screenplay, Anatole de Grunwald, from original idea by J. G. Brown. Editor, Gerald Turney-Smith; camera, Otto Heller, Brian Langley. At Warner, London, May 12, '48. Running time, **109 MINS.**

Ricki Merritt	Jean Kent
George Chester-Barratt	Roland Young
Mrs. Brawn	Kathleen Harrison
Joe Marsh	Derek Farr
Julia Chester-Barratt	Hazel Court
Steve Winter	Ronald Howard
Elsa	Paula Valenska
Frank	Robert Flemyng
Mary	Patricia Plunkett
Mrs. Taverner	Adrianne Allen
Len Phipps	Kenneth Griffith
Aunt Lottie	Marian Spencer
Yarrow	James McKechnie
Miss Slennett	Mary Jerrold
Head Waiter	Charles Goldner
Norma	Joan Dowling
Barman	Leslie Dwyer

Supposed to be 24 hours in Bond Street, this could just as easily be a day and night on Main Street anywhere. A few location shots don't justify the title. Fashioned to the "Grand Hotel" formula, there are four separate episodes linked by a slender framework. Three of the stories are old-fashioned and in novel form, the fourth is adult and amusing. There is much trashy stuff before the final episode, which could have been expanded to a full length film. And it redeems the picture from boredom and gives it some boxoffice chance. Some of cast has a little pull here, but with the exception of Roland Young they can mean nothing to U. S. audiences. Film has a slim future there.

Wedding of Hazel Court is the connecting link, her dress, her pearls, her veil and her flowers being the basis of the four stories. The wedding dress lends itself to an episode in a fashion establishment where one of the workers (nicely played by Kathleen Harrison) expecting a grandchild, becomes wrongly incensed against a customer and ruins her frock. Since the customer only wants it to greet a war-blind son who has regained his sight, all the workwomen volunteer to repair the damaged gown.

Blackmailers, pearls, other factors figure in subsequent episodes, final one having to do with an escaped prisoner-of-war, and the girl who befriended him. She comes to England day he's to be married. The principals in this episode, Young, Paula Valenska and Flemyng, play it for all it's worth.

There is little distinction about Gordon Parry's direction but he is hardly to blame. His handicap was an undistinguished script.

Cane.

The Fatal Night
(BRITISH)

London, May 6.

Columbia release of Anglofilm production. Stars Lester Ferguson. Directed by Mario Zampi. Screenplay by Gerald Butler, adapted by Kathleen Connors from story by Michael Arlen; editor, Giulio Zampi; music, Stanley Black; camera, Cedric Williams. At Hammer, London, May 5, '48. Running time, **50 MINS.**

Puce	Lester Ferguson
Geraldine	Jean Short
Cyril	Leslie Armstrong
Julia	Brenda Hogan
Tony	Patrick Macnee
Yokel	Aubrey Mallalieu

Made on a small budget ($56,000), this may find a place as a curtain raiser for family audiences. Whether the producers can make a profit that way is doubtful, as exhibs are unlikely to pay much for it since it can't be a boxoffice attraction on its own.

Story sticks fairly closely to the Arlen original. Dared to spend a night in an alleged haunted house by two Englishmen, an American settles down with a gun and a grisly thriller about two Victorian sisters. He dreams about the sisters and awakes to see a phantom in his room. He fires at it and then collapses in a faint. Seven years elapse. The Englishmen meet the American, tell him how they tricked him by loading the gun with blanks, when suddenly the American goes berserk. He is strangling one of them when warders from a nearby asylum arrive. The American has been a homicidal maniac for seven years.

Operatic tenor Lester Ferguson plays the American and warbles "Rigoletto" at the top of his voice in the dead of night when every precaution was taken to enter the house on tiptoe. He keeps repeating "It's a lot of hooey." Maybe he's right.

Cane.

The Calendar
(BRITISH)

London, May 26.

GFD release of J. Arthur Rank-Gainsborough production. Stars Greta Gynt, John McCallum. Directed by Arthur Crabtree. Screenplay, Geoffrey Kerr, from play by Edgar Wallace. Camera, Reg Wyer, Cyril J. Knowles. At Odeon, London, May 25, '48. Running time, **79 MINS.**

Wenda	Greta Gynt
Garry	John McCallum
Willie	Raymond Lovell
Mollie	Sonia Holm
Hillcott	Leslie Dwyer
John Dory	Charles Victor
Lord Forlingham	Felix Aylmer
Tony	Sydney King
Lawyer	Noel Howlett
Sir John Garth	Barry Jones
Inspond	Claude Bailey
Rainby	Desmond Roberts

Remake of Edgar Wallace's 19-year-old racing play (screened as "Bachelor's Folly" in 1932, with Herbert Marshall, Edna Best, Gordon Harker and Nigel Bruce) is moderate entertainment. Stars and Wallace's reputation may get it some business here, but its only chance in the U. S. is as a dualer. When first made it had novelty of horse-racing scenes, but these have now become commonplace, and the melodrama strikes an artificial note. More should have been made of the comedy angles.

Golddigger Wenda jilts racehorse owner Garry when he loses most of his money. She marries Willie whose sister Mollie trains Garry's horses. While drunk Garry falls in with the suggestion of his ex-burglar valet to "pull" his horse entered for an important race in order to get a better price for its next running. Burglary and forgery by the valet enable Garry to get out of his jam, and all ends well with his horse winning and Garry landing Mollie.

It's mostly old-fashioned melodrama which rarely rings true. For some inexplicable reason valet's burglary is done off screen, a situation that could have provided thrills and fun. Racing scenes are good, and additional interest is given by the documentary touch of the King and Queen arriving on the Ascot race course.

Acting of the principals calls for little comment. The minor players give a good account of themselves. Title of picture, referring to the racing calendar, is unexplained and will be misleading to most audiences.

Clem.

Marius
(FRENCH)

Siritzky release of Marcel Pagnol production, written by Pagnol. Stars Raimu, Pierre Fresnay, Charpin, Orane Demazis. Directed by Alexander Korda. Music, Vincent Scotto; English titles, Herman G. Weinberg. At Elysee, N. Y., May 11, '48. Running time, **127 MINS.**

Cesar	Raimu
Marius	Pierre Fresnay
Panisse	Charpin
Fanny	Orane Demazis
Honorine	Alida Rouffe
Mr. Brun	Robert Vattier
Pigueoisot	Michaelesco

(In French; English Titles)

This Marcel Pagnol production was first shown in the U. S. without English titles in 1933 at the 5th Avenue Playhouse, N. Y., where it died after a week. But the market for foreign pix has changed considerably since then. Fifteen years ago, VARIETY's reviewer, *Kauf*, said that "Marius" was "the finest French film to come over," but then paradoxically declared that "it's hopeless for U. S. consumption." Currently, it's slated for solid biz in the art houses.

For its revival, "Marius" has been refurbished with English titling and 25 minutes have been added to the original running time in the U. S. of 103 minutes. Initial part of Pagnol's trilogy on Marseilles life, film is full of the warmth and humor that typified "Fanny"—the second part of the trilogy which Siritzky, for some reason, released first. The pic's age is detectable only in occasional scratchiness of the sound track and slightly faded celluloid. In quality, however, it ranks among the top foreign offerings of the last few years.

Yarn concerns a waterfront love affair between Pierre Fresnay, a bartender's son with a yen for the sea, and Orane Demazis, a fishmonger's daughter. One of his best, though least known achievements, [now Sir] Alexander Korda directed this story with a simple and compelling honesty without the slightest taint of hokum.

Headed by the late Raimu, the cast of standout French thespers impart an earthy quality to their performances. Once again, Raimu, as the bartender, blends a profound pathos, and a vigorous sense of humor into a powerfully human portrait. Panisse, as an elderly suitor, matches Raimu in style and competence. Miss Demazis, while not a looker by Hollywood standards, is a sensitive actress with a tragic appeal. Fresnay is too theatrical but is checked by the film's overall quiet and leisurely mood.

Herm.

They Are Not Angels
(FRENCH)

Siritzky International release of French Pathe production. Stars Pierre Blanchar. Directed by Alexandre Esway. Screenplay, Joseph Kessel; camera, Nicolas Hayer; music, Maurice Thieriet; English titles, Charles Clement. At Ambassador, N. Y., May 21, '48. Running time, **123 MINS.**

Ferane	Pierre Blanchar
Paname	Raymond Bussieres
Ben Sassem	Jean Wall
Lt. de Carrizy	Christian Bertola
Baptiste	Rene Lefevre
Berthe Servais	Jeanne Crispin
Drobel	Pierre Louis
Le Gorille	Charles Moulin
Le Canaque	Mouloudji
Bouvier	Henri Nassiet
Veran	Nic Vogel
Brizeux	Andrieux
June	Daphne Courtney
Willy	John Howard
Molly	Pamela Sterling
Marc Intyre	Charles Rolfe

(In French; English Titles)

"They Are Not Angels," one of the few war films to come out of France since 1945, is slated for a good reception in the U. S. Story of a group of French paratroopers is narrated in a punchy, masculine style with plenty of familiar Hollywood melodramatics that cues it for general distribution here. Pic's quality and b.o. potential could be considerably improved by judicious slicing of about 25 minutes from its current two-hour running time.

Yarn's background is split between England and France with a liberal sprinkling of English actors and dialog in the film. Initial half covers the training preparation for a group of 400 partroopers who are designated to spearhead the invasion of the Nazi-held continent. The toughening-up process, the attempts to integrate some raw recruits into a group of vets, the boredom and anxiety before battle—all these facets are handled with straight realistic effectiveness.

Second half of the film, which concerns the combat action against the Germans after the paratroopers were landed in Brittany, is in the more hokey vein of melodramatic heroics. Menace of the enemy has not been delineated with sufficent actuality to provide a background of tension for this section of the yarn. The French commandos, moreover, engage in a series of bravado actions that generate excitement but lack conviction. This is a theatrical, not a real war.

Cast includes a flock of new French actors who deliver with verve and competence. The vet actor, Pierre Blanchar, gives a finely etched performance as the paratroopers' captain, although this role is not dominant. Raymond Bussieres, Nic Vogel and Pierre Louis, as rank-and-filers, contribute most to the film's violence and occasional humor. Group of English thespers, in bit parts, neatly underplay their lines in a documentary style.

Technically, film is marked by excellent lensing of the paratroopers' descent in mass formation. Background music, however, has a florid patriotic theme that doesn't add to the film's genuineness.

Herm.

Clandestine
(Les Clandestins)
(FRENCH-MADE)

J. H. Hoffberg release of Paul Pavaux production. Features Suzy Carrier, Georges Rollin, Samson Fainsilber. Directed by Andre E. Chotin. Screenplay, Pierre Le Stringuey; editor, Walter Klee; music, Jean Paquet. At Stanley theatre, N. Y., May 22, '48. Running time, **76 MINS.**

Yvonne	Suzy Carrier
Jean	Andre Reybas
Dr. Netter	Samson Fainsilber
Laurent	Georges Rollin
Priest	Constant Remy
Landlord	Guillaume De Sax

(In French; English Titles)

Lacking fresh and original treatment, this story of the French underground is just another adventure yarn. Picture's saleability will be limited to houses catering to lingual pix.

"Clandestine" shows Nazi brutality in its most elementary vein. Picture starts at a fast pace, with the Nazi capture of an underground newspaper and continues with the Germans liquidating hostages and torturing those who will not divulge information. In short, just another rehash.

Performances of fairly good calibre are turned in by Georges Rollin, as leader of the Maquis; Suzy Carrier, as the love interest for Rollin, and Andre Reybas as a recruit in the movement. The most rounded enactment is by Samson Fainsilber, as the Jewish medico captured by the Nazis. Constant Remy, as the priest who attempts to rescue hostages, also does well.

Andre E. Chotin's direction accents rapidity at the expense of characterization. Rest of the production comprises adequate sets and a good musical score by Jean Paquet. The English subtitles fill the language gap. *Jose.*

First Opera Film Festival
(ITALIAN)

Classic Pictures release of George Richfield production. Stars Tito Gobbi, Clio Elmo. Directed by E. Cancellieri. Music by La Scala Opera Company; English narration, Olin Downes. At Little Carnegie, N. Y., May 29, '48. Running time, 90 MINS.

"First Opera Film Festival" is a compilation of four standard operas in abbreviated versions which will have some appeal for the longhair music devotees. Except for the deletions, film presents the operas as they would be seen on the stage with no attempt to use the added scope of the camera for action and background. As a result, this importation is pictorially static and depends entirely upon the music to sustain interest. Film could probably be put to good use for schoolroom music appreciation courses.

High spots of Rossini's "William Tell," Mozart's "Marriage of Figaro," Donizetti's "Don Pasquale" and Bizet's "Carmen" are covered in this cinematic album. A group of thespers handle the various operatic roles in pantomime with members of the La Scala Opera Co. dubbing their voices. Dubbing technique is slipshod but there's compensation in a good soundtrack. Photography, however, is not adequately lighted.

Olin Downes, N. Y. Times music critic, explains the action in a narration that kids the corny operatic plots. At several points, his voice is superimposed on the singing in a manner that doesn't add to the pleasure of the music. *Herm.*

Miniature Reviews

"**Romance On the High Seas**" (Musical-Color) (WB). Gay tunefilm carrying high quota of entertainment.

"**Feudin', Fussin' and A-Fightin'**" (U) (Songs). Spritely comedy for good outlook business.

"**Coroner Creek**" (Color) (Col). Rough, tough western in Cinecolor. Strong action highlighted by one of best fights yet screened.

"**My Dog Rusty**" (Col). Sentimental entry in Columbia's series of kid-dog supporting features. Modest tear-jerker.

"**16 Fathoms Deep**" (Color) (Mono). Story of sponge fishing, in good color but slowly paced and only mildly exciting.

"**Germania Anno Zero**." Italian pic on German degradation is surefire for art situations.

"**Blind Desire**" (French) (Indie). Jean-Louis Barrault, Edwige Feuillere in disappointing love story about a temperamental musician-composer; mild returns indicated.

Romance on the High Seas
(COLOR—MUSICAL)
Hollywood, June 3.

Warner Bros. release of Alex Gottlieb (Michael Curtiz) production, directed by Curtiz. Stars Jack Carson, Janis Paige, Don De Fore, Doris Day; features Oscar Levant, S. Z. Sakall. Screenplay, Julius J. and Philip G. Epstein; added dialog, I. A. L. Diamond; story, S. Pondal Rios, Carlos A. Olivari; camera (Technicolor), Elwood Bredell; editor, Rudi Fehr; music, Jule Styne, Sammy Cahn. Tradeshown June 1, '48. Running time, 96 MINS.

Peter Virgil	Jack Carson
Elvira Kent	Janis Paige
Michael Kent	Don De Fore
Georgia Garrett	Doris Day
Oscar Farrar	Oscar Levant
Uncle Lazlo	S. Z. Sakall
Plinio	Fortunio Bonanova
Ship's Doctor	Eric Blore
Rio Hotel Clerk	Franklin Pangborn
Miss Medwick	Leslie Brooks
Travel Agent	William Bakewell
The Drunk	Johnny Berkes
Bartender	Kenneth Britton

Avon Long
Sir Lancelot
The Samba Kings
Page Cavanaugh Trio

"Romance on the High Seas" is slotted for wide popular acceptance. It's gay, slightly giddy, loaded with tunes, laughs and nonsense. Sturdy entertainment ingredients are displayed against a colorful production background aptly fitted to show off musical numbers and light story. Cast names are sturdy, auguring well for top bookings through all situations.

Score has eight tunes by Sammy Cahn and Jule Styne. Several already are catching radio popularity. Pop numbers are given strong selling by Doris Day, erstwhile orch chirp with sock film personality. Miss Day has five tunes, "I'm in Love," "It's You or No One," "It's Magic," "Put It in a Box" and "Two Lovers Met in the Night." In addition to easy listening, Miss Day clicks in her story character and should draw nifty fan response.

Plot is a fluffy one about a wife who suspects her husband of being a wolf. She arranges a South American cruise, but sends another girl under her name while she stays incognito in New York to do some domestic spying. The husband mistrusts her and sends a private detective on the cruise to watch out for two-timing. The pseudo-wife and the dick fall in love and complications that result rate beaucoup laughs.

Michael Curtiz' direction whips the story along swiftly, combining the chuckles and musical moments into fast-paced entertainment. The Epsteins' script is marked by breezy dialog and a number of hilarious sequences. One is bar scene where in Jack Carson and Oscar Levant become highly intoxicated without ever taking a drink.

Cast runs through the roles with evident enjoyment. Carson slaps home his scenes as the detective who falls for pseudo-wife Doris Day. The ever-loving couple gets solid interpretation from Janis Paige and Don De Fore. Levant rates some strong giggles as a quip-making pianist in love with Miss Day, and S. Z. Sakall is in for comedy as Miss Paige's uncle. Also showing up well are Fortunio Bonanova, Eric Blore, Franklin Pangborn, Leslie Brooks and Johnny Berkes.

There's plenty doing in the dance numbers by Busby Berkeley, with top nod going to Avon Long's specialty on "The Tourist Trade" against Cuban market place background. Sir Lancelot calypsos "In Trinidad," and Carson wraps up "Run, Run, Run." also a calypso.

Alex Gottlieb's production guidance gives showy presentation that favors eye appeal. Misses Paige and Day have been gorgeously gowned and make a beautiful appearance in Technicolor. Elwood Bredell's tinted lensing obtains the best from Anton Grot's striking art direction and the set decorations by Howard Winterbottom. Ray Heindorf orchestrated and conducted the music by Styne and Cahn. *Brog.*

Feudin', Fussin' and A-Fightin'
(SONGS)
Hollywood, June 5.

Universal release of Leonard Goldstein production. Stars Donald O'Connor, Marjorie Main, Percy Kilbride; features Penny Edwards, Joe Besser. Directed by George Sherman. Screenplay, D. D. Beauchamp from his Collier's mag story; camera, Irving Glassberg; editor, Edward Curtiss; music, Leith Stevens. Tradeshown June 4, '48. Running time, 78 MINS.

Wilbur McMurtry	Donald O'Connor
Maribel Matthews	Marjorie Main
Billy Caswell	Percy Kilbride
Libby Matthews	Penny Edwards
Sharkey Dolan	Joe Besser
Chauncey	Harry Shannon
Emory Tuttle	Fred Kohler, Jr.
Doc Overholt	Howland Chamberlin
Stage Driver	Edmund Cobb
Stage Passenger	Joel Friedkin
Guard	I. Stanford Jolley

"Feudin', Fussin' and A-Fightin'" is gay film fare that springs its laughs easily, making for lively, pleasant entertainment in general situations. The doings are sparked by Donald O'Connor, Marjorie Main and Percy Kilbride with broad playing suited to slaphappy story. Three familiar tunes and two ace dance numbers furnish the musical touches, blending ably with the comedy.

O'Connor goes to town on his solo number to the tune of "Me and My Shadow." Terping is sharp and has several moments that will bring gasps for unanticipated agility. Second dance piece is shared with Penny Edwards and is projected for pleasurable watching as team goes through vocals and footwork to "S'posin'." Third tune, the title number, is used at opening and closing for film, with the Sportsman Quartet handling the vocals.

O'Connor is seen as traveling salesman for nostrums who is unfortunate enough to demonstrate his fleet-footedness during a stopover in the town of Rimrock. Village is readying for its annual footrace with a rival town and lacks a runner. O'Connor is kidnapped and all the craft and wiles of the villagers turned loose to force him to give his all for Rimrock. The D. D. Beauchamp script, from his own story, gives everything a slaphappy touch that makes for strong laughs as directed by George Sherman. Latter's guidance is fast and excellently valued to point up the chuckles.

O'Connor makes an advantageous appearance, working hard and pleasing. Penny Edwards does an okay chore as the romantic interest. Two solid characterizations are in the seasoned hands of Miss Main, mayor of Rimrock, and Percy Kilbride, livery stable owner. Joe Besser, comic sheriff, Harry Shannon and Fred Kohler, Jr., rival town heavies, Howland Chamberlin, Edmund Cobb, Joel Friedkin, I. Stanford Jolley and others come through capably.

Leonard Goldstein's production has given this sturdy mounting on a medium budget, assuring good returns. The lensing by Irving Glassberg, editing, score and other technical factors are good assists. *Brog.*

Coroner Creek
(COLOR)
Hollywood, May 29.

Columbia release of Harry 'Joe' Brown (Producers Actors) production. Stars Randolph Scott, Marguerite Chapman; features George Macready, Sally Eilers, Edgar Buchanan. Directed by Ray Enright. Screenplay, Kenneth Gamet; adapted from novel by Luke Short; camera (Cinecolor), Fred H. Jackman, Jr.; score, Rudy Schrager; editor, Harvey Manger. Previewed May 27, '48. Running time, 89 MINS.

Chris Danning	Randolph Scott
Kate Hardison	Marguerite Chapman
Younger Miles	George Macready
Della Harms	Sally Eilers
Sheriff O'Hea	Edgar Buchanan
Abbie Miles	Barbara Reed
Andy West	Wallace Ford
Ernie Combs	Forrest Tucker
Leach Conover	William Bishop
Frank Yordy	Joe Sawyer
Walt Hardison	Russell Simpson
Stew Shallis	Douglas Fowley
Tip Henry	Lee Bennett
McCune	Forrest Taylor
Bill Arnold	Phil Schumaker
Ray Flanders	Warren Jackson

Columbia has a mighty solid western entry in "Coroner Creek." The stress is on deadly gunfighter action and it's rough, tough example of straight western fare that spares no punches. The melodramatic heroics have been given a Cinecolor garb that adds appeal and the general worth of this one for the outdoor trade has been heightened by some knock-down, drag-out fisticuffs that have rarely been matched on the screen.

Forthright direction by Ray Enright gives strong guidance to the Luke Short novel from which this one was adapted. Plotting follows the somewhat cryptic Short writing style but it all adds up in the end and Enright keeps it hitting hard throughout. Script by Kenneth Gamet is excellent, depicting the relentless pursuit of avenging gunman, Randolph Scott, as he tracks down the man behind an Indian raid on a stagecoach and theft of rich payroll loot.

Setting is the town of Coroner Creek, where the villain has established himself as a respected citizen through use of his stolen gold. Scott's efforts to smoke him out into the open lead to many scenes of deadly menace that will satisfy the most bloodthirsty fan. One of the peak moments of excitement is reached when Scott and Forrest Tucker, henchman of the villain, come together in a physical clash that ends with bloody heads and broken fists, leaving them crippled throughout the rest of the footage. It's a realistic staging guaranteed to sate the brute in the action seeker.

Film stresses characterization and the cast delivers. In addition to Scott's strong work, Marguerite Chapman appears to advantage in the femme lead. George Macready makes a menacing villain. Sally Eilers does well by a character not too clearly established and Edgar Buchanan's sheriff is topnotch: Barbara Reed, a femme souse; Wallace Ford, exceptionally good as a ranch character; Forrest Tucker, Joe Sawyer, Douglas Fowley, Lee Bennett and William Bishop are among the others who add capable performances.

Production supervision by Harry Joe Brown is expertly valued to make this one pay off. Scenic settings and other worthwhile dressings have been given ace lensing by Fred H. Jackman, Jr., and the editing by Harvey Manger is concise. *Brog.*

My Dog Rusty

Hollywood, June 5.
Columbia release of Wallace MacDonald production. Features Ted Donaldson, John Litel, Ann Doran, Mona Barrie, Whitford Kane, Jimmy Lloyd, Lewis L. Russell. Directed by Lew Landers. Screenplay, Brenda Weisberg; story, William B. Sackheim, Brenda Weisberg; based upon characters by Al Martin; camera, Vincent Farrar; editor, Jerome Thoms. At the Vogue, Hollywood, June 3, '48. Running time, 64 MINS.
Danny Mitchell...............Ted Donaldson
Hugh Mitchell....................John Litel
Mrs. Mitchell....................Ann Doran
Dr. Toni Cordell..................Mona Barrie
Mr. Tucker..................Whitford Kane
Rodney Pyle.................Jimmy Lloyd
Mayor Fulderwilder......Lewis L. Russell
Hebble.......................Harry Harvey
Frank Foley....................Olin Howlin
Bill Worden..................Ferris Taylor
Gerald Hebble............Mickey McGuire
Nip Worden..............Dwayne Hickman
Tuck Worden...............David Ackles
Squeeky Foley...............Teddy Infuhr
Mrs. Foley........Minta Durfee Arbuckle
Rusty. ....Flame

"My Dog Rusty" is another of Columbia's sentimental little sagas dealing with a child and his dog. It will fare no better no rworse than other entries in the series in the secondary bookings for which it is slated.

All the to-do in the Brenda Weisberg script deals with a kid whose habit of lying ruins his father's campaign for mayor. None of the plotting is particularly believeable and treads a saccharine path. The kid's meddling that brings temporary disgrace on the father, the parent's attitude toward an unruly son and the lack of reason for the son's disobedience makes for dull doings.

Ted Donaldson fails to register as the bad boy but the combination of kid and dog, in the latter instance the handsome Flame, is always good for certain type of family audience. John Litel and Ann Doran are okay as the father and mother, as are Mona Barrie and Whitford Kane, a blind man.

Lew Landers' direction overcomes, to some extent, the weak script. Producer Wallace Mac-Donald has haped the physical budget values in okay fashion. Technical credits are standard. *Brog.*

16 Fathoms Deep
(COLOR)

Hollywood, June 5.
Monogram release of Arthur Lake production, produced by James S. Burkett and Irving Allen; directed by Allen. Stars Lon Chaney, Jr., Arthur Lake, Lloyd Bridges, Eric Feldary, Tanis Chandler; features John Qualen, Ian MacDonald, Dickie Moore, Harry Cheshire. Screenplay, Max Trell; adaptation, Forrest Judd; from story, "16 Fathoms Under," by Eustace L. Adams; camera (Ansco), Jack Greenhalgh; editor, Charles Craft. Previewed June 3,
'48. Running time, 78 MINS.
Dimitri......................Lon Chaney
Pete.........................Arthur Lake
Douglas...................Lloyd Bridges
Alex.........................Eric Feldary
Simi.......................Tanis Chandler
Athos.......................John Qualen
Nick.......................Ian MacDonald
George.......................Dickie Moore
Miki.......................Harry Cheshire
Captain Brigers..............John Bleifer
Joe.........................Grant Means
Johnny.......................John Gonatos
Bus Driver..................Allen Mathews

"16 Fathoms Deep" is a mildly developed story of sponge fishing in the Gulf of Mexico. Chief interest lies in bacground and fact that it is the first feature film to be released in the new Ansco color process. Hues compare with other tint mediums and have a naturalness easy onm the eye.

Story is tied together with narration and spin off a full hour before any excitement is generated. This, coupled with slowly paced direction, makes for spotty interest. Lloyd Bridges does the narrating, portraying ex-Navy diver who hits the beach at Tarpon Springs in try to get on a sponge boat. He joins with a new boat owner and crew in the highly competitive industry and the doings follow a formula line in try for melodramatics.

The underwater sequences were filmed in Rainbow Springs, Fla., and Marineland Studios at St. Augustine, Fla. Menace, outside of human villainry, is supplied by deep-water denizens such as sharks and giant clams. Underwater shots have beauty but don't match supposed 16 fathoms deep location of action.

Lon Chaney, Jr., portrays the crooked sponge dealer whose henchmen try to best the new boat crew. Arthur Lake is in for broad comedy as camera-snapping tourist. Eric Feldary makes an adequate boat owner-diver and shares romance with Tanis Chandler. Bridges shows best, along with John Qualen, Dickie Moore and Harry Cheshire.

Film is presented as an Arthur Lake production for Monogram release. Irving Allen's direction would have brought off the melodramatics with more interest had the pace been sharpened. Jack Greenhalgh did the good color lensing and other credits are standard. *Brog.*

Germania Anno Zero
(Germany the Year Naught)
(ITALIAN)

Rome, May 30.
Universalia-GDB release of Teverfilm (Roberto Rossellini) production. Direction and original story by Rossellini; screenplay, Rossellini and Max Colpet. Camera, Robert Julliard; editor, Eraldo Da Roma. Previewed Rome, May 30, '48. Running time, 78 MINS.
Edmund.................Edmund Meschke
Edmund's Father.........Ernst Pittschau
Eva....................Ingetraud Hinzf
Karl-Heinz................Franz Grueger
Schoolteacher.................Eric Guehne

"Germany has backtracked 1948 years. It's now at naught — as if Christ weren't born, since they wanted to kill Him again. Therefore, don't seek traces of our civilization in this film. They've disappeared."

Film opens with this foreword. Not the slightest sign of comedy lightens the pic, being out of place in such a dark story. The film offers repulsive characters and episodes, too, because they're needed by the film's nature itself. Having resolved to mirror a world which has lost every moral rule, producer-director-writer Roberto Rossellini has done it without underscorings, in an extremely ob-

jective, cold manner, turning out more document than documentary —a film unique in motion picture history.

Comparison is impossible between this and previous Rossellini films. What "Open City" and "Paisan" had of heart and humanity is entirely gone here—at least for three-quarters of the footage. In his denial of all the screen is supposed to call for, Rossellini has gone to extremes.

Film deals with some objectionable material for U.S. standards. If censors don't frown, it will have surefire returns in art situations, even if larger exploitation seems hampered by the kind of story and lack of commercial entertainment in the accepted sense. German dialog also won't help, at least with Italian-language trade, although it adds to the film's authenticity.

Film deals with terrifying doings. There are boys in it who kill their parents and then commit suicide. There are girls—but they're prostitutes. There are school teachers—but they're of perverted natures. All this, on the terrifying background of bombed-out Berlin, where phantom-like people are living as they can, one selling black market goods which he immediately steals again, another playing for the Allies' enjoyment the record of one of Hitler's speeches among the ruins of the Chancery.

Film has a sequence of great poetry. When little Edmund Meschke, after having poisoned his father, meets the school teacher who suggested the crime to him and tells him about his deed, the man chases him, horrified. The boy can't understand why, but he realizes that something monstrous has happened. He walks along the ravaged streets of the city, made wretched by an inner conflict which the camera masterfully catches in every nuance at the right pitch.

This wandering, which leads to death, is handled like a game—a sinister, moving game. Now it's a stone the boy picks up and casts away, then it's a ball he throws back to other boys, now it's sliding for fun on a bombed roof-side, and finally it's his voluntary jump into the void and death. This episode, intensely breathtaking and done with superb artistry, is the best of the film and one of the best ever turned out.

Pic isn't acted but "lived." Pro and non-pro cast play it with uniform sincerity. Meschke is the most impressive of the lot, delivering a poignant, believable portrayal as the young disgraced hero. Photography by Robert Julliard keeps a constant balance between location shootings and studio scenes, latter being made extremely authentic by Piero Filippone's sets. Score by Renzo Rossellini always helps activate the drama. *Quat.*

Blind Desire
(La Part de L'Ombre)
(FRENCH)

Discina International Films release of Michel Safra-Andre Paulve production. Stars Jean-Louis Barrault, Edwige Feuillere. Directed by Jean Dellanoy. Screenplay, Charles Spaak, Jean Dellanoy; camera, Roger Hubert; music, George Auric; English titles, Bernard Friend. Previewed in N. Y., June 4, '48. Running time, 88 MINS.
Michel Kremer........Jean-Louis Barrault
Agnes Noblet............Edwige Feuillere
Robert Ancelot.................Jean Wall
Pierre Morin.............Raphael Patorni
Madame Berthe.................Line Noro
Fanny.....................Helene Vervors
Auguste.....................Yves Deniaud
Jerome Noblet.................Jean Yonnel

(*In French; English Titles*)

"Blind Desire" has two strikes on it for the U.S. Picture, firstly, is too strongly wrapped up with the careeer of a temperamental musician-composer—makes of this ilk having done big biz. Second handicap is lack of action and humor. Hence, this looks to do only moderately well at arty houses.

Exhibitors have Edwige Feuillere and Jean-Louis Barrault for name value, but that won't be enough. Story is of a violinist-composer who is thwarted in an early ambition, and it's not told particularly well. Jean Dellanoy, who directed, had a hand in scripting. Barrault, a musician with a touch of genius, is depicted running away from the easy-to-take attentions of Miss Feuillere, daughter of a noted musician. Ten years later she again plans to run off with him but the musician's mistress then interferes. Final meeting, 20 years after the first spat, finds Barrault's landlady, apparently his new sweetie, cutting off a final chance for the two to find happiness.

Miss Feuillere lends considerable beauty to the pic. Helene Vercors is especially fine as the mistress, while Line Noro makes a forceful landlady. Barrault gets too much footage.

Nice production values, excellent music by George Auric and a superbly staged concerthall sequence are some of the film's merits. *Wear.*

Miniature Reviews

"A Foreign Affair" (Par). Jean Arthur, John Lund and Marlene Dietrich in strong laugh film.

"Lulu Belle" (Col) (Songs). Dorothy Lamour in old play about a gal who romanced her way to Broadway.

"Beyond Glory" (Par). A kudo to the officer standards of West Point with Alan Ladd to sharpen boxoffice interest.

"Mickey" (Songs - Color) (EL). Minor yarn about a tomboy's awakening into young womanhood.

"Michael O'Halloran" (Mono) Sentimental story of youth that should find easy going in smaller, family-trade situations.

"My Sister And I" (GFD). Weak British thriller of little appeal.

"Portrait of Innocence" (French) (Siritzky). — French laugh vehicle; may please kid audiences but thin for adult audiences in foreign-language spots.

"Uneasy Terms" (Pathe). Lightweight British whodunit is mild entry.

"Razzia" (German) (Artkino). German-made meller of blackmarketeers is gripping fare.

A Foreign Affair
(SONGS)

Hollywood, June 11.

Paramount release of Charles Brackett production. Stars Jean Arthur, Marlene Dietrich, John Lund; features Millard Mitchell. Directed by Billy Wilder. Screenplay, Charles Brackett, Billy Wilder, Richard L. Breen; adaptation, Robert Harari; original story, David Shaw; camera, Charles B. Lang, Jr.; editor, Doane Harrison; songs, Frederick Hollander. Tradeshown in Los Angeles, June 11, '48. Running time, **115 MINS.**

Phoebe Frost....Jean Arthur
Erika Von Schluetow....Marlene Dietrich
Captain John Pringle....John Lund
Col. Rufus J. Plummer....Millard Mitchell
Hans Otto Birgel....Peter von Zerneck
Mike....Stanley Prager
Joe....Bill Murphy
First M.P....Gordon Jones
Second M.P....Freddie Steele
Pennecott....Raymond Bond
Giffin....Boyd Davis
Kraus....Robert Malcolm
Yandell....Charles Meredith
Salvatore....Michael Raffetto
Lieut. Hornby....James Larmore
Lieut. Colonel....Damien O'Flynn

"A Foreign Affair" is a witty satire developed around a Congressional investigation of GI morals in Germany. The humor to which such a theme lends itself has been given a stinging bite, even though presented broadly to tickle the risibilities. Boxoffice reaction should be strong.

Solons who take their probes seriously are likely to be uncomfortable in light of the Charles Brackett-Billy Wilder treatment of "Affair." While subject is handled for comedy, pair have managed to underlay the fun with an expose of human frailities and, to some extent, indicate a passive bitterness among the conquered in the occupied areas.

Jean Arthur is back in a topflight characterization after a considerable screen absence. As a spinsterish Congresswoman, she furnishes the distaff touch to an elemental girl-meets-boy angle in the story. The boy is John Lund, and his handling of the role of a fraternizing Army captain who warms up the femme solon should build a respectable fan following.

Marlene Dietrich personifies the eternal siren as an opportunist German femme who furnishes Lund with off-duty diversion. Also, she gives the Dietrich s.a. treatment to three Frederick Hollander tunes, lyrics of which completely express the cynical undertones of the film. Numbers are "Black Market," "Illusions" and "Ruins of Berlin."

Light musical moments spring from Miss Arthur's quaverings on "Iowa Corn Song," a "Deep in the Heart of Texas" treatment and "Meadowland."

Brackett, Wilder and Richard L. Breen have spotted their script with whiplash dialog that contrasts with almost slapstick style with which Wilder's direction plays some of the sequences. The combination is good but causes the laughs to tread too closely on a number of the catch lines. Plot deals with Congressional subcommittee which junkets to Berlin to investigate reports of prolific fraternization between GI's and frauleins. The probe tosses many a shock at Miss Arthur's unawakened feelings, and place takes on spicy interest when Lund makes a play for the Congresswoman to divert her from discovering his amatory affiliation with Miss Dietrich.

Millard Mitchell heads the featured players with a solid performance. As the colonel responsible for Lund and the committee from Washington, Mitchell reads into the role a lot of dry fun and bite. Stanley Prager and Bill Murphy are an expert pair of fraulein-chasing GI's. Gordon Jones and Freddie Steele are good as M.P.'s, and others in the cast deliver competently.

Much of the action is backgrounded against actual Berlin footage. Charles B. Lang does an ace lensing chore, and there are photographic assists from process work by Farciot Edouart and Dewey Wrigley, and the special effects by Gordon Jennings. *Brog.*

Lulu Belle
(SONGS)

Hollywood, June 12.

Columbia release of Benedict Bogeaus production. Stars Dorothy Lamour, George Montgomery; features Albert Dekker, Otto Kruger, Glenda Farrell, Greg McClure. Directed by Leslie Fenton. Screenplay, Everett Freeman; added dialog, Karl Lamb; based on play by Charles MacArthur and Edward Sheldon; camera, Ernest Laszlo; editor, James Smith; music, Henry Russell. Previewed June 9, '48. Running time, **86 MINS.**

Lulu Belle....Dorothy Lamour
George Davis....George Montgomery
Mark Brady....Albert Dekker
Harry Randolph....Otto Kruger
Molly Benson....Glenda Farrell
Butch Cooper....Greg McClure
Mrs. Randolph....Charlotte Wynters
Commissioner Dixon....Addison Richards
Duke Weaver....William Haade
Doctor....Ben Erway
Bartender....Clancy Cooper
Brady's Bodyguards.... John Indrisano, Bud Wiser
Captain Ralph....George Lewis
Maitre D'....Harry Hays Morgan
Wells....Jack Norman
Pearl....Martha Holliday

"Lulu Belle" is an old-fashioned ten-twent-thirt meller that seems likely to find the boxoffice going spotty. What returns it does rate will depend on Dorothy Lamour's name and type of exploitation used to attract the femmes to plot's bad-girl theme. It's a screen adaptation of the old Charles MacArthur-Edward Sheldon play, originally produced by David Belasco, and has undergone a film cleanup to dodge censors.

Miss Lamour gives considerable life to her title role. She also sells four tunes with a sultry personality, and songs listen well. Henry Russell cleffed "I'd Be Lost If I Ever Lost You," "Sweetie Pie" and the title tune. Others are the oldie "I Can't Tell Why I Love You," by Gus Edwards and Will D. Cobb, and "The Ace in the Hole," by George Mitchell and James Dempsey.

Script by Everett Freeman projects the career of Miss Lamour from her waterfront saloon days in Natchez to success in New Orleans and New York, goals achieved by conveniently placed male stepping stones. The blighting effect she has on the masculine elements in her climb upward is in keeping with obvious development of the tale and, except for the implied sinfulness of her use of charms, the interest isn't very strong.

George Montgomery's co-starring role is a complication of weakness and strength. As the young lawyer who gives up his fiancee and law practice in Natchez to elope with Lulu Belle, he doesn't have much to do. There's character weakness in the manner in which he sits back while the vamp progresses from lover to lover, and his only strength comes at the finale, when he walks off without her even though she is ready to settle down.

Progression of lovers starts with Greg McClure, a pugilist, then moves on to Albert Dekker, gambler, and Otto Kruger, railroad capitalist. Trio competently answer story demands. Glenda Farrell, Charlotte Wynters, Addison Richards, William Haade, Clancy Cooper, and George Lewis are among okay support.

Leslie Fenton's direction of the Benedict Bogeaus production isn't one of his better credits. Photography by Ernest Laszlo is hard on the eyes. Other technical values supplied under Bogeaus' supervision are in keeping with the period piece. *Brog.*

Beyond Glory

Hollywood, June 12.

Paramount release of Robert Fellows production. Stars Alan Ladd, Donna Reed; features George Macready, George Coulouris, Harold Vermilyea, Henry Travers. Directed by John Farrow. Screenplay, Jonathan Latimer, Charles Marquis Warren, William Wister Haines; camera, John F. Seitz; editor, Eda Warren; music score, Victor Young. Tradeshown at Los Angeles, June 11, '48. Running time, **82 MINS.**

Cadet "Rocky" Gilman....Alan Ladd
Ann Daniels....Donna Reed
Major General Bond....George Macready
Lew Proctor....George Coulouris
Raymond Denmore, Sr....Harold Vermilyea
Pop Dewing....Henry Travers
Dr. White....Luis Van Rooten
Captain Harry Daniels....Tom Neal
Raymond Denmore, Jr....Conrad Janis
Cora....Margaret Field
Miller....Paul Lees
Cadet Sgt. Eddie Loughlin....Dick Hogan
Thomas....Audie Murphy
Mrs. Daniels....Geraldine Wall
Mr. Julian....Charles Evans
A Cadet....Russell Wade
John Craig....Vincent Donahue
General Prescott....Steve Pendleton
Colonel Stoddard....Harland Tucker

"Beyond Glory" is a different approach to an Alan Ladd starring vehicle. The Paramount action star comes off rather well in a story characterization directed at kudosing West Point standards for officer candidates. His name on the marquee should attract good initial business. How well film does after that will depend upon fans' attitude towards a part that has only an implication of the muscle-flexing and swashbuckling usually associated with his name.

Story is one that demands close audience attention because of the flashback method of telling. It has interest that attracts, even though climax discloses a rather thin premise for plot motivation. Ladd is seen as a World War II veteran whose belief that he is responsible for the combat death of a buddy leads to his enrollment at West Point.

Plot opens with Ladd called from parade grounds to be a witness at reinstatement of a former cadet, discharged on Ladd's testimony. Little by little, details of Ladd's background, his drafting and rise in the Army, enrollment at the Point and love for his dead buddy's widow are brought to the front as the former cadet's attorney seeks to prove Ladd is a coward and unworthy of wearing a West Point uniform. Hinge of the charge is Ladd's own belief that he delayed an attack three minutes, giving the enemy time to blast his friend. Finale discloses Ladd was recovering from concussion caused by a near-miss of an enemy shell during the fatal period. His honor is restored to bring a happy ending.

Principal interest falls to Ladd, and he delivers competently. Donna Reed lends a quiet charm as the war widow who believes in Ladd. For once, George Macready isn't a heavy, depicting the West Point major general. Good character roles are filled by George Coulouris, Harold Vermilyea and Henry Travers. Conrad Janis is the discharged cadet. Tom Neal is good as Ladd's Army buddy, as is Dick Hogan. Luis Van Rooten as a doctor, Audie Murphy, another cadet, and others in the cast measure up to pic's demands.

John Farrow has given the picture well-rounded direction to hold interest. Original script by Jonathan Latimer, Charles Marquis Warren and William Wister Haines presents an attractive picture of plebe life and Academy aims.

Robert Fellows has climaxed his production with a clip of General Eisenhower delivering a graduation speech to a West Point class, a neat showmanly touch that matches other facets of his supervision. Among technical aids are photography by John F. Seitz, stirring musical direction by Victor Young and good editing that holds film to 82 minutes. *Brog.*

Mickey
(COLOR-SONGS)

Eagle Lion release of Aubrey Schenck production. Stars Lois Butler, Bill Goodwin, Irene Hervey, John Sutton; features Rose Hobart, Hattie McDaniel, Beverly Wills, Leon Tyler. Directed by Ralph Murphy. Screenplay, Muriel Roy Bolton and Agnes Christine Johnston; from novel, "Clementine," by Peggy Goodin; songs composed and adapted by Mario Silva and Randolph Van Scoyk; camera (Cinecolor), John W. Boyle; musical score, Marlin Skiles; musical director, Irving Friedman; editor, Norman Colbert. Previewed in N. Y., June 11, '48. Running time, **87 MINS.**

Mickey....Lois Butler
George Kelly....Bill Goodwin
Louise Williams....Irene Hervey
Ted Whitney....John Sutton
Lydia Matthews....Rose Hobart
Bertha....Hattie McDaniel
Hank Evans....Skippy Homeier
Cathy Williams....Beverly Wills
Robbie Matthews....Leon Tyler

Lois Butler, whom Eagle Lion is trying to build into a boxoffice name, is given little help in that direction by this production of "Mickey." Any promise or appeal the young actress may have is despite the picture, not because of it. Despite the use of color and apparent studio effort, "Mickey" is a minor item unlikely to draw at the wicket, impress or amuse audiences or exploit talent.

Miss Butler is an attractive and likeable youngster, with carrot colored hair (at least in this picture), suitably girlish figure, warm smile and a disarming directness. She has a pleasing soprano voice, though apparently not one appropriate for pop singing. Her dramatic ability is at least adequate for the modest demands of this vehicle; whether it's any more than that must wait more testing parts and pictures.

"Mickey," adapted from a novel called "Clementine," is a stilted and arch yarn about a tomboy's painful transition to young womanhood. The plot is elaborately contrived, the situations hackneyed, and the dialog painfully arch. Consequently, what might have been a touching story about a timeless subject is incredible, silly and a trifle irritating.

Instead of covering up the script's weakness, Ralph Murphy's direction accentuates the obvious. Bill Goodwin is plausible and sympathetic as the girl's understandably confused widower-father. Irene Hervey is good-looking and winning as the helpful next-door-visitor.

Rose Hobart is believable as a catty mama out to marry the heroine's father. Skippy Homeier seems authentic as a he-man teenager. Hattie McDaniel, Beverly Wills, Leon Tyler and John Sutton are acceptable in supporting parts. There are several semi-classic type songs in the picture, all sung by Miss Butler. The color photography is uneven and, for a lightweight picture, seems pretentious. *Hobe.*

Michael O'Halloran

Hollywood, June 12.

Monogram release of Julian Lesser-Frank Melford production. Stars Scotty Beckett, Allene Roberts; features Tommy Cook, Isabel Jewell, Charles Arnt, Jonathan Hale, Gladys Blake, Roy Gordon, Florence Aner, William Haade. Directed by John Rawlins. Screenplay, Emma Lazarus, from novel by Gene Stratton-Porter; camera, Jack McKenzie; editor, Merrill White; associate John Sheets; music direction, Lud Gluskin. Previewed in Hollywood, June 9, '48. Running time, 79 mins.

Michael.......Scotty Beckett
Lily.......Allene Roberts
Joey.......Tommy Cook
Mrs. Nelson.......Isabel Jewell
Doc Bruce.......Charles Arnt
Judge.......Jonathan Hale
Saleslady.......Cladys Blake
Dr. Carrell.......Roy Gordon
Mrs. Crawford.......Florence Auer
Detective.......William Haade
Ward Nurse.......Dorothy Granger
Doctor Johnson.......Douglas Evans
Student Nurse.......Beverly Jons
Officer Barker.......Greg Barton
Lounergan.......Lee Phelps
Officer Martin.......Harry Strang
Pete.......Bob Scott
Woman.......Ethyl Halls
Interne.......Ralph Brooks
Court Clerk.......Rob Haines

"Michael O'Halloran" is a sentimental offering with appeal to family trade in smaller situations. Film gains value because the makers have recognized it for what it is—a tearjerker—and stuck to a straight treatment. Production dress is good for the modest budget, and direction, playing and scripting carry interest.

Scotty Beckett does the title role as an orphan making his own as a newsboy. When Isabel Jewell, drunkard mother of Allene Roberts, a cripple, is injured, Beckett takes the girl to live with him. He arranges for a noted doctor to diagnose her affliction, finds out it's mental because of the mother's behavior. Beckett becomes involved with the law through aiding the girl, and she walks again to save him from punishment.

Erna Lazarus scripted from the Gene Stratton-Porter novel, and John Rawlins' direction unfolds it ably. Pacing is good. Beckett and Miss Roberts make an excellent teen-aged team. Tommy Cook, Beckett's pal, furnishes some lighter moments, and Charles Arnt shows up well as an understanding druggist. Miss Jewell's mother role is capably projected in keeping with film's mood. Jonathan Hale, Gladys Blake, Roy Gordon, Florence Auer, William Haade, Dorothy Granger and Beverly Jons are among others rating mention.

The Julian Lesser-Frank Melford production was lensed by Jack McKenzie, and all technical credits are in keeping with generally good effect obtained. *Brog.*

My Sister and I

(BRITISH)

London, June 9.

GFD release of J. Arthur Rank-Burnham production. Stars Sally Ann Howes, Barbara Mullen, Dermot Walsh. Directed by Harold Huth. Screenplay by A.R. Rawlinson, from Emery Bennett novel. Additional scenes and dialog, Joan Rees, Michael Medwin; editor, John Guthridge; camera, Harry Waxman. At Odeon, London, June 8, '48. Running time, 97 mins.

Robina Adams.......Sally Ann Howes
Graham Forbes.......Dermot Walsh
Mrs. Camelot.......Martita Hunt
Hypatia Foley.......Barbara Mullen
Roger Crisp.......Patrick Holt
Helena Forsythe.......Hazel Court
Ardath Bondage.......Joan Rees
Elsie.......Jane Hylton
Charlie.......Michael Medwin
Michael Marsh.......Rory McDermott
Hubert Bondage.......Hugh Miller
Horsnell.......Ian Wilson
Harry.......Niall Lawder
Phyllis.......Elizabeth Sydney
Pomfret.......Jack Vyvyan
Mrs. Pomfret.......Helen Goss
Colonel Thursby.......Stewart Rome
Miss Lippincot.......Olwyn Brooks

This is a feeble, high-schoolish production, with not much chance here or abroad.

Robina arrives at a provincial town as scenic designer at the local theatre run by elderly, freakish Mrs. Camelot as a memorial to her late husband. Actor Graham Forbes and lawyer Roger Crisp fall for Robina and all sorts of unexciting and uneventful happenings take place until Mrs. Camelot is found dead from gas poisoning. Mystery is unraveled uninterestingly.

Jane Hylton and Michael Medwin try their best. Rest of cast is so-so. Production too. *Cane.*

Portrait of Innocence

(FRENCH)

Siritzky International release of Pathe Films production. Stars Louise Carletti, Gilbert Gil. Directed by Louis Daquin. Screenplay, Hilero, Gaston Modot; camera Bachelet; English titles, Charles Clement. At Art theatre, N.Y., starting June 9, '48. Running time, 90 MINS.

Mariette.......Louise Carletti
M. Morin.......Gilbert Gil
Le Pere Finot.......Pierre Larquay
Le Commissaire.......Andre Brunot
Gros Charles.......Emile Genevoix
Gaston.......Bussieres
Pere de Laurent.......Coedel
Rozet.......Jean-Pierre Geffroy
Andre.......Georges Reygnier
Tom Mix.......Jean Buquet
Doudou.......Bernard Dayde

(In French; English Titles)

Marked by several good performances, the plot, execution or editing haven't made "Portrait of Innocence" strong enough to attract American audiences. It may appeal to youngsters but even with them, "Portrait" will prove tedious.

Picture is a rambling yarn about school kids who dig up odd jobs in their campaign to raise enough money to pay for a classroom window that was smashed accidentally by one of them. How they accomplish this, only to have a conniver rob them, forms the basis of the plot.

Louise Carletti, principal femme, does a nice job as the heart interest while Gilbert Gil, as the handsome schoolteacher, makes something of a rather unsympathetic role. Bussieres plays the thief who is brought to justice by the kids. Others are merely standard, with the kids doing okay. *Wear.*

Uneasy Terms

(BRITISH)

London, June 2.

Pathe Pictures release of British National-Louis H. Jackson production. Stars Michael Rennie; features Moira Lister, Faith B rook. Directed by Vernon Sewell. Screenplay, Peter Cheyney; editor, Monica Kimick; camera, Ernest Palmer. At Palace, London, June 1, '48. Running time, 83 MINS.

Slim Callaghan.......Michael Rennie
Corinne Alardyse.......Moira Lister
Viola Alardyse.......Faith Brook
Effie.......Joy Shelton
Patricia Alardyse.......Patricia Goddard
Inspector Gringell.......Barry Jones
Honoria Wymering.......Paul Carpenter
Donelly.......Nigel Patrick
Maysin.......Sydney Tafler
Sallins.......J.H. Roberts
Matron.......Joan Carol
La Valliere.......Mary Horn
Patrick.......Tony Quinn

Popular novelist Peter Cheyney sells his thrillers by the million. Having been persuaded to put one on the screen he should have allowed experts to adapt it and write the screenplay. Novel writing and scripting are different professions. His name may prove a slight draw, but the picture can only rate as a dualer here and has no prospects in America.

Private detective Slim Callaghan is offered an assignment, but when he arrives at the house he finds his client has been murdered. Two sisters are involved in the murder; there's a bit of blackmail, an outlandish story of a man married to both and not married to either; the conventional love affair between investigator and the good sister, and usual antagonism between police and private detective. It all adds up to an unexciting picture.

As Slim, Michael Rennie strives hard to give the detective some character, but is unsuccessful. All the others, with the exception of Paul Carpenter, who is worth noting, are stock-in-trade puppets. Production, is reminiscent of ancient silent melodramas. *Cane.*

Razzia

(Police Raid)

(GERMAN-MADE)

Artkino release of DEFA production. Stars Paul Bildt; features Elli Burgmer, Walter Gross, Friedhelm von Peterson. Directed by Werner Klingler. Screenplay, G. H. Peterson; camera, Friedel Behn-Grund, Eugen Klagemann; English titles, Charles Clement. At Stanley, N. Y., opening June 12, '48. Running time, 94 MINS.

Inspector Naumann.......Paul Bildt
Anna.......Eli Burgmer
Paul.......Walter Gross
Frau Naumann.......Agatha Poschmann
Karl Lorenz, Naumann's Asst.......Friedhelm von Petersen
Police Chief Lembke.......Hans Leibelt
Becker.......Klaus Holm
Goll.......Harry Frank
Yvonne.......Nina Konsta
Willi Vogel.......Heinz Welzel
Mierisch.......Arno Paulsen

(In German; English Titles)

Melodrama of postwar Germany and its black marketeers, this was produced in Soviet zone of Berlin and is one of first German-mades to come to U. S. since the war ended. Cast is virtually all-Teutonic, and technical crew is German, but supervision naturally was Soviet. "Razzia" is surprisingly fast, mainly because director Werner Klingler never forgot the melodramatic phases no matter how great the temptation to moralize on Berlin's black market operators and what it has done to the German people. Film should do well at foreign-language and arty theatres despite having a no-name cast for American audiences.

Strong direction and bright scripting are only surpassed by a thoroughly capable cast. Biggest criticism is that the editing could have been better. But even as is, it has pace, change of mood and humor besides dramatic potency.

Paul Bildt is fine as the inspector running down the black-market gang. Elli Burgmer does nicely as the daughter in love with Bildt's aide, Friedheim von Peterson. Latter chips in with a nicely rounded performance. Walter Gross, as the inspector's son, is a bit disappointing in an unsympathetic role. Agatha Poschman's typical German mother is okay. Heinz Welzel makes a corking blackmarket operator while Harry Frank, as the ringleader; Nina Konsta and Klaus Holm handle lesser parts skillfully.

Friedel Behn-Grund and Eugen Klagemann have done an excellent lensing job. *Wear.*

Folket I Simlangsdalen

(People from Simlangs Valley)

(SWEDISH)

Nordisk Tonefilm release of Ake Ohberg production. Stars Edvin Adolphsan, Eva Dahlbeck; features Karl-Henrik Fant, Barbro Nordin, Peter Lindgren. Directed by Ohberg. Screenplay, Harald Beijer; from novel by Fredrik Strom; camera, Goran Strindberg; music, Erland von Koch. At Astoria, Stockholm. Running time, 89 MINS.

Folkeson.......Edvin Adolphson
Ingrid.......Eva Dahlbeck
Sven.......Karl-Henrik Fant
Marit.......Barbro Nordin
Jan.......Peter Lindgren
Sibelius.......Carl Strom
Brand.......Arthur Fischer
Priest.......Sven Bergvall
Jonke.......Nils Hallberg
Berta.......Naima Wifstrand
Fia.......Fylgia Zadig
Sheriff.......David Eriksson

Adapted from a bestselling novel of Swedish farm life, "Folket I Simlangsdalen" has a good story, good acting and fine technical credits. Film abounds with well-drawn characterizations. Edwin Adolphson is excellent as the cruel master. Carl Strom has a sympathetic role, as champion of the poor people. Both players turn in top-notch performances. Balance of the cast also does well.

Direction of Ake Ohberg is impressive, as is his production. Goran Strindberg's lensing is good, too. "Folket" looks okay for the overseas trade and is a natural grosser in Scandinavian zones. *Winq.*

Var Sin Vag

(Different Roads)

(SWEDISH)

Europa Film release of Hasse Ekman Film production, directed and written by Ekman. Stars Ekman, Gunn Wallgren, Uno Henning; features Marianne Aminoff, Eva Dahlbeck, Hugo Jacobson, Gull Natorp, Hilda Bergstrom, Gunnar Bjornstrand, Gosta Cederlund, Stig Jarrel. Camera, Harald Berglund; music, Erik Baumann, Nathan Gorling. At Anglais, Stockholm. Running time, 110 MINS.

Tage Sundell.......Hasse Ekman
Birgit Sundell.......Gunn Wallgren
Dr. Holmberg.......Uno Henning
Sonja Collin.......Marianne Aminoff
Karin Brofeldt.......Eva Dahlbeck
Collin.......Hugo Jacobson
Mrs. Collin.......Gull Natorp
Mrs. Lundkvist.......Hilda Borgstrom
Professor.......Gosta Cederlund
Nils Brenner.......Stig Jarrel

"Var Sin Vag" is a firstrate comedy and ranks among the best films that its producer-writer-director-actor Hasse Ekman has done. It's a sure boxoffice entry in Scandinavia and has good chances for the world market as well. Picture is Ekman's last production for Europa before he left to join Terra Film.

Yarn revolves about Ekman, a

doctor, whose duties at a hospital keep him from his wife.

Cast turns in uniformly fine performances topped by portrayals contributed by Ekman and Henning. Former's direction and production values are also okay. Harald Berglund capably handled the camerawork. *Winq.*

Foreign Films

"Maj Pa Malo" (SWEDISH). Sandrew-Bauman Film release of Schamyl Bauman production. Stars Inga Landgre, Olof Bergstrom; features Ludde Gentzel, Bernhard Sonnerstedt, Ake Soderblom, Colbjorn Knudsen, Lilly Waestfeldt, Harry Ahlin, Jonsa Bengtsson. Directed by S. Bauman. Screenplay by Ragnar Arfvedsson. Camera, Sven Nykvist. At Grand, Stockholm. Running time, 74 MINS.

An okay Swedish comedy built on some popular songs by composer-singer Evert Taube. Film looks good for Scandinavia, and may do well in Swedish-language houses in U.S. Lensing by Sven Nykvist and acting by Inga Landgre are excellent. Background is western Sweden.

"Glada Paraden" (Happy Parade) (SWEDISH). Europa Film production and release. Stars Edvard Persson. Directed by Emil A. Lingheim. Commentary by Kar De Mumma. At Anglais, Stockholm. Running time, 100 MINS.

It is now 20 years since actor Edvard Persson started with his first talking-picture for Europa Film Co. To celebrate that event, the company arranged this film by cuttings from all his films since he started. It's a very interesting revue, and gives filmgoers of today a chance to see some old, very good Swedish actors. There's the late Fridolf Rhusin "the man who taught the Swedes to laugh"; the late Weyler Hildebrand, Nils Wahlbom and many others. Persson joined Europa Film when it started, and film is a cavalcade of the whole company. Persson is a good singer and the film is good entertainment. *Winq.*

"Anni" (AUSTRIAN). Styria-Bernal-Sascha release of Heinrich Haas production. Stars Elfie Mayerhofer, Siegfried Breuer; features Josef Meinrad, Anni Rosar. Scripted and directed by Max Neufeld; camera, Walter Riml; music, Alois Melichar, Robert Stolz and Peter Wehle. At Apollo, Vienna. Running time, 90 MINS.

Entertaining melodrama (with music) about the eternal triangle, with sufficient excitement and tension to the last moment. Elfie Mayerhofer looks beautiful and sings excellently. Siegfried Breuer measures up as heartbreaker. Josef Meinrad gives a credible interpretation of the unsuccessful lover. Supporting roles are brief but effectively handled. Lensing is good. *Maas.*

"Che Tempi!" (What Queer Times!) (ITALIAN). Fincine release of Taurus Film production. Stars Gilberto Govi; features Lea Padovani, Walter Chiari, Alberto Sordi. Directed by Giorgio Bianchi. Screenplay, Bianchi, Govi and Aldo De Benedetti from play by Emerico Valentinetti. Camera, Giuseppe La Torre. At Corso, Moderno and Margherita, Rome. Running time, 90 MINS.

Concerned with a miser's character, this story lacks wit and credibility. Production also lacks style and direction; needs pace. Gilberto Govi, a good thesp on the

stage, overacts here. Lea Padovani, Orson Welles' fiancee, is, as usual, attractive. *Quat.*

Miniature Reviews

"A Date With Judy" (M-G) (Songs-Color). Gay, infectious comedy with music based on radio characters; stout b.o.

"The Street With No Name" (20th-Fox). Powerful documentary-type film starring Richard Widmark and Mark Stevens; surefire b.o.

"Race Street" (RKO). George Raft, William Bendix in conventional underworld meller; moderate b.o.

"Mystery in Mexico" (RKO). Flip detective melodrama with Mexico City background for its mayhem. Okay double-biller.

"Man-Eater of Kumaon" (U). Sturdy entry for the exploitation market. Jungle-yarn of tiger-hunting with thrills.

"Canon City" (EL). Semi-documentary thriller of recent jailbreak at Canon City, Colo.; strong to smash biz assured.

A Date with Judy
(SONGS-COLOR)

Hollywood, June 18.

Metro release of Joe Pasternak production. Stars Wallace Beery, Jane Powell, Elizabeth Taylor, Carmen Miranda, Xavier Cugat, Robert Stack; features Scotty Beckett, Selena Royle, Leon Ames, Clinton Sundberg, George Cleveland. Directed by Richard Thorpe. Screenplay, Dorothy Cooper, Dorothy Kingsley; based on characters created by Aleen Leslie; camera (Technicolor), Robert Surtees; editor, Harold F. Kress; songs, Jimmy McHugh and Harold Adamson, Don Raye and Gene dePaul, Stella Unger and Alec Templeton. Tradeshown in Hollywood, June 17, '48. Running time, 113 MINS.

Melvin Colner Foster.......Wallace Beery
Judy Foster...................Jane Powell
Carol Pringle............Elizabeth Taylor
Rosita Conchellas........Carmen Miranda
Xavier Cugat........................Himself
Stephen I. Andrews.........Robert Stack
Ogden "Oogie" Pringle.....Scotty Beckett
Mrs. Foster................Selena Royle
Lucien T. Pringle............Leon Ames
Jameson.................Clinton Sundberg
Gramps...................George Cleveland
"Pop" Sam Scully.........Lloyd Corrigan
Randolph Foster............Jerry Hunter
Mitzi Hoffman.............Jean McLaren

"A Date With Judy" is loaded with youthful zest, making for gay, light entertainment. Based on the familiar air characters created by Aleen Leslie, yarn on film comes out as a tinted musical with all the factors that make for good box-office. There's a strong word-of-mouth potential and excellent cast names for the marquee to shove it along in all situations.

Joe Pasternak's production guidance is showmanly, backing the story with lush, but not ostentatious, trappings that provide top-notch setting for music and fun. Casting is particularly apt, both in youthful and character assignments, and each member delivers strongly under skillful direction by Richard Thorpe. Latter early establishes a good pace and blends the music and comedy together for general appeal to all type audiences.

Talented young Jane Powell registers appealingly with vocals on five numbers and for her comedy antics as wheelhorse of plot motivation. "It's a Most Unusual Day," by Jimmy McHugh and Harold Adamson, is opening number and also is reprised by Miss Powell for finale. Lighter numbers are "I'm Strictly On the Corny Side," by Stella Unger and Alec Templeton, and "Judaline," by Don Raye and Gene dePaul. "Through the Years" and "Love Is Where You Fnd It" round out her capable piping chores. Carmen Miranda gives her customary treatment to "Cooking With Glass" and "Quanto la Gusto," clicking strongly.

Locale is Santa Barbara, and

scripters Dorothy Cooper and Dorothy Kingsley present a romantic fable about young love and complications that holds interest. Plot concerns teen-age love affair between Miss Powell and Scotty Beckett which goes sour when the gal gets a crush on an older man, Robert Stack. It takes on another facet when Miss Powell suspects her father, Wallace Beery, of a romance with Miss Miranda, and the youngsters join forces to balk such a folly. Complications are neatly resolved for finale, but not before acting as a springboard for hearty laughs that feature footage.

Beery does an ace job, and with little of his customary mugging, as the father who's taking rhumba lessons so he can surprise his wife. Selena Royle, Elizabeth Taylor, rival for Stack's affections, makes a talented appearance. Her breath-taking beauty is complimented by the Technicolor lensing. Xavier Cugat plays himself neatly and gives musical backing to the Miranda songs. As Miss Powell's juvenile suitor, Scotty Beckett is standout. He is versatile on comedy and also abets Miss Powell on "Corny Side."

Rating mention for very capable performances are Miss Royle, Leon Ames, Clinton Sundberg, George Cleveland and Lloyd Corrigan.

Sturdy entertainment ingredients in this one have been given expert technical framing. Robert Surtees' photography, the art direction, musical arrangements, editing and other factors make for strong backing. *Brog.*

The Street With No Name

20th-Fox release of Samuel G. Engel production. Stars Mark Stevens, Richard Widmark; features Lloyd Nolan, Barbara Lawrence. Directed by William Keighley. Screenplay, Harry Kleiner; camera, Joe McDonald; editor, William Reynolds; music, Lionel Newman. Tradeshown N. Y., June 18, '48. Running time, 91 MINS.
Cordell.....................Mark Stevens
Alec Stiles.............Richard Widmark
Inspector Briggs.............Lloyd Nolan
Judy...................Barbara Lawrence
Chief Harmatz..................Ed Begley
Shivvy.....................Donald Buka
Matty...................Joseph Pevney
Cy Gordon.................John McIntire
Lt. Staller.............Walter Greaza
Commissioner Demory.......Howard Smith

A double-barreled gangster film, "The Street With No Name" ranks at the top of the list of documentary-type productions which have been rolling out of the 20th-Fox lot. This pic has a lean, tough surface wrapped around a nucleus of explosive violence. It should line 'em up at the wickets, proving that a good yarn can sell without a battery of star names.

"The Street With No Name" is a back street cutting across the U.S. on which the young punks of today develop into the bigtime mobsters of tomorrow. According to the preface, this pic is presumably pegged on a campaign to combat a current crime wave set in motion by a new group of teenage hoodlums. No time at all, however, is spent on sermonizing. The film's only discernible objective is to unfold a walloping story within 90 minutes of calculated brutality. Beneath its documentary exterior there lies a straight melodrama that harks back to the great gangster films of the early 1930's.

Richard Widmark, who twitched his way to stardom with his performance in "Kiss of Death," is the backbone of this film. As the leader of a gang of youngsters who operate with military science, Widmark commands complete interest with his interpretation of a psychotically ruthless character. His looks and personality have the latent menace of a loaded automatic. But Widmark needs slightly more scope than this film provides in order to break out of the conventional conception of the criminal type.

In neat contrast to Widmark, Mark Stevens plays the role of an all-American boy who, as an agent of the FBI, becomes a gang member. His efforts to collect the evidence for the police while exposing himself to the fate of a stoolpigeon provide the basis for the plot structure and tension. While this yarn is formula in outline, it's been dressed with enough clever twists to give it a new look.

Along a continuous line of fresh details, film includes a crackerjack fight sequence between Stevens and a professional pug, a glimpse into the FBI machinery and a slambang finale in which the cops and the hoodlums shoot it out in an industrial plant. Realistic backgrounds of underworld life also contribute heavily to the film's powerful impact.

In a secondary role, Lloyd Nolan, playing the same Inspector Briggs of the FBI of "The House on 92nd Street," delivers with his usual competence. Donald Buka and Joseph Pevney, as a couple of murderous hoods, give solid portrayals while Barbara Lawrence, as Widmark's moll, registers okay in a bit part. Down the line, the cast plays with documentary authenticity.

Herm.

Race Street
(SONGS)

RKO release of Nat Holt (Dore Schary) production. Stars George Raft, William Bendix, Marilyn Maxwell. Directed by Edwin L. Marin. Screenplay, Martin Rackin; songs, Don Raye, Gene De Paul, Ray Heindorf, Moe Jerome, Ted Koehler; camera, J. Roy Hunt; editor, Samuel E. Beetley. Tradeshown in N. Y., June 21, '48. Running time, 79 MINS.

Gannin	George Raft
Runson	William Bendix
Robbie	Marilyn Maxwell
Phil Dickson	Frank Faylen
Hal Towers	Henry Morgan
Elaine Gannin	Gale Robbins
Monty	Freddy Steele
Mike Hadley	Cully Richards
Easy	Russell Hicks
Al	Richard Powers
Nick	William Forrest
Herbie	Jim Nolan
Dixie	George Turner
Sam	Richard Benedict
Big Jack	Dean White
Stringy	Mack Gray

"Race Street" is a mild underworld meller that will do moderately good biz on the marquee strength of George Raft and William Bendix. While based on some hard-fisted ingredients, the film is handled too shyly and slowly to be clicko. Routine directorial treatment of a strictly formula story also serves to thin the impact.

Pic's main drawback lies in the scripting. Crammed with obviously bogus dialog, the screenplay makes up with repetition what it lacks in incident. "Race Street" is filled with bookie characters but there's not a single trace of a bangtail to enliven the proceedings. Most of the action takes place in hotel rooms and around nitery tables in the form of conversation. Pic, moreover, bends so far backwards to satisfy the guardians of morality with its respect-for-the-law message that it topples into incredibility.

Localed in San Francisco, yarn concerns the efforts of an "honest" bookie (Raft) to avenge the murder of his bookie pal who was knocked off by goons from a protection syndicate. A Frisco detective (Bendix), also on the trail of the killers, spends most of his time trying to persuade Raft to cooperate with the cops and stay out of trouble. But Raft insists that it's

not cricket for a bookie to blow whistles.

Romantic angles are injected via Marilyn Maxwell, a two-timer who holds hands with Raft while being linked up to the syndicate chieftain. Sequences in a nitery are occasions for two tuneful numbers, "Love That Boy" and "I'm in a Jam With Baby," which are delivered in good style by Gale Robbins and Cully Richards. Plot winds up with a slugfest in which Raft and Bendix, working together at last, send the mob to the cleaners. While delivering his final punch, Raft is fatally plugged. But the rest of his bookie pals can now ply their trades in peace.

Raft delivers another performance that will appeal to his fans. As a friendly cop, Bendix registers effectively for as long as his lines don't force him to be cute. Miss Maxwell handles the heavy role in competent fashion, while Frank Faylen, as the syndicate boss, is cut to a pattern. Rest of the cast handle themselves competently.

General production values are topflight with rich settings, expert lensing and smooth editing weighing heavily on the credit side.

Herm.

Mystery in Mexico

Hollywood, June 22.

RKO release of Sid Rogell production. Features William Lundigan, Jacqueline White, Ricardo Cortez, Tony Barrett, Jacqueline Dalya, Walter Reed. Directed by Robert Wise. Screenplay, Lawrence Kimble; story, Muriel Roy Bolton; camera, Jack Draper; editor, Samuel E. Beetley; music, Paul Sawtell. Tradeshown June 22, '48. Running time, 65 mins.

Steve	William Lundigan
Victoria	Jacqueline White
Norcross	Ricardo Cortez
Carlos	Tony Barrett
Dolores	Jacqueline Dalya
Glenn	Walter Reed
Swigart	Jose Torvay
Pancho	Jaime Jiminez
Pancho's Father	Antonia Frausto
Pancho's Mother	Dolores Camerillo
Commandant Rodriguez	Eduardo Casado
Floracita	Thalia Draper

"Mystery in Mexico" is okay program material. It's a story of stolen jewels, insurance detectives and mayhem filmed in Mexico City, the background locale. The treatment is a bit too flip at times, but good menace helps balance, and release intentions are fulfilled.

William Lundigan, insurance investigator, is sent to Mexico City when an operator disappears there after having worked on a stolen jewel case. Enroute via air he makes the acquaintance of Jacqueline White, the operator's sister. Romantic pursuit of the charmer is permitted to get a bit sticky but keeps the principals together, both on the same mission. Devious Latin ways of the heavies make Lundigan's work tough and he undergoes some solid punching before windup clears the heroine's brother and brings the villains to justice. Story gets a scenic lift from locale, and meller elements are made stronger as played against some of the rawer sections of Mexico City.

Robert Wise's direction has given the piece a good pace and develops sufficient thrills to maintain casual interest in the script. Sid Rogell's production, with Joseph Noriega as associate, is fitted to all market demands. Jack Draper contributes good photography.

Lundigan and Miss White make a good team, and femme also pipes a song chorus in Latin nitery. Ricardo Cortez is the suave heavy with endless henchmen. Tony Barrett contributes good characterization as a Mexican taxidriver on Cortez' payroll. Jacqueline Dalya and Walter Reed are capable. In-

teresting performances come from native performers, including young Jaime Jimenez, Antonio Frausto, Dolores Camerillo and Eduardo Casado.

Brog.

Man-Eater of Kumaon

Hollywood, June 18.

Universal release of Monty Shaff-Frank P. Rosenberg production. Stars Sabu, Wendell Corey, Joanne Page; features Morris Carnovsky, Argentina Brunetti, James Moss, Ted Hecht. Directed by Byron Haskin. Screenplay, Jeanne Bartlett, Lewis Meltzer; adaptation, Richard O. Hubler, Alden Nash; based on book, "Man-Eaters of Kumaon," by Jim Corbett; camera, William C. Mellor; editor, George Arthur; music, Hans J. Salter. Tradeshown in Hollywood, June 15, '48. Running time, 78 MINS.

Narain	Sabu
Dr. John Collins	Wendell Corey
Lali	Joanne Page
Ganga Ram	Morris Carnovsky
Sita	Argentina Brunetti
Panwah	James Moss
Native Doctor	Ted Hecht
Bearer	John Mansfield
Ox-Cart Driver	Eddie Das
Panwah's Father	Charles Wagenheim
Mother	Estelle Dodge
Farmers: Lal Chand Mehra, Phiroze Nazir, Virginia Ware.	
Villagers: Frank Lackteen, Jerry Riggio, Neyle Morrow, Ralph Moody, Alan Foster.	

Nifty exploitation values give "Man-Eater of Kumaon" good box-office prospects. The market hasn't had a jungle film with ballyhoo possibilities in some time, and this one is grooved for neat results if given showmanly handling. Picture has names of Sabu and Wendell Corey to help on the marquees and aid selling angles.

Production is a blend of authentic and studio-filmed footage, and plot deals with reformation of a society doctor while on a tiger-hunt in India. Although pace is leisurely, there are plenty of chills and thrills as the medico tracks down a man-eating tiger which is ravishing a native village at the foot of the Himalayas.

Film is rather loosely based on Jim Corbett's best seller of the same title, but scripters Jeanne Bartlett and Lewis Meltzer have given adaptation an okey basis upon which to string ballyhoo values.

Cast does an uniformly good job of projecting the native and straight characters under Byron Haskin's direction. Sabu and Joanne Page team effectively as a young native couple, and Wendell Corey is acceptable as the doctor who gets a new viewpoint on life through association with the villagers. Morris Carnovsky, village leader; James Moss, moppet orphaned by the tiger; Argentina Brunetti and others measure up to light demands on talent.

William C. Mellor's studio footage is blended neatly with jungle shots taken in India under direction of Bob Tansey. Score, editing and other technical aids measure up in helping to make this salable for the exploitation market. *Brog.*

Canon City

Eagle Lion release of Bryan Foy production (associate producer, Robert T. Kane). Directed by Crane Wilbur. Screenplay, Crane Wilbur; camera, John Alton; editor, Louis H. Sackin; special camera effects, George T. Teague. Tradeshown in N. Y., June 18, '48. Running time, 82 MINS.

Sherbondy	Scott Brady
Schwartzmiller	Jeff Corey
Heilman	Whit Bissell
New	Stanley Clements
Tolley	Charles Russell
Smalley	DeForest Kelley
Officer Gray	Ralph Byrd
Mrs. Oliver	Mabel Paige
Warden Roy Best	Himself
LaVergne	Alfred Linder
Trujillo	Richard Irving
Turley	Robert Bice
Freeman	Henry Branden
Hathaway	James Magill
Klinger	Ray Bennett
W. R. Williams	Robert Kellard
M. Oliver	Raymond Bond
Mr. George Bauer	John Doucette
Mrs. George Bauer	Eve Marsh

Eagle Lion has come up with a winner in "Canon City." It's the story of the actual jailbreak at Canon City, Colo., last December, in which 12 escaped prisoners either were recaptured or slain. Picture has strong exploitation possibilities.

Starting as a routine recital of Canon City and its widely-known pen, plot gradually focuses on an apparently innocent-looking, hardworking inmate. Then it's divulged he's making crude revolvers in his spare moments and gradually banding together 11 other conspirators for a break. Camera and story follow minute preparations for the break and then trails the 12 jailbirds as they attempt to gain their freedom. Then either their death or recapture.

Scott Brady looks like a comer on the basis of his performance as one of the prisoners. Jeff Corey is excellent as one of the chief conspirators. Ray Bennett makes an unusually fine ringleader, as a longtimer who conceives the break.

Roy Best, real-life warden at Canon City, is a natural in the warden role although not called on for much histrionics. Ralph Byrd, Mabel Paige, Eve Marsh and several others round out an unusually large, well-picked cast.

Crane Wilbur has scripted and directed with keen perception. Robert T. Kane has given this film the essential production values although most of the actual settings are in the Canon City pen itself. John Alton contributed sparkling lensing, and Louis H. Sackin's editing is likewise top-drawer. *Wear.*

Miniature Reviews

"Deep Waters" (20th). Sombre juve-delinquency film will need strong selling.

"Tap Roots" (U) (Color). Romantic costumer that swashbuckles through Civil War days in the South. General appeal good and b.o. outlook okay.

"Abbott & Costello Meet Frankenstein" (U). Comedy team battles Frankenstein's Monster, the Wolf Man, and Dracula. Good b.o.

"Oliver Twist" (GFD). Grade-A British version of Dickens' novel.

"The Black Arrow" (Col.) Robert Louis Stevenson's adventure novel is an entertaining blood and thunder-romance.

"The Timber Trail" (Rep) (Songs-Color). Average Monte Hale oatuner for horse opera circuit.

"Northwest Stampede" (Color) (EL). Joan Leslie, James Craig, Jackie Oakie in colorful western; okay biz.

"The Twisted Road" (RKO) Somber story of hopeless young love. Excellently done but no marquee values in title or cast names.

"The Betrayal" (Astor). All-Negro film is an overlong, naive drama, with limited audience appeal.

Deep Waters

Hollywood, June 25.

20th-Fox release of Samuel G. Engel production. Stars Dana Andrews, Jean Peters; features Cesar Romero, Dean Stockwell, Anne Revere, Ed Begley. Directed by Henry King. Screenplay, Richard Murphy, based on novel, "Spoonhandle," by Ruth Moore; camera, Joseph La Shelle; editor, Barbara McLean. Tradeshown in Hollywood June 25, '48. Running time, 86 MINS.

Hod Stillwell	Dana Andrews
Ann Freeman	Jean Peters
Joe Sanger	Cesar Romero
Danny Mitchell	Dean Stockwell
Mary McKay	Anne Revere
Josh Hovey	Ed Begley
Mrs. Freeman	Leona Powers
Molly Thatcher	Mae Marsh
Nick Driver	Will Geer
Druggist	Bruno Wick
Harris	Cliff Clark
Hopkins	Harry Tyler
Judge Tate	Raymond Greenleaf

"Deep Waters" will get by on strength of Dana Andrews' name and exploitation possibilities of its juvenile-delinquency theme, but will need pairing with a strong support on double bill. As pure entertainment film is too sombre-toned, and subject as presented doesn't always lend itself to more than average appeal.

Story is set against lobster-fishing background of Maine, where Henry King troupe spent month or more filming exteriors. It is here that Dean Stockwell, a "state boy"—an orphan taken over by state of Maine—is sent by juve authorities to home of Anne Revere, a hard-bitten but tender-hearted woman, as chore-boy. Story follows him as he gets into trouble for stealing a camera and selling it to a second-hand store, and efforts of Dana Andrews, lobsterman, to straighten him out and later to adopt him.

Interesting backgrounds are caught by camera, with whole film done in sepia, which gives it a particularly warm hue. Exciting sequence shows lobster boat driving through a storm to rescue of youngster, who is clinging onto overturned launch, with element of suspense entering as Andrews and Cesar Romero, his partner, nearly crash onto rocks after boy is picked up. Locations are fresh and new to movie-going public.

Subject has been presented too leisurely. Entire cast turns in workmanlike jobs, but fault lies in there being few highlights. Whatever acting honors there may be should go to young Stockwell. Andrews offers a straightforward performance, and so does Jean Peters, his co-star, although her part doesn't entirely ring true. Romero is excellent as a Portuguese fisherman, and Miss Revere, as usual, is persuasive. Ed Begley is good in smaller role.

Samuel G. Engel gave film appropriate physical values as producer, and King handled direction with eye to best effects, but both were somewhat stymied by subject.

Whit.

Tap Roots
(COLOR)

Hollywood, June 27.

Universal release of Walter Wanger production. Stars Van Heflin, Susan Hayward; features Boris Karloff, Julie London, Ward Bond, Richard Long, Whitfield Connor. Directed by George Marshall. Screenplay, Alan LeMay; added dialog, Lionel Wiggam; from novel by James Street; camera (Technicolor), Lionel Lindon, Winton C. Hoch; editor, Milton Carruth; music, Frank Skinner. Previewed in Hollywood June 22, '48. Running time, 108 MINS.

Keith Alexander	Van Heflin
Morna Dabney	Susan Hayward
Tishomingo	Boris Karloff
Aven Dabney	Julie London
Clay MacIvor	Whitfield Connor
Hoab Dabney	Ward Bond
Bruce Dabney	Richard Long
Reverend Kirkland	Arthur Shields
Dr. MacIntosh	Griff Barnett
Shellie	Sondra Rogers
Dabby	Ruby Dandridge
Sam Dabney	Russell Simpson

There's enough swash and buckle about "Tap Roots" to rate it good boxoffice in general situations. It never reaches epic proportions, is too long, and not always put together smoothly. However, the plot's high romance, the color lensing of the Civil War costumes, sex implications and broad action are salable values that will give it ticket-window attention to a good degree.

The George Marshall production for Walter Wanger Pictures, Inc., spins a fact-fiction tale of a Mississippi valley family that tried to stand against the south and, the north at the beginning of the war between the states. Marshall's direction points up the pulp-fiction quality of the narrative, giving sweep to the mass-action battle scenes. Characters are colorful, if unbelievable, and are generally well played, with a few exceptions.

Script by Alan LeMay is based on James Street's novel of the same title, and has necessarily, watered down some of the book's more salty moments. Plot deals with the Dabney family and its efforts to maintain a neutral valley in the south when the Civil War comes. No Union soldiers ride through the footage, battle action taking place between the diehard recruits of the Dabneys and the wearers of the grey.

Romantic conflict springs from characters of Van Heflin and Susan Hayward. Latter, fiery daughter of the Dabney tribe, gets her first emotional shakeup when Heflin, newspaper editor, decides she's the girl for him. There's plenty of smoldering sex in their scenes together—just about as much as the screen allows. That fact lends itself to exploitation, as does her sacrifice scene, when she goes to spend the night with a former fiance to give the Dabneys more time to draw their battle lines.

Miss Hayward benefits from a well-drawn character and plays it to the hilt. Heflin's ability overcomes difficulty of a role not clearly defined. Boris Karloff is excellent as an Indian friend of the family. Ward Bond misses on interpretation of the Dabney family head, and a number of his scenes should be cut entirely. Julie London, amorous younger sister who steals Whitfield Connor, Miss Hayward's fiance; Connor, Richard Long, Arthur Shields, Ruby Dandridge and Russell Simpson are among others who are capable.

Smoky Mountains location in North Carolina and Tennessee, where the Mississippi story was filmed, lends itself magnificently to the color lensing of Lionel Lindon and Winton C. Hoch. Scenic beauty makes for standout production dress.

Brog.

Abbott & Costello Meet Frankenstein

Hollywood, June 26.

Universal release of Robert Arthur production. Stars Bud Abbott, Lou Costello; features Lon Chaney, Bela Lugosi, Glenn Strange, Lenore Aubert, Jane Randolph. Directed by Charles T. Barton. Screenplay, Robert Lees, Frederic I. Rinaldo, John Grant; camera, Charles Van Enger; editor, Frank Gross; music, Frank Skinner. Previewed in Hollywood June 25, '48. Running time, 82 MINS.

Chick	Bud Abbott
Wilbur	Lou Costello
Lawrence Talbot	Lon Chaney
Dracula	Bela Lugosi
Monster	Glenn Strange
Sandra Mornay	Lenore Aubert
Joan Raymond	Jane Randolph
Mr. McDougal	Frank Ferguson
Dr. Stevens	Charles Bradstreet

"Abbott & Costello Meet Frankenstein" is a happy combination both for chills and laughs. The comedy team battles it out with the studio's roster of bogeymen in a rambunctious fracas that is funny and, at the same time, spine-tingling. Returns should please.

Stalking through the piece to add menace are such characters of horror as the Frankenstein Monster, the Wolf Man and Dracula. Their presence is a boxoffice perker, exploitation-wise. Production is showmanly shaped to take advantage of ballyhoo angles, and selling should be easy in general situations.

Loosely-knit script depicts a Monster growing weak. His master, Dracula, decides to transfer Costello's brain to the Frankenstein creation. As a lure, the batman uses wiles of Lenore Aubert to soften the fat man and maneuver him into proper setup. The dimwit finally catches on and, with expected heroics, does in the heavies in a hilarious chase finale. Through it all runs the Wolf Man as a sympathetic character who tries to warn the heroes against the plot but, unfortunately, proves a bit of menace himself whenever the moon rises and changes him into a killer.

Abbott and Costello work with less of their standard routines than usual, but keep the fun at high level. Bela Lugosi as Dracula; Glenn Strange, the Monster, and Lon Chaney, the Wolf Man, bulwark the chills and thrills. Miss Aubert, Dracula's tool; Jane Randolph, an insurance investigator; Frank Ferguson, operator of a horror museum, and Charles Bradstreet, a doctor, round out capable casting.

The Robert Arthur production is neatly tied together by Charles T. Barton's direction. Latter realizes on all the fun possible and misses no bets in sharpening blood-curdling sequences. Lensing, editing and other technical credits are good.

Brog.

Oliver Twist
(BRITISH)

London, June 23.

GFD release of J. Arthur Rank-Cineguild Ronald Neame production. Stars Robert Newton; features Alec Guinness, Kay Walsh, Francis L. Sullivan, Henry Stephenson. Directed by David Lean. Screenplay by Lean, Stanley Haynes, from Charles Dickens' novel. Editor, Jack Harris; music, Sir Arnold Bax; camera, Guy Green, Oswald Morris. At Odeon, London, June 22, '48. Running time, 116 MINS.

Bill Sikes	Robert Newton
Fagin	Alec Guinness
Nancy	Kay Walsh
Mr. Bumble	Francis L. Sullivan
Mrs. Corney	Mary Clare
Mr. Brownlow	Henry Stephenson
Oliver Twist	John Howard Davies
Monks	Ralph Truman
Artful Dodger	Anthony Newley
Oliver's Mother	Josephine Stuart
Mr. Sowerberry	Gibb McLaughlin
Mrs. Sowerberry	Kathleen Harrison
Mrs. Bedwin	Amy Veness
Bookseller	W. G. Fay
Chief of Police	Maurice Denham

From every angle this is a superb achievement. Dickens' devotees may object to condensing of the story and omission of some of the minor characters. But what is left still runs close to two hours, to hold the interest and satisfy. This one will win honors all around.

One of its merits is the absence of considerable unnecessary dialog, the child Oliver having the fewest lines ever allotted to so prominent a character. He has the wistful air of the typical Dickens waif and heads almost faultless casting for this second of Cineguild's Dickens screenings.

Camera work is on an exceptionally high level. Opening shots of a storm-swept sky and heavy clouds give an eerie quality that immediately grips the imagination. Josephine Stuart's delineation of a woman in labor pains, dragging herself across rain-sodden fields to a distant light that spells sanctuary, is unparalleled in its poignant realism.

Story is straightforward depiction of the foundling's life from his nameless birth in the workhouse, apprenticeship to a mortician, escape to London, corruption in the thieves' kitchen, rescue from the magistrate's court by his unknown grandfather, to his forcible return to Fagin's gang and subsequent rescue when Bill Sikes is run to earth for the murder of Nancy.

Alec Guinness gives a revoltingly faithful portrait of Fagin and Kay Walsh extracts just the right amount of viciousness overcome by pity in her delineation of Nancy. Robert Newton is a natural for the brutish Sikes and gets every ounce out of his opportunities. Henry Stephenson makes a gracious figure of Mr. Brownlow, who unwittingly befriends his own grandson. Francis L. Sullivan is suitably obnoxious as the Beadle and all other characters reveal discriminating judgment in casting.

Highlights of the production are the opening and closing shots, the dramatic ending showing the masses of citizens and a squad of police tracking down the murderer, being led to his hideout by his dog. And, of course, the famous "asking for more" scene when the poor mite goes up with his bowl for a second helping of gruel.

Clem.

The Black Arrow

Columbia release of Edward Small (Grant Whytock) production. Stars Louis Hayward, Janet Blair; features George Macready, Edgar Buchanan, Rhys Williams, Walter Kingsford, Lowell Gilmore, Halliwell Hobbes, Paul Cavanaugh, Ray Teal. Directed by Gordon Douglas. Screenplay, Richard Schayer, David P. Sheppard, Thomas Seller, from novel by Robert Louis Stevenson; camera, Charles Lawton; art direction, Stephen Goosson, A. Leslie Thomas; editor, Jerome Thoms. Previewed in N. Y., June 28, '48. Running time, 76 MINS.

Richard Shelton	Louis Hayward
Joanna Sedley	Janet Blair
Sir Daniel Brackley	George Macready
Lawless	Edgar Buchanan
Bennett Hatch	Rhys Williams
Sir Oliver Oates	Walter Kingsford
Duke of Gloucester	Lowell Gilmore
Bishop of Tilsbury	Halliwell Hobbes
Sir John Sedley	Paul Cavanaugh
Nick Appleyard	Ray Teal
Sir Harry Shelton	Russell Hicks
Sir William Catesby	Leslie Denison
Dame Carter	Betty Fairfax
Jailer	William Bevan

Using Robert Louis Stevenson's "The Black Arrow" for the takeoff, Columbia has made an action-filled cloak-and-dagger romance that should hold the customers for dual bills and secondary solos. The picture is virtually a western of lethal combat, hard riding, intrigue and deep-dyed villainy—all in when-knighthood-was-in-flower terms. Maybe it isn't exactly art, but it is good entertainment.

Of course, the romantic angle has been accented heavily in the translation from Stevenson's dispassionate narrative. The red-blooded hero returns from the 30 Years War to learn that his uncle has murdered his father to seize the House of York and has had the neighboring Lord of the House of Lancaster executed for the crime. And he understandably tumbles hard for the nifty Lancaster daughter.

The script properly emphasizes the dual elements of turbulence and love. The contending noblemen and their henchmen battle with bow-and-arrow, crossbow, lance, battleaxe, sword and dagger. They scramble through secret passages, over battlements and through forests. They push their horses to the limit of sweat-flecked flank. They match scheme with counter-scheme and boldness with brawn. And although the scoundrel tries to force the heroine to marry him to save her father from death, even he dies without a whimper when his plot backfires. Naturally, there's a proper clinch for the fadeout.

The production, direction and performances combine to carry out the double intention. Louis Hayward is rightly vigorous as the hero, while Janet Blair is the necessary eyeful as the maiden-in-distress. George Macready, Rhys Williams, Walter Kingsford and Ray Teal are convincing knaves, with Paul Cavanaugh and Edgar Buchanan as rebels against injustice. *Hobe.*

The Timber Trail

(SONGS—COLOR)

Republic release of Melville Tucker production. Stars Monte Hale, Lynne Roberts; features Foy Willing. Directed by Philip Ford. Screenplay, Bob Williams; songs, Tim Spencer, Ned Washington, Phil Ohman; camera (Trucolor), Reggie Lanning; editor, Tony Martinelli; musical director, Mort Glickman. Tradeshown N. Y., June 24, '48. Running time, 67 MINS.

Monte Hale	Monte Hale
Alice Baker	Lynne Roberts
Jed Baker	James Burke
Bart	Roy Barcroft
Ralph Baker	Francis Ford
Jordon Weatherbee	Robert Emmett Keane
Sheriff	Steve Darrell
Frank	Fred Graham
Walt	Wade Crosby
Telegraph Operator	Eddie Acuff
Themselves:	Foy Willing and the Riders of the Purple Sage

"The Timber Trail" is average fare for the oatuner circuit. Pic has been cut from the same Trucolored cloth used for its numerous predecessors in the Monte Hale series. It's filled with the usual brace of hoof-beating, six-shooting, knuckle-scraping and mustang-vocalizing, all encased in a corny yarn. This item will neither surprise nor disappoint the juve clientele.

Plot has the formula good guy vs. varmint angles, with Hale playing an itinerant cowboy who stops off in a badman's town to help a lady in distress. Latter, played by Lynne Roberts, is daughter of a stagecoach operator who is being driven out of business through a conspiracy of the local banker and a gang of toughies. Hale, after being framed, jailed and slugged to a fare-the-well, uncovers the culprits in a complicated ruse and delivers them slightly bruised to the sheriff.

Hale walks through his paces in standard style, handling both the action and crooning spots as a cinema cowboy hero should. Miss Roberts is adequate for the slight romantic byplay, while Robert Emmett Keane and Francis Ford make hissable heavies. Foy Willing and the Riders of the Purple Sage contribute a trio of pat prairie numbers in highly listenable manner. *Herm.*

Northwest Stampede

(COLOR)

Eagle Lion release of Albert S. Rogell production. Stars Joan Leslie, James Craig; features Jack Oakie, Chill Wills. Directed by Albert S. Rogell. Story and screenplay, Art Arthur, Lillie Hayward, suggested by Saturday Evening Post story, "Wild Horse Roundup," by Jean Muir; camera, John W. Boyle; editor, Philip Cahn; Cinecolor supervisor, Wilton Holm; special effects, R. O. Binger. Tradeshown in N. Y. June 25, '48. Running time, 79 MINS.

Chris Johnson	Joan Leslie
Dan Bennett	James Craig
Mike Kirby	Jack Oakie
Mileaway	Chill Wills
Mel Saunders	Victor Kilian
Bowles	Stanley Andrews
Barkis	Ray Bennett
Scrivner	Lane Chandler

"Northwest Stampede" is an outdoor animal-story thriller, the plot revolving around a white stallion and a police dog. Despite too much attention on these, film ultimately develops a fairly vivid he-man romance. Picture will delight the youngsters. It has some exciting photography of the Canadian Rockies, done in Cinecolor. But, boxoffice-wise, it does not rate much above the average western because of lack of top names. Exhibitors will have to lean on Joan Leslie, James Craig and Jack Oakie for marquee decoration, and it doesn't look like it's enough.

Photographed on location, for the most part, in the Canadian Rockies, story concerns a star rodeo performer (James Craig) who inherits his dad's big ranch near Calgary but continues to yearn a return to the rodeo arena. This brings him into conflict with his ranch foreman (Joan Leslie). She's stubborn in the belief that he should settle down and make the ranch a paying proposition. Offshoot of main plot has the new ranch owner striving to capture a white stallion, king of wild horses that ranges the mountains, and many times clashing with the girl. There are some authentic scenes of the Calgary Stampede, with events at this big Calgary rodeo dovetailing into the plot effectively. While much is made of the stallion and attempts to tame him, the police dog, Flame, comes close to stealing the picture.

Majestic views of the Canadian mountains form a backdrop to the action. Albert S. Rogell directed with maximum of action on this fairly routine plot, out the dialog is a handicap.

The ranch foreman is neatly portrayed by Miss Leslie, who, as the former cowgirl-rodeo star, lends charm to a rather difficult role. Only a few inanely-worded passages slow up her fine performance. Craig is too stilted in many scenes. Jack Oakie, as his sidekick, adds some droll humor, while Chill Wills makes a splendid character comedian.

Camera work represents outstanding effort by John W. Boyle, not only in following the plot carefully but in his remarkable shots of wild horses. Wilton Holm takes a bow for his strong Cinecolor supervision. *Wear.*

La Hosteria Del Caballito Blanco

("White Horse Inn")

(ARGENTINA)

Buenos Aires, June 8.

EMPA release of Emelco production. Directed by Benito Perojo. Stars Elisa Galve, Juan Carlos Thorry, Tilda Thamar; features Hector Calcagno, Susana Canales, Osvaldo Miranda. Screenplay, Gerardo Rinaldi; adapted by Juan Carlos Muello; dialog by Veribsky and Villalba Welsh. Music, J. Muller and Leo Benatzky; choreography, Margarita Wallman; camera, Pablo Tabernero. Running time, 90 MINS.

This production ran for five weeks in firstrun, grossing as well as any of the most publicized, star-studded Hollywood features, marking a record for an Argentine production. Filmed at the (for these parts) unusually high cost of $250,000, picture is important as index of what major local studios are aiming at to substitute for foreign productions, now that they can count on allout support from the Peron government (including loans up to 70% of production cost).

Coin has been thrown away prodigally on lavish (but not tasteful) decor, original costumes, crowd scenes with hordes of extras, and a galaxy of front-rank talent. Accent is on making a big splash. Director Benito Perojo is a master at megging crowd scenes, but he has overplayed here. Need is for more action, really bright dialog and less pompous pageantry. No value here for U. S. market.

Juan Carlos Thorry, who started his career as an orchestra crooner, sings several songs, dances and monopolizes the best scenes. Elisa Galve is beautiful but wooden as the femme lead, while Tilde Thamar gives a stereotyped version of the gold-digging vamp, helped out by exotic costumes. Brightest spot in this curious mixture is Susanita Canales, playing the ingenue schoolgirl sister of the heroine.

Plot, based on the old Leo Benatzky operetta, with Benatzky contributing music, revolves around Thorry, famous singer, who is enlisted by impetuous schoolgirls to boost custom at the White Horse Inn run by elder sister. Miss Galve. Thorry goes to the inn anonymously and makes a hit, both with patrons and manageress. His ex-girl friend, Miss Thamar, arrives unexpectedly with another boyfriend and creates a rift in the lute. After some confusing adventures all is cleared up, the vamp departing and the lovers united onstage.

Continuity is confusing, with camera pouncing from one sequence to another, apparently to give impression of vivid action, which entirely misfires. Despite all these defects this is a commendable effort on Emelco's part and a welcome change from the lugubrious melodramas so dear to local directors. Hollywood should take due note that this picture rates high in comparison to some of the not too successful pix exhibited here in the last months. The picture is now running in nabe theatres to record grosses. *Nid.*

The Twisted Road

(ONE SONG)

Hollywood, June 23.

RKO release of John Houseman production. Stars Cathy O'Donnell, Farley Granger, Howard Da Silva; features Jay C. Flippen, Helen Craig, Will Wright. Directed by Nicholas Ray. Screenplay, Charles Schnee; adaptation, Nicholas Ray; from the novel, "Thieves Like Us," by Edward Anderson; camera, George E. Diskant; editor, Sherman Todd; music, Leigh Harline; song, Richard M. Jones, Don Raye, Gene dePaul. Tradeshown in Hollywood, June 23, '48. Running time, 95 MINS.

Keechie	Cathy O'Donnell
Bowie	Farley Granger
Chickamaw	Howard Da Silva
T-Dub	Jay C. Flippen
Mattie	Helen Craig
Mobley	Will Wright
Singer	Marie Bryant
Hawkins	Ian Wolfe
Young Farmer	William Phipps
Hagenheimer	Harry Harvey

Underneath "The Twisted Road" is a moving, somber story of hopeless young love. Appeal is limited. There's no attempt at sugarcoating a happy ending, and yarn moves towards its inevitable, tragic climax without compromise. Honesty with which subject is treated, and the theme itself, mitigate against grosses, although development of some exploitable factors may aid.

A gifted team of young players stands out in making the performances thoroughly realistic. Farley G. Ranger and Cathy O'Donnell are in the lead roles, selling the portrayals with a sock. Both should have bright futures.

The script by Charles Schnee is based on Edward Anderson's novel, "Thieves Like Us," and tells the story of a young escaped convict who falls in love and marries a girl whose circumstances are little better than his own.

Nicholas Ray adapted the novel and directed, demonstrating a complete understanding of the characters. It's a firstrate job of moody storytelling. Howard Da Silva clicks as a ruthless, one-eyed bank robber, and Jay C. Flippen is equally topnotch for his delineation of a criminal. Helen Craig, Will Wright and Ian Wolfe give capable backing.

Production values supplied by John Houseman are in keeping with story background. The film's title is derived from song of same handle used in a nitery sequence, with Marie Bryant doing the vocals. *Brog.*

The Betrayal

Astor Pictures release of Oscar Micheaux production. Scripted and directed by Micheaux. Features Leroy Collins, Myra Stanton, Verlie Cowan, Harris Gaines, Yvonne Machen, Alice B. Russell. Camera, N. Spoor. At Mansfield, N. Y., June 24, '48. Running time, 183 MINS.

Ned Washington	Lou Vernon
Nelson Boudreaux	Edward Fraction
Martin Eden	Leroy Collins
Preble	Jessie Johnson
Jack Stewart	William Byrd
Deborah	Myra Stanton
Mrs. Bowles	Frances DeYoung
Joe Bowles	Arthur McCoo
Eunice	Vernettiea Moore
Jessie	Barbara Lee
Linda	Verlie Cowan
Aunt Mary	Alice B. Russell
Terry	Yvonne Machen
Mrs. Dewey	Gladys Williams
Broyle	Richard Lawrence
Dr. Lee	Harris Gaines
Crook	David Jones
Duval	Vernon B. Duncan
Glavis	Curley Killson
Bernadine	Sue McBride
Richards	Harold Mers

"The Betrayal" has some general interest because (a) it's an all-Negro acted-and-produced pic, and (b) because it touches honestly on some provocative racial themes. But that's all. Its amateurishness limits its appeal to Negro centers.

Oscar Michaeux, tripling as scripter-director-producer, has turned out an overlong, dull domestic drama about the tribulations of a young Negro farmer in the northwest.

Film, cut down from 3¼ hours to 183 minutes, is still much too long, especially when it constantly presents long scenes of sheer dialog and no action. The dialog is stilted and artificial. The acting is also inhibited. There is none of the natural, loose-swinging acting and speech which invariably make Negro personalities shine on stage or screen.

The film performs some service in discussing—quietly rather than sensationally — such matters as white and black intermarriage, caste system between light-skinned and dark Negroes, and economic hardships, all from the point of view of the Negro. But the sure professional hand is missing in treatment, performance or production.

Leroy Collins, as the young farmer who brings his schoolteacher wife to his Dakota farm to share his problems, is personable, but handicapped by script, direction and apparent inexperience. Verlie Cowan, as the wife who turns on him, and Myra Stanton, as the Creole Negro always in love with Collins, are also attractive but handicapped by similar failings.   Bron.

Miniature Reviews

"Key Largo" (WB). Potent gangster melodrama with Humphrey Bogart, Edward G. Robinson, Lauren Bacall.

"Thunderhoof" (Col). Program feature off the beaten path; okay supporter.

"The Walls of Jericho" (20th). Drama of politics and love in early Kansas will need strong selling. Good cast names.

"The Illegals" (Indie). Powerful documentary on the migration of Jewish d.p.'s from Europe to Palestine.

"Village Teacher" (Artkino). Routine Soviet film with limited prospects in foreign language houses.

Key Largo

Hollywood, July 3.

Warner Bros. release of Jerry Wald production. Stars Humphrey Bogart, Edward G. Robinson, Lauren Bacall; features Lionel Barrymore, Claire Trevor, Thomas Gomez. Directed by John Huston. Screenplay, Richard Brooks, John Huston; based on play by Maxwell Anderson; camera, Karl Freund; music, Max Steiner; editor, Rudi Fehr. Tradeshown at Los Angeles, July 2, '48. Running time, 100 MINS.
Frank M'Cloud...........Humphrey Bogart
Johnny Rocco.........Edward G. Robinson
Nora Temple................Lauren Bacall
James Temple............Lionel Barrymore
Gaye ....Claire Trevor
Curly ....Thomas Gomez
Toots ....Harry Lewis
Deputy Clyde Sawyer........John Rodney
Ziggy ....Marc Lawrence
Angel ....Dan Seymour
Ben Wade.....................Monte Blue
Henchman.................William Haade
Osceola-Baog............ } Silver Heels
                         } Rodric Red Wing

A tense film thriller has been developed from Maxwell Anderson's play, "Key Largo." It's a hard-hitting gangster yarn with enough marquee weight in the star names to kick it off strongly at the boxoffice. Emphasis is on tension in the telling, and effective use of melodramatic mood has been used to point up the suspense for audience satisfaction.

There are overtones of soapboxing on a better world but this is never permitted to interfere with basic plot, resulting in sturdy film fare for the meller fan. The Anderson play has been brought up to the postwar period by scripters Richard Brooks and John Huston, making a disillusioned veteran and a vice lord represent present-day problems in winning the peace. As noted, that particular theme doesn't interfere with essential aim of telling a gangster yarn.

Key West locale is an aid in stressing tension that carries through the plot. Atmosphere of the deadly, still heat of the keys, the threat of a hurricane and the menace of merciless gangsters make the suspense seem real, and Huston's direction stresses the mood of anticipation. These elements are further hammered home by Jerry Wald's production supervision and the skilled use of technical contributions.

Humphrey Bogart is seen as a veteran, stopping off at Key Largo to visit the family of a buddy killed in the war. He finds the run-down hotel taken over by a group of gangsters, who are waiting to exchange a load of counterfeit for real cash. Kept prisoners over a long day and night, during which a hurricane strikes, the best and the worst is brought out in the characters — fear, and the strength that comes from it, to the good, fear, and its weaknesses, for the evil. As the short span of hours come to a conclusion, Bogart

has found love and a new purpose in life.

The excitement generated is quiet, seldom rambunctious or slambang, although there are moments of high action. The performances are of uniform excellence and go a long way towards establishing credibility of the events. Bogart comes through with a solid performance. Edward G. Robinson has few equals at portraying swaggering racketeers and makes his character a standout. Lauren Bacall walks off with the straight assignment of a war widow, demonstrating ability to handle a character without a slink or a whistle.

Lionel Barrymore shows up strongly as the hotel owner. Claire Trevor gets her teeth into role of faded gangster moll, a character with plenty of opportunity to display acting talent. Thomas Gomez, Harry Lewis, Dan Seymour and William Haade make a swell bunch of henchmen for Robinson. John Rodney, deputy, Marc Lawrence, racketeer, and Monte Blue are among others rating mention.

Effective use of actual locale footage with studio - made scenes helps air of authenticity obtained by Wald's production. The fine lensing by Karl Freund, special effects, score, art direction and settings are strong contributors to mood.   Brog.

Thunderhoof

Hollywood, July 2.

Columbia release of Ted Richmond production. Features Preston Foster, Mary Stuart, William Bishop. Directed by Phil Karlson. Original screenplay, Hal Smith; added dialog, Kenneth Gamet; camera, Henry Freulich; editor, Jerome Thoms. At Pantages, Hollywood, June 30, '48. Running time, 76 MINS.

Scotty Mason..............Preston Foster
Margarita....................Mary Stuart
The Kid.....................William Bishop
Thunderhoof ....Himself

"Thunderhoof" attempts to be different from the usual supporting feature, and comes off rather well. Using small cast and outdoor locale, plot moves forward at an interesting pace, despite being overlength for its release intentions.

Story deals with three humans and how their characters are revealed during a hunt for a fabulous wild stallion in the Mexican wilderness. Preston Foster dreams of establishing a horse ranch in Texas. His wife, Mary Stuart, isn't sure of her love for her husband, and William Bishop is a weak youth making a play for the wife. Trio presents strange contrasts in the horse hunt and there is excitement in the clashes—human, animal and nature.

Equine handling title role adds considerable color and action to the doings as the focal point around which characterizations are developed. Also, he is responsible for the eventual saving of Foster and Miss Stuart after the death of Bishop. Plot line, in some ways, reminds of "Treasure of Sierra Madre," with the horse substituting for gold and ending happy rather than ironic.

Cast threesome gives individually good performances that help maintain interest. The Ted Richmond production is smooth and the outdoor setting has been filmed in sepia by Henry Freulich for another advantage. Phil Karlson's direction has developed the characterizations strongly in the Hal Smith script. Outside of an awkward length for double bill spot-

ting, "Thunderhoof" is a smart departure rrom formula program feature.   Brog.

The Walls of Jericho

Hollywood, July 3.

20th-Fox release of Lamar Trotti production. Stars Cornel Wilde, Linda Darnell, Anne Baxter, Kirk Douglas; features Ann Dvorak, Marjorie Rambeau, Henry Hull, Colleen Townsend, Barton MacLane, Griff Barnett, William Tracy, Art Baker. Directed by John M. Stahl. Screenplay, Lamar Trotti; based on novel by Paul Wellman; camera, Arthur Miller; editor, James B. Clark; music, Cyril Mockridge. Tradeshown July 1, '48. Running time, 111 MINS.
Dave.........................Cornel Wilde
Algeria......................Linda Darnell
Julia.........................Anne Baxter
Tucker Wedge................Kirk Douglas
Belle.........................Ann Dvorak
Mrs. Dunham.............Marjorie Rambeau
Jefferson Norman..............Henry Hull
Marjorie Ransome......Colleen Townsend
Gotch McCurdy...........Barton MacLane
Judge Hutto..................Griff Barnett
Cully Caxton................William Tracy
Peddigrew....................Art Baker
Tom Ransome..............Frank Ferguson
Nellie.......................Ann Morrison
Mrs. Hutto...................Hope Landin
Mrs. Ransome................Helen Brown
Andy McAdam..............Norman Leavitt
Judge Poster............Whitford Kane
Bailiff.............J. Farrell MacDonald
Mulliken.....................Dick Rich
Dr. Patterson................Will Wright

"The Walls of Jericho" is a leisurely screen drama of politics and love as practiced in Kansas early in the 20th century. Indications are that the boxoffice will be spotty. The Paul Wellman novel, from which film was adapted, has a number of exploitable angles that can be used to advantage in attracting the femmes. However, strong selling is necessary.

Characters are insufficiently established to give audiences a clear insight into what makes them tick. Footage is long and the leisurely pace used by John M. Stahl's direction makes for wavering interest. Players, within the limits of the treatment, are good, even adding a wallop to some of the more emotional scenes. Despite a number of good points, overall effect of film is flat.

Cornel Wilde and Anne Baxter are the principals around which the plot swings. He is a politically-minded country lawyer in love with her.

Miss Baxter is an attorney who returns that love although barred from consummation because of his marriage to a drunken spouse. Chief political antagonist to Wilde is Linda Darnell, ambitious wife of the town's publisher, Kirk Douglas. Through her wily, feminine tricks, Miss Darnell manges to estrange all friendships in the town, ruining reputations and besting her opponent until the law of averages catch up with her in the end.

As a Portia, Miss Baxter registers in her courtroom plea to save a girl accused of murder and to clear her own reputation, fouled through machinations of Miss Darnell. Her love scenes with Wilde also are good. His character is the most clearly motivated and, consequently, shows up strongly. Miss Darnell's reasoning is not sufficiently established but she graces the one-sided character with personal charm. Douglas works hard as the publisher used by his wife for her own advantage.

Ann Dvorak is seen as Wilde's wife and Marjorie Rambeau as the shrewish mother - in - law. Faring best among the featured players is Colleen Townsend, the young girl accused of murdering Barton MacLane, town bully. Griff Barnett, Art Baker, Frank Ferguson and Whitford Kane are among others rating mention.

Lamar Trotti produced from his own screenplay, faring better in supervision of physical values of the smalltown background than in the writing. Score is dotted with oldtime songs fitted to the era portrayed and Arthur Miller's photography is topnotch. Brog.

The Illegals
(DOCUMENTARY)

Mayer-Burstyn release of Meyer Levin production, directed, written and narrated by Levin. Camera, Jean-Paul Alphen, Bertrand Hesse; music, Wally Karveno-Pauquin. Previewed N. Y., June 28, '48. Running time, 60 MINS.

"The Illegals," a factual film depicting the exodus of Jewish displaced persons from Europe into Palestine, packs a terrific wallop. This is an authentic documentary made out of the tragic experience of real people in real situations. Whatever this pic's commercial fate will be, it's certain to endure in the historical record as a summation of this era's agony and hopes.

Like "My Father's House," Meyer Levin's initial production, this film will receive a good reception in carefully selected situations in most of the key cities. Heightened interest in the Palestinian question may widen its appeal to more general circles. However, the pic's unremitting sombreness and a few unavoidable flaws in lighting and lensing will probably restrict the playdates to a narrower field than the film deserves.

The best thing about "The Illegals" is that it never reaches for dramatic effects. Levin and his cameramen (recruited from European newsreel outfits) simply followed the movements of a group of refugees and let the facts speak eloquently for themselves. While the film is full of sympathy for the uprooted Jewish people, it scrupulously avoids violent partisanship in stating their case. It only propagandizes for the right of peoples to go freely to the land of their choosing.

The narrative thread is picked up in Poland where a young Jewish couple attempts to reconstruct their lives after being released from a Nazi labor camp. However, the universal rubble and the aftermath of anti-Semitism, which is sensitively suggested in the shrug of a Polish peasant's shoulders, forces their decision to go to Palestine. They join a larger group of emigrants and begin their dangerous underground trek across a continent where, ironically, virtually everything has been shattered except the frontiers.

The treatment of the final leg of their journey via boat from Italy to Haifa is a brilliant piece of camera reportage. The crowding of women and children aboard the tiny ship, the stifling discomfort below deck, the fear of detection by the British and the camaraderie and optimism of the refugees are drawn with poignant detail. Finally a British scouting plane flies over the ship and soon after, four heavy British cruisers are tagging the tiny vessel to Haifa. At this point, British authorities interned the refugees at Cyprus and put an end to the film. The abrupt finish of the picture is a masked but powerful thrust at the British.

Levin's background narration is tempered with judgment and restraint. Despite many provocations in the material, Levin skirts the pitfalls of over-emotionalism and poetic flights, which generally sound phoney. Bits of dialog within the film are dubbed into English with uneven results. Recordings of the Jewish folk songs, however, are excellent and add importantly to the film's hauntingly sad quality. Herm.

Village Teacher
(RUSSIAN)

Artkino release of Soyusdet production. Stars Vera Maretskaya. Directed by Mark Donskoy. Screenplay, Maria Smirnova; camera, Sergei Uresevsky. Tradeshown N. Y., July 1, '48. Running time, 97 MINS.
Varenka....................Vera Maretskaya
Martinov....................Dmitri Sagal
Voronov....................Vassili Maruta
School Watchman...........Pavel Olenev
Gymnasium Principal.......Roman Platt
                         { Volodya Lepeshinsky
Prov Voronov,........ { Dmitri Pavlov
Sergey Tsigankov...........Tolya Gonichev
Dunya....................Emma Balashova

(In Russian; English Titles)

"Village Teacher" is a mediocre film that will fare well only in the Russophile circuit. Pic is an overlong, sprawling and dull melange of Soviet patriotism and "bourgois" romance handled without conviction. Saddled by an all-powerful but capricious state censorship apparatus, Soviet producers are apparently finding it healthier to deal with "safe" ideas.

In external production values, this offering is almost as slick as one of Hollywood's top items. Technical finesse is found in the full lighting, expert outdoor camera work, solid interiors and fine makeup effects. Accomplished physical setup, however, only serves to highlight the pic's mechanical heart.

Undramatic yarn is concerned with the fictional biog of an idealistic young schoolteacher who leaves Moscow for a post in a Siberian village. Her career begins during the Czarist times and ranges until the end of the second World War. Her husband, first an underground revolutionist and then a political commissar, is killed in the war but she is rewarded by the successes of her students. Growth of the village and world developments during the teacher's lifetime are treated superficially with a crude tooting of the Soviet horn.

As the teacher, Vera Maretskaya registers as a credible performer who grows along with her role with a big lift from the makeup department. Dmitri Sagal, as her husband, is a typical storybook hero-revolutionist. The children provide the film's most natural and likable sequences. Herm.

Historia De Una Mala Mujer
(The Story of a Bad Woman)
(ARGENTINE)

Argentine Sono Film release and production. Directed by Luis Saslavsky. Stars Dolores del Rio. Adapted from an Oscar Wilde play by Pedro Miguel Obligado; camera, Alberto Etchebehere. At Ambassador, Buenos Aires. Running time, 90 MINS.
Miss Erlynne.............Dolores del Rio
Lady Windermere..........Maria Duval
Lord Arthur.............Francisco de Paula
Lord Darlington..........Fernando Lamas
Lord Windermere..........Alberto Closas
Duchess..................Amalia S. Arino

This is an unusually careful production for an Argentine-made picture and every effort has been made to live up to the prestige and marquee value of Dolores del Rio's name. But even this isn't enough to put the picture on a par with those of European or Hollywood studios. It's U. S. appeal is small.

Those of Oscar Wilde's original lines which have been allowed to remain in this very free adaptation of his "Lady Windermere's Fan" are entirely lost because the actors haven't mastered them. A great deal of sentimental melodrama has been added to the play, to explain Mrs. Erlynne's past and show her as sacrificing her great love for Lord Arthur, in order to save her daughter's happiness. In fact, maternal sacrifice is made the whole theme of the picture, with a finale different to that of the play, with Mrs. Erlynne selling her jewels, and in particular Lord Arthur's prized gift, before exiling herself from England.

Miss del Rio is moving and understandable in the role of Mrs. Erlynne, despite the studied artificiality of some of her poses. The Argentine cameramen are not always as kind to her as are the Mexicans, who are so much more skillful. Maria Duval is pleasing to the eye as Lady Windermere, and considering her previous thoroughly ingenue roles, gives a quite surprisingly good performance. Alberto Closas, Spanish legit actor, is the performer who seems most easy in his part. Other players act pretty stiffly. There are moments when the picture drags unbelievably, but relatively speaking it's the best turned out by local studios in a long time. Pic ran at the Ambassador for six weeks, with unprecedented grosses for a local production. Nid.

Foreign Films

"Il Fiacre N. 13" ("Cab No. 13") (ITALIAN). Minerva release of Excelsa production. Stars Marcel Herrand, Ginette Leclerc, Vera Carmi, Leonardo Cortese, Roldano Lupi, Pierre Larquey, Raymond Bussieres. Directed by Mario Mattoli. Screenplay, Mattoli, Leo Cattozzo, Andre Hugon, Raoul Andre, Jacques Rastler, from novel by Xavier de Montepin. Camera, Jan Stallich. At Europa and Galleria, Rome. Running time, 155 MINS.

Produced also in French version, this big-budgeted adaptation of the dusty melodrama by Xavier de Montepin is lacking in story interest. Lavish settings, gorgeous costumes and outstanding lenswork can't give life to puppet-like characters and old-fashioned intrigue. Script, direction and acting don't help much. Pic not a draw here, and unlikely elsewhere, except South-American markets. Quat.

Miniature Reviews

"Red River" (UA). Thrilling epic of the old west, potent boxoffice.
"That Lady In Ermine" Musicat-Color) (20th). With Betty Grable and Douglas Fairbanks, Jr.; solid b.o.
"Night Has a Thousand Eyes" (Par). Suspenseful thriller with high exploitation values.
"Texas, Brooklyn and Heaven" (UA). Romantic comedy with light marquee values; mild b.o.
"Shed No Tears" (EL). Minor melodrama for secondaries only. Dull development and slow pace.
"Train to Alcatraz" (Rep). Melodrama for secondary bookings. Okay plot and action.
"A Friend Will Come Tonight" (French) (Lopert). Michel Simon, Madeleine Sologne in World War 2 spy meller big for arty houses.

Red River
Hollywood, July 13.

United Artists release of Howard Hawks (Charles K. Feldman) production, directed by Hawks, co-directed, Arthur Rosson. Stars John Wayne, Montgomery Clift; features Joanne Dru, Walter Brennan, Coleen Gray, John Ireland, Noah Berry, Jr., Harry Carey, Sr., Harry Carey, Jr. Screenplay, Borden Chase, Charles Scheen; from Chase's Satevepost story; camera, Russell Harlan; editor, Christian Nyby; score and song, Dimitri Tiomkin. Previewed July 9, '48. Running time, 126 MINS.
Tom Dunson....................John Wayne
Matthew Garth...........Montgomery Clift
Tess Millay..............Joanne Dru
Groot Nadine.............Walter Brennan
Fen....................Coleen Gray
Cherry Valance..............John Ireland
Buster McGee.............Noah Beery, Jr.
Mr. Melville.............Harry Carey, Sr.
Dan Latimer.............Harry Carey, Jr.
Teeler Yacey....................Paul Fix
Matthew Garth (boy)........Mickey Kuhn
Quo....................Chief Yowlachie
Bunk Kenneally...........Ivan Parry
Walt Jergens....................Ray Hyke
Simms....................Hank Worden
Laredo....................Dan White
The Wrangler..............William Self
Old Leather..............Hal Taliaferro

"Red River" will take its place among the other big, boxoffice-important western epics that have come from Hollywood over the years. It's a spectacle of sweeping grandeur, as rugged and hard as the men and the times with which it deals.

Rough and tough with action, the film brawls and sprawls over two hours and six minutes of footage with such a tight, sure grip on the imagination that the few slow spots will not hinder its boxoffice reception. A money film from any angle—expensive to make but with an almost unlimited grossing potential—"Red River" is slotted for important playdates and bigtime returns.

Howard Hawks' production and direction have given a masterful interpretation to a story of the early west and the opening of the Chisholm Trail, over which Texas cattle were moved to Abilene to meet the railroad on its march across the country.

Also important to "Red River" is the introduction of a new star—Montgomery Clift. He is a young man who should have an important future in films. While "River" is his first bigtime screen job, actor's second venture, "The Search," is already screening.

Clift brings to the role of Matthew Garth a sympathetic personality that invites audience response. He reads the Garth character with an instinctive, nonchalant underplaying that is sock.

Hawks has loaded the film with mass spectacle and earthy scenes.

His try for naturalness in dialog between principals comes off well. The staging of physical conflict is deadly, equalling anything yet seen on the screen. Picture realistically depicts trail hardships; the heat, sweat, dust, storm and marauding Indians that bore down on the pioneers. Neither has Hawks overlooked sex, exponents being Joanne Dru and Coleen Gray. John Wayne has his best assignment to date and he makes the most of it.

Picture is not all tough melodrama. There's a welcome comedy relief in the capable hands of Walter Brennan. He makes his every scene stand out sharply, leavening the action with chuckles while maintaining a character as rough and ready as the next.

Sharing co-director credit with Hawks is Arthur Rosson. The pair have staged high excitement in the cattle stampedes and other scenes of mass action.

The first grade script was written by Borden Chase and Charles Schnee from Chase's Satevepost story. Russell Harlan's camera has captured breath-taking scenic beauty and the music score by Dimitri Tiomkin is an important contribution. *Brog.*

That Lady in Ermine

(COLOR—MUSICAL)

20th-Fox release of Ernst Lubitsch production, directed by Lubitsch. Stars Betty Grable, Douglas Fairbanks, Jr.; features Cesar Romero, Walter Abel, Reginald Gardiner, Harry Davenport. Screenplay, Samson Raphaelson; songs, Leo Robin, Frederick Hollander; score, Alfred Newman; camera (Technicolor), Leon Shamroy; editor, Dorothy Spencer. Tradeshown N. Y., July 10, '48. Running time, **89 MINS.**

Francesca and Angelina.......Betty Grable
Colonel and Duke...Douglas Fairbanks, Jr.
Mario..........................Cesar Romero
Major Horvath...................Walter Abel
Alberto...................Reginald Gardiner
Luigi.......................Harry Davenport
Theresa....................Virginia Campbell
Captain Novak.........Edmund MacDonald

With Betty Grable and Douglas Fairbanks, Jr., charging up the marquee voltage for this lush Technicolor musical, "That Lady in Ermine" has all the trappings of a boxoffice winner. This pic was temporarily cut short in the middle of shooting by the death of producer-director Ernst Lubitsch last November, but Otto Preminger finished it without any break in style. Preminger, at his own request—in tribute to Lubitsch—receives no billing in the credits.

Fanciful yarn of a Graustarkian princess and a Hungarian conqueror is treated with that light spoofing of romance associated with "the Lubitsch touch." That touch, however, is not sufficiently sustained to generate topnotch comedy. Several romantic sequences open in a farcical mood but wind up in a deadpan clinch, thereby muffling the laugh reaction.

This film is a departure from previous Grable musicals in its absence of any special production numbers. Score by lyricist Leo Robin and tunesmith Frederick Hollander is integrated directly into the action in the manner of contemporary legit musicals. One number, "This Is the Moment," is standout, while two others, "The Melody Has to Be Right" and "Ooh, What I'll Do!" are adequate.

Samson Raphaelson's screenplay is a tongue-in-cheek fairy tale about a married princess who saves her tiny mid-European country from invasion by bewitching the enemy's commander. But despite the martial ingredients and 19th Century plume-and-sabre flourishes, the story is lacking in movement.

Main comedy device is an ancestral gallery of portraits within the castle which becomes alive in face of the danger to their homeland. Miss Grable, also playing a medieval heroine who was in a predicament similar to that of her descendant, steps out of her frame and leads the amorous campaign against Douglas Fairbanks, Jr., a Hungarian colonel. Latter retreats under the confusion of double images but finally wins the princess' hand after she dumps her cowardly husband. Despite this switch, film exercises super-caution in not straying outside the censorship codes.

Top players, assisted by a solid supporting cast, play their parts to the hilt. Miss Grable registers strongly in lavish costumes, and handles the musical numbers and dancing chores in usual personable style. Fairbanks cuts a neat figure as the tough warrior who softens up under femme influence. Cesar Romero, as the chicken-hearted husband, furnishes the best comedy bits with his mugging and double-takes. Walter Abel, as Fairbanks' aide, and Reginald Gardiner, as one of the ancestors, also contribute firstrate performances.

Backgrounds for this tinter are tastefully dressed with superb camera handling extracting the maximum color values. *Herm.*

Night Has a Thousand Eyes

Hollywood, July 8.

Paramount release of Endre Bohem production. Stars Edward G. Robinson, Gail Russell, John Lund; features Virginia Bruce, William Demarest. Directed by John Farrow. Screenplay, Barre Lyndon, Jonathan Latimer; based on novel by Cornell Woolrich; camera, John F. Seitz; music, Victor Young; editor, Eda Warren. Tradeshown in Los Angeles, July 7, '48. Running time, **80 MINS.**

John Triton...........Edward G. Robinson
Jean Courtland...................Gail Russell
Elliott Carson.....................John Lund
Jenny.........................Virginia Bruce
Lieut. Shawn............William Demarest
Peter Vinson.................Richard Webb
Whitney Courtland...........Jerome Cowan
Dr. Walters...............Anslow Stevenson
Mr. Gilman................John Alexander
Melville Weston.............Roman Bohnen
Mr. Myers................Luis Van Rooten

Suspense is the dominating element in this thriller which follows a man who can foresee the future. Told in broad strokes of tenseness, picture can expect handsome returns with its strong exploitation possibilities.

Plot which might easily have gone overboard in handling, instead is a steadily-moving yarn of a mind-reader who eventually discovers the frightening fact that he he can actually tell what is to happen. Told in flashback form, story starts with Gail Russell about to commit suicide by jumping from a trestle onto a track in front of onrushing train, in terror after having been told by Edward G. Robinson, the diviner, that she will meet a violent death within a few days. Events in natural order then are narrated by Robinson, from time he learned he was gifted—or damned—with his inner sight to opening events, and occurrences that follow leading up to strong climax.

John Farrow's sure directorial hand is seen throughout unfolding of picture, scripted melodramatically by Barre Lyndon and Jonathan Latimer. Megger has maintained highly-charged atmosphere, and has able actor in Robinson to give credence to character. Robinson makes most of role, and has lovely support in Miss Russell. Jerome Cowan, Virginia Bruce, William Demarest and Roman Bohnen also contribute heftily to interest. John Lund, co-starred with Robinson and Miss Russell, isn't so fortunate, in evoking interest, but his role is necessary to plot.

Production reins were well handled by Endre Bohem. John F. Seitz' camera work, as well as Eda Warren's tight editing and Victor Young's atmosphere score, likewise contribute to film's qualities. *Whit.*

Texas, Brooklyn and Heaven

(ONE SONG)

United Artists release of Robert S. Golden production. Stars Guy Madison, Diana Lynn; features James Dunn, Michael Chekhov, Florence Bates, Lionel Stander. Directed by William Castle. Screenplay, Lewis Meltzer; based on story by Barry Benefield; song, "Texas, Brooklyn and Heaven," Ervin Drake, Jimmy Shirl; camera, William Mellor; editor, James Newcom; musical director, Emil Newman. Tradeshown N. Y. July 9, '48. Running time, **76 MINS.**

Eddie Tayloe......................Guy Madison
Perry Dunklin.....................Diana Lynn
Mike.............................James Dunn
The Bellhop................Lionel Stander
Mandy.......................Florence Bates
Gaboolian..................Michael Chekhov
Ruby Cheever...........Margaret Hamilton
Pearl Cheever.................Moyna Magill
Opal Cheever......................Irene Ryan
MacWirther..................Colin Campbell
Capt. Bjorn....................Clem Bevans
Carmody, the Cop............Roscoe Karns
The Agent..................William Frawley
Bernie.........................Alvin Hammer
Dr. Danson..................Erskine Sanford
McGonical.......................John Galidet
Policeman.......................James Burke
Thibault......................Guy Wilkerson
Copy Boy.....................Audie Murphy
Bartender.........................Tom Dugan

"Texas, Heaven and Brooklyn" is a rambling film that will have only a mild boxoffice impact. Lack of marquee weight will not help in overcoming other drawbacks of the production. Attempts to cash in on the two great national cliches of humor, Brooklyn and Texas, is treated in a plodding style with much hokey sentimentalism and few laughs.

Major flaw of this film is that the screenplay contains neither plot nor point. Story begins uncertainly, proceeds aimlessly and ends abruptly. Confusion of the pic is highlighted by a deficient editing job which leaves some sequences dangling in the middle, wholly unexplained. This glaring flaw was likely necessitated by heavy scissoring to bring the running time within dual bill needs.

This yarn is concerned with the adventures of a Texas lad, Guy Madison, who travels to New York to become a playwright. En route he teams up with a runaway Texas gal with a yen for the Brooklyn ozone. In New York, Diana Lynn adopts a pickpocket, Florence Bates, as her mother, and moves in with a trio of Flatbush spinsters. Story, which James Dunn, as a bartender, unfolds through long backflashes, travels through one flat scene at Coney Island and another in a whacky Brooklyn riding academy containing mechanical horses and camels. Sudden end to the film witnesses the romantic couple back in Texas riding the range.

Madison registers pleasantly but isn't given much to do. Miss Lynn is also likable personality but finds it tough-going through such awkward lines as "Brooklyn is a wondrous place indeed." Best thesping bits are supplied by Lionel Stander, as a lippy hotel porter, and Florence Bates, as the honest-faced dip. Dunn also does nicely in the bit part of the bartender.

One pleasant number, "Texas, Brooklyn and Heaven," is rendered in accompaniment of the credits. *Herm.*

Shed No Tears

Hollywood, July 10.

Eagle Lion release of Robert Frost production. Stars Wallace Ford, June Vincent; features Robert Scott, Frank Albertson, Richard Hogan, Elena Verdugo, Johnstone White. Directed by Jean Yarbrough. Screenplay, Brown Holmes, Virginia Cook; from novel by Don Martin; camera, Frank Redman; editor, Norman R. Cerf. At Vogue, Hollywood, June 9, '48. Running time, **70 MINS.**

Sam Grover...................Wallace Ford
Edna Grover...................June Vincent
Ray Belden......................Robert Scott
Huntington Stewart........Jonathan White
Tom Grover........................Dick Hogan
Hutton........................Frank Albertson

A minor entry for secondary bookings, "Shed No Tears" barely gets by. Overlong on footage and slowly developed, yarn fails to generate much interest for spectators. Sharper editing might help to fit it as filler material on dual bills in lesser situations.

Very mild screenplay deals with an insurance fraud and backfiring blackmail with cast trying hard but seldom succeeding in breathing life into plot. Dialog is trite and Jean Yarbrough's direction meandering.

June Vincent, the real heavy, talks husband Wallace Ford into faking death to collect a $50,000 insurance policy. Suspicions of Richard Hogan, Ford's son by an earlier marriage, upset the perfect scheme and the detective he hires takes a blackmail to bolster his regular fee. Windup has Ford appearing to shoot Miss Vincent's new love and, to a chorus of screaming lead and police sirens, a death leap from a 10-story window solves all the plot's problems.

Ford manages the most interest of the cast. Among others are Johnstone White, the blackmailing private eye, Robert Scott, Miss Vincent's new romance, and Frank Albertson. Stronger direction by Yarbrough could have given the Brown Holmes - Virginia Cook script a little lift. Production values achieved by Robert Frost are minor and lensing by Frank Redman is standard. *Brog.*

Train to Alcatraz

Hollywood, July 9.

Republic release of Lou Brock production. Stars Donald Barry, Janet Martin, William Phipps; features Roy Barcroft, June Storey, Jane Darwell, Milburn Stone, Chester Clute, Ralph Dunn, Richard Irving, John Alvin, Michael Carr. Directed by Philip Ford. Original screenplay, Gerald Geraghty; camera, Reggie Lanning; editor, Harold Minter. Previewed July 4, '48. Running time, **60 MINS.**

Forbes........................Donald Barry
Beatrice........................Janet Martin
Tommy Calligan............William Phipps
Grady..........................Roy Barcroft
Virginia.........................June Storey
Aunt Ella.....................Jane Darwell
Bart Kanin..................Milburn Stone
Conductor....................Chester Clute
U. S. Marshal..................Ralph Dunn
Anders.......................Richard Irving
Nick...............................John Alvin
Marty.........................Michael Carr
Mahaffey.........................Marc Krah
Hutchins.......................Denver Pyle
Geronimo...................Iron Eyes Cody
Reeves...............Kenneth MacDonald
George........................Harry Harvey
Edgar..........................Steven Baron
Hollister...........................Bob Stone
Billings......................Don Haggerty
McHenry..................John A. Doucette

"Train for Alcatraz" is a budget melodrama for secondary billings. Title is apt, plot being laid on a prison train, and action overcomes load of dialog to rate casual interest over the 60-minute running time.

The prison train is transporting group of convicts to Alcatraz and plot builds gradually through group's planning of an escape to climax in the blood-thirsty break for freedom. Flashback technique is used to establish sympathy for one of the cons, a young man with a bad record who is wrongfully convicted of murder. Before blow-off, his slate is cleaned by outside forces and the other convicts meet sudden death when they attempt to flee the train.

Donald Barry is the escape ringleader and William Phipps portrays the convict who was wronged. There's a suddenly developed romance between Phipps and Janet Martin, legit passenger on the train, and other chief femme role falls to June Storey, gunmoll who's aiding the escape plot. Roy Barcroft, guard; Ralph Dunn, U. S. marshal; and Chester Clute, timid conductor, give okay law-and-order characterizations. Among convicts showing up are Milburn Stone, John Alvin, Michael Carr, Marc Krah, Denver Pyle.

Philip Ford's direction of the Gerald Geraghty script keeps yarn moving forward at an okay pace and production values marshalled by Lou Brock within the limited budget are good. Lensing and other technical contributions are standard. *Brog.*

A Friend Will Come Tonight
(Un Ami Viendra Ce Soir)
(FRENCH)

Lopert Films release of Constantin Geftman production. Stars Michel Simon; features Madeleine Sologne, Louis Salou, Saturnin Fabre. Directed by Raymond Bernard. Screenplay, Jacques Companeez, Raymond Bernard from original by Companeez; camera, Robert Lefebvre; background music by Arthur Honegger. Previewed in N. Y., July 8, '48. Running time, 92 MINS.
Michel Lemaret..............Michel Simon
Helen Asselin..........Madeleine Sologne
Commissioner Martin.........Louis Salou
Commander Gerard...........Louis Salou
Philippe Prunier..........Saturnin Fabre
Dr. Tiller...................Paul Bernard
Dr. Lestrade..............Marcel Andre
Jacques Leroy.............Jacques Clancy
Pierre Ribault..............Daniel Gelin
Dr. Pigaut.............Claude Lehmann
The baroness.................Lily Mounet
Beatrice................Yvette Andreyor
Claire ....Cecilia Paroldi

(In French; English Titles)

A gripping, unusual spy meller, this is one of the better French contributions. Unfolded before a backdrop of Maquis underground operations in France during the last war, "A Friend Will Come Tonight" has action and an unusual amount of suspense. And with Michel Simon as star, it spells big boxoffice for arty theatres.

Story is mostly told in a private mental hospital of French Alpine region near Switzerland, at time the Nazis were prowling the sector in the fall of 1944. Yarn shows the German forces trying to locate among the inmates the brains of the underground.

Simon as a bewhiskered inmate, turns in another splendid characterization. His portrayal of a so-called world philosopher, as he fends off interrogations by the Nazi secret agent, furnish a highlight of the film. Scene winds up by Simon offering himself as the Maquis ringleader, and willing to be shot although not knowing what it's all about.

Madeleine Sologne impresses as the Jewish girl whose family has been wiped out by the Germans. Incidentally, she looks like a U. S. screen possibility.

Louis Salou is fine as the Maquis leader masquerading as hopelessly insane. Saturnin Fabre, Paul Bernard and Marcel Andre top the excellent supporting cast.

The unusual plot has been concocted by Jacques Companeez, with Director Raymond Bernard collab-

---

ing with him on the screenplay, Bernard's direction is topflight as is the lensing by Robert Lefebvre. Latter has done particularly well with outdoor camering. *Wear.*

Miniature Reviews

"The Velvet Touch" (RKO). Heavy drama of legit actress who kills her Svengali. Moderate b.o.

"Mr. Peabody and the Mermaid" (U). Lots of contented chuckles for males but light on femme appeal.

"The Babe Ruth Story" (Mono). Biopic with William Bendix as the Bambino. B.o. outlook excellent.

"The Checkered Coat" (20th). Program melodrama of psycho killer, for dualers.

"Eyes of Texas" (Color-Songs) (Rep). Roy Rogers oatuner packs enough action to rate big boxoffice.

"Daredevils in the Clouds" (Rep). Lightweight flying story for the duals.

"Lady at Midnight" (EL) Ordinary whodunit for secondary fare.

"My Brother's Keeper" (British) (GFD). New Sydney Box - Gainsborough-Rank meller, not big in U. S. market.

The Velvet Touch
(SONG)
Hollywood, July 16.

RKO release of Frederick Brisson (Edward Donahoe) production. Stars Rosalind Russell, Leo Genn, Claire Trevor, Sydney Greenstreet; features Leon Ames, Frank McHugh, Walter Kingsford, Dan Tobin, Lex Barker, Nydia Westman, Theresa Harris. Directed by John Gage. Screenplay, Leo Rosten; adaptation, Walter Reilly; story, William Mercer, Annabel Ross; camera, Joseph Walker; editor, Chandler House; score, Leigh Harline; song, Harline and Mort Greene. Tradeshown July 13, '48. Running time, 96 MINS.
Valérie Stanton.........Rosalind Russell
Michael Morrell...............Leo Genn
Marion Webster.............Claire Trevor
Captain Danbury.......Sydney Greenstreet
Gordon Dunning.............Leon Ames
Ernie Boyle...............Frank McHugh
Peter Gunther.........Walter Kingsford
Jeff Trent.................Dan Tobin
Paul Banton...............Lex Barker
Susan Crane.............Nydia Westman
Nancy...................Theresa Harris
Albert...................Irving Bacon
Pansy Dupont.............Esther Howard
Mr. Crouch.............Howard Hayden
Howard Forman...........William Erwin
Helen Adams..............Martha Hyer
Jimmy...................Steven Flagg
Terry...................Louis Mason
Sgt. Oliphant.............James Flavin
Mr. Soper...............Charles McAvoy
Eddie Brown................Dan Foster
Cast of "Hedda Gabler"
Hedda Gabler...........Rosalind Russell
Judge Brack...............Russell Hicks
George Tesman............James Todd
Mrs. Elvested.............Joyce Arling
Juliana Tesman...........Ida Schumaker
Ejlert Lovborg.............Phillip Barnes
Bertha...................Besse Wade

"The Velvet Touch" marks the initial independent production venture of star Rosalind Russell and hubby Frederick Brisson. Film has been given a glossy backing for selling by RKO as a top feature but indications are that returns will not be big. Excellent exploitation elements will aid in boosting grosses.

Chief distraction is the highly polished play-acting used on characters that carry no warmth or sympathy. Performances are showy professional work that demonstrate techniques but the people portrayed never get under the skin. Top role is a meaty one for a femme, acting-wise, and Miss Russell, uses all of her tricks to show off technical thespian skill.

Plot deals with a legit actress who, at the height of her career, kills the producer who had guided her to the top. Circumstance makes it possible for her to conceal her guilt and she permits another actress to be accused and driven to suicide. The Trilby-Svengali angle, as developed, carries no sympathy for the actress.

A bothersome conscience eventually leads her to confess although not legally tied to the crime.

Leo Rosten's script is loaded with glib, pat dialog. John Gage's direction is as showy as the trouping, without the depth needed to tie an audience more closely to the story. Among the players, Leo Genn presents an interesting personality as a man-of-the-world with whom Miss Russell falls in love. Claire Trevor is the distraught actress who is accused of killing the producer, her former lover.

Sydney Greenstreet portrays a police captain whose interest in the theatre makes him a natural to probe the crime. Leon Ames is the producer. Frank McHugh, Dan Tobin (columnist), Theresa Harris (maid), Irving Bacon, Esther Howard and others are capable.

Frederick Brisson and his associate producer, Edward Donahue, have given the picture excellent sight trappings as background for the drama. Also included is a play-within-a-play, characters doing "Hedda Gabler" as the finale piece which brings about Miss Russell's confession. A title tune by Mort Greene and Leigh Harline is used as music backing for opening screen credits. Joseph Walker's expert lensing heads up ace technical contributions. *Brog.*

Mr. Peabody and the Mermaid
(SONG)
Hollywood, July 10.

Universal release of Nunnally Johnson production. Stars William Powell, Ann Blyth; features Irene Hervey, Andrea King, Clinton Sundberg. Directed by Irving Pichel. Screenplay, Nunnally Johnson; from the novel, "Peabody's Mermaid," by Guy and Constance Jones; camera, Russell Metty; editor, Marjorie Fowler; song, Johnny Mercer, Robert Emmett Dolan. Previewed July 6, '48. Running time, 89 MINS.
Mr. Peabody..............William Powell
Mermaid ....Ann Blyth
Mrs. Polly Peabody..........Irene Hervey
Cathy Livingston...........Andrea King
Mike Fitzgerald.........Clinton Sundberg
Dr. Harvey...................Art Smith
Major Hadley...............Hugh French
Colonel Mandrake.........Lumsden Hare
Basil...................Fred Clark
Lieutenant...............James Logan
Wee Shop Clerk.............Mary Field
Mother...............Beatrice Roberts
Nurse...................Cynthia Corley
Waiter...................Tom Stevenson
Lady Trebshaw...........Mary Somerville
Waiter...................Richard Ryan
Boy...................Bobby Hyett
Sidney...................Ivan H. Browning

"Mr. Peabody and the Mermaid" is an object lesson in what could happen to males reaching the dangerous age of 50. As such it will afford a load of chuckles for the older masculine audiences but appeal isn't as strong for femmes. Film's title and whimsical theme are exploitation attractions that can aid grosses if backed by strong selling.

While story idea hasn't jelled as well as it might on celluloid, plot is intriguing, and dialog and situation are used to pleasantly prod the risibilities. As producer, Nunnally Johnson, with Gene Fowler, Jr., as associate, has furnished plenty of scenic values. Story locale is the British West Indies, with the island location, underwater scenes and general tropic flavor adding to the appeal.

Johnson's script, based on the novel, "Peabody's Mermaid" by Guy and Constance Jones, deals with a staid Bostonian who is ordered to spend the winter in the West Indies by his doctor. During a fishing interlude he hooks a mermaid in the tail, fetches her to his beach house and domiciles her in the fish pond. Through circumstance, no other cast principals catch a glimpse of more than the sea siren's tail, so his mermaid story—the most colossal fish yarn of all — makes for doubts of his sanity.

The aging Bostonian, just 50, falls in love with his finny charmer but in the end loses her to the sea again after as hectic a time imaginable in which his wife leaves him, he's suspect by island police and nearly drowns because of the siren's love for him.

William Powell plays the Bostonian with sly understanding and reaps a healthy crop of chuckles. His infatuation for the mermaid is understandable, particularly when the deep-sea denizen is such a charmer as Ann Blyth. Actress plays the role without a line of dialog, nearest approach being a hiss of anger at other femmes; yet, she gives it solid appeal.

Among some of the more delightful moments of comedy is Powell's purchase of the bra half of a femme swim suit and his efforts to explain its purpose to the mermaid. Aiding the purchase scene is some fancy work by Mary Field as the clerk.

Irene Hervey is especially good as Powell's wife, and Andrea King sparks a vampish role as a young lady attracted to the Bostonian. She also sings "The Caribbees," tune by Johnny Mercer and Robert Emmett Dolan. Clinton Sundberg milks neat role of resort press agent. Art Smith, a psychiatrist; Hugh French, Lumsden Hare, Fred Clark and others are good.

Direction by Irving Pichel keeps the mood pleasant and nicely spices the comedy. Russell Metty's photography is expert, and the underwater scenes lensed at Weekiwachee Spring, Fla., add value. Editing holds film to handy 89 minutes running time. *Brog.*

The Babe Ruth Story
(SONGS)
Hollywood, July 17.

Monogram release of Roy Del Ruth (Allied Artists) production, associate producer, Joe Kaufman. Stars William Bendix, Claire Trevor, Charles Bickford; features Sam Levene, William Frawley, Gertrude Niesen, Matt Briggs. Directed by Del Ruth. Screenplay, Bob Considine, George Callahan, from the book by Considine; camera, Philip Tannura; editor, Richard Heermance; music, Edward Ward; technical adviser, Pat Flaherty. Previewed July 15, '48. Running time, **106 MINS.**

Babe Ruth..................William Bendix
Claire Hodgson..................Claire Trevor
Brother Matthias..........Charles Bickford
Phil Conrad..........................Sam Levene
Jack Dunn....................William Frawley
Night Club Singer..........Gertrude Niesen
Miller Huggins....................Fred Lightner
Western Union Boy.......Stanley Clements
Babe Ruth (as a boy)...............Bobby Ellis
Balton..................................Lloyd Gough
Col. Ruppert..........................Matt Briggs
Dr. Menzies......................Paul Cavanagh
Bill Carrigan.......................Pat Flaherty
The Kid..................................Tony Taylor
Coach...................................Richard Lane
Mark Koenig.........................Mark Koenig
Sports Announcer.................Harry Wismer
Sports Announcer.......................Mel Allen
News Announcer...........H. V. Kaltenborn
Narrator..............................Knox Manning

America's baseball hero takes another turn at bat in what looks like a boxoffice home run, or at least a three-bagger. "The Babe Ruth Story" tells a fanciful, romanticized version of the life and deeds of the King of Swat, mixing screen license with fact to dish out a load of chuckles, tears and sentiment that should pay off.

Carrying the Allied Artists label for Monogram distribution, film is aimed at top percentage playing time in keeping with the hefty production budget. With the wealth of natural exploitation, coupled with the Babe Ruth name, there should be little trouble stirring up strong boxoffice interest. Early release to tie in with the national attention directed at diamond activities also is in the film's favor.

The screenplay picks up Ruth at the time he was taken from his father's Baltimore waterfront saloon and raised at the St. Mary's Industrial School for Boys. From there it gleans the highlights of his professional career, first as a bigtime pitcher and then as the Bambino of the mighty bat. His first start with the Baltimore Orioles, his career with the Boston Red Sox and then the New York Yankees and finally back to a slipping and aging Ruth who finished his diamond heroics with the Boston Braves. Considerable footage is given the Babe's present illness and long hospitalization. Opening and closing sequences, both on the long side, give a kudo to other diamond greats honored at Baseball's Hall of Fame at Cooperstown, N. Y., and the future that may await some present-day sandlotter.

In keeping with a national tendency to romanticize heroes, the Bob Considine-George Callahan script tosses out fact whenever screen license will do a more fanciful job of making Ruth the idol he has become to millions. Story shows him as a human, big-hearted and often brash character who captured the fancy of baseball fans because of his basic color.

Roy Del Ruth's direction milks every phase of the sympathetic treatment, combining warmth, tears and chuckles into a film that will sustain audience interest. William Bendix does an excellent job of the title role. While he's still Bendix, he gives the performance the color of Ruth and a reasonable facsimile of the Bambino's mannerism, batting stance and walk. The performance has a lot of heart in keeping with the script's line of development.

Claire Trevor gives one of her solid portrayals as Ruth's second wife (there's no mention of the first in the script). Charles Bickford pleases as Brother Matthias, the priest whose interest in Ruth as a boy carried through life.

Miller Huggins, the late manager of the Yankees, comes to life in the deft hands of Fred Lightner. Ruth as a boy is capably played by Bobby Ellis. Sam Levene does well as a sports writer pal of the Babe's, role being a composite of several. Rating mention, among the many good characterizations, are those by William Frawley, Stanley Clements, Matt Briggs, Paul Cavanagh, Pat Flaherty and Tony Taylor.

Del Ruth and his associate producer, Joe Kaufman, have given the film an excellent mounting. Gertrude Niesen's voice is an added production touch, lending sultry emphasis to vocals on "Nobody's Baby" and "Singing in the Rain." Other oldtime tunes are expertly done by The King's Men and the Mitchell Boychoir.

Good musical direction by Edward Ward, smooth lensing by Philip Tannura, and other technical credits measure up to making this an interesting, if semi-fictional, screen account of George Herman Ruth. *Brog.*

The Checkered Coat
Hollywood, July 17.

20th-Fox release of Sam Baerwitz (Belsam) production. Stars Tom Conway, Noreen Nash, Hurd Hatfield; features James Seay, Garry Owen, Marten Lamont, Rory Mallinson, Leonard Mudie. Directed by Edward L. Cahn. Screenplay, John C. Higgins; original, Seeleg Lester, Merwin Gerard; camera, Jackson Rose; editor, Paul Landres. At Grauman's Chinese, Hollywood, July 16, '48. Running time, **66 MINS.**

Dr. Michael Madden..........Tom Conway
Betty Madden..................Noreen Nash
Creepy..........................Hurd Hatfield
Capt. Dunhill...................James Seay
Prince............................Garry Owen
Fred Madden................Marten Lamont
Perkins.......................Rory Mallinson
Jerry...........................Leonard Mudie
Brownlee.........................Eddie Dunn
Marcus Anson..............John R. Hamilton
Bill Anson........................Fred Browne
Kim.............................Lee Tung Foo
Cafe Owner......................Julian Rivero
Singer...........................Dorothy Porter
Announcer.........................Sam Hayes
Bartender....................Dewey Robinson
Dr. Pryor.........................Lee Bonnell
Dr. Stevenson..................Russell Arms

"The Checkered Coat" averages out slightly better than the usual program filler feature by virtue of good performances. Otherwise, it's a small-budgeted meller aimed at lower half of the dualers. Running time of 66 minutes fits it handily into that bracket.

Plot projects some gruesome touches through interesting angle developed for the heavy, but needs sharper dialog and less pat story situations. Story concerns roundup of a psychopathic killer whose eventual downfall results from his cataleptic seizures. Edward L. Cahn's pacing of the melodramatics is good and performances give a lift to thriller elements under his helming.

Hurd Hatfield gets plenty of menace into his characterization of the crazy killer. Tom Conway is good as the doctor and Noreen Nash shows well as the wife. James Seay makes a credible police captain. There's a sharp character bit by Garry Owen. Marten Lamont, Lee Bonnell and others are capable. Film spots one tune, a television number on a barroom receiver, sung by Dorothy Porter.

The Sam Baerwitz production has stretched the budget dollar to good effect. Lensing by Jackson Rose, tight editing and other factors measure up. *Brog.*

Eyes of Texas
(COLOR—SONG)

Republic release of Edward J. White production. Stars Roy Rogers; features Andy Devine, Lynne Roberts, Bob Nolan and Sons of Pioneers. Directed by William Whitney. Original screenplay, Sloan Nibley; camera (Trucolor), Jack Marta; editor, Tony Martinelli. Tradeshown N. Y., July 16, '48. Running time, **71 MINS.**

Roy Rogers........................Roy Rogers
Penny Thatcher...............Lynne Roberts
Cookie Bullfincher..............Andy Devine
Hattie Waters....................Nana Bryant
Vic Rabin.........................Roy Barcroft
Frank Dennis...................Danny Morton
Thaddeus Cameron............Francis Ford
Pete...............................Pascale Perry
Sheriff.........................Stanley Blystone
Bob Nolan and Sons of Pioneers

Republic has packed plenty of action suspense into this typical outdoor opus. It has added Trucolor and the music and singing of Roy Rogers and Sons of Pioneers. Result is one of best Rogers oatuners in some time. Pic will be a strong entry wherever westerns are liked.

Usual formula has Rogers, as U. S. marshal, fighting an easy-money femme lawyer, but rings in a rather involved plot for a western. Woman barrister, who uses cowboy outlaws to carry out her orders, schemes to gain possession of a valuable ranch property with two killings resulting. She uses wild dogs (which she has trained to attack her victims) to carry out these slayings, thus appearing innocent of any wrongdoing. She claims it was wolves.

Plot has Rogers taming one of these wild police dogs and ultimately bringing all hands to justice. There's a hair-raising, running-gun fight as a climax that's loads different from the accepted ones.

Rogers and his horse, "Trigger," are as outstanding as ever, showing up particularly well in color. Lynne Roberts is markedly comely as the nurse who falls for Rogers. Andy Devine is the jovial western medico, playing it nearly straight for nice results.

Best tune done by Rogers and Sons of Pioneers is "Padre of Old San Antone" by Tim Spencer. Jack Marta has done a trim camera job while William Whitney's direction is topflight. The Trucolor job is okay for this western though not as contrasty as other color processes. *Wear.*

Daredevils of the Clouds

Republic release of Stephen Auer production. Stars Robert Livingston, Mae Clark, James Cardwell; features Grant Withers, Edward Gargan. Directed by George Blair. Screenplay, Norman S. Hall; original story, Ronald Davidson; camera, John MacBurnie; editor, Richard L. Van Enger. At New York theatre, N. Y., week July 13, '48. Running time, **60 MINS.**

Terry O'Rourke..........Robert Livingston
Kay Cameron.......................Mae Clark
Johnny Martin...............James Cardwell
Matt Conroy....................Grant Withers
Tapit Bowers.................Edward Gargan
Mitchell................................Ray Teal
Eddy Clark........................Jimmie Dodd
Douglas Harrison.............Pierre Watkin
Mollie............................Jayne Hazard
Joe.....................................Bob Wilke
Frank..............................Frank Melton
Jimmy............................Russell Arms
Sergeant..........................Hugh Prosser
Bartender.....................Charles Sullivan

"Daredevils of the Clouds" is an unpretentious actioner aimed at the dualers. Story is familiar stuff and cast names aren't strong enough to help the film's b.o. prospects. Returns will be similar to those garnered by the average programmer. Ballying the picture's flying sequences, however, might give the wicket an added whirl.

This is the oft-told tale of how a large airline seeks to absorb a smaller competitor. Latter is Polar Airways, headed by Robert Livingston, who's hard pressed to keep his line on a paying basis. Unknown to him, Trans-Global plants James Cardwell on the Polar payroll to get in some dirty work. After the usual yarn complications, the plot straightens out for a happy finale.

Cast contribs so-so performances in this Stephen Auer production. Livingston is a clear-cut airline operator. Mae Clark, a grounded pilot who becomes Polar's office manager, capably handles the heart interest. Cardwell is adequate as the undercover man while Grant Withers is a typical heavy. Supporting players offer little thesping lustre. Cameraman John MacBurnie's lensing is okay. George Blair's direction is fair. *Gilb.*

Lady at Midnight

Eagle Lion release of John Sutherland production. Stars Richard Denning, Frances Rafferty, Lora Lee Michel. Directed by Sherman Scott. Screenplay by Richard Sale from his original story; camera, Jack Greenhalgh; editor, Martin Cohn. Tradeshown July 16, '48. Running time, **61 MINS.**

Peter Wiggins..............Richard Denning
Ellen Wiggins..............Frances Rafferty
Tina Wiggins................Lora Lee Michel
Al Garrity...........................Ralph Dunn
Lydia Forsythe....................Nana Bryant
Freddy Forsythe..................Jack Searle
Ross Atherton....................Harlan Warde
Carolyn Sugar..................Claudia Drake
Willie Gold.........................Ben Welden

Routine whodunit never rises above its lightweight cast or humdrum story and production. It's strictly lower dual fare for there is not a name that is even faintly familiar to brighten the marquee.

Yarn concerns an adopted child and problems of a young wedded couple (he's a radio newscaster) to retain possession of said brat although they have had her as their own for some seven years. There is an unsolved murder in the first reel, and finally it appears that a scheming lawyer is at the core of several killings in his wild scheme to grab the youngster's fortune. There is the basis for a fruitful plot in this, but it is slaughtered here.

Jerky dialog is cluttered up with trite phrases as "open up in there," "you can say that again," "deliver that body to the morgue," etc. Lora Lee Michel, as the 7-year-old adopted girl, is too precocious though hinting some future possibilities in her less cute scenes. Frances Rafferty, as the young wife, is a looker but not particularly impressive as an actress. Richard Denning, the hubby, is earnest enough but that's all. Ralph Dunn, as the betting private sleuth, really breathes some life into the scenes in which he appears. Remainder of cast is undistinguished.

Some of the stilted performances appear to stem from ordinary directing by Sherman Scott. Jack Greenhalgh's lensing is up to standard. *Wear.*

My Brother's Keeper
(BRITISH)
London, July 14.

General Film Distributors' release of J. Arthur Rank-Gainsborough-Sydney Box production. Stars Jack Warner. Directed by Alfred Roome. Screenplay by Frank Harvey, Jr., from original story by Maurice Wiltshire; editor, Esmond Seal; camera, Gordon Lang, Frank Bassill. At Odeon. Running time, 96 MINS.
```
George Martin...............Jack Warner
Nora Lawrence...............Jane Hylton
Willie Stannard.............George Cole
Syd Evans...................Bill Owen
Ronnie Waring...............David Tomlinson
Meg Waring..................Yvonne Owen
Wainwright..................Raymond Lovell
Mrs. Martin.................Beatrice Varley
Mrs. Gully..................Amy Veness
Winnie Foreman..............Brenda Bruce
Beryl.......................Susan Shaw
Bert Foreman................John Boxer
Landlord....................Fred Groves
Brewster....................Garry Marsh
Harding.....................Wilfrid Hyde-White
```

A lack of names to put on the marquee is the greatest handicap this picture will have in the U. S. market. For though made on a modest budget, it develops a tense situation with action and excitement. In most spots here, Jack Warner's personality will be a telling factor, and "My Brother's Keeper" should do modestly.

Sydney Box has given many an opportunity to prove their worth in this production. Alfred Roome was promoted from the cutting room for this directorial assignment and has displayed a clear grasp of his new functions.

Film is by no means free of criticism. It takes too long to get under way, and in the opening stages dialog plays too important a part. But once it gets moving, film becomes a creditable thriller.

Plot is built around two escaped handcuffed prisoners, a hardened criminal and a frightened youth in trouble for the first time. Entire story is taken up with the relentless manhunt, emphasizing the bombast and confidence of one man and the terrified, miserable unwilling partner, who eventually gives himself up.

In his first starring part, Jack Warner departs from his customary comedian role and proves an all-round actor. Jane Hylton seems a girl of promise and turns in a neat performance as Warner's girl friend, but acting honors go to George Cole as the frightened accomplice.

The director makes good use of countryside locations. *Myro.*

Foreign Films

"My Hands Are Clay" (Irish). Egan Film Services release of Dublin Films—Patrick McCrossan production. Directed by Tommy Tomlinson. Original by John Patterson. Features Richard Aherne, Bernadette Leahy, Robert Dawson. At Adelphi, Dublin. Running time, 60 MINS.

First effort by new Irish setup fails to make the grade although exterior photography is of good quality. Story, told in flashback, is an amateurish melodrama of a child with talent as sculptor, nursing a jealous obsession through adolescent years, to be released from the obsession when he models a statue of the Blessed Virgin.

Direction is heavy and action slow, with small response from players, few of whom had previous screen experience. Dialog is inclined to drag. Picture, made on a reported budget of $80,000 is handicapped by story and lack of screencraft. *Swee.*

July 28, 1948

Miniature Reviews

"Good Sam" (McCarey-RKO). Gary Cooper - Ann Sheridan in overlong comedy; names should help it do biz.

"Sorry, Wrong Number" (Par). Radio's deadly suspense drama a real film chiller. B.o. outlook sturdy.

"Rusty Leads the Way" (Col). Staple supporting feature. Good entry in "Rusty" series.

"Adventures of Gallant Bess" (Color) (EL). Western; mainly lower dualers.

"Embraceable You." (WB). Mildly interesting drama for supporting positions.

"Blonde Ice" (FC). Mild meller with Leslie Brooks; modest support for duals.

Good Sam

RKO release of Rainbow (Leo McCarey) Production; directed by McCarey. Stars Gary Cooper, Ann Sheridan; features Ray Collins, Edmund Lowe, Joan Lorring, Clinton Sundberg. Screenplay, Ken Englund, from story by McCarey and John Klorer; camera, George Barnes; music, Robert Emmett Dolan; editor, James McKay; asst. director, Jesse Hibbs; special effects, Russell A. Cully. Previewed RKO 58th St., N.Y., July 26, '48. Running time, 114 MINS.
```
Sam Clayton.................Gary Cooper
Lu Clayton..................Ann Sheridan
Reverend Daniels............Ray Collins
H.C. Borden.................Edmund Lowe
Shirley Mae.................Joan Lorring
Nelson......................Clinton Sundberg
Mrs. Nelson.................Minerva Urecal
Chloe.......................Louise Beavers
Claude......................Dick Ross
Lain........................Lora Lee Michel
Butch.......................Bobby Dolan, Jr.
Mr. Butler..................Matt Moore
Mrs. Butler.................Netta Packer
Ruthie......................Ruth Roman
Mrs. Adams..................Carol Stevens
Joe Adams...................Todd Karns
Tramp.......................Irving Bacon
Tom.........................William Frawley
Banker......................Harry Hayden
```

Humility and goodness get a feverish workout in Leo McCarey's "Good Sam," a comedy exposition of virtue, its benedictions and the lack of them. With such names as Gary Cooper and Ann Sheridan for the marquee, and McCarey as the producer-director, "Good Sam" emerges as a wavering stalk of corn that frequently is reduced to merely a straw in the wind. It has potential boxoffice value because of the names involved, but too often does it strive too intensely but achieving nothing more than a vapid effect.

"Good Sam" is a comedy whose central character, played by Cooper, often slows the film's pace because of a languidness and too obviously premeditated performance in a pic that in itself is unusually long at just a few minutes under two hours. Sam, like the pants, made the picture too long.

"Good Sam" starts off promisingly with a number of gagged-up situations that click, however contrived, but with the pic's continuance there is the omniscient thought that here is a story that has bags under its gags. It is the story of Sam Clayton, the softest touch this side of the Marshall Plan. Sam co-signs bank loans for friends who never pay up; he lends his car to neighbors without knowing actually how he's going to get to work or the children to school. Sam loves everybody. In short, everyone sponges on him. And Lu, his wife, constantly harasses Sam to get some sense, especially when he loses the down payment on a house she always had set her chapeau for. But Sam is Sam, and

there's nothing Lu or anybody can do about it, and the moral presumably is that there can be great happiness in doing things for others, including the people from the Provident Loan Co.

"Good Sam" has a homespun air that perhaps will find considerable favor among the rusticates. Ann Sheridan, as something that might have stepped out of a Christian Dior salon instead of being an everlovin' wife and mother, is not always credible in a part that's unusual for her. Domestication is hardly Miss Sheridan's cinematic dish, no matter how authentic-looking are her scrambled eggs. Miss Sheridan has been given most of the gags, and much of the situational comedy payoffs revolve around her sharp retorts.

Cooper gives one of his standard performances—there are the wan smile, the gawky naivete and a sartorial manner that suggests Sam's pants need pressing, too.

Ray Collins, Edmund Lowe, Joan Lorring and Clinton Sundberg head the supporting players, all of whom satisfactorily fill their requirements.

McCarey has given the pic a top production all the way, and his direction is sharp in the comedy situations particularly. But the basic story yanks at its reins too often, defying any directorial control. There is an attempt to create too many situations in the basic narrative, and the defects are considerably the fault of the overlength. *Kahn.*

Sorry, Wrong Number
Hollywood, July 24.

Paramount release of Hal Wallis (Anatole Litvak) production; directed by Litvak. Stars Barbara Stanwyck, Burt Lancaster; features Ann Richards, Wendell Corey, Harold Vermilyea, Ed Begley. Original screenplay, Lucille Fletcher; based on her radio play; camera, Sol Polito; editor, Warren Low; score, Franz Waxman. Tradeshown July 22, '48. Running time, 89 MINS.
```
Leona Stevenson............Barbara Stanwyck
Henry Stevenson............Burt Lancaster
Sally Lord Dodge...........Ann Richards
Dr. Alexander..............Wendell Corey
Waldo Evans................Harold Vermilyea
James Cotterell............Ed Begley
Fred Lord..................Leif Erickson
Morano.....................William Conrad
Joe (Detective)............John Bromfield
Peter Lord.................Jimmy Hunt
Miss Jennings..............Dorothy Neumann
Harpootlian................Paul Fierro
```

"Sorry, Wrong Number" is a real chiller. Based on the w.k. radio drama of same title, picture is a top entry for the horror field. It should rate a handsome boxoffice return. The basic suspense of the ether show has been enlarged for sight values in the filming, and payoff reaps a load of spine-tingling menace.

Film is a fancily dressed co-production by Hal B. Wallis and Anatole Litvak. Pair has smoothly coordinated efforts to give strong backing to the Lucille Fletcher script, based on her radio play. Litvak's direction builds carefully, constantly heightening the tension to the nerve-wracking finale. It's an ace job of story guidance and player handling.

Plot, familiar to most radio listeners, deals with an invalid femme who overhears a murder scheme through crossed telephone lines. Alone in her home, the invalid tries to trace the call. She fails, and then tries to convince the police of the danger. She gradually comes to realize that it is her own death that is planned and tension mounts to the ruthless, deadly scene where the murderer does his job.

Characters have been more

roundly developed for filming because of the screen's greater flexibility and players realize perfectly on their assignments. What makes the characters tick is built up through flashbacks that detail motives and sharpen more suspenseful moments.

Barbara Stanwyck plays her role of the invalid almost entirely in bed. Her reading is sock, the actress giving an interpretation that makes the neurotic, selfish woman understandable. Same touch is used by Burt Lancaster to make audiences see through the role of the invalid's husband and how he came to plot her death. Both are very able.

Contributing capable performances are, among others, Ann Richards, who gives Miss Stanwyck her first inkling of the truth; Wendell Corey, physician; Harold Vermilyea, chemist; Ed Begley, the invalid's father; Leif Erickson and William Conrad. Some are seen only in bits but lend validity to the story.

Considerable emphasis is placed on the score by Franz Waxman, music being used to heighten and highlight the gradually mounting suspense. Sol Polito uses an extremely mobile camera for the same effect, sharpening the building terror with unusual angles and lighting. Warren Low's capable editing holds the picture to a tight 89 minutes. *Brog.*

Rusty Leads the Way

Hollywood, July 24.

Columbia release of Robert Cohn production. Features Ted Donaldson, Sharyn Moffett, John Litel, Ann Doran, Paula Raymond, Peggy Conevrse. Directed by Will Jason. Screenplay, Arthur Ross; story, Nedrick Young; based on characters created by Al Martin; camera, Vincent Farrar; editor, James Sweeney. At Pantages, July 22, '48. Running time, **58 MINS.**

Danny Mitchell............Ted Donaldson
Penny Waters............Sharyn Moffett
Hugh Mitchell............John Litel
Ethel Mitchell............Ann Doran
Louise Adams............Paula Raymond
Mrs. Waters............Peggy Converse
Harry Ainesworth............Harry Hayden
Mrs. Mungy............Ida Moore
Miss Davis............Mary Currier
Jack Coleman............Fred Sears
Gerald............Mickey McGuire
Squeaky............Teddy Infuhr
Nip............Wayne Hickman
Tuck............David Ackles
Rusty............Flame

"Rusty Leads the Way" is a better than average entry in the Columbia series. Stout trouping by moppets and generally inspiring motivation of the story overcome some dialog triteness and maintain interest for family trade.

Chief attention goes to moppets Ted Donaldson, Sharyn Moffett and the educated canine, Flame. Plot has young Donaldson solving the problems of Miss Moffett, a blind girl, through love and understanding.

Woven in the story effectively is the training of both seeing-eye dog and master. Sequences highlight interest and point up good plot motivation of Donaldson's kindness and efforts to restore a little girl's faith in life.

Will Jason's direction resolves the Arthur Ross script neatly and draws good performances from all concerned. John Litel and Ann Doran as young Donaldson's parents; Peggy Converse, the girl's mother; and others in the cast are credible.

The Robert Cohn production guidance shapes excellent values on a small budget. Expert lensing by Vincent Farrar, capable score, editing and other factors are in line with general effect achieved. *Brog.*

Adventures of Gallant Bess (COLOR)

Eagle-Lion release of Crestview production. Directed by Lew Landers. Screenplay, Matthew Rapf; camera (Cinecolor), William Bradford; editor, Harry Komer. Tradeshown N. Y., July 22, '48. Running time, **71 MINS.**

Ted Daniels............Cameron Mitchell
Penny Gray............Audrey Long
Woody............Fuzzy Knight
Bud Millerick............James Millican
Blake............John Harmon
Deputy............Ed Gargan
Doctor Gray............Harry V. Cheshire
Sheriff............Cliff Clark
Billie............Eevlynn Eaton
Bess............Herself

A superbly trained horse is the central figure in this animal-western. If the other characters had acquitted themselves as well, or the story had been more original, the potentialities of "Gallant Bess" might have turned out much higher. As is, it will take a whale of a selling job to move this picture past the secondary dual barrier.

Not that it is not fairly entertaining, mainly because Lew Landers' direction has made it so, but the same angle has been done so much better by other producers with at least a cast possessing more b.o. lure.

Cameron Mitchell comes through with firstrate performance as the wandering rodeo star who finally finds love by accident. His love for his trained horse is stressed, and some of the stunts the animal does are startling albeit sometimes dragged in. Dialog is comparatively bright for a western-type story.

Besides Mitchell and "Bess," Audrey Long does nicely as the comely gal with whom he falls in love. Fuzzy Knight contributes the chief comedy relief. Support is headed by James Millican. William Bradford does a tiptop job with his camera while the color work under Gar Gilbert's supervision (Cinecolor) is about the best with this tinter process to date. *Wear.*

Embraceable You

Hollywood, July 27.

Warner Bros. release of Saul Elkins production. Stars Dane Clark. Geraldine Brooks; features s.Z. Sakail, Wallace Ford, Richard Rober, Lina Romay, Douglas Kennedy, Mary Stuart, Philip Van Zandt, Rod Rogers. Directed by Felix Jacoves. Screenplay, Edna Anhalt; from story by Dietrich V. Hannekin and Aleck Block; camera, Carl Guthrie; editor, Thomas Reilly; music, William Lava. Tradeshown July 26, '48. Running time, 79 MINS.

Eddie............Dane Clark
Marie............Geraldine Brooks
Sammy............S.Z. Sakall
Ferria............Wallace Ford
Sig Kelch............Richard Rober
Libby............Lina Romay
Dr. Wirth............Douglas Kennedy
Miss Purdy............Mary Stuart
Matt............Philip Van Zandt
Bernie............Rod Rogers

"Embraceable You" is a mild supporting feature that deals with relatively unimportant people and events. Turned out with a moderate budget, it will find its level on lower rung of dual bills in majority of situations.

Plot is an odd combination of tender, hopeless love story of two ne'er-do-wells and a rather ordinary gangster yarn. Tearjerker romance will carry modest amount of attention for general run of femme audiences but this interest isn't strong enough to stretch over the 79 minutes' running time.

Dane Clark and Geraldine Brooks co-star as the ill-fated lovers. Both try hard and do manage to spark proceedings with sympathetic tug in romantic scenes. Otherwise, Miss Brooks is a bit too starry-eyed for her character and Clark has some clumsy tough-guy sequences that miss.

Script, by Edna Anhalt, deals with a young hood who is forced to take care of a girl he has struck down in a hit-run accident. Police can't legally tie him to the crime, and also suspect him of a connection with the murder of a gambler, but a kind cop makes him care for the girl because she's about to die from a blood clot developed by the accident. Just as the plot telegraphs, the boy falls in love with the girl and marries her in a sob finish as both try to find happiness before death strikes her down.

Wallace Ford is the tough but kind cop. S. Z. Sakall brings his usual tricks to role of Clark's friend and helps the script considerably. Richard Rober, a killer; Lina Romay and Philip Van Zandt, friends of Miss Brooks; Douglas Kennedy, a doctor, and others are adequate to light demands of script.

The Saul Elkins' budget production was directed by Felix Jacoves. Low-key lensing by Carl Guthrie contributes to somber mood. The William Lava score weaves the title tune, an old pop number, in and out of background music for nice nostalgic and romantic touch. *Brog.*

Blonde Ice

Film Classics production and release. Features Leslie Brooks, Robert Paige. Directed by Jack Bernhard. Screenplay by Kenneth Gamet from story by Whitman Chambers. At Rialto, N. Y., week July 24, '48. Running time, **73 MINS.**

Claire............Leslie Brooks
Les Burns............Robert Paige
Hack Doyle............Walter Sande
Carl Hanneman............John Holland
Al Herrick............James Griffith
Blackie............Russ Vincent
Mason............Michael Whalen
June............Mildred Coles
Murdock............Emory Parnell
Benson............Rory Mallinson
Mimi............Julie Gibson
Dr. Klippinger............David Leonard

This strictly lightweight meller is a weird conglomeration about a blonde murderess who seeks fortune and position through cold-blooded killings. It is not a nice story, and wastes the comely charms of Leslie Brooks, as the designing slayer. Picture has little for the marquee excepting the title and lurid pictures. Film, at best, is only lesser dual fare.

Plot spots Miss Brooks as a society editor who gains attention and wealth via a series of murders that take away her husbands and suitors. She even goes to the trouble of framing her only real sweetheart, a sports scribe. The wandering story finally is brought to an abrupt close when a noted criminal psychologist takes the icy blonde in hand. Out of a clear sky she confesses and tries to shoot her way to freedom, but only manages to kill herself.

Miss Brooks, who has the looks and enough ability for better roles, is surrounded by a fairly capable cast that appears to have been misdirected by Jack Bernhard. The story, of course, is too implausible to make much on the screen. Robert Paige does all he can with the role of the sports writer. Vehicle screams its limited production values. *Wear.*

Miniature Reviews

"Pitfall" (UA). Melodrama with only moderate entertainment values.

"Rachel and the Stranger" (RKO). Unexciting saga of a love triangle in pioneer days. Strong cast to help b.o.

"Two Guys from Texas" (Musical-Color) (WB) Entertaining musical about two errant nitery performers.

"The Spiritualist" (EL). Turhan Bay, Lynn Bari in unusual meller of mediums and murder.

"Fighting Back" (20th). Okay dualer.

"The Red Shoes" (British) (GFD). Meller with ballet back ground; too limited in audience appeal and too long for big U. S. biz.

"Variety Time" (RKO). Well-edited series of clips from many films made cohesive by Jack Paar's emceeing.

Pitfall

Hollywood, July 31.

United Artists release of Samuel Bischoff (Regal Films) production. Stars Dick Powell, Lizabeth Scott, Jane Wyatt; features Raymond Burr, John Litel, Byron Barr, Jimmy Hunt, Ann Doran, Selmer Jackson. Directed by Andre De Toth. Screenplay, Karl Kamb; based on novel, "The Pitfall" by Jay Dratler; camera, Harry Wild; editor, Walter Thompson; music, Louis Forbes Previewed July 30, '48. Running time, **85 MINS.**

John Forbes............Dick Powell
Mona Stevens............Lizabeth Scott
Sue Forbes............Jane Wyatt
MacDonald............Raymond Burr
District Attorney............John Litel
Bill Smiley............Byron Barr
Tommy Forbes............Jimmy Hunt
Maggie............Ann Doran
Ed Brawley............Selmer Jackson
Terry............Margaret Wells
Desk Sergeant............Dick Wassel

"Pitfall" never lives up to its promise of tight, suspenseful melodrama. It's a watered-down screen version of Jay Dratler's tough novel that loses an excellent idea for high dramatics somewhere along the production road. The promise of exciting stuff is always present, but never delivered. Just moderate b.o. attention is all it will rate.

Dick Powell, with a reputation for credible toughguy characterizations, has scant chance to get going in this one. He works well enough with material and has a few high spots but, on the whole, he disappoints as does the picture. Lizabeth Scott gets a bit more credence into her role. Soundest characterization is given by Jane Wyatt, who makes believable her wife role with an intelligent performance backed by the script's best dialog.

Screen adaptation of the Dratler novel presented a tough problem and only basic idea was lifted. That was still solid enough for sturdy film fare, but Karl Kamb has given it weak-kneed scripting and a tritely projected ending which Andre De Toth's direction doesn't help. Production sight values are excellent. Samuel Bischoff should have exercised the same care in insuring entertainment that would pay off on meller promises.

Powell is an insurance man, bored with his humdrum, clock-ruled life. This makes him a setup for Miss Scott's charms when he calls on her to collect gifts made by an absconder, now in jail. Their mutual attraction leads to one amorous night together and a guilty conscience. Raymond Burr, mountainous private eye, tries to make something of the incident because he has been spurned by Miss Scott. The something leads to Powell killing the absconder, paroled from jail and egged on to attack Powell by Burr. There's a full confession to the wife and the d.a., a lecture from both and ending finds Powell hopeful of renewing a happy married life.

Jimmy Hunt is cute as Powell's son and has been given equally cute lines. Burr is excellent. Litel has only one scene as the lecturing d.a. Byron Barr, the absconder, Ann Doran, Selmer Jackson and others have been given casual direction by De Toth.

Technical aids are topnotch; Harry Wild's camera work, score, editing, settings and art direction all representing expert craftsmanship. *Brog.*

Rachel and the Stranger
(SONGS)
Hollywood, Aug. 3.

RKO release of Richard H. Berger production. Stars Loretta Young, William Holden, Robert Mitchum; features Gary Gray, Tom Tully, Sara Haden, Frank Ferguson, Walter Baldwin, Regina Wallace. Directed by Norman Foster. Screenplay, Waldo Salt; from story, "Rachel" by Howard Fast; camera, Maury Gertsman; editor, Les Millbrook; songs, Roy Webb, Waldo Salt. Tradeshown at Los Angeles, Aug. 2, '48. Running time, 92 MINS.

Rachel .... Loretta Young
Big Davey .... William Holden
Jim .... Robert Mitchum
Davey .... Gary Gray
Parson Jackson .... Tom Tully
Mrs. Jackson .... Sara Haden
Mr. Green .... Frank Ferguson
Gallus .... Walter Baldwin
Mrs. Green .... Regina Wallace

"Rachel and the Stranger" plods an agreeable, if unexciting, entertainment path in narrating story of pioneer days and love in the wilderness. Star names are good, some marquee luster being provided by Loretta Young, William Holden and Robert Mitchum, which should sharpen b.o. response.

Mood of the picture is pleasant but is so even that interest isn't too strong. Dangers of pioneering in a wilderness, vaguely referred to as the northwest, could have been more excitingly depicted. Single incident of excitement—a strong one—is put off until the finale and has a socko Indian raid on a settler's homestead in the wilds.

Otherwise, narrative maintains its even pace in telling story of a pioneer who buys a bride to do the chores and teaches niceties of life to his motherless son. The bride is only a servant until a hunter, friend of the groom, appears and makes a play for her. Such attention sparks some interest in the husband and the triangle spins an anticipated course, with the Indian raid bringing the husband and wife together as lovers for the finale clinch.

Within the bounds of the script, everyone concerned do good, if not outstanding jobs. Even pace maintained by Norman Foster's direction is in keeping with writing but his handling of the night raid on the settler's cabin by redskins is solid action stuff. Flaming arrows and war whoops pinpoint pioneer danger but, unfortunately, there isn't enough of it in preceding footage.

Holden enacts the dour settler, so deeply in love with his dead wife he fails to appreciate, or even notice, the charms of his new bondswoman bride. Miss Young has only two costume changes and her makeup is true to role, but she makes some glamor shine through. Mitchum is the aimlessly wandering hunter—Romeo who, like the angel in "The Bishop's Wife," makes the husband aware of wifely charms by his own admiration of them. Gary Gray is good as Holden's wild young son. Others make only brief appearances.

There is an appeal to the five songs that aptly fit story demands. Mitchum lends an untutored pleasing vocal nonchalance to "Oh He Oh Hi Oh Ho," "Just Like Me" and "Foolish Pride." He joins with Miss Young on "Tall, Dark Stranger" and "Summer Song." All have a folksy flavor as cleffed by Roy Webb and Waldo Salt. Latter also was responsible for the script, from a story, "Rachel," by Howard Fast, and Webb did the smooth background score.

Richard H. Berger's production, under executive supervision of Jack J. Gross, utilizes exteriors almost completely, with the rustic cabin and a wilderness fort the only sets required. Scenic values are good and Maury Gertzman gave them sharp lensing. Editing holds the film to an adaptable 92 minutes. *Brog.*

Two Guys from Texas
(COLOR-MUSICAL))

Warner Bros. rel;ease of Alex Gottlieb production. Stars Dennis Morgan, Jack Carson; features Dorothy Malone, Penny Edwards. Directed by David Butler. Screenplay, I.A.L. Diamond and Allen Boretz, suggested by the play by Robert Sloane and Louis Pelletier; songs, Julie Styne, Sammy Chan; dances by Le Roy Prinz; musical director, Leo F. Forbstein; orchestral arrangements, Ray Heindorf; cartoon sequence directed by I. Freeleng; camera, (Technicolor), Arthur Edeson and William V. Skall; editor, Irene Morra. Previewed N.Y. July 28, '48. Running time, 86 mins.

Steve Carroll .... Dennis Morgan
Danny Foster .... Jack Carson
Joan Winston .... Dorothy Malone
Maggie Reed .... Penny Edwards
"Tex" Bennett .... Forrest Tucker
Dr. Straeger .... Fred Clark
Link Jessup .... Gerald Mohr
Jim Crocker .... John Alvin
"The Texan" .... Andrew Tombes
Pete Nash .... Monte Blue
Specialty .... Philharmonica Trio

This mistitled filmusical is about a couple of mediocre nitery song-and-dance men who go to, not come from, Texas to run afoul of misadventures and romance on a dude ranch. It's lightweight stuff, but unpretentious and moderately diverting, and should at least keep the customers seated until the top feature comes on.

In a modest way, "Two Guys from Texas" is a spoof of musical westerns, for it presents the broncho-bustin', gun-totin', frontier stuff as window dressing to give the big city dudes their money's worth. Also, there's a lampoon Hollywood cowboy number as well as some kidding - almost - on - the-square about swaggering Texans. The songs are tuneful, though undistinguished, the musical numbers are skillfully staged and pleasantly brief.

The opening song number, "Music in the Land," done by Dennis Morgan and Jack Carson supposedly bouncing over the Texas range in a aged Ford, is enjoyable. There's also a fairly good song and dance number, "I Don't Care If It Rains All Night," by Carson and Penny Edwards, but possibly the top musical spot is the hokum "I Want to Be a Cowboy in the Movies" duet by Morgan and Carson. Other songs are "Everyday I Love You a Little Bit More" and "Hankerin'."

In the comedy department there are a few good scenes, notably one in which the two girls and two boys prepare for bed in adjacent rooms, with their two conversations cleverly integrated for laughs. There's also some passably good slapstick, as the two performers flee jail and mix with a rodeo crowd in almost Keystone Kop fashion. A cartoon dream sequence is only mildly effective.

Nobody could take the plot seriously, of course, least of all the authors themselves, so there's no harm in the actors being casual about it. What matters is that there are the proper comedy situations, song cues, and the musical numbers and laugh lines are resoundingly put over. Visually, the picture is good, as the color photography capitalizes on the vivid ranch decor.

David Butler's direction suits the tempo to the style of the picture and the mood of the scene, skillfully avoiding lagging spots. Morgan is likable enough as the romantic lead, and Carson does some hilarious mugging as the comedy lead. Dorothy Malone has the requisite looks as the heroine, while Penny Edwards puts over the musical femme lead reasonably well, but occasionally hammers her song numbers a trifle. Forrest Tucker, Fred Clark and Andrew Tombes are notable in supporting parts. *Hobe.*

The Spiritualist

Eagle Lion release of Ben Stoloff production. Stars Turhan Bey, Lynn Bari, Cathy O'Donnell. Directed by Bernard Vorhaus. Screenplay, Muriel Roy Bolton and Ian Hunter from original by Crane Wilbur; camera, John Alton; editor, Norman Colbert. Tradeshown, N. Y., July 29, '48. Running time, 79 MINS.

Alexis .... Turhan Bey
Christine Faber .... Lynn Bari
Janet Burke .... Cathy O'Donnell
Martin Abbott .... Richard Carlson
Paul Faber .... Donald Curtis
Emily .... Virginia Gregg
Hoffman .... Harry Mendoza

Novel story, working in methods used by mediums to obtain high fees, turns out to be high tension melodrama. It has been expertly directed by Bernard Vorhaus from a whale of a yarn by Crane Wilbur. Helped by topflight performances by Turhan Bey, Lynn Bari and Cathy O'Donnell, "The Spiritualist" should prove strong boxoffice. Whether only passably stout or really big in most spots will depend on how sold, because picture is one that can be circused into real proportions.

Idea of mixing a spiritualist's machinations and usual spook screen sounds with a slambang murder plot has been worked out effectively. Miss Bari, as the rich, young widow, imagines being in contact with her deceased husband, who supposedly had died in an auto crash two years previously. That proves a workable thesis for seance expert Bey until he finds the mate, Donald Curtis, actually is alive. Also that the "dead" husband is plotting to get control of his wife's estate.

Ben Stoloff has given the picture magnificent production, with much action in and about a stately mansion perched high on a cliff overlooking the Pacific. Such setting makes for breath-taking scenes and obvious thrill sequences as the wife is lead along the top of the cliff while half-drugged. The odd sound effects, mysterious voices and other peculiar noises have been captured in one of the top sound-recording jobs of the year.

Bey chips in with probably his top performance as the money-grabbing medium while Miss Bari as the much-distressed wife who yens contact with her dead husband is also considerably better than in recent efforts. Miss O'Donnell does excellent work as the younger lass who seeks to save her sister, first from the spiritualist and then from her supposedly dead husband.

Curtis tops the support as the hubby who returns to life. Harry Mendoza does a neat job as the ex-magico, now a sleuth, who helps run down Bey's seance setup. Richard Carlson does well in the thankless role of a persistent suitor.

Besides Vorhaus' fine direction, picture is helped by sterling cameraing by John Alton and slick editing by Norman Colbert. The unusual photo effects are nicely done by George J. Teague. *Wear.*

Fighting Back
Hollywood, July 30.

Twentieth-Fox release of Sol M. Wurtzel production. Features Paul Langton, Jean Rogers, Gary Gray, Joe Sawyer, Morris Ankrum, John Jellogg, Daisy (canine). Directed by Mal St. Clair. Story and screenplay, John Stone; camera, Benjamin Kline; editor, William F. Claxton. At Grauman's Chinese, Hollywood, July 30, '48. Running time, 61 MINS.

Nick Sanders .... Paul Langton
June Sanders .... Jean Rogers
Jimmy Sanders .... Gary Gray
Sergeant Scudder .... Joe Sawyer
Mr. Higby .... Morris Ankrum
Sam Lang .... John Kellogg
Mrs. Higby .... Dorothy Christy
Larry Higby .... Tommy Ivo
Mrs. Winkle .... Lela Tyler
Colonel .... Pierre Watkin
Snuffy .... Daisy

"Fighting Back" never gets above its programmer classification but, in that bracket, is okay material. Plot is fairly plausible and fits the title. Dramatic elements come off best and would have been stronger but for distracting comedy hokum.

Story concerns ex-convict who starts on the straight and narrow after serving in the war. On parole, his attempts to provide a legal living for himself, his wife and son are going smoothly until an old criminal associate appears on the scene. Parolee becomes involved in the theft of a bracelet from his employer's wife. Bauble has been stolen by the canine, Daisy, at instructions of the former gangster pal, but inevitable happy ending rights all wrongs when the dog points out the real culprit.

Mal St. Clair's direction keeps the piece on the move and draws acceptable performances from the cast. Paul Langton handles his lead role pleasantly, as does Jean Rogers as his wife and Gary Gray, the son. Daisy will please the femmes and kiddies. John Kellogg is an okay villain. Joe Sawyer, policeman; Morris Ankrum, Dorothy Christy are among others in featured spots.

Production supervision by Sol M. Wurtzel has obtained good values for budget allotment, settings, art direction and other physical appurtenances being kept simple to fit struggling young couple's financial standing. *Brog.*

The Red Shoes
(Color)
(BRITISH)
London, July 27.

General Film Distributors release of J. Arthur Rank-Archers production. Stars Marius Goring, Anton Walbrook, Moira Shearer. Directed and written by Michael Powell, Emeric Pressburger; additional dialog by Keith Winter; editor, Reginald Mills. Music by Brian Easdale; ballets, Robert Helpmann; camera (Technicolor), Jack Cardiff, Christopher Challis. At Odeon, London, July 20, '48. Running time,

134 MINS.

Boris Lermontov.........Anton Walbrook
Julian Craster.............Marius Goring
Victoria Page..............Moira Shearer
Ljubov....................Leonide Massine
Ivan Boleslawsky.......Robert Helpmann
Ratov....................Albert Basserman
Livy....................Esmond Knight
Boronskaja..............Ludmilla Tcherina
Lord Oldham..........Derek Elphinstone
Lady Neston.................Irene Brown
Professor Palmer..........Austin Trevor
Madame Rambert.......Madame Rambert
Dimitri........................Eric Berry

The growing popularity of the ballet in Britain has been a post-war phenomenon, and undoubtedly influenced Powell and Presburger to produce this, their last for Rank. Although good ballet is assured boxoffice in London and possibly other big cities, its popularity in small towns and country districts is dubious. And in America, too, it will probably only attract a limited audience.

For the first 60 minutes, this is a commonplace backstage melodrama, in which temperamental ballerinas replace the more conventional showgirls. Then a superb ballet of the Red Shoes, based on a Hans Anderson fairy tale, is staged with breath-taking beauty, out-classing anything that could be done on the stage. It is a colorful sequence, full of artistry, imagination and magnificence. The three principal dancers, Moira, Shearer, Leonide Massine and Robert Helpmann, are beyond criticism.

Then the melodrama resumes, story being about the love of a ballerina for a young composer, thus incurring the severe displeasure of the ruthless Boris Lermontov, guiding genius of the ballet company. Caught up between her two loves, her husband and her dancing, the ballerina dances her way to death, echoing the theme of the Red Shoes ballet.

Although the story may be trite, there are many compensations, notably the flawless performance of Anton Walbrook, whose interpretation of the role of Lermontov is one of the best things he has done on the screen. Moira Shearer, glamorous red-head, who has already achieved fame as a ballerina, shows that she can act as well as dance, while Marius Goring, polished as ever, plays the young composer with enthusiasm.

The supporting roles have been carefully filled, including Esmond Knight, Eric Berry, Austin Trevor and Albert Basserman.

Other assets that can be chalked up are the wide variety of interesting locations—London, Paris, Monte Carlo, magnificent settings, firstclass Technicolor and some brilliant musical scores played by the Royal Philharmonic Orchestra with Sir Thomas Beecham as conductor. In spite of all this, the picture fails to come up to expectations. It will disappoint the ballet fans who won't be satisfied with a 15-minute show, and there isn't enough in the story for the general public to hold interest for two and a quarter hours.

Variety Time
(MUSICAL)

RKO release of George Bilson production. Leon Errol and Edgar Kennedy sequences directed by Hal Yates. Errol screenplay, Hal Law; Kennedy screenplay, Yates; Jack Paar material by Lee Solomon, Joseph Quillan; editors, Lee Millbrook, Edward W. Williams. Tradeshown, Aug. 2, '48. Running time, 59 MINS.

Cast: Jack Paar, Edgar Kennedy, Leon Errol, Frankie Carle & Orch., Pat Rooney, Miguelito Valdes, Harold & Lola, Jesse & James, Lynn, Royce & Vanya, Dorothy Granger, Jack Norton, Minerva Urecal, Florence Lake, Jack Rice, Dot Farley, Hal Conreid.

RKO in putting together a feature length film consisting of clips from out-of-circulation musicals, comedy shorts, sequences from silent films and faces left on the cutting room floor, have predestined such a release to the lower end of a dualler. However, the results coincide with the best video formula that's been found to date. "Variety Time" resembles closely the format that's been clicking on the Texaco Star Theatre, regarded by many as television's brightest program.

"Variety Time" is similar to the tele program, inasmuch as there's a good emcee (Jack Paar) tying together various song, dance, and specialty sequences. It's virtually perfect video fare. But sole drawbacks in selling this film to the 28 video stations now operating are the insufficiency of funds to buy current features and the low key photography in many sequences which would make parts of the picture not bright enough for the sets now on the market.

For theatres, the well-edited "Variety Time" will be mildly amusing. Although Jack Paar does a clever job of projecting the individual sequences, many will have the ring of familiarity, inasmuch as pictures they were taken from have been previously released. The Edgar Kennedy and Leon Errol shorts have already made the rounds as has the Miguelito Valdes "Babalu" clip with terping by Harold & Lola.

The vaude specialties are well staged with Pat Rooney doing his familiar "Daughter of Rosie O'Grady" tap, originally made for the Eddie Cantor pic, "Show Business;" Jesse and James hitting a good pace with their tray-balancing and acrohoofery, and Lynn, Royce & Vanya (team is now split with Vanya doing straight terping with Pierre D'Angelo) making a nice impression with comedy dancing. Frankie Carle's band contributes the "Carle Boogie."

The silent clips comprise a 1922 fashion newsreel, a William S. Hart western and a 1911 Biograph release, "Two Paths." Paar does an amusing commentary for all three. He also has a funny bit with Hal Conreid. Latter spoofs French cafe singers. *Jose.*

Miniature Reviews

"A Southern Yankee" (M-G), Wild and wacky Red Skelton comedy of a Yankee spy behind Confederate lines.

"Larceny" (U). Snappy melodrama, glibly dialoged and rapidly paced. Neat dual bill topper for general situations.

"Hollow Triumph" (EL). Good program melodrama starring Paul Henreid and Joan Bennett.

"Miraculous Journey" (Color - Song) (FC). Jungle drama that can be sold with exploitation.

"Phantom Valley" (Songs) (Col). Routine westerner for juve trade.

"Miracle in Harlem" (SG) (Sepiatone-Songs). All - Negro film for moderate grosses in colored houses.

A Southern Yankee
Hollywood, Aug. 10.

Metro release of Paul Jones production. Stars Red Skelton, Brian Donlevy; features Arlene Dahl, George Coulouris, Lloyd Gough, John Ireland, Minor Watson. Directed by Edward Sedgwick.. Screenplay, Harry Tugend; original by Melvin Frank and Norman Panama; camera, Ray June; editor, Ben Lewis. Tradeshown Aug. 5, '48. Running time, 90 MINS.

Aubrey Filmore................Red Skelton
Kurt Devlynn.................Brian Donlevy
Sallyann Weatharby...........Arlene Dahl
Major Jack Drumman....George Coulouris
Capt. Steve Lorford.........Lloyd Gough
Capt. Jed Calbern...........John Ireland
General Watkins............Minor Watson
Col. Weatharby..........Charles Dingle
Col. Clifford M. Baker........Art Baker
Fred Munsey................Reed Hadley
Mark Haskins...............Arthur Space
Hortense Dobson............Joyce Compton

About the only sense "A Southern Yankee" makes is that it has Red Skelton. That's enough. It's as wild and raucous a conglomeration of gags and belly-laughs as Skelton's recent "The Fuller Brush Man." The kiddies, the family and the general film fan will find it bait for the risibilities and respond with hearty ticket window payoff.

Production-wise, "Yankee" is an erratic jumble, pulled together only by a funny idea and Skelton's knack for clowning. That's a criticism that will mean little to those who lay the cash on the line at the boxoffice. Lack of smoothness probably can be attributed to fact that film had two directors and considerable re-working, with Edward Sedgwick drawing final director credit. Again, production faults mean little. It has Skelton and sock laughs. No more is needed.

Camera is seldom off Skelton as he presents an eager young man who wants to aid the Union army by being a spy. A lucky capture of the dreaded Confederate spy, Grey Spider, gives Skelton more than he bargains for. He's forced to go behind the Southern lines to deliver and pick up information while posing as the Spider. Naturally, there's a mush-mouthed daughter of the south with whom Skelton is smitten. The corn-pone is laid on thick as Skelton tries to pursue his romance, be a hero and keep a whole skin. It's all boisterous derring-do that has the laughs popping a mile-a-minute.

Harry Tugend's script from the original by Melvin Frank and Norman Panama is loaded with situations and gags tailored to Skelton's clowning and the uproar is so furiously paced that when the story often runs thin it doesn't matter.

Fact that Arlene Dahl as the south's own magnolia blossom makes her footage noticeable is a credit to her charms. Brian Donlevy is lost in the shuffle as a war-profiteering Southerner. Working hard to hold their own are George Coulouris, Lloyd Gough, John Ireland, Minor Watson, Art Baker, Reed Hadley and others.

Hurry - scurry production was guided by Paul Jones with technical assists from Ray June's photography; the art direction, score and special effects. *Brog.*

Larceny
Hollywood, Aug. 5.

Universal release of Leonard Goldstein (Aaron Rosenberg) production. Stars John Payne, Joan Caulfield, Dan Duryea, Shelley Winters; features Dorothy Hart, Patricia Alphin. Directed by George Sherman. Screenplay, Herbert F. Margolis, Louis Morheim, William Bowers; from novel, "The Velvet Fleece," by Lois Eby and John Fleming; camera, Irving Glassberg; editor, Frank Gross; music, Leith Stevens. Previewed Aug. 3, '48. Running time, 89 MINS.

Rick Maxon....................John Payne
Deborah Owens Clark......Joan Caulfield
Silky Randall................Dan Duryea
Tory....................Shelley Winters
Madeline..................Dorothy Hart
Max....................Richard Rober
Duke....................Dan O'Herlihy
Walter Vanderline..........Nicholas Joy
Charlie Jordan............Percy Helton
Mr. Owens................Walter Greaza
Waitress..................Patricia Alphin
Mr. McNulty..............Harry Antrim
Detective................Russ Conway
Mechanic..................Paul Brinegar
Master of Ceremonies.........Don Wilson

"Larceny" is a good melodrama for general situations. Its action is tough and fast, the dialog sharp and the development logical, indicating neat returns. Exploitable theme deals with bilking of war widows by confidence racketeers and is excellently supported by showmanly values.

Smooth scripting is marked by punchy dialog that lifts the melodrama formula into attention-holding class, and George Sherman's direction is rapid and pointed in building story and characterizations. Plot is one that could easily have fallen apart with less able direction and scripting.

Locale of yarn is a small Southern California city of wealthy inhabitants. A gang of confidence men move in to promote a phony war memorial for one of the town's heroes. They pick on the hero's widow, with the smoothy of the gang acting as front. The widow is a gullible gal and scheme moves forward easily until complications set in. The gang leader's girl goes for the smoothy and makes no bones about it. Her amatory interest in the front man, and his awakening love for the widow finally spoil the pitch. There's a slambang finish in which front man turns himself and the gang over to the police, an ending that has no happy twist.

John Payne does a good job as the gang's front man. Joan Caulfield is appealing, if a bit too gullible, as the widow. Dan Duryea turns in his customary tight-lipped characterization as the brains of the confidence gang. Shelley Winters will capture audience fancy with her bold, sexy portrayal of a girl on the make for Payne.

Nifty smaller characterizations are ably projected by Dorothy Hart, Patricia Alphin, Percy Helton, Richard Rober, Dan O'Herlihy and others. Helton's role is particularly well done.

Leonard Goldstein and his associate producer, Aaron Rosenberg, have backed the melodramatics with a strong framework. Lensing by Irving Glassberg capably displays the players and settitngs.

With exception of one abrupt cut, editing is smooth and holds film to tight 89 minutes. *Brog.*

Hollow Triumph

Eagle Lion release of Paul Henreid production. Stars Henreid and Joan Bennett; features Eduard Franz, Leslie Brooks, John Qualen, Mabel Paige, Herbert Rudley. Directed by Steve Sekely. Screenplay, Daniel Fuchs, based on novel by Murray Forbes; camera, John Alton; editor, Fred Allen; music, Sol Kaplan. Previewed N. Y. Aug. 5, '48. Running time, 83 MINS.

John Muller / Dr. Bartok ....Paul Henreid
Evelyn Hahn....Joan Bennett
Frederick Muller....Eduard Franz
Virginia Taylor....Leslie Brooks
Swangron....John Qualen
Charwoman....Mabel Paige
Marcy....Herbert Rudley
Coblenz....Charles Arnt
Aubrey, assistant....George Chandler
Artell, manager....Sid Tomack
Jerry....Alvin Hammer
Blonde....Ann Staunton
Clerk....Paul Burns
Deputy....Charles Trowbridge
Howard Anderson....Morgan Farley

Here is a suspenseful melodrama that comes close to out-twisting O. Henry. Liberal use of irony has been made in "Hollow Triumph." But so frequently has this literary artifice been employed that the overall story takes on a contrived, manufactured ring. Nevertheless, it is well qualified to hold up its end.

Producer of "Triumph," as well as its co-star, Paul Henreid has dealt himself a meaty, dual role. He's a renegade ex-medical student who carves his coin from stickups and confidence games rather than exercise his mental ability in more prosaic fields. On the lam with a big haul from a casino robbery, he discovers a prominent psychiatrist is a dead-ringer for his phiz. Henreid rubs out his double and assumes the latter's name as a sure means of shaking off pursuit by the casino operator. Preparatory to carrying out the impersonation, he romantically cultivates the physician's secretary, Joan Bennett. Later she becomes wise to the switch when it's executed, but her philosophic analysis of the situation prevents her from exposing him as an imposter.

Eventually the law of retribution asserts itself when Henreid himself is killed—killed by gunmen assigned to knock off the psychiatrist, an unsuccessful gambler in his after-office hours.

Also on the credit side are good production values and the marquee garnish afforded by the Henreid-Bennett combo. Former star turns in a believable performance in portraying both his parts. Miss Bennett isn't afforded the opportunity for any fancy histrionics, but does a job as a pretty secretary who's been short-changed on romance. Supporting players aid in sustaining the film's mood. Steve Sekely's direction is good as is the camerawork of John Alton. *Gilb.*

Miraculous Journey
(COLOR—ONE SONG)

Film Classics release of Sigmund Neufeld production. Stars Rory Calhoun; features Audrey Long, Virginia Grey. Directed by Peter Stewart. Screenplay, Fred Myton; camera (Cinecolor), Jack Greenhalgh; editor, Hollbrook N. Todd; song, Leo Erody, Lew Porter. Tradeshown N. Y. Aug. 4, '48. Running Time 83 MINS.

Larry....Rory Calhoun
Mary....Audrey Long
Patricia....Virginia Grey
Hermit....George Cleveland
Nick....Jim Bannon
Rene....June Storey
Kendricks....Thurston Hall
Jane....Carole Donne
Co-pilot....Tom Lane
Dog Flame....Himself
Jimmy the Crow....Himself

The familiar theme of collecting a cast of characters in the midst of a remote jungle and watching their reactions while close to nature comprises the subject matter of Film Classics' most ambitious release, "Miraculous Journey." Handsomely mounted with Cinecolor—one of the better jobs to date—the lush jungle scenery lends itself nicely to tinting a dualler.

There is considerable confusion in character delineation for best story results. There are some apparent contradictions and unexplainable character reversals so that several entities fail to stand up on their own.

On a plane forced down in the African jungle are a powerful financial figure, a spoiled heiress, an actress, a gangster, and a blind girl on her way for an operation to restore her sight. In addition there's the pilot and hostess. Soon after their arrival, an old gent marooned in the jungle for many years turns up, and shows the wreck survivors how to get along next to nature. As anticipated, the unsocial characters acquire humility and a different slant on life, and the unregenerate gangster gets rubbed out by a crocodile. They are eventually rescued when pilot Rory Calhoun makes his way out of the jungle and returns to the wreck via helicopter.

Calhoun, Audrey Long, latter as the blind girl, and Thurston Hall as the businessman, give probably the most consistent characterizations of those that survive the trip. There's a degree of muddling in the writing of the others.

The film itself can lend itself to exploitation that will hypo it beyond its actual worth. There are several angles that can be played up and thus create some curiosity at the boxoffice.

Peter Stewart's direction probably stems from the indecision of the writers on whether they wanted a picture with a moral or an action meller. The curious mixture of both incorporated into this setup doesn't lend itself to a cohesive story. *Jose.*

Phantom Valley
(SONGS)

Columbia release of Colbert Clark production. Stars Charles Starrett. Directed by Ray Nazarro. Original screenplay, J. Benton Cheney; camera, George F. Kelly; editor, Paul Borofsky; songs, Smiley Burnette. At New York, N. Y., Aug. 3, '48. Running time, 53 MINS.

Durango Kid....Charles Starrett
Smiley....Smiley Burnette
Janice Littlejohn....Virginia Hunter
Sam Littlejohn....Noel Franklin
Bob Reynolds....Robert W. Filmer
Crag Parker....Mike Conrad
Frazer....Don Murray
Jim Durant....Sam Flint
Ben Thiebold....Fred Sears

Latest in the Durango Kid series starring Charles Starrett, "Phantom Valley" gallops down a familiar trail of that-a-way chases and hard six-shooting. In all respects, film is an assembly-line oatuner cranked out for the juve trade for which it will serve as okay fare.

Pruned down to an economical 53 minutes, yarn concerns a feud between two gangs of ranchers and homesteaders with Starrett trying to maintain the peace as marshal. Some varmint, however, keeps stirring up trouble in an attempt to become baron of the valley. Finger of suspicion points at several prominent citizens but surprise climax reveals an innocent-looking gal as the culprit. Ungallantly, Starrett shoots her in the back to save the state time and trouble.

Starrett registers effectively as a square-jawed cowboy hero. Offering a broad type of comedy relief, Smiley Burnette also neatly warbles a couple of buckskin ballads with help of a good male quartet. Virginia Hunter is okay as the heavy, while rest of the cast is adequate in stock parts. *Herm.*

Miracle in Harlem
(SEPIATONE—SONGS)

Screen Guild release of Herald Pictures production by Jack Goldberg. Features Sheila Guyse, Stepin Fetchit. Directed by Jack Kemp. Screenplay, Vincent Valentini; camera, Don Melkames; music, John Gluskin. At Apollo, N. Y., week Aug. 6, '48. Running time, 69 MINS.

Julie Weston....Sheila Guyse
Swifty....Stepin Fetchit
Aunt Hattie....Hilda Offley
Reverend Jackson....Creighton Thompson
Jim Marshall....Kenneth Freeman
Bert Hallam....William Greaves
Alice Adams....Sybyl Lewis
Albert Marshall....Lawrence Criner
Phillip Manley....Jack Carter
Wilkinson....Milton Williams
Lt. Renard....Monte Hawley
Detectives....Ruble Blakey, Alfred Chester
Specialties by Savannah Churchill, Juanita Hall Choir, Lavada Carter, Norma Shepherd, Lynn Proctor Trio.

Herald Films, having produced a string of pictures with all-Negro casts, has apparently gotten itself into a groove from which it makes few departures. Formula of endowing a meller with musical sequences has been successful up to a point. However, that point as demonstrated in "Miracle in Harlem" has been worn down to the degree where some new departures are necessary if there's to be any respect from Negro audiences for film product with all-Negro casts.

The opening night audiences at Harlem's Apollo theatre didn't take too kindly to "Made in Harlem." Sequences which were intended to impart a warm glow were actually laughed at, and the gauche acting, directing and production were never taken seriously at any point.

Particularly appalling is the story line which drags religious themes into a routine murder yarn. Plot deals with an elderly widow who runs a candy shop which is taken over by a syndicate. After the widow and foster daughter are swindled out of the property, head of the syndicate is murdered and the foster-daughter is a prime suspect. She's ultimately cleared with the aid of a few implausible devices.

Herald has been using virtually a stock company with Sheila Guyse playing the lead in all their pictures. She's just about adequate for the assignment, while Hilda Offley shapes up a little better as the widow. Creighton Thompson, William Greaves and Kenneth Freeman do okay in supporting roles, while Stepin Fetchit manages some laughs as the slow-moving handy man.

The musical numbers are better handled than is the story. Savannah Churchill, Norma Shepherd and the Juanita Hall Choir provide tuneful relief in the proceedings.

Don Melkames' photography is passable. Dialog runs along well-established cliches. *Jose.*

Where Words Fail
(Donde Mueren las Palabras)
(ARGENTINE)

Lopert Films release of Artistas Argentinos Associados production. Stars Enrique Muino; features Dario Garzay, Italo Bertini. Directed by Hugo Fregonese. Screenplay, Ulysses Petit de Murat, Homero Manzi; camera, Jose M. Beltran. Previewed N. Y., July, 28, '48. Running time, 65 MINS.

Victorio....Enrique Muino
Carletti....Italo Bertini
Rogelio....Hector Mendez
Dario....Dario Garzay
Fedora....Linda Lorena
Maria....Aurelia Ferrer
Antonio....Rene Mugica
Boletero....Pablo Cumo
Aurora....Maria Hurtado
Leandro....Jose A. Vazquez
Director....Enrique Ferraro
Primera Ballerina....Maria Ruanova

This Argentine import is somber film fare whose boxoffice potentialities are decidedly meagre. Its strong musical background, buttressed with time-honored selections from Bach, Beethoven, Chopin, et al., may prove draw to some music lovers but a confused and gloomy plot militates against the picture's effectiveness as entertainment.

Told principally in flashback, "Where Words Fail" recounts the early struggles in the career of concert pianist Dario Garzay. A technique of using Garzay's voice in English to supply an explanatory narration supplements the printed English titles. But while this translatory method capably hurdles the language barrier, the elucidation merely serves to focus more emphasis on the dull yarn.

Picture boils down to a character study of Enrique Muino, a one-time symphony conductor, who sought, and temporarily found anonymity after the death of his ballerina daughter, Linda Lorena. While working as a night watchman in an opera house, Muino becomes acquainted with Garzay and for a time acts as his mentor. Later the watchman's true identity is revealed.

Cast in the meatiest role, Muino delivers a ponderous and stiff interpretation of the conscience-stricken conductor. So gruff and crotchety is his demeanor that seldom has he the audience's sympathy. Garzay is relatively colorless as the pianist although his solos on the instrument afford some of the few high spots in the film. Other of the pic's more interesting passages are scenes of the famed puppets of Podrecca and the orchestra and ballet of the Buenos Aires Philharmonic.

Supporting players are generally lustreless with the exception of Italo Bertini who manages to inject some authenticity into the part of the opera house manager. Hugo Fregonese's direction is heavy-handed. Both production values and Jose M. Beltran's camerawork are fair. Writers Ulysses Petit de Murat and Homero Manzi had a difficult subject to begin with. Their treatment doesn't make the theme any more plausible. *Gilb.*

En Svensk Tiger
(A Swedish Tiger)
(SWEDISH)

Stockholm, July 27.

Kungsfilm AB production and release. Stars Edvin Adolphson, Margareta Fahlen; features Sven Lindberg. Directed by Gustaf Edgren. Screenplay, Oscar Rydqvist, Gustav Edgren; camera, Martin Bodin. At Spegeln, Stockholm. Running time, 99 MINS.

Johan Tiger....Edvin Adolphsson
General Lucky....Edvin Adolphsson
Lena Andersson....Margareta Fahlen
Kurt Muller....Sven Lindgren
Hanna Andersson-Tiger..Marianne Lofgren
Wolff....Gunnar Bjornstrand
Dickman....Arnold Sjostrand
Captain Andersson....Erik Berglund
Leonard Stromlund....Fritiof Billquist
Swedish Minister....Olof Winnerstrand
Endahl....Tord Stal
Frans Fredriksson....Douglas Hage
Klara....Gull Natorp
Police Inspector....Henrik Schildt
British General....Gosta Cederlund
British Officer....Sture Djerf
Sub Lieutenant....Peter Winner

One of better films produced by the Swedish industry, "En Svensk Tiger" is a gripping espionage yarn revolving around the work done by agents of three countries in the past war. A dash of comedy helps in change of pace. Grosses on this entry will be surefire in Scandinavia and the picture's overall excellence makes it a prospect for the international market.

Despite an involved plot, the story threads are woven together well by scripters Oscar Rydqvist and Gustav Edgren. In essence the tale is built around the efforts of the British to mask Gen. Montgomery's movements prior to the European invasion. Edvin Adolphsson, a Swedish actor, is hired to impersonate the general in North Africa to mislead the Germans. With that mission accomplished, Adolphsson becomes snared in further intrigue as a passenger on a Swedish ship which the Germans are seeking to blow up through their agent, Sven Lindgren.

There are some minor story flaws and several action sequences are far-fetched.

As the actor who portrays Gen. Montgomery, Adolphsson is credible enough in handling his dual role. Supporting performances measure up. Lindberg contribs an able interpretation as German agent. Margareta Fahlen, cast as a Swedish counter-spy, registers well. Gustav Edgren, who collaborated on the script with Rydqvist, cleverly directed the film while camerawork of Martin Bodin also is good.   *Wing.*

Miniature Reviews

"Julia Misbehaves" (MG). Screwball comedy with strong laugh and · gross potential. Garson-Pidgeon for marquee.

"The Loves of Carmen" (Col) (Color). Bold, lusty screen fare, based upon the book, not the opera. Rita Hayworth's best and solid b.o.

"Luxury Liner" (Songs-Color) (M-G). Operatic and pop music combined with lightly diverting comedy.

"Isn't It Romantic" (Songs) (Par). Dull mixture of comedy and songs.

"Sofia" (Color-Songs) (FC). Highly topical treatise on Soviet intrigue lends solid exploitation angle and strong b.o. potential.

"Blondie's Reward" (Col). Above-average f o r s e r i e s; should be strong second feature.

"The Dead Don't Dream" (UA). Routine Hopalong Cassidy western.

"Urubu" (UA). Jungle adventure thriller okay for dualers and exploitation houses.

"Murderers Among Us" (Artkino). Adult postwar German film; moderate sureseater b.o.

"The Return of Wildfire" (SG). Sturdy outdoor action film for general situations. Better than average western.

Julia Misbehaves
(ONE SONG)
Hollywood, Aug. 17.

Metro release of Everett Riskin production. Stars Greer Garson, Walter Pidgeon; features Peter Lawford, Elizabeth Taylor, Cesar Romero, Lucile Watson, Nigel Bruce, Mary Boland, Reginald Owen. Directed by Jack Conway. Screenplay, William Ludwig, Harry Ruskin, Arthur Wimperis; adaptation, Gina Kaus, Monckton Hoffe; based on the novel, "The Nutmeg Tree," by Margery Sharp; camera, Joseph Ruttenberg; editor, John Dunning; song, Jerry Seelen and Hal Borne. Tradeshown Aug. 12, '48. Running time. 99 MINS.

Julia Packett	Greer Garson
Wm. Sylvester Packett	Walter Pidgeon
Ritchie Lorgan	Peter Lawford
Susan Packett	Elizabeth Taylor
Fred Ghenoccio	Cesar Romero
Mrs. Packett	Lucile Watson
Colonel Willowbrook	Nigel Bruce
Ma Ghenoccio	Mary Boland
Benjamin Hawkins	Reginald Owen
Lord Pennystone	Henry Stephenson
Vicar	Aubrey Mather
Hobson	Ian Wolfe
Pepito	Fritz Feld
Daisy	Phyllis Morris
Louise	Veda Ann Borg

"Julia Misbehaves" is a mighty undignified lady — and a mighty funny one. A riot of screwball slapstick that never takes itself seriously for a single moment, film is geared for grosses as hearty as its laughs. Greer Garson unbends in this one and the ballyhoo exploiting that unbending shapes it for big returns.

All forms of comedy but the subtle are used to spring the laughs that come from the frenetic antics of a middle-aged couple, long separated but bent on trying romance again. It's gag and situation farcing that's as artful as a slap in the face and answers all demands for escapist film fare.

Jack Conway's direction is fast and vigorous in walloping over the comedy. Laughs are piled on top of each other, making a lot of the dialog unheard and unnecessary, as the plot spends its course under Conway's snappy handling. When a gag line won't do it, Conway resorts to the physical for a howl and always gets results.

Miss Garson is punched, doused, muddied and tossed in her unbending process. She wears tights, takes a bubble bath, sings and generally acquits herself like a lady out to prove she can be hoydenish when necessary. She proves it and audiences will like the new Garson. As the other half of middle-aged team, Walter Pidgeon gives away no honors. He's pitching all the time and skillfully injects just the right amount of underplaying to balance broader delivery of his partner in fun. It's nigh perfect casting for the requirements of the roles.

The fun starts when Miss Garson, entertainer, receives an invitation to the wedding of her daughter, · Not having seen the girl since she was a baby, the mother journeys to France for the wedding. The father again becomes interested in mother and maneuvers her into trying marriage again, while the mother is maneuvering the daughter into casting off the fiance and eloping with another love.

Brief outline doesn't do justice to the fun packed into the script by William Ludwig, Harry Ruskin and Arthur Wimperis. En route to France, Miss Garson joins an acrobatic act, becomes involved with an elderly wolf, and generally has herself a time. In addition to the acro turn, a big laugh-getter, Pidgeon has his moments with a trained seal that makes for a socko sequence.

Elizabeth Taylor is the daughter who upsets her rich relatives when she elopes with an eager painter, elegantly portrayed by Peter Lawford. They shape up as a strong team of juves. Cesar Romero belts over an hilarious performance as an acrobat who goes for Miss Garson. It's a top job, rating a big hand.

Nigel Bruce is delightful as the elderly Romeo who pursues the heroine. Mary Boland registers strongly as the tipsy mother of the acrobats. Lucile Watson, Reginald Owen, Ian Wolfe and others add to the generally uproarious fun.

Everett Riskin's production guidance has shaped this for hefty returns on strength of showmanly values. The usual Metro elegance is found in production trappings that give smart physical framing to the comedy. Miss Garson's song, spotlighted during her acro stint, is "When You're Playing With Fire," and is delivered with unharmonious vocals, complete with gestures, for laughs.

Class lensing by Joseph Ruttenberg, art direction and settings, Adolphe Deutsch's music score, tight editing and special effects are among contributions that lend production polish.   *Brog.*

The Loves of Carmen
(MUSIC—COLOR)
Hollywood, Aug. 14.

Columbia release of Charles Vidor (Beckworth Corp.) production, directed by Vidor. Stars Rita Hayworth, Glenn Ford; features Ron Randell, Victor Jory, Luther Adler. Screenplay, Helen Deutsch; based on the story of "Carmen" by Prosper Merimee; camera (Technicolor), William Snyder; editor, Charles Nelson; score, Mario Castelnuovo-Tedesco. Tradeshown Aug. 12, '48. Running time. 95 MINS.

Carmen	Rita Hayworth
Don Jose	Glenn Ford
Andres	Ron Randell
Garcia	Victor Jory
Dancaire	Luther Adler
Colonel	Arnold Moss
Remendado	Joseph Buloff
Old Crone	Margaret Wycherly
Pablo	Bernard Nedell
Lucas	John Baragrey
Sergeant	Philip Van Zandt

Columbia has a potent piece of screen merchandise in "The Loves of Carmen." It is a bold screen adaptation of the Prosper Merimee novel that lends itself to the strongest type of exploitation. Such boxoffice factors as a socko title, sex, a colorful, lusty story and Rita Hayworth point the way to solid grosses.

Appeal is to both femme and male ticket buyers, sharpening b.o. prospects, and profits for both distributor and exhibitor should hit the upper brackets. Film carries the Beckworth Corp. label (a combination of the star's name and that of her daughter) and reflects considerable know-how in splashing the screen with a gusty, s.a. handling that will pay off.

As producer-director, Charles Vidor has made artful use of the story, the players and the color with which the plot is endowed. Under his handling, Miss Hayworth makes just about her best screen appearance. Her interpretation of Carmen, the beautiful gypsy without morals or conscience, is a socko s.a. reading, loaded with a personal magnetism. Carmen's not a nice creature and there's no attempt at soft-pedaling her wickedness or building sympathy.

Helen Deutsch did an adept job of scripting from the Merimee novel, moving the plot forward in development at a pace that holds interest as it builds to the inevitable finale wherein a fortune teller's prophecy that Carmen would die at the hands of the man she truly loves is fulfilled. Carmen's career of lovers, theft and murder is an operatic standard, but the film is drawn from the book with none of the opera's arias.

There is a musical score by Mario Castelnuovo-Tedesco that blends perfectly with the story's action. It never pounds or intrudes yet projects the mood with telling effect. The gypsy and Spanish music, the dances and one Latin tune done by Miss Hayworth are lilting moments that capture the fancy and please the ear.

Glenn Ford's character is the story pivot that poses moral of the dangers of falling in love with a conscienceless woman. He impresses in his tough moments, particularly in the deadly hand-to-hand knife duel with Carmen's outlaw husband. He uses his talent skillfully in depicting a man gone weak over love, and does these softer scenes so well they won't sit comfortably with masculine audiences.

Ford's opponent in the knife fight is Victor Jory. Latter is a menacing gypsy outlaw, sharpening the characterization and making it a standout performance. Luther Adler, Bernard Nedell and Joseph Buloff, members of the robber gang, contribute topnotch characters.

Arnold Moss, the colonel whose death in a sword fight sends Ford into outlawry; John Baragrey, the bullfighter whose dalliance with Carmen eventually leads to her stabbing by Ford and his death; Margaret Wycherly, the old crone who predicts Carmen's death, and Ron Randell are among others in the cast who contribute capably.

Wise use of Technicolor has been used in the lensing by William Snyder. Scenes have a breath-taking beauty without garishness, presenting pictorial splendor of early-day Seville settings and rocky mountain fastnesses. Costuming, choreography, art direction, set decorations all rate kudos.
         Brog.

Luxury Liner
(SONGS—COLOR)
Hollywood, Aug. 14.

Metro release of Joe Pasternak production. Stars George Brent, Jane Powell, Lauritz Melchior, Frances Gifford, Marina Koshetz, Xavier Cugat orch. Directed by Richard Whorf. Screenplay, Gladys Lehman, Richard Connell; camera (Technicolor), Robert Planck; editor, Robert J. Kern; musical direction, George Stoll. Tradeshown Aug. 11, '48. Running time, **97 MINS.**

Capt. Jeremy Bradford	George Brent
Polly Bradford	Jane Powell
Olaf Eriksen	Lauritz Melchior
Laura Dene	Frances Gifford
Zita Romanka	Marina Koshetz
Xavier Cugat	Himself
Denis Mulvy	Thomas E. Breen
Charles G. K. Worton	Richard Derr
Chief Officer Carver	John Ridgeley
The Pied Pipers	Themselves
Romo Vincent	Himself
Bertha	Connie Gilchrist

"Luxury Liner" wears the label popularly called light summer diversion. It mixes its songs and comedy rather skillfully and bedecks itself in lush Technicolor to make an elegant, flashy physical appearance. It should find the b.o. going pleasant on most bills.

Musical numbers are operatic and standard, with no new cleffing in the score. Lauritz Melchior gives a good account of himself on the long hair numbers with trilling assists from Jane Powell and Marina Koshetz. The vocals are smooth and the numbers interestingly presented. There's no feeling of crowding, despite 14 numbers being included in the score.

On the sock side is Melchior's "Siegmund's Liebeslied" solo and Miss Powell's "Gavotte" from "Manon." Others registering are "Spring Came Back to Vienna," "Aida," "Alouette," "Come Back to Sorrento," "Helan Gar," "Lohengrin's Abschied." Xavier Cugat gives bright workout to "Vamo a Rumbia" and "Con Maraccas," as well as ably backing "The Peanut Vendor," sung by Miss Powell as an operatic aria, "Sorrento," "Vienna" and "Ya Viechov Mlada."

Light story line plots action on a luxury liner. Miss Powell is the captain's daughter and stows away on George Brent's ship when he refuses her permission for a cruise to Rio. Papa's treatment of daughter by making her work her passage after being discovered springs laughs, and young lady's acting as Cupid's assistant in a romance between Brent and passenger Frances Gifford also adds to the fun.

The Joe Pasternak touch for pleasantly diverting froth combined with music is all over this one, making it easy to take. Richard Whorf's direction is capable, giving nice treatment to production numbers and putting the cast through the light moments interestingly. Gaining attention is the handling of "Alouette" sung by Miss Powell, Romo Vincent and the ship's galley staff as a novelty special. Presentation is tuneful and amusing. Another specialty is the Pied Pipers' rendition of "Yes, We Have No Bananas," quartet giving it nifty selling.

Miss Koshetz, as amorous opera singer, highlights a comedy scene with humorous treatment of "I've Got You Under My Skin" and otherwise aids the lighter moments. Brent acquits himself well as the captain and Miss Gifford pleases. Thomas E. Breen is good as a young ship's officer interested in Miss Powell. Latter's infectious personality and undeniable talent for song and comedy are a decided assist in making "Liner" diverting.

Lush art direction and settings have been beautifully lensed in color by Robert Planck. Georgie Stoll's musical direction is a tuneful contribution to pleasant mood maintained throughout. *Brog.*

Isn't It Romantic
(SONGS)

Hollywood, Aug. 17.

Paramount release of Daniel Dare production. Stars Veronica Lake, Mona Freeman, Billy De Wolfe, Mary Hatcher. Directed by Norman Z. McLeod. Screenplay, Theodore Strauss, Josef Mischel, Richard L. Breen; based on story by Jeannette Covert Nolan; camera, Lionel Lindon; songs, Jay Livingston, Ray Evans; editor, LeRoy Stone. Tradeshown Aug. 13, '48. Running time, **87 MINS.**

Candy	Veronica Lake
Susie	Mona Freeman
Rose	Mary Hatcher
Horace Frazier	Billy De Wolfe
Major Euclid Cameron	Roland Culver
Richard Brannon	Patric Knowles
Benjamin Logan	Richard Webb
Clarissa Thayer	Kathryn Givney
Hannibal	Larry Olsen
Abigail	Pearl Bailey

"Isn't It Romantic" isn't. It's a seldom diverting mixture of comedy and songs that misses.

Story idea, on its own, might have proved to be a mildly amusing period comedy, but the addition of dull songs and old-fashioned musical handling gives it a hybrid appearance. There's a spot of interest here and there but not enough to overcome the generally bad effect. An occasional line of dialog has spark and Billy De Wolfe has one good comedy scene. Pearl Bailey lends some importance to two unimportant tunes. Otherwise, it's quite static.

Locale of the turn-of-the-century costumer is an Indiana town where lives Roland Culver, still fighting the war between states, and his three daughters, Veronica Lake, Mona Freeman and Mary Hatcher. Culver is a southern gentleman above labor, consequently the family is broke. Film rolls awkwardly along through trite, contrived situations that have the daughters in and out of love, the old man falling for an oil scheme. Everything comes out okay for the finale but it's all much ado about nothing, not too brightly presented.

Norman Z. McLeod directed this celluloid medley under production supervision of Daniel Dare. Cast is adequate to demands but doesn't give a lift to proceedings. Five tunes, cleffed by Jay Livingston and Ray Evans, are included in the score and the two vocaled by Miss Bailey are "Won'rin' When" and "I Shoulda Quit When I Was Ahead."

Technical contributions are uniformly good in backing the story-tune melange. *Brog.*

Sofia
(COLOR-SONGS)

Film Classics release of ARPI production (Robert R. Presnell, Sr., John Reinhardt), directed by Reinhardt. Stars Gene Raymond, Sigrid Gurie; features Patricia Morison, Mischa Auer, George Baxter, Charles Rooner, Fernando Wagner. Screenplay, Frederick Stephani; camera (Cinecolor), William Clotheir; editor, Charles L. Kimball; songs, Serge and Karen Walter. Tradeshown N. Y. Aug. 11, '48. Running time, **83 MINS.**

Steve Roark	Gene Raymond
Linda Carlsen	Sigrid Gurie
Magda Onescu	Patricia Morison
Ali Imagu	Mischa Auer
Peter Goltzen	John Wengraf
James Braden	George Baxter
Dr. Stoyan	Charles Rooner
Dr. Viertel	Fernando Wagner
Ana Sokolova	Luz Alba
Marow	Egon Zappert
Bell Captain	Hamil Petroff
Brother Johannes	Peter O'Crotty
Lt. Comdr. Stark	John Kelly
Chodorov	Chel Lopez
Warden	Jose Torvay

With Soviet captives hopping out of consulate windows and testimony of derring-do unfolding in Washington as the current headliners, "Sofia" is promoted from the implausible to a strictly exploitable film, synchronized to the news of the day. Otherwise, the loose ends which keep dangling and utter improbabilities of this film of Russian intrigue in the Balkans would leave the customers unconvinced. Aided and abetted by vivid Cinecolor trappings, it will do good business in all but deluxe situations.

For the cloak-and-dagger student there's no explaining much that happens in "Sofia" except that it suited the conveniences of plot. Why sometimes the conspirators found it necessary to pass their mysterious messages by cake, carrier pigeon or invisible ink while at others they loudly and openly signal their intentions before the enemy at times assumes nonsensical hocus-pocus. To top it all, in the welter of plot and counterplot, two Yanks openly kidnap a brace of atomic scientists who are Russian prisoners and get away with it while cozily lingering behind the Iron Curtain.

Substitute for the Nazis of yore the Russian heavies of today, and what remains is a garden-type of cloak-and-dagger meller spiked with loads of action, if little plausibility. It relates the story of how a group of Americans, operating in satellite countries, rescue the aforesaid scientists and dispatch them to the U. S. In the course of it, one of the operators (Gene Raymond), an ex-O.S.S. officer, finds again in one of the atomic wizards (Sigrid Gurie) an old flame, and heads for the happy curtain clinch.

Several songs are piped by Patricia Morison, who plays a nitery chanteuse working both sides of espionage against the middle. Songs, however, are not given importance, since camera pans away frequently to uncover plot development. A surprisingly matured Raymond is nicely suited for the hard-bitten role he takes on. Miss Gurie's comparatively minor part presents no chances of ringing the bell. Other parts, tinging on the pure action, are workmanlike.

Production values are lush. Tinting shows a continuing improvement in net results of the Cinecolor process. Editing and cutting is n.s.g., since it misses coming up with cohesive and well-integrated footage. Direction, aside from some sorry lapses in continuity, is competently done to keep the action sprinting. *Wit.*

Blondie's Reward

Hollywood, Aug. 13.

Columbia production and release. Features Penny Singleton, Arthur Lake, Larry Simms, Marjorie Kent. Directed by Abby Berlin. Original screenplay, Edward Bernds, based on Chic Young comic strip; camera, Vincent Farrar; editor, Al Clark; music, Mischa Bakaleinikoff. Reviewed at Pantages, Aug. 12, '48. Running time, **65 MINS.**

Blondie	Penny Singleton
Dagwood	Arthur Lake
Alexander	Larry Simms
Cookie	Marjorie Kent
George Radcliffe	Jerome Cowan
Alice Dickson	Gay Nelson
Ted Scott	Ross Ford
Alvin	Danny Mummert
John Dickson	Paul Harvey
Ed Vance	Frank Jenks
Bill Cooper	Chick Chandler
Ollie	Jack Rice
Postman	Eddie Acuff
Mary	Alyn Lockwood
Officer Carney	Frank Sully
Cluett Day	Myron Healey
Leroy Blodgett	Chester Clute

Misadventures of Dagwood Bumstead with his boss again provide basis for latest in the "Blondie" films, which is one of better offerings in series. Original screenplay by Edward Bernds is directed for best comic effect by Abby Berlin, and Penny Singleton and Arthur Lake in familiar top roles do customary yeoman service for laughs. Comedy is strong supporter.

In line with past "Blondies," this one revolves around Dagwood getting in wrong with his boss, when he buys option on wrong property site, and then, in disgrace, proceeds to become further embroiled with employer by being blamed for socking prospective son-in-law of wealthy industrialist whom boss is trying to land as a client.

Scripter Bernds starts his yarn from this opening premise, or series of premises, and from then on piece lands Dagwood in one situation after another, with Blondie entering plot frequently to add her bit. Whole narrative has been carefully prepped, whenever there's corn being popped with eye to giggles, and adds up to good funfest. Jerome Cowan repeats with clever boss performance, Paul Harvey makes most of industrialist role, and Gay Nelson appears briefly but tellingly as his daughter. Danny Mummert, too, scores as boy next door, and Larry Simms and Marjorie Kent are the Bumstead moppets. *Whit.*

The Dead Don't Dream

United Artists release of Lewis J. Rachmil production. Stars William Boyd; features Rand Brooks, Andy Clyde. Directed by George Archainbaud. Screenplay, J. Benton Cheney, Bennett Cohen, Ande Lamb, based on Clarence E. Mulford stories. At New York theatre, N. Y., week Aug. 10, '48. Running time, **68 MINS.**

Cast: Boyd, Clyde, Brooks, Mary Sawdon, John Parrish, Leonard Penn, Francis McDonald, Bob Gabriel, Stanley Andrews, Forbes Murray.

"The Dead Don't Dream" is a routine entry in the Hopalong Cassidy series whose plot is composed of whodunit ingredients as well as a liberal sprinkling of elements found in all stock westerns. Picture will satisfy Bill Boyd fans and on the overall shapes up as an average filler for the double bills.

This time Boyd (Hopalong) ferrets out the mystery as to how three men were killed in a frontier hotel room. Before the killer is smoked out, there's a fair amount of action which varies in locale from mine tunnels to nocturnal chases hard by the hostelry. Andy Clyde supplies the comedy relief, while cast in the lone femme role is Mary Tucker.

Per usual, Boyd is a forthright upholder of the law and his supporting cast largely measures up to his workmanlike thesping. George Archainbaud directed at a breezy pace and camera work is standard. While writers J. Benton Cheney, Bennett Cohen and Ande Lamb aren't too original in adapting this yarn from the Clarence E. Mulford characters, this series has been flourishing a long time and the story barrel can't be expected to remain at the same high level.

Urubu

United Artists release of World Adventures production. Directed and photographed by George Breakston, Yorke Coplen. Story, Breakston; narration, Coplen; editor, Holbrook N. Todd; score, Albert Glasser. Tradeshown N. Y. Aug. 12, '48. Running time, **66 MINS.**

"Urubu," a photographic record of an expedition through the Matto Grosso jungle of Brazil, rates as solid fare for the exploitation houses. Pic offers the usual pegs for sensational ballyhoo in its lurid yarn, shots of prehistoric monsters and flock of primitive Indians, including an average quota of undraped native females. High interest level also makes this film a good supporting item for nabe situations.

Producers G e o r g e Breakston and Yorke Coplan fabricated several incredible twists for this jungle thriller, but, on the whole, the film keeps within reasonable bounds. Best parts of the film, which have an authentic look, are the shots of natural terrain with its varied and amazing forms of wild life. Fictional sequences, while obviously hokey, serve as an acceptable framework for the factual portions.

Yarn concerns the search for an English explorer who disappeared into the Brazilian interior many years ago. Accompanied by friendly natives, Breakston and Coplan cut their way through the Matto Grosso until they hit the land of the Urubus, an allegedly murderous tribe of Indians who have kidnapped a white girl.

Camerawork (without sound) is handled expertly throughout. Narration by Coplan, however, is full of cornily purple adjectives common to virtually all travelogs. Breakston and Coplan, the only two whites who appear in the film besides the unbilled girl, wisely underplay their performances onto a deadpan level. *Herm.*

Murderers Among Us
(GERMAN)

Artkino release of Defa production. Stars Hildegard Knef, Ernst Borchert. Written and directed by Wolfgang Staudt. Camera, Friedl Behn-Grund, Eugen Klagemann; score, Ernst Roters. Previewed N. Y., Aug. 9, '48. Running time, 80 MINS.

Susanna Wallner	Hildegard Knef
Dr. Hans Mertens	Ernst Borchert
Captain Bruckner	Arno Paulsen
Frau Bruckner	Erna Sellner
Herr Mondschein	Robert Forsch
Herr Timm	Albert Johann

(In German; English Titles)

The first postwar German production, "Murderers Among Us" ("Die Moerder Sind Unter Uns"), is a serious film concerned with the knotty problem of the individual German's guilt for Nazism. While not fully successful, either as drama or ideology, film is marked by a superb camera and montage technique recalling some of the firstrate German productions before the Nazi era. It is slated for moderately good reception in the sureseater circuit.

Framed against the ruins of Berlin, story is concerned with a young medico haunted into drunkenness by the memory of mass executions which were ordered by his captain in Poland. When the doctor once again meets the captain, now a kindly family man, he determines to kill the war criminal. At the last moment, however, the doctor's sweetheart intervenes to have the captain delivered up to the proper authorities. The final sequences in which the captain keeps shouting "I am not guilty" against kaleidoscopic shots of the war are the most effective and moving of the whole film.

Basic flaw of this film is the slow pace with which the story unfolds. Shallow sentimentalism in the romantic passages between the doctor and his girl friend also is damaging to this otherwise adult production. Although made in the Russian zone of Germany, the film is not weighted with heavy-handed propaganda. On the contrary, all

the questions which it raises are left unanswered.

Performances by the full cast measure up to the highest standards. Especially standout roles are turned in by Ernst Borchert, as the doctor; Arno Paulsen, as the captain, and Hildegard Knef, as the girl. Good score also contributes importantly to the film's sombre quality. *Herm.*

The Return of Wildfire
(SONG)

Hollywood, Aug. 13.

Screen Guild release of Carl K. Hittleman (Lippert) production. Stars Richard Arlen, Patricia Morison, Mary Beth Hughes. Directed by Ray Taylor. Screenplay, Betty Burbridge and Hittleman; camera (Sepiatone), Ernie Miller; editor, Paul Landres; music, Albert Glasser. Previewed Aug. 10, '48. Running time, 80 MINS.

Dobe	Richard Arlen
Pat Marlowe	Patricia Morison
Judy Marlowe	Mary Beth Hughes
Frank Keller	James Millican
Marty Quinn	Reed Hadley
Pancho	Chris-Pin Martin
"Pop" Marlowe	Stanley Andrews
Dirk	Holly Bane
Wildfire	Highland Dale

A creditable job has been done by all concerned in shaping this one for the general market. Returns should please. Rugged outdoor stuff has been beautifully lensed in Sepiatone and story has been given twists that lift it above usual western filmfare.

In addition to value of Sepiatone film makes good use of many clips of wild horse roundups and a bloody battle between two wild stallions.

Plotting concerns Reed Hadley's efforts to corner the horse market in a western valley. When rancher Stanley Andrews refuses to sell his stock he's murdered and the villain tries his scheme on the rancher's daughters, Patricia Morison and Mary Beth Hughes. Heavy's dirty work is upset when Richard Arlen, roving wrangler, comes to the aid of the girls and finale presents a slambang gun and fist fight between the hero and Hadley.

The sister team pleases, Miss Morison as the sensible prairie heroine with whom Arlen falls in love, and Miss Hughes as the more amorous of the pair, who injects s.a. into the western setting. There's a single tune, "Just An Old Sombrero," vocal by Miss Morison.

Hadley is a smooth heavy and James Millican, Chris-Pin Martin, Andrews and Holly Bane hold up their ends in the development. Highland Dale does the title role as a wild stallion.

Ray Taylor's direction has an actionful pace that gets best from the script by Betty Burbridge and Carl K. Hittleman. Latter also served as producer, making that function worthwhile. The outstanding lensing was contributed by Ernie Miller. *Brog.*

August 14
(RUSSIAN)
(Color—Documentary)

Artkino release of Central Studio production. Directed by Ilya Kopalin, Irina Setkina. Camera (Agfa), Mikhail Gleeder, Theodore Bunimovich; music, Arnold Roitman, David Shtilman. At Stanley, N. Y., week Aug. 14, '48. Running time, 68 MINS.

"August 14," photographed in 1947 by a crew of 50 Soviet cameramen just two years after the end of World War II, is an interesting documentary on Russian reconstruction. Of minor commercial value in the U. S., beyond the houses specializing in Russian im-

ports, this film, nevertheless, has considerable importance as a propaganda weapon.

Life among the Soviets, as these cameras carefully selected it, is teeming with health, happiness and energy. Sandwiched between panoramic shots of the varied Russian landscape, is the story of Russia's emergence from the war as a greater power than ever before. The message of strength is explicit in the shots of military maneuvers and reconstruction of the dams, factories, mines and homes in the postwar five-year plan.

Color photography, based on the so-called new Soviet tinting process (but actually it's the old German Agfa process), is uneven, ranging from sequences of brilliant hues to some of dullish grays. The background narration in English, done in Russia, has a restrained patriotic tone. *Herm.*

Miniature Reviews

"A Song Is Born" (Songs-Color) (RKO-Goldwyn). Danny Kaye, Virginia Mayo, top bandleaders in big b.o. comedy.

"One Touch of Venus" (Songs) (U). Gay musical fantasy with sock performance by Ava Gardner.

"An Act of Murder" (U). Fredric March, starred in controversial story on mercy killing. B. o. prospects good.

"Night Wind" (20th). Good programmer for the juvenile trade.

"I Surrender Dear" (Songs) (Col). Minor budget musical for secondary bookings.

"Joe Palooka in Winner Take All" (Mono). Good actioner for twin bills. Exciting ring footage.

"The Prairie" (SG). Better than average frontier fare.

"London Belongs To Me." (GFD). British-made melo, which turns to farce, doesn't quite come off.

"The Spirit and the Flesh" (Indie). Fair Italian-made import for art houses.

A Song Is Born
(COLOR; SONGS)

RKO release of Samuel Goldwyn production. Stars Danny Kaye; features Virginia Mayo, Hugh Herbert, J. Edward Bromberg, Steve Cochran, Felix Bressart, Benny Goodman, Louis Armstrong, Buck & Bubbles, Page Cavanaugh Trio, other bandleaders. Directed by Howard Hawks. Based on story, "From A to Z," by Thomas Monroe and Billy Wilder; camera, Gregg Toland; editor, Daniel Mandell; songs, Don Raye and Gene De Paul; musical direction, Emil Newman. Hugo Friedhofer; orchestrations, Sonny Burke. Previewed N. Y., Aug. 23, '48. Running time, 112 MINS.

Professor Hobart Frisbee	Danny Kaye
Honey Swanson	Virginia Mayo
Professor Magenbruch	Benny Goodman
Professor Twingle	Hugh Herbert
Tony Crow	Steve Cochran
Dr. Elfini	J. Edward Bromberg
Professor Gerkikoff	Felix Bressart
Professor Traumer	Ludwig Stossel
Professor Oddly	O. Z. Whitehead
Miss Bragg	Esther Dale
Miss Totten	Mary Field
Mr. Setter	Howland Chamberlin
Joe	Paul Langton
Adams	Sidney Blackmer
Monte	Ben Weldon
Ben	Ben Chasen
Louis	Peter Virgo
Bass	Harry Babasin
Drums	Louis Bellson
Guitar	Alton Hendrickson
Tommy Dorsey	Buck & Bubbles
Louis Armstrong	Page Cavanaugh Trio
Lionel Hampton	Golden Gate Quartet
Charlie Barnet	Russo & Samba Kings
Mel Powell	

"A Song Is Born" represents Danny Kaye's fourth and final picture under the banner of producer Samuel Goldwyn, with the comedian now at Warners. With a star-studded cast featuring some of the top name bandleaders and vaude acts in the country, plus the usual lush production mountings given by Goldwyn to the Kaye films, there's no question that "Song" will chalk up hefty grosses in all situations.

However, film represents a slight letdown from his previous efforts, largely because Kaye does none of the special songs usually penned for him by Sylvia Fine, his wife. Picture is a remake of Goldwyn's "Ball of Fire," released in 1941 and starring Gary Cooper and Barbara Stanwyck. Because the earlier edition is so recent, audiences will probably note the resemblance early in "Song," but it's doubtful that this will militate against the picture's acceptance. Most of Goldwyn's production crew worked on both films, including director Howard Hawks, cameraman Gregg Toland, editor Daniel Mandell, etc.

Charles Brackett and Billy Wilder screenplayed "Ball" from an original by Wilder and Thomas Monroe, but there's no screenplay credit given on "Song."

While "Ball" dealt with a group of stodgy old professors writing a new dictionary and the way a burlesque stripper tossed a bombshell into their work, "Song" presents a similar group of professors, only this time they're compiling a history of music and the stripper is a nitery thrush. Revised situation gives Goldwyn a chance to toss into the film the aforementioned name maestros and vaude acts whose work, for a change, is integrated neatly into the script. When Kaye is working with them before the cameras, in fact, the picture is standout entertainment. Last half of the picture, though, in which they get a semi-brushoff as Kaye becomes involved with a group of gangsters, drags by comparison.

Kaye himself does his usual neat thesping job as the youngest of the bachelor pedants, who gets his first intro to feminine wiles at the hands of a worldlywise nitery singer, played engagingly by Virginia Mayo. He demonstrates again that he's a real clown in the old tradition, handling the pathos as deftly as he does the comedy. It's difficult to understand, though, why he wasn't given a chance at his double-talk songs, always the high spot of his pictures. They're definitely missed in this one.

Script makes good use of the various musicians involved. They're spotlighted neatly at the beginning, as Kaye tours various Broadway niteries to get an idea of swing and jazz, which is completely unknown to the professorial group. They really click in several numbers in which they play together, result being a "dream band" seldom heard before. Benny Goodman, the only one not playing himself, is particularly standout as one of the professors. One sequence, in which he's invited by Mel Powell and Lionel Hampton to sit in on a number they played together when "members of Benny Goodman's band" is the comedy highpoint of the film.

Plot follows closely that of the earlier picture, with Miss Mayo hiding out in the monastic music foundation from the D.A.'s office, which wants her in connection with a murder committed by her gangster fiance. When Kaye falls in love with her, she plays along because the cops are hot on her trail. Gang chief gets sore, takes her back to the foundation to show her what a milquetoast Kaye actually is after she falls for him and then tries to marry her by force. Kaye and the bandleaders, in a contrived denouement, successfully foil the thugs and all ends happily.

Rest of the cast follow the comic's fine thesping under Hawks' capable touch for comedy. Miss Mayo, slimmer but beautiful as ever, surprises with some top acting in this one. Professors, including Hugh Herbert, J. Edward Bromberg, Felix Bressart, Ludwig Stossel and O. Z. Whitehead, milk their lines and situations for the maximum of laughs. Steve Cochran is sufficiently menacing as the gang chief. Buck and Bubbles, colored vaude act, turn in a couple of neat tricks as a pair of window-washers.

Two new songs cleffed for the film by Don Raye and Gene De Paul are good, with the title tune showing hit potentialities as groaned by Louis Armstrong with the "dream band" backing. It's the hot jive numbers played by the musicians, expertly arranged by Sonny Burke, though, that are standout. Rest of the production credits are up to the usual top Goldwyn standards, with Gregg Toland's Technicolor lensing especially good. *Stal.*

One Touch of Venus

(SONGS)

Hollywood, Aug. 21.

Universal release of Lester Cowan (John Beck) production. Stars Robert Walker, Ava Gardner, Dick Haymes; features Eve Arden, Olga San Juan, Tom Conway. Directed by William A. Seiter. Screenplay, Harry Kurnitz, Frank Tashlin; based on the musical of same title by S. J. Perelman, Odgen Nash and Kurt Weile; camera, Frank Planer; editor, Otto Ludwig; new songs, Ann Ronell; Previewed, Aug. 17, '48. Running time, 81 MINS.

Eddie Hatch .... Robert Walker
Venus .... Ava Gardner
Joe Grant .... Dick Haymes
Molly Stewart .... Eve Arden
Gloria .... Olga San Juan
Whitfield Savory .... Tom Conway
Corrigan .... James Flavin
Landlady .... Sara Allgood

"One Touch of Venus" comes to the screen as a pleasant comedy fantasy. Its theme of love is thoroughly exploited in a gay, saucy manner, told with rare good humor and infectious charm. Ava Gardner steps into the top ranks as the goddess, Venus. Hers is a sock impression, bountifully physical and alluring, delivered with a delightfully sly instinct for comedy.

Three of the songs from the original stage musical have been used, with new lyrics to fit the broadened theme. Merits of the stage piece gain additional worth in the screening. The film treatment is deft and racy, always clever at garnering the utmost in audience response.

The story of the love affair between goddess and a mortal is a blithe subject and the aura of romance casts a subtle influence that quickens the pulse. The good-humored handling of the plot is emphasized through William A. Seiter's good direction. He combines sly comedy with slapstick, slickly times the bits of business to create an effect of almost spontaneous and continuous mirth.

Plot, briefly, covers the romantic adventures of a department store window dresser, who, in a completely pixilated moment, kisses a statue of Venus and brings her to life for 24 hours. Those are eventful hours; Venus' aura of love casts a spell over all, bringing couples together and spreading happiness of romance. The script by Harry Kurnitz and Frank Tashlin is punctuated with snappy dialog and funny situation.

Robert Walker delivers a gifted comedy performance. An ingratiating personality and talent emphasize a performance that never lets down and never goes overboard, making his window dresser character real and earnest. Eve Arden, the store owner's glib secretary, gives another of her punchy deliveries, smartly shaded to catch the full worth of every throwaway line and situation.

Musical high spots please the ear and best is "Speak Low," from the original Kurt Weill-Odgen Nash score, reprised several times. Miss Gardner uses it too woo Walker and the magic of its spell is picked up in another part of the city by Dick Haymes in romancing Olga San Juan, pert clerk who loses Walker to the goddess but gains Haymes in the swap. The foursome are used for "Don't Look Now But My Heart Is Showing," tune spotting an amusement park production number and a breath-quickening love scene between Miss Gardner and Walker.

The three femmes bounce through "That's Him" for humorous results, completing film's musical portions that have had some new lyrics added by Ann Ronell.

Tom Conway is the wolfish department store owner and his apparent pleasure when he thinks he's making time with the goddess will be understandable to all males. Story setup permits Miss Gardner to work in goodness costume, a nightie and a slip, factors that will cause male response. For the femmes, she is given three slick, new-look outfits that are plenty smart.

Lester Cowan and his associate producer, John Beck, have given the story lush backing, but never let the trappings become ostentatious. It's a showmanly chore by both that realizes on the top entertainment values. The production elegance and the players have been brightly displayed by Frank Planer's photography. Editing is expert, holding the film to a fast 81 minutes. *Brog.*

An Act of Murder

Universal release of Jerry Bresler production. Stars Fredric March, Edmond O'Brien, Florence Eldridge, Geraldine Brooks; features Stanley Ridges, John McIntire, Frederic Tozere. Directed by Michael Gordon. Screenplay, Michael Blankfort and Robert Thoeren, based on novel, "Mills of God," by Ernest Lothar; camera, Hal Mohr; editor, Ralph Dawson; music, Daniele Amfitheatrof. Tradeshown N. Y., Aug. 19, '48. Running time, 91 MINS.

Judge Calvin Cooke .... Fredric March
David Douglas .... Edmond O'Brien
Catherine Cooke .... Florence Eldridge
Ellie Cooke .... Geraldine Brooks
Dr. Walter Morrison .... Stanley Ridges
Judge Ogden .... John McIntire
Charles Dayton .... Frederic Tozere
Judge Jim Wilder .... Will Wright
Mrs. Russell .... Virginia Brissac
Mr. Russell .... Francis McDonald
Julia .... Mary Servoss
Pearson .... Don Beddoe
Mr. Pope .... Clarence Muse

"An Act of Murder" is as adult and well-handled a picture as any that have come out of Hollywood in recent months. Universal went far out on a limb with this one by putting the subject of euthenasia, or mercy killing, squarely up to the audience and then taking a negative stand on the problem. Film, consequently, is very close to a documentary in theme, although it's given straight dramatic treatment.

Because euthanasia has been spotlighted in various newspaper stories recently, "Murder" is wide open to good exploitation selling. With the exception of Fredric March, the cast is relatively light on boxoffice names so that exhibs will have to rely mainly on ballyhoo to get 'em in. Once the ice is broken, though, word-of-mouth should catapult the film to good grosses in all situations.

Most sock aspect of "Murder" is the fine thesping turned in by all members of the cast under the adept direction of Michael Gordon. March, Edmond O'Brien, Florence Eldridge (who incidentally plays her real-life counterpart as March's wife) and Geraldine Brooks are standout, with Miss Eldridge, in particular, turning in a notable performance.

Screenplay by Michael Blankfort and Robert Thoeren is equally socko, maintaining the best qualities of Ernest Lothar's "Mills of God" novel but lightening the grim aspects of the film substantially for top audience reaction. March is a smalltown judge who decides his cases strictly on the letter of the law, ruling out any emotional considerations. Then, Miss Eldridge, as his wife, is stricken with a fatal disease accompanied by excruciating pain. Knowing she'll die soon anyway and tortured by the pain she's suffering, March decides to kill her by crashing their car over a cliff.

March's portrayal of the judge runs the full gamut of thesping and is consistent throughout. He's only slightly overshadowed by Miss Eldridge, who has the difficult part of the suffering wife down pat. O'Brien's splendid work, particularly in the final courtroom scene, should materially boost his boxoffice rating. Same goes for Geraldine Brooks as the daughter and Stanley Ridges as the doctor. Rest of the cast is equally good.

Producer Jerry Bresler has backgrounded the film with neat production trappings, with Daniele Amfitheatrof's score especially standout in hypoing the story's various themes. Hal Mohr's camera work is fine and Ralph Dawson has edited the film down to a tight 91 minutes. *Stal.*

Night Wind

20th-Fox release of Sol M. Wurtzel production. Features Charles Russell, Virginia Christine, Gary Gray. Directed by James Tinling. Original story, Robert G. North; screenplay, North and Arnold Belgard; camera, Benjamin Kline; editor, William F. Claxton. Previewed N. Y. Aug. 23, '48. Running time, 68 MINS.

Ralph Benson .... Charles Russell
Jean Benson .... Virginia Christine
Johnny Benson .... Gary Gray
Walters .... John Ridgely
Sheriff Hamilton .... James Burke
Dr. Ulding .... Konstantin Shayne
Barlow .... William Stelling
Wilson .... Guy Kingsford
John Steele .... Charles Lang
Margie Benson .... Deanna Woodruff
"Big Dan" .... Flame

A dog story, "Night Wind" is fine entertainment for juvenile audiences. Although adults will find the plot quite obvious, the yarn has the basic suspense that the Saturday matinee trade thrives upon.

Picture is built around the postwar life of Flame, a discharged Army German shepherd. Dog is idolized by moppet Gary Gray whose father was killed in the war. Canine supposedly was de-trained at his service exit. Nevertheless it's proved that he was the "killer" who snapped the necks of two alleged duck hunters. Writers Robert G. North and Arnold Belgard conveniently ease their way out of this by exposing the "hunters" as foreign spies. Hence, it was legal for the dog to kill.

In this modest Sol M. Wurtzel production, the cast does a uniformly good job. As a rocket researcher and stepfather to Gray, Charles Russell does a forthright portrayal. Gray is natural as the lad, while Virginia Christine is a typical mother whose only worries are whether the supper will get cold, etc. Flame, who has the role of "Big Dan," is a well-trained canine. Supporting cast is adequate.

Director James Tinling paced the situations nicely. Benjamin Kline's camerawork is good while production values are fair. "Night Wind" might well be the forerunner of a dog series for 20th on the basis of this effort. *Gilb.*

I Surrender Dear

(MUSICAL)

Hollywood, Aug. 21.

Columbia release of Sam Katzman production. Stars Gloria Jean, David Street; features Don McGuire, Alice Tyrrell, Robert Emmett Keane, Douglas Wood, The Novelites. Directed by Arthur Dreifuss. Original screenplay, M. Coates Webster; added dialog, Hal Collins; camera, Vincent Farrar; editor, Richard Fantl; musical director, Paul Mertz. At

Pantages, Hollywood, Aug. 19, '48. Running time, 67 MINS.
Patty Nelson.................Gloria Jean
Al Tyler.....................David Street
Tommy Tompkins...........Don McGuire
Trudy Clements..............Alice Tyrrell
Russ Nelson.......Robert Emmett Keane
R. H. Collins.............Douglas Wood
Mrs. Nelson...............Regina Wallace
George Rogers.............Byron Foulger
Disc Jockeys.............Jack Eigen / Dave Garroway / Peter Potter
The Novelites

A mildly amusing budget musical has been built around the song title, "I Surrender Dear." There's pleasant piping by Gloria Jean and David Street to help offset the ambling pace. It's all minor stuff but passable for the secondary market.

Plot has a disk jockey twist of orch leader turning platter twirler. It features romantic feud between Miss Jean and Street when latter turns jockey and eases her father out of his radio station job. It is all set up for the expected happy ending clinch and the finale production number. Film introduces three real-life disk jockeys, Jack Eigen, Peter Potter and Dave Garroway. Their brief footage is inserted in opening sequences, amounting to only a quick flash as story points establish platter-chatterer's salesmanship.

Score spots four songs, including the title number which Miss Jean vocals. She also does "How Can You Tell" and "Amado Mio," both by Allan Roberts and Doris Fisher. Street's vocals are on "When You Are in the Room." Two leads are best on tune work and only adequate otherwise.

Strong comedy trouping by Don McGuire and Alice Tyrrell capture some chuckles and Robert Emmett Keane and Douglas Wood as father and station owner, respectively, are okay. The Novelites are in for a comedy special that runs too long.

Production framework furnished by Sam Katzman is acceptable. Arthur Dreifuss' direction is slow.
Brog.

Joe Palooka in Winner Take All

Hollywood, Aug. 20.

Monogram release of Hal E. Chester production. Features Joe Kirkwood, Elyse Knox, William Frawley, Stanley Clements, John Shelton, Mary Beth Hughes, Sheldon Leonard. Directed by Reginald Le Borg. Screenplay, Stanley Rubin; added dialog, Monte V. Collins; camera, William Sickner; editor, Otho Lovering. Previewed at Hollywood, Aug. 19, '48. Running time, 64 MINS.
Joe Palooka..............Joe Kirkwood
Anne Howe...................Elyse Knox
Knobby Walsh..........William Frawley
Tommy.................Stanley Clements
Greg Tanner................John Shelton
Millie................Mary Beth Hughes
Herman...............Sheldon Leonard
Louie........................Frank Jenks
Henderson.....................Lyle Talbot
Waldo..........................Jack Roper
Canvas....................Eddie Gribbon
Taxi Driver...............Wally Vernon
Lt. Steve Mulford..........Ralph Sanford
Sportscaster......................Bill Martin
Bobo Walker............"Big" Ben Moroz
Sammy Talbot..............Hal Fieberling
Talbot's Manager..........William Ruhl
Doniger.......................Chester Clute
Reporters.............Douglas Fowley / Stanley Prager
Instructors..........Hugh Charles / Forrest Matthews
Mrs. Howard.............Gertrude Astor
Television Announcer.........Hal Gerard

Monogram's latest Joe Palooka adventure is film merchandize that will have a ready market. Entry maintains the consistent worth of the series, furnishing fans with exciting ring footage and the proper amount of comedy and melodrama. It's a strong programmer.

Title role is capably filled, physically, by Joe Kirkwood, whose appearance has the brawn of Ham Fisher's pen-and-ink hero. He handles his dukes ably, making believeable the ring sequences and generally proves satisfactory on all counts. Elyse Knox's Anne Howe character is appealing and William Frawley is good as the worrisome, slightly comic Knobby Walsh. Threesome teams well.

This time Palooka has his troubles with gamblers and a ward, the younger brother of a war pal. When gamblers fail to bring down the odds on Palooka's championship fight by threats, they use the ward and a phoney kidnapping to make the champ throw a fight. The ward gets over his peeve at Palooka in time for the hero to stage a last-minute comeback. It's all pat stuff, but neatly twisted in writing and direction to command audience interest.

There are a number of ring sequences, all solidly staged by John Indrisano. A standout one for laughs and thrills, is Palooka's go with a seven-foot boxer, "Big" Ben Moroz. The championship go between Kirkwood and Hal Fieberling is an authentic piece of action stuff.

Stanley Clements portrays the Palooka ward smartly, pointing up the assignment and giving film a decided lift. Sheldon Leonard is a joy as a dumb gambler with money, making for nifty laughs. Mary Beth Hughes and John Shelton are good as Leonard's partners. Others in the cast give capable support.

The Hal E. Chester production, directed by Reginald Le Borg, has been expertly mounted to get the most for budget dollar. Lensing, editing and other techinical credits reflect production care in hewing to an entertainment line that should give "Winner" plenty of playdates in its market. *Brog.*

The Prairie

Screen Guild release of Edward F. Finney (George Moskov) production. Stars Lenore Aubert, Alan Baxter; features Russ Vincent, Jack Mitchum. Directed by Frank Wisbar. Screenplay, Arthur St. Clare; camera, James S. Brown; editor, Douglas W. Bagier; music, Alexander Steinert. At New York, N. Y., Aug. 17, '48. Running time, 65 MINS.
Ellen Wade...............Lenore Aubert
Paul Hover....................Alan Baxter
Abiram White...............Russ Vincent
Asa Bush....................Jack Mitchum
Ishmael Bush...............Charles Evans
Esther Bush................Edna Holland
Eagle Feather.........Chief Thundercloud
Abner Bush.....................Fred Coby
Jess Bush.......................Bill Murphy
Gabe Bush.................David Gerber
Enoch Bush......................Don Lynch
Luke.......................George Morrell
Matoreeh..................Chief Yowlachie
Running Deer.............Jay Silverheels
Annie Morris....................Beth Taylor
Commentary by Frank Hemingway

The novels of James Fenimore Cooper have provided excellent screen fare for several decades. They usually have action, broad sweeps of motion and well-defined story lines, and "The Prairie" follows form. It's good frontier fare, a bit more adult than the general run of western and should fit on dual bills other than those presented on Saturday matinees.

Story concerns a covered-wagoning family into the newly opened Louisiana Purchase territory. It's a hard trek, made more difficult by Indians and danger of starvation. The entourage inherits an addition when two of the sons rescue a girl whose family has been wiped out by Indians. She splits the two male members of the clan, but is eventually won by Alan Baxter as an Army cartographer who turns up at strategic moments.

Cast is uniformally good with Lenore Aubert providing the romantic interest while Russ Vincent and Jack Mitchum do well as the feuding brothers. Charles Evans is excellent as the patriarch, and Baxter similarly does okay as the buckskin man of the hour.

Frank Wisbar's direction is a good blend of action and restraint. His introductions of set-tos are invariably timed after slow passages so that greater impact is registered. The screenplay by Arthur St. Clare is in a manner that lets the camera have greater say in the matter. The photography is okay and the musical background adequate. *Jose.*

London Belongs to Me
(BRITISH)

London, Aug. 12.

GFD release of J. Arthur Rank-individual-Launder-Gilliat production. Stars Richard Attenborough, Alastair Sim. Directed by Sidney Gilliat. Screenplay by Gilliat and J. B. Williams, from novel by Norman Collins; editor, Thelma Myers; camera, Wilkie Cooper, Ernie Steward. At Odeon, London. Running time, 112 MINS.
Percy Boon.......Richard Attenborough
Mr. Squales..................Alastair Sim
Uncle Henry...............Stephen Murray
Mrs. Josser..................Fay Compton
Mr. Josser..................Wylie Watson
Doris Josser....................Susan Shaw
Connie..........................Ivy St. Helier
Mrs. Vizzard....................Joyce Carey

Adapted from a bestseller by Norman Collins, it's doubtful whether this Launder-Gilliat production will repeat the success of the original novel. Starting out as tense melo it develops into broad farce, and many people may rightly resent being expected to laugh while a fight is being made for the life of a youth sentenced to death.

Set in a typical house in a typical street, the plot depicts the struggles and hopes of a group of ordinary people. They include a benign old couple with their attractive daughter, a widowed mother with her only son, a faded blonde who ekes out a pittance at a night club, and the landlady herself, slightly soured but almost falling for a fake spiritualist. All lead a humdrum existence until the young lad, in his desire to make some easy money and court the girl downstairs, gets involved in a murder and is sentenced to death.

Until now it has been a vigorous piece of melodrama, tense and exciting, and up to the standard expected from the Launder-Gilliat team. But without warning, and in questionable taste, the tempo changes and the organizing of a petition to save the life of the boy is treated as something meant to be hilariously funny. It doesn't come off.

Lack of consistency in the treatment unfortunately brings the film down to an average level. With its excellent characterizations, its meaty story and fine London backgrounds it should have been a firstrate thriller. But it isn't.

An exceptionally big cast handles the characterizations with skill, but top honors go to Richard Attenborough, living the part of the flashy youngster who wants to go places the easy way, and Alastair Sim, who just can't miss as the fake medium. Fay Compton, Wylie Watson and Susan Shaw are typical suburbanites, but Stephen Murray is more of a caricature than a character. *Myro.*

The Spirit and the Flesh
(ITALIAN)

Variety Film release of Lux (Mario Cancrini) production. Stars Gino Cervi, Dina Sassoli; features Ruggero Ruggeri, Enrico Glori, Luis Hurtado. Directed by Valentino Brosio. Screenplay, Canerini, from Alessandro Manzoni's novel; camera, Anchiso Brizzi; editors, Gino Brosio, Nathan Cy Braunstein, Clement Douneias; music, Ildebrando Pizzeti; English titles, John Erskine. Previewed N. Y. Aug. 11, '48. Running time, 105 MINS.
Renzo.............................Gino Cervi
Lucia..............................Dina Sassoli
Il Cardinale...............Ruggero Ruggeri
Don Abbondio.............Armando Falcone
Don Rodrigo..................Enrico Glori
L'Innominato.................Carlo Ninchi
Padre Christoforo.........Luis Hurtado
Perpetua...........................Ines Zacconi
Il Conte Attilio........Franco Scandurra
Agnese..........................Gilda Marchio
Il Griso..........................Dino Di Lucca
Ferrer..........................Enzo Biliotti

(In Italian; English Titles)

Adapted from a classic romantic novel by Alessandro Manzoni, "The Spirit and the Flesh" is a lengthy Italian import whose market appears to lie in carefully booked art house situations.

A wealth of pageantry has gone into this period piece, and the basically simple plot builds into a story of tremendous scope. Picture unfolds the struggle of youthful Gino Cervi to wed his betrothed, Dina Sassoli, despite the interference of Enrico Glori, the heavy.

Story is also a deeply religious one in which there is more than one concrete example where genuine faith is bound to save one from evil. Performances are uniformly good with Cervi, Miss Sassoli and Luis Hurtado (as the priest) standing out in particular. Direction of Valentino Brosio is fair as is the camerawork of Anchiso Brizzi. Production values are good.

Although a trio of editors worked on the print, the film's pace could have been speeded further by deletion of superfluous sequences that add nothing to the development of the plot. Creditable and lucid are John Erskine's English titles.

The Honorable Catherine
(FRENCH)

European Copyrights release of Marcel L'Herbier production. Stars Edwige Feuillere. Directed by Georges Lampin. Screenplay, S. H. Terac; camera, P. Montagel. At Elysee, N. Y., Aug. 21, '48. Running time, 85 MINS.
Catherine..................Edwige Feuillere
Pierre...........................Andre Luguet
Gisele...........................Claude Genia
Jacques...................Raymond Rouleau

(In French; English Titles)

"The Honorable Catherine" is one of those bad French mistakes that never should have been imported into this country. This pic attempts a genre of madcap comedy which only succeeds in being absurd. It will have no appeal for the usually discriminating art house clientele.

Disheveled yarn concerns a blackmailing femme who makes capital out of extra-marital shenanigans. In a complicated boudoir scene full of irate husbands and ducking wives, the blackmailer gets involved in a love affair with a young roue. But before the final clinch occurs, there are a series of wild episodes of pretended insanity which have little relevancy to the discernable plot.

Edwige Feuillere, who was seen last in the U.S. in her brilliant performance in "The Idiot," imparts verve to the role of the blackmailer but she can't cope with the zany situations. Andre Luguer registers as a conventional lover. Rest of the cast play in a broad style of comedy. *Herm.*

Miniature Reviews

"Rope" (Color) (WB). Technicolor shocker for the seeker of cinema thrills.

"An Innocent Affair" (Songs) (UA-Nasser). Fred MacMurray-Madeleine Carroll in straining comedy.

"For the Love of Mary" (Songs) (U). Breezy situation comedy which is Deanna Durbin's best in many a pic.

"Out of Storm" (Rep). Routine meller about a payroll robbery. Okay for some dualers.

"Nanook of the North" (Royal). New edition, with narrative and music, of classic documentary.

"Code of Scotland Yard" (Rep.). Well enacted murder yarn for the duallers.

"Bodyguard" (RKO). Neat cops-and-robber meller for dualers. Good action.

"In This Corner" (EL). Okay action programmer, mixing rehabilitation of veterans with prizering.

"Mr. Perrin and Mr. Traill" (British) (GFD). David Farrar. Yarn about British public schools; mild for U.S.

Rope
(COLOR)

Hollywood, Aug. 26.

Warner Bros. release of Alfred Hitchcock (Transatlantic Pictures) production, directed by Hitchcock. Stars James Stewart; features John Dall, Farley Granger, Sir Cedric Hardwicke, Constance Collier. Screenplay, Arthur Laurents; adapted by Hume Cronyn, from play by Patrick Hamilton; camera (Technicolor), Joseph Valentine, William V. Skall; editor, William H. Siegler; music, Leo F. Forbstein. Tradeshown, Aug. 24, '48. Running time, **80 MINS.**

Rupert Cadell	James Stewart
Brandon	John Dall
Philip	Farley Granger
Mr. Kentley	Sir Cedric Hardwicke
Mrs. Atwater	Constance Collier
Kenneth	Douglas Dick
Mrs. Wilson	Edith Evanson
David Kentley	William Hogan
Janet	Joan Chandler

"Rope" undoubtedly will be ballyhooed as a super-horror film. It is and in so being may defeat itself. It's a cold-blooded account of a wanton murder. The fastidious seeker of cinema thrills should be delighted with the ruthless way in which Alfred Hitchcock has displayed an unsavory subject, but acceptance by the general run of audiences, from whom the heavy b.o. coin comes, is unpredictable. It's definitely not for the kiddies.

Film has plenty of pegs upon which to hang strong exploitation and Warners can be expected to turn loose its full powers to ballyhoo this one. The type of selling should result in some big initial grosses, particularly in key situations where large groups of the morbidly curious can be attracted. The brutally uncompromising manner of presentation also may catch on, and if it does, general situations will pay off.

Critically, it seems that Hitchcock could have chosen a more entertaining subject with which to use the arresting camera and staging technique displayed in "Rope." Theme of a thrill murder, done for no reason but to satisfy a sadistical urge and intellectual vanity, is in questionable taste. Plot has its real-life counterpart in the infamous Loeb-Leopold case, and is based on the play by Patrick Hamilton.

Feature of the picture is that story action is continuous without time lapses. Action takes place within an hour and a half period and the film footage nearly duplicates the span, being 80 minutes. It is entirely confined to the murder apartment of two male dillettantes, intellectual morons who commit what they believe to be the perfect crime, then celebrate the deed with a gloulish supper served to the victim's relatives and friends from atop the chest in which the body is concealed.

Conventional camera closeups are omitted, Hitchcock using a soaring lens that moves without restraint through the apartment, zooming up to a player and then away, sometimes with a whirling-dervish effect that distracts. The continuous action and the extremely mobile camera are technical features of which industry craftsmen will make much, but to the layman audience effect is of a distracting interest that doesn't add to b.o. merits of the subject on which it is used.

To achieve his effects, Hitchcock put his cast and technicians through lengthy rehearsals before turning a camera. The method has paid off for presenting something different in production and does serve to emphasize the sordid story. An outstanding feature of the picture is the brilliant use of Technicolor and lighting shades that approximate real life. It will draw favorable critical comment.

Performances are class deliveries, characters remaining consistently true to type as the play unfolds. Hitchcock has managed a compelling suspense in telling a story which always can be anticipated, a neat trick of shudder-making with events that forecast their coming.

James Stewart, as the ex-professor who first senses the guilt of his former pupils and nibbles away at their composure with verbal barbs, does a commanding job. John Dall stands out as the egocentric who masterminds the killing and gloulish wake. Equally good is Farley Granger as the weakling partner in crime. Sir Cedric Hardwicke, the victim's father; Constance Collier, his aunt; Douglas Dick, a friend; Joan Chandler, fiancee; and William Hogan, the victim whose only scene is his strangling at film's opening, give capable accounts of themselves. Edith Evanson adds some contrasting humor as a maid serving the party.

Joseph Valentine and William V. Skall share the major camera credit, a most important contribution to the picture's unusualness. Credited also are Edward Fitzgerald, Paul G. Hill, Richard Emmons and Morris Rosen as operators of camera movement.

Brog.

An Innocent Affair
(SONGS)

United Artists release of James Nasser production. Stars Fred MacMurray and Madeleine Carroll; features Charles "Buddy" Rogers, Rita Johnson, Louise Allbritton, Alan Mowbray. Directed by Lloyd Bacon. Screenplay, Lou Breslow and Joseph Hoffman; camera, Edward Cronjager; music, Hans J. Salter; editor, Fred W. Berger; songs, Walter Kent and Kim Gannon; asst. director, Clarence Eurist. Previewed N. Y., Aug. 27, '48. Running time, **90 MINS.**

Vincent Doane	Fred MacMurray
Paula Doane	Madeleine Carroll
Claude Kimball	Charles "Buddy" Rogers
Eve Lawrence	Rita Johnson
Margot Fraser	Louise Allbritton
Ken St. Clari	Alan Mowbray
Maitre D'	"Prince" Mike Romanoff
T. D. Hendricks	Pierre Watkin
Gaylord	William Tannen
Lester Burnley	James Seay
Ted Burke	Matt McHugh
Hilda	Marie Blake
Vocalist	Susan Miller
Gladys	Anne Magel
Orchestra Leader	Eddie LeBaron
Doris	Jane Weeks

It's unfortunate that there could not have been a wiser choice for Madeleine Carroll in her comeback picture. "An Innocent Affair," in which she costars with Fred MacMurray, is a straining comedy of husband-wife jealousies that never fully justifies the obviously considerable effort that has gone into the production. Its business will depend on the cast name values, which also include, notably, the names of Charles "Buddy" Rogers and Rita Johnson.

"Affair" deals with an advertising man and his entanglement with a wealthy former flame whom he seeks to interest in the purchase of advertising for a company she controls. MacMurray is the ad man, and he veils the identity of the old sweetie to allay the suspicions of his wife (Miss Carroll). The latter learns of the "affair" anyway, and the complications that ensue are the result of the wife hiring a man with whom she would flirt so as to make the husband jealous. It's as complicated as all that.

Miss Carroll gives as creditable a performance as the story would permit; at the same time, the photography is not especially flattering to her. MacMurray garners some laughs in a couple of situations, but it remains for Alan Mowbray, in a restaurant scene, to nab the major guffaws with a standard situation that stands out in bold comedy relief.

Charles "Buddy" Rogers is also making a belated return to the screen, as a millionaire cigaret manufacturer who's one of the links in the four-ply romantic complications. Rogers retains much of the boyish charm and personality of his former film days, and there's little manifestation of the passing years in his appearance. Rita Johnson and Louise Allbritton haven't much to do effectively except wear some modishly tailored clothes.

There is little that direction could have done with the trite situations, and so director Lloyd Bacan can't be blamed too much. The film has some color in the presence of Mike Romanoff, the Beverly Hills restaurateur, who gives the pic a note of authenticity as the operator of the film's swank eatery. Walter Kent and Kim Gannon have written a couple of pop tunes as background.

Kahn.

For the Love of Mary
(SONGS)

Hollywood, Aug. 25.

Universal release of Robert Arthur production. Stars Deanna Durbin, Edmond O'Brien, Don Taylor, Jeffrey Lynn. Directed by Frederick De Cordova. Original screenplay, Oscar Brodney; camera, William Daniels; editor, Ted J. Kent; musical supervisor, Milton Schwarzwald. Tradeshown Aug. 25, '48. Running time, **90 MINS.**

Mary Peppertree	Deanna Durbin
Lt. Tom Farrington	Edmond O'Brien
David Paxton	Don Taylor
Phillip Manning	Jeffrey Lynn
Harvey Elwood	Ray Collins
Gustav Heindel	Hugo Haas
Justice Peabody	Harry Davenport
Timothy Peppertree	Griff Barnett
Miss Harkness	Katharine Alexander
Justice Van Sloan	James Todd
Adm. Walton	Morris Ankrum
Samuel Litchfield	Frank Conroy
Igor	Leon Belasco
Bertha	Louise Beavers
Justice Williams	Raymond Greenleaf
Justice Hastings	Charles Meredith
Mrs. Peabody	Adele Rowland
Marge	Mary Adams
Hilda	Adrienne Marden
Dorothy	Beatrice Roberts
Colonel Hedley	Harry Cheshire
Asst. Attorney General	Donald Randolph
Senator Benning	William Gould

Intriguing idea of the President of United States helping a White House telephone operator in her romantic problems is premise on which "For the Love of Mary" is constructed, and right well is it handled, too. Result is a delightful light comedy experience, with Deanna Durbin at her best in role of the operator whose troubles are usurped by both the President and justices of the U. S. Supreme Court for solution.

Star returns to the type of role and picture through which she first attracted public attention. Warbling a quintet of songs, the highlight is "Barber of Seville" excerpt which is given comedy treatment instead of being delivered as straight operatic rendition. Miss Durbin is allowed to cavort capriciously and with nothing more in mind by producers than an entertaining picture, which it is.

Miss Durbin scores on every count, timing her comedy to perfection and delivering strongly particularly with "Figaro." Of her male trio, Edmond O'Brien, Jeffrey Lynn and Don Taylor, latter finally wins her after having been the cause of all her difficulties. All are okay. Ray Collins does a bang-up job as the executive secretary; Hugo Haas is in for plenty of good comedy; and Harry Davenport registers as the Supreme Court justice who can't understand why Miss Durbin deserted his court.

Plot has been built up, and while the President is never seen or heard, his presence is felt throughout, particularly when his executive secretary enters the scene as proxy for the Chief Executive. Original screenplay by Oscar Brodney is cleverly devised, directed with quick awareness by Frederick De Cordova and produced by Robert Arthur with a sure eye for popular values.

Whit.

Out of the Storm

Republic production and release. Features James Lydon, Lois Collier, Marc Lawrence, Richard Travis. Directed by R. G. Springsteen. Screenplay, John K. Butler from story by Gordon Rigby; camera, John Mac Burnie; editor, Richard L. Van Enger. Tradeshown N. Y. Aug. 27, '48. Running time, **61 MINS.**

Donald Lewis	James Lydon
Ginny Powell	Lois Collier
Red Stubbins	Marc Lawrence
R. J. Ramsey	Richard Travis
Holbrook	Robert Emmett Keane
Martha Lewis	Helen Wallace
Chief Ryan	Harry Hayden
Arty Sorenson	Roy Barcroft
Mr. Evans	Charles Lane
Ginger	Iris Adrian
Al Weinstock	Byron Foulger
Mrs. Smith	Claire DuBrey
Maintenance Man	Smoki Whitfield
Plant Guard	Charlie Sullivan
Gus Clute	Rex Lease
Ed. Purcell	Edgar Dearing

Lightweight cops-and-robbers meller seeks to prove that crime does not pay. Cast lacks any name to brighten the marquee, but film may serve as lower half of twin bill in some locations.

There are so many implausible moments tossed in that one wonders what will happen next. Story of a modest-salaried clerk in a shipbuilding plant who tries to smuggle out $100,000 during a daring payroll robbery attempts to ring in some romance with little success. How the struggling clerk finally decides to go straight and return the missing money brings the film to an unusually dull ending.

James Lydon is the clerk who makes off with the 100G that's overlooked during the stickup. He doesn't fit too well into such a highly dramatic story and struggles too hard to make his character register. Lois Collier is not particularly effective as his sweetheart. Marc Lawrence makes a thoroughly hardboiled crook, leader of the holdup gang. Richard Travis, as an insurance sleuth, is so natural he seems out of place in such a yarn. *Wear.*

Nanook of the North

(DOCUMENTARY)

Royal Pictures (George Roth) release of Robert J. Flaherty production. This edition produced under supervision of Herbert Edwards from original 1922 release. Narrative by Ralph Schoolman, spoken by Berry Kroeger; score, Rudolf Schramm. At Sutton, N. Y., starting Aug. 19, '48. Running time, 55 MINS.

"Nanook of the North" is the granddaddy (or the Eskimo equivalent thereof) of all documentaries and widely extolled as the classic in its field. It was produced in 1920-21 by Robert J. Flaherty—who is still making documentaries, incidentally—under sponsorship of Revillon Freres, the furriers. It had been tucked away in the vaults since its original release in 1922, except for special showings. About 18 months ago Revillon was sold the idea of having it reedited and a commentary and music track added. It made its debut in this version in England with great success about a year ago under United Artists release, and is now having its U.S. preem under indie distribution auspices (George Roth).

Despite the comparatively primitive technique of almost 30 years ago and the natural difficulties of shooting a film in the frozen Hudson Bay wastelands, every minute of "Nanook" lives up to its reputation. Greatly enhanced by the commentary and the music, it should do okay in the art houses with proper selling and make a very unusual and acceptable bottom half of a double bill in almost any situation.

Yarn holds tremendous interest in detailing the life of an Eskimo family through the seasons of the year.

Ralph Schoolman's narrative hits the proper note. It treats the Eskimo with dignity, yet with a sense of humor, and it never gets pompous. Berry Kroeger likewise sticks to a simple, friendly, yet thoroughly dignified style in speaking the narration.

Shortcoming is in the editing, which was supervised, as was the making of this whole edition, by Herbert Edwards, head of the film division of the U. S. Dept. of State. The picture runs only 55 minutes, and is too brief—which gives a clue to the interest it holds. It has obviously been edited to be "fast."

Incidentally, the laboratory transposition of the 16 frames per second of the old silent projector to the 24 frames of the modern machine has been skillfully done to remove the jerkiness, which is scarcely visible to any but trained eyes. *Herb.*

Code of Scotland Yard

Republic release of George King production, directed by King. Stars Oscar Homolka; features Derek Farr, Muriel Pavlow. Screenplay, Katherine Strueby; camera, Hone Clendinning; editor, Manuel Del Campo; music, George Melachrino. Tradeshown N. Y. Aug. 30, '48. Running time, 60 MINS.

Descius Heiss	Oscar Homolka
Robert Graham	Derek Farr
Margaret Heiss	Muriel Pavlow
Archie Fellowes	Kenneth Griffith
Corder Morris	Manning Whiley
Mrs. Catt	Kathleen Harrison
Major Elliot	Garry Marsh
Professor Vanetti	Jan Van Loewen
Ruby Towser	Irene Handl
Inspector Robson	Johnnie Schofield

"Code of Scotland Yard," filmed with an all-British cast, is an excellently enacted story. Unfortunately, its effectiveness is marred by a choppy editing job which slows the picture's pace and leaves some sequences dangling mid-air. Even with this sharply blue-penciled version, film's story lines aren't hurt to any appreciable degree and the yarn can be sold on its blackmail and murder angles.

Oscar Homolka is well-cast as a seemingly respectable antique dealer who successfully conceals a background as an escaped Devil's Island convict who hits back at society by acting as a fence for a jewel robber. However, in order to protect his daughter's future as a concert violinist, he retires from illegal activities. Unfortunately, his shop assistant discovers Homolka's background, and blackmails him until demands become so extortionate that Homolka kills him. Homolka, in turn commits suicide, and a kindly Scotland yard official marks the case closed.

In support, Kenneth Griffith as the blackmailer, Muriel Pavlow as the daughter, and Derek Farr as her fiancee do creditable jobs. Garry Marsh gives the role of the Yard official a degree of smoothness.

Musical sequences are well done, with Frederic Grinke doing nicely on the solo violin, seemingly played by Miss Pavlow. The orchestral background is well-scored. *Jose.*

Bodyguard

Hollywood, Aug. 28.

RKO release of Sid Rogell production. Stars Lawrence Tierney, Priscilla Lane; features Philip Reed, June Clayworth, Elisabeth Risdon, Steve Brodie, Frank Fenton, Charles Cane. Directed by Richard O. Fleischer. Screenplay, Fred Niblo, Jr., Harry Essex; story, George W. George, Robert B. Altman; camera, Robert de Grasse; editor, Elmo Williams. Tradeshown Aug. 26, '48. Running time, 62 MINS.

Mike Carter	Lawrence Tierney
Doris Brewster	Priscilla Lane
Freddie Dysen	Philip Reed
Connie	June Clayworth
Gene Dysen	Elisabeth Risdon
Fenton	Steve Brodie
Lieut. Borden	Frank Fenton
Capt. Wayne	Charles Cane

"Bodyguard" is an adaptable melodrama, capable of going upstairs or downstairs on dual bills according to the situation. Action houses should find it a sturdy offering around which to swing a bill, and classier general situations can spot it advantageously as a supporter.

RKO's tough guy, Lawrence Tierney, is an okay character in this, even though suspected of murder and sundry misdeeds. A hot temper and ready fists get him bounced off the homicide squad and right into a frying pan of mayhem. A police lieutenant, a blackmailer is bumped off and Tierney is framed for the killing. Before he gets himself out of the scrape, he turns up evidence of a prior murder and hangs three killings on the real villain.

Script has good twists to keep interest alive in the more or less cops-and-robbers formula plot. A couple of scenes will give chuckles to avid newspaper readers. One has Tierney mixing a drink in favor of a glass of milk. Another has him denying he ever gets in fights. Fred Niblo, Jr., and Harry Essex did the neat scribbling from a story by George W. George and Robert B. Altman.

Direction by Richard O. Fleischer keeps the film on the move nicely spotting action and making development credible. Aiding Tierney clear himself of murder charges and expose a killer who took any means to safeguard his swindling in the meat packing trade is Priscilla Lane, the hero's sweetie and secretary in the police department.

Philip Reed is a capable heavy and Elisabeth Risdon, as the aunt he is defrauding, is good, June Clayworth, Steve Brodie, Frank Fenton and Charles Cane answer script demands favorably.

Producer Sid Rogell has turned this one out on a budget ample to carry the subject without overexpenditure on frills that do not matter. Technical assists are in keeping, including good lensing by Robert de Grasse; scoring by Paul Sawtell and Elmo Williams' tight editing. *Brog.*

The Secret Land

(DOCUMENTARY-COLOR)

Metro release of Orville O. Dull production. Stars Men and Ships of the U. S. Navy. Narrators, Comdr. Robert Montgomery (U.S.N.R.), Lieut. Robert Taylor (U.S.N.R.), Lieut. Van Heflin (A.A.F.-Ret.). Commentary written by Capt. Harvey S. Haislip (U.S.N.-Ret.), Comdr. William C. Park (U.S.N.R.); camera (Technicolor), by Navy, Marine Corps, Coast Guard and Army lensmen; editor, Comdr. Frederick Y. Smith (U.S.N.R.); score, Bronislau Kaper. Previewed in N. Y. Aug. 13, '48. Running time, 71 MINS.

A taut, pictorial account of the U. S. Navy's recent Antarctic expedition is "The Secret Land," which Metro is releasing for theatrical distribution. Beautifully photographed in Technicolor by cameramen from the four services, the film not only is a fine chronological record of the task force's mission but ranks also as a top adventure picture. Exhibitors will find this well worth booking.

As further selling points are the names of Robert Montgomery, Robert Taylor and Van Heflin. All former Navy and Army Air Force officers, the trio handle the narration although they're not seen on the screen. The film will do business at the boxoffice, but even more important, this documentary affords the general public (and taxpayers) a bird's eye view of just how the country's top naval brass plots out a multi-million dollar project.

Purpose of the mission, as is commonly known, was to map uncharted regions of Antarctica, geologically examine the terrain as well as test men, ships and equipment in the sub-zero climate. In view of the intricate preparation that undoubtedly went into "Operation Highjump," before it was launched, it's a mystery why more than one icebreaker was not assigned to the expedition.

This error was graphically demonstrated when the supply ships were midway across a several hundred mile pack ice barrier between them and Little America. At this point a Coast Guard icebreaker, which had been breaking a track, was forced to abandon its sister vessels in order to assist submarine to open water, thereupon causing an unanticipated delay in "Highjump's" time schedule. Other incidents further pointed up the value of specially-designed icebreakers.

Commentary written by Capt. Harvey S. Haislip and Comdr. William C. Park in general was lucid and ably complemented the photography. However, a description of the rescue of an officer who had fallen into the sea when a breeches buoy line parted was somewhat exaggerated in what appeared to be an attempt to insert false dramatic values into the scene. It was stated that in these waters a man lives for only eight minutes. He was saved in seven, prompting the comment that it was in the nick of time. In the last war some men torpedoed off Greenland in mid-winter survived even after several hours in the water.

Particularly well done was the editing of Frederick Y. Smith. Of the mountain of footage he undoubtedly was confronted with, he deftly made use of frequent clips of penguins, shots of King Neptune ceremonies when crossing the equator, as well as a few sequences of enlisted men and officers in their off-duty hours. These bits afforded a nice change of pace from the unreeling of the cold, factual details of the expedition itself. Orville O. Dull gave "Secret Land" a topflight production while Bronislau Kaper's musical score enhances the dramatic content of the film.

In This Corner

(ONE SONG)

Hollywood, Aug. 28.

Eagle-Lion release of David L. Stephenson (Arc) production. Stars Scott Brady; features Anabel Shaw, Jimmy Millican, Mary Meade, Charles D. Brown, Robert Bice. Directed by Charles F. Riesner. Screenplay, Burk Symon, Fred Niblo, Jr.; camera, Guy Roe; editor, Norman Colbert. Previewed Aug. 27, '48. Running time, 62 MINS.

Jimmy Weston	Scott Brady
Sally	Anabel Shaw
Doc Fuller	Chas. D. Brown
Tug Martin	Jimmy Millican
Birdie Bronson	Mary Meade
Commander Harris	Bob Bice
Television Announcer	Don Forbes
Barton, Announcer	Bill Kennedy
Dunkle	John Doucette
Tiny Reads	Cy Kendall

"In This Corner" proves an okay program feature, offering sufficient interest for the action houses. **Prizefight yarn has been mixed with theme of restoring war-marked veterans to normal activity and it all comes off well enough to stand up in its intended market.**

Smoother production and direction would have helped give the okay plot a stronger outlook, but even at that, budget limitations have been overcome with sufficient ingenuity to spin it along entertainingly despite the flaws.

Scott Brady, screen newcomer, makes a bid for attention and has the physical appearance to carry off role of vet who becomes a light heavyweight fighter. He looks like he has a chance with proper handling and more experience.

Yarn concerns Brady, discharged from Navy service, taking up fisticuffs for a livelihood. A crooked manager gets hold of him and shoves him along fast as a buildup for big gambling killing. When Brady won't go for a fixed fight, the gambler plot without him. He frames Brady to make it look like a punch has killed a sparring partner. This reawakens mental block Brady received during service when a blow from him killed a navy buddy. He loses the fight but next time around, just when Brady is taking a terrific beating, his girl friend rushes in with the supposedly dead man and saves the day.

Supporting Brady in his first star spot are Anabel Shaw, the girl friend; Jimmy Millican, the crooked manager; Mary Meade, latter's moll; Charles D. Brown, Brady's trainer; and Robert Bice, Navy commander. Cast has some awkward dialog to stumble through but otherwise measures up to demands.

Charles F. Riesner directed the David I. Stephenson production and standard lensing was contributed by Guy Roe. Editing is Jerky. One tune, "Out of the Blue," is injected for very minor results. *Brog.*

Mr. Perrin & Mr. Traill
(BRITISH)

London, Aug. 25.
General Film Distributors' release of J. Arthur Rank Two Cities Film production. Stars David Farrar, Marius Goring, Greta Gynt. Directed by Lawrence Huntington. Screenplay by L. A. G. Strong, from novel by Hugh Walpole; additional dialog by Tom Harrison; editor, Ralph Kemplen; camera, Erwin Hillier, Ray Sturgess. At Odeon, London. Running time, 92 MINS.
David Traill................David Farrar
Vincent Perrin...........Marius Goring
Isobel Lester................Greta Gynt
Moy-Thompson........Raymond Huntley
Birkland...................Edward Chapman
Mrs. Perrin..............Mary Jerrold
Comber....................Ralph Truman
Sir Joshua Varley........Finlay Currie
Clinton....................Maurice Jones
Dormer....................Lloyd Pearson
Mrs. Dormer..............May Macdonald
Mrs. Comber................Violet Lyel
White......................Archie Harradine

Hugh Walpole's typically English story of public school life is brought to the screen in leisurely fashion here, more emphasis being placed on characterization than on story. Not among the best of the author's works, the title means little to American audiences. Even though they may find something of appeal in the presentation of a facet of the British way of life, this looks mild for U. S. market.

The story of life at Benfield's College is in reality a story of British tradition, a story in which seniority takes first place. In this stuffy atmosphere comes David Farrar, fresh from the Commandos and full of enthusiasm, ready to lend a hand at sports and prove that he knew something of maths. But he had not reckoned with Marius Goring, whose 21 years at the college have filled him with tradition, who resents the new blood, and cannot forgive when he wins the one girl he had coveted.

It is in its characterization that this may score, and Goring's interpretation of the traditional teacher, whose background has been colored by his long association with the school, is one of the best things he has done on the screen. Not entirely gaining sympathy for his crass stupidity and petty jealousies, he typifies the staid and stuffy public school tradition, which is responsible for his untimely end.

On the other side of the fence is Farrar, smoothly competent in a role which does not make big demands, but making a very good romantic team with Greta Gynt.

Main settings of the film are the classroom. Direction needs tightening, and dialog is top heavy.
Myro.

Private Life of an Actor
(FRENCH)

Siritzky release of Union Cinematographique Lyonnaise production. Stars Sacha Guitry; written and directed by Guitry. Camera, N. Toporkoff; music, Louis Beydts; English titles, Charles Clements. Previewed N. Y., Aug. 30, '48. Running time, 100 MINS.
Lucien Guitry }
Sacha Guitry }..............Sacha Guitry
Catherine..................Lana Marconi
Antoinette..............Marguerite Pierry
Elise......................Pauline Carton
Maillard..................Jacques Baumer
Actor......................Robert Seller

(In French; English Titles)
Sacha Guitry's comeback to the postwar French cinema is a disappointment. "Private Life of an Actor," his first pic since being cleared of a collaborationist rap, is a prosaic biog of his father, Lucien Guitry, idol of the Paris legits around the turn of the century. Although the Guitrys, pere and fils, are reputed to have cut a fancy swath through French show biz, fore and aft of the footlights, this film only succeeds in making their lives singularly dull. It will draw a blank in the sureseater market.

Like his several successful prewar efforts, this film is a strictly one-man operation which Guitry wrote, directed and virtually plays single-handedly. But where his other pix were saved by wit, this film is drowned in sober gab. Guitry, in the person of his father, pontificates on love, morals, acting, playwrighting and even patriotism (returning, no doubt, a few pokes at his critics). But Guitry, as actor, is hamstrung by Guitry, as writer-director.

In relating the actor's life, the film shuttles between two settings —the dressing room and on stage. In the former, Guitry, senior, is beheld as an aging Romeo wooing susceptible young females with a conventional set of wiles. On stage, the actor is glimpsed posturing through about 20 of his great plays in magnificently hammy style. Neither of these facets are well handled cinematically. As a result, Guitry's omnipresence on the screen and soundtrack is magnified into an oppressive bore.

No one in the cast besides Guitry is permitted anything beyond a bit role, but these are uniformly well handled. Lana Marconi (Mrs. Sacha Guitry) registers nicely as a passing mistress as does Marguerite Pierry in a similar role. Both actresses, however, are completely overshadowed by the immensity of Guitry's varied, yet slightly monotonous characterizations.
Herm.

El Tambor de Tacuari
(The Drummer of Tacuari)
(ARGENTINE)

Buenos Aires, Aug. 2.
Emelco production and release. Stars Juan Carlo Barbieri; features Francisco Martinez Allende, Mario Vanarelli, Ricardo Canales, Norma Gimenez, Homero Carpena, Manolo Diaz, Leticia Scury, Jose L. Rodrigo. Directed by Carlos Borcosque. Adapted from story by Hugo MacDougall; camera, Humberto Peruzzi. At Gran Rex, Buenos Aires. Running time, 90 MINS.

First of a batch of historical pix, inspired by the Peron government's policy of boosting a nationalist spirit, every trick was tried to turn this into a boxoffice hit. But it is not. Film holds no interest for U. S. audiences.

Too bad so much coin and effort was wasted on such a puerile story. Not even the reconstruction of old Buenos Aires is convincing. The sets are obviously sets, and the melodrama is just as false.

The drummer of Tacuari is a youngster who flees from the despotic guardianship of a royalist uncle to join the patriots fighting for Argentine independence. Enlisted by General Belgrano as a drummer boy, he meets his patriot father on the field of Tacuari (historic battle won by the patriots). Both die heroically together.

Francisco Martinez Allende, as the drummer boy's father, carries off all the acting honors. Young Juan Carlos Barbieri is spontaneous and sincere as the drummer boy, but he is not an actor yet. A wonderful make-up job has been done on Mario Vanarelli as General Belgrano and he gives a genuine and authentic performance. The photography by Humberto Peruzzi is better than usual, especially the battle scenes. Director Carlos Borcosque relied on the help of army staff officers for these big battle scenes.

Previously Argentine studios have excelled at making historical pix but in this case Emelco, new to the game, has erred by trying to achieve a very bright light with a very small candle.
Nid.

Miniature Reviews

"Sealed Verdict" (Par). Draggy story of War Guilt trials. Ray Milland and newcomer Florence Marly starred.

"The Saxon Charm" (U-I). Sophisticated character study of a Broadway heel; Montgomery-Hayward will help b.o. will help b.o.

"My Dear Secretary" (UA-Popkin). Screwball comedy, hinging mainly on Keenan Wynn, that will score profitably.

"Station West" (RKO). Sturdy whodunit with period western background. Good b.o. prospects.

"Behind Locked Doors" (EL). Program melodrama with action localed in insane asylum. Okay supporter.

"Walk a Crooked Mile" (Col). Exciting yarn of atomic secrets and Red spies.

"Desperadoes of Dodge City" (Rep). Good Allan "Rocky" Lane actioner for the western trade.

"Kidnapped" (Mono). Mildly entertaining screen adaptation of the Robert Louis Stevenson classic with Roddy McDowall.

"Shanghai Chest" (Mono). Verbose murder-mystery featuring Roland Winters as Charlie Chan.

Sealed Verdict

Hollywood, Sept. 3.
Paramount release of Robert Fellows production. Stars Ray Milland, Florence Marly. Directed by Lewis Allen. Screenplay, Jonathan Latimer; based on novel by Lionel Shapiro; camera, Leo Tover; process photography, Farciot Edouart; special effects, Gordon Jennings; editor, Alma Macrorie; music, Hugo Friedhofer. Tradeshown Sept. 3, '48. Running time, 82 MINS.
Major Robert Lawson.....Ray Milland
Themis DeLisle..........Florence Marly
Captain Kinsella...Broderick Crawford
General Otto Steigmann......John Hoyt
Captain Lance Nissen.....John Ridgely
Jacob Meyersohn........Ludwig Donath
Slava Rodal..............Norbert Schiller
Lieutenant Parker..........Dan Tobin
Camilla Cameron.......Olive Blakeney
Captain Gribemont.......Marcel Journet
Private Clay Hockland..........Paul Lees
Mr. Elmer Hockland..........James Bell
Mrs. Cora Hockland.....Elizabeth Risdon
Colonel Pike.............Frank Conroy
Mrs. Emma Steigmann.......Celia Lovsky
Erika Wagner............June Jeffery
Maria Romanek...........Patricia Miller
Dr. Bossin.............Selmar Jackson
General Kirkwood.......Charles Evans

"Sealed Verdict" says a lot of things that need saying about unregenerate Nazis, but the telling is laborious and complicated and the headline values aren't what they were a year ago. Ray Milland, playing a GI prosecutor on the Judge Advocate General's staff in occupied Germany, may be counted on for some draw. Florence Marly, Czech import, is none too impressive in her U. S. debut, hampered as she is by unflattering photography.

Plot has its counterpart in the Nurenberg trials. Plagued by doubts that the Nazi suspect for whom he has secured a hanging sentence may be innocent, Milland goes overboard looking for evidence that may upset the hard-won guilty verdict. Rumors sweep through the underground that the Nazi, played brilliantly by John Hoyt, may not be strung up. Milland prevents the guy from becoming a "martyr" by removing from a deep scar in Hoyt's cheek a vial of poison the villain had planned taking before the sentence could be carried through.

Plethora of sub-plots makes the story drag. Miss Marly, suspected of being a Nazi sympathizer, because of her testimony in Hoyt's favor, is really a patriot, it develops. She had hobnobbed with Hoyt in order to get the goods on him. Audience sympathy is sidetracked with portrayal of Norbert Schiller as an anti-Nazi sadist who gets his kicks out of seeing the krauts executed. Paul Lees plays a GI who gets a fraulein "in trouble." He's killed in an accident and his parents, Elizabeth Risdon and James Bell, come over to Germany to adopt the half-jerry offspring. Pic's comparatively short running time isn't sufficient to develop the parade of characters convincingly.

Milland, looking properly harried, gives his usual stalwart performance, and gets considerable aid from Broderick Crawford, John Ridgely, Dan Tobin, Paul Lees, Frank Conroy and Charles Evans, on the side of law and order and Miss Marley and Schiller. James Bell and Elizabeth Risdon are excellent.

Exteriors aren't the novelty they were, but lensmen Leo Tover, Farciot Edouart and Gordon Jennings have achieved some remarkable shots and effects for the Jonathan Latimer screenplay. Robert Fellows production is truly distinctive in the casting and technical ends, and Lewis Allen's direction milked the involved script for all it is worth. *Mike.*

The Saxon Charm

(One Song)

Universal release of Jospeh Sistrom production. Stars Robert Montgomery, Susan Hayward, John Payen, Audrey Totter; features Henry Morgan, Harry Von Zell. Direction and screenplay Claude Binyon. Novel by Frederick Wokeman; camera. Milton Kramer; editor, Paul Weatherwax; music, Walter Scharf. Tradeshown N.Y. Aug. 27, '48. Running time 88 MINS.

Matt Saxon	Robert Montgomery
Janet Busch	Susan Hayward
Eric Busch	John Payne
Alma	Audrey Totter
Hermy	Henry Morgan
Zack Humber	Harry Von Zell
Dolly Humber	Cara Willaims
Captain Chatham	Chill Wills
Vivian Saxon	Heather Angel

"The Saxon Charm," based on Frederic Wakeman's so-so second novel, following his smash best-seller and cinematic hit in "The Hucksters," is a sophisticated and slick character study of a Broadway heel. Saddled, however, with an unpleasant theme and some ultra-smart talk about life and the theatre, this film may face tough sledding in the hinterlands despite the marquee pull of Robert Montgomery and Susan Hayward.

In the screenplay adaptation, Claude Binyon hewed closely to the novelistic style, depending too much on words and not enough on action. As a result, while the gab has brilliance, the film lacks pace and development. Directorially, Binyon, in his first megging job succeeds in composing several absorbingly acidulous sequences, but the film as a whole misses that mounting tension level or grand climax needed to wrap up both character and plot.

As Matt Saxon, the legit producer, Montgomery oozes with nastiness in his portrait of an egomaniac with less talent than gall. Montgomery is alternately smooth and violent, but always detestable. Only a superficial attempt is made, however, to probe the inner-springs of the Saxon character to supply the motivation for the viciousness.

Pic's yarn revolves around a group of people who are caught, and almost crushed, in a net of personal relations with Saxon. Topping the list is a novelist (John Payne) who gets his nerves frayed under pressure of revising his first play in accordance with Saxon's advice. Also caught up in the whirl of Saxon's whimsical insolence are the novelists's wife (Susan Hayward), Saxon's girl friend (Audrey Totter), and a commonplace billionaire legit angel (Harry Von Zell).

After running this crowd through a mill, Saxon gets his come-uppance when it's discovered that he's strictly a no-talent guy. At the fadeout, Saxon is completely isolated with a payoff shiner from his erstwhile novelist protege. This is the only relief to otherwise depressing spectacle of a scoundrel at work.

Solid performances by the rest of the cast help Montgomery carry the central load of the film. Montgomery ably projects the twisted elements in Saxon's personality although the lines don't permit a rounded, complex portrayal. As the stage-struck novelist, Payne draws sympathy in a well-turned thesping job.

Subordinate parts accorded to Susan Hayward and Audrey Totter are both handled competently. Miss Totter, who is not photographed to best advantage, executes the film's sole number, "I'm In the Mood for Love," in superb style against a nitery background. The Jimmy McHugh-Dorothy Fields oldie, incidentally, still rates as one of the top pop classics.

Production values in the film are buffed down to high sheen as evidenced in a number of elegant settings and overall slick technical execution. Walter Scharf's musical background is good. *Herm.*

My Dear Secretary

United Artists release of Harry M. Popkin (Leo C. Popkin) production. Stars Laraine Day, Kirk Douglas, Keenan Wynn, Helen Walker; features Rudy Vallee, Florence Bates. Directed and written by Charles Martin. Camera, Joseph Biroc; editor, Arthur H. Nadel; score, Heinz Roemheld. Previewed Loew's Orpheum, N. Y., Sept. 2, '48. Running time, 94 MINS.

Stephanie Gaylord	Laraine Day
Owen Waterbury	Kirk Douglas
Ronnie Hastings	Keenan Wynn
Elsie	Helen Walker
Charles Harris	Rudy Vallee
Mrs .Reeves	Florence Bates
Deveny	Alan Mowbray
Scott	Grady Sutton
Mary	Irene Ryan
Dawn O'Malley	Gale Robbins
Felicia	Virginia Hewitt
Taxi Driver	Abe Reynolds
Hilda Sneebacher	Jody Gilbert
Miss Pidgeon	Helene Stanley
Process Server	Joe Kirk
Publisher	Russell Hicks
Miss Gee	Gertrude Astor
Male Secretary	Martin Lamont

Harry M. Popkin, in his initial try for United Artists, has come up with a welcome batch of slapstick that should score nicely with the folks who like their gags broad and their situations whacky. Laraine Day and Kirk Douglas have the leading romantic roles, but they're just backdrops for the drolleries of Keenan Wynn, who should account for quite a few stubs through the chopper when the word-of-mouth on this one gets around.

There's not much story to "My Dear Secretary," even as whacky comedies go, and that's probably just as well, as long as the yaks come frequently. As a matter of fact, the film's one letdown is when the story gets in the way, about two-thirds through, and the guffaws are temporarily stymied behind the plot.

Charles Martin has both written and directed the tale, which finds Douglas highly-successful fiction writer with a penchant for sexretaries whose ability at shorthand and typing are understandably secondary. Wynn is a next-door neighbor who, aside from doing a bit of cooking and ironing for his pal, helps him cast the femmes for the late-evening dictation sessions. Miss Day, of course, is one who won't fall into the mold—and doesn't earn a mink coat. She marries the guy, instead.

The yarn itself is not one for the kiddies—although they'll get a load of laughs out of such Wynn business as his shirt-ironing routine and his baking of popovers. Unfortunately, however, there are also spaces when the natural Wynn comedy gets too diluted and Martin's script shows signs of his strain and struggle to thicken it up. Situations and gags, while generally on the original side, are too often forced.

Miss Day is a moderately competent comedienne but, in a peculiar blonde hair-do, looks hardly worth the trouble Douglas goes to to get her. Her vis-a-vis does a little better than she, but they both lack the full-spirited ease for this type of fast-moving screwballism. Fortunately, Wynn makes up for part of that lack and such minor characters as Florence Bates, Alan Mowbray and Irene Ryan, add the rest. Rudy Vallee is his usual unmoving self, and Helen Walker is an ex-secretary who plays a relatively minor role.

Direction, in keeping with the writing, is often breathless—until it gets tangled in the plot for that short midstretch. Likewise the editing, which is sometimes fast to the point of jumpiness.

Production, while showing signs of corner-cutting here and there, is plenty adequate for this type of film. It is justifiably proportioned to the picture's potentialities. *Herb.*

Station West

(SONGS)

Hollywood, Sept. 3.

RKO release of Robert Sparks production. Stars Dick Powell, Jane Greer; features Agnes Moorehead, Burl Ives, Tom Powers, Gordon Oliver, Steve Brodie, Guinn "Big Boy" Williams, Raymond Burr, Regis Toomey. Directed by Sidney Lanfield. Screenplay, Frank Fenton, Winston Miller; novel by Luke Short; camera, Harry J. Wild; editor, Frederic Knudtson; music, Heinz Roemheld; songs, Mort Greene, Leigh Harline. Tradeshown Sept. 1, '48. Running time, 91 MINS.

Haven	Dick Powell
Charlie	Jane Greer
Mrs. Caslon	Agnes Moorehead
Hotel Clerk	Burl Ives
Captain Iles	Tom Powers
Prince	Gordon Oliver
Stellman	Steve Brodie
Mick	Guinn "Big Boy" Williams
Mark Bristow	Raymond Burr
Goddard	Regis Toomey
Cook	Olin Howlin
Pianist	John Berkes
Jerry	Michael Steele
Pete	Dan White
Ben	John Kellogg
Bartender	John Doucette
Sheriff	Charles Middleton
Girl	Suzi Crandall

A zingy whodunit plot has been adapted to a western setting, giving "Station West" a modern touch that makes for good entertainment. B. o. returns should please. Story is one that could have worn a modern garb and is told in the popular style of private eye-versus-crook melodrama.

Sidney Lanfield's direction equips the film with a fast pace and tough action. The plot twists are accomplished with slick dialog, the punchlines provoking genuine chuckles of appreciation. Players enter into the spirit of the "new-look for westerns" style with which film has been clothed. Dick Powell, one of the screen's better tough guy investigators, gives a slick interpretation and Jane Greer makes for a luscious co-star in the actionful doings.

Topnotch script by Frank Fenton and Winston Miller, adapted from the Luke Short novel, concerns an undercover military investigator and his looksee into the murder of two soldiers at a western outpost. The crime boss of the prairie town is Miss Greer, a fact that adds complications, and pleasure, to Powell's work. In keeping with whodunit plots, there are plenty of red herrings around to keep Powell and the audience guessing before the swift finish is reached.

Picture is launched on a suspense keynote and mood is sustained throughout. There's a terrific fight between Powell and Guinn "Big Boy" Williams in early footage that establishes toughness of entire movement. Repartee that passes between principals gives a lighter touch that further emphasizes the building tension.

Two songs are advantageously spotted. Miss Greer takes able care of "Sometime Remind Me to Tell You." Burl Ives, laconic hotel keeper, injects his folk style on "The Sun is Shining Warm," reprised several times in score. Both tunes were cleffed by Mort Greene and Leigh Harline.

Backing the interesting work of the stars are Agnes Moorehead, Tom Powers, Gordon Oliver, Steve Brodie, Williams, Raymond Burr, Regis Toomey, Olin Howlin, John Berkes and others.

Film has been given smartly valued production supervision by Robert Sparks, who has geared it for a ready acceptance by ticket buyers. Class lensing by Harry J. Wild and an excellent score by Heinz Roemheld are slick assists. Editing is tight, in some instances so tight that motivation becomes a bit too cryptic, even for a cryptically-styled yarn. *Brog.*

Behind Locked Doors

Hollywood, Sept. 4.

Eagle Lion release of Eugene Ling (ARC) production. Stars Lucille Bremer, Richard Carlson; features Douglas Fowley, Ralf Harolde. Directed by Oscar Boetticher. Screenplay, Malvin Wald, Eugene Ling from story by Wald; camera, Guy Roe; editor, Norman Colbert. At Vogue, Hollywood, Sept. 3, '48. Running time, 61 MINS.

Kathy Lawrence	Lucille Bremer
Ross Stewart	Richard Carlson
Larson	Doug Fowley
Dr. Clifford Porter	Tom Browne Henry
Judge Drake	Herbert Heyes
Fred Hopps	Ralf Harolde
Madge Bennett	Gwen Donovan
Topper	Morgan Farley
Mr. Purvis	Trevor Bardette
Jim	Dickie Moore

"Behind Locked Doors" is an okay programmer. Its action is laid in a private sanitarium and there is nicely paced suspense in the development as directed by Oscar Boetticher. Production values are modest but expert for budget allotment and Eugene Ling shaped them to get the most for expenditure.

Plot deals with a private detective who has himself committed to a booby hatch where, it is suspected, a political crook is hiding from the police. His outside contact is a femme reporter, who poses as his wife and the pair are interested in a \$10,000 reward posted for the crook's arrest.

There is a gradually mounting suspense as Richard Carlson, private eye, gets nearer his objective, but before he can complete his job, the crook gets wise and finale winds up with gunplay and brutality as a dangerous patient gets loose and runs amok. Malvin Wald and Ling did the okay script from Wald's original.

Carlson and Lucille Bremer do

good teamwork in the top roles. Nice character work comes from Douglas Fowley as a sadistic sanitarium guard; Ralf Harolde as a sympathetic attendant; Herbert Heyes, the politician; Tom Browne Henry, Owen Donovan and others.

Photography, settings, editing and other technical functions measure up. *Brog.*

Walk a Crooked Mile

Hollywood, Sept. 4.

Columbia release of Edward Small (Grant Whytock) production. Stars Louis Hayward, Dennis O'Keefe; features Louise Allbritton, Carl Esmond, Onslow Stevens. Directed by Gordon Douglas. Screenplay, George Bruce; story, Bertram Millhauser; camera, George Robinson; editor, James E. Newcom; music, Paul Sawtell; narration, Reed Hadley. Previewed Aug. 31, '48. Running time, 90 MINS.

Philip Grayson	Louis Hayward
Daniel O'Hara	Dennis O'Keefe
Dr. Toni Neva	Louise Allbritton
Dr. Ritter Van Stolb	Carl Esmond
Igor Braun	Onslow Stevens
Krebs	Raymond Burr
Dr. Frederick Townsend	Art Baker
Dr. William Forrest	Lowell Gilmore
Anton Radchek	Philip Van Zandt
Dr. Romer Allen	Charles Evans
Carl Benish	Frank Ferguson
Alison	Jimmy Lloyd
Potter	Bert Davidson
Ivan	Paul Bryar
Feodore	Howard J. Negley
Curly	Crane Whitley
Adolph Mizner	Grandon Rhodes
Miller	Keith Richards
Landlady	Tamara Shayne
Narrator	Reed Hadley

The documentary technique gives a factual gloss to the high melodramatics of "Walk a Crooked Mile." Film is a solid example of action entertainment with a strong appeal to fans of rugged, exciting spy antics and super sleuthing. It will give a good account of itself at the boxoffice.

Exploitable material concerns atomic secrets and thefting of atom plans by a clever spy ring. It's timely, well told with a matter-of-fact air that heightens excitement. Crook wits are pitted against those of the FBI and Scotland Yard and the action is documented with details of methodical steps taken by law enforcement organizations to get their man.

A Southern California atom plant is losing its top secrets and the FBI and Scotland Yard, in the respective persons of Dennis O'Keefe and Louis Hayward, join forces to run down the criminals. Action swings to San Francisco and back to the southland, punching hard all the time under the knowledgable direction of Gordon Douglas. On-the-site filming of locales adds authenticity as Douglas spins the yarn along at a fast, engrossing pace.

George Bruce has loaded his script with nifty twists that add air of reality to the meller doings in the Bertram Millhauser story. Dialog is good and situations believably developed, even the highly contrived melodramatic finale. Documentary flavor is forwarded by Reed Hadley's credible narration chore.

Hayward and O'Keefe make an expert team of hard-working Government experts, and the featured players back stars' work with capable performances. Onslow Stevens, as kingpin of the "comrade" spy ring, and his aides, Raymond Burr, Philip Van Zandt, Charles Evans, Frank Ferguson, supply plenty of menace. Louise Allbriton, a suspected femme scientist; Carl Esmond, Art Baker, Tamara Shayne are among others who point up their work.

Grant Whytock has guided the Edward Small production for Columbia release with a showmanly style that is primed for strong exploitation selling. Paul Sawtell's score, outstanding lensing by George Robinson, smooth editing by James E. Newcom and other technical credits lend gloss to production. *Brog.*

Desperadoes of Dodge City

Hollywood, Sept. 4.

Republic release of Gordon Kay production. Stars Allan "Rocky" Lane; features Eddy Waller, Mildred Coles, Roy Barcroft, Tristram Coffin, William Phipps, James Craven. Directed by Philip Ford. Original screenplay, Bob Williams; camera, John MacBurnie; editor, Harold Minter. Previewed Sept. 1, '48. Running time, 60 MINS.

Allan "Rocky" Lane	Allan "Rocky" Lane
His Stallion	Black Jack
Nugget Clark	Eddy Waller
Gloria Lamoreaux	Mildred Coles
Homsteader	Roy Barcroft
Ace Durant	Tristram Coffin
Ted Loring	William Phipps
Cal Sutton	James Craven
Stockton	John Hamilton
Jim	Edward Cassidy
Henry	House Peters, Jr.
Pete	Dale Van Sickel
Mary	Peggy Wynne
Jake	Ted Mapes

"Desperadoes of Dodge City" measures up to all demands of the western market. Latest entry in the Allan "Rocky" Lane series from Republic, film is sturdy fodder for the Saturday juve trade.

This time Lane has to save a caravan of homesteaders from the murderous raids of a gang of badlands outlaws. He doesn't figure on doing it all by himself; the U. S. cavalry is to be called in an escort. The order for the cavalry action is swiped by the outlaw chief and Lane has a tough time trying to identify the crook and regain the military paper.

How he does it has been expertly set down in the Bob Williams script, and Philip Ford's direction insures plenty of rugged action. There's a bit more emphasis on characterization than in the usual western, but not enough to get in the way of the speedy pace. Lane's stallion, Black Jack, has a few tricky moments that will please the kiddies, and the supporting players measure up. Rating mention are Eddye Waller, Mildred Coles, Roy Barcroft, Tristram Coffin, William Phipps and James Craven.

Gordon Kay has given film good stock production values with full use made of outdoor setting by John MacBurnie's lensing. Editing holds film to fast 60 minutes. *Brog.*

Kidnapped

Hollywood, Sept. 4.

Monogram release of Lindsley Parsons (Roddy McDowall-Ace Herman) production. Stars Roddy McDowall; features Sue England, Dan O'Herlihy, Roland Winters, Jeff Corey. Directed by William Beaudine. Screenplay, W. Scott Darling; from Robert Louis Stevenson novel; camera, William Sickner; editor, Leonard W. Herman; music, Edward J. Kay. Previewed Sept. 2, '48. Running time, 81 MINS.

David Balfour	Roddy McDowall
Aileen Fairlie	Sue England
Alan Breck	Dan O'Herlihy
Captain Hoseason	Roland Winters
Shuan	Jeff Corey
Ebenezer	Houseley Stevenson
Rankeillor	Erskine Sanford
Fairlie	Alex Frazer
Innkeeper's Wife	Winefriede McDowall
Ransome	Bobby Anderson
Janet Clouston	Janet Murdoch
The Red Fox	Olaf Hytten
Mungo	Erville Alderson

Robert Louis Stevenson's swashbuckler of feuding Scots and foul play in the 18th century has lost a lot of its punch in the screen adaptation. "Kidnapped" is only mildly entertaining, telling its story with a too leisurely pace that keeps things at a walk for 81 minutes. Lesser situations will find it acceptable if coupled with strong exploitation. Otherwise, it's for supporting positions.

Sight values obtained on a light budget demonstrate plenty of production ingenuity and if similar resourcefulness had been used in unfolding the story, film would have been more promising. Lindsley Parsons rates a nod for production framework and slick twists that would indicate a higher budget but should have insured faster action for needed entertainment values.

The Stevenson classic concerns a young Scot who comes to claim an inheritance from his uncle. Latter has him kidnapped and shipped off to slavery but lad is saved by a political adventurer. The pair fight their way across country, picking up, en route, a young girl. After many narrow escapes, threesome confront the wicked uncle and secure the boy's estate.

Roddy McDowall portrays the young Scot and does well enough in the role. (Actor also served as associate producer with Ace Herman on the film.) Dan O'Herlihy is the political adventurer and Sue England the pert young miss who joins the safari across Scotland. Villainy is supplied by Roland Winters as Capt. Hoseason, Jeff Corey as the drunken mate, and Houseley Stevenson, the wicked uncle.

William Beaudine's direction has kept the action slow and missed on injecting sufficient swash and buckle in handling the W. Scott Darling script. William Sickner's camera has captured several artistic seascapes of a brigatine under full canvas and otherwise gives film a good lens dressing. *Brog.*

XIVth Olympiad—The Glory of Sport
(Color)
(BRITISH)

London, Sept. 1.

GFD release of Castleton Knight production. Camera, Stanley Sayer; editor, Roy Drew. Running time, 130 MINS.

Produced with sufficient speed to ensure topicality, this magnificent Technicolor record of the Olympic Games, completed within three weeks after event's conclusion, is at once a tribute not only to all the competitors but to all competing nations. Filmed without frills, the camera takes the place of the reporter in presenting a complete, comprehensive and memorable picture of the Games, without any suggestion of national bias and with a fairness worthy of comendation.

From the opening sequences in Greece, to the winter sports in St. Moritz, and finally through to the main attractions at Wembley Stadium, it's a spectacle of action and suspense, packing as much dramatic effect as the best studio productions. Inevitably, much has been omitted, but conversely the highlights of a crowded three weeks have been crammed into this opus, and any omissions of the camera are more than made good by the team of commentators, headed by Bill Stern, Ted Husing, Stewart MacPherson and other wellknown mike reporters, all of whom do their jobs efficiently, and without a suggestion of facetiousness.

British version, one of 16 being shown simultaneously throughout the world, puts the Games in their proper perspective. Americans who see it will be proud of the achievements of their countryfolk, but will also honor and pay tribute to the skill and courage of their competitors. *Myro.*

Shanghai Chest

Hollywood, Sept. 4.

Monogram release of James S. Burkett production. Features Roland Winters, Mantan Moreland, Deannie Best, John Alvin, Victor Sen Young, Tim Ryan. Directed by William Beaudine. Screenplay, W. Scott Darling and Sam Newman from story by Newman; camera, William Sickner; editors, Otto Lovering, Ace Herman. Reviewed Sept. 3, '48. Running time, 65 MINS.

Charlie Chan	Roland Winters
Birmingham	Mantan Moreland
Phyllis	Deannie Best
Vic Armstrong	John Alvin
Tommy Chan	Victor Sen Young
Lt. Ruark	Tim Ryan
Judge Armstrong	Pierre Watkin
D. A. Bronson	Russell Hicks
Pindello	Philip Van Zandt
Finley	George Eldredge
Willie	Willie Best
Ed Seward	Tristram Coffin
Mr. Grail	Milton Parsons
Cartwright	Edward Coke
Bates	Olaf Hytten
Walter Somervale	Erville Alderson
Officer Murphy	Charlie Sullivan
Custodian	Paul Scardon
Jailer	William Ruhl
Landlady	Lois Austin
Miss Lee	Chabing
Stacey	John Shay

Latest Charlie Chan is so loaded with pseudo-Chinese wisdom that thesps find it difficult to sweep through the maze into film's cloudy plot. "Shanghai Chest" will probably hold up in its intended lower rung rack though it is rather dull material.

Roland Winters particularly must have found the dialog very difficult to mouth during the greater part of film's 65-minute running time. Supporting players fight a static battle in their effort to stay abreast of the entangled, triple-murder plot. Deannie Best turns in the only really bad performance, but limited screen time reduces all the negations to a minimum.

W. Scott Darling and Sam Newman's screenplay brings Winters into scene with proverbs trained on a dead man who leaves his fingerprints in plain view after each of three murders. Detective eventually traces the culprit sporting the dead man's fingertips. Needless to say, he is always within firing range but never within suspicion.

William Beaudine did the utmost with his directional chores but plot's verbosity curtailed his power to bring in a sharp, low budget thriller to the screen. James S. Burkett's production leaves much to be desired. *Free.*

Miniature Reviews

"Johnny Belinda" (WB). Fine performances by Jane Wyman, Lew Ayres, others. B.o. outlook excellent.

"Apartment for Peggy" (Color) (20th). Heart-warming mixture of housing problems of G. I. student couple and philosophy. A b.o. standout.

'Miss Tatlock's Millions" (Par). Broad farce comedy, good entertainment, starring upcoming young players.

"Luck of the Irish" (20th). Tyrone Power, Anne Baxter in a whimsical tale about a leprechaun. Should do okay.

"Cry of the City" (20th), Exceptional chase melodrama with good b.o. outlook.

"The Girl from Manhattan" (UA). Dorothy Lamour, George Montgomery, Charles Laughton in trite story. Dull b.o.

"Smart Girls Don't Talk" (WB). Gangster actioner slowed by too much gabbing. Mild boxoffice prospects.

"Saraband for Dead Lovers." (British). Boff British historical romance in color, with Flora Robson, Francoise Rosay.

"Moonrise" (Rep). Morbid melodrama, well - made . but with limited appeal.

"The Gentleman From Nowhere" (Col). Okay dualer.

"Symphonie Pastorale" (French). Pierre Blanchar and Michele Morgan in solid sureseater b.o.

"Marriage In The Shadows" (Indie). German film's anti-Nazi theme is handled without originality.

Johnny Belinda

Hollywood, Sept. 25.

Warner Bros. release of Jerry Wald production. Stars Jane Wyman, Lew Ayres; features Charles Bickford, Agnes Moorehead, Stephen McNally, Jan Sterling, Rosalind Ivan. Directed by Jean Negulesco. Screenplay, Irmgard von Cube, Allen Vincent; from stage play by Elmer Harris; camera, Ted McCord; music, Max Steiner; editor, David Weisbart. Tradeshown Sept. 25, '48. Running time, 101 MINS.

Belinda	Jane Wyman
Dr. Robt. Richardson	Lew Ayres
Black McDonald	Charles Bickford
Aggie	Agnes Moorehead
Locky	Stephen McNally
Stella	Jan Sterling
Mrs. Poggety	Rosalind Ivan
Pacquet	Dan Seymour
Mrs. Lutz	Mabel Paige
Mrs. McKee	Ida Moore
Defense Attorney	Alan Napier
Ben	Monte Blue
Mountie	Douglas Kennedy
Interpreter	James Craven
Floyd McQuiggen	Richard Taylor
Fergus McQuiggen	Richard Walsh
Mrs. Tim Moore	Joan Winfield
Rector	Ian Wolfe
Judge	Holmes Herbert
Dr. Gray	Jonathan Hale
Tim Moore	Ray Montgomery

"Johnny Belinda" is a fine presentation of a tragedy with a happy ending. It is somber, tender, moving, told with a compelling sensitiveness that will capture critical attention. It will need selling but has the elements adaptable to high exploitation. There are a number of ten-twent-thirt 'meller angles that can be ballyhooed for strong response among the general public, particularly the femmes.

"Belinda" is a story that easily could have become a display of scenery-chewing theatrics. It has its theatrics but they spring from a rather earnest development of story fundamentals, tastefully handled. Jean Negulesco's direction never overplays the heartstrings, yet keeps them constantly twanging, and evidences a sympathetic instinct that is reflected in the performances.

Jane Wyman essays a daring role, in that she portrays a mute slattern completely devoid of film glamor. It is a personal success; a socko demonstration that an artist can shape a mood and sway an audience through projected emotions without a spoken word.

Without distracting from the impact she gives her role of the deaf and dumb girl, the character gains in strength from the principals who perform with her.

There are few actors who can convey the sincerity that Lew Ayres gives to the screen. There is an implication of theatric manners evident in earlier sequences, but this nonchalant shading is soon lost as he delves into the assignment of the doctor devoted to his deaf-mute patient—and patients who are anything but mute.

Plot essentials cover a deaf-mute girl, dwelling with her father and resentful aunt on a barren farm in Nova Scotia. To the small fishing-farming community comes a young doctor, idealistic and needing life away from the multitude. He becomes interested in helping the mute girl and makes her life easier by understanding and instruction in sight language.

A village romeo rapes her. She has a baby and events moves forward until the deaf-mute kills her ravisher when he tries to take the baby. She is tried for murder and saved at the finale by the confession of the rapist's wife.' The girl and her child find future happiness with the doctor.

Charles Bickford walks off with the assignment of Belinda's father. His handling of the part of the dour Scot farmer registers strongly, pulling audience interest all the way. Agnes Moorehead talentedly portrays the girl's aunt, whose sternness breaks when Belinda finds herself in trouble. It's another ace job in a strong lineup of strong performances.

Stephen McNally, the heavy; Jan Sterling, village belle and McNally's bride; Rosalind Ivan, Mabel Paige and Ida Moore; town gossips; Dan Seymour, village storekeeper; are among the many in the cast who back the principals with creditable work.

Jerry Wald's production supervision misses no bets in presenting the Irmgard von Cube-Allen Vincent script, from Elmer Harris' stage play, for outstanding attention. It is a class realization on story merits, top casting and exploitable material. Drab locale, somber yet picturesque, has been compellingly captured by Ted McCord's low key photography and the mood is further carried out by the excellent Max Steiner score. Editing makes the most of the leisurely, but never slow, pace and other technical credits are strong.
Brog.

Apartment for Peggy
(COLOR)

Hollywood, Sept. 8.

20th-Fox release of William Perlberg production. Stars Jeanne Crain, William Holden, Edmund Gwenn; features Gene Lockhart, Griff Barnett, Randy Stuart. Directed and written by George Seaton. Story, Faith Baldwin; camera (Technicolor), Harry Jackson; editor, Robert Simpson; music, David Raksin. Tradeshown Sept. 7, '48. Running time, 96 MINS.

Peggy	Jeanne Crain
Jason	William Holden
Prof. Henry Barnes	Edmund Gwenn
Prof. Edward Bell	Gene Lockhart
Dr. Conway	Griff Barnett
Dorothy	Randy Stuart
Ruth	Marion Marshall
Jeanne	Pati Behrs
Prof. Roland Pavin	Henri Letondal
Prof. T. J. Beck	Houseley Stevenson
Della	Helen Ford
Mrs. Landon	Almira Sessions
Prof. Collins	Charles Lane
Delivery Boy	Ronnold Burns
Jerry	Gene Nelson
Student	Bob Patten
Wife	Betty Ann Lynn
Nurses	{ Therese Lyon / Ann Staunton
Salesmen	{ Hal K. Dawson / Frank Scannell / Robert B. Williams

"Apartment for Peggy" is a worthy followup to 20th-Fox's fairy tale of last season, "A Miracle on 34th Street." Gently humorous and heart-warming, it spins a tale that builds audience affection as it develops. Grosses should be bright and will be particularly aided by word-of-mouth.

"Peggy" wears an unostentatious Technicolor garb to display its college background and story of G. I. life on the campus. It mixes housing problems with philosophy and has been treated by all concerned with gentle respect to make it charming entertainment.

The producer and director-scripter combination that made "Miracle" an entertaining study of human behavior, has repeated with "Peggy." As a team, William Perlberg and George Seaton sell the human interest with just the right amount of believeable hokum and heartstring tugs, and the cast plays it to the hilt.

Jeanne Crain is perfect casting for the young wife of William Holden, veteran studying under the G. I. bill. She gives the role a thoroughly believeable reading that comes off big and Holden's work matches. "Miracle's" Santa Claus, Edmund Gwenn, completes the star trio, socking over his professor of philosophy role with such deft understanding it's a joy to watch.

Seaton endows his script with modern dialog and quails not from using everyday expressions that usually are skirted in pictures. Miss Crain is pregnant, and says so. Dialog also has something to point up on postwar conditions for G.I.'s, and says it lucidly without preaching. The same goes for ignorance as the fount of trouble—personal or world—but the writing never mounts a soapbox to make its points, remembering always its entertainment aims.

Peggy is a spell-caster and injects her personality into the college, its profs and her husband, while giving them all more than she takes away. She talks Gwenn out of the use of his attic for a home, sways him away from a cherished suicide plan, and generally spreads love and joy on all whom she touches. Among a number of highlight scenes that Seaton's direction wallops over is the very funny one wherein Gwenn's friends believe he has taken sleeping pills and keep him walking, while all the time he's been given a mickey and wants to seek privacy.

A strong group of Gwenn's elderly cronies is composed of Gene Lockhart, Griff Barnett, Henri Letondal and Houseley Stevenson. They give a strong account in the entertainment, and particularly heartwarming are their musicales as they get together for fiddling and fluting. Randy Stuart, Charles Lane, Betty Ann Lynn, Almira Sessions, Marion Marshall, Pati Behrs and others furnish excellent support.

Production mounting has been expertly fitted to story's locale, and color lensing by Harry Jackson gives the physical values and the players a beautiful display. Special photographic effects are good and editing holds footage to 96 minutes.
Brog.

Miss Tatlock's Millions

Hollywood, Sept. 10.

Paramount release of Charles Brackett production. Stars John Lund, Wanda Hendrix, Barry Fitzgerald, Monty Woolley; features Ilka Chase, Robert Stack, Dorothy Stickney, Elizabeth Patterson. Directed by Richard Haydn. Screenplay, Charles Brackett, Richard L. Breen; suggested by play by Jacques Deval; camera, Charles B. Lang, Jr.; editor, Everett Douglas; score, Victor Young. Tradeshown Sept. 8, '48. Running time, 99 MINS.

Burke	John Lund
Nan Tatlock	Wanda Hendrix
Denno Noonan	Barry Fitzgerald
Miles Tatlock	Monty Woolley
Cassie Van Alen	Ilka Chase
Nickey Van Alen	Robert Stack
Emily Tatlock	Dorothy Stickney
Cora	Elizabeth Patterson
Dr. Mason	Leif Erickson
Clifford Tatlock	Dan Tobin
Kamamamalua	Hilo Hattie
Fergel	Richard Rancyd

Since slapstick is having its day in the current market, "Miss Tatlock's Millions" should give good account of itself at the box-office. It adds up to okay entertainment with a load of chuckles springing from the broad farcing style Richard Haydn has used for his first screen directing stint.

Basically, story and characters are much to-do about nothing, but the pace is fast, the dialog flip and sophisticated, and the playing expert. This gives the material a surface brightness that makes it look better than it is.

Haydn's directorial debut is creditable. He sets up his characters and situations to keep the chuckles rolling from the broad antics. Plot concerns a screwball family and the idiot heir to millions, with a number of tangent ramifications that keep the fun pot boiling.

John Lund and Wanda Hendrix team brightly in the principal roles and film receives major assists from Barry Fitzgerald, Monty Woolley, Ilka Chase and others. Fitzgerald, keeper of the idiot heir, has lost his charge, presumably in a fire in Hawaii. A reading of the will requires the looney's presence so Fitzgerald hires Lund, film stunt man, to masquerade as the cracked character. Lund does and falls in love with his "sister," Miss Hendrix, the only sane member of the Tatlock family.

Epigrams and insults fly fast and furious as plot unfolds with contrivances pointed toward bringing the heroine and hero together for a finale clinch. Romance is saved when the real heir appears, complete with native wife (Hilo Hattie) and a brood of offspring.

Haydn has given considerable footage to a display of the brawn of Lund and Robert Stack, romantic rivals, even to the point of neglecting Miss Hendrix in a bathing suit. However, the femmes shouldn't complain and Miss Hendrix's grownup costumes have style appeal. In addition to directing, Haydn cuts himself in for a very funny bit as an eccentric lawyer, using the name of Richard Rancyd.

In addition to principals named, suave performances are turned in by Dorothy Stickney, Elizabeth Patterson and Dan Tobin. Slapstick is run off to the accompaniment of a slick Victor Young score and camera work by Charles B. Lang, Jr., brightly displays lavish settings used to give the impression of a wealthy family. Charles Brackett's production supervision is expert, as always, as is his script collaboration with Richard L. Breen. · *Brog.*

Luck of the Irish

Twentieth-Fox release of Fred Kohlmar production. Stars Tyrone Power, Anne Baxter; features Cecil Kellaway, Lee J. Cobb, James Todd, Jayne Meadows. Directed by Henry Koster. Screenplay, Philip Dunne, based on novel by Guy and Constance Jones; music, Cyril Mockridge; camera, Joseph La Shelle; editor, J. Watson Webb, Jr. Tradeshown N. Y., Sept. 8, '48. Running time, 96 MINS.

Stephen Fitzgerald	Tyrone Power
Nora	Anne Baxter
Horace	Cecil Kellaway
D. C. Augur	Lee J. Cobb
Bill Clark	James Todd
Frances	Jayne Meadows
Taedy	J. M. Kerrigan
Higginbotham	Phil Brown
Cornelius	Charles Irwin
Augur's Secretary	Louise Lorimer
Clancy	Tim Ryan
Senator Ransom	Harry Antrim
Mrs. Augur	Margaret Wells
Butler	John Goldsworthy
Agency Manager	Dorothy Neumann
Secretary	Ruth Clifford
Receptionist	Douglas Gerrard
Greek Vendor	Tito Vuolo
Gentleman's Gentleman	Tom Stevenson
Milkman	Norman Leavitt
Irish Dancer	Frank Mitchell
Terrance	Bill Swingley
Captain of Waiters	Albert Morin
Cab Driver	Hollis Jewell
Hat Check Girl	Ann Frederick
Pickpocket	Eddie Parks
Subway Guard	John Roy
Bride	Claribel Bressel
Groom	Lee MacGregor
Singer	Jimmy O'Brien

Take some fantastic creature like a leprechaun, add to it a couple of stars like Tyrone Power and Anne Baxter, mix well with a whimsical story in modern dress, and the result should be a picture that could draw 'em all. But make the whimsy just a bit too contrived and the result is 20th-Fox's "Luck of the Irish," an entertaining little picture that misses just a bit.

With the names of Power, Miss Baxter and the catchy title, the film should have no trouble getting started in most situations. The word-of-mouth is the catch in this one. It all depends on whether the customers go for such things as a dyed-in-the-green leprechaun cavorting around Manhattan in the guise of a gentleman's gentleman. Same type of character in the current Broadway musical, "Finian's Rainbow," was acceptable, so maybe this one will be too.

Whether the customers go for the Irish type of pixie or not, they'll go for Cecil Kellaway, who plays the part in "Irish." Under the light comedy touch of director Henry Koster, Kellaway makes the character come to life in believable fashion. His every movement is tailored to the role and he's continually snatching scenes away from the stars. Irish mothers attempting to bring their kids up in the traditions of the auld sod may rebel at the leprechaun's persistent taste and apparently unquenchable thirst for good Scotch whiskey, but on Kellaway it looks good.

Power, after being saddled with the roles he had in "Nightmare Alley" and "Captain from Castile," has a part better suited to his talents as the political writer who befriends the leprechaun. Miss Baxter, on the other hand, seems wasted in a role that requires none of the heavy thesping with which she's made her mark. However, she carries off well the part of Power's vis-a-vis, making her Irish brogue sound authentic.

Story, adopted by Philip Dunne from a novel by Guy and Constance Jones, goes too far afield to be wholly believable. As a war correspondent who's freelanced around Europe after V-E Day, Power meets both the leprechaun and Miss Baxter, a native colleen, just before leaving Ireland to take a well-paying job in New York as ghost writer for a powerful publisher wishing to run for the Senate. Leprechaun, knowing Power is prostituting himself for money, turns up in N. Y. as his valet. Miss Baxter follows, the two of them work on Power and the denouement is obvious. Interspersed with the main plot are Power's half-hearted romance with the publisher's daughter and some notes on Irish folklore, showing how to trap a leprechaun and make him give up his w.k. pot of gold.

With the two stars and Kellaway taking the lead, the supporting cast follows through nicely. Talents of Lee J. Cobb, like those of Miss Baxter, seem wasted on the role of the publisher but, as usual, he turns in an ultra-neat performance. Jayne Meadows is sufficiently attractive and conniving as his daughter, out to trap Power and keep him in the family. James Todd, J. M. Kerrigan and Phil Brown are good in lesser roles.

Although the picture is no lush top-budgeter, in the modern idiom, producer Fred Kohlmar has limned it with some costly trappings. His use of a green-tinted film for all scenes supposedly shot in Ireland, incidentally, is a novel and well-executed stunt that should add exploitation value to the picture. Joseph La Sheele's camera direction is good, as is Cyril Mockridge's score. *Stal.*

Cry of the City

Hollywood, Sept. 11.

20th-Fox release of Sol C. Siegel production. Stars Victor Mature, Richard Conte; features Fred Clark, Shelley Winters, Betty Garde, Berry Kroeger, Tommy Cook, Debra Paget, Hope Emerson, Roland Winters, Walter Baldwin. Directed by Robert Siodmak. Screenplay, Richard Murphy; from novel by Henry Edward Helseth; camera, Lloyd Ahern; editor, Harmon Jones; music, Alfred Newman. Tradeshown Sept. 9, '48. Running time, 96 MINS.

Lt. Candella	Victor Mature
Martin Rome	Richard Conte
Lt. Collins	Fred Clark
Brenda	Shelley Winters
Mrs. Pruett	Betty Garde
Niles	Berry Kroeger
Tony	Tommy Cook
Teena Riconti	Debra Paget
Rose Given	Hope Emerson
Ledbetter	Roland Winters
Orvy	Walter Baldwin
Miss Boone	June Storey
Papa Roma	Tito Vuolo
Mama Roma	Mima Aguglia
Rosa	Dolores Castle
Rosa's Daughter	Claudette Ross
Perdita	Tiny Francone
Francesca	Elena Savonarola
Priest	Thomas Ingersoll
Julio	Vito Scotti
Dr. Veroff	Konstantin Shayne
Sullivan	Howard Freeman
Internes	Robert Karnes Charles Tannen
Caputo	Oliver Blake
Vaselli	Antonio Filauri
Vera	Joan Miller
Loomis	Ken Christy
Dr. Niklos	Emil Rameau
Mike	Eddie Parks
Counter Man	Charles Wagenheim
Mrs. Pruett's Mother	Kathleen Howard

The hard-hitting suspense of the chase formula has been given topnotch presentation in "Cry of the City." It's an exciting motion picture, credibly put together to wring out every bit of strong action and tension inherent in such a plot.

"City" gives Victor Mature a sturdy meller followup to "Kiss of Death," and again it's his constantly improving thespian stature that ties the yarn together, even though his character doesn't hog story interest. As Richard Widmark's role in "Kiss' was more colorful, so is Richard Conte's in "City," but it's Mature's playing that helps hold it on a credible path.

Robert Siodmak's penchant for shaping melodramatic excitement that gets through to an audience is realistically carried out in this one. By proper pacing and graphic handling he makes it believable and keeps the tension constantly mounting. Production-wise, Sol C. Siegel has been as showmanly, framing the action doings with authenticity.

The telling screenplay by Richand Murphy based on a novel, "The Chair for Martin Rome," by Henry Edward Helseth, presents Mature as a police lieutenant in homicide and Conte as a cop-killer—antagonists, although both sprung from New York's Italian sector. Essentially, plot deals with the police chase of Conte and events leading up to his demise at the hands of Mature in a climactic sidewalk duel. Both players get underneath the characters, making them real without high theatrics.

Characters are carefully spotted in script and by casting to maintain feeling of reality. Fred Clark is the laconic cop partner to Mature. Tito Vuolo and Mima Aguglia are perfect as parents of the killer, and Tommy Cook, the killer's kid brother, reads the part skillfully.

Shelley Winters sparks small assignment of a girl who drives the killer through the New York streets while an unlicensed doctor works desperately to patch up his wounds. There's a standout job by Hope Emerson, and Betty Garde, Berry Kroeger, Debra Paget, Roland Winters, Walter Baldwin, June Storey and others lend capable support.

Splendid photography of the New York locale and action has been turned in by Lloyd Ahern. Other technical credits are equally good, including tight editing, music score and special effects. *Brog.*

Girl From Manhattan

United Artists release of Benedict Bogeaus production. Stars Dorothy Lamour, George Montgomery, Charles Laughton; features Ernest Truex, Hugh Herbert, William Frawley, Constance Collier, Sara Allgood. Directed by Alfred E. Green. Original story and screenplay, Howard Estabrook; camera, Ernest Laszio; editor, James E. Smith; music, Heinz Roemheld. Tradeshown N. Y., Sept. 13, '48. Running time, 80 MINS.

Carol Maynard	Dorothy Lamour
Rev. Tom Walker	George Montgomery
The Bishop	Charles Laughton
Homer Purdy	Ernest Truex
Aaron Goss	Hugh Herbert
Mrs. Brooke	Constance Collier
Mr. Bernouti	William Frawley
Mrs. Beeler	Sara Allgood
Oscar Newsome	Frank Orth
Sam Griffin	Howard Freeman
Wilbur J. Birch	Raymond Largay
Monty	George Chandler
Dr. Moseby	Selmar Jackson
Old Woman	Adelaide De Walt Reynolds
Mr. Merkel	Maurice Cass
Jim Allison	Eddy Waller

"The Girl from Manhattan" is one of the weakest sisters out of Hollywood in some time. Despite the marquee names in the cast, the film is loaded down with a dull story, cliche dialog, stilted direction and poor thesping. It's for the double bills.

From the standpoint of constructive criticism, it's difficult to figure how a producer with the experience of Benedict Bogeaus and actors with the years of background held by Dorothy Lamour, Charles Laughton, Ernest Truex, et al, could come up with so dull a production. It's probably one of those things that looked good on paper but just couldn't make out on the screen.

Basic trouble lies in the script, an original by Howard Estabrook. Basically a story about a Yale All-American who becomes a small-town Protestant minister, it revives some of the trite situations which haven't been seen since "Way Down East" and "10 Nights in a Barroom." In this one, it's a beat-up old rooming house on which the mortgage is to be foreclosed by the villain, here in the guise of a realtor who stands to make a neat profit by selling the site for a new church and then selling the old church location as a new hotel site. Minister comes through with the necessary cash (out of his own savings, no less) to foil the villain at the last minute, and all's well.

With such a story line the cast could hardly have done better. Director Alfred E. Green apparently didn't help their cause. Miss Lamour, in the title role, is a New York model whose uncle, played by Truex, runs the boarding house. It's her second venture into straight dramatic roles (first was the recent "Lulabelle"). Laughton, as the local bishop, overacts. Montgomery does fairly well as the young minister. Truex, Hugh Herbert, William Frawley, Constance Collier and Sara Allgood are better in supporting roles.

Bogeaus' production trappings make it evident the film is no top-budgeter. Ernest Laszio's camera work and Heinz Roemheld's music are in keeping with the rest of the production. Editor James E. Smith has wisely held the running time down to 80 minutes. *Stal.*

Smart Girls Don't Talk

Warner Bros. release of Saul Elkins production. Stars Virginia Mayo, Bruce Bennett, Robert Hutton; features Richard Rober, Helen Westcott, Tom D'Andrea, Richard Benedict, Ben Welden, Richard Walsh. Directed by Richard Bare. Screenplay, William Sackheim; camera, Ted McCord; editor, Clarence Kolster; music, David Buttolph. Previewed Sept. 10, '48. Running time, 81 MINS.

Linda Vickers	Virginia Mayo
Marty Fain	Bruce Bennett
"Doc" Vickers	Robert Hutton
Sparky Lynch	Tom D'Andrea
Lieut. McReady	Richard Rober
Toni Peters	Helen Westcott
Cliff Saunders	Richard Benedict
Nelson Clark	Ben Welden
Johnny Warjak	Richard Walsh

This film would have packed a harder kick if the Burbank lot had hewed closer to the sense of the title, "Smart Girls Don't Talk." For the Warner Bros. opus which details the entanglement of a society gal with a contingent of mobster-gamblers is overloaded with too much talk of a curiously inept sort and given the short count of fast-clipped action. Despite an interesting story and adequate mountings, its over-talkiness spells mild b.o. returns.

Obviously, producer Saul Elkins intended the film to be a hard-hitting depiction of how gangsters kept a gambling den-nitery rolling by a series of murder and mayhem. Unfortunately, whenever the pic perks with a display of action, it gags on slack lines which obligato the gunplay.

The same weakness of dialog hampers the thesping of Virginia Mayo who fills in as the Park Avenuite tied to the mob. Miss Mayo, attractively photogenic as of yore, can't seem to throw herself into the spirit of the thing. Both she and Bruce Bennett, who plays the mobster chief, trip over attempts at conversational brightness which somehow miss coming off. Their lovemaking, too, is offhand and cursory.

Bennett is given a semi-sympathetic handling in the film which shows most of the foul doings committed by his aides without his specific knowledge. Treatment lends something three-dimentional to his characterization but the net result may be confused emotions to patrons who like their villains ebony-grained.

Richard Rober does excellently in the role of the thin-lipped sleuth who keeps his own counsel. Robert Hutton's slight part makes few emoting demands which are handled adequately. Other roles are nicely done.

Pic has an unpretentious production framework ample for the story it tells. Direction falls short of extracting the most from the scenes of violence spaced through the film, possibly because of curtailed footage devoted to them to fit in the chatter. Scissor might have been wielded more generously in editing. *Wit.*

Saraband for Dead Lovers

(BRITISH—COLOR)

London, Sept. 8.

GFD release of Ealing Studios-Michael Balcon production. Stars Francoise Rosay, Flora Robson, Joan Greenwood, Stewart Granger. Directed and designed by Basil Dearden, Michael Relph. Screenplay by John Dighton, Alexander Mackendrick, from novel by Helen Simpson. Editor, Michael Truman; music, Alan Rawsthorne; camera, Douglas Slocombe, Jeff Seaholme. At Rialto, London, Sept. 8, '48. Running time, 96 MINS.

Konigsmark .... Stewart Granger
Sophie Dorothea .... Joan Greenwood
Countess Platen .... Flora Robson
Electress Sophia .... Francoise Rosay
Elector Ernest Augustus .. Frederick Valk
Prince George Louis .... Peter Bull
Durer .... Anthony Quayle
Prince Charles .... Michael Gough
Frau Busche .... Megs Jenkins
Knesbeck .... Jill Balcon
Duke George William .... David Horne
Countess Eleanore .... Mercia Swinburne
Major Eck .... Cecil Trouncer
Count Platen .... Noel Howlett
Maria .... Barbara Leake
Lord of Misrule .... Miles Malleson

Colorful production, magnificent settings and costumes enhanced by unobtrusive use of Technicolor and a powerful melodramatic story of court intrigue at the House of Hanover in the early 18th century, add up to a firstrate piece of hokum entertainment. It should readily find favor on both sides of the Atlantic.

Taken from Helen Simpson's novel, the screenplay sincerely captures the atmosphere of the period. It tells the poignant story of the unhappy Princess Dorothea, compelled to marry against her will the uncouth Prince Louis to strengthen his title to the kingship of England. She's finally banished to end her life in the dismal castle of Ahlden when her plot to escape with the handsome Count Konigsmark is frustrated.

Without undue sentiment, and with emotion in the right key, the plot unfolds against the fascinating background of the Hanoverian court, with its intrigue and tragedies, its romances and miseries. Impressively mounted, with skillful handling of big crowds and a superbly staged carnival, it moves to its inevitable sombre climax of triumph on the one hand and despair on the other.

Reality is established by the excellent characterization of a well-chosen cast. Stewart Granger, as the Swedish Count Konigsmark, gives a performance that ranks with his best. Joan Greenwood is charming and colorful as the hapless Dorothea. Flora Robson is merciless as the arch intriguer at the court, who sends Konigsmark to his death and Dorothea to exile when she fails to capture the heart of the Swede. Francoise Rosay, Frederick Valk, Peter Bull and Miles Malleson act with restraint and conviction. *Myro.*

Moonrise

(SONGS)

Hollywood, Sept. 10.

Republic release of Charles Haas (Marshall Grant) production. Stars Dane Clark, Gail Russell, Ethel Barrymore; features Allyn Joslyn, Rex Ingram, Henry Morgan. Directed by Frank Borzage. Screenplay, Charles Haas; based on novel by Theodore Strauss; camera, John L. Russell; editor, Harry Keller; songs, Harry Tobias, William Lava, Theodore Strauss. At Paramount, Sept. 9, '48. Running time, 90 MINS.

Danny Hawkins .... Dane Clark
Gilly Johnson .... Gail Russell
Grandma .... Ethel Barrymore
Clem Otis .... Allyn Joslyn
Mose .... Rex Ingram
Billy Scripture .... Henry Morgan
Ken Williams .... David Street
Aunt Jessie .... Selena Royle
Jimmy Biff .... Harry Carey, Jr.
Judd Jenkins .... Irving Bacon
Jerry Sykes .... Lloyd Bridges
Uncle Joe Jingle .... Houseley Stevenson
Elmer .... Phil Brown
J. B. Sykes .... Harry V. Cheshire
Julie .... Lila Leeds

"Moonrise" is heavy melodrama, well made, but too drab. Film is adaptable to exploitation, which may aid some situations, but general outlook is not strong.

Sombre story has been unfolded leisurely by Frank Borzage's direction, in keeping with the almost morbid mood. He does manage several pulse-quickening suspense moments, though, particularly in the manhunt through swamp and southern countryside. Based on Theodore Strauss' novel of the same title, picture conerns itself with a boy marked and persecuted from childhood because his father had been hanged for murder.

Dane Clark is the tormented young man, who, in one frenzied moment, accidentally kills one of his persecutors. From then on, footage is concerned with his unhappy romance with a village school teacher and whether or not his crime will be found out. It is darkly dramatic, and had characters been a bit better rounded it could have come off solidly.

Gail Russell comes through best as the schoolteacher, honestly in love and troubled by her man's moody fear. Clark works hard with his character, and had the writing delved deeper would have appeared to better advantage. Ethel Barrymore has a six-minute bit in film's final 10 minutes, and gives it the expected assurance.

Allyn Joslyn is a good backwoods sheriff, and Rex Ingram stands out as a philosophical Negro swamp dweller, who talks out the tune, "Lonesome," by Strauss and William Lava. David Street, in small role as village orch leader, pleasingly pipes "The Moonrise Song," by Lava and Harry Tobias. Lloyd Bridges is the victim of Clark's righteous wrath, and among others who are good are Selena Royle, Irving Bacon, Houseley Stevenson and Henry Morgan, latter as a deaf mute.

Charles Haas production for Marshall Grant's indie company has given the film exactly valued physical dressing, but his scripting chore is less able. Low-key lensing by John L. Russell is expert. *Brog.*

The Gentleman From Nowhere

Hollywood, Sept. 11.

Columbia release of Rudolph C. Flothow production. Stars Warner Baxter; features Fay Baker, Luis Van Rooten, Charles Lane, Wilton Graff, Grandon Rhodes, Noel Madison. Directed by William Castle. Original screenplay, Edward Anhalt; camera, Vincent Farrar; editor, Henry Batista. At Pantages, Sept. 10, '48. Running time, 65 MINS.

Earl Donovan .... Warner Baxter
Catherine Ashton .... Fay Baker
Barton .... Luis Van Rooten
Fenmore .... Charles Lane
Larry Hendricks .... Wilton Graff
Edward Dixon .... Grandon Rhodes
Vincent Sawyer .... Noel Madison
Miss Kearns .... Victoria Horne
Bill Cook .... Don Haggerty
Henry Thompson .... William Forrest
Hoffman .... Pierre Watkin
Marshall .... Robert Emmett Keane

As a program melodrama, "The Gentleman From Nowhere" will prove okay in its market. Yarn is a bit involved for casual attention, but carries interest for the way it has been developed in direction and playing, even though devices used are standard.

Warner Baxter plays the title role as a man supposedly dead after having been involved in a robbery at a chemical plant years before. When he is hauled in by police for questioning in a warehouse robbery, an insurance detective is struck by his likeness to the dead man and seeks his aid in probing the old crime.

From there on, Baxter takes the reins in trying to clear his name so he can actually come back to life instead of posing as himself. Events move forward until Baxter proves he was framed for the crime and happy ending has a reconciliation with his wife.

Baxter, Fay Baker, the wife, and Luis Van Rooten, insurance detective do able performances that are backed up by the rest of the cast. William Castle's direction maintains a good pace, although lacking in excitement peaks, and character development is neatly worked out.

Production guidance by Rudolph C. Flothow shapes okay for light budget and technical credits are standard craftsmanship. *Brog.*

Symphonie Pastorale

(FRENCH)

Film International release of Pathe Cinema (Gibe) production. Stars Michele Morgan, Pierre Blanchar. Directed by Jean Delannoy. Screenplay, Pierre Bost, Jean Aurenche; adapted from Andre Gide novel by Delannoy and Aurenche; camera, Roger Corbeau, Armand Thirard; music, George Auric; English titles, Justin O'Brien. Previewed N. Y., Sept. 2, '48. Running time, 110 MINS.

Gertrude .... Michele Morgan
The Pastor .... Pierre Blanchar
Amelie .... Line Noro
Casteran .... Louvigny
Jacques .... Jean Desailly
Piette .... Andree Clement
Charlotte .... Rosine Luguet

(In French; English Titles)

Out of an obscure story by the Nobel prize-winning novelist, Andre Gide, the French studios have fashioned a superlative film that will rank among the top European successes shown in the U. S. since the war's end. "Symphonie Pastorale" is a tragic love story told with all the depth of an authentic work of art.

The title is ironic. Although unfolding within the pastoral quiet of a French mountainside village, the film is swept by a rising emotional turmoil that finally explodes in a shattering, inevitable denouement of anguish and death. The film has been fused together by director Jean Delannoy with sensitivity and restraint, aided by brilliant performances by Pierre Blanchar, Michele Morgan and Line Noro, an outstanding musical score by Georges Auric and superb photography.

This film is far removed from the conventional fudgy romances. It is, in all respects, an adult drama with exceedingly difficult elements that challenge the resources of understanding and sympathy. The theme involves the moral self-deception of a pastor whose love for a blind young girl turns from self-sacrifice into a smothering self-indulgence.

The story swivels around Blanchar who, as the pastor, assumes the task of rearing a blind orphan girl into womanhood. As she (Michele Morgan) matures, Blanchar transforms her into the obsessive center of his life. He becomes estranged from his wife who realizes before he does that his relationship with Miss Morgan is not entirely saintly. Out of jealousy he prevents his son from marrying the blind girl. And, out of fear of losing dependency upon him, Blanchar keeps putting off an operation to restore Miss Morgan's sight.

But with her sight restored, the girl only sees the misery which she unwittingly caused. In a smashing climactic sequence, following a poignant love scene between the pastor and Miss Morgan, the latter ends her confusion through suicide. Dragged out of the river, her wide-open eyes, now blind again, only then accuse Blanchar of his unuttered crimes against her.

Blanchar and Miss Morgan turn in powerful performances. Blanchar, in particular, draws an acute and persuasive portrait of an honest man unable to see or admit the deveil's hoof behind his saintly compassion. Line Noro, as the aging pastor's wife, also registers forcibly. The rest of the cast contribute importantly to a memorable film. *Herm.*

Marriage in the Shadows

(GERMAN)

Gramercy Films release of Defa production. Stars Paul Klinger, Ilse Stepat. Directed by Kurt Maetzig. Screenplay, Maetzig; adapted from novel by Hans Scheikart; camera, Friedel Behn-Grund, Eugen Klagemann; editor, Alice Ludwig; music, Wolfgang Zeller; English titles, Charles Clement. Previewed N. Y., Sept. 9, '48. Running time, 90 MINS.

Hans Wieland .... Paul Klinger
Elisabeth .... Ilse Steppat
Kurt Bernstein .... Alfred Balthoff
Dr. Herbert Blohm .... Claus Holm
Dr. Louis Silbermann .... Willi Prager
Fehrenbach .... Hans Leibelt
State Secretary .... Lothar Firmans
Gallenkamp .... Karl Hellmer

(In German; English Titles)

"Marriage in the Shadows," produced in Defa's Berlin studios early this year, is an uneven film that may arouse some interest in foreign language situations because of its theme. It represents the first time that Germany's slowly reviving cinema industry has dared to tackle the story of anti-Semitism during the Nazi nightmare. But other aspects of this film, unfortunately, tend to weaken the dramatic point.

The dominant flaw lies in the handling of the Nazi terror. Instead of a fresh slant born out of direct experience, Kurt Maetzig, film's writer and director, dishes out only a series of stereotypes. The Nazi psychosis and the Jewish tragedy are presented only as reflections of countless American and Russian pix on the same subject. This second-hand approach gives the film's tolerance message a peculiarly mechanical quality.

Yarn, based on an actual situation in Germany, recounts the tragic fate of a German actor and his Jewish wife who were ultimate victims of the racial purges. Beginning in 1933 when the Nazis were still underestimated, the film traces the couple's history until 1943 when an order for the deportation of all Jews forces them to commit suicide. While the bulk of the story is told conventionally, there is one graphic sequence of the Nazi hoodlums breaking up

Jewish shops and the final death scene is poignantly sad.

Paul Klinger, as the "Aryan" actor who marries his Jewish leading lady in defiance of the blood laws, registers strongly with an intense, but well-modulated performance. Ilse Steppat, as the wife, is adequate, although not wholly persuasive in the high-key emotive range. Claus Holm, as a shamefaced Nazi, and Alfred Balthoff, as a Jewish impresario, are stock characters falling patly into the film's cliches.

This production is also marred by the repetitive use of a primitive dissolve technique which gives the story a spasmodic continuity.
Herm.

We Live Again

Jewish Film Co. release of M. Babelfer-O. Fessler-A. Hamza-I. Holodenko-J. Weinfield production. Camera, Agai and Defassiaux: English titles, Charles Clement. At Stanley, N. Y., starting Sept. 4, '48. Running time, **55 MINS.**

(In Yiddish; English Titles)

This documentary, which is a strange compilation of long-familiar newsreel footage plus factual and travelog material, undoubtedly serves its purpose in pointing up the good work being done in France for children of Jewish parents killed by the Nazis. But for straight entertainment, it obviously has very limited appeal.

Picture is described as the first postwar Yiddish film; it hardly measures up to pre-war standards. Film is not apt to go over even with Jewish patrons because it's so slow and lacking in point of view.

Early sections of picture are made up of an odd collection of long-dated newsreel scenes of mass murders and arrests, and Nazi brutalities. This is soon bypassed as the vehicle becomes a travelog showing camps maintained for the unfortunate youngsters, shots being routine ones of the children eating, singing, bathing, playing and marching. Later sequences show older boys and girls learning a profession or trade.

The production is nicely scored, with Jewish and Palestinian modern and traditional folk songs and melodies done in excellent fashion. Narrative seems choppy, and Charles Clement did not have much chance on his job of adding English titles because so little occurs on the screen. There is no cohesive story; merely a cut-and-dried recital of what is being done to help these orphans get along in the world.

Film is being presented at the Stanley, N. Y., by the Central Commission for Child Welfare of the Union of Jews for Resistance and Mutual Aid in France. *Wear.*

The Loves of Don Juan
(ITALIAN)

Superfilm release of Scalera Films (Rome). Stars Adriano Rimoldi. Directed by Dina Falconi. Screenplay adapted from Mozart opera, "Don Giovanni"; camera, Otello Martelli. At Golden, N. Y., Sept. 1, '48. Running time, **92 MINS.**

Don Juan....Adriano Rimoldi
Anna....Dina Sassoli
Sganarello....Paolo Stoppa
Elvira....Elena Zareschi
Soccorito....Rina Morelli
The Gypsy....Elli Parvo
Imperia....Carla Candiani
Don Esteban....Giorgio Constantini
Don Pablo....Guglielmo Barnabo
Don Garcia....Cesare Fantoni
Pedrito....Vittorio Capanna

(In Italian; English Titles)

"The Loves of Don Juan" is one of those over-stuffed costume epics that used to roll out regularly from Italian studios before the war. Although a new production, this film shows no evidence of the immense strides forward made recently by Italo pic-makers. The story here is corny, the thesping is hammy and the direction compounds the dullness by a deadpan, overdrawn treatment.

Yarn is straight recital of the Don Juan legend which may be considered as a fictionalization of the Kinsey report. This film, however, succeeds in making sex a bore as the great lover is depicted dashing from one buxom wench to another over an obstacle course of outraged fathers, brothers and husbands. Finally, the boudoir merry-go-round breaks down when an indignant statute accidentally falls on Don Juan and kills him.

For all its defects, the film has at least one impressive aspect in its lush costuming and mammoth period settings. The background Mozart score will also please the longhair music fans if they can overlook the visual accompaniment.
Herm.

Nu Borjar Livet
(Life Starts Now)
(SWEDISH)

Svensk Filmindustri production and release. Stars Mai Zetterling, George Rydeberg; features Wanda Rothgardt, Hugo Bjorne, Bengt Ekelund, Ake Gronberg, Ivar Kage, Jan Molander, Sven-Erik Gamble, Erik Forslund. Directed by Gustaf Molander. Screenplay, Rune Lindstrom and Molander; camera, Ake Dahlquist; music, Erik Nordgren. At Roda Kvarn, Stockholm. Running time, **88 MINS.**

Vera Ullman....Mai Zetterling
Tore Gerhard....George Rydeberg
Dorrit Gerhard....Wanda Rothgardt
Eliasson....Hugo Bjorne
John Berg....Bengt Ekelund
Berra....Ake Gronberg
The Reverend....Ivar Kage
Svenne....Jan Molander
Platis....Sven-Erik Gamble
Detective....Helge Hagerman

An implausible story is unreeled in "Nu Borjar Livet." However, with Mai Zetterling's name to dress up the marquee coupled with a high-powered promotion campaign, the picture may do well enough in the Scandinavian market. Its appeal overseas is quite problematical.

Plot revolves around a minister who's unhappily married. He'd like to divorce his spouse, but fears the scandal. Jaded by his personal problems, he makes love to a young girl, Vera. First she falls for his charms, but later realizes her mistake and returns to her original boy friend. Disappointed, the cleric then commits suicide.

Although Miss Zetterling does well enough as Vera, she is miscast. George Rydeberg turns in a good performance as the minister. Top thesping laurels, however, go to Wanda Rothgardt, who capably handles the part of his wife. Gustav Molander, who collabed on the screenplay with Rune Lindstrom, ably directed the film. Camerawork of Ake Dahlqvist also measures up. *Winq.*

Miniature Reviews

"Road House" (Songs) (20th). Sturdy cast builds up uneven romantic meller into good b.o. fare.

"Sinister Journey" (UA). William Boyd in another Hopalong Cassidy western; okay for second slot of duals.

"Louisana Story" (Lopert). Robert Flaherty documentary pictorially impressive entertainment; should do good business for such type film.

"Jungle Patrol" (20th). Excellent budget feature wih Pacific war background. No names but can be ballyhooed.

"The Golden Eye" (Mono). Lightweight Charlie Chan; filler for twin bills.

"Son of God's Country" (Rep). Standard oater for Saturday matinee grinds.

Road House
(SONGS)

20th-Fox release of Edward Chodorov production. Stars Ida Lupino, Cornel Wilde, Celeste Holm, Richard Widmark. Directed by Jean Negulesco. Screenplay, Chodorov; story, Margaret Gruen and Oscar Saul; songs, Johnny Mercer and Harold Arlen, Lionel Newman and Dorcas Cochran; camera, Joseph La Shelle; editor, James B. Clark; music, Cyril Mockridge. Tradeshown N. Y. Sept. 20, '48. Running time, **95 MINS.**

Lily....Ida Lupino
Pete....Cornel Wilde
Susie....Celeste Holm
Jefty....Richard Widmark
Arthur....O. Z. Whitehead
Mike....Robert Karnes
Lefty....George Beranger
Sheriff....Ian MacDonald
Judge....Grandon Rhodes

A tough-skinned meller with romantic filling, "Road House" is slated for nice returns at the wickets. Film barely misses entry into the b.o. heavyweight class due to a screenplay which is tight at both ends but sags over a long center stretch. Strong cast and snappy exploitation possibilities, however, will help the pic's staying power.

Framed within a realistically intimate roadhouse setting, yarn reconstructs the triangle with an arrestingly psychotic twist supplied by Richard Widmark. For most of the way, director Jean Negulesco hurdles the script's over-length and internal weaknesses by building up conflict out of character studies of the principals. But the film finally bogs down in a lack of incident until a climactic shot-in-the-arm revives interest.

At the center of the story, turning in one of the best performances of her career is Ida Lupino, playing a lowdown blues warbler who finds herself in the middle between Widmark and Cornel Wilde. Widmark, the roadhouse operator, has a powerful yen for the singer but she prefers his general manager, Wilde. When Widmark discovers that his gal and his pal have been holding hands behind his back, he frames Wilde on a robbery rap.

Plenty of footage is consumed getting up to this point but interest perks with the unfolding of Widmark's insane scheme to get Wilde paroled into his custory in order to squeeze him on the psychological torture rack. The windup is an effectively violent sequence in which Wilde slugs Widmark to a fare-thee-well and then attempts to make a getaway with his gal through the north woods to Canada with gun-toting Widmark on their trail. The fox-and-hounds motif is tensely played until Miss Lupino puts a couple of slugs into Widmark in self-defense.

Miss Lupino's standout performance is highlighted by her firstrate handling of a brace of blues numbers, including "One for My Baby," "The Right Time" and "Again," all three being solid tunes. Her gravel-toned voice lacks range but has the more essential quality of style, along the lines of a femme Hoagy Carmichael. Widmark registers potently with one of his standard nasty portrayals but he's in danger of being typed, or stereotyped. Wilde also impresses favorably in a rough-and-tumble he-man role. In a spare-wheel part, Celeste Holm plays with her customary wit but she's never permitted to establish herself firmly in the pic.

Production is smartly dressed with modest, but neat backgrounds fully suitable to the yarn. Technical credits are topnotch with sharp camera work, smooth editing and a good background score helping to tie the film together.
Herm.

Sinister Journey

United Artists release of Lewis J. Rachmil production. Stars William Boyd. Directed by George Archainbaud. Screenplay, J. Benton Cheney, Bennett Cohen and Ande Lamb, based on characters created by Clarence E. Mulford. At New York, N. Y., week of Sept. 14, '48. Running time, **59 MINS.**

Hopalong Cassidy....William Boyd
California Carlson....Andy Clyde
Lucky Jenkins....Rand Brooks
Mrs. Garvin....Elaine Riley
Lee Garvin....John Kellogg

Hopalong Cassidy series continues to follow the same pat formula of these westerns in "Sinster Journey." And William Boyd continues to ride the range as the hero who always has time to right a wrong. This picture is for western fans in twin setups, being one of those lesser oat operas which generate business largely in smaller houses.

Boyd, who has hardly been out of the saddle since he first created the screen Hopalong character for Paramount years ago, has a more involved story than customary in "Journey." Squabble between an oldtime western railroad prexy and the young lad who elopes with his daughter is taken advantage of by the usual villian, with the innocent youth framed on a murder charge.

Boyd again makes the typical Hopalong character click but doesn't have as many actionful sequences as usual. Andy Clyde furnishes some comedy relief. John Kellogg makes an acceptable wronged youth, while Elaine Riley is the gal who falls for him. She's comely enough but no great shakes as an actress. Rand Brooks heads the supporting cast.

George Archainbaud has directed with more skill than is indicated, the major fault, of course, lying in the screenplay. *Wear.*

Louisiana Story

Lopert Films release of Robert Flaherty production, directed by Flaherty. Story, Robert and Frances Flaherty; score, Virgil Thomson; played by members of Philadelphia Orchestra, Eugene Ormandy conducting; camera, Richard Leacock; editor, Helen Van Dongen. Previewed N. Y. Sept. 18, '48. Running time, **77 MINS.**

Boy....Joseph Boudreaux
Father....Lionel Le Blanc
Mother....Mrs. E. Bienvenu
Driller....Frank Hardy
Boilerman....C. T. Guedry

Robert Flaherty's latest picture, "Louisiana Story," is a documentary-type story told almost purely in camera terms. It has a slender, appealing story, moments of agonizing suspense, vivid atmosphere and superlative photography. It should get excellent reviews and, if skillfully exploited, should do profitable business.

Filmed entirely in the bayou

country of Louisiana, the picture tells of the Cajun (Acadian) boy and his parents, who live by hunting and fishing in the alligator-infested swamps and streams, and of the oil-drilling crew that brings its huge derrick to sink a well. That's about all there is to the plot, but it suffices for an entertaining and generally moving film.

There probably aren't more than 100 lines of dialog in the entire picture—long sequences being told by the camera, with eloquent sound effects and Virgil Thomson's expressive music as background. There are no real heroes or villains (unless the terrifying alligators could be considered the latter). The simple Cajun family is friendly, and the oil-drilling crew is pleasant and likable.

There are exciting incidents as the youngster paddles his tiny boat through the lonely swamps with his pet racoon and is almost killed by the savage 'gator, until he finally captures and slays it in a spine-chilling struggle. On the other hand, the scenes around the floating derrick, as the crew drills for oil, caps a blowup of subterranean gas and ultimately gets the well installed, are graphic and engrossing.

The performances, apparently by the actual people themselves, seem unself-conscious and convincing. Whether any of the players would be effective under studio conditions may be another matter, but in these circumstances, they're all persuasive. The playing of the Philadelphia Orchestra musicians, under Eugene Ormandy's direction, adds considerably. Possibly the picture could be cut a bit more, including some seeming repeat shots, to shorten the running time for dual bookings.

Besides being excellent entertainment, "Louisiana Story" should be invaluable public relations material for Standard Oil of N. J., which contributed the necessary $200,000 production coin to Flaherty. The firm has no rights and no identification in the film, but stands to get across the idea that oil companies are beneficently public-spirited, their employees honest, industrious and amiable, and their operations productive and innocuous. *Hobe.*

Jungle Patrol

Hollywood, Sept. 17.

20th-Fox release of Frank Seltzer production. Features Kristine Miller, Arthur Franz. Directed by Joe Newman. Screenplay, Francis Swann; adaptation, Robertson White; based on play by William Bowers; camera, Mack Stengler; editor, Bert Jordan; song, Al Rinker, Floyd Huddleston. Tradeshown Sept. 15, '48. Running time, 71 MINS.

Jean....................Kristine Miller
Mace....................Arthur Franz
Skipper....................Ross Ford
Ham....................Tom Noonan
Minor....................Gene Reynolds
Dick....................Richard Jaeckel
Louie....................Mickey Knox
Derby....................Harry Lauter
Johnny....................Bill Murphy
Hanley....................G. Pat Collins

"Jungle Patrol" is a budget feature, but packs a lot more dramatic wallop than many of its big brothers. Starting with a good plot, all concerned have gone on from there to shape it as recommended drama. Cast carries no marquee brilliance, but is made up of young players who give a serious, realistic touch to this account of an incident in New Guinea during the Pacific War.

There are plenty of ballyhoo possibilities that may give the film a chance outside of its normal supporting classification. Picture is third of the Frank Seltzer productions for 20th-Fox release, and certainly the best of the trio.

Adapted from a play by William Bowers, Seltzer has been able to cut production corners and make the film more graphic by concentrating camera on the young character studies and only implying grueling, offstage air action. Sky fights between Nips and Yanks, as heard over Operations Radio, packs as much wallop as though actually viewed and intensify suspense. It's an offstage, legit effect that lends itself perfectly to the plot as well as picture-making economy.

Principals concerned are eight fliers, stationed at a temporary air strip near Port Moresby and charged with intercepting the Japs until a permanent strip can be completed. Boys have rung up a score of nearly 100 enemy planes without the loss of life. Tension continually mounts as the boys wonder when death will abandon its holiday and start decimating their ranks.

Francis Swann's script, adapted by Robertson White, sets up the moods for careful development by Joe Newman's direction. Mood isn't always stern. There's humor in the by-play between the fliers as they await their fate and the cast is uniformly outstanding in delivering performances that register strongly.

Kristine Miller brightens her role as USO entertainer visiting the lonely outpost and sings "Forever and Always" capably. The eight fliers are tellingly portrayed by Arthur Franz, Ross Ford, Tom Noonan, Gene Reynolds, Richard Jaeckel, Mickey Knox, Harry Lauter and Bill Murphy, each giving his part a feeling of reality. G. Pat Collins is good as the sergeant.

Camera work by Mack Stengler is expert in displaying jungle background and editing holds film to crisp 71 minutes. *Brog.*

The Golden Eye

Monogram release of James S. Burkett production. Features Roland Winters, Victor Sen Young. Directed by William Beaudine. Screenplay, W. Scott Darling, suggested by character created by Earl Derr Biggers; camera, William Sickner. At New York, N. Y., week of Sept. 14, '48. Running time, 69 MINS.

Charlie Chan ....Roland Winters
Birmingham ....Mantan Moreland
Tommy Chan ....Victor Sen Young
Lt. Ruark ....Tim Ryan
Bartlett ....Bruce Kellogg
Evelyn ....Wanda McKay
Driscoll ....Ralph Dunn
Manning ....Forrest Taylor
Teresa ....Evelyn Brent
Mrs. Driscoll ....Lois Austin

"The Golden Eye," another Charlie Chan meller, is hardly up to the standard of the series. Roland Winters is not particularly exciting or realistic as the new Charlie Chan. But the plot and direction also appear to be at fault. Film is of quickie calibre, strictly for padding out the dualers.

Chan's operations this time take him to a dude ranch and a gold mine in Arizona. Plot is of a supposedly mined-out shaft that suddenly becomes active. The secret ultimately is revealed of how the ore was actually smuggled from Mexico, then sold to the U. S. at an exorbitant price.

Winters is too listless as Chan although he's not helped much by the yarn. Victor Sen Young is acceptable as the detective's ambitious son. Mantan Moreland, as the chauffeur, provides a few humorous moments but milks each situation too long. Tim Ryan does well as a police lieutenant.

William Beaudine's direction is passable. *Wear.*

Son of God's Country

Hollywood, Sept. 17.

Republic release of Melville Tucker production. Stars Monte Hale; features Pamela Blake, Paul Hurst, Jim Nolan. Directed by R. G. Springsteen. Original screenplay, Paul Gangelin; added dialog, Bob Williams; camera, John MacBurnie; editor, Harry Keller. Previewed Sept. 15, '48. Running time, 60 MINS.

Monte Hale....................Monte Hale
Cathy Thornton...............Pamela Blake
Eli Walker....................Paul Hurst
Bill Sanger....................Jim Nolan
Frank Thornton....................Jay Kirby
Bigelow....................Steve Darrell
Tom Ford ....Francis McDonald
John Thornton............Jason Robards
Hagen....................Fred Graham

There's nothing unusual about "Son of God's Country." Stereotyped western fare, it boasts the usual amount of incredible cliches in action and dialog. However, it won't tax the kiddies, so will get by as Saturday matinee material.

Monte Hale is the hero who goes about his derringdo in too listless fashion. That land-grab plot is in again—there's a railroad coming through and the villain is trying to grab up all the ranches. Only variation is dating the action right after the war between the states so the heavy can blame the trouble on settlers from the south.

Director R. G. Springsteen keeps the oater formula running off at a standard pace and the cast responds in the same manner. As noted, Hale gives the impression of little enthusiasm for his heroics. Pamela Blake is an okay western femme lead. Paul Hurst, Jim Nolan, the heavy, and others are acceptable.

There's one tune, the traditional "Railroad Corral," crooned by Hale. Lensing and other production credits are adequate to demands made by Melville Tucker's supervision. *Brog.*

The Merry Chase
(ITALIAN)

Superfilm release of Minerva production. Stars Rossano Brazzi. Directed by Giorgio Blanchi. Camera, Massimo Terzano. At Golden, N. Y., starting Sept. 17, '48. Running time, 76 MINS.

Paola....................Clara Calamai
Andrea....................Nino Besotti
Guido....................Rossano Brazzi
Paola's Mother-in-law......Paola Borboni
Caesar....................Lauro Gazzolo

(In Italian; English Titles)

This Italian-made comedy is infinitely better than many imports being unveiled in the U. S. currently. Picture is rich farce, with yards of verbiage, some of it lost on any audience not understanding Italian. However, the adroit acting is not. And for Italo patrons it is hearty laugh material. Consequently, the film looks a solid bet for Italian-language spots and many arty theatres.

The idea of a canine romance, somewhat similar to the one used so effectively in "Emperor Waltz," is projected, but with unlike results. Also the mating of the two pekinese dogs is carried out with almost hammer-and-tong emphasis in this vehicle. Too, director Giorgio Blanchi made it mostly a framework on which to build the love affair between a pretty married woman and an embassy assistant. This rather torrid affair never gets past the kissing stage. The switch from farce to seriousness in the closing passages is a bit bewildering as Rossano Brazzi, the embassy aide, stalks off to his newly achieved consular post. But that seems a lesser flaw. The lighter moments are carried off with fine skill; as pointed out, undoubtedly much funnier in the original Italian than the English titles.

Touting Brazzi as "a new Valentino" is not far-fetched, since the handsome actor can act, has many of the American silent screen star's mannerisms and is extremely vivid in the love scenes. The principal osculatory clinch is a scorcher, and seemingly trimmed by censors. He is now under contract to David O. Selznick. Clara Calamai is remarkably good as the wedded beauty who nearly strays from the straight-and-narrow. She does excellent work despite being such a tall leading woman. Nino Besotti is highly satisfactory as the fussy, innocent little husband.

Heading the suport, Paola Borboni, as the wife's mother-in-law, and Lauro Gazzolo, the father-in-law, carry on a deft running word battle centering on their guessing about the handsome consular official's intentions in the home. Director Blanchi does a nice job, with other technical work of the production up to pre-war Italian standards. *Wear.*

Loves of Casanova
(SONGS — FRENCH)

Vog Film release of Sirius production. Stars Georges Guetary. Directed by Jean Boyer. Adapted by Marc G. Sauvajon; camera, Charles Suin; music, Rene Sylviano; lyrics, Vandair and Rouzaud; English titles, George Slocombe. At Ambassador, N. Y., Sept. 17, '48. Running time, 101 MINS.

Jean Casanova de Seingalt..........
Georges Guetary
Don Luis....................Aime Clariond
Dutch Merchant..............Jean Tissier
Genevieve............Helene Dassonville
Clotilde....................Noelle Norman
Coraline............Jacqueline Gauthier
Henriette..............Gisele Casadesus
Consuela................Claudette Falco
Esprit ....Dinan

(In French; English Titles)

"The Loves of Casanova" isn't likely to raise the blood-pressure even in the art houses. L'amour, l'amour can be pretty dull when piled on toujours with a trowel, and in this costume pic from 17th century France it is pretty ho-hum indeed.

Produced in France last year, film is a succession of romantic affairs between the legendary Casanova and a host of assorted femmes. The femmes are very attractive, and Georges Guetary, musical comedy star who plays Casanova, is an engaging rascal. But he hardly projects the fascination Casanova must have held for women, while the plot isn't much help in substantiating it. Story deals with Casanova's flight from Venice to Paris to seek his fortune, and tells it in a disjointed, musical-comedy vein, with Casanova bursting into song whenever things look blackest.

Not only is amour overexposed, but so is the camera work, with all the outdoor shots too bright and pale for good camera work. Subtitles suffer in the same way, often being illegible against indistinct backgrounds. Songs are pleasant and Gallic, and are sung agreeably by Guetary. Jean Tissier's performance as a Dutch banker, and Aime Clariond as Don Luis, are good, and a quintet of French good-lookers swoon about Casanova charmingly. Some duelling, intrigue and horse-riding give the pic a bit of action, but for the most part it plods along. *Bron.*

Lars Hard
(SWEDISH)

Stockholm, Sept. 7.

Sandrew-Bauman Film production and release. Stars George Fant, Adolf Jahr; features Elsa Widborg, Eva Dahlbeck, Ulla Smidje, Nine-Christine Jonsson, Hugo Bjorne. Directed by Hampe Faustman. Screenplay by Jan Fridegard, based on

his novel. Camera, Edlund; music. Er-
land von Koch. At Royal, Stockholm.
Running time, 87 MINS.
Lars Hard ....George Fant
His Father.................. Adolf Jahr
His mother............... Elsa Widborg
Inga...................... Eva Dahlbeck
Maj.................... Ulla Smidje
Eva ....Nine-Christine Jonsson
Sundwall .... Hugo Bjorne
The Driver............Torsten Bergstrom
His Wife.................. Rut Holm
Martha..........Anne-Marie Uddenberg

One of the better films of the
new season, "Lars Hard" looms as
a successful entry in Scandinavia
and has appeal for international
filmgoers as well. Fact that the
picture was adapted from a popular
novel by the author, Jan Fridegard,
should aid the film's prospects.

Yarn is set in a period of Swedish history when farm workers
were paid a pittance and looked
down on generally. George Fant,
one of them, is falsely charged
with having fathered the child of
a girl he scarcely knew, and serves
time in jail. On his release, he
discovers that everyone considers
him an outcast. Much of the subsequent footage is devoted to the
means he takes to rehabilitate
himself. Fant does a bang-up
portrayal of the wronged laborer
while supporting cast is proficient
under Hampe Faustman's direction.   Winq.

Pelota De Trapo
(Ragged Football)
(ARGENTINE)

Buenos Aires, Aug. 28.
SIFA production and release. Directed
by Leopoldo Torres Rios. Stars Armando
Bo, Santiago Arrieta, Orestes Caviglia,
Carmen Valdes, Graciela Lecube; features
Floren Delbene, Maria Luisa Robledo,
Mario Medrano, Semillita, Rodolfo Zenner,
Mabel Doran, Guillermo Stabile. Musical
score, Pedro Rubbione and Alberto Gnec-
co; camera, Alvaro Barreiro; script by
Ricardo Lorenzo and Jerry Gomez. At
the Metropolitan, Buenos Aires, Aug. 10,
'48. Running time, 110 MINS.

Produced by an independent
studio, which has relatively no financial resources, with what was
probably the most modest budget
of the year, this picture is establishing an unprecedented record
for a local production, not only at
the boxoffice, but from critics and
public. Already in its third week
at the Metropolitan, "Pelota de
Trapo" has beaten the record set
by "To Live in Peace" at the same
theatre last year, grossing $11,-
616.70 (U. S.) in the first week.

Human, unpretentious, the story
goes straight to the hearts of the
football-mad Argentine people. The
producers have put heart into it
instead of opulence. It's undoubtedly the most human of all Argentine pix to date. Although actors
of the calibre of Armando Bo and
Santiago Arrieta give a very good
account of themselves in the cast,
the acting honors are carried away
by juve football enthusiasts, all
newcomers to the screen, chosen
by director Torres Rios for the juvenile parts. Andres Poggio, as
Toscanito, especially draws attention.

Story, tells the tale of a youngster, born on the wrong side of the
tracks, whose one great joy in life
is his "team" of soccer players, who
meet for their games on an empty
lot, with only a rag football to practice with. The boy dreams of becoming a great football hero, acclaimed by millions of fans at the
Sunday matches, which fill Argentina's stadiums, who go to acclaim
what has become the country's favorite sport.

Picture has little interest for
U. S. fans, but has taken local ones

by storm, despite lack of the ballyhoo which has accompanied so
many of the deluxe productions of
major Argentine studios this year,
with such disappointing results.
While this picture is creating records in its Buenos Aires firstrun,
it's expected to do even better once
it goes out into the sticks. Nid.

Miniature Reviews

"Unfaithfully Yours" (20th).
Weak romantic comedy helped
by Harrison-Darnell names.
"The Winslow Boy" (Brit.
Lion). Ace British courtroom
drama, with Robert Donat, set
for good returns; ditto in U.S.
"Triple Threat" (Col). Mild
story formula woven around
news clips of football greats
in action. Secondary product.
"Sons of Adventure" (Rep).
Whodunit plot with Holly-
wood studio background.
Okay supporter.
"The Blind Goddess" (GFD).
British-made courtroom melo
should have fair draw.
"Eagle With Two Heads"
(Indie). Heavy-handed French
tragedy; weak sureseater.

Unfaithfully Yours

20th-Fox release of Preston Sturges
production; story and direction by
Sturges. Stars Rex Harrison, Linda Dar-
nell, Rudy Vallee, Barbara Lawrence;
features Kurt Kreuger, Lionel Stander.
Camera, Victor Milner; music, Alfred
Newman; editor, Robert Fritch. Trade-
shown, N. Y. Sept. 28, '48. Running
time, 105 MINS.
Sir Alfred de Carter.....Rex Harrison
Daphne de Carter........Linda Darnell
Barbara ....Barbara Lawrence
August Henschler..........Rudy Vallee
Anthony .... Kurt Kreuger
Hugo ....Lionel Stander
Sweeney .... Edgar Kennedy
House Detective..........Alan Bridge
Tailor ....Julius Tannen
Dr. Schultz................Torben Meyer
Jules ....Robert Greig
Mme. Pompadour.......Evelyn Beresford
Dowager ....Georgia Caine
Musician ....Harry Seymour
Telephone Operators,
     Isabel Jewell and Marion Marshall

Preston Sturges' initial assignment under his 20th-Fox pact is
an uneven laugh-maker with
enough marquee reserve power to
dent the b.o. A romantic comedy
that oscillates between sophistication and slapstick, "Unfaithfully
Yours" misses that stamp of originality which marked the scripting
and direction of Sturges' previous
films. The fabric of stale ideas
and antique gags out of which this
pic was spun is just barely hidden
by its glossy production casing.

The yarn is too slight to carry
the long running time. It's a takeoff on the suspicious husband-beau-
tiful wife formula which is stirred
up into a frothy pastry only on
occasion. With Rex Harrison playing a symphony orch leader,
Sturges executes some amusing
highjinks with serious music, but
the humor is mild and unsustained.
For most part, however, the laughs
depend on pratfalls. But even this
surefire tactic can be overworked.

The yarn unfolds via three long
revenge fantasies which race
through Harrison's brain while he
batons his way through a concert.
During a frenzied number by Rossini, there's a gruesome sequence
in which Harrison slashes his wife,
Linda Darnell, with a razor and
then pins the rap on her supposed
lover. Against a background of
Wagnerian music, he daydreams of
nobly renouncing his wife in favor
of the other man. Finally, against
a Tschaikowsky number, he imagines playing Russian roulette with
his rival in a test of passion.
Stylization of the fantasies would
have given these sequences that
comic energy which is lacking. Instead, these long passages are handled with such deadpan grimness
that Sturges' uncertainty over
whether to make this pic a comedy
or a meller becomes evident. The
dialog, moreover, is flat as, in such
overstrained lines as "there's a
thread of saffron in his character."

or as in such out-and-out cliches as
"you're as nutty as a fruitcake."
The flip, spontaneous quip is missing. The payoff scene in which
Harrison discovers his wife to be
innocent is also treated without
inventiveness.

Harrison's thesping is the pic's
strongest asset. In a versatile performance, he ranges from broad
comedy to high melodramatics
with a neat tongue-in-cheek mannerism. Miss Darnell, beautifully
photographed from all angles, is
competent in a straight role. Rudy
Vallee, as a stuffy brother-in-law,
and Lionel Stander, as a Russian-
accented impresario, also register
well in character bits. Barbara
Lawrence, as Vallee's wife, handles her smart-aleck lines acidly
while the rest of the cast delivers
strong support.   Herm.

The Winslow Boy
(BRITISH)

London, Sept. 23.
British Lion Film Corp. release of Lon-
don Films-Anatole de Grunwald produc-
tion. Stars Robert Donat; features Cedric
Hardwicke, Margaret Leighton. Directed
by Anthony Asquith. Screenplay by
Terence Rattigan, Anatole de Grunwald,
from stage play by Rattigan. Editor,
Gerald Turney Smith; music, William
Alwyn; camera, Frederick Young. At
Plaza, London, Sept. 22, '48. Running
time, 117 MINS.
Sir Robert Morton.........Robert Donat
Catherine Winslow....Margaret Leighton
Arthur Winslow....Cedric Hardwicke
Grace Winslow............Marie Lohr
Ronnie Winslow............Neil North
Dickie Winslow............Jack Watling
John Watherstone.......Frank Lawton
Colonel Watherstone....Nicholas Hannen
Desmond Curry...........Basil Radford
Violet ....Kathleen Harrison
Hamilton .... Evelyn Roberts
First Lord.............Walter Fitzgerald
Attorney-General ....Francis L. Sullivan
Watkinson..........Wilfrid Hyde White
Commander Flower....Ernest Thesiger
Admiral Springfield.......Lewis Casson

This is one of the finest pictures
to come from a British studio this
year. "The Winslow Boy," with its
star-studded cast, moving story and
emotional appeal, is a certain boxoffice winner for the home trade
and should do substantial business
with American audiences.

Terence Rattigan's story, based
on an actual incident that occurred
just before World War I, is typically British, and is a fine example
of the conception of British democracy. In essence, it's also a simple
story of a 13 year-old naval cadet,
expelled from school for the alleged theft of a dollar postal order.
The boy's father is certain of his
innocence and when he fails to
have the case reopened, invokes
the whole machinery of British democracy by arranging a full-scale
Parliamentary debate and subsequently bringing a successful action against the King.

It's more the father's conviction
of his son's innocence, rather than
the incident itself, which forms the
background of this well-knit story,
with sufficient emphasis on the
emotional angles to make it a sure
tearjerker. From its brisk opening
the plot quickly develops the main
theme, building up the fight for
justice through a series of incidents which are highlighted by the
interview between Sir Robert Morton, M.P., and famous attorney,
and the boy before he decides to
accept the brief. As the campaign
goes on through the House of Commons and law courts to its final
triumph, it brings hardship and
unhappiness to the Winslow family.
But a broken engagement or the
end of carefree college days mean
little when contrasted with the
satisfaction of knowing that justice
has been done.

A flawless cast portrays the principal characters to perfection, and
minor roles have been painstaking-

ly filled. Robert Donat, at the top of his form, makes Sir Robert Morton come to life with a portrayal that captures every mood of the subject. Sir Cedric Hardwicke commands sympathy for the Winslow father and Marie Lohr is faultless as his wife. There's a big future ahead for Neil North, who makes a terrific hit as the Winslow boy, standing up to a gruelling part and coming through with flying colors. Margaret Leighton and Jack Watling complete the members of the Winslow family, each performing with skill and sincerity. But Kathleen Harrison almost steals the picture, and has her greatest moment in breaking the news of the verdict to the family.

Anthony Asquith's polished direction, first rate production qualities, correct period atmosphere and fine backgrounds add up, with the story and acting, to make this British pic a handsome money-winner. *Myro.*

Triple Threat

Hollywood, Sept. 25.
Columbia release of Sam Katzman production. Features Richard Crane, Gloria Henry, Mary Stuart, John Litel, Pat Phelan, Joseph Crehan, Harry Wismer, Tom Harmon, Bob Kelley. Directed by Jean Yarbrough. Original screenplay, Joseph Carole, Don Martin; camera, Vincent Farrar; editor, Jerome Thoms. At Pantages, Sept. 23, '48. Running time 71 MINS.
Don Whitney .... Richard Crane
Ruth Nolan .... Gloria Henry
Marian Rutherford .... Mary Stuart
Coach Snyder .... John Litel
Joe Nolan .... Pat Phelan
Coach Miller .... Joseph Crehan
Mrs. Nolan .... Regina Wallace
Television Man .... Syd Saylor
Porter .... Dooley Wilson
Announcers: Harry Wismer, Tom Harmon, Bob Kelley.
Professional Football Players: Sammy Baugh, Paul Christman, Johnny Clement, "Bolev" Dancewicz, Bill Dudley, Paul Governali, "Indian" Jack Jacobs, Sid Luckman, Charles Trippi, Steve Van Buren, Bob Waterfield.

Now that fall and football are here it is only natural that the crop of "B" pigskinners should start turning up. "Triple Threat" offers no menace to any of its celluloid gridiron brothers. It's a programmer that constantly interrupts a trite, formula plot with news clips of name footballers in action. An occasional shot is interesting, but overall effect is dull.

Plot is the one about the reformation of a swellhead. Most of the players overcome, to some extent, weak dialog and situations. Richard Crane is the self-satisfied hero who takes his good opinion of himself from the college amateur field to the professional gridiron. There's a contrived romantic triangle that is an excuse for some bad ball playing on part of principals but difficulty is resolved just before the big game to make for the happy ending.

Jean Yarbrough's direction is only mildly effective and the players' work is on a par. Crane, John Litel, football coach, Gloria Henry, Mary Stuart and Pat Phelan are the principals and try hard. Brought into the footage for what amounts to only introductions are several football greats such as Sammy Baugh and Bob Waterfield. Their appearance makes little difference to film's values. Sportscasters Harry Wismer, Tom Harmon and Bob Kelley are spotted for some play-calling.

Associate producer Charles H. Schneer cut a lot of budget corners by use of news clips and had they been used to forward the story would have appeared to better advantage. Technical credits deliver standard craftsmanship. *Brog.*

Sons of Adventure

Hollywood, Sept. 25.
Republic release of Franklin Adreon production. Features Lynne Roberts, Russ Hayden, Gordon Jones. Directed by Yakima Canutt. Original screenplay, Franklin Adreon, Sol Shor; camera, John MacBurnie; editor, Harold Minter. At the Paramount, L. A., Sept. 23, '48. Running time, 60 MINS.
Jean .... Lynne Roberts
Steve .... Russ Hayden
Andy .... Gordon Jones
Sterling .... Grant Withers
Billy Wilkes .... George Chandler
Bennett .... Roy Barcroft
Peter Winslow .... John Newland
Laura .... Stephanie Bachelor
Paul Kenyon .... John Holland
Sam Hodges .... Gilbert Frye
Eddie .... Richard Irving
Glenda .... Joan Blair
Norton .... John Crawford
Harry .... Keith Richards
Whitey .... James Dale

"Sons of Adventure" stresses stunt man action that gives deceptive value to a thin plot. It will create no particular stir in the secondary market but serves its supporting purpose well enough. Republic studio background, with glimpses of films in the making, adds interest to the whodunit story.

Cast does well under the actionful guidance of Yakima Canutt, himself an ex-stunt man and therefore a good choice to direct a yarn that concerns the studio adventures of a man who performs the derring-do for screen heroes. A western star is killed on the set and stunter Russ Hayden does some amateur sleuthing to save his wartime buddy, Gordon Jones, from being accused of the murder. He runs the standard gauntlet of near escapes from death before putting the finger on the real villain.

Lynne Roberts pleases as a western stunt girl and Hayden handles his role easily. Jones, Grant Withers, George Chandler, Roy Barcroft, Stephanie Bachelor and John Holland are among others giving good characterizations.

Production helming takes full advantage of the studio background to give color to physical values. Franklin Adreon functioned better in the production capacity than he did in co-scripting light story with Sol Shor. Lensing is excellent and editing tight. *Brog.*

The Blind Goddess
(BRITISH)

London, Sept. 15.
GFD release of Gainsborough production. Stars Eric Portman, Anne Crawford, Hugh Williams, Michael Denison. Directed by Harold French. Screenplay by Muriel and Sydney Box from play by Patrick Hastings. Music, Bernard Grun; editor, Gordon Hales; camera, Ray Elton, Dudley Lovell. At Odeon, London, Sept. 14, '48. Running time, 88 MINS.
Sir John Dearing .... Eric Portman
Lady Brasted .... Anne Crawford
Lord Brasted .... Hugh Williams
Derek Waterhouse ..... Michael Denison
Lady Dearing .... Nora Swinburne
Mr. Mainwaring .... Raymond Lovell
Mary Dearing .... Claire Bloom
Judge .... Frank Cellier
Daphne Dearing .... Elspet Gray
Lord Brasted's Butler .. Maurice Denham
Count Mikla .... Martin Benson
Mario .... Martin Miller
Bertoni .... Marcel Poncin
Meyer .... Carl Jaffe
Morton .... Cecil Bevan

When a famous lawyer turns his hand to playwrighting it's a pretty safe bet he'll pick a subject with a predominant courtroom background. That's precisely what Sir Patrick Hastings, noted British attorney, has done with "The Blind Goddess," which he wrote originally for the stage, and he's gone all out for obvious melodrama which should achieve reasonably modest results at the boxoffice.

Author takes a simple situation, quickly builds up the plot and concentrates all his legal knowledge on the courtroom sequences. Lord Brasted is accused by his secretary of converting public funds to his own use, and when the latter reports the matter to the Prime Minister, an action is brought for criminal libel. Forged and stolen letters prove more convincing to the jury than the secretary's evidence, but once the trial is over the forgery and theft come to light, and his lordship takes the easy way out of suicide.

Film is very much a carbon copy of the original play, and in consequence suffers from its stagey atmosphere. But lack of movement is not of prime importance in this type of production, which is clearly designed to stress the melodramatic angles brought into full play during the trial scene. Acting matches the production, with Eric Portman very much at home as Sir John Dearing, who defends Brasted in the libel action and later unmasks the forgery. Hugh Williams is extremely solid as the Lord; Anne Crawford adequately suggests his scheming wife, and Michael Denison is somewhat insipid as the hero. *Myro.*

Eagle With Two Heads
(FRENCH)

Vog release of Georges Danciger & Alexandre Mnouchkine production. Stars Edwige Feuillere, Jean Marais. Directed by Jean Cocteau. Screenplay, Cocteau; camera, Christian Matras; music, Georges Auric; English titles, Noel Meadow. Previewed N. Y. Sept. 24, '48. Running time, 100 MINS.
The Queen .... Edwige Feuillere
Edith de Berg .... Sylvia Monfort
Stanislas .... Jean Marais
Felix de Willenstein ... Jean Debucourt
Count de Foehn ..... Jacques Varennes
Tony .... Abdallah
Rudy .... Gilles Queant
Geniz .... Maurice Nasil
Adams .... Edward Stirling

(In French; English Titles)

Jean Cocteau's "Eagle With Two Heads," which was a legit flop on Broadway last year, is also a dud in this French-imported film version. The script is unmanageable. It buries a tiny mouse of a story beneath a mountain of purple rhetoric and phony emotion. It's barely possible that Cocteau, l'enfant terrible of the Parisian avant garde, intended this film as a spoof on tragic romances, overplaying heavy drama into a sort of farce. If so, the point will be lost on U.S. audiences which will probably giggle at the wrong time.

The film plods laboriously through a yarn about an anarchist who comes to kill a Graustarkian queen but stays to become her lover. Fantastic coincidences such as making the assassin and the queen's dead husband carbon copies of each other, are mixed with a jumble of court intrigue into an indigestable stew. Cocteau's direction, which alternates between pretentious artiness and obviousness, is on a par with his scripting. His climactic touch of a love-death embrace between anarchist and queen is so corny, it's comical.

Everybody associated with this effort comes off badly. Cocteau, through his previous films, has proved himself to be an original film artist. Edwige Feuillere, one of France's standout actresses, is helpless in a role that keeps her pouting passionately throughout. Jean Marais, another talented thesper, is literally hamstrung by the direction. Finally, Georges

Auric, who picked up laurels for his brilliant music in "Symphonie Pastorale" and other French pix, has written a completely banal score. *Herm.*

Algo Flota Sobre El Agua
(Something Floats On the Water)
(MEXICAN)

Mexico City, Sept. 14.
Peliculas Nacionales release of Rudolph Loewenthal (Filmex) production. Stars Arturo de Cordoba, Elsa Aguirre, Amparo Morillo; features Fanny Schiller, Ruben Rojo, Gilberto Gonzalez, Joaquin Roche, Jr. Directed by Alfredo A. Crevenna. Adapted by Edmundo Baez and Egon Eis from novel by Lajos Zilahy. Camera, Agustin Martinez Solares. At Cine Mariscala, Mexico City. Running time, 91 MINS.

This picture is one of the best Mexican-made of 1948. Rudolph Loewenthal, who has had much pic experience in Europe, worked very hard and turned out a topper. The story, that of simple folk who live by the sea, should have wide interest because of its humanity. Dialog, unusually well done for a Mexican film, is forceful and real. Alfredo Crevenna's direction is fine and camera work by Augustin Martinez Solares is excellent.

Arturo de Cordoba does a fine bit of acting, and a new young actress, Amparo Morillo, does surprisingly well. Elsa Aguirre, only 17, shows immaturity. Fanny Schiller and Ruben Rojo give excellent support. *Grah.*

Miniature Reviews

"Hills of Home" (Color) (M-G). Edmund Gwenn in melodramatic tearjerker, with Lassie as added appeal; strong where Lassie pictures click.

"The Creeper" (20th). Okay horror feature for a spook bill where chills are being sold.

"Rogues' Regiment" (U). Chase melodrama with front page exploitation twist. Sturdy action fare.

"The Fallen Idol" (Lion). Ralph Richardson, Michele Morgan in ace British-made murder drama.

"Noose" (Pathe). British-made underworld comedy-drama, with Carole Landis, Joseph Calleia.

"Esther Waters" (GFD). British-made Victorian domestic drama, with horse-racing background.

"The Weaker Sex" (GFD). British drama of femmes during the war is on the weaker side.

Hills of Home
(COLOR)

Metro release of Robert Sisk production. Stars Edmund Gwenn and Lassie; features Donald Crisp, Janet Leigh, Rhys Williams. Directed by Fred M. Wilcox. Original screenplay, William Ludwig, suggested by Ian MacLaren sketches, "Doctor of the Old School"; camera (Technicolor), Charles Schoenbaum; editor, Ralph E. Winters. Tradeshown Oct. 1, '48. Running time, 97 MINS.

Dr. William MacLure ..... Edmund Gwenn
Drumsheugh ..... Donald Crisp
Tammas Milton ..... Tom Drake
Margit Mitchell ..... Janet Leigh
Mr. Milton ..... Rhys Williams
Hopps ..... Reginald Owen
Jaimie Soutar ..... Edmond Breon
Sir George ..... Alan Napier
Geordie ..... Hugh Green
Lord Kilspindle ..... Lumsden Hare
Belle Saunders ..... Eileen Erskine
David Mitchell ..... Victor Wood
Burnbrae ..... David Thursky
Dr. Weston ..... Frederick Worlock

This richly entertaining tear-jerker rises above being just another Lassie film. That is because of Edmund Gwenn's strong character study of a country doctor. Magnificent Technicolor adds further value. Film looks to reach top Lassie grosses, which is plenty okay for a picture of this type and budget. Title is meaningless, and if changed would help the box-office.

Robert Sisk's production combines enough of a dog story with straight melodrama to satisfy. Plot has Lasslie pushed around and depicted as a weakling afraid to go into the water until near the story's end. Earlier passages show Gwenn's untiring efforts to cure Lassie of this deadly fear.

While following the usual Lassie pattern half way through the vehicle, producers saw the strength to be derived by concentrating more on the sterling worth of the country medico to swing the yarn to a stirring climax. It shows the medico rushing about the country-side, saving lives, until old age finally brings the fatal accident.

There is the by-now familiar rescue with Lassie running for help to bring its injured master, the doctor, from the freezing storm—and swimming a raging stream to do it. A death-bed scene, burial and cemetery visitation are effective enough to please the most jaded.

Gwenn makes an ideal Scotch man of medicine. It is a solid delineation, measuring up to his finest previous efforts. Whole production is studded with Scottish accents, with Donald Crisp unusually excellent as the rich village friend of the doctor. Rhys Williams makes a rugged sheep raiser, being the closest thing to a villain in the piece.

Janet Leigh, only young femme in the picture, does well enough as the young student doctor's sweetheart. For a fairly new face to the screen, she comes through nicely, especially in a couple of more dramatic episodes. Tom Drake is nicely cast as this young medico. Reginald Owen makes the blustery innkeeper too much so. Lassie, of course, is the same smart canine-actor and not weighted down with the ostentatious makeup of some of the Scottish characters in this picture.

Tops among the large support cast are Edmond Breon, Alan Napier and Hugh Green. William Ludwig's original screenplay is a smooth writing job. Fred M. Wilcox directs intelligently, building up his climaxes with skill. Lensing by Charles Schoenbaum is top-flight throughout. *Wear.*

The Creeper

Hollywood, Oct. 2.

20th-Fox release of Ben Pivar (Reliance) production. Features Eduardo Ciannelli, Onslow Stevens, June Vincent, Ralph Morgan, Janis Wilson, John Baragrey. Directed by Jean Yarbrough. Screenplay, Maurice Tombragel; original, Don Martin; camera, George Robinson; editor, Saul A. Goodkind. At Grauman's Chinese, Hollywood, Oct. 1, '48. Running time, 63 MINS.

Dr. Van Glock ..... Eduardo Ciannelli
Dr. Bordon ..... Onslow Stevens
Gwen ..... June Vincent
Dr. Cavigny ..... Ralph Morgan
Nora ..... Janis Wilson
Dr. John Reade ..... John Baragrey
Inspector Fenwick ..... Richard Lane
Wong ..... Philip Ahn
Nurse ..... Lotte Stein
Porter ..... Ralph Peters
Andre ..... David Hoffman

Reliance Pictures has contrived a spook film that is an okay coupler for special Halloween or other chiller shows. Otherwise, it is a laboriously done, synthetic spine-tingler that shouldn't play double bills except with like fare. Pic is out of place in its local coupling with another 20th-Fox release, "Apartment for Peggy," making a bad teammate for "Peggy's" family and juve draw.

Plot concerns experiments with phosphorus, aimed at illuminating internal organs as an operational aid. Somewhere along the line, the experiments go haywire, with serum, developed from cats, turning those on whom it is used into maniacial felines (at least that's the inference gained from the vague plotting).

Menace comes when one doc wants to give up the experiments and another tries to carry them on. Three deaths, apparently caused by the clawing of a huge cat, spot the footage and suspects are strewn around generously. Shadowy lighting, false clues and sundry stock tricks of the horror subject do manage to stir up an occasional goose-bump, particularly for the highly susceptible or nervous.

Eduardo Ciannelli heads the featured cast but his role is only a small one as a red herring drawn across exposure of Onslow Stevens as the mad scientist. Hectic romance is taken care of by Janis Wilson and John Baragrey, while June Vincent and Ralph Morgan fill in as two of the victims.

Jean Yarbrough's direction of the Maurice Tombragel script manages a few eerie moments. Ben Pivar, as executive producer, supplies okay budget framework for the melodramatics. Lensing by George Robinson is good. *Brog.*

Rogues' Regiment
(SONGS)

Hollywood, Oct. 1.

Universal release of Robert Buckner production. Stars Dick Powell, Marta Toren, Vincent Price; features Stephen McNally, Carol Thurston, Edgar Barrier. Directed by Robert Florey. Screenplay, Robert Buckner, from original by Buckner and Florey; camera, Maury Gertsman; editor, Ralph Dawson; songs, Jack Brooks, Serge Walter. Previewed Sept. 28, '48. Running time, 85 MINS.

Whit Corbett ..... Dick Powell
Lili Maubert ..... Marta Toren
Mark Van Ratten ..... Vincent Price
Carl Reicher ..... Stephen McNally
Colonel Mauclaire ..... Edgar Barrier
Erich Heindorf ..... Henry Rowland
Li-Ho-Kay ..... Carol Thurston
Cobb ..... James Millican
Kao Pang ..... Richard Loo
Tran Duy Gian ..... Philip Ahn
Rycroft ..... Richard Fraser
Stein ..... Otto Reichow
Sam Latch ..... Kenny Washington
O'Hara ..... Dennis Dengate
Colonel Lemercier ..... Frank Conroy
Hazarat ..... Martin Garralaga
American Colonel ..... James F. Nolan

Neat action exploitation feature has been built around the still-missing Martin Bormann, rated as third-ranking Nazi wartime big-shot. In "Rogues' Regiment," dramatic license gives one version of what might have happened to him. Results are excellent for melodrama fans.

Name of Dick Powell is sufficient guarantee of some rough, tough doings and the script comes through. Writing is not too imaginative, but effectively integrates all of the standard tricks of the meller-suspense feature to keep the pic on the move and reasonably exciting.

The French Foreign Legion and a locale of Indo-China, skirmishes between Legionnaires and natives, double-dealing art collectors who are gunrunners and sloe-eyed exotic charmers, furnish colorful background for the U. S. Army's chase across a continent to get the missing Nazi.

Powell is the chaser and Stephen McNally the chased. Army Intelligence is handicapped by having no photo of the missing Nazi but clues place him in Indo-China. Powell joins the Legion, surmounts personal dangers and springs his trap. Legion-native clash is excellently staged, adding to excitement and there is strong menace supplied by Vincent Price as a gunrunning art collector.

Marta Toren lends charm and vocal two numbers as a Saigon nitery canary who is really a French agent. Tunes are "Just For a While," with English and German lyrics, and "Who Can Tell," both cleffed by Jack Brooks and Serge Walter.

McNally makes a good impression as the scurrying Nazi (script gives him the names of Bruner and Reicher instead of Bormann to permit dramatic license), and Henry Rowland shows up well as a cowardly ex-S. S. officer. Edgar Barrier, Carol Thurston, James Millican, Richard Loo, Philip Ahn and others are competent.

Robert Buckner and Robert Florey share writing credits, fashioning okay commercial feature to which Florey gives well-paced direction. Buckner's production framing is showwise to get the best values and lensing by Maury Gertsman is expert. Editing is good. *Brog.*

The Fallen Idol
(BRITISH)

London, Sept. 29.

British Lion release of London Films production. Stars Michele Morgan, Ralph Richardson. Directed by Carol Reed. Screenplay by Graham Greene; additional dialog by Lesley Storm, William Templeton. Editor, Oswald Hafenrichter; music, William Alwyn; camera, Georges Perinal, Dennis Coop. At Rialto, London, Sept. 29, '48. Running time, 94 MINS.

Baines ..... Ralph Richardson
Julie ..... Michele Morgan
Felipe ..... Bobby Henrey
Mrs. Baines ..... Sonia Dresdel
Det. Inspector Crowe ..... Denis O'Dea
Dr. Fenton ..... Walter Fitzgerald
First Secretary ..... Karel Stepanek
Mrs. Barrow ..... Joan Young
Mrs. Patterson ..... Danby Nichols
Detective Hart ..... Bernard Lee
Detective Lake ..... Jack Hawkins
Detective Davis ..... Geoffrey Keene
Clockwinder ..... Hay Petrie
Perry ..... James Hayter
Dr. Wilson ..... John Ruddock
Rose ..... Dora Bryan
Policeman "A" ..... Torin Thatcher

A fine sensitive story, a brillant new child star and a polished cast headed by Ralph Richardson and Michele Morgan, combine to make "The Fallen Idol" a satisfying piece of intelligent entertainment certain of success in Britain and worthy of widespread presentation in America.

Based on a short story by Graham Greene, the script, which won first prize at this year's Venice Festival for the best screenplay, develops the triangle drama with powerful dramatic force. Briefly, it's a story of the frustrated marriage of a butler, working at a foreign embassy in London, who's in love with an embassy typist. While the lovers are together, the wife, who has pretended to be in the country, comes in and after a hysterical row with her husband, accidentally falls and is killed.

Dominating the entire theme is young Felipe, son of the ambassador, who is left in the servants' care while the parents are away. The butler, Baines, and the boy are great friends, but Mrs. Baines and Felipe are not. When a police investigation suggests that the wife might have been murdered, Felipe lies for all he is worth to defend the butler, when the evidence of an accident is revealed, he tries in vain to tell the truth.

There's hardly a scene in the picture in which the kid, played by Bobby Henrey, doesn't appear and he comes through like a seasoned trouper. Setting the high standard for the acting is Ralph Richardson, whose masterly portrayal of the butler is a gratifying piece of work. Michele Morgan, with perfect restraint, wins sympathy for the "other woman" and Sonia Dresdel is typically hard and hysterical as the wronged wife. Dora Bryan stands out in a bit as a prostitute.

"The Fallen Idol" is unmistakably a director's picture, and Carol Reed has shown a complete understanding of the theme by extracting every ounce from the characters, as well as displaying a strong sense of humor and a clear conception of drama. Settings are excellent and the general production qualities are of a high standard. *Myro.*

Noose
(BRITISH)

London, Sept. 29.

Pathe release of Associated British Picture Corp.—Edward Dryhurst production. Stars Carole Landis, Derek Farr, Joseph Calleia. Directed by Edmond T. Greville. Screenplay by Richard Llewellyn, from his own play; editor, David Newhouse; music, Charles Williams; camera, Hone Glendinning. At Warner, London, Sept. 28, '48. Running time, 96 MINS.

Linda Medbury ..... Carole Landis

Sugiani ....Joseph Calleia
Captain Hoyle.............Derek Farr
Rendall ....Stanley Holloway
Bar Gorman................Nigel Patrick
Annie Foss.............Ruth Nixon
Mercia Lane ....Carol Van Derman
Pudd'n Bason..............John Slater
Basher..............Leslie Bradley
Editor..............Reginald Tate
Slush..................,......Edward Rigby
Greasy Anderson..........John Salew
Sergeant Brooks...........Robert Adair
The Barber.................Hay Petrie
Cosly................Uriel Porter
Nelly ....Ella Retford
Maffy..... ....Brenda Hogan

Gangsters, black - marketeers and smugglers congregate in Soho for this comedy-drama which deals with London's underworld army of racketeers. "Noose" is a nice subject to help fill the quota bill at home, but isn't likely to go too big in the export market, despite American names in leads.

From their night club in the heart of Soho, Sugiaini and his right-hand man, Bar Gorman, control a network of black market operations. They make the best five pound notes and gasoline coupons, operate a minor fleet for customs running and go in for smuggling. If someone gets too bothersome, he's put out of the way. Police are powerless and never have anything on Sugiani until an interfering newspaperwoman gets a lead on a murder and follows it through with the aid of a few hundred thugs to bring the racketeers to justice.

Depending more on characterization than on dramatic values, pic is noted for the excellent types who portray the underworld thugs. Joseph Calleia as Sugiani; Nigel Patrick as the irrepressible Bar Gorman, and Hay Petrie as the murderer, help lend color to the production. The late Carole Landis is attractive as the newspaperwoman who stumbles on a scoop and makes trouble for Sugiani. Teamed with her in providing the romantic interest is Derek Farr, who organizes and plans operation "Noose" with the aid of toughs from a boxing camp. *Myro.*

Esther Waters
(BRITISH)
London, Sept. 29.
GFD release of J. Arthur Rank-Wessex production. Stars Kathleen Ryan. Dirk Bogarde. Directed by Ian Dalrymple, Peter Proud. Screenplay by Michael Gordon, William Rose, from novel by George Moore; additional dialog, Gerard Tyrrell; editor, Brereton Porter; music, Dr. Gordon Jacob; camera, C. Pennington-Richards, H. E. Fowle. At Odeon, London, Sept. 28, '48. Running time, 108 MINS.
Esther Waters ....Kathleen Ryan
William Latch.............Dirk Bogarde
Fred Parsons..............Cyril Cusack
Randle ....Ivor Barnard
Mrs. Barfield.........Fay Compton
Sarah Tucker........Margaret Diamond
Mrs. Latch ....Mary Clare
Squire Barfield..........Julian D'Albie
Margaret Gale..........Shelagh Fraser
Joe Evans ....Harry Ross
Miss Peggy ....Lalage Lewis
Fred Archer..........Alexander Parker

This is another of those ponderous Victorian novels, this time from the pen of the Irish writer, George Moore, and perhaps his best-known work. The adapters have done a skillful job, lightening as far as possible a woeful story. Apart from appeal for its author, its main attraction will be to racing fans. Much of the action centers on the track, with Derby Day thrills culminating in the triumph of Fred Archer, the first American to win the event.

A young chapel-reared kitchen maid is seduced by a groom. The boy is quite willing to wed when he has enough put by, but is a born gambler and, after a rift with his sweetheart, clears out with another girl.

Years of drifting from place to place, boarding out her infant, is the girl's life, with heartache and misery telescoped through flashes of succeeding dates.

On the verge of marrying a preacher, Esther suddenly encounters her lover, now a flashy, prosperous bookmaker. He begs her to marry him for the sake of their son, and she settles down with him. Luck favors them for a while. Then the husband, now quite ill, gambles his savings on a horse, and dies, unaware that his last gamble has failed. His wife and child are reduced to penury again.

Kathleen Ryan is adequately pathetic and winsome as the wronged maiden and Dirk Bogarde gives an excellent performance as her betrayer. His death-bed scene is vivid dramatization, with the visions of the Derby race seen through his imagination, providing one of the most moving shots in the film. Color and effect are plentifully supplied with the track scenes at Epsom, and painstaking efforts succeed in bringing authentic atmosphere to the day and age. Supporting cast is commendable, but chief interest centers on the main characters. Miss Ryan has already achieved distinction with "Odd Man Out," but this is Bogarde's first screen stint and he comes through with high honors. *Clem.*

The Weaker Sex
(BRITISH)
London, Sept. 23.
GFD release of J. Arthur Rank-Two Cities Film (Paul Soskin) production. Stars Ursula Jeans, Cecil Parker. Joan Hopkins. Directed by Roy Baker. Screenplay by Esther McCracken, Soskin, adapted from Miss McCracken's play, "No Medals." Editor, Michael Joseph Stirling; camera, Erwin Hillier, Eric Besche; music, Arthur Wilkinson. At Leicester Square, London, Sept. 22, '48. Running time, 84 MINS.
Martha Dacre ....Ursula Jeans
Geoffrey Radcliffe..........Cecil Parker
Helen ....Joan Hopkins
Nigel ....Derek Bond
Lolly ....Lana Morris
Roddy ....John Stone
Mrs. Gaye..................Thora Hird
Benjie ....Digby Wolfe
Harriet ....Marian Spencer
Mrs. Maling............Dorothy Bramhall
Soldier ....Bill Owen
Capt. Dishart..........Kynaston Reeves

It's difficult to determine the motives which prompted Paul Soskin to make "The Weaker Sex," because it possesses very little in story values, and devotes a large part of its footage to recalling the war days without saying anything new. Presumably, it's meant to be a tribute to the long-suffering British housewife who still has to face queues and rationing, and as such may earn a sympathetic response from her opposite number in America.

The rambling story opens on the eve of D-Day, and Martha Dacre, like every other mother, is emotionally overwhelmed. After all, she's got a couple of daughters in the Wrens, a son and son-in-law in the Navy, and a couple of service men billeted on her. From that beginning one watches the progress of the Dacre family and its off-shoots, through the inevitable mining of the ship, and the marriage of mother and daughter to the billetees. Comes the end of the war, and with it the disillusionment that they aren't returning to a land of plenty; that distrust and suspicion still lurk in the background, and that a third world war is not beyond the realms of possibility.

Not by any means a powerful story, although the obvious emotional angles have been fully exploited and come into play in one or two strong scenes. Pic's main weakness, however, is its lack of action; it's almost the stage play transferred to celluloid and brought up to date by the authoress herself. As Mrs. Dacre, Ursula Jeans has a part which she handles with utmost ease; Cecil Parker is nicely cast as the naval officer whom she marries, and Lana Morris makes a satisfying starring debut as one of the Wrens. Major supporting roles are played with competence by an experienced cast but they are unable to redeem a subject which, while abounding in sincerity, is devoid of vitality. *Myrt.*

Always Another Dawn
Sydney, Sept. 24.
Universal-International release of Embassy Pictures (Tom McCreadie) production. Stars Charles Tingwell, Guy Doleman; features Queenie Ashton, Betty McDowell, Douglas Herald, Charles Zoll, Max Gibb. Directed by McCreadie. Original screenplay, Zelma Roberts; camera, George Malcolm. At Embassy, Sydney, Sept. 24, '48. Running time, 85 MINS.

This is Embassy Pictures' first break into the home production field. Producer-director Tom McCreadie runs an urban cinema near Sydney. Initial effort, cut to 30 minutes, would make a fairly good documentary. As is, however, it will probably get by locally, but won't have overseas draw.

Story is set around the exploits of the Royal Australian Navy and introduces the Coral Sea battle and other exploits during World War II. The local Navy cooperated with McCreadie for some good sea stuff. Otherwise there's not much to "Dawn." Dialog is stilted and has too many flag-waving speeches. Both Charles Tingwell and Guy Doleman show promise as screen players and may go places later. Rest of cast very weak.

This one won't put Aussie on the pic production map. *Rick.*

Foreign Films

"Marknadsafton" ("Carnival Evening") (SWEDISH). Sandrew-Bauman Film production and release. Stars Adolf Jahr, Emy Hagman; features Sigge Fyrst, Rut Holm, Carin Swenson, Bellan Roos. Directed by Ivar Johansson. Screenplay, Johansson; camera, Hilding Bladh; music, Charles Redland. At Grand, Stockholm. Running time, 78 MINS.

Based on a novel by w.k. Swedish author Wilhelm Moberg, "Marknadsafton" emerges as a fairly good film. It's a simple story of life in a Swedish province. Adolf Jahr tops the cast with a fine performance. Ivar Johansson's direction is capable as is lensing of Hilding Bladh. Picture undoubtedly will do will in Scandinavia, but its chances overseas will be confined to those familar with the Swedish tongue. *Wing.*

The Gallant Blade
(COLOR)
Columbia release of Irving Starr production. Stars Larry Parks, Marguerite Chapman; features Victor Jory, George MacReady. Directed by Henry Levin. Screenplay, Walter Ferris, Morton Grant; additional dialog, Wilfrid Pettitt; based on story by Ted Thomas and Edward Dein; camera (Cinecolor), Burnett Guffey, Charles Lawton; editor, Viola Lawrence; musical director, M. W. Stoloff; score, George Duning. Tradeshown N.Y., Oct. 11, '48. Running time, 81 MINS.
Lt. David Picard.............Larry Parks
Nanon de Lartigues.Marguerite Chapman
Marshall Mordore..............Victor Jory
General Cadeau........George MacReady
Madame Chauvignac.........Edith King
Paul Brissac................Michael Duane
General de la Garance....Onslow Stevens
Sergeant Jacques..........Peter Brocco
Major Lanier.............Tim Huntley
Henri ....Ross Ford
Georges ....Paul Campbell
Lawrence ....Fred Sears
Sergeant Martine........Nedrick Young
Duc d' Orleans.............Wilton Graff

"The Gallant Blade" is a de luxe swashbuckler slated for solid b.o. reception in all situations. Built along straight-action lines and aiming directly for the ready-made market for such fare, this pic can't miss with its pace, color and potent marquee values. Once again, as in Columbia's "The Swordsman," Larry Parks has a surefire role in a period costume saga whose escapist appeal will cut across all age levels.

Handsomely tinted, this film shows the best results achieved to date by the Cinecolor process. Careful attention to costuming, interior decorating and lighting and exterior shooting has made possible well-defined but naturalistic tinting. The expert color job is typical of the pic's overall production mounting, which has that luxurious, velvetine surface usually demanded for this type of entertainment.

Chief credit for this film's sturdy qualities, however, belongs to director Henry Levin. Aided by a straightforward script, Levin keeps the action rolling with headlong speed, cramming the celluloid with sword and gunplay, cross-country chases, intrigue and other stratagems to keep the customers, particularly the kids, in a boil. But while this pic doesn't contain a single subtle gesture, it also avoids crudity. It's hoss opera with fancy trimmings.

Cloak-and-dagger yarn is set in 17th Century France when, according to the script's loose history, a struggle broke out between the ruling warmongering faction and a group of peace-loving generals and soldiers. Victor Jory, as the heavy, attempts to crush the rebels by kidnapping a popular general, George MacReady, but Parks, as the latter's adjutant, stymies the plan by outwitting its execution and out-duelling his opponents in the nick of time.

Too close an examination of the plot mechanics is unnecessary, and besides, it's blocked by no less than four stirring fencing matches which compensate for any holes in the yarn. Romantic angles are injected via a love affair between Marguerite Chapman, Jory's espionage agent, and Parks, but the action never trips over this phase of the story.

As a bouncing swordsman, Parks delivers neatly by playing the heroics for all they are worth, but not more. Miss Chapman also registers with a neat performance that doesn't overstrain the emotions. Jory cops thesping honors with his smoothly sinister portrait of a court bigwig. MacReady also contributes a strong supporting performance and the rest of the large cast acquit themselves competently.

Herm.

No Minor Vices

Metro release of Enterprise (Lewis Milestone) production, directed by Milestone. Stars Dana Andrews, Lilli Palmer, Louis Jourdan; features Jane Wyatt, Norman Lloyd. Original screenplay, Arnold Manoff; editor, Robert Parrish; camera, George Barnes; music, Franz Waxman. Tradeshown, N. Y., Sept. 7, '48. Running time, 96 MINS.

Perry Aswell .... Dana Andrews
April Ashwell .... Lilli Palmer
Otavio Quaglini .... Louis Jourdan
Miss Darlington .... Jane Wyatt
Dr. Sturdivant .... Norman Lloyd
Mr. Zitzfleisch .... Bernard Gorcey
Mr. Felton .... Roy Roberts
Mrs. Felton .... Fay Baker
Gloria .... Sharon McManus
Mrs. Faraday .... Ann Doran
Bertram .... Beau Bridges
Cab Driver .... Frank Kreig
Receptionist .... Kay Williams
Genius .... Bobby Hyatt

"No Minor Vices," first Enterprise production to be released by Metro, is an attempt at the type of sophisticated comedy patterned originally by such cinema clicks as "It Happened One Night." Film is neatly paced and contains its quota of laughs but lacks the touch instilled in those earlier efforts. As a result, it will go okay in the key cities but may find it tough sledding in the hinterlands because of its hyper-sophistication. Picture will have to depend there strictly on its word of-mouth, since Dana Andrews, Lilli Palmer and Louis Jourdan haven't sufficient marquee lure for any really big payoff.

"Vices," marking Jourdan's second appearance in an American film, definitely sets up the French-born actor as a comedy star of first magnitude. He's cast as a Bohemian-type artist who almost wrecks the married life of Andrews and Miss Palmer. The role is in almost direct contrast to the harsh, romantic juvenile he played in David O. Selznick's "Paradine Case," his U. S. breaker-inner. Jourdan doesn't miss a bet in milking the script for every laugh available. Those newly-revealed talents, plus his s.a. appeal for the femmes, should make him a top boxoffice draw.

Arnold Manoff, who penned the original screenplay, had a good idea to start with but partially ruined its effectiveness by overdoing it. Particularly at fault is the over-usage of the off-camera "voices," supposed to be the consciences of the three leads. Eugene O'Neill employed this device best in his "Strange Interlude" and Manoff could have had equally good results, but overdid it. Effectiveness of Bernard Gorcey as a cigar-maker who watches the goings-on among the three stars from a window across the way is also partially negated by too constant usage.

Andrews is cast as a successful young pediatrician, who enjoys life to the full until he hooks up with Jourdon by inviting him to his offices to sketch some "real life." Painter immediately throws both the doctor's practice and private life into a turmoil by demonstrating, via his sketches, the real character of all with whom he comes into contact. He then makes a play for Miss Palmer (Andrews' wife), and the latter consents against his better judgment to let him portrait her. The green eye then rears its head in some hilarious sequences, but Jourdan gets a sudden change of heart and reveals in his painting that Andrews and his frau should stick together, and bows politely out of the picture.

Under the slick directorial touch of Lewis Milestone, who doubled from his producing job, the cast is good from the stars to the smallest bit player. Both Andrews and Miss Palmer, also switching from their usual heavier-type roles, shine with surprising comedic talents. Andrews is particularly good in one sequence where he imagines how best to break up a supposed tete-a-tete between Jourdan and his wife. Jane Wyatt is fine as Andrews' romantic nurse and Norman Lloyd dittoes as the doc's milquetoast assistant.

While the film isn't a spectacle by any means, Milestone has provided it with some expensive-looking production trappings, in keeping with its sophisticated formula. Camera work is excellent, as is Franz Waxman's score. The special photographic effects also rate a nod.

Stal.

Macbeth

Hollywood, Oct. 9.

Republican release of Mercury production (Orson Welles) directed by and starring Welles. Features Jeanette Nolan, Dan O'Herlihy, Roddy McDowall, Edgar Barrier, Alan Napier. From the play by William Shakespeare; camera, John L. Russell; editor, Louis Lindsay; score, Jacques Ibert, conducted by Efrem Kurtz. Previewed Oct. 7, '48. Running time, 106 MINS.

Macbeth .... Orson Welles
Lady Macbeth .... Jeanette Nolan
Macduff .... Dan O'Herlihy
Malcolm .... Roddy McDowall
Banquo .... Edgar Barrier
A Holy Father .... Alan Napier
Duncan .... Erskine Sanford
Ross .... John Dierkes
Lennox .... Keene Curtis
Lady Macduff .... Peggy Webber
Siward .... Lionel Braham
Young Siward .... Archie Heugly
Fleance .... Jerry Farber
Macduff Child .... Christopher Welles
Doctor .... Morgan Farley
Gentlewoman .... Lurene Tuttle
First Murderer .... Brainerd Duffield
Second Murderer .... William Alland
Seyton .... George Chirello
A Porter .... Gus Schilling
The Three .... Brainerd Duffield / Lurene Tuttle / Peggy Webber

William Shakespeare's "Macbeth" will survive its latest interpretation. Orson Welles' version undoubtedly is gratifying to the producer-director-star. To Bard purists it will be considerably less. On the art circuit, with emphasis on the Wellesian treatment, some initial interest can be stirred. Curiosity factor is strong regarding how Welles interprets Shakespeare, but results are not likely to please.

On the general situation route, "Macbeth" doesn't look like a commercial success. Shakespeare is b.o. only in some class versions when given specialized treatment in art spots. Latter is best hope for Welles' idea of Shakespeare—and it is such a personalized version that the controversy it might stir could mean extra ticket sales.

Production was comparatively inexpensive for this day of high costs—and looks it. Mood is as dour as the Scottish moors and crags that background the plot. Film is crammed with scenery-chewing theatrics in the best Shakespearean manner with Welles dominating practically every bit of footage. Only a few of the Bard's best lines are audible. The rest are lost in strained, dialectic gibbering that is only sound, not prose. At best, Shakepeare dialog requires close attention; but even intense concentration can't make intelligible the reading by Welles and others in the cast.

"Macbeth," the play, devotes considerable time to depicting femme influence on the male to needle his vanity and ambition into murder for a kingdom. "Macbeth," the film, devotes that footage to the male's reaction to the femme needling. Several Shakespeare characters have been turned into a Welles-introduced one, a Holy Father. There are similar bits of Wellesian license taken throughout, with which there would have been no quarrel had they been an improvement.

Welles introduces Jeanette Nolan as Lady Macbeth. Her reading is best in the "out, damned spot" scene. Dan O'Herlihy fares best as Macduff, his reading having the clearest ennunciation. Others are only adequate in tossing straight lines for Welles. Gloom of the play is aptly expressed in sackcloth costuming and fog-bound, barren settings against which "Macbeth" is played. Lensing is low-key, and full of trick angles that are distracting. Musical score by Jacques Ibert is excellent.

Brog.

Million Dollar Weekend

(SONGS)

Eagle Lion release of Masque (Matty Kemp) production. Stars Gene Raymond, Stephanie Paull, Francis Lederer; features Robert Warwick, Patricia Shay, James Craven, Royal Hawaiian Serenaders. Directed by Gene Raymond. Screenplay, Charles S. Belden; original story, Kemp and Raymond; camera, Paul Ivano; songs, Dorothy Daniels, Dorothy Roberts, Paul Koy. Previewed in N. Y. Oct. 7, '48. Running time, 73 MINS.

Nicholas Lawrence .... Gene Raymond
Cynthia Strong .... Stephanie Paull
Alan Marker .... Francis Lederer
Dave Dietrich .... Robert Warwick
Sally .... Patricia Shay
Dr. George Strong .... James Craven

Weighed down by an implausible story, "Million Dollar Weekend" is a passive dual entry. Its characters are unrealistic and a further handicap is the excessive attention to United Airlines, Napoleon brandy and name plaques of prominent San Francisco hotels. This frank amount of commercialism may irritate some exhibitors.

Original story of Gene Raymond and Matty Kemp, who directed and produced respectively, may have looked good on paper. All the action is compressed within a weekend. Worried over his business affairs, brokerage partner Raymond decides to flee to Shanghai with $1,000,000 of his firm's securities and cash. Aboard a plane en route to Honolulu, he becomes involved with two fellow passengers, widow Stephanie Paull, and Francis Lederer, who's trying to blackmail her.

In a series of clumsy mistakes, Raymond loses his haul to Lederer in an Hawaiian hotel. Chasing the thief back to San Francisco, he regains the loot after a long-anticipated fistic battle. Then feeling that he had wrongly absconded in the first place, returns to his office with the money. Final fadeout comes in Honolulu a month later, where both Raymond and Miss Paull had romantically agreed to meet again should their problems be adjusted.

Raymond appears strangely non-aggressive in view of Lederer's constant needling. When the fight does come, it's largely anti-climatic. Lederer tends to overplay his part of the blackmailer. Miss Paull's acting talents aren't particularly tested by a role which calls for her to emulate a clining-vine type with no resourcefulness whatsoever of her own.

Spliced into the footage are several musical sequences. Two numbers, "My Destiny" and "Where Have You Been?", by Dorothy Daniels and Dorothy Roberts, are mediocre material, as is "Heaven in Blue Hawaii" by Paul Koy. Raymond's direction is uneven while Matty Kemp's production values reflect a moderate budget. Paul Ivano's lensing is satisfactory.

Gilb.

The Strange Mrs. Crane

Hollywood, Oct. 9.

Eagle Lion release of John Sutherland production. Stars Marjorie Lord, Robert Shayne, Pierre Watkin, James Seay; features Ruthe Brady, Claire Whitney, Mary Gordon. Directed by Sherman Scott. Screenplay, Al Martin; original story, Frank Burt, Robert Libott; camera, Jack Greenhalgh; editor, Martin Cohn. At Vogue, Hollywood, Oct. 8, '48. Running time, 59 MINS.

Gina Crane .... Marjorie Lord
Floyd Durant .... Robert Shayne
Clinton Crane .... Pierre Watkin
Mark Emery .... James Seay
Barbara Arnold .... Ruthe Brady
Edna Emmerson .... Claire Whitney
Nora .... Mary Gordon
Marlow .... Chester Clute
Jennette Woods .... Dorothy Granger
McLean .... Charles Williams

"The Strange Mrs. Crane" is program melodrama that will just get by in supporting bookings. For all its meller implications, suspense and action are lacking.

Lightweight plot is the one about a former badger game expert now married to an elderly candidate for governor. When her former partner in crime shows up and tries blackmail, she murders him. Another femme is accused and tried for murder. The real killer is jury foreman and when the accused is convicted the court clerk gets a personal letter instead of the jury verdict. Letter hangs the rap on the politico's wife for the windup.

Cast troupes hard to get some life into the contrived plotting but trite dialog and situations are tough barriers to hurdle. Sherman Scott's direction suffers from same handicaps. Marjorie Lord is the femme crook turned respectable and Robert Shayne is her ex-partner. Ruthe Brady does the accused and Pierre Watkin is the old husband.

John Sutherland's production values are adequate to budget expenditure. Lensing and other technical credits are standard.

Brog.

Back Trail

Monogram release of Barney Sarecky production. Stars Johnny Mack Brown; features Raymond Hatton. Directed by Christy Cabanne. Screenplay, J. Benton Cheney. At New York theatre, N. Y., week Oct. 5, '48. Running time, 57 MINS.

Johnny	Johnny Mack Brown
Casoose	Raymond Hatton
Helen	Mildred Coles
Lacey	Marshall Reed
Terry	James Horne
Goofy	Snub Pollard
Frazer	Ted Adams
Gilmore	Pierce Lyden

"Back Trail" is a so-so Johnny Mack Brown oater. There are a minimum of chase scenes, and the fisticuff sequences are also seldom exciting, with none of the participants really cutting loose. This entry is strictly for the action situations and the Sat. mat trade.

There's a little blackmail mixed up in this tale. Saloonkeeper Pierce Lyden, who leads the outlaws, knows banker Ted Adams did a little time in stir in his younger days and threatens to expose him unless he kicks in with information on gold shipment departures. Suffice it that special investigator Brown gets to the bottom of all this in liesurely fashion.

Brown mechanically moves his dukes through a couple brawls with the outlaws. The former Alabama gridiron champ has been a lot more convincing in some of his previous outdoor sagas. Raymond Hatton is okay as his sidekick, while Lyden and Adams do as best they can with stereotyped roles. Producer Barney Sarecky eked this one out on an obviously slim budget. Christy Cabanne's direction is fair as is the lensing.

Gilb.

Appointment With Murder

Film Classics release of Falcon (Jack Bernhard) production. Directed by Bernhard. Stars John Calvert; features Catherine Craig, Jack Reitzen, Lyle Talbot. Screenplay, Don Martin; original story, Joel Malone, Harold Swanton, based on character created by Michael Arlen; camera, Walter Strenge; editor, Asa Boyd Clark; music, Karl Hajos. Previewed N. Y. Oct. 7, '48. Running time, 67 MINS.

Falcon	John Calvert
Lorraine	Catherine Craig
Norton	Jack Reitzen
Fred Muller	Lyle Talbot
Count Dalo	Robert Conte
Donatti	Fred Brocco
Minecci	Ben Welden
Farella	Carlos Schipa
Italian Woman	Ann Demitri
Customs Officer	Pat Lane
Butler	Eric Wilton
Baggage Clerk No. 1	Robert Nadell
Baggage Clerk No. 2	Michael Mark
Miss Connors	Carole Donne
Thug No. 1	Gene Carrick
Thug No. 2	Frank Richards
Guard	Carl Sklover
Detective	Jay Griffith
Hotel Clerk	Jack Chefe

As the latest in the "Falcon" series, "Appointment with Murder" is familiar action-mystery stuff. However, despite its pat plot, the film is fast moving and rates as a suitable entry to round out the lower half of the double bills.

There's an international background to the yarn which revolves around a brace of stolen paintings. This time, John Calvert as the Falcon, is an insurance investigator who's searching for the canvanses both in Hollywood and Italy in behalf of his employers who've paid off a claim on their loss.

Before the old masters are retrieved, Calvert has a busy time of it in outwitting culprit Jack Reitzen as well as analyzing the complicity of art gallery owner Catherine Craig in the matter. Although a mild amount of suspense is generated by Don Martin's screenplay, adapted from the Joel Malone and Harold Swanton original, most whodunit fans won't have any difficulty in anticipating the plot's movements.

Calvert is suave and forthright as the private investigator, Miss Craig seems rather youthful to be the proprietor of a swank art gallery, but handles her role competently enough. Reitzen is amply sinister as the thief. Lyle Talbot has little to do as the insurance company head. Supporting cast is generally adequate. Jack Bernhard's production values are good as is also his direction. Walter Strenge's camerawork measures up.

Gilb.

Without Prejudice
(RUSSIAN)

Artkino release of Popular Science Film Studios (U.S.S.R.) release. Stars Sergei Kurilov. Directed by Alexander Razumni. Screenplay, V. M. Volkenstein, Alexei Speshnev; camera, Boris Petrov; English titles, Charles Clement. At Stanley, N. Y., starting Oct. 9, '48. Running time, 90 MINS.

Nikolai Miklukho-Maclay	Sergei Kurilov
Margaret Robertson	Galina Grigoryeva
Thompson	Dmitri Budarov
Boy	Jim Komogorov
Dr. Brandler	Mikhail Astangov
Oor	Weyland Rodd
Maloo	Robert Robinson
Mr. Robertson	Andrei Maximov

(In Russian; English Titles)

This semi-documentary jungle yarn is purportedly based on the life of Nikolai Miklukho-Maclay, a 19th century Russian explorer and scientist. Story would have the audience believe he was first white man to set foot on the Maclay coast of New Guinea. Film is too elongated for what actually transpires on the screen but it may do okay in the few Russian-language theatres in the U. S.

Director Alexander Razumni obviously was overcome with the idea that he was directing a jungle opus, and the simple story is not helped by the annoyingly slow pace. American audiences will resent the corny flagwaving for the great Russian cause. Both Russian and Negro players appear in this but neither distinguish themselves particularly, and prove nothing that has not already been seen in American screen productions.

Plot has Sergei Kurilov, Moscow stage star, going to New Guinea to study the habits, lives and problems of natives. There is the by-now familiar stunt of having the native boy become ill, a touch of voodooism, etc., none of it done with much excitement.

Kurilov does nicely as the Russian explorer while Jim Komogorov, billed as the son of a Negro and a Russian woman, contributes a deft performance as the native boy who goes along with the explorer on his expedition. Weyland Rodd, credited with being a popular Negro actor in the Soviet Union, makes a nice characterization of the New Guinea tribal chief.

Alexander Razumni's direction is far from inspired and Boris Petrov's lensing is not up to usual Russian standard.

Wear.

When Love Calls
(Songs)
(ITALIAN)

Superfilm release of Scalera production. Stars Gino Bechi. Directed by Camillo Mastrocinque. Screenplay, Vittorio Novarese; camera, Arturo Gallea; editor, Fernando Tropea; music, Fernando Previtali. At Golden Cinema, N. Y., starting Oct. 8, '48. Running time, 106 MINS.

Claudio Tancredi	Gino Bechi
Anna Tancredi	Silvana Pampanini
Pacini	Aroldo Tieri
Emmy	Liliane Laine
Maestro Marconi	Carlo Romano
Squarcione	Gino Saltamerenda

(In Italian; English Titles)

"When Love Calls," despite some great singing by Gino Bechi, popular Italian baritone, is disappointing as compared with recent productions from Italy. It is one of those farce comedies with music and a liberal dose of sex that misses mainly because producers overlooked Bechi's vocal ability in favor of a lot of silly chasing over the countryside. Also, the rather torrid love sequences could have been developed instead of sidetracked in favor of this chase. Despite its very apparent flaws, this should be a good grosser in Italian-language houses because of its topflight singing.

Plot is too much reprise of the same theme — a temperamental operatic star always philandering and always getting into a row with his wife.

Sequence where Bechi goes carousing with the bandits and their girl friends is a real eye-opener for display of femme pulchritude. Even with obvious sharp scissoring by censors, it is about the warmest visual material to hit the screen in years. There are other risque moments but none compared to this episode.

Bechi is a personable screen actor but he is happiest when he is singing. His vocalizing is done so well it almost overcomes some of the obvious production errors. Silvana Pampanini, as his wife and femme lead in stage operas, does okay although overshadowed by several others. She is comely, as is Liliane Laine, the ballerina of the opera, who is his latest flame. Gino Saltamerenda contributes a skillful characterization of the bandit chief while the prettiest femme in the picture, the cafe entertainer, gets no program credit. Aroldo Tieri heads the big supporting cast.

Camillo Mastrocinque's direction fails to rise much above the Vittorio Novarese screenplay. Fernando Tropea's editing is humdrum.

Wear.

Miniature Reviews

"Joan of Arc" (Color) (Wanger-RKO). A smash.

"The Paleface" (Color) (Songs) (Par). Funny Bob Hope version of the stalwart western hero. Geared for laughs and good business.

"The Three Musketeers" (Color) (M-G). Multi-star cast in the Dumas classic. Socko excitement.

"June Bride" (WB). Bette Davis and Robert Montgomery in hilarious laughfest. Big b.o. potential.

"Kiss The Blood Off My Hands" (U). Grim melodrama with Burt Lancaster and Joan Fontaine; good b.o.

"The Return of October" (Color) (Col). Pert comedy drama, Glenn Ford, Terry Moore and Technicolor for general appeal.

"Disaster" (Par). Program actioner dealing with the steeplejack trade with murder meller angles.

"Marshal of Amarillo" (Rep). Standard Allan "Rocky" Lane western for the action houses.

"Smugglers Cove" (Mono). Another Leo Gorcey-Huntz Hall adventure. Good secondary product for series followers.

"Concert Magic" (Indie). Strong concert musical for art houses.

"Foolish Husbands" (French) (Siritzky). French farce that seldom jells; very mild U. S. returns indicated.

Joan of Arc

RKO release of Walter Wanger-Victor Fleming (Sierra Pictures) production, directed by Fleming. Stars Ingrid Bergman; features Jose Ferrer, Francis L. Sullivan, J. Carrol Naish, Ward Bond, Shepperd Strudwick, Hurd Hatfield, Gene Lockhart, John Emery, George Coulouris, John Ireland, Cecil Kellaway. Screenplay, Maxwell Anderson and Andrew Solt, based on Anderson's play, "Joan of Lorraine"; camera (Technicolor), Joseph Valentine; music, Hugo Friedhofer; music direction, Emil Newman; arrangements, Jerome Moross; vocals, Chas. Henderson with Roger Wagner Choir; art direction, Richard Day, asst. director, Slavko Vorkapich; editor, Frank Sullivan; special effects, Jack Cosgrove, John Fulton; 2d unit director, Horace Hough. Tradeshown N.Y. Oct. 18, '48. Running time, 150 MINS.

At Domremy, Joan's Birthplace in Lorraine

Jeanne d'Arc	Ingrid Bergman
Her Mother	Selena Royle
Her Father	Robert Barrat
Her Younger Brother	James Lydon
Her Older Brother	Rand Brooks

At Vaucouleurs

Her Uncle	Roman Bohnen
Catherine le Royer	Irene Rich
Henri le Royer	Nestor Paiva
Jean de Metz	Richard Derr
Bertrand de Poulengy	Ray Teal
Jean Fournier	David Bond
Constable of Clervaux	George Zucco
Sir Robert	George Coulouris

The Court of Charles VII at Chinon

Jean, Duke d'Alencon	John Emery
Georges de la Tremouille	Gene Lockhart
Archbishop of Rheims	Nicholas Joy
Charles de Bourbon	Richard Ney
Alain Chartier	Vincent Donahue
The Dauphin, Charles VII	Jose Ferrer

With the Army at Battle of Orleans

The Bastard of Orleans	Leif Erickson
Capt. Jean de la Boussac	John Ireland
Capt. Giles de Rais	Henry Brandon
Capt. Poton	Morris Ankrum
Capt. Raoul	Tom Brown Henry
Capt. Louis de Culan	Gregg Barton
Jean d'Aulon	Ethan Laidlaw
Father Pasquerel	Hurd Hatfield
La Hire	Ward Bond
Duke of Bedford	Frederic Worlock
Sir William Glasdale	Dennis Hoey
Duke of Burgundy	Colin Keith-Johnston
Countess of Luxembourg	Mary Currier
Burgundian Captain	Roy Roberts
Count of Luxembourg	J. Carrol Naish

The Trial at Rouen

Count-Bishop of Beauvais	Francis L. Sullivan
Father Massieu	Shepperd Strudwick
Bishop of Avranches	Taylor Holmes
Earl of Warwick	Alan Napier
Jean d'Estivet	Philip Bourneuf

Jean de la Fontaine ..... Aubrey Mather
Thomas de Courcelles ... Stephen Roberts
Isambard de la Pierre .... Herbert Rudley
Nicolas de Houppeville ... Frank Puglia
Guillaume Erard .... William Conrad
Jean Beaupere .... John Parrish
Nicolas Midi .... Victor Wood
Cardinal .... Houseley Stevenson
Prison Guard .... Jeff Corey
Her Executioner .... Bill Kennedy
Inquisitor of Rouen ...... Cecil Kellaway

"Joan of Arc" is a big picture in every respect. It has size, color, pageantry, a bold, historic bas-relief done up in the best 1948 Hollywood tradition. It has authority, conviction, an appeal to faith and a dedication to a cause that leaves little wanting. It has honesty, because whatever the captiousness about sensitive British feelings and even the more delicate ecclesiastic sensitivities, the more the auditor reviews it the more he becomes aware that few cinematic punches were pulled. And then, of course, "Joan of Arc" has Ingrid Bergman and a dream supporting cast.

It will do class and mass business. After the class runs—and a $4,600,000 negative cost necessitates such merchandising—it will click down the line. "Joan," in addition, should tap a new market of classroom and other educational-religioso segments. Its longevity for the 16m market is also obvious, and whether by accident or design, the breaking up of the film into five segments conjures up a strong new value for television presentation. This quintuplet cinematurgical device is an apparent transmutation of the Maxwell Anderson stage technique of subdividing the action into a celluloid approximation of five stage acts.

However, the prime concern right now of impresario Walter Wanger, producer-director Victor Fleming and star-copartner Ingrid Bergman are the theatrical rights. That $4,600,000 in this day and age of restricted domestic and foreign markets is quite an economic stake. It's the type of film which the trade and public, however, will recognize as noteworthy, distinguished and deserving of utmost financial support.

There are shortcomings to "Joan," of course, but these are negligible relatively. Miss Bergman makes her title role almost always convincing, even in those moments when the dialog or other screenwrighting is against her. For there are moments when, in other hands and under a less impressive sum total, that an untoward note might have crept in. An illustration of this is her peremptory edict against those time-honored heritages of soldiery—gambling, profanity and wenches. That carousing scene with the camp-followers is so much more vivid in its negative appeal that her relatively vacuous pronunciamento hasn't the positive conviction to support the dialog, as the loyal French suddenly recognize the Maid of Doremy.

In broad sweeps, director Fleming takes the Maid from her birthplace in Doremy in Lorraine to victory in Orleans, and her final ignominy when she is tried at Rouen for witchcraft and burned at the stake. It is to the credit of all that they have sustained the pitch even with common knowledge that there can be no "happy" ending, although the faith and the stoicism of the Maid is such as to endow the production, and all who will view it, with a new value.

There will, of course, be those who will look askance at the clergymen-peers whose political skullduggery and avarice transcended their ecclesiastic obligations, for their machinations in the prolonged trial at Rouen are completely lacking in piety. There may also be those who may question the credo that holy wars are to be condoned.

But since this is history translated in the modern idiom, but not to be interpreted, necessarily, as having bearing on the contemporaneous, the average film fan will view "Joan" in its fundamental light of an heroic chapter out of the world's annals, done in the most ultra and under most sympathetic Hollywood auspices.

Fleming has done an exciting job in blending the symbolism, the medieval warfront heroics, and the basic dramatic elements into a generally well-sustained whole. Whereas the trial, which pitches the Maid to the stake, is prolonged, he has not erred in moving Jeanne d'Arc from her birthplace in Lorraine in 1428 into Vaucouleurs where she finally interests the governor of that province into expediting her contact with The Dauphin. As the action moves from Vaucouleurs, the action moves from Vancouleurs, to the decadent Court of Charles VII (Jose Ferrer does an extremely effective job in painting the weak Dauphin), Fleming projects and progresses the action in broad shadings so as to make Joan's mission well nigh realistic.

There are certain misfires and false keynotes which militate against the desired consistency, such as Jose Ferrer's tiptop impersonation of The Dauphin, later to become the King of France, who makes his characterization so much the complete nitwit that the audience may well wonder at the complete obseisance of Joan to this weakling sovereign, regardless of the fact he is a symbol of the realm. The churchly gradations are also script shortcomings. Granted that "the voices" which have guided The Maid of Lorraine come from Valhalla the manner in which she is deserted in her darkest days—in her dungeon, beset by a would be rapacious gaoler, her ecclesiastic inquisitors, and at her final burning at the stake—is not moderated by any explanation why the sainted Joan is deprived of the same heavenly succor which attended her earlier days when this peasant maid was moved to become the warrior heroine of France. The trial, truly an inquisition, is a prolonged affair, historically and cinematically. Most of the dialog is punchy film-wise, and superb as a documentation for celluloid or other purposes.

The majesty of the earlier sequences is compelling almost all the way. When Joan edicts that "our strength is in our faith," when she leads her army in the Battle of Orleans, when she is betrayed by the Burgundians in calumny with the English, when in the earlier scenes she wins the grudging alliance of the Governor of Vaucouleurs and the courtiers at Chinon, Miss Bergman makes Joan a vivid albeit spiritual personality.

Whether captors or her allies, her supporting cast play their roles to the hilt. Jose Ferrer as the Dauphin, Francis L. Sullivan as the arch-heavy, J. Carrol Naish as her captor, the sympathetic Shepperd Strudwick as her bailiff, Ward Bond, Gene Lockhart, John Emery, George Coulouris, John Ireland, Cecil Kellaway, and a number of other standout players in relatively bit parts, make their chores stand out.

The color by Technicolor is magnificent. The production is lavish and looks every bit of its $4,000,000-plus. The pageantry and all the trappings bear the earmark of historic faithfulness, and there is an aura of authenticity and honesty about most of the unfolding as to impress "Joan" as truly extraordinary in every respect.

The picture bespeaks class, size and scope all the way. It's a much needed addition to the contemporaneous film scene, certain of reintensifying general interest in the American motion picture industry—still the world's leader, for all the sporadic excitements that, occasionally, but with no consistency, emanate from Italy or Britain. *Abel.*

The Paleface
(COLOR-SONGS)

Hollywood, Oct. 19.

Paramount release of Robert L. Welch production. Stars Bob Hope, Jane Russell; features Robert Armstrong, Iris Adrian, Robert Watson, Jack Searl, Joseph Vitale, Charles Trowbridge, Clem Bevans. Directed by Norman Z. McLeod. Original screenplay, Edmund Hartmann, Frank Tashlin; added dialog, Jack Rose; camera (Technicolor), Ray Rennahan; songs, Jay Livingston and Ray Evans, Joseph J. Lilley; score, Victor Young; editor, Ellsworth Hoagland. Tradeshown Oct. 19, '48. Running time, 91 MINS.

"Painless" Peter Potter .... Bob Hope
Calamity Jane .... Jane Russell
Terris .... Robert Armstrong
Pepper .... Iris Adrian
Toby Preston .... Robert Watson
Jasper Martin .... Jack Searl
Indian Scout .... Joseph Vitale
Governor Johnson ... Charles Trowbridge
Hank Billings .... Clem Bevans
Joe .... Jeff York
Commissioner Emerson . Stanley Andrews
Jeb .... Wade Crosby
Chief Yellow Feather .... Chief Yowlachie
Chief Iron Eyes .... Iron Eyes Cody
Village Gossip .... John Maxwell
Bartender .... Tom Kennedy
Wapato (Medicine Man) .. Henry Brandon
Lance .... Francis J. McDonald
Greg .... Frank Hagney
Pete .... Skelton Knaggs
Undertaker .... Olin Howland
First Patient .... George Chandler
Second Patient .... Nestor Paiva

"The Paleface" is a smart-aleck travesty on the west, told with considerable humor and bright gags. Bob Hope has been turned loose on a good script, whams his way through with sock results, and makes it add up to sturdy boxoffice. Production is a showmanly frame work for the antics, backed with high-gear action and fetching color lensing of the outdoor setting.

Setup is a natural for fun, and what holes might be found in the script are slickly glossed over to keep the western burlesque tickling the risibilities. Slow spots are few and far between. Audiences will like Hope's broad takeoff on all the swaggering oater heroes that ever stalked their gun prey down a western street; his cowardly heroics in an Indian raid; his fast quips and patsying for a gag.

Hope isn't all the film has to sell. There's Jane Russell as Calamity Jane, that rough, tough gal of the open west whose work as a Government agent causes Hope's troubles, but whose guns save him from harm and give him his hero reputation. She makes an able sparring partner for the Hope antics, and is a sharp eyeful in Technicolor.

"Buttons and Bows," by now a familiar to radio and record listeners, is top tune of the score's three pop numbers. Jay Livingston and Ray Evans cleffed and Hope renders as a plaintive love chant to Miss Russell. Team also authored "Meetcha 'Round the Corner," sung by Iris Adrian, but final editing gives it short shrift in the score. Miss Adrian also gives a torrid treatment to "Get a Man," by Joseph J. Lilley, in her role of entertainer at the Dirty Shame saloon.

Script by Edmund Hartmann and Frank Tashlin, with added dialog by Jack Rose, poses an amusing story idea—Hope as a correspondence school dentist touring the west in a covered wagon. He's having his troubles, but they're nothing compared to the grief that catches up with him when Calamity Jane seduces him into marriage so she can break up a gang smuggling rifles to the Indians. The standard perils of the epic western are dished out for comedy, with Hope the patsy. There are some unrelated, but funny, sequences, before the happy gag ending closes the saga of brave, bold empire builders.

Norman Z. McLeod's direction combines the slight gag with the oral to assure a fast payoff on every line and situation, and he keeps the pace marching forward briskly. Robert L. Welch, who received his comedy training in radio, lands his first film production credit on "Paleface," and it's a well-earned one. Showmanly production treatment and comedy knowhow keep things clicking in the proper vein for audience enjoyment.

Entering into spirit of fun are Robert Armstrong, Miss Adrian, Robert Watson, Jack Searl, Clem Bevans, Jeff York, Chief Yowlachie, Iron Eyes Cody and sundry oater characters. Olin Howland has a pip of a bit as a gleeful undertaker watching the film's gun fights.

Ray Rennahan was responsible for the glowing color lensing that adds dress to physical values, and Victor Young backs the fun with an excellent score. *Brog.*

The Three Musketeers
(COLOR)

Hollywood, ...

Metro release of Pandro S. Berman production. Stars Lana Turner, Gene Kelly, June Allyson, Van Heflin, Angela Lansbury; features Frank Morgan, Vincent Price, Keenan Wynn, John Sutton, Gig Young. Directed by George Sidney. Screenplay, Robert Ardrey; from Alexandre Dumas novel; camera (Technicolor), Robert Planck; editors, Robert J. Kern, George Boemler; score, Herbert Stothart, with themes by Tschaikowsky. Tradeshown .... Running time, 126 MINS.

Lady de Winter .... Lana Turner
D'Artagnan .... Gene Kelly
Constance .... June Allyson
Athos .... Van Heflin
Queen Anne .... Angela Lansbury
King Louis XIII .... Frank Morgan
Richelieu .... Vincent Price
Planchet .... Keenan Wynn
The Duke of Buckingham ... John Sutton
Porthos .... Gig Young
Aramis .... Robert Coote
Treville .... Reginald Owen
Rochefort .... Ian Keith
Kitty .... Patricia Medina
Albert .... Richard Stapley

Metro's "The Three Musketeers" is a swaggering, tongue-in-cheek treatment of picturesque fiction, extravagantly presented to capture the fancy of any high romanticist—and there are a lot of them. The Alexandre Dumas classic has always been a blood-quickener. It is even more so in its latest film version and, with a multi-star cast to brighten marquees, there is every indication it will cut a socko boxoffice swath right down the line.

Its footage is long, two hours and six minutes, but it is a rare instance when the pace slows down. The fanciful tale has been launched with a laugh, quickly swings into some of the most colorful and exciting sword duels yet staged for films as the pace is set for the imaginative adventures that feature the lives and loves of D'Artagnan and his three cronies. It is the complete Dumas novel, crammed with derring-do that makes for solid screen action.

There are acrobatics by Gene Kelly that would give the late, great Douglas Fairbanks pause. His first duel with Richelieu's cohorts is almost ballet, yet never loses the feeling of swaggering sword-play. It is a masterful mixture of dancing grace, acro-agility and sly horseplay of sock comedic punch. His escapades on castle rooftop, chandelier-swinging, wild rides and similar action follow the same pattern.

Kelly's broad interpretation, and the tongue-in-cheek mood of the entire film, is established in the opening sequence. While George Sidney's direction plays much of the footage straight, the key scenes tend toward chuckles as he affectionately kids such out-and-out pulp fiction. His direction is robust in sharpening the tremendous spectacle of duel, chase and mass clash. It is sly with humor in lightly burlesquing the romancing, and intensely dramatic in building serious moments.

Lana Turner is a perfect visualization of the sexy, wicked Lady de Winter, sharply contrasting with the sweet charm of June Allyson as the maid, Constance. The three king's musketeers of the title are dashingly portrayed by Van Heflin, Gig Young and Robert Coote as Athos, Porthos and Aramis, respectively. They belt over their parts in keeping with the style Kelly uses for D'Artagnan.

The Dumas tale concerns the four swordsmen of the king who dare to tangle with Richelieu in saving the royal family from the minister's political conniving. They escape every Richelieu plot with breathless daring as Dumas' highly romantic doings are sprawled across the screen in gorgeous Technicolor hues. It's the kind of swashbuckling that appeals to a broad audience.

Production-wise, Pandro S. Berman has overlooked no angles in dressing up "Musketeers" as a feast for the eyes and a stimulant for chimerical adventuring by an audience. He has done it with a lavish, sweeping approach that calls on showmanly and technical ingenuity to achieve the results that show on the screen.

Wise casting has Vincent Price bringing his suave leer and menace to the role of Richelieu. The part is short in the total footage, as is Queen Anne as portrayed by Angela Lansbury; King Louis by Frank Morgan; Planchet by Keenan Wynn; the Duke of Buckingham by John Sutton, and the other Dumas characters enacted by Reginald Owen, Ian Keith, Patricia Medina and Richard Stapley. Each lends the proper touch to sustain the adventurous movement.

Pictorial beauty of the settings, both indoor and out, has been fascinatingly captured by Robert Planck's camera. The dashing action, the beautiful femmes in lavish costumes and the spirit of adventure are heightened by the lensing. Another aid in making the film top commercial entertainment is the telling score by Herbert Stothart, using themes by Tschaikowsky. Score bridges any gap in movement without intruding itself as an oral distraction to the visual action. The editors had a job to trim the vast footage and yet keep the story together. Scissoring has been credibly done.

Brog.

June Bride

Hollywood, Oct. 19.

Warner Bros. release of Henry Blanke production. Stars Bette Davis, Robert Montgomery; features Fay Bainter, Betty Lynn, Tom Tully, Barbara Bates. Directed by Bretaigne Windust. Screenplay, Ranald MacDougall; based on play by Eileen Tighe, Graeme Lorimer; camera, Ted McCord; editor, Owen Marks; music, David Buttolph. Tradeshown, Oct. 19, 1948. Running time, 106 MINS.

Linda Gilman	Bette Davis
Carey Jackson	Robert Montgomery
Paula Winthrop	Fay Bainter
Boo Brinker	Betty Lynn
Mr. Brinker	Tom Tully
Jeanne Brinker	Barbara Bates
Carleton Towne	Jerome Cowan
Rosemary McNally	Mary Wickes
Luke Potter	James Burke
Bud Mitchell	Raymond Roe
Mrs. Brinker	Marjorie Bennett
Jim Mitchell	Ray Montgomery
Scott Davis	George O'Hanlon
Miss Rubens	Sandra Gould

After one film fumble, Bette Davis makes a recovery that should put her back on top. The switch from the heavy dramatics to which her followers have become inured, to hilarious gag and situation comedy is a stunt that comes off socko. The b.o. payoff should be big as there is boff word-of-mouth to help build ticket sales.

"June Bride" is a sometimes subtle, sometimes wacky, takeoff on home magazines and human nature. It has a starting hurdle as characters are set up, but once on its way never lets itself or the audience down. Bretaigne Windust's direction is always lively and extremely able at milking a line or situation, whether satire or antic, in filming the potent script by Ranald MacDougall.

Miss Davis presents a delightfully slicked up personality as a "through-with-love" home mag editor who does stereotyped articles on before-and-after houses and people. Robert Montgomery co-stars as a foreign correspondent assigned to aid Miss Davis when news becomes dull in Europe. His glib handling of the assignment sharpens many a scene in the film. Both give socko interpretations.

Basic concern of the plot is the off-again, on-again romance between Miss Davis and Montgomery, but other motivations share the interest. Heights of hilarity are spotted throughout the film. Among them is Montgomery's first encounter with hard cider and a face-flop in the snow; a husband's bewilderment as the housing experts discuss disposal of an antique marble bust while he is concerned about his wife, and the takeoff on how a mag staff gives the new look to a family and home still branded with the "McKinley-stinker" era trademark.

There's a solid portrayal of youth and budding romance in the characters so ably performed by Betty Lynn and Raymond Roe. They give their roles humor and heart-tug, and make them stand out. Barbara Bates and Ray Montgomery are good as the other young romance team.

Henry Blanke has cast the roles with care, resulting in solid performances that further the spirit of fun. Aiding Miss Davis as mag staffers are Fay Bainter, George O'Hanlon and Mary Wickes, a trio of stalwarts that register big. Tom Tully shines as the father of the family being made over, as does Marjorie Bennett as the mother. Jerome Cowan comes through as the mag publisher with a Machiavellian sense of humor. James Burke and Sandra Gould complete the able cast of funsters.

Lensing has been capably handled by Ted McCord to show off the players and physical properties to the best advantage. There's an unobtrusive score by David

Buttolph; expert editing and tastefully styled gowns by Edith Head among the other credits that are top level.

Brog.

Kiss the Blood Off My Hands

Universal release of Richard Vernon (Harold Hecht-Norma) production. Stars Joan Fontaine, Burt Lancaster; features Robert Newton. Directed by Norman Foster. Screenplay, Leonardo Bercovici; adaptation, Ben Maddow, Walter Bernstein; additional dialog, Hugh Gray; based on Gerald Butler novel; camera, Russell Metty; editor, Milton Carruth; music, Miklos Rozsa. Tradeshown N. Y. Oct. 8, '48. Running time, 79 MINS.

Jane Wharton	Joan Fontaine
Bill Saunders	Burt Lancaster
Harry Carter	Robert Newton
Tom Widgery	Lewis L. Russell
Landlady	Aminta Dyne
Mrs. Paton	Grizelda Hervey
Sea Captain	Jay Novello
Judge	Colin Keith-Johnston
Superintendent	Reginald Sheffield
Publican	Campbell Copelin
Tipster	Leland Hodgson
Young Father	Peter Hobbes

"Kiss the Blood Off My Hands," adapted from Gerald Butler's novel of postwar violence and demoralization, is an intensely moody melodrama with sufficient emotional kick to make it a good b.o. bet. The striking title, which promises a far greater scoop of excitement than what is delivered, will draw the male customers. But the film actually will find its heaviest appeal among the femme fans who will guzzle this sombre tale of ill-starred romance. The marquee duo of Joan Fontaine and Burt Lancaster also furnishes a substantial back-stop to the wickets.

The yarn concerns an uprooted vet of World War II whose life is shattered after he accidentally kills a man in a London pub. Although based on a formula plot, this film is lifted out of the run-of-the-mill class through Norman Foster's superior direction, first-rate thesping and well-integrated production mountings. Extra impact is lent to a middling screenplay by Foster's firm control over the film's pace and his achievement of a unified atmospheric quality. Excellent deep shadow camera work and minor key score by Miklos Rozsa add to the film's consistency.

The story opens explosively in a furious chase sequence with Lancaster, as the vet, making his getaway from the bobbies after a fatal brawl in a saloon. During his flight, he crosses paths with Joan Fontaine, a hospital worker, and, with credible plot development, they fall for each other. Lancaster then tries to go straight but is stymied by Robert Newton, a black marketeer who forces him into a hijacking deal under threats of exposing Lancaster to the police.

Latter portion of the film dips into sensationalism with Miss Fontaine stabbing Newton in her apartment while he's making a pass at her. Newton's death is coupled with a powerful cinematic image of goldfish, spilled from a broken aquarium, flapping around the corpse. This is an imaginative touch of horror which gives vividness to a conventional turn of the plot. In an effective windup which hews closely to the production code, Miss Fontaine and Lancaster make a dash for an outbound ship but finally decide to surrender to the cops.

Lancaster delivers a convincing and sympathetic portrayal of a

tough hombre who can't beat the bad breaks. Miss Fontaine performs with sensitivity and sincerity in a demanding role. As the heavy, Newton is properly oily and detestable. Rest of the cast only have bit parts which are handled competently.

Herm.

The Return of October
(COLOR)

Hollywood, Oct. 16.

Columbia release of Rudolph Mate production. Stars Glenn Ford, Terry Moore; features Albert Sharpe, James Gleason, Dame May Whitty, Henry O'Neill. Directed by Joseph H. Lewis. Screenplay, Melvin Frank, Norman Panama; story, Connie Lee, Karen DeWolf; camera (Technicolor), William Snyder; editor, Gene Havlick; music score, George Duning. Previewed Oct. 15, '48. Running time, 87 MINS.

Professor Bassett	Glenn Ford
Terry Ramsey	Terry Moore
Vince, the Tout	Albert Sharpe
Uncle Willie	James Gleason
Aunt Martha	Dame May Whitty
President Hotchkiss	Henry O'Neill
Mitchell	Frederic Tozere
Judge Northridge	Samuel S. Hinds
Therese	Nana Bryant
Dutton	Lloyd Corrigan
Colonel Wood	Roland Winters
Professor Stewart	Stephen Dunne
Benny	Gus Schilling
Little Max	Murray Alper
Big Louie	Horace MacMahon
Margaret	Victoria Horne
Jonathan	Byron Foulger
Tommy	Bill Pearson
Taylor	Russell Hicks
Detective	Robert Malcolm
Reporter	Ray Walker

"The Return of October" is a lot more fun than the title would indicate. It's pert, enjoyable and if sold strongly on entertainment content will return neat grosses. Audiences will like Terry Moore, comparative newcomer who shares top billing with Glen Ford. Technicolor also points up general audience appeal.

Story deals with a girl who believes her uncle's a horse. That doesn't sound like a particularly bright premise, but writing, direction and playing toss it off in a light, engaging manner that clicks. Fantasy angles have been avoided, wisely, and audiences will accept and enjoy the girl's belief.

Joseph H. Lewis' direction is slightly tongue-in-cheek in handling the Melvin Frank-Norman Panama script. Dialog is apt, the scenes are set up for neatly contrived twists, and the pace gallops. Horseracing scenes are thrilling and will have audience booting October (nee Uncle Willie) home as a Derby winner.

Plot breakdown has Terry Moore remembering her late Uncle Willie's statement that if he ever returned it would be as a horse to win the Derby. When she sees October, the nag reminds her of the departed and a chain reaction of events is launched that builds into infectious giggles. The girl is tried for insanity in a plot to obtain her estate. October (or Uncle Willie) wins the Derby and a psychology professor finds that facts aren't always what they appear.

Glenn Ford is the prof who makes the girl's fantasy the subject of a sensational book. Role is Ford's meat and he gives it a broad twist that adds plenty to the fun. Miss Moore makes an appealing heroine and has been fetchingly costumed in all manner of styles to rate eye attention. Backing the two stars is a strong supporting cast, including James Gleason, who's in briefly at the start as Uncle Willie; Albert Sharpe, a tout; Dame May Whitty, Henry O'Neill, Frederic Tozere, (the late) Samuel S. Hinds, Nana Bryant, Stephan Dunne, Gus Schilling, Murray Alper and Horace MacMahon.

Production guidance by Rudolph Mate maintains the whip hand on material and physical values, and along with others makes good entertainment. Camera work by William Snyder gives a lush color touch to smart settings and art direction. *Brog.*

Disaster

Hollywood, Oct. 19.

Paramount release of William Pine-William Thomas production. Features Richard Denning, Trudy Marshall. Directed by William H. Pine. Original screenplay, Thomas Ahearn; camera, Ellis W. Carter; editor, Howard Smith. Tradeshown Oct. 19, '48. Running time, 60 MINS.
Bill Wyatt	Richard Denning
Jerry Hansford	Trudy Marshall
Detective Dearborn	Damian O'Flynn
Pop Hansford	Will Wright
Sam Payne	James Millican
Frosty Davenport	Jack Lambert
Police Commissioner	Jonathan Hale

Pine-Thomas apparently set out to make a program action film dealing with the steeple-jack trade. Somewhere along the line a murder plot crept in for somewhat confusing results. However, sight thrills of height workers and general action idea make it okay material for supporting bookings.

Director William H. Pine permits his cast to spend too much time on dialog but sets up thriller moments nicely to give feeling of pace. Plot concerns structural steel worker on the lam to avoid arrest for murder. He takes a job with a steeplejack company, falls in love with the owner's daughter and for the finale risks capture to save the gal's father, who's trapped atop a building struck by a plane. Murder rap is cleared and love triumphs.

Richard Denning is the mysteriously-acting lead, dodging the law, and Trudy Marshall is the girl. Both give acceptable accounts. Will Wright's owner spot shows up best, James Millican, romantic rival, and Damian O'Flynn, detective, as well as others, likewise measure up to demands.

Straighter account of the trials and tribulations of the hero and less attempts at mystifying could have sharpened the plot. The Pine-Thomas producer function displays acumen in deft tricks to point up values on light budget. Lensing by Ellis W. Carter frameworks physical factors ably. *Brog.*

Marshal of Amarillo

Republic release of Gordon Kay production. Stars Allan "Rocky" Lane; features Eddy Waller, Mildred Cole, Clayton Moore, Roy Barcroft. Directed by Philip Ford. Original screenplay, Bob Williams; editor, Harold Minter; camera, John MacBurnie. At New York theatre, N. Y., week Oct. 12, '48. Running time, 60 MINS.
Allan "Rocky" Lane	Allan "Rocky" Lane
Nugget Clark	Eddy Waller
Marjorie Underwood	Mildred Cole
Art Crandall	Clayton Moore
Ben	Roy Barcroft
Frank Welch	Trevor Bardette
Mrs. Pettigrew	Minerva Urecal
Night Clerk	Denver Pyle
Hiram Short	Charles Williams
James Underwood	Tom Chatterton
Sam	Peter Perkins
Snodgrass	Tom London
Matilda	Lynn Castile

Standard oater fare, "Marshal of Amarillo" has the usual six gun shootin' matches and an ample supply of chases to keep the action fans content. Exhibs will find it an okay filler for the juve trade as well as suitable for rounding out the lower half of a dual in situations where gallopers find favor.

Formula story finds a wealthy gent from the east seized by the outlaws who are after his money. The thieves carry on their operations from a gloomy, desert hotel and are on the verge of grabbing the old boy's daughter in the inn when our Al'an "Rocky" Lane, in the title role, foils the plot. He bags the culprits, finds the cash and reunites father and daughter.

Best sequence of the film is in the final footage where Lane, instead of chasing the outlaws on hossback, commandeers a stage to overtake his adversaries who appropriately are using the same form of transportation. Lane is a forthright marshal, Eddy Waller is okay comedy relief while other players contrib adequate thesping.

Director Philip Ford keeps things moving at a brisk pace while Gordon Kay's production values are similar to that of the average outdoor saga. Cameraman John MacBurnie's lens work is competent as is Harold Minter's editing. *Gilb.*

Smugglers Cove

Hollywood, Oct. 16.

Monogram release of Jan Grippo production. Stars Leo Gorcey, Huntz Hall; features Gabriel Dell, Billy Benedict, David Gorcey, Benny Bartlett, Martin Kosleck, Paul Harvey, Amelita Ward, Jacqueline Dalya. Directed by William Beaudine. Screenplay, Edmond Seward, Tim Ryan; based on mag story by Talbert Josselyn; camera, Marcel Le Picard; editor, William Austin. At Grauman's Chinese, Oct. 16, '48. Running time, 66 MINS.
Slip (Terrence) Mahoney	Leo Gorcey
Sach	Huntz Hall
Gabe	Gabriel Dell
Whitey	Billy Benedict
Chuck	David Gorcey
Butch	Benny Bartlett
Count Petrov	Martin Kosleck
Terrence Mahoney, Esq	Paul Harvey
Teresa Mahoney	Amelita Ward
Sandra Hasso	Jacqueline Dalya
Digger	Eddie Gribbon
Captain Drum	Gene Stutenroth
Dr. Latka	Leonid Snegoff
Franz Leiber	John Bleifer
Karl	Andre Pola
Ryan	William Ruhl
Attorney Williams	Emmett Vogan
Messenger	Buddy Gorman

Leo Gorcey and Huntz Hall are at it again in another of their English-murdering minor epics. Results guarantee pleasure of followers—and those not too familiar with the slapstick derring-do staged by Monogram's tough kids. As a secondary, particularly in the action market, it's good material.

"Smugglers Cove" is a loosely-knit scramble of malaprops and adventure. It starts when Gorcey mistakenly receives letter notifying him of the inheritance of a Long Island estate. He and his gang trek to the manor, find it occupied by a gang smuggling aliens into the country. From then on, it's a juve screech-arouser of sliding doors; secret passageways and dungeons, with the tough kids, somehow, coming out on top.

The rough, but noble of heart characters fit Gorcey, Hall, Gabriel Dell, Billy Benedict, David Gorcey and Benny Bartlett like gloves and they wear them with swaggering aplomb. Martin Kosleck, Eddie Gribbon and others furnish the menace and Paul Harvey depicts a harassed business magnate who really inherits the estate. Amelita Ward is Harvey's daughter and Jacqueline Dalya sparks up spot as a Kosleck victim.

William Beaudine's direction gives the reins over to Gorcey and his pals for rough and rowdy results. Jan Grippo's production is good, keeping film aimed at pleasing in its market. Lensing, editing and other technical credits are standard. *Brog.*

Concert Magic

Hollywood, Oct. 19.

Morris Safier states rights release of a Paul Gordon-George Moskov Production. Directed by Gordon. Stars Yehudi Menuhin; features Jakob Gimpel, Eula Beal, Adolph Baller, Marguerita Campbell, Antal Dorati, Hollywood Symphony Orchestra. Musical adviser, Dr. Victor Clement; camera, Paul Ivano; editor, Douglas Bagier. Running time, 65 MINS.

"Concert Magic" brings to the screen a full-length concert devoid of plot and production embellishment. Picture was made for music lovers and should draw strong coin in art houses. Sets, in the entirety, are simple and unadorned. Only changes are in switches from one room to another. Costumes are merely ordinary day wear and formal night wear. Film features Yehudi Menuhin who is supported by Eula Beal, contralto; pianists Jakob Gimpel, Adolph Baller and Marguerita Campbell, and the Hollywood Symphony Orchestra conducted by Antal Dorati.

Menuhin plays five solos and one duet. Solo numbers are "Rondo Allegro" by Ludwig van Beethoven, "Malaguena" by Pablo Sarasate, "Scherzo Tarantelle" by Henri Wieniawski, "Hungarian Dances" by Johannes Brahms, "Labyrinth" by Pietro Locatelli and "Gypsy Airs" by Pablo Sarasate. Menuhin and Miss Beal duet "St. Matthew Passion" by Johann Sebastian Bach. She also sings Gounod's "Ave Maria," "Erl-King" by Franz Schubert and "None But the Lonely Heart" by Peter Ilich Tschaikowsky. Gimpel plays Felix Mendelssohn's "Los Illusions" and "Etude F Major" and "Etude E Major," "Waltz E Minor" by Frederic Chopin. Baller accompanies Menuhin and Miss Campbell accompanies Miss Beal.

Paul Gordon and George Moskov have, oddly enough, achieved the utmost in productional simplicity. Paul Ivano has done a magnificent job in lensing what could be referred to as inanimate objects. Camera angles and lighting perpetuate interest to the eye where ordinarily the only sustained interest would be to the ear. *Free.*

Foolish Husbands
(FRENCH)

Siritzky International release of Discina Film production. Stars Fernand Gravet and Pierre Renoir. Directed by Marcel L'Herbier. Screenplay, Armand Salacrou, from his original stageplay, "Histoire de Rire"; English titles, Charles Clement. At Ambassador, N.Y., starting Oct. 9. Running time, 99 MINS.
Fernand Gravet	Gerard
Micheline Presle	Adelaide
Marie Dea	Helene Donaldo
Pierre Renoir	Jules Donaldo
Bernard Lancret	Jean Louis Deshayes
Gilbert Gil	Achille Bailarson

(In French; English Titles)

Despite the presence of Fernand Gravet and Pierre Renoir, "Foolish Husbands" is lightweight French farce that also looks lightweight for the U. S. boxoffice.

Picture has to lean almost exclusively on the dialog to hold its audience. Because English titles are the sole guide for non-French speaking patrons, this represents a big void.

Like all French marital farces, this is loaded with snappy repartee. Yet this rapid chit-chat translated to Americanese in black-and-white screen titles becomes just so many words. All of the highly-spiced Gallic flavor is lost, leaving merely, one prolonged scene and episode after another.

Main thesis of Armand Salacrou's play, "Histoire de Rire," from which this was taken, is that marital infidelity, whether by husband or wife, never pays off. First, Gravet's wife tries a mild affair with an insipid youth she does not love on learning that her husband's friend is having an affair. The basic idea of having the wife away on a weekend, while the husband's favorite male companion is running away with a married woman, may have been okay on the stage, but here it lacks pace.

Neither Marcel L'Herbier's direction nor the Salacrou script comes anywhere near accepted French pre-war cinematic standards. Film, too, is lightweight on production values. Even Renoir, as the elderly philosophical husband, fails to save the aimless plot development. He has little to do until the film is nearly over, being held to a very subordinate role when the picture almost screams for somebody to give it a lift.

Gravet gives flashes of the talent which won him a pact some years ago with Metro, but his portrayal of the young husband is nearly as flighty as the direction. Bernard Lancret doesn't impress as the young lover who runs away with Renoir's wife. Micheline Presle overacts as Gravet's wife while Marie Dea does remarkably well as Renoir's philandering spouse. *Wear.*

Miniature Reviews

"Belle Starr's Daughter" (20th). Feature western that stretches itself too thin on action.

"Let's Live a Little" (EL). Pleasant madcap comedy with Hedy Lamarr, Robert Cummings.

"Black Eagle" (Col). Overlength supporting feature which could have clicked with more clarity in development.

"Night Time in Nevada" (Songs-Color) (Rep). Stout Roy Rogers oatuner slated for good playoff in that market.

"Woman Hater" (GFD). Mild British domestic farce.

"Sleeping Car to Trieste" (GFD). So-so British trainrobbery mystery.

Belle Starr's Daughter

Hollywood, Oct. 23.

20th-Fox release of Edward L. Alperson (Alson) production. Stars George Montgomery, Red Cameron, Ruth Roman; features Wallace Ford, Charles Kemper, William Phipps, Edith King. Directed by Lesley Selander. Original screenplay, W. R. Burnett; camera, William A. Sickner; editor, Jason Bernie. Tradeshown Oct. 22, '48. Running time, 86 MINS.

Tom Jackson ...... George Montgomery
Bob "Bittercreek" Yauntis .. Rod Cameron
Rose of Cimarron .... Ruth Roman
Bailey .... Wallace Ford
Gaffer .... Charles Kemper
Yuma .... William Phipps
Mrs. Allen .... Edith King
Bronc .... Jack Lambert
Slim .... Fred Libby
Belle Starr .... Isabel Jewell
Jed Purdy .... Larry Johns
Jim Davis .... Kenneth MacDonald

"Belle Starr's Daughter" spends too much time telling its story. It has sturdy range heroics but thrills are spaced by too much slow footage to have the punch they need for sustained interest. However, action names of George Montgomery and Rod Cameron will count in the selling and moderate returns can be expected.

Story has been filmed against fresh brackgrounds and the lensing is exceptionally good. Scenery is high and rugged to fit the plot, and adds to production values. It's a chase film, pitting stalwart western sheriff against a prairie baddie, with Montgomery and Cameron filling the respective roles. Plot ramifications bring in the daughter of Belle Starr for romance and a minor motivation, but forward movement hinges on the chase.

Lesley Selander's direction stresses characterization which, while good, tends to slow pace. He has staged a number of mass gun battles, such as the shoot 'em-up between Belle Starr's menaces and the forces of law in an early sequence. Tension doesn't draw too tight but is felt in several clashes between hero and heavy before good triumphs over evil at the finale.

Montgomery is a believable hero and Cameron makes a convincing heavy. Ruth Roman is good in the title role. Neat support comes from Wallace Ford, Charles Kemper, William Phipps, Jack Lambert. Role of Belle Starr is portrayed by Isabel Jewell in initial sequence to set up the plot.

Edward L. Alperson's production has the advantage of broad outdoor vistas of the location site where this one was filmed, and the sharp lensing is by William A. Sickner. Score, particularly for opening, has a dirge quality. Editing to trim the 86 minutes running time and tighten individual scenes would help. *Brog.*

Let's Live a Little

Eagle Lion release of United California (Eugene Frenke-Robert Cummings) production. Stars Hedy Lamarr, Robert Cummings; features Anna Sten. Directed by Richard Wallace. Screenplay, Albert J. Cohen, Jack Harvey; camera, Ernest Laszlo; editor, Arthur Hilton; score, Werner Heyman. Tradeshown N. Y. Oct. 21, '48. Running time, 85 MINS.

Dr. J. O. Loring .... Hedy Lamarr
Duke Crawford .... Robert Cummings
Michele Bennett .... Anna Sten
Dr. Richard Field .... Richard Shayne
Miss Adams .... Mary Treen
James Montgomery .... Harry Antrim

"Let's Live A Little," initial offering of United California Productions, is a madcap comedy romance which is entertaining without going anywhere in particular. Film will do moderately well at the nabe wickets but its texture is too lightweight for impressive results in the key firstruns.

First half of the pic is a brittle farce which trips sharply along as a takeoff on the advertising business. Although broad and exaggerated, this portion delivers laughs with pace and flashes of keen wit. Second half, however, weakens badly into flabby slapstick which considerably dims the overall brightness. Basic flaw lies in a script which apparently ran out of ideas after a fast and flip beginning.

Robert Cummings, co-partnered with Eugene Frenke in this new indie producing outfit, does a firstrate job in single-handedly squeezing out all the possible laughs. As a scatterbrain account exec, his mercurial mannerisms, mugging and double-takes register with broad appeal. Occasionally, he overstrains into cuteness in trying to save a weak line or sequence by unsupported antics, but generally Cummings shows good comedic control.

Thin yarn revolves around Cummings' attempt to keep out of an affair with one of his big, amorous clients (Anna Sten) while trying at the same time to sell her a fat advertising contract. The hectic two-faced dodging produces a mild case of hallucinations which drives Cummings into the arms of a femme psychiatrist (Hedy Lamarr). After a bizarre series of romantic misunderstandings which sends the psychiatrist daffy, Cummings finally lands his contract and weds the medico. Although a conventional clinch signalizes the fadeout, plenty of loose threads are still left dangling at the windup.

Miss Lamarr teams up nicely with Cummings in the romantic play but her straight role doesn't offer much maneuvering space for her talents. As the femme heavy, Anna Sten, in her first film in many years, shows a pleasant new facet of her personality in her cutups as a slinking siren. Richard Shayne, as Miss Lamarr's frustrated beau, also delivers nicely.

Production values, while not lavish are solid and polished. Director Richard Wallace, although handicapped by the screenplay, keeps the film rolling even through the slapstick marshlands. Film also has expert camera work, smooth editing and a competent musical score on the credit side. *Herm.*

The Angry God
(COLOR)

United Artists release of Edward J. Peskay production. Directed by Van Campen Heilner. Camera (Fullcolor), Luis Osorno Barona; music, Vernon Duke. At New York theatre, N. Y., week Oct. 19. '48. Running time, 57 MINS.

Of dubious entertainment value is "The Angry God." A fancy lobby display and a high powered exploitation campaign may bring the customers to the wicket, but after they've seen the film there'll be scant word of mouth. For despite its frequent scenes of an active volcano, the picture is merely a slow paced travelog in which a Mexican folk tale has been inserted.

Legend has to do with the love of Colima, the fire god, for a shapely femme mortal who already has a boy friend. When she rejects his unwanted attention, he causes the volcano to erupt in an act of vengeance. At that point the God of all creation decides Colima has gone far enough in his spite and imprisons him within the smoking mountain.

Dialog appears to have been dubbed in and the lines of the script hardly coincide with the general physical features of the native cast. Not much can be said for the acting. However, on the pulchritudinous side is Alicia Parla who has the role of the No. 1 maiden.

Filmed in Fullcolor, this tint process gives a coppery hue to both cast and scenery. A fiesta sequence was lensed well enough, but on the whole the camerawork is mediocre. Produced by Edward J. Peskay and directed by Van Campen Heilner, "Angry God" was shot in Michoacan, Mexico, nearby the famed Paricutin volcano which emerged from a farmer's cornfield several years ago. *Gill.*

Black Eagle

Hollywood, Oct. 23.

Columbia release of Robert Cohn production. Features William Bishop, Virginia Patten, Gordon Jones, James Bell, Trevor Bardette, Will Wright, Edmund MacDonald, Paul E. Burns. Directed by Robert Gordon. Screenplay, Edward Huebsch, Hal Smith; adaptation, Huebsch; based upon the O. Henry story, "The Passing of Black Eagle"; camera, Henry Freulich; editor, James Sweeney. At Pantages, Oct. 22, '48. Running time, 76 MINS.

Jason Bond .... William Bishop
Ginny Long .... Virginia Patton
Benjy Laughton .... Gordon Jones
Frank Hayden .... James Bell
Mike Long .... Trevor Bardette
Clancy .... Will Wright
Si .... Edmund MacDonald
Hank Daniels .... Paul E. Burns
The General .... Harry Cheshire
Chicken .... Al Eben
Sam .... Ted Mapes
Mort .... Richard Talmadge

"Black Eagle" fails to rate above supporting classification solely because of the confusion in development. What transpires is well done as far as performances are concerned but audiences will have only the vaguest notion of what it's all about. Lack of story clarity is a tough hurdle and what seems like an interesting plot fails to jump it.

Yarn is based on an O. Henry story which concerns a young man who tries to avoid people because they always cause trouble. Naturally, he walks right into a trouble setup when he boards a freight heading south. From that misstep he finds himself at first allied with a rancher intent on keep his word even though it means selling his horses at a loss. From there he is forced to swing to the other side in support of a crooked livestock agent. Rancher trouble is finally resolved and the young man scrams to rejoin his freight car cronies.

Cast does excellent work, and if the plot development had done a clearer job of telling the story, would have appeared to topnotch advantage. William Bishop is the rambling hero. Virginia Patton is the heroine. Gordon Jones, a rancher leading the fight against James Bell's skullduggery; Trevor Bardette, Will Wright, philosophical sheriff; Edmund MacDonald and others match the good performance delivered by Bishop.

Robert Gordon directed the Robert Cohn production and does well in the face of script handicaps. A good lensing job by Henry Freulich helps physical values of the essentially western layout. *Brog.*

Night Time in Nevada
(SONGS-COLOR)

Hollywood, Oct. 23.

Republic release of Edward J. White production. Stars Roy Rogers; features Adele Mara, Andy Devine, Bob Nolan and Sons of Pioneers. Directed by William Witney. Original screenplay, Sloan Nibley; camera (Trucolor), Jack Marta; editor, Tony Martinelli; score, Dale Butts; songs, Richard W. Pascoe, Will E. Dulmage and H. O'Reilly Clint, Tim Spencer, Edward Morrissey and Bob Nolan. At L. A. Paramount, Oct. 21, '48. Running time, 66 MINS.

Roy Rogers .... Roy Rogers
Joan Andrews .... Adele Mara
Cookie Bullfincher .... Andy Devine
Ran Farrell .... Grant Withers
Toni Bordon .... Marie Harmon
Casey .... Joseph Crehan
Jason Howley .... George Carleton
Mort Oakley .... Holly Bane
First Tramp .... Steve Darrell
Jim Andrews .... Jim Nolan
Second Tramp .... Hank Patterson
Bob Nolan and Sons of Pioneers

Roy Rogers sits easily in the saddle and wraps up songs and action to make "Night Time in Nevada" all that could be asked of western filmfare with music. It's a sturdy entry from his Republic stable and a certain fan pleaser. Film also has the best Trucolor hues yet used on the series.

Action tees off early under William Witney's fast direction with staging of cattle-train holdup. Grant Withers is out to obtain some quick cash so he can cover thefts from a trust fund belonging to Adele Mara. The cattle are Rogers' and he starts his manhunt to bring Withers to justice. Before the wild action climaxes in a death fight abroad a runaway truck, Rogers has tied Withers to the cattle and trust fund thefts, as well as a 20-year-old murder over a gold mine.

In between the strong movement, Rogers finds time to give a good vocal account of the title tune and traditional "Big Rock Candy Mountain." Latter is the best. Sons of the Pioneers and Bob Nolan support tuneful moments as well as figuring in the action. Their tunes are "Over Nevada" and "Sweet Laredo Lou."

Stout comedy work comes from Andy Devine as state police officer who aids Rogers' manhunt. Miss Mara is excellent in the femme lead. Distaff comedy comes from Marie Harmon as her friend. Aiding Withers' expert skullduggery is George Carleton.

Production framework supplied by Edward J. White gives good sight values to the action. Tony Martinelli's editing holds film to a tight 66 minutes and color lensing by Jack Marta is excellent. *Brog.*

Woman Hater

London, Oct. 14.

GFD release of J. Arthur Rank-Two Cities (William Sistrom) production. Stars Edwige Feuillere, Stewart Granger. Directed by Terence Young. Screenplay by Robert Westerby, Nicholas Phipps. Editor, Vera Campbell; camera, Andre Thomas, Norman Warwick. At Odeon, London, Oct. 13, '48. Running time, 105 MINS.

Terence, Lord Datchett Stewart Granger
Colette Marly .... Edwige Fenuillere
Claire .... Jeanne de Casalis
Jameson .... Ronald Squire

Dowager Lady Datchett ... Mary Jerrold
Robert................. David Hutcheson
Patrick.................... W. A. Kelly
Julia................. Georgina Cookson
Major............... Henry Edwards
Colonel Weston.......... Stewart Rome
George Spencer......... Valentine Dyall
Old Boy............... H. G. Stoker
Harris................. Michael Medwin

A farcical situation, based on the principle of what happens when two irresistible forces meet, has the potentiality of providing entertaining screen fare. In this case, the two forces are a man and woman, each avowed haters of the opposite sex, but their long drawn-out tussle is sorely in need of pruning if the producers have any designs on the American market.

Principal characters in this trivial piece are Lord Datchett, peer of the realm and member of the landed gentry, who quotes Diogenes to prove his dislike of women, and Colette Marly, famous star, who is bored with men and wants to be alone. To prove that all women are alike, Datchett offers the star the use of his country manor, pretends to be an agent on the estate, and becomes involved in a series of fairly obvious adventures before the inevitable happens.

Normally, farce doesn't call for much in story values, but relies on laughter-raising situations and snappy dialog. With "Woman Hater" the situations are too obviously contrived and the dialog so patently transparent that many of the frivolous interludes lose much of their value, and only serve to underline the thinness of the plot.

Departing from his customary role, Stewart Granger is very much at home in his lighthearted characterization of Lord Datchett, and endeavors to infuse some life into the picture. Edwige Feuillere, talented French star, romps through her part but is worthy of something better. Main support from Jeanne de Casalis and Ronald Squire, as maid and butler, is in experienced hands. *Myro.*

Sleeping Car to Trieste
(BRITISH)
London, Oct. 7.
GFD release of J. Arthur Rank-Two Cities (George H. Brown) production. Stars Jean Kent, Derrick de Marney, Albert Lieven, Paul Dupuis. Directed by John Paddy Carstairs. Screenplay by Allan Mackinnon, based on story by Clifford Grey. Editor, Sidney Stone; camera, Jack Hildyard, H.A.R. Thompson. At Leicester Square, London, Oct. 6, '48. Running time, 95 MINS.
Valya...................... Jean Kent
Zurta.................. Albert Lieven
George Grant....... Derrick de Marney
Jolif..................... Paul Dupuis
Joan Maxted.......... Rona Anderson
Tom Bishop ....- David Tomlinson
Sergeant West.......... Bonar Colleano
Alastair MacBain.......... Finlay Currie
Poirier.................. Coco Aslan
Poole.................... Alan Wheatley
Mills .... Hugh Burden
Denning............... David Hutcheson
Andree............... Claude Larue
Suzanne............... Zena Marshall
Randall............... Leslie Weston
Elvin.................. Michael Ward

Espionage dramas staged in transcontinental trains have been a good film standby for many a year, and the latest offering from the Rank stable, which is a remake of "Rome Express," offers little fresh in the way of screen entertainment. It lacks names and originality to have any hopes of earning more than modest support in the American market.

Picture is built up around the theft of a diary containing vital political information from a Paris diplomat. The thief is double-crossed by his accomplice, but both make for the express to Trieste on which, conveniently, one of the passengers is a police chief. Naturally enough, when the

search for the missing diary leads to the murder of the accomplice, the cop gets busy but his inquiries come to an abrupt end when the killer takes a nosedive in front of an oncoming train.

Although the film opens with a punch, too much time is taken in developing the motley assortment of characters on the train. Action virtually comes to a full stop while the various passengers are being established, and more than half the footage has passed through the projector before it begins to get lively.

Jean Kent and Albert Lieven put up an adequate show as the villans of the piece and the double-crossing member of the team is suitably suggested by Alan Wheatley. Derrick de Marney and Rona Anderson, planning an illicit holiday; Finlay Currie, as a pompous novelist, and Paul Dupuis, as the police chief, make up the interesting complement of travellers, and there is a breath of fresh air from Bonar Colleano as an American soldier. *Myro.*

S. O. S. Submarine
(ITALIAN)
Hollywood, Oct. 8.
Screen Guild release of C. Zanetti production written and directed by F. De Robertis. Previewed Oct. 7, '48. Running time, 71 MINS.

An interesting documentary feature, making for supporting subject off the beaten path. "S. O. S. Submarine," filmed with cooperation of the Italian Navy, apparently was made in pre-war days and at that time undoubtedly was propaganda for safety measures surrounding Italy's underwater fleet. Italian dialog has been obliterated and English dubbed in for U. S. release.

Showoff of safety devices is woven around slight story with typical foreign touches. Essentially, film deals with sub A-103 that runs into trouble just as it is finishing a 72-hour resistance test mission. Surfacing, sub is struck by a ship, a hole is torn in a forward section, the sub dives to bottom.

From then on it's a display of modern rescue techniques, both by sub occupants and the surface fleet. Even the non-technical minded will be held by rescue operations such use of escape tanks, divers working under water to mend the sub, the massing of tugs, seaplanes, PT boats and other crafts in a rush to the disaster scene.

Dubbed-in English dialog has been slickly done, even though not always in sync with lip movements. Lensing, uncredited, aids realistic values. Total running time of 71 minutes is a bit too long and there are a number of duplicate shots that could be trimmed to advantage. *Brog.*

The Street Calls
(La Calle Grita)
(ARGENTINE)
Buenos Aires, Sept. 30.
Artistas Argentinos Asociados production and release. Stars Enrique Muino, Angel Magana; features Patricia Castell, Florindo Ferrario, Hugo Pimentel, Diana Montes. Directed by Lucas Demare. Screenplay, Carlos A. Orlando. At Ambassador, Buenos Aires. Running time, 95 MINS.

This is an effort by director Lucas Demare to duplicate a top-flight U. S. picture, with the moral that all is not gold that glitters. The effort to make a carbon-copy turned out somewhat fuzzy but it contains some humor and a certain

amount of action, unusual for a native-made production. But real chance at showing life of an ordinary Buenos Aires city dweller was overlooked. Film has no interest for U. S. audiences but for local trade it's refreshing if for no other reason than that the comedy clicks.

Had there been less of "made-in-Hollywood" stamp on this, "Street Calls" might have been a great picture for this country and good overseas. As it is, the story of a young Bohemian peddler who tries to show a financial expert where his budgets don't run true to life turns out to be a jaunty yarn, but untrue to local ways.

Enrique Muino, as the capitalist, has a comparatively small role for him and has little chance to display his usual histronics. Angel Magana is overly enthusiastic as the young peddler, while Patricia Castell, a newcomer in the femme lead, shows acting promise but doesn't quite measure up as a screen beauty. Florindo Ferrario, the financier's secretary, is the least stilted person in the picture. Hugo Pimentel is never quite convincing as the financier's son while Diana Montes is okay as another secretary with little to do. *Nid.*

Miniature Reviews

"**The Snake Pit**" (20th). Class melodrama topped by smash performance by Olivia de Havilland. Big b.o.

"**You Gotta Stay Happy**" (U). High gear comedy with Joan Fontaine, James Stewart. Sturdy general appeal.

"**Bonnie Prince Charlie**" (color) (BL). Korda's $4,000,-000 spec long, ponderous and often boring.

"**The Countess of Monte Cristo**" (Songs) (U). Sonja Henie skating, but little else to recommand.

"**High Fury**" (UA). Madeline Carroll in modest budgeter with solid emotional kick; good b.o.

"**The Untamed Breed**" (Color) (Col). Mild western in Cinecolor, passable for the market.

"**The Plunderers**" (Color-Songs) (Rep). Good outdoor fare for general situations.

"**Leather Gloves**" (Col). Good prizefight supporting feature. Story twists help make it pleasant dual fare.

"**Jungle Goddess**" (SGS). White goddess in darkest Africa overly done and overly boring.

"**Quartet**" (GFD). Satisfying and sophisticated entertainment. Should go well with American audiences.

"**The Plot to Kill Roosevelt**" (UA). Crude British-made sensational spy yarn for U.S. exploitation circuit.

"**Four Steps in the Clouds**" (Italian). Charming import geared for hearty returns in art and language situations.

The Snake Pit
Hollywood, Nov. 2.
20th-Fox release of Anatole Litvak-Robert Bassler production, directed by Litvak. Stars Olivia de Havilland, Mark Stevens, Leo Genn; features Celeste Holm, Glenn Langan, Helen Craig, Leif Erickson, Beulah Bondi, Lee Patrick. Screenplay, Frank Partos, Millen Brand; based on novel by Mary Jane Ward; camera, Leo Tover; music, Alfred Neuman; editor, Dorothy Spencer. Tradeshown Oct. 20, '48. Running time, 107 MINS. .... ..
Virginia Cunningham..Olivia de Havilland
Robert Cunningham.......Mark Stevens
Dr. Kik....................Leo Genn
Grace..................Celeste Holm
Dr. Terry...............Glenn Langan
Miss Davis..............Helen Craig
Gordon.................Leif Erickson
Mrs. Greer..............Beulah Bondi
Asylum Inmate.............Lee Patrick
Dr. Curtis...........Howard Freeman
Mrs. Stuart...........Natalie Schafer
Ruth................Ruth Donnelly
Margaret.............Katherine Locke
Dr. Gifford...........Frank Conroy
Miss Hart..............Minna Gombell
Miss Bixby.............June Storey
Virginia (age 6)........Lora Lee Michel
Mr. Stuart............Damian O'Flynn
Valerie.................Ann Doran
Miss Vance.............Esther Somers
Miss Sommerville......Jacqueline de Wit
Hester................Betsy Blair
Miss Greene.............Lela Bliss
Lola.................Queenie Smith
Miss Seifert...........Virginia Brissac
Countess.............Grayce Hampton
Champion.............Dorothy Neumann
Singing Inmate..............Jan Clayton
Asylum Inmates: Isabel Jewell, Victoria Horne, Tamara Shayne, Grace Poggi.

"The Snake Pit" is a standout among class melodramas. Shaped by distinctive handling for the carriage trade, it also has the ingredients that make for popular boxoffice in general release. Morbid subjects, when properly presented, rate broad b.o. acceptance and "The Snake Pit" will be no exception.

Olivia de Havilland rises to new distinction with this. It is a memorable performance, both for fellow professionals and the discerning filmgoer, and certain to be the strongest talking point among the film's many potent word-of-mouth factors.

Producers Anatole Litvak and Robert Bassler started with a boff screenplay by Frank Partos and Millen Brand. As director, Litvak has given it hard, shocking reality in the filming. It is an adroit combination of realism and hokum, emotional but not maudlin. Picture is based on Mary Jane Ward's novel of insanity, a subject that would seem to make for doubtful screen fare, yet the skill in telling, playing and direction gives it a palliative treatment acceptable to picture audiences. What reluctance there might be by readers of the novel to see the shocker on film will be overcome by exploitation and word-of-mouth.

Picture probes into the processes of mental illness with a razor-sharp forthrightness, giving an open-handed display of the make-up of bodies without minds and the treatments used to restore intelligence. Clinical detail is stated with matter-of-fact clarity and becomes an important part of the melodramatics. That this phase of the picture is interesting bespeaks the general ability of those concerned with the filming.

Emotional peaks reach screaming tension and would have stretched nerves even tauter had not the music score been permitted to become noise. High volume music is a hokum trick that is not needed to point up the melodramatic moments in "Snake Pit," and can be easily corrected on the soundtrack. Otherwise the Alfred Newman music is used properly as a subtle bridge for the emotional going-on.

Miss de Havilland is seen as a young bride who goes insane and is committed to an institution for treatment. An understanding medico, Leo Genn, uses kindness and knowledge of mental ills to restore her. Just as a cure seems possible, she again plunges into a mental snake pit and starts all over on the road to insanity. Shock treatments, truth serum, and psychiatric probing gradually disclose the source of her trouble and bring her back to normalcy.

Scenes in the institution have a pathetic hopelessness as the inmates are depicted. Scenes will arouse some guilty chuckles from audiences as the grotesque characters go through their blank antics. There is a touching, tear-jerking sequence of a community sing in the asylum, with Jan Clayton vocalling "Going Home" in chorus with the inmates. Its only fault is that it goes one chorus too many.

Miss de Havilland's performance is likely to stand for a long time as a top gauge for judging femme histrionics. Genn goes about his part of the doctor with a quietness that gives it strength and Mark Stevens is excellent as Miss de Havilland's husband. Celeste Holm has only a brief bit as an inmate. Among those standing out in portrayals of insanity are Betsy Blair, Isabel Jewell, Beulah Bondi, Lee Patrick, Dorothy Neumann and Queenie Smith. Lending good support are Glenn Langhan, Helen Craig, Leif Erickson, Howard Freeman and others.

Technical credits are marked with the class that distinguishes the entire film. Lee Tover's photography is outstanding and special photographic effects by Fred Sersen add to the madness mood.

Brog.

You Gotta Stay Happy

Hollywood, Oct. 30.

Universal release of Karl Tunberg (Rampart-William Dozier) production. Stars Joan Fontaine, James Stewart; features Eddie Albert, Roland Young, Willard Parker, Percy Kilbride. Directed by H. C. Potter. Screenplay, Tunberg from Satevepost serial by Robert Carson; camera, Russell Metty; music, Daniele Amfitheatrof; editor, Paul Wetherwax. Previewed Oct. 26, '48. Running time, 100 MINS.

Dee Dee Dillwood	Joan Fontaine
Marvin Payne	James Stewart
Bullets Baker	Eddie Albert
Ralph Tutwiler	Roland Young
Henry Benson	Willard Parker
Mr. Racknell	Percy Kilbride
Mr. Caslon	Porter Hall
Georgia Goodrich	Marcy McGuire
Milton Goodrich	Arthur Walsh
Dick Hebert	William Bakewell
Dr. Blucher	Paul Cavanagh
Martin	Halliwell Hobbes
Jack Samuels	Stanley Prager
Aunt Martha	Mary Forbes
Mrs. Racknell	Edith Evanson
Barnabas	Peter Roman
Jud Tavis	Houseley Stevenson
Bank Watchman	Emory Parnell
Ted	Don Kohler
Nell	Bert Conway
Night Clerk	Hal K. Dawson
Mae	Vera Marshe
Curly	Jimmie Dodd
Eddie	Robert Rockwell
Joe	Joe

Apparently the cinema queens of heavy drama have started a trend to comedy. First Greer Garson, then Bette Davis, and now Joan Fontaine. As in the first two ventures, the change of pace comes off very happily for Miss Fontaine, giving "You Gotta Stay Happy" a neat boxoffice outlook. Her name, coupled with that of James Stewart, offers plenty of marquee gloss to give the picture initial impetus.

Fun content is good and, while the title is not a particularly bright tag to merchandise, it is apt enough to the plot. Script keeps the hokum pot boiling all the way and there are innumerable deft touches in writing and direction that make it a happy affair for light entertainment. From a mildly interesting start, picture picks up attention as it unfolds and delivers all that it promises in the way of chuckles.

Stewart is seen as an ex-Army flier battling his way in civilian life with a cargo plane company. A New York trip brings femme trouble when he is forced to play unwilling knight errant to a slightly wacky bride fleeing her stuffed-shirt groom on the wedding night. The gal talks him into taking her to California. It's an adventurous flight, with an assorted cargo such as a trained chimp, a corpse in a coffin, an absconder with his loot and an amorous pair of newlyweds.

A plane crash on the Oklahoma farm of Percy Kilbride gives Stewart and Miss Fontaine a chance to fall in love, have a misunderstanding and then make it all up in California when he reconciles himself to fact that she's not a poor, misguided girl who has gone wrong in the city but is an heiress.

Plot sounds like a lot of fluff, and it is, but comedy knowhow in bringing it to the screen, along with topnotch performances, makes it easy to take. Miss Fontaine and Stewart play it ably for laughs under the deft direction by H. C. Potter. Karl Tunberg functioned as producer and scripter, scoring on both chores. He also used the same skill in casting the roles and every performer adds punch to the doings.

Eddie Albert is extremely likeable as Stewart's flier pal. Kilbride (in a new version of Pa Kettle, complete with offspring), sharpens his country bumpkin role. Porter Hall is the absconder and makes it good for laughs. The newlyweds are pertly portrayed by Marcy McGuire and Arthur Walsh. Willard Parker, the groom deserted by Miss Fontaine; Roland Young, William Bakewell, Paul Cavanagh and others deliver strongly.

Picture is a Rampart production, presented by William Dozier for U release, and has been given a well-valued gloss to fit it for top billing in all situations. A humorous score by Daniele Amfitheatrof figures importantly and Russell Metty's lensing gives an expert display to the physical values.

Brog.

Bonnie Prince Charlie

(Color)

(BRITISH)

London, Nov. 1.

British Lion release of London Films (Sir Alexander Korda) Production. Stars David Niven, Margaret Leighton. Directed by Anthony Kimmins. Screenplay, Clemence Dane; camera (Technicolor), Robert Krasker, O. Borrodaile; editor, Grace Garland; music, Ian Whyte. Running time, 135 MINS.

Prince Charles Ed. Stuart	David Niven
Flora Macdonald	Margaret Leighton
Donald	Morland Graham
Blind Jamie	John Laurie
Clementina Walkinshaw	Judy Campbell
King James, III	Henry Oscar
Marquis of Tullibardine	Finlay Currie
Lord George Murray	Jack Hawkins
Cameron of Lochiel	Guy Lefeuvre
Macdonald of Keppoch	Franklin Dyall
Kinloch Moidart	Herbert Lomas
Macleod of Macleod	Ronald Adam
Macdonald of Armadale	Stuart Lindsell
Colonel O'Sullivan	John Longden
Glenaladale	Hector Ross
King George, II	Martin Miller
Duke of Cumberland	Elwyn Brook-Jones
Duke of Newcastle	G. H. Mulcaster
Captain Fergusson, R.N.	Charles Goldner
General Cope	Julien Mitchell
Lady Margaret Macdonald	Molly Rankin
Kingsburgh	James Hayter
Colonel Ker	Torin Thatcher
Young Alan of Moidart	Simon Lack
Clanranald	Tommy Duggan
Lieutenant Ingleby	Hugh Kelly
Mrs. Kingsburgh	Nell Ballantyne
Annie Kingsburgh	Patricia Fox

More than two years in the making, and reputed to have cost upwards of $4,000,000, the latest Alex Korda production from London Films is long, ponderous and often boring. Devoid of the spectacle and pageantry which was to have been expected from this historical drama, "Bonnie Prince Charlie" plods its dull and weary way through a series of meaningless adventures that follow the failure of the young pretender to recapture the throne for his exiled father. Despite the money expended, it is not a picture to enhance the prestige of Britain, and the producers cannot hope to recoup much of their cash outlay from the American market.

That it bears little resemblance to the history textbook is neither surprising nor disappointing, but there is cause for real regret in that a picture which occupied so much time on the studio floor apparently has little hope of earning more than a fraction of its original cost.

Of the two and a quarter hours spent in telling the story, only a small part is devoted to the battle of the Pretender against George of Hanover, and the rest of the screen time describes the Prince's exploits in outwitting the entire English army, and eventually making his way back to France. But even the battle scenes lack the spectacle and crowds, and despite the vivid Technicolor, are virtually colorless. As for the rest, it is nothing more than a familiar manhunt, lacking the suspense to capture the imagination.

It is unfair to criticize the acting by normal standards, as the leading players, competent though they may be, are given little scope. David Niven, for example, an accomplished actor, is entirely out of place and not even a blonde wig helps to provide the illusion that he is meant to be the young Prince Charles. Much the same can be said of Margaret Leighton, who plays the role of Flora Macdonald, the patriotic Highlander who helps the Prince to escape, and the other members of the cast who battle against unreasonable odds.

Myro.

The Countess of Monte Cristo

(SONGS)

Hollywood, Oct. 30.

Universal release of John Beck (Westwood) production. Stars Sonja Henie; features Michael Kirby, Olga San Juan, Dorothy Hart, Arthur Treacher, Freddie Trenkler. Directed by Frederick De Cordova. Screenplay, William Bowers; story, Walter Reisch; camera, Edward Cronjager; songs, Jack Brooks, Saul Chaplin; music, Walter Scharf; editor, Edward Curtiss. Previewed Oct. 29, '48. Running time, 76 MINS.

Karen	Sonja Henie
Jenny	Olga San Juan
Peg Manning	Dorothy Hart
Paul von Cram	Michael Kirby
Managing Director	Arthur Treacher
Count Holgar	Hugh French
Mr. Hansen	Ransom Sherman
Skating Specialty	Freddie Trenkler
Freddie	John James
Assistant Director	Arthur O'Connell
Joe	Joseph Crehan
Charlie	Ray Teal

"The Countess of Monte Cristo" is a passable Sonja Henie ice film. After a screen absence of nearly four years, the blade star could have used a stronger vehicle for a return. It's a fluffy to-do about nothing, mildly amusing at times.

Six skating numbers are spotted through the footage, all done with the expected Henie grace and skill but still not strong enough to overcome other handicaps. Some femme attention will be garnered by Michael Kirby, Miss Henie's real-life skating partner, who handles principal male interest in this. He films well and his personality pleases.

The John Beck production concerns itself with two Norwegian barmaids who get extra roles at an Oslo studio and then take off with film property to fake their way through a stay at a swank resort hotel. Miss Henie poses as the countess of the title and her buddy, Olga San Juan, becomes her personal maid. Mistaken identity theme is milked from all angles as the fable unfolds. There are suave crooks, rich lieutenants mistaken for doormen and sundry stock stunts carrying the slight story thread in between Miss Henie's production numbers.

Pertness of Olga San Juan gives some life to the story and she pleases with vocals on three tunes, "Count Your Blessings," "Who Believes in Santa Claus?" and "The Friendly Polka," all cleffed by Jack Brooks and Saul Chaplin. Dorothy Hart plays a character never made clear in the scripting and Arthur Treacher, resort host, manages some comedy touches.

Comedy ice specialty contributed by Freddie Trenker is one assist for the film. Frederick De Cordova's direction does its best with the "Student Prince," never-never land flavor of the William Bowers script. Physical production values are moderate and Edward Cronjager's lensing gives them an okay display.

Brog.

High Fury

United Artists release of Peak Film (Ivor McLaren) production. Stars Madeleine Carroll; features Ian Hunter, Michael Rennie. Directed by Harold French. Original screenplay, Harold French and Lesley Storm; camera, Derek Williams; editor, A. S. Bates, Walter Klee; score,

Dr. Bernard Grun. Tradeshown N. Y. Nov. 1, '48. Running time, 71 MINS.

Magda	Madeleine Carroll
Anton	Ian Hunter
Rudolph	Michael Rennie
Louise	Anne Marie Blanc
Roger	Michael McKeag
Joseph	Arnold Marle
Benno	Willi Fueter
Frederick	Max Haufler
Maria	Margarete Hoff
President	Gerard Kempinski

This is an appealing film about displaced war children which will generate nice response at the boxoffice. Produced on location in a Swiss mountain village, "High Fury" is warm, simple and sincere. Through excellent work by all concerned with this effort, the entertainment values have been stretched far beyond its modest budget resources.

This film has absorbed some of that realistic flavor found in superior continental productions. Against its authentic background, it unfolds a believable story with a cast that captures all the human nuances. Madeleine Carroll and Ian Hunter, the only two names known in the U. S., play with intelligence and sensitivity, setting the tone for the rest of the cast. Expert direction also neatly integrated into the story a flock of unprofessional kids and village characters, thereby erasing the line between fact and fiction.

Yarn is concerned with a war-orphaned French boy who, during the war, settled with a Swiss couple with conflicting feelings for him. The wife (Miss Carroll) wants to adopt him in order to save him from returning to a French orphanage. The husband (Michael Rennie), however, resents the boy and refuses to sign the adoption papers unless the wife signs over her property to him. But Rennie is a good-hearted heavy who, during a nerve-tingling Alpine climbing sequence, sacrifices his life to save the lad's. The climax, though slightly contrived to clear the way for a romance between Miss Carroll and the village doctor (Hunter), is fitted in with a minimum of artificiality.

In one of her most highly suitable roles, Miss Carroll plays with an emotional restraint and naturalness that blends her into the realistic settings. Hunter and Rennie, likewise, register as credible characters. As the young boy, Michael McKeag evokes sympathy with his suggestion of inward fear and torture. The rest of the cast play their bit roles to the hilt.

Added impact is given by first-rate outdoor camera work with striking shots of the Swiss peaks and a stirring score by Bernard Grun. *Herm.*

The Untamed Breed
(COLOR)

Hollywood, Oct. 29.

Columbia release of Harry Joe Brown production. Stars Sonny Tufts, Barbara Britton, George "Gabby" Hayes; features Edgar Buchanan, William Bishop, George E. Stone, Joe Sawyer, Gordon Jones. Directed by Charles Lamont. Screenplay, Tom Reed; based on Satevepost story by Eli Colter; camera (Cinecolor), Charles Lawton, Jr.; editor, Jerome Thoms. At the Vogue, Hollywood, Oct. 27, '48. Running time, 74 MINS.

Tom Kilpatrick	Sonny Tufts
Cherry Lucas	Barbara Britton
Windy Lucas	George "Gabby" Hayes
John Rambeau	Edgar Buchanan
Larch Keegan	William Bishop
Pablo	George E. Stone
Hoy Keegan	Joe Sawyer
Happy Keegan	Gordon Jones
Sheriff	James Kirkwood
Elisha Jones	Harry Tyler
Mrs. Jones	Virginia Brissac
Oklahoma	Reed Howes

The most exciting thing about "The Untamed Breed" is the title. It's a mildly active galloper that fails to get underway. What lure it will have at boxoffice will depend upon a familiar cast. Cinecolor gives it an okay production dress, but otherwise, it's run-of-the-mill.

There's no division between good and evil in the plot, script depending upon menace for antisocial attitude adopted by Pecos country ranchers towards a south Texan who wants them to improve their herds with a Brahma bull strain. Sonny Tufts is a misfit as the Texan with ambition, never making the role believable. Balance of cast fits better into outdoor characters but fails to give much of a lift to unfoldment.

Defter guidance in all departments might have made a good show out of the original story, but scripting, direction and playing is too formula to breed excitement. A modest thrill or two develops when the Brahma escapes and wreaks havoc on the ranches, and when Tufts has to catch and tame a wild horse to bring in the raging bull. A free-for-all between Tufts and William Bishop, former romantic rival, should have been a high spot. Instead, it's a ridiculously stagey melee with only comic values. That and other pitfalls prove too much for Charles Lamont's direction.

George "Gabby" Hayes plays his standard western character and does okay. Barbara Britton looks good in color as the heroine. Edgar Buchanan, Bishop, Joe Sawyer, Gordon Jones and others try hard. Production by Harry Joe Brown furnishes acceptable western settings for the plot and Charles Lawton, Jr., does justice by the scenery with his color lensing. *Brog.*

The Plunderers
(COLOR-SONGS)

Hollywood, Oct. 29.

Republic release of Joseph Kane production, directed by Kane. Stars Rod Cameron, Ilona Massey, Adrian Booth; features Forrest Tucker, George Cleveland, Grant Withers, Taylor Holmes, Paul Fix. Screenplay, Gerald Geraghty, Gerald Adams: based on an original by James Edward Grant; camera (Trucolor), Jack Marta; music, Dale Butts; editor, Arthur Roberts. Previewed Oct. 29, '48. Running time, 87 MINS.

John Drum	Rod Cameron
Lin Conner	Ilona Massey
Julie McCabe	Adrian Booth
Whit Lacey	Forrest Tucker
Sam Borden	George Cleveland
Tap Lawrence	Grant Withers
Eben Martin	Taylor Holmes
Calico	Paul Fix
Barnaby	Francis Ford
Sgt. Major	James Flavin
Cavalry Colonel	Russell Hicks
Old Dame	Maude Eburne
Pioneer Girl	Mary Ruth Wade
Sentry	Louis R. Faust

"The Plunderers" comes equipped with all the standard outdoor action appurtenances to measure up for the general situations. From the opening chase, it's a mixture of western formula on a large scale, filmed in color. The boxoffice attention should be satisfactory.

While film kicks off with a shoot-'em-up chase, the story-telling takes a little longer to get under way and some minutes have passed before action hits its best clip. Playing is good in a yarn that concerns an army officer working undercover to bring a tough outlaw and his gang to justice. Villain doesn't follow the accepted western pattern, being a rather likeable guy despite the way he earns his living.

Rod Cameron shows up excellently as the hero. Plot twist has him murdering a sheriff in opening sequences and it's some time before audiences will get wise that it is only a setup for him to get into the gang. He pits his wits against Forrest Tucker, who does an able heavy. Windup brings in an Indian raid, in which Tucker aids the law and escapes the rope when shot down by the redskins.

Femme interest is split between Ilona Massey and Adrian Booth, a couple of dancehall babes. Miss Massey enacts romantic partner opposite Cameron while Miss Booth is beloved by Tucker. Score includes two public domain tunes, "Walking Down Broadway" and "I'll Sing a Love Song," Miss Massey does the vocalling of special lyrics by Jack Elliott and Aaron Gonzales.

George Cleveland, for a change, is a smart sheriff, while Grant Withers is his dumb counterpart as deputy. Taylor Holmes is the respected townsman who's really backing the outlaws and Paul Fix enacts good characterization as Tucker's gun-slinging pal. Francis Ford and others add to the action bluster with which associate producer-director Joseph Kane has endowed this one.

Lensing by Jack Marta is expert and is done in an improving Trucolor process. Editing could have been smoother. *Brog.*

Leather Gloves

Hollywood, Oct. 30.

Columbia release of Richard Quine-William Asher production, directed by Quine and Asher. Features Cameron Mitchell, Virginia Grey, Jane Nigh, Sam Levene, Henry O'Neill, Blake Edwards. Screenplay, Brown Holmes; from Satevepost story by Richard English; camera, Henry Freulich; editor, Viola Lawrence. At Vogue, Hollywood, Oct. 27, '48. Running time, 75 MINS.

Dave Collins	Cameron Mitchell
Janet Gilbert	Virginia Grey
Cathy	Jane Nigh
Bernie	Sam Levene
Dudley	Henry O'Neill
Vince Reedy	Blake Edwards
Huerta Fernandez	Bob Castro
Mrs. Hubbard	Sally Corner
Mr. Hubbard	Stanley Andrews
Duke	Eddie Acuff
Referee	Ralph Volkie
Trimble	Walter Soderling

"Leather Gloves" makes for pleasant fare in the supporting slot. It's a prizefight yarn with twists, presented in a style to rate casual interest. Production represents good expenditure of budget coin in shaping picture as an okay entry for its market.

Performances are good, as is the direction, except for a midway lapse. Plot has a philosophical angle or two and the hero doesn't get the girl. Cameron Mitchell is excellent as a lightheavy pug on the bum who changes, for the better, the lives of several smalltown people with whom he comes in contact during one brief week.

Dual production job by Richard Quine and William Asher is carried over to double-stint on direction. They start the film rolling neatly and bring it to a strong conclusion, except for the middle sag, do well. Plot brings Mitchell to a small town. He talks his way on a fight card, falls for a girl and prepares to fake a loss to pick up some cash. He finds the girl goes for his opponent and gives the kid a licking so he'll get out of the fight game. Finale again has Mitchell on the move to other pastures.

Aiding Mitchell's good work are Virginia Grey, Jane Nigh, Sam Levene, Henry O'Neill, Blake Edwards and others. Okay scripting chore was turned in by Brown Holmes, story twists and dialog lifting it about level of ordinary prizefight plotting. Lensing is good, but editing lets footage run a bit too long for best double bill spotting. *Brog.*

Jungle Goddess

Hollywood, Oct. 29.

Screen Guild release of Lippert Production. Features George Reeves, Wanda McKay, Armida, Ralph Byrd. Directed by Lewis D. Collins. Screenplay, Joseph Pagano; editor, Norman Cerf; camera, Carl Berger. At Paramount, L. A., Oct. 28, '48. Running time, 62 MINS.

Mike Patton	George Reeves
Greta Vanderhorn	Wanda McKay
Wanama	Armida
Bob Simpson	Ralph Byrd
Oolonga, witch doctor	Smoki Whitfield
Yvonne	Dolores Castle
Nugara	Pudy Robles
Helen	Linda Johnson
Mrs. Fitzhugh	Helena Grant
Pilot	Fred Coby
Drummer	Onest Conley
Chief M'Benga	Zach Williams
Accompanist	Jack Carroll

"Jungle Goddess" got lost in a desert of dry performances and clammy direction. Screenplay is the same old white goddess among native tribesmen routine that has been run through innumerable times prior to this. There is no gold buried in this part of Africa.

Film gets under way when George Reeves and Ralph Byrd discover that Wanda McKay's father is offering a gigantic reward for her—dead or alive. Femme was last known to be aboard an airplane which crashed in the African jungles six years earlier. They find her living among the natives as tribe's top executioner. She condemns Byrd to die for slaying a native. He finally gets his in a new tangle with the natives while trying to break away for the plane. Reeves and Miss McKay manage to escape.

Featured trio, Reeves, Miss McKay and Bryd, turn in dull performances along with a cast of natives who belong anywhere but in "Jungle Goddess." Production values supplied by William Stephens are sorely lacking in the necessary stamina for pulling out an average film. Lewis D. Collins' direction falls by the wayside along with Joseph Pagano's screenplay. Lensing by Carl Berger adds nothing. *Free.*

Quartet

London, Oct. 27.

General Film Distributors' release of J. Arthur Rank (Gainsborough-Sydney Box) production. Stars Hermione Baddeley, Dirk Bogarde, Mervyn Johns, Cecil Parker, Basil Radford, Francoise Rosay, Susan Shaw, Linden Travers, Naunton Wayne, Mai Zetterling. Directed by Ken Annakin, Arthur Crabtree, Harold French, Ralph Smart. Screenplays by R. C. Sherriff; adapted from four stories by W. Somerset Maugham; camera, Ray Elton, Bernard Lewis; editor, Jean Barker; music, John Greenwood. At Odeon, London, Oct. 26. '48. Running time, 120 MINS.

The Facts of Life

Henry Garnet	Basil Radford
Leslie	Naunton Wayne
Ralph	Ian Fleming
Thomas	Jack Raine
Mrs. Garnet	Angela Baddeley
Branksome	James Robertson Justice
Nicky	Jack Watling
John	Nigel Buchanan
Jeanne	Mai Zetterling

The Alien Corn

George Bland	Dirk Bogarde
Sir Frederick Bland	Raymond Lovell
Lady Bland	Irene Browne
Paula	Honor Blackman
Uncle John	George Thorpe
Aunt Maud	Mary Hinton
Lea Makart	Francoise Rosay

The Kite

Prison Visitor	Bernard Lee
Governor	Frederick Leister
Prison Officer	George Merritt
Herbert Sunbury	George Cole
Herbert (boy)	David Cole
Beatrice Sunbury	Hermione Baddeley
Samuel Sudbury	Mervyn Johns
Betty	Susan Shaw
Reporter	Cyril Chamberlain

The Colonel's Lady

Colonel Peregrine	Cecil Parker
Mrs. Peregrine	Nora Swinburne
West	J. H. Roberts
1st Club Man	Claude Allister
2nd Club Man	Wilfred Hyde-White
Henry Dashwood	Ernest Thesiger
Duke of Heverel	Henry Edwards
Daphne	Linden Travers
Martin	Felix Aylmer
John Coleman	John Salew
Bannock	Lynn Evans

Railway Passenger .... Cyril Raymond
Henry Blane .... Clive Morton
Gushing Woman .... Margaret Withers

An original by Somerset Maugham, coupled with a script by R. C. Sherriff, is a safe guide to a piece of satisfying, sophisticated entertainment. In "Quartet" the satisfaction is multiplied four times, and each of the subjects that go to the making of this picture, although individualistic in theme and treatment, have 'the Maugham wit and sharpness of characterization as the connecting link. In Britain it is a prestige picture plus, and is by far the best to come from the Sydney Box outfit since "Seventh Veil." It also merits the approbation of American audiences who are always ready to show their appreciation of class entertainment.

Of the four stories that make up the film, the first and last are undoubtedly the most intriguing. "The Facts of Life" is a superbly told piece of a 19-year-old who disregards his father's advice on his first trip to Monte Carlo and outwits an obvious adventuress, and "The Colonel's Lady" is a delightful yarn of a Colonel's wife who causes much embarrassment to her husband by the publication of a book of verse purporting to describe her romantic experiences.

The intermediate two, while lacking the high level of the first and last, are certainly more than potboilers. An undergraduate son of a member of the landed gentry who hopes to become a professional pianist, provides the melodramatic theme of "The Alien Corn," while "The Kite" is an unusual story of a simple young man, very much under his mother's domination, who put his kite-flying before his wife and cheerfully goes to gaol when she wrecks his latest invention.

Individuality of story and treatment by separate casts and directors does not detract from the entertainment value of the finished article. Contrasting characters and plots add to the freshness and charm of the picture as a whole and, in effect, give the customers four complete pictures for their original stake. Direction and production throughout maintain an extraordinarily high level, and the casting, even down to the smallest bit, is uncannily accurate. Basil Radford and Naunton Wayne, always a perfect team, have the backing of Jack Watling and Mai Zetterling. Dirk Bogarde, supported by Raymond Lovell and Honor Blackman, take the honors for "The Alien Corn," in which Francoise Rosay excels in a small part. George Cole as the kite flier and Hermione Baddeley as his possessive mother carry the third subject, and Cecil Parker and Nora Swinburne are perfectly chosen as the Colonel and his wife.

Although off the beaten track, "Quartet" is a picture which deserves widespread popularity, and should go a long way to raise the standard of British product throughout America. *Myro.*

The Plot to Kill Roosevelt
(BRITISH)

United Artists release of Selected Films production. Stars Derek Farr, Marta Labarr. Directed by William Freshman. Previewed N. Y., Oct. 22, '48. Running time, 83 MINS.
Pemberton Grant .... Derek Farr
Natalie Trubetzin .... Marta Labarr
Paul Sherek ....,...... Manning Whiley

Aimed for the U. S. exploitation market by a British indie, "The Plot to Kill Roosevelt" spins a sensational yarn that'll even tax the credulity of the kids. Other facets of this production, from the thesping to the camera work, are equally hard to swallow in their crudity. Pic's sole asset lies in its title which may earn it a spot as dual program filler.

Fantastic plot is localed, for most part, in Teheran, meeting place of Roosevelt, Churchill and Stalin during the war years, where synthetic Arabs, Germans, Americans and Russians are shown engaged in espionage and military activities. Through an inexplicable bit of detective work, a British correspondent learns of a conspiracy by an international armaments ring to kill F.D.R. because his postwar peace plans would put them out of business. In cliffhanger style, the plot is foiled just as the varmints are about to set off the dynamite planted under the President's car.

The cast is of stock company calibre. Manning Whiley, as the villain, registers with the most competent performance, although his youth and his heavy role don't mix. Derek Farr, as the British journalist, and Marta Labarr, as a shadowy femme fatale, are barely adequate. Others in the cast border on the amateurish. *Herm.*

Four Steps in the Clouds
(ITALIAN)

Distinguished Films release of Alessandro Blasetti (Cines) production. Stars Gino Cervi, Adriana Benetti. Directed by Giuseppe Amato. Screenplay, C. Zavattini, P. Tellini and Amato; camera, Waclaw Vick; music, Alessandro Cicognini. Previewed N. Y., Oct. 27, '48. Running time, 88 MINS.
Paolo Bianchi .... Gino Cervi
Maria .... Adriana Benetti
Magnaghi .... Enrico Viarisio
Antonio .... Carlo Romano
Clara Bianchi ...,..... Giuditta Rissone
Conductor .... Lauro Gazzolo
1st Hurdy-gurdy Man Umberto Sacripanti
2d Hurdy-gurdy Man .... Silvio Bagolini
Father .... Aldo Silvani
Grandfather .... Giacinto Molteni
Station Master .... Armando Migliari
Passenger .... Arturo Bragaglia
Woman Passenger .... Pina Gallini
Another Passenger ...... Oreste Bilancia

"Four Steps in the Clouds" is one of the more charming Italian cinema imports. It's picture that will undoubtedly do well in the art and language houses and could conceivably entertain in other situations as part of a double bill.

The picture contains a high degree of clever cinematic exposition made possible by director Giuseppe Amato's deft touches of humor and colorful treatment of incident. Top performances by Adriana Benetti, Gino Cervi, Aldo Silvani and Giacinto Molteni produce an entertaining and altogether satisfying result.

Film has been playing to Continent for gratifying returns and Sir Alexander Korda has purchased the British remake rights. (Sir Ralph Richardson will play the Cervi role.)

The story treats of a girl approaching motherhood without benefit of clergy. She persuades a chance acquaintance to pose as her husband so that a place in the household of her strict parents can be insured. Deception, with its borderline situations always delicately handled, works out well until the father discovers a photograph of the man's family. With the ensuing confession, the father relents sufficiently to take care of his daughter.

It's apparent that the yarn could not have been treated as simply and as effectively if it were produced in Hollywood. Production code would demand that the girl be punished for her misdeed and consequently entire tone and character of the film would have to be changed.

Performances are of top cut. Adriana Benetti as the mother-to-be provides an excellent account of herself, but the best rounded performance is by Cervi who helps bring out the basic injustice and pathos of the entire situation. Portrayal indicates he could love the girl, but circumstances force him to return to his shrewish wife. Aldo Silvani as the stern parent, who is eventually touched by the kindness shown his daughter by a total stranger, gives a gratifying performance, while deft humor is displayed by Giacinto Molteni as the girl's grandfather.

Giuseppe Amato's direction contains a smooth pace and colorful embellishment of incident without marring the essential story line. English subtitles are okay.

There is only one detracting factor in the film. In editing for U.S. audiences one sequence has been eliminated in a jarring manner. The void is quite disturbing. *Jose.*

Monte Cassino
(ITALIAN)

Superfilm release of Pastor (Arturo Gemmiti) production, directed by Gemmiti. Screenplay, Gemmiti, Virgilio Sabel, Giovanni Paolucci; camera, Piero Portalupi, Vittorio Della Valle, Angelo Jannarelli; music, Adriano Lualdi; English titles, Charles Clement. Previewed N. Y., Oct. 27, '48. Running time, 93 MINS.
The Head Abbott .... Alberto C. Lolli
Don Martino .... Gilberto Severi
Don Eusebio .... Ubaldo Lay
Maria .... Zora Piazza
Alberto .... Pietro Bigerna
Marco .... Silverio Blasi
Carmela .... Vira Silenti
Capt. Richter .... Rodolpho Neuhaus
Antonio .... Livio Bussa
Father of Antonio .... Giuseppe Forli
Also a group of original survivors of Monte Cassino

(In Italian; English Titles)

"Monte Cassino" is a sombre, semi-documentary relating the various incidents that led up to the bombing of Monte Cassino Abbey during a decisive phase of the Italian campaign of the past war. It's a moving and touching film that should do well in the art houses.

Battle of Cassino was one of the most dramatic struggles of Gen. Mark Clark's Fifth Army in its drive to the north through the rugged Italian mountains. But another battle, almost equally as dramatic, was taking place within and nearby the walls of the 1,400-year-old abbey.

That fight was waged by the abbott, monks and brothers of the abbey against the German troops in the Cassino region who sought to prevent the monastery staff from administering to the needs of women, children, the aged and infirm, all of whom were helpless victims of the war about them.

Film has a ring of authenticity to it for the action is presented in chronological fashion dating from October, 1943, when fighting first approached Cassino village, up until the following March. That month brought the demise of the Abbey in a hail of American bombs.

As written, produced and directed by Arturo Gemmiti, "Monte Cassino" serves as a monument to the hapless refugees caught in the press of an army's offensive as well as a memorial to the monastery's staff. Sprinkled through this pictorial history are intricate characterizations of the abbott, a pair of youthful lovers and a German medical officer.

Onus for the abbey's destruction is placed upon the Germans for their failure to withdraw from the vicinity of Monte Cassino. Even after American planes distributed leaflets warning the monastery occupants that the structure would be bombed of necessity, the Nazi command refused to permit them to withdraw in time to escape. This and other incidents in the film lay the blame flatly on the German high command.

Despite the fact that "Monte Cassino" is evidently a straightforward account of the abbey's siege, its long running time tends to wring the dramatic values dry before the end of the footage. More judicious editing could have resulted in a speedier pace. Non-name cast handles its tasks adequately. Camera work of a trio of lensmen capably catches the grimness of the scarred, mountain terrain.

Inasmuch as the picture has a deeply religious background and was made with the cooperation of the Vatican, it's bound to have the backing of the church wherever screened. Exhibitors will also benefit by the public's general interest in the Cassino battle. For although the Fifth Army was sure that the heights of Monte Cassino were being used by the Germans for military purposes, the Americans were never able to prove it. *Gilb.*

Miniature Reviews

"When My Baby Smiles at Me" (Songs-Color) (20th). Smooth musical with nostalgic tunes, Betty Grable, Dan Dailey. Bright b.o. prospects.

"Every Girl Should Be Married" (RKO). Cary Grant, Franchot Tone in sock romantic comedy; surefire appeal.

"Blood On the Moon" (RKO) Adult-styled western drama away from usual action formula, which will hurt its b.o. chances.

"Racing Luck"(Col). Draggy racetrack entry lacks plot interest.

"Indian Agent" (RKO). Okay Tim Holt western for the Saturday matinee trade.

"West of Sonora" (Col). Average Charles Starrett ("Durango Kid") oatuner.

"The Guinea Pig" (Pathe). Sensitive British schoolboy study.

"No Room At the Inn" (Pathe). Grim British yarn about orphans in a Cockney boarding house. Limited draw.

"Scorned Flesh" (Italian). Story about a sailor and his tragic love; okay for foreign houses.

When My Baby Smiles at Me
(SONGS-COLOR)
Hollywood, Nov. 5.

20th-Fox release of George Jessel production. Stars Betty Grable, Dan Dailey; features Jack Oakie, June Havoc, Richard Arlen, James Gleason. Directed by Walter Lang. Screenplay, Lamar Trotti; adaptation, Elizabeth Reinhardt; from play, "Burlesque," by George Manker Watters, Arthur Hopkins; camera (Technicolor), Harry Jackson; editor, Barbara McLean; songs, Mack Gordon, Josef Myrow; musical direction, Alfred Newman. Tradeshown Nov. 3, '48. Running time. 98 MINS.

Bonny .... Betty Grable
Skid .... Dan Dailey
Bozo .... Jack Oakie
Gussie .... June Havoc
Harvey .... Richard Arlen
Lefty .... James Gleason
Bubbles .... Vanita Wade
Specialty Dancer .... Kenny Williams
Sylvia Marco .... Jean Wallace
Woman in Box .... Pati Behrs
Sam Harris .... Robert Emmett Keane
Midget .... Jerry Maren
Comic .... George "Bettlepuss" Lewis
Valet .... Tom Stevenson
Process Server .... Sam Bernard
Stage Manager .... Mauritz Hugo
Vendor .... Frank Scannell
Painters .... Tim Graham, Dave Morris

This 20th-Fox version of the old George Manker Watters-Arthur Hopkins "Burlesque" is a happy journey down memory lane. Stature is added through nostalgic quality gained in the aging. Packed with surefire old tunes, plus a couple of new ones, and filled with time-tested gags and laugh lines, it answers all requirements of the entertainment seeker. Technicolor adds lustre and marquee values are strong.

Producer George Jessel brings forth plenty of showmanship in tying up the entertainment. Showwise, he has picked his cast with care, and his affection for the old flesh shows is apparent in the touches given "When My Baby Smiles at Me." Score is studded with the memory treat of such songs as the title number, "Don't Bring Lulu," "Bye, Bye, Blackbird," "Birth of the Blues" and snatches of scores of others.

Betty Grable and Dan Dailey function strongly in the star spots, both trouping their roles and handling song and dance with a style that pleases. They fit easily into the burley atmosphere that permeates the production and give a

lift to the aging, but still fun, plot. Dailey is equally at home in dramatics, comedy and song-dance man routines. Miss Grable is more than an eyeful ornament to the story. She's a wow when interpreting a burley queen at work, and shows up well in the story sequences.

There's a lot of chorus curves and glamor to appeal to the males in the several production numbers. Costumes are visual treats, lending color to the numbers. From the title tune opener, sung by Dailey, through to new tunes by Mack Gordon and Josef Myrow, it's a musical feast wrapped around the corn and hokum of the burley gag and art. Best of the two new songs are "What Did I Do?," with Miss Grable on vocals. Other, also listenable, is "By the Way." Both are reprised with solos and production number backing.

Walter Lang's direction is lively and warm in handling the good script by Lamar Trotti. Screenplay follows closely the original play in telling of marital team of Skid and Bonny. When success goes to Skid's head, Bonny gets a divorce. Skid takes to the bottle, Bonny returns to straighten him out and there's a reconciliation for the finale.

Jack Oakie and June Havoc are perfectly at home in the atmosphere of this one and provide a lot of the punch that helps sell the show. Jimmy Gleason is good as the manager and Richard Arlen, rancher who goes for Miss Grable, pleases. Excellence of stars and feature players is reflected down the line by supporting performers.

Alfred Newman's musical direction is solid, as are the orchestral arrangements and vocal direction. A sharp, eye-filling lensing job has been turned in by Harry Jackson. Dance direction, settings and editing are commendable.

Every Girl Should Be Married

RKO release of Don Hartman (Dore Schary) production, directed by Hartman. Stars Cary Grant; features Franchot Tone, Diana Lynn, Betsy Drake, Alan Mowbray. Screenplay, Hartman and Stephen Morehouse Avery; camera, George S. Diskant; editor, Harry Marker; music, C. Bakaleinikoff. Tradeshown N. Y. Nov. 5, '48. Running time, 85 MINS.

Dr. Madison Brown .... Cary Grant
Roger Sanford .... Franchot Tone
Julie Hudson .... Diana Lynn
Anabel Sims .... Betsy Drake
Mr. Spitzer .... Alan Mowbray
Mary Nolan .... Elisabeth Risdon
Sam McNutt .... Richard Gaines
Gogarty .... Harry Hayden
Soda Clerk .... Chick Chandler
Violinist .... Leon Belasco
Pierre .... Fred Essler
Saleslady .... Anna Q. Nilsson

"Every Girl Should Be Married" is one of those rare comic delicacies that are always in good season at the b.o. Out of that venerable theme of the war between the sexes in which the remmes are the guileful aggressors, Don Hartman has fashioned a sparklingly witty comedy of modern manners which will set off a chain reaction of chuckles. With Cary Grant topping a superlative cast including Franchot Tone and a standout newcomer, Betsy Drake, this film will have a terrific payoff.

Script and direction, both handled by Hartman, are finely balanced in a clever pace and style cued for universal appeal. Although toned in smart dialog and subtle touches within a broad comedy situation, the pic nevertheless dodges the twin pitfalls of ultra-sophistication and corny slapstick. Starting off in a breezy flippancy, it rolls smoothly along in the same key throughout.

Miss Drake, a fresh personality with looks and talent who will generate plenty of word-of-mouth commendation, is the young gal set upon hooking an eligible bachelor. Accidentally bumping into Grant in a drugstore, she maps an elaborate pincer strategy after studiously gathering data on his habits and habitat. When this fails in a series of tactical reversals, she switches to piquing Grant with jealousy, using Tone, the boss of the department store in which she works, as the foil. But Grant still refuses to bite, maintaining an amused indifference that occasionally boils into irritation at the gal's persistence.

Her inventiveness, however, finally surmounts Grant's intransigeance. But before she can haul up the marriage license, Miss Drake is forced to sharpen the hook and pretty the bait. She enlists the whole town in her campaign to pressure her man to the altar. At the windup, she plays the winning trick by hiring a radio actor to pose as her home town flame coming to take her home. Grant relents, they clinch and with perfect timing, a preacher announces himself to work out the wedding details.

In a long part that keeps her within camera range for the full length of the film, Miss Drake's performance is a tour de force in the romantic comedy vein. She displays a remarkable range of expressiveness, going from pathos to frothiness with firm control. Grant, handling his lines with appropriate acidity, plays with skill and wit. Tone, in a brief role, and Diana Lynn, as Miss Drake's sidekick, both contribute strong support.

Matching the script's roguish air, this production is buffed down to a high polish although no lavish settings are evident. Topnotch camera work, expert editing and a gay background score integrate all aspects of this film for maximum impact. *Herm.*

Blood on the Moon
Hollywood, Nov. 6.

RKO release of Theron Warth production. Stars Robert Mitchum, Barbara Bel Geddes, Robert Preston; features Walter Brennan, Phyllis Thaxter, Frank Faylen, Tom Tully, Charles McGraw. Directed by Robert Wise. Screenplay, Lillie Hayward; adaptation, Harold Shumate, Luke Short, from a novel by Short; camera, Nicholas Musuraca; editor, Samuel E. Beetley. Tradeshown Nov. 5, '48. Running time, 86 MINS.

Jim Garry .... Robert Mitchum
Amy Lufton .... Barbara Bel Geddes
Tate Riling .... Robert Preston
Kris Barden .... Walter Brennan
Carol Lufton .... Phyllis Thaxter
Jake Pindalest .... Frank Faylen
John Lufton .... Tom Tully
Milo Sweet .... Charles McGraw
Joe Shotten .... Clifton Young
Frank Reardan .... Tom Tyler
Fred Barden .... George Cooper
Ted Elser .... Richard Powers
Cap Willis .... Bud Osborne
Nels Titterton .... Zon Murray
Bart Daniels .... Robert Bray

"Blood On the Moon" is a terse, tightly-drawn western drama. There's none of the formula approach to its story telling, a switch that doesn't add to its chances in the general market. However, name of Robert Mitchum promises some initial b.o. attention. For the connoisseur of adult western fiction there is appeal, but the average fan isn't likely to go for the understatement and gradually developed plotting.

Picture captures the crisp style used by Luke Short in writing his

western novels, and ticket buyers who like the different approach will find a load of excitement, deadly menace and high action. Performances are all above average, fitting ably into the mood sought by Robert Wise's direction. The Lillie Hayward script, from Harold Shumate's and Short's adaptation of the latter's novel, has none of the theatrical flamboyance of the commercial western plot, yet generates its own brand of interesting tension.

Plot deals with a Texas cowpoke who rides into a section of range country where ranchers and settlers are battling. Broke, he hires out his gun to an old friend, who is scheming with an Indian agent to acquire a cattle herd by promoting the feud. Ruthlessness of his friend finally awakens his conscience and he swings to the other side, finding new self-respect and love before the finale.

Mitchum is the cowpoke, a role he handles with skill under Wise's realistic direction. Barbara Bel Geddes registers strongly as the range heroine who first battles and then loves Mitchum. Robert Preston makes an oily villain, whose false charms fool Mitchum as well as the daughter of his chief rancher opponent, and the settlers. Walter Brennan, settler who loses his son in the feuding, Phyllis Thaxter, Tom Tully, Frank Faylen, Charles McGraw and others capably add to mood of the film.

Picture's pace has a false sense of leisureness that points up several tough moments of action. There is a deadly knock-down and drag-out fist fight between Mitchum and Preston; a long chase across snow-covered mountains and the climax gun battle between Preston's henchmen and Mitchum, Brennan and Miss Bel Geddes that are loaded with suspense wallop.

Theron Warth's production, under the executive supervision of Sid Rogell, has supplied topnotch scenic locations against which to film the story. Nicholas Musuraca's camerawork gives the physical values fine lensing. Editing is good. *Brog.*

He Walked by Night

Eagle Lion release of Bryan Foy production. Features Richard Basehart, Scott Brady. Directed by Alfred Werker. Screenplay, John C. Higgins, Crane Wilbur; additional dialog, Harry Essex; original story, Wilbur; camera, John Alton; editor, Alfred DeGaetano; music, Leonid Raab. Tradeshown N. Y. Nov. 4, '48. Running time, 79 MINS.

Davis Morgan .... Richard Basehart
Marty Brennan .... Scott Brady
Police Sergeant Breen ... Roy Roberts
Reeves .... Whit Bissell
Chuck Jones .... Jim Cardwell

Eagle Lion's production formula for action fare has clicked again. In "He Walked by Night," Bryan Foy has turned out another package of dynamite that will rank with "T-Men" and "Canon City" as surprising wicket spinners. This pic is a high tension crime meller, supercharged with violence but sprung with finesse. It can't miss.

Top credits for this film's wallop is shared equally by the several scripters, director Alfred Werker and a small, but superb cast headed by Richard Basehart. Produced on a relatively modest budget in this inflationary era, this pic rolls up all of its resources for firstrate quality impact. It accents the essential cinematic ingredients of plot, pace and characterization within a workable framework shorn of fol-de-rol trimmings.

Yarn is a straightforward documentary-style saga of a psychotic but brilliant killer who is tracked down through dogged detective work. Taken allegedly from the files of the Los Angeles police department, film opens with the brutal murder of a cop and follows through in detailing the criminal's career while the dragnet is closing in. There are no romantic angles in this all-male operation to slow matters down.

Starting in high gear, the film increases in momentum until the cumulative tension explodes in a powerful crime-doesn't-pay climax. Striking effects are achieved through counterpoint of the slayer's ingenuity in eluding the cops and the police efficiency in bringing him to book. High-spot of the film is the final sequence which takes place in L. A.'s storm drainage tunnel system where the killer tries to make his getaway, but fails after a resounding crossfire of automatics and tommyguns.

With this role, Basehart establishes himself as one of Hollywood's most talented finds in recent years. As the killer, he performs with emotional range and suppleness, delineating his psycho portrayal of a vicious character with complete persuasiveness. He heavily overshadows the rest of the cast, although Scott Brady, Roy Roberts and Jim Cardwell, as the detectives, deliver with high competence. Film is also marked by realistic camera work and a solid score. *Herm.*

Racing Luck

Hollywood, Nov. 5.

Columbia production and release. Features Gloria Henry, Stanley Clements, David Bruce, Paula Raymond, Harry Cheshire, Dooley Wilson, Ja/. Ingram, Nelson Leigh, Bill Cartledge, S.'d Saylor. Directed by William Berke. Screenplay, Joseph Carole, Al Martin, Harvey Gates; editor, Henry Batista; camera, Ira H. Morgan. At Vogue, L. A., Nov. 2, '48. Running time, 63 MINS.

Phyllis Warren .... Gloria Henry
Boots Warren .... Stanley Clements
Jeff Stuart .... David Bruce
Natalie Gunther .... Paula Raymond
Radcliffe Malone .... Harry Cheshire
Abe .... Dooley Wilson
George .... Jack Ingram
Hendricks .... Nelson Leigh
Joe .... Bill Cartledge
Pete .... Syd Saylor

A series of horseraces plus a mild sprinkling of the human animal and a dash of plot do not comprise entertainment. Inept formula was mixed for "Racing Luck" with catastrophic results. "Luck" rolls through 65-minutes at a mealy pace, failing to generate interest in races, humans or plot footage.

Thesps gather 'round for the old college try but to little avail. Gloria Henry, Stanley Clements and David Bruce follow director William Berke's wand very closely, but the magic stick is without power. Ensuing lineup pitches all the way.

Sam Katzman failed in his productional chores with a poor screenplay by Joseph Carole, Al Martin and Harvey Gates and director William Berke fails to give the pic a pace worthy of interest. Ira H. Morgan manages some good camera glances. *Free.*

Indian Agent

Hollywood, Nov. 9.

RKO release of Herman Schlom production. Stars Tim Holt; features Noah Beery, Jr., Richard Martin, Nan Leslie, Harry Woods. Director, Lesley Selander. Original screenplay, Norman Houston; camera, J. Roy Hunt; editor, Les Millbrook. Tradeshown Nov. 3, '48. Running time, 61 MINS.

Dave .... Tim Holt
Redfox .... Noah Beery, Jr.
Chito .... Richard Martin
Ellen .... Nan Leslie
Carter .... Harry Woods
Hutchins .... Richard Powers
Turquoise .... Claudia Drake
Nichols .... Robert Bray
Inky .... Lee White
Sheriff .... Bud Osborne
Wovoka .... Iron Eyes Cody

"Indian Agent" measures up as an okay Tim Holt saddle adventure. Wherever there's a demand for film gallopers this will fill the bill and appeal is particularly good for juve trade in Saturday matinee spots.

Plot deals with a crooked Indian agent, in cahoots with an equally crooked freighter. They scheme to divert food supplies destined for the reservation to the more lucrative gold field market. The redskins are unhappy but the scheme is working without a hitch until Holt and his buddy, Richard Martin, become suspicious and manage to deal out some stern, sixgun justice.

Holt is a good western hero, in appearance and actions, and Martin makes an excellent teammate to handle the lighter moments. Skullduggery is capably projected in the western manner by Harry Woods as the freighter and Richard Powers as the agent.

Script has a twist or two to give formula pattern a lift and Lesley Selander's direction keeps things racing along at the proper pace for an oater. Herman Schlom's production guidance furnishes good sight values for budget and lensing is expert.

Noah Beery, Jr., plays an Indian chief in this one and hasn't much to do. Also with little to do are Nan Leslie and Claudia Drake, since femme interest is kept to a minimum, which should please the kiddies. *Brog.*

West of Sonora

(SONGS)

Columbia release of Colbert Clark production. Stars Charles Starrett; features Smiley Burnette, Steve Darrell. Directed by Ray Nazarro. Original screenplay, Barry Shipman; camera, Ira H. Morgan; editor, Jerome Thoms. At New York theatre, N. Y., Nov. 2, '48. Running time, 55 MINS.

Steve Rollins / The Durango Kid .... Charles Starrett
Smiley Burnette .... Smiley Burnette
Black Murphy .... Steve Darrell
Sheriff Jeff Clinton ..... George Chesebro
Penelope Clinton .... Anita Castle
Sandy Clinton .... Hal Taliaferro
Brock .... Bob Wilke
Jack Bascom .... Emmett Lynn
Dickson .... Lynn Farr
The Sunshine Boys

"West of Sonora," another in the Charles Starrett (Durango Kid) series, generates a fair amount of ridin', shootin' and fightin'. There's some feudin', too, for the yarn hinges on a long standing quarrel between two grandfathers. An unpretentious oatuner, the film is average action fare for the duals and Sat. mat. trade.

Cast in his usual dual role, Starrett does yeoman work in patching up hard feelings between the maternal and paternal grandfathers of moppet Anita Castle. Former, who's suspected of being an outlaw, makes off with the girl. This touches off a posse hunt, an attempted lynching and a variety of gunplay. In his role of the Durango Kid, Starrett bags the true culprit paving the way for the customary happy finale.

Interspersed in the footage are several tunes contribbed by the four Sunshine Boys. Smiley Burnette also warbles a song and holds up the comedy end in so-so fashion. Starrett convinces as the champion of law and order while Steve Darrell and George Chesebro are okay as the rival grandpops.

Ray Nazarro's direction is standard. Production values of Colbert Clark reflect the maximum out of the low budget. Lensman Ira H. Morgan's photography is adequate while Jerome Thoms edited the film down to a concise 55 minutes. *Gilb.*

The Guinea Pig

(BRITISH)

London, Oct. 27.

Pathe release of Pilgrim Pictures-Filippo Del Giudice John Boulting) production. Stars Richard Attenborough, Sheila Sim. Directed by Roy Boulting. Screenplay by Bernard Miles, Warren Chetham Strode; adapted from stage play by Warren Chetham Strode. Editor, Richard Best; music, John Wooldridge; camera, Gilbert Taylor, Sheets Kelly. At Carlton, London. Running time, 98 MINS.

Jack Read .... Richard Attenborough
Lynne Hartley .... Sheila Sim
Mr. Read .... Bernard Miles
Mr. Hartley .... Cecil Trouncer
Nigel Lorraine .... Robert Flemyng
Mrs. Hartley .... Edith Sharpe
Mrs. Read .... Joan Hickson
Ronald Tracey .... Tim Bateson
Gregory .... Clive Baxter
Buckton .... Basil Cunard
Fitch .... John Forrest
Bessie .... Maureen Glynne
Lorna Beckett .... Brenda Hogan
Sir James Corfield .... Herbert Lomas
Miles Minor .... Anthony Newley

Typically British in flavor, Warren Chetham Strode's play of the rural schoolboy who is sent to an exclusive public school as an experiment, has been brought to the screen by the Boulting Bros. with sincerity and care. Not by any means in the big picture class, it should have a happy future at home, but the very nature of its insular theme is likely to restrict its success in the American market.

The guinea pig in the experiment is Jack Read, son of a suburban shopkeeper, whose admission into one of Britain's exclusive public schools brings him at once into conflict with tradition.

The role of Read provides Richard Attenborough with a human part, and it's a tribute to him that he looks every bit the schoolboy. First class performance is contributed by Cecil Trouncer as the unwilling but converted housemaster, and Sheila Sim as his daughter, and Robert Flemying as the tutor provide the not too obtrusive romantic interest. Bernard Miles and Joan Hickson, as the boy's parents, and Edith Sharpe, as the housemaster's wife, turn in effective sketches. *Myro.*

No Room at the Inn

(BRITISH)

London, Oct. 26.

Pathe release of British National (Ivan Foxwell-Louis H. Jackson) production. Stars Freda Jackson, Joy Shelton, Hermione Baddeley. Directed by Daniel Birt. Screenplay by Dylan Thomas, Ivan Foxwell, from play by Joan Temple. Editor, Charles Hasse; music, Hans May; camera, James Wilson, Moray Grant. At Warner, London, Oct. 25, '48. Running time, 82 MINS.

Mrs. Voray .... Freda Jackson
Judith Drave .... Joy Shelton
Mrs. Waters .... Hermione Baddeley
Norma Bates .... Joan Dowling
Mary O'Rane .... Ann Stephens
Rev. Allwroth .... Harcourt Williams
O'Rane .... Niall MacGinnis
Spiv Stranger .... Sydney Tafler
Burrells .... Frank Pettingell
Lily .... Betty Blackler
Irene .... Jill Gibbs
Ronnie .... Robin Netscher
Councillor Green .... Wylie Watson
Councillor Trouncer ...... James Hayter
News Editor .... Eliot Makeham

Reliance on legit material is almost becoming a chronic complaint with British producers nowadays. "No Room at the Inn" was a very successful West End stage play, and the picture version bears obvious traces of its theatrical origin, being restricted in settings and lacking in movement. Nonetheless, it isn't lacking in dramatic values, but its fate in America is predetermined by the overwhelming use of Cockney English, which dominates the entire script.

Retaining a close affinity to the original, it's a story of evacuee and orphaned children who are boarded out with a drunken woman, who feeds the kids on scraps while she soaks gin at the local public house. Gradually the youngsters are overwhelmed by the degradation and dirt, until they are saved when the landlady is killed in a drunken fury.

Relieved only by glimpses of Cockney wit, which wouldn't appeal outside this island, it's in the main a grim piece of entertainment, and sordid to a degree. Freda Jackson repeats her original stage success, her performance as the brutal landlady being a fine characterization. Ann Stephens, as the kid going wrong, and Joan Dowling, Robin Netscher, Betty Blackler and Jill Gibbs, as the unhappy boarders, excel. Hermione Baddeley turns in a fine study in a small incidental role and Joy Shelton makes the village schoolteacher a convincing character. *Myro.*

Scorned Flesh

(Statua Vivente)

(ITALIAN)

Foreign Screen release of Kino Film (Icillo Sterbini) production. Stars Laura Solari, Fosco Giachetti; features Camillo Pilotto, Lauro Gazzolo, Dhia Christiani, Guido Celano, Olga Solbelli, Checco Rossone. Directed by Camillo Mastrocinque. Story by Giorgio Pastina; camera, Aldo Tonti; music, Alessandro Cicognini; English titles, Rosemarie Ioppolo, Max De Alban; editor, James B. Cahoon. Previewed in N. Y. Nov. 3, '48. Running time, 105 MINS.

(In Italian; English Titles)

Obvious but interesting yarn about a wolfish sailor and a simple factory maid has several things to recommend it. Although film's appeal is limited largely to Italian-speaking trade, it will do okay in art houses catering to that trade.

Drawbacks to more general interest are a somewhat hackneyed story, its slow pace, some blurred or dark camera work and careless subtitling. Dialog is obviously loosely translated and doesn't do the script justice.

Yarn has a sailor (Fosco Giachetti) on the prowl, trying vainly to pick up a shy maid (Laura Solari), falling honestly in love with her and finding his affection reciprocated after they formally meet. She's killed in an accident on their wedding day, and the sailor takes to drink. Friends drag him off to a dive where he meets a dame (also played by Miss Solari), who startles him by her striking facial similarity to his dead love. Although he sets up housekeeping with her, he broods over his old love, and when taunted by the other, kills her.

Story isn't morbid, although the way it telegraphs its situations is a little trite. Picture has authentic mood and atmosphere for a good deal of appeal. Wharf and seacoast shots, and bistro interiors, lend much reality, and performances of cast are good. Miss Solari, doubling as the two lead femmes, is very attractive and strikingly contrasted in two dissimilar roles, handling both with skill. Giachetti's performance opposite is also superior. Camera catches some neat shots, but lighting is occasionally dull. *Bron.*

Long Is the Road
(GERMAN)

Lopert (Astoria) Films release of International Film Organization (Abraham Weinstein) production. Stars Israel Becker, Bettina Moissi, Berta Litwina; features Jakob Fischer. Directed by Herbert B. Fredersdorf. Mar_k Goldstein. Screenplay, Karl Georg Kulb and Israel Becker, based on original story by Becker; camera, Franz Koch; music, Lothar Bruhne. Previewed N. Y, Nov. 8, '48. Running time, 75 MINS.
David Jelin..............Israel Becker
Dora Berkowitz...........Bettina Moissi
Hanna Jelin...............Berta Litwina
Jakob Jelin..............Jakob Fischer
Senior Doctor............Otto Wernicke
2nd Doctor................Paul Dahlke
Farmer...............Alexander Bardini
Mr. Liebermann...........David Hart
Partisan................Mischa Nathan
Chodetzki................H. L. Fischer

(In Yiddish. German. Polish, English; English Titles)

First picture to be lensed in the American Occupation Zone of Germany, "Long Is the Road" is an honest and poignant story of the displaced persons in Europe looking for a homeland. Cast, though mostly professional actors, are nearly all D.P.s themselves and much of the story is said to be woven out of their own experiences. Film is a sure bet for the art house circuit, for which it's grooved in this country.

Original story centers around a single Jewish family from Warsaw, its uprooting by the war and subsequent determination to find a new place to live. Number of newsreel clips bridging the early sequences gives the picture a documentary form which sharply points up the theme. As such, the film represents honest propaganda for the European Jews' desire for a homeland in Palestine—which is emphasized currently by the battle in Israel. All-around excellence of the cast, story and direction, though, makes the picture able to stand on its own merits.

Screenplay, penned by Israel Becker and Karl Georg Kulb from an original by Becker, pulls no punches in getting across its point. Some of the concentration camp scenes are especially grim. Story has Becker, as the son, separated by the Nazis from his mother and father. He joins a Polish partisan troop, while the father is killed by the Germans as "unfit" and the mother is shifted from one labor camp to another. With the war over, the mother and son, after criss-crossing Europe in a search for each other, are finally reunited —but they still have no home. Interspersed with the main plot is a postwar romance between the son and a displaced German girl.

Becker does an admirable job in his dual capacity as writer-actor. Although far in appearance from the accepted Hollywood juve type, his fine thesping job will grow on the audience as the picture progresses. Equally standout is Berta Litwina as the mother. A Polish star before the war, Miss Litwina gives a finely-shaded characterization to the tragic role. Bettina Moissi. daughter of the former Max Reinhardt actor, Alexander Moissi, is appealing as the German girl. Jakob Fischer is fine as the father, and the rest of the cast, down to the smallest bit part, turn in good performances under the knowing direction of Herbert B. Fredersdorf and Marek Goldstein.

Dialog is mostly in Yiddish, but there's also considerable Polish, German and some English. English titles are adequate to follow the story. Production mountings are in keeping with the grim mood of the picture, which is also aided by the low key lighting and Lothar Bruhne's score, which includes several w.k. Yiddish folk tunes. Franz Koch's camera work, for the most part, is good. *Stal.*

Miniature Reviews

"**The Kissing Bandit**" (Musical-Color) (MG). Good songs and specialties but mild b.o. prospects.

"**The Accused**" (Par). Loretta Young, Robert Cummings. Wendell Corey in socko meller.

"**Dynamite**" (Par). Good action entry dealing with powder men in construction work.

"**The Boy With Green Hair**" (Songs-Color) (RKO) Poignant tolerance drama of kids. Good prestige draw.

"**Homicide for Three**" (Rep). Pleasant supporting melodrama with emphasis on lightness.

"**Borrowed Trouble**" (UA). Usual Hopalong Cassidy adventure with a dash of humor.

"**Mlle. Desiree**" (French). Sacha Guitry's fresh and daring technique promises healthy art theatre returns.

"**The Mozart Story**" (Music) (Austrian) (SG). New Vienna-made version of composer's life, good arty entry.

The Kissing Bandit
(MUSICAL-COLOR)
Hollywood, Nov. 13.

Metro release of Joe Pasternak production. Stars Frank Sinatra, Kathryn Grayson; features J. Carrol Naish, Mildred Natwick. Mikhail Rasumny, Billy Gilbert, Sono Osato; dance specialty, Ricardo Montalban, Ann Miller, Cyd Charisse; directed by Laslo Benedek. Original screenplay, Isobel Lennart, John Briard Harding; camera (Technicolor), Robert Surtees; editor, Adrienne Fazan; music, Nacio Herb Brown; lyrics, Earl Brent, Edward Heyman; dances, Stanley Donen. Tradeshown Nov. 10, '48. Running time, 100 MINS.
Ricardo..................Frank Sinatra
Teresa..................Kathryn Grayson
Chico...................J. Carrol Naish
Isabella...............Mildred Natwick
Don Jose...............Mikhail Rasumny
General Torro.............Billy Gilbert
Bianca....................Sono Osato
Colonel Gomez..........Clinton Sundberg
Count Belmonte.......Carleton G. Young
Juanita...................Edna Skinner
Mexican Guitarist.......Vincente Gomez

"The Kissing Bandit" burlesques the antics of the dashing hero of costume epics with varied results. It's a tunefilm in color with some recommended spots but overall grossing outlook isn't particularly bright. Songs are good, the specialty numbers outstanding and the story antic silly enough to rate some chuckles.

Title role is the exact opposite of the usual derring-do hero and casting of Frank Sinatra to play it sharpens the physical contrast. He's a milktoast from Boston who is forced to become a legendary early-California bandit who always kisses his femme victims.

Sinatra plays the role broadly and well enough. His clumsiness on horseback, his shyness at amour, and the general incongruity of his gauntness and lack of heft gives to the hero character a natural for laughs but it doesn't always come off. There are some titters and chuckles at the antics but no sock laughs. A little more directorial sublety in handling the story might have made the difference between spotty entertainment values and good, solid fun.

Music for the eight songs was cleffed by Nacio Herb Brown, with lyrics by Earl Brent and Edward Heyman. Tunes are effectively spotlighted and there are two used for production numbers. All please the ear and aid the story.

Sinatra's best is "Senorita," closely followed by "Siesta" and "If I Steal a Kiss." Kathryn Grayson shows up on "Love Is Where You Find It" (used in an earlier Metro release) and "Tomorrow Means Romance." She also works with Sinatra on "What's Wrong With Me" and "Senorita."

A production number highlight is Sono Osato vocaling "I Like You" and then segueing into a fiery whip dance that excites, Also exciting is "Nacio Herb Brown's Dance of Fury," outstandingly performed by Ricardo Montalban, Ann Miller and Cyd Charisse as an added specialty.

Original script by Isobel Lennart and John Briard Harding brings Sinatra to early California from Boston to take over the inn inherited from his father. The father was the original Kissing Bandit and his followers believe the son will step into the old man's shoes—in fact they force him to.

Major assists in helping to carry this one along come from J. Carrol Naish as henchman of Sinatra's, and Mikhail Rasumny, the cowardly governor of California. Their characters are hoked up sufficiently and are in experienced enough hands to please. Billy Gilbert is in for sneezes and Clinton Sundberg's comedy as the governor's aid is another assist.

Laslo Benedek's direction of the Joe Pasternak production strains too often to put over the story. Production flash given the picture is in the Pasternak style. Lush outdoor scenery, colorful costumes and the settings are fittingly displayed by Robert Surtees' Technicolor lensing. *Brog.*

The Accused
Hollywood, Nov. 13.

Paramount release of Hal B. Wallis production. Stars Loretta Young, Robert Cummings; features Wendell Corey, Sam Jaffe, Douglas Dick. Directed by William Dieterle. Screenplay, Ketti Frings; based on novel by June Truesdell; camera, Milton Krasner; score, Victor Young; editor, Warren Low. Tradeshown Nov. 12, '48. Running time, 101 MINS.
Wilma Tuttle.............Loretta Young
Warren Ford..........Robert Cummings
Lieut. Ted Dorgan.......Wendell Corey
Dr. Romley.................Sam Jaffe
Bill Perry.................Douglas Dick
Susan Duval............Suzanne Dalbert
Dean Rhodes.........George Spaulding
Mrs. Conner..............Sara Allgood
Jack Hunter..............Mickey Knox
Dr. Vinson.............Francis Pierlot
Miss Rice.................Ann Doran
Waitress..............Carole Mathews
Harry Brice...............Bill Mauch

"The Accused" exploits fear and emotional violence into a high grade melodrama for adult audiences. It is told with a grim intensity that will attract those who like their fare of stern stuff. Well above par in all departments, picture has a good boxoffice potential that will be aided by word-of-mouth and the excellent cast headed by Loretta Young.

The Ketti Frings screenplay is based on a novel by June Truesdell and is class scripting. Director William Dieterle, with a solid story foundation and an ace cast upon which to build, marches the melodrama along with a touch that keeps punching continually at audience emotions.

Miss Young's portrayal of the distraught professor plays strongly for sympathy. It's an intelligent delineation, gifting the role with life. She gets under the skin in bringing out the mental processes of an intelligent woman who knows she has done wrong but believes that her trail is so covered that murder will never out.

An unbalanced but attractive student is on the make for his professor. By guile he induces her to ride with him to the beach. He attempts to attack her and she, in a moment of surrender to violence, bashes his head in with a tire iron. The crime is concealed to make it look like he had died in a dive over the sea cliff. The stage setting for murder passes inspection by all but two, a smart homicide officer and the boy's guardian.

Police work, in the laboratory, by hunch and deduction bring the net closer to the professor and, in a nerve-rending scene staged by the officer, she confesses. There's never a point made that seems out of place, even the love that develops between the professor and the guardian, his attempts to spirit her away from harm before it is too late, and his courtroom defense of her only crime—fear—ring true.

Hal B. Wallis' sure production hand is stamped on the film. The casting of each role, the settings of campus, courtroom, police laboratory, beach, restaurants and the professor's small apartment, lend sense of reality to the film. Robert Cummings is unusually excellent as the guardian, co-starring with Miss Young. Wendell Corey's matter-of-fact police officer portrayal has a human quality that catches on. Douglas Dick registers strongly as the unbalanced student. Sam Jaffe, Suzanne Dalbert, Sara Allgood, Mickey Knox are among the others who back the fine work of the principals.

Dieterle's exceptionally potent direction and the mood he sustains is backed by Victor Young's top-notch music score. Class photography by Milton Krasner, and equally good art direction, sets and other technical credits, make this one measure up above par.

Brog.

Dynamite

Hollywood, Nov. 13.

Paramount release of William H. Pine-William Thomas production, directed by Pine. Features William Gargan, Virginia Welles, Richard Crane, Irving Bacon, Mary Newton. Original screenplay, Milton Raison; camera, Ellis W. Carter; editor, Howard Smith. Tradeshown Nov. 9, '48. Running time, 68 MINS.

Gunner Peterson	William Gargan
Mary	Virginia Welles
Johnny Brown	Richard Crane
Jake	Irving Bacon
Nellie Brown	Mary Newton
Hard Rock Mason	Frank Ferguson
Hank Gibbons	Douglass Dumbrille

The Pine-Thomas pattern for actionful accounts of dangerous occupations is well displayed in "Dynamite." Story is formula, tailored to deal with powder men and measures up to all demands of the general supporting feature market.

Principal aim of yarn is to weave some heroics around the men who earn their living blasting tunnels through mountains, helping to build bridges and sundry other outdoor projects. Pace is good and helps to breed a certain amount of excitement into the formula framework.

Direction by William H. Pine keeps the film on the move and the players performing in acceptable manner. Plot concerns a dynamite contractor, his daughter, and two powder monkeys who are rivals for her favor. There are some good explosion scenes and thrills, from the opening blast in which a man is killed, right down to the finale rescue of a powder man trapped in a tunnel.

William Gargan and Richard Crane are the rivals for Virginia Welles' affections, with Crane the winner. All acquit themselves in okay style. Richard Bacon is good as the contractor. Mary Newton, Frank Ferguson and Douglass Dumbrille answer all demands of their roles.

Production never tries to introduce values not fitting to the story or locales, a fact that also aided in keeping the budget down. Lensing by Ellis W. Carter and editing by Howard Smith are good. *Brog.*

The Boy With Green Hair

(SONGS—COLOR)

RKO release of Dore Schary (Stephen Ames) production. Stars Pat O'Brien, Robert Ryan, Barbara Hale, Dean Stockwell; features Richard Lyon, Walter Catlett, Samuel S. Hinds, Regis Toomey. Directed by Joseph Losey. Screenplay, Ben Barzman, Alfred Lewis Levitt; story, Betsy Beaton; camera (Technicolor), George Barnes; editor, Frank Doyle; song, Eden Ahbez; music, Leigh Harline; musical director, C. Bakaleinikoff. Tradeshown N. Y., Nov. 12, '48. Running time, 82 MINS.

Gramp	Pat O'Brien
Dr. Evans	Robert Ryan
Miss Brand	Barbara Hale
Peter	Dean Stockwell
Michael	Richard Lyon
"The King"	Walter Catlett
Dr. Knudson	Samuel S. Hinds
Mr. Davis	Regis Toomey
Mr. Piper	Charles Meredith
Barber	David Clarke
Red	Billy Sheffield
Danny	John Calkins
Timmy	Teddy Infuhr
Joey	Dwayne Hickman
Peggy	Eilene Janssen
Classmate	Curtis Jackson
Mr. Hammond	Charles Arnt

RKO has turned out an absorbing, sensitive story of tolerance and child understanding in "The Boy With Green Hair." Pic's intelligence, artistry and taste will draw fine critical comment to offset lack of marquee pull and weight of its theme. Although pic—a modest budgeter, despite the Technicolor cost—doesn't loom as a heavy grosser, it should make back its coin. Certainly it will redound to the industry's credit; RKO, and the film industry, deserve a lot of kudos for making it.

Film was made by Dore Schary for RKO before Howard Hughes gained control of the studio, and in its small way was one of the things that caused Schary to step out of the RKO setup. Pix had been completed, but Hughes ordered it re-edited and the tolerance theme taken out, on Hughes' general theory that films should entertain only and eschew social significance. Studio found that pic couldn't be re-edited, although it's reported to be toned down somewhat.

None of this intra-mural stuff is evident in the film's unreeling. In fact, the one questionable note in the film is a scene of bald preachment—a dream scene in a wood between the boy and a phantom group of war orphans—that could have been cut sharply. Otherwise, the film is a poignant, human-interest drama, and good entertainment all the way through.

What makes it so is the sensible screen treatment of a most unusual story, and two outstanding performances by Pat O'Brien and Dean Stockwell. Latter gives a beautifully restrained performance throughout as a sensitive, cruelly-treated boy. O'Brien has one of his best roles in a ream of films, giving a flavorsome, rich portrayal of a broken-down, onetime Irish magician and vauder, now a singing waiter, who furnishes a home and grandfatherly love to an orphaned waif.

Story is that of a war orphan, shifted around from one relative to another, who finally finds haven and security with the waiter in a small town. Then, one morning, he wakes to find his hair has turned green—and the world turns topsy-turvy about him. Other kids jeer at him; adults are perturbed; even the kindly milkman turns against him when accused of bringing it about through his product. Public opinion forces the boy to have his full head of hair shaven off, so that the kid runs away from home.

Through this parable about the unconscious cruelty of people to what is different, and the need of tolerance, runs another theme, that of anti-war preachment. When the boy meets children from war-orphan posters in a dream scene in the woods, and returns to annoy the townsfolk with the message that war is very bad—his green hair has thus acquired a meaning, to preach pacifism—the film hits a well-intentioned but false note. Otherwise, the social significance, the tolerance and anti-war themes, are served up palatably, to make this a superior, and very moving film.

Imagination and taste, in scripting and direction, show up constantly, in such scenes as the bitter one of the kid in the barber chair being shaved, with townsfolk crowded around the window outside; the terrible moment when he faces the school-kids after his hair has turned; the scene when his hair turns and the kid amuses himself with it in front of the bathroom mirror; the teacher trying to ease the situation by calling the role of the various types of hair among her students; the scene between O'Brien and Walter Catlett as "The King."

Last-named is one of the best light moments, with O'Brien delightfully rendering the song, "Tread on the Tail of the Coat." Film is never depressing or heavy, its clever treatment preventing that. Honest performances by Barbara Hale, Robert Ryan, Samuel S. Hinds, Regis Toomey and others in supporting roles also help greatly. Direction, photography, background music, all rate bows. *Bron.*

Homicide for Three

Hollywood, Nov. 11.

Republic release of Stephen Auer production. Features Audrey Long, Warren Douglas, Grant Withers. Directed by George Blair. Screenplay, Bradbury Foote; based on novel by Patrick Quentin; added dialog, Albert DeMond; camera, John MacBurnie; editor, Harry Keller. At the Paramount, L. A., Nov. 11, '48. Running time, 60 MINS.

Iris Duluth	Audrey Long
Lieut. Peter Duluth	Warren Douglas
Joe Hatch	Grant Withers
Emmanual Catt	Lloyd Corrigan
Mrs. Rose	Stephanie Bachelor
Bill Daggett	George Lynn
Rita Brown	Tala Birell
Timothy	Benny Baker
Capt. Webb	Joseph Crehan
Cab Driver	Sid Tomack
Doorman	Dick Elliott
Circus Doorman	Eddie Dunn
Desk Clerk	John Newland
Midget	Billy Curtis
Maid	Patsy Moran

"Homicide for Three" plays its melodramatics lightly and adds up to acceptable supporting fare. Flip treatment minimizes chills and thrills and develops a fairly glib pace that makes it mildly amusing.

Antics revolve around efforts of newlyweds to find a cozy spot for their honeymoon. Groom is a naval lieutenant on a 36-hour pass so things have to be rushed. Before finale is reached, there are only two hours of the pass left; two murders have been committed and a third nearly so, and the couple has had no privacy.

Plot is no heavy affair, despite melodramatic title, but is played with a lightness that gets it by under George Blair's direction. It gets underway when newlyweds are offered an apartment by a stranger, herself on her way to an elopement. Couple is plunged into murder for revenge against three femmes, all in show biz, who had been responsible for a previous prison term for the killers.

Audrey Long, as the bride, pleases pleasantly, and Warren Douglas is okay as the groom. Grant Withers and George Lynn are the killers. Lloyd Corrigan, Stephanie Bachelor, Tala Birell, latter showing up well in brief spot as a victim; Benny Baker and others give acceptable support.

Production values achieved for the budget dollar are excellent under Stephen Auer's supervision. Lensing, editing, and other technical credits are capable. *Brog.*

Borrowed Trouble

United Artists release of Lewis Rachmil production. Stars William Boyd; features Andy Clyde, Rand Brooks. Directed by George Archainbaud. At New York theatre, N. Y., Nov. 9, '48. Running time, 61 MINS.

Hopalong Cassidy	William Boyd
California Carlson	Andy Clyde
Lucky Jenkins	Rand Brooks
Mrs. Garvin	Elaine Riley
Lee Garvin	John Kellogg
Teacher	Helen Chapman

Hopalong Cassidy has a better than average adventure in "Borrowed Trouble." This long-running series of westerns has provided some good action-pieces for the double feature trade. However, elevation to the top rung of a bill for "Borrowed Trouble" seems unlikely even though the humorous situations make this film more palatable for general type audiences.

Bill Boyd, in his accustomed spot as Hopalong Cassidy, is faced with a different type problem. A prissy schoolmarm objects to the opening of a saloon next door to her place of operations. Boyd is sympathetic, but until the pedagog is kidnapped, he's unable to prevent the mixture of the three R's wth roulette and revelry. Boyd consequently rescues the teacher from the baddies and is instrumental in affecting a change of location for the saloon.

The cast with Andy Clyde, Rand Brooks and Helen Chapman gives an okay account and George Archainbaud's direction keeps the film moving at a good clip. The sets have the familiar look, but camera work is adequate. *Jose.*

The Mozart Story

(AUSTRIAN)

(Music)

Screen Guild release of Patrician Pictures production. Stars Hans Holt, Directed by Carl Hartl. Screenplay, Richard Billinger; additional dialog and sequences produced by Abrasha Haimson and directed by Frank Wisbar in Hollywood; music by Vienna Philharmonic orchestra. At Little Carnegie, N.Y., starting Nov. 13, '48. Running time, 91 MINS.

Wolfgang Amadeus Mozard	Hans Holt
Constance, his wife	Winnie Markus
Louise, her sister	Irene von Meyendorf
Ludwin von BVeethoven	Rene Deltger
Joseph Haydn	Edward Veddes
Antonio Salieri	Wilton Graff
Catherine Cavalleria	Carol Forman
Ruffini	Anthony Barr
Leopold	Walther Jansson
Mozard't Mother	Rosa Alback Rettas
Mother Weber	Anita Rosen
Sophia Weber	Thea Weiss
Joseph II	Curd Juergens
Strack	Paul Hoerbiger
Duke of Mannheim	John Siebert
Baron Gemmingen	Richard Eybner
Suessmeyer	Eric Nocowitz
Deinert	Theo Danagger
Albrechtaberger	Fred Imhoff
Hofer	Carl Bluhm

(Songs in German; English Dialog)

This Vienna-made version of Mozart's life is one of the better efforts. Its dialog is in English, the

American production firm having dubbed complete translation of original German speech for release in the U. S. Unfortunately, though, "Mozart Story" appears to have a limited American market. Film also is too leisurely in pace.

Dialog suffered in the translation; it is well spoken by uncredited American voices, verbiage being often stilted and too often not in keeping with the plot development. The additional footage intended to explain more fully why Mozart's genius was so little appreciated in his lifetime not only runs too long but looks like the padding that it is.

Hans Holt brings surprising vigor to the Mozart character, while Winnie Markus suffices as his wife. Irene von Meyerdorff is okay as the gal who ditches Mozart for an operatic career. Remainder of cast is passable.

The musical excerpts from "Magic Flute," "Abduction from Seraglio," "The Requiem," "Marriage of Figaro," and "Don Giovanni" provide some brighter moments. All this is backgrounded by the Vienna Philharmonic Orchestra, and aided by the Vienna State Opera. All of the singing is in German, and, oddly enough, does not seem incongruous with the cast spouting English dialog.

This version of Mozart's life emphasizes the happier passages, his early death being overshadowed here by the politico feud and his yen for his early sweetheart. Story has Mozart forced to turn out "Clemency of Titus," a full opera, in 18 days, this effort leading to his early demise. *Wear.*

Malacarne

("For the Love of Mariastella")
(ITALIAN)

Vesuvio film release of Sicilian Films Organization production. Features Mariella Lotti, Otello Tosi, Amedeo Nazzari. Directed by Natale Di Cristina. Screenplay, Ovidio Imara; story, Zucca Mercanti; camera, Giuseppe La Torre. Previewed N. Y., Oct. 8, '48. Running time, 103 MINS.

Mariastella	Mariella Lotti
Turi	Otello Tosi
Zu Bastiano	Amedeo Nazzari
Rais Pietro	Giovanni Grasso
Fifi the Hunchback	Umberto Spadaro
Donna Agatina	Margherita Nicosia
Rosolino	Carletto
Don Popo'	S. Chimenti
Donna Carmen	Rosetta Romano
The Poor Woman	Piera Paci
Don Crispino	Giovanni Baiardi
The Trapanese	Natale Cirino

and the little Simonello.

(In Italian; English Titles)

While the Sicilian-made film, "Malacarne," undoubtedly is technically inferior to American product, it has good dramatic values throughout a circuitous 103 minutes of running time. If edited down to stress the twin battles of a native fisherman—one against a sea monster, and the other a futile, romantic Odyssey — the picture's exploitational possibilities would be greatly enhanced. However, in the main it will find it a tough scramble to find playing time even in the houses with Italian patronage.

Yarn is localed in a small Sicilian fishing port, down on its luck for four years because a "sea monster" has driven the tuna away.

Tosi turns in the best performance. Thesping of other players is generally mediocre. Direction is often faulty. Camerawork gets in some nice seascapes on occasion. Film is bound to experience difficulty with both governmental as well as church censors. Clement Douenias' English titles are adequate.

Fremmande Hamn

(Strange Harbor)
(SWEDISH)

Stockholm, Oct. 27.

Sandrew-Bauman Film release of Rune Waldecrantz production. Stars George Fant, Adolf Jahr, Ilona Wieselmann; features Stig Jarrell, Ake Fridell, Fritiof Billquist, Costa Holmstrom, Carl Strom. Directed by Hampe Faustman. Screenplay, Herbert Grevenius, based on play by Joseph Kjellgren; camera, Calle Edlund; music, Carl Olof Anderberg. At Grand, Stockholm. Running time, 85 MINS.

Captain	Adolf Jahr
Hakon	George Fant
Mimi	Ilona Wieselmann
Espionage agent	Stig Jarrel
Steward	Ake Fridell
First mate	Fritiof Billquist
Second mate	Gosta Holmstrom
First engineer	Carl Strom
Second engineer	Bengt Sundmark
Jerker	Stig Johansson
Christian	Anders Borje
Masthugget	Josua Bengtsson
Gutten	Anders Andelius
Strandmark	Georg Skarstedt
Toivo	Henake Schubak

With an arms-smuggling yarn during the Spanish Civil War as its plot, "Fremmande Hamn" emerges as a compelling and stirring film. It lends itself naturally to exploitation and looms as a surefire grosser in Sweden. Overseas prospects are also lucrative.

Based on the late Joseph Kjellgren's play, "Unknown Swedish Soldier," the film is considerably better than the stage version. Celluloid medium has beautifully captured the salty flavor of the Polish port of Gdynia where a Swedish captain is at his wit's end trying to decide whether or not to sail for Spain with a munitions cargo.

Sandwiched in the story are several murders which take place near the sordid waterfront.

Thesping is well done by a long cast topped by Adolf Jahr, whose portrait of the captain is very realistic. George Fant turns in a striking portrayal as a sailor. Also excellent is Danish actress Ilona Wieselmann as the German refugee. Incidentally, this marks her debut in a Swedish film.

Hampe Faustman's direction keeps things moving at a swift pace in this Rune Waldecrantz production. Screenplay of Herbert Grevenius is a fine bit of scripting. *Winq.*

Little Melody from Vienna

("Kleine Melodie aus Wien")
(AUSTRIAN)

Vienna, Oct. 26.

Fritz Erban release of Excelsior Film production. Stars Paul Hoerbiger, Maria Andergast; features Annie Rosar, Fritz Imhoff, Fritz Lehmann, Theodor Danegger, Herta Dolezel. Directed by E. W. Emo Screenplay, Emo and Franz Tassie, from story by Fritz Koselka and Lillian Belmont; music, Robert Stolz; lyrics, Aldo Pinelli; camera, Fritz Woditzka. At Apollo, Vienna. Running time, 100 MINS.

"Little Melody From Vienna" is a richly entertaining picture which rises well above the quality of recent Austrian product. Aided by the fine score of Robert Stolz, the film should register at the b.o. in the local market and is a likely prospect for U. S. art house audiences.

Script displays a strong sense of humor and clear conception of dramatic housing problems in unfolding a touching tale of a war widow who lost her home. Housing office assigns her to two rooms in the house of a professor. Annoyed because he must share his quarters, he's very unpleasant toward the new occupant until he falls in love with her.

Maria Andergast wins sympathy as the pretty widow while Paul Hoerbiger stands out as the prof. Balance of the cast is adequate. Stolz's title number is a lilting tune, as are his "Violet Blue" and "Three Brownies."

Fritz Woditzke capably handled the lensing. Production values are standard. *Maass.*

Mlle. Desiree

(FRENCH)

Lopert Films release of C.C.F.C. (Sacha Guitry) production. Stars Guitry, Jean-Louis Barrault, Gaby Morlay, Genevieve Guitry. Directed and written by Guitry; camera, Jean Bachelet; music, Adolphe Borchard. Previewed, N. Y., Nov. 12, '48. Running time, 95 MINS.

First Part

Napoleon	Jean-Louis Barrault
Desiree	Genevieve Guitry
Bernadotte	Jacques Varenne
Julie	Yvette Lebon

Second Part

Napoleon	Sacha Guitry
Desiree	Gaby Morlay
Bernadotte	Jacques Varenne
Julie	Camille Fournier
Josephine	Lise Delamare
Jerome Bonaparte	Aime Clariond

(In French; English Titles)

In "Mlle. Desiree" Sacha Guitry has authored, produced and directed a film which must capture the industry's as well as patrons' attention for its witty flouting of the conventions of picture-making. Tossing the rules to the cutting room floor, Guitry changes actors in midstream. He halts the action to introduce and lavish praise on his scenery director, film editor and sound control man. He takes time out to flash on cast credits at the film's midway point.

The freshness of his approach, laced by typical Guitry irony and humor, wins its point and demonstrates the amazing flexibility of the film medium. As a result, "Mlle. Desiree" should cajole the fanciers of foreign-lingo pix to view his efforts by a plurality.

Guitry surefootedly takes his audience into his confidence, explaining the need for a second team because his characters are growing older. He even brings on Jean - Louis Barrault, depicting Napoleon of youthful days, to gain his okay before personally assuming the role and portray the stouter oldster of the Empire period.

Had he snowballed the charm and invention which brightens the film's first half, "Mlle. Desiree" would have been standout stuff. Unfortunately, even the story itself, at first an appealing portrayal of how a Marseillaise belle won and then lost the embryonic Napoleon, ultimately tangles itself into a snarl of meaningless court intrigue. When Guitry slackens the directorial reins to become Napoleon, the difference is sharply apparent.

Both Barrault and Guitry delineate Napoleon superbly. Barrault makes him quixotic, sensitive and expressive—clearly the coming man-of-the-hour. Guitry endows him with the powers and ironic strength of his maturer days of ascendancy. As commentator, Guitry is no less. He has the just-right touch of worldliness and well-tempered humor.

In the first-half title role, Genevieve Guitry is pert and winsome. Gaby Morlay, who later takes up the cudgels, is a bit too mousy to lend total conviction to the part of a femme fatale. Jacques Varenne has the distinction of being the only principal who plays throughout without benefit of a substitute. He captures a brilliant and headstrong Bernadotte.

Music of Adolphe Borchard thematically parallels the Gallic humor of the film. *Wit.*

Miniature Reviews

"That Wonderful Urge" (20th). Neat romantic comedy, starring Tyrone Power and Gene Tierney; strong b.o.

"Fighter Squadron" (Color) (WB). Red-blooded action feature of air aces and the European invasion. Strong commercial film-fare.

"Yellow Sky" (20th). Top-flight western drama with Gregory Peck, Anne Baxter, Richard Widmark.

"The Man from Colorado" (Color) (Col). Well-mounted action yarn, exploitation values hinge on spec and Glenn Ford.

"Bungalow 13" (20th). Tom Conway, Richard Cromwell in whodunit strictly as mild support on lower part of twinners.

"Unknown Island" (Color) (FC). Exploitation feature of modern-day adventurers and prehistoric animals.

"Harpoon" (SG). Alaskan drama that will hold up in lower rungs though it fails to fulfill its possibilities.

"Grand Canyon Trail" (Music-Color) (Rep). Roy Rogers riding to good returns in action situations.

"The Small Voice" (BL). Neat British psychological thriller.

"It's Hard To Be Good" (GFD). Mild British comedy with war-theme.

That Wonderful Urge

20th-Fox release of Fred Kohlmar production. Stars Tyrone Power, Gene Tierney; features Reginald Gardner, Arleen Whelan. Directed by Robert Sinclair. Screenplay, Jay Dratler; story, William R. Lipman, Frederick Stephani; camera, Charles G. Clarke; editor, Louis Loeffler; music, Cyril Mockridge; musical direction, Lionel Newman. Tradeshown, N. Y., Nov. 22, '48. Running time, 82 MINS.

Thomas Jefferson Tyler	Tyrone Power
Sara	Gene Tierney
Andre	Reginald Gardiner
Jessica	Arleen Whelan
Aunt Cornelia Farley	Lucile Watson
The Judge	Gene Lockhart
Duffy	Lloyd Gough
Attorney Ketchell	Porter Hall
Mr. Whitson	Richard Gaines
Attorney Rice	Taylor Holmes
Justice of the Peace	Chill Wills
Apartment House Keeper	Hope Emerson
Findlay	Frank Ferguson
Mr. Bissell	Charles Arnt
Barret	Francis Pierlot

With escapist comedies once again in their heyday of boxoffice favor, "That Wonderful Urge" can be marked down as a surefire laugh-winner and coin-snarer. It's one of the best in the current cycle of fluffy confections. Geared for gaiety, the film deftly spins its lightweight yarn into a zany and volatile romance for maximum impact. Teaming of Tyrone Power and Gene Tierney will provide the necessary marquee lift.

Mounted in a slick production, the screenplay is another variation of the poor - little - rich - girl theme against a newspaper background. But Jay Dratler has dressed up this script with enough new twists and smart dialog to give an old chestnut the flavor of a brand-new souffle. Robert Sinclair's direction has wrapped up this dish with a bouncing pace that never falters under the story's lack of weight.

Switching from his heavy romantic and adventure roles, Power makes the most of his comedy chances as a cynical reporter assigned to assassinate the character of a grocery chain heiress. Posing as a lover to get the inside story for his series, he becomes tangled in his own line and bait when the gal, Miss Tierney, snaps back and turns him into a national laughing-stock.

This is also one of Miss Tierney's most successful performances. Costumed to highlight her natural charms and rigged with peppery lines, she polishes off her role with considerable grace. Wreaking a woman's revenge on her tormentor, she gives a newsbeat to rival newspapermen by faking a claim of marriage to Power. Fired from his job for selling out to the enemy, Power works all the angles to extricate himself from her gag but can't prove that he's still a bachelor. At the finale, of course, there's a legitimate clinch with Power lying in bed reading the Kinsey report.

Solid support to the principals is delivered by Reginald Gardner, as a penniless count on the make for a fortune, and Gene Lockhart, as a sentimental judge who wants to reconcile the couple. Arleen Whelan and Lucile Watson, in briefer roles, also do nicely among a competent cast of secondary players.

Excellent camera work and a pointed musical score round off an ace production. *Herm.*

Fighter Squadron

(COLOR)

Hollywood, Nov. 17.

Warners release of Seton I. Miller production. Stars Edmond O'Brien, Robert Stack, John Rodney; features Tom D'Andrea, Henry Hull, James Holden, Walter Reed, Shepperd Strudwick, Arthur Space, Jack Larson, William McLean, Mickey McCardle. Directed by Raoul Walsh. Screenplay, Seton I. Miller; added dialog, Martin Rackin; camera (Technicolor), Sid Hickox, Wilfred M. Cline; editor, Christian Nyby; music, Max Steiner. Tradeshown in Hollywood, Nov. 16, '48. Running time, 94 MINS.

Major Ed Hardin	Edmond O'Brien
Capt. Stu Hamilton	Robert Stack
Col. Bill Brickley	John Rodney
Sergeant Dolan	Tom D'Andrea
Brig. Gen. Mike McCready	Henry Hull
Tennessee	James Holden
Capt. Duke Chappell	Walter Reed
Brig. Gen. M. Gilbert	Shepperd Strudwick
Major Sanford	Arthur Space
Shorty	Jack Larson
Wilbur	William McLean
Jacobs	Mickey McCardle

An exciting, red-blooded action feature has been woven around the grim realities of modern warfare in "Fighter Squadron," highly commercial feature with enough documentation and actual Air Force footage to stamp it with potent authenticity that should sell a lot of tickets.

Picture's time of action is the tense days of 1943-44, when the U. S. Air Force was paving the way for D-Day. It centers its story on one English-based squadron of fighter planes and pilots. The film thrives on deadly air action, and the AF combat footage that makes up a substantial part of the picture is a tingling reminder of World War II.

Combat footage has been interlaced into the high melodramatics of the story fiction to add a realistic flavor to the adventures of intrepid air aces, but the picture is not all grimness. Seton I. Miller, who wrote and produced, has given it a masculine humor that lightens the tension at the proper moments.

It opens with a light touch projected by a conniving sergeant, and then swings into a gripping, exciting sequence of battle-crippled fighter planes returning to base. That spacing of lightness and tension has been used throughout by Raoul Walsh's direction to keep the balance on entertainment for general audiences. Pilot horseplay, aground and aloft; the quietness with which they go about the deadly game of war; big brass, red tape, and the methodicalness of bigtime destruction are all graphically depicted.

It's an all-male picture, except for two brief scenes showing a sergeant, who uses the alias of "Kinsey," at work and in trouble. Femmes aren't missed, though. The gal back home and the one in London are constantly talked about by post-bound soldiers. Only "Kinsey" is able to break bounds, using an ingenious trick with black cats that is good for chuckles.

Cast is very able in portraying the assorted young men who live and die bravely. Edmond O'Brien, squadron leader, stands out, and there are strong assists from Robert Stack and John Rodney as flying mates. Principal light moments fall to the capable hands of Tom D'Andrea as the amorous sergeant. His comedy is backed by a perfect "sad sack" touch from William McLean as a lowly private.

Henry Hull, James Holden, Walter Reed and Shepperd Strudwick give life to their assignments. Jack Larson has only a short role but it realizes perfectly on the eager-beaver new pilot, scared before his first combat, but proud and sick after his first kill.

Walsh's knowhow in handling an action feature and Miller's ability in putting together a melodramatic yarn are strong foundation for giving "Fighter Squadron" stout b.o. prospects. Air battle scenes, the dogfights, strafings, explosions are brilliantly lensed in Technicolor, with Sid Hickox and Wilfred M. Cline sharing the top credit. Max Steiner's music score is excellent, and editing by Christian Nyby sharpens the action. *Brog.*

Yellow Sky

Hollywood, Nov. 19.

20th-Fox release of Lamar Trotti production. Stars Gregory Peck, Anne Baxter, Richard Widmark; features Robert Arthur, John Russell, Henry Morgan, James Barton, Charles Kemper. Directed by William A. Wellman. Screenplay, Lamar Trotti; based on story by W. R. Burnett; camera, Joe MacDonald; editor, Harmon Jones. Tradeshown Nov. 18, '48. Running time, 99 MINS.

Stretch	Gregory Peck
Mike	Anne Baxter
Dude	Richard Widmark
Bull Run	Robert Arthur
Lengthy	John Russell
Half Pint	Henry Morgan
Grandpa	James Barton
Walrus	Charles Kemper
Jed	Robert Adler
Lieutenant	Harry Carter
Bartender	Victor Kilian
Drunk	Paul Hurst
Rancher	Hank Worden
Indian	Jay Silverheels
Banker	William Gould
Bank Teller	Norman Leavitt
Colorado	Chief Yowlachie

A smart combination of talents makes "Yellow Sky" all that could be asked of an outdoor action drama. It's topgrade film fare with star values to help push ticket sales. Boxoffice looks strong. Marquee lineup of Gregory Peck, Anne Baxter and Robert Widmark, combined with a punchy story, should give this one a healthy ride through all situations.

Emphasis is on terse, tough action and the job of bringing the exceptionally good plot to the screen has been approached intelligently. Picture has a load of dramatic power of the kind seldom present in this type film and it's done in believable fashion by all concerned.

Setting for the story is the west of 1867 and the outdoor locations have been magnificently lensed as a telling backdrop for the dramatics. Lamar Trotti put together an ace screenplay from a story by W. R. Burnett, gave it dialog that rings true, and then proceeded with showmanly production guidance to make "Sky" a winner.

The direction by William A. Wellman is vigorous, potently emphasizing every element of suspense and action, and displaying the cast to the utmost advantage. There's never a faltering scene as sequence after sequence is unfolded at a swift pace. Plot outline traces a group of outlaws who rob a bank, flee across a desert and seek refuge in a ghost mining town. There they find a girl and her grandfather, learn they have gold and seek to steal it. Plot has a happy, believable ending, with three of the outlaws reforming and the others dead because of their greed.

There's many an earthy touch in the script and an understanding of the hungers of men; some for gold, some for women, and some for love and understanding. It is these touches and the manner in which they are approached through scripting, direction and playing that help to give the picture dramatic substance.

Peck shines as the outlaw leader and matching dramatic stride for stride with him is Miss Baxter as the ghost town girl. The emotional clash that sets up when these two strong characters meet has a smoldering s. a. wallop. Widmark steps out in another of his coldblooded killer delineations as Peck's doublecrossing partner in crime.

James Barton gives quality to his performance as the grandfather. Robert Arthur, John Russell, Henry Morgan, Charles Kemper and Robert Adler make their roles as outlaws important parts.

Manner of handling the solid music score by Alfred Newman is an example of the intelligent use of the film's varied talents. Music starts the dramatic scenes off and then fades out. It's a device that measurably increases mood and tension. (A previous 20th western, "Fury at Furnace Creek," used same trick, letting dramatics play alone to heighten effect.)

The standout photography was contributed by Joe MacDonald and the special effects by Fred Sersen are another top credit. Editing is tight, holding film to a swift 99 minutes. *Brog.*

The Man from Colorado

(COLOR)

Columbia release of Jules Schermer production. Stars Glenn Ford, William Holden; features Ellen Drew, Ray Collins, Edgar Buchanan, Jerome Courtland, James Millican, Jim Bannon, William Phillips. Directed by Henry Levin; original story, Borden Chase; screenplay, Robert D. Andrews, Ben Maddow; camera, William Snyder; editor, Charles Nelson; score George Duning. Tradeshown N. Y., Nov. 12, '48. Running time, 99 MINS.

Col. Owen Devereaux	Glenn Ford
Captain Del Stewart	William Holden
Caroline Emmett	Ellen Drew
Big Ed Carter	Ray Collins
Doc Merriam	Edgar Buchanan
Johnny Howard	Jerome Courtland
Sgt. Jericho Howard	James Millican
Nagel	Jim Bannon
York	Wm. "Bill" Phillips
Easy Jarrett	Denver Pyle
Dickson	James Bush
Morris	Mikel Conrad
Mutton McGuire	David Clarke
Jack Rawson	Ian MacDonald
Charlie Trumbull	Clarence Chase
Roger MacDonald	Stanley Andrews
Powers	Myron Healey
Parry	Craig Reynolds
Rebel Major	David York

While the action values of "The Man from Colorado" have been dissipated to some extent by the introduction of psychiatric motives, there's enough color and excitement to insure healthy returns for this post-Civil War western. Names of Glenn Ford and William Holden will aid the boxoffice. However, exhibitors will have to exploit the gunplay and spectacle items in order to entice better than usual boxoffice.

It's been generally presumed that high-action films were immune to psychiatric encroachment. It's a field that has a pre-sold audience which likes its riding and shooting in an unadulterated manner. "The Man from Colorado" will still get that patronage, but there's little likelihood of getting additional customers that might be enticed by the intellectualing of the film.

Story has Glenn Ford as a Civil War colonel who during the war years has developed a trigger-finger and kills for the love of it. With his mustering out of the Union Army, Ford is appointed a Federal judge in Colorado, where he hopes to settle down to normalcy. Instead he uses the law in the same manner he formerly used his six-shooter. He's ultimately rubbed out as the result of his misdeeds.

It's a difficult acting assignment for Ford, and he sometimes comes out second best to the script. The moments when his malaise grips him are overplayed. W. Holden plays Ford's adjutant throughout the war, taking on the job as Ford's marshal in order to set his friend straight. Holden sticks to him even when he knows that he ordered wiping out of a rebel band after it hoisted a white flag, and he tries to enforce Ford's martinet-like legal decisions when he knows it will lead to warfare. Ultimately, he deserts the post of marshal to join a band of former Army personnel who have been forced to become outlaws by Ford's decision taking away their gold-mining lands.

The rest of the cast do good jobs. Ellen Drew does well as the girl loved by Ford and Holden, marrying Ford only to desert him when she can no longer stand his trigger-happy mind. Ray Collins, as an understanding medico; Edgar Buchanan, Jerome Courtland, James Millican, Jim Bannon and William "Bill" Phillips, playing vets-turned-outlaws, provide some color to their roles.

The production is a well-turned affair, with Technicolor enhancing the film's values. Outdoor shots are particularly good, and sets and costumes are okay.

Henry Levin had to overcome some difficult problems inasmuch as he had to blend mental medicine with gunplay, and frequently had to subordinate one for the other. Under those circumstances it was virtually impossible to sustain a mood.

George Duning has fashioned an articulate score, and William Snyder's camera work is of top-drawer category. *Jose.*

Bungalow 13

20th-Fox release of Belsam production. Features Tom Conway, Margaret Hamilton, Richard Cromwell. Directed by Edward L. Cahn. Original screenplay, Richard G. Hubler, Sam Baerwitz; camera, Jackson Rose; editor, Lou Sackin. At New York, N. Y., week of Nov. 19, '48. Running time, 70 MINS.

Christopher Adams	Tom Conway
Mrs. Appleby	Margaret Hamilton
Patrick Macy	Richard Cromwell
Lt. Wilson	James Flavin
Alice Ashley	Marjorie Hoshelle
Gus Barton	Frank Cady
Jose Fernando	Eddie Acuff
Mrs. Barton	Jody Gilbert
Pedro Gomez	Juan Varro
Willie	Lyle Latell
Hibiscus	Mildred Coles
Mr. Eden	John Davidson

Tom Conway, who has done Bulldog Drummond and Falcon sleuth roles on the screen, strives hard to make something of this detective whodunit, but it's no dice. This meller of a private eye and missing jade stone only manages to mystify its audience without proving entertaining or half as gripping as most sleuth thrillers. Result is that it will be only mild material on lower half of twin bills.

"Bungalow 13" is loaded with victims who are knifed to death, plenty of shooting and a couple of rough-'n'-tumble fights. Yet it is dull, rambling (with many scenes supposed to depict outdoor scenes at night) and managing to become so involved as to characters suspected in the string of killings that few people will care who is guilty or why.

The Richard G. Hubler - Sam Baerwitz original smacks of any number of recent detective yarns. But the better portions of such yarns are not retained with enough force to mean much. Edward L. Cahn's direction also appears partly to blame, being unoriginal and routine for the most part.

Tom Conway is the private eye, who, per usual, helps the police unravel the mystery and put the finger on the guilty person. He is not altogether convincing but that possibly is partly because of the story and awkward story development. Richard Cromwell, back from a war stint in the Coast Guard, is miscast as a crook, being wasted on this lesser role. Marjorie Hoshelle is the only comely girl with much to do in the production, and she's bumped off early.

Margaret Hamilton, as an old-maidish detective story writer, supplies some comedy moments but the part hardly deserves as much footage as allotted to it. Support is mild, with James Flavin very bombastic and unrealistic as a police lieutenant.

Jackson Rose's camera work and Lou Sackin's editing are about on par with the mild standard of the whole production. *Wear.*

Unknown Island
(COLOR)

Hollywood, Nov. 15.

Film Classics release of Albert J. Cohen production. Features Virginia Grey, Philip Reed, Richard Denning, Barton MacLane, Richard Wessel, Daniel White, Philip Nazir. Directed by Jack Bernhard. Screenplay, Robert T. Shannon, Jack Harvey; original story, Shannon; camera (Cinecolor), Fred Jackman, Jr.; editor, Harry Gerstad; special effects, Howard A. Anderson, Ellis Burman. Previewed, Nov. 15, '48. Running time, 7[illegible] MINS.

Carole Lane	Virginia Grey
Ted Osborne	Philip Reed
John Fairbanks	Richard Denning
Captain Tarnowski	Barton MacLane
Sanderson	Richard Wessel
Edwards	Daniel White
Golab	Philip Nazir

"Unknown Island" is an exploitation adventure film with selling points to overcome its faults. Lensing of prehistoric animals in color and the ballyhoo that can be used to sell such a feature hold promise of fair boxoffice in specialized engagements.

Where film falls down is in the stilted direction and the incredible dialog used to tell the essentially okay thriller. Special effects created and photographed by Howard A. Anderson and Ellis Burman are imaginative. The monsters are frightening creations and should give enjoyable goosebumps to the audience that always seems to buy this type of show.

Jack Bernhard's direction moves the players slowly through a story about an assorted group of characters who go to a Pacific island to photograph, and maybe capture, the creatures that lived millions of years ago. Had Bernard sharpened his directorial pace and had scripters Robert T. Shannon and Jack Harvey used dialog instead of cliches, this one would have come off a great deal stronger.

Virginia Grey is the lone femme on the dangerous voyage and makes a pretty eyeful in Cinecolor. Part makes no other demands. Philip Reed is her fiance, more interested in his pictures than his gal. As a consequence, he loses her to Richard Denning, who had already been through one terrible experience with the prehistoric monsters. Barton MacLane appears as a tough, lustful ship captain who can't control his yens for booze or women, even in the face of violent death.

Picture dishes out a full complement of gore and violence in a to-the-death clash between a monsterous redhaired ape and a dinosaur, and there are other scenes where the assorted humans fight off the creatures with bullets and grenades. All of which are good ballyhoo stuff to help sell the picture.

Albert J. Cohen's production supervision has kept a watchful eye on the dollar, achieving good effects for coin spent. He should have been as careful in watching over the direction and script. Fred Jackman, Jr., did a good job of lensing. *Brog.*

Harpoon

Hollywood, Nov. 20.

Screen Guild Release of Danches production. Features John Bromfield, Alyce Louis, James Cardwell, Patricia Garrison, Jack George, Edgar Hinton, Frank Hagney, Hollis Bane. Directed by Ewing Scott. Screenplay by Girard Smith and Scott; camera, Frederick Gately; editor, Robert O. Crandall. Previewed Nov. 19, '48. Running time, 83 MINS.

Michael Shand	John Bromfield
Kitty Canon	Alyce Louis
Red Dorsett	James Cardwell
Christine McFee	Patricia Garrison
Rev. McFee	Jack George
Kirk Shand	Edgar Hinton
Red Dorsett, Sr	Frank Hagney
Kodiak	Hollis Bane
Patsy	Ruth Castle
Swede	Grant Means
Sally	Sally Davis
Fuzzy	James Martin
Lockerby	Willard Jillson
Prisoner	Gary Garrett
Whaler	Lee Elson
Whaler	Alex Sharp
Whaler	Lee Roberts

Lensed entirely in Alaska, "Harpoon" mixes some interesting location shots with a plausible plot. Though film will fare well enough in lower case situations, it lacks construction continuity and offers itself more as a series of sketches than a continuous story. Loose editing and unwieldly production are responsible.

Story gathers its strength from the hatred of Edgar Hinton for Frank Hagney. Hagney had shanghaied Hinton and beaten him brutally for a number of years before Hinton finally escaped. Never forgetting his hatred, Hinton married and brought up a son for the sole purpose of reaping retribution upon Hagney. Both Hinton and Hagney die but each of their sons carry on the grievances of the past.

John Bromfield and James Cardwell as the sons inject in the pic what spark is achieved. Pair pour their hatred upon each other for a full 65-minute through a series of fights, words and foul play. Bromfield enlists the forces of righteousness against Cardwell's envoys of evil and emerges the victor, claiming all the gold and Alyce Louis.

Ewing Scott's direction is taut, making the most of top sequences, and Frederick Gately's lensing offers interesting sea shots along with some good landscape angles. Screenplay developed by Paul Girard and Scott encased much stronger potential then film realized. *Free.*

Grand Canyon Trail
(SONGS-COLOR)

Republic release of Edward J. White production. Stars Roy Rogers; features Jane Frazee, Andy Devine. Directed by William Witney. Screenplay, Gerald Geraghty; camera (Trucolor), Reggie Lanning; editor, Tony Martinelli; music, Nathan Scott; songs, Jack Elliott, Foy Willing. Tradeshown N. Y. Nov. 18, '48. Running time, 67 MINS.

Roy Rogers	Roy Rogers
Carol Martin	Jane Frazee
Cookie Bullfincher	Andy Devine
Bill Regan	Robert Livingston
Dave Williams	Roy Barcroft
J. Malcolm Vanderpool	Charles Coleman
Ed Carruthers	Emmett Lynn
Mike Delsing	Ken Terrell
Sheriff	James Finlayson
Bannister	Tommy Coats
Foy Williams & Riders of Purple Sage	

Roy Rogers, topping a good cast in a well-turned color production, constitutes pre-sold boxoffice for the Saturday matinee trade and all situations where action yarns spell healthy returns. "Grand Canyon Trail" rides along at a lively gait, songs alternating with occasional dashes of humor, hard riding and plenty bursts from the six-shooters.

The film is handsomely embellished with good sets depicting a ghost town for added production values. It's one of the better sets seen in this type of western, and provides a reason for humor and action not too frequently seen in the cowpoke capers.

Story is built along comparatively simple lines having Rogers as a cowhand whose friends invest his savings in a doubtful silver-mining proposition. Inasmuch as the funds for which the stock was bought is borrowed from the bank, the venture must prove profit-making or else. Rogers eventually is instrumental in locating a mother lode.

Robert Livingston provides the bulk of the villainy as the mining engineer who seeks to swindle Rogers out of his holdings, and Jane Frazee provides the slim romantic interest as secretary to a financier who seeks to save her employer's silver holdings. Majority of the humorous touches are by Andy Devine as Rogers' buddy. Per usual, Foy Willing's Riders of the Purple Sage provide song and riding interludes.

The Trucolor camera work is okay although prints have a gaudy and uneven quality at times. *Jose.*

The Small Voice
(BRITISH)

London, Nov. 11.

British Lion release of Constellation Films-Anthony Havelock-Allan production. Stars Valerie Hobson, James Donald, Harold Keel. Directed by Fergus McDonnell. Screenplay by Derek Neame, Julian Orde, from novel by Robert Westerby; camera, Stan Pavey; editor, Manuel del Campo; music, Stanley Black. At Plaza, London, Nov. 10, '48. Running time, 83 MINS.

Eleanor	Valerie Hobson
Murray	James Donald
Boke	Harold Keel
Jim	David Greene
Frankie	Michael Balfour
Potter	Joan Young
Jenny	Angela Foulds
Ken	Glyn Dearman
Police Supt.	Norman Claridge
Inspector	Edward Evans
Maitland	Bill Shine
Dr. Mennell	Michael Horden
Joe Wallis	Edward Palmer
Collector	Lyn Evans

Anthony Havelock - Allan's first independent production since his breakaway from Cineguild is a neatly contrived thriller, strong in suspense values. Obviously made on a modest budget, its lack of star names to put on the marquee is clearly a handicap in selling the pic to American showmen, but it should make a worthwhile dualer.

Taken from the novel by Robert Westerby, the story depicts the emotional conflicts experienced by three escaped prisoners who keep a playwright and his wife prisoner in their own home while trying to elude the cops. Apart from the opening shots, there's little action, but there's a good quota of suspense developed from the main situation.

Because there is so little action, the pic has to rely on the actors for its effect. James Donald, as the playwright; Harold Keel, as the big shot, and David Greene and Michael Balfour as his two confederates, turn in meaty, convincing studies. Valerie Hobson is very effective as the wife who becomes reunited with her husband, but while lesser roles are well cast, the Welsh accent of many of the subsidiary characters may prove to be a deterrent in the U. S. *Myro.*

It's Hard To Be Good
(BRITISH)

London, Nov. 11.

GFD release of J. Arthur Rank-Two Cities film. Stars Anne Crawford, Jimmy Hanley. Directed by Jeffrey Dell. Screenplay by Dell; camera, Laurie Friedman; editor, Helga Cranston; music, Anthony Hopkins. At Odeon, London, Nov 10, '48. Running time, 93 MINS.

James	Jimmy Hanley
Mary	Anne Crawford
Williams	Raymond Huntley
Sergeant Todd	Geoffrey Keen
Budibent	Elwyn Brook Jones
Edward Beckett	David Horne
Alice Beckett	Joyce Carey
Ellen Beckett	Muriel Aked
Daphne	Lana Morris
Parkinson	Edward Rigby

Essentially British in its appeal, "It's Hard to be Good," although possessing a theme with tremendous possibilities, is treated in a light, frivolous manner, almost bordering on farce. It's a subject which should get by with native audiences, but be of little interest to American exhibs.

Central character in the plot is a young ex-Army officer who comes out of the service with lofty ideals and a Victoria Cross. Believing that the cure for all the ailments of the world is goodwill, he finds that every time he puts his theory to the test, the results are pretty disastrous.

Developed along more obvious slapstick lines, plot makes no attempt to come to grips with the issues raised, but prefers to poke gentle fun at the idealist. It's not a production which makes considerable demands on the cast. Jimmy Hanley and Anne Crawford make an attractive romantic team, with good support from Raymond Huntley and Geoffrey Keen. *Myro.*

Hamnstad
(Harbor City)
(SWEDISH)

Stockholm, Oct. 27.

Svensk Filmindustri production and release. Stars Christine Jonsson, Bengt Eklund; features Berta Hall, Erik Hell, Mimi Nelson, Birgitta Valberg, Hans Straat, Nils Dahlgren, Harry Ahlin, Nils Hallberg. Directed by Ingmar Bergman. Screenplay, Bergman, based on story by Olle Lensberg; camera, Gunnar Fischer; music, Erland von Koch. At Cosmorama and Kaparen, Gothenburg. Running time, 100 MINS.

Berit	Nine Christine Jonsson
Gosta	Bengt Eklund
Berit's mother	Berta Hall
Berit's father	Erik Hell
Gertrud	Mimi Nelson

Miss Velander	Birgitta Valberg
Velander	Hans Straat
Gertrud's father	Nils Dahlgren
Skaningen	Harry Ahlin
Gustav	Nils Hallberg
Mrs. Krona	Siv Ruud

Novel treatment handed the time - honored "boy - meets - girl" theme in "Hamnstad" lifts it out of the otherwise ordinary bracket. Picture has great b.o. prospects in Scandinavia and should do well abroad.

Sailor Bengt Eklund meets Nine Christine Jonsson at a Gothenburg dance hall, and falls for her. Lovers have several misunderstands. However, the situations adjust themselves and the fadeout finds them firmly reunited.

Competent direction of Ingmar Bergman as well as his crisp screenplay put plenty of entertainment values into the footage. Handling her first important role, Miss Jonsson registers auspiciously. Eklund is dashingly realistic as her vis-a-vis while supporting cast measures up. *Winq.*

The Man to Men
(D'Homme a Hommes)
(FRENCH)

Realisations D'Art Cinematographiques release of P. Albert and R.I.C. (Genveve) Production. Stars Jean-Louis Barrault, Bernard Blier, Helen Perdriere. Directed by Christian Jaque. Original screenplay by Charles Spaak and Christian Jaque. Camera, Christian Matras. At Hermitage, Nov. 19, '48. Running time, 112 MINS.

Henri Dunant	Jean Louis Barrault
Coquil't	Bernard Blier
Elsa Kastner	Helene Perdriere
Routorbe	Louis Seigner
Moynier	Abel Jacquin
General Dufour	Dennis D'Ines
La Mere De Dunant	Berthe Bovy
De Lormel	Maurice Escande
Napolean, III	Jean Debucourt
Cocher Piemontais	Fernand Rauzena
Docteur Basting	Groenenveld

France can be proud of this one. "Man to Men" is set for exportation to the states next month and should do well at the foreign film b.o. since it's one of France's best efforts. P. Albert, who produced "Grand Illusion," has surrounded himself with some of the best talent in France and the results are commendable. Though the motion picture is a tribute to Henri Dunant, founder of the International Red Cross, it is also a tribute to the acting ability of Jean-Louis Barrault.

Plot of the pic is thin and only skillful direction, acting and camerawork keep the interest high. Director Christian Jaque uses flashback technique, with Dunant himself telling his story. Coming back from Algeria to protest to Napoleon III about conditions in Africa, Dunant is caught in the Battle of Solferino where he witnesses the slaughter of POW's and wounded soldiers. After caring for the wounded, Dunant gets his idea for an International Red Cross which will be respected by all combatants. His efforts at first are stymied by the military commands of all powers, but after lobbying and politicking his Red Cross is finally recognized as an international symbol of peace to all men.

Best scenes in the pic are the realistic battles between the Prussians and the French. The focusing on the men wounded in these conflicts and hand to hand fighting makes exciting cinema, and Christian Matras can be credited with great camerawork.

Barrault's performance in this picture is the finest turned in by a French star this year. Bernard Blier, as Dunant's friend, also rates a nod for a great supporting role.

Jacque's deft direction, and sets by Robert Gys, contribute to effectiveness of the pic. The film was budgeted at $600,000, which makes it one of France's costliest endeavors. *Buch.*

Pa Dessa Skuldror
(On Those Shoulders)
(SWEDISH)

Stockholm, Nov. 1.

Nordisk Tonefilm release of Lennart Landheaim production. Stars Ulf Palme, Holger Lowenadler, Anita Bjork; features Marta Arbin, Kewe Hielm, Agneta Prytz, Ingrid Borthen, Carl Strom. Directed by Gosta Folke. Screenplay by Karl-Fredrik Bjorn from novel by Svend Edvin Salje; camera, Goran Strindberg; music, Erland von Koch. At Astoria, Stockholm. Running time, 103 MINS.

Kjell Loveng	Ulf Palme
Arvid Loveng	Holger Lowenadler
Birgit Larsson	Anita Bjork
Inga Loveng	Marta Arbin
Simon Loveng	Kewe Hielm
Edla	Agneta Prytz
Elin Tarp	Ingrid Borthen
Elis	Carl Strom
Sonja	Ragnvi Lindbladh
Andreasson	Oscar Ljung
Botvid	Carl Deurell
Aron	Erik Hell
Borje	Borje Mellwig
Tarp	John Norrman
Mans-Erik	Artur Cederborgh

This is an outstanding drama. To point up the advantages of rural life, the picture traces the career of a farm youth who returns to the countryside after giving the big city a whirl. It's the type of yarn that will prove a solid grosser for Scandinavian exhibitors, and chances are also good in the world market, especially in the U. S. and Britain.

In this adaptation from Svend Edvin Salje's novel, Ulf Palme returns to rebuild the farm to which his father, Holger Lowenadler, has become indifferent. When he's on the brink of success war intervenes. Later, with his soldiering over, he finds things are in a rut again.

Able cast is aided considerably by Gosta Folke's outstanding direction. Palme, in particular, racks up a sterling performance. Lowenadler, as the father, contributes an equally fine job in handling an unsympathetic role. Miss Bjork, who provides the romantic interest, also rates acclaim. Karl-Fredrik Bjorn's screenplay, camerawork of Goran Strindberg and Erland von Koch's music all combine to make "Pa Dessa Skuldror" one of the better Swedish films. *Winq.*

Foreign Films

novel, "Jorund Smed"; camera. Sten Dahlgren. At Royal, Stockholm. Running time, 86 MINS.

Fine lensing of Norwegian mountains and bays makes this interesting from a scenic point of view. However, aside from its pictorial asset "Dit Vindarna Bar" hasn't much to offer. Story revolves around a blacksmith's travels through the hills. Film may get by in Scandinavia with its mixed Norwegian and Swedish cast, but chances are dubious abroad. *Winq.*

Miniature Reviews

Decision of Christopher Blake

Warner Bros. release of Ranald MacDougall production. Stars Alexis Smith; features Robert Douglas, Ted Donaldson, Cecil Kellaway. Directed by Peter Godfrey. Screenplay, MacDougall, based on stage play by Moss Hart; camera, Karl Freund; editor, Frederick Richards; dialog director, Howard Lynn; music, Max Steiner; music director, Leo Forbstein. Tradeshown N. Y., Nov. 26, '48. Running time, 75 MINS.

Mrs. Blake	Alexis Smith
Mr. Blake	Robert Douglas
Judge Adamson	Cecil Kellaway
Christopher Blake	Ted Donaldson
Mr. Caldwell	John Hoyt
Courtroom Attendant	Harry Davenport
Clara	Mary Wickes
Mr. Kurlick	Art Baker
Miss McIntyre	Lois Maxwell
J. Roger Bascomb	Douglas Kennedy
Upton	Bert Hanlon

Moss Hart's stage play, with its title lengthened to "The Decision of Christopher Blake," has been converted into a passably interesting film by Ranald MacDougall. Lacking cast name value, with Alexis Smith as the top performer from a marquee standpoint, "Blake" is headed for only mild boxoffice returns, though not solely because of the lack of marquee values. The treatment of the subject matter—the fate of children of divorcing parents—doesn't have the depth to maintain major interest.

MacDougall did the adaptation, in addition to having produced the pic, which occasionally has some genuinely fine writing in its treatment of the conflicting emotions of a 13-year old faced with the prospect of whom to choose when his parents plan to divorce. It is the story of how the boy, overwhelmed by the confusions attendant to the situation, fancies himself as a subsequent subject of neglect by the parental decision. This facet of the story is cleverly contrived in several "dream" sequences.

Ted Donaldson is the boy, and he handles the role excellently. Miss Smith is the mother, and Robert Douglas the father, and each contributes competent performances. Cecil Kellaway is the kindly judge responsible for the reconciliation, and he, too, gives a workmanlike characterization. Supporting players who do well are Harry Davenport, Mary Wickes and John Hoyt.

Director Peter Godfrey has gotten a surprisingly sharp pace out of a story that could easily have been unwieldy, while the film's production standards are all top-bracket for what looks like a comparatively inexpensively budgeted yarn. *Kahn.*

Mexican Hayride

(ONE SONG)

Universal release of Robert Arthur production. Stars Bud Abbott, Lou Costello; features Virginia Grey, Luba Malina, John Hubbard. Directed by Charles T. Barton. Screenplay, Oscar Brodney, John Grant; based on the musical by Herbert and Dorothy Fields and Cole Porter; song, Jack Brooks and Walter Scharf; camera, Charles Van Enger; editor, Frank Gross; music, Walter Scharf. Tradeshown, N. Y., Nov. 30, '48. Running time, 77 MINS.

Harry Lambert	Bud Abbott
Joe Bascom	Lou Costello
Montana	Virginia Grey
Dagmar	Luba Malina
David Winthrop	John Hubbard
Senor Martinez	Pedro de Cordoba
Professor Ganzmeyer	Fritz Feld
Ed Mason	Tom Powers
Tim Williams	Pat Costello
Gus Adamson	Frank Fenton
Mariachi Leader	Chris Pin Martin
Reporter	Sidney Fields

Flores Brothers Trio

One more chapter in the zany cycle of Abbott & Costello reels off in "Mexican Hayride." Another chapter, another b.o. click. While not as strong an entry as the previous Frankenstein takeoff, this film has enough buffoonery and broad gagging to keep the A&C fans happy. It's standard fare for a ready-made audience.

Bearing only faint resemblance to the Cole Porter-Herbert & Dorothy Fields legit musical from which the title was taken, the film cuts its comic capers within a hokey but suitable south-of-the-border framework with an incidental musical background. Story values, as usual, are negligible with the whole production pegged onto Abbott's stooging to Costello's familiar idiom of low comedy.

Both the direction and screenplay attack on the strategy that if it's corny enough, it'll be funny. The result is a cornucopia of comedy situations which have become the trademark of Abbott & Costello since their vaude days. The single kernel of originality in this pic is a riotous bullfight sequence in which Costello clowns the bull into a stalemate.

Slight yarn revolves around a stock swindle scheme in which Costello is the fall guy for a gang of confidence men headed by Abbott. Chased out of the U. S. as a notorious confidence man, Costello gets trapped again by Abbott into fronting for a fake mining outfit in Mexico. But there's no further sense in the plot which serves only as a pretext for Costello's madcap mugging and antics.

The rest of the cast also roams through the film without any logic except to act as props for the A&C antics. Luba Malina, as a vague heavy, delivers one mediocre number, "Is It Yes, Or Is It No," in fair style. For some reason, the entire Cole Porter score in the original "Mexican Hayride" was bypassed for this ordinary tune by Jack Brooks and Walter Scharf. Virginia Grey and John Hubbard furnish the slight romantic angles adequately, while Fritz Feld gets in a solid turn as an elocution teacher. A flock of goodlooking extras dress up the backgrounds.

General production values are par for the A&C cycle. Excellent camera work, however, gives the pic a glossy finish with specially good trick shots evident in the bull-fight sequence. Editing and background musical score are competently handled. *Herm.*

3 Godfathers

(SONG-COLOR)

Hollywood, Nov. 19.

Metro release of John Ford-Merian C. Cooper (Argosy) production, directed by Ford. Stars John Wayne, Pedro Armendariz, Harry Carey, Jr.; features Ward Bond, Mae Marsh, Jane Darwell, Ben Johnson. Screenplay, Laurence Stallings, Frank S. Nugent; from story by Peter B. Kyne; camera (Technicolor), Winton Hoch; editor, Jack Murray. Tradeshown Nov. 17, '48. Running time, 106 MINS.

Bob Sangster	John Wayne
Pete	Pedro Armendariz
"The Kid"	Harry Carey, Jr.
"Buck" Perley Sweet	Ward Bond
Mrs. Perley Sweet	Mae Marsh
The Mother	Mildred Natwick
Miss Florie	Jane Darwell
Judge	Guy Kibbee
Ruby Latham	Dorothy Ford
Member of Posse	Ben Johnson

"3 Godfathers" is an unusual western, re-telling the age-old Christmas story and the reformation of man against a backdrop of desert wastes. While the off-the-beaten-path approach would indicate an appeal to the sophisticate, it will be the person who lives closer to his emotions who will get the most from it: i.e., the more general audience.

Critical appraisal will be varied, but there is a lot of tear-jerker stuff in the story to attract the average filmgoer. As usual with a John Ford production, a feature of the film is the use of the camera and the freshness of backgrounds. It also has other trademarks of the careful craftsman, striving for something a bit different but still with an eye on commercial factors.

The more critical ticket buyer will be disappointed that Ford doesn't quite achieve something that is distinctly different, but the general audience will find plenty of escape in the obvious play on the heartstrings and the extreme, deadly quiet action of the picture's first half.

John Wayne's name is a particularly bright marquee lure for the action fan, and the performance he delivers does him proud. However, it is Pedro Armendariz, in the more emotionally fluid character of a Mexican bandit, who comes through the most colorfully. Film also introduces Harry Carey, Jr., in his first big role, and the young man appeals strongly. [Picture, incidentally, is dedicated to his late father.]

Oddly enough, plot of "3 Godfathers" starts off with a similar story setup as another western soon to go into release (20th's "Yellow Sky"); bandits rob a bank and then take off across a great salt desert to escape the law, fight their way through great thirst and sandstorms. Desert location for both films appears the same.

From that point on, though, the Peter B. Kyne story on which script by Laurence Stallings and Frank S. Nugent is based, takes a different route. The three bandits, Wayne, Armendariz and Carey, Jr., reach a waterhole, find it dynamited. At the hole is a woman, ready to give birth. The bandits aid the delivery and vow to the dying woman to become the child's godfathers.

Film recounts their dangerous trek to re-cross the desert to save the child, using the biblical story of the three wise men journeying to Jerusalem as the motivation to turn the trio from evil ways and accept the responsibility of their new positions.

First half of the picture rings the bell as high class western action, done with a master's touch for mood and tension. Particularly pleasing is the character of a western sheriff who is smart, letting nature trap his bandits. Ward Bond is the sheriff and he gives the role life and not a little humor. Mae Marsh makes a choice assignment out of her part as Bond's wife. Jane Darwell, a bawdy water tank caretaker; Guy Kibbee, western justice, and Ben Johnson, bald posse member, are among others who show up well.

Carey, Jr., gives plaintive crooning to "Streets of Laredo" in a lullaby scene with the baby and has his big moment in his death scene when he lapses back to childhood to recite the Lord's Prayer.

The John Ford-Merian C. Cooper production has been impressively photographed by Winton Hoch. His camera paints desert scenes in glowing Technicolor with a touch that is breath-taking. The shimmering, intense heat of the desert locations is vividly reproduced on film. Other technical credits are stamped with quality. *Brog.*

Manhattan Angel

(SONGS)

Columbia release of Sam Katzman production. Stars Gloria Jean; features Ross Ford, Patricia White, Thurston Hall, Alice Tyrrell, Benny Baker, Russell Hicks, Fay Baker. Directed by Arthur Dreifuss. Screenplay, Albert Derr; story, George H. Plympton, Derr; camera, Ira H. Morgan; editor, Richard Fantl; songs, Dewey Bergman, Jack Segal, Oscar Hammerstein II, Ben Oakland, Robert Bilder, Herb Jeffries, Eddie Beal, Nick Castle. At Brooklyn Strand, Nov. 24, '48. Running time, 67 MINS.

Gloria Cole	Gloria Jean
Eddie Swenson	Ross Ford
Maggie Graham	Patricia White
Everett H. Burton	Thurston Hall
"Queenie" Walters	Alice Tyrrell
Aloysius Duff	Benny Baker
J. C. Rayland	Russell Hicks
Vi Langdon	Fay Baker
Elmer	Jimmy Lloyd
Toni	Toni Harper
Lester	Leonard Sues
Harry	Ralph Hodges
Mrs. Cole	Dorothy Vaughan
Miss Shelton	Isabel Withers
Esther	Peggy Wynne
Virginia Schuyler	Barbara Brier
Priscilla Lund	Ida Moore
Gus Davis	Robert Cherry

"Manhattan Angel" is saddled with a wobbly plot which intermittently drags its feet and signals its punches. The diluted entertainment quotient could have been thickened by more generous application and effective use of Gloria Jean's melodic powers. As it stands, the too-familiar pattern hit by this film makes it only so-so support for double-bill entries.

Film's to-do centers about the strivings of Miss Jean, copywriter in an ad agency, to save a youth center in Gotham's lower east side from replacement by a proposed factory building. In her efforts she tangles with an ill-tempered bachelor tycoon who happens to be both the agency's chief account and the owner of the factory. Before crossing the finishing mark, Miss Jean goes through some devious antics which make for plot development but little excitement.

Tight writing and better-barbed humor could have helped Miss Jean convert something titillating out of her scrapes, mishaps and final victory. But tired dialog for her and lack-lustre gags for Benny Butler and Alice Tyrrell fail to cop the necessary, gilt-edged guffaws. Sans freshness on story twists or bright writing, "Angel" never gets its wings.

Miss Jean's role would have been more rewarding if the script drafted her for more singing. The two numbers which she does take on ("It's a Wonderful, Wonderful Feeling" and "I'll Take Romance") are the only really bright spots in the pic. At that, her renditions are truncated to one or two choruses and little supporting background.

Thurston Hall does a likeable job as the choleric manufacturer. Other parts, however, are written either too obviously or colorlessly to score an impression. Ross Ford, for one, playing the boy friend, is confined to the borders of the monosyllable. Children scenes at the youth center fail to snare a factual, meaningful treatment.

Direction misses generating excitement and stumbles over an excessively long fashion sequence. Production values are ample for the economical operation. Editing could have employed the scissors more. *Wit.*

Vienna Philharmonic

Ambassador release of Eugen Sharin production of shorts. Features Vienna Philharmonic Orchestra. Directed by Leopold Hainisch. Previewed N. Y., Nov. 23, '48. Running time, 12 MINS. each.

These new 12-minute shorts of the Vienna Philharmonic Orchestra playing some of the great music classics, as well as the lighter operetta excerpts and waltzes, have great appeal. Shorts will draw in all the art houses, as well as in more general situations, while tele possibilities are excellent. Any longhair fan would be willing to take a Schubert "Unfinished" Symphony on TV once a week or so, for years at a stretch. (WCBS-TV, N. Y., has scheduled these pix for later this season).

Pix, filmed in Vienna or at Salzburg, show the world-famed Vienna symph under its various conductors, playing such works as Mozart's "Eine Kleine Nachtmusik," Offenbach's "Orpheus in Hades" Overture, first movement of Beethoven's Fifth Symphony, the Schubert "Unfinished," Johann Strauss' "Tales of the Vienna Woods," and Josef Strauss' "Music of the Spheres." Camera placed on an orchestra for 12 minutes may have a tendency towards monotony, but director Leopold Hainisch minimizes that by constantly shifting around to the various choirs handling the main themes, and by some excellent montage effects. Fact that camera lingers on the performers instead of wandering off into scenes of nature, keeps one's mind on the music. The occasional trick shots don't detract from the main attraction—which is the music.

Music is excellently performed, of course, but is well recorded too. There are no cheapening effects, idea being to present the world's music masterpieces as simply and tastefully as possible. Eighteen such symphony subjects have been filmed by producer Eugen Sharin.

Also shown at the N. Y. preview was a short of the Vienna Choir Boys in "Merry Christmas." Film is more pictorially interesting than the symph subjects, with a home background, showing the noted song group at work making toys, with some humorous touches added, in addition to their gifted carol singing. *Bron.*

Strike It Rich

Hollywood, Nov. 13.

Allied Artists release of Jack Wrather production. Stars Rod Cameron, Bonita Granville, Don Castle; features Stuart Erwin, Lloyd Corrigan. Directed by Lesley Selander. Screenplay, Francis Rosenwald; camera, Henry Sharp; editor, William Ziegler. Previewed in Hollywood, Nov. 12, '48. Running time, 81 MINS.

Duke Massey	Rod Cameron
Julie Brady	Bonita Granville
Tex Warren	Don Castle
Delbert Lane	Stuart Erwin
Matt Brady	Lloyd Corrigan
Mrs. Harkins	Ellen Corby
Carlton	Emory Parnell
Pap Jonathan	Harry Tyler
Mabel	Virginia Dale
Bull	William Haade
Mack	Edward Gargan
Postmaster	Robert Dudley

"Strike It Rich" is a sometimes engaging feature that gains interest from its oilfield locale and plot. Its best boxoffice level will be found in the smaller towns and situations, where it can go top-of-the-bill. Otherwise, it falls into the supporting classification.

Filmed entirely in the East Texas oilfields, with physical production values in keeping with the locale, yarn deals with wildcatters and oil sharpshooters who, often as not, ended up as millionaires. Story period runs from 1929 to the early '30s, climaxing with independent oilers' battle against prorata laws in force at that time.

Producer Jack Wrather, himself a bigtime oil lease operator, filmed the picture on his own East Texas properties, giving authentic settings to a story that follows a familiar pattern. Francis Rosenwald did the original script, basing it on actual events of the period.

Plot deals principally with a trio of rough and ready wildcatters who are always ready for a fight, a drink or to dig a well. After a falling out over ethics, Rod Cameron drifts west, taking with him as his bride, Bonita Granville. Staying behind in East Texas is Don Castle. The former partners both strike it rich after ups and downs. Cameron, vengeful and looking out for his pocketbook, promotes the prorata law. Miss Granville walks out on him, he sees the error of his way and saves the independents.

Mixed in with the routine story line are some tough fisticuffs (using obvious doubles) and a number of humorous situations expertly sharpened by Stuart Erwin as the third member of the trio. Pace is not always even as directed by Lesley Selander, but for general situations, the picture is an okay attraction, offering some locale novelty and the excitement of quick riches.

Lloyd Corrigan does well as a smalltown editor, and Ellen Corby rates laughs as a widow on the make for Erwin. The three stars make their assignments as convincing as possible, and small spots handled by Emory Parnell, Virginia Dale and Harry Tyler are okay.

Henry Sharp's lensing is excellent, and editing keeps film down to 81 minutes of footage. *Brog.*

Another Shore
(BRITISH)

London, Nov. 24.

GFD release of Ealing Studios-Michael Balcon production. Stars Robert Beatty, Moira Lister, Stanley Holloway. Directed by Charles Crichton. Screenplay by Walter Meade, from novel by Kenneth Reddin. Camera, Douglas Slocombe; editor, Bernard Gribble; music, Georges Auric. At Leicester Square, London, Nov. 23, '48. Running time, 77 MINS.

Gulliver .... Robert Beatty
Jennifer .... Moira Lister
Alastair .... Stanley Holloway
Yellow .... Michael Medwin
Nora .... Sheila Manahan
Coghlan .... Fred O'Donovan
Parkes .... Desmond Keane
Mrs. Gleeson .... Maureen Delaney
Boxer .... Dermot Kelly
Broderick .... Michael Golden
Fleming .... Michael O'Mahoney
Roger .... W. A. Kelly
Moore .... Wilfred Brambell

"Another Shore" is a competently-made pic with a smoothly-told story which should do steady, if moderate, business at the boxoffice with native audiences. Absence of star names for the marquee will be a handicap in the states, but its length should enable it to make the grade in the second feature class.

Dublin forms the background for this yarn of a young man named Gulliver with an ambition to settle in a South Sea island. Lacking the cash and unable to find a benefactor, he waits patiently at the city's most dangerous corners hoping for the opportunity of rescuing some wealthy person involved in an accident. By the time his victim comes along, however, Gulliver himself is trapped by a designing blonde which puts a finis to his Tahitian dreams.

Adroit direction takes full advantage of a neatly-developed script and maintains a steady but even pace. Comedy situations are effectively handled even though occasionally they are too obviously contrived. The production is carried by the three principal actors, with Robert Beatty as the day dreamer, Moira Lister as a very attractive and pleasing blonde, and Stanley Holloway as an irascible dissolute. They team together efficiently and are well supported by the other members of the cast. *Myro.*

Street Corner

Viro Pitcures release of George McCall-Wilshire Pictures production. Features Joseph Crehan, Marcia Mae Jones, John Treul. Directed by Albert Kelley. Story, Albert Kelley; screenplay, Jack Jungmeyer; camera, Virgil Miller; editor, John Faure. Previewed in N. Y., Nov. 26, '48. Running time, 68 MINS.

Dr. James Fenton .... Joseph Crehan
Lois Marsh .... Marcia Mae Jones
Bob Mason .... John Treul
Irene .... Billie Jean Eberhart
Hal .... John Duncan
Mrs. Marsh .... Jean Fenwick
Mr. Marsh .... Don Brodie
A Midwife .... Gretl DuPont
Kitty Mae .... Jan Sutton
Tom Brennan .... Milton Ross
Dr. Fenton's Nurse .... Jean Andren
Judge .... Stuart Holmes
District Attorney .... Sam Ash
Taxi Driver .... Eddie Gribben

"Street Corner" is a sex picture with real exploitation possibilities. As the sort of film that can be circused to the skies, it should make nice coin for exhibitors going for such pix. Picture is well-made for this type although obviously modestly budgeted.

Story unfolds a highschool romance that winds up in an affair following a graduation dance. The girl becomes pregnant, afraid to tell her mother, her sweetheart accidentally killed while on the way to marry her, then an abortion by a quack. Yarn parades the facts rather pointedly, with the running narration by the doctor helping make it convincing. Reluctance of parents to tell sex details to their children is pointed up, if a bit ineffectually.

Albert Kelley's direction is smoother than his original story. Joseph Crehan is standout as the family medico. Marcia Mae Jones is the 17-year-old who is sinned against; she isn't very effective. John Treul, as her highschool boyfriend, also is lightweight. Jean Fenwick, as the girl's mother, gives an uneven performance while Don Brodie, as the father, walks through his role. Stuart Holmes, screen vet, is seen briefly as the judge at the trial of the abortionist. Gretl DuPont contributes an excellent heavy protrayal as a "midwife" abortionist. *Wear.*

Miniature Reviews

"Words and Music" (M-G) (Musical-Color). Biog of Rodgers & Hart with roster of top names a b.o. sockeroo.

"Enchantment" (Goldwyn RKO). Romantic drama, starring David Niven and Teresa Wright. Femme draw.

"Letter to Three Wives" (20th). Another comedy winner from 20th; surefire.

"Chicken Every Sunday" (20th). Heartwarming and amusing family portrayal. Nice returns in the offing.

"Just William's Luck" (UA)... Meagre boxoffice values in this British import; may do for kids in some spots.

"Whispering Smith" (Color) (Par). Big-biceped western, toplining Alan Ladd and headed for great b.o.

"One Sunday Afternoon" (Color-Songs) (WB). Remake of "Strawberry Blonde" moderate b.o. prospect.

"So Dear to My Heart" (Music-Color) (RKO). One of Disney's best; potent fare.

"My Own True Love" (Par). Weak, war-theme meller, requiring hefty selling campaign.

"Family Honeymoon" (U). Good family comedy with Claudette Colbert and Fred MacMurray.

"Scott of the Antarctic" (GFD). John Mills stark Arctic semi-documentary, somewhat limited in appeal.

"An Old-Fashioned Girl" (Music) (EL). Gloria Jean clicks in standard Louisa May Alcott story; OK dualer.

"Here Come the Huggetts" (GFD). Weak British family drama.

Words and Music
(MUSICAL—COLOR)

Metro release of Arthur Freed production. Stars Mickey Rooney, Tom Drake, June Allyson, Perry Como, Judy Garland, Lena Horne, Gene Kelly and Ann Sothern; features Cyd Charisse, Betty Garrett, Janet Leigh, Mel Torme, Vera-Ellen, Richard Quine. Directed by Norman Taurog. Screenplay, based on lives and music of Richard Rodgers and Lorenz Hart, by Fred Finkelhoffe; story by Guy Bolton and Jean Holloway, adapted by Ben Feiner, Jr.; camera (Technicolor), Charles Rosher and Harry Stradling; editors, Albert Akst and Ferris Webster; musical director, Lennie Hayton; dances, Robert Alton. Tradeshown New York Dec. 1, '48. Running time, 119 MINS.

Herself .... June Allyson
Eddie Lorrison Anders .... Perry Como
Herself .... Judy Garland
Herself .... Lena Horne
Himself .... Gene Kelly
Lorenz "Larry" Hart .... Mickey Rooney
Joyce Harmon .... Ann Sothern
Richard "Dick" Rodgers .... Tom Drake
Herself .... Cyd Charisse
Peggy Lorgan McNeil .... Betty Garrett
Dorothy Feiner .... Janet Leigh
Herbert Fields .... Marshall Thompson
Himself .... Mel Torme
Herself .... Vera-Ellen
Mrs. Hart .... Jeanette Nolan
Ben Feiner, Jr .... Richard Quine
Shoe Clerk .... Clinton Sundberg
Herself .... Dee Turnell
Dr. Rodgers .... Harry Antrim
Mrs. Rodgers .... Ilka Gruning
Mr. Feiner .... Emory Parnell
Mrs. Feiner .... Helen Spring
James Fernby Kelly .... Edward Earle

Metro has made of the lives of Richard Rodgers and (the late) Lorenz Hart a slim but pleasant framework on which to hang some 22 of their most melodious and best-known tunes. To present them, it has corralled a lineup of performers that rate top-bracket for both marquee and entertainment values. An exhib could hardly ask for anything more. It's a stong boxoffice entry.

The saga of Rodgers and Hart itself is neither very interesting nor exceptional, unless it be in their early and continued success at turning out words and music for one top Broadway and Hollywood musical hit after another. Fred Finkelhoffe, therefore, in preparing his screenplay, acted wisely in reducing the biographical aspects to almost a minimum, using them only as a rack around which to weave production numbers, terp routines and lyric assignments. Only thing that could have been better from this standpoint would be even more drastic scissoring of the phoney romances of the boys and a straining out of the saccharine effort for a dramatic finale.

But that's minor to the overall lift the film gives. The tunes of this American Gilbert & Sullivan—as R&H have been dubbed—have an irrepressible froth and pleasantness. And, in this era of popular music nostalgia, even more listenable than when they were written are such toppers as "Where or when," "Lady Is a Tramp," "Mountain Greenery," "There's a Small Hotel," "With a Song in My Heart" and "My Heart Stood Still." These and other excerpts stem from such R&H hits as "Garrick Gaieties," "The Girl Friend," "Present Arms," "On Your Toes," "Babes in Arms," "I'd Rather Be Right," "I Married an Angel," "Boys from Syracuse," "Pal Joey" and "Jumbo."

Film is jampacked with musical numbers and Metro has gone right down its contract list, as well as reached outside, to find players to properly sing and dance them. Perry Como, Ann Sothern and Betty Garrett play character roles in the plot as a means of working in their numbers, but for the most part the warblers and terpers are just themselves. More or less skillfully rung in are June Allyson to do "Thou Swell" from "Connecticut Yankee," Judy Garland to do "Johnny One-Note" solo and "I Wish I Were in Love Again" with Mickey Rooney, Lena Horne to warble "Where or When" and "Lady Is a Tramp," Gene Kelly and Vera-Ellen to do a tremendously dramatic dance routine, "Slaughter on 10th Avenue;" Cyd Charisse to both sing and dance; and Mel Torme to pipe "Blue Moon."

Tom Drake plays the serious, businesslike and homeloving Rodgers, the melodist of the pair. Rooney plays Hart, giving the role at least some partial physical verisimilitude in that his tiny stature was a near-tragedy in the lyricist's life. Biog, as a matter of fact, sticks to truth about as closely as can be presented on the screen. While details are freely reshuffled, the yarn is strikingly sound from an overall psychological view, catching Hart's early zest for life and its gradual change to a tragic chase after a happiness he couldn't achieve, a chase that led to his death in 1943 at the age of 47.

Hart, who never married, but bounded about the world, was, of course, the more colorful of the pair and the camera faithfully catches that. Rooney plays Rooney, however, rather than Hart, almost turning the role into a burlesque. Drake imbues Rodgers with the dignity and modesty of a Rodgers—if not with the spark. Film doesn't go into the break between the pair, two years before Hart's death. It was at this time Rodgers teamed with Oscar Hammerstein II in their still-existent and fabulously successful words-and-music and legit production partnership which teed off with "Oklahoma!," and has rolled up grosses, as recently recounted in VARIETY, of more than $40,000,000.

Betty Garrett, in her second film, makes little out of the role of the gal Hart can't win; Ann Sothern doesn't score much better as the ditto in Rodgers' early life, while Janet Leigh turns in a pleasing job as the eventual Mrs. R.

Arthur Freed has gilded "Words and Music" with the customary production elegance of Metro musicals and director Norman Taurog has succeeded for the most part in keeping the pace swifter than normal in these biotunepix. Robert Alton, in conceiving and staging the musical numbers, rates a tally for keeping them simple and realistically within the bounds (well almost) of the legit theatre stages on which they are supposed to take place.

Special mention is due the Technicolor processing, which appears to have reached a final maturity in the realism and lack of gaudiness of the tinting. *Herb.*

Enchantment
(ONE SONG)

RKO release of Samuel Goldwyn production. Stars David Niven, Teresa Wright, Evelyn Keyes, Farley Granger; features Jayne Meadows, Leo G. Carroll, Philip Friend, Shepperd Strudwick, Henry Stephenson, Gigi Perreau. Directed by Irving Reis. Screenplay, John Patrick, from novel by Rumer Godden; music, Hugo Friedhofer; musical direction, Emil Newman; song, Don Raye and Gene De Paul; camera, Gregg Toland; editor, Daniel Mandell. Tradeshown N. Y., Dec. 2, '48. Running time, 102 MINS.

Gen. Sir Roland Dane........David Niven
Lark Ingoldsby............Teresa Wright
Grizel Dane................Evelyn Keyes
Pilot Pax Masterson......Farley Granger
Selina Dane..............Jayne Meadows
Proutie....................Leo G. Carroll
Pelham Dane................Philip Friend
Marchese Del Laudi..Shepperd Strudwick
Gen. Fitzgerald........Henry Stephenson
The Eye............Colin Keith-Johnston
Lark (as a child)............Gigi Perreau
Rollo (os a child).............Peter Miles
Selina (as a child)........Sherlee Collier
Pelham (as a child).....Warwick Gregson
Mrs. Sampson...........Marjorie Rhodes
Uncle Bunny..............Edmond Breon
Willoughby..........Gerald Oliver Smith
Jeweler.................Melville Cooper
Lance Corporal..........Dennis McCarthy
RAF Officer..........Gaylord Pendleton
Air Raid Warden........Matthew Boulton
Corporal....................Robin Hughes
Narrator..............William Johnstone

"Enchantment" is a slow, sentimental love story tailored for the femme trade. Latter will find it a satisfactory compendium of romance, heartache and nostalgia, to draw them to the boxoffice. Film looks like a modest budgeter, and with marquee draw of David Niven and Teresa Wright, can't miss.

Slow pace and lack of action may limit word-of-mouth plug, but on the other hand there are compensating selling points to push. These would include the excellent taste of the whole production; superb photography of the late Gregg Toland (this was his last camera job), and first-rate performances by a uniformly fine cast.

Story is a tale of two generations of lovers, and plot structure has it shifting constantly back and forth from one couple to the other. Evidence of the superiority of the production lies in the fact that this constant shifting isn't at all confusing. The dovetailing is done neatly, smoothly, without jar.

Yarn is primarily the story of two lovers separated by indecision, war and family dissension. It's told in flashback, through the eyes of a new generation of lovers, who almost make the same mistake. Latter are a Canadian flyer (Farley Granger) and American ambulance driver (Evelyn Keyes) who meet in London during the recent war at the home of the girl's uncle, Gen. Dane (David Niven). He's returned from India, after years of service, to a house of memories, still yearning for the girl (Teresa Wright) he let slip out of his hands.

Although performances by Miss Wright and Niven dominate the film, portrayals by Miss Keyes and Granger also stand out for their excellence. Another noteworthy performance is that of Gigi Perreau, as the orphaned waif, Lark, brought to the Dane home. Latter's child role is one of the most appealing in years for its honesty and restraint.

Miss Wright, as Lark grown up, sparks the picture with her portrayal of the mistreated foster-sister who never finds happiness, despite the loves of three men. Niven, either in his role of dashing young Army officer, or in authentic makeup as a crotchety old general, also dominates his scenes. Jayne Meadows is properly waspish and severe as the jealous older sister; Philip Friend is warming as the older Dane brother, and Shepperd Strudwick is appealing as the Italian marchese Lark finally marries. Leo G. Carroll, as the faithful servant, and Melville Cooper, in a bit part as a jeweler, make their roles stand out.

Picture throughout has the grace and appeal of a cameo, as it centers on the nostalgic past of the Dane house, with its memories of dances, party dresses and dashing Army costumes. *Bron.*

Letter to Three Wives

Twentieth-Fox release of Sol C. Siegel production. Stars Jeanne Crain, Linda Darnell, Ann Sothern; features Kirk Douglas, Paul Douglas, Barbara Lawrence, Jeffrey Lynn. Directed by Joseph L. Mankiewicz. Screenplay, Mankiewicz, adapted by Vera Caspary from novel by John Klempner; camera, Arthur Miller; editor, J. Watson Webb, Jr.; music, Alfred Newman. Tradeshown N. Y., Nov. 23, '48. Running time, 103 MINS.

Deborah Bishop..............Jeanne Crain
Lora May Hollingsway.....Linda Darnell
Rita Phipps..................Ann Sothern
George Phipps...............Kirk Douglas
Porter Hollingsway..........Paul Douglas
Babe..................Barbara Lawrence
Brad Bishop..................Jeffrey Lynn
Mrs. Finney............Connie Gilchrist
Mrs. Manleigh............Florence Bates
Mr. Manleigh..........Hobart Cavanaugh
Kathleen......................Patti Brady
Miss Hawkins................Ruth Vivian
Sadie........................Thelma Ritter
Old Man....................Stuart Holmes
Nick................George Offerman, Jr.
Character....................Ralph Brooks
Butler.....................James Adamson
Thomasino..................Joe Bautista
Waiter......................John Davidson
Messenger....................Carl Switzer

Twentieth-Fox, which has established a potent antidote for the current boxoffice dip with its high-grossing comedies the last couple of years, has done it again with "Letter to Three Wives." Film combines the slapstick antics of such as "Sitting Pretty" with the poignant appeal that made "Miracle on 34th Street" a winner and should thus emerge as a surefire b.o. champ in all situations. Star names, while possessing some marquee values, may not be strong enough to get the ball rolling without some heavy ballyhoo by exhibs, but once that opening-day audience is snared, the word-of-mouth should be terrific.

While the picture is standout in every aspect, there are two factors mainly responsible for its overall quality. One is the unique story, adapted from a John Klempner novel by Vera Caspary and given a nifty screenplay by Joseph L. Mankiewicz, doubling as director. Idea has three young housewives in Westchester, N. Y. (much of the film was shot on location in the east), all jealous of the same she-wolf who grew up with their husbands. The "other woman" addresses a letter to all three wives, explaining that she has run away with one of their spouses but without identifying which one. Through excellently contrived flashback techniques, the audience is then given a chance to figure out which one it is, before a surprise denouement explains all.

Other standout aspect is the fine film debut of legit actor Paul Douglas, late of the Broadway legit click, "Born Yesterday." Guy is the rugged type that will appeal to the femmes and also attract unanimous approval from the males. His role in "Wives" is that of a big, blustering but slightly dumb tycoon and he really gives it a ride with some neat character shading. He's equally good in the more serious romantic moments with Linda Darnell. This single role should establish strongly his Hollywood rep but Douglas should be careful not to get typed, since this role is already somewhat similar to his part in the "Born" legiter.

Rest of the cast, under Mankiewicz's ultra-comedic directorial talents, is equally good. Jeanne Crain, Miss Darnell and Ann Sothern, as the three fraus, each turns in a job as good as anything they've done in pix to date, with Miss Darnell in particular showing hitherto unrevealed thesping talents. Kirk Douglas, playing Miss Sothern's husband, is fine as the serious - minded literature prof who can't take his wife's soap-opera writing, and Jeffrey Lynn, in his first postwar role, does okay as Miss Crain's spouse. Barbara Lawrence is good in a lesser role as Miss Darnell's kid sister. Hilarious comedy support is lent by Thelma Ritter, as an outspoken maid.

Mankiewicz's screenplay is replete with sharp dialog. He aims barbed darts at many of the country's favorite institutions, including radio commercials and overly-ambitious labor unions, and makes them score with telling effect. Story is bridged by the off-screen voice of the she-wolf, who is built into a character resembling every man's dream gal by the dialog. Mankiewicz, wisely, never shows her.

Producer Sol C. Siegel has mounted the picture in line with its overall quality. Exterior shots of the Westchester locale, including the Hudson River, the now-defunct day steamers and the Bear Mountain resort, are well-handled and the interiors look expensive. Talking sound to bridge the flashbacks make good use of the Sonovox device. Camera work, under the supervision of Arthur Miller, is fine and the various moods are pointed up neatly by Alfred Newman's background scoring. *Stal.*

Chicken Every Sunday

20th-Fox release of William Perlberg production. Stars Dan Dailey, Celeste Holm; features Colleen Townsend, Alan Young, Natalie Wood, William Frawley, Connie Gilchrist, Veda Ann Borg, William Callahan, Porter Hall, Whitner Bissell, Katherine Emery. Directed by George Seaton. Screenplay, Seaton and Valentine Davies, adapted from play by Julius J. and Philip G. Epstein, from book by Rosemary Taylor; camera, Harry Jackson; editor, Robert Simpson. Previewed N. Y., Dec. 3, '48. Running time, 91 MINS.

Jim Hefferen....................Dan Dailey
Emily Hefferen..............Celeste Holm
Rosemary Hefferen....Colleen Townsend
Geoffrey Lawson..............Alan Young
Ruth.........................Natalie Wood
George Kirby............William Frawley
Millie Moon.............Connie Gilchrist
Harold Crandall........William Callahan
Rita Kirby..................Veda Ann Borg
Sam Howell.....................Porter Hall
Mr. Robinson.............Whitner Bissell
Mrs. Lawson............Katherine Emery
Harry Bowers..............Roy Roberts
Jake Barker................Hal K. Dawson
Mr. Sawyer..................Percy Helton
Miss Gilly......................Mary Field
Oliver.....................Anthony Sydes
Charley.......................H. T. Tsiang
Mr. Lawson.................Loren Raker
Deacon Wilson.........Junius Matthews
Bartender......................Dick Ryan
Nurse.......................Ruth Rickaby
Joe.........................Edward Keane
Harris.....................Jack Kirkwood
Blaine.....................Francis Pierlot
Hart........................Wilson Wood
Process Server..........Eddie Laughton
Moving Men..Frank Meredith, Jack Daley

Nostalgia racks up one more entertainment package in "Chicken Every Sunday." Latest in the tintype relays on family life in the crinoline era which is currently affording escape from these brash postwar years, "Chicken" is an endearing and entirely amusing study of goings-on in Tucson, Ariz., circa 1900. It's an adaptation—and also an improvement—on the play which rung up a moderate Broadway success four years ago. The film retains the play's humor content but jells tighter, promising a big payoff at the wickets.

"Chicken" is greatly enriched by the retention of salty characterizations exploited in the play, particularly those of the family's fringe of boarders. Its impact is further heightened by greater concentration on the husband-wife problems, mainly pop's inability to stay put in one business. Both producer William Perlberg and director George Seaton warrant the nod for canny use of situations and little touches of business which fatten an intrinsically slight story.

Deft employment of situation brightens the film throughout. Particularly risible is mother's belief that a sub-rosa amour is surreptitiously being staged in her house between two boarders. The frequent ma-pa debates over whether strange noises are the creaking footsteps of Mr. Robinson (Whitner Bissell) climbing the backstairs on his way to Mrs. Lawson's (Katherine Emery) room are nuggets of entertainment gold. Another standout bit is mother's insistence that a room be added to the house (to add another boarder) every time the titular breadwinner embarks on one more of his complex financial schemes.

Pic takes the form of a flashback with the opening sequence showing Mrs. Hefferen (Celeste Holm) indignantly seeking a divorce for non-support. From there, story hops back 20 years to take in their wedding and trace the family's rocky path through births, ventures and its accompanying mob of boarders. There is no doubt that ma, intent on security, still dotes on pa and that the latter (Dan Dailey) is a lovable and open-handed gent who is admired by his neighbors but destined for continual emersion in the hot-water kettle.

A new mortgage on the old homestead, arranged by the head of the family after the old one had been painfully liquidated, is the reason for mother's sudden decision to cut the nuptial ties. Sentimental but not obtrusive final scene sees ma call off her lawyers. She has then become convinced that pop may be no great shakes financially but is a whale of a success as a human being.

As Mr. and Mrs., Dailey and Miss Holm aid and abet each other handsomely, catching the spirit of light by-play which is the cardinal selling point of the film. Dailey's improvident but well-meaning father is warm, likeable and totally credible. Miss Holm wangles another thesping laurel by neatly combining the urge for security with softness and the sense of being an understanding hausfrau.

Gallery of supporting roles—ranging from the quixotic to the eccentric—are sharply etched to get the keenest edge of humor. Every one of the parts is a character—not too emphasized to strain credulity but different enough to make for color, change of pace and plot development.

As noted, Seaton's lively direction is a definite contributing factor to the pic's nice ability to keep events moving. Production values harmonize to the mood of the film—not over plush but integrated soundly as background to the happenings. *Wit.*

Just William's Luck
(BRITISH)

United Artists release of A. R. Shipman-David Coplan (James A. Carter) production. Features William Graham, Garry Marsh, Jane Welsh, Hugh Cross, Kathleen Stuart. Directed by Val Guest. Screenplay, Guest, based on characters created by Richmal Crompton; camera, Leslie Rowson; music, Robert Farnon. Tradeshown N. Y., Dec. 6, '48. Running time, 88 MINS.

William	William Graham
Mr. Brown	Garry Marsh
Mrs. Brown	Jane Welsh
Robert	Hugh Cross
Ethel	Kathleen Stuart
The Boss	Leslie Bradley
The Tramp	A. E. Matthews
Emily	Muriel Aked
Ginger	Brian Roper
Douglas	James Crabbe
Henry	Brian Weske
Violet Elizabeth	Audrey Manning
Gabrielle Gaye	Hy Hazell
Hubert Lane	Ivan Hyde
Hubert's Gang	Leslie Hazell
	Peter Davis
	John O'Horo
The Boss' Gang	Michael Medwin
	John Martel
	Ivan Craig
Tonks	Michael Balfour
The Glazier	John Powe
Hubert's Mother	Joan Hickson
Gabrielle's Secretary	Patricia Cutts
Masseur	Anna Marie

"Just William's Luck" is an inept, overlong schoolboy comedy that has little possibilities in U. S. houses, aside from an occasional booking for the Saturday juve trade.

Joint venture of A. R. Shipman and David Coplan (United Artists' managing director in Britain) is merely a collection of escapades perpetrated by a group of small boys. Ringleader of the lads is William Graham, in the title role. His cutups vex his parents and disrupt family life in general. However, in the final reel he regains the good graces of his elders by aiding police to bag a band of fur thieves.

Picture will get the wrong kind of laughs from American audiences because of the downright silliness of the situations. Playing make-believe games such as impersonating King Arthur's Knights of the Round Table is something all kids do, but it's questionable whether Yank moppets will develop any vicarious interest in the proceedings due to the accent of the British players.

Acting, on the whole, is fair. Graham does well enough as the errant urchin. Garry Marsh and Jane Welsh are okay as the parents. Val Guest, who directed from his own script, fails to bring much cohesion to the film's varied sequences. Leslie Rowson's camerawork is also mediocre with a chase scene badly lensed in particular in comparison to Hollywood standards. *Gilb.*

Whispering Smith
(COLOR)

Hollywood, Dec. 3.

Paramount release of Mel Epstein production. Stars Alan Ladd, Robert Preston, Donald Crisp; features Brenda Marshall, William Demarest, Fay Holden, Murvyn Vye, Frank Faylen. Directed by Leslie Fenton. Screenplay, Frank Butler, Karl Kamb, based on novel by Frank H. Spearman; camera (Technicolor), Ray Rennahan; special effects, Gordon Jennings, Farciot Edouart; editor, Archie Marshek; music, Adolph Deutsch. Tradesshown Dec. 2, '48. Running time, 88 MINS..

Whispering Smith	Alan Ladd
Murray Sinclair	Robert Preston
Barney Rebstock	Donald Crisp
Marian Sinclair	Brenda Marshall
Bill Dansing	William Demarest
Emmy Dansing	Fay Holden
Blake Barton	Murvyn Vye
Whitey Du Sang	Frank Faylen
George McCloud	John Eldredge

Alan Ladd inherits William S. Hart's spurs in "Whispering Smith" for a wild and woolly stint typical of hoss oprys of the good old days. Back on the screen for its third go-round, the old Frank H. Spearman yarn is again a cinch for top grosses by dint of a fine cast and expensive-looking color packaging.

Bad guys shoot Ladd's steed out from under him in the bangup teeoff. Film maintains its git-up-and-go pace as Ladd waylays the gang, bumping off two of them. When Robert Preston, his best friend, offers him a job as a foreman on Preston's ranch, Ladd nixes it because he doesn't care for Donald Crisp and several other of Preston's pals. Being a railroad detective, Ladd is also suspicious about Preston being able to afford a ranch on his freight-car overseer's salary.

Bounced by the road for overstepping his bounds on a wrecking crew job, Preston openly goes into business with Crisp's gang and is on hand during a holdup in which Frank Faylen, Crisp's triggerman, murders a postoffice employe. Ladd, who had tried to save Preston's job with the road, goes gunning for his old pal, and during the melee Faylen kills Crisp because the latter doublecrossed him. In one of those tense shoot-'em-up finales, Ladd gets Preston. Indications at the windup also point to Ladd's getting Brenda Marshall, Preston's wife. He loved the gal before Preston met her, it develops.

Trouping is excellent throughout, with the excepttion of Faylen's overdrawn stooge, and the tight Frank Butler-Karl Kamb script makes the old pulp stuff seem possessed of much more importance than it ever actually had. William Demarest and Fay Holden as a frontier couple who befriend Ladd give nice balance to the frantic thesping stints required of Ladd, Miss Marshall, Preston, Crisp and Murvyn Vye.

Leslie Fenton's guidance of the strong Mel Epstein production kept proceedings galloping along at a consistently fast pace, developing situations without any dillydallying. Indoor lensing gave the cast a slightly overbaked hue but Ray Rennahan's outdoor photography is all that could be asked of a galloper. There are some exceptionally good special effects work by Gordon Jennings and Farciot Edouart. Music by Adolph Deutsch and editing by Archie Marshek generally sustain high merit of the offering. *Mike.*

One Sunday Afternoon
(SONGS-COLOR)

Hollywood, Dec. 4.

Warner Bros. release of Jerry Wald production. Stars Dennis Morgan, Janis Paige, Don DeFore, Dorothy Malone; features Ben Blue, Oscar O'Shea, Alan Hale, Jr., George Neise. Directed by Raoul Walsh. Screenplay, Robert L. Richards; from play by James Hagan; camera (Technicolor), Sid Hickox, Wilfred M. Cline; editor, Christian Nyby; songs, Ralph Blane. Tradeshown Dec. 3, '48. Running time, 90 MINS.

Biff Grimes	Dennis Morgan
Virginia	Janis Paige
Hugo Barnstead	Don DeFore
Amy Lind	Dorothy Malone
Nick	Ben Blue
Toby	Oscar O'Shea
Marty	Alan Hale, Jr.
Chauncey	George Neise

Warners has revived its successful "Strawberry Blonde" for production as a musical under the original stage title, "One Sunday Afternoon." Despite Technicolor, period costumes and addition of music, it has not the zip and entertainment value of the first screen version.

Cast headliners this time are Dennis Morgan, Janis Paige, Don DeFore and Dorothy Malone, all good, but with the exception of Miss Malone, they fail to give the film that needed extra value that came from "Blonde's" performances by James Cagney, Rita Hayworth, Jack Carson and Olivia deHavilland in the same roles.

Script is taken from the James Hagan play that deals with young love and shenanigans in New York at the turn of the century. Flashback device is used to tell the story of Biff Grimes, who lost his girl and good name to a sharpshooting friend and then finds out that, despite the friend's wealth and position, his lot in life is really happier.

Raoul Walsh, who directed "Blonde," is again at the reins on this version. His pace is slow and interest lags. There are some valiant attempts at comedy by Ben Blue and amazon Dorothy Ford that rate an occasional laugh. Songs are injected ably but, with few exceptions, fail to capture the lilt of the period. New tunes, by Ralph Blane, are the title number, "I'll Forget You," "Girls Were Made to Take Care of Boys," "Amy, You're a Little Bit Old Fashioned" and "Sweet Corner Girl."

Miss Malone gives a spark to her role of Amy, who marries Dennis Morgan on the rebound after he's spurned by Janis Paige. Latter is the strawberry blonde of the piece who winds up a nagger married to city slicker Don DeFore. Smaller roles are essayed by Oscar O'Shea, Alan Hale, Jr., and George Neise

Jerry Wald's production trappings give the film excellent mounting, but overall supervision is not up to his usual par and boxoffice returns will be only moderate at best. Costumes and expertly valued settings have been given beautiful color lensing by Sid Hickox and Wilfred M. Cline. *Brog.*

So Dear to My Heart
(COLOR-SONGS)

Hollywood, Dec. 3.

RKO release of Walt Disney production; asosciate producer, Perce Pearce. Features Burl Ives, Beulah Bondi, Bobby Driscoll, Luana Patten, Harry Carey. Directors, Hamilton Luske, Harold Schuster. Screenplay, John Tucker Battle; adaptation, Maurice Rapf, Ted Sears; from story by Sterling North; camera (Technicolor), Winton C. Hoch; editing, Thomas Scott, Lloyd L. Richardson; score, Paul Smith; songs, Larry Morey, Don Raye, Gene De Paul, Irving Taylor, Bob Wells, Eliot Daniel, Ticker Freeman, Mel Torme. Tradeshown Dec. 3, '48. Running time, 82 MINS.

Jeremiah Kincaid	Bobby Driscoll
Granny Kincaid	Beulah Bondi
Uncle Hiram	Burl Ives
Tildy	Luana Patten
Judge	Harry Carey
Storekeeper	Raymond Bond
Storekeeper's son	Daniel Haight
Trainer	Matt Willis
Village cronie	Walter Soderling

Voices for cartoon characters: John Beal, Ken Carson, Bob Stanton, The Rhythmaires.

"So Dear to My Heart" stands right at the head of the class in Walt Disney's long line of paeans to childhood. Although only 20% cartoon, it's a firstrate job of sentimental storytelling by Hollywood's master animator. Sterling North's "live" story, inevitably inviting comparison to Metro's "The Yearling" of a few seasons back, is so heartwarming that the cartoons, excellent as they are, never overshadow. It's a must for kids and adults alike.

Animation and sprightly tunes, latter sung mostly by Burl Ives in an important role, are cleverly woven into the turn-of-the-century yarn about a moppet who settles for a black ram lamb when his dreams of owning a horse like Dan Patch aren't realized. His materialistic hopes for a County Fair blue ribbon for Danny the Ram are dashed when Danny runs away. Lad promises the Almighty that if Danny is returned he'll forget about prizes and concentrate on loving the animal. Child's granny provides a switch, when the ram is found, by revealing that she promised the Lord they'd go to the Fair. She has "known Him longer," it's explained, so off they go to cop a special award.

Beulah Bondi etches a memorable Granny. Bobby Driscoll's "Jeremiah" is one for the books — completely un - selfconscious, warm, human. Ives adds immeasurably, as village blacksmith, to the Brown County, Ind., doings. Luana Patten also accounts for some hearttugs as Driscoll's playmate, and the late Harry Carey, in his last screen stint, is the understanding stock judge.

There are plenty of laughs, suspense and good oldfashioned melodrama in the John Tucker Battle screenplay. Scrapbook narration technique, with a Wise Old Owl on hand to sermonize on "doing whatcha can with whatcha got," is nicely integrated by directors Hamilton Luske (cartoons) and Harold Schuster (screenplay). Title song is most hummable of the new tunes, others being "Ol' Dan Patch," "It's Whatcha Do with Whatcha Got," "Lavender Blue," "Stick-to-It-Ivity," "County Fair," and two public domainers, "Billy Boy" and "Sourwood Mountain."

Columbus, Robert Bruce and a caricature of the ram also show up in Driscoll's four animated daydreams, stepping out of the child's scrapbook of postcards and clippings like McGuffey's Reader characters come to life. Paul Smith's score is a constant delight, and the color work is nothing short of dazzling. High credits belong to Thomas Scott and Lloyd L. Richardson, for editing; John Ewing, art direction, and to the usual lengthy lineup of Disney artists and animators. *Mike.*

My Own True Love

Hollywood, Dec. 4.

Paramount release of Val Lewton production. Stars Phyllis Calvert, Melvyn Douglas; features Wanda Hendrix, Philip Friend, Binnie Barnes. Directed by Compton Bennett. Screenplay, Theodore

Strauss, Josef Mischel; camera, Charles B. Lang, Jr.; editor, LeRoy Stone; music, Robert Emmett Dolan. Tradeshown Nov. 29, '48. Running time, 93 MINS.

Joan Clews .... Phyllis Calvert
Clive Heath .... Melvyn Douglas
Sheila Heath .... Wanda Hendrix
Michael Heath .... Philip Friend
Geraldine .... Binnie Barnes
Kittredge .... Alan Napier
Iverson .... Arthur Shields
Mrs. Peach .... Phyllis Morris
A Corporal .... Richard Webb

Trite theme about the father and son who vie for the same woman is reprised in "My Own True Love," with rehabilitation of mentally and physically marred World War II vets tacked onto the triangle for timeliness. Ponderously handled and not too strong marquee-wise, it'll have a rough road at the b.o.

Strong film fare was indicated in the weepy Yolanda Foldes novel but it just doesn't get across. Melvyn Douglas plays a middle-aged Briton whose missing son, reportedly dead in a Jap prison camp, shows up just as a romance between Douglas and Phyllis Calvert, a mustered-out member of England's ATS corps, is warming up. Philip Friend, in role of the son, also falls for the girl.

Friend appears completely uninterested in living, having lost a leg. His father can't understand his pessism, but Miss Calvert, who was also a prisoner of war, is all compassion. She learns that Friend lost his Malayan wife and child to his captors, in adition to losing his leg. She announces that the wedding is cancelled, having decided to sacrifice her own happiness rather than witness her fiance's loss of his son. Then Friend attempts suicide, she convinces him that's a quitter's way out, and he goes off to Cambridge to continue his studies. Douglas and Miss Calvert are reunited.

Shorter running time would have helped things tremendously. As it stands, film is fully 20 minutes too long. Thesping, nonetheless, is thoroughly persuasive, from principals to a drunken corporal bit elegantly played by Richard Webb. Douglas and Miss Calvert are completely convincing, and Friend is excellent. Wanda Hendrix, as Douglas' daughter, struggles valiantly in her miscast niche. There's also staunch support from Binnie Barnes as Miss Calvert's ex-cellmate, Phyllis Morris as a charwoman, and Arthur Shields and Alan Napier as Douglas' cronies.

Val Lewton production is handsomely mounted, and lensing by Charles B. Lang, Jr., pars the fog-bound, gloomy Theodore Strauss-Josef Mischel script. Compton Bennett's direction wasn't helped too much by an unimaginative editing job. *Mike.*

Family Honeymoon

Universal release of John Beck-Z. Wayne Griffin production. Stars Claudette Colbert, Fred MacMurray. Directed by Claude Binyon. Screenplay, Dane Lussier, based on Homer Croy book; camera, William Daniels; editor, Multon Carruth; music, Milton Schwarzwald, Frank Skinner, David Tamkin; asst. director, Frank Shaw; special effects, David S. Horsley. Tradeshown N. Y., Dec. 6, '48. Running time, 90 MINS.

Katie Armstrong Jordan ... Claudette Colbert
Grant Jordan .... Fred MacMurray
Minna Fenster .... Rita Johnson
Arch Armstrong .... William Daniels
Zoe .... Gigi Perreau
Charlie .... Jimmy Hunt
Abner .... Peter Miles
Aunt Jo .... Lillian Bronson
Phyllis .... Hattie McDaniel
Fred .... Chill Wills
Mrs. Abercrombie .... Catharine Doucet
Richard Fenster .... Paul Harvey
Mr. Webb .... Irving Bacon
Taxi-driver .... Chick Chandler
Gas Station Attendant ...... Frank Jenks
Tom Roscoe .... Wally Brown

"Family Honeymoon" is one of those pleasant little family comedies, as the title indicates, which represents no major extraordinary talent expenditure, save for the co-stars, resolves no major issues, but emerges as a wholesome hour-and-a-half film divertissement. It will please generally, and should do a lot to perpetuate the Claudette Colbert-Fred MacMurray marquee values.

She's the attractive widow with three lively children and MacMurray's the college prof more familiar with botanical behaviorism but completely ignorant of childhood behaviorism. The fun stems from the five of them, including the 9 and 10-year-old boys and 7-year-old Zoe, going on the titular "Family Honeymoon." A combination of circumstances eliminates the bride's aunt as the stay-at-home guardian of the three children; likewise Hattie McDaniel includes herself out.

The honeymoon trip to the Grand Canyon is replete with genuine, unforced comedy situations running the gamut from the kids being left behind, or otherwise missing; the desire of the new stepfather to make himself acceptable to the three headstrong children; the other natural problems of adjustment; the travail of day-coach travel from this whistle-stop, where the errant children get lost; the backwoods folks' strange behaviorism (including a funny scene with the farmer set to trap the chicken-stealers, and another about skinning a skunk.) In between, MacMurray is sarcastically referred to as "that man" by the children; Rita Johnson, a predatory babe, snafus the honeymoon at the Grand Canyon; but it all comes out fine with a welcome-home party which looks headed for a real honeymoon.

The scripting is a compact job and director Claude Binyon, reunited with a couple of his former Paramount stars, Miss Colbert and MacMurray, for whom he has scripted in former years, handles the sum total with fine restraint. Underplaying the broader moments makes for a more solid comedy pattern all the way. The touches are natural and human; there's nothing intrusively spicy as the frustrations, attendant to the stars consummating their honeymoon, pile up.

The support likewise is in good key, even including the vamp who doesn't get too much out of bounds, although the personable Miss Johnson is a fetching eyeful for any honeymooning or non-honeymooning male. Paul Harvey, as her father, serves as a good brake in these sequences. Lillian Bronson is excellent as the understanding aunt (whose broken leg in a pre-wedding ceremony almost cancels the honeymoon trip). Gigi Perreau, Jimmy Hunt and Peter Miles are competent as the obstreperous children. *Abel.*

Scott of the Antarctic

(Color)

BRITISH

GFD release of Ealing Studios-Michael Balcon production. Stars John Mills; features Derek Bond, Harold Warrender, James Robertson Justice, Reginald Beckwith. Directed by Charles Frend. Screenplay by Walter Meade, Ivor Montagu; additional dialog by Mary Hayley Bell. Camera (Technicilor), Jack Cardiff, Osmond Borradaile, Geoffrey Unsworth; Editor, Peter Tanner; music, Vaughan Williams. At Empire, London, Nov. 29, '48. Running time, 111 MINS.

Capt. R. Scott .... John Mills
Kathleen Scott .... Diana Churchill
Dr. E. A. Wilson .... Harold Warrender
Oriana Wilson .... Anne Firth
Capt. L. Oates .... Derek Bond
Lieut. H. R. Bowers ... Reginald Beckwith
Taff Evans .... James Robertson Justice
Lieut. Teddy Evans .... Kenneth More
W. Lashly .... Norman Williams
P. O. T. Crean .... John Gregson
Surgeon E. Atkinson .... James McKechnie
Charles S. Wright .... Dennis Vance
P. O. P. Keohane .... Larry Burns
Dimitri .... Edward Lisak
Cecil Meares .... Melville Crawford
Bernard Day .... Christopher Lee
F. J. Hooper .... John Owers
Lieut. H. Pennell .... Bruce Seton
Herbert Ponting .... Clive Morton
E. McKenzie .... Sam Kydd

It would have been difficult to have found a more fitting subject for presentation at the Royal Command Film Performance than "Scott of the Antartic." The inspiring story of the ill-fated expedition to the South Pole has tremendous cinematic possibilities. In color, it should not only have been a magnificent eye-filling spectacle but also a stirring adventure. But the director's affinity to the documentary technique has robbed the subject of much of its intrinsic drama. While it's a picture which will enhance Britain's prestige, it doesn't fall into top category of boxoffice successes, and its appeal will be restricted to audiences interested in a chapter of British history.

Pic's greatest asset is the superb casting of John Mills in the title role. Obviously playing down the drama on directorial insistence, Mills' close resemblance to the famous explorer makes the character come to life.

Beginning with the preliminary arrangements for the expedition and Scott's tour of the country to raise necessary finance, the picture traces the adventures of the crew through the Antartic wastes, reaching their goal only to find that Amundsen had already planted the Norwegian flag on the South Pole. It is a grim journey, almost unrelieved in intensity, depicting the continuous battle against the elements, with agonizing incidents of the terror of the Antartic wastes.

Scott's discovery that he had been beaten in the race to the South Pole should have been a piece of poignant and moving drama. Instead, the five members of the expedition look very resolute, and very British, and philosophically begin the long trail home. Although depicted with fidelity, the agonies of the explorers on their homeward trek are presented with inadequate dramatization, with the result that the audience isn't emotionally affected when first one and then another succumbs to the Arctic terror.

From a spectacular point of view the production merits full credit. Except perhaps in a few opening shots, the technicolor is magnficent, and pictures the Antartic wastes with all their terrifying beauty.

Not only Johni Mills as Scott, but all other members of the expedition soft-pedal their respective parts. Harold Warrender, as Dr. Wilson, the scientist; Derek Bond, as Captain Oates, and Reginald Beckwith, as Lieut. Bowers, play their respective parts on a low but even key. They don't attempt to make glory out of their portrayals of real life heroes but choose to behave in the way the actual characters were believed to have behaved. They set the standard for the acting, which is faithfully followed by other members of the cast. *Myro.*

An Old-Fashioned Girl

(SONGS)

Eagle Lion release of Vinson production. Stars Gloria Jean; features Jimmy Lydon, John Hubbard, Frances Rafferty. Directed by Arthur Dreifuss. Adaptation and screenplay by Dreifuss, McElbert Moore, from Louisa May Alcott's story of same name; camera, Philip Tannura; editor, Arthur A. Brooks; songs by Charles Previn, Moore, Bobby Worth, Al Sendry. Tradeshown in N. Y., Dec. 2, '48. Running time, 82 MINS. ..

Polly Milton .... Gloria Jean
Tom Shaw .... Jimmy Lydon
Mr. Sydney .... John Hubbard
Frances Shaw .... Frances Rafferty
Maud Shaw ...... Mary Eleanor Donahue
Mrs. Shaw .... Irene Ryan
Mr. Shaw .... Douglas Wood
Trix Parker .... Barbara Brier
Miss Mills .... Claire Whitney
Emma Davenport .... Rosemary LaPlance
Miss Perkins .... Quenna Norla
Belle .... Shirley Mills
Irma .... Saundra Berkova
Farmer Brown .... Milton Kibbee

This is an immature adaptation of Louisa May Alcott's romantic story about the working girl who made good and shamed her rich relatives. "An Old-Fashioned Girl" is for audiences who like the "Little Women" type of yarn, since it's in much the same vein. Strictly for the duals.

Story of the poor girl who teaches music in Boston for a livelihood rather than depend on rich distant relations in the same city is entirely in the Alcott 19th century tradition of modes and manners. The little teacher gets shoved around, belittled and even temporarily thwarted of her lone romance. But she eventually gets her man.

Miss Jean's excellent singing goes far to smooth the rough spots. She does best with "Where" and "Kitchen Serenade," but the latter is all but murdered by some juvenile antics. With Miss Jean's maturity is revealed acting development, too. Saundra Berkova, as one of Miss Jean's pupils, impresses with F. Mendelssohn's "Violin Concerto." She combines looks with skill as a violinist.

Besides Miss Jean, John Hubbard breathes some life into this wooden vehicle as a successful businessman. Jimmy Lydon appears overly stupid as the college student. Frances Rafferty does well enough as the snobbish relative. Mary Eleanor Donahue, her kid sister, hints at promise in comedy relief.

Arthur Dreifuss' direction shapes up as too leisurely although the pace improves in the last half of the picture. He and McElbert Moore did the screenplay. Philip Tannura's lensing is a bright spot *Wear.*

Here Come the Huggetts

(BRITISH)

London, Nov. 25.

GFD release of J. Arthur Rank-Gainsborough (Betty E. Box) production. Features Jack Warner, Kathleen Harrison, Jane Hylton, Susan Shaw, Petula Clark. Directed by Ken Annakin. Screenplay by Mable and Denis Constanduros, Muriel and Sydney Box, Peter Rogers. Camera, Reg Wyer; editor, Gordon Hales. At Leicester Square, London, Nov. 24, '48. Running time, 93 MINS.

Father .... Jack Warner
Mother .... Kathleen Harrison
Jane .... Jane Hylton
Susan .... Susan Shaw
Pet .... Petula Clark
Jimmy .... Jimmy Hanley
Harold Hinchley .... David Tomlinson
Diana Hopkins .... Diana Dors
Peter Hawtrey .... Peter Hammond
Gowan .... John Blythe
Grandma .... Amy Veness
Mrs. Fisher .... Doris Hare
Mr. Campbell .... Clive Morton

First of a new family series from the Gainsborough Studios, "Here Come the Huggetts" is in ineffective production which will achieve little in the home market and less abroad.

Entire story about the various

Huggett family members, is built around a series of trivial adventures which fail to click. Scripting is bad, both in plot and dialog.

Kathleen Harrison and Jack Warner, both of whom are first rate artists, don't have a chance here. The three daughters played by Jane Hylton, Susan Shaw and Petula Clark have already proved they can do much better. Other members of the cast struggle with the inadequate material. *Myro.*

Miniature Reviews

"Siren of Atlantis" (UA). Fantastic adventure yarn with sharp exploitation pegs.

"Last of the Wild Horses" (SG). Good western for the action market.

"The Valiant Hombre" (UA). Routine Cisco Kid adventure.

"Because of Eve" (Indie). Childbirth clinical film strictly for the classroom.

"Savage Brigade" (French) (Indie). Charles Vanel in too talky, romantic meller; sub-par for French.

Siren of Atlantis

United Artists release of Seymour Nebenzal production. Stars Maria Montez, Jean-Pierre Aumont, Dennis O'Keefe. Directed and edited by Gregg G. Tallas. Screenplay, Rowland Leigh, Robert Lax; additional dialog, Thomas Job; based on novel by Pierre Benoit; camera, Karl Struss; music, Michel Michelet. Tradeshown N. Y., Dec. 10, '48. Running time, 75 MINS.

Antinea	Maria Montez
Andre St. Avit	Jean-Pierre Aumont
Jean Morhange	Dennis O'Keefe
Blades	Henry Daniell
Le Mesge	Morris Carnovsky
Cortot	Alexis Minotis
T'nit Zerga	Milada Mladova
Lindstrom	Allan Nixon
Eggali	Russ Conklin
Cegheir	Herman Boden
Hand Maiden	Margaret Martin

"Siren of Atlantis" is a fantastic adventure offering enough hot exploitation angles and a fair name cast for good boxoffice play outside of key firstruns. Pic is incredible in its discovery of a lost continent with hooded barbarians and a savage princess, but runs off with a sufficiently fast pace to satisfy the average customer in the market for wholly escapist fare.

Although a modest budgeter, production is marked by firstrate interiors and outdoor desert and mountain backgrounds. In fact, the physical dress of this pic, particularly the settings in the mythical Atlantis, lends a solidity to an otherwise lightweight yarn. Dialog and the thesping is frequently wooden, but director Gregg Tallas, who also edited, wisely keeps the accent on an exotic mood and melodramatic movement.

Yarn centers around a company of French Foreign Legionaires who find their way into Atlantis, a sunken civilization in Africa, but can't get out. Following in the footsteps of several other white men who entered this realm, Jean-Pierre Aumont, an officer, becomes daffy over the ruling queen, Maria Montez. Latter is a cruel and willful hussy who, as a practical joke, sets Aumont and his pal, Dennis O'Keefe, at each others throats in a jealous rage. Making his way back to his legion post, Aumont admits killing O'Keefe but is acquitted because nobody believes him. Production code requirements are satisfied when Aumont, still lovestruck, dies in the sand dunes while trying to find his way back to Atlantis.

In central role, Miss Montez is set off to best advantage by gauzy garb and handles her lines with appropriate suggestiveness. Aumont, however, falls short of a persuasive performance due largely to stilted lines and partly to over-acting. O'Keefe, as an ascetic army officer, also has difficulty in a strange part. Henry Daniell, as the queen's counsellor, does well in stock piece of sadism, while Morris Carnovsky and the rest of the supporting players appear only in walk-on roles.

Herm.

The Valiant Hombre

United Artists release of Philip N. Krasne production. Stars Duncan Renaldo, Leo Carillo; features John Litel, Stanley Andrews. Directed by Wallace Fox. Screenplay, Adele Buffington; based on character created by O. Henry; camera, Ernest Miller; editor, Martin Cohen; music, Albert Glasser. Tradeshown N. Y., Dec. 13. Running time, 60 MINS.

Cisco	Duncan Renaldo
Pancho	Leo Carrillo
Lon Lansdell	John Litel
Sheriff Dodge	Stanley Andrews
Paul Mason	John James
Linda Mason	Barbara Billingsley
Old Prospector	"Lasses" White

O. Henry's character creation, the Cisco Kid, isn't as colorful as he used to be. During the past few years, the films depicting the exploits of this fictional south-of-the-border Robin Hood, have become fairly stylized. In "The Valiant Hombre," the hard riding of Duncan Renaldo as the central character, the comedics of Leo Carillo as Pancho his constant companion, nor the villainy of John Litel, are sufficient to move this opus out of the classification of a secondary feature.

This time, Cisco becomes involved because of his attempt to locate the missing master of a cute dog. It develops that the hound's owner is a mining engineer who suddenly drops out of circulation after discovering a gold strike. Cisco and Pancho eventually locate the missing miner, after a sprightly gun-fest.

Renaldo turns in routine job as the Kid himself, while Carillo is held down by inept comedy material. Even his rendition of a comedy song dies because of weak lyrics. Litel, is competent as the villainous saloon keeper, while John James and Barbara Billingsley do well as the missing engineer and his sister, respectively.

Photography in "Hombre" is better than average. Several stills show up fleetingly with an arty quality, while the indoor scenes are well-lighted. Director Wallace Fox has kept the yarn moving and Albert Glasser has contrived an okay score. *Jose.*

Last of the Wild Horses

Hollywood, Dec. 11.

Screen Guild release of Carl K. Hittleman production. Stars James Ellison, Mary Beth Hughes, Jane Frazee; features Douglas Dumbrille. James Millican, Reed Hadley, Olin Howlin. Directed by Robert L. Lippert. Original screenplay, Jack Harvey; camera, Benjamin Cline; editor, Paul Landres. Previewed Dec. 9, '48. Running time, 84 MINS.

Duke Barnum	James Ellison
Terry Williams	Mary Beth Hughes
Jane Cooper	Jane Frazee
Charlie Cooper	Douglas Dumbrille
Sheriff Harrison	James Millican
Riley	Reed Hadley
Remedy Williams	Olin Howlin
Curly	Grady Sutton
Rocky Rockford	William Haade
Hank	Rory Mallison
Ferguson	Stanley Andrews

"Last of the Wild Horses" takes a bit too much footage to tell its story, but otherwise measures up as a good western for the action market. Further trimming of its 84 minutes would give it more zip and make it fit easier for twin bills.

Film has strong scenic values. Footage was lensed in Sepia Tone in the Rogue River Valley of Southern Oregon, and the backgrounds lend sturdy support. Story is more or less standard but handling helps smooth the more obvious points.

There's a touch of novelty in displaying film credits against shots of the finale fight, helping to establish action early before story flashes back to explain what the fisticuffs are all about. Plot deals with feud between a large rancher and his small neighbors, instigated by the big spreads crooked foreman. Trouble is over ranch's continual raids on a wild horse herd, with smaller outfits fearing herd will be depleted.

Into that setup comes James Ellison, who teams with the small ranchers against Douglas Dumbrille. Latter is murdered when he discovers the foreman's dirty work and Ellison is blamed. There's a trial, Ellison escapes and hunts down Reed Hadley, the heavy. They come together in a good rough and tumble brawl in a hayloft, making for a punchy finale.

Ellison shows up well as the hero, and Hadley is a slick villain. Femme interest is capably carried by Mary Beth Hughes and Jane Frazee, while considerable comedy values are injected by Olin Howlin. James Millican is a believeable sheriff. Others fill their parts well.

Robert L. Lippert functioned as executive producer and director of the Carl K. Hittleman production. He keeps the story on the move and, with the exception of over-length, has delivered acceptable western fare. Benjamin Cline did the excellent lensing. *Brog.*

Because of Eve

International Pictures release of William Daniels production. Features Joseph Crehan. Directed by Howard Bretherton. Story and screenplay, Larry Allen, Walter A. Lawrence; camera, Arthur Martinelli, Elmer Moss; editor, Dede Allen; narration, Sam Balter, Hy Averback. Previewed in N. Y., Dec. 9, '48. Running time, 67 MINS.

Doctor West	Joseph Crehan
Sally Stevens	Wanda McKay
Bob Stephens	John Parker
Nicholas Wilde	Robert Leaver

Just why this should be given any spot on theatre screens is difficult to comprehend. The picture, or portions of it, might be shown to college classes, only most schools of higher learning already cover the angles touched on in this film. Only in educational institutions, there is no attempt to disguise charts, slides, 16m pictures, etc., as theatrical fare.

This subject can only appeal to the uneducated—and even for them the theatre seems a poor place to have the subject of illegitimate children, venereal disease, some phases of married life and child birth paraded in front of them. And in such blatant form. The theatre, generally conceded to be a place of entertainment, seems an odd place for such a "clinical" picture. The average exhibitor will find little in this to further his reputation as a showman.

Film is being offered under the auspices of the Women's Research Guild, which is sponsoring it as part of its program to use every available media to combat juvenile delinquency.

Excuse is made that the picture will halt juvenile delinquency. Actually, the reaction probably will be to whet the appetites, especially among the people it would attract —those ignorant of social hygiene. This sordid story has the prospective husband and wife discussing with the family medico: (1) that she has previously had an illegitimate child, (2) that he has had venereal disease, (3) that both were innocent. It builds up from these premises with charts, stilted poses, operating room scenes, animated diagrams, etc. Some of the still shots of VD examples are particularly unsuited for the theatre. Nor are the detailed closeups of two infants born in a hospital.

Acting, directing and plot are sub-par. *Wear.*

Savage Brigade
(FRENCH)

Distinguished Films release of Franco-London Films production. Stars Charles Vanel. Directed by Marcel L'Herbier. Screenplay, Arnold Lipp; camera, Gerard Perrin; editor, Walter Klee. At Apollo, N. Y., week Dec. 2, '48. Running time, 87 MINS.

Col. Kalatjeff	Charles Vanel
Marie Kalatjeff	Vera Korene
Grand Duke	Roger Duchesne
Natasha	Lisette Lanvin
Boris Mirsky	Troubetskoy
Maximovitch	Jean Galland

(In French; English Titles)

The French producers apparently were just marking time when they turned out this odd little piece. It has suspense, some first-rate portrayals and snatches of action—yet "Savage Brigade" is a highly disappointing French display. Hence, it looks good for only modest returns in a few arty houses. Marcel L'Herbier, who has done some topflight French films about love and duty, is way below par with this picture.

Main reason for production's failure to jell is that the suspense is piled on too heavily. And the excuse for keeping the patrons up in the air so long is not particularly logical. French-made mainly concerns Russians and an affair between two Cossack officers of the first World War. Film has duel delayed 20 years because of war's outbreak.

There's also too much verbiage, with Charles Vanel, as the colonel, piling it on heavily. He's not that good.

Vanel is closely pursued for top laurels by Troubetskoy, the romantic lieutenant, who's always being sought by the comely damsels. Vera Korene, the colonel's wife, makes the earlier passages lead one to think the picture will prove exciting.

Film has strong production values but they seem wasted here. Gerard Perrin's camera job is not up to par. *Wear.*

Il Miracolo
(The Miracle)
(ITALIAN)

Rome, Dec. 7.

CEIAD release of Roberto Rossellini production. Stars Anna Magnani. Directed by Rossellini. Screenplay. Rossellini and Tullio Pinelli from original by Federico Fellini; camera, Aldo Tonti; music, Renzo Rossellini; editor, Eraldo Da Roma. At Rivoli, Rome. Running time, 37 MINS.

This short opus of Roberto Rossellini is touching and daring. "The Miracle" is the story of a pregnancy of a mentally-unbalanced shepherdess. Compromised by an unknown man whom she mistook for Saint Joseph, she believes she's going to give birth to the Savior. While the subject has been treated delicately it has enough to ruffle the Legion of Decency. In any case, it's strictly for the art houses.

Portraying the shepherdess, Anna Magnani is mocked and derided by the peasants. However, she ecstatically and heroically withstands their insults and when Christmas comes goes to the church steeple where she's delivered. Tale is brief, but is packed with sincerity and suspense.

In "The Miracle" Rossellini discloses a new side to his talent, tending to prove that even if his stories change, his originality and poetic gift remain constant. Strong help has been given him, nevertheless, by Miss Magnani, who looks both squalid and sublime as the shepherdess character requires. Camerawork of Aldo Tonti and Renzo Rossellini's score are adequate. Picture has been acquired

---

for U. S. distribution by Mayer & Burstyn. *Quat.*

Ladri Di Biciclette
(Bicycle Thieves)
(ITALIAN)

Rome, Dec. 6.

ENIC release of Vittorio De Sica production. Directed by De Sica. Screenplay, De Sica, Oreste Biancoli, Suso Cecchi D'Amico, Adolfo Franci, Gherardo Gherardi, Gerardo Guerrieri, Cesare Zavattini; story by Zavattini from a novel by Luigi Bartolini; camera, Carlo Montuori; music, Alessandro Cicognini; editor, Eraldo Da Roma. At Metropolitan and Barberini, Rome. Running time, 90 MINS.

Antonio	Lamberto Maggiorani
Maria	Lianella Carell
Bruno	Enzo Staiola
The Lady	Elena Altieri
The Thief	Vittorio Antonucci
Bajocco	Gino Saltamerenda
Amateur actor	Fausto Guerzoni

Vittorio De Sica, who made "Shoe Shine," has a rare gift of those queer productions which are practically nil for the domestic boxoffice, but terrific abroad. With a couple of scenes cut, this looks like an ideal U. S. entry.

This is the drama of a man whose bicycle has been stolen. He needs it for his bill-poster work, so that to retrieve it originally from the pawnbroker's shop when he finally got his job after long unemployment, he'd been compelled to pawn his bed sheets instead. Story is the search of the man and his child for the stolen bicycle, which represents the family food. It involves a chase of the thief through the city—a funny, dramatic, desperate chase which becomes bitterly significant when the hopeless hero, tries to steal a bicycle himself.

De Sica has taken a long, rich gallery of characters who, even when disagreeable, as they generally are, don't arouse dislike. Cast is headed by three non-professionals. Antonio Maggiorani hasn't the thesping ability of a seasoned player but he lives his part authentically. Lianella Carell does nicely as Maggiorani's wife (she's a newspaperwoman). Enzo Staiola's performance as the boy measures up to the highest standards. Class A lensing by Carlo Montuori, authentic settings by Antonio Traverso and impressive score by Alessandro Cicognini contribute to making the film exceptional. *Quat.*

Nach dem Sturm
(After the Storm)
(SWISS-AUSTRIAN)

Zurich, Nov. 17.

Elite Film release of Cordial Film production. Directed by Gustav Ucicky. Produced by Willy Wachtl. Screenplay, Peter Wyrsch, based on novol by Carl Zuckmayer; camera, Konstantin Tschet, Otto Ritter; music, Wal-Berg; editor, Herman Haller. At Urban, Zurich. Running time, 105 MINS.

Barbara von Trentini	Marte Harell
Father	Erwin Kaiser
Major Michael Sinclair	Nicholas Stuart
Thomas Esterer	Leopold Rudolph
Capt. Virginia Jenkins	Adrienne Gessner
Aichinger	Max Haufler
Gretel	Maria Schell

(In German and English)

This new Swiss-Austrian pic has been in production for more than six months and includes in its cast Viennese and Swiss players, as well as an American debutant, Nicholas Stuart. Lensing was done in Zurich, and in the Tessin, Italian Switzerland. U. S. chances are limited.

The story, by Carl Zuckmayer, is about a girl in post war Austria, who falls in love with an American major of the Occupation Army. The story offers good possibilities for a dramatic film, but is treated very conventionally and without

---

any personal touch. Director Gustav Ucicky did hardly more than routine work here. Also his choice of players wasn't a happy one.

Camera work by Konstantin Tschet is very good. The music by Wal-Berg contains an impressive piano concerto and a pop tune, "Somewhere. Some Time," which looks like a hit. *Mezo.*

Aux Yeux Du Souvenir
(To the Eyes of Memory)
(FRENCH)

Paris, Dec. 1.

Pathe release of Joseph Bercholz production. Directed by Jean Delannoy. Stars Michele Morgan, Jean Marais, Jean Chevrier. Screenplay by D'Henri Jeanson and Georges Neveux; music by George Auree; camera, Robert Le Febvre. At the Maragny, Paris, Nov. 30, '48. Running time, 140 MINS.

Claire Magny	Michele Morgan
Jaques Forestier	Jean Marais
Pierre Aubry	Jean Chevier
Paul Marcadour	Robert Nuonveau
Hostess	Colette Mars

This film is bound to make a lot of money in France, but b.o. reception abroad is questionable. Pic has enough stars, hokum and cliches to make it comparable to any good American melodrama. But unfortunately a foreign language picture has to be better than good to get a decent play in the states. It has to be an exceptional pix, and "Souvenir" is not exceptional.

The story is based on an occurence last year when an Air France plane flew from Rio to Dakar with two engines conked out. Using this to start with, the writers have written a corny love story to give Jean Marais, France's newest heart throb, and Michele Morgan, who has been in better pictures, an opportunity to make love to each other.

The picture is put together very well. Marais is fine, and Miss Morgan hasn't hurt Air France's public relations any.

Jean Delannoy, who directed "Symphony Pastorale" and "Eternal Retour," has done a good job, and Robert Le Febyre has used his cameras well. *Buch.*

Intill Helvetets Portar
(Till the Doors of Hell)
(SWEDISH)

Stockholm, Nov. 26.

Svensk Filmindustri release of Studio Film production. Stars Lars Hanson, Gunnel Brostrom, Olof Bergstrom; features Nils Dahlgren, Anna Lindahl, Arne Ragneborn, Georg Funkqvist, David Eriksson, Viktor Andersson, Erik Rosen. Directed by Goran Gentele. Screenplay, Sven Stolpe, Gosta Stevens; camera, Martin Bodin; music, John Hult. At Roda Kvarn, Stockholm. Running time, 98 MINS.

Victor Barring	Lars Hanson
Eva Barring	Gunnel Brostrom
Arne Hedberg	Olof Bergstrom
Dr. Barring	Nils Dahlgren
Margit Barring	Anna Lindahl
Bengt Barring	Arne Ragneborn
Dr. Kanzel	Georg Funkqvist
Ewers	David Eriksson
Ekman	Viktor Andersson
Doctor	Erik Rosen
Controller	Harry Ahlin
Chairman	Sven Bergvall

As its second production since its formation this year, Studio Film has turned out a meritorious picture with an atomic energy background. "Intill Helvetets Portar" is a well-written, well-directed entry for both the Scandinavian and world markets. Cast, too, does a bang-up job.

Story concerns Lars Hanson, who wins the Nobel prize for his work in atomic research. The award spurs him on in his tasks. However, when his assistants realize the frightful effect an atomic bomb might have upon world civilization, they attempt to stop him

---

from producing such an instrument.

Although Hanson hasn't appeared in a film for three years, his delineation of the scientist is a finely-etched piece of work. Under Goran Gentele's ace direction Gunnel Brostrom and Olof Bergstrom also rack up topflight performances as the assistants. Thesping of supporting players measure up. Cameraman Martin Bodin ably lensed the film. Much of the footage, incidentally, was shot at a prominent laboratory near Stockholm. *Winq.*

Foreign Films

"Janne Wangmans Bravader" ("The Adventures of Janne Wangman") (SWEDISH). Europa Film production and release. Stars Adolf Jahr; features Arthur Rolen, Ake Engfeldt, Rut Holm, Dagmar Olsson. Anders Borje. Directed by Gunnar Olsson. Screenplay, Karl Johan Radstrom, based upon novels by J. R. Sundstrom; camera, Karl-Erik Alberts. At Saga, Stockholm. Running time, 84 MINS.

Produced in Sweden last summer, "Janne Wangmans Bravader" is a fair comedy about a man's problems. Picture is typically Swedish, and while likely to do good business in Scandinavia, its chances abroad are meagre. Camcrawork of Karl-Erik Alberts is outstanding. *Winq.*

Miniature Reviews

"Act of Violence" (M-G). Melodrama as grim as title. Excellently done but for theatregoers who like stark drama.

"Whiplash" (WB). Formula fight game meller with Dane Clark, Alexis Smith, Zachary Scott; okay b.o.

"Angel of the Amazon" (Rep). Lusty exploitation entry for the action markets.

"Loaded Pistols" (Col). Gene Autry turns range detective for good results.

"Jungle Jim" (Col). Animal thriller with the Weissmuller name to carry it for juve patrons.

"Trouble Makers" (Mono). Excellent comedy - whodunit for the Bowery Boys fans; good supporter for twin bills.

"Look Before You Love" (GFD). Corny British romance, with Margaret Lockwood. Limited appeal.

"The Peaceful Years" (Pathe). British documentary on the 1919-39 period; good, but limited in appeal.

"Portrait From Life" (GFD). Poignant British-made drama of DP's, starring Mai Zetterling; will draw.

"Look Out Sister" (Astor). All-Negro hoss opr'y starring Louis Jordan; should rack up strong grosses.

Act of Violence

Hollywood, Dec. 18.
Metro release of William H. Wright production. Stars Van Heflin, Robert Ryan; features Janet Leigh, Mary Astor, Phyllis Thaxter. Directed by Fred Zinnemann. Screenplay, Robert L. Richards; story, Collier Young; camera, Robert Surtees; score, Bronislau Kaper; editor, Conrad A. Nervig. Tradeshown Dec. 15, '48. Running time, 82 MINS.
Frank R. Enley...............Van Heflin
Joe Parkson................Robert Ryan
Edith Enley................Janet Leigh
Pat ....Mary Astor
Ann ....Phyllis Thaxter
Johnny...................Berry Kroeger
Gavery...................Taylor Holmes
Fred ....Harry Antrim
Martha.................Connie Gilchrist
Pop ....Will Wright

The grim melodrama implied by its title is fully displayed in "Act of Violence." It is strong meat for the heavy drama addicts, tellingly produced and played to develop tight excitement. While its almost unrelieved grimness will find favor with ticket buyers who go for stark action, reception by fans who like lighter escapism in their film entertainment will be spotty.

The playing and direction catch plot aims and the characterizations are all topflight thesping. Van Heflin and Robert Ryan deliver punchy performances that give substance to the menacing terror of the Robert L. Richards script, taken from a story by Collier Young. Although not likely for wide popular reception, picture and the trouping click strongly, critically, to stand out in its class.

Fred Zinnemann's direction craftily builds the mood of tension that features the plot's manhunt. Heflin is the pursued and Ryan is the relentless, wouldbe killer. Story concerns two vets. Heflin has come out of the war with honors while his comrades, all but one, were killed in a Nazi prison camp. Ryan, crippled and vengeful, pursues Heflin to make him answer for betraying his buddies. Film realistically depicts the breakdown of Heflin's morale, clearly presents his reasons for the betrayal under the stress of war, and carries through to the tragic end that has him paying for his one past error

by giving his life for Ryan.

It's grim business, unrelieved by lightness, and the players belt over their assignments under Zinnemann's knowing direction. Janet Leigh points up her role as Heflin's worried but courageous wife, while Phyllis Thaxter does well by a smaller part as Ryan's girl. A standout is the brassy, blowzy femme created by Mary Astor—a woman of the streets who gives Heflin shelter during his wild flight from fate.

Taylor Holmes and Berry Kroeger show up strongly as ghoulish underworld characters who figure importantly in Heflin's eventual death. Harry Antrim, Connie Gilchrist and Will Wright complete the most able cast.

Productionwise, William H. Wright never allows the picture to deviate from the grim depiction of fear and revenge and its affects on man. The gripping mood of suspense is furthered by Bronislau Kaper's score and the ace lensing by Robert Surtees. Brog.

Whiplash
(SONGS)

Warner Bros. release of William Jacobs production. Stars Dane Clark, Alexis Smith, Zachary Scott; features Eve Arden, Jeffrey Lynn. Directed by Lew Seiler. Screenplay, Maurice Geraghty, Harriet Frank, Jr.; adaptation, Gordon Kahn; story, Kenneth Earl; songs, Dick Redmond, Fausto Curbelo, Johnny Camacho, Mick David; camera, Peverell Marley; editor, Frank Magee; musical director, Leo F. Forbstein. Tradeshown N. Y., Dec. 20, '48. Running time, 91 MINS.
Michael Gordon............Dane Clark
Laurie Durant............Alexis Smith
Rex Durant.............Zachary Scott
Chris ....Eve Arden
Dr. Arnold Vincent........Jeffrey Lynn
Sam ....S. Z. Sakall
Terrance O'Leary............Alan Hale
Costello ....Douglas Kennedy
Tex Sanders ....Ransom Sherman
Duke Carney ....Fred Steele
Trask ....Robert Lowell
Harkus ....Don McGuire

"Whiplash" is a formula fight game meller that'll pack a moderately good punch at the boxoffice. Name cast, slick production and merchandisable factors in the pug - underworld - nitery plot push this film over the hurdle of a routine screenplay. Pic, however, misses that knockout impact because of its switch away from the recent trend to ring realism back to synthetic toughness and heavy sentimental dosages.

A variation on the pix in which the fighters were either violinists or writers, this yarn has Dane Clark as an artist who's also handy with his dukes. Opening with a slashing fight in Madison Square Garden, N. Y., major portion of the film is narrated via flashback as Clark sits groggy in his corner wondering how it all happened. It started on the California coast where Clark, wielding his brushes, meets a mysterious femme, Alexis Smith, who runs out on him after a brief but intense romance.

He traces her back to New York where she's a singer in a nitery operated by her husband, Zachary Scott, and his mobsters. Scott, a former pug who was crippled in an auto crash, is hipped on managing a fighter who can fulfill his own yen to become world champion. Clark is the man for the job, and after some fight sequence montages, turns into a snarling killer in the ring out of pique at Miss Smith's apparent double-dealing. Meantime, Scott, getting wind of a repressed romance between his wife and his fighter, arranges to get Clark's head knocked off in a big bout. But Clark, despite a brain concussion, kayoes his opponent, and after Scott gets his

fatal comeuppance from Miss Smith's brother, both he and the gal renew their clinch in California's clime.

Numerous fight sequences hypo excitement but are handled in the contrived style in which every punch is a haymaker and every round sees at least a dozen knockdowns. Hokey atmosphere of the fights is also heightened by the obvious disparity of weights between Clark, who's a middleweight, and some of his opponents, who look like heavyweights.

Performances are generally marred by the cast's failure to dig deeply into their parts. Clark registers okay in the action scenes, but falters in the emotional register. Miss Smith turns in a creditable job, also neatly handling one good number, "Just For Now," in her nitery stint. Another rhythm number, "The Gal With a Spanish Drawl," is a throwaway. Scott and Jeffrey Lynn, as the brother, are pat in stock roles, while S. Z. Zakall contributes some effective comedy touches. Herm.

Angel on the Amazon

Republic release of John H. Auer production. Stars George Brent, Vera Ralston, Brian Aherne, Constance Bennett; features Fortunio Bonanova, Alfonso Bedoya, Gus Schilling, Richard Crane. Directed by Auer. Screenplay, Lawrence Kimble; original story, Earl Felton; camera, Reggie Lanning; editor, Richard L. Van Enger; music, Nathan Scott. Tradeshown, N. Y., Dec 15, '48. Running time, 86 MINS.
Jim Warburton............George Brent
Christine Ridgeway.......Vera Ralston
Anthony Ridgeway........Brian Aherne
Dr. Karen Lawrence..Constance Bennett
Sebastian Ortega........Fortunio Bonanova
Paulo ....Alfonso Bedoya
Dean Hartley ....Gus Schilling
Johnny MacMahon........Richard Crane
Jerry Adams..............Walter Reed
Frank Lane ....Ross Elliott
Dr. Jungmeyer......Konstantin Shayne

Republic has a lusty exploitation entry in "Angel on the Amazon." Fortified with an "eternal youth" theme, exciting jungle shots plus names of George Brent, Vera Ralston, Brian Aherne and Constance Bennett, picture seems assured of top returns in the action markets. A strong woman's angle is also present for the femme trade.

As screenplayed by Lawrence Kimble from Earl Felton's original, the story incorporates a number of cliches, and its situations are often telegraphed far in advance. However, these shortcomings might well be overlooked due to the film's pithy tropical scenes and colorful international background.

With locales skipping from the Amazon, to svelte Rio de Janeiro, the Riviera and finally Pasadena, Cal., "Angel" has been wrapped in well-appointed mountings by producer John H. Auer. Brazilian jungle is the favorite lair of Miss Ralston, who seeks its confines in an effort to soothe her remorse over the death of her daughter.

One of Miss Ralston's routine hunting expeditions is enlivened by a nearby plane crash. Piloted by George Brent, the transport has Miss Bennett, a doctor, among its passengers. Those aboard are saved by the huntress, and Brent subsequently falls for his rescuer. However, it later develops that Miss Ralston is already wed to Aherne, and her pristine beauty is merely the result of a cessation of her aging processes due to shock.

Another incident causes the "eternal youth" to be supplanted be greying hair and a lined phiz. For the fadeout Aherne deftly explains the whys and wherefores behind the change to Brent, who conveniently shifts his attentions to Miss Bennett. While Brent occa-

sionally is forthright as the lothario, his overall interpretation of the role lacks conviction. Miss Ralston is decorative in the dual part. Aherne does a standard portrayal in handing out fatherly advice, and Miss Bennett is okay. Other players give sturdy support.

Although Auer's production is nicely conceived, his direction fails to measure up. In trying to pack too much into the footage, the film's continuity and pacing suffer. Camerawork of Reggie Lanning is first rate as are most technical credits. Withal, solid showmanship and exploitation will sell this one. Gilb.

Loaded Pistols
(SONGS)

Hollywood, Dec. 18.
Columbia release of Armand Schaefer production. Stars Gene Autry, Barbara Britton; features Chill Wills, Jack Holt, Russell Arms, Robert Shayne, Vince Barnett. Directed by John English. Story and screenplay, Dwight Cummins, Dorothy Yost; camera, William Bradford; editor, Aaron Stell. At Vogue, Hollywood, Dec. 15, '48. Running time, 77 MINS.
Gene Autry ....Gene Autry
Mary Evans ....Barbara Britton
Sheriff Cramer ....Chill Wills
Dave Randall..............Jack Holt
Larry Evans.............Russell Arms
Don Mason ....Robert Shayne
Sam Gardner............Vince Barnett
Jake Harper...........Leon Weaver
Bill Otis ....Fred Kohler
Jim Hedge ....Clem Bevans
Rancher ....Sandy Sanders

Adult fans of Gene Autry should find "Loaded Pistols" to their liking. While the stock western ingredients are there, film treats them with more adult flavor. There's still enough of the shoot-'em-up action to satisfy the kiddies, though, so "Pistols" should find a ready acceptance in the tune-oater market.

Autry sings five numbers, two of them reprised, but musical spotting is so expertly done that action movement is never slowed. That's a major credit in itself for an oatuner. Title song is one of the numbers reprised and "Pretty Mary" is the other. "Blue Tail Fly," "When the Bloom Is On the Sage" and "A Boy from Texas" round out excellent musical moments.

The Dwight Cummins-Dorothy Yost script pictures Autry as an astute cowpoke who shields a boy wanted for murder while he tracks down the real killer. A shrewd sheriff and the murderous villain inject the menace that keeps Autry's manhunt from being too easy. Chase scenes are fast and thrills good. The climax, Autry tricks the killer into revealing himself, ties all loose threads together neatly.

There are some out of the ordinary western characterizations by the cast, all of which help to keep it from being run of the mill. Barbara Britton does well opposite Autry and Chill Wills' sheriff portrayal is a decided assist. Robert Shayne, heavy; Jack Holt, Russell Arms, and a neat prospector bit by Clem Bevans are factors on the credit side.

John English's direction of the Armand Schaefer production is competent in keeping footage on the move and interest whetted. Sepia-toned lensing adds quality to scenic backgrounds. Brog.

Jungle Jim

Hollywood, Dec. 18.
Columbia release of Sam Katzman production. Stars Johnny Weissmuller; features Virginia Grey, George Reeves, Lita Baron, Rick Vallin, Holmes Herbert. Directed by William Berke. Story and screenplay, Carroll Young; based on cartoon feature, "Jungle Jim"; camera,

Lester White: editor, Aaron Stell. At Vogue, Hollywood, Dec. 15, '48. Running time, 71 MINS.

Jungle Jim .... Johnny Weissmuller
Hilary Parker .... Virginia Grey
Bruce Edwards .... George Reeves
Zia .... Lita Baron
Kolu .... Rick Vallin
Commissioner Marsden .. Holmes Herbert
Chief Devil Doctor .... Tex Mooney

"Jungle Jim" is completely juvenile and for that reason should get by in the Saturday matinee market. While filling its purpose satisfactorily for the kiddie field, producers might have attracted a broader market had they given it a bit more adult interest.

Picture is a blend of animal stock shots and typical jungle thriller story. Each has a maximum of interest for the youthful film fan. Plot boils down to almost a Tarzan in clothes, making it fit aptly to the Johnny Weissmuller ability in the adventure field.

Chattering monkeys, roaring lions, stampeding elephants and slithering crocodiles furnish both comedy relief and thrills as Jungle Jim leads a safari on a hunt for a jungle pyramid for treasure and a witch doctor's poison that might prove useful in fighting infantile paralysis. Jungle Jim fights a leopard, a lion, a sea serpent and witch doctors with expected agility while looking after his human charges on the trek.

Virginia Grey fits uneasily into role of femme scientist and George Reeves doesn't have enough footage as the heavy who tries to do the safari dirt so he can seize the treasure. Lita Baron is an attractive jungle miss and Rick Vallin is adequate as the native guide.

This is the first of a new series for Weissmuller, which are to be based on the cartoon character. Sam Katzman's production values are good for release intentions, as is William Berke's direction. Lensing, editing and other technical credits are capable. *Brog.*

Trouble Makers

Hollywood, Dec. 17.

Monogram release of Jan Grippo production. Features Leo Gorcey, Huntz Hall, Gabriel Dell, Helen Parrish, Lionel Stander, John Ridgely, Frankie Darro, Billy Benedict. Directed by Reginald Le Borg. Screenplay, Edmond Seward, Tim Ryan, Gerald Schnitzer; original story, Gerald Schnitzer; camera, Marcel LePicard; editor, William Austin. At Grauman's Chinese, Hollywood, Dec. 16, '48. Running time, 66 MINS.

Slip .... Leo Gorcey
Sach .... Huntz Hall
Gabe Morino .... Gabriel Dell
Ann Prescott .... Helen Parrish
Hatchet Moran .... Lionel Stander
Silky .... John Ridgely
Feathers .... Frankie Darro
Whitey .... Billy Benedict
Chuck .... David Gorcey
Butch .... Benny Bartlett
Hennessey .... Fritz Feld
Louie .... Bernard Gorcey
Capt. Madison .... Cliff Clark
Jones .... William Ruhl
Lefty .... John Indrisano
Tailor .... Charles LaTorre
Morgue Keeper .... David Hoffman
Gimpy .... Pat Moran
Sam .... Herman Cantor
Newsboy .... Buddy Gorman
Hotel Clerk .... Maynard Holmes
Doorman .... Charles Coleman

"Trouble Makers" is a better than average Bowery Boys cutup from the Monogram studio. A whodunit with comedy, neatly scripted to please in the series' regular market, it will have no trouble making its way among the general situations.

Leo Gorcey and Huntz Hall are the prime trouble-makers, playing their lead roles a bit straighter than usual. Pair operate a sidewalk telescope business and when they witness a murder in a hotel blocks away their troubles commence. They enlist a cop friend to help smoke out the mystery. There are frameups, gambling raids and the menace of gang murder always present to keep suspense backing the comedy deliveries before Gorcey, Hall and cop pal Gabriel Dell clean up the mystery.

Two leads' antics are perfectly tuned to please their fans and others will find plenty to chuckle at, too. Dell and Helen Parrish carry off romantic implications, and excellent villainy is supplied by Lionel Stander, John Ridgely, Frankie Darro and others. Fritz Feld sharpens character of harassed hotel clerk.

Jan Grippo's production supervision ably realizes on necessary values to put this one over, and Reginald LeBorg's direction gives the script a snappy pace. Lensing and editing also are good. *Brog.*

Look Before You Love
(BRITISH)

London, Dec. 7.

GFD release of J. Arthur Rank-John Corfield production. Stars Margaret Lockwood, Griffith Jones, Norman Wooland. Directed by Harold Huth. Screenplay by Reginald Long, from story by Ketti Fring; camera, Harry Waxman, Harold Haysom; editor, John D. Guthridge; music, Bretton Byrd. At Leicester Square, London, Dec. 7, '48. Running time, 96 MINS.

Ann Markham .... Margaret Lockwood
Charles Kent .... Griffith Jones
Ashley Morehouse .... Norman Wooland
Bettina Colby .... Phyllis Stanley
Fosser .... Maurice Denham
Miller .... Frederick Piper
Johns .... Bruce Seton
Emile Garat .... Michael Medwin
Dowager .... Violet Farebrother

This is an overlong and somewhat corny love story that gives Margaret Lockwood a sympathetic role after her many "wicked lady" characterizations, in which she has been so successfully typed in the past. Its appeal will be limited to her fans, and admirers of Griffith Jones, on whose fatal charm the credulity of the story hinges. It may gratfy the out-of-town popular audiences, but its chances of success in any metropolis are scant.

While holding a responsible job at the British Embassy in Rio, Ann falls for Charlie, a good-looking wastrel with dubious credentials. She only learns on her wedding day that he is wanted for fraud, cardsharping etc., in different parts of the world. Secure in her love, and Charlie's promise of reform and getting an honest job, she persuades him to return to England. Trading on their steamship friendship with a young millionaire whom he has fleeced, Charlie gets $40,000 paid to clear out and leave Ann free for a divorce.

Mawkish sentiment vies with improbable situations, and acting is patchy and often stilted. Jones is the epitome of graceful villainy, and Norman Wooland is an agreeable millionaire. Best character cameo is turned in by Michael Medwin as a cockney "Frenchman." *Clem.*

The Peaceful Years
(BRITISH)

London, Dec. 14.

Pathe production and release. Produced by Peter Baylis. Narrated by Emlyn Williams; commentators, Stuart Hibberd, Maurice Denham, James McKechnie, Peter Madden, Ann Codrington, Betty Hardy. Music, Hal Evans. At New Gallery, London, Dec. 13, '48. Running time, 66 MINS.

Period between the two world wars was an eventful one in British history, and while not entirely insular in outlook, this documentary record of historic highlights is, of necessity, dominantly British. The period from 1919 to 1939, which saw the rise of fascism in Germany, Italy and Spain, the invasion of Manchuria, civil war in Spain, and terror in Abyssinia, could hardly be described as the "Peaceful Years." But this compilation picture gives a reasonably faithful, if inadequate, account of these turbulent times and although necessarily sketchy, has historic interest which may appeal to limited, but interested, audiences in the states.

Highlights of the period have been carefully selected by producer Peter Baylis and the pic is introduced and described by Emlyn Williams, aided by a number of experienced commentators. Many of the events depicted are of international interest, such as the Lindbergh crossing of the Atlantic, the 1929 Wall Street crisis, and Haille Selassie's appeal for his country at Geneva.

This is a page of history effectively told with the aid of well-preserved library shots and enlivened by a brisk and intelligent commentary. *Myro.*

Portrait From Life
(BRITISH)

London, Dec. 16.

GFD release of J. Arthur Rank-Gainsborough (Anthony Darnborough) production. Stars Mai Zetterling, Robert Beatty, Patrick Holt, Guy Rolfe, Herbert Lom. Directed by Terence Fisher. Screenplay by Frank Harvey, Jr., and Muriel and Sydney Box. Camera, Jack Asher; editor, V. Sagovsky; music, Benjamin Frankel. At Odeon, Marble Arch, London, Dec. 15, '48. Running time, 90 MINS.

Hildegarde .... Mai Zetterling
Lawrence .... Guy Rolfe
Ferguson .... Patrick Holt
Hendlmann .... Herbert Lom
Campbell Reid .... Robert Beatty
Lieutenant Keith .... Peter Murray
Menzel .... Arnold Marle
Mrs. Skinner .... Thora Hird
Coroner .... Eric Messiter
Supervisor .... Cyril Chamberlain

An unusual theme, strong dramatic angles, finely drawn characters and a first-rate performance by Mai Zetterling, are the features which combine to make "Portrait from Life" a much-better-than-average British picture. At home its boxoffice appeal is a certainty, and its interest is sufficiently wide to merit general support from American audiences.

In the main it is a simple story. A British officer on leave from Germany, and jilted by his girl friend, visits an art exhibition in Piccadilly and is fascinated by the portrait of a displaced person. His fascination is shared by an Austrian professor who is convinced that the girl in the picture is his daughter. The likeness between the portrait and a photograph of the professor's wife is so marked that the officer, on his return to Germany, carries out an intensive search through the various camps and eventually finds the girl. But she is in the camp with her "parents" and it takes a lot of insistence on the part of the officer before he establishes the fact that her camp father is a wanted Nazi and her real parent is the professor in London.

On cold analysis the plot may not mean a great deal, but in its development emphasis has been placed on the dramatic qualities and there is no belittling the success which has been achieved on this score. Story establishes a high degree of credibility and notwithstanding the contrived ending proves to be satisfying entertainment.

Very largely this is due to a flawless portrayal by Miss Zetterling who proves herself to be complete mistress of every situation. Hers is a moving performance, rich in appreciation and understanding and in keeping with the high tradition she has established in the past year or two. Her acting inevitably imposes a strain on other members of the cast, but Guy Rolfe as the officer who finds her, Robert Beatty as the artist who paints the original portrait, Herbert Lom as the Nazi who pretends to be her father, and Arnold Marle as the professor, prove themselves worthy of the test.

Atmosphere of the displaced persons' camp is every bit the genuine article and this is reinforced by the intelligent use of German dialog as and when necessary. It does not detract from following the story but adds conviction to the general theme. *Myro.*

Look Out Sister
(ALL-NEGRO MUSICAL)

Astor Pictures release of R. M. Savini (Berle Adams) production. Stars Louis Jordan, Suzette Harbin, Monte Hawley; features Glenn Allen, Tommy Southern, Jack Clisby. Directed and edited by Bud Pollard. Screenplay, John E. Gordon; camera, Carl Berger; songs, Louis Jordan, Leroy Hickman, Dallas Bartley, Don Wilson, Wilhelmina Grey, Sid Robbins, Benny Carter, Irving Gordon, Lee Penny, Dick Miles, Walter Bishop, Fleecie Moore, Ben Lorre, Jeff Dane. At Apollo, N. Y., week Dec. 17, '48. Running time, 64 MINS.

Louis Jordan .... Himself
Betty Scott .... Suzette Harbin
Mack Gordon .... Monte Hawley
Billy .... Glenn Allen
Cactus .... Tommy Southern
Pistol Pete .... Jack Clisby
Officer Lee / The Sheriff .... Maceo Sheffield
Dancer .... Peggy Thomas
Bathing Beauty .... Louise Franklin
Girl Exhibition Divers .... Anice Clark, Dorothy Seamans

Bob Scott and Louis Jordan's T-6

Trumpet .... Aaron Izenhall
Tenor Saxophone .... Paul Quinchette
Piano .... Wm. Doggett
Bass .... Wm. Hadnott
Drums .... Chris Colombus
Guitar .... James Jackson

A low-budget all-sepian entry, "Look Out Sister" is primed for okay b.o. results in houses whose patronage is predominantly Negro. Louis Jordan makes a fine marquee lure and his fans should be amply satisfied with the 11 tunes the saxophonist and his Tympany Six beat out in the course of the unreeling.

Story lends itself to humor for, through a "dream," Jordan fancies himself on a dude ranch. Whereupon the plot assumes the aspect of a standard western with "Two Gun" Jordan saving the hacienda from ignominious foreclosure in the nick of time.

More than half the film hangs upon Jordan's musikin' and he's in there solid with such aces as "Caldonia," "Don't Burn the Candle at Both Ends," and sundry blues numbers, among others. Picture, itself, comes off as a broad satire on the oaters although that may or may not have been the original intention of producer Berle Adams. Chase scene with Jordan clumsily bouncing on a nag with heavy, Monte Hawley, in hot pursuit is particularly ludicrous.

Tops in his musical chores, Jordan also rates a nod for his cowboy stint. Suzette Harbin shines as the heart interest, while Hawley is amusing as the baddie. Bob Scott, as co-owner of the ranch, registers well in contribbing some genuine horsemanship. Supporting players are adequate under Bud Pollard's routine direction. While production values are negligible, Jordan combo endows "Sister" with all the boxoffice appeal it needs. Novelty of a sepia western may also generate some interest. *Gilb.*

Parade Du Temps Perdu
(Parade of Lost Time)
(FRENCH)

Paris, Dec. 9.

Gaumont release of Cinephonic production, starring Noel Noel, Bernard Blier, Marguerite Deval, Jean Tissier. Directed by Jean Dreville. Written by Noel. Camera, Burel; music, Cloerec. At Gaumont, Paris. Running time, 90 MINS.
The Lecturer................Noel Noel
The Bores...Bernard Blier, Jean Tissier, R. Blancard, H. Cremieux, P. Frankeur

If France is looking for a picture to dub in English, this is it. Since a good part of the pic is a running commentary with not much mouth movement on the part of the actors, it shouldn't be difficult to make an English-speaking v e r s i o n. Fortunately it would be worth somebody's time and effort because it's a very funny film. It's b.o. material outside the art houses.

Noel Noel is to France what Charlie Chaplin is to the U. S. The comedian has scripted a fantasy about boring people that he and Moliere have known. In a lecture to the theatre audience Noel introduces these bores in several hilarious scenes. The mixture of slapstick and satire is very effective and the pace is very fast.

Since all the bores are universal characters it's just as easy to identify them in English as in French and the interspersed lectures with Noel literally throwing himself in and out of every scene is good fun and good cinema. All types of special effects are brought into play including puppets, television sets, blackboards and film cameras.

Noel has written a clever script full of wit and sense, and his acting is socko. Bernard Blier and the supporting cast are very funny. Jean Dreville's directing is tricky and well done. L. H. Burel on the cameras and Jean Feyte on the montage have done excellent work.
Buch.

Miniature Reviews

"Command Decision" (MG). Sock war film from the Broadway legit hit. Big name cast headed by Clark Gable, Walter Pidgeon, Van Johnson.

"Adventures of Don Juan" (Color) (WB). Swaggering costumer. Big b.o. prospects.

"Portrait of Jennie" (SRO). Romantic fantasy with special interest for the class filmgoer.

"Force of Evil" (Enterprise-MG). Static film on numbers racket; some b.o. from strong exploitation and John Garfield name.

"The Dark Past" (Col). William Holden in fine psychological thriller.

"Angel in Exile" (Rep). Action yarn with underlying religious motif for supporting situations.

"Gun Smugglers" (RKO). Average Tim Holt western. Okay for Saturday matinee trade.

"Incident" (Mono). Nicely done thriller for supporting positions in general release.

"Highway 13" (SG). Action melodrama p l o t t e d around trucking industry. OK dualer.

"What's On Your Mind" (Documentary) (Indie). Compilation of psycho-analytical shorts doesn't belong in average theatre; very mild even in arty houses.

Command Decision

Hollywood, Dec. 23.

Metro release of Sidney Franklin (Gottfried Reinhardt) production. Stars Clark Gable, Walter Pidgeon, Van Johnson, Brian Donlevy, Charles Bickford, John Hodiak. Edward Arnold; features Marshall Thompson, Richard Quine, Cameron Mitchell, Clinton Sundberg, Ray Collins. Directed by Sam Wood. Screenplay, William R. Laidlaw, George Froeschel; based on play by William Wister Haines; camera, Harold Rosson; music, Miklos Rozsa; editor, Harold F. Kress. Tradeshown Dec. 22, '48. Running time, 111 MINS.
Brig.-Gen. K.C. "Casey" Dennis ....
...........................Clark Gable
Maj.-Gen. Roland Goodlow Kane ....
.........................Walter Pidgeon
T/Sgt. Immanuel T. Evans Van Johnson
Brig.-Gen. Clifton I. Garnet Brian Donlevy
Elmer Brockhurst ....Charles Bickford
Col. Edward Martin ..... John Hodiak
Congr. Arthur Malcolm . Edward Arnold
Captain Bellpepper Lee..............
........................Marshall Thompson
Major George Rockton.... Richard Quine
Lieut. Ansel Goldberg Cameron Mitchell
Maj. Homer V. Prescott Clinton Sundberg
Major Desmond Lansing ... Ray Collins
Colonel Earnest Haley..Warner Anderson
Major Belding Davis ......John McIntire
Congressman Stone ....Moroni Olsen
James Carwood .... John Ridgely
Captain Lucius Malcolm Jenks ....
..........................Michael Steele
Congressman Watson ..... Edward Earle
Lieut. Col. Virgil Jackson Mack Williams
Major Garrett Davenport . James Millican

"Command Decision" is a literate war drama, presented with a class touch that means plenty of box-office dollars will come its way. It tells of World War II from the top level of heavy brass, but with a slant that makes the star-wearers human. There's no romance, and none is needed, as femmes still will be lured by the potent marquee flash furnished by the multiple male names.

"Decision's" footage is long, but the story comes through with a sock that grips. The stars, and even the minute bits, turn in worthy thesping to keep everything about the film on the class level.

In transferring the Broadway legit hit to the screen, producer Sidney Franklin and director Sam Wood have made it a faithful version. It's still laid, principally, in the GHQ of a bomber command and little attempt is made to broaden that essential locale. Where it gets its added sweep is in the lucid music score (which bows only to the bomber's roar) and in the graphic lensing that gives the story a movement not possible on stage.

Plot, by now familiar, deals chiefly with top level warfare; what makes generals tick and how they go about their deadly game; the political toadying necessary to keep the battles, and loses, coming through on schedule. The GI, too, will appreciate the human touch in the clay feet that the big brass wear.

Clark Gable walks off with a picture in which everyone of the cast stands out. His is a believeable delivery, interpreting the brigadier-general who must send his men out to almost certain death with an understanding that bespeaks his sympathy with the soldier—brass or dogface.

Walter Pidgeon is the real big brass—the trafficker with politicos, wheedling and conniving to keep his Air Force supplied with planes and men despite homefront cries against losses. He has never been better, even managing to make a mid-pic scene where he goes into a long history of the AF, its aims and ambitions, something more than a tiresome solo reading.

Van Johnson gives the GHQ-based tech sergeant just the proper touch of life to make it a sparklingly cynical reading of the thoughts and regard the real GI had for his bosses. It's a solid shift from the light, rah-rah boy type of role that first gave him prominence. There's a sock performance by Brian Donlevy as an armchair opportunist that figures importantly in the final evaluation of the playing.

Charles Bickford, the correspondent; John Hodiak, Gable's pilot friend; and Edward Arnold, a blabbermouth congressman, complete the star list. Individually, they boost their own stock and round out the top performances that are a distinguishing part of the film. In featured roles, Marshall Thompson has one scene as a drunken, mush-mouthed southern that is a wow; Clinton Sundberg's prissy public relations officer is a gem, and Richard Quine, Cameron Mitchell, and Ray Collins add to the general merit of the trouping.

Sam Wood's direction is articulate in endowing the film with the toughness of war and, at the same time, a sentiment that will click with the femmes. There are no phony touches in the drive for drama. Backing the potent script by William R. Laidlaw and George Froeschel, taken from the William Wister Haines play, is the polish of production knowhow furnished by Sidney Franklin's guidance in association with Gottfried Reinhardt.

The technical credits score solidly. Miklos Rozsa's score; the outstanding lensing by Harold Rosson; special effects by A. Arnold Gillespie and Warren Newcombe; authentic bomber command air base scenes and the other contributions are top craftsmanship that help in making this one a strong money film.
Brog.

Adventures of Don Juan
(Color)

Hollywood, Dec. 21

Warner Bros. release of Jerry Wald production. Stars Errol Flynn, Viveca Lindfors; features Robert Douglas, Alan Hale, Romney Brent, Ann Rutherford, Robert Warwick, Jerry Austin, Douglas Kennedy. Directed by Vincent Sherman. Screenplay, George Oppenheimer, Harry Kurnitz; from story by Herbert Dalmas; camera (Technicolor), Elwood Bredell; editor, Alan Crosland, Jr.; music, Max Steiner. Tradeshown Dec. 21, '48. Running time, 110 MINS.
Don Juan....................Errol Flynn
Queen Margaret.........Viveca Lindfors
Duke de Lorca..........Robert Douglas
Leporello ....Alan Hale
King Phillip III............Romney Brent
Donna Elena ....Ann Rutherford
Count De Polan.........Robert Warwick
Don Sebastian ....Jerry Austin
Don Rodrigo........Douglas Kennedy
Donna Carlotta........Jeanne Shepherd
Catherine .... Mary Stuart
Lady Diana ....Helen Westcott
Don Serafino ....Fortunio Bonanova
Lord Chalmers........Aubrey Mather
Duenna ....Una O'Connor
Captain Alvarez ....Raymond Burr
Catherine's Husband.......Tim Huntley
Innkeeper ....David Leonard
Don De Córdoba............Leon Belasco

A number of swashbuckling costume films have reached the screen recently. "Adventures of Don Juan" measures up among the best of them and is earmarked to return bright grosses. It adopts a tongue-in-cheek attitude towards the derringdo adventuring of its costumed hero without minimizing dashing high action.

The loves and escapades of the fabulous Don Juan are particularly adapted to the screen abilities of Errol Flynn and he gives them a flare that pays off strongly. The s. a. factor, as forthright as production code restrictions and reasonable good taste will permit, will play an important part in selling this one, along with the equally potent full measure of swordplay action that is dished out.

Amatory fires start burning with the opening scene and their smoldering presence is continually felt as Vincent Sherman's brisk direction puts the hero through his adventurous paces. It's all good fun, entertainment-wise, with escapist touches that stimulate the imagination.

Jerry Wald has wrapped the film in the eye-filling beauty of Technicolor and has assured other values that keep his production average high. The period piece lends itself to lush costumes, large-scale sets and massive mob scenes, giving it a bigness that will attract the boxoffice dollar.

Plot depicts Don Juan adventuring in England. Opening has him escaping an angry husband, only to become immediately involved again with another femme. This time his wooing ruins a state-arranged wedding and he's shipped off to Spain to face his angry monarch. The queen assigns him to post of instructor in the royal fencing academy, he discovers a plot against her majesty, instigated by a conniving prime minister. He takes time out from fencing and wooing to save the royal house and film ends with him off in pursuit of another pretty face.

Viveca Lindfors co-stars as the queen and she brings a compelling beauty to the role. It should help boost her stock among domestic film fans. Character is played straight and she skillfully portrays a queen who reluctantly, then openly, admits her attraction for the charming Don Juan. Her expreserve face and eyes say more than the dialog.

Sherman's direction captures the flavor of the script by George Oppenheimer and Harry Kurnitz, based on a story by Herbert Dalmas. He gives it fluid movement that excellently paces the high spots of duels and mass fights. Top action is reached in the deadly duel between Flynn and Robert Douglas, the crooked prime minister, climaxing with a long leap down a huge flight of castle stairs. It's spectacular stuff to wind up the many fights that spice the footage.

Douglas makes a perfect menace, playing the role suavely for major effect. Alan Hale turns in his usual competent work as Flynn's chief henchman and Romney Brent gets across the weak character of the king. Ann Rutherford, Robert Warwick, Jerry Austin, palace dwarf; Douglas Kennedy, Fortunio Bonanova, David Leonard, excellent as an innkeeper; and a bevy of costumed femme lookers aid in putting this one over.

Topnotch lensing in Technicolor by Elwood Bredell, an expert job of editing by Alan Crosland, Jr., the Max Steiner music score, and other technical contributions are first class. *Brog.*

Portrait of Jennie

(SONG-COLOR)

Hollywood, Dec. 21.

SRO release of David O. Selznick (David Hempstead) production. Stars Jennifer Jones, Joseph Cotten, Ethel Barrymore; features Lillian Gish, Cecil Kellaway, David Wayne, Albert Sharpe, Henry Hull, Florence Bates, Felix Bressart, Clem Bevans, Maude Simmons. Directed by William Dieterle. Screenplay, Paul Osborn, Peter Berneis; from book by Robert Nathan; adaptation, Leonard Bercovici; camera (with Technicolor sequence), Joseph August; special effects, Clarence Slifer; score, Dimitri Tiomkin; song, Bernard Herrmann; editor, Gerald Wilson. Previewed Dec. 23, '48. Running time, 86 MINS.

Eben Adams.... Joseph Cotten
Miss Spinney.... Ethel Barrymore
Mr. Matthews.... Cecil Kellaway
Jennie Appleton.... Jennifer Jones
Mrs. Jekes, the landlady.... Florence Bates
Mrs. Bunce, her friend.... Esther Somers
Gus O'Toole.... David Wayne
Mr. Moore.... Albert Sharpe
The Policeman.... John Farrell
The Old Doorman.... Felix Bressart
Clara Morgan.... Maude Simmons
Mother Mary of Mercy.... Lillian Gish
Captain Caleb Cobb.... Clem. Bevans
Another Old Mariner.... Robert Dudley
Eke.... Henry Hull

"Portrait of Jennie" is an unusual, artistic screen romance of the calibre to attract boxoffice attention in the class engagement. The showmanly ingredients usually associated with the David O. Selznick banner abound throughout, assuring bigtime exploitation. All phases of the production will be talked about, and plenty, which means hefty ticket sales in the top situations.

The story of an ethereal romance between two generations is told with style, taste and dignity. However, its very spiritual quality, no matter how tastefully done, lacks the earthy warmth needed to spellbind when it goes into the general situation where the exploitable tricks of multiple-sized screen and sound will not be available.

Figured on the class basis, though, "Jennie" is a thespian and technical delight. The performances are gifted with a make-believe skill that rings with quality and will attract the carriage trade looking for the unusual in story. Productionwise, there is the spectacular use of a twice normal size screen and added auditorium loudspeakers (for special engagements) to added noisy emphasis to a magnificently staged hurricane. It's a stunt that will be talked about.

Star value, plus the unusual angles, make the film a cinch for its class engagements, and the marquee names can't be discounted in attracting some initial trade when picture's general release comes up. Jennifer Jones' performance is a standout. Her miming ability gives a quality to the four ages she portrays—from a small girl through to flowering woman. Ingenuity in makeup also figures importantly in sharpening the portrayal.

William Dieterle has given the story sensitive direction and his guidance contributes considerably toward the top performances from the meticulously cast players.

It deals simply with an artist living in New York in the '30s. His work lacks depth and it is only when he meets a strange child in the park one day that inspiration to paint people comes. The elfish quality of the child stimulates a sketch. It is appreciated by art dealers and he builds the child's physical being in his mind until the next time she appears he sees her as a girl just entering her teens. Her growth moves into college years and then as a graduate while he, meantime, is discovering she is a person who has been dead for years. Before Jennie's preordained death in a Maine coast hurricane, he completes a portrait that is to bring him fame. Eventual realization of his strange visitation, and of the fact that woman and love are eternal, comes after he nearly loses his life in a storm that duplicates the one in which his beloved met her physical end.

Joseph Cotten endows the artist with a top performance, matching the compelling portrayal by Miss Jones. Ethel Barrymore, Cecil Kellaway, David Wayne, Henry Hull, Clem Bevans, Felix Bressart and every individual in this distinguished cast add their outstanding talents to the class worth of this film entry.

The photography by Joseph August is boffo, perfectly matching the artistic intents of the entire production. Of equal worth are the special photographic effects by Clarence Slifer, plus process and miniature photography by Paul Eagler. These technical credits, and the moving score by Dimitri Tiomkin, based on Claude Debussy themes, put the crowning touch of polish on the script by Paul Osborn and Peter Berneis, taken from Robert Nathan's book. There is a haunting song, ably cleffed by Bernard Herrmann, titled simply "Jennie's Song," that makes itself remembered. *Brog.*

Force of Evil

Hollywood, Dec. 24.

Metro release of Bob Roberts (Enterprise) production. Stars John Garfield; features Thomas Gomez, Marie Windsor, Beatrice Pearson. Directed by Abraham Polonsky. Screenplay, Polonsky and Ira Wolfert; based on novel, "Tucker's People," by Wolfert; camera, George Barnes, Jack Warren; music, David Raksin; editor, Art Seid. Tradeshown Dec. 20, '48. Running time, 78 MINS.

Joe Morse.... John Garfield
Doris Lowry.... Beatrice Pearson
Leo Morse.... Thomas Gomez
Ben Tucker.... Roy Roberts
Edna Tucker.... Marie Windsor
Fred Bauer.... Howland Chamberlin
Hobe Wheelock.... Paul McVey
Juice.... Jack Overman
Johnson.... Tim Ryan
Mary.... Barbara Woodell
Bunty.... Raymond Largay
Wally.... Stanley Prager
Frankie.... Beau Bridges
Badgley.... Allan Mathews
Egan.... Barry Kelley
Ficco.... Sheldon Leonard
Mrs. Bauer.... Jan Dennis
Mrs. Morse.... Georgia Backus
Two and Two.... Sid Tomack

"Force of Evil" fails to develop the excitement hinted at in the title. It's a missout for solid melodramatic entertainment, and will have to depend upon exceptionally strong exploitation and the value of the John Garfield name for boxoffice.

Makers apparently couldn't decide on the best way to present an expose of the numbers racket, winding up with neither fish nor fowl as far as hard-hitting racketeer meller is concerned. A poetic, almost allegorical, interpretation keeps intruding on the tougher elements of the plot. This factor adds no distinction and only makes the going tougher.

Garfield, as to be expected, comes through with a performance that gets everything out of the material furnished, but it's not enough to give this one more than a mild ride at the ticket window. Film also "introduces" Beatrice Pearson but she garners no great honors for herself. Others suffering from script and directorial confusion are Thomas Gomez, Roy Roberts, Marie Windsor and Howland Chamberlin.

Abraham Polonsky directed and co-scripted with Ira Wolfert, but his guidance lacks the touch needed for commercial success at the film b.o. Plot, based on Wolfert's novel, "Tucker's People," deals with the racketeers who fatten off the little person's nickels and dimes that daily are played on the numbers game. It is not a lucid expose as filmed.

Picture is an Enterprise Studios presentation being released by Metro. That distribution and the assured playdates mean that some coin will be returned, but film lacks the essentials necessary to swing it through all situations at a profit.

On the technical side, the Bob Roberts production fares better than story-wise. The physical mounting is expertly valued; the New York locale shots give authenticity; and lensing by George Barnes, while a bit on the arty side, displays skilled craftsmanship. Film bears evidence of having been put through the editing mill a number of times and present footage is held to 78 minutes. *Brog.*

The Dark Past

Columbia release of Buddy Adler production. Features William Holden, Nina Foch, Lee J. Cobb. Directed by Rudolph Mate. Adapted by Malvin Wald, Oscar Saul, from screenplay by Philip MacDonald, Michael Blankfort, Albert Duffy; based upon play, "Blind Alley," by James Warwick; camera, Joseph Walker; editor, Viola Lawrence. Tradeshown N. Y., Dec. 22, '48. Running time, 75 MINS.

Al Walker.... William Holden
Betty.... Nina Foch
Dr. Andrew Collins.... Lee J. Cobb
Laura Stevens.... Adele Jergens
Owen Talbot.... Stephen Dunne
Ruth Collins.... Lois Maxwell
Mike.... Berry Kroeger
Prof. Fred Linder.... Steven Geray
Frank Stevens.... Wilton Graff
Pete.... Robert Osterloh
Nora.... Kathryn Card
Bobby.... Bobby Hyatt
Agnes.... Ellen Corby
Sheriff.... Charles Cane
Williams.... Robert B., Williams

A crisp melodrama is "The Dark Past" which Columbia has remade from its 1939 release, "Blind Alley." Psychological thriller will prove solid supporting fare and its entertainment structure is sturdy enough to warrant going it alone in some situations. New version also points up the value of psychiatric treatment in combating juvenile delinquency.

Delinquency angle is the peg on which is hung the flashbacked central plot. As an example of what psychiatry can do for a criminal is graphically shown by college prof Lee J. Cobb who brings escaped convict William Holden to bay merely by probing into his mind to discover what impels him to be a murderer. When Holden realizes what has warped his brain, he finds he no longer can kill and proves an easy capture for the police.

Locale for Cobb's psychoanalysis is his own hunting lodge where his family and several guests have been taken prisoner by Holden and his accomplices. Under Rudolph Mate's skillful direction, the cast builds a firm aura of suspense in the grim period when the thugs hold the upper hand.

Always self-assured, the pipe-smoking Cobb racks up a neat portrayal of the medico. Holden is believable as the high-strung con on the lam. Nina Foch handles her role well as Holden's moll. Berry Kroeger, Robert Osterloh, Adele Jergens and other players lend strong support. Joseph Walker's camerawork is top quality while Buddy Adler embellished the pic with okay production values. *Gilb.*

Angel in Exile

Republic production and release. Stars John Carroll, Adele Mara; features Thomas Gomez, Barton MacLane, Alfonso Bedoya, Grant Williams. Directed by Allan Dwan, Phillip Ford. Screenplay, Charles Larson; photography, Reggie Lanning; music, Nathan Scott; editor, Arthur Roberts. Tradeshown N. Y. Dec. 23, '48. Running time, 90 MINS.

Charlie Dakin.... John Carroll
Raquel Chavez.... Adele Mara
Dr. Esteban Chavez.... Thomas Gomez
Max Giorgio.... Barton MacLane
Ysidro Alvarez.... Alfonso Bedoya
Sheriff.... Grant Withers
Carl Spitz.... Paul Fix
Ernie Coons.... Art Smith
Warden.... Tom Powers
Health Officer.... Ian Wolfe
J. H. Higgins.... Howland Chamberlin
Carmencita.... Elsa Lorraine Zepeda
Nurse.... Mary Currier

Introduction of a religious theme in "Angel in Exile" provides a more adult twist to what might have been a routine action yarn. The film is in keeping with a discernible religioso film cycle which has been evident in some of the newer releases. However, film still needs support in most situations.

"Angel's" story is based along comparatively simple lines with an O. Henryesque switch. John Carroll, playing a released convict, meets a loyal pal who has stached away a sizable hoard of stolen gold in an abandoned mine. They work the claim by mixing the gold dust with the sand from the mine, which makes it look like a legitimate operation. To the Mexicans in the nearby village, production of wealth from that mine, is construed as a miracle. They think a legendary angel has favored the village. The peons' faith gets Carroll around to their point of view and he reforms.

Action sequences are provided by Barton MacLane and Paul Fix as Carroll's former cronies who cut in on the loot. They're eventually liquidated, and the reward money on their heads and on the gold provides enough coin to rehabilitate the town.

Carroll gives a likable performance and does a convincing job of switching from a criminal to one who has found faith. Other good performances are by Thomas Gomez as the kindly village medico, and Adele Mara, his daughter, who provides the love interest.

Directors Allan Dwan and Phillip Ford have done well in blending the film's diverse elements into a believable yarn. The reformation scenes are handled excellently and film is well-gaited. Reggie Lanning's photography is good and music by Nathan Scott is frequently expressive. *Jose.*

Gun Smugglers

Hollywood, Dec. 29.

RKO release of Herman Schlom production. Stars Tim Holt; features Richard Martin, Martha Hyer, Gary Gray, Paul Hurst, Douglas Fowley. Directed by Frank McDonald. Original screenplay, Norman Houston; camera, J. Roy Hunt; editor, Les Millbrook. Tradeshown in N. Y., Dec. 28, '48. Running time, 61 MINS.
Tim Holt...................Tim Holt
Chito................Richard Martin
Judy...................Martha Hyer
Danny...................Gary Gray
Hasty...................Paul Hurst
Steve...................Douglas Fowley
Colonel Davis............Robert Warwick
Sheriff Shurlock..........Don Haggerty
Clancy...................Frank Sully
Dodge...................Robert Bray

"Gun Smugglers" is an average galloper from the Tim Holt stable at RKO. Juve interest is good and bookings should be okay in the Saturday matinee market.

Gary Gray plays a tough prairie urchin who is reformed by kindliness after his hero-worship of a bad big brother is responsible for a lot of killings and other trouble. The kid sharpens kiddie interest and Tim Holt carries off the adult lead with easy assurance.

Story deals with group of gun smugglers, led by Douglas Fowley, who hold up an army wagon train and steal a load of guns. Ambush is made possible by young Gray. The sergeant in charge of the train is broken out of the Army but his gentle treatment of the kid sets up the happy ending, where Holt battles it out with the baddies, the guns are recovered and the sergeant reinstated.

Richard Martin rides along for a number of chuckles as Holt's Irish-Spanish sidekick, and Martha Hyer fills slight role of femme lead. Paul Hurst is good as the sarg, and Fowley's villainy is up to his tough standard.

Frank McDonald's direction of the Herman Schlom production gives it an okay pace for the market, and sight values are aided by J. Roy Hunt's good lensing. *Brog.*

Incident

Hollywood, Dec. 21.

Monogram release of Harry Lewis-Hall Shelton (Master Films) production. Stars Jane Frazee, Warren Douglas, Robert Osterloh; features Joyce Compton, Anthony Caruso, Harry Lauter, Eddie Dunn. Directed by William Beaudine. Screenplay, Fred Niblo, Jr., Samuel Roeca; original story, Harry Lewis; camera, Marcel LePicard; editor, Ace Herman. Previewed in Hollywood, Dec. 21, '48. Running time, 68 MINS.
Joe Downey............Warren Douglas
Marion.................Jane Frazee
Slats..................Robert Osterloh
Joan...................Joyce Compton
Nails..................Anthony Caruso
Bill...................Harry Lauter
Lt. Madigan............Eddie Dunn
Knuckles...............Meyer Grace
Hartley................Harry Cheshire
Sally..................Lynn Millan
Rinsel.................Robert Emmett Keane
Sloan..................Pierre Watkin
Bugs...................Ralph Dunn
Freddie................John Shay

"Incident" is a well-paced thriller that will thoroughly satisfy in the supporting positions at which it is aimed. It's a yarn of gangsters, murder and love, all springing from a single, unexpected incident. Production polish is good for the budget and the cast troupes strongly to keep it interesting.

A mistake in identity rates Warren Douglas a beating by a muscleman. Douglas's curiosity leads him into a search to find out why he was mistaken for a gangster. Hunt leads him into murder and general rousting around, and leaves him at the finale hospital-bedded with gunshot wounds. He's satisfied, though. During the excitement, he falls in love and helps break up a gang of thieves.

Douglas and his girlfriend, Jane Frazee, go through their paces with zip, giving a good lift to proceedings. Also figuring expertly in the melodramatics are: Robert Osterloh, Anthony Caruso, Meyer Grace, Robert Emmett Keane and Ralph Dunn as the chief trouble makers. Joyce Compton, Harry Lauter and Eddie Dunn also show up well.

William Beaudine's direction keeps the action on the move and works up a nice measure of suspense without bearing down on heavy angles of the plot. Good script was written by Fred Niblo, Jr., and Samuel Roeca from an original by Harry Lewis. Production guidance by Lewis and Hall Shelton gets the most from a small budget. Marcel LePicard's lensing is a good assist, as is the editing by Ace Herman. *Brog.*

Highway 13

Hollywood, Dec. 23.

Screen Guild release of William Stephens production. Features Robert Lowery, Pamela Blake, Michael Whalen, Dan Seymour, Clem Bevans, Maris Wrixon. Directed by William Berke. Screenplay, Maurice Tombragel; original story, John Wilste; camera, Carl Berger; editor, Edward Mann. Previewed in Hollywood, Dec. 22, '48. Running time, 58 MINS.
Hank Wilson............Robert Lowery
Doris..................Pamela Blake
Frank Denton...........Michael Whalen
Kelleher...............Dan Seymour
Pops...................Clem Bevans
Miss Hadley............Maris Wrixon
Morris.................Tom Chatterton
Aunt Myrt..............Mary Gordon
George Montgomery...Gaylord Pendleton
Detective..............Lyle Talbot

"Highway 13," fast-moving programmer, gets a lot out of a small budget and goes about its thrill-making in a forthright fashion. Production values, trouping and direction all measure up to market demands.

Melodramatics are backgrounded against the trucking industry and a plot to wreck a big transportation company. There are flaming crashes, high-speed highway chases and sufficient mystery concerning the instigators of the accidents to hold audience attention.

Robert Lowery makes a capable appearance as a driver who gets mixed up in accidents and murder but who is eventually responsible for solution to the skullduggery. Pamela Blake is his comely gal friend. Michael Whalen, Clem Bevans and Maris Wrixon do well as the plotters who seek to gain control of the trucking company. Gaylord Pendleton, a private detective who's bumped off; Dan Seymour, insurance investigator, and others answer all demands.

William Berke's direction generates a fast pace to the melodramatics. William Stephens has obtained topnotch budget values. Lensing by Carl Berger fits the action pattern, and Edward Mann's editing keeps footage down to a tight 58 minutes. *Brog.*

What's On Your Mind
(DOCUMENTARY)

Oxford Films production and release. Compilation of four shots, being released as psycho-analytical film program. At Elysee, N. Y., starting Dec. 25. Running time, 87 MINS.

This loosely strung together group of shorts was planned originally for use by psychiatrists in probing emotional life with their patients. That is exactly where this belongs. Intending to show why people behave the way they do, it seems good only as an instrument for group psycho-therapy.

Any attempt to explain to the average theatre audience why certain individuals behave in specific ways under given circumstances obviously has to be handled with unusual skill to mean much. This does not for the most part.

The short titled "Feeling of Rejection," as done by the National Film Board of Canada, holds the most interest. It's the best made of the lot. Script by Bruce Ruddick seems adequate, as is Dennis Gilson's camera work. "Problems of Sleep" is a tired recital, produced by the Realist Film Unit of London, explaining the problems of getting youngsters to sleep peacefully and how to have their slumber undisturbed. Short has jerky continuity, pedantic approach and tedious treatment. A. E. Jeakins photography also is mild.

"Feeling of Inferiority," produced by Caravel Films, is the most inferior one of the four shorts. Canada's National Film Board also turned out the short, "What's On Your Mind," with supervision by Allan Memorial Institute of Psychiatry, but it's a bit too technical. *Wear.*